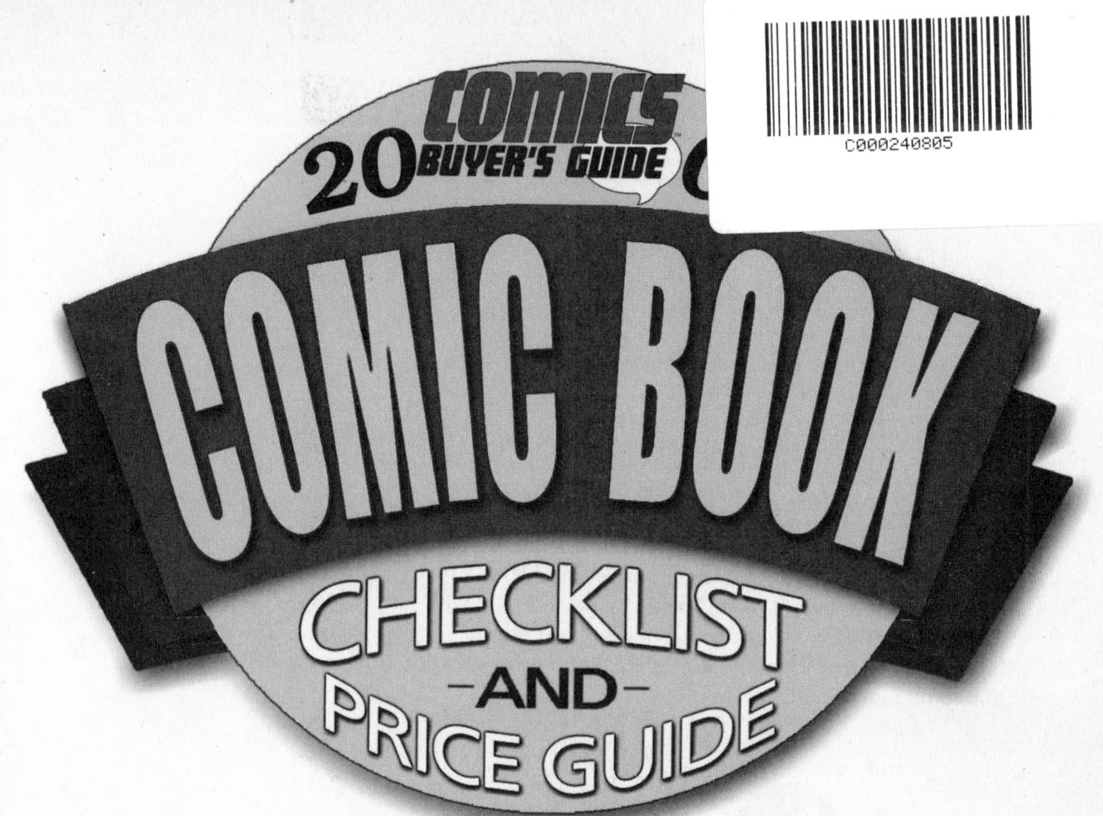

Maggie Thompson,
Brent Frankenhoff,
Peter Bickford,
& John Jackson Miller

Published by

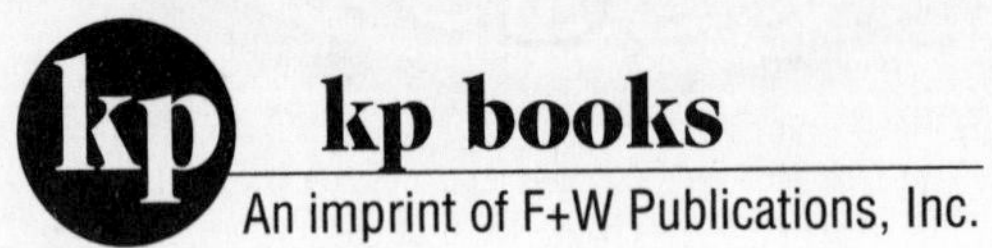

700 East State Street • Iola, WI 54990-0001
715-445-2214 • 888-457-2873

Please call or write for our free catalog.
Our toll-free number to place an order or obtain a free catalog is (800) 258-0929
or please use our regular business telephone (715) 445-2214.

Library of Congress Catalog Number: 1082-5649
ISBN: 0-87349-828-3

Printed in the United States of America

Acknowledgments

While there are four names on the cover of this latest edition, there are many other folks here at Krause Publications and in comics fandom to thank. As ever, there are so many of them to thank that we're bound to miss a few. To anyone who should be thanked but isn't (you know who you are): We're sorry, and you know we couldn't have done this without you.

First and foremost, without the copious contributions of *ComicBase* developer Peter Bickford, this edition simply wouldn't exist. While his research has often paralleled our own, he has also obtained information to which we didn't have access, just as our information has added many titles to his computerized comics database program.

The newest name on our cover, John Jackson Miller, has contributed tons of additional data to the database again this year in preparation for the recently released third edition of *The Standard Catalog of Comic Books*. Some of that information (including all sorts of new data on Harvey and Archie titles) has spilled over into this volume.

That brings us to the publishers and individual creators who provided copies of their titles, so that we could maintain a database based on actually published material. We thank them all and encourage others to do the same.

Thanks also to the readers of our previous editions who have been providing additional data on their favorite titles. This year again, special thanks goes to Howard Michaels Jr., Carl Tietz, and Harold Crump, who provided an ongoing stream of information to make our compendium of information even more detailed and precise.

Thanks to our own behind-the-scenes people, including: Brian Brogaard for designing the cover; Tammy Kuhnle and Scott Hippensteel, computer services; Sandy Morrison and Sally Olson in our book production department; Meredith Miller, Nate Melby, Mike Greenholdt, and Andrew Williams for data entry help; and the entire comics, toys, and games division at Krause Publications. An extra special thanks to Brent's wife, Kim, who understood when long weekends and evenings were required to finish data entry, proofreading, and preparation. (If this last sentence seems familiar, it's because she's put up with this sort of thing for the last several years.)

Most of all, we acknowledge the work of Don Thompson, who nursed this project through the last 11 years of his life. We miss you, Don.

And we thank you all.

Maggie Thompson
Brent Frankenhoff
John Jackson Miller
Iola, Wisconsin
October 12, 2004

And a special thanks to Darryl Buchanan of The Comic Sheet for his pricing analysis!

Contents

Introduction

By Maggie Thompson

This checklist and price guide is intended to function in a number of fashions.

There's more than one way to use it.

You can use it as a "have" list, in which you maintain an inventory of the comics you're collecting. (Make an "X" in the box for each one you have. If you don't use the "X" system, you can use your own symbols indicating what you please, including condition, in the open box. You can then see at a glance what you're still looking for of a title you want to collect.)

You can use it as a guide to show prices you can expect to pay for items, if you look for them in comics shops throughout the country, online, or at conventions. The prices listed are arrived at by surveying comics shops, online sales, convention sales, and mail-order houses.

With that information, our price guide reflects what a smart person with those choices would be willing to pay for a given issue.

You can use it as a guide for value, when you're buying or trading items. In that case, you'll want to keep in mind sales information you'll find on Page 9.

And you can carry it with you in your comics storage box, because it's sized to fit in a comics box.

Condition is vital.

Whether you're buying or selling comic books, one of the most important factors in setting the price is the condition of the material.

A scuffed, torn "reading copy" (that is, one that is suitable for reading but not for getting high prices at resale) will bring only a fraction of the price of a copy of the same issue which looks as though it has just come off the newsstand.

Picky collectors will even go through all the copies on a newsstand so as to buy the one in best condition. [Even a so-called "newsstand mint" copy of *Fantastic Four* #1 may have what is called "Marvel chipping" (a frayed right edge), since many of those early-'60s issues were badly cut by the printer.]

On the other hand, beat-up copies can provide bargains for collectors whose primary focus is *reading* the comic-book story. The same goes for reprints of comics which would otherwise be hard to find.

In fact, you may find prices on poor-condition copies even lower than the prices in this guide, depending on the attitude of the seller. It's a good time to get into collecting comics for the *fun* of it.

A major change in the comics-collecting world, CGC grading, has meant a huge jump in prices for certain hotly collected issues in almost-perfect condition. The third-party graders of Comics Guaranty LLC evaluate the condition of submitted copies and then encapsulate the graded issue in a labeled container. Because of the independent nature of the process and the reliability of the evaluating team, confidence in buying such items has meant a premium over the standard price in that condition.

For example, at press time, a CGC 9.4 (Near Mint) is bringing at auction *four times* our Near Mint price for non-encapsulated comics. More information on the company can be found on Page 14.

Our price guide is constantly evolving.

Each year, the most important changes in this guide from previous editions are, of course, the addition of countless chunks of data that we have compiled from consulting physical copies of the issues in question. (Thanks again to the many who helped.) Alone among checklists of Silver Age comics, this book contains original cover data and original pricing information for tens of thousands of comics.

We've also provided hundreds of new cover photos with enough additional information, we hope, to whet a collector's appetite. We want to provide the most accurate picture of what you, as a customer, can expect to pay for comics when you walk into a shop or comics convention with your want list.

Are There Any Questions?

Readers have been kind enough to ask many questions about our price guide. To help you make the best use of this volume, we're answering many of them here (and we're answering questions you **didn't** *ask, too, in an attempt to provide more information than you can possibly use).*

Collectors looking for series beginning with a creator's name will find the titles under the series' name with the creator's name in parentheses at the end. For example, *Kurt Busiek's Astro City* can be found under *Astro City (Kurt Busiek's).*
© 1995 Jukebox Productions.

Why do we need a price guide at all?

We've spent 23 years developing a guide so that buyers and sellers of back issues will have help knowing what a consumer with various buying choices can expect to pay, if he's looking — for example — for that issue that will complete his run of the two DC series of *Shade the Changing Man*. The collector will find that even the highest-priced issue in the best condition probably won't cost more than about $4 — and that's the sort of information that can motivate a casual reader to become a collector.

Moreover, we try to provide helpful information to people who purchase it in order to have a (yes) guide to buying comics. Pricing information is just *part* of what we offer. In fact, we are increasingly intrigued by the more detailed information you'll find in this book — where we provide original cover date and price information wherever we can locate it, along with character appearances.

Why can't I find a title in your list?

We're working constantly to expand the listings themselves and increase the information on those we already provide. Check out what we have included, and — if you have something we're not listing — please let us know the details!

We need to know the information as given in the indicia of the issue (that's the tiny print, usually on the first few pages, that gives the publishing information): the full title, the number, and the issue month and year — and the U.S. price given on the cover. If you find work by a creator on our abbreviations list that we haven't noted in this guide, please include that information. If there's a significant event (especially as given in the abbreviations list), please include that, too. This is an *annual* volume designed to consolidate our information — but our monthly *Comics Buyer's Guide* runs updated information (with commentary on recent sales activity), and we add to the data constantly — including updates to such market changes as the effects of CGC grading.

Check, too, on whether you're looking up the title as it appears in the indicia. For example, we list *The Vampire Lestat (Anne Rice's)*, not *Anne Rice's The Vampire Lestat*; we list *Mack Bolan: The Executioner (Don Pendleton's)*, not *Don Pendleton's Mack Bolan: The Executioner*. Many Marvel titles have adjectives. *Hulk*, for example, is listed as *Incredible Hulk*.

What's in this book?

This Silver Age and more recent price guide began as a quarterly update of activity in comics published since 1961, as reflected in prices comics shops were likely to charge. Moreover, the focus was pretty much limited to Silver Age super-hero titles — in fact, Silver Age super-hero titles *that were being published when the price guide began*. This meant that such titles as *OMAC*, a Silver Age title that starred a super-hero but was not still being published by 1983, didn't get listed in that earliest edition. It also meant that so-called "funny animal" titles, "war" titles, and the like were not included.

However, once the listings were begun (not by *Comics Buyer's Guide* staff, incidentally; the material was started for another publication), Don Thompson took over the compilation. From that point, every effort was made to include every issue of every comic book received in the office. However, since the entries were not on a database and had to be compressed to fit the space available, annotation, dates, and original prices were not usually part of the listing. On the other hand

(and because of Don's care, once he took over the project), material which was often overlooked by other reference publishers has been listed from the beginning in the *CBG* listings. *Concrete* and *Teenage Mutant Ninja Turtles*, for example, were first listed in *CBG*'s price listings.

And we continue to fill in remaining information whenever we get it. Our cooperative agreement with *ComicBase* has led to the inclusion of hundreds of new titles and issues, as well as a wealth of variant editions.

What is the "Silver Age?"

Comic-book collectors divide the history of comics into the "Golden Age" and the "Silver Age." "Golden Age" indicates the first era of comic-book production — the '30s and '40s. It was a time of incredible creation in the field, when such characters as Superman and Batman first appeared. It's the era *before* material in this price guide was published.

"Silver Age" is used to indicate a period of comic-book production of slightly less (nostalgic?) luster than that of the Golden Age. It is usually considered to have begun with the publication of the first revival of a '40s super-hero: the appearance of The Flash in *Showcase* #4 (Sep-Oct 1956). However, that was a lone appearance at the time, so this price guide concentrates on titles from the time Marvel reentered the super-hero field with the publication of *Fantastic Four* #1 (1961). Long-running titles such as *Batman, Superman,* and others have been extended back to mid-1956 for this edition.

This guide lists #8 and #10. Where's #9?

We haven't seen a copy and can't verify its existence. There was a time when comics collectors could safely assume that issue numbers would run in normal sequence, when no numbers were skipped and when there were no special numbers to confuse completists. That's not the case any more. What we need from those who want to help add to our information is confirmation that an item has *actually been published.*

This guide *does* include information on published material that was not widely distributed. Eternity's *Uncensored Mouse* #2, for example, was pulled from distribution after legal problems with The Walt Disney Company — but copies *do* exist. So few transactions involve it, however, that retailers have not yet established a standard price for the item.

So do you own all these comics?

No, many publishers and collectors have helped us over the years by sending photocopies of indicia, records of publication, annotations, and the like — all of which has permitted us to provide collectors with more information every year. What *ComicBase* and we cannot do — and *do* not do — is pull information from other price guides or from announcements of what is *scheduled* for publication. The former would not be proper; the latter leads to errors — the sort of errors that have been known to become imbedded in some price guides' information files.

This is also why information sometimes seems varied. Every effort has been made to make the notations consistent, but this list has more than 100,000 individual issues coordinated between *ComicBase* and Krause Publications, so this can be an arduous task. Nevertheless, we're whittling away at problems between issues of *Comics Buyer's Guide* and assorted other projects.

This title switched publishers. Why wasn't that noted?

Chances are that the publishers involved didn't give us the information. Again, if you have the information, please provide it to us for inclusion in the next edition.

Why do some of your listings say (first series), (second series), etc., while others have (Vol. 1), (Vol. 2), and so on? Is there a difference?

Although publishers may begin a series again at #1, they often don't update the volume number in the indicia, which leads to the (first series) and (second series) notations. If the volume number changes (and it's a clear change, as in the case of Marvel's "Heroes Reborn" and "Heroes Return" title restarts), that is what differentiates the series.

On the other hand, when the volume number changes each year (as was the case with some early Silver Age material) but the series number is ongoing in sequence (Vol. 2, #21), then we don't note that change. Marvel's return to original numbering for *Fantastic Four* and *Amazing Spider-Man* in mid-2003 has caused both titles' later listings, beginning with #500 for each, to revert to the respective title's first volume.

I've heard some of my squarebound comics referred to variously as "bookshelf format," "prestige format," and "Dark Knight format." What's the difference?

Various formats — usually reserved for special projects (mini-series and one-shots) — have different names, depending on the publisher. We use the term "prestige format" generically to indicate a fancier package than the average comic book. Marvel refers to some titles in upscale formats as "bookshelf format," whereas DC initially solicited some of its titles in the format of *Batman: The Dark Knight* as "Dark Knight format." Details of fancy formats can be widely varied.

I tried to sell my comics to a retailer, but he wouldn't even offer me 10% of the prices you list. Is he trying to cheat me? Are your prices wrong?

Remember, our prices are based on what an informed collector with some choices is willing to pay for a comic book, not necessarily what a shop is charging or paying for that comic book. A shop has huge overhead and needs to tailor its stock to match the interest shown by its customers. If no one locally is buying comics starring Muggy-Doo, Boy Cat, it doesn't matter that *Muggy-Doo, Boy Cat* is bringing high prices elsewhere in the country.

Comics listed at their original prices may be showing no movement in most comics shops. In such cases, a retailer won't usually be interested in devoting store space to such titles, no matter *how* nice they are or *how* much you're discounting them.

I'm a publisher, and I'd be willing to buy a hundred copies of my first issue at the price you list. I get calls from all over America from would-be buyers who would pay 10 times the price you give here for out-of-print issues of my comics. What's going on?

A publisher like you hears from faithful fans across the nation. A comics shop deals

It's probably going to be some time before any publisher surpasses *Zzz* for the final listing in our price guide.

© 2000 Alan Bunce.

with a market of one community or smaller. You're dealing with a narrow, focused market of aficionados of your product who are looking for the specific issues they're missing. And with more and more online offerings, those fans find it easier to seek you out.

As a result, a publisher who has back issues for sale may get higher prices than readers will find in this checklist.

It doesn't mean you're ripping off fans; it means fans looking to buy that material are competing within a nationwide pool; the Internet may eventually put everyone in the same pool.

***Can I just order the back-issue comics I want from* Comics Buyer's Guide?**

This price guide is just that: a guide to the average back-issue prices comics shops are likely to charge their customers.

We maintain no back-issue stock for sale; we leave that to retailers who specialize in back issues. (Start with your local shops. You'll be able to check out the variety of material available and take a look in advance at what you're buying.)

Comics Buyer's Guide itself is the magazine of the comic-book field. As such, it carries ads from retailers across the country. You can check those advertisements for specific back issues that you're looking for. You can even take out a "wanted" ad to locate particular items, if that appeals to you. Subscription information can be found at *www.comicsbuyersguide.com*.

If You're New to Collecting ...

If you've just begun to collect comic books, you may find some aspects confusing. Here are some terms and some basics. (Don't forget to check other introductory material in this book, as well.)

• **Cover variants:** These occur when publishers try to increase "collectibility" of and interest in a title by releasing an issue with an assortment of covers. This is in hopes that completists will want to buy multiple copies, instead of just one. (The practice has even spread to publications like *TV Guide*.) So how are these performing as "rare" back issues? So far: poorly. Prices may rise at the time of release, but they usually fall again relatively quickly.

The same thing goes for other gimmicky extras. *Slingers* and *Fathom* were released with variant interiors — and readership dropped.

• **Issue identification:** If you've found a box of old comics in the attic and wonder what to do next, the first thing to do is find out what you've got.

The same goes when you're looking for what you want to buy.

Here are some basics: Look at the copyright dates; if there are multiple dates, look at the *last* date. (If they're before 1950, chances are the comics are considered "Golden Age," and they're not covered in this price guide. Comics from the mid-1950s and later are Silver Age or more recent.)

Almost all comics are collected and identified by title and issue number. Look at the indicia, as outlined on page 7. That's what you'll use to find a specific issue in this or any other price guide. You'll want to check the issue title as given there — and the issue number.

• **Issue condition:** What does the comic book look like? Check pages 12 through 15 of our price guide to get a feel for the shape your comics are in. If they're beaten up, enjoy them for reading but don't expect to get a lot of money for them. For this reason, many beginning collectors focus on exactly such poor issues, getting the pleasure of reading without making a heavy investment.

• **Want to buy? To sell? To find out more about the field?** Check out page 9 for some indications.

• **Collecting with computer:** If you have a home computer, you'll find it increases your sources for buying and selling. (And *ComicBase* can help in your inventory.) Some sites of special interest include:

www.collect.com
www.comicsbuyersguide.com
www.ebay.com
www.amazon.com
www.bookfinder.com

But they're not the only spots comics collectors will find fascinating. Surf the Web to find more!

Happy collecting!

What's Next?

The Internet has gained in its importance to collectors, e-mail is connecting collectors around the world, a third-party grading service has led to incredible price variations in some back issues, and computers are permitting collectors, as well as retailers, to monitor what they've got, what condition it's in, and what they want to buy.

One advance we continue to work on is the expansion of the information in our files on as many back issues as possible. To that end, the assistance of Human Computing's *ComicBase* program has been invaluable. Our combined informational base has grown rapidly, and we look forward to an even greater mutual compilation of data. Collectors who choose to do so will be able to access the information in both electronic and printed form. Both companies have for years been in an aggressive program to improve and increase the data for collectors, and collectors today are already experiencing services not available in the 1900s.

Maggie Thompson

Inside our listings

Each title in the *Checklist and Price Guide* is identified by a unique title and a publisher name.

Issues are listed in numerical order, meaning "#0" and "negative number" issues appear out of sequence chronologically at the top of the listings, while DC's #1,000,000 issues appear just before their respective annuals.

Multiple printings are noted by a hyphen and the printing number following the issue number: **1-2, 1-3**, and so on.

Multiple covers are noted by a slash and letter following the issue number: **1/A, 1/B**, and so on.

Oddball versions of an issue are noted with the abbreviations at right: **1/GR,** for example, is the Golden Records variant of *Amazing Spider-Man* Vol. 1, #1. These are almost always explained in the text of the listing itself.

Most issues list a **month and year.** This is not the true publication date, but the date labeled on the comic book. Usually, it's the date in the indicia; occasionally, it's the date found on the cover. Where it's estimated but not known, we indicate with **ca.** for "circa."

(In a handful of cases, such as with Viz comics, we have been able to figure out true publication dates for issues which have no other such information.)

Abbreviations for many of the best-known creators can be found beginning on page 113. Most of the time, the use of an abbreviation indicates that that person was the artist on the particular issue. If it has a (c) after it, it means that creator was the cover artist; a (w) means that person was the writer.

Abbreviations appearing with issue numbers

Most are explained in their listings.

ACE	Wizard Ace Edition
AE	American Entertainment edition
AUT	Autographed
BL	Blue variation
AIM	Aim toothpaste giveaway
Anl	Annual
ASH	Ashcan
Dlx	Deluxe
DM	Direct Market edition
DOT	Dept. of Transportation giveaway
Fal	Fall
FAN	Fan magazine giveaway
GF	Gold foil edition
GIVE	Giveaway
GN	Graphic novel
Gold	Gold edition
GR	Golden Records variant
Giant	Giant Size
Hero	Hero magazine giveaway
HOL	Hologram edition
HS	Holiday Special
KS	King Size
LE	Limited edition
NT	New Testament
Nude	"Nude" edition
OT	Old Testament
PL	Platinum
PLND	Platinum "nude" edition
PR	Prestige edition
SC	Special cover
SD	Signed edition
SE	Special edition
SI	Silver edition
Smr	Summer
Spr	Spring
Win	Winter
YB	Yearbook

Abbreviations for such significant events as deaths, origins, appearances, *etc.*, can also be found in the list on page 113 and 114.

Photo Grading Guide

When comics are compared with the Photo Grading Guide, it's easy to see there are many comics which fall between categories in something of an infinite gradation. For example, a "Fair" condition comic book (which falls between "Good" and "Poor") may have a soiled, slightly damaged cover, a badly rolled spine, cover flaking, corners gone, tears, and the like. It is an issue with multiple problems but it is intact — and some collectors enjoy collecting in this grade for the fun of it. Tape may be present and is always considered a defect.

The condition of a comic book is a vital factor in determining its price.

MINT

(Abbreviated M, Mt)

This is a perfect comic book.

Its cover has full luster, with edges sharp and pages like new. There are no signs of wear or aging. It is not imperfectly printed or off-center. "Mint" means just what it says. **[The term for this grade is the same one used for CGC's 10.0 grade.]**

NEAR MINT

(Abbreviated NM)

This is a nearly perfect comic book.

Its cover shows barely perceptible signs of wear. Its spine is tight, and its cover has only minor loss of luster and only minor printing defects. Some discoloration is acceptable in older comics — as are signs of aging. **[The term for this grade is the same one used for CGC's 9.4 grade.]**

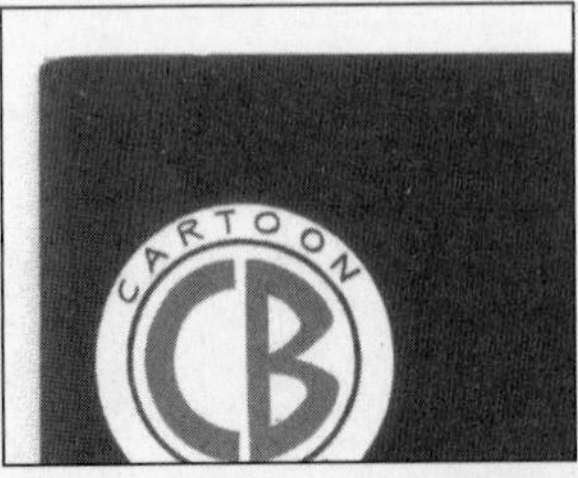

VERY FINE

(Abbreviated VF)

This is a nice comic book with beginning signs of wear.

There can be slight creases and wrinkles at the staples, but it is a flat, clean issue with definite signs of being read a few times. There is some loss of the original gloss, but it is in general an attractive comic book. **[The term for this grade is the same one used for CGC's 8.0 grade.]**

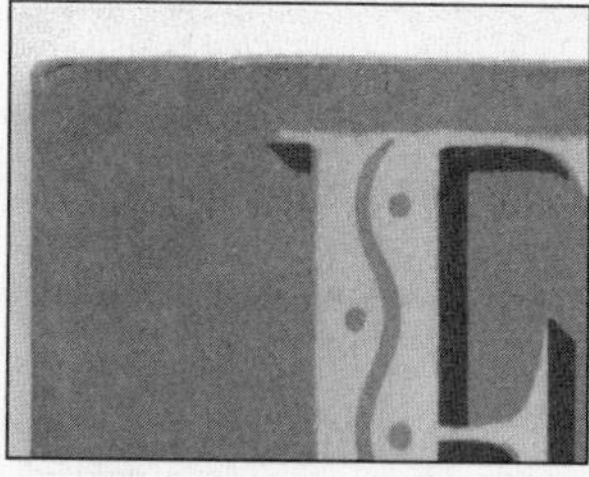

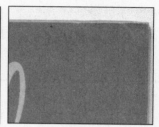

FINE

(Abbreviated F, Fn)

This comic book's cover is worn but flat and clean with no defacement.

There is usually no cover writing or tape repair. Stress lines around the staples and more rounded corners are permitted. It is a good-looking issue at first glance.**[The term for this grade is the same one used for CGC's 6.0 grade.]**

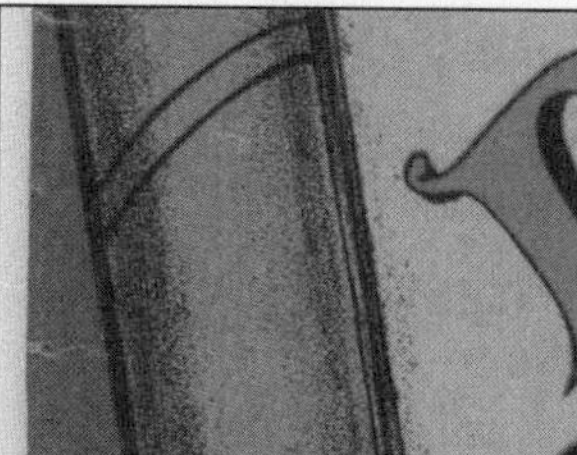

VERY GOOD

(Abbreviated VG, VGd)

Most of the original gloss is gone from this well-read issue.

There are minor markings, discoloration, and/or heavier stress lines around the staples and spine. The cover may have minor tears and/or corner creases, and spine-rolling is permissible. **[The term for this grade is the same one used for CGC's 4.0 grade.]**

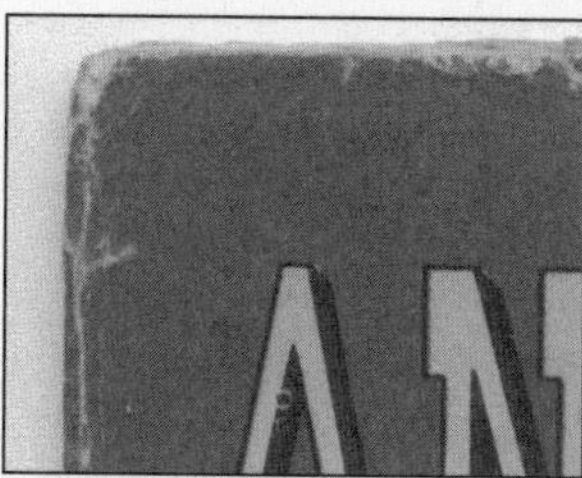

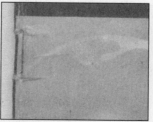

GOOD

(Abbreviated G, Gd)

This is a very worn comic book with nothing missing.

Creases, minor tears, rolled spine, and cover flaking are permissible. Older Golden Age comic books often come in this condition. **[The term for this grade is the same one used for CGC's 2.0 grade.]**

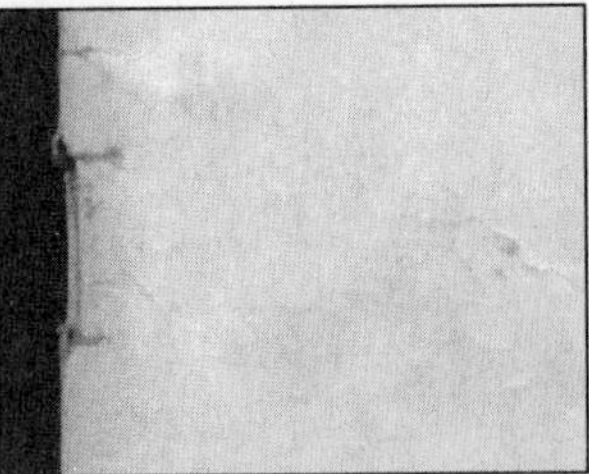

FAIR

(Abbreviated FA, Fr)

This comic book has multiple problems but is structurally intact.

Copies may have a soiled, slightly damaged cover, a badly rolled spine, cover flaking, corners gone, and tears. Tape may be present and is always considered a defect. **[The term for this grade is the same one used for CGC's 1.0 grade.]**

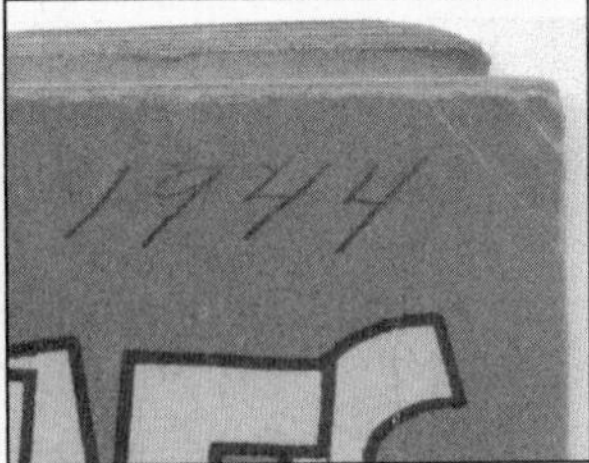

POOR

(Abbreviated P, Pr)

This issue is damaged and generally considered unsuitable for collecting.

While the copy may still contain some readable stories, major defects get in the way. Copies may be in the process of disintegrating and may do so with even light handling. **[The term for this grade is the same one used for CGC's 0.5 grade.]**

Guide to Defects

Theoretically, given a set of grading rules, determining the condition of a comic book should be simple. But flaws vary from item to item, and it can be difficult to pin one label on a particular issue — as with a sharp issue with a coupon removed. Another problem lies in grading historically significant vs. run-of-the-mill issues. The examples shown here represent specific defects listed. These defects need to be taken into account when grading, but should *not* be the sole determinant of a comic's grade. (For example, the copy with stamped arrival date, off-center staple is *not* in mint condition aside from those defects.)

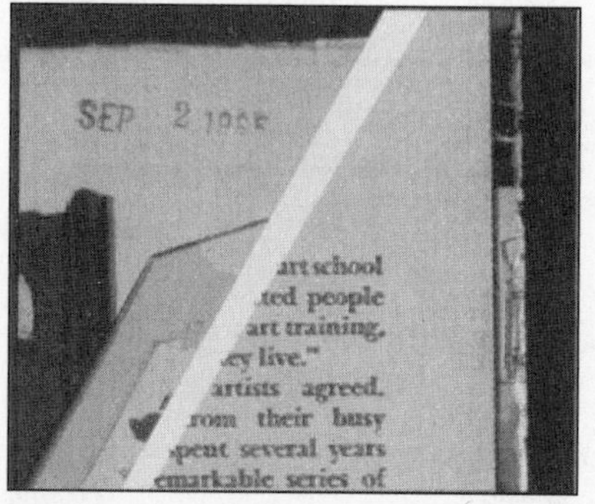

Stamped arrival date and **off-center cover and off-center stapling.**
Minor defects. Some will not call it "Mint"; some will.

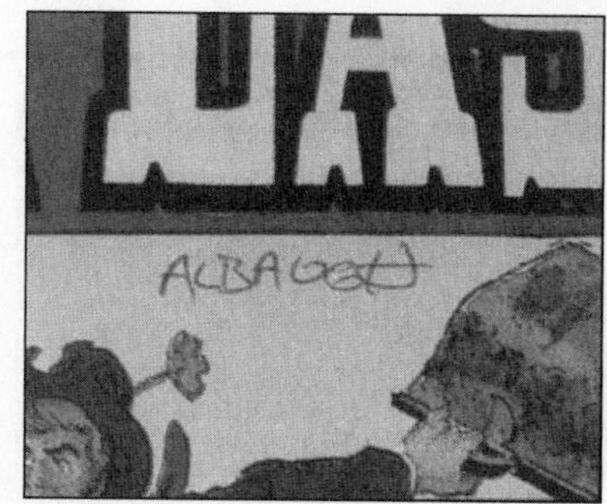

Writing defacing cover.
Marking can include filling in light areas or childish scribbling. Usually no better than "Good."

Subscription crease.
Comic books sent by mail were often folded down the middle, leaving a permanent crease. Definitely no better than "Very Good"; probably no better than "Good."

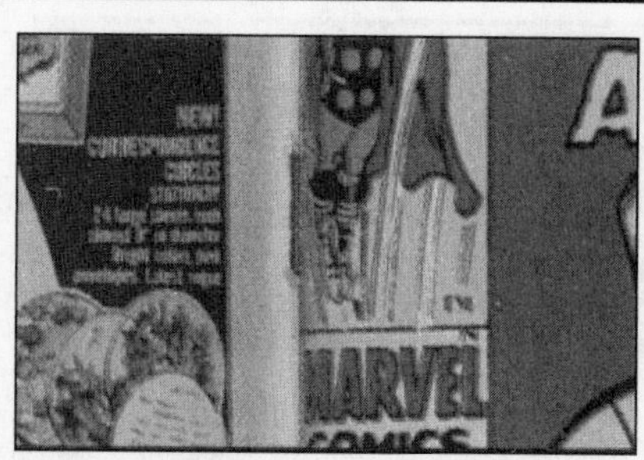

Rusty staple.
Caused by dampness during storage, rust stains around staples may be minor — or more apparent. No better than "Very Good."

Chunk missing.
Sizable piece missing from the cover (front or back).
No better than "Fair."

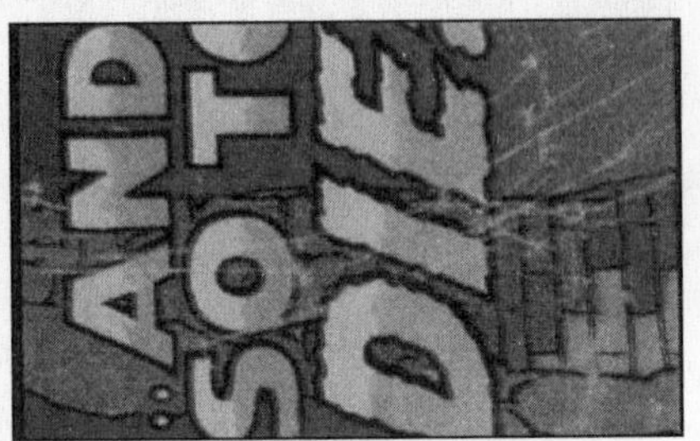

Multiple folds and wrinkles.
No better than "Fair" condition.

Tape.
This extreme example of tape damage is used to show *why* tape shouldn't be used on a comic book — or *any* book — for repairs. *All* tape (even so-called "magic" tape) ages badly — as does rubber cement. Use of tape usually means "Fair," at best.

Water damage.
Varies from simple page-warping to staining shown here on Jimmy's shirt. Less damage than this could be "Very Good"; this is no better than "Good."

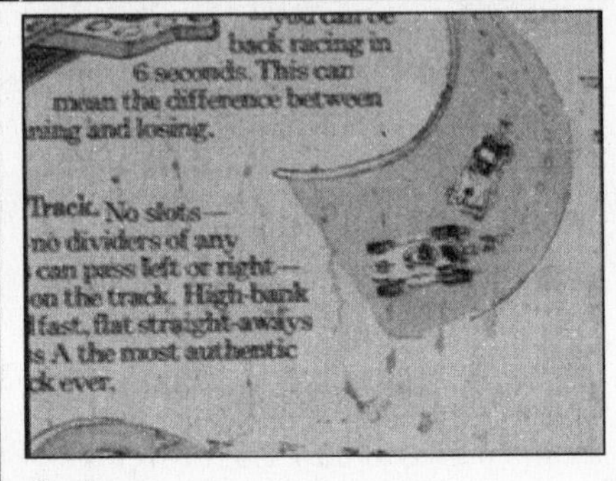

Stains.
Can vary widely, depending on cause. These look like mud — but food, grease, and the like also stain. No better than "Good."

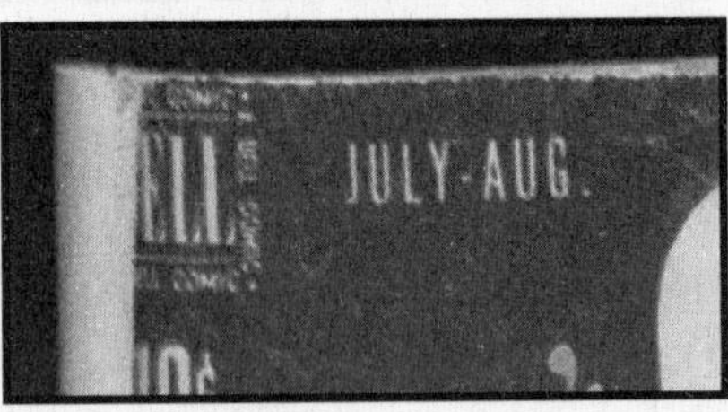

Rolled Spine.
Caused by folding back each page while reading — rather than opening the issue flat. Repeated folding permanently bent the spine. *May* be corrected, but the issue is no better than "Very Good."

Pricing:
Where art meets 21st Century computer science

Traditionally, comics price guides have relied solely on those "in-the-know" — advisors with recent experience in buying or selling comics.

While a method tried by most pricing publications at one time or another over the years, its shortcomings are readily apparent. Advisor information sometimes tended to be anecdotal, speaking in broad terms about entire lines rather than in specifics about particular issues in certain grades. Price guides often received advice in the form of spoken or written reports, rather than spreadsheets or other electronic formats likelier to deal in numerical detail.

And, too often, critics charged, advisors — most of whom were also retailers themselves — provided the prices they would have *liked* to have sold comics at, rather than the prices that they had *actually* sold comics at.

Wishful thinking (plus a simple business desire not to devalue their inventory) on behalf of advisors therefore tended to drive pricing in many guides up, up, up — even when prices were clearly falling for thousands of comic books.

The ***Comic Book Checklist and Price Guide*** determines a single Near-Mint price for each comic book through research by parties with no vested interest in seeing prices increase. Additionally, sales of CGC-graded copies are also analyzed, with the current sales ratios for non-encapsulated comics applied to the CGC prices to determine how the market is reacting.

Ungraded-copy price research

This volume includes a Near-Mint price for *each* of the comic books listed herein. The prices are the result of a combined effort by Human Computing, producers of *ComicBase,* and the staff of *Comics Buyer's Guide*.

Human Computing has set more than 1 million prices for comic books over the years. It's investigated every title at least once, usually multiple times over the years, rechecking whenever a new trend surfaces. Convention sales, mail-order sales, and shop prices throughout the United States are gathered on a continual basis.

Comics Buyer's Guide has used many of the same methods, including making reference to the largest sortable database of actual online transactions ever assembled in comics. Since 2000, the *Comics Buyer's Guide* staff has downloaded hundreds of thousands of completed transactions from the eBay auction service, including every single auction involving comic books graded by CGC.

These transactions are sorted by publisher, title, issue number, and grade, and a range of prices is determined. These transactions have been used to *inform*, rather than set, the prices for "unslabbed" comics seen herein. One or two transactions, even for a high-profile rare comic book, can't always be solely counted on to estimate the typical going rate everywhere else.

There are many price guides available for comics, some of which rely on each other so much that the prices all seem the same.

Those accustomed to that will find that prices in the ***Comic Book Checklist and Price Guide*** will look different, and often considerably different.

Our philosophy isn't to publish the highest prices we can find to make people feel better about their collections, but rather to publish the prices that smart collectors shopping at a variety of retail, convention, and online venues are likely to find.

If you're in a remote area with only one shop or the Internet to rely on, the prices you're likely to find will be higher.

Likewise, a comic book with some pedigree — having come from a famous collection — may also sell for more.

Graded vs. non-graded prices

Simply toughening grading standards and raising NM prices to reflect the high prices CGC-slabbed comics fetch is not a solution. From our observations, we can say that it is *not* generally the case that the high CGC prices have exerted upward influence on identical unslabbed copies.

Rather, there seem to be two separate markets developing with two separate sets of valuations.

In general, a Near Mint unslabbed comic book is fetching about what a slabbed VF/VF+ issue is bringing!

You can estimate CGC prices through the ratios we've developed. We've included a handy multiplier bar at the bottom of each page of the price guide to help determine prices in the other grades.

At presstime, the presence of a CGC slab and a Near-Mint (9.4) grade label on a random Near Mint comic book from before 1990 made that comic book *tend* to fetch **four** times our NM value in online auctions. The comic book on the border between Near Mint and Mint (CGC 9.8), brought **10.2 times** the NM value.

Using the Checklist and Price Guide

What's in the *Checklist and Price Guide*?

- English-language **comic books published and offered for sale in North America** for which we've been able to confirm existence.
- Many English-language **giveaway comic books** published in North America, including giveaways published by Marvel and DC.
- Many English-language **graphic novels** published in North America, hardcover and softcover, whose existence we've been able to confirm.
- **Magazines** that have a high percentage of comics content (such as *Cracked*).
- **Certain reference works** in comic-book size. (Such heavily illustrated encyclopedias as *The Official Handbook to the Marvel Universe* and *Who's Who in the DC Universe* are included.)
- Select other works of peculiar interest to comics collectors (such as *Newstime*, and *Marvel Age*.)

What's *not* in the *Checklist and Price Guide*?

- Some comic books released close to presstime. (Issues are entered into our database *en masse* according to publisher; our listings for, say, Marvel titles have issues more current than listings for some other publishers might.)
- Comic books whose existence we have not been able to confirm.
- Comics in languages other than English.
- Comics not published in North America.
- Paperback or hardcover reprints of comic strips not published in the dimensions of a comic book; *e.g.*, Fawcett *Peanuts* reprints.
- Certain reference works in comic-book size. (Works that are mostly prose, such as indexes to series, are generally excluded.)

Finding a title

The real, legal name of any comic book appears in its **indicia**, the block of small print usually found on the first or last inside page of most comics. **It does not necessarily match what's on the cover**; comics publishers have been known to relabel a single (or several) issues within a series for an editorial stunt, while never *really* changing the names of their series.

Drop proper names

Many titles have the name of one of their creators or the owner of a studio in their proper titles, such as *Kurt Busiek's Astro City*. In most cases, we have listed these comics in this manner: ***Astro City (Kurt Busiek's...)***.

There are a handful of cases where the series has only ever been identified by the name of a creator or studio, and in those few cases, such as ***Walt Disney's Comics & Stories***, we've left the title alone.

Alphabetization

We alphabetize titles as if there were no spaces in their names. Numbers are spelled out.

Multiple series with identical titles from the same publisher

When a publisher has used the same name for a series more than once, such as in the case of ***Amazing Spider-Man Vol. 1*** and ***Amazing Spider-Man Vol. 2***, we list those different titles in order of release with some indicator to differentiate them from each other. We generally, but not always, run them uninterrupted in order of their release.

Multiple series with identical titles from multiple publishers

When two or more publishers have published distinct and unrelated series with the same name, we generally run them in chronological order of release.

When a series changes publishers but does not interrupt its numbering, we tend to print them as separate listings but in consecutive chronological order.

CGC: Grading with confidence

Comics Buyer's Guide *broke the news on Comics Guaranty LLC, when the Certified Collectibles Group of companies announced it would serve the comic-book field. Today, CGC grading is widely used by online buyers and sellers to provide a standard on which both can agree.*

If you plan to have a comic book graded:

Information is available on the website, *www.CGCcomics.com*, and by calling (877) NM-COMIC. There are several levels of service. As of October 2004, the levels are:

• **Modern** (1975-today; value up to $200). Cost is $16 each, with a minimum of two graded. The price drops to $15 each for quantities of 10 or more.

• **Economy** (value of $0-$250). Cost is $29 each.

• **Standard** (value of $251-$1,000). Cost is $49 each.

• **Express** (value of $1,001-$4,000). Cost is $79 each.

• **Walkthru** (any value). Cost is 2.5% of Fair Market Value with a minimum charge of $110 and a maximum of $1,000 each.

Graders do not determine a value; they identify defects and place a grade on the comic book. This lets online buyers purchase items evaluated by a common standard — and identifies for buyer and seller such matters as whether issues have been restored.

If you plan to buy a CGC-graded comic book:

First, yes: You *can* remove the comic book from the sealed container. If you retain the container and paperwork with the comic book, CGC even offers a discount on re-encapsulation.

A summary is as follows, but note the descriptions are ***CBG***'s guidelines, *not* officially CGC's:

10.0 Mint
9.9 Mint
9.8 Near Mint/Mint
9.6 Near Mint+
9.4 Near Mint (almost invisible stress marks, very tiny color flecks, ever so slight corner blunting)
9.2 Near Mint-
9.0 Very Fine/Near Mint
8.5 Very Fine+
8.0 Very Fine (relatively flat cover, slight staple discoloration, 2 slight stress lines, 1/4-inch crease not breaking color, slight yellowing)
7.5 Very Fine-
7.0 Fine/Very Fine
6.5 Fine+
6.0 Fine (slight surface wear, a few stress marks or 1/4-inch spine split, read a few times)
5.5 Fine-
5.0 Very Good/Fine
4.5 Very Good+
4.0 Very Good (average used comic book, wear, center crease, slightly rolled spine, minor soiling, 1/4-inch triangle from corner or edge, store stamps, name stamps, minor tears and folds, minor tape)
3.5 Very Good-
3.0 Good/Very Good
2.5 Good+
2.0 Good (all pages and covers, small pieces missing inside, cover piece as much as 1/2-inch triangle, 2-inch spine split, abraded — but retains structural integrity)
1.8 Good-
1.5 Fair/Good
1.0 Fair (soiled, ragged, unattractive, spine split to 2/3 its length, staples gone, coupon clipped)

Now filter eBay for "CGC." And remember to check ***CBG*** for our latest market analyses.

— *Maggie Thompson*

Help us out!

Even in the unprecedented assemblage that is the **Checklist and Price Guide**, there are a great many facts that remain to be added. Even after years of adding data from our own comic books, we still have many we haven't gotten to yet.

We'll continue to make additions and revisions to the database, but we'd love to have your help. If you have any of the following information that we did not include for any comic book in (or not in) this directory, send it in:

- Title and issue number
- Publisher
- Publication date (as listed in the indicia)
- Cover price
- Page count (do not include covers)
- Whether it's color or black-and-white
- Titles of stories inside (note if any are text only)
- Writers whose works appear
- Artists whose works appear
- Cover artist
- Names of any people appearing on photo covers

Please send your findings (Excel files are acceptable) along with your name, address, and phone number to:

allcomics@krause.com

or to Brent Frankenhoff, 2005 Comic Book Checklist and Price Guide, 700 E. State St., Iola, WI 54990. All submissions become the property of Krause Publications. Please state the source of your information and provide only what you can find through your own original research.

For more information

In the summer of 2004, we produced the third edition of our *Standard Catalog of Comic Books*, a 1,584-page volume that listed as much information as we had in our database on more than 158,000 comics from before the Golden Age to the present.

Expanding on the line listings in this ***Checklist and Price Guide***, *The Standard Catalog* contains circulation data, CGC-grading information, full CGC auction results for more than 140,000 sales, distributor order numbers, and other information.

Copies of that tome are still available for collectors seeking additional data on their favorite comics. Simply call (800) 258-0929 and use order #SCOM3 to purchase the $34.99 softcover.

For still more suggested reading, see Page 791.

CGC Auction Prices Realized

In the year and a half prior to press time, we recorded the results of **every single eBay auction of a CGC-graded comic book**. We then removed all auctions for restored comics; all auctions that ended early; all auctions for more than one CGC comic book at a time; and all auctions that ended with no bids.

That left us with almost 100,000 completed auctions for CGC-graded comics. At right, we report the results of every combination of comic book and CGC grade that saw **five** or more closed auctions during the period from May 1, 2002-August 31, 2004.

We list the **unique name** of the comics title and **unique issue number**, as found in this edition of the *CBG Checklist & Price Guide* (or, in the case of comics from before 1961, *The Standard Catalog of Comic Books*). We then list the **grade of the comic book** being auctioned; the **number of different auctions** in that grade; the **lowest closing price**; the **average closing price**, and the **highest closing price**.

Adventures of Bob Hope

#9 8.5............5.........82.........**199**......300

In the sample above, there were 5 auctions for *Adventures of Bob Hope* #9 in 8.5 VF+. The average closing price was $199; the lowest was $82, and the highest was $300. Regard that the boldface price is an average and not the median; it will not necessarily be halfway between the low and high prices.

Aren't there a lot of issues missing? We only listed comics that had three or more auctions in a single grade — and, while CGC volume on eBay is high and growing higher, there simply weren't enough auctions to make our listing. *Amazing Spider-Man* is one of the most traded titles, for example, and issue #273 hasn't been sold online in any grade more than four times!

Did every one of these comics sell at these prices? No. A percentage of online auctions that end with bids don't sell because the bids don't reach the seller's "reserve price." On eBay, for example, reserve prices are set by sellers who aren't confident that their products will find their values.

We believe that, despite the fact that the comic books don't change hands, the closing prices of these auctions nonetheless demonstrate what the market would bear at any given moment. We can't say for sure whether auctioners, in general, set their reserve prices too high — but what we *can* say is that every auctioner who couldn't sell an item due to a reserve *did* overestimate what the market would bear.

A smaller percentage of auctions do not end in a transaction due to a failure of buyer and seller to come to terms — and, as such, we see the same comics coming up again for sale. That doesn't make the closing price less useful when it comes to determining what's going on in the market. (There are some auctions that end without transactions due to patently frivolous bids. We've removed those cases from the data set.)

Why are average sale prices for some grades higher than the average prices for the higher grades? This may be a consequence of the small number of auctions that took place. *Amazing Spider-Man* Vol. 1, #24 in 6.5 averaged $107 per auction, while #24 in 7.0 averaged only $95 per auction.

We see one possible reason why by looking at the auction volume: There have been three times as many auctions for 7.0 copies as there have been for 6.5 copies, suggesting that the greater availability of 7.0 copies depressed the price for them.

That's why we present you with not simply the average, but the high and low closing prices, as well as the number of auctions used to arrive at the price.

How reliable are these prices? These pages do exactly what we say they do: They report the ranges and averages offered online since the summer of 2002. Your future mileage may (and probably will) vary.

ISSUE	CGC GRADE	# of AUCTIONS	LOW CLOSE	AVG CLOSE	HIGH CLOSE
Abadazad					
#1	9.8	9	14	**21**	36
Action Comics					
#30	4.0	9	227	**325**	481
#42	4.0	5	202	**241**	275
#80	3.0	5	90	**105**	135
#84	6.5	7	78	**157**	275
#112	9.0	6	500	**630**	800
#220	8.0	5	175	**212**	265
#252	3.0	5	118	**159**	200
#267	7.5	5	181	**206**	240
#413	9.4	8	33	**51**	73
#500	9.4	5	16	**21**	25
#544	9.8	7	14	**30**	35
#584	9.6	11	11	**21**	26
#600	9.8	24	12	**32**	75
	9.6	10	10	**20**	34
#662	9.8	5	50	**66**	129
	9.6	6	9	**22**	48
	9.4	11	9	**15**	35
#700	9.8	9	10	**27**	50
#775	9.6	8	9	**26**	50
#811	9.8	5	11	**14**	16
#812	9.8	25	11	**25**	50
#812/2nd	9.8	25	11	**26**	35
#813	9.8	25	11	**25**	40
Adventure Comics					
#80	8.0	5	355	**796**	1,095
#109	3.5	5	39	**62**	78
#245	7.0	7	61	**75**	99
#256	2.0	8	13	**34**	53
#260	6.5	5	92	**151**	193
	3.5	5	34	**62**	88
#334	9.2	5	86	**119**	144
#381	9.0	5	51	**76**	100
#428	9.2	5	21	**57**	138
#431	9.2	9	33	**50**	76
	9.0	5	22	**30**	43
#432	9.6	7	64	**92**	128
	9.4	5	21	**58**	80
	9.0	5	20	**25**	30
#433	9.6	8	59	**94**	172
	9.4	20	26	**50**	86
Adventures of Bob Hope					
#9	8.5	5	82	**199**	300
Adventures of Superman					
#497	9.8	5	20	**33**	53
#500	9.8	5	16	**33**	70
#501	9.6	7	3	**8**	10
#624	9.8	5	10	**15**	26
#625	9.8	25	10	**31**	40
#625/2nd	9.8	23	9	**23**	32
#626	9.8	17	10	**27**	37
Adventures on the Planet of the Apes					
#1	9.6	6	50	**74**	120
Alias					
#1	9.8	16	17	**32**	86
	9.6	12	10	**20**	31

ISSUE	CGC GRADE	# of AUCTIONS	LOW CLOSE	AVG CLOSE	HIGH CLOSE
All-American Comics					
#62	8.0	6	158	**334**	427
#73	6.5	5	114	**154**	209
	5.5	6	103	**152**	204
All-Flash					
#1	8.0	5	4,372	**5,774**	7,000
#2	5.5	5	475	**569**	627
#13	8.5	6	305	**469**	704
All-Star Comics					
#5	8.5	5	2,050	**2,432**	2,600
	5.0	5	700	**758**	821
#6	9.0	6	1,900	**2,046**	2,227
	6.0	7	285	**624**	795
#7	9.0	5	2,225	**2,665**	3,050
#8	6.5	5	4,050	**5,460**	8,000
	5.5	6	4,055	**4,584**	5,250
#31	8.0	6	600	**651**	725
#33	7.5	5	1,200	**1,330**	1,601
#58	9.6	5	52	**75**	100
	9.4	15	19	**46**	86
All-Star Squadron					
#1	9.8	5	25	**51**	80
	9.6	12	6	**23**	37
	9.4	5	7	**14**	30
All-Star Western					
#5	9.6	8	31	**78**	117
	9.4	5	33	**56**	85
#10	9.4	5	644	**1,028**	1,494
	9.0	7	243	**364**	408
	8.0	6	66	**134**	203
#11	9.0	5	50	**98**	164
	7.5	5	16	**28**	50
Alpha Flight					
#1	9.8	25	14	**40**	150
	9.6	25	10	**23**	40
	9.4	9	12	**19**	32
#3	9.8	5	18	**23**	35
#13	9.8	6	7	**21**	35
#17	9.8	13	15	**22**	29
#33	9.8	5	35	**48**	73
	9.4	5	11	**28**	56
#34	9.8	8	20	**27**	36

ISSUE	CGC GRADE	# of AUCTIONS	LOW CLOSE	AVG CLOSE	HIGH CLOSE
Alpha Flight (Vol. 2)					
#1	9.8	7	15	**19**	25
Amazing Adult Fantasy					
#11	8.5	6	262	**394**	500
Amazing Adventures (Vol. 3)					
#1	9.4	7	72	**119**	167
	9.2	11	34	**46**	75
	9.0	5	30	**39**	44
#4	9.6	8	36	**46**	52
	9.4	9	25	**35**	60
	9.0	5	13	**21**	36
#5	9.2	5	10	**21**	32
#11	9.4	7	387	**588**	735
	9.2	8	148	**255**	566
	9.0	17	61	**131**	300
	8.5	6	57	**91**	113
#15	9.2	5	26	**33**	41
#34	9.8	5	26	**37**	51
Amazing Fantasy					
#15	7.5	15	5,380	**8,884**	14,500
	7.0	14	5,100	**6,766**	9,600
	6.5	8	5,000	**7,024**	9,999
	6.0	6	3,500	**4,745**	6,200
	5.5	16	3,180	**4,184**	6,100
	5.0	5	2,000	**2,902**	4,883
	4.5	15	1,632	**3,176**	4,500
	4.0	24	1,802	**2,653**	3,800
	3.5	25	1,400	**2,063**	2,900
	3.0	25	1,250	**1,747**	2,950
	2.5	13	1,226	**1,639**	1,999
	2.0	20	1,009	**1,305**	1,825
	1.5	9	810	**1,122**	1,500
	1.0	12	299	**786**	995
Amazing Spider-Man					
#1	9.0	8	18,100	**23,047**	26,500
	8.5	7	8,000	**10,387**	12,909
	8.0	17	5,888	**7,720**	10,000
	7.5	16	4,500	**6,296**	8,850
	7.0	8	3,000	**4,597**	6,100
	6.5	16	2,999	**3,787**	6,300
	6.0	16	2,025	**3,042**	4,050
	5.5	23	1,650	**2,585**	3,250
	5.0	25	1,918	**2,457**	3,850
	4.5	19	1,680	**2,175**	3,050
	4.0	25	1,026	**1,829**	2,800
	3.5	25	1,025	**1,483**	2,200
	3.0	25	730	**1,329**	1,925
	2.5	11	670	**984**	1,500
	2.0	12	500	**841**	1,100
	1.8	11	409	**728**	1,200
	1.5	13	410	**649**	1,010
	1.0	7	351	**607**	810
	0.5	8	81	**290**	566
#2	9.2	6	8,100	**8,595**	10,000
	9.0	7	2,250	**3,615**	5,352
	8.5	6	2,567	**3,053**	3,550
	8.0	5	1,948	**2,364**	3,150
	7.5	7	1,580	**1,866**	2,127
	6.5	10	449	**991**	1,358
	6.0	8	660	**877**	1,091
	5.0	6	496	**593**	661
	4.0	14	158	**505**	755
	3.5	10	294	**352**	412
	3.0	12	223	**350**	760
	2.5	10	177	**256**	310
	2.0	5	178	**287**	375
#3	9.0	15	3,050	**3,966**	5,150
	8.5	13	1,208	**2,244**	3,795
	8.0	10	1,750	**2,227**	2,734
	7.5	10	1,017	**1,523**	2,075
	7.0	17	831	**1,122**	1,525
	6.5	10	348	**730**	1,000
	5.5	8	233	**594**	810
	5.0	20	382	**586**	910
	4.5	16	375	**468**	657
	4.0	11	300	**400**	480
	3.5	8	300	**369**	450
	3.0	13	225	**319**	500
	2.5	10	200	**257**	325
	1.8	5	83	**136**	200
#4	8.5	7	1,630	**1,900**	2,222
	8.0	9	589	**1,454**	1,895
	7.5	18	810	**1,131**	1,650
	7.0	10	455	**671**	931
	6.5	7	481	**587**	699
	6.0	5	445	**528**	665
	5.0	20	203	**349**	560
	4.5	12	256	**324**	415
	4.0	17	132	**256**	362
	3.5	12	68	**180**	300
	3.0	11	153	**194**	270
	2.5	6	103	**145**	189
	1.5	5	68	**91**	113
#5	8.5	8	1,375	**1,957**	2,951
	8.0	7	1,230	**1,469**	1,800
	7.5	25	565	**792**	1,100
	6.5	12	407	**538**	750
	6.0	5	400	**481**	612
	5.5	12	297	**355**	415
	5.0	21	16	**301**	397
	4.5	12	153	**253**	340
	4.0	25	125	**234**	350
	3.5	10	108	**189**	255
	3.0	9	134	**200**	266
	2.5	7	81	**121**	134
#6	9.4	15	4,450	**6,787**	8,500
	9.0	10	750	**2,054**	2,763
	8.5	9	405	**1,234**	1,800
	8.0	5	765	**895**	1,060
	7.5	10	539	**757**	1,000
	7.0	11	410	**597**	835
	6.5	7	255	**403**	537
	6.0	16	256	**382**	585
	5.5	12	203	**324**	425
	5.0	20	193	**294**	433
	4.5	12	212	**280**	348
	4.0	18	131	**204**	262
	3.5	10	128	**179**	250

ISSUE	CGC GRADE	# of AUCTIONS	LOW CLOSE	AVG CLOSE	HIGH CLOSE
	3.0	8	104	**153**	205
	2.5	5	100	**140**	190
#7	9.0	5	510	**1,381**	1,847
	8.5	5	709	**876**	1,281
	8.0	8	521	**691**	861
	7.5	12	302	**470**	610
	7.0	20	184	**377**	610
	6.5	11	173	**308**	510
	6.0	8	114	**230**	360
	5.5	8	158	**240**	306
	5.0	11	67	**176**	225
	4.5	10	100	**149**	191
	4.0	18	37	**151**	225
	3.5	6	92	**127**	178
	3.0	7	90	**108**	135
	2.5	8	66	**96**	123
#8	9.4	8	2,550	**3,116**	5,000
	9.2	11	1,136	**1,647**	2,600
	9.0	7	899	**1,226**	1,350
	8.5	9	714	**842**	1,000
	8.0	9	455	**610**	750
	7.5	14	325	**467**	650
	7.0	14	276	**388**	600
	6.5	12	233	**300**	455
	6.0	13	153	**219**	300
	5.5	7	108	**201**	265
	5.0	10	105	**186**	251
	4.5	12	91	**146**	200
	4.0	17	78	**157**	309
	3.5	14	75	**101**	150
	3.0	5	73	**146**	310
#9	9.2	7	2,025	**2,597**	3,350
	9.0	5	1,275	**1,478**	1,625
	8.5	5	824	**985**	1,136
	8.0	12	605	**749**	1,175
	7.5	6	485	**633**	788
	7.0	14	255	**416**	540
	6.5	7	275	**390**	455
	6.0	10	218	**322**	415
	5.5	9	213	**252**	296
	5.0	6	187	**227**	286
	4.5	12	104	**189**	238
	4.0	15	120	**166**	260
	3.0	6	92	**151**	199
#10	9.0	10	610	**997**	1,375
	8.5	19	522	**719**	1,075
	8.0	9	355	**564**	700
	7.5	21	300	**398**	514
	7.0	14	201	**353**	510
	6.5	22	178	**262**	500
	6.0	14	163	**242**	330
	5.5	7	168	**180**	195
	5.0	10	128	**174**	282
	4.5	10	108	**149**	189
	4.0	21	96	**135**	225
	3.0	9	51	**82**	108
#11	8.0	8	303	**643**	997
	7.5	7	355	**423**	464
	7.0	8	199	**279**	350
	6.5	12	175	**275**	351
	6.0	9	93	**214**	399
	5.0	13	78	**142**	203
	4.5	5	75	**104**	148
	4.0	10	81	**112**	128
	3.5	6	77	**87**	112
#12	9.0	13	900	**1,111**	1,300
	8.5	7	163	**538**	785
	8.0	12	305	**407**	560
	7.5	12	208	**324**	405
	7.0	12	205	**300**	350
	6.5	11	133	**205**	275
	6.0	5	161	**200**	245
	5.0	7	51	**124**	203
	4.5	12	100	**130**	175
	4.0	10	58	**104**	134
	3.5	5	50	**81**	114
	3.0	8	56	**80**	120
#13	9.0	9	1,037	**1,390**	1,718
	8.5	7	599	**759**	915
	7.5	8	350	**417**	515
	7.0	17	132	**317**	530
	6.5	14	178	**263**	525
	6.0	5	180	**222**	267
	5.5	7	148	**199**	250
	5.0	5	109	**162**	200
	4.5	5	96	**123**	152
	4.0	12	74	**126**	198
	3.5	7	65	**96**	129
	3.0	5	69	**95**	125
#14	9.4	5	8,400	**9,500**	10,100
	9.2	12	2,950	**3,538**	4,150
	9.0	17	1,826	**2,365**	3,100
	8.5	18	1,034	**1,552**	2,395
	8.0	25	906	**1,244**	1,650
	7.5	25	381	**825**	1,425
	7.0	25	275	**705**	1,175
	6.5	25	299	**521**	875
	6.0	25	338	**460**	610
	5.5	25	265	**386**	675
	5.0	25	164	**338**	510
	4.5	25	109	**313**	450
	4.0	25	158	**275**	475
	3.5	14	154	**234**	340
	3.0	20	147	**198**	350
	2.5	7	111	**166**	249

ISSUE	CGC GRADE	# of AUCTIONS	LOW CLOSE	AVG CLOSE	HIGH CLOSE
Amazing Spider-Man (cont'd)					
#15	9.0	7	860	**1,146**	1,575
	8.5	5	547	**608**	638
	8.0	15	300	**440**	638
	7.5	9	100	**279**	411
	7.0	19	133	**239**	480
	6.0	13	117	**168**	216
	5.5	7	121	**163**	184
	4.5	6	77	**112**	150
	4.0	13	49	**99**	141
	3.5	5	71	**82**	100
#16	9.0	12	501	**752**	894
	8.5	6	364	**461**	655
	8.0	22	299	**386**	525
	7.5	11	202	**279**	401
	7.0	10	191	**246**	355
	6.5	8	173	**200**	250
	6.0	7	140	**175**	255
	5.0	7	97	**120**	175
	4.0	11	69	**87**	125
	3.5	5	78	**94**	110
#17	9.4	9	2,146	**3,136**	5,100
	9.2	10	985	**1,372**	1,750
	9.0	5	860	**942**	1,147
	8.5	11	370	**544**	675
	8.0	12	285	**404**	491
	7.5	7	255	**363**	460
	7.0	21	190	**272**	394
	6.5	19	125	**190**	292
	6.0	17	113	**165**	222
	5.5	6	96	**144**	182
	5.0	10	71	**111**	150
	4.5	12	69	**106**	203
	4.0	19	34	**90**	125
	3.5	8	50	**82**	120
	3.0	7	41	**60**	100
#18	9.4	5	1,025	**2,075**	2,800
	9.0	21	405	**594**	1,200
	8.5	10	337	**391**	455
	8.0	19	94	**298**	434
	7.0	18	113	**176**	250
	6.5	8	86	**143**	180
	4.5	11	50	**76**	100
	4.0	12	45	**71**	100
	3.5	6	31	**53**	80
#19	9.2	15	405	**591**	800
	9.0	22	203	**420**	600
	8.5	25	153	**274**	345
	8.0	25	151	**217**	295
	7.5	8	160	**189**	250
	7.0	11	129	**166**	225
	6.5	13	76	**109**	140
	6.0	5	96	**118**	166
	5.5	5	71	**85**	104
	5.0	9	42	**74**	100
	4.5	8	50	**66**	89
	4.0	5	44	**58**	86
#20	9.0	10	566	**714**	885
	8.5	12	300	**399**	460
	8.0	13	249	**359**	500
	7.5	18	89	**205**	331
	7.0	6	180	**207**	260
	6.5	11	120	**147**	178
	6.0	19	53	**129**	169
	5.5	5	98	**121**	174
	5.0	8	78	**92**	144
	4.5	6	78	**92**	105
	4.0	6	54	**68**	80
#21	9.2	8	404	**621**	820
	9.0	11	377	**432**	550
	8.5	6	240	**283**	355
	8.0	18	143	**224**	321
	7.5	14	124	**169**	205
	7.0	6	62	**129**	180
	5.5	6	48	**62**	74
	5.0	6	62	**81**	105
	4.5	6	27	**50**	73
#22	9.2	6	482	**584**	667
	9.0	10	275	**370**	441
	8.5	10	128	**230**	300
	8.0	20	115	**187**	262
	7.5	12	117	**170**	205
	7.0	11	91	**139**	175
	6.5	13	56	**80**	125
	6.0	6	51	**80**	104
	5.5	5	28	**46**	62
	5.0	12	26	**61**	100
#23	9.2	18	677	**970**	1,325
	9.0	11	366	**495**	600
	8.5	8	249	**361**	450
	8.0	25	129	**246**	350
	7.5	24	120	**186**	280
	7.0	22	67	**144**	262
	6.5	5	57	**128**	200
	6.0	24	49	**87**	125
	5.5	11	48	**74**	100
	5.0	16	51	**85**	128
	4.5	13	36	**57**	80
	4.0	5	49	**67**	77
#24	9.2	5	365	**497**	608
	9.0	13	250	**354**	450
	8.5	8	184	**231**	280
	8.0	10	149	**190**	230
	7.5	8	103	**145**	209
	7.0	15	51	**95**	150
	6.5	5	67	**107**	153
	5.5	6	43	**53**	85
	5.0	8	36	**50**	75
#25	9.2	8	332	**562**	755
	9.0	15	305	**405**	565
	8.5	10	177	**261**	360
	8.0	17	79	**174**	256
	7.5	18	103	**163**	255
	7.0	17	87	**131**	228
	6.5	9	89	**120**	204
	5.0	9	54	**66**	85
#26	9.0	9	355	**457**	687
	8.5	8	180	**304**	400
	8.0	13	157	**223**	301
	7.5	19	74	**134**	228

ISSUE	CGC GRADE	# of AUCTIONS	LOW CLOSE	AVG CLOSE	HIGH CLOSE
	7.0	9	72	**113**	152
	6.5	7	61	**101**	150
	6.0	11	53	**77**	100
	5.5	7	63	**77**	99
	4.5	12	32	**50**	77
	4.0	11	25	**45**	60
	3.5	6	35	**51**	70
#27	9.0	16	255	**414**	645
	8.5	10	204	**263**	350
	8.0	25	103	**209**	350
	7.5	12	97	**165**	380
	7.0	17	81	**130**	300
	6.5	9	16	**84**	122
	6.0	11	45	**74**	115
	5.0	16	51	**60**	75
	4.0	5	33	**38**	43
#28	9.0	16	500	**883**	1,380
	8.5	21	328	**520**	770
	8.0	11	103	**260**	400
	7.5	17	76	**269**	400
	7.0	25	71	**187**	305
	6.0	5	86	**116**	139
	5.5	11	50	**85**	123
	5.0	6	61	**71**	80
	4.5	11	29	**60**	100
	4.0	10	40	**49**	68
#29	9.4	5	700	**908**	1,000
	9.0	7	234	**290**	450
	8.5	14	133	**199**	256
	8.0	6	124	**145**	163
	7.5	11	51	**94**	131
	7.0	8	62	**106**	175
	6.5	7	45	**67**	96
	6.0	5	53	**65**	85
	4.5	5	38	**42**	47
	4.0	7	31	**39**	51
#30	9.8	5	21	**46**	69
	9.4	9	727	**967**	1,281
	9.2	25	228	**372**	503
	9.0	17	158	**230**	322
	8.5	19	129	**169**	302
	8.0	22	71	**122**	195
	7.5	15	27	**78**	138
	7.0	15	49	**77**	200
	4.5	7	25	**37**	53
	4.0	8	10	**29**	39
	3.5	7	25	**34**	50
#31	9.0	9	250	**333**	500
	8.5	9	138	**206**	265
	8.0	8	129	**183**	228
	7.5	7	51	**128**	213
	7.0	11	79	**100**	143
	6.5	6	51	**76**	100
	5.0	5	43	**55**	65
#32	9.4	8	545	**661**	999
	9.2	6	278	**350**	435
	9.0	13	162	**246**	372
	8.5	13	82	**144**	188
	8.0	12	99	**131**	169
	7.5	6	77	**115**	141
	7.0	8	53	**76**	103
	6.5	14	31	**59**	76
	5.0	7	30	**40**	50
	4.0	8	15	**27**	40
#33	9.6	19	576	**900**	1,414
	9.4	25	141	**589**	850
	9.2	21	226	**318**	386
	9.0	12	91	**247**	350
	8.5	12	125	**166**	218
	8.0	12	101	**157**	208
	7.5	6	96	**115**	143
	7.0	9	58	**100**	154
#34	9.4	5	847	**986**	1,275
	9.2	17	282	**414**	651
	9.0	21	104	**227**	310
	8.5	9	113	**171**	229
	8.0	16	92	**132**	220
	7.5	5	72	**91**	128
	7.0	6	51	**75**	92
	5.5	8	29	**43**	60
	5.0	7	19	**32**	40
#35	9.2	7	265	**395**	515
	9.0	19	125	**226**	338
	8.5	9	118	**153**	190
	8.0	11	91	**131**	207
	7.5	11	44	**72**	105
	7.0	10	57	**84**	118
	6.5	9	43	**53**	66
	5.0	5	24	**40**	53
#36	9.2	7	294	**399**	510
	9.0	17	135	**212**	316
	8.5	16	104	**146**	200
	8.0	21	51	**115**	215
	7.5	20	46	**81**	113
	7.0	14	41	**68**	87
	5.5	5	22	**35**	46
	5.0	5	27	**51**	86
	4.5	6	22	**30**	37
#37	9.2	10	99	**322**	442
	9.0	19	78	**201**	300
	8.5	11	104	**145**	220
	8.0	14	85	**114**	153
	7.5	5	76	**85**	102
	7.0	13	50	**68**	115
	5.0	8	28	**38**	55

Amazing Spider-Man (cont'd)

ISSUE	CGC GRADE	# of AUCTIONS	LOW CLOSE	AVG CLOSE	HIGH CLOSE
#38	9.4	10	547	**832**	1,080
	9.0	15	153	**216**	379
	8.5	24	61	**139**	225
	8.0	13	87	**116**	153
	7.5	11	51	**81**	140
	7.0	8	52	**73**	100
	6.0	10	37	**52**	77
	5.5	17	25	**40**	76
	4.5	7	25	**29**	37
	4.0	7	22	**31**	41
#39	9.6	5	3,050	**3,517**	4,800
	9.4	11	750	**1,442**	1,914
	9.2	18	455	**608**	750
	9.0	25	178	**368**	565
	8.5	15	183	**274**	365
	8.0	25	80	**201**	310
	7.5	13	100	**168**	213
	7.0	25	74	**117**	195
	6.5	15	55	**87**	135
	6.0	19	60	**84**	125
	5.5	10	46	**64**	91
	5.0	11	37	**60**	80
	4.5	10	31	**56**	77
	4.0	8	36	**50**	99
#40	9.4	19	711	**1,306**	1,950
	9.2	24	511	**709**	1,000
	9.0	25	305	**423**	695
	8.5	16	205	**280**	380
	8.0	25	178	**246**	338
	7.5	19	125	**179**	229
	7.0	13	79	**137**	190
	6.5	16	71	**101**	160
	6.0	22	57	**91**	150
	5.5	10	66	**80**	95
	5.0	5	51	**68**	86
	4.5	8	41	**54**	65
#41	9.4	12	999	**1,243**	1,611
	9.2	7	381	**537**	648
	9.0	12	257	**371**	455
	8.5	18	158	**235**	320
	8.0	11	96	**154**	230
	7.5	9	42	**141**	250
	7.0	12	59	**100**	150
	4.0	9	26	**45**	72
#42	9.6	8	910	**1,393**	1,750
	9.4	11	300	**781**	1,026
	9.2	19	205	**338**	570
	9.0	23	164	**218**	294
	8.5	17	40	**153**	200
	8.0	18	56	**122**	155
	7.5	10	61	**84**	128
	7.0	16	42	**66**	118
	6.5	9	41	**54**	70
	6.0	8	33	**52**	79
	4.5	5	23	**29**	35
	4.0	7	10	**21**	30
#43	9.4	7	375	**494**	635
	9.2	18	160	**241**	371
	9.0	15	119	**166**	245
	8.5	18	79	**106**	130
	8.0	13	59	**85**	135
	7.5	8	49	**72**	96
	7.0	8	38	**50**	80
#44	9.2	7	220	**332**	425
	9.0	10	113	**184**	300
	8.5	8	90	**131**	200
	8.0	7	53	**95**	125
	7.5	14	42	**62**	81
	7.0	12	35	**57**	90
	6.0	5	40	**46**	60
#45	9.4	14	382	**476**	626
	9.2	22	141	**230**	325
	9.0	25	31	**125**	188
	8.5	17	65	**96**	166
	8.0	16	51	**80**	127
	7.5	10	55	**65**	78
	7.0	12	39	**57**	86
	5.0	5	26	**36**	54
#46	9.0	14	143	**199**	335
	8.5	12	77	**114**	154
	8.0	18	59	**87**	150
	7.0	6	32	**67**	90
	5.0	7	28	**36**	46
#47	9.4	14	326	**412**	525
	9.2	22	140	**216**	315
	9.0	25	90	**144**	255
	8.5	15	51	**102**	160
	8.0	19	33	**74**	124
	7.5	11	16	**44**	62
	6.5	7	31	**49**	75
	6.0	5	31	**37**	45
#48	9.4	6	405	**470**	600
	9.2	22	128	**197**	306
	9.0	23	84	**143**	280
	8.5	11	71	**107**	130
	8.0	9	49	**75**	99
	7.0	7	38	**60**	92
	6.5	9	26	**38**	60
#49	9.2	20	158	**244**	410
	9.0	21	76	**134**	181
	8.5	13	65	**95**	175
	8.0	14	11	**76**	127
	7.5	13	29	**61**	100
	7.0	5	36	**45**	56
	6.5	10	31	**43**	61
#50	9.4	10	1,850	**2,561**	4,550
	9.2	20	900	**1,235**	1,525
	9.0	13	617	**742**	985
	8.5	25	311	**465**	718
	8.0	25	90	**340**	560
	7.5	25	98	**258**	350
	7.0	25	103	**209**	350
	6.5	18	100	**158**	305
	6.0	11	91	**133**	166
	5.5	14	72	**103**	178
	5.0	16	32	**88**	140
	4.5	7	68	**90**	173
	4.0	16	41	**66**	90
	3.0	6	37	**63**	75

ISSUE	CGC GRADE	# of AUCTIONS	LOW CLOSE	AVG CLOSE	HIGH CLOSE
#51	9.4	9	314	**701**	990
	9.2	16	234	**343**	599
	9.0	12	153	**228**	332
	8.5	15	97	**147**	210
	8.0	7	96	**122**	143
	7.5	8	57	**84**	114
	7.0	7	65	**84**	118
	6.5	8	13	**47**	75
	6.0	6	36	**56**	79
	5.5	5	11	**33**	50
	4.5	6	25	**35**	46
#52	9.0	9	76	**119**	178
	8.5	7	51	**82**	103
	8.0	5	51	**66**	76
	7.5	8	35	**52**	66
	7.0	7	35	**45**	61
#53	9.4	8	295	**435**	635
	9.2	14	168	**220**	303
	9.0	10	77	**115**	160
	8.5	6	54	**69**	105
	8.0	10	34	**60**	76
	7.5	10	34	**52**	70
	6.5	7	25	**39**	60
	4.0	5	25	**26**	30
#54	9.4	12	350	**459**	613
	9.2	14	100	**192**	352
	9.0	11	91	**119**	153
	8.5	14	56	**79**	114
	8.0	7	43	**54**	66
	7.5	9	36	**55**	80
	7.0	5	39	**50**	65
	5.0	5	25	**37**	52
#55	9.2	5	135	**203**	345
	9.0	11	70	**132**	200
	8.5	7	52	**78**	120
	8.0	5	51	**59**	74
	7.5	9	34	**45**	57
	6.0	8	23	**38**	51
#56	9.4	14	26	**354**	500
	9.2	25	70	**156**	232
	9.0	23	66	**105**	180
	8.5	9	36	**61**	81
	8.0	17	39	**64**	86
	7.5	11	12	**45**	61
	7.0	5	40	**50**	66
#57	9.4	22	188	**301**	494
	9.2	24	81	**130**	180
	9.0	9	77	**103**	150
	8.5	19	50	**68**	100
	8.0	9	42	**64**	100
	7.5	7	35	**48**	63
	7.0	6	32	**45**	77
#58	9.2	17	92	**153**	252
	9.0	16	67	**92**	110
	8.5	15	41	**71**	123
	8.0	11	19	**51**	72
	7.0	8	32	**39**	50
	4.5	5	20	**23**	25
#59	9.6	10	405	**624**	999
	9.4	25	125	**279**	395
	9.2	25	91	**155**	220
	9.0	25	67	**105**	158
	8.5	25	47	**81**	120
	8.0	16	44	**66**	96
	7.5	12	28	**48**	70
	7.0	10	41	**45**	52
#60	9.2	5	203	**234**	299
	9.0	6	92	**114**	150
	8.5	6	61	**76**	104
	7.0	10	25	**43**	70
#61	9.4	5	206	**291**	355
	9.2	12	114	**140**	193
	9.0	10	50	**94**	138
	8.5	13	45	**64**	95
	8.0	10	40	**54**	79
#62	9.4	25	175	**292**	411
	9.2	25	96	**144**	225
	9.0	12	10	**92**	125
	8.5	11	50	**64**	83
	8.0	9	41	**58**	71
	7.0	6	35	**43**	51
	6.0	6	26	**38**	66
#63	9.2	5	147	**285**	510
	9.0	9	10	**103**	140
	8.5	8	50	**79**	138
#64	9.6	19	280	**395**	595
	9.4	25	168	**237**	305
	9.2	25	50	**110**	199
	9.0	25	45	**84**	183
	8.5	23	38	**61**	111
	8.0	9	35	**48**	62
	7.5	12	29	**46**	70
	7.0	9	28	**37**	51
	6.0	5	21	**27**	34
#65	9.6	9	409	**567**	820
	9.4	14	10	**221**	295
	9.2	14	72	**115**	178
	9.0	12	50	**79**	110
	8.5	12	43	**55**	90
	8.0	9	38	**49**	71
	7.5	5	41	**46**	53
#66	9.6	6	440	**581**	810
	9.4	5	280	**348**	401
	9.2	13	103	**126**	163
	9.0	8	61	**80**	101
	8.5	15	2	**56**	81

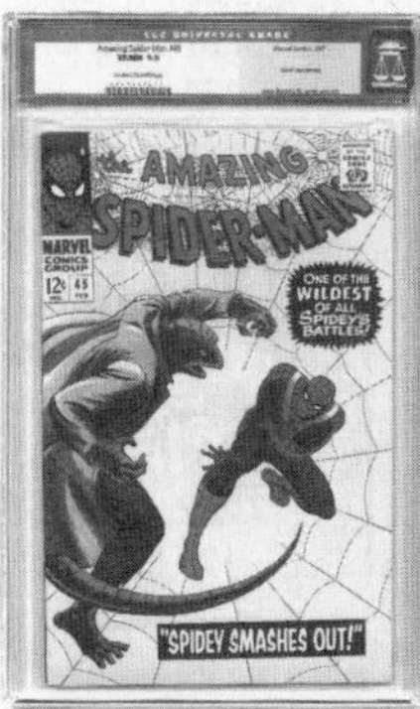

Amazing Spider-Man (cont'd)

ISSUE	CGC GRADE	# of AUCTIONS	LOW CLOSE	AVG CLOSE	HIGH CLOSE
	8.0	6	43	**51**	65
	7.5	10	12	**38**	49
	7.0	8	2	**34**	47
#67	9.6	7	305	**495**	695
	9.4	22	152	**239**	369
	9.2	21	50	**119**	203
	9.0	14	47	**90**	154
	8.0	12	32	**56**	103
	7.5	13	17	**43**	71
	7.0	6	23	**32**	39
	6.0	7	18	**27**	46
#68	9.6	5	403	**554**	788
	9.4	19	160	**233**	349
	9.2	24	70	**106**	175
	9.0	7	45	**74**	101
	8.5	7	37	**53**	90
	8.0	5	36	**55**	65
#69	9.4	13	19	**299**	535
	9.2	10	87	**146**	180
	9.0	13	67	**96**	150
	8.0	8	41	**52**	75
	7.0	6	26	**42**	56
#70	9.4	7	150	**280**	481
	9.2	9	99	**128**	175
	7.5	6	36	**47**	54
	7.0	6	25	**41**	55
#71	9.4	8	178	**277**	394
	9.2	11	74	**130**	175
	9.0	20	45	**82**	115
	8.5	7	44	**53**	62
	7.5	6	31	**42**	61
	5.0	7	15	**24**	31
#72	9.2	8	104	**141**	199
	9.0	9	60	**89**	113
	8.0	6	34	**50**	76
#73	9.4	11	144	**199**	293
	9.2	15	59	**113**	175
	9.0	15	67	**89**	165
	8.5	7	46	**64**	78
#74	9.0	6	40	**67**	90
	8.5	13	36	**59**	80
	8.0	10	26	**47**	75
#75	9.4	6	183	**268**	355
	9.2	7	97	**133**	204
	8.5	12	26	**61**	90
	8.0	8	41	**53**	70
#76	9.6	5	372	**607**	855
	9.2	10	100	**131**	189
	9.0	7	62	**78**	89
	8.5	5	42	**55**	69
#77	9.4	5	154	**232**	362
	9.2	9	93	**105**	119
	9.0	11	59	**85**	125
	8.5	7	42	**61**	85
	8.0	6	37	**43**	53
#78	9.4	6	191	**272**	361
	9.2	8	81	**123**	153
	9.0	6	64	**82**	120
	8.5	7	39	**60**	81
	8.0	6	32	**43**	52
#79	9.4	6	190	**248**	308
	9.2	6	95	**105**	129
	9.0	7	57	**74**	91
#80	9.2	12	79	**133**	415
#81	9.6	5	409	**582**	810
	9.4	11	111	**215**	294
	9.2	5	89	**112**	138
	9.0	6	50	**63**	81
	8.5	5	30	**39**	45
	8.0	9	29	**41**	62
#82	9.2	10	76	**109**	153
	9.0	11	52	**77**	120
#83	9.4	12	128	**209**	299
	9.0	10	45	**66**	90
	8.5	6	35	**51**	71
#84	9.4	6	152	**217**	250
	9.0	15	41	**74**	108
	8.5	8	42	**58**	90
#85	9.4	11	114	**224**	341
	9.2	6	64	**100**	130
#86	9.2	13	92	**127**	193
#87	9.4	8	231	**311**	405
	9.2	5	51	**101**	170
	9.0	11	45	**83**	128
	8.0	6	31	**41**	52
#88	9.4	9	169	**239**	305
	9.2	13	72	**106**	161
	9.0	12	40	**66**	83
	8.0	5	42	**52**	66
#89	9.2	7	119	**142**	185
	8.0	6	38	**51**	65
	7.5	6	21	**34**	46
#90	9.4	10	190	**310**	413
	9.2	10	100	**128**	224
	9.0	11	66	**93**	128
	8.5	5	47	**70**	84
	8.0	7	27	**42**	60
#91	9.6	8	325	**404**	637
	9.4	15	77	**189**	351
	9.2	9	39	**85**	143
	9.0	25	31	**60**	90
	8.5	11	31	**42**	52
	8.0	6	29	**38**	60
#92	9.4	12	190	**252**	357
	9.2	8	66	**115**	162
	9.0	5	51	**87**	105
	8.5	5	35	**45**	52
	8.0	5	26	**41**	51
#93	9.2	8	71	**116**	202
	9.0	7	40	**58**	76
	8.5	8	36	**49**	65
#94	9.4	20	61	**260**	450
	9.2	12	89	**129**	178
	9.0	9	65	**95**	122
	8.0	10	47	**52**	60
	7.0	8	18	**29**	56
#95	9.6	5	355	**492**	630
	9.4	25	99	**200**	300
	9.2	8	60	**81**	125

ISSUE	CGC GRADE	# of AUCTIONS	LOW CLOSE	AVG CLOSE	HIGH CLOSE
	8.0	6	27	**41**	70
#96	9.4	13	194	**335**	610
	9.2	11	104	**151**	181
	9.0	10	51	**99**	138
	8.5	15	48	**72**	100
	7.5	9	25	**46**	79
#97	9.6	19	415	**662**	1,039
	9.4	25	173	**289**	465
	9.2	25	57	**129**	199
	9.0	20	77	**110**	160
	8.5	16	45	**79**	125
	8.0	11	40	**65**	100
	7.5	7	31	**45**	67
	6.5	5	27	**33**	36
	6.0	7	26	**31**	40
#98	9.6	18	304	**540**	1,000
	9.4	25	198	**317**	1,250
	9.2	25	69	**144**	208
	9.0	23	51	**100**	125
	8.5	25	43	**74**	150
	8.0	15	41	**62**	120
	6.5	5	22	**32**	38
	6.0	6	17	**33**	71
	5.0	7	26	**36**	60
#99	9.4	6	181	**232**	290
	9.2	9	56	**79**	104
	9.0	8	56	**72**	103
	8.5	7	37	**48**	61
	7.0	5	21	**26**	33
#100	9.6	25	455	**740**	1,125
	9.4	25	245	**391**	762
	9.2	25	174	**218**	300
	9.0	25	108	**188**	300
	8.5	25	67	**129**	200
	8.0	25	42	**104**	150
	7.5	25	34	**80**	128
	7.0	15	46	**77**	204
	6.5	13	35	**54**	76
	6.0	8	34	**51**	91
	5.5	11	17	**44**	60
	5.0	11	27	**41**	51
	4.5	5	21	**32**	50
	4.0	6	10	**27**	41
#101	9.6	6	833	**1,195**	1,576
	9.4	9	332	**537**	875
	9.2	6	228	**261**	305
	9.0	11	134	**166**	195
	8.5	15	90	**114**	145
	8.0	9	53	**100**	160
	7.5	12	46	**78**	106
	7.0	6	58	**67**	80
	6.5	7	28	**44**	75
#102	9.4	12	335	**453**	548
	9.2	12	116	**160**	222
	9.0	25	74	**108**	150
	8.5	19	36	**74**	100
	8.0	14	36	**64**	91
	7.5	11	27	**42**	68
	7.0	9	32	**45**	72
#103	9.6	5	143	**217**	271
	9.4	7	103	**183**	257
	9.0	9	33	**59**	99
	8.5	5	32	**39**	47
#104	9.0	5	15	**47**	57
#105	9.6	17	108	**206**	430
	9.4	20	52	**100**	153
	9.2	9	43	**61**	99
	9.0	12	24	**43**	72
#106	9.2	9	40	**61**	124
	9.0	8	31	**50**	71
#107	9.6	9	153	**194**	305
	9.4	20	72	**111**	152
	9.2	15	38	**63**	110
	9.0	9	31	**42**	55
	8.5	8	20	**26**	36
#108	9.6	5	198	**279**	343
	9.4	17	72	**111**	148
	9.2	6	44	**59**	80
	9.0	9	20	**47**	65
#109	9.4	15	51	**112**	196
	9.2	12	40	**54**	78
	9.0	5	48	**50**	55
	8.5	10	13	**29**	50
#110	9.6	5	124	**218**	335
	9.4	14	94	**115**	148
	9.2	17	31	**58**	98
	9.0	8	31	**36**	42
	8.5	6	23	**35**	51
#111	9.4	13	76	**139**	230
#112	9.6	7	134	**204**	240
	9.4	6	77	**112**	203
	9.2	10	47	**73**	101
	9.0	7	28	**40**	68
	8.5	6	11	**23**	42
	8.0	5	28	**35**	49
	7.5	5	19	**21**	24
#113	9.6	5	165	**244**	360
	9.4	14	86	**138**	199
	9.2	10	13	**63**	100
	9.0	16	36	**46**	67
	8.5	10	20	**33**	75
#114	9.4	5	135	**164**	214
	9.2	5	36	**57**	100
#115	9.4	7	90	**136**	262
	9.2	17	36	**64**	134
	9.0	6	22	**41**	55

Amazing Spider-Man (cont'd)

ISSUE	CGC GRADE	# of AUCTIONS	LOW CLOSE	AVG CLOSE	HIGH CLOSE
#116	9.6	5	114	**183**	299
	9.4	16	36	**87**	158
	9.2	12	26	**62**	119
	9.0	7	25	**40**	61
	8.5	10	15	**24**	36
	8.0	9	12	**22**	43
#117	9.6	8	26	**143**	204
	9.4	24	52	**101**	150
	9.2	7	41	**55**	76
	9.0	9	25	**46**	70
	8.0	8	20	**24**	39
#118	9.6	6	150	**217**	386
	9.4	25	51	**93**	193
	9.2	20	12	**48**	77
	9.0	5	26	**35**	43
#119	9.6	7	305	**401**	518
	9.4	17	143	**198**	305
	9.2	25	66	**104**	135
	9.0	15	47	**83**	125
	8.5	6	19	**53**	80
	8.0	12	31	**57**	188
	6.5	5	16	**24**	30
#120	9.6	8	105	**278**	392
	9.4	25	76	**187**	295
	9.2	9	78	**104**	128
	9.0	19	53	**78**	103
	8.0	11	26	**51**	70
#121	9.6	13	910	**1,304**	1,600
	9.4	16	449	**617**	909
	9.2	25	154	**289**	550
	9.0	25	90	**219**	450
	8.5	25	110	**169**	275
	8.0	25	82	**129**	188
	7.5	14	75	**105**	153
	7.0	25	66	**103**	400
	6.5	9	51	**60**	77
	6.0	11	41	**80**	123
	5.5	7	43	**63**	81
	5.0	10	39	**51**	71
	4.5	8	25	**49**	81
	4.0	5	27	**37**	50
#122	9.6	20	750	**1,208**	2,127
	9.4	25	400	**523**	852
	9.2	25	200	**282**	425
	9.0	25	95	**215**	375
	8.5	25	75	**158**	300
	8.0	25	66	**145**	310
	7.5	25	51	**106**	165
	7.0	12	75	**101**	158
	6.5	14	61	**84**	133
	6.0	15	30	**62**	114
	5.5	7	41	**51**	61
	4.5	5	36	**42**	51
	4.0	8	31	**49**	69
#123	9.6	9	101	**229**	510
	9.4	10	82	**132**	204
	9.2	13	33	**53**	90
	9.0	7	26	**41**	76
	8.5	9	23	**34**	52
#124	9.4	10	79	**166**	249
	9.0	10	29	**56**	81
#125	9.6	6	174	**272**	401
	9.4	21	57	**114**	198
	9.2	10	38	**66**	128
	8.5	9	16	**24**	29
#126	9.6	14	71	**129**	178
	9.4	14	46	**75**	133
	9.2	23	22	**47**	136
	9.0	19	22	**34**	49
	8.5	12	14	**24**	40
#127	9.6	12	25	**174**	350
	9.4	12	61	**104**	180
	9.2	16	27	**48**	78
	9.0	8	16	**35**	60
	8.5	17	13	**27**	42
	7.5	8	10	**18**	25
#128	9.6	9	149	**216**	355
	9.4	14	39	**78**	135
	9.2	21	26	**42**	74
	9.0	17	17	**34**	57
	8.5	10	17	**26**	36
	8.0	5	13	**23**	30
	6.5	5	12	**15**	18
#129	9.6	25	1,026	**2,030**	3,025
	9.4	25	320	**929**	1,225
	9.2	25	250	**535**	735
	9.0	25	150	**411**	661
	8.5	25	143	**290**	400
	8.0	25	125	**218**	335
	7.5	25	67	**201**	306
	7.0	25	68	**160**	288
	6.5	20	61	**119**	168
	6.0	22	55	**115**	180
	5.5	8	64	**88**	113
	5.0	20	51	**103**	173
	4.5	11	51	**81**	129
	4.0	16	45	**72**	123
	3.0	7	32	**56**	84
#130	9.6	11	113	**158**	214
	9.4	21	34	**61**	102
	9.2	14	25	**41**	63
	8.0	5	16	**20**	27
#131	9.6	7	91	**164**	215
	9.4	15	38	**96**	188
	9.2	8	40	**54**	78
	8.5	5	16	**25**	32
#132	9.6	5	114	**178**	265
	9.4	11	45	**78**	180
	9.2	9	21	**42**	76
	8.5	5	22	**26**	32
#133	9.6	14	65	**147**	204
	9.4	15	41	**67**	178
	9.2	5	20	**37**	78
	8.5	5	20	**25**	31
#134	9.6	17	125	**225**	406
	9.4	18	57	**108**	225
	9.2	7	33	**47**	56
	9.0	9	11	**37**	61
#135	9.6	15	223	**348**	500

ISSUE	CGC GRADE	# of AUCTIONS	LOW CLOSE	AVG CLOSE	HIGH CLOSE
	9.4	22	76	**183**	277
	9.2	23	41	**80**	140
	9.0	19	16	**71**	144
	8.5	10	24	**41**	80
#136	9.6	22	218	**414**	908
	9.4	25	106	**201**	333
	9.2	23	51	**103**	169
	9.0	16	26	**77**	170
	8.5	12	29	**55**	94
	8.0	5	46	**51**	60
	7.5	7	21	**38**	65
	5.5	5	15	**21**	26
#137	9.6	12	99	**224**	305
	9.4	25	32	**94**	175
	9.2	9	32	**54**	75
	9.0	9	40	**48**	60
	8.5	6	14	**28**	37
	8.0	6	15	**25**	33
#138	9.8	6	154	**316**	600
	9.6	14	66	**116**	183
	9.4	18	31	**52**	103
	9.2	13	25	**36**	70
	9.0	5	15	**29**	50
	8.0	6	10	**18**	36
#139	9.6	5	89	**176**	282
	9.4	11	41	**75**	136
	9.2	6	34	**48**	60
	8.5	6	16	**28**	46
#140	9.4	11	33	**67**	138
	9.2	12	17	**30**	35
	8.0	5	23	**27**	31
#141	9.6	7	68	**154**	342
	9.4	22	28	**49**	83
	9.2	13	23	**37**	68
#142	9.4	19	32	**73**	230
	9.2	8	26	**39**	60
	9.0	6	20	**29**	50
#143	9.6	9	76	**101**	125
	9.4	9	26	**54**	82
	9.2	11	17	**32**	50
	9.0	5	23	**26**	34
#144	9.6	8	62	**106**	154
	9.4	14	40	**61**	114
	9.2	11	25	**41**	76
#145	9.4	21	32	**58**	113
	9.2	12	10	**34**	74
	9.0	10	10	**19**	29
#146	9.6	5	73	**130**	203
	9.4	19	26	**51**	90
	9.2	6	23	**34**	41
	8.5	7	11	**23**	48
#147	9.6	20	49	**96**	150
	9.4	25	25	**53**	91
	9.2	19	18	**30**	46
	9.0	6	16	**28**	36
	8.5	5	15	**23**	31
#148	9.4	10	69	**102**	161
	9.2	12	21	**41**	80
	8.5	5	17	**23**	35
	8.0	5	15	**23**	33
#149	9.6	6	185	**287**	427
	9.4	16	38	**111**	203
	9.2	13	38	**74**	127
	9.0	8	29	**48**	100
	7.5	5	11	**17**	21
#150	9.6	14	80	**195**	451
	9.4	15	29	**64**	110
	9.2	14	25	**40**	62
#151	9.4	11	50	**98**	230
	9.2	8	24	**35**	49
#152	9.6	16	35	**89**	223
	9.4	16	24	**44**	87
	9.2	6	22	**32**	50
#153	9.6	22	27	**72**	226
	9.4	17	23	**40**	57
	9.2	11	15	**25**	35
	9.0	7	5	**15**	22
	8.5	6	14	**21**	35
#154	9.6	23	38	**85**	218
	9.4	25	24	**38**	81
	9.2	13	11	**28**	65
#155	9.6	16	43	**78**	153
	9.4	25	11	**51**	200
	9.2	11	20	**31**	51
	9.0	5	16	**25**	36
	8.5	7	11	**21**	30
#156	9.4	14	9	**49**	292
	9.2	16	19	**27**	51
#157	9.6	19	47	**83**	153
	9.4	25	21	**48**	81
	9.2	12	19	**35**	80
	9.0	8	13	**25**	43
	8.5	7	14	**26**	50
#158	9.6	25	21	**53**	148
	9.4	25	14	**38**	91
	9.2	15	9	**21**	33
#159	9.8	5	150	**163**	180
	9.6	25	25	**66**	163
	9.4	15	26	**41**	58
	9.2	12	18	**24**	35
#160	9.4	12	20	**36**	71
	9.2	8	13	**21**	29
	8.5	6	10	**17**	27
#161	9.6	24	31	**91**	178
	9.4	18	27	**49**	80
	9.2	9	25	**31**	53

ISSUE	CGC GRADE	# of AUCTIONS	LOW CLOSE	AVG CLOSE	HIGH CLOSE
Amazing Spider-Man (cont'd)					
	9.0	5	13	**22**	36
#162	9.6	15	44	**81**	115
	9.4	18	33	**49**	90
	9.2	5	25	**30**	40
	9.0	9	16	**25**	35
#163	9.6	11	40	**64**	99
	9.4	11	25	**39**	86
	9.2	9	15	**23**	43
#164	9.4	8	25	**47**	90
#165	9.6	15	20	**73**	266
	9.4	13	16	**35**	82
#166	9.8	9	94	**145**	230
	9.6	25	27	**56**	114
	9.4	8	17	**31**	50
	9.2	7	16	**27**	39
#167	9.8	7	100	**160**	225
	9.6	24	25	**55**	123
	9.4	25	13	**28**	48
	9.2	7	9	**18**	25
#168	9.8	8	76	**133**	230
	9.6	25	25	**48**	100
	9.4	18	13	**28**	53
	9.2	6	12	**25**	40
	9.0	5	12	**14**	18
#169	9.8	9	120	**179**	230
	9.6	21	26	**57**	108
	9.4	10	16	**39**	90
	9.2	9	10	**22**	32
#170	9.6	25	29	**56**	80
	9.4	25	18	**29**	52
	9.2	5	15	**24**	34
#171	9.6	10	25	**55**	79
	9.4	19	9	**27**	51
	9.0	7	10	**18**	25
#172	9.6	13	25	**52**	105
	9.4	10	23	**34**	79
#173	9.4	9	27	**76**	214
#174	9.6	22	50	**81**	126
	9.4	25	20	**37**	84
	9.2	12	11	**27**	50
	9.0	10	15	**21**	41
#175	9.6	22	30	**67**	112
	9.4	25	22	**36**	68
	9.2	8	24	**36**	69
	9.0	5	13	**20**	25
	8.5	5	12	**14**	16
#176	9.4	19	21	**52**	107
	9.2	9	25	**38**	56
	9.0	8	14	**20**	29
#177	9.6	25	41	**69**	218
	9.4	24	15	**50**	103
	9.2	11	16	**26**	48
	9.0	12	18	**23**	31
#178	9.6	13	46	**76**	111
	9.4	22	18	**45**	84
	9.2	12	16	**28**	35
	9.0	6	21	**25**	30
#179	9.8	5	229	**257**	286
	9.6	20	36	**69**	123

ISSUE	CGC GRADE	# of AUCTIONS	LOW CLOSE	AVG CLOSE	HIGH CLOSE
	9.4	25	15	**43**	76
	9.2	9	20	**30**	45
	9.0	8	15	**26**	40
#180	9.6	25	26	**79**	156
	9.4	11	17	**47**	114
	9.2	17	16	**27**	40
	9.0	5	17	**31**	68
#181	9.6	14	29	**50**	98
	9.4	11	20	**33**	51
	9.2	5	16	**20**	28
#182	9.6	12	25	**51**	100
	9.4	16	8	**30**	81
#183	9.6	24	16	**40**	95
	9.4	13	20	**30**	76
#184	9.6	8	32	**75**	128
#185	9.6	24	24	**57**	141
	9.4	25	10	**27**	59
	9.2	8	13	**21**	34
#186	9.6	14	21	**50**	130
	9.4	8	20	**31**	59
#187	9.6	13	29	**65**	91
	9.4	12	20	**31**	42
	9.2	8	8	**34**	78
#188	9.6	14	37	**57**	103
	9.4	5	8	**26**	40
	9.2	5	23	**27**	33
	8.5	5	10	**19**	26
#189	9.8	5	79	**175**	203
	9.6	19	26	**45**	85
	9.4	21	14	**23**	32
	9.2	12	11	**22**	35
#190	9.8	10	77	**144**	299
	9.6	17	27	**47**	81
	9.4	12	24	**30**	41
#191	9.8	11	66	**130**	203
	9.6	25	23	**34**	55
	9.4	21	13	**22**	32
	9.2	6	15	**20**	33
#192	9.8	5	87	**134**	200
	9.6	25	13	**43**	104
	9.4	9	13	**23**	37
	9.2	12	15	**22**	69
#193	9.6	25	10	**43**	134
	9.4	20	15	**25**	44
#194	9.6	25	106	**174**	255
	9.4	25	35	**84**	175
	9.2	23	25	**50**	110
	9.0	14	18	**37**	70
	8.5	24	14	**29**	65
	8.0	7	21	**32**	49
#195	9.6	25	28	**60**	126
	9.4	11	14	**39**	96
	9.2	9	15	**23**	36
#196	9.6	15	21	**48**	105
	9.4	13	12	**24**	41
#197	9.8	6	71	**164**	265
	9.6	18	23	**42**	94
	9.4	9	11	**25**	33
	9.2	5	18	**20**	23
	9.0	5	10	**20**	26

ISSUE	CGC GRADE	# of AUCTIONS	LOW CLOSE	AVG CLOSE	HIGH CLOSE
#198	9.8	9	66	**103**	223
	9.6	24	25	**38**	81
	9.4	19	11	**25**	49
#199	9.8	5	72	**114**	165
	9.6	23	19	**44**	102
	9.4	14	14	**25**	40
	9.2	6	10	**17**	22
#200	9.8	25	67	**184**	482
	9.6	25	16	**54**	163
	9.4	25	11	**39**	68
	9.2	24	14	**28**	50
	9.0	10	15	**36**	84
	8.5	12	10	**18**	33
	7.0	6	10	**13**	23
#201	9.6	15	35	**82**	209
	9.4	15	18	**39**	68
#202	9.6	21	25	**61**	192
	9.4	16	14	**30**	50
	9.2	12	10	**20**	34
#203	9.6	11	30	**48**	91
#204	9.6	13	25	**42**	82
	9.4	11	19	**34**	60
#205	9.8	8	90	**138**	214
	9.6	17	22	**39**	70
	9.4	8	18	**24**	30
#206	9.6	20	16	**38**	68
	9.4	10	14	**23**	40
#207	9.8	8	92	**158**	245
	9.6	21	14	**33**	87
	9.4	7	14	**21**	26
	9.2	5	10	**15**	21
#208	9.6	19	2	**29**	77
#209	9.6	14	2	**40**	168
	9.4	5	17	**24**	30
#210	9.6	10	30	**58**	104
#211	9.6	21	11	**31**	52
#212	9.6	17	20	**35**	78
	9.4	5	13	**22**	39
#213	9.6	15	16	**26**	38
#214	9.6	7	16	**34**	78
	9.4	6	10	**18**	26
#215	9.6	21	17	**29**	66
	9.4	6	11	**22**	33
#216	9.6	6	22	**45**	81
#217	9.8	5	56	**116**	203
	9.6	13	20	**27**	48
	9.4	6	11	**19**	27
#218	9.8	7	51	**91**	154
	9.6	13	17	**36**	112
#219	9.6	5	25	**58**	113
#220	9.6	14	12	**29**	66
	9.4	6	14	**26**	47
#221	9.6	6	20	**51**	114
#222	9.6	13	17	**39**	71
#223	9.6	7	1	**24**	45
#224	9.4	8	13	**17**	25
#225	9.8	5	51	**91**	125
	9.6	9	10	**43**	114
#226	9.6	6	30	**67**	114
	9.4	6	20	**28**	35

ISSUE	CGC GRADE	# of AUCTIONS	LOW CLOSE	AVG CLOSE	HIGH CLOSE
#227	9.6	6	25	**32**	48
#228	9.6	5	20	**31**	50
#229	9.6	8	29	**52**	100
#230	9.6	5	26	**42**	88
	9.4	6	16	**23**	32
#231	9.4	6	11	**23**	34
#232	9.8	7	33	**70**	128
	9.6	6	21	**34**	60
#233	9.6	12	16	**27**	81
#234	9.6	10	19	**27**	44
#235	9.8	6	50	**84**	140
	9.6	6	20	**28**	33
#236	9.6	10	9	**30**	76
#237	9.6	11	20	**31**	58
	9.4	5	11	**18**	31
#238	9.8	21	235	**432**	667
	9.6	25	54	**150**	308
	9.4	25	33	**97**	202
	9.2	25	26	**63**	96
	9.0	25	16	**44**	100
	8.5	25	10	**34**	54
	8.0	21	15	**30**	45
	7.5	10	15	**26**	55
#239	9.8	25	64	**194**	311
	9.6	25	10	**58**	100
	9.4	25	21	**39**	65
	9.2	25	11	**27**	51
	9.0	11	16	**21**	30
	8.5	15	9	**19**	35
	8.0	6	10	**16**	25
#240	9.8	7	35	**67**	140
	9.6	13	15	**28**	70
	9.4	6	15	**19**	26
#241	9.8	13	27	**60**	158
	9.6	9	6	**27**	60
#242	9.8	6	37	**62**	81
	9.6	12	13	**23**	74
#243	9.8	15	26	**62**	114
	9.6	13	10	**26**	41
#244	9.8	19	27	**53**	117
	9.6	25	11	**27**	74
	9.4	9	16	**24**	40
#245	9.8	25	30	**55**	118
	9.6	24	15	**27**	51
	9.4	11	11	**21**	30
#246	9.6	8	20	**26**	30

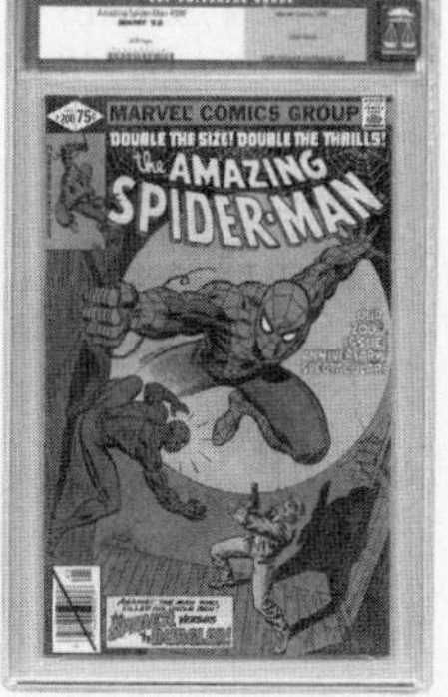

ISSUE	CGC GRADE	# of AUCTIONS	LOW CLOSE	AVG CLOSE	HIGH CLOSE
Amazing Spider-Man (cont'd)					
#247	9.6	6	13	**29**	54
#248	9.6	10	20	**25**	37
#249	9.6	15	15	**48**	232
	9.4	7	10	**20**	36
#250	9.8	9	38	**64**	100
	9.6	18	20	**39**	57
	9.4	10	13	**26**	45
	9.2	5	17	**25**	33
#251	9.6	16	15	**37**	138
	9.4	7	18	**24**	31
	9.2	5	12	**21**	34
#252	9.8	25	21	**199**	338
	9.6	25	30	**69**	154
	9.4	25	13	**40**	110
	9.2	25	15	**28**	51
	9.0	25	10	**23**	41
	8.5	15	10	**19**	30
	8.0	19	6	**16**	30
	7.5	8	0	**19**	50
	7.0	6	10	**14**	21
#253	9.8	25	18	**41**	90
	9.6	25	8	**21**	35
	9.4	6	11	**21**	31
#254	9.8	15	20	**39**	72
	9.6	25	10	**23**	41
	9.4	8	10	**20**	26
#255	9.8	25	15	**35**	114
	9.6	24	11	**22**	30
	9.4	16	10	**17**	25
#256	9.8	25	19	**42**	100
	9.6	25	12	**21**	32
	9.4	15	7	**16**	30
	9.2	6	2	**15**	28
#257	9.8	16	25	**48**	128
	9.6	9	10	**22**	30
	9.4	8	10	**16**	29
#258	9.8	25	12	**36**	80
	9.6	16	9	**25**	79
#259	9.8	16	22	**60**	130
	9.6	25	15	**27**	39
	9.4	10	10	**16**	28
#260	9.8	9	33	**66**	108
	9.6	21	13	**26**	46
	9.4	9	11	**21**	39
#261	9.6	21	15	**26**	37
	9.4	9	12	**20**	35
#262	9.8	23	20	**33**	71
	9.6	10	14	**25**	33
#263	9.8	8	25	**40**	68
	9.6	8	10	**19**	25
#264	9.8	17	20	**37**	90
	9.6	14	10	**20**	26
	9.4	12	10	**13**	21
#265	9.8	20	11	**42**	92
	9.6	20	23	**30**	48
	9.4	7	12	**19**	26
#266	9.6	15	11	**22**	38
	9.4	7	6	**11**	25
#267	9.8	13	25	**40**	96
	9.6	15	10	**21**	30
#268	9.8	23	25	**42**	114
	9.6	15	10	**20**	37
	9.4	11	8	**14**	24
#269	9.8	9	25	**49**	75
	9.6	16	15	**24**	35
#270	9.8	9	25	**59**	112
#271	9.4	5	10	**18**	26
#272	9.8	21	11	**39**	92
	9.6	13	9	**18**	40
#274	9.8	6	23	**40**	50
	9.6	6	13	**20**	25
#275	9.8	25	21	**52**	90
	9.6	25	13	**30**	70
	9.4	11	15	**21**	26
#276	9.8	7	30	**66**	112
	9.6	23	11	**26**	80
	9.4	7	19	**21**	24
#277	9.8	14	35	**61**	116
	9.6	16	10	**25**	45
#278	9.6	5	20	**26**	32
#279	9.6	9	15	**24**	39
#280	9.6	6	11	**23**	45
#282	9.8	6	27	**45**	78
	9.6	6	17	**24**	29
#283	9.8	19	21	**40**	118
	9.6	8	12	**21**	41
#284	9.6	5	20	**26**	33
	9.4	5	10	**18**	26
#285	9.8	12	30	**102**	325
	9.6	22	13	**25**	56
	9.4	8	10	**22**	40
#286	9.6	8	12	**26**	60
#287	9.8	11	35	**60**	100
	9.6	7	25	**30**	38
#288	9.8	8	34	**92**	180
	9.6	6	12	**24**	39
#289	9.8	11	71	**104**	150
	9.6	25	13	**34**	81
	9.4	20	10	**22**	52
	9.2	7	9	**20**	40
	9.0	9	10	**15**	20
#290	9.6	6	17	**24**	34
#292	9.8	21	11	**37**	60
	9.6	7	10	**21**	32
#293	9.8	9	41	**106**	150
	9.6	22	13	**25**	57
#294	9.6	8	21	**48**	87
	9.4	7	11	**22**	34
#295	9.6	7	16	**23**	37
	9.2	5	10	**12**	15
#296	9.8	7	25	**50**	80
	9.6	5	16	**28**	37
	9.4	5	10	**18**	35
#297	9.8	7	32	**63**	118
	9.6	6	20	**29**	53
#298	9.8	25	121	**187**	308
	9.6	25	26	**71**	250
	9.4	25	17	**41**	103
	9.2	25	14	**30**	61

ISSUE	CGC GRADE	# of AUCTIONS	LOW CLOSE	AVG CLOSE	HIGH CLOSE
	9.0	25	11	**26**	43
	8.5	13	10	**20**	50
	8.0	5	10	**19**	25
	7.0	6	15	**19**	23
#299	9.8	25	51	**159**	290
	9.6	25	21	**45**	76
	9.4	25	15	**34**	65
	9.2	18	17	**27**	41
	9.0	13	11	**19**	26
	8.5	11	10	**17**	26
#300	9.8	25	300	**716**	1,000
	9.6	25	62	**207**	310
	9.4	25	50	**106**	203
	9.2	25	25	**79**	133
	9.0	25	26	**61**	120
	8.5	25	14	**48**	81
	8.0	23	20	**39**	90
	7.5	15	20	**36**	81
	7.0	14	24	**35**	51
	6.5	7	12	**32**	56
	5.0	7	10	**28**	40
#301	9.6	25	21	**38**	63
	9.4	16	15	**22**	37
	9.2	10	13	**19**	30
	9.0	5	13	**17**	25
	8.5	7	8	**15**	25
	7.5	6	7	**10**	13
	7.0	5	1	**7**	15
#302	9.6	19	15	**25**	42
	9.4	11	10	**16**	21
#303	9.8	11	26	**52**	123
	9.6	22	13	**25**	35
	9.4	11	8	**18**	30
#304	9.6	14	17	**27**	40
	9.4	5	12	**15**	17
#305	9.6	12	16	**25**	35
#306	9.8	8	50	**62**	105
	9.6	25	8	**21**	30
	9.4	12	8	**17**	29
	8.5	5	2	**8**	10
#307	9.8	9	26	**47**	74
	9.6	20	14	**22**	33
	9.4	11	10	**17**	28
#308	9.6	9	16	**27**	44
	9.4	9	11	**18**	26
#309	9.8	5	23	**93**	168
	9.6	19	2	**22**	30
	9.4	6	11	**14**	16
#310	9.6	18	15	**28**	46
#311	9.8	7	32	**61**	100
	9.6	25	11	**24**	37
#312	9.8	25	31	**68**	130
	9.6	25	15	**26**	51
	9.4	16	11	**19**	38
	9.2	13	1	**14**	38
#313	9.8	17	26	**52**	80
	9.6	24	10	**23**	36
	9.4	15	10	**18**	28
#314	9.8	19	24	**51**	128
	9.6	15	15	**29**	73
	9.4	10	10	**15**	21
	9.2	5	9	**12**	15
#315	9.8	25	25	**48**	100
	9.6	23	15	**27**	43
	9.4	15	11	**20**	36
	8.5	7	1	**12**	20
#316	9.8	25	39	**69**	178
	9.6	24	15	**28**	41
	9.4	14	15	**22**	34
#317	9.6	21	10	**32**	61
	9.4	16	11	**20**	33
	9.2	5	10	**14**	17
#318	9.8	7	33	**45**	61
	9.6	18	15	**26**	36
	9.4	8	12	**23**	62
#319	9.8	17	25	**48**	158
	9.6	17	11	**24**	41
	9.4	8	12	**18**	29
#320	9.8	5	25	**89**	183
	9.6	23	15	**22**	34
	9.4	5	11	**12**	16
#321	9.8	16	20	**45**	86
	9.6	13	16	**22**	34
	9.4	6	10	**15**	21
#322	9.8	21	20	**34**	54
	9.6	19	15	**23**	41
	9.4	7	9	**18**	35
#323	9.8	20	25	**47**	156
	9.6	25	13	**24**	40
	9.4	7	5	**12**	18
#324	9.8	11	36	**84**	178
	9.6	19	15	**25**	40
	9.4	13	9	**18**	29
	9.2	5	8	**14**	20
#325	9.8	7	39	**78**	203
	9.6	14	19	**26**	45
	9.4	5	8	**11**	16
#326	9.8	6	16	**36**	51
	9.6	11	6	**19**	27
#327	9.8	12	10	**30**	50
	9.6	8	15	**22**	32
#328	9.8	25	21	**49**	101
	9.6	25	12	**25**	46
	9.4	25	6	**19**	35
#329	9.6	5	6	**20**	36
#330	9.8	25	10	**31**	65

ISSUE	CGC GRADE	# of AUCTIONS	LOW CLOSE	AVG CLOSE	HIGH CLOSE
Amazing Spider-Man (cont'd)					
	9.6	25	10	**17**	35
#331	9.8	22	4	**26**	60
	9.6	14	13	**20**	34
#333	9.6	11	15	**21**	30
#334	9.8	10	18	**27**	50
	9.6	5	15	**25**	34
#335	9.8	6	25	**41**	56
	9.6	6	10	**22**	36
#336	9.8	17	2	**26**	50
	9.6	10	9	**14**	34
#338	9.8	8	25	**32**	48
	9.6	9	10	**20**	34
#340	9.8	10	2	**36**	86
#342	9.8	8	23	**39**	75
	9.6	5	16	**26**	45
#343	9.8	13	16	**31**	57
	9.6	6	15	**23**	34
#344	9.8	11	30	**55**	81
	9.6	25	10	**24**	51
#345	9.8	24	23	**46**	89
	9.6	15	13	**24**	38
#346	9.8	6	25	**77**	115
#347	9.6	6	16	**22**	30
#348	9.8	6	25	**37**	77
#350	9.8	12	15	**30**	42
	9.6	17	10	**18**	26
#351	9.8	8	10	**31**	50
	9.6	5	10	**17**	20
#353	9.8	11	2	**27**	48
	9.6	6	13	**20**	25
#354	9.8	18	10	**27**	48
#356	9.8	6	1	**21**	42
#357	9.8	7	1	**30**	50
	9.6	5	18	**21**	25
#358	9.6	5	18	**23**	31
#359	9.8	9	25	**37**	56
#361	9.8	25	16	**67**	124
	9.6	25	10	**32**	61
	9.4	21	4	**21**	37
	9.2	5	9	**14**	21
#362	9.8	25	16	**32**	76
	9.6	21	11	**20**	34
#363	9.8	25	17	**30**	51
	9.6	25	10	**18**	29
	9.4	9	9	**14**	19
#364	9.8	10	12	**38**	79
#365	9.6	9	13	**21**	31
	9.4	9	7	**17**	41
#366	9.8	6	32	**49**	103
#367	9.8	5	25	**36**	57
#370	9.8	8	18	**37**	50
#374	9.8	8	19	**40**	108
#375	9.8	25	2	**27**	41
	9.6	14	10	**19**	31
#378	9.8	5	20	**32**	45
#379	9.8	8	13	**38**	73
#388	9.8	6	25	**43**	77
#400	9.6	12	12	**25**	41
	9.4	8	15	**21**	31

ISSUE	CGC GRADE	# of AUCTIONS	LOW CLOSE	AVG CLOSE	HIGH CLOSE
#499	9.8	7	10	**15**	21
#500	9.8	25	19	**36**	54
	9.6	11	12	**26**	59
#501	9.8	16	11	**18**	30
#502	9.8	5	14	**20**	30
	9.6	5	8	**9**	13
#504	9.8	7	18	**23**	30
#505	9.8	7	20	**24**	30
#509	9.8	6	35	**40**	45
Amazing Spider-Man (Vol. 2)					
#1	9.8	5	51	**108**	168
	9.6	6	45	**55**	64
	9.4	10	261	**614**	1,225
	9.0	6	123	**312**	500
	9.8	13	41	**74**	125
	9.6	21	21	**43**	99
	9.4	10	15	**24**	39
	9.8	25	22	**55**	128
	9.6	20	13	**26**	50
	9.4	5	14	**29**	55
#25	9.8	7	10	**30**	41
#30	9.8	25	15	**32**	66
	9.6	25	13	**24**	63
	9.4	15	10	**18**	49
	9.2	5	10	**23**	50
#31	9.8	22	10	**26**	44
	9.6	21	9	**17**	30
	9.4	5	8	**10**	15
#32	9.8	10	10	**27**	45
	9.6	9	7	**17**	25
	9.4	6	5	**14**	20
#33	9.6	12	8	**16**	21
#34	9.8	12	15	**26**	42
	9.6	7	13	**20**	30
#35	9.8	8	15	**40**	60
	9.6	13	10	**17**	30
	9.4	6	10	**16**	24
#36	9.9	23	130	**234**	400
	9.8	25	19	**85**	173
	9.6	25	7	**45**	123
	9.4	25	3	**35**	149
	9.2	20	15	**26**	51
	9.0	13	12	**29**	60
#37	9.8	11	16	**24**	46
	9.6	22	10	**16**	28
#38	9.6	20	9	**16**	26
	9.4	9	3	**11**	15
#39	9.6	15	5	**13**	16
	9.4	8	9	**12**	16
#40	9.6	16	10	**16**	27
#41	9.6	14	9	**13**	16
	9.4	6	10	**14**	25
#42	9.8	5	20	**28**	42
	9.6	8	10	**16**	33
#43	9.6	6	10	**16**	25
#45	9.6	5	10	**16**	21
#47	9.6	7	10	**15**	21
#50/DF	9.8	10	25	**39**	60
	9.6	22	9	**22**	71
#53/2nd	9.8	7	11	**24**	30

ISSUE	CGC GRADE	# of AUCTIONS	LOW CLOSE	AVG CLOSE	HIGH CLOSE
#55/2nd	9.8	5	17	**19**	20
#56/Sun	9.8	7	18	**22**	27
#57/Sun	9.8	5	18	**24**	27
#58/Sun	9.8	8	10	**16**	23
Amazing Spider-Man Annual					
#1	9.0	7	910	**1,350**	1,800
	8.5	10	416	**754**	960
	8.0	8	290	**485**	610
	7.5	8	255	**357**	450
	6.5	8	207	**252**	431
	6.0	7	71	**144**	191
	5.0	7	92	**130**	198
	3.5	6	21	**89**	130
#2	9.0	7	255	**313**	360
	8.5	11	148	**228**	375
	8.0	8	75	**115**	189
	7.5	9	50	**100**	183
	7.0	6	62	**113**	173
	5.5	6	21	**60**	88
#3	9.0	5	127	**153**	205
	8.0	5	68	**88**	115
#4	9.6	8	305	**531**	765
	9.4	10	103	**352**	660
	8.5	10	30	**76**	138
#5	9.4	9	91	**307**	494
	9.2	8	82	**132**	194
	9.0	6	51	**81**	105
	8.5	6	37	**65**	90
	8.0	5	24	**47**	66
#7	9.4	6	68	**128**	230
	9.2	5	41	**83**	108
#8	9.4	5	29	**90**	175
#9	9.4	13	68	**85**	123
#10	9.4	11	22	**33**	46
#11	9.6	7	11	**39**	58
	9.4	5	25	**31**	38
#12	9.6	7	24	**56**	81
	9.4	8	11	**27**	48
	9.2	8	18	**27**	46
#13	9.6	20	12	**35**	65
#14	9.6	8	19	**32**	50
	9.4	12	10	**27**	72
#15	9.8	8	51	**97**	159
	9.6	16	26	**43**	80
	9.4	10	20	**28**	45
#16	9.6	8	15	**23**	30
#18	9.8	13	9	**26**	68
	9.6	5	13	**19**	26
#21	9.8	24	34	**64**	153
	9.6	25	15	**27**	43
	9.4	7	10	**21**	44
#26	9.6	5	10	**13**	16
Amazing Spider-Man Vs. the Prodigy					
#0	9.6	11	16	**25**	50
	9.4	11	10	**17**	23
Ant					
#1	9.8	7	30	**32**	42
Aphrodite IX					
#2	9.8	18	10	**15**	23

ISSUE	CGC GRADE	# of AUCTIONS	LOW CLOSE	AVG CLOSE	HIGH CLOSE
Aquaman					
#1	7.0	5	238	**282**	350
	6.5	7	158	**263**	355
	6.0	7	101	**165**	200
	5.0	10	81	**141**	210
	4.5	6	62	**98**	128
Archer & Armstrong					
#2	9.8	5	13	**26**	40
Aspen					
#1	9.8	7	20	**35**	51
Aspen Sketchbook					
#1	9.8	8	21	**35**	66
Astonishing Tales					
#1	9.2	5	44	**51**	60
	9.0	8	21	**39**	51
#7	9.2	6	6	**12**	28
#8	9.4	6	41	**52**	81
#10	9.6	5	26	**41**	60
#25	9.6	25	132	**227**	331
	9.4	25	51	**94**	208
	9.2	11	35	**56**	120
	9.0	14	26	**46**	109
	8.5	10	11	**34**	81
#26	9.4	5	18	**41**	56
#28	9.6	6	25	**35**	47
#34	9.6	10	20	**34**	50
Astonishing X-Men					
#1	9.8	25	20	**47**	194
	9.6	13	15	**16**	21
#1/Cass	9.8	22	133	**177**	201
	9.6	14	52	**75**	100
#1/Dir	9.8	7	65	**75**	120
#1/Var	9.8	5	62	**79**	100
#2	9.8	10	10	**34**	41
#3	9.8	9	25	**29**	30
Astro Boy					
#1	7.5	8	78	**177**	260
Astro City					
#1	9.6	6	10	**14**	21

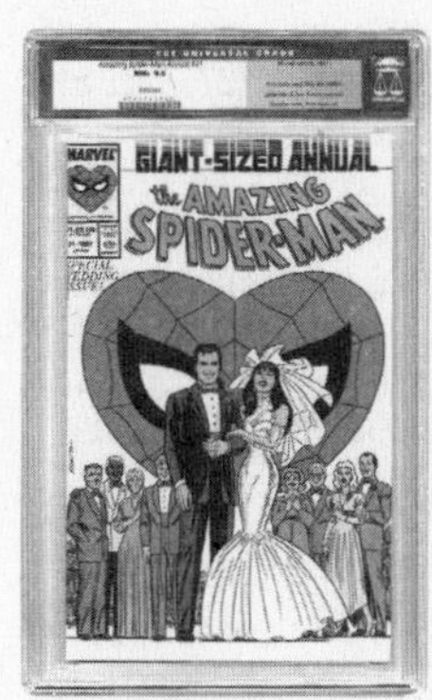

ISSUE	CGC GRADE	# of AUCTIONS	LOW CLOSE	AVG CLOSE	HIGH CLOSE
Atom					
#1	7.5	6	173	**351**	502
	6.5	8	123	**179**	250
	4.5	5	51	**100**	129
#2	9.0	7	102	**196**	280
#4	9.0	6	109	**146**	193
#7	8.5	7	31	**95**	135
#18	9.4	16	96	**211**	399
Atom and Hawkman					
#42	9.4	7	80	**121**	180
Atomic Comics					
#1	9.0	6	515	**818**	1,100
	8.0	13	300	**504**	844
	7.0	5	178	**388**	483
Aurora Comic Scenes					
#184	9.6	5	20	**23**	26
	9.4	5	12	**26**	45
#185	9.6	5	24	**30**	40
#186	9.6	8	16	**23**	40
#192	9.8	8	27	**45**	68
#193	9.8	7	25	**48**	103
Authority, The					
#1	9.6	9	11	**23**	46
	9.4	5	16	**20**	25
Avengers					
#1	8.0	7	1,325	**1,762**	2,247
	7.0	12	811	**1,060**	1,499
	6.5	13	500	**764**	1,200
	6.0	9	510	**663**	750
	5.5	15	410	**516**	610
	5.0	13	426	**536**	710
	4.5	7	406	**442**	478
	4.0	8	311	**382**	450
	3.5	13	203	**336**	460
	3.0	14	203	**288**	410
	1.5	7	51	**138**	204
#2	9.0	12	510	**834**	1,240
	8.5	7	453	**600**	800
	7.5	10	305	**367**	430
	7.0	9	205	**282**	400
	6.5	5	188	**232**	338
	6.0	11	150	**206**	306
	5.5	5	100	**132**	153
#3	8.5	6	400	**435**	505
	7.0	6	170	**227**	311
	6.0	5	152	**202**	301
	4.0	5	61	**78**	95
#4	9.2	13	1,350	**2,340**	3,500
	9.0	18	1,225	**1,705**	2,400
	8.5	8	712	**1,067**	1,415
	8.0	18	600	**939**	1,181
	7.5	13	500	**716**	911
	7.0	25	382	**552**	800
	6.5	16	330	**438**	625
	6.0	9	353	**401**	476
	5.5	14	275	**344**	431
	5.0	21	146	**297**	510

ISSUE	CGC GRADE	# of AUCTIONS	LOW CLOSE	AVG CLOSE	HIGH CLOSE
	4.5	19	153	**227**	304
	4.0	22	128	**211**	268
	3.0	8	100	**149**	198
	2.5	11	61	**140**	181
	2.0	7	102	**129**	163
	1.8	5	91	**100**	110
#4/GR	8.0	5	51	**155**	300
#5	8.5	9	52	**252**	338
	8.0	5	170	**207**	239
	7.0	7	128	**142**	154
#6	9.0	5	213	**284**	365
	8.5	7	173	**197**	234
#7	9.0	7	154	**276**	395
	8.0	7	91	**131**	178
	7.5	12	70	**95**	140
#8	7.0	7	82	**94**	109
	6.5	6	47	**130**	402
#9	8.0	5	146	**164**	188
#10	9.4	5	482	**657**	910
	9.2	5	325	**378**	450
	8.5	10	100	**134**	175
	8.0	14	83	**113**	150
	5.0	6	26	**51**	85
#11	9.2	11	365	**439**	510
	9.0	13	208	**267**	350
	8.0	5	135	**185**	250
	6.0	7	50	**64**	100
#12	9.2	10	192	**304**	614
	9.0	5	160	**182**	202
	8.5	13	49	**109**	160
	7.5	5	41	**59**	93
#13	9.2	8	153	**228**	380
	9.0	5	47	**137**	193
	7.5	5	31	**57**	89
	5.0	9	12	**26**	50
#14	9.2	5	219	**252**	300
	8.5	11	76	**95**	131
	8.0	8	30	**69**	100
	7.5	7	32	**50**	73
#15	9.4	8	203	**364**	660
	9.0	12	91	**137**	200
	8.5	10	51	**98**	160
	8.0	5	33	**62**	81
#16	8.0	10	58	**89**	125
#18	9.4	6	230	**389**	538
	9.2	5	124	**174**	230
	9.0	5	89	**135**	215
	8.0	8	30	**58**	75
#19	9.4	7	355	**533**	692
	9.0	6	95	**135**	167
#20	9.4	6	220	**336**	381
	9.2	6	61	**132**	185
	9.0	14	56	**81**	127
#22	9.2	10	93	**135**	199
	9.0	5	61	**76**	111
	8.5	8	40	**50**	75
#24	9.6	17	153	**217**	315
	9.4	20	100	**143**	204
	9.2	23	41	**77**	125
	9.0	9	34	**48**	62

ISSUE	CGC GRADE	# of AUCTIONS	LOW CLOSE	AVG CLOSE	HIGH CLOSE
#25	9.2	5	150	**185**	240
#26	8.0	6	31	**37**	42
#27	9.2	12	56	**98**	150
	8.5	9	32	**42**	59
#29	9.0	6	66	**80**	128
#30	9.2	5	85	**108**	169
#32	9.6	7	203	**299**	418
	9.4	14	99	**150**	200
#33	9.2	9	56	**83**	114
#36	9.2	7	52	**82**	125
#37	9.0	8	30	**55**	79
#39	9.0	5	25	**40**	57
#40	9.4	6	122	**155**	188
	9.2	6	52	**59**	71
#42	9.0	5	23	**44**	56
#44	9.0	5	43	**64**	130
#46	9.4	11	85	**125**	161
	9.0	5	41	**45**	49
#47	9.4	10	79	**151**	221
	9.2	6	52	**73**	95
	8.5	5	26	**34**	44
#48	9.4	11	57	**150**	204
	9.2	6	50	**89**	125
	9.0	8	40	**52**	80
#49	9.4	7	94	**130**	178
	9.2	8	50	**73**	104
	9.0	6	40	**47**	53
#50	9.4	14	76	**120**	175
	8.5	8	25	**32**	41
#52	9.4	10	123	**174**	322
	9.0	5	42	**49**	54
	8.5	5	38	**48**	75
#53	9.6	10	188	**349**	559
	9.4	7	189	**247**	363
	9.2	9	70	**93**	114
	9.0	11	63	**76**	100
	8.5	6	21	**43**	51
#54	9.4	5	110	**126**	146
#55	9.6	6	177	**228**	282
	9.4	14	77	**121**	183
	8.5	6	25	**35**	53
#56	9.4	5	133	**215**	365
#57	9.4	9	402	**445**	586
	9.2	19	163	**228**	320
	9.0	14	78	**146**	234
	8.5	12	71	**87**	132
	8.0	12	51	**76**	110
#58	9.4	14	180	**265**	355
	9.2	12	62	**109**	160
	9.0	7	56	**77**	110
	8.0	7	26	**45**	61
#59	9.0	6	45	**73**	143
#60	9.4	5	114	**161**	213
	7.5	5	13	**20**	23
#61	9.6	5	150	**168**	198
#62	9.0	5	36	**48**	62
#63	9.6	6	124	**241**	375
#64	9.6	5	174	**195**	233
	9.4	5	96	**114**	140
#65	9.4	7	86	**101**	120

ISSUE	CGC GRADE	# of AUCTIONS	LOW CLOSE	AVG CLOSE	HIGH CLOSE
#66	9.4	9	104	**121**	144
#70	8.5	5	25	**48**	71
#71	9.4	5	162	**220**	265
	9.0	5	53	**61**	68
	8.5	7	41	**55**	70
#74	9.8	6	215	**302**	462
#75	9.4	6	90	**100**	125
#76	9.6	8	124	**171**	250
	9.4	6	82	**96**	110
#81	9.4	7	66	**89**	109
	9.2	8	35	**49**	64
#82	9.4	7	88	**111**	205
#83	9.4	5	122	**153**	225
#85	9.4	9	55	**97**	135
#86	9.4	5	77	**100**	153
#88	9.6	7	91	**162**	252
	9.4	6	60	**95**	153
	9.2	7	39	**50**	65
#92	9.2	5	37	**63**	113
#93	9.4	6	361	**476**	587
	9.0	6	101	**161**	219
#95	9.4	5	100	**148**	177
#96	9.6	9	150	**216**	274
	9.4	8	103	**151**	202
	9.2	7	37	**64**	83
	9.0	6	25	**48**	76
#97	9.6	5	128	**193**	301
	9.4	5	92	**112**	153
#98	9.6	17	76	**121**	304
	9.4	22	43	**73**	105
	9.2	8	26	**44**	62
	8.5	6	16	**20**	27
#100	9.6	7	340	**440**	581
	9.4	14	153	**214**	322
	9.2	25	66	**105**	150
	9.0	21	46	**82**	149
	8.5	8	40	**55**	86
	8.0	9	32	**49**	61
#102	9.6	7	58	**75**	113
	9.4	6	41	**64**	119
#108	9.4	7	38	**48**	65
#111	9.4	5	71	**86**	100
#117	9.4	9	51	**77**	127
#134	9.2	5	15	**21**	28
#135	9.4	5	26	**38**	51
#136	9.4	5	26	**28**	31

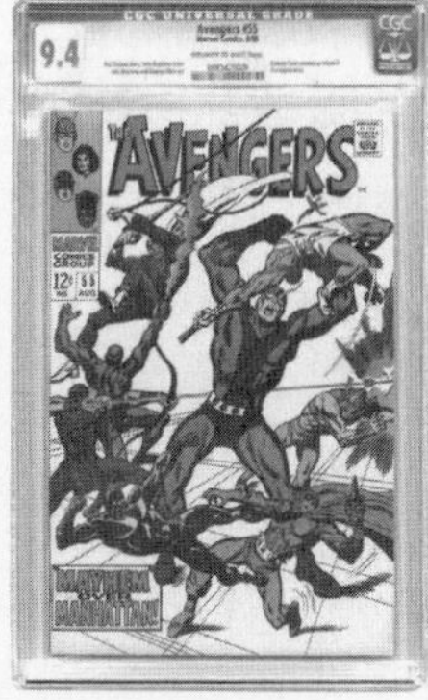

ISSUE	CGC GRADE	# of AUCTIONS	LOW CLOSE	AVG CLOSE	HIGH CLOSE
Avengers (cont'd)					
#137	9.6	6	29	**47**	73
#138	9.6	6	29	**41**	50
#139	9.6	20	20	**33**	47
#149	9.6	10	23	**44**	62
	9.4	9	19	**23**	40
#150	9.6	6	24	**34**	46
	9.4	8	16	**30**	45
#151	9.6	9	23	**45**	60
	9.4	5	22	**28**	34
#152	9.4	7	20	**26**	33
#161	9.6	7	30	**48**	89
#167	9.4	5	9	**16**	25
#170	9.4	6	1	**17**	29
#173	9.4	6	1	**16**	24
#179	9.6	6	21	**28**	35
#195	9.6	7	29	**36**	52
	9.4	5	15	**16**	18
#196	9.4	5	11	**26**	45
#200	9.6	22	10	**28**	52
#232	9.8	6	15	**24**	40
#236	9.8	5	11	**23**	35
#239	9.8	5	19	**22**	25
#249	9.8	5	15	**20**	25
#250	9.8	10	10	**17**	19
#258	9.8	5	15	**26**	34
#260	9.8	5	15	**23**	30
#263	9.8	5	22	**31**	50
#360	9.8	5	12	**17**	25
#500	9.8	10	23	**27**	40
Avengers (Vol. 3)					
#1/Sun	9.8	7	21	**35**	64
Avengers Annual					
#1	8.5	6	44	**71**	101
#7	9.6	11	66	**108**	152
	9.4	16	32	**50**	64
#10	9.8	22	64	**181**	300
	9.6	25	20	**56**	108
	9.4	25	19	**34**	60
	9.2	23	15	**24**	31
	9.0	10	14	**22**	38
	8.5	10	11	**16**	25
#11	9.8	5	20	**25**	31
#13	9.8	5	19	**23**	34
Avengers/JLA					
#2	9.9	12	20	**30**	40
	9.8	5	6	**16**	23
#4	10.0	20	70	**129**	201
	9.9	12	23	**43**	100
	9.8	11	20	**26**	35
Batgirl					
#1	9.8	19	20	**30**	44
	9.6	15	10	**22**	80
#2	9.4	6	5	**10**	18
Batgirl Special					
#1	9.6	5	15	**21**	25

ISSUE	CGC GRADE	# of AUCTIONS	LOW CLOSE	AVG CLOSE	HIGH CLOSE
Batman					
#3	6.5	5	911	**2,375**	2,800
#4	5.0	7	551	**1,041**	1,430
	3.5	5	456	**652**	859
#5	7.5	9	1,550	**2,045**	2,600
	7.0	5	1,527	**2,055**	3,150
#6	8.0	8	1,742	**1,952**	2,050
	7.0	7	1,050	**1,337**	1,625
#7	7.0	7	1,200	**1,515**	2,000
	5.0	5	595	**750**	1,000
#9	4.5	5	500	**571**	655
#10	7.5	5	1,102	**1,300**	1,595
#11	7.0	8	1,303	**2,037**	3,000
#13	7.5	9	315	**1,069**	1,999
	4.0	8	350	**392**	475
#15	7.0	6	600	**780**	1,000
#16	7.0	8	899	**1,422**	1,825
	6.0	6	605	**920**	1,099
#17	7.0	5	405	**588**	700
#18	6.0	5	330	**587**	765
#19	8.0	5	870	**935**	999
	6.0	5	320	**461**	600
	5.5	7	280	**344**	400
#20	7.0	5	575	**846**	1,240
#21	8.5	5	660	**792**	905
	6.5	7	306	**431**	595
	6.0	6	228	**281**	325
#22	9.0	5	760	**1,095**	1,300
	8.0	5	545	**674**	760
	7.5	6	440	**521**	643
	7.0	5	308	**418**	475
#23	7.5	8	664	**859**	1,076
	4.0	8	148	**314**	470
#24	9.2	5	1,500	**1,807**	2,303
	6.5	6	168	**294**	400
	6.0	5	177	**268**	350
#25	7.0	5	700	**835**	981
#26	8.0	18	548	**660**	839
	7.5	6	178	**496**	695
#27	9.0	9	1,101	**1,428**	1,900
#28	8.0	5	276	**677**	860
	6.0	5	306	**345**	399
	5.0	5	128	**191**	260
	4.0	7	128	**200**	269
#31	5.0	5	150	**311**	595
#32	6.0	5	181	**254**	355
#33	7.0	5	321	**384**	475
#34	7.0	7	256	**395**	480
#35	9.0	6	725	**896**	1,225
#36	9.0	5	455	**968**	1,325
	8.0	6	316	**493**	750
#39	4.5	5	142	**190**	265
#40	9.0	5	1,160	**1,432**	1,900
#43	7.0	6	337	**403**	599
#44	3.0	6	103	**163**	200
#47	4.5	7	383	**514**	695
#49	8.5	6	860	**1,061**	1,350
	5.0	6	255	**377**	630
#66	7.5	5	322	**403**	480
#100	7.5	8	900	**1,049**	1,375
	4.0	5	255	**280**	350

ISSUE	CGC GRADE	# of AUCTIONS	LOW CLOSE	AVG CLOSE	HIGH CLOSE
#104	7.5	5	153	**177**	195
#106	8.0	7	200	**296**	549
#136	7.5	5	75	**91**	116
#155	8.0	5	181	**216**	250
	7.0	10	72	**118**	175
#168	9.4	5	206	**345**	455
#171	9.0	5	393	**452**	540
	7.0	5	45	**118**	168
	6.0	6	60	**93**	118
#173	8.5	5	28	**51**	78
#180	9.4	12	103	**197**	302
#181	9.0	6	244	**296**	370
#189	9.6	5	700	**791**	937
#199	9.4	6	103	**190**	401
#200	9.4	20	154	**305**	463
	9.2	11	128	**173**	205
	9.0	13	76	**124**	163
	8.5	17	75	**91**	150
	8.0	10	47	**62**	81
	7.5	9	33	**57**	103
	6.5	6	30	**40**	58
	5.0	5	25	**40**	69
#218	9.4	5	118	**206**	305
#227	9.4	5	300	**353**	382
#232	9.6	14	300	**661**	1,025
	9.4	13	282	**389**	550
	9.2	14	158	**215**	290
	9.0	12	113	**187**	363
	8.5	10	70	**143**	228
	8.0	6	42	**112**	230
	7.5	6	43	**71**	109
	7.0	6	35	**53**	92
#234	9.4	6	304	**442**	611
	9.2	17	128	**200**	300
	9.0	13	91	**120**	160
	8.5	5	58	**83**	128
	7.5	5	26	**44**	67
#237	9.2	5	82	**130**	150
	9.0	5	63	**80**	98
#240	9.6	6	104	**119**	133
	9.4	12	42	**75**	201
#248	9.4	6	56	**86**	134
#251	9.4	5	200	**257**	325
	9.2	9	72	**97**	159
	9.0	6	41	**73**	100
	8.5	11	38	**48**	69
	8.0	6	22	**42**	66
	7.5	6	20	**23**	29
#253	9.2	5	26	**48**	66
#284	9.6	5	25	**36**	43
#286	9.4	6	31	**45**	60
#366	9.6	5	22	**33**	51
#400	9.6	7	36	**72**	110
	9.2	5	14	**21**	25
#404	9.8	20	65	**131**	331
	9.6	25	16	**31**	65
	9.4	25	10	**21**	57
	9.2	12	6	**13**	20
#405	9.8	9	22	**63**	135
	9.6	18	17	**36**	85
	9.4	8	10	**22**	40

ISSUE	CGC GRADE	# of AUCTIONS	LOW CLOSE	AVG CLOSE	HIGH CLOSE
#406	9.8	5	49	**61**	75
	9.6	13	8	**23**	41
#407	9.8	6	31	**59**	119
	9.6	14	20	**31**	79
#408	9.6	5	25	**35**	78
#426	9.6	19	15	**46**	90
	9.4	11	10	**23**	31
#428	9.6	25	23	**48**	99
	9.4	16	11	**23**	33
#429	9.8	6	26	**55**	81
#433	9.8	6	18	**26**	50
#434	9.8	5	6	**22**	35
#442	9.8	6	30	**38**	54
#450	9.8	5	10	**24**	36
#451	9.8	5	20	**25**	30
#488	9.6	5	10	**15**	22
#497	9.9	10	38	**78**	109
	9.8	25	10	**25**	41
	9.6	15	10	**14**	24
#500	9.6	10	8	**19**	28
#600	9.8	14	12	**24**	35
	9.6	8	11	**18**	30
#608	9.8	25	21	**45**	134
	9.6	25	1	**27**	80
	9.4	25	8	**18**	30
	9.2	9	11	**16**	21
	9.0	6	9	**15**	21
#608/2nd	9.8	25	40	**130**	305
	9.6	25	11	**43**	103
	9.2	10	11	**26**	41
#608/DF	9.8	11	29	**45**	70
#608/RRP	9.8	6	1,439	**2,000**	2,425
	9.6	15	660	**977**	1,299
	9.2	5	393	**551**	750
#609	9.8	25	11	**31**	70
	9.6	25	8	**17**	32
	9.4	8	11	**14**	22
#610	9.8	25	13	**24**	75
	9.6	25	1	**18**	36
	9.4	12	9	**12**	23
#611	9.8	25	16	**34**	75
	9.6	21	10	**18**	35
#612	9.8	25	20	**35**	113
	9.6	25	16	**23**	40
	9.4	14	11	**20**	28
#612/2nd	9.8	25	41	**76**	133
	9.6	25	21	**36**	128

ISSUE	CGC GRADE	# of AUCTIONS	LOW CLOSE	AVG CLOSE	HIGH CLOSE
Batman (cont'd)					
	9.4	8	20	**27**	36
#619/2nd	9.8	25	14	**23**	41
	9.6	5	12	**17**	20
#612/DF	9.8	9	26	**45**	90
#613	9.8	25	15	**30**	50
	9.6	21	9	**16**	27
#614	9.8	25	10	**27**	80
	9.6	25	10	**18**	30
#615	9.8	25	10	**27**	82
	9.6	15	10	**20**	31
#616	9.8	25	14	**32**	41
	9.6	6	15	**19**	27
#617	9.8	25	13	**23**	46
	9.6	17	7	**16**	25
#618	9.8	25	13	**27**	50
	9.6	15	8	**15**	20
#619	9.8	25	11	**28**	70
	9.6	25	1	**14**	35
	9.4	9	5	**11**	30
#620	9.8	15	10	**18**	24
#623	9.8	5	9	**12**	15
Batman Annual					
#1	8.0	6	375	**406**	499
	6.0	5	78	**136**	178
Batman Adventures					
#1	9.6	6	10	**13**	19
Batman and the Outsiders					
#1	9.8	9	18	**29**	57
Batman Family					
#5	9.4	5	15	**29**	39
Batman: Gotham Knights					
#1	9.8	16	13	**25**	45
#50	9.8	8	10	**17**	25
#51	9.8	5	6	**13**	18
Batman: Harley Quinn					
#0	9.8	8	23	**36**	52
Batman: Hush Double Feature					
#0	9.6	7	13	**22**	35
Batman: Legends of the Dark Knight					
#120	9.8	6	13	**19**	32
	9.6	8	9	**12**	20
Batman: Sword of Azrael					
#1	9.8	5	29	**45**	54
Batman: The Cult					
#1	9.8	19	11	**30**	69
#4	9.8	5	16	**23**	32
Batman: The Dark Knight Returns					
#1	9.8	25	23	**169**	295
	9.6	25	15	**53**	129
	9.4	25	10	**36**	55
	9.2	13	7	**35**	133
#2	9.8	17	25	**89**	178

ISSUE	CGC GRADE	# of AUCTIONS	LOW CLOSE	AVG CLOSE	HIGH CLOSE
	9.6	25	15	**32**	100
	9.4	17	15	**23**	50
#3	9.8	19	33	**70**	141
	9.6	25	13	**29**	49
	9.4	16	6	**18**	33
	9.2	9	6	**13**	24
#4	9.8	20	37	**69**	123
	9.6	25	6	**34**	72
	9.4	23	7	**17**	40
	9.2	9	10	**13**	19
Batman: The Killing Joke					
#0	9.8	25	21	**48**	99
	9.6	25	8	**22**	45
	9.4	12	13	**24**	40
#1	9.8	6	22	**31**	50
Batman: The Long Halloween					
#1	9.8	5	21	**29**	45
Batman vs. Predator					
#1	9.8	5	12	**26**	35
Battle Chasers					
#1	9.8	7	42	**65**	100
	9.6	12	10	**36**	60
Battle Classics					
#1	9.4	5	9	**18**	31
Battle of the Planets (Image)					
#1	9.8	25	10	**18**	92
	9.6	25	5	**16**	95
#1/DF	9.8	6	16	**20**	26
	9.6	7	10	**17**	20
Battle of the Planets (Gold Key)					
#1	9.6	14	32	**68**	100
Battlestar Galactica (Marvel)					
#1	9.8	25	19	**55**	100
	9.6	25	10	**27**	75
	9.4	9	10	**18**	33
#2	9.8	6	19	**28**	52
Bazooka Jules					
#2	9.8	6	16	**25**	35
Beware					
#12	5.5	5	41	**47**	55
Beware the Creeper					
#1	9.6	12	110	**241**	340
	9.4	15	103	**162**	270
	9.2	10	41	**87**	130
	9.0	10	43	**80**	110
	8.5	8	31	**48**	79
	8.0	5	36	**38**	42
Birds of Prey					
#8	9.6	8	53	**78**	125
	9.4	12	31	**54**	80
Bite Club					
#1	9.8	5	20	**22**	32
#2	9.9	5	23	**32**	39

ISSUE	CGC GRADE	# of AUCTIONS	LOW CLOSE	AVG CLOSE	HIGH CLOSE
Black Cat Comics					
#8	9.6	8	300	**542**	677
#28	9.4	5	305	**327**	362
Black Goliath					
#1	9.4	6	30	**47**	92
	9.0	6	10	**18**	29
Black Lightning					
#1	9.4	9	21	**38**	78
Black Magic (DC)					
#3	9.6	5	27	**42**	55
Black Panther					
#1	9.6	25	26	**73**	189
	9.4	25	11	**33**	59
	9.2	11	17	**30**	44
	9.0	6	15	**20**	26
Black Terror					
#16	5.0	5	66	**77**	104
Blackhawk					
#9	8.0	7	735	**1,229**	1,500
	5.5	5	228	**436**	775
Blitzkrieg					
#1	9.4	10	29	**55**	76
#4	9.6	12	18	**37**	81
Bloodshot					
#0	9.8	5	16	**31**	52
#1	9.8	14	15	**27**	45
Blue Beetle (Fox)					
#54	4.5	6	406	**491**	599
Blue Devil					
#1	9.8	6	19	**33**	53
Born					
#1	9.8	25	8	**30**	43
	9.6	11	9	**15**	24
#2	10.0	5	96	**131**	184
	9.8	8	10	**20**	34
Boy Comics					
#29	9.2	6	77	**117**	188
Boy Commandos					
#2	6.5	5	158	**287**	360
Brave and the Bold					
#28	4.0	10	103	**458**	610
	2.5	5	223	**288**	350
	2.0	5	276	**304**	365
#29	3.5	6	76	**137**	228
#30	7.0	5	255	**458**	565
	4.5	6	103	**163**	269
	4.0	10	56	**124**	250
	3.5	7	56	**96**	155
#34	8.0	15	735	**974**	1,376
	7.0	17	405	**529**	800
	6.5	8	105	**417**	610
	5.0	12	19	**127**	293
	4.5	13	61	**174**	280
	3.5	6	71	**141**	201
#41	9.0	6	94	**132**	181
#42	8.0	10	100	**174**	300
#44	7.0	5	79	**86**	99
#46	8.0	5	18	**34**	66
#51	7.0	6	30	**70**	118
#54	9.2	6	380	**512**	650
	9.0	5	305	**352**	450
	8.0	10	52	**160**	225
#57	9.4	5	355	**534**	768
#65	9.2	5	47	**85**	114
#68	9.2	5	88	**129**	158
#85	9.4	5	168	**272**	455
#87	9.0	5	34	**44**	55
#100	9.6	10	104	**158**	285
#102	9.4	6	51	**63**	76
#113	9.4	5	45	**62**	84
#136	9.4	5	10	**13**	16
#200	9.6	9	18	**32**	72
Brit					
#1	9.8	5	6	**9**	13
Buffy the Vampire Slayer					
#0.5	9.6	5	10	**19**	51
Cable					
#1	9.8	10	12	**22**	65
Cable/Deadpool					
#1	9.8	8	11	**20**	30
Cage					
#1	9.8	13	11	**19**	28
Caliber Presents					
#1	9.4	6	31	**54**	100
Call of Duty: The Brotherhood					
#1	9.8	14	2	**21**	40
	9.6	14	7	**16**	30
Captain 3-D					
#1	7.5	8	25	**46**	149

ISSUE	CGC GRADE	# of AUCTIONS	LOW CLOSE	AVG CLOSE	HIGH CLOSE
Captain Action					
#1	9.6	7	153	**271**	439
	9.4	7	84	**159**	259
	9.0	11	19	**72**	126
Captain America					
#100	9.6	21	621	**982**	1,376
	9.4	25	499	**645**	851
	9.2	18	223	**404**	510
	9.0	25	158	**330**	512
	8.5	25	168	**225**	331
	8.0	25	99	**193**	285
	7.5	25	61	**142**	235
	7.0	25	73	**105**	150
	6.5	13	61	**96**	154
	6.0	12	41	**74**	127
	5.5	13	46	**68**	109
	4.0	10	41	**55**	71
#101	9.4	13	128	**170**	274
	9.2	6	80	**112**	134
	8.5	8	33	**47**	65
	8.0	5	25	**40**	51
	7.5	6	31	**39**	50
#102	9.6	7	228	**266**	316
	9.4	18	83	**149**	261
	9.2	7	58	**90**	119
	9.0	6	46	**51**	61
	8.0	5	28	**36**	53
#103	9.4	9	98	**153**	200
	9.0	6	31	**56**	108
	8.5	9	28	**39**	49
#104	9.4	11	91	**131**	198
	9.2	13	45	**73**	118
	9.0	5	53	**62**	86
	8.5	9	25	**35**	49
	8.0	5	25	**27**	31
#105	9.4	6	105	**150**	210
	9.0	11	30	**44**	60
#106	9.4	18	75	**118**	158
	9.2	15	42	**62**	100
	9.0	6	38	**45**	55
#107	9.4	12	51	**129**	199
	9.2	10	49	**59**	70
	9.0	5	41	**56**	76
#108	9.6	10	99	**206**	305
	9.4	14	80	**126**	200
	9.2	11	37	**60**	83
	9.0	5	23	**53**	83
	8.5	5	25	**35**	46
#109	9.6	16	194	**288**	450
	9.4	25	90	**164**	275
	9.2	22	57	**95**	152
	9.0	18	45	**76**	153
	8.5	13	34	**52**	100
	8.0	6	26	**46**	60
	7.0	5	26	**30**	39
	6.5	6	11	**18**	27
#110	9.6	16	289	**461**	609
	9.4	17	151	**265**	410
	9.2	8	104	**148**	204
	9.0	10	72	**97**	128
	8.5	6	40	**72**	118
	8.0	8	33	**50**	70
#111	9.6	8	280	**434**	500
	9.4	10	180	**236**	280
	9.2	9	78	**119**	132
	9.0	10	51	**74**	96
	8.5	9	37	**61**	83
	8.0	13	34	**38**	43
#112	7.5	5	12	**24**	33
#113	9.6	9	305	**356**	522
	9.4	5	153	**215**	271
	9.2	11	51	**107**	170
	9.0	12	51	**82**	123
	8.0	9	35	**43**	56
#114	9.0	5	21	**38**	57
#115	9.4	5	86	**105**	130
#117	9.4	10	242	**336**	481
	9.2	9	123	**159**	208
	8.5	6	46	**68**	103
#120	9.2	5	21	**29**	45
#122	9.6	7	89	**130**	172
	9.4	6	50	**62**	86
#127	9.4	6	51	**62**	82
#128	9.4	8	41	**53**	66
#130	9.4	6	42	**55**	79
#133	9.6	12	31	**72**	133
	9.4	15	25	**44**	60
#137	9.6	6	144	**205**	295
	9.2	6	37	**50**	64
#143	9.6	5	154	**171**	209
	9.4	8	61	**91**	128
#168	9.4	6	51	**60**	81
#172	9.4	6	10	**38**	63
#175	9.6	6	36	**60**	92
#179	9.6	7	23	**37**	46
#190	9.6	5	19	**33**	59
#193	9.4	18	20	**26**	47
#199	9.4	5	7	**18**	27
#200	9.8	17	40	**71**	131
	9.6	24	15	**42**	131
	9.4	18	16	**24**	45
#204	9.4	5	13	**15**	19
#212	9.6	6	19	**27**	38
#216	9.6	8	10	**21**	36
#219	9.6	5	8	**16**	24
#241	9.4	9	25	**38**	62
	9.0	5	15	**19**	27
#252	9.8	7	18	**22**	28
#286	9.8	8	20	**40**	79
#383	9.6	8	10	**21**	29
Captain America (Vol. 2)					
#1	9.8	5	13	**20**	30
Captain America (Vol. 3)					
#1	9.8	16	18	**33**	60
#2/Sun	9.6	8	8	**17**	28
Captain America (Vol. 4)					
#1	9.6	5	10	**21**	30
	9.6	6	9	**12**	19

ISSUE	CGC GRADE	# of AUCTIONS	LOW CLOSE	AVG CLOSE	HIGH CLOSE
	9.8	25	10	**27**	100
	9.6	25	8	**18**	35
	9.4	5	11	**14**	20
Captain America & the Falcon					
#2	9.8	5	21	**24**	31
Captain America Annual					
#1	9.0	6	38	**43**	65
#8	9.8	9	76	**174**	300
	9.6	25	31	**49**	83
	9.4	25	14	**28**	46
	9.2	7	10	**17**	25
	9.0	5	10	**21**	31
Captain Atom					
#1	9.0	6	206	**250**	284
Captain Gallant					
#1	9.4	6	15	**36**	57
Captain Marvel					
#1	9.8	7	715	**987**	1,600
	9.6	22	255	**367**	600
	9.4	25	153	**235**	350
	9.2	16	42	**132**	175
	9.0	25	22	**107**	150
	8.5	20	23	**74**	138
	8.0	16	49	**70**	110
	7.5	17	41	**53**	80
	7.0	5	40	**57**	70
#2	9.8	5	276	**357**	475
	9.6	25	66	**121**	205
	9.4	25	37	**74**	118
	9.2	5	31	**48**	76
	8.5	5	14	**26**	40
#3	9.8	5	205	**256**	331
	9.6	7	99	**174**	263
	9.4	7	42	**75**	109
#5	8.5	6	10	**20**	36
#13	9.6	5	36	**73**	104
#26	9.4	5	69	**99**	125
#31	9.6	6	66	**87**	123
#32	9.6	6	31	**76**	103
	9.4	5	23	**40**	56
#33	9.4	8	45	**68**	105
#42	9.6	5	18	**33**	51
Captain Marvel (Vol. 4)					
#1	9.6	6	10	**19**	29
Captain Marvel Adventures					
#51	8.0	7	81	**173**	325
Captain Marvel Jr.					
#28	9.0	5	283	**329**	425
Captain Savage					
#1	9.2	5	26	**39**	53
Cat					
#1	9.4	7	100	**133**	160
Catwoman					
#2	9.8	14	13	**41**	115

ISSUE	CGC GRADE	# of AUCTIONS	LOW CLOSE	AVG CLOSE	HIGH CLOSE
	9.6	11	18	**26**	39
	9.4	7	3	**12**	18
Catwoman (Vol. 2)					
#1	9.8	25	15	**28**	56
	9.6	12	10	**16**	25
#2	9.8	5	20	**29**	37
Catwoman (Vol. 3)					
#1	9.8	17	10	**35**	103
	9.6	12	10	**18**	50
Cerebus the Aardvark					
#8	9.4	6	36	**46**	61
#21	9.4	7	22	**37**	56
Chamber of Chills					
#23	7.0	6	73	**112**	154
Chamber of Darkness					
#1	9.2	8	41	**63**	99
	9.0	5	21	**48**	70
Champions					
#1	9.6	22	38	**95**	203
	9.4	25	26	**49**	150
	9.2	20	9	**27**	44
	9.0	5	20	**27**	36
	8.5	6	10	**19**	25
Chaos Effect: Omega					
#0/Gld	9.4	5	21	**43**	71
Chastity: Theatre of Pain					
#1	9.8	5	11	**25**	51
Classic X-Men					
#1	9.6	5	16	**19**	26
Comic Cavalcade					
#16	9.0	7	305	**625**	749
Conan					
#1	9.8	25	17	**42**	61
	9.6	5	13	**15**	19
#1/2nd	9.8	8	20	**25**	35
#1/3rd	9.8	9	22	**25**	30
#2	9.8	13	20	**29**	37

Conan the Barbarian

ISSUE	CGC GRADE	# of AUCTIONS	LOW CLOSE	AVG CLOSE	HIGH CLOSE
#1	9.6	10	690	**1,154**	1,302
	9.4	25	410	**548**	760
	9.2	25	200	**276**	395
	9.0	25	144	**239**	400
	8.5	25	16	**148**	275
	8.0	25	80	**130**	294
	7.5	25	64	**93**	150
	7.0	25	51	**78**	142
	6.5	14	55	**79**	122
	6.0	12	43	**65**	100
	5.5	5	30	**59**	80
	4.5	5	44	**53**	66
#2	9.6	9	154	**260**	440
	9.4	10	111	**181**	228
	9.2	10	71	**85**	104
	9.0	13	41	**65**	96
	8.5	19	41	**58**	103
	8.0	7	45	**53**	68
	7.5	10	11	**34**	60
	6.5	5	16	**26**	36
#3	9.4	8	138	**287**	406
	9.2	19	84	**133**	198
	9.0	19	57	**99**	159
	8.5	11	27	**64**	85
	8.0	17	34	**66**	125
	7.5	9	37	**51**	62
#4	9.6	10	138	**212**	355
	9.4	16	73	**111**	178
	9.2	6	56	**71**	92
#5	9.4	5	90	**121**	156
	9.2	7	36	**63**	92
	9.0	11	28	**51**	93
#6	9.4	6	63	**106**	180
	9.2	6	26	**40**	50
	9.0	8	25	**41**	61
#7	9.6	10	103	**175**	233
	9.4	8	57	**88**	135
	9.2	10	36	**49**	61
#8	9.6	5	128	**161**	200
	9.4	6	79	**127**	203
#9	9.6	8	158	**192**	215
	9.4	7	68	**82**	113
	9.2	6	45	**53**	64
	9.0	8	27	**42**	57
#10	9.2	11	30	**59**	92
	9.0	8	37	**46**	60
	8.5	5	35	**39**	45
#11	9.6	8	153	**239**	345
	9.4	5	124	**152**	182
	9.2	6	32	**63**	89
#13	9.6	6	98	**141**	208
	9.4	7	51	**71**	87
#14	9.4	6	52	**84**	133
#15	9.6	14	76	**153**	355
	9.4	13	28	**69**	116
#16	9.6	7	113	**136**	163
	9.4	5	20	**65**	100
#17	9.6	14	33	**98**	150
#18	9.4	5	44	**73**	123
#19	9.4	6	45	**69**	90
#20	9.4	5	70	**101**	178
#21	9.4	5	61	**85**	104
	9.2	5	25	**31**	39
#22	9.0	5	25	**30**	36
#23	9.6	6	82	**119**	203
	9.4	25	49	**79**	125
	9.2	12	28	**37**	46
	9.0	9	24	**34**	51
#24	9.6	14	81	**150**	243
	9.4	25	51	**78**	105
	9.2	6	41	**58**	81
	9.0	7	19	**30**	51
	8.5	7	17	**28**	37
#37	9.6	12	42	**65**	114
	9.4	18	20	**42**	104
#44	9.0	5	6	**14**	22
#45	9.4	6	16	**33**	41
#47	9.6	5	25	**40**	56
#53	9.6	8	12	**28**	40
	9.4	5	10	**16**	21
#65	9.4	7	10	**16**	25
#66	9.6	5	10	**23**	35
#74	9.6	7	10	**27**	46
#79	9.6	5	16	**26**	50
#100	9.8	6	43	**64**	86
	9.6	24	12	**26**	98
	9.4	5	13	**26**	45

Conan the Barbarian Annual

ISSUE	CGC GRADE	# of AUCTIONS	LOW CLOSE	AVG CLOSE	HIGH CLOSE
#1	9.2	5	26	**34**	46
#4	9.6	5	12	**29**	51

Cougar, The

ISSUE	CGC GRADE	# of AUCTIONS	LOW CLOSE	AVG CLOSE	HIGH CLOSE
#1	9.6	9	19	**29**	45

Coup d'etat: Sleeper

ISSUE	CGC GRADE	# of AUCTIONS	LOW CLOSE	AVG CLOSE	HIGH CLOSE
#1	9.8	13	9	**19**	33

Coup d'etat: Stormwatch

ISSUE	CGC GRADE	# of AUCTIONS	LOW CLOSE	AVG CLOSE	HIGH CLOSE
#1	9.8	7	3	**9**	16

Coup d'etat: Wildcats

ISSUE	CGC GRADE	# of AUCTIONS	LOW CLOSE	AVG CLOSE	HIGH CLOSE
#1	9.8	6	3	**6**	17

Creatures on the Loose

ISSUE	CGC GRADE	# of AUCTIONS	LOW CLOSE	AVG CLOSE	HIGH CLOSE
#16	9.4	5	25	**28**	36
#17	9.6	6	36	**50**	77
#30	9.4	6	20	**85**	219

Crime Does Not Pay

ISSUE	CGC GRADE	# of AUCTIONS	LOW CLOSE	AVG CLOSE	HIGH CLOSE
#22	5.0	5	416	**609**	865

Crimefighters

ISSUE	CGC GRADE	# of AUCTIONS	LOW CLOSE	AVG CLOSE	HIGH CLOSE
#1	8.0	5	11	**141**	229

Crisis on Infinite Earths

ISSUE	CGC GRADE	# of AUCTIONS	LOW CLOSE	AVG CLOSE	HIGH CLOSE
#1	9.8	12	40	**53**	75
	9.6	25	10	**23**	65
	9.4	25	10	**16**	26
	9.2	7	9	**15**	20
	9.0	7	5	**11**	20
	8.5	5	6	**8**	11
#2	9.8	10	27	**46**	69

ISSUE	CGC GRADE	# of AUCTIONS	LOW CLOSE	AVG CLOSE	HIGH CLOSE
	9.6	6	8	**20**	25
#4	9.8	13	13	**34**	71
	9.6	7	11	**24**	36
#5	9.6	6	15	**24**	31
#6	9.8	9	26	**32**	38
	9.6	7	9	**19**	35
#7	9.8	25	22	**60**	100
	9.6	25	10	**26**	45
	9.4	21	8	**17**	46
#8	9.8	20	31	**68**	133
	9.6	25	7	**27**	61
	9.4	15	5	**20**	41
	9.2	8	11	**15**	31
#11	9.6	6	10	**23**	36
#12	9.6	12	13	**28**	50

Cry for Dawn

ISSUE	CGC GRADE	# of AUCTIONS	LOW CLOSE	AVG CLOSE	HIGH CLOSE
#1	9.2	6	30	**100**	153
#4	9.6	5	39	**68**	92
#5	9.6	9	43	**102**	275
#9	9.6	5	29	**61**	103

CSI: Crime Scene Investigation

ISSUE	CGC GRADE	# of AUCTIONS	LOW CLOSE	AVG CLOSE	HIGH CLOSE
#1	9.8	9	12	**21**	35

Cyblade/Shi

ISSUE	CGC GRADE	# of AUCTIONS	LOW CLOSE	AVG CLOSE	HIGH CLOSE
#1	9.6	6	10	**17**	25

Dagar the Invincible

ISSUE	CGC GRADE	# of AUCTIONS	LOW CLOSE	AVG CLOSE	HIGH CLOSE
#8	9.4	5	20	**27**	33

Danger Girl

ISSUE	CGC GRADE	# of AUCTIONS	LOW CLOSE	AVG CLOSE	HIGH CLOSE
#1	9.8	12	24	**79**	250
	9.6	23	15	**50**	105
	9.4	5	11	**23**	52
#1/Chrm	9.6	6	61	**65**	75
#2	9.8	7	20	**41**	104
	9.6	11	11	**24**	70
#4	9.6	6	10	**15**	21

Daredevil

ISSUE	CGC GRADE	# of AUCTIONS	LOW CLOSE	AVG CLOSE	HIGH CLOSE
#0.5	9.8	12	20	**36**	66
	9.6	9	14	**23**	31
#1	9.2	16	3,250	**5,671**	7,600
	9.0	20	2,342	**3,390**	5,100
	8.5	14	1,280	**2,147**	2,950
	8.0	20	1,275	**1,631**	2,550
	7.5	19	510	**1,376**	2,225
	7.0	25	716	**1,013**	1,599
	6.5	15	560	**721**	1,000
	6.0	25	456	**652**	911
	5.5	19	475	**593**	851
	5.0	24	400	**475**	585
	4.5	25	229	**424**	660
	4.0	25	203	**375**	516
	3.5	16	27	**294**	412
	3.0	20	178	**277**	380
	2.5	8	165	**245**	360
	1.8	6	103	**210**	307
#2	9.4	5	2,425	**2,975**	3,400
	9.2	9	985	**1,496**	1,924
	9.0	9	610	**852**	1,126
	8.0	10	120	**397**	560
	7.5	7	311	**376**	449
	7.0	11	76	**267**	330
	6.0	6	140	**184**	248
	5.5	8	102	**142**	178
	5.0	11	82	**127**	150
	4.0	8	77	**100**	120
#3	9.4	6	1,526	**1,934**	2,550
	9.0	14	358	**494**	728
	8.5	9	250	**325**	381
	8.0	12	194	**261**	400
	7.5	11	100	**165**	244
	7.0	11	26	**156**	250
	3.0	10	15	**39**	66
#4	9.4	10	827	**1,444**	2,601
	9.0	10	312	**382**	500
	8.0	6	155	**261**	510
	7.5	6	104	**155**	232
	7.0	13	61	**123**	177
	6.5	5	53	**105**	143
	5.0	5	57	**66**	82
	4.5	5	46	**61**	80
	4.0	9	36	**54**	76
#5	9.4	5	804	**1,097**	1,300
	9.2	9	300	**460**	600
	8.5	16	154	**208**	280
	8.0	8	85	**160**	236
	7.5	6	81	**108**	140
	7.0	6	61	**90**	122
	5.5	6	41	**60**	86
#6	9.4	5	675	**822**	1,026
	9.0	14	58	**220**	407
	8.5	5	100	**150**	213
	8.0	14	51	**113**	228
	7.5	8	79	**100**	150
	7.0	9	64	**76**	96
	6.5	10	41	**60**	77
	5.0	5	31	**47**	89
#7	9.0	9	380	**728**	1,200
	8.5	8	255	**418**	546
	8.0	9	80	**309**	457
	7.5	13	53	**214**	353
	7.0	6	148	**202**	310
	6.5	24	98	**133**	205
	5.5	6	27	**76**	110
	4.0	5	39	**66**	100
	3.0	5	28	**38**	50

ISSUE	CGC GRADE	# of AUCTIONS	LOW CLOSE	AVG CLOSE	HIGH CLOSE
Daredevil (cont'd)					
#8	9.4	10	500	**626**	785
	9.2	14	108	**246**	450
	9.0	7	154	**193**	300
	8.5	13	95	**148**	226
	8.0	11	61	**106**	128
	7.5	6	60	**78**	104
	7.0	15	46	**63**	97
	6.5	6	50	**56**	62
	6.0	6	29	**38**	50
	4.5	5	24	**31**	45
#9	9.6	6	565	**670**	723
	9.4	25	203	**408**	601
	9.2	18	169	**241**	350
	9.0	25	114	**172**	257
	8.5	8	86	**119**	150
	8.0	8	76	**87**	104
	7.5	8	50	**66**	92
	7.0	10	41	**59**	78
#10	9.2	9	200	**321**	475
	9.0	12	144	**179**	272
	8.0	8	80	**106**	143
	7.5	12	40	**70**	94
	7.0	6	44	**59**	85
	6.0	9	30	**43**	60
#11	9.4	6	285	**361**	481
	9.2	11	142	**222**	456
	9.0	9	90	**123**	169
	8.0	6	59	**68**	83
#12	8.0	6	46	**58**	70
#13	9.2	7	140	**260**	715
	9.0	9	56	**129**	224
	8.5	7	62	**87**	134
#14	9.0	7	67	**81**	100
	8.0	6	42	**60**	72
#15	9.4	8	178	**314**	450
	9.2	13	101	**142**	229
	8.5	6	47	**74**	118
	8.0	7	44	**50**	57
#16	9.4	6	99	**1,012**	2,184
	9.0	10	123	**249**	350
	8.5	10	105	**139**	180
	7.5	9	37	**92**	135
	7.0	6	51	**77**	138
#17	9.4	8	355	**586**	817
	9.0	11	104	**159**	212
	8.0	9	71	**89**	115
#18	9.4	14	75	**256**	340
	9.2	7	69	**129**	179
	9.0	8	70	**93**	128
#19	9.0	5	56	**87**	116
	8.0	5	35	**49**	89
	7.0	5	29	**116**	153
#20	8.5	13	41	**60**	76
#21	9.2	5	71	**93**	114
	7.5	5	29	**62**	178
#22	9.4	7	125	**182**	225
	9.2	5	69	**89**	131
#23	9.2	5	61	**114**	214
	8.5	6	28	**40**	52

ISSUE	CGC GRADE	# of AUCTIONS	LOW CLOSE	AVG CLOSE	HIGH CLOSE
#24	9.2	8	70	**108**	150
#25	9.4	5	123	**166**	194
	9.2	10	67	**91**	179
	9.0	8	41	**67**	95
	8.5	7	36	**49**	75
#26	9.4	5	179	**245**	300
	8.5	8	31	**45**	64
#27	9.4	11	154	**209**	331
	9.2	9	86	**119**	162
	9.0	14	51	**76**	203
	8.5	6	40	**49**	64
#28	9.4	6	140	**161**	179
	9.2	8	46	**79**	144
	9.0	8	35	**56**	85
	8.0	5	25	**31**	35
#30	9.4	12	109	**197**	294
	9.0	5	50	**58**	68
#32	9.6	5	23	**272**	402
	9.0	7	36	**49**	71
#33	9.4	5	105	**143**	168
	9.0	7	30	**44**	52
#34	9.4	5	103	**131**	184
	9.2	5	70	**87**	128
	8.5	5	27	**33**	50
#35	9.4	9	72	**135**	180
	8.0	9	11	**26**	35
#36	8.0	5	18	**34**	43
#37	9.4	6	180	**216**	260
	9.2	5	86	**100**	113
	7.0	6	15	**20**	28
#39	9.4	5	132	**166**	200
#40	9.4	5	85	**152**	243
	9.2	11	30	**50**	66
	9.0	7	30	**43**	57
	8.0	5	1	**24**	35
#41	9.4	10	66	**112**	184
	9.2	6	56	**67**	82
	9.0	5	42	**48**	51
#42	9.4	12	68	**119**	223
#43	9.4	24	104	**197**	362
	9.2	12	53	**82**	143
	8.0	6	30	**40**	56
#44	9.4	14	63	**103**	150
	9.2	10	41	**62**	100
	9.0	5	25	**38**	47
#45	9.4	22	60	**100**	175
	9.2	14	33	**52**	79
	8.5	7	25	**34**	47
#46	8.5	6	24	**26**	29
#47	9.4	5	62	**114**	153
	9.2	8	35	**44**	57
	9.0	6	31	**38**	56
	8.0	5	21	**23**	25
#48	9.4	5	99	**156**	204
#49	9.4	6	71	**109**	154
	9.2	7	35	**51**	62
	9.0	6	27	**36**	46
#50	9.4	6	104	**148**	204
	9.0	6	35	**47**	76
#51	9.2	5	36	**57**	76

ISSUE	CGC GRADE	# of AUCTIONS	LOW CLOSE	AVG CLOSE	HIGH CLOSE
#52	9.4	9	66	**125**	174
	8.5	5	21	**29**	40
	8.0	5	18	**63**	165
#53	9.4	17	51	**109**	260
#56	9.4	5	47	**80**	100
	9.2	6	27	**38**	50
#59	9.6	5	153	**195**	270
	9.4	6	51	**94**	138
	9.2	5	27	**45**	55
#60	9.4	6	65	**90**	114
#61	9.2	5	31	**52**	80
#62	9.2	5	25	**35**	50
#63	9.4	6	60	**89**	206
#67	9.4	6	56	**93**	142
#70	9.2	5	21	**49**	75
#71	9.2	5	20	**33**	51
#76	9.4	9	40	**60**	85
#77	9.6	11	120	**254**	651
	9.4	11	71	**112**	321
#78	9.4	8	50	**66**	78
#81	9.6	7	203	**314**	390
	9.4	11	83	**158**	282
	9.0	6	33	**42**	60
#84	9.2	7	23	**32**	41
#87	9.6	5	63	**105**	162
	9.4	5	41	**56**	77
#88	9.4	7	29	**43**	62
#90	9.4	8	40	**60**	81
#91	9.4	5	44	**63**	75
#95	9.4	6	62	**71**	86
#97	9.6	5	104	**106**	113
#98	9.4	9	27	**53**	72
#99	9.4	8	36	**73**	104
#100	9.4	7	45	**145**	325
	9.0	5	21	**25**	33
#103	9.2	5	27	**35**	61
#108	9.2	6	12	**24**	39
#126	9.6	7	49	**71**	95
#129	9.6	6	35	**56**	76
	9.4	5	11	**21**	39
#131	9.6	19	405	**540**	969
	9.4	25	138	**290**	599
	9.2	25	57	**163**	400
	9.0	25	45	**100**	165
	8.5	25	41	**74**	120
	8.0	21	30	**56**	103
	7.5	5	31	**58**	83
	7.0	14	26	**57**	103
	6.5	5	30	**39**	50
#132	9.8	5	228	**306**	430
	9.4	6	45	**86**	160
	9.0	15	13	**27**	75
#133	9.2	5	11	**20**	26
#135	9.4	6	18	**23**	28
#136	9.6	6	31	**40**	50
	9.4	10	18	**27**	43
#137	9.4	5	19	**26**	32
#139	9.6	7	28	**51**	77
	9.4	7	11	**21**	28
#140	9.6	8	22	**60**	136
#141	9.4	8	35	**59**	97
#145	9.6	7	18	**40**	79
#146	9.6	6	63	**103**	200
#147	9.6	5	27	**50**	92
#151	9.4	7	15	**24**	30
#155	9.6	5	26	**54**	84
#157	9.6	6	31	**49**	88
	9.4	6	18	**26**	39
#158	9.6	22	203	**344**	517
	9.4	25	79	**142**	350
	9.2	25	51	**88**	250
	9.0	25	30	**61**	114
	8.5	25	31	**46**	81
	8.0	16	25	**40**	65
	7.5	12	15	**26**	50
	7.0	14	13	**28**	41
	6.5	5	17	**28**	41
#159	9.6	15	14	**140**	304
	9.4	12	26	**69**	178
	9.2	10	14	**32**	51
	9.0	5	10	**17**	29
	8.5	8	15	**24**	35
	8.0	7	11	**16**	23
#160	9.6	21	37	**100**	255
	9.4	15	23	**53**	84
	9.2	7	25	**35**	55
	9.0	8	18	**25**	32
	8.5	7	11	**21**	35
#161	9.6	17	36	**99**	252
	9.4	21	25	**54**	125
	9.2	12	15	**30**	51
#163	9.6	6	168	**203**	275
	9.4	15	37	**79**	136
	9.2	12	20	**36**	66
	9.0	6	18	**24**	39
#164	9.8	6	103	**188**	326
	9.6	13	40	**76**	160
	9.4	18	15	**34**	81
	9.2	9	9	**19**	30
#165	9.0	7	1	**23**	86
#166	9.6	10	66	**100**	192
	9.4	7	26	**35**	52
	9.0	5	10	**11**	15
#167	9.6	17	38	**65**	99
	9.4	10	18	**29**	70

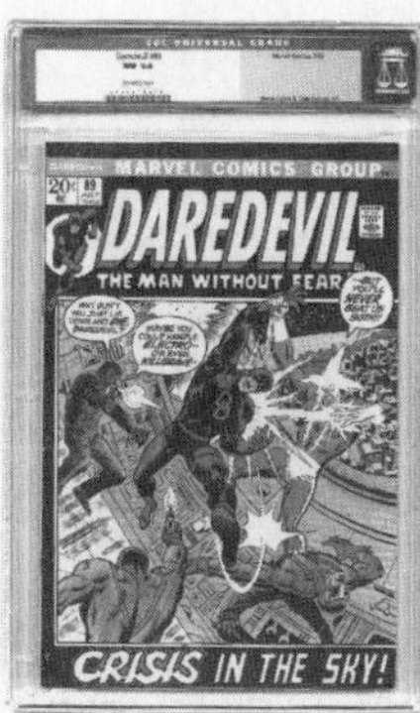

ISSUE	CGC GRADE	# of AUCTIONS	LOW CLOSE	AVG CLOSE	HIGH CLOSE
Daredevil (cont'd)					
#168	9.6	25	305	**560**	760
	9.4	25	153	**272**	514
	9.2	25	61	**118**	250
	9.0	25	45	**96**	169
	8.5	25	40	**70**	145
	8.0	25	36	**54**	74
	7.5	24	27	**47**	89
	7.0	9	25	**36**	59
#169	9.6	14	68	**138**	235
	9.4	10	41	**60**	129
	9.0	6	11	**18**	25
#170	9.6	10	46	**90**	153
	9.4	22	14	**28**	51
	9.2	5	10	**21**	30
#171	9.8	5	75	**197**	334
	9.4	11	13	**63**	203
	9.2	5	11	**17**	20
#172	9.8	5	80	**140**	248
	9.6	12	31	**81**	140
	9.4	13	19	**38**	103
#173	9.8	5	76	**114**	191
	9.6	11	27	**51**	147
	9.4	8	17	**21**	29
#174	9.8	6	66	**97**	138
	9.6	25	10	**36**	97
	9.4	18	18	**31**	72
	9.2	11	10	**17**	25
#175	9.6	25	13	**40**	100
	9.4	25	11	**25**	37
	9.2	9	10	**18**	35
#176	9.6	14	16	**43**	66
	9.4	8	21	**36**	53
	9.2	6	16	**21**	27
#177	9.8	7	46	**70**	113
	9.6	14	16	**38**	64
	9.4	8	20	**33**	66
#178	9.6	25	12	**39**	133
	9.4	17	13	**24**	39
#179	9.8	10	51	**75**	105
	9.6	25	20	**46**	175
	9.4	19	10	**24**	49
	9.2	14	8	**18**	36
	9.0	6	10	**11**	13
#180	9.8	25	20	**44**	125
	9.6	25	6	**30**	153
	9.4	25	6	**20**	46
	9.2	9	10	**12**	19
#181	9.8	25	41	**98**	250
	9.6	25	21	**48**	175
	9.4	25	14	**31**	90
	9.2	25	14	**29**	58
	9.0	24	10	**23**	52
	8.5	25	4	**20**	42
	7.5	5	13	**19**	30
#182	9.8	25	25	**53**	128
	9.6	25	12	**40**	153
	9.4	25	8	**18**	41
	9.2	9	10	**17**	25
	9.0	5	9	**12**	15
	8.5	9	4	**12**	20
#183	9.8	16	35	**66**	138
	9.6	25	10	**34**	214
	9.4	25	10	**21**	41
	9.2	12	10	**18**	26
	7.0	5	4	**8**	11
#184	9.8	16	31	**72**	202
	9.6	25	11	**26**	255
	9.4	25	8	**23**	56
	9.2	10	10	**13**	21
	9.0	8	10	**14**	22
	8.5	6	10	**16**	23
#185	9.8	17	25	**37**	69
	9.6	25	10	**27**	61
	9.4	20	10	**17**	25
	9.2	11	8	**14**	21
#186	9.9	5	71	**117**	205
	9.8	25	6	**27**	128
	9.6	25	10	**25**	214
	9.4	25	6	**20**	48
	9.2	6	10	**12**	16
#187	9.8	17	20	**43**	75
	9.6	25	14	**34**	133
	9.4	14	10	**20**	30
#188	9.8	16	12	**57**	150
	9.6	25	5	**33**	295
	9.4	9	11	**24**	73
#189	9.8	25	19	**43**	118
	9.6	25	11	**33**	158
	9.4	15	10	**18**	27
#190	9.8	25	25	**38**	114
	9.6	25	13	**25**	91
	9.4	15	10	**17**	32
	9.2	9	8	**14**	37
#191	9.8	25	18	**48**	123
	9.6	25	1	**29**	203
	9.4	15	5	**13**	21
#192	9.8	9	3	**23**	30
#193	9.8	9	13	**31**	86
	9.6	5	8	**14**	21
#194	9.8	5	17	**24**	30
	9.6	6	11	**16**	20
#195	9.8	11	15	**21**	27
	9.6	11	9	**21**	71
#196	9.8	25	33	**67**	128
	9.6	25	13	**30**	65
	9.4	24	14	**20**	30
	9.2	9	10	**17**	25
#197	9.6	7	18	**30**	50
#198	9.8	6	19	**30**	53
#199	9.8	5	22	**29**	38
#200	9.8	14	37	**76**	266
	9.6	20	13	**29**	47
	9.4	6	16	**24**	34
#201	9.8	9	15	**24**	35
	9.6	5	15	**18**	22
#202	9.8	13	13	**23**	37
#204	9.8	7	17	**22**	25
#205	9.8	10	16	**23**	26
#206	9.8	6	19	**24**	29

ISSUE	CGC GRADE	# of AUCTIONS	LOW CLOSE	AVG CLOSE	HIGH CLOSE
#207	9.8	11	17	**21**	29
#209	9.8	10	15	**27**	68
#210	9.8	5	17	**21**	25
#213	9.8	6	15	**30**	50
#215	9.8	7	10	**20**	25
#216	9.8	5	14	**22**	25
#217	9.8	6	17	**22**	25
#221	9.8	5	16	**20**	23
#222	9.8	5	16	**19**	25
#223	9.8	5	26	**36**	50
#224	9.8	5	10	**18**	25
#227	9.6	5	20	**34**	56
	9.4	9	10	**17**	35
#228	9.8	9	11	**30**	51
#232	9.8	5	20	**33**	49
#241	9.8	11	20	**31**	45
#249	9.6	5	21	**45**	90
#250	9.8	6	25	**27**	30
#251	9.9	5	25	**34**	43
#252	9.8	12	10	**20**	35
#254	9.6	5	31	**34**	42
	9.4	5	15	**23**	34
#257	9.8	7	18	**31**	50
	9.6	5	23	**30**	49
#265	9.8	5	18	**21**	26
#293	9.6	6	15	**18**	31
#300	9.8	9	1	**25**	62
	9.6	11	10	**21**	37
#323	9.8	5	20	**26**	30

Daredevil (Vol. 2)

ISSUE	CGC GRADE	# of AUCTIONS	LOW CLOSE	AVG CLOSE	HIGH CLOSE
#1	9.8	10	52	**127**	230
	9.6	25	17	**67**	153
	9.4	14	25	**41**	90
#2	9.6	6	25	**36**	66
#5	9.8	21	26	**66**	125
	9.6	6	18	**37**	51
#1	9.8	13	33	**136**	200
	9.6	25	21	**41**	100
	9.4	25	11	**34**	60
	9.2	10	9	**32**	86
	9.0	7	16	**28**	51
#2	9.8	11	20	**46**	66
	9.6	15	6	**20**	31
#3	9.8	10	31	**48**	76
	9.6	16	12	**22**	28
#4	9.8	6	25	**38**	51
	9.6	8	15	**22**	30
#5	9.8	9	33	**64**	88
	9.6	9	16	**28**	51
#6	9.8	15	18	**33**	50
	9.6	6	11	**23**	40
#7	9.8	12	13	**34**	50
	9.6	5	15	**34**	60
#8	9.6	5	15	**28**	40
#26	9.8	5	20	**24**	31
	9.4	5	6	**11**	15
#47	9.8	6	11	**20**	25
#49/DF	9.8	8	19	**22**	25
#50/DF	9.8	8	20	**27**	35
#51/DF	9.8	5	16	**19**	23

ISSUE	CGC GRADE	# of AUCTIONS	LOW CLOSE	AVG CLOSE	HIGH CLOSE
#54/Var	9.8	7	11	**17**	20
#56/Var	9.8	9	11	**15**	20
#57/Var	9.8	10	8	**14**	22

Daredevil Annual

ISSUE	CGC GRADE	# of AUCTIONS	LOW CLOSE	AVG CLOSE	HIGH CLOSE
#1	9.6	5	260	**362**	566
	9.4	14	71	**173**	243
	9.2	7	85	**115**	140
	9.0	5	62	**84**	120

Daredevil Comics

ISSUE	CGC GRADE	# of AUCTIONS	LOW CLOSE	AVG CLOSE	HIGH CLOSE
#19	7.5	5	179	**195**	199
#31	7.5	5	72	**199**	258

Daredevil: Father

ISSUE	CGC GRADE	# of AUCTIONS	LOW CLOSE	AVG CLOSE	HIGH CLOSE
#1	9.8	14	20	**24**	30

Daredevil: The Man Without Fear

ISSUE	CGC GRADE	# of AUCTIONS	LOW CLOSE	AVG CLOSE	HIGH CLOSE
#1	9.8	9	25	**37**	58
	9.4	9	5	**10**	16

Daredevil: The Target

ISSUE	CGC GRADE	# of AUCTIONS	LOW CLOSE	AVG CLOSE	HIGH CLOSE
#1	9.8	25	4	**14**	35
	9.6	9	9	**17**	35

Daredevil: Yellow

ISSUE	CGC GRADE	# of AUCTIONS	LOW CLOSE	AVG CLOSE	HIGH CLOSE
#1	9.8	21	10	**28**	55
	9.6	16	6	**17**	25

Darkchylde

ISSUE	CGC GRADE	# of AUCTIONS	LOW CLOSE	AVG CLOSE	HIGH CLOSE
#1	9.4	6	7	**19**	50

Dark Days

ISSUE	CGC GRADE	# of AUCTIONS	LOW CLOSE	AVG CLOSE	HIGH CLOSE
#1	9.8	16	10	**24**	35

Dark Knight Strikes Again

ISSUE	CGC GRADE	# of AUCTIONS	LOW CLOSE	AVG CLOSE	HIGH CLOSE
#1	9.9	24	22	**37**	57
	9.8	25	5	**16**	61
	9.6	13	3	**19**	50
#1/Var	9.8	12	15	**23**	35
#2	9.9	14	20	**32**	46
	9.8	25	8	**16**	25
	9.6	6	7	**15**	22
#3	9.8	15	10	**17**	35

Dark Mansion of Forbidden Love

ISSUE	CGC GRADE	# of AUCTIONS	LOW CLOSE	AVG CLOSE	HIGH CLOSE
#1	9.0	5	91	**117**	151
	8.5	5	48	**73**	103
	5.5	7	13	**21**	29

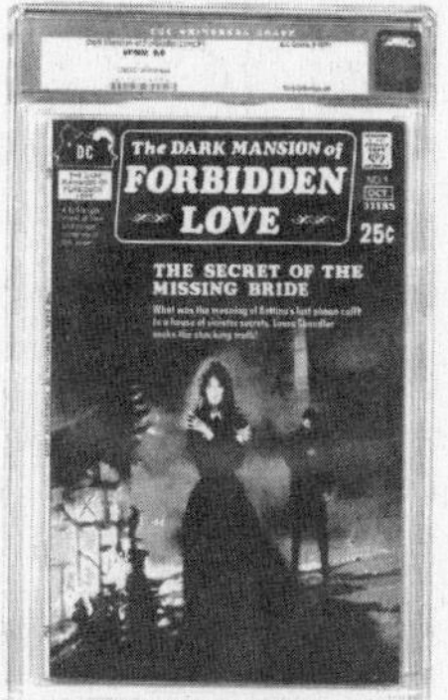

ISSUE	CGC GRADE	# of AUCTIONS	LOW CLOSE	AVG CLOSE	HIGH CLOSE
Darkness					
#1	9.8	11	10	**18**	27
#11	9.8	5	18	**22**	26
	9.6	5	10	**14**	22
Darkness (Vol. 2)					
#1	10.0	6	56	**111**	153
	9.8	16	10	**20**	35
Darkness/Incredible Hulk					
#1	9.8	5	19	**26**	40
Dark Shadows					
#4	9.4	5	38	**105**	153
Dawn					
#0.5	9.8	6	20	**21**	24
#1	9.8	9	26	**46**	75
	9.6	8	15	**46**	200
#1/Blk	9.8	5	34	**43**	50
Dazzler					
#1	9.8	10	26	**37**	50
	9.6	20	11	**23**	40
	9.4	7	10	**15**	23
#38	9.8	6	25	**29**	45
DC Comics Presents					
#1	9.6	9	26	**40**	56
	9.4	6	13	**26**	41
#26	9.6	18	26	**55**	125
	9.4	5	20	**39**	61
#47	9.6	7	41	**60**	121
	9.4	8	20	**26**	46
#87	9.8	6	15	**22**	27
DC 100 Page Super Spectacular					
#6	8.5	10	58	**100**	158
#15	9.4	7	33	**76**	104
#20	9.0	6	18	**33**	57
DC Special					
#1	9.2	6	78	**86**	103
	9.0	6	13	**42**	79
#6	9.4	5	42	**70**	94
#11	9.6	7	126	**157**	225
DC Special Series					
#16	9.2	6	31	**58**	99
DC Super-Stars					
#12	9.6	6	16	**29**	55
DC: The New Frontier					
#1	9.8	5	16	**18**	25
Deadpool					
#1	9.8	6	11	**28**	41
	9.6	5	10	**17**	33
Deadworld					
#1	9.6	7	12	**28**	79
Death Dealer					
#2	9.8	5	23	**27**	30

ISSUE	CGC GRADE	# of AUCTIONS	LOW CLOSE	AVG CLOSE	HIGH CLOSE
Deathmate Black					
#0	9.8	7	6	**25**	50
Debbi's Dates					
#1	9.2	5	45	**73**	100
Defenders					
#1	9.6	11	349	**577**	800
	9.4	25	193	**300**	501
	9.2	25	101	**133**	260
	9.0	25	41	**95**	153
	8.5	20	54	**78**	115
	8.0	14	45	**63**	96
	7.5	12	26	**45**	77
#3	9.2	6	32	**43**	50
#4	9.2	6	37	**55**	75
#9	9.4	8	53	**66**	86
	9.2	7	30	**40**	50
#10	9.4	25	147	**236**	370
	9.2	13	69	**95**	128
	9.0	5	57	**73**	111
	8.5	15	26	**55**	85
	7.5	5	20	**27**	34
#14	9.4	8	25	**43**	100
#15	9.4	8	26	**38**	60
#40	9.4	6	10	**17**	23
#100	9.6	7	13	**25**	45
Defenders Annual					
#1	9.4	6	36	**51**	65
Demon, The (1st Series)					
#1	9.2	12	31	**69**	150
Destructor					
#1	9.6	5	31	**44**	93
	9.4	8	12	**24**	51
Detective Comics					
#38	3.5	6	3,150	**4,331**	5,785
#45	6.5	8	560	**892**	1,500
#65	7.0	9	761	**1,013**	1,200
#80	4.5	5	155	**204**	249
#89	9.0	8	750	**867**	1,000
#102	4.5	5	158	**193**	228
#107	9.0	5	455	**659**	899
#111	8.5	10	300	**454**	566
#116	4.5	5	80	**99**	122
#119	8.5	7	307	**418**	549
#127	7.0	5	215	**230**	255
#140	4.5	5	525	**736**	895
	4.0	6	537	**772**	950
#225	6.5	5	1,051	**1,272**	1,536
	5.0	6	530	**730**	1,100
#229	7.0	5	159	**178**	205
#307	9.0	6	61	**93**	110
#356	9.0	6	44	**68**	130
#357	9.4	6	114	**163**	197
#359	9.0	5	213	**285**	465
#400	9.2	8	234	**316**	442
	9.0	7	178	**209**	280
#403	9.0	5	37	**46**	66
#405	9.0	5	32	**39**	50

ISSUE	CGC GRADE	# of AUCTIONS	LOW CLOSE	AVG CLOSE	HIGH CLOSE
#407	9.4	8	92	**175**	284
#410	9.2	9	50	**83**	103
#415	9.2	6	29	**49**	71
#430	9.4	8	30	**41**	60
#431	9.4	6	25	**43**	76
#443	9.2	6	30	**59**	123
#448	9.4	5	28	**34**	50
#469	9.6	6	22	**33**	72
#475	9.6	6	56	**82**	103
#476	9.6	5	54	**79**	90
	9.4	9	21	**46**	76
	9.0	6	18	**28**	42
#478	9.6	7	15	**29**	47
#479	9.6	12	20	**32**	53
	9.4	5	16	**23**	32
#491	9.6	6	16	**28**	39
#500	9.6	9	17	**28**	51
	9.4	8	9	**14**	21
#575	9.8	9	26	**60**	96
	9.6	15	18	**26**	49
#576	9.6	6	8	**26**	52
#577	9.8	6	33	**58**	104
	9.4	6	8	**12**	15
#578	9.6	14	11	**31**	78
	9.4	6	9	**17**	40

Devil Dinosaur

ISSUE	CGC GRADE	# of AUCTIONS	LOW CLOSE	AVG CLOSE	HIGH CLOSE
#1	9.8	10	42	**76**	100
	9.6	23	20	**31**	81
	9.4	13	10	**19**	31
	9.2	5	12	**14**	15

Devil May Cry

ISSUE	CGC GRADE	# of AUCTIONS	LOW CLOSE	AVG CLOSE	HIGH CLOSE
#1	9.8	5	25	**28**	36

Doc Savage (Marvel comic)

ISSUE	CGC GRADE	# of AUCTIONS	LOW CLOSE	AVG CLOSE	HIGH CLOSE
#1	8.5	5	25	**41**	59

Doctor Octopus: Negative Exposure

ISSUE	CGC GRADE	# of AUCTIONS	LOW CLOSE	AVG CLOSE	HIGH CLOSE
#1	9.8	9	11	**16**	22

Doctor Strange

ISSUE	CGC GRADE	# of AUCTIONS	LOW CLOSE	AVG CLOSE	HIGH CLOSE
#169	9.8	7	736	**819**	910
	9.6	25	255	**442**	663
	9.4	25	168	**263**	355
	9.2	23	87	**151**	225
	9.0	8	66	**104**	137
	8.5	7	67	**85**	104
	8.0	7	57	**73**	89
	7.0	7	31	**43**	52
	6.0	8	22	**32**	42
#170	9.4	6	85	**111**	142
	9.2	6	33	**46**	52
	9.0	5	29	**38**	50
#171	9.4	5	73	**125**	203
#172	9.4	8	76	**104**	150
	9.2	6	32	**53**	76
	8.5	5	16	**30**	40
#173	9.4	8	77	**113**	145
#176	9.2	5	27	**43**	53
#180	9.4	5	87	**122**	154

Doctor Strange (Vol. 2)

ISSUE	CGC GRADE	# of AUCTIONS	LOW CLOSE	AVG CLOSE	HIGH CLOSE
#1	9.8	9	338	**434**	510
	9.6	25	103	**156**	305
	9.4	25	53	**87**	156
	9.2	13	40	**50**	62
	9.0	12	32	**49**	80
#2	9.4	6	30	**83**	150
#15	9.6	8	16	**21**	33

Doctor Strange Annual

ISSUE	CGC GRADE	# of AUCTIONS	LOW CLOSE	AVG CLOSE	HIGH CLOSE
#1	9.4	7	12	**28**	40

Doctor Who

ISSUE	CGC GRADE	# of AUCTIONS	LOW CLOSE	AVG CLOSE	HIGH CLOSE
#1	9.8	8	12	**25**	50

Drama

ISSUE	CGC GRADE	# of AUCTIONS	LOW CLOSE	AVG CLOSE	HIGH CLOSE
#1	9.9	5	51	**94**	200
	9.8	8	21	**35**	46

Dreams of Darkchylde

ISSUE	CGC GRADE	# of AUCTIONS	LOW CLOSE	AVG CLOSE	HIGH CLOSE
#1	9.8	5	13	**17**	21

Dreams of Dawn

ISSUE	CGC GRADE	# of AUCTIONS	LOW CLOSE	AVG CLOSE	HIGH CLOSE
#0.5	9.8	10	15	**23**	53
	9.6	7	10	**19**	40

80 Page Giant

ISSUE	CGC GRADE	# of AUCTIONS	LOW CLOSE	AVG CLOSE	HIGH CLOSE
#1	8.0	8	145	**225**	325
#7	9.0	5	225	**275**	335
#8	9.2	12	152	**348**	575
	9.0	8	143	**267**	390
#12	9.4	5	153	**330**	429

Ekos Preview

ISSUE	CGC GRADE	# of AUCTIONS	LOW CLOSE	AVG CLOSE	HIGH CLOSE
#1	9.8	8	18	**32**	51

El Cazador

ISSUE	CGC GRADE	# of AUCTIONS	LOW CLOSE	AVG CLOSE	HIGH CLOSE
#1	9.8	7	20	**35**	50

Elektra

ISSUE	CGC GRADE	# of AUCTIONS	LOW CLOSE	AVG CLOSE	HIGH CLOSE
#1	9.8	8	23	**30**	50

Elektra (Vol. 2)

ISSUE	CGC GRADE	# of AUCTIONS	LOW CLOSE	AVG CLOSE	HIGH CLOSE
#1	9.8	25	16	**28**	50
	9.6	16	10	**18**	36
	9.4	5	7	**17**	25
#3	9.8	25	54	**141**	300
	9.6	25	28	**57**	149
	9.4	25	24	**44**	81
	9.2	18	13	**33**	60

ISSUE	CGC GRADE	# of AUCTIONS	LOW CLOSE	AVG CLOSE	HIGH CLOSE
Elektra: Assassin					
#1	9.8	10	26	**42**	50
	9.6	12	12	**21**	36
#2	9.8	9	17	**29**	37
Elfquest					
#1	9.8	10	13	**22**	30
Emergency!					
#1	9.6	6	38	**50**	71
Emma Frost					
#1	9.8	25	20	**34**	43
	9.6	5	14	**19**	28
#2	9.8	10	11	**24**	35
#3	9.8	7	23	**27**	35
Eternal Warrior					
#1/Gld	9.6	12	12	**38**	71
#2	9.8	8	16	**25**	35
Eternals					
#1	9.8	9	19	**105**	214
	9.6	25	17	**43**	140
	9.4	20	14	**28**	86
	9.2	6	10	**14**	17
	9.0	5	10	**19**	40
#1/30¢	9.4	5	52	**94**	152
Excalibur					
#1	9.8	17	11	**27**	43
	9.4	6	5	**11**	16
Excalibur Special Edition					
#0	9.8	6	2	**19**	35
Exciting Comics					
#43	9.2	7	307	**533**	725
#52	7.0	5	133	**161**	200
#64	7.0	5	103	**136**	200
Exiles					
#1	9.6	7	10	**19**	37
	9.4	6	6	**14**	25
Fables					
#1	9.8	15	25	**49**	117
	9.6	8	20	**31**	55
#6/RRP	9.4	5	27	**62**	125
Fantastic Four					
#1	4.5	13	1,800	**2,603**	4,371
	4.0	12	990	**2,045**	2,830
	3.5	5	1,275	**1,480**	1,825
	3.0	6	900	**1,034**	1,280
	2.5	10	710	**1,051**	1,700
	2.0	8	701	**954**	1,475
	1.8	10	660	**792**	960
#2	6.5	6	960	**1,191**	1,550
	5.0	6	532	**818**	1,000
	4.5	7	259	**601**	785
	4.0	5	307	**557**	725
	3.5	5	317	**427**	535
#3	5.0	7	404	**461**	610

ISSUE	CGC GRADE	# of AUCTIONS	LOW CLOSE	AVG CLOSE	HIGH CLOSE
	4.0	6	373	**413**	452
	2.5	8	180	**216**	296
#4	8.0	5	1,525	**1,738**	1,981
	7.0	5	500	**985**	1,277
	6.0	8	500	**653**	921
	5.5	5	481	**547**	660
	5.0	5	426	**495**	577
	4.5	6	387	**488**	675
	4.0	6	202	**354**	475
	3.5	7	296	**342**	425
#5	6.0	11	520	**856**	1,220
	5.0	7	325	**586**	700
	4.5	5	466	**542**	600
	4.0	11	337	**458**	641
	3.0	13	203	**302**	437
#6	9.0	6	1,324	**1,830**	2,425
	8.5	11	911	**1,327**	1,865
	6.5	10	183	**448**	660
	6.0	5	282	**412**	515
	5.0	9	259	**304**	360
	4.0	11	150	**199**	240
	3.5	6	138	**158**	178
	3.0	5	84	**135**	175
#7	7.5	9	406	**500**	597
	4.0	9	76	**127**	153
#8	4.5	6	91	**127**	160
	2.5	7	56	**78**	136
#9	7.5	5	425	**559**	650
	4.5	5	140	**180**	230
	4.0	6	82	**130**	261
#10	6.0	6	246	**295**	411
	5.0	6	136	**198**	249
	4.0	5	100	**149**	269
#12	7.5	6	521	**789**	1,200
	7.0	5	593	**721**	821
	6.5	7	515	**598**	760
	6.0	5	381	**479**	605
	4.5	6	174	**324**	441
#13	6.0	6	91	**210**	281
#14	9.0	7	398	**501**	610
	6.5	5	143	**175**	200
#15	7.0	6	153	**200**	300
#16	9.2	5	720	**1,227**	1,700
#17	7.5	5	117	**184**	238
#19	9.0	5	400	**462**	585
	8.5	9	228	**287**	340
#20	9.0	10	250	**423**	699
	6.5	7	73	**92**	129
	6.0	6	71	**92**	122
#21	9.0	12	280	**368**	567
#22	9.0	5	275	**370**	490
#24	9.2	5	287	**465**	666
	8.5	5	126	**178**	225
	4.5	6	21	**35**	53
#25	9.2	5	905	**1,287**	1,926
	8.0	6	300	**379**	430
	7.0	5	200	**225**	261
	3.0	6	13	**44**	66
#26	8.5	5	368	**390**	406
	8.0	11	214	**301**	415

ISSUE	CGC GRADE	# of AUCTIONS	LOW CLOSE	AVG CLOSE	HIGH CLOSE
	7.0	7	164	**202**	260
	6.5	7	73	**127**	178
#27	7.0	6	80	**100**	130
	6.0	7	60	**68**	90
#28	9.2	7	588	**819**	1,051
	9.0	9	436	**488**	585
	8.0	5	158	**231**	285
#29	9.2	5	228	**467**	890
#32	9.0	6	21	**181**	280
#33	9.2	6	258	**334**	414
	9.0	9	110	**192**	260
	8.5	8	97	**121**	165
#34	9.0	6	76	**144**	227
	6.0	5	32	**40**	48
#35	9.2	6	156	**248**	306
	9.0	5	121	**152**	164
	8.5	11	68	**101**	130
#36	9.2	9	263	**353**	410
	7.5	7	41	**53**	70
#37	9.2	5	188	**298**	390
#38	9.2	10	200	**275**	350
	8.0	11	46	**71**	100
#39	9.0	12	145	**200**	264
	8.5	6	94	**136**	183
	8.0	5	80	**103**	125
	7.5	6	51	**73**	124
	7.0	5	46	**53**	59
#40	8.0	9	56	**83**	94
#41	9.4	8	251	**408**	700
	9.2	12	54	**192**	325
	8.5	8	51	**79**	100
#42	9.2	10	110	**187**	300
	9.0	5	64	**116**	175
#43	9.2	5	218	**251**	300
#44	9.6	6	656	**727**	778
	9.4	24	210	**338**	535
	9.2	25	86	**126**	190
	9.0	16	76	**95**	125
	8.5	19	44	**66**	108
	8.0	8	44	**54**	67
	7.0	8	15	**30**	45
#45	9.0	7	125	**176**	210
	7.5	7	53	**65**	76
#46	9.4	14	104	**502**	1,225
	9.2	6	183	**206**	250
	9.0	11	39	**126**	160
	8.5	6	74	**94**	139
	7.0	5	23	**43**	70
#47	9.4	5	255	**386**	435
	9.0	5	77	**107**	139
	8.0	7	45	**59**	73
#48	9.6	16	1,525	**2,349**	3,250
	9.4	25	1,200	**1,650**	2,200
	9.2	25	835	**1,039**	1,360
	9.0	16	394	**761**	1,025
	8.5	25	405	**580**	870
	8.0	25	200	**470**	721
	7.5	25	203	**332**	595
	7.0	25	154	**296**	426
	6.5	25	148	**232**	305
	6.0	18	158	**210**	291
	5.5	25	99	**176**	250
	5.0	20	103	**148**	207
	4.5	25	91	**143**	400
	4.0	16	88	**115**	170
	3.5	16	36	**99**	182
	3.0	15	51	**82**	139
	2.0	8	26	**53**	78
#49	9.0	8	330	**419**	595
	8.5	8	194	**271**	363
	8.0	13	57	**159**	223
	7.5	10	92	**148**	200
	7.0	6	71	**93**	124
	4.5	5	36	**48**	60
	4.0	5	29	**53**	96
#50	9.2	10	647	**778**	925
	9.0	9	316	**409**	550
	8.0	13	129	**198**	266
	7.5	11	99	**143**	193
#51	9.2	8	152	**275**	370
#52	9.2	6	385	**456**	538
	9.0	8	234	**310**	455
	8.5	9	129	**172**	261
	8.0	9	101	**135**	190
	7.5	10	50	**83**	110
#53	9.4	7	390	**535**	625
	9.2	7	158	**228**	250
	8.5	15	68	**87**	130
	8.0	10	22	**50**	70
#54	9.4	9	226	**349**	504
	9.2	5	98	**152**	191
#55	9.4	8	643	**758**	900
	9.2	17	175	**299**	444
	9.0	12	118	**163**	201
	8.5	11	71	**102**	185
	8.0	10	49	**63**	95
	7.5	9	43	**74**	132
	7.0	6	39	**55**	67
	6.5	9	30	**34**	39
#56	6.5	8	18	**25**	35
#57	9.0	5	91	**121**	149
#58	9.6	6	511	**615**	750
	9.4	6	103	**325**	605
	9.2	12	74	**128**	204
	9.0	15	54	**76**	113
	8.5	6	25	**64**	115

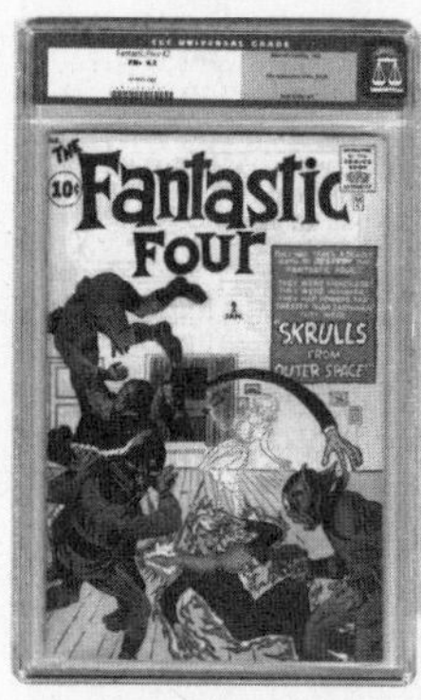

ISSUE	CGC GRADE	# of AUCTIONS	LOW CLOSE	AVG CLOSE	HIGH CLOSE
Fantastic Four (cont'd)					
	8.0	5	36	**44**	60
#59	9.6	10	360	**439**	512
	9.4	22	120	**222**	375
	9.2	22	65	**97**	130
	9.0	24	41	**67**	120
	8.0	9	40	**55**	100
	7.0	5	13	**31**	50
#60	9.4	12	140	**235**	286
	9.2	15	67	**109**	170
	9.0	10	50	**69**	91
	8.5	5	46	**66**	90
	7.5	6	31	**36**	45
#61	9.6	7	393	**528**	655
	9.4	10	170	**256**	456
	9.2	20	71	**100**	130
	9.0	6	46	**68**	96
#62	9.4	5	192	**236**	272
	9.2	19	51	**81**	120
	8.0	6	24	**38**	50
#63	9.4	7	195	**259**	350
	9.0	5	46	**62**	78
#64	9.4	9	149	**203**	300
	9.2	7	46	**79**	110
#65	9.2	7	67	**100**	169
	9.0	5	47	**62**	100
#66	9.4	6	340	**424**	511
	9.2	13	126	**185**	268
	9.0	5	77	**115**	151
	8.0	5	35	**61**	76
#67	9.4	5	244	**411**	505
	9.2	5	153	**192**	250
	9.0	13	51	**99**	150
	8.5	9	43	**68**	96
	8.0	7	36	**49**	61
	7.5	7	34	**44**	56
#68	9.4	11	125	**216**	305
	9.2	11	46	**77**	110
	8.0	5	31	**39**	46
#69	9.4	7	178	**222**	275
	9.2	9	49	**101**	130
	9.0	9	36	**60**	90
	8.0	11	24	**39**	59
#70	9.2	9	54	**94**	179
	9.0	6	41	**53**	78
#71	9.6	8	280	**432**	595
	9.4	7	115	**168**	228
	9.0	6	37	**63**	100
#72	9.4	6	255	**350**	405
	9.2	11	128	**182**	240
	9.0	6	65	**88**	110
	8.5	5	31	**62**	99
	7.5	9	32	**42**	60
	6.0	6	11	**22**	32
#73	9.6	5	338	**448**	600
	9.4	5	229	**298**	355
	9.2	6	71	**124**	218
	9.0	7	52	**80**	104
	7.5	5	26	**36**	51
#74	9.4	5	200	**303**	385

ISSUE	CGC GRADE	# of AUCTIONS	LOW CLOSE	AVG CLOSE	HIGH CLOSE
	9.2	13	77	**122**	204
#75	9.4	7	150	**189**	225
	9.2	5	76	**124**	151
	9.0	9	42	**66**	134
	8.5	5	39	**59**	103
#76	9.4	19	80	**160**	280
	9.2	11	56	**89**	120
	9.0	5	33	**57**	94
#77	9.4	9	144	**185**	235
	9.0	6	39	**68**	108
	8.5	8	28	**47**	77
#78	9.4	20	76	**119**	183
	9.2	21	34	**61**	99
	9.0	10	26	**34**	50
	8.0	5	21	**26**	35
#79	9.2	12	37	**72**	101
	9.0	6	41	**54**	79
	8.0	5	17	**25**	32
#80	9.0	7	36	**43**	50
#81	9.4	8	131	**161**	191
	9.2	5	36	**80**	133
	8.5	7	30	**39**	52
	8.0	5	23	**35**	45
#82	9.4	12	87	**135**	185
	9.2	18	41	**60**	105
	9.0	6	36	**47**	60
#83	9.4	13	76	**138**	255
	9.2	11	22	**52**	82
	7.5	5	20	**38**	79
#84	9.4	14	95	**153**	198
	9.2	11	49	**91**	153
#85	9.4	8	100	**143**	230
	9.2	9	41	**65**	101
#86	9.4	7	150	**186**	236
	9.2	5	50	**83**	150
	9.0	7	40	**55**	81
	8.0	5	21	**34**	45
	7.5	5	24	**30**	40
#87	9.4	8	122	**143**	178
#88	9.2	5	31	**57**	81
#89	9.4	6	108	**138**	188
	9.2	12	41	**59**	96
	9.0	6	26	**49**	113
#90	9.2	6	36	**54**	67
#91	9.4	8	96	**119**	148
	9.2	7	27	**54**	86
#92	9.4	5	74	**104**	135
	9.2	7	45	**61**	81
#93	9.2	12	41	**55**	82
#94	9.2	6	32	**51**	76
#95	9.4	8	97	**120**	139
	9.2	5	28	**48**	60
#96	9.2	5	27	**55**	111
#97	9.6	7	80	**201**	290
	9.4	5	79	**107**	154
	9.2	10	27	**43**	70
#98	9.6	6	183	**209**	232
	9.4	10	10	**88**	120
	9.2	9	29	**45**	65
#99	9.6	5	158	**247**	336

ISSUE	CGC GRADE	# of AUCTIONS	LOW CLOSE	AVG CLOSE	HIGH CLOSE
#100	9.6	6	405	**494**	609
	9.4	11	178	**248**	410
	9.2	23	80	**127**	175
	9.0	15	51	**83**	115
	8.5	9	33	**68**	114
	8.0	12	35	**61**	100
#102	9.4	7	63	**112**	178
	9.2	7	39	**59**	99
#104	9.4	7	100	**129**	150
#105	9.2	6	26	**47**	69
#106	9.4	7	46	**81**	128
#107	9.4	5	84	**120**	158
#108	9.6	11	99	**151**	196
	9.4	16	54	**82**	110
	9.0	5	22	**33**	62
	8.5	6	15	**20**	30
#110	9.4	10	35	**64**	108
#111	9.4	10	35	**75**	109
#112	9.4	5	566	**629**	760
	9.2	8	214	**273**	340
	9.0	19	108	**152**	225
	8.5	21	59	**94**	125
	8.0	11	42	**66**	93
	7.0	12	32	**47**	61
#113	9.4	6	69	**92**	128
#114	9.4	6	53	**105**	228
#115	9.4	5	51	**91**	152
#116	9.2	5	51	**100**	203
	9.0	6	31	**49**	61
	8.5	6	30	**36**	53
#118	9.4	5	54	**63**	82
#121	9.6	7	154	**187**	327
#122	9.4	5	110	**169**	311
	9.0	5	33	**40**	61
#123	9.4	8	71	**99**	180
	9.2	6	30	**50**	80
#126	9.4	7	54	**105**	149
#129	9.4	5	46	**78**	128
#130	9.4	6	26	**54**	91
#131	9.4	11	28	**52**	88
#139	9.4	6	19	**41**	56
	9.2	6	23	**32**	45
#140	9.6	7	42	**74**	191
	9.2	5	2	**20**	27
#141	9.4	5	40	**44**	50
#143	9.2	5	22	**33**	41
#144	9.6	6	52	**85**	184
#145	9.4	5	31	**49**	80
#146	9.4	5	26	**37**	46
#149	9.4	8	25	**36**	50
#150	9.6	7	51	**93**	126
	9.4	8	27	**45**	67
#153	9.4	8	26	**41**	60
#154	9.6	5	52	**70**	106
	9.4	6	20	**31**	37
#155	9.4	8	36	**75**	110
#156	9.6	9	12	**71**	92
	9.4	13	25	**42**	65
	9.2	6	15	**22**	28
#157	9.6	9	31	**77**	100
	9.4	15	28	**42**	60
#158	9.6	9	37	**48**	58
	9.4	7	24	**41**	60
#159	9.4	7	23	**33**	50
	9.2	5	19	**25**	41
#160	9.4	5	25	**27**	31
#165	9.6	6	28	**42**	51
	9.4	6	18	**21**	30
#166	9.6	5	44	**86**	118
#167	9.4	10	41	**67**	103
#168	9.6	5	35	**87**	120
#174	9.4	6	19	**31**	43
#175	9.6	6	28	**48**	79
	9.4	11	14	**31**	56
#183	9.6	5	19	**39**	61
	9.4	5	16	**21**	30
#184	9.6	5	14	**28**	39
#188	9.4	7	17	**29**	49
#190	9.4	5	18	**25**	44
#191	9.4	6	13	**19**	26
#199	9.6	8	16	**31**	50
#200	9.6	9	35	**66**	92
	9.4	9	22	**31**	41
	9.2	5	16	**30**	54
#207	9.6	5	11	**20**	35
#222	9.8	5	25	**43**	75
#229	9.6	8	13	**24**	36
#232	9.8	11	25	**33**	57
	9.6	12	16	**25**	41
#235	9.8	6	20	**33**	78
#236	9.6	13	11	**20**	31
	9.4	5	10	**16**	25
#238	9.8	7	20	**29**	52
#241	9.8	8	20	**29**	47
	9.6	5	11	**19**	32
#243	9.8	5	35	**54**	97
#244	9.8	5	24	**28**	35
#245	9.6	6	12	**21**	35
#246	9.8	11	21	**31**	69
#247	9.8	7	20	**26**	39
#249	9.8	7	15	**31**	49
#250	9.8	13	18	**38**	112
#251	9.8	6	23	**35**	76
#252	9.8	5	24	**27**	29
#253	9.8	7	24	**29**	47
#254	9.8	5	25	**30**	41

Fantastic Four (cont'd)

ISSUE	CGC GRADE	# of AUCTIONS	LOW CLOSE	AVG CLOSE	HIGH CLOSE
#255	9.8	10	20	**25**	29
#256	9.8	13	18	**40**	133
#258	9.8	6	25	**35**	68
#259	9.8	7	20	**29**	38
#260	9.8	8	24	**29**	39
#261	9.8	7	23	**33**	70
#263	9.8	8	25	**30**	38
#264	9.8	8	25	**30**	37
#265	9.8	12	20	**25**	34
#266	9.8	9	19	**24**	30
#268	9.8	9	23	**29**	37
#269	9.8	14	16	**24**	33
#270	9.8	16	18	**26**	40
#271	9.8	13	20	**26**	40
#272	9.8	9	16	**29**	70
#273	9.8	9	18	**24**	29
#274	9.8	8	21	**25**	33
#275	9.8	5	20	**23**	27
#276	9.8	9	25	**29**	42
#277	9.8	9	13	**26**	46
#278	9.8	9	25	**27**	35
#280	9.8	8	1	**18**	25
#282	9.8	6	25	**30**	51
#283	9.8	9	17	**25**	41
#284	9.8	9	15	**30**	61
#287	9.8	7	18	**26**	40
#292	9.8	6	25	**35**	63
#299	9.8	11	18	**23**	26
#300	9.8	15	1	**25**	45
#314	9.8	6	11	**21**	25
#347	9.6	20	1	**12**	20
#348	9.6	5	13	**20**	28
#349	9.8	5	24	**26**	30
#371	9.8	5	20	**36**	46
	9.6	5	10	**16**	35
#500	9.9	8	51	**86**	105
	9.8	25	16	**34**	61
	9.6	13	10	**20**	37

Fantastic Four (Vol. 2)

ISSUE	CGC GRADE	# of AUCTIONS	LOW CLOSE	AVG CLOSE	HIGH CLOSE
#1	9.2	9	118	**242**	434
	9.0	12	82	**146**	275
#1/2nd	8.5	9	78	**150**	255
	8.0	17	66	**123**	203
	7.5	10	52	**115**	250
	6.5	5	53	**123**	200
	9.6	6	13	**22**	35
	9.6	6	8	**16**	21
#1/Sun	9.4	11	10	**17**	25

Fantastic Four Annual

ISSUE	CGC GRADE	# of AUCTIONS	LOW CLOSE	AVG CLOSE	HIGH CLOSE
#1	9.0	11	482	**710**	1,000
	8.5	10	345	**555**	698
	8.0	7	350	**415**	505
	7.0	7	160	**292**	449
	3.5	7	51	**83**	100
#2	8.0	5	154	**211**	270
#3	9.0	6	134	**193**	255
	8.0	7	31	**79**	158
#4	8.5	7	58	**86**	118
#5	9.4	11	136	**250**	433
	9.2	10	96	**136**	206
	9.0	8	51	**82**	119
	8.5	7	26	**61**	99
	8.0	11	27	**48**	65
	7.5	6	10	**16**	25
#6	9.0	8	50	**62**	84
	8.5	5	28	**41**	75
#8	9.4	6	50	**74**	108
#18	9.8	5	20	**24**	30

Fantastic Four Roast

ISSUE	CGC GRADE	# of AUCTIONS	LOW CLOSE	AVG CLOSE	HIGH CLOSE
#1	9.8	7	21	**28**	38

Fantastic Four Special Edition

ISSUE	CGC GRADE	# of AUCTIONS	LOW CLOSE	AVG CLOSE	HIGH CLOSE
#1	9.8	5	20	**30**	40

Fantasy Masterpieces

ISSUE	CGC GRADE	# of AUCTIONS	LOW CLOSE	AVG CLOSE	HIGH CLOSE
#11	9.4	5	29	**50**	80

Fantasy Quarterly

ISSUE	CGC GRADE	# of AUCTIONS	LOW CLOSE	AVG CLOSE	HIGH CLOSE
#1	9.8	8	148	**229**	357
	9.6	5	95	**110**	129
	9.4	13	57	**119**	400

Fathom

ISSUE	CGC GRADE	# of AUCTIONS	LOW CLOSE	AVG CLOSE	HIGH CLOSE
#0	9.4	9	10	**20**	35
#1	9.8	6	28	**38**	50
	9.6	8	16	**25**	34
#1/Var	9.6	5	20	**25**	36
#3	9.8	6	15	**22**	28
#9	9.8	20	10	**32**	103
	9.6	11	10	**17**	31
#9/Var	9.6	8	13	**20**	34
#12	9.8	15	18	**28**	75
	9.6	7	11	**16**	20
#12/Var	9.8	11	17	**23**	31

Fathom Swimsuit Special

ISSUE	CGC GRADE	# of AUCTIONS	LOW CLOSE	AVG CLOSE	HIGH CLOSE
#1	9.8	6	23	**74**	306

Fear

ISSUE	CGC GRADE	# of AUCTIONS	LOW CLOSE	AVG CLOSE	HIGH CLOSE
#10	9.4	5	70	**115**	213
	9.2	6	34	**48**	72
#19	9.4	6	55	**111**	155
#20	9.6	5	90	**132**	178
	9.4	22	35	**87**	203
	9.2	7	24	**37**	46

Feature Comics

ISSUE	CGC GRADE	# of AUCTIONS	LOW CLOSE	AVG CLOSE	HIGH CLOSE
#80	9.2	5	143	**167**	200

Fight Comics

ISSUE	CGC GRADE	# of AUCTIONS	LOW CLOSE	AVG CLOSE	HIGH CLOSE
#1	6.0	7	91	**478**	710

Firestorm

ISSUE	CGC GRADE	# of AUCTIONS	LOW CLOSE	AVG CLOSE	HIGH CLOSE
#1	9.6	9	31	**49**	71
	9.4	7	24	**29**	36

Firestorm (Vol. 2)

ISSUE	CGC GRADE	# of AUCTIONS	LOW CLOSE	AVG CLOSE	HIGH CLOSE
#61	9.6	9	26	**49**	100
#61/Var	9.4	6	29	**45**	60

1st Issue Special

ISSUE	CGC GRADE	# of AUCTIONS	LOW CLOSE	AVG CLOSE	HIGH CLOSE
#1	9.6	18	13	**28**	43

ISSUE	CGC GRADE	# of AUCTIONS	LOW CLOSE	AVG CLOSE	HIGH CLOSE
#8	9.6	10	51	**102**	152
	9.4	25	22	**41**	66
	9.2	6	20	**23**	26

Flaming Carrot Comics

ISSUE	CGC GRADE	# of AUCTIONS	LOW CLOSE	AVG CLOSE	HIGH CLOSE
#4	9.6	7	25	**26**	36

Flash

ISSUE	CGC GRADE	# of AUCTIONS	LOW CLOSE	AVG CLOSE	HIGH CLOSE
#105	4.5	10	335	**570**	785
	4.0	5	362	**477**	556
	3.5	14	213	**352**	489
	2.0	6	183	**239**	282
#106	4.0	7	30	**187**	290
#109	6.5	5	108	**127**	148
#123	7.5	6	565	**638**	760
	7.0	17	178	**377**	630
	5.5	14	100	**204**	308
	5.0	6	113	**155**	183
	3.0	7	76	**108**	129
#129	6.5	6	41	**60**	74
#137	7.5	6	93	**129**	153
	6.5	9	38	**74**	110
	5.0	5	41	**49**	60
#138	8.5	7	73	**92**	115
#140	8.5	6	76	**100**	128
#145	9.2	6	78	**150**	202
	8.5	7	50	**62**	80
#148	9.2	5	118	**134**	158
#151	9.4	6	188	**295**	420
	9.0	5	105	**122**	145
#152	9.4	5	191	**232**	325
#155	8.0	5	33	**58**	77
#160	9.0	6	81	**89**	104
#166	9.2	5	81	**101**	134
	8.5	5	33	**63**	105
#167	9.4	5	118	**174**	240
#169	8.5	5	53	**66**	75
#175	9.4	5	160	**689**	1,275
	9.2	5	110	**277**	406
	9.0	11	80	**151**	239
	8.0	7	81	**100**	129
#177	9.2	5	26	**46**	72
#180	9.2	6	21	**33**	51
#181	9.4	6	32	**101**	148
#196	9.2	5	40	**99**	150
#197	9.8	5	33	**41**	65
#200	9.8	7	19	**93**	500
#219	9.4	5	56	**73**	78
#235	9.2	6	10	**17**	24
#350	9.6	5	6	**18**	30

Flash (Vol. 2)

ISSUE	CGC GRADE	# of AUCTIONS	LOW CLOSE	AVG CLOSE	HIGH CLOSE
#1	9.6	6	7	**24**	40
	9.4	7	17	**20**	25
#207	9.8	21	12	**33**	52
	9.6	6	10	**16**	23
#208	9.8	15	13	**21**	27
#209	9.8	15	20	**23**	29
#210	9.8	5	20	**22**	25

Flash Annual

ISSUE	CGC GRADE	# of AUCTIONS	LOW CLOSE	AVG CLOSE	HIGH CLOSE
#1	9.0	5	338	**391**	450

ISSUE	CGC GRADE	# of AUCTIONS	LOW CLOSE	AVG CLOSE	HIGH CLOSE
	8.5	6	208	**220**	249
	8.0	8	83	**172**	310

Flash Comics

ISSUE	CGC GRADE	# of AUCTIONS	LOW CLOSE	AVG CLOSE	HIGH CLOSE
#22	5.5	7	169	**223**	266

Flash Gordon

ISSUE	CGC GRADE	# of AUCTIONS	LOW CLOSE	AVG CLOSE	HIGH CLOSE
#1	9.4	10	49	**89**	175
#8	9.2	14	0	**22**	35

Forever People

ISSUE	CGC GRADE	# of AUCTIONS	LOW CLOSE	AVG CLOSE	HIGH CLOSE
#1	9.6	5	158	**269**	315
	9.4	13	81	**131**	175
	9.2	6	36	**58**	70
	9.0	13	10	**46**	75
	8.0	6	20	**26**	31

Formerly Known as the Justice League

ISSUE	CGC GRADE	# of AUCTIONS	LOW CLOSE	AVG CLOSE	HIGH CLOSE
#1	9.8	8	10	**16**	23

Four Color

ISSUE	CGC GRADE	# of AUCTIONS	LOW CLOSE	AVG CLOSE	HIGH CLOSE
#386	5.5	5	204	**258**	307
	3.5	5	91	**129**	170
#1237	7.0	6	18	**42**	100

Frankenstein (Monster of)

ISSUE	CGC GRADE	# of AUCTIONS	LOW CLOSE	AVG CLOSE	HIGH CLOSE
#1	9.4	25	10	**137**	256
	9.2	17	53	**75**	105
	9.0	11	32	**51**	100
	8.5	12	14	**32**	56

Frankenstein Mobster

ISSUE	CGC GRADE	# of AUCTIONS	LOW CLOSE	AVG CLOSE	HIGH CLOSE
#1	9.8	8	6	**9**	13

Freaks of the Heartland

ISSUE	CGC GRADE	# of AUCTIONS	LOW CLOSE	AVG CLOSE	HIGH CLOSE
#1	9.8	7	14	**19**	25

Freedom Fighters

ISSUE	CGC GRADE	# of AUCTIONS	LOW CLOSE	AVG CLOSE	HIGH CLOSE
#1	9.6	5	53	**96**	180
	9.4	5	25	**40**	59

From Hell

ISSUE	CGC GRADE	# of AUCTIONS	LOW CLOSE	AVG CLOSE	HIGH CLOSE
#11	9.8	5	18	**23**	30

Further Adventures of Indiana Jones

ISSUE	CGC GRADE	# of AUCTIONS	LOW CLOSE	AVG CLOSE	HIGH CLOSE
#1	9.8	5	20	**24**	28

Fury

ISSUE	CGC GRADE	# of AUCTIONS	LOW CLOSE	AVG CLOSE	HIGH CLOSE
#1	9.6	9	6	**10**	13

Gambit

ISSUE	CGC GRADE	# of AUCTIONS	LOW CLOSE	AVG CLOSE	HIGH CLOSE
#1	9.8	9	19	**23**	30

ISSUE	CGC GRADE	# of AUCTIONS	LOW CLOSE	AVG CLOSE	HIGH CLOSE
Generation X					
#1	9.8	10	8	**18**	26
	9.6	6	7	**10**	13
Gen13 Limited Series					
#1	9.6	7	7	**17**	25
Gen13					
#1	9.8	8	25	**55**	140
	9.6	8	10	**19**	26
Ghost Rider					
#1	9.6	5	25	**1,139**	2,126
	9.4	16	275	**527**	916
	9.2	23	128	**237**	400
	9.0	25	53	**142**	331
	8.5	14	79	**143**	515
	8.0	12	61	**103**	361
	7.0	6	46	**63**	91
	6.5	8	22	**38**	70
#2	9.4	6	61	**125**	175
	9.2	7	21	**38**	53
	8.0	5	25	**31**	37
#3	9.6	5	70	**130**	224
	9.4	6	56	**80**	125
#5	9.4	8	65	**89**	125
#8	9.4	5	41	**67**	129
#10	9.4	6	40	**59**	81
#16	9.6	5	45	**70**	114
#22	9.6	5	24	**41**	53
#47	9.6	7	15	**30**	54
#77	9.8	5	20	**38**	58
	9.6	5	10	**16**	20
#81	9.6	6	26	**62**	103
Ghost Rider (Vol. 2)					
#1	9.8	6	39	**50**	70
	9.6	16	16	**26**	46
	9.4	7	13	**20**	26
#15	9.8	23	12	**23**	40
Ghosts					
#1	8.5	7	26	**69**	100
#48	9.4	7	1	**10**	26
G.I. Combat					
#267	9.8	6	19	**23**	30
G.I. Joe					
#1	9.8	25	16	**189**	420
	9.6	25	25	**56**	103
	9.4	25	17	**33**	100
	9.2	23	10	**23**	36
	9.0	5	11	**20**	28
#2	9.8	5	13	**107**	188
	9.6	5	11	**56**	89
	9.4	5	7	**22**	51
#3	9.6	5	10	**34**	60
	9.4	6	6	**18**	28
#5	9.6	5	25	**43**	59
#21	9.6	8	156	**230**	302
	9.4	12	62	**100**	158
	9.2	11	23	**48**	100

ISSUE	CGC GRADE	# of AUCTIONS	LOW CLOSE	AVG CLOSE	HIGH CLOSE
	9.0	7	28	**48**	85
#27	9.4	6	10	**16**	30
#53	9.8	5	25	**37**	68
	9.6	5	10	**19**	35
#55	9.8	5	10	**26**	36
#95	9.4	7	7	**19**	31
#155	9.6	10	79	**121**	165
	9.4	12	36	**62**	79
G.I. Joe (Image)					
#1	9.8	25	8	**24**	63
	9.6	23	5	**16**	31
	9.4	9	9	**15**	25
	9.2	5	2	**9**	15
#2	9.8	22	10	**18**	31
	9.6	9	3	**10**	17
#3	9.8	9	9	**19**	30
#4	9.8	10	10	**18**	25
	9.6	6	10	**13**	22
G.I. Joe: Cobra Reborn					
#1	9.8	8	15	**20**	35
G.I. Joe: Front Line					
#1	9.8	5	10	**19**	40
G.I. Joe Special					
#1	9.8	6	103	**251**	456
	9.6	7	103	**155**	250
	9.4	8	30	**90**	128
G.I. Joe vs. Transformers					
#1	9.8	8	4	**28**	51
Giant-Size Avengers					
#1	9.6	7	128	**176**	208
Giant-Size Captain America					
#1	9.4	5	41	**69**	104
Giant-Size Chillers					
#1	9.6	6	128	**171**	200
	9.4	12	28	**86**	158
	9.2	10	14	**30**	50
Giant-Size Conan					
#1	9.4	6	31	**53**	90
	9.2	6	15	**31**	50
#4	9.6	10	21	**37**	53
	9.4	5	5	**15**	28
Giant-Size Creatures					
#1	9.4	6	61	**88**	180
	9.2	7	15	**40**	60
Giant-Size Defenders					
#1	9.4	12	36	**76**	111
	9.2	11	26	**40**	76
	9.0	6	21	**31**	52
	8.5	5	12	**25**	41
#3	9.4	5	40	**48**	52
Giant-Size Doc Savage					
#1	9.4	6	28	**37**	46
	9.2	5	13	**17**	21

ISSUE	CGC GRADE	# of AUCTIONS	LOW CLOSE	AVG CLOSE	HIGH CLOSE
Giant-Size Doctor Strange					
#1	9.6	6	32	**66**	102
	9.4	6	36	**47**	62
Giant-Size Dracula					
#5	9.4	6	51	**62**	75
Giant-Size Fantastic Four					
#2	9.4	7	36	**45**	63
#5	9.4	6	25	**35**	50
Giant-Size Hulk					
#1	9.4	8	62	**83**	115
	9.2	5	26	**40**	55
Giant-Size Invaders					
#1	9.6	9	83	**128**	202
	9.4	12	36	**58**	81
	9.0	6	11	**25**	50
Giant-Size Kid Colt					
#3	9.4	5	46	**76**	103
Giant-Size Man-Thing					
#1	9.6	5	56	**76**	115
#5	9.6	15	17	**42**	71
Giant-Size Spider-Man					
#1	9.4	7	75	**147**	305
	9.2	7	45	**50**	61
	9.0	10	25	**41**	52
	8.5	5	24	**28**	39
#2	9.4	10	31	**48**	75
#3	9.4	9	22	**48**	61
	9.2	5	21	**33**	62
#4	9.4	22	91	**159**	250
	9.2	24	31	**81**	130
	9.0	8	36	**54**	77
	8.5	8	11	**36**	50
	8.0	6	21	**31**	40
	7.5	12	15	**32**	60
#5	9.4	8	26	**50**	63
#6	9.6	7	67	**111**	175
	9.4	6	21	**58**	95
Giant-Size Super-Heroes					
#1	9.4	24	41	**82**	145
	9.2	8	31	**45**	56
	9.0	9	22	**40**	60
	8.5	5	18	**29**	51
	8.0	5	19	**25**	31
	7.5	5	13	**20**	28
Giant-Size Super-Stars					
#1	9.6	14	94	**134**	229
	9.4	15	46	**72**	91
	9.2	10	17	**47**	129
	9.0	5	26	**38**	56
	8.5	7	15	**20**	31
Giant-Size Super-Villain Team-Up					
#1	9.6	6	50	**72**	108
	9.4	6	50	**64**	88
#2	9.4	6	18	**30**	43

ISSUE	CGC GRADE	# of AUCTIONS	LOW CLOSE	AVG CLOSE	HIGH CLOSE
Giant-Size Thor					
#1	9.2	6	21	**28**	41
Giant-Size X-Men					
#1	9.6	25	1,600	**2,478**	3,302
	9.4	25	910	**1,494**	2,425
	9.2	25	610	**935**	1,375
	9.0	25	355	**601**	965
	8.5	25	285	**522**	950
	8.0	25	257	**408**	722
	7.5	25	153	**328**	500
	7.0	25	163	**268**	450
	6.5	25	169	**222**	295
	6.0	25	113	**197**	355
	5.5	21	104	**165**	250
	5.0	25	122	**162**	220
	4.5	22	73	**133**	192
	4.0	12	73	**116**	149
	3.5	7	58	**98**	131
	3.0	10	52	**87**	160
	2.5	5	57	**79**	91
#2	9.4	13	51	**118**	178
	9.2	9	47	**71**	93
	8.0	5	21	**33**	70
Godzilla					
#1	9.8	25	50	**84**	193
	9.6	25	21	**39**	75
	9.4	25	13	**26**	71
	9.2	12	6	**16**	23
	9.0	5	10	**13**	15
Great Comics					
#1	9.4	15	203	**415**	910
	9.2	7	205	**297**	480
Green Arrow					
#1	9.8	25	15	**31**	89
	9.6	25	3	**18**	45
	9.4	15	8	**14**	30
	9.2	5	10	**12**	19
#2	9.8	9	10	**18**	38
	9.6	11	5	**13**	27
	9.4	17	1	**7**	20
#100	9.8	9	11	**28**	45
#137	9.6	5	15	**17**	25
	9.4	7	4	**14**	25

Green Goblin

ISSUE	CGC GRADE	# of AUCTIONS	LOW CLOSE	AVG CLOSE	HIGH CLOSE
#1	9.8	8	13	**32**	109

Green Hornet Comics

ISSUE	CGC GRADE	# of AUCTIONS	LOW CLOSE	AVG CLOSE	HIGH CLOSE
#30	8.0	5	153	**198**	300
#40	9.0	6	88	**216**	307
#43	9.0	5	152	**194**	260

Green Lama

ISSUE	CGC GRADE	# of AUCTIONS	LOW CLOSE	AVG CLOSE	HIGH CLOSE
#7	9.0	5	134	**153**	176
	8.5	5	89	**119**	153

Green Lantern

ISSUE	CGC GRADE	# of AUCTIONS	LOW CLOSE	AVG CLOSE	HIGH CLOSE
#4	9.0	5	3,250	**7,583**	10,975
#20	7.5	5	425	**482**	531
#21	8.0	5	479	**613**	686
#25	8.0	5	510	**577**	695
#26	8.5	5	473	**648**	832

Green Lantern (Vol. 2)

ISSUE	CGC GRADE	# of AUCTIONS	LOW CLOSE	AVG CLOSE	HIGH CLOSE
#1	6.0	10	390	**609**	725
	4.5	7	306	**445**	675
	4.0	5	203	**311**	410
	2.5	5	173	**211**	275
#3	7.0	5	156	**177**	240
#12	7.5	5	40	**63**	105
#29	5.0	5	13	**22**	30
#35	9.4	5	39	**280**	363
#38	9.2	5	73	**98**	139
#40	9.2	10	422	**743**	950
	9.0	7	355	**427**	511
	8.5	7	103	**291**	516
	8.0	12	202	**258**	357
	7.5	11	158	**199**	261
	7.0	10	61	**133**	195
	6.5	8	86	**111**	150
	6.0	10	65	**99**	203
	4.0	9	34	**47**	57
#41	9.4	5	200	**263**	425
#45	9.0	8	48	**119**	173
	8.0	9	31	**71**	122
#54	8.0	5	25	**34**	42
#59	9.4	6	353	**447**	547
	9.2	13	144	**235**	349
	9.0	5	148	**169**	194
	8.5	14	69	**133**	195
	7.5	8	56	**85**	148
	5.0	5	24	**34**	55
#63	9.2	5	26	**63**	103
#64	9.4	5	91	**155**	263
	9.2	7	21	**44**	68
#66	9.4	8	90	**122**	203
#76	9.4	5	1,600	**2,009**	2,490
	9.2	8	635	**728**	860
	9.0	9	286	**414**	515
	8.0	9	148	**201**	305
	7.5	7	81	**128**	183
	7.0	5	71	**94**	138
	6.5	9	46	**66**	90
#77	9.4	5	228	**246**	260
#80	9.6	5	193	**352**	463
	9.0	7	39	**66**	105
	8.5	5	21	**33**	52
#81	9.2	7	31	**65**	104
#85	9.4	11	114	**189**	255
	9.2	7	77	**110**	150
	8.5	10	36	**59**	89
#86	9.4	8	104	**197**	255
	9.2	7	75	**109**	169
	9.0	10	47	**72**	112
#87	9.4	8	153	**205**	305
	9.2	5	68	**97**	146
	9.0	9	55	**66**	92
	8.5	7	30	**39**	50
#89	9.6	9	192	**274**	357
	9.2	13	26	**69**	109
#116	9.6	5	31	**50**	68
	9.4	7	13	**28**	41
#150	9.6	5	16	**33**	50
	9.4	5	10	**18**	25
#154	9.8	5	20	**30**	43

Green Lantern (Vol. 3)

ISSUE	CGC GRADE	# of AUCTIONS	LOW CLOSE	AVG CLOSE	HIGH CLOSE
#1	9.8	5	37	**62**	90
	9.6	7	10	**23**	36
#46	9.6	5	10	**15**	20
	9.4	6	9	**15**	25
#48	9.8	17	10	**31**	50
	9.6	11	10	**16**	21
#50	9.8	6	25	**36**	46
	9.6	7	10	**32**	78
	9.4	5	10	**19**	30
#81	9.8	5	25	**27**	33

Grendel

ISSUE	CGC GRADE	# of AUCTIONS	LOW CLOSE	AVG CLOSE	HIGH CLOSE
#1	9.2	8	17	**69**	100
	8.5	5	29	**42**	52
#2	9.6	5	81	**153**	250

Groo the Wanderer

ISSUE	CGC GRADE	# of AUCTIONS	LOW CLOSE	AVG CLOSE	HIGH CLOSE
#1	9.9	5	30	**68**	103
	9.8	25	19	**34**	104
	9.6	11	10	**29**	50
	9.4	8	14	**26**	67
#9	9.8	5	10	**23**	35

H.A.R.D. Corps

ISSUE	CGC GRADE	# of AUCTIONS	LOW CLOSE	AVG CLOSE	HIGH CLOSE
#1	9.8	8	16	**21**	25

H.R. Pufnstuf

ISSUE	CGC GRADE	# of AUCTIONS	LOW CLOSE	AVG CLOSE	HIGH CLOSE
#1	9.6	7	10	**201**	331

Harbinger

ISSUE	CGC GRADE	# of AUCTIONS	LOW CLOSE	AVG CLOSE	HIGH CLOSE
#0/Pnk	9.8	14	65	**122**	280
	9.6	15	39	**64**	125
	9.8	14	61	**221**	345
	9.6	14	51	**86**	128
	9.4	15	30	**60**	103
#1	9.6	10	40	**67**	101
	9.4	9	25	**46**	62
	9.2	9	16	**25**	35
#3	9.6	10	13	**27**	48
#4	9.6	5	28	**37**	53
#10	9.8	5	17	**28**	37

ISSUE	CGC GRADE	# of AUCTIONS	LOW CLOSE	AVG CLOSE	HIGH CLOSE
Harley Quinn					
#1	9.8	13	14	**23**	36
	9.6	16	10	**14**	21
Harvey Comic Hits					
#57	9.0	15	35	**95**	174
Harvey Hits					
#3	4.0	5	150	**230**	310
Hawk and the Dove					
#2	9.4	7	90	**121**	160
#6	9.4	5	36	**88**	125
Hawkeye					
#1	9.8	6	13	**15**	17
Hawkeye (Vol. 2)					
#1	9.8	5	6	**13**	16
Hawkman					
#1	9.4	5	10	**1,687**	3,600
	9.0	5	440	**555**	650
	8.5	13	263	**405**	473
	8.0	7	251	**285**	359
	7.5	5	191	**212**	245
	7.0	13	71	**170**	250
	5.5	9	51	**77**	110
	5.0	7	84	**100**	125
	4.0	7	38	**64**	104
#2	8.0	5	54	**86**	100
#3	9.4	5	130	**264**	350
#7	9.0	5	43	**79**	125
Hawkman (Vol. 4)					
#1	9.6	13	7	**13**	27
	9.4	16	6	**11**	21
	9.2	8	4	**9**	13
Hellboy Premiere Edition					
#0	9.8	7	11	**32**	50
Hellboy: Seed of Destruction					
#1	9.8	5	30	**53**	81
H-E-R-O					
#1	9.8	14	13	**25**	41
	9.6	6	10	**12**	20
Hero for Hire					
#1	9.4	10	320	**446**	760
	9.2	13	154	**210**	377
	9.0	13	77	**115**	162
	8.5	11	27	**67**	116
	8.0	5	36	**53**	80
	7.0	5	20	**28**	36
#2	9.4	8	27	**48**	75
Heroes, Inc. Presents Cannon					
#0	9.8	19	26	**58**	90
	9.6	9	19	**31**	46
	9.4	5	9	**14**	22
#1	9.6	5	30	**36**	43
Hi-Adventure Heroes					
#1	9.2	5	3	**42**	94

ISSUE	CGC GRADE	# of AUCTIONS	LOW CLOSE	AVG CLOSE	HIGH CLOSE
Horrific					
#3	6.5	6	405	**558**	825
House of Mystery					
#143	8.5	5	154	**178**	226
	8.0	5	62	**126**	200
#195	9.6	5	123	**279**	380
#200	9.4	5	24	**61**	128
#210	9.4	9	27	**44**	85
#243	9.4	6	1	**21**	36
House of Secrets					
#56	8.0	5	1	**28**	55
#92	9.2	10	525	**780**	1,077
	9.0	17	355	**511**	675
	8.5	25	250	**338**	495
	8.0	19	178	**292**	380
	7.5	24	143	**180**	250
	7.0	15	100	**148**	250
	6.5	18	42	**112**	213
	6.0	9	52	**118**	199
	5.5	6	76	**94**	118
	5.0	10	42	**63**	92
#95	9.4	8	66	**96**	145
#98	9.6	6	87	**146**	300
	9.2	6	21	**40**	60
#100	9.6	5	114	**154**	199
	9.4	6	81	**98**	125
#104	9.4	5	25	**42**	75
#121	9.8	6	54	**96**	143
#123	9.4	5	21	**34**	46
#140	9.4	5	20	**29**	39
Howard the Duck					
#1	9.6	8	61	**96**	150
	9.4	13	21	**42**	67
#3/30¢	9.4	6	14	**44**	61
#12	9.6	10	25	**41**	94
	9.4	9	21	**33**	49
	9.2	8	10	**24**	38
#13	9.6	18	30	**43**	64
	9.4	10	15	**23**	40
	9.2	8	9	**17**	26
Howard the Duck Annual					
#1	9.8	7	9	**32**	50

ISSUE	CGC GRADE	# of AUCTIONS	LOW CLOSE	AVG CLOSE	HIGH CLOSE
Hulk					
#1	9.6	10	16	**27**	40
	9.4	13	6	**17**	30
#1/DF	9.4	6	29	**73**	125
#1/Sun	9.6	25	16	**37**	74
#1/UD	9.8	6	22	**42**	81
#8	9.6	12	26	**46**	75
Hulk Gray					
#1	9.8	25	11	**23**	80
#3	9.8	8	10	**16**	30
#4	9.8	5	7	**10**	15
#5	9.8	12	7	**12**	25
Human Fly					
#1	9.8	19	39	**87**	213
	9.6	25	12	**29**	65
	9.4	8	13	**19**	25
I Love Lucy					
#5	8.0	13	25	**74**	179
Iceman					
#1	9.8	11	25	**29**	50
Identity Crisis					
#1	9.8	25	20	**26**	33
#2	9.8	13	20	**22**	25
Incredible Hulk					
#1	7.0	5	3,477	**4,605**	5,350
	6.5	9	2,900	**3,459**	4,200
	6.0	5	1,925	**2,592**	3,301
	5.5	5	2,177	**2,769**	3,395
	5.0	16	1,999	**2,327**	2,800
	4.5	13	1,300	**1,738**	2,750
	4.0	8	1,325	**1,685**	2,050
	3.5	6	1,100	**1,246**	1,338
	3.0	21	788	**1,171**	1,800
	2.5	11	700	**1,027**	1,450
	1.8	6	552	**689**	789
#2	5.5	8	488	**624**	730
	4.5	6	406	**508**	698
	4.0	6	308	**390**	500
	3.5	6	265	**329**	405
	3.0	19	133	**249**	411
#3	6.5	6	400	**524**	619
	5.5	5	357	**415**	487
	5.0	10	203	**401**	535
	1.8	5	68	**85**	96
#4	8.0	15	735	**923**	1,645
	7.5	13	430	**687**	850
	7.0	7	450	**600**	1,099
	6.5	5	280	**410**	510
	6.0	8	260	**351**	405
	5.5	6	201	**285**	340
	3.0	9	153	**208**	450
	2.0	11	76	**124**	154
#5	7.5	11	650	**748**	900
	7.0	5	504	**552**	710
	5.0	10	205	**271**	400
	4.0	6	159	**221**	260
	3.0	7	150	**180**	250
#6	8.0	5	1,000	**1,142**	1,625
	6.5	9	400	**499**	660
	6.0	8	317	**418**	510
	5.5	9	296	**369**	551
	5.0	5	305	**343**	360
	4.0	10	183	**247**	510
	3.5	7	165	**209**	317
	3.0	6	123	**168**	250
	2.0	5	67	**116**	155
#102	9.6	24	700	**1,013**	1,411
	9.4	25	283	**536**	949
	9.2	25	227	**310**	477
	9.0	25	158	**254**	355
	8.5	25	66	**168**	257
	8.0	25	68	**151**	250
	7.5	23	62	**115**	170
	7.0	17	45	**92**	190
	6.5	20	49	**80**	135
	6.0	21	45	**67**	101
	5.5	7	42	**62**	75
	5.0	7	31	**53**	80
	4.5	8	25	**47**	62
#103	9.4	5	229	**365**	512
	9.2	7	118	**148**	200
	8.5	6	51	**63**	76
	8.0	6	26	**41**	61
	7.5	5	32	**52**	72
#104	9.4	16	158	**286**	499
	9.2	6	120	**171**	261
	9.0	7	51	**98**	125
	8.5	5	51	**67**	80
	8.0	8	36	**61**	85
	7.5	10	39	**54**	69
	6.5	5	16	**29**	40
#105	9.6	5	349	**380**	411
	9.4	6	101	**268**	425
	9.2	11	82	**107**	133
	9.0	6	61	**80**	110
	8.0	5	26	**46**	66
	7.5	7	25	**38**	54
#106	9.6	6	355	**412**	465
	9.4	6	138	**195**	275
	9.2	7	68	**95**	188
	9.0	10	33	**64**	144
	8.5	11	21	**39**	76
	8.0	12	16	**34**	51
#107	9.6	9	103	**306**	475
	9.4	12	106	**171**	300
	9.2	20	51	**93**	150
	9.0	10	41	**63**	100
	8.5	8	21	**38**	60
	8.0	7	26	**40**	52
	7.5	6	20	**27**	38
#108	9.0	5	61	**73**	83
	8.5	5	11	**41**	60
	8.0	7	33	**42**	60
#109	9.4	11	96	**137**	199
	9.2	7	44	**77**	110
	8.0	8	20	**33**	41

ISSUE	CGC GRADE	# of AUCTIONS	LOW CLOSE	AVG CLOSE	HIGH CLOSE
#110	9.0	8	32	**56**	75
	8.5	5	25	**40**	66
	8.0	8	16	**31**	50
	7.5	5	20	**26**	33
#111	9.6	10	150	**247**	365
	9.4	17	39	**119**	200
	9.2	9	41	**69**	125
	8.5	6	25	**33**	56
#112	9.4	16	61	**129**	235
	9.2	10	35	**54**	66
	9.0	14	31	**52**	81
#113	9.2	6	41	**61**	96
	9.0	7	30	**41**	60
#115	9.6	5	230	**262**	310
	9.2	10	41	**59**	69
	9.0	5	41	**47**	53
	8.0	5	15	**22**	26
#116	9.6	6	138	**196**	225
	9.4	5	78	**112**	164
	9.2	12	48	**65**	90
	9.0	13	25	**43**	69
#117	9.4	8	56	**117**	172
	8.5	5	21	**39**	70
#119	9.2	6	37	**59**	80
#122	9.2	10	72	**120**	158
	9.0	9	61	**82**	104
	8.5	9	33	**72**	150
	8.0	12	23	**44**	65
#123	9.4	7	54	**83**	108
	9.0	8	25	**35**	45
#127	9.4	12	37	**64**	99
#129	9.0	5	16	**30**	39
#132	9.4	5	61	**101**	140
#134	9.6	17	46	**93**	175
	9.4	25	18	**58**	98
	9.2	5	25	**43**	52
#135	9.4	6	31	**55**	67
#141	9.4	17	189	**288**	454
	9.2	5	112	**148**	173
	9.0	6	53	**107**	163
#142	9.4	6	51	**82**	155
#146	9.2	5	24	**39**	51
#148	9.6	5	61	**86**	103
#161	9.6	6	103	**163**	206
	9.2	8	34	**48**	75
#162	9.6	6	305	**496**	761
	9.4	13	128	**206**	375
	9.2	10	81	**113**	164
#167	9.4	9	30	**50**	66
#170	9.6	10	45	**97**	153
#171	9.6	5	86	**165**	285
	9.2	5	35	**51**	78
#172	9.6	11	46	**153**	400
	9.4	9	61	**88**	110
	9.0	5	24	**48**	68
#173	9.4	6	29	**47**	62
#174	9.6	11	49	**76**	100
	9.4	5	19	**41**	61
#175	9.6	8	46	**77**	162
	9.4	7	36	**55**	101
#176	9.4	6	40	**47**	60
#177	9.4	8	36	**62**	101
#178	9.6	5	89	**177**	255
#179	9.4	8	36	**48**	60
#180	9.4	22	500	**664**	1,009
	9.2	21	203	**285**	425
	9.0	25	103	**199**	355
	8.5	25	71	**128**	248
	8.0	22	61	**117**	300
	7.5	19	47	**79**	120
	7.0	14	50	**80**	213
	6.5	7	37	**56**	83
	6.0	7	26	**38**	46
	4.0	5	30	**35**	41
#181	9.6	25	3,051	**4,176**	5,200
	9.4	25	1,450	**2,188**	3,262
	9.2	25	510	**1,225**	1,699
	9.0	25	306	**929**	1,199
	8.5	25	360	**695**	913
	8.0	25	305	**556**	800
	7.5	25	233	**456**	800
	7.0	25	193	**400**	599
	6.5	25	228	**360**	550
	6.0	25	197	**308**	425
	5.5	25	179	**260**	375
	5.0	25	125	**258**	586
	4.5	25	128	**220**	400
	4.0	22	118	**202**	277
	3.5	18	104	**184**	376
	3.0	10	104	**197**	330
	1.0	5	65	**130**	153
#182	9.6	5	431	**633**	750
	9.4	18	242	**353**	500
	9.2	20	32	**139**	250
	9.0	25	61	**112**	171
	8.5	14	24	**68**	100
	8.0	17	34	**63**	120
	7.5	18	25	**53**	92
	7.0	8	26	**45**	70
	6.5	9	16	**36**	57
#183	9.4	6	24	**45**	63
#185	9.2	5	14	**20**	23
#186	9.6	6	29	**50**	66
#190	9.6	9	37	**49**	90
#191	9.4	5	35	**46**	61
#194	9.4	12	10	**25**	51

ISSUE	CGC GRADE	# of AUCTIONS	LOW CLOSE	AVG CLOSE	HIGH CLOSE
Incredible Hulk (cont'd)					
	9.2	6	12	**18**	29
#195	9.6	5	49	**64**	100
#197	9.4	5	23	**52**	90
#198	9.4	5	21	**35**	56
#200	9.8	5	92	**209**	330
	9.6	25	28	**56**	103
	9.4	25	24	**39**	70
	9.2	16	11	**28**	41
	9.0	6	16	**23**	33
#201	9.6	5	26	**39**	55
#204	9.6	5	12	**26**	41
#210	9.4	5	19	**20**	21
#214	9.4	5	16	**27**	47
#231	9.4	6	15	**18**	24
#250	9.8	7	54	**133**	250
	9.6	17	19	**47**	74
	9.4	5	15	**27**	49
#264	9.8	6	7	**21**	29
#288	9.8	9	15	**23**	36
#290	9.8	5	1	**18**	25
#291	9.8	5	19	**23**	32
#295	9.8	12	2	**21**	29
#296	9.8	15	13	**23**	47
#297	9.8	9	11	**22**	34
#298	9.8	9	10	**21**	30
#300	9.8	23	20	**35**	54
	9.6	14	15	**30**	50
#301	9.8	7	10	**16**	25
#302	9.8	7	1	**22**	31
#304	9.6	5	10	**17**	25
#305	9.8	15	6	**21**	59
#306	9.8	8	10	**16**	20
#308	9.8	5	10	**22**	33
#310	9.8	11	10	**19**	26
#311	9.8	8	10	**19**	25
#312	9.8	5	17	**24**	30
#314	9.8	12	16	**25**	33
	9.6	5	15	**23**	38
#319	9.6	5	10	**15**	23
#330	9.8	10	54	**68**	101
	9.6	12	6	**25**	40
	9.4	9	12	**20**	31
#331	9.8	5	26	**57**	97
#340	9.8	25	163	**224**	365
	9.6	25	30	**65**	175
	9.4	25	25	**47**	85
	9.2	25	16	**33**	55
	9.0	24	12	**29**	70
	8.5	11	10	**24**	50
	8.0	5	11	**16**	20
	7.5	9	10	**26**	52
#367	9.6	8	10	**22**	37
#372	9.8	6	25	**34**	50
#377	9.8	18	20	**36**	75
	9.6	25	10	**19**	31
	9.4	5	10	**14**	15
#377/2nd	9.2	8	1	**6**	15
#392	9.8	6	11	**21**	30
#393	9.6	11	10	**13**	21
	9.4	8	1	**11**	20
#397	9.8	5	13	**17**	26
#400	9.8	17	13	**25**	34
#418	9.8	5	10	**16**	26
#449	9.4	10	8	**16**	25
Incredible Hulk (2nd series)					
#24	9.8	7	13	**61**	150
#25	9.8	8	16	**48**	71
#34	9.8	25	31	**72**	235
	9.6	25	15	**41**	90
	9.4	25	20	**33**	69
	9.2	9	11	**24**	35
#35	9.6	14	10	**22**	40
	9.4	18	10	**22**	49
#36	9.8	25	10	**33**	100
	9.6	7	15	**23**	31
	9.4	6	11	**15**	18
#37	9.6	6	10	**23**	44
	9.4	5	9	**14**	20
#38	9.8	9	20	**28**	40
	9.6	10	11	**20**	31
	9.4	10	8	**12**	18
#39	9.6	11	7	**13**	20
#40	9.6	6	10	**14**	20
	9.4	6	10	**10**	12
#41	9.8	16	12	**24**	41
#42	9.8	13	10	**19**	31
#43	9.8	10	10	**21**	43
	9.6	5	9	**15**	20
#44	9.8	8	11	**25**	50
	9.6	12	8	**12**	20
#45	9.6	6	9	**13**	20
	9.4	5	10	**12**	15
#46	9.6	16	9	**14**	20
#47	9.8	9	10	**18**	30
	9.6	6	9	**16**	23
#48	9.8	8	10	**17**	30
#49	9.8	8	15	**23**	40
#50	9.8	13	16	**39**	70
	9.6	25	8	**17**	30
#51	9.8	9	13	**21**	33
	9.6	7	10	**13**	19
	9.4	6	10	**14**	19
#52	9.8	7	10	**17**	25
#53	9.8	5	6	**16**	23
#54	9.8	6	10	**19**	33
#56	9.6	8	5	**10**	18
#57	9.6	7	10	**13**	19
#58	9.6	5	10	**13**	18
#60	9.8	7	15	**20**	23
#61	9.8	7	12	**17**	23
Incredible Hulk and Wolverine					
#1	9.6	6	16	**29**	37
Incredible Hulk Annual					
#1	9.6	15	472	**856**	1,275
	9.4	19	300	**415**	650
	9.2	16	108	**200**	330
	9.0	15	76	**147**	255

ISSUE	CGC GRADE	# of AUCTIONS	LOW CLOSE	AVG CLOSE	HIGH CLOSE
	8.5	12	61	**98**	173
	8.0	14	56	**82**	130
	4.0	7	5	**16**	31
#5	9.4	5	4	**36**	74

Incredible Hulk: Future Imperfect

ISSUE	CGC GRADE	# of AUCTIONS	LOW CLOSE	AVG CLOSE	HIGH CLOSE
#1	9.8	7	20	**30**	44

Incredible Hulk: The End

ISSUE	CGC GRADE	# of AUCTIONS	LOW CLOSE	AVG CLOSE	HIGH CLOSE
#1	9.8	25	25	**50**	100
	9.6	14	15	**26**	51

Incredible Hulk vs. Venom

ISSUE	CGC GRADE	# of AUCTIONS	LOW CLOSE	AVG CLOSE	HIGH CLOSE
#1	9.4	5	5	**14**	21
	9.2	5	11	**16**	21

Indiana Jones

ISSUE	CGC GRADE	# of AUCTIONS	LOW CLOSE	AVG CLOSE	HIGH CLOSE
#1	9.8	5	25	**35**	57

Inferno: Hellbound

ISSUE	CGC GRADE	# of AUCTIONS	LOW CLOSE	AVG CLOSE	HIGH CLOSE
#2	9.8	6	11	**18**	26

Inhumans, The

ISSUE	CGC GRADE	# of AUCTIONS	LOW CLOSE	AVG CLOSE	HIGH CLOSE
#1	9.8	8	13	**112**	203
	9.6	25	31	**52**	96
	9.4	23	19	**32**	50
	9.2	7	15	**29**	56
	9.0	13	12	**18**	27

Invaders (Gold Key)

ISSUE	CGC GRADE	# of AUCTIONS	LOW CLOSE	AVG CLOSE	HIGH CLOSE
#1	8.0	5	21	**32**	48

Invaders, The

ISSUE	CGC GRADE	# of AUCTIONS	LOW CLOSE	AVG CLOSE	HIGH CLOSE
#1	9.8	6	183	**326**	420
	9.6	25	55	**91**	183
	9.4	25	33	**61**	113
	9.2	10	20	**37**	81
	9.0	13	16	**25**	51
	8.5	5	16	**27**	35
#2	9.6	21	16	**37**	70
#5	9.6	10	22	**38**	55
#8	9.6	12	22	**33**	45
#9	9.6	13	20	**26**	35
#10	9.8	7	28	**48**	83
	9.6	20	14	**27**	57

Invaders Annual, The

ISSUE	CGC GRADE	# of AUCTIONS	LOW CLOSE	AVG CLOSE	HIGH CLOSE
#1	9.6	5	80	**119**	159
	9.2	8	23	**36**	77

Iron Fist

ISSUE	CGC GRADE	# of AUCTIONS	LOW CLOSE	AVG CLOSE	HIGH CLOSE
#1	9.6	25	183	**308**	510
	9.4	25	90	**142**	302
	9.2	25	41	**73**	140
	9.0	19	30	**48**	71
	8.5	11	27	**36**	52
	8.0	6	16	**30**	51
	7.5	7	12	**28**	39
#2	9.8	5	27	**193**	306
	9.6	20	33	**66**	110
	9.4	10	26	**36**	47
	9.2	12	15	**27**	40
	9.0	5	20	**23**	25
#3	9.6	9	51	**93**	164
	9.4	15	21	**39**	77
#4	9.6	23	31	**53**	118
	9.4	12	20	**30**	38
	9.0	6	11	**23**	40
#5	9.6	11	44	**70**	103
	9.4	10	17	**32**	50
	9.2	6	20	**23**	31
#6	9.6	7	51	**76**	113
#7	9.6	10	37	**66**	114
	9.2	8	9	**19**	25
#8	9.4	10	25	**45**	80
#9	9.6	12	31	**50**	105
	9.2	6	20	**23**	33
#10	9.4	5	29	**41**	61
#11	9.4	5	40	**44**	50
#13	9.4	10	20	**38**	72
#14	9.8	14	860	**1,520**	2,269
	9.6	25	203	**535**	900
	9.4	25	203	**315**	492
	9.2	25	116	**169**	265
	9.0	25	81	**140**	188
	8.5	24	57	**106**	300
	8.0	22	53	**83**	115
	7.5	19	36	**62**	88
	7.0	20	33	**56**	100
	6.5	6	42	**54**	83
	5.5	6	17	**39**	53
	5.0	5	26	**40**	56
#15	9.6	9	121	**186**	273
	9.4	25	50	**82**	158
	9.2	15	40	**50**	61
	9.0	5	32	**44**	59
	8.5	12	18	**26**	40
	8.0	8	11	**30**	45
	7.5	6	9	**15**	26

Iron Fist (Vol. 2)

ISSUE	CGC GRADE	# of AUCTIONS	LOW CLOSE	AVG CLOSE	HIGH CLOSE
#1	9.8	7	15	**27**	30

Iron Man

ISSUE	CGC GRADE	# of AUCTIONS	LOW CLOSE	AVG CLOSE	HIGH CLOSE
#1	9.6	17	812	**1,172**	1,650
	9.4	25	406	**833**	1,225
	9.2	25	150	**468**	679
	9.0	25	245	**415**	610
	8.5	25	203	**300**	575
	8.0	25	1	**236**	361

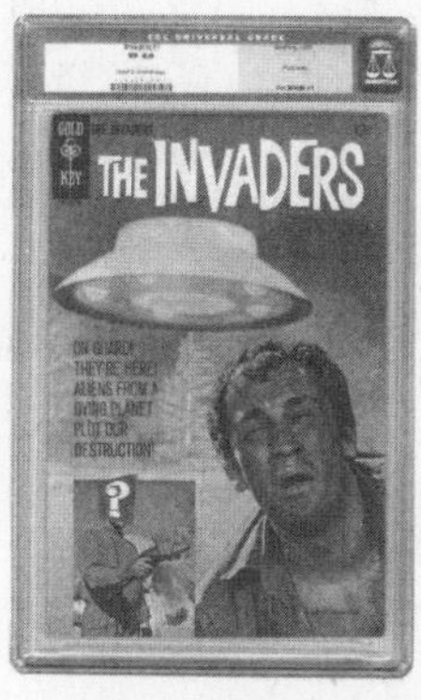

Iron Man (cont'd)

ISSUE	CGC GRADE	# of AUCTIONS	LOW CLOSE	AVG CLOSE	HIGH CLOSE
	7.5	25	103	**192**	295
	7.0	25	100	**167**	282
	6.5	18	82	**131**	183
	6.0	16	61	**105**	143
	5.5	8	61	**80**	100
	5.0	12	60	**91**	150
	4.5	8	63	**95**	128
	4.0	9	52	**79**	123
#2	9.8	18	425	**620**	1,000
	9.6	25	204	**315**	525
	9.4	25	104	**190**	330
	9.2	25	85	**130**	175
	9.0	19	76	**109**	150
	8.5	15	31	**78**	143
	8.0	14	43	**73**	119
	7.5	11	41	**64**	90
	4.0	5	17	**25**	32
#3	9.4	14	80	**167**	225
	9.2	12	51	**107**	169
	9.0	11	60	**89**	140
	8.5	5	31	**56**	81
	8.0	8	32	**50**	81
#4	9.4	8	83	**167**	230
	9.2	8	66	**108**	200
	8.5	14	27	**53**	75
#5	9.4	6	91	**171**	247
	9.2	10	31	**83**	125
	9.0	8	48	**67**	89
	8.5	7	36	**49**	71
	8.0	6	25	**40**	64
#6	9.4	10	100	**143**	228
	9.2	9	46	**68**	110
	8.5	7	27	**42**	55
#7	9.4	5	129	**168**	228
	9.0	12	37	**52**	80
	8.5	6	24	**42**	69
#8	9.4	11	86	**133**	190
	9.2	8	60	**90**	143
	9.0	5	34	**46**	63
	8.0	5	20	**34**	42
#9	9.4	7	128	**182**	250
	9.2	14	61	**77**	99
	8.0	11	22	**40**	62
#10	9.4	9	105	**151**	206
	9.2	8	46	**73**	93
#11	9.4	6	51	**118**	190
#12	9.4	8	46	**118**	225
	8.5	5	30	**33**	40
#13	9.6	7	143	**206**	370
#14	9.4	7	71	**119**	150
	9.0	9	22	**39**	53
#15	9.6	5	128	**174**	230
	9.4	16	26	**80**	140
	8.5	6	27	**33**	53
#21	9.4	6	49	**83**	100
#22	9.4	6	38	**64**	98
#23	9.6	5	72	**101**	139
#26	9.4	5	32	**65**	125
#27	9.4	6	50	**60**	76
#43	9.4	5	93	**105**	128
	9.2	5	41	**48**	61
#50	9.4	5	35	**42**	55
#55	9.6	8	500	**769**	1,109
	9.4	25	178	**403**	625
	9.2	18	131	**193**	325
	9.0	13	104	**155**	213
	8.5	8	82	**100**	124
	8.0	6	51	**63**	85
	6.0	5	33	**53**	90
#56	9.4	6	32	**53**	76
	9.2	6	21	**41**	51
#75	9.4	6	25	**30**	35
#76	9.4	5	36	**51**	90
#99	9.6	5	25	**38**	49
#100	9.6	10	32	**65**	104
	9.4	15	23	**44**	82
#100/35¢	8.0	5	51	**98**	183
#120	9.6	5	30	**35**	41
#150	9.8	5	58	**75**	92
	9.6	10	18	**27**	52
#177	9.8	7	10	**19**	26
#183	9.8	6	19	**21**	26
#184	9.8	7	12	**20**	35
#185	9.8	6	10	**19**	26
#192	9.8	7	22	**32**	62
#300	9.8	7	20	**25**	30

Iron Man and Sub-Mariner

ISSUE	CGC GRADE	# of AUCTIONS	LOW CLOSE	AVG CLOSE	HIGH CLOSE
#1	9.6	12	445	**571**	711
	9.4	18	225	**347**	520
	9.2	25	134	**199**	260
	9.0	25	107	**143**	270
	8.5	16	71	**109**	153
	8.0	18	51	**85**	124
	7.5	17	37	**71**	125
	7.0	9	34	**53**	68
	6.5	6	40	**47**	51
	6.0	9	17	**38**	61

Iron Man Annual

ISSUE	CGC GRADE	# of AUCTIONS	LOW CLOSE	AVG CLOSE	HIGH CLOSE
#1	9.6	8	144	**191**	271
#7	9.8	6	20	**22**	27

Isis

ISSUE	CGC GRADE	# of AUCTIONS	LOW CLOSE	AVG CLOSE	HIGH CLOSE
#1	9.6	10	26	**43**	67

Jimmy Wakely

ISSUE	CGC GRADE	# of AUCTIONS	LOW CLOSE	AVG CLOSE	HIGH CLOSE
#2	9.0	5	81	**242**	390

JLA

ISSUE	CGC GRADE	# of AUCTIONS	LOW CLOSE	AVG CLOSE	HIGH CLOSE
#1	9.8	8	35	**54**	103
	9.6	18	15	**27**	41
	9.4	8	11	**20**	25
#2	9.4	5	2	**13**	25
#3	9.6	6	11	**15**	25
#4	9.6	6	3	**15**	25
#5	9.6	5	10	**15**	19
	9.4	5	1	**14**	20
#6	9.6	9	1	**6**	20
#7	9.8	5	10	**14**	17
#8	9.6	6	10	**13**	18

ISSUE	CGC GRADE	# of AUCTIONS	LOW CLOSE	AVG CLOSE	HIGH CLOSE
#9	9.8	10	10	**14**	18
#10	9.6	5	13	**15**	22
#94	9.8	6	10	**15**	25

JLA/Avengers

ISSUE	CGC GRADE	# of AUCTIONS	LOW CLOSE	AVG CLOSE	HIGH CLOSE
#1	9.9	13	61	**103**	125
	9.8	25	9	**23**	45
	9.6	12	10	**15**	22
#2	10.0	7	125	**135**	150
	9.9	15	25	**54**	75
	9.8	16	10	**23**	40
#3	10.0	14	61	**126**	150
	9.9	17	32	**51**	65
	9.8	24	8	**19**	40
#4	9.8	7	20	**22**	25

John Carter, Warlord of Mars

ISSUE	CGC GRADE	# of AUCTIONS	LOW CLOSE	AVG CLOSE	HIGH CLOSE
#1	9.8	25	19	**54**	90
	9.6	25	16	**23**	38
	9.4	10	12	**20**	25

Joker, The

ISSUE	CGC GRADE	# of AUCTIONS	LOW CLOSE	AVG CLOSE	HIGH CLOSE
#1	9.6	25	41	**70**	164
	9.4	25	20	**50**	73
	9.2	7	15	**35**	55
	9.0	6	20	**30**	35
	8.5	7	13	**24**	35
#3	8.5	5	9	**14**	21
#4	9.4	7	10	**23**	53

Jonah Hex

ISSUE	CGC GRADE	# of AUCTIONS	LOW CLOSE	AVG CLOSE	HIGH CLOSE
#1	9.6	14	96	**165**	250
	9.4	25	50	**99**	153
	9.2	12	26	**54**	99
	9.0	14	12	**41**	80

Journey into Mystery

ISSUE	CGC GRADE	# of AUCTIONS	LOW CLOSE	AVG CLOSE	HIGH CLOSE
#1/GR	8.5	5	15	**19**	22
#83	8.0	6	2,929	**4,743**	6,228
	6.0	6	1,193	**1,708**	2,225
	5.0	8	660	**1,069**	1,326
	4.5	6	717	**848**	945
	4.0	6	325	**542**	655
	2.0	5	252	**346**	500
#85	6.5	5	159	**225**	357
#89	7.0	5	106	**194**	302
#96	8.5	7	51	**185**	338
#98	8.0	5	84	**127**	165
#100	9.0	6	225	**305**	350
#101	9.0	5	143	**178**	203
#106	8.5	6	103	**141**	199
#107	8.5	5	98	**116**	139
#108	9.0	6	160	**216**	275
#109	8.0	5	59	**101**	159
#111	9.2	6	153	**272**	590
#112	9.0	5	381	**459**	559
	8.0	15	156	**226**	332
#114	9.0	6	124	**237**	500
	8.0	6	51	**83**	106
#115	9.0	5	128	**177**	255
	8.5	6	47	**97**	139
#118	8.5	6	51	**102**	168
#120	9.0	5	91	**126**	195
	8.5	6	61	**81**	100
#121	9.4	10	137	**264**	430
	9.2	7	113	**155**	250
	9.0	5	94	**109**	149
	8.0	5	40	**70**	114
#122	8.0	9	28	**50**	72
#124	9.6	7	250	**351**	550
	9.4	22	114	**241**	310
	9.2	7	46	**115**	250
	8.5	6	31	**54**	70
	8.0	6	32	**51**	70
#125	8.5	6	65	**71**	79

Journey into Mystery (Vol. 2)

ISSUE	CGC GRADE	# of AUCTIONS	LOW CLOSE	AVG CLOSE	HIGH CLOSE
#83	9.0	7	80	**103**	125

Journey into Mystery Annual

ISSUE	CGC GRADE	# of AUCTIONS	LOW CLOSE	AVG CLOSE	HIGH CLOSE
#1	8.5	5	133	**172**	225

JSA

ISSUE	CGC GRADE	# of AUCTIONS	LOW CLOSE	AVG CLOSE	HIGH CLOSE
#1	9.6	10	10	**20**	36
	9.0	5	6	**11**	20
#23	9.8	15	17	**23**	28
	9.6	8	6	**13**	25
#57	9.8	5	6	**11**	18

Jumbo Comics

ISSUE	CGC GRADE	# of AUCTIONS	LOW CLOSE	AVG CLOSE	HIGH CLOSE
#22	4.0	6	56	**83**	110

Jungle Action

ISSUE	CGC GRADE	# of AUCTIONS	LOW CLOSE	AVG CLOSE	HIGH CLOSE
#8	9.4	5	26	**60**	105

Justice League

ISSUE	CGC GRADE	# of AUCTIONS	LOW CLOSE	AVG CLOSE	HIGH CLOSE
#1	9.8	7	33	**87**	189
	9.6	15	9	**22**	44
#3/Var	9.6	7	33	**73**	103
	9.4	7	23	**54**	75

Justice League Adventures

ISSUE	CGC GRADE	# of AUCTIONS	LOW CLOSE	AVG CLOSE	HIGH CLOSE
#1	9.8	8	8	**12**	21

Justice League of America

ISSUE	CGC GRADE	# of AUCTIONS	LOW CLOSE	AVG CLOSE	HIGH CLOSE
#1	6.5	6	656	**850**	999
	5.0	6	492	**605**	760
	4.5	9	322	**424**	575
	4.0	13	208	**356**	550
	3.0	5	170	**241**	305

ISSUE	CGC GRADE	# of AUCTIONS	LOW CLOSE	AVG CLOSE	HIGH CLOSE
Justice League of America (cont'd)					
#2	6.5	6	123	**186**	225
#3	3.5	7	42	**69**	100
#4	7.0	10	57	**121**	203
#5	6.5	5	61	**86**	110
#7	9.0	5	203	**333**	513
	8.5	6	136	**228**	299
#9	8.0	7	299	**337**	450
	6.5	7	51	**108**	160
#10	7.0	16	51	**80**	110
#15	9.2	5	154	**283**	394
	9.0	6	119	**168**	258
	8.5	6	57	**103**	148
#17	8.5	5	31	**59**	123
#18	9.0	5	180	**219**	255
#21	7.5	6	145	**164**	204
#22	6.0	6	37	**51**	66
#30	8.5	5	103	**130**	175
#35	9.2	7	122	**139**	153
#54	9.4	6	196	**236**	304
#56	9.2	9	128	**161**	200
#60	9.4	6	168	**198**	230
#63	9.4	5	118	**143**	175
#64	9.4	5	146	**183**	270
#65	9.2	6	61	**88**	128
#87	9.4	6	50	**91**	120
#111	9.4	5	81	**101**	129
#138	9.6	5	31	**63**	150
	9.4	7	16	**27**	35
#147	9.4	5	20	**30**	52
#193	9.8	5	18	**29**	40
	9.6	5	21	**27**	37
#228	9.8	8	17	**20**	25
#229	9.8	5	10	**20**	25
Justice League of America Annual					
#2	9.8	6	10	**22**	33
Ka'a'nga					
#13	4.0	5	26	**31**	38
Kamandi					
#1	9.6	25	56	**116**	211
	9.4	25	10	**68**	130
	9.2	14	22	**35**	46
	9.0	20	17	**38**	100
	8.5	12	13	**26**	41
	8.0	10	15	**21**	30
#18	9.8	10	23	**44**	100
Karate Kid					
#1	9.4	6	33	**46**	78
Ka-Zar					
#1	9.4	5	69	**134**	255
	9.2	10	19	**50**	94
Keen Detective Funnies (Vol. 2)					
#2	3.5	5	100	**136**	225
Kid Komics					
#9	6.5	5	175	**310**	425

ISSUE	CGC GRADE	# of AUCTIONS	LOW CLOSE	AVG CLOSE	HIGH CLOSE
King Conan					
#1	9.8	5	50	**68**	85
	9.6	6	22	**36**	62
	9.4	9	6	**24**	35
Kingdom Come					
#1	9.8	7	30	**37**	50
	9.6	8	14	**21**	26
#3	9.8	5	25	**42**	70
#4	9.8	5	25	**42**	71
Kiss Kiss Bang Bang					
#1	9.8	9	9	**22**	40
Kitty Pryde and Wolverine					
#1	9.8	10	17	**25**	37
	9.6	7	10	**19**	25
Knights 4					
#1	9.8	25	9	**21**	31
#2	9.8	9	17	**22**	28
#3	9.8	5	14	**20**	25
Kull the Conqueror					
#1	9.8	5	285	**404**	610
	9.6	11	93	**124**	174
	9.4	9	46	**77**	103
	9.2	5	41	**50**	64
#2	9.4	5	26	**42**	51
Lady Death II: Between Heaven & Hell					
#1	10.0	5	61	**97**	123
Lady Death in Lingerie					
#1	9.8	11	11	**28**	100
Lady Death: The Crucible					
#1	9.6	5	10	**15**	21
Lancelot Link, Secret Chimp					
#1	9.6	5	62	**78**	100
Last Starfighter					
#1	9.8	5	12	**19**	30
Laurel and Hardy					
#1	9.2	11	26	**49**	92
League of Extraordinary Gentlemen					
#1	9.8	15	29	**53**	154
	9.6	18	15	**31**	56
#2	9.8	7	15	**29**	60
#5	9.6	9	11	**127**	356
Legion of Super-Heroes					
#1	9.9	5	25	**36**	51
	9.8	13	10	**20**	26
#4	9.4	5	19	**24**	37
#38	9.8	5	26	**92**	300
	9.6	8	25	**26**	35
#300	9.8	15	1	**20**	33
Lobo					
#1	9.6	5	15	**23**	25

ISSUE	CGC GRADE	# of AUCTIONS	LOW CLOSE	AVG CLOSE	HIGH CLOSE
Logan's Run					
#1	9.6	13	14	**26**	36
	9.4	5	15	**23**	27
#3	9.8	7	18	**24**	40
Loki					
#1	9.8	6	28	**29**	32
Lone Ranger in Milk for Big Mike					
#0	9.6	8	31	**53**	90
	9.4	6	29	**37**	43
Lone Wolf and Cub					
#1	9.8	5	20	**30**	39
Longshot					
#1	9.8	14	25	**39**	60
#3	9.8	8	16	**28**	50
#5	9.8	5	12	**32**	50
Losers Special					
#1	9.8	5	15	**21**	25
Machine Man					
#1	9.8	10	26	**67**	120
	9.6	25	19	**29**	77
	9.4	24	11	**20**	37
Mad					
#1	7.5	5	1,728	**2,071**	2,300
	7.0	6	1,400	**1,671**	1,900
	3.0	8	332	**466**	775
#2	9.0	7	179	**721**	1,350
	8.5	7	675	**843**	1,025
	8.0	5	416	**530**	750
#4	8.0	11	255	**378**	565
Magneto					
#0/Gld	9.6	11	2	**56**	104
Magnus Robot Fighter (Valiant)					
#0	9.6	10	39	**63**	114
	9.4	6	21	**30**	42
#1	9.8	19	31	**98**	213
	9.6	14	19	**30**	61
	9.4	7	16	**26**	40
#2	9.6	7	14	**35**	108
#3	9.8	5	31	**62**	129
	9.6	6	11	**18**	26
#4	9.8	8	26	**67**	148
	9.6	5	14	**39**	120
#5	9.8	8	60	**97**	153
	9.6	7	18	**45**	69
#6	9.8	5	31	**59**	86
#10	9.8	5	21	**33**	41
#12	9.8	9	44	**138**	262
	9.6	11	33	**60**	109
	9.4	5	20	**27**	32
#21	9.8	10	16	**33**	76
Man from U.N.C.L.E					
#15	8.5	6	2	**13**	26
Man-Bat					
#1	9.6	10	27	**53**	76
	9.4	10	12	**31**	41

ISSUE	CGC GRADE	# of AUCTIONS	LOW CLOSE	AVG CLOSE	HIGH CLOSE
Man-Thing					
#1	9.8	5	523	**642**	960
	9.6	13	154	**260**	500
	9.4	22	6	**91**	159
	9.2	11	18	**64**	103
	9.0	18	10	**41**	90
	8.5	11	14	**33**	85
#5	9.6	6	14	**32**	43
Man-Thing (Vol. 2)					
#1	9.8	7	21	**63**	90
	9.6	16	10	**30**	91
	9.4	7	10	**14**	20
Marvel Age Spider-Man					
#1	9.8	6	15	**20**	25
Marvel and DC Present X-Men and Teen Titans					
#1	9.8	11	25	**46**	75
	9.6	9	20	**33**	50
	9.4	7	11	**17**	21
Marvel Authentix: Amazing Spider-Man					
#1	9.9	11	128	**194**	334
	9.8	25	36	**125**	615
Marvel Authentix: Amazing Spider-Man					
#1/Skch	9.8	7	50	**84**	144
Marvel Authentix: Astonishing X-Men					
#1	9.8	7	20	**66**	138
Marvel Authentix: Daredevil					
#1	10.0	15	200	**429**	960
	9.9	25	78	**156**	310
	9.8	25	47	**107**	338
Marvel Chillers					
#3	9.4	8	37	**48**	70
	9.2	6	21	**25**	31
Marvel Collectible Classics: Spider-Man					
#1	9.8	25	27	**106**	405
	9.6	11	23	**65**	178
Marvel Collectible Classics: X-Men					
#1	9.8	5	17	**33**	50

Marvel Comics Presents

ISSUE	CGC GRADE	# of AUCTIONS	LOW CLOSE	AVG CLOSE	HIGH CLOSE
#1	9.6	9	16	**24**	34
	9.4	6	13	**18**	28
#2	9.8	5	25	**32**	52
#72	9.8	5	33	**47**	76
	9.6	6	12	**20**	28
	9.4	6	10	**13**	18
#73	9.8	5	20	**25**	29
#81	9.8	6	10	**22**	39
#82	9.8	5	15	**20**	25
#83	9.8	6	10	**25**	39

Marvel Comics Super Special

ISSUE	CGC GRADE	# of AUCTIONS	LOW CLOSE	AVG CLOSE	HIGH CLOSE
#1	9.2	7	124	**184**	300

Marvel Fanfare

ISSUE	CGC GRADE	# of AUCTIONS	LOW CLOSE	AVG CLOSE	HIGH CLOSE
#1	9.8	13	26	**43**	79
	9.6	25	12	**22**	45
	9.4	5	10	**15**	26
#3	9.8	5	10	**12**	16
#11	9.8	5	10	**16**	25
#21	9.8	6	10	**24**	35

Marvel Feature

ISSUE	CGC GRADE	# of AUCTIONS	LOW CLOSE	AVG CLOSE	HIGH CLOSE
#1	9.6	12	430	**785**	1,132
	9.4	21	260	**394**	565
	9.2	13	51	**206**	300
	9.0	18	40	**127**	200
	8.5	16	51	**90**	158
	8.0	25	42	**91**	450
	7.0	5	32	**41**	56
#2	9.4	6	114	**175**	200
	9.2	6	47	**74**	103
	9.0	6	38	**52**	63
#3	9.6	7	69	**164**	228
	9.4	5	57	**87**	122
	9.2	5	31	**44**	59
#11	9.4	5	178	**226**	250
	9.2	11	38	**66**	100

Marvel Feature (Vol. 2)

ISSUE	CGC GRADE	# of AUCTIONS	LOW CLOSE	AVG CLOSE	HIGH CLOSE
#1	9.6	13	33	**66**	129
	9.4	5	22	**38**	62

Marvel Knights Spider-Man

ISSUE	CGC GRADE	# of AUCTIONS	LOW CLOSE	AVG CLOSE	HIGH CLOSE
#1	9.9	8	56	**86**	120
	9.8	25	16	**25**	69
#2	9.8	12	20	**21**	25

Marvel Mangaverse

ISSUE	CGC GRADE	# of AUCTIONS	LOW CLOSE	AVG CLOSE	HIGH CLOSE
#1	9.8	5	10	**16**	25

Marvel Mangaverse: Spider-Man

ISSUE	CGC GRADE	# of AUCTIONS	LOW CLOSE	AVG CLOSE	HIGH CLOSE
#1	9.6	6	10	**16**	25

Marvel Mangaverse: X-Men

ISSUE	CGC GRADE	# of AUCTIONS	LOW CLOSE	AVG CLOSE	HIGH CLOSE
#1	9.6	5	10	**11**	16

Marvel Mystery Comics

ISSUE	CGC GRADE	# of AUCTIONS	LOW CLOSE	AVG CLOSE	HIGH CLOSE
#13	4.0	13	720	**1,145**	1,725
#34	5.5	5	380	**489**	575
#73	8.0	5	481	**575**	670
#74	8.5	9	450	**624**	730

Marvel Premiere

ISSUE	CGC GRADE	# of AUCTIONS	LOW CLOSE	AVG CLOSE	HIGH CLOSE
#1	9.6	6	228	**319**	430
	9.4	25	34	**130**	251
	9.2	18	30	**52**	101
	9.0	9	27	**40**	51
	8.5	10	18	**38**	59
#2	9.6	16	50	**72**	154
	9.4	6	32	**44**	70
#3	9.0	5	12	**30**	43
#13	9.4	7	25	**34**	52
#15	9.6	8	485	**637**	730
	9.4	25	201	**306**	455
	9.2	25	75	**141**	240
	9.0	25	43	**97**	150
	8.5	8	25	**62**	90
	8.0	10	31	**48**	65
#20	9.6	7	50	**66**	81
	9.4	10	20	**35**	68
#22	9.4	6	15	**34**	63
#23	9.6	9	34	**47**	61
#24	9.4	8	15	**31**	49
#25	9.4	8	22	**51**	119
	9.2	8	11	**21**	30
#28	9.4	9	31	**53**	75
#40	9.4	5	12	**20**	25
#50	9.4	5	25	**32**	42

Marvel Presents

ISSUE	CGC GRADE	# of AUCTIONS	LOW CLOSE	AVG CLOSE	HIGH CLOSE
#1	9.6	9	25	**46**	81
#3	9.4	6	26	**48**	76

Marvel Preview

ISSUE	CGC GRADE	# of AUCTIONS	LOW CLOSE	AVG CLOSE	HIGH CLOSE
#2	9.4	6	100	**185**	305
	9.0	6	52	**87**	153

Marvels

ISSUE	CGC GRADE	# of AUCTIONS	LOW CLOSE	AVG CLOSE	HIGH CLOSE
#1	9.8	10	19	**27**	42
	9.6	11	5	**18**	30
#2	9.4	6	3	**13**	22
#3	9.8	8	15	**21**	27
#4	9.8	6	10	**17**	25

Marvel 1602

ISSUE	CGC GRADE	# of AUCTIONS	LOW CLOSE	AVG CLOSE	HIGH CLOSE
#1	9.8	25	10	**37**	71
	9.6	25	10	**17**	30
	9.4	6	10	**13**	20
#2	9.8	25	10	**21**	30
	9.6	5	10	**17**	23
#3	9.8	13	11	**27**	89
#4	9.8	13	10	**21**	35
#5	9.8	20	8	**20**	33
#6	9.9	5	80	**105**	150
	9.8	13	9	**18**	35
#7	9.8	7	10	**20**	28

Marvel Spotlight

ISSUE	CGC GRADE	# of AUCTIONS	LOW CLOSE	AVG CLOSE	HIGH CLOSE
#1	9.6	14	22	**140**	301
	9.4	11	30	**74**	105
	9.2	9	23	**37**	57
#2	9.6	6	760	**1,078**	1,526
	9.4	11	315	**482**	700
	9.2	12	175	**229**	310

ISSUE	CGC GRADE	# of AUCTIONS	LOW CLOSE	AVG CLOSE	HIGH CLOSE
	9.0	13	100	**149**	250
	8.5	16	51	**99**	150
	8.0	13	66	**87**	125
	7.5	6	49	**59**	76
	7.0	7	37	**50**	61
#3	9.4	5	67	**109**	177
	9.0	5	39	**74**	164
#4	9.4	12	37	**98**	150
#5	9.4	25	250	**940**	2,075
	9.2	25	200	**428**	809
	9.0	7	280	**345**	449
	8.5	18	126	**212**	338
	8.0	12	92	**156**	250
	7.5	14	61	**128**	220
	7.0	12	40	**86**	128
#6	9.6	6	183	**268**	430
	9.4	8	76	**153**	222
	9.2	5	50	**78**	104
	8.0	7	17	**26**	34
#8	9.4	12	53	**81**	133
#9	9.6	5	109	**181**	240
	9.4	7	69	**110**	151
#10	9.2	5	23	**40**	58
	8.5	5	12	**18**	25
#11	9.4	7	46	**72**	154
#12	9.2	6	28	**41**	65
#28	9.6	16	35	**83**	153
	9.4	21	21	**45**	120
	9.2	7	15	**26**	40
	9.0	5	6	**19**	30
#29	9.6	5	25	**40**	53
	9.4	9	15	**28**	36
#32	9.6	25	29	**62**	120
	9.4	12	19	**39**	60
	9.2	6	5	**23**	40

Marvel Super Action

ISSUE	CGC GRADE	# of AUCTIONS	LOW CLOSE	AVG CLOSE	HIGH CLOSE
#1	9.4	8	12	**27**	41

Marvel Super Hero Contest of Champions

ISSUE	CGC GRADE	# of AUCTIONS	LOW CLOSE	AVG CLOSE	HIGH CLOSE
#1	9.8	8	30	**47**	80

Marvel Super Heroes Secret Wars

ISSUE	CGC GRADE	# of AUCTIONS	LOW CLOSE	AVG CLOSE	HIGH CLOSE
#1	9.8	25	19	**50**	168
	9.6	22	11	**22**	40
	9.4	11	5	**15**	26
	9.2	5	7	**17**	26
#2	9.8	12	19	**34**	86
#4	9.8	19	9	**36**	60
#5	9.8	16	21	**31**	58
#6	9.8	7	25	**35**	54
#7	9.8	13	25	**36**	52
#8	9.8	25	40	**150**	405
	9.6	25	18	**42**	100
	9.4	25	6	**29**	60
	9.2	25	15	**23**	40
	9.0	13	13	**19**	25
	8.5	19	10	**16**	22
	7.0	17	2	**9**	16
#9	9.8	17	9	**25**	40

ISSUE	CGC GRADE	# of AUCTIONS	LOW CLOSE	AVG CLOSE	HIGH CLOSE
	9.6	9	10	**17**	25
#10	9.8	15	14	**28**	41
	9.6	6	6	**18**	28
#11	9.8	19	15	**26**	33
	9.6	6	3	**13**	26
#12	9.8	10	20	**30**	44
	9.6	8	9	**12**	15

Marvel Super-Heroes

ISSUE	CGC GRADE	# of AUCTIONS	LOW CLOSE	AVG CLOSE	HIGH CLOSE
#1	9.6	13	250	**334**	513
	9.4	24	104	**175**	285
	9.2	25	51	**102**	180
	9.0	17	31	**70**	109
	8.5	16	16	**54**	94
	8.0	8	27	**49**	75
	7.0	6	6	**25**	46
#12	9.4	7	202	**407**	610
	9.2	11	86	**152**	183
	9.0	10	49	**93**	153
	8.5	6	57	**71**	104
	8.0	8	32	**43**	63
	7.5	5	33	**42**	55
	6.5	5	19	**39**	75
#14	9.0	5	27	**53**	90

Marvel Team-Up

ISSUE	CGC GRADE	# of AUCTIONS	LOW CLOSE	AVG CLOSE	HIGH CLOSE
#1	9.4	6	575	**644**	725
	9.2	25	158	**213**	300
	9.0	15	91	**141**	225
	8.5	6	62	**89**	103
	8.0	16	23	**65**	100
	7.5	13	27	**47**	71
	7.0	5	36	**47**	57
	6.5	5	20	**34**	48
#2	9.8	5	248	**329**	400
	9.6	6	163	**192**	248
	9.4	10	71	**107**	189
	9.2	6	40	**55**	77
	9.0	8	30	**37**	61
#3	9.6	9	124	**168**	225
	9.4	23	59	**95**	160
	9.2	10	33	**57**	93
	8.5	5	21	**32**	51
#4	9.4	10	128	**172**	224
	9.2	6	75	**83**	93
	8.5	5	26	**36**	50
#6	9.4	5	36	**58**	78

ISSUE	CGC GRADE	# of AUCTIONS	LOW CLOSE	AVG CLOSE	HIGH CLOSE
Marvel Team-Up (cont'd)					
#8	9.6	8	75	**104**	175
	9.4	5	50	**67**	82
#9	9.4	7	38	**64**	100
#10	9.4	5	52	**78**	100
#13	9.4	9	25	**48**	80
#15	9.4	12	29	**63**	100
#16	9.6	7	33	**58**	72
#18	9.4	5	21	**51**	91
#19	9.6	5	35	**63**	99
	9.2	6	13	**19**	31
#20	9.4	6	51	**59**	76
#53	9.6	20	71	**123**	178
	9.4	21	45	**63**	120
	9.2	16	20	**30**	44
	9.0	6	1	**19**	26
	8.5	7	10	**17**	21
#57	9.6	7	10	**19**	30
#76	9.6	7	8	**22**	35
#81	9.6	6	15	**23**	30
#100	9.6	9	21	**31**	55
#117	9.6	20	17	**26**	41
#130	9.8	5	14	**25**	35
#135	9.6	5	8	**11**	15
#136	9.8	5	3	**23**	37
#139	9.8	5	15	**20**	30
#141	9.8	21	12	**56**	90
	9.6	12	20	**36**	91
#142	9.8	8	8	**20**	33
#144	9.8	11	1	**19**	30
#145	9.8	8	16	**25**	40
	9.6	5	6	**12**	21
#146	9.8	6	15	**26**	32
#147	9.8	8	9	**23**	32
#148	9.8	7	15	**26**	41
#150	9.8	6	25	**42**	85
Marvel Team-Up Annual					
#1	9.6	5	148	**197**	310
	9.4	19	80	**119**	180
	9.0	9	20	**33**	53
#7	9.8	9	6	**20**	26
Marvel Two-In-One					
#1	9.6	8	199	**415**	576
	9.4	16	143	**196**	276
	9.2	10	45	**69**	105
	9.0	6	41	**52**	64
	8.5	11	21	**34**	51
#2	9.4	7	13	**42**	60
#3	9.4	7	25	**40**	61
#7	9.4	7	16	**22**	42
Marvel Two-In-One Annual					
#2	9.6	14	44	**77**	131
	9.4	12	29	**52**	65
Marvel Universe: The End					
#1	9.8	6	16	**26**	47
Marville					
#1	9.8	7	11	**19**	25
	9.6	5	6	**14**	27

ISSUE	CGC GRADE	# of AUCTIONS	LOW CLOSE	AVG CLOSE	HIGH CLOSE
Master of Kung Fu					
#17	9.4	8	40	**57**	73
	9.2	7	14	**28**	45
#24	9.6	5	26	**32**	38
Masters of the Universe					
#1	9.8	25	9	**22**	94
	9.6	21	2	**21**	40
Meridian					
#1	9.8	5	20	**24**	31
Metal Men					
#1	8.0	7	280	**344**	405
Metamorpho					
#1	7.0	5	21	**27**	35
Michael Turner Presents: Aspen					
#1	9.8	5	14	**28**	41
Michael Turner's Soulfire					
#0	9.8	14	20	**24**	28
Micronauts					
#1	9.8	18	15	**41**	110
	9.6	25	7	**19**	55
	9.4	16	1	**16**	34
#37	9.6	5	6	**11**	15
#59	9.8	5	15	**21**	25
Micronauts Annual					
#1	9.8	6	18	**30**	40
Midnight Nation					
#0.5	9.8	5	6	**9**	10
Mighty Midget Comics (Captain Marvel Jr.)					
#11	9.4	16	80	**136**	316
Military Comics					
#21	6.5	6	95	**139**	200
#30	8.0	10	52	**153**	280
Millie the Model					
#135	9.6	6	26	**48**	65
Millie the Model Annual					
#5	9.4	5	34	**67**	110
Miracleman					
#1	9.6	20	21	**32**	50
	9.4	12	15	**28**	56
#2	9.6	5	16	**22**	29
#4	9.6	7	10	**14**	20
#12	9.4	7	10	**18**	26
#13	9.6	6	21	**28**	45
	9.4	7	14	**22**	28
#14	9.6	7	10	**35**	51
	9.4	5	12	**20**	25
	9.2	7	9	**22**	40
#15	9.6	22	95	**139**	203
	9.4	25	51	**86**	195
	9.2	16	50	**68**	127
#24	9.4	6	31	**38**	54

ISSUE	CGC GRADE	# of AUCTIONS	LOW CLOSE	AVG CLOSE	HIGH CLOSE
Miss Fury					
#7	9.0	5	406	**590**	788
Mister Miracle					
#1	9.6	8	121	**254**	430
	9.4	16	78	**150**	180
	9.2	10	32	**59**	85
#6	9.4	5	53	**73**	83
#8	9.4	5	18	**59**	80
#11	9.4	5	37	**47**	62
Modeling with Millie					
#36	9.6	7	35	**49**	65
	9.4	7	13	**37**	101
Moment of Silence					
#0	9.8	24	1	**15**	35
	9.6	10	10	**16**	32
Monolith					
#1	9.8	11	12	**16**	20
Monster Hunters					
#1	9.6	5	34	**50**	75
Moon Knight					
#1	9.8	8	4	**41**	78
	9.6	17	19	**32**	58
More Fun Comics					
#70	4.5	5	361	**428**	525
Morlock 2001					
#1	9.4	8	10	**30**	57
Ms. Marvel					
#1	9.6	23	23	**45**	85
	9.4	18	15	**28**	60
#5	9.6	7	8	**24**	73
#14	9.6	6	6	**16**	29
#17	9.6	7	22	**56**	89
	9.4	6	32	**39**	44
#18	9.4	5	63	**140**	255
	9.2	5	53	**94**	147
	9.0	8	17	**67**	123
Munsters, The					
#9	9.4	6	81	**139**	180
Mystery In Space					
#53	5.5	5	153	**222**	252
#70	5.0	10	16	**24**	36
#75	8.5	8	128	**165**	200
	8.0	5	108	**132**	150
	7.0	5	31	**40**	51
Mystic (CrossGen)					
#1	9.8	5	18	**23**	30
Mystique					
#1	9.8	25	22	**35**	51
	9.6	11	13	**21**	34
#2	9.8	9	11	**23**	35

ISSUE	CGC GRADE	# of AUCTIONS	LOW CLOSE	AVG CLOSE	HIGH CLOSE
Nam, The					
#1	9.8	6	22	**40**	95
	9.6	15	9	**17**	29
Nature Boy					
#5	8.5	8	39	**52**	80
New Adventures of Superboy					
#1	9.4	5	10	**18**	27
New Comics					
#6	3.5	6	103	**282**	414
New Gods					
#1	9.6	25	104	**176**	255
	9.4	25	54	**117**	193
	9.2	12	26	**58**	103
	9.0	12	20	**41**	75
	8.5	6	18	**30**	48
	8.0	11	11	**26**	46
	7.5	5	12	**22**	30
	7.0	5	13	**17**	25
#3	9.4	7	28	**45**	91
New Mutants					
#1	9.8	18	16	**47**	86
	9.6	25	11	**25**	51
	9.4	21	10	**16**	26
#87	9.8	10	100	**149**	223
	9.6	25	20	**41**	70
	9.4	25	15	**26**	40
	9.2	10	6	**16**	25
	9.0	6	10	**15**	21
#93	9.6	8	7	**19**	40
#94	9.6	6	10	**18**	35
#98	9.8	17	40	**110**	258
	9.6	25	13	**32**	60
	9.4	7	11	**26**	40
#100	9.6	11	5	**16**	40
New Mutants Special Edition					
#1	9.8	6	10	**23**	51
New Teen Titans					
#1	9.8	11	21	**65**	208
	9.8	19	13	**25**	45
	9.6	25	6	**48**	130
	9.6	13	12	**22**	31

ISSUE	CGC GRADE	# of AUCTIONS	LOW CLOSE	AVG CLOSE	HIGH CLOSE
New Teen Titans (cont'd)					
	9.4	10	12	**24**	35
	9.2	5	13	**23**	30
	8.5	13	2	**8**	12
#2	9.6	16	36	**75**	148
	9.0	13	1	**7**	13
#22	9.6	6	10	**19**	26
#26	9.8	5	9	**19**	29
#38	9.8	5	19	**25**	41
#39	9.8	6	21	**24**	30
New X-Men					
#1	9.8	6	20	**22**	25
#114	9.8	25	13	**32**	75
	9.6	25	8	**14**	26
	9.4	8	10	**22**	65
#147	9.8	6	12	**23**	40
#148	9.8	5	6	**17**	25
#150	9.8	18	21	**34**	48
#151	9.8	20	11	**24**	45
#152	9.8	20	10	**23**	64
#153	9.8	6	11	**22**	35
#154	9.8	5	14	**24**	28
John Byrne's Next Men					
#21	9.8	17	52	**294**	474
	9.6	21	51	**112**	203
	9.4	13	32	**71**	158
Nick Fury					
#1	9.8	8	672	**841**	1,028
	9.6	25	145	**348**	560
	9.4	25	53	**206**	355
	9.2	25	40	**134**	210
	9.0	25	56	**94**	128
	8.5	23	36	**77**	123
	8.0	14	32	**60**	83
	7.5	17	31	**52**	111
	7.0	10	34	**46**	60
	6.5	7	10	**30**	43
#2	9.6	10	29	**205**	292
	9.4	11	104	**137**	165
	9.2	16	43	**59**	90
	9.0	9	37	**51**	70
#3	9.2	10	51	**76**	123
	9.0	5	36	**50**	68
#4	9.4	5	113	**161**	213
	9.2	11	51	**88**	134
	9.0	11	37	**57**	83
#5	9.6	6	178	**250**	360
	9.4	13	76	**137**	230
	9.2	9	60	**78**	138
#6	9.4	18	70	**105**	138
	9.2	7	51	**70**	100
	9.0	10	32	**47**	75
#7	9.4	5	82	**113**	165
#8	9.4	6	73	**99**	133
#12	9.4	8	46	**82**	103
#15	9.4	9	104	**182**	250
	9.2	14	45	**98**	157
	9.0	9	50	**68**	79
	8.5	7	29	**50**	70

ISSUE	CGC GRADE	# of AUCTIONS	LOW CLOSE	AVG CLOSE	HIGH CLOSE
Nick Fury vs. S.H.I.E.L.D.					
#1	9.8	8	25	**31**	79
Night Nurse					
#1	9.0	5	85	**124**	158
	7.5	5	31	**47**	75
Nightwing					
#1	9.6	9	16	**35**	76
#2	9.6	16	1	**12**	30
#3	9.4	16	1	**8**	25
Ninjak					
#1	9.8	7	3	**17**	26
Not Brand Echh!					
#1	9.2	5	46	**59**	81
	9.0	11	25	**46**	69
Nova					
#1	9.8	12	100	**191**	304
	9.6	25	25	**48**	75
	9.4	16	15	**26**	35
	9.2	8	15	**19**	24
Nyx					
#1	9.8	12	22	**32**	45
OMAC					
#1	9.8	7	74	**126**	168
	9.6	13	15	**46**	78
	9.4	15	21	**41**	70
	9.2	7	13	**24**	45
	9.0	5	11	**21**	35
#7	9.4	5	10	**20**	38
Omega Men					
#1	9.8	6	19	**21**	25
#3	9.8	25	19	**37**	65
	9.6	25	10	**24**	79
	9.4	5	5	**13**	20
Omega the Unknown					
#1	9.4	5	23	**27**	31
100 Pages of Comics					
#1	8.0	11	210	**385**	680
Onslaught Marvel Universe					
#1	9.6	6	6	**11**	19
Our Army at War					
#124	9.0	6	23	**88**	193
#148	9.0	5	36	**73**	99
#238	9.6	5	47	**81**	180
#242	8.5	6	35	**81**	127
Out of this World					
#6	8.5	5	26	**78**	105
Outsiders					
#1	9.8	7	19	**37**	60
#6	9.8	5	6	**11**	15
Patsy and Hedy					
#104	9.8	6	34	**62**	100
	9.6	5	32	**68**	90

ISSUE	CGC GRADE	# of AUCTIONS	LOW CLOSE	AVG CLOSE	HIGH CLOSE
Pep Comics					
#2	7.0	10	14	**511**	900
Peter Parker: Spider-Man					
#1	9.8	9	22	**40**	103
#1/DF	9.8	5	51	**82**	100
	9.6	10	28	**53**	75
#1/Sun	9.8	7	27	**47**	75
	9.6	5	18	**25**	40
#29	9.4	5	10	**15**	18
#44	9.8	18	16	**34**	56
	9.6	13	8	**21**	43
#45	9.8	10	10	**21**	31
Phantom Stranger					
#1	9.2	7	51	**140**	220
#17	9.4	5	51	**74**	118
Phoenix					
#1	9.8	24	14	**33**	57
Phoenix (Atlas)					
#1	9.6	5	20	**32**	41
Pitt					
#1	9.8	14	18	**25**	43
	9.6	9	6	**12**	25
Planet Comics					
#30	8.5	5	485	**531**	599
#43	7.0	5	148	**173**	204
#48	9.0	5	415	**440**	477
#50	8.0	5	255	**288**	316
Planet of the Apes					
#1	9.8	8	184	**351**	710
	9.6	7	45	**90**	150
Plastic Man					
#4	7.5	11	103	**244**	405
Plop!					
#1	9.6	13	41	**72**	149
	9.4	8	29	**46**	80
#3	9.6	5	12	**33**	63
#4	9.8	5	33	**57**	105
	9.6	5	11	**29**	50
Pogo Possum					
#16	9.0	5	50	**104**	160
Popular Comics					
#97	7.0	5	52	**98**	169
Power Comics					
#2	3.5	5	103	**182**	289
Power Man and Iron Fist					
#57	9.4	5	27	**40**	52
#66	9.6	5	50	**79**	113
	9.4	10	25	**41**	69
	9.2	11	18	**22**	30
#106	9.8	5	16	**19**	25

ISSUE	CGC GRADE	# of AUCTIONS	LOW CLOSE	AVG CLOSE	HIGH CLOSE
Power Pack					
#1	9.8	6	10	**20**	32
Powers					
#1	9.8	5	19	**29**	54
Preacher					
#1	9.6	7	31	**44**	65
	9.4	5	15	**24**	44
Primer					
#2	9.6	12	41	**127**	203
	9.4	15	57	**81**	158
	9.2	14	21	**57**	152
	9.0	5	21	**42**	55
Prince Namor, the Sub-Mariner					
#1	9.8	15	15	**23**	45
Pulse					
#1	9.8	25	15	**25**	35
Punisher Limited Series					
#1	9.8	11	133	**234**	409
	9.6	25	28	**70**	151
	9.4	16	18	**44**	72
	9.2	8	16	**33**	56
	9.0	7	16	**24**	41
#2	9.6	24	19	**30**	78
	9.4	11	12	**18**	30
#3	9.6	12	25	**45**	114
	9.4	7	16	**24**	45
	9.2	6	9	**16**	24
#4	9.8	12	35	**78**	153
	9.6	19	16	**30**	52
	9.4	11	7	**18**	36
#5	9.8	9	50	**78**	105
	9.6	8	21	**35**	78
	9.4	5	15	**21**	25
	9.2	5	10	**15**	21
Punisher					
#1	9.8	14	57	**112**	178
	9.8	10	20	**34**	50
	9.8	10	19	**26**	30
	9.6	25	16	**39**	75
	9.6	10	7	**17**	31
	9.4	25	13	**27**	56
	9.2	9	10	**19**	28

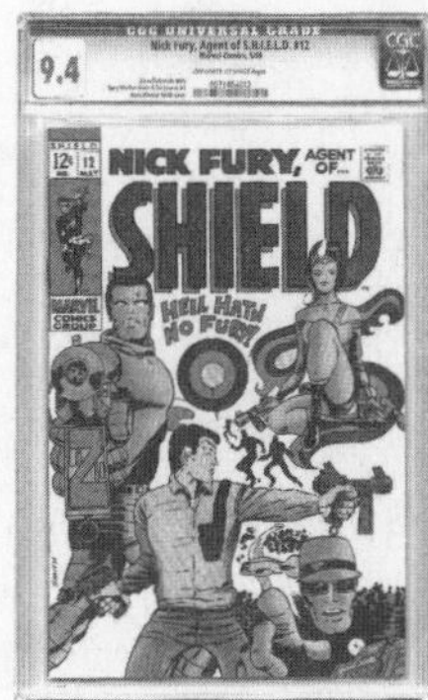

ISSUE	CGC GRADE	# of AUCTIONS	LOW CLOSE	AVG CLOSE	HIGH CLOSE
Punisher (cont'd)					
	9.0	7	11	**19**	23
#10	9.8	6	31	**42**	52
	9.6	7	20	**26**	35
Punisher (7th series/MAX)					
#1	9.8	25	13	**28**	40
#2	9.9	6	31	**45**	57
	9.8	14	10	**22**	40
#3	9.8	9	9	**20**	30
Punisher: The End					
#1	9.8	20	18	**23**	35
Punisher War Journal					
#1	9.8	12	25	**49**	80
	9.6	16	7	**17**	35
	9.4	6	12	**19**	24
#6	9.8	13	21	**40**	110
	9.6	24	10	**19**	33
#7	9.8	8	20	**28**	61
	9.6	12	8	**17**	36
	9.4	8	10	**14**	23
#15	9.6	6	4	**11**	17
Punisher: War Zone					
#1	9.8	18	8	**21**	30
	9.6	10	3	**13**	20
Purgatori					
#1	9.8	9	10	**28**	46
Purgatori: Vampire's Myth					
#1	9.8	9	10	**22**	40
Ragman					
#1	9.4	5	11	**19**	25
Rai					
#0	9.8	25	22	**31**	82
	9.6	17	9	**18**	36
#1	9.8	15	50	**90**	204
	9.6	19	14	**31**	78
	9.4	7	17	**20**	25
#2	9.8	5	21	**52**	72
	9.6	10	16	**29**	45
#3	9.8	13	50	**99**	213
	9.6	12	28	**48**	95
#4	9.6	22	25	**39**	83
	9.4	12	25	**34**	65
#8	9.8	13	11	**37**	79
Rawhide Kid					
#50	9.6	8	56	**118**	153
#56	9.4	8	40	**59**	86
Red Sonja					
#1	9.8	7	20	**83**	135
	9.6	24	25	**41**	60
	9.4	16	13	**33**	66
#3	9.8	5	31	**42**	55
#4	9.8	5	26	**38**	50
	9.6	5	16	**27**	40

ISSUE	CGC GRADE	# of AUCTIONS	LOW CLOSE	AVG CLOSE	HIGH CLOSE
Red Star					
#1	9.6	7	10	**19**	40
Red Wolf					
#1	9.4	7	70	**111**	255
Reptisaurus					
#4	9.0	7	22	**40**	69
Richard Dragon					
#1	9.8	5	17	**19**	20
Rima, The Jungle Girl					
#1	9.4	5	28	**40**	69
Ringo Kid					
#12	9.4	5	17	**36**	54
Rip Hunter Time Master					
#9	9.2	5	52	**87**	166
Rising Stars					
#1	9.8	6	20	**40**	60
	9.6	5	11	**19**	27
	9.4	7	10	**17**	27
#2	9.8	7	8	**16**	23
	9.6	6	1	**10**	18
#8	9.8	6	10	**16**	24
#12	9.8	5	10	**13**	17
Robin					
#121	9.8	12	11	**19**	35
#125	9.8	5	18	**23**	27
#126	9.8	11	24	**29**	37
Rogue					
#1	9.8	12	12	**18**	27
	9.6	5	1	**11**	23
Rogue (2nd series)					
#1	9.8	6	10	**14**	16
Rom					
#1	9.6	6	25	**43**	91
	9.4	5	20	**28**	46
#17	9.6	5	27	**41**	76
Ronin					
#1	9.8	12	18	**24**	35
#2	9.8	7	12	**22**	28
Rose and Thorn					
#1	9.8	6	12	**15**	23
Runaways					
#1	9.8	9	15	**25**	50
Sabretooth					
#1	9.8	7	9	**23**	30
Saga of the Swamp Thing					
#1	9.8	6	20	**26**	41
	9.6	10	10	**23**	45
#20	9.6	6	34	**41**	61
	9.4	5	20	**27**	30
#25	9.8	7	21	**33**	44

ISSUE	CGC GRADE	# of AUCTIONS	LOW CLOSE	AVG CLOSE	HIGH CLOSE
#34	9.6	5	10	**32**	55
#37	9.8	6	52	**110**	270
	9.6	9	36	**71**	164
	9.4	7	21	**53**	138
#41	9.8	6	15	**24**	36

Samson

ISSUE	CGC GRADE	# of AUCTIONS	LOW CLOSE	AVG CLOSE	HIGH CLOSE
#1	4.5	6	193	**288**	345

Sandman, The (1974)

ISSUE	CGC GRADE	# of AUCTIONS	LOW CLOSE	AVG CLOSE	HIGH CLOSE
#1	9.8	7	180	**247**	460
	9.6	20	43	**95**	204
	9.4	25	11	**49**	80
	9.2	14	21	**31**	50
	9.0	11	14	**25**	36
	8.5	6	10	**15**	20

Sandman (1989)

ISSUE	CGC GRADE	# of AUCTIONS	LOW CLOSE	AVG CLOSE	HIGH CLOSE
#1	9.6	25	31	**61**	106
	9.4	10	18	**40**	76
#8	9.4	5	13	**69**	255
#19/err	9.8	14	15	**29**	40

Savage Dragon (limited series)

ISSUE	CGC GRADE	# of AUCTIONS	LOW CLOSE	AVG CLOSE	HIGH CLOSE
#1	9.8	5	10	**20**	25

Savage Dragon

ISSUE	CGC GRADE	# of AUCTIONS	LOW CLOSE	AVG CLOSE	HIGH CLOSE
#1	9.8	6	16	**20**	25

Savage She-Hulk

ISSUE	CGC GRADE	# of AUCTIONS	LOW CLOSE	AVG CLOSE	HIGH CLOSE
#1	9.8	25	32	**80**	250
	9.6	25	13	**33**	91
	9.4	17	13	**26**	44

Savage Sword of Conan

ISSUE	CGC GRADE	# of AUCTIONS	LOW CLOSE	AVG CLOSE	HIGH CLOSE
#1	9.6	6	410	**480**	550
	9.4	7	163	**188**	218
	9.2	5	81	**98**	138
	9.0	8	47	**74**	110

Scion

ISSUE	CGC GRADE	# of AUCTIONS	LOW CLOSE	AVG CLOSE	HIGH CLOSE
#1	9.8	10	17	**32**	65

Sea Devils

ISSUE	CGC GRADE	# of AUCTIONS	LOW CLOSE	AVG CLOSE	HIGH CLOSE
#1	9.0	5	185	**584**	800
	8.0	7	203	**315**	391

Secret Origins

ISSUE	CGC GRADE	# of AUCTIONS	LOW CLOSE	AVG CLOSE	HIGH CLOSE
#1	9.4	6	36	**58**	79
	2.0	7	15	**24**	51

Secret Six

ISSUE	CGC GRADE	# of AUCTIONS	LOW CLOSE	AVG CLOSE	HIGH CLOSE
#1	9.2	11	31	**54**	98
#6	9.4	6	41	**59**	91

Secret Society of Super Villains

ISSUE	CGC GRADE	# of AUCTIONS	LOW CLOSE	AVG CLOSE	HIGH CLOSE
#1	9.6	16	13	**38**	118

Secret War

ISSUE	CGC GRADE	# of AUCTIONS	LOW CLOSE	AVG CLOSE	HIGH CLOSE
#1	9.8	25	21	**33**	61
#1/Comm	9.8	17	25	**34**	37
#2	9.8	5	40	**74**	180

Secret Wars II

ISSUE	CGC GRADE	# of AUCTIONS	LOW CLOSE	AVG CLOSE	HIGH CLOSE
#2	9.8	5	13	**18**	24

ISSUE	CGC GRADE	# of AUCTIONS	LOW CLOSE	AVG CLOSE	HIGH CLOSE
#3	9.8	9	6	**16**	46
#5	9.8	6	8	**18**	29

Secrets of Haunted House

ISSUE	CGC GRADE	# of AUCTIONS	LOW CLOSE	AVG CLOSE	HIGH CLOSE
#1	9.4	6	45	**125**	213

Sensation Comics

ISSUE	CGC GRADE	# of AUCTIONS	LOW CLOSE	AVG CLOSE	HIGH CLOSE
#24	7.0	5	228	**294**	429
#84	9.4	6	910	**1,060**	1,221
#108	3.5	6	76	**101**	130

Sensation Mystery

ISSUE	CGC GRADE	# of AUCTIONS	LOW CLOSE	AVG CLOSE	HIGH CLOSE
#112	4.0	5	46	**66**	98

Sensational Spider-Man

ISSUE	CGC GRADE	# of AUCTIONS	LOW CLOSE	AVG CLOSE	HIGH CLOSE
#0	9.8	9	10	**42**	85

Sgt. Fury

ISSUE	CGC GRADE	# of AUCTIONS	LOW CLOSE	AVG CLOSE	HIGH CLOSE
#1	4.0	7	183	**238**	275
	3.0	6	80	**147**	190
#4	8.5	5	83	**124**	195
#13	9.4	6	999	**1,763**	2,551
	9.2	6	445	**678**	1,000
	9.0	9	305	**372**	465
	7.5	6	118	**150**	200
	6.5	8	71	**90**	117
	6.0	7	63	**88**	158
#52	9.4	5	43	**62**	80
#70	9.2	5	9	**24**	36

Shade, the Changing Man

ISSUE	CGC GRADE	# of AUCTIONS	LOW CLOSE	AVG CLOSE	HIGH CLOSE
#1	9.6	6	12	**31**	51

Shadow, The

ISSUE	CGC GRADE	# of AUCTIONS	LOW CLOSE	AVG CLOSE	HIGH CLOSE
#1	9.6	15	63	**100**	169
	9.4	25	10	**46**	87
	9.2	9	19	**26**	40
	9.0	6	16	**22**	35
#3	9.6	5	10	**31**	42
#4	9.4	6	14	**33**	90

Shadowman

ISSUE	CGC GRADE	# of AUCTIONS	LOW CLOSE	AVG CLOSE	HIGH CLOSE
#1	9.8	13	10	**51**	78

Shanna the She-Devil

ISSUE	CGC GRADE	# of AUCTIONS	LOW CLOSE	AVG CLOSE	HIGH CLOSE
#1	9.2	5	21	**37**	56

Shazam

ISSUE	CGC GRADE	# of AUCTIONS	LOW CLOSE	AVG CLOSE	HIGH CLOSE
#1	9.8	11	100	**212**	300
	9.6	15	57	**128**	192

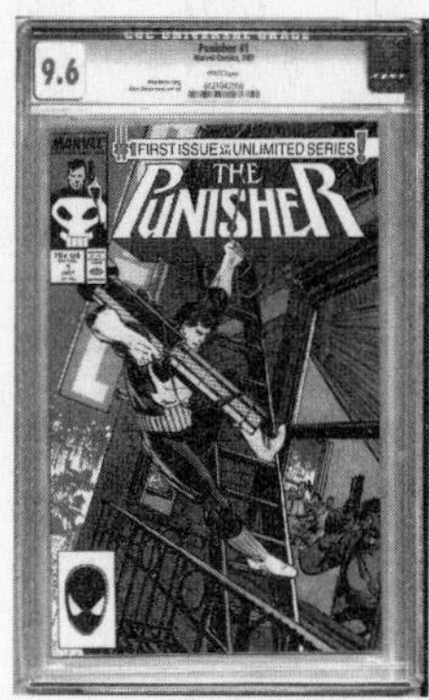

ISSUE	CGC GRADE	# of AUCTIONS	LOW CLOSE	AVG CLOSE	HIGH CLOSE
Shazam (cont'd)					
	9.4	21	25	**65**	140
	9.0	13	12	**30**	56
	7.5	5	9	**13**	21
#8	9.2	6	12	**35**	51
She-Hulk					
#1	9.8	19	16	**26**	43
Sherlock Holmes					
#1	9.4	5	15	**29**	48
Shield, The: Spotlight					
#1	9.8	6	6	**13**	35
Shock Suspenstories					
#1	5.0	9	82	**134**	224
	4.5	6	114	**132**	168
Shogun Warriors					
#1	9.8	12	17	**39**	79
	9.6	25	12	**27**	46
	9.4	9	10	**22**	31
Showcase					
#2	7.5	5	405	**583**	900
#4	6.5	11	3,075	**4,375**	6,017
	4.0	7	1,700	**2,145**	2,645
	1.0	5	100	**563**	800
#8	6.5	9	1,825	**2,341**	2,900
	6.0	5	1,225	**1,783**	2,216
#9	5.0	6	450	**921**	1,500
	4.0	7	255	**595**	806
	3.5	6	305	**456**	635
#10	3.5	5	102	**265**	405
#13	4.5	7	410	**523**	605
	4.0	5	380	**434**	499
#14	4.0	7	400	**432**	490
#17	4.5	5	106	**212**	300
#22	3.0	7	250	**336**	395
	2.0	5	153	**244**	400
#23	6.5	5	180	**316**	449
	4.0	6	101	**159**	280
#24	7.0	5	238	**517**	700
#27	7.5	7	160	**278**	360
#30	8.5	10	406	**560**	650
	7.0	10	154	**246**	349
	6.5	5	156	**191**	236
#34	8.5	5	798	**1,131**	1,899
	5.5	6	76	**163**	255
	4.5	5	130	**184**	295
	4.0	5	11	**104**	160
	3.5	8	48	**89**	143
	3.0	5	56	**78**	103
	2.5	5	37	**52**	75
#35	8.0	6	304	**378**	462
	7.5	5	114	**207**	354
	6.5	8	89	**125**	195
	5.5	17	33	**69**	109
#36	8.5	8	203	**329**	380
	8.0	5	200	**323**	500
	7.5	8	101	**160**	205

ISSUE	CGC GRADE	# of AUCTIONS	LOW CLOSE	AVG CLOSE	HIGH CLOSE
	7.0	13	76	**135**	170
#38	9.0	9	243	**354**	430
#42	9.0	5	87	**146**	180
#55	9.4	8	650	**804**	1,100
	8.0	5	76	**146**	250
	7.5	6	89	**96**	104
	7.0	6	51	**76**	100
#56	9.0	8	123	**140**	160
#58	9.4	5	243	**387**	575
	9.2	6	103	**183**	295
#60	9.2	14	203	**308**	456
	9.0	7	259	**286**	344
	8.5	12	80	**169**	250
	8.0	9	48	**142**	218
#61	9.4	5	304	**342**	393
	9.2	9	151	**204**	300
	9.0	7	104	**136**	155
	8.0	5	50	**71**	106
#73	9.4	12	193	**272**	360
	9.2	25	71	**132**	215
	9.0	11	13	**105**	211
	8.5	6	41	**55**	68
#74	9.6	5	174	**278**	500
	9.4	10	100	**149**	203
	9.2	5	61	**94**	117
#75	9.4	5	195	**264**	375
	9.2	7	103	**157**	255
#100	9.4	6	21	**32**	51
#101	9.4	7	13	**24**	54
Silver Streak Comics					
#8	7.0	6	154	**246**	399
Silver Surfer					
#1	9.8	10	32	**52**	73
	9.8	11	20	**23**	26
	9.6	7	2,076	**2,983**	4,100
	9.6	16	14	**30**	50
	9.4	25	788	**1,209**	2,650
	9.2	25	12	**613**	835
	9.0	25	311	**499**	925
	8.5	18	280	**356**	535
	8.0	25	218	**276**	350
	7.5	25	133	**210**	330
	7.0	17	118	**191**	308
	6.5	9	90	**139**	200
	6.0	15	55	**124**	165
	5.5	5	67	**83**	100
	5.0	12	71	**94**	129
	4.5	6	57	**79**	99
	4.0	8	55	**135**	406
	3.0	8	41	**62**	118
#2	9.6	9	455	**978**	1,525
	9.4	20	177	**351**	625
	9.2	25	128	**207**	390
	9.0	25	76	**151**	200
	8.5	6	83	**106**	139
	8.0	25	56	**92**	145
	7.5	14	45	**62**	86
	7.0	13	45	**60**	75
	6.5	8	30	**47**	61

ISSUE	CGC GRADE	# of AUCTIONS	LOW CLOSE	AVG CLOSE	HIGH CLOSE
#3	9.4	10	385	**533**	700
	9.2	11	180	**227**	275
	9.0	12	113	**178**	355
	8.5	24	62	**110**	169
	8.0	8	61	**89**	128
	7.5	7	51	**60**	73
	7.0	6	50	**67**	83
	6.0	6	25	**34**	44
#4	9.6	9	716	**1,603**	2,200
	9.4	25	334	**825**	1,550
	9.2	25	178	**487**	625
	9.0	23	304	**372**	455
	8.5	25	178	**276**	570
	8.0	25	169	**251**	350
	7.5	19	126	**188**	251
	7.0	21	104	**156**	200
	6.5	16	87	**111**	165
	6.0	14	83	**115**	155
	5.5	5	71	**82**	96
	5.0	18	60	**83**	114
	4.5	5	59	**67**	89
#5	9.4	24	153	**269**	379
	9.2	13	63	**159**	230
	9.0	9	63	**94**	150
	8.0	8	36	**68**	100
#6	9.4	9	190	**287**	525
	9.0	11	67	**98**	159
	8.5	6	54	**69**	89
#7	9.4	5	206	**379**	760
	9.2	7	50	**132**	282
	9.0	7	84	**133**	280
	8.5	6	25	**65**	100
	8.0	5	50	**61**	80
#8	9.2	6	97	**113**	130
	9.0	12	63	**83**	134
	8.5	5	50	**59**	80
	7.5	5	24	**33**	41
#9	9.6	5	306	**464**	700
	9.4	7	165	**231**	430
	9.0	7	70	**80**	97
#10	9.4	6	173	**204**	233
	9.2	7	66	**102**	173
	9.0	9	46	**70**	103
	8.5	7	36	**58**	70
	8.0	6	25	**45**	61
#11	9.6	5	305	**336**	359
	9.4	9	79	**253**	380
	9.2	6	124	**151**	189
	8.5	7	42	**63**	76
#12	9.4	6	138	**192**	228
#13	9.2	7	123	**132**	164
#14	9.4	6	317	**472**	710
	9.2	6	143	**193**	323
	9.0	7	98	**153**	208
	8.5	5	80	**104**	134
	5.5	5	16	**25**	30
#15	7.5	6	26	**35**	43
#16	9.4	5	141	**214**	325
	9.2	5	83	**109**	140
#17	9.4	7	133	**200**	294

ISSUE	CGC GRADE	# of AUCTIONS	LOW CLOSE	AVG CLOSE	HIGH CLOSE
	9.2	5	81	**114**	135
	9.0	10	60	**82**	105
	8.0	7	27	**43**	60
#18	9.2	5	98	**139**	162
	8.5	5	43	**55**	66
	7.0	5	21	**42**	87

Simpsons Comics

ISSUE	CGC GRADE	# of AUCTIONS	LOW CLOSE	AVG CLOSE	HIGH CLOSE
#3	9.6	5	11	**18**	20

Sinister House of Secret Love

ISSUE	CGC GRADE	# of AUCTIONS	LOW CLOSE	AVG CLOSE	HIGH CLOSE
#1	9.2	5	154	**208**	299
	8.0	8	35	**72**	115

Six Million Dollar Man

ISSUE	CGC GRADE	# of AUCTIONS	LOW CLOSE	AVG CLOSE	HIGH CLOSE
#1	9.8	5	77	**188**	375
	9.6	7	52	**88**	128
	9.4	17	29	**47**	103

Slam-Bang Comics

ISSUE	CGC GRADE	# of AUCTIONS	LOW CLOSE	AVG CLOSE	HIGH CLOSE
#1	3.5	5	100	**124**	153

Smurfs

ISSUE	CGC GRADE	# of AUCTIONS	LOW CLOSE	AVG CLOSE	HIGH CLOSE
#1	9.4	5	20	**20**	21
#3	9.6	5	20	**20**	21

Snappy Comics

ISSUE	CGC GRADE	# of AUCTIONS	LOW CLOSE	AVG CLOSE	HIGH CLOSE
#1	8.0	7	31	**88**	150

Sojourn

ISSUE	CGC GRADE	# of AUCTIONS	LOW CLOSE	AVG CLOSE	HIGH CLOSE
#1	9.8	17	42	**80**	158
	9.6	25	20	**32**	60
	9.4	11	11	**20**	26

Sojourn Prequel

ISSUE	CGC GRADE	# of AUCTIONS	LOW CLOSE	AVG CLOSE	HIGH CLOSE
#1	9.8	10	25	**42**	57
	9.6	5	16	**21**	27

Solar, Man of the Atom

ISSUE	CGC GRADE	# of AUCTIONS	LOW CLOSE	AVG CLOSE	HIGH CLOSE
#1	9.8	18	43	**120**	305
	9.6	18	20	**36**	80
#2	9.8	6	40	**64**	86
	9.6	7	18	**33**	68
#3	9.8	13	25	**64**	128
	9.6	6	25	**33**	41
#6	9.8	11	25	**44**	96
	9.6	5	17	**21**	25
#7	9.8	8	50	**98**	305
#8	9.8	9	28	**53**	99

ISSUE	CGC GRADE	# of AUCTIONS	LOW CLOSE	AVG CLOSE	HIGH CLOSE
Solar, Man of the Atom (cont'd)					
#10	9.6	18	28	**69**	255
	9.4	25	15	**31**	66
Son of Satan					
#1	9.4	12	32	**60**	153
	8.5	5	11	**16**	20
Space Ghost (Gold Key)					
#1	9.2	8	203	**406**	575
Space War					
#14	9.6	5	26	**76**	123
Spawn					
#1	9.9	19	25	**100**	203
	9.8	25	21	**42**	109
	9.6	25	10	**22**	154
	9.4	25	10	**16**	61
	9.2	20	10	**19**	61
	9.0	10	4	**12**	22
	8.5	6	1	**7**	16
	8.0	6	5	**7**	10
#2	9.8	15	16	**32**	60
	9.6	22	8	**16**	30
	9.4	9	12	**16**	25
#3	9.8	24	12	**25**	69
	9.6	14	9	**15**	35
	9.4	7	7	**10**	13
#4	9.8	25	10	**24**	41
	9.6	13	8	**15**	21
#5	9.8	6	19	**28**	41
	9.6	5	8	**17**	21
#6	9.8	5	25	**39**	71
	9.6	7	2	**14**	26
#7	9.6	5	3	**14**	25
#9	9.8	15	22	**35**	46
	9.6	5	6	**14**	17
	9.4	7	10	**12**	18
#10	9.8	5	16	**23**	30
	9.6	13	1	**17**	36
#11	9.6	8	1	**11**	19
#12	9.8	5	15	**25**	40
	9.6	5	10	**11**	17
#21	9.8	11	20	**35**	56
#100	9.8	20	10	**33**	75
	9.6	9	7	**16**	25
Spawn (black-and-white)					
#1	9.4	9	21	**69**	103
	9.2	5	15	**39**	61
Spawn: The Undead					
#1	9.8	18	10	**27**	38
Special Comics					
#1	5.0	5	355	**415**	455
Special Edition X-Men					
#1	9.8	8	25	**33**	40
	9.6	13	10	**25**	41
Special Marvel Edition					
#3	9.6	5	35	**46**	52

ISSUE	CGC GRADE	# of AUCTIONS	LOW CLOSE	AVG CLOSE	HIGH CLOSE
#15	9.8	7	660	**831**	1,082
	9.6	21	184	**262**	342
	9.4	25	103	**165**	229
	9.2	25	26	**69**	104
	9.0	25	12	**61**	120
	8.5	14	21	**30**	50
	8.0	7	13	**27**	41
#16	9.4	10	31	**64**	100
	9.2	9	15	**31**	50
Spectacular Spider-Man					
#1	9.8	25	86	**269**	515
	9.8	25	16	**26**	82
	9.6	25	28	**76**	153
	9.6	14	10	**16**	22
	9.4	25	14	**42**	81
	9.2	25	17	**36**	135
	9.0	25	15	**28**	51
	8.5	25	10	**25**	76
	8.0	23	8	**20**	47
	7.5	9	10	**18**	34
#2	9.8	5	4	**24**	33
	9.6	25	20	**36**	54
	9.4	11	16	**40**	175
	9.2	5	10	**15**	19
#3	9.8	19	25	**53**	100
	9.8	5	25	**29**	33
	9.6	25	10	**26**	45
	9.4	18	1	**14**	29
#4	9.8	8	26	**54**	77
	9.6	13	12	**35**	85
#5	9.6	7	30	**32**	38
	9.4	9	10	**17**	27
#6	9.8	8	42	**60**	100
	9.6	21	15	**25**	47
	9.4	8	10	**19**	28
#7	9.8	10	31	**66**	110
	9.6	25	11	**22**	35
#8	9.6	13	16	**26**	40
#9	9.6	15	13	**26**	37
#27	9.6	24	48	**74**	118
	9.4	10	31	**47**	90
#28	9.6	11	16	**44**	76
#58	9.8	5	20	**22**	25
	9.6	5	10	**19**	30
#81	9.8	9	16	**25**	40
#83	9.4	5	16	**29**	45
#90	9.8	5	21	**46**	92
	9.6	8	15	**20**	30
#91	9.8	5	14	**29**	65
#93	9.8	6	15	**22**	25
#96	9.8	11	11	**19**	28
#97	9.8	5	11	**19**	28
#100	9.8	6	25	**38**	51
#101	9.8	5	25	**41**	96
#107	9.8	7	13	**27**	46
#116	9.4	6	9	**13**	20
#147	9.6	7	11	**22**	37
#158	9.6	11	10	**20**	35
#189	9.8	5	14	**36**	81
	9.6	5	6	**22**	60

ISSUE	CGC GRADE	# of AUCTIONS	LOW CLOSE	AVG CLOSE	HIGH CLOSE
#200	9.8	25	13	**24**	43
	9.6	11	6	**17**	30
	9.4	12	10	**20**	67

Spectacular Spider-Man Annual

ISSUE	CGC GRADE	# of AUCTIONS	LOW CLOSE	AVG CLOSE	HIGH CLOSE
#1	9.6	11	14	**35**	90

Spectacular Spider-Man Magazine

ISSUE	CGC GRADE	# of AUCTIONS	LOW CLOSE	AVG CLOSE	HIGH CLOSE
#1	9.4	6	203	**289**	369
	9.2	9	85	**128**	169
	9.0	8	67	**85**	139
#2	9.6	18	233	**411**	760
	9.4	21	136	**199**	400
	9.2	9	104	**120**	136
	9.0	10	76	**109**	173
	8.5	10	41	**76**	139

Spectre, The

ISSUE	CGC GRADE	# of AUCTIONS	LOW CLOSE	AVG CLOSE	HIGH CLOSE
#1	9.4	8	15	**538**	788
	9.4	8	3	**11**	25
	9.2	7	129	**185**	305
	8.5	7	82	**109**	153
	6.5	9	21	**33**	41
#2	9.4	7	81	**132**	164
	9.2	15	41	**84**	133
#3	9.6	8	203	**275**	375
	9.4	10	88	**143**	232
	9.0	10	36	**60**	80
	8.0	5	21	**33**	52
#4	9.4	11	89	**151**	180
#6	9.4	5	76	**120**	175
#10	9.2	5	39	**69**	125

Speed Comics

ISSUE	CGC GRADE	# of AUCTIONS	LOW CLOSE	AVG CLOSE	HIGH CLOSE
#38	7.5	6	25	**115**	169

Spider-Man

ISSUE	CGC GRADE	# of AUCTIONS	LOW CLOSE	AVG CLOSE	HIGH CLOSE
#0.5	9.8	5	10	**29**	40
	9.6	7	10	**13**	24
#1	10.0	13	158	**531**	1,032
	9.9	25	43	**111**	300
	9.8	25	10	**31**	169
	9.6	25	10	**20**	80
	9.4	25	1	**20**	108
	9.2	18	8	**16**	26
	9.0	25	1	**15**	30
	8.5	17	3	**12**	17
	8.0	20	1	**9**	17
#1/Gld	9.8	25	29	**75**	220
	9.6	11	21	**41**	100
	9.4	6	15	**29**	67
	8.5	6	8	**16**	22
#1/Plt	9.6	5	80	**254**	380
	9.4	25	100	**163**	290
	9.2	25	75	**110**	238
	9.0	25	48	**99**	145
	8.5	20	38	**62**	103
	8.0	6	50	**66**	103
#1/G.UPC	9.8	11	251	**309**	349
	9.6	25	103	**171**	305
	9.4	25	51	**143**	298
	9.2	6	76	**114**	160

ISSUE	CGC GRADE	# of AUCTIONS	LOW CLOSE	AVG CLOSE	HIGH CLOSE
	9.0	15	51	**89**	140
#2	9.8	16	10	**26**	59
	9.6	13	7	**16**	37
#3	9.8	8	10	**24**	41
	9.6	7	8	**37**	96
#4	9.8	5	20	**29**	50
#5	9.6	7	13	**44**	89
#6	9.8	13	10	**32**	99
	9.6	13	10	**19**	25
#7	9.8	10	13	**23**	35
	9.6	25	10	**30**	89
#8	9.8	18	11	**45**	179
	9.6	10	11	**18**	25
#9	9.8	25	10	**32**	139
#10	9.8	16	10	**30**	139
	9.6	9	9	**12**	19
#11	9.6	5	6	**13**	17
#12	9.8	13	10	**23**	43
	9.6	5	12	**15**	21
#13	9.8	10	14	**35**	81
	9.6	5	11	**15**	20
#14	9.8	5	16	**22**	25
	9.6	8	10	**14**	16
#16	9.8	11	13	**24**	33
#17	9.6	5	19	**23**	26
#18	9.8	5	15	**23**	25
	9.6	5	9	**15**	25
#19	9.8	8	15	**26**	36
#22	9.8	7	10	**21**	27
#26	9.8	11	2	**23**	35
	9.6	7	7	**15**	25

Spider-Man and His Amazing Friends

ISSUE	CGC GRADE	# of AUCTIONS	LOW CLOSE	AVG CLOSE	HIGH CLOSE
#1	9.6	18	25	**47**	128

Spider-Man and the Hulk Special Edition

ISSUE	CGC GRADE	# of AUCTIONS	LOW CLOSE	AVG CLOSE	HIGH CLOSE
#0	9.6	8	23	**34**	60

Spider-Man and Wolverine

ISSUE	CGC GRADE	# of AUCTIONS	LOW CLOSE	AVG CLOSE	HIGH CLOSE
#1	9.6	11	12	**16**	20

Spider-Man/Black Cat

ISSUE	CGC GRADE	# of AUCTIONS	LOW CLOSE	AVG CLOSE	HIGH CLOSE
#1	9.8	25	10	**20**	50
	9.6	19	10	**15**	21
#2	9.8	25	6	**16**	33
	9.6	5	9	**12**	15
#3	9.6	5	8	**14**	26

ISSUE	CGC GRADE	# of AUCTIONS	LOW CLOSE	AVG CLOSE	HIGH CLOSE
Spider-Man: Blue					
#1	9.8	25	12	**23**	47
	9.6	18	8	**16**	45
#2	9.8	9	10	**21**	30
#3	9.8	8	9	**18**	26
#4	9.8	7	8	**13**	25
Spider-Man/Daredevil					
#1	9.8	14	20	**29**	40
	9.6	11	11	**20**	35
Spider-Man/Doctor Octopus					
#1	9.8	12	9	**23**	40
Spider-Man: Maximum Clonage Alpha					
#1	9.8	9	10	**19**	35
Spider-Man: Maximum Clonage Omega					
#1	9.8	10	1	**17**	27
Spider-Man: Official Movie Adaptation					
#1	9.8	25	8	**20**	40
Spider-Man: Quality of Life					
#1	9.8	9	10	**19**	25
	9.6	7	10	**11**	15
Spider-Man Special Edition					
#1	9.4	5	4	**24**	51
Spider-Man: Sweet Charity					
#1	9.8	6	15	**20**	25
Spider-Man 2099					
#1	9.8	12	8	**20**	26
Spider-Man Unlimited					
#1	9.8	25	10	**26**	52
	9.8	5	25	**33**	45
	9.6	7	11	**15**	23
	9.2	7	7	**10**	13
#2	9.8	6	18	**23**	29
Spider-Man vs. Wolverine					
#1	9.8	13	50	**120**	182
	9.6	25	19	**36**	81
	9.4	14	12	**25**	42
	9.2	7	10	**21**	35
	9.0	7	8	**14**	29
	8.0	6	3	**11**	20
Spider-Woman					
#1	9.8	15	64	**118**	183
	9.6	25	14	**29**	60
	9.4	25	11	**21**	40
	9.2	17	10	**17**	29
#38	9.8	5	28	**42**	68
	9.4	5	15	**18**	21
Spidey Super Stories					
#1	9.6	6	125	**169**	305
	9.4	6	31	**58**	91
	9.2	8	22	**38**	57
	9.0	8	26	**33**	50
#7	9.4	5	17	**23**	26

ISSUE	CGC GRADE	# of AUCTIONS	LOW CLOSE	AVG CLOSE	HIGH CLOSE
Stalker, The					
#1	9.6	5	25	**36**	56
Star Hunters					
#1	9.6	8	3	**19**	25
Star Spangled Comics					
#27	8.0	6	24	**192**	405
Star Spangled War Stories					
#139	8.5	5	39	**49**	57
#151	8.5	5	67	**94**	138
Star Trek (1st series/Gold Key)					
#12	9.4	11	22	**64**	114
#15	9.2	5	24	**61**	101
Star Trek (2nd series/Marvel)					
#1	9.8	10	31	**50**	110
	9.6	19	10	**28**	61
	9.4	10	10	**19**	26
Star Trek (3rd series/DC)					
#1	9.8	6	14	**25**	30
	9.6	7	25	**34**	89
	9.6	10	15	**23**	29
Star Wars					
#1	9.8	25	178	**345**	600
	9.6	25	21	**106**	204
	9.4	25	10	**59**	100
	9.2	25	17	**41**	75
	9.0	25	16	**31**	61
	8.5	16	18	**32**	50
	8.0	12	16	**26**	48
	7.5	7	11	**25**	51
#2	9.8	5	58	**105**	163
	9.6	25	20	**43**	100
	9.4	9	15	**31**	45
	9.0	6	8	**19**	30
#3	9.6	18	16	**49**	100
	9.4	9	14	**25**	45
	9.0	7	1	**16**	30
#4	9.6	8	29	**57**	103
	9.4	12	10	**22**	60
#5	9.2	18	2	**13**	30
#6	9.6	6	46	**66**	108
	9.4	11	6	**23**	51
#8	9.8	6	27	**35**	48
	9.6	8	21	**34**	56
#9	9.6	6	16	**33**	42
#10	9.6	9	11	**25**	42
#11	9.6	7	13	**25**	37
#12	9.6	5	24	**44**	77
#13	9.6	10	17	**30**	41
#14	9.6	9	20	**30**	52
#15	9.6	8	21	**41**	80
#16	9.6	11	9	**30**	51
#18	9.6	8	11	**30**	46
#23	9.4	7	9	**18**	42
#28	9.6	8	16	**26**	37
#39	9.6	9	1	**22**	42
#41	9.6	7	10	**29**	54

ISSUE	CGC GRADE	# of AUCTIONS	LOW CLOSE	AVG CLOSE	HIGH CLOSE
#43	9.6	10	6	**25**	42
	9.4	5	2	**12**	16
#44	9.6	15	6	**25**	48
#56	9.6	5	19	**25**	45
#65	9.8	5	25	**30**	48
#77	9.8	7	19	**27**	33
#84	9.8	5	19	**33**	41
#102	7.5	10	1	**3**	10
#103	8.5	5	1	**7**	15
#105	7.0	9	1	**2**	11
#107	9.6	7	75	**128**	228
	9.4	13	46	**73**	114
	9.2	9	23	**39**	51
	8.5	7	16	**31**	61
	8.0	6	10	**29**	41

Star Wars Annual

ISSUE	CGC GRADE	# of AUCTIONS	LOW CLOSE	AVG CLOSE	HIGH CLOSE
#1	9.9	6	108	**184**	311
	9.8	10	36	**82**	196
	9.6	11	19	**39**	82

Star Wars: Dark Empire

ISSUE	CGC GRADE	# of AUCTIONS	LOW CLOSE	AVG CLOSE	HIGH CLOSE
#1	9.8	7	20	**26**	35
	8.5	9	1	**4**	15
#3	9.2	16	1	**3**	9
#4	9.0	13	1	**2**	6
#5	9.4	14	1	**3**	8
	9.2	11	1	**2**	6
#6	9.2	16	1	**2**	8

Star Wars: Return of The Jedi

ISSUE	CGC GRADE	# of AUCTIONS	LOW CLOSE	AVG CLOSE	HIGH CLOSE
#1	9.6	9	8	**16**	23
#2	9.6	6	6	**12**	25
#4	9.8	7	5	**20**	26

Starfire

ISSUE	CGC GRADE	# of AUCTIONS	LOW CLOSE	AVG CLOSE	HIGH CLOSE
#1	9.6	11	10	**21**	40

Startling Comics

ISSUE	CGC GRADE	# of AUCTIONS	LOW CLOSE	AVG CLOSE	HIGH CLOSE
#1	5.0	11	203	**427**	677
#49	4.5	10	610	**763**	1,076

Strange Adventures

ISSUE	CGC GRADE	# of AUCTIONS	LOW CLOSE	AVG CLOSE	HIGH CLOSE
#14	4.0	5	22	**34**	52
#212	9.4	5	139	**166**	195
#213	9.4	7	31	**112**	165

Strange Suspense Stories

ISSUE	CGC GRADE	# of AUCTIONS	LOW CLOSE	AVG CLOSE	HIGH CLOSE
#1	7.0	6	103	**199**	275

Strange Tales

ISSUE	CGC GRADE	# of AUCTIONS	LOW CLOSE	AVG CLOSE	HIGH CLOSE
#97	7.5	7	280	**412**	587
#101	8.0	12	405	**650**	860
	7.5	6	255	**450**	575
	6.0	6	200	**234**	273
#102	8.0	6	185	**233**	260
	7.5	7	110	**143**	173
#105	9.0	5	297	**370**	430
#107	9.0	7	455	**524**	611
#109	9.0	7	202	**262**	300
	8.0	5	86	**105**	115
#110	9.0	6	1,005	**1,483**	1,825
	7.5	7	510	**587**	716
	5.0	5	173	**193**	205
	3.5	5	71	**140**	219
#114	9.0	9	391	**502**	700
#115	9.0	9	365	**556**	655
	4.5	12	37	**59**	101
#117	8.0	5	57	**75**	90
#121	8.0	5	39	**44**	48
#127	9.0	6	50	**122**	159
#133	9.0	7	33	**100**	178
#135	9.2	8	200	**316**	555
#138	9.4	13	66	**108**	258
	9.2	12	37	**61**	85
	9.0	7	23	**42**	68
#147	9.6	11	89	**131**	180
	9.2	5	42	**53**	80
#150	9.2	6	46	**62**	89
#159	9.2	6	57	**90**	140
#163	9.4	5	82	**155**	317
#167	9.4	5	205	**269**	316
	9.2	5	91	**114**	165
	9.0	5	55	**71**	80
	8.5	5	28	**40**	57
#178	9.6	16	27	**90**	178
	9.4	15	33	**45**	61
	9.2	7	17	**33**	58
#179	9.6	6	50	**80**	139
	9.4	5	26	**38**	49

Strange Tales Annual

ISSUE	CGC GRADE	# of AUCTIONS	LOW CLOSE	AVG CLOSE	HIGH CLOSE
#2	8.5	5	724	**767**	800
	7.5	10	153	**339**	511

Strange Worlds

ISSUE	CGC GRADE	# of AUCTIONS	LOW CLOSE	AVG CLOSE	HIGH CLOSE
#4	4.0	7	151	**185**	258

Street Fighter

ISSUE	CGC GRADE	# of AUCTIONS	LOW CLOSE	AVG CLOSE	HIGH CLOSE
#0/DF	9.8	6	10	**25**	45
#0/DF Sk	9.8	11	10	**17**	25
#1	9.8	8	25	**40**	50
#1/HF	9.8	7	16	**38**	50

Sub-Mariner

ISSUE	CGC GRADE	# of AUCTIONS	LOW CLOSE	AVG CLOSE	HIGH CLOSE
#1	9.8	13	25	**1,180**	1,750
	9.6	25	310	**505**	760
	9.4	25	205	**321**	455
	9.2	25	128	**202**	305
	9.0	25	75	**159**	260
	8.5	23	57	**114**	153

ISSUE	CGC GRADE	# of AUCTIONS	LOW CLOSE	AVG CLOSE	HIGH CLOSE
Sub-Mariner (cont'd)					
	8.0	19	51	**87**	140
	7.5	25	50	**77**	130
	7.0	12	45	**64**	100
	6.5	9	38	**55**	76
	6.0	12	26	**45**	78
#2	9.6	25	128	**193**	535
	9.4	25	73	**122**	201
	9.2	11	49	**65**	90
	9.0	5	50	**64**	90
	8.0	5	42	**51**	66
#3	9.4	6	103	**131**	155
	9.2	11	27	**48**	70
	9.0	5	37	**47**	60
#5	7.5	5	10	**25**	51
#6	9.6	5	139	**185**	225
	9.4	14	46	**88**	128
	9.2	10	37	**53**	75
	8.5	5	19	**21**	25
	8.0	7	14	**26**	36
#7	9.4	5	81	**89**	102
	9.2	8	36	**50**	75
#8	9.6	5	504	**586**	667
	9.4	6	150	**257**	376
	9.2	5	98	**121**	183
	9.0	10	66	**98**	134
	8.0	7	33	**43**	57
#10	9.2	5	29	**49**	60
#11	9.6	7	121	**185**	260
#12	9.4	5	66	**100**	128
#13	9.6	6	81	**133**	206
	9.2	5	36	**48**	55
#27	9.6	9	43	**63**	113
#28	9.4	5	33	**48**	60
#34	9.0	6	52	**65**	81
#35	9.2	8	61	**122**	182
#36	9.4	7	17	**48**	64
#44	9.2	6	11	**31**	46
#47	9.4	5	27	**76**	128
#49	9.4	5	34	**42**	51
#59	9.4	6	55	**75**	105
#62	9.6	6	50	**69**	95
#66	9.6	7	36	**61**	100
Sub-Mariner Comics					
#2	4.0	5	663	**903**	1,095
Sugar and Spike					
#96	9.4	7	40	**77**	195
Suicide Squad					
#1	9.4	8	1	**6**	15
Superboy					
#1	7.0	12	1,025	**1,702**	3,000
#3	4.5	5	225	**243**	256
#100	9.0	6	81	**173**	250
#137	9.2	5	25	**55**	76
#202	9.2	7	31	**44**	56
Super DC Giant					
#17	9.0	6	142	**257**	400

ISSUE	CGC GRADE	# of AUCTIONS	LOW CLOSE	AVG CLOSE	HIGH CLOSE
#23	9.2	5	27	**50**	85
#24	9.2	8	25	**32**	41
#25	9.2	6	1	**23**	46
Super Friends					
#1	9.4	8	20	**38**	50
Supergirl					
#1	9.4	6	56	**115**	156
	9.0	11	16	**35**	50
#75	9.8	7	20	**33**	50
	9.6	6	22	**32**	51
Superman					
#1	9.8	9	40	**60**	71
	9.6	11	10	**36**	75
#2	7.0	6	3,900	**4,741**	6,395
#4	4.5	5	500	**921**	1,395
#10	5.0	5	482	**583**	749
#11	7.0	5	770	**894**	1,100
#12	6.0	5	330	**497**	600
	4.5	5	335	**377**	461
	4.0	6	243	**285**	315
#13	4.0	6	263	**421**	545
#16	5.0	6	326	**354**	420
#24	5.0	6	360	**491**	651
#25	5.5	5	230	**285**	431
#27	6.0	5	198	**249**	317
#29	7.0	6	355	**410**	550
#30	7.0	11	527	**759**	1,100
#31	7.0	6	280	**310**	346
#35	8.0	8	105	**406**	700
	7.5	10	15	**346**	575
#36	8.5	5	237	**688**	1,225
	7.5	6	298	**440**	550
#39	6.0	5	195	**226**	280
#53	4.0	7	266	**369**	520
#75	9.8	10	48	**63**	92
	9.6	25	7	**30**	50
	9.4	14	10	**32**	128
	9.2	8	9	**16**	30
#75/Plt	9.2	6	31	**55**	77
#100	4.0	5	150	**241**	350
#192	9.4	5	72	**157**	228
#199	9.0	5	214	**417**	750
	8.0	9	46	**122**	199
#200	9.8	9	15	**28**	40
#201	9.8	8	15	**23**	34
#202	9.9	6	62	**89**	145
	9.8	25	10	**22**	40
#203	10.0	5	159	**201**	240
	9.9	6	54	**75**	90
	9.8	25	16	**23**	35
#204	9.9	20	66	**144**	285
	9.8	25	20	**32**	43
#205	9.8	25	20	**26**	33
	9.6	5	11	**16**	20
#206	9.8	13	19	**23**	25
#207	9.8	6	23	**23**	25
#233	9.4	8	302	**355**	510
#238	9.4	5	58	**71**	96

ISSUE	CGC GRADE	# of AUCTIONS	LOW CLOSE	AVG CLOSE	HIGH CLOSE
	9.2	5	29	**34**	40
#249	9.2	5	26	**41**	51
#252	9.4	5	166	**296**	400
#400	9.8	8	19	**40**	76
	9.6	8	13	**20**	27
Superman Annual					
#1	5.5	5	56	**80**	123
Superman/Batman					
#1	9.8	25	23	**47**	113
	9.6	25	16	**29**	90
	9.4	15	10	**21**	30
	9.2	5	13	**21**	28
#1/3rd	9.8	24	29	**43**	70
#1/RRP	9.6	21	225	**333**	550
	9.4	25	181	**259**	361
	9.2	15	133	**195**	300
	9.0	6	118	**159**	238
#3	9.8	20	17	**30**	37
	9.6	5	1	**8**	20
#4	9.8	20	13	**24**	41
#5	9.8	20	16	**26**	36
#6	9.8	13	15	**23**	33
#7	9.8	16	15	**24**	33
#8	9.8	25	17	**25**	100
	9.6	5	11	**15**	19
#8/2nd	9.8	25	19	**28**	40
#8/3rd	9.8	19	25	**25**	27
#9	9.8	24	18	**25**	33
#10	9.8	25	20	**29**	33
#11	9.8	22	20	**22**	30
Superman Family					
#165	9.4	5	31	**53**	82
#170	9.4	7	23	**35**	50
Superman: Red Son					
#1	9.8	25	31	**57**	123
	9.6	12	19	**30**	50
#2	9.8	8	25	**31**	40
#3	9.8	5	15	**31**	50
Superman's Girlfriend Lois Lane					
#66	9.0	5	21	**34**	47
#67	8.5	5	21	**32**	50
#70	8.0	6	103	**168**	214
#71	9.2	10	114	**181**	250
#117	9.4	5	30	**46**	61
Superman's Pal Jimmy Olsen					
#19	3.0	5	11	**18**	27
#137	9.4	7	29	**49**	72
#142	9.6	5	76	**118**	153
#145	9.2	5	16	**30**	51
#147	9.6	6	77	**103**	143
Superman: The Man of Steel					
#1	9.8	22	20	**34**	54
	9.6	15	6	**16**	31
#18	9.8	5	33	**51**	76
#19	9.8	8	13	**37**	56

ISSUE	CGC GRADE	# of AUCTIONS	LOW CLOSE	AVG CLOSE	HIGH CLOSE
Superman: The Wedding Album					
#1	9.8	25	13	**21**	31
Supernatural Thrillers					
#1	9.4	5	77	**101**	128
#4	9.4	7	26	**41**	60
#5	9.8	7	228	**336**	450
	9.6	9	113	**149**	225
	9.4	16	61	**101**	200
	9.2	6	41	**54**	95
	9.0	10	22	**44**	65
#9	9.6	5	43	**61**	80
Super Powers					
#1	9.8	9	19	**23**	26
#2	9.9	10	19	**33**	50
#3	9.8	6	15	**21**	26
Super-Team Family					
#1	9.4	5	19	**36**	50
Super-Villain Team-Up					
#1	9.6	25	26	**46**	113
	9.4	16	21	**38**	60
	9.2	5	16	**22**	30
	9.0	5	14	**22**	44
Supreme Power					
#1	9.8	25	20	**32**	81
	9.6	21	10	**18**	30
#2	9.8	9	8	**21**	27
#3	9.8	8	10	**19**	27
#5	9.8	5	13	**23**	35
#6	9.8	11	11	**19**	35
#7	9.8	6	15	**23**	30
Swamp Thing					
#1	9.8	25	10	**19**	33
	9.6	17	21	**430**	675
	9.4	25	154	**226**	350
	9.2	25	75	**122**	203
	9.0	25	51	**101**	415
	8.5	8	53	**77**	125
	8.0	10	25	**59**	100
	7.5	12	28	**42**	52
	5.0	5	10	**16**	21
#2	9.4	11	68	**109**	248
	9.2	5	40	**55**	92

ISSUE	CGC GRADE	# of AUCTIONS	LOW CLOSE	AVG CLOSE	HIGH CLOSE
Swamp Thing (cont'd)					
	9.0	5	26	**49**	75
	8.5	6	11	**27**	54
#3	9.4	10	25	**64**	100
	9.2	6	30	**38**	57
#4	9.6	5	94	**157**	240
	9.4	13	37	**63**	97
#5	9.4	7	38	**65**	108
	9.2	6	28	**35**	41
#6	9.6	6	89	**123**	178
	9.4	5	35	**50**	67
	9.2	8	20	**26**	41
#7	9.6	5	66	**123**	153
	9.4	12	61	**80**	114
	9.2	6	26	**42**	50
	9.0	8	23	**32**	40
	8.5	6	14	**25**	55
#8	9.6	9	51	**87**	160
	9.4	9	40	**48**	65
#9	9.6	21	41	**78**	113
	9.4	15	26	**46**	75
	9.2	8	21	**29**	36
	9.0	5	19	**25**	30
#10	9.6	12	60	**89**	125
#12	9.4	5	21	**29**	41
#17	9.4	5	17	**25**	39
#23	9.8	8	25	**28**	37
Sword of Sorcery					
#1	9.4	6	25	**32**	39
Tales from the Crypt					
#34	8.5	6	203	**274**	400
#38	5.5	5	64	**85**	107
Tales of Asgard					
#1	9.4	12	78	**117**	159
Tales of Evil					
#1	9.4	5	19	**32**	66
Tales of Ghost Castle					
#1	9.6	7	43	**83**	154
	9.4	17	15	**35**	50
Tales of Suspense					
#23	7.0	5	84	**99**	120
#27	8.0	7	85	**179**	318
#37	8.5	11	92	**151**	213
#39	7.5	11	1,825	**2,407**	3,630
	6.5	8	911	**1,159**	1,475
	5.5	12	500	**794**	1,625
	5.0	15	668	**890**	1,500
	4.5	8	481	**662**	936
	4.0	10	423	**532**	750
	3.5	13	279	**440**	537
	3.0	7	285	**412**	523
	1.5	5	178	**245**	305
#40	8.0	5	561	**767**	985
	6.5	6	270	**297**	338
	6.0	8	270	**351**	500
	5.0	5	203	**260**	305

ISSUE	CGC GRADE	# of AUCTIONS	LOW CLOSE	AVG CLOSE	HIGH CLOSE
	4.5	6	67	**128**	192
	3.0	5	67	**111**	142
#41	7.5	6	204	**321**	399
#42	9.0	6	147	**757**	1,416
	7.5	5	169	**211**	285
#43	8.0	7	220	**302**	375
#47	9.2	6	480	**802**	1,301
	9.0	9	256	**363**	711
#48	6.5	7	72	**92**	102
#49	8.0	7	211	**281**	483
	7.0	5	140	**181**	212
#52	8.5	7	175	**263**	348
#56	8.5	6	75	**114**	200
#57	8.0	7	153	**166**	180
#58	9.0	6	355	**415**	500
	7.5	9	56	**106**	150
	7.0	5	81	**108**	150
#59	9.2	6	399	**504**	587
	9.0	11	230	**329**	450
	8.5	12	150	**210**	326
	7.5	6	89	**119**	162
#61	9.2	6	124	**163**	199
#63	8.5	12	134	**166**	275
	8.0	6	114	**136**	150
#64	6.5	8	10	**35**	75
#65	8.5	5	56	**104**	131
#66	9.2	6	158	**230**	355
	8.5	5	76	**95**	113
	8.0	8	39	**72**	100
#67	9.0	7	72	**96**	149
#70	9.2	5	73	**118**	182
#71	9.2	14	61	**88**	138
#74	9.4	20	76	**138**	200
	9.2	5	57	**75**	93
	9.0	7	25	**47**	62
#80	9.4	8	133	**151**	179
	9.2	6	73	**93**	120
	9.0	8	56	**68**	76
#82	9.2	7	51	**86**	120
#83	9.4	6	134	**177**	225
	9.2	7	52	**59**	70
	9.0	5	43	**50**	57
	8.0	7	20	**31**	63
#85	9.4	9	94	**156**	214
	9.0	5	43	**53**	70
#86	9.4	6	134	**159**	181
#87	9.0	5	41	**59**	90
#88	9.2	11	46	**63**	87
	9.0	5	32	**44**	51
	6.0	6	1	**13**	22
#89	9.4	14	82	**140**	200
	9.2	8	50	**68**	96
#92	9.4	12	71	**149**	178
	9.2	5	54	**73**	89
#94	9.4	5	84	**173**	295
#96	9.4	7	102	**164**	192
#97	9.6	5	280	**357**	445
	9.2	6	46	**68**	82
#98	9.6	7	178	**252**	400
	9.4	6	150	**191**	225
	9.0	10	27	**53**	79

Tales of the Teen Titans

ISSUE	CGC GRADE	# of AUCTIONS	LOW CLOSE	AVG CLOSE	HIGH CLOSE
#42	9.8	5	15	**22**	36
#43	9.8	5	15	**22**	40
#44	9.8	16	29	**45**	100
	9.6	7	14	**28**	39
	9.4	6	13	**21**	30

Tales of the Unexpected

ISSUE	CGC GRADE	# of AUCTIONS	LOW CLOSE	AVG CLOSE	HIGH CLOSE
#79	9.0	5	25	**58**	83

Tales to Astonish

ISSUE	CGC GRADE	# of AUCTIONS	LOW CLOSE	AVG CLOSE	HIGH CLOSE
#7	7.5	7	16	**181**	320
#17	7.5	5	103	**150**	220
#27	6.0	5	684	**785**	953
	5.0	8	260	**509**	750
	2.5	12	175	**252**	381
#30	8.0	11	101	**138**	201
#35	7.0	7	356	**461**	565
	5.0	10	38	**190**	300
	3.5	5	108	**142**	210
#36	8.5	9	370	**481**	635
	8.0	7	255	**359**	467
	7.5	5	256	**280**	305
	7.0	6	149	**195**	250
	4.5	6	41	**73**	100
#38	5.0	6	46	**69**	99
#39	9.0	5	377	**423**	455
	8.5	5	88	**158**	260
#40	8.0	5	158	**211**	300
#44	8.0	5	228	**274**	325
	7.0	6	129	**166**	265
#45	9.2	5	228	**346**	465
#47	9.2	5	286	**321**	406
#49	8.0	7	103	**147**	230
#50	9.0	8	94	**155**	245
#51	9.2	10	170	**207**	250
	8.5	6	72	**93**	117
#54	7.5	5	27	**68**	168
#55	9.2	7	86	**162**	250
#56	9.2	6	158	**194**	222
	8.5	9	62	**88**	149
	7.5	5	39	**53**	86
#57	9.4	7	811	**1,057**	1,353
	7.0	7	77	**119**	201
#59	7.5	5	99	**142**	188
	7.0	5	79	**113**	145
#65	9.2	8	137	**178**	267
	8.5	5	42	**82**	130
#66	9.0	7	77	**116**	159
#67	8.5	5	65	**72**	80
#68	8.0	5	50	**56**	69
#70	9.0	7	73	**111**	147
	7.0	9	23	**39**	59
#78	7.5	5	10	**19**	31
#79	9.4	5	180	**217**	301
	9.2	5	82	**114**	178
	8.5	5	25	**61**	125
#83	9.0	5	28	**54**	70
	8.5	6	31	**38**	46
#84	9.4	6	128	**157**	190
	9.0	7	34	**58**	76
#86	9.4	9	96	**140**	203
#89	9.4	9	79	**159**	238
	9.2	6	60	**71**	82
	8.0	5	21	**29**	35
#91	9.2	7	72	**99**	121
#92	9.4	5	104	**158**	240
#93	9.2	17	57	**186**	301
	8.5	5	63	**81**	105
	7.5	6	38	**52**	60
#94	9.4	8	113	**131**	170
	9.2	7	31	**49**	57
	9.0	8	23	**49**	70
#95	9.4	5	128	**168**	226
#96	9.4	6	79	**125**	159
	9.2	7	42	**63**	99
#98	9.4	7	110	**138**	175
	9.2	6	53	**69**	82
	9.0	5	43	**53**	80
#100	9.6	5	457	**520**	611
	9.4	5	116	**165**	198
	9.2	8	70	**92**	114
	9.0	7	50	**75**	98
	8.0	9	26	**36**	46
#101	9.2	5	77	**101**	128
	9.0	9	40	**74**	120
	8.5	13	25	**56**	95
	8.0	6	24	**35**	40

Tarzan

ISSUE	CGC GRADE	# of AUCTIONS	LOW CLOSE	AVG CLOSE	HIGH CLOSE
#207	9.6	5	83	**118**	154
	9.4	9	23	**66**	123
	9.2	6	14	**34**	45

Tarzan (Lord of the Jungle)

ISSUE	CGC GRADE	# of AUCTIONS	LOW CLOSE	AVG CLOSE	HIGH CLOSE
#1	9.8	9	30	**59**	80
	9.6	23	10	**31**	72
	9.4	5	13	**21**	28

Taskmaster

ISSUE	CGC GRADE	# of AUCTIONS	LOW CLOSE	AVG CLOSE	HIGH CLOSE
#1	9.6	5	6	**8**	10

Teen Titans

ISSUE	CGC GRADE	# of AUCTIONS	LOW CLOSE	AVG CLOSE	HIGH CLOSE
#1	9.8	25	17	**42**	118
	9.6	6	11	**25**	39
	9.6	25	9	**26**	56
	5.0	6	43	**56**	75
#1/2nd	9.8	9	20	**30**	41
#1/4th	9.8	25	12	**25**	41

ISSUE	CGC GRADE	# of AUCTIONS	LOW CLOSE	AVG CLOSE	HIGH CLOSE
Teen Titans (cont'd)					
#1/Sk	9.8	10	25	**31**	35
#1/DF	9.8	6	21	**50**	90
#2	9.8	10	16	**32**	80
#2/2nd	9.8	6	14	**26**	40
#3	9.8	5	12	**22**	37
#4	9.8	11	11	**21**	37
#5	9.4	5	94	**148**	206
#6	9.8	5	14	**20**	30
#7	9.8	8	8	**17**	30
#8	9.8	6	10	**18**	29
	9.4	5	71	**128**	160
#9	9.8	7	6	**19**	24
#18	9.4	8	46	**97**	195
#40	9.6	6	19	**61**	93
Thanos					
#1	9.8	25	13	**24**	41
	9.6	5	12	**22**	56
Thanos Quest					
#1	9.8	8	22	**31**	51
The Thing!					
#16	9.4	8	168	**313**	440
	9.0	10	57	**142**	213
	8.5	5	48	**80**	125
	8.0	5	56	**91**	125
	7.5	6	16	**61**	111
Thing					
#1	9.8	15	35	**53**	77
	9.6	8	10	**24**	58
30 Days of Night					
#1	9.4	9	41	**85**	125
	9.2	5	51	**67**	95
#2	9.4	5	35	**54**	75
#3	9.8	21	21	**33**	51
	9.6	5	7	**25**	45
	9.4	5	8	**15**	23
Thor					
#126	8.0	7	36	**93**	163
	6.0	5	32	**40**	53
#127	9.0	5	68	**99**	120
#128	8.5	5	38	**56**	100
#132	9.8	8	208	**391**	650
	9.6	25	105	**182**	340
	9.4	25	46	**106**	178
	9.2	11	31	**55**	76
#134	9.4	8	135	**190**	238
#135	9.2	5	79	**103**	147
#138	9.0	6	36	**52**	85
#139	9.4	7	76	**124**	160
#140	9.0	5	38	**45**	51
	7.5	8	16	**27**	40
#141	9.4	7	103	**145**	180
#142	9.0	5	42	**52**	60
#146	9.4	5	96	**134**	199
	9.0	6	25	**43**	60
#147	9.4	8	86	**137**	178

ISSUE	CGC GRADE	# of AUCTIONS	LOW CLOSE	AVG CLOSE	HIGH CLOSE
#148	9.4	6	100	**162**	188
#149	9.4	5	85	**133**	185
	9.0	8	40	**46**	56
#151	9.4	8	76	**109**	158
#152	9.4	5	62	**99**	134
	9.2	9	34	**53**	68
#153	9.2	6	49	**60**	86
	9.0	10	25	**35**	50
#154	9.4	7	32	**85**	158
	9.0	6	39	**43**	46
#155	9.4	5	72	**112**	135
	8.5	6	24	**30**	55
#156	9.8	7	255	**397**	660
	9.6	7	95	**153**	235
	9.2	6	26	**47**	63
#157	9.2	6	34	**53**	65
#158	9.4	15	145	**183**	275
	9.2	9	36	**72**	135
	9.0	8	46	**59**	75
	8.5	9	24	**42**	90
#159	9.4	7	67	**111**	136
	9.2	9	29	**49**	84
	9.0	10	28	**45**	60
#161	9.4	8	51	**98**	145
#163	9.4	5	67	**95**	145
	9.0	6	16	**25**	28
#165	9.2	5	92	**103**	123
	8.0	10	23	**39**	61
#166	9.4	5	143	**186**	216
	9.2	10	42	**71**	91
	9.0	5	28	**49**	70
#169	9.0	5	43	**53**	71
#173	9.4	6	66	**78**	109
#175	9.4	7	50	**72**	100
#176	9.4	7	45	**78**	125
#180	9.6	7	115	**149**	213
#181	9.4	7	70	**115**	160
#182	9.8	17	114	**193**	445
	9.6	25	52	**84**	137
	9.4	7	39	**58**	82
#193	9.2	13	68	**106**	149
#194	9.4	5	30	**46**	69
#199	9.6	5	46	**69**	96
#222	9.6	6	23	**56**	123
#225	9.4	5	57	**94**	129
#226	9.4	7	30	**43**	104
#232	9.4	5	10	**30**	65
#234	9.6	7	16	**29**	38
#248	9.6	7	19	**26**	50
#249	9.6	9	15	**20**	30
#258	9.2	5	20	**21**	23
#337	9.8	9	62	**136**	229
	9.6	19	16	**29**	50
	9.4	5	14	**31**	53
#338	9.8	7	16	**25**	46
	9.6	8	13	**20**	27
#339	9.8	25	11	**17**	30
	9.6	7	11	**14**	22
#340	9.8	9	16	**24**	42
#341	9.8	12	14	**22**	30

ISSUE	CGC GRADE	# of AUCTIONS	LOW CLOSE	AVG CLOSE	HIGH CLOSE
#342	9.8	16	10	**17**	27
#343	9.8	7	11	**21**	30
#348	9.8	5	17	**22**	25
#350	9.8	5	14	**21**	33
#356	9.8	6	9	**22**	37

Thor (2nd series)

ISSUE	CGC GRADE	# of AUCTIONS	LOW CLOSE	AVG CLOSE	HIGH CLOSE
#1/Sun	9.6	9	16	**25**	51
#1/Sk	9.8	6	45	**64**	80

Thor: Vikings

ISSUE	CGC GRADE	# of AUCTIONS	LOW CLOSE	AVG CLOSE	HIGH CLOSE
#1	9.8	11	13	**19**	25

Thrilling Comics

ISSUE	CGC GRADE	# of AUCTIONS	LOW CLOSE	AVG CLOSE	HIGH CLOSE
#67	7.0	5	124	**138**	154

Thunda

ISSUE	CGC GRADE	# of AUCTIONS	LOW CLOSE	AVG CLOSE	HIGH CLOSE
#1	8.0	6	690	**841**	919

ThunderCats

ISSUE	CGC GRADE	# of AUCTIONS	LOW CLOSE	AVG CLOSE	HIGH CLOSE
#0	9.8	23	9	**15**	27
	9.6	8	8	**12**	19
#1	9.8	25	10	**18**	55
	9.6	12	10	**24**	60
	9.4	7	10	**26**	50

Tiny Tot Comics

ISSUE	CGC GRADE	# of AUCTIONS	LOW CLOSE	AVG CLOSE	HIGH CLOSE
#1	7.0	5	60	**114**	183

TMNT: Teenage Mutant Ninja Turtles

ISSUE	CGC GRADE	# of AUCTIONS	LOW CLOSE	AVG CLOSE	HIGH CLOSE
#1	9.8	5	23	**29**	34

Tomb of Dracula

ISSUE	CGC GRADE	# of AUCTIONS	LOW CLOSE	AVG CLOSE	HIGH CLOSE
#1	9.6	21	404	**549**	750
	9.4	25	215	**339**	550
	9.2	25	104	**168**	215
	9.0	25	73	**111**	175
	8.5	16	41	**74**	130
	8.0	20	43	**67**	120
	7.5	10	21	**46**	69
#2	9.6	7	125	**192**	275
	9.4	6	66	**127**	226
	9.2	9	31	**53**	75
	9.0	6	31	**50**	71
#4	8.0	6	12	**20**	30
#6	9.4	6	40	**89**	145
#8	9.4	5	33	**46**	61
	9.2	5	22	**29**	41
#9	9.4	8	21	**45**	75
#10	9.6	8	466	**659**	840
	9.4	16	225	**355**	600
	9.2	25	51	**158**	262
	9.0	8	76	**102**	138
	8.0	8	42	**82**	180
	7.5	6	16	**46**	71
#12	9.4	5	52	**102**	128
#13	9.4	5	61	**136**	175
#14	9.4	5	33	**59**	102
#17	9.4	8	23	**41**	71
#18	9.4	5	36	**53**	77
	9.2	6	21	**25**	35
#19	9.6	7	52	**112**	206
	9.4	6	21	**72**	169
#32	9.4	6	19	**39**	66
#38	9.4	5	10	**32**	51
#42	9.4	5	20	**27**	36
#58	8.0	5	1	**10**	25
#70	9.8	5	68	**193**	338
	9.6	20	30	**61**	126
	9.4	5	37	**46**	65

Tomb Raider

ISSUE	CGC GRADE	# of AUCTIONS	LOW CLOSE	AVG CLOSE	HIGH CLOSE
#0.5	9.8	6	16	**23**	48
#1	9.8	25	14	**26**	71
	9.6	25	10	**16**	41
	9.4	9	8	**12**	20
#2	9.6	8	8	**16**	25
#4	9.8	9	12	**18**	27
#7	9.6	6	1	**15**	24
#25/Plt	9.8	8	15	**33**	40
	9.6	6	15	**25**	40

Top 10

ISSUE	CGC GRADE	# of AUCTIONS	LOW CLOSE	AVG CLOSE	HIGH CLOSE
#1	9.8	5	10	**19**	30

Top Cat

ISSUE	CGC GRADE	# of AUCTIONS	LOW CLOSE	AVG CLOSE	HIGH CLOSE
#1	9.2	5	31	**128**	265

Top Comics Flintstones

ISSUE	CGC GRADE	# of AUCTIONS	LOW CLOSE	AVG CLOSE	HIGH CLOSE
#3	9.6	8	33	**49**	65
	9.4	6	31	**39**	55

Tor

ISSUE	CGC GRADE	# of AUCTIONS	LOW CLOSE	AVG CLOSE	HIGH CLOSE
#1	9.6	5	26	**45**	56
	9.4	6	10	**29**	61

Transformers

ISSUE	CGC GRADE	# of AUCTIONS	LOW CLOSE	AVG CLOSE	HIGH CLOSE
#1	9.8	8	23	**104**	250
	9.6	25	25	**83**	198
	9.4	11	16	**38**	66
	8.5	5	3	**8**	11
#2	9.8	9	19	**44**	77
	9.6	5	5	**17**	29
#3	9.6	5	28	**33**	45
#4	9.8	7	19	**31**	43
#5	9.8	8	21	**30**	41
	9.6	5	17	**22**	26
	9.2	6	1	**12**	24
#6	9.6	5	6	**17**	30
	9.4	5	18	**20**	25
#79	9.4	5	22	**34**	51

ISSUE	CGC GRADE	# of AUCTIONS	LOW CLOSE	AVG CLOSE	HIGH CLOSE
Transformers (cont'd)					
#80	9.4	7	39	**70**	125
	9.2	7	19	**31**	60
Transformers: Armada					
#1	10.0	5	109	**163**	220
	9.8	9	12	**20**	25
	9.9	9	26	**61**	113
	9.8	25	1	**25**	70
	9.6	25	5	**12**	25
Transformers Generation 1					
#0/Prv	9.8	11	17	**44**	150
	9.6	19	10	**33**	100
	9.4	7	11	**18**	31
#1	9.9	6	28	**63**	103
	9.8	25	3	**16**	71
	9.8	8	10	**23**	50
	9.6	25	3	**14**	41
	9.4	19	6	**15**	51
	9.2	5	3	**10**	28
#1/DF	9.8	6	6	**34**	56
	9.6	5	10	**18**	25
#1/HF	10.0	16	96	**237**	455
	9.9	25	32	**87**	153
	9.9	6	40	**63**	89
	9.8	25	10	**27**	82
	9.8	23	10	**25**	54
	9.6	25	2	**31**	46
	9.4	11	13	**21**	35
#1/Rtl	9.8	25	25	**58**	355
	9.8	20	24	**42**	71
	9.6	25	12	**52**	140
	9.4	25	24	**52**	82
#2	9.8	14	10	**21**	28
	9.6	25	2	**13**	21
	9.4	5	5	**7**	9
#3	9.8	15	5	**18**	26
	9.6	7	8	**14**	27
Transformers: The War Within					
#1	9.6	15	8	**17**	35
Trouble					
#1	9.8	24	11	**24**	40
	9.6	11	9	**12**	18
True 3-D					
#1	8.5	5	31	**40**	45
Truth: Red, White & Black					
#1	9.8	19	7	**21**	39
	9.6	15	6	**15**	25
#2	9.8	6	10	**18**	25
Turok, Dinosaur Hunter					
#1	9.8	11	6	**17**	27
	9.6	5	6	**12**	25
Twilight Zone					
#1	9.4	6	277	**334**	458
Two-Gun Kid					
#83	9.4	6	37	**50**	67

ISSUE	CGC GRADE	# of AUCTIONS	LOW CLOSE	AVG CLOSE	HIGH CLOSE
2001: A Space Odyssey					
#1	9.8	7	16	**66**	104
	9.6	25	16	**31**	57
	9.4	15	11	**20**	32
Ultimate Daredevil					
#1	9.8	9	10	**24**	40
Ultimate Daredevil and Elektra					
#1	9.8	25	14	**26**	63
	9.6	25	10	**18**	31
#2	9.8	11	10	**22**	40
	9.6	19	10	**17**	35
#3	9.6	13	0	**15**	35
#4	9.8	7	14	**26**	45
Ultimate Fantastic Four					
#1	9.9	8	108	**163**	229
	9.8	25	18	**26**	60
	9.6	25	10	**15**	25
	9.4	5	4	**14**	37
#1/DF	9.8	11	31	**54**	93
#2	10.0	5	203	**262**	300
	9.9	5	51	**106**	150
	9.8	25	16	**24**	35
#3	9.8	25	18	**22**	30
#4	9.8	25	16	**23**	30
#5	9.8	15	20	**23**	30
#6	9.8	15	19	**22**	25
#7	9.8	11	23	**26**	34
#8	9.8	7	20	**21**	22
#9	9.8	5	21	**22**	22
Ultimate Marvel Team-Up					
#1	9.8	25	15	**28**	60
	9.6	12	5	**13**	20
	9.4	5	6	**11**	15
#2	9.8	7	17	**29**	62
Ultimates					
#1	9.9	11	66	**101**	185
	9.8	25	16	**25**	103
	9.6	25	8	**16**	100
	9.4	22	1	**17**	67
	9.2	5	7	**10**	13
#2	9.8	25	21	**52**	90
	9.6	25	2	**21**	40
	9.4	10	10	**14**	18
#3	9.8	24	16	**37**	79
	9.6	24	7	**18**	25
	9.4	6	2	**10**	15
#4	9.8	25	16	**41**	81
	9.6	23	9	**20**	36
#5	9.8	7	52	**97**	180
	9.6	25	13	**27**	47
	9.4	15	10	**16**	30
#6	9.8	17	16	**31**	45
	9.6	17	1	**15**	25
	9.4	6	1	**9**	15
#7	9.8	25	9	**23**	51
	9.6	9	9	**17**	26
#8	9.8	25	10	**22**	43

ISSUE	CGC GRADE	# of AUCTIONS	LOW CLOSE	AVG CLOSE	HIGH CLOSE
	9.6	8	11	**17**	23
#9	9.8	7	25	**38**	45
	9.4	6	6	**12**	26
	9.2	5	4	**10**	18
#10	9.8	17	10	**22**	37
	9.6	6	6	**13**	20
#11	9.8	25	9	**20**	45
#12	9.8	10	19	**23**	30
#13	9.9	5	26	**36**	40
	9.8	7	10	**18**	23

Ultimate Six

ISSUE	CGC GRADE	# of AUCTIONS	LOW CLOSE	AVG CLOSE	HIGH CLOSE
#1	9.9	5	49	**94**	133
	9.8	23	15	**30**	60
	9.6	15	10	**13**	23
#2	9.9	7	40	**64**	75
	9.8	17	10	**18**	24
#4	9.8	8	10	**17**	25
#6	9.8	7	11	**16**	20

Ultimate Spider-Man

ISSUE	CGC GRADE	# of AUCTIONS	LOW CLOSE	AVG CLOSE	HIGH CLOSE
#0.5	9.8	25	16	**44**	199
	9.6	25	10	**20**	53
	9.4	25	10	**21**	76
	9.2	10	8	**18**	60
#0.5/WW	9.8	6	167	**221**	302
#1	9.8	25	40	**641**	910
	9.6	25	10	**201**	500
	9.4	25	11	**153**	242
	9.2	25	22	**94**	178
	9.0	10	7	**85**	198
	8.5	5	31	**64**	101
#1/2nd	9.6	11	10	**28**	66
	9.4	5	6	**17**	25
#1/DF	9.8	25	281	**422**	820
	9.6	25	85	**217**	317
	9.4	25	81	**137**	635
	9.2	11	74	**136**	305
#1/FC	9.9	9	25	**40**	150
	9.8	25	13	**31**	80
	9.6	19	8	**13**	25
	9.4	15	7	**12**	35
#1/Wh	9.8	25	325	**921**	2,550
	9.6	25	210	**278**	851
	9.4	25	163	**301**	426
	9.2	21	150	**221**	355
	9.0	6	178	**217**	300
#2	9.8	25	61	**137**	265
	9.6	25	21	**49**	200
	9.4	25	11	**43**	75
	9.2	15	21	**34**	51
#3	9.8	25	73	**267**	400
	9.6	25	16	**42**	103
	9.4	25	5	**31**	60
	9.2	20	8	**24**	46
#4	9.8	25	46	**164**	510
	9.6	25	16	**45**	91
	9.4	25	11	**30**	65
	9.2	8	12	**25**	35
#5	9.8	25	102	**230**	660
	9.6	25	26	**115**	169
	9.4	25	35	**65**	165
	9.2	16	33	**68**	99
#6	9.8	25	40	**210**	420
	9.6	25	16	**32**	100
	9.4	25	15	**28**	51
	9.2	7	12	**18**	27
#7	9.8	25	32	**66**	203
	9.6	25	11	**29**	65
	9.4	20	10	**20**	33
	9.2	6	15	**16**	21
#8	9.8	25	36	**62**	150
	9.6	25	14	**25**	50
	9.4	22	11	**21**	40
	9.2	10	5	**15**	25
#9	9.8	25	20	**39**	110
	9.6	25	10	**24**	40
#10	9.8	25	33	**57**	238
	9.6	25	9	**20**	72
	9.4	21	10	**16**	25
	9.2	5	8	**12**	16
#11	9.8	25	23	**52**	103
	9.6	25	10	**20**	72
	9.0	6	3	**8**	15
#12	9.8	25	25	**47**	90
	9.6	25	3	**20**	35
	9.4	21	10	**15**	25
#13	9.8	25	21	**59**	173
	9.6	25	13	**27**	80
	9.4	16	10	**17**	37
	9.2	5	10	**15**	17
#14	9.9	6	113	**150**	175
	9.8	25	14	**50**	153
	9.6	25	15	**21**	40
	9.4	9	9	**13**	22
#15	9.9	9	100	**114**	153
	9.8	25	6	**34**	87
	9.6	25	1	**19**	70
	9.4	7	12	**15**	16
#16	9.8	25	14	**31**	75
	9.6	25	2	**17**	33
	9.4	7	10	**12**	16
#17	9.8	25	21	**39**	70
	9.6	25	10	**20**	45
	9.4	18	6	**15**	25
#18	9.8	25	18	**36**	76
	9.6	25	6	**21**	50

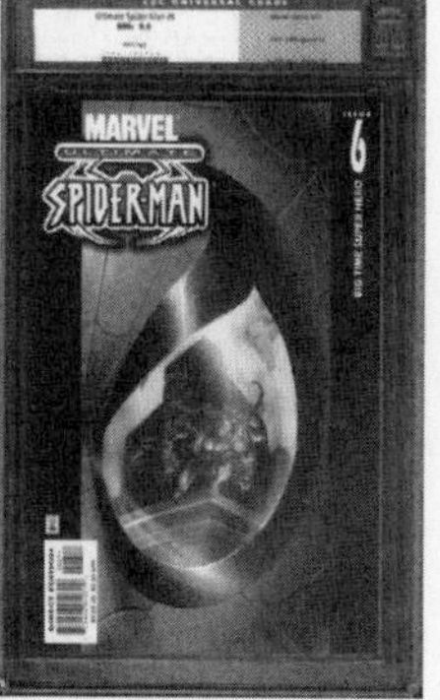

Ultimate Spider-Man (cont'd)

ISSUE	CGC GRADE	# of AUCTIONS	LOW CLOSE	AVG CLOSE	HIGH CLOSE
	9.4	5	10	**13**	16
#19	9.8	25	21	**37**	68
	9.6	25	1	**19**	41
#20	9.8	25	21	**39**	134
	9.6	25	10	**18**	30
	9.4	10	10	**13**	21
#21	9.8	25	18	**36**	81
	9.6	25	10	**17**	27
	9.4	6	10	**13**	16
#22	9.8	25	20	**38**	66
	9.6	25	10	**19**	25
	9.4	5	14	**16**	18
#23	9.8	25	20	**37**	103
	9.6	21	12	**17**	23
#24	9.8	25	10	**31**	71
	9.6	25	1	**17**	23
#25	9.8	25	16	**25**	90
	9.6	25	8	**21**	100
	9.2	5	7	**11**	19
#26	9.8	25	14	**26**	120
	9.6	13	10	**18**	33
	9.4	8	10	**14**	19
#27	9.8	25	11	**24**	81
	9.6	15	7	**17**	25
#28	9.8	25	18	**28**	60
	9.6	15	9	**16**	23
#29	10.0	5	100	**170**	243
	9.8	25	10	**22**	80
	9.6	25	1	**15**	23
#30	9.8	25	11	**25**	80
	9.6	21	6	**16**	30
#31	9.8	25	14	**25**	45
	9.6	21	1	**14**	21
#32	9.8	25	5	**25**	50
	9.6	17	10	**17**	28
#33	9.9	7	150	**202**	300
	9.8	25	20	**40**	90
	9.6	25	10	**24**	71
	9.4	25	7	**17**	33
	9.2	7	10	**17**	30
#34	9.8	25	6	**38**	70
	9.6	25	1	**19**	100
	9.4	15	8	**13**	25
#35	9.8	25	20	**35**	60
	9.6	25	6	**20**	38
	9.4	12	8	**13**	29
#36	9.8	25	15	**31**	65
	9.6	25	7	**18**	33
#37	9.8	25	21	**37**	46
	9.6	17	3	**16**	23
	9.4	6	10	**15**	22
#38	9.8	25	1	**28**	56
	9.6	25	9	**16**	22
#39	9.8	25	4	**23**	50
	9.6	25	7	**16**	24
#40	9.8	25	19	**31**	38
	9.6	7	10	**15**	22
#41	9.8	25	16	**25**	35
#42	9.8	14	18	**28**	38
#43	9.8	14	20	**30**	37
#44	9.8	20	16	**27**	40
#45	9.8	17	20	**27**	35
	9.2	5	6	**9**	13
#46	9.8	16	20	**29**	45
	9.6	8	10	**14**	17
#47	9.8	22	16	**23**	30
#49	9.8	15	16	**26**	35
	9.6	5	10	**15**	20
#50	9.9	12	90	**104**	125
	9.8	25	17	**30**	50
	9.6	7	15	**17**	19
#51	9.8	9	25	**32**	40
	9.6	5	10	**12**	17
#52	9.8	13	16	**25**	40
#53	9.8	18	16	**24**	36
#54	9.8	21	15	**23**	30
#55	9.8	24	17	**25**	34
#56	9.8	16	20	**25**	30
#57	9.8	7	23	**27**	31
#58	9.8	12	21	**31**	55
#59	9.8	13	27	**41**	50
#60	9.8	25	22	**24**	49
#61	9.8	18	20	**26**	32
#62	9.8	14	22	**24**	25
#63	9.8	6	24	**24**	24

Ultimate Spider-Man Special

ISSUE	CGC GRADE	# of AUCTIONS	LOW CLOSE	AVG CLOSE	HIGH CLOSE
#1	9.8	25	16	**32**	52
	9.6	22	11	**18**	30

Ultimate War

ISSUE	CGC GRADE	# of AUCTIONS	LOW CLOSE	AVG CLOSE	HIGH CLOSE
#1	9.9	9	50	**77**	150
	9.8	25	10	**19**	56
	9.6	25	6	**17**	29
	9.4	8	9	**14**	22
#2	9.8	11	10	**23**	45
	9.6	10	10	**18**	30
#3	9.8	5	20	**35**	49
	9.6	5	10	**14**	17

Ultimate X-Men

ISSUE	CGC GRADE	# of AUCTIONS	LOW CLOSE	AVG CLOSE	HIGH CLOSE
#0.5	9.8	25	13	**24**	37
	9.6	14	10	**19**	60
	9.4	22	6	**14**	20
#1	9.8	25	50	**157**	305
	9.6	25	23	**44**	184
	9.4	25	16	**33**	175
	9.2	14	16	**31**	66
	8.5	5	10	**15**	21
#1/DF	9.6	25	25	**75**	104
	9.4	22	21	**43**	62
	9.2	5	31	**50**	61
#1/Sk	9.8	8	203	**363**	476
	9.6	17	57	**132**	345
	9.4	10	65	**111**	150
#2	9.8	25	15	**80**	153
	9.6	25	16	**24**	40
	9.4	25	1	**18**	35
#3	9.8	25	17	**31**	57
	9.6	25	10	**20**	46

ISSUE	CGC GRADE	# of AUCTIONS	LOW CLOSE	AVG CLOSE	HIGH CLOSE
	9.4	6	8	**13**	18
#4	9.8	25	16	**29**	73
	9.6	11	10	**19**	28
	9.4	13	6	**11**	16
#5	9.8	20	20	**31**	47
	9.6	13	11	**16**	25
#6	9.8	13	19	**33**	50
	9.6	9	12	**17**	23
#7	9.8	20	19	**35**	75
	9.6	16	13	**18**	26
#8	9.8	9	16	**24**	29
	9.6	14	10	**14**	21
#9	9.8	9	15	**28**	47
	9.6	20	9	**16**	25
	9.4	5	10	**12**	15
#10	9.8	10	18	**24**	32
	9.6	17	1	**11**	20
	9.4	5	10	**12**	15
#11	9.8	25	10	**20**	41
	9.6	16	9	**13**	18
#12	9.8	14	14	**20**	27
	9.6	21	1	**12**	20
	9.4	5	10	**11**	13
#13	9.8	25	15	**25**	36
	9.6	12	10	**16**	29
#14	9.8	22	15	**24**	41
	9.6	20	9	**14**	24
#15	9.8	12	14	**22**	41
	9.6	21	7	**12**	17
#16	9.8	8	10	**21**	25
	9.6	10	3	**13**	17
	9.4	5	4	**8**	12
#17	9.8	7	14	**25**	39
	9.6	7	5	**13**	20
#18	9.8	13	1	**21**	38
	9.6	15	10	**14**	20
#19	9.8	14	11	**20**	31
#20	9.8	6	20	**27**	38
#21	9.8	6	20	**24**	32
#22	9.8	9	19	**22**	26
#23	9.8	5	10	**19**	25
#25	9.8	10	20	**34**	63
	9.6	7	14	**17**	23
#31	9.8	10	20	**23**	35
#32	9.8	5	20	**28**	36
#33	9.8	16	10	**21**	30
#34	9.8	25	10	**26**	50
	9.6	15	6	**15**	22
	9.4	7	10	**12**	17
#35	9.6	7	1	**9**	17
#36	9.9	5	36	**63**	100
	9.8	20	15	**23**	35
	9.6	6	1	**7**	13
#37	9.8	21	10	**21**	35
#38	9.8	9	15	**20**	25
#39	9.8	20	11	**19**	40
#40	9.8	23	10	**20**	30
#41	9.6	5	9	**10**	12
#42	9.8	10	11	**17**	25
#43	9.8	8	12	**18**	27
#46	9.8	6	23	**23**	25

ISSUE	CGC GRADE	# of AUCTIONS	LOW CLOSE	AVG CLOSE	HIGH CLOSE
Uncanny X-Men, The					
#142	9.8	25	128	**237**	404
	9.6	25	29	**73**	135
	9.4	25	21	**49**	80
	9.2	25	19	**32**	70
	9.0	17	13	**24**	31
	8.5	25	10	**21**	50
	8.0	8	13	**17**	23
	7.5	5	8	**15**	21
#143	9.8	25	66	**102**	206
	9.6	25	21	**44**	90
	9.4	25	17	**29**	52
	9.2	16	13	**21**	30
	9.0	11	10	**19**	25
	8.5	9	10	**16**	29
#144	9.8	10	50	**86**	130
	9.6	25	11	**33**	51
	9.4	18	15	**21**	31
#145	9.8	22	39	**59**	100
	9.6	25	12	**35**	60
	9.4	13	10	**24**	38
#146	9.8	21	26	**62**	134
	9.6	25	14	**32**	48
	9.4	17	10	**21**	33
	9.2	6	10	**17**	25
#147	9.8	25	31	**55**	82
	9.6	25	12	**30**	50
	9.4	7	18	**26**	45
#148	9.8	14	26	**60**	82
	9.6	25	16	**29**	45
	9.4	18	8	**17**	31
	9.2	9	10	**14**	20
#149	9.8	11	33	**59**	75
	9.6	25	18	**26**	45
	9.4	14	10	**19**	35
	9.2	11	7	**16**	23
#150	9.8	25	34	**53**	305
	9.6	25	16	**31**	70
	9.4	25	11	**21**	42
	9.2	11	10	**16**	26
	9.0	9	6	**13**	20
#151	9.8	9	39	**53**	75
	9.6	22	15	**25**	48
	9.4	18	7	**16**	29
	9.2	8	8	**18**	25
	9.0	7	11	**15**	20

ISSUE	CGC GRADE	# of AUCTIONS	LOW CLOSE	AVG CLOSE	HIGH CLOSE
Uncanny X-Men, The (cont'd)					
#152	9.6	25	15	**30**	50
	9.4	9	10	**18**	27
#153	9.8	7	50	**84**	116
	9.6	25	10	**28**	61
	9.4	6	11	**17**	20
#154	9.8	25	25	**49**	100
	9.6	18	15	**28**	61
	9.4	10	10	**18**	25
#155	9.8	5	50	**68**	108
	9.6	17	20	**29**	46
	9.4	7	10	**13**	20
#156	9.8	5	38	**63**	109
	9.6	22	14	**26**	56
	9.4	6	15	**20**	27
#157	9.8	21	30	**54**	113
	9.6	21	10	**25**	39
	9.4	16	10	**21**	43
#158	9.8	10	20	**93**	178
	9.6	25	20	**37**	77
	9.4	16	16	**24**	35
#159	9.6	12	18	**32**	50
	9.4	7	15	**26**	54
#160	9.8	9	33	**66**	100
	9.6	25	17	**27**	45
	9.4	7	10	**21**	30
#161	9.8	7	50	**72**	103
	9.6	16	21	**32**	51
#162	9.8	8	56	**90**	161
	9.6	25	16	**30**	59
	9.4	10	14	**22**	25
#163	9.8	6	42	**82**	198
	9.6	23	18	**27**	44
#164	9.6	17	17	**28**	46
	9.4	14	10	**24**	59
#165	9.8	9	37	**59**	109
	9.6	22	12	**25**	34
	9.4	6	13	**18**	26
	9.2	5	6	**13**	19
#166	9.8	13	45	**83**	143
	9.6	22	16	**27**	50
	9.4	5	17	**20**	23
	9.2	5	6	**12**	20
#167	9.8	8	30	**52**	78
	9.6	24	19	**30**	51
	9.4	5	10	**14**	17
#168	9.8	15	31	**73**	129
	9.6	21	16	**29**	43
#169	9.6	20	13	**27**	52
	9.4	9	10	**21**	36
	8.5	5	1	**8**	15
#170	9.8	13	33	**51**	88
	9.6	15	6	**26**	47
	9.4	5	10	**19**	39
#171	9.8	25	44	**78**	115
	9.6	25	22	**37**	70
	9.4	20	11	**21**	30
	9.2	7	9	**18**	26
	8.5	6	10	**15**	21
	7.5	5	1	**8**	15
#172	9.8	25	25	**41**	86
	9.6	25	10	**27**	71
	9.4	10	13	**21**	38
#173	9.8	18	40	**51**	113
	9.6	17	14	**27**	55
	9.4	12	10	**19**	32
#174	9.6	15	13	**29**	50
	9.4	6	7	**18**	40
#175	9.8	15	36	**65**	150
	9.6	22	14	**33**	153
	9.4	16	10	**21**	40
#176	9.8	25	20	**32**	69
	9.6	19	7	**22**	44
	9.4	7	1	**12**	21
#177	9.8	25	19	**41**	160
#178	9.8	23	25	**34**	59
	9.6	14	12	**25**	71
#179	9.9	8	25	**95**	159
	9.8	25	21	**35**	71
	9.6	15	6	**21**	31
	9.4	6	2	**13**	25
	9.2	5	2	**8**	11
#180	9.8	25	20	**34**	56
	9.6	14	1	**19**	35
#181	9.8	25	21	**35**	100
	9.6	11	15	**25**	38
#182	9.8	25	20	**30**	100
	9.6	19	11	**22**	35
#183	9.8	25	16	**37**	87
	9.6	12	10	**26**	46
#184	9.8	25	20	**36**	100
	9.6	17	16	**24**	41
	9.4	6	15	**20**	31
#185	9.8	25	25	**35**	75
	9.6	13	6	**23**	47
	9.4	7	8	**14**	25
#186	9.8	25	11	**31**	71
	9.6	24	4	**20**	40
	9.4	9	10	**14**	22
#187	9.8	20	21	**32**	56
	9.6	11	4	**20**	30
#188	9.8	25	21	**31**	84
	9.6	14	10	**22**	44
#189	9.8	17	23	**34**	50
	9.6	20	9	**21**	41
	9.4	8	8	**16**	27
	9.2	6	12	**16**	21
#190	9.8	13	26	**36**	50
	9.6	17	3	**22**	36
	9.4	7	10	**15**	20
	9.2	5	10	**13**	22
#191	9.8	25	11	**29**	66
	9.6	15	16	**25**	35
	9.4	6	10	**16**	23
#192	9.8	22	21	**31**	53
	9.6	11	11	**20**	25
	9.4	6	13	**15**	16
#193	9.8	25	21	**41**	175
	9.6	21	10	**21**	42
	9.4	6	10	**16**	21

ISSUE	CGC GRADE	# of AUCTIONS	LOW CLOSE	AVG CLOSE	HIGH CLOSE
#194	9.8	22	23	**37**	140
	9.6	9	10	**21**	40
#195	9.8	9	30	**36**	48
	9.6	17	15	**24**	40
#196	9.8	25	19	**31**	58
	9.6	13	16	**23**	36
#197	9.8	25	22	**32**	50
	9.6	9	12	**20**	28
	9.4	6	1	**14**	23
#198	9.8	25	25	**31**	45
	9.6	20	13	**18**	25
	9.4	7	16	**19**	23
#199	9.8	6	37	**45**	60
	9.6	8	16	**27**	52
#200	9.8	12	36	**52**	125
	9.6	25	15	**24**	50
	9.4	9	13	**19**	27
#201	9.8	10	55	**90**	181
	9.6	25	9	**30**	51
	9.4	8	14	**24**	50
#202	9.8	16	24	**32**	48
	9.6	8	17	**24**	35
#203	9.6	6	16	**20**	26
#204	9.8	5	21	**30**	40
	9.6	12	10	**17**	36
#205	9.8	10	48	**74**	123
	9.6	25	16	**31**	60
	9.4	12	10	**24**	50
#206	9.8	9	25	**40**	85
	9.6	10	13	**19**	30
#207	9.8	7	42	**59**	124
	9.6	5	16	**27**	38
	9.4	7	13	**19**	30
#208	9.8	9	24	**39**	61
	9.6	5	17	**23**	26
#209	9.8	5	25	**38**	50
	9.6	11	17	**21**	25
#210	9.8	7	28	**41**	50
	9.6	18	19	**31**	45
	9.2	5	10	**20**	25
#211	9.8	25	25	**55**	99
	9.6	25	12	**27**	50
	9.4	23	11	**19**	28
	9.2	12	10	**20**	29
#212	9.6	25	26	**39**	73
	9.4	25	6	**24**	51
	9.2	9	15	**21**	27
	9.0	5	10	**16**	25
#213	9.8	5	71	**103**	201
	9.6	25	20	**40**	65
	9.4	25	16	**26**	36
	9.2	13	12	**22**	37
	9.0	10	10	**19**	30
	5.0	6	1	**5**	10
#214	9.6	8	16	**22**	36
#215	9.6	10	15	**19**	25
#216	9.8	15	25	**30**	46
	9.6	6	20	**24**	33
#217	9.8	19	16	**30**	52
	9.6	14	13	**20**	35
#218	9.8	6	24	**30**	38
#219	9.8	13	20	**29**	49
	9.6	7	15	**22**	33
#221	9.8	11	36	**58**	140
	9.6	9	16	**30**	59
#222	9.8	23	32	**57**	101
	9.6	25	13	**32**	80
	9.4	11	15	**25**	50
	8.0	6	1	**9**	16
#225	9.8	6	32	**44**	79
	9.6	7	12	**18**	25
#227	9.8	13	11	**30**	75
	9.6	7	15	**23**	32
#228	9.8	8	25	**29**	40
	9.6	10	10	**17**	25
#229	9.6	5	10	**20**	36
#230	9.8	6	24	**26**	28
	9.6	6	13	**19**	36
#232	9.8	7	23	**33**	46
	9.6	5	12	**16**	20
#233	9.8	8	21	**30**	40
	9.6	5	11	**20**	25
#234	9.6	7	19	**27**	47
#235	9.6	6	16	**22**	30
#237	9.6	6	14	**35**	59
#238	9.6	7	15	**23**	52
#239	9.6	6	14	**23**	41
#241	9.8	9	23	**30**	40
	9.6	7	7	**19**	26
#242	9.8	5	28	**35**	41
	9.6	6	15	**18**	25
#243	9.8	15	11	**27**	86
#244	9.8	25	30	**70**	153
	9.6	25	8	**32**	55
	9.4	25	16	**23**	31
	9.2	14	13	**18**	25
	9.0	5	10	**12**	16
#245	9.8	12	12	**30**	43
#246	9.8	11	21	**28**	40
#247	9.8	19	16	**27**	52
	9.6	8	9	**17**	34
#248	9.8	25	15	**81**	187
	9.6	25	16	**33**	60
	9.4	25	15	**22**	35
	9.2	5	11	**17**	32
	9.0	12	6	**14**	20

ISSUE	CGC GRADE	# of AUCTIONS	LOW CLOSE	AVG CLOSE	HIGH CLOSE
Uncanny X-Men, The (cont'd)					
	8.0	5	7	**13**	24
#249	9.8	8	20	**27**	35
#250	9.8	8	16	**29**	46
	9.6	6	14	**19**	25
#251	9.8	6	36	**51**	86
#253	9.6	5	6	**17**	30
#256	9.8	18	26	**45**	91
	9.6	18	6	**22**	35
	9.4	8	5	**15**	22
	9.2	8	8	**11**	16
#257	9.8	16	25	**40**	61
	9.6	21	16	**22**	42
	9.4	7	10	**14**	31
#258	9.6	10	10	**23**	37
	9.4	5	10	**14**	17
#259	9.8	8	22	**25**	26
#260	9.8	7	20	**25**	27
#266	9.8	25	142	**238**	305
	9.6	25	32	**71**	200
	9.4	25	21	**50**	85
	9.2	25	17	**32**	53
	9.0	15	21	**35**	50
	8.5	5	12	**23**	32
#267	9.8	12	25	**66**	130
	9.6	17	17	**26**	51
	9.4	13	11	**22**	40
	9.2	7	10	**16**	20
#268	9.6	25	15	**32**	65
	9.4	25	6	**19**	36
	9.2	11	8	**13**	18
	9.0	7	10	**15**	21
	8.5	6	4	**9**	14
#270	9.6	6	16	**25**	44
	9.4	6	11	**17**	23
#272	9.8	8	21	**31**	41
#273	9.6	5	16	**28**	35
#274	9.8	9	25	**32**	49
#275	9.8	10	21	**29**	37
	9.6	14	15	**20**	28
	9.4	7	9	**14**	25
	9.2	6	8	**13**	16
#275/Gld	9.6	13	11	**33**	60
#276	9.6	5	15	**18**	22
#277	9.8	9	20	**26**	32
#279	9.8	5	20	**26**	30
#281	9.8	25	15	**30**	56
	9.6	16	9	**16**	34
#282	9.8	6	28	**48**	66
	9.6	12	15	**26**	50
	9.4	20	6	**16**	45
#283	9.8	25	23	**45**	81
	9.6	25	7	**21**	36
	9.4	11	10	**14**	23
#284	9.8	11	11	**24**	35
#288	9.8	5	20	**24**	28
#290	9.8	8	20	**25**	38
#300	9.8	20	16	**24**	41
	9.6	11	3	**15**	25
#304	9.8	12	20	**26**	36
ISSUE	CGC GRADE	# of AUCTIONS	LOW CLOSE	AVG CLOSE	HIGH CLOSE
#305	9.8	5	20	**25**	30
#306	9.8	6	20	**24**	30
#308	9.8	6	20	**24**	30
#311	9.8	5	21	**26**	30
#313	9.8	6	21	**26**	30
#316	9.8	6	20	**26**	35
#317	9.8	5	16	**27**	37
#342/Var	9.6	5	10	**15**	30
#350	9.8	6	30	**51**	66
	9.6	7	25	**32**	37
#390	9.8	10	22	**59**	101
	9.6	9	10	**23**	40
#394	9.8	19	15	**27**	49
	9.6	22	8	**20**	50
#400	9.6	20	1	**17**	46
#418	9.8	6	11	**16**	18
#422	9.6	7	7	**14**	18
#434	9.8	6	9	**20**	33
#435	9.8	5	10	**22**	30
#436	9.8	8	10	**21**	30
#439	9.8	8	9	**17**	30
#440	9.8	8	9	**18**	25
#442	9.8	5	10	**23**	30
#444	9.8	5	18	**22**	25
Uncanny X-Men Annual					
#1	9.4	19	120	**206**	330
	8.5	7	32	**56**	80
#2	9.2	5	36	**85**	208
	8.5	6	32	**39**	55
#3	9.8	5	79	**121**	170
	9.6	21	16	**46**	125
	9.4	14	15	**40**	72
	9.2	6	16	**22**	26
#4	9.6	5	17	**27**	41
	9.4	7	15	**25**	42
#5	9.8	6	36	**54**	103
	9.6	17	14	**25**	46
	9.2	5	10	**12**	17
#6	9.8	10	25	**42**	51
	9.6	10	10	**31**	61
#7	9.8	12	19	**29**	53
#8	9.8	15	12	**23**	31
#10	9.8	7	30	**64**	181
	9.6	6	13	**26**	51
#11	9.8	6	20	**28**	50
#14	9.8	15	20	**36**	84
	9.6	25	5	**21**	60
	9.4	9	10	**17**	25
	9.2	5	4	**10**	15
	8.5	6	5	**10**	13
2001	9.8	6	10	**15**	21
Uncle Sam Quarterly					
#7	7.5	6	163	**318**	460
Unexpected					
#119	9.6	7	42	**96**	152
#123	9.4	7	1	**39**	69
#133	9.4	6	38	**85**	129
#137	9.4	6	1	**20**	41

ISSUE	CGC GRADE	# of AUCTIONS	LOW CLOSE	AVG CLOSE	HIGH CLOSE
Unfunnies					
#1	9.8	17	6	**14**	25
Unity					
#0	9.8	18	2	**38**	125
	9.6	9	6	**17**	35
	9.4	5	2	**19**	60
#0/Rd	9.6	6	52	**84**	164
#1/Gld	9.8	9	23	**46**	71
	9.6	5	20	**27**	40
#1/Plt	9.8	10	21	**40**	99
	9.6	7	15	**23**	32
Universe X Spidey					
#1	9.6	5	16	**42**	61
Unusual Tales					
#32	9.4	8	43	**53**	71
	9.0	5	10	**28**	60
Vampirella					
#1	9.8	16	25	**41**	170
	9.6	18	6	**24**	50
	9.4	5	12	**22**	42
#4	9.4	8	15	**68**	250
Vampirella: Mike Mayhew Sketchbook					
#0	9.8	5	21	**24**	25
Vanguard					
#2	9.8	5	20	**23**	26
Vault of Horror					
#22	9.0	5	306	**391**	445
Vengeance Squad					
#1	9.4	6	11	**28**	50
Venom					
#1	9.8	25	15	**24**	51
	9.6	25	10	**18**	35
	9.4	5	7	**49**	200
#3	9.8	6	15	**22**	27
#6	9.8	6	25	**28**	35
Venom: Lethal Protector					
#1	9.8	25	10	**23**	68
	9.6	15	6	**11**	16
	9.4	9	9	**22**	51
#1 gold	9.8	6	41	**73**	104
	9.6	5	30	**43**	61
Vicki					
#3	9.4	5	38	**47**	60
Victory Comics					
#1	4.5	5	260	**345**	410
Wanted					
#1	9.8	21	16	**34**	46
#1/DRw	9.8	17	12	**30**	60
#1/DF	9.8	6	25	**35**	51
#1/Svtri	9.8	6	20	**36**	46
#1/Var	9.8	5	27	**37**	50
#1/WW	9.6	6	20	**33**	40
	9.4	5	16	**34**	71
#2	9.8	6	16	**49**	165
Warlock					
#1	9.6	5	243	**313**	400
	9.2	5	46	**54**	66
#9	9.6	8	22	**83**	148
	9.4	9	27	**41**	59
#10	9.6	11	36	**80**	163
	9.4	8	21	**42**	60
#11	9.6	8	31	**67**	99
	9.4	6	22	**28**	36
#12	9.6	6	22	**37**	50
	9.2	5	13	**16**	20
#13	9.6	12	21	**49**	85
#14	9.6	8	25	**47**	81
#15	9.4	5	10	**24**	47
Warlord					
#1	9.4	7	25	**41**	79
	9.0	7	10	**21**	50
Watchmen					
#1	9.6	17	26	**42**	78
	9.4	8	9	**18**	28
	9.2	7	12	**18**	25
#2	9.8	5	25	**33**	51
#6	9.8	5	25	**35**	44
#7	9.8	6	25	**32**	51
#12	9.8	13	21	**31**	50
	9.6	5	10	**19**	26
Weapon X					
#0.5	9.6	6	10	**12**	20
#1	9.8	5	20	**26**	35
	9.6	16	2	**13**	20
	9.4	6	3	**8**	10
Web of Spider-Man					
#1	9.8	25	51	**113**	321
	9.6	25	14	**34**	128
	9.4	25	10	**22**	41
	9.2	25	9	**21**	69
	9.0	22	10	**18**	47
	8.5	13	9	**14**	20
	8.0	6	2	**12**	20
	7.5	7	5	**11**	15
#2	9.8	25	19	**37**	75

ISSUE	CGC GRADE	# of AUCTIONS	LOW CLOSE	AVG CLOSE	HIGH CLOSE
Web of Spider-Man (cont'd)					
	9.6	14	10	**16**	25
#3	9.8	22	17	**33**	62
	9.6	12	13	**19**	25
#4	9.8	5	26	**33**	40
	9.6	9	12	**21**	30
#5	9.8	6	26	**35**	47
#6	9.8	5	25	**36**	66
#7	9.8	6	20	**36**	76
	9.6	7	4	**13**	16
#8	9.8	9	25	**31**	50
#29	9.8	8	39	**62**	96
	9.6	10	15	**23**	35
#90	9.6	10	8	**15**	25
#100	9.8	11	13	**23**	38
	9.6	6	12	**14**	20
Web of Spider-Man Annual					
#1	9.8	6	17	**33**	77
Weird Fantasy					
#11	7.0	6	90	**120**	175
#12	8.5	7	204	**272**	390
#15	9.0	8	230	**381**	465
Weird Mystery Tales					
#1	9.2	7	41	**50**	60
Weird War Tales					
#1	9.2	9	173	**247**	305
	9.0	10	112	**187**	249
	8.5	7	11	**118**	187
Weird Western Tales					
#12	9.6	6	158	**370**	709
	9.4	8	51	**147**	213
	9.2	7	52	**85**	118
#31	9.6	5	21	**41**	52
Weird Wonder Tales					
#1	9.4	5	27	**50**	79
Weird Worlds					
#1	9.4	5	22	**44**	65
Werewolf By Night					
#1	9.4	23	164	**273**	405
	9.2	22	78	**132**	183
	9.0	13	51	**96**	203
	8.5	9	40	**62**	109
	8.0	10	35	**52**	70
#3	9.6	7	69	**133**	179
	9.4	7	29	**52**	88
#4	9.2	7	16	**29**	50
#15	9.6	11	52	**100**	165
#16	9.4	5	26	**44**	85
#17	9.2	5	8	**17**	30
#20	9.6	8	31	**61**	123
#26	9.4	5	10	**29**	65
#30	9.4	6	17	**29**	38
#32	9.4	18	40	**241**	510
	9.2	8	105	**204**	535
	9.0	13	65	**103**	149
	8.5	12	30	**55**	100
#33	9.4	5	124	**145**	178
	9.2	7	22	**47**	65
West Coast Avengers					
#1	9.8	5	19	**40**	91
What If?					
#1	9.6	25	27	**53**	130
	9.4	25	20	**45**	125
	9.2	16	16	**26**	40
	9.0	5	19	**23**	28
	8.5	8	10	**17**	26
#2	9.8	9	25	**91**	200
	9.6	25	21	**38**	134
	9.4	10	16	**34**	86
	9.2	5	3	**12**	16
#3	9.6	19	15	**48**	90
	9.4	7	10	**26**	50
#8	9.6	7	16	**25**	46
#27	9.6	7	17	**26**	38
	9.4	10	13	**20**	28
#31	9.6	16	25	**57**	113
	9.4	11	14	**27**	45
#35	9.8	13	12	**32**	103
	9.6	25	4	**22**	32
	9.4	10	10	**15**	28
#45	9.8	5	19	**32**	66
#46	9.8	7	10	**24**	43
Whiz Comics					
#11	8.5	10	124	**191**	305
WildC.A.T.S.					
#1	9.6	5	5	**14**	25
#2	9.8	15	11	**16**	24
Wings Comics					
#1	6.0	6	306	**450**	595
#98	8.0	5	82	**110**	150
Witchblade					
#0.5	9.4	5	20	**31**	43
#1	9.8	25	37	**63**	125
	9.6	25	16	**38**	96
	9.4	18	11	**26**	42
	9.2	9	18	**28**	56
#2	9.6	5	20	**30**	41
	9.4	6	19	**24**	31
#3	9.4	5	13	**20**	25
#25	10.0	5	100	**215**	307
	9.8	12	18	**47**	210
	9.6	7	21	**29**	50
#50	9.8	8	12	**26**	34
#54	9.8	8	14	**19**	26
	9.6	7	18	**23**	33
#55	9.6	5	10	**12**	16
Witchblade/Tomb Raider					
#1	9.8	14	21	**30**	53
	9.6	6	14	**20**	26

ISSUE	CGC GRADE	# of AUCTIONS	LOW CLOSE	AVG CLOSE	HIGH CLOSE
Witchblade vs. Darkness					
#0.5	9.8	9	30	**32**	39
Witchblade/Wolverine					
#1	9.8	6	19	**24**	30
Witching Hour					
#1	9.4	6	360	**531**	920
	9.0	6	86	**122**	152
	7.5	5	41	**58**	77
#83	9.6	6	13	**19**	25
Wizard Ace Edition: Amazing Spider-Man					
#129	9.8	25	10	**25**	50
	9.6	21	10	**21**	99
	9.4	8	11	**24**	99
Wizard Ace Edition: Incredible Hulk					
#1	9.8	9	9	**16**	27
#181	9.8	24	19	**32**	56
	9.6	17	11	**35**	90
Wizard Ace Edition: Uncanny X-Men					
#94	9.8	13	6	**18**	28
	9.6	8	9	**15**	19
Wizard Ace Edition: Witchblade					
#1	9.8	6	36	**63**	81
Wolverine Limited Series					
#1	9.9	10	405	**756**	1,126
	9.8	25	67	**233**	650
	9.6	25	11	**66**	178
	9.4	25	7	**54**	86
	9.2	25	16	**32**	75
	9.0	25	15	**29**	60
	8.5	25	13	**23**	45
	8.0	18	4	**18**	38
	7.5	5	11	**18**	38
	7.0	11	11	**15**	19
#2	9.8	25	76	**125**	255
	9.6	25	8	**43**	101
	9.4	25	11	**30**	81
	9.2	25	13	**21**	33
	9.0	23	5	**17**	30
	8.5	16	5	**16**	32
#3	9.8	25	51	**112**	170
	9.6	25	1	**42**	92
	9.4	25	1	**32**	57
	9.2	25	0	**19**	36
	9.0	25	5	**15**	25
	8.5	11	7	**13**	23
	8.0	10	2	**14**	27
#4	9.8	25	66	**148**	316
	9.6	25	27	**57**	109
	9.4	25	8	**29**	56
	9.2	25	10	**19**	46
	9.0	19	11	**17**	26
	8.5	11	1	**13**	24
	8.0	6	1	**8**	13
Wolverine					
#1	9.8	25	30	**119**	220
	9.8	25	6	**28**	51
	9.6	25	18	**51**	108
	9.6	25	9	**16**	30
	9.4	25	10	**35**	80
	9.4	8	10	**15**	21
	9.2	25	9	**29**	69
	9.0	25	10	**26**	46
	8.5	25	6	**19**	40
	8.0	19	4	**16**	30
	7.5	8	5	**15**	25
	7.0	6	8	**14**	20
	4.0	8	4	**8**	15
#2	9.8	25	17	**49**	133
	9.8	14	15	**22**	32
	9.6	25	11	**27**	100
	9.6	5	11	**15**	20
	9.4	25	10	**20**	60
	9.2	5	7	**13**	20
	9.0	6	5	**10**	20
	8.5	5	5	**12**	25
#3	9.8	25	17	**39**	153
	9.8	10	16	**20**	23
	9.6	25	10	**24**	45
	9.4	8	9	**18**	40
#4	9.8	9	25	**49**	100
	9.6	13	15	**30**	71
	9.4	16	10	**17**	28
	9.2	5	11	**16**	20
#5	9.8	25	18	**37**	67
	9.6	16	12	**23**	35
	9.4	5	12	**15**	20
#6	9.8	22	12	**39**	101
	9.8	7	9	**20**	30
	9.6	8	13	**18**	25
	9.4	7	10	**13**	18
#7	9.8	8	40	**53**	75
	9.6	8	11	**20**	29
	9.4	5	10	**12**	16
#8	9.8	19	25	**53**	105
	9.8	7	10	**18**	26
	9.6	12	5	**28**	46
	9.4	6	10	**15**	17
	9.2	5	9	**18**	25
#9	9.8	10	20	**41**	71
	9.6	15	5	**17**	29
	9.4	5	11	**15**	20

ISSUE	CGC GRADE	# of AUCTIONS	LOW CLOSE	AVG CLOSE	HIGH CLOSE
Wolverine (cont'd)					
#10	9.8	25	20	**126**	260
	9.6	25	13	**44**	143
	9.4	25	20	**35**	59
	9.2	23	15	**27**	50
	9.0	15	11	**20**	36
	8.5	6	11	**16**	21
#11	9.8	9	10	**25**	44
	9.8	8	6	**12**	23
#12	9.8	10	10	**26**	45
#13	9.8	9	14	**30**	61
#14	9.8	8	10	**28**	57
#15	9.8	10	14	**24**	51
#16	9.8	8	13	**21**	40
#17	9.8	9	27	**39**	67
#20	9.8	6	14	**22**	25
#21	9.8	5	11	**30**	46
#41	9.8	17	19	**35**	60
	9.6	5	11	**15**	20
#42	9.8	5	19	**33**	66
#45	9.6	5	1	**17**	23
#47	9.8	8	13	**22**	36
#50	9.8	14	20	**46**	100
	9.6	8	10	**16**	25
	9.4	9	11	**19**	24
#62	9.8	6	20	**28**	36
#75	9.8	25	20	**35**	51
	9.6	10	13	**19**	27
	9.4	6	10	**13**	16
#100	9.6	8	16	**29**	41
	9.4	9	11	**22**	41
#131/Rcl	9.8	9	30	**53**	100
	9.6	18	12	**26**	43
#145	9.6	14	14	**29**	75
	9.4	5	10	**23**	50
#145/DF	9.6	6	16	**33**	50
#145/Nb	9.6	8	225	**269**	375
	9.6	5	158	**283**	500
	9.4	7	73	**142**	179
#146	9.6	5	13	**21**	36
#150	9.8	8	21	**33**	47
#166	9.8	5	53	**85**	128
	9.6	14	10	**22**	40
#175	9.8	5	16	**23**	28
#182	9.6	5	13	**14**	16
#189	9.6	5	10	**14**	17
Wolverine/Captain America					
#1	9.8	12	13	**18**	30
#2	9.8	8	9	**12**	20
#3	9.8	6	9	**14**	23
Wolverine/Hulk					
#1	9.6	14	8	**14**	26
	9.4	7	9	**12**	22
Wolverine/Punisher					
#1	9.8	5	10	**19**	27
Wolverine/Witchblade					
#1	9.8	10	17	**24**	39

ISSUE	CGC GRADE	# of AUCTIONS	LOW CLOSE	AVG CLOSE	HIGH CLOSE
Wolverine: The End					
#1	9.8	25	13	**38**	76
	9.6	25	11	**18**	31
	9.4	5	8	**21**	57
#1/WW	9.8	25	100	**220**	400
	9.6	25	46	**84**	234
	9.4	10	42	**65**	118
	9.2	8	24	**50**	79
#2	9.8	25	14	**28**	46
	9.6	5	10	**15**	23
#3	9.8	6	20	**26**	30
#4	9.8	6	20	**23**	27
Wolverine: The Origin					
#1	10.0	5	962	**1,442**	2,225
	9.9	23	148	**264**	355
	9.8	25	31	**72**	163
	9.6	25	13	**41**	136
	9.4	25	15	**28**	76
	9.2	25	17	**34**	69
	9.0	6	20	**28**	49
#1/DF	9.8	25	43	**95**	204
#2	9.9	6	158	**196**	225
	9.8	25	11	**29**	109
	9.6	25	7	**25**	87
	9.4	25	2	**17**	40
	9.2	13	11	**28**	90
	8.5	6	7	**13**	22
#2/DF	9.8	25	21	**58**	153
	9.6	8	21	**40**	70
#3	10.0	5	209	**321**	460
	9.9	25	34	**118**	375
	9.8	25	2	**24**	65
	9.6	25	8	**18**	36
	9.4	14	6	**17**	25
	9.2	9	10	**13**	17
	9.0	7	7	**9**	11
#4	9.9	10	51	**144**	240
	9.8	25	15	**33**	79
	9.6	25	3	**18**	41
	9.4	25	8	**14**	51
	9.2	9	6	**11**	20
#5	9.8	25	11	**30**	107
	9.6	25	3	**21**	44
	9.4	10	6	**13**	25
	9.2	10	1	**11**	18
#6	9.9	15	45	**102**	208
	9.8	25	7	**23**	63
	9.6	25	8	**18**	35
	9.4	10	8	**15**	25
Wonder Comics					
#17	5.5	6	128	**169**	273
Wonder Woman					
#1	9.8	6	50	**74**	90
	9.6	12	16	**25**	36
#90	9.8	8	20	**28**	37
#105	3.0	5	115	**148**	200
#134	9.2	5	133	**235**	450
#154	9.2	5	52	**171**	358

ISSUE	CGC GRADE	# of AUCTIONS	LOW CLOSE	AVG CLOSE	HIGH CLOSE
#164	7.5	5	23	**28**	36
#177	9.4	6	158	**270**	404
#190	9.4	5	51	**116**	220
#194	9.2	6	16	**36**	58
#199	9.4	17	108	**168**	226
	9.2	12	65	**82**	109
#200	9.8	15	16	**22**	35
	9.4	5	103	**183**	290
	9.0	7	35	**57**	78
	8.0	5	29	**38**	44
#206	9.4	6	34	**48**	80
#210	9.4	5	32	**49**	101
#214	9.2	5	44	**81**	129
#300	9.4	6	13	**22**	35

Wonderworld Comics

ISSUE	CGC GRADE	# of AUCTIONS	LOW CLOSE	AVG CLOSE	HIGH CLOSE
#4	6.5	5	143	**603**	957

World's Best Comics

ISSUE	CGC GRADE	# of AUCTIONS	LOW CLOSE	AVG CLOSE	HIGH CLOSE
#1	7.0	17	1,280	**2,903**	5,200

World's Finest Comics

ISSUE	CGC GRADE	# of AUCTIONS	LOW CLOSE	AVG CLOSE	HIGH CLOSE
#2	4.5	5	354	**492**	673
	3.0	5	203	**342**	485
#3	1.8	6	199	**245**	281
#8	6.5	6	250	**396**	610
#22	8.0	9	285	**404**	665
#23	7.0	6	189	**265**	330
#115	7.5	5	32	**41**	50
#130	9.0	6	16	**76**	129
#158	9.0	5	31	**38**	43
#162	9.2	7	8	**40**	66
#166	9.2	9	26	**57**	88
#169	9.0	5	29	**46**	57
#174	9.0	8	1	**36**	71
#177	9.2	5	26	**40**	65
#182	9.2	7	19	**35**	65
#198	9.2	5	89	**153**	250
#199	9.0	5	42	**62**	89
#225	9.4	6	50	**67**	109
#228	9.4	5	56	**79**	108

Worlds Unknown

ISSUE	CGC GRADE	# of AUCTIONS	LOW CLOSE	AVG CLOSE	HIGH CLOSE
#1	9.6	5	34	**127**	204
	9.4	5	27	**60**	76

Wulf The Barbarian

ISSUE	CGC GRADE	# of AUCTIONS	LOW CLOSE	AVG CLOSE	HIGH CLOSE
#2	9.4	5	10	**27**	51

X-Factor

ISSUE	CGC GRADE	# of AUCTIONS	LOW CLOSE	AVG CLOSE	HIGH CLOSE
#1	9.8	6	11	**69**	128
	9.6	21	15	**23**	35
	9.4	12	11	**15**	20
	9.2	9	9	**15**	22
#6	9.8	5	54	**89**	150
	9.6	6	18	**38**	50
	9.4	9	14	**19**	27
#24	9.6	18	11	**30**	79
#92	9.8	10	11	**17**	25

X-Files

ISSUE	CGC GRADE	# of AUCTIONS	LOW CLOSE	AVG CLOSE	HIGH CLOSE
#1	9.6	9	10	**24**	41

X-Force

ISSUE	CGC GRADE	# of AUCTIONS	LOW CLOSE	AVG CLOSE	HIGH CLOSE
#25	9.8	11	10	**18**	40
#116	9.6	13	5	**13**	27

X-Men (Vol. 1)

ISSUE	CGC GRADE	# of AUCTIONS	LOW CLOSE	AVG CLOSE	HIGH CLOSE
#1	8.5	11	4,001	**6,257**	8,552
	8.0	11	3,200	**3,992**	5,821
	7.5	22	1,976	**2,788**	3,950
	7.0	25	1,476	**2,564**	4,000
	6.5	13	1,434	**1,826**	2,500
	6.0	12	1,001	**1,505**	1,950
	5.5	18	1,092	**1,431**	1,921
	5.0	22	528	**1,218**	1,550
	4.5	20	731	**1,022**	1,525
	4.0	25	500	**864**	1,200
	3.5	25	203	**630**	825
	3.0	25	406	**596**	825
	2.5	16	358	**530**	750
	2.0	21	296	**428**	599
	1.8	10	300	**359**	450
	1.5	6	233	**351**	486
	1.0	8	196	**274**	330
#2	9.2	6	1,913	**2,607**	3,300
	9.0	7	1,525	**1,837**	2,400
	8.5	7	810	**1,002**	1,200
	8.0	15	800	**1,001**	1,350
	7.5	17	256	**615**	850
	7.0	17	255	**484**	775
	6.5	22	218	**392**	677
	6.0	16	178	**337**	522
	5.5	12	250	**328**	385
	5.0	5	253	**289**	360
	4.5	6	179	**221**	275
	4.0	23	103	**197**	300
	3.5	7	103	**164**	250
	3.0	14	100	**145**	199
	2.5	7	81	**147**	200
	2.0	6	63	**95**	105
#3	8.5	13	438	**588**	735
	8.0	16	203	**421**	610
	7.5	7	199	**331**	485
	7.0	8	229	**314**	390
	6.5	5	168	**218**	290
	5.0	10	110	**177**	339
	4.5	6	100	**148**	218
#4	9.4	7	3,100	**3,721**	5,000

X-Men (Vol. 1) (cont'd)

ISSUE	CGC GRADE	# of AUCTIONS	LOW CLOSE	AVG CLOSE	HIGH CLOSE
	8.5	7	500	**689**	910
	8.0	15	335	**450**	695
	7.5	8	280	**373**	513
	7.0	9	205	**289**	365
	6.0	7	156	**197**	228
	5.0	10	81	**130**	203
	4.5	12	60	**109**	166
	3.5	5	64	**91**	128
#5	9.4	7	1,501	**2,192**	3,151
	8.5	8	306	**452**	610
	8.0	9	288	**363**	500
	7.5	6	91	**223**	305
	6.0	5	125	**149**	168
#6	9.4	5	1,450	**2,065**	2,550
	9.2	6	535	**757**	911
	9.0	6	455	**552**	700
	8.0	14	229	**275**	350
	7.5	9	153	**193**	255
	7.0	9	111	**165**	204
	6.0	5	70	**99**	113
#7	9.0	6	416	**605**	835
	8.5	7	257	**343**	381
	8.0	9	68	**232**	300
	7.5	10	152	**191**	228
	7.0	6	124	**139**	180
	3.5	6	41	**47**	55
#8	9.0	13	328	**452**	700
	8.5	11	243	**298**	382
	8.0	9	177	**213**	280
	7.5	10	81	**146**	175
	7.0	18	77	**118**	200
	6.5	7	70	**100**	128
	5.0	8	42	**67**	91
	3.5	11	10	**35**	75
#9	9.2	12	432	**659**	810
	9.0	8	128	**402**	699
	8.5	10	234	**278**	319
	8.0	5	190	**233**	280
	7.5	8	143	**178**	265
	5.0	8	51	**66**	81
	4.0	6	44	**52**	71
#10	9.2	25	183	**530**	750
	9.0	12	99	**341**	541
	8.5	19	109	**250**	375
	8.0	18	133	**192**	220
	7.5	16	79	**134**	200
	6.5	9	20	**76**	105
	6.0	8	52	**81**	119
	5.0	5	45	**54**	60
	4.0	14	13	**35**	50
#11	9.0	5	429	**503**	563
	7.5	6	90	**106**	127
	6.5	5	76	**86**	95
	4.5	5	35	**49**	57
	2.0	6	11	**16**	25
#12	9.4	7	1,437	**2,052**	2,500
	9.0	6	380	**472**	569
	8.5	6	182	**348**	449
	8.0	12	191	**249**	356
	7.5	7	151	**196**	270
	5.0	8	29	**62**	106
	2.0	6	26	**38**	50
#13	9.0	10	182	**258**	346
	8.5	5	154	**224**	300
	8.0	11	51	**128**	166
	7.5	7	81	**118**	148
	7.0	5	61	**82**	97
	6.0	6	21	**55**	75
#14	9.4	14	708	**936**	1,278
	9.2	9	285	**489**	789
	9.0	12	213	**310**	440
	8.5	5	184	**225**	251
	8.0	14	76	**152**	235
	7.5	25	76	**121**	212
	7.0	9	67	**86**	119
	4.0	10	11	**38**	65
#15	8.5	16	138	**210**	325
	8.0	8	139	**153**	170
	7.5	10	26	**89**	114
	7.0	16	61	**87**	120
	6.5	5	43	**59**	69
	4.0	14	6	**24**	52
#16	9.4	9	505	**607**	722
	9.2	7	103	**267**	431
	9.0	7	175	**202**	250
	8.5	8	104	**136**	178
	7.0	13	46	**66**	103
	6.5	5	35	**49**	76
#17	9.0	6	202	**243**	316
	7.0	8	10	**40**	71
#18	8.0	10	71	**100**	154
	7.0	6	13	**32**	56
	6.0	7	40	**51**	75
#19	9.2	8	100	**280**	655
	9.0	17	100	**164**	266
	8.5	9	31	**107**	136
	7.0	6	46	**62**	90
	6.0	8	10	**28**	65
#20	9.4	13	100	**383**	600
	9.2	7	165	**256**	406
	8.5	13	71	**105**	150
	8.0	6	69	**94**	120
	7.0	5	41	**57**	75
#21	9.4	16	225	**341**	588
	9.2	19	82	**147**	208
	9.0	13	66	**128**	210
	8.5	14	18	**73**	100
	8.0	8	50	**71**	82
	7.5	7	36	**51**	78
#22	9.2	5	165	**282**	382
	9.0	6	77	**147**	210
#23	9.4	5	270	**376**	482
	9.2	12	128	**169**	262
	9.0	8	77	**105**	128
	8.5	6	63	**83**	110
#24	9.4	17	226	**335**	440
	9.0	6	76	**109**	134
	8.0	6	51	**68**	82
#25	9.4	6	220	**361**	443

ISSUE	CGC GRADE	# of AUCTIONS	LOW CLOSE	AVG CLOSE	HIGH CLOSE
	9.2	25	66	**145**	204
	9.0	11	63	**113**	138
	8.0	7	40	**58**	100
#26	9.4	14	260	**345**	480
	9.2	12	109	**167**	195
	9.0	10	71	**118**	170
	8.0	16	31	**58**	81
#27	9.4	7	310	**394**	525
	9.2	18	97	**159**	300
	9.0	17	71	**117**	203
	8.5	7	64	**79**	97
	8.0	7	40	**57**	90
	7.5	6	10	**33**	75
#28	9.2	16	228	**299**	420
	9.0	12	128	**193**	295
	8.5	14	81	**127**	156
	8.0	9	65	**97**	139
	6.5	7	31	**46**	75
	6.0	9	10	**41**	90
#29	9.4	10	250	**333**	442
	9.2	13	104	**152**	202
	9.0	11	46	**111**	200
	8.5	8	65	**96**	130
#30	9.4	7	230	**309**	402
	9.2	12	94	**166**	240
	9.0	9	69	**103**	133
	8.0	11	41	**61**	95
	7.5	8	19	**38**	53
	6.0	6	10	**20**	30
#31	9.2	6	90	**123**	160
	9.0	5	95	**103**	110
	8.0	6	44	**57**	71
	7.5	6	31	**40**	60
#32	9.6	7	128	**372**	602
	9.4	17	169	**281**	480
	9.2	13	101	**146**	210
	9.0	20	43	**111**	250
	8.5	8	55	**73**	111
	8.0	8	28	**50**	69
	6.0	6	26	**32**	36
#33	9.2	7	125	**152**	203
	9.0	7	85	**108**	136
	8.0	5	50	**62**	76
#34	9.2	6	108	**130**	159
	9.0	10	64	**94**	168
	8.0	5	52	**57**	61
#35	9.2	10	262	**350**	461
	9.0	14	121	**208**	275
	8.5	6	138	**157**	177
	7.5	12	62	**96**	193
	6.5	8	26	**52**	81
#36	9.4	6	200	**271**	330
	9.2	12	77	**120**	153
	9.0	19	46	**92**	135
	8.5	5	52	**65**	81
	7.0	5	11	**38**	58
#37	9.4	14	47	**236**	309
	9.2	14	51	**130**	204
	9.0	9	63	**106**	151
#38	9.4	6	270	**295**	325
	9.2	13	42	**151**	268
	9.0	11	90	**108**	130
	8.5	7	50	**68**	90
	8.0	8	36	**61**	94
#39	9.4	5	360	**487**	718
	9.2	5	129	**224**	367
	9.0	7	71	**116**	180
	8.5	6	65	**80**	91
	8.0	5	32	**48**	59
#40	9.6	10	41	**421**	875
	9.4	10	155	**233**	360
	9.2	9	81	**134**	205
	9.0	18	28	**85**	159
	8.5	10	49	**70**	115
	7.5	5	22	**34**	41
	7.0	6	21	**33**	45
#41	9.4	7	222	**299**	414
	9.0	5	71	**86**	100
	8.5	5	46	**72**	125
	8.0	6	42	**46**	51
	7.0	6	10	**17**	31
#42	9.0	6	69	**91**	125
#43	9.2	6	66	**136**	216
	8.0	6	33	**44**	51
#44	9.4	5	256	**340**	425
	9.0	6	47	**76**	100
#45	9.6	8	260	**344**	537
	9.4	25	123	**208**	431
	9.2	12	40	**98**	159
	9.0	14	53	**70**	110
	8.5	7	48	**57**	67
	7.5	6	11	**31**	40
#47	9.2	11	50	**105**	150
	8.5	5	32	**48**	57
	8.0	7	26	**36**	50
#48	9.2	6	82	**113**	178
	9.0	8	35	**67**	90
	8.5	7	46	**58**	80
#49	9.0	8	67	**87**	145
	8.5	9	51	**62**	78
#50	9.4	18	200	**316**	454
	9.2	21	75	**136**	229
	9.0	19	42	**79**	103
	8.5	10	55	**67**	90
	7.5	6	26	**41**	57
	7.0	8	26	**38**	46

ISSUE	CGC GRADE	# of AUCTIONS	LOW CLOSE	AVG CLOSE	HIGH CLOSE
X-Men (Vol. 1) (cont'd)					
	4.0	5	4	**9**	17
#51	9.4	9	178	**236**	326
	9.2	17	41	**121**	175
	9.0	11	36	**68**	101
	8.0	11	22	**44**	66
#52	9.4	5	154	**270**	345
	9.0	5	50	**76**	100
	8.5	5	39	**49**	61
	8.0	5	33	**40**	57
#53	9.4	5	292	**331**	440
	9.2	25	42	**113**	189
	9.0	12	61	**80**	119
	8.5	8	41	**56**	80
	8.0	5	28	**46**	52
#54	9.4	11	197	**260**	315
	9.2	9	65	**141**	198
	9.0	9	61	**83**	125
	8.5	7	20	**52**	86
	8.0	5	31	**42**	56
#55	9.6	6	380	**597**	795
	9.4	11	126	**236**	300
	9.2	7	56	**103**	140
	9.0	8	54	**78**	100
	8.5	7	50	**68**	89
	8.0	10	30	**44**	79
	7.5	6	30	**45**	100
#56	9.4	15	150	**317**	860
	9.2	16	46	**142**	204
	9.0	11	61	**76**	100
	8.5	11	31	**59**	75
	8.0	6	32	**44**	62
	7.5	5	33	**44**	53
#57	9.4	11	279	**334**	450
	9.2	7	128	**168**	205
	9.0	12	69	**80**	103
	8.5	5	45	**59**	68
	8.0	7	35	**44**	53
#58	9.4	6	304	**400**	550
	9.2	11	120	**216**	370
	9.0	17	91	**124**	164
	7.5	8	33	**44**	51
	6.0	5	22	**35**	44
	2.5	6	1	**13**	19
#59	9.0	5	84	**105**	120
#60	9.4	14	153	**277**	579
	9.2	8	75	**119**	148
	9.0	10	42	**77**	114
	8.5	8	36	**56**	70
	8.0	6	30	**42**	55
	7.0	5	21	**27**	35
#61	9.4	12	220	**282**	331
	9.2	9	88	**127**	160
	9.0	10	51	**75**	109
	8.5	7	36	**56**	104
	8.0	10	40	**51**	75
#62	9.0	6	77	**93**	112
	8.5	5	39	**56**	71
#63	9.2	7	123	**145**	200
	9.0	9	51	**81**	101
	8.5	6	30	**54**	76
#64	9.4	6	206	**286**	383
	9.2	7	103	**149**	210
	9.0	6	56	**97**	150
	7.5	6	19	**40**	64
#65	9.4	6	67	**235**	356
	9.2	6	100	**130**	171
	9.0	5	66	**92**	133
	8.5	6	54	**63**	70
#66	9.2	5	128	**153**	183
	9.0	6	63	**92**	110
#68	9.2	5	53	**78**	91
#69	9.4	6	93	**136**	158
	9.2	10	46	**87**	160
#70	9.4	10	104	**144**	203
#72	9.6	9	155	**226**	310
	9.4	5	113	**141**	168
	9.0	5	25	**35**	41
#74	9.4	8	53	**124**	203
#75	9.6	5	128	**225**	280
	9.0	8	27	**38**	50
#77	9.4	5	78	**113**	155
	9.0	5	42	**53**	61
#78	9.4	6	113	**148**	213
#80	9.4	6	81	**130**	250
#83	9.0	9	38	**49**	64
#85	9.2	6	27	**54**	80
#86	9.4	5	66	**111**	133
#87	8.5	5	21	**37**	43
#89	9.2	5	35	**53**	90
	9.0	11	16	**41**	66
#92	8.5	6	22	**28**	41
#94	9.6	13	3,600	**5,042**	6,988
	9.4	25	1,225	**1,927**	2,725
	9.2	25	430	**901**	1,335
	9.0	25	153	**618**	992
	8.5	25	230	**450**	625
	8.0	25	154	**330**	500
	7.5	25	99	**254**	405
	7.0	25	96	**204**	350
	6.5	25	81	**186**	405
	6.0	25	115	**169**	275
	5.5	25	98	**136**	188
	5.0	25	70	**114**	195
	4.5	19	78	**105**	148
	4.0	12	67	**97**	123
	3.5	9	51	**84**	140
	3.0	12	50	**78**	153
	2.5	10	35	**62**	104
#95	9.6	10	516	**695**	900
	9.4	25	250	**338**	600
	9.2	25	96	**187**	338
	9.0	25	75	**108**	218
	8.5	25	42	**93**	129
	8.0	19	33	**71**	115
	7.5	25	31	**55**	90
	7.0	12	34	**46**	71
	6.5	12	20	**42**	65
	5.5	7	22	**37**	45
	4.5	6	17	**32**	60

ISSUE	CGC GRADE	# of AUCTIONS	LOW CLOSE	AVG CLOSE	HIGH CLOSE
	4.0	5	17	**27**	30
#96	9.6	16	390	**467**	643
	9.4	25	148	**219**	300
	9.2	25	53	**102**	153
	9.0	25	30	**77**	125
	8.5	25	40	**67**	118
	8.0	20	21	**42**	62
	7.5	21	21	**37**	67
	7.0	18	16	**32**	50
	6.5	8	21	**31**	62
	6.0	5	16	**28**	45
	4.5	10	11	**19**	26
#97	9.6	20	285	**408**	611
	9.4	24	128	**209**	330
	9.2	25	76	**110**	160
	9.0	10	53	**72**	95
	8.5	11	45	**63**	88
	8.0	20	25	**49**	81
	7.5	11	25	**37**	56
	7.0	7	23	**30**	36
	6.5	6	18	**21**	24
	6.0	5	2	**21**	28
	5.5	5	16	**19**	21
#98	9.6	7	316	**459**	561
	9.4	25	52	**200**	305
	9.2	19	75	**105**	198
	9.0	19	27	**90**	250
	8.5	18	22	**62**	96
	7.5	8	21	**35**	45
	7.0	12	25	**38**	91
#99	9.6	17	228	**415**	610
	9.4	24	128	**185**	356
	9.2	15	75	**107**	150
	9.0	24	42	**67**	90
	8.5	14	45	**58**	95
	8.0	14	37	**50**	75
	7.5	13	17	**32**	60
	7.0	13	13	**28**	50
	6.5	5	20	**25**	29
#100	9.8	5	900	**1,329**	1,950
	9.6	25	325	**512**	760
	9.4	25	150	**225**	430
	9.2	25	86	**122**	178
	9.0	25	51	**94**	163
	8.5	25	37	**67**	102
	8.0	25	22	**55**	82
	7.5	25	18	**43**	76
	7.0	13	23	**36**	45
	6.5	6	12	**40**	90
	6.0	9	21	**31**	40
#101	9.6	25	265	**574**	860
	9.4	25	133	**232**	531
	9.2	25	70	**163**	310
	9.0	25	51	**100**	224
	8.5	13	34	**76**	130
	8.0	15	40	**76**	124
	7.5	10	31	**52**	103
	7.0	5	25	**46**	73
	6.5	9	26	**44**	69
#102	9.6	5	230	**303**	445
	9.4	23	76	**135**	228
	9.2	15	49	**76**	125
	9.0	17	25	**52**	109
	8.5	8	35	**46**	75
	8.0	8	16	**27**	41
#103	9.6	7	229	**307**	403
	9.4	25	75	**122**	229
	9.2	24	36	**59**	96
	9.0	20	25	**50**	125
	8.5	13	21	**36**	55
	8.0	8	13	**25**	32
#104	9.6	9	163	**232**	287
	9.4	25	41	**107**	160
	9.2	12	41	**67**	97
	9.0	12	28	**42**	62
	8.5	8	19	**38**	62
	8.0	10	17	**29**	46
	7.0	6	16	**21**	25
#105	9.6	25	129	**217**	350
	9.4	25	41	**96**	183
	9.2	25	30	**54**	125
	9.0	12	21	**43**	61
	8.5	13	20	**37**	56
	8.0	18	10	**26**	50
	7.5	5	10	**26**	51
#106	9.6	18	103	**185**	326
	9.4	25	41	**91**	225
	9.2	18	22	**43**	71
	9.0	11	26	**38**	54
	8.5	11	25	**33**	45
	7.5	7	16	**24**	46
#107	9.6	10	165	**266**	402
	9.4	15	72	**111**	147
	9.2	8	41	**67**	93
	9.0	8	29	**42**	54
	8.5	10	20	**35**	65
#108	9.6	25	104	**260**	565
	9.4	25	66	**131**	261
	9.2	25	51	**78**	106
	9.0	25	37	**64**	105
	8.5	21	34	**50**	71
	8.0	6	35	**44**	57
	7.5	9	9	**24**	36
	7.0	13	10	**25**	36
	6.0	5	13	**21**	35

X-Men (Vol. 1) (cont'd)

ISSUE	CGC GRADE	# of AUCTIONS	LOW CLOSE	AVG CLOSE	HIGH CLOSE
#109	9.6	14	170	**226**	360
	9.4	25	51	**110**	178
	9.2	21	25	**73**	110
	9.0	20	25	**51**	80
	8.5	13	26	**39**	61
	7.5	7	17	**29**	56
#110	9.6	25	96	**167**	255
	9.4	25	51	**73**	122
	9.2	20	25	**44**	100
	9.0	21	21	**39**	60
	8.5	6	20	**30**	48
	7.5	6	10	**21**	30
	7.0	8	11	**19**	27
#111	9.8	14	281	**384**	500
	9.6	20	81	**136**	213
	9.4	25	30	**76**	110
	9.2	21	23	**48**	75
	9.0	6	30	**45**	56
	8.5	10	20	**33**	50
	8.0	9	11	**21**	35
#112	9.6	14	89	**183**	286
	9.4	25	50	**74**	130
	9.2	16	35	**48**	74
	9.0	12	20	**34**	50
	8.5	9	24	**31**	51
	8.0	5	12	**20**	28
#113	9.6	21	113	**166**	257
	9.4	22	63	**80**	138
	9.2	7	36	**50**	71
	9.0	9	23	**40**	73
	8.5	18	15	**29**	61
#114	9.6	13	19	**278**	405
	9.4	18	12	**89**	140
	9.2	16	31	**44**	76
	9.0	17	23	**33**	51
	8.5	13	13	**24**	35
	8.0	7	21	**30**	50
	7.0	6	9	**17**	28
#115	9.6	18	89	**163**	228
	9.4	19	51	**80**	114
	9.2	16	26	**43**	54
	9.0	9	21	**37**	55
	8.5	16	16	**27**	38
	8.0	8	12	**22**	28
#116	9.6	13	128	**191**	277
	9.4	23	41	**69**	95
	9.2	14	25	**38**	66
	9.0	10	21	**27**	36
	8.5	6	11	**23**	36
	8.0	7	5	**20**	27
#117	9.6	25	75	**121**	193
	9.4	25	33	**60**	106
	9.2	25	26	**39**	56
	9.0	25	16	**27**	38
	8.5	10	13	**22**	35
	6.0	5	12	**13**	15
#118	9.6	25	26	**99**	209
	9.4	25	31	**54**	105
	9.2	25	15	**34**	51
	9.0	15	12	**26**	40
	8.5	7	6	**22**	46
	8.0	7	16	**24**	45
#119	9.8	16	174	**233**	325
	9.6	25	56	**99**	168
	9.4	25	31	**50**	150
	9.2	25	16	**33**	56
	9.0	12	14	**24**	31
	8.5	10	11	**28**	50
#120	9.6	8	262	**369**	515
	9.4	25	85	**123**	166
	9.2	25	32	**60**	130
	9.0	25	25	**42**	71
	8.5	16	19	**32**	43
	8.0	15	10	**27**	41
	7.5	8	16	**25**	36
	7.0	9	13	**20**	35
#121	9.6	25	103	**209**	356
	9.4	25	61	**99**	160
	9.2	25	30	**61**	118
	9.0	25	20	**49**	160
	8.5	23	21	**39**	75
	8.0	9	16	**29**	50
	7.5	9	15	**21**	30
	7.0	6	8	**18**	26
	6.0	6	8	**13**	21
#122	9.6	22	52	**126**	250
	9.4	25	28	**56**	103
	9.2	13	25	**43**	65
	9.0	11	15	**26**	40
	8.5	11	11	**25**	48
	8.0	5	16	**20**	22
	7.5	7	10	**18**	30
#123	9.6	25	51	**105**	203
	9.4	25	26	**49**	84
	9.2	11	18	**27**	42
	9.0	9	22	**29**	46
	8.5	7	12	**22**	38
#124	9.6	25	51	**109**	280
	9.4	25	26	**44**	80
	9.2	19	17	**27**	40
	9.0	8	12	**25**	40
	8.5	7	16	**23**	30
	8.0	15	7	**19**	28
	7.0	6	6	**14**	22
#125	9.8	14	183	**287**	495
	9.6	25	49	**92**	148
	9.4	25	36	**52**	81
	9.2	25	21	**36**	86
	9.0	13	18	**32**	76
#126	9.6	25	51	**85**	178
	9.4	25	27	**47**	65
	9.2	25	22	**31**	61
	9.0	7	21	**27**	35
	8.5	19	11	**21**	31
	8.0	10	10	**17**	26
#127	9.8	15	115	**220**	357
	9.6	25	41	**76**	153
	9.4	25	26	**43**	80
	9.2	25	14	**28**	46

ISSUE	CGC GRADE	# of AUCTIONS	LOW CLOSE	AVG CLOSE	HIGH CLOSE
	9.0	14	12	**22**	41
	8.5	6	15	**22**	31
	8.0	7	15	**18**	25
#128	9.6	25	73	**115**	223
	9.4	25	21	**45**	75
	9.2	18	21	**30**	43
	9.0	16	20	**29**	51
	8.5	11	8	**19**	36
	8.0	10	10	**19**	32
	7.0	5	12	**14**	17
#129	9.8	8	180	**314**	480
	9.6	25	61	**138**	275
	9.4	25	37	**63**	198
	9.2	25	24	**45**	100
	9.0	13	16	**32**	60
	8.5	11	14	**29**	45
	7.0	6	9	**22**	35
#130	9.6	25	36	**112**	281
	9.4	25	24	**66**	113
	9.2	25	12	**33**	51
	9.0	13	14	**26**	32
	8.5	14	6	**17**	30
	8.0	10	10	**19**	29
#131	9.6	25	53	**113**	249
	9.4	25	13	**52**	91
	9.2	21	18	**28**	51
	9.0	22	10	**24**	42
	8.5	13	4	**20**	33
	8.0	9	12	**17**	22
	7.5	6	10	**20**	40
	6.5	5	5	**8**	11
#132	9.8	5	179	**285**	411
	9.6	25	51	**86**	160
	9.4	25	25	**47**	75
	9.2	22	11	**28**	45
	9.0	11	17	**24**	35
	8.5	10	8	**18**	26
	8.0	5	11	**14**	20
#133	9.8	7	171	**253**	400
	9.6	25	54	**112**	179
	9.4	25	30	**53**	113
	9.2	18	23	**34**	58
	9.0	7	19	**27**	37
	8.5	8	8	**17**	25
#134	9.8	7	180	**326**	585
	9.6	25	53	**117**	213
	9.4	25	27	**50**	100
	9.2	22	21	**35**	62
	9.0	10	17	**29**	35
	8.5	14	11	**26**	61
	7.5	7	7	**14**	23
#135	9.8	25	143	**218**	434
	9.6	25	31	**89**	149
	9.4	25	29	**54**	101
	9.2	19	19	**32**	53
	9.0	9	20	**27**	34
	8.5	7	19	**23**	28
	6.5	5	3	**9**	17
#136	9.8	5	138	**300**	555
	9.6	25	44	**90**	180

ISSUE	CGC GRADE	# of AUCTIONS	LOW CLOSE	AVG CLOSE	HIGH CLOSE
	9.4	25	25	**42**	60
	9.2	25	20	**31**	56
	9.0	9	10	**24**	45
	8.5	6	10	**20**	25
#137	9.8	25	108	**256**	455
	9.6	25	41	**90**	221
	9.4	25	25	**53**	105
	9.2	25	16	**37**	90
	9.0	25	15	**29**	45
	8.5	20	15	**25**	46
	8.0	12	16	**24**	40
#138	9.8	20	120	**188**	280
	9.6	25	36	**58**	111
	9.4	25	6	**33**	66
	9.2	25	13	**26**	47
	9.0	22	9	**23**	36
	8.5	13	10	**18**	40
#139	9.6	25	25	**69**	125
	9.4	25	25	**45**	80
	9.2	25	16	**29**	50
	9.0	25	14	**26**	40
	8.5	8	11	**24**	38
	7.5	6	10	**20**	36
#140	9.8	8	55	**269**	404
	9.6	25	25	**70**	203
	9.4	25	15	**43**	100
	9.2	25	14	**29**	75
	9.0	16	10	**21**	40
	8.5	25	10	**20**	37
	8.0	7	13	**15**	19
	7.5	6	10	**15**	21
#141	9.8	25	193	**336**	566
	9.6	25	50	**94**	153
	9.4	25	25	**56**	105
	9.2	25	20	**36**	66
	9.0	16	18	**32**	64
	8.5	12	20	**29**	40
	8.0	7	13	**20**	27

X-Men (Vol. 2)

ISSUE	CGC GRADE	# of AUCTIONS	LOW CLOSE	AVG CLOSE	HIGH CLOSE
#1	9.8	25	10	**24**	80
	9.6	25	6	**16**	42
	9.4	9	6	**15**	40
	9.0	5	5	**9**	20
#2	9.8	15	11	**21**	30
	9.6	6	10	**16**	20

ISSUE	CGC GRADE	# of AUCTIONS	LOW CLOSE	AVG CLOSE	HIGH CLOSE
X-Men (Vol. 2) (cont'd)					
#3	9.8	5	19	**22**	25
#5	9.8	6	20	**32**	75
#6	9.8	5	12	**21**	29
#25	9.8	10	15	**37**	61
	9.6	22	10	**25**	45
	9.4	13	6	**16**	35
#100/DF	9.8	7	6	**33**	65
X-Men and the Micronauts					
#1	9.8	25	8	**19**	40
X-Men Unlimited					
#1	9.8	25	11	**21**	35
	9.6	6	10	**13**	19
X-Men: Alpha					
#1	9.8	17	10	**25**	65
	9.6	5	10	**18**	26
X-Men: Omega					
#1	9.8	12	10	**21**	32
X-Men: Prime					
#1	10.0	7	68	**134**	204
	9.9	8	25	**40**	50
	9.8	25	10	**20**	51
X-Men 2099					
#1	9.8	7	6	**18**	26
X-O Manowar					
#0	9.8	15	10	**21**	45
	9.6	5	10	**15**	26
#0/Gld	9.8	7	72	**122**	189

ISSUE	CGC GRADE	# of AUCTIONS	LOW CLOSE	AVG CLOSE	HIGH CLOSE
#1	9.8	22	10	**85**	154
	9.6	20	21	**36**	123
#2	9.8	9	16	**65**	153
	9.6	5	16	**23**	26
#3	9.8	9	21	**48**	76
#4	9.8	7	48	**64**	110
#5	9.8	5	37	**82**	145
#14	9.8	9	15	**28**	42
#15	9.8	6	10	**16**	23
X-Treme X-Men					
#1	9.6	8	11	**16**	21
Y: The Last Man					
#1	9.8	8	82	**142**	210
	9.6	16	34	**48**	75
	9.4	7	24	**32**	45
#4	9.4	5	1	**7**	15
Young Allies					
#2	7.0	6	520	**916**	1,275
#20	8.0	7	295	**497**	795
Young Love					
#107	9.0	8	26	**50**	65
Zip Comics					
#10	4.0	5	160	**196**	255
Zoo Funnies					
#2	9.4	5	77	**116**	182
Zoot Comics					
#7	8.0	7	290	**416**	52

Abbreviations

AA — Alfredo Alcala
AAd — Art Adams
AF — Al Feldstein
AM — Al Milgrom
AMo — Alan Moore
AN — Alex Nino
AR — Alex Raymond
AT — Angelo Torres
ATh — Alex Toth
AW — Al Williamson
BA — Brent Anderson
BB — Brian Bolland
BE — Bill Elder
BEv — Bill Everett
BG — Butch Guice
BH — Bob Hall
BK — Bernie Krigstein
BL — Bob Layton
BMc — Bob McLeod
BO — Bob Oksner
BS — Barry Smith
BSz — Bill Sienkiewicz
BT — Bryan Talbot
BW — Basil Wolverton
BWa — Bill Ward
BWi — Bob Wiacek
BWr — Berni Wrightson
CB — Carl Barks
CCB — C.C. Beck
CI — Carmine Infantino
CR — P. Craig Russell
CS — Curt Swan
CV — Charles Vess
DA — Dan Adkins
DC — Dave Cockrum
DD — Dick Dillin
DaG — Dave Gibbons
DG — Dick Giordano
DGr — Dan Green
DH — Don Heck
DN — Don Newton
DP — Don Perlin
DR — Don Rosa
DS — Dan Spiegle
DSt — Dave Stevens
EC — Ernie Colon
EL — Erik Larsen
FB — Frank Brunner
FF — Frank Frazetta
FG — Floyd Gottfredson
FGu — Fred Guardineer
FH — Fred Hembeck
FM — Frank Miller
FMc — Frank McLaughlin
FR — Frank Robbins
FS — Frank Springer
FT — Frank Thorne
GC — Gene Colan
GD — Gene Day
GE — George Evans
GI — Graham Ingels
GK — Gil Kane
GM — Gray Morrow
GP — George Pérez
GT — George Tuska
HC — Howard Chaykin
HK — Harvey Kurtzman
HT — Herb Trimpe
IN — Irv Novick
JA — Jim Aparo
JAb — Jack Abel
JB — John Buscema
JBy — John Byrne
JCr — Johnny Craig
JD — Jayson Disbrow
JDu — Jan Duursema
JJ — Jeff Jones
JK — Jack Kirby
JKa — Jack Kamen
JKu — Joe Kubert
JL — Jose Luis Garcia Lopez
JLee — Jim Lee
JM — Jim Mooney
JO — Joe Orlando
JOy — Jerry Ordway
JR — John Romita
JR2 — John Romita Jr.
JS — John Stanley
JSa — Joe Staton

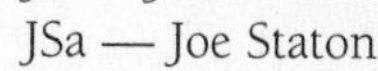

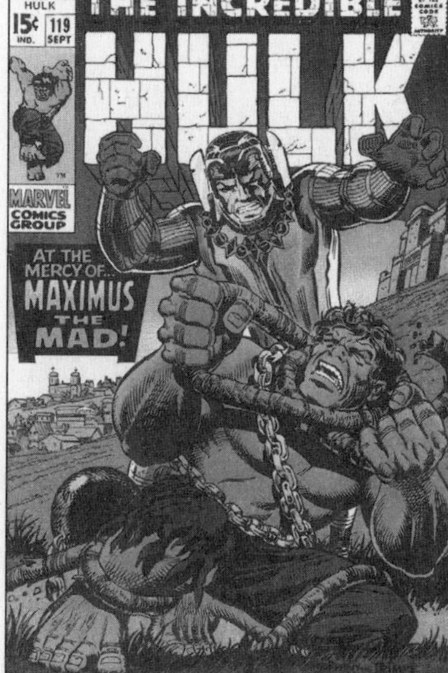

The entry for *Incredible Hulk* #119 reads: HT(c); SL (w); HT (a), which means Herb Trimpe was the cover and interior artist and Stan Lee was the writer.

JSe — John Severin
JSh — Jim Sherman
JSn — Jim Starlin
JSo — Jim Steranko
JSt — Joe Sinnott
KB — Kurt Busiek
KG — Keith Giffen
KGa — Kerry Gammill
KJ — Klaus Janson
KN — Kevin Nowlan
KP — Keith Pollard
KS — Kurt Schaffenberger
LMc — Luke McDonnell
MA — Murphy Anderson
MB — Matt Baker
MD — Mort Drucker
ME — Mark Evanier
MG — Michael Golden
MGr — Mike Grell
MGu — Mike Gustovich
MK — Mike Kaluta
MM — Mort Meskin
MN — Mike Nasser
MP — Mike Ploog
MR — Marshall Rogers
MW — Matt Wagner
MZ — Mike Zeck
NA — Neal Adams
NC — Nick Cardy
NG — Neil Gaiman
NR — Nestor Redondo
PB — Pat Broderick
PD — Peter David
PG — Paul Gulacy
PM — Pete Morisi
PS — Paul Smith
RA — Ross Andru
RB — Rich Buckler
RBy — Reggie Byers
RCo — Rich Corben
RE — Ric Estrada
RH — Russ Heath
RHo — Richard Howell
RK — Roy Krenkel
RL — Rob Liefeld
RM — Russ Manning
RMo — Ruben Moreira
RT — Romeo Tanghal
SA — Sergio Aragonés
SB — Sal Buscema
SD — Steve Ditko
SL — Stan Lee
SR — Steve Rude
SRB — Steve Rude
TA — Tony DeZuniga
TMc — Todd McFarlane
TP — Tom Palmer
TS — Tom Sutton
TVE — Trevor Von Eeden
TY — Tom Yeates
VM — Val Mayerik
WE — Will Eisner
WH — Wayne Howard
WK — Walt Kelly
WP — Wendy Pini
WS — Walter Simonson
WW — Wally Wood

Issue information (additional issue information appears on Page 11)

A — Appearance of
Aut — Autographed edition
C — Cameo of
D — Death of
DFE — Dynamic Forces Edition
Giant — Giant Size
HOL — Hologram cover
HS — Holiday Special
I — Introduction of
J — Joining of
JSA — Justice Society of America
L — Leaving of
M or W — Wedding of
N — New costume
nn — no number
O — Origin of
R — Revival or return of
rep. — reprint
SE — Special Edition
Smr — Summer Special
SS — Swimsuit Special
V — versus
1 — first appearance of
2 — second appearance of
3 — third appearance of

The entry for *Incredible Hulk* #180 reads: HT(c); HT, JAb (a); 1: Wolverine (cameo). A: Wendigo. Marvel Value Stamp #67: Cyclops, which means Herb Trimpe was the cover artist, he and Jack Abel were interior artists, Wolverine makes his first appearance in a cameo, Wendigo (who's also featured on the cover) makes an appearance, and the issue contains one of the Marvel Value Stamps issued in the mid-1970s, this one featuring Cyclops (who does not make an appearance in this issue).

N-MINT

A

A1 TRUE LIFE BIKINI CONFIDENTIAL, THE
ATOMEKA
- ❑1, b&w 6.95

A1 (VOL. 1)
ATOMEKA
- ❑1 1989 BB (c); AMo, NG (w); DaG, BSz (a) 6.00
- ❑2 1989 AMo, NG (w); MW, DaG, BB (a) 10.00
- ❑3 1990 BB (c); BB, AMo (w); BB (a) 6.00
- ❑4 1990 BB, AMo (w); BSz (a) 6.00
- ❑5 1991 JKu, JJ, NG (w); JKu, JJ (a) 8.00
- ❑6 1992 9.00
- ❑7 8.00

A1 (VOL. 2)
MARVEL / EPIC
- ❑1, ca. 1992 FM (w); CR (a) 6.00
- ❑2, ca. 1992 FM (w) 6.00
- ❑3, ca. 1992 6.00
- ❑4, ca. 1993 6.00

A', A
VIZ
- ❑1, b&w 15.95

ÄARDWOLF
AARDWOLF
- ❑1, Dec 1994 2.95
- ❑2, Feb 1995 2.95

AARON STRIPS
IMAGE
- ❑1, Apr 1997 2.95
- ❑2, Jun 1997 2.95
- ❑3, Aug 1997 2.95
- ❑4, Oct 1997; has "Aaron Warner's Year of the Monkey" back-up; goes to Amazing Aaron Productions 2.95
- ❑5, Jan 1999; continued numbering from Image series 2.95
- ❑6, Mar 1999 2.95

ABADAZAD
CROSSGEN
- ❑1, Feb 2004 2.95
- ❑1-2, Mar 2004 2.95
- ❑2, Mar 2004 2.95
- ❑3, Apr 2004 2.95
- ❑3-2, Apr 2004 2.95

ABBOTT & COSTELLO (CHARLTON)
CHARLTON
- ❑1, Feb 1968 30.00
- ❑2, Apr 1968 20.00
- ❑3, Jun 1968 20.00
- ❑4, Aug 1968 14.00
- ❑5, Oct 1968 14.00
- ❑6, Dec 1968 14.00
- ❑7, Mar 1969 14.00
- ❑8, Apr 1969 14.00
- ❑9, Jun 1969 14.00
- ❑10, Aug 1969 14.00
- ❑11, Oct 1969 12.00
- ❑12, Dec 1969; Abbott & Costello, Pie-In-The-Face Maze Page; Hearty Humor (text story); Abbott & Costello Game Page 12.00
- ❑13, Feb 1970 12.00
- ❑14, Apr 1970 12.00
- ❑15, Jun 1970; "Crazy Quiz", Joke Page; Ivan Inventorsky The Inventor "Build Your Private Beach" (text story); Maze Page 12.00
- ❑16, Aug 1970 12.00
- ❑17, Oct 1970; Nutty daisy poster; Haunted House Maze 12.00
- ❑18, Dec 1970 12.00
- ❑19, Feb 1971 12.00
- ❑20, Apr 1971 12.00
- ❑21, Jun 1971 12.00
- ❑22, Aug 1971 12.00

N-MINT

A.B.C. WARRIORS
FLEETWAY-QUALITY
- ❑1 1990 2.00
- ❑2 1990 2.00
- ❑3 1990 2.00
- ❑4 1990 2.00
- ❑5 1990 2.00
- ❑6 1990 2.00
- ❑7 1990 2.00
- ❑8 1990 2.00

ABC WARRIORS: KHRONICLES OF KHAOS
FLEETWAY-QUALITY
- ❑1 2.95
- ❑2 2.95
- ❑3 2.95
- ❑4 2.95

ABE SAPIEN DRUMS OF THE DEAD
DARK HORSE
- ❑1, Mar 1998; Hellboy back-up 2.95

A. BIZARRO
DC
- ❑1, Jul 1999 2.50
- ❑2, Aug 1999 2.50
- ❑3, Sep 1999 2.50
- ❑4, Oct 1999 2.50

A-BOMB
ANTARCTIC / VENUS
- ❑1, Dec 1993 2.95
- ❑2, Mar 1994 2.95
- ❑3, Jun 1994; Barr Girls story 2.95
- ❑4, Sep 1994; Barr Girls story 2.95
- ❑5, Dec 1994 2.95
- ❑6, Mar 1995 2.95
- ❑7, Jun 1995 2.95
- ❑8, Sep 1995 2.95
- ❑9, Nov 1995 2.95
- ❑10, Jan 1996 2.95
- ❑11, Mar 1996; Title page shows Vol. 2 #1 2.95
- ❑12, May 1996 2.95
- ❑13, Jul 1996 2.95
- ❑14, Sep 1996 2.95
- ❑15, Nov 1996 2.95
- ❑16, Jan 1997 2.95

ABOMINATIONS
MARVEL
- ❑1, Dec 1996; follows events in Hulk: Future Imperfect 1.50
- ❑2, Jan 1997 1.50
- ❑3, Feb 1997 1.50

ABRAHAM STONE (EPIC)
MARVEL / EPIC
- ❑1, Jul 1995 6.95
- ❑2, Aug 1995 6.95

ABSOLUTE VERTIGO
DC / VERTIGO
- ❑1, Win 1995 3.50

ABSOLUTE ZERO
ANTARCTIC
- ❑1, Feb 1995, b&w 3.50
- ❑2, May 1995, b&w 2.95
- ❑3, Aug 1995, b&w 2.95
- ❑4, Oct 1995, b&w 2.95
- ❑5, Dec 1995, b&w 2.95
- ❑6, Feb 1996, b&w 2.95

ABSURD ART OF J.J. GRANDVILLE, THE
TOME
- ❑1, b&w; no date of publication 2.50

ABYSS, THE
DARK HORSE
- ❑1, Aug 1989 2.50
- ❑2, Sep 1989 2.50

AC ANNUAL
AC
- ❑1 3.50
- ❑2 5.00

Charlton attempted to make Abbott & Costello hip and happening in their late 1960s comics series.

© 1969 Charlton

N-MINT

- ❑3 3.50
- ❑4 3.95

ACCELERATE
DC / VERTIGO
- ❑1, Aug 2000 2.95
- ❑2, Sep 2000 2.95
- ❑3, Oct 2000 2.95
- ❑4, Nov 2000 2.95

ACCIDENTAL DEATH, AN
FANTAGRAPHICS
- ❑1, Dec 1993, b&w 3.50

ACCIDENT MAN
DARK HORSE
- ❑1, ca. 1993 2.50
- ❑2, ca. 1993 2.50
- ❑3, ca. 1993 2.50

ACCLAIM ADVENTURE ZONE
ACCLAIM
- ❑1 1997; Ninjak on Cover 4.50
- ❑2 1997; Turok on Cover 4.50
- ❑3 1997; Turok and Dinosaur on Cover 4.50

ACE
HARRIER
- ❑1, b&w; no indicia 1.95

ACE COMICS PRESENTS
ACE
- ❑1, May 1987; Daredevil (Golden Age) vs. The Claw; Silver Streak 2.00
- ❑2, Jul 1987; Jack Bradbury 2.00
- ❑3, Sep 1987; The Golden Age of Klaus Nordling 2.00
- ❑4, Nov 1987; Lou Fine 2.00

ACE MCCOY
AVALON
- ❑1, b&w 2.95
- ❑2, b&w 2.95
- ❑3, b&w 2.95

ACE OF SPADES
ZUZUPETAL
- ❑1 2.50

ACES
ECLIPSE
- ❑1, Apr 1988 3.00
- ❑2 3.00
- ❑3 3.00
- ❑4 3.00
- ❑5 3.00

ACES HIGH (RCP)
RCP
- ❑1, Apr 1999 2.50
- ❑2, May 1999 2.50
- ❑3, Jun 1999 2.50
- ❑4, Jul 1999 2.50
- ❑5, Aug 1999 2.50
- ❑Annual 1; Collects Aces High #1-5 13.50

ACG CHRISTMAS SPECIAL
AVALON
- ❑1; Cover reads "Christmas Horror" 2.95

ACG'S CIVIL WAR
AVALON
- ❑1 1995 2.50

ACG'S HALLOWEEN SPECIAL
AVALON
- ❑1; Cover reads "Halloween Horror" 2.95

N-MINT

ACHILLES STORM: DARK SECRET
BRAINSTORM

- ❑1 ... 2.95
- ❑2 ... 2.95

ACHILLES STORM/RAZMATAZ
AJA BLU

- ❑1, Oct 1990 ... 2.25
- ❑2, Jan 1991 ... 2.25
- ❑3, May 1991 ... 2.25
- ❑4, Nov 1991 ... 2.25

ACID BATH CASE, THE
KITCHEN SINK

- ❑1 ... 4.95

ACK THE BARBARIAN
INNOVATION

- ❑1, b&w ... 2.25

ACME
FANDOM HOUSE

- ❑1 ... 3.00
- ❑2 ... 3.00
- ❑3 ... 3.00
- ❑4 ... 3.00
- ❑5 ... 3.00
- ❑6 ... 3.00
- ❑7 ... 3.00
- ❑8, Fal 1987 ... 2.00
- ❑9, Sum 1989 ... 3.00

ACME NOVELTY LIBRARY, THE
FANTAGRAPHICS

- ❑1, Win 1993 1: Jimmy Corrigan ... 10.00
- ❑1-2, Dec 1995; Jimmy Corrigan ... 3.95
- ❑2, Sum 1994; Quimby the Mouse ... 7.00
- ❑2-2, Sum 1995; Quimby the Mouse ... 4.95
- ❑3, Aut 1994; digest-sized; Blind Man ... 5.00
- ❑4, Win 1994; Sparky's Best Comics and Stories ... 5.00
- ❑4-2 ... 4.95
- ❑5; digest-sized; Jimmy Corrigan ... 3.95
- ❑6, Fal 1995; digest-sized; Jimmy Corrigan ... 3.95
- ❑7; Oversized; Book of Jokes ... 6.95
- ❑8, Win 1996; digest-sized; Jimmy Corrigan ... 4.75
- ❑9, Win 1997; digest-sized; Jimmy Corrigan ... 4.50
- ❑10, Spr 1998; digest-sized; Jimmy Corrigan ... 4.95
- ❑11, Fal 1998; digest-sized; Jimmy Corrigan ... 4.50
- ❑12, Spr 1999; digest-sized; Jimmy Corrigan ... 4.50
- ❑14, Aut 1999; Jimmy Corrigan ... 10.95

ACOLYTE, THE
MAD MONKEY

- ❑1, ca. 1993, b&w ... 3.95

ACTION COMICS
DC

- ❑0, Oct 1994; 1: Kenny Braverman. Peer Pressure, Part 4; ▲ 1994-40 ... 3.00
- ❑1-2; 2nd printing (giveaway, 1976?) FGu (w); FGu (a); O: Superman. 1: Zatara. 1: Superman. 1: Tex Thomson. 1: Lois Lane ... 18.00
- ❑1-3; 3rd printing (giveaway, 1983?) FGu (w); FGu (a); O: Superman. 1: Zatara. 1: Superman. 1: Tex Thomson. 1: Lois Lane ... 14.00
- ❑1-4; 4th printing (Nestle Quik 16-page giveaway, 1988) O: Superman ... 6.00
- ❑1-5; FGu (w); FGu (a); O: Superman. 1: Zatara. 1: Superman. 1: Tex Thomson. 1: Lois Lane. 5th printing (1992) ... 5.00
- ❑220, Sep 1956 ... 290.00
- ❑221, Oct 1956 ... 240.00
- ❑222, Nov 1956 ... 240.00
- ❑223, Dec 1956 ... 240.00
- ❑224, Jan 1957 ... 240.00
- ❑225, Feb 1957 ... 240.00
- ❑226, Mar 1957 ... 240.00
- ❑227, Apr 1957 ... 240.00
- ❑228, May 1957 ... 240.00
- ❑229, Jun 1957 ... 240.00
- ❑230, Jul 1957 ... 240.00
- ❑231, Aug 1957 ... 240.00
- ❑232, Sep 1957 CS (c) ... 240.00
- ❑233, Oct 1957 CS (c) ... 240.00
- ❑234, Nov 1957 CS (c) ... 240.00
- ❑235, Dec 1957 CS (c) ... 240.00
- ❑236, Jan 1958; CS (c); Tommy Tomorrow and Congo Bill/Janu the Jungle Boy back-ups ... 240.00
- ❑237, Feb 1958 CS (c) ... 240.00
- ❑238, Mar 1958 CS (c) ... 240.00
- ❑239, Apr 1958 CS (c) ... 240.00
- ❑240, May 1958; CS (c) ... 240.00
- ❑241, Jun 1958 CS (c); 1: Fortress of Solitude ... 250.00
- ❑242, Jul 1958 CS (c); O: Brainiac. 1: Kandor. 1: Brainiac ... 1200.00
- ❑243, Aug 1958 CS (c) ... 185.00
- ❑244, Sep 1958; CS (c); CS (a); Tommy Tomorrow and Congo Bill/Janu the Jungle Boy back-ups ... 185.00
- ❑245, Oct 1958 CS (c) ... 185.00
- ❑246, Nov 1958 CS (c) ... 185.00
- ❑247, Dec 1958 CS (c) ... 185.00
- ❑248, Jan 1959 CS (c); 1: Congorilla ... 185.00
- ❑249, Feb 1959 CS (c) ... 185.00
- ❑250, Mar 1959 CS (c) ... 185.00
- ❑251, Apr 1959; CS (c); Tommy Tomorrow; Legion ... 185.00
- ❑252, May 1959; CS (c); O: Supergirl. 1: Anti-Kryptonite. 1: Supergirl ... 1200.00
- ❑253, Jun 1959; CS (c); 2: Supergirl ... 425.00
- ❑254, Jul 1959 CS (c); A: Bizarro ... 325.00
- ❑255, Aug 1959 CS (c); 1: Bizarro Lois Lane ... 225.00
- ❑256, Sep 1959 CS (c) ... 100.00
- ❑257, Oct 1959 CS (c) ... 100.00
- ❑258, Nov 1959; CS (c); New Stars for Old Glory (PSA) ... 100.00
- ❑259, Dec 1959; CS (c); A: Superboy. Congorilla back-up ... 100.00
- ❑260, Jan 1960 CS (c) ... 100.00
- ❑261, Feb 1960 CS (c); O: Streaky the Supercat. 1: X-Kryptonite. 1: Streaky the Supercat ... 100.00
- ❑262, Mar 1960 CS (c) ... 90.00
- ❑263, Apr 1960 CS (c); O: Bizarro World ... 100.00
- ❑264, May 1960 CS (c) ... 80.00
- ❑265, Jun 1960 CS (c); CS (a) ... 80.00
- ❑266, Jul 1960 CS (c); CS (a) ... 80.00
- ❑267, Aug 1960 CS (c); 1: Chameleon Boy. 1: Colossal Boy. 1: Invisible Kid I (Lyle Norg) ... 250.00
- ❑268, Sep 1960 CS (c) ... 80.00
- ❑269, Oct 1960 CS (c) ... 80.00
- ❑270, Nov 1960 CS (c) ... 80.00
- ❑271, Dec 1960 CS (c) ... 65.00
- ❑272, Jan 1961 CS (c) ... 65.00
- ❑273, Feb 1961 CS (c); V: Mxyzptlk ... 65.00
- ❑274, Mar 1961 CS (c) ... 65.00
- ❑275, Apr 1961 CS (c) ... 65.00
- ❑276, May 1961; CS (c); JM (a); Triplicate Girl, Phantom Girl, Brainiac 5, Shrinking Violet, Bouncing Boy joins team ... 125.00
- ❑277, Jun 1961 CS (c) ... 60.00
- ❑278, Jul 1961 CS (c) ... 60.00
- ❑279, Aug 1961 CS (c) ... 60.00
- ❑280, Sep 1961 CS (c) ... 60.00
- ❑281, Oct 1961 CS (c) ... 60.00
- ❑282, Nov 1961 CS (c) ... 60.00
- ❑283, Dec 1961; CS (c); Legion of Super-Villains ... 60.00
- ❑284, Jan 1962; CS (c); Mon-El ... 60.00
- ❑285, Feb 1962; CS (c); NA (a); A: Legion of Super-Heroes. Supergirl goes public ... 100.00
- ❑286, Mar 1962; CS (c); Legion of Super-Villains ... 60.00
- ❑287, Apr 1962 CS (c); JM (a); A: Legion of Super-Heroes ... 60.00
- ❑288, May 1962; CS (c); Mon-El ... 60.00
- ❑289, Jun 1962 CS (c); JM (a); A: Legion of Super-Heroes ... 60.00
- ❑290, Jul 1962 CS, KS (c); CS (a); A: Legion of Super-Heroes ... 60.00
- ❑291, Aug 1962 CS (c); NA (a) ... 60.00
- ❑292, Sep 1962 CS (c); A: Superhorse (Comet) ... 60.00
- ❑293, Oct 1962 CS (c); O: Superhorse (Comet) ... 60.00
- ❑294, Nov 1962 CS (c); CS (a) ... 60.00
- ❑295, Dec 1962 CS (c); JM (a) ... 60.00
- ❑296, Jan 1963 CS (c); CS, JM (a) ... 60.00
- ❑297, Feb 1963 CS (c); JM (a) ... 60.00
- ❑298, Mar 1963 CS (c); CS, JM (a) ... 60.00
- ❑299, Apr 1963 CS (c) ... 60.00
- ❑300, May 1963; 300th anniversary issue CS (c) ... 50.00
- ❑301, Jun 1963 ... 50.00
- ❑302, Jul 1963 CS (a) ... 50.00
- ❑303, Aug 1963 CS (a) ... 50.00
- ❑304, Sep 1963 CS, JM (a); 1: Black Flame ... 50.00
- ❑305, Oct 1963 ... 50.00
- ❑306, Nov 1963 ... 50.00
- ❑307, Dec 1963 ... 50.00
- ❑308, Jan 1964 ... 50.00
- ❑309, Feb 1964; NA (a); A: Supergirl's parents. Legion ... 50.00
- ❑310, Mar 1964 1: Jewel Kryptonite ... 50.00
- ❑311, Apr 1964 ... 50.00
- ❑312, May 1964 ... 50.00
- ❑313, Jun 1964 A: Batman ... 50.00
- ❑314, Jul 1964 A: Batman ... 50.00
- ❑315, Aug 1964 ... 50.00
- ❑316, Sep 1964 ... 50.00
- ❑317, Oct 1964 ... 40.00
- ❑318, Nov 1964 ... 40.00
- ❑319, Dec 1964 ... 40.00
- ❑320, Jan 1965 ... 40.00
- ❑321, Feb 1965 CS (a) ... 40.00
- ❑322, Mar 1965 ... 40.00
- ❑323, Apr 1965 ... 40.00
- ❑324, May 1965 ... 40.00
- ❑325, Jun 1965 ... 40.00
- ❑326, Jul 1965 ... 40.00
- ❑327, Aug 1965; Imaginary Superman story ... 40.00
- ❑328, Sep 1965 ... 40.00
- ❑329, Oct 1965 ... 40.00
- ❑330, Nov 1965 ... 40.00
- ❑331, Dec 1965 ... 40.00
- ❑332, Jan 1966; Imaginary Superwoman Story ... 40.00
- ❑333, Feb 1966; Imaginary Superwoman Story ... 40.00
- ❑334, Mar 1966; Giant-sized issue O: Supergirl ... 60.00
- ❑335, Mar 1966 ... 30.00
- ❑336, Apr 1966 O: Akvar ... 30.00
- ❑337, May 1966 ... 30.00
- ❑338, Jun 1966 CS (a) ... 30.00
- ❑339, Jul 1966 CS, JM (a) ... 50.00
- ❑340, Aug 1966 1: Parasite ... 30.00
- ❑341, Sep 1966 A: Batman ... 30.00
- ❑342, Oct 1966 ... 30.00
- ❑343, Nov 1966 ... 30.00
- ❑344, Dec 1966 A: Batman ... 30.00
- ❑345, Jan 1967 A: Allen Funt ... 30.00
- ❑346, Feb 1967 ... 30.00
- ❑347, Apr 1967; Giant-sized issue; Supergirl; reprints Superman #140 and Action #290 and #293 ... 40.00
- ❑348, Mar 1967 ... 30.00
- ❑349, Apr 1967 ... 30.00
- ❑350, May 1967 JM (a) ... 30.00
- ❑351, Jun 1967 ... 30.00
- ❑352, Jul 1967 ... 30.00
- ❑353, Aug 1967 ... 30.00
- ❑354, Sep 1967 ... 30.00
- ❑355, Oct 1967 ... 30.00
- ❑356, Nov 1967 ... 30.00
- ❑357, Dec 1967 CS (a) ... 30.00
- ❑358, Jan 1968 CS (a) ... 30.00
- ❑359, Feb 1968 CS (a) ... 30.00
- ❑360, Mar 1968; Giant-sized issue; Supergirl ... 40.00

	N-MINT
❑361, Apr 1968	30.00
❑362, May 1968	30.00
❑363, Jun 1968	30.00
❑364, Jul 1968 KS (a); D: Superman	30.00
❑365, Aug 1968 D: Superman	30.00
❑366, Sep 1968 D: Superman	30.00
❑367, Oct 1968 CS (a)	30.00
❑368, Nov 1968 CS, JAb (a)	30.00
❑369, Dec 1968 CS, JAb (a)	30.00
❑370, Jan 1969 CS, JAb (a)	30.00
❑371, Feb 1969 CS, JAb (a)	30.00
❑372, Mar 1969 CS, JAb (a)	30.00
❑373, Apr 1969; Giant-sized issue; NA, CS (a); A: Supergirl. Giant size; Supergirl stories	40.00
❑374, Mar 1969 CS, JAb (a)	20.00
❑375, Apr 1969 CS, JAb (a); A: Batman	20.00
❑376, May 1969 CS, JAb (a)	20.00
❑377, Jun 1969; CS, JAb (a); Legion; Reprint from Adventure Comics #300	20.00
❑378, Jul 1969; CS, JAb (a); Legion	20.00
❑379, Aug 1969; CS, JAb (a); Legion	20.00
❑380, Sep 1969; CS (a); Legion	20.00
❑381, Oct 1969; CS (a); Legion	20.00
❑382, Nov 1969; CS (a); Legion	20.00
❑383, Dec 1969; CS (a); Legion	20.00
❑384, Jan 1970; CS (a); Legion	20.00
❑385, Feb 1970; CS (a); Legion	20.00
❑386, Mar 1970; CS (a); Legion	20.00
❑387, Apr 1970; CS (a); Legion	20.00
❑388, May 1970; CS (a); Legion; Reprints Legion story from Adventure Comics #302	20.00
❑389, Jun 1970; CS (a); Legion	20.00
❑390, Jul 1970; CS (a); Legion	20.00
❑391, Aug 1970; CS (a); Legion	20.00
❑392, Sep 1970; CS (a); Super-Sons; Last Legion of Super-Heroes	20.00
❑393, Oct 1970 CS (c); CS (a)	20.00
❑394, Nov 1970 CS (a)	20.00
❑395, Dec 1970 CS (a)	20.00
❑396, Jan 1971; MA, CS (a); Tales of the Fortress	20.00
❑397, Feb 1971; CS (a); Tales of the Fortress	20.00
❑398, Mar 1971 CS (a)	20.00
❑399, Apr 1971 CS (a)	20.00
❑400, May 1971 CS (a)	17.00
❑401, Jun 1971 CS (a)	17.00
❑402, Jul 1971; CS (a); Tales of the Fortress	17.00
❑403, Aug 1971; CS (a); Reprints from Adventure #310	17.00
❑404, Sep 1971; CS (a); Aquaman and Atom reprint stories	17.00
❑405, Oct 1971; CS (a); Aquaman and Vigilante reprint stories	17.00
❑406, Nov 1971; CS (c); ATh, CS (a); Atom and Flash story, part 1; reprinted from Brave and the Bold #53	17.00
❑407, Dec 1971; CS (c); ATh, CS (a); Atom and Flash story, part 2; reprinted from Brave and the Bold #53	15.00
❑408, Jan 1972; CS (c); GK, CS (a); reprints The Atom #9	15.00
❑409, Feb 1972; CS (a); Teen Titans reprint story	15.00
❑410, Feb 1972; CS (a); Teen Titans reprint story	13.00
❑411, Apr 1972; CS (a); O: Eclipso. Eclipso reprint story	13.00
❑412, May 1972; CS (a); Eclipso reprint story	12.00
❑413, Jun 1972; ATh, CS (a); Eclipso and Metamorpho reprint stories	12.00
❑414, Jul 1972 CS (a)	12.00
❑415, Aug 1972 CS (a)	12.00
❑416, Sep 1972 CS (a)	11.00
❑417, Oct 1972 CS (a)	11.00
❑418, Nov 1972 CS (a)	11.00
❑419, Dec 1972 CS (a); 1: Human Target	14.00
❑420, Jan 1973 CS (a)	11.00
❑421, Feb 1973; CS (a); Green Arrow begins	11.00
❑422, Mar 1973 CS (a)	11.00
❑423, Apr 1973 CS (a)	10.00
❑424, Jun 1973; MA, DG, CS (a); Green Arrow	10.00
❑425, Jul 1973 MA, DG, NA, CS (a)	19.00
❑426, Aug 1973 CS (a)	8.00
❑427, Sep 1973 CS (a)	8.00
❑428, Oct 1973 CS (a)	8.00
❑429, Nov 1973 CS (a)	8.00
❑430, Dec 1973; CS (a); Atom back-up	8.00
❑431, Jan 1974; CS (a); Green Arrow back-up	8.00
❑432, Feb 1974 CS (a)	8.00
❑433, Mar 1974 CS (a)	8.00
❑434, Apr 1974 CS (a)	8.00
❑435, May 1974 CS (a)	8.00
❑436, Jun 1974 CS (a)	8.00
❑437, Jul 1974; Giant-sized issue (100 pages); NC (c); MA, CI, GK, CS, RH, KS (a); Reprints Sea Devils #1, Mystery in Space #85, Western Comics #77, My Greatest Adventure #3, Doll Man #13; Appearance of Flash, Green Arrow, and Green Lantern	25.00
❑438, Aug 1974 CS (a)	8.00
❑439, Sep 1974; CS (a); Atom back-up	8.00
❑440, Oct 1974; MGr, CS (a); 1st Green Arrow by Mike Grell	25.00
❑441, Nov 1974; MGr, CS (a); A: Flash. Green Arrow back-up	12.00
❑442, Dec 1974 CS (a)	8.00
❑443, Jan 1975; Giant-sized issue (100 pages); NC (c); MA, CI, GK, CS, RH (a); 100-Page Super Spectacular; JLA, Sea Devils, Matt Savage, Adam Strange, Hawkman and Black Pirate; reprints stories from Sea Devils #3, Western	
❑Comics #78, Mystery in Space #87 and Sensation Comics #4	26.00
❑444, Feb 1975; CS (a); A: Green Lantern. Green Arrow back-up	7.00
❑445, Mar 1975 CS (a)	7.00
❑446, Apr 1975 CS (a)	7.00
❑447, May 1975 CS (a)	7.00
❑448, Jun 1975 CS (a)	7.00
❑449, Jul 1975; JK, CS (a); Green Arrow giant	7.00
❑450, Aug 1975 CS (a)	7.00
❑451, Sep 1975; CS (a); Green Arrow back-up	7.00
❑452, Oct 1975 CS (a)	7.00
❑453, Nov 1975; CS (a); Atom back-up	7.00
❑454, Dec 1975; CS (a); last Atom back-up	7.00
❑455, Jan 1976 CS (a)	6.00
❑456, Feb 1976; CS (a); Green Arrow/Black Canary back-up	6.00
❑457, Mar 1976; CS (a); Green Arrow/Black Canary back-up; Superman reveals ID to Pete Ross' son	6.00
❑458, Apr 1976; MGr, CS (a); 1: Blackrock. Green Arrow	6.00
❑459, May 1976 CS (a)	6.00
❑460, Jun 1976; CS (a); 1: Karb-Brak. Mxyzptlk back-up	6.00
❑461, Jul 1976; CS (a); V: Karb-Brak. Superman in colonial America; Bicentennial #30	6.00
❑462, Aug 1976 CS (a)	6.00
❑463, Sep 1976; CS (a); Bicentennial story	6.00
❑464, Oct 1976 CS (a)	6.00
❑465, Nov 1976 CS (a)	6.00
❑466, Dec 1976 CS (a)	5.00
❑467, Jan 1977 CS (a)	5.00
❑468, Feb 1977 CS (a)	5.00
❑469, Mar 1977 CS (a)	5.00
❑470, Apr 1977 CS (a)	5.00
❑471, May 1977 CS (a)	5.00
❑472, Jun 1977 CS (a); V: Faora Hu-Ul	5.00
❑473, Jul 1977 CS (a)	5.00
❑474, Aug 1977 CS (a)	5.00
❑475, Sep 1977 CS (a)	5.00
❑476, Oct 1977 CS (a)	5.00

Superman's first appearance in *Action Comics* #1 has been reprinted several times.

© 1992 DC Comics.

Original publication

© 1938 National Periodical Publications.

	N-MINT
❑477, Nov 1977 CS (a)	5.00
❑478, Dec 1977 CS (a)	5.00
❑479, Jan 1978 CS (a)	5.00
❑480, Feb 1978 CS (a)	5.00
❑481, Mar 1978 CS (a); 1: Supermobile. V: Amazo	5.00
❑482, Apr 1978 CS (a)	5.00
❑483, May 1978 CS (a); V: Amazo	5.00
❑484, Jun 1978; 40th anniversary; CS (a); Wedding of E-2 Superman and Lois Lane	5.00
❑485, Jul 1978 CS (a)	5.00
❑486, Aug 1978 CS (a)	5.00
❑487, Sep 1978 CS (a); O: Atom	5.00
❑488, Oct 1978 CS (a)	5.00
❑489, Nov 1978; CS (a); Atom back-up	5.00
❑490, Dec 1978 CS (a)	5.00
❑491, Jan 1979 CS (a)	5.00
❑492, Feb 1979 CS (a)	5.00
❑493, Mar 1979 CS (a)	5.00
❑494, Apr 1979 CS (a)	5.00
❑495, May 1979 CS (a); 1: Silver Banshee	5.00
❑496, Jun 1979 CS (a)	5.00
❑497, Jul 1979 CS (a)	5.00
❑498, Aug 1979 CS (a)	5.00
❑499, Sep 1979 CS (a)	5.00
❑500, Oct 1979; Giant-sized; CS (a); O: Superman. Superman's life	5.00
❑501, Nov 1979 CS (a)	5.00
❑502, Dec 1979 CS (a)	5.00
❑503, Jan 1980 CS (a)	5.00
❑504, Feb 1980 CS (a)	4.00
❑505, Mar 1980 CS (a)	4.00
❑506, Apr 1980 CS (a)	4.00
❑507, May 1980 CS (a)	4.00
❑508, Jun 1980 CS (a)	4.00
❑509, Jul 1980; JSn, CS, JSt (a); Radio Shack promo insert	4.00
❑510, Aug 1980 CS (a)	4.00
❑511, Sep 1980 CS (a)	4.00
❑512, Oct 1980; CS (a); Air Wave back-up	4.00
❑513, Nov 1980 CS (a)	4.00
❑514, Dec 1980 CS (a)	4.00
❑515, Jan 1981; CS (a); V: Vandal Savage. Atom back-up	4.00
❑516, Feb 1981; CS (a); V: Vandal Savage. Atom back-up	4.00
❑517, Mar 1981 CS (a)	4.00
❑518, Apr 1981; CS (a); Aquaman back-up	4.00
❑519, May 1981 CS (a)	4.00
❑520, Jun 1981 CS (a)	4.00
❑521, Jul 1981; CS (a); 1: Vixen. Atom, Aquaman back-up	4.00
❑522, Aug 1981; CS (a); Atom back-up	4.00
❑523, Sep 1981; CS (a); Atom back-up	4.00
❑524, Oct 1981; CS (a); Airwave and Atom back-up	4.00
❑525, Nov 1981 CS (a); 1: Neutron	4.00
❑526, Dec 1981 CS (a)	4.00
❑527, Jan 1982; CS (a); 1: Lord Satanis. Airwave, Aquaman back-up	4.00
❑528, Feb 1982; CS (a); A: Brainiac. Aquaman back-up	4.00
❑529, Mar 1982 CS (a)	4.00
❑530, Apr 1982 CS (a)	4.00
❑531, May 1982 CS (a)	4.00
❑532, Jun 1982 CS (a)	4.00

	N-MINT
❑533, Jul 1982 CS (a)	4.00
❑534, Aug 1982 CS (a)	4.00
❑535, Sep 1982 CS (a); A: Omega Men	4.00
❑536, Oct 1982 CS (a); A: Omega Men	4.00
❑537, Nov 1982; CS (a); Aquaman back-up; Masters of the Universe preview	4.00
❑538, Dec 1982 CS (a)	4.00
❑539, Jan 1983; GK, CS (a); Flash, Atom	4.00
❑540, Feb 1983; CS (a); Aquaman back-up	4.00
❑541, Mar 1983 CS (a)	4.00
❑542, Apr 1983 CS (a); V: Vandal Savage	4.00
❑543, May 1983 CS (a); V: Neutron	4.00
❑544, Jun 1983; 45th anniversary; DG, GK (c); GK, CS (a); O: Brainiac (New). O: Lex Luthor (New). 1: Brainiac (New). 1: Lex Luthor (New). 45th Anniversay issue; New Luthor and Braniac; Joe Shuster pin-up	4.00
❑545, Jul 1983 CS (a); V: New Brainiac	3.00
❑546, Aug 1983; CS (a); A: JLA, Titans	3.00
❑547, Sep 1983 CS (a)	3.00
❑548, Oct 1983 CS (a)	3.00
❑549, Nov 1983 CS (a)	3.00
❑550, Dec 1983 CS (a)	3.00
❑551, Jan 1984 CS (a); 1: Red Star (Starfire)	3.00
❑552, Feb 1984; CS (a); 1: Legion of Forgotten Heroes. A: Animal Man. Cave Carson, Congorilla, Suicide Squad, Animal Man, Rip Hunter, Immortal Man, Sea Devils, Dolphin	3.00
❑553, Mar 1984; CS (a); A: Legion of Forgotten Heroes. Cave Carson, Congorilla, Suicide Squad, Animal Man, Rip Hunter, Immortal Man, Sea Devils, Dolphin	3.00
❑554, Apr 1984; CS (a); Jerry and Joey create Superman	3.00
❑555, May 1984; CS (a); A: Supergirl. V: Parasite. Anniversary of Supergirl's debut in Action Comics; Continues in Supergirl #20	3.00
❑556, Jun 1984; CS (a); V: Vandal Savage. Neutron	3.00
❑557, Jul 1984 CS (a)	3.00
❑558, Aug 1984 CS (a)	3.00
❑559, Sep 1984 CS (a)	3.00
❑560, Oct 1984; CS (a); A: Ambush Bug	3.00
❑561, Nov 1984 CS (a)	3.00
❑562, Dec 1984 CS (a)	3.00
❑563, Jan 1985; CS (a); Ambush Bug vs. Mxyzptlk	3.00
❑564, Feb 1985 CS (a)	3.00
❑565, Mar 1985; CS (a); A: Ambush Bug	3.00
❑566, Apr 1985; CS (a); V: Captain Strong	3.00
❑567, May 1985 CS (a)	2.00
❑568, Jun 1985 CS (a)	2.00
❑569, Jul 1985 CS (a)	2.00
❑570, Aug 1985 CS (a)	2.00
❑571, Sep 1985 CS (a)	2.00
❑572, Oct 1985; MWa (w); CS (a); Mark Waid's first major comics work	2.00
❑573, Nov 1985; CS (a); MASK preview	2.00
❑574, Dec 1985 CS (a)	2.00
❑575, Jan 1986 CS (a)	2.00
❑576, Feb 1986 CS (a)	2.00
❑577, Mar 1986 CS (a)	2.00
❑578, Apr 1986 CS (a)	2.00
❑579, May 1986 CS (a)	2.00
❑580, Jun 1986 CS (a)	2.00
❑581, Jul 1986 CS (a)	2.00
❑582, Aug 1986 CS (a)	2.00
❑583, Sep 1986; AMo (w); CS (a); Continued from Superman #423; Last pre-Crisis on Infinite Earths Superman	2.00
❑584, Jan 1987; JBy (w); JBy, DG (a); A: Teen Titans; Post-Crisis Superman begins	2.00
❑585, Feb 1987; JBy, DG (a); A: Phantom Stranger	2.00
❑586, Mar 1987; JBy, DG (a); A: Orion. New Gods; "Legends" Chapter 19	2.00
❑587, Apr 1987; JBy, DG (a); A: Demon	2.00
❑588, May 1987; JBy, DG (a); A: Hawkman. Shadow War; Continued from Hawkman #10, continues in Hawkman #11 and Action #589	2.00
❑589, Jun 1987; JBy, DG (a); A: Green Lantern Corps	2.00
❑590, Jul 1987; JBy, DG (a); A: Metal Men. New Chemo	2.00
❑591, Aug 1987; JBy, DG (a); A: Superboy	2.00
❑592, Sep 1987; JBy, DG (a); A: Big Barda	2.00
❑593, Oct 1987; JBy, DG (a); A: Mr. Miracle	2.00
❑594, Nov 1987; JBy (a); A: Batman. Booster Gold; Continues in Booster Gold #23	2.00
❑595, Dec 1987; JBy (a); A: Batman. J'onn J'onzz	2.00
❑596, Jan 1988; JBy (a); A: Spectre. "Millennium" Week 4	2.00
❑597, Feb 1988; JBy (a); A: Lois Lane and Lana Lang	2.00
❑598, Mar 1988; JBy (a); 1: Checkmate	4.00
❑599, Apr 1988; JBy, RA (a); A: Metal Men. Bonus Book #1, Jimmy Olsen	2.00
❑600, May 1988; Giant-sized; GP, JBy (a); 50th Anniversary, 80-page Giant; Wonder Woman; pin-ups; "Genesis" prequel	5.00
❑601, Aug 1988; Superman, Blackhawk, Green Lantern, Deadman, Wild Dog, Secret Six; Action Comics begins weekly issues	2.00
❑602, Aug 1988; Superman, Blackhawk, Green Lantern, Deadman, Wild Dog, Secret Six	1.75
❑603, Aug 1988; Superman, Blackhawk, Green Lantern, Deadman, Wild Dog, Secret Six	1.75
❑604, Aug 1988; Superman, Blackhawk, Green Lantern, Deadman, Wild Dog, Secret Six	1.75
❑605, Aug 1988; Superman, Blackhawk, Green Lantern, Deadman, Wild Dog, Secret Six	1.75
❑606, Sep 1988; Superman, Blackhawk, Green Lantern, Deadman, Wild Dog, Secret Six	1.75
❑607, Sep 1988; Superman, Blackhawk, Green Lantern, Deadman, Wild Dog, Secret Six	1.75
❑608, Sep 1988; Superman, Blackhawk, Green Lantern, Deadman, Wild Dog, Secret Six	1.75
❑609, Sep 1988; BB (c); Superman, Black Canary, Green Lantern, Deadman, Wild Dog, Secret Six	1.75
❑610, Sep 1988; PD (w); CS (a); Superman, Phantom Stranger, Black Canary, Green Lantern, Deadman, Secret Six	1.75
❑611, Oct 1988; PD (w); Superman, Catwoman, Black Canary, Green Lantern, Deadman, Secret Six	1.75
❑612, Oct 1988; Superman, Catwoman, Black Canary, Green Lantern, Deadman, Secret Six	1.75
❑613, Oct 1988; Superman, Nightwing/Speedy, Phantom Stranger, Catwoman, Black Canary, Green Lantern	1.75
❑614, Oct 1988; Superman, Nightwing/Speedy, Phantom Stranger, Catwoman, Black Canary, Green Lantern	1.75
❑615, Oct 1988; Superman, Wild Dog, Blackhawk, Nightwing/Speedy, Black Canary, Green Lantern	1.75
❑616, Nov 1988; Superman, Wild Dog, Blackhawk, Nightwing/Speedy, Black Canary, Green Lantern	1.75
❑617, Nov 1988; Superman, Phantom Stranger, Wild Dog, Blackhawk, Nightwing/Speedy, Green Lantern	1.75
❑618, Nov 1988; Superman, Deadman, Wild Dog, Blackhawk, Nightwing/Speedy, Green Lantern	1.75
❑619, Nov 1988; Superman, Secret Six, Deadman, Wild Dog, Blackhawk, Green Lantern	1.75
❑620, Dec 1988; Superman, Secret Six, Deadman, Wild Dog, Blackhawk, Green Lantern	1.75
❑621, Dec 1988; Superman, Secret Six, Deadman, Wild Dog, Blackhawk, Green Lantern	1.75
❑622, Dec 1988; Superman, Starman, Secret Six, Wild Dog, Blackhawk, Green Lantern	1.75
❑623, Dec 1988; BA (c); BA (a); Superman, Deadman, Phantom Stranger, Shazam!, Secret Six, Green Lantern	1.75
❑624, Dec 1988; Superman, Black Canary, Deadman, Shazam!, Secret Six, Green Lantern	1.75
❑625, Dec 1988; Superman, Black Canary, Deadman, Shazam!, Secret Six, Green Lantern	1.75
❑626, Nov 1988; Superman, Black Canary, Deadman, Shazam!, Secret Six, Green Lantern	1.75
❑627, Nov 1988; Superman, Nightwing/Speedy, Black Canary, Secret Six, Green Lantern	1.75
❑628, Nov 1988; Superman, Blackhawk, Nightwing/Speedy, Black Canary, Secret Six, Green Lantern	1.75
❑629, Dec 1988; Superman, Blackhawk, Nightwing/Speedy, Black Canary, Secret Six, Green Lantern	1.75
❑630, Dec 1988; Superman, Blackhawk, Nightwing/Speedy, Black Canary, Secret Six, Green Lantern	1.75
❑631, Dec 1988; Superman, Phantom Stranger, Blackhawk, Nightwing/Speedy, Black Canary, Green Lantern	1.75
❑632, Dec 1988; Superman, Phantom Stranger, Blackhawk, Nightwing/Speedy, Black Canary, Green Lantern	1.75
❑633, Jan 1989; Superman, Phantom Stranger, Blackhawk, Nightwing/Speedy, Black Canary, Green Lantern	1.75
❑634, Jan 1989; Superman, Phantom Stranger, Blackhawk, Nightwing/Speedy, Black Canary, Green Lantern	1.75
❑635, Jan 1989; Superman, Blackhawk, Black Canary, Green Lantern; All characters in first story	1.75
❑636, Jan 1989; 1: new Phantom Lady. Superman, Phantom Lady, Wild Dog, Demon, Speedy, Phantom Stranger	1.75
❑637, Jan 1989; 1: Hero Hotline. Superman, Hero Hotline, Phantom Lady, Wild Dog, Demon, Speedy	1.75
❑638, Feb 1989; JK (c); JK, CS, TD (a); 2: Hero Hotline. Superman, Hero Hotline, Phantom Lady, Wild Dog, Demon, Speedy	1.75
❑639, Feb 1989; A: Hero Hotline. Superman, Hero Hotline, Phantom Lady, Wild Dog, Demon, Speedy	1.75
❑640, Feb 1989; A: Hero Hotline. Superman, Hero Hotline, Phantom Lady, Wild Dog, Demon, Speedy	1.75
❑641, Mar 1989; Superman, Phantom Stranger, Human Target, Phantom Lady, Wild Dog, Demon	1.75
❑642, Mar 1989; Superman, Green Lantern, Nightwing, Deadman, Guy Gardner in one story; Last weekly issue	1.75
❑643, Jul 1989; GP (a); Cover swipe from Superman #1; Title returns to Action Comics; Monthly issues begin again	1.75
❑644, Aug 1989 GP (a)	1.75
❑645, Sep 1989; GP (a); 1: Maxima. V: Maxima. Starman	1.75
❑646, Oct 1989 KG, GP (a)	1.75
❑647, Nov 1989; GP (a); O: Brainiac. Braniac Trilogy, Part 1	1.75
❑648, Dec 1989; GP (a); Braniac Trilogy, Part 2	1.75
❑649, Jan 1990; GP (a); Braniac Trilogy, Part 3	1.75
❑650, Feb 1990 JO, GP (a); A: Lobo	1.75
❑651, Mar 1990; V: Maxima. Day of the Krypton Man, Part 3	1.75
❑652, Apr 1990; Day of the Krypton Man, Part 6	1.75
❑653, May 1990	1.75

Condition price index: Multiply "NM prices" above by: **0.83 for Very Fine/Near Mint**
0.66 for Very Fine • 0.33 for Fine • 0.2 for Very Good • 0.125 for Good

N-MINT

❑654, Jun 1990; Batman 1.75

❑655, Jul 1990 .... 1.75

❑656, Aug 1990 .... 1.75

❑657, Sep 1990; Toyman 1.75

❑658, Oct 1990 CS (a); A: Sinbad 1.75

❑659, Nov 1990; Krisis of the Krimson Kryptonite, Part 3 .... 1.75

❑660, Dec 1990 D: Lex Luthor (fake death) 2.50

❑661, Jan 1991; Plastic Man; ▲ 1991-3 .... 1.75

❑662, Feb 1991; Clark Kent reveals Superman identity to Lois Lane ▲ 1991-6 .... 4.00

❑662-2, Feb 1991; Clark Kent reveals Superman identity to Lois Lane; ▲ 1991-6, 2nd Printing 1.50

❑663, Mar 1991; Superman in 1940s; JSA; ▲ 1991-9 .... 1.75

❑664, Apr 1991; A: Chronos. Dinosaurs; ▲ 1991-12 .... 1.75

❑665, May 1991; ▲ 1991-15 .... 1.75

❑666, Jun 1991; ▲ 1991-18 .... 1.75

❑667, Jul 1991; ▲ 1991-22 .... 2.00

❑668, Aug 1991; ▲ 1991-26 .... 1.75

❑669, Sep 1991; A: Thorn. ▲ 1991-30 1.75

❑670, Oct 1991; 1: Lex Luthor II. Armageddon; ▲ 1991-34 .... 1.75

❑671, Nov 1991; Blackout, Part 2; ▲ 1991-38 .... 1.75

❑672, Dec 1991; BMc (a); ▲ 1991-42 1.75

❑673, Jan 1992; BMc (a); V: Hellgrammite. ▲ 1992-4 .... 1.75

❑674, Feb 1992; BMc (a); Panic in the Sky, Prologue; Supergirl; ▲ 1992-8 1.75

❑675, Mar 1992; BMc (a); Panic in the Sky, Part 4; ▲ 1992-12 .... 1.75

❑676, Apr 1992; ▲ 1992-16 .... 1.75

❑677, May 1992; ▲ 1992-20 .... 1.75

❑678, Jun 1992; O: Luthor. ▲ 1992-24 2.00

❑679, Jul 1992; ▲ 1992-28 .... 1.75

❑680, Aug 1992; Blaze/Satanus War; ▲ 1992-32 .... 1.75

❑681, Sep 1992; V: Rampage. ▲ 1992-36 .... 1.75

❑682, Oct 1992; V: Hi-Tech. ▲ 1992-40 .... 1.75

❑683, Nov 1992; Doomsday; ▲ 1992-44 .... 2.50

❑683-2, Nov 1992; Doomsday; ▲ 1992-44, 2nd Printing 1.50

❑684, Dec 1992; Doomsday; ▲ 1992-48 .... 2.50

❑684-2, Dec 1992; Doomsday; ▲ 1992-48, 2nd Printing 1.50

❑685, Jan 1993; Funeral For a Friend, Part 2; ▲ 1993-4 .... 2.00

❑685-2, Jan 1993; Funeral For a Friend, Part 2; ▲ 1993-4, 2nd Printing 1.25

❑685-3, Jan 1993; Funeral For a Friend, Part 2; ▲ 1993-4, 3rd Printing 1.25

❑686, Feb 1993; Funeral For a Friend, Part 6; ▲ 1993-8 .... 2.00

❑687, Jun 1993; 1: alien Superman. A: ▲ 1993-12, 1st. Reign of the Supermen; ▲ 1993-12 .... 1.50

❑687/CS, Jun 1993; Reign of the Supermen; Eradicator; ▲ 1993-12; Die-cut cover 2.50

❑688, Jul 1993; Reign of the Supermen; Guy Gardner; ▲ 1993-16 ..... 2.00

❑689, Jul 1993; Reign of the Supermen; ▲ 1993-20 .... 2.00

❑690, Aug 1993; Reign of the Supermen; ▲ 1993-24 .... 2.00

❑691, Sep 1993; Reign of the Supermen; ▲ 1993-28 .... 2.00

❑692, Oct 1993; Clark Kent returns; ▲ 1993-32 .... 2.00

❑693, Nov 1993; ▲ 1993-36 .... 2.00

❑694, Dec 1993; V: Hi-Tech. ▲ 1993-40 .... 1.75

❑695, Jan 1994; A: Lobo. ▲ 1994-4 . 1.75

❑695/Variant, Jan 1994; A: Lobo. enhanced cover; ▲ 1994-4 .... 2.50

❑696, Feb 1994; Return of Doomsday; ▲ 1994-8 .... 1.75

N-MINT

❑697, Mar 1994; Bizarro's World, Part 3; ▲ 1994-12 .... 1.75

❑698, Apr 1994; ▲ 1994-16 .... 1.75

❑699, May 1994; The Battle for Metropolis ▲ 1994-20 .... 1.75

❑700, Jun 1994; Giant-size; The Fall Of Metropolis; Wedding of Pete Ross and Lana Lang; Destruction of the Daily Planet building; ▲ 1994-24 .. 3.25

❑700/Platinum, Jun 1994; Giant-size; No cover price; The Fall Of Metropolis; Wedding of Pete Ross and Lana Lang; Destruction of the Daily Planet building; ▲ 1994-24 .... 5.00

❑701, Jul 1994; Fall of Metropolis; ▲ 1994-28 .... 1.75

❑702, Aug 1994; V: Bloodsport. ▲ 1994-32 .... 1.75

❑703, Sep 1994; A: Liri Lee. A: Starro. Zero Hour; ▲ 1994-36 .... 1.75

❑704, Nov 1994; V: Eradictor and The Outsiders. Dead Again; ▲ 1994-44 1.75

❑705, Dec 1994; Dead Again; ▲ 1994-48 .... 1.75

❑706, Jan 1995; Supergirl; ▲ 1995-4 1.75

❑707, Feb 1995; V: Shadowdragon. ▲ 1995-8 .... 1.75

❑708, Mar 1995; A: Mister Miracle. ▲ 1995-12 .... 1.75

❑709, Apr 1995; V: Guy Gardner. ▲ 1995-16 .... 1.75

❑710, Jun 1995; Death of Clark Kent; ▲ 1995-20 .... 1.95

❑711, Jul 1995; D: Kenny Braverman (Conduit). Death of Clark Kent; ▲ 1995-24 .... 1.95

❑712, Aug 1995; ▲ 1995-29 .... 1.95

❑713, Sep 1995; ▲ 1995-33 .... 1.95

❑714, Oct 1995; A: Joker. ▲ 1995-37 1.95

❑715, Nov 1995; V: Parasite. ▲ 1995-42 1.95

❑716, Dec 1995; Trial of Superman; ▲ 1995-46 .... 1.95

❑717, Jan 1996; Trial of Superman; ▲ 1996-1 .... 1.95

❑718, Feb 1996; 1: Demolitia. ▲ 1996-5 .... 1.95

❑719, Mar 1996; A: Batman. ▲ 1996-9 .... 1.95

❑720, Apr 1996; Lois Lane breaks off engagement to Clark Kent; ▲ 1996-14 .... 2.00

❑720-2, Apr 1996; Lois Lane breaks off engagement to Clark Kent; ▲ 1996-14, 2nd Printing 1.95

❑721, May 1996; A: Mxyzptlk. ▲ 1996-18 .... 1.95

❑722, Jun 1996; ▲ 1996-22 .... 1.95

❑723, Jul 1996; ▲ 1996-27 .... 1.95

❑724, Aug 1996; O: Brawl. D: Brawl. ▲ 1996-31 .... 1.95

❑725, Sep 1996; V: Tolos. The Bottle City, Part 1; ▲ 1996-35 .... 1.95

❑726, Oct 1996; V: Barrage. ▲ 1996-40 .... 1.95

❑727, Nov 1996; Final Night; ▲ 1996-44 .... 1.95

❑728, Dec 1996; Hawaiian Honeymoon; ▲ 1996-49 .... 1.95

❑729, Jan 1997; A: Mr. Miracle, Big Barda. Power Struggle; ▲ 1997-3 . 1.95

❑730, Feb 1997; V: Superman Revenge Squad (Anomaly, Maxima, Misa, Barrage and Riot). ▲ 1997-8 .... 1.95

❑731, Mar 1997; V: Cauldron. ▲ 1997-12 .... 1.95

❑732, Apr 1997; V: Atomic Skull. more energy powers manifest; ▲ 1997-17 .... 1.95

❑733, May 1997; A: Ray. new uniform; Ray; ▲ 1997-21 .... 1.95

❑734, Jun 1997; Scorn vs. Rock; ▲ 1997-25 .... 1.95

❑735, Jul 1997; V: Saviour. ▲ 1997-29 1.95

❑736, Aug 1997; ▲ 1997-33 .... 1.95

❑737, Sep 1997; Jimmy pursued by Intergang; ▲ 1997-37 .... 1.95

❑738, Oct 1997; 1: Inkling. ▲ 1997-42 1.95

After nearly a year as a weekly series, *Action Comics* returned to a monthly format with #643, the cover of which paid homage to *Superman* #1.

N-MINT

❑739, Nov 1997; A: Sam Lane. V: Locksmith. Lois captured by Naga; ▲ 1997-46 .... 1.95

❑740, Dec 1997; V: Ripper. Face cover; ▲ 1997-50 .... 1.95

❑741, Jan 1998; A: Legion of Super-Heroes. ▲ 1998-4 .... 1.95

❑742, Mar 1998; Cover forms diptych with Superman: Man of Steel #77; ▲ 1998-10 .... 1.95

❑743, Apr 1998; Orgin of Inkling; ▲ 1998-14 .... 1.95

❑744, May 1998; Millennium Giants; ▲ 1998-18 .... 1.95

❑745, Jun 1998; V: Prankster. Toyman; ▲ 1998-23 .... 1.95

❑746, Jul 1998; V: Prankster. Toyman; ▲ 1998-27 .... 1.95

❑747, Aug 1998; A: Dominus. ▲ 1998-31 .... 1.95

❑748, Sep 1998; A: Waverider. V: Dominus. ▲ 1998-35 .... 1.95

❑749, Dec 1998; into Kandor; ▲ 1998-41 .... 2.00

❑750, Jan 1999; Giant-size; 1: Crazy-top. ▲ 1999-1 .... 2.00

❑751, Feb 1999; A: Lex Luthor. A: Geo-Force. A: DEO agents. ▲ 1999-6 ... 1.99

❑752, Mar 1999; A: Supermen of America. ▲ 1999-11 .... 1.99

❑753, Apr 1999; A: JLA. ▲ 1999-15 . 1.99

❑754, May 1999; V: Dominus. ▲ 1999-20 .... 1.99

❑755, Jul 1999; ▲ 1999-25 .... 1.99

❑756, Aug 1999; V: Doomslayers. ▲ 1999-30 .... 1.99

❑757, Sep 1999; Superman as Hawkman; ▲ 1999-34 .... 1.99

❑758, Oct 1999; V: Intergang. ▲ 1999-38 .... 1.99

❑759, Nov 1999; SB (a); A: Strange Visitor. ▲ 1999-42 .... 1.99

❑760, Dec 1999; ▲ 1999-49 .... 1.99

❑761, Jan 2000; A: Wonder Woman. ▲ 2000-4 .... 1.99

❑762, Feb 2000; ▲ 2000-9 .... 1.99

❑763, Mar 2000; ▲ 2000-13 .... 1.99

❑764, Apr 2000; ▲ 2000-17 .... 1.99

❑765, May 2000; Joker, Harley Quinn; ▲ 2000-21 .... 1.99

❑766, Jun 2000; ▲ 2000-25 .... 1.99

❑767, Jul 2000; ▲ 2000-29 .... 1.99

❑768, Aug 2000; A: Captain Marvel Jr.. A: Captain Marvel. A: Mary Marvel. ▲ 2000-33 .... 1.99

❑769, Sep 2000; ▲ 2000-37 .... 2.25

❑770, Oct 2000; Giant-size; A: Joker. ▲ 2000-42 .... 3.50

❑771, Nov 2000; A: Nightwing. ▲ 2000-46 .... 2.25

❑772, Dec 2000; A: Encantadora. A: Talia. ▲ 2000-50 .... 2.25

❑773, Jan 2001; ▲ 2001-5 .... 2.25

❑774, Feb 2001; ▲ 2001-9 .... 2.25

❑775, Mar 2001; Giant-size; ▲ 2001-13 3.75

❑776, Apr 2001; ▲ 2001-17 .... 2.25

❑777, May 2001; ▲ 2001-21 .... 2.25

❑775-2, Jul 2004; Second Printing ....

❑778, Jun 2001; ▲ 2001-25 .... 2.25

❑779, Jul 2001; ▲ 2001-29 .... 2.25

❑780, Aug 2001; ▲ 2001-33 .... 2.25

❑781, Sep 2001; ▲ 2001-37 .... 2.25

N-MINT

❑782, Oct 2001; ▲ 2001-41 .... 2.25
❑783, Nov 2001; ▲ 2001-45 .... 2.25
❑784, Dec 2001; ▲ 2001-49 .... 2.25
❑785, Jan 2002; ▲ 2002-4 .... 2.25
❑786, Feb 2002 .... 2.25
❑787, Mar 2002 .... 2.25
❑788, Apr 2002 .... 2.25
❑789, May 2002 .... 2.25
❑790, Jun 2002 .... 2.25
❑791, Jul 2002 .... 2.25
❑792, Aug 2002 .... 2.25
❑793, Sep 2002 .... 2.25
❑794, Oct 2002 .... 2.25
❑795, Nov 2002, KN (c) 2.25
❑796, Dec 2002 .... 2.25
❑797, Jan 2003 .... 2.25
❑798, Feb 2003 .... 2.25
❑799, Mar 2003 .... 2.25
❑800, Apr 2003 .... 3.95
❑801, May 2003 .... 2.25
❑802, Jun 2003 .... 2.25
❑803, Jul 2003 .... 2.25
❑804, Jun 2003 .... 2.25
❑805, Jul 2003 .... 2.25
❑806, Aug 2003 .... 2.25
❑807, Sep 2003 .... 2.25
❑808, Oct 2003 .... 2.25
❑809, Nov 2003 .... 2.25
❑810, Dec 2003 .... 2.25
❑811, Jan 2004 .... 5.00
❑812, Apr 2004 .... 8.00
❑813, May 2004 .... 2.25
❑814, Jun 2004 .... 2.50
❑815, Jul 2004 .... 2.50
❑816, Aug 2004 .... 2.50
❑817, Jul 2004 ....
❑1000000, Nov 1998 .... 3.00
❑Annual 1 1987; DG (a); Batman, female vampire; 1987 Annual 4.00
❑Annual 2 1989; JO, GP, CS (a); 1: The Eradicator. Matrix and Cat Grant bios; pin-up; 1989 Annual 3.00
❑Annual 3 1991; Armageddon 2001, Part 8; 1991 Annual 2.50
❑Annual 4 1992; Eclipso: The Darkness Within, Part 10; 1992 Annual 2.50
❑Annual 5 1993; JPH (w); 1: Loose Cannon. Bloodlines: Earthplague; 1993 Annual 2.50
❑Annual 6, ca. 1994; JBy (a); Elseworlds; 1994 Annual 2.95
❑Annual 7, ca. 1995; Year One; 1995 Annual 3.95
❑Annual 8, ca. 1996; A: Bizarro. Bizarro; Legends of the Dead Earth; 1996 Annual 2.95
❑Annual 9, ca. 1997; Pulp Heroes #9; 1997 Annual 3.95

A.C.T.I.O.N. FORCE (LIGHTNING)
LIGHTNING

❑1, Jan 1987 .... 1.75

ACTION GIRL COMICS
SLAVE LABOR

❑1, Oct 1994 .... 3.50
❑1-2, Feb 1996 .... 2.75
❑2, Jan 1995 .... 3.00
❑2-2, Oct 1995 .... 2.75
❑3, Apr 1995 .... 3.00
❑3-2, Feb 1996 .... 2.75
❑4, Jul 1995 .... 3.00
❑4-2, Jul 1996 .... 3.00
❑4-3 .... 3.00
❑5, Oct 1995 .... 3.00
❑6, Jan 1996 .... 2.75
❑6-2 .... 2.75
❑7, May 1996 .... 2.75
❑8, Jul 1996 .... 2.75
❑9 .... 2.75
❑10, Jan 1997 .... 2.75
❑11, May 1997, b&w 2.75
❑12, Jul 1997 .... 2.75
❑13, Oct 1997 .... 2.75
❑14, Jul 1998 .... 2.75

N-MINT

ACTION PLANET COMICS
ACTION PLANET

❑1, b&w; Black and white 3.95
❑2, Sep 2000, b&w 3.95
❑3, Sep 1997, b&w 3.95
❑Ashcan 1, b&w preview of series; "Philly Ashcan Ed."; Black and white 2.00
❑Giant Size 1, Oct 1998 .... 5.95

ACTIONS SPEAK (SERGIO ARAGONÉS)
DARK HORSE

❑1, Jan 2001 .... 2.99
❑2, Feb 2001 .... 2.99
❑3, Mar 2001 .... 2.99
❑4, Apr 2001 .... 2.99
❑5, May 2001 .... 2.99
❑6, Jun 2001 .... 2.99

ADA LEE
NBM

❑1 .... 9.95

A.D.A.M.
THE TOY MAN

❑1 .... 2.95
❑Ashcan 1; no cover price; preview ... 1.00

ADAM-12
GOLD KEY

❑1, Dec 1973 .... 20.00
❑2, Feb 1974 .... 15.00
❑3, Apr 1974 .... 12.00
❑4, Aug 1974 .... 12.00
❑5, Nov 1974 .... 12.00
❑6, Mar 1975 .... 10.00
❑7, May 1975 .... 10.00
❑8, Aug 1975 .... 10.00
❑9, Nov 1975 .... 10.00
❑10, Feb 1976 .... 10.00

ADAM AND EVE A.D.
BAM

❑1, Sep 1985 .... 1.50
❑2, Nov 1985 .... 1.50
❑3, Jan 1986 .... 1.50
❑4, Mar 1986 .... 1.50
❑5, May 1986 .... 1.50
❑6, Jul 1986 .... 1.50
❑7, Oct 1986 .... 1.50
❑8, Nov 1986 .... 1.50
❑9, Jan 1987 .... 1.50
❑10, Mar 1987 .... 1.50

ADAM BOMB COMICS
BLUE MONKEY

❑1, Sum 1999, b&w 2.00

ADAM STRANGE
DC

❑1, Mar 1990 .... 3.95
❑2, May 1990 .... 3.95
❑3, Jul 1990 .... 3.95

ADAM STRANGE ARCHIVES
DC

❑1, ca. 2004 .... 49.95

ADDAM OMEGA
ANTARCTIC

❑1, Jan 1997 .... 2.95
❑2, Apr 1997 .... 2.95
❑3, Jun 1997 .... 2.95
❑4, Aug 1997 .... 2.95

ADDAMS FAMILY EPISODE GUIDE
COMIC CHRONICLES

❑1, b&w; illustrated episode guide to original TV series 5.95

ADELE & THE BEAST
NBM

❑1, Jun 1990 .... 9.95

ADOLESCENT RADIOACTIVE BLACK BELT HAMSTERS, THE
ECLIPSE

❑1, b&w 2.00
❑1/Gold 1993; Gold edition; Published by Parody; 500 copies printed 2.95

N-MINT

❑1-2 .... 1.50
❑2, Spr 1986 .... 1.50
❑3, Jul 1986 .... 1.50
❑4, Nov 1986 .... 1.50
❑5, Feb 1987 .... 1.50
❑6, May 1987 .... 1.50
❑7, Aug 1987 .... 1.50
❑8, Oct 1987 .... 2.00
❑9, Jan 1988 .... 2.00

ADOLESCENT RADIOACTIVE BLACK BELT HAMSTERS CLASSICS
PARODY

❑1, Aug 1992, b&w; Reprints ARBBH in 3-D #1 .... 2.50
❑2, b&w; Reprints ARBBH in 3-D #2 . 2.50
❑3; Reprints ARBBH (Eclipse) #3 .... 2.50
❑4; Reprints ARBBH: Massacre the Japanese Invasion 2.50
❑5; Reprints ARBBH in 3-D #4; holiday cover 2.50

ADOLESCENT RADIOACTIVE BLACK BELT HAMSTERS IN 3-D
ECLIPSE

❑1, Jul 1986 .... 2.50
❑2, Sep 1986 .... 2.50
❑3, Nov 1986; aka Eclipse 3-D #13 ... 2.50
❑4, Dec 1986; aka Eclipse 3-D #14 .... 2.50

ADOLESCENT RADIOACTIVE BLACK BELT HAMSTERS: LOST AND ALONE IN NEW YORK
PARODY

❑1 .... 2.95

ADOLESCENT RADIOACTIVE BLACK BELT HAMSTERS MASSACRE THE JAPANESE INVASION
ECLIPSE

❑1, Aug 1989, b&w 2.50

ADOLESCENT RADIOACTIVE BLACK BELT HAMSTERS: THE LOST TREASURES
PARODY

❑1, b&w; Reprints portions of ARBBH (Eclipse) #9; cardstock cover 2.95

AD POLICE
VIZ

❑1, May 1994, b&w 14.95
❑1-2; 2nd printing with fold-out cover 12.95

ADRENALYNN
IMAGE

❑1, Aug 1999 .... 2.50
❑2, Oct 1999 .... 2.50
❑3, Dec 1999; Includes sketchbook pages 2.50
❑4, Feb 2000; Pin-up page 2.50

ADULT ACTION FANTASY FEATURING: TAWNY'S TALES
LOUISIANA LEISURE

❑1 .... 2.50
❑2 .... 2.50

ADULTS ONLY! COMIC MAGAZINE
INKWELL

❑1, Aug 1979 .... 2.50
❑2, Fal 1985 .... 2.50
❑3 .... 2.50

ADVANCED DUNGEONS & DRAGONS
DC

❑1, Dec 1988 .... 2.00
❑2, Jan 1989 .... 1.50
❑3, Feb 1989 .... 1.50
❑4, Mar 1989 .... 1.50
❑5, Apr 1989 .... 1.50
❑6, May 1989 .... 1.50
❑7, Jun 1989 .... 1.50
❑8, Jul 1989 .... 1.50
❑9, Aug 1989 .... 1.50
❑10, Sep 1989 .... 1.50
❑11, Oct 1989 .... 1.50
❑12, Nov 1989 .... 1.50
❑13, Dec 1989 .... 1.50

	N-MINT
❑14, Jan 1990	1.50
❑15, Feb 1990	1.50
❑16, Mar 1990	1.50
❑17, Apr 1990	1.50
❑18, May 1990	1.50
❑19, Jun 1990	1.50
❑20, Jul 1990	1.50
❑21, Aug 1990	1.50
❑22, Sep 1990	1.50
❑23, Nov 1990	1.50
❑24, Dec 1990	1.50
❑25, Jan 1991	1.50
❑26, Feb 1991	1.50
❑27, Mar 1991	1.50
❑28, Apr 1991	1.50
❑29, May 1991	1.50
❑30, Jun 1991	1.50
❑31, Jul 1991	1.50
❑32, Aug 1991	1.50
❑33, Sep 1991	1.50
❑34, Oct 1991	1.50
❑35, Nov 1991	1.50
❑36, Dec 1991	1.50
❑Annual 1, ca. 1990	3.00

ADVENTURE COMICS
DC

	N-MINT
❑228, Sep 1956	170.00
❑229, Oct 1956	170.00
❑230, Nov 1956	170.00
❑231, Dec 1956	170.00
❑232, Jan 1957	170.00
❑233, Feb 1957	170.00
❑234, Mar 1957	170.00
❑235, Apr 1957	170.00
❑236, May 1957	170.00
❑237, Jun 1957	170.00
❑238, Jul 1957	170.00
❑239, Aug 1957 CS (c)	170.00
❑240, Sep 1957	170.00
❑241, Oct 1957	170.00
❑242, Nov 1957	170.00
❑243, Dec 1957	170.00
❑244, Jan 1958	170.00
❑245, Feb 1958	170.00
❑246, Mar 1958	170.00
❑247, Apr 1958; O: Legion of Super-Heroes. 1: Legion of Super-Heroes, Cosmic Boy, Saturn Girl, Lightning Lad. Superboy joins team	4400.00
❑248, May 1958; Green Arrow	130.00
❑249, Jun 1958; Green Arrow	130.00
❑250, Jul 1958; Green Arrow	130.00
❑251, Aug 1958; Green Arrow	130.00
❑252, Sep 1958; Green Arrow	130.00
❑253, Oct 1958; Green Arrow; Robin meets Superboy	130.00
❑254, Nov 1958; Green Arrow	130.00
❑255, Dec 1958; 1: Red Kryptonite. Green Arrow	130.00
❑256, Jan 1959; JK (a); O: Green Arrow. Green Arrow	525.00
❑257, Feb 1959	125.00
❑258, Mar 1959	125.00
❑259, Apr 1959	125.00
❑260, May 1959 O: Aquaman	500.00
❑261, Jun 1959; Lois Lane meets Superboy	80.00
❑262, Jul 1959 O: Speedy	80.00
❑263, Aug 1959	80.00
❑264, Sep 1959; Aquaman and Green Arrow back-ups	80.00
❑265, Oct 1959 A: Superman	80.00
❑266, Nov 1959 A: Superman	80.00
❑267, Dec 1959 JM (a); 2: Legion of Super-Heroes	740.00
❑268, Jan 1960	80.00
❑269, Feb 1960 1: Aqualad	225.00
❑270, Mar 1960,A: Congorilla	80.00
❑271, Apr 1960, O: Lex Luthor. A: Congorilla	225.00
❑272, May 1960 A: Congorilla	65.00
❑273, Jun 1960 A: Congorilla	65.00
❑274, Jul 1960 A: Congorilla	65.00

	N-MINT
❑275, Aug 1960 O: Superman/Batman Team-up. A: Congorilla	145.00
❑276, Sep 1960 1: Sun Boy. A: Congorilla	65.00
❑277, Oct 1960 A: Congorilla	65.00
❑278, Nov 1960 A: Supergirl. A: Congorilla	65.00
❑279, Dec 1960 CS (a); 1: White Kryptonite. A: Congorilla	65.00
❑280, Jan 1961; A: Lori Lemaris. A: Congorilla. Superboy meets Lori Lemaris; Congo Bill, Aquaman/ Aqualad	65.00
❑281, Feb 1961; A: Congorilla. Congo Bill	60.00
❑282, Mar 1961 O: Starboy. 1: Starboy. A: Congorilla	95.00
❑283, Apr 1961 1: Phantom Zone. A: Congorilla	100.00
❑284, May 1961	60.00
❑285, Jun 1961; 1: Bizarro World. Tales of the Bizarro World	110.00
❑286, Jul 1961; 1: Bizarro Mxyzptlk. Tales of the Bizarro World	110.00
❑287, Aug 1961	60.00
❑288, Sep 1961 1: Dev-Em	60.00
❑289, Oct 1961	60.00
❑290, Nov 1961; O: Sun Boy. A: Legion of Super-Heroes. Sun Boy joins Legion of Super-Heroes	100.00
❑291, Dec 1961; Superboy	45.00
❑292, Jan 1962; Superboy	45.00
❑293, Feb 1962; CS (a); O: Mon-El. 1: Mon-El in Legion. 1: Legion of Super-Pets. Bizarro Luthor	100.00
❑294, Mar 1962; 1: Bizarro Marilyn Monroe. Superboy	90.00
❑295, Apr 1962; Superboy	45.00
❑296, May 1962; Superboy	45.00
❑297, Jun 1962; Superboy	45.00
❑298, Jul 1962; Superboy	45.00
❑299, Aug 1962; 1: Gold Kryptonite. Superboy; Bizarro world story	55.00
❑300, Sep 1962; 300th anniversary issue; Mon-El joins team; Legion of Super-Heroes begins as a regular back-up feature	200.00
❑301, Oct 1962 O: Bouncing Boy	70.00
❑302, Nov 1962; Legion	55.00
❑303, Dec 1962; 1: Matter-Eater Lad. Matter-Eater Lad joins team; Legion	55.00
❑304, Jan 1963; D: Lightning Lad. Legion	55.00
❑305, Feb 1963; Legion	55.00
❑306, Mar 1963; 1: Legion of Substitute Heroes. "Teen-age" Mxyzptlk	45.00
❑307, Apr 1963; 1: Element Lad. 1: Roxxas. Element Lad joins team; Legion	45.00
❑308, May 1963; 1: Lightning Lass. 1: Proty. Legion; Lightning Lass joins team	45.00
❑309, Jun 1963; Legion	45.00
❑310, Jul 1963; Legion	45.00
❑311, Aug 1963; 1: Legion of Super-Heroes Headquarters. A: Legion of Substitute Heroes. Legion	45.00
❑312, Sep 1963; D: Proty. Legion; Return of Lightning Lad	45.00
❑313, Oct 1963; CS (a); Legion	45.00
❑314, Nov 1963; Legion	45.00
❑315, Dec 1963; Legion	45.00
❑316, Jan 1964; CS (a); profile pages; Legion	45.00
❑317, Feb 1964; 1: Dream Girl. Dream Girl joins team; Legion	45.00
❑318, Mar 1964; Legion	45.00
❑319, Apr 1964; Legion	45.00
❑320, May 1964; Legion	45.00
❑321, Jun 1964; 1: Time Trapper. Legion	45.00
❑322, Jul 1964; Legion	45.00
❑323, Aug 1964; Legion	45.00
❑324, Sep 1964; 1: Duplicate Boy. 1: Heroes of Lallor (later Wanderers). Legion	40.00
❑325, Oct 1964; Legion	40.00
❑326, Nov 1964; Legion	40.00

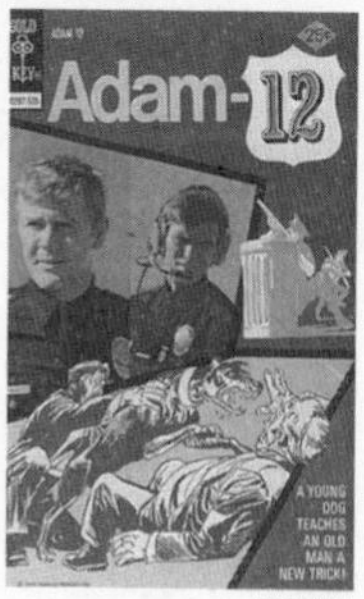

Like many other Gold Key TV-related comics, *Adam-12* sported photo covers.

© 1975 Gold Key.

	N-MINT
❑327, Dec 1964; 1: Timber Wolf. Timber Wolf joins team	40.00
❑328, Jan 1965; Legion	40.00
❑329, Feb 1965; JM (a); 1: Bizarro Legion of Super-Heroes. Legion	40.00
❑330, Mar 1965; JM (a); Dynamo Boy joins team; Legion	40.00
❑331, Apr 1965; JM (a); 1: Saturn Queen. Legion	40.00
❑332, May 1965; Legion	40.00
❑333, Jun 1965; Legion	40.00
❑334, Jul 1965; Legion	40.00
❑335, Aug 1965; 1: Magnetic Kid. 1: Starfinger. Legion	40.00
❑336, Sep 1965; Legion	40.00
❑337, Oct 1965; Legion; Wedding of Lightning Lad and Saturn Girl, Mon-El and Phantom Girl (fake weddings)	40.00
❑338, Nov 1965 1: Glorith. V: Time-Trapper, Glorith	40.00
❑339, Dec 1965; Legion	40.00
❑340, Jan 1966; CS (a); 1: Computo. D: one of Triplicate Girl's bodies. Legion	40.00
❑341, Feb 1966; CS (a); Legion	40.00
❑342, Mar 1966; CS (a); 1: Color Kid. Legion	40.00
❑343, Apr 1966; CS (a); Legion; reprints story from Superboy #90	40.00
❑344, May 1966; CS (a); Legion	40.00
❑345, Jun 1966; CS (a); 1: Khunds. D: Blockade Boy, Weight Wizard. Legion	40.00
❑346, Jul 1966; 1: Karate Kid, Princess Projectra, Ferro Lad. Karate Kid, Princess Projecta, Ferro Lad joins team	40.00
❑347, Aug 1966; CS (a); Legion	40.00
❑348, Sep 1966; O: Sunboy. 1: Doctor Regulus. V: Doctor Regulus. Legion	40.00
❑349, Oct 1966 1: Rond Vidar	40.00
❑350, Nov 1966; CS (a); 1: Mysa Nal. 1: Prince Evillo. Legion	40.00
❑351, Dec 1966 CS (a); 1: White Witch	50.00
❑352, Jan 1967; CS (a); 1: The Fatal Five. Legion	35.00
❑353, Feb 1967 CS (a); D: Ferro Lad	35.00
❑354, Mar 1967; CS (a); Legion	35.00
❑355, Apr 1967; CS (a); Adult Legion story	35.00
❑356, May 1967; CS (a); Legion	30.00
❑357, Jun 1967; CS (a); 1: Controllers. Legion	30.00
❑358, Jul 1967; Legion	30.00
❑359, Aug 1967; CS (a); Legion	30.00
❑360, Sep 1967; CS (a); Legion	30.00
❑361, Oct 1967; JM (a); A: Dominators. V: Unkillables. Legion	30.00
❑362, Nov 1967; V: Mantis Morlo. Legion	30.00
❑363, Dec 1967; V: Mantis Morlo. Legion	30.00
❑364, Jan 1968; CS (a); Legion	30.00
❑365, Feb 1968 NA, CS (a); 1: Shadow Lass	30.00
❑366, Mar 1968; NA (c); NA, CS (a); V: Validus. Legion; Shadow Lass joins Legion	30.00
❑367, Apr 1968; NA (c); CS (a); 1: The Dark Circle. Legion	25.00
❑368, May 1968; Legion	25.00
❑369, Jun 1968; 1: Mordru. Legion in Smallville	25.00
❑370, Jul 1968; Legion	25.00

N-MINT

❑371, Aug 1968; NA (a); 1: Chemical King. 1: Legion Academy. Legion; Colossal Boy leaves team 25.00
❑372, Sep 1968; NA (a); Legion; Chemical King joins Legion; Timber Wolf joins Legion 25.00
❑373, Oct 1968; Legion 22.00
❑374, Nov 1968; Legion 22.00
❑375, Dec 1968; NA (a); 1: Wanderers. 1: Quantum Queen. Legion 22.00
❑376, Jan 1969; Legion 22.00
❑377, Feb 1969; NA (c); NA (a); Legion 22.00
❑378, Mar 1969; NA (c); NA (a); Legion 22.00
❑379, Apr 1969; NA (c); NA (a); Legion 22.00
❑380, Apr 1969; CS (c); CS (a); Legion; Legion of Super-Heroes stories end 22.00
❑381, Jun 1969; Supergirl stories begin 58.00
❑382, Jul 1969 .... 22.00
❑383, Aug 1969 .... 22.00
❑384, Sep 1969 CS (c) 22.00
❑385, Oct 1969 .... 22.00
❑386, Nov 1969; A: Mxyzptlk. Supergirl 22.00
❑387, Dec 1969; V: Lex Luthor. Supergirl 22.00
❑388, Jan 1970; V: Lex Luthor. Supergirl 22.00
❑389, Feb 1970 .... 22.00
❑390, Apr 1970; Giant-size issue; 80-page Giant; All-Romance issue 22.00
❑391, Mar 1970 .... 22.00
❑392, Apr 1970 .... 22.00
❑393, May 1970 .... 22.00
❑394, Jun 1970 .... 22.00
❑395, Jul 1970 .... 22.00
❑396, Aug 1970 .... 22.00
❑397, Sep 1970 .... 22.00
❑398, Oct 1970 .... 22.00
❑399, Nov 1970; Black Canary 22.00
❑400, Dec 1970; 35th anniversary 22.00
❑401, Jan 1971 .... 21.00
❑402, Feb 1971; Supergirl loses powers 21.00
❑403, Apr 1971; Giant-size; CS (c); Death and rebirth of Lightning Lad (reprints from Adventure Comics #302, #305, #308, and #312; G-81 30.00
❑404, Mar 1971; Supergirl gets exo-skeleton 20.00
❑405, Apr 1971 .... 20.00
❑406, May 1971 .... 20.00
❑407, Jun 1971 .... 20.00
❑408, Jul 1971 .... 20.00
❑409, Aug 1971; reprints Legion story from Adventure #313; Supergirl gets new costume 20.00
❑410, Sep 1971 .... 20.00
❑411, Oct 1971 BO (a) 20.00
❑412, Nov 1971; BO (a); 1: Animal Man. Animal Man reprint; reprints Strange Adventures #180 .... 20.00
❑413, Dec 1971 BO (a) 20.00
❑414, Jan 1972 BO (a); A: Animal Man 20.00
❑415, Feb 1972; BO (a); Animal Man reprint 20.00
❑416, Mar 1972; Giant-size issue; a.k.a. DC 100-Page Super Spectacular #DC-10; all-women issue; wrap-around cover 18.00
❑417, Mar 1972 BO, FF (a) 13.00
❑418, Apr 1972; BO (a); also contains previously unpublished Golden Age Doctor Mid-Nite story, Black Canary 13.00
❑419, May 1972; BO (a); Black Canary 13.00
❑420, Jun 1972; CS (a); Animal Man reprint 13.00
❑421, Jul 1972; Animal Man reprint .. 13.00
❑422, Aug 1972 BO, GM (a) 13.00
❑423, Sep 1972 .... 13.00
❑424, Oct 1972 .... 13.00
❑425, Jan 1973 ATh (a); O: Captain Fear. 1: Captain Fear 13.00
❑426, Mar 1973 .... 13.00
❑427, May 1973 .... 13.00
❑428, Aug 1973 1: Black Orchid 28.00
❑429, Oct 1973 A: Black Orchid 15.00
❑430, Dec 1973 A: Black Orchid 15.00
❑431, Feb 1974 ATh, JA (a); A: Spectre 28.00
❑432, Apr 1974 .... 15.00

N-MINT

❑433, Jun 1974 JA (a); A: Spectre 15.00
❑434, Aug 1974 .... 12.00
❑435, Oct 1974; JA (a); A: Spectre. Aquaman back-up 12.00
❑436, Dec 1974; JA (a); A: Spectre. Aquaman back-up 10.00
❑437, Feb 1975 .... 10.00
❑438, Apr 1975 .... 10.00
❑439, Jun 1975 .... 8.00
❑440, Aug 1975 O: Spectre-New 8.00
❑441, Oct 1975 .... 8.00
❑442, Dec 1975 .... 6.00
❑443, Feb 1976; Seven Soldiers of Victory back-up; Aquaman 6.00
❑444, Apr 1976; Aquaman 6.00
❑445, Jun 1976 .... 6.00
❑446, Aug 1976; Bicentennial #31 .... 6.00
❑447, Oct 1976 .... 6.00
❑448, Nov 1976 .... 5.00
❑449, Jan 1977 .... 5.00
❑450, Mar 1977 .... 5.00
❑451, May 1977 .... 5.00
❑452, Jul 1977 .... 5.00
❑453, Sep 1977; A: Barbara Gordon. Superboy 5.00
❑454, Nov 1977 .... 5.00
❑455, Jan 1978 .... 5.00
❑456, Mar 1978 .... 5.00
❑457, May 1978 .... 5.00
❑458, Jul 1978 .... 5.00
❑459, Sep 1978; DN, JSa, JA (a); no ads; expands contents and raises price to $1 .... 3.50
❑460, Nov 1978 DN, SA, JSa (a) 3.50
❑461, Jan 1979; Giant-size issue; DN, JSa, JA (a); incorporates JSA story from unpublished All-Star Comics #75 .... 6.00
❑462, Mar 1979; Giant-size issue DG, JSa, JL (a); D: E-2 Batman 7.00
❑463, May 1979 FMc, DH, JSa, JL (a) 3.50
❑464, Jul 1979; contains previously unpublished Deadman story from Showcase #105 .... 3.50
❑465, Sep 1979 .... 3.50
❑466, Nov 1979; final JSA case before group retired in the '50s 3.50
❑467, Jan 1980 .... 3.50
❑468, Feb 1980 .... 3.50
❑469, Mar 1980 O: Starman III (Prince Gavyn). 1: Starman III (Prince Gavyn) 3.50
❑470, Apr 1980 O: Starman III (Prince Gavyn) 3.50
❑471, May 1980 .... 3.50
❑472, Jun 1980 .... 3.50
❑473, Jul 1980 .... 3.50
❑474, Aug 1980 .... 3.50
❑475, Sep 1980 .... 3.50
❑476, Oct 1980 .... 3.50
❑477, Nov 1980 .... 3.50
❑478, Dec 1980 .... 3.50
❑479, Mar 1981 1: Victoria Grant. 1: Christopher King 3.50
❑480, Apr 1981 .... 3.00
❑481, May 1981 .... 3.00
❑482, Jun 1981 .... 3.00
❑483, Jul 1981; Dial H for Hero 3.00
❑484, Aug 1981 .... 3.00
❑485, Sep 1981 .... 3.00
❑486, Oct 1981 .... 3.00
❑487, Nov 1981 .... 3.00
❑488, Dec 1981 .... 3.00
❑489, Jan 1982 .... 3.00
❑490, Feb 1982 .... 3.00
❑491, Sep 1982; digest size begins; Sandman 3.00
❑492, Oct 1982; Sandman 3.00
❑493, Nov 1982 A: Challengers of the Unknown 3.00
❑494, Dec 1982 A: Challengers of the Unknown 3.00
❑495, Jan 1983; A: Challengers of the Unknown. Sandman 3.00
❑496, Feb 1983; A: Challengers of the Unknown. Sandman 3.00

N-MINT

❑497, Mar 1983 A: Challengers of the Unknown 3.00
❑498, Apr 1983; Sandman 3.00
❑499, May 1983; Sandman, "Thor" 3.00
❑500, Jun 1983 .... 3.00
❑501, Jul 1983 .... 3.00
❑502, Aug 1983 .... 3.00
❑503, Sep 1983; Newsboy Legion 3.00

ADVENTURE COMICS (2ND SERIES)
DC

❑1, May 1999 .... 1.99
❑Giant Size 1, Oct 1998; Giant size; Wonder Woman, Captain Marvel, Superboy, Green Arrow, Legion, Supergirl, Bizarro 4.95

ADVENTURE OF THE COPPER BEECHES, THE
TOME

❑1; Reprints Cases of Sherlock Holmes #9 .... 2.50

ADVENTURERS, THE (AIRCEL)
AIRCEL

❑1; regular cover 2.00
❑1/Ltd.; skeleton cover; Limited ed ... 2.00
❑2 .... 2.00

ADVENTURERS, THE (BOOK 1)
ADVENTURE

❑0, ca. 1986 .... 1.50
❑1, ca. 1986 .... 1.50
❑1-2; published by Adventure 1.50
❑2, ca. 1986 .... 1.50
❑3, ca. 1986; no indicia 1.50
❑4, ca. 1986 .... 1.50
❑5, ca. 1986 .... 1.50
❑6, Jun 1987 .... 1.50
❑7, Jul 1987 .... 1.50
❑8, Sep 1987 .... 1.50
❑9, Oct 1987 .... 1.75
❑10, Nov 1987 .... 1.75

ADVENTURERS, THE (BOOK 2)
ADVENTURE

❑0, Jul 1988, b&w 1.95
❑1, Dec 1987; regular cover 1.50
❑1/Ltd., Dec 1987; Limited edition cover; Limited edition cover 1.50
❑2, Mar 1988 .... 1.50
❑3, Apr 1988 .... 1.50
❑4, Jun 1988 .... 1.50
❑5, Aug 1988 .... 1.50
❑6, Nov 1988 .... 1.50
❑7, Mar 1989, b&w 1.50
❑8 .... 1.50
❑9 .... 1.50
❑10 .... 1.50

ADVENTURERS, THE (BOOK 3)
ADVENTURE

❑1, Oct 1989; regular cover 2.25
❑1/Ltd., Oct 1989; Limited edition cover; Limited edition cover 2.25
❑2, Nov 1989 .... 2.25
❑3, Dec 1989 .... 2.25
❑4, Jan 1990 .... 2.25
❑5, Feb 1990 .... 2.25
❑6, Mar 1990 .... 2.25

ADVENTURES @ EBAY
EBAY

❑1, ca. 2000; eBay employee premium 1.00

ADVENTURES IN READING STARRING: THE AMAZING SPIDER-MAN
MARVEL

❑1, Sep 1990; Giveaway to promote literacy 1.00

ADVENTURES IN THE DC UNIVERSE
DC

❑1, Apr 1997; JLA 2.50
❑2, May 1997 O: The Flash III (Wally West) 2.00
❑3, Jun 1997; Batman vs. Poison Ivy; Wonder Woman vs. Cheetah 2.00

N-MINT

❑4, Jul 1997; Mr. Miracle; Green Lantern 2.00
❑5, Aug 1997; A: Ultra the Multi-Alien. Martian Manhunter 2.00
❑6, Sep 1997; Power Girl; Aquaman 2.00
❑7, Oct 1997; A: Clark Kent. A: Lois Lane. Marvel Family 2.00
❑8, Nov 1997; Question; Blue Beetle, Booster Gold 2.00
❑9, Dec 1997; Flash vs. Gorilla Grodd 2.00
❑10, Jan 1998; Legion of Super-Heroes 2.00
❑11, Feb 1998; Wonder Woman, Green Lantern 2.00
❑12, Mar 1998; JLA vs. Cipher 2.00
❑13, Apr 1998; Green Arrow; Impulse, Martian Manhunter 1.95
❑14, May 1998; Nightwing; Superboy, Flash 1.95
❑15, Jun 1998; Aquaman; Captain Marvel 1.95
❑16, Jul 1998; Green Arrow; Green Lantern 1.95
❑17, Aug 1998; Creeper; Batman 1.95
❑18, Sep 1998; JLA vs. Amazo 1.95
❑19, Oct 1998; Wonder Woman, Catwoman 1.99
❑Annual 1, Oct 1998; DG (a); Doctor Fate, Impulse, Superboy, Thorn, Mr. Miracle; events crossover with Superman Adventures Annual #1 and Batman & Robin Adventures Annual #2 3.95

ADVENTURES IN THE MYSTWOOD
BLACKTHORNE

❑1, Aug 1986 2.00

ADVENTURES IN THE RIFLE BRIGADE
DC / VERTIGO

❑1, Oct 2000 2.50
❑2, Nov 2000 2.50
❑3, Dec 2000 2.50

ADVENTURES IN THE RIFLE BRIGADE: OPERATION BOLLOCK
DC / VERTIGO

❑1, Oct 2001 2.50
❑2, Nov 2001 2.50
❑3, Dec 2001 2.50

ADVENTURES INTO THE UNKNOWN (A+)
A-PLUS

❑1, ca. 1991, b&w 2.50
❑2, ca. 1990 2.50
❑3 2.50
❑4 2.50

ADVENTURES MADE IN AMERICA
RIP OFF

❑0; Preview 2.75
❑1 2.75
❑2 2.75
❑3 2.75
❑4 2.75
❑5 2.75
❑6 2.75

ADVENTURES OF AARON
CHIASMUS

❑1 2.50
❑2, Jul 1995 2.50

ADVENTURES OF AARON (2ND SERIES)
IMAGE

❑1, Mar 1997 2.95
❑2, May 1997 2.95
❑3, Sep 1997; "Adventures of Dad" back-up 2.95
❑100, Jul 1997 2.95

ADVENTURES OF ADAM & BRYON
AMERICAN MULE

❑1, May 1998 2.50

ADVENTURES OF BAGBOY AND CHECKOUT GIRL, THE
ACETELYNE

❑Ashcan 1, Apr 2002 1.00

N-MINT

ADVENTURES OF BARON MUNCHAUSEN, THE
NOW

❑1, Jul 1989 2.00
❑2, Aug 1989 2.00
❑3, Sep 1989 2.00
❑4, Oct 1989 2.00

ADVENTURES OF BARRY WEEN, BOY GENIUS, THE
IMAGE

❑1, Mar 1999 2.95
❑2, Apr 1999; Jeremy turned into dinosaur 2.95
❑3, May 1999, at museum 2.95

ADVENTURES OF BARRY WEEN, BOY GENIUS 2.0, THE
ONI

❑1, Feb 2000, b&w 2.95
❑2, Mar 2000, b&w; in the old West 2.95
❑3, Apr 2000, b&w 2.95

ADVENTURES OF BAYOU BILLY, THE
ARCHIE

❑1, Sep 1989; Archie, Jughead, Betty, and Veronica public service announcement inside back cover 1.00
❑2, Nov 1989 1.00
❑3, Jan 1990 1.00
❑4, Apr 1990 1.00
❑5, Jun 1990 1.00

ADVENTURES OF BOB HOPE, THE
DC

❑41, Oct 1956 55.00
❑42, Dec 1956 55.00
❑43, Feb 1957 55.00
❑44, Apr 1957 55.00
❑45, Jun 1957 55.00
❑46, Aug 1957 55.00
❑47, Oct 1957 55.00
❑48, Dec 1957 55.00
❑49, Feb 1958 55.00
❑50, Apr 1958 55.00
❑51, Jun 1958 40.00
❑52, Aug 1958 40.00
❑53, Oct 1958 40.00
❑54, Dec 1958 40.00
❑55, Feb 1959 40.00
❑56, Apr 1959 40.00
❑57, Jun 1959 40.00
❑58, Aug 1959 40.00
❑59, Oct 1959 40.00
❑60, Dec 1959 40.00
❑61, Feb 1960 35.00
❑62, Apr 1960 35.00
❑63, Jun 1960 35.00
❑64, Aug 1960 35.00
❑65, Oct 1960 35.00
❑66, Dec 1960 35.00
❑67, Feb 1961 35.00
❑68, Apr 1961 35.00
❑69, Jun 1961 35.00
❑70, Aug 1961 35.00
❑71, Oct 1961 30.00
❑72, Dec 1961 30.00
❑73, Feb 1962 30.00
❑74, Apr 1962 MD (a) 30.00
❑75, Jun 1962 MD (a) 30.00
❑76, Aug 1962 MD (a) 30.00
❑77, Oct 1962 30.00
❑78, Dec 1962 30.00
❑79, Feb 1963 30.00
❑80, Apr 1963 30.00
❑81, Jun 1963 25.00
❑82, Aug 1963 MD (a) 25.00
❑83, Oct 1963 25.00
❑84, Dec 1963 25.00
❑85, Feb 1964 MD (a) 25.00
❑86, Apr 1964 25.00
❑87, Jun 1964 MD (a) 25.00
❑88, Aug 1964 25.00
❑89, Oct 1964 MD (a) 25.00
❑90, Dec 1964 MD (a) 25.00

The ongoing Legion of Super-Heroes features in *Adventure Comics* ended with #380.

© 1969 National Periodical Publications (DC).

N-MINT

❑91, Feb 1965 MD (a) 15.00
❑92, Apr 1965 15.00
❑93, Jun 1965 15.00
❑94, Aug 1965 A: Aquaman 15.00
❑95, Oct 1965 1: Super-Hip and monster faculty 15.00
❑96, Dec 1965 15.00
❑97, Feb 1966 15.00
❑98, Apr 1966 15.00
❑99, Jun 1966 15.00
❑100, Aug 1966; Super-Hip as President 15.00
❑101, Oct 1966 15.00
❑102, Dec 1966 15.00
❑103, Feb 1967 A: Batman, Nancy, Ringo Starr, Frank Sinatra, Stanley and his Monster 15.00
❑104, May 1967 15.00
❑105, Jun 1967 A: David Janssen, Dan Blocker, Ed Sullivan, Don Adams 15.00
❑106, Aug 1967 NA (c); NA (a) 25.00
❑107, Oct 1967 NA (c); NA (a) 25.00
❑108, Dec 1967 NA (c); NA (a) 25.00
❑109, Feb 1968 NA (c); NA (a) 25.00

ADVENTURES OF B.O.C., THE
INVASION

❑1, Nov 1986 1.50
❑2, Jan 1987 1.50
❑3, Mar 1987 1.50

ADVENTURES OF BROWSER & SEQUOIA, THE
SABERCAT

❑1, Aug 1999 2.95

ADVENTURES OF CAPTAIN AMERICA
MARVEL

❑1, Sep 1991 4.95
❑2, Nov 1991 4.95
❑3, Dec 1991 4.95
❑4, Jan 1992 4.95

ADVENTURES OF CAPTAIN JACK, THE
FANTAGRAPHICS

❑1, Jun 1986 2.00
❑2, Sep 1986 2.00
❑3, Oct 1986 2.00
❑4, Nov 1986 2.00
❑5, Dec 1986; no indicia 2.00
❑6, Jan 1987 2.00
❑7, Mar 1987 2.00
❑8, Jul 1987 2.00
❑9, Oct 1987 2.00
❑10, May 1988 2.00
❑11, Nov 1988 2.00
❑12, Jan 1989 2.00

ADVENTURES OF CAPTAIN NEMO, THE
RIP OFF

❑1, b&w 2.50

ADVENTURES OF CHRISSIE CLAUS, THE
HERO

❑1, Spr 1991 2.95
❑2, Jan 1994, w/ trading card 2.95

N-MINT

ADVENTURES OF CHUK THE BARBARIC
WHITE WOLF

❑1, Jul 1987 .... 1.50
❑2, Aug 1987, becomes Chuk the Barbaric 1.50

ADVENTURES OF CYCLOPS AND PHOENIX, THE
MARVEL

❑1, May 1994 .... 2.95
❑2, Jun 1994 .... 2.95
❑3, Jul 1994 .... 2.95
❑4, Aug 1994 .... 2.95

ADVENTURES OF DEAN MARTIN & JERRY LEWIS, THE
DC

❑1, Jul 1952 .... 550.00
❑2, Sep 1952 .... 275.00
❑3, Nov 1952 .... 140.00
❑4, Jan 1953 .... 140.00
❑5, Mar 1953 .... 140.00
❑6, May 1953 .... 140.00
❑7, Jul 1953 .... 140.00
❑8, Sep 1953 .... 140.00
❑9, Nov 1953 .... 140.00
❑10, Jan 1954 .... 140.00
❑11, Feb 1954 .... 90.00
❑12, Apr 1954 .... 90.00
❑13, May 1954 .... 90.00
❑14, Jul 1954 .... 90.00
❑15, Aug 1954 .... 90.00
❑16, Oct 1954 .... 90.00
❑17, Nov 1954 .... 90.00
❑18, Jan 1955 .... 90.00
❑19, Feb 1955 .... 90.00
❑20, Apr 1955 .... 75.00
❑21, May 1955 .... 75.00
❑22, Jul 1955 .... 75.00
❑23, Aug 1955 .... 75.00
❑24, Oct 1955 .... 75.00
❑25, Nov 1955 .... 75.00
❑26, Jan 1956 .... 75.00
❑27, Feb 1956 .... 75.00
❑28, Apr 1956 .... 75.00
❑29, May 1956 .... 75.00
❑30, Jul 1956 .... 75.00
❑31, Aug 1956 .... 55.00
❑32, Oct 1956 .... 55.00
❑33, Nov 1956 .... 55.00
❑34, Jan 1957 .... 55.00
❑35, Feb 1957 .... 55.00
❑36, Apr 1957 .... 55.00
❑37, May 1957 .... 55.00
❑38, Jul 1957 .... 55.00
❑39, Aug 1957 .... 55.00
❑40, Oct 1957; Series continues as The Adventures of Jerry Lewis 55.00

ADVENTURES OF DR. GRAVES
A-PLUS

❑1, b&w 2.50

ADVENTURES OF DOLO ROMY, THE
DÔLO BLUE

❑1 .... 2.95

ADVENTURES OF DORIS NELSON, ATOMIC HOUSEWIFE
JAKE COMICS

❑1, Aug 1996, b&w; reprints Doris Nelson, Atomic Housewife 2.95

ADVENTURES OF EDGAR MUDD AND ELAINE, THE
WET EARTH

❑1 .... 3.50

ADVENTURES OF EVIL & MALICE, THE
IMAGE

❑1, Jun 1999 .... 3.50
❑2, Aug 1999 .... 3.50
❑3, Nov 1999; cover says Oct, indicia says Nov 3.50

N-MINT

ADVENTURES OF FELIX THE CAT
HARVEY

❑1 .... 1.50

ADVENTURES OF FORD FAIRLANE, THE
DC

❑1, May 1990 .... 1.50
❑2, Jun 1990 .... 1.50
❑3, Jul 1990 .... 1.50
❑4, Aug 1990 .... 1.50

ADVENTURES OF JERRY LEWIS, THE
DC

❑41, Nov 1957; Series continued from Adventures of Dean Martin & Jerry Lewis 40.00
❑42, Jan 1958 .... 36.00
❑43, Feb 1958 .... 36.00
❑44, Apr 1958 .... 36.00
❑45, May 1958 .... 36.00
❑46, Jul 1958 .... 36.00
❑47, Aug 1958 .... 36.00
❑48, Oct 1958 .... 36.00
❑49, Nov 1958 .... 36.00
❑50, Jan 1959 .... 36.00
❑51, Mar 1959 .... 34.00
❑52, May 1959 .... 34.00
❑53, Jul 1959 .... 34.00
❑54, Sep 1959 .... 34.00
❑55, Nov 1959 .... 34.00
❑56, Jan 1960 .... 34.00
❑57, Mar 1960 .... 34.00
❑58, May 1960 .... 34.00
❑59, Jul 1960 .... 34.00
❑60, Sep 1960 .... 34.00
❑61, Nov 1960 .... 28.00
❑62, Jan 1961 .... 28.00
❑63, Mar 1961 .... 28.00
❑64, May 1961 .... 28.00
❑65, Jul 1961 .... 28.00
❑66, Sep 1961 .... 28.00
❑67, Nov 1961 .... 28.00
❑68, Jan 1962 .... 28.00
❑69, Mar 1962 .... 28.00
❑70, May 1962 .... 28.00
❑71, Jul 1962 .... 28.00
❑72, Sep 1962 MD (a) 28.00
❑73, Nov 1962 .... 28.00
❑74, Jan 1963; adapts It's Only Money 28.00
❑75, Mar 1963 .... 28.00
❑76, May 1963 .... 28.00
❑77, Jul 1963 .... 28.00
❑78, Sep 1963 .... 28.00
❑79, Nov 1963 1: Mr. Yes 28.00
❑80, Jan 1964 .... 28.00
❑81, Mar 1964 .... 25.00
❑82, May 1964 .... 25.00
❑83, Jul 1964; Frankenstein, Dracula, Werewolf 25.00
❑84, Sep 1964; Jerry becomes The Fearless Tarantula 25.00
❑85, Nov 1964 1: Renfrew 25.00
❑86, Jan 1965 BO (a) 25.00
❑87, Mar 1965 A: Renfrew 25.00
❑88, May 1965 1: Witch Kraft 25.00
❑89, Jul 1965 .... 25.00
❑90, Sep 1965 .... 25.00
❑91, Nov 1965 .... 25.00
❑92, Jan 1966 A: Superman 30.00
❑93, Mar 1966 .... 25.00
❑94, May 1966 .... 25.00
❑95, Jul 1966 .... 25.00
❑96, Sep 1966 .... 25.00
❑97, Nov 1966 A: Batman, Robin, Penguin, Riddler, Joker 35.00
❑98, Jan 1967 A: Ringo Starr, Ilya Kurakin (on stamps) 25.00
❑99, Mar 1967 .... 25.00
❑100, May 1967 1: Jerry Mess-terpiece pin-up 25.00
❑101, Jul 1967 NA (c); NA (a) 32.00
❑102, Sep 1967 NA (c); NA (a); A: The Beatles 55.00

N-MINT

❑103, Nov 1967 NA (c); NA (a) 32.00
❑104, Jan 1968 NA (c); NA (a) 32.00
❑105, Mar 1968 A: Superman, Lex Luthor 32.00
❑106, May 1968 .... 14.00
❑107, Jul 1968 .... 14.00
❑108, Sep 1968 .... 14.00
❑109, Nov 1968 .... 14.00
❑110, Jan 1969 .... 14.00
❑111, Mar 1969 .... 14.00
❑112, May 1969 A: Flash 14.00
❑113, Jul 1969 .... 14.00
❑114, Sep 1969 .... 14.00
❑115, Nov 1969 .... 14.00
❑116, Jan 1970 .... 14.00
❑117, Mar 1970 A: Wonder Woman 20.00
❑118, May 1970 .... 14.00
❑119, Jul 1970 .... 14.00
❑120, Sep 1970 .... 12.00
❑121, Nov 1970 .... 12.00
❑122, Jan 1971 .... 12.00
❑123, Mar 1971 .... 12.00
❑124, May 1971 .... 12.00

ADVENTURES OF KELLY BELLE: PERIL ON THE HIGH SEAS, THE
ATLANTIS

❑1 1996, b&w 2.95

ADVENTURES OF KOOL-AID MAN, THE
MARVEL

❑1, ca. 1983; giveaway; JR (c); DDC (a); 60 cent value on cover 1.00
❑5 .... 1.00

ADVENTURES OF LIBERAL MAN, THE
POLITICAL

❑1 .... 2.95
❑2 .... 2.95
❑3 .... 2.95
❑4, Jul 1996 .... 2.95
❑5, Sep 1996 .... 2.95
❑6, Oct 1996 .... 2.95
❑7, Nov 1996 .... 2.95

ADVENTURES OF LUTHER ARKWRIGHT, THE (VALKYRIE)
VALKYRIE

❑1, Oct 1987 BT (w); BT (a) 2.50
❑2, Dec 1987 BT (w); BT (a) 2.50
❑3, Feb 1988 BT (w); BT (a) 2.50
❑4, Apr 1988 BT (w); BT (a) 2.50
❑5, Jun 1988 BT (w); BT (a) 2.50
❑6, Aug 1988 BT (w); BT (a) 2.50
❑7, Oct 1988 BT (w); BT (a) 2.50
❑8, Dec 1988 BT (w); BT (a) 2.50
❑9, Feb 1989 BT (w); BT (a) 2.50
❑10, Apr 1989; BT (w); BT (a); Essays 2.50

ADVENTURES OF LUTHER ARKWRIGHT, THE (DARK HORSE)
DARK HORSE

❑1 1990; BT (w); BT (a); Reprints Adventures of Luther Arkwright (Valkyrie) #1 .... 2.50
❑2 1990; BT (w); BT (a); Reprints Adventures of Luther Arkwright (Valkyrie) #2 .... 2.00
❑3, May 1990; BT (w); BT (a); Reprints Adventures of Luther Arkwright (Valkyrie) #3 .... 2.00
❑4 1990; BT (w); BT (a); Reprints Adventures of Luther Arkwright (Valkyrie) #4 .... 2.00
❑5 1990; BT (w); BT (a); Reprints Adventures of Luther Arkwright (Valkyrie) #5 .... 2.00
❑6 1990; BT (w); BT (a); Reprints Adventures of Luther Arkwright (Valkyrie) #6 .... 2.00
❑7, Nov 1990; BT (w); BT (a); Reprints Adventures of Luther Arkwright (Valkyrie) #7 .... 2.00

N-MINT

❑8, Nov 1990; BT (w); BT (a); Reprints Adventures of Luther Arkwright (Valkyrie) #8 .... 2.00
❑9 1990; BT (w); BT (a); trading cards; Reprints Adventures of Luther Arkwright (Valkyrie) #9 .... 2.00

ADVENTURES OF MARK TYME, THE
JOHN SPENCER & CO.

❑1 .... 2.00
❑2 .... 2.00

ADVENTURES OF MR. PYRIDINE
FANTAGRAPHICS

❑1, b&w 2.50

ADVENTURES OF MISTY, THE
FORBIDDEN FRUIT

❑1, Apr 1991 .... 2.95
❑2, May 1991 .... 2.95
❑3, Jun 1991 .... 2.95
❑4, Jul 1991 .... 2.95
❑5, Aug 1991 .... 2.95
❑6, Oct 1991 .... 2.95
❑7, Dec 1991 .... 2.95
❑8, Feb 1992 .... 2.95
❑9, Apr 1992 .... 2.95
❑10, Jun 1992 .... 2.95
❑11, Aug 1992 .... 2.95
❑12, Oct 1992 .... 2.95

ADVENTURES OF MONKEY, THE
WOMP

❑1, Jul 1995 .... 2.00
❑2, Jun 1996 .... 2.00
❑3, Jun 1997 .... 2.00
❑4, Jun 1998; Freshmen back-up 2.00

ADVENTURES OF QUIK BUNNY
MARVEL

❑1 1984; giveaway; A: Spider-Man. 60 cent value on cover 3.00

ADVENTURES OF RHEUMY PEEPERS & CHUNKY HIGHLIGHTS, THE
ONI

❑1, Feb 1999 .... 2.95

ADVENTURES OF RICK RAYGUN, THE
STOP DRAGON

❑1, Sep 1986 .... 2.00
❑2, Oct 1986 .... 2.00
❑3, Fal 1986 .... 2.00
❑4, Nov 1986 .... 2.00
❑5, Jan 1987 .... 2.00

ADVENTURES OF ROBIN HOOD, THE
GOLD KEY

❑1, Mar 1974 .... 8.00
❑2, May 1974 .... 5.00
❑3, Jul 1974 .... 4.00
❑4, Aug 1974 .... 4.00
❑5, Sep 1974 .... 4.00
❑6, Nov 1974 .... 4.00
❑7, Jan 1975 .... 4.00

ADVENTURES OF ROMA
FORBIDDEN FRUIT

❑1, Jan 1993, b&w 3.50

ADVENTURES OF SNAKE PLISSKEN
MARVEL

❑1, Jan 1997, b&w and color 2.50

ADVENTURES OF SPENCER SPOOK, THE
ACE

❑1, Oct 1986; reprints stories from Giggle Comics #77 and Spencer Spook #102 .... 2.00
❑2, Dec 1986 .... 2.00
❑3, Jan 1987 .... 2.00
❑4, Mar 1987 .... 2.00
❑5 .... 2.00
❑6 .... 2.00

ADVENTURES OF SPIDER-MAN, THE
MARVEL

❑1, Apr 1996; A: Punisher. animated series adaptations 2.00
❑2, May 1996 V: Hammerhead 1.50

N-MINT

❑3, Jun 1996 A: X-Men. V: Mr. Sinister 1.50
❑4, Jul 1996 .... 1.50
❑5, Aug 1996 V: Rhino 1.50
❑6, Sep 1996; A: Thing. Human Torch 1.50
❑7, Oct 1996 V: Enforcers 1.50
❑8, Nov 1996 V: Kingpin 1.50
❑9, Dec 1996 .... 1.50
❑10, Jan 1997 V: Beetle 1.50
❑11, Feb 1997 A: Venom. V: Doctor Octopus and Venom 1.50
❑12, Mar 1997 A: Venom. V: Doctor Octopus and Venom 1.50

ADVENTURES OF STICKBOY, THE
STINKY ARMADILLO

❑1 .... 0.50

ADVENTURES OF SUPERBOY, THE
DC

❑19, Sep 1991; Series continued from Superboy (2nd Series) #18 .... 1.50
❑20, Oct 1991 JM (a); O: Knickknack 1.50
❑21, Nov 1991 .... 1.50
❑22, Dec 1991 CS (a) 1.50

ADVENTURES OF SUPERMAN
DC

❑0, Oct 1994; ▲ 1994-39 .... 2.50
❑424, Jan 1987 JOy (a) 2.50
❑425, Feb 1987 JOy (a) 2.00
❑426, Mar 1987; JOy (a); 1: Bibbo. Legends 2.00
❑427, Apr 1987 JOy (a) 2.00
❑428, May 1987 JOy (a) 2.00
❑429, Jun 1987 JOy (a) 2.00
❑430, Jul 1987 JOy (a) 2.00
❑431, Aug 1987 JOy (a) 2.00
❑432, Sep 1987 JOy (a); 1: Jose Delgado (Gangbuster) 2.00
❑433, Oct 1987 JOy (a) 2.00
❑434, Nov 1987 JOy (a); 1: Gangbuster 2.00
❑435, Dec 1987 JOy (a) 2.00
❑436, Jan 1988; JOy (a); Millennium 2.00
❑437, Feb 1988; JOy (a); V: Gangbuster. Millennium 2.00
❑438, Mar 1988 JOy (a); O: Brainiac II (Milton Moses Fine). 1: Brainiac II (Milton Moses Fine) 2.00
❑439, Apr 1988 JOy (a) 2.00
❑440, May 1988 JOy (a) 2.00
❑441, Jun 1988 JOy (a); V: Mxyzptlk 2.00
❑442, Jul 1988 JOy, JBy (a) 2.00
❑443, Aug 1988 JOy (a) 2.00
❑444, Sep 1988; JOy (a); Supergirl 2.00
❑445, Oct 1988 JOy (a) 2.00
❑446, Nov 1988 JOy (a); A: Gangbuster 2.00
❑447, Dec 1988 JOy (a) 2.00
❑448, Dec 1988 JOy (a) 2.00
❑449, Jan 1989; Invasion! 2.00
❑450, Jan 1989; Invasion! 2.00
❑451, Feb 1989 .... 2.00
❑452, Mar 1989 .... 2.00
❑453, Apr 1989 .... 2.00
❑454, May 1989 1: Draaga 2.00
❑455, Jun 1989 .... 2.00
❑456, Jul 1989 .... 2.00
❑457, Aug 1989 .... 2.00
❑458, Sep 1989; Jimmy as Elastic Lad 2.00
❑459, Oct 1989; Eradicator buried in Antarctic 2.00
❑460, Nov 1989 1: Fortress of Solitude 2.00
❑461, Dec 1989 .... 2.00
❑462, Jan 1990 .... 2.00
❑463, Feb 1990; A: Flash. Superman/Flash race 3.00
❑464, Mar 1990; V: Lobo. Krypton Man 2.00
❑465, Apr 1990; Krypton Man 2.00
❑466, May 1990 1: Hank Henshaw (becomes cyborg Superman) 3.00
❑467, Jun 1990; Batman 2.00
❑468, Jul 1990 .... 2.00
❑469, Aug 1990 1: Blaze 2.00
❑470, Sep 1990 .... 2.00
❑471, Oct 1990 A: Sinbad 2.00
❑472, Nov 1990 .... 2.00

Now adapted Terry Gilliam's movie *The Adventures of Baron Munchausen.*

© 1989 Now Comics.

N-MINT

❑473, Dec 1990; A: Green Lantern. Guy Gardner 2.00
❑474, Jan 1991 .... 2.00
❑475, Feb 1991; Wonder Woman; Batman, Flash 2.00
❑476, Mar 1991 1: The Linear Men. V: Linear Man 2.00
❑477, Apr 1991 A: Legion 2.00
❑478, May 1991 V: Dev-Em 2.00
❑479, Jun 1991 .... 2.00
❑480, Jul 1991; Giant-size 2.50
❑481, Aug 1991 .... 2.00
❑482, Sep 1991 V: Parasite 2.00
❑483, Oct 1991 1: Atomic Skull 2.00
❑484, Nov 1991; Blackout 2.00
❑485, Dec 1991; Blackout 2.00
❑486, Jan 1992 .... 2.00
❑487, Feb 1992 .... 2.00
❑488, Mar 1992 .... 2.00
❑489, Apr 1992 .... 2.00
❑490, May 1992 .... 2.00
❑491, Jun 1992 V: Metallo 2.00
❑492, Jul 1992; JOy (w); V: Agent Liberty. ▲ 1992-27 .... 2.00
❑493, Aug 1992 1: Lord Satanus. V: Blaze 2.00
❑494, Sep 1992 1: Kismet 2.00
❑495, Oct 1992 A: Forever People 2.00
❑496, Nov 1992; Mxyzptlk 3.00
❑496-2, Nov 1992 .... 2.00
❑497, Dec 1992; JOy (w); Doomsday; ▲ 1992-47 .... 3.00
❑497-2, Dec 1992; JOy (w); 2nd printing, ▲ 1992-47 .... 2.00
❑498, Jan 1993; JOy (w); ▲ 1993-3 .... 3.00
❑498-2, Jan 1993; JOy (w); ▲ 1993-3 .... 2.00
❑499, Feb 1993; JOy (w); ▲ 1993-7 .... 2.50
❑500, Jun 1993; JOy (w); begins return from dead 3.00
❑500/CS, Jun 1993; JOy (w); translucent cover; trading card; begins return from dead 3.50
❑500/Silver, Jun 1993; silver edition JOy (w) 20.00
❑501, Jun 1993; 1: Superboy (clone). ▲ 1993-15 .... 2.00
❑501/Variant, Jun 1993; 1: Superboy (clone). Die-cut cover; ▲ 1993-15 .... 2.00
❑502, Jul 1993; A: Supergirl. ▲ 1993-19 .... 1.75
❑503, Aug 1993; Superboy vs. Cyborg 1.75
❑504, Sep 1993 .... 1.75
❑505, Oct 1993; ▲ 1993-31 .... 1.75
❑505/Variant, Oct 1993; ▲ 1993-31, Special (prism) cover edition 2.50
❑506, Nov 1993 .... 1.50
❑507, Dec 1993 V: Bloodsport 1.50
❑508, Jan 1994; Challengers 1.50
❑509, Feb 1994 A: Auron 1.50
❑510, Mar 1994; Bizarro 1.50
❑511, Apr 1994 A: Guardian 1.50
❑512, May 1994 A: Guardian. V: Parasite 1.50
❑513, Jun 1994; ▲ 1994-23 .... 1.50
❑514, Jul 1994 .... 1.50
❑515, Aug 1994 V: Massacre 1.50
❑516, Sep 1994; A: Alpha Centurion. "Zero Hour" 1.50
❑517, Nov 1994 .... 1.50
❑518, Dec 1994 A: Darkseid 1.50

N-MINT

❑519, Jan 1995; V: Brainiac. Dead Again; ▲ 1995-3 ... 1.50
❑520, Feb 1995 A: Thorn ... 1.50
❑521, Mar 1995 A: Thorn ... 1.50
❑522, Apr 1995; Return of Metropolis ... 1.50
❑523, May 1995 ... 1.50
❑524, Jun 1995 ... 2.00
❑525, Jul 1995 ... 2.00
❑526, Aug 1995; Bloodsport vs. Bloodsport ... 2.00
❑527, Sep 1995; Alpha-Centurion returns ... 2.00
❑528, Oct 1995 ... 2.00
❑529, Nov 1995 ... 2.00
❑530, Dec 1995; SCU vs. Hellgrammite; "Trial of Superman/Underworld Unleashed" ... 2.00
❑531, Jan 1996; Cyborg Superman sentenced to a black hole; ▲ 1996-4 ... 2.00
❑532, Feb 1996; Return of Lori Lemaris; ▲ 1996-8 ... 2.00
❑533, Mar 1996; A: Impulse. ▲ 1996-12 ... 2.00
❑534, May 1996 ... 2.00
❑535, Jun 1996 ... 2.00
❑536, Jul 1996; Brainiac takes over Superman's body ... 2.00
❑537, Aug 1996 ... 2.00
❑538, Sep 1996; Clark Kent named acting managing editor; Perry White has cancer ... 2.00
❑539, Oct 1996 JOy (w); O: Anomaly. 1: Anomaly ... 2.00
❑540, Nov 1996; JOy (w); 1: Ferro. "Final Night"; ▲ 1996-43 ... 2.00
❑541, Dec 1996; A: Superboy. Clark shot by terrorists ... 2.00
❑542, Jan 1997 ... 2.00
❑543, Feb 1997 V: Superman Revenge Squad ... 2.00
❑544, Mar 1997; return of Intergang; ▲ 1997-11 ... 2.00
❑545, Apr 1997; V: Metallo. energy powers begin ... 2.00
❑546, May 1997; V: Metallo. new uniform ... 2.00
❑547, Jun 1997 A: Atom ... 2.00
❑548, Jul 1997 A: Phantom Stranger ... 2.00
❑549, Aug 1997 A: Newsboy Legion, Dingbats of Danger Street ... 2.00
❑550, Sep 1997; Giant-size; Jimmy's special airs ... 3.50
❑551, Oct 1997 V: Cyborg Superman ... 1.95
❑552, Nov 1997; V: Parasite. ▲ 1997-45 ... 1.95
❑553, Dec 1997; Face cover ... 1.95
❑554, Dec 1997 V: Ripper ... 1.95
❑555, Feb 1998; Superman Red vs. Superman Blue ... 1.95
❑556, Apr 1998; V: Millennium Guard. ▲ 1998-13 ... 1.95
❑557, May 1998; Millennium Giants ... 1.95
❑558, Jun 1998; set in Silver Age ... 1.95
❑559, Jul 1998; set in Silver Age ... 1.95
❑560, Aug 1998; A: Kismet. set in Silver Age ... 1.95
❑561, Sep 1998 V: Dominus ... 2.00
❑562, Oct 1998; D: Machine Gunn, Torcher. Daily Planet closed ... 2.00
❑563, Dec 1998; V: Cyborg. in Kandor ... 2.00
❑564, Feb 1999 JOy (w); A: Geo-Force ... 2.00
❑565, Mar 1999 JOy (w); A: D.E.O. agents. A: Justice League of America. A: Captain Boomerang. A: Metropolis Special Crimes Unit. A: Captain Cold ... 2.00
❑566, Apr 1999 JOy (w); A: Lex Luthor ... 2.00
❑567, May 1999; JOy (w); Lois' robot guardian returns; ▲ 1999-19 ... 2.00
❑568, Jun 1999; ▲ 1999-24 ... 2.00
❑569, Jul 1999; SCU forms meta-unit; ▲ 1999-28 ... 2.00
❑570, Sep 1999; Superman as protector of Rann ... 2.00
❑571, Oct 1999 V: Atomic Skull ... 2.00
❑572, Nov 1999; SB (a); A: Strange Visitor. V: War. ▲ 1999-41 ... 2.00
❑573, Dec 1999; ▲ 1999-47 ... 2.00
❑574, Jan 2000; ▲ 2000-2 ... 2.00
❑575, Feb 2000; ▲ 2000-6 ... 2.00
❑576, Mar 2000 ... 2.00
❑577, Apr 2000 ... 2.00
❑578, May 2000; ▲ 2000-19 ... 2.00
❑579, Jun 2000; ▲ 2000-23 ... 2.00
❑580, Jul 2000; ▲ 2000-27 ... 2.00
❑581, Aug 2000; V: Adversary. ▲ 2000-31; Lex Luthor announces candidacy for President ... 2.00
❑582, Sep 2000; ▲ 2000-35 ... 2.00
❑583, Oct 2000; ▲ 2000-40 ... 2.25
❑584, Nov 2000; 1: Devouris the Conqueror. A: Lord Satanus. ▲ 2000-44 ... 2.25
❑585, Dec 2000; A: Rampage. A: Adversary. A: Thorn. A: Prankster. ▲ 2000-48 ... 2.25
❑586, Jan 2001; ▲ 2000-52 ... 2.25
❑587, Feb 2001; ▲ 2001-7 ... 2.25
❑588, Mar 2001; ▲ 2001-11 ... 2.25
❑589, Apr 2001; ▲ 2001-15 ... 2.25
❑590, May 2001; ▲ 2001-19 ... 2.25
❑591, Jun 2001; ▲ 2001-23 ... 2.25
❑592, Jul 2001 ... 2.25
❑593, Aug 2001 ... 2.25
❑594, Sep 2001 ... 2.25
❑595, Oct 2001; ▲ 2001-39 ... 2.25
❑596, Nov 2001; ▲ 2001-43 ... 2.25
❑597, Dec 2001; ▲ 2001-47 ... 2.25
❑598, Jan 2002; ▲ 2002-6 ... 2.25
❑599, Feb 2002 ... 2.25
❑600, Mar 2002; Giant-size ... 3.95
❑601, Apr 2002 ... 2.25
❑602, May 2002 ... 2.25
❑603, Jun 2002 A: Super-Baby ... 2.25
❑604, Jul 2002 ... 2.25
❑605, Aug 2002 ... 2.25
❑606, Sep 2002 ... 2.25
❑607, Oct 2002 ... 2.25
❑608, Nov 2002 ... 2.25
❑609, Dec 2002 ... 2.25
❑610, Jan 2003 ... 2.25
❑611, Feb 2003 ... 2.25
❑612, Mar 2003 ... 2.25
❑613, Apr 2003 ... 2.25
❑614, May 2003 ... 2.25
❑615, Jun 2003 ... 2.25
❑616, Jul 2003 ... 2.25
❑617, Jun 2003 ... 2.25
❑618, Jul 2003 ... 2.25
❑619, Aug 2003 ... 2.25
❑620, Sep 2003 ... 2.25
❑621, Oct 2003 ... 2.25
❑622, Nov 2003 ... 2.25
❑623, Dec 2003 ... 2.25
❑624, Jan 2004 ... 5.00
❑625, Apr 2004 ... 2.25
❑626, May 2004 ... 2.25
❑627, Jun 2004 ... 2.50
❑628, Jul 2004 ... 2.50
❑629, Aug 2004 ... 2.50
❑630, Jul 2004
❑1000000, Nov 1998 A: Resurrection Man ... 3.00
❑Annual 1, Sep 1987 ... 3.00
❑Annual 2, Aug 1990; JBy (a); A: Lobo. L.E.G.I.O.N. '90 ... 3.00
❑Annual 3, Oct 1991 ... 3.00
❑Annual 4, ca. 1992 ... 3.00
❑Annual 5, ca. 1993 1: Sparx ... 3.00
❑Annual 6, ca. 1994; concludes in Superboy Annual #1 (1994); Elseworlds ... 2.95
❑Annual 7, ca. 1995; V: Kalibak. Year One ... 3.95
❑Annual 8, ca. 1996; Elseworlds; Legends of the Dead Earth ... 2.95
❑Annual 9, Sep 1997; Pulp Heroes ... 3.95

ADVENTURES OF TAD MARTIN, THE

Caliber

❑1 ... 2.50

ADVENTURES OF THE FLY

Archie / Radio

❑1, Aug 1959 JS, JK (a); O: Fly ... 220.00
❑2, Sep 1959; AW, JS, JK (a); Private Strong ... 140.00
❑3, Nov 1959 JD (a) ... 100.00
❑4, Jan 1960 ... 80.00
❑5, Mar 1960 ... 80.00
❑6, May 1960 ... 70.00
❑7, Jul 1960 ... 70.00
❑8, Sep 1960 ... 70.00
❑9, Nov 1960 ... 70.00
❑10, Jan 1961 ... 70.00
❑11, Mar 1961 ... 70.00
❑12, May 1961 ... 70.00
❑13, Jul 1961 ... 70.00
❑14, Sep 1961 ... 70.00
❑15, Oct 1961 ... 70.00
❑16, Nov 1961 ... 70.00
❑17, Jan 1962 ... 70.00
❑18, Mar 1962 ... 40.00
❑19, May 1962 ... 40.00
❑20, Jul 1962 ... 40.00
❑21, Sep 1962 ... 40.00
❑22, Oct 1962 ... 40.00
❑23, Nov 1962 ... 40.00
❑24, Feb 1963 ... 40.00
❑25, Apr 1963 ... 40.00
❑26, Jun 1963 ... 40.00
❑27, Aug 1963 ... 30.00
❑28, Oct 1963 ... 30.00
❑29, Jan 1964 ... 30.00
❑30, Oct 1964 ... 30.00
❑31, May 1965; becomes Fly Man ... 30.00

ADVENTURES OF THE JAGUAR

Archie / Radio

❑1, Sep 1961 ... 125.00
❑2, Oct 1961 ... 75.00
❑3, Nov 1961 ... 50.00
❑4, Jan 1962 ... 40.00
❑5, Mar 1962 ... 40.00
❑6, May 1962 ... 30.00
❑7, Jul 1962 ... 30.00
❑8, Aug 1962 ... 30.00
❑9, Sep 1962 ... 30.00
❑10, Nov 1962 ... 30.00
❑11, Mar 1963 ... 22.00
❑12, May 1963 ... 22.00
❑13, Aug 1963 ... 22.00
❑14, Oct 1963 ... 22.00
❑15, Nov 1963 ... 22.00

ADVENTURES OF THE LITTLE GREEN DINOSAUR, THE

Last Gasp

❑1, b&w ... 5.00
❑2, b&w ... 5.00

ADVENTURES OF THE MAD HUNDA DAY DAY, THE

Thaumaturge

❑1, Win 1995, b&w ... 2.00

ADVENTURES OF THE MASK

Dark Horse

❑1, Jan 1996 ... 2.50
❑2, Feb 1996 V: Walter ... 2.50
❑3, Mar 1996 ... 2.50
❑4, Apr 1996 1: Bombshell ... 2.50
❑5, May 1996 ... 2.50
❑6, Jun 1996 ... 2.50
❑7, Jul 1996 ... 2.50
❑8, Aug 1996; Milo dons the mask ... 2.50
❑9, Sep 1996; James Bond parody ... 2.50
❑10, Oct 1996 V: Walter ... 2.50
❑11, Nov 1996; Mask as Santa ... 2.50
❑12, Dec 1996 ... 2.50
❑Special 1, Oct 1996; Toys R Us Special Ed. Giveaway; newsprint cover ... 1.00

N-MINT

ADVENTURES OF THE OUTSIDERS, THE
DC

❑33, May 1986; Continued from Batman and the Outsiders #32 .... 1.00
❑34, Jun 1986 V: Masters of Disaster 1.00
❑35, Jul 1986 .... 1.00
❑36, Aug 1986 .... 1.00
❑37, Sep 1986 .... 1.00
❑38, Oct 1986 .... 1.00
❑39, Nov 1986 V: Nuclear Family 1.00
❑40, Dec 1986 JA (a); V: Nuclear Family 1.00
❑41, Jan 1987 JA (a); V: Force of July 1.00
❑42, Feb 1987 .... 1.00
❑43, Mar 1987 .... 1.00
❑44, Apr 1987 V: Duke of Oil 1.00
❑45, May 1987 V: Duke of Oil 1.00
❑46, Jun 1987 .... 1.00

ADVENTURES OF THEOWN, THE
PYRAMID

❑1 1986 .... 2.00
❑2 1986 .... 2.00
❑3 1986 .... 2.00

ADVENTURES OF THE SCREAMER BROTHERS
SUPERSTAR

❑1, Dec 1990 .... 1.50
❑2, Mar 1991 .... 1.50
❑3, Jun 1991 .... 1.50

ADVENTURES OF THE SCREAMER BROTHERS (VOL. 2)
SUPERSTAR

❑1, Aug 1991 .... 1.95
❑2 .... 1.95
❑3, Dec 1991 .... 1.95

ADVENTURES OF THE SUPER MARIO BROS.
VALIANT

❑1, Feb 1991 .... 4.00
❑2, Mar 1991; swimsuit issue 3.00
❑3, Apr 1991 .... 3.00
❑4, May 1991 .... 3.00
❑5, Jun 1991 .... 3.00
❑6, Jul 1991 .... 2.50
❑7, Aug 1991 .... 2.50
❑8, Sep 1991 .... 2.50
❑9, Oct 1991 .... 2.50

ADVENTURES OF THE THING, THE
MARVEL

❑1, Apr 1992; JBy (w); JBy, JSt (a); Reprints Marvel Two-In-One #50; Thing vs. Thing 1.50
❑2, May 1992 .... 1.50
❑3, Jun 1992 FM (a) 1.50
❑4, Jul 1992; A: Man-Thing. Reprints Marvel Two-In-One #77 .... 1.50

ADVENTURES OF THE VITAL-MAN
BUDGIE

❑1, Jun 1991, b&w 2.00
❑2 .... 2.00
❑3 .... 2.00
❑4 .... 2.00

ADVENTURES OF THE X-MEN, THE
MARVEL

❑1, Apr 1996; Wolverine vs. Hulk 2.00
❑2, May 1996 .... 1.50
❑3, Jun 1996 A: Spider-Man. V: Mr. Sinister 1.50
❑4, Jul 1996 .... 1.50
❑5, Aug 1996 V: Magneto 1.50
❑6, Sep 1996; Magneto vs. Apocalypse 1.25
❑7, Oct 1996 .... 1.25
❑8, Nov 1996 .... 1.25
❑9, Dec 1996 V: Vanisher 1.25
❑10, Jan 1997 V: Mojo 1.25
❑11, Feb 1997 A: Man-Thing 1.25
❑12, Mar 1997 .... 1.25

N-MINT

ADVENTURES ON SPACE STATION FREEDOM
TADCORPS

❑1; educational giveaway on International Space Station 2.50

ADVENTURES ON THE FRINGE
FANTAGRAPHICS

❑1, Mar 1992 .... 2.25
❑2, May 1992 .... 2.25
❑3, Jul 1992 .... 2.25
❑4, Oct 1992 .... 2.25
❑5, Feb 1993 .... 2.25

ADVENTURES ON THE PLANET OF THE APES
MARVEL

❑1, Oct 1975; JSn (c); JSn (a); Adapts movie 9.00
❑2, Nov 1975; Adapts movie 4.00
❑3 1976; Adapts movie 4.00
❑4 1976 .... 3.50
❑5, Apr 1976 .... 3.50
❑5/30 cent, Apr 1976; 30 cent price variant 20.00
❑6, Jun 1976 .... 4.00
❑6/30 cent, Jun 1976; 30 cent price variant 20.00
❑7, Aug 1976 .... 4.00
❑7/30 cent, Aug 1976; 30 cent price variant 20.00
❑8, Sep 1976 .... 4.00
❑9, Oct 1976; Adapts Beneath the Planet of the Apes 4.00
❑10, Nov 1976; AA (a); Adapts Beneath the Planet of the Apes 4.00
❑11, Dec 1976; AA (a); Adapts Beneath the Planet of the Apes; Destruction of Earth 4.00

ADVENTURE STRIP DIGEST
WCG

❑1, Aug 1994 .... 2.50
❑2, Apr 1995 .... 2.50
❑3 .... 2.50
❑4, Jun 1996 .... 2.50

ADVENTUROUS UNCLE SCROOGE MCDUCK, THE (WALT DISNEY'S...)
GLADSTONE

❑1, Jan 1998; CB (w); CB (a); reprints Barks' "The Twenty-Four Carat Moon" 2.50
❑2, Mar 1998; 50th anniversary of Uncle Scrooge 2.50

AEON FOCUS
AEON

❑1, Mar 1994; Justin Hampton's Twitch 2.95
❑2, Jun 1994; Colin Upton's Other Other Even Bigger Than Slightly Smaller That Got Bigger Big Thing 2.95
❑3, Oct 1994; Filthy Habits 2.95
❑4, Nov 1994; Ward Sutton's Ink Blot 2.95
❑5, ca. 1997 .... 2.95

AERTIMISAN: WAR OF SOULS
ALMAGEST

❑1, Nov 1997 .... 2.75
❑2, Jan 1998 .... 2.75

AESOP'S DESECRATED MORALS
MAGNECOM

❑1, b&w 2.95

AESOP'S FABLES
FANTAGRAPHICS

❑1, Spr 1991 .... 2.50
❑2, Fal 1991 .... 2.50
❑3, Win 1991 .... 2.50

AETERNUS
BRICK

❑1, Jun 1997 .... 2.95

AETOS THE EAGLE
ORPHAN UNDERGROUND

❑1, Sep 1994, b&w 2.50
❑2, Oct 1995, b&w 2.50

Jerry Lewis had several run-ins with gorillas during his comics career.
© 1965 National Periodical Publications (DC).

N-MINT

AETOS THE EAGLE (VOL. 2)
GROUND ZERO

❑1, Aug 1997 .... 3.00
❑2 .... 3.00
❑3 .... 3.00

AFFABLE TALES FOR YOUR IMAGINATON
LEE ROY BROWN

❑1, Jan 1987, b&w 3.00

AFTER APOCALYPSE
PARAGRAPHICS

❑1, May 1987 .... 1.95

AFTER DARK
MILLENNIUM

❑1 .... 2.95

AFTERMATH
PINNACLE

❑1, ca. 1986, b&w; sequel to Messiah 1.50

AFTERMATH (CHAOS)
CHAOS

❑1, ca. 2000 .... 2.95

AFTER/SHOCK: BULLETINS FROM GROUND ZERO
LAST GASP

❑1, b&w 2.00

AGAINST BLACKSHARD: 3-D: THE SAGA OF SKETCH, THE ROYAL ARTIST
SIRIUS

❑1 .... 2.25

AGENCY, THE
IMAGE

❑Ashcan 1/Gold; Ashcan preview ......
❑Ashcan 1; Ashcan preview ......
❑1/A, Aug 2001; Several figures standing on cover 2.50
❑1/B, Aug 2001; Woman sitting on cover 2.50
❑1/C, Aug 2001; Woman leaning on gun on cover 2.50
❑2, ca. 2001 .... 2.50
❑3, ca. 2001 .... 2.95
❑4, ca. 2001 .... 2.95
❑5, Feb 2002 .... 2.95
❑6, Mar 2002; Giant-size 4.95

AGENT, THE
MARVEL

❑1 .... 9.95

AGENT "00" SOUL
TWIST RECORDS

❑1; no price 5.00

AGENT AMERICA
AWESOME

❑Ashcan 1; Preview edition; 1: Coven. Series preempted by Marvel lawsuit 5.00

AGENT LIBERTY SPECIAL
DC

❑1 1991 .... 2.00

AGENTS
IMAGE

❑1, Apr 2003 .... 2.95
❑2, May 2003 .... 2.95
❑3, Jul 2003 .... 2.95
❑4, Aug 2003 .... 2.95

Condition price index: Multiply "NM prices" above by: **0.83 for Very Fine/Near Mint**
0.66 for Very Fine • 0.33 for Fine • 0.2 for Very Good • 0.125 for Good

N-MINT

❑5, Sep 2003 .... 2.95
❑6, Oct 2003 .... 2.95

AGENTS OF LAW
DARK HORSE

❑1, Mar 1995 .... 2.50
❑2 1995 .... 2.50
❑3 1995 .... 2.50
❑4 1995 .... 2.50
❑5 1995 .... 2.50
❑6, Sep 1995 .... 2.50

AGENT 13: THE MIDNIGHT AVENGER
TSR

❑1 .... 7.95

AGENT THREE ZERO
GALAXINOVELS

❑1; Galaxinovels w/ Trading Card and Poster 3.95

AGENT THREE ZERO: THE BLUE SULTAN'S QUEST/BLUE SULTAN-GALAXI FACT FILES
GALAXINOVELS

❑1; Flip-book; poster; trading card 2.95
❑1/Platinum; Platinum edition 2.95
❑2 .... 2.95
❑3 .... 2.95
❑4 .... 2.95

AGENT UNKNOWN
RENEGADE

❑1, Oct 1987 .... 2.00
❑2, Jan 1988 .... 2.00
❑3, Apr 1988 .... 2.00

AGENT X
MARVEL

❑1, Sep 2002 .... 2.25
❑2, Oct 2002 .... 2.25
❑3, Nov 2002 .... 2.25
❑4, Dec 2002 .... 2.25
❑5, Jan 2003 .... 2.25
❑6, Feb 2003 .... 2.25
❑7, Mar 2003 .... 2.99
❑8, Apr 2003 .... 2.99
❑9, May 2003 .... 2.99
❑10, Jun 2003 .... 2.99
❑11, Jul 2003 .... 2.99
❑12, Aug 2003 .... 2.99
❑13, Nov 2003 .... 2.99
❑14, Dec 2003 .... 2.99
❑15, Dec 2003 .... 2.99

AGE OF APOCALYPSE: THE CHOSEN
MARVEL

❑1 .... 2.50

AGE OF BRONZE
IMAGE

❑1, Nov 1998 .... 3.50
❑2, Jan 1999 .... 3.00
❑3, Mar 1999 .... 3.00
❑4, May 1999 .... 3.00
❑5, Oct 1999 .... 3.00
❑6, Jan 2000; cover says Dec, indicia says Jan 3.00
❑7, Mar 2000; cover says Apr, indicia says Mar 3.00
❑8, Aug 2000, b&w 3.50
❑9, Dec 2000; cover says Nov, indicia says Dec 3.50
❑10, Feb 2001 .... 3.50
❑11, Mar 2001 .... 3.50
❑12, Apr 2001 .... 3.50
❑13, May 2001 .... 3.50
❑14, Aug 2002 .... 3.50
❑15, Oct 2002 .... 3.50
❑16, Mar 2003 .... 3.50
❑17, Jul 2003 .... 3.50
❑18, Oct 2003 .... 3.50
❑19, Apr 2004 .... 3.50
❑Special 1, Jul 1999; cover says Jun, indicia says Jul 2.95
❑Special 2, May 2002; Behind the Scenes 3.50

N-MINT

AGE OF HEROES, THE
HALLOWEEN

❑1 1996, b&w 2.95
❑2 1996, b&w 2.95
❑3, Mar 1997 .... 2.95
❑4, May 1997 .... 2.95
❑5, Sep 1998 .... 2.95
❑Special 1; reprints Age of Heroes #1 and 2 (Halloween) 4.95
❑Special 2 .... 6.95

AGE OF HEROES, THE: WEX
IMAGE

❑1, Nov 1998, b&w 2.95

AGE OF INNOCENCE: THE REBIRTH OF IRON MAN
MARVEL

❑1 .... 2.50

AGE OF REPTILES
DARK HORSE

❑1, Nov 1993 .... 2.50
❑2, Dec 1993 .... 2.50
❑3, Jan 1994 .... 2.50
❑4, Feb 1994 .... 2.50

AGE OF REPTILES: THE HUNT
DARK HORSE

❑1, May 1996 .... 2.95
❑2, Jun 1996 .... 2.95
❑3, Jul 1996 .... 2.95
❑4, Aug 1996 .... 2.95
❑5, Sep 1996 .... 2.95

AGONY ACRES
AA2

❑1, May 1995 .... 2.95
❑1/Ashcan 1996 .... 2.50
❑2 1996 .... 2.95
❑3 1996, b&w 2.95
❑4 1996 .... 2.95
❑5 1996 .... 2.95

AHLEA
RADIO

❑1, Aug 1997 .... 2.95
❑2, Oct 1997 .... 2.95

AIDA-ZEE
NATE BUTLER

❑1 .... 1.50

AIDS AWARENESS
CHAOS CITY

❑1, ca. 1993, b&w 3.00

AIM (VOL. 2)
CRYPTIC

❑1 .... 1.95

AIRBOY
ECLIPSE

❑1, Jul 1986 O: Airboy II (modern). 1: Airboy II (modern). D: Airboy I (Golden Age) 2.00
❑2, Jul 1986 1: Skywolf (Golden Age, in modern era). 1: Marisa 1.50
❑3, Aug 1986 A: The Heap 1.50
❑4, Aug 1986 .... 1.50
❑5, Sep 1986; DSt (a); Return of Valkyrie 1.50
❑6, Sep 1986 1: Iron Ace (in modern age) 1.50
❑7, Oct 1986 .... 1.50
❑8, Oct 1986 .... 1.50
❑9, Nov 1986; Full-size issues begin O: Airboy (Golden Age). 1: Flying Fool (in modern age) 1.50
❑10, Nov 1986 1: Manic 1.25
❑11, Dec 1986; O: Airboy (Golden Age). O: Birdie. 1: Ito. Skywolf back-up .. 1.25
❑12, Dec 1986; 1: Kip Thorne. Iron Ace's identity revealed 1.25
❑13, Jan 1987; 1: Bald Eagle (in modern age). Airfighters back-up 1.25
❑14, Jan 1987 .... 1.25
❑15, Feb 1987 .... 1.25
❑16, Feb 1987 D: Manic 1.25
❑17, Mar 1987 1: Lacey Lyle. A: Harry Truman 1.25

N-MINT

❑18, Mar 1987 1: Black Angel (in modern age) 1.25
❑19, Apr 1987 V: Rats 1.25
❑20, Apr 1987 1: The Rats (in modern age). V: Rats 1.25
❑21, May 1987 GE (a); 1: Rat Mother 1.25
❑22, May 1987; 1: Lester Mansfield. 1: El Lobo Alado (Skywolf's father). Skywolf back-up story 1.25
❑23, Jun 1987 .... 1.25
❑24, Jun 1987 A: Heap 1.25
❑25, Jul 1987 O: Manure Man. 1: Manure Man. A: Heap 1.25
❑26, Jul 1987 1: Flying Dutchman (in modern age). 1: Road Rats 1.25
❑27, Aug 1987 .... 1.25
❑28, Aug 1987 1: Black Axis 1.25
❑29, Sep 1987 .... 1.25
❑30, Sep 1987 .... 1.25
❑31, Oct 1987 .... 1.25
❑32, Oct 1987 .... 1.25
❑33, Nov 1987 .... 1.75
❑34, Dec 1987 DS (a) 1.75
❑35, Jan 1988 .... 1.75
❑36, Feb 1988 .... 1.75
❑37, Mar 1988 .... 1.75
❑38, Apr 1988 .... 1.75
❑39, May 1988 .... 1.75
❑40, Jun 1988 .... 1.75
❑41, Jul 1988 .... 1.75
❑42, Aug 1988 .... 1.95
❑43, Sep 1988 .... 1.95
❑44, Oct 1988 .... 1.95
❑45, Nov 1988 .... 1.95
❑46, Jan 1989; Airboy Diary 1.95
❑47, Mar 1989; Airboy Diary 1.95
❑48, Apr 1989; Airboy Diary 1.95
❑49, Jun 1989; Airboy Diary 1.95
❑50, Oct 1989; Giant-size JKu (a) 4.95

AIRBOY MEETS THE PROWLER
ECLIPSE

❑1, Dec 1987 .... 1.95

AIRBOY-MR. MONSTER SPECIAL
ECLIPSE

❑1, Aug 1987 .... 1.75

AIRBOY VERSUS THE AIRMAIDENS
ECLIPSE

❑1, Jul 1988 .... 1.95

AIR FIGHTERS CLASSICS
ECLIPSE

❑1, Nov 1987; squarebound; cardstock cover; Reprints Air Fighters Comics#1 3.95
❑2, Jan 1988; Reprints Air Fighters Comics#2 .... 3.95
❑3, Mar 1988; Reprints Air Fighters Comics#3 .... 3.95
❑4; Reprints Air Fighters Comics#4 ... 3.95
❑5 1989; Reprints Air Fighters Comics#5 3.95
❑6; Reprints Air Fighters Comics#6 ... 3.95
❑7; Reprints Air Fighters Comics#7 ... 3.95

AIRFIGHTERS MEET SGT. STRIKE SPECIAL
ECLIPSE

❑1, Jan 1988 .... 1.95

AIRLOCK
ECLECTUS

❑1, Jun 1990, b&w 2.50
❑2, Jul 1991 .... 2.50
❑3, Oct 1991 .... 2.50

AIRMAIDENS SPECIAL
ECLIPSE

❑1, Aug 1987 .... 1.75

AIRMAN
MALIBU

❑1 .... 1.95

AIRMEN, THE
MANSION

❑1, Feb 1995, b&w 2.50

AIR RAIDERS
MARVEL / STAR

	N-MINT
❑1, Nov 1987	1.00
❑2, Dec 1987	1.00
❑3, Jan 1988	1.00
❑4, Feb 1988	1.00
❑5, Mar 1988	1.00

AIRTIGHT GARAGE, THE
MARVEL / EPIC

	N-MINT
❑1, Jul 1993	2.50
❑2, Aug 1993	2.50
❑3, Sep 1993	2.50
❑4, Oct 1993	2.50

AIR WAR STORIES
DELL

	N-MINT
❑1, Nov 1964	22.00
❑2, Dec 1965	14.00
❑3 1966	14.00
❑4 1966	14.00
❑5 1966	14.00
❑6 1966	14.00
❑7 1966	14.00
❑8; Final issue?	14.00

AIRWAVES
CALIBER

	N-MINT
❑1, Feb 1991	2.50
❑2 1991	2.50
❑3 1991	2.50
❑4 1991	2.50

A.K.A. GOLDFISH
CALIBER

	N-MINT
❑1; Joker	3.50
❑2; Ace	3.95
❑3, ca. 1995; Jack	3.95
❑4, ca. 1995; Queen	2.95
❑5, Mar 1996; King; cardstock cover	3.95

AKIKO
SIRIUS

	N-MINT
❑1, Mar 1996	6.00
❑2, Apr 1996	4.50
❑3, May 1996	4.00
❑4, Jun 1996	4.00
❑5 1996; no indicia	4.00
❑6, Aug 1996	3.50
❑7, Sep 1996	3.50
❑8, Oct 1996	3.50
❑9, Dec 1996	3.50
❑10, Jan 1997	3.50
❑11, Feb 1997	2.50
❑12, Mar 1997	2.50
❑13, Apr 1997	2.50
❑14, May 1997	2.50
❑15, Jul 1997	2.50
❑16, Aug 1997	2.50
❑17, Aug 1997; indicia says "Aug"	2.50
❑18, Sep 1997	2.50
❑19, Oct 1997; Beeba's story	2.50
❑20, Nov 1997; Beeba's story	2.50
❑21, Dec 1997	2.50
❑22, Jan 1998	2.50
❑23, Feb 1998	2.50
❑24, Mar 1998	2.50
❑25, May 1998	2.50
❑26, Jul 1998	2.50
❑27, Aug 1998	2.50
❑28, Oct 1998	2.50
❑29, Nov 1998	2.50
❑30, Dec 1998	2.50
❑31, Feb 1998	2.50
❑32, Mar 1998	2.50
❑33, May 1998	2.50
❑34, Jun 1999	2.50
❑35, Sep 1999, b&w	2.50
❑36, Oct 1999, b&w	2.50
❑37, Dec 1999, b&w	2.50
❑38, Feb 2000, b&w	2.50
❑39, May 2000, b&w	2.50
❑40, Aug 2000, b&w	2.95
❑41, Oct 2000, b&w	2.95
❑42 2001	0.00
❑43 2001	0.00
❑44 2001	0.00
❑45 2001	0.00
❑46 2001	0.00
❑47 2002	0.00
❑48 2002	0.00
❑49 2002	2.95
❑50, Jun 2003	3.50
❑51, Nov 2003	2.95

AKIKO ON THE PLANET SMOO
SIRIUS

	N-MINT
❑1, Dec 1995, b&w; Fold-out cover	5.00
❑1/HC, b&w; Hardcover edition	19.95
❑1-2, May 1998, b&w; cardstock cover	4.00
❑Fan ed. 1; free promotional giveaway	3.00

AKIKO ON THE PLANET SMOO: THE COLOR EDITION
SIRIUS

	N-MINT
❑1, Feb 2000; cardstock cover	4.95

AKIRA
MARVEL / EPIC

	N-MINT
❑1, Sep 1988	8.00
❑1-2 1988	4.00
❑2, Oct 1988	5.00
❑2-2 1988	4.00
❑3, Nov 1988	5.00
❑4, Dec 1988	4.00
❑5, Jan 1989	4.00
❑6, ca. 1989	4.00
❑7, ca. 1989	4.00
❑8, ca. 1989	4.00
❑9, ca. 1989	4.00
❑10, ca. 1989	4.00
❑11, ca. 1989	4.00
❑12, ca. 1989	4.00
❑13, ca. 1989	4.00
❑14, ca. 1989	4.00
❑15, ca. 1989	4.00
❑16, ca. 1989	4.00
❑17, ca. 1990	4.00
❑18, ca. 1990	4.00
❑19, ca. 1990	4.00
❑20, ca. 1990	4.00
❑21, ca. 1990	4.00
❑22, ca. 1990	4.00
❑23, ca. 1990	4.00
❑24, ca. 1990	4.00
❑25, ca. 1990	4.00
❑26, ca. 1990	4.00
❑27, ca. 1991	4.00
❑28, ca. 1991	4.00
❑29, ca. 1991	4.00
❑30, ca. 1991	4.00
❑31, ca. 1991	4.00
❑32, ca. 1992	4.00
❑33, ca. 1992	4.00
❑34, ca. 1994	4.00
❑35, ca. 1995	4.00
❑36 1995 A: Lady Miyako	4.00
❑37, ca. 1995	4.00
❑38, ca. 1995	4.00

A*K*Q*J
FANTAGRAPHICS

	N-MINT
❑1, Mar 1991, b&w; Captain Jack	2.75

ALADDIN (CONQUEST)
CONQUEST

	N-MINT
❑1, Feb 1993, b&w	2.95

ALADDIN (DISNEY'S...)
MARVEL

	N-MINT
❑1, Oct 1994	1.50
❑2, Nov 1994	1.50
❑3, Dec 1994	1.50
❑4, Jan 1995	1.50
❑5, Feb 1995	1.50
❑6, Mar 1995	1.50
❑7, Apr 1995	1.50
❑8, May 1995	1.50
❑9, Jun 1995	1.50
❑10, Jul 1995	1.50
❑11, Aug 1995	1.50

The Adventures of the Thing reprinted issues of *Marvel Two-in-One*.

© 1992 Marvel Comics.

THE ALAMO
ANTARCTIC

	N-MINT
❑1, Apr 2004	4.95

ALARMING ADVENTURES
HARVEY

	N-MINT
❑1, Oct 1962	40.00
❑2, Dec 1962	25.00
❑3, Feb 1963	20.00

ALBEDO (1ST SERIES)
THOUGHTS & IMAGES

	N-MINT
❑0, ca. 1986; Blue cover; 500 printed	8.00
❑0/A; Only 50 copies printed; White cover (yellow table)	30.00
❑0/B; Less than 500 copies printed; White cover (no yellow)	15.00
❑0-2; Blue cover	5.00
❑0-3; Blue cover	3.00
❑0-4, Dec 1986; Yellow cover from, blue cover back	2.50
❑1; 1: Usagi Yojimbo. Dark red cover	14.00
❑1/A; 1: Usagi Yojimbo. Bright red cover	10.00
❑1-2; 1: Usagi Yojimbo. Bright red cover	10.00
❑2, Nov 1984 2: Usagi Yojimbo	8.00
❑3, Apr 1985; Usagi Yojimbo back-up	5.00
❑4, Jul 1985; Usagi Yojimbo back-up	4.00
❑5, Oct 1985	4.00
❑6, Jan 1986	3.00
❑7, Mar 1986	3.00
❑8, Jul 1986	3.00
❑9, May 1987	2.00
❑10, Sep 1987; cardstock cover	2.00
❑11, Dec 1987	2.00
❑12, Mar 1988	2.00
❑13, Jun 1988	2.00
❑14, Spr 1989	2.00

ALBEDO (2ND SERIES)
ANTARCTIC

	N-MINT
❑1, Jun 1991	4.00
❑2, Sep 1991	3.00
❑3, Dec 1991	3.00
❑4, Mar 1992	3.00
❑5, Jun 1992	2.50
❑6, Sep 1992	2.50
❑7, Dec 1992	2.50
❑8, Mar 1993	2.50
❑9, Jun 1993	2.50
❑10, Oct 1993	2.75
❑Special 1, Jul 1993	2.95

ALBEDO (3RD SERIES)
ANTARCTIC

	N-MINT
❑1, Feb 1994	2.95
❑2, Oct 1994	2.95
❑3, Feb 1995	2.95
❑4, Jan 1996	2.95

ALBEDO (4TH SERIES)
ANTARCTIC

	N-MINT
❑1, Dec 1996	2.95
❑2, Jan 1999	2.99

ALBEDO (5TH SERIES)
ANTARCTIC

	N-MINT
❑1	2.99

N-MINT

ALBINO SPIDER OF DAJETTE
VEROTIK

❑1, ca. 1997 .... 2.95
❑2, Jun 1997 .... 2.95
❑0, ca. 1998 .... 2.95

AL CAPP'S LI'L ABNER: THE FRAZETTA YEARS
DARK HORSE

❑1, ca 2003 .... 18.95
❑2, ca 2003 .... 18.95
❑3, ca 2004 .... 18.95
❑4, ca 2004 .... 18.95

ALEC DEAR
MEDIOCRE CONCEPTS

❑1 1996, b&w; magazine-sized comic book with cardstock cover; no cover price 2.00

ALEC: LOVE AND BEERGLASSES
ESCAPE

❑1 .... 3.50

ALEX
FANTAGRAPHICS

❑1 .... 2.95
❑2, Apr 1994 .... 2.95
❑3, Jul 1994 .... 2.95
❑4, Oct 1994 .... 2.95
❑5, Nov 1994 .... 2.95
❑6, Jan 1995, b&w 2.95

ALEXIS (VOL. 2)
FANTAGRAPHICS / EROS

❑1 1995 .... 2.95
❑2, Jul 1995 .... 2.95
❑3 1995 .... 2.95
❑4 1995 .... 2.95
❑5, Mar 1996 .... 2.95

ALF
MARVEL

❑1, Mar 1988 .... 2.00
❑2, Apr 1988 .... 1.25
❑3, May 1988 .... 1.25
❑4, Jun 1988 .... 1.25
❑5, Jul 1988 .... 1.25
❑6, Aug 1988 .... 1.00
❑7, Sep 1988 .... 1.00
❑8, Oct 1988 .... 1.00
❑9, Nov 1988 .... 1.00
❑10, Dec 1988 .... 1.00
❑11, Jan 1989 .... 1.00
❑12, Feb 1989 .... 1.00
❑13, Mar 1989 .... 1.00
❑14, Apr 1989 .... 1.00
❑15, May 1989 .... 1.00
❑16, Jun 1989 .... 1.00
❑17, Jul 1989 .... 1.00
❑18, Aug 1989 .... 1.00
❑19, Sep 1989 .... 1.00
❑20, Oct 1989 .... 1.00
❑21, Nov 1989 .... 1.00
❑22, Nov 1989; X-Men parody 1.00
❑23, Dec 1989 .... 1.00
❑24, Dec 1989 .... 1.00
❑25, Jan 1990 .... 1.00
❑26, Feb 1990 .... 1.00
❑27, Mar 1990 .... 1.00
❑28, Apr 1990 .... 1.00
❑29, May 1990; "3-D" cover 1.00
❑30, Jun 1990 .... 1.00
❑31, Jul 1990 .... 1.00
❑32, Aug 1990 .... 1.00
❑33, Sep 1990 .... 1.00
❑34, Oct 1990 .... 1.00
❑35, Nov 1990 .... 1.00
❑36, Dec 1990 .... 1.00
❑37, Jan 1991 .... 1.00
❑38, Feb 1991 .... 1.00
❑39, Mar 1991 .... 1.00
❑40, Apr 1991 .... 1.00
❑41, May 1991 .... 1.00
❑42, Jun 1991 .... 1.00
❑43, Jul 1991 .... 1.00

N-MINT

❑44, Aug 1991; X-Men parody 1.00
❑45, Sep 1991 .... 1.00
❑46, Oct 1991 .... 1.00
❑47, Nov 1991 .... 1.00
❑48, Dec 1991 .... 1.00
❑49, Jan 1992 .... 1.00
❑50, Feb 1992; Giant-size 1.50
❑Annual 1, ca. 1988; Dynamic Forces edition 1.50
❑Annual 2, ca. 1989 .... 1.50
❑Annual 3, ca. 1990; TMNT parody ... 1.50
❑Holiday 1, Hol 1988; magazine-sized comic book with cardstock cover; Holiday Special #1; magazine-sized comic book with cardstock cover .. 1.50
❑Holiday 2, Hol 1989; Dynamic Forces edition; Holiday Special #2 .... 1.50
❑Spring 1; Spring Special 1.75

ALF COMICS MAGAZINE
MARVEL

❑1, Nov 1988; digest 2.00
❑2, Jan 1989; digest 2.00

ALIAS:
NOW

❑1, Jul 1990 .... 1.75
❑2, Aug 1990 .... 1.75
❑3, Sep 1990 .... 1.75
❑4, Oct 1990 .... 1.75
❑5, Nov 1990 .... 1.75

ALIAS (MARVEL)
MARVEL / MAX

❑1, Nov 2001 BMB (w) 3.50
❑2, Dec 2001 BMB (w) 3.00
❑3, Jan 2002 BMB (w) 3.00
❑4, Feb 2002 BMB (w) 3.00
❑5, Mar 2002 BMB (w) 3.00
❑6, Apr 2002 BMB (w) 3.00
❑7, May 2002 BMB (w) 3.00
❑8, Jun 2002 BMB (w) 3.00
❑9, Jul 2002 BMB (w) 3.00
❑10, Aug 2002 BMB (w) 3.00
❑11, Sep 2002 BMB (w) 2.99
❑12, Sep 2002 BMB (w) 2.99
❑13, Oct 2002 BMB (w) 2.99
❑14, Nov 2002 BMB (w) 2.99
❑15, Dec 2002 BMB (w) 2.99
❑16, Jan 2003 BMB (w) 2.99
❑17, Feb 2003 BMB (w) 2.99
❑18, Mar 2003 BMB (w) 2.99
❑19, Apr 2003 BMB (w) 2.99
❑20, May 2003 BMB (w) 2.99
❑21, May 2003 BMB (w) 2.99
❑22, Jul 2003 BMB (w); O: Jessica Jones 2.99
❑23, Aug 2003 BMB (w); O: Jessica Jones 2.99
❑24, Sep 2003 BMB (w) 2.99
❑25, Oct 2003 BMB (w) 2.99
❑26, Nov 2003 BMB (w) 2.99
❑27, Dec 2003 BMB (w) 2.99
❑28, Jan 2004 BMB (w) 2.99

ALI-BABA: SCOURGE OF THE DESERT
GAUNTLET

❑1 .... 3.50

ALICE IN LOST WORLD
RADIO

❑1 .... 2.95
❑2, ca. 2001 .... 2.95
❑3, ca. 2001 .... 2.95
❑4, ca. 2001 .... 2.95

ALIEN 3
DARK HORSE

❑1, Jun 1992 .... 2.50
❑2, Jun 1992 .... 2.50
❑3, Jun 1992 .... 2.50

ALIEN DUCKLINGS
BLACKTHORNE

❑1, Oct 1986 .... 2.00
❑2, Dec 1986 .... 2.00

N-MINT

❑3, Feb 1987 .... 2.00
❑4, Apr 1987 .... 2.00

ALIEN ENCOUNTERS (FANTACO)
FANTACO

❑1 1980 .... 1.50

ALIEN ENCOUNTERS (ECLIPSE)
ECLIPSE

❑1, Jun 1985 MGu (a) 2.00
❑2, Aug 1965 .... 2.00
❑3, Oct 1985 .... 2.00
❑4, Dec 1985 .... 2.00
❑5, Feb 1986 .... 2.00
❑6, Apr 1986; Story "Nada" used as basis for movie "They Live" 2.00
❑7, Jun 1986 RHo (a) 2.00
❑8, Aug 1986 .... 2.00
❑9, Oct 1986 .... 2.00
❑10, Dec 1986 TS, GM (a) 2.00
❑11, Feb 1987 .... 2.00
❑12, Apr 1987 .... 2.00
❑13, Jun 1987 .... 2.00
❑14, Aug 1987 .... 2.00

ALIEN FIRE
KITCHEN SINK

❑1, Jan 1987 .... 2.00
❑2, May 1987 .... 2.00
❑3, May 1987 .... 2.00

ALIEN FIRE: PASS IN THUNDER
KITCHEN SINK

❑1, May 1995, b&w; squarebound 6.95

ALIEN HERO
ZEN

❑1, Feb 1999; illustrated novella featuring Zen 8.95

ALIEN LEGION (VOL. 1)
MARVEL / EPIC

❑1, Apr 1984; Giant-size 2.00
❑2, Jun 1984 .... 1.50
❑3, Aug 1984 .... 1.50
❑4, Oct 1984 .... 1.50
❑5, Dec 1984 .... 1.50
❑6, Feb 1985 .... 1.50
❑7, Apr 1985 .... 1.50
❑8, Jun 1985 .... 1.50
❑9, Aug 1985 .... 1.50
❑10, Oct 1985 .... 1.50
❑11, Dec 1985 .... 1.50
❑12, Feb 1986 .... 1.50
❑13, Apr 1986 .... 1.50
❑14, Jun 1986 .... 1.50
❑15, Aug 1986 .... 1.50
❑16, Oct 1986 .... 1.50
❑17, Dec 1986 .... 1.50
❑18, Feb 1987 .... 1.50
❑19, Apr 1987 .... 1.50
❑20, Jun 1987 .... 1.50

ALIEN LEGION (VOL. 2)
MARVEL / EPIC

❑1, Oct 1987 .... 1.50
❑2, Dec 1987 .... 1.50
❑3, Feb 1988 .... 1.50
❑4, Apr 1988 .... 1.50
❑5, Jun 1988 .... 1.50
❑6, Aug 1988 .... 1.50
❑7, Oct 1988 .... 1.50
❑8, Dec 1988 .... 1.50
❑9, Feb 1989 .... 1.50
❑10, Apr 1989 .... 1.50
❑11, Jun 1989 .... 1.50
❑12, Aug 1989 .... 1.50
❑13, Oct 1989 .... 1.50
❑14, Dec 1989 .... 1.50
❑15, Feb 1990 .... 1.50
❑16, Apr 1990 .... 1.50
❑17, Jun 1990 .... 1.50
❑18, Aug 1990 .... 1.50

ALIEN LEGION: A GREY DAY TO DIE
MARVEL

❑1 .... 5.95

N-MINT

ALIEN LEGION: BINARY DEEP
MARVEL / EPIC

❑1, Sep 1993 .... 3.50

ALIEN LEGION: JUGGER GRIMROD
MARVEL / EPIC

❑1, Aug 1992 .... 5.95

ALIEN LEGION: ONE PLANET AT A TIME
MARVEL / EPIC

❑1, ca. 1993 .... 4.95
❑2, ca. 1993 .... 4.95
❑3, ca. 1993 .... 4.95

ALIEN LEGION: ON THE EDGE
MARVEL / EPIC

❑1, Nov 1990 .... 4.50
❑2, Dec 1990 .... 4.50
❑3, Jan 1991 .... 4.50

ALIEN LEGION: TENANTS OF HELL
MARVEL / EPIC

❑1, ca. 1991; cardstock cover 4.50
❑2, ca. 1991; cardstock cover 4.50

ALIEN NATION
DC

❑1, Dec 1988 .... 3.00

ALIEN NATION: A BREED APART
ADVENTURE

❑1, Nov 1990 .... 2.50
❑2, Dec 1990 .... 2.50
❑3, Jan 1991 .... 2.50
❑4, Mar 1991 .... 2.50

ALIEN NATION: THE FIRSTCOMERS
ADVENTURE

❑1, May 1991 .... 2.50
❑2, Jun 1991 .... 2.50
❑3, Jul 1991 .... 2.50
❑4, Aug 1991 .... 2.50

ALIEN NATION: THE LOST EPISODE
MALIBU

❑1 1992, b&w; squarebound; adapts second season opener 4.95

ALIEN NATION: THE PUBLIC ENEMY
ADVENTURE

❑1, Dec 1991 .... 2.50
❑2, Jan 1992 .... 2.50
❑3, Feb 1992 .... 2.50
❑4, Mar 1992 .... 2.50

ALIEN NATION: THE SKIN TRADE
ADVENTURE

❑1, Mar 1991 .... 2.50
❑2, Apr 1991 .... 2.50
❑3, May 1991 .... 2.50
❑4, Jun 1991 .... 2.50

ALIEN NATION: THE SPARTANS
ADVENTURE

❑1; Yellow 2.50
❑1/A 1990; Green 2.50
❑1/B 1990; Blue 2.50
❑1/C 1990; Red 2.50
❑1/Ltd. 1990 .... 3.00
❑2 1990 .... 2.50
❑3 1990 .... 2.50
❑4 1990 .... 2.50

ALIEN RESURRECTION
DARK HORSE

❑1, Oct 1997 .... 2.50
❑2, Nov 1997 .... 2.50

ALIENS, THE
GOLD KEY

❑1 .... 12.00
❑2 1982 .... 5.00

ALIENS (VOL. 1)
DARK HORSE

❑1, May 1988 .... 4.50
❑1-2 .... 2.50
❑1-3 .... 2.00
❑1-4 .... 2.00
❑1-5 .... 2.00

N-MINT

❑1-6 .... 2.00
❑2, Sep 1988 .... 3.50
❑2-2 .... 2.50
❑2-3 .... 2.00
❑2-4, Jul 1989 .... 2.00
❑3, Jan 1989 .... 2.50
❑3-3, Sep 1989 .... 2.00
❑3-2 .... 2.00
❑4, Mar 1989 .... 2.50
❑4-2 .... 2.00
❑5, Jun 1989 .... 2.50
❑5-2, Jun 1989 .... 2.00
❑6, Jul 1989 .... 2.50
❑6-2 .... 2.00

ALIENS (VOL. 2)
DARK HORSE

❑1, Aug 1989 .... 3.00
❑2, Dec 1989 .... 2.50
❑3, Mar 1990 .... 2.50
❑4, May 1990 .... 2.50

ALIENS: ALCHEMY
DARK HORSE

❑1, Oct 1997 .... 2.95
❑2, Nov 1997 .... 2.95
❑3, Nov 1997 .... 2.95

ALIENS: APOCALYPSE: THE DESTROYING ANGELS
DARK HORSE

❑1, Jan 1999 .... 2.95
❑2, Feb 1999 .... 2.95
❑3, Mar 1999 .... 2.95
❑4, Apr 1999 .... 2.95

ALIENS: BERSERKER
DARK HORSE

❑1, Jan 1995 .... 2.50
❑2, Feb 1995 .... 2.50
❑3, Mar 1995 .... 2.50
❑4, Apr 1995 .... 2.50

ALIENS: COLONIAL MARINES
DARK HORSE

❑1, Jan 1993 .... 2.50
❑2, Feb 1993 .... 2.50
❑3, Mar 1993 .... 2.50
❑4, Apr 1993 .... 2.50
❑5, May 1993 .... 2.50
❑6, Jun 1993 .... 2.50
❑7, Jul 1993 .... 2.50
❑8, Aug 1993 .... 2.50
❑9, Sep 1993 .... 2.50
❑10, Oct 1993 .... 2.50

ALIENS: EARTH ANGEL
DARK HORSE

❑1, Aug 1994 .... 2.95

ALIENS: EARTH WAR
DARK HORSE

❑1, Jun 1990 .... 3.00
❑1-2 .... 2.50
❑2, Jul 1990 .... 2.50
❑3, Sep 1990 .... 2.50
❑4, Oct 1990 .... 2.50

ALIEN SEX/MONSTER LUST
FANTAGRAPHICS / EROS

❑1, Apr 1992, b&w 2.50

ALIENS: GENOCIDE
DARK HORSE

❑1, Nov 1991 .... 2.50
❑2, Dec 1991 .... 2.50
❑3, Jan 1992 .... 2.50
❑4, Feb 1992 .... 2.50

ALIENS: GLASS CORRIDOR
DARK HORSE

❑1, Jun 1998 .... 2.95

ALIENS: HAVOC
DARK HORSE

❑1, Jun 1997 .... 2.95
❑2, Jul 1997 SA, CR (a) 3.95

Two of Eclipse's adventure heroes met in the *Airboy Meets The Prowler* one-shot.
© 1987 Eclipse.

N-MINT

ALIENS: HIVE
DARK HORSE

❑1, Feb 1992 .... 2.50
❑2, Mar 1992 .... 2.50
❑3, Apr 1992 .... 2.50
❑4, May 1992 .... 2.50

ALIENS: KIDNAPPED
DARK HORSE

❑1, Dec 1997 .... 2.50
❑2, Jan 1998 .... 2.50
❑3, Feb 1998 .... 2.50

ALIENS: LABYRINTH
DARK HORSE

❑1, Sep 1993 .... 2.50
❑2, Oct 1993 .... 2.50
❑3, Nov 1993 .... 2.50
❑4, Dec 1993 .... 2.50

ALIENS: LOVESICK
DARK HORSE

❑1, Dec 1996, b&w and color 2.95

ALIENS: MONDO HEAT
DARK HORSE

❑1, Feb 1996 .... 2.50

ALIENS: MONDO PEST
DARK HORSE

❑1 .... 2.95

ALIENS: MUSIC OF THE SPEARS
DARK HORSE

❑1, Jan 1994 .... 2.50
❑2, Feb 1994 .... 2.50
❑3, Mar 1994 .... 2.50
❑4, Apr 1994 .... 2.50

ALIENS: NEWT'S TALE
DARK HORSE

❑1, Jun 1992 .... 4.95
❑2, Aug 1992 .... 4.95

ALIENS: PIG
DARK HORSE

❑1, Mar 1997 .... 2.95

ALIENS/PREDATOR: THE DEADLIEST OF THE SPECIES
DARK HORSE

❑1, Jul 1993 .... 2.50
❑1/Ltd., Jul 1993; no cover price 4.00
❑2, Sep 1993 .... 2.50
❑3, Nov 1993 .... 2.50
❑4, Jan 1994 .... 2.50
❑5, Mar 1994 .... 2.50
❑6, May 1994 .... 2.50
❑7, Aug 1994 .... 2.50
❑8, Oct 1994 .... 2.50
❑9, Dec 1994 .... 2.50
❑10, Feb 1995 .... 2.50
❑11, May 1995 .... 2.50
❑12, Aug 1995 .... 2.50

ALIENS: PURGE
DARK HORSE

❑1, Aug 1997 .... 2.95

ALIENS: ROGUE
DARK HORSE

❑1, Apr 1993 .... 2.50
❑2, May 1993 .... 2.50
❑3, Jun 1993 .... 2.50
❑4, Jul 1993 .... 2.50

N-MINT

ALIENS: SACRIFICE
DARK HORSE

❑1, ca. 1993 .... 4.95

ALIENS: SALVATION
DARK HORSE

❑1, ca. 1993 .... 4.95

ALIENS: SALVATION AND SACRIFICE
DARK HORSE

❑1, Mar 2001 .... 12.95

ALIENS: SPECIAL
DARK HORSE

❑1, Jun 1997 .... 2.50

ALIENS: STALKER
DARK HORSE

❑1, Jun 1998 .... 2.50

ALIENS: STRONGHOLD
DARK HORSE

❑1, May 1994 .... 2.50
❑2, Jun 1994 .... 2.50
❑3, Jul 1994 .... 2.50
❑4, Sep 1994 .... 2.50

ALIENS: SURVIVAL
DARK HORSE

❑1, Feb 1998 .... 2.95
❑2, Mar 1998 .... 2.95
❑3, Apr 1998 .... 2.95

ALIENS: TRIBES
DARK HORSE

❑1 .... 11.95
❑1/HC; hardcover novel 24.95
❑1/Ltd.; Limited edition hardcover 75.00

ALIENS VS. PREDATOR
DARK HORSE

❑0, Jul 1990, b&w; reprints story from Dark Horse Presents #34-36 .... 4.00
❑1, Jun 1990 .... 4.00
❑1-2 .... 2.50
❑2, Aug 1990 .... 3.50
❑2-2 .... 2.50
❑3, Oct 1990 .... 3.00
❑3-2 .... 2.50
❑4, Dec 1990 .... 3.00
❑4-2 .... 2.50
❑Annual 1, Jul 1999 .... 4.95

ALIENS VS. PREDATOR: BOOTY
DARK HORSE

❑1, Jan 1996 .... 2.50

ALIENS VS. PREDATOR: DUEL
DARK HORSE

❑1, Mar 1995 .... 2.50
❑2, Apr 1995 .... 2.50

ALIENS VS. PREDATOR: ETERNAL
DARK HORSE

❑1, Jun 1998 .... 2.50
❑2, Jul 1998 .... 2.50
❑3, Aug 1998 .... 2.50
❑4, Sep 1998 .... 2.50

ALIENS VS. PREDATOR VS. THE TERMINATOR
DARK HORSE

❑1, Apr 2000 .... 2.95
❑2, May 2000 .... 2.95
❑3, Jun 2000 .... 2.95
❑4, Jul 2000 .... 2.95

ALIENS VS. PREDATOR: WAR
DARK HORSE

❑0 1995 .... 2.50
❑1 1995 .... 2.50
❑2, Jun 1995 .... 2.50
❑3, Jul 1995 .... 2.50
❑4, Aug 1995 .... 2.50

ALIENS VS. PREDATOR: XENOGENESIS
DARK HORSE

❑1, Dec 1999 .... 2.95
❑2, Jan 2000 .... 2.95

N-MINT

❑3, Feb 2000 .... 2.95
❑4, Mar 2000 .... 2.95

ALIENS: WRAITH
DARK HORSE

❑1, Jul 1998 .... 2.95

ALIENS: XENOGENESIS
DARK HORSE

❑1, Aug 1999 .... 2.95
❑2, Sep 1999 .... 2.95
❑3, Oct 1999 .... 2.95
❑4, Nov 1999 .... 2.95

ALIEN: THE ILLUSTRATED STORY
HM COMMUNICATIONS

❑1 .... 5.00

ALIEN WORLDS
PACIFIC

❑1, Dec 1982 AW, NR, VM (a) 2.50
❑2, May 1983 DSt (w); DSt (a) 2.00
❑3, Jul 1983 TY (a) 2.00
❑4, Sep 1983 AW, JJ, DSt (a) 2.00
❑5, Dec 1983 TY (a) 2.00
❑6, Feb 1984 FB (a) 2.00
❑7, ca. 1984 GM, GP, BA (a) 2.00
❑8, Nov 1984; AW (a); Eclipse Comics begins as publisher 2.00
❑9, Jan 1985 FB (a) 2.00
❑3D 1, Jul 1984; Full-size issues begin DSt (a) 2.00

ALIEN WORLDS (BLACKTHORNE)
BLACKTHORNE

❑1, b&w 5.95

ALISON DARE, LITTLE MISS ADVENTURES
ONI

❑1, Sep 2000, b&w 4.50

ALISTER THE SLAYER
MIDNIGHT

❑1, Oct 1995 .... 2.50

ALIZARIN'S JOURNAL
AVATAR

❑1, Mar 1999, b&w 3.50

ALLAGASH INCIDENT, THE
TUNDRA

❑1, Jul 1993 .... 2.95

ALL-AMERICAN COMICS (2ND SERIES)
DC

❑1, May 1999 A: Johnny Thunder. A: Green Lantern 2.00

ALLEGRA
IMAGE

❑1, Aug 1996 .... 2.50
❑1/Variant, Aug 1996; foil cover 2.50
❑2, Sep 1996 .... 2.50
❑3, Nov 1996 .... 2.50
❑4, Dec 1996 .... 2.50

ALLEY CAT
IMAGE

❑1, Jul 1999 .... 2.50
❑1/A, Jul 1999; Another Universe Edition; school girl cover 3.00
❑1/B, Jul 1999; Wizard World Edition; reclining with claws extended 2.50
❑2, Aug 1999 .... 2.50
❑2/A, Aug 1999; Monster Mart Edition; in red dress with stake in hand 2.50
❑3, Sep 1999; in front of grave 2.50
❑3/A, Sep 1999 .... 2.50
❑4, Oct 1999 .... 2.50
❑5, Dec 1999 .... 2.50
❑6, Feb 2000; with headdress 2.95
❑Ashcan 1, May 1999; Limited Preview Edition on cover; holding arms over head 2.95
❑Ashcan 1/A, May 1999; Dynamic Forces edition 3.00
❑Ashcan 1/B, May 1999; Dynamic Forces edition; front shot; Wizard World logo at bottom right 3.00

N-MINT

❑Ashcan 1/C, May 1999; Dynamic Forces edition; sketch cover 3.00
❑Ashcan 1/D, May 1999; Dynamic Forces edition; drawn color cover; kneeling on rooftop 3.00
❑Ashcan 1/E; Cover depicts claw outstretched, green background ....

ALLEY CAT LINGERIE EDITION
IMAGE

❑1, Oct 1999; photos and pin-ups; cardstock cover 4.95

ALLEY CAT VS. LADY PENDRAGON
IMAGE

❑1 2000 .... 3.00
❑1/A 2000; Wizard Mall variant; flipbook with Alley Cat Con Exclusive Preview 3.00

ALLEY OOP (DRAGON LADY)
DRAGON LADY

❑1 .... 5.95
❑2; time machine 6.95
❑3; Hercules 7.95

ALLEY OOP ADVENTURES
ANTARCTIC

❑1, Aug 1998 .... 2.95
❑2, Oct 1998 .... 2.95
❑3, Dec 1998 .... 2.95

ALLEY OOP QUARTERLY
ANTARCTIC

❑1, Sep 1999 .... 2.50
❑2, Dec 1999 .... 2.95
❑3, Mar 2000 .... 2.95

ALL GIRLS SCHOOL MEETS ALL BOYS SCHOOL
ANGEL

❑1 .... 3.00

ALL HALLOW'S EVE
INNOVATION

❑1 .... 4.95

ALLIANCE, THE
IMAGE

❑1, Aug 1995 .... 2.50
❑1/A, Aug 1995; variant cover 2.50
❑2, Sep 1995 .... 2.50
❑2/A, Sep 1995; variant cover 2.50
❑3, Nov 1995 .... 2.50
❑3/A, Nov 1995; variant cover 2.50

ALL NEW ADVENTURES OF THE MIGHTY CRUSADERS
ARCHIE / RED CIRCLE

❑1, Mar 1983 .... 1.00
❑2, May 1983 .... 1.00
❑3, Jul 1983, b&w; Title becomes Mighty Crusaders with #4 .... 1.00

ALL NEW COLLECTORS' EDITION
DC

❑53, Dec 1977; C-53 .... 26.00
❑54, Jan 1978; C-54 .... 12.00
❑55, Feb 1978; MGr (a); C-55; Legion; Wedding of Lightning Lad and Saturn Girl 15.00
❑56, Apr 1978; NA (w); NA (a); C-56 . 20.00
❑57, May 1978; C-57 .... 12.00
❑58, Jun 1978; RB, DG (a); C-58; Superman vs. Shazam 12.00
❑60, ca. 1978; C-60 .... 20.00
❑61, ca. 1979; C-61 .... 12.00
❑62, Mar 1979; C-62 .... 12.00

ALL NEW EXILES, THE
MALIBU / ULTRAVERSE

❑0, Sep 1995; "Black September"; Number infinity 1.50
❑0/Variant, Sep 1995; alternate cover; "Black September"; Number infinity 1.50
❑1, Oct 1995 .... 1.50
❑2, Nov 1995 .... 1.50
❑3, Dec 1995 .... 1.50
❑4, Jan 1996 .... 1.50
❑5, Feb 1996 .... 2.50
❑6, Mar 1996 .... 1.50

	N-MINT
❑7, Apr 1996	1.50
❑8, May 1996	1.50
❑9, Jun 1996	1.50
❑10, Jul 1996, alternate cover	1.50
❑11, Aug 1996, continues in UltraForce #12	1.50

ALL-NEW TENCHI MUYO PART 1
VIZ

	N-MINT
❑1, May 2002	2.95
❑2, Jun 2002	2.95
❑3, Jul 2002	2.95
❑4, Aug 2002	2.95
❑5, Sep 2002	2.95

ALL-NEW TENCHI MUYO PART 2
VIZ

	N-MINT
❑1, Oct 2002	2.95
❑2, Nov 2002	2.95
❑3, Dec 2002	2.95
❑4, Jan 2003	2.95
❑5, Feb 2003	2.95

ALL NEW UNDERGROUND COMIX
LAST GASP / ULTRAVERSE

	N-MINT
❑1	5.00
❑2	3.00
❑3	3.00
❑4	3.00
❑5; Two-Fisted Zombies	3.00

ALL-OUT WAR
DC

	N-MINT
❑1, Oct 1979 JKu (c); GE, RT (a); O: Viking Commando	3.00
❑2, Dec 1979	2.50
❑3, Feb 1980 JKu (c)	2.50
❑4, Apr 1980 JKu (c)	2.50
❑5, Jun 1980 JKu (c)	2.50
❑6, Aug 1980	2.50

ALLOY
PHENOMINAL CHILI

	N-MINT
❑Ashcan 1; White Ashcan edition 1: Alloy	0.50
❑Ashcan 1/A; Green ashcan edition 1: Alloy	0.50

ALL SHOOK UP
RIP OFF

	N-MINT
❑1, Jun 1990, b&w; earthquake	3.50

ALL-STAR COMICS
DC

	N-MINT
❑58, Feb 1976; WW, RE (a); 1: Power Girl. Power Girl joins team; regrouping of JSA; Series begins again after hiatus (1976)	12.00
❑59, Apr 1976 V: Brainwave, Per Degaton	6.00
❑60, Jun 1976 KG, WW (a); V: Vulcan	6.00
❑61, Aug 1976; KG, WW (a); V: Vulcan. Bicentennial #17	6.00
❑62, Oct 1976 KG, WW (a); A: E-2 Superman. V: Zanadu	6.00
❑63, Dec 1976 KG, WW (a); V: Injustice Gang, Solomon Grundy	6.00
❑64, Feb 1977 WW (a); A: Shining Knight. V: Vandal Savage	6.00
❑65, Apr 1977 WW (a); V: Vandal Savage	6.00
❑66, Jun 1977 BL, JSa (a); V: Icicle, Wizard, Thinker	8.00
❑67, Aug 1977 BL, JSa (a)	6.00
❑68, Oct 1977 BL, JSa (a); V: Psycho Pirate	6.00
❑69, Dec 1977; BL, JSa (a); 1: The Huntress II (Helena Wayne). Original JSA vs. New JSA	6.00
❑70, Feb 1978; BL, JSa (a); Huntress	6.00
❑71, Apr 1978 BL, JSa (a)	6.00
❑72, Jun 1978 V: Thorn, Sportsmaster, original Huntress	6.00
❑73, Aug 1978 JSa (a); V: Thorn, Sportsmaster, original Huntress	6.00
❑74, Oct 1978 JSa (a); V: Master Summoner	8.00

ALL STAR COMICS (2ND SERIES)
DC

	N-MINT
❑1, May 1999	2.95
❑2, May 1999	2.95
❑Giant Size 1, Sep 1999	4.95

ALL-STAR INDEX, THE
ECLIPSE / INDEPENDENT

	N-MINT
❑1, Feb 1987; background on members of the JSA and first four issues of All-Star Comics (1st series) and DC Special #29	2.00

ALL-STAR SQUADRON
DC

	N-MINT
❑1, Sep 1981 RB, JOy (a); 1: Danette Reilly (later Firebrand II)	4.00
❑2, Oct 1981 RB, JOy (a)	2.00
❑3, Nov 1981 RB, JOy (a)	2.00
❑4, Dec 1981 RB, JOy (a); 1: Dragon King	1.50
❑5, Jan 1982 RB, JOy (a); 1: Firebrand II (Danette Reilly)	1.50
❑6, Feb 1982	1.50
❑7, Mar 1982 JKu (a)	1.50
❑8, Apr 1982 O: Steel. V: Kung	1.50
❑9, May 1982 JKu (a); O: Baron Blitzkrieg	1.50
❑10, Jun 1982 JKu (a)	1.50
❑11, Jul 1982 JKu (a)	1.25
❑12, Aug 1982 JKu (a); V: Hastor	1.25
❑13, Sep 1982 JKu (a)	1.25
❑14, Oct 1982 JKu (a)	1.25
❑15, Nov 1982 JKu (a)	1.25
❑16, Dec 1982 JKu (a); V: Nuclear	1.25
❑17, Jan 1983; JKu (a); Trial of Robotman	1.25
❑18, Feb 1983 JKu (a); V: Villain from Valhalla	1.25
❑19, Mar 1983 V: Brainwave	1.25
❑20, Apr 1983 V: Brainwave	1.25
❑21, May 1983 1: Deathbolt. 1: Cyclotron. V: Cyclotron	1.25
❑22, Jun 1983	1.25
❑23, Jul 1983 1: Amazing Man	1.25
❑24, Aug 1983 1: Infinity Inc.. 1: Brainwave Jr.	1.25
❑25, Sep 1983 1: Infinity Inc.	1.25
❑26, Oct 1983 O: Infinity Inc.. 2: Infinity Inc.. 2: Jade	1.00
❑27, Nov 1983 A: Spectre	1.00
❑28, Dec 1983 A: Spectre	1.00
❑29, Jan 1984 A: Seven Soldiers of Victory	1.00
❑30, Feb 1984 V: Black Dragon Society	1.00
❑31, Mar 1984 A: Uncle Sam	1.00
❑32, Apr 1984	1.00
❑33, May 1984 O: Freedom Fighters	1.00
❑34, Jun 1984 V: Tsunami	1.00
❑35, Jul 1984; D: Red Bee. Hourman vs. Baron Blitzkrieg	1.00
❑36, Aug 1984 A: Captain Marvel	1.00
❑37, Sep 1984 A: Marvel Family	1.00
❑38, Oct 1984 A: Amazing Man	1.00
❑39, Nov 1984; A: Amazing Man. Junior JSA kit repro	1.00
❑40, Dec 1984; A: Monitor. Amazing Man vs. Real American	1.00
❑41, Jan 1985 O: Starman	1.00
❑42, Feb 1985	1.00
❑43, Mar 1985	1.00
❑44, Apr 1985 V: Night and Fog	1.00
❑45, May 1985 1: Zyklon	1.00
❑46, Jun 1985; Liberty Belle gets new powers	1.00
❑47, Jul 1985 TMc (a); O: Doctor Fate	3.00
❑48, Aug 1985; A: Shining Knight. Blackhawk	1.00
❑49, Sep 1985 A: Doctor Occult	1.00
❑50, Oct 1985; Double-size issue; A: Harbinger. Mr. Mind to Earth-2; Crisis; Uncle Sam and others to Earth-X; Steel to Earth-1	1.25
❑51, Nov 1985 V: Monster Society of Evil (Oom, Mr. Who, Ramulus, Nyola, Mr. Mind)	1.00
❑52, Dec 1985; A: Captain Marvel. Crisis	1.00
❑53, Jan 1986; Superman vs. Monster Society; Crisis	1.00
❑54, Feb 1986; V: Monster Society. Crisis	1.00
❑55, Mar 1986; V: Ultra-Humanite in 1980s. Crisis	1.00
❑56, Apr 1986; A: Seven Soldiers of Victory. Crisis	1.00
❑57, May 1986; Crisis	1.00
❑58, Jun 1986 A: Mekanique	1.00
❑59, Jul 1986 1: Aquaman in All-Star Squadron	1.00
❑60, Aug 1986; events of Crisis catch up with All-Star Squadron	1.00
❑61, Sep 1986 O: Liberty Belle	1.00
❑62, Oct 1986 O: Shining Knight	1.00
❑63, Nov 1986 O: Robotman	1.00
❑64, Dec 1986; retells Golden Age Superman story post-Crisis	1.00
❑65, Jan 1987 O: Johnny Quick	1.00
❑66, Feb 1987 O: Tarantula	1.00
❑67, Mar 1987; final issue: JSA's first case	1.00
❑Annual 1, Nov 1982 JOy (a); O: Atom, Wildcat, Guardian	1.25
❑Annual 2, Nov 1983 JOy (a); A: Infinity Inc.. D: Cyclotron	1.25
❑Annual 3, Sep 1984 DN, KG, JOy, GP (a); V: Ian Karkull	1.25

The *Aliens vs. Predator* comics have spawned, not only several mini-series, but also two computer videogames and 2004's *Alien vs. Predator* film.

© 1990 Universal Pictures and Dark Horse.

ALL-STAR WESTERN (2ND SERIES)
DC

	N-MINT
❑1, Sep 1970 CI (a); A: Pow-Wow Smith	30.00
❑2, Nov 1970	15.00
❑3, Jan 1971	15.00
❑4, Mar 1971	14.00
❑5, May 1971 DG, JA (a)	14.00
❑6, Jul 1971	9.00
❑7, Sep 1971	9.00
❑8, Nov 1971	9.00
❑9, Jan 1972	9.00
❑10, Mar 1972 SA (w); GM, TD, NC (a); 1: Jonah Hex	260.00
❑11, May 1972; Giant-size; GM, TD, NC (a); 2: Jonah Hex. Series continues as Weird Western Tales	70.00

ALL SUSPENSE
AVALON

	N-MINT
❑1 1998, b&w; reprints Nemesis and Mark Midnight stories	2.95

ALL THE RULES HAVE CHANGED
RIP OFF / ACG

	N-MINT
❑1	9.95

ALL THE WRONG PLACES
LASZLO / ACG

	N-MINT
❑1	2.95

ALL-THRILL COMICS
MANSION

	N-MINT
❑845; Actually #1	2.95

ALLY
ALLY-WINSOR

	N-MINT
❑1, Fal 1995, b&w	2.95
❑2	2.95
❑3; Flip-book	2.95

N-MINT

ALMURIC
DARK HORSE

❑1, Feb 1991 .... 10.95

ALONE IN THE DARK
IMAGE

❑1, Jul 2002, b&w and color 4.95
❑2, Mar 2003 .... 4.95

ALONE IN THE SHADE SPECIAL
ALCHEMY

❑1, b&w 2.00

ALPHABET
DARK VISIONS

❑1, Dec 1993 .... 2.50

ALPHA CENTURION SPECIAL
DC

❑1 .... 2.95

ALPHA FLIGHT
MARVEL

❑1, Aug 1983 JBy (c); JBy (w); JBy (a); 1: Wildheart (not identified)\. 1: Diamond Lil (not identified). 1: Puck, Marina 5.00
❑2, Sep 1983; JBy (w); JBy (a); O: Marina. O: Alpha Flight. 1: The Master. 1: Guardian I (James Hudson). Vindicator becomes Guardian I 4.00
❑3, Oct 1983 JBy (w); JBy (a); O: Marina. O: The Master. O: Alpha Flight 4.00
❑4, Nov 1983 JBy (w); JBy (a); O: Marina 4.00
❑5, Dec 1983 JBy (w); JBy (a); O: Elizabeth Twoyoungmen. 1: Elizabeth Twoyoungmen 4.00
❑6, Jan 1984; JBy (w); JBy (a); O: Shaman. all-white issue 4.00
❑7, Feb 1984 JBy (w); JBy (a); O: Snowbird 4.00
❑8, Mar 1984 JBy (w); JBy (a) 4.00
❑9, Apr 1984 JBy (w); JBy (a); O: Aurora. A: Thing 4.00
❑10, May 1984 JBy (w); JBy (a); O: Northstar. O: Sasquatch 4.00
❑11, Jun 1984 JBy (w); JBy (a); O: Sasquatch. 1: Wild Child. 1: Diamond Lil (identified) 3.00
❑12, Jul 1984; Double-size JBy (w); JBy (a); D: Guardian 3.00
❑13, Aug 1984 JBy (w); JBy (a); A: Wolverine 3.00
❑14, Sep 1984 JBy (w); JBy (a) 3.00
❑15, Oct 1984 JBy (w); JBy (a); A: Sub-Mariner 3.00
❑16, Nov 1984; JBy (w); JBy (a); A: Sub-Mariner. Wolverine cameo 3.00
❑17, Dec 1984; JBy (w); JBy (a); X-Men crossover; Wolverine cameo 3.00
❑18, Jan 1985 JBy (w); JBy (a) 3.00
❑19, Feb 1985 JBy (w); JBy (a); O: Talisman II (Elizabeth Twoyoungmen). 1: Talisman II (Elizabeth Twoyoungmen) 3.00
❑20, Mar 1985; JBy (w); JBy (a); New headquarters 1.50
❑21, Apr 1985 JBy (w); JBy (a); O: Diablo. V: Diablo 2.00
❑22, May 1985 JBy (w); JBy (a) 2.00
❑23, Jun 1985 JBy (w); JBy (a) 2.00
❑24, Jul 1985; Double-size JBy (w); JBy (a) 1.50
❑25, Aug 1985 JBy (w); JBy (a) 1.00
❑26, Sep 1985 JBy (w); JBy (a) 1.00
❑27, Oct 1985 JBy (w); JBy (a) 1.00
❑28, Nov 1985; JBy (w); JBy (a); Secret Wars II; Last Byrne issue 3.00
❑29, Dec 1985 A: Hulk 2.00
❑30, Jan 1986 .... 2.00
❑31, Feb 1986 .... 2.00
❑32, Mar 1986 .... 2.00
❑33, Apr 1986; SB (a); A: X-Men. Wolverine 2.00
❑34, May 1986; SB (a); O: Wolverine. Wolverine 2.50
❑35, Jun 1986; SB (a); Wolverine 1.50
❑36, Jul 1986; SB (a); Wolverine 1.50
❑37, Aug 1986; Wolverine 1.50
❑38, Sep 1986; Wolverine 1.50
❑39, Oct 1986; Wolverine 1.50
❑40, Nov 1986; Wolverine 1.50
❑41, Dec 1986; Wolverine 1.50
❑42, Jan 1987; Wolverine 1.50
❑43, Feb 1987; Wolverine 1.50
❑44, Mar 1987; D: Snowbird. Wolverine 1.50
❑45, Apr 1987; Wolverine 1.50
❑46, May 1987; Wolverine 3.00
❑47, Jun 1987; Wolverine 4.00
❑48, Jul 1987; Wolverine 1.50
❑49, Aug 1987; Wolverine 1.50
❑50, Sep 1987 .... 2.00
❑51, Oct 1987; JLee, (a); A: Wolverine. 1st Jim Lee work at Marvel 2.00
❑52, Nov 1987 A: Wolverine 2.00
❑53, Dec 1987 1: Laura Dean. A: Wolverine 2.00
❑54, Jan 1988 O: Laura Dean 3.00
❑55, Feb 1988 JLee (a) 2.00
❑56, Mar 1988 JLee (a); 1: The Dreamqueen 2.00
❑57, Apr 1988 JLee (a) 1.00
❑58, May 1988 JLee (a) 1.00
❑59, Jun 1988 JLee (a) 1.00
❑60, Jul 1988 JLee (a) 1.25
❑61, Aug 1988 JLee (a) 1.25
❑62, Sep 1988 JLee (a) 1.25
❑63, Oct 1988 .... 1.25
❑64, Nov 1988 .... 1.25
❑65, Dec 1988 .... 1.25
❑66, Jan 1989 .... 1.25
❑67, Feb 1989 O: The Dream Queen 1.25
❑68, Mar 1989 .... 1.25
❑69, Apr 1989 .... 1.25
❑70, May 1989 .... 1.25
❑71, Jun 1989 1: Llan the Sorcerer 1.25
❑72, Jul 1989 .... 1.25
❑73, Aug 1989 .... 1.25
❑74, Sep 1989 .... 1.25
❑75, Oct 1989; Double-size 2.00
❑76, Nov 1989 .... 1.50
❑77, Nov 1989 .... 1.50
❑78, Dec 1989 .... 1.50
❑79, Dec 1989; Acts of Vengeance 1.50
❑80, Jan 1990; Acts of Vengeance 1.50
❑81, Feb 1990 .... 1.50
❑82, Mar 1990 .... 1.50
❑83, Apr 1990 O: Talisman II (Elizabeth Twoyoungmen) 1.50
❑84, May 1990 .... 1.50
❑85, Jun 1990 .... 1.50
❑86, Jul 1990 .... 1.50
❑87, Aug 1990; JLee (c); JLee (a); 1: Windshear. Wolverine 2.00
❑88, Sep 1990; JLee (c); JLee (a); Wolverine; Guardian I reappears as cyborg 2.00
❑89, Oct 1990; JLee (c); JLee (a); Wolverine; Guardian returns 2.00
❑90, Nov 1990 JLee (c); JLee (a) 2.00
❑91, Dec 1990; Doctor Doom 1.75
❑92, Jan 1991 .... 1.75
❑93, Feb 1991 .... 1.75
❑94, Mar 1991; Fantastic 4 .... 1.75
❑95, Apr 1991 .... 1.75
❑96, May 1991 .... 1.75
❑97, Jun 1991 .... 1.75
❑98, Jul 1991 .... 1.75
❑99, Aug 1991 .... 1.75
❑100, Sep 1991 A: Galactus. A: Avengers 1.75
❑101, Oct 1991 .... 1.75
❑102, Nov 1991 1: Weapon Omega 1.75
❑103, Dec 1991 .... 1.75
❑104, Jan 1992 .... 1.75
❑105, Feb 1992 .... 1.75
❑106, Mar 1992; Northstar admits he's gay 3.00
❑106-2, Mar 1992; Northstar admits he's gay 2.00
❑107, Apr 1992 A: X-Factor 1.75
❑108, May 1992 .... 1.75
❑109, Jun 1992 .... 1.75
❑110, Jul 1992 .... 1.75
❑111, Aug 1992 PB (a) 1.75
❑112, Sep 1992 .... 1.75
❑113, Oct 1992 .... 1.75
❑114, Nov 1992 PB (a) 1.75
❑115, Dec 1992 1: Wyre 1.75
❑116, Jan 1993 PB (a) 1.75
❑117, Feb 1993 PB (a) 1.75
❑118, Mar 1993 PB (a); O: Wildheart. 1: Wildheart 1.75
❑119, Apr 1993 PB (a); V: Wrecking Crew 1.75
❑120, May 1993; PB (a); with poster . 2.25
❑121, Jun 1993 A: Spider-Man 1.75
❑122, Jul 1993 PB (a) 1.75
❑123, Aug 1993 PB (a) 1.75
❑124, Sep 1993; PB (a); Infinity Crusade 1.75
❑125, Oct 1993 .... 1.75
❑126, Nov 1993 .... 1.75
❑127, Dec 1993 .... 1.75
❑128, Jan 1994 .... 1.75
❑129, Feb 1994 .... 1.75
❑130, Mar 1994 .... 2.25
❑Annual 1, Sep 1986 .... 1.50
❑Annual 2, Dec 1987 .... 1.25
❑Special 1, Jun 1992; 1992 Special Edition (Vol. 2); A: Wolverine. No number on cover 2.50

ALPHA FLIGHT (VOL. 2)
MARVEL

❑-1, Jul 1997; Wedding of James Hudson and Heather McNeil; "Flashback" 2.00
❑1, Aug 1997; gatefold summary; wraparound cover 3.00
❑2, Sep 1997; gatefold summary; "Presenting: The Master of Chaos" on cover 2.00
❑2/A, Sep 1997; gatefold summary; alternate cover 2.00
❑3, Oct 1997; gatefold summary 2.00
❑4, Nov 1997; gatefold summary 2.00
❑5, Dec 1997; gatefold summary 2.00
❑6, Jan 1998; gatefold summary 1.99
❑7, Feb 1998; gatefold summary 1.99
❑8, Mar 1998; gatefold summary 1.99
❑9, Apr 1998; gatefold summary 1.99
❑10, May 1998; gatefold summary 1.99
❑11, Jun 1998; gatefold summary 1.99
❑12, Jul 1998; gatefold summary 1.99
❑13, Aug 1998; gatefold summary 1.99
❑14, Sep 1998; gatefold summary 1.99
❑15, Oct 1998; gatefold summary 1.99
❑16, Nov 1998; gatefold summary 1.99
❑17, Dec 1998; gatefold summary 1.99
❑18, Jan 1999; gatefold summary 1.99
❑19, Feb 1999 .... 1.99
❑20, Mar 1999 .... 1.99
❑Annual 1998, ca. 1998; Alpha Flight/ Inhumans '98; wraparound cover .. 3.50

ALPHA FLIGHT (VOL. 3)
MARVEL

❑1, May 2004 .... 2.99
❑2, Jun 2004 .... 2.99
❑3, Jul 2004 .... 0.00
❑4, Aug 2004 .... 2.99
❑5, Sep 2004 ....

ALPHA FLIGHT: IN THE BEGINNING
MARVEL

❑1, ca. 1997 .... 2.00

ALPHA FLIGHT SPECIAL
MARVEL

❑1, Jul 1991; Reprints Alpha Flight #97 2.00
❑2, Aug 1991; Reprints Alpha Flight #98 .... 2.00
❑3, Sep 1991; Reprints Alpha Flight #99 .... 2.00
❑4, Oct 1991; Reprints Alpha Flight #100 .... 2.00

ALPHA ILLUSTRATED
ALPHA PRODUCTIONS

❑0, Apr 1994, b&w; free; Preview 1.00
❑1, b&w 3.50

N-MINT

ALPHA KORPS
DIVERSITY
❑1, Sep 1996 .... 2.50
❑Ashcan 1; Preview issue 1.00

ALPHA TEAM OMEGA
FANTASY GRAPHICS
❑1, ca. 1983, b&w 0.50

ALPHA TRACK
FANTASY GENERAL
❑1, Feb 1985 .... 1.75
❑2 .... 1.75

ALPHA WAVE
DARKLINE
❑1 .... 1.75

ALTERED IMAGE
IMAGE
❑1, Apr 1998 .... 2.50
❑2, Jun 1998 .... 2.50
❑3, Oct 1998; cover says "Sep"; indicia says "Oct" 2.50

ALTERED REALITIES
ALTERED REALITY
❑1 .... 2.00

ALTER EGO
FIRST
❑1, May 1986 1: Alter Ego 1.50
❑2, Jul 1986 .... 1.50
❑3, Sep 1986 .... 1.50
❑4, Nov 1986 .... 1.50

ALTER EGO (HAMSTER)
HAMSTER
❑

ALTERNATE EXISTANCE
DRAGONMASTER
❑1 .... 1.25
❑2 .... 1.25

ALTERNATE HEROES
PRELUDE
❑1 .... 1.95

ALTERNATING CRIMES
ALTERNATING CRIMES
❑1, Fal 1996 .... 2.95
❑2, Fal 1997 .... 3.25

ALTERNATION
IMAGE
❑1, Mar 2004 .... 2.95
❑2, Mar 2004 .... 2.95
❑3, Apr 2004 .... 2.95
❑4, Aug 2004 .... 2.95

ALTERNATIVE COMICS
REVOLUTIONARY
❑1, Jan 1994; Pearl Jam/Cure/REM .. 2.50

ALTERNITY
NAVIGATOR
❑1, May 1992 .... 2.50

ALVAR MAYOR: DEATH AND SILVER
4WINDS
❑1, b&w 8.98

ALVIN
DELL
❑1, Oct 1962; 12-021-212 .... 25.00
❑2, Jan 1963; 12-021-303 .... 18.00
❑3, Apr 1963; 12-021-306 .... 15.00
❑4, Jul 1963; 12-021-309 .... 15.00
❑5, Oct 1963; 12-021-312 .... 15.00
❑6, Jan 1964; 12-021-403 .... 15.00
❑7, Apr 1964; 12-021-406 .... 15.00
❑8, Jul 1964; 12-021-409 .... 15.00
❑9, Oct 1964; 12-021-412 .... 15.00
❑10, Jan 1965 .... 15.00
❑11, Apr 1965 .... 12.00
❑12, Jul 1965 .... 12.00
❑13 1965 .... 12.00
❑14 1966 .... 12.00
❑15 1966 .... 12.00
❑16 1966 .... 12.00
❑17 1966 .... 12.00

N-MINT

❑18, Mar 1967 .... 12.00
❑19 .... 12.00
❑20, Oct 1969 .... 12.00
❑21, Oct 1970 .... 8.00
❑22 1971 .... 8.00
❑23, Jan 1972; 01-021-201 .... 8.00
❑24, Apr 1972; 01-021-204 .... 8.00
❑25 .... 8.00
❑26 .... 8.00
❑27, Jul 1973 .... 8.00
❑28, Oct 1973 .... 8.00

ALVIN AND THE CHIPMUNKS
HARVEY
❑1 .... 2.00
❑2 .... 1.50
❑3 .... 1.50
❑4 .... 1.50
❑5 .... 1.50

AMANDA AND GUNN
IMAGE
❑1, Apr 1997, b&w 2.95
❑2, Jun 1997, b&w 2.95
❑3, Aug 1997, b&w 2.95
❑4, Oct 1997, b&w 2.95

AMAZING ADULT FANTASY
MARVEL
❑7, Dec 1961; SL (w); SD (a); Series continued from Amazing Adventures #6 .... 600.00
❑8, Jan 1962 SL (w); SD (a) 475.00
❑9, Feb 1962 SL (w); SD (a) 425.00
❑10, Mar 1962 SL (w); SD (a) 425.00
❑11, Apr 1962 SL (w); SD (a) 425.00
❑12, May 1962 SL (w); SD (a) 425.00
❑13, Jun 1962 SL (w); SD (a) 425.00
❑13-2 SL (w); SD (a) 2.50
❑14, Jul 1962; SD (a); series continues as Amazing Fantasy; Professor X prototype; Series continued in Amazing Fantasy #15 .... 525.00

AMAZING ADVENTURE
MARVEL
❑1, Jul 1988; squarebound 4.95

AMAZING ADVENTURES (2ND SERIES)
MARVEL
❑1, Jun 1961; SL (w); SD (a); O: Doctor Droom. A: Doctor Droom. 1st appearance/origin Dr. Droom (first Marvel Silver Age superhero) 900.00
❑2, Jul 1961; SL (w); SD (a); A: Doctor Droom. Dr. Droom 525.00
❑3, Aug 1961; SL (w); SD (a); A: Doctor Droom. Dr. Droom 425.00
❑4, Sep 1961 SL (w); SD (a); A: Doctor Droom 425.00
❑5, Oct 1961 SL (w); SD (a); A: Doctor Droom 425.00
❑6, Nov 1961; SL (w); SD (a); A: Doctor Droom. Series continued in Amazing Adult Fantasy #7 .... 425.00

AMAZING ADVENTURES (3RD SERIES)
MARVEL
❑1, Aug 1970; JK (w); JB, JK (a); Inhumans 30.00
❑2, Sep 1970; Inhumans 20.00
❑3, Nov 1970; BEv (a); Black Widow; Inhumans 20.00
❑4, Jan 1971; BEv (a); Black Widow; Inhumans 20.00
❑5, Mar 1971 GC, BEv, NA (a) 20.00
❑6, May 1971; SB, DH, NA (a); Inhumans, Black Widow 20.00
❑7, Jul 1971; BEv, NA (a); Inhumans, Black Widow 20.00
❑8, Sep 1971; BEv, DH, NA (a); Inhumans, Black Widow 20.00
❑9, Nov 1971 BEv (a); A: Black Bolt .. 20.00
❑10, Jan 1972; Inhumans; Reprinted from Thor #146 .... 20.00
❑11, Mar 1972 O: Beast (in furry form). 1: Beast (in furry form) 106.00
❑12, May 1972; A: Beast. Iron Man ... 20.00

Legion of Super-Hero fans seeking the wedding of Lightning Lad and Saturn Girl should look for *All New Collectors' Edition* #C-55.

© 1978 National Periodical Publications (DC).

N-MINT

❑13, Jul 1972 1: Robert Buzz Baxter . 20.00
❑14, Sep 1972 .... 20.00
❑15, Nov 1972 O: Griffin. 1: Griffin 20.00
❑16, Jan 1973 .... 20.00
❑17, Mar 1973 .... 20.00
❑18, May 1973 HC, NA (a); O: Killraven. 1: Killraven 14.00
❑19, Jul 1973; Killraven 5.00
❑20, Sep 1973; HT (a); Killraven 5.00
❑21, Nov 1973; Killraven 5.00
❑22, Jan 1974; Killraven 5.00
❑23, Mar 1974; Killraven; Marvel Value Stamp #13: Dr. Strange 5.00
❑24, May 1974; HT (a); V: High Overlord. Killraven; Marvel Value Stamp #58: The Mandarin 5.00
❑25, Jul 1974; V: Skar. Killraven 5.00
❑26, Sep 1974; GC (a); Killraven: Marvel Value Stamp #96: Dr. Octopus .. 4.00
❑27, Nov 1974; JSn, CR, JSt (a); O: Killraven. Marvel Value Stamp #22: Man-Thing 4.00
❑28, Jan 1975; CR (a); O: Volcana. Killraven 4.00
❑29, Mar 1975; CR (a); Killraven 4.00
❑30, May 1975; CR (a); Killraven 4.00
❑31, Jul 1975; CR (a); Killraven 4.00
❑32, Sep 1975; CR (a); Killraven 4.00
❑33, Nov 1975; HT, CR (a); Killraven; Marvel Value Stamp #52: Quicksilver 4.00
❑34, Jan 1976; CR (a); D: Hawk. D: Grok. Killraven; Marvel Value Stamp B/10 . 4.00
❑35, Mar 1976; KG, CR, JAb (a); Killraven 4.00
❑36, May 1976; CR (a); Killraven 4.00
❑36/30 cent, May 1976; 30 cent regional price variant 20.00
❑37, Jul 1976 CR (a); O: Old Skull 4.00
❑37/30 cent, Jul 1976; CR (a); O: Old Skull. 30 cent regional price variant 20.00
❑38, Sep 1976; KG, CR (a); Killraven . 4.00
❑39, Nov 1976; CR (a); Killraven 4.00

AMAZING ADVENTURES (4TH SERIES)
MARVEL
❑1, Dec 1979; SL (w); JK (a); 1: the X-Men. Reprints first part of X-Men (1st Series) #1; 2nd story reprinted from X-Men (1st series) #38 .... 3.00
❑2, Jan 1980; SL (w); JK (a); O: Cyclops. Reprints second half of X-Men (1st Series) #1; 2nd story reprinted from X-Men (1st Series) #39 .... 2.00
❑3, Feb 1980; Reprinted from X-Men (first series) #2; 2nd story reprinted from X-Men (1st Series) #40 .... 2.00
❑4, Mar 1980; Reprinted from X-Men (first series) #2, retitled from "No One Can Stop the Vanisher"; 2nd story reprinted from X-Men (1st Series) #41 .... 2.00
❑5, Apr 1980; Reprinted from X-Men (first series) #3; 2nd story reprinted from X-Men (1st Series) #42 .... 2.00
❑6, May 1980; Reprinted from X-Men (first series) #3, retitled from "Beware, the Blob"; 2nd story reprinted from X-Men (1st Series) #43 .... 2.00
❑7, Jun 1980; Reprinted from X-Men (first series) #4; 2nd story reprinted from X-Men (1st Series) #44 .... 2.00

N-MINT

❑8, Jul 1980; Reprinted from X-Men (first series) #4, retitled from "The Brotherhood of Evil Mutants"; 2nd story reprinted from X-Men (1st Series) #45 .... 2.00
❑9, Aug 1980; Reprinted from X-Men (first series) #5, retitled from "Trapped: One X-Man"; 2nd story reprinted from X-Men (1st Series) #46 2.00
❑10, Sep 1980; Reprinted from X-Men (first series) #5; 2nd story reprinted from X-Men (1st Series) #47 .... 2.00
❑11, Oct 1980; Reprinted from X-Men (first series) #6; 2nd story reprinted from X-Men (1st Series) #48 .... 2.00
❑12, Nov 1980; Reprinted from X-Men (first series) #6, retitled from "Search for the Sub-Mariner"; 2nd story reprinted from Strange Tales #168 2.00
❑13, Dec 1980; Reprinted from X-Men (first series) #7 .... 2.00
❑14, Jan 1981; Reprinted from X-Men (first series) #8 .... 2.00

AMAZING ADVENTURES OF ACE INTERNATIONAL, THE
STARHEAD

❑1, Nov 1993, b&w 2.95

AMAZING ADVENTURES OF FRANK AND JOLLY (ALAN GROENING'S...)
PRESS THIS

❑1 .... 1.75
❑2 .... 1.75
❑3 .... 1.75
❑4 .... 1.75
❑5 .... 1.75
❑6 .... 1.75
❑7 .... 1.75
❑8 .... 1.75
❑9 .... 1.75

AMAZING ADVENTURES OF PROFESSOR JONES, THE
ANTARCTIC

❑1, Nov 1996 .... 2.95
❑2, Dec 1996 .... 2.95
❑3 .... 2.95
❑4 .... 2.95

AMAZING CHAN AND THE CHAN CLAN
GOLD KEY

❑1, May 1973 .... 14.00
❑2, Aug 1973 .... 9.00
❑3, Nov 1973 .... 9.00
❑4, Feb 1974 .... 9.00

AMAZING COMICS (MARVEL)
TIMELY

❑1, Fal 1944 .... 1600.00

AMAZING COMICS PREMIERES
AMAZING

❑1 1987 .... 1.95
❑2 1987 .... 1.95
❑3 1987 .... 1.95
❑4, Jul 1987 .... 1.95
❑5 1987; Stargrazers 1.95

AMAZING CYNICALMAN, THE
ECLIPSE

❑1, b&w 2.50

AMAZING FANTASY
MARVEL

❑15, Aug 1962, JK (c); SD, SL (w); SD, JK (a); O: Spider-Man. 1: Spider-Man. 32000.00
❑15-2, Aug 2002, Reprint packaged with Spider-Man movie DVD 5.00
❑16, Dec 1995; KB (w); cardstock cover; fills in gaps between Amazing Fantasy #15 and Amazing Spider-Man #1 .... 4.50
❑17, Jan 1996; KB (w); cardstock cover 4.50
❑18, Mar 1996; KB (w); cardstock cover 4.50

AMAZING FANTASY (2ND SERIES)
MARVEL

❑1, Aug 2004 .... 2.99

N-MINT

AMAZING HEROES SWIMSUIT SPECIAL
FANTAGRAPHICS

❑Annual 1990, Jun 1990, b&w 6.00
❑Annual 1991, Jun 1991 .... 8.00
❑Annual 1992, Jun 1992 .... 10.00
❑4, Mar 1993; published by Spoof Comics 3.95
❑5, Aug 1993; published by Spoof Comics 4.95

AMAZING HIGH ADVENTURE
MARVEL

❑1, Aug 1984 JSe (a) 2.50
❑2, Sep 1985 PS (a) 2.50
❑3, Oct 1986 .... 2.50
❑4, Nov 1986 .... 2.50
❑5, Dec 1986 .... 2.50

AMAZING SCARLET SPIDER, THE
MARVEL

❑1, Nov 1995 .... 1.95
❑2, Dec 1995 A: Joystick. A: Green Goblin IV 1.95
❑2/Direct ed., Dec 1995; Direct Edition 1.95

AMAZING SCREW-ON HEAD, THE
DARK HORSE

❑1, May 2002, b&w and color 2.99
❑1-2, Feb 2004 .... 2.99

AMAZING SPIDER-MAN, THE
MARVEL

❑-1, Jul 1997; Flashback 2.50
❑1, Mar 1963 SD (c); SD, SL (w); SD, JK (a); O: Spider-Man. 1: John Jameson. 1: J. Jonah Jameson. 1: Chameleon. A: Fantastic Four 27000.00
❑1/Golden Record; SD, SL (w); SD (a); O: Spider-Man. 1: J. Jonah Jameson. 1: Chameleon. A: Fantastic Four. Gold Records reprint 275.00
❑2, May 1963 SD (c); SD, SL (w); SD (a); 1: Mysterio (as alien). 1: Tinkerer. 1: Vulture 3400.00
❑3, Jul 1963 SD (c); SD, SL (w); SD (a); O: Doctor Octopus. 1: Doctor Octopus 3000.00
❑4, Sep 1963 SD (c); SD, SL (w); SD (a); O: Sandman (Marvel). 1: Betty Brant. 1: Sandman (Marvel) 2300.00
❑5, Oct 1963 SD (c); SD, SL (w); SD (a); V: Doctor Doom 2200.00
❑6, Nov 1963 SD (c); SD, SL (w); SD (a); O: The Lizard. 1: The Lizard 1600.00
❑7, Dec 1963 SD (c); SD, SL (w); SD (a); 2: The Vulture. V: Vulture 1100.00
❑8, Jan 1964 SD (c); SD, SL (w); SD (a); A: Human Torch. V: Flash Thompson. V: Living Brain 915.00
❑9, Feb 1964 SD (c); SD, SL (w); SD (a); O: Electro. 1: Doctor Bromwell. 1: Electro 1025.00
❑10, Mar 1964 SD (c); SD, SL (w); SD, JK (a); 1: Fancy Dan. 1: Big Man. 1: Montana. 1: Enforcers. 1: Ox 990.00
❑11, Apr 1964 SD (c); SD, SL (w); SD (a); 2: Doctor Octopus. V: Doctor Octopus 900.00
❑12, May 1964; SD (c); SD, SL (w); SD (a); V: Doctor Octopus. Spider-Man unmasked 750.00
❑13, Jun 1964 SD (c); SD, SL (w); SD (a); O: Mysterio. 1: Mysterio 975.00
❑14, Jul 1964 SD (c); SD, SL (w); SD (a); 1: Green Goblin I (Norman Osborn). A: Hulk. A: Enforcers 2200.00
❑15, Aug 1964 SD (c); SD, SL (w); SD (a); O: Kraven the Hunter. 1: Anna May Watson. 1: Kraven the Hunter. 1: Mary Jane Watson (name mentioned). A: Chameleon 1300.00
❑16, Sep 1964 SD (c); SD, SL (w); SD (a); 1: The Great Gambonnos. 1: Princess Python. A: Daredevil. V: Ringmaster and Circus of Crime 775.00
❑17, Oct 1964 SD (c); SD, SL (w); SD (a); 2: Green Goblin I (Norman Osborn). A: Torch. V: Green Goblin I (Norman Osborn) 775.00
❑18, Nov 1964 SD (c); SD, SL (w); SD (a); V: Sandman (Marvel) 510.00

N-MINT

❑19, Dec 1964 SD (c); SD, SL (w); SD (a); 1: MacDonald Mac Gargan [later becomes the Scorpion]. 1: Rock Gimpy. V: Sandman (Marvel). V: Enforcers 510.00
❑20, Jan 1965 SD (c); SD, SL (w); SD (a); O: The Scorpion. 1: The Scorpion 510.00
❑21, Feb 1965 SD (c); SD, SL (w); SD (a); 2: The Beetle. A: Torch. V: Beetle 510.00
❑22, Mar 1965 SD (c); SD, SL (w); SD (a); V: Ringmaster and Circus of Crime 510.00
❑23, Apr 1965 SD (c); SD, SL (w); SD (a); A: Green Goblin I (Norman Osborn). V: Green Goblin I (Norman Osborn) 510.00
❑24, May 1965 SD (c); SD, SL (w); SD (a); V: Mysterio 500.00
❑25, Jun 1965 SD (c); SD, SL (w); SD (a); 1: Spencer Smythe. 1: Spider-Slayers. 1: Mary Jane Watson (cameo-face not shown) 500.00
❑26, Jul 1965 SD (c); SD, SL (w); SD (a); 1: Crime-Master. 1: Patch. A: Green Goblin I (Norman Osborn) ... 500.00
❑27, Aug 1965 SD (c); SD, SL (w); SD (a); A: Green Goblin I (Norman Osborn). D: Crime-Master 500.00
❑28, Sep 1965; SD (c); SD, SL (w); SD (a); O: Molten Man. 1: Molten Man. 2: Spencer Smythe. Peter Parker graduates from high school 325.00
❑29, Oct 1965 SD (c); SD, SL (w); SD (a); 2: The Scorpion. V: The Scorpion 240.00
❑30, Nov 1965 SD (c); SD, SL (w); SD (a); V: Cat Burglar 240.00
❑31, Dec 1965; SD (c); SD, SL (w); SD (a); 1: Professor Warren. 1: Gwen Stacy. 1: Harry Osborn. 240.00
❑32, Jan 1966; SD (c); SD, SL (w); SD (a); Master Planner revealed as Doctor Octopus 195.00
❑33, Feb 1966 SD (c); SD, SL (w); SD (a); V: Doctor Octopus (as Master Planner) 195.00
❑34, Mar 1966 SD (c); SD, SL (w); SD (a); A: Green Goblin I (Norman Osborn). V: Kraven the Hunter 195.00
❑35, Apr 1966 SD (c); SD, SL (w); SD (a); 1: Spider Tracer. V: Molten Man 195.00
❑36, May 1966 SD (c); SD, SL (w); SD (a); 1: Looter (later Meteor Man in Marvel Team-Up #33) 195.00
❑37, Jun 1966 SD (c); SD, SL (w); SD (a); 1: Norman Osborn. A: Patch. V: Professor Mendel Stromm 195.00
❑38, Jul 1966 SD (c); SD, SL (w); SD (a); 2: Mary Jane Watson (cameo) 195.00
❑39, Aug 1966; JR (c); SL (w); JR (a); V: Green Goblin I (Norman Osborn). Green Goblin revealed as Norman Osborn 350.00
❑40, Sep 1966 JR (c); SL (w); JR (a); O: Green Goblin I (Norman Osborn) 350.00
❑41, Oct 1966 JR (c); SL (w); JR (a); 1: Rhino 300.00
❑42, Nov 1966 JR (c); SL (w); JR (a); A: Mary Jane Watson (first time her face is shown). A: Rhino 215.00
❑43, Dec 1966 JR (c); SL (w); JR (a); O: Rhino. V: Rhino 110.00
❑44, Jan 1967 JR (c); SL (w); JR (a); V: Lizard 110.00
❑45, Feb 1967 JR (c); SL (w); JR (a); V: Lizard 110.00
❑46, Mar 1967 JR (c); SL (w); JR (a); O: Shocker. 1: Shocker 160.00
❑47, Apr 1967 JR (c); SL (w); JR (a); V: Kraven the Hunter 110.00
❑48, May 1967 JR (c); SL (w); JR (a); V: second Vulture 110.00
❑49, Jun 1967 JR (c); SL (w); JR (a); V: Kraven the Hunter. V: Vulture 110.00
❑50, Jul 1967 JR (c); SL (w); JR (a); 1: Kingpin 575.00
❑51, Aug 1967 JR (a); O: Mysterio. 1: Robbie Robertson. 2: Kingpin. V: Kingpin 175.00
❑52, Sep 1967 JR (a); 1: Joe Robertson. D: Big Man (Frederick Foswell). V: Kingpin 100.00
❑53, Oct 1967 JR (a); V: Doctor Octopus 100.00

	N-MINT
❑54, Nov 1967 JR (a); V: Doctor Octopus	100.00
❑55, Dec 1967 JR (a); V: Doctor Octopus	100.00
❑56, Jan 1968 JR (a); 1: Captain Stacy. V: Doctor Octopus	100.00
❑57, Feb 1968 JR (a); A: Ka-Zar and Zabu	100.00
❑58, Mar 1968 JR (a); A: Ka-Zar and Zabu. V: Spencer Smythe. V: J. Jonah Jameson	80.00
❑59, Apr 1968 JR, SL (w); JR (a); 1: Doctor Winkler. 1: Slade. V: Kingpin (as Brainwasher)	90.00
❑60, May 1968 JR, SL (w); JR (a); 2: Doctor Winkler. 2: Slade. V: Kingpin	90.00
❑61, Jun 1968 JR, SL (w); JR (a); V: Kingpin	72.00
❑62, Jul 1968 JR, SL (w); JR (a); A: Medusa	72.00
❑63, Aug 1968 JR, SL (w); JR (a); V: both Vultures	150.00
❑64, Sep 1968 JR, SL (w); JR (a); V: Vulture	60.00
❑65, Oct 1968 JR, SL (w); JR (a)	60.00
❑66, Nov 1968 JR, SL (w); JR (a); A: Mysterio. V: Mysterio	85.00
❑67, Dec 1968 JR, SL (w); JR (a); 1: Randy Robertson. V: Mysterio	60.00
❑68, Jan 1969 JR, SL (w); JR, JM (a); 1: Louis Wilson. V: Kingpin	60.00
❑69, Feb 1969 JR, SL (w); JR, JM (a); V: Kingpin	70.00
❑70, Mar 1969 JR, SL (w); JR, JM (a); 1: Vanessa Fisk (Kingpin's wife-face not shown). V: Kingpin	70.00
❑71, Apr 1969 JR, SL (w); JR, JM (a); A: Quicksilver	70.00
❑72, May 1969 JR, SL (w); JB, JR (a); V: Shocker	90.00
❑73, Jun 1969 JR, SL (w); JB, JR (a); 1: Man-Mountain Marko. 1: Caesar Cicero. 1: Silvermane	50.00
❑74, Jul 1969 JR, SL (w); JR, JM (a); V: Man-Mountain Marko. V: Caesar Cicero. V: Silvermane	80.00
❑75, Aug 1969 JR, SL (w); JR, JM (a); V: Man-Mountain Marko. V: Caesar Cicero. V: Silvermane	60.00
❑76, Sep 1969 SL (w); JB, JR, JM (a); A: Human Torch. V: Lizard	60.00
❑77, Oct 1969 JR, SL (w); JB, JR, JM (a); A: Human Torch. V: Lizard	60.00
❑78, Nov 1969 JR2, SL (w); JB, JR, JM (a); 1: The Prowler	60.00
❑79, Dec 1969 SL (w); JB, JR, JM (a); 2: The Prowler. V: The Prowler. V: Prowler	60.00
❑80, Jan 1970 JR, SL (w); JB, JR (a); V: Chameleon	60.00
❑81, Feb 1970 JR, SL (w); JB, JR (a); O: The Kangaroo. 1: The Kangaroo	50.00
❑82, Mar 1970 JR, SL (w); JB, JR (a); O: Electro. V: Electro	50.00
❑83, Apr 1970 JR, SL (w); JR (a); 1: Richard Fisk ("The Schemer"). 1: Vanessa Fisk (Full-Kingpin's wife). V: Kingpin. V: Schemer	50.00
❑84, May 1970 JR, SL (w); JB, JR (a); V: Kingpin. V: Schemer	50.00
❑85, Jun 1970 JR, SL (w); JB, JR (a); V: Kingpin. V: Schemer	50.00
❑86, Jul 1970 JR, SL (w); JR, JM (a); O: Black Widow	50.00
❑87, Aug 1970; JR, SL (w); JR, JM (a); Peter reveals his secret identity	65.00
❑88, Sep 1970 SL (w); JR (a); A: Doctor Octopus. V: Doctor Octopus	65.00
❑89, Oct 1970 SL (w); GK, JR (a); A: Doctor Octopus. V: Doctor Octopus	65.00
❑90, Nov 1970 SL (w); GK (a); A: Doctor Octopus. D: Captain Stacy	65.00
❑91, Dec 1970 SL (w); GK, JR (a); 1: Sam Bullit	50.00
❑92, Jan 1971 SL (w); GK, JR (a); A: Sam Bullit. A: Iceman	50.00
❑93, Feb 1971 JR, SL (w); JR (a); A: Prowler	50.00
❑94, Mar 1971; JR, SL (w); SB, JR (a); O: Spider-Man. A: Beetle. Spider-Man's Origin retold	60.00
❑95, Apr 1971; JR, SL (w); SB, JR (a); Spider-Man goes to London	45.00

	N-MINT
❑96, May 1971; SL (w); GK (a); A: Green Goblin I (Norman Osborn). Drug topics not approved by CCA	85.00
❑97, Jun 1971; JR, SL (w); GK, JR (a); A: Green Goblin I (Norman Osborn). Drug topics not approved by CCA	85.00
❑98, Jul 1971; SL (w); GK (a); A: Green Goblin I (Norman Osborn). Drug topics not approved by CCA	85.00
❑99, Aug 1971 SL (w); GK (a); A: Johnny Carson	55.00
❑100, Sep 1971; 100th anniversary issue; SL (w); GK, JR (a); A: Green Goblin I (Norman Osborn). Peter grows four extra arms	150.00
❑101, Oct 1971 GK, SL (w); GK (a); 1: Morbius	120.00
❑101-2; GK, SL (w); GK (a); 1: Morbius. Metallic ink cover	2.50
❑102, Nov 1971; Giant-sized GK, SL (w); GK (a); O: Morbius. A: Lizard. A: Morbius	100.00
❑103, Dec 1971 GK, SL (w); GK (a); 1: Gog. V: Kraven the Hunter	45.00
❑104, Jan 1972 GK (w); GK (a); 2: Gog. V: Kraven the Hunter	90.00
❑105, Feb 1972 GK, SL (w); GK (a); V: Spider Slayer. V: Spencer Smythe	26.00
❑106, Mar 1972 JR, SL (w); JR (a); V: Spider Slayer. V: Spencer Smythe	26.00
❑107, Apr 1972 JR, SL (w); JR (a); V: Spider Slayer. V: Spencer Smythe	26.00
❑108, May 1972 JR, SL (w); JR (a); 1: Sha Shan. A: Flash Thompson	26.00
❑109, Jun 1972 JR, SL (w); JR (a); A: Doctor Strange	26.00
❑110, Jul 1972 JR, SL (w); JR (a); O: The Gibbon. 1: The Gibbon	26.00
❑111, Aug 1972 JR (w); JR (a); V: The Gibbon, Kraven the Hunter	26.00
❑112, Sep 1972 JR (w); JR (a); A: The Gibbon. V: Doctor Octopus	26.00
❑113, Oct 1972 JR (w); JSn, JR, JSt (a); 1: Hammerhead. V: Doctor Octopus	33.00
❑114, Nov 1972 JR (w); JSn, JR, JSt (a); O: Hammerhead. 1: Doctor Jonas Harrow	33.00
❑115, Dec 1972 JR (w); JR (a); V: Hammerhead, Doctor Octopus	33.00
❑116, Jan 1973; JR, SL (w); JR (a); 1: Smasher (was Man Monster). V: Richard Raleigh. Reprints Spectacular Spider-Man #1 ("Lo, This Monster") with some new art and dialogue; Man Monster renamed Smasher	22.00
❑117, Feb 1973; reprints story from Spectacular Spider-Man (magazine) #1 with updates; JR, SL (w); HT, JR (a); 1: Disruptor. Reprints Spectacular Spider-Man #1 ("Lo, This Monster") with some new art and dialogue; Man Monster renamed Smasher	22.00
❑118, Mar 1973; JR, SL (w); JR (a); V: Disruptor, Smasher. Reprints Spectacular Spider-Man #1 ("Lo, This Monster") with some new art and dialogue; Man Monster renamed Smasher	22.00
❑119, Apr 1973 JR (w); JR (a); A: Incredible Hulk. V: Hulk in Canada	47.00
❑120, May 1973 GK (w); GK, JR (a); A: Incredible Hulk. V: Hulk	47.00
❑121, Jun 1973 GK (w); GK, JR (a); D: Gwen Stacy. V: Green Goblin I (Norman Osborn)	150.00
❑122, Jul 1973 GK, SL (w); GK, JR (a); D: Green Goblin I (Norman Osborn)	150.00
❑123, Aug 1973 GK (w); GK, JR (a); A: Luke Cage	35.00
❑124, Sep 1973 GK (w); GK, JR (a); 1: Man-Wolf	35.00
❑125, Oct 1973 JR, RA (a); O: Man-Wolf	22.00
❑126, Nov 1973; JR, RA (a); A: Doctor Jonas Harrow. A: Human Torch. D: Kangaroo. Harry Osborn becomes Green Goblin	22.00
❑127, Dec 1973 JR, RA (a); V: third Vulture	22.00
❑128, Jan 1974 JR, RA (a); O: third Vulture	22.00

Alpha Flight

Marvel

The revelation of Alpha Flight member Northstar's homosexuality made national headlines in 1992.

© 1992 Marvel Comics.

	N-MINT
❑129, Feb 1974 GK, RA (a); 1: the Punisher. 1: Jackal	275.00
❑129/A, Apr 2002; Wizard Ace Edition	6.00
❑130, Mar 1974; JR, RA (a); 1: Spider-Mobile. V: Doctor Octopus. V: Hammerhead. V: Jackal. Marvel Value Stamp #2: Hulk	16.00
❑131, Apr 1974; GK, RA (a); V: Doctor Octopus. V: Hammerhead. Dr. Octopus, Hammerhead; Marvel Value Stamp #34: Mr. Fantastic	16.00
❑132, May 1974; GK, JR (a); V: Molten Man. Marvel Value Stamp #6: Thor	16.00
❑133, Jun 1974; JR, RA (a); V: Molten Man. Molten Man's relationship to Liz Allan revealed; Marvel Value Stamp #66: General Ross	16.00
❑134, Jul 1974; JR, RA (a); 1: Tarantula I (Anton Rodriguez). A: Punisher. Marvel Value Stamp #3: Conan	28.00
❑135, Aug 1974; JR, RA (a); O: Tarantula I (Anton Rodriguez). A: Punisher. Marvel Value Stamp #4: Thing	36.00
❑136, Sep 1974; JR, RA (a); 1: Green Goblin II (Harry Osborn). Marvel Value Stamp #95: Mole-Man	36.00
❑137, Oct 1974; GK, RA (a); 2: Green Goblin II (Harry Osborn). V: Green Goblin II (Harry Osborn). Marvel Value Stamp #99: Sandman	36.00
❑138, Nov 1974; GK, RA (a); O: The Mindworm. 1: The Mindworm. Peter moves in with Flash Thompson; Marvel Value Stamp #41: Gladiator	16.00
❑139, Dec 1974; GK, RA (a); 1: Grizzly. A: Jackal. Marvel Value Stamp #42: Man-Wolf	16.00
❑140, Jan 1975; GK, RA (a); O: Grizzly. 1: Gloria Grant. V: Jackal. Marvel Value Stamp #75: Morbius	16.00
❑141, Feb 1975; JR, RA (a); V: second Mysterio. Spider-Mobile sinks in Hudson Marvel Value Stamp #35: Killraven	16.00
❑142, Mar 1975 JR, RA (a); V: second Mysterio	16.00
❑143, Apr 1975 GK, RA (a); 1: Cyclone	16.00
❑144, May 1975; GK, RA (a); O: Cyclone. 1: Gwen Stacy clone. V: Cyclone. Marvel Value Stamp #17: Black Bolt	16.00
❑145, Jun 1975; GK, RA (a); A: Scorpion. V: Scorpion. Marvel Value Stamp #100: Galactus	16.00
❑146, Jul 1975; JR, RA (a); A: Scorpion. V: Jackal, Scorpion. Marvel Value Stamp #67: Cyclops	16.00
❑147, Aug 1975; JR, RA (a); V: Jackal, Tarantula. Marvel Value Stamp #42: Man-Wolf	16.00
❑148, Sep 1975; GK, RA (a); V: Jackal, Tarantula. Professor Warren revealed as Jackal	24.00
❑149, Oct 1975 GK, RA (a); 1: Ben Reilly. D: Jackal. D: Spider-clone (faked death)	40.00
❑150, Nov 1975; GK (a); A: Ben Reilly. Spider-Man attempts to determine if he is the clone or the original	16.00
❑151, Dec 1975; JR, RA (a); A: Ben Reilly. V: Shocker. Spider-Man disposes of clone's body (faked)	16.00
❑152, Jan 1976 GK, RA (a); V: Shocker	11.00
❑153, Feb 1976 GK, RA (a)	11.00
❑154, Mar 1976 SB, JR (a); V: Sandman (Marvel)	11.00

Condition price index: Multiply "NM prices" above by: **0.83 for Very Fine/Near Mint**
0.66 for Very Fine • 0.33 for Fine • 0.2 for Very Good • 0.125 for Good

	N-MINT
❑155, Apr 1976 SB, JR (a)	11.00
❑155/30 cent, Apr 1976; SB, JR (a); 30 cent regional price variant	20.00
❑156, May 1976 JR, RA (a); O: Mirage I (Desmond Charne). 1: Mirage I (Desmond Charne)	11.00
❑156/30 cent, May 1976, JR, RA (a); 30 cent regional price variant	20.00
❑157, Jun 1976; JR, RA (a); return of Doctor Octopus	11.00
❑157/30 cent, Jun 1976; JR, RA (a); 30 cent regional price variant; return of Doctor Octopus	20.00
❑158, Jul 1976; GK, RA (a); V: Doctor Octopus. Hammerhead regains physical form	11.00
❑158/30 cent, Jul 1976; GK, RA (a); 30 cent regional price variant; Hammerhead regains physical form	20.00
❑159, Aug 1976 GK, RA (a); 2: The Tinkerer. V: Doctor Octopus, Hammerhead	11.00
❑159/30 cent, Aug 1976; GK, RA (a); 30 cent regional price variant	20.00
❑160, Sep 1976; GK, RA (a); V: Tinkerer. return of Spider-Mobile	11.00
❑161, Oct 1976 GK, RA (a); A: Punisher. A: Nightcrawler	11.00
❑162, Nov 1976 RA (a); A: Punisher. A: Nightcrawler	11.00
❑163, Dec 1976 DC, RA (a); V: Kingpin	10.00
❑164, Jan 1977 JR, RA (a); V: Kingpin	10.00
❑165, Feb 1977 JR, RA (a); V: Stegron	6.50
❑166, Mar 1977 JR, RA (a); V: Lizard. V: Stegron	6.50
❑167, Apr 1977 JR, RA (a); 1: Will o' the Wisp	6.50
❑168, May 1977 RA (a); V: Will o' the Wisp	6.50
❑169, Jun 1977; AM, RA (a); J. Jonah Jameson acquires photos showing Spider-Man disposing of clone's(?) body	10.00
❑169/35 cent, Jun 1977; AM, RA (a); 35 cent regional price variant; J. Jonah Jameson acquires photos showing Spider-Man disposing of clone's(?) body	15.00
❑170, Jul 1977 RA (a); V: Doctor Faustus	6.50
❑170/35 cent, Jul 1977; RA (a); V: Doctor Faustus. 35 cent regional price variant	15.00
❑171, Aug 1977 RA (a); A: Nova	6.50
❑171/35 cent, Aug 1977; RA (a); 35 cent regional price variant	15.00
❑172, Sep 1977 RA (a); 1: Rocket Racer	6.50
❑172/35 cent, Sep 1977; RA (a); 1: Rocket Racer. 35 cent regional price variant	15.00
❑173, Oct 1977 RA (a); V: Molten Man	10.00
❑174, Nov 1977 RA (a); A: Punisher. V: Hitman	11.00
❑175, Dec 1977 RA (a); A: Punisher. V: Hitman	11.00
❑176, Jan 1978 RA (a); O: Green Goblin III (Doctor Barton Hamilton). 1: Green Goblin III (Doctor Barton Hamilton)	11.00
❑177, Feb 1978 RA (a); A: Green Goblin III (Doctor Barton Hamilton). V: Silvermane	15.00
❑178, Mar 1978 RA (a); A: Green Goblin III (Doctor Barton Hamilton). V: Silvermane	15.00
❑179, Apr 1978 RA (a); A: Green Goblin III (Doctor Barton Hamilton). V: Silvermane	15.00
❑180, May 1978 RA (a); A: Green Goblin III (Doctor Barton Hamilton). V: Silvermane	6.50
❑181, Jun 1978 SB, GK (a); O: Spider-Man	6.50
❑182, Jul 1978 RA (a); V: Rocket Racer	6.50
❑183, Aug 1978 RA (a); O: Big Wheel. 1: Big Wheel. D: Big Wheel. V: Tinkerer. V: Rocket Racer	6.50
❑184, Sep 1978 RA (a); 1: White Dragon II	6.50
❑185, Oct 1978; RA (a); V: Dragon Gangs. V: White Dragon II. Peter Parker graduates from college	6.50
❑186, Nov 1978 KP (a); V: Chameleon	6.50
❑187, Dec 1978 JSn (w); JSn, KP, BMc, JSt (a); A: Shield. A: Captain America. V: Electro	6.50
❑188, Jan 1979 KP, DC (a); O: Jigsaw. 1: Jigsaw. V: Jigsaw	6.50
❑189, Feb 1979 JBy (a); A: Man-Wolf	6.50
❑190, Mar 1979 JBy, KP, JM (a); A: Man-Wolf	6.50
❑191, Apr 1979 AM, KP (a); V: Spider Slayer. V: Spencer Smythe	6.00
❑192, May 1979 KP (a); D: Spencer Smythe. V: The Fly	6.00
❑193, Jun 1979 KP, JM (a); V: The Fly	6.00
❑194, Jul 1979 AM, KP (a); 1: Black Cat	23.00
❑195, Aug 1979; AM, KP, JM (a); O: Black Cat. Peter Parker informed of Aunt May's death (faked death)	8.00
❑196, Sep 1979 AM, KP, JM (a); D: Aunt May (faked death). V: Kingpin. V: Mysterio	6.00
❑197, Oct 1979 KP, JM (a); V: Kingpin	6.00
❑198, Nov 1979 SB, KP, JM (a); V: Mysterio	6.00
❑199, Dec 1979 SB, KP, JM (a); V: Mysterio	6.00
❑200, Jan 1980; Giant sized; KP, JR, JM (a); O: Spider-Man. D: unnamed burglar that shot Uncle Ben. Aunt May revealed to be alive	15.00
❑201, Feb 1980 KP, JR, JM (a); A: Punisher	9.00
❑202, Mar 1980 KP, JR, JM (a); A: Punisher	9.00
❑203, Apr 1980 FM (c); KP, FM, JR (a); 2: Dazzler. A: Dazzler	7.00
❑204, May 1980 KP, JR2 (a); A: Black Cat	7.00
❑205, Jun 1980 AM, KP (a); A: Black Cat	7.00
❑206, Jul 1980 AM, JBy (a)	7.00
❑207, Aug 1980 JM (a); V: Mesmero	5.00
❑208, Sep 1980 AM, JR2 (a); O: Fusion. 1: Lance Bannon. 1: Fusion	5.00
❑209, Oct 1980 O: Calypso. 1: Calypso. V: Kraven the Hunter	6.00
❑210, Nov 1980 JR2 (a); O: Madame Web. 1: Madame Web	6.00
❑211, Dec 1980 JR2, JM (a); A: Sub-Mariner	5.00
❑212, Jan 1981 JR2, JM (a); O: Sandman (Marvel). O: Hydro-Man. 1: Hydro-Man	5.00
❑213, Feb 1981 JR2, JM (a); V: Wizard	5.00
❑214, Mar 1981 JR2, JM (a); A: Sub-Mariner. V: Frightful Four	5.00
❑215, Apr 1981 JR2, JM (a)	5.00
❑216, May 1981 JR2, JM (a)	5.00
❑217, Jun 1981 JR2, JM (a)	5.00
❑218, Jul 1981 FM (c); JR2 (a)	5.00
❑219, Aug 1981 FM (c); JM (a)	5.00
❑220, Sep 1981 BMc (a); A: Moon Knight	6.00
❑221, Oct 1981	4.00
❑222, Nov 1981 BH (a)	4.00
❑223, Dec 1981 JR2 (a)	4.00
❑224, Jan 1982 JR2 (a)	4.00
❑225, Feb 1982 JR2, BWi (a); A: Foolkiller II (Greg Salinger)	4.00
❑226, Mar 1982 JR2 (a); A: Black Cat	6.00
❑227, Apr 1982 JR2, JM (a); A: Black Cat	4.00
❑228, May 1982 JR2 (a)	4.00
❑229, Jun 1982 JR2 (a)	6.00
❑230, Jul 1982 JR2 (a)	6.00
❑231, Aug 1982 JR2, JM (a)	6.00
❑232, Sep 1982 JR2 (a)	4.00
❑233, Oct 1982 JR2, JM (a)	4.00
❑234, Nov 1982; DGr, JR2 (a); Free 16 page insert-Marvel Guide to Collecting Comics	4.00
❑235, Dec 1982 JR2 (a); O: Will o' the Wisp	4.00
❑236, Jan 1983 JR2 (a); D: Tarantula I (Anton Rodriguez)	4.00
❑237, Feb 1983 BH (a)	4.00
❑238, Mar 1983; 1: Hobgoblin (Ned Leeds). Came with "Tattooz" temporary tattoo decal	35.00
❑239, Apr 1983 2: Hobgoblin	22.00
❑240, May 1983 BL, JR2 (a)	5.00
❑241, Jun 1983 JR2 (a); O: Vulture	5.00
❑242, Jul 1983 JR2 (a); V: Mad Thinker	5.00
❑243, Aug 1983 JR2 (a)	5.00
❑244, Sep 1983 JR2, KJ (a); A: Hobgoblin (cameo). V: Hobgoblin	5.00
❑245, Oct 1983; JR2 (a); Lefty Donovan becomes Hobgoblin	5.00
❑246, Nov 1983 JR2 (a)	4.00
❑247, Dec 1983 JR2 (a); V: Thunderball	4.00
❑248, Jan 1984 JR2 (a); V: Thunderball	4.00
❑249, Feb 1984 V: Hobgoblin	4.00
❑250, Mar 1984 JR2, KJ (a); A: Hobgoblin	6.00
❑251, Apr 1984; V: Hobgoblin. Last old costume	6.00
❑252, May 1984; new costume	16.00
❑253, Jun 1984 1: The Rose	6.00
❑254, Jul 1984 V: Jack O'Lantern	5.00
❑255, Aug 1984 V: Red Ghost	4.00
❑256, Sep 1984 O: Puma. 1: Puma. V: Puma	4.00
❑257, Oct 1984 2: Puma. A: Hobgoblin. V: Puma	4.00
❑258, Nov 1984 A: Hobgoblin	4.00
❑259, Dec 1984; O: Mary Jane Watson. A: Hobgoblin. Spider-Man back to old costume	4.00
❑260, Jan 1985 A: Hobgoblin. V: Hobgoblin	5.00
❑261, Feb 1985 A: Hobgoblin. V: Hobgoblin	5.00
❑262, Mar 1985; BL (w); BL (a); Spider-man unmasked	4.00
❑263, Apr 1985 1: Spider-Kid	4.00
❑264, May 1985	4.00
❑265, Jun 1985 1: Silver Sable	4.00
❑265-2 1: Silver Sable	2.00
❑266, Jul 1985 PD (w); SB (a)	4.00
❑267, Aug 1985 PD (w); BMc (a)	4.00
❑268, Sep 1985; A: Kingpin. A: Beyonder. Secret Wars II	4.00
❑269, Oct 1985 V: Firelord	4.00
❑270, Nov 1985 1: Kate Cushing (Peter Parker's supervisor at the Bugle). A: Avengers. V: Firelord	4.00
❑271, Dec 1985 V: Manslaughter	4.00
❑272, Jan 1986 SB (a); V: Slyde	4.00
❑273, Feb 1986; A: Puma. Secret Wars II	4.00
❑274, Mar 1986; A: Zarathos (the spirit of vengeance). V: Beyonder. Secret Wars II	5.00
❑275, Apr 1986; double-sized; O: Spider-Man. Hobgoblin story	5.00
❑276, May 1986 A: Hobgoblin. D: Fly	5.00
❑277, Jun 1986 V: Kingpin	4.00
❑278, Jul 1986 D: Wraith	4.00
❑279, Aug 1986; Jack O' Lantern versus Silver Sable	4.00
❑280, Sep 1986	3.00
❑281, Oct 1986; V: Sinister Syndicate. Jack O' Lantern cover/story	4.00
❑282, Nov 1986	4.00
❑283, Dec 1986 V: Absorbing Man. V: Titania	4.00
❑284, Jan 1987 A: Punisher	4.00
❑285, Feb 1987 A: Punisher. A: Hobgoblin	5.00
❑286, Mar 1986	5.00
❑287, Apr 1987 EL (a); A: Hobgoblin. A: Daredevil	5.00
❑288, May 1987 A: Hobgoblin	5.00
❑289, Jun 1987; double-sized issue; PD (w); 1: Hobgoblin II (Jason Macendale). Hobgoblin unmasked; Hobgoblin's identity revealed; Jack O' Lantern becomes Hobgoblin	5.00
❑290, Jul 1987; JR2 (a); Peter Parker proposes to Mary Jane	5.00
❑291, Aug 1987 JR2 (a); V: Spider-Slayer	5.00
❑292, Sep 1987 V: Spider Slayer	5.00

	N-MINT
❑293, Oct 1987 MZ (a); V: Kraven the Hunter	5.00
❑294, Nov 1987 MZ, BMc (a); D: Kraven. V: Kraven the Hunter	5.00
❑295, Dec 1987 BSz (a)	5.00
❑296, Jan 1988 V: Doctor Octopus	5.00
❑297, Feb 1988 V: Doctor Octopus	5.00
❑298, Mar 1988; TMc (a); 1: Venom (cameo). V: Chance I (Nicholas Powell). w/o costume	20.00
❑299, Apr 1988 TMc (a); 1: Venom (cameo). V: Chance I (Nicholas Powell)	15.00
❑300, May 1988; 25th anniversary; TMc (a); O: Venom. 1: Venom (Full). Last black costume for Spider-Man	45.00
❑300/A, May 1988; 25th anniversary; TMc (a); O: Venom. 1: Venom (Full). Chromium cover; Last black costume for Spider-Man	40.00
❑300/B, May 1988; 25th anniversary; TMc (a); O: Venom. 1: Venom (Full). Chromium cover; Last black costume for Spider-Man	30.00
❑301, Jun 1988 TMc (a)	9.00
❑302, Jul 1988 TMc (a)	9.00
❑303, Aug 1988 TMc (a); A: Silver Sable. A: Sandman	9.00
❑304, Sep 1988 TMc (a); V: The Fox	6.00
❑305, Sep 1988 TMc (a); V: The Prowler. V: The Fox	6.00
❑306, Oct 1988 TMc (a); V: Humbug	6.00
❑307, Oct 1988 TMc (a); O: Chameleon. V: Chameleon	6.00
❑308, Nov 1988 TMc (a); V: Taskmaster	6.00
❑309, Nov 1988 TMc (a)	6.00
❑310, Dec 1988 TMc (a); V: Killer Shrike	6.00
❑311, Jan 1989; TMc (a); V: Mysterio. Inferno	6.00
❑312, Feb 1989; TMc (a); V: Hobgoblin. V: Green Goblin. Inferno; Hobgoblin vs. Green Goblin II (Harry Osborn)	8.00
❑313, Mar 1989; TMc (a); V: Lizard. Inferno	5.00
❑314, Apr 1989 TMc (a)	5.00
❑315, May 1989 TMc (a); A: Venom. V: Venom	8.00
❑316, Jun 1989 TMc (a); A: Venom. V: Venom	8.00
❑317, Jul 1989 TMc (a); A: Venom. V: Venom	8.00
❑318, Aug 1989 TMc (a); A: Venom	6.00
❑319, Sep 1989 TMc (a)	6.00
❑320, Sep 1989 TMc (a); A: Silver Sable. V: Paladin	6.00
❑321, Oct 1989 TMc (a); A: Silver Sable	4.00
❑322, Oct 1989 TMc (a); A: Silver Sable. V: Ultimatum	4.00
❑323, Nov 1989 TMc (a); A: Silver Sable. V: Solo. V: Ultimatum	4.00
❑324, Nov 1989 TMc (c); TMc, EL (a); A: Sabretooth. V: Solo. V: Sabretooth	4.00
❑325, Nov 1989 TMc (a); A: Captain America. V: Red Skull	3.00
❑326, Dec 1989; V: Graviton. Acts of Vengeance	3.00
❑327, Dec 1989; EL (a); V: Magneto. cosmic Spider-Man; Acts of Vengeance	3.00
❑328, Jan 1990; TMc (a); Hulk; Acts of Vengeance; Last McFarlane Issue	5.00
❑329, Feb 1990; EL (a); V: Tri-Sentinel. Acts of Vengeance	3.00
❑330, Mar 1990 EL (a); A: Punisher. V: Punisher	3.00
❑331, Apr 1990 EL (a); A: Punisher. V: Punisher	3.00
❑332, May 1990 EL (a); A: Venom	3.00
❑333, Jun 1990 EL (a); A: Venom. V: Venom	3.00
❑334, Jul 1990; EL (a); V: Sinister Six (Doctor Octopus, Vulture, Electro, Sandman, Mysterio, Kraven the Hunter)	2.50
❑335, Jul 1990; EL (a); Sinister Six	2.50
❑336, Aug 1990; EL (a); Sinister Six	2.50
❑337, Aug 1990; EL (a); Sinister Six	2.50
❑338, Sep 1990; EL (a); Sinister Six	2.50

	N-MINT
❑339, Sep 1990; EL (a); Sinister Six	2.50
❑340, Oct 1990 EL (a)	2.50
❑341, Nov 1990; EL (a); V: Tarantula. Powerless; Spider-Man loses powers	2.50
❑342, Dec 1990; EL (a); V: Scorpion. Powerless	2.50
❑343, Jan 1991; EL (a); V: Scorpion. V: Tarantula. Spider-Man gets his powers back	2.50
❑344, Feb 1991 EL (a); 1: Cardiac. 1: Cletus Kassidy (later becomes Carnage)-cameo. V: Rhino	4.00
❑345, Mar 1991 A: Cletus Kassidy (later becomes Carnage)-full. V: Boomerang	3.00
❑346, Apr 1991 EL (a); A: Venom. V: Venom	3.00
❑347, May 1991 EL (a); A: Venom. V: Venom	3.00
❑348, Jun 1991 EL (a); A: Avengers	2.00
❑349, Jul 1991 EL (a)	2.00
❑350, Aug 1991 EL (a); V: Doctor Doom	2.00
❑351, Sep 1991 A: Nova. V: Tri-Sentinel	2.00
❑352, Oct 1991 A: Nova. V: Tri-Sentinel	2.00
❑353, Nov 1991 AM (w); A: Punisher. A: Moon Knight	2.00
❑354, Nov 1991 AM (w); A: Punisher. A: Moon Knight	2.00
❑355, Dec 1991 AM (w); A: Punisher. A: Moon Knight	2.00
❑356, Dec 1991 AM (w); A: Punisher. A: Moon Knight	2.00
❑357, Jan 1992 AM (w); A: Punisher. A: Moon Knight	2.00
❑358, Jan 1992 AM (w); A: Punisher. A: Moon Knight	4.00
❑359, Feb 1992	2.00
❑360, Mar 1992 O: Cardiac. 1: Carnage (cameo)	3.00
❑361, Apr 1992 1: Carnage (full appearance)	5.00
❑361-2; silver cover	1.50
❑362, May 1992 A: Carnage. A: Venom	4.00
❑362-2	1.50
❑363, Jun 1992 A: Carnage. A: Venom	4.00
❑364, Jul 1992; V: Shocker. Peter Parker's parents (false parents) appear	3.00
❑365, Aug 1992; PD (w); 1: Spider-Man 2099. Hologram cover; Peter Parker meets his (false) parents; Gatefold poster with Venom and Carnage; Lizard back-up story	5.00
❑366, Sep 1992 A: Red Skull. V: Red Skull	2.00
❑367, Oct 1992	2.00
❑368, Nov 1992 V: Spider-Slayers	2.00
❑369, Nov 1992 V: Spider-Slayers	2.00
❑370, Dec 1992 V: Spider-Slayers	2.00
❑371, Dec 1992 A: Black Cat. V: Spider-Slayers	2.00
❑372, Jan 1993 V: Spider-Slayers	2.00
❑373, Jan 1993 V: Spider-Slayers	2.00
❑374, Feb 1993 V: Venom	2.00
❑375, Mar 1993; 30th anniversary special; A: Venom. Metallic ink cover; Sets stage for Venom #1	5.00
❑376, Apr 1993 O: Cardiac. V: Cardiac, Styx and Stone	3.00
❑377, May 1993 V: Cardiac	3.00
❑378, Jun 1993 A: Carnage. A: Venom	3.00
❑379, Jul 1993 A: Carnage. A: Venom	3.00
❑380, Aug 1993 A: Carnage. A: Venom. V: Carnage. V: Demogoblin	3.00
❑381, Sep 1993 A: Hulk. V: Hulk	3.00
❑382, Oct 1993 A: Hulk. V: Hulk	3.00
❑383, Nov 1993	3.00
❑384, Dec 1993	3.00
❑385, Jan 1994	3.00
❑386, Feb 1994 V: Vulture	3.00
❑387, Mar 1994 V: Vulture	3.00
❑388, Apr 1994; Double-size D: Peter Parker's parents (false parents). V: Chameleon. V: Vulture	3.25
❑388/Variant, Apr 1994; Double-size; D: Peter Parker's parents (false parents). V: Vulture. foil cover	2.00

Three issues of *Amazing Spider-Man* dealing with drug abuse were not approved by the Comics Code Authority, although the stories did receive Code approval when they were reprinted a few years later.

© 1971 Marvel Comics.

	N-MINT
❑389, May 1994 V: Chameleon	3.00
❑390, Jun 1994	3.00
❑390/CS, Jun 1994	3.00
❑391, Jul 1994; V: Shriek. Aunt May suffers stroke	3.00
❑392, Aug 1994 V: Carrion. V: Shriek	3.00
❑393, Sep 1994; V: Carrion. V: Shriek. Carrion	3.00
❑394, Oct 1994 O: Ben Reilly. A: Ben Reilly	3.00
❑394/Variant, Oct 1994; Giant-size; O: Ben Reilly. A: Ben Reilly. enhanced cover	3.50
❑395, Nov 1994; V: Puma. continues in Spectacular Spider-Man #218	3.00
❑396, Dec 1994; A: Daredevil. V: Owl. V: Vulture. continues in Spectacular Spider-Man #219	3.00
❑397, Jan 1995; Double-size; V: Lizard. V: Doctor Octopus. flip book with illustrated story from The Ultimate Spider-Man back-up; continues in Spectacular Spider-Man #220	3.00
❑398, Feb 1995; V: Doctor Octopus. continues in Spectacular Spider-Man #221	3.00
❑399, Mar 1995; A: Scarlet Spider. A: Jackal. V: Jackal. continues in Spider-Man #56	3.00
❑400, Apr 1995 SL (w); JR2 (a); D: Aunt May (fake death)	6.00
❑400/A, Apr 1995; white cover edition (no ads, back-up story); SL (w); JR2 (a); D: Aunt May (fake death). white embossed cover	4.00
❑400/B, Apr 1995; SL (w); JR2 (a); D: Aunt May (fake death). Limited edition cover; 10,000 copies	6.00
❑401, May 1995 V: Kaine	1.50
❑402, Jun 1995 V: Traveller	1.50
❑403, Jul 1995 A: Carnage	1.50
❑404, Aug 1995	1.50
❑405, Sep 1995	1.50
❑406, Oct 1995; 1: Doctor Octopus II. OverPower cards inserted; (continues in Amazing Scarlet Spider)	1.50
❑407, Jan 1996 A: Silver Sable. A: Human Torch. A: Sandman	1.50
❑408, Feb 1996 V: Mysterio	1.50
❑409, Mar 1996 V: Rhino	1.50
❑410, Apr 1996 V: Cell 12	1.50
❑411, May 1996	1.50
❑412, Jun 1996	1.50
❑413, Jul 1996	1.50
❑414, Aug 1996 A: Delilah	1.50
❑415, Sep 1996; V: Sentinel. "Onslaught: Impact 2"	1.50
❑416, Oct 1996; post-Onslaught memories	1.50
❑417, Nov 1996	1.50
❑418, Dec 1996; birth of Peter and Mary Jane's baby; Return of Norman Osborn (face shown)	2.00
❑419, Jan 1997 V: Black Tarantula	1.50
❑420, Feb 1997 A: X-Man. D: El Uno	1.50
❑421, Mar 1997 O: The Dragonfly. 1: The Dragonfly	2.00
❑422, Apr 1997 O: Electro	2.00
❑423, May 1997 V: Electro	2.00
❑424, Jun 1997 A: Elektra. V: Elektra	2.00
❑425, Aug 1997	2.00
❑426, Sep 1997; gatefold summary	2.00

N-MINT

❑427, Oct 1997; gatefold summary; return of Doctor Octopus ... 2.00
❑428, Nov 1997; gatefold summary V: Doctor Octopus ... 2.00
❑429, Dec 1997; gatefold summary V: Absorbing Man ... 2.00
❑430, Jan 1998; gatefold summary A: Silver Surfer. V: Carnage ... 2.00
❑431, Feb 1998; gatefold summary A: Silver Surfer. V: Carnage ... 2.00
❑432, Mar 1998; gatefold summary ... 2.00
❑433, Apr 1998; gatefold summary ... 2.00
❑434, May 1998; gatefold summary . 2.00
❑435, Jun 1998; gatefold summary A: Ricochet ... 2.00
❑436, Jul 1998; gatefold summary ... 2.00
❑437, Aug 1998; gatefold summary A: Synch ... 2.00
❑438, Sep 1998; gatefold summary A: Daredevil ... 2.00
❑439, Sep 1998; gatefold summary A: Zack and Lana ... 2.00
❑440, Oct 1998; gatefold summary V: Molten Man ... 2.00
❑441, Nov 1998; gatefold summary A: Molten Man. D: Madame Web ... 2.00
❑500, Dec 2003; JR2 (a); numbering reverts to original series, adding in issues from Vol. 2 ... 3.50
❑501, Jan 2004 (c); JR2 (a) ... 2.99
❑502, Feb 2004 JR2 (a) ... 2.99
❑503, Mar 2004 ... 2.25
❑504, Apr 2004 JR2 (a) ... 2.25
❑505, May 2004 JR2 (a) ... 0.00
❑506, Jun 2004 JR2 (a) ... 2.25
❑507, Jul 2004 (c); JR2 (a) ... 2.25
❑508, Aug 2004 ... 2.25
❑509, Aug 2004 ... 2.25
❑509/A, Sep 2004; Director's Cut ...
❑510, Sep 2004 ...
❑Aim Giveaway 1, ca. 1980; Giveaway from Aim Toothpaste; A: Doctor Octopus. Spider-Man vs. Doctor Octopus ... 2.00
❑Aim Giveaway 2; Aim toothpaste giveaway A: Green Goblin ... 2.00
❑Annual 1 SD, SL (w); SD (a); 1: Sinister Six (Doctor Octopus, Vulture, Electro, Sandman, Mysterio, Kraven the Hunter) ... 700.00
❑Annual 2; Cover reads "King-Size Special"; SD, SL (w); SD (a); 1: Xandu. A: Doctor Strange. Reprints Amazing Spider-Man #1, 2, and 5, plus a new story ... 400.00
❑Annual 3, Nov 1966; Cover reads "King-Size Special"; DH, JR (a); A: Daredevil. A: Avengers. V: Hulk. New story; reprints Amazing Spider-Man #11 and 12 ... 115.00
❑Annual 4, Nov 1967; Cover reads "King-Size Special"; A: Torch. V: Mysterio. V: Wizard. Cover reads King-Size Special ... 90.00
❑Annual 5, Nov 1968; Cover reads "King-Size Special"; JR, SL (w); JR (a); 1: Peter Parker's parents. A: Red Skull. fate of Peter Parker's parents revealed ... 90.00
❑Annual 5-2; Cover reads "King-Size Special"; JR, SL (w); JR (a); 1: Peter Parker's parents. A: Red Skull. ... 2.50
❑Annual 6, Nov 1969; Cover reads "King-Size Special"; SD, SL (w); SD (a); reprints stories from Amazing Spider-Man #8, Annual #1 and Fantastic Four Annual #1 ... 35.00
❑Annual 7, Dec 1970; Cover reads "King-Size Special"; JR (c); SD, SL (w); SD, JR (a); reprints stories from Amazing Spider-Man #1, 2, and 38 ... 26.00
❑Annual 8, Dec 1971; Cover reads "King-Size Special"; SL (w); JR (a); A: Giant Man; reprints stories from Amazing Spider-Man #46 and 50 and Tales to Astonish #57 ... 26.00
❑Annual 9, ca. 1973; reprints Spectacular Spider-Man (magazine) #2; JR, SL (w); JR, JM (a); A: Hobgoblin. Cover reads King Size Special; reprinted with changes from Spectacular Spider-Man #2 ... 26.00
❑Annual 10, Sep 1976 GK (a); O: Human Fly. 1: Human Fly ... 10.00
❑Annual 11, Sep 1977 JR2, GK, DP (a) 10.00
❑Annual 12, Aug 1978; GK, JR (w); JBy, GK, JR (a); Reprints Hulk story from Amazing Spider-Man #119-120 ... 10.00
❑Annual 13, Nov 1979 JBy, KP, TD, JM (a); V: Doctor Octopus ... 10.00
❑Annual 14, Dec 1980 FM (w); FM (a); A: Doctor Strange. V: Doctor Doom 10.00
❑Annual 15, ca. 1981 FM (a); A: Punisher ... 7.00
❑Annual 16, ca. 1982 O: Captain Marvel II (Monica Rambeau). 1: Captain Marvel II (Monica Rambeau) ... 6.00
❑Annual 17, ca. 1983 ... 5.00
❑Annual 18, ca. 1984; Wedding of J. Jonah Jameson ... 5.00
❑Annual 19, ca. 1985 ... 5.00
❑Annual 20, ca. 1986 D: Blizzard ... 5.00
❑Annual 21, ca. 1987; newsstand edition; Wedding of Peter Parker and Mary Jane Watson ... 6.00
❑Annual 21/Direc, ca. 1987; Direct Market edition; Wedding of Peter Parker and Mary Jane Watson ... 6.00
❑Annual 22, ca. 1988 O: High Evolutionary. 1: Speedball. A: Daredevil . 4.00
❑Annual 23, ca. 1989; O: Spider-Man. Atlantis Attacks ... 3.00
❑Annual 24, ca. 1990 SD, GK, MZ (a); A: Ant-Man ... 3.00
❑Annual 25, ca. 1991; O: Spider-Man. Vibranium Vendetta; 1st solo Venom story ... 3.00
❑Annual 26, ca. 1998 1: Dreadnought 2000 ... 3.00
❑Annual 27, ca. 1993; 1: Annex. trading card ... 3.00
❑Annual 28, ca. 1994; Carnage ... 3.00
❑Annual 1996, ca. 1995 ... 3.00
❑Annual 1997, ca. 1996; V: Sundown. wraparound cover ... 3.00
❑Ashcan 1, b&w; ashcan edition; O: Spider-Man. ashcan ... 0.75

AMAZING SPIDER-MAN, THE (VOL. 2)
MARVEL

❑1, Jan 1999; JBy (a); wraparound cover ... 6.00
❑1/A, Jan 1999; JR2 (c); JBy, JR2 (a); Sunburst variant cover; DFE alternate cover, signed John Romita Jr . 12.00
❑1/B, Jan 1999; JBy (a); DFE alternate cover, signed Stan Lee ... 35.00
❑1/C, Jan 1999; JBy (a); Dynamic Forces Edition ... 5.00
❑1/D, Jan 1999; JBy (a); Signed ... 10.00
❑1/E, Jan 1999; Marvel Authentix edition JR2 (c); JBy, JR2 (a) ... 8.00
❑1/F, Jan 1999; JR2 (c); JBy (a); sunburst variant cover ... 6.00
❑2/A, Feb 1999; gatefold summary; JBy (a); V: Shadrac. new Spider-Man's identity revealed; Cover A: Skeleton grabbing Spider-Man ... 2.50
❑2/B, Feb 1999; gatefold summary; JBy (a); V: Shadrac. new Spider-Man's identity revealed; Cover B ... 2.50
❑3, Mar 1999 JBy (a); O: Shadrac ... 2.00
❑4, Apr 1999 JBy (a); A: Fantastic Four. V: Trapster. V: Sandman ... 2.00
❑5, May 1999 A: new Spider-Woman 2.00
❑6, Jun 1999 V: Spider-Woman ... 2.00
❑7, Jul 1999; Flash Thompson's fantasy ... 2.00
❑8, Aug 1999 V: Mysterio ... 2.00
❑9, Sep 1999 A: Doctor Octopus ... 2.00
❑10, Oct 1999 A: Doctor Octopus. V: Captain Power ... 2.00
❑11, Nov 1999 V: Blob ... 2.00
❑12, Dec 1999; Giant-size ... 3.00
❑13, Jan 2000 ... 2.00
❑14, Feb 2000 JBy (w); JBy, DGr (a) . 2.00
❑15, Mar 2000 JBy (w); JBy (a) ... 2.00
❑16, Apr 2000 ... 2.00
❑17, May 2000 ... 2.00
❑18, Jun 2000 ... 2.50
❑19, Jul 2000 EL (a); A: Venom ... 2.50
❑20, Aug 2000; EL (c); SL (w); SD, KP, JR, JM, EL (a); reprints Amazing Spider-Man (Vol. 1) #25, 58, and 192 . 4.50
❑21, Sep 2000 EL (c); EL (a); V: Spider-Slayers ... 2.25
❑22, Oct 2000 ... 2.25
❑23, Nov 2000 JR2 (a) ... 2.25
❑24, Dec 2000 JR2 (a) ... 2.25
❑25, Jan 2001; Speckle foil cover ... 4.00
❑25/A, Jan 2001, regular wraparound cover ... 3.00
❑26, Feb 2001 ... 2.25
❑27, Mar 2001 JR2 (a); A: Mr. Q. A: Mr. P 2.25
❑28, Apr 2001 ... 2.25
❑29, May 2001; Return of Mary Jane 2.25
❑30, Jun 2001 ... 5.00
❑31, Jul 2001 ... 2.00
❑32, Aug 2001 ... 4.00
❑33, Sep 2001 ... 4.00
❑34, Oct 2001 ... 4.00
❑35, Nov 2001 ... 4.00
❑36, Dec 2001 ... 10.00
❑36/DF, Dec 2001; 9/11 tribute issue; Dynamic Forces special edition ... 25.00
❑37, Jan 2002 ... 2.50
❑38, Feb 2002 JR2 (a) ... 2.50
❑39, ca. 2002 ... 2.50
❑40, Jun 2002 ... 2.25
❑41, Jul 2002 ... 4.00
❑42, Aug 2002 ... 3.00
❑43, Sep 2002 ... 3.00
❑44, Oct 2002 ... 2.25
❑45, Nov 2002 ... 2.25
❑46, Dec 2002 ... 2.25
❑47, Jan 2003 ... 2.25
❑48, Feb 2003 ... 2.25
❑49, Mar 2003 ... 2.25
❑50, Apr 2003 ... 5.00
❑51, May 2003 ... 2.25
❑52, Jun 2003 JR2 (c); JR2 (a) ... 2.25
❑53, Jul 2003, JR2 (c); JR2 (a); wraparound cover ... 2.25
❑54, Aug 2003 JR2 (a) ... 2.49
❑55, Sep 2003 JR2 (a) ... 2.49
❑56, Oct 2003 JR2 (a) ... 2.00
❑57, Oct 2003 (c); JR2 (a) ... 2.99
❑58, Nov 2003; (c); JR2 (a); numbering restarts at 500 under Vol. 1 ... 2.99
❑Annual 1999, Jun 1999; V: Trapster. V: Wizard. 1999 Annual ... 3.50
❑Annual 2000, ca. 2000 ... 3.50
❑Annual 2001, ca. 2001, Cover B ... 2.99

AMAZING SPIDER-MAN 30TH ANNIVERSARY POSTER MAGAZINE
MARVEL

❑1 ... 3.95

AMAZING SPIDER-MAN GIVEAWAYS
MARVEL

❑1; (two different, both #1) ... 4.00
❑2; Managing Materials ... 4.00
❑3, Feb 1977; Planned Parenthood giveaway; miniature; ... vs. The Prodigy! ... 4.00
❑4, ca. 1979; No issue number; All Detergent giveaway ... 6.00
❑5, child abuse; with New Mutants ... 4.00

AMAZING SPIDER-MAN, THE (LANCER)
LANCER

❑1; SD (a); "The Amazing Spider-Man Collector's Album" ... 15.00

N-MINT

AMAZING SPIDER-MAN, THE (PUBLIC SERVICE SERIES)
MARVEL

- ❑1, ca. 1990; TMc (c); TMc (a); Skating on Thin Ice! — 2.50
- ❑1-2, Feb 1993; US Edition; TMc (c); TMc (a); Skating on Thin Ice — 2.00
- ❑2, ca. 1993; TMc (a); Double Trouble! — 2.50
- ❑2-2, Feb 1993; US Edition; TMc (a); Double Trouble — 2.00
- ❑3, ca. 1991; TMc (a); Hit and Run! — 2.50
- ❑3-2, Feb 1993; US Edition; TMc (a); A: Ghost Rider. Hit and Run — 2.00
- ❑4, ca. 1992; TMc (a); 1: Turbine. Chaos in Calgary — 2.50
- ❑4-2, Feb 1993; US Edition; Chaos in Calgary — 2.00

AMAZING SPIDER-MAN, THE: SOUL OF THE HUNTER
MARVEL

- ❑1, Aug 1992 — 5.95

AMAZING SPIDER-MAN SUPER SPECIAL, THE
MARVEL

- ❑1, ca. 1995, Flip-book; two of the stories continue in Spider-Man Super Special #1; Amazing Scarlet Spider on other side — 4.00

AMAZING STRIP
ANTARCTIC

- ❑1, Feb 1994 — 2.95
- ❑2, Apr 1994; Indicia says April, cover says March — 2.95
- ❑3, Apr 1994 — 2.95
- ❑4, May 1994 — 2.95
- ❑5, Jun 1994 — 2.95
- ❑6, Jul 1994 — 2.95
- ❑7, Aug 1994 — 2.95
- ❑8, Sep 1994 — 2.95
- ❑9, Nov 1994 — 2.95
- ❑10, Dec 1994; #10 on cover, #4 in indicia (cover correct) — 2.95

AMAZING WAHZOO
SOLSON

- ❑1 1986 — 1.75

AMAZING WORLD OF SUPERMAN
DC

- ❑1 1973 — 4.00

AMAZING X-MEN
MARVEL

- ❑1, Mar 1995; Age of Apocalypse — 2.00
- ❑2, Apr 1995 — 2.00
- ❑3, May 1995 — 2.00
- ❑4, Jun 1995 — 2.00

AMAZON, THE
COMICO

- ❑1, Mar 1989 — 1.95
- ❑2, Apr 1989 — 1.95
- ❑3, May 1989 — 1.95

AMAZON
DC / AMALGAM

- ❑1, Apr 1996 — 1.95

AMAZON ATTACK 3-D
3-D ZONE

- ❑1, ca. 1990, b&w — 3.95

AMAZONS
FANTAGRAPHICS

- ❑1, b&w — 2.95

AMAZON TALES
FANTACO

- ❑1 — 2.95
- ❑2 — 2.95
- ❑3 — 2.95

AMAZON WARRIORS
AC

- ❑1 1989; b&w Reprint — 2.50

N-MINT

AMAZON WOMAN (1ST SERIES)
FANTACO

- ❑1 — 2.95
- ❑2 — 2.95

AMAZON WOMAN (2ND SERIES)
FANTACO

- ❑1 — 2.95
- ❑2 — 2.95
- ❑3 — 2.95
- ❑4 — 2.95

AMBER: NINE PRINCES IN AMBER (ROGER ZELAZNY'S...)
DC

- ❑1, ca. 1996; prestige format; adapts Zelazny story — 6.95
- ❑2, ca. 1996; prestige format; adapts Zelazny story — 6.95
- ❑3, ca. 1996; prestige format; adapts Zelazny story — 6.95

AMBER: THE GUNS OF AVALON (ROGER ZELAZNY'S...)
DC

- ❑1, ca. 1996; prestige format — 6.95
- ❑2, ca. 1996; prestige format — 6.95
- ❑3, ca. 1996; prestige format — 6.95

AMBUSH BUG
DC

- ❑1, Jun 1985 KG (w); KG (a) — 1.00
- ❑2, Jul 1985 KG (w); KG (a) — 1.00
- ❑3, Aug 1985 KG (w); KG (a) — 1.00
- ❑4, Sep 1985 KG (w); KG (a) — 1.00

AMBUSH BUG NOTHING SPECIAL
DC

- ❑1, Sep 1992 — 2.50

AMBUSH BUG STOCKING STUFFER
DC

- ❑1, Mar 1986 — 1.25

AMELIA RULES
RENAISSANCE

- ❑1, ca. 2001 — 2.95
- ❑2, ca. 2001 — 2.95
- ❑3, ca. 2001 — 2.95
- ❑4, ca. 2001 — 2.95

AMERICA AT WAR
FIRESIDE

- ❑1 — 30.00

AMERICAN, THE
DARK HORSE

- ❑1, Aug 1987, b&w — 1.50
- ❑2, Oct 1987 — 1.75
- ❑3, Dec 1987 — 1.75
- ❑4, Apr 1988 — 1.75
- ❑5, Jul 1988 — 1.75
- ❑6, Sep 1988 — 1.75
- ❑7, Oct 1988 — 1.75
- ❑8, Feb 1989 — 1.75
- ❑Special 1, b&w; Special edition — 2.25

AMERICAN BOOK, THE
DARK HORSE

- ❑1, Oct 1988, b&w — 5.95

AMERICAN CENTURY
DC / VERTIGO

- ❑1, May 2001 — 2.50
- ❑2, Jun 2001 — 2.50
- ❑3, Jul 2001 — 2.50
- ❑4, Aug 2001 — 2.50
- ❑5, Aug 2001 — 2.50
- ❑6, Sep 2001 — 2.50
- ❑7, Oct 2001 — 2.50
- ❑8, Nov 2001 — 2.50
- ❑9, Dec 2001 — 2.50
- ❑10, Jan 2002 — 2.50
- ❑11, Feb 2002 — 2.50
- ❑12, Mar 2002 — 2.50
- ❑13, Apr 2002 — 2.50
- ❑14, May 2002 — 2.50
- ❑15, Jun 2002 — 2.50
- ❑16, Aug 2002 — 2.50

The black costume Spider-Man received during Secret Wars turned out to be an alien symbiote that later became Venom.

© 1988 Marvel Comics

N-MINT

- ❑17, Sep 2002 — 2.50
- ❑18, Oct 2002 — 2.50
- ❑19 — 2.50
- ❑20 — 2.50
- ❑21 — 2.50
- ❑22 — 2.50
- ❑23, Apr 2003 — 2.75
- ❑24, May 2003 — 2.75
- ❑25, Jun 2003 — 2.75
- ❑26, Jul 2003 — 2.75
- ❑27, Sep 2003 — 2.75

AMERICAN FLAGG
FIRST

- ❑1, Oct 1983 HC (a); 1: Reuben Flagg — 2.50
- ❑2, Nov 1983 HC (a) — 2.00
- ❑3, Dec 1983 HC (a) — 2.00
- ❑4, Jan 1984 HC (a) — 2.00
- ❑5, Feb 1984 HC (w); HC (a) — 2.00
- ❑6, Mar 1984 HC (a) — 1.50
- ❑7, Apr 1984 HC (a) — 1.50
- ❑8, May 1984 HC (a) — 1.50
- ❑9, Jun 1984 HC (a) — 1.50
- ❑10, Jul 1984 HC (a) — 1.50
- ❑11, Aug 1984 HC (a) — 1.50
- ❑12, Sep 1984 HC (a) — 1.50
- ❑13, Oct 1984 HC (a) — 1.50
- ❑14, Nov 1984 PB (a) — 1.25
- ❑15, Dec 1984 HC (a) — 1.25
- ❑16, Jan 1985 HC (a) — 1.25
- ❑17, Feb 1985 HC (a) — 1.25
- ❑18, Mar 1985 HC (a) — 1.25
- ❑19, Apr 1985 HC (a) — 1.25
- ❑20, May 1985 HC (a) — 1.25
- ❑21, Jun 1985 AMo (w) — 1.25
- ❑22, Jul 1985 HC (c); AMo (w) — 1.25
- ❑23, Aug 1985 HC (c); AMo (w) — 1.25
- ❑24, Sep 1985 HC (c); AMo (w) — 1.25
- ❑25, Oct 1985 HC (c); AMo (w) — 1.25
- ❑26, Nov 1985 HC (c); AMo (w) — 1.25
- ❑27, Dec 1985 HC (c); AMo (w); HC (a) — 1.25
- ❑28, Apr 1986 HC, JSa (a) — 1.25
- ❑29, May 1986 HC, JSa (a) — 1.25
- ❑30, Jun 1986 HC, JSa (a) — 1.25
- ❑31, Jul 1986 HC (a); O: Bob Violence — 1.25
- ❑32, Aug 1986 HC (a) — 1.25
- ❑33, Sep 1986 — 1.25
- ❑34, Nov 1986 — 1.25
- ❑35, Dec 1986 — 1.25
- ❑36, Jan 1987 — 1.25
- ❑37, Feb 1987 — 1.25
- ❑38, Mar 1987 HC (a) — 1.25
- ❑39, Apr 1987 HC (a) — 1.25
- ❑40, May 1987 HC (a) — 1.25
- ❑41, Jun 1987 HC (a) — 1.25
- ❑42, Jul 1987 HC (a) — 1.25
- ❑43, Aug 1987 HC (a) — 1.25
- ❑44, Sep 1987 HC (a) — 1.25
- ❑45, Oct 1987 — 1.25
- ❑46, Nov 1987; HC (c); apology — 1.75
- ❑47, Dec 1987 HC (a) — 1.75
- ❑48, Jan 1988 HC (a) — 1.75
- ❑49, Feb 1988 HC (a) — 1.75
- ❑50, Mar 1988 HC (a) — 1.75
- ❑Special 1, Nov 1986; HC (w); HC (a); Special #1 — 1.75

N-MINT

AMERICAN FLAGG (HOWARD CHAYKIN'S...)
FIRST

- ❑1, May 1988 .... 2.00
- ❑2, Jun 1988 .... 1.75
- ❑3, Jul 1988 .... 1.75
- ❑4, Aug 1988 .... 1.75
- ❑5, Sep 1988 .... 1.75
- ❑6, Oct 1988 .... 1.95
- ❑7, Nov 1988 .... 1.95
- ❑8, Dec 1988 .... 1.95
- ❑9, Jan 1989 .... 1.95
- ❑10, Feb 1989 .... 1.95
- ❑11, Mar 1989 .... 1.95
- ❑12, Apr 1989 .... 1.95

AMERICAN FLYER
LAST GASP

- ❑1 .... 4.00
- ❑2 .... 4.00

AMERICAN FREAK: A TALE OF THE UN-MEN
DC / VERTIGO

- ❑1, Feb 1994 .... 2.00
- ❑2, Mar 1994 .... 2.00
- ❑3, Apr 1994 .... 2.00
- ❑4, May 1994 .... 2.00
- ❑5, Jun 1994 .... 2.00

AMERICAN HEROES
PERSONALITY

- ❑1, b&w 2.95

AMERICAN, THE: LOST IN AMERICA
DARK HORSE

- ❑1, Jul 1992 .... 2.50
- ❑2, Aug 1992 .... 2.50
- ❑3, Sep 1992 .... 2.50
- ❑4, Oct 1992 .... 2.50

AMERICAN PRIMITIVE
3-D ZONE

- ❑1, b&w; not 3-D 2.50

AMERICAN SPLENDOR
PEKAR

- ❑1 .... 15.00
- ❑2 .... 10.00
- ❑3 .... 8.00
- ❑4 .... 8.00
- ❑5 .... 8.00
- ❑6 .... 7.00
- ❑7 .... 7.00
- ❑8 .... 7.00
- ❑9 .... 7.00
- ❑10 .... 7.00
- ❑11 .... 6.00
- ❑12 .... 6.00
- ❑13 .... 6.00
- ❑14 .... 12.00
- ❑15 .... 6.00
- ❑17 .... 6.00

AMERICAN SPLENDOR: BEDTIME STORIES
DARK HORSE

- ❑1, Jun 2000 .... 3.95

AMERICAN SPLENDOR: COMIC-CON COMICS
DARK HORSE

- ❑1, Aug 1996, b&w 2.95

AMERICAN SPLENDOR: MUSIC COMICS
DARK HORSE

- ❑1, Nov 1997, b&w; collects Pekar's stories about music 2.95

AMERICAN SPLENDOR: ODDS & ENDS
DARK HORSE

- ❑1, Dec 1997, b&w; collects short pieces 2.95

AMERICAN SPLENDOR: ON THE JOB
DARK HORSE

- ❑1, May 1997, b&w 2.95

AMERICAN SPLENDOR: PORTRAIT OF THE AUTHOR IN HIS DECLINING YEARS
DARK HORSE

- ❑1, Apr 2001 .... 3.99

AMERICAN SPLENDOR: TERMINAL
DARK HORSE

- ❑1, Sep 1999 .... 2.95

AMERICAN SPLENDOR: TRANSATLANTIC COMICS
DARK HORSE

- ❑1, Jul 1998 .... 2.95

AMERICAN SPLENDOR: UNSUNG HERO
DARK HORSE

- ❑1, Aug 2002 .... 3.99
- ❑2, Sep 2002 .... 3.99
- ❑3, Oct 2002 .... 3.99

AMERICAN SPLENDOR: WINDFALL
DARK HORSE

- ❑1 1995, b&w 3.95
- ❑2, Oct 1995, b&w 3.95

AMERICAN SPLENDOR SPECIAL: A STEP OUT OF THE NEST
DARK HORSE

- ❑1, Aug 1994, b&w 2.95

AMERICAN TAIL, AN: FIEVEL GOES WEST
MARVEL

- ❑1 .... 1.25
- ❑2 .... 1.25
- ❑3, Feb 1992 .... 1.25

AMERICAN WOMAN
ANTARCTIC

- ❑1, Jun 1998 .... 2.95
- ❑2, Oct 1998 .... 2.95

AMERICA'S BEST COMICS
AMERICA'S BEST

- ❑Special 1 .... 6.95

AMERICA'S BEST COMICS PREVIEW
AMERICA'S BEST

- ❑1; AMo (w); KN (a); Included in Wizard #91 .... 1.50

AMERICA'S BEST COMICS SKETCHBOOK
DC / AMERICA'S BEST COMICS

- ❑1 .... 5.95

AMERICA'S BEST COMICS TP
DC

- ❑1, ca. 2003 .... 17.95

AMERICA'S BEST TV COMICS
ABC TV

- ❑1, ca. 1967; Giant-size; SL (w); JK, JR (a); promotional comic published by Marvel for ABC to promote Saturday morning cartoons 55.00

AMERICA VS. THE JUSTICE SOCIETY
DC

- ❑1, Jan 1985; Giant-size 1.50
- ❑2, Feb 1985 .... 1.00
- ❑3, Mar 1985; Wizard 1.00
- ❑4, Apr 1985; multiverse (Flash of Two Worlds) 1.00

AMERICOMICS
AC

- ❑1, Apr 1983 .... 2.00
- ❑2, Jun 1983 .... 2.00
- ❑3, Aug 1983 .... 2.00
- ❑4, Oct 1983 .... 2.00
- ❑5, Dec 1983 .... 2.00
- ❑6, Mar 1984 .... 2.00
- ❑Special 1, Jan 1983; Special 2.00

AMETHYST
DC

- ❑1, Jan 1985 RE (a); 1: Fire Jade 1.00
- ❑2, Feb 1985 .... 1.00
- ❑3, Mar 1985 .... 1.00
- ❑4, Apr 1985 .... 1.00
- ❑5, May 1985 .... 1.00
- ❑6, Jun 1985 .... 1.00
- ❑7, Jul 1985 .... 1.00
- ❑8, Aug 1985 .... 1.00
- ❑9, Sep 1985 .... 1.00
- ❑10, Oct 1985 .... 1.00
- ❑11, Nov 1985 .... 1.00
- ❑12, Dec 1985 .... 1.00
- ❑13, Feb 1986 A: Doctor Fate 1.00
- ❑14, Apr 1986 .... 1.00
- ❑15, Jun 1986 1: Child. 1: Flaw 1.00
- ❑16, Aug 1986 .... 1.00
- ❑Special 1, Oct 1986 .... 1.00

AMETHYST (MINI-SERIES)
DC

- ❑1, Nov 1987 .... 1.25
- ❑2, Dec 1987 .... 1.25
- ❑3, Jan 1988 .... 1.25
- ❑4, Feb 1988 .... 1.25

AMETHYST, PRINCESS OF GEMWORLD
DC

- ❑1, May 1983 O: Amethyst 1.00
- ❑2, Jun 1983 .... 1.00
- ❑3, Jul 1983 .... 1.00
- ❑4, Aug 1983 .... 1.00
- ❑5, Sep 1983 .... 1.00
- ❑6, Oct 1983 .... 1.00
- ❑7, Nov 1983 .... 1.00
- ❑8, Dec 1983 .... 1.00
- ❑9, Jan 1984 .... 1.00
- ❑10, Feb 1984 .... 1.00
- ❑11, Mar 1984 .... 1.00
- ❑12, Apr 1984 .... 1.00
- ❑Annual 1 .... 1.25

AMMO ARMAGEDDON
ATOMEKA

- ❑1 .... 4.95

AMNESIA
NBM

- ❑1 .... 9.95

AMORA (GRAY MORROW'S...)
FANTAGRAPHICS / EROS

- ❑1, Apr 1991, b&w 2.95

AMUSING STORIES
RENEGADE

- ❑1, Mar 1987, b&w 2.00

AMY PAPUDA
NORTHSTAR

- ❑1 .... 2.50
- ❑2 .... 2.50

AMY RACECAR COLOR SPECIAL
EL CAPITAN

- ❑1, Jul 1997 .... 2.95
- ❑2, ca. 1999 .... 3.50

ANARCHY COMICS
LAST GASP

- ❑1 .... 2.50
- ❑2 .... 2.50
- ❑3 .... 2.50
- ❑4 .... 2.50

ANARKY
DC

- ❑1, May 1999 .... 2.50
- ❑2, Jun 1999 .... 2.50
- ❑3, Jul 1999 .... 2.50
- ❑4, Aug 1999 .... 2.50
- ❑5, Sep 1999 .... 2.50
- ❑6, Oct 1999 .... 2.50
- ❑7, Nov 1999; Day of Judgment 2.50
- ❑8, Dec 1999 .... 2.50

ANARKY (MINI-SERIES)
DC

- ❑1, May 1997 .... 2.50
- ❑2, Jun 1997 .... 2.50
- ❑3, Jul 1997 .... 2.50
- ❑4, Aug 1997 .... 2.50

N-MINT

ANCIENT JOE
DARK HORSE

❑1, ca. 2001 ... 3.50
❑2, ca. 2001 ... 3.50
❑3, ca. 2002 ... 3.50

ANDROMEDA (ANDROMEDA)
ANDROMEDA

❑1, Mar 1995 ... 2.50
❑2, Apr 1995 ... 2.50

ANDROMEDA (SILVER SNAIL)
SILVER SNAIL

❑1 ... 2.00
❑2 ... 2.00
❑3 ... 2.00
❑4 ... 2.00
❑5 ... 2.00
❑6 ... 2.00

ANDY PANDA (GOLD KEY)
GOLD KEY / WHITMAN

❑1, Aug 1973 ... 4.00
❑2, Nov 1973 ... 2.50
❑3, Feb 1974 ... 2.50
❑4, May 1974 ... 2.50
❑5, Aug 1974 ... 2.00
❑6, Nov 1974 ... 2.00
❑7, Feb 1975 ... 2.00
❑8, May 1975 ... 2.00
❑9 1975 ... 2.00
❑10 1975 ... 2.00
❑11 1976 ... 2.00
❑12 1976 ... 2.00
❑13 1976 ... 2.00
❑14, Jul 1976 ... 2.00
❑15, Sep 1976 ... 2.00
❑16, Nov 1976 ... 2.00
❑17, Jan 1977 ... 2.00
❑18, Mar 1977 ... 2.00
❑19, May 1977 ... 2.00
❑20, Jul 1977 ... 2.00
❑21, Sep 1977 ... 2.00
❑22, Nov 1977 ... 2.00
❑23, Jan 1978 ... 2.00

A-NEXT
MARVEL

❑1, Oct 1998; next generation of Avengers ... 1.99
❑2/A, Nov 1998; Figures busting out of comic page on cover ... 1.99
❑2/B, Nov 1998; Earth Sentry flying on cover ... 1.99
❑3, Dec 1998 ... 1.99
❑4, Jan 1999 ... 1.99
❑5, Feb 1999 ... 1.99
❑6, Mar 1999 ... 1.99
❑7, Apr 1999 ... 1.99
❑8, May 1999 ... 1.99
❑9, Jun 1999 ... 1.99
❑10, Jul 1999 ... 1.99
❑11, Aug 1999 ... 1.99

ANGEL (2ND SERIES)
DARK HORSE

❑1, Nov 1999 ... 3.00
❑1/A, Nov 1999; Dynamic Forces goid logo variant ... 3.00
❑1/Variant, Nov 1999 ... 3.00
❑2, Dec 1999 ... 3.00
❑2/Variant, Dec 1999 ... 3.00
❑3, Jan 2000 ... 3.00
❑3/A, Jan 2000; Valentine's Day Edition; Dynamic Forces purple foil variant (white cover) ... 3.00
❑3/Variant, Jan 2000 ... 3.00
❑4, Feb 2000 ... 3.00
❑4/Variant, Feb 2000 ... 3.00
❑5, Mar 2000 ... 3.00
❑5/Variant, Mar 2000 ... 3.00
❑6, Apr 2000 ... 3.00
❑6/Variant, Apr 2000 ... 3.00
❑7, May 2000 ... 3.00

N-MINT

❑7/A, May 2000; Dynamic Forces Lucky 7 foil variant (limited to 1500 copies) ... 3.00
❑7/Variant, May 2000 ... 3.00
❑8, Jun 2000 ... 3.00
❑8/Variant, Jun 2000 ... 3.00
❑9, Jul 2000 ... 3.00
❑9/Variant, Jul 2000 ... 3.00
❑10, Aug 2000 ... 3.00
❑10/Variant, Aug 2000 ... 3.00
❑11, Sep 2000 ... 2.95
❑11/Variant, Sep 2000 ... 2.95
❑12, Oct 2000 ... 2.99
❑12/Variant, Oct 2000 ... 2.99
❑13, Nov 2000 ... 2.99
❑13/Variant, Nov 2000 ... 2.99
❑14, Dec 2000 ... 2.99
❑14/Variant, Dec 2000 ... 2.99
❑15, Feb 2001 ... 2.99
❑15/Variant, Feb 2001 ... 2.99
❑16, Mar 2001 ... 2.99
❑16/Variant, Mar 2001 ... 2.99
❑17, Apr 2001 ... 2.99
❑17/Variant, Apr 2001 ... 2.99

ANGEL (3RD SERIES)
DARK HORSE

❑1, Sep 2001 ... 2.99
❑1/Variant, Sep 2001 ... 2.99
❑2, Oct 2001 ... 2.99
❑2/Variant, Oct 2001 ... 2.99
❑3, Nov 2001 ... 2.99
❑3/Variant, Nov 2001 ... 2.99
❑4, May 2002 ... 2.99
❑4/Variant, May 2002 ... 2.99

ANGELA
IMAGE

❑1, Dec 1994 NG (w); A: Spawn ... 3.50
❑1/A, Dec 1994; NG (w); A: Spawn. Pirate Spawn cover ... 3.50
❑2, Jan 1995 NG (w); A: Spawn ... 3.00
❑3, Feb 1995 NG (w) ... 3.00

ANGELA/GLORY: RAGE OF ANGELS
IMAGE

❑1/A, Mar 1996 ... 2.50
❑1/B, Mar 1996 ... 2.50

ANGEL AND THE APE
DC

❑1, Nov 1968 ... 25.00
❑2, Jan 1969 ... 20.00
❑3, Mar 1969 ... 15.00
❑4, May 1969 ... 15.00
❑5, Jul 1969 ... 15.00
❑6, Sep 1969 ... 15.00
❑7, Nov 1969 ... 15.00

ANGEL AND THE APE (MINI-SERIES)
DC

❑1, Mar 1991 PF (w); PF (a) ... 1.25
❑2, Apr 1991 PF (a) ... 1.25
❑3, May 1991 PF (a) ... 1.25
❑4, Jun 1991 PF (a) ... 1.25

ANGEL AND THE APE (VERTIGO)
DC / VERTIGO

❑1, Oct 2001 ... 2.95
❑2, Nov 2001 ... 2.95
❑3, Dec 2001 ... 2.95
❑4, Jan 2002 ... 2.95

ANGEL FIRE
CRUSADE

❑1/A, Jun 1997; wraparound photo cover ... 2.95
❑1/B, Jun 1997; black background cover ... 2.95
❑1/C, Jun 1997; white background cover ... 2.95
❑2, Aug 1997 ... 2.95
❑3, Oct 1997, b&w ... 2.95

ANGEL GIRL
ANGEL

❑0 ... 2.95
❑0/Nude; Nude cover ... 5.00

A four-issue series of public-service comics featuring Spider-Man were issued in both U.S. and Canadian editions.

© 1993 Marvel Comics.

N-MINT

ANGEL GIRL: BEFORE THE WINGS
ANGEL

❑1, Aug 1997 ... 2.95

ANGEL GIRL VS. VAMPIRE GIRLS
ANGEL

❑1 ... 2.95
❑1/Nude; Nude edition ... 9.95

ANGELIC LAYER
TOKYOPOP

❑1, Jun 2002, b&w; printed in Japanese format ... 9.99

ANGEL LOVE
DC

❑1, Aug 1986 ... 1.00
❑2, Sep 1986 ... 1.00
❑3, Oct 1986 ... 1.00
❑4, Nov 1986 ... 1.00
❑5, Dec 1986 ... 1.00
❑6, Jan 1987 ... 1.00
❑7, Feb 1987 ... 1.00
❑8, Mar 1987 ... 1.00
❑Annual 1 ... 1.25
❑Special 1 ... 1.25

ANGEL OF DEATH
INNOVATION

❑1 ... 2.25
❑2 ... 2.25
❑3 ... 2.25
❑4 ... 2.25

ANGELS 750
ANTARCTIC

❑1, Apr 2004 ... 2.99

ANGELS OF DESTRUCTION
MALIBU

❑1, Oct 1996 ... 2.50

ANGER GRRRL
BLATANT

❑1, Jun 1999 ... 2.95

ANGRYMAN
CALIBER

❑1 ... 2.50
❑2 ... 2.50
❑3 ... 2.50

ANGRYMAN (2ND SERIES)
ICONOGRAFIX

❑1 ... 2.50
❑2 ... 2.50
❑3 ... 2.50

ANGRY SHADOWS
INNOVATION

❑1, ca. 1989, b&w ... 4.95

ANIMA
DC

❑0, Oct 1994; Series continued in Anima #8 ... 1.75
❑1, Mar 1994 ... 1.75
❑2, Apr 1994 ... 1.75
❑3, May 1994 ... 1.75
❑4, Jun 1994 ... 1.75
❑5, Jul 1994 ... 1.75
❑6, Aug 1994 ... 1.95
❑7, Sep 1994; Zero Hour ... 1.95
❑8, Nov 1994; Series continued from Anima #0 ... 1.95

	N-MINT
❑9, Dec 1994	1.95
❑10, Jan 1995	1.95
❑11, Feb 1995	1.95
❑12, Mar 1995	1.95
❑13, Apr 1995	1.95
❑14, Jun 1995	2.25
❑15, Jul 1995	2.25

ANIMAL CONFIDENTIAL
DARK HORSE

	N-MINT
❑1, May 1992, b&w	2.25

ANIMAL MAN
DC

	N-MINT
❑1, Sep 1988 BB (c)	4.00
❑2, Oct 1988 BB (c)	2.50
❑3, Nov 1988 BB (c)	2.00
❑4, Dec 1988 BB (c); A: B'wana Beast	2.00
❑5, Dec 1988; BB (c); Road Runner-Coyote	2.00
❑6, Jan 1989; BB (c); Invasion!	2.00
❑7, Jan 1989 BB (c)	2.00
❑8, Feb 1989 BB (c); V: Mirror Master	2.00
❑9, Mar 1989 BB (c); A: JLA	2.00
❑10, Apr 1989 BB (c); A: Vixen	2.00
❑11, May 1989 BB (c); A: Vixen	2.00
❑12, Jun 1989 BB (c); A: Vixen	2.00
❑13, Jul 1989 BB (c)	2.00
❑14, Aug 1989 BB (c)	2.00
❑15, Sep 1989 BB (c)	2.00
❑16, Oct 1989 BB (c)	2.00
❑17, Nov 1989 BB (c)	2.00
❑18, Dec 1989 BB (c)	2.00
❑19, Jan 1990 BB (c)	2.00
❑20, Feb 1990 BB (c)	2.00
❑21, Mar 1990 BB (c)	2.00
❑22, Apr 1990 BB (c)	2.00
❑23, May 1990; BB (c); A: Jason Blood. A: Phantom Stranger. Arkham Asylum story	2.00
❑24, Jun 1990 BB (c); A: Inferior Five	2.00
❑25, Jul 1990 BB (c)	2.00
❑26, Aug 1990; BB (c); Morrison puts himself in story	2.00
❑27, Sep 1990 BB (c)	2.00
❑28, Oct 1990 BB (c)	2.00
❑29, Nov 1990 BB (c); D: The Notional Man	2.00
❑30, Dec 1990 BB (c)	2.00
❑31, Jan 1991 BB (c)	2.00
❑32, Feb 1991 BB (c)	2.00
❑33, Mar 1991 BB (c)	2.00
❑34, Apr 1991 BB (c)	2.00
❑35, May 1991 BB (c)	2.00
❑36, Jun 1991 BB (c)	2.00
❑37, Jul 1991 BB (c)	2.00
❑38, Aug 1991; BB (c); Punisher parody	2.00
❑39, Sep 1991	2.00
❑40, Oct 1991	2.00
❑41, Nov 1991	2.00
❑42, Dec 1991	2.00
❑43, Jan 1992	2.00
❑44, Feb 1992	2.00
❑45, Mar 1992	2.00
❑46, Apr 1992	2.00
❑47, May 1992	2.00
❑48, Jun 1992	2.00
❑49, Jul 1992	2.00
❑50, Aug 1992; Giant-size	3.00
❑51, Sep 1992	2.00
❑52, Oct 1992	2.00
❑53, Nov 1992	2.00
❑54, Dec 1992	2.00
❑55, Jan 1993	2.00
❑56, Feb 1993; Giant-size	3.50
❑57, Mar 1993; Begin Vertigo line	2.00
❑58, Apr 1993	2.00
❑59, May 1993	2.00
❑60, Jun 1993 BB (c)	2.00
❑61, Jul 1993	2.00
❑62, Aug 1993	2.00
❑63, Sep 1993	2.00
❑64, Oct 1993	2.00
❑65, Nov 1993	2.00
❑66, Dec 1993	2.00
❑67, Jan 1994	2.00
❑68, Feb 1994	2.00
❑69, Mar 1994	2.00
❑70, Apr 1994	2.00
❑71, May 1994	1.95
❑72, Jun 1994	1.95
❑73, Jul 1994	1.95
❑74, Aug 1994	1.95
❑75, Sep 1994	1.95
❑76, Oct 1994	1.95
❑77, Nov 1994	1.95
❑78, Dec 1994	1.95
❑79, Jan 1995	1.95
❑80, Feb 1995	1.95
❑81, Mar 1995	1.95
❑82, Apr 1995	1.95
❑83, May 1995	2.25
❑84, Jun 1995	2.25
❑85, Jul 1995	2.25
❑86, Aug 1995	2.25
❑87, Sep 1995	2.25
❑88, Oct 1995	2.25
❑89, Nov 1995	2.25
❑Annual 1 BB (c)	4.00

ANIMAL MYSTIC
CRY FOR DAWN

	N-MINT
❑1; published by Cry For Dawn Productions	10.00
❑1/Ltd.; published by Cry For Dawn Productions; w/ alternate covers, 8 add'l pages (story, pin-ups; 1 Linsner pin-up)	10.00
❑1-2, May 1995, b&w; new cover; published by Sirius; new cover	5.00
❑2, Jun 1994, b&w 1: Klor	7.00
❑2-2, May 1995, b&w; New cover; art re-shot for superior reproduction	4.00
❑3, Oct 1994, b&w	5.00
❑3-2	3.00
❑4, Aug 1995, b&w	5.00
❑4/A, Aug 1995; Alternate centerfold	5.00
❑4/Ltd., Aug 1995; Limited edition with different covers and centerfold; Limited edition with different covers and centerfold; 1500 printed	5.00
❑4-2	4.00

ANIMAL MYSTIC WATER WARS
SIRIUS

	N-MINT
❑1, Jun 1996	2.95
❑2, Sep 1996	2.95
❑3, Jan 1997	2.95
❑4, Aug 1997	2.95
❑5, May 1998	2.95
❑6, Oct 1998	2.95
❑Ashcan 1; Preview edition	2.50

ANIMAL RIGHTS COMICS
STABUR

	N-MINT
❑1; Benefit comic for PETA	2.50

ANIMANIACS
DC

	N-MINT
❑1, May 1995 A: Pinky & The Brain	2.50
❑2, Jun 1995	2.00
❑3, Jul 1995	2.00
❑4, Aug 1995	2.00
❑5, Sep 1995	2.00
❑6, Oct 1995	2.00
❑7, Nov 1995	2.00
❑8, Dec 1995	2.00
❑9, Jan 1996; Pulp Fiction parody cover	2.00
❑10, Feb 1996; gratuitous pin-up cover	2.00
❑11, Mar 1996; Brain duplicates himself	1.75
❑12, Apr 1996	1.75
❑13, May 1996	1.75
❑14, Jun 1996	1.75
❑15, Jul 1996	1.75
❑16, Aug 1996; Wrestling issue	1.75
❑17, Sep 1996; Animaniacs judge a beauty contest	1.75
❑18, Oct 1996; All France issue	1.75
❑19, Nov 1996	1.75
❑20, Dec 1996; James Dean tribute	1.75
❑21, Jan 1997; Christmas issue	1.75
❑22, Feb 1997	1.75
❑23, Mar 1997	1.75
❑24, Apr 1997	1.75
❑25, May 1997; Anniversary issue	1.75
❑26, Jun 1997; Tales from the Crypt cover parody	1.75
❑27, Jul 1997; Slappy's plane is hijacked	1.75
❑28, Aug 1997; Star Trek parody; Science issue	1.75
❑29, Sep 1997	1.75
❑30, Oct 1997; "Electra Woman and Dyna Girl" parody	1.75
❑31, Nov 1997; 101 Dalmations parody	1.75
❑32, Dec 1997; Dot hosts a slumber party	1.95
❑33, Jan 1998; 1: Sakko Warner. Lost World cover	1.95
❑34, Feb 1998	1.95
❑35, Mar 1998 A: Freakazoid	1.95
❑36, Apr 1998	1.95
❑37, May 1998	1.95
❑38, Jun 1998; manga-style cover	1.95
❑39, Jul 1998 A: Alfred Nobel	1.95
❑40, Sep 1998; Spice Girls parody	1.95
❑41, Oct 1998; Little Nemo and Little Mermaid parodies	1.95
❑42, Nov 1998; Love Boat parody	1.99
❑43, Dec 1998; Pinky & the Brain	1.99
❑44, Jan 1999; Pinky & the Brain	1.99
❑45, Feb 1999; The Warner Twins; Featuring Pinky and the Brain	1.99
❑46, Mar 1999; Dot the Vampire Slayer; Featuring Pinky and the Brain	1.99
❑47, Apr 1999; Evita parody; Featuring Pinky and the Brain	1.99
❑48, May 1999	1.99
❑49, Jun 1999; literature issue; Featuring Pinky and the Brain; It's the Animaniacal Guide to the Classics!!	1.99
❑50, Jul 1999; Hello Nurse as superhero; Featuring Pinky and the Brain	1.99
❑51, Aug 1999; Featuring Pinky and the Brain	1.99
❑52, Sep 1999; football; Featuring Pinky and the Brain	1.99
❑53, Oct 1999; Featuring Pinky and the Brain	1.99
❑54, Nov 1999	1.99
❑55, Dec 1999; Featuring Pinky and the Brain	1.99
❑56, Jan 2000; Featuring Pinky and the Brain	1.99
❑57, Feb 2000	1.99
❑58, Mar 2000; Hello Nurse, Agent of H.U.B.B.A	1.99
❑59, Apr 2000; Featuring Pinky and the Brain	1.99
❑Holiday 1, Dec 1994; double-sized	2.00

ANIMATION COMICS
VIZ

	N-MINT
❑1	3.95
❑2	3.95
❑3	3.95
❑4; PokÈmon the Movie 2000	3.95

ANIMAX
MARVEL / STAR

	N-MINT
❑1, Dec 1986	1.00
❑2, Jan 1987	1.00
❑3, Feb 1987	1.00
❑4, Mar 1987	1.00

ANIMERICA EXTRA
VIZ

	N-MINT
❑1, ca. 1998	4.95
❑2, ca. 1998	4.95

ANIMERICA EXTRA (VOL. 2)
VIZ

	N-MINT
❑1, Jan 1999	4.95
❑2, Feb 1999	4.95
❑3, Mar 1999	4.95
❑4, Apr 1999	4.95
❑5, May 1999	4.95

N-MINT

❑6, Jun 1999 .... 4.95
❑7, Jul 1999 .... 4.95
❑8, Aug 1999 .... 4.95
❑9, Sep 1999 .... 4.95
❑10, Oct 1999 .... 4.95
❑11, Nov 1999 .... 4.95
❑12, Dec 1999 .... 4.95

ANIMERICA EXTRA (VOL. 3)
VIZ

❑1, Jan 2000 .... 4.95
❑2, Feb 2000 .... 4.95
❑3, Mar 2000 .... 4.95
❑4, Apr 2000 .... 4.95
❑5, May 2000 .... 4.95
❑6, Jun 2000; contains poster 4.95
❑7, Jul 2000 .... 4.95
❑8, Aug 2000 .... 4.95
❑9, Sep 2000 .... 4.95
❑10, Oct 2000 .... 4.95
❑11, Nov 2000 .... 4.95
❑12, Dec 2000 .... 4.95

ANIMERICA EXTRA (VOL. 4)
VIZ

❑1, Jan 2001 .... 4.95
❑2, Feb 2001 .... 4.95
❑3, Mar 2001 .... 4.95
❑4, Apr 2001 .... 4.95
❑5, May 2001 .... 4.95
❑6, Jun 2001 .... 4.95
❑7, Jul 2001 .... 4.95
❑8, Aug 2001 .... 4.95
❑9, Sep 2001 .... 4.95
❑10, Oct 2001 .... 4.95
❑11, Nov 2001 .... 4.95
❑12, Dec 2001 .... 4.95

ANIMERICA EXTRA (VOL. 5)
VIZ

❑1, Jan 2002 .... 4.95
❑2, Feb 2002 .... 4.95
❑3, Mar 2002 .... 4.95
❑4, Apr 2002 .... 4.95
❑5, May 2002 .... 4.95
❑6, Jun 2002 .... 4.95
❑7, Jul 2002 .... 4.95
❑8, Aug 2002 .... 4.95
❑9, Sep 2002 .... 4.95
❑10, Oct 2002 .... 4.95
❑11, Nov 2002 .... 4.95
❑12, Dec 2002 .... 4.95

ANIMERICA EXTRA (VOL. 6)
VIZ

❑1, Jan 2003 .... 4.95

ANIMISM
CENTURION

❑1, Jan 1987 .... 1.50

ANIVERSE, THE
WEEBEE

❑1, Oct 1987 .... 1.95
❑2, Dec 1987 .... 1.95

ANNEX
MARVEL

❑1, Aug 1994 .... 1.75
❑2, Sep 1994 .... 1.75
❑3, Oct 1994 .... 1.75
❑4, Nov 1994 .... 1.75

ANNIE
MARVEL

❑1, Oct 1982; Official movie adaptation 1.00
❑1/Special; Tabloid size 5.00
❑2, Nov 1982; Official movie adaptation 1.00

ANNIE SPRINKLE IS MISS TIMED
RIP OFF

❑1, Sep 1991 .... 2.50
❑2, Oct 1991 .... 2.50
❑3, Nov 1991 .... 2.50
❑4, Dec 1991 .... 2.50

N-MINT

ANOMALIES, THE
ABNORMAL FUN

❑1, Oct 2000 .... 2.95

ANOMALY
BUD PLANT

❑1 .... 8.00
❑2 .... 5.00
❑3 .... 5.00
❑4 .... 5.00

ANOMALY (BRASS RING)
BRASS RING

❑1 .... 3.95
❑2, Jun 2000 .... 3.95

ANOTHER CHANCE TO GET IT RIGHT
DARK HORSE

❑1 .... 9.95
❑1-2, Mar 1995 .... 9.95

ANOTHER DAY
RAISED BROW

❑1, Oct 1995, b&w 2.75
❑2, Aug 1997 .... 2.75

ANTABUSE
HIGH DRIVE

❑1 .... 2.50
❑2 .... 2.50

ANTARCTIC PRESS JAM 1996
ANTARCTIC

❑1, Dec 1996, b&w and color 2.95

ANTARES CIRCLE
ANTARCTIC

❑1 .... 1.95
❑2 .... 1.95

ANT BOY
STEELDRAGON

❑1 .... 1.75
❑2, Oct 1988 .... 1.75

ANT FARM
GALLANT

❑1, Jun 1998 .... 2.50
❑2 .... 2.50

ANTHRO
DC

❑1, Aug 1968 .... 24.00
❑2, Oct 1968 .... 18.00
❑3, Dec 1968 .... 18.00
❑4, Feb 1969 .... 18.00
❑5, Apr 1969 .... 18.00
❑6, Aug 1969 WW (a) 18.00

ANTICIPATOR, THE
FANTASY

❑1 .... 2.25

ANTIETAM: THE FIERY TRAIL
HERITAGE COLLECTION

❑1 1997 .... 3.50

ANTI-HITLER COMICS
NEW ENGLAND

❑1 .... 2.75
❑2 .... 2.75

ANTI-SOCIAL
HELPLESS ANGER

❑1, b&w 2.00
❑2 .... 2.50
❑3 .... 2.50
❑4 .... 2.75

ANTI SOCIAL FOR THE DISABLED
HELPLESS ANGER

❑1, b&w 5.00

ANTI SOCIAL JR.
HELPLESS ANGER

❑1, b&w 1.75

ANT-MAN'S BIG CHRISTMAS
MARVEL

❑1, Feb 2000; prestige format 5.95

ANTON'S DREKBOOK
FANTAGRAPHICS / EROS

❑1, Mar 1991, b&w 2.50

Harvey Pekar's slice-of-life *American Splendor* has been spotlighted by David Letterman.

© 1984 Harvey Pekar.

N-MINT

ANUBIS
SUPER CREW

❑1 .... 2.50

ANUBIS (2ND SERIES)
SUPER CREW

❑1 .... 2.95

ANYTHING BUT MONDAY
ANYTHING BUT MONDAY

❑1, Dec 1988 .... 2.00
❑2 .... 2.00

ANYTHING GOES!
FANTAGRAPHICS

❑1, Oct 1986 .... 2.00
❑2, Dec 1986 .... 2.00
❑3, Mar 1987 .... 2.00
❑4, May 1987 .... 2.00
❑5, Oct 1987; TMNT 2.00
❑6, Oct 1987, b&w 2.00

A-OK
ANTARCTIC

❑1, Sep 1992 .... 2.50
❑2, Nov 1992 .... 2.50
❑3, Jan 1993 .... 2.50
❑4, Mar 1993 .... 2.50

APACHE DICK
ETERNITY

❑1, Feb 1990 .... 2.25
❑2, Mar 1990 .... 2.25
❑3, Apr 1990 .... 2.25
❑4, May 1990 .... 2.25

APACHE SKIES
MARVEL

❑1, Sep 2002 ....
❑2, Oct 2002 ....
❑3, Nov 2002 ....
❑4, Dec 2002 ....

APACHE TRAIL
STEINWAY

❑1, Sep 1957 .... 58.00
❑2, Nov 1957 .... 36.00
❑3, Feb 1958 .... 36.00
❑4, Jun 1958 .... 36.00

APATHY KAT
EXPRESS / ENTITY

❑1, ca. 1995, b&w 2.50
❑2, ca. 1996 .... 2.75
❑3, ca. 1996 .... 2.75
❑4, ca. 1996 .... 2.75

APE CITY
ADVENTURE

❑1; Planet of the Apes story 2.50
❑2; Planet of the Apes story 2.50
❑3; Planet of the Apes story 2.50
❑4; Planet of the Apes story 2.50

APE NATION
ADVENTURE

❑1, Feb 1991; Alien Nation/Planet of Apes crossover 2.50
❑1/Ltd.; limited edition; Alien Nation/ Planet of the Apes crossover 4.00
❑2, Apr 1991; Alien Nation/Planet of the Apes crossover 2.00

N-MINT

❑3, May 1991; Alien Nation/Planet of the Apes crossover 2.00
❑4, Jun 1991; Alien Nation/Planet of the Apes crossover 2.00

APEX
Aztec

❑1, b&w 2.00

APEX PROJECT, THE
Stellar

❑1 1.00
❑2 1.00

APHRODISIA
Fantagraphics / Eros

❑1 2.95
❑2, Mar 1995 2.95

APHRODITE IX
Image

❑0, Mar 2001; Posterior shot on cover 2.00
❑0-2, Oct 2001 5.95
❑0/A, May 2001; Wizard Gold Foil Edition 9.00
❑0/B, May 2001; Wizard Blue Foil Edition 9.00
❑0/C, Mar 2001; Green foil behind logo 4.00
❑0/D, Mar 2001; Dynamic Forces Gold foil behind title 4.00
❑0/E, Mar 2001; Identical cover to #0; Limited to 250 4.00
❑0/F, Mar 2001; Limited to 50 4.00
❑1/A, Sep 2000; Aphrodite reclining against left edge of cover, gun up 4.00
❑1/B, Sep 2000; Aphrodite walking on metallic planks 2.50
❑1/C, Sep 2000; Red background, Aphrodite shooting on cover 2.50
❑1/D, Sep 2000; Green background, standing with guns up 2.50
❑1/E, Sep 2000; Tower records exclusive 5.00
❑1/F, Sep 2000; Tower records exclusive w/foil 5.00
❑1/G, Sep 2000; Wizard World exclusive 4.00
❑1/H, Sep 2000; Wizard World exclusive w/foil 4.00
❑1/I, Sep 2000; Chrome edition of 3,000; Dynamic Forces exclusive 5.00
❑2, Mar 2001 2.00
❑2/A; Graham Crackers comics exclusive 2.50
❑2/B; Blue Foil behind title; connects to Dynamic Forces Exclusive; Graham Crackers Comics/Midwest Comics Co. Exclusive 2.50
❑2/C; connects to Dynamic Forces Exclusive; Graham Crackers Comics/Midwest Comics Co. Exclusive; Green Foil behind title 2.50
❑2/D; Several characters in profile on cover; connects to Graham Crackers Comics/Midwest Comics Co. Exclusive; Dynamic Forces Exclusive 2.50
❑2/E; connects to Graham Crackers Comics/Midwest Comics Co. Exclusive; Dynamic Forces Exclusive 2.50
❑2/F; connects to Graham Crackers Comics/Midwest Comics Co. Exclusive; Dynamic Forces Exclusive 2.50
❑2/G; Blue Foil behind title; connects to Graham Crackers Comics/Midwest Comics Co. Exclusive; Exclusive/Wizard World Authentic 2.50
❑2/H; Blue Foil behind title; connects to Graham Crackers Comics/Midwest Comics Co. Exclusive; Dynamic Forces Exclusive/Wizard Authentic 2.50
❑2/I; connects to Graham Crackers Comics/Midwest Comics Co. Exclusive; Dynamic Forces Exclusive; Green Foil behind title 2.50
❑2/J; connects to Graham Crackers Comics/Midwest Comics Co. Exclusive; Dynamic Forces Exclusive; Green Foil behind title 2.50
❑2/K; connects to Graham Crackers Comics/Midwest Comics Co. Exclusive; Dynamic Forces Exclusive 2.50
❑3 2.00
❑4, Mar 2002; Double-size 4.00
❑4/A; sketch cover; Published/solicited by Jay Company Comics 4.95
❑Ashcan 1, Dec 2000; Convention Preview 6.00
❑Ashcan 1/Ltd.; Original color sketch and signature by Clarence Lansang; Solicited by Jay Company Comics 5.00

APOCALYPSE
Apocalypse

❑1 3.95
❑2 3.95
❑3 3.95
❑4 3.95
❑5 3.95
❑6 3.95
❑7; Makabre 3.95

APOCALYPSE: THE EYES OF DOOM
Kitchen Sink

❑1 14.95

APOLLO SMILE
Mixx

❑1, Jul 1998 3.50
❑2, Sep 1998 3.00

APPARITION, THE
Caliber

❑1 1996 2.95
❑2 1996 2.95
❑3 1996 2.95
❑4 1996 2.95
❑5 1996 2.95

APPARITION, THE: ABANDONED
Caliber

❑1 1995; prestige format 3.95

APPARITION, THE: VISITATIONS
Caliber

❑1, Aug 1995 3.95

APPLE, P.I.
Parrot Communications

❑1, Sep 1996; pronounced "Apple Pie" 1.00

APPLESEED BOOK 1
Eclipse

❑1, Sep 1988 7.00
❑2, Oct 1988 5.00
❑3, Nov 1988; Squarebound 5.00
❑4, Jan 1989 4.00
❑5, Feb 1989 4.00

APPLESEED BOOK 2
Eclipse

❑1, Feb 1989 5.00
❑2, Mar 1989 4.00
❑3, Apr 1989 3.50
❑4, May 1989 3.50
❑5, Jun 1989 3.50

APPLESEED BOOK 3
Eclipse

❑1, Aug 1989; Squarebound 4.00
❑2, Sep 1989 3.50
❑3, Oct 1989 3.50
❑4, Nov 1989 3.50
❑5, Dec 1989 3.50

APPLESEED BOOK 4
Eclipse

❑1, Jan 1991 3.50
❑2, Mar 1991 3.50
❑3, May 1991 3.50
❑4, Aug 1991 3.50

APPLESEED DATABOOK
Dark Horse

❑1, Apr 1994 3.50
❑2, May 1994; Flip-book; Squarebound 3.50

APRIL HORRORS
Rip Off

❑1, Sep 1993, b&w 2.95

AQUABLUE
Dark Horse

❑1, Nov 1989 6.95

AQUABLUE: THE BLUE PLANET
Dark Horse

❑1, Aug 1990 8.95

AQUA KNIGHT
Viz

❑1, ca. 2000 2.95
❑2, ca. 2000 3.50
❑3, ca. 2000 3.50
❑4, ca. 2000 3.50
❑5, ca. 2000 3.50
❑6, ca. 2000 3.50

AQUA KNIGHT PART 2
Viz

❑1, Oct 2000 3.50
❑2, Nov 2000 3.50
❑3, Dec 2000 3.50
❑4, Jan 2001 3.50
❑5, Feb 2001 3.50

AQUA KNIGHT PART 3
Viz

❑1, ca. 2001 3.50
❑2, ca. 2001 3.50
❑3, ca. 2001 3.50
❑4, ca. 2001 3.50
❑5, ca. 2001 3.50

AQUAMAN (1ST SERIES)
DC

❑1, Feb 1962 1: Quisp 410.00
❑2, Apr 1962 100.00
❑3, Jun 1962 55.00
❑4, Aug 1962 55.00
❑5, Oct 1962 55.00
❑6, Dec 1962 45.00
❑7, Feb 1963 45.00
❑8, Apr 1963 45.00
❑9, Jun 1963 45.00
❑10, Aug 1963 45.00
❑11, Oct 1963 1: Mera 45.00
❑12, Dec 1963 45.00
❑13, Feb 1964 40.00
❑14, Apr 1964 40.00
❑15, Jun 1964 40.00
❑16, Aug 1964 40.00
❑17, Oct 1964 50.00
❑18, Dec 1964; A: Justice League of America. Aquaman marries Mera 40.00
❑19, Feb 1965 30.00
❑20, Apr 1965 30.00
❑21, Jun 1965 1: Fisherman 30.00
❑22, Aug 1965 35.00
❑23, Oct 1965; Birth of Aquababy 35.00
❑24, Dec 1965 35.00
❑25, Feb 1966 35.00
❑26, Apr 1966 35.00
❑27, Jun 1966 35.00
❑28, Aug 1966 35.00
❑29, Oct 1966 1: Ocean Master 35.00
❑30, Dec 1966 35.00
❑31, Feb 1967 25.00
❑32, Apr 1967 25.00
❑33, Jun 1967 1: Aqua-Girl 25.00
❑34, Aug 1967 25.00
❑35, Oct 1967 1: Black Manta 20.00
❑36, Dec 1967 20.00
❑37, Feb 1968 20.00
❑38, Apr 1968 20.00
❑39, Jun 1968 20.00
❑40, Aug 1968 20.00
❑41, Oct 1968 20.00
❑42, Dec 1968 20.00
❑43, Feb 1969 20.00
❑44, Apr 1969 18.00
❑45, Jun 1969 18.00
❑46, Aug 1969 18.00
❑47, Oct 1969 58.00
❑48, Dec 1969 JA (a); O: Aquaman 18.00
❑49, Feb 1970 JA (a) 18.00
❑50, Apr 1970 NA (a); A: Deadman 18.00
❑51, Jun 1970 NA (a); A: Deadman 18.00
❑52, Aug 1970 NA (a); A: Deadman 29.00

	N-MINT
❑53, Oct 1970 JA (a)	15.00
❑54, Dec 1970 JA (a)	15.00
❑55, Feb 1971 JA (a)	15.00
❑56, Apr 1971 JA (a); O: Crusader. 1: Crusader	15.00
❑57, Aug 1977 JA (a)	15.00
❑58, Oct 1977 JA (a); O: Aquaman	15.00
❑59, Dec 1977	7.00
❑60, Feb 1978	7.00
❑61, Apr 1978	7.00
❑62, Jun 1978	7.00
❑63, Sep 1978	7.00

AQUAMAN (2ND SERIES)
DC

	N-MINT
❑1, Feb 1986; New costume	3.00
❑2, Mar 1986	2.50
❑3, Apr 1986	2.50
❑4, May 1986	2.50
❑Special 1, Jun 1988	2.50

AQUAMAN (3RD SERIES)
DC

	N-MINT
❑1, Jun 1989 KG, CS (a)	1.50
❑2, Jul 1989	1.50
❑3, Aug 1989	1.50
❑4, Sep 1989 CS (a)	1.50
❑5, Oct 1989	1.50
❑Special 1, Apr 1989; KG, CS (a); Legend of Aquaman	2.00

AQUAMAN (4TH SERIES)
DC

	N-MINT
❑1, Dec 1991	1.50
❑2, Jan 1992	1.00
❑3, Feb 1992	1.00
❑4, Mar 1992	1.00
❑5, Apr 1992	1.00
❑6, May 1992	1.25
❑7, Jun 1992	1.25
❑8, Jul 1992 A: Batman. V: Nicodemus	1.25
❑9, Aug 1992	1.25
❑10, Sep 1992	1.25
❑11, Oct 1992	1.25
❑12, Nov 1992	1.25
❑13, Dec 1992 A: Scavanger.	1.25

AQUAMAN (5TH SERIES)
DC

	N-MINT
❑0, Oct 1994; PD (w); Aquaman gets harpoon for arm	3.00
❑1, Aug 1994 PD (w)	3.00
❑2, Sep 1994; PD (w); V: Charybdis. Aquaman loses hand	3.00
❑3, Nov 1994 PD (w); V: Superboy	2.00
❑4, Dec 1994 PD (w); A: Lobo. V: Lobo	2.00
❑5, Jan 1995 PD (w)	2.00
❑6, Feb 1995 PD (w)	1.50
❑7, Mar 1995 PD (w)	1.50
❑8, Apr 1995 PD (w)	1.50
❑9, Jun 1995 PD (w)	1.75
❑10, Jul 1995 PD (w)	1.75
❑11, Aug 1995 PD (w)	1.75
❑12, Sep 1995; PD (w); Mera returns	1.75
❑13, Oct 1995 PD (w)	1.75
❑14, Nov 1995; PD (w); "Underworld Unleashed"	1.75
❑15, Dec 1995 PD (w)	1.75
❑16, Jan 1996 PD (w); V: Justice League	1.75
❑17, Feb 1996 PD (w)	1.75
❑18, Mar 1996 PD (w); O: Dolphin	1.75
❑19, Apr 1996; PD (w); Aqualad returns	1.75
❑20, May 1996 PD (w)	1.75
❑21, Jun 1996 PD (w)	1.75
❑22, Jul 1996 PD (w)	1.75
❑23, Aug 1996 PD (w); A: Sea Devils, Power Girl, Tsunami, Arion	1.75
❑24, Sep 1996 PD (w)	1.75
❑25, Oct 1996 PD (w)	1.75
❑26, Nov 1996; PD (w); "Final Night"	1.75
❑27, Dec 1996; PD (w); Aquaman declares war on Japan	1.75
❑28, Jan 1997 PD (w); A: Martian Manhunter	1.75
❑29, Feb 1997 PD (w); V: Black Manta	1.75
❑30, Mar 1997 PD (w)	1.75
❑31, Apr 1997 PD (w)	1.75
❑32, May 1997 PD (w); A: Swamp Thing	1.75
❑33, Jun 1997 PD (w)	1.75
❑34, Jul 1997 PD (w); V: Triton	1.75
❑35, Aug 1997; PD (w); A: Animal Man. V: Gamesman. Aquaman blind	1.75
❑36, Sep 1997 PD (w)	1.75
❑37, Oct 1997; PD (w); V: Parademons. "Genesis"	1.75
❑38, Nov 1997; PD (w); Poseidonis becomes a tourist attraction	1.75
❑39, Dec 1997; PD (w); A: Neptune Perkins. Face cover	2.00
❑40, Jan 1998 PD (w); V: Doctor Polaris	2.00
❑41, Feb 1998 PD (w); A: Maxima	2.00
❑42, Mar 1998 PD (w); V: Sea Wolf	2.00
❑43, Apr 1998; "Millennium Giants"	2.00
❑44, May 1998 A: Golden Age Flash. A: Sentinel	2.00
❑45, Jun 1998; Destruction of Poseidonis	2.00
❑46, Jul 1998	2.00
❑47, Aug 1998	2.00
❑48, Sep 1998	2.00
❑49, Oct 1998	2.00
❑50, Dec 1998 EL (c); EL (a)	2.00
❑51, Jan 1999 EL (c); EL (w); EL (a); A: King Noble	2.00
❑52, Feb 1999 EL (w); BSz, EL, JA (a); A: Fire Trolls. A: Mera. A: Lava Lord. A: Noble	2.00
❑53, Mar 1999 EL (w); EL (a); A: Superman. A: Shrapnel	2.00
❑54, Apr 1999 EL (w); EL (a); A: Sheeva the Mermaid. A: Landlovers. A: Blubber. A: Lagoon Boy	2.00
❑55, May 1999 EL (w); EL (a)	2.00
❑56, Jun 1999 EL (w); EL (a)	2.00
❑57, Jul 1999 EL (w); EL (a)	2.00
❑58, Aug 1999 EL (w); EL (a)	2.00
❑59, Sep 1999 EL (w); EL (a)	2.00
❑60, Oct 1999; EL (w); EL (a); Wedding of Tempest and Dolphin	2.00
❑61, Nov 1999	2.00
❑62, Dec 1999 EL (w)	2.00
❑63, Jan 2000	2.00
❑64, Feb 2000	2.00
❑65, Mar 2000	2.00
❑66, Apr 2000	2.00
❑67, May 2000	2.00
❑68, Jun 2000	2.00
❑69, Jul 2000	2.00
❑70, Aug 2000	2.00
❑71, Sep 2000 A: Warlord	2.50
❑72, Oct 2000	2.50
❑73, Nov 2000	2.50
❑74, Dec 2000	2.50
❑75, Jan 2001	2.50
❑1000000, Nov 1998	3.00
❑Annual 1, ca. 1995 A: Superman A: Wonder Woman	3.50
❑Annual 2, ca. 1996; Legends of the Dead Earth	2.95
❑Annual 3, Jul 1997; Pulp Heroes	3.95
❑Annual 4, Sep 1998; Ghosts	2.95
❑Annual 5, Sep 1999; JLApe	2.95

AQUAMAN (6TH SERIES)
DC

	N-MINT
❑1, Feb 2003; Aquaman receives water hand	2.50
❑2, Mar 2003	2.50
❑3, Apr 2003	2.50
❑4, May 2003	2.50
❑5, Jun 2003	2.50
❑6, Jul 2003	2.50
❑7, Aug 2003	2.50
❑8, Sep 2003	2.50
❑9, Oct 2003	2.50
❑10, Nov 2003	2.50
❑11, Dec 2003	2.50
❑12, Jan 2004	2.50
❑13, Feb 2004	2.50

Animaniacs has featured several cover parodies including this *Tales from the Crypt* rif.
© 1997 DC Comics and Warner Bros. Animation.

	N-MINT
❑14, Mar 2004	2.50
❑15, Apr 2004	12.00
❑16, May 2004	6.00
❑17, Jun 2004	6.00
❑18, Jul 2004	2.50
❑19, Aug 2004	2.50
❑20, Jul 2004	

AQUAMAN SECRET FILES
DC

	N-MINT
❑1, Dec 1998	4.95
❑2, Mar 2003	4.95

AQUAMAN: TIME AND TIDE
DC

	N-MINT
❑1, Dec 1993 PD (w); O: Aquaman	2.00
❑2, Jan 1994 PD (w)	2.00
❑3, Feb 1994 PD (w)	2.00
❑4, Mar 1994 PD (w); O: Ocean Master	2.00

AQUARIUM
CPM MANGA

	N-MINT
❑1/A, Apr 2000, b&w; wraparound cover	2.95
❑1/B, Apr 2000, b&w; alternate wraparound cover	2.95
❑2, ca. 2000, b&w	2.95
❑3, ca. 2000, b&w	2.95
❑4, ca. 2000, b&w	2.95
❑5, ca. 2000, b&w	2.95
❑6, ca. 2000, b&w	2.95

ARABIAN NIGHTS ON THE WORLD OF MAGIC: THE GATHERING
ACCLAIM / ARMADA

	N-MINT
❑1, Dec 1995	2.50
❑2	2.50

ARACHNOPHOBIA
DISNEY

	N-MINT
❑1	2.95

ARAGONÉS 3-D
3-D ZONE

	N-MINT
❑1; paperback	4.95

ARAKNIS
MUSHROOM

	N-MINT
❑0, Apr 1996; Published by Mystic	2.50
❑1, May 1995	2.50
❑2, ca. 1996	2.50
❑3, ca. 1996	2.50
❑4, ca. 1996	2.50
❑5, ca. 1996	2.50
❑6, ca. 1996	2.50

ARAK SON OF THUNDER
DC

	N-MINT
❑1, Sep 1981 O: Arak. 1: Angelica	1.00
❑2, Oct 1981 1: Malagigi	1.00
❑3, Nov 1981 1: Valda	1.00
❑4, Dec 1981	1.00
❑5, Jan 1982	1.00
❑6, Feb 1982	1.00
❑7, Mar 1982	1.00
❑8, Apr 1982	1.00
❑9, May 1982	1.00
❑10, Jun 1982	1.00
❑11, Jul 1982	1.00
❑12, Aug 1982	1.00
❑13, Sep 1982	1.00
❑14, Oct 1982	1.00
❑15, Nov 1982	1.00

	N-MINT
❑16, Dec 1982	1.00
❑17, Jan 1983	1.00
❑18, Feb 1983	1.00
❑19, Mar 1983	1.00
❑20, Apr 1983 O: Angelica	1.00
❑21, May 1983	1.00
❑22, Jun 1983	1.00
❑23, Jul 1983	1.00
❑24, Aug 1983	1.00
❑25, Sep 1983	1.00
❑26, Oct 1983	1.00
❑27, Nov 1983	1.00
❑28, Dec 1983	1.00
❑29, Jan 1984	1.00
❑30, Feb 1984	1.00
❑31, Mar 1984	1.00
❑32, Apr 1984	1.00
❑33, May 1984	1.00
❑34, Jun 1984	1.00
❑35, Jul 1984	1.00
❑36, Aug 1984	1.00
❑37, Sep 1984	1.00
❑38, Nov 1984	1.00
❑39, Dec 1984	1.00
❑40, Jan 1985	1.00
❑41, Feb 1985	1.00
❑42, Mar 1985	1.00
❑43, Apr 1985	1.00
❑44, May 1985	1.00
❑45, Jun 1985	1.00
❑46, Jul 1985	1.00
❑47, Aug 1985	1.00
❑48, Sep 1985	1.00
❑49, Oct 1985	1.00
❑50, Nov 1985; Giant-size	1.00
❑Annual 1	1.00

ARAMIS
COMICS INTERVIEW

	N-MINT
❑1	1.95
❑2	1.95
❑3	1.95

ARC (VOL. 2)
ARTS INDUSTRIA

	N-MINT
❑1, Apr 1994	

ARCADE
PRINT MINT

	N-MINT
❑1, Mar 1975	10.00
❑2, Jun 1975	8.00
❑3, Sep 1975	8.00
❑4	7.00
❑5	7.00
❑6, Jun 1976	7.00
❑7	5.00

ARCANA
DC / VERTIGO

	N-MINT
❑Annual 1, ca. 1994, "Children's Crusade"	4.00

ARCANA (WELLS & CLARK)
WELLS & CLARK

	N-MINT
❑1	3.00
❑2, Mar 1995	3.00
❑3, May 1995	3.00
❑4, Jul 1995	2.25
❑5, Sep 1995	2.25
❑6	2.25
❑7	2.25
❑8, Jul 1996	2.25
❑9, Sep 1996	2.25
❑10	2.25

ARCANE
ARCANE

	N-MINT
❑1	2.00
❑2; Fly in My Eye	9.95

ARCANE (2ND SERIES)
GRAPHIK

	N-MINT
❑1, b&w	1.25

ARCANUM
IMAGE

	N-MINT
❑0.5, Dec 1997	3.00
❑0.5/Gold, Dec 1997	5.00
❑1, Apr 1997	2.50
❑1/A, Apr 1997; variant cover	2.50
❑2, May 1997	2.50
❑2/A, May 1997; variant cover	2.50
❑3, Jun 1997	2.50
❑3/A, Jun 1997; variant cover	2.50
❑4, Jul 1997	2.50
❑4/A, Jul 1997; variant cover	2.50
❑5, Sep 1997	2.95
❑6, Nov 1997	2.95
❑7, Jan 1998	2.95
❑8, Feb 1998	2.95

ARCHANGEL
MARVEL

	N-MINT
❑1, Feb 1996, b&w; wraparound cover	2.50

ARCHANGELS: THE SAGA
ETERNAL

	N-MINT
❑1	2.50
❑1-2	2.50
❑2	2.50
❑3, Aug 1996	2.50
❑4	2.50
❑5	2.50
❑6	2.50
❑7	2.50
❑8	2.50

ARCHARD'S AGENTS
CROSSGEN

	N-MINT
❑1	2.95

ARCHER & ARMSTRONG
VALIANT

	N-MINT
❑0, Jul 1992 BL (w); O: Archer & Armstrong	2.50
❑0/Gold, Jul 1992; Gold edition BL (w); O: Archer & Armstrong	3.00
❑1, Aug 1992; FM (c); FM (a); Unity	2.50
❑2, Sep 1992; Unity	2.50
❑3, Oct 1992	2.50
❑4, Nov 1992	2.50
❑5, Dec 1992	2.50
❑6, Jan 1993	2.50
❑7, Feb 1993	2.50
❑8, Mar 1993; Double-sized: is also "Eternal Warrior #8"; 1: Timewalker (Ivar). Flip-book with Eternal Warrior #8	4.50
❑9, Apr 1993 BL (w); 1: Mademoiselle Noir	2.50
❑10, May 1993	2.50
❑11, Jun 1993 A: Solar	2.50
❑12, Jul 1993	2.50
❑13, Aug 1993	2.50
❑14, Sep 1993	2.50
❑15, Oct 1993	2.50
❑16, Nov 1993	2.50
❑17, Dec 1993	2.50
❑18, Jan 1994	2.50
❑19, Feb 1994	2.50
❑20, Mar 1994	2.50
❑21, Apr 1994 A: Shadowman	2.50
❑22, May 1994; trading card	2.50
❑23, Jun 1994	2.50
❑24, Aug 1994	2.50
❑25, Sep 1994 A: Eternal Warrior	2.50
❑26, Oct 1994; Flip-book with Eternal Warrior #26; indicia says August	2.75

ARCHIE
ARCHIE

	N-MINT
❑83, Nov 1956	44.00
❑84, Jan 1957	44.00
❑85, Mar 1957	44.00
❑86, May 1957	44.00
❑87, Jul 1957	44.00
❑88, Sep 1957	44.00
❑89, Nov 1957	44.00
❑90, Jan 1958	44.00
❑91, Mar 1958	34.00
❑92, May 1958	34.00
❑93, Jul 1958	34.00
❑94, Sep 1958	34.00
❑95, Oct 1958	34.00
❑96, Nov 1958	34.00
❑97, Dec 1958	34.00
❑98, Feb 1959	34.00
❑99, Mar 1959	34.00
❑100, Apr 1959	55.00
❑101, Jun 1959	22.00
❑102, Jul 1959	22.00
❑103, Aug 1959	22.00
❑104, Sep 1959	22.00
❑105, Nov 1959	22.00
❑106, Dec 1959	22.00
❑107, Feb 1960	22.00
❑108, Mar 1960	22.00
❑109, Apr 1960	22.00
❑110, Jun 1960	22.00
❑111, Jul 1960	22.00
❑112, Aug 1960	22.00
❑113, Sep 1960	22.00
❑114, Nov 1960	22.00
❑115, Dec 1960	22.00
❑116, Feb 1961	22.00
❑117, Mar 1961	22.00
❑118, Apr 1961	22.00
❑119, Jun 1961	22.00
❑120, Jul 1961	22.00
❑121, Aug 1961	16.00
❑122, Sep 1961	16.00
❑123, Nov 1961	16.00
❑124, Dec 1961	16.00
❑125, Feb 1962	16.00
❑126, Mar 1962	16.00
❑127, Apr 1962	16.00
❑128, Jun 1962	16.00
❑129, Jul 1962	16.00
❑130, Aug 1962	16.00
❑131, Sep 1962	16.00
❑132, Nov 1962	16.00
❑133, Dec 1962	16.00
❑134, Feb 1963	16.00
❑135, Mar 1963	16.00
❑136, Apr 1963	16.00
❑137, Jun 1963	16.00
❑138, Jul 1963	16.00
❑139, Aug 1963	16.00
❑140, Sep 1963	16.00
❑141, Nov 1963	13.00
❑142, Dec 1963	13.00
❑143, Feb 1964	13.00
❑144, Mar 1964	13.00
❑145, Apr 1964	13.00
❑146, Jun 1964	13.00
❑147, Jul 1964	13.00
❑148, Aug 1964	13.00
❑149, Sep 1964	13.00
❑150, Nov 1964	13.00
❑151, Dec 1964	8.50
❑152, Feb 1965	8.50
❑153, Mar 1965	8.50
❑154, Apr 1965	8.50
❑155, Jun 1965	8.50
❑156, Jul 1965	8.50
❑157, Aug 1965	8.50
❑158, Sep 1965	8.50
❑159, Nov 1965	8.50
❑160, Dec 1965	8.50
❑161, Feb 1966	8.50
❑162, Mar 1966	8.50
❑163, Apr 1966	8.50
❑164, Jun 1966	8.50
❑165, Jul 1966	8.50
❑166, Aug 1966	8.50
❑167, Sep 1966	8.50
❑168, Nov 1966	8.50
❑169, Dec 1966	8.50
❑170, Feb 1967	8.50
❑171, Mar 1967	8.50
❑172, Apr 1967	8.50
❑173, Jun 1967	8.50

	N-MINT
❑174, Jul 1967	8.50
❑175, Aug 1967	8.50
❑176, Sep 1967	8.50
❑177, Nov 1967	8.50
❑178, Dec 1967	8.50
❑179, Feb 1968	8.50
❑180, Mar 1968	8.50
❑181, Apr 1968	5.00
❑182, Jun 1968	5.00
❑183, Jul 1968	5.00
❑184, Aug 1968	5.00
❑185, Sep 1968	5.00
❑186, Nov 1968	5.00
❑187, Dec 1968	5.00
❑188, Feb 1969	5.00
❑189, Mar 1969	5.00
❑190, Apr 1969	5.00
❑191, Jun 1969	5.00
❑192, Jul 1969	5.00
❑193, Aug 1969	5.00
❑194, Sep 1969	5.00
❑195, Nov 1969	5.00
❑196, Dec 1969	5.00
❑197, Feb 1970	5.00
❑198, Mar 1970	5.00
❑199, Apr 1970	5.00
❑200, Jun 1970	5.00
❑201, Jul 1970	3.00
❑202, Aug 1970	3.00
❑203, Sep 1970	3.00
❑204, Nov 1970	3.00
❑205, Dec 1970	3.00
❑206, Feb 1971	3.00
❑207, Mar 1971	3.00
❑208, May 1971	3.00
❑209, Jun 1971	3.00
❑210, Jul 1971	3.00
❑211, Aug 1971	3.00
❑212, Sep 1971	3.00
❑213, Nov 1971	3.00
❑214, Dec 1971	3.00
❑215, Feb 1972	3.00
❑216, Mar 1972	3.00
❑217, Apr 1972	3.00
❑218, Jun 1972	3.00
❑219, Jul 1972	3.00
❑220, Aug 1972	3.00
❑221, Sep 1972	3.00
❑222, Nov 1972	3.00
❑223, Dec 1972	3.00
❑224, Feb 1973	3.00
❑225, Apr 1973	3.00
❑226, Jun 1973	3.00
❑227, Jul 1973	3.00
❑228, Aug 1973	3.00
❑229, Sep 1973	3.00
❑230, Nov 1973	3.00
❑231, Dec 1973	3.00
❑232, Feb 1974	3.00
❑233, Mar 1974	3.00
❑234, Apr 1974	3.00
❑235, Jun 1974	3.00
❑236, Jul 1974	3.00
❑237, Aug 1974	3.00
❑238, Sep 1974	3.00
❑239, Nov 1974	3.00
❑240, Dec 1974	3.00
❑241, Feb 1975	3.00
❑242, Mar 1975	3.00
❑243, Apr 1975	3.00
❑244, Jun 1975	3.00
❑245, Jul 1975	3.00
❑246, Aug 1975	3.00
❑247, Sep 1975	3.00
❑248, Nov 1975	3.00
❑249, Dec 1975	3.00
❑250, Feb 1976	3.00
❑251, Mar 1976	2.00
❑252, Apr 1976	2.00
❑253, Jun 1976	2.00
❑254, Jul 1976	2.00

	N-MINT
❑255, Aug 1976	2.00
❑256, Sep 1976	2.00
❑257, Nov 1976	2.00
❑258, Dec 1976	2.00
❑259, Feb 1977	2.00
❑260, Mar 1977	2.00
❑261, Apr 1977	2.00
❑262, Jun 1977	2.00
❑263, Jul 1977	2.00
❑264, Aug 1977	2.00
❑265, Sep 1977	2.00
❑266, Nov 1977	2.00
❑267, Dec 1977	2.00
❑268, Feb 1978	2.00
❑269, Mar 1978	2.00
❑270, Apr 1978	2.00
❑271, Jun 1978	2.00
❑272, Jul 1978	2.00
❑273, Aug 1978	2.00
❑274, Sep 1978	2.00
❑275, Nov 1978	2.00
❑276, Dec 1978	2.00
❑277, Feb 1979	2.00
❑278, Mar 1979	2.00
❑279, Apr 1979	2.00
❑280, May 1979	2.00
❑281, Jun 1979	2.00
❑282, Jul 1979	2.00
❑283, Aug 1979	2.00
❑284, Sep 1979	2.00
❑285, Oct 1979	2.00
❑286, Nov 1979	2.00
❑287, Dec 1979	2.00
❑288, Jan 1980	2.00
❑289, Feb 1980	2.00
❑290, Mar 1980	2.00
❑291, Apr 1980	2.00
❑292, May 1980	2.00
❑293, Jun 1980	2.00
❑294, Jul 1980	2.00
❑295, Aug 1980	2.00
❑296, Sep 1980	2.00
❑297, Oct 1980	2.00
❑298, Nov 1980	2.00
❑299, Dec 1980	2.00
❑300, Jan 1981	2.00
❑301, Feb 1981	1.50
❑302, Mar 1981	1.50
❑303, Apr 1981	1.50
❑304, May 1981	1.50
❑305, Jun 1981	1.50
❑306, Jul 1981	1.50
❑307, Aug 1981	1.50
❑308, Sep 1981	1.50
❑309, Oct 1981	1.50
❑310, Nov 1981	1.50
❑311, Dec 1981	1.50
❑312, Jan 1982	1.50
❑313, Feb 1982	1.50
❑314, Mar 1982	1.50
❑315, Apr 1982	1.50
❑316, May 1982	1.50
❑317, Jun 1982	1.50
❑318, Jul 1982	1.50
❑319, Sep 1982	1.50
❑320, Nov 1982	1.50
❑321, Jan 1983	1.50
❑322, Mar 1983	1.50
❑323, May 1983	1.50
❑324, Jul 1983	1.50
❑325, Sep 1983	1.50
❑326, Nov 1983	1.50
❑327, Jan 1984	1.50
❑328, Mar 1984	1.50
❑329, May 1984	1.50
❑330, Jul 1984	1.50
❑331, Sep 1984	1.50
❑332, Nov 1984	1.50
❑333, Jan 1985	1.50
❑334, Mar 1985	1.50
❑335, May 1985	1.50

Apathy Kat creator Harold Buchholz offers printing services to small publishers.

© 1995 Harold Buchholz.

	N-MINT
❑336, Jul 1985	1.50
❑337, Sep 1985	1.50
❑338, Nov 1985	1.50
❑339, Jan 1986	1.50
❑340, Mar 1986	1.50
❑341, May 1986	1.50
❑342, Jul 1986	1.50
❑343, Sep 1986	1.50
❑344, Nov 1986	1.50
❑345, Jan 1987	1.50
❑346, Mar 1987	1.50
❑347, May 1987	1.50
❑348, Jun 1987	1.50
❑349, Jul 1987	1.50
❑350, Aug 1987	1.50
❑351, Sep 1987	1.50
❑352, Oct 1987	1.50
❑353, Nov 1987	1.50
❑354, Jan 1988	1.50
❑355, Mar 1988	1.50
❑356, May 1988	1.50
❑357, Jun 1988	1.50
❑358, Jul 1988	1.50
❑359, Aug 1988	1.50
❑360, Sep 1988	1.50
❑361, Oct 1988	1.50
❑362, Nov 1988	1.50
❑363, Jan 1989	1.50
❑364, Feb 1989	1.50
❑365, Mar 1989	1.50
❑366, Apr 1989	1.50
❑367, May 1989	1.50
❑368, Jul 1989	1.50
❑369, Aug 1993	1.50
❑370, Sep 1989	1.50
❑371, Oct 1989	1.50
❑372, Nov 1989	1.50
❑373, Jan 1990	1.50
❑374, Feb 1990	1.50
❑375, Mar 1990	1.50
❑376, Apr 1990	1.50
❑377, May 1990	1.50
❑378, Jul 1990	1.50
❑379, Aug 1990	1.50
❑380, Sep 1990	1.50
❑381, Oct 1990	1.50
❑382, Nov 1990	1.50
❑383, Dec 1990	1.50
❑384, Feb 1991	1.50
❑385, Mar 1991	1.50
❑386, Apr 1991	1.50
❑387, May 1991	1.50
❑388, Jun 1991	1.50
❑389, Jul 1991	1.50
❑390, Aug 1991	1.50
❑391, Sep 1991	1.50
❑392, Oct 1991	1.50
❑393, Nov 1991	1.50
❑394, Dec 1991	1.50
❑395, Jan 1992	1.50
❑396, Feb 1992	1.50
❑397, Mar 1992	1.50
❑398, Apr 1992	1.50
❑399, May 1992	1.50
❑400, Jun 1992	1.50
❑401, Jul 1992	1.50
❑402, Aug 1992	1.50

Condition price index: Multiply "NM prices" above by: **0.83 for Very Fine/Near Mint**
0.66 for Very Fine • 0.33 for Fine • 0.2 for Very Good • 0.125 for Good

	N-MINT
❑403, Sep 1992	1.50
❑404, Oct 1992	1.50
❑405, Nov 1992	1.50
❑406, Dec 1992	1.50
❑407, Jan 1993	1.50
❑408, Feb 1993	1.50
❑409, Mar 1993	1.50
❑410, Apr 1993	1.50
❑411, May 1993	1.50
❑412, Jun 1993	1.50
❑413, Jul 1993	1.50
❑414, Aug 1993; prom poster	1.50
❑415, Sep 1993	1.50
❑416, Oct 1993	1.50
❑417, Nov 1993	1.50
❑418, Dec 1993	1.50
❑419, Jan 1994	1.50
❑420, Feb 1994	1.50
❑421, Mar 1994	1.50
❑422, Apr 1994	1.50
❑423, May 1994	1.50
❑424, Jun 1994	1.50
❑425, Jul 1994	1.50
❑426, Aug 1994	1.50
❑427, Sep 1994	1.50
❑428, Oct 1994	1.50
❑429, Nov 1994	1.50
❑430, Dec 1994	1.50
❑431, Jan 1995	1.50
❑432, Feb 1995	1.50
❑433, Mar 1995	1.50
❑434, Apr 1995	1.50
❑435, May 1995	1.50
❑436, Jun 1995	1.50
❑437, Jul 1995	1.50
❑438, Aug 1995	1.50
❑439, Sep 1995	1.50
❑440, Oct 1995	1.50
❑441, Nov 1995	1.50
❑442, Dec 1995; continues in Betty & Veronica #95	1.50
❑443, Jan 1996	1.50
❑444, Feb 1996	1.50
❑445, Mar 1996	1.50
❑446, Apr 1996	1.50
❑447, May 1996	1.50
❑448, Jun 1996	1.50
❑449, Jul 1996	1.50
❑450, Aug 1996	1.50
❑451, Sep 1996	1.50
❑452, Oct 1996	1.50
❑453, Nov 1996	1.50
❑454, Dec 1996	1.50
❑455, Jan 1997	1.50
❑456, Feb 1997	1.50
❑457, Mar 1997	1.50
❑458, Apr 1997	1.50
❑459, May 1997	1.50
❑460, Jun 1997	1.50
❑461, Jul 1997	1.50
❑462, Aug 1997	1.50
❑463, Sep 1997	1.50
❑464, Oct 1997	1.50
❑465, Nov 1997	1.50
❑466, Dec 1997	1.50
❑467, Jan 1998	1.75
❑468, Feb 1998	1.75
❑469, Mar 1998	1.75
❑470, Apr 1998	1.75
❑471, May 1998	1.75
❑472, Jun 1998	1.75
❑473, Jul 1998	1.75
❑474, Aug 1998	1.75
❑475, Sep 1998	1.75
❑476, Oct 1998	1.75
❑477, Nov 1998	1.75
❑478, Dec 1998	1.75
❑479, Jan 1999	1.75
❑480, Feb 1999	1.75
❑481, Mar 1999	1.75
❑482, Apr 1999	1.79

	N-MINT
❑483, May 1999	1.79
❑484, Jun 1999	1.79
❑485, Jul 1999	1.79
❑486, Aug 1999	1.79
❑487, Sep 1999	1.79
❑488, Oct 1999	1.75
❑489, Nov 1999	1.75
❑490, Dec 1999	1.75
❑491, Jan 2000	1.75
❑492, Feb 2000	1.75
❑493, Mar 2000	1.75
❑494, Apr 2000	1.75
❑495, May 2000	1.75
❑496, Jun 2000	1.75
❑497, Jul 2000	1.75
❑498, Aug 2000	1.75
❑499, Sep 2000	1.99
❑500, Oct 2000	1.99
❑501, Nov 2000	1.99
❑502, Dec 2000	1.99
❑503, Jan 2001	1.99
❑504, Feb 2001	1.99
❑505, Mar 2001	1.99
❑506, Apr 2001	1.99
❑507, May 2001	1.99
❑508, Jun 2001	1.99
❑509, Jul 2001	1.99
❑510, Aug 2001	1.99
❑511, Sep 2001	1.99
❑512, Oct 2001	1.99
❑513, Nov 2001	1.99
❑514, Nov 2001	2.19
❑515, Dec 2001	2.19
❑516, Jan 2002	2.19
❑517, Feb 2002	2.19
❑518, Mar 2002	2.19
❑519, Apr 2002	2.19
❑520, May 2002	2.19
❑521, Jun 2002	2.19
❑522, Jul 2002	2.19
❑523, ca. 2002	2.19
❑524, Aug 2002	2.19
❑525, Sep 2002	2.19
❑526, Oct 2002	2.19
❑527, Nov 2002	2.19
❑528, Dec 2002	2.19
❑529, Jan 2003	2.19
❑530, Feb 2003	2.19
❑531, Mar 2003	2.19
❑532, Apr 2003	2.19
❑533, May 2003	2.19
❑534, Jun 2003	2.19
❑535, Jul 2003	2.19
❑536, Jul 2003	2.19
❑537, Aug 2003	2.19
❑538, Sep 2003	2.19
❑539, Oct 2003	2.19
❑540, Nov 2003	2.19
❑541, Dec 2003	2.19
❑542, Jan 2004	2.19
❑543, Feb 2004	2.19
❑544, Mar 2004	2.19
❑545, Apr 2004 AM (a)	2.19
❑546, May 2004	2.19
❑547, Jun 2004	2.19
❑548, Jul 2004	2.19
❑Annual 7, ca. 1956	160.00
❑Annual 8, ca. 1957	135.00
❑Annual 9, ca. 1958	120.00
❑Annual 10, ca. 1959	110.00
❑Annual 11, ca. 1960	70.00
❑Annual 12, ca. 1961	60.00
❑Annual 13, ca. 1962	58.00
❑Annual 14, ca. 1963	50.00
❑Annual 15, ca. 1964	50.00
❑Annual 16, ca. 1965	26.00
❑Annual 17, ca. 1966	26.00
❑Annual 18, ca. 1967	22.00
❑Annual 19, ca. 1968	22.00
❑Annual 20, ca. 1969	14.00
❑Annual 21, ca. 1970	9.00

	N-MINT
❑Annual 22, ca. 1971	9.00
❑Annual 23, ca. 1972	8.00
❑Annual 24, ca. 1973	8.00
❑Annual 25, ca. 1974	8.00
❑Annual 26, ca. 1975	8.00

ARCHIE ALL CANADIAN DIGEST
ARCHIE

	N-MINT
❑1, Aug 1996; digest; reprints Archie stories set in Canada	2.00

ARCHIE AND FRIENDS
ARCHIE

	N-MINT
❑1, Dec 1992 A: Great Rondo. A: Hiram Lodge	3.00
❑2, Feb 1992	2.00
❑3, Apr 1992	2.00
❑4, Jun 1992	2.00
❑5, Aug 1992	2.00
❑6, Oct 1992 A: Sabrina	2.00
❑7, Mar 1993	2.00
❑8	2.00
❑9, Jun 1994	2.00
❑10, Aug 1994	2.00
❑11, Oct 1994	1.50
❑12, Dec 1994	1.50
❑13, Feb 1995	1.50
❑14, May 1995	1.50
❑15, Aug 1995	1.50
❑16, Nov 1995	1.50
❑17, Feb 1996	1.50
❑18, May 1996	1.50
❑19, Aug 1996; X-Men and E.R. parodies	1.50
❑20, Nov 1996	1.50
❑21, Feb 1997; The class puts on Romeo and Juliet	1.50
❑22, Apr 1997; Friends parody	1.50
❑23, Jun 1997	1.50
❑24, Aug 1997	1.50
❑25, Oct 1997	1.50
❑26, Dec 1997	1.50
❑27, Feb 1998	1.75
❑28, Apr 1998	1.75
❑29, Jun 1998; Pops opens a cyber-cafe	1.75
❑30, Aug 1998	1.75
❑31, Oct 1998	1.75
❑32, Dec 1998	1.75
❑33, Feb 1999	1.75
❑34, Apr 1999	1.75
❑35, Jun 1999	1.79
❑36, Aug 1999	1.79
❑37, Oct 1999	1.79
❑38, Dec 1999	1.79
❑39, Feb 2000	1.79
❑40, Apr 2000	1.79
❑41, Jun 2000	1.79
❑42, Aug 2000	1.99
❑43, Oct 2000	1.99
❑44, Dec 2000	1.99
❑45, Feb 2001	1.99
❑46, Apr 2001	1.99
❑47, Jun 2001	1.99
❑48, Sep 2001 A: Josie & the Pussycats	1.99
❑49, Oct 2001 A: Josie & the Pussycats	1.99
❑50, Nov 2001 A: Josie & the Pussycats	1.99
❑51, ca. 2001 A: Josie & the Pussycats	2.19
❑52, ca. 2001	2.19
❑53, Jan 2002 A: Josie & the Pussycats	2.19
❑54, ca. 2002	2.19
❑55, Apr 2002 A: Josie & the Pussycats	2.19
❑56, Jun 2002 A: Josie & the Pussycats	2.19
❑57, Jul 2002	2.19
❑58, Aug 2002 A: Josie & the Pussycats	2.19
❑59, Sep 2002	2.19
❑60, Oct 2002 A: Josie & the Pussycats	2.19
❑61, Oct 2002	2.19
❑62, Nov 2002	2.19
❑63, Dec 2002	2.19
❑64, Jan 2003	2.19
❑65, Feb 2003	2.19
❑66, Mar 2003	2.19
❑67, Apr 2003	2.19
❑68, May 2003	2.19

	N-MINT
❑69, Jun 2003	2.19
❑70, Jul 2003	2.19
❑71, Aug 2003	2.19
❑72, Sep 2003 AM (a)	2.19
❑73, Oct 2003	2.19
❑74, Oct 2003	2.19
❑75, Nov 2003	2.19
❑76, Dec 2003	2.19
❑77, Jan 2004	2.19
❑78, Feb 2004	2.19
❑79, Mar 2004	2.19
❑80, Apr 2004	2.19
❑81, May 2004	0.00
❑82, Jun 2004; Mr. Weatherbee's past revealed	0.00

ARCHIE AND ME
ARCHIE

	N-MINT
❑1, Oct 1964	125.00
❑2, Aug 1965	75.00
❑3, Sep 1965	45.00
❑4, Oct 1965	34.00
❑5, Dec 1965	34.00
❑6, Feb 1966	20.00
❑7, Apr 1966	20.00
❑8, Jun 1966	20.00
❑9, Aug 1966	20.00
❑10, Sep 1966	20.00
❑11, Oct 1966	12.00
❑12, Dec 1966	12.00
❑13, Feb 1967	12.00
❑14, Apr 1967	12.00
❑15, Jun 1967	12.00
❑16, Aug 1967	12.00
❑17, Oct 1967	12.00
❑18, Dec 1967	12.00
❑19, Feb 1968	12.00
❑20, Apr 1968	12.00
❑21, Jun 1968	8.00
❑22, Aug 1968	8.00
❑23, Sep 1968; Summer Camp issue	8.00
❑24, Oct 1968	8.00
❑25, Dec 1968; Election issue	8.00
❑26, Feb 1969; Christmas issue	8.00
❑27, Apr 1969	8.00
❑28, Jun 1969	8.00
❑29, Aug 1969	8.00
❑30, Sep 1969	8.00
❑31, Oct 1969	6.00
❑32, Dec 1969	6.00
❑33, Feb 1970	6.00
❑34, Apr 1970	6.00
❑35, Jun 1970	6.00
❑36, Aug 1970	6.00
❑37, Sep 1970; Japan's Expo 70	6.00
❑38, Oct 1970	6.00
❑39, Dec 1970	6.00
❑40, Feb 1971	6.00
❑41, Apr 1971	4.00
❑42, Jun 1971	4.00
❑43, Aug 1971	4.00
❑44, Sep 1971	4.00
❑45, Oct 1971	4.00
❑46, Dec 1971	4.00
❑47, Feb 1972	4.00
❑48, Apr 1972	4.00
❑49, Jun 1972	4.00
❑50, Aug 1972	4.00
❑51, Sep 1972	3.00
❑52, Oct 1972	3.00
❑53, Dec 1972	3.00
❑54, Feb 1973	3.00
❑55, Apr 1973	3.00
❑56, Jun 1973	3.00
❑57, Jul 1973	3.00
❑58, Aug 1973	3.00
❑59, Sep 1973	3.00
❑60, Oct 1973	3.00
❑61, Dec 1973	3.00
❑62, Jan 1974	3.00
❑63, Feb 1974	3.00
❑64, Apr 1974	3.00
❑65, Jun 1974	3.00
❑66, Jul 1974	3.00
❑67, Aug 1974	3.00
❑68, Sep 1974	3.00
❑69, Oct 1974	3.00
❑70, Dec 1974	3.00
❑71, Jan 1975	2.50
❑72, Feb 1975	2.50
❑73, Apr 1975	2.50
❑74, Jun 1975	2.50
❑75, Jul 1975	2.50
❑76, Aug 1975	2.50
❑77, Sep 1975	2.50
❑78, Oct 1975	2.50
❑79, Dec 1975	2.50
❑80, Jan 1976	2.50
❑81, Feb 1976	1.50
❑82, Apr 1976	1.50
❑83, Jun 1976	1.50
❑84, Jul 1976	1.50
❑85, Aug 1976	1.50
❑86, Sep 1976	1.50
❑87, Oct 1976	1.50
❑88, Dec 1976	1.50
❑89, Jan 1977	1.50
❑90, Feb 1977	1.50
❑91, Apr 1977	1.50
❑92, Jun 1977	1.50
❑93, Jul 1977	1.50
❑94, Aug 1977	1.50
❑95, Sep 1977	1.50
❑96, Oct 1977	1.50
❑97, Dec 1977	1.50
❑98, Jan 1978	1.50
❑99, Feb 1978	1.50
❑100, Apr 1978	1.50
❑101, Jun 1978	1.00
❑102, Jul 1978	1.00
❑103, Aug 1978	1.00
❑104, Sep 1978	1.00
❑105, Oct 1978	1.00
❑106, Dec 1978	1.00
❑107, Jan 1979	1.00
❑108, Feb 1979	1.00
❑109, Apr 1979	1.00
❑110, Jun 1979	1.00
❑111, Jul 1979	1.00
❑112, Aug 1979	1.00
❑113, Sep 1979	1.00
❑114, Oct 1979	1.00
❑115, Dec 1979	1.00
❑116, Jan 1980	1.00
❑117, Feb 1980	1.00
❑118, Apr 1980	1.00
❑119, Jun 1980	1.00
❑120, Jul 1980	1.00
❑121, Aug 1980	1.00
❑122, Sep 1980	1.00
❑123, Oct 1980	1.00
❑124, Dec 1980	1.00
❑125, Feb 1981	1.00
❑126, Apr 1981	1.00
❑127, ca. 1981	1.00
❑128, ca. 1981	1.00
❑129, ca. 1981	1.00
❑130, ca. 1981	1.00
❑131, ca. 1981	1.00
❑132, Feb 1982	1.00
❑133, Apr 1982	1.00
❑134, Jun 1982	1.00
❑135, Aug 1982	1.00
❑136, Oct 1982	1.00
❑137, Dec 1982	1.00
❑138, Feb 1983	1.00
❑139, May 1983	1.00
❑140, ca. 1983	1.00
❑141, ca. 1983	1.00
❑142, ca. 1983	1.00
❑143, Feb 1984 DDC (c)	1.00
❑144, Apr 1984	1.00
❑145, Jun 1984	1.00

The adventures of America's typical teen have been published continually for the past 60 years.

	N-MINT
❑146, Aug 1984	1.00
❑147, Oct 1984	1.00
❑148, Dec 1984	1.00
❑149, Feb 1985	1.00
❑150, Apr 1985	1.00
❑151, Jun 1985	1.00
❑152, Aug 1985	1.00
❑153, Oct 1985	1.00
❑154, Dec 1985	1.00
❑155, Feb 1986	1.00
❑156, Apr 1986	1.00
❑157, Jun 1986	1.00
❑158, Aug 1986	1.00
❑159, Oct 1986	1.00
❑160, Dec 1986	1.00
❑161, Feb 1987	1.00

ARCHIE ANNUAL DIGEST MAGAZINE
ARCHIE

	N-MINT
❑66, Jun 1995	1.75
❑67, Oct 1995	1.75
❑68, Apr 1997	1.79

ARCHIE... ARCHIE ANDREWS, WHERE ARE YOU? DIGEST MAGAZINE
ARCHIE

	N-MINT
❑1, Feb 1977	5.00
❑2, May 1977	3.00
❑3, Aug 1977	3.00
❑4, Nov 1977	3.00
❑5, Feb 1978	3.00
❑6, May 1978	3.00
❑7, Aug 1978	3.00
❑8, Nov 1978; JK (a); reprints story from Adventures of the Fly #1	3.00
❑9, Feb 1979	3.00
❑10, May 1979	3.00
❑11, Aug 1979	2.00
❑12, Nov 1979	2.00
❑13, Feb 1980	2.00
❑14, May 1980	2.00
❑15, Aug 1980	2.00
❑16, Nov 1980	2.00
❑17, Feb 1981	2.00
❑18, May 1981	2.00
❑19, Aug 1981	2.00
❑20, Nov 1981	2.00
❑21, Feb 1982	1.50
❑22, May 1982	1.50
❑23, Aug 1982	1.50
❑24, Nov 1982	1.50
❑25, Feb 1983	1.50
❑26, May 1983	1.50
❑27, Aug 1983	1.50
❑28, Oct 1983	1.50
❑29, Dec 1983	1.50
❑30, Feb 1984	1.50
❑31, Apr 1984	1.50
❑32, Jun 1984	1.50
❑33, Aug 1984	1.50
❑34, Oct 1984	1.50
❑35, Dec 1984	1.50
❑36, Feb 1985	1.50
❑37, Apr 1985	1.50
❑38, Jun 1985	1.50
❑39, Aug 1985	1.50
❑40, Oct 1985	1.50
❑41, Dec 1985	1.50

N-MINT

❑42, Feb 1986 .... 1.50
❑43, Apr 1986 .... 1.50
❑44, Jun 1986 .... 1.50
❑45, Aug 1986 .... 1.50
❑46, Oct 1986 .... 1.50
❑47, Dec 1986 .... 1.50
❑48, Feb 1987 .... 1.50
❑49, Apr 1987 .... 1.50
❑50, Jun 1987 .... 1.50
❑51, Aug 1987 .... 1.50
❑52, Oct 1987 .... 1.50
❑53, Dec 1987 .... 1.50
❑54, Feb 1988 .... 1.50
❑55, Apr 1988 .... 1.50
❑56, Jun 1988 .... 1.50
❑57, Aug 1988 .... 1.50
❑58, Oct 1988 .... 1.50
❑59, Dec 1988 .... 1.50
❑60, Feb 1989 .... 1.50
❑61, Apr 1989 .... 1.50
❑62, Jun 1989 .... 1.50
❑63, Aug 1989 .... 1.50
❑64, Oct 1989 .... 1.50
❑65, Dec 1989 .... 1.50
❑66, Feb 1990 .... 1.50
❑67, Apr 1990 .... 1.50
❑68, Jun 1990 .... 1.50
❑69, Aug 1990 .... 1.50
❑70, Oct 1990 .... 1.50
❑71, Dec 1990 .... 1.50
❑72, Feb 1991 .... 1.50
❑73, Apr 1991 .... 1.50
❑74, Jun 1991 .... 1.50
❑75, Aug 1991 .... 1.50
❑76, Oct 1991 .... 1.50
❑77, Dec 1991 .... 1.50
❑78, Feb 1992 .... 1.50
❑79, Apr 1992 .... 1.50
❑80, Jun 1992 .... 1.50
❑81, Aug 1992 .... 1.50
❑82, Oct 1992 .... 1.50
❑83, Dec 1992 .... 1.50
❑84, Jan 1993 .... 1.50
❑85, Feb 1993 .... 1.50
❑86, Apr 1993 .... 1.50
❑87, Jun 1993 .... 1.50
❑88, Aug 1993 .... 1.50
❑89, Oct 1993 .... 1.50
❑90, Dec 1993 .... 1.50
❑91, Feb 1994 .... 1.75
❑92, Mar 1994 .... 1.75
❑93, May 1994 .... 1.75
❑94, Jul 1994 .... 1.75
❑95, Sep 1994 .... 1.75
❑96, Nov 1994 .... 1.75
❑97, Jan 1995 .... 1.75
❑98, Feb 1995 .... 1.75
❑99, Apr 1995 .... 1.75
❑100, Jun 1995 .... 1.75
❑101, Aug 1995 .... 1.75
❑102, Oct 1995 .... 1.75
❑103, Dec 1995 .... 1.75
❑104, Jan 1996 .... 1.75
❑105, Mar 1996 .... 1.75
❑106, May 1996 .... 1.75
❑107, Aug 1996 .... 1.75
❑108, Nov 1996 .... 1.79
❑109, Feb 1997 .... 1.79
❑110, May 1997 .... 1.79
❑111, Sep 1997 .... 1.79
❑112, Nov 1997 .... 1.79
❑113, Feb 1998 .... 1.95
❑114, May 1998 .... 1.95
❑115, Sep 1998 .... 1.95
❑116, Nov 1998 .... 1.95
❑117, Feb 1999 .... 1.95

ARCHIE AS PUREHEART THE POWERFUL

ARCHIE

❑1, Sep 1966 .... 55.00
❑2 .... 35.00
❑3 .... 25.00
❑4, May 1967 .... 25.00
❑5, Aug 1967 .... 25.00
❑6, Nov 1967 .... 25.00

ARCHIE AT RIVERDALE HIGH

ARCHIE

❑1, Aug 1972 .... 42.00
❑2, Sep 1972 .... 22.00
❑3, Oct 1972 .... 16.00
❑4, Dec 1972 .... 16.00
❑5, Feb 1973 .... 16.00
❑6, Apr 1973 .... 11.00
❑7, Jun 1973 .... 11.00
❑8, Jul 1973 .... 11.00
❑9, Aug 1973 .... 11.00
❑10, Sep 1973 .... 11.00
❑11, Oct 1973 .... 8.00
❑12, Dec 1973 .... 8.00
❑13, Feb 1974 .... 8.00
❑14, Mar 1974 .... 8.00
❑15, Apr 1974 .... 8.00
❑16, Jun 1974 .... 8.00
❑17, Jul 1974 .... 8.00
❑18, Aug 1974 .... 8.00
❑19, Sep 1974 .... 8.00
❑20, ca. 1974 .... 8.00
❑21 .... 5.00
❑22, Feb 1975 .... 5.00
❑23, Mar 1975 .... 5.00
❑24, Apr 1975 .... 5.00
❑25, Jun 1975 .... 5.00
❑26, Jun 1975 .... 5.00
❑27, Aug 1975 .... 5.00
❑28, Sep 1975 .... 5.00
❑29, Oct 1975 .... 5.00
❑30, Nov 1975 .... 5.00
❑31, Dec 1975 .... 4.00
❑32, Jan 1976 .... 4.00
❑33, Feb 1976 .... 4.00
❑34, Mar 1976 .... 4.00
❑35, May 1976 .... 4.00
❑36, Jun 1976 .... 4.00
❑37, Jul 1976 .... 4.00
❑38, Aug 1976 .... 4.00
❑39, Sep 1976 .... 4.00
❑40, Oct 1976 .... 4.00
❑41, Dec 1976 .... 3.00
❑42, ca. 1977 .... 3.00
❑43, Mar 1977 .... 3.00
❑44, May 1977 .... 3.00
❑45, Jun 1977 .... 3.00
❑46, Jul 1977 .... 3.00
❑47, Aug 1977 .... 3.00
❑48, Sep 1977 .... 3.00
❑49, Oct 1977 .... 3.00
❑50, Dec 1977 .... 3.00
❑51, Jan 1978 .... 3.00
❑52, ca. 1978 .... 3.00
❑53, May 1978 .... 3.00
❑54, ca. 1978 .... 3.00
❑55, ca. 1978 .... 3.00
❑56, ca. 1978 .... 3.00
❑57, ca. 1978 .... 3.00
❑58, ca. 1978 .... 3.00
❑59, Dec 1978 .... 3.00
❑60, ca. 1979 .... 3.00
❑61, ca. 1979 .... 2.00
❑62, May 1979 .... 2.00
❑63, ca. 1979 .... 2.00
❑64, ca. 1979 .... 2.00
❑65, ca. 1979 .... 2.00
❑66, ca. 1979 .... 2.00
❑67, ca. 1979 .... 2.00
❑68, Dec 1979 .... 2.00
❑69, ca. 1980 .... 2.00
❑70, ca. 1980 .... 2.00
❑71, May 1980 .... 2.00
❑72, ca. 1980 .... 2.00
❑73, ca. 1980 .... 2.00
❑74, ca. 1980 .... 2.00
❑75, ca. 1980 .... 2.00
❑76, ca. 1980 .... 2.00
❑77, ca. 1980 .... 2.00
❑78, Feb 1981 .... 2.00
❑79, Apr 1981 .... 2.00
❑80, Jun 1981 .... 2.00
❑81, Aug 1981 .... 2.00
❑82, Oct 1981 .... 2.00
❑83, Dec 1981 .... 2.00
❑84, Feb 1982 .... 2.00
❑85, Apr 1982 .... 2.00
❑86, ca. 1982 .... 2.00
❑87 .... 2.00
❑88 .... 2.00
❑89 .... 2.00
❑90 .... 2.00
❑91, May 1983 DDC (c) 2.00
❑92, ca. 1983 DDC (c) 2.00
❑93, ca. 1983 .... 2.00
❑94 .... 2.00
❑95, Feb 1984 .... 2.00
❑96, Apr 1984; Teen smoking issue .. 2.00
❑97, Jun 1984 .... 2.00
❑98, Aug 1984 .... 2.00
❑99, Oct 1984 .... 2.00
❑100, Dec 1984; 100th anniversary issue 2.00
❑101, Feb 1985 .... 1.00
❑102, Apr 1985 .... 1.00
❑103, Jun 1985 .... 1.00
❑104, Aug 1985 .... 1.00
❑105, Oct 1985 .... 1.00
❑106, Dec 1985 .... 1.00
❑107, Feb 1986 .... 1.00
❑108, Apr 1986 .... 1.00
❑109, Jun 1986 .... 1.00
❑110, Aug 1986 DDC (c) 1.00
❑111, Oct 1986 .... 1.00
❑112, Dec 1986 .... 1.00
❑113, Feb 1986 DDC (c) 1.00
❑114, ca. 1987 .... 1.00

ARCHIE DIGEST MAGAZINE

ARCHIE

❑1, Aug 1973 .... 26.00
❑2, Oct 1973 .... 10.00
❑3, Dec 1973 .... 6.00
❑4, Feb 1974 .... 6.00
❑5, Apr 1974 .... 6.00
❑6, Jun 1974 .... 4.00
❑7, Aug 1974 .... 4.00
❑8, Oct 1974 .... 4.00
❑9, Dec 1974 .... 4.00
❑10, Feb 1975 .... 4.00
❑11, Apr 1975 .... 2.50
❑12, Jun 1975 .... 2.50
❑13, Aug 1975 .... 2.50
❑14, Oct 1975 .... 2.50
❑15, Dec 1975 .... 2.50
❑16, Feb 1976 .... 2.50
❑17, Apr 1976 .... 2.50
❑18, Jun 1976 .... 2.50
❑19, Aug 1976 .... 2.50
❑20, Oct 1976 .... 2.50
❑21, Dec 1976 .... 2.00
❑22, Feb 1977 .... 2.00
❑23, Apr 1977 .... 2.00
❑24, Jun 1977 .... 2.00
❑25, Aug 1977 .... 2.00
❑26, Oct 1977 .... 2.00
❑27, Dec 1977 .... 2.00
❑28, Feb 1978 .... 2.00
❑29, Apr 1978 .... 2.00
❑30, Jun 1978 .... 2.00
❑31, Aug 1978 .... 2.00
❑32, Oct 1978 .... 2.00
❑33, Dec 1978 .... 2.00
❑34, Feb 1979 .... 2.00
❑35, Apr 1979 .... 2.00
❑36, Jun 1979 .... 2.00
❑37, Aug 1979 .... 2.00

Condition price index: Multiply "NM prices" above by: **0.83 for Very Fine/Near Mint**
0.66 for Very Fine • 0.33 for Fine • 0.2 for Very Good • 0.125 for Good

	N-MINT
❑38, Oct 1979; Reprints Li'l Jinx story featuring comic-book collector paying $1,000 for old Red Circle comics	2.00
❑39, Dec 1979	2.00
❑40, Feb 1980	2.00
❑41, Apr 1980	2.00
❑42	2.00
❑43	2.00
❑44	2.00
❑45	2.00
❑46 1981	2.00
❑47 1981	2.00
❑48 1981	2.00
❑49 1981	2.00
❑50	2.00
❑51	1.50
❑52, Apr 1982	1.50
❑53	1.50
❑54	1.50
❑55	1.50
❑56	1.50
❑57	1.50
❑58 1983	1.50
❑59 1983	1.50
❑60 1983	1.50
❑61 1983	1.50
❑62	1.50
❑63	1.50
❑64	1.50
❑65	1.50
❑66, Jun 1984	1.50
❑67 1984	1.50
❑68	1.50
❑69	1.50
❑70	1.50
❑71	1.50
❑72 1985	1.50
❑73	1.50
❑74	1.50
❑75	1.50
❑76	1.50
❑77 1986	1.50
❑78	1.50
❑79	1.50
❑80	1.50
❑81	1.50
❑82 1987	1.50
❑83 1987	1.50
❑84 1987	1.50
❑85	1.50
❑86	1.50
❑87	1.50
❑88, Apr 1988	1.50
❑89 1988	1.50
❑90 1988	1.50
❑91 1988	1.50
❑92	1.50
❑93	1.50
❑94	1.50
❑95, Apr 1989	1.50
❑96	1.50
❑97	1.50
❑98	1.50
❑99	1.50
❑100	1.50
❑101	1.79
❑102	1.79
❑103 1990	1.79
❑104	1.79
❑105	1.79
❑106	1.79
❑107	1.79
❑108	1.79
❑109	1.79
❑110	1.79
❑111	1.79
❑112	1.79
❑113	1.79
❑114	1.79
❑115	1.79
❑116	1.79
❑117	1.79

	N-MINT
❑118 1992	1.79
❑119	1.79
❑120	1.79
❑121	1.79
❑122	1.79
❑123	1.79
❑124 1993	1.79
❑125	1.79
❑126	1.79
❑127	1.79
❑128	1.79
❑129	1.79
❑130	1.79
❑131, Dec 1994 DDC (c)	1.79
❑132, Feb 1995	1.79
❑133, Apr 1995	1.79
❑134, May 1995	1.79
❑135, Jul 1995	1.79
❑136, Sep 1995	1.79
❑137, Nov 1995	1.79
❑138, Jan 1996	1.79
❑139, Mar 1996	1.79
❑140, Apr 1996	1.79
❑141 1996	1.79
❑142 1996	1.79
❑143 1996	1.79
❑144, Dec 1996	1.79
❑145, Jan 1997	1.79
❑146, Mar 1997	1.79
❑147, Apr 1997	1.79
❑148, Jun 1997	1.79
❑149, Aug 1997	1.79
❑150, Sep 1997	1.79
❑151, Nov 1997	1.79
❑152, Jan 1998	1.95
❑153, Mar 1998	1.95
❑154, Apr 1998	1.95
❑155, Jun 1998	1.95
❑156, Jul 1998	1.95
❑157, Sep 1998	1.95
❑158, Oct 1998	1.95
❑159, Dec 1998	1.95
❑160, Jan 1999	1.95
❑161, Mar 1999	1.95
❑162, Apr 1999	1.99
❑163, Jun 1999	1.99
❑164, Jul 1999	1.99
❑165, Sep 1999	1.99
❑166, Oct 1999 DDC (c)	1.99
❑167, Nov 1999	1.99
❑168, Jan 2000	1.99
❑169, Feb 2000	1.99
❑170, Apr 2000	1.99
❑171, Jun 2000	1.99
❑172, Jul 2000	1.99
❑173, Aug 2000	2.19
❑174, Oct 2000	2.19
❑175, Nov 2000	2.19
❑176, Jan 2001	2.19
❑177, Feb 2001	2.19
❑178, Mar 2001	2.19
❑179, Apr 2001	2.19
❑180, Jun 2001	2.19
❑181, Jul 2001	2.19
❑182, Aug 2001	2.19
❑183, Sep 2001	2.19
❑184, Dec 2001	2.39
❑185, Jan 2002	2.39
❑186, Mar 2002	2.39
❑187, Apr 2002	2.39
❑188, May 2002	2.39
❑189, Jul 2002	2.39
❑190, Aug 2002	2.39
❑191, Oct 2002	2.39
❑192, Nov 2002	2.39
❑193, Dec 2002	2.39
❑194, Feb 2003	2.39
❑195, Mar 2003	2.39
❑196, Apr 2003	2.39
❑197, May 2003	2.39
❑198, Jul 2003	2.39

Archie's perpetual romantic triangle became a polygon when Cheryl Blossom was added to the mix.
© 1995 Archie Publications Inc.

	N-MINT
❑199, Aug 2003	2.39
❑200, Oct 2003	2.39
❑201, Nov 2003	2.39
❑202, Dec 2003	2.39
❑203, Jan 2004	2.39
❑204, Mar 2004	2.39
❑205, Apr 2004	2.39
❑206, Jun 2004	2.39
❑207, Jul 2004	2.39

ARCHIE GIANT SERIES MAGAZINE

ARCHIE

	N-MINT
❑1, Win 1954; Archie's Christmas Stocking (1954)	750.00
❑2, Win 1955; Archie's Christmas Stocking (1955)	475.00
❑3, Win 1956; Archie's Christmas Stocking (1956)	325.00
❑4, Win 1957; Archie's Christmas Stocking (1957)	325.00
❑5, Win 1958; Archie's Christmas Stocking (1958)	275.00
❑6, Win 1959; Archie's Christmas Stocking (1959)	275.00
❑7, Sep 1960; Katy Keene Holiday Fun	200.00
❑8, Oct 1960	200.00
❑9, Dec 1960	185.00
❑10, Jan 1961	185.00
❑11, Jun 1961	140.00
❑12, ca. 1961	125.00
❑13, ca. 1961	140.00
❑14, Dec 1961	110.00
❑15, Mar 1962	110.00
❑16, Jun 1962	125.00
❑17, Sep 1962	110.00
❑18, ca. 1962	125.00
❑19, ca. 1962	110.00
❑20, Jan 1963	100.00
❑21, ca. 1963	85.00
❑22, ca. 1963	60.00
❑23, ca. 1963	80.00
❑24, ca. 1963	60.00
❑25, ca. 1964	60.00
❑26, ca. 1964	80.00
❑27, Jun 1964	60.00
❑28, Sep 1964	80.00
❑29, ca. 1964	60.00
❑30, ca. 1964	60.00
❑31, ca. 1965	40.00
❑32, ca. 1965	40.00
❑33, ca. 1965	40.00
❑34, ca. 1965	40.00
❑35, ca. 1965; Series continued in #136	40.00
❑136, ca. 1965	40.00
❑137, ca. 1966	40.00
❑138, ca. 1966	40.00
❑139, ca. 1966	40.00
❑140, ca. 1966	40.00
❑141, ca. 1966	40.00
❑142, ca. 1966 O: Captain Pureheart .	45.00
❑143, ca. 1967	20.00
❑144, ca. 1967	20.00
❑145, ca. 1967	20.00
❑146, ca. 1967	20.00
❑147, ca. 1967	20.00
❑148, ca. 1967	20.00
❑149, ca. 1967	20.00
❑150, ca. 1967	20.00
❑151, ca. 1967	20.00

	N-MINT
❑152, Feb 1968	20.00
❑153, ca. 1968	20.00
❑154, ca. 1968	20.00
❑155, ca. 1968	20.00
❑156, ca. 1968	20.00
❑157, ca. 1968	20.00
❑158, ca. 1969	20.00
❑159, ca. 1969	20.00
❑160, ca. 1969	20.00
❑161, ca. 1969	12.00
❑162, ca. 1969	12.00
❑163, ca. 1969	12.00
❑164, ca. 1969	12.00
❑165, ca. 1969	12.00
❑166, ca. 1969	12.00
❑167, ca. 1970	12.00
❑168, ca. 1970	12.00
❑169, ca. 1970	12.00
❑170, ca. 1970	12.00
❑171, ca. 1970	12.00
❑172, ca. 1970	12.00
❑173, ca. 1970	12.00
❑174, ca. 1970	12.00
❑175, ca. 1970	12.00
❑176, ca. 1970	12.00
❑177, ca. 1970	12.00
❑178, ca. 1970	12.00
❑179, ca. 1971	12.00
❑180, ca. 1971	12.00
❑181, ca. 1971	10.00
❑182, ca. 1971	10.00
❑183, ca. 1971	10.00
❑184, ca. 1971	10.00
❑185, ca. 1971	10.00
❑186, ca. 1971	10.00
❑187, ca. 1971	10.00
❑188, ca. 1971	10.00
❑189, ca. 1971	10.00
❑190, ca. 1971	10.00
❑191, ca. 1972	10.00
❑192, ca. 1972	10.00
❑193, ca. 1972	10.00
❑194, ca. 1972	10.00
❑195, ca. 1972	10.00
❑196, ca. 1972	10.00
❑197, Jun 1972	10.00
❑198, ca. 1972	10.00
❑199, ca. 1972	10.00
❑200, ca. 1972	10.00
❑201, ca. 1972	8.00
❑202, ca. 1972	8.00
❑203, ca. 1972	8.00
❑204, ca. 1973	8.00
❑205, ca. 1973	8.00
❑206, ca. 1973	8.00
❑207, ca. 1973	8.00
❑208, ca. 1973	8.00
❑209, ca. 1973	8.00
❑210, Jun 1973	8.00
❑211, Jul 1973	8.00
❑212, Aug 1973	8.00
❑213, Sep 1973	8.00
❑214, Oct 1973	8.00
❑215, Nov 1973	8.00
❑216, Dec 1973	8.00
❑217, Jan 1974	8.00
❑218, Feb 1974	8.00
❑219, Mar 1974	8.00
❑220, Apr 1974	8.00
❑221, May 1974	6.00
❑222, Jun 1974	6.00
❑223, Jul 1974	6.00
❑224, Aug 1974	6.00
❑225, Sep 1974	6.00
❑226, Oct 1974	6.00
❑227, Nov 1974	6.00
❑228, Dec 1974	6.00
❑229, Jan 1975	6.00
❑230, Feb 1975	6.00
❑231, Mar 1975	6.00
❑232, Apr 1975	6.00

	N-MINT
❑233, May 1975	6.00
❑234, Jun 1975	6.00
❑235, ca. 1975	6.00
❑236, ca. 1975	6.00
❑237, ca. 1975	6.00
❑238, ca. 1975	6.00
❑239, ca. 1975	6.00
❑240, ca. 1975	6.00
❑241, ca. 1975	6.00
❑242, ca. 1976	6.00
❑243, ca. 1976	6.00
❑244, ca. 1976	6.00
❑245, ca. 1976	6.00
❑246, ca. 1976	6.00
❑247, ca. 1976	6.00
❑248, ca. 1976	6.00
❑249, ca. 1976	6.00
❑250, ca. 1976	6.00
❑251, ca. 1976; Series continued in #452	4.00
❑452, ca. 1976	3.00
❑453, ca. 1976	3.00
❑454, ca. 1976	3.00
❑455, Jan 1977	3.00
❑456, ca. 1977	3.00
❑457, ca. 1977	3.00
❑458, Jun 1977	3.00
❑459, ca. 1977	3.00
❑460, ca. 1977	3.00
❑461, ca. 1977	3.00
❑462, ca. 1977	3.00
❑463, ca. 1977	3.00
❑464, ca. 1977	3.00
❑465, ca. 1978	3.00
❑466, ca. 1978	3.00
❑467, ca. 1978	3.00
❑468, ca. 1978	3.00
❑469, ca. 1978	3.00
❑470, Jun 1978	3.00
❑471, Jul 1978	3.00
❑472, Aug 1978	3.00
❑473, Sep 1978	3.00
❑474, Oct 1978	3.00
❑475, Nov 1978	3.00
❑476, Dec 1978	3.00
❑477, Jan 1979	3.00
❑478, Feb 1979	3.00
❑479, Mar 1979	3.00
❑480, Apr 1979	3.00
❑481, May 1979	3.00
❑482, Jun 1979	3.00
❑483, ca. 1979	3.00
❑484, ca. 1979	3.00
❑485, ca. 1979	3.00
❑486, ca. 1979	3.00
❑487, ca. 1979	3.00
❑488, ca. 1979	3.00
❑489, ca. 1980	3.00
❑490, ca. 1980	3.00
❑491, ca. 1980	3.00
❑492, ca. 1980	3.00
❑493, ca. 1980; World of Jughead	3.00
❑494, ca. 1980	3.00
❑495, ca. 1980	3.00
❑496, ca. 1980	3.00
❑497, ca. 1980	3.00
❑498, ca. 1980	3.00
❑499, ca. 1980	3.00
❑500, ca. 1980	2.50
❑501, ca. 1981	2.50
❑502, ca. 1981	2.50
❑503, ca. 1981	2.50
❑504, ca. 1981	2.50
❑505, ca. 1981	2.50
❑506, ca. 1981	2.50
❑507, ca. 1981	2.50
❑508, ca. 1981	2.50
❑509, ca. 1981	2.50
❑510, ca. 1981	2.50
❑511, ca. 1981	2.50
❑512, ca. 1981	2.50

	N-MINT
❑513, ca. 1981	2.50
❑514, ca. 1982	2.50
❑515, ca. 1982	2.50
❑516, ca. 1982	2.50
❑517, ca. 1982	2.50
❑518, ca. 1982	2.50
❑519, ca. 1982	2.50
❑520, ca. 1982	2.50
❑521, ca. 1982	2.50
❑522, ca. 1982	2.50
❑523, ca. 1983	2.50
❑524, ca. 1983	2.50
❑525, ca. 1983	2.50
❑526, ca. 1983	2.50
❑527, ca. 1983	2.50
❑528, ca. 1983	2.50
❑529, ca. 1983	2.50
❑530, ca. 1983	2.50
❑531, ca. 1983	2.50
❑532, ca. 1983	2.50
❑533, ca. 1983	2.50
❑534, ca. 1984	2.50
❑535, ca. 1984	2.50
❑536, ca. 1984	2.50
❑537, ca. 1984	2.50
❑538, ca. 1984	2.50
❑539, ca. 1984	2.50
❑540, ca. 1984	2.50
❑541, ca. 1984	2.50
❑542, ca. 1984	2.50
❑543, ca. 1984	2.50
❑544, ca. 1984	2.50
❑545, ca. 1984	2.50
❑546, ca. 1984	2.50
❑547, ca. 1984	2.50
❑548, ca. 1984	2.50
❑549, ca. 1985	2.50
❑550, ca. 1985	2.50
❑551, ca. 1985	2.00
❑552, ca. 1985	2.00
❑553, ca. 1985	2.00
❑554, ca. 1985	2.00
❑555, ca. 1985	2.00
❑556, ca. 1986	2.00
❑557, ca. 1986	2.00
❑558, ca. 1986	2.00
❑559, ca. 1986	2.00
❑560, ca. 1986	2.00
❑561, ca. 1986	2.00
❑562, ca. 1986	2.00
❑563, ca. 1986	2.00
❑564, ca. 1986	2.00
❑565, ca. 1986	2.00
❑566, ca. 1986	2.00
❑567, ca. 1986	2.00
❑568, ca. 1986	2.00
❑569, ca. 1987	2.00
❑570, ca. 1987	2.00
❑571, ca. 1987	2.00
❑572, ca. 1987	2.00
❑573, ca. 1987	2.00
❑574, ca. 1987	2.00
❑575, ca. 1987	2.00
❑576, ca. 1987	2.00
❑577, ca. 1987	2.00
❑578, ca. 1987	2.00
❑579, ca. 1987	2.00
❑580, ca. 1988	2.00
❑581, ca. 1988	2.00
❑582, ca. 1988	2.00
❑583, ca. 1988	2.00
❑584, ca. 1988	2.00
❑585, ca. 1988	2.00
❑586, ca. 1988	2.00
❑587, ca. 1988	2.00
❑588, ca. 1988	2.00
❑589, ca. 1988	2.00
❑590, ca. 1988	2.00
❑591, ca. 1988	2.00
❑592, ca. 1989	2.00
❑593, ca. 1989	2.00

	N-MINT
❑594, ca. 1989	2.00
❑595, ca. 1989	2.00
❑596, ca. 1989	2.00
❑597, ca. 1989	2.00
❑598, ca. 1989	2.00
❑599, ca. 1989	2.00
❑600, ca. 1989	2.00
❑601, ca. 1989	1.50
❑602, ca. 1989	1.50
❑603, ca. 1990	1.50
❑604, ca. 1990	1.50
❑605, ca. 1990	1.50
❑606, ca. 1990	1.50
❑607, ca. 1990; Archie Giant Series Magazine Presents Little Archie A: Little Sabrina. A: Chester Punkett. A: South-Side Serpents. A: Mad Doctor Doom. A: Sue Stringly	1.50
❑608, ca. 1990	1.50
❑609, ca. 1990	1.50
❑610, ca. 1990	1.50
❑611, ca. 1990	1.50
❑612, ca. 1990	1.50
❑613, ca. 1990	1.50
❑614, Oct 1990; Pep Comics; Archie characters meet Archie Comics staff	1.50
❑615, ca. 1990	1.50
❑616, ca. 1990	1.50
❑617, ca. 1991	1.50
❑618, ca. 1991	1.50
❑619, ca. 1991	1.50
❑620, ca. 1991	1.50
❑621, ca. 1991	1.50
❑622, ca. 1991	1.50
❑623, ca. 1991	1.50
❑624, ca. 1991	1.50
❑625, ca. 1991	1.50
❑626, ca. 1992	1.50
❑627, ca. 1992	1.50
❑628, ca. 1992	1.50
❑629, ca. 1992	1.50
❑630, ca. 1992	1.50
❑631, Jun 1992	1.50
❑632, Jul 1992	1.50

ARCHIE MEETS THE PUNISHER

MARVEL

	N-MINT
❑1, Aug 1994; Archie cover	3.25

ARCHIE'S CHRISTMAS STOCKING (2ND SERIES)

ARCHIE

	N-MINT
❑1, Jan 1994; DDC (a); For 1993 holiday season	2.50
❑2; For 1994 holiday season	2.00
❑3; For 1995 holiday season	2.00
❑4; For 1996 holiday season	2.00
❑5; For 1997 holiday season	2.25
❑6; For 1998 holiday season	2.25
❑7; For 1999 holiday season	2.29

ARCHIE'S DATE BOOK

SPIRE

	N-MINT
❑1; religious	4.00

ARCHIE'S DOUBLE DIGEST MAGAZINE

ARCHIE

	N-MINT
❑1, Jan 1982	6.00
❑2, May 1982 DDC (c)	3.50
❑3, Jul 1982 DDC (c)	3.50
❑4, Oct 1982	3.50
❑5, Jan 1983	3.50
❑6, May 1983 DDC (c)	3.50
❑7, Jul 1983 DDC (c)	3.50
❑8, Oct 1983 DDC (c)	3.50
❑9, Jan 1984 DDC (c)	3.50
❑10, May 1984 DDC (c)	3.50
❑11, Jul 1984 DDC (c)	3.00
❑12, Sep 1984 DDC (c)	3.00
❑13, Nov 1984	3.00
❑14, Jan 1985	3.00
❑15, Mar 1985 DDC (c)	3.00
❑16, May 1985 DDC (c)	3.00
❑17, Jul 1985 DDC (c)	3.00
❑18, Sep 1985 DDC (c)	3.00
❑19, Nov 1985 DDC (c)	3.00
❑20, Jan 1986	3.00
❑21, Mar 1986 DDC (c)	3.00
❑22, May 1986 DDC (c)	3.00
❑23, Jul 1986 DDC (c)	3.00
❑24, Sep 1986 DDC (c)	3.00
❑25, Nov 1986 DDC (c)	3.00
❑26, Jan 1987 DDC (c)	3.00
❑27, Mar 1987 DDC (c)	3.00
❑28, May 1987 DDC (c)	3.00
❑29, Jul 1987 DDC (c)	3.00
❑30, Sep 1987 DDC (c)	3.00
❑31, Nov 1987 DDC (c)	3.00
❑32, Jan 1988 DDC (c)	3.00
❑33, Mar 1988 DDC (c)	3.00
❑34, May 1988 DDC (c)	3.00
❑35, Jul 1988 DDC (c)	3.00
❑36, Sep 1988 DDC (c)	3.00
❑37, Nov 1988 DDC (c)	3.00
❑38, Jan 1989 DDC (c)	3.00
❑39, Mar 1989 DDC (c)	3.00
❑40, May 1989 DDC (c)	3.00
❑41, Jul 1989	3.00
❑42, Sep 1989	3.00
❑43, Nov 1989	3.00
❑44, Jan 1990	3.00
❑45, Mar 1990	3.00
❑46, May 1990	3.00
❑47, Jul 1990	3.00
❑48, Sep 1990	3.00
❑49, Nov 1990	3.00
❑50, Jan 1991	3.00
❑51, Mar 1991	3.00
❑52, May 1991	3.00
❑53, Jul 1991	3.00
❑54, Sep 1991	3.00
❑55, Nov 1991	3.00
❑56, Dec 1991	3.00
❑57, Feb 1992	3.00
❑58, Apr 1992	3.00
❑59, Jun 1992	3.00
❑60, Aug 1992	3.00
❑61, Sep 1992	3.00
❑62, Nov 1992	3.00
❑63, Jan 1993	3.00
❑64, Mar 1993	3.00
❑65, May 1993	3.00
❑66, Jul 1993	3.00
❑67, Sep 1993	3.00
❑68, Oct 1993	3.00
❑69, Dec 1993	3.00
❑70, Feb 1994	3.00
❑71, Apr 1994	3.00
❑72, Jun 1994	3.00
❑73, Aug 1994	3.00
❑74, Oct 1994	3.00
❑75, Nov 1994	3.00
❑76, Jan 1995	3.00
❑77, Mar 1995	3.00
❑78, May 1995	3.00
❑79, Jul 1995	3.00
❑80, Aug 1995	2.75
❑81, Oct 1995	2.75
❑82, Dec 1995	2.75
❑83, Feb 1996	2.75
❑84, Apr 1996	2.75
❑85, May 1996	2.75
❑86, Jul 1996	2.75
❑87, Sep 1996	2.75
❑88, Oct 1996	2.75
❑89, Dec 1996	2.75
❑90, Feb 1997	2.75
❑91, Mar 1997	2.75
❑92, May 1997	2.75
❑93, Jul 1997	2.75
❑94, Aug 1997	2.75
❑95, Oct 1997	2.75
❑96, Dec 1997	2.75
❑97, Feb 1998	2.75
❑98, Mar 1998	2.75

Archie's Giant Series offered readers more stories for their money.

© 1968 Archie Publications Inc.

	N-MINT
❑99, May 1998	2.75
❑100, Jul 1998	2.75
❑101, Aug 1998	2.75
❑102, Sep 1998	2.75
❑103, Nov 1998 DDC (w)	2.95
❑104, Dec 1998	2.95
❑105, Feb 1999	2.95
❑106, Apr 1999	2.95
❑107, May 1999	2.99
❑108, Jun 1999	2.99
❑109, Aug 1999	2.99
❑110, Sep 1999	2.99
❑111, Nov 1999	2.95
❑112, Dec 1999	2.99
❑113, Feb 2000	2.95
❑114, Mar 2000	2.99
❑115, May 2000	2.95
❑116, Jul 2000	2.95
❑117, Aug 2000	3.19
❑118, Sep 2000	3.19
❑119, Nov 2000	3.19
❑120, Dec 2000	3.19
❑121, Jan 2001	3.19
❑122, Mar 2001	3.19
❑123, Apr 2001	3.29
❑124, May 2001	3.29
❑125, Jul 2001	3.29
❑126, Aug 2001	3.29
❑127, Sep 2001	3.29
❑128, Nov 2001	3.29
❑129, Dec 2001	3.29
❑130, Jan 2002	3.29
❑131, Mar 2002	3.29
❑132, Apr 2002	3.29
❑133, May 2002	3.29
❑134, Jul 2002	3.29
❑135, Aug 2002	3.29
❑136, Sep 2002	3.29
❑137, Nov 2002	3.29
❑138, Dec 2002	3.29
❑139, Jan 2003	3.59
❑140, Mar 2003	3.59
❑141, Apr 2003	3.59
❑142, May 2003	3.59
❑143, Jul 2003	3.59
❑144, Sep 2003	3.59
❑145, Oct 2003	3.59
❑146, Nov 2003	3.59
❑147, Jan 2004	3.59
❑148, Feb 2004 AM (a)	3.59
❑149, Mar 2004	3.59
❑150, May 2004 AM (a)	3.59
❑151, Jun 2004	3.59
❑152, Jul 2004	3.59

ARCHIE'S FAMILY ALBUM

SPIRE

	N-MINT
❑1	4.00

ARCHIE'S GIRLS BETTY & VERONICA

ARCHIE

	N-MINT
❑27, Nov 1956	165.00
❑28, Jan 1957	165.00
❑29, Mar 1957	165.00
❑30, May 1957	115.00
❑31, Jul 1957	115.00
❑32, Sep 1957	115.00
❑33, Nov 1957	115.00
❑34, Jan 1958	115.00

	N-MINT
❑35, Mar 1958	115.00
❑36, May 1958	115.00
❑37, Jul 1958	115.00
❑38, Sep 1958	115.00
❑39, Nov 1958	115.00
❑40, Jan 1959	85.00
❑41, Mar 1959	85.00
❑42, May 1959	85.00
❑43, Jul 1959	85.00
❑44, Aug 1959	85.00
❑45, Sep 1959	85.00
❑46, Oct 1959	85.00
❑47, Nov 1959	85.00
❑48, Dec 1959	85.00
❑49, Jan 1960	85.00
❑50, Feb 1960	85.00
❑51, Mar 1960	55.00
❑52, Apr 1960	55.00
❑53, May 1960	55.00
❑54, Jun 1960	55.00
❑55, Jul 1960	55.00
❑56, Aug 1960	55.00
❑57, Sep 1960	55.00
❑58, Oct 1960	55.00
❑59, Nov 1960	55.00
❑60, Dec 1960	55.00
❑61, Jan 1961	45.00
❑62, Feb 1961	45.00
❑63, Mar 1961	45.00
❑64, Apr 1961	45.00
❑65, May 1961	45.00
❑66, Jun 1961	45.00
❑67, Jul 1961	45.00
❑68, Aug 1961	45.00
❑69, Sep 1961	45.00
❑70, Oct 1961	45.00
❑71, Nov 1961	32.00
❑72, Dec 1961	32.00
❑73, Jan 1962	32.00
❑74, Feb 1962	32.00
❑75, Mar 1962	32.00
❑76, Apr 1962	32.00
❑77, May 1962	32.00
❑78, Jun 1962	32.00
❑79, Jul 1962	32.00
❑80, Aug 1962	32.00
❑81, Sep 1962	32.00
❑82, Oct 1962	32.00
❑83, Nov 1962	32.00
❑84, Dec 1962	32.00
❑85, Jan 1963	32.00
❑86, Feb 1963	32.00
❑87, Mar 1963	32.00
❑88, Apr 1963	32.00
❑89, May 1963	32.00
❑90, Jun 1963	32.00
❑91, Jul 1963	24.00
❑92, Aug 1963	24.00
❑93, Sep 1963	24.00
❑94, Oct 1963	24.00
❑95, Nov 1963	24.00
❑96, Dec 1963	24.00
❑97, Jan 1964	24.00
❑98, Feb 1964	24.00
❑99, Mar 1964	24.00
❑100, Apr 1964	24.00
❑101, May 1964	24.00
❑102, Jun 1964	24.00
❑103, Jul 1964	24.00
❑104, Aug 1964	24.00
❑105, Sep 1964	24.00
❑106, Oct 1964	24.00
❑107, Nov 1964	24.00
❑108, Dec 1964	24.00
❑109, Jan 1965	24.00
❑110, Feb 1965	24.00
❑111, Mar 1965	16.00
❑112, Apr 1965	16.00
❑113, May 1965	16.00
❑114, Jun 1965	16.00
❑115, Jul 1965	16.00
❑116, Aug 1965	16.00
❑117, Sep 1965	16.00
❑118, Oct 1965	16.00
❑119, Nov 1965	16.00
❑120, Dec 1965	16.00
❑121, Jan 1966	16.00
❑122, Feb 1966	16.00
❑123, Mar 1966	16.00
❑124, Apr 1966	16.00
❑125, May 1966	16.00
❑126, Jun 1966	16.00
❑127, Jul 1966	16.00
❑128, Aug 1966	16.00
❑129, Sep 1966	16.00
❑130, Oct 1966	16.00
❑131, Nov 1966	16.00
❑132, Dec 1966	16.00
❑133, Jan 1967	16.00
❑134, Feb 1967	16.00
❑135, Mar 1967	16.00
❑136, Apr 1967	16.00
❑137, May 1967	16.00
❑138, Jun 1967	16.00
❑139, Jul 1967	16.00
❑140, Aug 1967	16.00
❑141, Sep 1967	13.00
❑142, Oct 1967	13.00
❑143, Nov 1967	13.00
❑144, Dec 1967	13.00
❑145, Jan 1968	13.00
❑146, Feb 1968	13.00
❑147, Mar 1968	13.00
❑148, Apr 1968	13.00
❑149, May 1968	13.00
❑150, Jun 1968	13.00
❑151, Jul 1968	13.00
❑152, Aug 1968	13.00
❑153, Sep 1968	13.00
❑154, Oct 1968	13.00
❑155, Nov 1968	13.00
❑156, Dec 1968	13.00
❑157, Jan 1969	13.00
❑158, Feb 1969	13.00
❑159, Mar 1969	13.00
❑160, Apr 1969	13.00
❑161, May 1969	10.00
❑162, Jun 1969	10.00
❑163, Jul 1969	10.00
❑164, Aug 1969	10.00
❑165, Sep 1969	10.00
❑166, Oct 1969	10.00
❑167, Nov 1969	10.00
❑168, Dec 1969	10.00
❑169, Jan 1970	10.00
❑170, Feb 1970	10.00
❑171, Mar 1970	10.00
❑172, Apr 1970	10.00
❑173, May 1970	10.00
❑174, Jun 1970	10.00
❑175, Jul 1970	10.00
❑176, Aug 1970	10.00
❑177, Sep 1970	10.00
❑178, Oct 1970	10.00
❑179, Nov 1970	10.00
❑180, Dec 1970	10.00
❑181, Jan 1971	7.00
❑182, Feb 1971	7.00
❑183, Mar 1971	7.00
❑184, Apr 1971	7.00
❑185, May 1971	7.00
❑186, Jun 1971	7.00
❑187, Jul 1971	7.00
❑188, Aug 1971	7.00
❑189, Sep 1971	7.00
❑190, Oct 1971	7.00
❑191, Nov 1971	7.00
❑192, Dec 1971	7.00
❑193, Jan 1972	7.00
❑194, Feb 1972	7.00
❑195, Mar 1972	7.00
❑196, Apr 1972	7.00
❑197, May 1972	7.00
❑198, Jun 1972	7.00
❑199, Jul 1972	7.00
❑200, Aug 1972	7.00
❑201, Sep 1972	5.00
❑202, Oct 1972	5.00
❑203, Nov 1972	5.00
❑204, Dec 1972	5.00
❑205, Jan 1973	5.00
❑206, Feb 1973	5.00
❑207, Mar 1973	5.00
❑208, Apr 1973	5.00
❑209, May 1973	5.00
❑210, Jun 1973	5.00
❑211, Jul 1973	5.00
❑212, Aug 1973	5.00
❑213, Sep 1973	5.00
❑214, Oct 1973	5.00
❑215, Nov 1973	5.00
❑216, Dec 1973	5.00
❑217, Jan 1974	5.00
❑218, Feb 1974	5.00
❑219, Mar 1974	5.00
❑220, Apr 1974	5.00
❑221, May 1974	5.00
❑222, Jun 1974	5.00
❑223, Jul 1974	5.00
❑224, Aug 1974	5.00
❑225, Sep 1974	5.00
❑226, Oct 1974	5.00
❑227, Nov 1974	5.00
❑228, Dec 1974	5.00
❑229, Jan 1975	5.00
❑230, Feb 1975	5.00
❑231, Mar 1975	5.00
❑232, Apr 1975	5.00
❑233, May 1975	5.00
❑234, Jun 1975	5.00
❑235, Jul 1975	5.00
❑236, Aug 1975	5.00
❑237, Sep 1975	5.00
❑238, Oct 1975	5.00
❑239, Nov 1975	5.00
❑240, Dec 1975	5.00
❑241, Jan 1976	5.00
❑242, Feb 1976	5.00
❑243, Mar 1976	5.00
❑244, Apr 1976	5.00
❑245, May 1976	5.00
❑246, Jun 1976	5.00
❑247, Jul 1976	5.00
❑248, Aug 1976	5.00
❑249, Sep 1976	5.00
❑250, Oct 1976	5.00
❑251, Nov 1976	3.00
❑252, Dec 1976	3.00
❑253, Jan 1977	3.00
❑254, Feb 1977	3.00
❑255, Mar 1977	3.00
❑256, Apr 1977	3.00
❑257, May 1977	3.00
❑258, Jun 1977	3.00
❑259, Jul 1977	3.00
❑260, Aug 1977	3.00
❑261, Sep 1977	3.00
❑262, Oct 1977	3.00
❑263, Nov 1977	3.00
❑264, Dec 1977	3.00
❑265, Jan 1978	3.00
❑266, Feb 1978	3.00
❑267, Mar 1978	3.00
❑268, Apr 1978	3.00
❑269, May 1978	3.00
❑270, Jun 1978	3.00
❑271, Jul 1978	3.00
❑272, Aug 1978	3.00
❑273, Sep 1978	3.00
❑274, Oct 1978	3.00
❑275, Nov 1978	3.00
❑276, Dec 1978	3.00
❑277, Jan 1979	3.00

Condition price index: Multiply "NM prices" above by: **0.83 for Very Fine/Near Mint**
0.66 for Very Fine • 0.33 for Fine • 0.2 for Very Good • 0.125 for Good

	N-MINT
❑278, Feb 1979	3.00
❑279, Mar 1979	3.00
❑280, Apr 1979	3.00
❑281, May 1979	3.00
❑282, Jun 1979	3.00
❑283, Jul 1979	3.00
❑284, Aug 1979	3.00
❑285, Sep 1979	3.00
❑286, Oct 1979	3.00
❑287, Nov 1979	3.00
❑288, Dec 1979	3.00
❑289, Jan 1980	3.00
❑290, Feb 1980	3.00
❑291, Mar 1980	3.00
❑292, Apr 1980	3.00
❑293, May 1980	3.00
❑294, Jun 1980	3.00
❑295, Jul 1980	3.00
❑296, Aug 1980	3.00
❑297, Sep 1980	3.00
❑298, Oct 1980	3.00
❑299, Nov 1980	3.00
❑300, Dec 1980	3.00
❑301, Jan 1981	2.50
❑302, Feb 1981	2.50
❑303, Mar 1981	2.50
❑304, Apr 1981	2.50
❑305, May 1981	2.50
❑306, Jun 1981	2.50
❑307, Jul 1981	2.50
❑308, Aug 1981	2.50
❑309, Sep 1981	2.50
❑310, Oct 1981	2.50
❑311, Nov 1981	2.50
❑312, Dec 1981	2.50
❑313, Jan 1982	2.50
❑314, Feb 1982	2.50
❑315, Mar 1982	2.50
❑316, Apr 1982	2.50
❑317, May 1982	2.50
❑318, Jun 1982	2.50
❑319, Aug 1982	2.50
❑320, Oct 1982 1: Cheryl Blossom	8.00
❑321, Dec 1982	4.00
❑322, Feb 1983	3.00
❑323, Apr 1983	3.00
❑324, Jun 1983	2.50
❑325, Aug 1983	2.50
❑326, Oct 1983	2.50
❑327, Dec 1983	2.50
❑328, Feb 1984	2.50
❑329, Apr 1984	2.50
❑330, Jun 1984	2.50
❑331, Aug 1984	2.50
❑332, Oct 1984	2.50
❑333, Dec 1984	2.50
❑334, Feb 1985	2.50
❑335, Apr 1985	2.50
❑336, Jun 1985	2.50
❑337, Aug 1985	2.50
❑338, Oct 1985	2.50
❑339, Dec 1985	2.50
❑340, Feb 1986	2.50
❑341, Apr 1986	2.50
❑342, Jun 1986	2.50
❑343, Aug 1986	2.50
❑344, Oct 1986	2.50
❑345, Dec 1986	2.50
❑346, Feb 1987	2.50
❑347, Apr 1987	2.50
❑Annual 1, ca. 1953	525.00
❑Annual 2, ca. 1954	325.00
❑Annual 3, ca. 1955	265.00
❑Annual 4, ca. 1956	265.00
❑Annual 5, ca. 1957	250.00
❑Annual 6, ca. 1958	175.00
❑Annual 7, ca. 1959	150.00
❑Annual 8, ca. 1960	100.00

ARCHIE'S HOLIDAY FUN DIGEST MAGAZINE
ARCHIE

	N-MINT
❑1, Feb 1997	1.95
❑2, Feb 1998	1.95
❑3, Feb 1999	1.95
❑4, Feb 2000	1.99
❑5, Jan 2001	2.19
❑6, Jan 2002	2.19
❑7, Jan 2003	2.19
❑8, Dec 2003	2.39

ARCHIE'S JOKEBOOK MAGAZINE
ARCHIE

	N-MINT
❑24, Sep 1956	100.00
❑25, Nov 1956	100.00
❑26, Jan 1957	100.00
❑27, Mar 1957	100.00
❑28, May 1957	100.00
❑29, Jul 1957	100.00
❑30, Sep 1957	100.00
❑31, Nov 1957	75.00
❑32, Jan 1958	75.00
❑33, Mar 1958	75.00
❑34, May 1958	75.00
❑35, Jul 1958	75.00
❑36, Sep 1958	75.00
❑37, Nov 1958	75.00
❑38, Jan 1959	75.00
❑39, Mar 1959	75.00
❑40, May 1959	75.00
❑41, Jul 1959; NA (a); First pro work by Neal Adams	135.00
❑42, Sep 1959	65.00
❑43, Nov 1959	65.00
❑44, Jan 1960 NA (a)	70.00
❑45, Mar 1960 NA (a)	70.00
❑46, May 1960 NA (a)	70.00
❑47, Jul 1960 NA (a)	70.00
❑48, Sep 1960 NA (a)	70.00
❑49, Nov 1960	35.00
❑50, Dec 1960	35.00
❑51, Feb 1961	35.00
❑52, Apr 1961	35.00
❑53, May 1961	35.00
❑54, Jun 1961	35.00
❑55, Jul 1961	35.00
❑56, Aug 1961	35.00
❑57, Sep 1961	35.00
❑58, Oct 1961	35.00
❑59, Dec 1961	35.00
❑60, Feb 1962	35.00
❑61, Apr 1962	24.00
❑62, Jun 1962	24.00
❑63, Jul 1962	24.00
❑64, Aug 1962	24.00
❑65, Sep 1962	24.00
❑66, Oct 1962	24.00
❑67, Dec 1962	24.00
❑68, Feb 1963	24.00
❑69, Apr 1963	24.00
❑70, Jun 1963	24.00
❑71, Jul 1963	16.00
❑72, Aug 1963	16.00
❑73, Sep 1963	16.00
❑74, Oct 1963	16.00
❑75, Dec 1963	16.00
❑76, Feb 1964	16.00
❑77, Apr 1964	16.00
❑78, Jun 1964	16.00
❑79, Jul 1964	16.00
❑80, Aug 1964	16.00
❑81, Sep 1964	12.00
❑82, Oct 1964	12.00
❑83, Dec 1964	12.00
❑84, Jan 1965	12.00
❑85, Feb 1965	12.00
❑86, Mar 1965	12.00
❑87, Apr 1965	12.00
❑88, May 1965	12.00
❑89, Jun 1965	12.00
❑90, Jul 1965	12.00

Betty and Veronica have had several series separate from Archie.

© 2003 Archie Publications Inc.

	N-MINT
❑91, Aug 1965	8.00
❑92, Sep 1965	8.00
❑93, Oct 1965	8.00
❑94, Nov 1965	8.00
❑95, Dec 1965	8.00
❑96, Jan 1966	8.00
❑97, Feb 1966	8.00
❑98, Mar 1966	8.00
❑99, Apr 1966	8.00
❑100, May 1966	8.00
❑101, Jun 1966	5.00
❑102, Jul 1966	5.00
❑103, Aug 1966	5.00
❑104, Sep 1966	5.00
❑105, Oct 1966	5.00
❑106, Nov 1966	5.00
❑107, Dec 1966	5.00
❑108, Jan 1967	5.00
❑109, Feb 1967	5.00
❑110, Mar 1967	5.00
❑111, Apr 1967	5.00
❑112, May 1967	5.00
❑113, Jun 1967	5.00
❑114, Jul 1967	5.00
❑115, Aug 1967	5.00
❑116, Aug 1967	5.00
❑117, Oct 1967	5.00
❑118, Nov 1967	5.00
❑119, Dec 1967	5.00
❑120, Jan 1968	5.00
❑121, Feb 1968	3.00
❑122, Mar 1968	3.00
❑123, Apr 1968	3.00
❑124, May 1968	3.00
❑125, Jun 1968	3.00
❑126, Jul 1968	3.00
❑127, Aug 1968	3.00
❑128, Sep 1968	3.00
❑129, Oct 1968	3.00
❑130, Nov 1968	3.00
❑131, Dec 1968	3.00
❑132, Jan 1969	3.00
❑133, Feb 1969	3.00
❑134, Mar 1969	3.00
❑135, Apr 1969	3.00
❑136, May 1969	3.00
❑137, Jun 1969	3.00
❑138, Jul 1969	3.00
❑139, Aug 1969	3.00
❑140, Sep 1969	3.00
❑141, Oct 1969	3.00
❑142, Nov 1969	3.00
❑143, Dec 1969	3.00
❑144, Jan 1970	3.00
❑145, Feb 1970	3.00
❑146, Mar 1970	3.00
❑147, Apr 1970	3.00
❑148, May 1970	3.00
❑149, Jun 1970	3.00
❑150, Jul 1970	3.00
❑151, Aug 1970	2.00
❑152, Sep 1970	2.00
❑153, Oct 1970	2.00
❑154, Nov 1970	2.00
❑155, Dec 1970	2.00
❑156, Jan 1971	2.00
❑157, Feb 1971	2.00

Condition price index: Multiply "NM prices" above by: **0.83 for Very Fine/Near Mint**
0.66 for Very Fine • 0.33 for Fine • 0.2 for Very Good • 0.125 for Good

	N-MINT
❑158, Mar 1971	2.00
❑159, Apr 1971	2.00
❑160, May 1971	2.00
❑161, Jun 1971	2.00
❑162, Jul 1971	2.00
❑163, Aug 1971	2.00
❑164, Sep 1971	2.00
❑165, Oct 1971	2.00
❑166, Nov 1971	2.00
❑167, Dec 1971	2.00
❑168, Jan 1972	2.00
❑169, Feb 1972	2.00
❑170, Mar 1972	2.00
❑171, Apr 1972	2.00
❑172, May 1972	2.00
❑173, Jun 1972	2.00
❑174, Jul 1972	2.00
❑175, Aug 1972	2.00
❑176, Sep 1972	2.00
❑177, Oct 1972	2.00
❑178, Nov 1972	2.00
❑179, Dec 1972	2.00
❑180, Jan 1973	2.00
❑181, Feb 1973	1.50
❑182, Mar 1973	1.50
❑183, Apr 1973	1.50
❑184, May 1973	1.50
❑185, Jun 1973	1.50
❑186, Jul 1973	1.50
❑187, Aug 1973	1.50
❑188, Sep 1973	1.50
❑189, Oct 1973	1.50
❑190, Nov 1973	1.50
❑191, Dec 1973	1.50
❑192, Jan 1974	1.50
❑193, Feb 1974	1.50
❑194, Mar 1974	1.50
❑195, Apr 1974	1.50
❑196, May 1974	1.50
❑197, Jun 1974	1.50
❑198, Jul 1974	1.50
❑199, Aug 1974	1.50
❑200, Sep 1974	1.50
❑201, Oct 1974	1.00
❑202, Nov 1974	1.00
❑203, Dec 1974	1.00
❑204, Jan 1975	1.00
❑205, Feb 1975	1.00
❑206, Mar 1975	1.00
❑207, Apr 1975	1.00
❑208, May 1975	1.00
❑209, Jun 1975	1.00
❑210, Jul 1975	1.00
❑211, Aug 1975	1.00
❑212, Sep 1975	1.00
❑213, Oct 1975	1.00
❑214, Nov 1975	1.00
❑215, Dec 1975	1.00
❑216, Jan 1976	1.00
❑217, Feb 1976	1.00
❑218, Mar 1976	1.00
❑219, Apr 1976	1.00
❑220, May 1976	1.00
❑221, Jun 1976	1.00
❑222, Jul 1976	1.00
❑223, Aug 1976	1.00
❑224, Sep 1976	1.00
❑225, Oct 1976	1.00
❑226, Nov 1976	1.00
❑227, Dec 1976	1.00
❑228, Jan 1977	1.00
❑229, Feb 1977	1.00
❑230, Mar 1977	1.00
❑231, Apr 1977	1.00
❑232, May 1977	1.00
❑233, Jun 1977	1.00
❑234, Jul 1977	1.00
❑235, Aug 1977	1.00
❑236, Sep 1977	1.00
❑237, Oct 1977	1.00
❑238, Nov 1977	1.00
❑239, Dec 1977	1.00
❑240, Jan 1978	1.00
❑241, Feb 1978	1.00
❑242, Mar 1978	1.00
❑243, Apr 1978	1.00
❑244, May 1978	1.00
❑245, Jun 1978	1.00
❑246, Jul 1978	1.00
❑247, Aug 1978	1.00
❑248, Sep 1978	1.00
❑249, Oct 1978	1.00
❑250, Nov 1978	1.00
❑251, Dec 1978	1.00
❑252, Jan 1979	1.00
❑253, Feb 1979	1.00
❑254, Mar 1979	1.00
❑255, Apr 1979	1.00
❑256, May 1979	1.00
❑257, Jun 1979	1.00
❑258, Jul 1979	1.00
❑259, Aug 1979	1.00
❑260, Sep 1979	1.00
❑261, Oct 1979	1.00
❑262, Nov 1979	1.00
❑263, Dec 1979	1.00
❑264, Jan 1980	1.00
❑265, Feb 1980	1.00
❑266, Mar 1980	1.00
❑267, Apr 1980	1.00
❑268, May 1980	1.00
❑269, Jun 1980	1.00
❑270, Jul 1980	1.00
❑271, Aug 1980	1.00
❑272, Sep 1980	1.00
❑273, Nov 1980	1.00
❑274, Jan 1981	1.00
❑275, Mar 1981	1.00
❑276, May 1981	1.00
❑277, Jun 1981	1.00
❑278, Jul 1981	1.00
❑279, Aug 1981	1.00
❑280, Sep 1981	1.00
❑281, Oct 1981	1.00
❑282, Nov 1981	1.00
❑283, Jan 1982	1.00
❑284, Mar 1982	1.00
❑285, May 1982	1.00
❑286, Jul 1982	1.00
❑287, Sep 1982	1.00
❑288, Nov 1982	1.00

ARCHIE'S MADHOUSE
ARCHIE

	N-MINT
❑1, Sep 1959	175.00
❑2, Nov 1959	95.00
❑3, Jan 1960	68.00
❑4, Mar 1960	50.00
❑5, Jun 1960	50.00
❑6, Aug 1960	38.00
❑7, Sep 1960	38.00
❑8, Oct 1960	38.00
❑9, Dec 1960	38.00
❑10, Feb 1961	38.00
❑11, Apr 1961	26.00
❑12, Jun 1961	26.00
❑13, Aug 1961	26.00
❑14, Sep 1961	26.00
❑15, Oct 1961	26.00
❑16, Dec 1961	23.00
❑17, Feb 1962	23.00
❑18, Apr 1962	23.00
❑19, Jun 1962	23.00
❑20, Aug 1962	23.00
❑21, Sep 1962	18.00
❑22, Oct 1962 1: Sabrina the Teen-age Witch	100.00
❑23, Dec 1962	18.00
❑24, Feb 1963	18.00
❑25, Apr 1963	18.00
❑26, Jun 1963	14.00
❑27, Aug 1963	14.00
❑28, Sep 1963	14.00
❑29, Oct 1963	14.00
❑30, Dec 1963	14.00
❑31, Feb 1963	9.00
❑32, Apr 1964	9.00
❑33, Jun 1964	9.00
❑34, Aug 1964	9.00
❑35, Sep 1964	9.00
❑36, Oct 1964	9.00
❑37, Dec 1964	9.00
❑38, Feb 1965	9.00
❑39, Apr 1965	9.00
❑40, Jun 1965	9.00
❑41, Aug 1965	6.00
❑42, Sep 1965	6.00
❑43, Oct 1965	6.00
❑44, Dec 1965	6.00
❑45, Feb 1966	6.00
❑46, Apr 1966	6.00
❑47, Jun 1966	6.00
❑48, Aug 1966	6.00
❑49, Sep 1966	6.00
❑50, Oct 1966	6.00
❑51, Dec 1966	3.50
❑52, Feb 1967	3.50
❑53, Apr 1967	3.50
❑54, Jun 1967	3.50
❑55, Aug 1967	3.50
❑56, Sep 1967	3.50
❑57, Oct 1967	3.50
❑58, Dec 1967	3.50
❑59, Feb 1968	3.50
❑60, Apr 1968	3.50
❑61, Jun 1968	3.50
❑62, Aug 1968	3.50
❑63, Sep 1968	3.50
❑64, Oct 1968	3.50
❑65, Dec 1968; Series continues as Madhouse Ma-ad Jokes	3.50
❑66, Jan 1969	3.50
❑Annual 1, ca. 1962	65.00
❑Annual 2, ca. 1964	25.00
❑Annual 3, ca. 1965	15.00
❑Annual 4, ca. 1966	10.00
❑Annual 5, ca. 1968	10.00
❑Annual 6, ca. 1969	10.00

ARCHIE'S MYSTERIES
ARCHIE

	N-MINT
❑25, Feb 2003; Continues numbering from Archie's Weird Mysteries	2.19
❑26, Apr 2003	2.19
❑27, Jun 2003	2.19
❑28, Aug 2003	2.19
❑29, Sep 2003	2.19
❑30, Oct 2003	2.19
❑31, Nov 2003	2.19
❑32, Jan 2004	2.19
❑33, Mar 2004	2.19
❑34, May 2004	2.19

ARCHIE'S PAL JUGHEAD COMICS
ARCHIE

	N-MINT
❑46, Jun 1993; Series continued from Jughead #45	1.50
❑47, Jul 1993	1.50
❑48, Aug 1993	1.50
❑49, Sep 1993	1.50
❑50, Nov 1993	1.50
❑51, Dec 1993	1.50
❑52, Jan 1994	1.50
❑53, Feb 1994	1.50
❑54, Mar 1994	1.50
❑55, Apr 1994	1.50
❑56, May 1994	1.50
❑57, Jun 1994	1.50
❑58, Jul 1994	1.50
❑59, Aug 1994	1.50
❑60, Sep 1994	1.50
❑61, Oct 1994	1.50
❑62, Nov 1994	1.50
❑63, Dec 1994	1.50
❑64, Jan 1995	1.50
❑65, Feb 1995	1.50

	N-MINT
❑66, Mar 1995	1.50
❑67, Apr 1995	1.50
❑68, May 1995	1.50
❑69, Jun 1995	1.50
❑70, Jul 1995	1.50
❑71, Aug 1995	1.50
❑72, Sep 1995; Jellybean's real name revealed	1.50
❑73, Oct 1995	1.50
❑74, Nov 1995	1.50
❑75, Dec 1995	1.50
❑76, Jan 1996	1.50
❑77, Feb 1996	1.50
❑78, Mar 1996	1.50
❑79, Apr 1996	1.50
❑80, May 1996	1.50
❑81, Jun 1996	1.50
❑82, Jul 1996	1.50
❑83, Aug 1996	1.50
❑84, Sep 1996	1.50
❑85, Oct 1996	1.50
❑86, Nov 1996	1.50
❑87, Dec 1996	1.50
❑88, Jan 1997	1.50
❑89, Feb 1997 1: Trula Twist and J.U.S.T.	1.50
❑90, Mar 1997; Jughead asks Trula out	1.50
❑91, Apr 1997; Trula Twyst's true plan revealed	1.50
❑92, May 1997	1.50
❑93, Jun 1997 A: Trula Twyst	1.50
❑94, Jul 1997 A: Trula Twyst	1.50
❑95, Aug 1997	1.50
❑96, Sep 1997	1.50
❑97, Oct 1997 A: Trula Twyst	1.50
❑98, Nov 1997	1.50
❑99, Dec 1997 A: Trula Twyst	1.50
❑100, Jan 1998; continues in Archie #467	1.50
❑101, Feb 1998 1: Googie Gilmore	1.50
❑102, Mar 1998	1.50
❑103, Apr 1998	1.50
❑104, May 1998	1.50
❑105, Jun 1998	1.50
❑106, Jul 1998 A: Googie Gilmore	1.50
❑107, Aug 1998	1.50
❑108, Sep 1998	1.75
❑109, Oct 1998	1.75
❑110, Nov 1998	1.75
❑111, Dec 1998	1.75
❑112, Jan 1999 A: Trula Twyst	1.75
❑113, Feb 1999	1.75
❑114, Mar 1999 A: Trula Twyst	1.75
❑115, Apr 1999	1.75
❑116, May 1999	1.75
❑117, Jun 1999 A: Trula Twyst	1.75
❑118, Jul 1999 A: Trula Twyst	1.75
❑119, Aug 1999; Ethel gets Jughead's baby pictures	1.75
❑120, Sep 1999 A: Trula Twyst	1.75
❑121, Oct 1999	1.75
❑122, Nov 1999	1.75
❑123, Dec 1999	1.75
❑124, Jan 2000	1.75
❑125, Feb 2000	1.75
❑126, Apr 2000	1.75
❑127, May 2000	1.75
❑128, Jul 2000	1.99
❑129, Aug 2000	1.99
❑130, Sep 2000	1.99
❑131, Oct 2000	1.99
❑132, Dec 2000	1.99
❑133, Jan 2001	1.99
❑134, Feb 2001	1.99
❑135, Apr 2001	1.99
❑136, May 2001	1.99
❑137, Jul 2001	1.99
❑138, Aug 2001	1.99
❑139, Sep 2001	1.99
❑140, Dec 2001	2.19
❑141, Feb 2002	2.19
❑142, Apr 2002	2.19
❑143, Jun 2002	2.19
❑144, Aug 2002	2.19
❑145, Sep 2002	2.19
❑146, Oct 2002	2.19
❑147, Dec 2002	2.19
❑148, Feb 2003	2.19
❑149, Apr 2003	2.19
❑150, Jun 2003	2.19
❑151, Jul 2003	2.19
❑152, Sep 2003	2.19
❑153, Oct 2003	2.19
❑154, Dec 2003	2.19
❑155, Feb 2004	2.19
❑156, Apr 2004	2.19
❑157, Jun 2004	2.19

ARCHIE'S PALS 'N' GALS

ARCHIE

	N-MINT
❑1, ca. 1952	575.00
❑2, ca. 1954	290.00
❑3, ca. 1955	215.00
❑4, ca. 1956	185.00
❑5, ca. 1957	185.00
❑6, ca. 1958	135.00
❑7, ca. 1958	135.00
❑8, Spr 1959	80.00
❑9, Sum 1959	80.00
❑10, Fal 1959	80.00
❑11, Win 1959	45.00
❑12, Spr 1960	45.00
❑13, Sum 1960	45.00
❑14, Fal 1960	45.00
❑15, Win 1960	45.00
❑16, Spr 1961	45.00
❑17, Sum 1961	45.00
❑18, Fal 1961	45.00
❑19, Win 1961	45.00
❑20, Spr 1962	45.00
❑21, Sum 1962	22.00
❑22, Fal 1962	22.00
❑23, Win 1962	22.00
❑24, Spr 1963	22.00
❑25, Sum 1963	22.00
❑26, Fal 1963	22.00
❑27, Win 1963	22.00
❑28, Spr 1964	22.00
❑29, Sum 1964 A: The Beatles	45.00
❑30, Fal 1964	22.00
❑31, Win 1964	13.00
❑32, Spr 1965	13.00
❑33, Sum 1965	13.00
❑34, Fal 1965	13.00
❑35, Win 1965	13.00
❑36, Spr 1966	13.00
❑37, Sum 1966	13.00
❑38, Fal 1966	13.00
❑39, Win 1966	13.00
❑40, Spr 1967	13.00
❑41, Aug 1967	9.00
❑42, Oct 1967	9.00
❑43, Dec 1967	9.00
❑44, Feb 1968	9.00
❑45, Apr 1968	9.00
❑46, Jun 1968	9.00
❑47, Aug 1968	9.00
❑48, Oct 1968	9.00
❑49, Dec 1968	9.00
❑50, Feb 1969	9.00
❑51, Apr 1969	7.00
❑52, Jun 1969	7.00
❑53, Aug 1969	7.00
❑54, Oct 1969	7.00
❑55, Dec 1969	7.00
❑56, Feb 1970	7.00
❑57, Apr 1970	7.00
❑58, Jun 1970	7.00
❑59, Aug 1970	7.00
❑60, Oct 1970	7.00
❑61, Dec 1970	7.00
❑62, Feb 1971	7.00
❑63, Apr 1971	7.00
❑64, Jun 1971	7.00

A new member was added to the Archie cast when Jughead's sister, Jellybean, was born in 1993.

	N-MINT
❑65, Aug 1971	7.00
❑66, Oct 1971	7.00
❑67, Dec 1971	7.00
❑68, Feb 1972	7.00
❑69, Apr 1972	7.00
❑70, Jun 1972	7.00
❑71, Aug 1972	5.00
❑72, Sep 1972	5.00
❑73, Oct 1972	5.00
❑74, Dec 1972	5.00
❑75, Feb 1973	5.00
❑76, Apr 1973	5.00
❑77, Jun 1973	5.00
❑78, Jul 1973	5.00
❑79, Aug 1973	5.00
❑80, Sep 1973	5.00
❑81, Nov 1973	5.00
❑82, Dec 1973	4.00
❑83, Jan 1974	4.00
❑84, Apr 1974	4.00
❑85, Jun 1974	4.00
❑86, Jul 1974	4.00
❑87, Aug 1974	4.00
❑88, Sep 1974	4.00
❑89, Oct 1974	4.00
❑90, Nov 1974	4.00
❑91, Dec 1974	4.00
❑92, Mar 1975	4.00
❑93, Apr 1975	4.00
❑94, Jun 1975	4.00
❑95, Jul 1975	4.00
❑96, Aug 1975	4.00
❑97, Sep 1975	4.00
❑98, Oct 1975	4.00
❑99, Nov 1975	4.00
❑100, Dec 1975	4.00
❑101, Jan 1976	2.50
❑102, Feb 1976	2.50
❑103, Mar 1976	2.50
❑104, May 1976	2.50
❑105, Jun 1976	2.50
❑106, Jul 1976	2.50
❑107, Aug 1976	2.50
❑108, Sep 1976	2.50
❑109, Oct 1976	2.50
❑110, Dec 1976	2.50
❑111, Jan 1977	2.50
❑112, Mar 1977	2.50
❑113, May 1977	2.50
❑114, Jun 1977	2.50
❑115, Jul 1977	2.50
❑116, Aug 1977	2.50
❑117, Sep 1977	2.50
❑118, Oct 1977	2.50
❑119, Dec 1977	2.50
❑120, Jan 1978	2.50
❑121, Mar 1978	2.50
❑122, May 1978	2.50
❑123, Jun 1978	2.50
❑124, Jul 1978	2.50
❑125, Aug 1978	2.50
❑126, Sep 1978	2.50
❑127, Oct 1978	2.50
❑128, Dec 1978	2.50
❑129, Jan 1979	2.50
❑130, Mar 1979	2.50
❑131, May 1979	2.50

	N-MINT
❑132, Jun 1979	2.50
❑133, Jul 1979	2.50
❑134, Aug 1979	2.50
❑135, Sep 1979	2.50
❑136, Oct 1979	2.50
❑137, Dec 1979	2.50
❑138, Jan 1980	2.50
❑139, Mar 1980	2.50
❑140, May 1980	2.50
❑141, Jun 1980	2.50
❑142, Jul 1980	2.50
❑143, Aug 1980	2.50
❑144, Sep 1980	2.50
❑145, Oct 1980	2.50
❑146, Dec 1980	2.50
❑147, Jan 1981	2.50
❑148, Mar 1981	2.50
❑149, May 1981	2.50
❑150, Jun 1981	2.50
❑151, Jul 1981	2.00
❑152, Aug 1981	2.00
❑153, Sep 1981	2.00
❑154, Oct 1981	2.00
❑155, Dec 1981	2.00
❑156, Jan 1982	2.00
❑157, Mar 1982	2.00
❑158, May 1982	2.00
❑159, Jul 1982	2.00
❑160, Sep 1982	2.00
❑161, Nov 1982	2.00
❑162, Jan 1983	2.00
❑163, May 1983	2.00
❑164, Jul 1983	2.00
❑165, Sep 1983	2.00
❑166, Nov 1983	2.00
❑167, Jan 1984	2.00
❑168, Mar 1984	2.00
❑169, May 1984	2.00
❑170, Jul 1984	2.00
❑171, Sep 1984	2.00
❑172, Nov 1984	2.00
❑173, Jan 1985	2.00
❑174, Mar 1985	2.00
❑175, May 1985	2.00
❑176, Jul 1985	2.00
❑177, Sep 1985	2.00
❑178, Nov 1985	2.00
❑179, Jan 1986	2.00
❑180, Mar 1986	2.00
❑181, May 1986	2.00
❑182, Jul 1986	2.00
❑183, Sep 1986	2.00
❑184, Nov 1986	2.00
❑185, Jan 1987	2.00
❑186, Mar 1987	2.00
❑187, May 1987	2.00
❑188, Jun 1987	2.00
❑189, Jul 1987	2.00
❑190, Aug 1987	2.00
❑191, Sep 1987	2.00
❑192, Oct 1987	2.00
❑193, Nov 1987	2.00
❑194, Jan 1988	2.00
❑195, Mar 1988	2.00
❑196, May 1988	2.00
❑197, Jun 1988	2.00
❑198, Jul 1988	2.00
❑199, Aug 1988	2.00
❑200, Sep 1988	2.00
❑201, Oct 1988	1.50
❑202, Nov 1988	1.50
❑203, Jan 1989	1.50
❑204, Mar 1989	1.50
❑205, May 1989	1.50
❑206, Jun 1989	1.50
❑207, Jul 1989	1.50
❑208, Aug 1989	1.50
❑209, Sep 1989	1.50
❑210, Oct 1989	1.50
❑211, Nov 1989	1.50
❑212, Jan 1990	1.50
❑213, Mar 1990	1.50
❑214, May 1990	1.50
❑215, Jun 1990	1.50
❑216, Jul 1990	1.50
❑217, Aug 1990	1.50
❑218, Sep 1990	1.50
❑219, Nov 1990	1.50
❑220, Jan 1991	1.50
❑221, Mar 1991	1.50
❑222, May 1991	1.50
❑223, Jul 1991	1.50
❑224, Sep 1991	1.50

ARCHIE'S PALS 'N' GALS DOUBLE DIGEST
ARCHIE

	N-MINT
❑1	4.00
❑2	3.00
❑3	3.00
❑4	3.00
❑5	3.00
❑6	2.75
❑7	2.75
❑8	2.75
❑9, Jan 1995	2.75
❑10, Feb 1995	2.75
❑11, Apr 1995	2.75
❑12, Jun 1995	2.75
❑13, Aug 1995	2.75
❑14, Oct 1995	2.75
❑15, Dec 1995	2.75
❑16, Jan 1996	2.75
❑17, Mar 1996	2.75
❑18, May 1996	2.75
❑19, Jul 1996	2.75
❑20, Aug 1996	2.75
❑21, Oct 1996	2.75
❑22, Dec 1996	2.75
❑23, Jan 1997	2.75
❑24, Mar 1997	2.75
❑25, May 1997	2.75
❑26, Jul 1997	2.75
❑27, Aug 1997	2.75
❑28, Oct 1997	2.75
❑29, Dec 1997	2.75
❑30, Jan 1998	2.95
❑31, Mar 1998	2.95
❑32, May 1998	2.95
❑33, Jun 1998	2.95
❑34, Aug 1998	2.95
❑35, Sep 1998	2.95
❑36, Oct 1998	2.95
❑37, Dec 1998	2.95
❑38, Feb 1999	2.95
❑39, Apr 1999	2.95
❑40, May 1999	2.99
❑41, Jun 1999	2.99
❑42, Aug 1999	2.99
❑43, Sep 1999	2.99
❑44, Oct 1999	2.99
❑45, Dec 1999	2.99
❑46, Feb 2000	2.99
❑47, Mar 2000	2.99
❑48, May 2000	2.99
❑49, Jun 2000	3.19
❑50, Aug 2000	3.19
❑51, Sep 2000	3.19
❑52, Oct 2000	3.19
❑53, Dec 2000	3.19
❑54, Feb 2001	3.19
❑55, Mar 2001	3.19
❑56, May 2001	3.29
❑57, Jun 2001	3.29
❑58, Aug 2001	3.29
❑59, Sep 2001	3.29
❑60, Oct 2001	3.29
❑61, Dec 2001	3.29
❑62, Feb 2002	3.29
❑63, Mar 2002	3.29
❑64, May 2002	3.29
❑65, Jun 2002	3.29
❑66, Aug 2002	3.29
❑67, Sep 2002	3.29
❑68, Oct 2002	3.29
❑69, Dec 2002	3.29
❑70, Feb 2003	3.29
❑71, Mar 2003	3.59
❑72, May 2003	3.59
❑73, Jun 2003	3.59
❑74, Aug 2003	3.59
❑75, Sep 2003	3.59
❑76, Oct 2003	3.59
❑77, Sep 2003	3.59
❑78, Oct 2003	3.59
❑79, Dec 2003	3.59
❑80, Jan 2004	3.59
❑81, Feb 2004	3.59
❑82, Apr 2004	3.59
❑83, May 2004	3.59
❑84, Jun 2004	3.59

ARCHIE'S R/C RACERS
ARCHIE

	N-MINT
❑1, Sep 1989; Reggie appearance	2.00
❑2, Nov 1989	1.50
❑3, Jan 1990	1.50
❑4, Mar 1990	1.50
❑5, May 1990; Tennessee tribute corner box	1.50
❑6, Jul 1990; Kentucky tribute corner box	1.50
❑7, Sep 1990; Ohio tribute corner box	1.50
❑8, Nov 1990; Missouri tribute corner box	1.50
❑9, Jan 1991; Texas tribute cover box	1.50
❑10, Mar 1991	1.50

ARCHIE'S SPRING BREAK
ARCHIE

	N-MINT
❑1 1996	2.50
❑2 1997	2.50
❑3 1998	2.50
❑4 1999	2.50
❑5 2000	2.50

ARCHIE'S STORY & GAME DIGEST MAGAZINE
ARCHIE

	N-MINT
❑32, Jul 1995	2.00
❑33, Sep 1995	2.00
❑34, Mar 1996	2.00
❑35, May 1996	2.00
❑36, ca. 1996	2.00
❑37, Jan 1997	2.00
❑38, Aug 1997	2.00
❑39, Jan 1998	2.00

ARCHIE'S SUPER-HERO SPECIAL
ARCHIE / RED CIRCLE

	N-MINT
❑1, Jan 1979; JK (a); reprints Adventures of the Fly #2; reprints Double Life of Private Strong #1	3.00
❑2, Aug 1979; JK (a); reprints Double Life of Private Strong #1; reprints Double Life of Private Strong #2	3.00

ARCHIE'S SUPER TEENS
ARCHIE

	N-MINT
❑1 1994; poster	2.50
❑2 1995	2.50
❑3 1995	2.50
❑4 1996	2.50

ARCHIE'S TV LAUGH-OUT
ARCHIE

	N-MINT
❑1, Dec 1969	42.00
❑2, Mar 1970	24.00
❑3, Jun 1970	16.00
❑4, Sep 1970	16.00
❑5 1971	16.00
❑6 1971	12.00
❑7 1971; Josie and the Pussycats features begin	22.00
❑8, Aug 1971	12.00
❑9 1971	12.00
❑10 1971	12.00
❑11, Feb 1972	9.00
❑12, May 1972	9.00
❑13, Aug 1972	9.00

Condition price index: Multiply "NM prices" above by: **0.83 for Very Fine/Near Mint**
0.66 for Very Fine • 0.33 for Fine • 0.2 for Very Good • 0.125 for Good

	N-MINT
❑14, Sep 1972	9.00
❑15, Oct 1972	9.00
❑16, Dec 1972	9.00
❑17 1973	9.00
❑18 1973	9.00
❑19 1973	9.00
❑20 1973	9.00
❑21 1973	7.00
❑22, Oct 1973	7.00
❑23, Dec 1973	7.00
❑24, May 1974	7.00
❑25, Jul 1974	7.00
❑26, Aug 1974	7.00
❑27, Sep 1974	7.00
❑28, Oct 1974	7.00
❑29, Dec 1974	7.00
❑30, Feb 1975	7.00
❑31, May 1975	6.00
❑32, Jul 1975	6.00
❑33, Aug 1975	6.00
❑34, Sep 1975	6.00
❑35, Oct 1975	6.00
❑36, Dec 1975	6.00
❑37, Feb 1976	6.00
❑38, Mar 1976	6.00
❑39, Apr 1976	6.00
❑40, Jun 1976	6.00
❑41, Jul 1976	4.00
❑42, Aug 1976	4.00
❑43, Sep 1976	4.00
❑44, Nov 1976	4.00
❑45, Dec 1976	4.00
❑46, Feb 1977	4.00
❑47, Mar 1977	4.00
❑48, Apr 1977	4.00
❑49, Jun 1977	4.00
❑50, Jul 1977	4.00
❑51, Aug 1977	4.00
❑52, Sep 1977	4.00
❑53, Nov 1977	4.00
❑54, Dec 1977	4.00
❑55, Feb 1978	4.00
❑56, Mar 1978	4.00
❑57, Apr 1978	4.00
❑58, Jun 1978	4.00
❑59, Jul 1978	4.00
❑60, Aug 1978	4.00
❑61, Sep 1978	3.00
❑62, Nov 1978	3.00
❑63, Dec 1978	3.00
❑64, Feb 1979	3.00
❑65, Mar 1979	3.00
❑66, Apr 1979	3.00
❑67, Jun 1979	3.00
❑68, Jul 1979	3.00
❑69, Aug 1979	3.00
❑70, Sep 1979	3.00
❑71, Nov 1979	3.00
❑72, Dec 1979	3.00
❑73, Feb 1980	3.00
❑74, Mar 1980	3.00
❑75, Apr 1980	3.00
❑76, Jun 1980	3.00
❑77, Jul 1980	3.00
❑78, Aug 1980	3.00
❑79, Oct 1980	3.00
❑80, Feb 1981	3.00
❑81, May 1981	2.50
❑82, Aug 1981	2.50
❑83, Oct 1981	2.50
❑84, Feb 1982	2.50
❑85, May 1982	2.50
❑86, Aug 1982	2.50
❑87, Feb 1983	2.50
❑88, Apr 1983	2.50
❑89, Jun 1983 DDC (c)	2.50
❑90, Aug 1983 DDC (c)	2.50
❑91, Oct 1983 DDC (c)	2.50
❑92, Dec 1983 DDC (c)	2.50
❑93, Feb 1984	2.50
❑94, Apr 1984	2.50
❑95, Jun 1984	2.50
❑96, Aug 1984	2.50
❑97, Oct 1984	2.50
❑98, Dec 1984	2.50
❑99, Feb 1985	2.50
❑100, Apr 1985 DDC (a); A: Jackie Maxon	2.50
❑101, Jun 1985	2.50
❑102, Aug 1985	2.50
❑103, Oct 1985	2.50
❑104, Dec 1985	2.50
❑105, Feb 1986	2.50
❑106, Apr 1986	2.50

ARCHIE'S VACATION SPECIAL
ARCHIE

	N-MINT
❑1, Sum 1994 DDC (a)	2.50
❑2, Win 1995	2.50
❑3, Sum 1995	2.50
❑4, Sum 1996	2.50
❑5, Sum 1997	2.50
❑6, Sum 1998	2.50
❑7, Sum 1999	2.50
❑8, Sum 2000	2.50

ARCHIE'S WEIRD MYSTERIES
ARCHIE

	N-MINT
❑1, Feb 2000	2.00
❑2, Mar 2000	2.00
❑3, Apr 2000	2.00
❑4, May 2000	2.00
❑5, Jun 2000	2.00
❑6, Jul 2000	2.00
❑7, Aug 2000	2.00
❑8, Sep 2000	2.00
❑9, Oct 2000	2.00
❑10, Dec 2000	2.00
❑11, Feb 2001	2.00
❑12, Apr 2001	2.00
❑13, ca. 2001	2.00
❑14, ca. 2001	2.00
❑15, ca. 2001	2.00
❑16, ca. 2001	2.00
❑17	2.19
❑18, Feb 2002	2.19
❑19, Apr 2002	2.19
❑20, Jun 2002	2.19
❑21, Aug 2002	2.19
❑22, Sep 2002	2.19
❑23, Oct 2002	2.19
❑24, Dec 2002, Series changes to Archie's Mysteries	2.19
❑Ashcan 1; Giveaway from Diamond	1.00

ARCHIE 3000
ARCHIE

	N-MINT
❑1, May 1989	2.50
❑2, Jul 1989	2.00
❑3, Aug 1989	2.00
❑4, Oct 1989	2.00
❑5, Nov 1989	2.00
❑6, Jan 1990	1.00
❑7, Mar 1990	1.00
❑8, May 1990	1.00
❑9, Jul 1990	1.00
❑10, Aug 1990	1.00
❑11, Oct 1990	1.00
❑12, Nov 1990	1.00
❑13, Jan 1991	1.00
❑14, Mar 1991	1.00
❑15, May 1991	1.00

ARCOMICS PREMIERE
ARCOMICS

	N-MINT
❑1, Jul 1993, b&w; lenticular animation cover	2.95

ARCTIC COMICS
NICK BURNS

	N-MINT
❑1; souvenir	1.00

AREA 52
IMAGE

	N-MINT
❑1, Jan 2001	2.95
❑1/A, Jan 2001; Gold Foil Title	
❑1/B, Jan 2001; Red Foil Title	

Archie gave away promotional copies of *Archie's Weird Mysteries* in 1999.
© 1999 Archie Publications Inc.

	N-MINT
❑2, Mar 2001	2.95
❑3, Apr 2001	2.95
❑4, ca. 2001	2.95

AREA 88
ECLIPSE / VIZ

	N-MINT
❑1, May 1987	3.50
❑1-2	2.00
❑2, Jun 1987	2.50
❑2-2	2.00
❑3, Jun 1987	2.00
❑4, Jul 1987	2.00
❑5, Jul 1987	2.00
❑6, Aug 1987	2.00
❑7, Aug 1987	2.00
❑8, Sep 1987	2.00
❑9, Sep 1987	2.00
❑10, Oct 1987	2.00
❑11, Oct 1987	2.00
❑12, Nov 1987	2.00
❑13, Nov 1987	2.00
❑14, Dec 1987	2.00
❑15, Dec 1987	2.00
❑16, Jan 1988	2.00
❑17, Jan 1988	2.00
❑18, Feb 1988	2.00
❑19, Feb 1988	2.00
❑20, Mar 1988	2.00
❑21, Mar 1988	2.00
❑22, Apr 1988	2.00
❑23, Apr 1988	2.00
❑24, May 1988	2.00
❑25, May 1988	2.00
❑26, Jun 1988	2.00
❑27, Jun 1988	2.00
❑28, Jul 1988	2.00
❑29, Jul 1988	2.00
❑30, Aug 1988	2.00
❑31, Aug 1988	2.00
❑32, Sep 1988	2.00
❑33, Sep 1988	2.00
❑34, Oct 1988	2.00
❑35, Oct 1988	2.00
❑36, Nov 1988	2.00
❑37, Nov 1988	2.00
❑38, Dec 1988	2.00
❑39, Dec 1988	2.00
❑40, Jan 1989	2.00
❑41, Jan 1989	2.00
❑42, Feb 1989	2.00

AREALA: ANGEL OF WAR
ANTARCTIC

	N-MINT
❑1, Sep 1998	2.95
❑2, Nov 1998	2.95
❑3, Feb 1999	2.95
❑4, ca. 1999	2.99

ARENA
ALCHEMY

	N-MINT
❑1, b&w	1.50

ARGONAUTS, THE (ETERNITY)
ETERNITY

	N-MINT
❑1	1.95
❑2	1.95
❑3	1.95
❑4	1.95

N-MINT

ARGONAUTS, THE: SYSTEM CRASH
ALPHA PRODUCTIONS
❑1 .... 2.50
❑2 .... 2.50

ARGON ZARK!
ARCLIGHT
❑1 1997; based on on-line comics series 6.95

ARGUS
DC
❑1, Apr 1995 .... 1.50
❑2, Jun 1995 .... 1.50
❑3, Jul 1995 .... 1.50
❑4, Aug 1995 .... 1.50
❑5, Sep 1995 .... 1.50
❑6, Oct 1995 .... 1.50

ARIA
IMAGE
❑1, Jan 1999 .... 3.00
❑1/A, Jan 1999; white background cover 3.00
❑1/B, Jan 1999; Woman looking from balcony on cover 3.00
❑2, Apr 1999 .... 2.50
❑3, May 1999 .... 2.50
❑4/A, Nov 1999; Textured cover stock; Close-up shot of woman in green pointing at chest 2.50
❑4/B, Nov 1999; Variant cover with Angela 2.50
❑5, ca. 1999 .... 2.50
❑6, ca. 1999 .... 2.50
❑7, ca. 1999 .... 2.50
❑Ashcan 1, Nov 1998, b&w; preview issue 3.50

ARIA: A MIDWINTER'S DREAM
IMAGE
❑1, Jan 2002 .... 4.95

ARIA ANGELA
IMAGE
❑1/A, Feb 2000; Aria and Angela in profile on cover 2.95
❑1/B, Feb 2000; Aria sitting on stairs on cover 2.95
❑1/C, Feb 2000; Close-up on Aria (right half of 1/H cover in close-up) 2.95
❑1/D, Feb 2000; Woman walking through astral plane on cover 2.95
❑1/E, Feb 2000; Woman walking through astral plane on cover 2.95
❑1/F, Feb 2000; Two women, hawk on cover 2.95
❑1/G, Feb 2000; Tower records variant; Woman with sword (between legs) on cover 2.95
❑1/H, Feb 2000 .... 2.95
❑1/I, Feb 2000; chromium cover 2.95
❑2, Oct 2000 .... 2.95

ARIA ANGELA BLANC & NOIR
IMAGE
❑1, Apr 2000; Reprints Aria Angela #1 in black & white 2.95

ARIA BLANC & NOIR
IMAGE
❑1, Mar 1999; b&w reprint of Aria #1; wraparound cover 2.50
❑2, Mar 1999 .... 2.50

ARIA (MANGA)
ADV MANGA
❑1, ca 2004 .... 9.99

ARIANE & BLUEBEARD
ECLIPSE
❑1, ca. 1989, Part of Eclipse's Night Music Series 3.95

ARIANNE
SLAVE LABOR
❑1, May 1991 .... 4.95
❑2, Oct 1991 .... 2.95

ARIANNE (MOONSTONE)
MOONSTONE
❑1, Dec 1995, b&w 4.95

N-MINT

ARIA SUMMER'S SPELL
IMAGE
❑1, Mar 2002 ....
❑2, Jun 2002 ....

ARIA: THE SOUL MARKET
IMAGE
❑1, Mar 2001 .... 2.95
❑2, Apr 2001 .... 2.95
❑3, May 2001 .... 2.95
❑4, Jun 2001 .... 2.95
❑5, Jul 2001 .... 2.95
❑6, Aug 2001 .... 2.95

ARIA: THE USES OF ENCHANTMENT
IMAGE
❑1, Mar 2003 .... 2.95
❑2, Apr 2003 .... 2.95
❑3, Aug 2003 .... 2.95
❑4, Oct 2003 .... 2.95

ARIK KHAN (A+)
A-PLUS
❑1; b&w, reprint 2.50
❑2 .... 2.50

ARIK KHAN (ANDROMEDA)
ANDROMEDA
❑1, Sep 1977 .... 1.95
❑2 .... 1.95
❑3 .... 1.95

ARION, LORD OF ATLANTIS
DC
❑1, Nov 1982; JDu (a); Story continued from Warlord #62 .... 1.00
❑2, Dec 1982 JDu (a); 1: Mara 1.00
❑3, Jan 1983 JDu (a) 1.00
❑4, Feb 1983 JDu (a) 1.00
❑5, Mar 1983 JDu (a) 1.00
❑6, Apr 1983 JDu (a) 1.00
❑7, May 1983 JDu (a) 1.00
❑8, Jun 1983 .... 1.00
❑9, Jul 1983 .... 1.00
❑10, Aug 1983 .... 1.00
❑11, Sep 1983 .... 1.00
❑12, Oct 1983 JDu (a) 1.00
❑13, Nov 1983 .... 1.00
❑14, Dec 1983 .... 1.00
❑15, Jan 1984 .... 1.00
❑16, Feb 1984 .... 1.00
❑17, Mar 1984 .... 1.00
❑18, Apr 1984 .... 1.00
❑19, May 1984 .... 1.00
❑20, Jun 1984 .... 1.00
❑21, Jul 1984 .... 1.00
❑22, Aug 1984 .... 1.00
❑23, Sep 1984 .... 1.00
❑24, Oct 1984 .... 1.00
❑25, Nov 1984 .... 1.00
❑26, Dec 1984 .... 1.00
❑27, Jan 1985 .... 1.00
❑28, Feb 1985 .... 1.00
❑29, Mar 1985 .... 1.00
❑30, Apr 1985 .... 1.00
❑31, May 1985 .... 1.00
❑32, Jun 1985 .... 1.00
❑33, Jul 1985 .... 1.00
❑34, Aug 1985 .... 1.00
❑35, Sep 1985 .... 1.00
❑Special 1, ca. 1985; Special 1.00

ARION THE IMMORTAL
DC
❑1, Jul 1992 .... 1.50
❑2, Aug 1992 .... 1.50
❑3, Sep 1992 .... 1.50
❑4, Oct 1992 .... 1.50
❑5, Nov 1992 .... 1.50
❑6, Dec 1992 .... 1.50

ARISTOCATS, THE
GOLD KEY
❑1, Mar 1971; 30045-103; poster 3.50

N-MINT

ARISTOCRATIC X-TRATERRESTRIAL TIME-TRAVELING THIEVES
COMICS INTERVIEW
❑1, Feb 1987 .... 2.00
❑2, Apr 1987 .... 2.00
❑3, Jun 1987 .... 2.00
❑4, Aug 1987 .... 2.00
❑5, Oct 1987 .... 2.00
❑6, Dec 1987 .... 2.00
❑7, Feb 1988 .... 2.00
❑8, Apr 1988 .... 2.00
❑9, Jun 1988 .... 2.00
❑10, Aug 1988 .... 2.00
❑11, Oct 1988 .... 2.00
❑12, Dec 1988 .... 2.00

ARISTOCRATIC X-TRATERRESTRIAL TIME-TRAVELING THIEVES MICRO-SERIES
COMICS INTERVIEW
❑1, Aug 1986 .... 2.00
❑1-2 .... 2.00

ARISTOKITTENS, THE
GOLD KEY
❑1, Oct 1973 .... 16.00
❑2, Feb 1974 .... 10.00
❑3, Apr 1974 .... 8.00
❑4, Jul 1974 .... 8.00
❑5, Oct 1974 .... 8.00
❑6, Jan 1975 .... 6.00
❑7, Apr 1975 .... 6.00
❑8, Jul 1975 .... 6.00
❑9, Oct 1975 .... 6.00

ARIZONA: A SIMPLE HORROR
LONDON NIGHT
❑1 .... 3.00

ARKAGA
IMAGE
❑1, Sep 1997 .... 2.95
❑2, Nov 1997 .... 2.95

ARKANIUM
DREAMWAVE
❑1, Sep 2002 .... 2.95
❑2, Nov 2002 .... 2.95
❑3, Jan 2003 .... 2.95
❑4, Feb 2003 .... 2.95
❑5, Mar 2003 .... 2.95

ARKEOLOGY
VALKYRIE
❑1, Apr 1989; companion one-shot for The Adventures of Luther Arkwright 2.00

ARKHAM ASYLUM LIVING HELL
DC
❑1, May 2003 .... 2.50
❑2, Jun 2003 .... 2.50
❑3, Jul 2003 .... 2.50
❑4, Aug 2003 .... 2.50
❑5, Sep 2003 .... 2.50
❑6, Oct 2003 .... 2.50

ARLINGTON HAMMER IN: GET ME TO THE CHURCH ON TIME
ONE SHOT
❑1; comic for sale at conventions only 2.50

A.R.M.
ADVENTURE
❑1; Introduction by Larry Niven 2.50
❑2 .... 2.50
❑3 .... 2.50

ARMADILLO COMICS
RIP OFF
❑1 .... 2.50
❑2 .... 2.50

ARMAGEDDON
LAST GASP
❑1 .... 2.50
❑2 .... 2.50

N-MINT

ARMAGEDDON (CHAOS)
CHAOS

❑1, Oct 1999 ... 2.95
❑2, Nov 1999 ... 2.95
❑3, Dec 1999 ... 2.95
❑4, Jan 2000 ... 2.95

ARMAGEDDON 2001
DC

❑1, May 1991 ... 2.00
❑1-2, May 1991 ... 2.00
❑1-3, May 1991; 3rd printing (silver ink on cover) ... 2.00
❑2, Oct 1991; Monarch's ID revealed ... 2.00

ARMAGEDDON: INFERNO
DC

❑1, Apr 1992 ... 1.00
❑2, May 1992 ... 1.00
❑3, Jun 1992 ... 1.00
❑4, Jul 1992; JSA returns from limbo ... 1.00

ARMAGEDDON: THE ALIEN AGENDA
DC

❑1, Nov 1991 ... 1.00
❑2, Dec 1991 ... 1.00
❑3, Jan 1992 ... 1.00
❑4, Feb 1992 ... 1.00

ARMAGEDDON FACTOR, THE
AC

❑1, Jun 1987 ... 1.95
❑2, Aug 1987 ... 1.95
❑3 ... 1.95

ARMAGEDDON FACTOR, THE: THE CONCLUSION
AC

❑1 1990, b&w ... 3.95

ARMAGEDDONQUEST
STARHEAD

❑1 1994 ... 3.95
❑2 1994 ... 3.95

ARMAGEDDON RISING
MILLENNIUM

❑1 1997, b&w; special foil edition; features characters from Song of the Sirens ... 4.95

ARMAGEDDON SQUAD, THE
HAZE

❑1, b&w ... 1.50

ARMATURE
OLYOPTICS

❑1, Nov 1996 ... 2.95
❑2, Dec 1996 ... 2.95

ARMED AND DANGEROUS (ACCLAIM)
ACCLAIM / ARMADA

❑1, Apr 1996, b&w ... 2.95
❑2, May 1996, b&w ... 2.95
❑3, Jun 1996, b&w ... 2.95
❑4, Jul 1996, b&w ... 2.95
❑Special 1, Aug 1996, b&w; one-shot special; later indicias show this is really issue #5 of series ... 2.95

ARMED & DANGEROUS: HELL'S SLAUGHTERHOUSE
ACCLAIM

❑1 ... 2.95
❑2 ... 2.95
❑3 ... 2.95
❑4 ... 2.95

ARMED & DANGEROUS (KITCHEN SINK)
KITCHEN SINK

❑1, Jul 1995; magazine-sized graphic novel ... 9.95

ARMEN DEEP & BUG BOY
DILEMMA

❑2 1995, b&w; cardstock cover ... 2.50

ARMITAGE
FLEETWAY-QUALITY

❑1; cardstock cover ... 2.95
❑2; cardstock cover ... 2.95

N-MINT

ARM OF KANNON
TOKYOPOP

❑1, May 2004 ... 9.99

ARMOR
CONTINUITY

❑1 ... 2.00
❑2 ... 2.00
❑3 ... 2.00
❑4, Jul 1988 ... 2.00
❑5, Dec 1988 ... 2.00
❑6, Apr 1989 ... 2.00
❑7, Jan 1990 ... 2.00
❑8, Apr 1990 ... 2.00
❑9, Apr 1991 ... 2.00
❑10, Aug 1991 ... 2.00
❑11, Nov 1991 ... 2.00
❑12, Mar 1992 ... 2.00
❑13, Apr 1992 ... 2.00

ARMOR (2ND SERIES)
CONTINUITY

❑1, Apr 1993; wraparound foil cardstock cover; 2 trading cards ... 2.50
❑2, May 1993; trading card; diecut outer cover ... 2.50
❑3, Aug 1993 ... 2.50
❑4, Oct 1993 ... 2.50
❑5, Nov 1993 ... 2.50
❑6, Nov 1993 ... 2.50

ARMORED TROOPER VOTOMS
CPM

❑1, Jul 1996 ... 2.95

ARMORINES
VALIANT

❑0/Gold; Gold edition; gold edition ... 3.00
❑0, Feb 1993; "Fall Fling Preview Edition"; no cover price ... 2.00
❑1, Jun 1994 ... 2.25
❑2, Aug 1994 ... 2.25
❑3, Sep 1994 ... 2.25
❑4, Oct 1994 ... 2.25
❑5, Nov 1994; Continues from Harbinger #34 ... 2.25
❑6, Dec 1994 A: X-O ... 2.25
❑7, Jan 1995; wraparound cover ... 2.25
❑8, Feb 1995 ... 2.25
❑9, Mar 1995 ... 2.25
❑10, Apr 1995 ... 2.25
❑11, May 1995 ... 2.25
❑12, Jun 1995 ... 2.25

ARMORINES (VOL. 2)
ACCLAIM

❑1, Oct 1999 ... 3.95
❑2, Nov 1999 ... 3.95
❑3, Dec 1999 ... 3.95
❑4, Jan 2000 A: X-O Manowar ... 3.95

ARM'S LENGTH
THIRD WIND

❑1, Jul 2000, b&w ... 3.95

ARMY ANTS (MICHAEL T. DESING'S...)
MICHAEL T. DESING

❑8, b&w ... 2.50

ARMY OF DARKNESS
DARK HORSE

❑1 ... 12.00
❑2 ... 9.00
❑3, Oct 1993 ... 9.00

ARMY SURPLUS KOMIKZ FEATURING: CUTEY BUNNY
QUAGMIRE

❑1; Quagmire publishes ... 3.00
❑2 ... 2.50
❑3 ... 2.50
❑4 ... 2.50
❑5 1985, b&w; X-Men parody; Eclipse publishes ... 2.50

AROMATIC BITTERS, THE
TOKYOPOP

❑1, Mar 2004 ... 9.99

Area 88 was among the first Japanese manga stories adapted for U.S. audiences by Eclipse and Viz.

© 1987 Eclipse Enterprises and Viz Communications.

N-MINT

AROUND THE WORLD UNDER THE SEA
DELL

❑1, Dec 1966 ... 20.00

ARRGH!
MARVEL

❑1, Dec 1974 TS (a) ... 5.00
❑2, Feb 1975 TS (a) ... 4.00
❑3, May 1975 AA (a) ... 3.00
❑4, Jul 1975 ... 3.00
❑5, Sep 1975 RA (a) ... 3.00

ARROW
MALIBU

❑1 ... 1.95

ARROW ANTHOLOGY
ARROW

❑1, Nov 1997; The Fool, Jabberwocky, Great Scott, Night Streets, Battle Bot ... 3.95
❑2, Jan 1998; Simone & Ajax, Battle Bot, Night Streets, Miss Chevious, Dark Oz ... 3.95
❑3, Mar 1998; The Fool, Dragon Storm, Great Scott, Ninja Duck, Simone & Ajax, Samantha ... 3.95
❑4, Sep 1998; August, Land of Oz, Corhawk, Mr. Nightmare, Simone & Ajax ... 3.95
❑5 ... 3.95

ARROWMAN
PARODY

❑1, b&w ... 2.50

ARROWSMITH
DC / WILDSTORM

❑1, Jul 2003 ... 2.95
❑2, Aug 2003 ... 2.95
❑3, Sep 2003 ... 2.95
❑4, Nov 2003 ... 2.95
❑5, Jan 2004 ... 2.95
❑6, May 2004 ... 2.95

ARROWSMITH/ASTRO CITY
DC / WILDSTORM

❑1, Jun 2004 ... 2.95

ARROW SPOTLIGHT
ARROW

❑1 1998, b&w; Simone & Ajax ... 2.95

ARSENAL
DC

❑1, Oct 1998 ... 2.50
❑2, Nov 1998 ... 2.50
❑3, Dec 1998 ... 2.50
❑4, Jan 1999 ... 2.50

ARSENAL SPECIAL
DC

❑1 1996 ... 2.95

ARSENIC LULLABY
A. SILENT

❑1, Dec 1998 ... 5.00
❑2 1999 ... 2.50
❑3 1999 ... 2.50
❑4 1999 ... 2.50
❑5 1999 ... 2.50
❑6 2000 ... 2.50
❑7 2000 ... 2.50
❑8 2000 ... 2.50
❑9 2000 ... 2.50

Issue	N-MINT
❑10, May 2001	2.50
❑11, Jun 2001	2.50
❑12, Jul 2001	2.50
❑13, Jan 2002; No number on cover; Jan/Feb issue	2.50

ART & BEAUTY MAGAZINE
KITCHEN SINK

Issue	N-MINT
❑1, b&w; over-sized; cardstock cover	4.95

ARTBABE (VOL. 2)
FANTAGRAPHICS

Issue	N-MINT
❑1, May 1997	2.95
❑2, Nov 1997	2.95
❑3, Aug 1998	2.95
❑4, Apr 1999	2.95

ART D'ECCO
FANTAGRAPHICS

Issue	N-MINT
❑1, Jan 1990, b&w	2.50
❑2, b&w	2.50
❑3	2.75

ARTEMIS: REQUIEM
DC

Issue	N-MINT
❑1, Jun 1996	1.75
❑2, Jul 1996	1.75
❑3, Aug 1996	1.75
❑4, Sep 1996	1.75
❑5, Oct 1996	1.75
❑6, Nov 1996	1.75

ARTESIA
SIRIUS

Issue	N-MINT
❑1, Jan 1999	2.95
❑2, Feb 1999	2.95
❑3, Mar 1999	2.95
❑4, Apr 1999	2.95
❑5, May 1999	2.95
❑6, Jun 1999	2.95

ARTESIA AFIELD
SIRIUS

Issue	N-MINT
❑1, Jul 2000; wraparound cover	2.95
❑2, Aug 2000; wraparound cover	2.95
❑3, Sep 2000; wraparound cover	2.95
❑4, Oct 2000; wraparound cover	2.95

ARTESIA AFIRE
SIRIUS

Issue	N-MINT
❑1, Jun 2003	3.95
❑2, Jul 2003	3.95
❑3, Aug 2003	3.95
❑4, Oct 2003	3.95
❑5, Dec 2003	3.95
❑6, Mar 2004	3.95

ARTHUR KING OF BRITAIN
TOME

Issue	N-MINT
❑1, ca. 1993	2.95
❑2, ca. 1993	2.95
❑3	2.95
❑4	2.95
❑5	3.95

ARTHUR SEX
AIRCEL

Issue	N-MINT
❑1, b&w	2.50
❑2, b&w	2.50
❑3, Jul 1991, b&w	2.50
❑4, Aug 1991, b&w	2.50
❑5, Sep 1991, b&w	2.50
❑6, Oct 1991, b&w	2.50
❑7, Nov 1991, b&w	2.50
❑8, b&w	2.50

ARTILLERY ONE-SHOT
RED BULLET

Issue	N-MINT
❑1 1995, b&w	2.50

ARTISTIC COMICS
KITCHEN SINK

Issue	N-MINT
❑1, Aug 1995, b&w; adults only; new printing; squarebound	3.00
❑1-2	2.50

ARTISTIC LICENTIOUSNESS
STARHEAD

Issue	N-MINT
❑1, b&w	2.50
❑2, ca. 1994	2.95
❑3, ca. 1997, b&w	2.95

ART OF ABRAMS, THE
LIGHTNING

Issue	N-MINT
❑1, Dec 1996; b&w pin-ups	3.50

ART OF AUBREY BEARDSLEY, THE
TOME

Issue	N-MINT
❑1, b&w	2.95

ART OF HEATH ROBINSON
TOME

Issue	N-MINT
❑1, b&w	2.95

ART OF HOMAGE STUDIOS, THE
IMAGE

Issue	N-MINT
❑1 1993 JLee (a); 1: Gen13 (pin-ups, sketches)	5.50

ART OF JAY ANACLETO, THE
IMAGE

Issue	N-MINT
❑1, Apr 2002	5.95

ART OF JOSEPH MICHAEL LINSER
IMAGE

Issue	N-MINT
❑	

ART OF MARVEL COMICS
MARVEL

Issue	N-MINT
❑1, ca. 2004	29.99

ART OF MUCHA
TOME

Issue	N-MINT
❑1, ca. 1992, b&w	2.95

ART OF PULP FICTION, THE
A-LIST

Issue	N-MINT
❑1, Apr 1998	2.95

ART OF SPANKING, THE
NBM

Issue	N-MINT
❑1	17.95

ART OF USAGI YOJIMBO, THE
RADIO

Issue	N-MINT
❑1, Apr 1997	3.95
❑2, Jan 1998	3.95

ASCENSION
IMAGE

Issue	N-MINT
❑0; Included with Wizard Top Cow Special	3.00
❑0/Gold; Gold edition	3.00
❑0/Ltd.; Gold cover; Wizard "Certified Authentic"	4.00
❑0.5	4.00
❑1, Oct 1997	3.00
❑1/A, Oct 1997; Variant cover: Lucien holding head	3.00
❑1/B, Oct 1997; Fan club edition; Top Cow Fan Club exclusive	4.00
❑1/C, Oct 1997; American Entertainment exclusive	4.00
❑1/D, Oct 1997; Sendaway edition; angels on pile of bodies	3.00
❑2, Nov 1997	2.50
❑2/A, Nov 1997; American Entertainment exclusive	3.00
❑2/Gold, Nov 1997; Gold edition	3.00
❑3, Dec 1997	2.50
❑4, Feb 1998	2.50
❑5, Mar 1998	2.50
❑6, May 1998	2.50
❑7, Jul 1998	2.50
❑8, Aug 1998	2.50
❑9, Oct 1998	2.50
❑10, Nov 1998	2.50
❑11, Feb 1999	2.50
❑12, Apr 1999	2.50
❑13, May 1999	2.50
❑14, Jun 1999	2.50
❑15, Jul 1999	2.50
❑16, Jul 1999	2.50
❑17, Aug 1999	2.50
❑18, Sep 1999	2.50
❑19, Oct 1999	2.50
❑20, Nov 1999	2.50
❑21, Dec 1999; cover says Nov, indicia says Dec	2.95
❑22, Mar 2000	2.95
❑Ashcan 1, Jun 1997; Preview edition	4.00

ASH
EVENT

Issue	N-MINT
❑0, May 1996; "Present" edition; O: Ash. enhanced wraparound cover	3.50
❑0/A, May 1996; "Future" edition; O: Ash. alternate enhanced wraparound cover	3.50
❑0/B, May 1996; Red foil logo-Present edition	4.00
❑0/C, May 1996; Red foil logo-Future edition	4.00
❑0.5	2.50
❑0.5/Ltd.; Wizard authentic edition	4.00
❑0.5/Platinum; Platinum edition	4.00
❑1, Nov 1994 1: Ash	3.00
❑1/A, Nov 1994; 1: Ash. Commemorative Omnichrome cover	4.00
❑1/B, Nov 1994; 1: Ash. Dynamic Forces exclusive (DF on cover)	3.00
❑2	3.00
❑3, May 1995	3.00
❑4, Jul 1995	3.00
❑4/A; Red Edition	3.00
❑4/B; White edition	3.00
❑4/Gold; Gold edition	3.00
❑5, Sep 1995	3.00
❑6, Dec 1995	2.50
❑6/A, Dec 1995; alternate cover	2.50

ASH/22 BRIDES
EVENT

Issue	N-MINT
❑1, Dec 1996	2.95
❑2, Apr 1997	2.95

ASH: CINDER & SMOKE
EVENT

Issue	N-MINT
❑1, May 1997	2.95
❑2, Jun 1997	2.95
❑2/A, Jun 1997; variant cover	2.95
❑3, Jul 1997	2.95
❑3/A, Jul 1997; variant cover	2.95
❑4, Aug 1997	2.95
❑4/A, Aug 1997; variant cover	2.95
❑5, Sep 1997	2.95
❑5/A, Sep 1997; variant cover	2.95
❑6, Oct 1997	2.95
❑6/A, Oct 1997; variant cover	2.95

ASHEN VICTOR
VIZ

Issue	N-MINT
❑1, ca. 1997	2.95
❑2, ca. 1997	3.25
❑3, ca. 1997	2.95
❑4, ca. 1997	2.95

ASHES
CALIBER

Issue	N-MINT
❑1	2.50
❑2	2.50
❑3	2.50
❑4	2.50
❑5	2.50

ASH FILES, THE
EVENT

Issue	N-MINT
❑1, Mar 1997; background on series	2.95

ASH: FIRE AND CROSSFIRE
EVENT

Issue	N-MINT
❑1, Jan 1999 JRo (w)	2.95
❑1/A, Jan 1999 JRo (w)	5.00
❑2 1999 JRo (w)	2.95

ASHLEY DUST
KNIGHT

Issue	N-MINT
❑1	2.95
❑2, Dec 1994	2.95
❑3, Mar 1995	2.95

ASHPILE
SIDE SHOW

Issue	N-MINT
❑1	8.95

ASH: THE FIRE WITHIN
EVENT

	N-MINT
❑1, Sep 1996	2.95
❑2	2.95

ASKANI'SON
MARVEL

❑1, Jan 1996; cover says "Feb," indicia says "Jan"	2.95
❑2, Apr 1996; cover says "Mar", indicia says "Apr"	2.95
❑3, Apr 1996; cardstock wraparound cover	2.95
❑4, May 1996; cardstock wraparound cover	2.95

A SORT OF HOMECOMING
ALTERNATIVE

❑1	3.50
❑2, Feb 2004	3.50
❑3, May 2004	3.50

ASPEN EXTENDED EDITION
ASPEN

❑1, Mar 2004	5.99

ASPEN (MICHAEL TURNER PRESENTS)
ASPEN

❑1, Oct 2003	2.99
❑2, Nov 2003	2.99
❑3, Dec 2003	2.99

ASPEN SKETCHBOOK
ASPEN

❑1, Feb 2004	2.99

ASRIAL VS. CHEETAH
ANTARCTIC

❑1, Mar 1996	2.95
❑2, Apr 1996	2.95

ASSASSINATION OF MALCOLM X, THE
ZONE

❑1	2.95

ASSASSINETTE
POCKET CHANGE

❑1, ca. 1994; silver foil cover	2.50
❑2	2.50
❑3	2.50
❑4	2.50
❑5	2.50
❑6	2.50
❑7	2.50

ASSASSINS
DC / AMALGAM

❑1, Apr 1996	1.95

ASSASSINS INC.
SILVERLINE

❑1	1.95
❑2	1.95

ASSEMBLY
ANTARCTIC

❑1, Nov 2003	2.99
❑2, Dec 2003	3.50
❑3, Jan 2004	0.00

ASTER
EXPRESS / ENTITY

❑0, Oct 1994	2.95
❑1, Oct 1994, b&w	2.95
❑1/Gold, Oct 1994, b&w; Gold edition	3.00
❑2, Nov 1994; enhanced cardstock cover	2.95
❑3, Jan 1995	2.95
❑3/A, Jan 1995; alternate cover	2.95
❑3/B, Jan 1995; enhanced cover	2.95
❑Ashcan 1; no cover price; b&w preview	1.00

ASTER: THE LAST CELESTIAL KNIGHT
EXPRESS / ENTITY

❑1 1995, Chromium cover	3.75

ASTONISH!
WEHNER

❑1, b&w	2.00

ASTONISHING EXCITEMENT
ALL-JONH

	N-MINT
❑502	2.95
❑501	2.95
❑503	3.50

ASTONISHING TALES
MARVEL

❑1, Aug 1970; SL (w); JK, WW (a); A: Kraven the Hunter. Ka-Zar, Doctor Doom	36.00
❑2, Oct 1970; JK, WW (a); A: Kraven the Hunter. Ka-Zar, Doctor Doom	14.00
❑3, Dec 1970; WW (a); 1: Zaladane. Ka-Zar, Doctor Doom	14.00
❑4, Feb 1971; WW (a); Ka-Zar, Doctor Doom	14.00
❑5, Apr 1971; A: Red Skull. Ka-Zar, Doctor Doom	14.00
❑6, Jun 1971; 1: Mockingbird (as Bobbi Morse). Ka-Zar, Doctor Doom	10.00
❑7, Aug 1971; Ka-Zar, Doctor Doom	12.00
❑8, Oct 1971; Ka-Zar, Doctor Doom	13.00
❑9, Dec 1971; Ka-Zar	9.00
❑10, Feb 1972; SB (a); Ka-Zar	9.00
❑11, Apr 1972; O: Ka-Zar. Ka-Zar	9.00
❑12, Jun 1972; JB, NA, DA (a); A: Man-Thing. Ka-Zar	21.00
❑13, Aug 1972; RB, JB, DA (a); A: Man-Thing. Ka-Zar	4.00
❑14, Oct 1972; Ka-Zar; reprinted from Savage Tales #1 and Jungle Tales #2	4.00
❑15, Dec 1972; Ka-Zar	4.00
❑16, Feb 1973; Ka-Zar	4.00
❑17, Apr 1973; Ka-Zar	4.00
❑18, Jun 1973; Ka-Zar	4.00
❑19, Aug 1973; Ka-Zar	4.00
❑20, Oct 1973; Ka-Zar	4.00
❑21, Dec 1973; Reprinted from Amazing Adult Fantasy #9	4.00
❑22, Feb 1974; Reprinted from Strange Tales #74	4.00
❑23, Apr 1974; Reprinted from Strange Tales #89; Marvel Value Stamp #54: Shanna	4.00
❑24, Jun 1974; Marvel Value Stamp #18: Volstaag	4.00
❑25, Aug 1974; RB, GP (a); O: Deathlok I (Luther Manning). 1: Deathlok I (Luther Manning). 1st George Perez work; Marvel Value Stamp #68: Son of Satan	30.00
❑26, Oct 1974; A: Deathlok. Marvel Value Stamp #66: General Ross	9.00
❑27, Dec 1974; A: Deathlok. Marvel Value Stamp #22: Man-Thing	4.00
❑28, Feb 1975 A: Deathlok	4.00
❑29, Apr 1975; O: Guardians of the Galaxy. 1: Guardians of Galaxy. Reprinted from Marvel Super-Heroes #18	4.00
❑30, Jun 1975 RB, KP (a); A: Deathlok	4.00
❑31, Aug 1975; SL (w); RB, GC, KP (a); A: Deathlok. Reprinted from Silver Surfer #3	4.00
❑32, Nov 1976 A: Deathlok	4.00
❑33, Jan 1976 A: Deathlok	10.00
❑34, Mar 1976 A: Deathlok	4.00
❑35, May 1976 A: Deathlok	4.00
❑35/30 cent, May 1976; A: Deathlok. 30 cent regional price variant	20.00
❑36, Jul 1976 A: Deathlok	4.00
❑36/30 cent, Jul 1976; A: Deathlok. 30 cent regional price variant	20.00

ASTONISHING X-MEN
MARVEL

❑1, Mar 1995; DGr (a); Age of Apocalypse	2.50
❑2, Apr 1995 DGr (a)	2.00
❑3, May 1995 JPH (w); AM (a)	2.00
❑4, Jun 1995 AM (a)	2.00

ASTONISHING X-MEN (2ND SERIES)
MARVEL

❑1, Sep 1999	5.00
❑2, Oct 1999	2.50
❑3, Nov 1999	2.50

Bawdy adventures of King Arthur and his Knights of the Round Table were the focus of the adults-only title *Arthur Sex.*

© 1989 Aircel.

ASTONISHING X-MEN (3RD SERIES)
MARVEL

	N-MINT
❑1, Jul 2004	5.00
❑1/Cassaday, Jul 2004; John Cassaday cover	95.00
❑1/Del Otto, Jul 2004; Gabriel Del'Otto cover	12.00
❑1/A, Aug 2004; Director's Cut	3.99
❑2, Aug 2004	2.99
❑3, Sep 2004	

ASTOUNDING SPACE THRILLS
DAY 1

❑1, May 1998, b&w	2.95
❑2, Jul 1998, b&w	2.95
❑3, Jan 1999, b&w	2.95

ASTOUNDING SPACE THRILLS: THE COMIC BOOK
IMAGE

❑1, Apr 2000	2.95
❑2, Jul 2000	2.95
❑3, Sep 2000	2.95
❑4, Dec 2000	2.95
❑Giant Size 1, Oct 2001	4.95

ASTRIDER HUGO
RADIO

❑1, Jul 2000, b&w	3.95

ASTRO BOY (GOLD KEY)
GOLD KEY

❑1, Aug 1965	265.00

ASTRO BOY (DARK HORSE)
DARK HORSE

❑1, ca. 2002	9.95
❑2, ca. 2002	9.95
❑3, ca. 2002	9.95
❑4, ca. 2002	9.95
❑5, ca. 2002	9.95
❑6, ca. 2002	9.95
❑7, ca. 2002	9.95
❑8, ca. 2003	9.95
❑9, ca. 2003	9.95
❑10, ca. 2003	9.95
❑11, ca. 2003	9.95
❑12, ca. 2003	9.95
❑13, ca. 2003	9.95
❑14, ca. 2003	9.95
❑15, ca. 2003	9.95
❑16, ca. 2003	9.95
❑17, ca. 2003	9.95
❑18, ca. 2003	9.95
❑19, ca. 2003	9.95
❑20, ca. 2004	9.95
❑21, ca. 2004	9.95
❑22, ca. 2004	9.95
❑23 2004	9.95

ASTRO CITY LOCAL HEROS
DC

❑1, Feb 2003	2.95
❑2, Apr 2003	2.95
❑3, Jun 2003	2.95
❑4, Oct 2003	2.95
❑5, Dec 2003	2.95

N-MINT

ASTRO CITY (VOL. 1) (KURT BUSIEK'S...)
IMAGE

❑1, Aug 1995 ... 3.00
❑2, Sep 1995 ... 2.00
❑3, Oct 1995 ... 2.00
❑4, Nov 1995 ... 2.00
❑5, Dec 1995 ... 2.00
❑6, Jan 1996 ... 2.00

ASTRO CITY (VOL. 2) (KURT BUSIEK'S...)
IMAGE

❑0.5, Jan 2000; ARo (c); KB (w); BA (a); Wizard promotional item ... 3.00
❑0.5/Direct ed., Jan 1998; Direct Market edition; ARo (c); KB (w); BA (a); reprints "The Nearness of You" and "Clash of Titans" ... 3.00
❑1, Sep 1996 ARo (c); KB (w); BA (a) 4.00
❑1/3D, Dec 1997, Signed hardcover edition ARo (c); KB (w); BA (a) ... 5.00
❑2, Oct 1996 ARo (c); KB (w); BA (a); A: First Family ... 3.00
❑3, Nov 1996 ARo (c); KB (w); BA (a); A: Astra, First Family ... 3.00
❑4, Dec 1996 ARo (c); KB (w); BA (a); 1: Brian Kinney (The Altar Boy) (out of costume) ... 3.00
❑5, Jan 1997 ARo (c); KB (w); BA (a); O: The Altar Boy. 1: The Altar Boy (Brian Kinney in costume) ... 3.00
❑6, Feb 1997; ARo (c); KB (w); BA (a); 1: The Gunslinger. The Confessor revealed as vampire ... 3.00
❑7, Mar 1997 ARo (c); KB (w); BA (a); O: The Confessor I ... 2.50
❑8, Apr 1997 ARo (c); KB (w); BA (a); D: The Confessor I ... 2.50
❑9, May 1997 ARo (c); KB (w); BA (a); 1: The Confessor II ... 2.50
❑10, Oct 1997 ARo (c); KB (w); BA (a); O: Junkman. O: The Junkman ... 2.50
❑11, Nov 1997; ARo (c); KB (w); BA (a); 1: The Box. 1: The Jackson. Jack-in-the-Box vs. alternate versions ... 2.50
❑12, Dec 1997 ARo (c); KB (w); BA (a); 1: Jack-in-the-Box II (Roscoe James) ... 2.50
❑13, Feb 1998 ARo (c); KB (w); BA (a); O: Loony Leo. 1: Loony Leo ... 2.50
❑14, Apr 1998 ARo (c); KB (w); BA (a); O: Steeljack. 1: Steeljack ... 2.50
❑15, Dec 1998 ARo (c); KB (w); BA (a); 1: new Goldenglove. 2: Steeljack. A: Steeljack ... 2.50
❑16, Mar 1999 ARo (c); KB (w); BA (a); O: El Hombre ... 2.50
❑17, May 1999 ARo (c); KB (w); BA (a); O: The Mock Turtle ... 2.50
❑18, Aug 1999 ARo (c); KB (w); BA (a) 2.50
❑19, Nov 1999 ARo (c); KB (w); BA (a) 2.50
❑20, Jan 2000 ARo (c); KB (w); BA (a) 2.50
❑21, Mar 2000 ARo (c); KB (w); BA (a) 2.50
❑22, Aug 2000 ARo (c); KB (w); BA (a); O: Crimson Cougar. 1: Crimson Cougar ... 2.50

ASTROCOMICS
HARVEY

❑1; Giveaway from American Airlines; Reprints Harvey Comics stories ... 2.50

ASTRONAUTS IN TROUBLE: SPACE 1959
AIT

❑1 ... 2.50

ASTROTHRILL
CHEEKY

❑1, May 1999; cardstock cover; new material and reprints from Nemesister; CD ... 12.95

ASYLUM (MAXIMUM)
MAXIMUM

❑1, Dec 1995; Flip-book; Beanworld/Avengelyne flip covers ... 2.95
❑1/A, Dec 1995; Warchild/Doubletake flip covers ... 2.95
❑2, Jan 1996; Flip-book ... 2.95
❑3, Apr 1996; Flip-book ... 2.95
❑4, May 1996; Flip-book ... 2.95
❑5, Jun 1996 ... 2.95
❑6, Jul 1996 ... 2.95
❑7, Sep 1996 ... 2.95
❑8, Oct 1996 ... 2.95
❑9, Nov 1996 ... 2.95
❑10, Dec 1996 ... 2.95
❑11, Jan 1997 ... 2.99
❑12, Feb 1997 ... 2.99
❑13, Mar 1997 ... 2.99

ASYLUM (MILLENNIUM)
MILLENNIUM

❑1 ... 2.50
❑2 ... 2.50
❑3 ... 4.95

ASYLUM (NCG)
NEW COMICS

❑1, b&w ... 1.95
❑2 ... 2.25

ATARI FORCE
DC

❑1, Jan 1984 JL (a); 1: Dark Destroyer. 1: Babe. 1: Atari Force (in standard comics). 1: Dart. 1: Blackjak ... 1.00
❑2, Feb 1984 1: Martin Champion ... 1.00
❑3, Mar 1984 ... 1.00
❑4, Apr 1984 ... 1.00
❑5, May 1984 ... 1.00
❑6, Jun 1984 ... 1.00
❑7, Jul 1984 ... 1.00
❑8, Aug 1984 ... 1.00
❑9, Sep 1984 ... 1.00
❑10, Oct 1984 ... 1.00
❑11, Nov 1984 ... 1.00
❑12, Dec 1984 ... 1.00
❑13, Jan 1985 ... 1.00
❑14, Feb 1985 ... 1.00
❑15, Mar 1985 ... 1.00
❑16, Apr 1985 ... 1.00
❑17, May 1985 ... 1.00
❑18, Jun 1985 ... 1.00
❑19, Jul 1985 ... 1.00
❑20, Aug 1985 ... 1.00
❑Special 1 1986; Giant-size MR (a) ... 2.00

A-TEAM, THE
MARVEL

❑1, Mar 1984; based on TV series ... 2.00
❑2, Apr 1984 JM (a) ... 2.00
❑3, May 1984 ... 2.00

ATHENA
ANTARCTIC

❑0, Dec 1996; Antarctic publishes ... 2.95
❑1, Nov 1995; A.M. Press publishes . 2.95
❑2, Dec 1995 ... 2.95
❑3, Feb 1996 ... 2.95
❑4, Apr 1996 ... 2.95
❑5, Jun 1996 ... 2.95
❑6, Aug 1996 ... 2.95
❑7, Mar 1997, b&w ... 2.95
❑8, Apr 1997, b&w ... 2.95
❑9, May 1997, b&w ... 2.95
❑10, Jun 1997, b&w ... 2.95
❑11, Aug 1997, b&w ... 2.95
❑12, Sep 1997, b&w ... 2.95
❑13, Nov 1997, b&w ... 2.95
❑14, Dec 1997, b&w ... 2.95

ATHENA INC. THE BEGINNING
IMAGE

❑1, Jan 2001, b&w ... 5.95

ATHENA INC. THE MANHUNTER PROJECT
IMAGE

❑1 ...
❑1/A ...
❑Ashcan 1 ...
❑2/A, Apr 2002 ...
❑2/B, Apr 2002 ...
❑3/A, Aug 2002 ...
❑3/B, Aug 2002 ...
❑4/A, Oct 2002 ... 2.95
❑4/B, Oct 2002 ... 2.95
❑5/A, Jan 2003 ... 2.95
❑5/B, Jan 2003 ... 2.95
❑6/A, Apr 2003 ... 4.95
❑6/B, Apr 2003 ... 4.95

ATLANTIS CHRONICLES, THE
DC

❑1, Mar 1990 PD (w) ... 3.00
❑2, Apr 1990 PD (w) ... 3.00
❑3, May 1990 PD (w) ... 3.00
❑4, Jun 1990 PD (w) ... 3.00
❑5, Jul 1990 PD (w) ... 3.00
❑6, Aug 1990 PD (w) ... 3.00
❑7, Sep 1990 PD (w); O: Aquaman ... 3.00

ATLAS
DARK HORSE

❑1, Feb 1994 ... 2.50
❑2, Apr 1994 ... 2.50
❑3, Jun 1994 ... 2.50
❑4, Aug 1994 ... 2.50

ATLAS (AVATAR)
AVATAR

❑1/A, Aug 2002 ... 3.50
❑1/B, Aug 2002 ...
❑1/C, Aug 2002 ...
❑1/D, Aug 2002 ...
❑1/E, Aug 2002; M. Brooks cover ...
❑1/F, Aug 2002; Dealer incentive variant of #1/E; Platinum Foil title ...
❑1/G, Aug 2002; Judo Girl cover ...

ATOM, THE
DC

❑1, Jul 1962 MA, GK (a); 1: Plant Master ... 450.00
❑2, Sep 1962 MA, GK (a) ... 220.00
❑3, Nov 1962 MA, GK (a); 1: Chronos 170.00
❑4, Jan 1963 MA, GK (a) ... 125.00
❑5, Mar 1963 MA, GK (a) ... 125.00
❑6, May 1963 MA, GK (a) ... 90.00
❑7, Jul 1963 MA, GK (a); A: Hawkman 150.00
❑8, Sep 1963 MA, GK (a); A: Justice League of America ... 90.00
❑9, Nov 1963 MA, GK (a) ... 90.00
❑10, Jan 1964 MA, GK (a) ... 85.00
❑11, Mar 1964 MA, GK (a) ... 85.00
❑12, May 1964 MA, GK (a) ... 85.00
❑13, Jul 1964 ... 85.00
❑14, Sep 1964 ... 85.00
❑15, Nov 1964 ... 85.00
❑16, Jan 1965 MA, GK (a) ... 45.00
❑17, Mar 1965 MA, GK (a) ... 45.00
❑18, May 1965 MA, GK (a) ... 45.00
❑19, Jul 1965 MA, GK (a) ... 45.00
❑20, Sep 1965 MA, GK (a) ... 45.00
❑21, Nov 1965 ... 35.00
❑22, Jan 1966 ... 35.00
❑23, Mar 1966 ... 35.00
❑24, May 1966 ... 35.00
❑25, Jul 1966 ... 35.00
❑26, Sep 1966 1: Bug-Eyed Bandit ... 35.00
❑27, Nov 1966 V: Panther ... 35.00
❑28, Jan 1967 ... 35.00
❑29, Mar 1967 A: Atom I (Al Pratt) ... 90.00
❑30, May 1967 ... 35.00
❑31, Jul 1967 A: Hawkman ... 46.00
❑32, Sep 1967 ... 35.00
❑33, Nov 1967 ... 35.00
❑34, Jan 1968 ... 35.00
❑35, Mar 1968 GK (a) ... 35.00
❑36, May 1968 A: Atom I (Al Pratt) ... 45.00
❑37, Jul 1968 A: Hawkman ... 45.00
❑38, Sep 1968; Series continued in Atom and Hawkman #39 ... 3.00
❑Special 1, ca. 1993 ... 2.50
❑Special 2, ca. 1995; LMc (a); 1995 .. 2.50

ATOM AND HAWKMAN
DC

❑39, Oct 1968; JKu (a); Series continued from Atom #38 ... 30.00
❑40, Dec 1968 DD (a) ... 30.00

N-MINT

❑41, Feb 1969 .... 30.00
❑42, Apr 1969 .... 30.00
❑43, Jun 1969 JKu (a) 30.00
❑44, Aug 1969 .... 30.00
❑45, Oct 1969 .... 30.00

ATOM ANT
GOLD KEY

❑1, Jan 1966 .... 85.00

ATOM ARCHIVES, THE
DC

❑1, Collects early Atom appearances from Showcase #34-36, Atom #1-5 .... 49.95
❑2, ca. 2003 .... 49.95

ATOMIC AGE
MARVEL / EPIC

❑1, Nov 1990 .... 4.50
❑2, Dec 1990 .... 4.50
❑3, Jan 1991 .... 4.50
❑4, Feb 1991 .... 4.50

ATOMIC AGE TRUCKSTOP WAITRESS
FANTAGRAPHICS / EROS

❑1, Jul 1991, b&w 2.25

ATOMIC CITY TALES
KITCHEN SINK

❑1 1996 .... 2.95
❑2 1996 .... 2.95
❑3, Sep 1996 .... 2.95
❑Special 1 .... 2.95

ATOMIC MAN
BLACKTHORNE

❑1 1986 .... 1.75
❑2 1986 .... 1.75
❑3 1986 .... 1.75

ATOMIC MOUSE (VOL. 2)
CHARLTON

❑10, Sep 1985 .... 5.00
❑11, Nov 1985 .... 3.00
❑12, Jan 1986 .... 3.00
❑13, Mar 1986 .... 3.00

ATOMIC MOUSE (A+)
A+

❑1, ca. 1990 .... 2.50
❑2 1990 .... 2.50
❑3 1990 .... 2.50

ATOMICOW
VISION

❑1, Aug 1990 .... 2.50

ATOMIC RABBIT & FRIENDS
AVALON

❑1, b&w; reprints Charlton stories 2.50

ATOMICS, THE
AAA POP

❑1, Jan 2000 .... 2.95
❑2, Feb 2000 .... 2.95
❑3, Mar 2000 .... 2.95
❑4, Apr 2000 .... 2.95
❑5, May 2000 .... 2.95
❑6, Jun 2000 .... 2.95
❑7, Jul 2000 .... 2.95
❑8, Aug 2000 .... 2.95
❑9, Sep 2000 .... 2.95
❑10, Oct 2000 .... 2.95
❑11, Nov 2000 .... 2.95
❑12, Dec 2000 .... 3.50
❑13, Jan 2001 .... 3.50
❑14, Feb 2001 .... 3.50
❑15, Mar 2001 .... 3.50

ATOMIC TOYBOX
IMAGE

❑1, Nov 1999; cover says Dec, indicia says Nov 2.95
❑1/A, Nov 1999 .... 2.95
❑1/B, Nov 1999 .... 2.95

N-MINT

ATOMIK ANGELS (WILLIAM TUCCI'S...)
CRUSADE

❑1, May 1996 A: Freefall 2.95
❑1/Variant, May 1996; A: Freefall. variant cover 3.50
❑2, Jul 1996 .... 2.95
❑3, Sep 1996 .... 2.95
❑3/Variant, Sep 1996; alternate cover (orange background with Statue of Liberty) 3.50
❑4, Nov 1996; flipbook with Manga Shi 2000 preview 2.95
❑Special 1, Feb 1996, b&w; "The Intrepedition"; promotional comic for U.S.S. Intrepid 3.00

ATOM THE ATOMIC CAT
AVALON

❑1 .... 2.95

ATTACK (3RD SERIES)
CHARLTON

❑54, ca. 1958 .... 0.00
❑55, ca. 1959 .... 0.00
❑56, ca. 1959 .... 0.00
❑57, ca. 1959 .... 0.00
❑58, ca. 1959 .... 0.00
❑59, ca. 1959 .... 0.00
❑60, ca. 1959 .... 0.00
❑1 1962; No number in indicia or cover 25.00
❑2 1963 .... 15.00
❑3 1964 .... 12.00
❑4 1964 .... 12.00

ATTACK (4TH SERIES)
CHARLTON

❑1, Sep 1971 .... 7.00
❑2, Nov 1971 .... 4.00
❑3, Jan 1972 .... 4.00
❑4, Mar 1972 .... 3.00
❑5, May 1972 .... 3.00
❑6, Jul 1972 .... 2.50
❑7, Sep 1972 .... 2.50
❑8, Nov 1972 .... 2.50
❑9, Dec 1972 .... 2.50
❑10, Feb 1973 .... 2.50
❑11, May 1973 .... 2.50
❑12, Jul 1973 .... 2.50
❑13, Sep 1973 .... 2.50
❑14, Nov 1973 .... 2.50
❑15, Mar 1975 .... 2.50
❑16 .... 2.50
❑17, Sep 1979 .... 2.50
❑18, Nov 1979 .... 2.50
❑19, Jan 1980 .... 2.50
❑20, Mar 1980 .... 2.50
❑21, May 1980 .... 2.50
❑22 1980 .... 2.50
❑23 1980 .... 2.50
❑24 1980 .... 2.50
❑25, Dec 1980 .... 2.50
❑26, Feb 1981 .... 2.50
❑27, Apr 1981 .... 2.50
❑28, May 1981 .... 2.50
❑29, Jul 1981 .... 2.50
❑30, Sep 1981 .... 2.50
❑31, Nov 1981 .... 2.00
❑32, Jan 1982 .... 2.00
❑33, Mar 1982 .... 2.00
❑34, May 1982 .... 2.00
❑35, Jul 1982 .... 2.00
❑36, Sep 1982 .... 2.00
❑37, Nov 1982 .... 2.00
❑38, Jan 1983 .... 2.00
❑39, Mar 1983 .... 2.00
❑40, May 1983 .... 2.00
❑41, Jul 1983 .... 2.00
❑42, Sep 1983 .... 2.00
❑43 1983 .... 2.00
❑44 1984 .... 2.00
❑45 1984 .... 2.00
❑46 1984 .... 2.00

Collectors looking for series beginning with a creator's name will find the titles under the series' name with the creator's name in parentheses at the end.

N-MINT

❑47 1984 .... 2.00
❑48, Oct 1984 .... 2.00

ATTACK OF THE AMAZON GIRLS
FANTACO

❑1 .... 4.95

ATTACK OF THE MUTANT MONSTERS
A-PLUS

❑1, b&w 2.50

AT THE SEAMS
ALTERNATIVE

❑1, Jun 1997, b&w 2.95

ATTITUDE
NBM

❑1 .... 13.95

ATTITUDE LAD
SLAVE LABOR

❑1 .... 2.95

ATTU
4WINDS

❑1, b&w 9.95
❑2, b&w 9.95

AUGIE DOGGIE
GOLD KEY

❑1, Dec 1963 .... 45.00

AUGUST
ARROW

❑1 .... 2.95
❑2 .... 2.95
❑3 .... 2.95

AURORA COMIC SCENES
AURORA

❑181, ca. 1974; NA (a); really 181-140; small comic included in Aurora model kits (Tarzan) 25.00
❑182, ca. 1974; JR (a); really 182-140; small comic included in Aurora model kits (Amazing Spider-Man) .. 25.00
❑183, ca. 1974; GK (a); really 183-140; small comic included in Aurora model kits (Tonto) 25.00
❑184, ca. 1974; HT (a); really 184-140; small comic included in Aurora model kits (Incredible Hulk) 25.00
❑185, ca. 1974; CS (a); really 185-140; small comic included in Aurora model kits (Superman) 25.00
❑186, ca. 1974; DC (a); really 186-140; small comic included in Aurora model kits (Superboy) 25.00
❑187, ca. 1974; DG (a); really 187-140; small comic included in Aurora model kits (Batman) 25.00
❑188, ca. 1974; GK (a); really 188-140; small comic included in Aurora model kits (Lone Ranger) 25.00
❑192, ca. 1974; really 192-140; small comic included in Aurora model kits (Captain America) 25.00
❑193, ca. 1974; really 193-140; small comic included in Aurora model kits (Robin) 25.00

AUTHORITY, THE
DC / WILDSTORM

❑1, May 1999; wraparound cover 5.00
❑2, Jun 1999 .... 4.00
❑3, Jul 1999 .... 4.00
❑4, Aug 1999 .... 3.00

N-MINT

❑5, Oct 1999; cover says "Sep", indicia says "Oct" 3.00
❑6, Oct 1999 .... 3.00
❑7, Nov 1999 .... 3.00
❑8, Dec 1999 .... 3.00
❑9, Jan 2000 .... 3.00
❑10, Feb 2000 .... 3.00
❑11, Mar 2000 .... 2.50
❑12, Apr 2000 .... 2.50
❑13, May 2000 .... 2.50
❑14, Jun 2000 .... 2.50
❑15, Jul 2000 .... 2.50
❑16, Aug 2000 .... 2.50
❑17, Sep 2000 .... 2.50
❑18, Sep 2000 .... 2.50
❑19, Nov 2000 .... 2.50
❑20, Jan 2001 .... 2.50
❑21, Feb 2001 .... 2.50
❑22, Mar 2001 .... 2.50
❑23, Apr 2001 .... 2.50
❑24, May 2001 .... 2.50
❑25, Jun 2001 .... 2.50
❑26, Jul 2001 .... 2.50
❑27, Aug 2001 .... 2.50
❑28, Sep 2001 .... 2.50
❑29, Oct 2001 .... 2.50
❑Annual 2000, Dec 2000 .... 3.50

AUTHORITY (2ND SERIES)
DC / WILDSTORM

❑0, Aug 2003 .... 2.95
❑1, May 2003 .... 2.95
❑2, Jun 2003 .... 2.95
❑3, Jul 2003 .... 2.95
❑4, Aug 2003 .... 2.95
❑5, Sep 2003 .... 2.95
❑6, Oct 2003 .... 2.95
❑7, Nov 2003 .... 2.95
❑8, Dec 2003 .... 2.95
❑9, Jan 2004 .... 2.95
❑10, May 2004 .... 2.95
❑11, Jun 2004 .... 2.95
❑12, Jul 2004 .... 2.95
❑13, Aug 2004 .... 2.95

AUTHORITY/LOBO CHRISTMAS SPECIAL
DC / WILDSTORM

❑1, Dec 2003 .... 4.95

AUTHORITY: MORE KEV
DC / WILDSTORM

❑1, Jul 2004 .... 2.95
❑2, Aug 2004 .... 2.95

AUTOBIOGRAPHIX
DARK HORSE

❑1, ca. 2004 .... 14.95

AUTOMATIC KAFKA
WILDSTORM

❑1, Sep 2002 .... 2.95
❑2, Oct 2002 .... 2.95
❑3, Nov 2002 .... 2.95
❑4, Dec 2002 .... 2.95
❑5, Jan 2003 .... 2.95
❑6, Feb 2003 .... 2.95
❑7, Mar 2003 .... 2.95
❑8, Apr 2003 .... 2.95
❑9, May 2003 .... 2.95

AUTOMATON
IMAGE

❑1, Sep 1998 .... 2.95
❑2, Oct 1998; no month of publication 2.95
❑3, Nov 1998; no month of publication 2.95

AUTUMN
CALIBER

❑1, ca. 1995 .... 2.95
❑2, ca. 1995 .... 2.95
❑3 .... 2.95

AUTUMN ADVENTURES (WALT DISNEY'S)
DISNEY

❑1 .... 2.95

N-MINT

AUTUMN...EARTH
ACID RAIN

❑1 .... 2.50

AVALON
HARRIER

❑1, Oct 1986 .... 1.95
❑2, ca. 1986 .... 1.95
❑3, ca. 1987 .... 1.95
❑4, ca. 1987 .... 1.95
❑5, ca. 1987 .... 1.95
❑6, ca. 1987 .... 1.95
❑7, ca. 1987 .... 1.95
❑8, ca. 1987 .... 1.95
❑9, ca. 1987 .... 1.95
❑10, ca. 1987 .... 1.95
❑11, ca. 1987 .... 1.95
❑12, ca. 1987 .... 1.95
❑13, ca. 1987 .... 1.95
❑14, ca. 1988 .... 1.95

AVANT GUARD: HEROES AT THE FUTURE'S EDGE
DAY ONE

❑1, Mar 1994, b&w 2.50
❑2, Apr 1994, b&w 2.50
❑3, May 1994, b&w 2.50

AVATAARS: COVENANT OF THE SHIELD
MARVEL

❑1, Sep 2000 .... 2.99
❑2, Oct 2000 .... 2.99
❑3, Nov 2000 .... 2.99

AVATAR
DC

❑1 .... 3.50
❑2 .... 3.50
❑3 .... 3.50

AVELON
DRAWBRIDGE

❑1 1997 .... 2.95
❑2 .... 2.95
❑3 .... 2.95
❑4 .... 2.95
❑5 .... 2.95
❑6 .... 2.95
❑7 .... 2.95
❑8 .... 2.95
❑9 .... 2.95

AVENGEBLADE
MAXIMUM

❑1 .... 2.95
❑2 .... 2.95

AVENGELYNE (MINI-SERIES)
MAXIMUM

❑1, May 1995 RL (w); RL (a); O: Avengelyne. 1: Avengelyne 3.00
❑1/A, May 1995 RL (w); O: Avengelyne. 1: Avengelyne 3.00
❑1/Gold, May 1995; Gold edition RL (w); O: Avengelyne. 1: Avengelyne . 4.00
❑1/Variant, May 1995; RL (w); O: Avengelyne. 1: Avengelyne. chromium cover 3.50
❑2, Jun 1995; RL (w); polybagged with card 2.50
❑3/A, Jul 1995; RL (w); Avengelyne striking with sword on cover 2.50
❑3/B, Jul 1995; RL (w); Avengelyne standing with demons prominent on cover 2.50
❑Ashcan 1 RL (w) 3.50

AVENGELYNE (VOL. 2)
MAXIMUM

❑0, Oct 1996 .... 3.00
❑0.5 1996; Wizard promotional mail-in edition RL (w) 3.00
❑0.5/Platinum 1996; Platinum edition with certificate of authenticity (Wizard promo) RL (w) 3.50
❑1, Apr 1996 .... 3.00
❑1/Variant, Apr 1996; alternate cover (photo wraparound) 3.00

N-MINT

❑2, May 1996 1: Darkchylde 4.00
❑2/A, May 1996 1: Darkchylde 4.00
❑2/B, May 1996; 1: Darkchylde. Nude cover 5.00
❑3, Jun 1996 .... 2.50
❑4, Jul 1996 A: Cybrid 2.50
❑5, Aug 1996; RL (w); A: Cybrid. flip-book with Blindside preview 2.99
❑6, Sep 1996 RL (w) 2.99
❑7, Nov 1996 .... 2.99
❑8, Dec 1996 RL (w) 2.99
❑9, Jan 1997 .... 2.99
❑10, Feb 1997 RL (w) 2.99
❑11, Mar 1997 .... 2.99
❑11/Variant, Mar 1997; alternate cover (multiple characters behind Avengelyne) 2.99
❑12 .... 2.99
❑13 .... 2.99
❑14 .... 2.99
❑15 .... 2.99

AVENGELYNE (VOL. 3)
AWESOME

❑1, Mar 1999 .... 2.50

AVENGELYNE ARMAGEDDON
MAXIMUM

❑1, Dec 1996 .... 2.99
❑2, Jan 1997 .... 2.99
❑3, Feb 1997 .... 2.99

AVENGELYNE BIBLE
MAXIMUM

❑1, Oct 1996 .... 3.50

AVENGELYNE: DARK DEPTHS
AVATAR

❑0.5, Feb 2001 .... 3.00
❑0.5/A, Feb 2001 .... 3.00
❑0.5/B, Feb 2001 .... 3.00
❑0.5/C, Feb 2001 .... 3.00
❑1, Feb 2001 .... 3.50
❑1/A, Feb 2001 .... 3.50
❑1/B, Feb 2001 .... 3.50
❑1/C, Feb 2001 .... 3.50
❑1/D, Feb 2001 .... 3.50
❑1/E, Feb 2001 .... 3.50
❑2, Mar 2001 .... 3.50
❑2/A, Mar 2001 .... 3.50
❑2/B, Mar 2001 .... 3.50
❑2/C, Mar 2001 .... 3.50

AVENGELYNE: DEADLY SINS
MAXIMUM

❑1, Feb 1996 .... 2.95
❑1/Variant, Feb 1996; alternate cover (photo) 3.50
❑2, Mar 1996 .... 2.95

AVENGELYNE/GLORY
MAXIMUM

❑1, Sep 1995; wraparound chromium cover 3.95
❑1/Variant, Sep 1995; variant cover .. 3.95

AVENGELYNE/GLORY: THE GODYSSEY
MAXIMUM

❑1 .... 2.99
❑1/Variant 2.99

AVENGELYNE: POWER
MAXIMUM

❑1/A, Nov 1995; Red background on cover 2.50
❑1/B, Nov 1995; Blue background on cover 2.50
❑2, Dec 1995 .... 2.50
❑3, Jan 1996 .... 2.50

AVENGELYNE • PROPHET
MAXIMUM

❑1/A, May 1996; Close-up of faces on cover ....
❑1, May 1996 .... 2.95
❑2, Jun 1996 .... 2.95

Condition price index: Multiply "NM prices" above by: **0.83 for Very Fine/Near Mint**
0.66 for Very Fine • 0.33 for Fine • 0.2 for Very Good • 0.125 for Good

N-MINT

AVENGELYNE SWIMSUIT
Maximum

❑1, Aug 1995; Drawn cover; both drawn and photographed; n-ups ... 2.95
❑1/A, Aug 1995; Black swimsuit, dry hair, leaning against cliff on cover; pin-ups, both drawn and photographed ... 2.95
❑1/B, Aug 1995; Black suit, dry hair, sitting on cliff on cover; pin-ups, both drawn and photographed ... 2.95
❑1/C, Aug 1995; pin-ups, both drawn and photographed; White suit on cover ... 2.95
❑1/D, Aug 1995; Black suit, wet hair on cover; pin-ups, both drawn and photographed ... 2.95

AVENGELYNE/WARRIOR NUN AREALA
Maximum

❑1/A, Nov 1996; Avengelyne in front on cover ... 2.99
❑1/B, Nov 1996; Two women back-to-back on cover ... 2.99

AVENGERS, THE
Marvel

❑0; Wizard promotional edition ... 3.00
❑1, Sep 1963; JK, SL (w); JK (a); O: Avengers. 1st appearance/origin of the Avengers; Team consists of Thor, Ant-Man, Wasp, Hulk, and Iron Man 3560.00
❑1.5, Dec 1999; Issue #1-1/2 ... 3.00
❑2, Nov 1963; JK, SL (w); JK (a); 1: Space Phantom. Hulk leaves Avengers; Ant-Man becomes Giant-Man . 850.00
❑3, Jan 1964; JK, SL (w); JK (a); Avengers vs. Sub-Mariner and Hulk ... 475.00
❑4, Mar 1964; JK, SL (w); JK (a); 1: Baron Zemo. Captain America returns; Capt. America returns ... 1550.00
❑4/Golden Record, ca. 1966; Golden Records reprint ... 90.00
❑5, May 1964; JK, SL (w); JK (a); Hulk leaves team ... 250.00
❑6, Jul 1964 JK, SL (w); JK (a); 1: Masters of Evil ... 185.00
❑7, Aug 1964 JK, SL (w); JK (a) ... 185.00
❑8, Sep 1964 JK, SL (w); JK (a); O: Kang. 1: Kang ... 185.00
❑9, Oct 1964 SL (w); DH, JK (a); O: Wonder Man. 1: Wonder Man. D: Wonder Man ... 200.00
❑10, Nov 1964 SL (w); DH, JK (a); 1: Hercules. 1: Immortus ... 200.00
❑11, Dec 1964; SL (w); DH, JK (a); A: Spider-Man. Spider-Man ... 200.00
❑12, Jan 1965 SL (w); DH, JK (a); 1: Monk Keefer (later becomes Ape-Man I). V: Mole Man ... 125.00
❑13, Feb 1965 SL (w); DH, JK (a); 1: Count Nefaria ... 125.00
❑14, Mar 1965; JK, SL (w); JK (a); 1: Ogor and Kallusians. The Watcher . 125.00
❑15, Apr 1965; JK, SL (w); JK (a); D: Baron Zemo I (Heinrich Zemo). Death of Baron Zemo ... 125.00
❑16, May 1965; JK, SL (w); JK (a); Cap assembles new team of Hawkeye, Quicksilver, Scarlet Witch; New team begins: Captain America, Hawkeye, Quicksilver, and Scarlet Witch ... 125.00
❑17, Jun 1965 SL (w); JK (a) ... 100.00
❑18, Jul 1965 SL (w); DH, JK (a) ... 100.00
❑19, Aug 1965; SL (w); DH, JK (a); O: Hawkeye. 1: Swordsman. origin of Hawkeye ... 125.00
❑20, Sep 1965 SL (w); DH, WW (a); V: Swordsman ... 75.00
❑21, Oct 1965; SL (w); DH, JK (a); O: Power Man I (Erik Josten). 1: Power Man I (Erik Josten). Power Man ... 65.00
❑22, Nov 1965 SL (w); DH, JK (a) ... 65.00
❑23, Dec 1965 SL (w); DH, JK (a); 1: Ravonna ... 65.00
❑24, Jan 1966 SL (w); DH, JK (a); A: Kang. A: Doctor Doom. A: Princess Ravonna ... 65.00

N-MINT

❑25, Feb 1966 SL (w); DH, JK (a); A: Mr. Fantastic. A: Invisible Girl. A: Thing. A: Human Torch. A: Doctor Doom ... 65.00
❑26, Mar 1966 SL (w); DH, JK (a); A: Henry Pym. A: Puppet Master. A: Beetle. A: Tony Stark. A: Attuma. A: Sub-Mariner. A: The Wasp ... 65.00
❑27, Apr 1966 SL (w); DH, JK (a); A: Mr. Fantastic. A: Invisible Girl. A: Collector. A: Henry Pym. A: Beetle. A: Attuma ... 65.00
❑28, May 1966; SL (w); DH, JK (a); 1: The Collector. 1: Goliath. A: Beetle. Giant-Man becomes Goliath; Goliath rejoins Avengers; Wasp rejoins Avengers ... 50.00
❑29, Jun 1966; SL (w); DH, JK (a); 1: Hu Chen. 1: Doctor Yen. A: Black Widow. A: S.H.I.E.L.D.. A: Swordsman. Power Man I; Black Widow ... 50.00
❑30, Jul 1966; SL (w); DH, JK (a); 1: Doctor Franz Anton. 1: Keeper of the Flame. 1: Prince Rey. A: Black Widow. A: Power Man I. A: Hu Chen. A: Swordsman. Quicksilver & Scarlet Witch leave Avengers ... 50.00
❑31, Aug 1966 SL (w); DH, JK (a) ... 43.00
❑32, Sep 1966; SL (w); DH (a); 1: Sons of the Serpent. 1: Supreme Serpent I. 1: Bill Foster (Giant-Man II). A: Black Widow. A: Scarlet Witch. A: Quicksilver. A: Nick Fury. A: Tony Stark. Black Widow ... 43.00
❑33, Oct 1966; SL (w); DH (a); A: Black Widow. Black Widow ... 43.00
❑34, Nov 1966 SL (w); DH (a); O: Living Laser. 1: Living Laser. 1: Lucy Barton 43.00
❑35, Dec 1966 SL (w); DH (a); 1: Ultrana (off page). 2: Living Laser. 2: Lucy Barton. A: Black Widow. A: Bill Foster ... 43.00
❑36, Jan 1967; DH (a); 1: Ultroids. 1: Ultrana (full). 1: Ixar. A: Black Widow. Quicksilver & Scarlet Witch rejoin Avengers ... 43.00
❑37, Feb 1967; DH (a); 2: Ultroids. 2: Ultrana. 2: Ixar. A: Black Widow. Black Widow; Ultroids consolidate into giant robot Ultroid ... 43.00
❑38, Mar 1967; DH (a); A: Hercules. A: Black Widow. Hercules; Captain America leaves Avengers ... 43.00
❑39, Apr 1967; DH (a); A: Hercules. A: Black Widow. A: S.H.I.E.L.D.. A: Jasper Sitwell. A: Dum Dum Dugan. A: Nick Fury. A: Mad Thinker. Hercules 43.00
❑40, May 1967 DH (a); A: Hercules. A: Black Widow. A: Sub-Mariner. V: Sub-Mariner ... 43.00
❑41, Jun 1967; JB (a); 1: Colonel Ling. 2: Doctor Yen. A: Hercules. A: Black Widow. A: Dragon Man. A: Bill Foster. A: Diablo. Mr. Fantastic cameo; Human Torch cameo ... 43.00
❑42, Jul 1967; JB (a); V: Diablo, Dragon Man. Captain America rejoins the Avengers ... 43.00
❑43, Aug 1967 JB (a); 1: General Yuri Brushov. 1: Red Guardian I (Alexi Shostakov). A: Hercules. A: Black Widow. A: Edwin Jarvis. A: Colonel Ling ... 43.00
❑44, Sep 1967 JB (a); O: Red Guardian I (Alexi Shostakov). O: Black Widow (part). 2: Red Guardian I (Alexi Shostakov). A: Hercules. A: Black Widow. A: Colonel Ling. D: Red Guardian I (Alexi Shostakov) ... 43.00
❑45, Oct 1967; DH (w); DH (a); A: Super-Adaptoid. A: Iron Man I. A: Thor. V: Super-Adaptoid. Hercules joins team; Hercules joins Avengers; Black Widow retires ... 43.00
❑46, Nov 1967; 1: Whirlwind. Goliath regains Ant-Man powers ... 35.00
❑47, Dec 1967; D: Black Knight II (Nathan Garrett). New Black Knight (Dr. Dane Whitman) origin part 1 .. 35.00
❑48, Jan 1968; O: Aragorn. 1: Black Knight III (Dane Whitman). 1: Aragorn. New Black Knight (Dr. Dane Whitman) origin part 2 ... 35.00

The Authority turns many super-hero conventions on their head.

© 1999 WildStorm Productions. (DC)

N-MINT

❑49, Feb 1968; JB (a); A: Magneto. Quicksilver & Scarlet Witch leave Avengers; Goliath loses powers ... 35.00
❑50, Mar 1968; JB (a); Herculese leaves the Avengers ... 35.00
❑51, Apr 1968; JB (a); Thor, Iron Man; Goliath regains powers, new costume ... 35.00
❑52, May 1968; O: Grim Reaper. 1: Grim Reaper. Black Panther joins ... 38.00
❑53, Jun 1968 JB (a); A: X-Men ... 45.00
❑54, Jul 1968 JB (a); 1: Crimson Cowl 38.00
❑55, Aug 1968 JB (a); 1: Ultron-5 ... 38.00
❑56, Sep 1968 JB (a) ... 38.00
❑57, Oct 1968; JB (a); 1: The Vision II (android). First Vision ... 110.00
❑58, Nov 1968; JB (a); O: The Vision II (android). Origin of the Vision; The Vision joins the Avengers; Thor, Captain America, Iron Man ... 70.00
❑59, Dec 1968; JB (a); 1: Yellowjacket. Goliath becomes Yellowjacket ... 40.00
❑60, Jan 1969; JB (a); Yellowjacket marries Wasp; Captain America ... 40.00
❑61, Feb 1969; JB (a); Doctor Strange 30.00
❑62, Mar 1969 JB (a); 1: W'Kabi. 1: The Man-Ape ... 30.00
❑63, Apr 1969 GC (a); O: Goliath-New (Hawkeye). 1: Goliath-New (Hawkeye) ... 30.00
❑64, May 1969; GC (a); Black Widow; Hawkeye's identity revealed ... 30.00
❑65, Jun 1969 GC (a); O: Hawkeye ... 30.00
❑66, Jul 1969 ... 30.00
❑67, Aug 1969 ... 44.00
❑68, Sep 1969 SB (a) ... 22.00
❑69, Oct 1969; SB (a); 1: Grandmaster. 1: Nighthawk II (Kyle Richmond)-Full. First Nighthawk; Captain America and Black Panther rejoin ... 22.00
❑70, Nov 1969 SB (a) ... 22.00
❑71, Dec 1969; SB (a); 1: Invaders (prototype). Human Torch, Golden Age Captain America and Sub-Mariner; Black Knight joins Avengers ... 50.00
❑72, Jan 1970 SB (a); 1: Zodiac I. 1: Taurus. 1: Pisces I ... 23.00
❑73, Feb 1970; HT (a); Quicksilver, Scarlet Witch return; Yellowjacket and Wasp leave ... 23.00
❑74, Mar 1970 JB (a) ... 23.00
❑75, Apr 1970 JB (a); 1: Arkon ... 23.00
❑76, May 1970 JB (a) ... 23.00
❑77, Jun 1970 JB (a); 1: the Split-Second Squad ... 23.00
❑78, Jul 1970 JB (a) ... 23.00
❑79, Aug 1970 JB (a) ... 23.00
❑80, Sep 1970 JB (a); O: Red Wolf. 1: Red Wolf ... 23.00
❑81, Oct 1970 JB (a) ... 23.00
❑82, Nov 1970; JB (a); Daredevil ... 23.00
❑83, Dec 1970; JB (a); 1: Valkyrie. First Valkyrie ... 36.00
❑84, Jan 1971; JB (a); Black Knight's sword destroyed ... 23.00
❑85, Feb 1971 JB (a); 1: Whizzer II (Stanley Stewart). 1: Hawkeye II (Wyatt McDonald). 1: American Eagle II (James Dore Jr.). 1: Tom Thumb. 1: Doctor Spectrum I (Joe Ledger) ... 23.00
❑86, Mar 1971 JB, SB (a); 1: Brain-Child ... 23.00

	N-MINT
❑87, Apr 1971; O: Black Panther. Black Panther origin retold	40.00
❑88, May 1971 SB (a); 1: Psyklop	20.00
❑88-2 SB (a); 1: Psyklop	2.00
❑89, Jun 1971; SB (a); Kree/Skrull War part 1; Captain Marvel	20.00
❑90, Jul 1971; SB (a); Kree/Skrull War part 2; Captain Marvel origin retold	20.00
❑91, Aug 1971; SB (a); Kree/Skrull War part 3; Captain Marvel	20.00
❑92, Sep 1971; NA (c); SB, NA (a); Kree/Skrull War part 4; Captain Marvel	20.00
❑93, Nov 1971; Double-size; NA (a); Kree/Skrull War part 5; Captain Marvel	98.00
❑94, Dec 1971; JB, NA (a); 1: Mandroid armor. Kree/Skrull War part 6; Captain Marvel	35.00
❑95, Jan 1972; NA (a); O: Black Bolt. Kree/Skrull War part 7; Inhumans crosover with Amazing Adventures #5-8	35.00
❑96, Feb 1972; NA (a); Kree/Skrull War part 8; Captain Marvel	35.00
❑97, Mar 1972; NA (w); JB, BEv, SB, GK (a); Kree/Skrull War part 9; Captain Marvel	26.00
❑98, Apr 1972; 1: The Warhawks. Goliath becomes Hawkeye again	26.00
❑99, May 1972	26.00
❑100, Jun 1972; 100th anniversary issue; Black Knight regains magic sword	65.00
❑101, Jul 1972; RB (a); The Watcher	18.00
❑102, Aug 1972 RB (a)	18.00
❑103, Sep 1972 RB (a)	18.00
❑104, Oct 1972 RB (a)	18.00
❑105, Nov 1972 JB (a)	18.00
❑106, Dec 1972 RB, GT (a)	18.00
❑107, Jan 1973 JSn, GT, DC (a)	18.00
❑108, Feb 1973 DH (a)	18.00
❑109, Mar 1973; DH (a); 1: Imus Champion. Hawkeye leaves Avengers	18.00
❑110, Apr 1973; DH (a); A: X-Men. X-Men; crossover with Fantastic Four #132	22.00
❑111, May 1973; DH (a); A: X-Men. Daredevil	22.00
❑112, Jun 1973; DH (a); 1: Mantis. Black Widow leaves	18.00
❑113, Jul 1973; 1: The Living Bombs. D: The Living Bombs. Silver Surfer	13.00
❑114, Aug 1973; Silver Surfer	13.00
❑115, Sep 1973; D: The Living Bombs. Silver Surfer; Avengers and Defenders vs. Loki and Dormammu, part 1 - continues in Defenders #8	13.00
❑116, Oct 1973; Silver Surfer; Avengers and Defenders vs. Loki and Dormammu, part 3 - continues in Defenders #9	25.00
❑117, Nov 1973; Silver Surfer; Avengers and Defenders vs. Loki and Dormammu, part 5 - continues in Defenders #10	20.00
❑118, Dec 1973; Silver Surfer; Avengers and Defenders vs. Loki and Dormammu, part 7 - continues in Defenders #11	20.00
❑119, Jan 1974; Silver Surfer	12.00
❑120, Feb 1974 JSn, DH, JSt (a)	12.00
❑121, Mar 1974; JB (a); Marvel Value Stamp #84: Dr. Doom	12.00
❑122, Apr 1974; Marvel Value Stamp #71: Vision	12.00
❑123, May 1974; O: Mantis. Origin of Mantis, part 1; Marvel Value Stamp #4: Thing	12.00
❑124, Jun 1974; Origin of Mantis, part 2; Marvel Value Stamp #81: rhino	12.00
❑125, Jul 1974; A: Thanos. Thanos; Crossover with Captain Marvel #32 and 33; Marvel Value Stamp #69: Marvel Girl	12.00
❑126, Aug 1974; Marvel Value Stamp #46: Mysterio	12.00
❑127, Sep 1974; SB, FF (a); 1: Ultron-7. A: Fantastic Four. A: Inhumans. continues in Fantastic Four #150 (wedding of Crystal and Quicksilver); Marvel Value Stamp #13: Dr. Strange	12.00
❑128, Oct 1974; SB (a); Marvel Value Stamp #70: Super Skrull	12.00
❑129, Nov 1974; SB (a); Marvel Value Stamp #88: Leader	12.00
❑130, Dec 1974; SB (a); 1: The Slasher. V: Titanium Man, Radioactive Man, Crimson Dynamo, Slasher. Marvel Value Stamp #96: Dr. Octopus	12.00
❑131, Jan 1975; SB (a); Immortus; Marvel Value Stamp #70: Super Skrull	8.00
❑132, Feb 1975; SB (a); Iron Man dies (resurrected in Giant-Size Avengers #3); Marvel Value Stamp #78: Owl	8.00
❑133, Mar 1975; SB (a); origin of the Vision and Golden Age Human Torch, part 1	8.00
❑134, Apr 1975; SB (a); O: Vision II (android). origin of the Vision and Golden Age Human Torch, part 2	8.00
❑135, May 1975; GT (a); O: Moondragon. O: Vision II (android)-real origin. origin of the Vision and Golden Age Human Torch, part 3	8.00
❑136, Jun 1975; reprints with changes Amazing Adventures #12	8.00
❑137, Jul 1975; GT (a); membership becomes Beast, Iron Man, Moondragon, Thor, Wasp and Yellowjacket	8.00
❑138, Aug 1975 GT (a)	8.00
❑139, Sep 1975 GT (a)	8.00
❑140, Oct 1975; GT (a); Vision and Scarlet Witch return	8.00
❑141, Nov 1975; GP (a); 1: Golden Archer II (Wyatt McDonald). Squadron Sinister	8.00
❑142, Dec 1975; GP (a); Rawhide Kid, Two-Gun Kid, Kid Colt, Night Rider	8.00
❑143, Jan 1976 GP (a)	8.00
❑144, Feb 1976; GP (a); O: Hellcat. 1: Hellcat	8.00
❑145, Mar 1976 DH (a)	5.50
❑146, Apr 1976; KP, DH (a); Falcon	5.50
❑146/30 cent, Apr 1976; KP, DH (a); Falcon; 30 cent regional price variant	20.00
❑147, May 1976; Hellcat	5.50
❑147/30 cent, May 1976; Hellcat; 30 cent regional price variant	20.00
❑148, Jun 1976 1: Cap'n Hawk	5.50
❑148/30 cent, Jun 1976; 1: Cap'n Hawk. 30 cent regional price variant	15.00
❑149, Jun 1976	5.50
❑149/30 cent, Jun 1976; 30 cent regional price variant	15.00
❑150, Aug 1976; GP (a); New team: Captain America, Iron Man, Yellowjacket, Wasp, Beast, Vision II (android), and Scarlet Witch; Partial Reprint from Avengers #16, retitled from "The Old Order Changeth"	5.50
❑150/30 cent, Aug 1976; GP (a); New team: Captain America, Iron Man, Yellowjacket, Wasp, Beast, Vision II (android), and Scarlet Witch; Partial Reprint from Avengers #16, retitled from "The Old Order Changeth"	15.00
❑151, Sep 1976; GP (a); New Avengers lineup: Beast, Captain America, Iron Man, Scarlet Witch, Vision, Wasp, Yellowjacket; Wonder Man comes back from dead, new costume	5.50
❑152, Oct 1976 1: Black Talon II	5.50
❑153, Nov 1976	5.50
❑154, Dec 1976	5.50
❑155, Jan 1977	5.50
❑156, Feb 1977 1: Tyrack	8.00
❑157, Mar 1977	5.50
❑158, Apr 1977	5.50
❑159, May 1977 SB (a)	5.50
❑160, Jun 1977	5.50
❑160/35 cent, Jun 1977; 35 cent regional price variant	15.00
❑161, Jul 1977 GP, JBy (a)	5.50
❑161/35 cent, Jul 1977; GP, JBy (a); 35 cent regional price variant	15.00
❑162, Aug 1977 GP, JBy (a); O: Jocasta. 1: Jocasta	5.50
❑162/35 cent, Aug 1977; GP, JBy (a); 35 cent regional price variant	15.00
❑163, Sep 1977 GP, JBy (a)	5.50
❑164, Oct 1977 GP, JBy (a)	5.50
❑165, Nov 1977 JBy (a)	5.50
❑166, Dec 1977 JBy (a)	5.50
❑167, Jan 1978 JBy (a)	5.00
❑168, Feb 1978 JBy (a)	5.00
❑169, Mar 1978 JBy (a)	5.00
❑170, Apr 1978 JBy (a)	5.00
❑171, May 1978 JBy (a)	5.00
❑172, Jun 1978	5.00
❑173, Jul 1978	5.00
❑174, Aug 1978	5.00
❑175, Sep 1978	5.00
❑176, Oct 1978	5.00
❑177, Nov 1978	5.00
❑178, Dec 1978 CI, JBy (a)	5.00
❑179, Jan 1979 JM (a); 1: The Monolith. 1: The Stinger II	5.00
❑180, Feb 1979 JM (a)	5.00
❑181, Mar 1979; GP, JBy, TD (a); New team: Captain America, Falcon, Iron Man, Beast, Vision II (android), and Scarlet Witch	4.50
❑182, Apr 1979 JBy (a)	5.00
❑183, May 1979 JBy (a)	5.00
❑184, Jun 1979 JBy (a)	5.00
❑185, Jul 1979 JBy (a); O: Scarlet Witch. O: Quicksilver. 1: Chthon (in human body)	5.00
❑186, Aug 1979 JBy (a)	5.00
❑187, Sep 1979 JBy (a); 1: Chthon (in real human form)	5.00
❑188, Oct 1979 JBy, DGr, FS (a)	5.00
❑189, Nov 1979 JBy (a)	5.00
❑190, Dec 1979; JBy (a); Daredevil	5.00
❑191, Jan 1980 GP, JBy (a)	5.00
❑192, Feb 1980	5.00
❑193, Mar 1980 FM, BMc (c); SB, DGr (a)	5.00
❑194, Apr 1980 GP (a)	5.00
❑195, May 1980 GP (a); 1: Taskmaster	5.00
❑196, Jun 1980 GP (a); O: Taskmaster	5.00
❑197, Jul 1980 CI (a)	5.00
❑198, Aug 1980 GP (a)	5.00
❑199, Sep 1980 GP (a)	5.00
❑200, Oct 1980; double-sized; GP, DGr (a); Ms. Marvel leaves team	7.00
❑201, Nov 1980 GP (a)	2.50
❑202, Dec 1980 GP (a); V: Ultron	2.50
❑203, Jan 1981 CI (a)	2.50
❑204, Feb 1981 DN (a); A: Yellow Claw	2.50
❑205, Mar 1981 A: Yellow Claw	2.50
❑206, Apr 1981 GC (a)	2.50
❑207, May 1981 GC (a)	2.50
❑208, Jun 1981 GC (a)	2.50
❑209, Jul 1981	2.50
❑210, Aug 1981 GC, DG (a)	2.50
❑211, Sep 1981; GC, DG (a); Moon Knight, Dazzler; New team begins	2.50
❑212, Oct 1981 BH (c)	2.50
❑213, Nov 1981; BH (c); BH (a); Yellowjacket's court martial; Yellowjacket leaves	2.50
❑214, Dec 1981 BH (c); BH (a); A: Ghost Rider	3.00
❑215, Jan 1982 A: Silver Surfer	2.50
❑216, Feb 1982 A: Silver Surfer	2.50
❑217, Mar 1982; BH (c); BH (a); Yellowjacket jailed; Yellowjacket & Wasp return	3.00
❑218, Apr 1982 DP (a)	3.00
❑219, May 1982 BH (c); BH (a); A: Drax	2.00
❑220, Jun 1982 BH (c); BH (a); A: Drax. D: Drax the Destroyer	2.00
❑221, Jul 1982; BH (c); BH (a); Hawkeye rejoins; She-Hulk joins; Wolverine on cover, not in issue	2.00
❑222, Aug 1982 V: Masters of Evil	2.00
❑223, Sep 1982 A: Ant-Man	2.00

	N-MINT
❑224, Oct 1982; Tony Stark/Wasp romance	2.00
❑225, Nov 1982 1: Balor. A: Black Knight	3.00
❑226, Dec 1982 1: Valinor. A: Black Knight	2.00
❑227, Jan 1983; SB (a); O: Yellowjacket. O: Ant-Man. O: Goliath. O: Wasp. O: Giant-Man. O: Avengers. Captain Marvel II joins team; Captain Marvel II (female) joins team	2.00
❑228, Feb 1983 AM (a)	2.00
❑229, Mar 1983 AM (a); V: Egghead	2.00
❑230, Apr 1983; AM (a); D: Egghead. Yellowjacket leaves	2.00
❑231, May 1983; AM (a); Iron Man leaves	2.00
❑232, Jun 1983; AM (a); A: Starfox. Starfox (Eros) joins	2.00
❑233, Jul 1983 JBy (w); JBy, JSt (a)	2.00
❑234, Aug 1983 AM (a); O: Scarlet Witch. O: Quicksilver	2.00
❑235, Sep 1983 V: Wizard	2.00
❑236, Oct 1983; AM (a); Spider-Man; New logo	2.00
❑237, Nov 1983; AM (a); Spider-Man	2.00
❑238, Dec 1983 AM (a); O: Blackout I (Marcus Daniels)	2.00
❑239, Jan 1984 AM (a); A: David Letterman. D: Blackout I (Marcus Daniels)	2.00
❑240, Feb 1984; AM (a); A: Spider-Woman. Spider-Woman revived	2.00
❑241, Mar 1984 AM (a); A: Spider-Woman	2.00
❑242, Apr 1984 AM (a)	2.00
❑243, May 1984 AM (a)	2.00
❑244, Jun 1984 AM (a); V: Dire Wraiths	2.00
❑245, Jul 1984 AM (a); V: Dire Wraiths	2.00
❑246, Aug 1984 AM (a); A: Sersi	2.00
❑247, Sep 1984 AM (a); A: Uni-Mind	2.00
❑248, Oct 1984 AM (a); A: Eternals	2.00
❑249, Nov 1984 AM (a); A: Fantastic Four	2.00
❑250, Dec 1984; AM (a); Maelstrom	2.50
❑251, Jan 1985 BH (c); BH (a)	1.75
❑252, Feb 1985 BH (c); BH (a)	1.75
❑253, Mar 1985 BH (a)	1.75
❑254, Apr 1985 BH (c); BH (a)	1.75
❑255, May 1985 JB (a)	1.75
❑256, Jun 1985; JB (a); Savage Land	1.75
❑257, Jul 1985 JB (a); 1: Nebula	1.75
❑258, Aug 1985; Spider-Man vs. Firelord	1.75
❑259, Sep 1985 V: Skrulls	1.75
❑260, Oct 1985; JB (a); A: Nebula. Secret Wars II	1.75
❑261, Nov 1985; JB (a); Secret Wars II	1.75
❑262, Dec 1985 JB (a); A: Sub-Mariner	1.75
❑263, Jan 1986 1: X-Factor. D: Melter	3.00
❑264, Feb 1986	1.75
❑265, Mar 1986; JB (a); Secret Wars II	1.75
❑266, Apr 1986; JB (a); Secret Wars II Epilogue	1.50
❑267, May 1986 JB (a); V: Kang	1.50
❑268, Jun 1986 JB (a); V: Kang	1.50
❑269, Jul 1986 JB (a); O: Rama-Tut. V: Kang	1.50
❑270, Aug 1986 JB (a); A: Namor	1.50
❑271, Sep 1986 JB (a)	1.50
❑272, Oct 1986 JB (a); A: Alpha Flight	1.50
❑273, Nov 1986 JB (a)	1.50
❑274, Dec 1986 JB (a)	1.50
❑275, Jan 1987 JB (a)	1.50
❑276, Feb 1987 JB (a)	1.50
❑277, Mar 1987 JB (a); D: Blackout	1.50
❑278, Apr 1987 JB (a)	1.50
❑279, May 1987	1.50
❑280, Jun 1987 BH (a)	1.50
❑281, Jul 1987	1.50
❑282, Aug 1987 V: Neptune	1.50
❑283, Sep 1987	1.50
❑284, Oct 1987; on Olympus	1.50
❑285, Nov 1987 V: Zeus	1.50
❑286, Dec 1987 JB (a); V: Super Adaptoid	1.50
❑287, Jan 1988 JB (a); V: Fixer	1.50
❑288, Feb 1988 JB (a); V: Sentry Sinister	1.50
❑289, Mar 1988 JB (a); V: Super Adaptoid, Sentry Sinister, Machine Man, Tess-One, Fixer	1.50
❑290, Apr 1988 JB (a)	1.50
❑291, May 1988 JB (a)	1.50
❑292, Jun 1988 JB (a); 1: Leviathan III (Marina). D: Leviathan III (Marina)	1.50
❑293, Jul 1988 JB (a); 1: Nebula. D: Marina. D: Marrina	1.50
❑294, Aug 1988; JB (a); Captain Marvel leaves team; Capt. Marvel leaves team	1.50
❑295, Sep 1988 JB (a)	1.50
❑296, Oct 1988 JB (a)	1.50
❑297, Nov 1988; JB (a); D: Doctor Druid. Thor, Black Knight, She-Hulk leaves team; She-Hulk, Thor, and Black Knight leave	1.50
❑298, Dec 1988; JB (a); Inferno	1.50
❑299, Jan 1989; JB (a); Inferno	1.50
❑300, Feb 1989; 300th anniversary issue; JB (a); Inferno; new team; Thor Joins	2.00
❑301, Mar 1989 BH (c); BH (a)	1.50
❑302, Apr 1989 RB (a)	1.50
❑303, May 1989 RB (a)	1.50
❑304, Jun 1989 RB (a); 1: Portal. A: Puma. V: U-Foes	1.50
❑305, Jul 1989 JBy (w); JBy (a)	1.50
❑306, Aug 1989 JBy (w)	1.50
❑307, Sep 1989 JBy (w)	1.50
❑308, Oct 1989 JBy (w)	1.50
❑309, Nov 1989 JBy (w); TP (a)	1.50
❑310, Nov 1989 JBy (w)	1.50
❑311, Dec 1989; JBy (w); TP (a); "Acts of Vengeance"	1.50
❑312, Dec 1989; JBy (w); TP (a); "Acts of Vengeance"	1.50
❑313, Jan 1990; JBy (w); "Acts of Vengeance"	1.50
❑314, Feb 1990; JBy (w); Spider-Man	1.50
❑315, Mar 1990; JBy (w); TP (a); Spider-Man; Spider-Man x-over	1.50
❑316, Apr 1990; JBy (w); Spider-Man	1.50
❑317, May 1990; JBy (w); Spider-Man	1.50
❑318, Jun 1990; Spider-Man	1.50
❑319, Jul 1990	1.50
❑320, Aug 1990 A: Alpha Flight	1.50
❑321, Aug 1990	1.50
❑322, Sep 1990 A: Alpha Flight	1.50
❑323, Sep 1990 A: Alpha Flight	1.50
❑324, Oct 1990	1.50
❑325, Oct 1990	1.50
❑326, Nov 1990 1: Rage	1.50
❑327, Dec 1990	1.50
❑328, Jan 1991 O: Rage. O: Turbo	1.50
❑329, Feb 1991	1.50
❑330, Mar 1991	1.50
❑331, Apr 1991	1.50
❑332, May 1991	1.50
❑333, Jun 1991 HT (a)	1.50
❑334, Jul 1991	1.50
❑335, Aug 1991	1.50
❑336, Aug 1991	1.50
❑337, Sep 1991	1.50
❑338, Sep 1991	1.50
❑339, Oct 1991	1.50
❑340, Oct 1991	1.50
❑341, Nov 1991	1.50
❑342, Dec 1991 A: New Warriors	1.50
❑343, Jan 1992	1.50
❑344, Feb 1992	1.50
❑345, Mar 1992; Operation: Galactic Storm, Part 5	1.50
❑346, Apr 1992; Operation: Galactic Storm, Part 12	1.50
❑347, May 1992; D: Supreme Intelligence (apparent death). Operation: Galactic Storm, Part 19; Conclusion to Operation: Galactic Storm	2.00
❑348, Jun 1992	1.50
❑349, Jul 1992	1.50

Captain America was the second Golden Age Marvel character to be revived in the Silver Age.

© 1964 Marvel Comics.

	N-MINT
❑350, Aug 1992; Dbl. Size; Gatefold covers	2.50
❑351, Aug 1992	1.25
❑352, Sep 1992 V: Grim Reaper	1.25
❑353, Sep 1992 V: Grim Reaper	1.25
❑354, Oct 1992 V: Grim Reaper	1.25
❑355, Oct 1992	1.25
❑356, Nov 1992	1.25
❑357, Dec 1992	1.25
❑358, Jan 1993	1.25
❑359, Feb 1993	1.25
❑360, Mar 1993; foil cover	2.95
❑361, Apr 1993	1.25
❑362, May 1993	1.25
❑363, Jun 1993; Silver embossed cover	2.95
❑364, Jul 1993	1.25
❑365, Aug 1993	1.25
❑366, Sep 1993; sculpted foil cover	3.95
❑367, Oct 1993 A: Sersi. A: Black Knight	1.25
❑368, Nov 1993	1.25
❑369, Dec 1993; sculpted foil cover	2.95
❑370, Jan 1994	1.25
❑371, Feb 1994 MGu, TP (a)	1.25
❑372, Mar 1994	1.25
❑373, Apr 1994	1.25
❑374, May 1994; cards	1.25
❑375, Jun 1994; Giant-size; D: Proctor. poster; Dane Whitman and Sersi leave the Avengers	2.00
❑375/CS, Jun 1994; Giant-size; D: Proctor. Dane Whitman and Sersi leave the Avengers	2.50
❑376, Jul 1994	1.50
❑377, Aug 1994	1.50
❑378, Sep 1994	1.50
❑379, Oct 1994	1.50
❑379/A, Oct 1994; Double-feature with Giant-Man	2.50
❑380, Nov 1994 V: High Evolutionary	1.50
❑380/A, Nov 1994; second indicia gives name as "Marvel Double Feature ... The Avengers/Giant Man"	2.50
❑381, Dec 1994 TP (a)	1.50
❑381/A, Dec 1994; TP (a); second indicia gives name as "Marvel Double Feature ... The Avengers/Giant Man"	2.50
❑382, Jan 1995 TP (a)	1.50
❑382/A, Jan 1995; TP (a); second indicia gives name as "Marvel Double Feature ... The Avengers/Giant Man"	2.50
❑383, Feb 1995 MGu (a)	1.50
❑384, Mar 1995	1.50
❑385, Apr 1995	1.50
❑386, May 1995	1.50
❑387, Jun 1995	1.50
❑388, Jul 1995	1.50
❑389, Aug 1995	1.50
❑390, Sep 1995	1.50
❑391, Oct 1995	1.50
❑392, Nov 1995; Mantis returns	1.50
❑393, Dec 1995; A: Tony Stark. "The Crossing"; Wasp critically injured	1.50
❑394, Jan 1996; 1: New Wasp. "The Crossing"	1.50
❑395, Feb 1996 D: Tony Stark	1.50
❑396, Mar 1996	1.50
❑397, Apr 1996	1.50
❑398, May 1996	1.50
❑399, Jun 1996	1.50

	N-MINT
❑400, Jul 1996; MWa (w); wraparound cover	4.00
❑401, Aug 1996 MWa (w); A: Magneto, Rogue	2.50
❑402, Sep 1996; MWa (w); "Onslaught: Impact 2"; story continues in X-Men #56 and Onslaught: Marvel	2.50
❑Annual 1, Sep 1967; Cover reads "King-Size Special"; DH (a); A: Hercules. A: Iron Man I. A: Mandarin. A: Black Widow. A: Edwin Jarvis. A: Power Man I. A: Living Laser. A: Thor	85.00
❑Annual 2, Sep 1968; Cover reads "King-Size Special"	26.00
❑Annual 3, Sep 1969; Cover reads "King-Size Special"; Reprinted from Avengers #4 and Tales of Suspense #66, #67, and #68 respectively	26.00
❑Annual 4, Jan 1971; Cover reads "King-Size Special"; O: Moondragon. Reprinted from Avengers #5 & #6 respectively	23.00
❑Annual 5, Jan 1972; Cover reads "King-Size Special"; DH, JK (a); Cover reads King Size Special; Reprinted from Avengers #8 and 11	10.00
❑Annual 6, ca. 1976 GP (a); V: Nuklo	7.00
❑Annual 7, ca. 1977; JSn, JSt (a); D: Gamora. D: Warlock. Warlock	14.00
❑Annual 8, ca. 1978 GP (a); A: Ms. Marvel	6.00
❑Annual 9, ca. 1979 DN (a)	4.00
❑Annual 10, ca. 1981; MG (a); 1: Rogue. 1: Destiny. X-Men	20.00
❑Annual 11, ca. 1982 AM (a)	3.50
❑Annual 12, ca. 1983 A: Inhumans	3.50
❑Annual 13, ca. 1984 SD, JBy (a); D: Nebulon	3.50
❑Annual 14, ca. 1985 JBy (a)	3.50
❑Annual 15, ca. 1986 SD (a)	3.50
❑Annual 16, ca. 1987	3.50
❑Annual 17, ca. 1988	3.00
❑Annual 18, ca. 1989; Atlantis Attacks	2.50
❑Annual 19, ca. 1990; KB (w); RHo, HT (a); Terminus	2.50
❑Annual 20, ca. 1991; Subterranean Wars	2.50
❑Annual 21, ca. 1992; HT (a); O: Terminatrix. 1: Terminatrix. Citizen Kang	2.50
❑Annual 22, ca. 1993; AM, MGu (a); 1: Bloodwraith. trading card; Polybagged with trading card	2.95
❑Annual 23, ca. 1994 AM, JB (a)	2.95

AVENGERS (VOL. 2)
MARVEL

	N-MINT
❑1, Nov 1996; RL (c); RL (a); Thor revived	3.00
❑1/A, Nov 1996; RL (a); alternate cover; Thor revived	3.00
❑2, Dec 1996 JPH, RL (w); A: Mantis. V: Kang	2.00
❑3, Jan 1997 JPH, RL (w); A: Mantis, Nick Fury	2.00
❑4, Feb 1997 JPH, RL (w); V: Hulk	2.00
❑5, Mar 1997; JPH (w); RL (a); Thor vs. Hulk	2.00
❑5/A, Mar 1997; JPH (w); RL (a); White cover; Thor vs. Hulk	2.00
❑6, Apr 1997; JPH, RL (w); continues in Iron Man #6	1.95
❑7, May 1997 JPH, RL (w); V: Lethal Legion (Enchantress, Wonder Man, Ultron 5, Executioner, Scarlet Witch)	1.95
❑8, Jun 1997	1.95
❑9, Jul 1997 V: Masters of Evil	1.95
❑10, Aug 1997; gatefold summary V: dopplegangers	1.95
❑11, Sep 1997; gatefold summary D: Thor. V: Loki	1.95
❑12, Oct 1997; cover forms quadtych with Fantastic Four #12, Iron Man #12, and Captain America #12	2.99
❑13, Nov 1997; cover forms quadtych with Fantastic Four #13, Iron Man #13, and Captain America #13	1.95

AVENGERS (VOL. 3)
MARVEL

	N-MINT
❑0; Promotional edition included with Wizard	2.00
❑1, Feb 1998; gatefold summary	4.00
❑1/A; chromium cover	6.00
❑1/B, Jul 1998; Avengers Rough Cut; cardstock cover	4.00
❑1/C, Feb 1998; gatefold summary; alternate cover	4.00
❑2, Mar 1998; gatefold summary	3.00
❑2/Variant, Mar 1998; gatefold summary; alternate cover	3.00
❑3, Apr 1998	2.50
❑4, May 1998; New team announced gatefold summary; New team begins	2.50
❑5, Jun 1998; gatefold summary	2.50
❑6, Jul 1998; gatefold summary	2.00
❑7, Aug 1998; gatefold summary; Warbird leaves	2.00
❑8, Sep 1998; gatefold summary	2.00
❑9, Oct 1998; gatefold summary	2.00
❑10, Nov 1998; Anniversary issue	2.00
❑11, Dec 1998; gatefold summary	2.00
❑12, Jan 1999; double-sized; Continued from Thunderbolts #22; wraparound cover	3.00
❑12/A, Jan 1999; Continued from Thunderbolts #22; DFE alternate cover	12.00
❑12/B, Jan 1999, Headshot cover (white background); Continued from Thunderbolts #22	5.00
❑12/Variant, Jan 1999; Continued from Thunderbolts #22; DFE alternate cover	7.00
❑13, Feb 1999	2.00
❑14, Mar 1999; Return of Beast to team	2.00
❑15, Apr 1999	2.00
❑16, May 1999	2.00
❑16/A, May 1999, 1 in 4 variant cover (purple background with team charging)	2.00
❑17, Jun 1999	2.00
❑18, Jul 1999	2.00
❑19, Aug 1999	2.00
❑20, Sep 1999	2.00
❑21, Oct 1999	2.00
❑22, Oct 1999	2.00
❑23, Dec 1999; Wonder Man versus Vision	2.00
❑24, Jan 2000	2.00
❑25, Feb 2000; Giant-size	3.00
❑26, Mar 2000	2.00
❑27, Apr 2000	2.00
❑28, May 2000	2.00
❑29, Jun 2000	2.25
❑30, Jul 2000	2.25
❑31, Aug 2000	2.25
❑32, Sep 2000	2.25
❑33, Oct 2000	2.25
❑34, Nov 2000; double-sized issue	2.99
❑35, Dec 2000	2.25
❑36, Jan 2001	2.25
❑37, Feb 2001	2.25
❑38, Mar 2001; Slashback issue; price reduced	1.99
❑39, Apr 2001	2.25
❑40, May 2001	2.25
❑41, Jun 2001	2.25
❑42, Jul 2001	2.25
❑43, Aug 2001	2.25
❑44, Sep 2001	2.25
❑45, Oct 2001	2.25
❑46, Nov 2001	2.25
❑47, Dec 2001	2.25
❑48, Jan 2002	3.50
❑49, Feb 2002	2.25
❑50, Mar 2002	2.99
❑51, Apr 2002, wraparound cover	2.25
❑52, May 2002, wraparound cover	2.25
❑53, Jun 2002, wraparound cover	2.25
❑54, Jul 2002, wraparound cover	2.25
❑55, Aug 2002, wraparound cover	2.25
❑56, Sep 2002, wraparound cover	2.25
❑57, Oct 2002, wraparound cover	2.25
❑58, Nov 2002, wraparound cover	2.25
❑59, Dec 2002, wraparound cover	2.25
❑60, Jan 2003, wraparound cover	2.25
❑61, Feb 2003, wraparound cover	2.25
❑62, Feb 2003, wraparound cover	2.25
❑63, Mar 2003, wraparound cover	2.25
❑64, Apr 2003	2.25
❑65, May 2003	2.25
❑66, Jun 2003	2.25
❑67, Jul 2003	2.25
❑68, Aug 2003	2.25
❑69, Sep 2003	2.25
❑70, Oct 2003	2.25
❑71, Nov 2003	2.25
❑72, Nov 2003	2.25
❑73, Dec 2003	2.25
❑74, Jan 2004	2.25
❑75, Feb 2004	2.25
❑76, Feb 2004	2.25
❑77, Mar 2004	2.25
❑78, Apr 2004	2.25
❑79, Apr 2004	2.25
❑80, May 2004	2.25
❑81, Jun 2004	2.99
❑82, Jul 2004	2.99
❑83, Jul 2004	2.25
❑84, Aug 2004	2.25
❑85, Sep 2004	
❑Annual 1998, ca. 1998; gatefold summary; wraparound cover	2.99
❑Annual 1999, Jul 1999; Jarvis' story	3.50
❑Annual 2000, ca. 2000, wraparound cover	3.50
❑Annual 2001, ca. 2001; wraparound cover	2.99

AVENGERS CASEBOOK
MARVEL

	N-MINT
❑1999, ca. 1999	2.99

AVENGERS, THE: CELESTIAL QUEST
MARVEL

	N-MINT
❑1, Sep 2001	2.50
❑2, Oct 2001	2.50
❑3, Nov 2001	2.50
❑4, Dec 2001	2.50
❑5, Jan 2002	2.50
❑6, Feb 2002	2.50
❑7, Mar 2002	2.50
❑8, Apr 2002	3.50

AVENGERS: DEATH TRAP, THE VAULT
MARVEL

	N-MINT
❑1, Sep 1991; also published as Venom: Deathtrap - The Vault	9.95

AVENGERS FOREVER
MARVEL

	N-MINT
❑1, Dec 1998	2.99
❑1/WF, Dec 1998; Westfield alternate cover	4.95
❑2, Jan 1999	2.99
❑3, Feb 1999	2.99
❑4/A, Mar 1999; Avengers of Tomorrow cover	2.99
❑4/B, Mar 1999; Kang in the Old West cover	2.99
❑4/C, Mar 1999; Avengers throughout time cover	2.99
❑4/D, Mar 1999; Avengers of the '50s cover	2.99
❑5, Apr 1999	2.99
❑6, May 1999	2.99
❑7, Jun 1999	2.99
❑8, Jul 1999	2.99
❑9, Aug 1999	2.99
❑10, Oct 1999	2.99
❑11, Jan 2000	2.99
❑12, Feb 2000	2.99

AVENGERS (GOLD KEY)
GOLD KEY

	N-MINT
❑1; based on TV series	60.00

N-MINT

AVENGERS ICONS: THE VISION
MARVEL

❑1 ... 2.99
❑2 ... 2.99
❑3 ... 2.99
❑4 ... 2.99

AVENGERS INFINITY
MARVEL

❑1/DF, Sep 2000; Dynamic Forces variant (Thor brandishing hammer) ....
❑1, Sep 2000 ... 2.99
❑2, Oct 2000 ... 2.99
❑3, Nov 2000 ... 2.99
❑4, Dec 2000 ... 2.99

AVENGERS/JLA
DC

❑2, Oct 2003 ... 5.95
❑4, May 2004 ... 5.95

AVENGERS LEGENDS
MARVEL

❑1 ... 0.00
❑2, ca. 2003 ... 19.95
❑3, ca. 2004 ... 16.99

AVENGERS LOG
MARVEL

❑1, Feb 1994 ... 1.95

AVENGERS SPOTLIGHT
MARVEL

❑21, Aug 1989; Starfox; Series continued from Solo Avengers #20 ... 1.00
❑22, Sep 1989; Swordsman ... 1.00
❑23, Oct 1989; Vision ... 1.00
❑24, Nov 1989 A: Trickshot ... 1.00
❑25, Nov 1989 A: Crossfire. A: Mockingbird. A: Trickshot ... 1.00
❑26, Dec 1989; "Acts of Vengeance" .. 1.00
❑27, Dec 1989; AM (a); "Acts of Vengeance" ... 1.00
❑28, Jan 1990; "Acts of Vengeance" .. 1.00
❑29, Feb 1990; "Acts of Vengeance" .. 1.00
❑30, Mar 1990; new Hawkeye costume 1.00
❑31, Apr 1990 ... 1.00
❑32, May 1990 ... 1.00
❑33, Jun 1990 ... 1.00
❑34, Jul 1990 ... 1.00
❑35, Aug 1990 A: Gilgamesh ... 1.00
❑36, Sep 1990 ... 1.00
❑37, Oct 1990 BH (a) ... 1.00
❑38, Nov 1990 ... 1.00
❑39, Dec 1990 ... 1.00
❑40, Jan 1991 ... 1.00

AVENGERS STRIKE FILE
MARVEL

❑1, Jan 1994 ... 1.75

AVENGERS: THE CROSSING
MARVEL

❑1, Sep 1995; Chromium cover ... 4.95

AVENGERS: THE TERMINATRIX OBJECTIVE
MARVEL

❑1, Sep 1993; Holo-grafix cover; U.S.Agent, Thunderstrike, War Machine ... 2.50
❑2, Oct 1993; New Avengers vs. Old Avengers ... 1.25
❑3, Nov 1993 ... 1.25
❑4, Dec 1993 ... 1.25

AVENGERS: THE ULTRON IMPERATIVE
MARVEL

❑1, Oct 2001 ... 5.99

AVENGERS/THUNDERBOLTS
MARVEL

❑1, May 2004 (c); KB (w) ... 2.99
❑2, Jun 2004 (c); KB (w) ... 2.99
❑3, Jun 2004 (c); KB (w) ... 2.99
❑4, Aug 2004 ... 299.00
❑5, Aug 2004 ... 2.99

N-MINT

AVENGERS: TIMESLIDE
MARVEL

❑1, Feb 1996; enhanced wraparound cardstock cover ... 4.95

AVENGERS TWO: WONDER MAN & BEAST
MARVEL

❑1, May 2000 ... 2.99
❑2, Jun 2000 ... 2.99
❑3, Jul 2000 ... 2.99

AVENGERS/ULTRAFORCE
MARVEL

❑1, Oct 1995; continues in UltraForce/Avengers #1; Foil logo ... 3.95

AVENGERS: ULTRON UNLEASHED
MARVEL

❑1, Aug 1999; collects Avengers (1st series) #57-58 and #170-171 ... 3.50

AVENGERS: UNITED THEY STAND
MARVEL

❑1, Nov 1999 ... 2.99
❑2, Dec 1999 ... 1.99
❑3, Jan 2000 ... 1.99
❑4, Feb 2000 ... 1.99
❑5, Mar 2000 ... 1.99
❑6, Apr 2000 ... 1.99
❑7, May 2000 ... 1.99

AVENGERS UNIVERSE
MARVEL

❑1, Aug 2000 ... 2.99
❑2, Sep 2000 ... 2.99
❑3, Oct 2000 ... 2.99
❑4, Nov 2000; reprints Iron Fist: Wolverine #1; indicia is for Iron Fist: Wolverine #1 ... 2.99
❑5, Dec 2000; reprints Iron Fist: Wolverine #2; indicia is for Iron Fist: Wolverine #2 ... 2.99
❑6, Jan 2001; reprints Iron Fist: Wolverine #3; indicia is for Iron Fist: Wolverine #3 ... 2.99

AVENGERS UNPLUGGED
MARVEL

❑1, Oct 1995 ... 1.25
❑2, Dec 1995; A: Gravitron. Untold Tales of Spider-Man #4 ... 1.00
❑3, Dec 1996; Luna; Black Widow ... 1.00
❑4, Feb 1996; Wedding of Thunderball and Titania; Peter David appears as reverend in story; Untold Tales of Spider-Man #8 ... 1.00
❑5, Jun 1996 A: Captain Marvel ... 1.00
❑6, Aug 1996 ... 1.00

AVENGERS WEST COAST
MARVEL

❑47, Aug 1989 ... 1.00
❑48, Sep 1989 ... 1.00
❑49, Oct 1989 ... 1.00
❑50, Nov 1989; Golden Age Human Torch returns ... 1.00
❑51, Nov 1989 ... 1.00
❑52, Dec 1989 ... 1.00
❑53, Dec 1989; "Acts of Vengeance" .. 1.00
❑54, Jan 1990; Fantastic Four #1 cover homage; "Acts of Vengeance" ... 1.00
❑55, Feb 1990; "Acts of Vengeance" .. 1.00
❑56, Mar 1990 ... 1.00
❑57, Apr 1990 ... 1.00
❑58, May 1990 ... 1.00
❑59, Jun 1990 ... 1.00
❑60, Jul 1990 ... 1.00
❑61, Aug 1990 ... 1.00
❑62, Sep 1990 ... 1.00
❑63, Oct 1990 ... 1.00
❑64, Nov 1990 ... 1.00
❑65, Dec 1990 ... 1.00
❑66, Jan 1991 ... 1.00
❑67, Feb 1991 ... 1.00
❑68, Mar 1991 ... 1.00
❑69, Apr 1991 ... 1.00
❑70, May 1991 ... 1.00
❑71, Jun 1991 ... 1.00

Kurt Busiek and George Pérez recast Marvel's super-hero team, trimming the roster in 1998.

© 1998 Marvel Characters Inc.

N-MINT

❑72, Jul 1991 ... 1.00
❑73, Aug 1991 ... 1.00
❑74, Sep 1991 ... 1.00
❑75, Oct 1991; Double-size issue ... 1.50
❑76, Nov 1991 ... 1.00
❑77, Dec 1991 ... 1.00
❑78, Jan 1992 ... 1.00
❑79, Feb 1992 ... 1.25
❑80, Mar 1992; Galactic Storm ... 1.25
❑81, Apr 1992; Galactic Storm ... 1.25
❑82, May 1992; Galactic Storm ... 1.25
❑83, Jun 1992 ... 1.25
❑84, Jul 1992 ... 1.25
❑85, Aug 1992 ... 1.25
❑86, Sep 1992 ... 1.25
❑87, Oct 1992 ... 1.25
❑88, Nov 1992 ... 1.25
❑89, Dec 1992 ... 1.25
❑90, Jan 1993 ... 1.25
❑91, Feb 1993 ... 1.25
❑92, Mar 1993 ... 1.25
❑93, Apr 1993 ... 1.25
❑94, May 1993 ... 1.25
❑95, Jun 1993 ... 1.25
❑96, Jul 1993 ... 1.25
❑97, Aug 1993 ... 1.25
❑98, Sep 1993 ... 1.25
❑99, Oct 1993 ... 1.25
❑100, Nov 1993; sculpted foil cover .. 1.25
❑101, Dec 1993 ... 1.25
❑102, Jan 1994 ... 1.25
❑Annual 4, ca. 1989; see West Coast Avengers for previous Annuals; "Atlantis Attacks" ... 2.00
❑Annual 5, ca. 1990; "Terminus Factor" 2.00
❑Annual 6 ... 2.00
❑Annual 7, ca. 1992 ... 2.25
❑Annual 8; Polybagged with trading card 2.95

AVENUE D
FANTAGRAPHICS

❑1, b&w ... 3.50

AVENUE X
PURPLE SPIRAL

❑1, ca. 1992 ... 2.50
❑2, ca. 1992 ... 2.50
❑3, ca. 1992 ... 3.00

AVIGON
IMAGE

❑1, Oct 2000 ... 5.95

A-V IN 3-D
AARDVARK-VANAHEIM

❑1, Dec 1984; glasses ... 3.00

AWAKENING, THE
IMAGE

❑1, Oct 1997 ... 2.95
❑2, Dec 1997 ... 2.95
❑3, Feb 1998 ... 2.95
❑4, Apr 1998 ... 2.95

AWAKENING COMICS
AWAKENING COMICS

❑1 1997 ... 3.50
❑2, Nov 1997 A: Cerebus the Aardvark. A: Cerebus ... 3.50

N-MINT

❑3, Aug 1998; wraparound cover; "The Everwinds Awakening War" 2.95
❑4, Nov 1998 1: Melvin G. Moose, Private Eye 2.95

AWAKENING COMICS 1999
AWAKENING COMICS

❑1 1999, b&w 3.50

AWESOME ADVENTURES
AWESOME

❑1/A, Aug 1999; Woman standing (full length) on cover 2.50
❑1/B, Aug 1999; Woman standing (3/4 length) on cover 2.50

AWESOME HOLIDAY SPECIAL
AWESOME

❑1, Dec 1997; Flip cover; Youngblood side has gold foil logo 2.50

AWESOME MAN
ASTONISH

❑1 2002 .... 2.95
❑2, Aug 2003 .... 3.50

AWESOME PREVIEW
AWESOME

❑1 1997; ARo (c); ARo (a); b&w and color previews of upcoming Awesome series given out at Comic-Con International: San Diego '97 .... 1.00

AWKWARD
SLAVE LABOR

❑1 .... 4.95

AWKWARD UNIVERSE
SLAVE LABOR

❑1, Dec 1995 .... 9.95

AXA (ECLIPSE)
ECLIPSE

❑1, ca. 1987 .... 2.00
❑2 1987, b&w 2.00

AXED FILES
EXPRESS / PARODY

❑1 1995, b&w 2.50

AXEL PRESSBUTTON
ECLIPSE

❑1, Nov 1984 .... 2.00
❑2, Jan 1985 .... 2.00
❑3, Mar 1985 .... 2.00
❑4, May 1985 .... 2.00
❑5, Jul 1985; Continues as Pressbutton 2.00
❑6, Jul 1985 .... 2.00

AXIS ALPHA
AXIS

❑1, Feb 1994 .... 2.50

AXIS MUNDI
AMAZE INK

❑2, Dec 1996, b&w; no indicia; wraparound cover 2.95

AZ
COMICO

❑1, b&w 1.50
❑2, b&w 1.50

AZRAEL
DC

❑1, Feb 1995 .... 2.00
❑2, Mar 1995 .... 2.00
❑3, Apr 1995 .... 2.00
❑4, May 1995 .... 2.00
❑5, Jun 1995 .... 2.00
❑6, Jul 1995 .... 2.00
❑7, Aug 1995 .... 2.00
❑8, Sep 1995 .... 2.00
❑9, Oct 1995 .... 2.00
❑10, Nov 1995; "Underworld Unleashed" 2.00
❑11, Dec 1995 .... 1.95
❑12, Jan 1996 .... 1.95
❑13, Feb 1996 .... 1.95
❑14, Mar 1996 .... 1.95
❑15, Mar 1996; Marked as Contagion, Part 4 on cover 1.95
❑16, Apr 1996 .... 1.95

N-MINT

❑17, May 1996 .... 1.95
❑18, Jun 1996 .... 1.95
❑19, Jul 1996 .... 1.95
❑20, Aug 1996 .... 1.95
❑21, Sep 1996 .... 1.95
❑22, Oct 1996 .... 1.95
❑23, Oct 1996 .... 1.95
❑24, Dec 1996 .... 1.95
❑25, Jan 1997 .... 1.95
❑26, Feb 1997 .... 1.95
❑27, Mar 1997 .... 1.95
❑28, Apr 1997 .... 1.95
❑29, May 1997 .... 1.95
❑30, Jun 1997 .... 1.95
❑31, Jul 1997 .... 1.95
❑32, Aug 1997 .... 1.95
❑33, Sep 1997 .... 1.95
❑34, Oct 1997; "Genesis" 1.95
❑35, Nov 1997 .... 1.95
❑36, Dec 1997; Face cover 1.95
❑37, Jan 1998 .... 1.95
❑38, Feb 1998 .... 1.95
❑39, Mar 1998 .... 1.95
❑40, Apr 1998; continues in Detective Comics #720 .... 1.95
❑41, May 1998 .... 1.95
❑42, Jun 1998 .... 1.95
❑43, Jul 1998 .... 1.95
❑44, Aug 1998 .... 1.95
❑45, Sep 1998 .... 2.25
❑46, Oct 1998 .... 1.99
❑47, Dec 1998; Signed extra-sized flip-book; Title changes to "Azrael: Agent of the Bat"; "Road to No Man's Land"; flipbook with Batman: Shadow of the Bat #80 (true title) 3.95
❑47/Ltd., Dec 1998 .... 6.00
❑48, Jan 1999; "Road to No Man's Land"; Batman cameo 2.25
❑49, Feb 1999; "Road to No Man's Land" 2.25
❑50, Mar 1999; "No Man's Land" 2.25
❑51, Apr 1999; "No Man's Land"; new costume 2.25
❑52, May 1999; "No Man's Land" 2.25
❑53, Jun 1999; "No Man's Land" 2.25
❑54, Jul 1999; "No Man's Land" 2.25
❑55, Aug 1999; "No Man's Land" 2.25
❑56, Sep 1999; "No Man's Land" 2.25
❑57, Oct 1999; "No Man's Land" 2.25
❑58, Nov 1999; "No Man's Land"; Day of Judgment 2.25
❑59, Dec 1999; No Man's Land 2.25
❑60, Jan 2000; No Man's Land 2.25
❑61, Feb 2000 .... 2.25
❑62, Mar 2000 .... 2.25
❑63, Apr 2000 .... 2.25
❑64, May 2000 .... 2.25
❑65, Jun 2000 .... 2.25
❑66, Jul 2000 .... 2.25
❑67, Aug 2000 .... 2.25
❑68, Sep 2000 .... 2.25
❑69, Oct 2000 .... 2.50
❑70, Nov 2000 .... 2.50
❑71, Dec 2000 .... 2.50
❑72, Jan 2001 .... 2.50
❑73, Feb 2001 .... 2.50
❑74, Mar 2001 .... 2.50
❑75, Apr 2001; Giant-size 3.95
❑76, May 2001 .... 2.50
❑77, Jun 2001 .... 2.50
❑78, Jul 2001 .... 2.50
❑79, Aug 2001 .... 2.50
❑80, Sep 2001 .... 2.50
❑81, Oct 2001 .... 2.50
❑82, Nov 2001 .... 2.50
❑83, Dec 2001; Joker: Last Laugh crossover 2.50
❑84, Jan 2002 .... 2.50
❑85, Feb 2002 .... 2.50
❑86, Mar 2002 .... 2.50
❑87, Apr 2002 .... 2.50
❑88, May 2002 .... 2.50

N-MINT

❑89, Jun 2002 .... 2.50
❑91, Aug 2002 ....
❑90, Jul 2002 .... 2.50
❑92, Sep 2002 ....
❑93, Oct 2002 ....
❑94, Nov 2002 ....
❑95, Dec 2002 ....
❑96, Jan 2003 ....
❑97, Feb 2003 ....
❑98, Mar 2003 ....
❑99, Apr 2003 .... 2.95
❑100, May 2003 .... 2.95
❑1000000, Nov 1998; becomes Azrael: Agent of the Bat 3.00
❑Annual 1, ca. 1995; Year One; 1995 Annual 3.95
❑Annual 2, ca. 1996; Legends of the Dead Earth 2.95
❑Annual 3, ca. 1997; Pulp Heroes 3.95

AZRAEL/ASH
DC

❑1, ca. 1997 .... 4.95

AZRAEL PLUS
DC

❑1, Dec 1996 .... 2.95

AZTEC ACE
ECLIPSE

❑1, Mar 1984; Giant-size 1: Aztec Ace 2.50
❑2 1984 .... 2.00
❑3 1984 .... 2.00
❑4 1984 .... 2.00
❑5 1984 .... 2.00
❑6 1984 .... 2.00
❑7 1984 .... 2.00
❑8 1984 .... 2.00
❑9, Jan 1985 .... 2.00
❑10 1985 .... 2.00
❑11 1985 .... 2.00
❑12 1985 .... 2.00
❑13 1985 .... 2.00
❑14 1985 .... 2.00
❑15, Sep 1985 .... 2.00

AZTEC ANTHROPOMORPHIC AMAZONS
ANTARCTIC

❑1, Mar 1994, b&w 2.75

AZTEC OF THE CITY
EL SALTO

❑1, May 1993 .... 2.25

AZTEC OF THE CITY (VOL. 2)
EL SALTO

❑1 1996 .... 2.50
❑2, May 1996 .... 2.50

AZTEK: THE ULTIMATE MAN
DC

❑1, Aug 1996 .... 1.75
❑2, Sep 1996 .... 1.75
❑3, Oct 1996 .... 1.75
❑4, Nov 1996 .... 1.75
❑5, Dec 1996 .... 1.75
❑6, Jan 1997 .... 1.75
❑7, Feb 1997 .... 1.75
❑8, Mar 1997 .... 1.75
❑9, Apr 1997 .... 1.75
❑10, May 1997 .... 1.75

AZUMANGA DAIOH
ADV MANGA

❑1, ca 2003 .... 9.99
❑2, ca 2003 .... 9.99
❑3, ca 2004 .... 9.99
❑4, ca 2004 .... 9.99

B

BABE
DARK HORSE / LEGEND

❑1, Jul 1994 .... 2.50
❑2, Aug 1994 .... 2.50

N-MINT

❑3, Sep 1994 .... 2.50
❑4, Oct 1994 .... 2.50

BABE 2
DARK HORSE / LEGEND

❑1, Mar 1995 .... 2.50
❑2, Apr 1995 .... 2.50

BABES OF BROADWAY
BROADWAY

❑1, May 1996; pin-ups and previews of upcoming Broadway series 2.95

BABEWATCH
EXPRESS / PARODY

❑1 1995, b&w 2.50
❑1/A 1995 .... 2.95

BABY ANGEL X
BRAINSTORM

❑1, b&w 2.95

BABY HUEY DIGEST
HARVEY

❑1 .... 1.75

BABY HUEY IN 3-D
BLACKTHORNE

❑1 .... 2.50

BABY HUEY THE BABY GIANT
HARVEY

❑1, Sep 1956 .... 150.00
❑2, Nov 1956 .... 85.00
❑3, Jan 1957 .... 48.00
❑4, Mar 1957 .... 36.00
❑5, May 1957 .... 36.00
❑6, Jul 1957 .... 20.00
❑7, Sep 1957 .... 20.00
❑8, Nov 1957 .... 20.00
❑9, Jan 1958 .... 20.00
❑10, Mar 1958 .... 20.00
❑11, ca. 1958 .... 15.00
❑12, ca. 1958 .... 15.00
❑13, ca. 1958 .... 15.00
❑14, ca. 1958 .... 15.00
❑15, ca. 1958 .... 15.00
❑16, Feb 1959 .... 15.00
❑17, Apr 1959 .... 15.00
❑18, Jun 1959 .... 15.00
❑19, Aug 1959 .... 15.00
❑20, Oct 1959 .... 15.00
❑21, Dec 1959 .... 12.00
❑22, Feb 1960 .... 12.00
❑23, Apr 1960 .... 12.00
❑24, ca. 1960 .... 12.00
❑25, ca. 1960 .... 12.00
❑26, ca. 1960 .... 12.00
❑27, ca. 1960 .... 12.00
❑28, Nov 1960 .... 12.00
❑29, Dec 1960 .... 12.00
❑30, Jan 1961 .... 12.00
❑31, Feb 1961 .... 9.00
❑32, Mar 1961 .... 9.00
❑33, Apr 1961 .... 9.00
❑34, May 1961 .... 9.00
❑35, Jun 1961 .... 9.00
❑36, Jul 1961 .... 9.00
❑37, Aug 1961 .... 9.00
❑38, Sep 1961 .... 9.00
❑39, Oct 1961 .... 9.00
❑40, Nov 1961 .... 9.00
❑41, Dec 1961 .... 6.00
❑42, Jan 1962 .... 6.00
❑43, Feb 1962 .... 6.00
❑44, Mar 1962 .... 6.00
❑45, Apr 1962 .... 6.00
❑46, Jun 1962 .... 6.00
❑47, Aug 1962 .... 6.00
❑48, Oct 1962 .... 6.00
❑49, Dec 1962 .... 6.00
❑50, Feb 1963 .... 6.00
❑51, Apr 1963 .... 4.00
❑52, Jun 1963 .... 4.00
❑53, Aug 1963 .... 4.00
❑54, Oct 1963 .... 4.00

N-MINT

❑55, Dec 1963 .... 4.00
❑56, Feb 1964 .... 4.00
❑57, Apr 1964 .... 4.00
❑58, Jun 1964 .... 4.00
❑59, Aug 1964 .... 4.00
❑60, Oct 1964 .... 4.00
❑61, Dec 1964 .... 4.00
❑62, Feb 1965 .... 4.00
❑63, Apr 1965 .... 4.00
❑64, Jun 1965 .... 4.00
❑65, Aug 1965 .... 4.00
❑66, Oct 1965 .... 4.00
❑67, Dec 1965 .... 4.00
❑68, Feb 1966 .... 4.00
❑69, Apr 1966 .... 4.00
❑70, Jun 1966 .... 4.00
❑71, Aug 1966 .... 2.50
❑72, Oct 1966 .... 2.50
❑73, Dec 1966 .... 2.50
❑74, Feb 1967 .... 2.50
❑75, Apr 1967 .... 2.50
❑76, Jun 1967 .... 2.50
❑77, Aug 1967 .... 2.50
❑78, Oct 1967 .... 2.50
❑79, Dec 1967 .... 2.50
❑80, Dec 1968; Giant-size 2.50
❑81, Feb 1969; Giant-size 2.50
❑82, Apr 1969; Giant-size 2.50
❑83, Jun 1969; Giant-size 2.50
❑84, Aug 1969; Giant-size 2.50
❑85, Oct 1969; Giant-size 2.50
❑86, Dec 1969; Giant-size 2.50
❑87, Feb 1970; Giant-size 2.50
❑88, Apr 1970; Giant-size 2.50
❑89, Jun 1970; Giant-size 2.50
❑90, Aug 1970; Giant-size 2.50
❑91, Oct 1970; Giant-size 2.50
❑92, Dec 1970; Giant-size 2.50
❑93, Feb 1971; Giant-size 2.50
❑94, Apr 1971; Giant-size 2.50
❑95, Jun 1971; Giant-size 2.50
❑96, Aug 1971; Giant-size 2.50
❑97, Oct 1971; Giant-size 2.50
❑98, Oct 1972 .... 2.50
❑99 .... 2.50
❑100, Oct 1990; Series begins again after hiatus 1.00
❑101 .... 1.00
❑102 .... 1.00

BABY HUEY (VOL. 2)
HARVEY

❑1 1991 .... 1.25
❑2, Jan 1992 .... 1.25
❑3, Apr 1992 .... 1.25
❑4, Aug 1992 .... 1.25
❑5, Nov 1992 .... 1.25
❑6, Mar 1993 .... 1.25
❑7, Jun 1993 .... 1.25
❑8 .... 1.25
❑9 .... 1.25

BABYLON 5
DC

❑1, Jan 1995 .... 5.00
❑2, Feb 1995 .... 4.00
❑3, Mar 1995 .... 3.50
❑4, Apr 1995 .... 3.50
❑5, Jun 1995 .... 3.00
❑6, Jul 1995 .... 3.00
❑7, Aug 1995 .... 3.00
❑8, Sep 1995 .... 2.50
❑9, Oct 1995 .... 2.50
❑10, Nov 1995 .... 2.50
❑11, Dec 1995 .... 2.50

BABYLON 5: IN VALEN'S NAME
DC

❑1, Mar 1998 .... 3.50
❑2, Apr 1998 .... 3.00
❑3, May 1998 .... 3.00

DC's *Babylon 5* focused on the adventures of Commander Jeffrey Sinclair, rather than his successor, John Sheridan.

N-MINT

BABYLON CRUSH
BONEYARD

❑1, May 1995; cardstock cover, b&w 2.95
❑2, Jul 1995; cardstock cover, b&w 2.95
❑3, Oct 1995, b&w 2.95
❑4 .... 2.95
❑Xmas 1, Jan 1998 .... 2.95

BABY'S FIRST DEADPOOL BOOK
MARVEL

❑1, Dec 1998; children's-book style stories 2.99

BABY SNOOTS
GOLD KEY

❑1, Aug 1970 .... 12.00
❑2, Nov 1970 .... 10.00
❑3, Feb 1971 .... 8.00
❑4, May 1971 .... 6.00
❑5, Aug 1971 .... 6.00
❑6, Nov 1971 .... 6.00
❑7, Feb 1972 .... 6.00
❑8, May 1972 .... 6.00
❑9, Aug 1972 .... 6.00
❑10, Nov 1972 .... 6.00
❑11, Feb 1973 .... 6.00
❑12, May 1973 .... 6.00
❑13, Aug 1973 .... 5.00
❑14, Nov 1973 .... 5.00
❑15, Feb 1974 .... 5.00
❑16, May 1974 .... 5.00
❑17, Aug 1974 .... 5.00
❑18, Nov 1974 .... 5.00
❑19, Feb 1975 .... 5.00
❑20, May 1975 .... 5.00
❑21, Aug 1975 .... 5.00
❑22, Nov 1975 .... 5.00

BABY, YOU'RE REALLY SOMETHING!
FANTAGRAPHICS / EROS

❑1, b&w 2.50

BACCHUS COLOR SPECIAL
DARK HORSE

❑1, Apr 1995 .... 3.25

BACCHUS (EDDIE CAMPBELL'S...)
EDDIE CAMPBELL

❑1, May 1999 .... 6.00
❑1-2 .... 3.00
❑2 .... 4.00
❑3 .... 4.00
❑4 .... 3.50
❑5 .... 3.50
❑6 .... 3.00
❑7 .... 3.00
❑8, Dec 1995 .... 3.00
❑9, Jan 1996 .... 3.00
❑10, Feb 1996 .... 3.00
❑11, Mar 1996 .... 3.00
❑12, Apr 1996 .... 3.00
❑13, May 1996 .... 3.00
❑14, Jun 1996 .... 3.00
❑15, Jul 1996 .... 3.00
❑16, Aug 1996 .... 3.00
❑17, Sep 1996 .... 3.00
❑18, Oct 1996, b&w 3.00
❑19, Nov 1996 .... 3.00
❑20, Dec 1996 .... 3.00
❑21, Jan 1997 .... 2.95
❑22, Feb 1997 .... 2.95

N-MINT

❑23, Mar 1997 ... 2.95
❑24, ca. 1997 ... 2.95
❑25, ca. 1997 ... 2.95
❑26, ca. 1997 ... 2.95
❑27, Aug 1997 ... 2.95
❑28, Sep 1997 ... 2.95
❑29, Oct 1997 ... 2.95
❑30, Nov 1997 ... 2.95
❑31, Dec 1997 ... 2.95
❑32, ca. 1998 ... 2.95
❑33, ca. 1998 ... 2.95
❑34, Apr 1998 ... 2.95
❑35, ca. 1998 ... 2.95
❑36, ca. 1998 ... 2.95
❑37, ca. 1998 ... 2.95
❑38, Sep 1998 ... 2.95
❑39, Oct 1998 ... 2.95
❑40, Dec 1998 ... 2.95
❑41, Jan 1999 ... 2.95
❑42, Feb 1999 ... 2.95

BACCHUS (HARRIER)
HARRIER

❑1 ... 5.00
❑2 ... 4.00

BACHELOR FATHER
DELL

❑2, Nov 1962 ... 50.00

BACK DOWN THE LINE
ECLIPSE

❑1 ... 8.95

BACKLASH
IMAGE

❑1, Nov 1994; Double cover ... 2.50
❑2, Dec 1994 ... 2.50
❑3, Jan 1995 ... 2.50
❑4, Feb 1995 ... 2.50
❑5, Feb 1995 ... 2.50
❑6, Mar 1995 ... 2.50
❑7, Apr 1995 ... 2.50
❑8, May 1995; bound-in trading cards ... 2.50
❑9, Jun 1995 ... 2.50
❑10, Jul 1995; indicia says Jul, cover says Aug ... 2.50
❑11, Aug 1995 ... 2.50
❑12, Sep 1995; indicia says Sep, cover says Oct ... 2.50
❑13, Nov 1995 ... 2.50
❑14, Nov 1995; indicia says Nov, cover says Dec ... 2.50
❑15, Dec 1995; indicia says Dec, cover says Jan ... 2.50
❑16, Jan 1996; indicia says Jan, cover says Feb ... 2.50
❑17, Feb 1996 ... 2.50
❑18, Mar 1996 ... 2.50
❑19, Apr 1996 ... 2.50
❑20, May 1996 ... 2.50
❑21, Jun 1996 ... 2.50
❑22, Jul 1996 ... 2.50
❑23, Aug 1996 ... 2.50
❑24, Sep 1996 ... 2.50
❑25, Nov 1996; Giant-size ... 2.50
❑26, Nov 1996 ... 2.50
❑27, Dec 1996 ... 2.50
❑28, Jan 1997 ... 2.50
❑29, Feb 1997 ... 2.50
❑30, Mar 1997 ... 2.50
❑31, Apr 1997 ... 2.50
❑32, May 1997 ... 2.50

BACKLASH & TABOO'S AFRICAN HOLIDAY
DC / WILDSTORM

❑1, Sep 1999 ... 5.95

BACKLASH/SPIDER-MAN
IMAGE

❑1, Aug 1996 ... 2.50
❑1/A, Aug 1996; crossover with Marvel, cover says Jul, indicia says Aug ... 2.50
❑1/B, Aug 1996; alternate cover, crossover with Marvel, cover says Jul, indicia says Aug ... 2.50
❑2, Oct 1996; crossover with Marvel ... 2.50

BACKPACK MARVELS: AVENGERS
MARVEL

❑1, Jan 2001 ... 6.95

BACKPACK MARVELS: X-MEN
MARVEL

❑1, Nov 2000 ... 6.95
❑2, Nov 2000; Reprints Uncanny X-Men #167-173 ... 6.95

BACK TO THE FUTURE
HARVEY

❑1, Nov 1991 GK (c); GK (a) ... 1.50
❑2, Nov 1991 ... 1.50
❑3, Jan 1992 ... 1.50
❑4, Jun 1992 ... 1.50
❑Special 1; Universal Studios-Florida giveaway ... 1.00

BACK TO THE FUTURE: FORWARD TO THE FUTURE
HARVEY

❑1, Oct 1992 ... 1.50
❑2, Nov 1992 ... 1.50
❑3, Jan 1993 ... 1.50

BAD APPLES
HIGH IMPACT

❑1, Jan 1997 ... 2.95
❑2, ca. 1997 ... 2.95

BAD ART COLLECTION, THE
SLAVE LABOR

❑1, Apr 1996; Oversized ... 1.95

BADAXE
ADVENTURE

❑1 ... 1.00
❑2 ... 1.00
❑3 ... 1.00

BAD BOY
ONI

❑1, Dec 1997; oversized one-shot ... 4.95

BAD COMICS
CAT-HEAD

❑1, b&w ... 2.75

BAD COMPANY
FLEETWAY-QUALITY

❑1 ... 1.50
❑2 ... 1.50
❑3 ... 1.50
❑4 ... 1.50
❑5 ... 1.50
❑6 ... 1.50
❑7 ... 1.50
❑8 ... 1.50
❑9 ... 1.50
❑10 ... 1.50
❑11 ... 1.50
❑12 ... 1.50
❑13 ... 1.50
❑14 ... 1.50
❑15 ... 1.50
❑16 ... 1.75
❑17 ... 1.75
❑18 ... 1.75
❑19 ... 1.75

BADE BIKER & ORSON
MIRAGE

❑1, Nov 1986 ... 1.50
❑2, Jan 1987 ... 1.50
❑3, Mar 1987 ... 1.50
❑4, Jun 1987 ... 1.50

BAD EGGS, THE
ACCLAIM / ARMADA

❑1, Jun 1996 ... 2.95
❑2, Jul 1996 ... 2.95
❑3, Aug 1996 ... 2.95
❑4, Sep 1996 ... 2.95
❑5, Sep 1996; cover says Oct, indicia says Sep ... 2.95
❑6, Nov 1996; shoplifting instructions on cover ... 2.95
❑7, Dec 1996 ... 2.95
❑8, Jan 1997 ... 2.95

BADGE
VANGUARD

❑1 1981 ... 2.95

BADGER
CAPITAL

❑1, Oct 1983 SR (a); 1: Badger. 1: Ham ... 4.00
❑2, Feb 1984 ... 2.50
❑3, Mar 1984 ... 2.50
❑4, Apr 1984 ... 2.50
❑5, May 1985; First Comics begins publishing ... 2.50
❑6, Jul 1985 ... 2.00
❑7, Sep 1985 ... 2.00
❑8, Nov 1985 ... 2.00
❑9, Jan 1986 ... 2.00
❑10, Mar 1986 ... 2.00
❑11, May 1986 ... 2.00
❑12, Jun 1986 ... 2.00
❑13, Jul 1986 ... 2.00
❑14, Aug 1986 ... 2.00
❑15, Sep 1986 ... 2.00
❑16, Oct 1986 ... 2.00
❑17, Nov 1986 ... 2.00
❑18, Dec 1986 ... 2.00
❑19, Jan 1987 ... 2.00
❑20, Feb 1987 ... 2.00
❑21, Mar 1987 ... 2.00
❑22, Apr 1987 ... 2.00
❑23, May 1987 ... 2.00
❑24, Jun 1987 ... 2.00
❑25, Jul 1987 ... 2.00
❑26, Aug 1987; Roach Wrangler ... 2.00
❑27, Sep 1987; Roach Wrangler ... 2.00
❑28, Oct 1987 ... 2.00
❑29, Nov 1987 ... 2.00
❑30, Dec 1987 ... 2.00
❑31, Jan 1988 ... 2.00
❑32, Feb 1988 ... 2.00
❑33, Mar 1988 ... 2.00
❑34, Apr 1988 ... 2.00
❑35, May 1988 ... 2.00
❑36, Jun 1988 ... 2.00
❑37, Jul 1988 ... 2.00
❑38, Aug 1988 ... 2.00
❑39, Sep 1988 ... 2.00
❑40, Oct 1988 ... 2.00
❑41, Nov 1988 ... 2.00
❑42, Dec 1988 ... 2.00
❑43, Jan 1989 ... 2.00
❑44, Feb 1989 1: Steve Marmel (The Hilariator-in comics) ... 2.00
❑45, Mar 1989 ... 2.00
❑46, Apr 1989 ... 2.00
❑47, May 1989 ... 2.00
❑48, Jun 1989 ... 2.00
❑49, Jul 1989 ... 2.00
❑50, Aug 1989; Double-size ... 3.95
❑51, Sep 1989 ... 2.00
❑52, Oct 1989 ... 3.00
❑53, Nov 1989 ... 3.00
❑54, Dec 1989 ... 3.00
❑55, Jan 1990 ... 2.00
❑56, Feb 1990 ... 2.00
❑57, Mar 1990 ... 2.00
❑58, Apr 1990 ... 2.00
❑59, May 1990 ... 2.00
❑60, Jun 1990 ... 2.00
❑61, Jul 1990 ... 2.00
❑62, Aug 1990 ... 2.00
❑63, Sep 1990 ... 2.00
❑64, Oct 1990 ... 2.25
❑65, Nov 1990 ... 2.25
❑66, Dec 1990 ... 2.25
❑67, Jan 1991 ... 2.25
❑68, Feb 1991 ... 2.25
❑69, Mar 1991 ... 2.25
❑70, Apr 1991 ... 2.25

N-MINT

BADGER (VOL. 2)
FIRST

❑1, May 1991; Badger Bedlam 4.95

BADGER (VOL. 3)
IMAGE

❑1, May 1997, b&w; indicia says #78 in series 2.95
❑2, Jun 1997, b&w; indicia says #79 in series 2.95
❑3, Jul 1997, b&w; indicia says #80 in series 2.95
❑4, Aug 1997, b&w; indicia says #81 in series 2.95
❑5, Sep 1997, b&w; indicia says #82 in series 2.95
❑6, Oct 1997, b&w; indicia says #83 in series 2.95
❑7, Nov 1997, b&w; indicia says #84 in series 2.95
❑8, Dec 1997, b&w; indicia says #85 in series 2.95
❑9, Jan 1998, b&w; indicia says #86 in series 2.95
❑10, Feb 1998, b&w; indicia says #87 in series 2.95
❑11, Apr 1998, b&w; indicia says #88 in series 2.95

BADGER GOES BERSERK
FIRST

❑1, Sep 1989 .... 2.00
❑2, Oct 1989 .... 2.00
❑3, Nov 1989 .... 2.00
❑4, Dec 1989 .... 2.00

BADGER: SHATTERED MIRROR
DARK HORSE

❑1, Jul 1994 .... 2.50
❑2, Aug 1994 .... 2.50
❑3, Sep 1994 .... 2.50
❑4, Oct 1994 .... 2.50

BADGER: ZEN POP FUNNY-ANIMAL VERSION
DARK HORSE

❑1, Jul 1994 .... 2.50
❑2, Aug 1994 .... 2.50

BAD GIRLS
DC

❑1, Aug 2003 .... 2.50
❑2, Sep 2003 .... 2.50
❑3, Oct 2003 .... 2.50
❑4, Nov 2003 .... 2.50
❑5, Dec 2003 .... 2.50

BAD GIRLS (BILL WARD'S...)
FORBIDDEN FRUIT

❑1 .... 1.50

BAD GIRLS OF BLACKOUT
BLACKOUT

❑0 1995 .... 3.50
❑1 1995 .... 3.50
❑Annual 1, ca. 1995 .... 3.50

BAD HAIR DAY
SLAB-O-CONCRETE

❑1; Postcard Comic 1.00

BAD IDEAS
IMAGE

❑1, Apr 2004 .... 5.95

BAD KITTY
CHAOS

❑1, Feb 2001 .... 2.99
❑1/A, Mar 2001; Alternate cover (nude w/cat) 2.99
❑Ashcan 1; 1,000 copies printed ....
❑2, Mar 2001 .... 2.99
❑3, Apr 2001 .... 2.99

BAD KITTY: MISCHIEF NIGHT
CHAOS

❑1, Nov 2001; Events take place after Lady Death/Bad Kitty #1 .... 3.00
❑1/A, Nov 2001; Events take place after Lady Death/Bad Kitty #1 .... 2.99

N-MINT

❑1/B, Nov 2001; Events take place after Lady Death/Bad Kitty #1; Posing next to car on white background 2.99
❑1/C, Nov 2001; Events take place after Lady Death/Bad Kitty #1; Posing next to car on white background 2.99
❑1/D, Nov 2001; Otherwise same as #1 2.99

BADLANDS
DARK HORSE

❑1, Jul 1991 .... 2.50
❑2 .... 2.50
❑3 .... 2.50
❑4 .... 2.50
❑5 .... 2.50
❑6 .... 2.50

BAD LUCK AND RICK DEES SENTINEL OF JUSTICE
KING COMICS

❑1, Feb 1994 .... 2.95

BAD MEAT
FANTAGRAPHICS / EROS

❑1, Jul 1991, b&w 2.25
❑2 .... 2.25

BAD NEWS
FANTAGRAPHICS

❑3, b&w 3.50

BADROCK
IMAGE

❑1/A, Mar 1995 .... 1.75
❑1/B, Mar 1995 .... 1.75
❑1/C, Mar 1995 .... 1.75
❑2 .... 1.75
❑3 .... 1.75
❑Annual 1, Jul 1995 .... 2.95

BADROCK & COMPANY
IMAGE

❑1, Sep 1994 .... 2.50
❑2, Oct 1994 .... 2.50
❑3, Nov 1994 .... 2.50
❑4, Dec 1994 .... 2.50
❑5, Jan 1995 .... 2.50
❑6, Oct 1995; cover says Feb 95, indicia says Oct 94 .... 2.50
❑Special 1, Sep 1994; San Diego Comic-Con edition 2.50

BADROCK/WOLVERINE
IMAGE

❑1/A, Jun 1996 .... 4.95
❑1/B, Jun 1996 .... 4.95
❑1/C, Jun 1996 .... 4.95
❑1/D, Jun 1996 .... 4.95

BAKER STREET
CALIBER

❑1, Mar 1989 .... 2.50
❑2 .... 2.50
❑3 .... 2.50
❑4 .... 2.50
❑5 .... 2.50
❑6 .... 2.50
❑7 .... 2.50
❑8 .... 2.50
❑9 .... 2.50
❑10 .... 2.50

BAKER STREET GRAFFITI
CALIBER

❑1, b&w 2.50

BAKER STREET SKETCHBOOK
CALIBER

❑1 .... 3.95

BALANCE OF POWER
MU

❑1, b&w 2.50
❑2 .... 2.50
❑3, Mar 1991 .... 2.50
❑4, Jul 1991 .... 2.50

BALDER THE BRAVE
MARVEL

❑1, Nov 1985 SB (a) 1.00
❑2, Jan 1986 .... 1.00

A bickering couple on the verge of divorce overcame their differences when they acquired super-powers and had to work together to overcome a threat to Earth in *Ball and Chain*.

© 2000 WildStorm Productions (Homage).

N-MINT

❑3, Mar 1986 .... 1.00
❑4, May 1986 .... 1.00

BALLAD OF HALO JONES, THE
FLEETWAY-QUALITY

❑1, Sep 1987; AMo (w); 1: Halo Jones. Reprints The Ballad of Halo Jones from 2000 A.D 1.50
❑2, Oct 1987 AMo (w) 1.50
❑3 AMo (w) 1.50
❑4 AMo (w) 1.50
❑5 AMo (w) 1.50
❑6 AMo (w) 1.50
❑7 AMo (w) 1.50
❑8 AMo (w) 1.50
❑9 AMo (w) 1.50
❑10 AMo (w) 1.50
❑11 AMo (w) 1.50
❑12 AMo (w) 1.50

BALLAD OF UTOPIA, THE
BLACK DAZE

❑1, Aug 1998 .... 2.95
❑2, Sep 1999 .... 2.95
❑3, Nov 1999 .... 2.95

BALL AND CHAIN
DC / HOMAGE

❑1, Nov 1999 .... 2.50
❑2, Dec 1999 .... 2.50
❑3, Jan 2000 .... 2.50
❑4, Feb 2000 .... 2.50

BALLISTIC
IMAGE

❑1, Sep 1995 .... 2.50
❑2, Oct 1995 .... 2.50
❑3, Nov 1995 .... 2.50

BALLISTIC ACTION
IMAGE

❑1, May 1996; pin-ups 2.95

BALLISTIC IMAGERY
IMAGE

❑1, Jan 1996 .... 2.50
❑2 .... 2.50

BALLISTIC STUDIOS SWIMSUIT SPECIAL
IMAGE

❑1, May 1995; pin-ups 2.95

BALLISTIC/WOLVERINE
TOP COW

❑1, Feb 1997; crossover with Marvel, continues in Wolverine/Witchblade 3.50

BALLOONATIKS, THE
BEST

❑1, Oct 1991 .... 2.50

BAMBI
DELL

❑3, Apr 1956, reprints Four-Color #186 30.00
❑3/A, Apr 1956, 15 cent regional price variant; reprints Four-Color #186 ... 50.00

BAMBI (WALT DISNEY...)
WHITMAN

❑1; Reprint of 1942 story 2.50

BAMBI AND HER FRIENDS
FRIENDLY

❑1, Jan 1991 .... 2.50
❑2, Feb 1991 .... 2.50

Condition price index: Multiply "NM prices" above by: **0.83 for Very Fine/Near Mint**
0.66 for Very Fine • 0.33 for Fine • 0.2 for Very Good • 0.125 for Good

	N-MINT
❑3, Mar 1991	2.95
❑4, Apr 1991	2.95
❑5, May 1991	2.95
❑6, Jun 1991	2.95
❑7, Jul 1991	2.95
❑8, Aug 1991	2.95
❑9, Sep 1991	2.95

BAMBI IN HEAT
FRIENDLY

❑1 ... 2.95
❑2 ... 2.95
❑3 ... 2.95

BAMBI THE HUNTER
FRIENDLY

❑1 ... 2.95
❑2 ... 2.95
❑3, Mar 1992 ... 2.95
❑4 ... 2.95
❑5 ... 2.95

BAMM-BAMM AND PEBBLES FLINTSTONE
GOLD KEY

❑1, ca. 1964 ... 75.00

BANANA SPLITS, THE (HANNA BARBERA...)
GOLD KEY

❑1, Jun 1969 1: Snorky (in comics). 1: Fleegle (in comics). 1: Drooper (in comics). 1: Bingo (in comics) ... 30.00
❑2, Apr 1970 ... 18.00
❑3, Jul 1970 ... 14.00
❑4, Oct 1970 ... 14.00
❑5, Jan 1971 ... 14.00
❑6, Apr 1971 ... 12.00
❑7, Jul 1971 ... 12.00
❑8, Oct 1971 ... 12.00

BANDY MAN, THE
CALIBER

❑1 1996, b&w ... 2.95
❑2, Nov 1996, b&w ... 2.95
❑3, ca. 1997, b&w ... 2.95

BANG GANG
FANTAGRAPHICS / EROS

❑1, b&w ... 2.50

BANGS AND THE GANG
SHHWINNG

❑1, Feb 1994, b&w ... 2.95

BANISHED KNIGHTS
IMAGE

❑1, Dec 2001; no cover price ... 6.50
❑1/A, Dec 2001 ... 3.00
❑1/B, Dec 2001 ... 3.00
❑2/A, Feb 2002 ... 3.00
❑2/B, Feb 2002 ... 3.00

BANZAI GIRL
SIRIUS

❑1 2002 ... 2.95
❑2 2002 ... 2.95
❑3, Feb 2003 ... 2.95
❑4, May 2003 ... 2.95
❑Annual 1, Jan 2004 ... 3.50

BAOH
VIZ

❑1 ... 3.50
❑2 ... 3.00
❑3 ... 3.00
❑4 ... 3.00
❑5 ... 3.00
❑6 ... 3.00
❑7 ... 3.00
❑8 ... 3.00

BARABBAS
SLAVE LABOR

❑1, Aug 1986 ... 1.50
❑2, Nov 1985 ... 1.50

BARBARIAN COMICS
CALIFORNIA

❑1, ca. 1972 ... 3.00
❑2, ca. 1973 ... 2.50

BARBARIANS
ATLAS-SEABOARD

❑1, Jun 1975 O: Andrax. 1: Ironjaw ... 6.00

BARBARIANS (AVALON)
AVALON

❑1 ... 2.95
❑2 ... 2.95

BARBARIANS AND BEAUTIES
AC

❑1 1990 ... 2.75

BARBARIC TALES
PYRAMID

❑1 ... 1.70
❑2 ... 1.70

BARBARIENNE (FANTAGRAPHICS)
FANTAGRAPHICS / EROS

❑2, b&w ... 2.50
❑3, b&w ... 2.50

BARBARIENNE (HARRIER)
HARRIER

❑1, Mar 1987 ... 2.00
❑2 ... 2.00
❑3 ... 2.00
❑4 ... 2.00
❑5 ... 2.00
❑6 V: Cuirass ... 2.00
❑7 V: Cuirass ... 2.00
❑8 V: Cuirass ... 2.00

BARBIE
MARVEL

❑1, Jan 1991 ... 3.00
❑1/A, Jan 1991 ... 3.00
❑2, Feb 1991 ... 2.00
❑3, Mar 1991 ... 2.00
❑4, Apr 1991 ... 2.00
❑5, May 1991 ... 2.00
❑6, Jun 1991 ... 1.50
❑7, Jul 1991 ... 1.50
❑8, Aug 1991 ... 1.50
❑9, Sep 1991 ... 1.50
❑10, Oct 1991 ... 1.50
❑11, Nov 1991 ... 1.50
❑12, Dec 1991 ... 1.50
❑13, Jan 1992 ... 1.50
❑14, Feb 1992 ... 1.50
❑15, Mar 1992 ... 1.50
❑16, Apr 1992 ... 1.50
❑17, May 1992 ... 1.50
❑18, Jun 1992 ... 1.50
❑19, Jul 1992 ... 1.50
❑20, Aug 1992 ... 1.50
❑21, Sep 1992 ... 1.50
❑22, Oct 1992 ... 1.50
❑23, Nov 1992 ... 1.50
❑24, Dec 1992 ... 1.50
❑25, Jan 1993 ... 1.50
❑26, Feb 1993 ... 1.50
❑27, Mar 1993 ... 1.50
❑28, Apr 1993 ... 1.50
❑29, May 1993 ... 1.50
❑30, Jun 1993 ... 1.50
❑31, Jul 1993 ... 1.50
❑32, Aug 1993 GM (a) ... 1.50
❑33, Sep 1993 ... 1.50
❑34, Oct 1993 A: Teresa ... 1.50
❑35, Nov 1993 ... 1.50
❑36, Dec 1993 ... 1.50
❑37, Jan 1994 ... 1.50
❑38, Feb 1994 ... 1.50
❑39, Mar 1994 ... 1.50
❑40, Apr 1994 ... 1.50
❑41, May 1994 ... 1.50
❑42, Jun 1994 ... 1.50
❑43, Jul 1994 ... 1.50
❑44, Aug 1994 ... 1.50
❑45, Sep 1994 ... 1.50
❑46, Oct 1994 ... 1.50
❑47, Nov 1994 ... 1.50
❑48, Dec 1994 ... 1.50
❑49, Jan 1995 ... 1.50
❑50, Feb 1995; Giant-size ... 2.25
❑51, Mar 1995 ... 1.50
❑52, Apr 1995 ... 1.50
❑53, May 1995 ... 1.50
❑54, Jun 1995 ... 1.50
❑55, Jul 1995 ... 1.50
❑56, Aug 1995 ... 1.50
❑57, Sep 1995 ... 1.50
❑58, Oct 1995 ... 1.50
❑59, Nov 1995 ... 1.50
❑60, Dec 1995 ... 1.50
❑61, Jan 1996 ... 1.50
❑62, Feb 1996; Nutcracker Suite references ... 1.50
❑63, Mar 1996 ... 1.50

BARBIE AND KEN
DELL

❑1, May 1962 ... 200.00
❑2, Aug 1962 ... 150.00
❑3, May 1963 ... 150.00
❑4, Aug 1963 ... 150.00
❑5, Nov 1963 ... 165.00

BARBIE FASHION
MARVEL

❑1, Jan 1991 ... 3.00
❑1/A, Jan 1991 ... 3.00
❑2, Feb 1991 ... 2.00
❑3, Mar 1991 ... 2.00
❑4, Apr 1991 ... 1.50
❑5, May 1991 ... 1.50
❑6, Jun 1991 ... 1.50
❑7, Jul 1991 ... 1.50
❑8, Aug 1991 ... 1.50
❑9, Sep 1991 ... 1.50
❑10, Oct 1991 ... 1.50
❑11, Nov 1991 ... 1.50
❑12, Dec 1991 ... 1.50
❑13, Jan 1992 ... 1.50
❑14, Feb 1992 ... 1.50
❑15, Mar 1992 ... 1.50
❑16, Apr 1992 ... 1.50
❑17, May 1992 ... 1.50
❑18, Jun 1992 ... 1.50
❑19, Jul 1992 ... 1.50
❑20, Aug 1992 ... 1.50
❑21, Sep 1992 ... 1.50
❑22, Oct 1992 ... 1.50
❑23, Nov 1992 ... 1.50
❑24, Dec 1992 ... 1.50
❑25, Jan 1993 ... 1.50
❑26, Feb 1993 ... 1.50
❑27, Mar 1993 ... 1.50
❑28, Apr 1993 ... 1.50
❑29, May 1993 ... 1.50
❑30, Jun 1993 ... 1.50
❑31, Jul 1993 GM (a) ... 1.50
❑32, Aug 1993 ... 1.50
❑33, Sep 1993 ... 1.50
❑34, Oct 1993 ... 1.50
❑35, Nov 1993 ... 1.50
❑36, Dec 1993 ... 1.50
❑37, Jan 1994 ... 1.50
❑38, Feb 1994 ... 1.50
❑39, Mar 1994 ... 1.50
❑40, Apr 1994 ... 1.50
❑41, May 1994 ... 1.50
❑42, Jun 1994 ... 1.50
❑43, Jul 1994 ... 1.50
❑44, Aug 1994 ... 1.50
❑45, Sep 1994 ... 1.50
❑46, Oct 1994 ... 1.50
❑47, Nov 1994 ... 1.50
❑48, Dec 1994 ... 1.50
❑49, Jan 1995 ... 1.50
❑50, Feb 1995; Giant-size ... 2.25
❑51, Mar 1995 ... 1.50

N-MINT

❑52, Apr 1995 .... 1.50
❑53, May 1995 .... 1.50
❑54 .... 1.50
❑55 .... 1.50

BARBI TWINS ADVENTURES, THE
TOPPS
❑1, Jul 1995; Flip-book 2.50

BARB WIRE
DARK HORSE
❑1, Apr 1994 .... 2.50
❑2, May 1994 .... 2.50
❑3, Jun 1994 .... 2.50
❑4, Aug 1994 .... 2.50
❑5, Sep 1994 .... 2.50
❑6, Oct 1994 .... 2.50
❑7, Nov 1994 .... 2.50
❑8, Jan 1995 .... 2.50
❑9, Feb 1995 .... 2.50

BARB WIRE: ACE OF SPADES
DARK HORSE
❑1, May 1996 .... 2.95
❑2, Jun 1996 .... 2.95
❑3, Jul 1996 .... 2.95
❑4, Sep 1996 .... 2.95

BARB WIRE COMICS MAGAZINE SPECIAL
DARK HORSE
❑1, May 1996; magazine-sized adaptation of movie, b&w, poster 3.50

BARB WIRE MOVIE SPECIAL
DARK HORSE
❑1, May 1996; adapts movie 3.95

BAR CRAWL OF THE DAMNED
MORTCO
❑1 1997, b&w 2.50

BAREFOOTZ FUNNIES
KITCHEN SINK
❑1, b&w 3.00
❑2, b&w 2.00
❑3, b&w 2.00

BAREFOOTZ THE COMIX BOOK STORIES (HOWARD CRUSE'S...)
RENEGADE
❑1 A: Dolly. A: Barefootz. A: Headrack 2.50

BARF
REVOLUTIONARY
❑1, Apr 1990, b&w 1.95
❑2, Jun 1990, b&w 2.50
❑3, Sep 1990, b&w 2.50

BARNEY AND BETTY RUBBLE
CHARLTON
❑1, Jan 1973 .... 15.00
❑2, Jan 1973 .... 10.00
❑3, Mar 1973 .... 6.00
❑4, May 1973 .... 6.00
❑5, Jul 1973 .... 6.00
❑6, Sep 1973 .... 6.00
❑7, May 1974 .... 6.00
❑8, Jul 1974 .... 6.00
❑9, Sep 1974 .... 6.00
❑10, Nov 1974 .... 6.00
❑11, Feb 1975 .... 6.00
❑12, Mar 1975 .... 5.00
❑13, May 1975 .... 5.00
❑14, Jun 1975 .... 5.00
❑15, Aug 1975 .... 5.00
❑16, Oct 1975 .... 5.00
❑17, Dec 1975 .... 5.00
❑18, Feb 1976 .... 5.00
❑19, Apr 1976 .... 5.00
❑20, Jun 1976 .... 5.00
❑21, Aug 1976 .... 5.00
❑22, Oct 1976 .... 5.00
❑23, Dec 1976 .... 5.00

BARNEY THE INVISIBLE TURTLE
AMAZING
❑1 .... 1.95

N-MINT

BARNUM HC
DC
❑1, May 2003 .... 0.00

BARR GIRLS, THE
ANTARCTIC / VENUS
❑1, b&w 2.95

BARRON STOREY'S WATCH ANNUAL (VOL. 2)
VANGUARD
❑1; b&w anthology, squarebound 5.95

BARRY WINDSOR-SMITH: STORYTELLER
DARK HORSE
❑1, Oct 1996 .... 4.95
❑1/Variant, Oct 1996; alternate cover (logoless), cover with logos appears as back cover 4.95
❑2, Nov 1996 .... 4.95
❑3, Dec 1996 .... 4.95
❑4, Jan 1997 .... 4.95
❑5, Feb 1997 .... 4.95
❑6, Mar 1997 .... 4.95
❑7, May 1997 .... 4.95
❑8, Jun 1997 .... 4.95
❑9, Jul 1997 .... 4.95

BAR SINISTER
WINDJAMMER / ACCLAIM
❑1, Jun 1995 .... 2.50
❑2, Jul 1995 .... 2.50
❑3, Aug 1995 .... 2.50
❑4, Sep 1995 .... 2.50

BARTMAN
BONGO
❑1, ca. 1993; Silver ink cover 4.00
❑2, ca. 1994 .... 3.00
❑3, ca. 1994; trading card 3.00
❑4, ca. 1995 .... 2.50
❑5, ca. 1995 1: Lisa the Conjuror. 1: The Great Maggeena 2.50
❑6, ca. 1995 0: Bart Dog. 1: Bart Dog 2.50

BASEBALL CLASSICS
PERSONALITY
❑1 .... 2.95
❑2 .... 2.95

BASEBALL COMICS
KITCHEN SINK
❑1, May 1991; trading cards 3.95
❑2; cards on back cover 2.95

BASEBALL COMICS (PERSONALITY)
PERSONALITY
❑1 .... 2.95
❑2 .... 2.95

BASEBALL GREATS
DARK HORSE
❑1, Oct 1992; Jimmy Piersall, with cards 2.95
❑2; Bob Gibson 2.95
❑3; 2 trading cards 2.95

BASEBALL HALL OF SHAME IN 3-D
BLACKTHORNE
❑1 .... 2.50

BASEBALL LEGENDS
REVOLUTIONARY
❑1, Mar 1992, b&w; Babe Ruth 2.50
❑2, Apr 1992, b&w; Ty Cobb 2.50
❑3, May 1992, b&w; Ted Williams 2.50
❑4, Jun 1992, b&w; Mickey Mantle 2.50
❑5, Jul 1992, b&w; Joe Dimaggio 2.50
❑6, Aug 1992, b&w; Jackie Robinson 2.50
❑7, Sep 1992, b&w; Sandy Koufax 2.50
❑8, Oct 1992, b&w; Willie Mays 2.50
❑9, Nov 1992, b&w; Honus Wagner 2.50
❑10, Dec 1992; Roberto Clemente 2.75
❑11, Jan 1993; Yogi Berra 2.75
❑12, Feb 1993; Billy Martin 2.75
❑13, Mar 1993; Hank Aaron 2.95
❑14, Apr 1993, b&w; Carl Yastrzemski 2.95
❑15, May 1993, b&w; Satchel Paige 2.95
❑16, Jun 1993, b&w; Johnny Bench 2.95

Howard Cruse's underground *Barefootz* strips were collected by Kitchen Sink in three issues.
© 1975 Howard Cruse.

N-MINT

❑17, Jul 1993, b&w; Shoeless Joe Jackson 2.95
❑18, Aug 1993, b&w; Lou Gehrig 2.95
❑19, Sep 1993, b&w; Casey Stengel 2.95

BASEBALL'S GREATEST HEROES
MAGNUM
❑1, Dec 1991; Mickey Mantle 2.50
❑2 .... 2.50

BASEBALL SLUGGERS
PERSONALITY
❑1 .... 2.95
❑2 .... 2.95
❑3 .... 2.95
❑4 .... 2.95

BASEBALL SUPERSTARS COMICS
REVOLUTIONARY
❑1, Nov 1991; Nolan Ryan 2.50
❑2, Feb 1992; Bo Jackson 2.50
❑3, Mar 1992; Ken Griffey Jr 2.50
❑4, Apr 1992; Pete Rose 2.50
❑5, May 1992; Rickey Henderson 2.50
❑6, Jun 1992; Jose Canseco 2.50
❑7, Jul 1992; Cal Ripkin Jr 2.50
❑8, Aug 1992; Carlton Fisk 2.50
❑9, Sep 1992; George Brett 2.50
❑10, Oct 1992; Darryl Strawberry 2.50
❑11, Nov 1992; Frank Thomas 2.50
❑12, Dec 1992; Ryne Sandberg 2.75
❑13, Jan 1993; Kirby Puckett 2.75
❑14, Feb 1993; Roberto and Sandi Alomar 2.75
❑15, Mar 1993; Roger Clemens 2.95
❑16, Apr 1993, b&w; Mark McGuire 2.95
❑17, May 1993, b&w; Avery/Glavine 2.95
❑18, Jun 1993, b&w; Dennis Eckersley 2.95
❑19, Jul 1993, b&w; Dave Winfield 2.95
❑20, Aug 1993, b&w; Jim Abbott 2.95

BASEBALL THRILLS 3-D
3-D ZONE
❑1 .... 2.95

BASICALLY STRANGE
JOHN C.
❑1, Nov 1982 WW (w); ATh, FT, WW (a) 4.00

BASTARD
VIZ
❑1, Dec 2001 .... 3.95
❑2, Jan 2002 .... 3.95
❑3, Feb 2002 .... 3.95
❑4, Mar 2002 .... 3.95
❑5, Apr 2002 .... 3.95
❑6, May 2002 .... 3.95
❑7, Jun 2002 .... 3.95
❑8, Jul 2002 .... 3.95
❑9, Aug 2002 .... 3.95
❑10, Sep 2002 .... 3.95
❑11, Oct 2002 .... 3.95
❑12, Nov 2002 .... 3.95
❑13, Dec 2002 .... 3.95
❑14, Jan 2003 .... 3.95
❑15, Feb 2003 .... 3.95

BASTARD SAMURAI
IMAGE
❑1, Apr 2002 .... 2.95
❑2, Jun 2002 .... 2.95
❑3, Aug 2002 .... 2.95

N-MINT

BASTARD TALES
Baboon Books

❑1 1998, b&w 2.95

BAT, THE (APPLE)
Apple

❑1, Mar 1994, b&w 2.50

BATBABE
Spoof

❑2 2.50

BATCH
Caliber

❑1, b&w 2.95

BATGIRL
DC

❑1, Apr 2000 4.00
❑1-2, Apr 2000 3.00
❑2, May 2000 3.50
❑3, Jun 2000 3.50
❑4, Jul 2000 3.50
❑5, Aug 2000 3.50
❑6, Sep 2000 3.00
❑7, Oct 2000 3.00
❑8, Nov 2000 3.00
❑9, Dec 2000 3.00
❑10, Jan 2001 3.00
❑11, Feb 2001 2.50
❑12, Mar 2001; Officer Down 2.50
❑13, Apr 2001 2.50
❑14, May 2001 2.50
❑15, Jun 2001 2.50
❑16, Jul 2001 2.50
❑17, Aug 2001 2.50
❑18, Sep 2001 2.50
❑19, Oct 2001 2.50
❑20, Nov 2001 2.50
❑21, Dec 2001 2.50
❑22, Jan 2002 2.50
❑23, Feb 2002 2.50
❑24, Mar 2002 2.50
❑25, Apr 2002; Giant-size 3.25
❑26, May 2002 2.50
❑27, Jun 2002 2.50
❑28, Jul 2002 2.50
❑29, Aug 2002 2.50
❑30, Sep 2002 2.50
❑31, Oct 2002 2.50
❑32, Nov 2002 2.50
❑33, Dec 2002 2.50
❑34, Jan 2003 2.50
❑35, Feb 2003 2.50
❑36, Mar 2003 2.50
❑37, Apr 2003 2.50
❑38, May 2003 2.50
❑39, Jun 2003 2.50
❑40, Jul 2003 2.50
❑41, Aug 2003 2.50
❑42, Sep 2003 2.50
❑43, Oct 2003 2.50
❑44, Nov 2003 2.50
❑45, Dec 2003 2.50
❑46, Jan 2004 2.50
❑47, Feb 2004 2.50
❑48, Mar 2004 2.50
❑49, Apr 2004 2.50
❑50, May 2004 2.50
❑51, Jun 2004 2.50
❑52, Jul 2004 2.50
❑53, Aug 2004 2.50
❑54, Jul 2004
❑Annual 1, ca. 2002; 1: Aruna; Planet DC 4.00

BATGIRL ADVENTURES, THE
DC

❑1, Feb 1998 V: Harley Quinn, Poison Ivy 3.50

BATGIRL SECRET FILES AND ORIGINS
DC

❑1, Aug 2002 4.95

N-MINT

BATGIRL SPECIAL
DC

❑1, Jul 1988 3.00

BATGIRL: YEAR ONE
DC

❑1, Feb 2003 2.95
❑2, Mar 2003 2.95
❑3, Apr 2003 2.95
❑4, May 2003 2.95
❑5, Jun 2003 2.95
❑6, Jul 2003 2.95
❑7, Aug 2003 2.95
❑8, Sep 2003 2.95
❑9, Oct 2003 2.95

BATHING MACHINE
C&T

❑1, b&w 2.50
❑2 1.50
❑3 1.50

BATHROOM GIRLS
Modern

❑1 1997, b&w 2.95
❑2 1998, b&w 2.95

BAT LASH
DC

❑1, Nov 1968 25.00
❑2, Jan 1969 15.00
❑3, Mar 1969 15.00
❑4, May 1969 15.00
❑5, Jul 1969 15.00
❑6, Sep 1969 15.00
❑7, Nov 1969 SA (w); NC (a) 15.00

BATMAN
DC

❑0,Oct 1994 2.50
❑102, Sep 1956 400.00
❑103, Oct 1956 400.00
❑104, Dec 1956 400.00
❑105, Feb 1957 2: Batwoman 490.00
❑106, Mar 1957 400.00
❑107, Apr 1957 400.00
❑108, Jun 1957 400.00
❑109, Jul 1957 400.00
❑110, Sep 1957 A: Joker. V: Joker 425.00
❑111, Oct 1957 290.00
❑112, Dec 1957 1: The Signalman 290.00
❑113, Feb 1958 1: Fatman 290.00
❑114, Mar 1958 290.00
❑115, Apr 1958 290.00
❑116, Jun 1958 290.00
❑117, Jul 1958 290.00
❑118, Sep 1958 290.00
❑119, Oct 1958 290.00
❑120, Dec 1958 290.00
❑121, Feb 1959 O: Mr. Zero (later Mr. Freeze). 1: Mr. Zero (later Mr. Freeze) 375.00
❑122, Mar 1959 225.00
❑123, Apr 1959 A: Joker 220.00
❑124, Jun 1959 195.00
❑125, Aug 1959 195.00
❑126, Sep 1959 195.00
❑127, Oct 1959 A: Joker. A: Superman 240.00
❑128, Dec 1959 195.00
❑129, Feb 1960 O: Robin I (Dick Grayson) 250.00
❑130, Mar 1960 A: Lex Luthor. A: Bat-Hound ("Ace") 195.00
❑131, Apr 1960 1: 2nd Batman 145.00
❑132, Jun 1960 130.00
❑133, Aug 1960 130.00
❑134, Sep 1960 130.00
❑135, Oct 1960 130.00
❑136, Dec 1960 A: Joker. V: Joker 215.00
❑137, Feb 1961 A: Mr. Marvel 140.00
❑138, Mar 1961 140.00
❑139, Apr 1961 1: Batgirl (Golden Age) 140.00
❑140, Jun 1961 A: Joker 140.00
❑141, Aug 1961 140.00
❑142, Sep 1961 140.00
❑143, Oct 1961 140.00

N-MINT

❑144, Dec 1961 A: Joker 140.00
❑145, Feb 1962 A: Joker 140.00
❑146, Mar 1962 110.00
❑147, May 1962 110.00
❑148, Jul 1962 A: Joker 140.00
❑149, Aug 1962 110.00
❑150, Oct 1962 110.00
❑151, Nov 1962 90.00
❑152, Dec 1962 A: Joker 100.00
❑153, Feb 1963 85.00
❑154, Mar 1963 85.00
❑155, Apr 1963 1: Penguin (in Silver Age) 300.00
❑156, Jun 1963 85.00
❑157, Aug 1963 85.00
❑158, Sep 1963 85.00
❑159, Nov 1963 A: Joker 85.00
❑160, Dec 1963 85.00
❑161, Feb 1964 85.00
❑162, Mar 1964 85.00
❑163, May 1964 A: Joker 85.00
❑164, Jun 1964 85.00
❑165, Aug 1964 85.00
❑166, Sep 1964 85.00
❑167, Nov 1964 85.00
❑168, Dec 1964 85.00
❑169, Feb 1965 A: Penguin 90.00
❑170, Mar 1965 85.00
❑171, May 1965 CI (a) 450.00
❑172, Jun 1965 75.00
❑173, Aug 1965 75.00
❑174, Sep 1965 75.00
❑175, Nov 1965 75.00
❑176, Dec 1965; 80-Page Giant A: Joker 85.00
❑177, Dec 1965 75.00
❑178, Feb 1966 75.00
❑179, Mar 1966 A: Riddler 120.00
❑180, May 1966 60.00
❑181, Jun 1966 1: Poison Ivy 175.00
❑182, Aug 1966 A: Joker 60.00
❑183, Aug 1966; TV show reference . 60.00
❑184, Sep 1966 60.00
❑185, Nov 1966; 80-Page Giant 60.00
❑186, Nov 1966 A: Joker 60.00
❑187, Dec 1966; 80-Page Giant A: Joker 65.00
❑188, Jan 1967 40.00
❑189, Feb 1967 1: The Scarecrow (in Silver Age) 115.00
❑190, Mar 1967 A: Penguin 45.00
❑191, May 1967 40.00
❑192, Jun 1967 40.00
❑193, Aug 1967; 80-Page Giant 70.00
❑194, Aug 1967 40.00
❑195, Sep 1967 40.00
❑196, Nov 1967 40.00
❑197, Dec 1967 A: Catwoman 100.00
❑198, Jan 1968; 80-Page Giant O: Batman. A: Joker 80.00
❑199, Feb 1968 40.00
❑200, Mar 1968 NA (a); O: Robin I (Dick Grayson). O: Batman. A: Joker 100.00
❑201, May 1968 A: Joker 35.00
❑202, Jun 1968 30.00
❑203, Aug 1968; 80-Page Giant 30.00
❑204, Aug 1968 30.00
❑205, Sep 1968 30.00
❑206, Nov 1968 30.00
❑207, Dec 1968 30.00
❑208, Jan 1969; 80-Page Giant O: Batman (new origin) 30.00
❑209, Jan 1969 30.00
❑210, Mar 1969 30.00
❑211, May 1969 30.00
❑212, Jun 1969 30.00
❑213, Aug 1969; Giant-size; O: Robin I (Dick Grayson-new origin). A: Joker. Joker reprint 45.00
❑214, Aug 1969 30.00
❑215, Sep 1969 30.00
❑216, Nov 1969 30.00
❑217, Dec 1969 30.00

	N-MINT
❑218, Feb 1970; Giant-size	50.00
❑219, Feb 1970 NA (a)	50.00
❑220, Mar 1970 NA (a)	30.00
❑221, May 1970 NA (a)	30.00
❑222, Jun 1970 NA (a); A: The Beatles	50.00
❑223, Aug 1970; Giant-size; CS (c); MA (a); Reprints stories from Batman #79 & #93, Detective #196 & #248, and Sunday strips from August 8 through September 17, 1944	40.00
❑224, Aug 1970 NA (a)	30.00
❑225, Sep 1970 NA (a)	30.00
❑226, Nov 1970 NA (a)	30.00
❑227, Dec 1970; NA (a); Robin back-up	30.00
❑228, Feb 1971; Giant-size; MA (a); giant	40.00
❑229, Feb 1971	30.00
❑230, Mar 1971	30.00
❑231, May 1971	30.00
❑232, Jun 1971 DG, NA (a); O: Batman. 1: Ra's Al Ghul	100.00
❑233, Aug 1971; Giant-size; giant	30.00
❑234, Aug 1971 CI, NA (a); 1: Two-Face (in Silver Age)	115.00
❑235, Sep 1971 CI (a)	17.00
❑236, Nov 1971 NA (a)	17.00
❑237, Dec 1971 NA (a); 1: The Reaper	75.00
❑238, Jan 1972; Giant-size; JKu, NA (a); a.k.a. DC 100-Page Super Spectacular #DC-8, wraparound cover	65.00
❑239, Feb 1972 RB, NA (a)	17.00
❑240, Mar 1972 RB, NA (a)	17.00
❑241, May 1972 RB, NA (a)	17.00
❑242, Jun 1972 RB (a)	17.00
❑243, Aug 1972; DG, NA (a); Ra's al Ghul	40.00
❑244, Sep 1972; DG, NA (a); Ra's al Ghul	40.00
❑245, Oct 1972 FM (c); DG, NA, IN (a)	40.00
❑246, Dec 1972	15.00
❑247, Feb 1973	15.00
❑248, Apr 1973	15.00
❑249, Jun 1973	15.00
❑250, Jul 1973	15.00
❑251, Sep 1973 NA (a); A: Joker	60.00
❑252, Sep 1973	14.00
❑253, Nov 1973	14.00
❑254, Feb 1974; 100 Page giant NA, GK (a)	32.00
❑255, Apr 1974; 100 Page giant CI, DG, NA, GK (a)	32.00
❑256, Jun 1974; 100 Page giant	32.00
❑257, Aug 1974; 100 Page giant	32.00
❑258, Oct 1974; 100 Page giant	32.00
❑259, Dec 1974; 100 Page giant	32.00
❑260, Feb 1975; 100 Page giant A: Joker	32.00
❑261, Mar 1975; 100 Page giant	32.00
❑262, Apr 1975; Giant-size	13.00
❑263, May 1975	9.00
❑264, Jun 1975 DG (a); V: Devil Dayre	9.00
❑265, Jul 1975	9.00
❑266, Aug 1975; A: Catwoman. Catwoman goes back to old costume	9.00
❑267, Sep 1975	8.00
❑268, Oct 1975	8.00
❑269, Nov 1975	8.00
❑270, Dec 1975	8.00
❑271, Jan 1976	8.00
❑272, Feb 1976	8.00
❑273, Mar 1976	8.00
❑274, Apr 1976	8.00
❑275, May 1976	8.00
❑276, Jun 1976	8.00
❑277, Jul 1976; Bicentennial #11	8.00
❑278, Aug 1976	8.00
❑279, Sep 1976	8.00
❑280, Oct 1976	8.00
❑281, Nov 1976	8.00
❑282, Dec 1976	8.00
❑283, Jan 1977 V: Omega	8.00
❑284, Feb 1977	8.00
❑285, Mar 1977	8.00
❑286, Apr 1977 A: Joker	12.00
❑287, May 1977	9.00
❑288, Jun 1977	9.00

	N-MINT
❑289, Jul 1977	9.00
❑290, Aug 1977	9.00
❑291, Sep 1977 A: Joker	9.00
❑292, Oct 1977	9.00
❑293, Nov 1977 A: Lex Luthor. A: Superman	9.00
❑294, Dec 1977 A: Joker	9.00
❑295, Jan 1978	8.00
❑296, Feb 1978 V: Scarecrow	8.00
❑297, Mar 1978	8.00
❑298, Apr 1978	8.00
❑299, May 1978	8.00
❑300, Jun 1978; Double-size	15.00
❑301, Jul 1978	7.00
❑302, Aug 1978	7.00
❑303, Sep 1978	7.00
❑304, Oct 1978	7.00
❑305, Nov 1978	7.00
❑306, Dec 1978	7.00
❑307, Jan 1979	7.00
❑308, Feb 1979	7.00
❑309, Mar 1979	7.00
❑310, Apr 1979	7.00
❑311, May 1979	7.00
❑312, Jun 1979	7.00
❑313, Jul 1979	7.00
❑314, Aug 1979	7.00
❑315, Sep 1979	7.00
❑316, Oct 1979	7.00
❑317, Nov 1979	7.00
❑318, Dec 1979 1: Firebug	7.00
❑319, Jan 1980	7.00
❑320, Feb 1980	7.00
❑321, Mar 1980 A: Catwoman. A: Joker	7.00
❑322, Apr 1980	7.00
❑323, May 1980	7.00
❑324, Jun 1980	7.00
❑325, Jul 1980	7.00
❑326, Aug 1980 1: Arkham Asylum	7.00
❑327, Sep 1980	7.00
❑328, Oct 1980	7.00
❑329, Nov 1980	7.00
❑330, Dec 1980	7.00
❑331, Jan 1981 1: Electrocutioner	7.00
❑332, Feb 1981; 1st solo Catwoman story	8.00
❑333, Mar 1981	7.00
❑334, Apr 1981	7.00
❑335, May 1981	7.00
❑336, Jun 1981	7.00
❑337, Jul 1981	7.00
❑338, Aug 1981	7.00
❑339, Sep 1981	7.00
❑340, Oct 1981	7.00
❑341, Nov 1981	7.00
❑342, Dec 1981	7.00
❑343, Jan 1982	7.00
❑344, Feb 1982	7.00
❑345, Mar 1982	7.00
❑346, Apr 1982 V: Two-Face	7.00
❑347, May 1982	7.00
❑348, Jun 1982	7.00
❑349, Jul 1982	7.00
❑350, Aug 1982	7.00
❑351, Sep 1982	7.00
❑352, Oct 1982	7.00
❑353, Nov 1982 A: Joker	5.00
❑354, Dec 1982	7.00
❑355, Jan 1983	7.00
❑356, Feb 1983	7.00
❑357, Mar 1983 1: Killer Croc. 1: Jason Todd	9.00
❑358, Apr 1983	7.00
❑359, May 1983 A: Joker	7.00
❑360, Jun 1983	7.00
❑361, Jul 1983 1: Harvey Bullock	7.00
❑362, Aug 1983	7.00
❑363, Sep 1983	7.00
❑364, Oct 1983	7.00
❑365, Nov 1983	7.00
❑366, Dec 1983 1: Jason Todd in Robin costume. A: Joker	6.00

Batman's origins, like those of many other DC heroes, were retold during October 1994's "Zero Month" event.

© 1994 DC Comics.

	N-MINT
❑367, Jan 1984	7.00
❑368, Feb 1984 DN, AA (a); 1: Robin II (Jason Todd)	8.00
❑369, Mar 1984 V: Deadshot	6.00
❑370, Apr 1984	6.00
❑371, May 1984 V: Catman	5.00
❑372, Jun 1984	5.00
❑373, Jul 1984 V: Scarecrow	5.00
❑374, Aug 1984 V: Penguin	5.00
❑375, Sep 1984 V: Mr. Freeze	5.00
❑376, Oct 1984	5.00
❑377, Nov 1984	5.00
❑378, Dec 1984 V: Mad Hatter	5.00
❑379, Jan 1985 V: Mad Hatter	5.00
❑380, Feb 1985	5.00
❑381, Mar 1985	5.00
❑382, Apr 1985 GK (c); A: Catwoman	5.00
❑383, May 1985	5.00
❑384, Jun 1985 V: Calendar Man	5.00
❑385, Jul 1985	5.00
❑386, Aug 1985 1: Black Mask	5.00
❑387, Sep 1985 V: Black Mask	5.00
❑388, Oct 1985 V: Mirror Master. V: Capt. Boomerang. V: Captain Boomerang	5.00
❑389, Nov 1985 A: Catwoman	5.00
❑390, Dec 1985 A: Catwoman	5.00
❑391, Jan 1986 A: Catwoman	5.00
❑392, Feb 1986	5.00
❑393, Mar 1986	5.00
❑394, Apr 1986	5.00
❑395, May 1986	5.00
❑396, Jun 1986	5.00
❑397, Jul 1986 V: Two-Face	5.00
❑398, Aug 1986 A: Catwoman. V: Two-Face.	5.00
❑399, Sep 1986	5.00
❑400, Oct 1986; Anniversary edition	10.00
❑401, Nov 1986; V: Magpie. Legends	4.00
❑402, Dec 1986	4.00
❑403, Jan 1987	4.00
❑404, Feb 1987 FM (w); O: Batman. 1: Catwoman (new)	5.00
❑405, Mar 1987; FM (w); Year One	6.00
❑406, Apr 1987; FM (w); Year One	5.00
❑407, May 1987; FM (w); Year One	5.00
❑408, Jun 1987 O: Jason Todd (new origin)	5.00
❑409, Jul 1987	3.00
❑410, Aug 1987 V: Two-Face	3.00
❑411, Sep 1987	3.00
❑412, Oct 1987 O: Mime. 1: Mime	3.00
❑413, Nov 1987	3.00
❑414, Dec 1987; JSn (w); JA (a); Millennium	3.00
❑415, Jan 1988; Millennium	3.00
❑416, Feb 1988 JA (a); A: Nightwing	3.00
❑417, Mar 1988 MZ (c); 1: KGBeast. V: KGBeast	5.00
❑418, Apr 1988 MZ (c); V: KGBeast	4.00
❑419, May 1988 MZ (c); V: KGBeast	4.00
❑420, Jun 1988 MZ (c); V: KGBeast	4.00
❑421, Jul 1988	3.00
❑422, Aug 1988	3.00
❑423, Sep 1988 TMc (c); DC (a)	3.00
❑424, Oct 1988	3.00
❑425, Nov 1988	3.00
❑426, Dec 1988	6.00
❑427, Dec 1988 D: Robin, newsstand	6.00

	N-MINT
❑427/Direct ed., Dec 1988 D: Robin, direct sale	4.00
❑428, Jan 1989; D: Robin II (Jason Todd). Robin declared dead	6.00
❑429, Jan 1989 JSn (w); JA (a)	4.00
❑430, Feb 1989	3.00
❑431, Mar 1989	2.00
❑432, Apr 1989	2.00
❑433, May 1989 JBy (w); JBy, JA (a)	2.00
❑434, Jun 1989 JBy (w); JBy, JA (a)	2.00
❑435, Jul 1989 JBy (w); JBy, JA (a)	2.00
❑436, Aug 1989	2.50
❑436-2	1.25
❑437, Aug 1989 PB (a)	2.00
❑438, Sep 1989	2.00
❑439, Sep 1989	2.00
❑440, Oct 1989 JA (a); 1: Timothy Drake	2.00
❑441, Nov 1989	2.00
❑442, Dec 1989 1: Robin III (Timothy Drake)	2.50
❑443, Jan 1990	1.50
❑444, Feb 1990 JA (a); V: Crimesmith	1.50
❑445, Mar 1990 JA (a); 1: NKVDemon. V: NKVDemon	1.50
❑446, Apr 1990 V: NKVDemon	1.50
❑447, May 1990 V: NKVDemon	1.50
❑448, Jun 1990 V: Penguin	1.50
❑449, Jun 1990 V: Penguin	1.50
❑450, Jul 1990 V: Joker	1.50
❑451, Jul 1990 V: Joker	1.50
❑452, Aug 1990 V: Riddler	1.50
❑453, Aug 1990 V: Riddler	1.50
❑454, Sep 1990 V: Riddler	1.50
❑455, Oct 1990	1.50
❑456, Nov 1990	1.50
❑457, Dec 1990; 1: new Robin costume. Timothy Drake as Robin	2.50
❑457/Direct ed., Dec 1990; with #000 on indicia	3.00
❑457-2, Dec 1990; Timothy Drake as Robin	2.00
❑458, Jan 1991 1: Harold	1.50
❑459, Feb 1991	1.50
❑460, Mar 1991; A: Catwoman	1.50
❑461, Apr 1991; A: Catwoman	1.50
❑462, May 1991	1.50
❑463, Jun 1991	1.50
❑464, Jul 1991	1.50
❑465, Jul 1991; Robin	1.50
❑466, Aug 1991; Robin	1.50
❑467, Aug 1991; A: Robin. Covers form triptych	1.50
❑468, Sep 1991; A: Robin. Covers form triptych	1.50
❑469, Sep 1991; A: Robin. Covers form triptych	1.50
❑470, Oct 1991; War of the Gods	1.50
❑471, Nov 1991	1.50
❑472, Dec 1991	1.50
❑473, Jan 1992	1.50
❑474, Feb 1992; Anton Furst's Gotham City	1.50
❑475, Mar 1992 V: Two-Face. V: Scarface. V: Ventriloquist	1.50
❑476, Apr 1992	1.50
❑477, May 1992	1.50
❑478, May 1992	1.50
❑479, Jun 1992	1.50
❑480, Jun 1992 JA (a)	1.50
❑481, Jul 1992 JA (a)	1.50
❑482, Jul 1992 JA (a)	1.50
❑483, Aug 1992 JA (a)	1.50
❑484, Sep 1992	1.50
❑485, Oct 1992	1.50
❑486, Nov 1992 V: Metalhead	1.50
❑487, Dec 1992	1.25
❑488, Jan 1993; JA (a); Robin trains Azrael	2.50
❑489, Feb 1993 JA (a); 1: Azrael (as Batman). A: Bane	2.50
❑490, Mar 1993; JA (a); Riddler on Venom	2.50

	N-MINT
❑491, Apr 1993; JA (a); Knightfall prequel	2.50
❑492, May 1993	2.50
❑492/Silver, May 1993; Silver edition printing	4.50
❑492-2, May 1993	2.00
❑493, May 1993 V: Mr. Zsasz	3.00
❑494, Jun 1993 JA (a); V: Scarecrow	2.00
❑495, Jun 1993 JA (a); V: Poison Ivy	2.00
❑496, Jul 1993 JA (a); V: Joker	2.00
❑497, Jul 1993; JA (a); partial overlay outer cover; Bane cripples Batman	3.00
❑497-2, Jul 1993; JA (a); 2nd Printing, also has partial overlay; Bane cripples Batman	2.00
❑498, Aug 1993; JA (a); Azrael takes on role of Batman	2.00
❑499, Sep 1993 JA (a)	2.00
❑500, Oct 1993; Giant-size; JA (a); Azrael vs. Bane, with poster	2.00
❑500/CS, Oct 1993; Giant-size; JA (a); diecut; two-level cover; Azrael vs. Bane; Collector's set	4.00
❑501, Nov 1993	2.00
❑502, Dec 1993	2.00
❑503, Jan 1994 A: Catwoman	2.00
❑504, Feb 1994 A: Catwoman	2.00
❑505, Mar 1994	2.00
❑506, Apr 1994	2.00
❑507, May 1994	2.00
❑508, Jun 1994 D: Abattoir	2.00
❑509, Jul 1994	2.00
❑510, Aug 1994	2.00
❑511, Sep 1994; A: Batgirl. Zero Hour, A: Batgirl	2.00
❑512, Nov 1994 MGu, RT (a)	2.00
❑513, Dec 1994 MGu, RT (a)	2.00
❑514, Jan 1995	2.00
❑515, Feb 1995; Return of Bruce Wayne as Batman	2.00
❑515/Variant, Feb 1995; Embossed cover; Return of Bruce Wayne as Batman	4.00
❑516, Mar 1995	2.00
❑517, Apr 1995	2.00
❑518, May 1995 V: Black Mask	2.00
❑519, Jun 1995	2.00
❑520, Jul 1995	2.00
❑521, Aug 1995 V: Killer Croc	2.00
❑522, Sep 1995 V: Killer Croc, Swamp Thing	2.00
❑523, Oct 1995 V: Scarecrow	2.00
❑524, Nov 1995 V: Scarecrow	2.00
❑525, Dec 1995; V: Mr. Freeze. Underworld Unleashed	2.00
❑526, Jan 1996	2.00
❑527, Feb 1996 V: Two-Face	2.00
❑528, Mar 1996	2.00
❑529, Apr 1996	2.00
❑530, May 1996; Glow-in-the-dark cover	1.95
❑530/Variant, May 1996; Glow-in-the-dark cover	2.50
❑531, Jun 1996; Glow-in-the-dark cover	1.95
❑531/Variant, Jun 1996; Glow-in-the-dark cover	2.50
❑532, Jul 1996; Glow-in-the-dark cover	1.95
❑532/Variant, Jul 1996; glow-in-the-dark cardstock cover	2.50
❑533, Aug 1996 JA (a)	2.00
❑534, Sep 1996	2.00
❑535, Oct 1996; self-contained story, V: The Ogre and The Ape	2.00
❑535/Variant, Oct 1996; V: The Ogre and The Ape. Die-cut cover; self-contained story	4.00
❑536, Nov 1996; Final Night	2.00
❑537, Dec 1996 A: Man-Bat. V: Man-Bat	2.00
❑538, Jan 1997 A: Man-Bat	2.00
❑539, Feb 1997	2.00
❑540, Mar 1997 A: Spectre	2.00
❑541, Apr 1997 A: Spectre	2.00
❑542, May 1997	2.00
❑543, Jun 1997	2.00

	N-MINT
❑544, Jul 1997 A: Demon	2.00
❑545, Aug 1997 A: Demon	2.00
❑546, Sep 1997 A: Demon	2.00
❑547, Oct 1997; Genesis	2.00
❑548, Nov 1997 V: Penguin	2.00
❑549, Dec 1997; V: Penguin. Face cover	2.00
❑550, Jan 1998 2: Chase	3.00
❑550/Variant, Jan 1998 2: Chase	3.50
❑551, Feb 1998 A: Ragman	2.00
❑552, Mar 1998 A: Ragman	2.00
❑553, Apr 1998; KJ (a); continues in Azrael #40	2.00
❑554, May 1998 KJ (a); V: Quakemaster, continues in Batman: Huntress-Spoiler - Blunt Trauma #1	2.00
❑555, Jun 1998; V: Ratcatcher. Aftershock	2.00
❑556, Jul 1998; Aftershock	2.00
❑557, Aug 1998; SB (a); Aftershock, A: Ballistic	2.00
❑558, Sep 1998; Aftershock	2.00
❑559, Oct 1998; Aftershock	2.00
❑560, Dec 1998; Road to No Man's Land, Bruce Wayne testifies	2.00
❑561, Jan 1999; JA (a); Road to No Man's Land, Bruce Wayne testifies	2.00
❑562, Feb 1999; JA (a); A: Mayor Grange. Road to No Man's Land, Gotham City is cut off	2.00
❑563, Mar 1999; A: Oracle. V: Joker. No Man's Land	3.00
❑564, Apr 1999; A: Scarecrow. A: Huntress. No Man's Land	2.50
❑565, May 1999; No Man's Land	2.00
❑566, Jun 1999; A: Superman. No Man's Land	2.00
❑567, Jul 1999; No Man's Land	2.00
❑568, Aug 1999; BSz (a); A: Poison Ivy. No Man's Land V: Clayface	2.00
❑569, Sep 1999; No Man's Land	2.00
❑570, Oct 1999; V: Joker. No Man's Land	2.00
❑571, Nov 1999; V: Bane. No Man's Land	2.00
❑572, Dec 1999; No Man's Land	2.00
❑573, Jan 2000; No Man's Land	2.00
❑574, Feb 2000; No Man's Land	2.00
❑575, Mar 2000	2.00
❑576, Apr 2000	2.00
❑577, May 2000	2.00
❑578, Jun 2000	2.00
❑579, Jul 2000	2.00
❑580, Aug 2000 V: Orca	2.25
❑581, Sep 2000 V: Orca	2.25
❑582, Oct 2000	2.25
❑583, Nov 2000	2.25
❑584, Dec 2000	2.25
❑585, Jan 2001	2.25
❑586, Feb 2001	2.25
❑587, Mar 2001	2.25
❑588, Apr 2001	2.25
❑589, May 2001	2.25
❑590, Jun 2001	2.25
❑591, Jul 2001	2.25
❑592, Aug 2001	2.25
❑593, Sep 2001	2.25
❑594, Oct 2001	2.25
❑595, Nov 2001	2.25
❑596, Dec 2001; Joker: Last Laugh crossover	2.25
❑597, Jan 2002	2.25
❑598, Feb 2002	2.25
❑599, Mar 2002	2.25
❑600, Apr 2002; Giant-size anniversary issue	3.95
❑601, May 2002	2.25
❑602, Jun 2002	2.25
❑603, Jul 2002	2.25
❑604, Aug 2002	2.25
❑605, Sep 2002	2.25
❑606, Oct 2002	2.25
❑607, Nov 2002	2.25
❑608, Dec 2002 JPH (w); JLee (a)	5.00
❑608-2, Dec 2002	2.25

N-MINT

❑608/DF, Dec 2002; Dynamic Forces signed edition 5.00
❑608/RRP, Dec 2002; Retailer incentive promo (aka RRP edition); alternate cover with no cover price 400.00
❑609, Jan 2003 JPH (w); JLee (a) 4.00
❑610, Feb 2003 JPH (w); JLee (a) 2.25
❑611, Mar 2003 JPH (w); JLee (a) 2.25
❑612, Apr 2003; JPH (w); JLee (a); A: Superman. alternate cover with no cover price 2.25
❑612-2, Apr 2003; alternate cover with no cover price 2.25
❑613, May 2003; JPH (w); JLee (a); alternate cover with no cover price 2.25
❑614, Jun 2003 .... 2.25
❑615, Jul 2003 .... 2.25
❑616, Aug 2003 .... 2.25
❑617, Sep 2003 .... 3.00
❑618, Oct 2003 .... 3.00
❑619, Nov 2003 O: Batman 5.00
❑620, Dec 2003 .... 2.25
❑621, Jan 2004 .... 2.25
❑622, Feb 2004 .... 2.25
❑623, Mar 2004 .... 2.25
❑624, Apr 2004 .... 2.25
❑625, May 2004 .... 2.25
❑626, Jun 2004 .... 2.25
❑627, Jul 2004 .... 2.25
❑628, Jul 2004 .... 2.25
❑629, Aug 2004 .... 2.25
❑630, Sep 2004 ....
❑1000000, Nov 1998 SB (a) 3.00
❑Annual 1, ca. 1961 CS (a); O: The Batcave 540.00
❑Annual 1-2, ca. 1999; O: The Batcave. cardstock cover; Reprint 5.50
❑Annual 2, ca. 1961 .... 275.00
❑Annual 3, Sum 1962; 80-Page Giant 215.00
❑Annual 4, Win 1963; 80-Page Giant 110.00
❑Annual 5, Sum 1963; 80-Page Giant 110.00
❑Annual 6, Win 1964 .... 85.00
❑Annual 7, Sum 1964 .... 85.00
❑Annual 8 1982 A: Ra's Al Ghul 7.00
❑Annual 9 1985 JOy, PS, AN (a) 6.00
❑Annual 10 1986 .... 6.00
❑Annual 11 1987 AMo (w) 6.00
❑Annual 12 1988 .... 5.00
❑Annual 13 1989; Who's Who entries 5.00
❑Annual 14 1990 O: Two-Face 3.00
❑Annual 15 1991 A: Joker 3.00
❑Annual 15-2 1991 .... 2.00
❑Ann 15-3/Silver 1991 .... 2.00
❑Annual 16 1992; A: Joker. Eclipso ... 3.00
❑Annual 17 1993; 1: Ballistic. Bloodlines: Earthplague 3.00
❑Annual 18 1994; Elseworlds 3.00
❑Annual 19 1995; O: Scarecrow. Year One 4.00
❑Annual 20 1996; Legends of the Dead Earth 3.00
❑Annual 21 1997; Pulp Heroes 3.95
❑Annual 22 1998; Ghosts 2.95
❑Annual 23, Sep 1999; JLApe 2.95
❑Annual 24, Oct 2000 JA (a); 1: The Boggart 3.50
❑Giant Size 1, Aug 1998 KJ, DGry (w); KJ (a) 4.95
❑Giant Size 2, Oct 1999 SB (a) 4.95
❑Giant Size 3, Jul 2000 BSz, JSa (a) . 5.95

BATMAN: TERROR
DC

❑1, ca. 2003 .... 12.95

BATMAN 3-D
DC

❑1, ca. 1990 .... 9.95

BATMAN ABSOLUTION SC
DC

❑0 .... 0.00

BATMAN ADVENTURES
DC

❑1, Apr 2003 .... 2.25
❑2, May 2003 .... 2.25

N-MINT

❑3, Jun 2003 .... 2.25
❑4, Jul 2003 .... 2.25
❑5, Aug 2003 .... 2.25
❑6, Sep 2003 .... 2.25
❑7, Oct 2003 .... 2.25
❑8, Nov 2003 .... 2.25
❑9, Dec 2003 .... 2.25
❑10, Jan 2004 .... 2.25
❑11, Apr 2004 .... 2.25
❑12, May 2004 .... 2.25
❑13, Jun 2004 .... 2.25
❑14, Jul 2004 .... 2.25
❑15, Aug 2004 .... 2.25
❑16, Sep 2004 ....

BATMAN ADVENTURES, THE
DC

❑1, Oct 1992; A: Penguin. based on animated series, V: Penguin 3.00
❑1/Silver, Oct 1992; silver edition 2.00
❑2, Nov 1992 A: Catwoman. V: Catwoman 2.00
❑3, Dec 1992 A: Joker. V: Joker 2.00
❑4, Jan 1993; Robin 2.00
❑5, Feb 1993 A: Scarecrow. V: Scarecrow 2.00
❑6, Mar 1993 .... 2.00
❑7, Apr 1993 V: Killer Croc 2.00
❑7/CS, Apr 1993; trading card, V: Killer Croc 2.00
❑8, May 1993 .... 2.00
❑9, Jun 1993 .... 2.00
❑10, Jul 1993 V: Riddler 2.00
❑11, Aug 1993 V: Man-Bat 1.50
❑12, Sep 1993; Batgirl 1.50
❑13, Oct 1993 .... 1.50
❑14, Nov 1993; Robin 1.50
❑15, Dec 1993 .... 1.50
❑16, Jan 1994 A: Joker. V: Joker 1.50
❑17, Feb 1994 .... 1.50
❑18, Mar 1994; Batgirl-Robin 1.50
❑19, Apr 1994 V: Scarecrow 1.50
❑20, May 1994 .... 1.50
❑21, Jun 1994; Holiday special A: Catwoman. V: Man-Bat. V: Mr. Freeze . 1.50
❑22, Jul 1994 V: Two-Face 1.50
❑23, Aug 1994 V: Poison Ivy 1.50
❑24, Sep 1994 .... 1.50
❑25, Oct 1994; Giant-size A: Lex Luthor. A: Superman 2.50
❑26, Nov 1994 A: Batgirl 1.50
❑27, Dec 1994 .... 1.50
❑28, Jan 1995 A: Harley Quinn 1.50
❑29, Feb 1995 V: Ra's Al Ghul 1.50
❑30, Mar 1995 O: The Perfesser. O: Mister Nice. O: Mastermind (DC) .. 1.50
❑31, Apr 1995 .... 1.50
❑32, Jun 1995 .... 1.50
❑33, Jul 1995 .... 1.75
❑34, Aug 1995 A: Catwoman. V: Hugo Strange 1.75
❑35, Sep 1995 A: Catwoman. V: Hugo Strange 1.75
❑36, Oct 1995 A: Catwoman. V: Hugo Strange 1.75
❑Annual 1 1994 MW (a) 2.95
❑Annual 2 1995 A: The Demon 3.50
❑Holiday 1, Jan 1995; gatefold summary V: Mr. Freeze 2.95

BATMAN ADVENTURES, THE: MAD LOVE
DC

❑1, Feb 1994 O: Harley Quinn. A: Joker 7.50
❑1-2 1994; prestige format O: Harley Quinn. A: Joker 5.50

BATMAN ADVENTURES, THE: THE LOST YEARS
DC

❑1, Jan 1998; fills in time between first and second Batman animated series 2.00
❑2, Feb 1998 A: Robin II 2.00
❑3, Mar 1998 V: Two-Face 2.00
❑4, Apr 1998 .... 2.00
❑5, May 1998 A: Nightwing 2.00

Bane, a super-criminal who had learned Batman's secret identity, broke the Caped Crusader's back in *Batman* #497.

© 1993 DC Comics.

N-MINT

BATMAN/ALIENS
DARK HORSE

❑1, Mar 1997; prestige format; BWr (a); crossover with DC 5.00
❑2, Apr 1997; prestige format; BWr (a); crossover with DC 5.00

BATMAN/ALIENS II TP
DC

❑1, ca. 2003 .... 14.95

BATMAN/ALIENS II
DC-DARK HORSE

❑1 2003 .... 5.95
❑2 2003 .... 5.95
❑3 2003 .... 5.95

BATMAN: A LONELY PLACE OF DYING
DC

❑

BATMAN AND OTHER DC CLASSICS
DC

❑1, ca. 1989, KG (w); GP, BB, FM (a); O: Batman. Includes guide to collecting comics by Don & Maggie Thompson 2.00

BATMAN AND ROBIN ADVENTURES, THE
DC

❑1, Nov 1995 .... 3.00
❑2, Dec 1995 V: Two-Face 2.00
❑3, Jan 1996 V: Riddler 2.00
❑4, Feb 1996 V: Penguin 2.00
❑5, Mar 1996 V: Joker 2.00
❑6, May 1996 .... 1.75
❑7, Jun 1996 V: Scarface 1.75
❑8, Jul 1996; Robin is enslaved by Poison Ivy 1.75
❑9, Aug 1996; Batgirl versus Talia 1.75
❑10, Sep 1996 V: Ra's Al Ghul 1.75
❑11, Oct 1996 .... 1.75
❑12, Nov 1996 V: Bane 1.75
❑13, Dec 1996 V: Scarecrow 1.75
❑14, Jan 1997 .... 1.75
❑15, Feb 1997 A: Deadman 1.75
❑16, Mar 1997 A: Catwoman 1.75
❑17, Apr 1997 .... 1.75
❑18, May 1997 V: Joker 1.75
❑19, Jun 1997 .... 1.75
❑20, Jul 1997 .... 1.75
❑21, Aug 1997; JSa (a); Batgirl vs. Riddler 1.75
❑22, Sep 1997 V: Two-Face 1.75
❑23, Oct 1997 V: Killer Croc 1.75
❑24, Nov 1997 V: Poison Ivy 1.75
❑25, Dec 1997; Giant-size; V: Ra's Al Ghul. Face cover 2.95
❑Annual 1, Nov 1996; sequel to Batman: Mask of the Phantasm 2.95
❑Annual 2, Nov 1997; JSa (a); A: Zatara. A: Zatanna. ties in with Adventures in the DC Universe Annual #1 and Superman Adventures Annual #1 .. 3.95

BATMAN AND ROBIN ADVENTURES, THE: SUB-ZERO
DC

❑1 1998; cover says 98; adapts direct-to-video movie; indicia says 97 ...... 3.95

Condition price index: Multiply "NM prices" above by: **0.83 for Very Fine/Near Mint**
0.66 for Very Fine • 0.33 for Fine • 0.2 for Very Good • 0.125 for Good

N-MINT

BATMAN AND ROBIN: THE OFFICIAL ADAPTATION OF THE WARNER BROS. MOTION PICTURE
DC

❑1, ca. 1997; prestige format 5.95

BATMAN & SUPERMAN ADVENTURES: WORLD'S FINEST
DC

❑1 1997; prestige format; adapts 90-minute special 6.95

BATMAN AND SUPERMAN: WORLD'S FINEST
DC

❑1, Apr 1999; prestige format 2.50
❑1/Autographed 18.95
❑2, May 1999 .... 2.00
❑3, Jun 1999 V: Joker 2.00
❑4, Jul 1999 .... 2.00
❑5, Aug 1999 A: Batgirl 2.00
❑6, Sep 1999 A: Bat-Mite. A: Mr. Mxyzptlk 2.00
❑7, Oct 1999 .... 2.00
❑8, Nov 1999 .... 2.00
❑9, Dec 1999 .... 2.00
❑10, Jan 2000 .... 2.00

BATMAN AND THE OUTSIDERS
DC

❑1, Aug 1983 O: Geo-Force. 1: Baron Bedlam 3.00
❑2, Sep 1983 JA (a); V: Baron Bedlam 2.00
❑3, Oct 1983 JA (a); V: Agent Orange 2.00
❑4, Nov 1983 JA (a) 2.00
❑5, Dec 1983 JA (a); A: New Teen Titans 2.00
❑6, Jan 1984 .... 1.50
❑7, Feb 1984 .... 1.50
❑8, Mar 1984 .... 1.50
❑9, Apr 1984 1: Masters of Disaster . 1.50
❑10, May 1984 V: Masters of Disaster 1.50
❑11, Jun 1984 O: Katana 1.50
❑12, Jul 1984 O: Katana 1.50
❑13, Aug 1984 .... 1.50
❑14, Oct 1984 V: Maxie Zeus 1.50
❑15, Nov 1984 V: Maxie Zeus 1.50
❑16, Dec 1984 .... 1.50
❑17, Jan 1985 .... 1.50
❑18, Feb 1985 .... 1.50
❑19, Mar 1985 .... 1.50
❑20, Apr 1985 1: Syonide II 1.50
❑21, May 1985 .... 1.50
❑22, Jun 1985 .... 1.50
❑23, Jul 1985 .... 1.50
❑24, Aug 1985 .... 1.50
❑25, Sep 1985 .... 1.50
❑26, Oct 1985 V: Kobra 1.50
❑27, Nov 1985 .... 1.50
❑28, Dec 1985 .... 1.50
❑29, Jan 1986 .... 1.50
❑30, Feb 1986 .... 1.50
❑31, Mar 1986 .... 1.50
❑32, Apr 1986; Series continues as Adventures of the Outsiders; Batman leaves 1.50
❑Annual 1, ca. 1984 FM (c); FM (a); 1: Force of July. 1: Major Victory 2.00
❑Annual 2, ca. 1985; JA (a); Wedding of Metamorpho and Sapphire Stag 2.00

BATMAN: ARKHAM ASYLUM - TALES OF MADNESS
DC

❑1, May 1998 .... 2.95

BATMAN: ARROW, RING AND BAT
DC

❑1, ca. 2003 .... 19.95

BATMAN: A WORD TO THE WISE
DC

❑1; (DC giveaway) 1.25

BATMAN: BANE
DC

❑1, Jul 1997; prestige format one-shot, cover is part of quadtych 4.95

BATMAN: BANE OF THE DEMON
DC

❑1, Mar 1998 .... 1.95
❑2, Apr 1998 .... 1.95
❑3, May 1998 .... 1.95
❑4, Jun 1998 .... 1.95

BATMAN: BATGIRL
DC

❑1, Jul 1997; prestige format one-shot; cover is part of quadtych 4.95

BATMAN: BATGIRL (GIRLFRENZY)
DC

❑1, Jun 1998; Girlfrenzy; one-shot, V: Mr. Zsasz 1.95

BATMAN BEYOND
DC

❑1, Nov 1999; adapts first episode 2.50
❑2, Dec 1999; adapts first episode 2.00
❑3, Jan 2000 V: Blight 2.00
❑4, Feb 2000 A: Demon 1.99
❑5, Mar 2000 .... 1.99
❑6, Apr 2000 .... 1.99
❑7, May 2000 .... 1.99
❑8, Jun 2000 .... 1.99
❑9, Jul 2000 .... 1.99
❑10, Aug 2000 V: Golem 1.99
❑11, Sep 2000 .... 1.99
❑12, Oct 2000 V: Terminal 1.99
❑13, Nov 2000 A: Scarecrow. A: Batgirl 1.99
❑14, Dec 2000 A: Demon 1.99
❑15, Jan 2001 .... 1.99
❑16, Feb 2001 .... 1.99
❑17, Mar 2001 .... 1.99
❑18, Apr 2001 .... 1.99
❑19, May 2001 .... 1.99
❑20, Jun 2001 .... 1.99
❑21, Jul 2001 .... 1.99
❑22, Aug 2001 .... 1.99
❑23, Sep 2001 .... 1.99
❑24, Oct 2001 .... 1.99

BATMAN BEYOND (MINI-SERIES)
DC

❑1, Mar 1999; O: Batman II (Terry McGuiness). adapts first episode .. 2.50
❑2, Apr 1999; O: Batman II (Terry McGuiness). A: Derek Powers. adapts first episode 2.00
❑3, May 1999 V: Blight 2.00
❑4, Jun 1999 JSa (a); A: Demon 2.00
❑5, Jul 1999 .... 2.00
❑6, Aug 1999 JSa (a) 2.00

BATMAN BEYOND: RETURN OF THE JOKER
DC

❑1, Feb 2001 .... 2.95

BATMAN BEYOND SPECIAL ORIGIN ISSUE
DC

❑1, Jun 1999; Free 1.00

BATMAN BLACK AND WHITE
DC

❑1, Jun 1996, b&w JLee (c); HC, JKu (a) 3.50
❑2, Jul 1996, b&w FM (c) 3.00
❑3, Aug 1996, b&w MW, BSz, KJ (a) . 3.00
❑4, Sep 1996, b&w ATh (c) 3.00

BATMAN: BLACKGATE
DC

❑1, Jan 1997 .... 3.95

BATMAN: BLACKGATE, ISLE OF MEN
DC

❑1, Apr 1998; one-shot, continues in Batman: Shadow of the Bat #74 .... 2.95

BATMAN: BOOK OF THE DEAD
DC

❑1, Jun 1999 .... 4.95
❑2, Jul 1999 .... 4.95

BATMAN: BULLOCK'S LAW
DC

❑1, Aug 1999 .... 4.95

BATMAN/CAPTAIN AMERICA
DC

❑1 1996; prestige format crossover with Marvel, Elseworlds; prestige format crossover with Marvel; Elseworlds ... 5.95

BATMAN: CASTLE OF THE BAT
DC

❑1 1994; prestige format; Elseworlds 5.95

BATMAN: CATWOMAN DEFIANT
DC

❑1; prestige format; cover forms diptych with Batman: Penguin Triumphant ... 5.00

BATMAN: CHILD OF DREAMS
DC

❑1/Variant, ca. 2003 .... 19.95
❑1/HC, ca. 2003 .... 24.95

BATMAN CHRONICLES, THE
DC

❑1, Jun 1995; Giant-size BSz (a) 4.00
❑2, Sep 1995 .... 3.50
❑3, Dec 1995 BB (c); BSz (a); O: Mr. Zsasz. A: Riddler. A: Killer Croc 3.50
❑4, Mar 1996 A: Hitman 4.00
❑5, Jun 1996 HC (c); O: Oracle 3.50
❑6, Sep 1996 CS (a) 3.50
❑7, Dec 1996 JO (c); JA (a); A: Superman 3.50
❑8, Mar 1997 SB (a); V: Ra's Al Ghul . 3.50
❑9, Jun 1997; Movie poster cover 3.50
❑10, Sep 1997 BSz (a) 3.50
❑11, Dec 1997 .... 3.50
❑12, Mar 1998 BSz, KJ (a) 3.50
❑13, Jun 1998 SB, DG (a) 3.00
❑14, Sep 1998; Aftershock 3.00
❑15, Dec 1998; A: Man-Bat. A: Green Lantern. A: Question. A: Oracle. team-up issue 3.00
❑16, Mar 1999; A: Renee Montoya. A: Batgirl. A: Two Face. No Man's Land 3.00
❑17, Jun 1999; BSz (a); No Man's Land; Man-Bat's child 3.00
❑18, Sep 1999; DGry (w); No Man's Land 3.00
❑19, Dec 1999 .... 3.00
❑20, Mar 2000 DGry (w) 3.00
❑21, Jun 2000 .... 2.95
❑22, Sep 2000 .... 2.95
❑23, Dec 2000 KN (w); KN (a) 2.95

BATMAN CHRONICLES GALLERY, THE
DC

❑1, May 1997; pin-ups 3.50

BATMAN CHRONICLES: THE GAUNTLET
DC

❑1 1997; prestige format; 1st Robin solo adventure 4.95

BATMAN: CITY OF LIGHT
DC

❑1, Dec 2003 .... 2.95
❑2, Jan 2004 .... 2.95
❑3, Feb 2004 .... 2.95
❑4, Mar 2004 .... 2.95
❑5, Apr 2004 .... 2.95
❑6, May 2004 .... 2.95
❑7, Jun 2004 .... 2.95
❑8, Jul 2004 .... 2.95

BATMAN: CULT
DC

❑1, ca. 2003 .... 19.95

BATMAN/DAREDEVIL
DC

❑1 2000 .... 5.95

BATMAN: DARK ALLEGIANCES
DC

❑1 1996 .... 5.95

Condition price index: Multiply "NM prices" above by: **0.83 for Very Fine/Near Mint • 0.66 for Very Fine • 0.33 for Fine • 0.2 for Very Good • 0.125 for Good**

N-MINT

BATMAN: THE DARK KNIGHT ADVENTURES
DC

❑1 ... 7.95

BATMAN: DARK KNIGHT GALLERY
DC

❑1, Jan 1996; pin-ups ... 3.50

BATMAN: DARK KNIGHT OF THE ROUND TABLE
DC

❑1, ca. 1999; prestige format; Elseworlds story ... 4.95
❑2, ca. 1999; prestige format; Elseworlds story ... 4.95

BATMAN: DARK VICTORY
DC

❑0, ca. 1999; Wizard giveaway ... 1.00
❑1, Dec 1999; prestige format ... 5.00
❑2, Jan 2000; cardstock cover ... 3.00
❑3, Feb 2000; cardstock cover ... 3.00
❑4, Mar 2000; cardstock cover ... 3.00
❑5, Apr 2000; cardstock cover ... 3.00
❑6, May 2000; cardstock cover ... 3.00
❑7, Jun 2000; cardstock cover ... 3.00
❑8, Jul 2000; cardstock cover ... 3.00
❑9, Aug 2000; cardstock cover ... 3.00
❑10, Sep 2000; cardstock cover ... 3.00
❑11, Oct 2000; cardstock cover ... 3.00
❑12, Nov 2000; cardstock cover ... 3.00
❑13, Dec 2000; prestige format ... 3.00

BATMAN: DAY OF JUDGMENT
DC

❑1, Nov 1999 ... 3.95

BATMAN: DEATH AND THE MAIDENS
DC

❑1, Oct 2003 ... 2.95
❑2, Nov 2003 ... 2.95
❑3, Dec 2003 ... 2.95
❑4, Jan 2004 ... 2.95
❑5, Feb 2004 ... 2.95
❑6, Mar 2004 ... 2.95
❑7, Apr 2004 ... 2.95
❑8, Jun 2004 ... 2.95
❑9, Jun 2004 ... 2.95

BATMAN/DEATHBLOW: AFTER THE FIRE
DC

❑1, May 2002 ... 5.95
❑2, Jun 2002 ... 5.95
❑3, Oct 2002 ... 5.95

BATMAN: DEATH OF INNOCENTS
DC

❑1, Dec 1996; one-shot about the dangers of landmines and unexploded ordnance ... 3.95

BATMAN/DEMON
DC

❑1 1996; prestige format one-shot ... 4.95

BATMAN/DEMON: A TRAGEDY
DC

❑1 2000 ... 5.95

BATMAN: DOA
DC

❑1, Jan 2000 ... 6.95

BATMAN FAMILY, THE
DC

❑1, Oct 1975 ... 14.00
❑2, Dec 1975 ... 10.00
❑3, Feb 1976 ... 8.00
❑4, Apr 1976 CI (a); A: Fatman ... 8.00
❑5, Jun 1976 ... 8.00
❑6, Aug 1976 ... 8.00
❑7, Sep 1976 ... 6.00
❑8, Nov 1976 ... 6.00
❑9, Jan 1977 A: Duela Dent ... 7.00
❑10, Mar 1977 ... 7.00
❑11, May 1977 ... 7.00
❑12, Jul 1977 ... 7.00
❑13, Sep 1977 A: Man-Bat. V: Outsider ... 5.00

N-MINT

❑14, Oct 1977 ... 5.00
❑15, Dec 1977 ... 5.00
❑16, Feb 1978 ... 5.00
❑17, Apr 1978 ... 7.00
❑18, Jun 1978 ... 7.00
❑19, Aug 1978 ... 7.00
❑20, Oct 1978 ... 7.00

BATMAN: FAMILY
DC

❑1, Dec 2002 ... 2.95
❑2, Jan 2003 ... 2.95
❑3, Jan 2003 ... 2.95
❑4, Jan 2003 ... 2.95
❑5, Jan 2003 ... 2.95
❑6, Feb 2003 ... 2.95
❑7, Feb 2003 ... 2.95
❑8, Feb 2003 ... 2.95

BATMAN FOREVER: THE OFFICIAL COMIC ADAPTATION OF THE WARNER BROS. MOTION PICTURE
DC

❑1 1995 ... 3.95
❑1/Prestige; movie adaptation, prestige format ... 5.95

BATMAN: FULL CIRCLE
DC

❑1, ca. 1991, b&w; prestige format ... 6.00

BATMAN GALLERY, THE
DC

❑1 ... 2.95

BATMAN: GCPD
DC

❑1, Aug 1996 ... 2.25
❑2, Sep 1996 ... 2.25
❑3, Oct 1996 ... 2.25
❑4, Nov 1996 ... 2.25

BATMAN: GHOSTS
DC

❑1 1995; prestige format one-shot ... 4.95

BATMAN: GORDON OF GOTHAM
DC

❑1, Jun 1998 ... 1.95
❑2, Jul 1998 ... 1.95
❑3, Aug 1998 ... 1.95
❑4, Sep 1998 ... 1.95

BATMAN: GORDON'S LAW
DC

❑1, Dec 1996 ... 1.95
❑2, Jan 1997 ... 1.95
❑3, Feb 1997 ... 1.95
❑4, Mar 1997 ... 1.95

BATMAN: GOTHAM ADVENTURES
DC

❑1, Jun 1998; based on animated series, Joker has a price on his head ... 3.00
❑2, Jul 1998 V: Two-Face ... 2.50
❑3, Aug 1998; cover is toy package mock-up ... 2.50
❑4, Sep 1998 V: Catwoman ... 2.50
❑5, Oct 1998 ... 2.50
❑6, Nov 1998 A: Deadman ... 2.50
❑7, Dec 1998 ... 2.50
❑8, Jan 1999 1: Hunchback. A: Batgirl ... 2.50
❑9, Feb 1999 A: League of Assassins. A: Batgirl. V: Sensei ... 2.50
❑10, Mar 1999 A: Joker. A: Nightwing. A: Harley Quinn. A: Robin III (Timothy Drake) ... 2.50
❑11, Apr 1999 A: Riddler. V: Riddler ... 2.00
❑12, May 1999 V: Two-Face ... 2.00
❑13, Jun 1999 A: final ... 2.00
❑14, Jul 1999 V: Harley Quinn ... 2.00
❑15, Aug 1999 A: Bane. V: Venom ... 2.00
❑16, Sep 1999; Alfred is kidnapped ... 2.00
❑17, Oct 1999 ... 2.00
❑18, Nov 1999 A: Man-Bat ... 2.00
❑19, Dec 1999 ... 2.00
❑20, Jan 2000 ... 2.00
❑21, Feb 2000 ... 2.00
❑22, Mar 2000 ... 2.00

The adventures of teen-ager Terry McGinnis, who takes on the mantle of Batman in the future, are covered in *Batman Beyond*.

© 2000 DC Comics and Warner Bros. Animation.

N-MINT

❑23, Apr 2000 ... 2.00
❑24, May 2000 ... 2.00
❑25, Jun 2000 ... 2.00
❑26, Jul 2000 ... 2.00
❑27, Aug 2000 ... 2.00
❑28, Sep 2000 ... 2.00
❑29, Oct 2000 JSa (a) ... 2.00
❑30, Nov 2000 ... 2.00
❑31, Dec 2000 A: Joker ... 2.00
❑32, Jan 2001 ... 2.00
❑33, Feb 2001 ... 2.00
❑34, Mar 2001 ... 2.00
❑35, Apr 2001 ... 2.00
❑36, May 2001 ... 2.00
❑37, Jun 2001 A: Joker ... 2.00
❑38, Jul 2001 ... 2.00
❑39, Aug 2001 ... 2.00
❑40, Sep 2001 ... 2.00
❑41, Oct 2001 ... 2.00
❑42, Nov 2001 ... 2.00
❑43, Dec 2001 ... 2.00
❑44, Jan 2002 A: Two-Face ... 2.00
❑45, Feb 2002 ... 2.00
❑46, Mar 2002 ... 2.00
❑47, Apr 2002 ... 2.00
❑48, May 2002 ... 2.00
❑49, Jun 2002 ... 2.00
❑50, Jul 2002 ... 2.00
❑51, Aug 2002 ... 2.00
❑52, Sep 2002 ... 2.00
❑53, Oct 2002 ... 2.25
❑54, Nov 2002 ... 2.25
❑55, Dec 2002 ... 2.25
❑56, Jan 2003 ... 2.25
❑57, Feb 2003 ... 2.25
❑58, Mar 2003 ... 2.25
❑59, Apr 2003 ... 2.25
❑60, May 2003 ... 2.25

BATMAN: GOTHAM BY GASLIGHT
DC

❑1, ca. 1989, prestige format; CR (a); first Elseworlds story; Victorian-era Batman; Prelude by Robert Bloch ... 4.00

BATMAN GOTHAM CITY SECRET FILES
DC

❑1, Apr 2000 ... 4.95

BATMAN: GOTHAM KNIGHTS
DC

❑1, Mar 2000 ... 3.00
❑2, Apr 2000 ... 2.50
❑3, May 2000 ... 2.50
❑4, Jun 2000 ... 2.50
❑5, Jul 2000 ... 2.50
❑6, Aug 2000 ... 2.50
❑7, Sep 2000 ... 2.50
❑8, Oct 2000 ... 2.50
❑9, Nov 2000 ... 2.50
❑10, Dec 2000 ... 2.50
❑11, Jan 2001 ... 2.50
❑12, Feb 2001 ... 2.50
❑13, Mar 2001 ... 2.50
❑14, Apr 2001 ... 2.50
❑15, May 2001 ... 2.50
❑16, Jun 2001 ... 2.50
❑17, Jul 2001 ... 2.50
❑18, Aug 2001 ... 2.50

N-MINT

❑19, Sep 2001 .... 2.50
❑20, Oct 2001 .... 2.50
❑21, Nov 2001 .... 2.50
❑22, Dec 2001; Joker: Last Laugh crossover 2.50
❑23, Jan 2002 .... 2.50
❑24, Feb 2002 .... 2.50
❑25, Mar 2002 .... 2.50
❑26, Apr 2002 .... 2.50
❑27, May 2002 .... 2.50
❑28, Jun 2002 .... 2.50
❑29, Jul 2002 .... 2.50
❑30, Aug 2002 .... 2.50
❑31, Sep 2002 .... 2.50
❑32, Oct 2002 .... 2.75
❑33, Nov 2002 .... 2.75
❑34, Dec 2002 .... 2.75
❑35, Jan 2003 .... 2.75
❑36, Feb 2003 .... 2.75
❑37, Mar 2003 .... 2.75
❑38, Apr 2003 .... 2.75
❑39, May 2003 .... 2.75
❑40, Jun 2003 .... 2.75
❑41, Jul 2003 .... 2.75
❑42, Aug 2003 .... 2.75
❑43, Sep 2003 .... 2.75
❑44, Oct 2003 .... 2.75
❑45, Nov 2003 .... 2.75
❑46, Dec 2003 .... 2.75
❑47, Jan 2004 .... 2.75
❑48, Feb 2004 .... 2.75
❑49, Mar 2004 .... 2.75
❑50, Apr 2004 .... 2.75
❑51, May 2004 .... 2.75
❑52, Jun 2004 .... 2.75
❑52-2, Jul 2004; 2nd printing 2.95
❑53, Jul 2004 .... 2.95
❑54, Aug 2004 .... 2.95
❑55, Sep 2004 ....

BATMAN: GOTHAM NOIR
DC

❑1, May 2001; Elseworlds 6.95

BATMAN/GREEN ARROW: THE POISON TOMORROW
DC

❑1 1992; prestige format 6.00

BATMAN/GRENDEL (1ST SERIES)
DC / COMICO

❑1, ca. 1993; prestige format MW (a) 6.00
❑2, ca. 1993; MW (a); Index title: Grendel/Batman: Devil's Masque; prestige format, cover indicates Grendel/Batman 6.00

BATMAN/GRENDEL (2ND SERIES)
DC / DARK HORSE

❑1, Jun 1996; Batman/Grendel: Devil's Bones; prestige format crossover with Dark Horse; concludes in Grendel/Batman: Devil's Dance 5.00
❑2, Jul 1996; prestige format; MW (w); MW (a); Grendel/Batman: Devil's Dance; continued from Batman/Grendel: Devil's Bones 5.00

BATMAN: HARLEY & IVY
DC / WILDSTORM

❑1, Jun 2004 .... 2.50
❑2, Jul 2004 .... 2.50
❑3, Aug 2004 .... 2.50

BATMAN: HARLEY QUINN
DC

❑1, ca. 1999; prestige format ARo (c); ARo (a) 12.00
❑1-2 ARo (c); ARo (a) 6.00

BATMAN: HAUNTED GOTHAM
DC

❑1 2000; prestige format; Elseworlds 4.95
❑2 2000; prestige format; Elseworlds 4.95
❑3 2000; prestige format; Elseworlds 4.95
❑4 2000; prestige format; Elseworlds 4.95

N-MINT

BATMAN/HELLBOY/STARMAN
DC / DARK HORSE

❑1, Jan 1999 .... 3.00
❑1/Autographed, Jan 1999 .... 10.00
❑2, Feb 1999 .... 3.00

BATMAN: HOLLYWOOD KNIGHT
DC

❑1, Apr 2001; Elseworlds 2.50
❑2, May 2001; Elseworlds 2.50
❑3, Jun 2001; Elseworlds 2.50

BATMAN: HOLY TERROR
DC

❑1, Oct 1991; prestige format; Elseworlds 5.00

BATMAN: HONG KONG
DC

❑1, ca. 2003 .... 24.95

BATMAN/HOUDINI: THE DEVIL'S WORKSHOP
DC

❑1; prestige format; Elseworlds 4.50

BATMAN/HUNTRESS: CRY FOR BLOOD
DC

❑1, Jun 2000 .... 2.50
❑2, Jul 2000 .... 2.50
❑3, Aug 2000 .... 2.50
❑4, Sep 2000 .... 2.50
❑5, Oct 2000 .... 2.50
❑6, Nov 2000 .... 2.50

BATMAN: HUSH DOUBLE FEATURE
DC

❑1 2003; Reprints Batman #608-609 4.95

BATMAN: I, JOKER
DC

❑1, Oct 1998; prestige format; Elseworlds 4.95

BATMAN: IN DARKEST KNIGHT
DC

❑1, ca. 1994, prestige format; Elseworlds; Bruce Wayne as Green Lantern 4.95

BATMAN: JOKER'S APPRENTICE
DC

❑1, May 1999 .... 3.95

BATMAN/JOKER: SWITCH
DC

❑1, ca. 2003 .... 12.95

BATMAN: JOKER TIME
DC

❑1; prestige format 4.95
❑2; prestige format 4.95
❑3; prestige format 4.95

BATMAN/JUDGE DREDD: DIE LAUGHING
DC

❑1; prestige format; Joker in Mega-City One 4.95
❑2; prestige format; Joker in Mega-City One 4.95

BATMAN/JUDGE DREDD: J UDGMENT ON GOTHAM
DC

❑1 .... 5.95

BATMAN/JUDGE DREDD: THE ULTIMATE RIDDLE
DC

❑1; prestige format 5.00

BATMAN/JUDGE DREDD: VENDETTA IN GOTHAM
DC

❑1 1993 .... 6.00

BATMAN: LEAGUE OF BATMEN
DC

❑1, Jun 2001 .... 5.95
❑2, Jul 2001 .... 5.95

N-MINT

BATMAN: LEGENDS OF THE DARK KNIGHT
DC

❑0, Oct 1994 .... 2.50
❑1, Nov 1989; Outer cover comes in four different colors (yellow, blue, orange, pink); poster 3.00
❑2, Dec 1989 .... 2.75
❑3, Jan 1990 .... 2.75
❑4, Feb 1990 .... 2.75
❑5, Mar 1990 .... 2.75
❑6, Apr 1990 KJ (a) 2.50
❑7, May 1990 KJ (a) 2.50
❑8, Jun 1990 KJ (a) 2.50
❑9, Jul 1990 KJ (a) 2.50
❑10, Aug 1990 KJ (a) 2.50
❑11, Sep 1990 PG, TD (a) 2.50
❑12, Oct 1990 PG, TD (a) 2.50
❑13, Nov 1990 PG, TD (a) 2.50
❑14, Dec 1990 PG, TD (a) 2.50
❑15, Feb 1991 PG, TD (a) 2.50
❑16, Mar 1991; Tie-in to Bane/Knights End 3.50
❑17, Apr 1991; Tie-in to Bane/Knights End 2.50
❑18, May 1991; Tie-in to Bane/Knights End 2.50
❑19, Jun 1991; Tie-in to Bane/Knights End 2.50
❑20, Jul 1991; Tie-in to Bane/Knights End 2.50
❑21, Aug 1991 .... 2.00
❑22, Sep 1991 .... 2.00
❑23, Oct 1991 .... 2.00
❑24, Nov 1991 GK (a) 2.00
❑25, Dec 1991 GK (a) 2.00
❑26, Jan 1992 GK (a) 2.00
❑27, Feb 1992; Gotham City Visions by Anton Furst feature 2.50
❑28, Mar 1992; MW (a); Two-Face 2.00
❑29, Apr 1992; MW (a); Two-Face 2.00
❑30, May 1992; MW (a); Two-Face 2.00
❑31, Jun 1992 BA (a) 2.00
❑32, Jun 1992 JRo (w) 2.00
❑33, Jul 1992 JRo (w) 2.00
❑34, Jul 1992 JRo (w) 2.00
❑35, Aug 1992 .... 2.00
❑36, Aug 1992 .... 2.00
❑37, Aug 1992; Series continues as Batman: Legends of the Dark Knight 2.00
❑38, Oct 1992 A: Bat-Mite 2.00
❑39, Nov 1992 BT (a) 2.00
❑40, Dec 1992 BT (w); BT (a) 2.00
❑41, Jan 1993 .... 2.00
❑42, Feb 1993 CR (a) 2.00
❑43, Mar 1993 CR (a) 2.00
❑44, Apr 1993 .... 2.00
❑45, May 1993 .... 2.00
❑46, Jun 1993 RH (a); A: Catwoman. V: Catwoman. V: Catman 2.00
❑47, Jul 1993 RH (a); A: Catwoman. V: Catwoman. V: Catman 2.00
❑48, Aug 1993 RH (a); A: Catwoman. V: Catwoman. V: Catman 2.00
❑49, Aug 1993 RH (a); A: Catwoman. V: Catwoman. V: Catman 2.00
❑50, Sep 1993; Giant-size; A: Joker. foil cover 4.00
❑51, Sep 1993 JKu (c) 2.00
❑52, Oct 1993 .... 2.00
❑53, Oct 1993 .... 2.00
❑54, Nov 1993 .... 2.00
❑55, Dec 1993 .... 2.00
❑56, Jan 1994 .... 2.00
❑57, Feb 1994 .... 2.00
❑58, Mar 1994 .... 2.00
❑59, Apr 1994 .... 2.00
❑60, May 1994 .... 2.00
❑61, Jun 1994 .... 2.00
❑62, Jul 1994 .... 2.00
❑63, Aug 1994 .... 2.00
❑64, Sep 1994 .... 2.00
❑65, Nov 1994 JSa (a); A: Joker. V: Joker 2.00
❑66, Dec 1994 JSa (a); A: Joker. V: Joker 2.00

N-MINT

❑67, Jan 1995 JSa (a); A: Joker. V: Joker 2.00
❑68, Feb 1995 JSa (a); V: Joker 2.00
❑69, Mar 1995 MZ (a) 2.00
❑70, Apr 1995 MZ (a) 2.00
❑71, May 1995 2.00
❑72, Jun 1995 2.00
❑73, Jul 1995 2.00
❑74, Aug 1995 2.00
❑75, Sep 1995 2.00
❑76, Oct 1995 2.00
❑77, Nov 1995 2.00
❑78, Dec 1995 2.00
❑79, Jan 1996 2.00
❑80, Feb 1996 2.00
❑81, Mar 1996 2.00
❑82, May 1996 2.00
❑83, Jun 1996 2.00
❑84, Jul 1996 2.00
❑85, Aug 1996 2.00
❑86, Sep 1996 2.00
❑87, Oct 1996 2.00
❑88, Nov 1996 2.00
❑89, Dec 1996 O: Clayface (Matt Hagen) 2.00
❑90, Jan 1997 2.00
❑91, Feb 1997 2.00
❑92, Mar 1997 2.00
❑93, Apr 1997 2.00
❑94, May 1997; three eras of Batman 2.00
❑95, Jun 1997 2.00
❑96, Jul 1997 2.00
❑97, Aug 1997 2.00
❑98, Sep 1997 2.00
❑99, Oct 1997 2.00
❑100, Nov 1997; Double-size; ARo (c); JRo (w); ARo, FM, CS, KJ (a); O: Robin I and Robin II, pin-up gallery. O: Robin I and Robin II. A: Joker. pin-up gallery 4.50
❑101, Dec 1997; Face cover; 100 years in the future 2.00
❑102, Jan 1998 JRo (w) 2.00
❑103, Feb 1998 JRo (w) 2.00
❑104, Mar 1998 JRo (w) 2.00
❑105, Apr 1998 2.00
❑106, May 1998; Gordon vs. Joker 2.00
❑107, Jun 1998 2.00
❑108, Jul 1998 2.00
❑109, Aug 1998 V: Riddler 2.00
❑110, Sep 1998 V: Riddler 2.00
❑111, Oct 1998 V: Riddler 2.00
❑112, Nov 1998 2.00
❑113, Dec 1998 2.00
❑114, Jan 1999 2.00
❑115, Feb 1999; LMc (a); The Darkness 2.00
❑116, Apr 1999; A: Scarecrow. A: Huntress. No Man's Land 2.00
❑117, May 1999; V: Penguin. No Man's Land 2.00
❑118, Jun 1999; No Man's Land 2.00
❑119, Jul 1999; A: Two-Face. No Man's Land 2.00
❑120, Aug 1999; 1: Batgirl III (in costume). A: Huntress. A: Nightwing. A: Robin. No Man's Land 3.50
❑121, Sep 1999; V: Mr. Freeze. No Man's Land 2.00
❑122, Oct 1999; PG (a); A: Lynx. No Man's Land 2.00
❑123, Nov 1999; No Man's Land 2.00
❑124, Dec 1999; No Man's Land 2.00
❑125, Jan 2000; No Man's Land; Batman attempts to reveal identity to Commissioner Gordon 2.00
❑126, Feb 2000; DGry (w); No Man's Land 2.00
❑127, Mar 2000 2.00
❑128, Apr 2000 2.00
❑129, May 2000 2.00
❑130, Jun 2000 2.00
❑131, Jul 2000 2.00
❑132, Aug 2000 JRo (a); A: Silver St. Cloud 2.00
❑133, Sep 2000 JRo (a); A: Silver St. Cloud 2.25

N-MINT

❑134, Oct 2000 JRo (a); A: Silver St. Cloud 2.25
❑135, Nov 2000 JRo (a) 2.25
❑136, Dec 2000 JRo (a) 2.25
❑137, Jan 2001 PG (a) 2.25
❑138, Feb 2001 PG (a) 2.25
❑139, Mar 2001 PG (a) 2.25
❑140, Apr 2001 PG (a) 2.25
❑141, May 2001 PG (a) 2.25
❑142, Jun 2001 JA (a) 2.25
❑143, Jul 2001 JA (a) 2.25
❑144, Aug 2001 JA (a) 2.25
❑145, Sep 2001 JA (a) 2.25
❑146, Oct 2001 2.25
❑147, Nov 2001 2.25
❑148, Dec 2001 2.25
❑149, Jan 2002 TVE (a) 2.25
❑150, Feb 2002 TVE (a) 2.25
❑151, Mar 2002 TVE (a) 2.25
❑152, Apr 2002 TVE (a) 2.25
❑153, May 2002 TVE (a) 2.25
❑154, Jun 2002 2.25
❑155, Jul 2002 2.25
❑156, Aug 2002 2.25
❑157, Sep 2002 2.25
❑158, Oct 2002 2.50
❑159, Nov 2002 2.50
❑160, Dec 2002 2.50
❑161, Jan 2003 2.50
❑162, Feb 2003 2.50
❑163, Mar 2003 2.50
❑164, Apr 2003 2.50
❑165, May 2003 2.50
❑166, Jun 2003 2.50
❑167, Jul 2003 2.50
❑168, Aug 2003 2.50
❑169, Sep 2003 2.50
❑170, Oct 2003 2.50
❑171, Nov 2003 2.50
❑172, Dec 2003 2.50
❑173, Jan 2004 2.50
❑174, Feb 2004 2.50
❑175, Mar 2004 2.50
❑176, Apr 2004 2.50
❑177, May 2004 (c); DGry (w) 2.50
❑178, Jun 2004 2.50
❑179, Jul 2004 2.50
❑180, Aug 2004 2.50
❑181, Sep 2004
❑Annual 1, Dec 1991 MG, KG, DS, JA (a) 4.50
❑Annual 2, ca. 1992; Wedding of James Gordon 3.50
❑Annual 3, ca. 1993 GM, LMc (a); 1: Cardinal Sin 3.50
❑Annual 4, ca. 1994 MWa (w); JSa (a) 3.50
❑Annual 5, ca. 1995; O: Man-Bat. Year One 3.95
❑Annual 6, ca. 1996; Legends of the Dead Earth 2.95
❑Annual 7, ca. 1997; A: Balloon Buster. Pulp Heroes 3.95
❑Special 1, ca. 1993; prestige format 6.95

BATMAN: LEGENDS OF THE DARK KNIGHT: JAZZ
DC

❑1, Apr 1995 2.50
❑2, May 1995 2.50
❑3, Jun 1995 2.50

BATMAN: MADNESS A LEGENDS OF THE DARK KNIGHT HALLOWEEN SPECIAL
DC

❑1; prestige format 4.95

BATMAN: MANBAT
DC

❑1, prestige format; Elseworlds 5.00
❑2, prestige format; Elseworlds 5.00
❑3, prestige format; Elseworlds 5.00

Four cover variants were offered for *Batman: Legends of the Dark Knight* #1 to increase sales for retailers who had heavily overordered on the title.

© 1989 DC Comics.

N-MINT

BATMAN: MASK OF THE PHANTASM-THE ANIMATED MOVIE
DC

❑1; newstand 2.95
❑1/Prestige; slick paper 4.95

BATMAN: MASQUE
DC

❑1, Jan 1997; prestige format; Elseworlds; Phantom of the Opera theme; prestige format, Elseworlds, Phantom of the Opera theme 6.95

BATMAN: MASTER OF THE FUTURE
DC

❑1, ca. 1991 5.95

BATMAN: MR. FREEZE
DC

❑1, May 1997; prestige format; cover is part of quadtych 4.95

BATMAN: MITEFALL
DC

❑1; prestige format; prestige format one-shot 4.95

BATMAN: NEVERMORE
DC

❑1, Jun 2003 2.50
❑2, Jul 2003 2.50
❑3, Aug 2003 2.50
❑4, Sep 2003 2.50
❑5, Oct 2003 2.50

BATMAN/NIGHTWING: BLOODBORNE
DC

❑1, Mar 2002, prestige format 5.95

BATMAN: NO LAW AND A NEW ORDER
DC

❑1; collects Batman: No Man's Land #1, Batman #563, Batman: Shadow of the Bat #83, and Detective Comics #730 5.95

BATMAN: NO MAN'S LAND
DC

❑0, Dec 1999 4.95
❑1, Mar 1999 ARo (c); ARo (a) 2.95
❑1/Autographed, Mar 1999 ARo (c); ARo (a) 17.95
❑1/Variant, Mar 1999; ARo (c); ARo (a); lenticular animation cover 3.95
❑2 2.95
❑3 2.95
❑4 2.95

BATMAN: NO MAN'S LAND GALLERY
DC

❑1, Jul 1999; pin-ups 3.95

BATMAN: NO MAN'S LAND SECRET FILES
DC

❑1, Dec 1999 4.95

BATMAN: NOSFERATU
DC

❑1, May 1999; prestige format; Elseworlds 5.95

BATMAN OF ARKHAM, THE
DC

❑1 5.95

Condition price index: Multiply "NM prices" above by: **0.83 for Very Fine/Near Mint**
0.66 for Very Fine • 0.33 for Fine • 0.2 for Very Good • 0.125 for Good

N-MINT

BATMAN: ORDER OF THE BEASTS
DC
❑1, Jul 2004 .... 6.95

BATMAN: ORPHEUS RISING
DC
❑1, Oct 2001 .... 2.50
❑2, Nov 2001 .... 2.50
❑3, Dec 2001 .... 2.50
❑4, Jan 2002 .... 2.50
❑5, Feb 2002 .... 2.50

BATMAN: OUR WORLDS AT WAR
DC
❑1, Aug 2001 .... 2.95

BATMAN: OUTLAWS
DC
❑1, Sep 2000 .... 4.95
❑2, Oct 2000 .... 4.95
❑3, Nov 2000 .... 4.95

BATMAN: PENGUIN TRIUMPHANT
DC
❑1; prestige format; JSa (a); cover forms diptych with Batman: Catwoman Defiant 5.00

BATMAN/PHANTOM STRANGER
DC
❑1, Dec 1997; prestige format 5.00

BATMAN PLUS
DC
❑1, Feb 1997 .... 2.95

BATMAN: POISON IVY
DC
❑1, Jul 1997; prestige format; O: Poison Ivy. A: Croc. A: Batman. Cover is part of quadtych 5.00

BATMAN/POISON IVY: CAST SHADOWS
DC
❑1, ca 2004 .... 6.95

BATMAN/PREDATOR III
DC
❑1, Nov 1997 .... 1.95
❑2, Dec 1997 .... 1.95
❑3, Jan 1998 .... 1.95
❑4, Feb 1998 .... 1.95

BATMAN/PUNISHER: LAKE OF FIRE
DC / MARVEL
❑1 1994 .... 5.00

BATMAN: REIGN OF TERROR
DC
❑1, Feb 1999; prestige format; Elseworlds 4.95

BATMAN RETURNS: THE OFFICIAL COMIC ADAPTATION OF THE WARNER BROS. MOTION PICTURE
DC
❑1; Comic adaptation of Warner Bros. Movie 4.00
❑1/Prestige; prestige format; Comic adaptation of Warner Bros. Movie . 6.00

BATMAN: RIDDLER: THE RIDDLE FACTORY
DC
❑1; prestige format; cover forms diptych with Batman: Two-Face - Crime and Punishment 4.95

BATMAN: ROOMFUL OF STRANGERS
DC
❑1, Apr 2004 .... 5.95

BATMAN: RUN, RIDDLER, RUN
DC
❑1 1992; prestige format 5.00
❑2 1992; prestige format 5.00
❑3 1992; prestige format 5.00

BATMAN/SCARECROW 3-D
DC
❑1, Dec 1998; with glasses 3.95
❑1/Variant, Dec 1998 .... 7.50

N-MINT

BATMAN/SCARFACE: A PSYCHODRAMA
DC
❑1, Mar 2001 .... 5.95

BATMAN: SCAR OF THE BAT
DC
❑1; prestige format; Elseworlds 4.95

BATMAN: SCOTTISH CONNECTION
DC
❑1; prestige format 5.95

BATMAN SECRET FILES
DC
❑1, Oct 1997; background information 4.95

BATMAN: SEDUCTION OF THE GUN
DC
❑1, Feb 1993; Special edition on gun control; dedicated to John Reisenbach (Son of DC editor slain in gun killing) 3.50

BATMAN: SHADOW OF THE BAT
DC
❑0, O: Batman. falls between issues #31 and 32 .... 2.50
❑1, Last Arkham 2.50
❑1/CS, Jun 1992; collector's set 3.50
❑2, Last Arkham 2.75
❑3, Last Arkham 2.75
❑4, Last Arkham 2.75
❑5, Oct 1992 .... 2.75
❑6, Nov 1992 .... 2.50
❑7, Dec 1992 .... 2.50
❑8, Jan 1993; Misfits 2.50
❑9, Feb 1993 .... 2.50
❑10, Mar 1993 .... 2.50
❑11, Apr 1993 .... 2.50
❑12, May 1993 .... 2.50
❑13, Jun 1993 .... 2.50
❑14, Jul 1993 JSa (a) 2.50
❑15, Aug 1993 JSa (a) 2.50
❑16, Sep 1993 V: Scarecrow 2.50
❑17, Sep 1993 V: Scarecrow 2.50
❑18, Oct 1993 V: Scarecrow 2.50
❑19, Oct 1993 V: Tally Man 2.50
❑20, Nov 1993 V: Tally Man 2.50
❑21, Nov 1993 .... 2.50
❑22, Dec 1993 .... 2.50
❑23, Jan 1994 .... 2.50
❑24, Feb 1994 .... 2.50
❑25, Mar 1994 A: Joe Public 2.50
❑26, Apr 1994 V: Clayface 2.50
❑27, May 1994 .... 2.50
❑28, Jun 1994 .... 2.50
❑29, Jul 1994; Giant-size 2.50
❑30, Aug 1994 .... 2.50
❑31, Sep 1994; Zero Hour, R: Alfred as detective 2.50
❑32, Nov 1994 .... 2.50
❑33, Dec 1994 .... 2.50
❑34, Jan 1995 .... 2.50
❑35, Feb 1995 .... 2.50
❑35/Variant, Feb 1995; enhanced cover 2.95
❑36, Mar 1995 A: Black Canary 2.00
❑37, Apr 1995 .... 2.00
❑38, May 1995 .... 2.00
❑39, Jun 1995 V: Anarky 2.00
❑40, Jul 1995 V: Anarky 2.00
❑41, Aug 1995 .... 2.00
❑42, Sep 1995 .... 2.00
❑43, Oct 1995 .... 2.00
❑44, Nov 1995 .... 2.00
❑45, Dec 1995; Wayne Manor history 2.00
❑46, Jan 1996 .... 2.00
❑47, Feb 1996 .... 2.00
❑48, Mar 1996; trading card bound in 2.00
❑49, Apr 1996 .... 2.00
❑50, May 1996 .... 2.00
❑51, Jun 1996 .... 2.00
❑52, Jul 1996 .... 2.00
❑53, Aug 1996 A: Huntress 2.00
❑54, Sep 1996 .... 2.00
❑55, Oct 1996 KJ (a) 2.00

N-MINT

❑56, Nov 1996 V: Poison Ivy 2.00
❑57, Dec 1996 V: Poison Ivy 2.00
❑58, Jan 1997 V: Floronic Man 2.00
❑59, Feb 1997 V: Scarface 2.00
❑60, Mar 1997 V: Scarface 2.00
❑61, Apr 1997 JA (a) 2.00
❑62, May 1997 V: Two-Face 2.00
❑63, Jun 1997 V: Two-Face 2.00
❑64, Jul 1997 .... 2.00
❑65, Aug 1997 .... 2.00
❑66, Sep 1997 .... 2.00
❑67, Oct 1997 .... 2.00
❑68, Nov 1997 .... 2.00
❑69, Dec 1997 A: Fate 2.00
❑70, Jan 1998 A: Fate 2.00
❑71, Feb 1998 .... 2.00
❑72, Mar 1998 1: Drakken 2.00
❑73, Apr 1998; continues in Nightwing #19 .... 2.00
❑74, May 1998; continues in Batman Chronicles #12 .... 2.00
❑75, Jun 1998; V: Clayface. V: Mr. Freeze. Aftershock 2.00
❑76, Jul 1998; Aftershock 2.00
❑77, Aug 1998; Aftershock 2.00
❑78, Sep 1998; Aftershock 2.00
❑79, Oct 1998; Aftershock 2.00
❑80, Dec 1998; Road to No Man's Land; flipbook with Azrael: Agent of the Bat #47 .... 2.00
❑80/Ltd., Dec 1998; Extra-sized flipbook 4.00
❑81, Jan 1999; A: Jeremiah Arkham. Road to No Man's Land 2.00
❑82, Feb 1999; Road to No Man's Land 2.00
❑83, Mar 1999; 1: new Batgirl. No Man's Land 9.00
❑84, Apr 1999; A: Scarecrow. A: Huntress. A: Batgirl. No Man's Land 2.00
❑85, May 1999; A: Batgirl. V: Penguin. No Man's Land 2.00
❑86, Jun 1999; No Man's Land 2.00
❑87, Jul 1999; A: Two-Face. No Man's Land 2.00
❑88, Aug 1999; BSz (a); A: Poison Ivy. V: Clayface. No Man's Land; continues in Batman #568 .... 2.00
❑89, Sep 1999; V: Killer Croc. No Man's Land 2.00
❑90, Oct 1999; PG (a); A: Lynx. No Man's Land 2.00
❑91, Nov 1999 .... 2.00
❑92, Dec 1999; DGry (w); No Man's Land 2.00
❑93, Jan 2000; BSz (a); No Man's Land 2.00
❑94, Feb 2000 .... 2.00
❑1000000, Nov 1998; Aftershock 3.00
❑Annual 1, ca. 1993 TVE (a); 1: Joe Public 4.00
❑Annual 2, ca. 1994; JSa (a); Elseworlds 3.95
❑Annual 3, ca. 1995; O: Poison Ivy. Year One 3.95
❑Annual 4, Nov 1996; Legends of the Dead Earth; 1996 Annual 2.95
❑Annual 5, Oct 1997; V: Poison Ivy. 1997 Annual; Pulp Heroes 3.95

BATMAN-SPAWN: WAR DEVIL
DC
❑1; prestige format; crossover with Image 4.95

BATMAN SPECIAL
DC
❑1, ca. 1984, MG (a) 2.50

BATMAN/SPIDER-MAN
DC
❑1, Oct 1997; prestige format; crossover with Marvel 4.95

BATMAN: SPOILER/HUNTRESS: BLUNT TRAUMA
DC
❑1, May 1998 .... 2.95
❑2 .... 2.95
❑3 .... 2.95
❑4 .... 2.95

N-MINT

BATMAN/SUPERMAN/ WONDERWOMAN TRINITY
DC

❑1, Aug 2003 .... 6.95
❑2, Oct 2003 .... 6.95
❑3, Dec 2003 .... 6.95

BATMAN/SUPERMAN WORLD'S FINEST TP
DC

❑1, ca. 2003 .... 19.95

BATMAN: SWORD OF AZRAEL
DC

❑1, Oct 1992; 1: Azrael. Wraparound, gatefold cover 4.00
❑1/Silver, Oct 1992; silver edition 2.00
❑2, Nov 1992 .... 3.00
❑2/Silver, Nov 1992; silver edition 2.00
❑3, Dec 1992 .... 3.00
❑3/Silver, Dec 1992; silver edition 2.00
❑4, Jan 1993 .... 2.50
❑4/Silver, Jan 1993; silver edition 2.00

BATMAN/TARZAN: CLAWS OF THE CAT-WOMAN
DARK HORSE

❑1, Sep 1999 .... 2.95
❑2, Oct 1999 .... 2.95
❑3, Nov 1999 .... 2.95
❑4, Dec 1999 .... 2.95

BATMAN: TENSES
DC

❑1, Oct 2003 .... 6.95
❑2 2003 .... 6.95

BATMAN: THE ABDUCTION
DC

❑1, Jun 1998; prestige format; Batman kidnapped by aliens 5.95

BATMAN: THE ANKH
DC

❑1, Jan 2002 .... 5.95
❑2, Feb 2002 .... 5.95

BATMAN: THE BLUE, THE GREY, AND THE BAT
DC

❑1 1992; prestige format; Elseworlds 5.95

BATMAN: THE BOOK OF SHADOWS
DC

❑1; prestige format 5.95

BATMAN: THE CULT
DC

❑1, Aug 1988 JSn (w); JSn, BWr (a) . 4.00
❑2, Sep 1988 JSn (w); JSn, BWr (a) . 4.00
❑3, Oct 1988 JSn (w); JSn, BWr (a) .. 4.00
❑4, Nov 1988 JSn (w); JSn, BWr (a) . 4.00

BATMAN: THE DARK KNIGHT
DC

❑1, Mar 1986; FM (w); FM (a); Square-bound 25.00
❑1-2, Mar 1986 FM (w); FM (a) 7.00
❑1-3 FM (w); FM (a) 5.00
❑2, Mar 1986 FM (w); FM (a) 9.00
❑2-2, ca. 1986 FM (w); FM (a) 3.00
❑2-3 FM (w); FM (a) 3.00
❑3, ca. 1986 FM (w); FM (a); D: Joker (future) 6.00
❑3-2 FM (w); FM (a); D: Joker (future) 3.00
❑4, ca. 1986 FM (w); FM (a); D: Alfred (future) 5.00

BATMAN: THE DOOM THAT CAME TO GOTHAM
DC

❑1, Nov 2000 .... 4.95
❑2, Dec 2000 .... 4.95
❑3, Jan 2001 .... 4.95

BATMAN: THE HILL
DC

❑1, May 2000 .... 2.95

N-MINT

BATMAN: THE KILLING JOKE
DC

❑1, Jul 1988; prestige format; BB (c); AMo (w); BB (a); O: Joker. V: Joker. first printing; green logo 7.00
❑1-2; prestige format; BB (c); AMo (w); BB (a); O: Joker. V: Joker. second printing; pink logo 5.50
❑1-3; prestige format; BB (c); AMo (w); BB (a); O: Joker. V: Joker. third printing; yellow logo 5.00
❑1-4; prestige format; BB (c); AMo (w); BB (a); O: Joker. V: Joker. fourth printing; orange logo 5.00
❑1-5; prestige format BB (c); AMo (w); BB (a); O: Joker. V: Joker 5.00
❑1-6; prestige format BB (c); AMo (w); BB (a); O: Joker. V: Joker 5.00
❑1-7; prestige format BB (c); AMo (w); BB (a); O: Joker. V: Joker 5.00
❑1-8; prestige format BB (c); AMo (w); BB (a); O: Joker. V: Joker 5.00

BATMAN: THE LONG HALLOWEEN
DC

❑1, Dec 1996; prestige format JPH (w) 8.50
❑2, Jan 1997; JPH (w); V: Solomon Grundy. cardstock cover 6.50
❑3, Feb 1997; JPH (w); V: Joker. cardstock cover 5.50
❑4, Mar 1997; JPH (w); V: Joker. cardstock cover 5.00
❑5, Apr 1997; JPH (w); A: Catwoman. A: Poison Ivy. cardstock cover 4.50
❑6, May 1997; JPH (w); V: Poison Ivy. cardstock cover 4.50
❑7, Jun 1997; JPH (w); V: Riddler. cardstock cover 3.50
❑8, Jul 1997; JPH (w); V: Scarecrow. cardstock cover 3.50
❑9, Aug 1997; JPH (w); cardstock cover 3.50
❑10, Sep 1997; JPH (w); A: Catwoman. V: Scarecrow. V: Mad Hatter. cardstock cover 3.50
❑11, Oct 1997; JPH (w); O: Two-Face. cardstock cover 3.50
❑12, Nov 1997; JPH (w); D: Maroni. cardstock cover; identity of Holiday revealed 3.50
❑13, Dec 1997; prestige format JPH (w); 1: Holiday. V: Arkham inmates 5.50

BATMAN: THE OFFICIAL COMIC ADAPTATION OF THE WARNER BROS. MOTION PICTURE
DC

❑1; regular edition; JOy (a); newsstand format; Comic adaptation of Warner Bros. Movie 3.00
❑1/Prestige; prestige format; Comic adaptation of Warner Bros. Movie . 5.00

BATMAN: THE 10-CENT ADVENTURE
DC

❑1, Mar 2002 .... 1.00

BATMAN: THE ULTIMATE EVIL
DC

❑1; prestige format; adapts Andrew Vachss novel 6.00
❑2; prestige format; adapts Andrew Vachss novel 6.00

BATMAN: THRILLKILLER
DC

❑1; collects Thrillkiller #1-3 and Thrillkiller '62 .... 12.95

BATMAN: TOYMAN
DC

❑1, Nov 1998 .... 2.25
❑2, Dec 1998 .... 2.25
❑3, Jan 1999; Wordless issue 2.25
❑4, Feb 1999 .... 2.25

BATMAN: TURNING POINTS
DC

❑1, Jan 2001 .... 2.50
❑2, Jan 2001 .... 2.50
❑3, Jan 2001 .... 2.50
❑4, Jan 2001 .... 2.50
❑5, Jan 2001 .... 2.50

The Joker's origin was updated by Alan Moore and Brian Bolland in the prestige-format one-shot *Batman: The Killing Joke.*
© 1988 DC Comics.

N-MINT

BATMAN: TWO-FACE: CRIME AND PUNISHMENT
DC

❑1; prestige format; cover forms diptych with Batman: Riddler - The Riddle Factory 4.95

BATMAN: TWO FACES
DC

❑1, Nov 1998; Elseworlds 4.95
❑1/Ltd., Nov 1998; Signed edition 10.00

BATMAN: TWO-FACE STRIKES TWICE
DC

❑1 JSa (a) 5.00
❑2 .... 5.00

BATMAN: VENGEANCE OF BANE II
DC

❑1 .... 4.00

BATMAN: VENGEANCE OF BANE SPECIAL
DC

❑1, Jan 1993 O: Bane. 1: Bane 4.00

BATMAN VERSUS PREDATOR
DC / DARK HORSE

❑1, ca. 1991; DaG (w); newsstand 2.50
❑1/A, ca. 1991; prestige format; trading cards; Batman on front cover 5.00
❑1/B, ca. 1991; prestige format; trading cards; Predator on front; Batman on back cover 5.00
❑2, ca. 1992; DaG (w); newsstand 2.50
❑2/Prestige, ca. 1992; prestige format; DaG (w); pin-ups 5.00
❑3, ca. 1992; DaG (w); newsstand 2.50
❑3/Prestige, ca. 1992; prestige format DaG (w) 5.00

BATMAN VERSUS PREDATOR II: BLOODMATCH
DC / DARK HORSE

❑1; Crossover, no year in indicia 2.50
❑2; Crossover 2.50
❑3; Crossover 2.50
❑4; Crossover 2.50

BATMAN VS. THE INCREDIBLE HULK
DC

❑1, Fal 1981; oversized, (DC Special Series #27) 2.50
❑1-2; 2nd Printing, comics-sized 3.95

BATMAN VILLAINS SECRET FILES
DC

❑1, Oct 1998 .... 4.95

BATMAN: WAR ON CRIME
DC

❑1, Nov 1999 .... 9.95
❑1-2 .... 9.95

BATMAN/WILDCAT
DC

❑1, Apr 1997 .... 2.25
❑2, May 1997 .... 2.25
❑3, Jun 1997 .... 2.25

BAT, THE (MARY ROBERTS RINEHART'S)
ADVENTURE

❑1, Aug 1992, b&w 2.50

N-MINT

BAT MEN
AVALON
❑1 2.95

BATS, CATS & CADILLACS
NOW
❑1, Oct 1990 2.00
❑2, Nov 1990 2.00

BAT-THING
DC / AMALGAM
❑1, Jun 1997 1.95

BATTLE ANGEL ALITA PART 1
VIZ
❑1, Jul 1992 1: Alita 4.00
❑2, Aug 1992 3.50
❑3, Sep 1992 3.50
❑4, Oct 1992 3.00
❑5, Nov 1992 3.00
❑6, Dec 1992 3.00
❑7, Jan 1993 3.00
❑8, Feb 1993 3.00
❑9, Mar 1993 3.00

BATTLE ANGEL ALITA PART 2
VIZ
❑1, Apr 1993 3.00
❑2, May 1993 2.75
❑3, Jun 1993 2.75
❑4, Jul 1993 2.75
❑5, Aug 1993 2.75
❑6, Sep 1993 2.75
❑7, Oct 1993 2.75

BATTLE ANGEL ALITA PART 3
VIZ
❑1, Nov 1993 2.75
❑2, Dec 1993 2.75
❑3, Jan 1994 2.75
❑4, Feb 1994 2.75
❑5, Mar 1994 2.75
❑6, Apr 1994 2.75
❑7, May 1994 2.75
❑8, Jun 1994 2.75
❑9, Jul 1994 2.75
❑10, Aug 1994 2.75
❑11, Sep 1994 2.75
❑12, Oct 1994 2.75
❑13, Nov 1994 2.75

BATTLE ANGEL ALITA PART 4
VIZ
❑1, Dec 1994 2.75
❑2, Jan 1995 2.75
❑3, Feb 1995 2.75
❑4, Mar 1995 2.75
❑5, Apr 1995 2.75
❑6, May 1995 2.75
❑7, Jun 1995 2.75

BATTLE ANGEL ALITA PART 5
VIZ
❑1, Jul 1995 2.75
❑2, Aug 1995 2.75
❑3, Sep 1995 2.75
❑4, Oct 1995 2.75
❑5, Nov 1995 2.75
❑6, Dec 1995 2.75
❑7, Jan 1996 2.95

BATTLE ANGEL ALITA PART 6
VIZ
❑1, Feb 1996 2.95
❑2, Mar 1996 2.95
❑3, Apr 1996 2.95
❑4, May 1996 2.95
❑5, Jun 1996 2.95
❑6, Jul 1996 2.95
❑7, Aug 1996 2.95
❑8, Sep 1996 2.95

BATTLE ANGEL ALITA PART 7
VIZ
❑1, Oct 1996 2.95
❑2, Nov 1996 2.95
❑3, Dec 1996 2.95
❑4, Jan 1997 2.95
❑5, Feb 1997 2.95
❑6, Mar 1997 2.95
❑7, Apr 1997 2.95
❑8, May 1997 2.95

BATTLE ANGEL ALITA PART 8
VIZ
❑1, Jun 1997 2.95
❑2, Jul 1997 2.95
❑3, Aug 1997 2.95
❑4, Sep 1997 2.95
❑5, Oct 1997 2.95
❑6, Nov 1997 2.95
❑7, Dec 1997 2.95
❑8, Jan 1998 2.95
❑9, Feb 1998 2.95

BATTLE ANGEL ALITA: LAST ORDER PART 1
VIZ
❑1, Sep 2002 2.95
❑2, Oct 2002 2.95
❑3, Nov 2002 2.95
❑4, Dec 2002 2.95
❑5, Jan 2003 2.95
❑6, Feb 2003 2.95

BATTLE ARMOR
ETERNITY
❑1, Oct 1988 1.95
❑2 1.95
❑3 1.95

BATTLE AXE
COMICS INTERVIEW
❑1, b&w 2.50

BATTLEAXES
DC / VERTIGO
❑1, May 2000 2.50
❑2, Jun 2000 2.50
❑3, Jul 2000 2.50
❑4, Aug 2000 2.50

BATTLE AXIS
INTREPID
❑1, Feb 1993 2.95

BATTLE BEASTS
BLACKTHORNE
❑1 1.75
❑2 1.50
❑3 1.50
❑4 1.75

BATTLE BINDER PLUS
ANTARCTIC / VENUS
❑1, Nov 1994 2.95
❑2, Dec 1994 2.95
❑3, Jan 1995 2.95
❑4, Feb 1995 2.95
❑5, Mar 1995 2.95
❑6, Apr 1995 2.95

BATTLE CHASERS
IMAGE / CLIFFHANGER
❑1, Apr 1998 5.00
❑1/A, Apr 1998; alternate cover, logo on back side of wraparound cover 8.00
❑1/B, Apr 1998; Limited holochrome cover (limited to 5,000 copies); Wrap-around 16.50
❑1/C, Apr 1998; Gold "Come on, take a peek" cover (Monika) 14.00
❑1-2, Apr 1998 3.00
❑2, May 1998 4.00
❑2/A, May 1998; Special "omnichrome" cover from Dynamic Forces 5.00
❑2/B, May 1998; Battlechrome edition 6.00
❑3, Jul 1998 3.00
❑4/A, four alternate back covers form quadtych 2.50
❑4/B, Old man on cover 2.50
❑4/C, four alternate back covers form quadtych 2.50
❑4/D, Oct 1998; four alternate back covers form quadtych 2.50
❑5, May 1999 2.50
❑6, Aug 1999 2.50
❑7, Jan 2001 2.50
❑8, May 2001 2.50
❑9, Jun 2001; Flip book with bonus story 3.50
❑Ashcan 1, Aug 1998; Preview edition 1: Battle Chasers 5.00
❑Ashcan 1/Gold, Aug 1998; Preview edition; 1: Battle Chasers. Gold logo 7.00
❑Deluxe 1, Dec 1999; A Gathering of Heroes hardcover 24.95

BATTLE CLASSICS
DC
❑1, Oct 1978 4.00

BATTLEFIELD ACTION
CHARLTON
❑16; Continued from Foreign Intrigues #15 28.00
❑17 13.00
❑18, Mar 1958 10.00
❑19, May 1958 10.00
❑20, Jul 1958 10.00
❑21, Sep 1958 9.00
❑22, Dec 1958 9.00
❑23 1959 9.00
❑24 1959 9.00
❑25, Jul 1959 9.00
❑26, Sep 1959; Swimming pool contest 9.00
❑27 1959 9.00
❑28, Jan 1960 9.00
❑29 1960 9.00
❑30, Jun 1960 9.00
❑31 7.00
❑32 7.00
❑33 7.00
❑34 7.00
❑35 1961 7.00
❑36 1961 7.00
❑37 1961 7.00
❑38, Nov 1961 7.00
❑39, Dec 1961 7.00
❑40, Feb 1962 7.00
❑41, May 1962 6.00
❑42, ca. 1962 6.00
❑43, ca. 1962 6.00
❑44, ca. 1962 6.00
❑45, Jan 1963 6.00
❑46, Mar 1963 6.00
❑47, May 1963 6.00
❑48, Jul 1963 6.00
❑49, Sep 1963 6.00
❑50, Nov 1963 6.00
❑51, Jan 1964 5.00
❑52, ca. 1964 5.00
❑53, Jun 1964 5.00
❑54, ca. 1964 5.00
❑55, Nov 1964 5.00
❑56, Jan 1965 5.00
❑57, ca. 1965 5.00
❑58, Jul 1965 5.00
❑59, ca. 1965 5.00
❑60, Oct 1965 5.00
❑61, Mar 1963 5.00
❑62, Feb 1966; Last issue of 1960s run 5.00
❑63, Jul 1980; Series begins again 2.50
❑64, Sep 1980 2.50
❑65, Nov 1980 2.50
❑66, Jan 1981 2.50
❑67, Mar 1981 2.50
❑68, Apr 1981 2.50
❑69, Jun 1981 2.50
❑70, Aug 1981 2.50
❑71, Oct 1981 2.50
❑72, Dec 1981 2.50
❑73, Feb 1982 2.50
❑74, Apr 1982 2.50
❑75, Jun 1982 2.50
❑76, Aug 1982 2.50
❑77, Oct 1982 2.50
❑78, Dec 1982 2.50
❑79, Feb 1983 2.50
❑80, Apr 1983 2.50
❑81, Jun 1983 2.50

N-MINT

- ❑82, Aug 1983 ... 2.50
- ❑83, Oct 1983 ... 2.50
- ❑84, Dec 1983; Reprints from Foxhole #6 ("Boidie" & "Steven"), and #5 ("Stiff") ... 2.50
- ❑85 1984 ... 2.50
- ❑86 1984 ... 2.50
- ❑87 1984 ... 2.50
- ❑88, Sep 1984 ... 2.50
- ❑89, Nov 1984 ... 2.50

BATTLE FOR A THREE DIMENSIONAL WORLD
3-D Cosmic

- ❑1, ca. 1982, b&w; JK (a); no cover price ... 2.50

BATTLEFORCE
Blackthorne

- ❑1 ... 1.75
- ❑2, b&w ... 1.75

BATTLE GIRLZ
Antarctic

- ❑1, ca. 2002, b&w ... 2.99

BATTLE GODS: WARRIORS OF THE CHAAK
Dark Horse

- ❑1, Apr 2000 ... 2.95
- ❑2, May 2000 ... 2.95
- ❑3, Jun 2000 ... 2.95

BATTLEGROUND EARTH
Best

- ❑1, b&w ... 2.50
- ❑2, b&w ... 2.50

BATTLE GROUP PEIPER
Tome

- ❑1, b&w ... 2.95

BATTLE OF THE PLANETS
Gold Key / Whitman

- ❑1, Jun 1979 ... 12.00
- ❑2, Aug 1979 ... 6.00
- ❑3, Oct 1979 ... 6.00
- ❑4, Dec 1979 ... 6.00
- ❑5, Feb 1980 ... 6.00
- ❑6, Apr 1980 ... 5.00
- ❑7, ca. 1980 ... 5.00
- ❑8, ca. 1980 ... 5.00
- ❑9, Dec 1980 ... 5.00
- ❑10, Feb 1981 ... 5.00

BATTLE OF THE PLANETS (IMAGE)
Image

- ❑0.5, Jul 2003; Black & white cover ... 3.00
- ❑0.5/Gold; Black & white cover ... 5.00
- ❑1/A, Aug 2002 ARo (c) ... 3.00
- ❑1/B, Aug 2002 ... 3.00
- ❑1/C, Aug 2002 ... 3.00
- ❑1/D, Aug 2002 ... 3.00
- ❑1/E, Aug 2002; ARo (c); Holofoil cover ... 3.00
- ❑1/F, Aug 2002; Wizard World 2002 Convention Edition, limited to 5,000 copies ... 3.00
- ❑1/G, Aug 2002; ARo (c); Limited to 7,000 copies; DFE red foil cover ... 3.00
- ❑1/H, Aug 2002; ARo (c); Limited to 2,000 copies; DFE blue foil cover ... 3.00
- ❑1/I, Aug 2002; ARo (c); Limited to 1,978 copies; DFE gold foil cover ... 3.00
- ❑1/J, Aug 2002; "Virgin" cover without price or logo ... 3.00
- ❑1/K, Aug 2002; Black & white cover ... 3.00
- ❑2, Sep 2002 ... 2.99
- ❑2/Variant, Sep 2002; Animation cover; Limited to 5,000 copies ... 3.00
- ❑2/A, Sep 2002; 2002 San Diego Convention exclusive; Limited to 1,000 copies ... 3.00
- ❑2/B, Sep 2002; "Virgin" cover without price or logo ... 3.00
- ❑3, Oct 2002 ARo (c) ... 2.99
- ❑4, Nov 2002 ... 2.99
- ❑5, Dec 2002 ... 2.99
- ❑6, Feb 2003 ... 2.99
- ❑7, Mar 2003 ... 2.99
- ❑7/A, Mar 2003; Retailer incentive; variant cover ... 5.00
- ❑8, Apr 2003 ... 2.99
- ❑9, May 2003 ... 2.99
- ❑10, Jun 2003 ... 2.99
- ❑11, Jul 2003 ... 2.99
- ❑12, Aug 2003 ... 4.99

BATTLE OF THE PLANETS: JASON
Image

- ❑1, Jun 2003 ... 4.99

BATTLE OF THE PLANETS: MANGA
Image

- ❑1, Oct 2003 ... 2.99
- ❑2, Nov 2003 ... 2.99
- ❑3, Dec 2003 ... 2.99

BATTLE OF THE PLANETS: MARK
Image

- ❑1, May 2003 ... 4.99

BATTLE OF THE PLANETS/ THUNDERCATS
Image

- ❑1, May 2003 ... 4.99

BATTLE OF THE PLANETS/ WITCHBLADE
Image

- ❑1, Feb 2003 ... 5.95

BATTLE OF THE ULTRA-BROTHERS
Viz

- ❑1 ... 4.95
- ❑2 ... 4.95
- ❑3 ... 4.95
- ❑4 ... 4.95
- ❑5 ... 4.95

BATTLEPOPE
Funk-O-Tron

- ❑1, Jun 2000, b&w ... 2.95
- ❑2, Jul 2000, b&w ... 2.95
- ❑3, Aug 2000, b&w ... 2.95
- ❑4, Sep 2000, b&w ... 2.95
- ❑5, Mar 2001, b&w; A.K.A. Battle Pope Shorts #1 ... 2.95
- ❑6, Jun 2001, b&w; A.K.A. Battle Pope: Mayhem #1 ... 2.95
- ❑7, Jul 2001, b&w; A.K.A. Battle Pope: Mayhem #2 ... 2.95

BATTLESTAR GALACTICA 1999 TOUR BOOK
Realm

- ❑1/A, May 1999 ... 2.99
- ❑1/B, May 1999; Dynamic Forces Edition, no cover price; Dynamic Forces Edition, no cover price ... 3.00
- ❑1/C, May 1999; white background cover ... 3.00

BATTLESTAR GALACTICA: APOLLO'S JOURNEY
Maximum

- ❑1, Apr 1995 ... 2.95

BATTLESTAR GALACTICA EVE OF DESTRUCTION PRELUDE
Realm

- ❑1, ca. 2000 ... 3.99

BATTLESTAR GALACTICA: JOURNEY'S END
Maximum

- ❑1, Aug 1996 ... 2.99
- ❑2, Sep 1996 ... 2.99
- ❑3, Oct 1996 ... 2.99
- ❑4, Nov 1996 ... 2.99

BATTLESTAR GALACTICA (MARVEL)
Marvel

- ❑1, Mar 1979; Pilot movie adaptation; reformatted from Marvel Super Special #8 ... 4.00
- ❑1-2; 20 Yahren reunion edition; reprint ... 5.00
- ❑2, Apr 1979; Pilot movie adaptation; reformatted from Marvel Super Special #8 ... 3.00

Battle Chasers #4 had four alternate covers. The back covers assembled into one larger image.
© 1998 Image.

N-MINT

- ❑3, May 1979; Pilot movie adaptation; reformatted from Marvel Super Special #8 ... 3.00
- ❑4, Jun 1979; Adapts first hour-long episode of TV series ... 3.00
- ❑5, Jul 1979; Adapts second hour-long episode of TV series ... 3.00
- ❑6, Aug 1979; First original comics story ... 3.00
- ❑7, Sep 1979; Adama trapped in Memory Machine ... 3.00
- ❑8, Oct 1979; Young Adama on Scorpia; fill-in issue ... 3.00
- ❑9, Nov 1979 ... 3.00
- ❑10, Dec 1979; PB (a); Flashback story ... 3.00
- ❑11, Jan 1980 KJ (a) ... 2.00
- ❑12, Feb 1980; Adama leaves Memory Machine ... 2.00
- ❑13, Mar 1980 ... 2.00
- ❑14, Apr 1980; Muffit Two is melted ... 2.00
- ❑15, May 1980; KJ (a); Boomer discovers Adama's wife alive ... 2.00
- ❑16, Jun 1980 ... 2.00
- ❑17, Jul 1980; Red "Hulks" ... 2.00
- ❑18, Aug 1980; Red "Hulks" ... 2.00
- ❑19, Sep 1980; Starbuck returns ... 2.00
- ❑20, Oct 1980 ... 2.00
- ❑21, Nov 1980 BA (a) ... 2.00
- ❑22, Dec 1980 ... 2.00
- ❑23, Jan 1981; Last issue ... 2.00

BATTLESTAR GALACTICA (MAXIMUM)
Maximum

- ❑1, Jul 1995 ... 2.50
- ❑2, Aug 1995 ... 2.50
- ❑3, Sep 1995 ... 2.50
- ❑4, Nov 1995 ... 2.50
- ❑Special 1, Jan 1997 ... 2.99

BATTLESTAR GALACTICA (REALM)
Realm

- ❑1/A, Dec 1997; Spaceships cover ... 2.99
- ❑1/B, Dec 1997; Cylons cover ... 2.99
- ❑2, Jan 1998 ... 2.99
- ❑3, Mar 1998 ... 2.99
- ❑3/Variant, Mar 1998; alternate cover (eyes in background) ... 2.99
- ❑4, ca. 1998 ... 2.99
- ❑5, ca. 1998 ... 2.99

BATTLESTAR GALACTICA: SEARCH FOR SANCTUARY
Realm

- ❑1, Sep 1998 ... 2.99
- ❑Special 1, Sep 1998 ... 3.99

BATTLESTAR GALACTICA: SEASON III
Realm

- ❑1, Jun 1999 ... 2.99
- ❑1/A, Jun 1999; Special Convention Edition ... 5.00
- ❑1/B, Jun 1999 ... 4.99
- ❑2, Jul 1999 ... 4.99

BATTLESTAR GALACTICA: STARBUCK
Maximum

- ❑1 ... 2.50
- ❑2 ... 2.50
- ❑3, Mar 1996 ... 2.50

Condition price index: Multiply "NM prices" above by: **0.83 for Very Fine/Near Mint**
0.66 for Very Fine • 0.33 for Fine • 0.2 for Very Good • 0.125 for Good

N-MINT

BATTLESTAR GALACTICA: THE COMPENDIUM
MAXIMUM

❏1, Feb 1997, b&w 2.95

BATTLESTAR GALACTICA: THE ENEMY WITHIN
MAXIMUM

❏1, Nov 1995 .... 2.50
❏2 .... 2.50
❏3, Feb 1996 .... 2.95
❏3/Variant, Feb 1996; alternate cover 2.95

BATTLESTONE
IMAGE

❏1 .... 2.50
❏1/A, Nov 1994 .... 2.50
❏1/B, Nov 1994; alternate cover 2.50
❏2, Dec 1994 .... 2.50

BATTLETECH
MALIBU

❏0 .... 2.95

BATTLETECH (BLACKTHORNE)
BLACKTHORNE

❏1, Oct 1997 .... 2.00
❏2, b&w 2.00
❏3, b&w 2.00
❏4, b&w 2.00
❏5, b&w 2.00
❏6, b&w 2.00

BATTLETECH: FALLOUT
MALIBU

❏1 .... 2.50
❏2 .... 2.50
❏3 .... 2.50
❏4 .... 2.50

BATTLETECH IN 3-D
BLACKTHORNE

❏1 .... 2.50

BATTLETIDE
MARVEL

❏1, Dec 1992 .... 1.75
❏2, Jan 1993 .... 1.75
❏3, Feb 1993 .... 1.75
❏4, Mar 1993 .... 1.75

BATTLETIDE II
MARVEL

❏1, Aug 1993; Embossed cover 2.50
❏2, Sep 1993 .... 1.75
❏3, Oct 1993 .... 1.75
❏4, Nov 1993 .... 1.75

BATTLE TO THE DEATH
IMPERIAL

❏1, b&w 1.50
❏2 .... 1.50
❏3 .... 1.50

BATTLE VIXENS
TOKYOPOP

❏1, Apr 2004 .... 9.99

BATTLEZONES: DREAM TEAM 2
MALIBU

❏1, Mar 1996; pin-ups of battles between Malibu and Marvel characters 3.95

BATTRON
NEC

❏1, b&w 2.75
❏2, b&w 2.75

BATTRON'S 4 QUEENS: GUNS, BABES & INTRIGUE
COMMODE

❏1 .... 3.50

BAY CITY JIVE
DC / WILDSTORM

❏1, Jul 2001 .... 2.95
❏1/A, Jul 2001; alternate cover 2.95
❏2, Aug 2001 .... 2.95
❏3, Sep 2001 .... 2.95

N-MINT

BAYWATCH COMIC STORIES
ACCLAIM / ARMADA

❏1 .... 4.95
❏2 .... 4.95
❏3 .... 4.95
❏4 .... 4.95

BAZOOKA JULES
COM.X

❏1, ca. 2001 .... 2.99
❏2, ca. 2001 .... 2.95

B-BAR-B RIDERS
AC

❏1 FF (a) 2.00

BEACH HIGH
BIG

❏1, Feb 1997; illustrated text story, one-shot 3.25

BEACH PARTY
ETERNITY

❏1; b&w pin-ups 2.50

BEAGLE BOYS, THE
GOLD KEY

❏1, Nov 1964 .... 22.00
❏2, Nov 1965 .... 16.00
❏3, Aug 1966 .... 16.00
❏4, Nov 1966 .... 16.00
❏5, Feb 1967 .... 16.00
❏6, May 1967 .... 12.00
❏7 .... 12.00
❏8, Oct 1968 .... 12.00
❏9, Apr 1970 .... 12.00
❏10 .... 12.00
❏11 .... 8.00
❏12, Sep 1971 .... 8.00
❏13 .... 8.00
❏14, Sep 1972 .... 8.00
❏15 .... 8.00
❏16, Apr 1973 A: Uncle Scrooge 8.00
❏17, Jul 1973 .... 8.00
❏18, Oct 1973 .... 8.00
❏19, Jan 1974 .... 8.00
❏20, Apr 1974 .... 8.00
❏21, Jul 1974 .... 6.00
❏22, Oct 1974 .... 6.00
❏23, Jan 1975 .... 6.00
❏24, Apr 1975 .... 6.00
❏25, Jul 1975 .... 6.00
❏26, Oct 1975 .... 6.00
❏27, Jan 1976 .... 6.00
❏28, Mar 1976 .... 6.00
❏29, May 1976 .... 6.00
❏30, Jul 1976 .... 6.00
❏31, Sep 1976 .... 4.00
❏32, Nov 1976 .... 4.00
❏33, Jan 1977 .... 4.00
❏34, Apr 1977 .... 4.00
❏35, Jun 1977 .... 4.00
❏36, Aug 1977 .... 4.00
❏37, Sep 1977 .... 4.00
❏38, Oct 1977 .... 4.00
❏39, Dec 1977 .... 4.00
❏40, Jan 1978 .... 4.00
❏41, Apr 1978 .... 3.00
❏42, Jun 1978 .... 3.00
❏43, Aug 1978 .... 3.00
❏44, Sep 1978 .... 3.00
❏45, Oct 1978 .... 3.00
❏46, Dec 1978 .... 3.00
❏47 .... 3.00

BEAGLE BOYS VERSUS UNCLE SCROOGE, THE
WHITMAN

❏1, Mar 1979 .... 6.00
❏2, Apr 1979 .... 5.00
❏3, May 1979 .... 4.00
❏4, Jun 1979 .... 4.00
❏5, Jul 1979 .... 4.00
❏6, Aug 1979 .... 4.00
❏7, Sep 1979 .... 4.00
❏8, Oct 1979 .... 3.00

N-MINT

❏9, Nov 1979 .... 3.00
❏10, Dec 1979 .... 3.00
❏11, Jan 1980 .... 3.00
❏12, Feb 1980 .... 3.00

BEANY AND CECIL
DELL

❏1, Jul 1962 .... 75.00
❏2, Oct 1962 .... 60.00
❏3, Jan 1963 .... 60.00
❏4, Apr 1963 .... 60.00
❏5, Jul 1963 .... 60.00

BEAR
SLAVE LABOR

❏1, ca. 2003 .... 2.95
❏2, ca. 2003 .... 2.95
❏3, ca. 2003 .... 2.95
❏4, ca. 2004 .... 2.95
❏5, ca. 2004 .... 2.95

BEARFAX FUNNIES
TREASURE

❏1 .... 2.75

BEARSKIN: A GRIMM TALE
THECOMIC.COM

❏1, b&w; no cover price 1.50

BEAST, THE
MARVEL

❏1, May 1997 .... 2.50
❏2, Jun 1997 .... 2.50
❏3, Jul 1997 .... 2.50

BEAST BOY
DC

❏1, Jan 2000 .... 2.95
❏2, Feb 2000 .... 2.95
❏3, Mar 2000 .... 2.95
❏4, Apr 2000 .... 2.95

B.E.A.S.T.I.E.S.
AXIS

❏1, Apr 1994 .... 1.95

BEAST WARRIORS OF SHAOLIN
PIED PIPER

❏1, Jul 1987 .... 1.95
❏2 .... 1.95
❏3 .... 1.95

BEATLES, THE (DELL)
DELL

❏1, Sep 1964 .... 440.00

BEATLES EXPERIENCE, THE
REVOLUTIONARY

❏1, Mar 1991 .... 2.50
❏2, May 1991 .... 2.50
❏3, Jul 1991 .... 2.50
❏4, Sep 1991 .... 2.50
❏5, Nov 1991 .... 2.50
❏6, Jan 1992 .... 2.50
❏7, Mar 1992 .... 2.50
❏8, May 1992 .... 2.50

BEATLES, THE (PERSONALITY)
PERSONALITY

❏1, b&w 5.00
❏1/Ltd.; limited edition, b&w 8.00
❏2, b&w 4.00

BEATLES VS. THE ROLLING STONES, THE
CELEBRITY

❏1, May 1992 .... 2.95

BEATRIX
VISION

❏1 .... 2.95
❏2, Mar 1997 .... 2.95

BEAUTIES & BARBARIANS
AC

❏1 WW (a) 1.50

BEAUTIFUL PEOPLE
SLAVE LABOR

❏1, Apr 1994; Oversized 4.50

Condition price index: Multiply "NM prices" above by: **0.83 for Very Fine/Near Mint**
0.66 for Very Fine • 0.33 for Fine • 0.2 for Very Good • 0.125 for Good

BEAUTIFUL STORIES FOR UGLY CHILDREN
DC / PIRANHA

	N-MINT
❑1	2.50
❑2	2.50
❑3	2.50
❑4	2.50
❑5	2.50
❑6	2.50
❑7	2.50
❑8	2.50
❑9	2.50
❑10	2.50
❑11	2.50
❑12	2.50
❑13	2.50
❑14	2.50
❑15	2.50
❑16	2.50
❑17	2.50
❑18	2.50
❑19	2.50
❑20	2.50
❑21	2.50
❑22	2.50
❑23	2.50
❑24	2.50
❑25	2.50
❑26	2.50
❑27	2.50
❑28	2.50
❑29	2.50
❑30	2.50

BEAUTY AND THE BEAST
DISNEY

	N-MINT
❑1	2.50
❑1/Direct ed.; squarebound	4.95

BEAUTY AND THE BEAST (DISNEY'S...)
DISNEY

	N-MINT
❑1, Sep 1994	1.50
❑2, Oct 1994	1.50
❑3, Nov 1994	1.50
❑4, Dec 1994	1.50
❑5, Jan 1995	1.50
❑6, Feb 1995	1.50
❑7, Mar 1995	1.50
❑8, Apr 1995	1.50
❑9, May 1995	1.50
❑10, Jun 1995	1.50
❑11, Jul 1995	1.50
❑12, Aug 1995	1.50
❑13, Sep 1995	1.50
❑Holiday 1; digest; based on direct-to-video feature	4.50

BEAUTY AND THE BEAST (INNOVATION)
INNOVATION

	N-MINT
❑1, May 1993	2.50
❑1/CS	3.95
❑2, Jun 1993	2.50
❑3, Jul 1993	2.50
❑4, Aug 1993	2.50
❑5, Sep 1993	2.50
❑6, Oct 1993; indicia says Jul, should be Oct	2.50

BEAUTY AND THE BEAST (MARVEL)
MARVEL

	N-MINT
❑1, Dec 1984 DP (a)	2.00
❑2, Feb 1985 DP (a)	2.00
❑3, Apr 1985 DP (a)	2.00
❑4, Jun 1985 DP (a)	2.00

BEAUTY AND THE BEAST: NIGHT OF BEAUTY
FIRST

	N-MINT
❑1, Mar 1990	5.95

BEAUTY AND THE BEAST: PORTRAIT OF LOVE
FIRST

	N-MINT
❑1, May 1989	5.95

BEAUTY AND THE BEAST (STAN SHAW'S...)
DARK HORSE

	N-MINT
❑1	4.95

BEAUTY OF THE BEASTS
MU

	N-MINT
❑1, Nov 1991, b&w	2.50
❑2, May 1992, b&w	2.50
❑3, Jul 1993	2.50

BEAVIS & BUTT-HEAD
MARVEL

	N-MINT
❑1, Mar 1994 1: Beavis & Butt-Head (in comics). A: Punisher	2.50
❑1-2, Mar 1994	1.95
❑2, Apr 1994	2.50
❑3, May 1994 JR (a)	2.50
❑4, Jun 1994	2.50
❑5, Jul 1994	2.50
❑6, Aug 1994	2.00
❑7, Sep 1994	2.00
❑8, Oct 1994	2.00
❑9, Nov 1994	2.00
❑10, Dec 1994	2.00
❑11, Jan 1995	2.00
❑12, Feb 1995	2.00
❑13, Mar 1995	2.00
❑14, Apr 1995	2.00
❑15, May 1995	2.00
❑16, Jun 1995	2.00
❑17, Jul 1995	2.00
❑18, Aug 1995	2.00
❑19, Sep 1995	2.00
❑20, Oct 1995	2.00
❑21, Nov 1995	2.00
❑22, Dec 1995	2.00
❑23, Jan 1996	2.00
❑24, Feb 1996	2.00
❑25, Mar 1996	2.00
❑26, Apr 1996	2.00
❑27, May 1996	2.00
❑28	2.00

BECK & CAUL INVESTIGATIONS
CALIBER

	N-MINT
❑1, Jan 1994	2.95
❑2, Mar 1994	2.95
❑3, May 1994	2.95
❑4, Aug 1994	2.95
❑5	2.95
❑Annual 1, May 1995	3.50

BEDLAM!
ECLIPSE

	N-MINT
❑1, Aug 1985	1.75
❑2, Sep 1985	1.75

BEDLAM (CHAOS)
CHAOS

	N-MINT
❑1, Sep 2000	2.95
❑1/Variant, Sep 2000	2.95

BEELZELVIS
SLAVE LABOR

	N-MINT
❑1, Feb 1994	2.95

BEEP BEEP
DELL

	N-MINT
❑4, Feb 1960	24.00
❑5, May 1960	24.00
❑6, Aug 1960	24.00
❑7, Nov 1960	24.00
❑8, Feb 1961	24.00
❑9, May 1961	24.00
❑10, Aug 1961	16.00
❑11, Nov 1961	16.00
❑12, Feb 1962	16.00
❑13, May 1962	16.00
❑14, Aug 1962	16.00

BEEP BEEP, THE ROAD RUNNER (GOLD KEY)
GOLD KEY

	N-MINT
❑1, Oct 1966	28.00
❑2, Jan 1967	26.00
❑3, Apr 1967	20.00
❑4, Jul 1967	20.00
❑5, Oct 1967	20.00
❑6, Jan 1968	15.00
❑7, Apr 1968	15.00
❑8, Jul 1968	15.00
❑9, Oct 1968	15.00
❑10, Feb 1969	15.00
❑11, Apr 1969	15.00
❑12, Jun 1969	15.00
❑13, Aug 1969	15.00
❑14, Oct 1969	15.00
❑15, Dec 1969	15.00
❑16, Feb 1970	10.00
❑17, Apr 1970	10.00
❑18, Jun 1970	10.00
❑19, Aug 1970	10.00
❑20, Oct 1970	10.00
❑21, Dec 1970	10.00
❑22, Feb 1971	10.00
❑23, Apr 1971	10.00
❑24, Jun 1971	10.00
❑25, Aug 1971	10.00
❑26, Oct 1971	10.00
❑27, Dec 1971	10.00
❑28, Feb 1972	10.00
❑29, Apr 1972	10.00
❑30, Jun 1972	10.00
❑31, Aug 1972	10.00
❑32, Oct 1972	10.00
❑33, Dec 1972	10.00
❑34, Feb 1973	10.00
❑35, Apr 1973	10.00
❑36, Jun 1973	10.00
❑37, Aug 1973	10.00
❑38, Sep 1973	10.00
❑39, Oct 1973	10.00
❑40, Dec 1973	10.00
❑41, Feb 1974	8.00
❑42, Apr 1974	8.00
❑43, Jun 1974	8.00
❑44, Aug 1974	8.00
❑45, Sep 1974	8.00
❑46, Oct 1974	8.00
❑47, Dec 1974	8.00
❑48, Feb 1975	8.00
❑49, Apr 1975	8.00
❑50, Jun 1975	8.00
❑51, Jul 1975	8.00
❑52, Aug 1975	8.00
❑53, Oct 1975	8.00
❑54, Dec 1975	8.00
❑55, Jan 1976	8.00
❑56, Mar 1976	8.00
❑57, May 1976	8.00
❑58, Jul 1976	8.00
❑59, Sep 1976	8.00
❑60, Oct 1976	6.00
❑61, Nov 1976	6.00
❑62, Jan 1977	6.00
❑63, Mar 1977	6.00
❑64, May 1977	6.00
❑65, Jul 1977	6.00
❑66, Sep 1977	6.00
❑67, Oct 1977	6.00
❑68, Nov 1977	6.00
❑69, Jan 1978	6.00
❑70, Mar 1978	6.00

Uncle Scrooge's arch-enemies, The Beagle Boys, had their own Gold Key series.

© 1972 Walt Disney Productions.

N-MINT

❑71, May 1978 ... 6.00
❑72, Jul 1978 ... 6.00
❑73, Sep 1978 ... 6.00
❑74, Oct 1978 ... 6.00
❑75, Nov 1978 ... 6.00
❑76, Jan 1979 ... 6.00
❑77, Mar 1979 ... 6.00
❑78, Apr 1979 ... 6.00
❑79, May 1979 ... 6.00
❑80, Jun 1979 ... 3.00
❑81, Jul 1979 ... 3.00
❑82, Aug 1979 ... 3.00
❑83, Sep 1979 ... 3.00
❑84, Oct 1979 ... 3.00
❑85, Nov 1979 ... 3.00
❑86, Dec 1979 ... 3.00
❑87, Jan 1980 ... 3.00
❑88, Feb 1980 ... 3.00
❑89, Apr 1980 ... 3.00
❑90, Jul 1980 ... 3.00
❑91, Aug 1980 ... 3.00
❑92, Sep 1980 ... 3.00
❑93, Oct 1980 ... 3.00
❑94, Feb 1981 ... 3.00
❑95 1981 ... 3.00
❑96 1981 ... 3.00
❑97, Sep 1981 ... 3.00
❑98 1981 ... 3.00
❑99 1981 ... 3.00
❑100 1982 ... 3.00
❑101, Apr 1982 ... 3.00
❑102 1982 ... 3.00
❑103 1982 ... 3.00
❑104 1982 ... 3.00
❑105, ca. 1983 ... 3.00

BEER & ROAMING IN LAS VEGAS
SLAVE LABOR

❑1, ca. 1998, b&w ... 2.95
❑Ashcan 1 ... 1.00

BEER NUTZ
TUNDRA

❑1 ... 2.95
❑2 ... 2.00
❑3, b&w ... 2.25

BEETHOVEN
HARVEY

❑1, Mar 1994 ... 1.50
❑2, May 1994 ... 1.50
❑3, Jul 1994 ... 1.50

BEETLE BAILEY (VOL. 1)
DELL

❑5, Apr 1956; Earlier issues appeared as Four Color #469, #521, #552, and #622 ... 24.00
❑6, Jun 1956 ... 24.00
❑7, Aug 1956 ... 24.00
❑8, Nov 1956 ... 24.00
❑9, Feb 1957 ... 24.00
❑10, May 1957 ... 24.00
❑11, Aug 1957 ... 18.00
❑12, Nov 1957 ... 18.00
❑13, Feb 1958 ... 18.00
❑14, Apr 1958 ... 18.00
❑15, Jun 1958 ... 18.00
❑16, Aug 1958 ... 18.00
❑17, Oct 1958 ... 18.00
❑18, Dec 1958 ... 18.00
❑19, Feb 1959 ... 18.00
❑20, Apr 1959 ... 18.00
❑21, Jun 1959 ... 14.00
❑22, Aug 1959 ... 14.00
❑23, Oct 1959 ... 14.00
❑24, Dec 1959 ... 14.00
❑25, Feb 1960 ... 14.00
❑26, Apr 1960 ... 14.00
❑27, Jun 1960 ... 14.00
❑28 1960 ... 14.00
❑29 1960 ... 14.00
❑30 1960 ... 14.00
❑31, Mar 1961 ... 10.00

N-MINT

❑32, May 1961 ... 10.00
❑33, Jul 1961 ... 10.00
❑34, Sep 1961 ... 10.00
❑35, Nov 1961 ... 10.00
❑36, Jan 1962 ... 10.00
❑37, Mar 1962 ... 10.00
❑38, May 1962 ... 10.00
❑39, Nov 1962 ... 10.00
❑40, Feb 1963 ... 10.00
❑41, May 1963 ... 8.00
❑42, Aug 1963 ... 8.00
❑43, Nov 1963 ... 8.00
❑44, Feb 1964 ... 8.00
❑45, May 1964 ... 8.00
❑46, Aug 1964 ... 8.00
❑47, Nov 1964 ... 8.00
❑48, Feb 1965 ... 8.00
❑49, May 1965 ... 8.00
❑50, Aug 1965 ... 8.00
❑51, Nov 1965 ... 7.00
❑52, Feb 1966 ... 7.00
❑53, May 1966; Last Dell/Gold Key issue ... 7.00
❑54, Aug 1966; First King issue ... 7.00
❑55, Oct 1966 ... 7.00
❑56, Dec 1966 ... 7.00
❑57, Feb 1967 ... 7.00
❑58, Apr 1967 ... 7.00
❑59, Jun 1967 ... 7.00
❑60, Jul 1967 ... 7.00
❑61, Aug 1967 ... 6.00
❑62, Sep 1967 ... 6.00
❑63 1968 ... 6.00
❑64 1968 ... 6.00
❑65 1968 ... 6.00
❑66 1968; Last King issue ... 6.00
❑67, Feb 1969; First Charlton issue ... 6.00
❑68, Apr 1969 ... 6.00
❑69, Jun 1969 ... 6.00
❑70, ca. 1969 ... 6.00
❑71, Oct 1969 ... 4.00
❑72, Nov 1969 ... 4.00
❑73, Jan 1970 ... 4.00
❑74, Mar 1970 ... 4.00
❑75, May 1970 ... 4.00
❑76, Jul 1970 ... 4.00
❑77, Sep 1970 ... 4.00
❑78, Nov 1970 ... 4.00
❑79, Jan 1971 ... 4.00
❑80, Mar 1971 ... 4.00
❑81, May 1971 ... 4.00
❑82, Jul 1971 ... 4.00
❑83, Sep 1971 ... 4.00
❑84, Oct 1971 ... 4.00
❑85, Nov 1971 ... 4.00
❑86, Dec 1971 ... 4.00
❑87, Jan 1972 ... 4.00
❑88, Mar 1972 ... 4.00
❑89, Apr 1972 ... 4.00
❑90, Jun 1972 ... 4.00
❑91, Jul 1972 ... 4.00
❑92, Aug 1972 ... 4.00
❑93, Oct 1972 ... 4.00
❑94, Nov 1972 ... 4.00
❑95, Dec 1972 ... 4.00
❑96, Jan 1973 ... 4.00
❑97, Mar 1973 ... 4.00
❑98, Apr 1973 ... 4.00
❑99, Jun 1973 ... 4.00
❑100, Jul 1973 ... 4.00
❑101, Aug 1973 ... 3.00
❑102, Oct 1973 ... 3.00
❑103, Nov 1973 ... 3.00
❑104 1974 ... 3.00
❑105, May 1974 ... 3.00
❑106, Jul 1974 ... 3.00
❑107, Oct 1974 ... 3.00
❑108 1974 ... 3.00
❑109 1975 ... 3.00
❑110, Apr 1975 ... 3.00
❑111, Jun 1975 ... 3.00

N-MINT

❑112, Sep 1975 ... 3.00
❑113 1975 ... 3.00
❑114 1976 ... 3.00
❑115, Mar 1976 ... 3.00
❑116, May 1976 ... 3.00
❑117, Jul 1976 ... 3.00
❑118, Sep 1976 ... 3.00
❑119; Last Charlton issue ... 3.00
❑120, Apr 1978; Returns to Gold Key ... 3.00
❑121, Jun 1978 ... 3.00
❑122, Aug 1978 ... 3.00
❑123, Oct 1978 ... 3.00
❑124, Dec 1978 ... 3.00
❑125, Feb 1979 ... 3.00
❑126, Apr 1979 ... 3.00
❑127, Jun 1979 ... 3.00
❑128, Aug 1979 ... 3.00
❑129, Oct 1979 ... 3.00
❑130, Dec 1979 ... 3.00
❑131, Feb 1980 ... 3.00
❑132, Apr 1980 ... 3.00

BEETLE BAILEY (VOL. 2)
HARVEY

❑1, Sep 1992 ... 2.00
❑2, Jan 1993 ... 2.00
❑3, Apr 1993 ... 2.00
❑4, Jul 1993 ... 2.00
❑5, Oct 1993 ... 2.00
❑6, Jan 1994 ... 2.00
❑7, Apr 1994 ... 2.00
❑8, Jun 1994 ... 2.00
❑9, Aug 1994 ... 2.00
❑Giant Size 1 ... 2.25
❑Giant Size 2 ... 2.25

BEETLE BAILEY BIG BOOK
HARVEY

❑2 ... 2.00

BEETLEJUICE
HARVEY

❑1 ... 1.50
❑2 ... 1.50

BEETLEJUICE: CRIMEBUSTERS ON THE HAUNT
HARVEY

❑1 ... 1.50

BEETLEJUICE: ELLIOT MESS AND THE UNWASHABLES
HARVEY

❑1 ... 1.50
❑2, Oct 1992 ... 1.50
❑3, Nov 1992 ... 1.50

BEETLEJUICE HOLIDAY SPECIAL
HARVEY

❑1, Feb 1992 ... 1.50

BEETLEJUICE IN THE NEITHERWORLD
HARVEY

❑1 ... 1.50
❑2 ... 1.50

BEFORE THE FANTASTIC FOUR: BEN GRIMM AND LOGAN
MARVEL

❑1, Jul 2000 ... 2.99
❑2, Aug 2000 ... 2.99
❑3, Sep 2000 ... 2.99
❑4, Oct 2000 ... 2.99

BEFORE THE FF: REED RICHARDS
MARVEL

❑1, Sep 2000 ... 2.99
❑2, Oct 2000 ... 2.99
❑3, Dec 2000 ... 2.99
❑4, Dec 2000 ... 2.99

BEFORE THE FF: THE STORMS
MARVEL

❑1, Dec 2000 ... 2.99
❑2, Jan 2001 ... 2.99
❑3, Feb 2001 ... 2.99

N-MINT

BEHOLD 3-D
Edge Group

❑1 .... 3.95

BELIEVE IN YOURSELF PRODUCTIONS
Believe in Yourself Productions

❑1/Ashcan; Cardstock cover. Includes 6 page story only available in Ashcan format with 14 pin-u 1.00
❑1/B; Sapphire Edition. Only 25 made 1.00
❑1/Ltd 1.00

BELLA DONNA
Pinnacle

❑1, b&w 1.75

BEN CASEY FILM STORIES
Gold Key

❑1, ca. 1962 .... 55.00

BENEATH THE PLANET OF THE APES
Gold Key

❑1, Dec 1970 .... 35.00

BENZANGO OBSCURO
Starhead

❑1 .... 2.75

BENZINE
Antarctic

❑1, Oct 2000 .... 4.95
❑2, Nov 2000 .... 4.95
❑3, Dec 2000 .... 4.95
❑4, Jan 2001 .... 4.95
❑5, Feb 2001 .... 4.95
❑6, Mar 2001 .... 4.95
❑7, May 2001 .... 4.95

BEOWULF
DC

❑1, May 1975 1: Grendel (monster). 1: Beowulf 3.00
❑2, Jul 1975 .... 3.00
❑3, Sep 1975 .... 1.50
❑4, Nov 1975 .... 1.50
❑5, Jan 1976 .... 1.50
❑6, Mar 1976 .... 1.50

BEOWULF (THECOMIC.COM)
Comic.Com

❑1, ca. 1999 .... 4.95
❑2 1999 .... 4.95
❑3 1999 .... 4.95

BERLIN
Drawn & Quarterly

❑1, Apr 1996 .... 2.50
❑2, Jul 1996 .... 2.50
❑3, Feb 1997 .... 2.50
❑4, Feb 1998 .... 2.50
❑5, ca. 1998 .... 2.95
❑6, ca. 1999 .... 2.95
❑7, Apr 2000, b&w; smaller than normal comic book 2.95
❑8, b&w 2.95

BERNIE WRIGHTSON, MASTER OF THE MACABRE
Pacific

❑1, Jun 1983; BWr (w); BWr (a); Edgar Allen Poe adaptation ("The Black Cat") 2.50
❑2, Aug 1983 BWr (w); BWr (a) 2.50
❑3, Aug 1983 BWr (w); BWr (a) 2.50
❑4, Aug 1984 BWr (w); BWr (a) 2.50
❑5, Nov 1984 BWr (w); BWr (a) 2.50

BERSERK
Dark Horse

❑1, ca. 2003 .... 13.95
❑2, ca. 2004 .... 13.95
❑3, ca. 2004 .... 13.95

BERZERKER
Gauntlet

❑1, Feb 1993; Medina 2.95
❑2 .... 2.95
❑3 .... 2.95
❑4 .... 2.95
❑5 .... 2.95

N-MINT

BERZERKERS
Image

❑1, Aug 1995 .... 2.50
❑1/Variant, Aug 1995; alternate cover 2.50
❑2, Sep 1995 .... 2.50
❑3, Oct 1995 .... 2.50

BEST CELLARS
Out of the Cellar

❑1 .... 2.50

BEST OF BARRON STOREY'S W.A.T.C.H. MAGAZINE
Vanguard

❑1, Dec 1993 .... 2.95

BEST OF DARK HORSE PRESENTS, THE
Dark Horse

❑1, b&w 5.95
❑2, b&w 8.95

BEST OF DC, THE
DC

❑1, Sep 1979 .... 5.00
❑2, Nov 1979 .... 4.00
❑3, Jan 1980 .... 4.00
❑4, Mar 1980 .... 4.00
❑5, May 1980 .... 4.00
❑6, Jul 1980 .... 4.00
❑7, Sep 1980; Superboy 4.00
❑8, Nov 1980; Superman, Other Identities 4.00
❑9, Jan 1981 .... 4.00
❑10, Mar 1981 .... 4.00
❑11, Apr 1981 .... 4.00
❑12, May 1981 .... 4.00
❑13, Jun 1981 .... 4.00
❑14, Jul 1981 .... 4.00
❑15, Aug 1981; Superboy 4.00
❑16, Sep 1981; Superman Anniversaries 4.00
❑17, Oct 1981 .... 4.00
❑18, Nov 1981 .... 4.00
❑19, Dec 1981; Superman, Imaginary Stories 4.00
❑20, Jan 1982 .... 4.00
❑21, Feb 1982; Justice Society 4.00
❑22, Mar 1982; Sandman 4.00
❑23, Apr 1982 .... 4.00
❑24, May 1982; Legion 4.00
❑25, Jun 1982 .... 4.00
❑26, Jul 1982; Brave and the Bold 4.00
❑27, Aug 1982; Superman vs. Luthor 4.00
❑28, Sep 1982 .... 4.00
❑29, Oct 1982 .... 4.00
❑30, Nov 1982; Batman 4.00
❑31, Dec 1982; Justice League 4.00
❑32, Jan 1983; Superman 4.00
❑33, Feb 1983 .... 4.00
❑34, Mar 1983; Metal Men 4.00
❑35, Apr 1983; Year's Best 82 .... 4.00
❑36, May 1983; Superman vs. Kryptonite 4.00
❑37, Jun 1983 .... 4.00
❑38, Jul 1983 .... 4.00
❑39, Aug 1983 .... 4.00
❑40, Sep 1983; Superman, Krypton 4.00
❑41, Oct 1983 .... 4.00
❑42, Nov 1983 .... 4.00
❑43, Dec 1983 .... 4.00
❑44, Jan 1984; Legion 4.00
❑45, Feb 1984; Binky 4.00
❑46, Mar 1984; Jimmy Olsen 4.00
❑47, Apr 1984 .... 4.00
❑48, May 1984 .... 4.00
❑49, Jun 1984 .... 4.00
❑50, Jul 1984; Superman 4.00
❑51, Aug 1984 .... 4.00
❑52, Sep 1984; Year's Best 83 .... 4.00
❑53, Oct 1984 .... 4.00
❑54, Nov 1984 .... 4.00
❑55, Dec 1984 .... 4.00
❑56, Jan 1985; Superman 4.00
❑57, Feb 1985; Legion 4.00

Several issues of *The Best of DC* contained *Sugar & Spike* reprints.

© 1982 DC Comics.

N-MINT

❑58, Mar 1985; Superman Jrs 4.00
❑59, Apr 1985; Superman 4.00
❑60, May 1985 .... 4.00
❑61, Jun 1985 .... 4.00
❑62, Jul 1985; Batman 4.00
❑63, Aug 1985 .... 4.00
❑64, Sep 1985; Legion 4.00
❑65, Oct 1985; Sugar & Spike 4.00
❑66, Nov 1985; Superman 4.00
❑67, Dec 1985 .... 4.00
❑68, Jan 1986; Sugar & Spike 4.00
❑69, Feb 1986; Year's Best 85 .... 4.00
❑70, Mar 1986; Binky's Buddies 4.00

BEST OF DONALD DUCK AND UNCLE SCROOGE, THE
Gold Key

❑1, Nov 1964; Reprints stories from Four Color Comics #189 and 408 (Donald Duck) 50.00
❑2, Sep 1967; CB (a); Reprints stories from Four Color Comics #256 (Donald Duck) and Uncle Scrooge #7 and 8 .. 50.00

BEST OF DORK TOWER
Dork Storm

❑1, ca. 2001, b&w 2.00

BEST OF FURRLOUGH
Antarctic

❑1, Jan 1995, b&w 3.95
❑2 .... 3.95

BEST OF GOLD DIGGER
Antarctic

❑Annual 1, May 1999, b&w 2.99

BEST OF NORTHSTAR, THE
Northstar

❑1, b&w 1.95

BEST OF THE BRAVE AND THE BOLD, THE
DC

❑1, Oct 1988; Batman, Green Arrow .. 2.50
❑2, Nov 1988; Batman, Flash 2.50
❑3, Dec 1988; Batman, Aquaman 2.50
❑4, Dec 1988; Batman, Creeper 2.50
❑5, Jan 1989; Batman, House of Mystery 2.50
❑6, Jan 1989; Batman, Teen Titans 2.50

BEST OF THE BRITISH INVASION
Revolutionary

❑1, Sep 1993, b&w 2.50
❑2, Jan 1994, b&w 2.50

BEST OF TRIBUNE CO., THE
Dragon Lady

❑1 .... 2.95
❑2 .... 2.95
❑3 .... 2.95
❑4; (becomes Thrilling Adventure Strips) 2.95

BEST OF WALT DISNEY COMICS, THE
Western

❑1, ca. 1974; 96170; Reprints stories from Four Color Comics #62 (Donald Duck) 15.00
❑2, ca. 1974; 96171 .... 12.00

Condition price index: Multiply "NM prices" above by: **0.83 for Very Fine/Near Mint**
0.66 for Very Fine • 0.33 for Fine • 0.2 for Very Good • 0.125 for Good

N-MINT

❑3, ca. 1974; 96172; Reprints stories from Four Color Comics #386 and 495 (Uncle Scrooge) and Uncle Scrooge #7 ..... 12.00
❑4, ca. 1974; 96173; Reprints stories from Four Color Comics #159 and 178 (Donald Duck) 12.00

BETA SEXUS
FANTAGRAPHICS / EROS

❑1, b&w 2.75
❑2, Jul 1994, b&w 2.75

BETTA: TIME WARRIOR
IMMORTAL / EROS

❑1 ..... 2.95
❑2 ..... 2.95
❑3 ..... 2.95

BETTI COZMO
ANTARCTIC

❑1, Apr 1999 ..... 2.99
❑2, Jun 1999 ..... 2.99

BETTIE PAGE COMICS
DARK HORSE

❑1, Mar 1996; one-shot, cardstock cover 3.95

BETTIE PAGE COMICS: SPICY ADVENTURE
DARK HORSE

❑1, Jan 1997 ..... 2.95

BETTIE PAGE: QUEEN OF THE NILE
DARK HORSE

❑1, Dec 1999 ..... 2.95
❑2, Feb 2000 ..... 2.95
❑3, Apr 2000 ..... 2.95

BETTY
ARCHIE

❑1, Sep 1992 ..... 4.00
❑2, Oct 1992 ..... 2.00
❑3, Dec 1992 ..... 2.00
❑4, Feb 1993 ..... 2.00
❑5, Apr 1993 ..... 2.00
❑6, Jun 1993 ..... 1.50
❑7, Aug 1993 ..... 1.50
❑8, Sep 1993 ..... 1.50
❑9, Oct 1993 ..... 1.50
❑10, Nov 1993 ..... 1.50
❑11, Dec 1993 ..... 1.50
❑12, Feb 1994 ..... 1.50
❑13, Apr 1994 ..... 1.50
❑14, Jun 1994 ..... 1.50
❑15, Jul 1994 ..... 1.50
❑16, Aug 1994 ..... 1.50
❑17, Sep 1994 ..... 1.50
❑18, Oct 1994 ..... 1.50
❑19, Nov 1994 ..... 1.50
❑20, Dec 1994 ..... 1.50
❑21, Jan 1995 ..... 1.50
❑22, Feb 1995 ..... 1.50
❑23, Mar 1995 ..... 1.50
❑24, Apr 1995 ..... 1.50
❑25, May 1995 ..... 1.50
❑26, Jun 1995 ..... 1.50
❑27, Jul 1995 ..... 1.50
❑28, Aug 1995 ..... 1.50
❑29, Sep 1995 ..... 1.50
❑30, Oct 1995 ..... 1.50
❑31, Nov 1995 ..... 1.50
❑32, Dec 1995 ..... 1.50
❑33, Jan 1996 ..... 1.50
❑34, Feb 1996 ..... 1.50
❑35, Mar 1996 ..... 1.50
❑36, Apr 1996 ..... 1.50
❑37, May 1996 ..... 1.50
❑38, Jun 1996 ..... 1.50
❑39, Jul 1996 ..... 1.50
❑40, Aug 1996 ..... 1.50
❑41, Sep 1996 ..... 1.50
❑42, Oct 1996; cover has reader sketches of Betty 1.50
❑43, Nov 1996 ..... 1.50
❑44, Dec 1996 ..... 1.50
❑45, Jan 1997 ..... 1.50
❑46, Feb 1997 ..... 1.50
❑47, Mar 1997 ..... 1.50
❑48, Apr 1997 ..... 1.50
❑49, May 1997 ..... 1.50
❑50, Jun 1997 ..... 1.50
❑51, Jul 1997 ..... 1.50
❑52, Aug 1997 ..... 1.50
❑53, Sep 1997 ..... 1.50
❑54, Oct 1997 ..... 1.50
❑55, Nov 1997 ..... 1.50
❑56, Dec 1997; return of Polly Cooper 1.50
❑57, Jan 1998 ..... 1.75
❑58, Feb 1998; Virtual Pets 1.75
❑59, Mar 1998 ..... 1.75
❑60, Apr 1998 ..... 1.75
❑61, May 1998 ..... 1.75
❑62, Jun 1998 ..... 1.75
❑63, Jul 1998 ..... 1.75
❑64, Aug 1998 ..... 1.75
❑65, Sep 1998 ..... 1.75
❑66, Oct 1998 ..... 1.75
❑67, Nov 1998 ..... 1.75
❑68, Dec 1998 ..... 1.75
❑69, Jan 1999 ..... 1.75
❑70, Feb 1999 ..... 1.75
❑71, Mar 1999 ..... 1.75
❑72, Apr 1999 ..... 1.79
❑73, May 1999 ..... 1.79
❑74, Jun 1999 ..... 1.79
❑75, Jul 1999 ..... 1.79
❑76, Aug 1999 ..... 1.79
❑77, Sep 1999 ..... 1.79
❑78, Oct 1999 ..... 1.79
❑79, Nov 1999 ..... 1.79
❑80, Dec 1999 ..... 1.79
❑81, Jan 2000 ..... 1.79
❑82, Feb 2000 ..... 1.79
❑83, Mar 2000 ..... 1.79
❑84, Apr 2000 ..... 1.79
❑85, May 2000 ..... 1.79
❑86, Jun 2000 ..... 1.79
❑87, Jul 2000 ..... 1.99
❑88, Aug 2000 ..... 1.99
❑89, Sep 2000 ..... 1.99
❑90, Oct 2000 ..... 1.99
❑91, Nov 2000 ..... 1.99
❑92, Dec 2000 ..... 1.99
❑93, Jan 2001 ..... 1.99
❑94, Feb 2001 ..... 1.99
❑95, Mar 2001 ..... 1.99
❑96, Apr 2001 ..... 1.99
❑97, May 2001 ..... 1.99
❑98, Jun 2001 ..... 1.99
❑99, Jul 2001 ..... 1.99
❑100, Aug 2001 ..... 1.99
❑101, Sep 2001 ..... 1.99
❑102, Oct 2001 ..... 1.99
❑103, Oct 2001 ..... 2.19
❑104, Nov 2001 ..... 2.19
❑105, Dec 2001 ..... 2.19
❑106, Jan 2002 ..... 2.19
❑107, Feb 2002 ..... 2.19
❑108, Mar 2002 ..... 2.19
❑109, Apr 2002 ..... 2.19
❑110, May 2002 ..... 2.19
❑111, Jun 2002 ..... 2.19
❑112, Jul 2002 ..... 2.19
❑113, Aug 2002 ..... 2.19
❑114, Sep 2002 ..... 2.19
❑115, Oct 2002 ..... 2.19
❑116, Oct 2002 ..... 2.19
❑117, Nov 2002 ..... 2.19
❑118, Dec 2002 ..... 2.19
❑119, Jan 2003 ..... 2.19
❑120, Feb 2003 ..... 2.19
❑121, Mar 2003 ..... 2.19
❑122, Apr 2003 ..... 2.19
❑123, May 2003 ..... 2.19
❑124, Jun 2003 ..... 2.19
❑125, Jul 2003 ..... 2.19
❑126, Aug 2003 ..... 2.19
❑127, Sep 2003 ..... 2.19
❑128, Oct 2003 ..... 2.19
❑129, Oct 2003 ..... 2.19
❑130, Nov 2003 ..... 2.19
❑131, Dec 2003 ..... 2.19
❑132, Jan 2004 ..... 2.19
❑133, Feb 2004 ..... 2.19
❑134, Mar 2004 ..... 2.19
❑135, Apr 2004 ..... 2.19
❑136, May 2004 ..... 2.19
❑137, Jul 2004 ..... 2.19

BETTY & ME
ARCHIE

❑1, Aug 1965 ..... 65.00
❑2, Nov 1965 ..... 40.00
❑3, Aug 1966 ..... 24.00
❑4, Oct 1966 ..... 24.00
❑5, Dec 1966 ..... 24.00
❑6, Feb 1967 ..... 15.00
❑7, Apr 1967 ..... 15.00
❑8, Jun 1967 ..... 15.00
❑9, Aug 1967 ..... 15.00
❑10, Oct 1967 ..... 15.00
❑11, Dec 1967 ..... 10.00
❑12, Feb 1968 ..... 10.00
❑13, Apr 1968 ..... 10.00
❑14, Jun 1968 ..... 10.00
❑15, Aug 1968 ..... 10.00
❑16, Sep 1968 ..... 10.00
❑17, Oct 1968 ..... 10.00
❑18, Dec 1968 ..... 10.00
❑19, Feb 1969 ..... 10.00
❑20, Apr 1969 ..... 10.00
❑21, Jun 1969 ..... 7.00
❑22, Aug 1969 ..... 7.00
❑23, Sep 1969 ..... 7.00
❑24, Oct 1969 ..... 7.00
❑25, Dec 1969 ..... 7.00
❑26, Feb 1970 ..... 7.00
❑27, Apr 1970 ..... 7.00
❑28, Jun 1970 ..... 7.00
❑29, Aug 1970 ..... 7.00
❑30, Sep 1970 ..... 7.00
❑31, Oct 1970 ..... 6.00
❑32, Dec 1970 ..... 6.00
❑33, Feb 1971 ..... 6.00
❑34, Apr 1971 ..... 6.00
❑35, Jun 1971 ..... 6.00
❑36, Aug 1971 ..... 6.00
❑37, Sep 1971 ..... 6.00
❑38, Oct 1971 ..... 6.00
❑39, Dec 1971 ..... 6.00
❑40, Feb 1972 ..... 6.00
❑41, Apr 1972 ..... 5.00
❑42, Jun 1972 ..... 5.00
❑43, Aug 1972 ..... 5.00
❑44, Sep 1972 ..... 5.00
❑45, Oct 1972 ..... 5.00
❑46, Dec 1972 ..... 5.00
❑47, Feb 1973 ..... 5.00
❑48, Apr 1973 ..... 5.00
❑49, Jun 1973 ..... 5.00
❑50, Jul 1973 ..... 5.00
❑51, Aug 1973 ..... 4.00
❑52, Sep 1973 ..... 4.00
❑53, Oct 1973 ..... 4.00
❑54, Dec 1973 ..... 4.00
❑55, Feb 1974 ..... 4.00
❑56, Apr 1974 ..... 4.00
❑57, Jun 1974 ..... 4.00
❑58, Jul 1974 ..... 4.00
❑59, Aug 1974 ..... 4.00
❑60, Sep 1974 ..... 4.00
❑61, Oct 1974 ..... 3.00
❑62, Dec 1974 ..... 3.00
❑63, Feb 1975 ..... 3.00
❑64, Mar 1975 ..... 3.00
❑65, Apr 1975 ..... 3.00
❑66, May 1975 ..... 3.00
❑67, Jul 1975 ..... 3.00

	N-MINT
❑68, Aug 1975	3.00
❑69, Sep 1975	3.00
❑70, Oct 1975	3.00
❑71, Dec 1975	2.00
❑72, Feb 1976	2.00
❑73, Mar 1976	2.00
❑74, Apr 1976	2.00
❑75, May 1976	2.00
❑76, Jul 1976	2.00
❑77, Aug 1976	2.00
❑78, Sep 1976	2.00
❑79, Oct 1976	2.00
❑80, Dec 1976	2.00
❑81, Feb 1977	2.00
❑82, Mar 1977	2.00
❑83, Apr 1977	2.00
❑84, May 1977	2.00
❑85, Jul 1977	2.00
❑86, Aug 1977	2.00
❑87, Sep 1977	2.00
❑88, Oct 1977	2.00
❑89, Dec 1977	2.00
❑90, Feb 1978	2.00
❑91, Mar 1978	2.00
❑92, Apr 1978	2.00
❑93, May 1978	2.00
❑94, Jul 1978	2.00
❑95, Aug 1978	2.00
❑96, Sep 1978	2.00
❑97, Oct 1978	2.00
❑98, Dec 1978	2.00
❑99, Feb 1979	2.00
❑100, Mar 1979	2.00
❑101, Apr 1979	2.00
❑102, May 1979	2.00
❑103, Jul 1979	2.00
❑104, Aug 1979	2.00
❑105, Sep 1979	2.00
❑106, Oct 1979	2.00
❑107, Dec 1979	2.00
❑108, Feb 1980	2.00
❑109, Mar 1980	2.00
❑110 1980	2.00
❑111 1980	2.00
❑112 1980	2.00
❑113 1980	2.00
❑114	2.00
❑115	2.00
❑116	2.00
❑117	2.00
❑118	2.00
❑119	2.00
❑120	2.00
❑121	2.00
❑122	2.00
❑123	2.00
❑124	2.00
❑125	2.00
❑126 1982	2.00
❑127 1982	2.00
❑128 1982	2.00
❑129 1982	2.00
❑130 1982	2.00
❑131 1982	2.00
❑132, Jan 1983	2.00
❑133 1983	2.00
❑134, Jul 1983	2.00
❑135, Sep 1983	2.00
❑136, Nov 1983	2.00
❑137, Jan 1984	2.00
❑138, Mar 1984	2.00
❑139, May 1984	2.00
❑140, Jul 1984	2.00
❑141, Sep 1984	2.00
❑142, Nov 1984	2.00
❑143, Jan 1985	2.00
❑144, Mar 1985	2.00
❑145, May 1985	2.00
❑146, Jul 1985	2.00
❑147, Sep 1985	2.00
❑148, Nov 1985	2.00

	N-MINT
❑149, Jan 1986	2.00
❑150, Mar 1986	2.00
❑151, May 1986	1.50
❑152, Jul 1986	1.50
❑153, Sep 1986	1.50
❑154, Nov 1986	1.50
❑155, Jan 1987	1.50
❑156, Mar 1987	1.50
❑157, May 1987	1.50
❑158, Jun 1987	1.50
❑159, Jul 1987	1.50
❑160, Aug 1987	1.50
❑161, Sep 1987	1.50
❑162, Oct 1987	1.50
❑163, Dec 1987	1.50
❑164, Jan 1988	1.50
❑165, Mar 1988	1.50
❑166, May 1988	1.50
❑167, Jun 1988	1.50
❑168, Jul 1988	1.50
❑169, Aug 1988	1.50
❑170, Sep 1988	1.50
❑171, Oct 1988	1.50
❑172, Jan 1989	1.50
❑173, Mar 1989	1.50
❑174, May 1989	1.50
❑175, Jun 1989	1.50
❑176, Jul 1989	1.50
❑177, Aug 1989	1.50
❑178, Sep 1989 A: Veronica Lodge	1.50
❑179, Oct 1989	1.50
❑180, Jan 1990	1.50
❑181, Mar 1990	1.50
❑182, May 1990	1.50
❑183, Jun 1990	1.50
❑184, Jul 1990	1.50
❑185, Aug 1990	1.50
❑186, Sep 1990	1.50
❑187, Oct 1990	1.50
❑188, Jan 1991	1.50
❑189, Mar 1991	1.50
❑190, May 1991	1.50
❑191, Jul 1991	1.50
❑192, Aug 1991	1.50
❑193, Sep 1991	1.50
❑194, Oct 1991	1.50
❑195, Nov 1991	1.50
❑196, Jan 1992	1.50
❑197, Mar 1992	1.50
❑198, May 1992	1.50
❑199, Jul 1992	1.50
❑200, Aug 1992	1.50

BETTY AND VERONICA
ARCHIE

	N-MINT
❑1, Jun 1987	6.00
❑2 1987	4.00
❑3 1987	4.00
❑4	3.00
❑5	3.00
❑6	3.00
❑7	3.00
❑8 1988	3.00
❑9 1988	3.00
❑10 1988	3.00
❑11 1988	2.50
❑12 1988	2.50
❑13 1988	2.50
❑14	2.50
❑15	2.50
❑16	2.50
❑17	2.50
❑18	2.50
❑19	2.50
❑20 1989	2.50
❑21 1989	2.00
❑22 1989	2.00
❑23 1989	2.00
❑24 1989	2.00
❑25 1989	2.00
❑26	2.00
❑27	2.00

Betty's resourcefulness shines in her solo series.

	N-MINT
❑28 1990	2.00
❑29 1990	2.00
❑30, May 1990	2.00
❑31 1990	2.00
❑32 1990	2.00
❑33 1990	2.00
❑34 1990	2.00
❑35 1990	2.00
❑36	2.00
❑37 1991	2.00
❑38 1991	2.00
❑39 1991	2.00
❑40 1991	2.00
❑41 1991	2.00
❑42 1991	2.00
❑43 1991	2.00
❑44 1991	2.00
❑45 1991	2.00
❑46 1991	2.00
❑47, Jan 1992	2.00
❑48, Feb 1992	2.00
❑49, Mar 1992	2.00
❑50, Apr 1992	2.00
❑51, May 1992	1.50
❑52, Jun 1992	1.50
❑53, Jul 1992	1.50
❑54, Aug 1992	1.50
❑55, Sep 1992	1.50
❑56, Oct 1992	1.50
❑57, Nov 1992	1.50
❑58, Dec 1992	1.50
❑59, Jan 1993	1.50
❑60, Feb 1993	1.50
❑61, Mar 1993	1.50
❑62, Apr 1993	1.50
❑63, May 1993	1.50
❑64, Jun 1993	1.50
❑65, Jul 1993	1.50
❑66, Aug 1993 DDC (a)	1.50
❑67, Sep 1993	1.50
❑68, Oct 1993	1.50
❑69, Nov 1993	1.50
❑70, Dec 1993	1.50
❑71, Jan 1994	1.50
❑72, Feb 1994	1.50
❑73, Mar 1994	1.50
❑74, Apr 1994	1.50
❑75, May 1994	1.50
❑76, Jun 1994	1.50
❑77, Jul 1994	1.50
❑78, Aug 1994	1.50
❑79, Sep 1994	1.50
❑80, Oct 1994	1.50
❑81, Nov 1994	1.50
❑82, Dec 1994	1.50
❑83, Jan 1995	1.50
❑84, Feb 1995	1.50
❑85, Mar 1995	1.50
❑86, Apr 1995	1.50
❑87, May 1995	1.50
❑88, Jun 1995	1.50
❑89, Jul 1995	1.50
❑90, Aug 1995	1.50
❑91, Sep 1995	1.50
❑92, Oct 1995	1.50
❑93, Nov 1995	1.50
❑94, Dec 1995	1.50

N-MINT

- ❑95, Jan 1996; concludes in Archie's PalJughead #76 .... 1.50
- ❑96, Feb 1996 .... 1.50
- ❑97, Mar 1996 .... 1.50
- ❑98, Apr 1996 .... 1.50
- ❑99, May 1996 .... 1.50
- ❑100, Jun 1996 .... 1.50
- ❑101, Jul 1996 .... 1.50
- ❑102, Aug 1996 .... 1.50
- ❑103, Sep 1996 .... 1.50
- ❑104, Oct 1996 .... 1.50
- ❑105, Nov 1996 .... 1.50
- ❑106, Dec 1996 .... 1.50
- ❑107, Jan 1997 .... 1.50
- ❑108, Feb 1997 .... 1.50
- ❑109, Mar 1997 .... 1.50
- ❑110, Apr 1997 .... 1.50
- ❑111, May 1997 .... 1.50
- ❑112, Jun 1997 .... 1.50
- ❑113, Jul 1997 .... 1.50
- ❑114, Aug 1997 .... 1.50
- ❑115, Sep 1997 .... 1.50
- ❑116, Oct 1997 .... 1.50
- ❑117, Nov 1997 .... 1.50
- ❑118, Dec 1997 .... 1.50
- ❑119, Jan 1998 .... 1.75
- ❑120, Feb 1998 .... 1.75
- ❑121, Mar 1998 .... 1.75
- ❑122, Apr 1998 .... 1.75
- ❑123, May 1998 .... 1.75
- ❑124, Jun 1998 .... 1.75
- ❑125, Jul 1998 .... 1.75
- ❑126, Aug 1998 .... 1.75
- ❑127, Sep 1998 DDC (a) 1.75
- ❑128, Oct 1998 .... 1.75
- ❑129, Nov 1998 DDC (a) 1.75
- ❑130, Dec 1998 .... 1.75
- ❑131, Jan 1999 .... 1.75
- ❑132, Feb 1999 .... 1.75
- ❑133, Mar 1999 DDC (a) 1.75
- ❑134, Apr 1999 .... 1.79
- ❑135, May 1999 DDC (a) 1.79
- ❑136, Jun 1999 .... 1.79
- ❑137, Jul 1999 .... 1.79
- ❑138, Aug 1999 .... 1.79
- ❑139, Sep 1999 .... 1.79
- ❑140, Oct 1999 .... 1.79
- ❑141, Nov 1999 .... 1.79
- ❑142, Dec 1999 .... 1.79
- ❑143, Jan 2000 .... 1.79
- ❑144, Feb 2000 .... 1.79
- ❑145, Mar 2000 .... 1.79
- ❑146, Apr 2000 .... 1.79
- ❑147, May 2000 .... 1.79
- ❑148, Jun 2000 .... 1.79
- ❑149, Jul 2000 .... 1.99
- ❑150, Aug 2000 .... 1.99
- ❑151, Sep 2000 .... 1.99
- ❑152, Oct 2000 .... 1.99
- ❑153, Nov 2000 .... 1.99
- ❑154, Dec 2000 .... 1.99
- ❑155, Jan 2001 .... 1.99
- ❑156, Feb 2001 .... 1.99
- ❑157, Mar 2001 .... 1.99
- ❑158, Apr 2001 .... 1.99
- ❑159, May 2001 .... 1.99
- ❑160, May 2001 .... 1.99
- ❑161, Jun 2001 .... 1.99
- ❑162, Jul 2001 .... 1.99
- ❑163, Aug 2001 .... 1.99
- ❑164, Sep 2001 .... 1.99
- ❑165, Oct 2001 .... 1.99
- ❑166, Nov 2001 .... 2.19
- ❑167, Dec 2001 .... 2.19
- ❑168, Jan 2002 .... 2.19
- ❑169, Feb 2002 .... 2.19
- ❑170, Mar 2002 .... 2.19
- ❑171, Apr 2002 .... 2.19
- ❑172, Apr 2002 .... 2.19
- ❑173, May 2002 .... 2.19
- ❑174, Jun 2002 .... 2.19
- ❑175, Jul 2002 .... 2.19
- ❑176, Aug 2002 .... 2.19
- ❑177, Sep 2002 .... 2.19
- ❑178, Oct 2002 .... 2.19
- ❑179, Nov 2002 .... 2.19
- ❑180, Dec 2002 .... 2.19
- ❑181, Jan 2003 .... 2.19
- ❑182, Feb 2003 .... 2.19
- ❑183, Mar 2003 .... 2.19
- ❑184, Apr 2003 .... 2.19
- ❑185, Apr 2003 .... 2.19
- ❑186, May 2003 .... 2.19
- ❑187, Jun 2003 .... 2.19
- ❑188, Jul 2003 .... 2.19
- ❑189, Aug 2003 .... 2.19
- ❑190, Sep 2003 .... 2.19
- ❑191, Oct 2003 .... 2.19
- ❑192, Nov 2003 .... 2.19
- ❑193, Dec 2003 .... 2.19
- ❑194, Jan 2004 .... 2.19
- ❑195, Feb 2004 .... 2.19
- ❑196, Mar 2004 .... 2.19
- ❑197, Mar 2004 .... 2.19
- ❑198, May 2004 .... 2.19
- ❑199, Jun 2004 .... 2.19
- ❑200, Jul 2004 .... 2.19

BETTY & VERONICA ANNUAL DIGEST MAGAZINE

ARCHIE

- ❑12, Jan 1995 .... 1.75
- ❑13, Sep 1995 .... 1.75
- ❑14, Feb 1996 .... 1.75
- ❑15, Jul 1996 .... 1.75
- ❑16, Aug 1997 .... 1.79

BETTY AND VERONICA COMICS DIGEST

ARCHIE

- ❑1, Aug 1982 .... 9.00
- ❑2, Nov 1982 .... 5.00
- ❑3, Feb 1983 .... 5.00
- ❑4, May 1983 .... 4.00
- ❑5, Aug 1983 .... 4.00
- ❑6, Nov 1983 .... 4.00
- ❑7, Feb 1984 .... 4.00
- ❑8, May 1984 .... 4.00
- ❑9, Aug 1984 .... 4.00
- ❑10, Nov 1984 .... 4.00
- ❑11, Feb 1985 .... 3.00
- ❑12, Apr 1985 .... 3.00
- ❑13, Jun 1985 .... 3.00
- ❑14, Aug 1985 .... 3.00
- ❑15, Oct 1985 .... 3.00
- ❑16, Dec 1985 .... 3.00
- ❑17, Feb 1986 .... 3.00
- ❑18, Apr 1986 .... 3.00
- ❑19, Jun 1986 .... 3.00
- ❑20, Aug 1986 .... 3.00
- ❑21, Oct 1986 .... 3.00
- ❑22, Dec 1986 .... 3.00
- ❑23, Feb 1987 .... 3.00
- ❑24, Apr 1987 .... 3.00
- ❑25, Jun 1987 .... 3.00
- ❑26, Aug 1987 .... 3.00
- ❑27, Nov 1987 .... 3.00
- ❑28, Jan 1988 .... 3.00
- ❑29, Mar 1988 .... 3.00
- ❑30, May 1988 .... 3.00
- ❑31, Jul 1988 .... 2.50
- ❑32, Sep 1988 .... 2.50
- ❑33, Nov 1988 .... 2.50
- ❑34, Jan 1989 .... 2.50
- ❑35, Mar 1989 .... 2.50
- ❑36, May 1989 .... 2.50
- ❑37, Jul 1989 .... 2.50
- ❑38, Sep 1989 .... 2.50
- ❑39, Nov 1989 .... 2.50
- ❑40, Jan 1990 .... 2.50
- ❑41, Mar 1990 .... 2.50
- ❑42, May 1990 .... 2.50
- ❑43, Jul 1990; becomes Betty and Veronica Digest Magazine 2.50

N-MINT

BETTY AND VERONICA DIGEST MAGAZINE

ARCHIE

- ❑44, Sep 1990 .... 2.50
- ❑45, Nov 1990 .... 2.50
- ❑46, Jan 1991 .... 2.50
- ❑47, Mar 1991 .... 2.50
- ❑48, May 1991 .... 2.50
- ❑49, Jul 1991 .... 2.50
- ❑50, Sep 1991 .... 2.50
- ❑51, Nov 1991 .... 2.00
- ❑52, ca. 1992 .... 2.00
- ❑53, ca. 1992 .... 2.00
- ❑54, ca. 1992 .... 2.00
- ❑55, ca. 1992 .... 2.00
- ❑56, ca. 1992 .... 2.00
- ❑57, ca. 1992 .... 2.00
- ❑58, ca. 1992 .... 2.00
- ❑59, ca. 1992 .... 2.00
- ❑60, Feb 1993 .... 2.00
- ❑61, Apr 1993 .... 2.00
- ❑62, Jun 1993 .... 2.00
- ❑63, Aug 1993 .... 2.00
- ❑64, Oct 1993 .... 2.00
- ❑65, Dec 1993 .... 2.00
- ❑66, Feb 1994 .... 2.00
- ❑67, Apr 1994 .... 2.00
- ❑68, ca. 1994 .... 2.00
- ❑69, Jul 1994 .... 2.00
- ❑70, ca. 1994 .... 2.00
- ❑71, ca. 1994 .... 2.00
- ❑72, Jan 1995 .... 2.00
- ❑73, Mar 1995 .... 2.00
- ❑74, Apr 1995 .... 2.00
- ❑75, Jun 1995 .... 2.00
- ❑76, Aug 1995 .... 2.00
- ❑77, Oct 1995 .... 2.00
- ❑78, Dec 1995 .... 2.00
- ❑79, Feb 1996 .... 2.00
- ❑80, Apr 1996 .... 2.00
- ❑81, Jun 1996 .... 2.00
- ❑82, Jul 1996 .... 2.00
- ❑83, Sep 1996 .... 2.00
- ❑84, Nov 1996 .... 2.00
- ❑85, Jan 1997 .... 2.00
- ❑86, Feb 1997 .... 2.00
- ❑87, Apr 1997 .... 2.00
- ❑88, Jun 1997 .... 2.00
- ❑89, Jul 1997 .... 2.00
- ❑90, Sep 1997 .... 2.00
- ❑91, Oct 1997 .... 2.00
- ❑92, Dec 1997 .... 2.00
- ❑93, Feb 1998 .... 2.00
- ❑94, Apr 1998 .... 2.00
- ❑95, May 1998 .... 2.00
- ❑96, Jul 1998 .... 2.00
- ❑97, Aug 1998 .... 2.00
- ❑98, Sep 1998 .... 2.00
- ❑99, Nov 1998 DDC (a) 2.00
- ❑100, Dec 1998 .... 2.00
- ❑101, Feb 1999 .... 2.00
- ❑102, Apr 1999 .... 2.00
- ❑103, May 1999 .... 2.00
- ❑104, Jul 1999 .... 2.00
- ❑105, Aug 1999 .... 2.00
- ❑106, Sep 1999 .... 2.00
- ❑107, Nov 1999 .... 2.00
- ❑108, Sep 1999 .... 2.00
- ❑109, Feb 2000 .... 2.00
- ❑110, Apr 2000 .... 2.00
- ❑111, May 2000 .... 2.00
- ❑112, Jul 2000 .... 2.19
- ❑113, Aug 2000 .... 2.19
- ❑114, Oct 2000 .... 2.19
- ❑115, Nov 2000 .... 2.19
- ❑116, Dec 2000 .... 2.19
- ❑117, Feb 2001 .... 2.19
- ❑118, Apr 2001 .... 2.19
- ❑119, May 2001 .... 2.19
- ❑120, Jun 2001 .... 2.19
- ❑121, Aug 2001 .... 2.19

	N-MINT
❑122, Sep 2001	2.19
❑123, Oct 2001	2.19
❑124, Dec 2001	2.19
❑125, Jan 2002	2.19
❑126, Mar 2002	2.19
❑127, Apr 2002	2.19
❑128, May 2002	2.19
❑129, Jul 2002	2.19
❑130, Aug 2002	2.19
❑131, Oct 2002	2.19
❑132, Nov 2002	2.19
❑133, Dec 2002	2.19
❑134, Feb 2003	2.19
❑135, Mar 2003	2.39
❑136, Apr 2003	2.39
❑137, May 2003	2.39
❑138, Jul 2003	2.39
❑139, Aug 2003	2.39
❑140, Sep 2003	2.39
❑141, Oct 2003	2.39
❑142, Dec 2003	2.39
❑143, Jan 2004	2.39
❑144, Mar 2004	2.39
❑145, Apr 2004	2.39
❑146, May 2004	2.39
❑147, Jul 2004	2.39

BETTY AND VERONICA DOUBLE DIGEST

Archie

	N-MINT
❑1, Jun 1987	8.00
❑2, Aug 1987	5.00
❑3, Oct 1987	5.00
❑4, Dec 1987	4.00
❑5, Feb 1988	4.00
❑6, Apr 1988	4.00
❑7, Jun 1988	4.00
❑8, Aug 1988	4.00
❑9, Oct 1988	4.00
❑10, Dec 1988	4.00
❑11, Feb 1989	3.00
❑12, Apr 1989	3.00
❑13, Jun 1989	3.00
❑14, Aug 1989	3.00
❑15, Oct 1989	3.00
❑16, Dec 1989	3.00
❑17, Feb 1990	3.00
❑18, Apr 1990	3.00
❑19, Jun 1990	3.00
❑20, Aug 1990	3.00
❑21, Oct 1990	3.00
❑22, Dec 1990	3.00
❑23, Feb 1991	3.00
❑24, Apr 1991	3.00
❑25, Jun 1991	3.00
❑26, Aug 1991	3.00
❑27, Oct 1991	3.00
❑28, Nov 1991	3.00
❑29, Jan 1992	3.00
❑30, Mar 1992	3.00
❑31, May 1992	3.00
❑32, Jul 1992	3.00
❑33, Sep 1992	3.00
❑34, Oct 1992	3.00
❑35, Dec 1992	3.00
❑36, Feb 1993	3.00
❑37, Apr 1993	3.00
❑38, Jun 1993	3.00
❑39, Aug 1993	3.00
❑40, Sep 1993	3.00
❑41, Nov 1993	3.00
❑42, Jan 1994	3.00
❑43, Apr 1994	3.00
❑44, May 1994	3.00
❑45, Jul 1994	3.00
❑46, Aug 1994	3.00
❑47, Oct 1994	3.00
❑48, Dec 1994 DDC (c)	3.00
❑49, Feb 1995	3.00
❑50, Apr 1995	3.00
❑51, Jun 1995	3.00
❑52, Aug 1995	3.00
❑53, Sep 1995	3.00
❑54, Nov 1995	3.00
❑55, Jan 1996	3.00
❑56, Mar 1996	3.00
❑57, Apr 1996	3.00
❑58, Jun 1996	3.00
❑59, Aug 1996	3.00
❑60, Oct 1996	3.00
❑61, Nov 1996	3.00
❑62, Jan 1997	3.00
❑63, Mar 1997	3.00
❑64, Apr 1997	3.00
❑65, Jun 1997	3.00
❑66, Aug 1997	3.00
❑67, Sep 1997	3.00
❑68, Nov 1997	3.00
❑69, Jan 1998	3.00
❑70, Mar 1998	3.00
❑71, Apr 1998	3.00
❑72, Jun 1998	3.00
❑73, Jul 1998	3.00
❑74, Sep 1998	3.00
❑75, Oct 1998	3.00
❑76, Dec 1998	3.00
❑77, Jan 1999	3.00
❑78, Mar 1999	3.00
❑79, Apr 1999	3.00
❑80, Jun 1999	3.00
❑81, Jul 1999	3.00
❑82, Sep 1999	3.00
❑83, Oct 1999	3.00
❑84, Dec 1999	3.00
❑85, Jan 2000	3.00
❑86, Mar 2000	3.00
❑87, Apr 2000	3.00
❑88, Jun 2000	3.00
❑89, Jul 2000	3.00
❑90, Sep 2000	3.19
❑91, Oct 2000	3.19
❑92, Nov 2000	3.19
❑93, Jan 2001	3.19
❑94, Feb 2001	3.19
❑95, Apr 2001	3.29
❑96, Jun 2001	3.29
❑97, Jul 2001	3.29
❑98, Sep 2001	3.29
❑99, Oct 2001	3.29
❑100, Nov 2001	3.29
❑101, Dec 2001	3.29
❑102, Feb 2002	3.29
❑103, Mar 2002	3.29
❑104, Apr 2002	3.29
❑105, Jun 2002	3.29
❑106, Jul 2002	3.29
❑107, Sep 2002	3.29
❑108, Oct 2002	3.29
❑109, Nov 2002	3.59
❑110, Dec 2002	3.59
❑111, Feb 2003	3.59
❑112, Mar 2003	3.59
❑113, Apr 2003	3.59
❑114, Jun 2003	3.59
❑115, Jul 2003	3.59
❑116, Sep 2003	3.59
❑117, Oct 2003	3.59
❑118, Nov 2003	3.59
❑119, Dec 2003	3.59
❑120, Feb 2004	3.59
❑121, Mar 2004	3.59
❑122, Apr 2004	3.59

BETTY AND VERONICA SPECTACULAR

Archie

	N-MINT
❑1, Oct 1992	4.00
❑2	3.00
❑3, May 1993	3.00
❑4 1993	2.50
❑5, Oct 1993	2.50
❑6, Feb 1994	2.00
❑7, Apr 1994	2.00
❑8, May 1994	2.00

The Archie digests collect several stories from the past in an easy-to-carry package.
© 2003 Archie Publications Inc.

	N-MINT
❑9, Jul 1994	2.00
❑10, Sep 1994	2.00
❑11, Nov 1994	2.00
❑12, Jan 1995	2.00
❑13, Feb 1995	2.00
❑14, Apr 1995	2.00
❑15, Jul 1995	2.00
❑16, Oct 1995	2.00
❑17, Jan 1996	2.00
❑18, Apr 1996	2.00
❑19, Jul 1996	2.00
❑20, Oct 1996	2.00
❑21, Jan 1997; Betty becomes a fashion model	2.00
❑22, Mar 1997	2.00
❑23, May 1997	2.00
❑24, Jul 1997; Betty and Veronica set up web pages	2.00
❑25, Sep 1997	2.00
❑26, Nov 1997	2.00
❑27, Feb 1998	2.00
❑28, Mar 1998	2.00
❑29, May 1998	2.00
❑30, Jul 1998	2.00
❑31, Sep 1998	2.00
❑32, Nov 1998; Betty and Veronica are maids for each other	2.00
❑33, Jan 1999; talent competition	2.00
❑34, Mar 1999	2.00
❑35, May 1999; Swing issue	2.00
❑36, Jul 1999	2.00
❑37, Sep 1999	2.00
❑38, Nov 1999	2.00
❑39, Jan 2000	2.00
❑40, Mar 2000	2.00
❑41, May 2000	2.00
❑42, Jul 2000	2.00
❑43, Sep 2000	2.00
❑44, Nov 2000	2.00
❑45, Jan 2001	2.00
❑46, Mar 2001	2.00
❑47, May 2001	2.00
❑48, Jul 2001	2.00
❑49, Sep 2001	2.00
❑50, Nov 2001	2.00
❑51, Jan 2002	2.00
❑52, Mar 2002	2.00
❑53, May 2002	2.00
❑54, Jul 2002	2.00
❑55, Sep 2002	2.00
❑56, Nov 2002	2.00
❑57, Jan 2003	2.00
❑58, Mar 2003	2.20
❑59, May 2003	2.20
❑60, Jul 2003	2.20
❑61, Sep 2003	2.19
❑62, Nov 2003	2.19
❑63, Dec 2003	2.19
❑64, Feb 2004	2.19
❑65, May 2004	2.19
❑66, Jul 2004	2.19

BETTY & VERONICA SUMMER FUN

Archie

	N-MINT
❑1, Sum 1994	3.00
❑2, Sum 1995	2.50
❑3, Sum 1996	2.50
❑4, Sum 1997	2.50

Condition price index: Multiply "NM prices" above by: **0.83 for Very Fine/Near Mint**
0.66 for Very Fine • 0.33 for Fine • 0.2 for Very Good • 0.125 for Good

N-MINT

❑5, Sum 1998 2.25
❑6, Sum 1999 2.29

BETTY BOOP 3-D
BLACKTHORNE

❑1, Nov 1986 2.50

BETTY BOOP'S BIG BREAK
FIRST

❑1 5.95

BETTY IN BONDAGE: BETTY MAE
SHUNGA

❑1 6.95

BETTY IN BONDAGE (TEO JONELLI'S...)
SHUNGA

❑1, b&w 3.00
❑2, b&w 3.00
❑3, b&w 3.00
❑4, b&w 3.00
❑5 3.00
❑6 3.00
❑7 3.00
❑8 3.00
❑Annual 1; 1993 Annual 5.95
❑Annual 2; 1994 Annual 5.95
❑Annual 3; 1995 Annual 5.95

BETTY PAGE 3-D COMICS
3-D ZONE

❑1 3.95

BETTY PAGE 3-D PICTURE BOOK, THE
3-D ZONE

❑1; photos, adult 3.95

BETTY PAGE CAPTURED JUNGLE GIRL 3-D
3-D ZONE

❑1; photos 3.95

BETTY PAGES, THE
PURE IMAGINATION

❑1; DSt (a); Ward, photos 6.00
❑1-2 5.00
❑2 5.00
❑2-2 5.00
❑3 5.00
❑4 5.00
❑5, Win 1989 4.50
❑6 4.50
❑7 4.50
❑8 4.50
❑9 5.00

BETTY PAGE: THE 50'S RAGE
ILLUSTRATION

❑1/A, Jan 1993; tame cover 3.25
❑1/B, Jan 1993; Adult cover 3.25
❑2/A; tame cover 3.25
❑2/B; Adult cover 3.25

BETTY'S DIARY
ARCHIE

❑1, Apr 1986 4.00
❑2 1986 2.50
❑3 1986 2.50
❑4 1986 2.50
❑5 1986 2.50
❑6 1986 2.00
❑7 1987 2.00
❑8 1987 2.00
❑9 1987 2.00
❑10, Aug 1987 2.00
❑11, Sep 1987 1.50
❑12, Oct 1987 1.50
❑13 1987 1.50
❑14 1987 1.50
❑15 1988 1.50
❑16 1988 1.50
❑17 1988 1.50
❑18 1988 1.50
❑19 1988 1.50
❑20 1988 1.50
❑21 1988 1.50
❑22 1988 1.50
❑23 1989 1.50
❑24 1989 1.50
❑25 1989 1.50
❑26 1989 1.50
❑27 1989 1.50
❑28 1989 1.50
❑29 1989 1.50
❑30 1989 1.50
❑31 1990 1.50
❑32 1990 1.50
❑33 1990 1.50
❑34 1990 1.50
❑35 1990 1.50
❑36 1990 1.50
❑37 1990 1.50
❑38 1990 1.50
❑39 1991 1.50
❑40 1991 1.50

BETTY'S DIGEST MAGAZINE
ARCHIE

❑1, Nov 1996 2.00
❑2, Nov 1997 2.00

BETWEEN THE SHEETS
TOKYOPOP

❑1, May 2003, b&w; printed in Japanese format 9.99

BEVERLY HILLBILLIES, THE
DELL

❑1, Apr 1963 60.00
❑2, Jul 1963 38.00
❑3, Oct 1963 28.00
❑4, Jan 1964 24.00
❑5, Apr 1964 24.00
❑6, Jul 1964 18.00
❑7, Oct 1964 18.00
❑8, Jan 1965 18.00
❑9, Apr 1965 18.00
❑10, ca. 1965; Not a photo cover; cartoon Clampetts appear on cover, but actors' names still listed with them 18.00
❑11, Dec 1965 15.00
❑12, Mar 1966 15.00
❑13, Jun 1966 15.00
❑14, Sep 1966 15.00
❑15, Dec 1966 15.00
❑16, Mar 1967 15.00
❑17, May 1967 15.00
❑18, Aug 1967 12.00
❑19, Oct 1969; Same cover as #1 12.00
❑20, Oct 1970 12.00
❑21, Oct 1971 12.00

BEWARE (MARVEL)
MARVEL

❑1, Mar 1973; "Witch" reprinted from Tales of Suspense #27 8.00
❑2, May 1973 5.00
❑3, Jul 1973 5.00
❑4, Sep 1973 5.00
❑5, Nov 1973 5.00
❑6, Jan 1974 5.00
❑7, Mar 1974 5.00
❑8, May 1974; Series continued in Tomb of Darkness #9 5.00

BEWARE THE CREEPER
DC

❑1, Jun 1968 SD (a) 40.00
❑2, Aug 1968 SD (a) 25.00
❑3, Oct 1968 SD (a) 25.00
❑4, Dec 1968 SD (a) 25.00
❑5, Feb 1969 SD (a) 25.00
❑6, Apr 1969 SD (a) 25.00

BEWARE THE CREEPER (2ND SERIES)
DC

❑1, Jun 2003 2.95
❑2, Jul 2003 2.95
❑3, Aug 2003 2.95
❑4, Sep 2003 2.95
❑5, Oct 2003 2.95

BEWITCHED
DELL

❑1, Apr 1965 85.00
❑2, Jul 1965 50.00
❑3, Oct 1965 40.00
❑4, Mar 1966 40.00
❑5, Jun 1966 40.00
❑6, Sep 1966 40.00
❑7, Dec 1966 40.00
❑8, Mar 1967 40.00
❑9, Apr 1967 40.00
❑10, Jul 1967 40.00
❑11, Oct 1967 30.00
❑12, Oct 1968 30.00
❑13, Jan 1969 30.00
❑14, Oct 1969 30.00

BEYOND (BLUE)
BLUE

❑1, Jun 1996 2.95

BEYOND COMMUNION
CALIBER

❑1 2.95

BEYOND MARS
BLACKTHORNE

❑1, Jan 1989, b&w 2.00
❑2, Feb 1989, b&w 2.00
❑3, Mar 1989 2.00
❑4, ca. 1989 2.00
❑5, ca. 1989 2.00

BEYOND THE GRAVE
CHARLTON

❑1, Jul 1975 6.50
❑2, Oct 1975 4.00
❑3, Dec 1975 4.00
❑4, Feb 1976 3.00
❑5 3.00
❑6, Jun 1976 2.50
❑7 2.50
❑8 2.50
❑9 2.50
❑10, Aug 1983 2.50
❑11 1983 2.50
❑12 1983 2.50
❑13, Feb 1984 2.50
❑14, Apr 1984 2.50
❑15, Jun 1984 2.50
❑16, Aug 1984 2.50
❑17 2.50

BICENTENNIAL GROSS-OUTS
YENTZER AND GONIF

❑1, Jul 1976

BIFF BANG POW!
PAISANO

❑1 2.95
❑2, Feb 1992 2.95

BIG
DARK HORSE

❑1, Mar 1989; adaptation 2.50

BIG BAD BLOOD OF DRACULA
APPLE

❑1; reprints, b&w 2.75
❑2 2.95

BIG BANG COMICS: ROUND TABLE OF AMERICA
IMAGE

❑1, Mar 2004 3.95

BIG BANG COMICS (VOL. 1)
CALIBER / BIG BANG

❑0, May 1995, b&w and color ARo (c); ARo (a) 3.50
❑1, Spr 1994, b&w 2.50
❑2, Sum 1994, b&w 2.50
❑3, Oct 1994, b&w 2.50
❑4, Feb 1995, b&w 2.50

Condition price index: Multiply "NM prices" above by: **0.83 for Very Fine/Near Mint**
0.66 for Very Fine • 0.33 for Fine • 0.2 for Very Good • 0.125 for Good

N-MINT

BIG BANG COMICS (VOL. 2)
IMAGE

❑1, May 1996; Mighty Man, Knight Watchman, Doctor Weird 3.00
❑2, Jun 1996; Silver Age Shadowhawk, Knight Watchman, The Badge 2.75
❑3, Jul 1996; Knight Watchman, Ultiman, Thunder Girl 2.75
❑4, Sep 1996 .... 2.75
❑5, Oct 1996; origins issue 2.95
❑6, Nov 1996 CS (c); CS (a) 2.95
❑7, Dec 1996; Mighty Man vs. Mighty Man 2.95
❑8, Jan 1997 1: Mister U.S. 2.95
❑9, Mar 1997; A: Sphinx. A: Blitz. Showplace 2.95
❑10, May 1997 .... 2.95
❑11, Jul 1997; Knight Watchman vs. Faulty Towers 2.95
❑12, Sep 1997 A: Savage Dragon 2.95
❑13, Aug 1997; cover says Jul, indicia says Aug 2.95
❑14, Oct 1997 A: Savage Dragon 2.95
❑15, Oct 1997; Doctor Weird vs. Bog Swamp Demon, cover says Dec, indicia says Oct/Nov 2.95
❑16, Jan 1998; Thunder Girl 2.95
❑17, Feb 1998; Shadow Lady 2.95
❑18, Apr 1998 DC (c); DC (a); A: Savage Dragon, Pantheon of Heroes 2.95
❑19, Jun 1998; O: The Beacon II (Doctor Julia Gardner). O: The Hummingbird. O: The Beacon I (Scott Martin). cover says Apr, indicia says Jun 2.95
❑20, Jul 1998; A: Dimensioneer. A: Knight Watchman. A: The Blitz. A: The Sphinx. photo back cover 2.95
❑21, Aug 1998; Shadow Lady 2.95
❑22, Sep 1998; Knight Watchman 2.95
❑23, Nov 1998; Tales of the Sphinx, Book 2 .... 3.95
❑24, Apr 1999; The Big Bang History of Comics 2.95
❑25, Jun 1999 .... 2.95
❑26, Jul 1999 .... 2.95
❑27, Oct 1999; The Big Bang History of Comics, Part 2 .... 3.95
❑28, Dec 1999; Knight Watchman 3.95
❑29, Feb 2000 .... 3.95
❑30, Mar 2000 .... 3.95
❑31, Apr 2000 .... 3.95
❑32, Jun 2000 .... 3.95
❑33, Jul 2000 .... 3.95
❑34, Aug 2000 .... 3.95
❑35, Jan 2001 .... 3.95

BIG BANG (RED CALLOWAY'S...)
ZOO ARSONIST

❑1 .... 2.95

BIG BANG SUMMER SPECIAL
IMAGE

❑1, Aug 2003 .... 4.95

BIG BLACK KISS
VORTEX

❑1, Sep 1989 HC (w); HC (a) 3.95
❑2, Oct 1989 HC (w); HC (a) 3.95
❑3, Nov 1989 HC (w); HC (a) 3.95

BIG BLACK THING (COLIN UPTON'S...)
UPTON

❑1, b&w 3.25

BIG BLOWN BABY
DARK HORSE

❑1, Aug 1996 .... 2.95
❑2, Sep 1996 .... 2.95
❑3, Oct 1996 .... 2.95
❑4, Nov 1996 .... 2.95

BIG BLUE COUCH COMIX
COUCH

❑1, b&w 2.00

BIG BOOB BONDAGE
ANTARCTIC / VENUS

❑1, Jan 1997; b&w pin-ups, adult 2.95

N-MINT

BIG BRUISERS
IMAGE

❑1, Jul 1996 .... 3.50

BIG DADDY DANGER
DC

❑1, Oct 2002 .... 2.95
❑2, Nov 2002 .... 2.95
❑3, Dec 2002 .... 2.95
❑4, Jan 2003 .... 2.95
❑5, Feb 2003 .... 2.95
❑6, Mar 2003 .... 2.95
❑7, Apr 2003 .... 2.95
❑8, May 2003 .... 2.95
❑9, Jun 2003 .... 2.95

BIG DOG FUNNIES
RIP OFF

❑1, Jun 1992 .... 2.50

BIG FUNNIES
RADIO

❑1, ca. 2001 .... 3.95
❑2, ca. 2001 .... 3.99
❑3, ca. 2001 .... 3.99

BIGGER: WILL RISON & THE DEVIL'S CONCUBINE
FREE LUNCH

❑1, Dec 1998 .... 2.95

BIGG TIME
DC / VERTIGO

❑1 .... 14.95

BIG GUY AND RUSTY THE BOY ROBOT, THE
DARK HORSE / LEGEND

❑1, Jul 1995 FM (w) 10.00
❑2, Aug 1995 FM (w) 10.00

BIG HAIR PRODUCTIONS
IMAGE

❑1, Mar 2000 .... 3.50
❑2, Apr 2000 .... 3.50

BIG LOU
SIDE SHOW

❑1 .... 2.95

BIG MONSTER FIGHT
KIDGANG COMICS

❑0 .... 2.50
❑1 .... 2.50

BIG MOUTH
STARHEAD

❑1, b&w 2.95
❑2, b&w 2.95
❑3 .... 2.95
❑4 .... 2.95
❑5; no indicia, b&w 2.95
❑6, Dec 1996 .... 2.95
❑7, Jan 1998 .... 2.95

BIG NUMBERS
MAD LOVE

❑1 .... 5.50
❑2; Final published issue 5.50

BIG O PART 1
VIZ

❑1, Feb 2002 .... 3.50
❑2, Mar 2002 .... 3.50
❑3, Apr 2002 .... 3.50
❑4, May 2002 .... 3.50
❑5, Jun 2002 .... 3.50

BIG O PART 2
VIZ

❑1, Jul 2002 .... 3.50
❑2, Aug 2002 .... 3.50
❑3, Sep 2002 .... 3.50
❑4, Oct 2002 .... 3.50

BIG O PART 3
VIZ

❑1, Nov 2002 .... 3.50
❑2, Dec 2002 .... 3.50
❑3, Jan 2003 .... 3.50
❑4, Feb 2003 .... 3.50

The misadventures of the Clampett family were chronicled in Dell's *The Beverly Hillbillies.*

© 1963 Filmways and Dell.

N-MINT

BIG O PART 4
VIZ

❑1, Mar 2003 .... 3.50
❑2, Apr 2003 .... 3.50
❑3, May 2003 .... 3.50

BIG PRIZE, THE
ETERNITY

❑1, May 1988, b&w 1.95
❑2, Aug 1985, b&w 1.95

BIG TIME
DELTA

❑1, Mar 1996 .... 1.95

BIG TOP BONDAGE
FANTAGRAPHICS / EROS

❑1, b&w 2.50

BIG TOWN (MARVEL)
MARVEL

❑1, Jan 2001; A: X-Men. A: Avengers. says Fantastic Four Big Town on cover; alternate Marvel history 3.50
❑2, Feb 2001 A: Hulk. A: Avengers. A: Sub-Mariner 3.50
❑3, Mar 2001 A: Hulk. A: Avengers. A: Sub-Mariner 3.50
❑4, Apr 2001 A: Hulk. A: Avengers. A: Sub-Mariner 3.50

BIG VALLEY, THE
DELL

❑1, ca. 1966 .... 40.00
❑2, ca. 1966 .... 25.00
❑3, ca. 1967 .... 25.00
❑4, ca. 1967 .... 25.00
❑5, ca. 1967 .... 25.00
❑6, ca. 1967 .... 25.00

BIJOU FUNNIES
KITCHEN SINK

❑1 .... 85.00
❑1-2 .... 30.00
❑2 1970 .... 30.00
❑3 .... 25.00
❑3-2 .... 15.00
❑3-3 .... 10.00
❑4 1972 .... 25.00
❑5 .... 20.00
❑6 .... 18.00
❑7 .... 18.00
❑8 1973 .... 18.00
❑8-2 .... 4.00

BIKER MICE FROM MARS
MARVEL

❑1, Nov 1993 O: The Biker Mice From Mars 2.00
❑2, Dec 1993 O: The Biker Mice From Mars 2.00
❑3, Jan 1994 .... 2.00

BIKINI ASSASSIN TEAM, THE
CATFISH

❑1 .... 2.50

BIKINI BATTLE 3-D
3-D ZONE

❑1 .... 3.95

BILL & TED'S BOGUS JOURNEY
MARVEL

❑1, Sep 1991 .... 2.95

Condition price index: Multiply "NM prices" above by: **0.83 for Very Fine/Near Mint**
0.66 for Very Fine • 0.33 for Fine • 0.2 for Very Good • 0.125 for Good

N-MINT

BILL & TED'S EXCELLENT ADVENTURE MOVIE ADAPTATION
DC

❑1; adapts movie, wraparound cover, no cover price ... 1.50

BILL & TED'S EXCELLENT COMIC BOOK
MARVEL

❑1, Dec 1991 ... 1.50
❑2, Jan 1992 ... 1.50
❑3, Feb 1992 ... 1.50
❑4, Mar 1992 ... 1.50
❑5, Apr 1992 ... 1.50
❑6, May 1992 ... 1.50
❑7, Jun 1992 ... 1.50
❑8, Jul 1992 ... 1.50
❑9, Aug 1992 ... 1.50
❑10, Sep 1992 ... 1.50
❑11, Oct 1992 ... 1.50
❑12, Nov 1992 ... 1.50

BILL, THE GALACTIC HERO
TOPPS

❑1, Jul 1994; prestige format, based on Harry Harrison novel series ... 4.95
❑2, Sep 1994 ... 4.95
❑3, Nov 1994 ... 4.95

BILLI 99
DARK HORSE

❑1 ... 3.50
❑2 ... 3.50
❑3 ... 3.50
❑4 ... 3.50

BILL THE BULL: BURNT CAIN
BONEYARD

❑1, Jul 1992 ... 4.95
❑2 ... 4.95
❑3 ... 4.95

BILL THE BULL: ONE SHOT, ONE BOURBON, ONE BEER
BONEYARD

❑1, Dec 1994 ... 2.95
❑2, indicia says Mar 94, a misprint ... 2.95

BILL THE CLOWN
SLAVE LABOR

❑1, Feb 1992, b&w; 2nd Printing, b&w ... 2.50
❑1-2, 2nd Printing, b&w ... 2.95

BILL THE CLOWN: COMEDY ISN'T PRETTY
SLAVE LABOR

❑1, Nov 1992, b&w ... 2.50

BILL THE CLOWN: DEATH & CLOWN WHITE
SLAVE LABOR

❑1, Sep 1993, b&w ... 2.95

BILLY BOY THE SICK LITTLE FAT KID
ASYLUM

❑1, ca. 2001 ... 2.95

BILLY COLE
CULT

❑1, Jun 1994, b&w ... 2.75
❑2 ... 2.75
❑3 ... 2.75
❑4 ... 2.75

BILLY DOGMA
MODERN

❑1, Apr 1997 ... 2.95
❑2, Aug 1997 ... 2.95
❑3, Dec 1997 ... 2.95

BILLY JOE VAN HELSING: REDNECK VAMPIRE HUNTER
ALPHA

❑1 ... 2.50

BILLY NGUYEN, PRIVATE EYE
ATTITUDE

❑1, Mar 1988 ... 2.00
❑2 ... 2.00
❑3 ... 2.00

N-MINT

BILLY NGUYEN, PRIVATE EYE (VOL. 2)
CALIBER

❑1, b&w ... 2.50

BILLY RAY CYRUS
MARVEL MUSIC

❑1; prestige format ... 5.95

BILLY THE KID
CHARLTON

❑9, Nov 1957; Series continued from Masked Raider #8 ... 58.00
❑10, Dec 1957 ... 35.00
❑11 1958; Double-size ... 40.00
❑12 1958 ... 30.00
❑13 1958 AW (a) ... 40.00
❑14 1958 ... 30.00
❑15 1958 O: Billy the Kid ... 40.00
❑16 ... 40.00
❑17 1959 ... 30.00
❑18 1959 ... 30.00
❑19 1959 ... 30.00
❑20 1959 ... 35.00
❑21 1959 ... 35.00
❑22 ... 35.00
❑23 1960 ... 20.00
❑24 1960 ... 35.00
❑25 1960 ... 35.00
❑26 1960 ... 35.00
❑27 ... 20.00
❑28 1961 ... 20.00
❑29 1961 ... 20.00
❑30 1961 ... 20.00
❑31 1961 ... 14.00
❑32, Jan 1962 ... 14.00
❑33, Apr 1962 ... 14.00
❑34 1962 ... 14.00
❑35 1962 ... 14.00
❑36 ... 14.00
❑37 1963 ... 14.00
❑38 1963 ... 14.00
❑39 1963 ... 14.00
❑40 1963 ... 14.00
❑41 ... 8.00
❑42 ... 8.00
❑43 1964 ... 8.00
❑44 1964 ... 8.00
❑45 1964 ... 8.00
❑46 1964 ... 8.00
❑47 ... 8.00
❑48 ... 8.00
❑49 1965 ... 8.00
❑50 1965 ... 8.00
❑51 1965 ... 7.00
❑52 1965 ... 7.00
❑53 1965 ... 7.00
❑54 1966 ... 7.00
❑55 1966 ... 7.00
❑56 1966 ... 7.00
❑57 1966 ... 7.00
❑58, Nov 1966 ... 7.00
❑59, Jan 1967 ... 7.00
❑60, Mar 1967 ... 7.00
❑61 1967 ... 5.00
❑62 ... 5.00
❑63 ... 5.00
❑64 ... 5.00
❑65 ... 5.00
❑66 ... 5.00
❑67 ... 5.00
❑68 ... 5.00
❑69, Nov 1968 ... 5.00
❑70, Jan 1969 ... 5.00
❑71, Mar 1969 ... 4.00
❑72, May 1969 ... 4.00
❑73, Jul 1969 ... 4.00
❑74, Sep 1969 ... 4.00
❑75, Nov 1969 ... 4.00
❑76, Jan 1970 ... 4.00
❑77, Mar 1970 ... 4.00
❑78, May 1970 ... 4.00
❑79, Jul 1970 ... 4.00

N-MINT

❑80, Sep 1970 ... 4.00
❑81, Nov 1970 ... 3.50
❑82, Jan 1971 ... 3.50
❑83, Mar 1971 ... 3.50
❑84, May 1971 ... 3.50
❑85, Jul 1971 ... 3.50
❑86, Sep 1971 ... 3.50
❑87, Nov 1971 ... 3.50
❑88, Dec 1971 ... 3.50
❑89 1972 ... 3.50
❑90, Mar 1972 ... 3.50
❑91, Apr 1972 ... 3.50
❑92 1972 ... 3.50
❑93 1972 ... 3.50
❑94, Aug 1972 ... 3.50
❑95, Oct 1972 ... 3.50
❑96, Nov 1972 ... 3.50
❑97, Dec 1972 ... 3.50
❑98, Jan 1973 ... 3.50
❑99, Feb 1973 ... 3.50
❑100, Mar 1973 ... 3.50
❑101 1973 ... 3.00
❑102 1973 ... 3.00
❑103, Aug 1973; Spanish lesson text piece; no credits listed ... 3.00
❑104 1973 ... 3.00
❑105 1973 ... 3.00
❑106 1974 ... 3.00
❑107, May 1974 ... 3.00
❑108 1974 ... 3.00
❑109 1974 ... 3.00
❑110 1974 ... 3.00
❑111, Feb 1975 ... 3.00
❑112, Apr 1975 ... 3.00
❑113 1975 ... 3.00
❑114, Oct 1975 ... 3.00
❑115, Dec 1975 ... 3.00
❑116 1976 ... 3.00
❑117 1976 ... 3.00
❑118 1976 ... 3.00
❑119 1976 ... 3.00
❑120, Oct 1976 ... 3.00
❑121 ... 3.00
❑122 ... 3.00
❑123 ... 3.00
❑124 ... 3.00
❑125 ... 3.00
❑126, Jan 1979 ... 3.00
❑127 1979 ... 3.00
❑128 1979 ... 3.00
❑129 1979 ... 3.00
❑130, Aug 1979 ... 3.00
❑131, Sep 1979 ... 3.00
❑132, Oct 1979 ... 3.00
❑133, Dec 1979 ... 3.00
❑134, Feb 1980 ... 3.00
❑135 ... 3.00
❑136 ... 3.00
❑137 ... 3.00
❑138 ... 3.00
❑139 ... 3.00
❑140 ... 3.00
❑141 ... 3.00
❑142 ... 3.00
❑143 ... 3.00
❑144, Oct 1981 ... 3.00
❑145 ... 3.00
❑146 ... 3.00
❑147 ... 3.00
❑148 ... 3.00
❑149 ... 3.00
❑150 ... 3.00
❑151 ... 3.00
❑152 ... 3.00
❑153 ... 3.00

BINKY
DC

❑72, May 1970; Series continued from "Leave it to Binky #71" ... 7.00
❑73, Jul 1970 ... 7.00
❑74, Sep 1970 ... 7.00

N-MINT

❑75, Nov 1970 .... 7.00
❑76, Jan 1971 .... 6.00
❑77, Mar 1971 .... 6.00
❑78, May 1971 .... 6.00
❑79, Jul 1971 .... 6.00
❑80, Sep 1971 .... 6.00
❑81, Nov 1971; Final issue of original series 6.00
❑82, Sum 1977; 1977 one-shot revival 3.00

BINKY'S BUDDIES
DC

❑1, Jan 1969 .... 26.00
❑2, Mar 1969 .... 16.00
❑3, May 1969 .... 12.00
❑4, Jul 1969 .... 10.00
❑5, Sep 1969 .... 10.00
❑6, Nov 1969 .... 10.00
❑7, Jan 1970 .... 10.00
❑8, Mar 1970 .... 10.00
❑9, May 1970 .... 10.00
❑10, Jul 1970 .... 10.00
❑11, Sep 1970 .... 10.00
❑12, Nov 1970 .... 10.00

BIO 90
BULLET

❑1, Aug 1992, b&w 2.50

BIO-BOOSTER ARMOR GUYVER
VIZ

❑1 .... 4.00
❑2 .... 3.50
❑3 .... 3.50
❑4 .... 3.50
❑5 .... 3.50
❑6 .... 3.00
❑7 .... 3.00
❑8 .... 3.00
❑9 .... 3.00
❑10 .... 3.00
❑11 .... 3.00
❑12 .... 3.00

BIO-BOOSTER ARMOR GUYVER PART 2
VIZ

❑1, Oct 1994 .... 3.00
❑2, Nov 1994 .... 3.00
❑3, Dec 1994 .... 3.00
❑4, Jan 1995 .... 3.00
❑5, Feb 1995 .... 3.00
❑6, Mar 1995 .... 3.00

BIO-BOOSTER ARMOR GUYVER PART 3
VIZ

❑1, Apr 1995 .... 2.75
❑2, May 1995 .... 2.75
❑3, Jun 1995 .... 2.75
❑4, Jul 1995 .... 2.75
❑5, Aug 1995 .... 2.75
❑6, Sep 1995 .... 2.75
❑7, Oct 1995 .... 2.75

BIO-BOOSTER ARMOR GUYVER PART 4
VIZ

❑1, Nov 1995 .... 2.75
❑2, Dec 1995 .... 2.75
❑3, Jan 1996 .... 2.95
❑4, Feb 1996 .... 2.95
❑5, Mar 1996 .... 2.95
❑6, Apr 1996 .... 2.95

BIO-BOOSTER ARMOR GUYVER PART 5
VIZ

❑1, May 1996 .... 2.95
❑2, Jun 1996 .... 2.95
❑3, Jul 1996 .... 2.95
❑4, Aug 1996 .... 2.95
❑5, Sep 1996 .... 2.95
❑6, Oct 1996 .... 2.95
❑7, Nov 1996 .... 2.95

N-MINT

BIO-BOOSTER ARMOR GUYVER PART 6
VIZ

❑1, Dec 1996 .... 2.95
❑2, Jan 1997 .... 2.95
❑3, Feb 1997 .... 2.95
❑4, Mar 1997 .... 2.95
❑5, Apr 1997 .... 2.95
❑6, May 1997 .... 2.95

BIOLOGIC SHOW, THE
FANTAGRAPHICS

❑0, Oct 1994, b&w; magazine; cardstock cover 2.95
❑1, Jan 1995, b&w 2.75

BIONEERS
MIRAGE

❑1, Aug 1994 .... 2.75
❑2 .... 2.75
❑3 .... 2.75

BIONIC DOG
HUGO REX

❑1 .... 3.25

BIONICLE
DC

❑1, ca. 2001 .... 2.25
❑2 2001 .... 2.25
❑3, Oct 2001 .... 2.25
❑4 2002 .... 2.25
❑5, Apr 2002 .... 2.25
❑6, May 2002 .... 2.25
❑7 2002 .... 2.25
❑8 2002 .... 2.25
❑9, Dec 2002 .... 2.25

BIONIC WOMAN, THE
CHARLTON

❑1, Oct 1977 .... 9.00
❑2, Feb 1978 .... 4.00
❑3, Mar 1978 .... 4.00
❑4, May 1978 .... 4.00
❑5, Jun 1978 .... 4.00

BIONIX
MAXIMUM

❑1, ca. 1996 .... 2.99

BIRDLAND
FANTAGRAPHICS / EROS

❑1, b&w 1.95
❑2 .... 2.25
❑3 .... 2.25

BIRDLAND (VOL. 2)
FANTAGRAPHICS / EROS

❑1, Jun 1994, b&w 2.95

BIRDS OF PREY
DC

❑1, Jan 1999 A: Hellhound. A: Oracle 4.00
❑1/Autographed, Jan 1999 A: Hellhound. A: Oracle 8.00
❑2, Feb 1999 A: Hellhound. A: Black Canary. A: Jackie Pajamas 3.00
❑3, Mar 1999 A: Hellhound. A: Black Canary 3.00
❑4, Apr 1999 A: Ravens. A: Kobra 3.00
❑5, May 1999 A: Ravens 3.00
❑6, Jun 1999 .... 3.00
❑7, Jul 1999 .... 3.00
❑8, Aug 1999 A: Nightwing 40.00
❑9, Sep 1999 .... 3.00
❑10, Oct 1999 .... 3.00
❑11, Nov 1999 DG (a) 3.00
❑12, Dec 1999 .... 3.00
❑13, Jan 2000 .... 3.00
❑14, Feb 2000 .... 3.00
❑15, Mar 2000 .... 3.00
❑16, Apr 2000 BG (a); A: Joker 3.00
❑17, May 2000 BG (a) 3.00
❑18, Jun 2000 BG (a) 3.00
❑19, Jul 2000 BG (a) 3.00
❑20, Aug 2000 BG (a) 3.00
❑21, Sep 2000 BG (a) 3.00
❑22, Oct 2000 BSz, BG (a) 3.00

Marvel's *Bill & Ted's Excellent Comic Book* was collected in new trade paperbacks by Slave Labor Graphics in 2004.

© 1991 Marvel Comics

N-MINT

❑23, Nov 2000 BG (a) 3.00
❑24, Dec 2000 BG (a) 3.00
❑25, Jan 2001 BG (a) 3.00
❑26, Feb 2001 BG (a) 3.00
❑27, Mar 2001 .... 3.00
❑28, Apr 2001 BG (a) 3.00
❑29, May 2001 BG (a) 3.00
❑30, Jun 2001 BG (a) 3.00
❑31, Jul 2001 .... 2.50
❑32, Aug 2001 .... 2.50
❑33, Sep 2001 BG (a) 2.50
❑34, Oct 2001 BG (a) 2.50
❑35, Nov 2001 .... 2.50
❑36, Dec 2001 .... 2.50
❑37, Jan 2002 .... 2.50
❑38, Feb 2002 .... 2.50
❑39, Mar 2002 .... 2.50
❑40, Apr 2002 .... 2.50
❑41, May 2002 .... 2.50
❑42, Jun 2002 .... 2.50
❑43, Jul 2002 .... 2.50
❑44, Aug 2002 .... 2.50
❑45, Sep 2002 .... 2.50
❑46, Oct 2002 .... 2.50
❑47, Nov 2002 .... 2.50
❑48, Dec 2002 .... 2.50
❑49, Jan 2003 .... 2.50
❑50, Feb 2003 .... 2.50
❑51, Mar 2003 .... 2.50
❑52, Apr 2003 .... 2.50
❑53, May 2003 .... 2.50
❑54, Jun 2003 .... 2.50
❑55, Jul 2003 .... 2.50
❑56, Aug 2003 .... 2.50
❑57, Sep 2003 .... 2.50
❑58, Oct 2003 .... 2.50
❑59, Nov 2003 .... 2.50
❑60, Dec 2003 .... 2.50
❑61, Jan 2004 .... 2.50
❑62, Feb 2004 .... 2.50
❑63, Mar 2004 .... 2.50
❑64, Apr 2004 .... 2.50
❑65, May 2004 .... 2.50
❑66, Jun 2004 .... 2.50
❑67, Jul 2004 .... 2.50
❑68, Aug 2004 .... 2.50
❑69, Sep 2004 ....
❑70, Sep 2004 ....

BIRDS OF PREY: BATGIRL
DC

❑1, Feb 1998 .... 3.00

BIRDS OF PREY: CATWOMAN
DC

❑1, Feb 2003 .... 5.95
❑2, Mar 2003 .... 5.95

BIRDS OF PREY: MANHUNT
DC

❑1, Sep 1996 .... 2.25
❑2, Oct 1996 .... 2.00
❑3, Nov 1996 .... 2.00
❑4, Dec 1996 SB (a) 2.00

BIRDS OF PREY: REVOLUTION
DC

❑1, Apr 1997 .... 2.95

N-MINT

BIRDS OF PREY: SECRET FILES 2003
DC
❑1, Jun 2003 ..... 4.95

BIRDS OF PREY: THE RAVENS
DC
❑1, Jun 1998; Girlfrenzy 1.95

BIRDS OF PREY: WOLVES
DC
❑1, Oct 1997 ..... 2.95

BIRTH CAUL
EDDIE CAMPBELL
❑1, ca. 1999 ..... 5.95

BIRTHDAY RIOTS, THE
NBM
❑1 ..... 14.95

BIRTHRIGHT
FANTAGRAPHICS
❑1 ..... 2.50
❑2 ..... 2.50
❑3 ..... 2.50

BIRTHRIGHT (TSR)
TSR
❑1 ..... 1.50

BIRTH RITE
CONGRESS
❑1 ..... 2.50
❑2 ..... 2.50
❑3 ..... 2.50
❑4 ..... 2.50

BISHOP
MARVEL
❑1, Dec 1994; foil cover 2.95
❑2, Jan 1995 ..... 2.95
❑3, Feb 1995 ..... 2.95
❑4, Mar 1995 ..... 2.95

BISHOP THE LAST X-MAN
MARVEL
❑1, Oct 1999 ..... 2.99
❑2, Nov 1999 ..... 2.99
❑3, Dec 1999 ..... 2.99
❑4, Jan 2000 ..... 2.99
❑5, Feb 2000 ..... 2.99
❑6, Mar 2000 ..... 2.99
❑7, Apr 2000 ..... 2.99
❑8, May 2000 ..... 2.99
❑9, Jun 2000 ..... 2.99
❑10, Jul 2000 ..... 2.99
❑11, Aug 2000 ..... 2.99
❑12, Sep 2000; double-sized 2.99
❑13, Oct 2000 ..... 2.25
❑14, Nov 2000 ..... 2.25
❑15, Dec 2000 ..... 2.25
❑16, Jan 2001 ..... 2.25

BISHOP: XSE
MARVEL
❑1, Jan 1998; gatefold summary 2.50
❑2, Feb 1998; gatefold summary 2.50
❑3, Mar 1998 ..... 2.50

BISLEY'S SCRAPBOOK
ATOMEKA
❑1 ..... 2.50

BITCH IN HEAT
FANTAGRAPHICS / EROS
❑1, Mar 1997 ..... 2.95
❑2 ..... 2.95
❑3 ..... 2.95
❑4 ..... 2.95
❑5, Jul 1998 ..... 2.95
❑6, Sep 1998 ..... 2.95
❑7, Jan 1999 ..... 2.95
❑8, Apr 1999 ..... 2.95
❑9, ca. 1999 ..... 2.95
❑10, ca. 2000 ..... 2.95

BITE CLUB
DC / VERTIGO
❑1, May 2004 ..... 2.95
❑2, Jun 2004 ..... 0.00

N-MINT

❑3, Aug 2004 ..... 2.95
❑4, Sep 2004 .....

BITS AND PIECES
MORTIFIED
❑1, Nov 1994 ..... 3.00

BITTER CAKE
TIN CUP
❑1, b&w 2.00

BIZARRE 3-D ZONE
BLACKTHORNE
❑1, Jul 1986 ..... 2.25
❑2 ..... 2.25
❑3 ..... 2.25
❑4 ..... 2.25
❑5, Jul 1986; #1 on cover 2.25

BIZARRE ADVENTURES
MARVEL
❑25, Mar 1981; A: Black Widow. Lethal Ladies; Was Marvel Preview 2.50
❑26, May 1981; King Kull 2.50
❑27, Jul 1981; X-Men 4.00
❑28, Oct 1981; FM (w); FM (a); A: Elektra. Unlikely Heroes 3.00
❑29, Dec 1981; Stephen King; Horror 2.50
❑30 1982; Paradox; Tomorrow 2.50
❑31 1982; FM (a); After the Violence Stops 2.50
❑32, Aug 1982; Thor and other Gods 2.50
❑33 1982; 1: Varnae. Dracula; Zombie; Horror 2.50
❑34, Feb 1983; gatefold summary; AM (w); AM, PS (a); A: Howard the Duck. Format changes to comic book 2.50

BIZARRE FANTASY
FLASHBACK
❑0 ..... 2.50
❑0/Autographed; 1500 copies printed 9.95
❑1 ..... 2.50
❑2 ..... 2.50

BIZARRE HEROES
KITCHEN SINK
❑1, May 1990; parody, b&w 2.50

BIZARRE HEROES (DON SIMPSON'S...)
FIASCO
❑0, Dec 1994 ..... 2.95
❑1, May 1994 ..... 3.25
❑2, Jun 1994 ..... 2.95
❑3, Jul 1994 ..... 2.95
❑4, Aug 1994 ..... 2.95
❑5, Sep 1994 ..... 2.95
❑6, Oct 1994 ..... 2.95
❑7, Nov 1994 ..... 2.95
❑8, Dec 1994 ..... 2.95
❑9 ..... 2.95
❑10 ..... 2.95
❑11 ..... 2.95
❑12 ..... 2.95
❑13 ..... 2.95
❑14, Oct 1995; Title changes to Bizarre Heroes 2.95
❑15, Jan 1996 O: The Slick 2.95

BIZARRE SEX
KITCHEN SINK
❑1 ..... 15.00
❑2 ..... 9.00
❑3; White "remove this outer cover at your own risk" cover 7.00
❑4; White "remove this outer cover at your own risk" cover 5.00
❑4-2; White "remove this outer cover at your own risk" cover 4.00
❑4-3 ..... 4.00
❑5 ..... 5.00
❑6 ..... 5.00
❑7 ..... 5.00
❑8 ..... 5.00
❑9, Aug 1981, b&w 1: Omaha 18.00

N-MINT

BIZARRO COMICS!
DC
❑1; hardcover 19.95
❑1/Variant, ca. 2003 ..... 19.95

BIZZARIAN
IRONCAT
❑1, ca. 2000 ..... 2.95
❑2, ca. 2000 ..... 2.95
❑3, ca. 2000 ..... 2.95
❑4, ca. 2000 ..... 2.95
❑5, ca. 2001 ..... 2.95
❑6, ca. 2001 ..... 2.95
❑7, ca. 2001 ..... 2.95
❑8, ca. 2001 ..... 2.95

B. KRIGSTEIN SAMPLER, A
INDEPENDENT
❑1 BK (c); BK (w); BK (a) 2.50

BLAB!
KITCHEN SINK
❑8, Sum 1995; odd-sized anthology 16.95
❑9, Fal 1997; odd-sized anthology 18.95
❑10, Fal 1998; odd-sized anthology 19.95

BLACK & WHITE (MINI-SERIES)
IMAGE
❑1, Oct 1994 ..... 1.95
❑2, Nov 1994 ..... 1.95
❑3, Jan 1995 ..... 1.95

BLACK & WHITE
IMAGE
❑1, Feb 1996 ..... 2.50
❑Ashcan 1; No cover price; ashcan preview of series 1.00

BLACK & WHITE (VIZ)
VIZ
❑1, Aug 1999 ..... 3.25
❑2 1999 ..... 3.25
❑3 1999 ..... 3.25

BLACK AND WHITE BONDAGE
VEROTIK
❑1 ..... 4.95

BLACK AND WHITE COMICS
APEX NOVELTIES
❑1 ..... 4.00

BLACK AND WHITE THEATER
DOUBLE M
❑1, Jun 1996, b&w 2.95
❑2, b&w 2.95

BLACK ANGEL
VEROTIK
❑1, Sep 1996; prestige format; reprints Golden Age stories 9.95

BLACK AXE
MARVEL
❑1, Apr 1993 ..... 1.75
❑2, May 1993 ..... 1.75
❑3, Jun 1993 ..... 1.75
❑4, Jul 1993 ..... 1.75
❑5, Aug 1993 ..... 1.75
❑6, Sep 1993 ..... 1.75
❑7, Oct 1993 ..... 1.75

BLACKBALL COMICS
BLACKBALL
❑1, Mar 1994 ..... 3.00

BLACK BOOK (BRIAN BOLLAND'S...)
ECLIPSE
❑1 BB (a) 2.00

BLACK BOW
ARTLINE
❑1 ..... 2.50

BLACKBURNE COVENANT
DARK HORSE
❑1, Jun 2003 ..... 2.99
❑2, Jul 2003 ..... 2.99
❑3, Aug 2003 ..... 2.99
❑4, Sep 2003 ..... 2.99

BLACK CANARY
DC

	N-MINT
❑1, Jan 1993 TVE (a)	2.00
❑2, Feb 1993 TVE (a)	2.00
❑3, Mar 1993 TVE (a)	2.00
❑4, Apr 1993 TVE (a)	2.00
❑5, May 1993 TVE (a)	2.00
❑6, Jun 1993 TVE (a)	2.00
❑7, Jul 1993 TVE (a)	2.00
❑8, Aug 1993 A: The Ray	2.00
❑9, Sep 1993 TVE (a)	2.00
❑10, Oct 1993 TVE (a)	2.00
❑11, Nov 1993 TVE (a)	2.00
❑12, Dec 1993	2.00

BLACK CANARY (MINI-SERIES)
DC

	N-MINT
❑1, Nov 1991 TVE (a)	2.50
❑2, Dec 1991 TVE (a)	2.50
❑3, Jan 1992 TVE (a)	2.50
❑4, Feb 1992 TVE (a)	2.50

BLACK CANARY/ORACLE: BIRDS OF PREY
DC

	N-MINT
❑1	3.95

BLACK CAT (THE ORIGINS)
LORNE-HARVEY

	N-MINT
❑1; color and b&w; reprints Black Cat and Sad Sack strips; text feature on Alfred Harvey	3.50

BLACK CAT THE WAR YEARS
RECOLLECTIONS

	N-MINT
❑1; Golden Age reprints, b&w	1.00

BLACK CONDOR
DC

	N-MINT
❑1, Jun 1992 O: Black Condor II. 1: Black Condor II	1.50
❑2, Jul 1992	1.25
❑3, Aug 1992	1.25
❑4, Sep 1992	1.25
❑5, Oct 1992	1.25
❑6, Nov 1992	1.25
❑7, Dec 1992	1.25
❑8, Jan 1993 MGu (a)	1.25
❑9, Feb 1993	1.25
❑10, Mar 1993 A: The Ray	1.25
❑11, Apr 1993	1.25
❑12, May 1993 A: Batman	1.25

BLACK CROSS: DIRTY WORK
DARK HORSE

	N-MINT
❑1, Apr 1997	2.95

BLACK CROSS SPECIAL
DARK HORSE

	N-MINT
❑1, Jan 1988, b&w	2.50
❑1-2	1.75

BLACK DIAMOND
AC

	N-MINT
❑1, May 1983	2.00
❑2, Jul 1983	2.00
❑3, Dec 1983	2.00
❑4, Feb 1984	2.00
❑5, May 1984	2.00

BLACK DIAMOND EFFECT, THE
BLACK DIAMOND EFFECT

	N-MINT
❑1	3.00
❑2, Oct 1991	3.10
❑3	3.10
❑4	3.10
❑5	3.10
❑6, Dec 1992	3.00
❑7	3.10

BLACK DRAGON, THE
MARVEL / EPIC

	N-MINT
❑1, May 1985	3.00
❑2, Jun 1985	2.50
❑3, Jul 1985	2.50
❑4, Aug 1985	2.50
❑5, Sep 1985	2.00
❑6, Oct 1985	2.00

BLACK FLAG (IMAGE)
IMAGE

	N-MINT
❑1, Jun 1994, b&w; Fold-out cover	1.95
❑Ashcan 1; Preview edition	1.95

BLACK FLAG (MAXIMUM)
MAXIMUM

	N-MINT
❑0, Jul 1995	2.50
❑1, Jan 1995	2.50
❑2/A, Feb 1995; Woman on cover	2.50
❑2/B; Variant cover with man	2.50
❑3, Mar 1995	2.50
❑4/A, cover has black background	2.50
❑4/B, cover has white background	2.50

BLACK FOREST
IMAGE

	N-MINT
❑1, ca 2003	9.95

BLACK GOLIATH
MARVEL

	N-MINT
❑1, Feb 1976 GT (a); O: Black Goliath	15.00
❑2, Apr 1976	5.00
❑2/30 cent, Apr 1976; 30-cent regional price variant	20.00
❑3, Jun 1976	4.00
❑3/30 cent, Jun 1976; 30-cent regional price variant	20.00
❑4, Aug 1976	4.00
❑4/30 cent, Aug 1976; 30-cent regional price variant	20.00
❑5, Nov 1976	4.00

BLACKHAWK (1ST SERIES)
DC

	N-MINT
❑105, Oct 1956	105.00
❑106, Nov 1956	105.00
❑107, Dec 1956	105.00
❑108, Jan 1957; DC begins publishing (formerly Quality)	325.00
❑109, Feb 1957	130.00
❑110, Mar 1957	110.00
❑111, Apr 1957	110.00
❑112, May 1957	110.00
❑113, Jun 1957	110.00
❑114, Jul 1957	110.00
❑115, Aug 1957	110.00
❑116, Sep 1957	110.00
❑117, Oct 1957	110.00
❑118, Nov 1957 FF (a)	135.00
❑119, Dec 1957	85.00
❑120, Jan 1958	85.00
❑121, Feb 1958	85.00
❑122, Mar 1958	85.00
❑123, Apr 1958	85.00
❑124, May 1958	85.00
❑125, Jun 1958	85.00
❑126, Jul 1958	85.00
❑127, Aug 1958	85.00
❑128, Sep 1958	85.00
❑129, Oct 1958	85.00
❑130, Nov 1958	85.00
❑131, Dec 1958	65.00
❑132, Jan 1959	65.00
❑133, Feb 1959 1: Lady Blackhawk	65.00
❑134, Mar 1959	65.00
❑135, Apr 1959	65.00
❑136, May 1959	65.00
❑137, Jun 1959	65.00
❑138, Jul 1959	65.00
❑139, Aug 1959	65.00
❑140, Sep 1959	65.00
❑141, Oct 1959	50.00
❑142, Nov 1959	50.00
❑143, Dec 1959	50.00
❑144, Jan 1960	50.00
❑145, Feb 1960	50.00
❑146, Mar 1960	50.00
❑147, Apr 1960	50.00
❑148, May 1960	50.00
❑149, Jun 1960	50.00
❑150, Jul 1960	48.00
❑151, Aug 1960	48.00
❑152, Sep 1960	48.00
❑153, Oct 1960	48.00

Marvel Preview changed its title to *Bizarre Adventures* with #25, which focused on The Black Widow.

© 1981 Marvel Comics.

	N-MINT
❑154, Nov 1960	48.00
❑155, Dec 1960	48.00
❑156, Jan 1961	48.00
❑157, Feb 1961	48.00
❑158, Mar 1961	48.00
❑159, Apr 1961	48.00
❑160, May 1961	48.00
❑161, Jun 1961	48.00
❑162, Jul 1961	48.00
❑163, Aug 1961	48.00
❑164, Sep 1961 O: Blackhawks. O: Blackhawk	60.00
❑165, Oct 1961	48.00
❑166, Nov 1961	48.00
❑167, Dec 1961	22.00
❑168, Jan 1962	22.00
❑169, Feb 1962	22.00
❑170, Mar 1962	22.00
❑171, Apr 1962	22.00
❑172, May 1962	22.00
❑173, Jun 1962	22.00
❑174, Jul 1962	22.00
❑175, Aug 1962	22.00
❑176, Sep 1962	22.00
❑177, Oct 1962	22.00
❑178, Nov 1962	22.00
❑179, Dec 1962	22.00
❑180, Jan 1963	22.00
❑181, Feb 1963	16.00
❑182, Mar 1963	16.00
❑183, Apr 1963	16.00
❑184, May 1963	16.00
❑185, Jun 1963	16.00
❑186, Jul 1963	16.00
❑187, Aug 1963	16.00
❑188, Sep 1963	16.00
❑189, Oct 1963 O: Blackhawks	16.00
❑190, Nov 1963	16.00
❑191, Dec 1963	16.00
❑192, Jan 1964	16.00
❑193, Feb 1964	16.00
❑194, Mar 1964	16.00
❑195, Apr 1964	16.00
❑196, May 1964; Biographies of Dick Dillon and Chuck Cuidera (Blackhawk artists)	16.00
❑197, Jun 1964; new look	16.00
❑198, Jul 1964 O: Blackhawks. O: Blackhawk	16.00
❑199, Aug 1964	16.00
❑200, Sep 1964	16.00
❑201, Oct 1964	15.00
❑202, Nov 1964	15.00
❑203, Dec 1964 O: Chop-Chop	15.00
❑204, Jan 1965	15.00
❑205, Feb 1965	15.00
❑206, Mar 1965	15.00
❑207, Apr 1965	15.00
❑208, May 1965	15.00
❑209, Jun 1965	15.00
❑210, Jul 1965	15.00
❑211, Aug 1965	15.00
❑212, Sep 1965	15.00
❑213, Oct 1965	15.00
❑214, Nov 1965	15.00
❑215, Dec 1965	15.00
❑216, Jan 1966	15.00
❑217, Feb 1966	15.00

	N-MINT
❑218, Mar 1966	15.00
❑219, Apr 1966	15.00
❑220, May 1966	15.00
❑221, Jun 1966	15.00
❑222, Jul 1966	15.00
❑223, Aug 1966	15.00
❑224, Sep 1966	15.00
❑225, Oct 1966	15.00
❑226, Nov 1966	15.00
❑227, Dec 1966	15.00
❑228, Jan 1967	30.00
❑229, Feb 1967	15.00
❑230, Mar 1967; Blackhawks become super-heroes; New costumes	15.00
❑231, Apr 1967; Blackhawks as super-heroes	15.00
❑232, May 1967; Blackhawks as super-heroes	15.00
❑233, Jun 1967; Blackhawks as super-heroes	15.00
❑234, Jul 1967; Blackhawks as super-heroes	15.00
❑235, Aug 1967; Blackhawks as super-heroes	15.00
❑236, Sep 1967; Blackhawks as super-heroes	15.00
❑237, Nov 1967; Blackhawks as super-heroes	15.00
❑238, Jan 1968; Blackhawks as super-heroes	15.00
❑239, Mar 1968; Blackhawks as super-heroes	15.00
❑240, May 1968; Blackhawks as super-heroes	15.00
❑241, Jul 1968; Blackhawks as super-heroes	15.00
❑242, Sep 1968; Blackhawks back to old costumes	15.00
❑243, Nov 1968; Last issue of 1960s run	15.00
❑244, Feb 1976; GE (a); New issues begin with old # sequence	4.00
❑245, Apr 1976	4.00
❑246, Jun 1976	4.00
❑247, Aug 1976; Bicentennial #25	4.00
❑248, Sep 1976	4.00
❑249, Nov 1976	4.00
❑250, Jan 1977 D: Chuck	4.00
❑251, Oct 1982	4.00
❑252, Nov 1982 DS (a); V: War Wheel	4.00
❑253, Dec 1982	4.00
❑254, Jan 1983	4.00
❑255, Feb 1983	4.00
❑256, Mar 1983	4.00
❑257, Apr 1983 HC (c)	4.00
❑258, May 1983 HC (c)	4.00
❑259, Jun 1983 HC (c)	4.00
❑260, Jul 1983 HC (c); ME (w); HC (a)	4.00
❑261, Aug 1983	3.00
❑262, Sep 1983 HC (c); ME (w); DS (a)	3.00
❑263, Oct 1983 GK (c); V: War Wheel	3.00
❑264, Nov 1983	3.00
❑265, Dec 1983	3.00
❑266, Jan 1984	3.00
❑267, Feb 1984	3.00
❑268, Mar 1984	3.00
❑269, Apr 1984 1: Killer Shark I (General Haifisch)	3.00
❑270, May 1984	3.00
❑271, Jul 1984	3.00
❑272, Sep 1984	3.00
❑273, Nov 1984 HC (c)	3.00

BLACKHAWK (2ND SERIES)
DC

	N-MINT
❑1, Mar 1988; HC (w); HC (a); no mature readers advisory	3.50
❑2, Apr 1988 HC (w); HC (a)	3.50
❑3, May 1988 HC (w); HC (a)	3.50

BLACKHAWK (3RD SERIES)
DC

	N-MINT
❑1, Mar 1989	2.00
❑2, Apr 1989	1.75
❑3, May 1989	1.75
❑4, Jun 1989	1.75
❑5, Aug 1989	1.75
❑6, Sep 1989	1.50
❑7, Oct 1989; Double-size WE (a)	2.50
❑8, Nov 1989	1.50
❑9, Dec 1989	1.50
❑10, Jan 1990	1.50
❑11 1990	1.50
❑12 1990	1.50
❑13 1990	1.50
❑14 1990	1.50
❑15 1990	1.50
❑16 1990	1.50
❑Annual 1, ca. 1989	2.95
❑Special 1, ca. 1992	3.50

BLACK HEART: ASSASSIN
IGUANA

	N-MINT
❑1	2.95

BLACK HEART BILLY
SLAVE LABOR

	N-MINT
❑1, Mar 2000, b&w	2.95

BLACK HOLE
KITCHEN SINK

	N-MINT
❑1	3.50
❑2, Nov 1995	3.50
❑3, Jul 1996	3.50
❑4, Jun 1997	3.50
❑5, Mar 1998	3.95
❑6, Dec 1998	4.50
❑7, ca. 1999	4.50
❑8, ca. 2000	4.50
❑9, ca. 2001	4.50

BLACK HOLE, THE (WALT DISNEY...)
WHITMAN

	N-MINT
❑1, Mar 1980	2.00
❑2, May 1980	2.00
❑3, Jul 1980	2.00
❑4, Sep 1980	2.00

BLACK HOOD
DC / IMPACT

	N-MINT
❑1, Dec 1991	1.00
❑2, Jan 1992	1.00
❑3, Feb 1992	1.00
❑4, Mar 1992	1.00
❑5, Apr 1992	1.00
❑6, May 1992	1.00
❑7, Jun 1992	1.00
❑8, Aug 1992	1.00
❑9, Sep 1992	1.00
❑10, Oct 1992	1.00
❑11, Nov 1992	1.00
❑12, Dec 1992	1.00
❑Annual 1; trading card	1.50

BLACK HOOD, THE (RED CIRCLE)
ARCHIE / RED CIRCLE

	N-MINT
❑1, Jun 1983 ATh, GM (a)	3.00
❑2, Aug 1983 ATh, GM (a)	2.00
❑3, Oct 1983 ATh, GM (a)	2.00

BLACKJACK
DARK ANGEL

	N-MINT
❑1, Sep 1996	2.95
❑2, Oct 1996	2.95
❑3, Jan 1997	2.95
❑4 1997	2.95
❑Special 1, Sep 1998	3.50

BLACKJACK (VOL. 2)
DARK ANGEL

	N-MINT
❑1, Apr 1997	2.95
❑2, Feb 1998	2.95

BLACK JACK (VIZ)
VIZ

	N-MINT
❑Special 1	3.25

BLACK KISS
VORTEX

	N-MINT
❑1, Jun 1988 HC (w); HC (a)	2.50
❑1-2 HC (w); HC (a)	2.00
❑1-3 HC (w); HC (a)	2.00
❑2, Jul 1988 HC (w); HC (a)	2.50
❑2-2 HC (w); HC (a)	2.00
❑3, Aug 1988 HC (w); HC (a)	2.00
❑4, Sep 1988; HC (w); HC (a); polybagged with black insert card covering actual cover	2.00
❑5, Oct 1988 HC (w); HC (a)	2.00
❑6, Nov 1988 HC (w); HC (a)	2.00
❑7, Dec 1988 HC (w); HC (a)	2.00
❑8, Jan 1989; HC (w); HC (a); indicia says 88 (misprint)	2.00
❑9, Feb 1989; HC (w); HC (a); indicia says 88 (misprint)	2.00
❑10, Mar 1989; HC (w); HC (a); indicia says 88 (misprint)	2.00
❑11, May 1989 HC (w); HC (a)	2.00
❑12, Jul 1989 HC (w); HC (a)	2.00

BLACK KNIGHT (LTD. SERIES)
MARVEL

	N-MINT
❑1, Jun 1990 TD (a); O: Black Knight III (Dane Whitman). O: Black Knight I (Sir Percy). O: Black Knight II (Nathan Garrett)	2.00
❑2, Jul 1990 A: Captain Britain	1.50
❑3, Aug 1990 RB (a); 1: new Valkyrie. A: Doctor Strange	1.50
❑4, Sep 1990 A: Doctor Strange. A: Valkyrie	1.50

BLACK KNIGHT: EXODUS
MARVEL

	N-MINT
❑1, Dec 1996	2.50

BLACK LAMB, THE
DC / HELIX

	N-MINT
❑1, Nov 1996	2.50
❑2, Dec 1996	2.50
❑3, Jan 1997	2.50
❑4, Feb 1997	2.50
❑5, Mar 1997	2.50
❑6, Apr 1997	2.50

BLACK LIGHTNING (1ST SERIES)
DC

	N-MINT
❑1, Apr 1977 TVE, FS (a); O: Black Lightning. 1: Black Lightning	7.00
❑2, May 1977	5.00
❑3, Jul 1977	5.00
❑4, Sep 1977	5.00
❑5, Nov 1977	5.00
❑6, Jan 1978 1: Syonide I	5.00
❑7, Mar 1978	5.00
❑8, Apr 1978	5.00
❑9, May 1978	5.00
❑10, Jul 1978	5.00
❑11, Sep 1978 A: The Ray	5.00

BLACK LIGHTNING (2ND SERIES)
DC

	N-MINT
❑1, Feb 1995	2.50
❑2, Mar 1995	2.00
❑3, Apr 1995	2.00
❑4, May 1995	2.00
❑5, Jun 1995	2.00
❑6, Jul 1995 A: Gangbuster	2.75
❑7, Aug 1995 A: Gangbuster	2.25
❑8, Sep 1995	2.25
❑9, Oct 1995	2.25
❑10, Nov 1995	2.25
❑11, Dec 1995	2.25
❑12, Jan 1996	2.25
❑13, Feb 1996	2.25

BLACK MAGIC (DC)
DC

	N-MINT
❑1, Nov 1973	7.50
❑2, Dec 1973	4.00
❑3, Apr 1974	4.00
❑4, Jun 1974 JK (a)	4.00
❑5, Aug 1974	4.00
❑6, Oct 1974	4.00
❑7, Dec 1974	4.00
❑8, Feb 1975	4.00
❑9, Apr 1975	4.00

BLACK MAGIC (ECLIPSE)
ECLIPSE

	N-MINT
❑1, Apr 1990; Japanese, b&w	3.50
❑2, Jun 1990	2.75

	N-MINT
❑3, Aug 1990	2.75
❑4, Oct 1990	2.75

BLACKMASK
DC

	N-MINT
❑1	4.95
❑2	4.95
❑3	4.95

BLACKMASK (EASTERN)
EASTERN

	N-MINT
❑1 1988, Translated by Franz Hankel	1.75
❑2 1988	1.75
❑3 1988	1.75

BLACK MIST
CALIBER

	N-MINT
❑1, ca. 1994	2.95
❑2, ca. 1994	2.95
❑3, ca. 1994	2.95
❑4, ca. 1994	2.95

BLACK MIST: BLOOD OF KALI
CALIBER

	N-MINT
❑1, Jan 1998	2.95
❑2, ca. 1998	2.95
❑3, ca. 1998	2.95

BLACKMOON
U.S.COMICS

	N-MINT
❑1 1985 O: Blackmoon	2.00
❑2	2.00
❑3	2.00

BLACK OPS
IMAGE

	N-MINT
❑1, Jan 1996	2.50
❑2, Feb 1996	2.50
❑3, Mar 1996	2.50
❑4, Apr 1996	2.50
❑5/A, Jun 1996	2.50
❑5/B, Jun 1996; alternate cover	2.50

BLACK ORCHID
DC / VERTIGO

	N-MINT
❑1, Sep 1993	2.50
❑1/Platinum, Sep 1993; Platinum edition	5.00
❑2, Oct 1993	2.25
❑3, Nov 1993	2.25
❑4, Dec 1993	2.25
❑5, Jan 1994	2.25
❑6, Feb 1994	2.00
❑7, Mar 1994	2.00
❑8, Apr 1994	2.00
❑9, May 1994	2.00
❑10, Jun 1994	2.00
❑11, Jul 1994	2.00
❑12, Aug 1994	2.00
❑13, Sep 1994	2.00
❑14, Oct 1994	2.00
❑15, Nov 1994	2.00
❑16, Dec 1994	2.00
❑17, Jan 1995	1.95
❑18, Feb 1995	1.95
❑19, Mar 1995	1.95
❑20, Apr 1995	1.95
❑21, May 1995	2.25
❑22, Jun 1995	2.25
❑Annual 1; Children's Crusade	4.00

BLACK ORCHID (MINI-SERIES)
DC

	N-MINT
❑1 1988; NG (w); 1st Neil Gaiman U.S. comics work	5.00
❑2 1989 NG (w); A: Batman	5.00
❑3 1989 NG (w)	5.00

BLACK PANTHER
MARVEL

	N-MINT
❑1, Jan 1977 JK (a)	9.00
❑2, Mar 1977 JK (w); JK (a)	6.00
❑3, May 1977 JK (a)	5.00
❑4, Jul 1977 JK (a)	5.00
❑5, Sep 1977 JK (a)	5.00
❑5/35 cent, Sep 1977; JK (a); 35 cent regional price variant	15.00
❑6, Nov 1977 JK (c); JK (w); JK (a)	5.00
❑7, Jan 1978 JK (a)	5.00
❑8, Mar 1978 JK (a)	5.00
❑9, May 1978 JK (a)	5.00
❑10, Jul 1978 JK (a)	5.00
❑11, Sep 1978 JK (a)	4.00
❑12, Nov 1978 JK (a)	4.00
❑13, Jan 1979	4.00
❑14, Mar 1979	4.00
❑15, May 1979 JK (a); A: Klaw	4.00

BLACK PANTHER (VOL. 2)
MARVEL

	N-MINT
❑1, Nov 1998; gatefold summary	5.00
❑1/Variant, Nov 1998; DFE alternate cover	7.00
❑2/A, Dec 1998; gatefold summary	4.00
❑2/B, Dec 1998; gatefold summary	4.00
❑3, Jan 1999; gatefold summary; A: Fantastic Four	3.00
❑4, Feb 1999 A: Mephisto	3.00
❑5, Mar 1999 A: Mephisto	3.00
❑6, Apr 1999 V: Kraven the Hunter	3.00
❑7, May 1999	3.00
❑8, Jun 1999	3.00
❑9, Jul 1999	3.00
❑10, Aug 1999	3.00
❑11, Sep 1999	3.00
❑12, Oct 1999	3.00
❑13, Dec 1999	3.00
❑14, Jan 2000	3.00
❑15, Feb 2000	3.00
❑16, Mar 2000	3.00
❑17, Apr 2000	3.00
❑18, May 2000	3.00
❑19, Jun 2000	3.00
❑20, Jul 2000	3.00
❑21, Aug 2000	2.50
❑22, Sep 2000	2.50
❑23, Oct 2000	2.50
❑24, Nov 2000	2.50
❑25, Dec 2000	2.50
❑26, Jan 2001 A: Storm	2.50
❑27, Feb 2001	2.50
❑28, Mar 2001	2.50
❑29, Apr 2001	2.50
❑30, May 2001; A: Captain America. World War II story	2.50
❑31, Jun 2001	2.50
❑32, Jul 2001	2.50
❑33, Aug 2001	2.50
❑34, Sep 2001	2.50
❑35, Oct 2001	2.50
❑36, Nov 2001	2.50
❑37, Dec 2001	2.50
❑38, Jan 2002	2.50
❑39, Feb 2002	2.50
❑40, Mar 2002	2.50
❑41, Apr 2002	2.50
❑42, May 2002	2.50
❑43, Jun 2002	2.50
❑44, Jul 2002, wraparound cover	2.50
❑45, Aug 2002, wraparound cover	2.50
❑46, Aug 2002, wraparound cover	2.50
❑47, Sep 2002, wraparound cover	2.50
❑48, Oct 2002, wraparound cover	2.50
❑49, Nov 2002, wraparound cover	2.50
❑50, Dec 2002, wraparound cover	2.50
❑51, Jan 2003, wraparound cover	2.50
❑52, Feb 2003, wraparound cover	2.50
❑53, Mar 2003, wraparound cover	2.50
❑54, Apr 2003	2.99
❑55, May 2003	2.99
❑56, May 2003	2.99
❑57, Jun 2003	2.99
❑58, Jun 2003	2.99
❑59, Jul 2003	2.99
❑60, Jul 2003	2.99
❑61, Sep 2003	2.99
❑62, Sep 2003	2.99

BLACK PANTHER (LTD. SERIES)
MARVEL

	N-MINT
❑1, Jul 1988	2.00
❑2, Aug 1988	2.00

After more than seven years, the Blackhawks returned with new adventures.

© 1976 National Periodical Publications (DC).

	N-MINT
❑3, Sep 1988	2.00
❑4, Oct 1988	2.00

BLACK PANTHER: PANTHER'S PREY
MARVEL

	N-MINT
❑1, May 1991	4.95
❑2, Jun 1991	4.95
❑3, Aug 1991	4.95
❑4, Oct 1991	4.95

BLACK PEARL, THE
DARK HORSE

	N-MINT
❑1, Sep 1996	3.50
❑2, Oct 1996	3.00
❑3, Nov 1996	3.00
❑4, Dec 1996	3.00
❑5, Jan 1997	3.00

BLACK PHANTOM
AC

	N-MINT
❑1, b&w	2.50
❑2	2.50
❑3, b&w	2.75

BLACK SABBATH
ROCK-IT / MALIBU

	N-MINT
❑1, Feb 1994	3.95

BLACK SCORPION
SPECIAL STUDIO

	N-MINT
❑1, b&w	2.75
❑2, b&w	2.75
❑3, b&w	2.75

BLACK SEPTEMBER
MALIBU / ULTRAVERSE

	N-MINT
❑1, events affect the Infinity issues of the other Ultraverse titles	2.00

BLACKSTAR
IMPERIAL

	N-MINT
❑1	2.00
❑2	2.00

BLACKSTONE, THE MAGICIAN DETECTIVE FIGHTS CRIME
EC

	N-MINT
❑1 1947	440.00

BLACK SUN
WILDSTORM

	N-MINT
❑1, Nov 2002	2.95
❑2, Dec 2002	2.95
❑3, Jan 2003	2.95
❑4, Feb 2003	2.95
❑5, Mar 2003	2.95
❑6	2.95

BLACK SUN: X-MEN
MARVEL

	N-MINT
❑1, Nov 2000	2.99
❑1/A, Nov 2000; Dynamic Forces cover	6.00
❑2, Nov 2000	2.99
❑3, Nov 2000	2.99
❑4, Nov 2000	2.99
❑5, Nov 2000	2.99

BLACK TERROR, THE (ECLIPSE)
ECLIPSE

	N-MINT
❑1, Oct 1989	4.95
❑1/Autographed, Oct 1989	3.50
❑2, Mar 1990	4.95
❑2/Autographed, Mar 1990	3.50
❑3, Jun 1990	4.95
❑3/Autographed, Jun 1990	3.50

N-MINT

BLACKTHORNE'S 3 IN 1
BLACKTHORNE
- ❑1, Nov 1986 .... 1.75
- ❑2, Feb 1987 .... 1.75

BLACKTHORNE'S HARVEY FLIP BOOK
BLACKTHORNE
- ❑1, b&w 2.00

BLACK TIDE
IMAGE
- ❑1/A, Nov 2001; Grey background; 3 figures standing on cover 2.95
- ❑1/B, Nov 2001; 2 figures charging on cover 2.95
- ❑1/C, Nov 2001; Sun in background; 3 figures posing on cover 2.95
- ❑2, Jan 2002 .... 2.95
- ❑3, Mar 2002 .... 2.95
- ❑4, May 2002 .... 2.95

BLACK TIDE (VOL 2)
AVATAR
- ❑1 .... 2.95
- ❑1/A 2.95
- ❑1/C; Wrap-Around cover 2.95
- ❑2 .... 2.95
- ❑2/A 2.95
- ❑3 .... 2.95
- ❑3/A 2.95
- ❑4 .... 2.95
- ❑4/A 2.95
- ❑5, May 2003 .... 2.95
- ❑5/A, May 2003 .... 2.95
- ❑6, Jun 2003 .... 2.95
- ❑6/A, Jun 2003 .... 2.95
- ❑7, Sep 2003 .... 2.95
- ❑7/A, Sep 2003 .... 2.95
- ❑8, Nov 2003 .... 2.95
- ❑8/A, Nov 2003 .... 2.95
- ❑9, Feb 2004 .... 2.95
- ❑9/A, Feb 2004 .... 2.95

BLACK WEB
INKS
- ❑1 .... 2.95

BLACK WIDOW
MARVEL
- ❑1, Jun 1999 .... 3.50
- ❑2, Jul 1999 .... 3.00
- ❑3, Aug 1999 .... 3.00

BLACK WIDOW (VOL. 2)
MARVEL
- ❑1, Jan 2001 .... 2.99
- ❑2, Feb 2001 .... 2.99
- ❑3, May 2001 .... 2.99

BLACK WIDOW: PALE LITTLE SPIDER
MARVEL
- ❑1, Jun 2002 .... 2.99
- ❑2, Jul 2002 .... 2.99
- ❑3, Aug 2002 .... 2.99
- ❑4, Sep 2002 .... 2.99

BLACK WIDOW: WEB OF INTRIGUE
MARVEL
- ❑1, Jun 1999; collects Marvel Fanfare #10-13 .... 3.50

BLACKWULF
MARVEL
- ❑1, Jun 1994; Embossed cover 2.50
- ❑2, Jul 1994 .... 1.50
- ❑3, Aug 1994 .... 1.50
- ❑4, Sep 1994 .... 1.50
- ❑5, Oct 1994 .... 1.50
- ❑6, Nov 1994 .... 1.50
- ❑7, Dec 1994 .... 1.50
- ❑8, Jan 1995 .... 1.50
- ❑9, Feb 1995 .... 1.50
- ❑10, Mar 1995 .... 1.50

BLACK ZEPPELIN (GENE DAY'S...)
RENEGADE
- ❑1, Apr 1985 GD (w); GD (a) 2.00
- ❑2 .... 2.00
- ❑3 .... 2.00

N-MINT

- ❑4 .... 2.00
- ❑5 .... 2.00

BLADE (BUCCANEER)
BUCCANEER
- ❑1, Dec 1989 .... 2.00
- ❑2 .... 2.00

BLADE (1ST SERIES)
MARVEL
- ❑1, May 1997; giveaway GC, TP (a); O: Blade 1.50

BLADE (2ND SERIES)
MARVEL
- ❑1, Mar 1998 .... 3.50

BLADE (3RD SERIES)
MARVEL
- ❑1, Oct 1998; gatefold summary 2.99

BLADE (4TH SERIES)
MARVEL
- ❑1, Nov 1998; gatefold summary 3.50
- ❑2/A, Dec 1998; gatefold summary; cover says Nov, indicia says Dec 2.99
- ❑2/B, Dec 1998 .... 2.99
- ❑3, Jan 1999; gatefold summary; cover says Dec, indicia says Jan 2.99
- ❑4 .... 2.99

BLADE OF SHURIKEN
ETERNITY
- ❑1, May 1987 .... 1.95
- ❑2, Jul 1987 .... 1.95
- ❑3, Sep 1987 .... 1.95
- ❑4, Nov 1987 .... 1.95
- ❑5, Jan 1988 .... 1.95

BLADE OF THE IMMORTAL
DARK HORSE
- ❑1, Jun 1996 .... 3.50
- ❑2, Jul 1996 .... 3.00
- ❑3, Aug 1996 .... 3.00
- ❑4, Sep 1996 .... 3.00
- ❑5, Oct 1996 .... 3.00
- ❑6, Nov 1996 .... 2.95
- ❑7, Dec 1996 .... 2.95
- ❑8, Jan 1997 .... 2.95
- ❑9, Apr 1997; Giant-size SA (a) 3.95
- ❑10, May 1997; Giant-size DG (a) 3.95
- ❑11, Jun 1997; Giant-size GK (a) 3.95
- ❑12, Jul 1997 .... 2.95
- ❑13, Aug 1997 .... 2.95
- ❑14, Sep 1997 .... 2.95
- ❑15, Oct 1997 .... 2.95
- ❑16, Nov 1997 .... 2.95
- ❑17, Dec 1997 .... 2.95
- ❑18, Jan 1998 .... 2.95
- ❑19, Mar 1998 .... 2.95
- ❑20, Apr 1998 .... 2.95
- ❑21, May 1998 .... 2.95
- ❑22, Jun 1998 .... 2.95
- ❑23, Jul 1998 .... 2.95
- ❑24, Aug 1998 .... 2.95
- ❑25, Sep 1998 .... 2.95
- ❑26, Oct 1998 .... 2.95
- ❑27, Nov 1998 .... 2.95
- ❑28, Dec 1998 .... 2.95
- ❑29, Jan 1999 .... 2.95
- ❑30, Feb 1999 .... 2.95
- ❑31, Mar 1999 .... 2.95
- ❑32, Apr 1999 .... 2.95
- ❑33, May 1999 .... 2.95
- ❑34, Jun 1999 .... 3.95
- ❑35, Jul 1999 .... 2.95
- ❑36, Aug 1999 .... 3.95
- ❑37, Sep 1999 .... 3.95
- ❑38, Oct 1999 .... 3.95
- ❑39, Nov 1999 .... 2.99
- ❑40, Dec 1999 .... 2.99
- ❑41, Jan 2000 .... 2.99
- ❑42, Feb 2000 .... 2.99
- ❑43, Mar 2000 .... 2.99
- ❑44, Apr 2000 .... 2.99
- ❑45, May 2000 .... 2.99
- ❑46, Jun 2000 .... 2.99

N-MINT

- ❑47, Jul 2000 .... 2.99
- ❑48, Aug 2000 .... 2.99
- ❑49, Sep 2000 .... 2.99
- ❑50, Oct 2000 .... 2.99
- ❑51, Nov 2000 .... 2.99
- ❑52, Dec 2000 .... 2.99
- ❑53, Jan 2001 .... 2.99
- ❑54, Feb 2001 .... 2.99
- ❑55, Mar 2001 .... 2.99
- ❑56, Apr 2001 .... 2.99
- ❑57, May 2001 .... 2.99
- ❑58, Jun 2001 .... 2.99
- ❑59, Jul 2001 .... 2.99
- ❑60, Aug 2001 .... 2.99
- ❑61, Sep 2001 .... 2.99
- ❑62, Oct 2001 .... 2.99
- ❑63, Nov 2001 .... 2.99
- ❑64, Dec 2001 .... 2.99
- ❑65, Feb 2002 .... 2.99
- ❑66, Mar 2002 .... 2.99
- ❑67, Apr 2002 .... 2.99
- ❑68, May 2002 .... 2.99
- ❑69, Jun 2002 .... 2.99
- ❑70, Jul 2002 .... 2.99
- ❑71, Aug 2002 .... 2.99
- ❑72, Sep 2002 .... 2.99
- ❑73, Nov 2002 .... 2.99
- ❑74, Dec 2002 .... 2.99
- ❑75, Jan 2003 .... 2.99
- ❑76, Feb 2003 .... 2.99
- ❑77, Mar 2003 .... 2.99
- ❑78, Apr 2003 .... 2.99
- ❑79, Jun 2003 .... 2.99
- ❑80, Jul 2003 .... 2.99
- ❑81, Aug 2003 .... 2.99
- ❑82, Sep 2003 .... 2.99
- ❑83, Oct 2003 .... 2.99
- ❑84, Nov 2003 .... 2.99
- ❑85, Dec 2003 .... 2.99
- ❑86, Jan 2004 .... 2.99
- ❑87, Feb 2004 .... 2.99
- ❑88, Apr 2004 .... 2.99
- ❑89, Jul 2004 .... 2.99
- ❑90, Aug 2004 .... 2.99

BLADE RUNNER
MARVEL
- ❑1, Oct 1982 AW (a) 1.50
- ❑2, Nov 1982 BA (c); AW, BA (a) 1.00

BLADE: SINS OF THE FATHER
MARVEL
- ❑1, Oct 1998 .... 5.99

BLADESMEN, THE
BLUE COMET
- ❑0, b&w 2.00
- ❑1, b&w 2.00
- ❑2 .... 2.00

BLADE: THE VAMPIRE-HUNTER
MARVEL
- ❑1, Jul 1994; foil cover 2.95
- ❑2, Aug 1994 .... 1.95
- ❑3, Sep 1994 .... 1.95
- ❑4, Oct 1994 .... 1.95
- ❑5, Nov 1994 .... 1.95
- ❑6, Dec 1994 .... 1.95
- ❑7, Jan 1995 .... 1.95
- ❑8, Feb 1995 .... 1.95
- ❑9, Mar 1995 .... 1.95
- ❑10, Apr 1995 .... 1.95

BLADE: VAMPIRE HUNTER
MARVEL
- ❑1, Dec 1999 .... 3.50
- ❑2, Jan 2000 .... 2.50
- ❑3, Feb 2000 .... 2.50
- ❑4, Mar 2000 .... 2.50
- ❑5, Apr 2000 .... 2.50
- ❑6, May 2000 .... 2.50

BLADE 2: MOVIE ADAPTATION
MARVEL
- ❑1, May 2002, b&w 5.95

N-MINT

BLAIR WHICH? (SERGIO ARAGONÉS')
DARK HORSE
- ❑1, Dec 1999 .... 2.95

BLAIR WITCH CHRONICLES, THE
ONI
- ❑1, Mar 2000, b&w 2.95
- ❑2, Apr 2000 .... 2.95
- ❑3, Jun 2000 .... 2.95
- ❑4, Jul 2000 .... 2.95

BLAIR WITCH: DARK TESTAMENTS
IMAGE
- ❑1, Oct 2000 .... 2.95

BLAIR WITCH PROJECT, THE
ONI
- ❑1, Aug 1999; prequel to movie 10.00
- ❑1-2 .... 3.00

BLANCHE GOES TO HOLLYWOOD
DARK HORSE
- ❑1, b&w 2.95

BLANCHE GOES TO NEW YORK
DARK HORSE
- ❑1, Nov 1992, b&w 2.95

BLARNEY
DISCOVERY
- ❑1; cardstock cover, b&w 2.95

BLAST CORPS
DARK HORSE
- ❑1, Oct 1998; based on Nintendo 64 games 2.50

BLASTERS SPECIAL
DC
- ❑1, May 1989 .... 2.00

BLAST-OFF
HARVEY
- ❑1, Oct 1965 AW, JK (w); AW, JK (a); A: The Three Rocketeers 28.00

BLAZE
MARVEL
- ❑1, Aug 1994; silver enhanced cover 2.95
- ❑2, Sep 1994 .... 1.95
- ❑3, Oct 1994 .... 1.95
- ❑4, Nov 1994 .... 1.95
- ❑5, Dec 1994 .... 1.95
- ❑6, Jan 1995 .... 1.95
- ❑7, Feb 1995 .... 1.95
- ❑8, Mar 1995 .... 1.95
- ❑9, Apr 1995 .... 1.95
- ❑10, May 1995 .... 1.95
- ❑11, Jun 1995 .... 1.95
- ❑12, Jul 1995 .... 1.95

BLAZE: LEGACY OF BLOOD
MARVEL
- ❑1, Dec 1993 .... 1.75
- ❑2, Jan 1994 .... 1.75
- ❑3, Feb 1994 .... 1.75
- ❑4, Mar 1994 .... 1.75

BLAZE OF GLORY
MARVEL
- ❑1, Feb 2000; biweekly mini-series 2.95
- ❑2, Feb 2000 .... 2.95
- ❑3, Mar 2000 .... 2.95
- ❑4, Mar 2000 .... 2.99

BLAZING BATTLE TALES
SEABOARD / ATLAS
- ❑1, Jul 1975 .... 2.50

BLAZING COMBAT
WARREN
- ❑1, Oct 1965; FF (c); FF (a); scarcer 90.00
- ❑2 1965 FF (c); FF (a) 30.00
- ❑3 1966 FF (c); FF (a) 30.00
- ❑4 1966 FF (c); FF (a) 30.00
- ❑Annual 1 .... 45.00

BLAZING COMBAT (APPLE)
APPLE
- ❑1 .... 4.50
- ❑2, b&w 4.50

N-MINT

BLAZING COMBAT: WORLD WAR I AND WORLD WAR II
APPLE
- ❑1 .... 3.75
- ❑2, Jun 1994 .... 3.75

BLAZING FOXHOLES
FANTAGRAPHICS / EROS
- ❑1, Sep 1994 .... 2.95
- ❑2 .... 2.95
- ❑3, Jan 1995 .... 2.95

BLAZING WESTERN (AC)
AC
- ❑1, b&w 2.50

BLAZING WESTERN (AVALON)
AVALON
- ❑1, ca. 1997, b&w 2.75

BLEAT
SLAVE LABOR
- ❑1, Aug 1995 .... 2.95

BLEEDING HEART
FANTAGRAPHICS
- ❑1 .... 2.50
- ❑2, Spr 1992 .... 2.50
- ❑3 .... 2.50
- ❑4 .... 2.50
- ❑5, Aug 1993 .... 2.50

BLINDSIDE
IMAGE
- ❑1, Feb 1998; video game magazine in comic-book format 1.00
- ❑1/A, Aug 1996 .... 2.50
- ❑1/B, Aug 1996; white background cover 2.50
- ❑2, Sep 1996 .... 1.00
- ❑3, Dec 1996 .... 1.00
- ❑4 1997 .... 1.00
- ❑5 1997 .... 1.00
- ❑6 1997 .... 1.00
- ❑7 1997 .... 1.00

BLINK
MARVEL
- ❑1, Mar 2001 .... 2.99
- ❑2, Apr 2001 .... 2.99
- ❑3, May 2001 .... 2.99
- ❑4 .... 2.99

BLIP
MARVEL
- ❑1, Feb 1983; video game magazine in comic-book format 1.00
- ❑2, Mar 1983 .... 1.00
- ❑3, Apr 1983 .... 1.00
- ❑4, May 1983 .... 1.00
- ❑5, Jun 1983 .... 1.00
- ❑6, Jul 1983 .... 1.00
- ❑7, Aug 1983 .... 1.00

BLIP (BARDIC)
BARDIC
- ❑1, Feb 1998 .... 1.25

BLIP AND THE C.C.A.D.S.
AMAZING
- ❑1 .... 2.00
- ❑2 .... 2.00

BLISS ALLEY
IMAGE
- ❑1, Jul 1997 .... 2.95
- ❑2, Sep 1997 .... 2.95

BLITE
FANTAGRAPHICS
- ❑1, b&w 2.25

BLITZ
NIGHTWYND
- ❑1 .... 2.50
- ❑2 .... 2.50
- ❑3 .... 2.50
- ❑4 .... 2.50

Sergio Aragonés poked gentle fun at the phenomenon of the independent film *The Blair Witch Project* with his *Blair Which?* one-shot.

N-MINT

BLITZKRIEG
DC
- ❑1, Jan 1976 RE (a) 16.00
- ❑2, Mar 1976 .... 8.00
- ❑3, May 1976 RE (a) 6.00
- ❑4, Jul 1976; Bicentennial #20 .... 6.00
- ❑5, Sep 1976 .... 6.00

BLOKHEDZ
IMAGE
- ❑1, Dec 2003 .... 2.95

BLONDE, THE
FANTAGRAPHICS / EROS
- ❑1 .... 2.50
- ❑2 .... 2.50
- ❑3 .... 2.50

BLONDE ADDICTION
BLITZWEASEL
- ❑1 .... 2.95
- ❑2 .... 2.95
- ❑3 .... 2.95
- ❑4; flip-book with Blonde Avenger's Subplots 2.95

BLONDE AVENGER
BLITZ WEASEL
- ❑27/A 3.95
- ❑27/B 3.95

BLONDE AVENGER, THE (MINI-SERIES)
FANTAGRAPHICS / EROS
- ❑1, Mar 1993 .... 2.75
- ❑2, ca. 1993 .... 2.75
- ❑3 .... 2.75
- ❑4, Apr 1994 .... 2.75

BLONDE AVENGER: CROSSOVER CRAZZEEE
BLITZWEASEL
- ❑1 .... 3.95

BLONDE AVENGER MONTHLY
BLITZWEASEL
- ❑1, Mar 1996, b&w 4.00
- ❑2, Apr 1996 .... 3.00
- ❑3, May 1996 .... 2.95
- ❑4, Jun 1996 .... 2.95
- ❑5 .... 2.95
- ❑6 .... 2.95

BLONDE AVENGER ONE-SHOT SPECIAL: THE SPYING GAME
BLITZWEASEL
- ❑1, Mar 1996, b&w 2.95

BLONDE, THE: BONDAGE PALACE
FANTAGRAPHICS / EROS
- ❑1 .... 2.95
- ❑2 .... 2.95
- ❑3 .... 2.95
- ❑5, May 1994 .... 2.95

BLONDIE COMICS
DAVID MCKAY
- ❑94, Sep 1956 .... 9.00
- ❑95, Oct 1956 .... 9.00
- ❑96, Nov 1956 .... 9.00
- ❑97, Dec 1956 .... 9.00
- ❑98, Jan 1957 .... 9.00
- ❑99, Feb 1957 .... 9.00

N-MINT

❑100, Mar 1957; 100th anniversary issue ... 10.00
❑101, Apr 1957 ... 8.00
❑102, May 1957 ... 8.00
❑103, Jun 1957 ... 8.00
❑104, Jul 1957 ... 8.00
❑105, Aug 1957 ... 8.00
❑106, Sep 1957 ... 8.00
❑107, Oct 1957 ... 8.00
❑108, Nov 1957 ... 8.00
❑109, Dec 1957 ... 8.00
❑110 1958 ... 8.00
❑111 1958 ... 8.00
❑112 1958 ... 8.00
❑113 1958 ... 8.00
❑114 1958 ... 8.00
❑115 1958 ... 8.00
❑116 1958 ... 8.00
❑117 1958 ... 8.00
❑118 1958 ... 8.00
❑119 1958 ... 8.00
❑120 1958 ... 8.00
❑121, Jan 1959 ... 8.00
❑122, Feb 1959 ... 8.00
❑123, Mar 1959 ... 8.00
❑124, Apr 1959 ... 8.00
❑125 1959; Double-size ... 9.00
❑126 1959 ... 8.00
❑127 1959 ... 8.00
❑128 1959 ... 8.00
❑129 1959 ... 8.00
❑130 ... 8.00
❑131 ... 7.00
❑132 ... 7.00
❑133 1960 ... 7.00
❑134 1960 ... 7.00
❑135 1960 ... 7.00
❑136 1960 ... 7.00
❑137 1960 ... 7.00
❑138 1960 ... 7.00
❑139 1960 ... 7.00
❑140 1960 ... 7.00
❑141 ... 8.00
❑142 ... 8.00
❑143 ... 8.00
❑144, Apr 1961 ... 8.00
❑145 ... 8.00
❑146 ... 8.00
❑147 ... 8.00
❑148 ... 8.00
❑149 ... 8.00
❑150 ... 8.00
❑151 ... 8.00
❑152 ... 8.00
❑153 ... 8.00
❑154 ... 8.00
❑155 ... 8.00
❑156 ... 8.00
❑157 ... 8.00
❑158 ... 8.00
❑159, Nov 1963 ... 8.00
❑160, Mar 1965 ... 8.00
❑161 1965 ... 8.00
❑162, Sep 1965 ... 8.00
❑163, Nov 1965 ... 8.00
❑164, Aug 1966; King Features Syndicate begins publishing ... 8.00
❑165 1966 ... 8.00
❑166 ... 8.00
❑167 ... 8.00
❑168 1967 ... 5.00
❑169 1967 ... 5.00
❑170 1967 ... 5.00
❑171 1967 ... 5.00
❑172 1967 ... 5.00
❑173 1967 ... 5.00
❑174 1967 ... 5.00
❑175, Dec 1967 ... 5.00
❑176 ... 5.00
❑177, Feb 1969 ... 5.00
❑178 1969 ... 5.00
❑179 1969 ... 5.00
❑180, Aug 1969 ... 5.00
❑181 1969 ... 4.00
❑182 ... 4.00
❑183 1970 ... 4.00
❑184 1970 ... 4.00
❑185 1970 ... 4.00
❑186 1970 ... 4.00
❑187, Sep 1970 ... 4.00
❑188 ... 4.00
❑189 ... 4.00
❑190 1971 ... 4.00
❑191 1971 ... 4.00
❑192 1971 ... 4.00
❑193 1971 ... 4.00
❑194 1971 ... 4.00
❑195 ... 4.00
❑196 1972 ... 4.00
❑197, Apr 1972 ... 4.00
❑198 1972 ... 4.00
❑199, Jul 1972 ... 4.00
❑200, Oct 1972; Anniversary issue ... 4.00
❑201 ... 3.00
❑202 1973 ... 3.00
❑203 1973 ... 3.00
❑204 1973 ... 3.00
❑205, Jul 1973 ... 3.00
❑206, Sep 1973 ... 3.00
❑207 1974 ... 3.00
❑208, May 1974 ... 3.00
❑209 1974 ... 3.00
❑210, Oct 1974 ... 3.00
❑211 1974 ... 3.00
❑212, Feb 1975 ... 3.00
❑213 1975 ... 3.00
❑214, Jun 1975 ... 3.00
❑215, Sep 1975 ... 3.00
❑216 1975 ... 3.00
❑217 1976 ... 3.00
❑218 1976 ... 3.00
❑219 1976 ... 3.00
❑220 1976 ... 3.00
❑221 1976 ... 3.00
❑222, Nov 1976 ... 3.00

BLOOD
FANTACO
❑1, b&w ... 3.95

BLOOD AND GLORY
MARVEL
❑1; Embossed cover ... 5.95
❑2 ... 5.95
❑3 ... 5.95

BLOOD & KISSES
FANTACO
❑1 ... 2.95
❑2 ... 3.95

BLOOD & ROSES ADVENTURES
KNIGHT
❑1, May 1995, b&w ... 2.95

BLOOD & ROSES: FUTURE PAST TENSE
SKY
❑1, Dec 1993; Silver logo regular edition ... 2.25
❑1/Ashcan; ashcan edition ... 3.00
❑1/Gold; Gold logo ... 3.00
❑2 ... 2.25

BLOOD & ROSES: SEARCH FOR THE TIME-STONE
SKY
❑1 ... 2.50
❑1/Ashcan ... 3.00
❑2 ... 2.50

BLOOD AND SHADOWS
DC / VERTIGO
❑1 ... 5.95
❑2 ... 5.95
❑3 ... 5.95
❑4 ... 5.95

BLOOD AND THUNDER
CONQUEST
❑1, b&w ... 2.95

BLOOD & WATER
SLAVE LABOR
❑1, Oct 1991, b&w ... 2.95

BLOOD AND WATER (DC)
DC / VERTIGO
❑1, May 2003 ... 2.95
❑2, Jun 2003 ... 2.95
❑3, Jul 2003 ... 2.95
❑4, Aug 2003 ... 2.95
❑5, Sep 2003 ... 2.95

BLOOD: A TALE
MARVEL / EPIC
❑1 1987 ... 3.25
❑2 1987 ... 3.25
❑3 1987 ... 3.25
❑4 1987 ... 3.25

BLOOD: A TALE (VERTIGO)
DC / VERTIGO
❑1, Nov 1996 ... 2.95
❑2, Dec 1996 ... 2.95
❑3, Jan 1997 ... 2.95
❑4, Feb 1997 ... 2.95

BLOODBATH
DC
❑1, Dec 1993 ... 3.50
❑2, Dec 1993 ... 3.50

BLOOD BOUNTY
HIGHLAND
❑1 ... 2.00

BLOODBROTHERS
ETERNITY
❑1 ... 1.95
❑2 ... 1.95
❑3 ... 1.95
❑4 ... 1.95

BLOODCHILDE
MILLENNIUM
❑1, Dec 1994 ... 2.50
❑2, Feb 1995 ... 2.50
❑3, May 1995 ... 2.50
❑4, Jul 1995 ... 2.95

BLOOD CLUB
KITCHEN SINK
❑2; Cover says "Blood Club Featuring Big Baby" ... 5.95

BLOODFANG
EPITAPH
❑0, Mar 1996 ... 2.50
❑1 ... 2.50

BLOOD FEAST
ETERNITY
❑1, b&w; tame cover ... 2.50
❑1/Variant, b&w; Explicit cover ... 2.50
❑2, b&w ... 2.50
❑2/Variant, b&w; Explicit cover ... 2.50

BLOOD FEAST: THE SCREENPLAY
ETERNITY
❑1, b&w; not comics ... 4.95

BLOODFIRE
LIGHTNING
❑0, May 1994; Giant-size ... 3.50
❑0/A, Jun 1994; Giant-size; Yellow logo on cover ... 3.50
❑1, Mar 1993, b&w; promotional copy ... 3.50
❑1/Platinum, Jun 1993; platinum ... 3.50
❑1/Variant, Jun 1993; red foil ... 3.50
❑2, Jul 1993 ... 2.95
❑8, Jan 1994 ... 2.95
❑3, Aug 1993 ... 2.95
❑4, Sep 1993 ... 2.95
❑5, Oct 1993; trading card ... 2.95
❑6, Nov 1993 ... 2.95
❑7, Dec 1993 ... 2.95
❑9, Feb 1994 ... 2.95
❑10, Mar 1994 ... 2.95

N-MINT

❑11, Apr 1994 .... 2.95
❑12, May 1994 .... 2.95

BLOODFIRE/HELLINA
LIGHTNING

❑1, Aug 1995 .... 3.00
❑1/Nude, Aug 1995; Nude edition 4.00
❑1/Platinum; Platinum edition 3.00

BLOOD GOTHIC
FANTACO

❑1 .... 4.95
❑2 .... 4.95

BLOODHOUND
DC

❑1, Sep 2004 .... 2.95

BLOODHUNTER
BRAINSTORM

❑1, Oct 1996, b&w; cardstock cover . 2.95

BLOOD IS THE HARVEST
ECLIPSE

❑1, Jul 1992 .... 2.50
❑2 .... 2.50
❑3 .... 2.50
❑4 .... 2.50

BLOOD JUNKIES
ETERNITY

❑1 .... 2.50
❑2 .... 2.50

BLOOD LEGACY: THE STORY OF RYAN
IMAGE

❑1, Jul 2000 .... 2.50
❑2, Aug 2000 .... 2.50
❑3, Sep 2000 .... 2.50
❑4, Nov 2000 .... 2.50

BLOOD LEGACY/ YOUNG ONES ONE SHOT
IMAGE

❑1, Apr 2003 .... 4.99

BLOODLETTING (1ST SERIES)
FANTACO

❑1 .... 2.95

BLOODLETTING (2ND SERIES)
FANTACO

❑1 .... 3.95
❑2 .... 3.95

BLOODLINES
AIRCEL

❑1; Aircel publishes 2.50
❑2 .... 2.50
❑3; Blackburn begins as publisher 2.50
❑4 .... 2.50
❑5 .... 2.50
❑6 .... 2.50

BLOODLINES: A TALE FROM THE HEART OF AFRICA
MARVEL / EPIC

❑1, ca. 1992 .... 5.95

BLOODLUST
SLAVE LABOR

❑1, Dec 1990 .... 2.25

BLOOD 'N' GUTS
AIRCEL

❑1, Nov 1990, b&w 2.50
❑2 .... 2.50
❑3 .... 2.50
❑4 .... 2.50

BLOOD OF DRACULA
APPLE

❑1, Nov 1987 .... 2.00
❑2, Dec 1987 .... 2.00
❑3, Jun 1988 .... 2.00
❑4, Jul 1988 .... 2.00
❑5, Aug 1988 .... 2.00
❑6, Sep 1988 .... 2.00
❑7, Oct 1988 .... 2.00
❑8, Nov 1988 .... 2.00
❑9, Jan 1989 .... 2.00

N-MINT

❑10, Mar 1989 .... 2.00
❑11, May 1989 .... 2.00
❑12, Jun 1989 .... 2.00
❑13, Jul 1989 BWr (a) 2.00
❑14, Sep 1989 BWr (a) 2.25
❑15, Nov 1989; flexidisc 3.75
❑16, May 1990 BWr (a) 2.25
❑17, Jul 1990 BWr (a) 2.25
❑18, Sep 1990 BWr (a) 2.25
❑19, Mar 1991 BWr (a) 2.25

BLOOD OF THE INNOCENT
WARP

❑1 .... 2.00
❑2 .... 2.00
❑3 .... 2.00
❑4 .... 2.00

BLOOD PACK
DC

❑1, Mar 1995 .... 1.50
❑2, Apr 1995 .... 1.50
❑3, May 1995 .... 1.50
❑4, Jun 1995 .... 1.50

BLOODPOOL
IMAGE

❑1, Aug 1995 .... 2.50
❑1/Variant, Aug 1995; alternate cover 2.50
❑2, Sep 1995 .... 2.50
❑3, Oct 1995 .... 2.50
❑4, Nov 1995 .... 2.50
❑Special 1, Mar 1996; Special 2.50

BLOOD REIGN
FATHOM

❑1 .... 2.95
❑2, Sep 1991 .... 2.95
❑3, Oct 1991 .... 2.95

BLOODSCENT
COMICO

❑1, Oct 1988 .... 2.00

BLOODSEED
MARVEL

❑1, Oct 1993 .... 1.95
❑2, Nov 1993; Gold cover; nudity; Final issue (series was rescheduled as 2-issue series) 1.95

BLOODSHED
DAMAGE!

❑1 .... 2.95
❑1/Ltd.; no cover price, b&w 2.95
❑2 .... 2.95
❑3, ca. 1994; no cover price; cardstock cover 2.95
❑Ashcan 1, ca. 1997; no cover price; "Promo Edition" on cover; retailer promotional item 2.00

BLOODSHOT
VALIANT

❑0, Mar 1994; O: Bloodshot. A: Eternal Warrior. chromium cover 3.50
❑0/Gold, Mar 1994; Gold edition; O: Bloodshot. A: Eternal Warrior. no cover price 5.00
❑1, Feb 1993; DP (a); Metallic embossed foil cover 3.50
❑2, Mar 1993 V: X-O Manowar 2.50
❑3, Apr 1993 .... 2.25
❑4, May 1993 A: Eternal Warrior 2.25
❑5, Jun 1993 A: Rai. A: Eternal Warrior 2.25
❑6, Jul 1993 DP (a); 1: Ninjak 2.25
❑7, Aug 1993 A: Ninjak 2.25
❑8, Sep 1993 .... 2.25
❑9, Oct 1993 .... 2.25
❑10, Nov 1993 .... 2.25
❑11, Dec 1993 .... 2.25
❑12, Jan 1994 DP (a) 2.25
❑13, Feb 1994 .... 2.25
❑14, Mar 1994 .... 2.25
❑15, Apr 1994 .... 2.25
❑16, May 1994; trading card 2.25
❑17, Jun 1994 A: H.A.R.D.Corps 2.25
❑18, Aug 1994 .... 2.25

Blitzkrieg featured World War II stories told from the German point of view.
© 1976 National Periodical Publications (DC).

N-MINT

❑19, Sep 1994 .... 2.25
❑20, Oct 1994; Chaos Effect 2.25
❑21, Nov 1994 V: Ax 2.25
❑22, Dec 1994 .... 2.25
❑23, Jan 1995 .... 2.25
❑24, Feb 1995 .... 2.25
❑25, Mar 1995 .... 2.25
❑26, Apr 1995 .... 2.25
❑27, May 1995 .... 2.25
❑28, May 1995 V: Ninjak 2.25
❑29, Jun 1995; Valiant becomes Acclaim imprint 2.25
❑30, Jul 1995; Birthquake 2.25
❑31, Jul 1995; Birthquake 2.25
❑32, Aug 1995; Birthquake 2.25
❑33, Aug 1995; Birthquake 2.25
❑34, Sep 1995 .... 2.50
❑35, Sep 1995 V: Rampage 2.50
❑36, Oct 1995 MGr, BA (a) 2.50
❑37, Oct 1995 BA (a) 2.50
❑38, Nov 1995 .... 2.50
❑39, Nov 1995 .... 2.50
❑40, Dec 1995 .... 2.50
❑41, Dec 1995 .... 2.50
❑42, Jan 1996 .... 2.50
❑43, Jan 1996 .... 2.50
❑44, Feb 1996 .... 2.50
❑45, Mar 1996 .... 2.50
❑46, Apr 1996 .... 2.50
❑47, May 1996 .... 2.50
❑48, May 1996 .... 2.50
❑49, Jun 1996 .... 2.50
❑50, Jul 1996 .... 2.50
❑51, Aug 1996 .... 2.50
❑Yearbook 1, ca. 1994; Yearbook (annual) #1 .... 3.95

BLOODSHOT (VOL. 2)
ACCLAIM

❑1, Jul 1997 .... 2.50
❑1/Variant, Jul 1997; alternate painted cover 2.50
❑2, Aug 1997 .... 2.50
❑3, Sep 1997 .... 2.50
❑4, Oct 1997 .... 2.50
❑5, Nov 1997; Steranko tribute cover 2.50
❑6, Dec 1997 .... 2.50
❑7, Jan 1998 V: X-O Manowar 2.50
❑8, Feb 1998 V: X-O Manowar 2.50
❑9, Mar 1998 .... 2.50
❑10, Apr 1998; in Area 51 .... 2.50
❑11, May 1998 .... 2.50
❑12, Jun 1998; No cover date; indicia says Feb 2.50
❑13, Jul 1998 .... 2.50
❑14, Aug 1998 .... 2.50
❑15, Sep 1998 .... 2.50
❑16, Oct 1998 .... 2.50
❑Ashcan 1, Mar 1997; No cover price; b&w preview of upcoming series 1.00

BLOODSTONE
MARVEL

❑1, Dec 2001 .... 2.99
❑2, Jan 2002 .... 2.99
❑3, Feb 2002 .... 2.99
❑4, Mar 2002 .... 2.99

N-MINT

BLOODSTREAM
IMAGE

- ❑1, Jan 2004 .... 2.95
- ❑2, Mar 2004 .... 2.95

BLOODSTRIKE
IMAGE

- ❑1, Apr 1993; RL (a); 1: Tag. 1: Deadlock. 1: Shogun. 1: Col. Cabbot. 1: Fourplay. fading blood cover 3.00
- ❑2, Jun 1993 1: Lethal 2.00
- ❑3, Jul 1993 .... 2.00
- ❑4, Oct 1993 KG (w) 2.00
- ❑5, Nov 1993 1: Noble. A: Supreme .. 2.00
- ❑6, Dec 1993; Chapel becomes team leader 2.00
- ❑7, Jan 1994 A: Chapel 2.00
- ❑8, Feb 1994 .... 2.00
- ❑9, Mar 1994 .... 2.00
- ❑10, Apr 1994 .... 2.00
- ❑11, Jul 1994 .... 2.00
- ❑12, Aug 1994 .... 2.00
- ❑13, Aug 1994 .... 2.50
- ❑14, Sep 1994 .... 2.50
- ❑15, Oct 1994 .... 2.50
- ❑16, Nov 1994 .... 2.50
- ❑17, Dec 1994 .... 2.50
- ❑18, Jan 1995; polybagged with trading card 2.50
- ❑19, Feb 1995; polybagged 2.50
- ❑20, Mar 1995 .... 2.50
- ❑21, Apr 1995 .... 2.50
- ❑22, May 1995 .... 2.50
- ❑23 .... 2.50
- ❑24 .... 2.50
- ❑25, May 1994; Images of Tomorrow; Published out of sequence as a preview of the future 1.95

BLOODSTRIKE ASSASSIN
IMAGE

- ❑0, Oct 1995 .... 2.50
- ❑1/A, Jun 1995 .... 2.50
- ❑1/B, Jun 1995; alternate cover 2.50
- ❑2, Jul 1995 .... 2.50
- ❑3, Aug 1995 .... 2.50
- ❑4 .... 2.50

BLOODSUCKER
FANTAGRAPHICS / EROS

- ❑1, b&w 2.50

BLOOD SWORD, THE
JADEMAN

- ❑1, Aug 1988 .... 1.95
- ❑2, Sep 1988 .... 1.95
- ❑3, Oct 1988 .... 1.95
- ❑4, Nov 1988 .... 1.95
- ❑5, Dec 1988 .... 1.95
- ❑6, Jan 1989 .... 1.95
- ❑7, Feb 1989 .... 1.95
- ❑8, Mar 1989 .... 1.95
- ❑9, Apr 1989 .... 1.95
- ❑10, May 1989 .... 1.95
- ❑11, Jun 1989 .... 1.95
- ❑12, Jul 1989 .... 1.95
- ❑13, Aug 1989 .... 1.95
- ❑14, Sep 1989 .... 1.95
- ❑15, Oct 1989 .... 1.95
- ❑16, Nov 1989 .... 1.95
- ❑17, Dec 1989 .... 1.95
- ❑18, Jan 1990 .... 1.95
- ❑19, Feb 1990 .... 1.95
- ❑20, Mar 1990 .... 1.95
- ❑21, Apr 1990 .... 1.95
- ❑22, May 1990 .... 1.95
- ❑23, Jun 1990 .... 1.95
- ❑24, Jul 1990 .... 1.95
- ❑25, Aug 1990 .... 1.95
- ❑26, Sep 1990 .... 1.95
- ❑27, Oct 1990 .... 1.95
- ❑28, Nov 1990 .... 1.95
- ❑29, Dec 1990 .... 1.95
- ❑30, Jan 1991 .... 1.95
- ❑31, Feb 1991 .... 1.95

N-MINT

- ❑32, Mar 1991 .... 1.95
- ❑33, Apr 1991 .... 1.95
- ❑34, May 1991 .... 1.95
- ❑35, Jun 1991 .... 1.95
- ❑36, Jul 1991 .... 1.95
- ❑37, Aug 1991 .... 1.95
- ❑38, Sep 1991 .... 1.95
- ❑39, Oct 1991 .... 1.95
- ❑40, Nov 1991 .... 1.95
- ❑41, Dec 1991 .... 1.95
- ❑42, Jan 1992 .... 1.95

BLOOD SWORD DYNASTY
JADEMAN

- ❑1, Sep 1989 .... 1.25
- ❑2, Oct 1989 .... 1.25
- ❑3, Nov 1989 .... 1.25
- ❑4, Dec 1989 .... 1.25
- ❑5, Jan 1990 .... 1.25
- ❑6, Feb 1990 .... 1.25
- ❑7, Mar 1990 .... 1.25
- ❑8, Apr 1990 .... 1.25
- ❑9, May 1990 .... 1.25
- ❑10, Jun 1990 .... 1.25
- ❑11, Jul 1990 .... 1.25
- ❑12, Aug 1990 .... 1.25
- ❑13, Sep 1990 .... 1.25
- ❑14, Oct 1990 .... 1.25
- ❑15, Nov 1990 .... 1.25
- ❑16, Dec 1990 .... 1.25
- ❑17, Jan 1991 .... 1.25
- ❑18, Feb 1991 .... 1.25
- ❑19, Mar 1991 .... 1.25
- ❑20, Apr 1991 .... 1.25
- ❑21, May 1991 .... 1.25
- ❑22, Jun 1991 .... 1.25
- ❑23, Jul 1991 .... 1.25
- ❑24, Aug 1991 .... 1.25
- ❑25, Sep 1991 .... 1.25
- ❑26, Oct 1991 .... 1.25
- ❑27, Nov 1991 .... 1.25
- ❑28, Dec 1991 .... 1.25
- ❑29, Jan 1992 .... 1.25

BLOOD SYNDICATE
DC / MILESTONE

- ❑1, Apr 1993 TVE (a); 1: Blood Syndicate. 1: Rob Chaplik 1.50
- ❑1/CS, Apr 1993; TVE (a); 1: Blood Syndicate. 1: Rob Chaplik. poster, trading card 2.95
- ❑2, May 1993 1: Boogieman. V: Holocaust 1.50
- ❑3, Jun 1993 1: MOM. A: Boogieman 1.50
- ❑4, Jul 1993 D: Tech-9 .... 1.50
- ❑5, Aug 1993 1: Demon Fox. 1: John Wing. 1: Kwai 1.50
- ❑6, Sep 1993 .... 1.50
- ❑7, Oct 1993 1: Edmund. 1: Cornelia 1.50
- ❑8, Nov 1993 1: Kwai 1.50
- ❑9, Dec 1993 O: Blood Syndicate. 1: Templo 1.50
- ❑10, Jan 1994; Giant-size; 1: Bubbasaur. Metallic ink cover 2.50
- ❑11, Feb 1994; Aquamaria joins Blood Syndicate 1.50
- ❑12, Mar 1994 1: The Rat Congress .. 1.50
- ❑13, Apr 1994 1: The White Roaches 1.50
- ❑14, May 1994 .... 1.50
- ❑15, Jun 1994 .... 1.50
- ❑16, Jul 1994 A: Superman 1.50
- ❑17, Aug 1994 .... 1.75
- ❑18, Sep 1994 .... 1.75
- ❑19, Oct 1994 .... 1.75
- ❑20, Nov 1994 A: Shadow Cabinet 1.75
- ❑21, Dec 1994 .... 1.75
- ❑22, Jan 1995 .... 1.75
- ❑23, Feb 1995 .... 1.75
- ❑24, Mar 1995 .... 1.75
- ❑25, Apr 1995; Giant-size; Tech-9 returns 2.95
- ❑26, May 1995 .... 1.75
- ❑27, Jun 1995 .... 1.75
- ❑28, Jul 1995 .... 2.50

N-MINT

- ❑29, Aug 1995 .... 1.00
- ❑30, Sep 1995 .... 2.50
- ❑31, Oct 1995 .... 2.50
- ❑32, Nov 1995 .... 2.50
- ❑33, Dec 1995 .... 0.99
- ❑34, Jan 1996 .... 2.50
- ❑35, Feb 1996 .... 3.50

BLOODTHIRST: TERMINUS OPTION
ALPHA PRODUCTIONS

- ❑1, b&w 2.50
- ❑2 .... 2.50

BLOODTHIRST: THE NIGHTFALL CONSPIRACY
ALPHA

- ❑1 .... 2.50
- ❑2 .... 2.50

BLOODTHIRSTY PIRATE TALES
BLACK SWAN

- ❑1 .... 2.50
- ❑2 .... 2.50
- ❑3, Win 1995 .... 2.50
- ❑4, Fal 1996 .... 2.50
- ❑5, Spr 1997 .... 2.50
- ❑6, Win 1997 .... 2.50
- ❑7 .... 2.50
- ❑8 .... 2.50

BLOOD TIES
FULL MOON

- ❑1, ca. 1991 .... 2.25

BLOODWING
ETERNITY

- ❑1, Jan 1988 .... 1.95
- ❑2, Feb 1988 .... 1.95
- ❑3, Mar 1988 .... 1.95
- ❑4, Apr 1988 .... 1.95
- ❑5, May 1988 .... 1.95
- ❑6 .... 1.95

BLOODWULF
IMAGE

- ❑1, Feb 1995; five different covers 2.50
- ❑2, Mar 1995 .... 2.50
- ❑3, Apr 1995 .... 2.50
- ❑4, May 1995 .... 2.50
- ❑Summer 1, Aug 1995; Summer Special 2.50

BLOODY BONES & BLACKEYED PEAS
GALAXY

- ❑1 .... 1.00

BLOODYHOT
PARODY

- ❑1 .... 2.95

BLOODY MARY
DC / HELIX

- ❑1, Oct 1996 .... 2.25
- ❑2, Nov 1996 .... 2.25
- ❑3, Dec 1996 .... 2.25
- ❑4, Jan 1997 .... 2.25

BLOODY MARY: LADY LIBERTY
DC / HELIX

- ❑1, Sep 1997 .... 2.50
- ❑2, Oct 1997 .... 2.50
- ❑3, Nov 1997 .... 2.50
- ❑4, Dec 1997 .... 2.50

BLOODY SCHOOL
CURTIS COMIC

- ❑1 .... 2.95

BLUE
IMAGE

- ❑1, Aug 1999 .... 2.50
- ❑2, Apr 2000 .... 2.50

BLUEBEARD
SLAVE LABOR

- ❑1, b&w 2.95
- ❑2, b&w 2.95
- ❑3, b&w 2.95

N-MINT

BLUE BEETLE (VOL. 2)
CHARLTON

❑1, Jun 1964 SD (a) 45.00
❑2, Sep 1964 SD (a) 30.00
❑3, Nov 1964 SD (a) 20.00
❑4, Jan 1965 SD (a) 20.00
❑5, Apr 1965 SD (a) 20.00

BLUE BEETLE (VOL. 3)
CHARLTON

❑50, Jul 1965 22.00
❑51, Aug 1965 22.00
❑52, Oct 1965 SD (a) 22.00
❑53, Dec 1965 SD (a) 22.00
❑54, Feb 1966 22.00
❑1, Jun 1967 SD (c); SD (a) 45.00
❑2, Aug 1967 SD (c); SD (w); SD (a) 30.00
❑3, Oct 1967 SD (c); SD (w); SD (a) 22.00
❑4, Dec 1967 SD (c); SD (w); SD (a) 22.00
❑5, Nov 1968, SD (a) 22.00

BLUE BEETLE (DC)
DC

❑1, Jun 1986 O: Blue Beetle. V: Firefist 1.00
❑2, Jul 1986 O: Firefist. V: Firefist 1.00
❑3, Aug 1986 V: Madmen 1.00
❑4, Sep 1986 V: Doctor Alchemy 1.00
❑5, Oct 1986 A: Question 1.00
❑6, Nov 1986 A: Question 1.00
❑7, Dec 1986 A: Question. D: Muse 1.00
❑8, Jan 1987 V: Calculator 1.00
❑9, Feb 1987; Legends 1.00
❑10, Mar 1987; V: Chronos. Legends 1.00
❑11, Apr 1987 A: Teen Titans 1.00
❑12, May 1987 A: Teen Titans 1.00
❑13, Jun 1987 A: Teen Titans 1.00
❑14, Jul 1987 1.00
❑15, Aug 1987 1.00
❑16, Sep 1987 1.00
❑17, Oct 1987 1.00
❑18, Nov 1987 1.00
❑19, Dec 1987 1.00
❑20, Jan 1988; Millennium 1.00
❑21, Feb 1988; Millennium 1.00
❑22, Mar 1988 1.00
❑23, Apr 1988 1.00
❑24, May 1988 1.00

BLUE BLOCK
KITCHEN SINK

❑1 2.95

BLUE BULLETEER, THE
AC

❑1, b&w O: Blue Bulleteer 2.50

BLUE DEVIL
DC

❑1, Jun 1984 O: Blue Devil 1.00
❑2, Jul 1984 V: Shockwave 1.00
❑3, Aug 1984 V: Metallo 1.00
❑4, Sep 1984 A: Zatanna 1.00
❑5, Oct 1984 A: Zatanna 1.00
❑6, Nov 1984 1: Bolt 1.00
❑7, Dec 1984 V: Bolt. V: Trickster 1.00
❑8, Jan 1985 V: Bolt. V: Trickster 1.00
❑9, Feb 1985 V: Bolt. V: Trickster 1.00
❑10, Mar 1985 1.00
❑11, Apr 1985 1.00
❑12, May 1985 A: Demon 1.00
❑13, Jun 1985 A: Green Lantern. A: Zatanna 1.00
❑14, Jul 1985 1: Kid Devil 1.00
❑15, Aug 1985 1.00
❑16, Sep 1985 1.00
❑17, Oct 1985; Crisis 1.00
❑18, Nov 1985; Crisis 1.00
❑19, Dec 1985 1.00
❑20, Jan 1986 1.00
❑21, Feb 1986 1.00
❑22, Mar 1986 1.00
❑23, Apr 1986 A: Firestorm 1.00
❑24, May 1986 1.00
❑25, Jun 1986 1.00
❑26, Jul 1986 V: Green Gargoyle 1.00

N-MINT

❑27, Aug 1986 1.00
❑28, Sep 1986 1.00
❑29, Oct 1986 1.00
❑30, Nov 1986; Double-size V: Flash's Rogues' Gallery 1.25
❑31, Dec 1986; Giant-size 1.25
❑Annual 1, Nov 1985 1.25

BLUE HOLE
CHRISTINE SHIELDS

❑1 2.95

BLUE ICE
MARTYR

❑1 2.50

BLUE LILY, THE
DARK HORSE

❑1, Mar 1993 3.95
❑2 3.95
❑3 3.95
❑4 3.95

BLUE LOCO
KITCHEN SINK

❑1, Feb 1997; cardstock cover 5.95

BLUE MONDAY: ABSOLUTE BEGINNERS
ONI

❑1, ca. 2001 2.95
❑2, ca. 2001 2.95
❑3, ca. 2001 2.95
❑4, ca. 2001 2.95

BLUE MONDAY: LOVECATS
ONI

❑1, ca. 2002 2.95

BLUE MONDAY: THE KIDS ARE ALRIGHT
ONI

❑1, ca. 2000 2.95
❑2, ca. 2000 2.95
❑3, ca. 2000 2.95

BLUE MOON
MU

❑1, Sep 1992 2.50
❑2, Nov 1992 2.50
❑3, Feb 1993 2.50
❑4, May 1993 2.50
❑5, Dec 1993 2.50

BLUE MOON (VOL. 2)
AEON

❑1, Aug 1994, b&w 2.95

BLUE NOTEBOOK, THE
NBM

❑1 13.95

BLUE RIBBON COMICS (VOL. 2)
ARCHIE / RED CIRCLE

❑1, Nov 1983; SD (c); AW, JK (a); Red Circle publishes 2.50
❑2, Nov 1983 RB (c); AN (a) 1.50
❑3, Dec 1983 1.50
❑4, Jan 1984 1.50
❑5, Feb 1984; A: Steel Sterling. All reprinted from "The Double Life of Private Strong" #1 1.50
❑6, Mar 1984 1.50
❑7, Apr 1984 RB (w); TD (a) 1.50
❑8, May 1984 1.50
❑9, Jun 1984 1.50
❑10, Jul 1984 1.50
❑11, Aug 1984 1.50
❑12, Sep 1984 1.50
❑13, Oct 1984 1.50
❑14, Dec 1984 1.50

B-MOVIE PRESENTS
B-MOVIE

❑1 1.70
❑2 1.70
❑3 1.70
❑4 1.70

Bloodshot's nanite-enhanced blood was collected and handed down through the centuries until it was used to give a Rai his powers in the 41st century.

© 1994 Voyager Communications Inc. (Valiant).

N-MINT

BOARD OF SUPERHEROS
NOT AVAILABLE

❑1 1.00

BOBBY BENSON'S B-BAR-B RIDERS
AC

❑1, ca. 1990, b&w 2.75

BOBBY RUCKERS
ART

❑1 2.95

BOBBY SHERMAN
CHARLTON

❑1, Feb 1972 15.00
❑2, Mar 1972 10.00
❑3, May 1972 10.00
❑4, Jun 1972 10.00
❑5, Jul 1972 10.00
❑6, Sep 1972 10.00
❑7, Oct 1972 10.00

BOB, THE GALACTIC BUM
DC

❑1, Feb 1995 2.00
❑2, Mar 1995 2.00
❑3, Apr 1995 2.00
❑4, Jun 1995 2.00

BOB MARLEY, TALE OF THE TUFF GONG
MARVEL

❑1 5.95
❑2 5.95
❑3 5.95

"BOB'S" FAVORITE COMICS
RIP OFF

❑1, b&w 2.50
❑1-2, b&w 2.50
❑1-3, b&w 2.50

BOB STEELE WESTERN (AC)
AC

❑1, b&w 2.75

BODY BAGS
DARK HORSE / BLANC NOIR

❑1, Sep 1996 3.50
❑2, Oct 1996 3.00
❑3, Nov 1996 3.00
❑4, Jan 1997 3.00
❑Ashcan 1 3.00

BODY COUNT (AIRCEL)
AIRCEL

❑1; TMNT storyline 2.25
❑2; TMNT storyline 2.25
❑3; TMNT storyline 2.25
❑4; TMNT storyline 2.25

BODYCOUNT (IMAGE)
IMAGE

❑1, Mar 1996 2.50
❑2, Apr 1996 2.50
❑3, May 1996 2.50
❑4 2.50

BODY DOUBLES
DC

❑1, Oct 1999 2.50
❑2, Nov 1999 2.50
❑3, Dec 1999 2.50
❑4, Jan 2000 2.50

Condition price index: Multiply "NM prices" above by: **0.83 for Very Fine/Near Mint**
0.66 for Very Fine • 0.33 for Fine • 0.2 for Very Good • 0.125 for Good

N-MINT

BODY DOUBLES (VILLAINS)
DC
❑1, Feb 1998; New Year's Evil 2.00

BODYGUARD
AIRCEL
❑1, Sep 1990, b&w; intro by Todd McFarlane 2.50
❑2, Oct 1990, b&w 2.50
❑3, Nov 1990, b&w 2.50

BODY PAINT
FANTAGRAPHICS / EROS
❑1 .... 2.95
❑2, Jun 1995 .... 2.95

BODY SWAP, THE
ROGER MASON
❑1 .... 2.95

BOFFO IN HELL
NEATLY CHISELED FEATURES
❑1 .... 2.50

BOFFO LAFFS
PARAGRAPHICS
❑1; first hologram cover 2.50
❑2 .... 1.95
❑3 .... 1.95
❑4 .... 1.95
❑5 .... 1.95

BOFFY THE VAMPIRE LAYER
FANTAGRAPHICS / EROS
❑1, ca. 2000 .... 2.95
❑2, ca. 2000 .... 2.95
❑3, ca. 2001 .... 2.95

BOGIE MAN, THE
FAT MAN
❑1 .... 2.50
❑2 .... 2.50
❑3 .... 2.50
❑4 .... 2.50

BOGIE MAN, THE: CHINATOON
ATOMEKA
❑1 .... 2.95
❑2 .... 2.95
❑3 .... 2.95
❑4 .... 2.95

BOGIE MAN, THE: THE MANHATTAN PROJECT
TUNDRA
❑1, Jul 1992 .... 4.95

BOG SWAMP DEMON
HALL OF HEROES
❑1, Aug 1996 .... 2.50
❑2, Oct 1996; no indicia 2.50
❑3, Dec 1996 .... 2.50
❑4, Mar 1997 .... 2.50

BOHOS
IMAGE
❑1, May 1998; cover says Jun, indicia says May 2.95
❑2, Jun 1998 .... 2.95
❑3, Jul 1998; no month of publication 2.95

BO JACKSON VS. MICHAEL JORDAN
CELEBRITY
❑1 .... 2.95
❑2 .... 2.95

BOLD ADVENTURE
PACIFIC
❑1 .... 2.00
❑2 .... 2.00
❑3 .... 2.00

BOLT AND STARFORCE SIX
AC
❑1, Jul 1984 .... 1.75

BOLT SPECIAL
AC
❑1 .... 2.00

N-MINT

BOMARC
NIGHTWYND
❑1 .... 2.50
❑2 .... 2.50
❑3 .... 2.50

BOMBA
DC
❑1, Sep 1967 1: Bomba 16.00
❑2, Nov 1967 .... 8.00
❑3, Jan 1968 .... 8.00
❑4, Mar 1968 .... 8.00
❑5, May 1968 .... 8.00
❑6, Jul 1968 .... 8.00
❑7, Sep 1968 .... 8.00

BOMBAST
TOPPS
❑1, Apr 1993; Savage Dragon, #1 - Factory bagged 2.95

BOMBASTIC
SCREAMING DODO
❑1, Nov 1996 .... 2.50
❑2, Feb 1997 .... 2.50
❑3, May 1997 .... 2.50
❑4, Aug 1997 .... 2.50
❑5, Dec 1997; cardstock cover 2.50

BONAFIDE
BONAFIDE
❑0-2, Mar 1994 .... 3.95
❑0 .... 3.95

BONANZA
GOLD KEY
❑1, Dec 1962 .... 110.00
❑2, Mar 1963 .... 75.00
❑3, Jun 1963 .... 50.00
❑4, Sep 1963 .... 50.00
❑5, Dec 1963 .... 50.00
❑6, Feb 1964 .... 32.00
❑7, Apr 1964 .... 32.00
❑8, Jun 1964 .... 32.00
❑9, Aug 1964 .... 32.00
❑10, Oct 1964 .... 32.00
❑11, Dec 1964 .... 22.00
❑12, Feb 1965 .... 22.00
❑13, Apr 1965 .... 22.00
❑14, Jun 1965 .... 22.00
❑15, Aug 1965 .... 22.00
❑16, Oct 1965 .... 22.00
❑17, Dec 1965 .... 22.00
❑18, Feb 1966 .... 22.00
❑19, Apr 1966 .... 22.00
❑20, Jun 1966 .... 22.00
❑21, Aug 1966 .... 15.00
❑22, Oct 1966 .... 15.00
❑23, Feb 1967 .... 15.00
❑24, May 1967 .... 15.00
❑25, Aug 1967 .... 15.00
❑26, Nov 1967 .... 15.00
❑27, Feb 1968 .... 15.00
❑28, May 1968 .... 15.00
❑29, Aug 1968 .... 15.00
❑30, Nov 1968 .... 15.00
❑31, Feb 1969 .... 12.00
❑32, May 1969 .... 12.00
❑33, Aug 1969 .... 12.00
❑34, Nov 1969 .... 12.00
❑35, Feb 1970 .... 12.00
❑36, May 1970 .... 12.00
❑37, Aug 1970 .... 12.00

BONDAGE CONFESSIONS
FANTAGRAPHICS / EROS
❑1 .... 2.95
❑2 .... 2.95
❑3 .... 2.95
❑4, Nov 1998 .... 2.95

BONDAGE FAIRIES
ANTARCTIC / VENUS
❑1, Mar 1994 .... 4.00
❑1-2, May 1994 .... 2.95
❑1-3, Aug 1994 .... 2.95

N-MINT

❑1-4, Jan 1995 .... 2.95
❑2, Apr 1994 .... 4.00
❑2-2, Jun 1994 .... 2.95
❑2-3, Oct 1994 .... 2.95
❑2-4, Apr 1995 .... 2.95
❑3, May 1994 .... 3.25
❑3-2, Sep 1994 .... 2.95
❑3-3, Dec 1994 .... 2.95
❑4, Jun 1994 .... 3.25
❑4-2, Nov 1994 .... 2.95
❑4-3, Jan 1995 .... 2.95
❑5, Jul 1994 .... 3.25
❑5-2, Nov 1994 .... 2.95
❑5-3, Feb 1995 .... 2.95
❑6, Aug 1994 .... 2.95
❑6-2, Feb 1995 .... 2.95

BONDAGE FAIRIES EXTREME
FANTAGRAPHICS / EROS
❑1, Oct 1999 .... 3.50
❑2, Nov 1999 .... 3.50
❑3, Dec 1999 .... 3.50
❑4, Jan 2000 .... 3.50
❑5, Feb 2000 .... 3.50
❑6, Mar 2000 .... 3.50
❑7, Apr 2000 .... 3.50
❑8, May 2000 .... 3.95
❑9, Jun 2000 .... 3.50
❑10, Jul 2000 .... 3.50
❑11, Sep 2000 .... 3.50
❑12, Oct 2000 .... 3.50
❑13, Nov 2000 .... 3.95
❑14, ca. 2000 .... 3.50

BONDAGE GIRLS AT WAR
FANTAGRAPHICS / EROS
❑1 1996 .... 2.95
❑2 1996 .... 2.95
❑3 1996 .... 2.95
❑4 1996 .... 2.95
❑5, Feb 1997 .... 2.95
❑6, ca. 1997 .... 2.95

BONE
CARTOON BOOKS
❑1, Jul 1991, b&w; 1: Phoney Bone. 1: Smiley Bone. 1: Fone Bone. 3000 printed 80.00
❑1-2 1: Phoney Bone. 1: Fone Bone .. 8.00
❑1-3 1: Phoney Bone. 1: Fone Bone .. 3.00
❑1-4, Jan 1993 1: Phoney Bone. 1: Fone Bone 3.00
❑1-5; 1: Phoney Bone. 1: Fone Bone. fifth printing 3.00
❑1-6; 1: Phoney Bone. 1: Fone Bone. sixth printing 3.00
❑1-7; 1: Phoney Bone. 1: Fone Bone. seventh printing 3.00
❑1-8; 1: Phoney Bone. 1: Fone Bone. eighth printing 3.00
❑1-9, 1: Phoney Bone. 1: Fone Bone. Image reprint 3.00
❑2, Sep 1991, b&w 1: Thorn 45.00
❑2-2 1: Thorn 6.00
❑2-3, Jan 1993 1: Thorn 3.00
❑2-4 1: Thorn 3.00
❑2-5; 1: Thorn. fifth printing 3.00
❑2-6; 1: Thorn. sixth printing 3.00
❑2-7; 1: Thorn. seventh printing 3.00
❑2-8, Image reprint 3.00
❑3, Dec 1991, b&w 25.00
❑3-2 .... 3.00
❑3-3, Jan 1993 .... 3.00
❑3-4 .... 3.00
❑3-5; fifth printing 3.00
❑3-6; sixth printing 3.00
❑3-7; seventh printing 3.00
❑3-8, Image reprint 3.00
❑4, Mar 1992, b&w 16.00
❑4-2, Sep 1992 .... 3.00
❑4-3, Image reprint 3.00
❑4-4 .... 3.00
❑4-5 .... 3.00
❑4-6 .... 3.00
❑5, Jun 1992, b&w 12.00

N-MINT

❑5-2, Sep 1992; Image reprint 3.00
❑5-3, Image reprint 3.00
❑5-4 .... 3.00
❑5-5 .... 3.00
❑5-6 .... 3.00
❑5-7 .... 3.00
❑6, Nov 1992, b&w 7.00
❑6-2 .... 3.00
❑6-3, Image reprint 3.00
❑6-4 .... 3.00
❑6-5 .... 3.00
❑6-6 .... 3.00
❑7, Dec 1992, b&w 7.00
❑7-2 .... 3.00
❑7-3, Image reprint 3.00
❑7-4 .... 3.00
❑7-5 .... 3.00
❑8, Feb 1993, b&w 7.00
❑8-2 .... 3.00
❑8-3 .... 3.00
❑8-4 .... 3.00
❑8-5; fifth printing 3.00
❑8-6; sixth printing 3.00
❑8-7, Image reprint 3.00
❑9, Jul 1993, b&w 4.00
❑9-2 .... 3.00
❑9-3, Image reprint 3.00
❑9-4 .... 3.00
❑10, Sep 1993, b&w 3.50
❑10-2 .... 2.95
❑10-3, Image reprint 2.95
❑11, Dec 1993, b&w 3.50
❑11-2, Image reprint 2.95
❑12, Feb 1994, b&w 3.50
❑12-2, Image reprint 2.95
❑12-3 .... 2.95
❑13, Mar 1994, b&w 3.50
❑13-2, Image reprint 2.95
❑13.5; Wizard promotional edition 3.50
❑13.5/Gold; Gold edition 3.50
❑14, May 1994, b&w 2.95
❑14-2, Image reprint 2.95
❑15, Aug 1994, b&w 2.95
❑15-2, Image reprint 2.95
❑16, Oct 1994, b&w 2.95
❑16-2, Image reprint 2.95
❑17, Jan 1995, b&w 2.95
❑17-2, Image reprint 2.95
❑18, Apr 1995, b&w 2.95
❑18-2, Image reprint 2.95
❑19, Jun 1995, b&w 2.95
❑19-2, Image reprint 2.95
❑20, Oct 1995, b&w; moves to Image 2.95
❑20-2, Image reprint 2.95
❑21, Dec 1995, b&w; Image begins as publisher 2.95
❑22, Feb 1996, b&w 2.95
❑23, May 1996, b&w 1: Baby Rat Creature 2.95
❑24, Jun 1996, b&w 2.95
❑25, Aug 1996, b&w 2.95
❑26, Dec 1996, b&w 2.95
❑27, Apr 1997, b&w; Phoney captures Red Dragon; series returns to Cartoon Books 2.95
❑28, Aug 1997, b&w; Cartoon Books begins as publisher 2.95
❑29, Nov 1997, b&w 2.95
❑30, Jan 1998, b&w 2.95
❑31, Apr 1998, b&w 2.95
❑32, Jun 1998, b&w 2.95
❑33, Aug 1998, b&w 2.95
❑34, Dec 1998, b&w 2.95
❑35, Mar 1999, b&w 2.95
❑36, May 1999, b&w 2.95
❑37, Aug 1999, b&w; cover says Sep, indicia says Aug 2.95
❑38/A, Aug 2000, b&w 2.95
❑38/B, Aug 2000, b&w; FM (c); FM (a); alternate cover 2.95
❑38/C, Aug 2000, b&w; ARo (c); ARo (a); alternate cover 2.95
❑39, Oct 2000, b&w 2.95

N-MINT

❑40, Jan 2001, b&w 2.95
❑41, Mar 2001, b&w 2.95
❑42, May 2001, b&w 2.95
❑43, Jul 2001, b&w 2.95
❑44, Sep 2001, b&w 2.95
❑45 2001 .... 2.95
❑46 2001 .... 2.95
❑47 2002 .... 2.95
❑48 2002 .... 2.95
❑49 2002 .... 2.95
❑50 2002 .... 2.95
❑51 2002 .... 2.95
❑52 2003 .... 3.00
❑53 2003 .... 3.00
❑54 2003 .... 3.00
❑55, Jun 2004 .... 3.00
❑Special 1; Special edition 2.00

BONE SOURCEBOOK
Image

❑1/A, Nov 1995, b&w; No cover price; promotional handout 2.00
❑1/B, Nov 1995; San Diego Comic-Con edition 2.00

BONES
Malibu

❑1 .... 1.95
❑2 .... 1.95
❑3, Oct 1987 .... 1.95
❑4, Nov 1987 .... 1.95

BONE SAW
Tundra

❑1, b&w 14.95

BONESHAKER
Caliber

❑1, ca. 1994, b&w; Collects serial from Negative Burn 3.50

BONEYARD
NBM

❑1, ca. 2001 .... 2.95
❑2, ca. 2001 .... 2.95
❑3, ca. 2001 .... 2.95
❑4, ca. 2002 .... 2.95
❑5, ca. 2002 .... 2.95
❑6 .... 2.95
❑7 .... 2.95
❑8 .... 2.95

BONEYARD PRESS 1993 TOURBOOK
Boneyard

❑1; Distributor giveaway previewing Boneyard Press books 1.50

BONGO SPECIAL EDITION
Bongo

❑1; hardcover collection of Simpsons #1, Bartman #1, Itchy&Scratchy #1, Radioactive Man #1 (1000 copies) 20.00

BOOF (ICONOGRAFIX)
Iconografix

❑1, b&w 2.50

BOOF (IMAGE)
Image

❑1, Jul 1994 .... 1.95
❑1/A, Jul 1994; alternate cover 1.95
❑2, Aug 1994 .... 1.95
❑2/A, Aug 1994; alternate cover 1.95
❑3, Sep 1994 .... 1.95
❑3/A, Sep 1994; alternate cover 1.95
❑4, Oct 1994 .... 1.95
❑5, Nov 1994 .... 1.95
❑6, Dec 1994 .... 1.95

BOOF AND THE BRUISE CREW
Image

❑1, Jul 1994 .... 1.95
❑1/A, Jul 1994; alternate cover 1.95
❑2, Aug 1994 .... 1.95
❑2/A, Aug 1994; alternate cover 1.95
❑3, Sep 1994 .... 1.95
❑3/A, Sep 1994; alternate cover 1.95
❑4, Oct 1994 .... 1.95

AC has reprinted some adventures of *Bobby Benson's B-Bar-B Riders* from the 1950s.

© 1997 AC.

N-MINT

❑5, Nov 1994 .... 1.95
❑6, Dec 1994 .... 1.95

BOOGEYMAN (SERGIO ARAGONÉS')
Dark Horse

❑1, Jun 1998 .... 2.95
❑2, Jul 1998 .... 2.95
❑3, Aug 1998 .... 2.95
❑4, Sep 1998 .... 2.95

BOOGIEMAN, THE
Rion

❑1, b&w 1.50

BOOK
Dreamsmith

❑1, May 1998, b&w 3.50
❑2, Jun 1998 .... 3.50

BOOK OF ANGELS
Caliber

❑1, ca. 1997, b&w; cardstock cover 3.95

BOOK OF BALLADS AND SAGAS, THE
Green Man

❑1 1996, b&w 2.95
❑2 1996, b&w 2.95
❑3, Jun 1996, b&w 3.50
❑4, Dec 1996, b&w 3.50

BOOK OF FATE, THE
DC

❑1, Feb 1997 .... 2.25
❑2, Mar 1997 .... 2.25
❑3, Apr 1997 .... 2.25
❑4, May 1997 .... 2.25
❑5, Jun 1997 .... 2.25
❑6, Jul 1997; continues in Night Force #8 .... 2.25
❑7, Aug 1997 .... 2.25
❑8, Sep 1997 .... 2.25
❑9, Oct 1997 .... 2.25
❑10, Nov 1997 .... 2.25
❑11, Dec 1997; Face cover 2.25
❑12, Jan 1998 .... 2.50

BOOK OF NIGHT, THE
Dark Horse

❑1, Jul 1987 CV (w); CV (a) 2.50
❑2, Aug 1987 CV (w); CV (a) 2.00
❑3, Sep 1987 CV (w); CV (a) 2.00

BOOK OF SPELLS
Double Edge

❑1 .... 2.00
❑2, Sep 1994 .... 2.00
❑3 .... 2.00
❑4 .... 2.00

BOOK OF THE DAMNED: A HELLRAISER COMPANION (CLIVE BARKER'S...)
Marvel / Epic

❑1, Oct 1991 .... 4.95
❑2, Apr 1992 .... 4.95
❑3 .... 4.95
❑4 .... 4.95

BOOK OF THE DEAD
Marvel

❑1, Dec 1993 MP (a) 2.00
❑2, Jan 1994 GM, HC, MP (a) 2.00
❑3, Feb 1994 MP (a) 2.00
❑4, Mar 1994 MP (a) 2.00

N-MINT

BOOK OF THE TAROT
CALIBER / TOME
- ❑1, b&w 3.95

BOOK OF THOTH, THE
CIRCLE
- ❑1, Jun 1995 2.50

BOOKS OF FAERIE, THE
DC / VERTIGO
- ❑1, Mar 1997 2.50
- ❑2, Apr 1997 2.50
- ❑3, May 1997 2.50

BOOKS OF FAERIE, THE: AUBERON'S TALE
DC / VERTIGO
- ❑1, Aug 1998 2.50
- ❑2, Sep 1998 2.50
- ❑3, Oct 1998 2.50

BOOKS OF FAERIE, THE: MOLLY'S STORY
DC / VERTIGO
- ❑1, Sep 1999 2.50
- ❑2, Oct 1999 2.50
- ❑3, Nov 1999 2.50
- ❑4, Dec 1999 2.50

BOOKS OF LORE: SPECIAL EDITION
PEREGRINE ENTERTAINMENT
- ❑1, Sep 1997, b&w; cardstock cover, b&w 2.95
- ❑1/Ltd., Collector's Edition, bagged with poster and limited and regular editions of #1 5.00
- ❑2, Nov 1997 2.95

BOOKS OF LORE: STORYTELLER
PEREGRINE ENTERTAINMENT
- ❑1 2.95

BOOKS OF LORE: THE KAYNIN GAMBIT
PEREGRINE ENTERTAINMENT
- ❑0, Dec 1998 2.95
- ❑1, Nov 1998 2.95
- ❑1/Variant, Nov 1998; alternate cover 2.95
- ❑2, Jan 1999 2.95
- ❑3, Mar 1999 2.95
- ❑Ashcan 1, Jul 1998; b&w preview of Books Of Lore: The Kaynin Gambit 3.00

BOOKS OF MAGIC, THE (MINI-SERIES)
DC
- ❑1, Dec 1990 NG (w); 1: Timothy Hunter 4.00
- ❑2, Jan 1991 NG (w) 4.00
- ❑3, Feb 1991 NG (w); CV (a) 4.00
- ❑4, Mar 1991; NG (w); Paul Johnson 4.00

BOOKS OF MAGIC, THE
DC / VERTIGO
- ❑1, May 1994 3.00
- ❑1/Silver, May 1994; Silver (limited promotional) edition; no cover price 4.00
- ❑2, Jun 1994 2.50
- ❑3, Jul 1994 2.50
- ❑4, Aug 1994 2.50
- ❑5, Sep 1994 2.50
- ❑6, Oct 1994 2.50
- ❑7, Nov 1994 2.50
- ❑8, Dec 1994 2.50
- ❑9, Jan 1995 2.50
- ❑10, Feb 1995 2.50
- ❑11, Mar 1995 2.50
- ❑12, Apr 1995 2.50
- ❑13, May 1995 2.50
- ❑14, Jul 1995 2.50
- ❑15, Aug 1995 2.50
- ❑16, Sep 1995 2.50
- ❑17, Oct 1995 2.50
- ❑18, Nov 1995 2.50
- ❑19, Dec 1995 2.50
- ❑20, Jan 1996 2.50
- ❑21, Feb 1996 2.50
- ❑22, Mar 1996 2.50
- ❑23, Apr 1996 2.50
- ❑24, May 1996 2.50
- ❑25, Jun 1996 A: Death (Sandman) 2.50
- ❑26, Jul 1996 2.50
- ❑27, Aug 1996 2.50
- ❑28, Sep 1996 2.50
- ❑29, Oct 1996 2.50
- ❑30, Nov 1996 2.50
- ❑31, Dec 1996 2.50
- ❑32, Jan 1997 2.50
- ❑33, Feb 1997 2.50
- ❑34, Mar 1997 2.50
- ❑35, Apr 1997 2.50
- ❑36, May 1997 2.50
- ❑37, Jun 1997 2.50
- ❑38, Jul 1997 2.50
- ❑39, Aug 1997 2.50
- ❑40, Sep 1997 2.50
- ❑41, Oct 1997 2.50
- ❑42, Nov 1997 2.50
- ❑43, Dec 1997 2.50
- ❑44, Jan 1998 2.50
- ❑45, Feb 1998 2.50
- ❑46, Mar 1998 2.50
- ❑47, Apr 1998 2.50
- ❑48, May 1998 2.50
- ❑49, Jun 1998 2.50
- ❑50, Jul 1998; preview of issue #51 2.50
- ❑51, Aug 1998 2.50
- ❑52, Sep 1998 2.50
- ❑53, Oct 1998 2.50
- ❑54, Nov 1998 2.50
- ❑55, Dec 1998 2.50
- ❑56, Jan 1999 A: Cain 2.50
- ❑57, Feb 1999; Books of Faerie back-up 2.50
- ❑58, Mar 1999; Books of Faerie back-up 2.50
- ❑59, Apr 1999; Books of Faerie back-up 2.50
- ❑60, May 1999 2.50
- ❑61, Jun 1999 2.50
- ❑62, Jul 1999; Books of Faerie back-up 2.50
- ❑63, Aug 1999 2.50
- ❑64, Sep 1999 2.50
- ❑65, Oct 1999 2.50
- ❑66, Nov 1999 2.50
- ❑67, Dec 1999 2.50
- ❑68, Jan 2000 2.50
- ❑69, Feb 2000 2.50
- ❑70, Mar 2000 2.50
- ❑71, Apr 2000 2.50
- ❑72, May 2000 2.50
- ❑74, Jul 2000 2.50
- ❑73, Jun 2000 2.50
- ❑75, Aug 2000 2.50
- ❑Annual 1, Feb 1997; 1997 Annual 3.95
- ❑Annual 2, Feb 1998; 1998 Annual 3.95
- ❑Annual 3, Jun 1999; 1999 Annual 3.95

BOOKS OF MAGICK: LIFE DURING WARTIME
DC / VERTIGO
- ❑1, Sep 2004 2.95

BOOM BOOM
AEON
- ❑1, b&w 2.50
- ❑2, Sep 1994, b&w 2.50
- ❑3 2.50
- ❑4, ca. 1995 2.50

BOONDOGGLE
KNIGHT
- ❑1, Mar 1995 2.95
- ❑2, Jul 1995, b&w 2.95
- ❑3, Nov 1995 2.95
- ❑4, Jan 1996, b&w 2.95
- ❑Special 1, Nov 1996, b&w 2.95

BOOSTER GOLD
DC
- ❑1, Feb 1986 1: Booster Gold. V: Blackguard 1.00
- ❑2, Mar 1986 1: Mindancer 1.00
- ❑3, Apr 1986 1.00
- ❑4, May 1986 1.00
- ❑5, Jun 1986 1.00
- ❑6, Jul 1986 A: Superman 1.00
- ❑7, Aug 1986 A: Superman 1.00
- ❑8, Sep 1986 A: Legion 1.00
- ❑9, Oct 1986 A: Legion 1.00
- ❑10, Nov 1986 1.00
- ❑11, Dec 1986 1.00
- ❑12, Jan 1987 1.00
- ❑13, Feb 1987 1.00
- ❑14, Mar 1987; back to future 1.00
- ❑15, Apr 1987 1.00
- ❑16, May 1987 1: Booster Gold International 1.00
- ❑17, Jun 1987 A: CheshireHawk 1.00
- ❑18, Jul 1987 1.00
- ❑19, Aug 1987 V: Rainbow Raider 1.00
- ❑20, Sep 1987; blind 1.00
- ❑21, Oct 1987 1.00
- ❑22, Nov 1987 A: Justice League International 1.00
- ❑23, Dec 1987 A: Superman 1.00
- ❑24, Jan 1988; Millennium 1.00
- ❑25, Feb 1988; Millennium; final issue 1.00

BOOTS OF THE OPPRESSOR
NORTHSTAR
- ❑1, Apr 1993 2.95

BORDERGUARD
ETERNITY
- ❑1, Nov 1987 1.95
- ❑2, Dec 1987 1.95

BORDERLINE
KARDIA
- ❑1, Jun 1992 2.25

BORDER WORLDS (VOL. 1)
KITCHEN SINK
- ❑1, Jul 1986; Reprinted from Megaton Man 1.95
- ❑2, Sep 1986 1.95
- ❑3, Nov 1986 1.95
- ❑4, Jan 1987 1.95
- ❑5, Apr 1987 1.95
- ❑6, Jun 1987 1.95
- ❑7, Aug 1987; pages 4-5 transposed 2.00
- ❑7/A; Corrected edition; corrected 2.00

BORDER WORLDS (VOL. 2)
KITCHEN SINK
- ❑1, b&w 2.00

BORIS' ADVENTURE MAGAZINE
NICOTAT
- ❑1, Aug 1988, b&w; Rocketeer Adventure Magazine parody 2.00
- ❑2, Punishbear 2.95
- ❑3, Sep 1996 2.95
- ❑4, BlackBear 2.95

BORIS KARLOFF TALES OF MYSTERY
GOLD KEY
- ❑3, Apr 1963 25.00
- ❑4, Jul 1963 20.00
- ❑5, Oct 1963 20.00
- ❑6, Jan 1964 20.00
- ❑7, Sep 1964 18.00
- ❑8, Dec 1965 18.00
- ❑9, Mar 1965 WW (a) 30.00
- ❑10, Jun 1965 15.00
- ❑11, Sep 1965 22.00
- ❑12, Dec 1965; back cover pin-up 15.00
- ❑13, Mar 1966 12.00
- ❑14, Jun 1966 12.00
- ❑15, Sep 1966 15.00
- ❑16, Dec 1966 12.00
- ❑17, Mar 1967 12.00
- ❑18, Jun 1967 12.00
- ❑19, Sep 1967 12.00
- ❑20, Dec 1967 12.00
- ❑21, Mar 1968 JJ (a) 18.00
- ❑22, Jun 1968 10.00
- ❑23, Sep 1968; 10053-809 10.00
- ❑24, Dec 1968 10.00
- ❑25, Mar 1969 10.00
- ❑26, Jun 1969 10.00
- ❑27, Sep 1969 10.00

Condition price index: Multiply "NM prices" above by: **0.83 for Very Fine/Near Mint**
0.66 for Very Fine • 0.33 for Fine • 0.2 for Very Good • 0.125 for Good

	N-MINT
❑28, Dec 1969	10.00
❑29, Feb 1970	10.00
❑30, May 1970	10.00
❑31, Aug 1970	8.50
❑32, Nov 1970	8.50
❑33, Feb 1971	8.50
❑34, Apr 1971	8.50
❑35, Jun 1971	8.50
❑36, Aug 1971	8.50
❑37, Oct 1971	8.50
❑38, Dec 1971	8.50
❑39, Feb 1972	8.50
❑40, Apr 1972	8.50
❑41, Jun 1972	7.50
❑42, Oct 1972	7.50
❑43, Dec 1972	7.50
❑44, Feb 1973	7.50
❑45, Apr 1973	7.50
❑46, May 1973	7.50
❑47, Jun 1973	7.50
❑48, Jul 1973	7.50
❑49, Aug 1973; 90053-308	7.50
❑50, Oct 1973	7.50
❑51, Dec 1973	6.00
❑52, Feb 1974	6.00
❑53, Apr 1974	6.00
❑54, Jun 1974	6.00
❑55, Jul 1974	6.00
❑56, Aug 1974	6.00
❑57, Oct 1974	6.00
❑58, Dec 1974	6.00
❑59, Feb 1975	6.00
❑60, Apr 1975	5.00
❑61, ca. 1975	5.00
❑62, ca. 1975	5.00
❑63, Aug 1975	5.00
❑64, Oct 1975	5.00
❑65, Dec 1975	5.00
❑66, Feb 1976	5.00
❑67, Apr 1976	5.00
❑68, Jun 1976	5.00
❑69, ca. 1976	5.00
❑70, Sep 1976	5.00
❑71, ca. 1976	5.00
❑72, Dec 1976	5.00
❑73, ca. 1977	5.00
❑74, Apr 1977	5.00
❑75, ca. 1977	3.00
❑76, ca. 1977	3.00
❑77, ca. 1977	3.00
❑78, Oct 1977	3.00
❑79, ca. 1977	3.00
❑80, Feb 1978	3.00
❑81, Apr 1978	3.00
❑82, ca. 1978	3.00
❑83, Aug 1978	3.00
❑84, Sep 1978	3.00
❑85, Oct 1978	3.00
❑86, Nov 1978	3.00
❑87, Dec 1978	3.00
❑88, Jan 1979	3.00
❑89, Feb 1979	3.00
❑90, ca. 1979	3.00
❑91, May 1979	3.00
❑92, Jul 1979	3.00
❑93, Aug 1979	3.00
❑94, Sep 1979	3.00
❑95, Oct 1979	3.00
❑96, Nov 1979	3.00
❑97, Feb 1980	3.00

BORIS KARLOFF THRILLER
GOLD KEY

	N-MINT
❑1, Oct 1962	55.00
❑2, Jan 1963	40.00

BORIS THE BEAR
DARK HORSE

	N-MINT
❑1, ca. 1986, b&w	3.00
❑1-2 1986, b&w	1.75
❑2, ca. 1986, b&w V: Transformers	2.25
❑3, ca. 1986, b&w; Boris takes on Marvel Comics for Jack Kirby	2.50
❑4, ca. 1986, b&w; O: Boris the Bear. two different covers; Man of Steel parody cover (far shot)	2.50
❑4/A, ca. 1986, Man of Steel parody cover (close-up)	1.50
❑5, b&w; Swamp Thing parody	2.50
❑6, b&w; Batman parody	2.50
❑7, b&w; Elfquest parody	2.25
❑8, b&w	2.25
❑9, b&w; G.I. Joe parody; Wacky Squirrel backup	2.25
❑10, May 1987, b&w; G.I. Joe parody continues; Wacky Squirrel backup .	2.25
❑11, Jun 1987, b&w; DA (a); T.H.U.N.D.E.R. Agents	2.25
❑12, Jul 1987, b&w; Boris' Birthday; Last Dark Horse issue	2.25
❑13, Nov 1987, b&w; 1: Punishbear. Drug abuse issue; First Nicotat issue, remaining issues scarce	2.25
❑14, Dec 1987, b&w V: Number Two	2.25
❑15, ca. 1988, b&w	2.25
❑16, Mar 1988, b&w; Indiana Jones parody	2.25
❑17, ca. 1988, b&w; BlackHawk parody; Sininju Coneys back-up	2.25
❑18, ca. 1988, b&w; Spider-Slayer (Spider-Man) parody	2.25
❑19, Sep 1988, b&w; The Old Swap Shop back-up	2.25
❑20, Nov 1988, b&w; The Old Swap Shop back-up	2.25
❑21, Feb 1989, b&w; The Old Swap Shop back-up	2.00
❑22, Apr 1989, b&w; Kraven the Hunter/Sonny and Cher parody	2.00
❑23, May 1989, b&w	2.00
❑24, Jul 1989, b&w; Bingo Glumm back-up	2.00
❑25, b&w A: Southern Squadron	2.00
❑26, Jul 1990, b&w; A: Beardevil. Tom & Jerry parody	2.00
❑27, Oct 1990, b&w	2.00
❑28, ca. 1990, b&w	2.00
❑29, Jan 1991, b&w	2.00
❑30, Apr 1991, b&w; Gulf War issue/parody	2.50
❑31, Jun 1991, b&w	2.50
❑32, Jul 1991, b&w; Dinosaurs; very scarce	2.50
❑33, Sep 1991, b&w; very scarce	2.50
❑34, Nov 1991, b&w; A: BlackBear. #1 of 4, but series cancelled; very scarce	2.50

BORIS THE BEAR INSTANT COLOR CLASSICS
DARK HORSE

	N-MINT
❑1, Jul 1987; 1: Boris the Bear. Reprints Boris the Bear #1 in color	2.00
❑2, Aug 1987	2.00
❑3, Dec 1987	2.00

BORN
MARVEL / MAX

	N-MINT
❑1, Aug 2003; cardstock cover; Vietnam	3.50
❑2, Sep 2003; cardstock cover; Vietnam	3.50
❑3, Oct 2003; cardstock cover; Vietnam	3.50
❑4, Nov 2003; cardstock cover; Vietnam	3.50

BORN AGAIN
SPIRE

	N-MINT
❑1; Chuck Colson	3.50

BORN TO KILL
AIRCEL

	N-MINT
❑1, May 1991, b&w	2.50
❑2	2.50
❑3	2.50

BOSTON BOMBERS, THE
CALIBER

	N-MINT
❑1	2.50
❑2	2.50
❑3	2.50
❑4	2.50
❑5	2.50

After a short run at Image, Cartoon Books resumed publication of *Bone* in 1997.

© 1997 Jeff Smith (Cartoon Books).

	N-MINT
❑6	2.50
❑Special 1, ca. 1997	3.95

BOULEVARD OF BROKEN DREAMS
FANTAGRAPHICS

	N-MINT
❑1	3.95

BOUND AND GAGGED
ICONOGRAFIX

	N-MINT
❑1	2.50

BOUND IN DARKNESS: INFINITY ISSUE
CFD

	N-MINT
❑1, b&w	2.50

BOUNTY
CALIBER

	N-MINT
❑1	2.50
❑2	2.50
❑3	2.50

BOUNTY OF ZONE-Z
SUNSET STRIPS

	N-MINT
❑1	2.50

BOX
FANTAGRAPHICS / EROS

	N-MINT
❑1	2.25
❑2	2.25
❑3	2.25
❑4	2.25
❑5	2.25
❑6	2.25

BOXBOY
SLAVE LABOR

	N-MINT
❑1, Aug 1993	1.00
❑1-2, May 1995	1.25
❑2, Jul 1995	1.25

BOX OFFICE POISON
ANTARCTIC

	N-MINT
❑0; Collects stories from mini-comics	4.00
❑1, Oct 1996	8.00
❑2, Dec 1996	5.00
❑3, Feb 1997	4.00
❑4, Mar 1997	4.00
❑5, ca. 1997	3.00
❑6, ca. 1997	3.00
❑7, Nov 1997	3.00
❑8, Feb 1998; cover says Feb 97, indicia says Feb 98	2.95
❑9, Apr 1998; cover says May, indicia says Apr	2.95
❑10, Jul 1998	2.95
❑11, Oct 1998	2.95
❑12, Dec 1998; wraparound cover	2.95
❑13, Feb 1999	2.99
❑14, Jun 1999	2.99
❑15, Aug 1999	2.99
❑16 1999	2.99
❑17 2000	2.99
❑18, ca. 2000	2.99
❑20, Aug 2000, b&w	2.99
❑SS 1, May 1997; Super Special	4.95

BOX OFFICE POISON: KOLOR KARNIVAL
ANTARCTIC

	N-MINT
❑1, May 1999; cover says Apr, indicia says May; Kolor Karnival	3.50

N-MINT

BOY AND HIS 'BOT, A
Now

❑1, Jan 1987; digest-sized ... 1.95

BOY COMMANDOS (2ND SERIES)
DC

❑1, Oct 1973; JK (a); Reprinted from Detective Comics #66 ("Sphinx") and Boy Commandos #1 ("Heroes") ... 4.00
❑2, Dec 1973; JK (a); Reprinted from Boy Commandos #2 & #6 respectively ... 3.00

BOZO: THE WORLD'S MOST FAMOUS CLOWN (LARRY HARMON'S...)
Innovation

❑1; some reprint; Reprints Four Color Comics #285 ... 6.00

BOZZ CHRONICLES, THE
Marvel / Epic

❑1, Dec 1985 O: Bozz. 1: Bozz ... 2.00
❑2, Feb 1986 ... 2.00
❑3, Apr 1986 ... 2.00
❑4, Jun 1986 ... 2.00
❑5, Aug 1986 ... 2.00
❑6, Oct 1986 ... 2.00

BPRD: A PLAGUE OF FROGS
Dark Horse

❑1, Mar 2004 ... 2.99
❑2, Apr 2004 ... 2.99
❑3, May 2004 ... 2.99
❑4, Aug 2004 ... 2.99

BPRD: DARK WATERS
Dark Horse

❑1, Jul 2003 ... 2.99

BPRD: HOLLOW EARTH
Dark Horse

❑1, Jan 2002 ... 2.99
❑2, Apr 2002 ... 2.99
❑3, Jun 2002 ... 2.99

BPRD: NIGHT TRAIN
Dark Horse

❑1, Sep 2003 ... 2.99

BPRD: SOUL OF VENICE
Dark Horse

❑1, May 2003 ... 2.99

BPRD: THERE'S SOMETHING UNDER MY BED
Dark Horse

❑1, Nov 2003 ... 2.99

BRADLEYS, THE
Fantagraphics

❑1, Apr 1999 ... 2.95
❑2, May 1999 ... 2.95
❑3, Jul 1999 ... 2.95

BRADY BUNCH
Dell

❑1, ca. 1970 ... 45.00
❑2, ca. 1970 ... 30.00

BRAGADE
Parody

❑1, Mar 1993 ... 2.50

BRAINBANX
DC / Helix

❑1, Mar 1997 ... 2.50
❑2, Apr 1997 ... 2.50
❑3, May 1997 ... 2.50
❑4, Jun 1997 ... 2.50
❑5, Jul 1997 ... 2.50
❑6, Aug 1997 ... 2.50

BRAIN BAT 3-D
3-D Zone

❑1, ca. 1992, b&w; No cover price; Oversized ... 3.95

BRAIN BOY
Dell

❑2 A: Series numbering continued from ... 65.00
❑3 ... 50.00
❑4, ca. 1963 ... 45.00
❑5, Jun 1963 ... 45.00
❑6, ca. 1963 ... 45.00

N-MINT

BRAIN CAPERS
Fantagraphics

❑1 ... 3.95

BRAIN FANTASY
Last Gasp

❑1 ... 3.00

BRAIN, THE (I.W.)
I.W.

❑1, Sep 1958 ... 12.00
❑2 ... 9.00
❑3 ... 9.00
❑4 ... 9.00
❑5; Exists? ... 9.00
❑6; Exists? ... 9.00
❑7; Exists? ... 9.00
❑8 ... 9.00
❑9 ... 9.00
❑10, ca. 1963 ... 9.00
❑11; Exists? ... 8.00
❑12; Exists? ... 8.00
❑13; Exists? ... 8.00
❑14; Exists? ... 8.00
❑15; Exists? ... 8.00
❑16; Exists? ... 8.00
❑17 ... 8.00
❑18 ... 8.00

BRAINTRUST KOMICKS
Spoon

❑1, Mar 1993 ... 2.75

BRAND NEW YORK
Mean

❑1, Jul 1997, b&w and red; cardstock cover ... 3.95
❑2 ... 3.95

BRASS
Image

❑1, Aug 1996 ... 2.50
❑1/Deluxe, Aug 1996; Folio edition ... 4.50
❑2, Sep 1996 ... 2.50
❑3, May 1997 ... 2.50

BRASS (WILDSTORM)
DC / Wildstorm

❑1, Aug 2000 ... 2.50
❑2, Sep 2000 ... 2.50
❑3, Oct 2000 ... 2.50
❑4, Nov 2000 ... 2.50
❑5, Dec 2000 ... 2.50
❑6, Jan 2001 ... 2.50

BRATH
CrossGen

❑1, Mar 2003 ... 2.95
❑2, Apr 2003 ... 2.95
❑3, May 2003 ... 2.95
❑4, Jun 2003 ... 2.95
❑5, Jul 2003 ... 2.95
❑6, Aug 2003 ... 2.95
❑7, Sep 2003 ... 2.95
❑8, Oct 2003 ... 2.95
❑9, Nov 2003 ... 2.95
❑10, Dec 2003 ... 2.95
❑11, Jan 2004 ... 2.95
❑12, Feb 2004 ... 2.95
❑13, Apr 2004 ... 2.95
❑14, May 2004 ... 2.95

BRATPACK
King Hell

❑1, Aug 1990, b&w 1: Doctor Blasphemy. 1: Luna. 1: Kid Vicious. 1: Wild Boy ... 3.00
❑1-2 1: Doctor Blasphemy. 1: Luna. 1: Kid Vicious. 1: Wild Boy ... 3.00
❑1-3 1: Doctor Blasphemy. 1: Luna. 1: Kid Vicious. 1: Wild Boy ... 3.00
❑2, Nov 1990 ... 2.95
❑3, Jan 1991 ... 2.95
❑4, Mar 1991 ... 2.95
❑5, May 1991 ... 2.95

N-MINT

BRAT PACK/MAXIMORTAL SUPER SPECIAL
King Hell

❑1, Sep 1996 ... 2.95

BRATS BIZARRE
Marvel / Epic

❑1, May 1994 ... 2.50
❑2, Jun 1994 ... 2.50
❑3, Jul 1994; trading card ... 2.50
❑4, Aug 1994 ... 2.50

BRAVE AND THE BOLD, THE
DC

❑1, Aug 1955; JKu (a); Viking Prince, Golden Gladiator, Silent Knight Vi .. 2600.00
❑2, Oct 1955; Viking Prince, Golden Gladiator, Silent Knight ... 1100.00
❑3, Dec 1955; Viking Prince, Golden Gladiator, Silent Knight ... 675.00
❑4, Feb 1956; Viking Prince, Golden Gladiator, Silent Knight ... 625.00
❑5, Apr 1956; Robin Hood, Silent Knight, Viking Prince ... 625.00
❑6, Jun 1956; JKu (a); Robin Hood, Silent Knight, Golden Gladiator ... 425.00
❑7, Aug 1956; JKu (a); Robin Hood, Silent Knight, Viking Prince ... 425.00
❑8, Oct 1956; JKu (a); Robin Hood, Silent Knight, Golden Gladiator ... 425.00
❑9, Dec 1956; JKu (a); Robin Hood, Silent Knight, Viking Prince ... 425.00
❑10, Feb 1957; JKu (a); Robin Hood, Silent Knight, Viking Prince ... 425.00
❑11, Apr 1957; JKu (a); Robin Hood, Silent Knight, Viking Prince ... 340.00
❑12, Jun 1957; JKu (a); Robin Hood, Silent Knight, Viking Prince ... 340.00
❑13, Sep 1957; JKu (a); Robin Hood, Silent Knight, Viking Prince ... 340.00
❑14, Nov 1957; JKu (a); Robin Hood, Silent Knight, Viking Prince ... 340.00
❑15, Jan 1958; JKu (a); Robin Hood, Silent Knight, Viking Prince ... 340.00
❑16, Mar 1958; JKu (a); Silent Knight, Viking Prince ... 340.00
❑17, May 1958; JKu (a); Silent Knight, Viking Prince ... 340.00
❑18, Jul 1958; JKu (a); Silent Knight, Viking Prince ... 340.00
❑19, Sep 1958; JKu (a); Silent Knight, Viking Prince ... 340.00
❑20, Nov 1958; JKu (a); Silent Knight, Viking Prince ... 340.00
❑21, Jan 1959; JKu (a); Silent Knight, Viking Prince ... 340.00
❑22, Mar 1959; JKu (a); Silent Knight, Viking Prince ... 340.00
❑23, May 1959; JKu (a); O: Viking Prince. Viking Prince ... 390.00
❑24, Jul 1959; JKu (a); Viking Prince 340.00
❑25, Sep 1959 1: The Suicide Squad (Golden Age) ... 425.00
❑26, Nov 1959 2: Suicide Squad ... 330.00
❑27, Jan 1960 A: Suicide Squad ... 330.00
❑28, Mar 1960; 1: Justice League of America. 1: Starro the Conqueror. 1: Snapper Carr ... 2500.00
❑29, May 1960; 2: Justice League of America ... 1320.00
❑30, Jul 1960; 1: Amazo. 1: Professor Ivo. A: Justice League of America .. 1100.00
❑31, Sep 1960 1: Cave Carson ... 350.00
❑32, Nov 1960; Cave Carson ... 200.00
❑33, Jan 1961; Cave Carson ... 200.00
❑34, Mar 1961 JK, JKu (a); 1: Thanagar. 1: Byth. 1: Hawkwoman II (Shayera Thal). 1: Hawkman II (Katar Hol) ... 1300.00
❑35, May 1961; JK, JKu (a); 1: Matter Master. Hawkman ... 350.00
❑36, Jul 1961; JK, JKu (a); 1: Shadow-Thief. Hawkman ... 350.00
❑37, Sep 1961; Suicide Squad ... 250.00
❑38, Nov 1961; Suicide Squad ... 225.00
❑39, Jan 1962; Suicide Squad ... 225.00
❑40, Mar 1962; Cave Carson ... 140.00
❑41, May 1962; Cave Carson ... 140.00
❑42, Jul 1962 JK, JKu (a); A: Hawkman 300.00

N-MINT

❑43, Sep 1962 JK, JKu (a); O: Hawkman (Silver Age). 1: Manhawks 350.00
❑44, Nov 1962 JK, JKu (a); A: Hawkman 260.00
❑45, Jan 1963; CI (a); Strange Sports Stories 60.00
❑46, Mar 1963; CI (a); Strange Sports Stories 60.00
❑47, May 1963; CI (a); Strange Sports Stories 60.00
❑48, Jul 1963; CI (a); Strange Sports Stories 60.00
❑49, Sep 1963; CI (a); Strange Sports Stories 60.00
❑50, Nov 1963; Green Arrow; Team-ups begin 175.00
❑51, Jan 1964; Aquaman, Hawkman; Early Hawkman/Aquaman team-up 225.00
❑52, Mar 1964; JK (a); Sgt. Rock 125.00
❑53, May 1964; ATh (a); Atom & Flash 125.00
❑54, Jul 1964 O: Teen Titans. 1: Teen Titans 250.00
❑55, Sep 1964; Metal Men, Atom 45.00
❑56, Nov 1964; 1: Wynde. Flash 45.00
❑57, Jan 1965 O: Metamorpho. 1: Metamorpho 145.00
❑58, Mar 1965 2: Metamorpho. 65.00
❑59, May 1965; Batman; Batman/Green Lantern team-up 75.00
❑60, Jul 1965; 1: Wonder Girl (Donna Troy). Teen Titans 85.00
❑61, Sep 1965; MA (a); O: Starman I (Ted Knight). O: Black Canary. 85.00
❑62, Nov 1965; MA (a); Starman, Black Canary 85.00
❑63, Jan 1966; Supergirl 32.00
❑64, Mar 1966; A: Eclipso. Batman ... 50.00
❑65, May 1966; Doom Patrol 22.00
❑66, Jul 1966; Metamorpho, Metal Men 22.00
❑67, Sep 1966; CI (a); Batman, Flash; Batman in all remaining issues 40.00
❑68, Nov 1966; A: Joker. Metamorpho 40.00
❑69, Jan 1967; Green Lantern 40.00
❑70, Mar 1967; Hawkman 40.00
❑71, May 1967; Green Arrow 40.00
❑72, Jul 1967; CI (a); Spectre 40.00
❑73, Sep 1967; Aquaman, Atom 35.00
❑74, Nov 1967; Metal Men 35.00
❑75, Jan 1968; Spectre 35.00
❑76, Mar 1968; Plastic Man 35.00
❑77, May 1968 ..... 35.00
❑78, Jul 1968; 1: Copperhead. Wonder Woman 35.00
❑79, Sep 1968; NA (a); A: Deadman. Deadman 45.00
❑80, Nov 1968; NA (a); A: Creeper. Creeper 50.00
❑81, Jan 1969; NA (a); A: Deadman. Flash 50.00
❑82, Mar 1969 NA (a); O: Ocean Master. A: Deadman 50.00
❑83, May 1969; NA (a); Titans 60.00
❑84, Jul 1969; NA (a); Sgt. Rock 50.00
❑85, Sep 1969; NA (a); Green Arrow; Green Arrow gets new costume 50.00
❑86, Nov 1969; NA (a); Deadman 50.00
❑87, Jan 1970; Wonder Woman 20.00
❑88, Mar 1970; Wildcat 20.00
❑89, May 1970; Phantom Stranger ... 20.00
❑90, Jul 1970; Adam Strange 20.00
❑91, Sep 1970; Black Canary 18.00
❑92, Nov 1970; Bat Squad 18.00
❑93, Jan 1971; NA (a); House of Mystery 30.00
❑94, Mar 1971; Titans 18.00
❑95, May 1971; Plastic Man 15.00
❑96, Jul 1971; Sgt. Rock 15.00
❑97, Sep 1971; Wildcat 15.00
❑98, Nov 1971; Phantom Stranger 15.00
❑99, Jan 1972; NC (a); Flash 15.00
❑100, Mar 1972; Double-size; NA (a); Green Arrow 30.00
❑101, May 1972; Metamorpho 12.00
❑102, Jul 1972; NA (a); Titans 15.00
❑103, Oct 1972; Metal Men 12.00
❑104, Dec 1972; JA (a); Deadman 12.00

N-MINT

❑105, Feb 1973; JA (a); Wonder Woman 12.00
❑106, Apr 1973; JA (a); Green Arrow 12.00
❑107, Jul 1973; Black Canary 12.00
❑108, Sep 1973; JA (a); Sgt. Rock 12.00
❑109, Nov 1973; JA (a); Demon 12.00
❑110, Jan 1974; JA (a); Wildcat 12.00
❑111, Mar 1974; JA (a); Joker 18.00
❑112, May 1974; 100 Page giant; Mr. Miracle 18.00
❑113, Jul 1974; 100 Page giant; JA (a); Metal Men 18.00
❑114, Sep 1974; 100 Page giant; JA (a); Aquaman 18.00
❑115, Nov 1974; 100 Page giant JA (a); O: Viking Prince 18.00
❑116, Jan 1975; 100 Page giant; JA (a); Spectre 18.00
❑117, Mar 1975; 100 Page giant; JA (a); Sgt. Rock; reprints Secret Six #1 ... 18.00
❑118, Apr 1975; JA (a); Wildcat, Joker 18.00
❑119, Jun 1975; JA (a); Man-Bat 6.00
❑120, Jul 1975; JA (a); Kamandi, 68 pgs., reprints Secret Six #2; Kamandi 6.00
❑121, Sep 1975; JA (a); Metal Men ... 6.00
❑122, Oct 1975; Swamp Thing 6.00
❑123, Dec 1975; JA (a); Plastic Man, Metamorpho 6.00
❑124, Jan 1976; JA (a); Sgt. Rock 6.00
❑125, Mar 1976; JA (a); Flash 6.00
❑126, Apr 1976; JA (a); Aquaman 6.00
❑127, Jun 1976; JA (a); Wildcat 6.00
❑128, Jul 1976; JA (a); Mr. Miracle; Bicentennial #19 ..... 6.00
❑129, Sep 1976; Green Arrow/Joker . 11.00
❑130, Oct 1976; Green Arrow/Joker .. 11.00
❑131, Dec 1976; JA (a); A: Catwoman. Wonder Woman 6.00
❑132, Feb 1977; JA (a); Kung Fu Fighter 4.00
❑133, Apr 1977; JA (a); Deadman 4.00
❑134, May 1977; JA (a); Green Lantern 4.00
❑135, Jul 1977; JA (a); Metal Men 4.00
❑136, Sep 1977; Green Arrow, Metal Men 4.00
❑137, Oct 1977; Demon 4.00
❑138, Nov 1977; JA (a); Mr. Miracle . 4.00
❑139, Jan 1978; JA (a); Hawkman 4.00
❑140, Mar 1978; JA (a); Wonder Woman 4.00
❑141, May 1978; Black Canary, Joker 10.00
❑142, Jul 1978; JA (a); Aquaman 4.00
❑143, Sep 1978 JA (a); O: Human Target 4.00
❑144, Nov 1978; JA (a); Green Arrow 4.00
❑145, Dec 1978; JA (a); Phantom Stranger 4.00
❑146, Jan 1979; JA (a); E-2 Batman/Unknown Soldier 4.00
❑147, Feb 1979 JA (a); A: Doctor Light 4.00
❑148, Mar 1979; Plastic Man 4.00
❑149, Apr 1979; JA (a); Teen Titans .. 4.00
❑150, May 1979; JA (a); Superman .. 4.00
❑151, Jun 1979; JA (a); Flash 4.00
❑152, Jul 1979; JA (a); Atom 4.00
❑153, Aug 1979; DN (a); Red Tornado 4.00
❑154, Sep 1979; JA (a); Metamorpho 4.00
❑155, Oct 1979; JA (a); Green Lantern 4.00
❑156, Nov 1979; DN (a); Doctor Fate 4.00
❑157, Dec 1979; JA (a); Kamandi, continues story from Kamandi #59 ..... 4.00
❑158, Jan 1980; JA (a); Wonder Woman 4.00
❑159, Feb 1980; JA (a); Ra's al Ghul . 4.00
❑160, Mar 1980; JA (a); Supergirl 4.00
❑161, Apr 1980; JA (a); Adam Strange 4.00
❑162, May 1980; JA (a); Sgt. Rock ... 4.00
❑163, Jun 1980; DG (a); Black Lightning 4.00
❑164, Jul 1980; JL (a); A: Hawkgirl. A: Hawkman. Hawkman 4.00
❑165, Aug 1980; DN (a); Man-Bat 4.00
❑166, Sep 1980; DS, TD (a); 1: Nemesis. Black Canary 4.00
❑167, Oct 1980; DC, DA (a); Blackhawk 4.00
❑168, Nov 1980; JA (a); Green Arrow 4.00
❑169, Dec 1980; JA (a); Zatanna 4.00

The Boston Bombers featured a world war set on an alternate Earth where zeppelins were still in use.
© 1990 Caliber.

N-MINT

❑170, Jan 1981; JA (a); Nemesis 4.00
❑171, Feb 1981; GC, JL (a); Scalphunter 4.00
❑172, Mar 1981; CI (a); Firestorm 4.00
❑173, Apr 1981; JA (a); Guardians 4.00
❑174, May 1981; JA (a); Green Lantern 4.00
❑175, Jun 1981; JA (a); Lois Lane 4.00
❑176, Jul 1981; JA (a); Swamp Thing 4.00
❑177, Aug 1981; JA (a); Elongated Man 4.00
❑178, Sep 1981; JA (a); Creeper 4.00
❑179, Oct 1981; Legion 4.00
❑180, Nov 1981; JA (a); Spectre, Nemesis 3.00
❑181, Dec 1981; JA (a); Hawk & Dove, Nemesis 3.00
❑182, Jan 1982; JA (a); E-2 Robin 3.00
❑183, Feb 1982; CI (a); Riddler, Nemesis 3.00
❑184, Mar 1982; JA (a); Huntress 3.00
❑185, Apr 1982; Green Lantern 3.00
❑186, May 1982; JA (a); Hawkman, Nemesis 3.00
❑187, Jun 1982; JA (a); Metal Men, Nemesis 3.00
❑188, Jul 1982; JA (a); Rose & Thorn 3.00
❑189, Aug 1982; JA (a); Thorn, Nemesis 3.00
❑190, Sep 1982; JA (a); Adam Strange, Nemesis 3.00
❑191, Oct 1982; JA (a); A: Penguin. A: Nemesis. Joker 8.00
❑192, Nov 1982; JA (a); V: Mr. IQ. Superboy 3.00
❑193, Dec 1982 JA (a); D: Nemesis .. 3.00
❑194, Jan 1983; CI (a); V: Double-X. V: Rainbow Raider. Flash; V: Rainbow Raider, Double-X 3.00
❑195, Feb 1983; JA (a); I...Vampire ... 3.00
❑196, Mar 1983; JA (a); Ragman 3.00
❑197, Apr 1983; Catwoman; Wedding of Earth-2 Batman & Earth-2 Catwoman 4.00
❑198, May 1983; Karate Kid 3.00
❑199, Jun 1983; RA (a); Spectre 3.00
❑200, Jul 1983; Giant-size; JA (a); 1: Halo. 1: Katana. 1: Geo-Force. 1: Outsiders. E-1 and E-2 Batman 7.00
❑Annual 1; SD, CI (a); Revival issue (2001) 5.95

BRAVE AND THE BOLD, THE (MINI-SERIES)
DC

❑1, Dec 1991 MGr (w) 2.50
❑2, Jan 1992 MGr (w) 2.00
❑3, Feb 1992 MGr (w) 2.00
❑4, Mar 1992 MGr (w) 2.00
❑5, May 1992 MGr (w) 2.00
❑6, Jun 1992 MGr (w) 2.00

BRAVE OLD WORLD
DC / VERTIGO

❑1, Feb 2000 ..... 2.50
❑2, Mar 2000 ..... 2.50
❑3, Apr 2000 ..... 2.50
❑4, May 2000 ..... 2.50

BRAVESTARR IN 3-D
BLACKTHORNE

❑1 ..... 2.50
❑2 ..... 2.50

BRAVO FOR ADVENTURE
DRAGON LADY

❑1 ..... 5.95

Condition price index: Multiply "NM prices" above by: **0.83 for Very Fine/Near Mint**
0.66 for Very Fine • 0.33 for Fine • 0.2 for Very Good • 0.125 for Good

N-MINT

BRAVURA PREVIEW BOOK
MALIBU / BRAVURA
- ❑0, Jan 1995; JSn, HC (w); JSn, HC, GK (a); Coupon redemption promotion 3.00
- ❑1, Nov 1993; No cover price; 1994 Preview book 1.50
- ❑2, Aug 1994; 1995 Preview book (#1 on cover) 1.50

BREAKDOWNS
INFINITY
- ❑1, Oct 1986, b&w 1.70

BREAKFAST AFTER NOON
ONI
- ❑1, May 2000, b&w 2.95
- ❑2, Aug 2000, b&w 2.95
- ❑3, Sep 2000, b&w 2.95
- ❑4, Nov 2000, b&w 2.95
- ❑5, Dec 2000, b&w 2.95
- ❑6, Jan 2001, b&w 2.95

BREAKNECK BLVD. (MOTION)
MOTION
- ❑0, Feb 1994, b&w 2.50
- ❑1, Jul 1994, b&w 2.50
- ❑2, Sep 1994, b&w 2.50

BREAKNECK BLVD. (SLAVE LABOR)
SLAVE LABOR
- ❑1, Jul 1995 .... 2.95
- ❑2, Oct 1995 .... 2.95
- ❑3, Jan 1996 .... 2.95
- ❑4, May 1996 .... 2.95
- ❑5, Aug 1996 .... 2.95
- ❑6, Dec 1996 .... 2.95

BREAK THE CHAIN
MARVEL MUSIC
- ❑1; polybagged with KRS-1 cassette tape 6.95

BREAK-THRU
MALIBU
- ❑1, Dec 1993 GP (a) 2.50
- ❑1/Ltd., Dec 1993; Ultra Limited; foil logo 4.00
- ❑2, Jan 1994 GP (a) 2.50

BREATHTAKER
DC
- ❑1, Jul 1990 1: The Man. 1: Breathtaker 5.00
- ❑2, Aug 1990 .... 5.00
- ❑3, Sep 1990 O: Breathtaker 5.00
- ❑4, Oct 1990 .... 5.00

'BREED
MALIBU / BRAVURA
- ❑1, Jan 1994 .... 2.50
- ❑2, Feb 1994 .... 2.50
- ❑3, Mar 1994 .... 2.50
- ❑4, Apr 1994 .... 2.50
- ❑5, May 1994 .... 2.50
- ❑6, Jun 1994 .... 2.50

'BREED II
MALIBU / BRAVURA
- ❑1, Nov 1994 .... 2.95
- ❑2, Dec 1994 .... 2.95
- ❑3, Jan 1995 .... 2.95
- ❑4, Feb 1995 .... 2.95
- ❑5, Mar 1995 .... 2.95
- ❑6, Apr 1995 .... 2.95

BRENDA LEE'S LIFE STORY
DELL
- ❑1, Sep 1962 .... 50.00

BRENDA STARR (AVALON)
AVALON
- ❑1 .... 2.95
- ❑2 .... 2.95

BRENDA STARR CUT-OUTS AND COLORING BOOK
BLACKTHORNE
- ❑1 .... 6.95

N-MINT

BRICKMAN
HARRIER
- ❑1 .... 1.95

BRIDGMAN'S CONSTRUCTIVE ANATOMY
A-LIST
- ❑1, Apr 1998, b&w 2.95

BRIGADE (MINI-SERIES)
IMAGE
- ❑1, Aug 1992 .... 2.00
- ❑1/Gold, Aug 1992; Gold edition 2.00
- ❑2, Oct 1992 .... 3.50
- ❑2/Gold, Oct 1992; Gold edition 3.50
- ❑3, Feb 1993 .... 2.00
- ❑4, Jul 1993; flip side of Youngblood #5 .... 2.00

BRIGADE
IMAGE
- ❑0, Sep 1993; RL (w); 1: Warcry. gatefold cover 2.00
- ❑1, May 1993 RL (w); 1: Boone. 1: Hacker 2.00
- ❑2, Jun 1993, RL (w) 2.00
- ❑2/A, Jun 1993, foil alternate cover 2.95
- ❑3, Sep 1993; RL (w); 1: Roman. Indicia says Volume 1 instead of Volume 2 .... 2.00
- ❑4, Oct 1993 .... 2.00
- ❑5, Nov 1993 .... 2.00
- ❑6, Dec 1993 1: Worlok. 1: Coral 1.95
- ❑7, Feb 1994 .... 1.95
- ❑8, Mar 1994 .... 1.95
- ❑9, Apr 1994 .... 1.95
- ❑10, Jun 1994 .... 1.95
- ❑11, Aug 1994 A: WildC.A.T.s 1.95
- ❑12, Sep 1994 A: WildC.A.T.s 2.50
- ❑13, Oct 1994 .... 2.50
- ❑14, Nov 1994 .... 2.50
- ❑15, Dec 1994 .... 2.50
- ❑16, Jan 1995 .... 2.50
- ❑17, Feb 1995 .... 2.50
- ❑18, Mar 1995 .... 2.50
- ❑18/Variant, Mar 1995; alternate cover 2.50
- ❑19, Apr 1995 A: Glory 2.50
- ❑20/A, May 1995 A: Glory 2.50
- ❑20/B, May 1995; A: Glory. alternate cover 2.50
- ❑21, Jun 1995; Funeral of Shadowhawk 2.50
- ❑22, Jul 1995 .... 2.50
- ❑25, May 1994; Images of Tomorrow; Published out of sequence as a preview of the future 1.95
- ❑26, Jun 1994; Published out of sequence as a preview of the future 1.95
- ❑27, Jul 1994 .... 2.50

BRIGADE (AWESOME)
AWESOME
- ❑1, Jul 2000 .... 2.99

BRIGADE SOURCEBOOK
IMAGE
- ❑1, Aug 1994 .... 2.95

BRIK HAUSS
BLACKTHORNE
- ❑1, Jul 1987 .... 1.75

BRILLIANT BOY
CIRCUS
- ❑1, Jan 1997 .... 2.95
- ❑2, Mar 1997 .... 2.50
- ❑3, May 1997 .... 2.50
- ❑4 .... 2.50
- ❑5 .... 2.50

BRINKE OF DESTRUCTION
HIGH-TOP
- ❑1, Dec 1995 .... 2.95
- ❑1/CS, Dec 1995; packaged with audio tape 6.99
- ❑2 .... 2.95
- ❑3, Jan 1997 .... 2.95
- ❑Special 1 .... 6.95

BRINKE OF DISASTER
HIGH-TOP
- ❑1, Sep 1996 .... 2.25

N-MINT

BRINKE OF ETERNITY
CHAOS
- ❑1, Apr 1994 .... 2.75

BRIT
IMAGE
- ❑1, Jul 2003 .... 4.95

BRIT-CIT BABES
FLEETWAY-QUALITY
- ❑1 .... 5.95

BRIT/COLD DEATH ONE SHOT
IMAGE
- ❑1, Jan 2004 .... 4.95

BROADWAY BABES
AVALON
- ❑1; reprints Moronica stories, b&w 2.95

BROADWAY VIDEO SPECIAL COLLECTORS EDITION
BROADWAY
- ❑1, Promotional giveaway; 1150 copies printed; cardstock cover 1.00

BROID
ETERNITY
- ❑1, May 1990, b&w 2.75
- ❑2 .... 2.25
- ❑3 .... 2.25
- ❑4 .... 2.25

BROKEN AXIS
ANTARCTIC
- ❑1, b&w 2.95

BROKEN FENDER
TOP SHELF PRODUCTIONS
- ❑1, ca. 1997, b&w 2.95
- ❑2, b&w 2.95

BROKEN HALO: IS THERE NOTHING SACRED?
BROKEN HALOS
- ❑2, Oct 1998, b&w 2.95
- ❑2/Nude, Oct 1998, b&w; nude cover edition; Nude cover edition 4.95

BROKEN HEROES
SIRIUS
- ❑1, Mar 1998 .... 2.50
- ❑2, Apr 1998 .... 2.50
- ❑3, May 1998 .... 2.50
- ❑4, Jun 1998 .... 2.50
- ❑5, Jul 1998 .... 2.50
- ❑6, Aug 1998 .... 2.50
- ❑7, Sep 1998 .... 2.50
- ❑8, Oct 1998 .... 2.50
- ❑9, Nov 1998 .... 2.50
- ❑10, Dec 1998 .... 2.50
- ❑11, Jan 1999 .... 2.50
- ❑12, Feb 1999 .... 2.50

BRONX
ETERNITY
- ❑1 .... 2.50
- ❑2 .... 2.50
- ❑3 .... 2.50

BROOD TROUBLE IN THE BIG EASY
MARVEL
- ❑1, Aug 1993; Collects X-Men (2nd Series) #8-9, Ghost Rider (2nd Series) #26-27 .... 6.95

BROOKLYN DREAMS
DC / PARADOX
- ❑1 1994, b&w 4.95
- ❑2 1994, b&w 4.95
- ❑3 1994, b&w 4.95
- ❑4 1994, b&w 4.95

BROTHERHOOD, THE
MARVEL
- ❑1, Jul 2001 .... 2.25
- ❑2, Aug 2001 .... 2.25
- ❑3, Sep 2001 .... 2.25
- ❑4, Oct 2001 .... 2.25
- ❑5, Nov 2001 .... 2.25
- ❑6, Dec 2001 .... 2.25
- ❑7, Jan 2002 .... 2.25

N-MINT

❑8, Feb 2002 .... 2.25
❑9, Mar 2002 .... 2.25

BROTHERMAN
BIG CITY

❑1 .... 2.00
❑2 .... 2.00
❑3 .... 2.00
❑4 .... 2.00
❑5 .... 2.00
❑6 .... 2.00
❑7 .... 2.00
❑8 .... 2.00

BROTHER MAN: DICTATOR OF DISCIPLINE
BIG CITY

❑11, Jul 1996; magazine-sized 2.95

BROTHER POWER, THE GEEK
DC

❑1, Sep 1968 1: Brother Power, the Geek 30.00
❑2, Nov 1968 .... 20.00

BROTHERS OF THE SPEAR
GOLD KEY

❑1 .... 20.00
❑2 .... 10.00
❑3, Dec 1972 .... 6.00
❑4, ca. 1973 .... 6.00
❑5, ca. 1973 .... 6.00
❑6, ca. 1973 .... 4.00
❑7 .... 4.00
❑8 .... 4.00
❑9, Jun 1974 .... 4.00
❑10, ca. 1974 .... 4.00
❑11 .... 4.00
❑12 .... 4.00
❑13 .... 4.00
❑14 .... 4.00
❑15, ca. 1975 .... 4.00
❑16, Nov 1975 .... 4.00
❑17, ca. 1976; Original series ends (1976) 4.00
❑18, ca. 1982; One-shot continuation of series (1982) 2.50

BRUCE LEE
MALIBU

❑1, Jul 1994 .... 2.95
❑2, Aug 1994 .... 2.95
❑3, Sep 1994 .... 2.95
❑4, Oct 1994 .... 2.95
❑5, Nov 1994 .... 2.95
❑6, Dec 1994 .... 2.95

BRUCE WAYNE: AGENT OF S.H.I.E.L.D.
MARVEL / AMALGAM

❑1, Apr 1996 .... 1.95

BRU-HED
SCHISM

❑1, Mar 1994 1: Bru-Hed. 1: Grrim & Grritty 3.00
❑1/Ashcan; Test-Market Ashcan edition 1: Bru-Hed. 1: Grrim & Grritty 3.00
❑1/Variant, Mar 1994; metallic foil logo on cover 2.50
❑2, Jul 1994, b&w 2.50
❑3, b&w; D: Grrim & Grritty. 2.50
❑4 .... 2.50
❑Ashcan 1; Test-Market Ashcan edition; 1: Bru-Hed. 1: Grrim & Grritty. ashcan, b&w 4.00

BRU-HED'S BREATHTAKING BEAUTIES
SCHISM

❑1 1995, b&w pin-ups, cardstock cover 2.50

BRU-HED'S BUNNIES, BADDIES & BUDDIES
SCHISM

❑1 .... 2.50

N-MINT

BRU-HED'S GUIDE TO GETTIN' GIRLS NOW!
SCHISM

❑1 .... 2.95
❑2 .... 2.50

BRUISER
ANTHEM

❑1, Feb 1994 .... 2.45

BRUISER, THE
MYTHIC

❑1, No cover price 2.50

BRUNNER'S BEAUTIES
FANTAGRAPHICS / EROS

❑1; pin-ups, adult, b&w 4.95

BRUTE, THE
ATLAS-SEABOARD

❑1, Feb 1975 O: Brute. 1: Brute 7.00
❑2, Apr 1975 .... 5.00
❑3, Jul 1975 .... 5.00

BRUTE FORCE
MARVEL

❑1, Aug 1990 .... 1.00
❑2, Sep 1990 .... 1.00
❑3, Oct 1990 .... 1.00
❑4, Nov 1990 .... 1.00

B-SIDES
MARVEL

❑1, Nov 2002, b&w 3.50
❑2, Dec 2002 .... 2.99
❑3, Jan 2003 .... 2.99

BUBBLEGUM CRISIS: GRAND MAL
DARK HORSE

❑1, Mar 1994 .... 2.50
❑2, Apr 1994 .... 2.50
❑3, May 1994 .... 2.50
❑4, Jun 1994 .... 2.50

BUCKAROO BANZAI
MARVEL

❑1, Dec 1984 .... 1.00
❑2, Feb 1985 .... 1.00

BUCK GODOT, ZAP GUN FOR HIRE
PALLIARD

❑1, Jul 1993 PF (w); PF (a) 3.50
❑2, Nov 1993 PF (w); PF (a) 3.00
❑3, Apr 1994 PF (w); PF (a) 2.95
❑4, Aug 1994 PF (w); PF (a) 2.95
❑5, Sep 1995 PF (w); PF (a) 2.95
❑6, Oct 1995 PF (w); PF (a) 2.95
❑7, Aug 1997 PF (w); PF (a) 2.95
❑8, Mar 1998 PF (w); PF (a) 2.95

BUCK ROGERS
GOLD KEY / WHITMAN

❑1, Oct 1964; Gold Key publishes 36.00
❑2, Aug 1979 .... 5.00
❑3, Sep 1979 .... 4.00
❑4, Oct 1979 .... 4.00
❑5, Dec 1979 .... 3.00
❑6, Feb 1980 .... 3.00
❑7, Apr 1980; Series begins under Whitman imprint 3.00
❑8, ca. 1980 .... 3.00
❑9, ca. 1980 .... 3.00
❑10 .... 3.00
❑11, Feb 1981 .... 3.00
❑12, Jul 1981 .... 3.00
❑13, Oct 1981 .... 3.00
❑14, Feb 1982 .... 3.00
❑15, ca. 1982 .... 3.00
❑16, May 1982 .... 3.00

BUCK ROGERS COMICS MODULE
TSR

❑1; Listed as 1 of 3 .... 2.95
❑2 .... 2.95
❑3 .... 2.95
❑4 .... 2.95
❑5 .... 2.95
❑6 .... 2.95
❑7 .... 2.95

The android Amazo was introduced in *The Brave and the Bold* #30.
© 1960 National Periodical Publications (DC).

N-MINT

❑8 .... 2.95
❑9 .... 2.95

BUCKY O'HARE
CONTINUITY

❑1, Jan 1991 .... 2.50
❑2, May 1991 .... 2.00
❑3, Jul 1991 .... 2.00
❑4, Dec 1991 .... 2.00
❑5, Mar 1992 .... 2.00

BUDDHA ON THE ROAD
AEON

❑1, Aug 1996 .... 2.95
❑2, Nov 1996 .... 2.95
❑3, Feb 1997 .... 2.95
❑4, May 1997 .... 2.95
❑5, Sep 1997 .... 2.95
❑6, Mar 1997, Indicia says 1997, should be 1998 .... 2.95

BUFFALO WINGS
ANTARCTIC

❑1, Sep 1993, b&w 2.50
❑2, Nov 1993, b&w 2.75

BUFFY THE VAMPIRE SLAYER
DARK HORSE

❑0.5; Wizard promotional edition 4.00
❑0.5/Gold; Wizard promotional edition; Gold logo 8.00
❑0.5/Platinum; Wizard promotional edition; Platinum logo 10.00
❑1, Sep 1998; no month of publication 5.00
❑1/A, Sep 1998; Another Universe foil logo variant 10.00
❑1/B, Sep 1998; Another Universe edition; depicts Buffy holding gate without foil logo 5.00
❑1/Gold, Sep 1998; Gold art cover with gold foil logo 10.00
❑1/Variant, Sep 1998 .... 10.00
❑1-2, Feb 1999 .... 4.00
❑2, Oct 1998 .... 4.00
❑2/Variant, Oct 1998 .... 5.00
❑3, Nov 1998; no month of publication 5.00
❑3/Variant, Nov 1998 .... 5.00
❑4, Dec 1998 .... 4.00
❑4/Variant, Dec 1998 .... 4.00
❑5, Jan 1999 .... 4.00
❑5/Variant, Jan 1999 .... 4.00
❑6, Feb 1999 .... 3.50
❑6/Variant, Feb 1999 .... 3.50
❑7, Mar 1999 .... 3.50
❑7/Variant, Mar 1999 .... 3.50
❑8, Apr 1999 .... 3.50
❑8/Variant, Apr 1999 .... 3.50
❑9, May 1999 .... 3.50
❑9/Variant, May 1999 .... 3.50
❑10, Jun 1999; teen magazine-style cover; teen magazine-style cover 3.50
❑10/Variant, Jun 1999 .... 3.50
❑11, Jul 1999 .... 3.50
❑11/Variant, Jul 1999 .... 3.50
❑12, Aug 1999 .... 3.50
❑12/Variant, Aug 1999 .... 3.50
❑13, Sep 1999 .... 3.50
❑13/Variant, Sep 1999 .... 3.50
❑14, Oct 1999 .... 3.50
❑14/Variant, Oct 1999 .... 3.50
❑15, Nov 1999 .... 3.50

N-MINT

❑15/Variant, Nov 1999 .... 3.50
❑16, Dec 1999 .... 3.50
❑16/Variant, Dec 1999 .... 3.50
❑17, Jan 2000 .... 3.50
❑17/Variant, Jan 2000 .... 3.50
❑18, Feb 2000 .... 3.50
❑18/Variant, Feb 2000 .... 3.50
❑19, Mar 2000 .... 3.50
❑19/Variant, Mar 2000 .... 3.50
❑20, Apr 2000 .... 3.50
❑20/Variant, Apr 2000 .... 3.00
❑21, May 2000 .... 3.00
❑21/Variant, May 2000 .... 3.00
❑22, Jun 2000 .... 3.00
❑22/Variant, Jun 2000 .... 3.00
❑23, Jul 2000 .... 3.00
❑23/Variant, Jul 2000 .... 3.00
❑24, Aug 2000 .... 3.00
❑24/Variant, Aug 2000 .... 3.00
❑25, Sep 2000 .... 3.00
❑25/Variant, Sep 2000 .... 3.00
❑26, Oct 2000 .... 3.00
❑26/Variant, Oct 2000 .... 3.00
❑27, Nov 2000 .... 3.00
❑27/Variant, Nov 2000 .... 3.00
❑28, Dec 2000 .... 3.00
❑28/Variant, Dec 2000 .... 3.00
❑29, Jan 2001 .... 3.00
❑29/Variant, Jan 2001 .... 3.00
❑30, Feb 2001 .... 3.00
❑30/Variant, Feb 2001 .... 3.00
❑31, Mar 2001 .... 3.00
❑31/Variant, Mar 2001 .... 3.00
❑32, Apr 2001 .... 3.00
❑32/Variant, Apr 2001 .... 3.00
❑33, May 2001 .... 3.00
❑33/Variant, May 2001 .... 3.00
❑34, Jun 2001 .... 3.00
❑34/Variant, Jun 2001 .... 3.00
❑35, Jul 2001 .... 3.00
❑35/Variant, Jul 2001 .... 3.00
❑36, Aug 2001 .... 3.00
❑36/Variant, Aug 2001 .... 3.00
❑37, Sep 2001 .... 3.00
❑37/Variant, Sep 2001 .... 3.00
❑38, Oct 2001 .... 3.00
❑38/Variant, Oct 2001 .... 3.00
❑39, Nov 2001 .... 3.00
❑39/Variant, Nov 2001 .... 3.00
❑40, Dec 2001 .... 3.00
❑40/Variant, Dec 2001 .... 3.00
❑41, Jan 2002 .... 3.00
❑41/Variant, Jan 2002 .... 3.00
❑42, Feb 2002 .... 3.00
❑42/Variant, Feb 2002 .... 3.00
❑43, Mar 2002 .... 3.00
❑43/Variant, Mar 2002 .... 3.00
❑44, Apr 2002 .... 3.00
❑44/Variant, Apr 2002 .... 3.00
❑45, May 2002 .... 3.00
❑45/Variant, May 2002 .... 3.00
❑46, Jun 2002 .... 3.00
❑46/Variant, Jun 2002 .... 3.00
❑47, Jul 2002 .... 3.00
❑47/Variant, Jul 2002 .... 3.00
❑48, Aug 2002 .... 3.00
❑48/Variant, Aug 2002 .... 3.00
❑49, Sep 2002 .... 3.00
❑49/Variant, Sep 2002 .... 3.00
❑50, Oct 2002 .... 3.50
❑50/Variant, Oct 2002 .... 3.50
❑51, Nov 2002 .... 3.00
❑51/Variant, Nov 2002 .... 3.00
❑52, Dec 2002 .... 3.00
❑52/Variant, Dec 2002 .... 3.00
❑53, Jan 2003 .... 3.00
❑53/Variant, Jan 2003 .... 3.00
❑54, Feb 2003 .... 3.00
❑55, Mar 2003 .... 3.00
❑56, Apr 2003 .... 3.00
❑57, May 2003 .... 3.00

N-MINT

❑58, Jun 2003 .... 2.99
❑59, Jul 2003 .... 2.99
❑60, Aug 2003 .... 2.99
❑61, Sep 2003 .... 2.99
❑62, Oct 2003 .... 2.99
❑63, Nov 2003 .... 2.99
❑Annual 1999, Aug 1999; square-bound; 1999 Annual 5.50

BUFFY THE VAMPIRE SLAYER: ANGEL
DARK HORSE

❑1, May 1999 .... 4.00
❑1/Variant, May 1999 .... 4.00
❑2, Jun 1999 .... 3.50
❑2/Variant, Jun 1999 .... 3.50
❑3, Jul 1999 .... 3.50
❑3/Variant, Jul 1999 .... 3.50

BUFFY THE VAMPIRE SLAYER: CHAOS BLEEDS
DARK HORSE

❑1, Jun 2003 .... 2.99

BUFFY THE VAMPIRE SLAYER: GILES
DARK HORSE

❑1, Oct 2000 .... 3.00
❑1/Variant, Oct 2000 .... 3.00

BUFFY THE VAMPIRE SLAYER: HAUNTED
DARK HORSE

❑1, Dec 2001 .... 3.00
❑2, Jan 2002 .... 3.00
❑3, Feb 2002 .... 3.00
❑4, Mar 2002 .... 3.00

BUFFY THE VAMPIRE SLAYER: JONATHAN
DARK HORSE

❑1, Jan 2001 .... 3.00
❑1/Variant, Jan 2001 .... 3.00
❑1/Gold, Jan 2001 .... 10.00
❑1/Platinum, Jan 2001 .... 20.00

BUFFY THE VAMPIRE SLAYER: LOST AND FOUND
DARK HORSE

❑1, Mar 2002, b&w 3.00

BUFFY THE VAMPIRE SLAYER: LOVER'S WALK
DARK HORSE

❑1, Feb 2001 .... 3.00
❑1/Variant, Feb 2001 .... 3.00
❑1/DF, Feb 2001 .... 10.00

BUFFY THE VAMPIRE SLAYER: OZ
DARK HORSE

❑1, Jul 2001 .... 3.00
❑1/Variant, Jul 2001 .... 3.00
❑2, Aug 2001 .... 3.00
❑2/Variant, Aug 2001 .... 3.00
❑3, Sep 2001 .... 3.00
❑3/Variant, Sep 2001 .... 3.00

BUFFY THE VAMPIRE SLAYER: REUNION
DARK HORSE

❑1, Jun 2002, b&w 3.50

BUFFY THE VAMPIRE SLAYER: SPIKE AND DRU
DARK HORSE

❑1, Apr 1999 .... 2.95
❑2, May 1999 .... 2.95
❑3, Jun 1999 .... 2.95
❑3/Variant, Dec 2000 .... 2.95

BUFFY THE VAMPIRE SLAYER, TALES OF THE SLAYERS
DARK HORSE

❑1/Variant, Oct 2002 .... 3.50
❑1, Oct 2002 .... 3.50

N-MINT

BUFFY THE VAMPIRE SLAYER: THE ORIGIN
DARK HORSE

❑1, Jan 1999 .... 3.50
❑1/Ltd., Jan 1999; Limited edition foil cover 15.00
❑1/Variant, Jan 1999 .... 4.00
❑2, Feb 1999 .... 2.95
❑2/Variant, Feb 1999 .... 2.95
❑3, Mar 1999 .... 2.95
❑3/Variant, Mar 1999 .... 2.95

BUFFY THE VAMPIRE SLAYER: WILLOW & TARA
DARK HORSE

❑1, Apr 2001 .... 5.00
❑1/Variant, Apr 2001 .... 5.00

BUFFY THE VAMPIRE SLAYER: WILLOW & TARA: WILDERNESS
DARK HORSE

❑1, Aug 2002 .... 2.99
❑2, Sep 2002 .... 2.99

BUG (MARVEL)
MARVEL

❑1, Mar 1997 .... 2.99

BUG (PLANET-X)
PLANET-X

❑1 .... 1.50

BUG & STUMP
AAARGH!

❑1, Aut 1993, b&w; Australian, distributed in U.S 2.95
❑2, Spr 1994, b&w; Australian, distributed in U.S 2.95

BUGBOY
IMAGE

❑1, Jun 1998, b&w 3.95

B.U.G.G.'S
ACETYLENE COMICS

❑Ashcan 1 .... 2.25
❑1 .... 2.25
❑2 .... 2.25

B.U.G.G.'S (VOL. 2)
ACETYLENE COMICS

❑1/A 2.50
❑1 .... 2.25
❑2 .... 2.25
❑3/A; Fighting on cover, orange stripe down center 2.50
❑3; Woman posing on cover 2.50
❑4 .... 2.50

BUGHOUSE (CAT-HEAD)
CAT-HEAD

❑1, ca. 1994, b&w 2.95
❑2, Nov 1994, b&w 2.95
❑3, Jun 1995, b&w 2.95
❑4, ca. 1996, b&w; cardstock cover 2.95
❑5, Spr 1997, b&w 2.95

BUG-HUNTERS
TRIDENT

❑1, b&w 5.95

BUGS BUNNY (GOLD KEY)
GOLD KEY

❑86, Oct 1962 .... 7.00
❑87, Dec 1962 .... 7.00
❑88, Mar 1963 .... 7.00
❑89, Jun 1963 .... 7.00
❑90, Sep 1963 .... 7.00
❑91, Dec 1963 .... 7.00
❑92, Mar 1964 .... 7.00
❑93, May 1964 .... 7.00
❑94, Jul 1964 .... 7.00
❑95, Sep 1964 .... 7.00
❑96, Nov 1964 .... 7.00
❑97, Jan 1965 .... 7.00
❑98, Mar 1965 .... 7.00
❑99, May 1965 .... 7.00
❑100, Jul 1965 .... 7.00
❑101, Sep 1965 .... 7.00
❑102, Nov 1965 .... 6.00

	N-MINT
❑103, Jan 1966	6.00
❑104, Mar 1966	6.00
❑105, May 1966	6.00
❑106, Jul 1966	6.00
❑107, Sep 1966	6.00
❑108, Nov 1966	6.00
❑109, Jan 1967	6.00
❑110, Mar 1967	6.00
❑111, May 1967	6.00
❑112, Jul 1967	6.00
❑113, Sep 1967	6.00
❑114, Nov 1967	6.00
❑115, Jan 1968	6.00
❑116, Mar 1968	6.00
❑117, May 1968	6.00
❑118, Jul 1968	6.00
❑119, Sep 1968	6.00
❑120, Nov 1968	6.00
❑121, Jan 1969	6.00
❑122, Mar 1969	6.00
❑123, May 1969	6.00
❑124, Jul 1969	6.00
❑125, Sep 1969	6.00
❑126, Nov 1969	6.00
❑127, Jan 1970	6.00
❑128, Mar 1970	6.00
❑129, May 1970	6.00
❑130, Jul 1970	6.00
❑131, Sep 1970	6.00
❑132, Nov 1970	6.00
❑133, Jan 1971	6.00
❑134, Mar 1971	6.00
❑135, May 1971	6.00
❑136, Jul 1971	6.00
❑137, Sep 1971	6.00
❑138, Oct 1971	6.00
❑139, Dec 1971	6.00
❑140, Jan 1971	6.00
❑141, Mar 1972	6.00
❑142, May 1972	6.00
❑143, Jul 1972	6.00
❑144, Sep 1972	6.00
❑145, Oct 1972	6.00
❑146, Dec 1972	6.00
❑147, Jan 1973	6.00
❑148, Mar 1973	6.00
❑149, May 1973	6.00
❑150, Jul 1973	6.00
❑151, Aug 1973	5.00
❑152, Sep 1973	5.00
❑153, Nov 1973	5.00
❑154, Jan 1974	5.00
❑155, Mar 1974	5.00
❑156, May 1974	5.00
❑157, Jul 1974	5.00
❑158, Aug 1974	5.00
❑159, Sep 1974	5.00
❑160, Nov 1974	5.00
❑161, Jan 1975	5.00
❑162, Mar 1975	5.00
❑163, May 1975	5.00
❑164, Jul 1975	5.00
❑165, Aug 1975	5.00
❑166, Sep 1975	5.00
❑167, Oct 1975	5.00
❑168, Nov 1975	5.00
❑169, Jan 1976	5.00
❑170, Mar 1976	5.00
❑171, Apr 1976	5.00
❑172, May 1976	5.00
❑173, Jun 1976	5.00
❑174, Jul 1976	5.00
❑175, Aug 1976	5.00
❑176, Sep 1976	5.00
❑177, Oct 1976	5.00
❑178, Nov 1976	5.00
❑179, Dec 1976	5.00
❑180, Jan 1977	5.00
❑181, Feb 1977	5.00
❑182, Mar 1977	5.00
❑183, Apr 1977	5.00
❑184, May 1977	5.00
❑185, Jun 1977	5.00
❑186, Jul 1977	5.00
❑187, Aug 1977	5.00
❑188, Sep 1977	5.00
❑189, Oct 1977	5.00
❑190, Nov 1977	5.00
❑191, Dec 1977	5.00
❑192, Jan 1978	5.00
❑193, Feb 1978	5.00
❑194, Mar 1978	5.00
❑195, Apr 1978	5.00
❑196, May 1978	5.00
❑197, Jun 1978	5.00
❑198, Jul 1978	5.00
❑199, Aug 1978	5.00
❑200, Sep 1978	5.00
❑201, Oct 1978	3.00
❑202, Nov 1978	3.00
❑203, Dec 1978	3.00
❑204, Jan 1979	3.00
❑205, Feb 1979	3.00
❑206, Mar 1979	3.00
❑207, Apr 1979	3.00
❑208, May 1979	3.00
❑209, Jun 1979	3.00
❑210, Jul 1979	3.00
❑211, Aug 1979	3.00
❑212, Sep 1979	3.00
❑213, Oct 1979	2.00
❑214, Nov 1979	2.00
❑215, Dec 1979	2.00
❑216, Jan 1980	2.00
❑217, Feb 1980	2.00
❑218, Mar 1980	2.00
❑219, ca. 1980	2.00
❑220, ca. 1980	2.00
❑221, Sep 1980	2.00
❑222, Nov 1980	2.00
❑223, Jan 1981	2.00
❑224, Mar 1981	2.00
❑225, Jun 1981	2.00
❑226, Jul 1981	2.00
❑227, Aug 1981	2.00
❑228, Sep 1981	2.00
❑229, Oct 1981	2.00
❑230, Nov 1981	2.00
❑231, Dec 1981	2.00
❑232, ca. 1982	2.00
❑233, ca. 1982	2.00
❑234, ca. 1982	2.00
❑235, ca. 1982	2.00
❑236, ca. 1982	2.00
❑237, ca. 1982	2.00
❑238, ca. 1982	2.00
❑239, ca. 1982	2.00
❑240, ca. 1982	2.00
❑241, ca. 1982	2.00
❑242	2.00
❑243	2.00
❑244, ca. 1983	2.00
❑245	2.00

BUGS BUNNY
DC

❑1, Jun 1990	2.00
❑2, Jul 1990	1.50
❑3, Aug 1990	1.50

BUGS BUNNY AND PORKY PIG
DELL

❑1, ca. 1965	26.00

BUGS BUNNY MONTHLY, THE
DC

❑1	1.95
❑2	1.95
❑3	1.95

BUGS BUNNY WINTER FUN
GOLD KEY

❑1, Dec 1967	30.00

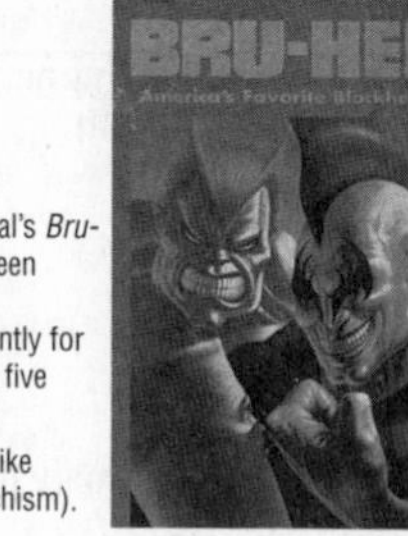

Mike Pascal's *Bru-Hed* has been published independently for more than five years.

© 1994 Mike Pascal (Schism).

BUG'S GIFT, A
DISCOVERY

	N-MINT
❑1	1.95

BULLDOG
FIVE STAR

❑1	2.95

BULLET CROW, FOWL OF FORTUNE
ECLIPSE

❑1	2.00
❑2	2.00

BULLETPROOF
KNOWN ASSOCIATES

❑1, b&w	3.95

BULLETPROOF COMICS
WET PAINT GRAPHICS

❑1	2.25
❑2, May 1999	2.25
❑3, Sep 1999	2.25

BULLETPROOF MONK
IMAGE

❑1, Nov 1998	3.00
❑2, Dec 1998	3.00
❑3, Jan 1999	3.00

BULLETPROOF MONK: TALES OF THE BULETPROOF MONK
IMAGE

❑1, Mar 2003	2.95

BULLETS AND BRACELETS
MARVEL / AMALGAM

❑1, Apr 1996	1.95

BULLWINKLE
DELL

❑1, Jul 1962	100.00

BULLWINKLE AND ROCKY (GOLD KEY)
GOLD KEY

❑1, Nov 1962	90.00
❑2, Feb 1963	68.00
❑3, Apr 1972	45.00
❑4, Jul 1972	40.00
❑5, Sep 1972	40.00
❑6, Jan 1973	28.00
❑7, Apr 1973	28.00
❑8, Jul 1973	28.00
❑9, Oct 1973	28.00
❑10, Jan 1974	28.00
❑11, Apr 1974; Last issue of original run	28.00
❑12, Jun 1976; Series picks up after hiatus	14.00
❑13, Sep 1976	20.00
❑14, Dec 1976	16.00
❑15, Mar 1977	10.00
❑16, Jun 1977	10.00
❑17, Sep 1977	10.00
❑18, Dec 1977	10.00
❑19	10.00
❑20	10.00
❑21	8.00
❑22	8.00
❑23, Oct 1979	8.00
❑24, Dec 1979	8.00
❑25	8.00

N-MINT

BULLWINKLE AND ROCKY (CHARLTON)
CHARLTON
- ❑1, Jul 1970; poster ... 30.00
- ❑2, Sep 1970 ... 18.00
- ❑3, Nov 1970 ... 15.00
- ❑4, Jan 1971 ... 12.00
- ❑5, Mar 1971 ... 12.00
- ❑6, May 1971 ... 12.00
- ❑7, Jul 1971 ... 12.00

BULLWINKLE AND ROCKY (STAR)
MARVEL / STAR
- ❑1, Nov 1987 ... 2.00
- ❑2, Jan 1988 ... 1.50
- ❑3, Mar 1988 ... 1.50
- ❑4, May 1988 ... 1.50
- ❑5, Jul 1988 ... 1.50
- ❑6, Sep 1988 ... 1.50
- ❑7, Nov 1988 ... 1.50
- ❑8, Jan 1989; Marvel publishes ... 1.50
- ❑9, Mar 1989 ... 1.50

BULLWINKLE & ROCKY (BLACKTHORNE)
BLACKTHORNE
- ❑1 ... 2.50
- ❑2 ... 2.50
- ❑3 ... 2.50
- ❑3D 1, Mar 1987 ... 2.50

BULLWINKLE FOR PRESIDENT IN 3-D
BLACKTHORNE
- ❑1, Mar 1987, b&w; no cover price ... 2.50

BULLWINKLE MOTHER MOOSE NURSERY POMES
DELL
- ❑1, May 1962 ... 85.00

BUMBERCOMIX
STARHEAD
- ❑1; Giveaway from arts festival ... 1.00

BURIAL OF THE RATS (BRAM STOKER'S...)
ROGER CORMAN'S COSMIC COMICS
- ❑1 ... 2.50
- ❑2, May 1995 ... 2.50

BURIED TERROR
NEC
- ❑1, Mar 1995 ... 2.75

BURIED TREASURE
PURE IMAGINATION
- ❑1 ... 5.95
- ❑2 ... 5.95
- ❑3; moves to Caliber ... 5.95

BURIED TREASURE (2ND SERIES)
CALIBER
- ❑1; reprints, b&w ... 2.50
- ❑2 ... 2.50
- ❑3; reprints Frankenstein ... 2.50
- ❑4 ... 2.50

BURKE'S LAW
DELL
- ❑1, Jan 1964 ... 24.00
- ❑2, ca. 1964 ... 20.00
- ❑3, Mar 1965 ... 20.00

BURRITO
ACCENT!
- ❑1, Jan 1995 ... 2.75
- ❑2, Apr 1995 ... 2.75
- ❑3, Jul 1995 ... 2.75
- ❑4, Nov 1995 ... 2.75
- ❑5, Jul 1996 ... 2.75

BUSHIDO
ETERNITY
- ❑1, Jul 1988 ... 1.95
- ❑2 ... 1.95
- ❑3 ... 1.95
- ❑4 ... 1.95

N-MINT

BUSHIDO BLADE OF ZATOICHI WALRUS
SOLSON
- ❑1 ... 2.00
- ❑2, ca. 1987, b&w ... 2.00

BUSHWHACKED
FANTAGRAPHICS / EROS
- ❑1 ... 2.95

BUSTER
CRISIS
- ❑1 ... 2.50
- ❑2 ... 2.50

BUSTER THE AMAZING BEAR
URSUS
- ❑1, Aug 1992; says Aug 93 on cover, Aug 92 in indicia; Surprise Poster Insert ... 2.50
- ❑2, Oct 1993 ... 2.50
- ❑2-2, Oct 1994 ... 2.50
- ❑3, Jan 1994 ... 2.50
- ❑4, May 1994 ... 2.50
- ❑5, Nov 1994 ... 2.50

BUSTLINE COMBAT
FANTAGRAPHICS / EROS
- ❑1, May 1999 ... 2.95

BUTCHER, THE
DC
- ❑1, May 1990 1: John Butcher ... 2.50
- ❑2, Jun 1990 ... 2.00
- ❑3, Jul 1990 ... 2.00
- ❑4, Aug 1990 ... 2.00
- ❑5, Sep 1990 ... 2.00

BUTCHER KNIGHT
IMAGE
- ❑1/A, Dec 2000; Demon's teeth cover ... 2.50
- ❑1/B, Dec 2000; Woman standing next to demon on cover ... 2.50
- ❑1/C, Dec 2000; Woman posing on demon on cover ... 2.50
- ❑1/D, Dec 2000; White cover ... 2.50
- ❑2, Jan 2001 ... 2.50
- ❑3, Apr 2001 ... 2.95
- ❑4, May 2001 ... 2.95

BUTT BISCUIT
FANTAGRAPHICS
- ❑1 ... 2.25
- ❑2 ... 2.25
- ❑3, Sep 1992 ... 2.25

BUTTERSCOTCH
FANTAGRAPHICS / EROS
- ❑1 ... 2.50
- ❑2 ... 2.50
- ❑3 ... 2.50

BUTTON MAN: THE KILLING GAME
KITCHEN SINK
- ❑1, Aug 1995; oversized graphic novel ... 15.95

BUZ SAWYER QUARTERLY
DRAGON LADY
- ❑1, Nov 1986 ... 5.95
- ❑2, Apr 1987 ... 5.95
- ❑3, Apr 1987 ... 5.95

BUZZ
KITCHEN SINK
- ❑1 ... 2.95
- ❑2 ... 2.95
- ❑3 ... 2.95

BUZZ, THE
MARVEL
- ❑1, Jul 2000 ... 2.99
- ❑2, Aug 2000 ... 2.99
- ❑3, Sep 2000 ... 2.99

BUZZ AND COLONEL TOAD
BELMONT
- ❑1 ... 2.50
- ❑2 ... 2.50
- ❑3, Jan 1998 ... 2.50

N-MINT

BUZZARD
CAT-HEAD
- ❑1 ... 3.00
- ❑2, Oct 1990 ... 3.00
- ❑3 ... 3.00
- ❑4 ... 3.00
- ❑5 ... 3.00
- ❑6, Aug 1992 ... 3.00
- ❑7, Feb 1993 ... 3.00
- ❑8 ... 3.00
- ❑9 ... 3.00
- ❑10 ... 3.00
- ❑11 ... 3.25
- ❑12 ... 3.50
- ❑13 ... 3.50
- ❑14 ... 3.50
- ❑15 ... 3.50
- ❑16 ... 3.50
- ❑17 ... 3.50
- ❑18 ... 3.75
- ❑19 ... 3.75
- ❑20 ... 3.75

BUZZBOY
SKYDOG
- ❑1, May 1998 ... 2.95
- ❑2, Aug 1998 ... 2.95
- ❑3, Oct 1998 ... 2.95
- ❑4, Win 1998 ... 2.95

BY BIZARRE HANDS
DARK HORSE
- ❑1, Apr 1994 ... 2.50
- ❑2, May 1994 ... 2.50
- ❑3, Jun 1994 ... 2.50

BY BIZARRE HANDS (JOE LANSDALE'S)
AVATAR
- ❑1, Apr 2004 ... 3.50
- ❑2, May 2004 ... 3.50

BY THE TIME I GET TO WAGGA WAGGA
HARRIER
- ❑1 ... 1.50

C

C•23
IMAGE
- ❑1, Apr 1998 ... 2.50
- ❑2, May 1998 ... 2.50
- ❑3, Jun 1998; bound-in card ... 2.50
- ❑4, Jul 1998 ... 2.50
- ❑5, Aug 1998 ... 2.50
- ❑6, Sep 1998 ... 2.50
- ❑7, Oct 1998 ... 2.50
- ❑8, Nov 1998 ... 2.50
- ❑8/Variant, Nov 1998; alternate cover (group) ... 2.50

CABBOT: BLOODHUNTER
MAXIMUM
- ❑1, Jan 1997 ... 2.50

CABINET OF DR. CALIGARI, THE
MONSTER
- ❑1, Apr 1992 ... 2.25
- ❑2, Jun 1992 ... 2.25
- ❑3, Sep 1992 ... 2.25

CABLE
MARVEL
- ❑-1, Jul 1997; JRo (w); Flashback; Alpha Flight, Vol. 2 preview ... 2.25
- ❑1, May 1993; Embossed cover ... 4.00
- ❑2, Jun 1993 ... 2.50
- ❑3, Jul 1993 AM, PS, TP, KGa, KJ, BWi (a) ... 2.50
- ❑4, Aug 1993 RL (a) ... 2.50
- ❑5, Nov 1993 ... 2.50
- ❑6, Dec 1993 A: Other. A: Sinsear ... 2.50
- ❑7, Jan 1994 ... 2.50
- ❑8, Feb 1994 ... 2.50

N-MINT

❑9, Mar 1994 A: Omega Red 2.50
❑10, Apr 1994 .... 2.50
❑11, May 1994 A: Colossus 2.25
❑12, Jun 1994 .... 2.25
❑13, Jul 1994 .... 2.25
❑14, Aug 1994 .... 2.25
❑15, Sep 1994 .... 2.25
❑16, Oct 1994 .... 2.25
❑16/Variant, Oct 1994; Prismatic foil cover 4.00
❑17, Nov 1994 .... 1.50
❑17/Deluxe, Nov 1994; Deluxe edition 2.00
❑18, Dec 1994 .... 1.50
❑18/Deluxe, Dec 1994; Deluxe edition 2.00
❑19, Jan 1995 .... 1.50
❑19/Deluxe, Jan 1995; Deluxe edition 2.00
❑20, Feb 1995 A: X-Men 1.50
❑20/Deluxe, Feb 1995; Deluxe edition; JPH (w); A: X-Men. A Legion Quest Addendum 2.00
❑21, Jul 1995 .... 2.00
❑22, Aug 1995 .... 2.00
❑23, Sep 1995 .... 2.00
❑24, Oct 1995; no issue number on cover 2.00
❑25, Nov 1995; Giant-size; JPH (w); enhanced wraparound fold-out card-stock cover; 25th Issue Extravaganza 4.00
❑26, Dec 1995 A: Weapon X 2.00
❑27, Jan 1996 V: Sugar Man 2.00
❑28, Feb 1996 V: Sugar Man 2.00
❑29, Mar 1996 JPH (w) 2.00
❑30, Apr 1996; JPH (w); A: X-Man. Cable meets X-Man 2.00
❑31, May 1996 V: X-Man 2.00
❑32, Jun 1996 .... 2.00
❑33, Jul 1996 .... 2.00
❑34, Aug 1996 V: Hulk 2.00
❑35, Sep 1996 V: Apocalypse 2.00
❑36, Oct 1996 .... 2.00
❑37, Nov 1996 A: Weapon X 2.00
❑38, Dec 1996 JPH (w); A: Micronauts 2.00
❑39, Jan 1997 JPH (w); A: Micronauts 2.00
❑40, Feb 1997 .... 2.00
❑41, Mar 1997 A: Bishop 2.00
❑42, Apr 1997 .... 2.00
❑43, May 1997 .... 2.00
❑44, Jun 1997 JRo (w) 2.00
❑45, Aug 1997; gatefold summary; Operation Zero Tolerance 2.00
❑46, Sep 1997; gatefold summary; JRo (w); Operation Zero Tolerance 2.00
❑47, Oct 1997; gatefold summary; Operation Zero Tolerance 2.00
❑48, Nov 1997; gatefold summary 2.00
❑49, Dec 1997; gatefold summary 2.00
❑50, Jan 1998; Giant-size 2.95
❑51, Feb 1998; gatefold summary 1.99
❑52, Mar 1998; gatefold summary 1.99
❑53, Apr 1998; gatefold summary 1.99
❑54, May 1998; gatefold summary A: Black Panther. V: Klaw 1.99
❑55, Jun 1998; gatefold summary A: Domino 1.99
❑56, Jul 1998; gatefold summary 1.99
❑57, Aug 1998; gatefold summary 1.99
❑58, Sep 1998; gatefold summary 1.99
❑59, Oct 1998; gatefold summary V: Zzzax 1.99
❑60, Nov 1998; gatefold summary 1: Agent 18 .... 1.99
❑61, Nov 1998; gatefold summary; captured by S.H.I.E.L.D 1.99
❑62, Dec 1998; gatefold summary A: Nick Fury 1.99
❑63, Jan 1999; gatefold summary A: Stryfe. V: Stryfe 1.99
❑64, Feb 1999; gatefold summary O: Cable. A: Ozymandias 1.99
❑65, Mar 1999 1: Acidroid. A: Rachel Summers 1.99
❑66, Apr 1999 .... 1.99
❑67, May 1999 A: Avengers 1.99
❑68, Jun 1999 A: Avengers 1.99

N-MINT

❑69, Jul 1999 .... 1.99
❑70, Aug 1999 .... 1.99
❑71, Sep 1999 V: Hound Master 1.99
❑72, Oct 1999 .... 1.99
❑73, Nov 1999 .... 1.99
❑74, Dec 1999 .... 1.99
❑75, Jan 2000 .... 2.25
❑76, Feb 2000 .... 2.25
❑77, Mar 2000 .... 2.25
❑78, Apr 2000 .... 2.25
❑79, May 2000 .... 2.25
❑80, Jun 2000 .... 2.25
❑81, Jul 2000 .... 2.25
❑82, Aug 2000 .... 2.25
❑83, Sep 2000 .... 2.25
❑84, Oct 2000 .... 2.25
❑85, Nov 2000 .... 2.25
❑86, Dec 2000 .... 2.25
❑87, Jan 2001 .... 2.25
❑88, Feb 2001 A: Nightcrawler 2.25
❑89, Mar 2001 .... 2.25
❑90, Apr 2001 .... 2.25
❑91, May 2001 .... 2.25
❑92, Jun 2001 .... 2.25
❑93, Jul 2001 .... 2.25
❑94, Aug 2001 .... 2.25
❑95, Sep 2001 .... 2.25
❑96, Oct 2001 .... 2.25
❑97, Nov 2001 .... 2.25
❑98, Dec 2001 .... 2.25
❑99, Jan 2002 .... 2.25
❑100, Feb 2002; Giant-size 3.99
❑101, Mar 2002 .... 2.25
❑102, Apr 2002 .... 2.25
❑103, May 2002 .... 2.25
❑104, Jun 2002 .... 2.25
❑105, Jul 2002 .... 2.25
❑106, Aug 2002 .... 2.25
❑107, Sep 2002 .... 2.25
❑Annual 1998, Sep 1998; Cable/ Machine Man '98; continues in Machine Man/Bastion '98; wrap-around cover 2.99
❑Annual 1999, Sep 1999 V: Sinister .. 3.50

CABLE: BLOOD AND METAL
MARVEL

❑1, Oct 1992 JR2 (a) 3.50
❑2, Nov 1992 JR2 (a) 3.00

CABLE/DEADPOOL
MARVEL

❑1, May 2004 .... 2.99
❑2, Jun 2004 .... 2.99
❑3, Jul 2004 .... 2.99
❑4, Aug 2004 .... 2.99
❑5, Sep 2004 ....

CABLE: SECOND GENESIS
MARVEL

❑1, Sep 1999; collects New Mutants #1-2 and X-Force #1 .... 3.99

CABLE TV
PARODY

❑1, b&w 2.50

CADAVERA
MONSTER

❑1, b&w 1.95
❑2, b&w 1.95

CADILLACS & DINOSAURS
MARVEL / EPIC

❑1, Nov 1990; Reprints Xenozoic Tales #1 in color 2.50
❑2, Dec 1990; Reprints Xenozoic Tales #2 in color 2.50
❑3, Jan 1991; Reprints Xenozoic Tales #3 in color 2.50
❑4, Feb 1991; Reprints Xenozoic Tales #4 in color 2.50
❑5, Mar 1991; Reprints Xenozoic Tales #5 in color 2.50
❑6, Apr 1991; Reprints Xenozoic Tales #6 in color 2.50
❑3D 1, Jul 1992; 100 Page giant 3.95

Topps issued two *Cadillacs & Dinosaurs* series to tie in with CBS' animated series.

© 1994 Mark Schultz and Topps.

N-MINT

CADILLACS & DINOSAURS (KITCHEN SINK)
KITCHEN SINK

❑1, Dec 1993 .... 4.00

CADILLACS & DINOSAURS (VOL. 2)
TOPPS

❑1, Feb 1994 .... 2.50
❑1/Variant, Feb 1994; foil cover 2.95
❑2, Mar 1994 .... 2.50
❑2/Deluxe, Mar 1994; poster by Moebius 2.50
❑3, Apr 1994 .... 2.50
❑3/Deluxe, Apr 1994; poster 2.50
❑4, Jun 1994 .... 2.50
❑4/Variant, Jun 1994 .... 2.50
❑5, Aug 1994 .... 2.50
❑6, Oct 1994 .... 2.50
❑7, Dec 1994 .... 2.50
❑8, Feb 1995 .... 2.50
❑9, Apr 1995 .... 2.50
❑10, Jun 1995 .... 2.50

CAFFEINE
SLAVE LABOR

❑1, Jan 1996 .... 2.95
❑2, Apr 1996 .... 2.95
❑3, Jul 1996 .... 2.95
❑4, Nov 1996 .... 2.95
❑5, Jan 1997 .... 2.95
❑6, Apr 1997 .... 2.95
❑7, Jul 1997; flip book 2.95
❑8, Nov 1997 .... 2.95
❑9, Jan 1998 .... 2.95
❑10, Apr 1998 .... 2.95

CAGE
MARVEL

❑1, Apr 1992 .... 1.00
❑2, May 1992 .... 1.00
❑3, Jun 1992 .... 1.00
❑4, Jul 1992 .... 1.00
❑5, Aug 1992 .... 1.00
❑6, Sep 1992 .... 1.00
❑7, Oct 1992 .... 1.00
❑8, Nov 1992 .... 1.00
❑9, Dec 1992 .... 1.00
❑10, Jan 1993 .... 1.00
❑11, Feb 1993 .... 1.00
❑12, Mar 1993; Giant-size; Iron Fist .. 1.00
❑13, Apr 1993 .... 1.00
❑14, May 1993 .... 1.00
❑15, Jun 1993 .... 1.00
❑16, Jul 1993 .... 1.00
❑17, Aug 1993 .... 1.00
❑18, Sep 1993 .... 1.00
❑19, Oct 1993 .... 1.00
❑20, Nov 1993 .... 1.00

CAGE (2ND SERIES)
MARVEL / MAX

❑1, Mar 2002 .... 2.99
❑2, May 2002 .... 2.99
❑3, Jul 2002 .... 2.99
❑4, Aug 2002 .... 2.99
❑5, Sep 2002 .... 2.99

CAGED HEAT 3000
ROGER CORMAN'S COSMIC COMICS

❑1 .... 2.50
❑2 .... 2.50

N-MINT

CAGES
TUNDRA

❑1, b&w ... 5.00
❑2, b&w ... 4.00
❑3, b&w ... 4.00
❑4 ... 4.00
❑5 ... 4.00
❑6 ... 4.00
❑7 ... 4.00
❑8 ... 4.00
❑9 ... 4.00
❑10 ... 5.00

CAIN
HARRIS

❑1; trading card ... 2.95
❑2, Oct 1993; two alternate covers ... 2.95

CALCULATED RISK
GENESIS

❑1, Mar 1990, b&w ... 2.00

CALIBER CHRISTMAS, A (1ST SERIES)
CALIBER

❑1 ... 5.95

CALIBER CHRISTMAS, A (2ND SERIES)
CALIBER

❑1, Dec 1989; Crow; sampler ... 3.95

CALIBER CORE
CALIBER

❑0, b&w; intro to imprint ... 2.95
❑Ashcan 1, b&w; No cover price; intro to imprint ... 1.00

CALIBER PRESENTS
CALIBER

❑1, Jan 1989, b&w; Crow ... 15.00
❑2 1989, b&w ... 2.50
❑3 1989, b&w ... 2.50
❑4 1989, b&w ... 2.50
❑5 1989, b&w ... 2.50
❑6, Aug 1989 ... 2.50
❑7, Nov 1989, b&w ... 2.50
❑8 ... 2.00
❑9 ... 2.50
❑10 ... 2.95
❑11 ... 2.95
❑12 ... 2.50
❑13 ... 2.95
❑14 ... 2.50
❑15, Sep 1990 ... 3.50
❑16 ... 3.50
❑17 ... 3.50
❑18 ... 3.50
❑19 ... 3.50
❑20 ... 3.50
❑21 ... 3.50
❑22 ... 3.50
❑23 ... 3.50
❑24 ... 3.50

CALIBER PRESENTS: CINDERELLA ON FIRE
CALIBER

❑1, ca. 1994, b&w ... 2.95

CALIBER PRESENTS: GENERATOR COMICS
CALIBER

❑1, b&w ... 2.95

CALIBER PRESENTS: HYBRID STORIES
CALIBER

❑1, b&w ... 2.95

CALIBER PRESENTS: PETIT MAL
CALIBER

❑1, b&w ... 2.95

CALIBER PRESENTS: ROMANTIC TALES
CALIBER

❑1, ca. 1995, b&w ... 2.95

N-MINT

CALIBER PRESENTS: SEPULCHER OPUS
CALIBER

❑1, ca. 1993, b&w ... 2.95

CALIBER PRESENTS: SOMETHING INSIDE
CALIBER

❑1, b&w ... 3.50

CALIBER PRESENTS: SUB-ATOMIC SHOCK
CALIBER

❑1, b&w ... 2.95

CALIBER SPOTLIGHT
CALIBER

❑1, May 1995; b&w anthology with A.K.A. Goldfish, Kabuki, Kilroy is Here, Oz, and previews ... 2.95

CALIBRATIONS (1ST SERIES)
CALIBER

❑1, b&w ... 1.00
❑2 ... 1.00
❑3 ... 1.00
❑4 ... 1.00
❑5 ... 1.00

CALIBRATIONS (3RD SERIES)
CALIBER

❑1, Jun 1996; preview of The Lost and Atmospherics ... 1.00
❑2, Jul 1996 ... 1.00
❑3, Aug 1996 ... 1.00
❑4, Sep 1996 ... 1.00
❑5, Oct 1996 ... 1.00

CALIFORNIA COMICS
CALIFORNIA

❑1 ... 5.00
❑2 ... 4.00

CALIFORNIA GIRLS
ECLIPSE

❑1, Jun 1987 ... 2.00
❑2, Jul 1987 ... 2.00
❑3, Aug 1987 ... 2.00
❑4, Sep 1987 ... 2.00
❑5, Oct 1987 ... 2.00
❑6, Nov 1987 ... 2.00
❑7, Dec 1987 ... 2.00
❑8, Jan 1988 ... 2.00

CALIFORNIA RAISINS IN 3-D, THE
BLACKTHORNE

❑1, Dec 1987; a.k.a. Blackthorne in 3-D #31 ... 2.50
❑1-2 ... 2.50
❑1-3 ... 2.50
❑2 ... 2.50
❑3 ... 2.50
❑4 ... 2.50
❑5 ... 2.50

CALIGARI 2050
MONSTER

❑1, Apr 1992 ... 2.25
❑2 ... 2.25
❑3 ... 2.25

CALL, THE
MARVEL

❑1, Jun 2003 ... 2.25
❑2, Jul 2003 ... 2.25
❑3, Aug 2003 ... 2.25
❑4, Sep 2003; cardstock cover ... 2.25

CALLED FROM DARKNESS
ANARCHY

❑1-2 ... 2.95
❑1 ... 2.95

CALL ME PRINCESS
CPM

❑1, May 1999, b&w ... 2.95
❑1/A, May 1999, b&w ... 2.95
❑2 1999, b&w ... 2.95
❑3 1999, b&w ... 2.95
❑4 1999, b&w ... 2.95

N-MINT

❑5 1999, b&w ... 2.95
❑6 1999, b&w ... 2.95

CALL OF DUTY: THE BROTHERHOOD
MARVEL

❑1, Aug 2002 ... 2.25
❑2, Sep 2002 ... 2.25
❑3, Oct 2002 ... 2.25
❑4, Nov 2002 ... 2.25
❑5, Dec 2002 ... 2.25
❑6, Jan 2003 ... 2.25

CALL OF DUTY: THE PRECINCT
MARVEL

❑1, Sep 2002 ... 2.25
❑2, Oct 2002 ... 2.25
❑3, Nov 2002 ... 2.25
❑4, Dec 2002 ... 2.25
❑5, Jan 2003 ... 2.25

CALL OF DUTY: THE WAGON
MARVEL

❑1, Oct 2002 ... 2.25
❑2, Nov 2002 ... 2.25
❑3, Dec 2002 ... 2.25
❑4, Jan 2003 ... 2.25

CAMBION
SLAVE LABOR

❑1, Dec 1995 ... 2.95
❑2, Feb 1996 ... 2.95
❑3, Feb 1997, b&w; Published by Moonstone ... 2.95

CAMELOT ETERNAL
CALIBER

❑1 ... 2.50
❑2 ... 2.50
❑3 ... 2.50
❑4 ... 2.50
❑5 ... 2.50
❑6 ... 2.50
❑7 ... 2.50
❑8 ... 2.50

CAMELOT 3000
DC

❑1, Dec 1982 BB (a); O: Merlin. O: Arthur ... 2.50
❑2, Jan 1983 BB (a) ... 2.00
❑3, Feb 1983 BB (a) ... 2.00
❑4, Mar 1983 BB (a) ... 2.00
❑5, Apr 1983 BB (a) ... 2.00
❑6, Jul 1983 BB (a) ... 2.00
❑7, Aug 1983 BB (a) ... 2.00
❑8, Sep 1983 BB (a) ... 2.00
❑9, Dec 1983 BB (a) ... 2.00
❑10, Mar 1984 BB (a) ... 2.00
❑11, Jul 1984 BB (a) ... 2.00
❑12, Apr 1985 BB (a) ... 2.00

CAMP CANDY
MARVEL

❑1, May 1990 ... 1.00
❑2, Jun 1990 ... 1.00
❑3, Jul 1990 ... 1.00
❑4, Aug 1990 ... 1.00
❑5, Sep 1990 ... 1.00
❑6, Oct 1990 ... 1.00
❑7, Nov 1990 ... 1.00

CAMPING WITH BIGFOOT
SLAVE LABOR

❑1, Sep 1995 ... 2.95

CANADIAN ROCK SPECIAL
REVOLUTIONARY

❑1, Apr 1994, b&w; Rush ... 2.50

CANCER: THE CRAB BOY
SABRE'S EDGE

❑1 ... 2.95
❑2 ... 2.95
❑3 ... 2.95
❑4 ... 2.95
❑5 ... 2.95

CANDIDATE GODDESS, THE
TOKYOPOP

	N-MINT
❑1, Apr 2004	9.99

CANDIDE REVEALED
FANTAGRAPHICS / EROS

	N-MINT
❑1, b&w	2.25

CANNIBALIS
RAGING RHINO

	N-MINT
❑1, b&w	2.95

CANNON
FANTAGRAPHICS / EROS

	N-MINT
❑1, Feb 1991, b&w WW (w); WW (a)	2.75
❑1-2 WW (a)	2.95
❑2, Mar 1991, b&w WW (w); WW (a)	2.95
❑2-2 WW (a)	2.95
❑3, Apr 1991 WW (w); WW (a); O: Madame Toy. O: Sue Stevens	2.95
❑3-2 WW (a); O: Madame Toy. O: Sue Stevens	2.95
❑4, May 1991 WW (w); WW (a)	2.95
❑5, Jun 1991 WW (w); WW (a)	2.95
❑6, Jul 1991 WW (w); WW (a)	2.95
❑7, Aug 1991 WW (w); WW (a)	2.95
❑8, Sep 1991 WW (w); WW (a)	2.95

CANNON GOD EXAXXION
DARK HORSE

	N-MINT
❑1, Nov 2001; Stage 1.1	2.99
❑2, Dec 2001; Stage 1.2	2.99
❑3, Jan 2002; Stage 1.3	2.99
❑4, Feb 2002; Stage 1.4	2.99
❑5, Mar 2002; Stage 1.5	2.99
❑6, Apr 2002; Stage 1.6	2.99
❑7, May 2002; Stage 1.7	2.99
❑8, Jun 2002; Stage 1.8	2.99
❑9, Sep 2002; 48 pages; Stage 2.1	3.99
❑10, Oct 2002; Stage 2.2	3.50
❑11, Nov 2002	3.50
❑12, Dec 2002	3.50
❑13, Jan 2003	3.50
❑14, Jun 2003	3.50
❑15, Jul 2003	2.99
❑16, Aug 2003	2.99
❑17, Sep 2003	2.99
❑18, Oct 2003	2.99
❑19, Nov 2003	2.99
❑20, Dec 2003	2.99

CAPE CITY
DIMENSION X

	N-MINT
❑1, b&w	2.75
❑2, b&w	2.75

CAPER
DC

	N-MINT
❑1, Dec 2003	2.95
❑2, Jan 2004	2.95
❑3, Feb 2004	2.95
❑4, Mar 2004	2.95
❑5, Apr 2004	2.95
❑6, May 2004	2.95
❑7, Jun 2004	2.95
❑8, Jul 2004	2.95
❑9, Aug 2004	2.95
❑10, Sep 2004	

CAPES
IMAGE

	N-MINT
❑1, Oct 2003	3.50
❑2, Nov 2003	3.50
❑3, Dec 2003	3.50

CAPITAL CAPERS PRESENTS
BLT

	N-MINT
❑1, Oct 1994, b&w	2.95

CAP'N OATMEAL
ALL AMERICAN

	N-MINT
❑1, b&w	2.25

CAP'N QUICK & A FOOZLE
ECLIPSE

	N-MINT
❑1, Jul 1984	1.50
❑2, Mar 1985	1.50
❑3; Title changes to The Foozle	1.50

CAPTAIN ACTION
KARL ART

	N-MINT
❑0; preview of ongoing series; Insert in Space Bananas #1	1.95

CAPTAIN ACTION (DC)
DC

	N-MINT
❑1, Nov 1968 WW (a); O: Captain Action	58.00
❑2, Jan 1969 GK, WW (a)	35.00
❑3, Mar 1969 GK, WW (a)	35.00
❑4, May 1969 GK (a)	35.00
❑5, Jul 1969 GK, WW (a)	35.00

CAPTAIN AMERICA (VOL. 1)
MARVEL

	N-MINT
❑100, Apr 1968; JK (a); A: Avengers. Series continued from Tales of Suspense #99	210.00
❑101, May 1968 JK (a); 1: 4th Sleeper	55.00
❑102, Jun 1968 JK (a)	35.00
❑103, Jul 1968; JK (a); A: Red Skull. Agent 13's identity revealed as Sharon Carter	35.00
❑104, Aug 1968 JK (a); V: Red Skull	35.00
❑105, Sep 1968 JK (a); V: Batroc	35.00
❑106, Oct 1968 SL (w); JK (a)	35.00
❑107, Nov 1968 SL (w); JK (a); 1: Doctor Faustus. A: Red Skull	35.00
❑108, Dec 1968 JK (a)	35.00
❑109, Jan 1969 SL (w); JK (a); O: Captain America	35.00
❑109-2, ca. 1994, JK (a); O: Captain America. Reprint	2.50
❑110, Feb 1969; JSo (a); 1: Viper II (as Madame Hydra). 1: Viper. A: Hulk. A: Rick Jones. Rick Jones dons Bucky costume	57.00
❑111, Mar 1969 JSo (a)	50.00
❑112, Apr 1969; GT, JK (a); O: Viper II (as Madame Hydra). O: Captain America. album	35.00
❑113, May 1969; JSo (a); Avengers	48.00
❑114, Jun 1969 JR (a)	26.00
❑115, Jul 1969	26.00
❑116, Aug 1969	26.00
❑117, Sep 1969 GC, JSt (a); 1: Falcon	45.00
❑118, Oct 1969 SL (w); GC, JSt (a); A: Falcon	16.00
❑119, Nov 1969 SL (w); GC, JSt (a); A: Falcon	16.00
❑120, Dec 1969 SL (w); GC, JSt (a); A: Falcon	16.00
❑121, Jan 1970 SL (w); GC (a); O: Captain America	16.00
❑122, Feb 1970 SL (w); GC (a)	16.00
❑123, Mar 1970 SL (w); GC (a); 1: Suprema (later becomes Mother Night)	16.00
❑124, Apr 1970 SL (w); GC (a)	16.00
❑125, May 1970 SL (w); GC (a)	16.00
❑126, Jun 1970 SL (w); GC (a); 1: Diamond Head. A: Falcon	16.00
❑127, Jul 1970 SL (w); GC (a)	16.00
❑128, Aug 1970 SL (w); GC (a)	15.00
❑129, Sep 1970 SL (w); GC (a)	15.00
❑130, Oct 1970 SL (w); GC (a)	15.00
❑131, Nov 1970 SL (w); GC (a)	15.00
❑132, Dec 1970 SL (w); GC (a)	15.00
❑133, Jan 1971; SL (w); GC (a); O: Modok. Falcon becomes Captain America's partner	15.00
❑134, Feb 1971 SL (w); GC (a)	15.00
❑135, Mar 1971 JR (c); SL (w); GC (a)	15.00
❑136, Apr 1971 SL (w); GC (a)	15.00
❑137, May 1971 GC, BEv (a); A: Spider-Man	20.00
❑138, Jun 1971 JR (a); A: Spider-Man	20.00
❑139, Jul 1971 SL (w); GC, JR (a)	15.00
❑140, Aug 1971 JR (a); O: Grey Gargoyle	15.00
❑141, Sep 1971 SL (w); JR (a)	15.00
❑142, Oct 1971 JR (a); V: Grey Gargoyle	15.00
❑143, Nov 1971; Giant-size JR (a)	15.00
❑144, Dec 1971 JR (a)	15.00
❑145, Jan 1972 GK (a)	15.00

Camelot 3000 was DC's first maxi-series to be sold only through comics shops.
© 1982 DC Comics.

	N-MINT
❑146, Feb 1972 SB (a)	15.00
❑147, Mar 1972	15.00
❑148, Apr 1972	15.00
❑149, May 1972 SB (a)	15.00
❑150, Jun 1972	15.00
❑151, Jul 1972	15.00
❑152, Aug 1972 SB (a)	15.00
❑153, Sep 1972 1: Bucky III (Jack Monroe). 1: Captain America IV. V: Red Skull	15.00
❑154, Oct 1972	15.00
❑155, Nov 1972 SB (a); O: Captain America II (Jack Monroe). O: Captain America	15.00
❑156, Dec 1972	15.00
❑157, Jan 1973	10.00
❑158, Feb 1973	10.00
❑159, Mar 1973	10.00
❑160, Apr 1973 1: Solarr	10.00
❑161, May 1973 SB (a)	10.00
❑162, Jun 1973 SB (a); O: Sharon Carter	10.00
❑163, Jul 1973 SB (a); 1: Dave Cox	10.00
❑164, Aug 1973 1: Nightshade	10.00
❑165, Sep 1973 SB (a)	10.00
❑166, Oct 1973 SB (a)	10.00
❑167, Nov 1973 SB (a)	10.00
❑168, Dec 1973 SB (a); 1: Phoenix I (Helmut Zemo). A: Baron Zemo (Helmut). D: Phoenix I (Helmut Zemo)	12.00
❑169, Jan 1974 1: Moonstone I (Lloyd Bloch)-cameo	10.00
❑170, Feb 1974 SB (a); 1: Moonstone I (Lloyd Bloch)-full	10.00
❑171, Mar 1974; Marvel Value Stamp #50: Black Panther	10.00
❑172, Apr 1974; SB (a); A: X-Men. A: Banshee. Marvel Value Stamp #43: Enchantress	10.00
❑173, May 1974; SB (a); A: X-Men. Marvel Value Stamp #61: Red Ghost	10.00
❑174, Jun 1974; SB (a); A: X-Men. Marvel Value Stamp #48: Kraven	10.00
❑175, Jul 1974; SB (a); A: X-Men. Marvel Value Stamp #77: Swordsman	10.00
❑176, Aug 1974; SB (a); Marvel Value Stamp #15: Iron Man	7.00
❑177, Sep 1974; SB (a); recalls origin and quits; Marvel Value Stamp #26: Mephisto	7.00
❑178, Oct 1974; SB (a); Marvel Value Stamp #89: Hammerhead	7.00
❑179, Nov 1974; SB (a); Marvel Value Stamp #52: Quicksilver	7.00
❑180, Dec 1974; SB (a); O: Nomad. 1: Nomad (Steve Rogers). 1: Viper II. Marvel Value Stamp #61: Red Ghost	7.00
❑181, Jan 1975; SB (a); O: Captain America (new). 1: Captain America (new). Marvel Value Stamp #46 Mysterio	7.00
❑182, Feb 1975; Marvel Value Stamp #36: Ancient One	7.00
❑183, Mar 1975; D: Captain America (new). Steve Rogers becomes Captain America again	7.00
❑184, Apr 1975; Marvel Value Stamp #94: Electro	5.00
❑185, May 1975	5.00
❑186, Jun 1975 O: Falcon (real origin)	5.00
❑187, Jul 1975	5.00
❑188, Aug 1975 SB (a)	5.00
❑189, Sep 1975 FR (a)	5.00

	N-MINT
❑190, Oct 1975 FR (a)	5.00
❑191, Nov 1975 FR (a)	5.00
❑192, Dec 1975; FR (a); 1: Karla Sofen (becomes Moonstone). Marvel Value Stamp #56: Rawhide Kid	5.00
❑193, Jan 1976 JK (w); JK (a)	5.00
❑194, Feb 1976 JK (w); JK (a)	5.00
❑195, Mar 1976 JK (w); JK (a)	5.00
❑196, Apr 1976 JK (w); JK (a)	5.00
❑196/30 cent, Apr 1976; JK (w); JK (a); 30 cent regional price variant	20.00
❑197, May 1976 JK (w); JK (a)	5.00
❑197/30 cent, May 1976; JK (w); JK (a); 30 cent regional price variant	20.00
❑198, Jun 1976 JK (w); JK (a)	5.00
❑198/30 cent, Jun 1976, JK (w); JK (a); 30 cent regional price variant	20.00
❑199, Jul 1976 JK (w); JK (a)	5.00
❑199/30 cent, Jul 1976; JK (w); JK (a); 30 cent regional price variant	20.00
❑200, Aug 1976; 200th anniversary issue JK (w); JK (a)	6.00
❑200/30 cent, Aug 1976; JK (w); JK (a); 30 cent regional price variant	20.00
❑201, Sep 1976 JK (w); JK (a)	4.00
❑202, Oct 1976 JK (a)	4.00
❑203, Nov 1976 JK (w); JK (a)	4.00
❑204, Dec 1976 JK (w); JK (a)	4.00
❑205, Jan 1977 JK (w); JK (a)	4.00
❑206, Feb 1977 JK (w); JK (a); 1: Donna Maria Puentes	4.00
❑207, Mar 1977 JK (w); JK (a)	4.00
❑208, Apr 1977 JK (w); JK (a); 1: Arnim Zola	4.00
❑209, May 1977 JK (w); JK (a); 1: Arnim Zola. 1: Doughboy	4.00
❑210, Jun 1977 JK (w); JK (a)	4.00
❑211, Jul 1977 JK (w); JK (a)	4.00
❑211/35 cent, Jul 1977; JK (w); JK (a); 35 cent regional price variant	15.00
❑212, Aug 1977 JK (w); JK (a)	4.00
❑213, Sep 1977 JK (w); JK (a)	4.00
❑214, Oct 1977 JK (w); JK (a)	4.00
❑215, Nov 1977 GK (a)	4.00
❑216, Dec 1977; GK (a); Reprinted from Strange Tales #114	4.00
❑217, Jan 1978 JB (a); 1: Quasar (Marvel Man). 1: Blue Streak	4.00
❑218, Feb 1978 SB (a)	4.00
❑219, Mar 1978 SB (a)	4.00
❑220, Apr 1978 SB, GK (a)	4.00
❑221, May 1978 SB, GK (a)	4.00
❑222, Jun 1978 SB (a)	4.00
❑223, Jul 1978 SB, JBy (a)	4.00
❑224, Aug 1978 MZ (a); 1: Señor Muerte II (Philip Garcia)	4.00
❑225, Sep 1978 SB (a)	4.00
❑226, Oct 1978 SB (a)	4.00
❑227, Nov 1978 SB (a)	4.00
❑228, Dec 1978 SB (a)	4.00
❑229, Jan 1979 SB (a); A: Marvel Man (Quasar)	4.00
❑230, Feb 1979 SB, DP (a); A: Hulk. V: Hulk	4.00
❑231, Mar 1979 SB, DP (a); V: Grand Director	4.00
❑232, Apr 1979 SB, DP (a)	4.00
❑233, May 1979 SB, DP (a); D: Sharon Carter	4.00
❑234, Jun 1979 A: Daredevil	4.00
❑235, Jul 1979 SB, FM, JAb (a); A: Daredevil	4.00
❑236, Aug 1979 SB, DP (a); D: Captain America IV	4.00
❑237, Sep 1979; SB, DP (a); 1: Anna Kappelbaum. 1: Joshua Cooper. 1: Copperhead. 1: Mike Farrel. Steve moves to Brooklyn	4.00
❑238, Oct 1979 JBy (a)	4.00
❑239, Nov 1979 JBy (a)	4.00
❑240, Dec 1979	4.00
❑241, Jan 1980 FM (c); FM (a); A: Punisher	4.00
❑242, Feb 1980 DP, JSt (a)	4.00
❑243, Mar 1980 RB, GP, DP (a)	4.00
❑244, Apr 1980 FM (c); FM, DP (a)	4.00

	N-MINT
❑245, May 1980 FM (a)	4.00
❑246, Jun 1980 GP (a)	4.00
❑247, Jul 1980 JBy (a); 1: Machinesmith	4.00
❑248, Aug 1980 JBy (a); 1: Bernie Rosenthal	4.00
❑249, Sep 1980 JBy (a); O: Machinesmith	4.00
❑250, Oct 1980 JBy (a)	4.00
❑251, Nov 1980 JBy (a)	4.00
❑252, Dec 1980 JBy (a)	4.00
❑253, Jan 1981 JBy (a); 1: Joe Chapman (becomes Union Jack III). D: Union Jack II (Brian Falsworth)	4.00
❑254, Feb 1981 JBy (a); O: Union Jack III (Joe Chapman). 1: Union Jack III (Joe Chapman). D: Baron Blood. D: Union Jack I (Lord Falsworth)	4.00
❑255, Mar 1981; 40th anniversary FM (c); JBy, FM (a); O: Captain America. 1: Sarah Rogers (Steve's mother)	4.00
❑256, Apr 1981 GC (a)	2.00
❑257, May 1981 A: Hulk	2.00
❑258, Jun 1981 MZ (a)	2.00
❑259, Jul 1981 MZ (a)	2.00
❑260, Aug 1981 AM (w); AM (a)	2.00
❑261, Sep 1981 MZ (a)	2.00
❑262, Oct 1981 MZ (a)	2.00
❑263, Nov 1981 MZ (a)	2.00
❑264, Dec 1981; MZ (a); A: X-Men. X-Men cameo	2.00
❑265, Jan 1982 MZ (a); A: Nick Fury & Spider-Man	2.00
❑266, Feb 1982 MZ (a)	2.00
❑267, Mar 1982 MZ (a); 1: Everyman	2.00
❑268, Apr 1982 MZ (a)	2.00
❑269, May 1982 MZ (a); 1: Team America	2.00
❑270, Jun 1982 MZ (a)	2.00
❑271, Jul 1982	2.00
❑272, Aug 1982 MZ (a); 1: Vermin	3.00
❑273, Sep 1982 MZ (a)	2.00
❑274, Oct 1982 MZ (a); D: General Samuel "Happy Sam" Sawyer	2.00
❑275, Nov 1982; MZ (a); Bernie Rosenthal learns Cap's identity	2.00
❑276, Dec 1982; MZ (a); 1: Baron Zemo II (Helmut Zemo). Later becomes Citizen V	4.00
❑277, Jan 1983 MZ (a)	2.00
❑278, Feb 1983 MZ (a)	2.00
❑279, Mar 1983 MZ (a)	2.00
❑280, Apr 1983 MZ (a)	2.00
❑281, May 1983 MZ (a); A: Jack Monroe	2.00
❑282, Jun 1983 MZ (a); 1: Joseph Rogers (Steve's father). 1: Nomad II (Jack Monroe)	3.00
❑282-2, Jun 1983; MZ (a); 1: Nomad II (Jack Monroe). silver ink	2.00
❑283, Jul 1983 MZ (a); 2: Nomad (Jack Monroe)	2.00
❑284, Aug 1983 MZ (a); A: Patriot (Jeffrey Mace)	2.00
❑285, Sep 1983 SB, MZ (a); D: Patriot (Jeffrey Mace). V: Porcupine	2.00
❑286, Oct 1983 MZ (a); A: Deathlok	3.00
❑287, Nov 1983 MZ (a); A: Deathlok	3.00
❑288, Dec 1983 MZ (a); A: Deathlok	3.00
❑289, Jan 1984; MZ (a); A: Bernie America. Assistant Editors' Month	2.00
❑290, Feb 1984; JBy (a); 1: Black Crow (in crow form). A: Mother Night. Zemo	2.00
❑291, Mar 1984 JBy (c); HT (a)	2.00
❑292, Apr 1984 O: Black Crow. 1: Black Crow (in human form)	2.00
❑293, May 1984	2.00
❑294, Jun 1984	2.00
❑295, Jul 1984	2.00
❑296, Aug 1984	2.00
❑297, Sep 1984	2.00
❑298, Oct 1984 O: Red Skull	2.00
❑299, Nov 1984 O: Red Skull	2.00
❑300, Dec 1984 MZ (a); V: Red Skull	2.00
❑301, Jan 1985	2.00

	N-MINT
❑302, Feb 1985 1: Machete	2.00
❑303, Mar 1985 V: Batroc	2.00
❑304, Apr 1985	2.00
❑305, May 1985 A: Captain Britain	2.00
❑306, Jun 1985 A: Captain Britain	2.00
❑307, Jul 1985 1: Madcap	2.00
❑308, Aug 1985; JBy (a); Secret Wars II	2.00
❑309, Sep 1985; O: Madcap. V: Madcap. Nomad leaves team	2.00
❑310, Oct 1985 1: Diamondback. 1: Rattler. 1: Cottonmouth II. 1: Serpent Society. 1: Bushmaster. 1: Asp II (Cleo)	2.00
❑311, Nov 1985 V: Super-Adaptoid	2.00
❑312, Dec 1985 O: Flag-Smasher. 1: Flag-Smasher	2.00
❑313, Jan 1986 JBy (a)	2.00
❑314, Feb 1986	2.00
❑315, Mar 1986 D: Porcupine. V: Serpent Society	2.00
❑316, Apr 1986	2.00
❑317, May 1986	2.00
❑318, Jun 1986 D: The Blue Streak. D: Death-Adder	2.00
❑319, Jul 1986 D: Bird-Man II	2.00
❑320, Aug 1986 V: Scourge	2.00
❑321, Sep 1986 MZ (a); 1: Ultimatum	2.00
❑322, Oct 1986 1: Super-Patriot	2.00
❑323, Nov 1986 MZ (a); 1: Super-Patriot II (later becomes USAgent)	2.00
❑324, Dec 1986	2.00
❑325, Jan 1987 MZ (a); 1: Slug	2.00
❑326, Feb 1987 MZ (a)	2.00
❑327, Mar 1987 MZ (a)	2.00
❑328, Apr 1987 MZ (a); O: Demolition-Man. 1: Demolition-Man	2.00
❑329, May 1987 MZ (a)	2.00
❑330, Jun 1987 MZ (a); A: Demolition-Man	2.00
❑331, Jul 1987 MZ (a)	2.00
❑332, Aug 1987; MZ (a); Steve Rogers quits as Captain America	3.00
❑333, Sep 1987; MZ (a); 1: Captain America VI (John Walker). John Walker (Super-Patriot II) becomes Captain America	2.00
❑334, Oct 1987 MZ (a); 1: Bucky IV (Lemar Hoskins)	2.00
❑335, Nov 1987 1: Watchdogs	2.00
❑336, Dec 1987 MZ (a)	2.00
❑337, Jan 1988 MZ (a); 1: Fer-de-Lance. 1: The Captain. 1: Puff Adder	2.00
❑338, Feb 1988 D: Professor Power	2.00
❑339, Mar 1988; Fall of Mutants	2.00
❑340, Apr 1988	2.00
❑341, May 1988 1: Left-Winger. 1: Rock Python (cameo). 1: Battle Star. A: Iron Man	2.00
❑342, Jun 1988 1: Rock Python (full appearance)	2.00
❑343, Jul 1988 1: Quill	2.00
❑344, Aug 1988; Giant-size	2.00
❑345, Sep 1988	2.00
❑346, Oct 1988	2.00
❑347, Nov 1988 D: Left-Winger	2.00
❑348, Dec 1988 V: Flag Smasher	2.00
❑349, Jan 1989	2.00
❑350, Feb 1989; Giant-size; The Captain and Super-Patriot fight for title of Captain America	3.00
❑351, Mar 1989 A: Nick Fury. D: Watchdog	2.00
❑352, Apr 1989 1: Machete. A: Soviet Super Soldiers	2.00
❑353, May 1989 A: Soviet Super Soldiers	2.00
❑354, Jun 1989; 1: U.S. Agent. A: Fabian Stankowitz. Super-Patriot becomes USAgent	2.00
❑355, Jul 1989 RB (a)	2.00
❑356, Aug 1989 AM (a); 1: Mother Night	2.00
❑357, Sep 1989; CBG Fan Awards parody ballot	2.00
❑358, Sep 1989 A: John Jameson	2.00
❑359, Oct 1989 1: Crossbones (cameo)	2.00

Condition price index: Multiply "NM prices" above by: **0.83 for Very Fine/Near Mint**
0.66 for Very Fine • 0.33 for Fine • 0.2 for Very Good • 0.125 for Good

N-MINT

❑360, Oct 1989 1: Crossbones (full appearance) 2.00
❑361, Nov 1989 .... 2.00
❑362, Nov 1989 .... 2.00
❑363, Nov 1989 .... 2.00
❑364, Dec 1989 .... 2.00
❑365, Dec 1989; Acts of Vengeance .. 2.00
❑366, Jan 1990; Acts of Vengeance .. 2.00
❑367, Feb 1990; Acts of Vengeance; Red Skull vs. Magneto 2.00
❑368, Mar 1990 O: Machinesmith 2.00
❑369, Apr 1990 1: Skeleton Crew 2.00
❑370, May 1990 .... 2.00
❑371, Jun 1990 .... 2.00
❑372, Jul 1990 .... 2.00
❑373, Jul 1990 .... 2.00
❑374, Aug 1990 .... 2.00
❑375, Aug 1990 .... 2.00
❑376, Sep 1990 .... 2.00
❑377, Sep 1990 .... 2.00
❑378, Oct 1990 .... 2.00
❑379, Nov 1990 O: Nefarius. 1: Nefarius. A: Quasar. V: Nefarius 2.00
❑380, Dec 1990 .... 2.00
❑381, Jan 1991 .... 2.00
❑382, Feb 1991 .... 2.00
❑383, Mar 1991; 50th anniversary issue JLee (c); JLee (a) 3.00
❑384, Apr 1991 A: Jack Frost 2.00
❑385, May 1991 .... 2.00
❑386, Jun 1991 A: U.S. Agent 2.00
❑387, Jul 1991; Red Skull back-up stories 2.00
❑388, Jul 1991; 1: Impala. Red Skull back-up stories 2.00
❑389, Aug 1991; Red Skull back-up stories 2.00
❑390, Aug 1991 .... 2.00
❑391, Sep 1991 .... 2.00
❑392, Sep 1991 .... 2.00
❑393, Oct 1991 .... 2.00
❑394, Nov 1991 .... 2.00
❑395, Dec 1991 .... 2.00
❑396, Jan 1992 1: Jack O'Lantern II . 2.00
❑397, Feb 1992 .... 2.00
❑398, Mar 1992; Galactic Storm 2.00
❑399, Apr 1992; Galactic Storm 2.00
❑400, May 1992; O: Cutthroat. O: Diamondback. Double-gatefold cover; Galactic Storm; reprints Avengers #4 3.00
❑401, Jun 1992 .... 2.00
❑402, Jul 1992 1: Dredmund Druid. A: Wolverine 2.00
❑403, Jul 1992 2: Dredmund Druid. A: Wolverine 2.00
❑404, Aug 1992 A: Wolverine 2.00
❑405, Aug 1992 A: Wolverine 2.00
❑406, Sep 1992 A: Wolverine 2.00
❑407, Sep 1992 A: Wolverine. A: Cable 2.00
❑408, Oct 1992 D: Cutthroat 2.00
❑409, Nov 1992 .... 2.00
❑410, Dec 1992 .... 2.00
❑411, Jan 1993 .... 2.00
❑412, Feb 1993 .... 2.00
❑413, Mar 1993 V: Modam 2.00
❑414, Apr 1993; Savage Land 2.00
❑415, May 1993 .... 2.00
❑416, Jun 1993 .... 2.00
❑417, Jul 1993 .... 2.00
❑418, Aug 1993 .... 2.00
❑419, Sep 1993 A: Silver Sable 2.00
❑420, Oct 1993 A: Nomad. A: Blazing Skull. A: Viper 2.00
❑420/CS, Oct 1993; Includes copy of Dirt Magazine A: Nomad. A: Blazing Skull. A: Viper 3.00
❑421, Nov 1993 A: Nomad 2.00
❑422, Dec 1993 .... 2.00
❑423, Jan 1994 V: Namor 2.00
❑424, Feb 1994 .... 2.00
❑425, Mar 1994; Giant-size 3.00
❑425/Variant, Mar 1994; Giant-size; Foil-embossed cover 3.00
❑426, Apr 1994 .... 2.00

N-MINT

❑427, May 1994 .... 2.00
❑428, Jun 1994 .... 2.00
❑429, Jul 1994 1: Kono the Sumo 2.00
❑430, Aug 1994 .... 2.00
❑431, Sep 1994 1: Free Spirit 2.00
❑432, Oct 1994 .... 2.00
❑433, Nov 1994 .... 2.00
❑434, Dec 1994 1: Jack Flag 2.00
❑435, Jan 1995 V: new Cobra 2.00
❑436, Feb 1995 .... 2.00
❑437, Mar 1995 .... 2.00
❑438, Apr 1995 1: Cap-Armor 2.00
❑439, May 1995 V: Death-Stalker 2.00
❑440, Jun 1995 .... 2.00
❑441, Jul 1995 .... 2.00
❑442, Aug 1995 .... 2.00
❑443, Sep 1995 D: Captain America . 2.00
❑444, Oct 1995; MWa (w); Title changes to Steve Rogers, Captain America; Red Skull brings Cap back to life; Return of Sharon Carter 3.00
❑445, Nov 1995; MWa (w); Return of Sharon Carter; Cap revived 2.00
❑446, Dec 1995 MWa (w); A: Red Skull 2.00
❑447, Jan 1996 MWa (w) 2.00
❑448, Feb 1996; Giant-size MWa (w) 3.00
❑449, Mar 1996 MWa (w) 2.00
❑450, Apr 1996; MWa (w); Title returns to Captain America; Cap's American citizenship is revoked 2.00
❑450/A, Apr 1996; MWa (w); alternate cover 2.00
❑451, May 1996 MWa (w) 2.00
❑452, Jun 1996 MWa (w) 2.00
❑453, Jul 1996; MWa (w); Cap's citizenship restored 2.00
❑454, Aug 1996 MWa (w) 2.00
❑Annual 1, ca. 1971; Cover reads "King-Size Special"; Reprints from Tales of Suspense #63, 69-71, 75 .... 30.00
❑Annual 2, Jan 1972; Cover reads "King-Size Special"; GC, GT, JK (a); Reprints from Tales of Suspense #72-74; Not Brand Ecch #3 .... 10.00
❑Annual 3, ca. 1976 JK (a) 7.00
❑Annual 4, ca. 1977 JK (a); 1: Slither. 1: Crucible (Marvel) 7.00
❑Annual 5, ca. 1981 FM (c); FM (a) .. 3.00
❑Annual 6, ca. 1982; Four Caps 3.00
❑Annual 7, ca. 1983; O: Kubik (Cosmic Cube). 3.00
❑Annual 8, ca. 1986 A: Wolverine 12.00
❑Annual 9, ca. 1990 A: Iron Man 3.00
❑Annual 10, ca. 1991 DH (a); O: Captain America. O: Bushmaster 3.00
❑Annual 11, ca. 1992; Citizen Kang ... 3.00
❑Annual 12, ca. 1993; 1: Battling Bantam. Polybagged with trading card 3.00
❑Annual 13, ca. 1994 V: Red Skull 3.00
❑Ashcan 1; ashcan edition; no indicia; Mini "Ashcan" preview 1.00
❑Special 1, Feb 1984; Special Edition #1; JSo (c); JSo (a); reprint of Steranko issues 4.00
❑Special 2, Mar 1984, Special Edition #2; JSo (c); JSo (a); reprint of Steranko issues; Double-gatefold cover 4.00

CAPTAIN AMERICA (VOL. 2)
MARVEL

❑1, Nov 1996; Steve Rogers regains memories of WW II action; Captain America jumping forward on cover 3.00
❑1/A, Nov 1996; Variant cover (flag background) 3.00
❑1/B, Nov 1996; variant cover 3.00
❑2, Dec 1996 .... 2.00
❑3, Jan 1997 .... 2.00
❑4, Feb 1997 .... 2.00
❑5, Mar 1997 .... 2.00
❑6, Apr 1997 .... 2.00
❑7, May 1997 .... 2.00
❑8, Jun 1997 .... 2.00
❑9, Jul 1997 .... 2.00
❑10, Aug 1997; gatefold summary 2.00
❑11, Sep 1997; gatefold summary 2.00

Flag-Smasher, a psychotic ex-soldier, was introduced in *Captain America* #312.
© 1985 Marvel Comics.

N-MINT

❑12, Oct 1997; gatefold summary; cover forms quadtych with Avengers #12, Iron Man #12; and Fantastic Four #12 .... 2.00
❑13, Nov 1997; gatefold summary 2.00
❑Ashcan 1, Mar 1995; Collector's Preview 2.00
❑Ashcan 1/A; Special Comicon Edition; No cover price; preview of Vol. 2 ... 1.00

CAPTAIN AMERICA (VOL. 3)
MARVEL

❑1, Jan 1998; gatefold summary; follows events in Heroes Return; Cap in Japan; wraparound cover 3.50
❑1/A, Jan 1998; gatefold summary; alternate cover; follows events in Heroes Return; Cap in Japan 3.50
❑2, Feb 1998; gatefold summary; Cap loses his shield 2.50
❑2/A, Feb 1998; variant cover 2.50
❑3, Mar 1998; gatefold summary 2.00
❑4, Apr 1998; gatefold summary; true identity of Sensational Hydra revealed 2.00
❑5, May 1998; gatefold summary; Cap replaced by Skrull 2.00
❑6, Jun 1998; gatefold summary; Skrulls revealed 2.00
❑7, Jul 1998; gatefold summary 2.00
❑8, Aug 1998; gatefold summary; Cap's shield destroyed; continues in Quicksilver #10 .... 2.00
❑9, Sep 1998; gatefold summary; Cap gets new virtual shield 2.00
❑10, Oct 1998; gatefold summary; Nightmare 2.00
❑11, Nov 1998; gatefold summary 2.00
❑12, Dec 1998; double-sized; wraparound cover 2.00
❑12/Ltd., Dec 1998 .... 6.00
❑13, Jan 1999; gatefold summary 2.00
❑14, Feb 1999; gatefold summary 2.00
❑15, Mar 1999 .... 2.00
❑16, Apr 1999 .... 2.00
❑17, May 1999 .... 2.00
❑18, Jun 1999 .... 2.00
❑19, Jul 1999 .... 2.00
❑20, Aug 1999; Sgt. Fury back-up (b&w) 2.00
❑21, Sep 1999; Sgt. Fury back-up (b&w) 2.00
❑22, Oct 1999; Cap's shield restored 2.00
❑23, Nov 1999 .... 2.00
❑24, Dec 2000 .... 2.00
❑25, Jan 2000; Giant-size 3.00
❑26, Feb 2000 .... 2.25
❑27, Mar 2000 .... 2.25
❑28, Apr 2000 .... 2.25
❑29, May 2000 .... 2.25
❑30, Jun 2000 .... 2.25
❑31, Jul 2000 .... 2.25
❑32, Aug 2000; World War II story 2.25
❑33, Sep 2000 .... 2.25
❑34, Oct 2000 .... 2.25
❑35, Nov 2000 .... 2.25
❑36, Dec 2000 .... 2.25
❑37, Jan 2001 .... 2.25
❑38, Feb 2001 .... 2.25
❑39, Mar 2001 .... 2.25
❑40, Apr 2001 .... 2.25
❑41, May 2001 .... 2.25
❑42, Jun 2001 .... 2.25

N-MINT

❑43, Jul 2001 .... 2.25
❑44, Aug 2001 .... 2.25
❑45, Sep 2001 .... 2.25
❑46, Oct 2001 .... 2.25
❑47, Nov 2001 .... 2.25
❑48, Dec 2001 .... 2.25
❑49, Jan 2002 .... 2.25
❑50, Feb 2002 .... 5.95
❑Annual 1998, ca. 1998; wraparound cover 3.50
❑Annual 1999, ca. 1999 .... 3.50
❑Annual 2000, ca. 2000; continued from Captain America #35 .... 3.50
❑Annual 2001, ca. 2001 .... 2.99

CAPTAIN AMERICA (VOL. 4)
MARVEL

❑1, Jun 2002 .... 4.00
❑1/A, Jun 2002 .... 4.00
❑2, Jul 2002 .... 3.00
❑3, Aug 2002 .... 3.00
❑4, Sep 2002 .... 3.00
❑5, Oct 2002 .... 3.00
❑6, Dec 2002 .... 3.00
❑7, Feb 2003 .... 3.00
❑8, Mar 2003 .... 3.00
❑9, Apr 2003 .... 3.00
❑10, May 2003 .... 3.00
❑11, Jun 2003 .... 3.00
❑12, Jun 2003 .... 3.00
❑13, Jul 2003 .... 3.00
❑14, Aug 2003 .... 3.00
❑15, Sep 2003 .... 3.00
❑16, Oct 2003 .... 3.00
❑17, Nov 2003 .... 3.00
❑18, Nov 2003 .... 3.00
❑19, Dec 2003 .... 3.00
❑20, Jan 2004 .... 3.00
❑21, Feb 2004 .... 3.00
❑22, Mar 2004 .... 3.00
❑23, Apr 2004 .... 3.00
❑24, May 2004 .... 3.00
❑25, Jun 2004 .... 3.00
❑26, Jul 2004 .... 0.00
❑27, Aug 2004 .... 2.99
❑28, Aug 2004 .... 2.99
❑29, Sep 2004 ....

CAPTAIN AMERICA AND THE CAMPBELL KIDS
MARVEL

❑1, ca. 1980; giveaway 3.00

CAPTAIN AMERICA & THE FALCON
MARVEL

❑1, May 2004 .... 2.99
❑2, Jun 2004 .... 2.99
❑3, Jul 2004 .... 0.00
❑4, Aug 2004 .... 2.99
❑5, Sep 2004 ....

CAPTAIN AMERICA: DEAD MAN RUNNING
MARVEL

❑1, Mar 2002 .... 2.99
❑2, Apr 2002 .... 2.99
❑3, May 2002 .... 2.99

CAPTAIN AMERICA: DEATHLOK LIVES!
MARVEL

❑1; Reprints from Captain America #286-288 .... 4.95

CAPTAIN AMERICA: DRUG WAR
MARVEL

❑1, Apr 1993 .... 2.00

CAPTAIN AMERICA GOES TO WAR AGAINST DRUGS
MARVEL

❑1, ca. 1990; Anti-drug giveaway PD (w) 1.00

CAPTAIN AMERICA: MEDUSA EFFECT
MARVEL

❑1, Mar 1994 .... 2.95

N-MINT

CAPTAIN AMERICA/NICK FURY: BLOOD TRUCE
MARVEL

❑1, Feb 1995; prestige format one-shot 5.95

CAPTAIN AMERICA/NICK FURY: THE OTHERWORLD WAR
MARVEL

❑1, Oct 2001 .... 6.95

CAPTAIN AMERICA: SENTINEL OF LIBERTY
MARVEL

❑1, Sep 1998; gatefold summary; wraparound cover 1.99
❑1/Variant, Sep 1988; Roughcut edition 2.99
❑2, Oct 1998; gatefold summary; Invaders 1.99
❑3, Nov 1998; gatefold summary; Invaders 1.99
❑4, Dec 1998; gatefold summary; Invaders 1.99
❑5, Jan 1999; gatefold summary; Tales of Suspense tribute 1.99
❑6, Feb 1999; double-sized; Tales of Suspense tribute 2.99
❑7, Mar 1999; Bicentennial story 1.99
❑8, Apr 1999 .... 1.99
❑9, May 1999 .... 1.99
❑10, Jun 1999 .... 1.99
❑11, Jul 1999 .... 1.99
❑12, Aug 1999 .... 2.99

CAPTAIN AMERICA: THE LEGEND
MARVEL

❑1, Sep 1996; background on Cap and his supporting cast; wraparound cover 4.00

CAPTAIN AMERICA: THE MOVIE SPECIAL
MARVEL

❑1, May 1992 .... 3.50

CAPTAIN AMERICA: WHAT PRICE GLORY
MARVEL

❑1, May 2003 .... 2.99
❑2, May 2003 .... 2.99
❑3, May 2003 .... 2.99
❑4, May 2003 .... 2.99

CAPTAIN ATOM (CHARLTON)
CHARLTON

❑78, Dec 1965; O: Captain Atom. Series continued from Strange Suspense Stories #77 .... 40.00
❑79, Mar 1966 .... 25.00
❑80, May 1966 SD (a) 25.00
❑81, Jul 1966 .... 25.00
❑82, Sep 1966 .... 25.00
❑83, Nov 1966 1: Ted Kord (Blue Beetle) 25.00
❑84, Jan 1967 1: Captain Atom (new) 25.00
❑85, Mar 1967 .... 25.00
❑86, Jun 1967 .... 20.00
❑87, Aug 1967; SD (a); Nightshade back-up story 20.00
❑88, Oct 1967 .... 20.00
❑89, Dec 1967 .... 20.00

CAPTAIN ATOM (DC)
DC

❑1, Mar 1987; PB (a); O: Captain Atom. New costume 1.00
❑2, Apr 1987 .... 1.00
❑3, May 1987 O: Captain Atom (fake origin) 1.00
❑4, Jun 1987 .... 1.00
❑5, Jul 1987 A: Firestorm 1.00
❑6, Aug 1987 V: Doctor Spectro 1.00
❑7, Sep 1987 .... 1.00
❑8, Oct 1987 A: Plastique 1.00
❑9, Nov 1987 .... 1.00
❑10, Dec 1987 .... 1.00
❑11, Jan 1988; A: Firestorm. Millennium 1.00
❑12, Feb 1988 1: Major Force 1.00
❑13, Mar 1988 .... 1.00
❑14, Apr 1988 .... 1.00

N-MINT

❑15, May 1988 V: Major Force 1.00
❑16, Jun 1988 A: JLI 1.00
❑17, Jul 1988 A: Swamp Thing 1.00
❑18, Aug 1988 .... 1.00
❑19, Sep 1988 .... 1.00
❑20, Oct 1988 A: Blue Beetle 1.00
❑21, Nov 1988 .... 1.00
❑22, Dec 1988; Plastique vs. Nightshade 1.00
❑23, ca. 1988; V: Ghost. no month of publication 1.00
❑24, ca. 1989; Invasion!; no month of publication 1.00
❑25, Jan 1989; Invasion!; no month of publication 1.00
❑26, Feb 1989 O: Captain Atom. A: JLA 1.00
❑27, Mar 1989 PB (a); O: Captain Atom 1.00
❑28, Apr 1989 O: Captain Atom. V: Ghost 1.00
❑29, May 1989 .... 1.00
❑30, Jun 1989 .... 1.00
❑31, Jul 1989 V: Rocket Red 1.00
❑32, Aug 1989 .... 1.00
❑33, Sep 1989; Batman; new costume 1.00
❑34, Oct 1989 V: Doctor Spectro 1.00
❑35, Nov 1989; A: Major Force. back to old costume 1.00
❑36, Dec 1989 .... 1.00
❑37, Jan 1990 .... 1.00
❑38, Feb 1990 V: Black Racer 1.00
❑39, Mar 1990 .... 1.00
❑40, Apr 1990 .... 1.00
❑41, May 1990 .... 1.00
❑42, Jun 1990 .... 1.00
❑43, Jul 1990 .... 1.00
❑44, Aug 1990 A: Plastique 1.00
❑45, Sep 1990 .... 1.00
❑46, Oct 1990; Superman 1.00
❑47, Nov 1990 .... 1.00
❑48, Dec 1990 .... 1.00
❑49, Jan 1991; Trial of Plastique 1.00
❑50, Feb 1991; Giant-size D: Megala 2.00
❑51, Mar 1991 .... 1.00
❑52, Apr 1991 .... 1.00
❑53, May 1991 .... 1.00
❑54, Jun 1991 .... 1.00
❑55, Jul 1991 .... 1.00
❑56, Aug 1991 .... 1.00
❑57, Sep 1991 .... 1.00
❑Annual 1, ca. 1988; 1: Major Force. V: Major Force. says 88 on cover, 87 in indicia 1.25
❑Annual 2, ca. 1989 V: Queen Bee 1.50

CAPTAIN BRITAIN
MARVEL UK

❑1, Jan 1985 O: The Free-Fall Warriors 2.50
❑2, Feb 1985, b&w; No logo, Gold cover 2.00
❑3, Mar 1985, b&w; No logo, Gold cover 2.00
❑4, Apr 1985, b&w; No logo, Gold cover 2.00
❑5, May 1985, b&w; No logo, Gold cover 2.00
❑6, Jun 1985, b&w; No logo, Gold cover 2.00
❑7, Jul 1985, b&w; No logo, Gold cover 2.00
❑8, Aug 1985, b&w; No logo, Gold cover 2.00
❑9, Sep 1985, b&w; No logo, Gold cover 2.00
❑10, Oct 1985, b&w; No logo, Gold cover 2.00
❑11, Nov 1985, b&w; No logo, Gold cover 2.00
❑12, Dec 1985, b&w; No logo, Gold cover 2.00
❑13, Jan 1986, b&w; No logo, Gold cover 2.00
❑14, Feb 1986 .... 2.00

CAPTAIN CANUCK
COMELY

❑1, Jul 1975 .... 3.00
❑2; no month of publication 2.00
❑3; no month of publication 2.00
❑4, Aug 1979; New publisher 1.50
❑5, Sep 1979 .... 1.50
❑6, Nov 1979 .... 1.50
❑7, Jan 1980 .... 1.50
❑8, Mar 1980 .... 1.50
❑9, May 1980; says Jun on cover; May in indicia 1.50

N-MINT

❑10, Aug 1980 ... 1.50
❑11, Oct 1980 ... 1.50
❑12, Dec 1980 ... 1.50
❑13, Feb 1981 ... 1.50
❑14, Apr 1981 ... 1.50

CAPTAIN CANUCK FIRST SUMMER SPECIAL
COMELY

❑1, Sep 1980 ... 1.50

CAPTAIN CANUCK REBORN
SEMPLE

❑0, Sep 1993 ... 1.50
❑1, Jan 1994 ... 2.50
❑1/Gold; Gold polybagged edition with trading cards ... 2.95
❑2, Jul 1994 ... 2.50
❑3, b&w; strip reprints; cardstock cover ... 2.50

CAPTAIN CARROT AND HIS AMAZING ZOO CREW
DC

❑1, Mar 1982 A: Superman. A: Starro 1.50
❑2, Apr 1982 AA (a) ... 1.00
❑3, May 1982 ... 1.00
❑4, Jun 1982 ... 1.00
❑5, Jul 1982 A: Oklahoma Bones ... 1.00
❑6, Aug 1982 V: Bunny from Beyond 1.00
❑7, Sep 1982 A: Bow-zar the Barbarian 1.00
❑8, Oct 1982 1: Z-Building (Zoo Crew's Headquarters) ... 1.00
❑9, Nov 1982; A: Terrific Whatzie. A: Three Mouseketeers. Masters of the Universe preview ... 1.00
❑10, Dec 1982 ... 1.00
❑11, Jan 1983 ... 1.00
❑12, Feb 1983; 1: Little Cheese. 1st Art Adams art ... 1.00
❑13, Mar 1983 ... 1.00
❑14, Apr 1983; Justa Lotta Animals .. 1.00
❑15, May 1983; Justa Lotta Animals . 1.00
❑16, Jun 1983 ... 1.00
❑17, Jul 1983 ... 1.00
❑18, Aug 1983 ... 1.00
❑19, Sep 1983 V: Frogzilla ... 1.00
❑20, Nov 1983 A: Changeling. V: Gorilla Grodd ... 1.00

CAPTAIN CONFEDERACY (STEELDRAGON)
STEELDRAGON

❑1 ... 1.50
❑2 ... 1.50
❑3 ... 1.50
❑4 ... 1.50
❑5 ... 1.50
❑6, Sum 1987 ... 1.50
❑7, Aut 1987 ... 1.75
❑8, Win 1987 ... 1.75
❑9, Spr 1988 ... 1.75
❑10, Jun 1988 ... 1.75
❑11, Jun 1988 ... 1.75
❑12, Oct 1988 ... 1.75
❑Special 1, Sum 1987 ... 1.75
❑Special 2, Sum 1987 ... 1.75

CAPTAIN CONFEDERACY (EPIC)
MARVEL / EPIC

❑1, Nov 1991 ... 2.00
❑2, Dec 1991 ... 2.00
❑3, Jan 1992 ... 2.00
❑4, Feb 1992 ... 2.00

CAPTAIN COSMOS, THE LAST STARVEYOR
YBOR CITY

❑1 ... 2.95

CAPTAIN CRAFTY
CONCEPTION

❑1, Jun 1994, b&w; wraparound cover 2.50
❑2, Win 1994, b&w; wraparound cover 2.50
❑2.5, Apr 1998 ... 1.00

N-MINT

CAPTAIN CRAFTY COLOR SPECTACULAR
CONCEPTION

❑1, Aug 1996; wraparound cover ... 2.50
❑2, Dec 1996; wraparound cover ... 2.50

CAPTAIN CRUSADER
TPI

❑1, Aug 1990 ... 1.25

CAPTAIN CULT
HAMMAC

❑1, b&w; 1st appearance of Captain Cult ... 2.00

CAPTAIN DINGLEBERRY
SLAVE LABOR

❑1, Aug 1998 ... 2.95
❑2, Sep 1998 ... 2.95
❑3, Oct 1998 ... 2.95
❑4 1998 ... 2.95
❑5, Jan 1999 ... 2.95
❑6, Feb 1999 ... 2.95

CAPTAIN EO 3-D
ECLIPSE

❑1, Aug 1987; oversized (11x17) ... 5.00

CAPTAIN FORTUNE
RIP OFF

❑1 ... 2.95
❑2 ... 3.25
❑3 ... 3.25
❑4 ... 3.25

CAPTAIN GLORY
TOPPS

❑0, Apr 1993; trading card ... 2.95
❑1, Apr 1993 ... 2.95

CAPTAIN GRAVITY
PENNY-FARTHING

❑1, Dec 1998 ... 2.75
❑1/Autographed, Dec 1998 ... 3.50
❑2, Jan 1999 ... 2.75
❑3, Feb 1999 ... 2.75
❑4, Mar 1999 ... 2.75

CAPTAIN GRAVITY: ONE TRUE HERO
PENNY-FARTHING

❑1, Aug 1999 ... 2.95

CAPTAIN HARLOCK
ETERNITY

❑1, b&w; Character created by Leiji Matsumoto ... 2.50
❑2 ... 2.50
❑3 ... 2.50
❑4 ... 2.50
❑5 ... 2.50
❑6 ... 2.50
❑7 ... 2.50
❑8 ... 2.50
❑9 ... 2.50
❑10 ... 2.50
❑11 ... 2.50
❑12 ... 2.50
❑13 ... 2.50
❑Holiday 1, b&w; prestige format ... 2.50

CAPTAIN HARLOCK: DEATHSHADOW RISING
ETERNITY

❑1 ... 2.25
❑2 ... 2.25
❑3 ... 2.25
❑4 ... 2.25
❑5 ... 2.25
❑6 ... 2.25

CAPTAIN HARLOCK: THE FALL OF THE EMPIRE
ETERNITY

❑1 ... 2.50
❑2, Aug 1992 ... 2.50
❑3 ... 2.50
❑4 ... 2.50

Air Force Captain Nathaniel Adam gained superpowers and was hurled forward in time during a military experiment with alien metal and a nuclear device.

© 1987 DC Comics.

N-MINT

CAPTAIN HARLOCK: THE MACHINE PEOPLE
ETERNITY

❑1 ... 2.50
❑2 ... 2.50
❑3 ... 2.50
❑4 ... 2.50

CAPTAIN JOHNER & THE ALIENS
VALIANT

❑1, May 1995; reprints back-ups from Magnus, Robot Fighter (Gold Key) #1-7; cardstock cover ... 2.95
❑2, May 1995; reprints back-ups from Magnus, Robot Fighter (Gold Key); cardstock cover ... 2.95

CAPTAIN JUSTICE
MARVEL

❑1, ca. 1988; TV show ... 1.25
❑2, Apr 1988; TV show ... 1.25

CAPTAIN MARVEL (1ST SERIES)
MARVEL

❑1, May 1968; GC (a); Indicia: Marvel's Space-Born Superhero: Captain Marvel ... 60.00
❑2, Jun 1968 GC (a); A: Sub-Mariner. V: Skrull ... 24.00
❑3, Jul 1968 GC (a); V: Skrull ... 20.00
❑4, Aug 1968 GC (a); A: Sub-Mariner. V: Sub-Mariner ... 20.00
❑5, Sep 1968 DH (a) ... 15.00
❑6, Oct 1968 DH (a) ... 15.00
❑7, Nov 1968 DH (a); V: Quasimodo . 15.00
❑8, Dec 1968 DH (a); 1: Aakon (alien race) ... 15.00
❑9, Jan 1969 DH (a) ... 15.00
❑10, Feb 1969 DH (a) ... 13.00
❑11, Mar 1969 D: Una ... 13.00
❑12, Apr 1969 ... 13.00
❑13, May 1969 ... 13.00
❑14, Jun 1969 A: Iron Man ... 13.00
❑15, Aug 1969 ... 13.00
❑16, Sep 1969 ... 13.00
❑17, Oct 1969; GK, DA (c); GK, DA (a); O: Rick Jones retold. new costume; crossover with Captain America #114-116 ... 13.00
❑18, Nov 1969 ... 13.00
❑19, Dec 1969; GK, DA (a); series goes on hiatus ... 13.00
❑20, Jun 1970 GK, DA (c); GK, DA (a) 13.00
❑21, Aug 1970; A: Hulk. series goes on hiatus ... 13.00
❑22, Sep 1972; V: Megaton. Title changes to Captain Marvel after hiatus 13.00
❑23, Nov 1972 V: Megaton ... 13.00
❑24, Jan 1973 ... 13.00
❑25, Mar 1973; JSn (a); Thanos War begins ... 25.00
❑26, May 1973; JSn (a); A: Thanos. Thing; Masterlord revealed as Thanos 25.00
❑27, Jul 1973; JSn (a); 1: Death (Mar-vel). A: Thanos. death of Super Skrull 25.00
❑28, Sep 1973; AM, JSn (a); A: Thanos. Avengers ... 25.00
❑29, Nov 1973; AM, JSn (a); O: Kronos. A: Thanos. Captain Marvel gets new powers ... 12.00
❑30, Jan 1974 AM, JSn (a); A: Thanos. V: Controller ... 12.00

N-MINT

❑31, Mar 1974; JSn (a); 1: ISAAC. A: Thanos. Avengers ... 12.00
❑32, May 1974; JSn (a); O: Moondragon. O: Drax. A: Thanos. Rick Jones vs. Thanos; continued in Avengers #125; Marvel Value Stamp #19: Balder, Hogun, Fandral ... 12.00
❑33, Jul 1974; JSn (a); O: Thanos. Thanos War ends; continued from Avengers #125; Marvel Value Stamp #6: Thor ... 12.00
❑34, Sep 1974; JSn, JAb (a); 1: Nitro. Captain Marvel contracts cancer (will eventually die from it); Marvel Value Stamp #25: Torch ... 6.00
❑35, Nov 1974; AA (a); V: Living Laser. Ant-Man, Wasp; Marvel Value Stamp #1: Spider-Man ... 3.00
❑36, Jan 1975; JSn (a); A: Thanos. Watcher; Marvel Value Stamp #25: Torch ... 3.00
❑37, Mar 1975; AM (w); Watcher ... 3.00
❑38, May 1975; AM (w); Trial of the Watcher ... 3.00
❑39, Jul 1975; AM (w); 1: Aron the Rogue Watcher. Watcher (Uatu) ... 3.00
❑40, Sep 1975; AM (w); Watcher ... 3.00
❑41, Nov 1975; AM (w); A: Supreme Intelligence. V: Ronan. Marvel Value Stamp #2: Hulk ... 3.00
❑42, Jan 1976 AM (w); V: Stranger ... 3.00
❑43, Mar 1976 AM (a); V: Drax ... 3.00
❑44, May 1976 AM (w); V: Drax ... 3.00
❑44/30 cent, May 1976; AM (w); V: Drax. 30 cent regional price variant ... 20.00
❑45, Jul 1976 AM (w) ... 3.00
❑45/30 cent, Jul 1976; AM (w); 30 cent regional price variant ... 20.00
❑46, Sep 1976 1: Supremor ... 3.00
❑47, Nov 1976 A: Human Torch. V: Sentry Sinister ... 3.00
❑48, Jan 1977 1: Cheetah (Esteban Carracus). V: Cheetah. V: Sentry Sinister ... 3.00
❑49, Mar 1977 V: Ronan ... 3.00
❑50, May 1977 AM (a); 1: Doctor Minerva. A: Avengers. A: Adaptoid ... 3.00
❑51, Jul 1977 V: Mercurio ... 3.00
❑52, Sep 1977 ... 3.00
❑53, Nov 1977 ... 3.00
❑54, Jan 1978 ... 3.00
❑55, Mar 1978 V: Death-Grip ... 3.00
❑56, May 1978 PB (a); V: Death-Grip ... 3.00
❑57, Jul 1978; PB, BWi (a); A: Thanos. V: Thor. (flashback) ... 3.00
❑58, Sep 1978 V: Drax ... 3.00
❑59, Nov 1978 1: Elysius. V: Drax ... 3.00
❑60, Jan 1979 ... 3.00
❑61, Mar 1979 PB (a) ... 3.00
❑62, May 1979 ... 3.00

CAPTAIN MARVEL (2ND SERIES)
MARVEL

❑1, Nov 1989; New Captain Marvel (Monica Rambeau) gets her powers back ... 2.00

CAPTAIN MARVEL (3RD SERIES)
MARVEL

❑1, Feb 1994 ... 2.00

CAPTAIN MARVEL (4TH SERIES)
MARVEL

❑1, Dec 1995; enhanced cardstock cover ... 2.95
❑2, Jan 1996 ... 1.95
❑3, Feb 1996 ... 1.95
❑4, Mar 1996 ... 1.95
❑5, Apr 1996 ... 1.95
❑6, May 1996 ... 1.95

CAPTAIN MARVEL (5TH SERIES)
MARVEL

❑0; Wizard promotional edition ... 3.00
❑1, Jan 2000; PD (w); Regular cover (space background w/rocks) ... 3.00
❑1/A, Jan 2000; PD (w); 1: 10 ratio. Variant cover (Marvel against white background) ... 4.00
❑2, Feb 2000 PD (w); A: Wendigo. A: Moondragon. A: Hulk ... 2.50
❑3, Mar 2000 PD (w); A: Wendigo. A: Moondragon. A: Hulk. A: Drax. D: Lorraine ... 2.50
❑4, Apr 2000 PD (w); A: Moondragon. A: Drax ... 2.50
❑5, May 2000; PD (w); A: Moondragon. A: Drax. in microverse ... 2.50
❑6, Jun 2000 PD (w) ... 2.50
❑7, Jul 2000 ... 2.50
❑8, Aug 2000 ... 2.50
❑9, Sep 2000 PD (w); A: Super Skrull. A: Silver Surfer ... 2.50
❑10, Oct 2000 ... 2.50
❑11, Nov 2000 PD (w); JSn (a); A: Moondragon. A: Silver Surfer. A: Mar-Vell ... 2.50
❑12, Dec 2000 PD (w) ... 2.50
❑13, Jan 2001 PD (w) ... 2.50
❑14, Feb 2001 ... 2.50
❑15, Mar 2001 PD (w) ... 2.50
❑16, Apr 2001 PD (w) ... 2.50
❑17, May 2001 PD (w); JSn (a); A: Thor ... 2.50
❑18, Jun 2001 ... 2.50
❑19, Jul 2001 ... 2.50
❑20, Aug 2001 ... 2.50
❑21, Sep 2001 ... 2.50
❑22, Oct 2001 ... 2.50
❑23, Nov 2001 ... 2.50
❑24, Dec 2001 ... 2.50
❑25, Jan 2002 ... 2.50
❑26, Feb 2002 ... 2.50
❑27, Mar 2002 ... 2.50
❑29, Apr 2002 ... 2.50
❑28, Mar 2002 ... 2.50
❑30, May 2002 ... 2.50
❑31, Jun 2002 ... 2.50
❑32, Jul 2002 ... 2.50
❑33, Aug 2002 ... 2.50
❑34, Sep 2002 ... 2.50
❑35, Oct 2002 ... 2.50

CAPTAIN MARVEL (6TH SERIES)
MARVEL

❑1, Nov 2002 ... 2.25
❑2, Dec 2002 ... 2.25
❑3, Jan 2003 ... 2.25
❑4, Feb 2003 ... 2.25
❑5, Mar 2003 ... 2.99
❑6, Apr 2003 ... 2.99
❑7, May 2003 ... 2.99
❑8, Jun 2003 ... 2.99
❑9, Jul 2003 ... 2.99
❑10, Jul 2003 ... 2.99
❑11, Aug 2003 ... 2.99
❑12, Sep 2003 ... 2.99
❑13, Oct 2003 ... 2.99
❑14, Oct 2003 ... 2.99
❑15, Nov 2003 ... 2.99
❑16, Jan 2004 ... 2.99
❑17, Feb 2004 ... 2.99
❑18, Mar 2004 ... 2.99
❑19, Apr 2004 ... 2.99
❑20, May 2004 ... 2.99
❑21, May 2004 ... 2.99
❑22, Jun 2004 ... 2.99
❑23, Jul 2004 ... 2.99
❑24, Aug 2004 ... 2.99
❑25, Sep 2004 ...

CAPTAIN NAUTICUS & THE OCEAN FORCE
EXPRESS / ENTITY

❑1, May 1994 ... 2.95
❑1/Ltd., Oct 1994; limited promotional edition ... 2.95
❑2, Dec 1994; for The National Maritime Center Authority ... 2.95

CAPTAIN NICE
GOLD KEY

❑1, Nov 1967 ... 35.00

CAPTAIN N: THE GAME MASTER
VALIANT

❑1 ... 1.95
❑2 ... 1.95
❑3 ... 1.95
❑4 ... 1.95
❑5 ... 1.95
❑6 ... 1.95

CAPTAIN OBLIVION
HARRIER

❑1, Aug 1987 ... 1.95

CAPTAIN PARAGON
AC

❑1, Dec 1983 ... 1.50
❑2 ... 1.50
❑3 ... 1.50
❑4 ... 1.50

CAPTAIN PARAGON AND THE SENTINELS OF JUSTICE
AC

❑1 ... 1.75
❑2 ... 1.75
❑3 ... 1.75
❑4 ... 1.75
❑5; O: Captain Paragon. Title changes to Sentinels of Justice ... 1.75
❑6 ... 1.75

CAPTAIN PHIL
STEELDRAGON

❑1 ... 1.50

CAPTAIN PLANET AND THE PLANETEERS
MARVEL

❑1, Oct 1991; TV ... 1.00
❑2, Nov 1991 ... 1.00
❑3, Dec 1991 ... 1.00
❑4, Jan 1992 ... 1.00
❑5, Feb 1992 ... 1.00
❑6, Mar 1992 ... 1.00
❑7, Apr 1992 ... 1.00
❑8, Jun 1992 ... 1.00
❑9, Jul 1992 ... 1.00
❑10, Aug 1992 ... 1.00
❑11, Sep 1992 ... 1.00
❑12, Oct 1992 ... 1.00

CAPTAIN POWER AND THE SOLDIERS OF THE FUTURE
CONTINUITY

❑1, Aug 1988; newsstand cover: Captain Power standing ... 2.00
❑1/Direct ed. 1988; direct-sale cover: Captain Power kneeling ... 2.00
❑2, Jan 1989 ... 2.00

CAPTAIN SALVATION
STREETLIGHT

❑1 ... 1.95

CAPTAIN SATAN
MILLENNIUM

❑1; Flip-book format ... 2.95
❑2; Flip-book format ... 2.95

CAPT. SAVAGE AND HIS LEATHERNECK RAIDERS
MARVEL

❑1, Jan 1968 O: Captain Savage and his Leatherneck Raiders. A: Sgt. Fury ... 15.00
❑2, Mar 1968 O: Hydra. V: Baron Strucker ... 10.00
❑3, May 1968 V: Baron Strucker, Hydra ... 9.00
❑4, Jul 1968 V: Baron Strucker ... 9.00
❑5, Aug 1968 ... 9.00
❑6, Sep 1968 A: Izzy Cohen ... 8.00
❑7, Oct 1968 A: Ben Grimm ... 8.00
❑8, Nov 1968; (becomes Captain Savage) ... 8.00
❑9, Dec 1968; Title changes to Captain Savage (and his Battlefield Raiders) ... 8.00
❑10, Jan 1969 ... 8.00
❑11, Feb 1969; A: Sgt. Fury. D: Baker. Story continued in Sgt. Fury #64 ... 6.00
❑12, Mar 1969 ... 6.00
❑13, Apr 1969 DH (a) ... 6.00
❑14, May 1969 DH (a) ... 6.00
❑15, Jul 1969; DH (a); Title changes to Capt. Savage ... 6.00

Condition price index: Multiply "NM prices" above by: **0.83 for Very Fine/Near Mint**
0.66 for Very Fine • 0.33 for Fine • 0.2 for Very Good • 0.125 for Good

N-MINT

❑16, Sep 1969 DH (a) 6.00
❑17, Nov 1969 .... 6.00
❑18, Jan 1970 .... 6.00
❑19, Mar 1970 .... 6.00

CAPTAIN'S JOLTING TALES
ONE SHOT

❑1, Aug 1991 .... 2.95
❑2, Oct 1991 .... 3.50
❑3; trading card 3.50
❑3/Deluxe, Dec 1992 .... 3.50
❑4 .... 3.50

CAPTAIN STERNN: RUNNING OUT OF TIME
KITCHEN SINK

❑1, Sep 1993, b&w BWr (w); BWr (a) 5.50
❑2, Dec 1993, b&w BWr (w); BWr (a) 5.00
❑3, Mar 1994 BWr (w); BWr (a) 5.00
❑4, May 1994 BWr (w); BWr (a) 5.00
❑5, Sep 1994 BWr (w); BWr (a) 5.00

CAPT. STORM
DC

❑1, Jun 1964 O: Captain Storm 28.00
❑2, Aug 1964 .... 18.00
❑3, Oct 1964 .... 18.00
❑4, Dec 1964 .... 18.00
❑5, Feb 1965 .... 18.00
❑6, Apr 1965 .... 14.00
❑7, Jun 1965 .... 12.00
❑8, Aug 1965 .... 12.00
❑9, Oct 1965 .... 12.00
❑10, Dec 1965 .... 12.00
❑11, Feb 1966 .... 12.00
❑12, Apr 1966 .... 12.00
❑13, Jun 1966 .... 12.00
❑14, Aug 1966 .... 12.00
❑15, Oct 1966 .... 12.00
❑16, Dec 1966 .... 9.00
❑17, Feb 1967 .... 9.00
❑18, Apr 1967 .... 9.00

CAPTAIN TAX TIME
PAUL HAYNES COMICS

❑1 .... 4.00

CAPTAIN THUNDER AND BLUE BOLT
HERO

❑1 1987 .... 1.95
❑2, Oct 1987 .... 1.95
❑3 1988 .... 1.95
❑4 1988 .... 1.95
❑5 1988 .... 1.95
❑6 .... 1.95
❑7 1989 .... 1.95
❑8 .... 1.95
❑9 .... 1.95
❑10 .... 1.95

CAPTAIN THUNDER AND BLUE BOLT (VOL. 2)
HERO

❑1, Aug 1992 .... 3.50
❑2 .... 3.50

CAPTAIN VENTURE AND THE LAND BENEATH THE SEA
GOLD KEY

❑1, Oct 1968 .... 26.00
❑2, Oct 1969 DS (a) 18.00

CAPTAIN VICTORY AND THE GALACTIC RANGERS
PACIFIC

❑1, Nov 1981 .... 1.00
❑2, Jan 1982 .... 1.00
❑3, Mar 1982 .... 1.00
❑4, May 1982; Goozlebobber 1.00
❑5, Jul 1982; Goozlebobber 1.00
❑6, Sep 1982; Goozlebobber 1.00
❑7, Oct 1982; Martius Klavus 1.00
❑8, Dec 1982; Martius Klavus 1.00
❑9, Feb 1983; Martius Klavus 1.00
❑10, Apr 1983 .... 1.00
❑11, Jun 1983 .... 1.00
❑12, Oct 1983 .... 1.00

N-MINT

❑13, Jan 1984; indicia lists title as Captain Victory 1.50
❑Special 1, Oct 1983 .... 1.50

CAPTAIN VICTORY AND THE GALACTIC RANGERS (MINI-SERIES)
JACK KIRBY

❑1, Jul 2000, b&w; no cover price 2.95
❑2, Sep 2000 .... 2.95
❑3, Nov 2000 .... 2.95

CAPTAIN WINGS COMPACT COMICS
AC

❑1 .... 3.95
❑2 .... 3.95

CARAVAN KIDD
DARK HORSE

❑1, Jul 1992 .... 2.50
❑2, Aug 1992 .... 2.50
❑3, Sep 1992 .... 2.50
❑4, Oct 1992 .... 2.50
❑5, Nov 1992 .... 2.50
❑6, Dec 1992 .... 2.50
❑7, Jan 1993 .... 2.50
❑8, Feb 1993 .... 2.50
❑9, Mar 1993 .... 2.50
❑10, Apr 1993 .... 2.50

CARAVAN KIDD PART 2
DARK HORSE

❑1, May 1993 .... 2.50
❑2, Jun 1993 .... 2.50
❑3, Jul 1993 .... 2.95
❑4, Aug 1993 .... 2.50
❑5, Sep 1993 .... 2.50
❑6, Oct 1993 .... 2.50
❑7 .... 2.50
❑8 .... 2.50
❑9, Mar 1994 .... 2.50
❑10, Apr 1994 .... 2.50

CARAVAN KIDD PART 3
DARK HORSE

❑1, May 1994 .... 2.50
❑2, Jun 1994 .... 2.50
❑3, Jul 1994 .... 2.50
❑4, Aug 1994 .... 2.50
❑5, Sep 1994 .... 2.50
❑6, Oct 1994 .... 2.50
❑7, Nov 1994 .... 2.95
❑8, Dec 1994 .... 2.50

CARBON KNIGHT
LUNAR

❑1 .... 2.95
❑2 .... 2.95

CARDCAPTOR SAKURA COMIC
MIXX

❑1, ca. 2000 .... 2.95
❑2, ca. 2000 .... 2.95
❑3 2000 .... 2.95
❑4 2000 .... 2.95
❑5 2000 .... 2.95
❑6 2000 .... 2.95
❑7 2000 .... 2.95
❑8 2000 .... 2.95
❑9 2000 .... 2.95
❑10 2000 .... 2.95
❑11 2000 .... 2.95
❑12 2000 .... 2.95
❑13, ca. 2001 .... 2.95
❑14 2001 .... 2.95
❑15 2001 .... 2.95
❑16 2001 .... 2.95
❑17 2001 .... 2.95
❑18 2001 .... 2.95
❑19 2001 .... 2.95
❑20 2001 .... 2.95
❑21 2001 .... 2.95
❑22 2001 .... 2.95
❑23 2001 .... 2.95
❑24, Jan 2002 .... 2.95
❑25, Feb 2002 .... 2.95
❑26, Mar 2002 .... 2.95

Captain Marvel's first encounter with the explosive super-villain Nitro would eventually lead to the hero's death.

© 1974 Marvel Comics.

N-MINT

❑27, Apr 2002 .... 2.95
❑28, May 2002 .... 2.99
❑29, Jun 2002 .... 2.99
❑30, Jul 2002 .... 2.99
❑31, Aug 2002 .... 2.99
❑32, Sep 2002 .... 2.99
❑33, Oct 2002 .... 2.99
❑34, Nov 2002 .... 2.99

CARDCAPTOR SAKURA: MASTER OF THE CLOW
TOKYOPOP

❑1, Aug 2002, b&w; printed in Japanese format 9.99

CARE BEARS
MARVEL / STAR

❑1, Nov 1985 .... 1.00
❑2, Jan 1986 .... 1.00
❑3, Mar 1986 .... 1.00
❑4, May 1986 .... 1.00
❑5, Jul 1986 .... 1.00
❑6, Sep 1986 .... 1.00
❑7, Nov 1986 .... 1.00
❑8, Jan 1987 .... 1.00
❑9, Mar 1987 .... 1.00
❑10, May 1987 .... 1.00
❑11, Jul 1987 .... 1.00
❑12, Sep 1987 .... 1.00
❑13, Nov 1987 A: Madballs 1.00
❑14, Jan 1988 .... 1.00
❑15, Mar 1988 .... 1.00
❑16, May 1988 .... 1.00
❑17, Jul 1988 .... 1.00
❑18, Sep 1988 .... 1.00
❑19, Nov 1988 .... 1.00
❑20, Jan 1989 .... 1.00

CAR 54 WHERE ARE YOU?
DELL

❑2, Aug 1962 .... 75.00
❑3, Oct 1962 .... 45.00
❑4, Dec 1962 .... 40.00
❑5, Mar 1963 .... 40.00
❑6, Jun 1963 .... 35.00
❑7, Sep 1963 .... 35.00

CARL AND LARRY CHRISTMAS SPECIAL
COMICS INTERVIEW

❑1, b&w 2.25

CARMEN
NBM

❑1 .... 10.95

CARMILLA
AIRCEL

❑1, Feb 1991, b&w; outer paper wrapper to cover nude cover 2.50
❑2, Mar 1991, b&w 2.50
❑3, Apr 1991, b&w 2.50
❑4, b&w 2.50
❑5, b&w 2.50
❑6, b&w 2.50

CARNAGE
ETERNITY

❑1 .... 1.95

CARNAGE: IT'S A WONDERFUL LIFE
MARVEL

❑1, Oct 1996 .... 1.95

N-MINT

CARNAGE: MINDBOMB
MARVEL

❑1, Feb 1996; foil cover 2.95

CARNAL COMICS PRESENTS DEMI'S WILD KINGDOM ADVENTURE
REVISIONARY

❑1, Sep 1999, b&w; no cover price ... 3.50

CARNAL COMICS PRESENTS GINGER LYNN IS TORN
REVISIONARY

❑1, Sep 1999, b&w; Drawn cover 3.50
❑1/A, Sep 1999, b&w; adult 3.50

CARNEYS, THE
ARCHIE

❑1, Sum 1994 .... 2.00

CARNOSAUR CARNAGE
ATOMEKA

❑1 .... 4.95

CARTOON CARTOONS
DC

❑1, Mar 2001 .... 2.25
❑2, Apr 2001 .... 2.00
❑3, May 2001 .... 2.00
❑4, Jun 2001 .... 2.00
❑5, Jul 2001 .... 2.00
❑6, Aug 2001 .... 2.00
❑7, Sep 2001 .... 2.00
❑8, Jan 2002 .... 2.00
❑9, Mar 2002 .... 2.00
❑10, May 2002 .... 2.00
❑11, Jun 2002 .... 2.00
❑12, Sep 2002 .... 2.00
❑13, Nov 2002 .... 2.25
❑14, Jan 2003 .... 2.25
❑15, Mar 2003 .... 2.25
❑16, May 2003 .... 2.25
❑17, Jun 2003 .... 2.25
❑18, Jul 2003 .... 2.25
❑19, Jul 2003 .... 2.25
❑20, Aug 2003 .... 2.25
❑21, Sep 2003 .... 2.25
❑22, Oct 2003 .... 2.25
❑23, Nov 2003 .... 2.25
❑24, Dec 2003 .... 2.25
❑25, Jan 2004 .... 2.25
❑26, Feb 2004 .... 2.25
❑27, Apr 2004 .... 2.25
❑28, May 2004 .... 2.25
❑29, Jun 2005 .... 2.25
❑30, Jul 2004 .... 2.25
❑31, Aug 2004 .... 2.25
❑32, Sep 2004 ....

CARTOON HISTORY OF THE UNIVERSE, THE
RIP OFF

❑1, b&w; cardstock cover 4.50
❑2, b&w; cardstock cover 3.50
❑3, b&w; cardstock cover 3.50
❑4, b&w; cardstock cover 3.50
❑5, b&w; cardstock cover 3.50
❑6, b&w; cardstock cover 2.50
❑7, b&w; cardstock cover 2.50
❑8, b&w 2.95
❑9, b&w 2.95

CARTOONIST, THE
SIRIUS / DOG STAR

❑1, b&w; collects strips 2.95

CARTOON NETWORK
DC

❑1; Giveaway from DC Comics to promote comics; Reprints stories from Cartoon Networks Presents #6 ...... 1.00

CARTOON NETWORK CHRISTMAS SPECTACULAR
ARCHIE

❑1 .... 2.00

N-MINT

CARTOON NETWORK PRESENTS
DC

❑1, Aug 1997; Dexter's Laboratory, Top Cat 2.00
❑2, Sep 1997; Space Ghost, Yogi Bear 2.00
❑3, Oct 1997; Hanna-Barbera crossover with Mr. Peebles, Ranger Smith, Officer Dibble, Mr. Twiddle, and Colonel Fusby; Wally Gator back-up; Cartoon All-Stars 2.00
❑4, Nov 1997; Dial M for Monkey 2.00
❑5, Dec 1997; A: Birdman, Herculoids. Toonami 2.00
❑6, Jan 1998; Cow and Chicken 2.00
❑7, Feb 1998; Wacky Races 2.00
❑8, Mar 1998; Fighting Monkies; Johnny Bravo 2.00
❑9, Apr 1998; A: Herculoids, Birdman. Toonami 2.00
❑10, May 1998; Cow & Chicken 2.00
❑11, Jun 1998; Wacky Races 2.00
❑12, Aug 1998; Cartoon All-Stars; Peter Potamus 2.00
❑13, Sep 1998; Toonami, Birdman, Herculoids 2.00
❑14, Oct 1998; Cow and Chicken 2.00
❑15, Nov 1998; Wacky Races 1.99
❑16, Dec 1998; Cartoon All-Stars; Top Cat 1.99
❑17, Jan 1999; Toonami, Herculoids, Galaxy Trio; Toonami 1.99
❑18, Feb 1999; Cartoon All-Stars; Fun-tastic Treasure Hunt 1.99
❑19, Mar 1999; Cow and Chicken 1.99
❑20, Apr 1999; Cartoon All-Stars; Hong Kong Phooey, Atom Ant, Secret Squirrel 1.99
❑21, May 1999; Toonami, Blue Falcon and Dyno-Mutt, Galtar and the Golden Lance; Toonami 1.99
❑22, Jun 1999; A: Yogi Bear. A: Quick Draw McGraw. A: Magilla Gorilla. A: Boo Boo Bear. A: El Kabonng. A: Ranger Jones. A: Ranger Smith. Cartoon All-Stars; Baba Looey 1.99
❑23, Jul 1999; Jabberjaw, Speed Buggy, Captain Caveman; Jabberjaw; Speed Buggy; Captain Caveman 1.99
❑24, Aug 1999; Scrappy-Doo 1.99

CARTOON NETWORK PRESENTS SPACE GHOST
ARCHIE

❑1, Mar 1997 .... 2.00

CARTOON NETWORK STARRING
DC

❑1, Sep 1999; The Powerpuff Girls ... 3.00
❑2, Oct 1999 1: Johnny Bravo (in comics) 3.00
❑3, Nov 1999 .... 2.00
❑4, Dec 1999; Space Ghost 2.00
❑5, Jan 2000 .... 2.00
❑6, Feb 2000 .... 2.00
❑7, Mar 2000 .... 2.00
❑8, Apr 2000 .... 2.00
❑9, May 2000; Space Ghost 2.00
❑10, Jun 2000 .... 2.00
❑11, Jul 2000 .... 2.00
❑12, Aug 2000 .... 2.00
❑13, Sep 2000 .... 2.00
❑14, Oct 2000; Johnny Bravo 2.00
❑15, Nov 2000; Space Ghost 2.00
❑16, Dec 2000; Cow and Chicken 2.00
❑17, Jan 2001; Johnny Bravo 2.00
❑18, Feb 2001; Space Ghost 2.00

CARTOON QUARTERLY
GLADSTONE

❑1; Mickey Mouse 5.00

CARTOON TALES (DISNEY'S...)
DISNEY

❑1, ca. 1992 .... 2.95
❑2, ca. 1992; 21809; Darkwing Duck 2.95
❑3, ca. 1992; 21810; Tale Spin: Surprise in the Skies; Reprints stories from Disney's Tale Spin #4, 6 .... 2.95
❑4; Beauty and the Beast 2.95

N-MINT

CARTUNE LAND
MAGIC CARPET

❑1, b&w 1.50
❑2, Jul 1987, b&w 1.50

CARVERS
IMAGE

❑1, Oct 1998 .... 2.95
❑2, Nov 1998 .... 2.95
❑3, Dec 1998 .... 2.95

CAR WARRIORS
MARVEL / EPIC

❑1, Jun 1991 .... 2.25
❑2, Jul 1991 .... 2.25
❑3, Aug 1991 .... 2.25
❑4, Sep 1991 .... 2.25

CASA HOWHARD
NBM

❑1 .... 10.95

CASANOVA
AIRCEL

❑1, b&w 2.50
❑2, b&w 2.50
❑3, b&w 2.50
❑4, b&w 2.50
❑5, b&w 2.50
❑6, b&w 2.50
❑7, b&w 2.50
❑8, b&w 2.50
❑9, Nov 1991, b&w 2.95
❑10, b&w 2.95

CASEFILES: SAM & TWITCH
IMAGE

❑1, Jun 2003 .... 2.50
❑2, Aug 2003 .... 2.50
❑3, Sep 2003 .... 2.50
❑4, Oct 2003 .... 2.50
❑5, Nov 2003 .... 2.50
❑6, Dec 2003 .... 2.50
❑7, Mar 2004 .... 2.50
❑8, Apr 2004 .... 2.50

CASE MORGAN, GUMSHOE PRIVATE EYE
FORBIDDEN FRUIT

❑1, b&w 2.95
❑2, b&w 2.95
❑3, b&w 2.95
❑4, b&w 2.95
❑5, b&w 2.95
❑6, b&w 2.95
❑7, b&w 2.95
❑8, b&w 2.95
❑9, b&w 2.95
❑10, b&w 2.95
❑11, b&w 3.50

CASE OF BLIND FEAR, A
ETERNITY

❑1, Jan 1989, b&w; Sherlock Holmes, Invisible Man 1.95
❑2, Apr 1989, b&w; Sherlock Holmes, Invisible Man 1.95
❑3, b&w; Sherlock Holmes, Invisible Man 1.95
❑4, b&w; Sherlock Holmes, Invisible Man 1.95

CASES OF SHERLOCK HOLMES
RENEGADE

❑1, May 1986, b&w; Renegade publishes 2.00
❑2, Jul 1986, b&w 2.00
❑3, Sep 1986 .... 2.00
❑4, Nov 1986 .... 2.00
❑5, Jan 1987 .... 2.00
❑6, Mar 1987 .... 2.00
❑7, May 1987 .... 2.00
❑8, Jul 1987 .... 2.00
❑9, Sep 1987 .... 2.00
❑10, Nov 1987 .... 2.00
❑11, Jan 1988 .... 2.00
❑12, Mar 1988 .... 2.00
❑13, May 1988 .... 2.00

N-MINT

❑14, Jul 1988 .... 2.00
❑15, Sep 1988 .... 2.00
❑16, Nov 1988, b&w; Northstar begins as publisher 2.25
❑17, Jan 1989, b&w 2.25
❑18, Mar 1989, b&w 2.25
❑19, May 1989 .... 2.25
❑20, Jul 1989 .... 2.25
❑21, Sep 1989 .... 2.25
❑22, Nov 1989 .... 2.25
❑23, Jan 1990 .... 2.25
❑24, Mar 1990 .... 2.25

CASEY JONES & RAPHAEL
MIRAGE

❑1, Oct 1994 .... 2.75
❑2, Nov 1994; Exists? 2.75
❑3, Dec 1994; Exists? 2.75
❑4, Jan 1995; Exists? 2.75
❑5, Feb 1995; Exists? 2.75

CASEY JONES: NORTH BY DOWNEAST
MIRAGE

❑1, May 1994 .... 2.75
❑2, Jul 1994 .... 2.75

CASPER ADVENTURE DIGEST
HARVEY

❑1, Oct 1992 .... 2.00
❑2, Dec 1992 .... 1.75
❑3, Jan 1993 .... 1.75
❑4, Apr 1993 .... 1.75
❑5, Jul 1993 .... 1.75
❑6, Oct 1993 .... 1.75
❑7 .... 1.75
❑8 .... 1.75

CASPER AND FRIENDS
HARVEY

❑1, ca. 1991 .... 1.50
❑2, ca. 1991 .... 1.50
❑3, ca. 1992 .... 1.50
❑4, ca. 1992 .... 1.50
❑5, ca. 1992 .... 1.50

CASPER AND FRIENDS MAGAZINE
MARVEL

❑1, Mar 1997; magazine 3.99
❑2, May 1997; magazine 3.99
❑3, Jul 1997; magazine 3.99

CASPER AND THE GHOSTLY TRIO
HARVEY

❑1, Nov 1972 .... 20.00
❑2, Jan 1973 .... 15.00
❑3, Mar 1973 .... 15.00
❑4, May 1973 .... 15.00
❑5, Jul 1973 .... 12.00
❑6, Sep 1973 .... 12.00
❑7, Nov 1973 .... 12.00
❑8, Aug 1990 .... 1.50
❑9, Oct 1990 .... 1.50
❑10, Dec 1990 .... 1.50

CASPER & WENDY
HARVEY

❑1, Sep 1972; Alice in Wonderland 9.00
❑2, Nov 1972 .... 5.00
❑3, Jan 1973 .... 4.00
❑4, Mar 1973 .... 4.00
❑5, May 1973 .... 4.00
❑6, Jul 1973 .... 3.00
❑7, Sep 1973 .... 3.00
❑8, Nov 1973 .... 3.00

CASPER DIGEST MAGAZINE
HARVEY

❑1 .... 2.50
❑2 .... 2.00
❑3 .... 2.00
❑4 .... 2.00
❑9, Sep 1989 .... 2.00
❑10, Feb 1990 .... 2.00
❑11, May 1990 .... 2.00
❑12, Jul 1990 .... 2.00
❑13, Aug 1990 .... 2.00

N-MINT

CASPER DIGEST MAGAZINE (VOL. 2)
HARVEY

❑1, Sep 1991 .... 2.00
❑2, Jan 1992 .... 1.75
❑3, Apr 1992 .... 1.75
❑4, Jul 1992; indicia says Casper Digest 1.75
❑5, Nov 1992 .... 1.75
❑6, Feb 1993 .... 1.75
❑7, May 1993 .... 1.75
❑8, Aug 1993 .... 1.75
❑9, Nov 1993 .... 1.75
❑10, Feb 1994 .... 1.75
❑11, May 1994 .... 1.75
❑12, Jul 1994 .... 1.75
❑13, Aug 1994 .... 1.75
❑14, Nov 1994 .... 1.75

CASPER ENCHANTED TALES DIGEST
HARVEY

❑1, May 1992 .... 2.00
❑2, Sep 1992 .... 1.75
❑3 1993 .... 1.75
❑4, Jun 1993 .... 1.75
❑5, Sep 1993 .... 1.75
❑6, Dec 1993 .... 1.75
❑7 1994 .... 1.75
❑8, Jun 1994 .... 1.75
❑9, Aug 1994 .... 1.75
❑10, Oct 1994 .... 1.75

CASPER GHOSTLAND
HARVEY

❑1, ca. 1992 .... 1.50

CASPER GIANT SIZE
HARVEY

❑1 .... 2.25
❑2 .... 2.25
❑3 .... 2.25
❑4 .... 2.25

CASPER IN 3-D
BLACKTHORNE

❑1, Win 1988 .... 2.50

CASPER SPACE SHIP
HARVEY

❑1, Aug 1972 .... 16.00
❑2, Oct 1972 .... 13.00
❑3, Dec 1972 .... 13.00
❑4, Feb 1973 .... 10.00
❑5, Apr 1973 .... 10.00

CASPER THE FRIENDLY GHOST (2ND SERIES)
HARVEY

❑1, Mar 1991 .... 2.00
❑2, May 1991 .... 1.50
❑3, Jul 1991 .... 1.50
❑4, Sep 1991 .... 1.50
❑5, Nov 1991 .... 1.50
❑6, Jan 1992 .... 1.50
❑7, Mar 1992 .... 1.50
❑8 1992 .... 1.50
❑9 1992 .... 1.50
❑10 1992 .... 1.50
❑11, Dec 1992 .... 1.50
❑12 1993 .... 1.50
❑13 1993 .... 1.50
❑14 1993 .... 1.50
❑15, Oct 1993 .... 1.50
❑16, Nov 1993 .... 1.50
❑17, Dec 1993 .... 1.50
❑18, Jan 1994 .... 1.50
❑19, Feb 1994 .... 1.50
❑20, Mar 1994 .... 1.50
❑21, Apr 1994 .... 1.50
❑22, May 1994 .... 1.50
❑23, Jun 1994 .... 1.50
❑24, Jul 1994 .... 1.50
❑25, Aug 1994 .... 1.50
❑26, Sep 1994 .... 1.50
❑27, Oct 1994 .... 1.50
❑28, Nov 1994 .... 1.50
❑Giant Size 1 .... 2.25

Hanna-Barbera's animal keepers, including Mr. Twiddle, Ranger Smith, Mr. Peebles, Officer Dibble, and Colonel Fusby, met for the first time in *Cartoon Network Presents* #3.

© 1997 DC Comics and Hanna-Barbera Productions.

N-MINT

❑Giant Size 2 .... 2.25
❑Giant Size 3 .... 2.25
❑Giant Size 4 .... 2.25

CASPER THE FRIENDLY GHOST BIG BOOK
HARVEY

❑1 .... 2.00
❑2 .... 2.00
❑3 .... 2.00

CASTLE WAITING
OLIO

❑1, b&w 4.50
❑1-2 .... 3.50
❑1-3 .... 3.50
❑2, b&w 3.00
❑2-2 .... 3.00
❑3, ca. 1997, b&w; Akiko pin-up 3.00
❑3-2 .... 3.00
❑4, b&w; Scott Roberts pin-up 3.00
❑4-2 .... 3.00
❑5, Mar 1998, b&w 3.00
❑5-2 .... 3.00
❑6, May 1998, b&w; profiles of 12 Witches begins 3.00
❑7, Oct 1998, b&w 3.00
❑8, Jan 1999, b&w; Hiatus issue 3.00
❑Ashcan 1; Limited ashcan edition given away (20 printed) 10.00

CASTLE WAITING (CARTOON BOOKS)
CARTOON BOOKS

❑1, Jul 2000, b&w; follows events of Olio series 3.00
❑2, Oct 2000 .... 3.00
❑3, Dec 2000 .... 3.00
❑4, Mar 2001 .... 3.00

CASUAL HEROES
IMAGE

❑1, Apr 1996 .... 2.25

CAT, THE
MARVEL

❑1, Nov 1972; WW (a); O: Cat. 1: Cat. Cat later becomes Tigra 22.00
❑2, Jan 1973 .... 15.00
❑3, Apr 1973 A: Contains letter by Frank Miller (1st Miller 12.00
❑4, Jun 1973 .... 10.00

CAT, THE (AIRCEL)
AIRCEL

❑1, b&w 2.50
❑2, b&w 2.50

CATALYST: AGENTS OF CHANGE
DARK HORSE

❑1, Feb 1994; cardstock cover with foil logo 2.00
❑2, Mar 1994 .... 2.00
❑3, Apr 1994 .... 2.00
❑4, May 1994 .... 2.00
❑5 .... 2.00
❑6, Aug 1994 .... 2.00
❑7, Sep 1994 .... 2.00

CAT & MOUSE
EF GRAPHICS

❑1, Jan 1989, b&w and color; part color 2.00
❑1-2 .... 1.75

N-MINT

CAT & MOUSE (AIRCEL)
Aircel

- ❑1, Mar 1990, b&w 2.25
- ❑2, Apr 1990, b&w 2.25
- ❑3, May 1990, b&w 2.25
- ❑4, Jun 1990, b&w 2.25
- ❑5, Jul 1990, b&w 2.25
- ❑6, Aug 1990, b&w 2.25
- ❑7, Sep 1990, b&w 2.25
- ❑8, Oct 1990, b&w 2.25
- ❑9, Nov 1990, b&w 2.25
- ❑10, Dec 1990, b&w 2.25
- ❑11, Jan 1991, b&w 2.25
- ❑12, Feb 1991, b&w 2.25
- ❑13, Mar 1991, b&w 2.25
- ❑14, Apr 1991, b&w 2.25
- ❑15, May 1991, b&w 2.25
- ❑16, Jun 1991, b&w 2.25
- ❑17, Aug 1991, b&w 2.25
- ❑18, Sep 1991, b&w 2.25

CAT CLAW
Eternity

- ❑1, Sep 1990, b&w 2.50
- ❑1-2 2.50
- ❑2, Nov 1990 2.50
- ❑3, Jan 1991 2.50
- ❑4, Feb 1991 2.50
- ❑5, Apr 1991 2.50
- ❑6, Jun 1991 2.50
- ❑7 2.50
- ❑8 2.50
- ❑9 2.50

CATFIGHT
Insomnia

- ❑1, Mar 1995, b&w 2.75
- ❑1/Gold; Gold edition 3.00

CATFIGHT: DREAM INTO ACTION
Lightning

- ❑1, Mar 1996; Creed Guest Star 2.75

CATFIGHT: DREAM WARRIOR
Lightning

- ❑1 2.75

CATFIGHT: ESCAPE FROM LIMBO
Lightning

- ❑1, Nov 1996 2.75

CATFIGHT: SWEET REVENGE
Lightning

- ❑1, Apr 1997, b&w; alternate cover B 2.95

CATHARSIS
Being

- ❑1, Oct 1994 2.50

CATNIP
Side Show

- ❑1 2.95

CATSEYE
Manic

- ❑1, Dec 1998 2.50
- ❑2 1999 2.50
- ❑3 1999 2.50
- ❑4 1999 2.50
- ❑5 1999 2.50
- ❑6 1999 2.50
- ❑7 1999 2.50
- ❑8 1999 2.50

CATSEYE AGENCY
Rip Off

- ❑1, Sep 1992, b&w 2.50
- ❑2, Oct 1992, b&w 2.50

CAT, T.H.E. (DELL)
Dell

- ❑1, ca. 1967 18.00
- ❑2, ca. 1967 12.00
- ❑3, ca. 1967 12.00
- ❑4, Oct 1967 12.00

CATTLE BRAIN
Itchy Eyeball

- ❑1, b&w 2.75
- ❑2, b&w 2.75
- ❑3, b&w 2.75

CATWOMAN (1ST SERIES)
DC

- ❑1, Feb 1989 O: Catwoman (new origin) 3.00
- ❑2, Mar 1989 2.50
- ❑3, Apr 1989 2.00
- ❑4, May 1989 2.00

CATWOMAN (2ND SERIES)
DC

- ❑0, Oct 1994 O: Catwoman 2.00
- ❑1, Aug 1993 O: Catwoman 4.00
- ❑2, Sep 1993 3.00
- ❑3, Oct 1993 2.50
- ❑4, Nov 1993 2.50
- ❑5, Dec 1993 2.50
- ❑6, Jan 1994 2.50
- ❑7, Feb 1994 2.50
- ❑8, Mar 1994 2.50
- ❑9, Apr 1994 2.50
- ❑10, May 1994 2.50
- ❑11, Jun 1994 2.00
- ❑12, Jul 1994 2.00
- ❑13, Aug 1994 2.00
- ❑14, Sep 1994; Zero Hour 2.00
- ❑15, Nov 1994 2.00
- ❑16, Dec 1994 2.00
- ❑17, Jan 1995 2.00
- ❑18, Feb 1995 2.00
- ❑19, Mar 1995 2.00
- ❑20, Apr 1995 2.00
- ❑21, May 1995 2.00
- ❑22, Jul 1995 2.00
- ❑23, Aug 1995 2.00
- ❑24, Sep 1995 2.00
- ❑25, Oct 1995; Giant-size A: Psyba-Rats. A: Robin 2.00
- ❑26, Nov 1995 2.00
- ❑27, Dec 1995 2.00
- ❑28, Jan 1996 2.00
- ❑29, Feb 1996 2.00
- ❑30, Mar 1996 2.00
- ❑31, Mar 1996 2.00
- ❑32, Apr 1996 2.00
- ❑33, May 1996 2.00
- ❑34, Jun 1996 2.00
- ❑35, Jul 1996 2.00
- ❑36, Aug 1996 2.00
- ❑37, Sep 1996 2.00
- ❑38, Oct 1996 2.00
- ❑39, Nov 1996 2.00
- ❑40, Dec 1996 V: Two-Face, Penguin 2.00
- ❑41, Jan 1997 2.00
- ❑42, Feb 1997 1: Cybercat 2.00
- ❑43, Mar 1997 A: She-Cat 2.00
- ❑44, Apr 1997 2.00
- ❑45, May 1997 2.00
- ❑46, Jun 1997 V: Two-Face 2.00
- ❑47, Jul 1997 V: Two-Face 2.00
- ❑48, Aug 1997 2.00
- ❑49, Sep 1997 2.00
- ❑50, Oct 1997 2.00
- ❑50/A, Oct 1997; yellow logo 2.95
- ❑50/B, Oct 1997; purple logo 2.95
- ❑51, Nov 1997 V: Huntress 2.00
- ❑52, Dec 1997; Face cover 2.00
- ❑53, Jan 1998 2.00
- ❑54, Feb 1998; DGry (w); self-contained story; 1st Devin Grayson script 2.00
- ❑55, Mar 1998; DGry (w); self-contained story 2.00
- ❑56, Apr 1998; continues in Robin #52 2.00
- ❑57, May 1998; V: Poison Ivy. continues in Batman: Arkham Asylum - Tales of Madness #1 2.00
- ❑58, Jun 1998 V: Scarecrow 2.00
- ❑59, Jul 1998 V: Scarecrow 2.00
- ❑60, Aug 1998 V: Scarecrow 2.00
- ❑61, Sep 1998 2.00
- ❑62, Oct 1998 A: Nemesis 2.00
- ❑63, Dec 1998 V: Joker 2.00
- ❑64, Jan 1999 DGry (w); A: Joker. A: Batman. V: Joker 2.00
- ❑65, Feb 1999 DGry (w); A: Scarecrow. A: Joker. A: Batman. V: Joker 2.00
- ❑66, Mar 1999 DGry (w) 2.00
- ❑67, Apr 1999 DGry (w) 2.00
- ❑68, May 1999; DGry (w); V: Body Doubles. Lady Vic 2.00
- ❑69, Jun 1999 DGry (w); A: Trickster 2.00
- ❑70, Jul 1999 DGry (w) 2.00
- ❑71, Aug 1999 DGry (w) 2.00
- ❑72, Sep 1999; DGry (w); No Man's Land 2.00
- ❑73, Oct 1999; No Man's Land 2.00
- ❑74, Nov 1999; No Man's Land 2.00
- ❑75, Dec 1999; No Man's Land 2.00
- ❑76, Jan 2000; No Man's Land 2.00
- ❑77, Feb 2000 2.00
- ❑78, Mar 2000 2.00
- ❑79, Apr 2000 2.00
- ❑80, May 2000 2.00
- ❑81, Jun 2000 2.00
- ❑82, Jul 2000 2.00
- ❑83, Aug 2000 2.25
- ❑84, Sep 2000 2.25
- ❑85, Oct 2000 2.25
- ❑86, Nov 2000 2.25
- ❑87, Dec 2000 2.25
- ❑88, Jan 2001 2.25
- ❑89, Feb 2001 2.25
- ❑90, Mar 2001 2.25
- ❑91, Apr 2001 2.25
- ❑92, May 2001 2.25
- ❑93, Jun 2001 2.25
- ❑94, Jul 2001 2.25
- ❑1000000, Nov 1998 3.00
- ❑Annual 1, ca. 1994; Elseworlds 3.50
- ❑Annual 2, ca. 1995; Year One 3.95
- ❑Annual 3, ca. 1996; Legends of the Dead Earth 2.95
- ❑Annual 4, ca. 1997; Pulp Heroes 3.95

CATWOMAN (3RD SERIES)
DC

- ❑1, Jan 2002 3.00
- ❑2, Feb 2002 2.50
- ❑3, Mar 2002 2.50
- ❑4, Apr 2002 2.50
- ❑5, May 2002 2.50
- ❑6, Jun 2002 2.50
- ❑7, Jul 2002 2.50
- ❑8, Aug 2002 2.50
- ❑9, Sep 2002 2.50
- ❑10, Oct 2002 2.50
- ❑11, Nov 2002 2.50
- ❑12, Dec 2002 2.50
- ❑13, Jan 2003 2.50
- ❑14, Feb 2003 2.50
- ❑15, Mar 2003 2.50
- ❑16, Apr 2003 2.50
- ❑17, May 2003 2.50
- ❑18, Jun 2003 2.50
- ❑19, Jul 2003 2.50
- ❑20, Aug 2003 2.50
- ❑21, Sep 2003 2.50
- ❑22, Oct 2003 2.50
- ❑23, Nov 2003 2.50
- ❑24, Dec 2003 2.50
- ❑25, Jan 2004 2.50
- ❑26, Feb 2004 2.50
- ❑27, Mar 2004 2.50
- ❑28, Apr 2004 PG (c); PG (a) 2.50
- ❑29, May 2004 2.50
- ❑30, Jun 2004 2.50
- ❑31, Jul 2004 2.50
- ❑32, Aug 2004 2.50
- ❑33, Jul 2004

CATWOMAN: CROOKED LITTLE TOWN
DC

- ❑1, ca. 2003 14.95

Condition price index: Multiply "NM prices" above by: **0.83 for Very Fine/Near Mint**
0.66 for Very Fine • 0.33 for Fine • 0.2 for Very Good • 0.125 for Good

N-MINT

CATWOMAN: GUARDIAN OF GOTHAM
DC

❑1, ca. 1999 .... 5.95
❑2, ca. 1999 .... 5.95

CATWOMAN PLUS
DC

❑1, Nov 1997; continues in Robin Plus #2 .... 2.95

CATWOMAN SECRET FILES AND ORIGINS
DC

❑1, Nov 2002 .... 4.95

CATWOMAN: SELINA'S BIG SCORE
DC

❑1 .... 24.95
❑1/Variant, ca. 2003 .... 17.95

CATWOMAN/VAMPIRELLA: THE FURIES
DC

❑1, Feb 1997, prestige format; crossover with Harris 4.95

CATWOMAN/WILDCAT
DC

❑1, Aug 1998 .... 2.50
❑2, Sep 1998 .... 2.50
❑3, Oct 1998 .... 2.50
❑4, Nov 1998 .... 2.50

CAVE BANG
FANTAGRAPHICS / EROS

❑1, Oct 1996 .... 2.95
❑2, Jul 2000 .... 2.95

CAVE GIRL
AC

❑1 .... 2.95

CAVE KIDS
GOLD KEY

❑1, Feb 1963 .... 35.00
❑2, ca. 1963 .... 18.00
❑3, Nov 1963 .... 15.00
❑4, Mar 1964 .... 15.00
❑5, Jun 1964 .... 15.00
❑6, Sep 1964 .... 12.00
❑7, Dec 1964 .... 12.00
❑8, Mar 1965 .... 12.00
❑9, Jun 1965 .... 12.00
❑10, Sep 1965 .... 12.00
❑11, Dec 1965 .... 12.00
❑12, Mar 1966 .... 12.00
❑13, Jun 1966 .... 9.00
❑14, Sep 1966 .... 9.00
❑15, Dec 1966 .... 9.00
❑16, Mar 1967 .... 9.00

CAVEMAN
CAVEMAN

❑1, Apr 1998 .... 3.50
❑2, Jun 1998 .... 3.50
❑3, Aug 1998 .... 3.50
❑4, Oct 1998 .... 3.50
❑GN 1, b&w; graphic novel 9.95

CAVEWOMAN
BASEMENT

❑1, Jan 1994, b&w 26.00
❑2, ca. 1994, b&w 20.00
❑3, Jul 1994, b&w 15.00
❑4, Nov 1994, b&w 12.00
❑5, b&w 10.00
❑6, b&w 10.00

CAVEWOMAN COLOR SPECIAL
AVATAR

❑1 .... 3.50

CAVEWOMAN: MISSING LINK
BASEMENT

❑1, Sep 1997, b&w 2.95
❑2, Nov 1997, b&w 2.95

CAVEWOMAN: ODYSSEY
CALIBER

❑1 ....

N-MINT

CAVEWOMAN ONE-SHOT
BASEMENT

❑1, Apr 2001, Klyde & Meriem 4.00

CAVEWOMAN: PANGAEAN SEA
AVATAR

❑Ashcan 1, Oct 1999 .... 4.95

CAVEWOMAN: RAIN
BASEMENT

❑1, ca. 1996 .... 3.00
❑1-2 .... 2.95
❑1-3 .... 2.95
❑2 .... 3.50
❑2-2 .... 2.95
❑2-3 .... 2.95
❑3, ca. 1997 .... 3.50
❑3-2 .... 2.95
❑4 .... 3.00
❑4-2 .... 2.95
❑5, Nov 1996 .... 3.00
❑5-2 .... 2.95
❑6, Feb 1997 .... 3.00
❑7, May 1997 .... 3.00
❑8, Sep 1997 .... 3.00

CAVEWOMAN: RAPTOR
BASEMENT

❑1, Jul 2002 .... 3.25

CECIL KUNKLE (2ND SERIES)
DARKLINE

❑1 .... 3.50
❑2 .... 3.50
❑3, b&w; Santa cover 2.00

CECIL KUNKLE (CHARLES A. WAGNER'S...)
RENEGADE

❑1, May 1986, b&w 2.00

CELESTIAL MECHANICS: THE ADVENTURES OF WIDGET WILHELMINA JONES
INNOVATION

❑1, Dec 1990, b&w 2.25
❑2, Feb 1991, b&w 2.25
❑3, b&w 2.25

CELESTINE
IMAGE

❑1, May 1996 .... 2.50
❑1/Variant, May 1996; alternate cover 2.50
❑2, Jun 1996 .... 2.50

CELL
ANTARCTIC

❑1, Sep 1996, b&w 2.95
❑2, Nov 1996, b&w 2.95
❑3, Jan 1997, b&w 2.95

CEMENT SHOOZ
HORSE FEATHERS

❑1, Sep 1991 .... 2.50

CENOTAPH
NORTHSTAR

❑1 .... 3.95

CENTRIFUGAL BUMBLE-PUPPY
FANTAGRAPHICS

❑1, b&w 2.25
❑2, b&w 2.25
❑3, b&w 2.25
❑4, b&w 2.25
❑5, b&w 2.25
❑6, b&w 2.25
❑7 .... 2.25
❑8 .... 2.50

CENTURIONS
DC

❑1, Jun 1987 O: Centurions 1.00
❑2, Jul 1987 DH (a); O: Centurions 1.00
❑3, Aug 1987 .... 1.00
❑4, Sep 1987 .... 1.00

CENTURY: DISTANT SONS
MARVEL

❑1, Feb 1996 .... 2.95

A portion of *Cerebus*' third major storyline, in which the barbarian aardvark abused his papal powers, was reprinted in *Cerebus: Church & State*.

© 1992 Dave Sim and Gerhard (Aardvark-Vanaheim).

N-MINT

CEREAL KILLINGS
FANTAGRAPHICS

❑1, Mar 1992, b&w 2.50
❑2, b&w 2.50
❑3, b&w 2.50
❑4, b&w 2.50
❑5, b&w 2.50

CEREBUS BI-WEEKLY
AARDVARK-VANAHEIM

❑1, Dec 1988, b&w A: Reprints Cerebus the Aardvark #1 .... 1.50
❑2, Dec 1988, b&w; Reprints Cerebus the Aardvark #2 .... 1.50
❑3, Dec 1988, b&w; Reprints Cerebus the Aardvark #3 .... 1.50
❑4, Jan 1989, b&w; Reprints Cerebus the Aardvark #4 .... 1.50
❑5, Jan 1989, b&w; Reprints Cerebus the Aardvark #5 .... 1.50
❑6, Feb 1989, b&w; Reprints Cerebus the Aardvark #6 .... 1.50
❑7, Feb 1989, b&w; Reprints Cerebus the Aardvark #7 .... 1.50
❑8, Mar 1989, b&w; Reprints Cerebus the Aardvark #8 .... 1.50
❑9, Mar 1989, b&w; Reprints Cerebus the Aardvark #9 .... 1.50
❑10, Apr 1989, b&w; Reprints Cerebus the Aardvark #10 .... 1.50
❑11, Apr 1989, b&w; Reprints Cerebus the Aardvark #11 .... 1.50
❑12, May 1989, b&w; Reprints Cerebus the Aardvark #12 .... 1.50
❑13, May 1989, b&w; Reprints Cerebus the Aardvark #13 .... 1.50
❑14, May 1989, b&w; Reprints Cerebus the Aardvark #14 .... 1.50
❑15, Jun 1989, b&w; Reprints Cerebus the Aardvark #15 .... 1.50
❑16, Jun 1989, b&w; Reprints Cerebus the Aardvark #16 .... 1.50
❑17, Jul 1989, b&w; 1: Hepcats. Reprints Cerebus the Aardvark #17 with new material 4.00
❑18, Jul 1989, b&w; Reprints Cerebus the Aardvark #18 .... 1.50
❑19, Aug 1989, b&w; Reprints Cerebus the Aardvark #19 .... 1.50
❑20, Aug 1989, b&w; 1: Milk & Cheese. Reprints Cerebus the Aardvark #20 with new material 6.00
❑21, Sep 1989, b&w; Reprints Cerebus the Aardvark #21 .... 1.50
❑22, Sep 1989, b&w; Reprints Cerebus the Aardvark #22 .... 1.50
❑23, Oct 1989, b&w; Reprints Cerebus the Aardvark #23 .... 1.50
❑24, Oct 1989, b&w; Reprints Cerebus the Aardvark #24 .... 1.50
❑25, Nov 1989, b&w; Reprints Cerebus the Aardvark #25 .... 1.50
❑26, Nov 1989, b&w; Reprints Cerebus the Aardvark "Prince Silverspoon" strips from The Buyer's Guide for Comic Fandom no indicia or cover number 1.50

CEREBUS: CHURCH & STATE
AARDVARK-VANAHEIM

❑1, Feb 1991, b&w; Reprints Cerebus the Aardvark #51 .... 2.00
❑2, Feb 1991, b&w; Reprints Cerebus the Aardvark #52 .... 2.00

N-MINT

❑3, Mar 1991, b&w; Reprints Cerebus the Aardvark #53 ... 2.00
❑4, Mar 1991, b&w; Reprints Cerebus the Aardvark #54 ... 2.00
❑5, Apr 1991, b&w; Reprints Cerebus the Aardvark #55 ... 2.00
❑6, Apr 1991, b&w; Reprints Cerebus the Aardvark #56 ... 2.00
❑7, May 1991, b&w; Reprints Cerebus the Aardvark #57 ... 2.00
❑8, May 1991, b&w; Reprints Cerebus the Aardvark #58 ... 2.00
❑9, Jun 1991, b&w; Reprints Cerebus the Aardvark #59 ... 2.00
❑10, Jun 1991, b&w; Reprints Cerebus the Aardvark #60 ... 2.00
❑11, Jul 1991, b&w; Reprints Cerebus the Aardvark #61 ... 2.00
❑12, Jul 1991, b&w; Reprints Cerebus the Aardvark #62 ... 2.00
❑13, Aug 1991, b&w; Reprints Cerebus the Aardvark #63 ... 2.00
❑14, Aug 1991, b&w; Reprints Cerebus the Aardvark #64 ... 2.00
❑15, Sep 1991, b&w; Reprints Cerebus the Aardvark #65 ... 2.00
❑16, Sep 1991, b&w; Reprints Cerebus the Aardvark #66 ... 2.00
❑17, Oct 1991, b&w; Reprints Cerebus the Aardvark #67 ... 2.00
❑18, Oct 1991, b&w; Reprints Cerebus the Aardvark #68 ... 2.00
❑19, Nov 1991, b&w; Reprints Cerebus the Aardvark #69 ... 2.00
❑20, Nov 1991, b&w; Reprints Cerebus the Aardvark #70 ... 2.00
❑21, Dec 1991, b&w; Reprints Cerebus the Aardvark #71 ... 2.00
❑22, Dec 1991, b&w; Reprints Cerebus the Aardvark #72 ... 2.00
❑23, Jan 1992, b&w; Reprints Cerebus the Aardvark #73 ... 2.00
❑24, Jan 1992, b&w; Reprints Cerebus the Aardvark #74 ... 2.00
❑25, Feb 1992, b&w; Reprints Cerebus the Aardvark #75 ... 2.00
❑26, Feb 1992, b&w; Reprints Cerebus the Aardvark #76 ... 2.00
❑27, Mar 1992, b&w; Reprints Cerebus the Aardvark #77 ... 2.00
❑28, Mar 1992, b&w; Reprints Cerebus the Aardvark #78 ... 2.00
❑29, Apr 1992, b&w; Reprints Cerebus the Aardvark #79 ... 2.00
❑30, Apr 1992, b&w; Reprints Cerebus the Aardvark #80 ... 2.00

CEREBUS COMPANION
WIN-MILL

❑1, Dec 1993, b&w ... 3.95
❑2, Dec 1994, b&w ... 3.95

CEREBUS GUIDE TO SELF PUBLISHING
AARDVARK-VANAHEIM

❑1, Nov 1997, b&w; collects Sim text pieces on the subject from Cerebus ... 3.95

CEREBUS: GUYS PARTY PACK
AARDVARK-VANAHEIM

❑1, b&w; Reprints Cerebus the Aardvark #201-204 ... 3.95

CEREBUS HIGH SOCIETY
AARDVARK-VANAHEIM

❑1, Feb 1990, b&w ... 2.00
❑2, Feb 1990, b&w ... 2.00
❑3, Mar 1990, b&w ... 2.00
❑4, Mar 1990, b&w ... 2.00
❑5, Apr 1990, b&w ... 2.00
❑6, Apr 1990, b&w ... 2.00
❑7, May 1990, b&w ... 2.00
❑8, May 1990, b&w ... 2.00
❑9, Jun 1990, b&w ... 2.00
❑10, Jun 1990, b&w ... 2.00
❑11, Jul 1990, b&w ... 2.00
❑12, Jul 1990, b&w ... 2.00
❑13, Aug 1990, b&w ... 2.00
❑14, Aug 1990, b&w ... 2.00
❑15, Sep 1990, b&w ... 2.00
❑16, Sep 1990, b&w ... 2.00
❑17, Oct 1990, b&w ... 2.00
❑18, Oct 1990, b&w ... 2.00
❑19, Nov 1990, b&w ... 2.00
❑20, Nov 1990, b&w ... 2.00
❑21, Dec 1990, b&w ... 2.00
❑22, Dec 1990, b&w ... 2.00
❑23, Jan 1991, b&w ... 2.00
❑24, Jan 1991, b&w ... 2.00
❑25, Feb 1991, b&w ... 2.00

CEREBUS JAM
AARDVARK-VANAHEIM

❑1, Apr 1985, b&w ... 3.00

CEREBUS THE AARDVARK
AARDVARK-VANAHEIM

❑0, Jun 1993, b&w; Reprints Cerebus the Aardvark #51, 112/113, 137/138 ... 4.00
❑0/Gold, b&w; Reprints Cerebus the Aardvark #51, 112/113, 137/138; Gold logo on cover ... 6.00
❑1, Dec 1977, b&w; 1: Cerebus. genuine; Low circulation ... 850.00
❑1/CF, b&w; Counterfeit edition (glossy cover stock on inside cover); 1: Cerebus. Low circulation ... 60.00
❑2 1978, b&w ... 225.00
❑3 1978, b&w 1: Red Sophia ... 175.00
❑4 1978, b&w 1: Elrod the Albino ... 150.00
❑5, Aug 1978, b&w ... 70.00
❑6, Oct 1978, b&w 1: Jaka ... 60.00
❑7, Dec 1978, b&w ... 35.00
❑8, Feb 1979, b&w ... 35.00
❑9, Apr 1979, b&w ... 35.00
❑10, Jun 1979, b&w ... 35.00
❑11, Aug 1979, b&w 1: Captain Cockroach ... 14.00
❑12, Oct 1979, b&w ... 14.00
❑13, Dec 1979, b&w ... 14.00
❑14, Mar 1980, b&w 1: Lord Julius ... 14.00
❑15, Apr 1980, b&w ... 14.00
❑16, May 1980, b&w ... 18.00
❑17, Jun 1980, b&w ... 15.00
❑18, Jul 1980, b&w ... 15.00
❑19, Aug 1980, b&w ... 15.00
❑20, Sep 1980, b&w ... 15.00
❑21, Oct 1980, b&w; 1: Weisshaupt. Low circulation ... 12.00
❑22, Nov 1980, b&w; no cover price ... 12.00
❑23, Dec 1980, b&w ... 6.00
❑24, Jan 1981, b&w ... 6.00
❑25, Mar 1981, b&w ... 6.00
❑26, May 1981, b&w ... 6.00
❑27, Jun 1981, b&w ... 6.00
❑28, Jul 1981, b&w ... 6.00
❑29, Aug 1981, b&w 1: Elf ... 6.00
❑30, Sep 1981, b&w ... 6.00
❑31, Oct 1981, b&w 1: Astoria ... 6.00
❑32, Nov 1981, b&w; First "Unique Story" backup ... 5.00
❑33, Dec 1981, b&w ... 5.00
❑34, Jan 1982, b&w ... 5.00
❑35, Feb 1982, b&w ... 5.00
❑36, Mar 1982, b&w ... 5.00
❑37, Apr 1982, b&w ... 5.00
❑38, May 1982, b&w ... 5.00
❑39, Jun 1982, b&w ... 5.00
❑40, Jul 1982, b&w ... 5.00
❑41, Aug 1982, b&w ... 4.00
❑42, Sep 1982, b&w ... 4.00
❑43, Oct 1982, b&w ... 4.00
❑44, Nov 1982, b&w; sideways ... 4.00
❑45, Dec 1982, b&w; sideways ... 4.00
❑46, Jan 1983, b&w; sideways ... 4.00
❑47, Feb 1983, b&w; sideways ... 4.00
❑48, Mar 1983, b&w; sideways ... 4.00
❑49, Apr 1983, b&w; rotating issue ... 4.00
❑50, May 1983, b&w ... 4.00
❑51, Jun 1983, b&w; Low circulation ... 6.00
❑52, Jul 1983, b&w ... 4.00
❑53, Aug 1983, b&w 1: Wolveroach (cameo) ... 4.00
❑54, Sep 1983, b&w 1: Wolveroach (full story). A: Wolveroach ... 4.00
❑55, Oct 1983, b&w A: Wolveroach ... 4.00
❑56, Nov 1983, b&w 1: Normalman. A: Wolveroach ... 4.00
❑57, Dec 1983, b&w 2: Normalman ... 4.00
❑58, Jan 1984, b&w ... 3.00
❑59, Feb 1984, b&w ... 3.00
❑60, Mar 1984, b&w ... 3.00
❑61, Apr 1984, b&w; A: Flaming Carrot. Flaming Carrot ... 4.00
❑62, May 1984, b&w; A: Flaming Carrot. Flaming Carrot ... 4.00
❑63, Jun 1984, b&w ... 2.50
❑64, Jul 1984, b&w ... 2.50
❑65, Aug 1984, b&w; Gerhard begins as background artist ... 2.50
❑66, Sep 1984, b&w ... 2.50
❑67, Oct 1984, b&w ... 2.50
❑68, Nov 1984, b&w ... 2.50
❑69, Dec 1984, b&w ... 2.50
❑70, Jan 1985, b&w ... 2.50
❑71, Feb 1985, b&w; Last "Unique Story" backup ... 2.50
❑72, Mar 1985, b&w ... 2.50
❑73, Apr 1985, b&w ... 2.50
❑74, May 1985, b&w ... 2.50
❑75, Jun 1985, b&w ... 2.50
❑76, Jul 1985, b&w ... 2.50
❑77, Aug 1985, b&w ... 2.50
❑78, Sep 1985, b&w ... 2.50
❑79, Oct 1985, b&w ... 2.50
❑80, Nov 1985, b&w ... 2.50
❑81, Dec 1985, b&w ... 2.50
❑82, Jan 1986, b&w ... 2.50
❑83, Feb 1986, b&w ... 2.50
❑84, Mar 1986, b&w ... 2.50
❑85, Apr 1986, b&w ... 2.50
❑86, May 1986, b&w ... 2.50
❑87, Jun 1986, b&w ... 2.50
❑88, Jul 1986, b&w ... 2.50
❑89, Aug 1986, b&w ... 2.50
❑90, Sep 1986, b&w ... 2.50
❑91, Oct 1986, b&w ... 2.50
❑92, Nov 1986, b&w ... 2.50
❑93, Dec 1986, b&w ... 2.50
❑94, Jan 1987, b&w ... 2.50
❑95, Feb 1987, b&w ... 2.50
❑96, Mar 1987, b&w ... 2.50
❑97, Apr 1987, b&w ... 2.50
❑98, May 1987, b&w ... 2.50
❑99, Jun 1987, b&w 1: Cirin ... 2.50
❑100, Jul 1987, b&w ... 2.50
❑101, Aug 1987, b&w ... 2.00
❑102, Sep 1987, b&w ... 2.00
❑103, Oct 1987, b&w ... 2.00
❑104, Nov 1987, b&w A: Flaming Carrot ... 2.00
❑105, Dec 1987, b&w ... 2.00
❑106, Jan 1988, b&w ... 2.00
❑107, Feb 1988, b&w ... 2.00
❑108, Mar 1988, b&w ... 2.00
❑109, Apr 1988, b&w ... 2.00
❑110, May 1988, b&w ... 2.00
❑111, Jun 1988, b&w ... 2.00
❑112, Jul 1988, b&w; Double-issue #112 and #113 ... 2.00
❑114, Sep 1988, b&w ... 2.00
❑115, Oct 1988, b&w ... 2.00
❑116, Nov 1988, b&w ... 2.00
❑117, Dec 1988, b&w ... 2.00
❑118, Jan 1989, b&w ... 2.00
❑119, Feb 1989, b&w ... 2.00
❑120, Mar 1989, b&w ... 2.00
❑121, Apr 1989, b&w ... 2.00
❑122, May 1989, b&w ... 2.00
❑123, Jun 1989, b&w ... 2.00
❑124, Jul 1989, b&w ... 2.00
❑125, Aug 1989, b&w ... 2.00
❑126, Sep 1989, b&w ... 2.00
❑127, Oct 1989, b&w ... 2.00
❑128, Nov 1989, b&w ... 2.00
❑129, Dec 1989, b&w ... 2.00

	N-MINT
❑130, Jan 1990, b&w	2.00
❑131, Feb 1990, b&w	2.00
❑132, Mar 1990, b&w	2.00
❑133, Apr 1990, b&w	2.00
❑134, May 1990, b&w	2.00
❑135, Jun 1990, b&w	2.00
❑136, Jul 1990, b&w	2.00
❑137, Aug 1990, b&w	2.25
❑138, Sep 1990, b&w	2.25
❑139, Oct 1990, b&w	2.25
❑140, Nov 1990, b&w	2.25
❑141, Dec 1990, b&w	2.25
❑142, Jan 1991, b&w	2.25
❑143, Feb 1991, b&w	2.25
❑144, Mar 1991, b&w	2.25
❑145, Apr 1991, b&w	2.25
❑146, May 1991, b&w	2.25
❑147, Jun 1991, b&w	2.25
❑148, Jul 1991, b&w	2.25
❑149, Aug 1991, b&w	2.25
❑150, Sep 1991, b&w	2.25
❑151, Oct 1991, b&w	2.25
❑152, Nov 1991, b&w	2.25
❑153, Dec 1991, b&w	2.25
❑154, Jan 1992, b&w	2.25
❑155, Feb 1992, b&w	2.25
❑156, Mar 1992, b&w	2.25
❑157, Apr 1992, b&w	2.25
❑158, May 1992, b&w	2.25
❑159, Jun 1992, b&w	2.25
❑160, Jul 1992, b&w	2.25
❑161, Aug 1992, b&w; Bone back-up	2.25
❑162, Sep 1992, b&w	2.25
❑163, Oct 1992, b&w	2.25
❑164, Nov 1992, b&w	2.25
❑165, Dec 1992, b&w	2.25
❑165-2, Dec 1992, b&w	2.25
❑166, Jan 1993, b&w	2.25
❑167, Feb 1993, b&w	2.25
❑168, Mar 1993, b&w	2.25
❑169, Apr 1993, b&w	2.25
❑170, May 1993, b&w	2.25
❑171, Jun 1993, b&w	2.25
❑172, Jul 1993, b&w	2.25
❑173, Aug 1993, b&w	2.25
❑174, Sep 1993, b&w	2.25
❑175, Oct 1993, b&w	2.25
❑176, Nov 1993, b&w	2.25
❑177, Dec 1993, b&w	2.25
❑178, Jan 1994, b&w	2.25
❑179, Feb 1994, b&w	2.25
❑180, Mar 1994, b&w	2.25
❑181, Apr 1994, b&w	2.25
❑182, May 1994, b&w	2.25
❑183, Jun 1994, b&w	2.25
❑184, Jul 1994, b&w	2.25
❑185, Aug 1994, b&w	2.25
❑186, Sep 1994, b&w	2.25
❑187, Oct 1994, b&w	2.25
❑188, Nov 1994, b&w	2.25
❑189, Dec 1994, b&w	2.25
❑190, Jan 1994, b&w	2.25
❑191, Feb 1994, b&w	2.25
❑192, Mar 1994, b&w	2.25
❑193, Apr 1994, b&w	2.25
❑194, May 1995, b&w	2.25
❑195, Jun 1995, b&w	2.25
❑196, Jul 1995, b&w	2.25
❑197, Aug 1995, b&w	2.25
❑198, Sep 1995, b&w	2.25
❑199, Oct 1995, b&w	2.25
❑200, Nov 1995, b&w; Patty Cake back-up	2.25
❑201, Dec 1995, b&w	2.25
❑202, Jan 1996, b&w	2.25
❑203, Feb 1996, b&w	2.25
❑204, Mar 1996, b&w	2.25
❑205, Apr 1996, b&w	2.25
❑206, May 1996, b&w	2.25
❑207, Jun 1996, b&w	2.25
❑208, Jul 1996, b&w	2.25

	N-MINT
❑209, Aug 1996, b&w	2.25
❑210, Sep 1996, b&w	2.25
❑211, Oct 1996, b&w	2.25
❑212, Nov 1996, b&w	2.25
❑213, Dec 1996, b&w	2.25
❑214, Jan 1997, b&w	2.25
❑215, Feb 1997, b&w	2.25
❑216, Mar 1997, b&w	2.25
❑217, Apr 1997, b&w	2.25
❑218, May 1997, b&w	2.25
❑219, Jun 1997, b&w	2.25
❑220, Jul 1997, b&w	2.25
❑221, Aug 1997, b&w	2.25
❑222, Sep 1997, b&w	2.25
❑223, Oct 1997, b&w	2.25
❑224, Nov 1997, b&w	2.25
❑225, Dec 1997, b&w	2.25
❑226, Jan 1998, b&w	2.25
❑227, Feb 1998, b&w	2.25
❑228, Mar 1998, b&w	2.25
❑229, Apr 1998, b&w	2.25
❑230, May 1998, b&w A: Jaka	2.25
❑231, Jun 1998, b&w	2.25
❑232, Jul 1998, b&w	2.25
❑233, Aug 1998, b&w	2.25
❑234, Sep 1998, b&w	2.25
❑235, Oct 1998, b&w	2.25
❑236, Nov 1998, b&w	2.25
❑237, Dec 1998, b&w	2.25
❑238, Jan 1999, b&w	2.25
❑239, Feb 1999, b&w	2.25
❑240, Mar 1999, b&w	2.25
❑241, Apr 1999, b&w	2.25
❑242, May 1999, b&w	2.25
❑243, Jun 1999, b&w	2.25
❑244, Jul 1999, b&w	2.25
❑245, Aug 1999, b&w	2.25
❑246, Sep 1999, b&w	2.25
❑247, Oct 1999, b&w	2.25
❑248, Nov 1999, b&w	2.25
❑249, Dec 1999, b&w	2.25
❑250, Jan 2000, b&w	2.25
❑251, Feb 2000, b&w	2.25
❑252, Mar 2000, b&w	2.25
❑253, Apr 2000, b&w	2.25
❑254, May 2000, b&w	2.25
❑255, Jun 2000, b&w	2.25
❑256, Jul 2000, b&w	2.25
❑257, Aug 2000, b&w	2.25
❑258, Sep 2000, b&w	2.25
❑259, Oct 2000, b&w	2.25
❑260, Nov 2000, b&w	2.25
❑261, Dec 2000, b&w	2.25
❑262, Jan 2001, b&w	2.25
❑263, Feb 2001, b&w	2.25
❑264, Mar 2001, b&w	2.25
❑265, Apr 2001, b&w	2.25
❑266, May 2001, b&w	2.25
❑267, Jun 2001, b&w	2.25
❑268, Jul 2001, b&w 1: The Three Wise Fellows	2.25
❑269, Aug 2001, b&w	2.25
❑270, Sep 2001, b&w	2.25
❑271, Oct 2001, b&w	2.25
❑272, Nov 2001, b&w 1: Rabbi	2.25
❑273, Dec 2001, b&w	2.25
❑274, Jan 2002, b&w	2.25
❑275, Feb 2002, b&w	2.25
❑276, Mar 2002, b&w	2.25
❑277, Apr 2002, b&w	2.25
❑278, May 2002, b&w	2.25
❑279, Jun 2002, b&w	2.25
❑280, Jul 2002, b&w	2.25
❑281, Aug 2002, b&w	2.25
❑282, Sep 2002, b&w	2.25
❑283, Oct 2002, b&w	2.25
❑284, Nov 2002, b&w	2.25
❑285, Dec 2002, b&w	2.25
❑286, Jan 2003, b&w	2.25
❑287, Feb 2003, b&w	2.25
❑288, Mar 2003, b&w	2.25

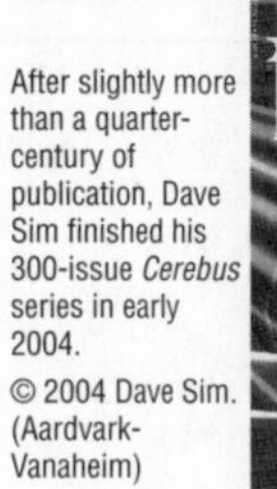

After slightly more than a quarter-century of publication, Dave Sim finished his 300-issue *Cerebus* series in early 2004.

© 2004 Dave Sim. (Aardvark-Vanaheim)

	N-MINT
❑289, Apr 2003	2.25
❑290, May 2003	2.25
❑291, Jun 2003	2.25
❑292, Jul 2003	2.25
❑293, Aug 2003	2.25
❑294, Sep 2003	2.25
❑295, Oct 2003	2.25
❑296, Nov 2003	2.25
❑297, Dec 2003	2.25
❑298, Jan 2004	2.25
❑299, Feb 2004	2.25
❑300, Mar 2004 D: Cerebus	2.25

CEREBUS WORLD TOUR BOOK
AARDVARK-VANAHEIM

❑1, b&w	3.00

CERES CELESTIAL LEGEND PART 1
VIZ

❑1, Jun 2001	3.25
❑2, Jul 2001	2.95
❑3, Aug 2001	2.95
❑4, Sep 2001	2.95
❑5, Oct 2001	2.95
❑6, Nov 2001	2.95

CERES CELESTIAL LEGEND PART 2
VIZ

❑1, Dec 2001	2.95
❑2, Jan 2002	2.95
❑3, Feb 2002	2.95
❑4, Mar 2002	2.95
❑5, Apr 2002	2.95
❑6, May 2002	2.95

CERES CELESTIAL LEGEND PART 3
VIZ

❑1, Jun 2002	2.95
❑2, Jul 2002	3.50
❑3, Aug 2002	3.50
❑4, Sep 2002	3.50

CERES CELESTIAL LEGEND PART 4
VIZ

❑1, Oct 2002	3.50
❑2, Nov 2002	3.50
❑3, Dec 2002	3.50
❑4, Jan 2003	3.50

CERES CELESTIAL LEGEND PART 5
VIZ

❑1, Feb 2003	3.50

CHADZ FRENDZ
SMILING FACE

❑1, Jan 1998	1.50

CHAINGANG
NORTHSTAR

❑1, b&w	2.50
❑2	2.50

CHAIN GANG WAR
DC

❑1, Jul 1993; Foil embossed cover	2.50
❑1/Silver, Jul 1993; Silver promotional edition	2.50
❑2, Aug 1993	1.75
❑3, Sep 1993	1.75
❑4, Oct 1993	1.75
❑5, Nov 1993; Embossed cover	2.50
❑6, Dec 1993	1.75
❑7, Jan 1994	1.75
❑8, Feb 1994	1.75

N-MINT

❑9, Mar 1994 ... 1.75
❑10, Apr 1994 ... 1.75
❑11, May 1994 ... 1.75
❑12, Jun 1994; End of Chain Gang ... 1.75

CHAINSAW VIGILANTE
NEC

❑1 ... 3.50
❑1/A; Orange cover ... 5.00
❑1/B; Gold foil cover ... 6.00
❑1/C; Pseudo-3D "platinum" foil cover ... 6.00
❑2 ... 2.75
❑3 ... 2.75

CHAINS OF CHAOS
HARRIS

❑1, Nov 1994 ... 2.95
❑2, Dec 1994 ... 2.95
❑3, Jan 1995 ... 2.95

CHAKAN
RAK

❑1, b&w ... 4.00

CHALLENGERS OF THE FANTASTIC
MARVEL / AMALGAM

❑1, Jun 1997 ... 2.00

CHALLENGERS OF THE UNKNOWN
DC

❑1, May 1958 JK (a) ... 1850.00
❑2, Jul 1958 JK (a) ... 725.00
❑3, Sep 1958 JK (a) ... 600.00
❑4, Nov 1958 JK, WW (a) ... 500.00
❑5, Jan 1959 JK, WW (a) ... 500.00
❑6, Mar 1959 JK, WW (a) ... 475.00
❑7, May 1959 JK, WW (a) ... 475.00
❑8, Jul 1959 JK, WW (a) ... 475.00
❑9, Sep 1959 ... 275.00
❑10, Nov 1959 ... 275.00
❑11, Jan 1960 ... 185.00
❑12, Mar 1960 ... 185.00
❑13, May 1960 ... 185.00
❑14, Jul 1960 O: Multi-Man. 1: Multi-Man ... 185.00
❑15, Sep 1960 ... 185.00
❑16, Nov 1960 ... 110.00
❑17, Jan 1961 ... 110.00
❑18, Mar 1961 1: Cosmo (Challengers of the Unknown's Pet) ... 110.00
❑19, May 1961 ... 110.00
❑20, Jul 1961 ... 110.00
❑21, Sep 1961 ... 65.00
❑22, Nov 1961 ... 65.00
❑23, Jan 1962 ... 65.00
❑24, Mar 1962 ... 65.00
❑25, May 1962 ... 65.00
❑26, Jul 1962 ... 65.00
❑27, Sep 1962 ... 65.00
❑28, Nov 1962 ... 65.00
❑29, Jan 1963 ... 65.00
❑30, Mar 1963 ... 65.00
❑31, May 1963 O: Challengers of the Unknown ... 75.00
❑32, Jul 1963 ... 40.00
❑33, Sep 1963 ... 40.00
❑34, Nov 1963 O: Multi-Woman. 1: Multi-Woman ... 40.00
❑35, Jan 1964 ... 40.00
❑36, Mar 1964 ... 40.00
❑37, May 1964 ... 40.00
❑38, Jul 1964 ... 40.00
❑39, Sep 1964 ... 40.00
❑40, Nov 1964 ... 40.00
❑41, Jan 1965 ... 24.00
❑42, Mar 1965 ... 24.00
❑43, May 1965; Challengers of the Unknown get new uniforms ... 24.00
❑44, Jul 1965 ... 24.00
❑45, Sep 1965 ... 24.00
❑46, Nov 1965 ... 24.00
❑47, Jan 1966 ... 24.00
❑48, Mar 1966 A: The Doom Patrol ... 24.00
❑49, May 1966 ... 24.00
❑50, Jul 1966 1: Villo ... 24.00
❑51, Sep 1966 A: Sea Devils. V: Sponge Man ... 20.00
❑52, Nov 1966 ... 20.00
❑53, Jan 1967 ... 20.00
❑54, Mar 1967 ... 20.00
❑55, May 1967 1: Tino Manarry. D: Red Ryan ... 20.00
❑56, Jul 1967 ... 20.00
❑57, Sep 1967 ... 20.00
❑58, Nov 1967 V: Neutro ... 20.00
❑59, Jan 1968 ... 20.00
❑60, Mar 1968; Red Ryan returns ... 20.00
❑61, May 1968 ... 7.00
❑62, Jul 1968 ... 7.00
❑63, Sep 1968 ... 7.00
❑64, Nov 1968; JK (a); O: Challengers of the Unknown. reprints Showcase #6 ... 7.00
❑65, Jan 1969; JK (a); O: Challengers of the Unknown. reprints Showcase #6 ... 7.00
❑66, Mar 1969 ... 7.00
❑67, May 1969 ... 7.00
❑68, Jul 1969 ... 7.00
❑69, Sep 1969 1: Corinna ... 7.00
❑70, Nov 1969 ... 7.00
❑71, Jan 1970 ... 7.00
❑72, Mar 1970 ... 7.00
❑73, May 1970 ... 7.00
❑74, Jul 1970 NA (a); A: Deadman ... 14.00
❑75, Sep 1970; JK (a); V: Ultivac. reprints Showcase #7 ... 7.00
❑76, Nov 1970; Reprints stories from Challengers of the Unknown #2 & #3 ... 7.00
❑77, Jan 1971; reprints Showcase #12 ... 7.00
❑78, Feb 1973; Reprints stories from Challengers of the Unknown #6 & #7 ... 7.00
❑79, Apr 1973; JKu (c); reprints stories from Challengers of the Unknown #1 and 2 ... 7.00
❑80, Jul 1973; reprints Showcase #11; series goes on hiatus for four years ... 7.00
❑81, Jul 1977 ... 6.00
❑82, Aug 1977 A: Swamp Thing ... 5.00
❑83, Oct 1977 ... 5.00
❑84, Dec 1977 ... 5.00
❑85, Feb 1978 A: Deadman, Swamp Thing ... 5.00
❑86, Apr 1978 A: Deadman, Swamp Thing ... 5.00
❑87, Jul 1978 KG (a); A: Deadman, Swamp Thing, Rip Hunter ... 5.00

CHALLENGERS OF THE UNKNOWN (2ND SERIES)
DC

❑1, Feb 1997; new team ... 2.25
❑2, Mar 1997 ... 2.25
❑3, Apr 1997 ... 2.25
❑4, May 1997 ... 2.25
❑5, Jun 1997 ... 2.25
❑6, Jul 1997; concludes in Scare Tactics #8 ... 2.25
❑7, Aug 1997; return of original Challengers ... 2.25
❑8, Sep 1997 ... 2.25
❑9, Oct 1997 ... 2.25
❑10, Nov 1997 ... 2.25
❑11, Dec 1997; Face cover ... 2.25
❑12, Jan 1998 ... 2.25
❑13, Feb 1998 ... 2.25
❑14, Mar 1998 ... 2.25
❑15, Apr 1998; Millennium Giants; continues in Superman #134 ... 2.25
❑16, May 1998; tales of the original Challengers ... 2.25
❑17, Jun 1998 ... 2.25
❑18, Jul 1998 ... 2.50

CHALLENGERS OF THE UNKNOWN (MINI-SERIES)
DC

❑1, Mar 1991 ... 1.75
❑2, Apr 1991 ... 1.75
❑3, May 1991 ... 1.75
❑4, Jun 1991 ... 1.75
❑5, Jul 1991 ... 1.75
❑6, Aug 1991 ... 1.75
❑7, Sep 1991 ... 1.75
❑8, Oct 1991 ... 1.75

CHALLENGERS OF THE UNKNOWN (2ND MINI-SERIES)
DC

❑1, Aug 2004 ... 2.95
❑2, Sep 2004 ... 2.95

CHAMBER OF CHILLS
MARVEL

❑1, Nov 1972 ... 8.00
❑2, Jan 1973 ... 5.00
❑3, Mar 1973 ... 4.00
❑4, May 1973 ... 4.00
❑5, Jul 1973 ... 4.00
❑6, Sep 1973 ... 4.00
❑7, Nov 1973 ... 4.00
❑8, Jan 1974 ... 4.00
❑9, Mar 1974 ... 4.00
❑10, May 1974 ... 4.00
❑11, Jul 1974; Reprints story from Tales of Suspense #28 ... 3.00
❑12, Sep 1974 ... 3.00
❑13, Nov 1974 ... 3.00
❑14, Jan 1975 ... 3.00
❑15, Mar 1975 ... 3.00
❑16, May 1975 ... 3.00
❑17, Jul 1975 ... 3.00
❑18, Sep 1975; Reprints story from Tales to Astonish #11 ... 3.00
❑19, Nov 1975; Reprints story from Tales to Astonish #26 ... 3.00
❑20, Jan 1976 ... 3.00
❑21, Mar 1976 ... 3.00
❑22, May 1976; Reprints story from Tales to Astonish #26 ... 3.00
❑22/30 cent, May 1976; Reprint story from Tales to Astonish #26; 30 cent regional price variant ... 20.00
❑23, Jul 1976 ... 3.00
❑23/30 cent, Jul 1976 ... 8.00
❑24, Sep 1976 ... 3.00
❑25, Nov 1976 ... 3.00

CHAMBER OF CLUES
HARVEY

❑27, Feb 1955; A: Kitty Carson. A: Kerry Drake. Continued from Chamber of Chills #26 ... 30.00
❑28, Apr 1955 ... 25.00

CHAMBER OF DARKNESS
MARVEL

❑1, Oct 1968 SL (w); JB, DH (a) ... 30.00
❑2, Dec 1968 ... 8.00
❑3, Feb 1969 ... 8.00
❑4, Apr 1969; Conan try-out ... 17.00
❑5, Jun 1969 ... 8.00
❑6, Aug 1969 ... 8.00
❑7, Oct 1969; BWr (a); 1st Bernie Wrightson work; reprints story from Tales to Astonish #13 ... 20.00
❑8, Dec 1969 ... 8.00
❑1/Special 1972; Special Edition ... 20.00

CHAMBER OF EVIL
COMAX

❑1 ... 2.95

CHAMPION, THE
SPECIAL STUDIO

❑1, b&w ... 2.50

CHAMPION OF KATARA, THE
MU

❑1, Jan 1992, b&w ... 2.50
❑2, Apr 1992 ... 2.50

CHAMPION OF KATARA: DUM-DUMS & DRAGONS, THE
MU

❑1, Jun 1995, b&w ... 2.95
❑2, Jul 1995, b&w ... 2.95
❑3, Aug 1995, b&w ... 2.95

N-MINT

CHAMPIONS CLASSICS
Hero

❑1 .... 1.00
❑13, Oct 1993; b&w reprint 3.95
❑14, Jan 1994; b&w reprint 3.95

CHAMPIONS CLASSICS/FLARE ADVENTURES
Hero

❑2; flip-format 2.95
❑3; flip-format 2.95
❑4; flip-format 3.50
❑5; flip-format 3.50
❑6; flip-format 3.50
❑7; flip-format 3.50

CHAMPIONS (ECLIPSE)
Eclipse

❑1, Jun 1986 .... 1.25
❑2, Sep 1986 .... 1.25
❑3, Oct 1986 .... 1.25
❑4, Nov 1986 .... 1.25
❑5, Feb 1987 .... 1.25
❑6, Feb 1987 .... 1.25

CHAMPIONS (HERO)
Hero

❑1, Sep 1987; 1 Madame Synn; 1 The Galloping Galooper 1.95
❑2, Oct 1987; 1 Black Enchantress; 1 The Fat Man 1.95
❑3, Nov 1987; O: Flare. 1 Icicle; 1 Sparkplug 1.95
❑4, Dec 1987; 1 Exo-Skeleton Man; 1 Pulsar 1.95
❑5, Jan 1988 .... 1.95
❑6, Feb 1988; 1 Mechanon 1.95
❑7, Mar 1988 .... 1.95
❑8, May 1988 O: Foxbat 1.95
❑9, Jun 1988; (also was Flare #0) 1.95
❑10, Jul 1988 .... 1.95
❑11, Sep 1988 .... 1.95
❑12, Oct 1988 .... 1.95
❑13 .... 1.95
❑14 .... 1.95
❑15, b&w 3.95
❑Annual 1, Dec 1988 O: Giant. O: Dark Malice 2.75
❑Annual 2 .... 3.95

CHAMPIONS, THE (MARVEL)
Marvel

❑1, Oct 1975 DH (a); O: The Champions. 1: The Champions. A: Venus .. 12.00
❑2, Jan 1976 .... 6.00
❑3, Feb 1976 .... 6.00
❑4, Mar 1976 .... 5.00
❑5, Apr 1976 DH (a); O: Rampage (Marvel). 1: Rampage (Marvel). A: Ghost Rider 5.00
❑5/30 cent, Apr 1976; DH (a); 30 cent regional price variant 20.00
❑6, Jun 1976 .... 4.00
❑6/30 cent, Jun 1976; 30 cent regional price variant 20.00
❑7, Aug 1976 .... 4.00
❑7/30 cent, Aug 1976; 30 cent regional price variant 20.00
❑8, Oct 1976 GK, BH (a) 4.00
❑9, Dec 1976 GK, BH (a); V: Darkstar, Titanium Man, Crimson Dynamo ... 4.00
❑10, Jan 1977 DC, BH (a) 4.00
❑11, Feb 1977 JBy (a) 4.00
❑12, Mar 1977 JBy (a) 4.00
❑13, May 1977 JBy (a) 4.00
❑14, Jul 1977 JBy (a); 1: Swarm 4.00
❑14/35 cent, Jul 1977; JBy (a); 1: Swarm. 35 cent regional price variant 15.00
❑15, Sep 1977 JBy (a) 4.00
❑15/35 cent, Sep 1977; JBy (a); 35 cent regional price variant 15.00
❑16, Nov 1977 JBy, BH (a); A: Doctor Doom 4.00
❑17, Jan 1978 JBy, GT (a); V: Sentinels 4.00

N-MINT

CHAMPION SPORTS
DC

❑1, Nov 1973 .... 5.00
❑2, Jan 1974 .... 3.50
❑3, Mar 1974 .... 3.50

CHANGE COMMANDER GOKU (1ST SERIES)
Antarctic

❑1, Oct 1993 .... 2.95
❑2, Nov 1993 .... 2.95
❑3, Dec 1993 .... 2.95
❑4, Jan 1994 .... 2.95
❑5, Feb 1994 .... 2.95

CHANGE COMMANDER GOKU 2
Antarctic

❑1, Sep 1996 .... 2.95
❑2, Nov 1996 .... 2.95
❑3, Jan 1997 .... 2.95
❑4, Mar 1997 .... 2.95

CHANGES
Tundra

❑1 .... 7.95

CHANNEL ZERO
Image

❑1, Feb 1998 .... 2.95
❑2, Apr 1998 .... 2.95
❑3, Jun 1998 .... 2.95
❑4, Aug 1998 .... 2.95
❑5, Nov 1998 .... 2.95
❑6, Feb 1999 .... 2.95

CHANNEL ZERO: DUPE
Image

❑1, Jan 1999, b&w 2.95

CHAOS! BIBLE, THE
Chaos

❑1, Nov 1995 .... 3.50

CHAOS! CHRONICLES
Chaos

❑1, Feb 2000 .... 3.50

CHAOS EFFECT, THE: ALPHA
Valiant

❑1, ca. 1994; giveaway; BL (w); A: Timewalker. no cover price 1.00
❑1/Gold, ca. 1994; Gold edition BL (w); A: Timewalker 2.00

CHAOS EFFECT, THE: EPILOGUE
Valiant

❑1, Dec 1994; Magnus in 20th century; cardstock cover 2.95
❑2, Jan 1995; Magnus in 20th century; cardstock cover 2.95

CHAOS EFFECT, THE: OMEGA
Valiant

❑1, Nov 1994; Magnus in 20th century; cardstock cover 2.25
❑1/Gold, Nov 1994; Gold edition; Magnus in 20th century; cardstock cover 3.00
❑2, Nov 1994; BL (w); Omega 2.25
❑2/Gold, Nov 1994; Gold edition BL (w) 2.50

CHAOS EFFECT, THE: BETA
Valiant

❑1 .... 2.25

CHAOS! GALLERY
Chaos!

❑1, Aug 1997; pin-ups 2.95

CHAOS! PRESENTS JADE
Chaos

❑1, May 2001 .... 2.99
❑2, Jun 2001 .... 2.99
❑3, Jul 2001 .... 2.99
❑4, Aug 2001 .... 2.99

CHAOS! QUARTERLY
Chaos

❑1 .... 4.95
❑2 .... 4.95
❑3 .... 3.95

A group of folks who had it in for The Challengers of the Unknown was formed in *Challengers of the Unknown* #42.

© 1965 National Periodical Publications (DC).

N-MINT

CHAPEL
Image

❑1, Feb 1995 .... 2.50
❑2, Mar 1995 .... 2.50
❑2/Variant, Mar 1995; Alternate cover; Chapel firing right, white lettering in logo 2.50

CHAPEL (VOL. 2)
Image

❑1, Aug 1995 .... 2.50
❑1/Variant, Aug 1995; alternate cover 2.50
❑2, Sep 1995 .... 2.50
❑3, Oct 1995 .... 2.50
❑4, Nov 1995; Babewatch 2.50
❑5, Dec 1995 .... 2.50
❑6, Feb 1996 .... 2.50
❑7, Apr 1996 .... 2.50

CHAPEL (MINI-SERIES)
Image

❑1 .... 2.50
❑2, Mar 1995 .... 2.50

CHARLEMAGNE
Defiant

❑0, Feb 1994; giveaway 1.00
❑1, Mar 1994 .... 3.25
❑2, Apr 1994 .... 2.50
❑3, May 1994 .... 2.50
❑4, Jun 1994 .... 2.50
❑5, Jul 1994 .... 2.50
❑6 .... 2.50
❑7 .... 2.50
❑8 .... 2.50

CHARLES BURNS' MODERN HORROR SKETCHBOOK
Kitchen Sink

❑1 .... 6.95

CHARLIE CHAN (ETERNITY)
Eternity

❑1, Mar 1989; b&w strip reprint 1.95
❑2, Mar 1989; b&w strip reprint 1.95
❑3, Apr 1989; b&w strip reprint 1.95
❑4, May 1989; b&w strip reprint 1.95
❑5, Jul 1989 .... 2.25
❑6, Aug 1989 .... 2.25

CHARLIE THE CAVEMAN
Fantasy General

❑1, b&w 2.00

CHARLTON ACTION FEATURING STATIC
Charlton

❑11, Oct 1985 .... 1.50
❑12, Dec 1985 .... 1.50

CHARLTON BULLSEYE
Charlton

❑1, Jun 1981 .... 3.00
❑2, Jul 1981 .... 2.00
❑3, Sep 1981 .... 2.00
❑4, Nov 1981 .... 2.00
❑5, Jan 1982 .... 2.00
❑6, Mar 1982 .... 2.00
❑7, May 1982 A: Captain Atom 2.00
❑8, Jul 1982 .... 2.00
❑9, Sep 1982 GD (w); GD (a) 2.00
❑10, Dec 1982 .... 2.00

N-MINT

CHARLTON CLASSICS
CHARLTON
❑1, Apr 1980 .... 3.00
❑2, Jun 1980 .... 2.00
❑3, Aug 1980 .... 2.00
❑4, Oct 1980 .... 2.00
❑5, Dec 1980 .... 2.00
❑6, Feb 1981 .... 2.00
❑7, Apr 1981 .... 2.00
❑8, Jun 1981; Hercules; Joe Gill story, Sam Glanzman art credits; Tom Sutton script and art 2.00
❑9, Aug 1981 .... 2.00

CHARLTON PREMIERE (VOL. 1)
CHARLTON
❑19, Jul 1967 .... 20.00

CHARLTON PREMIERE (VOL. 2)
CHARLTON
❑1, Sep 1967; Restarted; Vol. 1, #19 was the end of Marine War Heroes 6.00
❑2, Nov 1967 .... 4.00
❑3, Jan 1968 .... 4.00
❑4, May 1968 .... 4.00

CHARLTON SPORT LIBRARY: PROFESSIONAL FOOTBALL
CHARLTON
❑1, Win 1969 .... 35.00

CHASE
DC
❑1, Feb 1998; bound-in trading cards 2.50
❑2, Mar 1998 A: Bolt, Sledge, Killer Frost, Copperhead 2.50
❑3, Apr 1998 .... 2.50
❑4, May 1998 A: Clock King 2.50
❑5, Jun 1998 A: Klarion 2.50
❑6, Jul 1998 .... 2.50
❑7, Aug 1998 .... 2.50
❑8, Sep 1998 .... 2.50
❑9, Oct 1998 A: Green Lantern 2.50
❑1000000, Nov 1998 .... 3.00

CHASER PLATOON
AIRCEL
❑1, Feb 1991, b&w 2.25
❑2, Mar 1991, b&w 2.25
❑3, Apr 1991, b&w 2.25
❑4, May 1991, b&w 2.25
❑5, b&w 2.25
❑6, b&w 2.25

CHASING DOGMA
IMAGE
❑1 .... 14.95

CHASSIS (VOL. 1)
MILLENNIUM / EXPAND
❑1; foil logo 2.95
❑1-2, May 1997 .... 2.95
❑2 .... 2.95
❑3, Apr 1998 .... 2.95

CHASSIS (VOL. 2)
HURRICANE
❑0 .... 2.95
❑1, Jun 1998 .... 2.95
❑2, Sep 1998 .... 2.95
❑3, Jan 1999 .... 2.95

CHASSIS (VOL. 3)
IMAGE
❑0, Apr 1999; background information 2.95
❑1, Nov 1999 .... 2.95
❑1/A, Nov 1999; Alternate cover with Chassis standing against blueprint background 2.95
❑2, Dec 1999 .... 2.95
❑3, Mar 2000 .... 2.95
❑4, Mar 2000 .... 2.95

CHASTITY
CHAOS!
❑0.5, Jan 2001 .... 2.95

N-MINT

CHASTITY: LUST FOR LIFE
CHAOS!
❑1/DF, May 1999; Dynamic Forces cover (falling with two outstretched swords)
❑1/Ltd., May 1999
❑1, May 1999 .... 3.50
❑2, Jun 1999 .... 2.95

CHASTITY: REIGN OF TERROR
CHAOS!
❑1, Oct 2000 .... 2.95

CHASTITY: ROCKED
CHAOS!
❑1, Nov 1998 .... 2.95
❑2, Dec 1998 .... 2.95
❑3, Jan 1999 .... 2.95
❑4, Feb 1999 .... 2.95

CHASTITY: THEATRE OF PAIN
CHAOS!
❑1, Feb 1997 .... 2.95
❑1/Variant, Feb 1997; Onyx Premium Edition; cardstock cover 4.00
❑2, Apr 1997 .... 2.95
❑3, Jun 1997; back cover pin-up 2.95
❑3/Variant, Jun 1997; Final Curtain Edition; No cover price; Limited Engagement 4.00

CHEAPSKIN
FANTAGRAPHICS / EROS
❑1, b&w 2.95

CHECKMATE (GOLD KEY)
GOLD KEY
❑1, ca. 1962 .... 30.00
❑2, ca. 1963 .... 20.00

CHECKMATE
DC
❑1, Apr 1988 .... 1.25
❑2, May 1988 .... 1.25
❑3, Jun 1988 .... 1.25
❑4, Jul 1988 .... 1.25
❑5, Aug 1988 .... 1.25
❑6, Sep 1988 .... 1.25
❑7, Oct 1988 .... 1.25
❑8, Nov 1988 .... 1.25
❑9, Dec 1988 .... 1.25
❑10, Win 1988 .... 1.25
❑11, Hol 1988; Invasion! First Strike . 1.25
❑12, Feb 1989; Invasion! Aftermath .. 1.25
❑13, Mar 1989 .... 1.50
❑14, Apr 1989 .... 1.50
❑15, May 1989; continues in Suicide Squad #27 .... 1.50
❑16, May 1989; continues in Suicide Squad #28 .... 1.50
❑17, Jun 1989; continues in Manhunter #14 .... 1.50
❑18, Jun 1989; continues in Suicide Squad #30 .... 1.50
❑19, Jul 1989 .... 1.50
❑20, Aug 1989 .... 1.50
❑21, Oct 1989 .... 1.50
❑22, Nov 1989 .... 1.50
❑23, Dec 1989 .... 1.50
❑24, Jan 1990 .... 1.50
❑25, Feb 1990 .... 1.50
❑26 .... 1.50
❑27 .... 1.50
❑28, Jun 1990 .... 1.50
❑29, Jul 1990 .... 1.50
❑30, Aug 1990 .... 1.50
❑31, Oct 1990 .... 1.50
❑32, Dec 1990 .... 1.50
❑33 1991 .... 1.50

CHECK-UP
FANTAGRAPHICS
❑1, b&w 2.75

CHEECH WIZARD
LAST GASP
❑1 .... 3.00

N-MINT

CHEERLEADERS FROM HELL
CALIBER
❑1, b&w 2.50

CHEESE HEADS, THE
TRAGEDY STRIKES
❑1, b&w; second edition 2.50
❑1-2, b&w; second edition 2.95
❑2, b&w 2.50
❑3 .... 2.95
❑4 .... 2.95
❑5 .... 2.95

CHEESE WEASEL
SIDE SHOW
❑1; Color cover 2.95
❑2; Black & white covers begin 2.95
❑3 .... 2.95
❑4 .... 2.95
❑5 .... 2.95
❑6 .... 2.95
❑7 .... 2.95

CHEESE WEASEL: INNOCENT UNTIL PROVEN GUILTY
SIDE SHOW
❑1 .... 9.95

CHEETA POP SCREAM QUEEN
ANTARCTIC / VENUS
❑1, May 1994 .... 2.95
❑2, Nov 1994 .... 2.95
❑3, Jan 1995 .... 2.95
❑4, Mar 1995 .... 2.95
❑5, May 1995 .... 2.95

CHEETA POP (VOL. 2)
FANTAGRAPHICS / EROS
❑1 .... 2.95
❑2 .... 2.95
❑3, Jan 1996 .... 2.95

CHEMICAL WARFARE
CHECKER COMICS
❑1, b&w 2.95
❑2, Sum 1998, b&w 2.95
❑3 .... 2.95

CHEQUE, MATE, THE
FANTAGRAPHICS
❑1, b&w 3.50

CHERRY
LAST GASP
❑1, ca. 1982; 1: Cherry Poptart. 1977 8.00
❑1-2; 1: Cherry Poptart. 1982 .... 4.00
❑2 .... 4.00
❑3; Title changes to Cherry; indicia says Cherry (nee Poptart) 4.00
❑4 .... 3.50
❑5 .... 3.50
❑6 .... 3.50
❑7 .... 3.50
❑8; Oz parody Land of Woz 3.50
❑9 .... 3.50
❑10 .... 3.50
❑11; 3-D issue; 3-D issue 4.00
❑11-2; Kitchen Sink reprint 4.00
❑12, Sum 1991; Cherry goes to Iraq . 3.00
❑13; Last Cherry issue from Last Gasp 3.00
❑14, Feb 1993; O: Cherry. moves to Kitchen Sink; 1st issue at Kitchen Sink 3.00
❑15, Nov 1993 .... 3.00
❑16, Nov 1994 .... 3.00
❑17, Apr 1995; TMNT parody 3.00
❑18, Oct 1995 .... 3.00
❑19, Sep 1996; moves to Cherry Comics 3.00
❑20, Mar 1999; was Kitchen Sink 3.00

CHERRY DELUXE
CHERRY
❑1, Aug 1998, b&w 4.00

CHERRY'S JUBILEE
TUNDRA
❑1 .... 2.95
❑2 .... 2.95

N-MINT

❑3 ... 2.95
❑4 ... 2.95

CHERYL BLOSSOM (1ST SERIES)
ARCHIE

❑1, Sep 1995 ... 2.50
❑2, Oct 1995 ... 2.00
❑3, Nov 1995 ... 2.00

CHERYL BLOSSOM (2ND SERIES)
ARCHIE

❑1, Jul 1996 DDC (a) ... 2.00
❑2, Aug 1996 ... 1.50
❑3, Sep 1996 ... 1.50

CHERYL BLOSSOM (3RD SERIES)
ARCHIE

❑1, Apr 1997 ... 2.00
❑2, May 1997 ... 1.50
❑3, Jun 1997 ... 1.50
❑4, Aug 1997 ... 1.50
❑5, Sep 1997 ... 1.50
❑6, Oct 1997 ... 1.50
❑7, Nov 1997 ... 1.50
❑8, Jan 1998 ... 1.75
❑9, Feb 1998 ... 1.75
❑10, Mar 1998 ... 1.75
❑11, Apr 1998 ... 1.75
❑12, May 1998 ... 1.75
❑13, Jun 1998 ... 1.75
❑14, Aug 1998 ... 1.75
❑15, Sep 1998; cover forms triptych with issue #16 and #17 ... 1.75
❑16, Oct 1998 ... 1.75
❑17, Nov 1998 ... 1.75
❑18, Jan 1999; Cheryl as super-model with readers' fashions ... 1.75
❑19, Feb 1999 ... 1.75
❑20, Mar 1999 ... 1.75
❑21, Apr 1999 ... 1.79
❑22, May 1999 ... 1.79
❑23, Jun 1999 ... 1.79
❑24, Aug 1999 ... 1.79
❑25, Sep 1999 ... 1.79
❑26, Oct 1999 ... 1.79
❑27, Nov 1999 ... 1.79

CHERYL BLOSSOM GOES HOLLYWOOD
ARCHIE

❑1, Dec 1996 ... 1.50
❑2, Jan 1997 ... 1.50
❑3, Feb 1997 ... 1.50

CHERYL BLOSSOM SPECIAL
ARCHIE

❑1 ... 2.00
❑2 ... 2.00
❑3 ... 2.00
❑4 ... 2.00

CHESTY SANCHEZ
ANTARCTIC

❑1, Nov 1995, b&w ... 2.95
❑2, Mar 1996, b&w ... 2.95
❑3 ... 2.95
❑Special 1, Feb 1999, b&w; Super Special Edition; collects two-issue series; cardstock cover ... 5.99

CHEVAL NOIR
DARK HORSE

❑1, Aug 1989, b&w DSt (c) ... 3.50
❑2, Oct 1989, b&w DSt (c) ... 3.50
❑3 ... 3.50
❑4 1990 ... 3.50
❑5, Mar 1990 BB (a) ... 3.50
❑6 1990 BB (w); BB (a) ... 3.50
❑7 1990 DSt (c) ... 3.50
❑8 1990 ... 3.50
❑9 1990 ... 3.50
❑10 1990 ... 3.50
❑11 1990 ... 3.50
❑12 1990 ... 3.50
❑13 1990 ... 3.50
❑14 ... 3.50
❑15 1991 ... 3.50

N-MINT

❑16 1991; trading cards ... 3.75
❑17 1991; trading cards ... 3.50
❑18 1991; trading cards ... 3.50
❑19 1991; trading cards ... 3.50
❑20 1991 ... 3.50
❑21 1991 ... 3.50
❑22 1991 ... 3.50
❑23 1991 ... 3.50
❑24 1991 ... 3.50
❑25 1991 ... 3.50
❑26, Jan 1992 ... 3.50
❑27, Feb 1992 ... 2.95
❑28, Mar 1992 ... 2.95
❑29, Apr 1992 ... 2.95
❑30, May 1992 ... 2.95
❑31, Jun 1992 ... 2.95
❑32, Jul 1992 ... 2.95
❑33, Aug 1992 ... 2.95
❑34, Sep 1992 ... 2.95
❑35, Oct 1992 ... 2.95
❑36, Nov 1992 ... 2.95
❑37, Dec 1992 ... 2.95
❑38, Jan 1993 ... 2.95
❑39, Feb 1993 ... 2.95
❑40, Mar 1993 ... 2.95
❑41, Apr 1993 ... 2.95
❑42, May 1993 ... 2.95
❑43, Jun 1993 ... 2.95
❑44, Jul 1993 ... 2.95
❑45, Aug 1993 ... 2.95
❑46, Sep 1993 ... 2.95
❑47, Oct 1993 ... 2.95
❑48, Nov 1993 ... 2.95
❑49, Dec 1993 ... 2.95
❑50, Jan 1994 ... 2.95

CHIAROSCURO
DC / VERTIGO

❑1, Jul 1995 ... 2.50
❑2, Aug 1995 ... 2.50
❑3, Sep 1995 ... 2.50
❑4, Oct 1995 ... 2.50
❑5, Nov 1995 ... 2.50
❑6, Dec 1995 ... 2.50
❑7, Jan 1996 ... 2.50
❑8, Feb 1996 ... 2.50
❑9, Mar 1996 ... 2.95
❑10, Apr 1996 ... 2.95

CHI CHIAN
SIRIUS

❑1, Oct 1997 ... 2.95
❑2, Dec 1997, b&w; Rough & Pulpy cover ... 2.95
❑2-2 ... 2.95
❑2-3, b&w; Rough & Pulpy cover ... 2.95
❑3, Feb 1998 ... 2.95
❑4, Apr 1998 ... 2.95
❑5, Jun 1998 ... 2.95
❑6, Aug 1998 ... 2.95

CHICK MAGNET
VOLUPTUOUS

❑1 ... 2.95

CHILDHOOD'S END
IMAGE

❑1, Oct 1997, b&w ... 2.95
❑2, Nov 1997 ... 2.95
❑3, Dec 1997 ... 2.95
❑4, Jan 1998 ... 2.95
❑5, Feb 1998 ... 2.95

CHILDREN OF FIRE
FANTAGOR

❑1 ... 2.00
❑2 ... 2.00
❑3 ... 2.00

CHILDREN OF THE FALLEN ANGEL
ACE

❑1, Feb 1997 ... 2.95

Two of the movies featuring killer doll Chucky were adapted by Innovation.

© 1991 Innovative Corporation (Innovation).

N-MINT

CHILDREN OF THE NIGHT
NIGHTWYND

❑1, b&w ... 2.50
❑2, b&w ... 2.50
❑3, b&w ... 2.50
❑4, b&w ... 2.50

CHILDREN OF THE VOYAGER
MARVEL

❑1, Sep 1993; Embossed cover ... 2.95
❑2, Oct 1993 ... 1.95
❑3, Nov 1993 ... 1.95
❑4, Dec 1993 ... 1.95

CHILDREN'S CRUSADE, THE
DC / VERTIGO

❑1, Dec 1993 NG (w) ... 4.50
❑2, Jan 1994 NG (w) ... 4.00

CHILD'S PLAY 2: THE OFFICIAL MOVIE ADAPTATION
INNOVATION

❑1; Adapted from the screenplay by Don Mancini ... 2.50
❑2 ... 2.50
❑3 ... 2.50

CHILD'S PLAY 3
INNOVATION

❑1 ... 2.50
❑2 ... 2.50
❑3 ... 2.50
❑4 ... 2.50

CHILD'S PLAY: THE SERIES
INNOVATION

❑1 ... 2.50
❑2 ... 2.50
❑3 ... 2.50
❑4 ... 2.50
❑5 ... 2.50

CHILLER
MARVEL / EPIC

❑1 ... 3.00
❑2 ... 3.00

CHILLING TALES OF HORROR (1ST SERIES)
STANLEY

❑1 ... 12.00
❑2, Aug 1969 ... 10.00
❑3 ... 10.00
❑4 ... 10.00
❑5 ... 10.00
❑6 ... 10.00
❑7 ... 10.00

CHILLING TALES OF HORROR (2ND SERIES)
STANLEY

❑1 ... 9.00
❑2/A, Feb 1971 ... 8.00
❑2/B ... 8.00
❑3 ... 6.00
❑4 ... 6.00
❑5 ... 6.00

CHIMERA
CROSSGEN

❑1, Mar 2003 ... 2.95
❑2, Apr 2003 ... 2.95
❑3, May 2003 ... 2.95
❑4, Jul 2003 ... 2.95

N-MINT

CHINAGO AND OTHER STORIES
TOME

❑1, b&w 2.50

CHINA SEA
NIGHTWYND

❑1, b&w 2.50
❑2, b&w 2.50
❑3, b&w 2.50
❑4, b&w 2.50

CHIPMUNKS & SQUIRRELS
ORIGINAL SYNDICATE

❑1, Dec 1994 .... 5.95

CHIP 'N' DALE (2ND SERIES)
GOLD KEY

❑1, May 1967 .... 20.00
❑2, Aug 1968 .... 12.00
❑3, Apr 1969 .... 8.00
❑4, Aug 1969 .... 8.00
❑5, Dec 1969 .... 8.00
❑6, Mar 1970 .... 5.00
❑7, Jun 1970 .... 5.00
❑8, Sep 1970 .... 5.00
❑9, Dec 1970 .... 5.00
❑10, Mar 1971 .... 5.00
❑11, Jun 1971 .... 5.00
❑12, Sep 1971 .... 5.00
❑13, Dec 1971 .... 5.00
❑14, Mar 1972 .... 5.00
❑15, May 1972 .... 5.00
❑16, Jul 1972 .... 5.00
❑17, Sep 1972 .... 5.00
❑18, Nov 1972 .... 5.00
❑19, Jan 1973 .... 5.00
❑20, Mar 1973 .... 5.00
❑21, May 1973 .... 3.00
❑22, Jul 1973 .... 3.00
❑23, Sep 1973 .... 3.00
❑24, Nov 1973 .... 3.00
❑25, Jan 1974 .... 3.00
❑26, Mar 1974 .... 3.00
❑27, May 1974 .... 3.00
❑28, Jul 1974 .... 3.00
❑29, Sep 1974 .... 3.00
❑30, Nov 1974 .... 3.00
❑31, Jan 1975 .... 3.00
❑32, Mar 1975 .... 3.00
❑33, May 1975 .... 3.00
❑34, Jul 1975 .... 3.00
❑35, Sep 1975 .... 3.00
❑36, Nov 1975 .... 3.00
❑37, Jan 1976 .... 3.00
❑38, Mar 1976 .... 3.00
❑39, May 1976 .... 3.00
❑40, Jul 1976 .... 3.00
❑41, Aug 1976 .... 2.50
❑42, Sep 1976 .... 2.50
❑43, Nov 1976 .... 2.50
❑44, Jan 1977 .... 2.50
❑45, Mar 1977 .... 2.50
❑46, May 1977 .... 2.50
❑47, Jul 1977 .... 2.50
❑48, Aug 1977 .... 2.50
❑49, Nov 1977 .... 2.50
❑50, Jan 1978 .... 2.50
❑51, Mar 1978 .... 2.50
❑52, May 1978 .... 2.50
❑53, Jul 1978 .... 2.50
❑54, Sep 1978 .... 2.50
❑55, Nov 1978 .... 2.50
❑56, Jan 1979 .... 2.50
❑57, Mar 1979 .... 2.50
❑58, May 1979 .... 2.50
❑59, Jul 1979 .... 2.50
❑60, Aug 1979 .... 2.50
❑61, Sep 1979 .... 2.50
❑62, Oct 1979 .... 2.50
❑63, Nov 1979 .... 2.50
❑64, Feb 1980 .... 2.50
❑65, Apr 1980 .... 2.50
❑66, Jun 1980 .... 2.50
❑67, Aug 1980 .... 2.50
❑68 1980 .... 2.50
❑69 1981 .... 2.50
❑70 1981 .... 2.50
❑71, Jun 1981 .... 2.50
❑72, Aug 1982 .... 2.50
❑73, Oct 1982 .... 2.50
❑74, Dec 1982 .... 2.50
❑75, Feb 1982 .... 2.50
❑76 1982 .... 2.50
❑77 1982 .... 2.50
❑78 .... 2.50
❑79 .... 2.50
❑80 .... 2.50
❑81 .... 2.50
❑82 .... 2.50
❑83 .... 2.50

CHIP 'N' DALE (ONE-SHOT)
DISNEY

❑1 .... 3.50

CHIP 'N' DALE RESCUE RANGERS (DISNEY'S...)
DISNEY

❑1, Jun 1990 .... 1.50
❑2, Jul 1990 .... 1.50
❑3, Aug 1990 .... 1.50
❑4, Sep 1990 .... 1.50
❑5, Oct 1990 .... 1.50
❑6, Nov 1990 .... 1.50
❑7, Dec 1990 .... 1.50
❑8, Jan 1991 .... 1.50
❑9, Feb 1991 .... 1.50
❑10, Mar 1991 .... 1.50
❑11, Apr 1991 .... 1.50
❑12, May 1991 .... 1.50
❑13, Jun 1991 .... 1.50
❑14, Jul 1991 .... 1.50
❑15, Aug 1991 .... 1.50
❑16, Sep 1991 .... 1.50
❑17, Oct 1991 .... 1.50
❑18, Nov 1991 .... 1.50
❑19, Dec 1991 .... 1.50

CHIPS AND VANILLA
KITCHEN SINK

❑1, Jun 1988, b&w 1.75

CHIRALITY
CPM

❑1, Mar 1997 .... 2.95
❑2, Apr 1997; Carol reveals morph power 2.95
❑3, May 1997 .... 2.95
❑4, Jun 1997 .... 2.95
❑5, Jul 1997 .... 2.95
❑6, Aug 1997 .... 2.95
❑7, Sep 1997 .... 2.95
❑8, Oct 1997 .... 2.95
❑9, Nov 1997 .... 2.95
❑10, Dec 1997 .... 2.95
❑11, Jan 1998 .... 2.95
❑12, Feb 1998 .... 2.95
❑13, Mar 1998 .... 2.95
❑14, Apr 1998 .... 2.95
❑15, May 1998 .... 2.95
❑16, Jun 1998 .... 2.95
❑17, Jul 1998 .... 2.95
❑18, Aug 1998 .... 2.95

CHIRÖN
HAMMAC

❑1, b&w; Hammac Publications 2.00
❑2, b&w; Hammac Publications 2.00
❑3, b&w; Alpha Productions takes over 2.00

C.H.I.X.
IMAGE

❑1, Jan 1998; Bad Girl parody comic book 2.50
❑1/Variant, Jan 1998; X-Ray edition; Bad Girl parody comic book; Comic Cavalcade alternate 2.50

C.H.I.X. THAT TIME FORGOT
IMAGE

❑1, Aug 1998 .... 2.95

CHOBITS
TOKYOPOP

❑1, Apr 2003, b&w; printed in Japanese format 9.99
❑2, Jul 2002, b&w; printed in Japanese format 9.99
❑3, Oct 2002, b&w; printed in Japanese format 9.99

CHOICES
ANGRY ISIS

❑1 .... 4.00

CHOKE, THE
ANUBIS

❑1 .... 2.95
❑2 .... 2.95
❑2/Ltd., Centaur cover 2.95
❑Annual 1, Jul 1994 .... 2.75

CHOPPER: EARTH, WIND & FIRE
FLEETWAY-QUALITY

❑1; cardstock cover 2.95
❑2 .... 2.95

CHOPPER: SONG OF THE SURFER
FLEETWAY-QUALITY

❑1 .... 9.95

CHOSEN, THE
MARTINEZ

❑1, Jul 1995; cover indicates Premiere Issue 2.50

CHOSEN (DARK HORSE)
DARK HORSE

❑1, Feb 2004 .... 2.99
❑1-2, Feb 2004 .... 2.99
❑2, Apr 2004 .... 2.99

CHRISTIAN COMICS & GAMES MAGAZINE
AIDA-ZEE

❑0, b&w 3.50
❑1, b&w 3.50

CHRISTINA WINTERS: AGENT OF DEATH
FANTAGRAPHICS / EROS

❑1 .... 2.95
❑2, Mar 1995 .... 2.95

CHRISTMAS CLASSICS (WALT KELLY'S...)
ECLIPSE

❑1, Dec 1987; Peter Wheat 1.75

CHRISTMAS WITH SUPERSWINE
FANTAGRAPHICS

❑1, b&w 2.00

CHRISTMAS WITH THE SUPER-HEROES
DC

❑1, Dec 1988; MA, DG, FM, NA, DD, CS, NC, JL (a); Reprints stories from DC Special Series #21, Justice League of America #110; Teen Titans #13; DC Comics Presents #67, and Batman #219; Mark Waid editorial . 3.00
❑2, Dec 1989; DaG, JBy, ES (w); GM, JBy, DG, ES (a); New stories; Mark Waid editorial; Cover says 1989, indicia says 1988 .... 3.00

CHROMA-TICK, THE
NEW ENGLAND

❑1, Feb 1992; trading cards; Reprints The Tick #1 in color 3.95
❑2, Jun 1992; "Special Edition #2"; trading cards 3.95
❑3, Aug 1992 .... 3.50
❑4, Oct 1992; Bush cover 3.50
❑4/A, Oct 1992; Perot cover 3.50
❑4/B, Oct 1992; Clinton cover 3.50
❑5 .... 3.50
❑6, Jun 1993 .... 3.50
❑7 .... 3.50

N-MINT

❑8 .... 3.50
❑9 .... 3.50

CHROME
HOT COMICS

❑1, Oct 1986 .... 1.50
❑2, Oct 1986; Reprints indicia from issue #1 .... 1.50
❑3, Mar 1987 .... 1.50

CHROMIUM MAN, THE
TRIUMPHANT

❑0, Apr 1994 .... 2.50
❑1, Jan 1994 .... 2.50
❑1/Ashcan 1994; ashcan edition 2.50
❑2 1994; indicia not updated through issue #7; says Jan 94; Violent Past 2.50
❑3 1994 .... 2.50
❑4 1994; Unleashed! 2.50
❑5 1994; Unleashed! 2.50
❑6 1994 .... 2.50
❑7 1994 .... 2.50
❑8, Mar 1994 .... 2.50
❑9, Mar 1994 .... 2.50
❑10, May 1994 .... 2.50
❑11 .... 2.50
❑12 .... 2.50
❑13 .... 2.50
❑14 .... 2.50
❑15 .... 2.50

CHROMIUM MAN, THE: VIOLENT PAST
TRIUMPHANT

❑1 .... 2.50
❑2 .... 2.50

CHRONIC APATHY
ILLITERATURE

❑1, Aug 1995, b&w 2.95
❑2, Sep 1995, b&w 2.95
❑3, Oct 1995, b&w 2.95
❑4, Dec 1995, b&w 2.95

CHRONIC IDIOCY
CALIBER

❑1, b&w 2.50
❑2, b&w 2.50
❑3, b&w 2.50

CHRONICLES OF CORUM, THE
FIRST

❑1, Jan 1987 .... 2.00
❑2, Mar 1987 .... 2.00
❑3, May 1987 .... 2.00
❑4, Jul 1987 .... 2.00
❑5, Sep 1987 .... 2.00
❑6, Nov 1987 .... 2.00
❑7, Jan 1988 .... 2.00
❑8, Mar 1988 .... 2.00
❑9, May 1988 .... 2.00
❑10, Jul 1988 .... 2.00
❑11, Sep 1988 .... 2.00
❑12, Nov 1988 .... 2.00

CHRONICLES OF CRIME AND MYSTERY: SHERLOCK HOLMES
NORTHSTAR

❑1, b&w 2.25

CHRONICLES OF PANDA KHAN, THE
ABACUS

❑1 .... 1.50
❑2 .... 1.50
❑3 .... 1.50
❑4 .... 1.50

CHRONO CRUSADE
ADV MANGA

❑1, ca 2004 .... 9.99

CHRONOS
DC

❑1, Mar 1998 .... 2.50
❑2, Apr 1998 .... 2.50
❑3, May 1998 .... 2.50
❑4, Jun 1998 D: original Chronos 2.50
❑5, Jul 1998 .... 2.50

N-MINT

❑6, Aug 1998; A: Tattooed Man. funeral of original Chronos 2.50
❑7, Sep 1998 .... 2.50
❑8, Oct 1998 .... 2.50
❑9, Dec 1998 A: Destiny 2.50
❑10, Jan 1999 A: Azrael 2.50
❑11, Feb 1999 .... 2.50
❑1000000, Nov 1998 A: Hourman 3.00

CHRONOWAR
DARK HORSE / MANGA

❑1, Aug 1996, b&w 2.95
❑2, Sep 1996, b&w 2.95
❑3, Oct 1996, b&w 2.95
❑4, Nov 1996, b&w 2.95
❑5, Dec 1996, b&w 2.95
❑6, Jan 1997, b&w 2.95
❑7, Feb 1997, b&w 2.95
❑8, Mar 1997, b&w 2.95
❑9, Apr 1997, b&w 2.95

CHUCK NORRIS
MARVEL / STAR

❑1, Jan 1987 SD (a) 1.50
❑2, Mar 1987 SD (a) 1.25
❑3, May 1987 SD (a) 1.25
❑4, Jul 1987 .... 1.25
❑5, Sep 1997 .... 1.25

CHUK THE BARBARIC
AVATAR

❑3; no color cover 1.25

CHYNA
CHAOS!

❑1, Sep 2000 .... 2.95
❑1/Variant, Sep 2000; Special cover 2.95

CINDERALLA
VIZ

❑1, Jun 2002 .... 15.95

CINDER AND ASHE
DC

❑1, May 1988 .... 1.75
❑2, Jun 1988 .... 1.75
❑3, Jul 1988 .... 1.75
❑4, Aug 1988 .... 1.75

CINNAMON EL CICLO
DC

❑1, Oct 2003 .... 2.50
❑2, Nov 2003 .... 2.50
❑3, Dec 2003 .... 2.50
❑4, Jan 2004 .... 2.50
❑5, Feb 2004 .... 2.50

CIRCLE UNLEASHED, THE
EPOCH

❑1, May 1995 .... 3.00

CIRCLE WEAVE, THE: APPRENTICE TO A GOD
ABALONE

❑1, b&w 2.00
❑2, b&w 2.00

CIRCUS WORLD
HAMMAC

❑1, b&w 2.50
❑2 .... 2.50
❑3 .... 2.50

CITIZEN V AND THE V-BATTALION
MARVEL

❑1, Jun 2001 .... 2.99
❑2, Jul 2001 .... 2.99
❑3, Aug 2001 .... 2.99

CITIZEN V AND THE V BATTALION: THE EVERLASTING
MARVEL

❑1, Apr 2002 .... 2.99
❑2, May 2002 .... 2.99
❑3, Jun 2002 .... 2.99
❑4, Jul 2002 .... 2.99

CITY OF HEROES
DARK HORSE

❑1; no cover price ....

Jay Hosler shares his field of scholastic expertise with others in the educational *Clan Apis*.

© 1998 Jay Hosler (Active Synapse).

N-MINT

CITY OF SILENCE
IMAGE

❑1, May 2000 .... 2.50
❑2, Jun 2000 .... 2.50
❑3, Jul 2000 .... 2.50

CLAIR VOYANT
LIGHTNING

❑1, Jun 1996, b&w 3.50

CLAN APIS
ACTIVE SYNAPSE

❑1, b&w; educational comic about bees 2.95
❑2 .... 2.95
❑3 .... 2.95
❑4 .... 2.95
❑5, Apr 1999, b&w 3.95

CLANDESTINE
MARVEL

❑1, Oct 1994; foil cover 2.95
❑2, Nov 1994 .... 2.50
❑3, Dec 1994 .... 2.50
❑4, Jan 1995 .... 2.50
❑5, Feb 1995 .... 2.50
❑6, Mar 1995 .... 2.50
❑7, Apr 1995 .... 2.50
❑8, May 1995 .... 2.50
❑9, Jun 1995 .... 2.50
❑10, Jul 1995 .... 2.50
❑11, Aug 1995 .... 2.50
❑12, Sep 1995 .... 2.50
❑Ashcan 1, Oct 1994; Preview 1.50

CLASH
DC

❑1, ca. 1991 .... 4.95
❑2, ca. 1991 .... 4.95
❑3, ca. 1991 .... 4.95

CLASSIC ADVENTURE STRIPS
DRAGON LADY

❑1, May 1985; King of the Royal Mounted 4.00
❑2, Jul 1985; Red Ryder 4.00
❑3, Sep 1985; Dickie Dare, Flash Gordon 4.00
❑4, Nov 1985; FR (w); FR (a); Buz Sawyer; Johnny Hazard; Steve Canyon 4.00
❑5, Jan 1986; Wash Tubbs 4.00
❑6, Mar 1986; Mandrake the Magician, Johnny Hazard, Rip Kirby 4.00
❑7, Jul 1986; Buz Sawyer 4.00
❑8, Oct 1986 .... 4.00
❑9, Jan 1987 .... 4.00
❑10, Apr 1987 MA (w); MA (a) 4.00

CLASSIC GIRLS
ETERNITY

❑1, b&w 2.50
❑2, b&w 2.50
❑3, b&w 2.50
❑4, b&w 2.50

CLASSIC JONNY QUEST: SKULL & DOUBLE CROSSBONES
ILLUSTRATED PRODUCTIONS

❑1, Mar 1996; smaller than normal size comic book; No cover price; inserted with Jonny Quest videos 1.00

Condition price index: Multiply "NM prices" above by: **0.83 for Very Fine/Near Mint**
0.66 for Very Fine • 0.33 for Fine • 0.2 for Very Good • 0.125 for Good

N-MINT

CLASSIC JONNY QUEST: THE QUETONG MISSILE MYSTERY
ILLUSTRATED PRODUCTIONS
❑1, Mar 1996; smaller than normal size comic book; No cover price; inserted with Jonny Quest videos 1.00

CLASSIC PUNISHER
MARVEL
❑1, Dec 1989, b&w; prestige format; Reprints Punisher stories from Marvel Preview #2, Marvel Super Action #1 ..... 4.95

CLASSICS ILLUSTRATED (FIRST)
FIRST
❑1, Feb 1990 ..... 4.00
❑2, Feb 1990 ..... 4.00
❑3, Feb 1990 ..... 4.00
❑4, Feb 1990 BSz (c); BSz (a) 4.00
❑5, Mar 1990 ..... 4.00
❑6, Mar 1990 CR (a) 4.00
❑7, Apr 1990 DS (a) 4.00
❑8, Apr 1990 JK (a) 4.00
❑9, May 1990 MP (a) 4.00
❑10, Jun 1990 ..... 4.00
❑11, Jul 1990 ..... 4.00
❑12, Aug 1990 ..... 4.00
❑13, Oct 1990 ..... 4.00
❑14, Sep 1990 CR (a) 4.00
❑15, Nov 1990 ..... 4.00
❑16, Dec 1990 JSa (w); JSa (a) 4.00
❑17 1991 ..... 4.00
❑18 1991 ..... 4.00
❑19, Feb 1991 ..... 4.00
❑20, Mar 1991 ..... 4.00
❑21 1991 ..... 4.00
❑22 1991 ..... 4.00
❑23, Apr 1991 ..... 4.00
❑24, May 1991 ..... 4.00
❑25, May 1991 ..... 4.00
❑26, Jun 1991 ..... 4.00
❑27 ..... 4.00

CLASSICS ILLUSTRATED STUDY GUIDE
ACCLAIM
❑1 1997; All Quiet on the Western Front 4.99
❑2 1997; Around the World in 80 Days 4.99
❑3, Sep 1997; The Call of the Wild 4.99
❑4 1997; Captains Courageous 4.99
❑5 1997; A Christmas Carol 4.99
❑6 1997; The Count of Monte Cristo 4.99
❑7, Aug 1997; David Copperfield 4.99
❑8 1997; Doctor Jekyll and Mr. Hyde 4.99
❑9 1997; Don Quixote 5.25
❑10 1997; Faust 4.99
❑11 1997; Frankenstein 4.99
❑12 1997; Great Expectations 4.99
❑13, Sep 1997; The Hunchback of Notre Dame 4.99
❑14 1997; The Iliad 4.99
❑15 1997; The Invisible Man 4.99
❑16, Aug 1997; Julius Caesar 4.99
❑17, Aug 1997; The Jungle Book 4.99
❑18 1997; Kidnapped 4.99
❑19 1997; Kim 4.99
❑20 1997; The Last of the Mohicans 4.99
❑21, Sep 1997; Lord Jim 4.99
❑22, Aug 1997; The Man in the Iron Mask 4.99
❑23 1997; The Master of Ballantrae 4.99
❑24, Apr 1997; A Midsummer Night's Dream 4.99
❑25, Apr 1997; Moby Dick 4.99
❑26 1997; new adaptation of Narrative of the Life of Frederick Douglass 4.99
❑27 1997; The Prince and the Pauper 4.99
❑28, Aug 1997; Pudd'nhead Wilson 4.99
❑29, Sep 1997; Robinson Crusoe 4.99
❑30 1997; new adaptation of The Scarlet Pimpernel 4.99
❑31 1997; Silas Marner 4.99
❑32 1997; War of the Worlds 4.99
❑33 1997; Wuthering Heights 4.99
❑34, Feb 1997 ..... 4.99
❑35 1997 ..... 4.99
❑36, Feb 1997 ..... 4.99
❑37, Jul 1997 ..... 4.99
❑38, Feb 1997 ..... 4.99

CLASSIC STAR WARS
DARK HORSE
❑1, Aug 1992 ..... 4.00
❑2, Sep 1992 ..... 3.50
❑3, Oct 1992 ..... 3.50
❑4, Nov 1992 ..... 3.25
❑5, Dec 1992 AW (a) 3.25
❑6, Jan 1993 AW (a) 3.00
❑7, Feb 1993 AW (a) 3.00
❑8, Apr 1993; AW (a); trading card 3.00
❑9, May 1993 AW (a) 3.00
❑10, Jun 1993 ..... 3.00
❑11, Aug 1993 ..... 3.00
❑12, Sep 1993 ..... 3.00
❑13, Oct 1993 ..... 3.00
❑14, Nov 1993 ..... 3.00
❑15, Jan 1994 ..... 3.00
❑16, Feb 1994 ..... 3.00
❑17, Mar 1994 ..... 3.00
❑18, Apr 1994 ..... 3.00
❑19, May 1994 ..... 3.00
❑20, Jun 1994; Giant-size 3.50

CLASSIC STAR WARS: A NEW HOPE
DARK HORSE
❑1, Jun 1994; prestige format; Collects Star Wars (Marvel) #1-3 ..... 3.95
❑2, Jul 1994; prestige format; Collects Star Wars (Marvel) #4-6 ..... 3.95

CLASSIC STAR WARS: DEVILWORLDS
DARK HORSE
❑1, Aug 1996 ..... 2.50
❑2, Sep 1996 ..... 2.50

CLASSIC STAR WARS: HAN SOLO AT STARS' END
DARK HORSE
❑1, Mar 1997; adapts Brian Daley novel; cardstock cover 2.95
❑2, Apr 1997; adapts Brian Daley novel; cardstock cover 2.95
❑3, May 1997; adapts Brian Daley novel; cardstock cover 2.95

CLASSIC STAR WARS: RETURN OF THE JEDI
DARK HORSE
❑1, Oct 1994; AW (a); polybagged with trading card 3.50
❑2, Nov 1994 AW (a) 3.95

CLASSIC STAR WARS: THE EARLY ADVENTURES
DARK HORSE
❑1, Aug 1994 ..... 2.50
❑2, Sep 1994 ..... 2.50
❑3, Oct 1994 ..... 2.50
❑4, Nov 1994 ..... 2.50
❑5, Dec 1994 ..... 2.50
❑6, Jan 1995 ..... 2.50
❑7, Feb 1995 ..... 2.50
❑8, Mar 1995 ..... 2.50
❑9, Apr 1995 ..... 2.50

CLASSIC STAR WARS: THE EMPIRE STRIKES BACK
DARK HORSE
❑1, Aug 1994; prestige format 3.95
❑2, Sep 1994; prestige format 3.95

CLASSIC STAR WARS: THE VANDELHELM MISSION
DARK HORSE
❑1, Mar 1995 ..... 2.50

CLASSIC X-MEN
MARVEL
❑1, Sep 1986 ..... 6.00
❑2, Oct 1986; DC (a); Reprints X-Men (1st Series) #94 ..... 4.00
❑3, Nov 1986 ..... 3.00
❑4, Dec 1986 ..... 3.00
❑5, Jan 1987 ..... 3.00
❑6, Feb 1987 ..... 2.50
❑7, Mar 1987 ..... 2.50
❑8, Apr 1987 ..... 2.50
❑9, May 1987 ..... 2.50
❑10, Jun 1987 ..... 2.50
❑11, Jul 1987 ..... 2.50
❑12, Aug 1987 ..... 2.50
❑13, Sep 1987 ..... 2.50
❑14, Oct 1987 ..... 2.50
❑15, Nov 1987 ..... 2.50
❑16, Dec 1987 ..... 2.50
❑17, Jan 1988 ..... 2.50
❑18, Feb 1988 ..... 2.50
❑19, Mar 1988 ..... 2.50
❑20, Apr 1988 ..... 2.50
❑21, May 1988 ..... 2.50
❑22, Jun 1988 FM (a) 2.50
❑23, Jul 1988 ..... 2.50
❑24, Aug 1988 ..... 2.50
❑25, Sep 1988 ..... 2.50
❑26, Oct 1988 ..... 2.50
❑27, Nov 1988 ..... 2.50
❑28, Dec 1988 ..... 2.50
❑29, Jan 1989 ..... 2.50
❑30, Feb 1989 ..... 2.00
❑31, Mar 1989; JBy (a); Reprints X-Men (1st Series) #125 ..... 2.00
❑32, Apr 1989 ..... 2.00
❑33, May 1989 ..... 2.00
❑34, Jun 1989 ..... 2.00
❑35, Jul 1989 ..... 2.00
❑36, Aug 1989 ..... 2.00
❑37, Sep 1989 ..... 2.00
❑38, Oct 1989 ..... 2.00
❑39, Nov 1989 ..... 2.00
❑40, Nov 1989 ..... 2.00
❑41, Dec 1989 ..... 2.00
❑42, Dec 1989 ..... 2.00
❑43, Jan 1990 ..... 2.00
❑44, Feb 1990 ..... 2.00
❑45, Mar 1990; Series continued in X-Men Classic #46 ..... 2.00

CLAUS
DRACO
❑1, Dec 1997 ..... 2.95
❑2, Feb 1998 ..... 2.95

CLAWS
CONQUEST
❑1, b&w 2.95

CLAW THE UNCONQUERED
DC
❑1, Jun 1975 1: Claw the Unconquered 3.50
❑2, Aug 1975 ..... 2.50
❑3, Oct 1975 ..... 2.00
❑4, Dec 1975 ..... 2.00
❑5, Feb 1976 ..... 2.00
❑6, Apr 1976 ..... 2.00
❑7, Jun 1976 ..... 2.00
❑8, Aug 1976; Bicentennial #18 ..... 2.00
❑9, Oct 1976 O: Claw the Unconquered 2.00
❑10, May 1978 ..... 2.00
❑11, Jul 1978 ..... 2.00
❑12, Sep 1978 ..... 2.00

CLEM: MALL SECURITY
SPIT TAKE
❑0, ca. 1997, b&w 2.00

CLEOPATRA
RIP OFF
❑1, Feb 1992, b&w 2.50

CLERKS: THE COMIC BOOK
ONI
❑1, Feb 1998 KSm (w) 5.00
❑1-2 KSm (w) 3.00
❑1-3 KSm (w) 3.00
❑1-4, May 1998 ..... 3.00
❑2 ..... 3.00
❑Holiday 1, Dec 1998, b&w; Double-size KSm (w) 3.00

Condition price index: Multiply "NM prices" above by: **0.83 for Very Fine/Near Mint**
0.66 for Very Fine • 0.33 for Fine • 0.2 for Very Good • 0.125 for Good

N-MINT

CLETUS AND FLOYD SHOW, THE
ASYLUM
- ❑1, Mar 2002 ... 2.95

CLF: CYBERNETIC LIBERATION FRONT
ANUBIS
- ❑1 ... 2.75

CLICK!
NBM
- ❑1 ... 10.95
- ❑2 ... 12.95
- ❑3 ... 12.95
- ❑4 ... 10.95

CLIFFHANGER!
IMAGE
- ❑1, ca. 1997 ... 3.00

CLIFFHANGER COMICS
AC
- ❑1, ca. 1989, b&w; Tom Mix Western; Don Winslow serial (photo-text)
- ❑ ... 2.50
- ❑2, ca. 1989, b&w; Tom Mix Western 2.50

CLIFFHANGER COMICS (2ND SERIES)
AC
- ❑1/A 1990, b&w; new and reprint ... 2.75
- ❑2/A, Aug 1990, b&w; new and reprint 2.75

CLIMAXXX
AIRCEL
- ❑1, Apr 1991 ... 3.50
- ❑2, May 1991 ... 3.50
- ❑3, Jun 1991 ... 3.50
- ❑4, Jul 1991 ... 3.50

CLINT
TRIGON
- ❑1, Sep 1986 ... 1.50
- ❑2, Jan 1987 ... 1.50

CLINT: THE HAMSTER TRIUMPHANT
ECLIPSE
- ❑1, b&w ... 1.50
- ❑2, b&w ... 1.50

CLOAK & DAGGER
MARVEL
- ❑1, Jul 1985 ... 2.00
- ❑2, Sep 1985 TD (a) ... 1.50
- ❑3, Nov 1985 TD (a); A: Spider-Man . 1.50
- ❑4, Jan 1986; Secret Wars II ... 1.50
- ❑5, Mar 1985 TD (a); O: Mayhem. 1: Mayhem ... 1.25
- ❑6, May 1985 TD (a) ... 1.25
- ❑7, Jul 1985 TD (a) ... 1.25
- ❑8, Sep 1985 TD (a) ... 1.25
- ❑9, Nov 1985 TD (a) ... 1.25
- ❑10, Jan 1986 TD (a) ... 1.25
- ❑11, Mar 1986; Giant-size TD (a) ... 1.50

CLOAK AND DAGGER IN PREDATOR AND PREY
MARVEL
- ❑1; prestige format ... 5.95

CLOAK & DAGGER (LTD. SERIES)
MARVEL
- ❑1, Oct 1983 TD (a); 1: Brigid O'Reilly 2.95
- ❑2, Nov 1983 TD (a) ... 2.95
- ❑3, Dec 1983 TD (a) ... 2.00
- ❑4, Jan 1984 TD (a); O: Cloak & Dagger 2.00

CLOCK!
TOP SHELF
- ❑3, b&w ... 2.95

CLOCKMAKER
IMAGE
- ❑1, Feb 2003 ... 2.50
- ❑2, Mar 2003 ... 2.50
- ❑3, May 2003 ... 2.50
- ❑4, Jun 2003 ... 2.50

CLOCKMAKER ACT 2
IMAGE
- ❑1 2003 ... 4.95
- ❑2, Aug 2004 ... 4.95

N-MINT

CLONEZONE SPECIAL
DARK HORSE
- ❑1, b&w ... 2.00

CLOUDFALL
IMAGE
- ❑1, Dec 2003 ... 4.95

CLOVER HONEY
FANTAGRAPHICS
- ❑

CLOWN: NOBODY'S LAUGHING NOW, THE
FLEETWAY-QUALITY
- ❑1 ... 4.95

CLOWNS
YAHOO PRO
- ❑1 ... 3.00

CLOWNS, THE
DARK HORSE
- ❑1, Apr 1998, b&w; adapts Leoncavallo opera ... 2.95

CLYDE CRASHCUP
DELL
- ❑1, Aug 1963 ... 90.00
- ❑2 1963 ... 65.00
- ❑3, May 1964 ... 48.00
- ❑4, Jun 1964 ... 48.00
- ❑5, Sep 1964 ... 48.00

COBALT 60
TUNDRA
- ❑1 ... 4.95
- ❑2 ... 4.95

COBALT BLUE
POWER
- ❑1, Jan 1978 MGu (a) ... 2.00

COBALT BLUE (INNOVATION)
INNOVATION
- ❑1, Sep 1989 MGu (a) ... 2.00
- ❑2, Oct 1989 MGu (a) ... 2.00
- ❑GN 1; KP (a); Graphic novel ... 5.95

COBRA
VIZ
- ❑1 ... 2.95
- ❑2 ... 2.95
- ❑3 ... 2.95
- ❑4 ... 2.95
- ❑5 ... 2.95
- ❑6 ... 2.95
- ❑7 ... 3.25
- ❑8 ... 3.25
- ❑9 ... 3.25
- ❑10 ... 3.25
- ❑11 ... 3.25
- ❑12 ... 3.25

CODA
CODA
- ❑1 ... 2.00
- ❑2 ... 2.00
- ❑3 ... 2.00
- ❑4 ... 2.00

CODE BLUE
IMAGE
- ❑1, Apr 1998 ... 2.95

CODENAME: DANGER
LODESTONE
- ❑1, Aug 1985 RB (a) ... 2.00
- ❑2, Oct 1985 ... 1.75
- ❑3, Jan 1986 PS (a) ... 1.75
- ❑4, May 1986 ... 1.75

CODENAME: FIREARM
MALIBU
- ❑0, Jun 1995, b&w ... 2.95
- ❑1, Jun 1995, b&w ... 2.95
- ❑2, Jul 1995, b&w ... 2.95
- ❑3, Jul 1995, b&w ... 2.95
- ❑4, Aug 1995, b&w ... 2.95
- ❑5, Aug 1995, b&w ... 2.95

The further adventures of Kevin Smith's creations can be found in *Clerks: The Comic Book.*

© 1998 Kevin Smith and Oni Press.

N-MINT

CODENAME: GENETIX
MARVEL
- ❑1, Feb 1993 ... 1.75
- ❑2, Mar 1993 ... 1.75
- ❑3, Apr 1993 ... 1.75
- ❑4, May 1993 ... 1.75

CODENAME: KNOCKOUT
DC / VERTIGO
- ❑0, Jun 2001 ... 2.50
- ❑1, Jul 2001 ... 2.50
- ❑2, Aug 2001 ... 2.50
- ❑3, Sep 2001 ... 2.50
- ❑4, Oct 2001 ... 2.50
- ❑5, Nov 2001 ... 2.50
- ❑6, Dec 2001 ... 2.50
- ❑7, Jan 2002 ... 2.50
- ❑8, Feb 2002 ... 2.50
- ❑9, Mar 2002 ... 2.50
- ❑10, Apr 2002 ... 2.50
- ❑11, May 2002 ... 2.50
- ❑12, Jun 2002 ... 2.50
- ❑13, Jul 2002 ... 2.50
- ❑14, Aug 2002 ... 2.50
- ❑15, Sep 2002 ... 2.50
- ❑16, Oct 2002 ... 2.75
- ❑17, Nov 2002 ... 2.75
- ❑18, Dec 2002 ... 2.75
- ❑19, Feb 2003 ... 2.75
- ❑20, Mar 2003 ... 2.75
- ❑21, Apr 2003 ... 2.75
- ❑22, May 2003 ... 2.75
- ❑23, Jun 2003 ... 2.75

CODE NAME NINJA
SOLSON
- ❑1, b&w ... 2.00

CODENAME: SCORPIO
ANTARCTIC
- ❑1, Oct 1996, b&w ... 2.95
- ❑2, Apr 1997, b&w ... 2.95
- ❑3, Jul 1997, b&w ... 2.95
- ❑4, Sep 1997, b&w ... 2.95

CODENAME: SPITFIRE
MARVEL
- ❑10, Jul 1987; Series continued from Spitfire and the Troubleshooters #9 1.00
- ❑11, Aug 1987 ... 1.00
- ❑12, Sep 1987 ... 1.00
- ❑13, Oct 1987 ... 1.00

CODENAME: STRIKEFORCE
SPECTRUM
- ❑1, Jun 1984 ... 1.50

CODENAME: STRYKE FORCE
IMAGE
- ❑0, Jun 1995; indicia says Jun, cover says Jul ... 2.50
- ❑1, Jan 1994 ... 2.50
- ❑1/Gold, Jan 1994; Gold promotional edition ... 3.00
- ❑1/Variant, Jan 1994; blue embossed edition ... 2.50
- ❑2, Mar 1994 ... 1.95
- ❑3, Apr 1994 ... 1.95
- ❑4, Jun 1994 ... 1.95
- ❑5, Jul 1994 ... 1.95
- ❑6, Aug 1994 ... 1.95
- ❑7, Oct 1994 ... 1.95

N-MINT

❑8/A, Nov 1994; same cover, different poster 1.95
❑8/B, Nov 1994; same cover, different poster 1.95
❑8/C, Nov 1994; same cover, different poster 1.95
❑9, Dec 1994 ..... 1.95
❑10, Jan 1995 ..... 1.95
❑11, Mar 1995 ..... 1.95
❑12, Apr 1995 ..... 1.95
❑13, May 1995 ..... 2.25
❑14, Aug 1995 ..... 2.25

CODE OF HONOR
MARVEL

❑1, Jan 1997 ..... 5.95
❑2, Mar 1997 ..... 5.95
❑3, Apr 1997 ..... 5.95
❑4, May 1997 ..... 5.95

CODY STARBUCK
STAR*REACH

❑1 ..... 2.00

CO-ED SEXXTASY
FANTAGRAPHICS / EROS

❑1, Dec 1999 ..... 3.50
❑2, Jan 2000 ..... 3.50
❑3, Feb 2000 ..... 3.50
❑4, Mar 2000 ..... 3.50
❑5, Apr 2000 ..... 3.50
❑6, May 2000 ..... 3.50
❑7, Jun 2000 ..... 3.50
❑8, Jul 2000 ..... 3.50
❑9, Aug 2000 ..... 3.50
❑10, Sep 2000 ..... 3.50
❑11, Oct 2000 ..... 3.50

COFFIN, THE
ONI

❑1, Sep 2000, b&w 2.95

COFFIN BLOOD
MONSTER

❑1, b&w 3.95

COLD BLOODED
NORTHSTAR

❑1, b&w 2.95
❑2, Sep 1993, b&w 2.95
❑3, Dec 1993, b&w 4.95

COLD-BLOODED CHAMELEON COMMANDOS
BLACKTHORNE

❑1 ..... 1.50
❑2 ..... 1.50
❑3 ..... 1.50
❑4 ..... 1.50
❑5 ..... 1.50

COLD BLOODED: THE BURNING KISS
NORTHSTAR

❑1, Nov 1993, b&w; cardstock cover 4.95

COLD EDEN
LEGACY

❑4, Nov 1995, b&w; cover says Feb 96, indicia says Nov 95 ..... 2.35

COLLECTION
ETERNITY

❑1 ..... 2.95

COLLECTOR'S DRACULA, THE
MILLENNIUM

❑1 ..... 3.95
❑2 ..... 3.95

COLLECTORS GUIDE TO THE ULTRAVERSE
MALIBU / ULTRAVERSE

❑1, Aug 1994 ..... 1.00

COLLIER'S
FANTAGRAPHICS

❑1, b&w 2.75
❑2, b&w 3.25

N-MINT

COLONIA
COLONIA

❑1, Oct 1998, b&w 2.95
❑1-2, b&w 2.95
❑2, b&w 2.95
❑3, b&w 2.95
❑4 ..... 2.95
❑5 ..... 2.95
❑6 ..... 2.95
❑7 ..... 2.95
❑8 ..... 2.95

COLORS IN BLACK
DARK HORSE

❑1, Mar 1995 ..... 2.95
❑2 1995 ..... 2.95
❑3 1995 ..... 2.95
❑4 1995 ..... 2.95

COLOSSUS
MARVEL

❑1, Oct 1997; gatefold summary 2.99

COLOSSUS: GOD'S COUNTRY
MARVEL

❑1; prestige format 6.95

COLOUR OF MAGIC, THE (TERRY PRATCHETT'S...)
INNOVATION

❑1 ..... 2.50
❑2 ..... 2.50
❑3 ..... 2.50
❑4 ..... 2.50

COLT SPECIAL
AC

❑1, Aug 1985 ..... 1.50

COLUMBUS
DARK HORSE

❑1, b&w 2.50

COLVILLE
KING INK

❑1, Sep 1997, b&w 3.00

COMBAT (IMAGE)
IMAGE

❑1, Jan 1996 ..... 2.50
❑2, Jan 1996 ..... 2.50

COMBAT KELLY (2ND SERIES)
MARVEL

❑1, Jun 1972; O: Combat Kelly. Combat Kelly becomes leader of Dum-Dum Dugan's Deadly Dozen (from Sgt. Fury #98) 10.00
❑2, Aug 1972 ..... 6.00
❑3, Oct 1972 O: Combat Kelly 6.00
❑4, Dec 1972 A: Sgt. Fury and his Howling Commandos 4.00
❑5, Feb 1973 ..... 4.00
❑6, Apr 1973 ..... 4.00
❑7, Jun 1973 ..... 4.00
❑8, Aug 1973 ..... 4.00
❑9, Oct 1973; D: Deadly Dozen. Combat Kelly leaves team 4.00

COMBAT ZONE
AVALON

❑1, b&w 2.95

COME AGAIN
FANTAGRAPHICS / EROS

❑1, Feb 1997 ..... 2.95
❑2, May 1997 ..... 2.95

COMET, THE (RED CIRCLE)
ARCHIE / RED CIRCLE

❑1, Oct 1983 ..... 1.00
❑2, Dec 1983 ..... 1.00

COMET, THE (IMPACT)
DC / IMPACT

❑1, Jul 1991 ..... 1.00
❑2, Aug 1991 ..... 1.00
❑3, Sep 1991 ..... 1.00
❑4, Oct 1991 ..... 1.00
❑5, Nov 1991 ..... 1.00
❑6, Dec 1991 ..... 1.00

N-MINT

❑7, Jan 1992 ..... 1.00
❑8, Feb 1992 ..... 1.00
❑9, Mar 1992 ..... 1.00
❑10, Apr 1992; trading card 1.00
❑11, May 1992 ..... 1.00
❑12, Jun 1992 ..... 1.00
❑13, Jul 1992 ..... 1.00
❑14, Aug 1992 ..... 1.00
❑15, Sep 1992 ..... 1.00
❑16, Oct 1992 ..... 1.00
❑17, Nov 1992 ..... 1.00
❑18, Dec 1992 ..... 1.00
❑Annual 1; trading card 2.00

COMET TALES
ROCKET

❑1 ..... 1.00
❑2 ..... 1.00
❑3 ..... 1.00

COMIC BOOK
MARVEL / SPUMCO

❑1, ca. 1996; oversized anthology 6.95
❑2, ca. 1997; oversized anthology 6.95

COMIC BOOK CONFIDENTIAL
SPHINX

❑1, ca. 1988, b&w; giveaway promo for documentary film of same name; No cover price; Film promo 2.00

COMIC BOOK HEAVEN
SLAVE LABOR

❑1 ..... 2.00
❑2 ..... 2.00

COMIC BOOK TALENT SEARCH, THE
SILVERWOLF

❑1, Feb 1987 ..... 1.50

COMICO BLACK BOOK, THE
COMICO

❑1, ca. 1987 ..... 2.00

COMICO CHRISTMAS SPECIAL
COMICO

❑1, Dec 1988 ..... 2.50

COMICO COLLECTION
COMICO

❑1; 10 comics & Grendel: Devil's Vagary 9.95

COMICS AND STORIES
DARK HORSE

❑1, Apr 1996; Wolf & Red 2.95
❑2, May 1996 ..... 2.95
❑3, Jun 1996; Bad Luck Blackie 2.95
❑4, Jan 1997; Screwball Squirrel 2.95

COMICS ARE DEAD
SLAP HAPPY

❑1 1999, b&w 4.95

COMICS ARTIST SHOWCASE, THE
SHOWCASE

❑1 ..... 1.00

COMICS FOR STONERS
JASON NEUMAN

❑1 .....

COMICS' GREATEST WORLD
DARK HORSE

❑1, Jun 1993; preview copy of Comics' Greatest World: X; 1500 printed 1.00

COMICS' GREATEST WORLD: ARCADIA
DARK HORSE

❑1, Jun 1993; FM (c); FM (a); 1: X. X; Arcadia, Week 1 ..... 2.00
❑1/Ltd., Jun 1993; limited edition for Heroes World Distribution; FM (c); FM (a); enhanced cardstock cover; X 2.50
❑2, Jun 1993; Pit Bulls; Arcadia, Week 2 ..... 1.00
❑3, Jun 1993; 1: Ghost. Ghost; Arcadia, Week 3 ..... 3.00
❑4; Monster; continues in Comics' Greatest World - Golden City; Arcadia, Week 4 ..... 1.00

Condition price index: Multiply "NM prices" above by: **0.83 for Very Fine/Near Mint • 0.66 for Very Fine • 0.33 for Fine • 0.2 for Very Good • 0.125 for Good**

N-MINT

COMICS' GREATEST WORLD: CINNABAR FLATS
DARK HORSE

❑1, Jun 1993; Division 13; Vortex, Week 1 ... 1.00
❑1/A, Aug 1993; limited edition for American Distribution; Division 13; Vortex, Week 1; cardstock cover ... 2.50
❑1/Ltd., Aug 1993; limited edition; Division 13; cardstock cover ... 2.50
❑2, Jun 1993; Hero Zero; Vortex, Week 2 ... 1.00
❑3, Jun 1993; King Tiger; Vortex, Week 3 ... 1.00
❑4, Jun 1993; Out of the Vortex; continues in Out of the Vortex (Comics' Greatest World...), Week 4 ... 1.00

COMICS' GREATEST WORLD: GOLDEN CITY
DARK HORSE

❑1, Jul 1993; JO (c); Rebel; Golden City, Week 1 ... 1.00
❑1/Ltd.; limited edition for Heroes World Distribution; JO (c); enhanced cardstock cover; Rebel; Golden City, Week 1 ... 2.50
❑2, Jul 1993; Mecha; Golden City, Week 2 ... 1.00
❑3, Jul 1993; Titan; Golden City, Week 3 ... 1.00
❑4, Aug 1993; JDu (a); continues in Comics' Greatest World - Steel Harbor; Catalyst: Agents of Change; Golden City, Week 4 ... 1.00

COMICS' GREATEST WORLD SOURCEBOOK
DARK HORSE

❑1, Mar 1993 ... 1.00

COMICS' GREATEST WORLD: STEEL HARBOR
DARK HORSE

❑1, Aug 1993; PG (a); 1: Barb Wire. Barb Wire; Steel Harbor, Week 1 ... 2.50
❑2; The Machine; Steel Harbor, Week 2 1.00
❑3, Aug 1993; Wolf Gang; Steel Harbor, Week 3 ... 1.00
❑4, Aug 1993; Motorhead; continues in Comics' Greatest World - Cinnabar Flats; Steel Harbor, Week 4 ... 1.00

COMICS 101 PRESENTS
CHEAP THRILLS

❑1, Aug 1994, b&w; two covers, one inside the other ... 1.50

COMING OF APHRODITE
HERO

❑1, b&w ... 3.95

COMIX BOOK
MARVEL

❑1, ca. 1974; 1974 ... 10.00
❑2, ca. 1974 ... 8.00
❑3, ca. 1975 ... 8.00
❑4, ca. 1975 ... 5.00
❑5, ca. 1975 ... 5.00

COMMAND REVIEW
THOUGHTS & IMAGES

❑1, Jul 1986, b&w; collects stories from Albedo #1-4 ... 4.00
❑2, Aug 1987, b&w; collects stories from Albedo #5-8 ... 4.00
❑3, b&w ... 5.00
❑4, Jan 1994 ... 4.95

COMMIES FROM MARS
LAST GASP

❑1 ... 2.00
❑2 ... 2.00
❑3 ... 2.00
❑4 ... 2.00
❑5 ... 2.00
❑6 ... 2.50

COMMON GROUNDS
IMAGE

❑1, Jan 2004 ... 2.99
❑2, Feb 2004 ... 2.99

N-MINT

❑3, Mar 2004 ... 2.99
❑4, Apr 2004 ... 2.99
❑5, Jun 2004 ... 2.99
❑6, Aug 2004 ... 2.99

COMMUNION
FANTAGRAPHICS / EROS

❑1, b&w ... 2.75

COMPLETE CHEECH WIZARD
RIP OFF

❑1, Oct 1986, b&w; Vaughn Bodé ... 2.25
❑2, Jan 1987, b&w; Vaughn Bodé ... 2.25
❑3, May 1987, b&w and color; Vaughn Bodé ... 2.50
❑4, Nov 1987, b&w and color; Vaughn Bodé ... 2.50

COMPLETE FRANK MILLER SPIDER-MAN
MARVEL / VERTIGO

❑0 ... 0.00

COMPLETELY BAD BOYS
FANTAGRAPHICS

❑1, b&w ... 2.50

COMPLEX CITY
BETTER

❑1, Oct 2000 ... 2.50
❑2, Dec 2000 ... 2.50
❑3, Mar 2001 ... 2.50
❑4, May 2001 ... 2.50

COMPU-M.E.C.H.
MONOLITH

❑1, Oct 1999 ... 2.75
❑2, Jul 2000 ... 2.75
❑3, ca. 2004; squarebound ... 7.95
❑4, ca. 2004; squarebound ... 7.95
❑5, ca. 2004; squarebound ... 7.95
❑6, ca. 2004; squarebound ... 7.95
❑7, ca. 2004; squarebound ... 7.95
❑8, ca. 2004; squarebound ... 7.95
❑9, ca. 2004; squarebound ... 7.95
❑10, ca. 2004; squarebound ... 7.95

CONAN
MARVEL

❑1, Aug 1995; cardstock cover ... 2.95
❑2, Sep 1995; cardstock cover ... 2.95
❑3, Oct 1995; cardstock cover ... 2.95
❑4, Nov 1995; A: Rune. cardstock cover ... 2.95
❑5, Dec 1995; A: yeti. cardstock cover 2.95
❑6, Jan 1996; cardstock cover ... 2.95
❑7, Feb 1996 V: Man of Iron ... 2.95
❑8, Mar 1996; cardstock cover ... 2.95
❑9, Apr 1996; cardstock cover ... 2.95
❑10, May 1996; cardstock cover ... 2.95
❑11, Jun 1996; cardstock cover ... 2.95
❑12, Jul 1996 ... 2.95

CONAN (DARK HORSE)
DARK HORSE

❑1, Feb 2004 ... 10.00
❑1-2, Aug 2004; re-print ... 2.99
❑2, Mar 2004 ... 2.99
❑2-2, Aug 2004; re-print ... 2.99
❑3, Apr 2004 ... 2.99
❑4, Jun 2004 ... 2.99
❑5, Aug 2004 ... 2.99

CONAN CLASSIC
MARVEL

❑1, Jun 1994; Reprints Conan the Barbarian #1 ... 1.50
❑2, Jul 1994 ... 1.50
❑3, Aug 1994 ... 1.50
❑4, Sep 1994 ... 1.50
❑5, Oct 1994 ... 1.50
❑6, Nov 1994 ... 1.50
❑7, Dec 1994 ... 1.50
❑8, Jan 1995 ... 1.50
❑9, Feb 1995 ... 1.50
❑10, Mar 1995 ... 1.50
❑11, Apr 1995 ... 1.50

Atlas war hero Combat Kelly was revived by Marvel in the early 1970s to lead The Deadly Dozen.

© 1972 Marvel Comics.

N-MINT

CONAN: DEATH COVERED IN GOLD
MARVEL

❑1, Sep 1999 ... 2.99
❑3, Nov 1999 ... 2.99

CONAN: FLAME AND THE FIEND
MARVEL

❑1, Aug 2000 ... 2.99
❑2, Sep 2000 ... 2.99
❑3, Oct 2000 ... 2.99

CONAN: RETURN OF STYRM
MARVEL

❑1, Sep 1998; gatefold summary ... 2.99
❑2, Oct 1998; gatefold summary ... 2.99
❑3, Nov 1998; gatefold summary ... 2.99

CONAN: RIVER OF BLOOD
MARVEL

❑1, Jun 1998 ... 2.50
❑2, Jul 1998 ... 2.50
❑3, Aug 1998 ... 2.50

CONAN SAGA
MARVEL

❑1, May 1987, b&w ... 3.00
❑2, Jun 1987 ... 2.50
❑3, Jul 1987 ... 2.50
❑4, Aug 1987 ... 2.50
❑5, Sep 1987 ... 2.50
❑6, Oct 1987 ... 2.50
❑7, Nov 1987 ... 2.50
❑8, Dec 1987 ... 2.50
❑9, Jan 1988 ... 2.50
❑10, Feb 1988 ... 2.50
❑11, Mar 1988 ... 2.50
❑12, Apr 1988 ... 2.50
❑13, May 1988 ... 2.50
❑14, Jun 1988 ... 2.50
❑15, Jul 1988 ... 2.50
❑16, Aug 1988 ... 2.50
❑17, Sep 1988 ... 2.50
❑18, Oct 1988 ... 2.50
❑19, Nov 1988 ... 2.50
❑20, Dec 1988 ... 2.50
❑21, Jan 1989 ... 2.50
❑22, Feb 1989 ... 2.50
❑23, Mar 1989 ... 2.50
❑24, Apr 1989 ... 2.50
❑25, May 1989 ... 2.50
❑26, Jun 1989 ... 2.50
❑27, Jul 1989 ... 2.50
❑28, Aug 1989, b&w ... 2.50
❑29, Sep 1989, b&w ... 2.50
❑30, Oct 1989, b&w ... 2.50
❑31, Nov 1989, b&w ... 2.50
❑32, Dec 1989, b&w ... 2.50
❑33, Dec 1989, b&w ... 2.50
❑34, Jan 1990, b&w ... 2.50
❑35, Feb 1990, b&w ... 2.50
❑36, Mar 1990, b&w ... 2.50
❑37, Apr 1990, b&w ... 2.50
❑38, May 1990, b&w ... 2.50
❑39, Jun 1990, b&w ... 2.50
❑40, Jul 1990, b&w ... 2.50
❑41, Aug 1990, b&w ... 2.50
❑42, Sep 1990, b&w ... 2.50
❑43, Oct 1990, b&w ... 2.50
❑44, Nov 1990, b&w ... 2.50
❑45, Dec 1990, b&w ... 2.50

	N-MINT
❑46, Jan 1991, b&w	2.50
❑47, Feb 1991, b&w	2.50
❑48, Mar 1991, b&w	2.50
❑49, Apr 1991, b&w	2.50
❑50, May 1991, b&w	2.50
❑51, Jun 1991, b&w	2.50
❑52, Jul 1991, b&w	2.50
❑53, Aug 1991, b&w	2.50
❑54, Sep 1991, b&w JB (a)	2.50
❑55, Oct 1991, b&w JB (a)	2.50
❑56, Nov 1991, b&w JB (a)	2.50
❑57, Dec 1991, b&w FB (a)	2.50
❑58, Jan 1992, b&w	2.50
❑59, Feb 1992, b&w	2.50
❑60, Mar 1992, b&w JB (a)	2.50
❑61, Apr 1992, b&w JB (a)	2.50
❑62, May 1992, b&w JB (a)	2.50
❑63, Jun 1992, b&w JB (a)	2.50
❑64, Jul 1992, b&w	2.50
❑65, Aug 1992, b&w JB (a)	2.50
❑66, Sep 1992, b&w	2.50
❑67, Oct 1992, b&w JB (a)	2.50
❑68, Nov 1992, b&w JB (a)	2.50
❑69, Dec 1992, b&w	2.50
❑70, Jan 1993, b&w	2.50
❑71, Feb 1993, b&w JB (a)	2.50
❑72, Mar 1993, b&w JB, MP (a)	2.50
❑73, Apr 1993, b&w JB (a)	2.50
❑74, May 1993, b&w JB (a)	2.50
❑75, Jun 1993; poster, handbook	4.00
❑76, Jul 1993, b&w	2.25
❑77, Aug 1993, b&w	2.25
❑78, Sep 1993, b&w	2.25
❑79, Oct 1993, b&w; JB, FT, NA (a); A: Red Sonja. Reprints Conan the Barbarian #43-45	2.25
❑80, Nov 1993, b&w JB (a)	2.25
❑81, Dec 1993, b&w JB (a)	2.25
❑82, Jan 1994, b&w JB (a)	2.25
❑83, Feb 1994, b&w	2.25
❑84, Mar 1994, b&w	2.25
❑85, Apr 1994, b&w	2.25
❑86, May 1994, b&w JB (a)	2.25
❑87, Jun 1994, b&w JB (a)	2.25
❑88, Jul 1994, b&w JB (a)	2.25
❑89, Aug 1994, b&w JB (a)	2.25
❑90, Sep 1994, b&w	2.25
❑91, Oct 1994, b&w HC (a)	2.25
❑92, Nov 1994, b&w JB (a)	2.25
❑93, Dec 1994, b&w JB (a)	2.25
❑94, Jan 1995, b&w JB (a)	2.25
❑95, Feb 1995, b&w JB (a)	2.25
❑96, Mar 1995, b&w; JB (a); Reprints Conan the Barbarian #101-103 in black and white	2.25
❑97, Apr 1995, b&w JB (a)	2.25

CONAN: SCARLET SWORD

MARVEL

	N-MINT
❑1, Dec 1998; gatefold summary	2.99
❑2, Jan 1999; gatefold summary	2.99
❑3, Feb 1999	2.99

CONAN THE ADVENTURER

MARVEL

	N-MINT
❑1, Jun 1994; Embossed foil cover	2.00
❑2, Jul 1994	1.50
❑3, Aug 1994	1.50
❑4, Sep 1994	1.50
❑5, Oct 1994	1.50
❑6, Nov 1994	1.50
❑7, Dec 1994	1.50
❑8, Jan 1995	1.50
❑9, Feb 1995	1.50
❑10, Mar 1995	1.50
❑11, Apr 1995	1.50
❑12, May 1995	1.50
❑13, Jun 1995	1.50
❑14, Jul 1995	1.50

CONAN THE BARBARIAN

MARVEL

	N-MINT
❑1, Oct 1970; DA (a); O: Conan. 1: Conan. A: Kull. Hyborian Age map	150.00
❑2, Dec 1970	45.00
❑3, Feb 1971; TS (a); low dist	55.00
❑4, Apr 1971 TS, SB (a)	26.00
❑5, May 1971 TS (a)	26.00
❑6, Jun 1971	26.00
❑7, Jul 1971; 1: Thoth Amon. Howard story	26.00
❑8, Aug 1971	26.00
❑9, Aug 1971	26.00
❑10, Oct 1971; Giant-size A: King Kull	35.00
❑11, Nov 1971; Giant-size	35.00
❑12, Dec 1971	16.00
❑13, Jan 1972	16.00
❑14, Mar 1972; 1: Elric. Michael Moorcock characters	16.00
❑15, May 1972; A: Elric. Michael Moorcock characters	16.00
❑16, Jul 1972; TS (a); reprinted from Savage Tales #1 and Chamber of Darkness #4	16.00
❑17, Aug 1972 GK (a)	16.00
❑18, Aug 1972 GK (a)	16.00
❑19, Oct 1972	16.00
❑20, Nov 1972	16.00
❑21, Dec 1972	16.00
❑22, Jan 1973; reprinted from Conan the Barbarian #1	16.00
❑23, Feb 1973 TS, GK (a); 1: Red Sonja	20.00
❑24, Mar 1973; A: Red Sonja. 1st full Red Sonja story	16.00
❑25, Apr 1973 TS, JB, GK (a)	10.00
❑26, May 1973 JB (a)	8.00
❑27, Jun 1973 JB (a)	8.00
❑28, Jul 1973 TS, JB, GK (a)	8.00
❑29, Aug 1973 TS, JB, GK (a)	8.00
❑30, Sep 1973 TS, JB, GK (a)	8.00
❑31, Oct 1973 JB (a)	7.00
❑32, Nov 1973 JB (a)	7.00
❑33, Dec 1973 JB (a)	7.00
❑34, Jan 1974 JB (a)	7.00
❑35, Feb 1974 JB (a)	7.00
❑36, Mar 1974; JB (a); Marvel Value Stamp #10: Power Man	7.00
❑37, Apr 1974; TS, NA (a); Marvel Value Stamp #8: Captain America	9.00
❑38, May 1974; Marvel Value Stamp #30: Grey Gargoyle	5.00
❑39, Jun 1974; JB (a); Marvel Value Stamp #72: Lizard	5.00
❑40, Jul 1974; RB (a); Marvel Value Stamp #31: Modok	5.00
❑41, Aug 1974; JB, GK (a); Marvel Value Stamp #91: Hela	5.00
❑42, Sep 1974; JB, GK (a); Marvel Value Stamp #24: Falcon	5.00
❑43, Oct 1974; JB, GK (a); Red Sonja; Marvel Value Stamp #55: Medusa	5.00
❑44, Nov 1974; JB (a); Red Sonja; Marvel Value Stamp #71: Vision	5.00
❑45, Dec 1974 NA (a)	5.00
❑46, Jan 1975 JB (a)	5.00
❑47, Feb 1975 JB (a)	5.00
❑48, Mar 1975 JB (a); O: Conan	5.00
❑49, Apr 1975; JB (a); Marvel Value Stamp #80: Ghost Rider	5.00
❑50, May 1975 JB (a)	5.00
❑51, Jun 1975 JB (a); V: Unos	5.00
❑52, Jul 1975 JB (a)	5.00
❑53, Aug 1975 JB (a)	5.00
❑54, Sep 1975 JB (a)	5.00
❑55, Oct 1975 JB (a)	5.00
❑56, Nov 1975 JB (a)	5.00
❑57, Dec 1975 MP (a)	5.00
❑58, Jan 1976 JB (a); 2: of Bélit	5.00
❑59, Feb 1976 JB (a); O: Bélit	5.00
❑60, Mar 1976 JB (a)	5.00
❑61, Apr 1976 JB (a)	5.00
❑61/30 cent, Apr 1976; 30 cent regional price variant	20.00
❑62, May 1976 JB (a)	5.00
❑62/30 cent, May 1976; 30 cent regional price variant	20.00
❑63, Jun 1976 JB (a)	5.00
❑63/30 cent, Jun 1976; 30 cent regional price variant	20.00
❑64, Jul 1976 AM, JSn (a)	5.00
❑64/30 cent, Jul 1976; 30 cent regional price variant	20.00
❑65, Aug 1976 JB, GK (a)	5.00
❑65/30 cent, Aug 1976; 30 cent regional price variant	20.00
❑66, Sep 1976 JB, GK (a); V: Dagon	5.00
❑67, Oct 1976; JB, GK (a); A: Red Sonja. Red Sonja	5.00
❑68, Nov 1976; JB, GK (a); A: Red Sonja. (continued from Marvel Feature #7)	5.00
❑69, Dec 1976	5.00
❑70, Jan 1977 JB (a)	5.00
❑71, Feb 1977 JB (a)	5.00
❑72, Mar 1977 JB (a)	5.00
❑73, Apr 1977 JB (a)	5.00
❑74, May 1977 JB (a)	5.00
❑75, Jun 1977 JB (a)	5.00
❑75/35 cent, Jun 1977	3.00
❑76, Jul 1977 JB (a)	5.00
❑77, Aug 1977 JB (a)	5.00
❑77/35 cent, Aug 1977	3.00
❑78, Sep 1977 JB (a)	5.00
❑79, Oct 1977 HC (a)	5.00
❑80, Nov 1977 HC (a)	5.00
❑81, Dec 1977 HC (a)	5.00
❑82, Jan 1978 HC (a)	5.00
❑83, Feb 1978 HC (a)	5.00
❑84, Mar 1978 JB (a); 1: Zula	5.00
❑85, Apr 1978 JB (a); O: Zula	5.00
❑86, May 1978 JB (a)	5.00
❑87, Jun 1978; JB (a); Reprints Savage Sword of Conan #3 in color	5.00
❑88, Jul 1978; JB (a); Return of Belit	5.00
❑89, Aug 1978 JB (a); V: Thoth-Amon	5.00
❑90, Sep 1978 JB (a)	5.00
❑91, Oct 1978 JB (a)	5.00
❑92, Nov 1978 JB (a)	5.00
❑93, Dec 1978; JB (a); Belit regains throne	5.00
❑94, Jan 1979 JB (a)	4.00
❑95, Feb 1979 JB (a)	4.00
❑96, Mar 1979 JB (a)	4.00
❑97, Apr 1979 JB (a)	4.00
❑98, May 1979 JB (a)	4.00
❑99, Jun 1979 JB (a)	4.00
❑100, Jul 1979; Double-size issue TS, JB (a); D: Bélit	4.00
❑101, Aug 1979 JB (a)	2.00
❑102, Sep 1979 JB (a)	2.00
❑103, Oct 1979 JB (a)	2.00
❑104, Nov 1979 JB (a)	2.00
❑105, Dec 1979 JB (a)	2.00
❑106, Jan 1980 JB (a)	2.00
❑107, Feb 1980 JB (a)	2.00
❑108, Mar 1980 JB (a)	2.00
❑109, Apr 1980 JB (a)	2.00
❑110, May 1980 JB (a)	2.00
❑111, Jun 1980 JB (a)	2.00
❑112, Jul 1980 JB (a)	2.00
❑113, Aug 1980 JB (a)	2.00
❑114, Sep 1980 JB (a)	2.00
❑115, Oct 1980; double-sized JB (a)	2.00
❑116, Nov 1980 JB, NA (a)	2.00
❑117, Dec 1980 JB (a)	2.00
❑118, Jan 1981 JB (a)	2.00
❑119, Feb 1981 JB (a)	2.00
❑120, Mar 1981 JB (a)	2.00
❑121, Apr 1981 JB (a)	2.00
❑122, May 1981 JB (a)	2.00
❑123, Jun 1981 JB (a)	2.00
❑124, Jul 1981 JB (a)	2.00
❑125, Aug 1981 JB (a)	2.00
❑126, Sep 1981 JB (a)	2.00
❑127, Oct 1981 JB (a)	2.00
❑128, Nov 1981 GK (c); GK (a)	2.00
❑129, Dec 1981	2.00

N-MINT

❑130, Jan 1982 GK (a) ... 2.00
❑131, Feb 1982 GK (a) ... 2.00
❑132, Mar 1982 GK (a) ... 2.00
❑133, Apr 1982 GK (a) ... 2.00
❑134, May 1982 GK (a) ... 2.00
❑135, Jun 1982 ... 2.00
❑136, Jul 1982 JB (a) ... 2.00
❑137, Aug 1982 AA (a) ... 2.00
❑138, Sep 1982 VM (a) ... 2.00
❑139, Oct 1982 VM (a) ... 2.00
❑140, Nov 1982 JB (a) ... 2.00
❑141, Dec 1982 JB (a) ... 2.00
❑142, Jan 1983 JB (a) ... 2.00
❑143, Feb 1983 JB (a) ... 2.00
❑144, Mar 1983 JB (a) ... 2.00
❑145, Apr 1983 JB (a) ... 2.00
❑146, May 1983 JB (a) ... 2.00
❑147, Jun 1983 JB (a) ... 2.00
❑148, Jul 1983 JB (a) ... 2.00
❑149, Aug 1983 JB (a) ... 2.00
❑150, Sep 1983 JB (a) ... 2.00
❑151, Oct 1983 JB (a) ... 2.00
❑152, Nov 1983 JB (a) ... 2.00
❑153, Dec 1983 JB (a) ... 2.00
❑154, Jan 1984; Assistant Editors' Month ... 2.00
❑155, Feb 1984 JB (a) ... 2.00
❑156, Mar 1984 JB (a) ... 2.00
❑157, Apr 1984 JB (a) ... 2.00
❑158, May 1984 JB (a) ... 2.00
❑159, Jun 1984 JB (a) ... 2.00
❑160, Jul 1984 ... 2.00
❑161, Aug 1984 JB (a) ... 2.00
❑162, Sep 1984 JB (a) ... 2.00
❑163, Oct 1984 JB (a) ... 2.00
❑164, Nov 1984 ... 2.00
❑165, Dec 1984 JB (a) ... 2.00
❑166, Jan 1985 JB (a) ... 2.00
❑167, Feb 1985 JB (a) ... 2.00
❑168, Mar 1985 JB (a) ... 2.00
❑169, Apr 1985 JB (a) ... 2.00
❑170, May 1985 JB (a) ... 2.00
❑171, Jun 1985 JB (a) ... 2.00
❑172, Jul 1985 JB (a) ... 2.00
❑173, Aug 1985 JB (a) ... 2.00
❑174, Sep 1985 JB (a) ... 2.00
❑175, Oct 1985 JB (a) ... 2.00
❑176, Nov 1985 JB (a) ... 2.00
❑177, Dec 1985 JB (a) ... 2.00
❑178, Jan 1986 JB (a) ... 2.00
❑179, Feb 1986 JB (a) ... 2.00
❑180, Mar 1986 JB (a) ... 2.00
❑181, Apr 1986 JB (a) ... 2.00
❑182, May 1986 JB (a) ... 2.00
❑183, Jun 1986 JB (a) ... 2.00
❑184, Jul 1986 ... 2.00
❑185, Aug 1986 ... 2.00
❑186, Sep 1986 ... 2.00
❑187, Oct 1986 JB (a) ... 2.00
❑188, Nov 1986 ... 2.00
❑189, Dec 1986 ... 2.00
❑190, Jan 1987 ... 2.00
❑191, Feb 1987 ... 2.00
❑192, Mar 1987 ... 2.00
❑193, Apr 1987 ... 2.00
❑194, May 1987 ... 2.00
❑195, Jun 1987 ... 2.00
❑196, Jul 1987 ... 2.00
❑197, Aug 1987 ... 2.00
❑198, Sep 1987 ... 2.00
❑199, Oct 1987 ... 2.00
❑200, Nov 1987; 200th issue anniversary ... 2.00
❑201, Dec 1987 ... 2.00
❑202, Jan 1988 ... 2.00
❑203, Feb 1988 ... 2.00
❑204, Mar 1988 ... 2.00
❑205, Apr 1988 ... 2.00
❑206, May 1988 ... 2.00
❑207, Jun 1988 ... 2.00
❑208, Jul 1988 ... 2.00
❑209, Aug 1988 ... 2.00

N-MINT

❑210, Sep 1988 ... 2.00
❑211, Oct 1988 ... 2.00
❑212, Nov 1988 ... 2.00
❑213, Dec 1988 ... 2.00
❑214, Jan 1989 ... 2.00
❑215, Feb 1989 ... 2.00
❑216, Mar 1989 ... 2.00
❑217, Apr 1989 ... 2.00
❑218, May 1989 ... 2.00
❑219, Jun 1989 ... 2.00
❑220, Jul 1989 ... 2.00
❑221, Aug 1989 ... 2.00
❑222, Sep 1989 ... 2.00
❑223, Oct 1989 ... 2.00
❑224, Nov 1989 ... 2.00
❑225, Nov 1989 ... 2.00
❑226, Dec 1989 ... 2.00
❑227, Dec 1989 ... 2.00
❑228, Jan 1990 ... 2.00
❑229, Feb 1990 ... 2.00
❑230, Mar 1990 ... 2.00
❑231, Apr 1990 ... 2.00
❑232, May 1990; starts over ... 2.00
❑233, Jun 1990 ... 2.00
❑234, Jul 1990 ... 2.00
❑235, Aug 1990 ... 2.00
❑236, Sep 1990 ... 2.00
❑237, Oct 1990 ... 2.00
❑238, Nov 1990 ... 2.00
❑239, Dec 1990 ... 2.00
❑240, Jan 1991 ... 2.00
❑241, Feb 1991 TMc (c); TMc (a) ... 2.00
❑242, Mar 1991 JLee (c); JLee (a) ... 2.00
❑243, Apr 1991; Red Sonja ... 2.00
❑244, May 1991; Red Sonja ... 2.00
❑245, Jun 1991; Red Sonja ... 2.00
❑246, Jul 1991; Red Sonja ... 2.00
❑247, Aug 1991; Red Sonja ... 2.00
❑248, Sep 1991; Red Sonja ... 2.00
❑249, Oct 1991; Red Sonja ... 2.00
❑250, Nov 1991; 250th issue anniversary ... 2.00
❑251, Dec 1991 ... 2.00
❑252, Jan 1992 ... 2.00
❑253, Feb 1992 ... 2.00
❑254, Mar 1992 ... 2.00
❑255, Apr 1992 ... 2.00
❑256, May 1992 ... 2.00
❑257, Jun 1992 V: Thoth-Amon ... 2.00
❑258, Jul 1992; returns to Cimmeria ... 2.00
❑259, Aug 1992 ... 2.00
❑260, Sep 1992 ... 2.00
❑261, Oct 1992 ... 2.00
❑262, Nov 1992 ... 2.00
❑263, Dec 1992 ... 2.00
❑264, Jan 1993 ... 2.00
❑265, Feb 1993 ... 2.00
❑266, Mar 1993 ... 2.00
❑267, Apr 1993 ... 2.00
❑268, May 1993 ... 2.00
❑269, Jun 1993 ... 2.00
❑270, Jul 1993 ... 2.00
❑271, Aug 1993 ... 2.00
❑272, Sep 1993 ... 2.00
❑273, Oct 1993 A: Lord of the Purple Lotus ... 2.00
❑274, Nov 1993 ... 2.00
❑275, Dec 1993 ... 2.50
❑Annual 1, ca. 1973; Cover reads "King-Size Special"; Reprints Conan the Barbarian #2 and 4 ... 10.00
❑Annual 2, Jan 1976 JB (a) ... 6.00
❑Annual 3, ca. 1977; JB, HC, NA (a); A: King Kull. Reprints Savage Sword of Conan #2 ... 6.00
❑Annual 4, ca. 1978; JB (a); King Conan story ... 2.00
❑Annual 5, ca. 1979 JB (a) ... 2.00
❑Annual 6, ca. 1981 JB (a) ... 2.00
❑Annual 7, ca. 1982 JB (a) ... 1.50
❑Annual 8, ca. 1983 VM (a) ... 1.50
❑Annual 9, ca. 1984 ... 1.50

Marvel began adapting the adventures of Robert E. Howard's Cimmerian with a sword in 1970.

© 1970 Marvel Comics and Robert E. Howard Enterprises.

N-MINT

❑Annual 10, ca. 1985 ... 1.50
❑Annual 11, ca. 1986 ... 1.50
❑Annual 12, ca. 1987 ... 1.50
❑Special 1 ... 2.50

CONAN THE BARBARIAN (VOL. 2)

MARVEL

❑1, Jul 1997 ... 2.50
❑2, Aug 1997 ... 2.50
❑3, Oct 1997 ... 2.50

CONAN THE BARBARIAN MOVIE SPECIAL

MARVEL

❑1, Oct 1982 JB (w); JB (a) ... 1.00
❑2, Nov 1982 JB (w); JB (a) ... 1.00

CONAN THE BARBARIAN: THE USURPER

MARVEL

❑1, Dec 1997; gatefold summary; gatefold cover ... 2.50
❑2, Jan 1998; gatefold summary ... 2.50
❑3, Feb 1988 ... 2.50
❑4, Mar 1988 ... 2.50

CONAN THE DESTROYER

MARVEL

❑1, Jan 1985 ... 1.00
❑2, Mar 1985 ... 1.00

CONAN THE KING

MARVEL

❑20, Jan 1984; Continued from King Conan #19 ... 1.50
❑21, Mar 1984 ... 1.50
❑22, May 1984 ... 1.50
❑23, Jul 1984 ... 1.50
❑24, Sep 1984 ... 1.50
❑25, Nov 1984 ... 1.50
❑26, Jan 1985 ... 1.50
❑27, Mar 1985 ... 1.50
❑28, May 1985 ... 1.50
❑29, Jul 1985 ... 1.50
❑30, Sep 1985 ... 1.50
❑31, Nov 1985 ... 1.50
❑32, Jan 1986 ... 1.50
❑33, Mar 1986 ... 1.50
❑34, May 1986 ... 1.50
❑35, Jul 1986 ... 1.50
❑36, Sep 1986 ... 1.50
❑37, Nov 1986 ... 1.50
❑38, Jan 1987 ... 1.50
❑39, Mar 1987 ... 1.50
❑40, May 1987 ... 1.50
❑41, Jul 1987 ... 1.50
❑42, Sep 1987 ... 1.50
❑43, Nov 1987 ... 1.50
❑44, Jan 1988 ... 1.50
❑45, Mar 1988 ... 1.50
❑46, May 1988 ... 1.50
❑47, Jul 1988 ... 1.50
❑48, Sep 1988 ... 1.50
❑49, Nov 1988 ... 1.50
❑50, Jan 1989 ... 1.50
❑51, Mar 1989 ... 1.50
❑52, May 1989 ... 1.50
❑53, Jul 1989 ... 1.50
❑54, Sep 1989 ... 1.50
❑55, Nov 1989 ... 1.50

N-MINT

CONAN: THE LORD OF THE SPIDERS
MARVEL

❑1, Mar 1998; gatefold summary; gatefold cover 2.50
❑2, Apr 1998; gatefold summary 2.50
❑3, May 1998; gatefold summary 2.50

CONAN THE SAVAGE
MARVEL

❑1, Aug 1995; b&w magazine 2.95
❑2, Sep 1995; b&w magazine 2.95
❑3, Oct 1995; b&w magazine 2.95
❑4, Nov 1995; b&w magazine; indicia gives title as Conan 2.95
❑5, Dec 1995; b&w magazine 2.95
❑6, Jan 1996; b&w magazine 2.95
❑7, Feb 1996; b&w magazine 2.95
❑8, Mar 1996; b&w magazine 2.95
❑9, Apr 1996; b&w magazine 2.95
❑10, May 1996; b&w magazine 2.95
❑11, Jun 1996 .... 2.95
❑12, Jul 1996 .... 2.95

CONAN VS. RUNE
MARVEL

❑1, Nov 1995 .... 2.95

CONCRETE
DARK HORSE

❑1, Mar 1987 .... 2.50
❑1-2 .... 1.50
❑2, Jun 1987 .... 2.00
❑3, Aug 1987 O: Concrete 2.00
❑4, Oct 1987 O: Concrete 2.00
❑5, Dec 1987 .... 2.00
❑6, Feb 1988 .... 2.00
❑7, Apr 1988 .... 2.00
❑8, Jun 1988 .... 2.00
❑9, Sep 1988 .... 2.00
❑10 .... 2.00
❑Hero ed. 1; Hero Special edition; Included with Hero Illustrated #23 .... 1.00

CONCRETE: A NEW LIFE
DARK HORSE

❑1, Oct 1989; b&w reprint 2.95

CONCRETE CELEBRATES EARTH DAY
DARK HORSE

❑1, Apr 1990; Moebius 3.50

CONCRETE COLOR SPECIAL
DARK HORSE

❑1, Feb 1989; reprint in color 2.95

CONCRETE: ECLECTICA
DARK HORSE

❑1, Apr 1993; wraparound cover from 1992 WonderCon program book ... 2.95
❑2, May 1993; wraparound cover 2.95

CONCRETE: FRAGILE CREATURE
DARK HORSE

❑1, Jun 1991; wraparound cover 2.50
❑2, Jul 1991; wraparound cover 2.50
❑3, Aug 1991; wraparound cover 2.50
❑4, Feb 1992; wraparound cover 2.50

CONCRETE JUNGLE: THE LEGEND OF THE BLACK LION
ACCLAIM

❑1, Apr 1998 .... 2.50

CONCRETE: KILLER SMILE
DARK HORSE / LEGEND

❑1, Jul 1994 .... 2.95
❑2, Aug 1994 .... 2.95
❑3, Sep 1994 .... 2.95
❑4, Oct 1994 .... 2.95

CONCRETE: LAND & SEA
DARK HORSE

❑1, Feb 1989, b&w; reprints first two Concrete stories with additional material; wraparound cardstock cover 2.95

CONCRETE: ODD JOBS
DARK HORSE

❑1, Jul 1990; b&w reprint; Collects Concrete #5-6 .... 3.50

N-MINT

CONCRETE: STRANGE ARMOR
DARK HORSE

❑1, Dec 1997 .... 2.95
❑2, Jan 1998 .... 2.95
❑3, Mar 1998 .... 2.95
❑4, Apr 1998 .... 2.95
❑5, May 1998 .... 2.95

CONCRETE: THINK LIKE A MOUNTAIN
DARK HORSE / LEGEND

❑1, Mar 1996, b&w 2.95
❑2, Apr 1996 .... 2.95
❑3, May 1996 .... 2.95
❑4, Jun 1996 .... 2.95
❑5, Jul 1996 .... 2.95
❑6, Aug 1996 .... 2.95
❑Ashcan 1, b&w; promotional give-away for mini-series 1.00

CONDOM-MAN
AAAAHH!!

❑1; Gold ink limited edition 3.95

CONDORMAN (WALT DISNEY)
WHITMAN

❑1, Nov 1981 .... 2.00
❑2, Dec 1981 .... 2.00
❑3, Jan 1982 .... 2.00

CONEHEADS
MARVEL

❑1, Jun 1994 .... 1.75
❑2, Jul 1994 .... 1.75
❑3, Aug 1994 .... 1.75
❑4, Sep 1994 .... 1.75

CONFESSIONS OF A CEREAL EATER
NBM

❑1 2000, b&w 2.95
❑2 2000, b&w 2.95
❑3 2000, b&w 2.95

CONFESSIONS OF A TEENAGE VAMPIRE: THE TURNING
SCHOLASTIC

❑1, Jul 1997; digest 4.99

CONFESSIONS OF A TEENAGE VAMPIRE: ZOMBIE SATURDAY NIGHT
SCHOLASTIC

❑1, Jul 1997; digest 4.99

CONFESSOR, THE (DEMONICUS EX DEO)
DARK MATTER

❑1, b&w 2.95

CONFIDENTIAL CONFESSIONS
TOKYOPOP

❑1, Jul 2003, b&w; printed in Japanese format 9.99

CONFRONTATION, THE
SACRED ORIGIN

❑1, Jul 1997 .... 2.95
❑2, Oct 1997 .... 2.95
❑3 1997 .... 2.95
❑4 1998 .... 2.95
❑Special 1; Convention exclusive edition 5.00

CONGO BILL (VERTIGO)
DC / VERTIGO

❑1, Oct 1999 .... 2.95
❑2, Nov 1999 .... 2.95
❑3, Dec 1999 .... 2.95
❑4, Jan 2000 .... 2.95

CONGORILLA
DC

❑1, Nov 1992 .... 2.00
❑2, Dec 1992 .... 1.75
❑3, Jan 1993 .... 1.75
❑4, Feb 1993 .... 1.75

CONJURORS
DC

❑1, Apr 1999; Elseworlds story 2.95
❑2, May 1999; Elseworlds story 2.95
❑3, Jun 1999; Elseworlds story 2.95

N-MINT

CONQUEROR
HARRIER

❑1, Aug 1984 .... 1.75
❑2, Oct 1984 .... 1.75
❑3, Dec 1984 .... 1.75
❑4, Feb 1985 .... 1.75
❑5, Apr 1985 .... 1.75
❑6, Jun 1985 .... 1.75
❑7, Aug 1985 .... 1.75
❑8, Oct 1985 .... 1.75
❑9, Dec 1985 .... 1.75
❑Special 1; Special edition (1987) 1.95

CONQUEROR OF THE BARREN EARTH
DC

❑1, Feb 1983 .... 1.00
❑2, Mar 1983 .... 1.00
❑3, Apr 1983 .... 1.00
❑4, May 1983 .... 1.00

CONQUEROR UNIVERSE
HARRIER

❑1 .... 2.75

CONSERVATION CORPS
ARCHIE

❑1, Aug 1993 .... 1.25
❑2, Sep 1993 .... 1.25
❑3, Nov 1993 .... 1.25

CONSPIRACY
MARVEL

❑1, Feb 1998 .... 2.99
❑2, Mar 1998 .... 2.99

CONSPIRACY COMICS
REVOLUTIONARY

❑1, Oct 1991; Marilyn Monroe 2.50
❑2, Feb 1992, b&w; John F. Kennedy 2.50
❑3, Jul 1992, b&w; Robert F. Kennedy 2.50

CONSTELLATION GRAPHICS
STAGES

❑1 .... 1.50
❑2 .... 1.50

CONSTRUCT
CALIBER

❑1 .... 2.95
❑2 .... 2.95
❑3 .... 2.95
❑4 .... 2.95
❑5 .... 2.95
❑6 .... 2.95

CONTAMINATED ZONE, THE
BRAVE NEW WORDS

❑1, Apr 1991, b&w 2.50
❑2 1991, b&w 2.50
❑3 1991, b&w 2.50

CONTEMPORARY BIO-GRAPHICS
REVOLUTIONARY

❑1, Dec 1991, b&w; Stan Lee 2.50
❑2, Apr 1992, b&w; Boris Yeltsin 2.50
❑3, May 1992, b&w; Gene Roddenberry 2.50
❑4, Jun 1992; Pee Wee Herman 2.50
❑5, Sep 1992, b&w; David Lynch 2.50
❑6, Oct 1992; Ross Perot 2.50
❑7, Dec 1992, b&w; Spike Lee 2.50
❑8, Jun 1993, b&w; Image story 2.50

CONTENDER COMICS SPECIAL
CONTENDER

❑1, b&w 1.00

CONTEST OF CHAMPIONS II
MARVEL

❑1, Sep 1999; Iron Man vs. Psylocke; Iron Man vs. X-Force 2.50
❑2, Sep 1999; Human Torch vs. Spider-Girl, Storm, She-Hulk; Mr. Fantastic vs. Hulk 2.50
❑3, Oct 1999; Thor vs. Storm; Cable vs. Scarlet Witch; New Warriors vs. Slingers 2.50
❑4, Nov 1999; Black Panther vs Captain America 2.50
❑5, Nov 1999; Rogue vs Warbird 2.50

N-MINT

CONTINÜM PRESENTS
CONTINÜM

❑1, Oct 1988 .... 1.75
❑2, Fal 1989 .... 1.75

CONTRACTORS
ECLIPSE

❑1, Jun 1987, b&w 2.00

CONVOCATIONS: A MAGIC: THE GATHERING GALLERY
ACCLAIM / ARMADA

❑1, Jan 1995; pin-ups; reproduces covers from several Magic mini-series 2.50

COOL WORLD
DC

❑1, Apr 1992 .... 1.75
❑2, May 1992 .... 1.75
❑3, Jun 1992 .... 1.75
❑4, Sep 1992 .... 1.75

COOL WORLD MOVIE ADAPTATION
DC

❑1 .... 3.50

COP CALLED TRACY, A
AVALON

❑1 .... 2.95
❑2 .... 2.95
❑3 .... 2.95
❑4 .... 2.95
❑5 .... 2.95
❑6 .... 2.95
❑7 .... 2.95
❑8 .... 2.95
❑9 .... 2.95
❑10 .... 2.95
❑11 .... 2.95
❑12 .... 2.95
❑13 .... 2.95
❑14 .... 2.95
❑15 .... 2.95
❑16 .... 2.95
❑17 .... 2.95
❑18 .... 2.95
❑19 .... 2.95
❑20 .... 2.95
❑21 .... 2.95
❑22 .... 2.95

COPS
DC

❑1, Aug 1988; Giant-size 1.00
❑2, Sep 1988 .... 1.00
❑3, Oct 1988 .... 1.00
❑4, Nov 1988 .... 1.00
❑5, Dec 1988 .... 1.00
❑6, Win 1988; Winter, 1988 .... 1.00
❑7, Hol 1988; Holdays, 1988 .... 1.00
❑8, Jan 1989 .... 1.00
❑9, Feb 1989 .... 1.00
❑10, Mar 1989 .... 1.00
❑11, Apr 1989 .... 1.00
❑12, May 1989 .... 1.00
❑13, Jun 1989 .... 1.00
❑14, Jul 1989 .... 1.00
❑15, Aug 1989 .... 1.00

COPS: THE JOB
MARVEL

❑1, Jun 1992 .... 1.25
❑2, Jul 1992 .... 1.25
❑3, Aug 1992 .... 1.25
❑4, Sep 1992 .... 1.25

COPYBOOK TALES, THE
SLAVE LABOR

❑1, Jul 1996, b&w 2.95
❑2, Oct 1996, b&w 2.95
❑3, Jan 1997, b&w 2.95
❑4, Apr 1997, b&w 2.95
❑5, Jul 1997, b&w 2.95
❑6, Aug 1997; Cover swipe of X-Men (1st Series) #141 .... 2.95

N-MINT

CORBEN SPECIAL, A
PACIFIC

❑1, May 1984, Adapted From Edgar Allan Poe 1.50

CORBO
SWORD IN STONE

❑1 .... 1.75

CORMAC MAC ART
DARK HORSE

❑1, Jul 1989, b&w 1.95
❑2, Aug 1989, b&w 1.95
❑3, Mar 1990, b&w 1.95
❑4, Apr 1990, b&w 1.95

CORNY'S FETISH
DARK HORSE

❑1, Apr 1998, b&w 4.95

CORPORATE CRIME COMICS
KITCHEN SINK

❑1 .... 2.50
❑2 .... 2.50

CORTEZ AND THE FALL OF THE AZTECS
TOME

❑1, b&w 2.95
❑2, b&w 2.95

CORTO MALTESE: BALLAD OF THE SALT SEA
NBM

❑1 .... 2.95
❑2 .... 2.95
❑3 .... 2.95
❑4 .... 2.95

CORUM: THE BULL AND THE SPEAR
FIRST

❑1 .... 1.50
❑2 .... 1.50
❑3 .... 1.50
❑4 .... 1.50

CORVUS REX: A LEGACY OF SHADOWS
CROW

❑1, Feb 1996, b&w; Prologue 1.95

COSMIC BOOK, THE
ACE

❑1 .... 1.95

COSMIC BOY
DC

❑1, Dec 1986; KG (a); Legends Spin-Off, Part 4 .... 1.00
❑2, Jan 1987; Legends Spin-Off, Part 8 .... 1.00
❑3, Feb 1987; Legends Spin-Off, Part 13 .... 1.00
❑4, Mar 1987; V: Time Trapper. Legends Spin-Off, Part 20 .... 1.00

COSMIC HEROES
ETERNITY

❑1, b&w; Buck Rogers 1.95
❑2, b&w; Buck Rogers 1.95
❑3, b&w; Buck Rogers 1.95
❑4, b&w; Buck Rogers 1.95
❑5, b&w; Buck Rogers 1.95
❑6, b&w; Buck Rogers 1.95
❑7 .... 2.25
❑8 .... 2.25
❑9 .... 2.95
❑10 .... 3.50
❑11 .... 3.95

COSMIC KLITI
FANTAGRAPHICS / EROS

❑1, b&w 2.25

COSMIC ODYSSEY
DC

❑1, Nov 1988 .... 3.50
❑2, Dec 1988 .... 3.50
❑3, Dec 1988 .... 3.50
❑4, Jan 1989 .... 3.50

Former senatorial speechwriter Ronald Lithgow's brain was transplanted into an alien stone body in Paul Chadwick's *Concrete*.

© 1987 Paul Chadwick and Dark Horse.

N-MINT

COSMIC POWERS
MARVEL

❑1, Mar 1994; Thanos 2.50
❑2, Apr 1994; Terrax 2.50
❑3, May 1994; Jack of Hearts & Ganymede 2.50
❑4, Jun 1994 .... 2.50
❑5, Jul 1994; Morg 2.50
❑6, Aug 1994; Tyrant 2.50

COSMIC POWERS UNLIMITED
MARVEL

❑1, May 1995 .... 3.95
❑2, Aug 1995; indicia says Aug; cover says Sep 3.95
❑3, Dec 1995 .... 3.95
❑4, Feb 1996 .... 3.95
❑5, May 1996 .... 3.95

COSMIC RAY
IMAGE

❑1/A, Jun 1999; green sunglasses cover 2.95
❑1/B, Jun 1999; Murderer or Hero cover 2.95
❑2, Aug 1999 .... 2.95
❑3, Oct 1999 .... 2.95

COSMIC STELLER REBELLERS
HAMMAC

❑1 .... 1.50
❑2 .... 1.50

COUGAR, THE
ATLAS-SEABOARD

❑1, Apr 1975 .... 2.00
❑2, Jul 1975 O: Cougar 2.00

COUNTDOWN
DC / WILDSTORM

❑1, Jun 2000 .... 2.95
❑2, Jul 2000 .... 2.95
❑3, Aug 2000 .... 2.95
❑4, Sep 2000 .... 2.95
❑5, Oct 2000 .... 2.95
❑6, Nov 2000 .... 2.95
❑7, Dec 2000 .... 2.95
❑8, Jan 2001 .... 2.95

COUNT DUCKULA
MARVEL

❑1, Jan 1989 .... 1.00
❑2, Feb 1989 .... 1.00
❑3, Mar 1989 .... 1.00
❑4, Apr 1989; Danger Mouse 1.00
❑5, May 1989; Danger Mouse 1.00
❑6, Jun 1989; Danger Mouse 1.00
❑7, Jul 1989; Danger Mouse 1.00
❑8, Aug 1989; Geraldo Rivera 1.00
❑9, Sep 1989 .... 1.00
❑10, Oct 1989 .... 1.00
❑11, Nov 1989 .... 1.00
❑12, Dec 1989 .... 1.00
❑13, Jan 1990 .... 1.00
❑14, Feb 1990 .... 1.00
❑15, Mar 1990 .... 1.00

COUNTER OPS
ANTARCTIC

❑1, Mar 2003 .... 3.95
❑2, Apr 2003 .... 3.95
❑3, May 2003 .... 3.95
❑4, Jun 2003 .... 3.95

N-MINT

COUNTERPARTS
TUNDRA

❑1, Jan 1993, b&w 2.95
❑2, Mar 1993, b&w 2.95
❑3 .... 2.95

COUP D'ETAT (MINI SERIES)
DC / WILDSTORM

❑1, Apr 2004 .... 2.95
❑2, Apr 2004 .... 2.95
❑3, Apr 2004 .... 2.95
❑4, Apr 2004 .... 2.95

COUP D'ETAT
DC / WILDSTORM

❑1, May 2004 .... 2.95

COUP D'ETAT: AFTERWORD
DC / WILDSTORM

❑1, ca. 2004 .... 2.95

COUPLE OF WINOS, A
FANTAGRAPHICS

❑1, ca. 1991, b&w 2.25

COURAGEOUS MAN ADVENTURES
MOORDAM

❑1, b&w; Mr. Beat back-up 2.95
❑2, b&w 2.95
❑3 .... 2.95

COURTNEY CRUMRIN & THE NIGHT THINGS
ONI

❑1, Mar 2002 .... 2.95
❑2, Apr 2002 .... 2.95
❑3, May 2002 .... 2.95
❑4, Jun 2002 .... 2.95

COURTSHIP OF EDDIE'S FATHER
DELL

❑1, Jan 1970 .... 30.00
❑2, May 1970 .... 24.00

COURTYARD (ALAN MOORE'S)
AVATAR

❑1, Feb 2003 .... 3.50
❑1/A, Feb 2003 .... 3.95
❑2, Mar 2003 .... 3.50
❑2/A, Mar 2003 .... 3.95

COUTOO
DARK HORSE

❑1, b&w 3.50

COVEN, THE
AWESOME

❑1/A, Aug 1997; RL (c); JPH (w); RL (a); "Butt" cover 2.50
❑1/B, Aug 1997; JPH (w); Man with flaming hands on cover; Red border 2.50
❑1/C, Aug 1997; JPH (w); "Wizard Authentic" cover 3.00
❑1/D, Aug 1997; JPH (w); Team on cover; White border 2.50
❑1/E, Aug 1997; Dynamic Forces edition; RL (c); JPH (w); RL (a); Chromium cover otherwise same as 1/A 2.50
❑1/F, Aug 1997; 1" Edition; JPH (w); Flip book with Kaboom 1+ 2.50
❑1/G, Aug 1997; JPH (w); "Flame Hands" cover 2.50
❑1-2 1997; "Fan Appreciation Edition"; JPH (w); Is really 2nd Printing 2.50
❑2, Sep 1997 JPH (w) 2.50
❑2/Gold, Sep 1997; Gold edition limited to 5000 copies JPH (w) 2.50
❑3, Oct 1997 JPH (w) 2.50
❑3/A, Oct 1997; JPH (w); Red foil logo on cover 2.50
❑4, Nov 1998 JPH (w) 2.50
❑5, Jan 1998 JPH (w) 2.50
❑5/A, Jan 1998; JPH (w); Variant cover, woman, ghouls standing in water 2.50
❑6, Feb 1998 JPH (w) 2.50

N-MINT

COVEN, THE (VOL. 2)
AWESOME

❑1, Jan 1999; regular cover: Woman with glowing gloves facing forward 2.50
❑1/A, Jan 1999; Chrome ("Covenchrome") edition with certificate of authenticity; Two team-members flying on cover with white Coven logo 2.50
❑1/B, Jan 1999; Variant "scratch" cover by Ian Churchill 2.50
❑1/C, Jan 1999; Gold edition 2.50
❑1/D, Jan 1999; "Spellcaster" cover by Rob Liefeld 2.50
❑1/E, Jan 1999; "Black Mass" cover 2.50
❑1/F, Jan 1999; Dynamic Forces exclusive cover with two women surfing 2.50
❑2, Feb 1999 .... 2.50
❑3, Mar 1999 .... 2.50
❑4, Apr 1999 .... 2.50

COVEN BLACK AND WHITE
AWESOME

❑1, Sep 1998 .... 2.95

COVEN: DARK ORIGINS
AWESOME

❑1, Jun 1999 .... 2.50

COVEN, THE: FANTOM
AWESOME

❑1, Feb 1998 JPH (w) 3.00
❑1/Gold, Feb 1998; JPH (w); Gold logo 3.00

COVEN OF ANGELS
JITTERBUG

❑1, Nov 1995 .... 4.00
❑2 .... 4.00
❑Ashcan 1; Ashcan edition with Linsner cover 8.00

COVEN 13
NO MERCY

❑1, Aug 1997 .... 2.50

COVEN, THE: TOOTH AND NAIL
AVATAR

❑1 .... 2.95
❑1/Ltd.; White foil-embossed leatherette cover; No indicia 29.95

COVENTRY
FANTAGRAPHICS

❑1, Nov 1996, b&w; cardstock cover 3.95
❑2, Mar 1997, b&w; cardstock cover 3.95
❑3, Jul 1997, b&w; cardstock cover 3.95

COW
MONSTERPANTS

❑1 .... 1.99
❑2 .... 1.99
❑3 .... 1.99

COW-BOY
OGRE

❑1, b&w 4.00

COWBOY IN AFRICA
GOLD KEY

❑1, Mar 1968 .... 40.00

COWBOY LOVE (AVALON)
AVALON

❑1, b&w 2.95

COW SPECIAL, THE (VOL. 2)
IMAGE

❑1, Jun 2001, b&w; Spring/Summer issue 2.95

COYOTE
MARVEL / EPIC

❑1, Apr 1983 O: Coyote 2.50
❑2, Jun 1983 .... 2.00
❑3, Sep 1983 .... 2.00
❑4, Jan 1984 .... 1.50
❑5, Apr 1984 .... 1.50
❑6, Jun 1984 .... 1.50
❑7, Jul 1984 SD (a) 1.50
❑8, Oct 1984 SD (a) 1.50
❑9, Dec 1984 SD (a) 1.50
❑10, Jan 1985 .... 1.50

N-MINT

❑11, Mar 1985; TMc (a); 1st Todd McFarlane art 2.50
❑12, May 1985 TMc (a) 2.00
❑13, Jul 1985 TMc (a) 2.00
❑14, Sep 1985 TMc (a); A: Badger 1.50
❑15, Nov 1985 .... 1.50
❑16, Jan 1986 .... 1.50

CRABBS
CAT-HEAD

❑1, b&w 3.75

CRACK BUSTERS
SHOWCASE

❑1, Nov 1986 .... 1.95
❑2 .... 1.95

CRACKED
GLOBE

❑1, Feb 1958 .... 125.00
❑2, Apr 1958 .... 60.00
❑3, Jun 1958 .... 35.00
❑4, Aug 1958 .... 35.00
❑5, Oct 1958 .... 35.00
❑6, Dec 1958 .... 20.00
❑7, Feb 1959 .... 20.00
❑8, ca. 1959 .... 20.00
❑9, ca. 1959 .... 20.00
❑10, ca. 1959 .... 20.00
❑11, ca. 1959 .... 12.00
❑12 .... 12.00
❑13 .... 12.00
❑14, Jun 1960 .... 12.00
❑15, Aug 1960 .... 12.00
❑16, ca. 1960 .... 12.00
❑17 .... 12.00
❑18, ca. 1961 .... 12.00
❑19, ca. 1961 .... 12.00
❑20, ca. 1961 .... 12.00
❑21 .... 10.00
❑22, ca. 1962 .... 10.00
❑23, ca. 1962 .... 10.00
❑24, ca. 1962 .... 10.00
❑25, Jul 1962 .... 10.00
❑26 .... 10.00
❑27 .... 10.00
❑28, ca. 1963 .... 10.00
❑29, ca. 1963 .... 10.00
❑30, ca. 1963 .... 10.00
❑31, Sep 1963 .... 8.00
❑32 .... 8.00
❑33 .... 8.00
❑34 .... 8.00
❑35, ca. 1964 .... 8.00
❑36, ca. 1964 .... 8.00
❑37, ca. 1964 .... 8.00
❑38, ca. 1964 .... 8.00
❑39 .... 8.00
❑40 .... 8.00
❑41 .... 8.00
❑42 .... 8.00
❑43, May 1965 .... 8.00
❑44, ca. 1965 .... 8.00
❑45, ca. 1965 .... 8.00
❑46 1965 .... 8.00
❑47 .... 8.00
❑48 .... 8.00
❑49 .... 8.00
❑50 .... 8.00
❑51, ca. 1966 .... 5.00
❑52, ca. 1966 .... 5.00
❑53, ca. 1966 .... 5.00
❑54 1966 .... 5.00
❑55, Sep 1966 .... 5.00
❑56 .... 5.00
❑57 .... 5.00
❑58 .... 5.00
❑59 1967 .... 5.00
❑60 1967 .... 5.00
❑61, Jul 1967 .... 5.00
❑62, Aug 1967 .... 5.00
❑63, Sep 1967 .... 5.00
❑64, Oct 1967 .... 5.00
❑65, Nov 1967 .... 5.00

	N-MINT
❑66	5.00
❑67 1968	5.00
❑68 1968	5.00
❑69 1968	5.00
❑70 1968	5.00
❑71 1968	5.00
❑72 1968	5.00
❑73 1968	5.00
❑74, Jan 1969	5.00
❑75 1969	5.00
❑76, May 1969	5.00
❑77 1969	5.00
❑78 1969	5.00
❑79 1969	5.00
❑80 1969	5.00
❑81 1969	5.00
❑82, Jan 1970	5.00
❑83 1970	5.00
❑84 1970	5.00
❑85 1970	5.00
❑86 1970	5.00
❑87, Sep 1970	5.00
❑88, Oct 1970	5.00
❑89, Nov 1970	5.00
❑90, Jan 1971	5.00
❑91, Mar 1971	5.00
❑92, May 1971	5.00
❑93, Jul 1971	5.00
❑94, Aug 1971	5.00
❑95, Sep 1971	5.00
❑96, Oct 1971	5.00
❑97, Nov 1971	5.00
❑98, Jan 1972	5.00
❑99, Mar 1972	5.00
❑100, May 1972	5.00
❑101, Jul 1972	4.00
❑102, Aug 1972	4.00
❑103, Sep 1972	4.00
❑104, Oct 1972	4.00
❑105, Nov 1972	4.00
❑106, Jan 1973	4.00
❑107, Mar 1973	4.00
❑108, May 1973	4.00
❑109, Jul 1973	4.00
❑110, Aug 1973	4.00
❑111, Sep 1973	4.00
❑112, Oct 1973	4.00
❑113, Nov 1973	4.00
❑114, Jan 1974	4.00
❑115, Mar 1974	4.00
❑116, May 1974	4.00
❑117, Jul 1974	4.00
❑118, Aug 1974	4.00
❑119, Sep 1974	4.00
❑120, Oct 1974	4.00
❑121, Nov 1974	4.00
❑122, Jan 1975	4.00
❑123, Mar 1975	4.00
❑124, May 1975	4.00
❑125, Jul 1975	4.00
❑126, Aug 1975	4.00
❑127, Sep 1975	4.00
❑128, Oct 1975	4.00
❑129, Nov 1975	4.00
❑130, Jan 1976 BWa, JSe (a)	4.00
❑131, Mar 1976 BWa, JSe (a)	4.00
❑132, May 1976	4.00
❑133, Jul 1976 BWa, JSe (a)	4.00
❑134, Aug 1976	4.00
❑135, Sep 1976 BWa, JSe (a)	4.00
❑136, Oct 1976 BWa, JSe (a)	4.00
❑137, Nov 1976	4.00
❑138, Dec 1976	4.00
❑139, Jan 1977	4.00
❑140, Mar 1977 BWa, JSe (a)	4.00
❑141, May 1977	4.00
❑142, Jul 1977	4.00
❑143, Aug 1977	4.00
❑144, Sep 1977	4.00
❑145, Oct 1977	4.00
❑146, Nov 1977	4.00
❑147, Dec 1977	4.00
❑148, Jan 1978	4.00
❑149, Mar 1978	4.00
❑150, May 1978	4.00
❑151, Jul 1978	3.00
❑152, Aug 1978	3.00
❑153, Sep 1978	3.00
❑154, Oct 1978	3.00
❑155, Nov 1978	3.00
❑156, Dec 1978	3.00
❑157, Jan 1979	3.00
❑158, Mar 1979	3.00
❑159, May 1979	3.00
❑160, Jul 1979	3.00
❑161, Aug 1979	3.00
❑162, Sep 1979 BWa, JSe (a)	3.00
❑163, Oct 1979	3.00
❑164, Nov 1979	3.00
❑165, Dec 1979	3.00
❑166, Jan 1980	3.00
❑167, Mar 1980	3.00
❑168, May 1980	3.00
❑169, Jul 1980	3.00
❑170, Aug 1980	3.00
❑171, Sep 1980	3.00
❑172, Oct 1980	3.00
❑173, Nov 1980	3.00
❑174, Dec 1980	3.00
❑175, Jan 1981	3.00
❑176, Mar 1981	3.00
❑177, May 1981	3.00
❑178, Jul 1981	3.00
❑179, Aug 1981	3.00
❑180, Sep 1981	3.00
❑181, Oct 1981	3.00
❑182, Nov 1981	3.00
❑183, Dec 1981	3.00
❑184, Jan 1982	3.00
❑185, Mar 1982	3.00
❑186, May 1982	3.00
❑187, Jul 1982	3.00
❑188, Aug 1982	3.00
❑189, Sep 1982	3.00
❑190, Oct 1982	3.00
❑191, Nov 1982 BWa (a)	3.00
❑192, Jan 1983	3.00
❑193, Mar 1983	3.00
❑194, May 1983	3.00
❑195, Jul 1983	3.00
❑196, Aug 1983	3.00
❑197, Sep 1983	3.00
❑198, Oct 1983	3.00
❑199, Nov 1983	3.00
❑200, Dec 1983	3.00
❑201, Jan 1984	2.50
❑202, Mar 1984	2.50
❑203, May 1984	2.50
❑204, Jul 1984	2.50
❑205, Aug 1984	2.50
❑206, Sep 1984	2.50
❑207, Oct 1984	2.50
❑208, Nov 1984	2.50
❑209, Jan 1985	2.50
❑210, Mar 1985	2.50
❑211, May 1985	2.50
❑212, Jul 1985	2.50
❑213, Aug 1985	2.50
❑214, Sep 1985	2.50
❑215, Oct 1985	2.50
❑216, Nov 1985	2.50
❑217, Dec 1985	2.50
❑218, Jan 1986	2.50
❑219, Mar 1986	2.50
❑220, May 1986	2.50
❑221, Jul 1986	2.50
❑222, Aug 1986	2.50
❑223, Sep 1986	2.50
❑224, Oct 1986	2.50
❑225, Nov 1986	2.50
❑226, Mar 1987	2.50
❑227, May 1987	2.50

Several WildStorm series crossed over in 2004's *Coup D'Etat*.
© 2004 WildStorm Productions Inc. (DC)

	N-MINT
❑228, Jul 1987	2.50
❑229, Aug 1987	2.50
❑230, Sep 1987	2.50
❑231, Oct 1987	2.50
❑232, Nov 1987	2.50
❑233, Jan 1988	2.50
❑234, Mar 1988	2.50
❑235, May 1988	2.50
❑236, Jul 1988	2.50
❑237, Aug 1988	2.50
❑238, Sep 1988	2.50
❑239, Oct 1988	2.50
❑240, Nov 1988	2.50
❑241, Dec 1988	2.50
❑242, Jan 1989	2.50
❑243, Mar 1989	2.50
❑244, May 1989	2.50
❑245, Jul 1989	2.50
❑246, Aug 1989	2.50
❑247, Sep 1989	2.50
❑248, Oct 1989	2.50
❑249, Nov 1989	2.50
❑250, Dec 1989	2.50
❑251, Jan 1990	2.00
❑252, Mar 1990	2.00
❑253, May 1990	2.00
❑254, Jul 1990	2.00
❑255, Aug 1990	2.00
❑256, Sep 1990	2.00
❑257, Oct 1990	2.00
❑258, Nov 1990	2.00
❑259, Dec 1990	2.00
❑260, Jan 1991	2.00
❑261, Mar 1991	2.00
❑262, May 1991	2.00
❑263, Jul 1991	2.00
❑264, Aug 1991	2.00
❑265, Sep 1991	2.00
❑266, Oct 1991	2.00
❑267, Nov 1991	2.00
❑268, Dec 1991	2.00
❑269, Jan 1992	2.00
❑270, Mar 1992	2.00
❑271, May 1992	2.00
❑272, Jul 1992	2.00
❑273, Aug 1992	2.00
❑274, Sep 1992	2.00
❑275, Oct 1992	2.00
❑276, Nov 1992	2.00
❑277, Dec 1992	2.00
❑278, Jan 1993	2.00
❑279, Mar 1993	2.00
❑280, May 1993	2.00
❑281, Jul 1993	2.00
❑282, Aug 1993	2.00
❑283, Sep 1993	2.00
❑284, Oct 1993	2.00
❑285, Nov 1993	2.00
❑286, Dec 1993	2.00
❑287, Jan 1994	2.00
❑288, Mar 1994	2.00
❑289, May 1994	2.00
❑290, Jul 1994	2.00
❑291, Aug 1994; b&w magazine	2.00
❑292, Sep 1994; b&w magazine	2.00
❑293, Oct 1994	2.00
❑294, Nov 1994; b&w magazine	2.00

Condition price index: Multiply "NM prices" above by: **0.83 for Very Fine/Near Mint**
0.66 for Very Fine • 0.33 for Fine • 0.2 for Very Good • 0.125 for Good

	N-MINT
❑295, Dec 1994; b&w magazine	2.00
❑296, Jan 1995; b&w magazine	2.00
❑297, Mar 1995; b&w magazine	2.00
❑298, May 1995	2.00
❑299, Jul 1995	2.00
❑300, Aug 1995	2.00
❑301, Sep 1995	2.00
❑302, Oct 1995; b&w magazine	2.00
❑303, Nov 1995	2.00
❑304, Dec 1995	2.00
❑305, Jan 1996	2.00
❑306, Mar 1996; b&w magazine	2.00
❑307, ca. 1996	2.00
❑308, ca. 1996	2.00
❑309, Aug 1996	2.00
❑310, Sep 1996	2.00
❑311, Oct 1996	2.00
❑312, Nov 1996	2.00
❑313	2.00
❑314 1997	2.00
❑315, Mar 1997	2.00
❑316 1997	2.00
❑317 1997	2.00
❑318, Aug 1997	2.00
❑319	2.00
❑320	2.00
❑321	2.00
❑322	2.00
❑323	2.00
❑324	2.00
❑325	2.00
❑326	2.00
❑327	2.00
❑328; JSe (a); Simpsons, South Park, King of the Hill parody	2.00
❑329	2.00
❑330	2.00
❑331	2.00
❑332	2.00
❑333	2.00
❑334	2.00
❑335	2.00
❑336	2.00
❑337	2.00
❑338	2.00
❑339	2.00
❑340	2.00
❑341	2.00
❑342	2.00
❑343	2.00
❑Annual 1	7.00
❑Annual 2	5.00
❑Annual 3	5.00
❑Annual 4	4.00
❑Annual 5	4.00
❑Annual 6	4.00
❑Annual 7	4.00
❑Annual 8	4.00
❑Annual 9; JSe (a); 1975 Annual	4.00

CRACKED COLLECTORS' EDITION
GLOBE

	N-MINT
❑4	10.00
❑5	8.00
❑6	6.00
❑7	6.00
❑8 1975	6.00
❑9 1975	6.00
❑10 1975	6.00
❑11 1975	5.00
❑12 1975	5.00
❑13 1976	5.00
❑14 1976	5.00
❑15 1976	5.00
❑16 1976	5.00
❑17 1976	5.00
❑18 1976	5.00
❑19	5.00
❑20	5.00
❑21	5.00
❑22	5.00
❑23	5.00
❑24	5.00
❑25	5.00
❑26	5.00
❑27	5.00
❑28	5.00
❑29	5.00
❑30	5.00
❑31	4.00
❑32	4.00
❑33	4.00
❑34	4.00
❑35	4.00
❑36	4.00
❑37	4.00
❑38	4.00
❑39	4.00
❑40	4.00
❑41, May 1981	4.00
❑42	4.00
❑43	4.00
❑44	4.00
❑45	4.00
❑46	4.00
❑47	4.00
❑48	4.00
❑49	4.00
❑50	4.00
❑51	3.00
❑52	3.00
❑53	3.00
❑54	3.00
❑55	3.00
❑56	3.00
❑57	3.00
❑58	3.00
❑59	3.00
❑60	3.00
❑61	3.00
❑62	3.00
❑63	3.00
❑64	3.00
❑65	3.00
❑66	3.00
❑67	3.00
❑68	3.00
❑69	3.00
❑70	3.00
❑71	3.00
❑72, Sep 1987	3.00
❑73, Jan 1988	3.00
❑74 1988	3.00
❑75 1988	3.00
❑76 1988	3.00
❑77 1989	3.00
❑78 1989	3.00
❑79 1989	3.00
❑80 1989	3.00
❑81 1990	3.00
❑82 1990	3.00
❑83 1990	3.00
❑84 1990	3.00
❑85 1991	3.00
❑86 1991	3.00
❑87 1991	3.00
❑88 1991	3.00
❑89 1992	3.00
❑90 1992	3.00
❑91 1992	3.00
❑92 1992	3.00
❑93 1993	3.00
❑94 1993	3.00
❑95 1993	3.00
❑96 1993	3.00
❑97, Jan 1994; 35th Anniversary issue	3.00
❑98, Apr 1994	3.00
❑99, Jul 1994	3.00
❑100, Oct 1994	3.00
❑101, Jan 1995; b&w magazine	3.00
❑102, Apr 1995	3.00
❑103, Jul 1995	3.00
❑104, Oct 1995	3.00
❑105, Jan 1996	3.00
❑106, Apr 1996	3.00
❑107, Jul 1996	3.00
❑108, Oct 1996	3.00
❑109, Jan 1997	3.00
❑110, Apr 1997	3.00

CRAP
FANTAGRAPHICS

	N-MINT
❑1, Aug 1993	2.50
❑2, Oct 1993	2.50
❑3, Feb 1994	2.50
❑4, May 1994	2.50
❑5, Aug 1994	2.50

CRASH DUMMIES
HARVEY

	N-MINT
❑1 1994	1.50
❑2 1994	1.50
❑3, Jun 1994	1.50

CRASH METRO & THE STAR SQUAD
ONI

	N-MINT
❑1, May 1999, b&w	2.95

CRASH RYAN
MARVEL / EPIC

	N-MINT
❑1, Oct 1984	1.50
❑2, Nov 1984	1.50
❑3, Dec 1984	1.50
❑4, Jan 1985	1.50

CRAY BABY ADVENTURES SPECIAL, THE
ELECTRIC MILK

	N-MINT
❑1	2.95

CRAY-BABY ADVENTURES, THE: WRATH OF THE PEDIDDLERS
DESTINATION ENTERTAINMENT

	N-MINT
❑1, b&w	2.95

CRAZY (MARVEL)
MARVEL

	N-MINT
❑1, Feb 1973; reprints Not Brand Ecch	14.00
❑2, Apr 1973; reprints Not Brand Ecch #6	8.00
❑3, Jun 1973; reprints Not Brand Ecch #7	8.00

CRAZY (MAGAZINE)
MARVEL

	N-MINT
❑1, Oct 1973	12.00
❑2 1973	6.00
❑3, Mar 1974	5.00
❑4, May 1974	5.00
❑5, Jul 1974	5.00
❑6, Aug 1974	3.00
❑7, Oct 1974	3.00
❑8, Dec 1974	3.00
❑9, Feb 1975	3.00
❑10, Apr 1975	3.00
❑11, Jun 1975	3.00
❑12, Aug 1975	3.00
❑13, Oct 1975	3.00
❑14, Nov 1975	3.00
❑15, Jan 1976	3.00
❑16, Mar 1976	2.00
❑17, May 1976	2.00
❑18, Jul 1976	2.00
❑19, Aug 1976	2.00
❑20, Oct 1976	2.00
❑21, Nov 1976	2.00
❑22, Jan 1977	2.00
❑23 1977	2.00
❑24 1977	2.00
❑25 1977	2.00
❑26, Jun 1977	2.00
❑27, Jul 1977	2.00
❑28, Aug 1977	2.00
❑29, Sep 1977	2.00
❑30, Oct 1977	2.00
❑31, Nov 1977	2.00
❑32, Dec 1977	2.00
❑33, Jan 1978	2.00
❑34, Feb 1978	2.00
❑35, Mar 1978	2.00
❑36, Apr 1978	2.00
❑37, May 1978	2.00

Condition price index: Multiply "NM prices" above by: **0.83 for Very Fine/Near Mint**
0.66 for Very Fine • 0.33 for Fine • 0.2 for Very Good • 0.125 for Good

	N-MINT
❑38, Jun 1978	2.00
❑39, Jul 1978	2.00
❑40, Aug 1978	2.00
❑41, Sep 1978	2.00
❑42, Sep 1978	2.00
❑43, Oct 1978	2.00
❑44, Nov 1978	2.00
❑45, Dec 1978	2.00
❑46, Jan 1979	2.00
❑47, Feb 1979	2.00
❑48, Mar 1979	2.00
❑49, Apr 1979	2.00
❑50, May 1979	2.00
❑51, Jun 1979	2.00
❑52, Jul 1979	2.00
❑53, Aug 1979	2.00
❑54, Sep 1979	2.00
❑55, Oct 1979	2.00
❑56, Nov 1979	2.00
❑57, Dec 1979	2.00
❑58, Jan 1980	2.00
❑59, Feb 1980	2.00
❑60, Mar 1980	2.00
❑61, Apr 1980	2.00
❑62, May 1980	2.00
❑63, Jun 1980	2.00
❑64, Jul 1980	2.00
❑65, Aug 1980	2.00
❑66, Sep 1980; "Creatures" parodizes Journey into Mystery #51	2.00
❑67, Oct 1980	2.00
❑68, Nov 1980	2.00
❑69, Dec 1980	2.00
❑70, Jan 1981	2.00
❑71, Feb 1981	2.00
❑72, Mar 1981	2.00
❑73, Apr 1981	2.00
❑74, May 1981	2.00
❑75, Jun 1981	2.00
❑76, Jul 1981	2.00
❑77, Aug 1981	2.00
❑78, Sep 1981	2.00
❑79, Oct 1981	2.00
❑80, Nov 1981	2.00
❑81, Dec 1981	2.00
❑82, Jan 1982; parodies Amazing Spider-Man #8	2.00
❑83, Feb 1982; Raiders of the Lost Ark parody	2.00
❑84, Mar 1982	2.00
❑85, Apr 1982	2.00
❑86, May 1982	2.00
❑87, Jun 1982	2.00
❑88, Jul 1982	2.00
❑89, Aug 1982	2.00
❑90, Sep 1982	2.00
❑91, Oct 1982; Blade Runner parody	2.00
❑92, Dec 1982; Star Trek II parody	2.00
❑93, Feb 1983	2.00
❑94, Apr 1983	2.00

CRAZY BOB
Blackbird

❑1, b&w	2.75
❑2, b&w	2.00

CRAZYFISH PREVIEW
Crazyfish

❑1	0.50
❑2	0.50

CRAZYMAN
Continuity

❑1, Apr 1992; enhanced cover	3.95
❑2, May 1992	2.50
❑3, Jul 1992	2.50

CRAZYMAN (2ND SERIES)
Continuity

❑1, May 1993; Die-cut comic book	3.95
❑2, Dec 1993	2.50
❑3, Dec 1993	2.50
❑4, Jan 1994; indicia says #3	2.50

N-MINT

CREATURE
Antarctic

❑1, Oct 1997, b&w	2.95
❑2, Dec 1997, b&w	2.95

CREATURE COMMANDOS
DC

❑1, May 2000	2.50
❑2, Jun 2000	2.50
❑3, Jul 2000	2.50
❑4, Aug 2000	2.50
❑5, Sep 2000	2.50
❑6, Oct 2000	2.50
❑7, Nov 2000	2.50
❑8, Dec 2000	2.50

CREATURE FEATURES
Mojo

❑1, b&w; prestige format one-shot	4.95

CREATURES OF THE ID
Caliber

❑1, Jan 1990, b&w 1: Madman (Frank Einstein).	12.00

CREATURES ON THE LOOSE
Marvel

❑10, Mar 1971; SL (w); BWr, JK (a); Title changes to Creatures on the Loose; first King Kull story; Series continued from Tower of Shadows #9; "Trull" reprints story from Tales to Astonish #21	9.00
❑11, May 1971; reprints story from Tales to Astonish #23	3.50
❑12, Jul 1971; reprints story from Journey into Mystery #69	3.50
❑13, Sep 1971; reprints stories from Tales to Astonish #25 & #28	3.50
❑14, Nov 1971; reprints story from Tales to Astonish #33	3.50
❑15, Jan 1972	3.50
❑16, Mar 1972 GK (a); O: Gullivar Jones, Warrior of Mars.	3.50
❑17, May 1972 GK (a); A: Gullivar Jones, Warrior of Mars.	3.50
❑18, Jul 1972 RA (a); A: Gullivar Jones, Warrior of Mars.	3.50
❑19, Sep 1972 JM (a); A: Gullivar Jones, Warrior of Mars.	3.50
❑20, Nov 1972 GM (a); A: Gullivar Jones, Warrior of Mars.	4.00
❑21, Jan 1973 JSo (c); GM, JSo (a); A: Gullivar Jones, Warrior of Mars.	4.00
❑22, Mar 1973 VM (a); A: Thongor.	3.00
❑23, May 1973 VM (a); A: Thongor.	3.00
❑24, Jul 1973 VM (a); A: Thongor.	3.00
❑25, Sep 1973 VM (a); A: Thongor.	3.00
❑26, Nov 1973 VM (a); A: Thongor.	3.00
❑27, Jan 1974 VM (a); A: Thongor.	3.00
❑28, Mar 1974; A: Thongor. Marvel Value Stamp #15: Iron Man	3.00
❑29, May 1974; A: Thongor. Marvel Value Stamp #37: Watcher	3.00
❑30, Jul 1974; A: Man-Wolf. Marvel Value Stamp #65: Iceman	3.00
❑31, Sep 1974; GT (a); A: Man-Wolf. Marvel Value Stamp #30: Grey Gargoyle	3.00
❑32, Nov 1974; A: Man-Wolf. Marvel Value Stamp #34: Mr. Fantastic	3.00
❑33, Jan 1975; A: Man-Wolf. Marvel Value Stamp #24: Falcon	3.00
❑34, Mar 1975 A: Man-Wolf.	3.00
❑35, May 1975 A: Man-Wolf.	3.00
❑36, Jul 1975; A: Man-Wolf. Marvel Value Stamp #73: Kingpin	3.00
❑37, Sep 1975 A: Man-Wolf.	3.00
❑King Size 1; King-size special	5.00

CREECH, THE
Image

❑1, Oct 1997	1.95
❑1/A, Oct 1997; alternate cover	1.95
❑2, Nov 1997	2.50
❑3, Dec 1997	2.50

The three comic-book issues of *Crazy* reprinted stories from *Not Brand Ecch*.

© 1973 Marvel Comics.

N-MINT

CREECH, THE: OUT FOR BLOOD
Image

❑1, Jul 2001	4.95
❑2, Sep 2001	4.95

CREED (1ST SERIES)
Hall of Heroes

❑1	4.00
❑2, Dec 1994	3.00

CREED (2ND SERIES)
Lightning

❑1, Sep 1995, b&w; reprints Hall of Heroes #1 and #2 with corrections; Black and white	3.00
❑1/A, Sep 1995, color	3.00
❑1/B, Sep 1995; Purple edition	3.00
❑1/Platinum, Sep 1995; Collectorís edition; enhanced cover	3.00
❑2, Jan 1996	3.00
❑2/Platinum, Jan 1996; Platinum edition; alternate cover	4.00
❑3, Jul 1996; bagged with trading card	3.00
❑3/Platinum; Platinum edition	3.00

CREED: CRANIAL DISORDER
Lightning

❑1, Nov 1996	3.00
❑2, Nov 1996; alternate cover, cover says Dec, indicia says Nov	3.00
❑3, Apr 1997; alternate cover	3.00

CREED: MECHANICAL EVOLUTION
Gearbox

❑1, Sep 2000	2.95

CREED/TEENAGE MUTANT NINJA TURTLES
Lightning

❑1, May 1996	3.00

CREED: THE GOOD SHIP AND THE NEW JOURNEY HOME
Lightning

❑1, Jul 1997, b&w	2.95

CREED USE YOUR DELUSION
Avatar

❑1, Jan 1998	3.00
❑2, Feb 1998	3.00

CREED: UTOPIATE
Image

❑1, Jan 2002	2.95
❑2/A, Mar 2002; Indicia is from #1	2.95
❑2/B, Mar 2002; Indicia is from #1	2.95
❑3, Aug 2002	2.95
❑4 2002	2.95

CREEPER, THE
DC

❑1, Dec 1997	2.50
❑2, Jan 1998	2.50
❑3, Feb 1998	2.50
❑4, Mar 1998	2.50
❑5, Apr 1998	2.50
❑6, May 1998	2.50
❑7, Jun 1998 V: Joker.	2.50
❑8, Jul 1998 A: Batman.	2.50
❑9, Aug 1998	2.50
❑10, Sep 1998	2.50
❑11, Oct 1998	2.50
❑1000000, Nov 1998	3.00

N-MINT

CREEPS
IMAGE

❑1, Oct 2001 .... 2.95
❑2 .... 2.95
❑3, Feb 2002 .... 2.95
❑4, May 2002 .... 2.95

CREEPSVILLE
GO-GO

❑1, b&w; trading cards 2.95
❑2, b&w; trading cards 2.95
❑3 .... 2.95
❑4 .... 2.95
❑5 .... 2.95

CREEPY TALES
PINNACLE

❑1 1975 .... 1.75

CREEPY: THE LIMITED SERIES
DARK HORSE

❑1, ca. 1992, b&w; prestige format 4.00
❑2, ca. 1992, b&w; prestige format KB (w) 4.00
❑3, ca. 1992, b&w; prestige format RHo, PD (w); JM (a) 4.00
❑4, ca. 1992, b&w; prestige format 4.00
❑FB 1993, ca. 1993; KB (w); A: Vampirella. 1993 "Fearbook"; Relaunch of Vampirella for '90s 12.00

CREMATOR
CHAOS

❑1, Dec 1998 .... 2.95
❑2, Dec 1999 .... 2.95
❑3, Jan 1999 .... 2.95
❑4, Feb 1999 .... 2.95
❑5, Apr 1999 .... 2.95

CRESCENT
B-LINE

❑0, May 1996 .... 1.00

CRESCENT MOON
TOKYOPOP

❑1, May 2004 .... 9.99

CREW, THE
MARVEL

❑1, Jul 2003 .... 2.50
❑2, Aug 2003 .... 2.50
❑3, Sep 2003 .... 2.50
❑4, Oct 2003 .... 2.99
❑5, Nov 2003 .... 2.99
❑6, Dec 2003 .... 2.99
❑7, Jan 2004 .... 2.99

CRIME & JUSTICE
AVALON

❑1, Mar 1998, b&w 2.95

CRIME AND PUNISHMENT MARSHAL LAW TAKES MANHATTAN
MARVEL / EPIC

❑1, ca. 1989, prestige format 4.95

CRIMEBUSTER
AC

❑0 .... 2.95

CRIMEBUSTER CLASSICS
AC

❑1 .... 3.50

CRIME CLASSICS
ETERNITY

❑1, Jul 1988; The Shadow 1.95
❑2, Jul 1988; The Shadow 1.95
❑3, Aug 1988; The Shadow 1.95
❑4, Sep 1989; The Shadow 1.95
❑5, Jan 1989; The Shadow 1.95
❑6, Feb 1989; The Shadow 1.95
❑7, Mar 1989; The Shadow 1.95
❑8, Apr 1989; The Shadow 1.95
❑9, May 1989; The Shadow 1.95
❑10, Jun 1989; The Shadow 1.95
❑11, Aug 1989; The Shadow 1.95
❑12, Sep 1989; The Shadow 1.95
❑13, Oct 1989; The Shadow 1.95

N-MINT

CRIME CLINIC
SLAVE LABOR

❑1, Nov 1995 .... 2.95
❑2, May 1995 .... 2.95

CRIME PATROL (GEMSTONE)
GEMSTONE

❑1, Apr 2000; Reprints Crime Patrol #1 (#7) 2.50
❑2, May 2000; Reprints Crime Patrol #2 (#8) 2.50
❑3, Jun 2000; Reprints Crime Patrol #3 (#9) 2.50
❑4, Jul 2000; Reprints Crime Patrol #4 .... 2.50
❑5, Aug 2000; Reprints Crime Patrol #5 .... 2.50
❑Annual 1, ca. 2000; Collects issues #1-5 .... 13.50

CRIME PAYS
BONEYARD

❑1, Oct 1996, b&w 2.95
❑2, Sep 1997 .... 2.95

CRIME-SMASHER (BLUE COMET)
BLUE COMET

❑Special 1, Jul 1987 .... 2.00

CRIME SUSPENSTORIES (RCP)
GEMSTONE

❑1, Nov 1992; HK, JCr, WW, GI (w); HK, JCr, WW, GI (a); Reprints Crime SuspenStories (EC) #1 .... 2.00
❑2, Nov 1992; Reprints Crime SuspenStories (EC) #2 .... 2.00
❑3, Feb 1993; Reprints Crime SuspenStories (EC) #3 .... 2.00
❑4, May 1993; JCr, JKa, GI (w); JCr, JKa, GI (a); Reprints Crime SuspenStories (EC) #4 .... 2.00
❑5, Aug 1993; Reprints Crime SuspenStories (EC) #5 .... 2.00
❑6, Nov 1993; Reprints Crime SuspenStories (EC) #6 .... 2.00
❑7, Feb 1994; Reprints Crime SuspenStories (EC) #7 .... 2.00
❑8, May 1994; Reprints Crime SuspenStories (EC) #8 .... 2.00
❑9, Aug 1994; Reprints Crime SuspenStories (EC) #9 .... 2.00
❑10, Nov 1994; Reprints Crime SuspenStories (EC) #10 .... 2.00
❑11, Feb 1995; Reprints Crime SuspenStories (EC) #11 .... 2.00
❑12, May 1995; Reprints Crime SuspenStories (EC) #12 .... 2.00
❑13, Aug 1995; Reprints Crime SuspenStories (EC) #13 .... 2.00
❑14, Nov 1995; Reprints Crime SuspenStories (EC) #14 .... 2.00
❑15, Feb 1996; Ray Bradbury story; Reprints Crime SuspenStories (EC) #15 .... 2.00
❑16, May 1996; AW, JO, JCr, JKa (w); AW, JO, JCr, JKa (a); Reprints Crime SuspenStories (EC) #16 .... 2.50
❑17, Aug 1996; AW, JCr, FF, BE, JKa (w); AW, JCr, FF, BE, JKa (a); Ray Bradbury story; Reprints Crime SuspenStories (EC) #17 .... 2.50
❑18, Nov 1996; JCr, BE, JKa (w); JCr, BE, JKa (a); Reprints Crime SuspenStories (EC) #18 .... 2.50
❑19, Feb 1997; GE, JCr (w); GE, JCr (a); Reprints Crime SuspenStories (EC) #19 .... 2.50
❑20, May 1997; Reprints Crime SuspenStories (EC) #20 .... 2.50
❑21, Aug 1997; Reprints Crime SuspenStories (EC) #21 .... 2.50
❑22, Nov 1997; Reprints Crime SuspenStories (EC) #22 .... 2.50
❑23, Feb 1998; Reprints Crime SuspenStories (EC) #23 .... 2.50
❑24, May 1998; JO, BK, JKa (a); Reprints Crime SuspenStories (EC) #24 .... 2.50
❑25, Aug 1998; GE, BK, JKa (a); Reprints Crime SuspenStories (EC) #25 .... 2.50
❑26, Nov 1998; JO, JKa (a); Reprints Crime SuspenStories (EC) #26 .... 2.50

N-MINT

❑27, Feb 1999; GE, BK, JKa, GI (a); Reprints Crime SuspenStories (EC) #27 .... 2.50
❑Annual 1; Reprints Crime SuspenStories (EC) #1-5 .... 8.95
❑Annual 2; Reprints Crime SuspenStories (EC) #6-10 .... 9.95
❑Annual 3; Reprints Crime SuspenStories (EC) #11-15 .... 9.95
❑Annual 4; Reprints Crime SuspenStories (EC) #15-19 .... 10.50
❑Annual 5; Reprints Crime SuspenStories (EC) #20-23 .... 10.95
❑Annual 6; Reprints Crime SuspenStories (EC) #24-27 .... 10.95

CRIMINAL MACABRE
DARK HORSE

❑1, May 2003 .... 2.99
❑2, Jun 2003 .... 2.99
❑3, Jul 2003 .... 2.99
❑4, Aug 2003 .... 2.99
❑5, Sep 2003 .... 2.99

CRIMSON
IMAGE / CLIFFHANGER

❑1, May 1998; Several figures on cover, one in cowboy hat smoking 3.50
❑1/A, May 1998; Boy covered in blood/rain 3.50
❑1/B, May 1998; chromium cover; Three figures on ledge 6.00
❑1/C, May 1998; Dynamic Forces chromium edition with certificate of authenticity; Boy in graveyard; chromium cover 6.00
❑2, May 1998 .... 3.00
❑2/A, Jun 1998; alternate cover (vampire) 6.00
❑2/B, Jun 1998; Crimson chrome edition 6.00
❑3, Jun 1998 .... 3.00
❑3/A, Jul 1998; alternate cover (red background) 3.50
❑4, Jul 1998 .... 2.50
❑5, Aug 1998 .... 2.50
❑6, Sep 1998 .... 2.50
❑7, Dec 1998 .... 2.50
❑7/A, Nov 1998; DFE Hard-to-Get Foil covers pack 15.00
❑7/B, Dec 1998; alternate cover (angels) 3.00
❑7/C, Dec 1998; alternate cover (archway) 3.00
❑8, Dec 1999 .... 2.50
❑9, Mar 1999 .... 2.50
❑10, May 1999 .... 2.50
❑11, Jun 1999 .... 2.50
❑12, Aug 1999 .... 2.50
❑13, Dec 1999 .... 2.50
❑14, Jan 2000 .... 2.50
❑15, Feb 2000 .... 2.50
❑16, Mar 2000 .... 2.50
❑17, Apr 2000 .... 2.50
❑18, Jul 2000 .... 2.50
❑19, Sep 2000 .... 2.50
❑20, Oct 2000 .... 2.50
❑21, Nov 2000 .... 2.50
❑22, Dec 2000 .... 2.50
❑23, Jan 2001 .... 2.50
❑24, Apr 2001 .... 2.50
❑Special 1 .... 6.95
❑Special 1/A; European cover 8.00
❑Special 1/Autog; DFE alternate cover 7.00
❑Special 1/Varia; DFE alternate cover 7.00

CRIMSON AVENGER
DC

❑1, Jun 1988 .... 1.50
❑2, Jul 1988 .... 1.50
❑3, Aug 1988 MGu (a) 1.50
❑4, Sep 1988 MGu (a) 1.50

CRIMSON DREAMS
CRIMSON

❑1 .... 2.00
❑2 .... 2.00
❑3 .... 2.00

N-MINT

❑4 .... 2.00
❑5 .... 2.00
❑6 .... 2.00
❑7, ca. 1985 .... 2.00
❑8, ca. 1986 .... 2.00
❑9, Sum 1986 .... 2.00
❑10, ca. 1986 .... 2.00
❑11, ca. 1986 .... 2.00

CRIMSON DYNAMO
MARVEL / EPIC

❑1, Oct 2003 .... 2.50
❑2, Nov 2003 .... 2.50
❑3, Dec 2003 .... 2.50
❑4, Jan 2004; Going Up! 2.50
❑5, Jan 2004; Retells origin of Crimson Dynamo; price erroneously printed as $2.99, retailers charged $2.50 .... 2.95
❑6, May 2004 .... 2.50

CRIMSON LETTERS
ADVENTURE

❑1; Adventurers b&w 2.25

CRIMSON NUN, THE
ANTARCTIC

❑1, May 1997 .... 2.95
❑2, Jul 1997 .... 2.95
❑3, Sep 1997 .... 2.95
❑4, Nov 1997 .... 2.95

CRIMSON PLAGUE
EVENT

❑1, Jun 1997 .... 2.95
❑1/Ltd., Jun 1997; alternate limited edition only sold at 1997 Heroes Con 5.00

CRIMSON PLAGUE (GEORGE PÉREZ'S...)
IMAGE

❑1, Jun 2000 .... 2.95
❑2, Aug 2000 .... 2.50

CRIMSON: SCARLET X BLOOD ON THE MOON
DC / CLIFFHANGER

❑1, Oct 1999 .... 3.95

CRIMSON SOURCEBOOK
WILDSTORM

❑1, Nov 1999 .... 2.95

CRISIS ON INFINITE EARTHS
DC

❑1, Apr 1985; wraparound cover 5.00
❑2, May 1985 .... 4.00
❑3, Jun 1985 .... 3.00
❑4, Jul 1985 .... 3.00
❑5, Aug 1985 .... 3.00
❑6, Sep 1985 .... 3.00
❑7, Oct 1985; Double-size 5.00
❑8, Nov 1985 .... 5.00
❑9, Dec 1985 .... 4.00
❑10, Jan 1986 .... 4.00
❑11, Feb 1986 .... 4.00
❑12, Mar 1986 .... 5.00

CRISIS ON MULTIPLE EARTHS
DC

❑1; Collects stories from Justice League of America #21-22, 29-30, 37ñ38, 46ñ47 .... 14.95
❑2, ca. 2003 .... 14.95
❑3, ca. 2004 ....

CRISP
CRISP BISCUIT

❑1, Apr 1997 .... 3.00
❑2, Apr 1998 .... 3.00

CRISP BISCUIT
CRISP BISCUIT

❑1, Jul 1991 .... 2.00

CRISTIAN DARK
DARQUE

❑1 1993 .... 2.50
❑2 1993 .... 2.50
❑3, Dec 1993 .... 2.50

N-MINT

CRITICAL ERROR
DARK HORSE

❑1, Jul 1992; color reprint of silent story from The Art of John Byrne .. 2.50

CRITICAL MASS
MARVEL / EPIC

❑1, Jan 1989 .... 4.95
❑2, Feb 1989 .... 4.95
❑3, Mar 1989 .... 4.95
❑4, Apr 1989 .... 4.95
❑5, May 1989 .... 4.95
❑6, Jun 1989 .... 4.95
❑7, Jul 1989 .... 4.95

CRITTERS
FANTAGRAPHICS

❑1, Jun 1986, b&w A: Usagi Yojimbo. 10.00
❑2, Jul 1986; Captain Jack debut 3.00
❑3, Aug 1986 A: Usagi Yojimbo. 8.00
❑4, Sep 1986 .... 3.00
❑5, Oct 1986 .... 3.00
❑6, Nov 1986 A: Usagi Yojimbo. 5.00
❑7, Dec 1986 A: Usagi Yojimbo. 5.00
❑8, Jan 1987 .... 3.00
❑9, Feb 1987 .... 3.00
❑10, Mar 1987 A: Usagi Yojimbo. 4.00
❑11, Apr 1987 .... 3.00
❑12, May 1987 .... 3.00
❑13, Jun 1987; Gnuff story; Birthright II story 3.00
❑14, Jul 1987 A: Usagi Yojimbo. 3.00
❑15, Aug 1987 .... 3.00
❑16, Sep 1987 .... 3.00
❑17, Oct 1987 .... 3.00
❑18, Nov 1987; indicia says Sep 87 .. 3.00
❑19, Dec 1987 .... 3.00
❑20, Jan 1988 .... 3.00
❑21, Feb 1988 .... 2.50
❑22, Mar 1988; Watchmen parody cover; indicia repeated from issue #21 .... 2.50
❑23, Apr 1988 AMo (w) 3.95
❑24, May 1988 .... 2.50
❑25, Jun 1988 .... 2.50
❑26, Jul 1988 .... 2.50
❑27, Aug 1988 .... 2.50
❑28, Sep 1988 .... 2.50
❑29, Oct 1988 .... 2.50
❑30, Nov 1988 .... 2.50
❑31, Dec 1988 .... 2.50
❑32, Jan 1989 .... 2.50
❑33, Feb 1989 .... 2.50
❑34, Mar 1989 .... 2.50
❑35, Apr 1989 .... 2.50
❑36, May 1989 .... 2.50
❑37, Jun 1989 .... 2.50
❑38, Jul 1989; 1: Stinz. Usagi Yojimbo 2.50
❑39, Aug 1989; Fission Chicken 2.50
❑40, Aug 1989 .... 2.50
❑41, Sep 1989; Platypus 2.00
❑42, Sep 1989; Captain Jack 2.00
❑43 1989 .... 2.00
❑44 1989 .... 2.00
❑45 1989 .... 2.00
❑46 1989 .... 2.00
❑47 1990 .... 2.00
❑48 1990 .... 2.00
❑49 1990 .... 2.00
❑50 1990 .... 4.95
❑Special 1, Jan 1988; A: Usagi Yojimbo. Special #1 .... 2.00

CRITTURS
MU

❑0, Nov 1992 .... 2.50

CROMWELL STONE
DARK HORSE

❑1, b&w 3.50

CROSS
DARK HORSE

❑0, Oct 1995 .... 2.95
❑1, Nov 1995 .... 2.95
❑2, Dec 1995 .... 2.95

Marshal Law visited The Big Apple and its super-powered citizens in *Crime and Punishment: Marshal Law Takes Manhattan.*

© 1989 Epic.

N-MINT

❑3, Jan 1996 .... 2.95
❑4, Feb 1996 .... 2.95
❑5, Mar 1996 .... 2.95
❑6, Apr 1996 .... 2.95

CROSS AND THE SWITCHBLADE, THE
SPIRE

❑1; Based on the book, The Cross and the Switchblade 3.00

CROSSED SWORDS
K-Z

❑1, Dec 1986 .... 1.00

CROSSFIRE
ECLIPSE

❑1, May 1984 DS, ME (w); DS (a) 2.50
❑2, Jun 1984 DS (a) 1.75
❑3, Jul 1984 DS (a) 1.75
❑4, Aug 1984 DS (a) 1.75
❑5, Sep 1984 DS (a) 1.75
❑6, Nov 1984 DS (a) 1.75
❑7, Dec 1984 DS (a) 1.75
❑8, Jan 1985 DS (a) 1.75
❑9, Mar 1985 DS (a) 1.75
❑10, Apr 1985 DS (a) 1.75
❑11, May 1985 DS (a) 1.75
❑12, Jun 1985; DSt (c); DS (a); Marilyn Monroe story, cover 1.75
❑13, Jul 1985 DS (a) 1.75
❑14, Aug 1985 DS (a) 1.75
❑15, Oct 1985 DS (a) 1.75
❑16, Jan 1986 BA (c); BA, DS (a) 1.75
❑17, Mar 1986 DS (a) 1.75
❑18, Jan 1987; Black & white issues begin 1.75
❑19, Feb 1987 .... 1.75
❑20, Mar 1987 .... 1.75
❑21, Apr 1987 .... 1.75
❑22, Jun 1987 .... 1.75
❑23, Jul 1987 .... 1.75
❑24, Aug 1987 .... 1.75
❑25, Oct 1987 .... 1.75
❑26, Feb 1988 .... 1.75

CROSSFIRE AND RAINBOW
ECLIPSE

❑1, Jun 1986 .... 1.25
❑2, Jul 1986 .... 1.25
❑3, Aug 1986 .... 1.25
❑4, Sep 1986 .... 1.25

CROSSGEN CHRONICLES
CROSSGEN

❑1, Jun 2000; lead-in to ongoing CrossGen series; background info on creators and series 3.95
❑2, Mar 2001 .... 3.95
❑3, Jun 2001 .... 3.95
❑4, Sep 2001 .... 3.95
❑5, Dec 2001 .... 3.95
❑6, Mar 2002; The First 3.95
❑7, May 2002; Negation 3.95

CROSSGEN SAMPLER
CROSSGEN

❑1, Feb 2000; No cover price; previews of upcoming series 1.00

CROSSOVERS
CROSSGEN

❑1, Feb 2003 .... 2.95
❑2, Mar 2003 .... 2.95

Condition price index: Multiply "NM prices" above by: **0.83 for Very Fine/Near Mint**
0.66 for Very Fine • 0.33 for Fine • 0.2 for Very Good • 0.125 for Good

N-MINT

❑3, Apr 2003 .... 2.95
❑4, May 2003 .... 2.95
❑5, Jun 2003 .... 2.95
❑6, Jul 2003 .... 2.95
❑7, Oct 2003 .... 2.95
❑8, Nov 2003 .... 2.95
❑9, Dec 2003 .... 2.95

CROSSROADS
FIRST

❑1, Jul 1988; Sable, Whisper 3.50
❑2, Aug 1988; Sable, Badger 3.50
❑3, Sep 1988; Badger, Luther Ironheart 3.50
❑4, Oct 1988; Grimjack, Judah 3.50
❑5, Nov 1988; Grimjack, Nexus, Dreadstar 3.50

CROW, THE (CALIBER)
CALIBER

❑1, Feb 1989; O: The Crow. b&w (10, 000 print run) 15.00
❑1-2; O: The Crow. 2nd Printing (5, 000 print run) 3.50
❑1-3; O: The Crow. 3rd printing (5, 000 print run) 3.00
❑2, Mar 1989; (7000 print run) 12.00
❑2-2, Dec 1989; 2nd Printing (5, 000 print run) 3.50
❑2-3, Jun 1990; 3rd printing (5, 000 print run) 3.00
❑3, Aug 1989; (5000 print run) 10.00
❑3-2; 2nd Printing (5, 000 print run) 3.50
❑4, ca. 1989; only printing (12, 000 print run) 10.00

CROW, THE (TUNDRA)
TUNDRA

❑1, Jan 1992, b&w; prestige format .. 4.95
❑2, Mar 1992, b&w; prestige format . 4.95
❑3, May 1992, b&w; prestige format 4.95
❑4 .... 4.95

CROW, THE (IMAGE)
IMAGE

❑1, Feb 1999 .... 3.00
❑1/A, Feb 1999; gravestones 3.00
❑2, Mar 1999 .... 2.50
❑3, Apr 1999 .... 2.50
❑4, May 1999 .... 2.50
❑5, Jun 1999 .... 2.50
❑6, Jul 1999 .... 2.50
❑7, Aug 1999 .... 2.50
❑8, Sep 1999 .... 2.50
❑9, Oct 1999 .... 2.50
❑10, Nov 1999 .... 2.50

CROW, THE: CITY OF ANGELS
KITCHEN SINK

❑1, Jul 1996; adapts movie 2.95
❑1/Variant, Jul 1996; adapts movie ... 2.95
❑2, Aug 1996; adapts movie 2.95
❑2/Variant, Aug 1996; adapts movie . 2.95
❑3, Sep 1996 .... 2.95
❑3/Variant, Sep 1996 .... 2.95

CROW, THE: DEAD TIME
KITCHEN SINK

❑1, Jan 1996, b&w 2.95
❑2, Feb 1996 .... 2.95
❑3, Mar 1996 .... 2.95

CROW, THE: FLESH & BLOOD
KITCHEN SINK

❑1, May 1996, b&w 2.95
❑2, Jun 1996, b&w 2.95
❑3, Jul 1996, b&w 2.95

CROW OF THE BEARCLAN
BLACKTHORNE

❑1, Oct 1986 .... 1.50
❑2 1987 .... 1.50
❑3 1987 .... 1.50
❑4 1987 .... 1.50
❑5 1987 .... 1.50
❑6, Mar 1988 .... 1.50

N-MINT

CROW, THE: WAKING NIGHTMARES
KITCHEN SINK

❑1, Jan 1997, b&w 2.95
❑2, Jan 1998, b&w 2.95
❑3, Feb 1998, b&w 2.95
❑4, May 1998, b&w 2.95

CROW, THE: WILD JUSTICE
KITCHEN SINK

❑1, Oct 1996, b&w 2.95
❑2, Nov 1996, b&w 2.95
❑3, Dec 1996, b&w 2.95

CROZONIA
IMAGE

❑1 .... 2.95

CRUCIAL FICTION
FANTAGRAPHICS

❑1, Mar 1992, b&w 2.50
❑2, b&w 2.25
❑3, b&w 2.25

CRUCIBLE
DC / IMPACT

❑1, Feb 1993 MWa (w) 1.50
❑2, Mar 1993 .... 1.25
❑3, Apr 1993 .... 1.25
❑4, May 1993 .... 1.25
❑5, Jun 1993 .... 1.25
❑6, Jul 1993 .... 1.25

CRUEL AND UNUSUAL
DC / VERTIGO

❑1, Jun 1999 .... 2.95
❑2, Jul 1999 .... 2.95
❑3, Aug 1999 .... 2.95
❑4, Sep 1999 .... 2.95

CRUEL & UNUSUAL PUNISHMENT
STARHEAD

❑1, Nov 1993, b&w 2.50
❑2, Oct 1994, b&w 2.95

CRUEL WORLD
FANTAGRAPHICS

❑1, b&w 3.50

CRUSADERS
GUILD

❑1; Title continued in Southern Nights #2 .... 1.00

CRUSADERS, THE
DC / IMPACT

❑1, May 1992 .... 1.00
❑2, Jun 1992 .... 1.00
❑3, Jul 1992 .... 1.00
❑4, Aug 1992 .... 1.00
❑5, Sep 1992 .... 1.00
❑6, Oct 1992 .... 1.00
❑7, Nov 1992 .... 1.00
❑8, Dec 1992 .... 1.00

CRUSADES, THE
DC / VERTIGO

❑1, May 2001 .... 2.50
❑2, Jun 2001 .... 2.50
❑3, Jul 2001 .... 2.50
❑4, Aug 2001 .... 2.50
❑5, Sep 2001 .... 2.50
❑6, Oct 2001 .... 2.50
❑7, Nov 2001 .... 2.50
❑8, Dec 2001 .... 2.50
❑9, Jan 2002 .... 2.50
❑10, Feb 2002 .... 2.50
❑11, Mar 2002 .... 2.50
❑12, Apr 2002 .... 2.50
❑13, May 2002 .... 2.50
❑14, Jun 2002 .... 2.50
❑15, Jul 2002 .... 2.50
❑16, Aug 2002 .... 2.50
❑17, Sep 2002 .... 2.50
❑18, Oct 2002 .... 2.95
❑19, Nov 2002 .... 2.95
❑20, Dec 2002 .... 2.95

N-MINT

CRUSADES, THE: URBAN DECREE
DC / VERTIGO

❑1, Apr 2001 .... 3.95

CRUSH
AEON

❑1, Nov 1995, b&w; cardstock cover 2.95
❑2, Dec 1995, b&w; cardstock cover . 2.95
❑3, Jan 1996, b&w; cardstock cover . 2.95
❑4, Feb 1996, b&w; cardstock cover . 2.95

CRUSH (DARK HORSE)
DARK HORSE

❑1, Oct 2003 .... 2.99
❑2, Dec 2003 .... 2.99
❑3, Feb 2004 .... 2.99
❑4, Mar 2004 .... 2.99

CRUSH, THE
IMAGE

❑1, Jan 1996; cover says Mar, indicia says Jan 2.25
❑2, Apr 1996 .... 2.25
❑3, May 1996 .... 2.25
❑4, Jun 1996 .... 2.25
❑5, Jul 1996 .... 2.25

CRUSHER JOE
IRONCAT

❑1 1999 .... 2.25
❑2 1999 .... 2.25
❑3, Mar 1999 .... 2.25

CRUST
TOP SHELF

❑1, b&w; no cover date 3.00

CRUX
CROSSGEN

❑1, May 2001 .... 2.95
❑2, Jun 2001 .... 2.95
❑3, Jul 2001 .... 2.95
❑4, Aug 2001 .... 2.95
❑5, Sep 2001 .... 2.95
❑6, Oct 2001 .... 2.95
❑7, Nov 2001 .... 2.95
❑8, Dec 2001 .... 2.95
❑9, Jan 2002 .... 2.95
❑10, Feb 2002 .... 2.95
❑11, Mar 2002 .... 2.95
❑12, Apr 2002 .... 2.95
❑13, May 2002 .... 2.95
❑14, Jun 2002 .... 2.95
❑15, Jul 2002 .... 2.95
❑16, Aug 2002 .... 2.95
❑17, Sep 2002 .... 2.95
❑18, Oct 2002 .... 2.95
❑19, Nov 2002 .... 2.95
❑20, Dec 2002 .... 2.95
❑21, Jan 2003 .... 2.95
❑22, Feb 2003 .... 2.95
❑23, Mar 2003 .... 2.95
❑24, Apr 2003 .... 2.95
❑25, May 2003 .... 2.95
❑26, Jun 2003 .... 2.95
❑27, Jul 2003 .... 2.95
❑28, Aug 2003 .... 2.95
❑29, Nov 2003 .... 2.95
❑30, Nov 2003 .... 2.95
❑31, Dec 2003 .... 2.95
❑32, Dec 2003 .... 2.95
❑33, Feb 2004 .... 2.95

CRY FOR DAWN
CRY FOR DAWN

❑1, Apr 1989, b&w 1: Dawn. 45.00
❑1/A; Black light edition 15.00
❑1/CF; Counterfeit version of #1; Has blotchy tones on cover 2.25
❑1-2 1: Dawn. 20.00
❑1-3 1: Dawn. 18.00
❑2, ca. 1990 .... 30.00
❑2-2 .... 15.00
❑3 .... 25.00
❑4, Win 1991 .... 15.00
❑4/Autographed, Win 1991 .... 30.00
❑5, b&w 15.00

N-MINT

❑5/Autographed 25.00
❑5-2 ..... 8.00
❑6, Fal 1991, b&w 15.00
❑6/Autographed, Fal 1991 ..... 25.00
❑7, b&w 15.00
❑7/Autographed 15.00
❑8, Win 1992, b&w 10.00
❑8/Autographed, Win 1992 ..... 15.00
❑9, Spr 1992, b&w 10.00
❑9/Autographed, Spr 1992 ..... 15.00

CRYING FREEMAN PART 1
Viz

❑1 1989; O: The 108 Dragons. O: Emu Hino. 1: Crying Freeman 4.00
❑2 1: Ryuji The Blade 4.00
❑3 ..... 4.00
❑4 1990 O: Crying Freeman 4.00
❑5 1990; Crying Freeman gets tattooed 4.00
❑6 1990 ..... 4.00
❑7 1990 ..... 4.00
❑8 1990 ..... 4.00

CRYING FREEMAN PART 2
Viz

❑1 1990 ..... 4.00
❑2 ..... 4.00
❑3 ..... 4.00
❑4 D: Koh Tokugen. D: Kitche. 4.00
❑5 ..... 4.00
❑6 D: Old Man Venus. D: Old Man Earth. D: Old Man Jupiter. D: Old Man Saturn. D: Old Man Mars 4.00
❑7 D: Shikeb 4.00
❑8 ..... 4.00
❑9 1991 O: Muramasa 4.00

CRYING FREEMAN PART 3
Viz

❑1 1991 1st issue in color 5.50
❑2, color 5.00
❑3, color 5.00
❑4, color 5.00
❑5, color 5.00
❑6, color 5.00
❑7, color 5.00
❑8, color 5.00
❑9, color; D: Detective Nitta. color 5.00
❑10 1992, color 5.00

CRYING FREEMAN PART 4
Viz

❑1 ..... 5.00
❑2 ..... 5.00
❑3 ..... 5.00
❑4 ..... 3.00
❑5 ..... 3.00
❑6 ..... 3.00
❑7 ..... 3.00
❑8 ..... 3.00

CRYING FREEMAN PART 5
Viz

❑1, b&w 2.75
❑2, b&w 2.75
❑3, b&w 2.75
❑4, b&w 2.75
❑5, b&w 2.75
❑6, b&w 2.75
❑7, b&w 2.75
❑8, b&w 2.75
❑9, b&w 2.75
❑10, b&w 2.75
❑11, b&w 2.75

CRYPT
Image

❑1, Aug 1995 ..... 2.50
❑2, Oct 1995 ..... 2.50

CRYPTIC TALES
Showcase

❑1 ..... 1.95

N-MINT

CRYPTIC WRITINGS OF MEGADETH
Chaos!

❑1, Sep 1997; Necro Limited Premium Edition; comics adaptation of Megadeath songs; alternate cardstock cover 2.95
❑2, Dec 1997; comics adaptation of Megadeath songs 2.95

CRYPT OF C*M
Fantagraphics / Eros

❑1, Feb 1999 ..... 2.95

CRYPT OF DAWN
Sirius

❑1, Oct 1996 ..... 3.50
❑1/Ltd., Oct 1996 ..... 6.00
❑2, Apr 1997 ..... 3.00
❑3, Feb 1998 ..... 3.00
❑4, Jun 1998; color story 2.95
❑5, Nov 1998 ..... 2.95
❑6, Mar 1999 ..... 2.95

CRYPT OF SHADOWS
Marvel

❑1, Jan 1973; BW (a); Reprints Adventures into Terror #7 ..... 8.00
❑2, Mar 1973 ..... 5.00
❑3, May 1973 ..... 5.00
❑4, Jul 1973 ..... 4.00
❑5, Sep 1973 ..... 4.00
❑6, Oct 1973 ..... 3.00
❑7, Nov 1973 ..... 3.00
❑8, Jan 1974 ..... 3.00
❑9, Mar 1974 ..... 3.00
❑10, May 1974 ..... 3.00
❑11, Jul 1974 ..... 3.00
❑12, Sep 1974 ..... 3.00
❑13, Oct 1974 ..... 3.00
❑14, Nov 1974 ..... 3.00
❑15, Jan 1975 ..... 3.00
❑16, Mar 1975 ..... 3.00
❑17, May 1975 ..... 3.00
❑18, Jul 1975; Reprints Tales to Astonish #11 ..... 3.00
❑19, Sep 1975 ..... 3.00
❑20, Oct 1975; Reprints Tales of Suspense #29 ..... 3.00
❑21, Nov 1975 ..... 3.00

CRYSTAL BALLS
Fantagraphics / Eros

❑1 ..... 2.95
❑2, Sep 1995 ..... 2.95

CRYSTAL BREEZE UNLEASHED
High Impact

❑1, Oct 1996, b&w; no cover price ... 3.00

CRYSTAL WAR, THE
Atlantis

❑1 ..... 3.50

CSI: BAD RAP
Idea & Design Works

❑1, ca. 2003 ..... 6.00
❑2, ca. 2003 ..... 4.00
❑3, ca. 2003 ..... 4.00
❑4, ca. 2004 ..... 4.00
❑5, ca. 2004 ..... 4.00

CSI: CRIME SCENE INVESTIGATION
Idea & Design Works

❑1 2003 ..... 12.00
❑1/A 2003 ..... 7.00
❑2 2003 ..... 5.00
❑2/A 2003 ..... 5.00
❑3 2003 ..... 3.99
❑3/A 2003 ..... 5.00
❑4 2003 ..... 3.99
❑4/A 2003 ..... 5.00
❑5 2003 ..... 3.99
❑5/A 2003 ..... 5.00

CSI: DEMON HOUSE
Idea & Design Works

❑1, ca. 2004 ..... 5.00
❑2, ca. 2004 ..... 4.00
❑3, ca. 2004 ..... 4.00

Several of Spire's comics adapted stories of Christians in action, including *The Cross and the Switchblade*, *The Hiding Place*, and *God's Smuggler*.
© 1971 Spire.

N-MINT

CTHULHU (H.P. LOVECRAFT'S...)
Millennium

❑1 ..... 2.50
❑1/CS; trading cards 3.50
❑2; trading cards 2.50
❑3 ..... 2.50

CUCKOO
Green Door

❑1, b&w; cardstock cover 2.75
❑2, Win 1996, b&w; cardstock cover 2.75
❑3, Spr 1997, b&w; cardstock cover . 2.75
❑4, Sum 1997, b&w; cardstock cover 2.75
❑5, Fal 1997, b&w; cardstock cover .. 2.75

CUD
Fantagraphics

❑1, b&w 3.00
❑2, b&w 2.50
❑3, b&w 2.50
❑4, b&w 2.50
❑5, b&w 2.50
❑6, b&w 2.50
❑7, Aug 1994, b&w 2.50

CUDA
Avatar

❑1/C, Oct 1998; Woman bathing on cover 3.50
❑1/B, Oct 1998; Nude cover 3.50
❑1/A, Oct 1998; Woman battling man on cover 3.50
❑1, Oct 1998; wraparound cover 3.50

CUDA B.C.
Rebel

❑1 ..... 2.00

CUD COMICS
Dark Horse

❑1, Nov 1995, b&w 2.95
❑2, Jan 1996, b&w 2.95
❑3, Mar 1996, b&w 2.95
❑4, Jun 1996 ..... 2.95
❑5, Sep 1996, b&w 2.95
❑6, Dec 1996, b&w 2.95
❑7, Apr 1997, b&w 2.95
❑8, Sep 1997, b&w 2.95
❑Ashcan 1; Ashcan promotional give-away from comic con appearances 1.00

CUIRASS
Harrier

❑1, b&w 1.95

CULT TELEVISION
Zone

❑1, Nov 1992 ..... 2.95

CULTURAL JET LAG
Fantagraphics

❑1, Jul 1991, b&w 2.50

CULTURE VULTURES, THE
Iconografix

❑1 ..... 2.95

CUPID'S REVENGE
Fantagraphics / Eros

❑1 ..... 2.95
❑2 ..... 2.95

CURIO SHOPPE, THE
Phoenix

❑1, Mar 1995, b&w 2.50

Condition price index: Multiply "NM prices" above by: **0.83 for Very Fine/Near Mint**
0.66 for Very Fine • 0.33 for Fine • 0.2 for Very Good • 0.125 for Good

N-MINT

CURSED
IMAGE

- ❑1, Oct 2003 ... 2.99
- ❑2, Nov 2003 ... 2.99
- ❑3, Dec 2003 ... 2.99
- ❑4, Jan 2004 ... 2.99

CURSED WORLDS SOURCE BOOK
BLUE COMET

- ❑1 ... 2.95

CURSE OF DRACULA, THE
DARK HORSE

- ❑1, Jul 1998 ... 2.95
- ❑2, Aug 1998 ... 2.95
- ❑3, Sep 1998 ... 2.95

CURSE OF DREADWOLF
LIGHTNING

- ❑1, Sep 1994, b&w ... 2.75

CURSE OF RUNE
MALIBU

- ❑1, May 1995 ... 2.50
- ❑2, Jun 1995, b&w; no indicia ... 2.50
- ❑3, Jul 1995, b&w ... 2.50
- ❑4, Aug 1995, b&w ... 2.50

CURSE OF THE MOLEMEN
KITCHEN SINK

- ❑1, color ... 4.95

CURSE OF THE SHE-CAT
AC

- ❑1, Feb 1989, b&w ... 2.50

CURSE OF THE SPAWN
IMAGE

- ❑1, Sep 1996; b&w promo ... 3.00
- ❑1/A, Sep 1996, b&w; softcover; promo ... 4.00
- ❑2, Oct 1996 ... 3.00
- ❑3, Nov 1996 ... 3.00
- ❑4, Dec 1996 ... 2.50
- ❑5, Dec 1996 ... 2.50
- ❑6, Feb 1997 ... 2.50
- ❑7, Mar 1997 ... 2.50
- ❑8, Apr 1997 ... 2.50
- ❑9, May 1997 A: Angela. ... 2.50
- ❑10, Jun 1997 A: Angela. ... 2.50
- ❑11, Aug 1997 A: Angela. ... 2.50
- ❑12, Sep 1997 ... 2.50
- ❑13, Oct 1997 ... 2.50
- ❑14, Nov 1997 ... 2.50
- ❑15, Dec 1997 ... 2.50
- ❑16, Jan 1998 ... 2.00
- ❑17, Feb 1998 ... 2.00
- ❑18, Mar 1998 ... 2.00
- ❑19, Apr 1998 ... 2.00
- ❑20, May 1998 ... 2.00
- ❑21, Jun 1998 ... 2.00
- ❑22, Jul 1998 ... 2.00
- ❑23, Aug 1998 ... 2.00
- ❑24, Sep 1998 ... 1.95
- ❑25, Oct 1998 ... 1.95
- ❑26, Nov 1998 ... 1.95
- ❑27, Dec 1998 ... 1.95
- ❑28, Feb 1999 TMc (a) ... 1.95
- ❑29, Mar 1999 TMc (a) ... 1.95

CURSE OF THE WEIRD
MARVEL

- ❑1, Dec 1993; RH (a); Reprints stories from Adventures in Terror #4, Astonishing Tales #10, others ... 1.50
- ❑2, Jan 1994 ... 1.50
- ❑3, Feb 1994 BW, RH (a) ... 1.50
- ❑4, Mar 1994 ... 1.50

CURSE OF THE ZOMBIE
MARVEL

- ❑4 ... 1.25

CUTEGIRL
NOT AVAILABLE

- ❑1 ... 0.50
- ❑2 ... 0.50

N-MINT

CUTTING CLASS
B COMICS

- ❑1, Sep 1995 ... 2.00

CUTTING EDGE
MARVEL

- ❑1, Dec 1995; continued from The Incredible Hulk #436; continues in The Incredible Hulk #437 ... 2.95

CYBER 7
ECLIPSE

- ❑1, Mar 1989, b&w; Japanese ... 2.00
- ❑2, Apr 1989, b&w; Japanese ... 2.00
- ❑3, May 1989, b&w; Japanese ... 2.00
- ❑4, Jun 1989, b&w; Japanese ... 2.00
- ❑5, Jul 1989, b&w; Japanese ... 2.00
- ❑6, Aug 1989, b&w; Japanese ... 2.00
- ❑7, Sep 1989, b&w; Japanese ... 2.00

CYBER 7 BOOK TWO
ECLIPSE

- ❑1, Oct 1989, b&w; Japanese ... 2.00
- ❑2, Nov 1989, b&w; Japanese ... 2.00
- ❑3, Dec 1989, b&w; Japanese ... 2.00
- ❑4, Jan 1990, b&w; Japanese ... 2.00
- ❑5, Mar 1990, b&w; Japanese ... 2.00
- ❑6, Apr 1990, b&w; Japanese ... 2.00
- ❑7, May 1990, b&w; Japanese ... 2.00
- ❑8, Jun 1990, b&w; Japanese ... 2.00
- ❑9, Sep 1990, b&w; Japanese ... 2.00
- ❑10, Nov 1990, b&w; Japanese ... 2.00

CYBER CITY: PART 1
CPM

- ❑1, Sep 1995; adapts anime ... 2.95
- ❑2, Sep 1995; adapts anime ... 2.95

CYBER CITY: PART 2
CPM

- ❑1, Oct 1995; adapts anime ... 2.95
- ❑2, Nov 1995; adapts anime ... 2.95

CYBER CITY: PART 3
CPM

- ❑1, Dec 1995; adapts anime ... 2.95
- ❑2, Jan 1996; adapts anime ... 2.95

CYBERCOM, HEART OF THE BLUE MESA
MATRIX

- ❑1, Dec 1987, b&w ... 2.00

CYBER CRUSH: ROBOTS IN REVOLT
FLEETWAY-QUALITY

- ❑1, Sep 1991 ... 1.95
- ❑2, Oct 1991 ... 1.95
- ❑3, Nov 1991 ... 1.95
- ❑4, Dec 1991 ... 1.95
- ❑5, Feb 1992 ... 1.95
- ❑6, Mar 1992 ... 1.95
- ❑7, Apr 1992 ... 1.95
- ❑8, May 1992 ... 1.95
- ❑9, Jun 1992 ... 1.95
- ❑10, Jul 1992 ... 1.95
- ❑11, Aug 1992 ... 1.95
- ❑12, Sep 1992 ... 1.95
- ❑13, Oct 1992 ... 1.95
- ❑14, Nov 1992 ... 1.95

CYBERELLA
DC / HELIX

- ❑1, Sep 1996 ... 2.25
- ❑2, Oct 1996 ... 2.25
- ❑3, Nov 1996 ... 2.25
- ❑4, Dec 1996 ... 2.25
- ❑5, Jan 1997 ... 2.25
- ❑6, Feb 1997 ... 2.25
- ❑7, Mar 1997 ... 2.50
- ❑8, Apr 1997 ... 2.50
- ❑9, May 1997 ... 2.50
- ❑10, Jun 1997 ... 2.50
- ❑11, Jul 1997 ... 2.50
- ❑12, Aug 1997 ... 2.50

CYBERFARCE
PARODY

- ❑1, b&w ... 2.50

N-MINT

CYBER FEMMES
SPOOF

- ❑1 ... 2.95

CYBERFORCE (VOL. 1)
IMAGE

- ❑1, Oct 1992 1: Cyberforce. ... 3.00
- ❑2, Mar 1993 ... 2.50
- ❑3, May 1993 A: Pitt. ... 2.00
- ❑4, Jul 1993; foil cover ... 2.00

CYBERFORCE (VOL. 2)
IMAGE

- ❑0, Sep 1993 O: Cyberforce. ... 2.50
- ❑1, Nov 1993 ... 2.50
- ❑1/Gold, Gold edition ... 3.00
- ❑1-2, Nov 1993 ... 1.25
- ❑2, Feb 1994 ... 2.50
- ❑2/Platinum, Feb 1994; Platinum edition; foil-embossed outer wrap ... 3.00
- ❑3, Mar 1994 ... 2.50
- ❑3/Gold, Mar 1994; Gold edition ... 2.50
- ❑4, Apr 1994 ... 2.50
- ❑5, Jun 1994 ... 2.50
- ❑6, Jul 1994 ... 2.00
- ❑7, Sep 1994 ... 2.00
- ❑8, Oct 1994; TMc (a); Image X-Month ... 2.50
- ❑9, Dec 1994 ... 2.50
- ❑10, Feb 1995 ... 2.50
- ❑10/Gold, Feb 1995; Gold edition ... 2.50
- ❑10/Platinum, Feb 1995; Platinum edition ... 2.50
- ❑10/Variant, Feb 1995; alternate cover ... 2.50
- ❑11, Mar 1995 ... 2.00
- ❑12, Apr 1995 ... 2.00
- ❑13, Jun 1995 ... 2.50
- ❑14, Jul 1995 ... 2.50
- ❑15, Aug 1995 ... 2.50
- ❑16, Nov 1995 ... 2.50
- ❑17, Dec 1995 ... 2.25
- ❑18, Jan 1996 ... 2.50
- ❑18/A, Jan 1996; alternate cover ... 2.50
- ❑19, Feb 1996 ... 2.50
- ❑20, Mar 1996 ... 2.50
- ❑21, May 1996 ... 2.50
- ❑22, May 1996 ... 2.50
- ❑23, Jun 1996 ... 2.50
- ❑24, Jun 1996 ... 2.50
- ❑25, Aug 1996; enhanced wraparound cardstock cover ... 3.95
- ❑26, Sep 1996 ... 2.50
- ❑27, Oct 1996 ... 2.50
- ❑27/Variant, Oct 1996; A: Ash. alternate cover ... 2.50
- ❑28, Nov 1996 A: Gabriel (from Ash). ... 2.50
- ❑29, Dec 1996 ... 2.50
- ❑30, Feb 1997 ... 2.50
- ❑31, Mar 1997 ... 2.50
- ❑32, Apr 1997 ... 2.50
- ❑33, May 1997 ... 2.50
- ❑34, Jul 1997 ... 2.50
- ❑35, Sep 1997 ... 2.50
- ❑Annual 1, Mar 1995 ... 2.50
- ❑Annual 2, Aug 1996 ... 2.95

CYBERFORCE ORIGINS
IMAGE

- ❑1, Jan 1995 O: Cyblade. ... 2.50
- ❑1/Gold, Jan 1995; Gold edition O: Cyblade. ... 3.00
- ❑1-2, Mar 1996 O: Cyblade. ... 1.25
- ❑2, Feb 1995 O: Stryker. ... 2.50
- ❑3, Nov 1995 O: Impact. ... 2.50

CYBERFORCE, STRYKE FORCE: OPPOSING FORCES
IMAGE

- ❑1, Sep 1995 ... 2.50
- ❑2, Oct 1995 ... 2.50

CYBERFORCE UNIVERSE SOURCEBOOK
IMAGE

- ❑1, Aug 1994 ... 2.50
- ❑2, Feb 1995 ... 2.50

Condition price index: Multiply "NM prices" above by: **0.83 for Very Fine/Near Mint**
0.66 for Very Fine • 0.33 for Fine • 0.2 for Very Good • 0.125 for Good

N-MINT

CYBERFROG (HARRIS)
HARRIS

❑1/A, Feb 1996; Alternate cover (titles along left side) 2.95
❑0, Mar 1997 .... 3.00
❑0/A, Mar 1997 .... 3.00
❑2/A; Alternate cover ("Wax the Kutyack!") 2.95
❑1, Feb 1996 .... 3.00
❑3/A; Alternate cover (rendered) 2.95
❑4/A; Alternate cover (holding manís face against wall) 2.95
❑2 1996 .... 3.00
❑3 1996 .... 3.00
❑4 1996 .... 3.00

CYBERFROG: RESERVOIR FROG
HARRIS

❑1, Sep 1996 .... 2.95
❑1/A 2.95
❑2, Oct 1996 .... 2.95
❑2/A 2.95

CYBERFROG: 3RD ANNIVERSARY SPECIAL
HARRIS

❑1, Jan 1997, b&w; Reprints from Hall of Heroes 2.50
❑2, Feb 1997, b&w; Reprints from Hall of Heroes 2.50

CYBERFROG VS CREED
HARRIS

❑1, Jul 1997 .... 2.95

CYBERGEN
CFD

❑1, Jan 1996 .... 2.50

CYBERHAWKS
PYRAMID

❑1, Jul 1987, b&w 1.80
❑2, b&w 1.80

CYBERLUST
AIRCEL

❑1, b&w 2.95
❑2, b&w 2.95
❑3, b&w 2.95

CYBERNARY
IMAGE

❑1, Nov 1995 .... 2.50
❑2, Dec 1995 .... 2.50
❑3, Jan 1996 .... 2.50
❑4, Feb 1996 .... 2.50
❑5, Mar 1996 .... 2.50

CYBERNARY 2.0
DC / WILDSTORM

❑1, Sep 2001 .... 2.95
❑2, Oct 2001 .... 2.95
❑3, Nov 2001 .... 2.95
❑4, Dec 2001 .... 2.95
❑5, Jan 2002 .... 2.95
❑6, Apr 2002 .... 2.95

CYBERPUNK (BOOK 1)
INNOVATION

❑1 .... 1.95
❑2 .... 1.95

CYBERPUNK (BOOK 2)
INNOVATION

❑1 .... 2.25
❑2 .... 2.25

CYBERPUNK GRAPHIC NOVEL
INNOVATION

❑1 .... 6.95

CYBERPUNK: THE SERAPHIM FILES
INNOVATION

❑1 .... 2.50
❑2 .... 2.50

CYBERPUNX
IMAGE

❑1/A, Mar 1996; Woman with purple/white costume at bottom of cover . 2.50
❑1/B, Mar 1996; Man with green hair at bottom of cover 2.50

N-MINT

❑1/C, Mar 1996; variant cover 2.50
❑1/D, Mar 1996; variant cover 2.50

CYBERRAD (1ST SERIES)
CONTINUITY

❑1, Jan 1991 .... 2.00
❑2, Apr 1991 .... 2.00
❑3, May 1991 .... 2.00
❑4, Jun 1991 .... 2.00
❑5; glow cover 2.00
❑6, Nov 1991; foldout poster 2.00
❑7, Mar 1992 .... 2.00

CYBERRAD (2ND SERIES)
CONTINUITY

❑1, Nov 1992; Hologram cover 2.95
❑1/A, Nov 1992; With regular cover .. 2.00

CYBERRAD DEATHWATCH 2000
CONTINUITY

❑1, Apr 1993; trading card 2.50
❑2, Jul 1993; trading card; indicia drops Deathwatch 2000 .... 2.50

CYBER REALITY COMIX
WONDER COMIX

❑1, Fal 1994 .... 3.95
❑2, Win 1995 .... 3.95

CYBERSEXATION
ANTARCTIC / VENUS

❑1, Mar 1997, b&w 2.95

CYBERSPACE 3000
MARVEL

❑1, Jul 1993; Glow-in-the-dark cover 2.95
❑2, Aug 1993 .... 1.75
❑3, Sep 1993 .... 1.75
❑4, Oct 1993 .... 1.75
❑5, Nov 1993 .... 1.75
❑6, Dec 1993 .... 1.75
❑7, Jan 1994 .... 1.75
❑8, Feb 1994 .... 1.75

CYBERSUIT ARKADYNE
IANUS

❑1, b&w 2.50
❑2, b&w 2.50
❑3, Jun 1992, b&w 2.50
❑4 .... 2.50
❑5 .... 2.50
❑6 .... 2.50

CYBERTRASH AND THE DOG
SILVERLINE

❑1, May 1998 .... 2.95

CYBERZONE
JET-BLACK GRAFIKS

❑1, Jul 1994 .... 2.50
❑2, Sep 1994 .... 2.50
❑3, Dec 1994 .... 2.50
❑4, Mar 1995 .... 2.50
❑5, May 1995 .... 2.50
❑6, Sep 1995 .... 2.50
❑7, Feb 1996 .... 2.50
❑8 .... 2.50

CYBLADE/GHOST RIDER
MARVEL

❑1, Jan 1997; crossover with Top Cow; continues in Ghost Rider/Ballistic .. 2.95

CYBLADE/SHI: THE BATTLE FOR INDEPENDENTS
IMAGE

❑1 1: Witchblade. 5.00
❑1/A; 1: Witchblade. alternate cover; crossover; concludes in Shi/Cyblade: The Battle for Independents #2 .... 6.00
❑1/B; crossover; concludes in Shi/Cyblade: The Battle for Independents #2; San Diego Preview 6.00
❑1/CS; boxed set; crossover with Crusade; also contains Shi/Cyblade: The Battle for Independents #2 .... 15.00
❑Ashcan 1, ca. 1995; preview of crossover with Crusade 3.00

The one-shot *Cutting Edge* had a story that occurred between the events of *Incredible Hulk* #436 and #437.

© 1995 Marvel Characters Inc.

N-MINT

CYBOARS
VINTAGE

❑1, Aug 1996 .... 1.95
❑1/A, Aug 1996, color; alternate cover 1.95

CYBORG, THE COMIC BOOK
CANNON

❑1, Jun 1989 .... 1.00

CYBRID
MAXIMUM

❑1, Jul 1995 .... 2.95

CYCLOPS
MARVEL

❑1, Oct 2000 .... 2.50
❑2, Nov 2000 .... 2.50
❑3, Dec 2000 .... 2.50
❑4, Jan 2001 .... 2.50

CYCOPS
COMICS INTERVIEW

❑1, Jun 1988, b&w 1.95
❑2, Sum 1988, b&w 1.95
❑3, b&w 1.95

CY-GOR
IMAGE

❑1, Jul 1999 .... 2.50
❑2, Aug 1999 .... 2.50
❑3, Sep 1999 .... 2.50
❑4, Oct 1999 .... 2.50
❑5, Nov 1999 .... 2.50

CYLINDERHEAD
SLAVE LABOR

❑1, Feb 1989, b&w 1.95

CYNDER
IMMORTELLE

❑1 .... 2.50
❑2 .... 2.50
❑3 .... 2.50
❑Annual 1, Nov 1996 .... 2.95

CYNDER/HELLINA SPECIAL
IMMORTELLE

❑1, Nov 1996 .... 2.95

CYNOSURE
CYNOSURE

❑1, Nov 1994 .... 1.95

CYNTHERITA
SIDE SHOW

❑1 .... 2.95

CZAR CHASM
C&T

❑1, b&w 2.00
❑2, b&w 2.00

D

DADAVILLE
CALIBER

❑1, b&w 2.95

DAEMONIFUGE: THE SCREAMING CAGE
BLACK LIBRARY

❑1, Mar 2002 .... 2.50
❑2 .... 2.50
❑3 .... 2.50

N-MINT

DAEMON MASK
AMAZING

❑1 ... 1.95

DAEMONSTORM
CALIBER

❑1 1997, b&w; TMc (c); Partial color ... 3.95
❑Ashcan 1, b&w; preview of upcoming series ... 1.00

DAFFY
DELL / GOLD KEY/WHITMAN

❑7, Oct 1956 ... 18.00
❑8, Jan 1957 ... 18.00
❑9, Apr 1957 ... 18.00
❑10, Jul 1957 ... 18.00
❑11, Oct 1957 ... 10.00
❑12, Jan 1958 ... 10.00
❑13, Apr 1958 ... 10.00
❑14, Jul 1958 ... 10.00
❑15, Oct 1958 ... 10.00
❑16, Jan 1959 ... 10.00
❑17, Apr 1959 ... 10.00
❑18, Jul 1959 ... 10.00
❑19, Oct 1959 ... 10.00
❑20, Jan 1960 ... 10.00
❑21, Apr 1960 ... 7.00
❑22, Jul 1960 ... 7.00
❑23, Oct 1960 ... 7.00
❑24, Mar 1961 ... 7.00
❑25, Jun 1961 ... 7.00
❑26, Sep 1961 ... 7.00
❑27, Dec 1961 ... 7.00
❑28 1962 ... 7.00
❑29 1962 ... 7.00
❑30, Jul 1962 ... 7.00
❑31 1962 ... 7.00
❑32 1963 ... 7.00
❑33, Jun 1963 ... 7.00
❑34, Sep 1963 ... 7.00
❑35, Nov 1963 ... 7.00
❑36, Mar 1964 ... 7.00
❑37, Jun 1964 ... 7.00
❑38, Sep 1964 ... 7.00
❑39, Dec 1964 ... 7.00
❑40, Mar 1965 ... 7.00
❑41, Jun 1965 ... 5.00
❑42, Sep 1965 ... 5.00
❑43, Dec 1965 ... 5.00
❑44, Mar 1966 ... 5.00
❑45, Jun 1966 ... 5.00
❑46, Sep 1966 ... 5.00
❑47, Dec 1966 ... 5.00
❑48, Mar 1967 ... 5.00
❑49, Jun 1967 ... 5.00
❑50, Sep 1967 ... 5.00
❑51, Dec 1967 ... 5.00
❑52, Mar 1968 ... 5.00
❑53, Jun 1968 ... 5.00
❑54, Sep 1968 ... 5.00
❑55, Dec 1968 ... 5.00
❑56, Mar 1969 ... 5.00
❑57, May 1969 ... 5.00
❑58, Jul 1969 ... 5.00
❑59, Sep 1969 ... 5.00
❑60, Nov 1969 ... 5.00
❑61, Jan 1970 ... 4.00
❑62, Mar 1970 ... 4.00
❑63, May 1970 ... 4.00
❑64, Jul 1970 ... 4.00
❑65, Sep 1970 ... 4.00
❑66, Nov 1970 ... 4.00
❑67, Jan 1971 ... 4.00
❑68, Mar 1971 ... 4.00
❑69, May 1971 ... 4.00
❑70, Jul 1971 ... 4.00
❑71, Sep 1971 ... 4.00
❑72, Nov 1971 ... 4.00
❑73, Jan 1972 ... 4.00
❑74, Mar 1972 ... 4.00
❑75, May 1972 ... 4.00
❑76, Jul 1972 ... 4.00
❑77, Aug 1972 ... 4.00
❑78, Oct 1972 ... 4.00
❑79, Dec 1972 ... 4.00
❑80, Feb 1973 ... 4.00
❑81, Apr 1973 ... 2.50
❑82, Jun 1973 ... 2.50
❑83, Aug 1973 ... 2.50
❑84, Oct 1973 ... 2.50
❑85, Dec 1973 ... 2.50
❑86, Feb 1974 ... 2.50
❑87, Apr 1974 ... 2.50
❑88, Jun 1974 ... 2.50
❑89, Aug 1974 ... 2.50
❑90, Oct 1974 ... 2.50
❑91, Dec 1974 ... 2.50
❑92, Feb 1975 ... 2.50
❑93, Apr 1975 ... 2.50
❑94, Jun 1975 ... 2.50
❑95, Aug 1975 ... 2.50
❑96, Sep 1975 ... 2.50
❑97, Oct 1975 ... 2.50
❑98, Dec 1975 ... 2.50
❑99, Feb 1976 ... 2.50
❑100, Apr 1976 ... 2.50
❑101, Jun 1976 ... 2.00
❑102, Jul 1976 ... 2.00
❑103, Aug 1976 ... 2.00
❑104, Oct 1976 ... 2.00
❑105, Dec 1976 ... 2.00
❑106, Feb 1977 ... 2.00
❑107, Apr 1977 ... 2.00
❑108, Jun 1977 ... 2.00
❑109, Jul 1977 ... 2.00
❑110, Aug 1977 ... 2.00
❑111, Oct 1977 ... 2.00
❑112, Dec 1977 ... 2.00
❑113, Feb 1978 ... 2.00
❑114, Apr 1978 ... 2.00
❑115, Jun 1978 ... 2.00
❑116, Jul 1978 ... 2.00
❑117, Aug 1978 ... 2.00
❑118, Oct 1978 ... 2.00
❑119, Dec 1978 ... 2.00
❑120, Feb 1979 ... 2.00
❑121, Apr 1979 ... 2.00
❑122, Jun 1979 ... 2.00
❑123, Aug 1979 ... 2.00
❑124, Oct 1979 ... 2.00
❑125, Dec 1979 ... 2.00
❑126, Feb 1980 ... 2.00
❑127, Apr 1980 ... 2.00
❑128, Jun 1980 ... 2.00
❑129, Aug 1980 ... 2.00
❑130, Oct 1980 ... 2.00
❑131, Dec 1980 ... 2.00
❑132, Jan 1981 ... 2.00
❑133, Feb 1981 ... 2.00
❑134, Mar 1981 ... 2.00
❑135, Jul 1981 ... 2.00
❑136, Nov 1981 ... 2.00
❑137, Dec 1981 ... 2.00
❑138, Jan 1982 ... 2.00
❑139, Feb 1982 ... 2.00
❑140, Mar 1982 ... 2.00
❑141, Apr 1982 ... 2.00
❑142 1982 ... 2.00
❑143 1982 ... 2.00
❑144 1983 ... 2.00
❑145 1983 ... 2.00

DAFFY QADDAFI
COMICS UNLIMITED

❑1 1986, b&w; A: Oliver North. A: Moammar Qaddafi. A: Daffy Duck. A: Ronald Reagan. Nancy Reagan cameo ... 2.00

DAGAR THE INVINCIBLE (TALES OF SWORD AND SORCERY...)
GOLD KEY

❑1, Oct 1972 O: Dagar. 1: Scorpio. 1: Ostellon. ... 8.00
❑2, Jan 1973 ... 4.00
❑3, Apr 1973 1: Graylin. ... 3.00
❑4, Jul 1973 ... 3.00
❑5, Oct 1973 ... 3.00
❑6, Jan 1974; Dark Gods story ... 2.50
❑7, Apr 1974 ... 2.50
❑8, Jul 1974 ... 2.50
❑9, Oct 1974 ... 2.50
❑10, Jan 1975 ... 2.50
❑11, Apr 1975 ... 2.50
❑12, Jul 1975 ... 2.50
❑13, Oct 1975 ... 2.50
❑14, Jan 1976 ... 2.50
❑15, Apr 1976 ... 2.50
❑16, Jul 1976 ... 2.50
❑17, Oct 1976 ... 2.50
❑18, Dec 1976; Final issue of original run (1976) ... 2.50
❑19, Apr 1982; O: Dagar. One-shot revival: 1982; Reprints Dagar #1 ... 2.00

DAHMER'S ZOMBIE SQUAD
BONEYARD

❑1, Feb 1993 ... 3.95

DAI KAMIKAZE!
NOW

❑1, Jun 1987; Preview of Speed Racer ... 1.50
❑1-2, Sep 1987 ... 1.75
❑2, Jul 1987 ... 1.50
❑3, Aug 1987 ... 1.50
❑4, Oct 1987 ... 1.50
❑5, Nov 1987 ... 1.75
❑6, Dec 1987 ... 1.75
❑7, Jan 1988 ... 1.75
❑8, Feb 1988 ... 1.75
❑9, Mar 1988 ... 1.75
❑10, Apr 1988 ... 1.75
❑11, Jun 1988 ... 1.75
❑12, Jul 1988 ... 1.75

DAIKAZU
GROUND ZERO

❑1, b&w ... 1.50
❑1-2, b&w ... 1.50
❑2, b&w ... 1.50
❑2-2, b&w ... 1.50
❑3, Jul 1988, b&w ... 1.50
❑4, b&w ... 1.50
❑5, b&w ... 1.50
❑6, b&w ... 1.50
❑7, b&w ... 1.50
❑8, b&w ... 1.75

DAILY BUGLE
MARVEL

❑1, Dec 1996, b&w ... 2.50
❑2, Jan 1997, b&w ... 2.50
❑3, Feb 1997, b&w ... 2.50

DAILY PLANET INVASION! EXTRA
DC

❑1; newspaper ... 2.00

DAIMONS
CRY FOR DAWN

❑1 ... 2.50

DAISY AND DONALD
GOLD KEY

❑1, May 1973; CB (a); A: June. A: May. A: April. Reprints story from Walt Disney's Comics #308 ... 12.00
❑2, Aug 1973 ... 6.00
❑3, Nov 1973 ... 4.00
❑4, Jan 1974; CB (a); Reprints story from Walt Disney's Comics #224 ... 4.00
❑5, May 1974 ... 4.00
❑6, Aug 1974 ... 4.00
❑7, Nov 1974 ... 4.00
❑8, Jan 1975 ... 4.00
❑9, Mar 1975 ... 4.00
❑10, May 1975 ... 4.00
❑11, Jul 1975 ... 3.00
❑12, Sep 1975 ... 3.00
❑13, Nov 1975 ... 3.00
❑14, Jan 1976 ... 3.00
❑15, Mar 1976 ... 3.00

N-MINT

❑16, May 1976 .... 3.00
❑17, Jul 1976 .... 3.00
❑18, Aug 1976 .... 3.00
❑19, Sep 1976 .... 3.00
❑20, Nov 1976 .... 3.00
❑21, Jan 1977 .... 3.00
❑22, Mar 1977 .... 3.00
❑23, May 1977 .... 3.00
❑24, Jul 1977 .... 3.00
❑25, Aug 1977 .... 3.00
❑26, Sep 1977 .... 3.00
❑27, Nov 1977 .... 3.00
❑28, Jan 1978 .... 3.00
❑29, Mar 1978 .... 3.00
❑30, May 1978 .... 3.00
❑31, Jul 1978 .... 2.50
❑32, Aug 1978 .... 2.50
❑33, Sep 1978 .... 2.50
❑34, Nov 1978 .... 2.50
❑35, Jan 1979 .... 2.50
❑36, Mar 1979 .... 2.50
❑37, May 1979 .... 2.50
❑38, Jul 1979 .... 2.50
❑39, Aug 1979 .... 2.50
❑40, Sep 1979 .... 2.50
❑41, Nov 1979 .... 2.50
❑42, Mar 1980 .... 2.50
❑43, Apr 1980 .... 2.50
❑44, May 1980 .... 2.50
❑45, Jun 1980 .... 2.50
❑46, Oct 1980 .... 2.50
❑47, Dec 1980 .... 2.50
❑48 1981 .... 2.50
❑49 1981 .... 2.50
❑50, Aug 1981 .... 2.50
❑51, Oct 1981 .... 2.50
❑52, Dec 1981 .... 2.50
❑53, Feb 1982 .... 2.50
❑54 .... 2.50
❑55 .... 2.50
❑56 .... 2.50
❑57 .... 2.50
❑58 .... 2.50
❑59, Jul 1984 .... 2.50

DAKOTA NORTH
MARVEL

❑1, Jun 1986 .... 1.50
❑2, Aug 1986 .... 1.50
❑3, Oct 1986 .... 1.50
❑4, Dec 1986 .... 1.50
❑5, Feb 1987 .... 1.50

DAKTARI
DELL

❑1, Jul 1967 .... 35.00
❑2, Nov 1967; Yale Summers' name misspelled on cover 30.00
❑3, Oct 1968; Yale Summers' name misspelled again on cover, a different way; same for Hedley Mattingly; no interior ads 30.00
❑4, Oct 1969; Cover from #1 reused . 30.00

DALGODA
FANTAGRAPHICS

❑1, Aug 1984, b&w 2.25
❑2, Dec 1984, b&w 1.50
❑3, Feb 1985, b&w 1.50
❑4, Apr 1985, b&w 1.50
❑5, Jun 1985, b&w 2.00
❑6, Oct 1985, b&w 2.00
❑7, Jan 1986, b&w 2.00
❑8, Apr 1986, b&w 2.00

DALKIEL: THE PROPHECY
VEROTIK

❑1, Aug 1998; cardstock cover 3.95

DAM
DAM

❑1 .... 2.95

N-MINT

DAMAGE
DC

❑0, Oct 1994; Follows Damage #6 .... 1.95
❑1, Apr 1994 .... 1.75
❑2, May 1994 .... 1.75
❑3, Jun 1994 .... 1.75
❑4, Jul 1994 .... 1.75
❑5, Aug 1994; Iron Munro 1.95
❑6, Sep 1994; A: New Titans. Zero Hour 1.95
❑7, Nov 1994 .... 1.95
❑8, Dec 1994 .... 1.95
❑9, Jan 1995 A: Iron Munro. 1.95
❑10, Feb 1995 A: Iron Munro. 1.95
❑11, Mar 1995 .... 1.95
❑12, Apr 1995 .... 1.95
❑13, Jun 1995 .... 2.25
❑14, Jul 1995 A: Ray. 2.25
❑15, Aug 1995 .... 2.25
❑16, Sep 1995 .... 2.25
❑17, Oct 1995 .... 2.25
❑18, Nov 1995; Underworld Unleashed 2.25
❑19, Dec 1995 .... 2.25
❑20, Jan 1996 .... 2.25

DAMAGE CONTROL (VOL. 1)
MARVEL

❑1, May 1989 A: Spider-Man. A: Thor. 1.50
❑2, Jun 1989 A: Doctor Doom. 1.00
❑3, Jul 1989 A: Iron Man. 1.00
❑4, Aug 1989; A: Wolverine. Inferno . 1.00

DAMAGE CONTROL (VOL. 2)
MARVEL

❑1, Dec 1989; A: Captain America. A: Thor. Acts of Vengeance 1.50
❑2, Dec 1989; A: Punisher. Acts of Vengeance 1.00
❑3, Jan 1990; A: She-Hulk. Acts of Vengeance 1.00
❑4, Feb 1990; A: Punisher. A: Shield. A: Captain America. A: Thor. Acts of Vengeance 1.00

DAMAGE CONTROL (VOL. 3)
MARVEL

❑1, Jun 1991 .... 1.50
❑2, Jul 1991 .... 1.00
❑3, Aug 1991 .... 1.00
❑4, Sep 1991 .... 1.00

DAME PATROL
SPOOF

❑1, b&w 2.95

DAMLOG
PYRAMID

❑1, b&w 2.00

DAMNATION
FANTAGRAPHICS

❑1, Sum 1994, b&w; magazine 2.95

DAMNED
IMAGE

❑1, Jun 1997 .... 2.50
❑2, Jul 1997 .... 2.50
❑3, Aug 1997 .... 2.50
❑4, Sep 1997 .... 2.50

DANCE OF LIFEY DEATH
DARK HORSE

❑1, Jan 1994 .... 3.95

DANCE PARTY DOA
SLAVE LABOR

❑1, Nov 1993 .... 3.95

DANCES WITH DEMONS
MARVEL

❑1, Sep 1993; Embossed foil cover ... 2.95
❑2, Oct 1993 .... 1.95
❑3, Nov 1993 .... 1.95
❑4, Dec 1993 .... 1.95

DANGER GIRL
IMAGE / CLIFFHANGER

❑1, Mar 1998 .... 3.50
❑1/A, Mar 1998; chromium cover 5.00
❑1/B, Mar 1998; magazine-sized 20.00

Daisy's nieces, April, May, and June, made an appearance in the first issue of *Daisy and Donald*.

© 1973 Walt Disney Productions and Gold Key.

N-MINT

❑1/C, Mar 1998, Tour Edition; Woman holding rifle, white background Tour Edition 6.00
❑1/D, Mar 1988; Chromium a-go-go cover 40.00
❑2, May 1998 .... 3.00
❑2/A, May 1998; Special holochrome cover 8.00
❑2/B, May 1988; Dynamic Forces cover, later recalled 25.00
❑2/Gold, May 1998; Gold logo 6.00
❑3, Aug 1998; White background, 3 girls on cover 3.00
❑3/A, Aug 1998; Girls surrounding guy, knife cover 3.00
❑3/B, Aug 1998; "Filled to the Brim with Danger" cover 3.00
❑4, Dec 1998 .... 3.00
❑4/A, Dec 1998; alternate cover (purple background) 3.00
❑5, Jul 1999 .... 2.50
❑5/A, Jul 1999; Dynamic Forces variant; Woman in red bikini 6.00
❑5/B, Jul 1999; Dynamic Forces variant; Woman in blue bikini 6.00
❑6, Dec 1999 .... 2.50
❑6/A, Dec 1999; DFE gold foil edition 8.00
❑6/Gold, Dec 1999; DFE gold foil edition 5.00
❑7, Feb 2001 .... 5.95
❑Ashcan 1; Preview edition 5.00
❑Ashcan 1/Gold; Preview edition; Gold logo 6.00
❑Special 1, Feb 2000 .... 3.50

DANGER GIRL 3-D
DC

❑1, Apr 2003 .... 4.95

DANGER GIRL: HAWAIIAN PUNCH
DC

❑1, May 2003 .... 4.95

DANGER GIRL KAMIKAZE
DC / WILDSTORM

❑1, Nov 2001 .... 2.95
❑2, Dec 2001 .... 2.95

DANGER GIRL SKETCHBOOK
DC / WILDSTORM

❑1 .... 6.95

DANGER GIRL: VIVA LAS DANGER
DC

❑1, Jan 2004 .... 4.95

DANGEROUS TIMES
EVOLUTION

❑1 .... 1.75
❑1-2 .... 1.75
❑2 .... 1.75
❑2-2 .... 1.75
❑3 .... 1.95
❑3-2 .... 1.95
❑4 .... 1.95
❑4-2 .... 1.95
❑5 .... 1.95
❑5-2 .... 1.95
❑6 .... 1.95
❑6-2 .... 2.25

DANGER RANGER
CHECKER

❑1, Sum 1998 .... 1.95
❑2 1998 .... 1.95

N-MINT

DANGER TRAIL (MINI-SERIES)
DC

❑1, Apr 1993 1.50
❑2, May 1993 1.50
❑3, Jun 1993 1.50
❑4, Jul 1993 1.50

DANGER UNLIMITED
DARK HORSE / LEGEND

❑1, Feb 1994 2.00
❑2, Mar 1994 2.00
❑3, Apr 1994 2.00
❑4, May 1994 2.00

DAN TURNER: ACE IN THE HOLE
ETERNITY

❑1, b&w 2.50

DAN TURNER: DARK STAR OF DEATH
ETERNITY

❑1, b&w 2.50

DAN TURNER: HOMICIDE HUNCH
ETERNITY

❑1, Jul 1991, b&w 2.50

DAN TURNER: STAR CHAMBER
ETERNITY

❑1, Sep 1991, b&w 2.50

DARBY O'GILL AND THE LITTLE PEOPLE
GOLD KEY

❑1, Jan 1970; Reprints Four Color Comics (2nd Series) #1024 20.00

D'ARC TANGENT
FFANTASY FFACTORY

❑1, Aug 1982 2.00

DAREDEVIL
MARVEL

❑-1, Jul 1997; GC (a); Flashback 2.25
❑1, Apr 1964; SL (w); BEv (a); O: Daredevil. 1: Karen Page. 1: Battling Jack Murdock. 1: Daredevil. 1: Foggy Nelson. D: Battling Jack Murdock. 2100.00
❑2, Jun 1964 SL (w); JO (a); A: Fantastic Four. V: Electro. 560.00
❑3, Aug 1964 JO (a); O: Owl. 1: Owl. 450.00
❑4, Oct 1964 JO (a); O: The Purple Man. 1: The Purple Man. V: Killgrave. 350.00
❑5, Dec 1964 WW (a); V: Masked Matador. 250.00
❑6, Feb 1965 WW (a); 1: Mister Fear I (Zoltan Drago). V: Fellowship of Fear. 200.00
❑7, Apr 1965 WW (a); 1: red costume. A: Sub-Mariner. 225.00
❑8, Jun 1965 WW (a); O: Stilt Man. 1: Stilt Man. 135.00
❑9, Aug 1965 WW (a) 135.00
❑10, Oct 1965 WW (a); 1: Ape-Man I (Gordon Monk Keefer). 1: Frog-Man I (Francois LeBlanc). 1: Ani-Men. 1: Cat-Man I (Townshend Horgan). 1: Bird-Man I (Henry Hawk). 135.00
❑11, Dec 1965 JK, JR (a) 85.00
❑12, Jan 1966 2: Ka-Zar. 85.00
❑13, Feb 1966 JK, JR (a); O: Ka-Zar. 85.00
❑14, Mar 1966 A: Ka-Zar. 85.00
❑15, Apr 1966 JR (a) 85.00
❑16, May 1966 JR (a); 1: Masked Marauder. A: Spider-Man. 120.00
❑17, Jun 1966 JR (a); A: Spider-Man. 120.00
❑18, Jul 1966 JR (a); O: Gladiator I (Melvin Potter). 1: Gladiator I (Melvin Potter). 60.00
❑19, Aug 1966 JR (a); A: Gladiator I (Melvin Potter). 60.00
❑20, Sep 1966 GC (a); V: Owl. 55.00
❑21, Oct 1966 GC (a); V: Owl. 50.00
❑22, Nov 1966 SL (w); GC (a) 50.00
❑23, Dec 1966 GC (a) 50.00
❑24, Jan 1967 GC (a); A: Ka-Zar. 50.00
❑25, Feb 1967 GC (a) 50.00
❑26, Mar 1967 GC (a) 50.00
❑27, Apr 1967 GC (a); A: Spider-Man. 50.00
❑28, May 1967 GC (a) 45.00
❑29, Jun 1967 SL (w); GC (a) 45.00
❑30, Jul 1967 GC (a); A: Thor. 45.00

N-MINT

❑31, Aug 1967; GC (a); Cobra 40.00
❑32, Sep 1967 GC (a) 40.00
❑33, Oct 1967 SL (w); GC (a) 40.00
❑34, Nov 1967 GC (a) 40.00
❑35, Dec 1967 GC (a); A: Invisible Girl. V: Trapster. 40.00
❑36, Jan 1968 GC (a); A: Fantastic Four. A: Doctor Doom. 40.00
❑37, Feb 1968 GC (a); A: Doctor Doom. V: Doctor Doom. 40.00
❑38, Mar 1968 SL (w); GC (a); A: Fantastic Four. A: Doctor Doom. 40.00
❑39, Apr 1968 GC (a); 1: Exterminator (later Death-Stalker). 40.00
❑40, May 1968 SL (w); GC (a) 40.00
❑41, Jun 1968 SL (w); GC (a) D: Mike Murdock (Daredevil's "twin brother"). 40.00
❑42, Jul 1968 GC (a); 1: Jester. 40.00
❑43, Aug 1968 GC (a); O: Daredevil. V: Captain America. 45.00
❑44, Sep 1968 GC (a) 30.00
❑45, Oct 1968; GC (a); Characters drawn on Statue of Liberty photo 30.00
❑46, Nov 1968 GC (a) 30.00
❑47, Dec 1968 GC (a) 30.00
❑48, Jan 1969 GC (a) 30.00
❑49, Feb 1969 GC (a); 1: Samuel Starr Saxon. 30.00
❑50, Mar 1969 33.00
❑51, Apr 1969 A: Captain America. 33.00
❑52, May 1969 A: Black Panther. 33.00
❑53, Jun 1969 GC (a); O: Daredevil. 20.00
❑54, Jul 1969 GC (a); 1: Mister Fear II (Samuel Starr Saxon). A: Spider-Man. 20.00
❑55, Aug 1969 GC (a) 20.00
❑56, Sep 1969 GC (a) 20.00
❑57, Oct 1969; GC (a); Daredevil reveals identity to Karen Page 20.00
❑58, Nov 1969 GC (a) 20.00
❑59, Dec 1969 GC (a) 20.00
❑60, Jan 1970 GC (a) 20.00
❑61, Feb 1970 GC (a) 20.00
❑62, Mar 1970 GC (a); O: Nighthawk II (Kyle Richmond). 20.00
❑63, Apr 1970 GC (a) 20.00
❑64, May 1970 GC (a) 20.00
❑65, Jun 1970 GC (a) 20.00
❑66, Jul 1970 GC (a) 20.00
❑67, Aug 1970 GC (a) 20.00
❑68, Sep 1970 GC (a) 20.00
❑69, Oct 1970 GC (a); 1: William Carver (Thunderbolt). 20.00
❑70, Nov 1970 GC (a) 20.00
❑71, Dec 1970 GC (a) 20.00
❑72, Jan 1971 GC (a); 1: Tagak the Leopard Lord. 17.00
❑73, Feb 1971 GC (a) 17.00
❑74, Mar 1971 GC (a) 17.00
❑75, Apr 1971 GC (a) 17.00
❑76, May 1971 GC (a) 17.00
❑77, Jun 1971 GC (a) 17.00
❑78, Jul 1971 GC (a) 17.00
❑79, Aug 1971 GC (a) 17.00
❑80, Sep 1971 GC (a) 17.00
❑81, Nov 1971; GC (a); A: Human Torch. giant; reprints story from Strange Tales #132 25.00
❑82, Dec 1971 GC (a) 17.00
❑83, Jan 1972 V: Mr. Hyde. 17.00
❑84, Feb 1972 GC (a) 14.00
❑85, Mar 1972 14.00
❑86, Apr 1972 14.00
❑87, May 1972 14.00
❑88, Jun 1972 GC (a); O: Black Widow. 14.00
❑89, Jul 1972 14.00
❑90, Aug 1972 14.00
❑91, Sep 1972 1: Mister Fear III (Larry Cranston). 14.00
❑92, Oct 1972 GC (a) 14.00
❑93, Nov 1972 14.00
❑94, Dec 1972 14.00
❑95, Jan 1973 14.00
❑96, Feb 1973 14.00

N-MINT

❑97, Mar 1973 GC (a); 1: Dark Messiah. 1: Disciples of Doom. 14.00
❑98, Apr 1973 14.00
❑99, May 1973; story continues in Avengers #110 14.00
❑100, Jun 1973; 100th anniversary issue GC (a); 1: Angar the Screamer. 30.00
❑101, Jul 1973 8.00
❑102, Aug 1973 8.00
❑103, Sep 1973 DH (a); O: Ramrod I. 1: Ramrod I. 8.00
❑104, Oct 1973 8.00
❑105, Nov 1973 O: Moondragon. 1: Moondragon. A: Thanos. 8.00
❑106, Dec 1973 DH (a); 1: Black Spectre (female group). A: Black Widow. 8.00
❑107, Jan 1974 SB (a); A: Captain Marvel. 8.00
❑108, Mar 1974; Marvel Value Stamp #22: Man-Thing 8.00
❑109, May 1974; Story continues in Marvel Two-In-One #3; Marvel Value Stamp #52: Quicksilver 8.00
❑110, Jun 1974; GC (a); Marvel Value Stamp #51: Bucky Barnes 8.00
❑111, Jul 1974; 1: Silver Samurai. Marvel Value Stamp #70: Super Skrull. 8.00
❑112, Aug 1974; Marvel Value Stamp #63: Sub-Mariner 8.00
❑113, Sep 1974; Marvel Value Stamp #85: Lilith 8.00
❑114, Oct 1974; 1: Death-Stalker. Marvel Value Stamp #7: Werewolf 8.00
❑115, Nov 1974; Marvel Value Stamp #35: Killraven 8.00
❑116, Dec 1974; Marvel Value Stamp #95: Mole-Man 8.00
❑117, Jan 1975; Marvel Value Stamp #88: Leader 8.00
❑118, Feb 1975; DH (a); 1: Blackwing. Marvel Value Stamp #28: Hawkeye 8.00
❑119, Mar 1975 8.00
❑120, Apr 1975; Marvel Value Stamp #99: Sandman 8.00
❑121, May 1975 8.00
❑122, Jun 1975 8.00
❑123, Jul 1975 8.00
❑124, Aug 1975 GC, KJ (a); 1: Blake Tower. 1: Copperhead. 8.00
❑125, Sep 1975 KJ (a) 8.00
❑126, Oct 1975 KJ (a); 1: Torpedo. 8.00
❑127, Nov 1975; KJ (a); Marvel Value Stamp #80: Ghost Rider 8.00
❑128, Dec 1975 KJ (a) 8.00
❑129, Jan 1976 KJ (a) 8.00
❑130, Feb 1976 KJ (a) 8.00
❑131, Mar 1976; KJ (a); O: Bullseye. First Bullseye 50.00
❑132, Apr 1976 15.00
❑132/30 cent, Apr 1976; 30 cent regional variant 20.00
❑133, May 1976 1: Mind-Wave. 6.00
❑133/30 cent, May 1976; 30 cent regional variant 20.00
❑134, Jun 1976 6.00
❑134/30 cent, Jun 1976; 30 cent regional variant 20.00
❑135, Jul 1976 6.00
❑135/30 cent, Jul 1976; 30 cent regional variant 20.00
❑136, Aug 1976 JB (a) 6.00
❑136/30 cent, Aug 1976; 30 cent regional variant 20.00
❑137, Sep 1976 JB (a) 6.00
❑138, Oct 1976 JBy (a); A: Ghost Rider. A: Death's Head (monster). 6.00
❑139, Nov 1976 SB (a) 6.00
❑140, Dec 1976 SB (a) 6.00
❑141, Jan 1977 GK (a) 6.00
❑142, Feb 1977 JB (a); V: Cobra, Mr. Hyde. 6.00
❑143, Mar 1977 6.00
❑144, Apr 1977 6.00
❑145, May 1977 GT, JM (a) 6.00
❑146, Jun 1977 GK (a); A: Bullseye. V: Bullseye. 6.00
❑147, Jul 1977 GK, KJ (a) 6.00

	N-MINT
❑147/35 cent, Jul 1977; GK, KJ (a); 35 cent regional price variant	15.00
❑148, Sep 1977 GK, KJ (a)	6.00
❑148/35 cent, Sep 1977, GK, KJ (a); 35 cent regional variant	15.00
❑149, Nov 1977 CI, KJ (a)	6.00
❑150, Jan 1978 CI, KJ (a); 1: Paladin.	6.00
❑151, Mar 1978; GK, KJ (a); Daredevil reveals identity to Heather Glenn	6.00
❑152, May 1978 CI, KJ (a); A: Paladin.	6.00
❑153, Jul 1978 1: Ben Urich.	6.00
❑154, Sep 1978 GC (a)	6.00
❑155, Nov 1978; FR (a); Black Widow returns	6.00
❑156, Jan 1979 GC (a); A: 1960's Daredevil.	6.00
❑157, Mar 1979 GC, KJ (a); 1: Bird-Man II (Achille DiBacco). 1: Cat-Man II (Sebastian Patane). 1: Ape-Man II (Roy McVey).	6.00
❑158, May 1979; FM (w); FM (a); O: Death-Stalker. D: Cat-Man II (Sebastian Patane). D: Ape-Man II (Roy McVey). D: Death-Stalker. V: Death-stalker. First Miller Daredevil	40.00
❑159, Jul 1979 FM (a); A: Bullseye. V: Bullseye.	16.00
❑160, Sep 1979 FM (a); V: Bullseye.	12.00
❑161, Nov 1979 FM (a); V: Bullseye.	12.00
❑162, Jan 1980 SD (a)	9.00
❑163, Mar 1980 FM (a)	18.00
❑164, May 1980 FM (a)	11.00
❑165, Jul 1980 FM (a)	11.00
❑166, Sep 1980 FM (a)	11.00
❑167, Nov 1980 FM (a)	11.00
❑168, Jan 1981; FM (w); FM (a); O: Elektra. 1: Elektra.	60.00
❑169, Mar 1981 FM (w); FM (a); A: Elektra. V: Bullseye.	16.00
❑170, May 1981 FM (w); FM (a); V: Bullseye.	10.00
❑171, Jun 1981 FM (w); FM (a)	12.00
❑172, Jul 1981 FM (w); FM (a)	7.00
❑173, Aug 1981 FM (w); FM (a)	7.00
❑174, Sep 1981 FM (w); FM (a)	7.00
❑175, Oct 1981 FM (w); FM (a)	7.00
❑176, Nov 1981 FM (w); FM (a); 1: Stick. A: Elektra.	7.00
❑177, Dec 1981 FM (w); FM (a); A: Elektra.	7.00
❑178, Jan 1982 FM (w); FM (a); A: Elektra.	6.00
❑179, Feb 1982 FM (w); FM (a); A: Elektra.	6.00
❑180, Mar 1982 FM (w); FM (a); A: Elektra.	6.00
❑181, Apr 1982; double-sized; FM (w); FM (a); D: Elektra. V: Bullseye. Punisher cameo out of costume	10.00
❑182, May 1982 FM (w); FM (a); A: Punisher. V: Punisher.	4.00
❑183, Jun 1982 FM (w); FM (a); A: Punisher. V: Punisher.	4.00
❑184, Jul 1982 FM (w); FM (a); A: Punisher. V: Punisher.	4.00
❑185, Aug 1982 FM (w); FM, KJ (a)	4.00
❑186, Sep 1982 FM (w); FM, KJ (a)	4.00
❑187, Oct 1982 FM (w); FM, KJ (a); A: Black Widow.	4.00
❑188, Nov 1982 FM (w); FM, KJ (a)	4.00
❑189, Dec 1982 FM (w); FM, KJ (a); D: Stick.	4.00
❑190, Jan 1983; Double-size FM (w); FM, KJ (a); O: Elektra. A: Elektra.	3.00
❑191, Feb 1983 FM (w); FM (a)	3.00
❑192, Mar 1983 KJ (a)	3.00
❑193, Apr 1983 KJ (a)	3.00
❑194, May 1983 KJ (a)	3.00
❑195, Jun 1983 KJ (a)	3.00
❑196, Jun 1983 KJ (a); A: Wolverine.	5.00
❑197, Aug 1983 KJ (a); V: Bullseye.	3.00
❑198, Sep 1983	3.00
❑199, Oct 1983	3.00
❑200, Nov 1983 JBy (c); V: Bullseye.	3.00
❑201, Dec 1983 A: Black Widow.	3.00
❑202, Jan 1984	3.00

	N-MINT
❑203, Feb 1984 1: Trump.	3.00
❑204, Mar 1984 LMc (a)	3.00
❑205, Apr 1984	3.00
❑206, May 1984	3.00
❑207, Jun 1984	3.00
❑208, Jul 1984	3.00
❑209, Aug 1984	3.00
❑210, Sep 1984	3.00
❑211, Oct 1984	3.00
❑212, Nov 1984	3.00
❑213, Dec 1984	3.00
❑214, Jan 1985	3.00
❑215, Feb 1985 A: Two-Gun Kid.	3.00
❑216, Mar 1985	3.00
❑217, Apr 1985 FM (c)	3.00
❑218, May 1985 SB (a)	3.00
❑219, Jun 1985 FM (w); SB, FM (a)	3.00
❑220, Jul 1985	3.00
❑221, Aug 1985	3.00
❑222, Sep 1985 A: Black Widow.	3.00
❑223, Oct 1985; Secret Wars II	3.00
❑224, Nov 1985 V: Sunturion.	3.00
❑225, Dec 1985 V: Vulture.	3.00
❑226, Jan 1986 FM (w); FM (a)	3.00
❑227, Feb 1986 FM (w); A: Kingpin.	3.00
❑228, Mar 1986 FM	3.00
❑229, Apr 1986 FM (w); 1: Sister Maggie.	3.00
❑230, May 1986 FM	3.00
❑231, Jun 1986 FM	3.00
❑232, Jul 1986 FM	3.00
❑233, Aug 1986 FM	3.00
❑234, Sep 1986 SD (a)	3.00
❑235, Oct 1986 SD (a)	3.00
❑236, Nov 1986	3.00
❑237, Dec 1986	3.00
❑238, Jan 1987 SB (a); A: Sabretooth.	3.00
❑239, Feb 1987	3.00
❑240, Mar 1987	3.00
❑241, Apr 1987 TMc (a)	3.00
❑242, May 1987 KP (a)	3.00
❑243, Jun 1987	3.00
❑244, Jul 1987	3.00
❑245, Aug 1987 A: Black Panther.	3.00
❑246, Sep 1987	3.00
❑247, Oct 1987 KP (a)	3.00
❑248, Nov 1987 A: Wolverine.	3.00
❑249, Dec 1987 A: Wolverine.	4.00
❑250, Jan 1988 JR2 (a); 1: Bullet.	3.00
❑251, Feb 1988 JR2 (a)	3.00
❑252, Mar 1988; double-sized; JR2 (a); Fall of Mutants	3.00
❑253, Apr 1988 JR2 (a)	3.00
❑254, May 1988; JR2 (a); O: Typhoid Mary. 1: Typhoid Mary.	6.00
❑255, Jun 1988 JR2 (a); 2: Typhoid Mary.	2.50
❑256, Jul 1988; JR2 (a); A: Typhoid Mary.	2.50
❑257, Aug 1988 JR2 (a); A: Punisher.	2.50
❑258, Sep 1988 O: Bengal. 1: Bengal.	3.00
❑259, Oct 1988 JR2 (a); A: Typhoid Mary.	3.00
❑260, Nov 1988; double-sized JR2 (a)	3.00
❑261, Dec 1988 JR2 (a); A: Human Torch.	3.00
❑262, Jan 1989; JR2 (a); Inferno	3.00
❑263, Feb 1989; JR2 (a); Inferno	3.00
❑264, Mar 1989 SD (a)	3.00
❑265, Apr 1989; JR2 (a); Inferno	3.00
❑266, May 1989 JR2 (a)	3.00
❑267, Jun 1989 JR2 (a)	3.00
❑268, Jul 1989 JR2 (a)	3.00
❑269, Aug 1989 JR2 (a)	3.00
❑270, Sep 1989 JR2 (a); O: Blackheart. 1: Blackheart. A: Spider-Man.	3.00
❑271, Oct 1989 JR2 (a)	3.00
❑272, Nov 1989 JR2 (a); 1: Shotgun II.	3.00
❑273, Nov 1989 JR2 (a)	3.00
❑274, Dec 1989 JR2 (a)	3.00
❑275, Dec 1989; JR2 (a); Acts of Vengeance	3.00

A year after the sixth issue and more than two and a half years after its first, *Danger Girl* ended its first story arc with #7.

© 1999 J. Scott Campbell and Image.

	N-MINT
❑276, Jan 1990; JR2 (a); Acts of Vengeance	3.00
❑277, Feb 1990	3.00
❑278, Mar 1990 JR2 (a)	3.00
❑279, Apr 1990 JR2 (a)	3.00
❑280, May 1990 JR2 (a)	3.00
❑281, Jun 1990; JR2 (a); Silver Surfer cameo	3.00
❑282, Jul 1990 A: Silver Surfer.	3.00
❑283, Aug 1990 A: Captain America.	3.00
❑284, Sep 1990	3.00
❑285, Oct 1990	3.00
❑286, Nov 1990	3.00
❑287, Dec 1990	3.00
❑288, Jan 1991	3.00
❑289, Feb 1991	3.00
❑290, Mar 1991	3.00
❑291, Apr 1991	3.00
❑292, May 1991 A: Punisher.	3.00
❑293, Jun 1991 A: Punisher.	3.00
❑294, Jul 1991	3.00
❑295, Aug 1991 A: Ghost Rider.	3.00
❑296, Sep 1991	1.50
❑297, Oct 1991 A: Typhoid Mary. V: Typhoid Mary.	1.50
❑298, Nov 1991	1.50
❑299, Dec 1991	1.50
❑300, Jan 1992; double-sized; Kingpin deposed	3.00
❑301, Feb 1992 V: Owl.	1.50
❑302, Mar 1992 V: Owl.	1.50
❑303, Apr 1992 V: Owl.	1.50
❑304, May 1992	1.50
❑305, Jun 1992 1: Surgeon General.	1.50
❑306, Jul 1992	1.50
❑307, Aug 1992	1.50
❑308, Sep 1992	1.50
❑309, Oct 1992	1.50
❑310, Nov 1992	1.50
❑311, Dec 1992	1.50
❑312, Jan 1993	1.50
❑313, Feb 1993	1.50
❑314, Mar 1993	1.50
❑315, Apr 1993 V: Mr. Fear.	1.50
❑316, May 1993	1.50
❑317, Jun 1993 V: Stiltman.	1.50
❑318, Jul 1993 V: Stiltman. V: Devil-Man.	1.50
❑319, Aug 1993; first printing (white); Elektra returns	2.50
❑319-2, Aug 1993; 2nd Printing (black); Elektra returns	1.25
❑320, Sep 1993; A: Silver Sable. red costume destroyed; New costume	2.00
❑321, Oct 1993	2.00
❑321/Variant, Oct 1993; Special glow-in-the-dark cover	3.00
❑322, Nov 1993	2.00
❑323, Dec 1993 V: Venom.	2.00
❑324, Jan 1994	2.00
❑325, Feb 1994; Double-size; D: Hell-spawn. poster	3.00
❑326, Mar 1994	1.50
❑327, Apr 1994	1.50
❑328, May 1994	1.50
❑329, Jun 1994	1.50
❑330, Jul 1994; Gambit	1.50
❑331, Aug 1994	1.50
❑332, Sep 1994	1.50

N-MINT

❑333, Oct 1994 ... 1.50
❑334, Nov 1994 ... 1.50
❑335, Dec 1994 ... 1.50
❑336, Jan 1995 ... 1.50
❑337, Feb 1995 ... 1.50
❑338, Mar 1995 ... 1.50
❑339, Apr 1995 ... 1.50
❑340, May 1995 ... 1.50
❑341, Jun 1995 ... 1.50
❑342, Jul 1995 ... 1.50
❑343, Aug 1995 ... 1.50
❑344, Sep 1995; Yellow and red-costumed Daredevil returns ... 2.00
❑345, Oct 1995; Red-costumed Daredevil returns; OverPower card inserted ... 2.00
❑346, Nov 1995 ... 2.00
❑347, Dec 1995; Identity of both Daredevils revealed ... 2.00
❑348, Jan 1996; A: Sister Maggie. A: Stick. cover says Dec, indicia says Jan ... 2.00
❑349, Feb 1996 AW (a); A: Sister Maggie. A: Stick. ... 2.00
❑350, Mar 1996; Giant-size; Daredevil switches back to red costume ... 2.95
❑350/Variant, Mar 1996; Giant-size; gold ink on cover; Daredevil switches back to red costume ... 3.50
❑351, Apr 1996 1: The Vice Cop. ... 2.00
❑352, May 1996 A: Bullseye. V: Bullseye. ... 2.00
❑353, Jun 1996 V: Mr. Hyde. ... 2.00
❑354, Jul 1996 A: Spider-Man. ... 1.50
❑355, Aug 1996 V: Pyro. ... 1.50
❑356, Sep 1996 V: Enforcers. ... 1.50
❑357, Oct 1996 V: Enforcers. ... 1.50
❑358, Nov 1996 V: Mysterio. ... 1.50
❑359, Dec 1996 ... 1.50
❑360, Jan 1997 V: Absorbing Man. ... 1.50
❑361, Feb 1997 A: Black Widow. ... 1.50
❑362, Mar 1997 ... 1.99
❑363, Apr 1997 GC (a); 1: Insomnia. V: Insomnia. ... 1.95
❑364, May 1997 ... 1.95
❑365, Jun 1997 V: Molten Man. ... 1.99
❑366, Aug 1997; gatefold summary AW, GC (a) ... 1.99
❑367, Sep 1997; gatefold summary GC (a) ... 1.99
❑368, Oct 1997; gatefold summary GC (a); V: Omega Red. ... 1.99
❑369, Nov 1997; gatefold summary ... 1.99
❑370, Dec 1997; gatefold summary GC (a); A: Black Widow. ... 1.99
❑371, Jan 1998; gatefold summary; Ghost Rider ... 1.99
❑372, Feb 1998; gatefold summary A: Ghost Rider. ... 1.99
❑373, Mar 1998; gatefold summary ... 1.99
❑374, Apr 1998; gatefold summary ... 1.99
❑375, May 1998; Giant-size V: Mr. Fear. ... 2.95
❑376, Jun 1998; gatefold summary; Matt sent deep undercover, regains eyesight ... 1.99
❑377, Jul 1998; gatefold summary; Matt as Laurent Levasseur with new costume ... 1.99
❑378, Aug 1998; gatefold summary ... 1.99
❑379, Sep 1998; gatefold summary; Matt regains his identity and loses sight ... 1.99
❑380, Oct 1998; Giant-size A: Kingpin. ... 2.99
❑Annual 1, Sep 1967; Cover reads "King-Size Special"; GC (a) ... 40.00
❑Annual 2, Feb 1971; Cover reads "King-Size Special" ... 9.00
❑Annual 3, Jan 1972; Cover reads "King-Size Special"; JR (a); Reprints Daredevil #16-17 ... 9.00
❑Annual 4, ca. 1976 ... 6.00
❑Annual 5; JR2 (a); Cover # of 4, seems to be a mistake; Atlantis Attacks; 1989 annual ... 4.00
❑Annual 6; TS (a); Lifeform ... 3.00
❑Annual 7, ca. 1991; O: Crippler. 1: Crippler. Von Strucker Gambit ... 2.50
❑Annual 8, ca. 1992 ... 2.50
❑Annual 9, ca. 1993; O: Devourer. 1: Devourer. trading card ... 2.95
❑Annual 10 ... 2.95
❑Annual 1997, Sep 1997; gatefold summary; Daredevil/Deadpool '97; combined annuals for Daredevil and Deadpool ... 2.99

DAREDEVIL (VOL. 2)
Marvel

❑0.5, Nov 1998; gatefold summary ... 6.00
❑1, Nov 1998; gatefold summary ... 8.50
❑1/Ltd., Nov 1998; DFE alternate cover signed ... 12.00
❑1/Variant, Nov 1998; DFE alternate cover ... 6.00
❑2/A, Dec 1998; gatefold summary ... 4.00
❑2/B, Dec 1998 ... 4.00
❑3, Jan 1999; gatefold summary; Matt quits law firm ... 3.00
❑4, Feb 1999 ... 3.00
❑5, Mar 1999; Bullseye cover ... 3.00
❑5/A, Mar 1999; Black/white/red cover ... 3.00
❑6, Apr 1999 ... 3.00
❑7, May 1999 ... 3.00
❑8, Jun 1999; Karen's funeral ... 3.00
❑9, Dec 1999 ... 3.00
❑10, Mar 2000 ... 3.00
❑11, May 2000 ... 3.00
❑12, Jun 2000 ... 3.00
❑13, Oct 2000; Trial of Kingpin ... 3.00
❑14, Mar 2001 ... 3.00
❑15, Apr 2001 ... 3.00
❑16, May 2001 ... 3.00
❑17, Jun 2001 ... 3.00
❑18, Jul 2001 ... 3.00
❑19, Aug 2001 ... 3.00
❑20, Sep 2001 ... 3.00
❑21, Oct 2001 ... 2.99
❑22, Oct 2001 ... 2.99
❑23, Nov 2001 ... 2.99
❑24, Nov 2001 ... 2.99
❑25, Dec 2001 ... 2.99
❑26, Jan 2002 ... 2.99
❑27, Feb 2002 ... 2.99
❑28, Mar 2002; Silent issue ... 2.99
❑29, Apr 2002 ... 2.99
❑30, May 2002 ... 2.99
❑31, Jun 2002 ... 2.99
❑32, Jul 2002 ... 2.99
❑33, Aug 2002, Has part 3 of Spider-Man/Jay Leno team-up ... 2.99
❑34, Sep 2002 ... 2.99
❑35, Oct 2002 ... 2.99
❑36, Nov 2002 ... 2.99
❑37, Dec 2002 ... 2.99
❑38, Dec 2002 ... 2.99
❑39, Jan 2003 ... 2.99
❑40, Feb 2003 ... 2.99
❑41, Mar 2003 ... 1.00
❑42, Apr 2003 ... 2.99
❑43, Apr 2003 ... 2.99
❑44, Apr 2003 ... 2.99
❑45, May 2003 ... 2.99
❑46, Jun 2003 ... 2.99
❑47, Jul 2003 ... 2.99
❑48, Aug 2003 ... 2.99
❑49, Sep 2003 ... 2.99
❑50, Oct 2003 ... 2.99
❑51, Nov 2003 ... 2.99
❑52, Nov 2003 ... 2.99
❑53, Dec 2003 ... 2.99
❑54, Jan 2004 ... 2.99
❑55, Feb 2004 ... 2.99
❑56, Mar 2004 ... 2.99
❑57, Apr 2004 ... 2.99
❑58, May 2004 ... 2.99
❑59, Jun 2004 ... 2.99
❑60, Jul 2004 ... 2.99
❑61, Aug 2004 ... 2.99
❑62, Sep 2004 ... 2.99

DAREDEVIL/BATMAN
Marvel

❑1, ca. 1997; prestige format; crossover with DC ... 5.99

DAREDEVIL/BLACK WIDOW: ABATTOIR
Marvel

❑1 ... 14.95

DAREDEVIL: FATHER
Marvel

❑1, Jun 2004 ... 3.50

DAREDEVIL LEGENDS
Marvel

❑1, ca. 2003 ... 14.99
❑2, ca. 2003 ... 17.95
❑3, ca. 2003 ... 16.95
❑4, ca. 2003 ... 19.99

DAREDEVIL: NINJA
Marvel

❑1, Dec 2000 ... 2.99
❑1/A, Dec 2000 ... 2.99
❑2, Jan 2001 ... 2.99
❑3, May 2001 ... 2.99

DAREDEVIL/PUNISHER: CHILD'S PLAY
Marvel

❑1 ... 4.95

DAREDEVIL/SHI
Marvel

❑1, Feb 1997; AW (a); crossover with Crusade ... 3.00

DAREDEVIL/SPIDER-MAN
Marvel

❑1, Jan 2001 ... 2.99
❑1/A, Jan 2000 ... 2.99
❑2, Feb 2001 ... 2.99
❑3, Mar 2001 ... 2.99
❑4, Apr 2001 ... 2.99

DAREDEVIL THE MAN WITHOUT FEAR
Marvel

❑1, Oct 1993; FM (w); AW, JR2 (a); O: Daredevil. Partial foil cover ... 3.50
❑2, Nov 1993; FM (w); AW, JR2 (a); Partial foil cover ... 3.50
❑3, Dec 1993; FM (w); AW, JR2 (a); cardstock cover ... 3.50
❑4, Jan 1994; FM (w); AW, JR2 (a); Partial foil cover ... 3.00
❑5, Feb 1994; FM (w); AW, JR2 (a); cardstock cover ... 3.00

DAREDEVIL: THE TARGET
Marvel

❑1, Jan 2003 ... 3.50

DAREDEVIL VS. VAPORA
Marvel

❑1; Fire-prevention comic ... 1.25

DAREDEVIL: YELLOW
Marvel

❑1, Aug 2001 ... 3.50
❑2, Sep 2001 ... 3.50
❑3, Oct 2001 ... 3.50
❑4, Nov 2001 ... 3.50
❑5, Dec 2001 ... 3.50
❑6, Jan 2002 ... 3.50

DARERAT/TADPOLE
Mighty Pumpkin

❑1, Feb 1987, b&w; parody of Frank Miller's Daredevil work; flip book with Tadpole: Prankster back-up; color poster ... 1.95

DARIA JONTAK
JMJ

❑1, Jan 2001 ... 4.99

DARING ADVENTURES
B Comics

❑1 1993 ... 2.00
❑2, Jul 1993 ... 2.00
❑3 1993 ... 2.00

N-MINT

DARING ADVENTURES
I.W.

❑9, ca. 1963 20.00
❑10, ca. 1963 20.00
❑11, ca. 1964 20.00
❑12, ca. 1964 40.00
❑13, ca. 1964 20.00
❑14, ca. 1964 20.00
❑15, ca. 1964 20.00
❑16, ca. 1964 20.00
❑17, ca. 1964 20.00
❑18, ca. 1964 20.00

DARING ESCAPES
IMAGE

❑1, Sep 1998 2.50
❑1/Variant, Sep 1998; alternate cover 2.50
❑2, Oct 1998 2.50
❑3, Nov 1998 2.50
❑4, Dec 1998 2.50

DARING NEW ADVENTURES OF SUPERGIRL, THE
DC

❑1, Nov 1982 CI (a); O: Supergirl. 1: Psi. 2.50
❑2, Dec 1982 2.00
❑3, Jan 1983 1: The Council. 2.00
❑4, Feb 1983 1: The Gang. 1.50
❑5, Mar 1983 1.50
❑6, Apr 1983 1: Matrix-Prime. 1.50
❑7, May 1983 1.50
❑8, Jun 1983 1: Reactron. A: The Doom Patrol. 1.50
❑9, Jul 1983 A: The Doom Patrol. 1.50
❑10, Aug 1983 1.50
❑11, Sep 1983 1.50
❑12, Oct 1983 1.50
❑13, Nov 1983; 1: Blackstarr. New costume; Series continues "Supergirl" 1.50

DARK, THE (VOL. 1)
CONTINUÜM

❑1, Jun 1993, blue foil cover 2.00
❑1/Variant, Jun 1993; red foil cover 2.00
❑1-2, Jun 1993; blue foil cover 2.00
❑1-3, Oct 1993, blue foil cover 2.00
❑2, Jul 1993 2.00
❑3, Aug 1993; GP (c); GP (a); foil cover 2.00
❑3/Autographed, Aug 1993; GP (a); foil cover 2.00
❑4, Sep 1993 2.00
❑5, Feb 1994 2.00
❑6, Mar 1994 2.00
❑7, Jul 1994 2.00
❑7-2, Jul 1994; blue foil cover 2.00

DARK, THE (VOL. 2)
CONTINUÜM

❑1, Jan 1995 2.00
❑1/A, Jan 1995; enhanced cover 2.50
❑2, Feb 1995 2.25
❑3, Mar 1995 2.50
❑4, Apr 1995 2.50

DARK, THE (AUGUST HOUSE)
AUGUST HOUSE

❑1, May 1995; enhanced cover 2.50
❑2, Mar 1995 2.50

DARK ADVENTURES
DARKLINE

❑1 1.25
❑2 1.75
❑3 1.50
❑4 1.25

DARK ANGEL (1ST SERIES)
BONEYARD

❑1, May 1997, b&w 2.25
❑2, Sep 1991 2.25
❑3, Oct 1991 2.25

N-MINT

DARK ANGEL (2ND SERIES)
MARVEL

❑6, Dec 1992; Title changes to Dark Angel; Series continued from Hell's Angel #5 1.75
❑7, Jan 1993 1.75
❑8, Feb 1993 1.75
❑9, Apr 1993 1.75
❑10, May 1993 1.75
❑11, Jun 1993 1.75
❑12, Jul 1993 1.75
❑13, Aug 1993 1.75
❑14, Sep 1993 1.75
❑15, Oct 1993 1.75
❑16, Nov 1993 1.75
❑17, Dec 1993 1.75

DARK ANGEL (3RD SERIES)
BONEYARD

❑1 1997 4.95
❑2, Aug 1997 1.95
❑3, Sep 1997 1.95

DARK ANGEL (4TH SERIES)
CPM MANGA

❑1 2.95
❑2, Jun 1999 2.95
❑3, Jul 1999 2.95
❑4, Aug 1999 2.95
❑5, Sep 1999 2.95
❑6, Oct 1999 2.95
❑7, Nov 1999 2.95
❑8, Dec 1999 2.95
❑9, Jan 2000 2.95
❑10, Feb 2000 2.95
❑11, Mar 2000 2.95
❑12, Apr 2000 2.95
❑13, May 2000 2.95
❑14, Jun 2000 2.95
❑15, Jul 2000 2.95
❑16, Aug 2000 2.95
❑17, Sep 2000 2.95
❑18, Oct 2000 2.95
❑19, Nov 2000 2.95
❑20, Dec 2000 2.95
❑21, Jan 2001 2.95
❑22, Feb 2001 2.95
❑23, Mar 2001 2.95
❑24, Apr 2001 2.95
❑25, May 2001 2.95
❑26, Jun 2001 2.95
❑27, Jul 2001 2.95
❑28, Aug 2001 2.95
❑29, Sep 2001 2.95

DARK ANGEL: PHOENIX RESURRECTION
IMAGE

❑1, May 2000 2.95
❑2, Aug 2000 2.95
❑3, Mar 2001 2.95
❑4, Oct 2001 2.95

DARK ASSASSIN
SILVERWOLF

❑1, Feb 1987, b&w; cardstock cover. 1.50

DARKCHYLDE (IMAGE)
IMAGE

❑0/A, Mar 1998 2.50
❑0/B, Mar 1998, b&w; Variant Cover Another Universe 2.50
❑0/C, Mar 1998 2.50
❑0.5, Aug 1997; Wizard 1/2 edition; purple background, girl sitting on skull 3.00
❑0.5/Variant, Aug 1997; Wizard 1/2 edition; Black background, demoness 3.00
❑1 3.00
❑1/American Ent; American Entertainment variant 3.00
❑1/B; Magazine-style variant 4.00
❑1/C; San Diego Comic-Con variant (Darkchylde with wings standing on front); Flip-book with Glory/Angela #1 3.00

The Punisher was a frequent guest-star in *Daredevil*.

© 1982 Marvel Comics.

N-MINT

❑2 2.50
❑2/A; Spider-Web/Moon variant cover 2.50
❑3 2.50
❑3/A; All-white variant 2.50
❑4/A, Mar 1997; was Maximum Press title; Image begins as publisher 2.50
❑4/B, Mar 1997; "Fear" Edition; alternate cover; Image begins as publisher 2.50
❑5/A, Sep 1997; variant cover 2.50
❑5/B, Sep 1997; alternate cover 2.50
❑5/C, Sep 1997; alternate cover 2.50
❑Ashcan 1; Preview edition 2.50
❑Ashcan 1/Gold; Preview edition; Gold logo 3.00
❑Ashcan 1/Ltd. 5.00

DARKCHYLDE (MAXIMUM)
MAXIMUM

❑1, Jun 1996 3.00
❑2, Jul 1996 2.50
❑3, Sep 1996 2.50

DARKCHYLDE REMASTERED
IMAGE

❑0, Mar 1998 2.50
❑1/A, May 1997; reprints Darkchylde #1 with corrections 2.50
❑1/B, May 1997; alternate cover; reprints Darkchylde #1 with corrections 2.50
❑2, Sep 1998; reprints Darkchylde #2 with corrections 2.50
❑3, Nov 1998; reprints Darkchylde #3 with corrections 2.50

DARKCHYLDE SUMMER SWIMSUIT SPECTACULAR
DC / WILDSTORM

❑1, Aug 1999; pin-ups 3.95

DARKCHYLDE THE DIARY
IMAGE

❑1/A, Jun 1997; pin-ups with diary entries 2.50
❑1/B, Jun 1997; alternate cover; pin-ups with diary entries 2.50
❑1/C, Jun 1997; alternate cover; pin-ups with diary entries 2.50
❑1/D, Jun 1997; alternate cover; pin-ups with diary entries 2.50

DARKCHYLDE: THE LEGACY
IMAGE

❑1, Aug 1998; cardstock cover 2.50
❑1/A, Aug 1998; DFE alternate chrome cover 4.00
❑1/Variant, Aug 1998; DFE alternate chrome cover 4.00
❑2, Dec 1998 2.50
❑2/Variant, Dec 1998; alternate cover 2.50
❑3, Jun 1999 2.50

DARK CLAW ADVENTURES
DC / AMALGAM

❑1, Jun 1997 1.95

DARK CONVENTION BOOK, THE
CONTINUÜM

❑1 1.95

DARK CROSSINGS: DARK CLOUD RISING
IMAGE

❑1, Sep 2003 5.95

N-MINT

DARK CROSSINGS
IMAGE
- ❑1, Jun 2000 .... 5.95
- ❑2, Oct 2000 .... 5.95

DARK CROSSINGS: DARK CLOUDS OVERHEAD
IMAGE
- ❑1, Jun 2000; prestige format; cover says Dark Crossings: Dark Clouds Rising 5.95

DARK CRYSTAL, THE
MARVEL
- ❑1, Apr 1983 .... 1.25
- ❑2, May 1983 .... 1.25

DARK DAYS: A 30 DAYS OF NIGHT SEQUEL
IDEA & DESIGN WORKS
- ❑1, ca. 2003 .... 8.00
- ❑2, ca. 2003 .... 5.00
- ❑3, ca. 2003 .... 4.00
- ❑4, ca. 2003 .... 4.00
- ❑5, ca. 2003 .... 4.00
- ❑6, ca. 2004 .... 4.00

DARK DESTINY
ALPHA
- ❑1, Nov 1994, b&w; cardstock cover 3.50

DARKDEVIL
MARVEL
- ❑1, Nov 2000 .... 2.99
- ❑2, Dec 2000 .... 2.99
- ❑3, Jan 2001 .... 2.99

DARK DOMINION
DEFIANT
- ❑1, Oct 1993 .... 2.50
- ❑2, Nov 1993 .... 2.50
- ❑3, Dec 1993 .... 2.50
- ❑4, Jan 1994 .... 2.50
- ❑5, Feb 1994 .... 2.50
- ❑6, Mar 1994 .... 2.50
- ❑7, Apr 1994 .... 2.50
- ❑8, May 1994 .... 2.50
- ❑9, Jun 1994 .... 2.50
- ❑10, Jul 1994 .... 2.50
- ❑11, Aug 1994 .... 2.50
- ❑12, Sep 1994 .... 2.50
- ❑13, Oct 1994 .... 2.50

DARKER IMAGE
IMAGE
- ❑1, Mar 1993 RL, JLee (a); 1: Maxx. 1: Deathblow. 2.50
- ❑1/Gold, Mar 1993; RL, JLee (a); 1: Maxx. 1: Deathblow. Gold logo 4.00
- ❑1/Ltd., Mar 1993; White limited edition cover; RL, JLee (a); 1: Maxx. 1: Deathblow. 4.00

DARK FANTASY
APPLE
- ❑1, Sep 1992, b&w 2.75

DARK FRINGE, THE
BRAINSTORM
- ❑2, Dec 1996, b&w 2.95

DARK GUARD
MARVEL
- ❑1, Oct 1993; 1: The Time Guardian. Prism cover 2.95
- ❑2, Nov 1993 .... 1.75
- ❑3, Dec 1993 .... 1.75
- ❑4, Jan 1994 .... 1.75
- ❑5 .... 1.75

DARKHAWK
MARVEL
- ❑1, Mar 1991 O: Darkhawk. 1: Darkhawk. A: Hobgoblin. 2.00
- ❑2, Apr 1991 A: Hobgoblin. A: Spider-Man. 1.50
- ❑3, May 1991 A: Hobgoblin. A: Spider-Man. 1.50
- ❑4, Jun 1991 .... 1.50
- ❑5, Jul 1991 .... 1.50
- ❑6, Aug 1991 A: Daredevil. A: Captain America. 1.50
- ❑7, Sep 1991 .... 1.50
- ❑8, Oct 1991 .... 1.50
- ❑9, Nov 1991 A: Punisher. 1.50
- ❑10, Dec 1991 .... 1.50
- ❑11, Jan 1992 .... 1.50
- ❑12, Feb 1992 V: Tombstone. 1.50
- ❑13, Mar 1992 A: Venom. 1.50
- ❑14, Apr 1992 A: Venom. 1.50
- ❑15, May 1992 .... 1.25
- ❑16, Jun 1992 V: Peristrike Force. 1.25
- ❑17, Jul 1992 V: Peristrike Force. 1.25
- ❑18, Aug 1992 .... 1.25
- ❑19, Sep 1992 A: Spider-Man. 1.25
- ❑20, Oct 1992 A: Sleepwalker. A: Spider-Man. 1.25
- ❑21, Nov 1992 O: Darkhawk. 1.25
- ❑22, Dec 1992 A: Ghost Rider. 1.25
- ❑23, Jan 1993 .... 1.25
- ❑24, Feb 1993 .... 1.25
- ❑25, Mar 1993; Double-size; O: Darkhawk armor. foil cover 2.95
- ❑26, Apr 1993 A: New Warriors. 1.25
- ❑27, May 1993 .... 1.25
- ❑28, Jun 1993 .... 1.25
- ❑29, Jul 1993 .... 1.25
- ❑30, Aug 1993; Infinity Crusade crossover 1.25
- ❑31, Sep 1993; Infinity Crusade crossover 1.25
- ❑32, Oct 1993 .... 1.25
- ❑33, Nov 1993 .... 1.25
- ❑34, Dec 1993 .... 1.25
- ❑35, Jan 1994 A: Venom. 1.25
- ❑36, Feb 1994 A: Venom. 1.25
- ❑37, Mar 1994 A: Venom. 1.25
- ❑38, Apr 1994 .... 1.25
- ❑39, May 1994 .... 1.50
- ❑40, Jun 1994 .... 1.50
- ❑41, Jul 1994 .... 1.50
- ❑42, Aug 1994 .... 1.50
- ❑43, Sep 1994 .... 1.50
- ❑44, Oct 1994 .... 1.50
- ❑45, Nov 1994 .... 1.50
- ❑46, Dec 1994 .... 1.50
- ❑47, Jan 1995 .... 1.50
- ❑48, Feb 1995 .... 1.50
- ❑49, Mar 1995 .... 1.50
- ❑50, Apr 1995; Giant-size 2.50
- ❑Annual 1 .... 2.50
- ❑Annual 2 1: Dreamkiller. 2.95
- ❑Annual 3 .... 2.95

DARKHOLD
MARVEL
- ❑1/CS, Oct 1992; Midnight Sons 2.75
- ❑2, Nov 1992 .... 1.75
- ❑3, Dec 1992 .... 1.75
- ❑4, Jan 1993 .... 1.75
- ❑5, Feb 1993 .... 1.75
- ❑6, Mar 1993 .... 1.75
- ❑7, Mar 1993 .... 1.75
- ❑8, Apr 1993 .... 1.75
- ❑9, May 1993 .... 1.75
- ❑10, Jun 1993 .... 1.75
- ❑11, Jul 1993; Double-cover 1.75
- ❑12, Aug 1993 .... 1.75
- ❑13, Sep 1993; Missing CCA approval stamp 1.75
- ❑14, Oct 1993 .... 1.75
- ❑15, Nov 1993 .... 1.75
- ❑16, Dec 1993 .... 1.75

DARK HORSE CLASSICS: ALIENS VERSUS PREDATOR
DARK HORSE
- ❑1, Feb 1997; Reprints Aliens Vs. Predator #1 with new cover 2.95
- ❑2, Mar 1997; Reprints Aliens Vs. Predator #2 with new cover 2.95
- ❑3, Apr 1997; Reprints Aliens Vs. Predator #3 with new cover 2.95
- ❑4, May 1997; Reprints Aliens Vs. Predator #4 with new cover 2.95
- ❑5, Jun 1997; Reprints Aliens Vs. Predator #5 with new cover 2.95
- ❑6, Jul 1997; Reprints Aliens Vs. Predator #6 with new cover 2.95

DARK HORSE CLASSICS: GODZILLA
DARK HORSE
- ❑1, Apr 1998 .... 2.95

DARK HORSE CLASSICS: GODZILLA: KING OF THE MONSTERS
DARK HORSE
- ❑1, Jul 1998 .... 2.95
- ❑2, Aug 1998; Can G-Force Survive? In the Grip of Godzilla! 2.95
- ❑3, Sep 1998; No Blast from the Past-Godzilla Rules! 2.95
- ❑4, Oct 1998 .... 2.95
- ❑5, Nov 1998 .... 2.95
- ❑6, Dec 1998 .... 2.95

DARK HORSE CLASSICS: STAR WARS: DARK EMPIRE
DARK HORSE
- ❑1, Mar 1997 .... 2.95
- ❑2, Apr 1997 .... 2.95
- ❑3, May 1997 .... 2.95
- ❑4, Jun 1997 .... 2.95
- ❑5, Jul 1997 .... 2.95
- ❑6, Aug 1997 .... 2.95

DARK HORSE CLASSICS: TERROR OF GODZILLA
DARK HORSE
- ❑1, Aug 1998; Translation by Mike Richardson and Randy Stradley of Viz Communications 2.95
- ❑2, Sep 1998; Translation by Mike Richardson and Randy Stradley of Viz Communications 2.95
- ❑3, Oct 1998; Translation by Mike Richardson and Randy Stradley of Viz Communications 2.95
- ❑4, Nov 1998 .... 2.95
- ❑5, Dec 1998 .... 2.95
- ❑6, Jan 1999 .... 2.95

DARK HORSE COMICS
DARK HORSE
- ❑1, Aug 1992; 1: Time Cop. wraparound gatefold cover; Predator, RoboCop, Time Cop, Renegade 3.50
- ❑2, Sep 1992; RoboCop, Renegade, Time Cop, Predator 2.50
- ❑3, Oct 1992 .... 2.50
- ❑4, Nov 1992; Aliens, Predator, Indiana Jones, Mad Dogs 2.50
- ❑5, Dec 1992; Aliens, Predator, Indiana Jones, Mad Dogs 2.50
- ❑6, Jan 1993; RoboCop, Predator, Indiana Jones, Mad Dogs 2.50
- ❑7, Feb 1993; RoboCop, Star Wars, Mad Dogs, Predator 5.00
- ❑8, Mar 1993; 1: X. RoboCop, James Bond, Star Wars 5.00
- ❑9, Apr 1993; 2: X. James Bond, Star Wars, RoboCop 4.00
- ❑10, May 1993; X, Predator, Godzilla, James Bond 3.00
- ❑11, Jul 1993; Predator, Godzilla, James Bond, Aliens 2.50
- ❑12, Aug 1993; Aliens, Predator 2.50
- ❑13, Sep 1993; Aliens, Predator, Thing from Another World 2.50
- ❑14, Oct 1993; Predator, The Mark, Thing from Another World 2.50
- ❑15, Nov 1993 .... 2.50
- ❑16, Dec 1993 .... 2.50
- ❑17, Jan 1994 .... 2.50
- ❑18, Feb 1994; Aliens, Star Wars: Droids, Predator 2.50
- ❑19, Mar 1994; X, Aliens, Star Wars: Droids 2.50
- ❑20, Apr 1994 .... 2.50
- ❑21, May 1994 .... 2.50
- ❑22, Jun 1994 .... 2.50
- ❑23, Jul 1994; Aliens, The Machine 2.50
- ❑24, Aug 1994 .... 2.50
- ❑25, Sep 1994; Flip-book 2.50

Condition price index: Multiply "NM prices" above by: **0.83 for Very Fine/Near Mint**
0.66 for Very Fine • 0.33 for Fine • 0.2 for Very Good • 0.125 for Good

N-MINT

DARK HORSE DOWN UNDER
DARK HORSE

❑1, Jun 1994, b&w 2.50
❑2, Aug 1994, b&w 2.50
❑3, Oct 1994, b&w 2.50

DARK HORSE MAVERICK 2000
DARK HORSE

❑0, Jul 2000 .... 3.95

DARK HORSE MAVERICK 2001
DARK HORSE / MAVERICK

❑1, Jul 2001 .... 4.99

DARK HORSE MONSTERS
DARK HORSE

❑1, Feb 1997; Reprinted from Dark Horse Presents #33 & #47 .... 2.95

DARK HORSE PRESENTS
DARK HORSE

❑1, Jul 1986 1: Concrete. A: Black Cross. 4.00
❑1-2 1: Concrete. A: Black Cross. 2.25
❑1-3; Commemorative edition; 1: Concrete. A: Black Cross. green border 2.25
❑1-4; silver border 2.25
❑2 1986, b&w 2: Concrete. 2.50
❑3, Nov 1986 A: Concrete. 2.50
❑4, Jan 1987 A: Concrete. 2.50
❑5, Feb 1987 A: Concrete. 2.00
❑6, Apr 1987 A: Concrete. 2.00
❑7, May 1987 .... 2.00
❑8, Jun 1987 A: Concrete. 2.00
❑9, Jul 1987 .... 2.00
❑10, Sep 1987 1: The Mask. A: Concrete. 3.00
❑11, Oct 1987 2: The Mask. 2.50
❑12, Nov 1987 A: Concrete. A: The Mask. 2.50
❑13, Dec 1987 A: The Mask. 2.50
❑14, Jan 1987 A: Concrete. A: The Mask. 2.50
❑15, Feb 1988 A: The Mask. 2.50
❑16, Mar 1988 A: Concrete. A: The Mask. 2.50
❑17, Apr 1988; Spume, Muzzi & Woim, Roachmill 2.00
❑18, Jun 1988 A: Concrete. A: The Mask. 2.50
❑19, Jul 1988 A: The Mask. 2.00
❑20, Aug 1988; Double Size A: Flaming Carrot. A: Concrete. A: The Mask. .. 2.00
❑21, Aug 1988 A: The Mask. 2.00
❑22, Sep 1988 1: Duckman. 2.00
❑23, Oct 1988 .... 2.00
❑24, Nov 1988; O: Aliens. 1: Aliens. .. 5.00
❑25, Dec 1988 .... 2.00
❑26, Jan 1989 .... 2.00
❑27, Feb 1989 .... 2.00
❑28, Mar 1989; Double Size; Concrete, Mr. Monster 3.00
❑29, Apr 1989 .... 2.00
❑30, May 1989 .... 2.00
❑31, Jul 1989; Duckman 2.00
❑32, Jul 1989; Giant-size A: Concrete. 3.50
❑33, Aug 1989; Giant-size 2.50
❑34, Aug 1989; Aliens 3.00
❑35, Dec 1989; Predator, Heartbreakers, A Tough Nut To Crack, Aliens .. 3.00
❑36, Oct 1989; Aliens vs. Predator; regular cover 3.00
❑36/A, Oct 1989; Aliens vs. Predator; Painted cover 3.00
❑37, Nov 1989 .... 2.00
❑38, Apr 1990 A: Concrete. 2.00
❑39, May 1990 .... 2.00
❑40, Jun 1990; Giant-size MW (a) 3.00
❑41, Jul 1990 .... 2.00
❑42, Aug 1990; Aliens 2.00
❑43, Sep 1990; Aliens 2.00
❑44, Oct 1990 .... 2.00
❑45, Nov 1990 MW (a) 2.00
❑46, Nov 1990; Predator, Bacchus, Crash Ryan 2.00
❑47, Jan 1991; monsters 2.00
❑48, Feb 1991; Black Cross, Roachmill, Concrete, Mr. Monster 2.00
❑49, Mar 1991 .... 2.00
❑50, Apr 1991 .... 2.00
❑51, Jun 1991 FM (w); FM (a) 2.00
❑52, Jul 1991 FM (w); FM (a) 2.00
❑53, Aug 1991 FM (w); FM (a) 2.00
❑54, Sep 1991 JBy (w); GM, JBy, FM (a); 1: Next Men. 3.00
❑55, Oct 1991 JBy, FM (w); JBy, FM (a); 2: Next Men. 2.25
❑56, Nov 1991; Double-size; FM (w); JBy, FM (a); Aliens 3.95
❑57, Dec 1991; Giant-size FM (w); JBy, FM (a) 3.50
❑58, Jan 1992 FM (w); FM (a) 2.00
❑59, Feb 1992 FM (w); FM (a) 2.50
❑60, Mar 1992 FM (w); FM (a) 2.50
❑61, Apr 1992 FM (w); FM (a) 2.50
❑62, May 1992 FM (w); FM (a) 2.50
❑63, Jun 1992 FM 2.50
❑64, Jul 1992 .... 2.50
❑65, Sep 1992 .... 2.50
❑66, Sep 1992 ES (a) 2.50
❑67, Nov 1992; Double-size issue CR, ES (a); A: Zoo-Lou. 3.95
❑68, Dec 1992; Predator: Race War .. 2.50
❑69, Feb 1993; Predator: Race War .. 2.50
❑70, Mar 1993 .... 2.50
❑71, Apr 1993 .... 2.50
❑72, Apr 1993 .... 2.50
❑73, Jun 1993 .... 2.50
❑74, Jun 1993 .... 2.50
❑75, Jul 1993 CV (a) 2.50
❑76, Aug 1993 .... 2.50
❑77, Sep 1993 .... 2.50
❑78, Oct 1993 .... 2.50
❑79, Nov 1993 .... 2.50
❑80, Dec 1993 .... 3.00
❑81, Jan 1994 .... 2.50
❑82, Feb 1994 .... 2.50
❑83, Mar 1994 .... 2.50
❑84, Apr 1994 .... 2.50
❑85, May 1994 .... 2.50
❑86, Jun 1994 .... 2.50
❑87, Jul 1994 .... 2.50
❑88, Aug 1994; Hellboy 2.50
❑89, Sep 1994; Hellboy 2.50
❑90, Oct 1994 .... 2.50
❑91, Nov 1994 .... 2.50
❑92, Dec 1994 A: Too Much Coffee Man. 2.50
❑93, Jan 1995 A: Too Much Coffee Man. 2.50
❑94, Feb 1995 .... 2.50
❑95, Mar 1995 A: Too Much Coffee Man. 2.50
❑96, Apr 1995 .... 2.50
❑97, May 1995 .... 2.50
❑98, Jun 1995 .... 2.50
❑99, Jul 1995 .... 2.50
❑100.1, Aug 1995; FM, DSt (c); FM, DSt (w); FM, DSt (a); Issue 100 #1 ...... 2.50
❑100.2, Aug 1995; Issue 100 #2: Hellboy cover and story 2.50
❑100.3, Aug 1995; Issue 100 #3; Concrete cover and story 2.50
❑100.4, Aug 1995; DaG (c); FM (w); Martha Washington story; Issue 100 #4 . 2.50
❑100.5, Aug 1995; Issue 100 #5 ...... 2.50
❑101, Sep 1995 BWr (a); A: Aliens. .. 2.50
❑102, Oct 1995 .... 2.50
❑103, Nov 1995; JK (a); Kirby centerfold; Mr. Painter, One-Trick Rip-Off, The Pink Tornado, Hairball 2.95
❑104, Dec 1995 .... 2.95
❑105, Jan 1996 .... 2.95
❑106, Feb 1996 .... 2.95
❑107, Mar 1996 .... 2.95
❑108, Apr 1996 .... 2.95
❑109, May 1996 .... 2.95
❑110, Jun 1996 .... 2.95
❑111, Jul 1996 .... 2.95
❑112, Aug 1996 .... 2.95
❑113, Sep 1996 .... 2.95

Deathblow and The Maxx were introduced in *Darker Image #1*.
© 1993 Image.

N-MINT

❑114, Oct 1996; FM (w); FM (a); Star Slammers, Lance Blastoff, Lowlife, Trypto the Acid Dog 2.95
❑115, Nov 1996; FM (c); Doctor Spin, The Creep, Lowlife, Trypto the Acid Dog 2.95
❑116, Dec 1996; Fat Dog Mendoza, Trypto the Acid Dog, Doctor Spin .. 2.95
❑117, Jan 1997; GC (a); Aliens, Trypto the Acid Dog, Doctor Spin 2.95
❑118, Feb 1997; Monkeyman & O'Brien, Hectic Planet, Trypto the Acid Dog, Doctor Spin 2.95
❑119, Mar 1997; Monkeyman & O'Brien, Hectic Planet, Trout, Predator 2.95
❑120, Apr 1997; One Last Job, The Lords of Misrule, Trout, Hectic Planet 2.95
❑121, May 1997; Jack Zero, Aliens, The Lords of Misrule, Trout 2.95
❑122, Jun 1997; Jack Zero, Imago, Trout, The Lords of Misrule 2.95
❑123, Jul 1997; Imago, Jack Zero, Trout 2.95
❑124, Aug 1997; Predator, Jack Zero, Outside, Inside 2.95
❑125, Sep 1997 .... 2.95
❑126, Oct 1997 .... 2.95
❑127, Nov 1997; Nocturnals, Metalfer, Stiltskin, Blue Monday 2.95
❑128, Jan 1998; Dan & Larry, Metalfer, Stiltskin 2.95
❑129, Feb 1998 .... 2.95
❑130, Mar 1998; Dan & Larry, Wanted Man, Mary Walker: The Woman 2.95
❑131, Apr 1998; Girl Crazy, The Fall, Dan & Larry, Boogie Picker 2.95
❑132, Apr 1998; The Fall, Dan & Larry, Dirty Pair 2.95
❑133, May 1998; Carson of Venus, The Fall, Dirty Pair, Blue Monday 2.95
❑134, Jul 1998 .... 2.95
❑135, Sep 1998; Carson of Venus, The Mark, The Fall, The Ark 3.50
❑136, Oct 1998; The Ark, Spirit of the Badlander 2.95
❑137, Nov 1998; Predator, The Ark, My Vagabond Days 2.95
❑138, Dec 1998; Terminator, The Moth, My Vagabond Days 2.95
❑139, Jan 1999; Roachmill, Saint Slayer 2.95
❑140, Feb 1999; Aliens, Usagi Yojimbo, Saint Slayer 2.95
❑141, Mar 1999; Buffy the Vampire Slayer 2.95
❑142, Apr 1999; 1: Doctor Gosburo Coffin. Codex Arcana 2.95
❑143, May 1999; TY (w); TY (a); Tarzan: Tales of Pellucidar 2.95
❑144, Jun 1999; The Vortex, Burglar Girls, Galactic Jack 2.95
❑145, Jul 1999; Burglar Girls 2.95
❑146, Sep 1999; Aliens vs Predator .. 2.95
❑147, Oct 1999; Ragnok 2.95
❑148, Oct 1999 .... 2.95
❑149, Dec 1999 .... 2.95
❑150, Jan 2000; Giant-size 4.50
❑151, Feb 2000, b&w 2.95
❑152, Mar 2000, b&w 2.95
❑153, Apr 2000, b&w; Flipbook 2.95
❑154, May 2000, b&w 2.95
❑155, Jul 2000, b&w 2.95

N-MINT

❑156, Aug 2000, b&w ... 2.95
❑157, Sep 2000, b&w; Last issue of the series. ... 2.95
❑Annual 1997, Feb 1998, b&w; GM (a); cover says 1997, indicia says 1998 ... 4.95
❑Annual 1998, Sep 1998, b&w; Hellboy, Buffy, Skeleton Key, The Ark, My Vagabond Days, Infirmary ... 4.95
❑Annual 1999, Aug 1999; SA, ME (w); SA (a); Dark Horse Jr. ... 4.95
❑Annual 2000, Jun 2000; Flip-book PD (w); ... 4.95

DARK HORSE PRESENTS: ALIENS
DARK HORSE

❑1, ca. 1992; color reprints; Reprints Aliens stories from Dark Horse Presents ... 4.95
❑1/A, ca. 1992; Promotion only ... 4.95

DARK ISLAND
DAVDEZ

❑1, May 1998, b&w ... 2.95
❑2, Jun 1998, b&w ... 2.95
❑3, Jul 1998, b&w ... 2.50

DARK KNIGHT STRIKES AGAIN, THE
DC

❑1, ca. 2001; FM (a); Only DK2 on cover ... 7.95
❑1/A, ca. 2001; Full title on cover; Variant cover edition ... 9.00
❑2, ca. 2002; FM (a); Only DK2 on cover ... 7.95
❑2/A, ca. 2002; Full title on cover; Variant cover edition ... 9.00
❑3, ca. 2002; FM (a); Only DK2 on cover ... 7.95
❑3/A, ca. 2002; Full title on cover; Variant cover edition ... 9.00

DARKLIGHT: PRELUDE
SIRIUS

❑1, Jan 1994, b&w ... 2.95
❑2, b&w ... 2.95
❑3, b&w ... 2.95

DARKLON THE MYSTIC
PACIFIC

❑1, Nov 1983 ... 2.00

DARKMAN (MAGAZINE)
MARVEL

❑1, Sep 1990, b&w; Magazine size ... 2.25

DARK MANSION OF FORBIDDEN LOVE, THE
DC

❑1, Sep 1971 TD (a) ... 100.00
❑2, Nov 1971 ... 35.00
❑3, Jan 1972 DH (a) ... 35.00
❑4, Mar 1972; Series continued in Forbidden Tales of Dark Mansion #5 ... 35.00

DARKMAN (VOL. 1)
MARVEL

❑1, Oct 1990 BH (c); BH (a) ... 2.00
❑2, Nov 1990 BH (c); BH (a) ... 1.50
❑3, Dec 1990 BH (c); BH (a) ... 1.50

DARKMAN (VOL. 2)
MARVEL

❑1, Apr 1993 ... 3.95
❑2, May 1993 ... 2.95
❑3, Jun 1993 ... 2.95
❑4, Jul 1993 ... 2.95
❑5, Aug 1993 ... 2.95
❑6, Sep 1993 ... 2.95

DARKMINDS
IMAGE

❑0.5, May 1999 ... 2.50
❑1, Jul 1998 ... 3.50
❑1/Gold, Aug 1998; DFE gold foil edition ... 4.00
❑1/Variant, Jul 1998; alternate cover (solo figure) ... 3.50
❑1-2 ... 2.50
❑2, Aug 1998 ... 3.00
❑2/Variant, Aug 1998; alternate cover ... 3.00
❑3, Sep 1998 ... 3.00
❑3/Variant, Sep 1998; alternate cover ... 3.00
❑4, Oct 1998; cover says Dec, indicia says Oct ... 3.00
❑5, Nov 1998 ... 2.50
❑6, Dec 1998 ... 2.50
❑7, Feb 1999 ... 2.50
❑8, Apr 1999 ... 2.50

DARKMINDS (VOL. 2)
IMAGE

❑0, Jul 2000 ... 2.50
❑1, Feb 2000 ... 2.50
❑2, Mar 2000 ... 2.50
❑3, Apr 2000 ... 2.50
❑4, May 2000 ... 2.50
❑5, Jun 2000 ... 2.50
❑6, Sep 2000 ... 2.50
❑7, Oct 2000 ... 2.50
❑8, Nov 2000 ... 2.50
❑9, Feb 2001 ... 2.50
❑10, Apr 2001 ... 2.50

DARKMINDS: MACROPOLIS
IMAGE

❑1/A ... 2.95
❑1/B ... 2.95
❑2/A, Mar 2002 ... 2.95
❑2/B, Mar 2002 ... 2.95

DARKMINDS: MACROPOLIS VOL 2
DREAMWAVE

❑1, Sep 2003 ... 2.95
❑2, Oct 2003 ... 2.95
❑3, Dec 2003 ... 2.95

DARKMINDS/WITCHBLADE
IMAGE

❑1, Aug 2000 ... 5.95

DARK MOON PROPHESY
DARK MOON PRODUCTIONS

❑1, May 1995; free color and b&w preview of Dark Moon line ... 1.00

DARK NEMESIS (VILLAINS)
DC

❑1, Feb 1998; New Year's Evil ... 1.95

DARKNESS, THE
TOP COW / IMAGE

❑0 ... 3.00
❑0.5, ca. 1996; Wizard mail-away promotion ... 3.00
❑0.5/Variant, ca. 1996; Christmas cover; Wizard mail-away promotion ... 3.00
❑0.5-2, Mar 2001 ... 2.95
❑1, Dec 1996 ... 3.00
❑1/A, Dec 1996; Dark cover variant ... 3.00
❑1/B, Dec 1996, Wizard Ace edition; Variant ... 3.00
❑1/C, Dec 1996; Fan club edition ... 3.00
❑1/Gold, Dec 1996; Gold edition ... 3.00
❑1/Platinum, Dec 1996, Platinum edition ... 8.00
❑2, Jan 1997 ... 3.00
❑3, Mar 1997 ... 3.00
❑4, May 1997 ... 3.00
❑5, Jun 1997 ... 3.00
❑6, Jul 1997 ... 3.00
❑7, Aug 1997 ... 2.50
❑7/A, Aug 1997; Variant cover with Michael Turner and babes ... 2.50
❑8, Oct 1997 ... 2.50
❑8/A, Oct 1997; alternate cover ... 2.50
❑8/B, Oct 1997; alternate cover ... 2.50
❑8/C, Oct 1997; alternate cover ... 2.50
❑9, Nov 1997 ... 2.50
❑9/A, Nov 1997; alternate cover ... 2.50
❑10, Dec 1997 ... 2.50
❑10/A, Dec 1997; alternate cover (gold) ... 2.50
❑10/B, Dec 1997; alternate cover (gold) ... 2.50
❑11/A, Jan 1998; chromium cover ... 8.00
❑11/B, Jan 1998 ... 2.50
❑11/C, Jan 1998 ... 2.50
❑11/D, Jan 1998 ... 2.50
❑11/E, Jan 1998 ... 2.50
❑11/F, Jan 1998 ... 2.50
❑11/G, Jan 1998 ... 2.50
❑11/H, Jan 1998 ... 2.50
❑11/I, Jan 1998 ... 2.50
❑11/J, Jan 1998, Museum Edition ... 2.50
❑12, Feb 1998 ... 2.50
❑13, Mar 1998 ... 2.50
❑14, Apr 1998 ... 2.50
❑15, Jun 1998 ... 2.50
❑16, Jul 1998 ... 2.50
❑17, Sep 1998 O: Magdalena. ... 2.50
❑18, Nov 1998 ... 2.50
❑19, Jan 1999 ... 2.50
❑20/A, Apr 1999; Regular Cover (with Darklings) ... 2.50
❑20/B, Apr 1999, Museum Edition ... 2.50
❑20/C, Apr 1999; Alternate Cover (With Darklings) ... 2.50
❑21, May 1999 ... 2.50
❑22, Jun 1999 ... 2.50
❑23, Jul 1999 ... 2.50
❑24, Aug 1999 ... 2.50
❑25, Sep 1999 ... 3.99
❑25/A, Sep 1999, Chrome Holofoil variant ... 20.00
❑26, Oct 1999 ... 2.50
❑27, Oct 1999 ... 2.50
❑28, Jan 2000 ... 2.50
❑29 2000 ... 2.50
❑30, Apr 2000 ... 2.50
❑31, May 2000 ... 2.50
❑32, Jul 2000 ... 2.50
❑33, Aug 2000 ... 2.50
❑34, Oct 2000 ... 2.50
❑35, Nov 2000 ... 2.50
❑36, Dec 2000 ... 2.50
❑37, Feb 2001 ... 2.50
❑38, Apr 2001 ... 2.50
❑39, May 2001 ... 2.50
❑40, Aug 2001 ... 2.50
❑Ashcan 1, Jul 1996; No cover price; preview of upcoming series ... 3.00
❑Ashcan 1/A; Prelude; "Wizard Authentic" variant ... 3.00
❑Deluxe 1; Deluxe edition; Reprints The Darkness #1-6; Slipcased ... 14.95

DARKNESS (VOL. 2)
IMAGE

❑1, Dec 2002 ... 2.99
❑1/A, Dec 2002; Black and White ... 2.99
❑1/B, Dec 2002; DF Cover ... 2.99
❑1/C, Dec 2002; Holofoil Cover ... 2.99
❑1/D, Dec 2002; Sketch Cover ... 2.99
❑2, Feb 2003 ... 2.99
❑3, Apr 2003 ... 2.99
❑4, Jun 2003 ... 2.99
❑5, Sep 2003 ... 2.99
❑6, Nov 2003 ... 2.99
❑7, Apr 2004 ... 2.99
❑8, Apr 2004 ... 2.99
❑9, May 2004 ... 2.99
❑10, May 2004 ... 2.99
❑11, Jun 2004 ... 2.99
❑12, Aug 2004 ... 2.99

DARKNESS/BATMAN, THE
IMAGE

❑1, Aug 1999 ... 5.95

DARKNESS COLLECTED EDITION
IMAGE

❑1, Oct 2003 ... 4.95

DARKNESS/HULK
IMAGE

❑1, Jul 2004 ... 5.00

DARKNESS INFINITY
IMAGE

❑1, Aug 1999 ... 3.50

DARKNESS: MEGACON ISSUE
IMAGE

❑1, Aug 2003 ... 0.00

DARKNESS/PAINKILLER JANE
IMAGE

❑Ashcan 1 ... 3.00
❑Ashcan 1/A; variant cover ... 3.00

N-MINT

DARKNESS PRELUDE
IMAGE

❑0, Jan 2003; Dynamic Foces Exclusive — 4.00
❑0/A, Jan 2003 — 4.00

DARKNESS, THE: SPEAR OF DESTINY
IMAGE

❑1, Apr 2000; Collects The Darkness #15-18 — 12.95

DARKNESS: WANTED DEAD ONE SHOT
IMAGE

❑1, Aug 2003 — 2.99

DARKNESS/WITCHBLADE SPECIAL
IMAGE

❑1, Dec 1999 — 3.95

DARK OZ
ARROW

❑1 1997 — 2.75
❑2 1997 — 2.75
❑3 1998 — 2.75
❑4 1998 — 2.75
❑5 1998; indicia says 97, a misprint — 2.75

DARK RAT
MAVERICK PULP COMIX

❑1, Sep 1997, b&w — 2.50

DARK REALM
IMAGE

❑1, Oct 2000 — 2.95
❑2, Dec 2000 — 2.95
❑3, Feb 2001 — 2.95
❑4, Jun 2001 — 2.95

DARK REGIONS
WHITE WOLF

❑1, Feb 1987 — 1.75
❑2 — 1.75
❑3, May 1987 — 1.75

DARKSEID (VILLAINS)
DC

❑1, Feb 1998; New Year's Evil — 1.95

DARK SHADOWS (GOLD KEY)
GOLD KEY

❑1, Mar 1969; based on TV series — 145.00
❑1/A; based on TV series; without poster — 50.00
❑2, Aug 1969 — 55.00
❑3, Nov 1969 — 50.00
❑4, Feb 1970 — 40.00
❑5, May 1970 — 40.00
❑6, Aug 1970 — 32.00
❑7, Nov 1970 — 32.00
❑8, Feb 1971 — 32.00
❑9, May 1971 — 32.00
❑10, Aug 1971 — 32.00
❑11, Nov 1971 — 30.00
❑12, Feb 1972 — 30.00
❑13, Apr 1972 — 30.00
❑14, Jun 1972; Painted cover — 30.00
❑15, Aug 1972 — 30.00
❑16, Oct 1972 — 24.00
❑17, Dec 1972 — 24.00
❑18, Feb 1973 — 24.00
❑19, Apr 1973 — 24.00
❑20, Jun 1973 — 24.00
❑21, Aug 1973 — 18.00
❑22, Oct 1973 — 18.00
❑23, Dec 1973 — 18.00
❑24, Feb 1974 — 18.00
❑25, Apr 1974 — 18.00
❑26, Jun 1974 — 18.00
❑27, Aug 1974 — 18.00
❑28, Oct 1974 — 18.00
❑29, Dec 1974 — 18.00
❑30, Feb 1975 — 18.00
❑31, Apr 1975 — 15.00
❑32, Jun 1975 — 15.00
❑33, Aug 1975 — 15.00
❑34 — 15.00
❑35, Feb 1975 — 15.00

N-MINT

DARK SHADOWS (INNOVATION)
INNOVATION

❑1, Jun 1992; TV series — 3.00
❑2, Aug 1992; TV series — 2.50
❑3, Nov 1992; TV series — 2.50
❑4, Spr 1993; TV series — 2.50
❑5, Jun 1993; Book 2, #1 — 2.50
❑5/Autographed, Jun 1993; Book 2, #1 — 2.50
❑6, Jun 1993; Book 2, #2 — 2.50
❑7, Jun 1993; Book 2, #3 — 2.50
❑8; Book 2, #4 — 2.50
❑9; Book 3 #1 — 2.50

DARK SHRINE
ANTARCTIC

❑1, May 1999 — 2.99
❑2, Jun 1999 — 2.50

DARK SHRINE GALLERY
BASEMENT

❑1 — 3.25

DARKSIDE BLUES
ADV MANGA

❑1 — 0.00

DARKSIDE BLUES
ADV MANGA

❑1, Mar 2004 — 14.98

DARKSTARS, THE
DC

❑0, Oct 1994; Series continued in Darkstars #24 — 2.00
❑1, Oct 1992 — 1.75
❑2, Nov 1992 — 1.75
❑3, Dec 1992 — 1.75
❑4, Jan 1993 — 1.75
❑5, Feb 1993 — 1.75
❑6, Mar 1993 — 1.75
❑7, Apr 1993 — 1.75
❑8, May 1993 — 1.75
❑9, Jun 1993 — 1.75
❑10, Jun 1993 — 1.75
❑11, Aug 1993 — 1.75
❑12, Sep 1993 — 1.75
❑13, Oct 1993 — 1.75
❑14, Nov 1993 — 1.75
❑15, Dec 1993 — 1.75
❑16, Jan 1994 — 1.75
❑17, Feb 1994 — 1.75
❑18, Mar 1994 — 1.75
❑19, Apr 1994; Flash — 1.75
❑20, May 1994; Flash — 1.75
❑21, Jun 1994 — 1.75
❑22, Jul 1994 — 1.75
❑23, Aug 1994; Series continued in Darkstars #0, Donna Troy joins Darkstars — 1.95
❑24, Sep 1994; Zero Hour — 1.95
❑25, Nov 1994 — 1.95
❑26, Dec 1994 — 1.95
❑27, Jan 1995 — 1.95
❑28, Feb 1995 — 1.95
❑29, Mar 1995 — 1.95
❑30, Apr 1995 — 1.95
❑31, Jun 1995 — 2.25
❑32, Jul 1995 — 2.25
❑33, Aug 1995 — 2.25
❑34, Sep 1995 — 2.25
❑35, Oct 1995 — 2.25
❑36, Nov 1995 — 2.25
❑37, Dec 1995 — 2.25
❑38, Jan 1996 — 2.25

DARK TALES OF DAILY HORROR
ANTARCTIC

❑1, Feb 1994, b&w — 2.95

DARK VISIONS
PYRAMID

❑1, Nov 1986 — 2.00
❑2 — 2.00

DARKWING DUCK
DISNEY

❑1 — 1.50
❑2 — 1.50

A Buffy the Vampire Slayer story appears in *Dark Horse Presents* #141.

© 1999 Dark Horse Comics and WB Television.

N-MINT

❑3 — 1.50
❑4 — 1.50

DARKWING DUCK LIMITED SERIES (DISNEY'S...)
DISNEY

❑1, Nov 1991 — 1.50
❑2, Dec 1991 — 1.50
❑3, Jan 1992 — 1.50
❑4, Feb 1992 — 1.50

DARK WOLF
ETERNITY

❑1 1988, b&w — 1.95
❑2 1988, b&w — 1.95
❑3 1988, b&w — 1.95
❑4 1988, b&w — 1.95
❑5, Jun 1988, b&w — 1.95
❑6 1988, b&w — 1.95
❑7 1988, b&w — 1.95
❑8 1988, b&w — 1.95
❑9, b&w — 1.95
❑10, b&w — 1.95
❑11, b&w — 1.95
❑12, b&w — 1.95
❑13, b&w — 1.95
❑14, b&w — 1.95
❑Annual 1, b&w — 2.25

DARK WOLF (VOL. 2)
MALIBU

❑1 — 1.95
❑2 — 1.95
❑3 — 1.95
❑4 — 1.95

DARQUE PASSAGES
VALIANT

❑1, Jan 1994 — 2.00

DARQUE PASSAGES (VOL. 2)
ACCLAIM

❑1, Apr 1998 — 2.50
❑2, Jan 1998; No cover date; indicia says Jan — 2.50
❑3, Feb 1998; No cover date; indicia says Feb — 2.50

DARQUE RAZOR
LONDON NIGHT

❑1, Oct 1997 — 3.00

DART
IMAGE

❑1, Feb 1996 — 2.50
❑1/A, Feb 1996; alternate cover — 2.50
❑2, Apr 1996 — 2.50
❑3, May 1996 — 2.50

DATE WITH DEBBI
DC

❑1, Feb 1969 — 16.00
❑2, Apr 1969 — 12.00
❑3, Jun 1969 — 10.00
❑4, Aug 1969 — 10.00
❑5, Oct 1969 — 10.00
❑6, Dec 1969 — 10.00
❑7, Feb 1970 — 10.00
❑8, Apr 1970 — 10.00
❑9, Jun 1970 — 10.00
❑10, Aug 1970 — 10.00
❑11, Oct 1970 — 10.00
❑12, Dec 1970 — 10.00

	N-MINT
❑13, Feb 1971	12.00
❑14, Apr 1971	12.00
❑15, Jun 1971	12.00
❑16, Aug 1971	12.00
❑17, Oct 1971	12.00
❑18, ca. 1972	10.00

DAUGHTERS OF TIME 3-D
3-D Zone

	N-MINT
❑1	3.95

DAVID & GOLIATH
Image

	N-MINT
❑1, Sep 2003	2.95
❑2, Dec 2003	2.95
❑3, Jun 2004	2.95

DAVID CASSIDY
Charlton

	N-MINT
❑1, Feb 1972	25.00
❑2, Mar 1972	16.00
❑3, May 1972	16.00
❑4 1972	16.00
❑5, Aug 1972	16.00
❑6, Sep 1972	14.00
❑7, Oct 1972	14.00
❑8, Nov 1972	14.00
❑9, Dec 1972	14.00
❑10, Feb 1973	12.00
❑11, Mar 1973	12.00
❑12, May 1973	12.00
❑13, Jul 1973	12.00
❑14, Sep 1973	12.00

DAVID CHELSEA IN LOVE
Eclipse

	N-MINT
❑1, b&w	3.50
❑2, b&w	3.50
❑3, b&w	3.50
❑4, b&w	3.50

DAVY CROCKETT
Gold Key

	N-MINT
❑1, ca. 1963	100.00
❑2, Nov 1969	20.00

DAWN
Sirius Entertainment

	N-MINT
❑0.5, ca. 1996; Wizard mail-away	3.00
❑0.5/Variant, ca. 1996; Wizard mail-away; "Hey Kids" Variant cover	5.00
❑1, Jul 1995	3.00
❑1/A, Jul 1995; blacklight edition; "Black light" cover	5.00
❑1/B, Jul 1995; "White Trash" edition; Look Sharp Edition	5.00
❑1/C, Jul 1995; "Look Sharp" edition; Kids	5.00
❑2, Sep 1995	3.00
❑2/A, Sep 1995; Signed, limited edition; Mystery Book	6.00
❑3, ca. 1996	3.00
❑3/A, ca. 1996; Signed, limited edition	6.00
❑4, ca. 1996	3.00
❑4/A, ca. 1996; Signed, limited edition	5.00
❑5, Sep 1996	3.00
❑5/A, Sep 1996; Signed, limited edition	5.00
❑6, Oct 1996	3.00
❑6/A, Oct 1996; Signed, limited edition	5.00

DAWN 2004 CON SKETCHBOOK ONE-SHOT
Image

	N-MINT
❑1, May 2004	2.95

DAWN CONVENTION SKETCH BOOK
Image

	N-MINT
❑1, Apr 2003	2.95

DAWN: CONVENTION SKETCHBOOK
Image

	N-MINT
❑1, Mar 2002	2.95

DAWN TENTH ANNIVERSARY SPECIAL
Sirius Entertainment

	N-MINT
❑1, Sep 1999	2.95

DAWN: THE RETURN OF THE GODDESS
Sirius Entertainment

	N-MINT
❑1, Apr 1999	2.95
❑1/Ltd., Apr 1999	8.00
❑2, May 1999	2.95
❑3, Nov 1999	2.95
❑4, Jul 2000	2.95

DAWN: THREE TIERS
Image

	N-MINT
❑1, Jul 2003	2.95
❑2, Sep 2003	2.95
❑3, Feb 2004	2.95

DAYDREAMERS
Marvel

	N-MINT
❑1, Aug 1997; gatefold summary; teams Howard the Duck, Man-Thing, Franklin Richards, Leech, Artie, and Tana	2.50
❑2, Sep 1997; gatefold summary	2.50
❑3, Oct 1997; gatefold summary	2.50

DAY OF JUDGMENT
DC

	N-MINT
❑1, Nov 1999	2.50
❑2, Nov 1999	2.50
❑3, Nov 1999	2.50
❑4, Nov 1999	2.50
❑5, Nov 1999; Hal Jordan becomes Spectre	2.50

DAY OF JUDGMENT SECRET FILES
DC

	N-MINT
❑1, Nov 1999; background on participants in event	4.95

DAY OF THE DEFENDERS
Marvel

	N-MINT
❑1, Mar 2001	3.50

DAYS OF WRATH
Apple

	N-MINT
❑1, b&w	2.75
❑2, b&w	2.75
❑3, b&w	2.75
❑4, Jun 1994, b&w	2.75

DAZZLER
Marvel

	N-MINT
❑1, Mar 1981; JR2 (a); O: Dazzler. A: X-Men. First Marvel direct market-only comic	2.00
❑2, Apr 1981 JR2, AA (a); A: X-Men.	1.50
❑3, May 1981 BA (c); JR2, BA (a); A: Doctor Doom. V: Doctor Doom.	1.00
❑4, Jun 1981 FS (a); V: Doctor Doom.	1.00
❑5, Jul 1981 1: Blue Shield.	1.00
❑6, Aug 1981	1.00
❑7, Sep 1981	1.00
❑8, Oct 1981	1.00
❑9, Nov 1981	1.00
❑10, Dec 1981 A: Galactus.	1.00
❑11, Jan 1982 A: Galactus.	1.00
❑12, Feb 1982	1.00
❑13, Mar 1982	1.00
❑14, Apr 1982	1.00
❑15, May 1982 FS (a)	1.00
❑16, Jun 1982 FS (a)	1.00
❑17, Jul 1982; FS (a); Angel	1.00
❑18, Aug 1982 FS (a)	1.00
❑19, Sep 1982	1.00
❑20, Oct 1982	1.00
❑21, Nov 1982; Double-size	1.00
❑22, Dec 1982 A: Rogue. V: Rogue.	1.00
❑23, Jan 1983	1.00
❑24, Feb 1983	1.00
❑25, Mar 1983	1.00
❑26, May 1983	1.00
❑27, Jul 1983 BSz (c)	1.00
❑28, Sep 1983 BSz (c); A: Rogue.	1.00
❑29, Nov 1983	1.00
❑30, Jan 1984 BSz (c)	1.00
❑31, Mar 1984 BSz (c)	1.00
❑32, Jun 1984 BSz (c); A: Inhumans.	1.00
❑33, Aug 1984 BSz (c)	1.00
❑34, Oct 1984 BSz (c)	1.00
❑35, Jan 1985 BSz (c)	1.00
❑36, Mar 1985 JBy (c)	1.00
❑37, May 1985	1.00
❑38, Jul 1985 A: X-Men.	1.00
❑39, Sep 1985	1.00
❑40, Nov 1985; Secret Wars II	1.00
❑41, Jan 1986	1.00
❑42, Mar 1986	1.00

DC 100-PAGE SUPER SPECTACULAR: WORLD'S GREATEST SUPER-HEROES
DC

	N-MINT
❑1, Jul 2004	6.95

DC CHALLENGE
DC

	N-MINT
❑1, Nov 1985 ME (w); GC (a)	1.50
❑2, Dec 1985	1.50
❑3, Jan 1986 CI (a)	1.50
❑4, Feb 1986 GK, KJ (a)	1.50
❑5, Mar 1986 DaG (a)	1.50
❑6, Apr 1986	1.50
❑7, May 1986 JSa (a)	1.50
❑8, Jun 1986 DG (a)	1.50
❑9, Jul 1986 DH (a)	1.50
❑10, Aug 1986 CS (a)	1.50
❑11, Sep 1986 KG, RT (a)	1.50
❑12, Oct 1986 GP (a)	2.00

DC COMICS PRESENTS
DC

	N-MINT
❑1, Jul 1978; JL, DA (a); Flash	3.00
❑2, Sep 1978; JL, DA (a); Flash	3.00
❑3, Oct 1978; JL (a); Adam Strange	2.00
❑4, Dec 1978; JL (a); Metal Men	2.00
❑5, Jan 1979; MA (a); Aquaman	2.00
❑6, Feb 1979; CS (a); Green Lantern	2.00
❑7, Mar 1979; DD (a); Red Tornado	2.00
❑8, Apr 1979; MA (a); Swamp Thing	2.00
❑9, May 1979; JSa (a); Wonder Woman	2.00
❑10, Jun 1979; JSa (a); Sgt. Rock	2.00
❑11, Jul 1979; JSa (a); Hawkman	2.00
❑12, Aug 1979; RB, DG (a); Mr. Miracle	2.00
❑13, Sep 1979; DG, DD (a); Legion of Super-Heroes	2.00
❑14, Oct 1979; DG, DD (a); Superboy	1.50
❑15, Nov 1979; JSa (a); Atom	1.50
❑16, Dec 1979; Black Lightning	1.50
❑17, Jan 1980; JL (a); Firestorm	1.50
❑18, Feb 1980; DD (a); Zatanna	1.50
❑19, Mar 1980; JSa (a); Batgirl	1.50
❑20, Apr 1980; JL (a); Green Arrow	1.50
❑21, May 1980; JSa (a); Elongated Man	1.50
❑22, Jun 1980; Captain Comet	1.50
❑23, Jul 1980; JSa (a); Doctor Fate	1.50
❑24, Aug 1980; JL (a); Deadman	1.50
❑25, Sep 1980; Phantom Stranger	1.50
❑26, Oct 1980; JSn (w); JSn, GP (a); 1: New Teen Titans. 1: Raven. 1: Starfire II (Koriand'r). 1: Cyborg. Green Lantern	7.00
❑27, Nov 1980; JSn (a); 1: Mongul. Martian Manhunter; Congorilla back-up	2.50
❑28, Dec 1980; JSn (a); V: Mongul. Supergirl; Johnny Thunder Lawman back-up	1.50
❑29, Jan 1981; JSn, RT (a); Spectre	1.50
❑30, Feb 1981; CS (a); Black Canary	1.50
❑31, Mar 1981; DG, JL (a); Robin; Robotman back-up	1.50
❑32, Apr 1981; Wonder Woman	1.50
❑33, May 1981; Captain Marvel	1.50
❑34, Jun 1981; Marvel Family	1.50
❑35, Jul 1981; CS (a); Man-Bat	1.50
❑36, Aug 1981; JSn (a); Starman	1.50
❑37, Sep 1981; JSn, RT (a); Hawkgirl; Rip Hunter back-up	1.50
❑38, Oct 1981; D: Crimson Avenger. Flash	1.50
❑39, Nov 1981 JSn (a); A: Toyman.	1.50
❑40, Dec 1981; Metamorpho	1.50
❑41, Jan 1982; 1: new Wonder Woman. A: Joker.	2.25

Condition price index: Multiply "NM prices" above by: **0.83 for Very Fine/Near Mint**
0.66 for Very Fine • 0.33 for Fine • 0.2 for Very Good • 0.125 for Good

N-MINT

❑42, Feb 1982; Unknown Soldier; Golden Age Sandman back-up 1.25
❑43, Mar 1982; CS (a); Legion 1.25
❑44, Apr 1982; A: Joker. Dial 'H' for Hero 2.25
❑45, May 1982; RB (a); Firestorm 1.25
❑46, Jun 1982 1: Global Guardians. 1.25
❑47, Jul 1982 1: Masters of Universe. 1.25
❑48, Aug 1982; Aquaman; Black Pirate back-up 1.25
❑49, Sep 1982; RB (a); Captain Marvel 1.25
❑50, Oct 1982; CS (a); Clark Kent 1.25
❑51, Nov 1982; FMc (a); Atom 1.25
❑52, Dec 1982; KG (a); 1: Ambush Bug. Doom Patrol 2.50
❑53, Jan 1983; 1: Atari Force. House of Mystery 1.00
❑54, Feb 1983; DN (a); Green Arrow, Black Canary 1.00
❑55, Mar 1983; A: Superboy. V: Parasite. Air Wave 1.00
❑56, Apr 1983; CS (a); 1: Maaldor the Darklord. Power Girl 1.00
❑57, May 1983; Atomic Knights 1.00
❑58, Jun 1983; GK (c); CS (a); 1: The Untouchables (DC). Robin, Elongated Man 1.00
❑59, Jul 1983; KG (a); Legion of Super-Heroes, Ambush Bug 1.00
❑60, Aug 1983; Guardians of the Universe 1.00
❑61, Sep 1983; OMAC 1.00
❑62, Oct 1983; Freedom Fighters 1.00
❑63, Nov 1983; Amethyst 1.00
❑64, Dec 1983; Kamandi 1.00
❑65, Jan 1984; Madame Xanadu 1.00
❑66, Feb 1984; JK (a); 1: Blackbriar Thorn. Demon 1.00
❑67, Mar 1984; V: Toyman. Santa Claus 1.00
❑68, Apr 1984; MA, CS (a); Vixen 1.00
❑69, May 1984; IN (a); Blackhawk 1.00
❑70, Jun 1984; Metal Men 1.00
❑71, Jul 1984; CS (a); Bizarro 1.00
❑72, Aug 1984; Phantom Stranger, Joker 1.50
❑73, Sep 1984; CI (a); Flash 1.00
❑74, Oct 1984; Hawkman 1.00
❑75, Nov 1984; Arion 1.00
❑76, Dec 1984; A: Monitor. Wonder Woman 1.00
❑77, Jan 1985; 1: The Forgotten Villains. Animal Man, Dolphin, Congorilla, Cave Carson, Immortal Man, Rip Hunter, Rick Flagg 3.00
❑78, Feb 1985; Animal Man, Dolphin, Congorilla, Cave Carson, Immortal Man, Rip Hunter, Rick Flagg 3.00
❑79, Mar 1985; Clark Kent 1.00
❑80, Apr 1985; Legion; 1.00
❑81, May 1985; V: Kobra. Ambush Bug 1.00
❑82, Jun 1985; Adam Strange 1.00
❑83, Jul 1985; Outsiders 1.00
❑84, Aug 1985; Challengers of the Unknown 1.00
❑85, Sep 1985; AMo (w); Swamp Thing 8.00
❑86, Oct 1985; V: Blackstarr. Crisis; Supergirl 1.00
❑87, Nov 1985; 1: Superboy of Earth-Prime. Crisis 1.00
❑88, Dec 1985; Crisis 1.00
❑89, Jan 1986; Omega Men 1.00
❑90, Feb 1986; O: Captain Atom. Firestorm 1.00
❑91, Mar 1986; Captain Comet 1.00
❑92, Apr 1986; Vigilante 1.00
❑93, May 1986; Plastic Man, Elongated Man, Elastic Lad 1.00
❑94, Jun 1986; Harbinger, Lady Quark, Pariah 1.00
❑95, Jul 1986; Hawkman 1.00
❑96, Aug 1986; Blue Devil 1.00
❑97, Sep 1986; Double-size A: Bizarro. A: Mxyzptlk. V: Phantom Zone Criminals. 1.25
❑Annual 1, ca. 1982; RB (a); Superman & E-2 Superman 3.00
❑Annual 2, ca. 1983 O: Superwoman. 1: Superwoman. 3.00
❑Annual 3, ca. 1984; Doctor Sivana gains the Shazam! powers 3.00
❑Annual 4, ca. 1985 A: Superwoman. 3.00

DC COMICS PRESENTS: BATMAN
DC

❑1, Sep 2004 2.50

DC COMICS PRESENTS: GREEN LANTERN
DC

❑1, Sep 2004 2.50

DC COMICS PRESENTS: HAWKMAN
DC

❑1, Sep 2004 2.50

DC COMICS PRESENTS: MYSTERY IN SPACE
DC

❑1, Sep 2004 2.50

DC FIRST: BATGIRL/JOKER
DC

❑1, Jul 2002 3.50

DC FIRST: FLASH/SUPERMAN
DC

❑1, Jul 2002 3.50

DC FIRST: GREEN LANTERN/GREEN LANTERN
DC

❑1, Jul 2002 3.50

DC FIRST: SUPERMAN/LOBO
DC

❑1, Jul 2002 3.50

DC GRAPHIC NOVEL
DC

❑1; Star Raiders 5.95
❑2; Warlords 5.95
❑3; Medusa Chain 5.95
❑4; Hunger Dogs 5.95
❑5; Me and Joe Priest 5.95
❑6; Metalzoic 6.95
❑7; Space Clusters 5.95

DC/MARVEL: ALL ACCESS
DC

❑1, Dec 1996; A: Superman, Spider-Man, Venom. crossover with Marvel 2.95
❑2, Jan 1997; A: Jubilee, Robin, Two-Face, Scorpion. crossover with Marvel 2.95
❑3, Jan 1997; A: Jubilee, Robin, Batman, Doctor Strange, Scorpion, JLA, X-Men. crossover with Marvel 2.95
❑4, Feb 1997; A: JLA, X-Men, Doctor Strangefate, Amalgam universe. crossover with Marvel 2.95

DC 100 PAGE SUPER SPECTACULAR
DC

❑4, ca. 1971; Weird Mystery Tales; back cover pin-up 120.00
❑5, ca. 1971; BO, MD, RE (a); Love Stories; back cover pin-up 400.00
❑5-2; Replica edition; BO, MD, RE (a); Love Stories 7.00
❑6, ca. 1971; World's Greatest Super-Heroes; reprints JLA #21-22; wraparound cover 120.00
❑7, Dec 1971; really DC-7; a.k.a. Superman #245; back cover pin-up 50.00
❑8, Jan 1972; really DC-8; a.k.a. Batman #238; wraparound cover 65.00
❑9, Feb 1972; really DC-9; a.k.a. Our Army at War #242; Sgt. Rock, wraparound cover 65.00
❑10, Mar 1972; really DC-10; a.k.a. Adventure Comics #416; Supergirl; wraparound cover 45.00
❑11, Apr 1972; really DC-11; a.k.a. Flash #214; wraparound cover 45.00
❑12, May 1972; really DC-12; a.k.a. Superboy #185; wraparound cover 45.00
❑13, Jun 1972; really DC-13; a.k.a. Superman #252; wraparound cover 45.00
❑14, Feb 1973; really DC-14; Batman; wraparound cover 40.00

Teen sensation David Cassidy had his own Charlton comic book in the early 1970s.

© 1972 Charlton.

N-MINT

❑15, Mar 1973; really DC-15; Superboy; back cover pin-up 40.00
❑16, Apr 1973; really DC-16; Sgt. Rock; back cover cover gallery 30.00
❑17, Jun 1973; really DC-17; JLA; back cover cover gallery 30.00
❑18, Jul 1973; Superman's 35th anniversary; NC (c); MA, GK, CS (a); really DC-18; back cover cover gallery; Superman cast, Golden Age Atom, TNT, Hourman, Captain Triumph; Reprints from Superman #25, #97, & #162, Flash Comics #90, Atom #8, World's Finest Comics #5, Adventure #57, and Crack Comics #42 30.00
❑19, Aug 1973; JKu (c); RM (a); really DC-19; Tarzan; back cover pin-up 30.00
❑20, Sep 1973; O: Two-Face. really DC-20; Batman; back cover cover gallery 30.00
❑21, Oct 1973; really DC-21; Superboy; back cover cover gallery 30.00
❑22, Nov 1973; really DC-22; Flash; Super Specs become part of individual series beginning with Shazam! #8 10.00

DC ONE MILLION
DC

❑1, Nov 1998 2.00
❑1/Variant, Nov 1998; Signed edition 14.99
❑2, Nov 1998 2.00
❑3, Nov 1998 2.00
❑4, Nov 1998 2.00
❑Giant Size 1, Aug 1999; 80-Page Giant 4.95

DC SAMPLER
DC

❑1, Sep 1983; Promotional giveaway; CI (a); no cover price 1.50
❑2, Sep 1984; Promotional giveaway; FH, JL (a); No cover price; Atari Force, etc. 1.00
❑3; Promotional giveaway; FH (c); AMo (w); FH (a); No cover price; The Saga of the Swamp Thing, etc. 1.00

DC SCIENCE FICTION GRAPHIC NOVEL
DC

❑1; Hell on Earth 5.95
❑2; Nightwings 5.95
❑3 5.95
❑4; Merchants Venus 5.95
❑5 5.95
❑6; Magic Goes Away 5.95
❑7; Sand Kings 5.95

DC SILVER AGE CLASSICS ACTION COMICS
DC

❑252; reprints Action Comics #252 1.00

DC SILVER AGE CLASSICS ADVENTURE COMICS
DC

❑247; reprints Adventure Comics #247 1.00

DC SILVER AGE CLASSICS DETECTIVE COMICS
DC

❑225; reprints Detective Comics #225 1.00
❑327; reprints Detective Comics #327 1.00

N-MINT

DC SILVER AGE CLASSICS GREEN LANTERN
DC

❑76; reprints Green Lantern #76 .... 1.00

DC SILVER AGE CLASSICS HOUSE OF SECRETS
DC

❑92; reprints House of Secrets #92 .. 1.00

DC SILVER AGE CLASSICS SHOWCASE
DC

❑4; reprints Showcase #4 .... 1.00
❑22; reprints Showcase #22 .... 1.00

DC SILVER AGE CLASSICS SUGAR & SPIKE
DC

❑99; not a reprint; first publication of Sugar and Spike #99 .... 2.00

DC SILVER AGE CLASSICS THE BRAVE AND THE BOLD
DC

❑28; 1: JLA. 1: The Justice League of America. reprints The Brave and the Bold #28 .... 1.25

DC SPECIAL
DC

❑1, Dec 1968; CI (a); Flash, Batman, Adam Strange 30.00
❑2, Mar 1969; teen 20.00
❑3, Jun 1969; ATh, GK, JM (a); All female issue; Wonder Woman, Green Lantern/Star Sapphire, Green Arrow/ Black Canary, Supergirl/Black Flame; Reprints stories from Green Lantern (2nd series) #16 and Action #304 .. 20.00
❑4, Sep 1969; JK (a); Partial reprint from Tales of the Unexpected #16 . 20.00
❑5, Dec 1969 .... 20.00
❑6, Mar 1970 .... 20.00
❑7, Jun 1970; Strange Sports 20.00
❑8, Sep 1970; Wanted 20.00
❑9, Dec 1970 .... 20.00
❑10, Feb 1971 .... 20.00
❑11, Apr 1971; Monsters 20.00
❑12, Jun 1971; JKu, RH, IN (a); Viking Prince 20.00
❑13, Aug 1971; Strange Sports 20.00
❑14, Oct 1971; Giant-size; Wanted: The World's Most Dangerous Villains .. 20.00
❑15, Dec 1971; Giant-size; O: Woozy Winks. O: Plastic Man (Golden Age). Plastic Man reprints 25.00
❑16, Spr 1975; CI, RA (a); Gorillas 10.00
❑17, Sum 1975 .... 10.00
❑18, Nov 1975; Earth-Shaking Stories 10.00
❑19, Jan 1976 .... 10.00
❑20, Mar 1976; Green Lantern 10.00
❑21, May 1976; Monsters, War That Time Forgot 10.00
❑22, Jul 1976; Three Musketeers, Robin Hood 10.00
❑23, Sep 1976; Three Musketeers, Robin Hood 10.00
❑24, Oct 1976; Robin Hood, Viking Prince 10.00
❑25, Dec 1976; Robin Hood, Viking Prince 10.00
❑26, Feb 1977; Enemy Ace 10.00
❑27, Apr 1977; Captain Comet 10.00
❑28, Jun 1977; Batman; new Legion of Super-Heroes story 10.00
❑29, Sep 1977 BL, JSa (a); O: Justice Society of America (Secret Origin). 10.00

DC SPECIAL BLUE RIBBON DIGEST
DC

❑1, Apr 1980; Legion of Super Heroes 5.00
❑2, Jun 1980; Flash 4.00
❑3, Aug 1980; Justice Society 4.00
❑4, Oct 1980; Green Lantern 4.00
❑5, Dec 1980; Secret Origins 4.00
❑6, Jan 1981; AA, TD, JA (a); House of Mystery 3.00
❑7, Mar 1981; Flying Tigers, Haunted Tank, War That Time Forgot, Enemy Ace 3.00
❑8, Apr 1981; Legion 3.00
❑9, May 1981; The Atom 3.00
❑10, Jun 1981; Warlord 3.00
❑11, Jul 1981; Justice League, Justice Society, Seven Soldiers 3.00
❑12, Aug 1981; Haunted Tank 3.00
❑13, Sep 1981; Strange Sports 3.00
❑14, Oct 1981; Science Fiction 3.00
❑15, Nov 1981; Superboy, Green Lantern, Batman 3.00
❑16, Dec 1981; Green Lantern/Green Arrow 3.00
❑17, Jan 1982; Mystery 3.00
❑18, Feb 1982; Sgt. Rock 4.00
❑19, Mar 1982; Reprints My Greatest Adventure #80 and Doom Patrol #86, 90 and 91 .... 3.00
❑20, Apr 1982; Mystery 7.00
❑21, May 1982; JK (a); War 3.00
❑22, Jun 1982; Secret Origins 3.00
❑23, Jul 1982; Green Arrow 3.00

DC SPECIAL SERIES
DC

❑1, Sep 1977; FMc, MN, DD, JR, IN (a); 5-Star Super-Hero Spectacular 6.00
❑2, Sep 1977; BWr (a); Swamp Thing reprint; Swamp Thing 4.00
❑3, Oct 1977; JK (a); Sgt. Rock 4.00
❑4, Oct 1977; Unexpected Annual 4.00
❑5, Nov 1977; A: Superman. A: Luthor. A: Brainiac. a.k.a. Superman Spectacular; first DC Dollar Comic; Superman, Luthor 4.00
❑6, Nov 1977; JLA 3.00
❑7, Dec 1977; Ghosts 3.00
❑8, Feb 1978; DG (a); Brave & Bold .. 3.00
❑9, Mar 1978; SD, RH (a); Wonder Woman vs. Hitler 8.00
❑10, Apr 1978; MN (a); Super-Heroes 3.00
❑11, May 1978; MA, WW, KS, IN (a); A: Johnny Quick. Flash; a.k.a. Flash Spectacular 3.00
❑12, Jun 1978; Secrets of Haunted House 3.00
❑13, Jul 1978; Sgt. Rock 3.00
❑14, Jul 1978; Swamp Thing reprint . 3.00
❑15, Aug 1978; Batman, Ra's al Ghul 3.00
❑16, Sep 1978 RH (a); D: Jonah Hex. 14.00
❑17, Sep 1979; Swamp Thing reprint 2.00
❑18, Oct 1979; digest Sgt. Rock 2.00
❑19, Oct 1979; digest; O: Wonder Woman. Secret Origins 2.50
❑20, Jan 1980; BWr (a); Swamp Thing reprint; a.k.a. Original Swamp Thing Saga 2.50
❑21, Mar 1980; FM (a); Batman; Legion; 1st Frank Miller Batman 14.00
❑22, Sep 1980; G.I. Combat 3.00
❑23, Feb 1981; digest; Flash 3.00
❑24, Feb 1981; Flash 3.00
❑25, Sum 1981; treasury-sized; Superman II movie adaptation 3.00
❑26, Sum 1981; treasury-sized; RA, RT (a); Superman's Fortress 3.00
❑27, Dec 1981; treasury-sized; Batman vs. The Incredible Hulk 14.00

DC SPOTLIGHT
DC

❑1, Sep 1985 JL (c) 1.00

DC SUPER-STARS
DC

❑1, Mar 1976; Double-size; NC (a); Teen Titans reprint 6.00
❑2, Apr 1976; Double-size; Space 3.00
❑3, May 1976; CS (a); A: Legion of Super-Heroes. Superman; Reprints Legion of Super-Heroes story from Adventure Comics #354 and #355 . 4.00
❑4, Jun 1976 .... 2.00
❑5, Jul 1976; Flash; Bicentennial #33 2.00
❑6, Aug 1976 .... 2.00
❑7, Sep 1976 .... 2.00
❑8, Oct 1976; Reprints Showcase #15 4.00
❑9, Nov 1976; Man Behind the Gun ... 2.00
❑10, Dec 1976; A: Joker. Sports stories and Batman story 5.00
❑11, Jan 1977 .... 2.00
❑12, Feb 1977 .... 2.00
❑13, Mar 1977 SA (a) 2.00
❑14, May 1977 O: Doctor Light. O: Brainiac. O: Two-Face. O: Gorilla Grodd. O: Shark. 4.00
❑15, Jul 1977; war stories 4.00
❑16, Sep 1977 DN, BL (a); 1: Star Hunters. 3.00
❑17, Nov 1977; BL, JSa (w); BL, MGr, JSa (a); O: Green Arrow. O: The Huntress II (Helena Wayne). 1: The Huntress II (Helena Wayne). Secret Origins; Revealed that Earth-2 Batman had married Earth-2 Catwoman; Legion story 16.00
❑18, Jan 1978; Deadman, Phantom Stranger 2.00

DC: THE NEW FRONTIER
DC

❑1, Jan 2004 .... 6.95
❑2, Apr 2004 .... 6.95
❑3, May 2004 .... 6.95
❑4, Jul 2004 .... 6.95
❑5, Sep 2004 .... 6.95

DC 2000
DC

❑1 2000 .... 6.95
❑2 2000 .... 6.95

DCU HEROES SECRET FILES
DC

❑1, Feb 1999 .... 4.95

DC UNIVERSE CHRISTMAS, A
DC

❑1 .... 19.95

DC UNIVERSE HOLIDAY BASH
DC

❑1, Jan 1997; Preview edition; JA, MWa (w); SB, KN (a); Holiday special for 1996 season 3.95
❑2, Jan 1998; prestige format; Holiday special for 1997 season 4.95
❑3, Jan 1999; Signed edition; Holiday special for 1998 season 4.95

DC UNIVERSE: TRINITY
DC

❑1, Aug 1993; foil cover 2.95
❑2, Sep 1993; foil cover 2.95

DCU VILLAINS SECRET FILES
DC

❑1, Apr 1999 .... 4.95

D-DAY
AVALON

❑1 .... 2.95

DEAD, THE
ARROW

❑1 .... 2.95
❑1/A; alternate cover 2.95
❑2 .... 2.95
❑3 .... 2.95

DEAD, THE (2ND SERIES)
ARROW

❑1 .... 2.95

DEAD AIR
SLAVE LABOR

❑1 .... 5.95

DEADBEATS
CLAYPOOL

❑1, Jun 1992 RHo (w); RHo (a) 4.00
❑2, Jul 1992 RHo (w); RHo (a) 3.00
❑3, Sep 1992 RHo (w); RHo (a) 3.00
❑4, Oct 1992 RHo (w); RHo (a) 3.00
❑5, Sep 1993 RHo (w); RHo (a) 3.00
❑6, Mar 1994 RHo (w); RHo (a) 2.50
❑7, Jun 1994 RHo (w); RHo (a) 2.50
❑8, Aug 1994 RHo (w); RHo (a) 2.50
❑9, Nov 1994 .... 2.50

N-MINT

❑10, Jan 1995 2.50
❑11, Mar 1995 2.50
❑12, May 1995 2.50
❑13, Jul 1995 2.50
❑14, Sep 1995 2.50
❑15, Nov 1995 2.50
❑16, Jan 1996 2.50
❑17, Mar 1996 2.50
❑18, May 1996 2.50
❑19, Jul 1996 2.50
❑20, Sep 1996 2.50
❑21, Nov 1996 2.50
❑22, Jan 1997 2.50
❑23, Mar 1997 2.50
❑24, May 1997 2.50
❑25, Jul 1997 2.50
❑26, Sep 1997 RHo (w); 2.50
❑27, Nov 1997 RHo (w); 2.50
❑28, Jan 1998 RHo (w); RHo (a) 2.50
❑29, Mar 1998 2.50
❑30, May 1998 2.50
❑31, Jul 1998 2.50
❑32, Oct 1998 2.50
❑33, Dec 1998 2.50
❑34, Feb 1999 2.50
❑35, Apr 1999 2.50
❑36, Jun 1999 2.50
❑37, Aug 1999 2.50
❑38, Oct 1999 2.50
❑39, Dec 1999 2.50
❑40, Feb 2000 2.50
❑41, Apr 2000 2.50
❑42, Jun 2000 2.50
❑43, Aug 2000 RHo (w); 2.50
❑44, Oct 2000 2.50
❑45, Dec 2000 2.50
❑46, Feb 2001 2.50
❑47, Apr 2001 2.50
❑48, Jun 2001 2.50
❑49, Aug 2001 2.50
❑50, Oct 2001 2.50
❑51, Dec 2001 2.50
❑52, Feb 2002 2.50
❑53, Apr 2002 2.50
❑54, Jun 2002 2.50
❑55, Aug 2002 2.50
❑56, Oct 2002 2.50
❑57, Dec 2002 2.50
❑58, Feb 2003 2.50
❑59, Apr 2003 2.50

DEAD CLOWN
MALIBU

❑1, Oct 1996 2.50
❑2 2.50
❑3, Feb 1994 2.50

DEAD CORPS(E)
DC / HELIX

❑1, Sep 1998 2.50
❑2, Oct 1998 2.50
❑3, Nov 1998 2.50
❑4, Dec 1998 2.50

DEADENDERS
DC / VERTIGO

❑1, Mar 2000 2.50
❑2, Apr 2000 2.50
❑3, May 2000 2.50
❑4, Jun 2000 2.50
❑5, Jul 2000 2.50
❑6, Aug 2000 2.50
❑7, Sep 2000 2.50
❑8, Oct 2000 2.50
❑9, Nov 2000 2.50
❑10, Dec 2000 2.50
❑11, Jan 2001 2.50
❑12, Feb 2001 2.50
❑13, Mar 2001 2.50
❑14, Apr 2001 2.50
❑15, May 2001 2.50
❑16, Jun 2001 2.50

N-MINT

DEADFACE
HARRIER

❑1, ca. 1987 5.00
❑2, ca. 1987 4.00
❑3, ca. 1987 3.00
❑4, ca. 1987 3.00
❑5, ca. 1987 3.00
❑6, ca. 1987 2.50
❑7, ca. 1987 2.50
❑8, ca. 1987 2.50

DEADFACE: DOING THE ISLANDS WITH BACCHUS
DARK HORSE

❑1, Jul 1991, b&w 2.95
❑2, Aug 1991, b&w 2.95
❑3, Sep 1991, b&w 2.95

DEADFACE: EARTH, WATER, AIR, AND FIRE
DARK HORSE

❑1 1992, b&w 2.50
❑2 1992, b&w 2.50
❑3 1992, b&w 2.50
❑4 1992, b&w 2.50

DEAD FOLKS (LANSDALES & TRUMAN'S)
AVATAR

❑1, Mar 2003 3.50
❑1/A, Mar 2003; Wrap Cover 3.95
❑2, May 2003 3.50
❑2/A, May 2003; Wrap Cover 3.95
❑3, Jul 2003 3.50

DEADFORCE (ANTARCTIC)
ANTARCTIC

❑1, May 1999, b&w 2.50
❑2, Jun 1999 2.50
❑Ashcan 1 1.00

DEADFORCE (STUDIONOIR)
STUDIO NOIR

❑1, Jul 1996, b&w 2.50

DEAD GRRRL: DEAD AT 21
BONEYARD

❑1, Apr 1998 2.95

DEAD IN THE WEST
DARK HORSE

❑1, Oct 1993, b&w 3.95
❑2, Mar 1994, b&w 3.95

DEAD KID ADVENTURES
KNIGHT

❑1, Jul 1998 2.95

DEAD KILLER
CALIBER

❑1 2.95

DEAD KING: BURNT
CHAOS

❑1, May 1998 2.95
❑2, Jun 1998 2.95
❑3, Jul 1998 2.95
❑4, Aug 1998 2.95

DEADLINE (MARVEL)
MARVEL

❑1, Jun 2002 2.99
❑2, Jul 2002 2.99
❑3, Aug 2002 2.99
❑4, Sep 2002 2.99

DEADLINE USA
DARK HORSE

❑1, Sep 1991, b&w 3.95
❑2, b&w 3.95
❑3, b&w 3.95
❑4 3.95
❑5 A: Gwar. 3.95
❑6 3.95
❑7 3.95
❑8 3.95

DEADLY DUO, THE
IMAGE

❑1, Nov 1994 2.50

DC 100 Page Super Spectacular #5, which focused on romance stories, was reprinted in 2001.

© 1971 National Periodical Publications Inc. (DC).

N-MINT

❑2, Dec 1994 2.50
❑3, Jan 1995 2.50

DEADLY DUO, THE (2ND SERIES)
IMAGE

❑1, Jul 1995 2.50
❑2, Aug 1995 2.50
❑3, Sep 1995 2.50
❑4, Oct 1995 2.50

DEADLY FOES OF SPIDER-MAN
MARVEL

❑1, May 1991; AM, KGa (a); Punisher, Rhino, Kingpin, others appear 1.50
❑2, Jun 1991 AM, KGa (a) 1.50
❑3, Jul 1991 AM (a) 1.50
❑4, Aug 1991 AM (a) 1.50

DEADLY HANDS OF KUNG FU
MARVEL

❑1, Apr 1974 JSn (w); 16.00
❑2, Jun 1974 8.00
❑3, Aug 1974 6.00
❑4, Sep 1974 6.00
❑5, Oct 1974 6.00
❑6, Nov 1974 5.00
❑7, Dec 1974 5.00
❑8, Jan 1975 5.00
❑9, Feb 1975 5.00
❑10, Mar 1975 5.00
❑11, Apr 1975 4.00
❑12, May 1975 4.00
❑13, Jun 1975 4.00
❑14, Jul 1975 4.00
❑15, Aug 1975 4.00
❑16, Sep 1975 4.00
❑17, Oct 1975 4.00
❑18, Nov 1975 4.00
❑19, Dec 1975 4.00
❑20, Jan 1976 4.00
❑21, Feb 1976 3.00
❑22, Mar 1976 3.00
❑23, Apr 1976 3.00
❑24, May 1976 3.00
❑25, Jun 1976 3.00
❑26, Jul 1976 3.00
❑27, Aug 1976 3.00
❑28, Sep 1976 3.00
❑29, Oct 1976 3.00
❑30, Nov 1976 3.00
❑31, Dec 1976 3.00
❑32, Jan 1977 3.00
❑33, Feb 1977 3.00
❑Special 1 1974 3.00

DEADMAN (1ST SERIES)
DC

❑1, May 1985 CI, NA (a) 2.50
❑2, Jun 1985 NA (a) 2.50
❑3, Jul 1985 NA (a) 2.50
❑4, Aug 1985 NA (a) 2.50
❑5, Sep 1985 NA (a) 2.50
❑6, Oct 1985 NA (a) 2.50
❑7, Nov 1985 NA (a) 2.50

DEADMAN (2ND SERIES)
DC

❑1, Mar 1986 JL (a) 2.00
❑2, Apr 1986 JL (a) 2.00
❑3, May 1986 JL (a) 2.00
❑4, Jun 1986 JL (a) 2.00

N-MINT

DEADMAN (3RD SERIES)
DC

❑1, Feb 2002 ... 2.50
❑2, Mar 2002 ... 2.50
❑3, Apr 2002 ... 2.50
❑4, May 2002 ... 2.50
❑5, Jun 2002 ... 2.50
❑6, Jul 2002 ... 2.50
❑7, Aug 2002 ... 2.50
❑8, Sep 2002 ... 2.50
❑9, Oct 2002 ... 2.50

DEADMAN: DEAD AGAIN
DC

❑1, Oct 2001 ... 2.50
❑2, Oct 2001 ... 2.50
❑3, Oct 2001 ... 2.50
❑4, Oct 2001 ... 2.50
❑5, Oct 2001 ... 2.50

DEADMAN: EXORCISM
DC

❑1; prestige format ... 4.95
❑2; prestige format ... 4.95

DEADMAN: LOVE AFTER DEATH
DC

❑1, Dec 1989; prestige format ... 3.95
❑2, Jan 1990; prestige format ... 3.95

DEAD OF NIGHT
MARVEL

❑1, Dec 1973 JSt (w); JSt (a) ... 35.00
❑2, Feb 1974 ... 12.00
❑3, Apr 1974 ... 12.00
❑4, Jun 1974 ... 12.00
❑5, Aug 1974 ... 12.00
❑6, Oct 1974 ... 12.00
❑7, Dec 1974 ... 12.00
❑8, Feb 1975 ... 12.00
❑9, Apr 1975 ... 12.00
❑10, Jun 1975 ... 12.00
❑11, Aug 1975 1: Scarecrow. ... 16.00

DEAD OR ALIVE: A CYBERPUNK WESTERN
DARK HORSE

❑1, Apr 1998 ... 2.50
❑2, May 1998 ... 2.50
❑3, Jun 1998 ... 2.50
❑4, Jul 1998 ... 2.50

DEADPAN
ICHOR

❑1, Mar 1995 ... 3.95

DEADPOOL
MARVEL

❑-1, Jul 1997; O: Deadpool. Flashback ... 2.25
❑0; Included as giveaway with Wizard Magazine ... 1.50
❑1, Jan 1997; wraparound cover ... 4.00
❑2, Feb 1997 ... 3.00
❑3, Mar 1997 A: Siryn. ... 2.50
❑4, Apr 1997 A: Hulk. V: Hulk. ... 2.50
❑5, May 1997 ... 2.00
❑6, Jun 1997 ... 2.00
❑7, Aug 1997; gatefold summary ... 2.00
❑8, Sep 1997; gatefold summary ... 2.00
❑9, Oct 1997; gatefold summary ... 2.00
❑10, Nov 1997; gatefold summary; A: Great Lakes Avengers. back-up feature on making of Deadpool #11 ... 2.00
❑11, Dec 1997; gatefold summary; A: Great Lakes Avengers. Deadpool and Blind Al interact with Amazing Spider-Man #47 ... 2.00
❑12, Jan 1998; gatefold summary; parody of Faces of the DC Universe month ... 2.00
❑13, Feb 1998; gatefold summary ... 2.00
❑14, Mar 1998; gatefold summary ... 2.00
❑15, Apr 1998; gatefold summary ... 2.00
❑16, May 1998; gatefold summary ... 2.00
❑17, Jun 1998; gatefold summary ... 2.00
❑18, Jul 1998; gatefold summary V: Ajax. ... 2.00
❑19, Aug 1998; gatefold summary V: Ajax. ... 2.00
❑20, Sep 1998; gatefold summary ... 2.00
❑21, Oct 1998; gatefold summary ... 2.00
❑22, Nov 1998; gatefold summary A: Cable. ... 2.00
❑23, Dec 1998; gatefold summary; wraparound cover ... 2.99
❑24, Jan 1999; gatefold summary A: Tiamat. A: Cosmic Messiah. ... 1.99
❑25, Feb 1999 A: Tiamat. A: Captain America. ... 2.99
❑26, Mar 1999 ... 1.99
❑27, Apr 1999 A: Wolverine. V: Doc Bong. ... 1.99
❑28, May 1999 ... 1.99
❑29, Jun 1999 ... 1.99
❑30, Jul 1999 ... 1.99
❑31, Aug 1999 ... 1.99
❑32, Sep 1999 ... 1.99
❑33, Oct 1999 ... 1.99
❑34, Nov 1999 ... 1.99
❑35, Dec 1999 ... 2.25
❑36, Jan 2000 ... 2.25
❑37, Feb 2000 ... 2.25
❑38, Mar 2000 ... 2.25
❑39, Apr 2000 ... 2.25
❑40, May 2000 ... 2.25
❑41, Jun 2000 ... 2.25
❑42, Jul 2000 ... 2.25
❑43, Aug 2000 ... 2.25
❑44, Sep 2000 ... 2.25
❑45, Oct 2000 ... 2.25
❑46, Nov 2000 ... 2.25
❑47, Dec 2000 ... 2.25
❑48, Jan 2001 ... 2.25
❑49, Feb 2001 ... 2.25
❑50, Mar 2001 ... 2.25
❑51, Apr 2001; A: Kid Deadpool. Detective Comics #39 cover homage ... 2.25
❑52, May 2001 ... 2.25
❑53, Jun 2001 ... 2.25
❑54, Jul 2001 ... 2.25
❑55, Aug 2001 ... 2.25
❑56, Sep 2001 ... 2.25
❑57, Oct 2001 ... 2.25
❑58, Nov 2001 ... 2.25
❑59, Dec 2001 ... 2.25
❑60, Jan 2002 ... 2.25
❑61, Feb 2002 ... 2.25
❑62, Mar 2002 ... 2.25
❑63, Apr 2002 ... 2.25
❑64, May 2002 ... 2.25
❑65, Jun 2002 ... 2.25
❑66, Jul 2002 ... 2.25
❑67, Aug 2002 ... 2.25
❑68, Sep 2002 ... 2.25
❑69, Oct 2002 ... 2.25
❑Annual 1998, ca. 1988; gatefold summary; Deadpool/Death '98; wraparound cover ... 2.99

DEADPOOL (LTD. SERIES)
MARVEL

❑1, Aug 1994 MWa (w); ... 3.00
❑2, Sep 1994 MWa (w); ... 2.50
❑3, Oct 1994 MWa (w); ... 2.50
❑4, Nov 1994 MWa (w); ... 2.50

DEADPOOL TEAM-UP
MARVEL

❑1, Dec 1998; gatefold summary; Secret Wars II tie-in ... 2.99

DEADPOOL: THE CIRCLE CHASE
MARVEL

❑1, Aug 1993; Embossed cover ... 2.50
❑2, Sep 1993 ... 2.00
❑3, Oct 1993 ... 2.00
❑4, Nov 1993 ... 2.00

DEADSHOT
DC

❑1, Nov 1988 O: Deadshot. ... 1.50
❑2, Dec 1988 ... 1.50
❑3, Win 1988 ... 1.50
❑4, Hol 1988 ... 1.50

DEADTIME STORIES
NEW COMICS

❑1, Oct 1987, b&w ... 1.75

DEADWALKERS
AIRCEL

❑1/A, Jan 1991; "gross" cover ... 2.50
❑1/B, Jan 1991; "not-so-gross" cover ... 2.50
❑2, Feb 1991 ... 2.50
❑3, Mar 1991 ... 2.50
❑4, Apr 1991 ... 2.50

DEADWORLD (VOL. 1)
ARROW

❑1, ca. 1986, b&w; Arrow publishes ... 3.00
❑2 ... 2.50
❑3 ... 2.50
❑4 ... 2.50
❑5 ... 2.50
❑6 ... 2.50
❑7 ... 2.50
❑8 ... 2.50
❑9 ... 2.50
❑10, b&w; Caliber begins as publisher ... 2.50
❑11, b&w ... 2.50
❑12, b&w ... 2.50
❑13, b&w ... 2.50
❑14, b&w ... 2.50
❑15, b&w ... 2.50
❑16, b&w ... 2.50
❑17, b&w ... 2.50
❑18, b&w ... 2.50
❑19, b&w ... 2.50
❑20, b&w ... 2.50
❑21, b&w ... 2.50
❑22, b&w ... 2.50
❑23, b&w ... 2.50
❑24, b&w ... 2.50
❑25, b&w ... 2.50
❑26, b&w ... 2.50

DEADWORLD (VOL. 2)
CALIBER

❑1, ca. 1993, b&w; Giant-size ... 3.50
❑2, b&w ... 3.00
❑3, b&w ... 3.00
❑4, b&w ... 3.00
❑5, b&w ... 3.00
❑6, b&w ... 3.00
❑7, b&w ... 2.95
❑8, b&w ... 2.95
❑9, b&w ... 2.95
❑10, b&w ... 2.95
❑11, b&w ... 2.95
❑12, b&w ... 2.95
❑13, b&w ... 2.95
❑14, b&w ... 2.95
❑15, b&w ... 2.95

DEADWORLD ARCHIVES
CALIBER

❑1, b&w ... 2.50
❑2, b&w ... 2.50
❑3, b&w ... 2.50

DEADWORLD: BITS AND PIECES
CALIBER

❑1, b&w ... 2.95

DEADWORLD CHRONICLES: PLAGUE
CALIBER

❑1 ... 2.95

DEADWORLD: DAEMONSTORM
CALIBER

❑1 ... 3.95

DEADWORLD: NECROPOLIS
CALIBER

❑1 ... 3.95

DEADWORLD: TO KILL A KING
CALIBER

❑1; Sinergy as flip-book ... 2.95
❑1/Ltd.; limited edition ... 5.95

N-MINT

❑2 .... 2.95
❑3 .... 2.95

DEAR JULIA
BLACK EYE

❑1 .... 3.50
❑2 .... 3.50
❑3, Feb 1997 .... 3.50
❑4 .... 3.50

DEATH3
MARVEL

❑1, Sep 1993; Embossed cover 2.95
❑2, Oct 1993 .... 1.75
❑3, Nov 1993 .... 1.75
❑4, Dec 1993 .... 1.75

DEATH & CANDY
FANTAGRAPHICS

❑1, Win 1999 .... 3.95

DEATH & TAXES: THE REAL COSTS OF LIVING
PARODY

❑1, b&w 2.50

DEATHANGEL
LIGHTNING

❑1/A, Dec 1997 .... 2.95
❑1/B, Dec 1997; alternate cover 2.95

DEATH: AT DEATH'S DOOR
DC / VERTIGO

❑1, ca. 2003 .... 9.95

DEATHBLOW
IMAGE

❑0, Aug 1996 JLee (a) 2.50
❑1, Apr 1993; JLee (w); JLee (a); 1: Cybernary. Black varnish cover; Cybernary #1 as flip-book 3.00
❑2, Aug 1993; JLee (w); JLee (a); Cybernary #2 as flip-book 2.50
❑3, Feb 1994; 1: Cisco. Cybernary #3 as flip-book 3.00
❑4, Apr 1994 .... 2.00
❑5, May 1994 .... 2.00
❑5/A, May 1994; Variant cover edition; alternate cover 2.00
❑6, Jun 1994 .... 1.95
❑7, Jul 1994 .... 1.95
❑8, Aug 1994 .... 1.95
❑9, Oct 1994 .... 1.95
❑10, Nov 1994; wraparound cover 2.50
❑11, Dec 1994 .... 2.50
❑12, Jan 1995 .... 2.50
❑13, Feb 1995 .... 2.50
❑14, Mar 1995 .... 2.50
❑15, Apr 1995 .... 2.50
❑16, May 1995; bound-in trading cards 1.95
❑16/Variant, May 1995 .... 2.50
❑17, Jun 1995 .... 2.50
❑17/A, Jun 1995; Chicago Comicon limited edition 2.50
❑18, Jul 1995 .... 2.50
❑19, Sep 1995 .... 2.50
❑20, Oct 1995 .... 2.50
❑21, Nov 1995 A: Gen13. .... 2.50
❑22, Dec 1995 .... 2.50
❑23, Jan 1996 .... 2.50
❑24, Feb 1996 A: Grifter. 2.50
❑25, Mar 1996 .... 2.50
❑26, Mar 1996 .... 2.50
❑27, Apr 1996 .... 2.50
❑28, Jul 1996 .... 2.50
❑28/Variant, Jul 1996; alternate cover 2.50
❑29, Aug 1996 .... 2.50

DEATHBLOW: BYBLOWS
WILDSTORM

❑1, Nov 1999 .... 2.95
❑2, Dec 1999 .... 2.95
❑3, Jan 2000 .... 2.95

DEATHBLOW/WOLVERINE
IMAGE

❑1, Sep 1996; crossover with Marvel 2.50
❑2, Feb 1997; crossover with Marvel 2.50

N-MINT

DEATH BY CHOCOLATE
SLEEPING GIANT

❑1, Mar 1996, b&w 2.50

DEATH BY CHOCOLATE: SIR GEOFFREY AND THE CHOCOLATE CAR
SLEEPING GIANT

❑1, b&w 2.50

DEATH BY CHOCOLATE: THE METABOLATORS
SLEEPING GIANT

❑1, b&w 2.50

DEATH CRAZED TEENAGE SUPERHEROES
ARF! ARF!

❑1 .... 1.50
❑2 .... 1.50

DEATH DEALER
VEROTIK

❑1, Jul 1995 FF (c); FF (a) 6.00
❑2, May 1996 .... 6.95
❑3, Apr 1997 .... 6.95
❑4, Jul 1997 .... 6.95

DEATH DREAMS OF DRACULA
APPLE

❑1, b&w 2.50
❑2, b&w 2.50
❑3, b&w 2.50
❑4, b&w 2.50

DEATH GALLERY, A
DC / VERTIGO

❑1; portraits 3.00

DEATH HAWK
ADVENTURE

❑1, b&w 1.95
❑2, b&w 1.95
❑3, b&w 1.95

DEATH HUNT
ETERNITY

❑1, b&w 1.95

DEATHLOK (1ST SERIES)
MARVEL

❑1, Jul 1990 .... 3.95
❑2, Aug 1990 .... 3.95
❑3, Sep 1990 .... 3.95
❑4, Oct 1990 .... 3.95

DEATHLOK (2ND SERIES)
MARVEL

❑1, Jul 1991; Silver ink cover 2.50
❑2, Aug 1991 A: Forge. 2.00
❑3, Sep 1991 V: Doctor Doom. 2.00
❑4, Oct 1991 .... 2.00
❑5, Nov 1991; X-Men & Fantastic Four crossover 2.00
❑6, Dec 1991; Punisher crossover 2.00
❑7, Jan 1992; Punisher crossover 2.00
❑8, Feb 1992; Punisher crossover 2.00
❑9, Mar 1992 A: Ghost Rider. V: Ghost Rider. 2.00
❑10, Apr 1992 A: Ghost Rider. V: Ghost Rider. 2.00
❑11, May 1992 1: High-Tech. 1.75
❑12, Jun 1992 .... 1.75
❑13, Jul 1992 .... 1.75
❑14, Aug 1992 O: Deathlok III (Luther Manning). 1.75
❑15, Sep 1992 .... 1.75
❑16, Oct 1992 .... 1.75
❑17, Nov 1992 .... 1.75
❑18, Dec 1992 .... 1.75
❑19, Jan 1993; O: Siege. 1: Siege. foil cover 2.25
❑20, Feb 1993 .... 1.75
❑21, Mar 1993 .... 1.75
❑22, Apr 1993 .... 1.75
❑23, May 1993 .... 1.75
❑24, Jun 1993 .... 1.75
❑25, Jul 1993; A: Black Panther. foil cover 1.75

Many issues of *DC Special Series* can also be found under their individual title names, including #5, which is also known as the 1977 *Superman Spectacular*, DC's first Dollar Comic.

© 1977 National Periodical Publications Inc. (DC).

N-MINT

❑26, Aug 1993 A: Hobgoblin. 1.75
❑27, Sep 1993 .... 1.75
❑28, Oct 1993; A: Timestream. A: Goddess. Infinity Crusade crossover 1.75
❑29, Nov 1993 .... 1.75
❑30, Dec 1993 .... 1.75
❑31, Jan 1994 .... 1.75
❑32, Feb 1994 .... 1.75
❑33, Mar 1994 .... 1.75
❑34, Apr 1994 .... 1.75
❑Annual 1, ca. 1992 .... 2.50
❑Annual 2, ca. 1993; O: Tracer. 1: Tracer. Polybagged 2.95
❑Special 1, May 1991; reprints Deathlok (1st series) #1 .... 2.00
❑Special 2, Jun 1991; reprints Deathlok (1st series) #2 .... 2.00
❑Special 3, Jun 1991; reprints Deathlok (1st series) #3 .... 2.00
❑Special 4, Jun 1991; reprints Deathlok (1st series) #4 .... 2.00

DEATHLOK (3RD SERIES)
MARVEL

❑1, Sep 1999 .... 2.00
❑2, Oct 1999 .... 1.99
❑3, Nov 1999 .... 1.99
❑4, Nov 1999 .... 1.99
❑5, Dec 1999 .... 1.99

DEATHMARK
LIGHTNING

❑1, Dec 1994, b&w 2.95

DEATHMASK
FUTURE

❑1, Apr 2003 .... 2.99
❑2, Jun 2003 .... 2.99
❑3, Jul 2003 .... 2.99

DEATHMATE
IMAGE / VALIANT

❑1, Sep 1993; BL (w); crossover; prologue; silver cover 2.95
❑1/Gold, Sep 1993; Gold cover (limited promotional edition); BL (w); Gold cover (limited promotional edition); Prologue 4.00
❑2, Sep 1993; JLee (a); 1: Fairchild. 1: Burn-Out. 1: Gen13 (full). 1: Freefall. Black 3.00
❑2/Gold, Sep 1993; Gold edition 1: Gen13 (full). 6.00
❑3, Sep 1993; Yellow; cover says Oct, indicia says Sep 4.95
❑3/Gold, Sep 1993; Gold edition; Yellow 6.00
❑4, Oct 1993; Blue 4.95
❑4/Gold, Oct 1993; Gold edition; Blue 6.00
❑5, Nov 1993; Red 4.95
❑5/Gold, Nov 1993; Gold edition; Red 6.00
❑6, Feb 1994; BL (w); Epilogue; silver cover 2.95
❑6/Gold, Feb 1994; Gold edition 4.00
❑Ashcan 1, Aug 1993; ashcan edition 1.00

DEATH METAL
MARVEL

❑1, Jan 1994 .... 1.95
❑2, Feb 1994 .... 1.95
❑3, Mar 1994 .... 1.95
❑4, Apr 1994 .... 1.95

N-MINT

DEATH METAL VS. GENETIX
MARVEL

❑1, Dec 1993 ... 2.95
❑2, Jan 1994 ... 2.95

DEATH OF ANGEL GIRL, THE
ANGEL

❑1 ... 2.95

DEATH OF ANTISOCIALMAN, THE
NOT AVAILABLE

❑1 ... 0.50
❑2 ... 0.50
❑3 ... 0.50
❑4 ... 0.50
❑5 ... 0.50
❑6 ... 0.50
❑7 ... 0.50
❑8 ... 0.50
❑9 ... 0.50
❑10 ... 0.50

DEATH OF LADY VAMPRÉ
BLACKOUT

❑1 ... 2.95

DEATH OF STUPIDMAN, THE
PARODY

❑1 ... 3.50

DEATH OF SUPERBABE
SPOOF

❑1, b&w ... 3.95

DEATH OF VAMPIRELLA
HARRIS

❑1, Feb 1997; Memorial Edition; Chromium cover; Green logo ... 15.00
❑1/Variant, Feb 1997; Holofoil chromium edition; 750 copies printed; Yellow logo ... 15.00

DEATH RACE 2020
COSMIC

❑1, Apr 1995; sequel to Corman film ... 2.50
❑2, May 1995 ... 2.50
❑5, Aug 1995 ... 2.50

DEATH RATTLE (VOL. 2)
KITCHEN SINK

❑1, Oct 1985 ... 2.00
❑2, Dec 1985 ... 2.00
❑3, Feb 1986 ... 2.00
❑4 ... 2.00
❑5 ... 2.00
❑6, b&w; Black and white; Listed as #5 in indicia ... 2.00
❑7, b&w ... 2.00
❑8, Dec 1986 ... 2.00
❑9, Jan 1987 ... 2.00
❑10, Mar 1987 ... 2.00
❑11, May 1987 ... 2.00
❑12, Jul 1987 ... 2.00
❑13, Nov 1987 ... 2.00
❑14, Jan 1988 ... 2.00
❑15, Mar 1988 ... 2.00
❑16, May 1988 ... 2.00
❑17, Jul 1988 ... 2.00
❑18, Oct 1988 ... 2.00

DEATH RATTLE (VOL. 3)
KITCHEN SINK

❑1, Oct 1995, b&w ... 2.95
❑2, Dec 1995, b&w ... 2.95
❑3, Feb 1996 ... 2.95
❑4, Apr 1996 ... 2.95
❑5, Jun 1996, b&w ... 2.95
❑6 ... 2.95

DEATHROW
HEROIC / BLUE COMET

❑1, Sep 1993, b&w ... 2.50

DEATH'S HEAD
MARVEL

❑1, Dec 1988 ... 1.75
❑2, Jan 1989 ... 1.75
❑3, Feb 1989 ... 1.75
❑4, Mar 1989 ... 1.75
❑5, Apr 1989 ... 1.75
❑6, May 1989 ... 1.75
❑7, Jun 1989 ... 1.75
❑8, Jul 1989 ... 1.75
❑9, Aug 1989 ... 1.75
❑10, Sep 1989 ... 1.75

DEATH'S HEAD II (VOL. 1)
MARVEL

❑1, Mar 1992 1: Death's Head II. D: Death's Head. ... 2.50
❑1-2, Mar 1992; 1: Death's Head II. D: Death's Head. Silver ink cover ... 1.75
❑2, Apr 1992 ... 2.00
❑2-2, Apr 1992; Silver ink cover ... 1.75
❑3, May 1992 1: Tuck. ... 2.00
❑4, Jun 1992 A: Wolverine. A: Captain America. ... 2.00

DEATH'S HEAD II (VOL. 2)
MARVEL

❑1, Dec 1992; A: X-Men. gatefold cover ... 2.00
❑2, Jan 1993 A: X-Men. ... 2.00
❑3, Feb 1993 A: X-Men. ... 2.00
❑4, Mar 1993 A: X-Men. ... 2.00
❑5, Apr 1993 ... 1.75
❑6, May 1993 ... 1.95
❑7, Jun 1993 ... 1.95
❑8, Jul 1993 ... 1.95
❑9, Aug 1993 ... 1.95
❑10, Sep 1993 ... 1.95
❑11, Oct 1993 1: Death's Head III. A: Doctor Necker. A: Charnel. ... 1.95
❑12, Nov 1993 ... 1.95
❑13, Dec 1993 ... 1.95
❑14, Jan 1994; Prelude to Death's Head Gold #1; foil cover ... 2.95
❑15, Feb 1994 ... 1.95
❑16, Mar 1994 ... 1.95

DEATH'S HEAD II & THE ORIGIN OF DIE-CUT
MARVEL

❑1, Aug 1993; foil cover ... 2.95
❑2, Sep 1993 ... 1.75

DEATH'S HEAD II GOLD
MARVEL

❑1; foil cover ... 3.95

DEATH SHRIKE
BRAINSTORM

❑1, Jul 1993, b&w ... 2.95

DEATHSNAKE, THE
FANTAGRAPHICS / EROS

❑1, Aug 1994 ... 2.95
❑2, Oct 1994, b&w ... 2.95

DEATHSTROKE THE TERMINATOR
DC

❑0, Oct 1994 ... 2.00
❑1, Aug 1991 O: Deathstroke the Terminator. ... 3.00
❑1-2 O: Deathstroke the Terminator. ... 1.75
❑2, Sep 1991 ... 2.00
❑3, Oct 1991 ... 2.00
❑4, Nov 1991 V: Ravager. ... 2.00
❑5, Dec 1991 ... 2.00
❑6, Jan 1992 ... 2.00
❑7, Feb 1992; Batman ... 2.00
❑8, Mar 1992; Batman ... 2.00
❑9, Apr 1992; 1: Vigilante III (Pat Trayce). Batman ... 2.00
❑10, Jun 1992 ... 2.00
❑11, Jun 1992; Vigilante ... 2.00
❑12, Jul 1992 MG (a) ... 2.00
❑13, Aug 1992 ... 2.00
❑14, Sep 1992 ... 2.00
❑15, Oct 1992 ... 2.00
❑16, Nov 1992 D: Deathstroke the Terminator. ... 2.00
❑17, Dec 1992; Deathstroke the Terminator revived ... 2.00
❑18, Jan 1993 ... 2.00
❑19, Feb 1993; Quarac destroyed ... 2.00
❑20, Mar 1993 ... 1.75
❑21, Apr 1993 ... 1.75
❑22, May 1993 ... 1.75
❑23, May 1993 ... 1.75
❑24, Jun 1993 ... 1.75
❑25, Jun 1993 ... 1.75
❑26, Jul 1993 ... 1.75
❑27, Aug 1993 ... 1.75
❑28, Sep 1993 ... 1.75
❑29, Oct 1993 ... 1.75
❑30, Nov 1993 ... 1.75
❑31, Dec 1993 ... 1.75
❑32, Jan 1994 ... 1.75
❑33, Feb 1994 ... 1.75
❑34, Mar 1994 ... 1.75
❑35, Apr 1994 ... 1.75
❑36, May 1994 ... 1.75
❑37, Jun 1994 ... 1.75
❑38, Jul 1994 A: Vigilante III (Pat Trayce). A: Vigilante. ... 1.95
❑39, Aug 1994; A: Green Arrow. Title becomes "Deathstroke the Hunted" ... 1.95
❑40, Sep 1994 ... 1.95
❑41, Nov 1994 ... 1.95
❑42, Dec 1994 ... 1.95
❑43, Jan 1995 ... 1.95
❑44, Feb 1995 ... 1.95
❑45, Mar 1995 ... 1.95
❑46, Apr 1995 ... 1.95
❑47, May 1995 ... 1.95
❑48, Jun 1995 ... 2.25
❑49, Jul 1995 ... 2.25
❑50, Aug 1995; Giant-size; Title changes to Deathstroke ... 3.50
❑51, Sep 1995 ... 2.25
❑52, Oct 1995 GP (a); A: Hawkman. ... 2.25
❑53, Nov 1995 ... 2.25
❑54, Dec 1995 ... 2.25
❑55, Jan 1996 ... 2.25
❑56, Feb 1996 ... 2.25
❑57, Mar 1996 ... 2.25
❑58, Apr 1996 V: Joker. ... 2.25
❑59, May 1996 ... 2.25
❑60, Jun 1996 ... 2.25
❑Annual 1, ca. 1992 A: Vigilante. ... 3.50
❑Annual 2, ca. 1993 1: Gunfire. ... 3.50
❑Annual 3, ca. 1994; Elseworlds ... 3.95
❑Annual 4 1995; Year One ... 3.95

DEATH TALKS ABOUT LIFE
DC / VERTIGO

❑1 NG (w); ... 1.50

DEATH: THE HIGH COST OF LIVING
DC / VERTIGO

❑1, Mar 1993 NG (w); ... 3.00
❑1/Platinum; Platinum edition NG (w); ... 6.00
❑2, Apr 1993 NG (w); ... 3.00
❑3, May 1993; regular edition NG (w); ... 3.00
❑3/A, May 1993; with error ... 3.00

DEATH: THE TIME OF YOUR LIFE
DC / VERTIGO

❑1, Apr 1996 NG ... 3.50
❑2, May 1996 NG ... 3.00
❑3, Jun 1996 NG ... 3.00

DEATHWATCH
HARRIER

❑1, Jul 1987 ... 1.95

DEATHWISH
MILESTONE / DC

❑1, Dec 1994 ... 2.50
❑2, Jan 1995 ... 2.50
❑3, Feb 1995 ... 2.50
❑4, Mar 1995 ... 2.50

DEATHWORLD
ADVENTURE

❑1, Nov 1990, b&w ... 2.50
❑2, Dec 1990, b&w ... 2.50
❑3, Jan 1991, b&w ... 2.50
❑4, Feb 1991, b&w ... 2.50

DEATHWORLD BOOK II
ADVENTURE

❑1, Apr 1991, b&w ... 2.50
❑2, May 1991, b&w ... 2.50

N-MINT

❑3, Jun 1991, b&w 2.50
❑4, Jul 1991, b&w 2.50

DEATHWORLD BOOK III
ADVENTURE

❑1, Aug 1991, b&w 2.50
❑2, Sep 1991, b&w 2.50
❑3, Nov 1991, b&w 2.50
❑4, Dec 1991, b&w 2.50

DEATH WRECK
MARVEL

❑1, Jan 1994 1.95
❑2, Feb 1994 1.95
❑3, Mar 1994 1.95
❑4, Apr 1994 1.95

DEBBIE DOES COMICS
AIRCEL

❑1, b&w 2.95

DEBBIE DOES DALLAS
AIRCEL

❑1, Mar 1991 2.50
❑1/3D 3.95
❑1-2 2.50
❑2, Apr 1991 2.50
❑3, May 1991 2.50
❑4, Jun 1991 2.50
❑5, Jul 1991 2.50
❑6 1991 2.50
❑7, Oct 1991 2.50
❑8, Nov 1991 2.50
❑9, Dec 1991 2.95
❑10 1992 2.95
❑11 1992 2.95
❑12 1992 2.95
❑13 1992 2.95
❑14 1992 2.95
❑15 2.95
❑16 2.95
❑17 2.95
❑18 2.95

DEBBI'S DATES
DC

❑1, May 1969 30.00
❑2, Jul 1969 18.00
❑3, Sep 1969 18.00
❑4, Nov 1969 18.00
❑5, Jan 1970 18.00
❑6, Mar 1970 30.00
❑7, May 1970 18.00
❑8, Jul 1970 18.00
❑9, Sep 1970 18.00
❑10, Nov 1970 18.00
❑11, Jan 1971 18.00

DECADE
DARK HORSE

❑1 12.95

DECADE OF DARK HORSE, A
DARK HORSE

❑1, Jul 1996, b&w and color; Sin City, Predator, Grendel stories 2.95
❑2, Aug 1996; Star Wars, Ghost, Trekker stories 2.95
❑3, Sep 1996, b&w and color; Aliens, Outlanders, Nexus, The Mask stories 2.95
❑4, Oct 1996; b&w and color, Concrete, Black Cross, Exon Depot, Godzilla stories, final issue 2.95

DECAPITATOR (RANDY BOWEN'S...)
DARK HORSE

❑1, Jun 1998 2.95
❑2, Jul 1998 2.95
❑3, Aug 1998 2.95
❑4, Sep 1998 2.95

DECEPTION, THE
IMAGE

❑1, ca. 1999 2.95
❑2, ca. 1999 2.95
❑3, ca. 1999 2.95

DECORATOR, THE
FANTAGRAPHICS / EROS

❑1, b&w 2.50

N-MINT

DECOY
PENNY-FARTHING

❑1, Mar 1999 2.75
❑1/Autographed, Mar 1999 3.25
❑2, Apr 1999 2.75
❑3, May 1999 2.75
❑4, Jun 1999 2.75

DEE DEE
FANTAGRAPHICS / EROS

❑1, Jul 1996, b&w 2.95

DEEP, THE
MARVEL

❑1, Nov 1977 CI (c); CI (a) 1.50

DEEP BLACK
CHAOS!

❑1/A, Aug 1997; No cover price; b&w pencilled pin-ups 2.00
❑1/B, Aug 1997; b&w pencilled pin-ups; all-white cardstock cover 2.00

DEEPEST DIMENSION
REVOLUTIONARY

❑1, Jun 1993 2.50
❑2, Aug 1993 2.50

DEEP GIRL
ARIEL BORDEAUX

❑1 2.50
❑2 2.50
❑3 1.50
❑4 2.50
❑5 2.50

DEEP TERROR
AVALON

❑1, b&w 2.95

DEE VEE
DEE VEE

❑1, Feb 1997 2.95
❑5, Feb 1998, b&w; wraparound cover 2.95
❑6, Apr 1998, b&w; wraparound cover 2.95
❑7, Jun 1998, b&w; wraparound cover 2.95

DEFCON 4
IMAGE

❑1/A, Feb 1996; wraparound cover 2.50
❑1/B, Feb 1996; alternate wraparound cover 2.50
❑2, Mar 1996 2.50
❑3, Jun 1996; cover says May, indicia says Jun 2.50
❑4, Sep 1996 2.50
❑5 1996 2.50

DEFENDERS, THE (DELL)
DELL

❑1 26.00
❑2, Feb 1963 16.00

DEFENDERS, THE
MARVEL

❑1, Aug 1972; SB (c); SB (a); Team consists of Doctor Strange, Hulk, and Sub-Mariner 80.00
❑2, Oct 1972; SB (c); SB (a); A: Silver Surfer. Silver Surfer joins Defenders 32.00
❑3, Dec 1972; GK (c); SB, JM (a); A: Silver Surfer. Black Knight 26.00
❑4, Feb 1973; SB (c); FMc, SB (a); Valkyrie joins Defenders 26.00
❑5, Apr 1973 SB (c); FMc, SB (a); D: Omegatron. 26.00
❑6, Jun 1973 SB (c); FMc, SB (a) 16.00
❑7, Aug 1973; (c); SB (a); A: Hawkeye. 16.00
❑8, Sep 1973; SB (c); FMc, SB (a); A: Avengers. Avengers and Defenders vs. Loki and Dormammu, part 2 - continues in Avengers #116 (continued from Avengers #115) 16.00
❑9, Oct 1973; SB (c); FMc, SB (a); A: Avengers. Avengers and Defenders vs. Loki and Dormammu, part 4 - continues in Avengers #117 16.00
❑10, Nov 1973; SB (c); SB (a); A: Avengers. Avengers and Defenders vs. Loki and Dormammu, part 6 - continues in Avengers #118 45.00

Jim Lee was the artist on the first few issues of *Deathblow.*

© 1993 Jim Lee and Image.

N-MINT

❑11, Dec 1973; SB (c); SB (a); A: Avengers. Avengers and Defenders vs. Loki and Dormammu, part 8, continued from Avengers #118; Hawkeye, Silver Surfer and Sub-Mariner leave Defenders 9.00
❑12, Feb 1974; (c); SB, JAb (a); Hulk fights Xemnu the Titan 9.00
❑13, May 1974; SB, KJ (c); SB, KJ (a); 1: Nebulon. Nighthawk; Marvel Value Stamp #86: Zemo 9.00
❑14, Jul 1974; (c); SB, DGr (a); Nighthawk joins Defenders 9.00
❑15, Sep 1974; SB (c); SB, KJ (a); A: Magneto. V: Magneto. Professor X; Nighthawk new costume; Marvel Value Stamp #8: Captain America 10.00
❑16, Oct 1974; GK (c); SB (a); A: Magneto. Professor X; Marvel Value Stamp #44: Absorbing Man 10.00
❑17, Nov 1974; (c); SB, DGr (a); 1: Bulldozer. Luke Cage; Marvel Value Stamp #20: Brother Voodoo 6.50
❑18, Dec 1974; SB (c); SB, DGr (a); O: Bulldozer. V: Wrecking Crew. Luke Cage 6.50
❑19, Jan 1975; (c); SB, KJ (a); Luke Cage; Marvel Value Stamp #98: Puppet Master 6.50
❑20, Feb 1975; SB (c); SB (a); A: Thing. origin of Valkyrie; Marvel Value Stamp #31: Mordo 7.00
❑21, Mar 1975; SB, KJ (c); SB (a); The Headmen introduced 6.00
❑22, Apr 1975; GK (c); SB (a); The Sons of the Serpent 6.00
❑23, May 1975; GK, KJ (c); SB (a); Yellowjacket; Marvel Value Stamp #78: Owl 6.00
❑24, Jun 1975; GK, KJ (c); SB, BMc (a); A: Daredevil. A: Son of Satan. Luke Cage, Yellowjacket 6.00
❑25, Jul 1975; (c); SB, JAb (a); A: Daredevil. Luke Cage, Daredevil, Daimon Hellstorm, Yellowjacket 6.50
❑26, Aug 1975; SB (c); SB (a); A: Guardians of the Galaxy. Continued from Giant-Size Defenders #5 7.00
❑27, Sep 1975; SB (c); SB (a); 1: Starhawk II (Aleta)-cameo. A: Guardians of the Galaxy. 7.00
❑28, Oct 1975; (c); SB (a); 1: Starhawk II (Aleta)-full. A: Guardians of the Galaxy. Starhawk 7.00
❑29, Nov 1975; (c); SB (a); A: Guardians of the Galaxy. Starhawk 7.00
❑30, Dec 1975 (c); JAb (a) 4.00
❑31, Jan 1976 GK (c); SB, JM (a) 4.00
❑32, Feb 1976 GK, KJ (c); SB, JM (a); O: Nighthawk II (Kyle Richmond). 4.00
❑33, Mar 1976 GK (c); SB, JM (a) 4.00
❑34, Apr 1976 RB, DA (c); SB, JM (a); V: Nebulon. 4.00
❑34/30 cent, Apr 1976; RB, DA (c); SB, JM (a); V: Nebulon. 30 cent regional price variant 20.00
❑35, May 1976 GK (c); SB, KJ (a); 1: Red Guardian II (Doctor Tanja Belinskya). 4.00
❑35/30 cent, May 1976; GK (c); SB, KJ (a); 1: Red Guardian II (Doctor Tanja Belinskya). 30 cent regional price variant 20.00
❑36, Jun 1976 GK (c); SB, KJ (a) 4.00
❑36/30 cent, Jun 1976; GK (c); SB, KJ (a); 30 cent regional price variant 20.00

Condition price index: Multiply "NM prices" above by: **0.83 for Very Fine/Near Mint**
0.66 for Very Fine • 0.33 for Fine • 0.2 for Very Good • 0.125 for Good

	N-MINT
❑37, Jul 1976 GK (c); SB, KJ (a)	4.00
❑37/30 cent, Jul 1976; GK (c); SB, KJ (a); 30 cent regional price variant	20.00
❑38, Aug 1976 SB (c); SB, KJ (a)	4.00
❑38/30 cent, Aug 1976, SB (c); SB, KJ (a); 30 cent regional price variant	5.00
❑39, Sep 1976 (c); SB, KJ (a)	4.00
❑40, Oct 1976 GK, KJ (c); SB, KJ (a)	4.00
❑41, Nov 1976 GK, KJ (c); SB, KJ (a)	4.00
❑42, Dec 1976 (c); KG, KJ (a)	4.00
❑43, Jan 1977 AM, JK (c); KG, KJ (a)	4.00
❑44, Feb 1977; (c); KG, KJ (a); Hellcat joins Defenders	4.00
❑45, Mar 1977 JK (c); KG, KJ (a)	4.00
❑46, Apr 1977 (c); KG, KJ (a)	4.00
❑47, May 1977; (c); KG, KJ (a); Moon Knight	4.00
❑48, Jun 1977 (c); KG, DGr (a); O: Zodiac II.	4.00
❑49, Jul 1977 (c); KG (a); O: Zodiac II.	4.00
❑50, Aug 1977 KG (a); O: Zodiac II.	4.00
❑50/A, Aug 1977	8.00
❑51, Sep 1977; GP (c); KG, KJ (a); 1: Ringer I (Anthony Davis). A: Moon Knight. Moon Knight	4.00
❑52, Oct 1977 GK (c); KG (a); O: Presence. 1: Presence. A: Hulk. V: Sub-Mariner.	4.00
❑53, Nov 1977 GP, BWi (c); MG, KG, DC (a); 1: Lunatik.	4.00
❑54, Dec 1977 (c); MG, KG, BMc (a)	4.00
❑55, Jan 1978 GK (c); Cl, KJ (a); O: Red Guardian II (Doctor Tanja Belinskya).	4.00
❑56, Feb 1978 (c); Cl, KJ (a)	4.00
❑57, Mar 1978 (c); DGr, GT, DC (a)	4.00
❑58, Apr 1978 (c); DGr, KJ (a)	4.00
❑59, May 1978 (c); DGr (a)	4.00
❑60, Jun 1978 (c); DGr (a)	4.00
❑61, Jul 1978 (c)	4.00
❑62, Aug 1978 BL, JR2 (c); SB, JM (a)	4.00
❑63, Sep 1978 JSt (c); SB, JM (a)	4.00
❑64, Oct 1978 SB (c); SB, DP (a)	4.00
❑65, Nov 1978 DP (a)	4.00
❑66, Dec 1978 SB (c)	4.00
❑67, Jan 1979 (c)	4.00
❑68, Feb 1979 (c); HT (a)	4.00
❑69, Mar 1979 (c); AM, HT (a)	4.00
❑70, Apr 1979 (c); HT (a); A: Lunatik. V: Lunatik.	4.00
❑71, May 1979 HT (c); HT, JAb (a); O: Lunatik.	4.00
❑72, Jun 1979 HT (c); HT (a); A: Lunatik.	4.00
❑73, Jul 1979 HT (c); HT (a); A: Foolkiller II (Greg Salinger).	4.00
❑74, Aug 1979; HT (c); HT (a); A: Foolkiller II (Greg Salinger). Nighthawk II resigns from Defenders	4.00
❑75, Sep 1979 HT (c); HT (a); A: Foolkiller II (Greg Salinger).	4.00
❑76, Oct 1979 RB (c); HT (a); O: Omega.	4.00
❑77, Nov 1979 RB (c); AM, HT (a); D: James-Michael Starling (Omega the Unknown's counterpart).	4.00
❑78, Dec 1979; HT (a); Original Defenders return	4.00
❑79, Jan 1980 RB (c); HT (a)	4.00
❑80, Feb 1980 RB (c); DGr, HT (a)	4.00
❑81, Mar 1980 RB (c); HT, JAb (a)	4.00
❑82, Apr 1980 RB (c); DP, JSt (a)	4.00
❑83, May 1980 RB (c); DP (a)	4.00
❑84, Jun 1980 RB (c); DP (a)	4.00
❑85, Jul 1980 RB (c); DP, JM (a)	4.00
❑86, Aug 1980 RB (c); DP (a)	4.00
❑87, Sep 1980 (c); DP (a)	4.00
❑88, Oct 1980 MN (c); DP (a)	4.00
❑89, Nov 1980 MN (c); DP (a)	4.00
❑90, Dec 1980; RB (c); DP (a); Daredevil	4.00
❑91, Jan 1981; RB (c); DP (a); Daredevil	4.00
❑92, Feb 1981 DP (a)	4.00
❑93, Mar 1981 DP, JSt (a)	2.50
❑94, Apr 1981 MG (c); DP, JSt (a); 1: Gargoyle.	2.50
❑95, May 1981 PB (c); DP, JSt (a); O: Gargoyle. A: Dracula.	2.50
❑96, Jun 1981 MG (c); DP, JSt (a); A: Ghost Rider.	2.50
❑97, Jul 1981 AM (c); DP, JSt (a)	2.50
❑98, Aug 1981 MR (c); DP, JSt (a)	2.50
❑99, Sep 1981 AM (c); DP, JSt (a)	2.50
❑100, Oct 1981; Giant-size; AM (c); DP, JSt (a); giant	2.50
❑101, Nov 1981 AM (c); DP, JSt (a); A: Silver Surfer.	2.00
❑102, Dec 1981 AM (c); DP, JSt, JAb (a)	2.00
❑103, Jan 1982 AM (c); DP, JSt (a); O: Null the Living Darkness. 1: Null the Living Darkness.	2.00
❑104, Feb 1982 AM (c); DP, JSt (a)	2.00
❑105, Mar 1982 AM (c); DP, JSt (a)	2.00
❑106, Apr 1982 AM (c); AM, DP, JAb (a); A: Daredevil. D: Nighthawk II (Kyle Richmond).	2.00
❑107, May 1982 AM (c); AM, DP (a); A: Enchantress.	2.00
❑108, Jun 1982 AM, DP (c); AM, DP, JSt (a)	2.00
❑109, Jul 1982 AM (c); DP, JSt (a)	2.00
❑110, Aug 1982 AM (c); DP (a)	2.00
❑111, Sep 1982 AM (c); DP (a)	2.00
❑112, Oct 1982 BA (c); DP, MGu (a); 1: Power Princess. 1: Nuke I (Albert Gaines).	2.00
❑113, Nov 1982 DP (c); DP (w); DP, MGu (a)	2.00
❑114, Dec 1982 AM, DP (c); DP (w); DP, MGu (a)	2.00
❑115, Jan 1983 DP (c); DP (a)	2.00
❑116, Feb 1983 DP (c); DP (a)	2.00
❑117, Mar 1983 DP, JAb (c); DP, JAb (a)	2.00
❑118, Apr 1983 AM, DP (c); DP (a)	2.00
❑119, May 1983 SB, JAb (a); 1: Yandroth II.	2.00
❑120, Jun 1983 DP, JAb (c); DP, JAb (a)	2.00
❑121, Jul 1983 DP (c); DP (w); DP, JAb (a)	2.00
❑122, Aug 1983 BA, DP (c); DP (a)	2.00
❑123, Sep 1983 BSz (c); DP (a); 1: Cloud.	2.00
❑124, Oct 1983 DP (a)	2.00
❑125, Nov 1983; double-sized; BSz (c); DP (a); 1: Mad-Dog. New Team begins: Valkyrie, Beast, Iceman, Angel, Gargoyle, and Moondragon	2.00
❑126, Dec 1983 MZ (c); O: Leviathan I (Edward Cobert). 1: Leviathan I (Edward Cobert).	2.00
❑127, Jan 1984 MZ (c); SB (a)	2.00
❑128, Feb 1984 KN (c)	2.00
❑129, Mar 1984 BG (c); DP (a); A: New Mutants. V: New Mutants.	2.00
❑130, Apr 1984 MZ (a)	2.00
❑131, May 1984 BSz (c)	1.50
❑132, Jun 1984 DP (a)	1.50
❑133, Jul 1984 KN (c); 1: Manslaughter (cameo).	1.50
❑134, Aug 1984 KN (c); DP (a); 1: Manslaughter (full appearance).	1.50
❑135, Sep 1984 BSz (c); DP (a)	1.50
❑136, Oct 1984 DP (a)	1.50
❑137, Nov 1984 KN (c); DP (a)	1.50
❑138, Dec 1984 DP (a); O: Moondragon.	1.50
❑139, Jan 1985; DP (a); Series continues as The New Defenders	1.50
❑140, Feb 1985 DP (a)	1.50
❑141, Mar 1985 DP (a)	1.50
❑142, Apr 1985 DP (a)	1.50
❑143, May 1985 BA (c); DP (a); O: Moondragon. 1: Runner. 1: Dragon of the Moon. 1: Andromeda.	1.50
❑144, Jun 1985 DP (a)	1.50
❑145, Jul 1985 DP (a); A: Johnny Blaze.	1.50
❑146, Aug 1985 LMc (a)	1.50
❑147, Sep 1985; DP (a); Sgt. Fury and His Howling Defenders on both cover and in indicia	1.50
❑148, Oct 1985 SB (a)	1.50
❑149, Nov 1985 KN (c); DP (a); O: Andromeda.	1.50
❑150, Dec 1985; double-sized DP (a); O: Cloud.	1.50
❑151, Jan 1986 KN (c); DP (a)	1.50
❑152, Feb 1986; double-sized; DP (a); O: Manslaughter. Secret Wars II	1.50
❑Annual 1, Nov 1976 (c); SB, KJ (a); O: Hulk.	15.00

DEFENDERS (VOL. 2)
MARVEL

	N-MINT
❑1, Mar 2001	2.99
❑2, Apr 2001	2.25
❑3, May 2001	2.25
❑4, Jun 2001	2.25
❑5, Jul 2001	2.25
❑6, Aug 2001	2.25
❑7, Sep 2001	2.25
❑8, Oct 2001	2.25
❑9, Nov 2001	2.25
❑10, Dec 2001	2.25
❑11, Jan 2002	2.25
❑12, Feb 2002	3.50

DEFENDERS OF DYNATRON CITY
MARVEL

	N-MINT
❑1, Feb 1992	1.25
❑2, Mar 1992	1.25
❑3, Apr 1992	1.25
❑4, May 1992	1.25
❑5, Jun 1992	1.25
❑6, Jul 1992	1.25

DEFENDERS OF THE EARTH
MARVEL / STAR

	N-MINT
❑1, Jan 1987; Flash Gordon, Mandrake, Phantom	1.00
❑2, Mar 1987; Flash Gordon, Mandrake, Phantom	1.00
❑3, May 1987; Flash Gordon, Mandrake, Phantom	1.00
❑4, Jul 1987	1.00

DEFENSELESS DEAD, THE
ADVENTURE

	N-MINT
❑1, Feb 1991, b&w; based on Larry Niven story	2.50
❑2, ca. 1991, b&w; based on Larry Niven story	2.50
❑3, ca. 1991, b&w; based on Larry Niven story	2.50

DEFIANCE
IMAGE

	N-MINT
❑1, Feb 2002	3.50
❑2, Apr 2002	2.95
❑3, Jun 2002	2.95
❑4, Sep 2002	2.95
❑5, Nov 2002; variant cover	2.95
❑6, Mar 2003; variant cover	2.95
❑7, Apr 2003; variant cover	2.95
❑8, Jul 2003	2.95

DEFIANT GENESIS
DEFIANT

	N-MINT
❑1, Oct 1993; no cover price	1.00

DEFINITION
SLAVE LABOR

	N-MINT
❑1, Aug 1997, b&w; Oversized	12.95

DEITY (VOL. 1)
IMAGE

	N-MINT
❑0, May 1998, exclusive New Dimension Comics edition; Flip cover	6.00
❑0/A, May 1998	3.00
❑1, Sep 1997; White background on cover	3.00
❑1/A, Sep 1997; variant cover	3.00
❑2, Oct 1997; Regular cover (power blasts)	3.00
❑2/A, Oct 1997; variant cover; Brandishing gun, sword	3.00
❑3, Nov 1997; Regular cover (brown background, bandages on face)	2.95
❑3/A, Nov 1997; variant cover; Cyborg girl	3.50
❑4, Dec 1997	2.95
❑4/A, Dec 1997; variant cover	3.00
❑5, Feb 1998	2.95
❑5/A, Feb 1998; variant cover	3.00

N-MINT

❑6, Apr 1998; Girl with backpack on cover 2.95
❑6/A, Apr 1998; variant cover 3.00

DEITY (VOL. 2)
IMAGE

❑1, Sep 1998; Flipbook preview of Catseye 2.95
❑1/A, Sep 1998; Variant cover with blue background, wielding sword 2.95
❑1/B, Sep 1998; Variant cover with monster threatening 2.95
❑1/C, Sep 1998; Variant cover with gratuitous bathing suit, cleavage 2.95
❑2, Nov 1998 .... 2.95
❑3, Jan 1999 .... 2.95
❑4, Jan 1999 .... 2.95
❑5, May 1999 .... 2.95
❑Ashcan 1, Jun 1998; Special Preview edition 2.95

DEITY: REVELATIONS
IMAGE

❑1, Jul 1999; Woman on floating skateboard, figures in background 2.95
❑1/A, Jul 1999; variant cover: woman holding her face on cover 2.95
❑1/B, Jul 1999; variant cover 2.95
❑2, Sep 1999; variant cover 2.95
❑3, Nov 1999 .... 2.95
❑4, Jan 2000 .... 2.95

DEJA VU
FANTACO

❑1, Flip cover 2.95

DEJA VU (RADIO COMIX)
RADIO

❑1, Nov 2000, Flip cover 2.95

DELIA CHARM
RED MENACE

❑1 .... 2.95
❑2 .... 2.95

DELICATE CREATURES
IMAGE

❑1/HC 16.95

DELIRIUM
METRO

❑1 .... 2.00

DELTA SQUADRON
ANDERPOL

❑1 .... 2.00

DELTA TENN
ENTERTAINMENT

❑1, Jul 1987 .... 1.50
❑2, Sep 1987 .... 1.50
❑3, Nov 1987 .... 1.50
❑4, Jan 1988 .... 1.50
❑5, Mar 1988 .... 1.50
❑6, May 1988 .... 1.50
❑7, Jul 1988 .... 1.50
❑8, Sep 1988 .... 1.50
❑9, b&w 1.50
❑10, b&w 1.50

DELTA, THE ULTIMATE DIFFERENCE
APEX ONE

❑1, Oct 1997, b&w; no cover price 2.00
❑2, Fal 1998, b&w; cardstock cover 2.95

DEMENTED: SCORPION CHILD
DMF

❑1, Nov 2000 .... 2.95
❑2, Dec 2000 .... 2.95
❑3, Jan 2001 .... 2.95
❑4, Feb 2001 .... 2.95
❑5, Mar 2001 .... 2.95

DEMI'S WILD KINGDOM ADVENTURE
OPUS

❑1, Mar 2000, b&w; squarebound 9.95

DEMI THE DEMONESS
RIP OFF

❑1, Mar 1993 .... 2.50
❑1-2; Rip-Off publishes 2.95
❑2, Nov 1993 .... 2.95

N-MINT

❑3, Mar 1995; flip-book with Kit-Ra back-up 2.95
❑4 .... 3.25
❑5 .... 2.95
❑6, Jun 2002; Carnal Comics publishes 5.95
❑Special 1; "Choose your own adventure"-style special 5.95

DEMOLITION MAN
DC

❑1, Nov 1993 .... 1.75
❑2, Dec 1993 .... 1.75
❑3, Jan 1994 .... 1.75
❑4, Feb 1994 .... 1.75

DEMON, THE (1ST SERIES)
DC

❑1, Aug 1972; JK (a); O: Etrigan. 1: Jason Blood. 1: Etrigan. 1: Randu Singh. 35.00
❑2, Oct 1972 JK (a) 12.00
❑3, Nov 1972; JK (w); JK (a); Batman 10.00
❑4, Dec 1972 JK (a) 10.00
❑5, Jan 1973 JK (a) 9.00
❑6, Feb 1973 JK (a) 9.00
❑7, Mar 1973 JK (a); 1: Klarion the Witch Boy. 9.00
❑8, Apr 1973 JK (a) 9.00
❑9, Jun 1973 JK (a) 9.00
❑10, Jul 1973 JK (a) 7.00
❑11, Aug 1973 JK (a) 7.00
❑12, Sep 1973 JK (a) 7.00
❑13, Oct 1973 JK (a) 7.00
❑14, Nov 1973 JK (a) 7.00
❑15, Dec 1973 JK (a) 7.00
❑16, Jan 1974 JK (a) 7.00

DEMON, THE (2ND SERIES)
DC

❑1, Jan 1987 MW (w); MW (a) 2.00
❑2, Feb 1987 MW (a) 2.00
❑3, Mar 1987 MW (a) 2.00
❑4, Apr 1987 MW (w); MW (a) 2.00

DEMON, THE (3RD SERIES)
DC

❑0, Oct 1994 O: Jason Blood. O: Etrigan. 2.00
❑1, Jul 1990 .... 4.00
❑2, Aug 1990 .... 2.50
❑3, Sep 1990; Batman 2.50
❑4, Oct 1990 .... 2.25
❑5, Nov 1990 .... 2.25
❑6, Dec 1990 .... 2.25
❑7, Jan 1991 .... 2.25
❑8, Feb 1991; Batman 2.25
❑9, Mar 1991 .... 2.25
❑10, Apr 1991 .... 2.25
❑11, May 1991 .... 3.00
❑12, Jun 1991 A: Lobo. 2.00
❑13, Jul 1991 A: Lobo. 2.00
❑14, Aug 1991 A: Lobo. 2.00
❑15, Sep 1991 A: Lobo. 2.00
❑16, Oct 1991 .... 2.00
❑17, Nov 1991; War of the Gods 2.00
❑18, Dec 1991 .... 2.00
❑19, Jan 1992; Double-size; Lobo poster 2.50
❑20, Feb 1992 .... 2.00
❑21, Mar 1992 .... 2.00
❑22, Apr 1992 .... 2.00
❑23, May 1992; Robin 2.00
❑24, Jun 1992; Robin 2.00
❑25, Jul 1992 .... 1.50
❑26, Aug 1992 .... 1.50
❑27, Sep 1992 .... 1.50
❑28, Oct 1992; Superman 1.50
❑29, Nov 1992 .... 1.75
❑30, Dec 1992 .... 1.75
❑31, Jan 1993 .... 1.75
❑32, Feb 1993 .... 1.75
❑33, Mar 1993 .... 1.75
❑34, Apr 1993; Lobo 1.75
❑35, May 1993; Lobo 1.75
❑36, Jun 1993 .... 1.75

Image's Gen^{13} was introduced in the Image-Valiant crossover *Deathmate*.

© 1993 Image and Voyager Communications Inc. (Valiant).

N-MINT

❑37, Jul 1993 .... 1.75
❑38, Aug 1993 .... 1.75
❑39, Sep 1993 .... 1.75
❑40, Oct 1993 .... 1.75
❑41, Nov 1993 .... 1.75
❑42, Dec 1993 .... 1.75
❑43, Jan 1994 A: Hitman. 3.50
❑44, Feb 1994 A: Hitman. 3.00
❑45, Mar 1994 A: Hitman. 3.00
❑46, Apr 1994 A: Haunted Tank. 1.75
❑47, May 1994 A: Haunted Tank. 1.75
❑48, Jun 1994 .... 1.95
❑49, Jul 1994 .... 1.95
❑50, Aug 1994; Giant-size 2.95
❑51, Sep 1994 .... 1.95
❑52, Nov 1994 A: Hitman. 1.95
❑53, Dec 1994 A: Hitman. 1.95
❑54, Jan 1995 A: Hitman. 1.95
❑55, Feb 1995 .... 1.95
❑56, Mar 1995 .... 1.95
❑57, Apr 1995 .... 1.95
❑58, May 1995 .... 1.95
❑Annual 1, ca. 1992 .... 3.00
❑Annual 2, ca. 1993 1: Hitman. 12.00

DEMON BEAST INVASION
CPM / BARE BEAR

❑1, Oct 1996, b&w; wraparound cover 2.95

DEMON BEAST INVASION: THE FALLEN
CPM / BARE BEAR

❑1, Sep 1998, b&w 2.95
❑2, Oct 1998, b&w 2.95

DEMONBLADE
NEW COMICS

❑1, b&w 1.95

DEMON DREAMS
PACIFIC

❑1, Feb 1984 .... 1.50
❑2, May 1984 .... 1.50

DEMON DRIVEN OUT
DC / VERTIGO

❑1, Nov 2003 .... 2.50
❑2, Dec 2003 .... 2.50
❑3, Jan 2004 .... 2.50
❑4, Feb 2004 .... 2.50
❑5, Mar 2004 .... 2.50
❑6, Apr 2004 .... 2.50

DEMONGATE
SIRIUS

❑1, May 1996 .... 2.50
❑2, Jun 1996 .... 2.50
❑3, Jul 1996 .... 2.50
❑4 1996 .... 2.50
❑5, Oct 1996 .... 2.50
❑6, Nov 1996 .... 2.50
❑7, Dec 1996 .... 2.50
❑8, Jan 1997 .... 2.50
❑9, Feb 1997, b&w 2.50

DEMON GUN
CRUSADE

❑1, Jun 1996, b&w 2.95
❑2, Sep 1996, b&w 2.95
❑3, Jan 1997, b&w 2.95

DEMON-HUNTER
ATLAS-SEABOARD

	N-MINT
❑1, Sep 1975 RB (w); RB (a); 1: Gideon Cross.	2.00

DEMON HUNTER (AIRCEL)
AIRCEL

	N-MINT
❑1, Mar 1989, b&w	1.95
❑2, Apr 1989, b&w	1.95
❑3, May 1989, b&w	1.95
❑4, Jun 1989, b&w	1.95

DEMON HUNTER (DAVDEZ)
DAVDEZ

	N-MINT
❑1, Aug 1998	2.50

DEMONIC TOYS
ETERNITY

	N-MINT
❑1, Jan 1992	2.50
❑2	2.50
❑3	2.50
❑4	2.50

DEMONIQUE
LONDON NIGHT

	N-MINT
❑1, Oct 1994, b&w	3.00
❑2 1995	3.00
❑3 1995	3.00
❑4 1995	3.00

DEMONIQUE: ANGEL OF NIGHT
LONDON NIGHT

	N-MINT
❑1, Jul 1997	3.00

DEMON ORORON, THE
TOKYOPOP

	N-MINT
❑1, Apr 2004	9.99

DEMON REALM
MEDEIA

	N-MINT
❑0	2.50

DEMONS & DARK ELVES
WEIRDWORX

	N-MINT
❑1, b&w	2.95

DEMON'S BLOOD
ODYSSEY

	N-MINT
❑1	2.00

DEMONSLAYER
IMAGE

	N-MINT
❑1, Nov 1999	2.95
❑2, Dec 1999	2.95
❑3, Jan 2000	2.95

DEMONSLAYER (NEXT)
NEXT

	N-MINT
❑0; Tower Records cover	2.95

DEMONSLAYER (VOL. 2)
IMAGE

	N-MINT
❑1, Jun 2000	2.95
❑2, Jul 2000	2.95
❑3, Aug 2000	2.95

DEMON'S TAILS
ADVENTURE

	N-MINT
❑1, b&w	2.50
❑2, b&w	2.50
❑3, b&w	2.50
❑4, b&w	2.50

DEMON WARRIOR, THE
EASTERN

	N-MINT
❑1, Aug 1987, b&w	1.50
❑2 1987, b&w	1.50
❑3 1987, b&w	1.50
❑4 1988, b&w	1.50
❑5, b&w	1.50
❑6, b&w	1.50

DEMONWARS: EYE FOR AN EYE (RA SALVATORE'S)
CROSSGEN

	N-MINT
❑1, Jun 2003	2.95
❑2, Jul 2003	2.95
❑3, Aug 2003	2.95
❑4, Sep 2003	2.95
❑5, Oct 2003	2.95

DEMONWARS: TRIAL BY FIRE (R.A. SALVATORE'S...)
CROSSGEN

	N-MINT
❑1, Jan 2003	2.95
❑2, Feb 2003	2.95
❑3, Mar 2003	2.95
❑4, Apr 2003	2.95
❑5, May 2003	2.95

DEN
FANTAGOR

	N-MINT
❑1	3.00
❑2	3.00
❑3	3.00
❑4	3.00
❑5	3.00
❑6	2.50
❑7	2.50
❑8	2.50
❑9 AN (a)	2.50
❑10	2.50

DENIZENS OF DEEP CITY
KITCHEN SINK

	N-MINT
❑1, ca. 1988, b&w	2.00
❑2, ca. 1988, b&w	2.00
❑3, ca. 1988, b&w	2.00
❑4, ca. 1988, b&w	2.00
❑5, ca. 1988, b&w	2.00
❑6, ca. 1988, b&w	2.00
❑7, ca. 1988, b&w	2.00
❑8, ca. 1988, b&w	2.00
❑9, ca. 1988	2.00

DENNIS THE MENACE (FAWCETT)
STANDARD

	N-MINT
❑19, Nov 1956	45.00
❑20, Jan 1957	45.00
❑21, Mar 1957	35.00
❑22, May 1957	35.00
❑23, Jul 1957	35.00
❑24, Sep 1957	35.00
❑25, Nov 1957	35.00
❑26, Jan 1958	35.00
❑27, Mar 1958	35.00
❑28, May 1958	35.00
❑29, Jul 1958	35.00
❑30, Sep 1958	35.00
❑31, Nov 1958	25.00
❑32	25.00
❑33 1959	25.00
❑34 1959	25.00
❑35, May 1959	25.00
❑36 1959	25.00
❑37 1959	25.00
❑38, Sep 1959	25.00
❑39, Nov 1959	25.00
❑40, Jan 1960	25.00
❑41, Mar 1960	18.00
❑42, May 1960	18.00
❑43, Jun 1960	18.00
❑44 1960	18.00
❑45, Sep 1960	18.00
❑46 1960	18.00
❑47	18.00
❑48	18.00
❑49 1961	18.00
❑50 1961	18.00
❑51 1961	14.00
❑52 1961	14.00
❑53 1961	14.00
❑54	14.00
❑55	14.00
❑56 1962	14.00
❑57 1962	14.00
❑58 1962	14.00
❑59	14.00
❑60, Jul 1962	14.00
❑61 1962	14.00
❑62 1962	14.00
❑63	14.00
❑64	14.00
❑65, Mar 1963	14.00
❑66, May 1963	14.00
❑67, Jul 1963	14.00
❑68, Sep 1963	14.00
❑69, Nov 1963	14.00
❑70, Jan 1964	14.00
❑71, Mar 1964	10.00
❑72, May 1964	10.00
❑73, Jul 1964	10.00
❑74, Sep 1964	10.00
❑75, Nov 1964	10.00
❑76, Jan 1965	10.00
❑77, Mar 1965	10.00
❑78, May 1965	10.00
❑79, Jul 1965	10.00
❑80, Sep 1965	10.00
❑81, Nov 1965	10.00
❑82, Jan 1966	10.00
❑83, Mar 1966	10.00
❑84, May 1966	10.00
❑85, Jul 1966	10.00
❑86, Sep 1966	10.00
❑87, Nov 1966	10.00
❑88, Jan 1967	10.00
❑89, Mar 1967	10.00
❑90, May 1967	10.00
❑91, Jul 1967	6.00
❑92, Sep 1967	6.00
❑93, Nov 1967	6.00
❑94, Jan 1968	6.00
❑95, Mar 1968	6.00
❑96, May 1968	6.00
❑97, Jul 1968	6.00
❑98, Sep 1968	6.00
❑99, Nov 1968	6.00
❑100, Jan 1969	6.00
❑101, Mar 1969	4.00
❑102, May 1969	4.00
❑103, Jul 1969	4.00
❑104, Sep 1969	4.00
❑105, Nov 1969	4.00
❑106, Jan 1970	4.00
❑107, Mar 1970	4.00
❑108, May 1970	4.00
❑109, Jul 1970	4.00
❑110, Sep 1970	4.00
❑111, Nov 1970	4.00
❑112, Jan 1971	4.00
❑113, Mar 1971	4.00
❑114, May 1971	4.00
❑115, Jul 1971	4.00
❑116, Sep 1971; anti-pollution issue	4.00
❑117, Nov 1971	4.00
❑118, Jan 1972	4.00
❑119, Mar 1972	4.00
❑120, May 1972	4.00
❑121, Jul 1972	3.00
❑122, Sep 1972	3.00
❑123, Nov 1972	3.00
❑124, Jan 1973	3.00
❑125, Mar 1973	3.00
❑126, May 1973 A: Gina.	3.00
❑127, Jul 1973	3.00
❑128, Sep 1973	3.00
❑129, Nov 1973	3.00
❑130, Jan 1974	3.00
❑131, Mar 1974	3.00
❑132, May 1974	3.00
❑133, Jul 1974	3.00
❑134, Sep 1974	3.00
❑135, Nov 1974	3.00
❑136, Jan 1975	3.00
❑137, Mar 1975	3.00
❑138, May 1975	3.00
❑139, Jul 1975	3.00
❑140, Sep 1975; at Winchester mansion	3.00
❑141, Nov 1975	2.00
❑142, Jan 1976	2.00
❑143, Mar 1976	2.00
❑144, May 1976	2.00
❑145, Jun 1976	2.00

Condition price index: Multiply "NM prices" above by: **0.83 for Very Fine/Near Mint**
0.66 for Very Fine • 0.33 for Fine • 0.2 for Very Good • 0.125 for Good

N-MINT

- ❑146, Jul 1976 .... 2.00
- ❑147, Sep 1976 .... 2.00
- ❑148, Nov 1976 .... 2.00
- ❑149, Jan 1977 .... 2.00
- ❑150, Mar 1977 .... 2.00
- ❑151, May 1977 .... 2.00
- ❑152, Jul 1977 .... 2.00
- ❑153, Sep 1977 .... 2.00
- ❑154, Nov 1977 .... 2.00
- ❑155, Jan 1978 .... 2.00
- ❑156, Mar 1978 .... 2.00
- ❑157, May 1978 .... 2.00
- ❑158, Jul 1978 .... 2.00
- ❑159, Sep 1978 .... 2.00
- ❑160, Nov 1978 .... 2.00
- ❑161, Jan 1979 .... 2.00
- ❑162, Mar 1979 .... 2.00
- ❑163, May 1979 .... 2.00
- ❑164, Jul 1979 .... 2.00
- ❑165, Sep 1979 .... 2.00
- ❑166, Nov 1979 .... 2.00

DENNIS THE MENACE (MARVEL)
MARVEL

- ❑1, Nov 1981 .... 2.00
- ❑2, Dec 1981 .... 1.50
- ❑3, Jan 1982 .... 1.50
- ❑4, Feb 1982 .... 1.50
- ❑5, Mar 1982 .... 1.50
- ❑6, Apr 1982 .... 1.50
- ❑7, May 1982 .... 1.50
- ❑8, Jun 1982 .... 1.50
- ❑9, Jul 1982 .... 1.50
- ❑10, Aug 1982 .... 1.50
- ❑11, Sep 1982 .... 1.50
- ❑12, Oct 1982 .... 1.50
- ❑13, Nov 1982 .... 1.50

DENNIS THE MENACE AND HIS FRIENDS
FAWCETT

- ❑1, ...and Joey (#2 on cover) 12.00
- ❑2, ...and Ruff (#2 on cover) 12.00
- ❑3, Oct 1969, ...and Mr. Wilson (#1 on cover) 12.00
- ❑4, ...and Margaret (#1 on cover) 12.00
- ❑5, Jan 1970, ...and Margaret (#5 on cover) 8.00
- ❑6, Jun 1970; Joey 5.00
- ❑7, Aug 1970 .... 5.00
- ❑8, Oct 1970 .... 5.00
- ❑9, Jan 1971 .... 5.00
- ❑10, Jun 1971 .... 5.00
- ❑11, Aug 1971 .... 4.00
- ❑12, Oct 1971; Mr. Wilson 4.00
- ❑13, Jan 1972; Margaret 4.00
- ❑14, Jun 1972 .... 4.00
- ❑15, Aug 1972; Ruff 4.00
- ❑16, Oct 1972; Mr. Wilson 4.00
- ❑17, Jan 1973 .... 4.00
- ❑18, Jun 1973; Joey 4.00
- ❑19, Aug 1973 .... 4.00
- ❑20, Oct 1973 .... 4.00
- ❑21, Jan 1974 .... 3.00
- ❑22, Jun 1974; Joey 3.00
- ❑23, Aug 1974 .... 3.00
- ❑24, Oct 1974 .... 3.00
- ❑25, Jan 1975 .... 3.00
- ❑26, Jun 1975 .... 3.00
- ❑27, Aug 1975 .... 3.00
- ❑28, Oct 1975 .... 3.00
- ❑29, Jan 1976; ...and Margaret (#29) 3.00
- ❑30, Jun 1976 .... 3.00
- ❑31, Aug 1976 .... 3.00
- ❑32, Oct 1976 .... 3.00
- ❑33, Jan 1977 .... 3.00
- ❑34, Jun 1977 .... 3.00
- ❑35, Aug 1977; Ruff 3.00
- ❑36, Oct 1977 .... 3.00
- ❑37, Oct 1977 .... 3.00
- ❑38, Apr 1978; digest size begins 2.50
- ❑39, Jun 1978 .... 2.50
- ❑40, Aug 1978 .... 2.50

N-MINT

- ❑41, Oct 1978; Reprints first Margaret story; Screamy Mimi story; Chub story 2.50
- ❑42, Apr 1979 .... 2.50
- ❑43, Jun 1979; Reprints 24 of 26 Dennis Alphabet stories, omitting A and B 2.50
- ❑44, Jul 1979 .... 2.50
- ❑45, Oct 1979 .... 2.50
- ❑46, Apr 1980 .... 2.50

DENNIS THE MENACE BIG BONUS SERIES
FAWCETT

- ❑10, Feb 1980 .... 3.00
- ❑11, Apr 1980 .... 3.00

DENNIS THE MENACE BONUS MAGAZINE SERIES
FAWCETT

- ❑76, Jan 1970; Series continued from Dennis the Menace (Giants) #75 .... 8.00
- ❑77, Feb 1970 .... 8.00
- ❑78, Mar 1970 .... 8.00
- ❑79, Apr 1970 .... 8.00
- ❑80, May 1970 .... 8.00
- ❑81, Jun 1970 .... 8.00
- ❑82, Jun 1970 .... 8.00
- ❑83, Jul 1970 .... 8.00
- ❑84, Jul 1970; at the circus 8.00
- ❑85, Aug 1970 .... 8.00
- ❑86, Oct 1970; Christmas 8.00
- ❑87, Oct 1970 .... 8.00
- ❑88, Jan 1971 .... 8.00
- ❑89, Feb 1971 .... 8.00
- ❑90, Mar 1971 .... 8.00
- ❑91, Apr 1971 .... 7.00
- ❑92, May 1971 .... 7.00
- ❑93, Jun 1971 .... 7.00
- ❑94, Jun 1971 .... 7.00
- ❑95, Jul 1971 .... 7.00
- ❑96, Jul 1971 .... 7.00
- ❑97, Aug 1971 .... 7.00
- ❑98, Oct 1971; Christmas 7.00
- ❑99, Oct 1971 .... 7.00
- ❑100, Jan 1972 .... 7.00
- ❑101, Feb 1972 .... 7.00
- ❑102, Mar 1972 .... 7.00
- ❑103, Apr 1972; Short Stuff Special 7.00
- ❑104, May 1972 .... 7.00
- ❑105, Jun 1972 .... 7.00
- ❑106, Jun 1972 .... 7.00
- ❑107, Jul 1972 .... 7.00
- ❑108, Jul 1972 .... 7.00
- ❑109, Aug 1972 .... 7.00
- ❑110, Oct 1972; Christmas 7.00
- ❑111, Oct 1972; Christmas 7.00
- ❑112, Jan 1973; Go-Go Special 7.00
- ❑113, Feb 1973 .... 7.00
- ❑114, Mar 1973 .... 7.00
- ❑115, Apr 1973 .... 7.00
- ❑116, May 1973 .... 7.00
- ❑117, Jun 1973 .... 7.00
- ❑118, Jun 1973 .... 7.00
- ❑119, Jul 1973; Summer Number and state flags 7.00
- ❑120, Jul 1973 .... 7.00
- ❑121, Aug 1973 .... 6.00
- ❑122, Oct 1973 .... 6.00
- ❑123, Oct 1973 .... 6.00
- ❑124, Jan 1974 .... 6.00
- ❑125, Feb 1974 .... 6.00
- ❑126, Mar 1974 .... 6.00
- ❑127, Apr 1974 .... 6.00
- ❑128, May 1974 .... 6.00
- ❑129, Jun 1974 .... 6.00
- ❑130, Jun 1974 .... 6.00
- ❑131, Jul 1974 .... 6.00
- ❑132, Jul 1974 .... 6.00
- ❑133, Aug 1974 .... 6.00
- ❑134, Oct 1974; Christmas 6.00
- ❑135, Oct 1974 .... 6.00
- ❑136, Jan 1975 .... 6.00
- ❑137, Feb 1975 .... 6.00
- ❑138, Mar 1975 .... 6.00

Tommy Monahagan was transformed into Hitman in *The Demon Annual* #2.

© 1993 DC Comics.

N-MINT

- ❑139, Apr 1975 .... 6.00
- ❑140, May 1975 .... 6.00
- ❑141, Jun 1975 .... 6.00
- ❑142, Jun 1975 .... 6.00
- ❑143, Jul 1975 .... 6.00
- ❑144, Jul 1975 .... 6.00
- ❑145, Aug 1975 .... 6.00
- ❑146, Oct 1975; Christmas 6.00
- ❑147, Oct 1975 .... 6.00
- ❑148, Jan 1976 .... 6.00
- ❑149, Feb 1976 .... 6.00
- ❑150, Mar 1976 .... 6.00
- ❑151, Apr 1976 .... 4.00
- ❑152, May 1976 .... 4.00
- ❑153, Jun 1976 .... 4.00
- ❑154, Jun 1976 .... 4.00
- ❑155, Jul 1976 .... 4.00
- ❑156, Jul 1976 .... 4.00
- ❑157, Aug 1976 .... 4.00
- ❑158, Oct 1976 .... 4.00
- ❑159, Oct 1976 .... 4.00
- ❑160, Jan 1977 .... 4.00
- ❑161 1977 .... 4.00
- ❑162 1977 .... 4.00
- ❑163 1977 .... 4.00
- ❑164 1977 .... 4.00
- ❑165 1977 .... 4.00
- ❑166 1977 .... 4.00
- ❑167, Jun 1977 .... 4.00
- ❑168 1977 .... 4.00
- ❑169 1977 .... 4.00
- ❑170 1977 .... 4.00
- ❑171 1977 .... 3.00
- ❑172, Jan 1978 .... 3.00
- ❑173, Feb 1978 .... 3.00
- ❑174, Mar 1978 .... 3.00
- ❑175, Apr 1978 .... 3.00
- ❑176, May 1978 .... 3.00
- ❑177, Jun 1978 .... 3.00
- ❑178, Jun 1978 .... 3.00
- ❑179, Jul 1978 .... 3.00
- ❑180, Jul 1978 .... 3.00
- ❑181, Aug 1978 .... 3.00
- ❑182, Oct 1978 .... 3.00
- ❑183, Oct 1978 .... 3.00
- ❑184, Jan 1979 .... 3.00
- ❑185, Feb 1979 .... 3.00
- ❑186, Mar 1979 .... 3.00
- ❑187, Apr 1979 .... 3.00
- ❑188, May 1979 .... 3.00
- ❑189, Jun 1979 .... 3.00
- ❑190, Jun 1979 .... 3.00
- ❑191, Jul 1979 .... 3.00
- ❑192, Jul 1979 .... 3.00
- ❑193, Aug 1979 .... 3.00
- ❑194, Oct 1979 .... 3.00

DENNIS THE MENACE COMICS DIGEST
MARVEL

- ❑1; DC logo placed on cover in error by World Color Press; reprints 20.00
- ❑2; reprints 1.25
- ❑3; reprints 1.25

N-MINT

DENNIS THE MENACE POCKET FULL OF FUN
FAWCETT

❑1, ca. 1969 ... 25.00
❑2 1969 ... 20.00
❑3 1969 ... 20.00
❑4 1970 ... 20.00
❑5 1970 ... 20.00
❑6 1970 ... 20.00
❑7 1971 ... 20.00
❑8 1971 ... 20.00
❑9 1971 ... 20.00
❑10 1971 ... 20.00
❑11 1972 ... 15.00
❑12 1972 ... 15.00
❑13 1972 ... 15.00
❑14 1972 ... 15.00
❑15 1973 ... 15.00
❑16 1973 ... 15.00
❑17 1973 ... 10.00
❑18 1973; Holiday cover ... 10.00
❑19 ... 10.00
❑20 ... 10.00
❑21 ... 10.00
❑22 ... 10.00
❑23 ... 10.00
❑24 ... 10.00
❑25 ... 10.00
❑26 ... 10.00
❑27 ... 10.00
❑28 ... 10.00
❑29 ... 10.00
❑30 ... 10.00
❑31 ... 10.00
❑32 ... 10.00
❑33 ... 10.00
❑34 ... 10.00
❑35 ... 10.00
❑36 1977 ... 10.00
❑37, Jan 1978 ... 10.00
❑38, Apr 1978 ... 10.00
❑39, May 1978 ... 10.00
❑40, Jun 1978 ... 10.00
❑41, Aug 1978 ... 10.00
❑42, Sep 1978 ... 10.00
❑43, Jan 1979 ... 10.00
❑44 1979 ... 10.00
❑45 1979 ... 10.00
❑46 1979 ... 10.00
❑47, Jul 1979 ... 10.00
❑48 1979 ... 10.00
❑49 1980 ... 10.00
❑50 1980 ... 10.00

DER VANDALE
INNERVISION

❑1, b&w ... 2.50
❑1/Variant, b&w; alternate cover ... 2.50
❑2 ... 2.50
❑3 ... 2.50

DESCENDANTS OF TOSHIN
ARROW

❑1, Apr 1999, b&w ... 2.95

DESCENDING ANGELS
MILLENNIUM

❑1 ... 2.95

DESERT PEACH, THE
THOUGHTS & IMAGES

❑1, Jul 1988, b&w; Thoughts & Images publishes ... 10.00
❑2, Feb 1989, b&w ... 6.00
❑3, Jan 1990, b&w; Goes to Mu Press ... 4.00
❑4, Mar 1990, b&w; First Mu Issue ... 4.00
❑5, Jun 1990, b&w; MU Press begins publishing ... 4.00
❑6, Aug 1990, b&w ... 4.00
❑7, Sep 1990 ... 3.00
❑8, Nov 1990 ... 3.00
❑9, Dec 1990 ... 3.00
❑10, Feb 1991 ... 3.00
❑11, Jun 1991 ... 3.00
❑12, Aug 1991 ... 2.50
❑13, Oct 1991 ... 2.50
❑14, Dec 1991 ... 2.50
❑15, Feb 1992 ... 2.50
❑16, Apr 1992 ... 2.50
❑17, Aug 1992, b&w; Giant-size ... 3.95
❑18, Aug 1992, b&w; Last Mu Press issue ... 2.50
❑19, ca. 1993, b&w; aka Desert Peach: Self-Propelled Target; Aeon begins publishing ... 4.95
❑20, ca. 1993, b&w; aka Desert Peach: Fever Dream ... 4.95
❑21, Jun 1994, b&w ... 4.95
❑22, Nov 1994, b&w ... 4.95
❑23, Jun 1995, b&w; a.k.a. The Desert Peach: Visions ... 2.95
❑24, Sep 1995, b&w; a.k.a. The Desert Peach: Ups and Downs ... 2.95
❑25, ca. 1996; Last Aeon issue; moves to A Fine Line ... 2.95
❑26, ca. 1997, b&w; a.k.a. The Desert Peach: Miki; first issue from A Fine Line; cardstock cover ... 2.95
❑27, ca. 1997 ... 2.95
❑28, Aug 1998 ... 2.95
❑29, Apr 2000 ... 2.95
❑30, Jun 2001 ... 2.95

DESERT STORM JOURNAL
APPLE

❑1; Hussein on cover ... 2.75
❑1/A; Schwartzkopf on cover ... 2.75
❑2, b&w ... 2.75
❑3, b&w ... 2.75
❑4, b&w ... 2.75
❑5, b&w ... 2.75
❑6, b&w ... 2.75
❑7, b&w ... 2.75
❑8, b&w ... 2.75

DESERT STORM: SEND HUSSEIN TO HELL!
INNOVATION

❑1 ... 2.95

DESERT STREAMS
DC / PIRANHA

❑1 ... 5.95

DESPAIR
PRINT MINT

❑1, ca. 1969 ... 10.00

DESPERADOES
IMAGE

❑1, Sep 1997 ... 2.50
❑1-2, Sep 1997 ... 2.50
❑2, Oct 1997 ... 2.95
❑3, Nov 1997 ... 2.95
❑4, Dec 1997 ... 2.95
❑5, Jun 1998 ... 2.95

DESPERADOES: EPIDEMIC!
DC / WILDSTORM

❑1, Nov 1999; prestige format ... 5.95

DESPERADOES: QUIET OF THE GRAVE
DC / HOMAGE

❑1, Jul 2001 ... 2.95
❑2, Aug 2001 ... 2.95
❑3, Sep 2001 ... 2.95
❑4, Oct 2001 ... 2.95
❑5, Nov 2001 ... 2.95

DESPERATE TIMES
IMAGE

❑0, Jan 2004 ... 3.50
❑1, Jun 1998 ... 2.95
❑2, Aug 1998 ... 2.95
❑3, Oct 1998 ... 2.95
❑4, Dec 1998 ... 2.95

DESPERATE TIMES (VOL 2)
IMAGE

❑1, Apr 2004 ... 2.95

DESSO-LETTE
FOLLIS BROTHERS

❑1, Jul 1997 ... 2.95

DESTINY: A CHRONICLE OF DEATHS FORETOLD
DC / VERTIGO

❑1, ca. 1997; prestige format ... 5.95
❑2, ca. 1997; prestige format ... 5.95
❑3, ca. 1997; prestige format ... 5.95

DESTINY ANGEL
DARK FANTASY

❑1 ... 3.95

DESTROY!!
ECLIPSE

❑1, Nov 1986, b&w; oversize ... 4.95
❑1/3D; 3-D ... 3.00

DESTROY ALL COMICS
SLAVE LABOR

❑1, Nov 1994; Oversized ... 3.50
❑2, Feb 1995; Oversized ... 3.50
❑3, Aug 1995; Oversized ... 3.50
❑4, Jan 1996; Oversized ... 3.50
❑5, Apr 1996; Oversized ... 3.50

DESTROYER DUCK
ECLIPSE

❑1, Feb 1982 ME (w); SA, VM, JK (a); O: Destroyer Duck. 1: Groo. 1: Destroyer Duck. ... 4.00
❑2, Jan 1983 VM, JK (a) ... 1.50
❑3, Jun 1983 VM, JK (a) ... 1.50
❑4, Oct 1983 VM, JK (a) ... 1.50
❑5, Dec 1983 VM, JK (a) ... 1.50
❑6, Mar 1984 VM (a) ... 1.50
❑7, May 1984 FM (c); VM (a) ... 1.50

DESTROYER, THE (MAGAZINE)
MARVEL

❑1, Nov 1989 O: Remo Williams. ... 3.00
❑2, Dec 1989 ... 2.50
❑3, Dec 1989 ... 2.50
❑4, Jan 1990 SD (a) ... 2.50
❑5, Feb 1990 ... 2.50
❑6, Mar 1990 ... 2.50
❑7, Apr 1990 ... 2.50
❑8, May 1990 ... 2.50

DESTROYER, THE (VOL. 2)
MARVEL

❑1, Mar 1991 ... 1.95

DESTROYER, THE (VOL. 3)
MARVEL

❑1, Dec 1991 ... 1.95
❑2, Jan 1992 ... 1.95
❑3, Feb 1992 ... 1.95
❑4, Mar 1992 ... 1.95

DESTROYER, THE (VALIANT)
VALIANT

❑1, Apr 1995; cover says #0 ... 2.95

DESTRUCTOR, THE
ATLAS-SEABOARD

❑1, Feb 1975 SD, WW (a); O: Destructor. ... 2.00
❑2, Apr 1975 SD, WW (a) ... 2.00
❑3, Jun 1975 SD (a) ... 2.00
❑4, Aug 1975 ... 2.00

DETECTIVE, THE: CHRONICLES OF MAX FACCIONI
CALIBER

❑1 ... 2.95

DETECTIVE COMICS
DC

❑0, Oct 1994 O: Batarangs. O: Batmobile. O: Batman. ... 2.50
❑235, Sep 1956 O: Batman. ... 565.00
❑236, Oct 1956 ... 325.00
❑237, Nov 1956 ... 275.00
❑238, Dec 1956 ... 275.00
❑239, Jan 1957 ... 275.00
❑240, Feb 1957 ... 275.00
❑241, Mar 1957 ... 210.00
❑242, Apr 1957 ... 210.00
❑243, May 1957 ... 210.00
❑244, Jun 1957 ... 210.00
❑245, Jul 1957 ... 210.00

Condition price index: Multiply "NM prices" above by: **0.83 for Very Fine/Near Mint**
0.66 for Very Fine • 0.33 for Fine • 0.2 for Very Good • 0.125 for Good

	N-MINT
❑246, Aug 1957 1: Diane Meade (Martian Manhunter's girlfriend).	210.00
❑247, Sep 1957 1: Professor Ivo.	210.00
❑248, Oct 1957	210.00
❑249, Nov 1957 A: Batwoman.	210.00
❑250, Dec 1957	210.00
❑251, Jan 1958; Roy Raymondand John Jones/Manhunter from Mars back-ups	210.00
❑252, Feb 1958	210.00
❑253, Mar 1958	210.00
❑254, Apr 1958	210.00
❑255, May 1958	210.00
❑256, Jun 1958	210.00
❑257, Jul 1958	210.00
❑258, Aug 1958	210.00
❑259, Sep 1958; 1: Calendar Man. Roy Raymond and John Jones/Manhunter from Mars back-ups	210.00
❑260, Oct 1958	210.00
❑261, Nov 1958 1: Doctor Double X.	165.00
❑262, Dec 1958	165.00
❑263, Jan 1959	165.00
❑264, Feb 1959	165.00
❑265, Mar 1959 O: Batman. A: Joker.	275.00
❑266, Apr 1959	165.00
❑267, May 1959 O: Bat-Mite. 1: Bat-Mite.	210.00
❑268, Jun 1959	165.00
❑269, Jul 1959	165.00
❑270, Aug 1959	165.00
❑271, Sep 1959 O: Martian Manhunter.	175.00
❑272, Oct 1959	125.00
❑273, Nov 1959; Martian Manhunter reveals his identity	160.00
❑274, Dec 1959	125.00
❑275, Jan 1960	125.00
❑276, Feb 1960 A: Bat-Mite. A: Batwoman.	125.00
❑277, Mar 1960	125.00
❑278, Apr 1960	125.00
❑279, May 1960	125.00
❑280, Jun 1960	125.00
❑281, Jul 1960	100.00
❑282, Aug 1960	100.00
❑283, Sep 1960	100.00
❑284, Oct 1960	100.00
❑285, Nov 1960 A: Batwoman.	100.00
❑286, Dec 1960 A: Batwoman.	100.00
❑287, Jan 1961 O: Martian Manhunter.	100.00
❑288, Feb 1961	100.00
❑289, Mar 1961	100.00
❑290, Apr 1961	100.00
❑291, May 1961	100.00
❑292, Jun 1961 A: Batwoman.	100.00
❑293, Jul 1961	100.00
❑294, Aug 1961	100.00
❑295, Sep 1961	100.00
❑296, Oct 1961	100.00
❑297, Nov 1961	100.00
❑298, Dec 1961 1: Clayface II (Matt Hagen).	175.00
❑299, Jan 1962	70.00
❑300, Feb 1962	70.00
❑301, Mar 1962	70.00
❑302, Apr 1962 A: Batwoman.	70.00
❑303, May 1962	70.00
❑304, Jun 1962	70.00
❑305, Jul 1962	70.00
❑306, Aug 1962	70.00
❑307, Sep 1962 A: Batwoman.	70.00
❑308, Oct 1962	70.00
❑309, Nov 1962 A: Batwoman.	70.00
❑310, Dec 1962	70.00
❑311, Jan 1963 1: Cat-Man (DC). A: Batwoman.	70.00
❑312, Feb 1963	70.00
❑313, Mar 1963	70.00
❑314, Apr 1963	70.00
❑315, May 1963	70.00
❑316, Jun 1963	70.00
❑317, Jul 1963	70.00
❑318, Aug 1963 A: Batwoman.	70.00
❑319, Sep 1963	70.00

	N-MINT
❑320, Oct 1963	70.00
❑321, Nov 1963 A: Batwoman.	70.00
❑322, Dec 1963	70.00
❑323, Jan 1964	70.00
❑324, Feb 1964	70.00
❑325, Mar 1964 A: Batwoman.	70.00
❑326, Apr 1964	70.00
❑327, May 1964; 25th anniversary; CI (a); symbol change; 300th Batman in Detective Comics	140.00
❑328, Jun 1964 D: Alfred.	150.00
❑329, Jul 1964	60.00
❑330, Aug 1964	60.00
❑331, Sep 1964	53.00
❑332, Oct 1964 A: Joker.	50.00
❑333, Nov 1964	40.00
❑334, Dec 1964 A: Joker.	40.00
❑335, Jan 1965	40.00
❑336, Feb 1965	40.00
❑337, Mar 1965	40.00
❑338, Apr 1965	40.00
❑339, May 1965	40.00
❑340, Jun 1965	40.00
❑341, Jul 1965 A: Joker.	52.00
❑342, Aug 1965	40.00
❑343, Sep 1965	40.00
❑344, Oct 1965	40.00
❑345, Nov 1965 1: Blockbuster.	40.00
❑346, Dec 1965	40.00
❑347, Jan 1966	40.00
❑348, Feb 1966	40.00
❑349, Mar 1966	40.00
❑350, Apr 1966	40.00
❑351, May 1966 1: Cluemaster.	40.00
❑352, Jun 1966; Elongated Man back-up	40.00
❑353, Jul 1966	40.00
❑354, Aug 1966 1: Doctor Tzin-Tzin.	40.00
❑355, Sep 1966	40.00
❑356, Oct 1966; Alfred returns	40.00
❑357, Nov 1966	40.00
❑358, Dec 1966 1: Spellbinder.	40.00
❑359, Jan 1967 1: Batgirl (Barbara Gordon).	40.00
❑360, Feb 1967	40.00
❑361, Mar 1967	40.00
❑362, Apr 1967 A: Riddler.	40.00
❑363, May 1967 A: Batgirl (Barbara Gordon).	40.00
❑364, Jun 1967 A: Batgirl (Barbara Gordon).	40.00
❑365, Jul 1967 A: Joker.	70.00
❑366, Aug 1967	40.00
❑367, Sep 1967	40.00
❑368, Oct 1967	40.00
❑369, Nov 1967; NA (a); Robin teams with Batgirl; Elongated Man back-up	60.00
❑370, Dec 1967; GK, BK (a); Elongated Man	40.00
❑371, Jan 1968 A: Batgirl (Barbara Gordon).	40.00
❑372, Feb 1968	40.00
❑373, Mar 1968 A: Riddler.	40.00
❑374, Apr 1968	40.00
❑375, May 1968	40.00
❑376, Jun 1968; Elongated Man back-up	40.00
❑377, Jul 1968	40.00
❑378, Aug 1968	40.00
❑379, Sep 1968	40.00
❑380, Oct 1968	40.00
❑381, Nov 1968	30.00
❑382, Dec 1968	30.00
❑383, Jan 1969	30.00
❑384, Feb 1969	30.00
❑385, Mar 1969	30.00
❑386, Apr 1969	30.00
❑387, May 1969; 1: Batman. Reprints Detective Comics #27	60.00
❑388, Jun 1969 A: Joker.	45.00
❑389, Jul 1969	24.00
❑390, Aug 1969	24.00
❑391, Sep 1969	20.00
❑392, Oct 1969 FR (w); MA, GK (a); 1: Jason Bard.	20.00

While a majority of them appeared in every issue, the name of only one of Dennis the Menace's friends was featured on the cover of each issue of *Dennis the Menace and His Friends*.

© 1976 Fawcett and Hank Ketcham.

	N-MINT
❑393, Nov 1969	20.00
❑394, Dec 1969	20.00
❑395, Jan 1970 MA, DG, NA, GK (a)	30.00
❑396, Feb 1970 NA (c); GK (a); A: Batgirl.	20.00
❑397, Mar 1970 NA (a)	30.00
❑398, Apr 1970	20.00
❑399, May 1970	20.00
❑400, Jun 1970 GC, NA (a); O: Man-Bat. 1: Man-Bat.	60.00
❑401, Jul 1970	18.00
❑402, Aug 1970 NA (a)	30.00
❑403, Sep 1970; NA (c); GK (a); Robin	18.00
❑404, Oct 1970; DG, NA, GK (a); Batgirl	28.00
❑405, Nov 1970	18.00
❑406, Dec 1970	18.00
❑407, Jan 1971 NA (a); A: Man-Bat.	30.00
❑408, Feb 1971 NA (a)	30.00
❑409, Mar 1971 NA (c); DG, IN (a)	18.00
❑410, Apr 1971; DH, DG, NA (a); Batgirl	30.00
❑411, May 1971 1: Talia.	18.00
❑412, Jun 1971	18.00
❑413, Jul 1971 DG (a)	18.00
❑414, Aug 1971; Giant-size	18.00
❑415, Sep 1971; Giant-size	18.00
❑416, Oct 1971; Giant-size	18.00
❑417, Nov 1971; Giant-size	18.00
❑418, Dec 1971; Giant-size	18.00
❑419, Jan 1972; Giant-size	18.00
❑420, Feb 1972; Giant-size	18.00
❑421, Mar 1972; Giant-size; DH (a); Batgirl story	18.00
❑422, Apr 1972; Giant-size	18.00
❑423, May 1972; Giant-size	18.00
❑424, Jun 1972; Giant-size	18.00
❑425, Jul 1972	16.00
❑426, Aug 1972	16.00
❑427, Sep 1972	16.00
❑428, Oct 1972 DD (a)	12.00
❑429, Nov 1972	12.00
❑430, Dec 1972	12.00
❑431, Jan 1973	12.00
❑432, Feb 1973	12.00
❑433, Mar 1973	12.00
❑434, Apr 1973 RB (a); 1: The Spook.	12.00
❑435, Jul 1973	12.00
❑436, Sep 1973	12.00
❑437, Nov 1973 JA (a); 1: Manhunter.	18.00
❑438, Jan 1974; Manhunter	28.00
❑439, Mar 1974; O: Manhunter. Manhunter	28.00
❑440, May 1974; Manhunter	28.00
❑441, Jul 1974; Manhunter	28.00
❑442, Sep 1974; Manhunter	28.00
❑443, Nov 1974 D: Manhunter.	28.00
❑444, Jan 1975	28.00
❑445, Mar 1975	28.00
❑446, Apr 1975; RB, JA (a); 1: Sterling Silversmith. Hawkman back-up	8.00
❑447, May 1975	8.00
❑448, Jun 1975	8.00
❑449, Jul 1975	8.00
❑450, Aug 1975	8.00
❑451, Sep 1975	6.00
❑452, Oct 1975; JL (a); Hawkman back-up	6.00
❑453, Nov 1975	6.00
❑454, Dec 1975 JL (a)	6.00
❑455, Jan 1976 JL (a)	6.00

	N-MINT
❑456, Feb 1976	6.00
❑457, Mar 1976; O: Batman. Elongated Man back-up	6.00
❑458, Apr 1976	6.00
❑459, May 1976	6.00
❑460, Jun 1976	6.00
❑461, Jul 1976; Bicentennial #29	6.00
❑462, Aug 1976	6.00
❑463, Sep 1976 1: Black Spider. 1: the Calculator.	6.00
❑464, Oct 1976	6.00
❑465, Nov 1976; TD (a); Elongated Man	6.00
❑466, Dec 1976 TD, MR (a)	9.00
❑467, Jan 1977 TD, MR (a)	9.00
❑468, Mar 1977 TD, MR (a)	9.00
❑469, May 1977 AM, MR (a); 1: Doctor Phosphorus.	5.00
❑470, Jun 1977 AM, MR (a); A: Hugo Strange.	5.00
❑471, Aug 1977 MR (a); A: Hugo Strange.	8.00
❑472, Sep 1977 MR (a)	8.00
❑473, Oct 1977 MR (a)	8.00
❑474, Dec 1977 MR (a)	8.00
❑475, Feb 1978 MR (a); A: Joker.	15.00
❑476, Mar 1978 MR (a); A: Joker.	15.00
❑477, May 1978 MR (a)	7.00
❑478, Jul 1978 MR (a); 1: Clayface III (Preston Payne).	7.00
❑479, Sep 1978 RB, MR (a); 1: The Fadeaway Man.	7.00
❑480, Nov 1978 DN, MA (a)	5.00
❑481, Dec 1978; Double-size DN, JSn, CR, MR, DA (a)	7.00
❑482, Feb 1979; Double-size JSn, HC, DG, CR (a)	5.00
❑483, Apr 1979; Double-size DN, MG, DG, DA (a); 1: Maxie Zeus.	7.00
❑484, Jun 1979; Double-size O: Robin I (Dick Grayson).	5.00
❑485, Aug 1979; Double-size	4.00
❑486, Oct 1979; Double-size	4.00
❑487, Dec 1979; Double-size	4.00
❑488, Feb 1980; Double-size	4.00
❑489, Apr 1980; Double-size; Batgirl forgets Batman and Robin's secret identities	4.00
❑490, May 1980; Double-size	4.00
❑491, Jun 1980; Double-size	4.00
❑492, Jul 1980; Double-size	4.00
❑493, Aug 1980; Double-size	4.00
❑494, Sep 1980; Double-size 1: Crime Doctor.	4.00
❑495, Oct 1980; Double-size	4.00
❑496, Nov 1980	4.00
❑497, Dec 1980	4.00
❑498, Jan 1981	4.00
❑499, Feb 1981	4.00
❑500, Mar 1981; 500th anniversary issue CI, DG, TY, JKu (a); A: Deadman, Slam Bradley, Hawkman, Robin.	5.00
❑501, Apr 1981	4.00
❑502, May 1981	4.00
❑503, Jun 1981 JSn (a)	4.00
❑504, Jul 1981 JSn (a); A: Joker.	6.00
❑505, Aug 1981	4.00
❑506, Sep 1981	4.00
❑507, Oct 1981	4.00
❑508, Nov 1981	4.00
❑509, Dec 1981	4.00
❑510, Jan 1982	4.00
❑511, Feb 1982 1: Mirage (DC).	4.00
❑512, Mar 1982	4.00
❑513, Apr 1982	4.00
❑514, May 1982	4.00
❑515, Jun 1982	4.00
❑516, Jul 1982	4.00
❑517, Aug 1982	4.00
❑518, Sep 1982 1: Velvet Tiger.	4.00
❑519, Oct 1982	4.00
❑520, Nov 1982	4.00
❑521, Dec 1982	4.00
❑522, Jan 1983	4.00
❑523, Feb 1983	4.00

	N-MINT
❑524, Mar 1983 2: Jason Todd.	5.00
❑525, Apr 1983	4.00
❑526, May 1983 DN, AA (a)	4.00
❑527, Jun 1983	4.00
❑528, Jul 1983	4.00
❑529, Aug 1983	4.00
❑530, Sep 1983	4.00
❑531, Oct 1983	4.00
❑532, Nov 1983 A: Joker.	4.00
❑533, Dec 1983	4.00
❑534, Jan 1984 V: Poison Ivy.	4.00
❑535, Feb 1984 2: Robin II (Jason Todd). V: Crazy Quilt.	5.00
❑536, Mar 1984 V: Deadshot.	4.00
❑537, Apr 1984	4.00
❑538, May 1984 V: Catman.	4.00
❑539, Jun 1984 V: Catman.	4.00
❑540, Jul 1984 V: Scarecrow.	4.00
❑541, Aug 1984	4.00
❑542, Sep 1984 V: Nocturna.	4.00
❑543, Oct 1984	4.00
❑544, Nov 1984	4.00
❑545, Dec 1984	4.00
❑546, Jan 1985	4.00
❑547, Feb 1985	4.00
❑548, Mar 1985	4.00
❑549, Apr 1985 AMo (w);	4.00
❑550, May 1985; AMo (w); Green Arrow back-up	4.00
❑551, Jun 1985 V: Calendar Man.	4.00
❑552, Jul 1985	4.00
❑553, Aug 1985 V: Black Mask.	4.00
❑554, Sep 1985	4.00
❑555, Oct 1985 V: Mirror Master. V: Captain Boomerang.	4.00
❑556, Nov 1985	4.00
❑557, Dec 1985	4.00
❑558, Jan 1986	4.00
❑559, Feb 1986 A: Catwoman. A: Green Arrow. A: Black Canary.	4.00
❑560, Mar 1986 1: Steelclaw.	4.00
❑561, Apr 1986	4.00
❑562, May 1986	4.00
❑563, Jun 1986 V: Two-Face.	4.00
❑564, Jul 1986 D: Steelclaw. V: Two-Face.	4.00
❑565, Aug 1986	3.00
❑566, Sep 1986 A: Joker.	3.00
❑567, Oct 1986 JSn (a)	3.00
❑568, Nov 1986; Legends	3.00
❑569, Dec 1986 A: Catwoman. A: Joker. V: Joker.	4.00
❑570, Jan 1987 A: Joker.	4.00
❑571, Feb 1987 V: Scarecrow.	3.00
❑572, Mar 1987; Giant-size A: Slam Bradley.	4.00
❑573, Apr 1987 V: Mad Hatter.	2.50
❑574, May 1987 O: Batman.	3.00
❑575, Jun 1987	3.50
❑576, Jul 1987 TMc (a)	3.00
❑577, Aug 1987 TMc (a)	3.00
❑578, Sep 1987 TMc (a)	3.00
❑579, Oct 1987 V: Two-Face.	2.00
❑580, Nov 1987 V: Two-Face.	2.00
❑581, Dec 1987 V: Two-Face.	2.00
❑582, Jan 1988; Millennium	2.00
❑583, Feb 1988 1: Ventriloquist.	2.00
❑584, Mar 1988	2.00
❑585, Apr 1988	2.00
❑586, May 1988 V: Rat-catcher.	2.00
❑587, Jun 1988	2.00
❑588, Jul 1988	2.00
❑589, Aug 1988; Bonus Book #5	2.00
❑590, Sep 1988	2.00
❑591, Oct 1988	2.00
❑592, Nov 1988	2.00
❑593, Dec 1988	2.00
❑594, Dec 1988 1: Joe Potato.	2.00
❑595, Jan 1989; Bonus Book; Invasion!	2.00
❑596, Jan 1989	2.00
❑597, Feb 1989	2.00
❑598, Mar 1989; Double-size	3.00
❑599, Apr 1989	2.50

	N-MINT
❑600, May 1989; Double-size FM (a)	3.00
❑601, Jun 1989 A: Demon.	2.00
❑602, Jul 1989 A: Demon.	2.00
❑603, Aug 1989 A: Demon.	2.00
❑604, Sep 1989; poster	2.00
❑605, Sep 1989	2.00
❑606, Oct 1989	2.00
❑607, Oct 1989	2.00
❑608, Nov 1989 1: Anarky.	2.00
❑609, Dec 1989 2: Anarky.	2.00
❑610, Jan 1990; Penguin	2.00
❑611, Feb 1990; Penguin	1.50
❑612, Mar 1990; Catman, Catwoman	1.50
❑613, Apr 1990	1.50
❑614, May 1990	1.50
❑615, Jun 1990; Penguin	1.50
❑616, Jun 1990	1.50
❑617, Jul 1990 A: Joker.	1.50
❑618, Jul 1990	1.50
❑619, Aug 1990	1.50
❑620, Aug 1990	1.50
❑621, Sep 1990	1.50
❑622, Oct 1990	1.50
❑623, Nov 1990	1.50
❑624, Dec 1990	1.50
❑625, Jan 1991	1.50
❑626, Feb 1991	1.50
❑627, Mar 1991; A: Batman's 600th. giant	3.00
❑628, Apr 1991	1.50
❑629, May 1991	1.50
❑630, Jun 1991	1.50
❑631, Jul 1991	1.50
❑632, Jul 1991	1.50
❑633, Aug 1991	1.50
❑634, Aug 1991	1.50
❑635, Sep 1991	1.50
❑636, Sep 1991	1.50
❑637, Oct 1991	1.50
❑638, Nov 1991 JA (a)	1.50
❑639, Dec 1991 JA (a)	1.50
❑640, Jan 1992 JA (a)	1.50
❑641, Feb 1992; JA (a); Anton Furst's Gotham City designs	1.50
❑642, Mar 1992 JA (a); V: Scarface.	1.50
❑643, Apr 1992 JA (a)	1.50
❑644, May 1992	1.50
❑645, Jun 1992	1.50
❑646, Jul 1992	1.50
❑647, Aug 1992	1.50
❑648, Aug 1992	1.50
❑649, Sep 1992	1.50
❑650, Sep 1992	1.50
❑651, Oct 1992	1.50
❑652, Oct 1992 A: The Huntress III (Helena Bertinelli).	1.50
❑653, Nov 1992 A: The Huntress III (Helena Bertinelli).	1.50
❑654, Dec 1992	1.50
❑655, Jan 1993 V: Ulysses.	1.50
❑656, Feb 1993 A: Bane.	2.50
❑657, Mar 1993	2.50
❑658, Apr 1993	2.50
❑659, May 1993	2.50
❑659-2, May 1993	1.25
❑660, May 1993	2.00
❑661, Jun 1993	2.00
❑662, Jun 1993	2.00
❑663, Jul 1993	2.00
❑664, Aug 1993	2.00
❑665, Aug 1993	2.00
❑666, Sep 1993	2.00
❑667, Oct 1993	1.50
❑668, Nov 1993	1.50
❑669, Dec 1993	1.50
❑670, Jan 1994 V: Mr. Freeze.	1.50
❑671, Feb 1994	1.50
❑672, Mar 1994	1.50
❑673, Apr 1994 V: Joker.	1.50
❑674, May 1994	1.50
❑675, Jun 1994	1.50

Condition price index: Multiply "NM prices" above by: **0.83 for Very Fine/Near Mint**
0.66 for Very Fine • 0.33 for Fine • 0.2 for Very Good • 0.125 for Good

	N-MINT
❑675/Platinum, Jun 1994; Platinum edition; no cover price	3.00
❑675/Variant, Jun 1994; premium edition; Special cover	2.95
❑676, Jul 1994; Giant-size	2.50
❑677, Aug 1994 V: Nightwing.	1.50
❑678, Sep 1994; O: Batman. Zero Hour	1.50
❑679, Nov 1994 V: Ratcatcher.	1.50
❑680, Dec 1994 V: Two-Face.	1.50
❑681, Jan 1995	1.50
❑682, Feb 1995	1.50
❑682/Variant, Feb 1995; enhanced cover	2.50
❑683, Mar 1995 V: Penguin.	1.50
❑684, Apr 1995	1.50
❑685, May 1995	1.50
❑686, Jun 1995 A: Huntress. A: Nightwing.	2.00
❑687, Jul 1995	2.00
❑688, Aug 1995	2.00
❑689, Sep 1995	2.00
❑690, Oct 1995 V: Firefly.	2.00
❑691, Nov 1995; V: Spellbinder. Underworld Unleashed	2.00
❑692, Dec 1995; Underworld Unleashed	2.00
❑693, Jan 1996 1: Allergent. A: Poison Ivy.	2.00
❑694, Feb 1996 A: Poison Ivy. V: Allergent.	2.00
❑695, Mar 1996	2.00
❑696, Apr 1996	2.00
❑697, Jun 1996 V: Two-Face.	2.00
❑698, Jul 1996 V: Two-Face.	2.00
❑699, Jul 1996	2.00
❑700, Aug 1996; Anniversary issue	3.50
❑700/Variant, Aug 1996; Anniversary issue; cardstock outer wrapper	5.00
❑701, Sep 1996 V: Bane.	2.00
❑702, Oct 1996	2.00
❑703, Nov 1996; Final Night	2.00
❑704, Dec 1996; self-contained story	2.00
❑705, Jan 1997 V: Riddler. V: Cluemaster.	2.00
❑706, Feb 1997 A: Riddler. V: Riddler.	2.00
❑707, Mar 1997 V: Riddler.	2.00
❑708, Apr 1997 BSz (a)	2.00
❑709, May 1997 BSz (a)	2.00
❑710, Jun 1997 BSz (a)	2.00
❑711, Jul 1997	2.00
❑712, Aug 1997	2.00
❑713, Sep 1997	2.00
❑714, Oct 1997 V: Firefly.	2.00
❑715, Nov 1997 A: J'onn J'onzz.	2.00
❑716, Dec 1997; JA (a); Face cover	2.00
❑717, Jan 1998	2.00
❑718, Feb 1998 BMc (a); V: Finch.	2.00
❑719, Mar 1998 JA (a)	2.50
❑720, Apr 1998; continues in Catwoman #56	3.50
❑721, May 1998; continues in Catwoman #57	3.00
❑722, Jun 1998; JA (a); Aftershock	2.50
❑723, Jul 1998; continues in Robin #55	2.00
❑724, Aug 1998; Aftershock	2.00
❑725, Sep 1998; Aftershock	2.00
❑726, Oct 1998; A: Joker. Aftershock	1.95
❑727, Dec 1998; A: Nightwing. A: Robin. Road to No Man's Land	1.99
❑728, Jan 1999; A: Nightwing. A: Robin. Road to No Man's Land	1.99
❑729, Feb 1999; A: Nightwing. A: Robin. A: Commissioner Gordan. Road to No Man's Land	1.99
❑730, Mar 1999; A: Scarface. No Man's Land	1.99
❑731, Apr 1999; A: Scarecrow. A: Huntress. No Man's Land	1.99
❑732, May 1999; A: Batgirl. No Man's Land	1.99
❑733, Jun 1999; No Man's Land	1.99
❑734, Jul 1999; A: Batgirl. No Man's Land	1.99
❑735, Aug 1999; BSz (a); A: Poison Ivy. V: Clayface. No Man's Land	1.99
❑736, Sep 1999; No Man's Land	1.99

	N-MINT
❑737, Oct 1999; V: Joker. V: Harley Quinn. No Man's Land	1.99
❑738, Nov 1999; No Man's Land	1.99
❑739, Dec 1999; No Man's Land	1.99
❑740, Jan 2000; No Man's Land	1.99
❑741, Feb 2000 D: Sarah.	2.50
❑742, Mar 2000	1.99
❑743, Apr 2000	1.99
❑744, May 2000	1.99
❑745, Jun 2000	1.99
❑746, Jul 2000	1.99
❑747, Aug 2000	2.50
❑748, Sep 2000	2.50
❑749, Oct 2000	2.50
❑750, Nov 2000; Giant-size	4.95
❑751, Dec 2000	2.50
❑752, Jan 2001	2.50
❑753, Feb 2001	2.50
❑754, Mar 2001	2.50
❑755, Apr 2001	2.50
❑756, May 2001	2.50
❑757, Jun 2001	2.50
❑758, Jul 2001	2.50
❑759, Aug 2001	2.50
❑760, Sep 2001	2.50
❑761, Oct 2001	2.50
❑762, Nov 2001	2.50
❑763, Dec 2001; Joker: Last Laugh crossover	2.50
❑764, Jan 2002	2.50
❑765, Feb 2002	2.50
❑766, Mar 2002	2.50
❑767, Apr 2002	2.50
❑768, May 2002	2.50
❑769, Jun 2002	2.50
❑770, Jul 2002	2.50
❑771, Aug 2002	2.50
❑772, Sep 2002	2.50
❑773, Oct 2002	2.75
❑774, Nov 2002	2.75
❑775, Dec 2002	3.50
❑776, Jan 2003	2.75
❑777, Feb 2003	2.75
❑778, Mar 2003	2.75
❑779, Apr 2003	2.75
❑780, May 2003	2.75
❑781, Jun 2003	2.75
❑782, Jul 2003	2.75
❑783, Aug 2003	2.75
❑784, Sep 2003	2.75
❑785, Oct 2003	2.75
❑786, Nov 2003	2.75
❑787, Dec 2003	2.75
❑788, Jan 2004	2.75
❑789, Feb 2004	2.75
❑790, Mar 2004	2.75
❑791, Apr 2004	2.75
❑792, May 2004	2.75
❑793, Jun 2004	2.75
❑794, Jul 2004	2.75
❑795, Aug 2004	2.95
❑796, Sep 2004	2.95
❑1000000, ca. 1998	3.00
❑1000000/Variant, ca. 1998; Signed	14.99
❑Annual 1, ca. 1988; TD, KJ (a); V: Penguin. ca. 1988; Fables	5.00
❑Annual 2, ca. 1989; Who's Who entries	4.00
❑Annual 3, ca. 1990	2.50
❑Annual 4, ca. 1991; Armageddon 2001	2.50
❑Annual 5, ca. 1992; V: Joker. Eclipso	2.75
❑Annual 6, ca. 1993; 1: Geist. 1993 Annual; Bloodlines	2.50
❑Annual 7, ca. 1994; Elseworlds	2.95
❑Annual 8, ca. 1995; O: Riddler. Year One	3.95
❑Annual 9, ca. 1996; Legends of the Dead Earth; 1996 annual	2.95
❑Annual 10, ca. 1997; SB (a); Pulp Heroes	3.95

Harley Quinn made one of her early appearances in the mainstream DC universe in *Detective Comics* #737.

© 1999 DC Comics.

DETECTIVES, THE
Alpha Productions

	N-MINT
❑1, Apr 1993, b&w	4.95

DETECTIVES, INC.: A TERROR OF DYING DREAMS
Eclipse

❑1, Jun 1987; GC (a); sepia	2.00
❑2, Sep 1987; GC (a); sepia	2.00
❑3, Dec 1987; GC (a); sepia	2.00

DETECTIVES INC. (MICRO-SERIES)
Eclipse

❑1, Apr 1985 MR (a)	2.00
❑2, Apr 1985 MR (a)	2.00

DETENTION COMICS
DC

❑1, Oct 1996; Robin, Superboy, and Warrior stories	3.50

DETONATOR
Chaos!

❑1, Dec 1994	2.75
❑2, Jan 1994	2.75

DETOUR
Alternative

❑1, Oct 1997, b&w	2.95

DETROIT! MURDER CITY COMIX
Kent Myers

❑1 1993, b&w	3.00
❑2 1994, b&w	2.50
❑3 1994, b&w	2.50
❑4, Jun 1994, b&w	2.95
❑5, Aug 1994, b&w	2.95
❑6, Jan 1995, b&w A: Iggy Pop.	2.95
❑7, May 1995, b&w	2.95

DEVASTATOR
Image

❑1, ca. 1998, b&w	2.95
❑2, ca. 1998, b&w	2.95
❑3, ca. 1998	2.95

DEVIANT
Antarctic / Venus

❑1, Mar 1999, b&w	2.99

DEVIL CHEF
Dark Horse

❑1, Jul 1994, b&w	2.50

DEVIL DINOSAUR
Marvel

❑1, Apr 1978 JK (w); JK (a); O: Devil Dinosaur. 1: Devil Dinosaur. 1: Moon Boy.	5.00
❑2, May 1978 JK (a)	3.50
❑3, Jun 1978 JK (a)	2.50
❑4, Jul 1978 JK (a)	2.50
❑5, Aug 1978 JK (a)	2.50
❑6, Sep 1978 JK (a)	2.50
❑7, Oct 1978 JK (a)	2.50
❑8, Nov 1978 JK (a)	2.50
❑9, Dec 1978 JK (a)	2.50

DEVIL DINOSAUR SPRING FLING
Marvel

❑1, Jun 1997	2.99

DEVILINA
Atlas-Seaboard

❑1, Jan 1975, b&w; magazine	9.00
❑2, May 1975, b&w; magazine	12.00

N-MINT

DEVIL JACK
Doom Theater
❑1, Jul 1995 .... 2.95
❑2 .... 2.95

DEVILMAN
Verotik
❑1, Jun 1995 .... 3.50
❑2 .... 3.00
❑3 .... 3.00
❑4 .... 2.95
❑5 .... 2.95
❑6 .... 3.50

DEVIL MAY CRY
Dreamwave
❑1, Mar 2004 .... 3.95
❑1-2, Mar 2004 .... 3.95

DEVIL'S ANGEL, THE
Fantagraphics / Eros
❑1 .... 2.95

DEVIL'S BITE
Boneyard
❑1 .... 2.95
❑2; Indicia lists as #1 .... 2.95

DEVIL'S DUE STUDIOS PREVIEWS 2003
Image
❑1, Mar 2003 .... 1.00

DEVIL'S FOOTPRINTS
Dark Horse
❑1, Mar 2003 .... 2.99
❑2, Apr 2003 .... 2.99
❑3, May 2003 .... 2.99
❑4, Jul 2003 .... 2.99

DEVIL'S REIGN
Image
❑0.5, ca. 1996; Wizard mail-in 3.00
❑0.5/Autographed, ca. 1996; Signed, limited edition 3.00
❑0.5/Platinum, ca. 1996; Platinum edition 3.00

DEVLIN
Maximum
❑1, Apr 1996 .... 2.50

DEVLIN DEMON: NOT FOR NORMAL CHILDREN
Dublin
❑1 .... 2.95

DEWEY DESADE
Item
❑1 .... 3.50
❑2 .... 3.50
❑Ashcan 1; Promotional, mini-ashcan (4 x 2) 0.25

DEXTER'S LABORATORY
DC
❑1, Sep 1999 .... 2.50
❑2, Oct 1999 A: Mandark. 2.00
❑3, Nov 1999; Dexter's robot takes his place 2.00
❑4, Dec 1999 .... 2.00
❑5, Jan 2000 .... 2.00
❑6, Feb 2000 .... 2.00
❑7, Mar 2000 .... 2.00
❑8, Apr 2000 .... 2.00
❑9, May 2000 .... 2.00
❑10, Jun 2000 .... 2.00
❑11, Jul 2000 .... 1.99
❑12, Aug 2000 .... 1.99
❑13, Sep 2000 .... 1.99
❑14, Oct 2000 .... 1.99
❑15, Nov 2000 .... 1.99
❑16, Dec 2000 .... 1.99
❑17, Jan 2001 .... 1.99
❑18, Feb 2001 .... 1.99
❑19, Mar 2001 .... 1.99
❑20, Apr 2001 .... 1.99
❑21, May 2001 .... 1.99
❑22, Jun 2001 .... 1.99
❑23, Jul 2001 .... 1.99

N-MINT

❑24, Aug 2001 .... 1.99
❑25, Sep 2001 .... 0.50
❑26, Oct 2001 .... 1.99
❑27, Nov 2001 .... 1.99
❑28, Dec 2001 .... 1.99
❑29, Jan 2002 .... 1.99
❑30, Aug 2002 ....
❑31, Oct 2002 .... 2.25
❑32, Dec 2002 .... 2.25
❑33, Feb 2004 .... 2.25
❑34, Apr 2004 .... 2.25

DHAMPIRE: STILLBORN
DC / Vertigo
❑1, Sep 1996; prestige format 5.95

DIABLO: TALES OF SANCTUARY
Dark Horse
❑1, Nov 2001, Several characters in profile on cover 5.95

DIA DE LOS MUERTOS (SERGIO ARAGONÉS')
Dark Horse
❑1, Oct 1998; Day of the Dead stories 2.95

DIATOM
Photographics
❑1, Apr 1995, b&w; prestige format; fumetti 4.95
❑2 .... 4.95
❑3 .... 4.95

DICK DANGER
Olsen
❑1, Jan 1998 .... 2.95
❑2 .... 2.95
❑3 .... 2.95
❑4 .... 2.95
❑5 .... 2.95

DICK TRACY (BLACKTHORNE)
Blackthorne
❑1, Jun 1986 .... 5.95
❑2, Jun 1986 .... 5.95
❑3, Jul 1986 .... 6.95
❑4, Aug 1986 .... 6.95
❑5, Oct 1986 .... 6.95
❑6, Oct 1986 .... 6.95
❑7, Dec 1986 .... 6.95
❑8, Jan 1987 .... 6.95
❑9, Jan 1987 .... 6.95
❑10, Feb 1987 .... 6.95
❑11, Mar 1987 .... 6.95
❑12, Apr 1987 .... 6.95
❑13, May 1987 .... 6.95
❑14, Jun 1987 .... 6.95
❑15, Jul 1987 .... 6.95
❑16, Aug 1987 .... 6.95
❑17, Sep 1987 .... 6.95
❑18, Sep 1987 .... 6.95
❑19, Oct 1987 .... 6.95
❑20, Oct 1987 .... 6.95
❑21, Nov 1987 .... 6.95
❑22, Nov 1987 .... 6.95
❑23, Nov 1987 .... 6.95
❑24, Dec 1987 .... 6.95

DICK TRACY (DISNEY)
Disney
❑1; newsstand format 2.95
❑1/Direct ed.; prestige format 4.95
❑2; newsstand format 2.95
❑2/Direct ed.; prestige format 5.95
❑3; newsstand format 2.95
❑3/Direct ed.; prestige format 5.95

DICK TRACY 3-D
Blackthorne
❑1, Jul 1986 .... 2.50

DICK TRACY ADVENTURES (GLADSTONE)
Gladstone
❑1, Sep 1991 .... 4.95

N-MINT

DICK TRACY ADVENTURES (HAMILTON)
Hamilton
❑1, b&w 3.95

DICK TRACY CRIMEBUSTER
Avalon
❑1 .... 2.95
❑2 .... 2.95
❑3 .... 2.95
❑4 .... 2.95

DICK TRACY DETECTIVE
Avalon
❑1 .... 2.95
❑2 .... 2.95
❑3 .... 2.95
❑4 .... 2.95

DICK TRACY MONTHLY (BLACKTHORNE)
Blackthorne
❑1, May 1986 .... 2.50
❑2, Jun 1986 .... 2.00
❑3, Jul 1986 .... 2.00
❑4, Aug 1986 .... 2.00
❑5, Sep 1986 .... 2.00
❑6, Oct 1986 .... 2.00
❑7, Nov 1986 .... 2.00
❑8, Dec 1986 .... 2.00
❑9, Jan 1987 .... 2.00
❑10, Feb 1987 .... 2.00
❑11, Mar 1987 .... 2.00
❑12, Apr 1987; no month in indicia ... 2.00
❑13, May 1987 .... 2.00
❑14, Jun 1987 .... 2.00
❑15, Jul 1987 .... 2.00
❑16 1988 .... 2.00
❑17 1988 .... 2.00
❑18 1988 .... 2.00
❑19 1988 .... 2.00
❑20 1988 .... 2.00
❑21 1988 .... 2.00
❑22 1988 .... 2.00
❑23 1988 .... 2.00
❑24 1988 .... 2.00
❑25 1988; Series continues as Dick Tracy Weekly 2.00

DICK TRACY SPECIAL
Blackthorne
❑1, Jan 1988 .... 2.95
❑2, Mar 1988 .... 2.95
❑3, May 1988 .... 2.95

DICK TRACY: THE EARLY YEARS
Blackthorne
❑1, Aug 1987 .... 6.95
❑2, Oct 1987 .... 6.95
❑3, Apr 1988 .... 6.95
❑4 .... 2.95

DICK TRACY "UNPRINTED STORIES"
Blackthorne
❑1, Sep 1987 .... 2.95
❑2, Nov 1987 .... 2.95
❑3, Jan 1988 .... 2.95
❑4, Jun 1988 .... 2.95

DICK TRACY WEEKLY
Blackthorne
❑26, Jan 1988 .... 2.00
❑27, Jan 1988 .... 2.00
❑28, Jan 1988 .... 2.00
❑29, Jan 1988 .... 2.00
❑30, Feb 1988 .... 2.00
❑31, Feb 1988 .... 2.00
❑32, Feb 1988 .... 2.00
❑33, Feb 1988 .... 2.00
❑34, Mar 1988 .... 2.00
❑35, Mar 1988 .... 2.00
❑36, Mar 1988 .... 2.00
❑37, Mar 1988 .... 2.00
❑38, Jun 1988 .... 2.00
❑39, Jun 1988 .... 2.00
❑40, Jun 1988 .... 2.00
❑41, Jun 1988 .... 2.00

N-MINT

❑42, Jul 1988 2.00
❑43, Jul 1988 2.00
❑44, Jul 1988 2.00
❑45, Jul 1988 2.00
❑46, Aug 1988 2.00
❑47, Aug 1988 2.00
❑48, Aug 1988 2.00
❑49, Aug 1988 2.00
❑50, Sep 1988 2.00
❑51, Sep 1988 2.00
❑52, Sep 1988 2.00
❑53, Sep 1988 2.00
❑54, Oct 1988 2.00
❑55, Oct 1988 2.00
❑56, Oct 1988 2.00
❑57, Oct 1988 2.00
❑58, Oct 1988 2.00
❑59, Oct 1988 2.00
❑60, Nov 1988 2.00
❑61, Nov 1988 2.00
❑62, Nov 1988 2.00
❑63, Nov 1988 2.00
❑64, Nov 1988 2.00
❑65, Nov 1988 2.00
❑66, Dec 1988 2.00
❑67, Dec 1988 2.00
❑68, Dec 1988 2.00
❑69, Dec 1988 2.00
❑70, Jan 1989 2.00
❑71, Jan 1989 2.00
❑72, Jan 1989 2.00
❑73, Jan 1989 2.00
❑74, Feb 1989 2.00
❑75, Feb 1989 2.00
❑76, Feb 1989 2.00
❑77, Feb 1989 2.00
❑78, Mar 1989 2.00
❑79, Mar 1989 2.00
❑80, Mar 1989 2.00
❑81, Mar 1989 2.00
❑82, Apr 1989 2.00
❑83, Apr 1989 2.00
❑84, Apr 1989 2.00
❑85, Apr 1989 2.00
❑86, May 1989 2.00
❑87, May 1989 2.00
❑88, May 1989 2.00
❑89, May 1989 2.00
❑90, Jun 1989 2.00
❑91, Jun 1989 2.00
❑92, Jun 1989 2.00
❑93, Jun 1989 2.00
❑94, Aug 1989 2.00
❑95, Aug 1989 2.00
❑96, Aug 1989 2.00
❑97, Aug 1989 2.00
❑98, Sep 1989 2.00
❑99, Sep 1989 2.00

DICK WAD
SLAVE LABOR

❑1, Sep 1993, b&w 2.50

DICTATORS: HITLER
ANTARCTIC

❑1, Apr 2004 2.99

DIEBOLD
SILENT PARTNERS

❑1 1996, b&w 2.95
❑2 1996, b&w 2.95

DIE-CUT
MARVEL

❑1, Nov 1993; diecut cover 2.50
❑2, Dec 1993 1.75
❑3, Jan 1994 1.75
❑4, Feb 1994 1.75

DIE-CUT VS. G-FORCE
MARVEL

❑1, Nov 1993; Holo-Grafx cover 2.75
❑2, Dec 1993; foil cover 2.75

N-MINT

DIESEL
ANTARCTIC

❑1, Apr 1997 2.95

DIGIMON DIGITAL MONSTERS
DARK HORSE

❑1, May 2000 2.95
❑2, May 2000 2.95
❑3, May 2000 2.95
❑4, May 2000 2.95
❑5, Aug 2000 2.95
❑6, Sep 2000 2.95
❑7, Sep 2000 2.95
❑8, Sep 2000 2.95
❑9, Sep 2000 2.99
❑10, Oct 2000 2.99
❑11, Nov 2000 2.99
❑12, Nov 2000 2.99

DIGIMON TAMERS
TOKYOPOP

❑1, Apr 2004 9.99

DIGITAL DRAGON
PEREGRINE ENTERTAINMENT

❑1, Jan 1999, b&w 2.95
❑2, Apr 1999, b&w 2.95

DIGITEK
MARVEL

❑1, Dec 1992 2.00
❑2, Jan 1993 2.00
❑3, Feb 1993 2.00
❑4, Mar 1993 2.00

DIK SKYCAP
RIP OFF

❑1, Dec 1991, b&w 2.50
❑2, May 1992, b&w 2.50

DILEMMA PRESENTS
DILEMMA

❑1, Oct 1994, b&w 2.50
❑2, b&w; Flip-book 2.50
❑3, Apr 1995, b&w; Flip-book 2.50
❑4, b&w; Flip-book 2.50

DILTON'S STRANGE SCIENCE
ARCHIE

❑1, May 1989 2.00
❑2, Aug 1989 1.50
❑3, Nov 1989 1.50
❑4, Feb 1990 1.50
❑5, May 1990 1.50

DIMENSION 5
EDGE

❑1, Oct 1995, b&w 3.95

DIMENSION X
KARL ART

❑1, b&w 3.50

DIMENSION Z
PYRAMID

❑1 2.00
❑2 2.00

DIMM COMICS PRESENTS
DIMM

❑Ashcan 0, Jan 1996, b&w; ashcan promotional comic 1.00
❑Ashcan 1, May 1996, b&w; ashcan promotional comic 1.00

DIM-WITTED DARRYL
SLAVE LABOR

❑1, Jun 1998, b&w 2.95
❑2 2.95
❑3 2.95

DINGLEDORFS, THE
SKYLIGHT

❑1, b&w 2.75

DINKY ON THE ROAD
BLIND BAT

❑1, Jun 1994, b&w 1.95

DINO ISLAND
MIRAGE

❑1, Feb 1993; covers form diptych 2.75
❑2, Mar 1993; covers form diptych 2.75

Newspaper strips featuring Chester Gould's master detective were reprinted in Blackthorne's *Dick Tracy Weekly.*

© 1988 Tribune Media and Blackthorne.

N-MINT

DINO-RIDERS
MARVEL

❑1, Mar 1989 1.50
❑2, Apr 1989 1.50
❑3, May 1989 1.50

DINOSAUR BOP
MONSTER

❑1, b&w 2.50
❑2, b&w 2.50

DINOSAUR ISLAND
MONSTER

❑1, b&w 2.50

DINOSAUR MANSION
EDGE

❑1, b&w; no indicia 2.95

DINOSAUR REX
UPSHOT

❑1 2.00
❑2, b&w 2.00
❑3, b&w 2.00

DINOSAURS
HOLLYWOOD

❑1; TV based 3.00
❑2; TV based 3.00

DINOSAURS ATTACK!
ECLIPSE

❑1; trading cards 3.95
❑2 3.95
❑3 3.95

DINOSAURS, A CELEBRATION
MARVEL / EPIC

❑1, ca. 1992; Horns and Heavy Armor 4.95
❑2, ca. 1992; Bone heads and Duck-bills 4.95
❑3, ca. 1992; Egg stealers and Earth shakers 4.95
❑4, ca. 1992; Terrible Claws and Tyrants 4.95

DINOSAURS FOR HIRE (ETERNITY)
ETERNITY

❑1, Mar 1988, b&w 2.00
❑1/3D; 3-D 2.95
❑1-2, Mar 1988 1.95
❑2, Jun 1988 1.95
❑3 1.95
❑4 1.95
❑5 1.95
❑6 1.95
❑7 1.95
❑8 1.95
❑9 1.95

DINOSAURS FOR HIRE (MALIBU)
MALIBU

❑1, Feb 1993 1.95
❑2, Mar 1993 1.95
❑3, Apr 1993 1.95
❑4, May 1993 1.95
❑5, Jun 1993 2.50
❑6, Jul 1993; Jurassic Park parody cover 2.50
❑7, Aug 1993 2.50
❑8, Sep 1993 2.50
❑9, Oct 1993 2.50
❑10, Nov 1993; Comics' Greatest World parody cover 2.50

N-MINT

❑11, Dec 1993 .... 2.50
❑12, Feb 1994; Ultraverse parody cover 2.50

DINOSAURS FOR HIRE: DINOSAURS RULE!
ETERNITY

❑1; Dinosaurs Rule! 5.95

DINOSAURS FOR HIRE FALL CLASSIC
ETERNITY

❑1, Nov 1988, b&w; Fall Classic; Elvis 2.25

DINOSAURS FOR HIRE: GUNS 'N' LIZARDS
ETERNITY

❑1; Guns 'n' Lizards 5.95

DIORAMAS: LOVE STORY
IMAGE

❑1, ca 2004 .... 12.95

DIRECTORY TO A NONEXISTENT UNIVERSE
ECLIPSE

❑1, Dec 1987 .... 2.00

DIRE WOLVES: A CHRONICLE OF THE DEADWORLD
CALIBER

❑1, b&w 3.95

DIRTBAG
TWIST N SHOUT

❑1, ca. 1993 .... 2.95
❑2, ca. 1993 .... 2.95
❑3, Nov 1993 .... 2.95
❑4, Dec 1993 .... 2.95
❑5, ca. 1994 .... 2.95
❑6 .... 2.95
❑7 .... 2.95

DIRTY DOZEN, THE
DELL

❑1, Oct 1967; 12-180-710 .... 25.00

DIRTY PAIR
ECLIPSE

❑1, Dec 1988, b&w 4.00
❑2, Jan 1989, b&w 3.00
❑3, Feb 1989, b&w 3.00
❑4, Mar 1989, b&w 3.00

DIRTY PAIR II
ECLIPSE

❑1, May 1989, b&w 2.50
❑2, Aug 1989, b&w 2.50
❑3, Nov 1989 .... 2.50
❑4, Feb 1990 .... 2.50
❑5, May 1990 .... 2.50

DIRTY PAIR III
ECLIPSE

❑1, Aug 1990, b&w 2.25
❑2, Nov 1990, b&w 2.25
❑3, Feb 1991 .... 2.25
❑4, May 1991 .... 2.25
❑5, Aug 1991 .... 2.25

DIRTY PAIR (4TH SERIES)
VIZ

❑1 .... 4.95
❑2 .... 4.95
❑3 .... 4.95
❑4 .... 4.95
❑5 .... 4.95

DIRTY PAIR: DANGEROUS ACQUAINTANCES
DARK HORSE / MANGA

❑1, b&w 2.95
❑2, b&w 2.95
❑3, b&w 2.95
❑4, b&w 2.95
❑5, b&w 2.95

DIRTY PAIR, THE: FATAL BUT NOT SERIOUS
DARK HORSE / MANGA

❑1, Jul 1995 .... 2.95
❑2, Aug 1995 .... 2.95
❑3, Sep 1995 .... 2.95
❑4, Oct 1995 .... 2.95
❑5, Nov 1995 .... 2.95

DIRTY PAIR, THE: RUN FROM THE FUTURE
DARK HORSE / MANGA

❑1, Jan 2000 .... 2.95
❑1/A, Jan 2000; alternate cover 2.95
❑2, Feb 2000 .... 2.95
❑3, Mar 2000 .... 2.95
❑4, Apr 2000 .... 2.95

DIRTY PAIR, THE: SIM HELL
DARK HORSE / MANGA

❑1 1993, b&w 2.95
❑2 1993, b&w 2.95
❑3 1993, b&w 2.95
❑4 1993, b&w 2.95
❑5 1993 .... 2.95

DIRTY PAIR, THE: SIM HELL REMASTERED
DARK HORSE / MANGA

❑1, May 2001 .... 2.99
❑2, Jun 2001 .... 2.99
❑3, Jul 2001 .... 2.99
❑4, Aug 2001 .... 2.99

DIRTY PAIR, THE: START THE VIOLENCE
DARK HORSE

❑1/A, Sep 1999 .... 2.95
❑1/B, Sep 1999; variant cover 2.95

DIRTY PICTURES
AIRCEL

❑1, Apr 1991, b&w 2.50
❑2, b&w 2.50
❑3, b&w 2.50

DIRTY PLOTTE
DRAWN AND QUARTERLY

❑1 .... 2.50
❑2 .... 2.50
❑3 .... 2.50
❑4 .... 2.50
❑5 .... 2.50
❑6 .... 2.50
❑7 .... 2.95
❑8 .... 2.95
❑9 .... 2.95
❑10, Nov 1996 .... 3.50

DISAVOWED
DC / WILDSTORM

❑1, Mar 2000 .... 2.50
❑2, Apr 2000 .... 2.50
❑3, May 2000 .... 2.50
❑4, Jun 2000 .... 2.50
❑5, Jul 2000 .... 2.50
❑6, Aug 2000 .... 2.50

DISCIPLES, THE
IMAGE

❑1, Apr 2001 .... 2.95
❑2, Jun 2001 .... 2.95

DISHMAN
ECLIPSE

❑1, Sep 1988, b&w 2.50

DISNEY AFTERNOON, THE
MARVEL

❑1, Nov 1994; Darkwing Duck, Bonkers, Goof Troop, Tailspin 2.00
❑2, Dec 1994 .... 1.50
❑3, Jan 1995 .... 1.50
❑4, Feb 1995 .... 1.50
❑5, Mar 1995 .... 1.50
❑6, Apr 1995 .... 1.50
❑7, May 1995 .... 1.50
❑8, Jun 1995 .... 1.50
❑9, Jul 1995 .... 1.50
❑10, Aug 1995 .... 1.50

DISNEY COMIC HITS
MARVEL

❑1, Oct 1995; Pocahontas 2.00
❑2, Nov 1995; Timon and Pumbaa 2.00
❑3, Dec 1995 A: Pocahontas. A: Captain John Smith. 2.00
❑4, Jan 1996; Adapts Toy Story 2.00
❑5, Feb 1996; Winter Wonderland 2.00
❑6, Mar 1996 .... 2.00
❑7, Apr 1996 .... 2.00
❑8, May 1996 .... 2.00
❑9, Jun 1996 .... 2.00
❑10, Jul 1996; adapts Hunchback of Notre Dame 2.00
❑11, Aug 1996; Hunchback of Notre Dame 2.00
❑12, Sep 1996; The Little Mermaid 2.00
❑13, Oct 1996; adapts Aladdin and the King of Thieves 2.00
❑14, Nov 1996; Timon & Pumbaa 2.00
❑15, Dec 1996; Toy Story adventures 2.00
❑16, Jan 1997; adapts 101 Dalmations 2.00

DISNEYLAND BIRTHDAY PARTY (WALT DISNEY'S...)
GLADSTONE

❑1, ca. 1985; CB (a); Reprints Disneyland Birthday Party (Giant), Uncle Scrooge Goes to Disneyland 10.00
❑1/A; digest 10.00

DISNEY MOVIE BOOK
DISNEY

❑1; Roger Rabbit in Tummy Trouble 7.95

DISNEY'S ACTION CLUB
ACCLAIM

❑1; digest; Hercules, Hunchback, Lion King, Aladdin, Toy Story, Mighty Ducks 4.50
❑2 .... 4.50
❑3 .... 4.50
❑4; digest; Mighty Ducks, Toy Story, Aladdin, Hercules stories 4.50
❑5 .... 4.50
❑6 .... 4.50
❑7, Jun 1997 .... 4.50

DISNEY'S COLOSSAL COMICS
DISNEY

❑1 .... 2.00

DISNEY'S COLOSSAL COMICS COLLECTION
DISNEY

❑1; digest 2.00
❑2; digest 2.00
❑3; digest 2.00
❑4; digest 2.00
❑5; digest 2.00
❑6; digest 2.00
❑7; digest 2.00
❑8; digest 2.00
❑9; digest 2.00
❑10; digest 2.00

DISNEY'S COMICS IN 3-D
DISNEY

❑1 .... 2.95

DISNEY'S ENCHANTING STORIES
ACCLAIM

❑1 .... 4.50
❑2; Pocahontas 4.50
❑3; Beauty & The Beast 4.50
❑4; 101 Dalmations 4.50

DISOBEDIENT DAISY
FANTAGRAPHICS / EROS

❑1, Aug 1995, b&w 2.95
❑2, Oct 1995, b&w 2.95

DISTANT SOIL, A (1ST SERIES)
WARP

❑1 1983 .... 8.00
❑2 1984 .... 5.00
❑3 1984 .... 4.00
❑4 1984 .... 4.00
❑5 1985 .... 4.00
❑6, Jun 1985; Standard comic size 1: Panda Khan. 3.00
❑7, Sep 1985 .... 3.00
❑8, Dec 1985 .... 3.00
❑9, Mar 1986 .... 3.00

N-MINT

DISTANT SOIL, A (2ND SERIES)
ARIA

❑1 1991 .... 5.00
❑1-2 .... 3.00
❑1-3 .... 2.00
❑1-4 .... 1.75
❑2 .... 3.00
❑2-2 .... 1.75
❑3 1992 .... 3.00
❑3-2 .... 1.75
❑4 1993 .... 2.00
❑4-2 .... 1.75
❑5 1993 .... 1.75
❑6 .... 1.75
❑7 1994 .... 1.75
❑8, Jun 1994 .... 1.75
❑9 1994 .... 2.50
❑10 .... 2.50
❑11, Apr 1995 .... 2.50
❑12, Nov 1995 .... 2.50
❑13, Jun 1996 .... 2.95
❑14, Aug 1996 .... 2.95
❑15, Aug 1996; Image begins as publisher 2.95
❑16, Oct 1996 .... 2.95
❑17, Dec 1996 .... 2.95
❑18, Feb 1997 .... 2.95
❑19, Apr 1997 .... 2.95
❑20, Jun 1997 .... 2.95
❑21, Sep 1997 .... 2.95
❑22, Dec 1997 .... 2.95
❑23, Feb 1998 .... 2.95
❑24, Apr 1998 .... 2.95
❑25, Jun 1998; double-sized NG (w); 3.95
❑25/Ltd., Jun 1998; 15th anniversary issue NG (w); 8.00
❑26, Nov 1998; Christmas cover; not Christmas story 2.95
❑27, Apr 1999 .... 2.95
❑28, Jul 1999 .... 3.95
❑29, Dec 1999 .... 3.95
❑30, Aug 2000 .... 3.95
❑31, Jan 2001 .... 3.95
❑32, May 2001 .... 3.95
❑33, Aug 2001 .... 3.95
❑34, Sep 2001; Giant-size 4.95
❑35 .... 0.00
❑36, Oct 2003 .... 4.50

DISTRICT X
MARVEL

❑1, Jul 2004 .... 0.00
❑2, Aug 2004 .... 2.99
❑3, Sep 2004 ....

DITKO PACKAGE
DITKO

❑1; squarebound 8.95

DIVA GRAFIX & STORIES
STARHEAD

❑1, Nov 1993, b&w 3.95
❑2, b&w 3.95

DIVAS
CALIBER

❑1, b&w 2.50
❑2, b&w 2.50
❑3, b&w 2.50
❑4, b&w 2.50

DIVINE INTERVENTION/GEN13
DC / WILDSTORM

❑1, Nov 1999 .... 2.50

DIVINE INTERVENTION/WILDCATS
DC / WILDSTORM

❑1, Nov 1999 .... 2.50

DIVINE RIGHT
IMAGE

❑1, Sep 1997 JLee (w); JLee (a) 3.00
❑1/A, Sep 1997; JLee (w); JLee (a); variant cover 3.00
❑1/B, Sep 1997; JLee (c); JLee (w); JLee (a); American Entertainment variant; Christy Blaze with flag in background 3.00

N-MINT

❑1/C, Sep 1997; Bagged edition JLee (c); JLee (w); JLee (a) 3.00
❑1/D, Sep 1997; Spanish edition; alternate cover 2.50
❑1/E, Sep 1997; Voyager pack with preview of Stormwatch 2.50
❑2, Oct 1997; JLee (w); JLee (a); Sword battle scene on cover 3.00
❑2/Variant, Oct 1997; alternate cover; fight scene 2.50
❑3, Nov 1997 JLee (w); JLee (a); A: Fairchild. 2.50
❑3/Variant, Nov 1997; no cover price on outer cover 2.50
❑4, Dec 1997; JLee (w); JLee (a); White cover w/blue figure (no Fairchild) .. 2.50
❑4/Variant, Dec 1997; JLee (w); JLee (a); Variant cover (Fairchild) 2.50
❑5, Feb 1998 JLee (w); JLee (a) 2.50
❑5/Variant, Feb 1998; Pacific Comicon variant cover edition; JLee (w); JLee (a) 2.50
❑6, Aug 1998 JLee (w); JLee (a) 2.50
❑7, Dec 1998 JLee (w); JLee (a) 2.50
❑8, Jan 1999 JLee (w); JLee (a) 2.50
❑8/Variant, Jan 1999; alternate cover 2.50
❑9, Jul 1999 JLee (w); JLee (a) 2.50
❑10, Oct 1999 JLee (w); JLee (a) 2.50
❑11, Nov 1999 JLee (w); JLee (a) 2.50
❑Ashcan 1, Jul 1997; JLee (w); JLee (a); 1: Divine Right. Team on cover 3.00
❑Ashcan 1/A, Jul 1997; JLee (w); JLee (a); 1: Divine Right. variant cover: Faraday typing, woman's leg in foreground 3.00

DIVISION 13
DARK HORSE

❑1, Sep 1994 .... 2.50
❑2, Oct 1994 .... 2.50
❑3, Dec 1994 .... 2.50
❑4, Jan 1995, b&w 2.50

DIXIE ROAD
NBM

❑1 .... 10.95
❑2 .... 10.95

DJANGO AND ANGEL
CALIBER

❑1, b&w 2.50
❑2, b&w 2.50
❑3, b&w 2.50
❑4, b&w 2.50
❑5, b&w 2.50

DNAGENTS
ECLIPSE

❑1, Mar 1983 .... 2.50
❑2, Apr 1983 ME (w) 2.00
❑3, May 1983 ME (w) 2.00
❑4, Jul 1983 .... 2.00
❑5, Aug 1983 .... 2.00
❑6, Oct 1983 .... 1.75
❑7, Nov 1983 .... 1.75
❑8, Jan 1984 .... 1.75
❑9, Feb 1984 .... 1.75
❑10, Mar 1984 .... 1.75
❑11, May 1984 .... 1.75
❑12, May 1984 .... 1.75
❑13, Jun 1984 .... 1.75
❑14, Jul 1984 .... 1.75
❑15, Aug 1984 EL (a) 1.75
❑16, Sep 1984 .... 1.75
❑17, Dec 1984 .... 1.75
❑18, Jan 1985 .... 1.75
❑19, Feb 1985 .... 1.75
❑20, Mar 1985 .... 1.75
❑21, Apr 1985 .... 1.75
❑22, May 1985 .... 1.75
❑23, Jun 1985 .... 1.75
❑24, Jul 1985 DSt (c) 1.75
❑3D 1, Jan 1986; 3-Dminensional DNAgents 2.50

DNAGENTS SUPER SPECIAL
ANTARCTIC

❑1, Apr 1994, b&w 3.50

Panda Khan made his first appearance in *A Distant Soil* (1st series) #6.
© 1985 Colleen Doran, etc.

N-MINT

D-N-ANGEL
TOKYOPOP

❑1, Apr 2004 .... 9.99

D.O.A.
SAVING GRACE

❑1 .... 1.00

DOC CHAOS: THE STRANGE ATTRACTOR
VORTEX

❑1, Apr 1990 .... 3.00
❑2 1990 .... 3.00
❑3 1990 .... 3.00

DOC SAMSON
MARVEL

❑1, Jan 1996 .... 1.95
❑2, Feb 1996 .... 1.95
❑3, Mar 1996 .... 1.95
❑4, Apr 1996 .... 1.95

DOC SAVAGE (GOLD KEY)
GOLD KEY

❑1, Nov 1966; 10192-611 .... 38.00

DOC SAVAGE (MARVEL)
MARVEL

❑1, Oct 1972; RA, JM (a); adapts Man of Bronze 6.00
❑2, Dec 1972; adapts Man of Bronze . 3.50
❑3, Feb 1973; adapts Death in Silver . 3.00
❑4, Apr 1973; adapts Death in Silver . 3.00
❑5, Jun 1973; adapts The Monsters .. 3.00
❑6, Aug 1973; GK (c); RA (a); adapts The Monsters 3.00
❑7, Oct 1973; adapts Brand of the Werewolf 3.00
❑8, Jan 1974; adapts Brand of the Werewolf 3.00

DOC SAVAGE (MARVEL MAGAZINE)
MARVEL

❑1, Aug 1975 .... 6.00
❑2, Oct 1975 .... 4.00
❑3, Jan 1976 .... 4.00
❑4, Apr 1976 .... 4.00
❑5, Jul 1976 .... 4.00
❑6, Oct 1976 .... 3.00
❑7, Jan 1977 .... 3.00
❑8, Spr 1977 .... 3.00

DOC SAVAGE (MINI-SERIES)
DC

❑1, Nov 1987 .... 2.00
❑2, Dec 1987 .... 2.00
❑3, Jan 1988 .... 2.00
❑4, Feb 1988 .... 2.00

DOC SAVAGE (DC)
DC

❑1, Nov 1988 .... 2.00
❑2, Dec 1988 .... 2.00
❑3, Dec 1988 .... 2.00
❑4, Jan 1989 .... 2.00
❑5, Jan 1989 .... 2.00
❑6, Mar 1989 .... 2.00
❑7, Apr 1989 .... 2.00
❑8, May 1989 .... 2.00
❑9, Jun 1989 .... 2.00
❑10, Jul 1989 .... 2.00
❑11, Aug 1989 V: John Sunlight. 2.00
❑12, Sep 1989 V: John Sunlight. 2.00
❑13, Oct 1989 V: John Sunlight. 2.00

N-MINT

❑14, Nov 1989 V: John Sunlight. 2.00
❑15, Dec 1989 ...... 2.00
❑16, Jan 1990 ...... 2.00
❑17, Feb 1990; Shadow 2.00
❑18, Mar 1990; Shadow 2.00
❑19, May 1990 ...... 2.00
❑20, Jun 1990 ...... 2.00
❑21, Jul 1990 ...... 2.00
❑22, Aug 1990 ...... 2.00
❑23, Sep 1990 ...... 2.00
❑24, Oct 1990 ...... 2.00
❑Annual 1, ca. 1989 ...... 3.50

DOC SAVAGE: CURSE OF THE FIRE GOD
DARK HORSE

❑1, Sep 1995 ...... 2.95
❑2, Oct 1995 ...... 2.95
❑3, Nov 1995 ...... 2.95
❑4, Dec 1995 ...... 2.95

DOC SAVAGE: DEVIL'S THOUGHTS
MILLENNIUM

❑1 ...... 2.50
❑2 ...... 2.50
❑3 ...... 2.50

DOC SAVAGE: DOOM DYNASTY
MILLENNIUM

❑1 ...... 2.00
❑2 ...... 2.00

DOC SAVAGE: MANUAL OF BRONZE
MILLENNIUM

❑1, Aug 1992 ...... 2.50

DOC SAVAGE: REPEL
MILLENNIUM

❑1; only issue ever released 2.50

DOC SAVAGE: THE MAN OF BRONZE
MILLENNIUM

❑1 ...... 2.50
❑2 ...... 2.50
❑3 ...... 2.50
❑4 ...... 2.50

DOC STEARN...MR. MONSTER
ECLIPSE

❑1, Jan 1985; 1: Mr. Monster. Reprints Mr. Monster story from Vanguard Illustrated #7 ...... 2.50
❑2, Aug 1985 DSt (c) 2.00
❑3, Oct 1985 ...... 2.00
❑4, Dec 1985 ...... 2.00
❑5, Feb 1986 ...... 2.00
❑6, Jun 1986 ...... 2.00
❑7, Dec 1986 ...... 2.00
❑8, Mar 1987 ...... 2.00
❑9, Apr 1987 A: Wolff & Byrd. 2.00
❑10, Jun 1987; BW, AMo (w); BW (a); 6-D 2.00

DOCTOR FATE (2ND MINI-SERIES)
DC

❑1, Oct 2003 ...... 2.50
❑2, Nov 2003 ...... 2.50
❑3, Dec 2003 ...... 2.50
❑4, Jan 2004 ...... 2.50
❑5, Feb 2004 ...... 2.50

DR. ANDY
ALLIANCE

❑1, Aug 1994, b&w 2.50

DR. ATOMIC
LAST GASP

❑1 ...... 5.00
❑2 ...... 4.00
❑3 ...... 4.00
❑4 ...... 3.00
❑5 ...... 3.00
❑6 ...... 3.00

DOCTOR BANG
RIP OFF

❑1, Feb 1992, b&w 2.50

DOCTOR BOOGIE
MEDIA ARTS

❑1 ...... 1.75

N-MINT

DOCTOR CHAOS
TRIUMPHANT

❑1; Unleashed! 2.50
❑2; Unleashed! 2.50
❑3, Jan 1994 ...... 2.50
❑4, Feb 1994 ...... 2.50
❑5, Mar 1994 ...... 2.50
❑6, Mar 1994 ...... 2.50
❑7 1994 ...... 2.50
❑8 1994 ...... 2.50
❑9 1994 ...... 2.50
❑10 1994 ...... 2.50
❑11 1994 ...... 2.50
❑12 1994 ...... 2.50

DOCTOR CYBORG
ATTENTION!

❑1, b&w 1: Doctor Cyborg. 2.95
❑1/Ashcan, b&w; Preview edition of Doctor Cyborg #1; 1: Doctor Cyborg. 1.00
❑2, b&w 2.95
❑3, b&w 2.95

DOCTOR DOOM'S REVENGE
MARVEL

❑1, ca. 1989, giveaway comic included with computer game from Paragon Software 1.00

DOCTOR FATE (1ST MINI-SERIES)
DC

❑1, Jul 1987 KG (a) 2.00
❑2, Aug 1987 KG (a) 2.00
❑3, Sep 1987 KG (a) 2.00
❑4, Oct 1987 KG (a); 1: Doctor Fate II (Eric Strauss & Linda Strauss). D: Doctor Fate I (Kent Nelson). 2.00

DOCTOR FATE
DC

❑1, Dec 1988 ...... 2.00
❑2, Jan 1989 ...... 1.25
❑3, Jan 1989 ...... 1.25
❑4, Feb 1989 ...... 1.25
❑5, Apr 1989 ...... 1.25
❑6, May 1989 ...... 1.75
❑7, Jun 1989 ...... 1.75
❑8, Jul 1989 ...... 1.75
❑9, Aug 1989 ...... 1.75
❑10, Sep 1989 ...... 1.75
❑11, Nov 1989 ...... 1.50
❑12, Dec 1989 ...... 1.50
❑13, Jan 1990 ...... 1.50
❑14, Feb 1990 ...... 1.50
❑15, Mar 1990 ...... 1.50
❑16, Apr 1990 ...... 1.50
❑17, May 1990 ...... 1.50
❑18, Jun 1990 ...... 1.50
❑19, Jul 1990 ...... 1.50
❑20, Aug 1990 ...... 1.50
❑21, Oct 1990 ...... 1.50
❑22, Nov 1990 ...... 1.50
❑23, Dec 1990 ...... 1.50
❑24, Jan 1991 ...... 1.50
❑25, Feb 1991 ...... 1.50
❑26, Mar 1991 ...... 1.50
❑27, Apr 1991 ...... 1.50
❑28, May 1991 ...... 1.50
❑29, Jun 1991 ...... 1.50
❑30, Jul 1991 ...... 1.50
❑31, Aug 1991 ...... 1.50
❑32, Sep 1991; War of the Gods 1.75
❑33, Oct 1991; War of the Gods 1.75
❑34, Nov 1991 ...... 1.75
❑35, Dec 1991 ...... 1.75
❑36, Jan 1992 ...... 1.75
❑37, Feb 1992 ...... 1.75
❑38, Mar 1992 ...... 1.75
❑39, Apr 1992 ...... 1.75
❑40, May 1992 ...... 1.75
❑41, Jun 1992 ...... 1.75
❑Annual 1, Nov 1989 ...... 2.95

N-MINT

DOCTOR FAUSTUS
ANARCHY

❑1, b&w 2.95
❑2 1994, b&w 2.95
❑Ashcan 1; b&w 2.00

DOCTOR FRANKENSTEIN'S HOUSE OF 3-D
3-D ZONE

❑1, ca. 1992, Oversized; Oversized 4.00

DR. FU MANCHU
I.W.

❑1, ca. 1964 ...... 45.00

DR. GIGGLES
DARK HORSE

❑1 1992 ...... 2.50
❑2 1992 ...... 2.50

DOCTOR GORPON
ETERNITY

❑1, b&w 2.50
❑2, b&w 2.50
❑3, Aug 1991, b&w 2.50

DR. GOYLE SPECIAL
ARROW

❑1, b&w 2.95

DOCTOR! I'M TOO BIG!
NBM

❑1 ...... 10.95

DR. JEKYLL AND MR. HYDE
NBM

❑1 ...... 15.95

DR. KILDARE
DELL

❑2 1962 ...... 50.00
❑3, Oct 1962 ...... 40.00
❑4, Dec 1962 ...... 40.00
❑5, Mar 1963 ...... 40.00
❑6, Jun 1963 ...... 40.00
❑7, Sep 1963 ...... 40.00
❑8, Oct 1964 ...... 40.00
❑9, Apr 1965 ...... 40.00

DOCTOR MID-NITE
DC

❑1, ca. 1999; D.O.A. 5.95
❑2, ca. 1999 ...... 5.95
❑3, ca. 1999 ...... 5.95

DR. RADIUM AND THE GIZMOS OF BOOLA-BOOLA
SLAVE LABOR

❑1, Jan 1992, b&w 4.95

DR. RADIUM, MAN OF SCIENCE
SLAVE LABOR

❑1, Oct 1992, b&w 2.50
❑2, Jan 1993, b&w 2.50
❑3, Jul 1993 ...... 2.95
❑4, Jan 1994 ...... 2.95
❑5, Jan 1995, b&w 2.95

DR. ROBOT SPECIAL
DARK HORSE

❑1, Apr 2000 ...... 2.95

DOCTOR SOLAR, MAN OF THE ATOM
GOLD KEY

❑1, Oct 1962; O: Doctor Solar. 1: Doctor Solar (out of costume). 1st Gold Key comic 100.00
❑2, Dec 1962 1: Professor Harbinger. 45.00
❑3, Mar 1963 ...... 30.00
❑4, Jun 1963 ...... 30.00
❑5, Sep 1963 1: Doctor Solar (in costume). 30.00
❑6, Nov 1963 ...... 22.00
❑7, Mar 1964; Painted cover 22.00
❑8, Jul 1964 ...... 22.00
❑9, Oct 1964 ...... 22.00
❑10, Jan 1965 ...... 22.00
❑11, Mar 1965 ...... 16.00
❑12, May 1965; makes multiple versions of self 16.00
❑13, Jul 1965 ...... 16.00
❑14, Sep 1965; Painted cover 16.00

	N-MINT
❑15, Dec 1965 O: Doctor Solar.	20.00
❑16, Jun 1966; Painted cover	16.00
❑17, Sep 1966	16.00
❑18, Dec 1966	16.00
❑19, Apr 1967	16.00
❑20, Jul 1967	16.00
❑21, Oct 1967	12.00
❑22, Jan 1968	12.00
❑23, Apr 1968	12.00
❑24, Jul 1968	12.00
❑25, Oct 1968	12.00
❑26, Jan 1969	12.00
❑27, Apr 1969; End of original series	12.00
❑28, Apr 1981; Series begins again (1981)	3.50
❑29 1981	3.50
❑30, Feb 1982 A: Magnus, Robot Fighter (Gold Key).	3.50
❑31, Mar 1982 A: Magnus, Robot Fighter (Gold Key).	3.50

DR. SPECK
Bug Books

	N-MINT
❑1, b&w	2.95
❑2, b&w	2.95
❑3, b&w	2.95
❑4, b&w	2.95

DOCTOR STRANGE (1ST SERIES)
Marvel

	N-MINT
❑169, Jun 1968; DA (a); O: Doctor Strange. Series continued from Strange Tales #168	100.00
❑170, Jul 1968 DA (a); V: Nightmare.	40.00
❑171, Aug 1968 DA (a)	32.00
❑172, Sep 1968 GC (a); V: Dormammu.	32.00
❑173, Oct 1968 GC (a); V: Dormammu.	32.00
❑174, Nov 1968 GC (a); 1: Satannish.	32.00
❑175, Dec 1968 GC (a)	32.00
❑176, Jan 1969 GC (a)	32.00
❑177, Feb 1969 GC (a); 1: new costume.	26.00
❑178, Mar 1969 GC (a); A: Black Knight.	26.00
❑179, Apr 1969; SD (a); A: Spider-Man. reprints Amazing Spider-Man Annual #2	26.00
❑180, May 1969 GC (a); A: Eternity.	26.00
❑181, Jun 1969 GC (a)	26.00
❑182, Sep 1969 GC (a); V: Juggernaut.	26.00
❑183, Nov 1969 GC (a)	26.00

DOCTOR STRANGE (2ND SERIES)
Marvel

	N-MINT
❑1, Jun 1974; FB, DG (a); Marvel Value Stamp #23: Sgt. Fury	25.00
❑2, Aug 1974; FB, DG (a); 1: Silver Dagger. A: Defenders. Marvel Value Stamp #5: Dracula	12.00
❑3, Sep 1974; FB, DG (a); V: Dormammu. reprints with changes Strange Tales #126 and 127; Marvel Value Stamp #14: Living Mummy	6.00
❑4, Oct 1974; FB, DG (a); Marvel Value Stamp #33:Invisible Girl	6.00
❑5, Nov 1974; FB, DG (a); O: Silver Dagger. Marvel Value Stamp #76: Dormammu	6.00
❑6, Dec 1974; GC (a); Marvel Value Stamp #37: Watcher	5.00
❑7, Apr 1975 GC (a)	5.00
❑8, Jun 1975 GC (a); O: Clea.	5.00
❑9, Aug 1975 GC (a); O: Clea.	5.00
❑10, Oct 1975 GC (a)	5.00
❑11, Dec 1975 GC (a)	3.00
❑12, Feb 1976 GC (a)	3.00
❑13, Apr 1976 GC (a)	3.00
❑13/30 cent, Apr 1976; 30 cent regional price variant	20.00
❑14, May 1976 GC (a)	3.00
❑14/30 cent, May 1976; 30 cent regional price variant	20.00
❑15, Jun 1976 GC (a)	3.00
❑15/30 cent, Jun 1976; 30 cent regional price variant	20.00
❑16, Jul 1976 GC (a)	3.00
❑16/30 cent, Jul 1976; 30 cent regional price variant	20.00
❑17, Aug 1976 GC (a)	3.00
❑17/30 cent, Aug 1976; 30 cent regional price variant	20.00
❑18, Sep 1976 GC (a)	3.00
❑19, Oct 1976 GC, AA (a); 1: Xander.	3.00
❑20, Dec 1976	3.00
❑21, Feb 1977; O: Doctor Strange. reprinted from Doctor Strange (1st series) #169	2.50
❑22, Apr 1977	2.50
❑23, Jun 1977	2.50
❑23/35 cent, Jun 1977; 35 cent regional price variant	15.00
❑24, Aug 1977	2.50
❑24/35 cent, Aug 1977; 35 cent regional price variant	15.00
❑25, Oct 1977	2.50
❑25/35 cent, Oct 1977; 35 cent regional price variant	15.00
❑26, Dec 1977	2.00
❑27, Feb 1978	2.00
❑28, Apr 1978	2.00
❑29, Jun 1978 TS (a)	2.00
❑30, Aug 1978 TS (a)	2.00
❑31, Oct 1978 TS (a)	2.00
❑32, Dec 1978	2.00
❑33, Feb 1979	2.00
❑34, Apr 1979	2.00
❑35, Jun 1979	2.00
❑36, Aug 1979 GC, DGr (a)	2.00
❑37, Oct 1979	2.00
❑38, Dec 1979 GC, DGr (a)	2.00
❑39, Feb 1980	2.00
❑40, Apr 1980	2.00
❑41, Jun 1980	2.00
❑42, Aug 1980	2.00
❑43, Oct 1980	2.00
❑44, Dec 1980	2.00
❑45, Feb 1981	2.00
❑46, Apr 1981 FM (c); FM (a)	2.00
❑47, Jun 1981	2.00
❑48, Aug 1981 A: Brother Voodoo.	2.00
❑49, Oct 1981 A: Baron Mordo.	2.00
❑50, Dec 1981 A: Baron Mordo.	2.00
❑51, Feb 1982	2.00
❑52, Apr 1982	2.00
❑53, Jun 1982	2.00
❑54, Aug 1982 PS, BA (a)	2.00
❑55, Oct 1982 MG (a)	2.00
❑56, Dec 1982 PS (a)	2.00
❑57, Feb 1983 KN (a)	2.00
❑58, Apr 1983 DGr (a)	2.00
❑59, Jun 1983 DGr (a)	2.00
❑60, Aug 1983 DGr (a); A: Dracula.	2.00
❑61, Oct 1983 DGr (a); A: Dracula.	2.00
❑62, Dec 1983 A: Dracula.	2.00
❑63, Feb 1984	2.00
❑64, Apr 1984	2.00
❑65, Jun 1984 PS (a)	2.00
❑66, Aug 1984 PS (a)	2.00
❑67, Oct 1984	2.00
❑68, Dec 1984 PS (a)	2.00
❑69, Feb 1985 PS (a)	2.00
❑70, Apr 1985	2.00
❑71, Jun 1985 PS (a); O: Umar.	2.00
❑72, Aug 1985 PS (a)	2.00
❑73, Oct 1985 PS (a)	2.00
❑74, Dec 1985; 1: Ecstasy. Secret Wars II	2.00
❑75, Feb 1986 SB (a); O: Wong (Doctor Strange's manservant).	2.00
❑76, Apr 1986	2.00
❑77, Jun 1986	2.00
❑78, Aug 1986; New costume	2.00
❑79, Oct 1986	2.00
❑80, Dec 1986	2.00
❑81, Feb 1987	2.00
❑Annual 1, ca. 1976	2.00
❑Special 1, Mar 1983 FB (a)	3.00

Gold Key's first super-hero comic book was *Doctor Solar, Man of the Atom.*

© 1963 Gold Key.

DOCTOR STRANGE (3RD SERIES)
Marvel

	N-MINT
❑1, Feb 1999	2.99
❑2, Mar 1999	2.99
❑3, Apr 1999	2.99
❑4, May 1999	2.99

DOCTOR STRANGE CLASSICS
Marvel

	N-MINT
❑1, Mar 1984 SD (a)	2.00
❑2, Apr 1984 SD (a)	2.00
❑3, May 1984	2.00
❑4, Jun 1984	2.00

DOCTOR STRANGE/GHOST RIDER SPECIAL
Marvel

	N-MINT
❑1, Apr 1991; reprints Doctor Strange #28; Continued from Ghost Rider 12	1.50

DOCTOR STRANGE: SHAMBALLA
Marvel

	N-MINT
❑1, ca. 1986	5.95

DOCTOR STRANGE: SORCERER SUPREME
Marvel

	N-MINT
❑1, Nov 1988	3.00
❑2, Jan 1989; Inferno	2.00
❑3, Mar 1989	2.00
❑4, May 1989	1.50
❑5, Jul 1989	1.50
❑6, Aug 1989	1.50
❑7, Sep 1989	1.50
❑8, Oct 1989 O: Satannish. O: Mephisto.	1.50
❑9, Nov 1989	1.50
❑10, Dec 1989 A: Morbius.	1.50
❑11, Dec 1989; A: Hobgoblin. Acts of Vengeance	1.50
❑12, Dec 1989; Acts of Vengeance	1.50
❑13, Jan 1990; Acts of Vengeance	1.50
❑14, Feb 1990; vampires	1.50
❑15, Mar 1990; Amy Grant cover (unauthorized, caused Marvel to be sued); vampires	3.00
❑16, Apr 1990; vampires	1.50
❑17, May 1990; vampires	1.50
❑18, Jun 1990; vampires	1.50
❑19, Jul 1990 GC (a)	1.50
❑20, Aug 1990	1.50
❑21, Sep 1990	1.50
❑22, Oct 1990 O: Umar.	1.50
❑23, Nov 1990	1.50
❑24, Dec 1990	1.50
❑25, Jan 1991	1.50
❑26, Feb 1991; werewolf	1.50
❑27, Mar 1991; werewolf	1.50
❑28, Apr 1991; Ghost Rider crossover	1.50
❑29, May 1991	1.50
❑30, Jun 1991	1.50
❑31, Jul 1991; Infinity Gauntlet	1.50
❑32, Aug 1991; Infinity Gauntlet	1.50
❑33, Sep 1991; Infinity Gauntlet	1.50
❑34, Oct 1991; Infinity Gauntlet	1.50
❑35, Nov 1991; Infinity Gauntlet	1.50
❑36, Dec 1991; Infinity Gauntlet; Prelude to Warlock & the Infinity Watch #1	1.50
❑37, Jan 1992 A: Silver Surfer.	1.50
❑38, Feb 1992	1.75
❑39, Mar 1992	1.75

N-MINT

- ❑40, Apr 1992 ..... 1.75
- ❑41, May 1992; Wolverine 1.75
- ❑42, Jun 1992; Galactus 1.75
- ❑43, Jul 1992 ..... 1.75
- ❑44, Aug 1992 ..... 1.75
- ❑45, Sep 1992 ..... 1.75
- ❑46, Oct 1992 ..... 1.75
- ❑47, Nov 1992 ..... 1.75
- ❑48, Dec 1992 ..... 1.75
- ❑49, Jan 1993 ..... 1.75
- ❑50, Feb 1993; Prelude to Secret Defenders #1; Prism cover 2.95
- ❑51, Mar 1993 ..... 1.75
- ❑52, Apr 1993 A: Morbius. 1.75
- ❑53, May 1993 ..... 1.75
- ❑54, Jun 1993 ..... 1.75
- ❑55, Jul 1993 ..... 1.75
- ❑56, Aug 1993 ..... 1.75
- ❑57, Sep 1993 ..... 1.75
- ❑58, Oct 1993 A: Urthona. 1.75
- ❑59, Nov 1993 ..... 1.75
- ❑60, Dec 1993; Spot varnish cover ... 1.75
- ❑61, Jan 1994 ..... 1.75
- ❑62, Feb 1994 ..... 1.75
- ❑63, Mar 1994 ..... 1.75
- ❑64, Apr 1994 ..... 1.75
- ❑65, May 1994 ..... 1.75
- ❑66, Jun 1994 ..... 1.95
- ❑67, Jul 1994 ..... 1.95
- ❑68, Aug 1994 ..... 1.95
- ❑69, Sep 1994 ..... 1.95
- ❑70, Oct 1994 A: Hulk. 1.95
- ❑71, Nov 1994 A: Hulk. 1.95
- ❑72, Dec 1994 ..... 1.95
- ❑73, Jan 1995 ..... 1.95
- ❑74, Feb 1995 ..... 1.95
- ❑75, Mar 1995; Giant-size 2.50
- ❑75/Variant, Mar 1995; Giant-size; Holo-grafix cover 3.50
- ❑76, Apr 1995 ..... 1.95
- ❑77, May 1995 ..... 1.95
- ❑78, Jun 1995 ..... 1.95
- ❑79, Jul 1995 ..... 1.95
- ❑80, Aug 1995; indicia changes to Doctor Strange, Sorcerer Supreme for remainder of run 1.95
- ❑81, Sep 1995 ..... 1.95
- ❑82, Oct 1995 ..... 1.95
- ❑83, Nov 1995 ..... 1.95
- ❑84, Dec 1995 A: Mordo. 1.95
- ❑85, Jan 1996 O: Mordo. 1.95
- ❑86, Feb 1996 ..... 1.95
- ❑87, Mar 1996 D: Mordo. 1.95
- ❑88, Apr 1996 ..... 1.95
- ❑89, May 1996 ..... 1.95
- ❑90, Jun 1996 ..... 1.95
- ❑Annual 1 ..... 2.50
- ❑Annual 2, ca. 1992 ..... 2.25
- ❑Annual 3, ca. 1993; trading card 2.95
- ❑Annual 4, ca. 1994 ..... 2.95
- ❑Ashcan 1, ca. 1995, b&w; no indicia 0.75

DR. STRANGE VS. DRACULA
MARVEL

- ❑1, Mar 1994 ..... 1.75

DOCTOR STRANGE: WHAT IS IT THAT DISTURBS YOU STEPHEN?
MARVEL

- ❑1, Oct 1997; squarebound 5.99

DOCTOR STRANGEFATE
DC / AMALGAM

- ❑1, Apr 1996 ..... 1.95

DOCTOR TOM BRENT, YOUNG INTERN
CHARLTON

- ❑1, Feb 1963 ..... 15.00
- ❑2, Apr 1963 ..... 10.00
- ❑3, Jun 1963 ..... 10.00
- ❑4, Aug 1963 ..... 10.00
- ❑5, Oct 1963 ..... 10.00

N-MINT

DR. TOMORROW
ACCLAIM

- ❑1, May 1997 ..... 2.50
- ❑2, Jun 1997 ..... 2.50
- ❑3, Jul 1997 ..... 2.50
- ❑4, Aug 1997 ..... 2.50
- ❑5, Sep 1997 ..... 2.50
- ❑6, Oct 1997 ..... 2.50
- ❑7, Nov 1997; Tomorrow and Mushroom Cloud go to Vietnam 2.50
- ❑8, Dec 1997 ..... 2.50
- ❑9, Jan 1998; No cover date; indicia says Jan 98 ..... 2.50
- ❑10, Feb 1998; No cover date; indicia says Jan 98 ..... 2.50
- ❑11, Mar 1998 ..... 2.50
- ❑12, Apr 1998 ..... 2.50

DOCTOR WEIRD
CALIBER / BIG BANG

- ❑1, Oct 1994, b&w 2.95
- ❑2, May 1995, b&w 2.95
- ❑Special 1, Feb 1994, b&w 3.95

DR. WEIRD (VOL. 2)
OCTOBER

- ❑1, Oct 1997 ..... 2.95
- ❑2, Jul 1998 ..... 2.95

DOCTOR WHO
MARVEL

- ❑1, Oct 1984; DaG (a); BBC TV series; Reprint from Doctor Who Monthly (British) 3.00
- ❑2, Nov 1984; DaG (a); Reprint from Doctor Who Monthly (British) 2.00
- ❑3, Dec 1984; DaG (a); Reprint from Doctor Who Monthly (British) 2.00
- ❑4, Jan 1985; Reprint from Doctor Who Monthly (British) 2.00
- ❑5, Feb 1985; Reprint from Doctor Who Monthly (British) 2.00
- ❑6, Mar 1985; Reprint from Doctor Who Monthly (British) 2.00
- ❑7, Apr 1985; Reprint from Doctor Who Monthly (British) 2.00
- ❑8, May 1985; Reprint from Doctor Who Monthly (British) 2.00
- ❑9, Jun 1985; Reprint from Doctor Who Monthly (British) 2.00
- ❑10, Jul 1985; Reprint from Doctor Who Monthly (British) 2.00
- ❑11, Aug 1985; Reprint from Doctor Who Monthly (British) 1.50
- ❑12, Sep 1985; Reprint from Doctor Who Monthly (British) 1.50
- ❑13, Oct 1985; Reprint from Doctor Who Monthly (British) 1.50
- ❑14, Nov 1985; Reprint from Doctor Who Monthly (British) 1.50
- ❑15, Dec 1985; Reprint from Doctor Who Monthly (British) 1.50
- ❑16, Jan 1986; Reprint from Doctor Who Monthly (British) 1.50
- ❑17, Feb 1986; Reprint from Doctor Who Monthly (British) 1.50
- ❑18, Mar 1986; Reprint from Doctor Who Monthly (British) 1.50
- ❑19, Apr 1986; Reprint from Doctor Who Monthly (British) 1.50
- ❑20, May 1986; Reprint from Doctor Who Monthly (British) 1.50
- ❑21, Jun 1986; Reprint from Doctor Who Monthly (British) 1.50
- ❑22, Jul 1986; Reprint from Doctor Who Monthly (British) 1.50
- ❑23, Aug 1986; Reprint from Doctor Who Monthly (British) 1.50

DR. WONDER
OLD TOWN

- ❑1, Jun 1996, b&w 2.95
- ❑2, Jul 1996, b&w 2.95
- ❑3, Aug 1996, b&w 2.95
- ❑4, Oct 1996, b&w 2.95
- ❑5, Fal 1997, b&w; magazine-sized ... 2.95

N-MINT

DOCTOR ZERO
MARVEL / EPIC

- ❑1, Apr 1988 BSz (c); BSz (a) 1.50
- ❑2, Jun 1988 BSz (c) 1.50
- ❑3, Aug 1988 ..... 1.50
- ❑4, Oct 1988 ..... 1.50
- ❑5, Dec 1988 ..... 1.50
- ❑6, Feb 1989 ..... 1.50
- ❑7, Apr 1989 DS (a) 1.50
- ❑8, Jun 1989 ..... 1.50

DOC WEIRD'S THRILL BOOK
PURE IMAGINATION

- ❑1 AW, ATh, FF (a) 2.00
- ❑2; WW (a); Jack Cole 2.00
- ❑3 WW (a) 2.00

DODEKAIN
ANTARCTIC

- ❑1, Nov 1994, b&w 2.95
- ❑2, Dec 1994, b&w 2.95
- ❑3, Jan 1995, b&w 2.95
- ❑4, Feb 1995, b&w 2.95
- ❑5, Mar 1995, b&w 2.95
- ❑6, Apr 1995, b&w 2.95
- ❑7, May 1995, b&w 2.95
- ❑8, Jun 1995, b&w 2.95

DODGES BULLETS
IMAGE

- ❑1, ca 2004 ..... 9.95

DO-DO MAN
EDGE

- ❑1 ..... 2.99

DOG BOY
FANTAGRAPHICS

- ❑1 ..... 2.00
- ❑2, Apr 1987 ..... 1.75
- ❑3, May 1987 ..... 1.75
- ❑4 ..... 1.75
- ❑5 ..... 1.75
- ❑6 ..... 1.75
- ❑7, Sep 1987 ..... 1.75
- ❑8 ..... 1.75
- ❑9 ..... 1.75

DOG MOON
DC / VERTIGO

- ❑1 ..... 6.95

DOGS OF WAR
DEFIANT

- ❑1, Apr 1994 ..... 2.50
- ❑2, May 1994 ..... 2.50
- ❑3, Jun 1994 ..... 2.50
- ❑4, Jul 1994 ..... 2.50
- ❑5, Aug 1994 ..... 2.50
- ❑6, Sep 1994 ..... 2.50
- ❑7, Oct 1994 ..... 2.50
- ❑8, Nov 1994 ..... 2.50

DOG SOUP
DOG SOUP

- ❑1, b&w 2.50

DOGS-O-WAR
CRUSADE

- ❑1, Jun 1996, b&w 2.95
- ❑2, Jul 1996, b&w 2.95
- ❑3, Jan 1997, b&w 2.95

DOG T.A.G.S.: TRAINED ANIMAL GUN SQUADRON
BUGGED OUT

- ❑1, Jun 1993, b&w 1.95

DOGWITCH
SIRIUS

- ❑1 ..... 2.95
- ❑2 ..... 2.95
- ❑3 ..... 2.95
- ❑4, Feb 2003 ..... 2.95
- ❑5, May 2003 ..... 2.95
- ❑6, Jul 2003 ..... 2.95
- ❑7, Oct 2003 ..... 2.95
- ❑8, Nov 2003 ..... 2.95
- ❑9, Jan 2004 ..... 2.95

N-MINT

❑10, Mar 2004 ..... 2.95
❑11, May 2004 ..... 2.95

DOIN' TIME WITH OJ
BONEYARD

❑1, Dec 1994, b&w 3.50

DOJINSHI
ANTARCTIC

❑1, Oct 1992, b&w 2.95
❑2, Dec 1992, b&w 2.95
❑3, Feb 1993, b&w 2.95
❑4, Apr 1993, b&w 2.95

DOLL
RIP OFF

❑1, Feb 1989, b&w 3.00
❑2, Mar 1989, b&w 2.50
❑3, May 1989, b&w 2.50
❑4, Feb 1990, b&w 2.50
❑5, Mar 1991, b&w 2.50
❑6, May 1991, b&w 2.50
❑7, Jun 1991, b&w 2.50
❑8, Sep 1992, b&w 2.95

DOLLMAN (MINI-SERIES)
ETERNITY

❑1, Nov 1991; movie tie-in 2.50
❑2 1992; movie tie-in 2.50
❑3 1992; movie tie-in 2.50
❑4 1992; movie tie-in 2.50

DOLL PARTS
SIRIUS

❑1, Oct 2000, b&w 2.95

DOLLS
SIRIUS

❑1, Jun 1996 ..... 2.95

DOLLZ, THE
IMAGE

❑1/A, Apr 2001; Two girls facing monster on cover 2.95
❑1/B, Apr 2001; Dynamic Forces cover: Girl posing with bunny, gun 2.95
❑1/C, Apr 2001; Alternate cover (figures include girl holding bunny) 2.95
❑1/D, Apr 2001; Girls posing with large face in background 2.95
❑1/E, Apr 2001; Nighttime fight scene on cover 2.95
❑2, Jun 2001 ..... 2.95

DOME: GROUND ZERO, THE
DC / HELIX

❑1; prestige format; computer-generated 7.95

DOMINATION FACTOR: AVENGERS
MARVEL

❑1, Nov 1999; says 1.2 on cover, 1 in indicia 2.50
❑2, Nov 1999; says 2.4 on cover, 2 in indicia 2.50

DOMINATION FACTOR: FANTASTIC FOUR
MARVEL

❑1, Dec 1999; cover forms diptych with Domination Factor: Avengers #1 ..... 2.50
❑2, Dec 1999; says 2.3 on cover, 2 in indicia 2.50

DOMINION
ECLIPSE

❑1, ca. 1990, b&w; Japanese 3.00
❑2, ca. 1990, b&w; Japanese 2.50
❑3, ca. 1991, b&w; Japanese 2.50
❑4, ca. 1991, b&w; Japanese 2.00
❑5, ca. 1991, b&w; Japanese 2.00
❑6, ca. 1991, b&w; Japanese 2.00

DOMINION (DARK HORSE)
IMAGE

❑1, Feb 2003 ..... 2.95
❑2, May 2003 ..... 2.95

DOMINION: CONFLICT 1
DARK HORSE / MANGA

❑1, Mar 1996, b&w 2.95
❑2, Apr 1996, b&w 2.95
❑3, May 1996, b&w 2.95

N-MINT

❑4, Jun 1996, b&w 2.95
❑5, Jul 1996, b&w 2.95
❑6, Aug 1996, b&w 2.95

DOMINION: PHANTOM OF THE AUDIENCE
DARK HORSE

❑1 ..... 2.50

DOMINIQUE: FAMILY MATTERS
CALIBER

❑1, b&w 2.95

DOMINIQUE: KILLZONE
CALIBER

❑1, ca. 1995, b&w 2.95

DOMINIQUE: PROTECT AND SERVE
CALIBER

❑1, ca. 1995, b&w 2.95

DOMINIQUE: WHITE KNUCKLE DRIVE
CALIBER

❑1, b&w 2.95

DOMINO
MARVEL

❑1, Jan 1997 ..... 2.00
❑2, Feb 1997 V: Deathstrike. 2.00
❑3, Mar 1997 ..... 2.00

DOMINO (2ND SERIES)
MARVEL

❑1, Jun 2003 ..... 2.50
❑2, Jun 2003; cardstock cover 2.50
❑3, Jul 2003; cardstock cover 2.50
❑4, Aug 2003; cardstock cover 2.50

DOMINO CHANCE
CHANCE

❑1, May 1982, b&w 2.50
❑1-2, b&w 1.50
❑2, Jul 1982, b&w 2.00
❑3, Sep 1982, b&w 2.00
❑4 1983, b&w 2.00
❑5, Jul 1983, b&w 2.00
❑6 1984, b&w 2.00
❑7 1984, b&w 1: Gizmo. 2.00
❑8 1985, b&w 2: Gizmo. 2.00
❑9 1985, b&w 2.00

DOMINO CHANCE: ROACH EXTRAORDINAIRE
AMAZING

❑1 ..... 1.95

DOMINO LADY
FANTAGRAPHICS / EROS

❑1, Dec 1990, b&w 1.95
❑2, Jan 1991, b&w 1.95
❑3, Mar 1991, b&w 1.95

DOMINO LADY'S JUNGLE ADVENTURE
FANTAGRAPHICS / EROS

❑1, b&w 2.75
❑2, b&w 2.75
❑3, Nov 1992, b&w 2.75

DOMU: A CHILD'S DREAM
DARK HORSE / MANGA

❑1, Mar 1995 ..... 5.95
❑2, Apr 1995 ..... 5.95
❑3, May 1995 ..... 5.95

DONALD AND MICKEY
GLADSTONE

❑19, Sep 1993 ..... 1.50
❑20, Nov 1993 ..... 2.95
❑21, Jan 1994 ..... 1.50
❑22, Mar 1994 ..... 1.50
❑23, May 1994 ..... 1.50
❑24, Jul 1994 ..... 1.50
❑25, Sep 1994 ..... 2.95
❑26, Nov 1994; newsstand distribution by Marvel 1.50
❑27, Jan 1995 ..... 1.50
❑28, Mar 1995 ..... 1.50
❑29, May 1995 ..... 1.50
❑30, Jul 1995 ..... 1.50

Dr. Tomorrow paid homage to different comics eras by telling its stories in each era's style, beginning with the Golden Age.

© 1997 Acclaim.

N-MINT

DONALD AND SCROOGE
DISNEY

❑1, ca. 1992 ..... 1.75
❑2, ca. 1992 ..... 1.75
❑3, ca. 1992 ..... 1.75

DONALD DUCK (WALT DISNEY'S...)
DELL / GOLD KEY

❑50, Nov 1956 ..... 35.00
❑51, Jan 1967 ..... 35.00
❑52, Mar 1957 CB (a) 90.00
❑53, May 1957 ..... 30.00
❑54, Jul 1957 ..... 30.00
❑55, Sep 1957 ..... 30.00
❑56, Nov 1957 ..... 30.00
❑57, Jan 1958 ..... 30.00
❑58, Mar 1958 ..... 30.00
❑59, May 1958 CB (a) 80.00
❑60, Jul 1958 CB (a) 80.00
❑61, Sep 1958 ..... 25.00
❑62, Nov 1958 ..... 25.00
❑63, Jan 1959 ..... 25.00
❑64, Mar 1959 ..... 25.00
❑65, May 1959 ..... 25.00
❑66, Jul 1959 ..... 25.00
❑67, Sep 1959 ..... 25.00
❑68, Nov 1959 CB (a) 70.00
❑69, Jan 1960 ..... 25.00
❑70, Mar 1960 ..... 25.00
❑71, May 1960 ..... 20.00
❑72, Jul 1960 ..... 20.00
❑73, Sep 1960 ..... 20.00
❑74, Nov 1960 ..... 20.00
❑75, Jan 1961 ..... 20.00
❑76, Mar 1961 ..... 20.00
❑77, May 1961 ..... 20.00
❑78, Jul 1961 ..... 20.00
❑79, Sep 1961 ..... 20.00
❑80, Nov 1961 ..... 20.00
❑81, Jan 1962 ..... 20.00
❑82, Mar 1962 ..... 20.00
❑83, May 1962 ..... 20.00
❑84, Jul 1962 ..... 20.00
❑85, Sep 1962; Gold Key imprints begin 18.00
❑86, Nov 1962 ..... 18.00
❑87, Jan 1963 ..... 18.00
❑88, Mar 1963 ..... 18.00
❑89, May 1963 ..... 18.00
❑90, Jul 1963 ..... 18.00
❑91, Sep 1963 ..... 18.00
❑92, Nov 1963 ..... 18.00
❑93, Jan 1964 ..... 18.00
❑94, Mar 1964 ..... 18.00
❑95, May 1964 ..... 18.00
❑96, Jul 1964 ..... 18.00
❑97, Sep 1964 ..... 18.00
❑98, Nov 1964 ..... 18.00
❑99, Jan 1965; Reprints story from Donald Duck #46 ..... 18.00
❑100, Mar 1965 ..... 18.00
❑101, May 1965 ..... 16.00
❑102, Jul 1965 ..... 16.00
❑103, Sep 1965 ..... 16.00
❑104, Nov 1965 ..... 16.00
❑105, Jan 1966 ..... 16.00
❑106, Mar 1966 ..... 16.00
❑107, May 1966 ..... 16.00

	N-MINT
❑108, Jul 1966	16.00
❑109, Sep 1966	16.00
❑110, Nov 1966	16.00
❑111, Jan 1967	16.00
❑112, Mar 1967	16.00
❑113, May 1967	16.00
❑114, Jul 1967	16.00
❑115, Sep 1967	16.00
❑116, Nov 1967	16.00
❑117, Jan 1968	16.00
❑118, Mar 1968	16.00
❑119, May 1968	16.00
❑120, Jul 1968	16.00
❑121, Sep 1968	12.00
❑122, Nov 1968	12.00
❑123, Jan 1969	12.00
❑124, Mar 1969	12.00
❑125, May 1969	12.00
❑126, Jul 1969	12.00
❑127, Sep 1969	12.00
❑128, Nov 1969	12.00
❑129, Jan 1970	12.00
❑130, Mar 1970	12.00
❑131, May 1970	12.00
❑132, Jul 1970	12.00
❑133, Sep 1970	12.00
❑134, Nov 1970; Reprints stories from Donald Duck #52 and Walt Disney's Comics #194	12.00
❑135, Jan 1971; Reprints stories from Uncle Scrooge #27 and Walt Disney's Comics #198	12.00
❑136, Mar 1971	10.00
❑137, May 1971	10.00
❑138, Jul 1971	10.00
❑139, Sep 1971	10.00
❑140, Nov 1971	10.00
❑141, Jan 1972	10.00
❑142, Mar 1972	10.00
❑143, May 1972	10.00
❑144, Jul 1972	10.00
❑145, Sep 1972	10.00
❑146, Nov 1972	10.00
❑147, Jan 1973	10.00
❑148, Mar 1973	10.00
❑149, May 1973	10.00
❑150, Jul 1973	10.00
❑151, Sep 1973	9.00
❑152, Oct 1973	9.00
❑153, Nov 1973	9.00
❑154, Jan 1974; Reprints story from Donald Duck #46	9.00
❑155, Mar 1974	9.00
❑156, May 1974	9.00
❑157, Jul 1974; Reprints story from Donald Duck #45	9.00
❑158, Sep 1974	9.00
❑159, Oct 1974; Reprints story from Walt Disney's Comics #192	9.00
❑160, Nov 1974; Reprints story from Donald Duck #26	9.00
❑161, Jan 1975	8.00
❑162, Mar 1975	8.00
❑163, May 1975	8.00
❑164, Jul 1975	8.00
❑165, Sep 1975	8.00
❑166, Oct 1975	8.00
❑167, Nov 1975	8.00
❑168, Jan 1976	8.00
❑169, Mar 1976	8.00
❑170, Apr 1976	8.00
❑171, May 1976	6.00
❑172, Jun 1976	6.00
❑173, Jul 1976	6.00
❑174, Aug 1976	6.00
❑175, Sep 1976	6.00
❑176, Oct 1976	6.00
❑177, Nov 1976	6.00
❑178, Dec 1976	6.00
❑179, Jan 1977	6.00
❑180, Feb 1977	6.00
❑181, Mar 1977	6.00
❑182, Apr 1977	6.00

	N-MINT
❑183, May 1977; Reprints story from Donald Duck #138	6.00
❑184, Jun 1977	6.00
❑185, Jul 1977	6.00
❑186, Aug 1977	6.00
❑187, Sep 1977	6.00
❑188, Oct 1977; Reprints story from Donald Duck #68	6.00
❑189, Nov 1977	6.00
❑190, Dec 1977	6.00
❑191, Jan 1978	4.00
❑192, Feb 1978; Reprints stories from Donald Duck #60 and Walt Disney's Comics #226 and 234	4.00
❑193, Mar 1978	4.00
❑194, Apr 1978	4.00
❑195, May 1978	4.00
❑196, Jun 1978	4.00
❑197, Jul 1978	4.00
❑198, Aug 1978	4.00
❑199, Sep 1978	4.00
❑200, Oct 1978	4.00
❑201, Nov 1978; Reprints story from Christmas Parade (Dell) #26	4.00
❑202, Dec 1978	4.00
❑203, Jan 1979	4.00
❑204, Feb 1979	4.00
❑205, Mar 1979	4.00
❑206, Apr 1979	4.00
❑207, May 1979	4.00
❑208, Jun 1979	4.00
❑209, Jul 1979	4.00
❑210, Aug 1979	4.00
❑211, Sep 1979	3.00
❑212, Oct 1979	3.00
❑213, Nov 1979	3.00
❑214, Dec 1979	3.00
❑215, Jan 1980	3.00
❑216, Feb 1980	3.00
❑217, Mar 1980; Whitman begins as publisher	3.00
❑218, Apr 1980	3.00
❑219, May 1980	3.00
❑220, Jun 1980	3.00
❑221, Aug 1980	3.00
❑222, Oct 1980	3.00
❑223, Dec 1980	3.00
❑224, Jan 1981	3.00
❑225, Feb 1981	3.00
❑226, Mar 1981	3.00
❑227, Apr 1981	3.00
❑228, May 1981	3.00
❑229, Jun 1981	3.00
❑230, Jul 1981	3.00
❑231, Aug 1981	3.00
❑232, Sep 1981	3.00
❑233, Oct 1981	3.00
❑234, Nov 1981	3.00
❑235, Dec 1981	3.00
❑236, Jan 1982	3.00
❑237, Feb 1982	3.00
❑238, Mar 1982	3.00
❑239, Apr 1983	3.00
❑240, May 1982	3.00
❑241, Apr 1982	3.00
❑242, May 1983	3.00
❑243, Mar 1984	3.00
❑244, Apr 1984	3.00
❑245, Jul 1984; Last issue of original run	3.00
❑246, Oct 1986; CB (a); Series begins again (1986); Gladstone publishes	8.00
❑247, Nov 1986 CB (a)	5.00
❑248, Dec 1986 CB (a)	5.00
❑249, Jan 1987 CB (a)	5.00
❑250, Feb 1987; CB (a); reprints 1st Barks comic	8.00
❑251, Mar 1987 CB (a)	4.00
❑252, Apr 1987 CB (a)	4.00
❑253, May 1987 CB (a)	4.00
❑254, Jun 1987	4.00
❑255, Jul 1987	4.00
❑256, Aug 1987	4.00

	N-MINT
❑257, Sep 1987; CB (a); forest fire	4.00
❑258, Oct 1987 CB (a)	4.00
❑259, Nov 1987 CB (a)	4.00
❑260, Dec 1987 CB (a)	4.00
❑261, Jan 1988 CB (a)	3.00
❑262, Mar 1988 CB (a)	3.00
❑263, Jun 1988 CB (a)	3.00
❑264, Jul 1988 CB (a)	3.00
❑265, Aug 1988	3.00
❑266, Sep 1988	3.00
❑267, Oct 1988	3.00
❑268, Nov 1988	3.00
❑269, Jan 1989	3.00
❑270, Mar 1989	3.00
❑271, Apr 1989; says Jun on cover, Apr in indicia	2.50
❑272, Jul 1989	2.50
❑273, Aug 1989	2.50
❑274, Sep 1989	2.50
❑275, Oct 1989; CB, WK (a); Donocchio	2.50
❑276, Nov 1989 CB (a)	2.50
❑277, Jan 1990 CB (a)	2.50
❑278, Mar 1990 CB, DR (a)	2.50
❑279, May 1990; CB (a); Series ends again (1990)	2.50
❑280, Sep 1993; Series begins again (1993)	1.50
❑281, Nov 1993	1.50
❑282, Jan 1994 CB (a)	1.50
❑283, Mar 1994 DR (a)	1.50
❑284, May 1994 CB (a)	1.50
❑285, Jul 1994 CB (a)	1.50
❑286, Sep 1994; Giant-size; Donald Duck's 60th	3.00
❑287, Nov 1994	1.50
❑288, Jan 1995 CB (a)	1.50
❑289, Mar 1995	1.50
❑290, May 1995	1.50
❑291, Jul 1995	1.50
❑292, Sep 1995	1.50
❑293, Nov 1995	1.50
❑294, Jan 1996 CB (a)	1.50
❑295, Mar 1996; newsprint covers begin	1.50
❑296, May 1996	1.50
❑297, Jul 1996	1.50
❑298, Sep 1996	1.50
❑299, Nov 1996	1.50
❑300, Jan 1997	1.50
❑301, Mar 1997; newsprint covers end	1.50
❑302, May 1997 CB (c); CB (a)	1.95
❑303, Jul 1997	1.95
❑304, Sep 1997 CB (a)	1.95
❑305, Nov 1997 CB (w); CB (a)	1.95
❑306, Jan 1998	1.95
❑307, Mar 1998	1.95

DONALD DUCK AND FRIENDS (GEMSTONE)

GEMSTONE

	N-MINT
❑308, Sep 2003	2.95
❑309, Oct 2003	2.95
❑310, Nov 2003	2.95
❑311, Dec 2003	2.95
❑312, Jan 2004	2.95
❑313, Feb 2004	2.95
❑314, Mar 2004	2.95
❑315, Apr 2004	2.95
❑316, May 2004	2.95
❑317, Jun 2004	2.95

DONALD DUCK ADVENTURES (GEMSTONE)

GEMSTONE

	N-MINT
❑1, Jul 2003	7.95
❑2, Oct 2003	7.95
❑3, Dec 2003	7.95
❑4, Feb 2004	7.95
❑5, Mar 2004	7.95
❑6, Jun 2004	7.95

N-MINT

DONALD DUCK ADVENTURES (DISNEY)
Disney

❑1, Jun 1990 DR (w); DR (a) 2.50
❑2, Jul 1990 CB (a) 2.00
❑3, Aug 1990 .... 2.00
❑4, Sep 1990 CB (a) 2.00
❑5, Oct 1990 .... 2.00
❑6, Nov 1990 .... 2.00
❑7, Dec 1990 .... 2.00
❑8, Jan 1991 .... 2.00
❑9, Feb 1991; CB (a); reprint of 1: Uncle Scrooge 2.00
❑10, Mar 1991 .... 2.00
❑11, Apr 1991; Mad #1 cover parody 2.00
❑12, May 1991 .... 2.00
❑13, Jun 1991 .... 2.00
❑14, Jul 1991 CB (a) 2.00
❑15, Aug 1991 .... 2.00
❑16, Sep 1991 .... 2.00
❑17, Oct 1991 .... 2.00
❑18, Nov 1991 .... 2.00
❑19, Dec 1991 .... 2.00
❑20, Jan 1992 .... 2.00
❑21, Feb 1992; CB (a); golden Christmas tree 1.50
❑22, Mar 1992 DR (a) 1.50
❑23, Apr 1992 CB (a) 1.50
❑24, May 1992 DR (a) 1.50
❑25, Jun 1992; map piece 1.50
❑26, Jul 1992; CB (a); map piece 1.50
❑27, Aug 1992; CB (a); map piece 1.50
❑28, Sep 1992; Olympics 1.50
❑29, Oct 1992 .... 1.50
❑30, Nov 1992 .... 1.50
❑31, Dec 1992 .... 1.50
❑32, Jan 1993 .... 1.50
❑33, Feb 1993 .... 1.50
❑34, Mar 1993; DR (a); Return of Super-Duck 1.50
❑35, Apr 1993 CB (a) 1.50
❑36, May 1993 CB (a) 1.50
❑37, Jun 1993 CB, DR (a) 1.50
❑38, Jul 1993 .... 1.50
❑39, Aug 1993 .... 1.50
❑40, Sep 1993 .... 1.50
❑41, Oct 1993 .... 1.50
❑42, Nov 1993 CB (c) 1.50
❑43 1993 .... 1.50
❑44, Dec 1993; Gladstone resumes publishing its series 1.50

DONALD DUCK ADVENTURES (GLADSTONE)
Gladstone

❑1, Nov 1987 CB (a) 2.50
❑2, Jan 1988 CB (a) 2.00
❑3, Mar 1988 CB (a) 2.00
❑4, May 1988 CB (a) 2.00
❑5, Jul 1988 CB, DR (a) 2.00
❑6, Aug 1988 CB (a) 1.50
❑7, Sep 1988 CB (a) 1.50
❑8, Oct 1988 CB, DR (a) 1.50
❑9, Nov 1988 CB (a) 1.50
❑10, Dec 1988 CB (a) 1.50
❑11, Feb 1989 CB (a) 1.50
❑12, May 1989 CB, DR (a) 1.50
❑13, Jul 1989 DR (c); CB (a) 1.50
❑14, Aug 1989 CB (a) 1.50
❑15, Sep 1989 CB (a) 1.50
❑16, Oct 1989 CB (a) 1.50
❑17, Nov 1989 CB (a) 1.50
❑18, Dec 1989 CB (a) 1.50
❑19, Feb 1990 CB (a) 1.50
❑20, Apr 1990; CB (a); series goes on hiatus during Disney run 1.50
❑21, Aug 1993 DR (c); CB (a) 1.50
❑22, Oct 1993 CB (a) 1.50
❑23, Dec 1993 DR (c) 1.50
❑24, Feb 1994 .... 1.50
❑25, Apr 1994 .... 1.50
❑26, Jun 1994 CB (a) 2.95
❑27, Aug 1994 .... 1.50

N-MINT

❑28, Oct 1994; CB (a); cover uses portion of Barks painting 1.50
❑29, Dec 1994; newsstand distribution by Marvel 1.50
❑30, Feb 1995 CB (a) 2.95
❑31, Apr 1995 .... 1.50
❑32, Jun 1995 .... 1.50
❑33, Aug 1995 CB (a) 1.95
❑34, Oct 1995; newsprint covers begin 1.50
❑35, Dec 1995 .... 1.50
❑36, Feb 1996 .... 1.50
❑37, Apr 1996 .... 1.50
❑38, Jun 1996 .... 1.50
❑39, Aug 1996 .... 1.50
❑40, Oct 1996 .... 1.50
❑41, Dec 1996 .... 1.50
❑42, Feb 1997 .... 1.50
❑43, Apr 1997; newsprint covers end 1.50
❑44, Jun 1997 .... 1.95
❑45, Aug 1997 .... 1.95
❑46, Oct 1997 .... 1.95
❑47, Dec 1997 CB (a) 1.95
❑48, Feb 1998 .... 1.95

DONALD DUCK & MICKEY MOUSE
Gladstone

❑1, Sep 1995 .... 1.50
❑2, Nov 1995 .... 1.50
❑3, Jan 1996 .... 1.50
❑4, Mar 1996 .... 1.50
❑5, May 1996 .... 1.50
❑6, Jul 1996 .... 1.50
❑7, Sep 1996 .... 1.50

DONALD DUCK BEACH PARTY (WALT DISNEY'S...)
Dell

❑1, ca. 1954; Reprints story from Walt Disney's Comics #45 .... 100.00
❑2, Jul 1955 .... 65.00
❑3, Jul 1956 .... 55.00
❑4, ca. 1957 .... 55.00
❑5, Jul 1958 .... 55.00
❑6, ca. 1959 .... 55.00

DONATELLO TEENAGE MUTANT NINJA TURTLE
Mirage

❑1, Aug 1986, b&w 2.00

DONIELLE: ENSLAVED AT SEA
Raging Rhino

❑1, b&w 2.95
❑2, b&w 2.95
❑3, b&w 2.95
❑4, b&w 2.95
❑5 1993 .... 2.95
❑6 .... 2.95
❑7 .... 2.95
❑8 .... 2.95
❑9 .... 2.95

DONNA MATRIX
Reactor

❑1, Aug 1993; O: Donna Matrix. 1: Donna Matrix. computer-generated 3.50

DONNA MIA
Avatar

❑1, Dec 1996 .... 3.00
❑2, Jan 1997 .... 3.00
❑3, Feb 1997 .... 3.00

DONNA'S DAY
Slab-O-Concrete

❑1; Postcard comic book 1.00

DOOFER
Fantagraphics

❑1, b&w 2.75

DOOFUS
Fantagraphics

❑1, Dec 1994, b&w 2.75
❑2, Spr 1997, b&w 2.75

The strange numbering on the covers of *Domination Factor: Avengers* and *Domination Factor: Fantastic Four* indicated the order in which the issues were to be read.

© 1999 Marvel Characters Inc.

N-MINT

DOOM
Marvel

❑1, Oct 2000 .... 2.99
❑2, Nov 2000 .... 2.99
❑3, Dec 2000 .... 2.99

DOOM FORCE SPECIAL
DC

❑1, Jul 1992; X-Force parody 2.95

DOOM PATROL, THE (1ST SERIES)
DC

❑86, Mar 1964; 1: Monsieur Mallah. 1: The Brain. 1: Madame Rouge. Series continued from My Greatest Adventure #85 .... 70.00
❑87, May 1964 .... 48.00
❑88, Jun 1964 O: The Chief. 40.00
❑89, Aug 1964 .... 40.00
❑90, Sep 1964 .... 40.00
❑91, Nov 1964 1: Mento. 38.00
❑92, Dec 1964 .... 38.00
❑93, Feb 1965 .... 38.00
❑94, Mar 1965 .... 38.00
❑95, May 1965 .... 38.00
❑96, Jun 1965 .... 38.00
❑97, Aug 1965 1: Garguax. 38.00
❑98, Sep 1965 .... 38.00
❑99, Nov 1965 1: Changeling. 45.00
❑100, Dec 1965 O: Changeling. 50.00
❑101, Feb 1966 .... 25.00
❑102, Mar 1966 A: Challengers of the Unknown. 25.00
❑103, May 1966 .... 25.00
❑104, Jun 1966 .... 25.00
❑105, Aug 1966 .... 25.00
❑106, Sep 1966 O: Negative Man. 25.00
❑107, Nov 1966 .... 25.00
❑108, Dec 1966 .... 25.00
❑109, Feb 1967 .... 25.00
❑110, Mar 1967 .... 25.00
❑111, May 1967 .... 25.00
❑112, Jun 1967 .... 25.00
❑113, Aug 1967 .... 25.00
❑114, Sep 1967 .... 25.00
❑115, Nov 1967 .... 25.00
❑116, Dec 1967 .... 25.00
❑117, Feb 1968; reprints story from Tales of the Unexpected #3 .... 25.00
❑118, Mar 1968 .... 25.00
❑119, May 1968 .... 25.00
❑120, Jun 1968 .... 25.00
❑121, Aug 1968 JO (a); D: The Doom Patrol. 45.00
❑122, Feb 1973; Reprints begin (1973); From DP #76 and 89 .... 2.00
❑123, Apr 1973; From DP #95; Premiani biography 2.00
❑124, Jul 1973; From DP #90 .... 2.00

DOOM PATROL (2ND SERIES)
DC

❑1, Oct 1987; The Doom Patrol returns from their supposed deaths 2.50
❑2, Nov 1987 .... 1.50
❑3, Dec 1987 1: Rhea Jones. 1: Lodestone. 1.50
❑4, Jan 1988 O: Lodestone. 1.50
❑5, Feb 1988 .... 1.50
❑6, Mar 1988 EL (a) 1.50
❑7, Apr 1988 1: Shrapnel. 1.50

N-MINT

❑8, May 1988 EL (a) 1.50
❑9, Jun 1988; Bonus Book 1.50
❑10, Jul 1988 A: Superman. 1.50
❑11, Aug 1988 .... 1.50
❑12, Sep 1988 .... 1.50
❑13, Oct 1988 .... 1.50
❑14, Nov 1988 1: Dorothy Spinner. A: Power Girl. 1.50
❑15, Dec 1988 V: Animal-Vegetable-Mineral Man. 1.50
❑16, Dec 1988 .... 1.50
❑17, Jan 1989; D: Celsius. Invasion! . 1.50
❑18, Jan 1989; Invasion! 1.50
❑19, Feb 1989; 1: Crazy Jane. 1st Grant Morrison; New, very strange direction for The Doom Patrol 3.00
❑20, Mar 1989 1: The Scissormen. ... 2.00
❑21, Apr 1989 .... 2.00
❑22, May 1989 .... 2.00
❑23, Jun 1989 .... 2.00
❑24, Jul 1989 .... 2.00
❑25, Aug 1989 .... 2.00
❑26, Sep 1989 1: The Brotherhood of Dada. 2.00
❑27, Nov 1989 .... 2.00
❑28, Dec 1989 .... 2.00
❑29, Jan 1990; JL (a); Superman cover 2.00
❑30, Feb 1990 .... 2.00
❑31, Apr 1990 .... 2.00
❑32, May 1990 .... 2.00
❑33, Jun 1990 .... 2.00
❑34, Jul 1990 .... 2.00
❑35, Aug 1990 1: Danny the Street. 1: Flex Mentallo. 2.00
❑36, Sep 1990 .... 2.00
❑37, Oct 1990 .... 2.00
❑38, Nov 1990 .... 2.00
❑39, Dec 1990 .... 2.00
❑40, Jan 1991 .... 2.00
❑41, Feb 1991 .... 2.00
❑42, Mar 1991 O: Flex Mentallo. 1: The Fact. 2.00
❑43, Apr 1991 .... 2.00
❑44, May 1991 1: The Candlemaker. . 2.00
❑45, Jul 1991 .... 2.00
❑46, Aug 1991 .... 2.00
❑47, Sep 1991 .... 2.00
❑48, Oct 1991 .... 2.00
❑49, Nov 1991 .... 2.00
❑50, Dec 1991; Giant-size BB (a) 2.50
❑51, Jan 1992 1: Yankee Doodle Dandy. 2.00
❑52, Feb 1992 .... 1.75
❑53, Mar 1992; Fantastic Four parody 1.75
❑54, Apr 1992 .... 1.75
❑55, May 1992 .... 1.75
❑56, Jun 1992 .... 1.75
❑57, Jul 1992; Giant-size 2.50
❑58, Aug 1992 .... 1.75
❑59, Sep 1992 .... 1.75
❑60, Oct 1992 .... 1.75
❑61, Nov 1992 .... 1.75
❑62, Dec 1992 .... 1.75
❑63, Jan 1993 .... 1.75
❑64, Mar 1993; Begins Vertigo line ... 1.75
❑65, Apr 1993 .... 1.75
❑66, May 1993 .... 1.95
❑67, Jun 1993 .... 1.95
❑68, Jul 1993 .... 1.95
❑69, Aug 1993 .... 1.95
❑70, Sep 1993; Partial photo cover ... 1.95
❑71, Oct 1993 .... 1.95
❑72, Nov 1993 .... 1.95
❑73, Dec 1993 .... 1.95
❑74, Jan 1994 .... 1.95
❑75, Feb 1994 .... 1.95
❑76, Mar 1994 .... 1.95
❑77, Apr 1994 .... 1.95
❑78, May 1994 .... 1.95
❑79, Jun 1994 .... 1.95
❑80, Jul 1994 .... 1.95
❑81, Aug 1994 .... 1.95
❑82, Sep 1994 .... 1.95
❑83, Oct 1994 .... 1.95
❑84, Nov 1994 .... 1.95
❑85, Dec 1994 .... 1.95
❑86, Jan 1995 .... 1.95
❑87, Feb 1995 .... 1.95
❑Annual 1, ca. 1988 .... 1.50
❑Annual 2, ca. 1994; Children's Crusade 3.95

DOOM PATROL (3RD SERIES)
DC

❑1, Dec 2001 .... 3.00
❑2, Jan 2002 .... 2.50
❑3, Feb 2002 .... 2.50
❑4, Mar 2002 .... 2.50
❑5, Apr 2002 .... 2.50
❑6, May 2002 .... 2.50
❑7, Jun 2002 .... 2.50
❑8, Jul 2002 .... 2.50
❑9, Aug 2002 .... 2.50
❑10, Sep 2002 .... 2.50
❑11, Oct 2002 .... 2.50
❑12, Nov 2002 .... 2.50
❑13, Dec 2002 .... 2.50
❑14, Jan 2003 .... 2.50
❑15, Feb 2003 .... 2.50
❑16, Mar 2003 .... 2.50
❑17, Apr 2003 .... 2.50
❑18, May 2003 .... 2.50
❑19, Jun 2003 .... 2.50
❑20, Jul 2003 .... 2.50
❑21, Aug 2003 .... 2.50
❑22, Sep 2003 .... 2.50

DOOM PATROL (4TH SERIES)
DC

❑1, Aug 2004 .... 2.95
❑2, Sep 2004 .... 2.95

DOOM PATROL AND SUICIDE SQUAD SPECIAL
DC

❑1, Feb 1988 EL (a) 2.00

DOOMSDAY + 1 (AVALON)
AVALON

❑1 .... 2.95
❑2 .... 2.95

DOOMSDAY + 1 (CHARLTON)
CHARLTON

❑1, Jul 1975 JBy (a) 8.00
❑2, Sep 1975 JBy (a) 5.00
❑3, Nov 1975 JBy (a) 4.00
❑4, Jan 1976 JBy (a) 4.00
❑5, Mar 1976 JBy (a) 4.00
❑6, May 1976 JBy (a) 4.00
❑7, Jun 1978; JBy (a); Reprints Doomsday + 1 #1 .... 3.00
❑8, Sep 1978; JBy (a); Reprints Doomsday + 1 #2 .... 3.00
❑9, Nov 1978; JBy (a); Reprints Doomsday + 1 #3 .... 3.00
❑10, Jan 1979; JBy (a); Reprints Doomsday + 1 #4 .... 3.00
❑11 1979; JBy (a); Reprints Doomsday + 1 #5 .... 3.00
❑12 1979; JBy (a); Reprints Doomsday + 1 #6 .... 3.00

DOOMSDAY ANNUAL
DC

❑1, ca. 1995 .... 3.95

DOOMSDAY SQUAD, THE
FANTAGRAPHICS

❑1, Aug 1986 JBy (a) 2.00
❑2 JBy (a) 2.00
❑3 JBy (a); A: Usagi Yojimbo. 3.00
❑4 JBy (a) 2.00
❑5 JBy (a) 2.00
❑6 JBy (a) 2.00
❑7 JBy (a) 2.00

DOOM'S IV
IMAGE

❑0.5, Dec 1994; Preview promotional edition 2.50
❑1, Jul 1994 RL (w); 2.50
❑1/A, Jul 1994; RL (w); Alternate cover with left half of yellow two-part picture 2.50
❑1/B, Jul 1994; RL (w); Alternate cover with right half of yellow two-part picture 2.50
❑2, Aug 1994 .... 2.50
❑2/A, Aug 1994 .... 2.50
❑3, Sep 1994 .... 2.50
❑4, Oct 1994 .... 2.50

DOOM: THE EMPEROR RETURNS
MARVEL

❑1, Jan 2002 .... 2.50
❑2, Feb 2002 .... 2.50
❑3, Mar 2002 .... 2.50

DOOM 2099
MARVEL

❑1, Jan 1993; PB (a); 1: Doom 2099. Metallic ink cover 2.50
❑2, Feb 1993 PB (a) 1.75
❑3, Mar 1993 PB (a) 1.75
❑4, Apr 1993 PB (a) 1.75
❑5, May 1993 1: Fever. 1.75
❑6, Jun 1993 PB (a) 1.50
❑7, Jul 1993 PB (a) 1.50
❑8, Aug 1993 PB (a) 1.50
❑9, Sep 1993 .... 1.50
❑10, Oct 1993; PB (a); A: Xandra. Covers of Doom 2099 10-12 combine to form triptych 1.50
❑11, Nov 1993; PB (a); Covers of Doom 2099 10-12 combine to form triptych 1.25
❑12, Dec 1993; PB (a); Covers of Doom 2099 10-12 combine to form triptych 1.25
❑13, Jan 1994 .... 1.25
❑14, Feb 1994 PB (a) 1.25
❑15, Mar 1994 PB (a) 1.25
❑16, Apr 1994 .... 1.25
❑17, May 1994 PB (a) 1.25
❑18, May 1994; PB (a); D: Radian. poster 1.50
❑19, Jul 1994 PB (a) 1.50
❑20, Aug 1994 .... 1.50
❑21, Sep 1994 PB (a) 1.50
❑22, Oct 1994 PB (a) 1.50
❑23, Nov 1994 PB (a) 1.50
❑24, Dec 1994 PB (a) 1.50
❑25, Jan 1995; Giant-size; PB (a); regular cover 2.25
❑25/Variant, Jan 1995; Giant-size; PB (a); Embossed foil cover 2.95
❑26, Feb 1995 PB (a) 1.50
❑27, Mar 1995 PB (a) 1.50
❑28, Apr 1995 .... 1.95
❑29, May 1995 .... 1.95
❑29/Variant, May 1995; enhanced acetate overlay cover 3.50
❑30, Jun 1995 .... 1.95
❑31, Jul 1995 .... 1.95
❑32, Aug 1995 .... 1.95
❑33, Sep 1995 .... 1.95
❑34, Oct 1995 .... 1.95
❑35, Nov 1995 .... 1.95
❑36, Dec 1995 .... 1.95
❑37, Jan 1996 .... 1.95
❑38, Feb 1996 .... 1.95
❑39, Mar 1996 JB (a) 1.95
❑39/Variant, Mar 1996; Special cover 3.50
❑40, Apr 1996; JB (a); Doom 2099 comes to present 1.95
❑41, May 1996 V: Namor. V: Daredevil. 1.95
❑42, Jun 1996 V: Fantastic Four. 1.95
❑43, Jul 1996; story continues in Fantastic Four 2099 #7 .... 1.95
❑44, Aug 1996; continues in 2099: World of Tomorrow 1.95

DOORMAN (CALIBER)
CALIBER

❑1 .... 2.95

DOORMAN (CULT)
CULT

❑1, b&w; Double-cover 2.95
❑2, b&w 2.50

N-MINT

❑3, b&w 2.50
❑4, b&w 2.95
❑Ashcan 1 1.00

DOORMAN: FAMILY SECRETS
CALIBER

❑1 2.95

DOORWAY TO NIGHTMARE
DC

❑1, Feb 1978 VM (a) 3.00
❑2, Apr 1978 2.00
❑3, Jun 1978 2.00
❑4, Aug 1978 2.00
❑5, Oct 1978 2.00

DOPE COMIX
KITCHEN SINK

❑1 5.00
❑2 3.00
❑3 3.00
❑4 3.00
❑5 3.00

DOPIN' DAN
LAST GASP

❑1, Apr 1972 5.00
❑2 3.00
❑3 3.00

DORIS NELSON: ATOMIC HOUSEWIFE
JAKE COMICS

❑1, Dec 1995, b&w 2.75

DORK
SLAVE LABOR

❑1, Jun 1993, b&w 3.00
❑1-2, Aug 1995, b&w 2.75
❑1-3, Mar 1997, b&w 2.75
❑2, May 1994, b&w 2.50
❑2-2, Jan 1996, b&w 2.75
❑3, Aug 1995, b&w 2.75
❑3-2, Sep 1996, b&w 2.75
❑4, Mar 1997, b&w 2.75
❑5, Jan 1998, b&w 2.95
❑6, May 1998, b&w 2.95
❑7, Aug 1999, b&w 2.95
❑8, Sep 2000, b&w 3.50
❑9, Aug 2001 2.95

DORK HOUSE COMICS
PARODY

❑1 2.50

DORKIER IMAGES
PARODY

❑1, Mar 1993; Standard edition 2.50
❑1/Variant; gold, silver, blue edition 3.00

DORK TOWER
CORSAIR

❑1, Jul 1998 4.00
❑2, Oct 1998 3.00
❑3, Jan 1999 3.00
❑4, May 1999; Star Wars 3.00
❑5, Jul 1999; Babylon 5 2.95
❑6 1999 2.95
❑7, Jan 2000 2.95
❑8, Mar 2000 2.95
❑9, Aug 2000, b&w; switches to Dork Storm 2.95
❑10, Aug 2000 2.95
❑11, Sep 2000 2.95
❑12, Nov 2000 2.95
❑13, Feb 2001 2.95
❑14 2001 2.95
❑15 2001 2.95
❑16 2001 2.99
❑17 2002 2.99
❑18 2002 2.99
❑19 2002 2.99
❑20 2002 2.99
❑21 2002 2.99
❑22 2002 2.99

N-MINT

DOUBLE DRAGON
MARVEL

❑1, Jul 1991 1.00
❑2, Aug 1991 1.00
❑3, Sep 1991 1.00
❑4, Oct 1991 1.00
❑5, Nov 1991 1.00
❑6, Dec 1991 1.00

DOUBLE EDGE: ALPHA
MARVEL

❑1, Aug 1995; Chromium cover; Punisher 4.95

DOUBLE EDGE: OMEGA
MARVEL

❑1, Oct 1995; enhanced wraparound cover; Punisher 4.95

DOUBLE IMAGE
IMAGE

❑1, Feb 2001; Flip-book 2.95
❑2, Mar 2001; Had two different front covers and was NOT a flipbook. 2.95
❑3, Apr 2001; Flip-book 2.95
❑4, May 2001; Flip-book 2.95
❑5, Jun 2001; Flip-book 2.95

DOUBLE IMPACT
HIGH IMPACT

❑1, Mar 1995; No cover price; no indicia; gray polybag; preview of Double Impact #3 and 4; San Diego Comic-Con ed. 3.95
❑1/Ltd., Mar 1995; No cover price; no indicia; black polybag; letters pages and pin-ups; limited to 5000 3.95
❑2, May 1995 3.00
❑3, Jul 1995 3.00
❑5, Nov 1995 3.00
❑4, Sep 1995 3.00

DOUBLE IMPACT (VOL. 2)
HIGH IMPACT

❑0, Dec 1996 2.95
❑1 1997; Chromium cover 4.00
❑2 1997 3.00
❑3 1997 3.00
❑4 1997 3.00
❑5 1997 3.00
❑6 1997 3.00
❑7, May 1996 3.00

DOUBLE IMPACT: ART ATTACK
ABC

❑1 3.00
❑1/A; China & Jazz Nude Edition 4.00
❑1/B; Nude Jazz Edition 4.00

DOUBLE IMPACT: ASSASSINS FOR HIRE
HIGH IMPACT

❑1, Apr 1997, b&w; Hard Core! Edition; cardstock cover 2.95

DOUBLE IMPACT BIKINI SPECIAL
HIGH IMPACT

❑1, Sep 1998, b&w; pin-ups 3.00

DOUBLE IMPACT: FROM THE ASHES
HIGH IMPACT

❑1, b&w 3.00
❑2, b&w; says Swedish Erotika Vol. 5 on cover 5.95

DOUBLE IMPACT/HELLINA
ABC

❑1, Jan 1998, b&w; crossover with Lightning 3.00
❑1/Autographed, Mar 1996, b&w; Signed, limited edition nude cover 4.00
❑1/Gold, Mar 1996; Gold nude cover 5.00
❑1/Nude, Jan 1998; Nude cover 3.00
❑1/Variant, Mar 1996; Nude cover 3.00

DOUBLE IMPACT: ONE STEP BEYOND
HIGH IMPACT

❑1, Sep 1998 3.00
❑1/Variant; Leather cover 20.00

Gladstone's *Donald Duck Adventures* took a two-and-a-half-year hiatus, while Disney published its own separately numbered series.

© 1990 Walt Disney Productions.

N-MINT

DOUBLE IMPACT: RAISING HELL
ABC

❑1, Sep 1997, b&w 2.95
❑1/Nude, Sep 1997, b&w; nude cover 3.50

DOUBLE IMPACT: RAW
ABC

❑1, Nov 1997; cardstock cover 2.95
❑1/A, Nov 1997; Eurotika Edition; no cover price 4.00
❑1/Nude, Nov 1997; Eurotika Edition; nude cover 4.00
❑1-2 3.50
❑2, ca. 1998 3.00
❑2/Nude, ca. 1998; nude cover 3.00
❑3, ca. 1998 3.00

DOUBLE IMPACT: RAW (VOL. 2)
ABC

❑1/Nude, Sep 1998; Nude cover 3.00

DOUBLE IMPACT: SUICIDE RUN
HIGH IMPACT

❑1, Jun 1997 3.00
❑1/A, Jun 1997 4.00
❑1/Leather, Jun 1997; no cover price 4.00
❑1/Nude, Jun 1997 4.00

DOUBLE IMPACT: TRIGGER HAPPY
HIGH IMPACT

❑1, ca. 1997 3.00
❑1/B, ca. 1997; Jazz Edition 3.00
❑1/Ltd., ca. 1997; Gold edition; No cover price; limited to 300 copies 4.00

D.P.7
MARVEL

❑1, Nov 1986 1.00
❑2, Dec 1986 1.00
❑3, Jan 1987 1.00
❑4, Feb 1987 1.00
❑5, Mar 1987 1.00
❑6, Apr 1987 1.00
❑7, May 1987 1.00
❑8, Jun 1987 1.00
❑9, Jul 1987 1.00
❑10, Aug 1987 1.00
❑11, Sep 1987 1.00
❑12, Oct 1987 1.00
❑13, Nov 1987 1.00
❑14, Dec 1987 1.00
❑15, Jan 1988 1.00
❑16, Feb 1988 1.00
❑17, Mar 1988 1.00
❑18, Apr 1988 1.00
❑19, May 1988 1.00
❑20, Jun 1988 1.00
❑21, Jul 1988 1.00
❑22, Aug 1988 1.00
❑23, Sep 1988 1.00
❑24, Oct 1988 1.00
❑25, Nov 1988 1.00
❑26, Dec 1988 1.00
❑27, Jan 1989 1.00
❑28, Feb 1989 1.00
❑29, Mar 1989 1.00
❑30, Apr 1989 1.00
❑31, May 1989 1.00
❑32, Jun 1989 1.00
❑Annual 1, Nov 1987 1.00

N-MINT

DRACULA (ETERNITY)
ETERNITY

❑1 ... 2.50
❑1-2 ... 2.50
❑2, b&w ... 2.50
❑3, b&w ... 2.50
❑4, b&w ... 2.50

DRACULA (BRAM STOKER'S...)
TOPPS

❑1, Oct 1992 ... 2.95
❑1/Variant, Oct 1992; no cover price . 3.50
❑2, Nov 1992 ... 2.95
❑3, Dec 1992 ... 2.95
❑4, Jan 1993 ... 2.95

DRACULA 3-D
3-D ZONE

❑1 ... 3.95

DRACULA CHRONICLES, THE
TOPPS

❑1 ... 2.50
❑2 ... 2.50
❑3 ... 2.50

DRACULA IN HELL
APPLE

❑1, Jan 1992, b&w ... 2.50
❑2, b&w ... 2.50

DRACULA LIVES! (MAGAZINE)
MARVEL

❑1, Jun 1973 ... 5.00
❑2, Aug 1973 O: Dracula. ... 4.00
❑3, Oct 1973 A: Soloman Kane. ... 3.00
❑4, Jan 1974; title changes to Dracula Lives! ... 3.00
❑5, Mar 1974; adapts Bram Stoker novel ... 3.00
❑6, May 1974 ... 3.00
❑7, Jul 1974 ... 3.00
❑8, Sep 1974 ... 3.00
❑9, Nov 1974 ... 3.00
❑10, Jan 1975 ... 3.00
❑11, Mar 1975 ... 3.00
❑12, May 1975 ... 3.00
❑13, Jul 1975 ... 3.00
❑Annual 1, ca. 1975, b&w; magazine 3.00

DRACULA: LORD OF THE UNDEAD
MARVEL

❑1, Dec 1998; gatefold summary ... 2.99
❑2, Dec 1998; gatefold summary ... 2.99
❑3, Dec 1998; gatefold summary ... 2.99

DRACULA: RETURN OF THE IMPALER
SLAVE LABOR

❑1, Jul 1993 ... 2.95
❑2, Jan 1994 ... 2.95
❑3, Mar 1994 ... 2.95
❑4, Oct 1994 ... 2.95

DRACULA'S DAUGHTER
FANTAGRAPHICS / EROS

❑1, b&w ... 2.50

DRACULA: THE LADY IN THE TOMB
ETERNITY

❑1, b&w ... 2.50

DRACULA: THE SUICIDE CLUB
ADVENTURE

❑1, Aug 1992 ... 2.50
❑2, Sep 1992 ... 2.50
❑3, Oct 1992 ... 2.50
❑4, Nov 1992 ... 2.50

DRACULA VERSUS ZORRO
TOPPS

❑1, Oct 1993 TY (a) ... 4.00
❑2, Nov 1993 TY (a) ... 3.50

DRACULA VERSUS ZORRO (VOL. 2)
TOPPS

❑1, Apr 1994 ... 5.95

DRACULA VERSUS ZORRO (VOL. 3)
IMAGE

❑1, Sep 1998 ... 2.95
❑2, Oct 1998 ... 2.95

N-MINT

DRACULA: VLAD THE IMPALER
TOPPS

❑1; trading cards ... 2.95
❑2; trading cards ... 2.95
❑3; trading cards ... 2.95

DRACULINA (2ND SERIES)
DRACULINA

❑1 ... 2.50

DRACULINA'S COZY COFFIN
DRACULINA

❑1, b&w; no indicia ... 2.50
❑2, b&w; no indicia ... 2.50

DRAFT, THE
MARVEL

❑1, Jul 1988; D.P.7, Nightmask ... 2.00

DRAGON
COMICS INTERVIEW

❑1, Aug 1987; weekly ... 1.75
❑2, Aug 1987; weekly ... 1.75
❑3, Aug 1987; weekly ... 1.75
❑4, Aug 1987; weekly ... 1.75

DRAGON (2ND SERIES)
IMAGE

❑1, Mar 1996 ... 2.00
❑2, Apr 1996 ... 2.00
❑3, May 1996 ... 2.00
❑4, Jun 1996 ... 2.00
❑5, Jul 1996 A: Badrock. ... 2.00

DRAGON ARMS
ANTARCTIC

❑1, Dec 2002 ... 3.50
❑2, Jan 2003 ... 3.50
❑3, Feb 2003 ... 3.50
❑4, Mar 2003 ... 3.50
❑5, Apr 2003 ... 3.50
❑6, May 2003 ... 3.50

DRAGON ARMS: CHAOS BLADE
ANTARCTIC

❑1, Jan 2004 ... 2.99
❑2 2004 ... 2.99
❑3, May 2004 ... 2.99

DRAGONBALL
VIZ

❑1, Mar 1998; 'Manga Style' Edition . 4.00
❑2, Apr 1998; 'Manga Style' Edition .. 3.50
❑3, May 1998; 'Manga Style' Edition . 3.50
❑4, Jun 1998; 'Manga Style' Edition .. 3.50
❑5, Jul 1998; 'Manga Style' Edition ... 3.50
❑6, Aug 1998; 'Manga Style' Edition . 3.50
❑7, Sep 1998; 'Manga Style' Edition .. 3.50
❑8, Oct 1998 ... 3.00
❑9, Nov 1998 ... 3.00
❑10, Dec 1998 ... 3.00
❑11, Jan 1999 ... 3.00
❑12, Feb 1999 ... 3.00

DRAGONBALL PART 2
VIZ

❑1, Mar 1999 ... 4.00
❑2, Apr 1999 ... 3.00
❑3, May 1999 ... 3.00
❑4, Jun 1999 ... 3.00
❑5, Jul 1999 ... 3.00
❑6, Aug 1999 ... 3.00
❑7, Sep 1999 ... 3.00
❑8, Oct 1999 ... 3.00
❑9, Nov 1999 ... 2.95
❑10, Dec 1999 ... 2.95
❑11, Jan 2000 ... 2.95
❑12, Feb 2000 ... 2.95
❑13, Mar 2000 ... 2.95
❑14, Apr 2000 ... 2.95
❑15, May 2000 ... 2.95

DRAGONBALL PART 3
VIZ

❑1, Jun 2000 ... 2.95
❑2, Jul 2000 ... 2.95
❑3, Aug 2000 ... 2.95
❑4, Sep 2000 ... 2.95
❑5, Oct 2000 ... 2.95

N-MINT

❑6, Nov 2000 ... 2.95
❑7, Dec 2000 ... 2.95
❑8, Jan 2001 ... 2.95
❑9, Feb 2001 ... 2.95
❑10, Mar 2001 ... 2.95
❑11, Apr 2001 ... 2.95
❑12, May 2001 ... 2.95
❑13, Jun 2001 ... 2.95
❑14, Jul 2001 ... 2.95

DRAGONBALL PART 4
VIZ

❑1, Aug 2001 ... 2.95
❑2, Sep 2001 ... 2.95
❑3, Oct 2001 ... 2.95
❑4, Nov 2001 ... 2.95
❑5, Dec 2001 ... 2.95
❑6, Jan 2002 ... 2.95
❑7, Feb 2002 ... 2.95
❑8, Mar 2002 ... 2.95
❑9, Apr 2002 ... 2.95
❑10, May 2002 ... 2.95

DRAGONBALL PART 5
VIZ

❑1, Jun 2002 ... 2.95
❑2, Jul 2002 ... 2.95
❑3, Aug 2002 ... 2.95
❑4, Sep 2002 ... 2.95
❑5, Oct 2002 ... 2.95
❑6, Nov 2002 ... 2.95
❑7, Dec 2002 ... 2.95

DRAGONBALL PART 6
VIZ

❑1, Jan 2003 ... 3.50
❑2, Feb 2003 ... 3.50

DRAGONBALL Z
VIZ

❑1, Mar 1998 ... 4.00
❑2, Apr 1998 ... 3.50
❑3, May 1998 ... 3.50
❑4, Jun 1998 ... 3.50
❑5, Jul 1998 ... 3.50
❑6, Aug 1998 ... 3.00
❑7, Sep 1998 ... 3.00
❑8, Oct 1998 ... 3.00
❑9, Nov 1998 ... 3.00
❑10, ca. 1998 ... 3.00

DRAGONBALL Z PART 2
VIZ

❑1, Dec 1998; 'Manga Style' Edition .. 3.50
❑2, Jan 1999; 'Manga Style' Edition .. 3.00
❑3, Feb 1999; 'Manga Style' Edition .. 3.00
❑4, Mar 1999; 'Manga Style' Edition .. 3.00
❑5, Apr 1999; 'Manga Style' Edition .. 3.00
❑6, May 1999; 'Manga Style' Edition . 2.95
❑7, Jun 1999; 'Manga Style' Edition .. 2.95
❑8, Jul 1999 ... 2.95
❑9, Aug 1999 ... 2.95
❑10, Sep 1999 ... 2.95
❑11, Oct 1999 ... 2.95
❑12, Nov 1999 ... 2.95
❑13, Dec 1999 ... 2.95
❑14, Jan 2000 ... 2.95

DRAGONBALL Z PART 3
VIZ

❑1, Feb 2000 ... 2.95
❑2, Mar 2000 ... 2.95
❑3, Apr 2000 ... 2.95
❑4, May 2000 ... 2.95
❑5, Jun 2000 ... 2.95
❑6, Jul 2000 ... 2.95
❑7, Aug 2000 ... 2.95
❑8, Sep 2000 ... 2.95
❑9, Oct 2000 ... 2.95
❑10, Nov 2000 ... 2.95

DRAGONBALL Z PART 4
VIZ

❑1, Dec 2000 ... 2.95
❑2, Jan 2001 ... 2.95
❑3, Feb 2001 ... 2.95

	N-MINT
❑4, Mar 2001	2.95
❑5, Apr 2001	2.95
❑6, May 2001	2.95
❑7, Jun 2001	2.95
❑8, Jul 2001	2.95
❑9, Aug 2001	2.95
❑10, Sep 2001	2.95
❑11, Oct 2001	2.95
❑12, Nov 2001	2.95
❑13, Dec 2001	2.95

DRAGONBALL Z PART 5
VIZ

❑1, Jan 2002	2.95
❑2, Feb 2002	2.95
❑3, Mar 2002	2.95
❑4, Apr 2002	2.95
❑5, May 2002	2.95
❑6, Jun 2002	2.95
❑7, Jul 2002	2.95
❑8, Aug 2002	2.95
❑9, Sep 2002	2.95
❑10, Oct 2002	2.95
❑11, Nov 2002	2.95
❑12, Dec 2002	2.95

DRAGON, THE: BLOOD & GUTS
IMAGE

❑1, Mar 1995	2.50
❑2, Apr 1995	2.50
❑3, May 1995	2.50

DRAGON CHIANG
ECLIPSE

❑1, ca. 1991, b&w; nn, cardstock cover	3.95

DRAGONFIRE (VOL. 1)
NIGHTWYND

❑1, b&w	2.50
❑2, b&w	2.50
❑3, b&w	2.50
❑4, b&w	2.50

DRAGONFIRE (VOL. 2)
NIGHTWYND

❑1, b&w	2.50
❑2, b&w	2.50
❑3, b&w	2.50
❑4, b&w	2.50

DRAGONFIRE: THE CLASSIFIED FILES
NIGHTWYND

❑1, b&w	2.50
❑2, b&w	2.50
❑3, b&w	2.50
❑4, b&w	2.50

DRAGONFIRE: THE EARLY YEARS
NIGHT WYND

❑1, b&w	2.50
❑2, b&w	2.50
❑3, b&w	2.50
❑4, b&w	2.50
❑5, b&w	2.50
❑6, b&w	2.50
❑7, b&w	2.50
❑8, b&w	2.50

DRAGONFIRE: UFO WARS
NIGHTWYND

❑1, b&w	2.50
❑2, b&w	2.50
❑3, b&w	2.50

DRAGONFLIGHT
ECLIPSE

❑1, Feb 1991	4.95
❑2 1991	4.95
❑3 1991; Anne McCaffrey	4.95

DRAGON FLUX
ANTARCTIC

❑2, Jun 1996, b&w	2.95
❑3, Nov 1996, b&w	2.95

DRAGONFLY
AC

	N-MINT
❑1, Aug 1985	1.75
❑2	1.75
❑3	1.75
❑4	1.75
❑5	1.75
❑6, Feb 1987	1.75
❑7, Jul 1987	1.75
❑8	1.95

DRAGONFORCE
AIRCEL

❑1, ca. 1988, b&w O: Dragonforce. O: Alloy. 1: Kohl. 1: Maire. 1: Dragonforce. 1: Alloy. 1: Kamikaze. 1: Sental.	2.00
❑2, ca. 1988, b&w	2.00
❑3, ca. 1988, b&w	2.00
❑4, ca. 1988, b&w	2.00
❑5, ca. 1988, b&w	2.00
❑6, ca. 1988, b&w	2.00
❑7, ca. 1989, b&w	2.00
❑8, ca. 1989, b&w	2.00
❑9, ca. 1989, b&w	2.00
❑10, ca. 1989, b&w	2.00
❑11, ca. 1989, b&w	2.00
❑12, ca. 1989, b&w	2.00
❑13, ca. 1989, b&w	2.00

DRAGONFORCE CHRONICLES
AIRCEL

❑1, ca. 1989, b&w	2.95
❑2, ca. 1989, b&w	2.95
❑3, ca. 1989, b&w	2.95
❑4, ca. 1989, b&w	2.95
❑5, ca. 1989, b&w	2.95

DRAGONHEART
TOPPS

❑1, May 1996	2.95
❑2, Jun 1996	4.95

DRAGON KNIGHTS (SLAVE LABOR)
SLAVE LABOR / AMAZE INK

❑1, Aug 1998, b&w	1.75
❑2	1.75
❑3	1.75

DRAGON KNIGHTS (TOKYOPOP)
TOKYOPOP

❑1, Mar 2002, b&w; printed in Japanese format	9.99

DRAGON LADY
DRAGON LADY

❑1; King of Mounted	6.95
❑2; Red Ryder	6.95
❑3; Captain Easy	5.95
❑4; Secret Agent X-9	5.95
❑5; Brick Bradford	5.95
❑6; Secret Agent X-9	5.95
❑7; Captain Easy	5.95
❑8; Terry	5.95

DRAGONLANCE
DC

❑1, Dec 1988	2.00
❑2, Win 1988	1.50
❑3, Hol 1988	1.25
❑4, Jan 1989	1.25
❑5, Feb 1989	1.25
❑6, Mar 1989	1.50
❑7, Apr 1989	1.50
❑8, Jun 1989	1.50
❑9, Jul 1989	1.50
❑10, Aug 1989	1.50
❑11, Sep 1989	1.50
❑12, Oct 1989	1.50
❑13, Nov 1989	1.50
❑14, Dec 1989	1.50
❑15, Jan 1990	1.50
❑16, Feb 1990	1.50
❑17, Mar 1990	1.50
❑18, Apr 1990	1.50
❑19, May 1990	1.50
❑20, Jun 1990	1.50
❑21, Jul 1990	1.50

Evan Dorkin's *Dork* is an anthology containing such features as "Milk and Cheese," "The Murder Family," "Fisher Price Theater," and "Myron, The Living Voodoo Doll."

© 1994 Evan Dorkin and Slave Labor.

	N-MINT
❑22, Aug 1990	1.50
❑23, Oct 1990	1.50
❑24, Nov 1990	1.75
❑25, Dec 1990	1.75
❑26, Jan 1991	1.75
❑27, Feb 1991	1.75
❑28, Mar 1991	1.75
❑29, Apr 1991	1.75
❑30, May 1991	1.75
❑31, Jun 1991	1.75
❑32, Jul 1991	1.75
❑33, Aug 1991	1.75
❑34, Sep 1991	1.75

DRAGONLANCE COMIC BOOK
TSR

❑1	1.00

DRAGONLANCE SAGA
TSR

❑1	9.95
❑2	9.95
❑3	9.95
❑4	9.95
❑5	9.95

DRAGON LINES
MARVEL / EPIC

❑1, May 1993; Embossed cover	2.50
❑2, Jun 1993	1.95
❑3, Jul 1993	1.95
❑4, Aug 1993	1.95

DRAGON LINES: WAY OF THE WARRIOR
MARVEL / EPIC

❑1, Nov 1993	2.25
❑2, Jan 1994	2.25

DRAGON OF THE VALKYR
RAK

❑1, b&w	1.75
❑2	1.75
❑3	1.75

DRAGON QUEST
SILVERWOLF

❑1, b&w	2.00
❑2	2.00

DRAGONRING
AIRCEL

❑1 1986, b&w	2.00
❑2 1986, b&w	2.00
❑3 1986, b&w	2.00
❑4 1986, b&w	2.00
❑5 1986, b&w	2.00
❑6 1986, b&w	2.00

DRAGONRING (VOL. 2)
AIRCEL

❑1 1986	2.00
❑2 1987	2.00
❑3 1987	2.00
❑4 1987	2.00
❑5 1987	2.00
❑6 1987	2.00
❑7 1987	2.00
❑8 1987	2.00
❑9 1987	2.00
❑10 1987	2.00
❑11 1987	2.00
❑12 1987	2.00

N-MINT

- ❑13 1987 ... 2.00
- ❑14 1988 ... 2.00
- ❑15 1988 ... 2.00

DRAGONROK SAGA, THE
HANTHERCRAFT

- ❑1 ... 2.50
- ❑2 ... 2.50
- ❑3 ... 2.50
- ❑4 ... 2.50
- ❑5 ... 2.50
- ❑6 ... 2.50
- ❑7 ... 2.50
- ❑8 ... 2.50
- ❑9 ... 2.50
- ❑10 ... 2.50

DRAGON'S BANE
HALL OF HEROES

- ❑1 ... 2.50
- ❑Ashcan 1; Chicago Comic Con Ashcan limited to 100 copies ... 4.95

DRAGON'S CLAWS
MARVEL

- ❑1, Jul 1988 1: Dragon's Claws. ... 1.50
- ❑2, Aug 1988 ... 1.50
- ❑3, Sep 1988 ... 1.50
- ❑4, Oct 1988 ... 1.50
- ❑5, Nov 1988 1: Death's Head I. ... 2.00
- ❑6, Dec 1988 ... 1.75
- ❑7, Jan 1989 ... 1.75
- ❑8, Feb 1989 ... 1.75
- ❑9, Mar 1989 ... 1.75
- ❑10, Apr 1989 ... 1.75

DRAGONS IN THE MOON
AIRCEL

- ❑1, Oct 1990, b&w ... 2.50
- ❑2, Oct 1990, b&w ... 2.50
- ❑3, Oct 1990, b&w ... 2.50
- ❑4, Oct 1990, b&w ... 2.50

DRAGON'S LAIR: SINGE'S REVENGE
CROSSGEN

- ❑1, Sep 2003 ... 2.95
- ❑2, Nov 2003 ... 2.95
- ❑3, Nov 2003 ... 2.95

DRAGONSLAYER
MARVEL

- ❑1, Oct 1981 ... 1.50
- ❑2, Nov 1981 ... 1.50

DRAGON'S STAR
MATRIX

- ❑1, Dec 1986 ... 2.00
- ❑2 1987 ... 2.00
- ❑3 1987 ... 2.00

DRAGON'S STAR 2
CALIBER

- ❑1 1994 ... 2.95
- ❑2 1994 ... 2.95
- ❑3 ... 2.95

DRAGON'S TEETH
DRAGON'S TEETH

- ❑1, b&w ... 2.95

DRAGON STRIKE
MARVEL

- ❑1, Feb 1994 ... 1.50

DRAGONSTRIKE PRIME
ILLUSION

- ❑2, Dec 1996, b&w ... 1.95

DRAGON WARS, THE
IRONCAT

- ❑1, Apr 1998 ... 2.95
- ❑2, May 1998 ... 2.95
- ❑3, Jun 1998 ... 2.95
- ❑4, Jul 1998 ... 2.95
- ❑5, Aug 1998 ... 2.95
- ❑6, Sep 1998 ... 2.95
- ❑7, Oct 1998 ... 2.95

N-MINT

DRAG-STRIP HOTRODDERS
CHARLTON

- ❑1, Sum 1963 ... 40.00
- ❑2, ca. 1964 ... 25.00
- ❑3, ca. 1964 ... 25.00
- ❑4, Jun 1965 ... 25.00
- ❑5, Aug 1965 ... 25.00
- ❑6, Oct 1965 ... 25.00
- ❑7, Dec 1965 ... 25.00
- ❑8, Feb 1966 ... 25.00
- ❑9, Apr 1966 ... 25.00
- ❑10, Jun 1966 ... 25.00
- ❑11, Aug 1966 ... 25.00
- ❑12, Oct 1966 ... 25.00
- ❑13, Dec 1966 ... 25.00
- ❑14, Mar 1967 ... 25.00
- ❑15, Jun 1967 ... 25.00
- ❑16, Aug 1967; Later issues published as World of Wheels ... 25.00

DRAKE: DEMON BOX
IMAGE

- ❑1, Dec 2003 ... 2.50

DRAKKON WARS, THE
REALM

- ❑0, Jul 1997; Battlestar Galactica story written by Richard Hatch ... 2.99

DRAKUUN
DARK HORSE / MANGA

- ❑1, Feb 1997 ... 2.95
- ❑2, Mar 1997 ... 2.95
- ❑3, Apr 1997 ... 2.95
- ❑4, May 1997 ... 2.95
- ❑5, Jun 1997 ... 2.95
- ❑6, Jul 1997 ... 2.95
- ❑7, Aug 1997 ... 2.95
- ❑8, Sep 1997 ... 2.95
- ❑9, Oct 1997 ... 2.95
- ❑10, Nov 1997 ... 2.95
- ❑11, Dec 1997 ... 2.95
- ❑12, Jan 1998 ... 2.95
- ❑13, Feb 1998 ... 2.95
- ❑14, Mar 1998 ... 2.95
- ❑15, Apr 1998 ... 2.95
- ❑16, May 1998 ... 2.95
- ❑17, Jun 1998 ... 2.95
- ❑18, Jul 1998 ... 2.95
- ❑19, Oct 1998 ... 2.95
- ❑20, Nov 1998 ... 2.95
- ❑21, Dec 1998 ... 2.95
- ❑22, Jan 1999 ... 2.95
- ❑23, Feb 1999 ... 2.95
- ❑24, Mar 1999 ... 2.95

DRAMA
SIRIUS ENTERTAINMENT

- ❑1, Jun 1994, Chronium Cover ... 4.00
- ❑1/Ltd., Chronium Cover; limited to 1400 copies; signed by Linsner; w/ trading cards & Art Plate of Authenticity in an illustrated envelope ... 12.00

DRAWING ON YOUR NIGHTMARES: HALLOWEEN 2003 SPECIAL
DARK HORSE

- ❑1, Oct 2003 ... 2.99

DRAWN & QUARTERLY
DRAWN & QUARTERLY

- ❑1 1990, b&w ... 3.00
- ❑2 1990 ... 3.00
- ❑3, Jan 1991 ... 3.50
- ❑4, Mar 1991 ... 3.75
- ❑5 1991 ... 3.75
- ❑6 1991 ... 3.75
- ❑7 1992 ... 3.75
- ❑8, Apr 1992, b&w ... 3.75

DREADLANDS
MARVEL / EPIC

- ❑1, ca. 1992 ... 3.95
- ❑2, ca. 1992 ... 3.95
- ❑3, ca. 1992 ... 3.95
- ❑4, ca. 1992 ... 3.95

N-MINT

DREAD OF NIGHT
HAMILTON

- ❑1, b&w ... 3.95
- ❑2, b&w ... 3.95

DREADSTAR
MARVEL / EPIC

- ❑1, Nov 1982; JSn (c); JSn (w); JSn (a); Story continued from Epic Illustrated #15 ... 2.50
- ❑2, Jan 1983; JSn (c); JSn (w); JSn (a); O: Willow. Willow ... 2.00
- ❑3, Mar 1983; JSn (c); JSn (w); JSn (a); Lord Papal ... 2.00
- ❑4, May 1983 JSn (c); JSn (w); JSn (a) 2.00
- ❑5, Jul 1983 JSn (c); JSn (w); JSn (a) 2.00
- ❑6, Sep 1983 JSn (c); JSn (w); JSn (a) 1.75
- ❑7, Nov 1983 JSn (c); JSn (w); JSn (a) 1.75
- ❑8, Jan 1984 JSn (c); JSn (w); JSn (a) 1.75
- ❑9, Mar 1984 JSn (c); JSn (w); JSn (a) 1.75
- ❑10, Apr 1984 JSn (c); JSn (w); JSn (a) 1.75
- ❑11, Jun 1984 JSn (c); JSn (w); JSn (a) 1.75
- ❑12, Jul 1984; JSn (c); JSn (w); JSn (a); New costume ... 1.75
- ❑13, Aug 1984 JSn (c); JSn (w); JSn (a) 1.75
- ❑14, Oct 1984; JSn (c); JSn (w); JSn (a); Fights Lord Papal ... 1.75
- ❑15, Nov 1984 JSn (c); JSn (w); JSn (a) 1.75
- ❑16, Dec 1984 JSn (c); JSn (w); JSn (a) 1.50
- ❑17, Feb 1985 JSn (c); JSn (w); JSn (a) 1.50
- ❑18, Apr 1985 JSn (c); JSn (w); JSn (a) 1.50
- ❑19, Jun 1985 JSn (c); JSn (w); JSn (a) 1.50
- ❑20, Aug 1985 JSn (c); JSn (w); JSn (a) ... 1.50
- ❑21, Oct 1985 JSn (c); JSn (w); JSn (a) 1.50
- ❑22, Dec 1985 JSn (c); JSn (w); JSn (a) 1.50
- ❑23, Feb 1986 JSn (c); JSn (w); JSn (a) 1.50
- ❑24, Apr 1986 JSn (c); JSn (w); JSn (a) 1.50
- ❑25, Jun 1986 JSn (c); JSn (w); JSn (a) 1.50
- ❑26, Aug 1986 JSn (c); JSn (w); JSn (a) 1.50
- ❑27, Nov 1986; JSn (c); JSn (w); JSn (a); First Comics begins publishing 1.75
- ❑28, Jan 1987 JSn (c); JSn (w); JSn (a) 1.75
- ❑29, Mar 1987 JSn (c); JSn (w); JSn (a) 1.75
- ❑30, May 1987 JSn (c); JSn (w); JSn (a) 1.75
- ❑31, Jul 1987 JSn (c); JSn (w); JSn (a) 1.75
- ❑32, Sep 1987 JSn (c); JSn (w); JSn (a) 1.75
- ❑33, Nov 1987 JSn (c); JSn (w); JSn (a) 1.75
- ❑34, Jan 1988 JSn (c); JSn (w); JSn (a) 1.75
- ❑35, Mar 1988 JSn (c); JSn (w); JSn (a) 1.75
- ❑36, May 1988 JSn (c); JSn (w); JSn (a) 1.75
- ❑37, Jul 1988 JSn (c); JSn (w); JSn (a) 1.75
- ❑38, Sep 1988 JSn (c); JSn (w); JSn (a) 1.75
- ❑39, Nov 1988 JSn (c); JSn (w); JSn (a) 1.95
- ❑40, Jan 1989 JSn (c); JSn (w); JSn (a) 1.95
- ❑41, Mar 1989; PD (w); Peter David writing starts ... 1.95
- ❑42, May 1989 PD ... 1.95
- ❑43, Jun 1989 PD ... 1.95
- ❑44, Jul 1989 PD ... 1.95
- ❑45, Aug 1989 PD ... 1.95
- ❑46, Sep 1989 PD ... 1.95
- ❑47, Oct 1989 PD ... 1.95
- ❑48, Nov 1989 PD ... 1.95
- ❑49, Dec 1989 PD ... 1.95
- ❑50, Jan 1990; Double-size; PD (w); Embossed cover ... 2.75
- ❑51, Feb 1990 PD ... 1.95
- ❑52, Mar 1990 PD ... 1.95
- ❑53, Apr 1990 PD ... 1.95
- ❑54, May 1990 PD ... 1.95
- ❑55, Jun 1990 PD ... 2.25
- ❑56, Jul 1990 PD ... 2.25
- ❑57, Aug 1990 PD ... 2.25
- ❑58, Sep 1990 PD ... 2.25
- ❑59, Oct 1990 PD ... 2.25
- ❑60, Nov 1990 PD ... 2.25
- ❑61, Dec 1990 PD ... 2.25
- ❑62, Jan 1991 PD ... 2.25
- ❑63, Feb 1991 PD ... 2.25
- ❑64, Mar 1991 PD ... 2.25
- ❑Annual 1, ca. 1983 JSn (a) ... 2.00

N-MINT

DREADSTAR (MALIBU)
MALIBU / BRAVURA

❑0.5, Mar 1994; Promotional edition included in Hero Illustrated 2.00
❑1, Apr 1994 PD 2.50
❑2, May 1994 PD 2.50
❑3, Jun 1994 PD 2.50
❑4, Sep 1994 PD 2.50
❑5, Oct 1994 PD (w); D: Dreadstar (Vanth). 2.50
❑6, Jan 1995 PD 2.50

DREADSTAR & CO.
MARVEL / EPIC

❑1, Jul 1985 JSn (c); JSn (w); JSn (a) 1.00
❑2, Aug 1985 JSn (c); JSn (w); JSn (a) 1.00
❑3, Sep 1985 JSn (c); JSn (w); JSn (a) 1.00
❑4, Oct 1985 JSn (c); JSn (w); JSn (a) 1.00
❑5, Nov 1985 JSn (c); JSn (w); JSn (a) 1.00
❑6, Dec 1985 JSn (c); JSn (w); JSn (a) 1.00

DREAM ANGEL
ANGEL ENTERTAINMENT

❑0, Fal 1996, b&w 2.95

DREAM ANGEL AND ANGEL GIRL
ANGEL

❑1 .... 3.00

DREAM ANGEL: THE QUANTUM DREAMER
ANGEL

❑0 .... 2.95
❑1 .... 2.95
❑2 .... 2.95

DREAM CORRIDOR (HARLAN ELLISON'S...)
DARK HORSE

❑1, Mar 1995 JBy (a) 3.50
❑2, Apr 1995 JBy (a) 3.25
❑3, May 1995 JBy (a) 3.00
❑4, Jun 1995 JBy (a) 3.00
❑5, Aug 1995 .... 3.00
❑6, Sep 1995 .... 3.00
❑Special 1, Jan 1995; prestige format 5.00
❑Special 1-2, Sep 1995; prestige format 4.95

DREAM CORRIDOR QUARTERLY (HARLAN ELLISON'S...)
DARK HORSE

❑1, Aug 1996; prestige format 5.95

DREAMER, THE
DC

❑1, Jun 2000 .... 7.95

DREAMERY, THE
ECLIPSE

❑1, Dec 1986, b&w 2.00
❑2, Feb 1987, b&w; Lela Dowling bio 2.00
❑3, Apr 1987, b&w; Councilman Stinz story; Donna Barr bio 2.00
❑4, Jun 1987, b&w 2.00
❑5, Aug 1987, b&w 2.00
❑6, Oct 1987, b&w 2.00
❑7, Dec 1987, b&w 2.00
❑8, Feb 1988, b&w 2.00
❑9, Apr 1988, b&w; Young Stinz story 2.00
❑10, Jun 1988, b&w; Young Stinz story 2.00
❑11, Aug 1988, b&w; Young Stinz story 2.00
❑12, Oct 1988, b&w; Councilman Stinz story 2.00
❑13, Dec 1988, b&w; Councilman Stinz story 2.00
❑14, Feb 1989, b&w; Cover reads "The Ninjery" 2.00

DREAMING, THE
DC / VERTIGO

❑1, Jun 1996 .... 3.00
❑2, Jul 1996 .... 2.50
❑3, Aug 1996 .... 2.50
❑4, Sep 1996 .... 2.50
❑5, Oct 1996 .... 2.50
❑6, Nov 1996 .... 2.50
❑7, Dec 1996 .... 2.50

N-MINT

❑8, Jan 1997; self-contained story; cover says Nov 96, indicia says Jan 97 ...... 2.50
❑9, Feb 1997 .... 2.50
❑10, Mar 1997 .... 2.50
❑11, Apr 1997 .... 2.50
❑12, May 1997 .... 2.50
❑13, Jun 1997 .... 2.50
❑14, Jul 1997 .... 2.50
❑15, Aug 1997 .... 2.50
❑16, Sep 1997 .... 2.50
❑17, Oct 1997 .... 2.50
❑18, Nov 1997 .... 2.50
❑19, Dec 1997 .... 2.50
❑20, Jan 1998 .... 2.50
❑21, Feb 1998 .... 2.50
❑22, Mar 1998 .... 2.50
❑23, Apr 1998 .... 2.50
❑24, May 1998 .... 2.50
❑25, Jun 1998 .... 2.50
❑26, Jul 1998 .... 2.50
❑27, Aug 1998 .... 2.50
❑28, Sep 1998; House of Mystery burns down 2.50
❑29, Oct 1998 .... 2.50
❑30, Nov 1998 .... 2.50
❑31, Dec 1998 .... 2.50
❑32, Jan 1999 .... 2.50
❑33, Feb 1999 .... 2.50
❑34, Mar 1999 .... 2.50
❑35, Apr 1999 .... 2.50
❑36, May 1999 .... 2.50
❑37, Jun 1999 .... 2.50
❑38, Jul 1999 .... 2.50
❑39, Aug 1999 .... 2.50
❑40, Sep 1999 .... 2.50
❑41, Oct 1999 .... 2.50
❑42, Nov 1999 .... 2.50
❑43, Dec 1999 .... 2.50
❑44, Jan 2000 .... 2.50
❑45, Feb 2000 .... 2.50
❑46, Mar 2000 .... 2.50
❑47, Apr 2000 .... 2.50
❑48, May 2000 .... 2.50
❑49, Jun 2000 .... 2.50
❑50, Jul 2000 .... 2.50
❑51, Aug 2000 .... 2.50
❑52, Sep 2000 .... 2.50
❑53, Oct 2000 .... 2.50
❑54, Nov 2000 .... 2.50
❑55, Dec 2000 .... 2.50
❑56, Jan 2001 .... 2.50
❑57, Feb 2001 .... 2.50
❑58, Mar 2001 .... 2.50
❑59, Apr 2001 .... 2.50
❑60, May 2001 .... 2.50
❑Special 1, Jul 1998; wraparound cover 5.95

DREAMLAND CHRONICLES
ASTONISH

❑1, Mar 2004 .... 3.50

DREAM-QUEST OF UNKNOWN KADATH, THE (H.P. LOVECRAFT'S...)
MOCK MAN

❑1 .... 2.95
❑1-2, Mar 1998 .... 2.95
❑2 .... 2.95
❑3 .... 2.95
❑4 .... 2.95
❑5 .... 2.95

DREAMS CANNOT DIE!
MARK'S GIANT ECONOMY SIZE

❑1, Jun 1996; Trade Paperback 17.95

DREAMS 'N' SCHEMES OF COL. KILGORE
SPECIAL STUDIO

❑1, Mar 1991, b&w 2.50
❑2, May 1991, b&w 2.50

The Lord of the Undead took on the defender of Old California in three separate Topps series.

© 1993 Topps.

N-MINT

DREAMS OF A DOG
RIP OFF

❑1, May 1990, b&w 2.00
❑2, Jun 1992, b&w 2.50

DREAMS OF EVERYMAN
RIP OFF

❑1, Jun 1992 .... 2.50

DREAMS OF THE DARKCHYLDE
DARKCHYLDE

❑1, Oct 2000 .... 3.50
❑1/A, Oct 2000; variant cover 3.50
❑1/B, Oct 2000; chromium cover 10.00
❑1/C, Oct 2000; Dynamic Forces cover 6.00
❑1/D, Oct 2000; DFE blue foil cover ... 7.00
❑1/E, Oct 2000; DFE chrome cover 10.00
❑1/F, Oct 2000; Tower Records cover 5.00
❑2, Nov 2000; Tower Records cover . 3.00
❑3, Dec 2000; Tower Records cover .. 3.00
❑4, Mar 2001; Tower Records cover . 2.95
❑5, ca. 2001; Tower Records cover ... 2.95
❑6, Sep 2001; Tower Records cover .. 2.95

DREAM TEAM
MALIBU

❑1, Jul 1995; Malibu/Marvel Pin-ups . 4.95

DREAMTIME
BLIND BAT

❑1, May 1995, b&w 2.50
❑2, b&w; no indicia 2.50

DREAMWALKER (DREAMWALKER)
DREAMWALKER

❑1, ca. 1996, b&w 2.95
❑2, ca. 1996, b&w 2.95
❑3, ca. 1996, b&w 2.95
❑4, ca. 1996, b&w 2.95
❑5, ca. 1996, b&w 2.95

DREAMWALKER (CALIBER)
CALIBER / TAPESTRY

❑1, Dec 1996, b&w 2.95
❑2, Feb 1997, b&w 2.95
❑3 1997, b&w 2.95
❑4, Jul 1997, b&w 2.95
❑5, Sep 1997, b&w 2.95
❑6, Jul 1998, b&w 2.95

DREAMWALKER (AVATAR)
AVATAR

❑0, Nov 1998, b&w 3.00

DREAMWALKER (MARVEL)
MARVEL

❑1 .... 6.95

DREAMWALKER: AUTUMN LEAVES
AVATAR

❑1, Sep 1999, b&w 3.00
❑2, Oct 1999, b&w 3.00

DREAMWALKER: CAROUSEL
AVATAR

❑1, Mar 1999, b&w 3.00
❑2, Apr 1999, b&w 3.00

DREAMWALKER: SUMMER RAIN
AVATAR

❑1, Jul 1999, b&w 3.00

DREAM WEAVER
ROBERT LANKFORD

❑1, Aug 1987 .... 1.95

N-MINT

DREAM WEAVERS
Golden Realm Unlimited
❑1 .... 1.50
❑2 .... 1.50

DREAM WOLVES
Dramenon
❑1, b&w 3.00
❑2, Dec 1994, b&w; cardstock cover 3.00
❑3, Jan 1995, b&w; cardstock cover . 3.00
❑4, Feb 1995, b&w 3.00

DREAM WOLVES SWIMSUIT BIZARRE
Gothic
❑0, Dec 1995 .... 3.00

DREDD BY BISLEY
Fleetway-Quality
❑1 .... 5.95

DREDD RULES!
Fleetway-Quality
❑1 .... 3.50
❑2 .... 3.00
❑3 .... 3.00
❑4 .... 3.00
❑5 .... 3.00
❑6 .... 2.95
❑7 .... 2.95
❑8 .... 2.95
❑9 .... 2.95
❑10 .... 2.95
❑11 .... 2.95
❑12 .... 2.95
❑13 .... 2.95
❑14 V: Santa. 2.95
❑15 .... 2.95
❑16 .... 2.95
❑17 .... 2.95
❑18 .... 2.95
❑19 .... 2.95
❑20 .... 2.95

DRIFTER
Brainstorm
❑1, b&w 2.95

DRIFTERS
Infinity
❑1, Oct 1986 .... 2.00

DRIFTERS, THE
Cornerstone
❑1, b&w 2.00

DRIVE-IN (JOE LANSDALE'S)
Avatar
❑1, Nov 2003 .... 3.50
❑1/A, Nov 2003; Wrap Cover 3.95
❑2, Dec 2003 .... 3.50
❑3, Jan 2004 .... 3.95
❑3/A, Jan 2004; Wrap Cover 3.50
❑4, Mar 2004 .... 3.50

DROIDS
Marvel / Star
❑1, Apr 1986 .... 3.00
❑2, Jun 1986 JR (a) 2.00
❑3, Aug 1986 .... 2.00
❑4, Oct 1986 .... 2.00
❑5, Dec 1986 .... 2.00
❑6, Feb 1987; A New Hope told from droids' p.o.v. 2.00
❑7, Apr 1987; A New Hope told from droids' p.o.v. 2.00
❑8, Jun 1987; A New Hope told from droids' p.o.v. 2.00

DROOL MAGAZINE
Co. & Sons
❑1 .... 3.00

DROOPY
Dark Horse
❑1, Oct 1995; Screwball Squirrel back-up 2.50
❑2, Nov 1995; Wolf and Red back-up 2.50
❑3, Dec 1995; Screwball Squirrel back-up 2.50

N-MINT

DROPSIE AVENUE: THE NEIGHBORHOOD
Kitchen Sink
❑1, Jun 1995, b&w 15.95

DRUID
Marvel
❑1, May 1995 .... 2.50
❑2, Jun 1995 .... 1.95
❑3, Jul 1995 .... 1.95
❑4, Aug 1995 .... 1.95

DRUNKEN FIST
Jademan
❑1, Aug 1988 .... 1.95
❑2, Sep 1988 .... 1.95
❑3, Oct 1988 .... 1.95
❑4, Nov 1988 .... 1.95
❑5, Dec 1988 .... 1.95
❑6, Jan 1989 .... 1.95
❑7, Feb 1989 .... 1.95
❑8, Mar 1989 .... 1.95
❑9, Apr 1989 .... 1.95
❑10, May 1989 .... 1.95
❑11, Jun 1989 .... 1.95
❑12, Jul 1989 .... 1.95
❑13, Aug 1989 .... 1.95
❑14, Sep 1989 .... 1.95
❑15, Oct 1989 .... 1.95
❑16, Nov 1989 .... 1.95
❑17, Dec 1989 .... 1.95
❑18, Jan 1990 .... 1.95
❑19, Feb 1990 .... 1.95
❑20, Mar 1990 .... 1.95
❑21, Apr 1990 .... 1.95
❑22, May 1990 .... 1.95
❑23, Jun 1990 .... 1.95
❑24, Jul 1990 .... 1.95
❑25, Aug 1990 .... 1.95
❑26, Sep 1990 .... 1.95
❑27, Oct 1990 .... 1.95
❑28, Nov 1990 .... 1.95
❑29, Dec 1990 .... 1.95
❑30, Jan 1991 .... 1.95
❑31, Feb 1991 .... 1.95
❑32, Mar 1991 .... 1.95
❑33, Apr 1991 .... 1.95
❑34, May 1991 .... 1.95
❑35, Jun 1991 .... 1.95
❑36, Jul 1991 .... 1.95
❑37, Aug 1991 .... 1.95
❑38, Sep 1991 .... 1.95
❑39, Oct 1991 .... 1.95
❑40, Nov 1991 .... 1.95
❑41, Dec 1991 .... 1.95
❑42, Jan 1992 .... 1.95
❑43, Feb 1992 .... 1.95
❑44, Mar 1992 .... 1.95
❑45, Apr 1992 .... 1.95
❑46, May 1992 .... 1.95
❑47, Jun 1992 .... 1.95
❑48, Jul 1992 .... 1.95
❑49, Aug 1992 .... 1.95
❑50, Sep 1992 .... 1.95
❑51, Oct 1992 .... 1.95
❑52, Nov 1992 .... 1.95
❑53, Dec 1992 .... 1.95
❑54, Jan 1993 .... 1.95

DRY ROT
Zolton
❑1, b&w 2.95

DUCK AND COVER
Cat-Head
❑1, b&w 2.00
❑2, b&w 2.00

DUCKBOTS
Blackthorne
❑1, Feb 1987 .... 2.00
❑2 .... 2.00

N-MINT

DUCKMAN
Dark Horse
❑1, Sep 1990, b&w 1: Duckman. 2.00
❑2, b&w 2.00
❑Special 1, Apr 1990, b&w 2.00

DUCKMAN (TOPPS)
Topps
❑1, Nov 1994 .... 2.50
❑2, Dec 1994 .... 2.50
❑3, Mar 1995 .... 2.50
❑4, Mar 1995 .... 2.50
❑5, May 1995 .... 2.50
❑6 .... 2.50

DUCKMAN: THE MOB FROG SAGA
Topps
❑1, Nov 1994 .... 2.50
❑2, Dec 1994 .... 2.50
❑3, Feb 1995 .... 2.50

DUCKTALES (GLADSTONE)
Gladstone
❑1, Oct 1988 CB (a) 2.00
❑2, Nov 1988 .... 1.50
❑3, Jan 1989 .... 1.50
❑4, Feb 1989 .... 1.50
❑5, Apr 1989 .... 1.50
❑6, May 1989 .... 1.50
❑7, Jul 1989 .... 1.50
❑8, Aug 1989 .... 1.50
❑9, Oct 1989 CB (a) 1.50
❑10, Nov 1989 CB (a) 1.50
❑11, Jan 1990 CB (a) 1.50
❑12, Mar 1990 CB (a) 1.50
❑13, May 1990 CB (a) 1.50

DUCKTALES (DISNEY'S...)
Disney
❑1, Jun 1990 .... 2.00
❑2, Jul 1990 .... 1.50
❑3, Aug 1990 V: Magica de Spell. 1.50
❑4, Sep 1990 .... 1.50
❑5, Oct 1990 .... 1.50
❑6, Nov 1990 .... 1.50
❑7, Dec 1990 .... 1.50
❑8, Jan 1991 .... 1.50
❑9, Feb 1991 .... 1.50
❑10, Mar 1991 .... 1.50
❑11, Apr 1991 .... 1.50
❑12, May 1991 .... 1.50
❑13, Jun 1991 .... 1.50
❑14, Jul 1991 .... 1.50
❑15, Aug 1991 .... 1.50
❑16, Sep 1991 .... 1.50
❑17, Oct 1991 .... 1.50
❑18, Nov 1991 .... 1.50

DUCKTALES: THE MOVIE
Disney
❑1; adaptation 5.95

DUDLEY DO-RIGHT
Charlton
❑1, Aug 1970 .... 25.00
❑2, Oct 1970 .... 15.00
❑3, Dec 1970 .... 12.00
❑4, Feb 1971 .... 10.00
❑5, Apr 1971 .... 10.00
❑6, Jun 1971 .... 10.00
❑7, Aug 1971 .... 10.00

DUEL MASTERS
Dreamwave
❑1, Nov 2003 .... 2.95
❑1/DF, Nov 2003; Holofoil Cover 5.95
❑1/A, Dec 2003 .... 2.95
❑2, Dec 2003 .... 2.95
❑3, Jan 2004 .... 2.95
❑3-2, Mar 2004 .... 2.95
❑4, Apr 2004 .... 2.95
❑5, May 2004 .... 3.95

DUMB-ASS EXPRESS
McMann & Tate
❑1; slightly oversized 2.95

N-MINT

DUMM $2099
PARODY

❑1; Cover forms triptych with Rummage $2099, Pummeler $2099 ... 2.95

DUNE
MARVEL

❑1, Apr 1985 BSz (a) ... 1.50
❑2, May 1985 BSz (a) ... 1.50
❑3, Jun 1985 BSz (a) ... 1.50

DUNG BOYS, THE
KITCHEN SINK

❑1, Apr 1996, b&w ... 2.95
❑2, May 1996; nude cover with black bars ... 2.95
❑3, Jun 1996 ... 2.95

DUNGEON
NBM

❑1, ca. 2002, Several characters in profile on cover ... 2.95

DUNGEONEERS, THE
SILVERWOLF

❑1 ... 1.50
❑2, Oct 1986 ... 1.50
❑3, Nov 1986 ... 1.50
❑4 ... 1.50

DUNGEONS & DRAGONS: WHERE SHADOWS FALL
KENZER AND COMPANY

❑1, Aug 2003 ... 3.50
❑2, Oct 2003 ... 3.50
❑3, Dec 2003 ... 3.50
❑4, Feb 2004 ... 3.50

DUPLEX PLANET ILLUSTRATED
FANTAGRAPHICS

❑1, Jan 1993, b&w ... 2.95
❑2 1993 ... 2.50
❑3 1993 ... 2.50
❑4 1993 ... 2.50
❑5 1993 ... 2.95
❑6 1994 ... 2.95
❑7 1994, b&w ... 2.50
❑8, May 1994, b&w ... 2.50
❑9, Jul 1994, b&w ... 2.50
❑10, Sep 1994, b&w ... 2.50
❑11, Dec 1994 ... 2.50
❑12 1995 ... 2.50
❑13 1995 ... 2.50
❑14 1995 ... 2.50
❑15, Apr 1996, b&w ... 4.95

DURANGO KID, THE
AC

❑1; some color ... 2.50
❑2, b&w ... 2.75
❑3 ... 4.95

DUSK
DEADWOOD

❑1, b&w; cardstock cover ... 3.00

DUSTY STAR
IMAGE

❑0, Apr 1997, b&w; collects stories from Negative Burn #28 and #37 ... 2.95
❑1, Jun 1997, b&w ... 2.95

DV8
DC / WILDSTORM

❑0, Dec 1998 ... 3.00
❑0.5, Jan 1997; Wizard 1/2 Promotional edition ... 3.00
❑0.5/A, Jan 1997; Wizard 1/2 Promotional edition; variant cover ... 3.00
❑0.5/Gold, Jan 1997; Wizard 1/2 "Authentic Gold" promotional edition ... 3.00
❑0.5/Platinum, Jan 1997; Wizard 1/2 Platinum promotional edition; Wizard promotional item; platinum version ... 3.00
❑1/A, Aug 1996 ... 3.00
❑1/B, Aug 1996 ... 3.00
❑1/C, Aug 1996 ... 3.00
❑1/D, Aug 1996 ... 3.00
❑1/E, Aug 1996 ... 3.00
❑1/F, Aug 1996 ... 3.00
❑1/G, Aug 1996 ... 3.00
❑1/H, Aug 1996 ... 3.00
❑2, Nov 1996 ... 2.50
❑3, Dec 1996 ... 2.50
❑4, Jan 1997 ... 2.50
❑5, Feb 1997 ... 2.50
❑6, Mar 1997 ... 2.50
❑7, Apr 1997; cover says May, indicia says Apr ... 2.50
❑8, May 1997; cover says Jun, indicia says May ... 2.50
❑9, Jun 1997 ... 2.50
❑10, Jul 1997 ... 2.50
❑11, Sep 1997 ... 2.50
❑12, Oct 1997 ... 2.50
❑13, Nov 1997 ... 2.50
❑14/A, Dec 1997; Has woman on cover ... 2.50
❑14/B, Dec 1997; Whole group on cover; white background ... 2.50
❑14/C, Dec 1997; Voyager pack with preview of Danger Girl ... 5.00
❑15, Jan 1998 ... 2.50
❑16, Feb 1998 ... 2.50
❑17, Apr 1998 ... 2.50
❑18, May 1998 ... 2.50
❑19, Jun 1998 ... 2.50
❑20, Jul 1998 ... 2.50
❑21, Aug 1998 ... 2.50
❑22, Sep 1998 ... 2.50
❑22/A, Sep 1998; alternate cover (white background) ... 2.50
❑23, Oct 1998 ... 2.50
❑24, Nov 1998 ... 2.50
❑25, Dec 1998 ... 2.50
❑26, May 1999 ... 2.50
❑27, Jun 1999 ... 2.50
❑28, Jul 1999 ... 2.50
❑29, Aug 1999 ... 2.50
❑30, Sep 1999 ... 2.50
❑31, Oct 1999 ... 2.50
❑32, Nov 1999 ... 2.50
❑Annual 1, Jan 1998 ... 2.95
❑Annual 1999, Mar 1999; continued from Gen13 Annual 1999; wraparound cover ... 3.50

DV8 RAVE
IMAGE

❑1, Jul 1996 ... 2.00

DV8 VS. BLACK OPS
IMAGE

❑1, Oct 1997 ... 2.50
❑2, Nov 1997 ... 2.50
❑3, Dec 1997 ... 2.50

DYKE'S DELIGHT
FANNY

❑1 ... 2.95
❑2 ... 2.95

DYLAN DOG
DARK HORSE

❑1, Mar 1999 ... 4.95
❑2, Apr 1999 ... 4.95
❑3, May 1999 ... 4.95
❑4, Jun 1999 ... 4.95
❑5, Jul 1999 ... 4.95
❑6, Aug 1999 ... 4.95

DYNAMIC CLASSICS
DC

❑1, Sep 1978 ... 2.50

DYNAMO
TOWER

❑1, Aug 1966 WW (a) ... 35.00
❑2, Oct 1966 WW (a) ... 25.00
❑3, Mar 1967 WW (a) ... 25.00
❑4, Jun 1967 WW (a) ... 25.00

DYNAMO JOE
FIRST

❑1, May 1986 ... 1.50
❑2, Jun 1986 ... 1.25
❑3, Jul 1986 ... 1.25
❑4, Feb 1987 ... 1.25

Members of *Sandman*'s supporting cast, as well as the "hosts" of *House of Mystery* and *House of Secrets*, appeared in *The Dreaming*.

© 1996 DC Comics (Vertigo).

N-MINT

❑5, Mar 1987 ... 1.25
❑6, Apr 1987 ... 1.25
❑7, May 1987 ... 1.25
❑8, Jun 1987 ... 1.25
❑9, Jul 1987 ... 1.25
❑10, Aug 1987 ... 1.25
❑11, Sep 1987 ... 1.25
❑12, Oct 1987 ... 1.75
❑13, Nov 1987 ... 1.75
❑14, Dec 1987 ... 1.75
❑15, Jan 1988 ... 1.75
❑Special 1, Jan 1987 ... 1.25

DYNOMUTT
MARVEL

❑1, Nov 1977; Scooby Doo ... 6.00
❑2, Jan 1978; Scooby Doo ... 4.00
❑3, Mar 1978; Scooby Doo ... 3.00
❑4, May 1978; Scooby Doo ... 3.00
❑5, Jul 1978; Scooby Doo ... 3.00
❑6, Sep 1978; Scooby Doo ... 3.00

DYSTOPIK SNOMEN
SLAVE LABOR

❑1, Oct 1994; was college newspaper strip ... 4.95

DYSTOPIK SNOMEN (VOL. 2)
SLAVE LABOR

❑1, Sep 1995 ... 1.50
❑2, Dec 1995 ... 1.75

E

EAGLE (CRYSTAL)
CRYSTAL

❑1, Sep 1986 ... 1.50
❑1/Ltd., Sep 1986; limited edition ... 1.50
❑2 ... 1.50
❑3 1987 ... 1.50
❑4, Apr 1987 ... 1.50
❑5, May 1987 ... 1.50
❑6, Jun 1987; Adam Hughes pin-up (his first major comics work) ... 1.50
❑7, Jul 1987 ... 1.50
❑8, Aug 1987 ... 1.50
❑9, Sep 1987 ... 1.50
❑10, Oct 1987 ... 1.50
❑11, Nov 1987 ... 1.50
❑12, Dec 1987 ... 1.50
❑13, Jan 1988 ... 1.50
❑14, Feb 1988 ... 1.50
❑15, Mar 1988 ... 1.50
❑16, May 1988 ... 1.50
❑17 1988, b&w ... 1.95
❑18, Sep 1988, b&w ... 1.95
❑19, Oct 1988, b&w ... 1.95
❑20, b&w ... 1.95
❑21 1989, b&w ... 1.95
❑22 1989, b&w ... 1.95
❑23 1989 ... 2.25

EAGLE (COMIC ZONE)
COMIC ZONE

❑1, b&w ... 2.75
❑2, b&w ... 2.75
❑3, b&w ... 2.75

N-MINT

EAGLES DARE
AAGER

❑1 .... 1.95
❑2, Sep 1994 .... 1.95

EAGLE: THE DARK MIRROR SAGA
COMIC ZONE

❑1, Jan 1992 .... 2.75
❑2 .... 2.75
❑3 .... 2.75

EARLY DAYS OF THE SOUTHERN KNIGHTS
COMICS INTERVIEW

❑1 1986 .... 4.95
❑1-2 .... 4.95
❑2, Feb 1987 .... 4.95
❑3, Jul 1987 .... 4.95
❑4 1987 .... 4.95
❑5 1988 .... 5.95
❑6, Nov 1988 .... 6.50
❑7, Jan 1989 .... 6.95
❑8, Mar 1989 .... 6.95

EARTH C.O.R.E.
INDEPENDENT

❑1 .... 1.95

EARTH 4
CONTINUITY

❑1 .... 2.50
❑2, Dec 1993 .... 2.50
❑3 .... 2.50
❑4, Jan 1994 .... 2.50

EARTH 4 (VOL. 2)
CONTINUITY

❑1, Dec 1993 .... 2.50
❑2, Dec 1993 .... 2.50
❑3, Dec 1993 .... 2.50
❑4, Jan 1994 .... 2.50

EARTH 4 DEATHWATCH 2000
CONTINUITY

❑0, Apr 1993; Trading Cards 2.50
❑1, Apr 1993; trading cards; indicia says #0, a misprint 2.50
❑2, May 1993; trading card 2.50
❑3, Aug 1993; trading card; Deathwatch 2000 dropped from indicia .. 2.50

EARTHLORE
ETERNITY

❑1 .... 2.00
❑2 .... 2.00

EARTHWORM JIM
MARVEL

❑1, Dec 1995; based on video game . 2.25
❑2, Jan 1996 .... 2.25
❑3, Feb 1996 .... 2.25
❑4, Mar 1996 .... 2.25

EARTH X
MARVEL

❑0, Mar 1999 ARo (c); ARo (w); ARo (a) 4.00
❑0/A, Mar 1999; ARo (c); ARo (w); ARo (a); A: X-51. A: Watcher. Covers of series form giant picture 5.00
❑0/B, Mar 1999; ARo (c); ARo (w); ARo (a); A: X-51. A: Watcher. Covers of series form giant picture 4.00
❑0/C, Mar 1999; ARo (c); ARo (w); ARo (a); A: X-51. A: Watcher. DFE alternate cover 5.00
❑1, Apr 1999; ARo (c); ARo (w); ARo (a); A: Inhumans. A: Hydra. Covers of series form giant picture 3.00
❑1/A, Apr 1999; ARo (c); ARo (w); ARo (a); A: Inhumans. A: Hydra. Covers of series form giant picture 5.00
❑1/B, Apr 1999; ARo (w); A: Inhumans. A: Hydra. DFE alternate cover 3.50
❑1/C, Apr 1999; ARo (w); A: Inhumans. A: Hydra. DFE alternate cover 5.00
❑2, May 1999 ARo (c); ARo (w); ARo (a) 2.99
❑3, Jun 1999 ARo (c); ARo (w); ARo (a) 2.99
❑4, Jul 1999 ARo (c); ARo (w); ARo (a) 2.99
❑5, Aug 1999 ARo (c); ARo (w); ARo (a) 2.99
❑6, Sep 1999 ARo (c); ARo (w); ARo (a) 2.99
❑7, Oct 1999 ARo (c); ARo (w); ARo (a) 2.99
❑8, Nov 1999 ARo (c); ARo (w); ARo (a) 2.99
❑9, Dec 1999 ARo (c); ARo (w); ARo (a) 2.99
❑10 2000 ARo (c); ARo (w); ARo (a) . 2.99
❑11, Mar 2000 ARo (c); ARo (w); ARo (a) 2.99
❑12, Apr 2000 ARo (c); ARo (w); ARo (a) 2.99
❑13, Jun 2000; ARo (c); ARo (w); ARo (a); "X" issue 3.99

EARTH X SKETCHBOOK
MARVEL

❑1, Mar 1999 .... 4.50

EAST MEETS WEST
INNOVATION

❑1, Apr 1990 .... 2.50

EAT-MAN
VIZ

❑1, Aug 1997, b&w 2.95
❑2, Sep 1997, b&w 2.95
❑3, Oct 1997, b&w 2.95
❑4, Nov 1997, b&w 2.95
❑5, Dec 1997, b&w 2.95
❑6, Jan 1997, b&w 2.95

EAT-MAN SECOND COURSE
VIZ

❑1, Feb 1998, b&w 2.95
❑2, Mar 1998, b&w 3.50
❑3, Apr 1998, b&w 3.50
❑4, May 1998, b&w 3.25
❑5, b&w 2.95

EB'NN
NOW

❑3, Jun 1986 .... 1.50
❑4, Aug 1986 .... 1.50
❑5, Nov 1986 .... 1.50
❑6, Jan 1987 .... 1.50

EB'NN THE RAVEN
CROWQUILL

❑1 .... 3.00
❑2 .... 3.00

EBONY WARRIOR
AFRICA RISING

❑1, Apr 1993 .... 1.95

E.C. CLASSIC REPRINTS
EAST COAST COMIX

❑1, May 1973; AF (w); GE, JO, GI (a); Reprints Crypt of Terror #1 (a series meant to have been launched when EC ceased publishing horror) 4.00
❑2; AF (w); AW, JO, WW, JKa (a); Reprints Weird Science #15 .... 3.00
❑3; Reprints Shock SuspenStories #12 3.00
❑4; Reprints Haunt of Fear #12 .... 3.00
❑5; Reprints Weird Fantasy #13 .... 3.00
❑6; GE, BK (a); Reprints Crime SuspenStories #25 .... 3.00
❑7; Reprints Vault of Horror #26 .... 3.00
❑8; Reprints Shock SuspenStories #6 3.00
❑9; Reprints Two-Fisted Tales #34 ..... 3.00
❑10; Reprints Haunt of Fear #23 .... 3.00
❑11; Reprints Weird Science #12 .... 3.00
❑12, ca. 1976; Reprints Shock SuspenStories #2 .... 3.00

EC CLASSICS
COCHRAN

❑1 .... 5.00
❑2 .... 5.00
❑3 .... 5.00
❑4 .... 5.00
❑5; AW (a); Reprints from Weird Fantasy #14, 15, 16, 17 .... 5.00
❑6 .... 5.00

ECHO
IMAGE

❑0, Jul 2000 .... 2.50
❑1, Mar 2000 .... 2.95
❑2, Apr 2000 .... 2.50
❑3, May 2000 .... 2.50
❑4, Jun 2000 .... 2.50
❑5, Sep 2000 .... 2.50

ECHO OF FUTUREPAST
CONTINUITY

❑1, May 1984 .... 2.95
❑2 1984 .... 2.95
❑3, Nov 1984 .... 2.95
❑4, Feb 1985 .... 2.95
❑5, Apr 1985 .... 2.95
❑6, Jul 1985 .... 2.95
❑7, Aug 1985 .... 2.95
❑8, Dec 1985 .... 2.95
❑9, Jan 1986 .... 2.95

ECLIPSE GRAPHIC ALBUM SERIES
ECLIPSE

❑1, Oct 1978; PG (a); Sabre 7.00
❑1-2; PG (a); Sabre 6.00
❑1-3; Sabre: 10th anniversary; PG (a); Sabre 5.95
❑2, Nov 1979; CR (w); CR (a); Night Music 5.00
❑3, May 1980; MR (a); Detectives, Inc. 6.95
❑4; GC (a); Stewart the Rat 5.95
❑5; JSn (w); JSn (a); The Price 7.00
❑6; MR (a); I am Coyote 6.00
❑7; DSt (w); DSt (a); The Rocketeer .. 8.00
❑7/HC; Hardcover edition; DSt (w); DSt (a); Hardcover; The Rocketeer 19.95
❑7-2; DSt (w); DSt (a); The Rocketeer 7.95
❑7-3; DSt (w); DSt (a); The Rocketeer 9.00
❑8; Zorro 6.00
❑9, Feb 1987; Somerset Holmes; The Sacred and the Profane 14.00
❑10, Mar 1987; BA (a); Sacred & Profane; Somerset Holmes 14.00
❑10/HC, Mar 1987; Hardcover edition; BA (a); Hardcover; Somerset Holmes 24.95
❑11 1987; Floyd Farland 25.00
❑12, Jul 1987; Silverheels 7.95
❑12/HC, Jul 1987, b&w; Hardcover edition; Silverheels 14.95
❑12/Ltd., Jul 1987; Signed hardcover; Silverheels 24.95
❑13; The Sisterhood of Steel 9.00
❑14; Samurai, Son of Death 5.00
❑15; Twisted Tales 3.95
❑16; Air Fighters Classics #1 .... 4.50
❑17; PG (a); Valkyrie: Prisoner of the Past 6.95
❑18; Air Fighters Classics #2 .... 4.50
❑19; Scout: Four Monsters; Collects Scout #1-7 .... 14.95
❑20; Air Fighters Classics #3 .... 4.50
❑21; XYR "choose your own adventure" game 3.95
❑22; Alien Worlds 5.00
❑23; Air Fighters Classics #4 .... 4.50
❑24; Heartbreak Comics; Heartbreak . 5.00
❑25; ATh (w); ATh (a); Alex Toth's Zorro #1 .... 9.00
❑26; ATh (w); ATh (a); Alex Toth's Zorro #2 .... 9.00
❑27; She; Fast Fiction 6.00
❑28; AMo (w); DaG, BSz, TY (a); Brought to Light 9.00
❑29; JK (w); JK (a); Miracleman Book One 15.00
❑30; AMo (w); BSz, JK (a); Real Love: The Best of Simon & Kirby Romance Comics 9.00
❑30/HC, b&w; Hardcover edition; AMo (w); BSz (a) 30.00
❑31; Pigeons from Hell 7.00
❑31/Ltd.; Limited hardcover edition .. 30.00
❑32; HK, JK (w); HK, JK (a); Teenaged Dope Slaves & Reform School Girls 9.95
❑33; Bogie 9.95
❑34; Air Fighters Classics #5 .... 3.95
❑35; Into the Shadow of the Sun, Rael 7.95
❑36; CR (a); Ariane & Bluebeard 4.95
❑37; Air Fighters Classics #6 .... 3.95
❑38; Doctor Watchstop 8.95
❑39; MGr (a); James Bond 007: Permission to Die 1 .... 4.95
❑40; MGr (a); James Bond 007: Permission to Die 2 .... 4.95

N-MINT

❑41; MGr (a); James Bond 007: Permission to Die 3 ..... 4.95
❑42; MGr (a); James Bond 007: Licence to Kill 8.95
❑43; Tapping the Vein #1 ..... 7.95
❑44; Hobbit #1 ..... 5.95
❑45; Toadswart 10.95
❑46; Tapping the Vein #2 ..... 7.95
❑47; Scout: Mount Fire 14.95
❑48; Moderne Man Comics 9.95
❑49; Tapping the Vein #3 ..... 6.95
❑50; Miracleman Book Two 12.95
❑51; Tapping the Vein 4 ..... 7.95
❑52; James Bond 007: Permission to Die #3 ..... 4.95

ECLIPSE MAGAZINE
ECLIPSE

❑1, May 1981, b&w 2.95
❑2, Jul 1981 ..... 2.95
❑3, Nov 1981 ..... 2.95
❑4, Jan 1982 ..... 2.95
❑5, Mar 1982 ..... 2.95
❑6, Jul 1982 ..... 2.95
❑7, Nov 1982 ..... 2.95
❑8, Jan 1983 ..... 2.95

ECLIPSE MONTHLY
ECLIPSE

❑1, Aug 1983 ..... 2.00
❑2, Sep 1983 ..... 2.00
❑3, Oct 1983 ..... 2.00
❑4, Jan 1984 ..... 1.50
❑5, Feb 1984 ..... 1.50
❑6, Mar 1984 ..... 1.50
❑7, Apr 1984 ..... 1.50
❑8, May 1984 ..... 1.50
❑9, Jun 1984 ..... 1.50
❑10, Jul 1984 ..... 1.50

ECLIPSO
DC

❑1, Nov 1992 ..... 2.00
❑2, Dec 1992 KG (a) 1.75
❑3, Jan 1993 KG (a) 1.75
❑4, Feb 1993 KG, LMc (a) 1.50
❑5, Mar 1993 KG, LMc (a) 1.50
❑6, Apr 1993 KG, LMc (a) 1.25
❑7, May 1993 KG (a) 1.25
❑8, Jun 1993 ..... 1.25
❑9, Jul 1993 ..... 1.25
❑10, Aug 1993 ..... 1.25
❑11, Sep 1993 ..... 1.25
❑12, Oct 1993 ..... 1.25
❑13, Nov 1993 ..... 1.25
❑14, Dec 1993 ..... 1.25
❑15, Jan 1994 ..... 1.50
❑16, Feb 1994 ..... 1.50
❑17, Mar 1994 ..... 1.50
❑18, Apr 1994 A: Spectre. 1.50
❑Annual 1, ca. 1993 1: Prism. 2.50

ECLIPSO: THE DARKNESS WITHIN
DC

❑1, Jul 1992; KG (w); KG (a); Without plastic gem (newsstand version) 2.50
❑1/Direct ed., Jul 1992; Direct Market edition; KG (w); KG (a); plastic diamond glued to cover 3.00
❑2, Jul 1992 ..... 2.50

ECTOKID
MARVEL

❑1, Sep 1993; Foil embossed cover 2.50
❑2, Oct 1993 ..... 1.75
❑3, Nov 1993 ..... 1.75
❑4, Dec 1993 ..... 1.75
❑5, Jan 1994 ..... 1.75
❑6, Feb 1994 ..... 1.75
❑7, Mar 1994 ..... 1.75
❑8, Apr 1994 ..... 1.75
❑9, May 1994 ..... 1.75

ECTOKID UNLEASHED!
MARVEL

❑1, Oct 1994 ..... 2.95

N-MINT

ED
3CG COMICS

❑1, Mar 1997, b&w 2.95

EDDY CURRENT
MAD DOG

❑1, Jul 1987 ..... 2.50
❑2, Sep 1987 ..... 2.50
❑3, Oct 1987 ..... 2.50
❑4, Nov 1987 ..... 2.50
❑5, Jan 1988 ..... 2.50
❑6, Feb 1988 ..... 2.50
❑7, Apr 1988 A: Amazing Broccoli. 2.50
❑8, Jun 1988 ..... 2.50
❑9, Jul 1988 ..... 2.50
❑10, Sep 1988 ..... 2.50
❑11, Nov 1988 ..... 2.50
❑12, Dec 1988 ..... 2.50

EDEN DESCENDANTS, THE
QUESTER ENTERTAINMENT

❑1, b&w; cardstock cover 3.95

EDEN MATRIX, THE
ADHESIVE

❑1/A 2.95
❑1/B 2.95

EDEN'S TRAIL
MARVEL

❑1, Jan 2003 ..... 2.99
❑2, Feb 2003 ..... 2.99
❑3, Mar 2003 ..... 2.99
❑4, Apr 2003 ..... 2.99
❑5, May 2003 ..... 2.99

EDGAR ALLAN POE
ETERNITY

❑1 1988, b&w; Black Cat 1.95
❑2 1988, b&w; Pit & Pendulum 1.95
❑3, Dec 1988, b&w; Red Death 1.95
❑4 1989, b&w; Rue Morgue 1.95
❑5 1989, b&w; Tell-Tale Heart 1.95

EDGE
BRAVURA / MALIBU

❑1, Jul 1994 ..... 2.50
❑2, Aug 1994 ..... 2.50
❑3, Apr 1995 ..... 2.95
❑4 ..... 2.95

EDGE OF CHAOS
PACIFIC

❑1, Jul 1983 GM (a) 1.00
❑2, Oct 1984; GM (a); Adam Kubert's first major comics work 1.00
❑3, Jan 1983 GM (a) 1.00

EEK! THE CAT
HAMILTON

❑1, Feb 1994; TV show 1.95
❑2, Mar 1994; TV show 1.95
❑3, Apr 1994; TV show 1.95

EERIE (I.W.)
I.W.

❑1 ..... 24.00
❑2 ..... 17.00

EERIE QUEERIE!
TOKYOPOP

❑1, Mar 2004 ..... 9.99

EERIE TALES
SUPER

❑12; Reprints(?) 15.00

EGON
DARK HORSE

❑1, Jan 1998 ..... 2.95
❑2 ..... 2.95

EGYPT
DC / VERTIGO

❑1, Aug 1995 ..... 2.50
❑2, Sep 1995 ..... 2.50
❑3, Oct 1995 ..... 2.50
❑4, Nov 1995 ..... 2.50
❑5, Dec 1995 ..... 2.50
❑6, Jan 1996 ..... 2.50
❑7, Feb 1996 ..... 2.50

East Coast Comix issued a series of reprints of classic E.C. comics in the early 1970s.

© 1974 East Coast Comix and E.C.

N-MINT

EHLISSA
HIGHLAND GRAPHICS

❑1, Nov 1992; Color on cover 2.00
❑1-2; Black & white cover 2.00
❑1-3; Black & white cover 2.00
❑2, Dec 1992; Color on cover 2.00
❑2-2; Black & white cover 2.00
❑3, Jan 1993; Color on cover 2.00
❑3-2; Black & white cover 2.00
❑4, Mar 1993; Color on cover 2.00
❑4-2; Black & white cover 2.00
❑5, Mar 1993; Color on cover 2.00
❑5-2; Black & white cover 2.00
❑6; Color on cover 2.00
❑6-2; Black & white cover 2.00
❑7; Color on cover 2.00
❑7-2; Black & white cover 2.00
❑8, May 1993; Color on cover 2.00
❑8-2; Black & white cover 2.00
❑9, Jul 1993; Color on cover 2.00
❑9-2; Black & white cover 2.00
❑10 1993; Color on cover 2.00
❑10-2; Black & white cover 2.00
❑11 1993; Color on cover 2.00
❑11-2; Black & white cover 2.00
❑12 1993; Color on cover 2.00
❑12-2; Black & white cover 2.00
❑13 1993; Color on cover 2.00
❑13-2; Black & white cover 2.00
❑14, Jan 1994; Color on cover 2.00
❑14-2; Black & white cover 2.00
❑15, Feb 1994; Color on cover 2.00
❑15-2; Black & white cover 2.00
❑16, Mar 1994; Color on cover 2.00
❑16-2; Black & white cover 2.00
❑17, Apr 1994; Color on cover 2.00
❑17-2; Black & white cover 2.00
❑18, May 1994; Color on cover 2.00
❑18-2; Black & white cover 2.00
❑19, Jun 1994; Color on cover 2.00
❑19-2; Black & white cover 2.00
❑20, Jul 1994; Color on cover 2.00
❑20-2; Black & white cover 2.00
❑21, Aug 1994 ..... 2.00
❑22, Sep 1994 ..... 2.00
❑23, Oct 1994 ..... 2.00
❑24, Nov 1994 ..... 2.00
❑25, Dec 1994 ..... 2.00
❑26, Jan 1995 ..... 2.00
❑27, Feb 1995 ..... 2.00
❑28, Mar 1995 ..... 2.00
❑29, Apr 1995 ..... 2.00
❑30, May 1995 ..... 2.00
❑31, Jun 1995; has #27's indicia 2.00
❑32 ..... 2.00
❑33 ..... 2.00

EIGHTBALL
FANTAGRAPHICS

❑1 ..... 10.00
❑1-2 ..... 5.00
❑1-3 ..... 3.50
❑1-4 ..... 3.00
❑2 ..... 6.00
❑3 ..... 5.00
❑4 ..... 5.00
❑5 ..... 4.00
❑6 ..... 4.00

N-MINT

❑7 4.00
❑8 4.00
❑9 3.00
❑10 3.00
❑11 3.00
❑12, Nov 1993 3.00
❑13 3.00
❑14 3.00
❑15 3.00
❑16, Nov 1995; cardstock cover 4.00
❑17 2.95
❑18, Mar 1997 2.95
❑19, May 1998 3.95
❑20, Feb 1999; cardstock cover 4.50
❑21, Feb 2000 4.95
❑22, Aug 2001 2.95
❑23 2.95

EIGHTH WONDER, THE
DARK HORSE

❑1, Nov 1997, b&w; cover says The 8th Wonder, indicia says The Eighth Wonder 2.95

EIGHT LEGGED FREAKS
WILDSTORM

❑1, Sep 2002, Several characters in profile on cover 6.95

80 PAGE GIANT MAGAZINE
DC

❑1, Aug 1964; Superman; Imaginary stories 295.00
❑2, Sep 1964; Jimmy Olsen 125.00
❑3, Sep 1964; Lois Lane 125.00
❑4, Oct 1964; CI (a); Flash 125.00
❑5, Nov 1964; Batman 125.00
❑6, Jan 1965; Superman 125.00
❑7, Feb 1965; Sgt. Rock 125.00
❑8, Mar 1965; Secret Origins 125.00
❑9, Apr 1965; CI (c); MA, CI (a); Flash; reprints stories from Showcase #14, and Flash #106, 108, 117, and 123 125.00
❑10, May 1965; Superboy 125.00
❑11, Jun 1965; Superman 125.00
❑12, Jul 1965; Batman 80.00
❑13, Aug 1965; Jimmy Olsen 80.00
❑14, Sep 1965; Lois Lane 80.00
❑15, Oct 1965; Batman/Superman 80.00

EKOS PREVIEW
ASPEN

❑1, Jan 2004 4.00

EL CAZADOR
CROSSGEN

❑1, Oct 2003 2.95
❑1-2, Nov 2003 2.95
❑2, Nov 2003 2.95
❑3, Dec 2003 2.95
❑4, Jan 2004 2.95
❑4-2, Feb 2004 2.95
❑5, Mar 2004 2.95
❑6, May 2004 2.95

EL CAZADOR: BLACKJACK TOM
CROSSGEN

❑1, Apr 2004 2.95

EL DIABLO
DC

❑1, Aug 1989; Double-size 2.50
❑2, Sep 1989 1.50
❑3, Oct 1989 1.50
❑4, Dec 1989 1.50
❑5, Jan 1990 1.50
❑6, Feb 1990 1.50
❑7, Mar 1990 1.75
❑8, Apr 1990 1.75
❑9, May 1990 1.75
❑10, Jun 1990 1.75
❑11, Jul 1990 1.75
❑12, Aug 1990; Golden Age Vigilante 2.00
❑13, Sep 1990 2.00
❑14, Oct 1990 2.00
❑15, Dec 1990 2.00
❑16, Jan 1991 2.00

N-MINT

EL DIABLO (MINI-SERIES)
DC / VERTIGO

❑1, Mar 2001 2.50
❑2, Apr 2001 2.50
❑3, May 2001 2.50
❑4, Jun 2001 2.50

ELECTRIC FEAR
SPARKS

❑1, Win 1984 1.50
❑2, Spr 1986 1.50

ELECTRIC GIRL
MIGHTY GREMLIN

❑1, May 1998 3.50
❑2, Spr 1999 2.95
❑3, Sum 1999 2.95

ELECTRIC WARRIOR
DC

❑1, May 1986 1.50
❑2, Jun 1986 1.50
❑3, Jul 1986 1.50
❑4, Aug 1986 1.50
❑5, Sep 1986 1.50
❑6, Oct 1986 1.50
❑7, Nov 1986 1.50
❑8, Dec 1986 1.50
❑9, Jan 1987 1.50
❑10, Feb 1987 1.50
❑11, Mar 1987 1.50
❑12, Apr 1987 1.50
❑13, May 1987 1.50
❑14, Jun 1987 1.50
❑15, Jul 1987 1.50
❑16, Aug 1987 1.50
❑17, Sep 1987 1.50
❑18, Oct 1987 1.50

ELECTROPOLIS
IMAGE

❑1, May 2001 2.95
❑2, Jun 2001 2.95
❑3, Dec 2001 2.95

ELEKTRA (1ST SERIES)
MARVEL

❑1, Mar 1995; enhanced cover 3.25
❑2, Apr 1995; enhanced cover 3.25
❑3, May 1995; enhanced cover 3.25
❑4, Jun 1995; enhanced cover 3.25

ELEKTRA (2ND SERIES)
MARVEL

❑-1, Jul 1997; A: Daredevil. Flashback 2.25
❑1, Nov 1996 3.00
❑1/A, Nov 1996; variant cover 3.00
❑2, Dec 1996 V: Bullseye. 2.50
❑3, Jan 1997 2.50
❑4, Feb 1997 2.00
❑5, Mar 1997 2.00
❑6, Apr 1997 V: Razorfist. 2.00
❑7, May 1997 2.00
❑8, Jun 1997 2.00
❑9, Aug 1997; gatefold summary 2.00
❑10, Sep 1997; gatefold summary 2.00
❑11, Oct 1997; gatefold summary A: Daredevil. 2.00
❑12, Nov 1997; gatefold summary A: Daredevil. 2.00
❑13, Dec 1997; gatefold summary A: Daredevil. 2.00
❑14, Jan 1998; gatefold summary 2.00
❑15, Feb 1998; gatefold summary 2.00
❑16, Mar 1998; gatefold summary A: Shang-Chi. 2.00
❑17, Apr 1998; gatefold summary 2.00
❑18, May 1998; gatefold summary 2.00
❑19, Jun 1998; gatefold summary 2.00

ELEKTRA (3RD SERIES)
MARVEL / MAX

❑1, Sep 2001 3.50
❑2, Oct 2001 2.99
❑2/A, Oct 2001 2.99
❑3, Nov 2001 2.99

N-MINT

❑3/Nude, Nov 2001, b&w; Recalled due to interior nudity 15.00
❑4, Dec 2001 2.99
❑5, Jan 2002 2.99
❑6, Feb 2002; Silent issue 2.99
❑7, Mar 2002 2.99
❑8, Apr 2002 2.99
❑9, May 2002 2.99
❑10, Jun 2002 2.99
❑11, Aug 2002 2.99
❑12, Sep 2002 2.99
❑13, Oct 2002 2.99
❑14, Nov 2002 2.99
❑15, Dec 2002 2.99
❑16, Jan 2003 2.99
❑17, Jan 2003 2.99
❑18, Feb 2003 2.99
❑19, Feb 2003 2.99
❑20, Mar 2003 2.99
❑21, Jun 2003 2.99
❑22, Jun 2003 2.99
❑23, Jul 2003 TP (a) 2.99
❑24, Aug 2003 TP (a) 2.99
❑25, Sep 2003; cardstock cover 2.99
❑26, Oct 2003 2.99
❑27, Nov 2003 (c) 2.99
❑28, Dec 2003 2.99
❑29, Jan 2004 2.99
❑30, Feb 2004 2.99
❑31, Mar 2004 2.99
❑32, Apr 2004 2.99
❑33, May 2004 2.99
❑34, May 2004 2.99
❑35, Jun 2004 2.99

ELEKTRA & WOLVERINE: THE REDEEMER
MARVEL

❑1, Jan 2002 5.95
❑2, Feb 2002 5.95
❑3, Mar 2002 5.95

ELEKTRA: ASSASSIN
MARVEL / EPIC

❑1, Aug 1986 FM (w); BSz, FM (a) 3.00
❑2, Sep 1986 FM (w); BSz, FM (a) 2.50
❑3, Oct 1986 FM (w); BSz, FM (a) 2.50
❑4, Nov 1986 FM (w); BSz, FM (a) 2.50
❑5, Dec 1986 FM (w); BSz, FM (a) 2.50
❑6, Jan 1987 FM (w); BSz, FM (a) 2.50
❑7, Feb 1987 FM (w); BSz, FM (a) 2.50
❑8, Mar 1987; FM (w); BSz, FM (a); Relatively scarce 3.00

ELEKTRA/CYBLADE
IMAGE

❑1, Mar 1997; crossover with Marvel; concludes in Silver Surfer/Weapon Zero 2.95
❑1/A, Mar 1997; Alternate cover 2.95

ELEKTRA: GLIMPSE & ECHO
MARVEL

❑1, Sep 2002, Several characters in profile on cover 2.99
❑2, Oct 2002 2.99
❑3, Nov 2002 2.99
❑4, Dec 2002 2.99

ELEKTRA LIVES AGAIN
MARVEL / EPIC

❑1, Mar 1991; hardcover 24.95

ELEKTRA MEGAZINE
MARVEL

❑1, Nov 1996; Reprints Elektra stories from Daredevil 3.95
❑2, Nov 1996; Reprints Elektra stories from Daredevil 3.95

ELEKTRA SAGA, THE
MARVEL

❑1, Feb 1984; FM (w); FM (a); Daredevil reprint 4.00
❑2, Mar 1984; FM (w); FM (a); Daredevil reprint 3.50

N-MINT

❑3, Apr 1984; FM (w); FM (a); Daredevil reprint 3.50
❑4, May 1984; FM (w); FM (a); Daredevil reprint 3.50

ELEMENTALS (VOL. 1)
COMICO

❑1 1984 .... 2.50
❑2 1985 .... 2.00
❑3 1985 .... 2.00
❑4, Jun 1985 .... 2.00
❑5, Dec 1985 .... 2.00
❑6, Feb 1986 .... 1.50
❑7, Apr 1986 .... 1.50
❑8, Jun 1986 .... 1.50
❑9, Aug 1986 .... 1.50
❑10, Oct 1986 .... 1.50
❑11, Dec 1986 .... 1.50
❑12, Feb 1987 .... 1.50
❑13, Apr 1987 .... 1.50
❑14, Jun 1987 .... 1.50
❑15, Jul 1987 .... 1.50
❑16, Aug 1987 .... 1.50
❑17, Sep 1987 .... 1.50
❑18, Oct 1987 .... 1.50
❑19, Nov 1987 .... 1.50
❑20, Dec 1987 .... 1.50
❑21, Jan 1988 .... 1.50
❑22, Feb 1988 .... 1.50
❑23, Mar 1988 .... 1.75
❑24, Apr 1988 .... 1.75
❑25, May 1988 .... 1.75
❑26, Jun 1988 .... 1.75
❑27, Jul 1988 .... 1.75
❑28, Aug 1988 .... 1.75
❑29, Sep 1988 .... 1.75
❑Special 1, Mar 1986; Child abuse special 2.00
❑Special 2, Jan 1989 .... 1.95

ELEMENTALS (VOL. 2)
COMICO

❑1, Mar 1989 .... 2.50
❑2, Apr 1989 .... 2.00
❑3, May 1989 .... 2.00
❑4, Jun 1989 .... 2.50
❑5, Jul 1989 .... 2.50
❑6, Aug 1989 .... 2.50
❑7, Sep 1989 .... 2.50
❑8, Oct 1989 .... 2.50
❑9, Nov 1989 .... 2.50
❑10, Dec 1989 .... 2.50
❑11, Jan 1990 .... 2.50
❑12, Feb 1990 .... 2.50
❑13, Mar 1990 .... 2.50
❑14, May 1990 .... 2.50
❑15, Jul 1990 .... 2.50
❑16, May 1991 .... 2.50
❑17, May 1991 .... 2.50
❑18, Jun 1991 .... 2.50
❑19, Aug 1991 .... 2.50
❑20, Oct 1991 .... 2.50
❑21, Nov 1991 .... 2.50
❑22, Mar 1992 .... 2.50
❑23, May 1992 1: New Monolith. 2.50
❑24, Aug 1992 .... 2.50
❑25, Nov 1992 .... 2.50
❑26, Apr 1993 .... 2.50
❑27; Never published? 2.50
❑28; Never published? 2.50
❑29; Never published? 2.50
❑30; Never published? 2.50
❑31; Never published? 2.50
❑32; Never published? 2.50
❑33; Never published? 2.50
❑34; Never published? 2.50
❑35; Never published? 2.50
❑36; Never published? 2.50
❑37; Never published? 2.50
❑38; Never published? 2.50
❑39; Never published? 2.50
❑40; Never published? 2.50
❑41; Never published? 2.50

N-MINT

ELEMENTALS (VOL. 3)
COMICO

❑1, Dec 1995; Bagged w/ card 2.95
❑2, ca. 1996 .... 2.95
❑3, May 1996 .... 2.95

ELEMENTALS: GHOST OF A CHANCE
COMICO

❑1, Dec 1995 .... 5.95

ELEMENTALS: HOW THE WAR WAS WON
COMICO

❑1, Jun 1996 .... 2.95
❑2, Aug 1996 .... 2.95

ELEMENTALS LINGERIE
COMICO

❑1, May 1996; pin-ups 2.95

ELEMENTALS SEX SPECIAL
COMICO

❑1/Gold, Oct 1991; Gold edition 3.50
❑1, Oct 1991 .... 2.95
❑2, Jun 1992 .... 2.95
❑3, Sep 1992 .... 2.95
❑4, Feb 1993 .... 2.95

ELEMENTALS SEX SPECIAL (2ND SERIES)
COMICO

❑1, b&w and color 2.95

ELEMENTAL'S SEXY LINGERIE SPECIAL
COMICO

❑1/A, Jan 1993; without poster 2.95
❑1/B, Jan 1993 .... 5.95

ELEMENTALS SWIMSUIT SPECTACULAR 1996
COMICO

❑1/Gold, Jun 1996; Gold edition; pin-ups 3.50
❑1, Jun 1996; pin-ups 2.95

ELEMENTALS: THE VAMPIRES' REVENGE
COMICO

❑1, Jun 1996 .... 2.95
❑2, Jun 1996; Gold edition 3.00

ELEVEN OR ONE
SIRIUS ENTERTAINMENT

❑1, Apr 1995; reprints new story from Angry Christ Comics tpb 4.00
❑1-2 .... 3.00

ELFHEIM
NIGHTWYND

❑1 1991, b&w 2.50
❑2, b&w 2.50
❑3, b&w 2.50
❑4, b&w 2.50

ELFHEIM (VOL. 2)
NIGHTWYND

❑1, b&w 2.50
❑2, b&w 2.50
❑3, b&w 2.50
❑4, b&w 2.50

ELFHEIM (VOL. 3)
NIGHTWYND

❑1, b&w 2.50
❑2, b&w 2.50
❑3, b&w 2.50
❑4, b&w 2.50

ELFHEIM (VOL. 4)
NIGHTWYND

❑1, b&w 2.50
❑2, b&w 2.50

ELFHEIM: DRAGON DREAM (VOL. 5)
NIGHT WYND

❑1 .... 2.50
❑2 .... 2.50
❑3 .... 2.50
❑4 .... 2.50

A modern-day version of the Western defender El Diablo had a short-lived series from 1989 to 1991.

© 1989 DC Comics.

N-MINT

ELFIN ROMANCE
MT. WILSON

❑1, Feb 1994, b&w 1.50
❑2, Apr 1994, b&w 1.50
❑3, Apr 1994, b&w 1.50
❑4, Jun 1994, b&w 2.00
❑5, Aug 1994, b&w 2.00
❑6, Oct 1994, b&w 1.75
❑7, Dec 1996, b&w 3.25

ELFLORD
AIRCEL

❑1, Feb 1986, b&w 2.00
❑1-2 .... 2.00
❑2, Mar 1986 .... 2.00
❑2-2 .... 2.00
❑3, Apr 1986 .... 2.00
❑4, May 1986 .... 2.00
❑5, Jun 1986 .... 2.00
❑6, Jul 1986 .... 2.00
❑7, Aug 1986; Never published? 2.00
❑8, Sep 1986; Never published? 2.00

ELFLORD (2ND SERIES)
AIRCEL

❑1, Oct 1986 .... 2.00
❑2, Nov 1986 .... 2.00
❑3, Dec 1986 .... 2.00
❑4, Jan 1987 .... 2.00
❑5, Feb 1987 .... 2.00
❑6, Mar 1987 .... 2.00
❑7, Apr 1987 .... 2.00
❑8, May 1987 .... 2.00
❑9, Jun 1987 .... 2.00
❑10, Jul 1987 .... 2.00
❑11, Aug 1987 .... 2.00
❑12, Sep 1987 .... 2.00
❑13, Oct 1987 .... 2.00
❑14, Nov 1987 .... 2.00
❑15, Dec 1987 .... 2.00
❑15.5 1988; The Falcon Special 2.00
❑16, Jan 1988 .... 2.00
❑17, Feb 1988 .... 2.00
❑18, Mar 1988 .... 2.00
❑19 1988 .... 2.00
❑20 1988 .... 2.00
❑21 1988; double-sized 4.95
❑22 1988 .... 1.95
❑23 1988 .... 1.95
❑24 1988 .... 1.95
❑25 1988 .... 1.95
❑26, Dec 1988 .... 1.95
❑27, Jan 1989 .... 1.95
❑28 1989 .... 1.95
❑29 1989 .... 1.95
❑30 1989 .... 1.95
❑31 1989 .... 1.95

ELFLORD (3RD SERIES)
NIGHT WYND

❑1, b&w 2.50
❑2, b&w 2.50
❑3, b&w 2.50
❑4, b&w 2.50

ELFLORD (4TH SERIES)
WARP

❑1, Jan 1997, b&w 2.95
❑2, Feb 1997, b&w 2.95

N-MINT

❑3, Mar 1997, b&w ... 2.95
❑4, Apr 1997, b&w ... 2.95

ELFLORD (5TH SERIES)
WARP

❑1, Sep 1997, b&w ... 2.95
❑2, Oct 1997, b&w ... 2.95
❑3, Nov 1997, b&w ... 2.95
❑4, Dec 1997, b&w ... 2.95
❑5, Jan 1997 ... 2.95
❑6, Feb 1997 ... 2.95
❑7, Mar 1997 ... 2.95

ELFLORD CHRONICLES, THE
AIRCEL

❑1, Oct 1990, b&w ... 2.50
❑2, Oct 1990, b&w ... 2.50
❑3, Nov 1990, b&w ... 2.50
❑4, Dec 1990, b&w ... 2.50
❑5, Jan 1991, b&w ... 2.50
❑6, Feb 1991, b&w ... 2.50
❑7, Mar 1991, b&w ... 2.75
❑8, Apr 1991 ... 2.75
❑9 ... 2.75
❑10 ... 2.75
❑11 ... 2.75
❑12 ... 2.75

ELFLORD: DRAGON'S EYE
NIGHT WYND

❑1, ca. 1993 ... 2.50
❑2, ca. 1993 ... 2.50
❑3, ca. 1993 ... 2.50

ELFLORD THE RETURN
MAD MONKEY

❑1, ca. 1996 ... 6.96

ELFLORD: THE RETURN OF THE KING
NIGHT WYND

❑1 ... 2.50
❑2 ... 2.50
❑3 ... 2.50
❑4 ... 2.50

ELFLORE
NIGHTWYND

❑1, b&w ... 2.50
❑2, b&w ... 2.50
❑3, b&w ... 2.50
❑4, b&w ... 2.50

ELFLORE (VOL. 2)
NIGHTWYND

❑1, b&w ... 2.50
❑2, b&w ... 2.50
❑3, b&w ... 2.50
❑4, b&w ... 2.50

ELFLORE: HIGH SEAS
NIGHT WYND

❑1 ... 2.50
❑2 ... 2.50
❑3 ... 2.50

ELFLORE (VOL. 3)
NIGHTWYND

❑1, b&w ... 2.50
❑2, b&w ... 2.50
❑3, b&w ... 2.50
❑4, b&w ... 2.50

ELFQUEST
WARP

❑1, Apr 1979 WP (w); WP (a) ... 32.00
❑1-2 WP (w); WP (a) ... 12.00
❑1-3 WP (w); WP (a) ... 8.00
❑1-4 WP (w); WP (a) ... 5.00
❑2, Aug 1978 WP (w); WP (a) ... 18.00
❑2-2 WP (w); WP (a) ... 6.00
❑2-3 WP (w); WP (a) ... 4.00
❑2-4 WP (w); WP (a) ... 3.00
❑3, Dec 1978 WP (w); WP (a) ... 18.00
❑3-2 WP (w); WP (a) ... 3.00
❑3-3 WP (w); WP (a) ... 3.00
❑3-4 WP (w); WP (a) ... 3.00
❑4, Apr 1979 WP (w); WP (a) ... 16.00
❑4-2 WP (w); WP (a) ... 5.00
❑4-3 WP (w); WP (a) ... 4.00
❑4-4 WP (w); WP (a) ... 2.50
❑5, Aug 1979 WP (w); WP (a) ... 16.00
❑5-2 WP (w); WP (a) ... 3.00
❑5-3 WP (w); WP (a) ... 3.00
❑6, Jan 1980 WP (w); WP (a) ... 13.00
❑6-2 WP (w); WP (a) ... 4.00
❑6-3 WP (w); WP (a) ... 3.00
❑7, May 1980 WP (w); WP (a) ... 10.00
❑7-2 WP (w); WP (a) ... 4.00
❑7-3 WP (w); WP (a) ... 3.00
❑8, Sep 1980 WP (w); WP (a) ... 10.00
❑8-2 WP (w); WP (a) ... 4.00
❑8-3 WP (w); WP (a) ... 3.00
❑9, Feb 1981 WP (w); WP (a) ... 10.00
❑9-2 WP (w); WP (a) ... 4.00
❑9-3 WP (w); WP (a) ... 3.00
❑10, Jun 1981 WP (w); WP (a) ... 7.50
❑11, Oct 1981 WP (w); WP (a) ... 7.50
❑12, Feb 1982 WP (w); WP (a) ... 7.50
❑13, Jun 1982 WP (w); WP (a) ... 7.50
❑14, Oct 1982 WP (w); WP (a) ... 7.50
❑15, Feb 1983 WP (w); WP (a) ... 7.50
❑16, Jun 1983 WP (w); WP (a) ... 10.00
❑17, Oct 1983; WP (w); WP (a); Elf orgy ... 7.00
❑18, Feb 1984 WP (w); WP (a) ... 7.00
❑19, Jun 1984 WP (w); WP (a) ... 7.00
❑20, Oct 1984 WP (w); WP (a) ... 7.00
❑21, Feb 1985; WP (w); WP (a); all letters issue ... 7.00

ELFQUEST (VOL. 2)
WARP

❑1, May 1996 ... 6.00
❑2, Jun 1996 ... 5.00
❑3, Jul 1996 ... 5.00
❑4, Aug 1996 ... 5.00
❑5, Sep 1996 ... 5.00
❑6, Nov 1996 ... 5.00
❑7, Dec 1996 ... 5.00
❑8, Jan 1997 ... 5.00
❑9, Feb 1997 ... 5.00
❑10, Mar 1997 ... 5.00
❑11, Apr 1997 ... 4.95
❑12, May 1997 ... 4.95
❑13, Jun 1997 ... 4.95
❑14, Jul 1997 ... 4.95
❑15, Aug 1997 ... 4.95
❑16, Sep 1997 ... 4.95
❑17, Oct 1997 ... 4.95
❑18, Nov 1997 ... 4.95
❑19, Dec 1997 ... 4.95
❑20, Jan 1998 ... 4.95
❑21, Feb 1998 ... 4.95
❑22, Mar 1998 ... 4.95
❑23, Apr 1998 ... 4.95
❑24, May 1998 ... 4.95
❑25, Jun 1998; needlepoint style cover 4.95
❑26, Jul 1998 ... 4.95
❑27, Aug 1998 ... 4.95
❑28, Sep 1998 ... 4.95
❑29, Oct 1998 ... 4.95
❑30, Nov 1998 ... 4.95
❑31, Dec 1998; Christmas cover ... 4.95
❑32, Jan 1999 ... 2.95
❑33, Feb 1999 ... 2.95

ELFQUEST (EPIC)
MARVEL / EPIC

❑1, Aug 1985 WP (w); WP (a) ... 3.50
❑2, Sep 1985 WP (w); WP (a) ... 2.50
❑3, Oct 1985 WP (w); WP (a) ... 2.50
❑4, Nov 1985 WP (w); WP (a) ... 2.50
❑5, Dec 1985 WP (w); WP (a) ... 2.50
❑6, Jan 1986 WP (w); WP (a) ... 2.25
❑7, Feb 1986 WP (w); WP (a) ... 2.25
❑8, Mar 1986 WP (w); WP (a) ... 2.25
❑9, Apr 1986 WP (w); WP (a) ... 2.25
❑10, May 1986 WP (w); WP (a) ... 2.25
❑11, Jun 1986 WP (w); WP (a) ... 2.00
❑12, Jul 1986 WP (w); WP (a) ... 2.00
❑13, Aug 1986 WP (w); WP (a) ... 2.00
❑14, Sep 1986 WP (w); WP (a) ... 2.00
❑15, Oct 1986 WP (w); WP (a) ... 2.00
❑16, Nov 1986 WP (w); WP (a) ... 2.00
❑17, Dec 1986 WP (w); WP (a) ... 2.00
❑18, Jan 1987 WP (w); WP (a) ... 2.00
❑19, Feb 1987 WP (w); WP (a) ... 2.00
❑20, Mar 1987 WP (w); WP (a) ... 2.00
❑21, Apr 1987 WP (w); WP (a) ... 1.50
❑22, May 1987 WP (w); WP (a) ... 1.50
❑23, Jun 1987 WP (w); WP (a) ... 1.50
❑24, Jul 1987 WP (w); WP (a) ... 1.50
❑25, Aug 1987 WP (w); WP (a) ... 1.50
❑26, Sep 1987 WP (w); WP (a) ... 1.50
❑27, Oct 1987 WP (w); WP (a) ... 1.50
❑28, Nov 1987 WP (w); WP (a) ... 1.50
❑29, Dec 1987 WP (w); WP (a) ... 1.50
❑30, Jan 1988 WP (w); WP (a) ... 1.50
❑31, Feb 1988 WP (w); WP (a) ... 1.50
❑32, Mar 1988 WP (w); WP (a) ... 1.50

ELFQUEST (WARP REPRINTS)
WARP

❑1, May 1989 ... 2.00
❑2, Jun 1989 ... 2.00
❑3, Jul 1989 ... 2.00
❑4, Aug 1989 ... 2.00

ELFQUEST 25TH ANNIVERSARY EDITION
DC

❑1, Sep 2003 ... 2.95

ELFQUEST: BLOOD OF TEN CHIEFS
WARP

❑1, Aug 1993 ... 2.50
❑2, Sep 1993 ... 2.50
❑3, Nov 1993 ... 2.50
❑4, Jan 1994 ... 2.50
❑5, Mar 1994 ... 2.50
❑6, May 1994 ... 2.50
❑7, Jun 1994 ... 2.50
❑8, Jul 1994 ... 2.50
❑9, Aug 1994 ... 2.50
❑10, Sep 1994 ... 2.50
❑11, Oct 1994 ... 2.50
❑12, Nov 1994 ... 2.50
❑13, Dec 1994 ... 2.50
❑14, Jan 1995 ... 2.50
❑15, Feb 1995 ... 2.50
❑16, Apr 1995 ... 2.50
❑17, May 1995 ... 2.50
❑18, Jun 1995 ... 2.50
❑19, Aug 1995; contains Elfquest timeline ... 2.50
❑20, Sep 1995 ... 2.50

ELFQUEST: HIDDEN YEARS
WARP

❑1, May 1992 ... 3.00
❑2, Jul 1992 ... 2.50
❑3, Sep 1992; This story was previewed in Harbinger #11 (character reads it as in a comic book) ... 2.50
❑4, Nov 1992 ... 2.50
❑5, Jan 1993 ... 2.50
❑6, Mar 1993 ... 2.50
❑7, May 1993 ... 2.50
❑8, Jul 1993 ... 2.50
❑9, Sep 1993 ... 2.50
❑9.5, Nov 1993; double-sized JBy (a) ... 2.95
❑10, Jan 1994 ... 2.50
❑11, Mar 1994 ... 2.50
❑12, Apr 1994 ... 2.50
❑13, May 1994 ... 2.50
❑14, Jun 1994 WP (w) ... 2.50
❑15, Jul 1994 ... 2.50
❑16, Aug 1994 ... 2.50
❑17, Oct 1994 ... 2.50
❑18, Dec 1994 ... 2.50
❑19, Jan 1995 ... 2.50
❑20, Apr 1995 ... 2.50
❑21, May 1995 ... 2.50
❑22, Jul 1995 ... 2.50
❑23, Aug 1995; contains Elfquest timeline ... 2.50
❑24, Sep 1995 ... 2.50
❑25, Oct 1995, b&w ... 2.50

N-MINT

- ❑26, Dec 1995, b&w ... 2.50
- ❑27, Jan 1996, b&w ... 2.50
- ❑28, Feb 1996, b&w ... 2.50
- ❑29, Mar 1996, b&w ... 2.50

ELFQUEST: JINK
WARP

- ❑1, Nov 1994 ... 2.50
- ❑2, Dec 1994 ... 2.50
- ❑3, Jan 1995 WP (w) ... 2.50
- ❑4, Apr 1995 ... 2.50
- ❑5, May 1995 ... 2.50
- ❑6, Jul 1995; contains Elfquest world map ... 2.50
- ❑7, Aug 1995; contains Elfquest timeline ... 2.50
- ❑8, Oct 1995; b&w for remainder of series ... 2.50
- ❑9, Nov 1995 ... 2.50
- ❑10, Dec 1995 ... 2.50
- ❑11, Jan 1996 ... 2.50
- ❑12, Feb 1996 ... 2.50

ELFQUEST: KAHVI
WARP

- ❑1, Oct 1995 ... 2.25
- ❑2, Nov 1995 ... 2.25
- ❑3, Dec 1995 ... 2.25
- ❑4, Jan 1996 ... 2.25
- ❑5, Feb 1996 ... 2.25
- ❑6, Mar 1996 ... 2.25

ELFQUEST: KINGS CROSS
WARP

- ❑1, Nov 1997, b&w ... 2.95
- ❑2, Dec 1997, b&w ... 2.95

ELFQUEST: KINGS OF THE BROKEN WHEEL
WARP

- ❑1, Jun 1990 WP (a) ... 2.50
- ❑2, Aug 1990 WP (a) ... 2.00
- ❑3, Sep 1990 WP (a) ... 2.00
- ❑4, Dec 1990 WP (a) ... 2.00
- ❑5, Feb 1991 WP (a) ... 2.00
- ❑6, May 1991 WP (a) ... 2.00
- ❑7, Aug 1991 WP (a) ... 2.00
- ❑8, Nov 1991 WP (a) ... 2.00
- ❑9, Feb 1992 WP (a) ... 2.00

ELFQUEST: METAMORPHOSIS
WARP

- ❑1, Apr 1996 ... 2.95

ELFQUEST: NEW BLOOD
WARP

- ❑1, Aug 1992; gatefold summary; JBy (a); "Elfquest Summer Special" ... 5.00
- ❑2, Oct 1992 ... 2.50
- ❑3, Dec 1992 ... 2.50
- ❑4, Feb 1993 ... 2.50
- ❑5, Apr 1993 ... 2.50
- ❑6, Jun 1993 ... 2.50
- ❑7, Jul 1993 ... 2.50
- ❑8, Aug 1993 ... 2.50
- ❑9, Sep 1993 ... 2.50
- ❑10, Oct 1993 ... 2.50
- ❑11, Nov 1993 ... 2.25
- ❑12, Dec 1993 ... 2.25
- ❑13, Jan 1994 ... 2.25
- ❑14, Feb 1994 ... 2.25
- ❑15, Mar 1994 ... 2.25
- ❑16, Apr 1994 ... 2.25
- ❑17, May 1994 ... 2.25
- ❑18, Jun 1994 ... 2.25
- ❑19, Jul 1994 ... 2.25
- ❑20, Aug 1994 ... 2.25
- ❑21, Sep 1994 ... 2.25
- ❑22, Oct 1994 ... 2.25
- ❑23, Nov 1994 ... 2.25
- ❑24, Dec 1994 ... 2.25
- ❑25, Jan 1995 ... 2.25
- ❑26, Feb 1995 ... 2.25
- ❑27, Apr 1995 ... 2.50
- ❑28, May 1995 ... 2.50
- ❑29, Jul 1995 ... 2.50

N-MINT

- ❑30, Aug 1995; contains Elfquest timeline ... 2.50
- ❑31, Sep 1995 ... 2.50
- ❑32, Oct 1995 ... 2.50
- ❑33, Nov 1995 ... 2.50
- ❑34, Dec 1995 ... 2.25
- ❑35, Jan 1996 ... 2.25
- ❑Special 1, Jul 1993 JBy (a) ... 3.95

ELFQUEST: SHARDS
WARP

- ❑1, Aug 1994 WP (w) ... 2.50
- ❑2, Sep 1994 WP (w) ... 2.50
- ❑3, Oct 1994 WP (w) ... 2.50
- ❑4, Nov 1994 WP (w) ... 2.50
- ❑5, Dec 1994 WP (w) ... 2.50
- ❑6, Jan 1995 WP (w) ... 2.25
- ❑7, Mar 1995 WP (w) ... 2.25
- ❑8, May 1995 WP (w) ... 2.25
- ❑9, Jun 1995 WP (w) ... 2.50
- ❑10, Aug 1995; WP (w); contains Elfquest timeline ... 2.50
- ❑11, Sep 1995 WP (w) ... 2.50
- ❑12, Oct 1995 WP (w) ... 2.50
- ❑13, Dec 1995 ... 2.25
- ❑14, Feb 1996 ... 2.25
- ❑15, Apr 1996 ... 2.25
- ❑16, Jun 1996 ... 2.25
- ❑Ashcan 1; ashcan preview/ San Diego Comic-Con premium ... 1.00

ELFQUEST: SIEGE AT BLUE MOUNTAIN
WARP / APPLE

- ❑1, Mar 1987, b&w WP (w); WP, JSa (a) ... 3.00
- ❑1-2 WP (w); WP (a) ... 2.50
- ❑2, May 1987 WP (w); WP, JSa (a) ... 3.00
- ❑2-2 WP (w); WP (a) ... 2.25
- ❑2-3, b&w ... 3.00
- ❑3, Jul 1987 WP (w); WP, JSa (a) ... 2.50
- ❑3-2 WP (w); WP (a) ... 2.00
- ❑4, Sep 1987 WP (w); WP, JSa (a) ... 2.50
- ❑5, Nov 1987 WP (w); WP, JSa (a) ... 2.50
- ❑6, Aug 1988 WP (w); WP, JSa (a) ... 2.50
- ❑7, Oct 1988 WP (w); WP, JSa (a) ... 2.50
- ❑8, Dec 1988 WP (w); WP, JSa (a) ... 2.50

ELFQUEST: THE GRAND QUEST
DC

- ❑1, ca. 2004 ... 9.95
- ❑2, ca. 2004 ... 9.95
- ❑3, ca. 2004 ... 9.95

ELFQUEST: THE REBELS
WARP

- ❑1, Nov 1994 ... 2.50
- ❑2, Dec 1994 ... 2.25
- ❑3, Jan 1995 ... 2.25
- ❑4, Mar 1995 ... 2.25
- ❑5, Apr 1995 ... 2.25
- ❑6, Jun 1995 ... 2.25
- ❑7, Jul 1995; contains Elfquest world map ... 2.25
- ❑8, Sep 1995 ... 2.25
- ❑9, Oct 1995 ... 2.25
- ❑10, Nov 1995 ... 2.25
- ❑11, Jan 1996 ... 2.25
- ❑12, Feb 1996 ... 2.25

ELFQUEST: TWO-SPEAR
WARP

- ❑1, Oct 1995 ... 2.25
- ❑2, Nov 1995 ... 2.25
- ❑3, Dec 1995 ... 2.25
- ❑4, Jan 1996 ... 2.25
- ❑5, Feb 1996 ... 2.25

ELFQUEST: WAVEDANCERS
WARP

- ❑1, Dec 1993 O: The Wavedancers. ... 2.25
- ❑2, Feb 1994 ... 2.25
- ❑3, Apr 1994 ... 2.25
- ❑4, Jun 1994 ... 2.25
- ❑5, Aug 1994 ... 2.25
- ❑6, Oct 1994 ... 2.25
- ❑Special 1 ... 2.25

Wendy and Richard Pini's *Elfquest* has spawned an upcoming animated feature and a line of action figures.

© 1979 Father Tree Press (Warp Graphics).

N-MINT

ELFQUEST: WORLDPOOL
WARP

- ❑1, Jul 1997, b&w ... 2.95

ELF-THING
ECLIPSE

- ❑1, Mar 1987, b&w ... 1.50

ELFTREK
DIMENSION

- ❑1, Jul 1986; parody of Star Trek, Elfquest ... 1.75
- ❑2, Oct 1986; parody of Star Trek, Elfquest ... 1.75

ELF WARRIOR
ADVENTURE

- ❑1, Feb 1987 ... 1.95
- ❑2 ... 1.95
- ❑3 ... 1.95
- ❑4; Published by Quadrant ... 1.95

EL GATO NEGRO
AZTECA

- ❑1, Oct 1993, b&w ... 2.00
- ❑2, Sum 1994, b&w ... 2.00
- ❑3, Fal 1995, b&w ... 2.00
- ❑4 ... 2.50

EL GAUCHO
NBM

- ❑1 ... 20.95

EL-HAZARD
VIZ

- ❑1, Apr 1997 ... 2.95

EL HAZARD: THE MAGNIFICENT WORLD PART 1
VIZ

- ❑1, Sep 2000 ... 2.95
- ❑2, Oct 2000 ... 2.95
- ❑3, Nov 2000 ... 2.95
- ❑4, Dec 2000 ... 2.95
- ❑5, Jan 2001 ... 2.95

EL HAZARD: THE MAGNIFICENT WORLD PART 2
VIZ

- ❑1, Feb 2001 ... 2.95
- ❑2, Mar 2001 ... 2.95
- ❑3, Apr 2001 ... 2.95
- ❑4, May 2001 ... 2.95
- ❑5, Jun 2001 ... 2.95

EL HAZARD: THE MAGNIFICENT WORLD PART 3
VIZ

- ❑1, Jul 2001 ... 2.95
- ❑2, Aug 2001 ... 2.95
- ❑3, Sep 2001 ... 2.95
- ❑4, Oct 2001 ... 2.95
- ❑5, Nov 2001 ... 2.95
- ❑6, Dec 2001 ... 2.95

ELIMINATOR, THE
MALIBU / ULTRAVERSE

- ❑0, Apr 1995; Collects Eliminator appearances from Ultraverse Premiere ... 2.95
- ❑1, May 1995; 7th Infinity Gem revealed ... 2.50
- ❑1/Variant, May 1995; Black cover edition; Black cover edition; 7th Infinity Gem revealed ... 3.95

N-MINT

- ❑2, Jun 1995 .... 2.50
- ❑3, Jul 1995 .... 2.50

ELIMINATOR (ETERNITY)
ETERNITY

- ❑1, b&w 2.50
- ❑2, b&w 2.50
- ❑3, b&w 2.50

ELIMINATOR FULL COLOR SPECIAL
ETERNITY

- ❑1, Oct 1991 .... 2.95

ELONGATED MAN
DC

- ❑1, Jan 1992 .... 1.25
- ❑2, Feb 1992 .... 1.00
- ❑3, Mar 1992 .... 1.00
- ❑4, Apr 1992 .... 1.00

ELRIC
PACIFIC

- ❑1, Apr 1983 CR (a) 2.00
- ❑2, Aug 1983 CR (a) 1.75
- ❑3, Oct 1983 CR (a) 1.75
- ❑4, Dec 1983 CR (a) 1.75
- ❑5, Feb 1984 CR (a) 1.75
- ❑6, Apr 1984 CR (a) 1.75

ELRIC (TOPPS)
TOPPS

- ❑0, ca. 1996 NG (w); CR (a) 3.50
- ❑1, ca. 1996 .... 2.95
- ❑2, ca. 1996 .... 2.95
- ❑3, ca. 1996 .... 2.95
- ❑4, ca. 1996 CR (w); CR (a) 2.95

ELRIC: SAILOR ON THE SEAS OF FATE
FIRST

- ❑1, Jun 1985 .... 2.00
- ❑2, Aug 1985 .... 1.75
- ❑3, Oct 1985 .... 1.75
- ❑4, Dec 1985 .... 1.75
- ❑5, Feb 1986 .... 1.75
- ❑6, Apr 1986 .... 1.75
- ❑7, Jun 1986 .... 1.75

ELRIC: STORMBRINGER
DARK HORSE / TOPPS

- ❑1, ca. 1997 .... 2.95
- ❑2, ca. 1997 .... 2.95
- ❑3, ca. 1997 .... 2.95
- ❑4, ca. 1997 .... 2.95
- ❑5, ca. 1997 .... 2.95
- ❑6, ca. 1997 .... 2.95
- ❑7, ca. 1997 .... 2.95

ELRIC: THE BANE OF THE BLACK SWORD
FIRST

- ❑1, Aug 1988 .... 2.00
- ❑2, Oct 1988 .... 2.00
- ❑3, Dec 1988 .... 2.00
- ❑4, Feb 1989 .... 2.00
- ❑5, Apr 1989 .... 2.00
- ❑6, Jun 1989 .... 2.00

ELRIC: THE VANISHING TOWER
FIRST

- ❑1, Aug 1987 .... 1.75
- ❑2, Oct 1987 .... 1.75
- ❑3, Dec 1987 .... 1.75
- ❑4, Feb 1988 .... 1.75
- ❑5, Apr 1988 .... 1.75
- ❑6, Jun 1988 .... 1.75

ELRIC: WEIRD OF THE WHITE WOLF
FIRST

- ❑1, Oct 1986 .... 1.75
- ❑2, Dec 1986 .... 1.75
- ❑3, Feb 1987 .... 1.75
- ❑4, Apr 1987 .... 1.75
- ❑5, Jun 1987 .... 1.75

ELSEWHERE PRINCE, THE
MARVEL / EPIC

- ❑1, May 1990 .... 1.95
- ❑2, Jun 1990 .... 1.95

N-MINT

- ❑3, Jul 1990 .... 1.95
- ❑4, Aug 1990 .... 1.95
- ❑5, Sep 1990 .... 1.95
- ❑6, Oct 1990 .... 1.95

ELSEWORLDS 80-PAGE GIANT
DC

- ❑1, Aug 1999; U.S. copies destroyed, only released in England; less than 700 copies estimated to exist 110.00

ELSEWORLD'S FINEST
DC

- ❑1, ca. 1997; prestige format; Superman and Batman in the 1920s; Elseworlds story 4.95
- ❑2, ca. 1997; prestige format; Superman and Batman in the 1920s 4.95

ELSEWORLD'S FINEST: SUPERGIRL & BATGIRL
DC

- ❑1, ca. 1998; prestige format 5.95
- ❑1/Ltd., ca. 1998; ca. 1998; Signed ... 18.95

ELVEN
MALIBU / ULTRAVERSE

- ❑0, Oct 1994 1: Elven. 2.95
- ❑1, Feb 1995 A: Prime. 2.25
- ❑1/Ltd., Feb 1995; Limited foil edition A: Prime. 2.50
- ❑2, Mar 1995 .... 2.25
- ❑3, Apr 1995 .... 2.25
- ❑4, May 1995 .... 2.25

ELVIRA, MISTRESS OF THE DARK
CLAYPOOL

- ❑1, May 1993 .... 4.00
- ❑2, Jun 1993 KB (w) 3.00
- ❑3, Jul 1993 KB (w) 3.00
- ❑4, Aug 1993 .... 3.00
- ❑5, Sep 1993 KB (w) 3.00
- ❑6, Oct 1993 .... 3.00
- ❑7, Nov 1993 KB (w) 3.00
- ❑8, Dec 1993 .... 3.00
- ❑9, Jan 1994 KB (w) 3.00
- ❑10, Feb 1994 KB (w) 3.00
- ❑11, Mar 1994 KB (w) 2.75
- ❑12, Apr 1994 .... 2.75
- ❑13, May 1994 .... 2.75
- ❑14, Jun 1994 .... 2.75
- ❑15, Jul 1994 .... 2.75
- ❑16, Aug 1994 .... 2.75
- ❑17, Sep 1994 .... 2.75
- ❑18, Oct 1994 .... 2.75
- ❑19, Nov 1994 .... 2.75
- ❑20, Dec 1994 .... 2.75
- ❑21, Jan 1995 .... 2.50
- ❑22, Feb 1995 .... 2.50
- ❑23, Mar 1995 .... 2.50
- ❑24, Apr 1995 .... 2.50
- ❑25, May 1995 KB (w) 2.50
- ❑26, Jun 1995 .... 2.50
- ❑27, Jul 1995 .... 2.50
- ❑28, Aug 1995 .... 2.50
- ❑29, Sep 1995 .... 2.50
- ❑30, Oct 1995 .... 2.50
- ❑31, Nov 1995 .... 2.50
- ❑32, Dec 1995 .... 2.50
- ❑33, Jan 1996 .... 2.50
- ❑34, Feb 1996 .... 2.50
- ❑35, Mar 1996 .... 2.50
- ❑36, Apr 1996 .... 2.50
- ❑37, May 1996 .... 2.50
- ❑38, Jun 1996 .... 2.50
- ❑39, Jul 1996 A: Portia Prinz. 2.50
- ❑40, Aug 1996 .... 2.50
- ❑41, Sep 1996 .... 2.50
- ❑42, Oct 1996 .... 2.50
- ❑43, Nov 1996 .... 2.50
- ❑44, Dec 1996 .... 2.50
- ❑45, Jan 1997 .... 2.50
- ❑46, Feb 1997 .... 2.50
- ❑47, Mar 1997 .... 2.50
- ❑48, Apr 1997 .... 2.50
- ❑49, May 1997 .... 2.50

N-MINT

- ❑50, Jun 1997 .... 2.50
- ❑51, Jul 1997 .... 2.50
- ❑52, Aug 1997 .... 2.50
- ❑53, Sep 1997 .... 2.50
- ❑54, Oct 1997 .... 2.50
- ❑55, Nov 1997 .... 2.50
- ❑56, Dec 1997 .... 2.50
- ❑57, Jan 1998 .... 2.50
- ❑58, Feb 1998 .... 2.50
- ❑59, Mar 1998 .... 2.50
- ❑60, Apr 1998 .... 2.50
- ❑61, May 1998 .... 2.50
- ❑62, Jun 1998 .... 2.50
- ❑63, Jul 1998 .... 2.50
- ❑64, Aug 1998 .... 2.50
- ❑65, Sep 1998 .... 2.50
- ❑66, Oct 1998 .... 2.50
- ❑67, Nov 1998 .... 2.50
- ❑68, Dec 1998 .... 2.50
- ❑69, Jan 1999 .... 2.50
- ❑70, Feb 1999 .... 2.50
- ❑71, Mar 1999 .... 2.50
- ❑72, Apr 1999 .... 2.50
- ❑73, May 1999 .... 2.50
- ❑74, Jun 1999 .... 2.50
- ❑75, Jul 1999 .... 2.50
- ❑76, Aug 1999 .... 2.50
- ❑77, Sep 1999 .... 2.50
- ❑78, Oct 1999 .... 2.50
- ❑79, Nov 1999 .... 2.50
- ❑80, Dec 1999 .... 2.50
- ❑81, Jan 2000 .... 2.50
- ❑82, Feb 2000 .... 2.50
- ❑83, Mar 2000 .... 2.50
- ❑84, Apr 2000 .... 2.50
- ❑85, May 2000 .... 2.50
- ❑86, Jun 2000 .... 2.50
- ❑87, Jul 2000 .... 2.50
- ❑88, Aug 2000 RHo (w) 2.50
- ❑89, Sep 2000 .... 2.50
- ❑90, Oct 2000 RHo (w) 2.50
- ❑91, Nov 2000 .... 2.50
- ❑92, Dec 2000 .... 2.50
- ❑93, Jan 2001 .... 2.50
- ❑94, Feb 2001 .... 2.50
- ❑95, Mar 2001 .... 2.50
- ❑96, Apr 2001 .... 2.50
- ❑97, May 2001 .... 2.50
- ❑98, Jun 2001 .... 2.50
- ❑99, Jul 2001 .... 2.50
- ❑100, Aug 2001 .... 2.50
- ❑101, Sep 2001 .... 2.50
- ❑102, Oct 2001 .... 2.50
- ❑103, Nov 2001 .... 2.50
- ❑104, Dec 2001 .... 2.50
- ❑105, Jan 2002 .... 2.50
- ❑106, Feb 2002 .... 2.50
- ❑107, Mar 2002 .... 2.50
- ❑108, Apr 2002 .... 2.50
- ❑109, May 2002 .... 2.50
- ❑110, Jun 2002 .... 2.50
- ❑111, Jul 2002 .... 2.50
- ❑112, Aug 2002 .... 2.50
- ❑113, Sep 2002 .... 2.50
- ❑114, Oct 2002 .... 2.50
- ❑115, Nov 2002 .... 2.50
- ❑116, Dec 2002 .... 2.50
- ❑117, Jan 2003 .... 2.50
- ❑118, Feb 2003 .... 2.50
- ❑119, Mar 2003 .... 2.50
- ❑120, Apr 2003 .... 2.50
- ❑121, May 2003 .... 2.50

ELVIRA'S HOUSE OF MYSTERY
DC

- ❑1, Jan 1986; Double-size 2.50
- ❑2, Apr 1986 .... 2.00
- ❑3, May 1986 .... 2.00
- ❑4, Jun 1986 .... 2.00
- ❑5, Jul 1986 .... 2.00
- ❑6, Aug 1986; sideways issue 2.00
- ❑7, Sep 1986; science-fiction issue ... 2.00

N-MINT

- ❑8, Oct 1986 ... 2.00
- ❑9, Nov 1986 ... 2.00
- ❑10, Dec 1986 A: Cain. ... 2.00
- ❑11, Jan 1987; Double-size DSt (c) .. 2.50
- ❑Special 1, ca. 1987; Christmas stories 2.00

ELVIS MANDIBLE, THE
DC / PIRANHA

- ❑1, ca. 1990, b&w ... 3.50

ELVIS PRESLEY EXPERIENCE, THE
REVOLUTIONARY

- ❑1, Aug 1992, b&w ... 2.50
- ❑2, Oct 1992, b&w ... 2.50
- ❑3, Jan 1993, b&w ... 2.50
- ❑4, Feb 1993, b&w ... 2.50
- ❑5, Jul 1993, b&w ... 2.50
- ❑6, Aug 1993, b&w ... 2.50
- ❑7, Apr 1994, b&w ... 2.50

ELVIS SHRUGGED
REVOLUTIONARY

- ❑1, Feb 1992, b&w ... 2.50
- ❑2, Aug 1992, b&w ... 2.50
- ❑3, Apr 1992, b&w ... 3.95

EL ZOMBO
DARK HORSE

- ❑1, Apr 2004 ... 2.99
- ❑2, May 2004 ... 2.99

E-MAN (1ST SERIES)
CHARLTON

- ❑1, Oct 1973 O: E-Man. ... 4.00
- ❑2, Dec 1973 ... 2.50
- ❑3, Jun 1974 ... 2.50
- ❑4, Aug 1974 ... 2.50
- ❑5, Nov 1974 ... 2.50
- ❑6, Jan 1975 JBy (a) ... 2.50
- ❑7, Mar 1975 JBy (a) ... 2.50
- ❑8, May 1975; JBy (a); Nova becomes E-Man's partner ... 2.50
- ❑9, Jul 1975 JBy (a) ... 2.50
- ❑10, Sep 1975 JBy (a) ... 2.50

E-MAN (2ND SERIES)
FIRST

- ❑1, Apr 1983 JSa (a); O: E-Man. ... 2.00
- ❑2, Jun 1983; JSa (a); A: F-Men. X-Men parody ... 1.50
- ❑3, Jun 1983 JSa (a) ... 1.50
- ❑4, Jul 1983 JSa (a) ... 1.50
- ❑5, Aug 1983 JSa (a) ... 1.50
- ❑6, Sep 1983 JSa (a); O: E-Man. ... 1.25
- ❑7, Oct 1983 JSa (a) ... 1.25
- ❑8, Nov 1983 JSa (a) ... 1.25
- ❑9, Dec 1983 JSa (a) ... 1.25
- ❑10, Jan 1984 JSa (a); O: Nova Kane. 1.25
- ❑11, Feb 1984 JSa (a) ... 1.25
- ❑12, Mar 1984 JSa (a) ... 1.25
- ❑13, Apr 1984 JSa (a) ... 1.25
- ❑14, May 1984 JSa (a) ... 1.25
- ❑15, Jun 1984 JSa (a) ... 1.25
- ❑16, Jul 1984 JSa (a) ... 1.25
- ❑17, Aug 1984 JSa (a) ... 1.25
- ❑18, Sep 1984 JSa (a) ... 1.25
- ❑19, Oct 1984 JSa (a) ... 1.25
- ❑20, Nov 1984 JSa (a) ... 1.25
- ❑21, Dec 1984 JSa (a) ... 1.25
- ❑22, Feb 1985 JSa (a) ... 1.25
- ❑23, Apr 1985 JSa (a) ... 1.25
- ❑24, Jun 1985 JSa (a); O: Michael Mauser. ... 1.25
- ❑25, Aug 1985 JSa (a) ... 1.25

E-MAN (3RD SERIES)
COMICO

- ❑1, Sep 1989 ... 2.75

E-MAN (4TH SERIES)
COMICO

- ❑1, Jan 1990 ... 2.50
- ❑2, Feb 1990 ... 2.50
- ❑3, Mar 1990 ... 2.50

E-MAN (5TH SERIES)
ALPHA

- ❑1, Oct 1993 ... 2.75

N-MINT

E-MAN RETURNS
ALPHA PRODUCTIONS

- ❑1, Mar 1994, b&w ... 2.75

EMBLEM
ANTARCTIC / VENUS

- ❑1, May 1994, b&w ... 3.50
- ❑2, Jun 1994, b&w ... 2.95
- ❑3, Jul 1994, b&w ... 2.95
- ❑5, Oct 1994, b&w ... 2.95
- ❑6, Nov 1994, b&w ... 2.95
- ❑7, Dec 1994, b&w ... 2.95
- ❑8, Feb 1995, b&w ... 2.95

EMBRACE
LONDON NIGHT

- ❑1, Jun 1997 ... 3.00
- ❑1/Ltd.; Signed, promotional edition . 4.00

EMERALDAS
ETERNITY

- ❑1, Nov 1990, b&w ... 2.25
- ❑2, b&w ... 2.25
- ❑3, b&w ... 2.25
- ❑4, b&w ... 2.25

EMERGENCY!
CHARLTON

- ❑1, Jun 1976 JBy (a) ... 20.00
- ❑2, Aug 1976 ... 16.00
- ❑3, Oct 1976 ... 14.00
- ❑4, Dec 1976; Scarce ... 16.00

EMERGENCY! (MAGAZINE)
CHARLTON

- ❑1, Jun 1976 NA (c); NA (a) ... 30.00
- ❑2, Aug 1976 ... 25.00
- ❑3, Oct 1976 ... 22.00
- ❑4, Dec 1976 ... 22.00

EMISSARY
STRATEIA

- ❑1, Jul 1998 ... 2.50

EMMA DAVENPORT
LOHMAN HILLS

- ❑1, Apr 1995, b&w ... 3.00
- ❑2, Jun 1995, b&w ... 2.75
- ❑3, Aug 1995, b&w ... 2.75
- ❑4, Oct 1995, b&w ... 2.75
- ❑5, Dec 1995, b&w ... 2.75
- ❑6, Feb 1996, b&w ... 2.75
- ❑7, Apr 1996, b&w ... 2.75
- ❑8, Feb 1996, b&w; crossover with Femforce ... 2.75

EMMA FROST
MARVEL

- ❑1, Aug 2003 ... 2.50
- ❑2, Sep 2003 ... 2.50
- ❑3, Oct 2003 ... 2.50
- ❑4, Dec 2003 ... 2.50
- ❑5, Jan 2004 ... 2.50
- ❑6, Feb 2004 ... 2.50
- ❑7, Mar 2004 ... 2.50
- ❑8, Apr 2004 ... 2.99
- ❑9, May 2004 ... 2.99
- ❑10, Jun 2004 ... 2.99
- ❑11, Jul 2004 ... 2.99
- ❑12, Aug 2004 ... 2.99
- ❑13, Sep 2004

EMPIRE
ETERNITY

- ❑1, Mar 1988 ... 1.95
- ❑2, Apr 1988 ... 1.95
- ❑3, May 1988 ... 1.95
- ❑4, Jun 1988 ... 1.95

EMPIRE (IMAGE)
IMAGE

- ❑1, May 2000 ... 2.50
- ❑2, Sep 2000 ... 2.50

EMPIRE (DC)
DC

- ❑0, Jul 2003 ... 4.95
- ❑1, Sep 2003 ... 2.50
- ❑2, Sep 2003 ... 2.50
- ❑3, Oct 2003 ... 2.50

The worlds of *Star Trek* and *Elfquest* met (in a way) in the 1986 two-issue parody series, *Elftrek*.

© 1986 Dimension Graphics.

N-MINT

- ❑4, Dec 2003 ... 2.50
- ❑5, Dec 2003 ... 2.50
- ❑6, Jan 2004 ... 2.50

EMPIRE LANES (NORTHERN LIGHTS)
NORTHERN LIGHTS

- ❑1, Dec 1986 ... 1.75
- ❑2 ... 1.75
- ❑3 ... 1.75
- ❑4 ... 1.75

EMPIRE LANES (KEYLINE)
KEYLINE

- ❑1 ... 1.75

EMPIRE LANES (VOL. 2)
KEYLINE

- ❑1 ... 2.95

EMPIRES OF NIGHT
REBEL

- ❑1, Dec 1993, b&w ... 2.25
- ❑2 ... 2.25
- ❑3 ... 2.25
- ❑4 ... 2.25

EMPTY LOVE STORIES
SLAVE LABOR

- ❑1, Nov 1994, b&w ... 2.95
- ❑2, Aug 1996, b&w ... 2.95

EMPTY LOVE STORIES (2ND SERIES)
FUNNY VALENTINE

- ❑1, Jul 1998, b&w; reprints Slave Labor issue ... 2.95
- ❑Special 1, Jan 1998, b&w ... 2.95

EMPTY SKULL COMICS
FANTAGRAPHICS

- ❑1, Apr 1996, b&w; Oversized; card-stock cover ... 4.95

EMPTY ZONE
SIRIUS

- ❑1 ... 2.50
- ❑2 ... 2.50
- ❑3 ... 2.50
- ❑4 ... 2.50

EMPTY ZONE (2ND SERIES)
SIRIUS

- ❑1, ca. 1998 ... 2.95
- ❑2, ca. 1998 ... 2.95
- ❑3, ca. 1998 ... 2.95
- ❑4, ca. 1998 ... 2.95
- ❑5, ca. 1998 ... 2.95
- ❑6, ca. 1998 ... 2.95
- ❑7, ca. 1998 ... 2.95
- ❑8, ca. 1998 ... 2.95

EMPTY ZONE: TRANCEMISSIONS
SIRIUS

- ❑1 ... 2.95

ENCHANTED
SIRIUS

- ❑1, ca. 1997 ... 2.95
- ❑2, ca. 1997 ... 2.95
- ❑3, ca. 1997 ... 2.95

ENCHANTED (VOL. 2)
SIRIUS

- ❑1 ... 2.95
- ❑2 ... 2.95
- ❑3 ... 2.95

Condition price index: Multiply "NM prices" above by: **0.83 for Very Fine/Near Mint**
0.66 for Very Fine • 0.33 for Fine • 0.2 for Very Good • 0.125 for Good

N-MINT

ENCHANTED VALLEY
BLACKTHORNE
- ❑1, May 1997 .... 1.75
- ❑2 .... 1.75

ENCHANTED WORLDS
BLACKMORE
- ❑1, b&w 2.75

ENCHANTER
ECLIPSE
- ❑1, Oct 1985 .... 2.00
- ❑2, Nov 1985 .... 2.00
- ❑3, Dec 1985 .... 2.00
- ❑4, Jan 1986 .... 2.00
- ❑5, Feb 1986 .... 2.00
- ❑6, Mar 1986 .... 2.00
- ❑7, Apr 1986 .... 2.00
- ❑8, May 1986 .... 2.00

ENCHANTER: APOCALYPSE MOON
EXPRESS / ENTITY
- ❑1, b&w; illustrated novella 2.95

ENCHANTER: PRELUDE TO APOCALYPSE
EXPRESS
- ❑1, b&w 2.50
- ❑2, b&w 2.50
- ❑3, b&w 2.50

ENCHANTERS, THE
HIDDEN POET
- ❑1, Jun 1996 .... 2.50

ENCYCLOPÆDIA DEADPOOLICA, THE
MARVEL
- ❑1, Dec 1998; Deadpool reference 2.99

END, THE: IN THE BEGINNING
AFC
- ❑1, Jun 2000, b&w 2.95

ENDLESS GALLERY, THE
DC / VERTIGO
- ❑1; pin-ups; Introduction by Neil Gaiman 3.50

ENEMY
DARK HORSE
- ❑1, May 1994 .... 2.50
- ❑2, Jun 1994 .... 2.50
- ❑3, Jul 1994 .... 2.50
- ❑4, Aug 1994 .... 2.50
- ❑5, Sep 1994 .... 2.50

ENEMY ACE SPECIAL
DC
- ❑1, Oct 1990; JKu (a); reprints Showcase and Our Army at War 3.00

ENEMY ACE: WAR IDYLL
DC
- ❑1, ca. 1990; prestige format 4.95

ENEMY ACE: WAR IN HEAVEN
DC
- ❑1, May 2001 .... 5.95
- ❑2, Jun 2001 .... 5.95

ENFORCE
REOCCURRING IMAGES
- ❑1 .... 2.95

ENGINEHEAD
DC
- ❑1, May 2004 .... 2.50
- ❑2, Jun 2004 .... 2.50
- ❑3, Aug 2004 .... 2.50

ENIGMA
DC / VERTIGO
- ❑1, Mar 1993 .... 2.50
- ❑2, Apr 1993 .... 2.50
- ❑3, May 1993 .... 2.50
- ❑4, Jun 1993 .... 2.50
- ❑5, Jul 1993 .... 2.50
- ❑6, Aug 1993 .... 2.50
- ❑7, Sep 1993 .... 2.50
- ❑8, Oct 1993 .... 2.50

N-MINT

ENO & PLUM
ONI
- ❑1, Mar 1998, b&w 2.95

ENTROPY TALES
ENTROPY
- ❑1 .... 1.50
- ❑2 .... 1.50
- ❑3 .... 1.50
- ❑4 .... 1.50

ENTS
MANIC
- ❑1, b&w 2.50
- ❑2, b&w 2.50
- ❑3, b&w 2.50

EO
REBEL
- ❑1 .... 3.00
- ❑1/Ltd.; Limited "Premier" edition 3.00
- ❑2 .... 3.00
- ❑2/Ltd.; limited edition 3.00
- ❑3 .... 3.00
- ❑4 .... 3.00

EPIC ANTHOLOGY
MARVEL / EPIC
- ❑1, Apr 2004; Sleepwalker, Young Ancient One, and Strange Magic stories 5.99

EPIC ILLUSTRATED
MARVEL / EPIC
- ❑1, Spr 1980 FF (c); WP, JSn, FF (a); 1: Dreadstar. A: Silver Surfer. 6.00
- ❑2, Sum 1980 .... 4.00
- ❑3, Aut 1980; Aut 1980 .... 4.00
- ❑4, Win 1980 .... 4.00
- ❑5, Apr 1981 .... 3.00
- ❑6, Jun 1981 .... 3.00
- ❑7, Aug 1981 .... 3.00
- ❑8, Oct 1981 .... 3.00
- ❑9, Dec 1981 .... 3.00
- ❑10, Feb 1982 .... 3.00
- ❑11, Apr 1982 .... 3.00
- ❑12, Jun 1982 .... 3.00
- ❑13, Aug 1982 .... 3.00
- ❑14, Oct 1982 .... 3.00
- ❑15, Dec 1982 .... 3.00
- ❑16, Feb 1983 .... 3.00
- ❑17, Apr 1983 .... 3.00
- ❑18, Jun 1983 .... 3.00
- ❑19, Aug 1983 .... 3.00
- ❑20, Oct 1983 .... 3.00
- ❑21, Dec 1983 .... 3.00
- ❑22, Feb 1984 .... 3.00
- ❑23, Apr 1984 .... 3.00
- ❑24, Jun 1984 .... 3.00
- ❑25, Aug 1984 .... 3.00
- ❑26, Oct 1984 .... 3.00
- ❑27, Dec 1984 .... 3.00
- ❑28, Feb 1985 .... 3.00
- ❑29, Apr 1985 .... 3.00
- ❑30, Jun 1985 .... 3.00
- ❑31, Aug 1985 .... 3.00
- ❑32, Oct 1985 .... 3.00
- ❑33, Dec 1985 .... 3.00
- ❑34, Feb 1986 .... 3.00

EPIC LITE
MARVEL / EPIC
- ❑1, Sep 1991 .... 4.50

EPSILON WAVE, THE
INDEPENDENT
- ❑1, Oct 1985; Independent Comics publishes 1.50
- ❑2, Dec 1985 .... 1.50
- ❑3, Feb 1986 .... 1.50
- ❑4, Apr 1986 .... 1.50
- ❑5, May 1986; Elite begins as publisher 1.75
- ❑6, Jun 1986 .... 1.75
- ❑7, Aug 1986 .... 1.75
- ❑8 1986 .... 1.75

N-MINT

EQUINE THE UNCIVILIZED
GRAPHXPRESS
- ❑1, b&w 2.00
- ❑2 .... 2.00
- ❑3 .... 2.00
- ❑4 .... 2.00
- ❑5 .... 2.00
- ❑6 .... 2.00

EQUINOX CHRONICLES
INNOVATION
- ❑1, b&w 2.25
- ❑2, b&w 2.25

ERADICATOR
DC
- ❑1, Aug 1996 .... 1.75
- ❑2, Sep 1996 .... 1.75
- ❑3, Oct 1996 .... 1.75

ERADICATORS, THE
SILVERWOLF
- ❑1, May 1986 .... 1.50
- ❑2, Jul 1986 .... 1.50
- ❑3, Aug 1986 .... 1.50
- ❑4, Sep 1986 .... 1.50

ERADICATORS, THE (VOL. 2)
SILVERWOLF
- ❑1, Aug 1989, b&w; Cover says September 2.00
- ❑2, Apr 1990, b&w 2.00

ERIC PRESTON IS THE FLAME
B-MOVIE
- ❑1 .... 1.00

ERNIE
KITCHEN SINK
- ❑1; comics 2.00

EROS FORUM
FANTAGRAPHICS / EROS
- ❑1, b&w 2.50
- ❑3, b&w 2.95

EROS GRAPHIC ALBUM
FANTAGRAPHICS / EROS
- ❑1 .... 9.95
- ❑2 .... 12.95
- ❑3 .... 10.95
- ❑4 .... 10.95
- ❑5 .... 14.95
- ❑6 .... 16.95
- ❑7 .... 12.95
- ❑8 .... 12.95
- ❑9 .... 9.95
- ❑10 .... 12.95
- ❑11 .... 11.95
- ❑12 .... 12.95
- ❑13 .... 12.95
- ❑14 .... 14.95
- ❑15 .... 14.95
- ❑16 .... 14.95
- ❑17 .... 15.95
- ❑18 .... 12.95
- ❑19 .... 14.95
- ❑20 .... 12.95
- ❑21 .... 14.95
- ❑22 .... 14.95
- ❑23 .... 12.95
- ❑24 .... 12.95
- ❑25 .... 16.95
- ❑26 .... 13.95
- ❑27 .... 11.95
- ❑28 .... 16.95
- ❑29 .... 16.95
- ❑30 .... 13.95
- ❑31 .... 19.95
- ❑32 .... 16.95
- ❑33 .... 16.95
- ❑34; Buffy Collection 14.95
- ❑35 .... 14.95
- ❑36 .... 19.95
- ❑37 .... 19.95
- ❑38 .... 19.95
- ❑39 .... 19.95

N-MINT

❑40 .... 19.95
❑41 .... 19.95
❑42 .... 19.95
❑43 .... 16.95
❑44 .... 16.95

EROS HAWK
FANTAGRAPHICS / EROS

❑1 .... 2.75
❑2 .... 2.75
❑3 .... 2.75
❑4 .... 2.75

EROS HAWK III
FANTAGRAPHICS / EROS

❑1, Jul 1994, b&w 2.75

EROTICA (VAUGHN BODÉ'S...)
FANTAGRAPHICS

❑

EROTIC FABLES & FAERIE TALES
FANTAGRAPHICS / EROS

❑1, b&w 2.50
❑2, b&w 2.50

EROTICOM
CALIBER

❑1 .... 2.50

EROTICOM II
CALIBER

❑1, ca. 1994, b&w; pin-ups, many swiped from Playboy's Book of Lingerie 2.95

EROTIC ORBITS
COMAX

❑1, b&w 2.95

EROTIC TALES
AIRCEL

❑1, b&w 2.95
❑2, b&w 2.95
❑3, b&w 2.95

EROTIC WORLDS OF FRANK THORNE, THE
FANTAGRAPHICS / EROS

❑1, Oct 1990; FT (w); FT (a); sexy cover 2.95
❑1/A, Oct 1990; FT (w); FT (a); Violent cover 2.95
❑2 FT (w); FT (a) 2.95
❑3 FT (w); FT (a) 2.95
❑4 FT (w); FT (a) 2.95
❑5 FT (w); FT (a) 2.95
❑6 FT (w); FT (a) 2.95

EROTIQUE
AIRCEL

❑1, b&w 2.50

ERSATZ PEACH, THE
AEON

❑1, Jul 1995; see also The Desert Peach; Charity fund-raiser; Desert Peach stories by various artists and writers 7.95

ESC
COMICO

❑1 1996 .... 2.95
❑2, Sep 1996 .... 2.95
❑3 1996 .... 2.95
❑4 1997 .... 2.95

ESCAPADE IN FLORENCE
GOLD KEY

❑1, Jan 1963 .... 40.00

ESCAPE TO THE STARS
SOLSON

❑1 .... 1.75

ESPERS
ECLIPSE

❑1, Jul 1986 .... 3.00
❑2, Sep 1986 .... 2.00
❑3, Nov 1986 BB (c); BB (a) 2.00
❑4, Feb 1987 .... 2.00
❑5, Apr 1987; Story continued in Interface #1 .... 2.00

N-MINT

ESPERS (VOL. 2)
HALLOWEEN

❑1 1996, b&w 3.50
❑2 1996, b&w 3.00
❑3 1997, b&w 3.00
❑4 1997, b&w 3.00
❑5 1997, b&w 3.00
❑6 1997 .... 3.00

ESPERS (VOL. 3)
IMAGE

❑1 1997, b&w 3.50
❑2 1997, b&w 3.00
❑3, Aug 1997, b&w 3.00
❑4 1997, b&w 3.00
❑5 1997, b&w 3.00
❑6 1997, b&w 3.00
❑7 1998, b&w 3.00
❑8 1998 .... 3.00
❑9 .... 3.00

ESPIONAGE
DELL

❑1 .... 18.00
❑2 .... 15.00

ESSENTIAL ELFQUEST, THE
WARP

❑1, Apr 1995; giveaway; WP (w); Free Preview 1.50

ESSENTIAL VERTIGO: SWAMP THING
DC / VERTIGO

❑1, Nov 1996; AMo (w); Reprints Saga of the Swamp Thing #21 .... 3.00
❑2, Dec 1996; AMo (w); Reprints Saga of the Swamp Thing #22 .... 2.50
❑3, Jan 1997; AMo (w); Reprints Saga of the Swamp Thing #23 .... 2.50
❑4, Feb 1997; AMo (w); Reprints Saga of the Swamp Thing #24 .... 2.50
❑5, Mar 1997; AMo (w); Reprints Saga of the Swamp Thing #25 .... 2.50
❑6, Apr 1997; Reprints Saga of the Swamp Thing #26 .... 2.00
❑7, May 1997; Reprints Saga of the Swamp Thing #27 .... 2.00
❑8, Jun 1997; Reprints Saga of the Swamp Thing #28 .... 2.00
❑9, Jul 1997; Reprints Saga of the Swamp Thing #29 .... 2.00
❑10, Aug 1997; AA (a); Reprints Saga of the Swamp Thing #30 .... 2.00
❑11, Sep 1997; Reprints Saga of the Swamp Thing #31 .... 2.00
❑12, Oct 1997; Reprints Saga of the Swamp Thing #32 .... 2.00
❑13, Nov 1997; AMo (w); Reprints Saga of the Swamp Thing #32 .... 2.00
❑14, Dec 1997; AMo (w); Reprints Saga of the Swamp Thing #34 .... 2.00
❑15, Jan 1998; Reprints Saga of the Swamp Thing #34 .... 2.00
❑16, Feb 1998; Reprints Saga of the Swamp Thing #35 .... 2.00
❑17, Mar 1998; Reprints Saga of the Swamp Thing #36 .... 2.00
❑18, Apr 1998; Reprints Saga of the Swamp Thing #37 .... 2.00
❑19, May 1998; Reprints Saga of the Swamp Thing #38 .... 2.00
❑20, Jun 1998; Reprints Saga of the Swamp Thing #39 .... 2.00
❑21, Jul 1998; Reprints Saga of the Swamp Thing #40 .... 2.00
❑22, Aug 1998; AA (a); Reprints Saga of the Swamp Thing #41 .... 2.00
❑23, Sep 1998; Reprints Saga of the Swamp Thing #42 .... 2.25
❑24, Oct 1998 .... 2.25

ESSENTIAL VERTIGO: THE SANDMAN
DC / VERTIGO

❑1, Aug 1996; NG (w); Reprints Sandman #1 .... 3.00
❑2, Sep 1996; NG (w); Reprints Sandman #2 .... 2.50
❑3, Oct 1996; NG (w); Reprints Sandman #3 .... 2.50

The adventures of Los Angeles paramedics John Gage and Roy Desoto were chronicled in comic-book form by Charlton.

© 1976 Charlton.

N-MINT

❑4, Oct 1996; NG (w); Reprints Sandman #4 .... 2.50
❑5, Dec 1996; NG (w); Reprints Sandman #5 .... 2.50
❑6, Jan 1997; NG (w); Reprints Sandman #6 .... 2.00
❑7, Feb 1997; NG (w); Reprints Sandman #7 .... 2.00
❑8, Mar 1997; NG (w); 1: Death (Sandman). Reprints Sandman #8 .... 2.00
❑9, Apr 1997; NG (w); Reprints Sandman #9 .... 2.00
❑10, May 1997; NG (w); Reprints Sandman #10 .... 2.00
❑11, Jun 1997; NG (w); Reprints Sandman #11 .... 2.00
❑12, Jul 1997; NG (w); Reprints Sandman #12 .... 2.00
❑13, Aug 1997; NG (w); Reprints Sandman #13 .... 2.00
❑14, Sep 1997; NG (w); Reprints Sandman #14 .... 2.00
❑15, Oct 1997; NG (w); Reprints Sandman #15 .... 2.00
❑16, Nov 1997; NG (w); Reprints Sandman #16 .... 2.00
❑17, Dec 1997; NG (w); Reprints Sandman #17 .... 2.00
❑18, Jan 1998; NG (w); Reprints Sandman #18 .... 2.00
❑19, Feb 1998; NG (w); CV (a); Reprints Sandman #19 .... 2.00
❑20, Mar 1998; NG (w); Reprints Sandman #20 .... 2.00
❑21, Apr 1998; NG (w); Reprints Sandman #21 .... 1.95
❑22, May 1998; NG (w); Reprints Sandman #22 .... 1.95
❑23, Jun 1998; NG (w); Reprints Sandman #23 .... 1.95
❑24, Jul 1998; NG (w); Reprints Sandman #24 .... 1.95
❑25, Aug 1998; NG (w); Reprints Sandman #25 .... 1.95
❑26, Sep 1998; NG (w); Reprints Sandman #26 .... 2.25
❑27, Oct 1998; NG (w); Reprints Sandman #27 .... 2.25
❑28, Nov 1998; NG (w); Reprints Sandman #28 .... 2.25
❑29, Dec 1998; NG (w); Reprints Sandman #29 .... 2.25
❑30, Jan 1999; NG (w); Reprints Sandman #30 .... 2.25
❑31, Feb 1999; NG (w); Reprints Sandman #31 .... 2.25
❑32, Mar 1999; NG (w); BT (a); Reprints Sandman Special #1 .... 4.50

ESTABLISHMENT, THE
DC / WILDSTORM

❑1, Nov 2001 .... 3.00
❑2, Dec 2001 .... 2.50
❑3, Jan 2002 .... 2.50
❑4, Feb 2002 .... 2.50
❑5, Mar 2002 .... 2.50
❑6, Apr 2002 .... 2.50
❑7, May 2002 .... 2.50
❑8, Jun 2002 .... 2.50
❑9, Jul 2002 .... 2.50
❑10, Aug 2002 .... 2.50
❑11, Sep 2002 .... 2.50

	N-MINT
❑12, Oct 2002	2.50
❑13, Nov 2002	2.50

ETC
DC / Piranha

	N-MINT
❑1	2.50
❑2	2.50
❑3	2.50
❑4	2.50
❑5	2.50

ETERNAL, THE
Marvel / MAX

	N-MINT
❑1, Aug 2003	2.99
❑2, Sep 2003	2.99
❑3, Oct 2003	2.99
❑4, Nov 2003	2.99
❑5, Dec 2003	2.99
❑6, Jan 2004	2.99

ETERNAL ROMANCE
Best Destiny

	N-MINT
❑1, Feb 1997, b&w	3.00
❑2, May 1997, b&w	2.50
❑3, Dec 1997	2.50
❑4, Jul 1998	2.50

ETERNAL ROMANCE LABOR OF LOVE SKETCHBOOK
Best Destiny

	N-MINT
❑1; Labor of Love sketchbook. 250 printed	2.50

ETERNALS, THE
Marvel

	N-MINT
❑1, Jul 1976; JK (w); JK (a); O: Eternals. 1: Kro. 1: Margo Damian. 1: Brother Tode. 1: Ikaris. 1st appearance	3.50
❑1/30 cent, Jul 1976; JK (w); JK (a); O: Eternals. 1: Kro. 1: Margo Damian. 1: Brother Tode. 1: Ikaris. 30 cent regional price variant; 1st appearance	25.00
❑2, Aug 1976 JK (w); JK (a); 1: Ajak. 1: Arishem the Judge.	2.50
❑2/30 cent, Aug 1976; JK (w); JK (a); 1: Ajak. 1: Arishem the Judge. 30 cent regional price variant	20.00
❑3, Sep 1976 JK (w); JK (a); 1: Sersi.	2.50
❑4, Oct 1976 JK (w); JK (a); 1: Gammenon the Gatherer.	2.50
❑5, Nov 1976 JK (w); JK (a); 1: Makkari. 1: Zuras (Thena).	2.50
❑6, Dec 1976 JK (w); JK (a)	2.00
❑7, Jan 1977 JK (w); JK (a); 1: Nezarr.	2.00
❑8, Feb 1977 JK (w); JK (a); 1: Karkas.	2.00
❑9, Mar 1977 JK (w); JK (a); 1: Sprite I.	2.00
❑10, Apr 1977 JK (w); JK (a)	2.00
❑11, May 1977 JK (w); JK (a); 1: Aginar.	2.00
❑12, Jun 1977 JK (w); JK (a); 1: Uni-Mind.	2.00
❑13, Jul 1977 JK (w); JK (a); 1: Gilgamesh. 1: One Above All.	2.00
❑13/35 cent, Jul 1977; JK (w); JK (a); 1: Gilgamesh. 1: One Above All. 35 cent regional price variant	15.00
❑14, Aug 1977 JK (w); JK (a); A: Hulk.	2.00
❑14/35 cent, Aug 1977; JK (w); JK (a); A: Hulk. 35 cent regional price variant	15.00
❑15, Sep 1977 JK (w); JK (a); A: Hulk.	2.00
❑16, Oct 1977 JK (w); JK (a)	2.00
❑17, Nov 1977 JK (w); JK (a)	2.00
❑18, Dec 1977 JK (w); JK (a)	2.00
❑19, Jan 1978 JK (w); JK (a); 1: Ziran.	2.00
❑Annual 1, Oct 1977 JK (w); JK (a)	2.00

ETERNALS, THE (LTD. SERIES)
Marvel

	N-MINT
❑1, Oct 1985; Giant-size 1: Khoryphos.	1.50
❑2, Nov 1985 1: Ghaur.	1.00
❑3, Dec 1985	1.00
❑4, Jan 1986	1.00
❑5, Feb 1986	1.00
❑6, Mar 1986	1.00
❑7, Apr 1986	1.00
❑8, May 1986	1.00
❑9, Jun 1986	1.00
❑10, Jul 1986 O: Ghaur. D: Margo Damian.	1.00
❑11, Aug 1986	1.00
❑12, Sep 1986; Giant-size	1.25

ETERNALS: THE HEROD FACTOR
Marvel

	N-MINT
❑1, Nov 1991	2.50

ETERNAL THIRST
Alpha Productions

	N-MINT
❑3, b&w	1.95
❑4, b&w	1.95
❑5, b&w	1.95

ETERNAL WARRIOR
Valiant

	N-MINT
❑1, Aug 1992; FM (c); FM (a); Unity	3.00
❑1/Gold Foil, Aug 1992; FM (c); FM (a); Gold foil logo (dealer promotion)	12.50
❑2, Sep 1992; Unity	2.50
❑3, Oct 1992 A: Armstrong.	2.50
❑4, Nov 1992 1: Bloodshot (cameo).	2.50
❑5, Dec 1992 A: Bloodshot.	2.50
❑6, Jan 1993 V: Master Darque.	2.25
❑7, Feb 1993	2.25
❑8, Mar 1993; Double-size; combined with Archer & Armstrong #8	4.50
❑9, Apr 1993	2.25
❑10, May 1993	2.25
❑11, Jun 1993	2.25
❑12, Jul 1993	2.25
❑13, Aug 1993 V: Eternal Enemy.	2.25
❑14, Sep 1993 A: Bloodshot.	2.25
❑15, Oct 1993 A: Bloodshot.	2.25
❑16, Nov 1993	2.25
❑17, Dec 1993	2.25
❑18, Jan 1994	2.25
❑19, Feb 1994 A: Doctor Mirage.	2.25
❑20, Mar 1994	2.25
❑21, Apr 1994	2.25
❑22, May 1994; trading card	2.25
❑23, Jun 1994	2.25
❑24, Aug 1994 V: Immortal Enemy.	2.25
❑25, Sep 1994 A: Archer & Armstrong.	2.25
❑26, Oct 1994; indicia says August; Flip-book with Archer & Armstrong #26	2.75
❑27, Nov 1994	2.25
❑28, Dec 1994	2.25
❑29, Jan 1995	2.25
❑30, Feb 1995	2.25
❑31, Mar 1995	2.25
❑32, Apr 1995	2.25
❑33, May 1995	2.25
❑34, Jun 1995	2.25
❑35, Jul 1995; Birthquake; outer white cover with warning	2.50
❑36, Jul 1995; Birthquake	2.50
❑37, Aug 1995	2.50
❑38, Aug 1995 V: Spider Queen.	2.50
❑39, Sep 1995	2.50
❑40, Sep 1995	2.50
❑41, Oct 1995	2.50
❑42, Oct 1995	2.50
❑43, Nov 1995	2.50
❑44, Nov 1995	2.50
❑45, Dec 1995	2.50
❑46, Dec 1995	2.50
❑47, Jan 1996	2.50
❑48, Jan 1996	2.50
❑49, Feb 1996	2.50
❑50, Mar 1996 A: Geomancer.	2.50
❑Special 1, Feb 1996	2.50
❑Yearbook 1, ca. 1993; cardstock cover	3.95
❑Yearbook 2, ca. 1994; cardstock cover	3.95

ETERNAL WARRIOR: FIST AND STEEL
Acclaim / Valiant

	N-MINT
❑1, May 1996	2.50
❑2, Jun 1996	2.50

ETERNAL WARRIORS
Acclaim / Valiant

	N-MINT
❑1, Jun 1997	3.95
❑1/Variant, Jun 1997; alternate painted cover	3.95
❑Ashcan 1, Feb 1997, b&w; No cover price; preview of Time and Treachery one-shot	1.00

ETERNAL WARRIORS: ARCHER & ARMSTRONG
Acclaim / Valiant

	N-MINT
❑1, Dec 1997; price stickered on cover	3.95

ETERNAL WARRIORS BLACKWORKS
Acclaim / Valiant

	N-MINT
❑1, Mar 1998	3.95

ETERNAL WARRIORS: DIGITAL ALCHEMY
Acclaim / Valiant

	N-MINT
❑1, Sep 1997	3.95

ETERNAL WARRIORS: MOG
Acclaim / Valiant

	N-MINT
❑1, Mar 1998	3.95

ETERNAL WARRIOR SPECIAL
Acclaim / Valiant

	N-MINT
❑1, Feb 1996; Eternal Warrior in WW II	2.50

ETERNAL WARRIORS: THE IMMORTAL ENEMY
Acclaim / Valiant

	N-MINT
❑1; Final issue of VH-2 universe	3.95

ETERNAL WARRIORS: TIME AND TREACHERY
Acclaim / Valiant

	N-MINT
❑1, ca. 1997	3.95

ETERNITY SMITH (VOL. 1)
Renegade

	N-MINT
❑1, Sep 1986	1.50
❑2, Nov 1986	1.50
❑3, Jan 1987	1.50
❑4, Mar 1987	1.50
❑5, May 1987	1.50

ETERNITY SMITH (VOL. 2)
Hero

	N-MINT
❑1, Sep 1987	1.95
❑2, Oct 1987	1.95
❑3, Nov 1987	1.95
❑4, Dec 1987	1.95
❑5, Jan 1988	1.95
❑6, Feb 1988	1.95
❑7, Apr 1988	1.95
❑8, Jun 1988	1.95
❑9, Aug 1988	1.95

ETERNITY TRIPLE ACTION
Eternity

	N-MINT
❑1, b&w	2.50
❑2, b&w	2.50
❑3, b&w	2.50
❑4, b&w	2.50

EUDAEMON, THE
Dark Horse

	N-MINT
❑1, Aug 1993	2.50
❑2	2.50
❑3	2.50

EUGENUS
Eugenus

	N-MINT
❑1, b&w	3.50
❑2, b&w	3.50
❑3	2.50

EUREKA
Radio

	N-MINT
❑1, Apr 2000, b&w	2.95
❑2, Jul 2000, b&w	2.95
❑3, Sep 2000, b&w	2.95

EUROPA AND THE PIRATE TWINS
Powder Monkey

	N-MINT
❑1, Oct 1996, b&w	2.95
❑1/A, Oct 1996, b&w; no cover price	2.95
❑Ashcan 1, Mar 1996, b&w; No cover price; smaller than normal comic	1.00

N-MINT

EVANGELINE SPECIAL
LODESTONE

❑1 ... 2.00

EVANGELINE (VOL. 1)
COMICO

❑1, ca. 1984 1: Evangeline. ... 2.50
❑2, ca. 1984 ... 2.00

EVANGELINE (VOL. 2)
FIRST

❑1, May 1987 ... 2.50
❑2, Jul 1987 ... 2.00
❑3, Sep 1987 ... 2.00
❑4, Nov 1987 ... 2.00
❑5, Jan 1988 ... 2.00
❑6, Mar 1988 ... 2.00
❑7, May 1988 ... 2.00
❑8, Jul 1988 ... 2.00
❑9, Sep 1988 ... 2.00
❑10, Nov 1988 ... 2.00
❑11, Jan 1989 ... 2.00
❑12, Mar 1989 ... 2.00

EVEL KNIEVEL
MARVEL

❑1; giveaway ... 10.00

EVEN MORE SECRET ORIGINS 80-PAGE GIANT
DC

❑1, ca. 2003 ... 6.95

E.V.E. PROTOMECHA
IMAGE

❑1 ... 2.50
❑1/A, Alternate Cover Finch ... 2.50
❑1/Gold; Gold Cover ... 2.50
❑1/Hologram; Holofield ... 2.50
❑2 ... 2.50
❑3, May 2000 ... 2.50
❑4, Nov 2000 ... 2.50
❑5 ... 2.50
❑6, Sep 2000 ... 2.50

EVERQUEST: THE RUINS OF KUNARK
DC / WILDSTORM

❑1, Feb 2002, Several characters in profile on cover ... 5.95

EVERQUEST: TRANSFORMATION
DC

❑1, Aug 2002, Several characters in profile on cover ... 5.95

EVERWINDS
SLAVE LABOR / AMAZE INK

❑1, Aug 1997, b&w ... 2.95
❑2, Oct 1997, b&w ... 2.95
❑3, Dec 1997, b&w ... 2.95
❑4, Mar 1998 ... 2.95

EVERY DOG HAS HIS DAY
SHIGA

❑1 ... 2.00

EVERYMAN, THE
MARVEL / EPIC

❑1, Nov 1991 ... 4.50

EVIL ERNIE (ETERNITY)
ETERNITY

❑1, ca. 1991, b&w O: Evil Ernie. 1: Evil Ernie. 1: Lady Death. ... 12.00
❑1/Ltd.; Limited edition reprint (1992) O: Evil Ernie. 1: Evil Ernie. 1: Lady Death. ... 6.00
❑2, ca. 1992, b&w ... 5.00
❑3, ca. 1992, b&w ... 4.00
❑4, ca. 1992, b&w ... 4.00
❑5, ca. 1992, b&w ... 4.00

EVIL ERNIE (CHAOS!)
CHAOS!

❑0 ... 3.00
❑0/Platinum; Platinum edition ... 5.00
❑1, Jul 1998 ... 3.00
❑2, Aug 1998 ... 3.00
❑3, Sep 1998 ... 3.00
❑4, Oct 1998 ... 3.00
❑5, Nov 1998 ... 2.95

N-MINT

❑6, Dec 1998 ... 2.95
❑7, Jan 1999 ... 2.95
❑8, Feb 1999 ... 2.95
❑9, Mar 1999 ... 2.95
❑10, Apr 1999 ... 2.95

EVIL ERNIE: BADDEST BATTLES
CHAOS

❑1, Jan 1997 ... 1.50
❑1/Variant, Jan 1997; Splatterfest Premium Edition cover ... 1.50

EVIL ERNIE: DEPRAVED
CHAOS!

❑1, Jul 1999 ... 2.95
❑2, Aug 1999 ... 2.95
❑3, Sep 1999 ... 2.95

EVIL ERNIE: DESTROYER
CHAOS!

❑1, Oct 1997 ... 2.95
❑2, Nov 1997 ... 2.95
❑3, Dec 1997 ... 2.95
❑4, Jan 1998 ... 2.95
❑5, Feb 1998 ... 2.95
❑6, Mar 1998 ... 2.95
❑7, Apr 1998 ... 2.95
❑8, May 1998 ... 2.95
❑9, Jun 1998 ... 2.95
❑Ashcan 1, Sep 1997 ... 2.50

EVIL ERNIE: NEW YEAR'S EVIL
CHAOS!

❑1 ... 5.00

EVIL ERNIE: PIECES OF ME
CHAOS!

❑1, Nov 2000, b&w ... 2.95
❑1/Variant, Nov 2000; Chromium Mega-Premium Edition; Limited to 2,500 ... 2.95

EVIL ERNIE: REVENGE
CHAOS!

❑0 ... 2.50
❑1, Oct 1994 ... 3.00
❑1/Deluxe, Oct 1994; Master of Annihilation premium edition ... 4.00
❑1/Ltd., Oct 1994; Glow-in-the-dark limited edition ... 4.00
❑2 1994 ... 3.00
❑3, Jan 1995 ... 2.50
❑4, Feb 1995 ... 2.50

EVIL ERNIE: STRAIGHT TO HELL
CHAOS!

❑1, Oct 1995; Coffin fold-out cover ... 3.00
❑1/A, Oct 1995; chromium cover ... 4.00
❑2, Dec 1995 ... 3.00
❑3, Feb 1996 ... 3.00
❑4, Apr 1996 ... 3.00
❑5, Jun 1996 ... 3.00

EVIL ERNIE: THE LOST SKETCHES
CHAOS

❑Ashcan 1, Jul 2001 ... 1.00

EVIL ERNIE: THE RESURRECTION
CHAOS!

❑1, ca. 1993 O: Evil Ernie. ... 4.00
❑1/Gold, ca. 1993; Gold promotional edition O: Evil Ernie. ... 5.00
❑2, ca. 1994 ... 3.50
❑3, ca. 1994 ... 3.50
❑4, ca. 1994 A: Lady Death. ... 3.00
❑Ashcan 1, ca. 1993 ... 5.00

EVIL ERNIE VS. THE MOVIE MONSTERS
CHAOS!

❑1/A, ca. 1997; TerrorVision cover ... 2.95
❑1, ca. 1997 ... 3.00

EVIL ERNIE VS. THE SUPER HEROES
CHAOS!

❑1, Aug 1995 O: Evil Ernie. ... 3.00
❑1/Variant, Aug 1995; premium edition (10, 000 copies); O: Evil Ernie. no cover price ... 3.00
❑2, Sep 1998 ... 2.95

A family of immortals hatched Machiavellian plans to help the Earth in Acclaim's series of *Eternal Warriors* one-shots.

© 1997 Acclaim.

N-MINT

EVIL ERNIE: WAR OF THE DEAD
CHAOS!

❑1, Nov 1999 ... 2.95
❑2, Dec 1999 ... 2.95
❑3, Jan 2000 ... 2.95

EVIL ERNIE: YOUTH GONE WILD
CHAOS!

❑1, Nov 1996, b&w; reprints Eternity's Evil Ernie ... 1.95
❑2, Dec 1996, b&w; reprints Eternity's Evil Ernie ... 1.95
❑3, Jan 1997, b&w; reprints Eternity's Evil Ernie ... 1.95
❑4, Feb 1997, b&w; reprints Eternity's Evil Ernie ... 1.95
❑5, Mar 1997, b&w; reprints Eternity's Evil Ernie ... 1.95
❑Special 1; "Director's Cut" #1 ... 4.95

EVIL EYE
FANTAGRAPHICS

❑1, Jun 1998 ... 2.95
❑2, Oct 1998 ... 2.95
❑3, Apr 1999 ... 2.95

EVILMAN SAVES THE WORLD
MOONSTONE

❑1, Jul 1996, b&w ... 2.95

EVO
IMAGE

❑1, Feb 2003 ... 2.99

EWOKS
MARVEL / STAR

❑1, May 1985 ... 3.00
❑2, Jul 1985 ... 2.00
❑3, Sep 1985 ... 2.00
❑4, Nov 1985 ... 2.00
❑5, Jan 1986 ... 2.00
❑6, Mar 1986 ... 2.00
❑7, May 1986 ... 2.00
❑8, Jul 1986 ... 2.00
❑9, Sep 1986 ... 2.00
❑10, Nov 1986 ... 2.00
❑11, Jan 1987 ... 2.00
❑12, Mar 1987 ... 2.00
❑13, May 1987 ... 2.00
❑14, Jul 1987 ... 2.00

EXCALIBUR
MARVEL

❑-1, Jul 1997; Flashback ... 2.00
❑1, Oct 1988 ... 2.50
❑2, Nov 1988 1: Tweedledope (in America). 1: Kylun. ... 2.00
❑3, Dec 1988 ... 2.00
❑4, Jan 1989; 1: Jester (in America). 1: Red Queen (in America). 1: The Crazy Gang (in America). 1: Executioner (in America). 1: Knave (in America). ... 2.00
❑5, Feb 1989 ... 2.00
❑6, Mar 1989; Inferno ... 1.75
❑7, Apr 1989; Inferno ... 1.75
❑8, May 1989 ... 1.75
❑9, Jun 1989 ... 1.75
❑10, Jul 1989 ... 1.75
❑11, Aug 1989 ... 1.75
❑12, Sep 1989 ... 1.75
❑13, Oct 1989 ... 1.75
❑14, Nov 1989 ... 1.75
❑15, Nov 1989 ... 1.75

Condition price index: Multiply "NM prices" above by: **0.83 for Very Fine/Near Mint**
0.66 for Very Fine • 0.33 for Fine • 0.2 for Very Good • 0.125 for Good

N-MINT

❑16, Dec 1989 .... 1.75
❑17, Dec 1989 .... 1.75
❑18, Jan 1990 .... 1.75
❑19, Feb 1990 .... 1.75
❑20, Mar 1990 .... 1.75
❑21, Apr 1990 .... 1.75
❑22, May 1990 .... 1.75
❑23, Jun 1990 .... 1.75
❑24, Jul 1990 .... 1.75
❑25, Aug 1990 .... 1.75
❑26, Aug 1990 .... 1.75
❑27, Aug 1990 A: Nth Man. 1.75
❑28, Sep 1990 .... 1.75
❑29, Sep 1990 .... 1.75
❑30, Oct 1990 .... 1.75
❑31, Nov 1990 .... 1.75
❑32, Dec 1990; with $1.75 price 1.75
❑32/A, Dec 1990; with $1.50 price 1.75
❑33, Jan 1991 .... 1.75
❑34, Feb 1991 .... 1.75
❑35, Mar 1991 .... 1.75
❑36, Apr 1991; Outlaws 1.75
❑37, May 1991 .... 1.75
❑38, Jun 1991 .... 1.75
❑39, Jul 1991 .... 1.75
❑40, Aug 1991 .... 1.75
❑41, Sep 1991 .... 1.75
❑42, Oct 1991 .... 1.75
❑43, Nov 1991 .... 1.75
❑44, Nov 1991 1: Micromax. 1.75
❑45, Dec 1991 1: Necrom. 1.75
❑46, Jan 1992 .... 1.75
❑47, Feb 1992 1: Cerise. 1.75
❑48, Mar 1992 1: Feron. 1.75
❑49, Apr 1992 .... 1.75
❑50, May 1992; Double-size; O: Feron. glow in the dark cover 2.75
❑51, Jun 1992 .... 1.75
❑52, Jul 1992 O: Phoenix III (Rachel Summers). A: X-Men. 1.75
❑53, Aug 1992 A: Spider-Man. 1.75
❑54, Sep 1992 .... 1.75
❑55, Oct 1992 .... 1.75
❑56, Nov 1992 A: X-Men. 1.75
❑57, Nov 1992 .... 1.75
❑58, Dec 1992 .... 1.75
❑59, Dec 1992 .... 1.75
❑60, Jan 1993 .... 1.75
❑61, Jan 1993 .... 1.75
❑62, Feb 1993 .... 1.75
❑63, Mar 1993 .... 1.75
❑64, Apr 1993 .... 1.75
❑65, May 1993 .... 1.75
❑66, Jun 1993 .... 1.75
❑67, Jul 1993 .... 1.75
❑68, Aug 1993 A: Starjammers. 1.75
❑69, Sep 1993 .... 1.75
❑70, Oct 1993 O: Cerise. A: Starjammers. A: Shi'Ar. 1.75
❑71, Nov 1993; Hologram cover; Fatal Attractions, Finale 3.50
❑72, Dec 1993 .... 1.75
❑73, Jan 1994 .... 1.75
❑74, Feb 1994 .... 1.75
❑75, Mar 1994; Giant-size 1: Britannic. 2.25
❑75/Variant, Mar 1994; Giant-size; 1: Britannic. Holo-grafix cover 3.50
❑76, Apr 1994 .... 1.75
❑77, May 1994 .... 1.95
❑78, Jun 1994 .... 1.95
❑79, Jul 1994 .... 1.95
❑80, Aug 1994 .... 1.95
❑81, Sep 1994 .... 1.95
❑82, Oct 1994; Giant-size 2.50
❑82/Variant, Oct 1994; Giant-size; foil cover 3.50
❑83, Nov 1994 .... 1.50
❑83/Deluxe, Nov 1994; Deluxe edition 1.95
❑84, Dec 1994 .... 1.50
❑84/Deluxe, Dec 1994; Deluxe edition 1.95
❑85, Jan 1995 .... 1.50
❑85/Deluxe, Jan 1995; Deluxe edition 1.95

N-MINT

❑86, Feb 1995 .... 1.95
❑86/Deluxe, Feb 1995; Deluxe edition 1.95
❑87, Jul 1995 .... 1.95
❑88, Aug 1995 .... 1.95
❑89, Sep 1995 .... 1.95
❑90, Oct 1995; OverPower cards inserted 1.95
❑91, Nov 1995 .... 1.95
❑92, Dec 1995 A: Colossus. A: Pete Wisdom. 1.95
❑93, Jan 1996; Rahne's past 1.95
❑94, Feb 1996 .... 1.95
❑95, Mar 1996 A: X-Man. 1.95
❑96, Apr 1996 .... 1.95
❑97, May 1996 .... 1.95
❑98, Jun 1996 .... 1.95
❑99, Jul 1996 .... 1.95
❑100, Aug 1996; Giant-size; wrap-around cover 2.95
❑101, Sep 1996 .... 1.95
❑102, Oct 1996; bound-in trading cards 1.95
❑103, Nov 1996 .... 1.95
❑104, Dec 1996 .... 1.95
❑105, Jan 1997 KG (w) 1.95
❑106, Feb 1997 .... 1.95
❑107, Mar 1997 .... 1.95
❑108, Apr 1997 .... 1.95
❑109, May 1997 V: Spiral. 1.95
❑110, Jun 1997 .... 1.99
❑111, Aug 1997; gatefold summary 1.99
❑112, Sep 1997; gatefold summary 1.99
❑113, Oct 1997; gatefold summary A: High Evolutionary. 1.99
❑114, Nov 1997; gatefold summary 1.99
❑115, Dec 1997; gatefold summary 1.99
❑116, Jan 1998; gatefold summary 1.99
❑117, Feb 1998; gatefold summary 1.99
❑118, Mar 1998; gatefold summary 1.99
❑119, Apr 1998; gatefold summary V: Nightmare. 1.99
❑120, May 1998; gatefold summary 1.99
❑121, Jun 1998; gatefold summary 1.99
❑122, Jul 1998; gatefold summary V: Prime Sentinels. 1.99
❑123, Aug 1998; gatefold summary V: Mimic. 1.99
❑124, Sep 1998; gatefold summary; Captain Britain's bachelor party 1.99
❑125, Oct 1998; Giant-size; Wedding of Captain Britain, Meggan 3.00
❑Annual 1, ca. 1993; 1: Ghath. trading card 2.95
❑Annual 2, ca. 1994; 1994 Annual; ca. 1994 .... 2.95

EXCALIBUR (MINI-SERIES)

MARVEL

❑1, Feb 2001 .... 2.99
❑2, Mar 2001 .... 2.99
❑3, Apr 2001 .... 2.99

EXCALIBUR (2ND SERIES)

MARVEL

❑1, Jul 2004 .... 2.99
❑2, Aug 2004 .... 2.99
❑3, Sep 2004

EXCALIBUR: AIR APPARENT

MARVEL

❑1, Dec 1991; Air Apparent Special Edition 4.95

EXCALIBUR: MOJO MAYHEM

MARVEL

❑1, Dec 1989 .... 4.50

EXCALIBUR: SWORD OF POWER

MARVEL

❑1, Feb 2002 .... 2.99
❑2, Mar 2002 .... 2.99
❑3, Apr 2002 .... 2.99
❑4, May 2002 .... 2.99

EXCALIBUR: THE POSSESSION

MARVEL

❑1, Jul 1991 .... 2.95

N-MINT

EXCALIBUR: THE SWORD IS DRAWN

MARVEL

❑1, ca. 1987; prestige format O: Excalibur. 1: Excalibur. 4.00
❑1-2 1: Excalibur. 3.50
❑1-3 1: Excalibur. 3.50

EXCALIBUR: WEIRD WAR III

MARVEL

❑1, Dec 1990 .... 9.95

EXCALIBUR: XX CROSSING

MARVEL

❑1, May 1992; indicia says May, cover says Jul 2.50

EXCITING X-PATROL

MARVEL / AMALGAM

❑1, Jun 1997 .... 1.95

EXEC, THE

COMICS CONSPIRACY

❑1, Feb 2001, Several characters in profile on cover 3.95

EXHIBITIONIST, THE

FANTAGRAPHICS / EROS

❑1 .... 2.75
❑2, Aug 1994 .... 2.75

EXILE

EYEBALL SOUP DESIGNS

❑1, May 1996, b&w; cardstock cover 2.95
❑2, Jul 1996, b&w; cardstock cover 2.95

EXILED, THE

EXILED

❑1, Jan 1998 .... 2.75
❑2, Apr 1998 .... 2.75
❑3, Jun 1998; cover says 98, indicia says 97 .... 2.75

EXILE EARTH

RIVER CITY

❑1, ca. 1994 .... 1.95
❑2, ca. 1994 .... 1.95

EXILES (MALIBU)

MALIBU

❑1, Aug 1993, b&w 1: The Exiles. 2.00
❑1/Variant, Aug 1993, b&w; 1: The Exiles. Hologram cover 5.00
❑2, Sep 1993 .... 2.00
❑3, Oct 1993; Rune 2.50
❑4, Nov 1993 D: Exiles. 2.00

EXILES (MARVEL)

MARVEL

❑1, Aug 2001 .... 2.99
❑2, Sep 2001 .... 2.25
❑3, Oct 2001 .... 2.25
❑4, Nov 2001 .... 2.25
❑5, Dec 2001 .... 2.25
❑6, Jan 2002 .... 2.25
❑7, Feb 2002 .... 2.25
❑8, Mar 2002 .... 2.25
❑9, Apr 2002 .... 2.25
❑10, Apr 2002 .... 2.25
❑11, May 2002 .... 2.25
❑12, Jun 2002 .... 2.25
❑13, Jul 2002 .... 2.25
❑14, Aug 2002 .... 2.25
❑15, Sep 2002 .... 2.25
❑16, Oct 2002 .... 2.25
❑17, Nov 2002 .... 2.25
❑18, Dec 2002 .... 2.25
❑19, Jan 2003 .... 2.25
❑20, Feb 2003 .... 2.25
❑21, Mar 2003 .... 2.25
❑22, Apr 2003 .... 2.25
❑23, May 2003 .... 2.25
❑24, Jun 2003 .... 2.25
❑25, Jun 2003 .... 2.99
❑26, Jul 2003 .... 2.99
❑27, Jul 2003 .... 2.99
❑28, Aug 2003 .... 2.99
❑29, Sep 2003 .... 2.99
❑30, Sep 2003 .... 2.99
❑31, Oct 2003; Avengers turned into vampires 2.99

Condition price index: Multiply "NM prices" above by: **0.83 for Very Fine/Near Mint**
0.66 for Very Fine • 0.33 for Fine • 0.2 for Very Good • 0.125 for Good

N-MINT

❑32, Oct 2003 .... 2.99
❑33, Nov 2003 .... 2.99
❑34, Nov 2003 .... 2.99
❑35, Dec 2003 .... 2.99
❑36, Dec 2003 .... 2.99
❑37, Jan 2004 .... 2.99
❑38, Feb 2004 .... 2.99
❑39, Feb 2004 .... 2.99
❑40, Mar 2004 .... 2.99
❑41, Apr 2004 .... 2.99
❑42, May 2004 .... 2.99
❑43, May 2004 .... 2.99
❑44, May 2004 .... 2.99
❑45, Jun 2004 .... 2.99
❑46, Jul 2004 .... 2.99
❑47, Jul 2004 .... 2.99
❑48, Aug 2004 .... 2.99
❑49, Sep 2004 ....

EXILES (ALPHA)
ALPHA PRODUCTIONS

❑1, b&w 1.95

EXIT (VOL. 2)
CALIBER

❑1 .... 2.95
❑2 .... 2.95
❑3 .... 2.95
❑4 .... 2.95
❑5 .... 2.95

EXIT 6
PLASTIC SPOON

❑1, Aug 1998, b&w 2.95
❑2/Ashcan, Aug 1998; preview of upcoming issue 2.95
❑3, Jan 1999 .... 2.95
❑3/Ashcan, Aug 1998; preview of upcoming issue 2.95

EXIT FROM SHADOW
BRONZE MAN

❑4; indicia has name change, cover doesn't; was Secret Killers 2.95

EX-LIBRIS EROTICIS
NBM

❑1 .... 9.95

EX MACHINA
DC

❑1, Aug 2004 .... 2.95
❑2, Sep 2004 ....

EX-MUTANTS (AMAZING)
PIED PIPER / AMAZING

❑1 .... 2.00
❑2 .... 2.00
❑3 .... 2.00
❑4 .... 2.00
❑5 A: New Humans. 2.00
❑6, Jul 1987 .... 2.00
❑7 .... 2.00
❑8 .... 2.00
❑Special 1, Spr 1987, b&w 2.00

EX-MUTANTS (ETERNITY)
ETERNITY

❑1, ca. 1986 .... 2.00
❑2 .... 2.00
❑3 .... 2.00
❑4, Oct 1988 RL (c) 2.00
❑5 1988 .... 2.00
❑6 1988 .... 2.00
❑7 1988 .... 2.00
❑8, Jan 1989 .... 2.00
❑9, Feb 1989 .... 2.00
❑10 .... 2.00
❑11 .... 2.00
❑12 .... 2.00
❑13 .... 2.00
❑14 .... 2.00
❑15 .... 1.95
❑Annual 1, Mar 1998 .... 1.95

N-MINT

EX-MUTANTS (MALIBU)
MALIBU

❑1, Nov 1992 O: Ex-Mutants. 2.00
❑1/Variant, Nov 1992; O: Ex-Mutants. shiny cover 2.50
❑2, Dec 1992 .... 1.95
❑3, Jan 1993 .... 1.95
❑4, Feb 1993 .... 1.95
❑5, Mar 1993 .... 1.95
❑6, Apr 1993 .... 1.95
❑7, May 1993 .... 1.95
❑8, Jun 1993 .... 1.95
❑9, Jul 1993 .... 1.95
❑10, Aug 1993 .... 1.95
❑11, Sep 1993; Crossover with Dinosaurs for Hire and Protectors 1.95
❑12, Oct 1993; Crossover with Dinosaurs for Hire and Protectors 2.25
❑13, Nov 1993; Genesis begins publishing 2.25
❑14, Dec 1993; Genesis 2.25
❑15, Jan 1994; Genesis 2.25
❑16, Feb 1994; Genesis 2.25
❑17, Mar 1994; Genesis 2.50
❑18, Apr 1994; Genesis 2.50

EX-MUTANTS MICROSERIES: ERIN (LAWRENCE & LIM'S...)
PIED PIPER

❑1, b&w 1.95

EX-MUTANTS PIN-UP BOOK
ETERNITY

❑1 .... 1.95

EXODUS REVELATION
EXODUS

❑1, Nov 1994, b&w; no cover price 1.00

EXOSQUAD
TOPPS

❑0, Jan 1994; cardstock cover 1.00

EXOTICA
CRY FOR DAWN

❑1, b&w 4.00
❑2, Nov 1993 .... 3.00

EXOTIC FANTASY
FANTAGRAPHICS / EROS

❑1, b&w; sketches 4.95
❑2, b&w; sketches 4.95
❑3, b&w; sketches 4.95

EXPERIENCE, THE
AIRCEL

❑1, b&w 3.25

EXPLORERS
EXPLORER

❑1, ca. 1996, b&w 2.95
❑2, ca. 1996, b&w 2.95
❑3, ca. 1996, b&w 2.95

EXPLORERS OF THE UNKNOWN
ARCHIE

❑1, Jun 1990 .... 1.00
❑2, Aug 1990 .... 1.00
❑3, Oct 1990 .... 1.00
❑4, Dec 1990 .... 1.00
❑5, Feb 1991 .... 1.00
❑6, Apr 1991 .... 1.00

EXPLORERS (VOL. 2)
CALIBER / TAPESTRY

❑1, ca. 1996, b&w 2.95
❑2, ca. 1996, b&w 2.95

EXPOSE
CRACKED PEPPER

❑1, Dec 1993, b&w 2.50

EXPOSURE
IMAGE

❑1, Nov 1999 .... 2.50
❑2, Dec 1999 .... 2.50
❑2/A, Dec 1999 .... 2.50
❑3, Jan 2000 .... 2.50
❑4, Feb 2000 .... 2.50
❑5, Mar 2000 .... 3.50
❑6, Apr 2000 .... 3.50

Excalibur paid tribute to Edgar Rice Burroughs' John Carter of Mars series during its "Cross-Time Caper."
© 1989 Marvel Comics.

N-MINT

EXQUISITE CORPSE
DARK HORSE

❑1; Yellow issue 2.50
❑2; Red Issue 2.50
❑3; Green Issue 2.50

EXTINCT!
NEW ENGLAND

❑1, b&w 3.50
❑2, b&w 3.50

EXTINCTIONERS
SHANDA FANTASY ARTS

❑1, Apr 1999, b&w 2.95
❑2 .... 2.95

EXTINCTION EVENT
DC / WILDSTORM

❑1, Sep 2003 .... 2.50
❑2, Oct 2003 .... 2.50
❑3, Nov 2003 .... 2.50
❑4, Dec 2003 .... 2.50
❑5, Jan 2004 .... 2.50

EXTRA! (GEMSTONE)
GEMSTONE

❑1, Jan 2000 .... 2.50
❑2, Feb 2000 .... 2.50
❑3, Mar 2000 .... 2.50
❑4, Apr 2000 .... 2.50
❑5, May 2000 .... 2.50
❑Annual 1 .... 13.50

EXTRA TERRESTRIAL TRIO, THE
SMILING FACE

❑1, ca. 1995, b&w 2.95

EXTREME (IMAGE)
IMAGE

❑0, Aug 1993 RL (w); RL (a) 2.50
❑0/A, Aug 1993 RL (w); RL (a) 2.50
❑0/B, Aug 1993; San Diego Con edition RL (w); RL (a) 2.50
❑0/Gold, Aug 1993; Gold edition RL (w); RL (a) 3.00
❑Holiday 1; "Extreme Hero" promotional edition from Hero Magazine; RL (w); RL (a); no cover price 1.00

EXTREME (CURTIS)
CURTIS

❑1 .... 2.95

EXTREME DESTROYER EPILOGUE
IMAGE

❑1, Jan 1996 .... 2.50

EXTREME DESTROYER PROLOGUE
IMAGE

❑1, Jan 1996; bagged with card 2.50

EXTREME JUSTICE
DC

❑0, Jan 1995 .... 2.00
❑1, Feb 1995 .... 1.75
❑2, Mar 1995 .... 1.75
❑3, Apr 1995 .... 1.75
❑4, May 1995 .... 1.75
❑5, Jun 1995 .... 1.75
❑6, Jul 1995 .... 1.75
❑7, Aug 1995 .... 1.75
❑8, Sep 1995 .... 1.75
❑9, Oct 1995 1: Zan and Jayna. 1.75
❑10, Nov 1995 .... 1.75
❑11, Dec 1995 .... 1.75

N-MINT

❑12, Jan 1996 .... 1.75
❑13, Feb 1996 V: Monarch. 1.75
❑14, Mar 1996 .... 1.75
❑15, Apr 1996 .... 1.75
❑16, May 1996 .... 1.75
❑17, Jun 1996 .... 1.75
❑18, Jul 1996 .... 1.75

EXTREMELY SILLY
ANTARCTIC

❑1 .... 3.00

EXTREMELY SILLY (VOL. 2)
ANTARCTIC

❑1, Nov 1996, b&w; Star Trek parody 1.25

EXTREMELY YOUNGBLOOD
IMAGE

❑1, Sep 1996 .... 3.50

EXTREME PREJUDICE
IMAGE

❑0, Nov 1994 .... 2.50

EXTREME PREVIEWS
IMAGE

❑1, Mar 1996 .... 1.00

EXTREME PREVIEWS 1997
IMAGE

❑1; No cover price; pin-ups 1.00

EXTREME SACRIFICE
IMAGE

❑1, Jan 1995; Prelude, polybagged with trading card 2.50
❑2, Jan 1995; Epilogue 2.50

EXTREMES OF VIOLET
BLACKOUT

❑0 .... 2.95
❑1 .... 2.95
❑2, Mar 1995 .... 2.95

EXTREME SUPER CHRISTMAS SPECIAL
IMAGE

❑1, Dec 1994 .... 2.95

EXTREME SUPER TOUR BOOK
IMAGE

❑1 .... 1.00
❑1/Gold; Gold edition 2.00

EXTREME TOUR BOOK
IMAGE

❑1; no cover price 2.50
❑1/Gold; Gold edition 2.50

EXTREMIST, THE
DC / VERTIGO

❑1, Sep 1993 1: The Extremist. 2.50
❑1/Platinum, Sep 1993; Platinum edition 1: The Extremist. 4.00
❑2, Oct 1993 .... 2.50
❑3, Nov 1993 .... 2.50
❑4, Dec 1993 .... 2.50

EYE, THE
HAMSTER

❑Special 1, Jun 1999; Special edition 2.95

EYEBALL KID, THE
DARK HORSE

❑1, b&w 1: Eyeball Kid (in comic books). 2.50
❑2, b&w 2.50
❑3, b&w 2.50

EYEBEAM
ADHESIVE

❑1, b&w; strip reprints 2.50
❑2, ca. 1994, b&w; strip reprints 2.50
❑3, ca. 1994, b&w; strip reprints 2.50
❑4, b&w; strip reprints 2.50
❑5, b&w; strip reprints 2.50

EYE OF MONGOMBO
FANTAGRAPHICS

❑1, b&w 2.00
❑2, b&w 2.00
❑3, b&w 2.00
❑4, b&w 2.00
❑5, b&w 2.00

N-MINT

❑6 1991, b&w 2.00
❑7, Dec 1991, b&w 2.25

EYE OF THE BEHOLDER
NBM

❑1 .... 10.95

EYE OF THE STORM
RIVAL

❑1, Dec 1994 .... 2.95

EYE OF THE STORM ANNUAL
DC / WILDSTORM

❑1, Sep 2003 .... 4.95

F

FAANS
SIX HANDED

❑1, b&w 2.95

FABLES
DC / VERTIGO

❑1, Jul 2002 .... 3.50
❑2, Aug 2002 .... 3.00
❑3, Sep 2002 .... 3.00
❑4, Oct 2002 .... 2.75
❑5, Nov 2002 .... 2.50
❑6, Dec 2002 .... 2.50
❑6/RRP, Dec 2002; Retailer Representative Program variant 15.00
❑7, Jan 2003 .... 2.50
❑8, Feb 2003 .... 2.50
❑9, Mar 2003 .... 2.50
❑10, Apr 2003 .... 2.50
❑11, May 2003 .... 2.50
❑12, Jun 2003 .... 2.50
❑13, Jul 2003 .... 2.50
❑14, Aug 2003 .... 2.50
❑15, Sep 2003 .... 2.50
❑16, Oct 2003 .... 2.50
❑17, Nov 2003 .... 2.50
❑18, Dec 2003 .... 2.50
❑19, Jan 2004 .... 2.50
❑20, Feb 2004 .... 2.50
❑21, Mar 2004 .... 2.50
❑22, Apr 2004 .... 2.50
❑23, May 2004 .... 2.50
❑24, Jun 2004 .... 2.50
❑25, Jul 2004 .... 2.50
❑26, Aug 2004 .... 2.50
❑27, Sep 2004 ....

FABLES BY THE BROTHERS DIMM
DIMM

❑1, Apr 1995, b&w 1.50

FABLES: LAST CASTLE
DC / VERTIGO

❑1, ca. 2003 .... 5.00

FABULOUS FURRY FREAK BROTHERS, THE
RIP OFF

❑0; 1985 Compilation 2.95
❑1, b&w; Collected Adventures of the...; 1971 .... 55.00
❑1-2; Collected Adventures of the...; 1980 .... 2.95
❑1-3 2002, Collected Adventures of the... .... 3.95
❑2, b&w; Further Adventures of the... .... 35.00
❑2-2; Further Adventures of the...; 1989 .... 2.95
❑3, b&w; A Year Passes Like Nothing With... .... 15.00
❑4, ca. 1975, b&w; Brother Can You Spare 75¢ For... .... 13.00
❑5, ca. 1977, b&w; Fabulous Furry Freak Brothers 10.00
❑6, b&w; Six Snappy Sockeroos From the Archives Of... .... 4.00
❑7, b&w 2.00
❑8 .... 2.00
❑9 .... 2.00
❑10 .... 2.00
❑11 .... 2.95

N-MINT

❑12, b&w 2.95
❑13, b&w; reprints stories from High Times 2.95

FACE (PARADOX)
DC / VERTIGO

❑1, Jan 1995 .... 4.95

FACTION PARADOX
IMAGE

❑1, Aug 2003 .... 2.95
❑2, Nov 2003 .... 3.50

FACTOR-X
MARVEL

❑1, Mar 1995; AM (a); Age of Apocalypse 2.00
❑2, Apr 1995 .... 2.00
❑3, May 1995 .... 2.00
❑4, Jun 1995 .... 2.00

FACULTY FUNNIES
ARCHIE

❑1, Jun 1989 .... 4.00
❑2, Sep 1989 .... 2.50
❑3, Dec 1989 .... 2.50
❑4, Mar 1990 .... 2.50
❑5, May 1990 .... 2.50

FAERIE CODEX
RAVEN

❑1, b&w 2.95
❑2, b&w 2.95
❑3, Dec 1997, b&w 2.95

FAFHRD AND THE GRAY MOUSER
MARVEL / EPIC

❑1, Oct 1990 .... 4.50
❑2 .... 4.50
❑3 .... 4.50
❑4 .... 4.50

FAILED UNIVERSE
BLACKTHORNE

❑1, Dec 1986 .... 1.75

FAIRY TALES OF THE BROTHERS GRIMM
NBM

❑1 .... 15.95

FAITH (LIGHTNING)
LIGHTNING

❑1/A, Jul 1997, b&w 2.95

FAITH
DC / VERTIGO

❑1, Nov 1999 .... 2.50
❑2, Dec 1999 .... 2.50
❑3, Jan 2000 .... 2.50
❑4, Feb 2000 .... 2.50
❑5, Mar 2000 .... 2.50

FAITH: A FABLE
CARBON-BASED BOOKS

❑1, Jan 2000, b&w; Trade Paperback; smaller than normal comic book ... 8.95

FAKE
TOKYOPOP

❑1, May 2003, b&w; printed in Japanese format 9.99

FALCON
MARVEL

❑1, Nov 1983 PS (a) 2.00
❑2, Dec 1983 PS (c); PS (a) 2.00
❑3, Jan 1984 .... 2.00
❑4, Feb 1984 .... 2.00

FALL, THE (BIG BAD WORLD)
BIG BAD WORLD

❑1, b&w 3.00

FALL, THE (CALIBER)
CALIBER

❑1, b&w 2.95

FALLEN, THE
NBM

❑1 .... 8.95

N-MINT

FALLEN ANGEL
DC

❑1, Sep 2003 PD (w) 2.50
❑2, Oct 2003 PD (w) 2.50
❑3, Nov 2003 PD (w) 2.50
❑4, Dec 2003 PD (w) 2.50
❑5, Jan 2004 PD (w) 2.50
❑6, Feb 2004 PD (w) 2.50
❑7, Mar 2004 PD (w) 2.50
❑8, Apr 2004 2.50
❑9, May 2004 PD (w) 2.50
❑10, Jun 2004 2.50
❑11, Jul 2004 2.95
❑12, Aug 2004 2.95
❑13, Sep 2004

FALLEN ANGEL ON THE WORLD OF MAGIC: THE GATHERING
ACCLAIM / ARMADA

❑1, May 1996; prestige format; polybagged with Fallen Angel card 5.95

FALLEN ANGELS
MARVEL

❑1, Apr 1987 2.00
❑2, May 1987 1.50
❑3, Jun 1987 1: Chance II. 1.50
❑4, Jul 1987 1.50
❑5, Aug 1987 D: Don. 1.50
❑6, Sep 1987 1.50
❑7, Oct 1987 1.50
❑8, Nov 1987 1.50

FALLEN EMPIRES ON THE WORLD OF MAGIC: THE GATHERING
ACCLAIM / ARMADA

❑1, Sep 1995; polybagged with pack of Fallen Empires cards 2.75
❑2, Oct 1995; polybagged with sheet of creature tokens 2.75

FALLING MAN, THE
IMAGE

❑1, Feb 1998, b&w 2.95

FALLOUT 3000 (MIKE DEODATO'S...)
CALIBER

❑1 2.95

FALLS THE GOTHAM RAIN
COMICO

❑1 4.95

FAMILY AFFAIR
GOLD KEY

❑1, Jan 1970 24.00
❑2, Apr 1970 20.00
❑3, Jul 1970 14.00
❑4, Oct 1970 14.00

FAMILY MAN
DC / PARADOX

❑1, b&w; digest 4.95
❑2, b&w; digest 4.95
❑3, b&w; digest 4.95

FAMOUS FEATURES (JERRY IGER'S...)
PACIFIC

❑1, Jul 1984; Flamingo 2.50

FAMOUS FIRST EDITION
DC

❑4, Nov 1974; really F-4; reprints Whiz Comics #2 13.00
❑5, Jan 1975; really F-5; reprints Batman #1 10.00
❑6, May 1975; really F-6; reprints Wonder Woman #1 10.00
❑7, Jul 1975; really F-7; reprints All-Star #3 12.00
❑8, Sep 1975; really F-8; reprints Flash Comics #1 9.00
❑26; 1: Superman. really C-26; reprints Action Comics #1 9.00
❑28; really C-28; reprints Detective Comics #1; reprints Detective Comics #27 9.00

N-MINT

❑30; 1: Wonder Woman. really C-30; reprints Sensation Comics #1 9.00
❑61, Mar 1979; really C-61; reprints Superman #1 9.00

FANA
COMAX

❑1, b&w 2.95

FANA THE JUNGLE GIRL
COMAX

❑1, b&w 2.95

FANBOY
DC

❑1, Mar 1999 2.50
❑2, Apr 1999 2.50
❑3, May 1999 2.50
❑4, Jun 1999; Our Army at War take-off 2.50
❑5, Jul 1999 2.50
❑6, Aug 1999 2.50

FANDOM CONFIDENTIAL
KITCHEN SINK

❑1 2.95

FANG (SIRIUS)
SIRIUS ENTERTAINMENT

❑1, Feb 1995 2.95
❑2, Apr 1995 2.95
❑3, Jun 1995 2.95

FANG (CONQUEST)
CONQUEST

❑1, b&w 2.95

FANG (TANGRAM)
TANGRAM

❑1, b&w 2.95

FANG: TESTAMENT
SIRIUS ENTERTAINMENT

❑1 2.50
❑2 2.50
❑3 2.50
❑4 2.50

FANGRAPHIX
FANGRAPHIX

❑1 1.95
❑2 1.95
❑3 1.95

FANGS OF THE COBRA
MYTHIC

❑1, Win 1996; color and b&w 2.95

FANNY
FANNY

❑1 3.00
❑2 3.00
❑3, b&w 3.95

FANNY HILL
SHUNGA

❑1, b&w 2.50

FANTAESCAPE
ZINZINNATI

❑1, Jun 1988 1.75

FANTAGOR
LAST GASP

❑1 3.00
❑2 3.00
❑3 3.00

FANTASCI
APPLE

❑1, b&w 2.00
❑2, b&w 2.00
❑3, b&w; Apple Comics publisher Begins 2.00
❑4 2.00
❑5 1.75
❑6 1.75
❑7 1.75
❑8, Jul 1988 1.75
❑9 1.95

FANTASTIC ADVENTURES (ACE)
ACE

❑1, Mar 1987 1.75

DC's oversized *Famous First Editions* reprinted key DC comics from the Golden Age.

© 1975 National Periodical Publications Inc. (DC).

N-MINT

❑2, Jun 1987 1.75
❑3, Oct 1987 1.75

FANTASTIC FABLES (BASIL WOLVERTON'S...)
DARK HORSE

❑1, Oct 1993, b&w 2.50
❑2 2.50

FANTASTIC FANZINE
ARROW

❑1 1.50
❑2 1.50
❑3 1.50

FANTASTIC FIVE
MARVEL

❑1, Oct 1999 1.99
❑2, Nov 1999 1.99
❑2/A, Nov 1999; variant cover 1.99
❑3, Dec 1999 1.99

FANTASTIC FORCE
MARVEL

❑1, Nov 1994; O: Fantastic Force. 1: Fantastic Force. foil cover 2.50
❑2, Dec 1994 2.00
❑3, Jan 1995 2.00
❑4, Feb 1995 1.75
❑5, Mar 1995 1.75
❑6, Apr 1995 1.75
❑7, May 1995 1.75
❑8, Jun 1995 1.75
❑9, Jul 1995 1.75
❑10, Aug 1995 1.75
❑11, Sep 1995 1.75
❑12, Oct 1995 1.75
❑13, Nov 1995; She-Hulk joins team 1.75
❑14, Dec 1995 A: She-Hulk. A: Black Panther. A: Human Torch. A: Wakanda. 1.75
❑15, Jan 1996; Team disbands; cover says Jan 95, indicia says Jan 96 1.75
❑16, Feb 1996 1.75
❑17, Mar 1996 1.75
❑18, Apr 1996 1.75

FANTASTIC FOUR (VOL. 1)
MARVEL

❑1, Nov 1961; JK, SL (w); JK (a); O: Fantastic Four, Mole Man. 1: Fantastic Four, Mole Man. 16000.00
❑1/Golden Record, JK, SL (w); JK (a); Golden Record reprint 100.00
❑2, Jan 1962, JK, SL (w); JK (a); O: The Fantastic Four. 1: The Skrulls. 3400.00
❑3, Mar 1962, JK, SL (w); JK (a); 1: Fantasti-Copter. 1: The Miracle Man (Marvel). 1: Fantasti-Car. 1: Pogo Plane. 1: Baxter Building. Fantastic Four wear uniforms for first time 2350.00
❑4, May 1962, JK, SL (w); JK (a); 1: Sub-Mariner (in Silver Age). 1: Giganto. D: Giganto. 2500.00
❑5, Jul 1962, JK, SL (w); JK (a); O: Doctor Doom. 1: Doctor Doom. 3250.00
❑6, Sep 1962, JK, SL (w); JK (a); 1: The Yancy Street Gang (name only). A: Doctor Doom. Doctor Doom & Sub-Mariner vs. Fantastic Four 1500.00
❑7, Oct 1962, JK, SL (w); JK (a); 1: Kurrgo. 1: The Xantha. 775.00
❑8, Nov 1962, JK, SL (w); JK (a); 1: Puppet Master. 1: Alicia Masters. 765.00

N-MINT

❑9, Dec 1962, JK, SL (w); JK (a); A: Sub-Mariner. 740.00
❑10, Jan 1963, JK, SL (w); JK (a); 1: The Ovoids. 1: Jack Kirby (as character in story). 1: Stan Lee (as character in story). A: Doctor Doom. V: Doctor Doom. 740.00
❑11, Feb 1963 JK, SL (w); JK (a); O: Fantastic Four. O: Impossible Man. 1: Willie Lumpkin (Fantastic Four's mailman)-Silver Age. 1: Impossible Man. 1: The Popuppians. 565.00
❑12, Mar 1963; JK, SL (w); JK (a); 1: The Wrecker I (Dr. Karl Kort). V: Hulk. Thing fights Hulk for 1st time 1125.00
❑13, Apr 1963 JK, SL (w); JK (a); O: Red Ghost. 1: Red Ghost. 1: The Watcher. 460.00
❑14, May 1963 JK, SL (w); JK (a); A: Sub-Mariner. V: Puppet Master. V: Sub-Mariner. 310.00
❑15, Jun 1963 JK, SL (w); JK (a); 1: Awesome Android. 1: Mad Thinker. 310.00
❑16, Jul 1963 JK (a); A: Ant Man. A: Doctor Doom. A: The Wasp. V: Doctor Doom. 310.00
❑17, Aug 1963 JK (a); A: Ant Man. A: Doctor Doom. V: Doctor Doom. 310.00
❑18, Sep 1963; JK (a); O: Super-Skrull. 1: Super-Skrull. 310.00
❑19, Oct 1963 JK (a); O: Rama-Tut. 1: Rama-Tut. 310.00
❑20, Nov 1963; JK (a); O: Molecule Man. 1: Molecule Man. A: Watcher. 310.00
❑21, Dec 1963 JK (a); O: Hate-Monger. 1: Hate-Monger. A: Nick Fury. 210.00
❑22, Jan 1964 JK (a); V: Mole Man. 150.00
❑23, Feb 1964 JK (a); A: Doctor Doom. V: Doctor Doom. 150.00
❑24, Mar 1964 JK (a); 1: Moloids. 150.00
❑25, Apr 1964; JK (a); A: Rick Jones. A: Avengers. V: Hulk. first mention of Thing's Aunt Petunia; Hulk Battles Thing 375.00
❑26, May 1964 JK (a); A: Rick Jones. A: Avengers. V: Hulk. 375.00
❑27, Jun 1964 JK (a); A: Doctor Strange. V: Sub-Mariner. 150.00
❑28, Jul 1964 JK (a); A: X-Men. V: Puppet Master. V: Mad Thinker. 180.00
❑29, Aug 1964 JK (a); A: Watcher. V: Red Ghost. 100.00
❑30, Sep 1964 JK (a); O: Diablo. 1: Diablo. 100.00
❑31, Oct 1964 JK (a); A: Avengers. V: Mole Man. 100.00
❑32, Nov 1964 JK (a); 1: Sue and Johnny's parents (Franklin and Mary). V: Super-Skrull. 100.00
❑33, Dec 1964; JK (a); 1: Attuma. A: Sub-Mariner. 100.00
❑34, Jan 1965 JK (a); 1: Thomas Gideon (later becomes Glorian). 100.00
❑35, Feb 1965 JK (a); O: Dragon Man. 1: Dragon Man. V: Diablo. 100.00
❑36, Mar 1965; JK (a); O: Frightful Four. 1: Frightful Four. 1: Medusa. 100.00
❑37, Apr 1965 JK (a) 100.00
❑38, May 1965; JK (a); 1: Trapster I (Peter Petruski). A: Frightful Four. Paste-Pot Pete becomes Trapster I 100.00
❑39, Jun 1965; JK (a); A: Daredevil. A: Doctor Doom. V: Doctor Doom. 100.00
❑40, Jul 1965 JK (a); A: Daredevil. V: Doctor Doom. 100.00
❑41, Aug 1965 JK (a); V: Frightful Four. 80.00
❑42, Sep 1965 JK (a); V: Frightful Four. 80.00
❑43, Oct 1965 JK (a); V: Frightful Four. V: Doctor Doom. 80.00
❑44, Nov 1965 SL (w); JK (a); 1: Gorgon. A: Dragon Man. A: Medusa. 80.00
❑45, Dec 1965 JK (a); 1: Karnak. 1: Inhumans. 1: Crystal. 1: Triton. 1: Lockjaw. 1: Black Bolt. A: Trapster I. A: Sandman. V: Maximus. V: Dragon Man. 100.00
❑46, Jan 1966 JK, SL (w); JK (a); A: Inhumans. 90.00
❑47, Feb 1966 JK, SL (w); JK (a); 1: Maximus. A: Inhumans. V: Maximus. 80.00

N-MINT

❑48, Mar 1966; JK, SL (w); JK (a); 1: Galactus. 1: Silver Surfer. A: Inhumans. 750.00
❑49, Apr 1966; JK, SL (w); JK (a); A: Galactus. A: Silver Surfer. A: Watcher. V: Galactus. 250.00
❑50, May 1966; JK, SL (w); JK (a); 1: Wyatt Wingfoot. A: Galactus. A: Silver Surfer. A: Watcher. V: Galactus. Galactus 265.00
❑51, Jun 1966 JK, SL (w); JK (a); 1: Negative Zone. 50.00
❑52, Jul 1966 JK, SL (w); JK (a); 1: Black Panther. 150.00
❑53, Aug 1966; JK, SL (w); JK (a); O: Black Panther. O: Klaw. 1: Klaw. 120.00
❑54, Sep 1966 JK, SL (w); JK (a); O: Prester John. 1: Prester John. A: Inhumans. A: Black Panther. 80.00
❑55, Oct 1966; JK, SL (w); JK, JSt (a); A: Silver Surfer. Thing vs. Silver Surfer 150.00
❑56, Nov 1966 JK, SL (w); JK (a); O: Klaw. V: Klaw. 80.00
❑57, Dec 1966 JK, SL (w); JK, JSt (a); A: Inhumans. A: Doctor Doom. V: Doctor Doom. V: Wizard. V: Sandman. 80.00
❑58, Jan 1967 JK, SL (w); JK, JSt (a); A: Doctor Doom. A: Lockjaw. A: Silver Surfer. V: Doctor Doom. 80.00
❑59, Feb 1967 JK, SL (w); JK, JSt (a); A: Inhumans. A: Silver Surfer. V: Doctor Doom. 60.00
❑60, Mar 1967 JK, SL (w); JK, JSt (a); A: Inhumans. A: Black Panther. A: Doctor Doom. A: Silver Surfer. A: Watcher. V: Doctor Doom. 60.00
❑61, Apr 1967 JK, SL (w); JK (a); A: Inhumans. A: Silver Surfer. V: Sandman. 60.00
❑62, May 1967 JK, SL (w); JK (a); 1: Blastaar. A: Sandman. 60.00
❑63, Jun 1967 JK, SL (w); JK (a); V: Blastaar. V: Sandman. 60.00
❑64, Jul 1967 JK, SL (w); JK (a); 1: Supreme Intelligence. 60.00
❑65, Aug 1967 JK, SL (w); JK (a); 1: Kree. 1: Kree Supreme Intelligence. 1: Ronan the Accuser. 60.00
❑66, Sep 1967; JK, SL (w); JK (a); O: The Enclave. O: Him (later Warlock). 1: Him (later Warlock). 1: The Enclave (unnamed). A: Crystal. 90.00
❑66-2, Sep 1967; JK (a); 1: Him (later Warlock); 1: The Enclave (unnamed) 2.00
❑67, Oct 1967; JK, SL (w); JK (a); O: Him (later Warlock). A: Him (later Warlock). 90.00
❑67-2, Oct 1967 JK (a) 2.00
❑68, Nov 1967 JK, SL (w); JK (a); V: Mad Thinker. 50.00
❑69, Dec 1967 JK, SL (w); JK (a); V: Mad Thinker. 50.00
❑70, Jan 1968 JK, SL (w); JK (a); V: Mad Thinker. 50.00
❑71, Feb 1968 JK, SL (w); JK (a); V: Mad Thinker. 45.00
❑72, Mar 1968 JK, SL (w); JK (a); A: Silver Surfer. 75.00
❑73, Apr 1968 JK, SL (w); JK (a); A: Daredevil. A: Spider-Man. A: Thor. V: Doctor Doom. 75.00
❑74, May 1968 JK, SL (w); JK (a); A: Galactus. A: Silver Surfer. V: Galactus. 75.00
❑75, Jun 1968 JK, SL (w); JK (a); A: Galactus. A: Silver Surfer. V: Galactus. 42.00
❑76, Jul 1968 JK, SL (w); JK (a); A: Silver Surfer. V: Galactus. V: Psycho-Man. 42.00
❑77, Aug 1968 JK, SL (w); JK (a); A: Silver Surfer. V: Galactus. V: Psycho-Man. 42.00
❑78, Sep 1968 JK, SL (w); JK (a); V: Wizard. 42.00
❑79, Oct 1968 JK, SL (w); JK (a); V: Mad Thinker. 42.00
❑80, Nov 1968 JK, SL (w); JK (a) 42.00

N-MINT

❑81, Dec 1968; JK, SL (w); JK (a); V: Wizard. Crystal joins Fantastic Four 35.00
❑82, Jan 1969 JK, SL (w); JK (a); A: Inhumans. V: Maximus. 35.00
❑83, Feb 1969 JK, SL (w); JK (a); A: Inhumans. V: Maximus. 35.00
❑84, Mar 1969 JK, SL (w); JK (a); A: Doctor Doom. V: Doctor Doom. 35.00
❑85, Apr 1969 JK, SL (w); JK (a); A: Doctor Doom. V: Doctor Doom. 35.00
❑86, May 1969 JK, SL (w); JK (a); A: Doctor Doom. V: Doctor Doom. 35.00
❑87, Jun 1969 JK, SL (w); JK (a); A: Doctor Doom. V: Doctor Doom. 35.00
❑88, Jul 1969 JK, SL (w); JK (a); V: Mole Man. 35.00
❑89, Aug 1969 JK, SL (w); JK (a); V: Mole Man. 27.00
❑90, Sep 1969 JK, SL (w); JK (a); V: Mole Man. 27.00
❑91, Oct 1969 JK, SL (w); JK (a); 1: Torgo. 27.00
❑92, Nov 1969 JK, SL (w); JK (a); 2: Torgo. V: Torgo. 27.00
❑93, Dec 1969 JK, SL (w); JK (a); A: Torgo. V: Torgo. 27.00
❑94, Jan 1970 JK, SL (w); JK (a); 1: Agatha Harkness. V: Trapster. V: Wizard. V: Sandman. 27.00
❑95, Feb 1970 JK, SL (w); JK (a); 1: The Monocle. 27.00
❑96, Mar 1970 JK, SL (w); JK (a); V: Mad Thinker. 27.00
❑97, Apr 1970 JK, SL (w); JK (a) 27.00
❑98, May 1970 JK, SL (w); JK (a); A: Neil Armstrong. 27.00
❑99, Jun 1970 JK, SL (w); JK (a); A: Inhumans. 27.00
❑100, Jul 1970; anniversary; JK, SL (w); JK (a); V: Lots of villains. Doctor Doom, Sandman, Sub-Mariner, others appear 60.00
❑101, Aug 1970 JK, SL (w); JK (a); 1: Gimlet. 1: Top Man. 27.00
❑102, Sep 1970 JR (c); JK, SL (w); JK (a); A: Magneto. A: Sub-Mariner. V: Magneto. 27.00
❑103, Oct 1970 JR, SL (w); JR (a); 2: Agatha Harkness. A: Richard M. Nixon. A: Magneto. A: Sub-Mariner. V: Magneto. 27.00
❑104, Nov 1970 SL (w); JR (a); A: Richard M. Nixon. A: Magneto. A: Sub-Mariner. V: Magneto. 22.00
❑105, Dec 1970 SL (w); JR (a); 1: The "monster" (Larry Rambow). 1: Dr. Phillip Zolten Rambow. 22.00
❑106, Jan 1971 JR, SL (w); JR (a); 2: The "monster" (Larry Rambow). 2: Dr. Phillip Zolten Rambow. 22.00
❑107, Feb 1971 SL (w); JB (a); 1: Janus (the scientist). 22.00
❑108, Mar 1971 JK, JR, SL (w); JB, JK (a); 2: Janus (the scientist). 22.00
❑109, Apr 1971 SL (w); JB (a); A: Captain Marvel. D: Janus (the scientist). V: Annihilus. 22.00
❑110, May 1971 SL (w); JB (a); A: Joe Robertson. A: J. Jonah Jameson. V: Annihilus. 22.00
❑111, Jun 1971 SL (w); JB (a); 1: Collins (landlord of Baxter building). A: Joe Robertson. A: Peter Parker. A: Hulk. A: J. Jonah Jameson. 22.00
❑112, Jul 1971; SL (w); JB (a); 2: Collins. A: Bruce Banner. A: Hulk. A: J. Jonah Jameson. Thing vs. Hulk 90.00
❑113, Aug 1971 SL (w); JB (a); 1: Overmind. A: Bruce Banner. A: The Watcher. 21.00
❑114, Sep 1971 SL (w); JB (a); 2: Overmind. A: The Watcher. V: Overmind. 21.00
❑115, Oct 1971 SL (w); JB (a); O: Overmind. 1: The Eternals (a.k.a. Eternians). A: The Watcher. 21.00
❑116, Nov 1971; Giant-size JB (a); O: Stranger. A: The Stranger. A: The Watcher. A: Edwin Jarvis. A: Doctor Doom. 14.00

Condition price index: Multiply "NM prices" above by: **0.83 for Very Fine/Near Mint**
0.66 for Very Fine • 0.33 for Fine • 0.2 for Very Good • 0.125 for Good

	N-MINT
❑117, Dec 1971 JB (a); 1: Chiron. 1: Asmodeus. A: Crystal. A: Diablo. A: Kaliban. V: Diablo.	14.00
❑118, Jan 1972 JB (a); 1: Reed Richards of Earth-A. 1: Ben Grimm of Earth-A. 1: Sue Storm Grimm of Earth-A. A: Crystal. A: Diablo. A: Lockjaw. V: Diablo.	14.00
❑119, Feb 1972 JB (a); A: Black Panther. A: Klaw. V: Klaw.	14.00
❑120, Mar 1972 JB, SL (w); JB (a); 1: Air-Walker (robot form). A: General T. E. "Thunderbolt" Ross. V: Air-Walker Automaton.	14.00
❑121, Apr 1972 JB, SL (w); JB (a); 2: Air-Walker (robot form). A: Galactus. A: Silver Surfer. V: Air-Walker Automaton.	30.00
❑122, May 1972 SL (w); JB (a); A: Galactus. A: Silver Surfer. V: Galactus.	30.00
❑123, Jun 1972 SL (w); JB (a); A: General Ross. A: Galactus. A: Richard M. Nixon. A: Silver Surfer. V: Galactus.	30.00
❑124, Jul 1972 SL (w); JB (a)	18.00
❑125, Aug 1972 SL (w); JB (a)	18.00
❑126, Sep 1972 JB (a); O: Fantastic Four.	18.00
❑127, Oct 1972 JB (a); V: Mole Man.	18.00
❑128, Nov 1972 JB (a); V: Tyrannus. V: Mole Man.	18.00
❑129, Dec 1972 JB (a); 1: Thundra. A: Medusa.	18.00
❑130, Jan 1973 JB (a); 2: Thundra. A: Inhumans. V: Trapster. V: Thundra. V: Wizard. V: Sandman.	12.00
❑131, Feb 1973 JB (c); RA (a); 1: Omega (the ultimate Alpha Primitive). A: Inhumans. V: Maximus.	12.00
❑132, Mar 1973; JB (a); V: Maximus. Medusa Joins	12.00
❑133, Apr 1973 JB (c); V: Trapster. V: Thundra. V: Wizard. V: Sandman.	12.00
❑134, May 1973 JB (a); V: Dragon Man.	12.00
❑135, Jun 1973 JB (a); V: Dragon Man.	12.00
❑136, Jul 1973 JB (a); V: Shaper of Worlds.	12.00
❑137, Aug 1973 JB (a); V: Shaper of Worlds.	12.00
❑138, Sep 1973 JB (a); V: Miracle Man.	12.00
❑139, Oct 1973 JB (a); V: Miracle Man.	12.00
❑140, Nov 1973 RB (c); JB (a); O: Annihilus. V: Annihilus.	12.00
❑141, Dec 1973 JR (c); JB (a); V: Annihilus.	12.00
❑142, Jan 1974 RB (a); 1: Darkoth the Death-Demon. V: Doctor Doom.	12.00
❑143, Feb 1974 GK (c); RB (a); V: Doctor Doom.	12.00
❑144, Mar 1974; RB (a); A: Doctor Doom. V: Doctor Doom. Marvel Value Stamp #39: Iron Fist	12.00
❑145, Apr 1974; GK (c); RA (a); Doctor Doom. Marvel Value Stamp #9: Captain Marvel	12.00
❑146, May 1974; GK (c); RA (a); Marvel Value Stamp #91: Hela	12.00
❑147, Jun 1974; RB (a); A: Sub-Mariner. Marvel Value Stamp #82: Mary Jane	12.00
❑148, Jul 1974 RB (a); V: Frightful Four.	12.00
❑149, Aug 1974; RB (a); Marvel Value Stamp #78: Owl	12.00
❑150, Sep 1974; GK (c); RB (a); A: Inhumans. A: Avengers. Wedding of Crystal and Quicksilver; Marvel Value Stamp #27: Black Widow	12.00
❑151, Oct 1974; RB (a); O: Thundra. 1: Mahkizmo. Marvel Value Stamp #21: Kull	9.00
❑152, Nov 1974; RB (a); Marvel Value Stamp #23: Sgt. Fury	9.00
❑153, Dec 1974; GK (c); RB (a); V: Mahkizmo. Marvel Value Stamp #62: Plunderer	9.00
❑154, Jan 1975; GK (c); partial reprint of Strange Tales #127; Marvel Value Stamp #100: Galactus	9.00
❑155, Feb 1975; RB (a); A: Silver Surfer. V: Doctor Doom. Marvel Value Stamp #16: Shang-Chi	13.00

	N-MINT
❑156, Mar 1975 RB (a); A: Doctor Doom. A: Silver Surfer. V: Doctor Doom.	13.00
❑157, Apr 1975 RB (a); A: Doctor Doom. A: Silver Surfer. V: Doctor Doom.	13.00
❑158, May 1975 RB (a); V: Xemu.	8.00
❑159, Jun 1975; RB (a); A: Inhumans. V: Xemu. Marvel Value Stamp #84: Dr. Doom	8.00
❑160, Jul 1975; GK (c); JB (a); V: Arkon. Marvel Value Stamp #32: Red Skull	8.00
❑161, Aug 1975 RB (a); A: Valeria. A: Reed Richards of Earth-A. A: Sue Grimm of Earth-A. A: Ben Grimm of Earth-A. A: Lockjaw. A: Phineas.	10.00
❑162, Sep 1975 RB (a); A: Albert E. DeVoor. A: The "Old One". A: Valeria. A: Reed Richards of Earth-A. A: Gaard (Johnny Storm of Earth-A, reconstructed). A: Arkon. A: Ben Grimm of Earth-A. A: Phineas.	10.00
❑163, Oct 1975 RB (a); A: Albert E. DeVoor. A: Reed Richards of Earth-A. A: Gaard (Johnny Storm of Earth-A, reconstructed). A: Arkon.	10.00
❑164, Nov 1975 JK (c); GP (a); 1: Crusader (a.k.a. Marvel Boy). 1: Frankie Raye.	10.00
❑165, Dec 1975 GP (a); O: Crusader (a.k.a. Marvel Boy). D: Crusader.	10.00
❑166, Jan 1976 RB (c); GP (a); A: Hulk. A: Puppet Master. V: Hulk.	10.00
❑167, Feb 1976 JK (c); GP (a); A: Hulk. A: Puppet Master. V: Hulk.	10.00
❑168, Mar 1976; RB (a); A: Wreaker. Thing replaced by Luke Cage (Power Man)	10.00
❑169, Apr 1976 RB (a); A: Luke Cage.	10.00
❑169/30 cent, Apr 1976; RB (a); A: Luke Cage. 30 cent regional price variant	20.00
❑170, May 1976 GP (a); A: Luke Cage.	10.00
❑170/30 cent, May 1976; GP (a); A: Luke Cage. 30 cent regional price variant	20.00
❑171, Jun 1976 JK (c); RB, GP (a); 1: Gorr. V: Galactus.	6.00
❑171/30 cent, Jun 1976; JK (c); RB, GP (a); 1: Gorr. V: Galactus. 30 cent regional price variant	20.00
❑172, Jul 1976 JK (c); GP (a); 2: Gorr. A: Galactus. A: The High Evolutionary. A: The Destroyer. V: Galactus.	6.00
❑172/30 cent, Jul 1976; JK (c); GP (a); 2: Gorr. A: Galactus. A: The High Evolutionary. A: The Destroyer. V: Galactus. 30 cent regional price variant	20.00
❑173, Aug 1976 JK (c); JB (a); A: Galactus. A: Gorr. A: The High Evolutionary. A: Torgo. V: Galactus.	6.00
❑173/30 cent, Aug 1976; JK (c); JB (a); A: Galactus. A: Gorr. A: The High Evolutionary. A: Torgo. V: Galactus. 30 cent regional price variant	20.00
❑174, Sep 1976 JK (c); JB (a); A: Galactus. A: Gorr. A: The High Evolutionary. A: Torgo. V: Galactus.	6.00
❑175, Oct 1976 JK (c); JB (a); A: Galactus. A: The Impossible Man. A: Gorr. A: The High Evolutionary. V: Galactus.	6.00
❑176, Nov 1976 JK (c); GP (a); A: The Impossible Man. A: Roy Thomas. A: Stan Lee. A: Jack Kirby. V: Trapster. V: Wizard. V: Sandman.	6.00
❑177, Dec 1976 JK (c); GP (a); O: Texas Twister. 1: Texas Twister. 1: Captain Ultra. A: Tigra. A: Impossible Man. V: Trapster. V: Brute. V: Wizard. V: Sandman.	6.00
❑178, Jan 1977 JR (c); GP (a); A: The Impossible Man. A: Brute. V: Trapster. V: Brute. V: Wizard. V: Sandman.	6.00
❑179, Feb 1977 AM (c); 1: Metalloid. A: Tigra. A: Thundra. A: Reed Richards of Counter-Earth. A: Impossible Man. A: Annihilus. A: Mad Thinker. V: Annihilus. V: Mad Thinker.	6.00
❑180, Mar 1977; JK (c); JK, SL (w); JK (a); reprints FF #101	6.00

John Byrne retold The Fantastic Four's origin in the team's 20th anniversary issue.
© 1981 Marvel Comics.

	N-MINT
❑181, Apr 1977 JK (c); A: Reed Richards of Counter-Earth. A: Annihilus. V: Reed Richards of Counter-Earth. V: Annihilus. V: Mad Thinker.	6.00
❑182, May 1977 V: Reed Richards of Counter-Earth. V: Annihilus. V: Mad Thinker.	6.00
❑183, Jun 1977 GP (c); SB (a); A: Tigra. A: Thundra. A: Impossible Man. A: Brute. A: Annihilus. A: Mad Thinker. V: Brute. V: Annihilus. V: Mad Thinker.	6.00
❑183/35 cent, Jun 1977; 35 cent regional price variant	15.00
❑184, Jul 1977 GP (a); A: Tigra. A: Thundra. A: Impossible Man.	6.00
❑184/35 cent, Jul 1977; 35 cent regional price variant	15.00
❑185, Aug 1977 GP (a); 1: Nicholas Scratch. 2: New Salem's Witches. A: Impossible Man.	5.00
❑185/35 cent, Aug 1977; 35 cent regional price variant	15.00
❑186, Sep 1977 GP (a); O: New Salem's Witches. 2: Nicholas Scratch. A: Impossible Man.	5.00
❑186/35 cent, Sep 1977; GP (a); O: New Salem's Witches. 2: Nicholas Scratch. A: Impossible Man. 35 cent regional price variant	15.00
❑187, Oct 1977 GP (a); A: Molecule Man. A: Klaw. A: Impossible Man. V: Molecule Man. V: Klaw.	5.00
❑188, Nov 1977 GP (a); A: The Watcher. A: Molecule Man. A: Impossible Man. V: Molecule Man. V: Klaw.	5.00
❑189, Dec 1977; KP (c); JK, SL (w); JK (a); reprints FF Annual #4	5.00
❑190, Jan 1978; JK (c); SB (a); Thing recounts FF's career	5.00
❑191, Feb 1978; GP (a); A: Plunderer. A: Thundra. V: Plunderer. Fantastic Four resign	5.00
❑192, Mar 1978 GP (a); A: Texas Twister.	5.00
❑193, Apr 1978 KP (w); KP (a); O: Darketh the Death-Demon. 1: Victor Von Doom II (not face). A: Diablo. A: Impossible Man. V: Diablo.	5.00
❑194, May 1978 GP (c); KP (w); KP (a); A: Darketh. A: Diablo. A: Impossible Man. A: Sub-Mariner. V: Diablo.	5.00
❑195, Jun 1978 GP (c); KP (a); 2: Victor Von Doom II (not face). A: Lord Vashti. A: Impossible Man. A: Sub-Mariner.	5.00
❑196, Jul 1978; GP (c); KP (a); A: Victor Von Doom II. A: Doctor Doom.	5.00
❑197, Aug 1978; GP (c); KP (a); A: Red Ghost. A: Victor Von Doom II. A: Dr. Doom. A: Nick Fury. V: Red Ghost. V: Doctor Doom. Reed Richards gets powers back	5.00
❑198, Sep 1978; JB (c); KP (a); A: Prince Zorba. A: Victor Von Doom II. A: Doctor Doom. V: Doctor Doom. Team gets together to fight Doctor Doom	5.00
❑199, Oct 1978 KP (a); O: Victor Von Doom II. A: Prince Zorba. A: Doctor Doom. D: Victor Von Doom II.	5.00
❑200, Nov 1978; KP (a); A: Doctor Doom. V: Doctor Doom. Prince Zorba	5.00
❑201, Dec 1978 KP (a); A: Prince Zorba. A: Quasimodo.	4.00

Condition price index: Multiply "NM prices" above by: **0.83 for Very Fine/Near Mint**
0.66 for Very Fine • 0.33 for Fine • 0.2 for Very Good • 0.125 for Good

N-MINT

❑202, Jan 1979 JB, KP (a); A: Iron Man. A: Quasimodo. A: Tony Stark. 4.00
❑203, Feb 1979 KP (a) 4.00
❑204, Mar 1979 KP (a); 1: Queen Adora (of Xandar). 1: Skrull X. A: Man-Wolf. A: The Watcher. A: Monocle. A: Edwin Jarvis. A: Spider-Man. 4.00
❑205, Apr 1979 KP (a); 1: Thoran Rul (Protector). 2: Queen Adora (of Xandar). A: The Watcher. A: Monocle. A: Emperor Dorrek. 4.00
❑206, May 1979 KP (a) 4.00
❑207, Jun 1979 SB (a); 1: The Enclave (identified). A: Barney Bushkin. A: Medusa. A: Monocle. A: Spider-Man. 4.00
❑208, Jul 1979 SB (a); O: Protector. A: Nova. A: Sphinx. A: Queen Adora. A: Comet. A: Diamondhead. A: Thoran Rul (Protector). A: Crimebuster. A: Doctor Sun. A: Powerhouse. 4.00
❑209, Aug 1979 JBy (a); 1: Herbie. ... 4.00
❑210, Sep 1979 JBy (a); 2: Herbie. A: Galactus. 4.00
❑211, Oct 1979 JBy (a); 1: Terrax the Tamer. A: Galactus. A: The Watcher. 4.00
❑212, Nov 1979 JBy (a); A: Galactus. A: Sphinx. A: The Watcher. A: Sayge. A: Skrull X. 4.00
❑213, Dec 1979 JBy (a); A: Galactus. A: Sphinx. A: The Watcher. A: Sayge. 4.00
❑214, Jan 1980 JBy (a); A: Queen Adora. A: Dum Dum Dugan. D: Skrull X. 4.00
❑215, Feb 1980 JBy (a) 4.00
❑216, Mar 1980 JBy (a) 4.00
❑217, Apr 1980 JBy (a); A: Dazzler. ... 4.00
❑218, May 1980; JBy, JSt (a); Continued from Peter Parker, the Spectacular Spider-Man #42 .... 4.00
❑219, Jun 1980 .... 4.00
❑220, Jul 1980 JBy (w); JBy (a); O: Fantastic Four. 4.00
❑221, Aug 1980 JBy (a) 4.00
❑222, Sep 1980 BSz, JSt (a) 4.00
❑223, Oct 1980 .... 4.00
❑224, Nov 1980 .... 4.00
❑225, Dec 1980 BSz (a); A: Thor. 4.00
❑226, Jan 1981 BSz (a) 4.00
❑227, Feb 1981 BSz (a) 4.00
❑228, Mar 1981 BSz, JSt (a) 4.00
❑229, Apr 1981 BSz, JSt (a) 4.00
❑230, May 1981 BSz, JSt (a) 4.00
❑231, Jun 1981 BSz, JSt (a) 4.00
❑232, Jul 1981 JBy (c); JBy (w); JBy (a) 4.00
❑233, Aug 1981 JBy (c); JBy (w); JBy (a) 4.00
❑234, Sep 1981 JBy (c); JBy (w); JBy (a) 4.00
❑235, Oct 1981 JBy (c); JBy (w); JBy (a); V: Ego. 4.00
❑236, Nov 1981; 20th Anniversary Issue JBy (c); JBy (w); JBy (a); O: Fantastic Four. V: Doctor Doom. 4.00
❑237, Dec 1981 JBy (c); JBy (w); JBy (a); 1: Julie Angel. 4.00
❑238, Jan 1982 JBy (c); JBy (w); JBy (a); O: Frankie Raye. A: Aunt Petunia. 4.00
❑239, Feb 1982 JBy (c); JBy (w); JBy (a) 4.00
❑240, Mar 1982 JBy (c); JBy (w); JBy (a); 1: Luna. 2.50
❑241, Apr 1982 JBy (c); JBy (w); JBy (a); A: Black Panther. 2.50
❑242, May 1982 JBy (c); JBy (w); JBy (a); A: Daredevil. 2.50
❑243, Jun 1982 JBy (c); JBy (w); JBy (a) 2.50
❑244, Jul 1982; JBy (c); JBy (w); JBy (a); 1: Nova II (Frankie Raye). Frankie Raye becomes herald of Galactus .. 2.50
❑245, Aug 1982 JBy (c); JBy (w); JBy (a) 2.50
❑246, Sep 1982 JBy (c); JBy (w); JBy (a) 2.50
❑247, Oct 1982 JBy (c); JBy (w); JBy (a); 1: Kristoff Vernard. 2.50
❑248, Nov 1982 JBy (c); JBy (w); JBy (a) 2.50
❑249, Dec 1982 JBy (c); JBy (w); JBy (a); V: Gladiator. 2.50
❑250, Jan 1983; Double-size; JBy (c); JBy (w); JBy (a); A: X-Men. A: Captain America. A: Spider-Man. X-Men appearance (Skrulls impersonating) 3.00
❑252, Mar 1983; JBy (c); JBy (w); JBy (a); sideways format 2.50

N-MINT

❑251, Feb 1983, JBy (c); JBy (w); JBy (a); Negative Zone 2.50
❑253, Apr 1983 JBy (c); JBy (w); JBy (a) 2.50
❑254, May 1983 JBy (c); JBy (w); JBy (a); A: She-Hulk. 2.50
❑255, Jun 1983 JBy (c); JBy (w); JBy (a) 2.50
❑256, Jul 1983 JBy (c); JBy (w); JBy (a) 2.50
❑257, Aug 1983 JBy (c); JBy (w); JBy (a) 2.50
❑258, Sep 1983 JBy (c); JBy (w); JBy (a) 2.50
❑259, Oct 1983 JBy (c); JBy (w); JBy (a) 2.50
❑260, Nov 1983; JBy (c); JBy (w); JBy (a); A: Doctor Doom. A: Silver Surfer. D: Terrax. Silver Surfer, Doctor Doom 3.00
❑261, Dec 1983 JBy (c); JBy (w); JBy (a); A: Silver Surfer. A: Watcher. 2.50
❑262, Jan 1984; JBy (c); JBy (w); JBy (a); O: Galactus. Trial of Reed Richards; John Byrne appears in story . 2.50
❑263, Feb 1984 JBy (a) 2.50
❑264, Mar 1984; JBy (w); JBy (a); V: Karisma. Cover swipe of Fantastic Four #1 .... 2.50
❑265, Apr 1984; JBy (a); 1: Lyja (as Alicia Masters). 1: Roberta the Receptionist. She-Hulk joins Fantastic Four (replaces Thing, who left in Secret Wars) 2.50
❑266, May 1984 JBy (w); JBy, KGa (a) 2.50
❑267, Jun 1984; JBy (a); Sue has a miscarriage 2.50
❑268, Jul 1984 JBy (a); A: Hulk. A: Doctor Octopus. 2.50
❑269, Aug 1984 JBy (w); JBy (a); 1: Terminus. 2.50
❑270, Sep 1984 JBy (w); JBy (a); V: Terminus. 2.50
❑271, Oct 1984 JBy (w); JBy (a) 2.50
❑272, Nov 1984 JBy (w); JBy (a); 1: Nathaniel Richards (Reed's father). 2.50
❑273, Dec 1984 JBy (w); JBy (a); O: Kang. 2.50
❑274, Jan 1985; JBy (w); JBy (a); Thing solo story; alien costume freed 2.50
❑275, Feb 1985 JBy (w); JBy (a) 2.50
❑276, Mar 1985 JBy (w); JBy (a) 2.50
❑277, Apr 1985 JBy (w); JBy (a) 2.50
❑278, May 1985; JBy (w); JBy (a); O: Doctor Doom. Kristoff becomes second Doctor Doom 2.50
❑279, Jun 1985 JBy (w); JBy (a) 2.50
❑280, Jul 1985; JBy (w); JBy (a); 1: Hate-Monger III ("H.M. Unger"). Sue becomes Malice 2.50
❑281, Aug 1985 JBy (w); JBy (a) 2.50
❑282, Sep 1985; JBy (w); JBy (a); Secret Wars II 2.50
❑283, Oct 1985 JBy (w); JBy (a) 2.50
❑284, Nov 1985; JBy (w); JBy (a); Invisible Girl becomes Invisible Woman 2.50
❑285, Dec 1985; JBy (w); JBy (a); Secret Wars II 2.50
❑286, Jan 1986; JBy (w); JBy (a); 2: X-Factor. A: X-Men. return of Jean Grey 3.00
❑287, Feb 1986 JBy (w); JBy (a); A: Doctor Doom. 2.00
❑288, Mar 1986; JBy (a); A: Doctor Doom. Secret Wars II; Doctor Doom vs. Beyonder 2.00
❑289, Apr 1986 JBy (a); D: Basilisk I (Basil Elks). 2.00
❑290, May 1986 JBy (w); JBy (a) 2.00
❑291, Jun 1986 JBy (w); JBy (a) 2.00
❑292, Jul 1986 JBy (w); JBy (a); A: Nick Fury. 2.00
❑293, Aug 1986 JBy (a) 2.00
❑294, Sep 1986 JOy (a) 2.00
❑295, Nov 1986 JOy (a) 2.00
❑296, Nov 1986; Double-size; Thing comes back 2.50
❑297, Dec 1986 JB, SB (a) 2.00
❑298, Jan 1987 JB, SB (a) 2.00
❑299, Feb 1987 .... 2.00
❑300, Mar 1987; JB, SB (a); Wedding of Johnny Storm and Alicia; "Alicia" later revealed to be Lyja (a Skrull) .. 2.50
❑301, Apr 1987 JB (a) 2.00

N-MINT

❑302, May 1987 JB, SB (a) 2.00
❑303, Jun 1987 JB (a) 2.00
❑304, Jul 1987; JB, JSt (a); Reed and Sue take leave of absence 2.00
❑305, Aug 1987 JB, JSt (a) 2.00
❑306, Sep 1987 A: Ms. Marvel (Sharon Ventura). 2.00
❑307, Oct 1987; Crystal and new Ms. Marvel joins team 2.00
❑308, Nov 1987 JB, JSt (a); 1: Fasaud. 2.00
❑309, Dec 1987 JB, JSt (a) 2.00
❑310, Jan 1988; Ms. Marvel becomes She-Thing 2.00
❑311, Feb 1988 .... 2.00
❑312, Mar 1988; A: Doctor Doom. Fall of Mutants 2.00
❑313, Apr 1988 .... 2.00
❑314, May 1988 KP, JSt (a); V: Belasco. 2.00
❑315, Jun 1988 KP, JSt (a) 2.00
❑316, Jul 1988 KP, JSt (a) 2.00
❑317, Aug 1988 .... 2.00
❑318, Sep 1988; Doctor Doom 2.00
❑319, Oct 1988; Giant-size; Doctor Doom vs. Beyonder; Beyonder returns, merges with Molecule Man 2.50
❑320, Nov 1988; Thing vs. Hulk 2.00
❑321, Dec 1988; 1: Aron the Rogue Watcher. Ms. Marvel vs. She-Hulk . 1.50
❑322, Jan 1989; Inferno 1.50
❑323, Feb 1989; Inferno 1.50
❑324, Mar 1989; KP (a); Inferno 1.50
❑325, Apr 1989 RB (a) 1.50
❑326, May 1989; Reed and Sue return to team 1.50
❑327, Jun 1989; Thing reverts to human form 1.50
❑328, Jul 1989 KP (a) 1.50
❑329, Aug 1989 RB (a) 1.50
❑330, Sep 1989 RB (a); V: Doom. 1.50
❑331, Oct 1989 RB (a); V: Ultron. 1.50
❑332, Nov 1989 RB (a) 1.50
❑333, Nov 1989 RB (a) 1.50
❑334, Dec 1989; Acts of Vengeance .. 1.50
❑335, Dec 1989; RB (a); Acts of Vengeance 1.50
❑336, Jan 1990; Acts of Vengeance .. 1.50
❑337, Feb 1990 .... 2.00
❑338, Mar 1990 .... 2.00
❑339, Apr 1990 .... 2.00
❑340, May 1990 .... 2.00
❑341, Jun 1990 .... 2.00
❑342, Jul 1990 A: Spider-Man. 2.00
❑343, Aug 1990 .... 2.00
❑344, Sep 1990 .... 2.00
❑345, Oct 1990 .... 2.00
❑346, Nov 1990 .... 2.00
❑347, Dec 1990 A: Hulk. A: Ghost Rider. A: Wolverine. A: Spider-Man. 2.50
❑347-2, Dec 1990 A: Hulk. A: Ghost Rider. A: Wolverine. 1.50
❑348, Jan 1991 A: Hulk. A: Ghost Rider. A: Wolverine. A: Spider-Man. 2.50
❑348-2, Jan 1991 .... 1.50
❑349, Feb 1991 A: Punisher. A: Hulk. A: Ghost Rider. A: Wolverine. A: Spider-Man. 2.50
❑350, Mar 1991; Giant-size; A: Doctor Doom. Return of Thing 2.50
❑351, Apr 1991 .... 2.00
❑352, May 1991; Reed and Doctor Doom battle through time 2.00
❑353, Jun 1991 .... 2.00
❑354, Jul 1991 .... 2.00
❑355, Aug 1991 AM (a) 2.00
❑356, Sep 1991; Alicia is Skrull; Fantastic Four vs. New Warriors 2.00
❑357, Oct 1991; 1: Lyja (in true form). Skrull's identity revealed as Lyja 2.00
❑358, Nov 1991; 30th Anniversary Issue; O: Paibok the Power Skrull. 1: Paibok the Power Skrull. Die-cut cover 2.50
❑359, Dec 1991; 1: Devos the Devastator. The real Alicia returns 1.50
❑360, Jan 1992 .... 1.50
❑361, Feb 1992; Doctor Doom 1.50

Condition price index: Multiply "NM prices" above by: **0.83 for Very Fine/Near Mint**
0.66 for Very Fine • 0.33 for Fine • 0.2 for Very Good • 0.125 for Good

	N-MINT
❑362, Mar 1992	1.50
❑363, Apr 1992 O: Occulus. 1: Occulus.	1.50
❑364, May 1992	1.50
❑365, Jun 1992	1.50
❑366, Jul 1992	1.50
❑367, Aug 1992	1.50
❑368, Sep 1992	1.50
❑369, Oct 1992	1.50
❑370, Nov 1992 1: Lyja the Lazerfist.	1.50
❑371, Dec 1992; All-white embossed cover	3.00
❑371-2, Dec 1992; red embossed cover	2.50
❑372, Jan 1993	1.25
❑373, Feb 1993 A: Silver Sable.	1.25
❑374, Mar 1993; Spider-Man, Hulk, Ghost Rider, Wolverine team up again; Secret Defenders crossover	1.25
❑375, Apr 1993; Prism cover	3.00
❑376, May 1993; Franklin returns from future as a young man	1.25
❑377, Jun 1993; 1: Huntara. Secret Defenders crossover	1.25
❑378, Jul 1993	1.25
❑379, Aug 1993	1.50
❑380, Sep 1993	1.50
❑381, Oct 1993 A: Hunger. D: Mister Fantastic (apparent death). D: Doctor Doom.	3.00
❑382, Nov 1993	2.00
❑383, Dec 1993	1.25
❑384, Jan 1994 A: Ant-Man (Scott Lang).	1.25
❑385, Feb 1994	1.25
❑386, Mar 1994; 1: Egg (Lyja's baby). Birth of Lyja's baby	1.25
❑387, Apr 1994	1.25
❑387/Variant, Apr 1994; diecut cover	3.00
❑388, May 1994; A: Avengers. cards	1.50
❑389, Jun 1994	1.50
❑390, Jun 1994 A: Galactus.	1.50
❑391, Aug 1994 A: Galactus.	1.50
❑392, Sep 1994	1.50
❑393, Oct 1994; A: Puppet Master. Nathaniel Richards takes over Latveria	1.50
❑394, Nov 1994	1.50
❑394/CS, Nov 1994; polybagged with 16-page Marvel Action Hour preview, acetate print, and other items	2.95
❑395, Dec 1994 A: Wolverine.	1.50
❑396, Jan 1995	1.50
❑397, Feb 1995 V: Aron.	1.50
❑398, Mar 1995	1.50
❑398/Variant, Mar 1995; foil cover	2.50
❑399, Apr 1995	1.50
❑399/Variant, Apr 1995; enhanced cardstock cover	2.50
❑400, May 1995; Giant-size; foil cover	3.95
❑401, Jun 1995	1.50
❑402, Jul 1995; A: Thor. Atlantis Rising	1.50
❑403, Aug 1995	1.50
❑404, Sep 1995	1.50
❑405, Oct 1995; A: Iron Man 2020. A: Conan. A: Red Raven. A: Young Allies. A: Zarko. A: Green Goblin. The Thing becomes human	1.50
❑406, Nov 1995; 1: Hyperstorm. Return of Doctor Doom	1.50
❑407, Dec 1995; Return of Reed Richards	1.50
❑408, Jan 1996 V: Hyperstorm.	1.50
❑409, Feb 1996; The Thing's face is healed	1.50
❑410, Mar 1996 O: Kristoff.	1.50
❑411, Apr 1996 A: Inhumans. V: Black Bolt.	1.50
❑412, May 1996	1.50
❑413, Jun 1996; Franklin Richards becomes a child again	1.50
❑414, Jul 1996 O: Hyperstorm.	1.50
❑415, Aug 1996; Franklin captured by Onslaught	2.00
❑416, Sep 1996; Giant-size; Series continues in Fantastic Four Vol. 2; wraparound cover	3.50

	N-MINT
❑500, Sep 2003; 71st issue of Vol. 3/ 500th Issue of ongoing run; numbering restarts at 500 adding in issues from Vol. 2 and Vol. 3	3.50
❑500/CS, Sep 2003	3.50
❑501, Oct 2003 MWa (w)	2.25
❑502, Oct 2003 MWa (w)	2.99
❑503, Nov 2003 MWa (w)	2.99
❑504, Nov 2003 MWa (w)	2.99
❑505, Dec 2003 MWa (w)	2.99
❑506, Jan 2003 MWa (w)	2.99
❑507, Jan 2004 MWa (w)	2.99
❑508, Feb 2004 MWa (w)	2.99
❑509, Mar 2004	2.25
❑510, Apr 2004 MWa (w)	2.99
❑511, May 2004 MWa (w)	2.25
❑512, Jun 2004 MWa (w)	2.99
❑513, Jul 2004 MWa (w)	2.99
❑514, Aug 2004	2.25
❑515, Sep 2004	
❑516, Sep 2004	
❑Annual 1, ca. 1963; JK (a); O: Fantastic Four. O: Sub-Mariner. 1: Krang. A: Spider-Man. A: Doctor Doom. A: Sub-Mariner. V: Sub-Mariner. Spider-Man; reprints FF #1	425.00
❑Annual 2, ca. 1964; O: Doctor Doom. 1: Boris. reprints FF #5	250.00
❑Annual 3, ca. 1965; Wedding of Reed Richards and Susan Storm; Virtually all Marvel super-heroes appear; reprints FF #6 and 11	100.00
❑Annual 4, Nov 1966; JK, SL (w); JK (a); 1: Quasimodo. Return of Golden Age Human Torch; reprints FF #25 and 26	55.00
❑Annual 5, Nov 1967 JK, SL (w); JK (a); 1: Psycho-Man. A: Inhumans. A: Inhumans, Black Panther.	70.00
❑Annual 6, Nov 1968 JK, SL (w); JK (a); 1: Franklin Richards. 1: Annihilus.	45.00
❑Annual 7, Nov 1969; JK, SL (w); JK (a); reprints FF #1, FF Annual #2	18.00
❑Annual 8, Dec 1970; JK (a); reprints FF Annual #1	12.00
❑Annual 9, Dec 1971; JK, SL (w); JK (a); reprints stories from FF #43, Annual #3, and Strange Tales #131	10.00
❑Annual 10, ca. 1973; JK, SL (w); JK (a); reprints stories from FF Annual #3 and 4; Reprints wedding of Reed and Sue Richards	8.00
❑Annual 11, ca. 1976 JK (c); JB (a); A: The Watcher. A: Invaders. V: Invaders.	6.00
❑Annual 12, ca. 1977 KP, BH (a); A: Karnak. A: Sphinx. A: Medusa. A: Crystal. A: Triton. A: Quicksilver. A: Lockjaw. A: Gorgon. A: Black Bolt.	5.00
❑Annual 13, ca. 1978 SB (a); A: Daredevil. A: Mole Man.	5.00
❑Annual 14, ca. 1979 GP (a)	5.00
❑Annual 15, ca. 1980; GP (a); Skrulls	3.00
❑Annual 16, ca. 1982 SD, JBy (a)	3.00
❑Annual 17, ca. 1983 JBy (w); JBy (a)	3.00
❑Annual 18, ca. 1984; JBy (w); Kree-Skrull War	3.00
❑Annual 19, ca. 1985 JBy (a); A: Avengers.	3.00
❑Annual 20, ca. 1986	3.00
❑Annual 21, ca. 1988	3.00
❑Annual 22, ca. 1989; RB (a); Atlantis Attacks	3.00
❑Annual 23, ca. 1990 1: Kosmos.	3.00
❑Annual 24, ca. 1991; O: Fantastic Four. A: Guardians of Galaxy. Korvac Quest	2.50
❑Annual 25, ca. 1992; HT (a); 1: Temptress. Citizen Kang	2.50
❑Annual 26, ca. 1993; HT (a); 1: Wildstreak. Polybagged with trading card	3.00
❑Annual 27, ca. 1994; MGu (a); 1994 Annual	3.00
❑Special 1; JBy (a); Reprints Sub-Mariner vs. Fantastic Four from Annual #1 with added material	2.50
❑Ashcan 1; ashcan edition O: Fantastic Four.	1.00

Fantasy Masterpieces (Vol. 1) reprinted stories from Marvel's Golden Age, when the company was known as Timely.

© 1966 Marvel Comics.

FANTASTIC FOUR (VOL. 2)

MARVEL

	N-MINT
❑1, Nov 1996; JLee (w); JLee (a); O: Fantastic Four (new origin). AKA Fantastic Four Vol. 1, #417	4.00
❑1/A, Nov 1996; JLee (w); JLee (a); O: Fantastic Four (new origin). AKA Fantastic Four Vol. 1, #417; alternate cover	3.00
❑1/B, Nov 1996; JLee (w); JLee (a); AKA Fantastic Four Vol. 1, #417	3.50
❑2, Dec 1996; JLee (w); JLee (a); V: Namor. AKA Fantastic Four Vol. 1, #418	2.00
❑3, Jan 1997; JLee (w); JLee (a); A: Avengers. V: Namor. AKA Fantastic Four Vol. 1, #419	2.00
❑4, Feb 1997; JLee (w); JLee (a); A: Black Panther. A: Doctor Doom. V: Doctor Doom. AKA Fantastic Four Vol. 1, #420	2.00
❑4/A, Feb 1997; JLee (w); JLee (a); AKA Fantastic Four Vol. 1, #420	2.00
❑5, Mar 1997; JLee (w); JLee (a); V: Doctor Doom. AKA Fantastic Four Vol. 1, #421	2.00
❑6, Apr 1997; JLee (w); JLee (a); A: Silver Surfer. V: Super Skrull. AKA Fantastic Four Vol. 1, #422; continues in Avengers #6	2.00
❑7, May 1997; JLee (w); A: Galactus. A: Wolverine. A: Blastaar. AKA Fantastic Four Vol. 1, #423	2.00
❑8, Jun 1997; JLee (w); A: Inhumans. AKA Fantastic Four Vol. 1, #424	2.00
❑9, Jul 1997; A: Inhumans. A: Firelord. AKA Fantastic Four Vol. 1, #425	2.00
❑10, Aug 1997; gatefold summary; A: Inhumans. AKA Fantastic Four Vol. 1, #426	2.00
❑11, Sep 1997; gatefold summary; V: Terrax. AKA Fantastic Four Vol. 1, #427	2.00
❑12, Oct 1997; gatefold summary; AKA Fantastic Four Vol. 1, #428; covers forms quadtych with Avengers #12, Iron Man #12, and Captain America #12	2.99
❑13, Nov 1997; gatefold summary; A: StormWatch. A: Wetworks. A: WildC.A.T.s. AKA Fantastic Four Vol. 1, #429; covers forms quadtych with Avengers #13, Iron Man #13, and Captain America #13	2.00

FANTASTIC FOUR (VOL. 3)

MARVEL

	N-MINT
❑1, Jan 1998; Giant-size; AKA Fantastic Four Vol. 1, #430; Cover has green background with team facing forward	3.00
❑1/A, Jan 1998; gatefold summary; AKA Fantastic Four Vol. 1, #430; alternate cover	4.00
❑2, Feb 1998; gatefold summary; AKA Fantastic Four Vol. 1, #431	3.00
❑2/A, Feb 1998; gatefold summary; AKA Fantastic Four Vol. 1, #431; alternate cover	3.00
❑3, Mar 1998; gatefold summary; 1: Crucible. AKA Fantastic Four Vol. 1, #432	3.00
❑4, Apr 1998; gatefold summary; 1: Billie the Postman. A: Silver Surfer. V: Terminus. AKA Fantastic Four Vol. 1, #433	2.50

Condition price index: Multiply "NM prices" above by: **0.83 for Very Fine/Near Mint**
0.66 for Very Fine • 0.33 for Fine • 0.2 for Very Good • 0.125 for Good

	N-MINT
❑5, May 1998; gatefold summary; V: Crucible. AKA Fantastic Four Vol. 1, #434	2.50
❑6, Jun 1998; gatefold summary; A: Iron Fist. AKA Fantastic Four Vol. 1, #435; Thing vs. Technet	2.25
❑7, Jul 1998; gatefold summary; V: Warwolves. AKA Fantastic Four Vol. 1, #436	2.25
❑8, Aug 1998; gatefold summary; AKA Fantastic Four Vol. 1, #437	2.25
❑9, Sep 1998; gatefold summary; A: Spider-Man. AKA Fantastic Four Vol. 1, #438	2.25
❑10, Oct 1998; gatefold summary; V: Trapster. AKA Fantastic Four Vol. 1, #439	2.25
❑11, Nov 1998; gatefold summary; A: Her. AKA Fantastic Four Vol. 1, #440	2.25
❑12, Dec 1998; gatefold summary; V: Her. V: Crucible. AKA Fantastic Four Vol. 1, #441; wraparound cover	2.25
❑13, Jan 1999; gatefold summary; V: Ronan. AKA Fantastic Four Vol. 1, #442	2.25
❑14, Feb 1999; gatefold summary; A: Ronan the Accuser. V: Ronan. AKA Fantastic Four Vol. 1, #443	2.25
❑15, Mar 1999; A: Kree. A: S.H.I.E.L.D.. A: Shi'Ar. A: Iron Man. A: Ronan the Accuser. A: Watcher. V: Ronan. AKA Fantastic Four Vol. 1, #444; Iron Man crossover, Part 1	2.25
❑16, Apr 1999; A: Kree. V: Kree. AKA Fantastic Four Vol. 1, #445	2.25
❑17, May 1999; AKA Fantastic Four Vol. 1, #446	2.25
❑18, Jun 1999; AKA Fantastic Four Vol. 1, #447	2.25
❑19, Jul 1999; V: Annihilus. AKA Fantastic Four Vol. 1, #448	2.25
❑20, Aug 1999; AKA Fantastic Four Vol. 1, #449	2.25
❑21, Sep 1999; AKA Fantastic Four Vol. 1, #450	2.00
❑22, Oct 1999; AKA Fantastic Four Vol. 1, #451	2.00
❑23, Nov 1999; AKA Fantastic Four Vol. 1, #452	2.00
❑24, Dec 1999; AKA Fantastic Four Vol. 1, #453	2.00
❑25, Jan 2000; Giant-size; AKA Fantastic Four Vol. 1, #454	3.00
❑26, Feb 2000; AKA Fantastic Four Vol. 1, #455	2.25
❑27, Mar 2000; AKA Fantastic Four Vol. 1, #456	2.25
❑28, Apr 2000; AKA Fantastic Four Vol. 1, #457	2.25
❑29, May 2000; AKA Fantastic Four Vol. 1, #458	2.25
❑30, Jun 2000; AKA Fantastic Four Vol. 1, #459	2.25
❑31, Jul 2000; AKA Fantastic Four Vol. 1, #460	2.25
❑32, Aug 2000; AKA Fantastic Four Vol. 1, #461	2.25
❑33, Sep 2000; AKA Fantastic Four Vol. 1, #462	2.25
❑34, Oct 2000; AKA Fantastic Four Vol. 1, #463	2.25
❑35, Nov 2000; AKA Fantastic Four Vol. 1, #464	3.25
❑36, Dec 2000; A: Daredevil. A: Spider-Man. A: Diablo. AKA Fantastic Four Vol. 1, #465	2.25
❑37, Jan 2001; AKA Fantastic Four Vol. 1, #466	2.25
❑38, Feb 2001; AKA Fantastic Four Vol. 1, #467	2.25
❑39, Mar 2001; A: Grey Gargoyle. A: Avengers. AKA Fantastic Four Vol. 1, #468; Thing can switch from rock form to human and back	2.25
❑40, Apr 2001; AKA Fantastic Four Vol. 1, #469; Baxter Building reopens	2.25
❑41, May 2001; JPH (w); A: First. AKA Fantastic Four Vol. 1, #470; First appearance of Hellscout	2.25
❑42, Jun 2001; AKA Fantastic Four Vol. 1, #471	2.25
❑43, Jul 2001; AKA Fantastic Four Vol. 1, #472	2.25
❑44, Aug 2001; AKA Fantastic Four Vol. 1, #473	2.25
❑45, Sep 2001; AKA Fantastic Four Vol. 1, #474	2.25
❑46, Oct 2001; AKA Fantastic Four Vol. 1, #475	2.25
❑47, Nov 2001; AKA Fantastic Four Vol. 1, #476	2.25
❑48, Dec 2001; AKA Fantastic Four Vol. 1, #477	2.25
❑49, Jan 2002; AKA Fantastic Four Vol. 1, #478	2.25
❑50, Feb 2002; AKA Fantastic Four Vol. 1, #479	3.99
❑51, Mar 2002; AKA Fantastic Four Vol. 1, #480	3.50
❑52, Apr 2002; AKA Fantastic Four Vol. 1, #481	2.25
❑53, May 2002; AKA Fantastic Four Vol. 1, #482	3.25
❑54, Jun 2002; AKA Fantastic Four Vol. 1, #483	3.50
❑55, Jul 2002, AKA Fantastic Four Vol. 1, #484	2.25
❑56, Aug 2002, AKA Fantastic Four Vol. 1, #485	2.25
❑57, Aug 2002, AKA Fantastic Four Vol. 1, #486	2.25
❑58, Sep 2002, AKA Fantastic Four Vol. 1, #487	2.25
❑59, Oct 2002, AKA Fantastic Four Vol. 1, #488	2.25
❑60, Oct 2002, AKA Fantastic Four Vol. 1, #489	1.00
❑61, Nov 2002, AKA Fantastic Four Vol. 1, #490	2.25
❑62, Dec 2002, AKA Fantastic Four Vol. 1, #491	2.25
❑63, Jan 2003, AKA Fantastic Four Vol. 1, #492	2.25
❑64, Feb 2003, AKA Fantastic Four Vol. 1, #493	2.25
❑65, Mar 2003, AKA Fantastic Four Vol. 1, #494	2.25
❑66, Apr 2003; AKA Fantastic Four Vol. 1, #495	2.25
❑67, May 2003; AKA Fantastic Four Vol. 1, #496	2.25
❑68, Jun 2003; MWa (w); AKA Fantastic Four Vol. 1, #497	2.25
❑69, Jul 2003, MWa (w); AKA Fantastic Four Vol. 1, #498	2.25
❑70, Aug 2003 MWa (w)	2.25
❑71, Sep 2003; MWa (w); 71st/500th Issue; numbering restarts at 500 under volume 1	3.50
❑Annual 1998, ca. 1998; Fantastic Four/Fantastic 4 '98; alternate universe FF	3.50
❑Annual 1999, ca. 1999; Fantastic Four/Fantastic 4 '99	3.50
❑Annual 2001, ca. 2001	2.99

FANTASTIC FOUR: ATLANTIS RISING

MARVEL

	N-MINT
❑1, Jun 1995; Atlantis rises from sea; acetate outer cover	3.95
❑2, Jul 1995; acetate outer cover	3.95
❑Ashcan 1, May 1995; Collector's Preview	2.25

FANTASTIC FOUR: FIREWORKS

MARVEL

	N-MINT
❑1, Jan 1999; Marvel Remix	2.99
❑2, Feb 1999; Marvel Remix	2.99
❑3, Mar 1999; Marvel Remix	2.99

FANTASTIC FOUR LEGENDS

MARVEL

	N-MINT
❑1, Sep 2003	13.99

FANTASTIC FOUR: 1 2 3 4

MARVEL

	N-MINT
❑1, Oct 2001	2.99
❑2, Nov 2001	2.99
❑3, Dec 2001	2.99
❑4, Jan 2002	2.99

FANTASTIC FOUR ROAST

MARVEL

	N-MINT
❑1, May 1982; Celebrates 20th Anniversary of Fantastic Four FH (w); MA, FH, MG, JB, FM, TD (a)	2.00

FANTASTIC FOUR SPECIAL

MARVEL

	N-MINT
❑1, May 1984; JBy (c); reprints FF Annual #1	3.00

FANTASTIC FOUR: THE LEGEND

MARVEL

	N-MINT
❑1, Oct 1996; highlights of group's history	3.95

FANTASTIC FOUR: THE WORLD'S GREATEST COMICS MAGAZINE

MARVEL

	N-MINT
❑1, Feb 2001; EL (c); EL (w); KG, EL (a); set after events of Fantastic Four (Vol. 1) #100	3.00
❑2, Mar 2001 MG (c); EL (w); KG, EL (a)	2.99
❑3, Apr 2001 EL (w); KG, EL, ES (a)	2.99
❑4, May 2001	2.99
❑5, Jun 2001	2.99
❑6, Jul 2001	2.99
❑7, Aug 2001	2.99
❑8, Sep 2001	2.99
❑9, Oct 2001	2.99
❑10, Nov 2001	2.99
❑11, Dec 2001	2.99
❑12, Jan 2002	2.99

FANTASTIC FOUR 2099

MARVEL

	N-MINT
❑1, Jan 1996; enhanced wraparound cover	3.95
❑2, Feb 1996 JB (a)	2.00
❑3, Mar 1996 AW (a)	2.00
❑4, Apr 1996 AW (a); A: Spider-Man 2099.	2.00
❑5, May 1996; A: Doctor Strange. Joe Kelly's first major comics work	2.00
❑6, Jun 1996 A: Spider-Man 2099. A: Doctor Strange.	2.00
❑7, Jul 1996 A: Doom 2099. V: Attuma.	2.00
❑8, Aug 1996 A: Doom 2099.	2.00

FANTASTIC FOUR UNLIMITED

MARVEL

	N-MINT
❑1, Mar 1993 HT (a)	4.50
❑2, Jun 1993 HT (a)	4.00
❑3, Sep 1993 HT (a)	4.00
❑4, Dec 1993; HT (a); Thing vs. Hulk	3.95
❑5, Mar 1994 HT (a)	3.95
❑6, Jun 1994 HT (a); V: Namor.	3.95
❑7, Sep 1994; HT (a); V: early Marvel monsters. wraparound cover	3.95
❑8, Dec 1994 V: Doom.	3.95
❑9, Mar 1995 HT (a)	3.95
❑10, Jul 1995	3.95
❑11, Sep 1995 A: Inhumans.	3.95
❑12, Dec 1995; HT (a); A: Hyperstorm. A: Doctor Doom. how Reed and Doom vanished; wraparound cover	3.95

FANTASTIC FOUR UNPLUGGED

MARVEL

	N-MINT
❑1, Sep 1995	1.25
❑2, Nov 1995; reading of Reed Richards' will	1.00
❑3, Jan 1996	1.00
❑4, Mar 1996; Flip book with Untold Tales of Spider-Man #7	1.00
❑5, May 1996 V: Blastaar.	1.00
❑6, Jul 1996	1.00

FANTASTIC FOUR: UNSTABLE MOLECULES

MARVEL

	N-MINT
❑1, Mar 2003	2.99
❑2, Apr 2003	2.99
❑3, May 2003	2.99
❑4, Jun 2003	2.99

FANTASTIC FOUR VS. X-MEN

MARVEL

	N-MINT
❑1, Feb 1987	2.50
❑2, Mar 1987	2.50

N-MINT

❑3, Apr 1987 ... 2.50
❑4, May 1987 ... 2.50

FANTASTIC PANIC
ANTARCTIC

❑1, Aug 1993 ... 3.00
❑2, Oct 1993 ... 3.00
❑3, Dec 1993 ... 3.00
❑4, Feb 1994 ... 3.00
❑5, Apr 1994 ... 3.00
❑6, Jun 1994 ... 3.00
❑7, Aug 1994 ... 3.00
❑8, Oct 1994 ... 3.00

FANTASTIC PANIC (VOL. 2)
ANTARCTIC

❑1, Nov 1995 ... 2.95
❑2, Jan 1996 ... 2.95
❑3, Mar 1996 ... 2.95
❑4, May 1996 ... 2.95
❑5, Jul 1996 ... 2.95
❑6, Sep 1996 ... 2.95
❑7, Nov 1996 ... 2.95
❑8, Dec 1996 ... 2.95

FANTASTIC VOYAGE
GOLD KEY

❑1, Aug 1969 ... 25.00
❑2, Dec 1969 ... 16.00

FANTASTIC VOYAGES OF SINDBAD
GOLD KEY

❑1, Oct 1965; pin-up on back cover .. 18.00
❑2, Jun 1967 ... 12.00

FANTASY FEATURES
AC

❑1 1987 ... 1.75
❑2 1987 ... 1.95

FANTASY GIRLS
COMAX

❑1, b&w ... 2.50

FANTASY MASTERPIECES (VOL. 1)
MARVEL

❑1, Feb 1966; SD, DH, JK (a); Golden Age reprints ... 75.00
❑2, Apr 1966; SD, DH, JK (a); Golden Age reprints; Fin Fang Foom ... 30.00
❑3, Jun 1966; Golden Age reprints; Captain America, other Golden Age super-heroes appear ... 15.00
❑4, Aug 1966; Golden Age reprints; Captain America, other Golden Age super-heroes appear ... 12.00
❑5, Oct 1966; Golden Age reprints; Captain America, other Golden Age super-heroes appear ... 12.00
❑6, Dec 1966; Golden Age reprints; Captain America, other Golden Age super-heroes appear ... 12.00
❑7, Feb 1967; Golden Age reprints; Captain America, other Golden Age super-heroes appear ... 12.00
❑8, Apr 1967; Golden Age reprints; Sub-Mariner vs. Human Torch (original) ... 13.00
❑9, Jun 1967; O: Human Torch (original). Golden Age reprints; Reprints Marvel Comics #1 ... 12.00
❑10, Aug 1967; O: All Winners Squad. 1: All Winners Squad. Golden Age reprints; Reprints All Winners #19 ... 10.00
❑11, Oct 1967; O: Toro. Series continues as Marvel Super-Heroes; Reprints Human Torch #1 ... 10.00

FANTASY MASTERPIECES (VOL. 2)
MARVEL

❑1, Dec 1979; SL (w); Silver Surfer reprint ... 6.00
❑2, Jan 1980; SL (w); Reprints Silver Surfer (Vol. 1) #2 ... 3.50
❑3, Feb 1980; SL (w); Reprints Silver Surfer (Vol. 1) #3 ... 3.00
❑4, Mar 1980; SL (w); Reprints Silver Surfer (Vol. 1) #4 ... 3.00
❑5, Apr 1980; SL (w); Reprints Silver Surfer (Vol. 1) #5 ... 3.00
❑6, May 1980; SL (w); JB (a); Reprints Silver Surfer (Vol. 1) #6 ... 2.50

N-MINT

❑7, Jun 1980; SL (w); Reprints Silver Surfer (Vol. 1) #7 ... 2.50
❑8, Jul 1980; SL (w); Reprints Silver Surfer (Vol. 1) #8 ... 2.50
❑9, Aug 1980; SL (w); Reprints Silver Surfer (Vol. 1) #9 ... 2.50
❑10, Sep 1980; SL (w); JB (a); Reprints Silver Surfer (Vol. 1) #10 ... 2.50
❑11, Oct 1980 ... 2.00
❑12, Nov 1980 ... 2.00
❑13, Dec 1980 ... 2.00
❑14, Jan 1981 ... 2.00

FANTASY QUARTERLY
INDEPENDENT PUB. SYND.

❑1, Spr 1978, b&w; 1: Elfquest. back-up story with art by Sim ... 55.00

FAREWELL, MOONSHADOW
DC / VERTIGO

❑1, Jan 1997; prestige format ... 7.95

FAREWELL TO WEAPONS
MARVEL / EPIC

❑1 ... 2.25

FARSCAPE: WAR TORN
DC / WILDSTORM

❑1, Apr 2002 ... 4.95
❑2, May 2002 ... 4.95

FAR WEST
ANTARCTIC

❑1, Nov 1998 ... 2.95
❑2, Jan 1999 ... 2.95
❑3, Mar 1999 ... 2.95
❑4, May 1999 ... 2.95

FASHION IN ACTION
ECLIPSE

❑Summer 1, Aug 1986; gatefold summary ... 2.00
❑WS 1; anniversary ... 2.00

FASHION POLICE, THE
BRYCE ALAN

❑1 ... 2.50

FAST FORWARD
DC / PIRANHA

❑1; phobias ... 4.95
❑2; family ... 4.95
❑3; Storytellers ... 4.95

FASTLANE ILLUSTRATED
FASTLANE

❑0.5; Giveaway at 1994 San Diego Comicon ... 1.50
❑1, Sep 1994, b&w ... 2.50
❑2, Jun 1995, b&w ... 2.50
❑3, Jul 1996, b&w; wraparound cover ... 2.50

FAST WILLIE JACKSON
FITZGERALD PERIODICALS

❑1, Oct 1976 ... 24.00
❑2, Dec 1976 ... 16.00
❑3, Feb 1977 ... 16.00
❑4, Apr 1977 ... 16.00
❑5, Jun 1977 ... 16.00
❑6, Aug 1977 ... 16.00
❑7, Sep 1977; Last issue ... 16.00

FATAL BEAUTY
ILLUSTRATION

❑Ashcan 1/A, Jun 1996; Adult cover . 3.95

FAT ALBERT
GOLD KEY

❑1, Mar 1974 ... 12.00
❑2, Jun 1974 ... 8.00
❑3, Sep 1974 ... 7.00
❑4, Dec 1974 ... 7.00
❑5, Feb 1975 ... 7.00
❑6, Apr 1975 ... 6.00
❑7, Jun 1975 ... 6.00
❑8, Aug 1975 ... 6.00
❑9, Oct 1975 ... 6.00
❑10, Dec 1975 ... 6.00
❑11, Feb 1976 ... 4.00
❑12, Apr 1976 ... 4.00
❑13, Jun 1976 ... 4.00

Fat Freddy's Comics & Stories spun off from *The Fabulous Furry Freak Brothers.*
© 1983 Gilbert Shelton (Rip Off)

N-MINT

❑14, Aug 1976 ... 4.00
❑15, Oct 1976 ... 4.00
❑16, Dec 1976 ... 4.00
❑17, Feb 1977 ... 4.00
❑18, Apr 1977 ... 4.00
❑19, Jun 1977 ... 4.00
❑20, Aug 1977 ... 4.00
❑21, Oct 1977 ... 4.00
❑22, Dec 1977 ... 4.00
❑23, Feb 1978 ... 4.00
❑24, Apr 1978 ... 4.00
❑25, Jun 1978 ... 4.00
❑26, Aug 1978 ... 4.00
❑27, Oct 1978 ... 4.00
❑28, Dec 1978 ... 4.00
❑29, Feb 1979 ... 4.00

FATALE
BROADWAY

❑1, Jan 1996; Embossed cover ... 2.50
❑2, Feb 1996 ... 2.50
❑3, Mar 1996 ... 2.50
❑4, May 1996 ... 2.50
❑5, Jul 1996 ... 2.95
❑6, Oct 1996 ... 2.95
❑Ashcan 1, Sep 1995, b&w; giveaway preview edition ... 1.00

FAT DOG MENDOZA
DARK HORSE

❑1, Dec 1992, b&w ... 2.50

FATE
DC

❑0, Oct 1994 O: Doctor Fate IV (Jared Stevens). 1: Doctor Fate IV (Jared Stevens). D: Doctor Fate III (Kent & Inza Nelson). ... 2.50
❑1, Nov 1994 O: Doctor Fate IV (Jared Stevens). ... 2.50
❑2, Dec 1994 ... 2.00
❑3, Jan 1995 ... 2.00
❑4, Feb 1995 ... 2.00
❑5, Mar 1995 ... 2.00
❑6, Apr 1995 ... 2.00
❑7, May 1995 ... 2.00
❑8, Jun 1995 ... 2.25
❑9, Jul 1995 ... 2.25
❑10, Aug 1995 ... 2.25
❑11, Sep 1995 ... 2.25
❑12, Oct 1995 A: Sentinel. ... 2.25
❑13, Nov 1995; Underworld Unleashed 2.25
❑14, Dec 1995 ... 2.25
❑15, Jan 1996 ... 2.25
❑16, Feb 1996 ... 2.25
❑17, Mar 1996 ... 2.25
❑18, May 1996 ... 2.25
❑19, Jun 1996 ... 2.25
❑20, Jul 1996 ... 2.25
❑21, Aug 1996 ... 2.25
❑22, Sep 1996; Kent and Inza Nelson go to heaven ... 2.25

FATE OF THE BLADE
DREAMWAVE

❑1, Aug 2002 ... 2.95
❑2, Oct 2002 ... 2.95
❑3, Nov 2002 ... 2.95
❑4, Jan 2003 ... 2.95
❑5, Feb 2003 ... 2.95

N-MINT

FATE'S FIVE
INNERVISION
❑1, b&w 2.50
❑2 2.50
❑3 2.50
❑4 2.50

FAT FREDDY'S COMICS & STORIES
RIP OFF
❑1, Dec 1983 3.00
❑2, Dec 1985 2.50

FAT FURY SPECIAL
AVALON
❑1, b&w; reprints Herbie stories 2.95

FATHER & SON
KITCHEN SINK
❑1, Jul 1995, b&w 2.75
❑2, Sep 1995, b&w 2.75
❑3, Dec 1995, b&w 2.75
❑4, Jan 1996, b&w 2.75
❑Ashcan 1, Jul 1995; ashcan edition limited to 200, b&w 2.00
❑Special 1, b&w; "Like, Special #1" 3.95

FATHOM (1ST SERIES)
COMICO
❑1, May 1987 1.50
❑2, Jun 1987 1.50
❑3, Jul 1987; wraparound cover 1.50

FATHOM (2ND SERIES)
COMICO
❑1, Nov 1992 2.50
❑2, Apr 1993 2.50
❑3, Jun 1993 2.50

FATHOM (3RD SERIES)
IMAGE
❑0; Wizard Promotional Edition: Given away with subsrciption to Wizard; Issue #0, with gold logo, had Jan. '00 in the indica and Feb. on the cover. 3.00
❑0/A; Green holografix cover 3.00
❑0/B; Wizard authentic edition 3.00
❑0.5 3.00
❑0.5/A, Feb 2003; Gold foil variant 4.00
❑1/A, Aug 1998; Variant covers, some pages 3.00
❑1/B, Aug 1998, b&w; Fathom standing underwater; Variant covers, some pages, bubbles 3.00
❑1/C, Aug 1998; Fathom, dolphins on cover w/inset close-up 3.00
❑1/D; Museum edition; Limited to 50 copies. 115.00
❑2, Sep 1998 3.00
❑2/A; Museum edition 100.00
❑3, Oct 1998 3.00
❑3/Variant; Monster Edition: No cover price 3.00
❑4, Mar 1999 2.50
❑5, May 1999 2.50
❑6, Jun 1999 2.50
❑7, Aug 1999 2.50
❑8, Sep 1999 2.50
❑9, Oct 1999 2.50
❑9/A; Holofoil edition 8.00
❑9/B; Platinum Holofoil edition 7.00
❑9/C; Aspen on outcropping 5.00
❑9/D; Green logo variant w/Aspen on rock outcropping 8.50
❑10, Jan 2000 2.50
❑10/A; Perfect 10 DFE Alternate cover 4.00
❑10/B; Perfect 10 DFE Alternate cover with Gold Stamp and certificate of authenticity 5.00
❑11, Apr 2000 2.50
❑12, Jul 2000; Witchblade in background, Fathom crawling on cover 2.50
❑12/A 6.00
❑12/B; Holofoil edition 6.00
❑12/C; DF Alternate edition 5.00
❑12/D; DF Alternate edition with certificate of authenticity; Gold logo 8.00
❑13 2002 2.50
❑13/A; Dynamic Forces variant with Certificate of Authenticity 5.00
❑13/B; Dynamic Forces gold foil variant; Limited to 999 copies 15.00
❑13/C; Dynamic Forces blue foil variant; Limited to 999 copies 15.00
❑14 2002 2.50
❑14/A; Pittsburgh Convention exclusive 6.00
❑Deluxe 1; Collects Fathom #1-9 24.95

FATHOM: EAST & WEST COAST TOUR BOOKS
IMAGE
❑1, Jan 2004 3.00

FATHOM (MICHAEL TURNER'S...): KILLIAN'S TIDE
IMAGE
❑1, Apr 2001 3.00
❑2, Jun 2001 3.00
❑3/A, Sep 2001; Blue background on cover 3.00
❑3/B, Sep 2001; Dark background on cover, skull reflected in water 3.00
❑4/A, Nov 2001 3.00
❑4/B, Nov 2001 3.00

FATHOM PREVIEW SPECIAL
IMAGE
❑1, ca. 1998 3.00

FATHOM SWIMSUIT SPECIAL
IMAGE
❑1, May 1999 2.95
❑2000, Dec 2000 2.95

FATMAN, THE HUMAN FLYING SAUCER
LIGHTNING
❑1, Apr 1967 35.00
❑2, Jun 1967 25.00
❑3, Sep 1967 25.00

FAT NINJA, THE
SILVERWOLF
❑1, b&w 1.50
❑2, b&w 1.50
❑3, b&w 1.50
❑4, b&w 1.50
❑5, b&w 1.50

FATT FAMILY, THE
SIDE SHOW
❑1, b&w 2.95

FAULTLINES
DC / VERTIGO
❑1, May 1997 2.50
❑2, Jun 1997 2.50
❑3, Jul 1997 2.50
❑4, Aug 1997 2.50
❑5, Sep 1997 2.50
❑6, Oct 1997 2.50

FAUNA REBELLION, THE
FANTAGRAPHICS
❑1, Mar 1990, b&w 2.00
❑2, Apr 1990, b&w 2.00
❑3, b&w 2.00

FAUST
NORTHSTAR
❑1, ca. 1989 8.00
❑1-2 4.00
❑1-3 3.00
❑2, ca. 1989 6.00
❑2-2 4.00
❑2-3 3.00
❑3, ca. 1989 5.00
❑3-2 3.00
❑4 4.00
❑4-2 3.00
❑5, Aug 1989 4.00
❑5-2 3.00
❑6, Nov 1989; becomes Rebel title 3.50
❑6-2 2.50
❑7 3.50
❑7-2; gatefold cover 2.50
❑8 3.50
❑8-2 2.50
❑9 3.00
❑9-2 2.50
❑10 3.00
❑10-2 2.50
❑11 2.50
❑Special 1, ca. 1988 10.00

FAUST 777: THE WRATH
AVATAR
❑0, Dec 1998 3.00
❑1, ca. 1998 3.00
❑1/A, ca. 1998; wraparound cover 3.50
❑2, ca. 1998 3.00
❑3, ca. 1998 3.00

FAUST: THE BOOK OF M
AVATAR
❑1 3.00

FEAR
MARVEL
❑1, Nov 1970 65.00
❑2, Jan 1971 25.00
❑3, Mar 1971 15.00
❑4, Jul 1971 SD, JK, JSt (a) 15.00
❑5, Nov 1971 SD (a) 15.00
❑6, Feb 1972 SL (w); SD, DH (a) 15.00
❑7, May 1972 15.00
❑8, Jun 1972 15.00
❑9, Aug 1972 15.00
❑10, Oct 1972; HC (a); Man-Thing stories begin ("Adventures into Fear") 25.00
❑11, Dec 1972; Man-Thing 15.00
❑12, Feb 1973; Man-Thing 9.00
❑13, Apr 1973; Man-Thing 9.00
❑14, Jun 1973; Man-Thing 9.00
❑15, Aug 1973; Man-Thing 9.00
❑16, Sep 1973; Man-Thing 9.00
❑17, Oct 1973; V: Wundarr. Man-Thing 9.00
❑18, Nov 1973; Man-Thing 9.00
❑19, Dec 1973; 1: Howard the Duck. Man-Thing 25.00
❑20, Feb 1974; PG (a); Morbius stories begin 18.00
❑21, Apr 1974; Morbius; Marvel Value Stamp #77: Swordsman 7.00
❑22, Jun 1974; Morbius; Marvel Value Stamp #49: Odin 7.00
❑23, Aug 1974; CR (a); A: Morbius. 1st Russell art; Marvel Value Stamp #86: Zemo 7.00
❑24, Oct 1974; A: Blade the Vampire Slayer. V: Blade. Morbius; Marvel Value Stamp #38: Red Sonja 10.00
❑25, Dec 1974; Morbius 7.00
❑26, Feb 1975; Morbius; Marvel Value Stamp #75: Morbius 7.00
❑27, Apr 1975; V: Simon Stroud. Morbius 7.00
❑28, Jun 1975; FR (a); Morbius 7.00
❑29, Aug 1975 DH (a); A: Helleyes. A: Simon Stroud. A: Morbius. 7.00
❑30, Oct 1975; Morbius 7.00
❑31, Dec 1975; Morbius; Marvel Value Stamp #75: Morbius 7.00

FEAR EFFECT: RETRO HELIX
IMAGE
❑1, Mar 2002
❑1/Gold, Mar 2002

FEAR EFFECT SPECIAL
IMAGE
❑1, May 2000 2.95

FEATHER
IMAGE
❑1, Aug 2003 2.95
❑2, Oct 2003 2.95
❑3, Dec 2003 2.95
❑4, Feb 2004 2.95
❑5, Jun 2004 5.95

FEDS 'N' HEADS
PRINT MINT
❑1 8.00

Condition price index: Multiply "NM prices" above by: **0.83 for Very Fine/Near Mint**
0.66 for Very Fine • 0.33 for Fine • 0.2 for Very Good • 0.125 for Good

N-MINT

FEEDERS
Dark Horse

❑1, Oct 1999 2.95

FEELGOOD FUNNIES
Rip Off

❑1 3.00

FELICIA HARDY: THE BLACK CAT
Marvel

❑1, Jul 1994 1.50
❑2, Aug 1994 1.50
❑3, Sep 1994 1.50
❑4, Oct 1994 1.50

FELIX THE CAT (2ND SERIES)
Dell

❑1, ca. 1962 35.00
❑2, Jan 1963 24.00
❑3, Apr 1963 24.00
❑4, Jul 1963 24.00
❑5, Oct 1963 24.00
❑6, Jan 1964 24.00
❑7, Apr 1964 24.00
❑8, Jul 1964 24.00
❑9, Oct 1964 24.00
❑10, Jan 1965 24.00
❑11, Apr 1965 24.00
❑12, Jul 1965 24.00

FELIX THE CAT (3RD SERIES)
Harvey

❑1, Sep 1991 2.00
❑2, Nov 1991 1.25
❑3, Jan 1992 1.25
❑4, Mar 1992 1.25
❑5, Jun 1992 1.25
❑6, Sep 1992 1.25
❑7, Jan 1993 1.25

FELIX THE CAT AND FRIENDS
Felix

❑1, ca. 1994 1.95
❑2, ca. 1994 1.95
❑3, ca. 1994 1.95
❑4, ca. 1994 1.95
❑5, ca. 1994 1.95

FELIX THE CAT BIG BOOK (VOL. 2)
Harvey

❑1, Sep 1992 1.95

FELIX THE CAT BLACK & WHITE
Felix

❑1 1.95
❑2 1.95
❑3 1.95
❑4 1.95
❑5 1.95
❑6 1.95
❑7 2.25
❑8 2.25

FELIX THE CAT DIGEST MAGAZINE
Harvey

❑1 1.75

FELON
Image

❑1, Nov 2001 2.95
❑2, Jan 2002 2.95
❑3, Feb 2002 2.95
❑4, Apr 2002 2.95

FEM 5
Express / Parody

❑1/A; variant cover 2.95
❑1/B; variant cover 2.95
❑1/C; variant cover 2.95
❑1/D; variant cover 2.95
❑2 2.95

FEMALE SEX PIRATES
Friendly

❑1 2.95

FEM FANTASTIQUE
AC

❑1, Jul 1988, b&w 1.95

N-MINT

FEMFORCE
AC

❑1, ca. 1985 O: Femforce. 4.00
❑2 1986 3.50
❑3 1986 3.00
❑4 1986 3.00
❑5 1986 3.00
❑6, Feb 1987 2.50
❑7, May 1987 2.50
❑8, Jul 1987 2.50
❑9, Aug 1987 2.50
❑10 2.50
❑11, Mar 1988 2.50
❑12, May 1988 2.50
❑13, May 1988 2.50
❑14 1988 2.50
❑15, Aug 1988 2.50
❑16 1988 2.50
❑17, Jan 1989 2.50
❑18 1989 2.50
❑19, Apr 1989 2.50
❑20 1989, b&w 2.50
❑21 1989, b&w 2.50
❑22 1989, b&w 2.50
❑23 1990, b&w 2.50
❑24, Apr 1990, b&w 2.50
❑25, May 1990, b&w 2.50
❑26, Jun 1990, b&w 2.50
❑27, Jul 1990, b&w 2.50
❑28, Aug 1990, b&w 2.50
❑29, Sep 1990, b&w 2.50
❑30, Oct 1990, b&w 2.50
❑31, Nov 1990 2.75
❑32, Dec 1990 2.75
❑33, Jan 1991 2.75
❑34, Feb 1991 2.75
❑35, Mar 1991 2.75
❑36, Apr 1991 2.75
❑37, May 1991 2.75
❑38, Jun 1991 2.75
❑39, Jul 1991 2.75
❑40, Aug 1991 2.75
❑41, Sep 1991 2.75
❑42, Oct 1991 2.75
❑43, Nov 1991; Includes pull-out comic, Rocketman and Jet Girl #0 . 2.75
❑44, Dec 1991 2.75
❑45, Jan 1992 2.75
❑46, Feb 1992 2.75
❑47, Mar 1992 2.75
❑48, Apr 1992 2.75
❑49, May 1992 2.75
❑50, Jun 1992; color; Includes flexi-disc 2.95
❑51, Jul 1992 2.75
❑52, Aug 1992 2.75
❑53 2.75
❑54 2.75
❑55 2.75
❑56 2.75
❑57 2.75
❑58 O: Microman. 2.75
❑59 2.75
❑60 2.75
❑61 2.75
❑62 2.75
❑63 2.95
❑64 2.95
❑65 2.95
❑66 2.95
❑67 2.95
❑68 2.95
❑69 2.95
❑70 2.95
❑71 2.95
❑72 2.95
❑73 2.95
❑74 2.95
❑75 2.95
❑76 2.95
❑77 2.95
❑78 2.95

New adventures of Felix the Cat and his friends appeared in Felix Comics' *Felix the Cat Black & White*.

© 1998 Felix Publications.

N-MINT

❑79 2.95
❑80 V: Iron Jaw. 2.95
❑81 2.95
❑82 2.95
❑83 2.95
❑84 2.95
❑85 2.95
❑86 2.95
❑87; 10th anniversary issue A: AC staff. 2.95
❑88 2.95
❑89 2.95
❑90 2.95
❑91 2.95
❑92 2.95
❑93 2.95
❑94 2.95
❑95 2.95
❑96 2.95
❑97, b&w 2.95
❑98, b&w; subtitled in Spanish 2.95
❑99, b&w 2.95
❑100, b&w; photo back cover 3.95
❑100/CS 6.90
❑101, b&w 4.95
❑102, b&w 4.95
❑103, b&w 4.95
❑104, b&w 4.95
❑105, b&w 4.95
❑106, b&w 4.95
❑107 4.95
❑108 4.95
❑109 4.95
❑110/A; Rayda on cover 2.95
❑110/B; Femforce on cover 2.95
❑111 2.95
❑112 2.95
❑113 2.95
❑114 2.95
❑115 0.00
❑116 0.00
❑117 0.00
❑118 0.00
❑119 0.00
❑120 0.00
❑121 0.00
❑122, Jan 2004 6.95
❑Special 1, Nov 1984 1.50

FEMFORCE FRIGHTBOOK
AC

❑1, b&w 2.95

FEMFORCE IN THE HOUSE OF HORROR
AC

❑1, b&w 2.50

FEMFORCE: NIGHT OF THE DEMON
AC

❑1, b&w 2.75

FEMFORCE: OUT OF THE ASYLUM SPECIAL
AC

❑1, Aug 1987, b&w 2.50

FEMFORCE PIN UP PORTFOLIO
AC

❑1 2.50
❑2 2.50
❑3 2.50

N-MINT

❑4, Dec 1991 .... 5.00
❑5 .... 5.00

FEMFORCE UNCUT
AC

❑1 .... 9.95

FEMFORCE UP CLOSE
AC

❑1, Apr 1992; Nightveil 3.00
❑2, Jul 1992; Stardust 3.00
❑3; Dragonfly 3.00
❑4 O: She Cat. 2.95
❑5; Blue Bulleteer 2.95
❑6; Ms. Victory 2.95
❑7; Ms. Victory 2.95
❑8; Tara, Garganta 2.95
❑9; Synn 2.95
❑10, b&w; Yankee Girl 2.95
❑11, b&w; Nightveil 2.95

FEMME MACABRE
LONDON NIGHT

❑1 .... 2.95

FEMME NOIRE
CAT-HEAD

❑1 .... 1.75
❑2 .... 1.75

FENRY
RAVEN

❑1 .... 6.95

FERRET (1ST SERIES)
MALIBU

❑1, ca. 1992 .... 1.95

FERRET, THE (2ND SERIES)
MALIBU

❑1, May 1993 .... 1.95
❑1/Variant, May 1993; die-cut 2.50
❑2, Jun 1993 .... 2.50
❑3, Jul 1993 .... 2.50
❑4, Aug 1993 .... 2.50
❑5, Sep 1993 .... 2.25
❑6, Oct 1993 .... 2.25
❑7, Nov 1993 .... 2.25
❑8, Dec 1993 .... 2.25
❑9, Jan 1994 .... 2.25
❑10, Feb 1994 .... 2.25

FEUD
MARVEL / EPIC

❑1, Jul 1993; embossed cardstock cover 2.50
❑2, Aug 1993 .... 1.95
❑3, Sep 1993 .... 1.95
❑4, Oct 1993 .... 1.95

FEVER
WONDER COMIX

❑1, b&w 1.95

FEVER DREAMS
KITCHEN SINK

❑1 .... 3.00

FEVER IN URBICAND
NBM

❑1 .... 12.95

F5
IMAGE

❑1, Apr 2000; Giant-size 2.95
❑2, Jun 2000 .... 2.50
❑3, Aug 2000 .... 2.50
❑4, Oct 2000 .... 2.50
❑Ashcan 1, Jan 2000; Preview issue . 2.50

F5 ORIGIN
DARK HORSE

❑1, Nov 2001, Several characters in profile on cover 2.99

FIFTH FORCE FEATURING HAWK AND ANIMAL, THE
ANTARCTIC

❑1, Apr 1999 .... 1.99
❑2, Jul 1999 .... 2.50

N-MINT

FIFTIES TERROR
ETERNITY

❑1, Oct 1988, b&w 2.00
❑2, Nov 1988, b&w 2.00
❑3, Dec 1988, b&w 2.00
❑4, Jan 1989, b&w 2.00
❑5, Feb 1989, b&w 2.00
❑6, Mar 1989, b&w 2.00

FIGHT FOR TOMORROW
DC / VERTIGO

❑1, Nov 2002, Several characters in profile on cover 2.50
❑2, Dec 2002 .... 2.50
❑3, Jan 2003 .... 2.50
❑4, Feb 2003 .... 2.50
❑5, Mar 2003 .... 2.50
❑6, Apr 2003 .... 2.50

FIGHTIN' 5
CHARLTON

❑28, Jul 1964; Continued from Space War (Vol. 2) #27 .... 20.00
❑29, Oct 1964 .... 10.00
❑30, Dec 1964 .... 10.00
❑31, Feb 1965 .... 9.00
❑32, May 1965 .... 9.00
❑33, Jul 1965 .... 9.00
❑34, Sep 1965 .... 9.00
❑35, Nov 1965 .... 9.00
❑36, Jan 1966 .... 9.00
❑37, May 1966 .... 9.00
❑38, Jul 1966 .... 9.00
❑39, Sep 1966 .... 9.00
❑40, Nov 1966 1: The Peacemaker. ... 18.00
❑41, Jan 1967 .... 10.00
❑42, Oct 1981 .... 3.00
❑43, Dec 1981 .... 3.00
❑44, Feb 1982 .... 3.00
❑45, Apr 1982 .... 3.00
❑46, Jun 1982 .... 3.00
❑47, Aug 1982 .... 3.00
❑48, Oct 1982 .... 3.00
❑49, Dec 1982 .... 3.00

FIGHTIN' AIR FORCE
CHARLTON

❑3, Feb 1956 .... 32.00
❑4, ca. 1956 .... 20.00
❑5, ca. 1956 .... 20.00
❑6 .... 15.00
❑7 .... 15.00
❑8 .... 15.00
❑9 .... 15.00
❑10 .... 15.00
❑11 .... 12.00
❑12, ca. 1957 .... 12.00
❑13, Dec 1958 .... 12.00
❑14, ca. 1959 .... 12.00
❑15, ca. 1959 .... 12.00
❑16, ca. 1959 .... 12.00
❑17, ca. 1959 .... 12.00
❑18, ca. 1959 .... 12.00
❑19 .... 12.00
❑20 .... 12.00
❑21 .... 8.00
❑22 .... 8.00
❑23, Oct 1960 .... 8.00
❑24, Dec 1960 .... 8.00
❑25, Feb 1961 .... 8.00
❑26, Apr 1961 .... 8.00
❑27, Jun 1961 .... 8.00
❑28, Aug 1961 .... 8.00
❑29, Oct 1961 .... 8.00
❑30, Dec 1961 .... 8.00
❑31, Mar 1962 .... 8.00
❑32, May 1962 .... 8.00
❑33, Jul 1962 .... 8.00
❑34, Sep 1962 .... 8.00
❑35, Nov 1962 DG (c) 8.00
❑36, Jan 1963 .... 8.00
❑37, Mar 1963 .... 8.00
❑38, May 1963 .... 8.00
❑39, Jul 1963 .... 8.00

N-MINT

❑40, Sep 1963 .... 8.00
❑41, Nov 1963 .... 8.00
❑42, Jan 1964 .... 8.00
❑43, Mar 1964 .... 8.00
❑44, Jun 1964 .... 8.00
❑45, Sep 1964 .... 8.00
❑46, Nov 1964 .... 8.00
❑47, Jan 1965 .... 8.00
❑48, ca. 1965 .... 8.00
❑49, Jul 1965 .... 8.00
❑50, Aug 1965 A: American Eagle. 8.00
❑51, Oct 1965 A: American Eagle. 8.00
❑52, Dec 1965 A: American Eagle. 8.00
❑53, Mar 1966 A: American Eagle. 8.00

FIGHTIN' ARMY
CHARLTON

❑16, Jan 1956 .... 24.00
❑17 1956 .... 18.00
❑18 1956 .... 18.00
❑19 1957 .... 18.00
❑20 1957 .... 18.00
❑21, Jul 1957 .... 15.00
❑22, Oct 1957 .... 15.00
❑23 1958 .... 15.00
❑24 1958 .... 15.00
❑25, Feb 1959 .... 15.00
❑26, Apr 1959 .... 15.00
❑27, Jun 1959 .... 15.00
❑28, Aug 1959 .... 15.00
❑29, Oct 1959 .... 15.00
❑30, Dec 1959 .... 15.00
❑31, Jan 1960 .... 12.00
❑32, Feb 1960 .... 12.00
❑33, Mar 1960 .... 12.00
❑34, Apr 1960 .... 12.00
❑35, May 1960 .... 12.00
❑36, Jul 1960 .... 12.00
❑37, Sep 1960 .... 12.00
❑38, Nov 1960 .... 12.00
❑39, Jan 1961 .... 12.00
❑40, Mar 1961 .... 12.00
❑41, May 1961 .... 10.00
❑42, ca. 1961 .... 10.00
❑43, ca. 1961 .... 10.00
❑44, Dec 1961 .... 10.00
❑45, ca. 1962 .... 10.00
❑46, May 1962 .... 10.00
❑47, ca. 1962 .... 10.00
❑48, ca. 1962 .... 10.00
❑49, Nov 1962 .... 10.00
❑50, Jan 1963 .... 10.00
❑51, ca. 1963 .... 8.00
❑52, ca. 1963 .... 8.00
❑53, Jul 1963 .... 8.00
❑54, Sep 1963 .... 8.00
❑55, Nov 1963 .... 8.00
❑56 1964 .... 8.00
❑57, Mar 1964 .... 8.00
❑58, Jun 1964 .... 8.00
❑59, ca. 1964 .... 8.00
❑60 1964 .... 8.00
❑61 1965 .... 8.00
❑62, Mar 1965 .... 8.00
❑63, Jun 1965 .... 8.00
❑64, Aug 1965 .... 8.00
❑65, Oct 1965 .... 8.00
❑66 1965 .... 8.00
❑67, Mar 1966 .... 8.00
❑68, May 1966 .... 8.00
❑69, Jul 1966 .... 8.00
❑70, Sep 1966 .... 8.00
❑71, Nov 1966 .... 8.00
❑72, Jan 1967 .... 8.00
❑73, Mar 1967 .... 8.00
❑74, ca. 1967 .... 8.00
❑75, Aug 1967 .... 8.00
❑76, Oct 1967; Lonely War of Capt. Willy Schultz begins 10.00
❑77, Dec 1967 .... 6.00
❑78, Feb 1968 .... 6.00
❑79, May 1968 .... 6.00

	N-MINT
❑80, Jul 1968	6.00
❑81, Sep 1968	6.00
❑82, Nov 1968	6.00
❑83, Jan 1969	6.00
❑84, Mar 1969	6.00
❑85, May 1969	6.00
❑86, Jul 1969	6.00
❑87, Sep 1969	6.00
❑88, Nov 1969	6.00
❑89, Jan 1970	6.00
❑90, Mar 1970	6.00
❑91, May 1970	6.00
❑92, Jul 1970	6.00
❑93, Sep 1970	6.00
❑94, Nov 1970	6.00
❑95, Jan 1971	6.00
❑96, Mar 1971	6.00
❑97, May 1971	6.00
❑98, Jul 1971	6.00
❑99, Sep 1971	6.00
❑100, Nov 1971	6.00
❑101, Jan 1972	5.00
❑102, Mar 1972	5.00
❑103, May 1972	5.00
❑104, Jul 1972	5.00
❑105, Sep 1972	5.00
❑106, Nov 1972	5.00
❑107, Jan 1973	5.00
❑108, Mar 1973	5.00
❑109, May 1973	5.00
❑110, Jul 1973	5.00
❑111, Sep 1973	5.00
❑112, Nov 1973	5.00
❑113, May 1974	5.00
❑114, Jul 1974	5.00
❑115, Sep 1974	5.00
❑116, Nov 1974	5.00
❑117, Feb 1975	5.00
❑118, ca. 1975	5.00
❑119, Jun 1975	5.00
❑120, Sep 1975	5.00
❑121, Nov 1975	4.00
❑122 1976	4.00
❑123, ca. 1976	4.00
❑124, May 1976	4.00
❑125, ca. 1976	4.00
❑126, Oct 1976	4.00
❑127, Dec 1976	4.00
❑128, Sep 1977	4.00
❑129, Nov 1977	4.00
❑130, Feb 1978	4.00
❑131, Mar 1978	4.00
❑132, Apr 1978	4.00
❑133, Jun 1978	4.00
❑134, Sep 1978; has Iron Corporal story	4.00
❑135, Nov 1978	4.00
❑136	4.00
❑137, ca. 1979	4.00
❑138, May 1979	4.00
❑139, Jul 1979	4.00
❑140, Aug 1979	4.00
❑141, ca. 1979	4.00
❑142, Nov 1979	4.00
❑143	4.00
❑144, Feb 1980	4.00
❑145, Apr 1980	4.00
❑146, Jul 1980	4.00
❑147, Sep 1980	4.00
❑148, Nov 1980	4.00
❑149, Jan 1981	4.00
❑150, Mar 1981	4.00
❑151, Apr 1981	3.00
❑152, Jun 1981	3.00
❑153, Aug 1981	3.00
❑154, Oct 1981	3.00
❑155, Dec 1981	3.00
❑156, Feb 1982	3.00
❑157, Apr 1982	3.00
❑158, Jun 1982	3.00
❑159, Aug 1982	3.00

	N-MINT
❑160, Oct 1982	3.00
❑161, Dec 1982	3.00
❑162, Feb 1983	3.00
❑163, Apr 1983	3.00
❑164, Jun 1983	3.00
❑165, Aug 1983	3.00
❑166, Oct 1983	3.00
❑167	3.00
❑168	3.00
❑169, May 1984	3.00
❑170, Jul 1984	3.00
❑171, Sep 1984	3.00
❑172, Nov 1984	3.00

FIGHTING AMERICAN (MINI-SERIES)
DC

❑1, Feb 1994 O: Fighting American.	2.00
❑2, Mar 1994	2.00
❑3, Apr 1994	2.00
❑4, May 1994	2.00
❑5, Jun 1994	2.00
❑6, Jul 1994	2.00

FIGHTING AMERICAN (AWESOME)
AWESOME

❑1/A, Aug 1997; Diving at guns, bayonets on cover	2.50
❑1/B, Aug 1997; Holding flag on cover	2.50
❑1/C, Aug 1997; Comics Cavalcade regular edition (two heroes diving toward a gun at lower left corner)	2.50
❑1/D, Aug 1997; Comics Cavalcade Liberty Gold Foil Edition	15.95
❑2, Oct 1997	2.50
❑3, Dec 1997	2.50

FIGHTING AMERICAN: DOGS OF WAR
AWESOME

❑1, Sep 1998 JSn (w)	2.50
❑1/A, Sep 1998; 98 Tour Edition cover; JSn (w)	3.00

FIGHTING AMERICAN: RULES OF THE GAME
AWESOME

❑1, Nov 1997	2.50
❑1/A, Nov 1997; Fighting American standing on cover	2.50
❑1/B, Nov 1997; Woman pointing gun on cover	2.50

FIGHTING AMERICAN SPECIAL COMICON EDITION
AWESOME

❑1, ca. 1997; No cover price; b&w preview of upcoming series given out at Comic-Con International: San Diego 1997	1.00

FIGHTING FEM CLASSICS
FORBIDDEN FRUIT

❑1, b&w	3.50

FIGHTING FEMS
FORBIDDEN FRUIT

❑1, b&w	3.50
❑2, b&w	3.50

FIGHTIN' MARINES
CHARLTON

❑21	16.00
❑22	16.00
❑23	16.00
❑24, ca. 1957	16.00
❑25, Mar 1958; Giant-size	36.00
❑26, ca. 1958; Giant-size	40.00
❑27, ca. 1958	16.00
❑28	16.00
❑29	16.00
❑30, Jun 1959	13.00
❑31, Aug 1959	13.00
❑32, ca. 1959	13.00
❑33, Jan 1960	13.00
❑34, Mar 1960	13.00
❑35, May 1960	13.00
❑36, Jul 1960	13.00
❑37, Sep 1960	13.00
❑38, Nov 1960	13.00
❑39, Jan 1961	13.00

"The Lonely War of Captain Willy Schultz," a realistic depiction of World War II as seen through the eyes of one soldier, began in *Fightin' Army* #76.

© 1967 Charlton.

	N-MINT
❑40, Mar 1961	10.00
❑41, May 1961	10.00
❑42, Jul 1961	10.00
❑43, Sep 1961	10.00
❑44, Nov 1961	10.00
❑45, Feb 1962	10.00
❑46, Apr 1962	10.00
❑47, Jun 1962	10.00
❑48, Aug 1962	10.00
❑49, Oct 1962	10.00
❑50, Dec 1962	10.00
❑51, Feb 1963	7.00
❑52, Apr 1963	7.00
❑53, Jun 1963	7.00
❑54, Aug 1963	7.00
❑55 1963	7.00
❑56 1963	7.00
❑57 1964	7.00
❑58, May 1964	7.00
❑59, Jul 1964	7.00
❑60, Oct 1964	7.00
❑61 1964	7.00
❑62, Feb 1965	7.00
❑63, May 1965	7.00
❑64, Jul 1965	7.00
❑65, Sep 1965	7.00
❑66, Nov 1965	7.00
❑67, Jan 1966	7.00
❑68, Mar 1966	7.00
❑69, ca. 1966	7.00
❑70, Aug 1966	7.00
❑71 1966	6.00
❑72 1966	6.00
❑73 1967	6.00
❑74 1967	6.00
❑75, Jul 1967	4.00
❑76, Sep 1967	4.00
❑77, Nov 1967	4.00
❑78, Jan 1968 1: Shotgun Harker. 1: The Chicken.	4.00
❑79, ca. 1968	4.00
❑80, Jul 1968	4.00
❑81, Sep 1968	4.00
❑82, Nov 1968; Giant-size	6.00
❑83, Jan 1969	4.00
❑84, Mar 1969	4.00
❑85, May 1969	4.00
❑86, Jul 1969	4.00
❑87, Sep 1969	4.00
❑88, Nov 1969	4.00
❑89, Jan 1970	4.00
❑90, Mar 1970	4.00
❑91, May 1970	3.50
❑92, Jul 1970	3.50
❑93, Sep 1970	3.50
❑94, Nov 1970	3.50
❑95, Jan 1971	3.50
❑96, Mar 1971	3.50
❑97, May 1971	3.50
❑98, Jul 1971	3.50
❑99, Sep 1971	3.50
❑100, Nov 1971	3.50
❑101, Jan 1972	3.00
❑102, Mar 1972	3.00
❑103, Apr 1972	3.00
❑104, Jun 1972	3.00
❑105, Aug 1972; Don Perlin cover	3.00

	N-MINT
❑106, Oct 1972	3.00
❑107, Dec 1972; Nicolas A. Lascia cover	3.00
❑108, Jan 1973	3.00
❑109, Mar 1973	3.00
❑110, Apr 1973	3.00
❑111, Jun 1973	3.00
❑112, ca. 1973	3.00
❑113, ca. 1973	3.00
❑114, Oct 1973	3.00
❑115 1973	3.00
❑116, Jan 1974	3.00
❑117, Jun 1974	3.00
❑118, ca. 1974	3.00
❑119, Nov 1974	3.00
❑120, Jan 1975	3.00
❑120-2, ca. 1975; reprints Charlton #120	1.50
❑121, Mar 1975	3.00
❑122, ca. 1975	3.00
❑123, May 1975	3.00
❑124, ca. 1975	3.00
❑125, ca. 1975	3.00
❑126, ca. 1975	2.50
❑127, Jan 1976	2.50
❑128, Mar 1976	2.50
❑129, May 1976	2.50
❑130, Jul 1976	2.50
❑131, Sep 1976	2.50
❑132, Nov 1976	2.50
❑133, Oct 1977	2.50
❑134, Dec 1977	2.50
❑135, Feb 1978	2.50
❑136, Apr 1978	2.50
❑137, Jun 1978	2.50
❑138, Aug 1978	2.50
❑139, Oct 1978	2.50
❑140	2.50
❑141	2.50
❑142, ca. 1979	2.50
❑143, ca. 1979	2.50
❑144, Jul 1979	2.50
❑145, ca. 1979	2.50
❑146, ca. 1979	2.50
❑147, Dec 1979	2.50
❑148, Jan 1980	2.50
❑149, Mar 1980	2.50
❑150, May 1980	2.50
❑151, ca. 1980	2.00
❑152, Oct 1980	2.00
❑153, Dec 1980	2.00
❑154, Jan 1981	2.00
❑155, Mar 1981	2.00
❑156, May 1981	2.00
❑157, Jul 1981	2.00
❑158, Sep 1981	2.00
❑159, Oct 1981	2.00
❑160, Dec 1981	2.00
❑161, Feb 1982	2.00
❑162, Apr 1982	2.00
❑163, Jul 1982	2.00
❑164, Sep 1982	2.00
❑165, Nov 1982	2.00
❑166, Jan 1983	2.00
❑167, Mar 1983	2.00
❑168, May 1983	2.00
❑169, Jul 1983	2.00
❑170, Sep 1983	2.00
❑171, Nov 1983	2.00
❑172, Jan 1984	2.00
❑173, Mar 1984	2.00
❑174, May 1984	2.00
❑175, Jul 1984	2.00
❑176, Sep 1984	2.00

FIGHTIN' NAVY
CHARLTON

	N-MINT
❑74, ca. 1956	24.00
❑75	18.00
❑76	18.00
❑77	18.00
❑78	18.00
❑79	18.00
❑80	18.00
❑81	15.00
❑82, Mar 1958	15.00
❑83, Sep 1958	15.00
❑84	15.00
❑85	15.00
❑86	15.00
❑87, ca. 1959	15.00
❑88, ca. 1959	15.00
❑89, ca. 1959	15.00
❑90, ca. 1959	15.00
❑91, ca. 1959	12.00
❑92, ca. 1959	12.00
❑93, ca. 1959	12.00
❑94, ca. 1959	12.00
❑95, ca. 1959	12.00
❑96, Jan 1960	12.00
❑97	12.00
❑98	12.00
❑99, Jul 1961	12.00
❑100, Sep 1961	12.00
❑101, Nov 1961	8.00
❑102, Jan 1962	8.00
❑103, Apr 1962	8.00
❑104, ca. 1962	8.00
❑105, Aug 1962	8.00
❑106, ca. 1962	8.00
❑107, ca. 1962	8.00
❑108, ca. 1963	8.00
❑109, ca. 1963	8.00
❑110, ca. 1963	8.00
❑111, Aug 1963	8.00
❑112, ca. 1963	8.00
❑113, ca. 1963	8.00
❑114, Feb 1964	8.00
❑115, May 1964	8.00
❑116, ca. 1964	8.00
❑117, ca. 1964	8.00
❑118, ca. 1964	8.00
❑119, Feb 1965	8.00
❑120, May 1965	8.00
❑121, ca. 1965	5.00
❑122, ca. 1965	5.00
❑123, Dec 1965	5.00
❑124, Jan 1966	5.00
❑125, ca. 1966; Last issue of original run	5.00
❑126, Aug 1983; Series begins again	2.00
❑127, Oct 1983	2.00
❑128, Dec 1983	2.00
❑129, Feb 1984	2.00
❑130, Apr 1984	2.00
❑131, Jun 1984	2.00
❑132, Aug 1984	2.00
❑133, Oct 1984	2.00

FIGHT MAN
MARVEL

	N-MINT
❑1, Jun 1993	2.00

FIGHT THE ENEMY
TOWER

	N-MINT
❑1, Aug 1966	22.00
❑2, Oct 1966	16.00
❑3	16.00

FIGMENTS
BLACKTHORNE

	N-MINT
❑1	1.75
❑2	1.75

FIGMENTS UNLIMITED
GRAPHIK

	N-MINT
❑1	1.25
❑2	1.25
❑3	1.25

FILES OF MS. TREE, THE
RENEGADE

	N-MINT
❑1, Jun 1984, b&w	6.00
❑2, Sep 1985, b&w	6.00
❑3, b&w	6.00

FILIBUSTING COMICS
FANTAGRAPHICS

	N-MINT
❑1, Jan 1995, b&w; Parody of Understanding Comics; b&w pin-ups, cardstock cover	2.75

FILTH, THE
DC / VERTIGO

	N-MINT
❑1, Aug 2002	2.95
❑2, Sep 2002	2.95
❑3, Oct 2002	2.95
❑4, Nov 2002	2.95
❑5, Dec 2002	2.95
❑6, Jan 2003	2.95
❑7, Feb 2003	2.95
❑8, Mar 2003	2.95
❑9, Apr 2003	2.95
❑10, Jun 2003	2.95
❑11, Jul 2003	2.95
❑12, Aug 2003	2.95
❑13, Sep 2003	2.95

FILTHY ANIMALS
RADIO

	N-MINT
❑1, Aug 1997	2.95
❑2 1998	2.95
❑3, Aug 1998	2.95
❑4	2.95

FILTHY HABITS
AEON

	N-MINT
❑1, Jul 1996, b&w	2.95
❑2, Nov 1996, b&w	2.95
❑3, Feb 1997, b&w	2.95

FINAL CYCLE, THE
DRAGON'S TEETH

	N-MINT
❑1, b&w	1.75
❑2, b&w	1.75
❑3, b&w	1.75
❑4, b&w	1.75

FINAL MAN, THE
C&T

	N-MINT
❑1, b&w	1.50

FINAL NIGHT, THE
DC

	N-MINT
❑1, Nov 1996	2.50
❑2, Nov 1996	2.00
❑3, Nov 1996	2.00
❑4, Nov 1996 D: Hal Jordan.	2.00

FINAL TABOO
AIRCEL

	N-MINT
❑1, b&w	2.50
❑2, b&w	2.50

FINALS
DC / VERTIGO

	N-MINT
❑1, Sep 1999	2.95
❑2, Oct 1999	2.95
❑3, Nov 1999	2.95
❑4, Dec 1999	2.95

FINDER
LIGHTSPEED

	N-MINT
❑1, Nov 1996, b&w; wraparound cover	4.00
❑2, Jan 1997, b&w	3.50
❑3, Mar 1997, b&w	3.50
❑4, May 1997, b&w	3.50
❑5, Jul 1997, b&w	3.50
❑6, Sep 1997, b&w	3.50
❑7, Nov 1997, b&w	3.50
❑8	3.50
❑9	3.50
❑10	3.50
❑11	3.50
❑12	3.50
❑13	3.50
❑14	3.50
❑15, Dec 1999	2.95
❑16, Feb 2000	2.95
❑17, May 2000	2.95
❑18	2.95
❑19	2.95
❑20	2.95
❑21	2.95

N-MINT

❑22, May 2001; Fight Scene 2.95
❑23, Jul 2001 2.95
❑24, Nov 2001
❑25, Jan 2002
❑26, Mar 2002
❑27, Jul 2002
❑28, Sep 2002
❑29, Nov 2002
❑30, Jan 2003
❑Ashcan 1 1.00

FINDER FOOTNOTES
LIGHTSPEED

❑1 6.00

FINIEOUS TREASURY, THE
TSR

❑1; magazine-sized 3.00

FINK, INC.
FINK, INC.

❑1 3.50

FIRE
CALIBER

❑1, b&w 2.95
❑2, b&w 2.95

FIREARM
MALIBU / ULTRAVERSE

❑0, Aug 1993; with videotape 14.95
❑1, Sep 1993 2.25
❑1/Ltd.; limited promotional edition; foil cover 3.00
❑2, Oct 1993; Rune 2.50
❑3, Nov 1993 1.95
❑4, Dec 1993; Break-Thru 1.95
❑5, Jan 1994 1.95
❑6, Feb 1994 1.95
❑7, Mar 1994 1.95
❑8, May 1994 1.95
❑9, Jun 1994 1.95
❑10, Jul 1994 3.50
❑11, Aug 1994; Flipbook with Ultraverse Premiere #5 1.95
❑12, Sep 1994 1.95
❑13, Oct 1994 1.95
❑14, Nov 1994 1.95
❑15, Dec 1994 1.95
❑16, Jan 1995 1.95
❑17, Feb 1995 1.95
❑18, Mar 1995 1.95
❑19, Apr 1995 1.95

FIREBRAND
DC

❑1, Feb 1996 O: Firebrand III (Alex Sanchez). 1: Firebrand III (Alex Sanchez). 2.00
❑2, Mar 1996 1.75
❑3, Apr 1996 1.75
❑4, May 1996 1.75
❑5, Jun 1996 1.75
❑6, Jul 1996 1.75
❑7, Aug 1996 1.75
❑8, Sep 1996 1.75
❑9, Oct 1996 1.75

FIREBREATHER
IMAGE

❑1, Jan 2003 2.95
❑2, Feb 2003 2.95
❑3, Mar 2003 2.95
❑4, Apr 2003 2.95

FIRE FROM HEAVEN
IMAGE

❑0.5 1.00
❑1, Mar 1996; wraparound cover 2.50
❑2, Jul 1996 2.50

FIRE SALE
RIP OFF

❑1, Dec 1989, b&w; benefit 2.50

FIRESTAR
MARVEL

❑1, Mar 1986 O: Firestar. A: X-Men. A: New Mutants. 1.50
❑2, Apr 1986 A: Wolverine. 1.50

N-MINT

❑3, May 1986 1.00
❑4, Jun 1986 1.00

FIRESTORM
DC

❑1, Mar 1978 AM, JR (a); O: Firestorm. 1: Firestorm. 3.00
❑2, Apr 1978 AM (a) 2.00
❑3, Jun 1978 AM (a); 1: Killer Frost. 2.00
❑4, Aug 1978 AM (a) 2.00
❑5, Oct 1978 AM (a) 2.00

FIRESTORM (SERIES)
DC

❑1, Jul 2004 2.50
❑2, Aug 2004 2.50
❑3, Sep 2004
❑33, Sep 2004

FIRESTORM, THE NUCLEAR MAN
DC

❑65, Nov 1987; A: Green Lantern. A: new Firestorm. Series continued from Fury of Firestorm #64 1.00
❑66, Dec 1987 A: Green Lantern. 1.00
❑67, Jan 1988; Millennium 1.00
❑68, Feb 1988; Millennium 1.00
❑69, Mar 1988 1.00
❑70, Apr 1988 1.00
❑71, May 1988 1.00
❑72, Jun 1988 1.00
❑73, Jul 1988 A: Soyuz. 1.00
❑74, Aug 1988 1.00
❑75, Sep 1988 1.00
❑76, Oct 1988 A: Firehawk. V: Brimstone. 1.00
❑77, Nov 1988 1.00
❑78, Dec 1988 1.00
❑79; no cover date 1.00
❑80; A: Firehawk, Power Girl. No cover date; Invasion! 1.00
❑81, Jan 1989; A: Soyuz. Invasion! Aftermath 1.00
❑82, Feb 1989 1.00
❑83, Mar 1989 1.00
❑84, Apr 1989 1.00
❑85, May 1989; new Firestorm 1.00
❑86, Jun 1989 1.00
❑87, Jul 1989 1.00
❑88, Aug 1989 1.00
❑89, Sep 1989 1.00
❑90, Oct 1989 1: Naiad. 1.00
❑91, Nov 1989 1.00
❑92, Dec 1989 1.00
❑93, Jan 1990 1.00
❑94, Feb 1990 1.00
❑95, Mar 1990 1.00
❑96, Apr 1990 1.00
❑97, May 1990 1.00
❑98, Jun 1990 1.00
❑99, Jul 1990 1.00
❑100, Aug 1990; Giant-size 2.95
❑Annual 5 1.25

FIRE TEAM
AIRCEL

❑1, b&w 2.50
❑2, Jan 1991, b&w 2.50
❑3, Feb 1991, b&w 2.50
❑4, b&w 2.50
❑5, b&w 2.50
❑6, b&w 2.50

FIRKIN
KNOCKABOUT

❑1 2.50
❑2 2.50
❑6, b&w 2.50

FIRST, THE
CROSSGEN

❑1, Dec 2000 3.25
❑2, Jan 2001 3.00
❑3, Feb 2001 3.00
❑4, Mar 2001 3.00
❑5, Apr 2001 3.00
❑6, May 2001 2.95

Introduced on the animated *Spider-Man and His Amazing Friends*, Firestar had her own four-issue mini-series in 1986, where an attempt was made to shoehorn her into Marvel continuity.

© 1986 Marvel Comics.

N-MINT

❑7, Jun 2001 2.95
❑8, Jul 2001 2.95
❑9, Aug 2001 2.95
❑10, Sep 2001 2.95
❑11, Oct 2001 2.95
❑12, Nov 2001 2.95
❑13, Dec 2001 2.95
❑14, Jan 2002 2.95
❑15, Feb 2002 2.95
❑16, Mar 2002 2.95
❑17, Apr 2002 2.95
❑18, May 2002 2.95
❑19, Jun 2002 2.95
❑20, Jul 2002 2.95
❑21, Aug 2002 2.95
❑22, Sep 2002 2.95
❑23, Oct 2002 2.95
❑24, Nov 2002 2.95
❑25, Dec 2002 2.95
❑26, Jan 2003 2.95
❑27, Feb 2003 2.95
❑28, Mar 2003 2.95
❑29, Apr 2003 2.95
❑30, May 2003 2.95
❑31, Jun 2003 2.95
❑32, Jul 2003 2.95
❑33, Aug 2003 2.95
❑34, Sep 2003 2.95
❑35, Nov 2003 2.95
❑36, Dec 2003 2.95
❑37, Dec 2003 2.95

FIRST ADVENTURES
FIRST

❑1, Dec 1985 1.25
❑2, Jan 1986 1.25
❑3, Feb 1986 1.25
❑4, Mar 1986 1.25
❑5, Apr 1986 1.25

1ST FOLIO
PACIFIC

❑1, Mar 1984; Joe Kubert School 1.50

FIRST GRAPHIC NOVEL
FIRST

❑

1ST ISSUE SPECIAL
DC

❑1, Apr 1975; JK (c); JK (w); JK (a); 1: Atlas. 4.00
❑2, May 1975; Green Team 4.00
❑3, Jun 1975; Metamorpho 4.00
❑4, Jul 1975; (c); Lady Cop 4.00
❑5, Aug 1975; JK (c); JK (w); JK (a); 1: Manhunters. 1: Manhunter II (Mark Shaw). 4.00
❑6, Sep 1975; JK (c); JK (w); JK (a); Dingbats 4.00
❑7, Oct 1975; (c); SD (a); A: Creeper. 4.00
❑8, Nov 1975; MGr (c); MGr (w); MGr (a); O: Warlord. 1: Deimos. 1: Skartaris. 1: Warlord. 10.00
❑9, Dec 1975; JKu (c); A: Doctor Fate. 4.00
❑10, Jan 1976; (c); Outsiders 4.00
❑11, Feb 1976; MGr (c); AM (a); Code Name: Assassin 4.00

N-MINT

- ❑12, Mar 1976; JKu (c); O: Starman II (Mikaal Tomas). 1: Starman II (Mikaal Tomas). 4.00
- ❑13, Apr 1976; (c); Return of the New Gods 5.00

FIRST KINGDOM, THE
BUD PLANT

- ❑1 .... 3.00
- ❑2 .... 2.50
- ❑3 .... 2.50
- ❑4 .... 2.50
- ❑5 .... 2.50
- ❑6 .... 2.00
- ❑7 .... 2.00
- ❑8 .... 2.00
- ❑9 .... 2.00
- ❑10 .... 2.00
- ❑11 .... 2.00
- ❑12 .... 2.00
- ❑13 .... 2.00
- ❑14 .... 2.00
- ❑15 .... 2.00
- ❑16 .... 2.00
- ❑17 .... 2.00
- ❑18 .... 2.00
- ❑19 .... 2.00
- ❑20 .... 2.00
- ❑21 .... 2.00
- ❑22 .... 2.00
- ❑23 .... 2.00
- ❑24 .... 2.00

FIRST KISS
CHARLTON

- ❑1, Dec 1957 DG (a) 45.00
- ❑2, Feb 1958 .... 28.00
- ❑3, May 1958 DG (a) 22.00
- ❑4, ca. 1958 .... 18.00
- ❑5, ca. 1958 .... 18.00
- ❑6, ca. 1958 DG (a) 13.00
- ❑7, ca. 1959 DG (a) 13.00
- ❑8, ca. 1959 .... 13.00
- ❑9, ca. 1959 .... 13.00
- ❑10, Sep 1959 .... 13.00
- ❑11, Nov 1959 .... 12.00
- ❑12, Jan 1960 DG (a) 12.00
- ❑13, Mar 1960 DG (a) 12.00
- ❑14, May 1960 DG (a) 12.00
- ❑15, Jul 1960 .... 12.00
- ❑16, Sep 1960 .... 12.00
- ❑17, Nov 1960 .... 12.00
- ❑18, Jan 1961 .... 12.00
- ❑19, Mar 1961 .... 12.00
- ❑20, May 1961 .... 12.00
- ❑21, Jul 1961 .... 8.00
- ❑22, Sep 1961 .... 8.00
- ❑23, Nov 1961 .... 8.00
- ❑24, ca. 1962 .... 8.00
- ❑25, ca. 1962 .... 8.00
- ❑26, ca. 1962 .... 8.00
- ❑27, ca. 1962 .... 8.00
- ❑28, ca. 1962 .... 8.00
- ❑29, Dec 1962 DG (c) 8.00
- ❑30, Feb 1963 DG (a) 8.00
- ❑31, Apr 1963 .... 8.00
- ❑32, Jun 1963 DP (a) 8.00
- ❑33, Aug 1963 .... 8.00
- ❑34, Oct 1963 .... 8.00
- ❑35, Dec 1963 DG (c) 8.00
- ❑36, ca. 1964 .... 8.00
- ❑37, ca. 1964 DG (c) 8.00
- ❑38, ca. 1964 DG (c) 8.00
- ❑39, ca. 1964 DG (c) 8.00
- ❑40, ca. 1965 DG (c) 8.00

FIRST MAN
IMAGE

- ❑1, Jun 1997; cover says 1st Man, indicia says First Man 2.50

FIRST SIX PACK
FIRST

- ❑1, Jul 1987 .... 1.00
- ❑2 JSn, HC, MGr (w); PS, LMc (a) 1.00

N-MINT

FIRST TRIP TO THE MOON
AVALON

- ❑1, b&w; reprints Charlton story 2.50

FIRST WAVE
ANDROMEDA

- ❑1, Dec 2000 .... 2.99

FISHMASTERS
SLAVE LABOR

- ❑1, May 1994; adapts TV show 2.95

FISH POLICE (VOL. 1)
FISHWRAP

- ❑1, Dec 1985; Indicia title: Inspector Gill of the Fish Police 1.25
- ❑1-2; Indicia changed to "Fish Police" 1.25
- ❑2, Feb 1986 .... 1.25
- ❑3, Apr 1986 .... 1.25
- ❑4, Jun 1986 .... 1.50
- ❑5, Aug 1986 .... 1.50
- ❑6 1986 .... 1.50
- ❑7, Feb 1987; indicia says Feb 86 .... 1.50
- ❑8 1987 .... 1.50
- ❑9 1987 .... 1.50
- ❑10 1987 .... 1.50
- ❑11 1987 .... 1.50

FISH POLICE, THE (VOL. 2)
COMICO

- ❑5 1987 .... 1.75
- ❑6 1987 .... 1.75
- ❑7 .... 1.75
- ❑8 .... 1.75
- ❑9 .... 1.75
- ❑10 1988 .... 1.75
- ❑11 1988 .... 1.75
- ❑12 1988 .... 1.75
- ❑13 1988 .... 1.75
- ❑14, Dec 1988 .... 1.75
- ❑15 .... 1.75
- ❑16 .... 1.75
- ❑17, Jun 1989 .... 2.50
- ❑18, Aug 1989, b&w; Black & white format begins, Apple Comics 2.25
- ❑19, Oct 1989, b&w 2.25
- ❑20, Mar 1990, b&w 2.25
- ❑21 1990, b&w 2.25
- ❑22 1990, b&w 2.25
- ❑23 1990, b&w 2.25
- ❑24 1990, b&w 2.25
- ❑25, Nov 1990, b&w 2.25
- ❑26, b&w 2.25
- ❑Special 1, ca. 1987 .... 2.25

FISH POLICE (MARVEL)
MARVEL

- ❑1, Oct 1992, b&w 1.25
- ❑2, Nov 1992, b&w 1.25
- ❑3, Dec 1992, b&w 1.25
- ❑4, Jan 1993, b&w 1.25
- ❑5, Feb 1993, b&w 1.25
- ❑6, Mar 1993 .... 1.25

FISH SHTICKS
APPLE

- ❑1, Nov 1991, b&w 2.00
- ❑2, b&w 2.00
- ❑3, May 1992, b&w 2.00
- ❑4, b&w 2.00
- ❑5, b&w 2.00
- ❑6, b&w 2.00

FISSION CHICKEN
FANTAGRAPHICS

- ❑1, ca. 1990, b&w 2.00
- ❑2, b&w 2.00
- ❑3, b&w 2.00
- ❑4, b&w 2.00

FISSION CHICKEN: PLAN NINE FROM VORTOX
MU

- ❑1, Jul 1994 .... 3.95

N-MINT

FIST OF GOD, THE
ETERNITY

- ❑1, May 1988 .... 2.25
- ❑2, Jul 1988 .... 1.95
- ❑3, Sep 1988 .... 1.95
- ❑4, Nov 1988 .... 1.95

FIST OF THE NORTH STAR
VIZ

- ❑1 .... 2.95
- ❑2 .... 2.95
- ❑3 .... 2.95
- ❑4 .... 2.95
- ❑5 .... 2.95
- ❑6 .... 2.95
- ❑7 .... 2.95
- ❑8 .... 2.95

FIST OF THE NORTH STAR PART 2
VIZ

- ❑1 .... 2.75
- ❑2 .... 2.75
- ❑3 .... 2.95
- ❑4 .... 2.95
- ❑5 .... 2.95
- ❑6 .... 2.95
- ❑7 .... 2.95
- ❑8 .... 2.95

FIST OF THE NORTH STAR PART 3
VIZ

- ❑1 .... 2.95
- ❑2 .... 2.95
- ❑3, Sep 1996 .... 2.95
- ❑4, Oct 1996 .... 2.95
- ❑5, Nov 1996 .... 2.95

FIST OF THE NORTH STAR PART 4
VIZ

- ❑1, Dec 1996 .... 2.95
- ❑2, Jan 1997 .... 2.95
- ❑3, Feb 1997 .... 2.95
- ❑4, Mar 1997 .... 2.95
- ❑5 .... 2.95
- ❑6 .... 2.95
- ❑7 .... 2.95

FIVE LITTLE COMICS
SCOTT MCCLOUD

- ❑1 .... 4.00

FIVE YEARS OF PAIN
BONEYARD

- ❑1, Jan 1997 .... 3.95

FLAG FIGHTERS
IRONCAT

- ❑1, Sep 1997, b&w 2.95
- ❑2 1997, b&w 2.95
- ❑3, Nov 1997, b&w 2.95
- ❑4 .... 2.95
- ❑5 .... 2.95

FLAMEHEAD
JNCO

- ❑0 ....

FLAME, THE (AJAX)
AJAX

- ❑1; 1: Flame II 285.00
- ❑2 .... 165.00
- ❑3 .... 150.00

FLAME TWISTERS
BROWN STUDY

- ❑1, Oct 1994, b&w 2.50
- ❑2, Mar 1995, b&w 2.50

FLAMING CARROT (KILLIAN)
KILIAN

- ❑1, Sum 1981; magazine 35.00

FLAMING CARROT COMICS
AARDVARK-VANAHEIM

- ❑1, May 1984; 1: Flaming Carrot. Aardvark-Vanaheim publishes 26.00
- ❑2, Jul 1984 .... 15.00
- ❑3, Sep 1984 .... 12.00
- ❑4, Nov 1984 .... 10.00
- ❑5, Jan 1985 .... 8.00

N-MINT

❑6, Mar 1985; becomes Flaming Carrot Comics 8.00
❑7, May 1985; Renegade begins publishing 7.00
❑8, Aug 1985 .... 5.00
❑9, Oct 1985 .... 5.00
❑10, Dec 1985 .... 4.00
❑11, Mar 1986 .... 4.00
❑12, May 1986 .... 4.00
❑13, Jul 1986 .... 3.00
❑14, Oct 1986 .... 3.00
❑15, Jan 1987 .... 3.00
❑15/A, Jan 1987; no cover price 4.00
❑16, Jun 1987 1: Mystery Men. 4.00
❑17, Jul 1987 A: Mystery Men. 3.00
❑18, Jun 2001; Dark Horse begins publishing 3.00
❑19, Jun 2001 .... 3.00
❑20, Nov 1988 .... 3.00
❑21, Spr 1989 .... 3.00
❑22, Jun 1989 .... 3.00
❑23, Nov 1989 .... 3.00
❑24, Apr 1990 .... 3.00
❑25, Apr 1991 A: Teenage Mutant Ninja Turtles. 3.50
❑26, Jun 1991 A: Teenage Mutant Ninja Turtles. 2.50
❑27; TMc (c); A: Mystery Men. A: Teenage Mutant Ninja Turtles. no indicia 2.50
❑28, Aug 1992 .... 2.50
❑29, Oct 1992 .... 2.50
❑30, Dec 1992; brown background ... 2.50
❑30/A, Dec 1992; blue background ... 2.50
❑31, Oct 1994; A: Herbie. Story originally scheduled for Herbie (Dark Horse) #3 .... 2.50
❑Annual 1, Jan 1997, b&w; A: Mystery Men. 1997 Annual; cardstock cover 5.00

FLAMING CARROT STORIES
DARK HORSE

❑1; "Version A" 5.00

FLARE
HERO

❑1, Nov 1988 .... 2.75
❑2, Dec 1988 .... 2.75
❑3, Jan 1989 .... 2.75

FLARE (VOL. 2)
HERO

❑1 .... 3.00
❑2 .... 3.00
❑3, Jan 1989 .... 3.00
❑4, Sum 1991 .... 2.75
❑5; Eternity Smith 2.75
❑6, Sep 1991 .... 2.75
❑7, Nov 1991 .... 2.75
❑8, b&w 2.75
❑9, b&w 2.75
❑10, b&w 2.75
❑11, Apr 1993, b&w 2.75
❑12, Jun 1993, b&w 2.75
❑13, Aug 1993, b&w 2.75
❑14, Oct 1993, b&w 2.75
❑15, Jan 1994 .... 2.75
❑16 .... 2.75
❑Annual 1, b&w 4.50

FLARE ADVENTURES
HERO

❑1 .... 1.25
❑2; Flip-book format with Champions Classics #2 .... 2.95
❑3; Flip-book format with Champions Classics #3 .... 2.95
❑4, b&w; Flip-book format with Champions Classics #4 .... 3.95
❑5, b&w; Flip-book format with Champions Classics #5 .... 3.95
❑6, b&w; Flip-book format with Champions Classics #6 .... 3.95
❑7, b&w; Flip-book format with Champions Classics #7 .... 3.95
❑8, b&w; Flip-book format with Champions Classics #8 .... 3.95
❑9, b&w; Flip-book format 3.95

N-MINT

❑10, b&w; Flip-book format 3.95
❑11, b&w; Flip-book format 3.95
❑12, b&w; Flip-book format 3.95
❑13, b&w; Flip-book format 3.95

FLARE FIRST EDITION
HERO

❑1; contents will vary 3.50
❑2; contents will vary 3.50
❑3, b&w 3.50
❑4, b&w 4.50
❑5, b&w 4.50
❑6, b&w 3.95
❑7, b&w 3.95
❑8, b&w 3.95
❑9; Sparkplug 3.95
❑10 .... 3.95
❑11, Oct 1993, b&w 3.95

FLASH, THE (1ST SERIES)
DC

❑105, Feb 1959; CI (a); O: Flash II (Barry Allen). 1: Mirror Master. numbering continued from Flash Comics 3850.00
❑106, May 1959 CI (a); O: Pied Piper. O: Gorilla Grodd. 1: Gorilla City. 1: Gorilla Grodd. 1: The Pied Piper. ... 1100.00
❑107, Jul 1959 CI (a); 2: Gorilla Grodd. 650.00
❑108, Sep 1959 CI (a); A: Gorilla Grodd. 600.00
❑109, Nov 1959 CI (a) 440.00
❑110, Jan 1960 MA, CI (a); O: Kid Flash. 1: Weather Wizard. 1: Kid Flash. 800.00
❑111, Mar 1960 CI (a); 2: Kid Flash. . 275.00
❑112, May 1960 CI (a); O: Elongated Man. 1: Elongated Man. 300.00
❑113, Jul 1960 CI (a); O: Trickster. 1: Trickster. 275.00
❑114, Aug 1960 CI (a); O: Captain Cold. 200.00
❑115, Sep 1960 MA, CI (a) 175.00
❑116, Nov 1960 CI (a) 175.00
❑117, Dec 1960 MA, CI (a); O: Captain Boomerang. 1: Captain Boomerang. 200.00
❑118, Feb 1961 CI (a) 175.00
❑119, Mar 1961; CI (a); Wedding of Elongated Man and Sue Dearborn . 175.00
❑120, May 1961 CI (a) 175.00
❑121, Jun 1961 CI (a) 135.00
❑122, Aug 1961 CI (a); O: Top, The. 1: Top, The. 135.00
❑123, Sep 1961; CI (a); O: Flash I (Jay Garrick). O: Flash II (Barry Allen). 1: Earth-2 (as an alternate Earth). A: Flash I (Jay Garrick). 1st meeting between Golden and Silver Age Flashes; First Alley Award winner: Best Cover, Best Single Issue of a Comic Book, Best Story 625.00
❑124, Nov 1961 CI (a) 90.00
❑125, Dec 1961 CI (a); 1: cosmic treadmill. 100.00
❑126, Feb 1962 CI (a) 100.00
❑127, Mar 1962 CI (a) 100.00
❑128, May 1962 CI (a); O: Abra Kadabra. 1: Abra Kadabra. 100.00
❑129, Jun 1962 CI (a); A: Flash I (Jay Garrick). 200.00
❑130, Aug 1962 CI (a) 100.00
❑131, Sep 1962 CI (a); A: Green Lantern. 100.00
❑132, Nov 1962 CI (a) 100.00
❑133, Dec 1962 CI (a) 100.00
❑134, Feb 1963 CI (a) 100.00
❑135, Mar 1963 CI (a) 100.00
❑136, May 1963 CI (a) 100.00
❑137, Jun 1963; CI (a); A: Flash I (Jay Garrick). Vandal Savage 200.00
❑138, Sep 1963 CI (a) 90.00
❑139, Sep 1963 CI (a); O: Professor Zoom. 1: Professor Zoom. 100.00
❑140, Nov 1963 CI (a); O: Heat Wave. 1: Heat Wave. 90.00
❑141, Dec 1963 CI (a) 90.00
❑142, Feb 1964 CI (a) 90.00
❑143, Mar 1964 CI (a) 90.00
❑144, May 1964 CI (a) 90.00
❑145, Jun 1964 CI (a) 90.00
❑146, Aug 1964 CI (a) 90.00

The Silver Age adventures of The Flash continued the numbering of the Golden Age *Flash Comics*, making #109 really only the *fifth* issue of the Silver Age series.

© 1959 National Periodical Publications Inc. (DC).

N-MINT

❑147, Sep 1964 CI (a) 90.00
❑148, Nov 1964 CI (a); V: Captain Boomerang. 90.00
❑149, Dec 1964 CI (a) 90.00
❑150, Feb 1965 CI (a) 90.00
❑151, Mar 1965 CI (a); A: Flash I (Jay Garrick). 75.00
❑152, May 1965 CI (a) 55.00
❑153, Jun 1965 CI (a) 55.00
❑154, Aug 1965 CI (a) 55.00
❑155, Sep 1965 CI (a) 55.00
❑156, Nov 1965 CI (a) 55.00
❑157, Dec 1965 CI (a) 55.00
❑158, Feb 1966 CI (a) 55.00
❑159, Mar 1966 CI (a) 55.00
❑160, Apr 1966; Giant-size CI (a) 75.00
❑161, May 1966 CI (a) 35.00
❑162, Jun 1966 CI (a) 35.00
❑163, Aug 1966 CI (a) 35.00
❑164, Sep 1966 CI (a) 35.00
❑165, Nov 1966; CI (a); Wedding of Flash II (Barry Allen) and Iris West 65.00
❑166, Dec 1966 CI (a) 35.00
❑167, Feb 1967 CI (a); O: Flash II (Barry Allen). 1: Mopee. 35.00
❑168, Mar 1967 .... 35.00
❑169, May 1967; Giant-size O: Flash II (Barry Allen). 70.00
❑170, Jun 1967 .... 35.00
❑171, Jun 1967 V: Doctor Light. 35.00
❑172, Aug 1967 .... 35.00
❑173, Sep 1967 .... 35.00
❑174, Nov 1967; V: Rogue's Gallery. Flash II reveals identity to wife 35.00
❑175, Dec 1967; Flash II races Superman 130.00
❑176, Feb 1968 .... 35.00
❑177, Mar 1968 .... 35.00
❑178, May 1968; Giant-size 35.00
❑179, May 1968; Flash visits DC Comics 35.00
❑180, Jun 1968 .... 35.00
❑181, Aug 1968 .... 30.00
❑182, Sep 1968 .... 30.00
❑183, Nov 1968 .... 30.00
❑184, Dec 1968 .... 30.00
❑185, Feb 1969 .... 30.00
❑186, Mar 1969 .... 30.00
❑187, May 1969; Giant-size 35.00
❑188, May 1969 .... 25.00
❑189, Jun 1969 JKu (c) 25.00
❑190, Aug 1969 .... 25.00
❑191, Sep 1969 .... 20.00
❑192, Nov 1969 .... 20.00
❑193, Dec 1969 .... 20.00
❑194, Feb 1970 .... 20.00
❑195, Mar 1970 .... 20.00
❑196, May 1970; Giant-size 35.00
❑197, May 1970 .... 20.00
❑198, Jun 1970 .... 20.00
❑199, Aug 1970 .... 20.00
❑200, Sep 1970 .... 20.00
❑201, Nov 1970 .... 14.00
❑202, Dec 1970 .... 14.00
❑203, Feb 1971 .... 14.00
❑204, Mar 1971 .... 14.00
❑205, May 1971; Giant-size 14.00
❑206, May 1971 .... 14.00
❑207, Jun 1971 .... 14.00

	N-MINT
❑208, Aug 1971; Giant-size; Elongated Man back-up	14.00
❑209, Sep 1971; Giant-size V: Captain Boomerang. V: Trickster.	14.00
❑210, Dec 1971; Giant-size; in future	14.00
❑211, Dec 1971; Giant-size; Golden Age Flash back-up	14.00
❑212, Feb 1972	14.00
❑213, Mar 1972	14.00
❑214, Apr 1972; CI (a); O: Metal Men. a.k.a. DC 100-Page Super Spectacular #DC-11; wraparound cover; reprints O: Metal Men; Reprints Showcase #37	14.00
❑215, May 1972; A: Golden Age Flash. V: Vandal Savage. giant	14.00
❑216, Jun 1972	14.00
❑217, Sep 1972; FMc, DG, NA, IN (a); Green Lantern/Green Arrow back-up; Green Arrow back-up	14.00
❑218, Nov 1972 NA (a)	14.00
❑219, Jan 1973; NA (a); last Green Arrow back-up	14.00
❑220, Mar 1973	10.00
❑221, May 1973	10.00
❑222, Aug 1973	10.00
❑223, Oct 1973; NA (a); Green Lantern back-up	10.00
❑224, Dec 1973	10.00
❑225, Feb 1974	10.00
❑226, Apr 1974 NA (a); V: Captain Cold.	15.00
❑227, Jun 1974	10.00
❑228, Aug 1974	10.00
❑229, Oct 1974; 100 Page giant V: Rag Doll.	16.00
❑230, Dec 1974 V: Doctor Alchemy.	10.00
❑231, Feb 1975	10.00
❑232, Apr 1975; 100 Page giant	19.00
❑233, May 1975; 100 Page giant	8.00
❑234, Jun 1975	8.00
❑235, Aug 1975 A: Green Lantern. A: Golden Age Flash. V: Vandal Savage.	8.00
❑236, Sep 1975 A: Doctor Fate. A: Golden Age Flash.	8.00
❑237, Nov 1975 A: Green Lantern.	8.00
❑238, Dec 1975	4.00
❑239, Feb 1976	4.00
❑240, Mar 1976	4.00
❑241, May 1976	4.00
❑242, Jun 1976	4.00
❑243, Aug 1976	4.00
❑244, Sep 1976	4.00
❑245, Nov 1976	4.00
❑246, Jan 1977	4.00
❑247, Mar 1977	4.00
❑248, Apr 1977	4.00
❑249, May 1977	4.00
❑250, Jun 1977 1: Golden Glider. V: Golden Glider.	4.00
❑251, Aug 1977	4.00
❑252, Sep 1977	4.00
❑253, Sep 1977	4.00
❑254, Oct 1977 V: Rogue's Gallery.	4.00
❑255, Nov 1977	4.00
❑256, Dec 1977 V: Rogue's Gallery.	4.00
❑257, Jan 1978	4.00
❑258, Feb 1978	4.00
❑259, Mar 1978	4.00
❑260, Apr 1978	4.00
❑261, May 1978	4.00
❑262, Jun 1978 V: Golden Glider.	4.00
❑263, Jul 1978 V: Golden Glider.	4.00
❑264, Aug 1978	4.00
❑265, Sep 1978	4.00
❑266, Oct 1978	4.00
❑267, Nov 1978	4.00
❑268, Dec 1978	4.00
❑269, Jan 1979	4.00
❑270, Mar 1979	4.00
❑271, Mar 1979 RB (a)	3.50
❑272, Apr 1979 RB (a)	3.50
❑273, May 1979 RB (a)	3.50
❑274, Jun 1979 RB (a)	3.50

	N-MINT
❑275, Jul 1979 D: Iris West Allen (Flash II's wife).	3.50
❑276, Aug 1979 A: JLA.	3.50
❑277, Sep 1979 A: JLA.	3.50
❑278, Oct 1979	3.50
❑279, Nov 1979	3.50
❑280, Dec 1979	3.50
❑281, Jan 1980	3.50
❑282, Feb 1980	3.50
❑283, Mar 1980	3.50
❑284, Apr 1980	3.50
❑285, May 1980	3.50
❑286, Jun 1980 1: Rainbow Raider.	3.50
❑287, Jul 1980	3.50
❑288, Aug 1980	3.50
❑289, Sep 1980; GP, DH (a); O: Firestorm. George Perez's first work at DC	5.00
❑290, Oct 1980 GP (a); A: Firestorm.	3.00
❑291, Nov 1980	3.00
❑292, Dec 1980	3.00
❑293, Jan 1981 A: Firestorm.	3.00
❑294, Feb 1981	3.00
❑295, Mar 1981 V: Gorilla Grodd.	3.00
❑296, Apr 1981	3.00
❑297, May 1981	3.00
❑298, Jun 1981	3.00
❑299, Jul 1981	3.00
❑300, Aug 1981; Giant-size; CI (a); O: Flash. A: New Teen Titans. wraparound cover	5.00
❑301, Sep 1981	3.00
❑302, Oct 1981	3.00
❑303, Nov 1981	3.00
❑304, Dec 1981 1: Colonel Computron.	3.00
❑305, Jan 1982	3.50
❑306, Feb 1982 CI, KG (a)	3.50
❑307, Mar 1982; CI, KG (a); Doctor Fate back-up	2.50
❑308, Apr 1982 CI, KG (a)	2.50
❑309, May 1982 CI, KG (a)	2.50
❑310, Jun 1982 CI, KG (a)	2.50
❑311, Jul 1982 CI, KG (a)	2.50
❑312, Aug 1982 CI, KG (a); 1: Creed Phillips.	2.50
❑313, Sep 1982 CI, KG (a)	2.50
❑314, Oct 1982 1: The Eradicator.	2.50
❑315, Nov 1982	2.50
❑316, Dec 1982	2.50
❑317, Jan 1983	2.50
❑318, Feb 1983 CI (a); 1: Big Sir.	2.50
❑319, Mar 1983	2.50
❑320, Apr 1983	2.50
❑321, May 1983	2.50
❑322, Jun 1983; V: Reverse Flash.	2.50
❑323, Jul 1983; V: Reverse Flash.	2.50
❑324, Aug 1983	2.50
❑325, Sep 1983	2.50
❑326, Oct 1983	2.50
❑327, Nov 1983	2.50
❑328, Dec 1983	2.50
❑329, Jan 1984 V: Gorilla Grodd.	2.50
❑330, Feb 1984	2.50
❑331, Mar 1984 CI (a); A: Gorilla Grodd.	2.50
❑332, Apr 1984 A: Green Lantern.	2.50
❑333, May 1984	2.50
❑334, Jun 1984	2.50
❑335, Jul 1984	2.50
❑336, Aug 1984	2.50
❑337, Sep 1984 V: Pied Piper.	2.50
❑338, Oct 1984 V: Big Sir.	2.50
❑339, Nov 1984 V: Big Sir.	2.50
❑340, Dec 1984; Trial begins	2.50
❑341, Jan 1985	2.50
❑342, Feb 1985	2.50
❑343, Mar 1985	2.50
❑344, Apr 1985 O: Kid Flash.	2.50
❑345, May 1985	2.50
❑346, Jun 1985	2.50
❑347, Jul 1985	2.50
❑348, Aug 1985	2.50
❑349, Sep 1985	2.50
❑350, Oct 1985; Double-size	6.50

	N-MINT
❑Annual 1, Dec 1963; O: Elongated Man. O: Kid Flash. Golden-Age Flash story	400.00
❑Annual 1-2, Nov 2001, Replica edition; O: Elongated Man. O: Kid Flash. 80 pages; Golden-Age Flash story	6.95

FLASH (2ND SERIES)
DC

	N-MINT
❑0, Oct 1994 O: Flash III (Wally West).	4.00
❑1, Jun 1987; Wally West as Flash	5.00
❑2, Jul 1987 V: Vandal Savage.	3.00
❑3, Aug 1987 1: Tina McGee. V: Kilg%re.	2.50
❑4, Sep 1987 V: Kilg%re.	2.50
❑5, Oct 1987	2.50
❑6, Nov 1987	2.50
❑7, Dec 1987 1: Red Trinity.	2.50
❑8, Jan 1988; Millennium	2.50
❑9, Feb 1988; 1: Chunk. Millennium	2.50
❑10, Mar 1988	2.50
❑11, Apr 1988	2.50
❑12, May 1988; Bonus Book #2	2.50
❑13, Jun 1988 V: Vandal Savage.	2.50
❑14, Jul 1988 V: Vandal Savage.	2.50
❑15, Aug 1988 GP (c)	2.50
❑16, Sep 1988 GP (c)	2.50
❑17, Oct 1988 GP (c)	2.50
❑18, Nov 1988	2.50
❑19, Dec 1988; Bonus Book #9	2.50
❑20	2.50
❑21; Invasion!	2.00
❑22, Jan 1989; A: Manhunter. Invasion!	2.00
❑23, Feb 1989	2.00
❑24, Mar 1989	2.00
❑25, Apr 1989	2.00
❑26, May 1989	2.00
❑27, Jun 1989	2.00
❑28, Jul 1989	2.00
❑29, Aug 1989 A: Phantom Lady.	2.00
❑30, Sep 1989	2.00
❑31, Oct 1989	1.50
❑32, Nov 1989	1.50
❑33, Dec 1989	1.50
❑34, Jan 1990	1.50
❑35, Feb 1990 V: Turtle.	1.50
❑36, Mar 1990	1.50
❑37, Apr 1990	1.50
❑38, May 1990	1.50
❑39, Jun 1990	1.50
❑40, Jul 1990	1.50
❑41, Aug 1990	1.50
❑42, Sep 1990	1.50
❑43, Oct 1990	1.50
❑44, Nov 1990 V: Gorilla Grodd.	1.50
❑45, Dec 1990 V: Gorilla Grodd.	1.50
❑46, Jan 1991 A: Vixen.	1.50
❑47, Feb 1991 A: Vixen. V: Gorilla Grodd.	1.50
❑48, Mar 1991	1.50
❑49, Apr 1991	1.50
❑50, May 1991; Giant size	2.50
❑51, Jun 1991	1.50
❑52, Jul 1991	1.50
❑53, Aug 1991; Superman	1.50
❑54, Sep 1991	1.50
❑55, Oct 1991; War of the Gods	1.50
❑56, Nov 1991; Icicle	1.50
❑57, Dec 1991; Icicle	1.50
❑58, Jan 1992	1.50
❑59, Feb 1992 A: Power Girl.	1.50
❑60, Mar 1992 FMc (a)	1.50
❑61, Apr 1992	1.50
❑62, May 1992 MWa (w); O: Flash.	2.00
❑63, May 1992 O: Flash.	2.00
❑64, Jun 1992 O: Flash.	1.50
❑65, Jun 1992 O: Flash.	1.50
❑66, Jul 1992; Aquaman	1.50
❑67, Aug 1992 V: Abra Kadabra.	1.50
❑68, Sep 1992 V: Abra Kadabra.	1.50
❑69, Oct 1992 A: Green Lantern. V: Hector Hammond. V: Gorilla Grodd.	1.50

Condition price index: Multiply "NM prices" above by: **0.83 for Very Fine/Near Mint**
0.66 for Very Fine • 0.33 for Fine • 0.2 for Very Good • 0.125 for Good

	N-MINT
❑70, Nov 1992 A: Green Lantern. V: Hector Hammond. V: Gorilla Grodd.	1.50
❑71, Dec 1992 V: Doctor Alchemy.	1.50
❑72, Jan 1993	1.50
❑73, Feb 1993 A: Jay Garrick.	1.50
❑74, Mar 1993	1.50
❑75, Apr 1993	1.50
❑76, May 1993	1.50
❑77, Jun 1993	1.50
❑78, Jul 1993	1.50
❑79, Jul 1993; Giant-size MWa (w)	2.50
❑80, Aug 1993; regular cover	1.50
❑80/Variant, Aug 1993; foil cover	2.50
❑81, Sep 1993 A: Nightwing. A: Starfire.	1.50
❑82, Oct 1993 A: Nightwing. A: Starfire.	1.50
❑83, Oct 1993	1.50
❑84, Nov 1993 V: Razer.	1.50
❑85, Dec 1993 V: Razer.	1.50
❑86, Jan 1994	1.50
❑87, Feb 1994	1.50
❑88, Mar 1994 MWa (w)	2.00
❑89, Apr 1994 MWa (w)	2.00
❑90, May 1994 MWa (w)	2.00
❑91, Jun 1994 MWa (w)	4.00
❑92, Jul 1994 MWa (w); 1: Impulse.	8.00
❑93, Aug 1994 MWa (w); 2: Impulse.	5.00
❑94, Sep 1994; MWa (w); Zero Hour	3.00
❑95, Nov 1994	3.00
❑96, Dec 1994	2.00
❑97, Jan 1995 MWa (w)	2.00
❑98, Feb 1995	2.00
❑99, Mar 1995	2.00
❑100, Apr 1995; Giant-size	3.00
❑100/Variant, Apr 1995; Giant-size; Holo-grafix cover	4.00
❑101, May 1995	2.00
❑102, Jun 1995 V: Mongul.	2.00
❑103, Jul 1995	2.00
❑104, Aug 1995	2.00
❑105, Sep 1995 V: Mirror Master.	2.00
❑106, Oct 1995; return of Frances Kane	2.00
❑107, Nov 1995; A: Captain Marvel. Underworld Unleashed	2.00
❑108, Dec 1995	2.00
❑109, Jan 1996; continues in Impulse #10	2.00
❑110, Feb 1996; MWa (w); continues in Impulse #11	2.00
❑111, Mar 1996 MWa (w)	2.00
❑112, Apr 1996 MWa (w); A: John Fox.	2.00
❑113, May 1996	2.00
❑114, Jun 1996 A: Don and Dawn Allen.	2.00
❑115, Jul 1996	2.00
❑116, Aug 1996	2.00
❑117, Sep 1996; Flash returns to present	2.00
❑118, Oct 1996 MWa (w)	2.00
❑119, Nov 1996; MWa (w); Final Night	2.00
❑120, Dec 1996; MWa (w); A: Trickster. Wally West asked to leave Keystone	2.00
❑121, Jan 1997 MWa (w); V: Top.	2.00
❑122, Feb 1997; MWa (w); Flash becomes a commuting super-hero	2.00
❑123, Mar 1997 MWa (w)	2.00
❑124, Apr 1997 MWa (w); V: Major Disaster.	2.00
❑125, May 1997 V: Major Disaster.	2.00
❑126, Jun 1997; V: Major Disaster. return of Rogues Gallery	2.00
❑127, Jul 1997 A: Neron. A: Jay Garrick. V: Soulless Rogues Gallery.	2.00
❑128, Aug 1997 A: Wonder Woman. A: Superman. A: Martian Manhunter. A: Green Lantern. V: Soulless Rogues Gallery.	2.00
❑129, Sep 1997 V: Neron.	2.00
❑130, Oct 1997; Wally has his legs broken	2.00
❑131, Nov 1997; Wally gets new costume	2.00
❑132, Dec 1997; A: Mirror Master. Face cover	1.95
❑133, Jan 1998 V: Mirror Master.	1.95

	N-MINT
❑134, Feb 1998 A: Thinker. A: Wildcat. A: Johnny Thunder. A: Ted Knight. A: Sentinel. A: Jay Garrick.	1.95
❑135, Mar 1998; cover forms triptych with Green Arrow #130 and Green Lantern #96	1.95
❑136, Apr 1998 A: Krakkl.	1.95
❑137, May 1998	1.95
❑138, Jun 1998	1.95
❑139, Jul 1998 D: Linda Park.	1.95
❑140, Aug 1998; Linda's funeral	1.95
❑141, Sep 1998 V: Black Flash.	1.95
❑142, Oct 1998; Wedding of Wally and Linda	1.95
❑143, Dec 1998 V: Cobalt Blue.	1.99
❑144, Jan 1999 O: Cobalt Blue.	1.99
❑145, Feb 1999 MWa (w); A: Cobalt Blue.	1.99
❑146, Mar 1999 MWa (w); A: Cobalt Blue.	1.99
❑147, Apr 1999 MWa (w); A: Reverse Flash. A: Cobalt Blue.	1.99
❑148, May 1999 MWa (w); A: Barry Allen.	1.99
❑149, Jun 1999; MWa (w); Crisis ending changed	1.99
❑150, Jul 1999; MWa (w); Wally vs. Anti-Monitor	2.95
❑151, Aug 1999; MWa (w); Teen Titans adventure	1.99
❑152, Sep 1999 MWa (w)	1.99
❑153, Oct 1999 MWa (w); V: Folded Man.	1.99
❑154, Nov 1999; new Flash reveals identity	1.99
❑155, Dec 1999 MWa (w)	1.99
❑156, Jan 2000 MWa (w)	1.99
❑157, Feb 2000	1.99
❑158, Mar 2000	1.99
❑159, Apr 2000 MWa (w)	1.99
❑160, May 2000	1.99
❑161, Jun 2000 A: JSA. A: Flash I (Jay Garrick).	1.99
❑162, Jul 2000	1.99
❑163, Aug 2000	2.25
❑164, Sep 2000	2.25
❑165, Oct 2000	2.25
❑166, Nov 2000	2.25
❑167, Dec 2000	2.25
❑168, Jan 2001	2.25
❑169, Feb 2001	2.25
❑170, Mar 2001	2.25
❑171, Apr 2001	2.25
❑172, May 2001	2.25
❑173, Jun 2001	2.25
❑174, Jul 2001; 1: Tar Pit	2.25
❑175, Aug 2001	2.25
❑176, Sep 2001	2.25
❑177, Oct 2001	2.25
❑178, Nov 2001	2.25
❑179, Dec 2001; Joker: Last Laugh crossover	2.25
❑180, Jan 2002	2.25
❑181, Feb 2002	2.25
❑182, Mar 2002	2.25
❑183, Apr 2002 1: Trickster II (Axel Walker).	2.25
❑184, May 2002	2.25
❑185, Jun 2002	2.25
❑186, Jul 2002	2.25
❑187, Aug 2002	2.25
❑188, Sep 2002	2.25
❑189, Oct 2002	2.25
❑190, Nov 2002	2.25
❑191, Dec 2002	2.25
❑192, Jan 2003	2.25
❑193, Feb 2003	2.25
❑194, Mar 2003	2.25
❑195, Apr 2003	2.25
❑196, May 2003	2.25
❑197, Jun 2003	2.25
❑198, Jul 2003	2.25
❑199, Aug 2003	2.25
❑200, Sep 2003	3.50

With his top speed reduced to Mach 1, Wally West took on the mantle of The Flash after *Crisis on Infinite Earths*.

© 1987 DC Comics.

	N-MINT
❑201, Oct 2003	2.25
❑202, Nov 2003	2.25
❑203, Dec 2003	2.25
❑204, Jan 2004	2.25
❑205, Feb 2004	2.25
❑206, Mar 2004	2.25
❑207, Apr 2004	5.00
❑208, May 2004	2.25
❑209, Jun 2004	2.25
❑210, Jul 2004	2.25
❑210-2, Aug 2004	2.25
❑211, Aug 2004	2.25
❑212, Sep 2004	
❑1000000, Nov 1998 MWa (w)	3.00
❑Annual 1, ca. 1987	3.00
❑Annual 2; Private Lives	2.00
❑Annual 3; Who's Who entries	2.25
❑Annual 4	2.25
❑Annual 5	2.75
❑Annual 6 1: Argus.	2.50
❑Annual 7; Elseworlds	2.95
❑Annual 8, ca. 1995; Year One	3.50
❑Annual 9, ca. 1996; Legends of the Dead Earth	2.95
❑Annual 10, ca. 1997; DG (a); Pulp Heroes; 1997 Annual	3.95
❑Annual 11, ca. 1998; A: Johnny Quick. Ghosts; 1998 Annual	3.95
❑Annual 12, Oct 1999; JLApe; 1999 Annual	2.95
❑Annual 13, Sep 2000; 2000 Annual; Planet DC	3.50
❑Giant Size 1, Aug 1998 JBy, MWa (w); JBy (a); A: Flash II (Barry Allen). A: Lightning. A: Flash III (Wally West). A: Jesse Quick. A: Impulse. A: Flash I (Jay Garrick). A: Captain Boomerang. A: Flash IV (John Fox).	4.95
❑Giant Size 2, Apr 1999	4.95
❑Special 1; 50th anniversary issue; JKu (c); CI (a); 1: John Fox. 3 Flashes	3.50
❑TV 1 1991; A: Kid Flash. TV Special; Stories about TV show Flash	3.95

FLASH & GREEN LANTERN: THE BRAVE AND THE BOLD
DC

❑1, Oct 1999	2.50
❑2, Nov 1999	2.50
❑3, Dec 1999	2.50
❑4, Jan 2000	2.50
❑5, Feb 2000	2.50
❑6, Mar 2000	2.50

FLASHBACK
SPECIAL

❑1	3.00
❑2	3.00
❑3, ca. 1974	3.00
❑4 1974	3.00
❑5 1974	3.00
❑6 1974	3.00
❑7 1974	3.00
❑8 1974	3.00
❑9 1974	3.00
❑10, ca. 1974	3.00
❑11 1974	3.00
❑12 1974	3.00
❑13 1974	3.00
❑14, ca. 1974	3.00
❑15	3.00

	N-MINT
❑16	3.00
❑17	3.00
❑18	3.00
❑19	3.00
❑20	3.00
❑21	3.00
❑22	3.00
❑23	3.00
❑24	3.00
❑25	3.00
❑26	3.00
❑27	3.00

FLASH GORDON (GOLD KEY ONE-SHOT)
GOLD KEY

❑1, Jun 1965; Dinosaur cover ... 26.00

FLASH GORDON (DC)
DC

❑1, Jun 1988 ... 2.00
❑2, Jul 1988 ... 1.50
❑3, Aug 1988 ... 1.50
❑4, Sep 1988 ... 1.50
❑5, Oct 1988 ... 1.50
❑6, Nov 1988 ... 1.50
❑7, Dec 1988 ... 1.50
❑8, Win 1988 ... 1.50
❑9, Hol 1988 ... 1.50

FLASH GORDON (MARVEL)
MARVEL

❑1, Jun 1995; wraparound cardstock cover ... 2.95
❑2, Jul 1995; wraparound cardstock cover ... 2.95

FLASH GORDON: THE MOVIE
GOLDEN PRESS

❑1 AW (a) ... 2.50

FLASH/GREEN LANTERN: FASTER FRIENDS
DC

❑1; prestige format; continued from Green Lantern/Flash: Faster Friends ... 4.95

FLASH: OUR WORLDS AT WAR
DC

❑1, Oct 2001 ... 2.95

FLASH PLUS
DC

❑1, Jan 1997 ... 2.95

FLASH SECRET FILES, THE
DC

❑1, Nov 1997; bios on major cast members and villains; timeline ... 4.95
❑2, Nov 1999; updates on cast ... 4.95
❑3, Nov 2001 ... 4.95

FLASH, THE: IRON HEIGHTS
DC

❑1, Oct 2001 ... 5.95

FLASHMARKS
FANTAGRAPHICS

❑1, b&w ... 2.95

FLASHPOINT
DC

❑1, Dec 1999; Elseworlds ... 2.95
❑2, Jan 2000 ... 2.95
❑3, Feb 2000 ... 2.95

FLATLINE COMICS PRESENTS...
FLATLINE

❑1, Dec 1993 ... 2.50

FLAXEN
DARK HORSE

❑1; photo back cover ... 2.95

FLAXEN: ALTER EGO
CALIBER

❑1, Mar 1995 ... 2.95

FLEENER
ZONGO

❑1, b&w ... 2.95
❑2, Dec 1996, b&w ... 2.95
❑3, b&w ... 2.95

FLESH
FLEETWAY-QUALITY

❑1 ... 2.95
❑2 ... 2.95
❑3 ... 2.95
❑4 ... 2.95

FLESH & BLOOD
BRAINSTORM

❑1; Partial foil cover ... 2.95
❑1/Ashcan; Ashcan preview from 1995 Philadelphia Comic Con ... 1.00

FLESH & BLOOD: PRE-EXISTING CONDITIONS
BLINDWOLF

❑1 ... 2.95

FLESH AND BONES
UPSHOT

❑1 ... 2.00
❑2 ... 2.00
❑3 ... 2.00
❑4 ... 2.00

FLESH CRAWLERS
KITCHEN SINK

❑1, ca. 1994 ... 2.50
❑2, Jan 1995 ... 2.50
❑3, Feb 1995 ... 2.50

FLESH GORDON
AIRCEL

❑1, Mar 1992 ... 2.95
❑2, Apr 1992 ... 2.95
❑3, May 1992 ... 2.95
❑4, Jun 1992 ... 2.95

FLESHPOT
FANTAGRAPHICS / EROS

❑1, Oct 1997 ... 2.95

FLEX MENTALLO
DC / VERTIGO

❑1, Jun 1996 ... 10.00
❑2, Jul 1996; EC parody cover ... 8.00
❑3, Aug 1996; Dark Knight parody cover ... 8.00
❑4, Sep 1996 ... 8.00

FLICKERING FLESH
BONEYARD

❑1, Mar 1993 ... 2.50

FLICKER'S FLEAS
FIFTH WHEEL

❑1 ... 3.00

FLINCH
DC / VERTIGO

❑1, Jun 1999 JLee (a) ... 3.00
❑2, Jul 1999 BSz (a) ... 2.50
❑3, Aug 1999 ... 2.50
❑4, Sep 1999 PG (a) ... 2.50
❑5, Oct 1999 ... 2.50
❑6, Nov 1999 ... 2.50
❑7, Dec 1999 DGry (w) ... 2.50
❑8, Jan 2000 ... 2.50
❑9, Feb 2000 ... 2.50
❑10, Mar 2000 ... 2.50
❑11, Apr 2000 ... 2.50
❑12, May 2000 ... 2.50
❑13 2000 ... 2.50
❑14, Sep 2000 BWr (a) ... 2.50
❑15, Nov 2000 ... 2.50
❑16, Jan 2001 ... 2.50

FLINT ARMBUSTER JR. SPECIAL
ALCHEMY

❑1, b&w ... 2.95

FLINTSTONE KIDS, THE
MARVEL / STAR

❑1, Aug 1987 ... 2.00
❑2, Oct 1987 ... 1.50
❑3, Dec 1987 ... 1.50
❑4, Feb 1988 ... 1.50
❑5, Apr 1988 ... 1.50
❑6, Jun 1988 ... 1.50
❑7, Aug 1988 ... 1.50
❑8, Oct 1988 ... 1.50
❑9, Dec 1988 ... 1.50
❑10, Feb 1989 ... 1.50
❑11, Apr 1989 ... 1.50

FLINTSTONES 3-D
BLACKTHORNE

❑1, Apr 1987; a.k.a. Blackthorne 3-D #19 ... 2.50
❑2, Fal 1987; a.k.a. Blackthorne 3-D #22 ... 2.50
❑3 ... 2.50
❑4 ... 2.50

FLINTSTONES, THE (MARVEL)
MARVEL

❑1, Oct 1977 ... 5.00
❑2, Dec 1977 ... 3.00
❑3, Feb 1978 ... 3.00
❑4, Apr 1978 ... 3.00
❑5, Jun 1978 ... 3.00
❑6, Aug 1978 ... 3.00
❑7, Oct 1978 ... 3.00
❑8, Dec 1978 ... 3.00
❑9, Feb 1979 ... 3.00

FLINTSTONES, THE (HARVEY)
HARVEY

❑1, Sep 1992 ... 2.50
❑2, Jan 1993 ... 2.00
❑3, ca. 1993 ... 2.00
❑4, Sep 1993 ... 2.00
❑5, Oct 1993 ... 2.00
❑6, Nov 1993 ... 2.00
❑7, Dec 1993 ... 2.00
❑8, Jan 1994 ... 2.00
❑9, Feb 1994 ... 2.00
❑10, Mar 1994 ... 2.00
❑11, Apr 1994 ... 2.00
❑12, May 1994 ... 2.00
❑13, Jun 1994 ... 2.00

FLINTSTONES, THE (ARCHIE)
ARCHIE

❑1, Sep 1995 ... 2.00
❑2, Oct 1995 ... 1.50
❑3, Nov 1995 ... 1.50
❑4, Dec 1995 ... 1.50
❑5, Jan 1996 ... 1.50
❑6, Feb 1996 ... 1.50
❑7, Mar 1996 ... 1.50
❑8, Apr 1996 ... 1.50
❑9, May 1996 ... 1.50
❑10, Jun 1996 ... 1.50
❑12, Aug 1996 ... 1.50
❑13, Sep 1996 ... 1.50
❑14, Oct 1996 ... 1.50
❑15, Nov 1996 ... 1.50
❑16, Dec 1996 ... 1.50
❑17, Jan 1997 ... 1.50
❑18, Feb 1997; Fred becomes a cartoonist ... 1.50
❑19, Mar 1997 A: Great Gazoo. ... 1.50
❑20, Apr 1997 ... 1.50
❑21, May 1997 ... 1.50
❑22, Jun 1997 A: Gruesomes. ... 1.50

FLINTSTONES AND THE JETSONS, THE
DC

❑1, Aug 1997 ... 2.00
❑2, Sep 1997 ... 2.00
❑3, Oct 1997; Spacely turned into baby ... 2.00
❑4, Nov 1997; Gazoo turns Fred and Barney into women ... 2.00
❑5, Dec 1997; Judy and Elroy throw a party ... 2.00
❑6, Jan 1998 ... 2.00
❑7, Feb 1998; Spies issue ... 2.00
❑8, Mar 1998; Kung Fu issue ... 2.00
❑9, Apr 1998 ... 2.00
❑10, May 1998 ... 2.00
❑11, Jun 1998; Time travel ... 2.00
❑12, Jul 1998 ... 2.00
❑13, Aug 1998 ... 2.00
❑14, Oct 1998 ... 2.00
❑15, Nov 1998; Super-Fred ... 2.00
❑16, Dec 1998 ... 2.00

N-MINT

❑17, Jan 1999 .... 2.00
❑18, Feb 1999; A: Great Gazoo. It's A Wonderful Life homage 2.00
❑19, Mar 1999; Jetsons Bizarro story 2.00
❑20, Apr 1999 .... 2.00
❑21, May 1999; Fred and George switch places 1.99

FLINTSTONES AT THE NEW YORK WORLD'S FAIR
DELL
❑1, ca. 1964 .... 48.00

FLINTSTONES BIG BOOK, THE
HARVEY
❑1 .... 1.95
❑2 .... 1.95

FLINTSTONES BIGGER AND BOULDER
GOLD KEY
❑1, Nov 1962 .... 65.00
❑2, Jun 1966 .... 45.00

FLINTSTONES DOUBLEVISION, THE
HARVEY
❑1, Sep 1994; polybagged with double vision glasses, adaptation of movie 2.95

FLINTSTONES GIANT SIZE
HARVEY
❑2, ca. 1992 .... 2.50
❑3, ca. 1993 .... 2.50

FLINTSTONES WITH PEBBLES AND BAMM-BAMM, THE
GOLD KEY
❑1, Nov 1965; Regular paper (non-glossy) cover 50.00

FLIPPER
GOLD KEY
❑1, Apr 1966 .... 25.00
❑2, Nov 1966 .... 18.00
❑3, Nov 1967 .... 18.00

FLOATERS
DARK HORSE
❑1, Sep 1993, b&w 2.50
❑2, Oct 1993, b&w 2.50
❑3, Nov 1993, b&w 2.50
❑4, Dec 1993, b&w 2.50
❑5, Jan 1994 .... 2.50

FLOCK OF DREAMERS
KITCHEN SINK
❑1, Nov 1997, b&w 12.95

FLOOD RELIEF
MALIBU
❑1; Ultraverse Red Cross giveaway ... 5.00

FLOWERS
DRAWN AND QUARTERLY
❑1 .... 2.95

FLOWERS ON THE RAZORWIRE
BONEYARD
❑1, b&w 2.95
❑2, b&w 2.95
❑3, b&w 2.95
❑4, Nov 1994, b&w 2.95
❑5, May 1995, b&w 2.95
❑6, May 1995, b&w 2.95
❑7, Oct 1995, b&w 2.95
❑8, b&w 2.95
❑9, b&w 2.95
❑10, Apr 1997, b&w 2.95

FLY, THE (ARCHIE)
ARCHIE / RED CIRCLE
❑1, May 1983 .... 3.00
❑2, Jul 1983 .... 1.50
❑3, Oct 1983 .... 1.50
❑4, Dec 1983 SD (a) 1.50
❑5, Feb 1984 .... 1.50
❑6, Apr 1984 .... 1.50
❑7, Jun 1984 .... 1.50
❑8, Aug 1984 .... 1.50
❑9, Oct 1984 .... 1.50

N-MINT

FLY, THE (IMPACT)
DC / IMPACT
❑1, Aug 1991 .... 1.25
❑2, Sep 1991 .... 1.00
❑3, Oct 1991 .... 1.00
❑4, Nov 1991 .... 1.00
❑5, Dec 1991 .... 1.00
❑6, Jan 1992 .... 1.00
❑7, Feb 1992 .... 1.00
❑8, Mar 1992 .... 1.00
❑9, Apr 1992 .... 1.00
❑10, May 1992 .... 1.00
❑11, Jun 1992 .... 1.25
❑12, Jul 1992 .... 1.25
❑13, Aug 1992 .... 1.25
❑14, Sep 1992 .... 1.25
❑15, Oct 1992 .... 1.25
❑16, Nov 1992 .... 1.25
❑17, Dec 1992 .... 1.25
❑Annual 1; trading card 2.00

FLY MAN
ARCHIE / RADIO
❑32, Jul 1965; Series continued from Adventures of the Fly #31 .... 18.00
❑33, Sep 1965 .... 16.00
❑34, Nov 1965 .... 16.00
❑35, Jan 1966 .... 16.00
❑36, Mar 1966 O: The Web. 16.00
❑37, May 1966 .... 16.00
❑38, Jul 1966 .... 16.00
❑39, Sep 1966; Series continued in Mighty Comics #40 .... 16.00

FLYING COLORS 10TH ANNIVERSARY SPECIAL
FLYING COLORS
❑1, Sep 1998 .... 2.95

FLYING NUN
DELL
❑1, Feb 1968 .... 32.00
❑2, May 1968 .... 20.00
❑3, Aug 1968 .... 20.00
❑4 .... 20.00

FLYING SAUCERS (DELL)
DELL
❑1, Apr 1967 .... 26.00
❑2, Jul 1967 .... 15.00
❑3, Oct 1967 .... 15.00
❑4, Nov 1967 .... 15.00
❑5, Oct 1969 .... 15.00

FOCUS
DC
❑1, Sum 1987; BSz, GP (a); no cover price 1.00

FOES
RAM
❑1 .... 1.95

FOG CITY COMICS
STAMPART
❑1 .... 1.00

FOODANG
CONTINUÜM
❑1, Jul 1994, b&w; foil cover 1.95
❑Ashcan 1; Ashcan promotional edition; 1: Foodang. Previews Foodang #1; Flip Book with The Dark Ashcan #1 .... 1.00

FOODANG (2ND SERIES)
AUGUST HOUSE
❑1, Jan 1995; oversized trading card; enhanced cover 2.50

FOOD FIRST COMICS
IFDP
❑1 .... 3.00
❑1-2 .... 3.00
❑1-3 .... 3.00

FOOFUR
MARVEL / STAR
❑1, Aug 1987 .... 1.00
❑2, Oct 1987 .... 1.00
❑3, Dec 1987 .... 1.00

Stories featuring the modern stone-age family and the first family of the future can be found in DC's *The Flintstones and The Jetsons.*

© 1997 DC Comics and Hanna-Barbera Productions.

N-MINT

❑4, Feb 1988 .... 1.00
❑5, Apr 1988 .... 1.00
❑6, Jun 1988 .... 1.00

FOOLKILLER
MARVEL
❑1, Oct 1990 O: FoolKiller III. 1: FoolKiller III (Kurt Gerhardt). A: Greg Salinger (FoolKiller II). 2.00
❑2, Nov 1990 .... 2.00
❑3, Dec 1990; cover says Nov, indicia says Dec 2.00
❑4, Jan 1991 .... 2.00
❑5, Feb 1991 TD (a) 2.00
❑6, Apr 1991 TD (a) 2.00
❑7 1991 .... 2.00
❑8, Jul 1991; A: Spider-Man. 2.00
❑9 1991 .... 2.00
❑10 1991 .... 2.00

FOOT SOLDIERS, THE
DARK HORSE
❑1, Jan 1996 .... 2.95
❑2, Feb 1996 .... 2.95
❑3, Mar 1996 .... 2.95
❑4, Apr 1996 .... 2.95

FOOT SOLDIERS (VOL. 2)
IMAGE
❑1, Sep 1997, b&w 2.95
❑2, Nov 1997, b&w 2.95
❑3, Jan 1998, b&w 2.95
❑4, Mar 1998, b&w 2.95
❑5, May 1998, b&w 2.95

FOOZLE, THE
ECLIPSE
❑1 1985 .... 1.75
❑2 1985 .... 1.75
❑3, Aug 1985; Reprints original Foozle Story in color 1.75

FORBIDDEN FRANKENSTEIN
FANTAGRAPHICS / EROS
❑1, b&w 2.25
❑2, b&w 2.50

FORBIDDEN KINGDOM, THE
EASTERN
❑1, Nov 1987, b&w 1.95
❑2, Jan 1988, b&w 1.95
❑3, Mar 1988, b&w 1.95
❑4, May 1988, b&w 1.95
❑5, Jul 1988, b&w 1.95
❑6, b&w 1.95
❑7, b&w 1.95
❑8, b&w 1.95

FORBIDDEN KNOWLEDGE
LAST GASP
❑1 .... 4.00

FORBIDDEN KNOWLEDGE: ADVENTURE BEYOND THE DOORWAY TO SOULS WITH RADICAL DREAMER
MARK'S GIANT ECONOMY SIZE
❑1, b&w; infinity cover 3.50

FORBIDDEN PLANET
INNOVATION
❑1, May 1992 .... 2.50
❑2, Jul 1992 .... 2.50
❑3, Sep 1992 .... 2.50
❑4, Spr 1993 .... 2.50

N-MINT

FORBIDDEN SUBJECTS
ANGEL

- ❑0 ... 2.95
- ❑0/A; Nude edition A ... 3.95
- ❑0/B; Nude edition B ... 3.95

FORBIDDEN SUBJECTS: CANDY KISSES
ANGEL

- ❑1; Censored cover ... 3.00
- ❑1/B; Adult cover ... 3.00

FORBIDDEN TALES OF DARK MANSION
DC

- ❑5, Jun 1972; Series continued from The Dark Mansion of Forbidden Love #4 ... 10.00
- ❑6, Aug 1972 ... 10.00
- ❑7, Oct 1972 JO (w); HC, TD (a) ... 10.00
- ❑8, Dec 1972 ... 10.00
- ❑9, Feb 1973 ... 10.00
- ❑10, Apr 1973 ... 8.00
- ❑11, Jul 1973 ... 8.00
- ❑12, Sep 1973 ... 8.00
- ❑13, Nov 1973 ... 8.00
- ❑14, Jan 1974 ... 8.00
- ❑15, Mar 1974 ... 8.00

FORBIDDEN VAMPIRE
ANGEL

- ❑0 ... 2.95

FORBIDDEN WORLDS
ACG

- ❑47, Oct 1956 ... 54.00
- ❑48, Nov 1956 ... 54.00
- ❑49, Dec 1956 ... 54.00
- ❑50, Jan 1957 ... 54.00
- ❑51, Feb 1957 ... 45.00
- ❑52, Mar 1957 ... 45.00
- ❑53, Apr 1957 ... 45.00
- ❑54, May 1957 ... 45.00
- ❑55, Jun 1957 ... 45.00
- ❑56, Jul 1957 ... 45.00
- ❑57, Aug 1957 ... 45.00
- ❑58, Sep 1957 ... 45.00
- ❑59, Oct 1957 ... 45.00
- ❑60, Nov 1957 ... 45.00
- ❑61, Dec 1957 ... 40.00
- ❑62, Jan 1958 ... 40.00
- ❑63, Feb 1958 ... 40.00
- ❑64, Mar 1958 ... 40.00
- ❑65, Apr 1958 ... 40.00
- ❑66, May 1958 ... 40.00
- ❑67, Jun 1958 ... 40.00
- ❑68, Jul 1958 ... 40.00
- ❑69, Aug 1958 ... 40.00
- ❑70, Sep 1958 ... 40.00
- ❑71, Oct 1958 ... 35.00
- ❑72, Nov 1958 ... 35.00
- ❑73, Dec 1958 1: Herbie. ... 275.00
- ❑74, Jan 1959 ... 35.00
- ❑75, Feb 1959 ... 35.00
- ❑76, Mar 1959 ... 35.00
- ❑77, Apr 1959 ... 35.00
- ❑78, May 1959 ... 35.00
- ❑79, Jun 1959 ... 35.00
- ❑80, Jul 1959 ... 35.00
- ❑81, Aug 1959 ... 24.00
- ❑82, Sep 1959 ... 24.00
- ❑83, Oct 1959; reprints begin ... 24.00
- ❑84, Nov 1959 ... 24.00
- ❑85, Jan 1960 ... 24.00
- ❑86, Mar 1960; Flying saucer cover ... 30.00
- ❑87, May 1960 ... 24.00
- ❑88, Jul 1960 ... 24.00
- ❑89, Aug 1960 ... 24.00
- ❑90, Sep 1960 ... 24.00
- ❑91, Oct 1960 ... 20.00
- ❑92, Nov 1960 ... 20.00
- ❑93, Jan 1961 ... 20.00
- ❑94, Mar 1961 A: Herbie. ... 55.00
- ❑95, May 1961 ... 20.00
- ❑96, Jul 1961 ... 20.00
- ❑97, Aug 1961 ... 20.00
- ❑98, Sep 1961 ... 20.00
- ❑99, Oct 1961 ... 20.00
- ❑100, Nov 1961 CCB (a) ... 20.00
- ❑101, Jan 1962 ... 16.00
- ❑102, Mar 1962 ... 16.00
- ❑103, May 1962 ... 16.00
- ❑104, Jul 1962 ... 16.00
- ❑105, Aug 1962 ... 16.00
- ❑106, Sep 1962 ... 16.00
- ❑107, Oct 1962 ... 16.00
- ❑108, Nov 1962 ... 16.00
- ❑109, Jan 1963 ... 16.00
- ❑110, Mar 1963 A: Herbie. ... 35.00
- ❑111, May 1963 ... 16.00
- ❑112, Jul 1963 ... 16.00
- ❑113, Aug 1963 ... 16.00
- ❑114, Sep 1963 A: Herbie. ... 35.00
- ❑115, Oct 1963 ... 16.00
- ❑116, Nov 1963 A: Herbie. ... 30.00
- ❑117, Jan 1964 ... 16.00
- ❑118, Mar 1964 ... 16.00
- ❑119, May 1964 ... 16.00
- ❑120, Jul 1964 ... 16.00
- ❑121, Aug 1964 ... 12.00
- ❑122, Sep 1964 ... 12.00
- ❑123, Oct 1964 ... 12.00
- ❑124, Nov 1964 ... 12.00
- ❑125, Jan 1965 O: Magicman. 1: Magicman. ... 25.00
- ❑126, Mar 1965 ... 12.00
- ❑127, May 1965 ... 12.00
- ❑128, Jul 1965 A: Magicman. ... 14.00
- ❑129, Aug 1965 ... 12.00
- ❑130, Sep 1965 A: Magicman. ... 14.00
- ❑131, Oct 1965 ... 12.00
- ❑132, Nov 1965 ... 12.00
- ❑133, Jan 1966 ... 12.00
- ❑134, Mar 1966 ... 12.00
- ❑135, May 1966 ... 12.00
- ❑136, Jul 1966 ... 12.00
- ❑137, Aug 1966 ... 12.00
- ❑138, Sep 1966 ... 12.00
- ❑139, Oct 1966 ... 12.00
- ❑140, Nov 1966 ... 12.00
- ❑141, Jan 1967 ... 10.00
- ❑142, Mar 1967 ... 10.00
- ❑143, May 1967 ... 10.00
- ❑144, Jul 1967 ... 10.00
- ❑145, Aug 1967 ... 10.00

FORBIDDEN WORLDS (A+)
A-PLUS

- ❑1, b&w ... 2.50

FORBIDDEN WORLDS (AVALON)
AVALON

- ❑1 ... 2.95

FORBIDDEN X ANGEL
ANGEL

- ❑1 ... 2.95

FORBIDDEN ZONE
GALAXY ENTERTAINMENT

- ❑1 ... 5.95

FORCE 10
CROW

- ❑1 1: Impel. ... 2.50
- ❑1/Ashcan; Flux. 1: Armadillos. 1: Spook. 1: Rukh. 1: Lodestar. 1: Teknik. 1: Leprechaun. 1: Force 10. ... 3.00

FORCE OF BUDDHA'S PALM, THE
JADEMAN

- ❑1, ca. 1988 ... 2.00
- ❑2, ca. 1988 ... 1.95
- ❑3, ca. 1988 ... 1.95
- ❑4, ca. 1988 ... 1.95
- ❑5, ca. 1988 ... 1.95
- ❑6, ca. 1989 ... 1.95
- ❑7, ca. 1989 ... 1.95
- ❑8, ca. 1989 ... 1.95
- ❑9, ca. 1989 ... 1.95
- ❑10, ca. 1989 ... 1.95
- ❑11, ca. 1989 ... 1.95
- ❑12, ca. 1989 ... 1.95
- ❑13, ca. 1989 ... 1.95
- ❑14, ca. 1989 ... 1.95
- ❑15, ca. 1989 ... 1.95
- ❑16, ca. 1989 ... 1.95
- ❑17, ca. 1989 ... 1.95
- ❑18, ca. 1990 ... 1.95
- ❑19, ca. 1990 ... 1.95
- ❑20, ca. 1990 ... 1.95
- ❑21, ca. 1990 ... 1.95
- ❑22, ca. 1990 ... 1.95
- ❑23, ca. 1990 ... 1.95
- ❑24, ca. 1990 ... 1.95
- ❑25, ca. 1990 ... 1.95
- ❑26, ca. 1990 ... 1.95
- ❑27, ca. 1990 ... 1.95
- ❑28, ca. 1990 ... 1.95
- ❑29, ca. 1990 ... 1.95
- ❑30, ca. 1991 ... 1.95
- ❑31, ca. 1991 ... 1.95
- ❑32, ca. 1991 ... 1.95
- ❑33, ca. 1991 ... 1.95
- ❑34, ca. 1991 ... 1.95
- ❑35, ca. 1991 ... 1.95
- ❑36, ca. 1991 ... 1.95
- ❑37, ca. 1991 ... 1.95
- ❑38, ca. 1991 ... 1.95
- ❑39, ca. 1991 ... 1.95
- ❑40, ca. 1991 ... 1.95
- ❑41, ca. 1991 ... 1.95
- ❑42, ca. 1992 ... 1.95
- ❑43, Feb 1992 ... 1.95
- ❑44, Mar 1992 ... 1.95
- ❑45 ... 1.95
- ❑46, Apr 1992 ... 1.95
- ❑47, May 1992 ... 1.95
- ❑48, Jun 1992 ... 1.95
- ❑49, Jul 1992 ... 1.95
- ❑50, Sep 1992 ... 1.95
- ❑51, Oct 1992 ... 1.95
- ❑52, Nov 1992 ... 1.95
- ❑53, Dec 1992 ... 1.95
- ❑54, Jan 1993 ... 1.95
- ❑55, Feb 1993 ... 1.95

FORCE SEVEN
LONE STAR

- ❑1, Aug 1999 ... 2.95
- ❑2, Sep 1999 ... 2.95
- ❑3, Mar 2000 ... 2.95

FORCE WORKS
MARVEL

- ❑1, Jul 1994; Giant-size; Pop-up cover ... 3.95
- ❑2, Aug 1994 ... 1.50
- ❑3, Sep 1994 ... 1.50
- ❑4, Oct 1994 ... 1.50
- ❑5, Nov 1994 ... 1.50
- ❑5/CS, Nov 1994; with sericel ... 2.95
- ❑6, Dec 1994 ... 1.50
- ❑7, Jan 1995 ... 1.50
- ❑8, Feb 1995 ... 1.50
- ❑9, Mar 1995 ... 1.50
- ❑10, Apr 1995 ... 1.50
- ❑11, May 1995 ... 1.50
- ❑12, Jun 1995 ... 2.50
- ❑13, Jul 1995 ... 1.50
- ❑14, Aug 1995 ... 1.50
- ❑15, Sep 1995 ... 1.50
- ❑16, Oct 1995 ... 1.50
- ❑17, Nov 1995 ... 1.50
- ❑18, Dec 1995 ... 1.50
- ❑19, Jan 1996 ... 1.50
- ❑20, Feb 1996 ... 1.50
- ❑21, Mar 1996 ... 1.50
- ❑22, Apr 1996 ... 1.50
- ❑Ashcan 1; ashcan edition ... 0.75

FOREPLAY
NBM

- ❑1 ... 18.95

N-MINT

FORE/PUNK
PARODY
- ❑1/A; punk cover ... 2.50
- ❑1/B; fore cover ... 2.50

FORETERNITY
ANTARCTIC
- ❑1, Jul 1997, b&w ... 2.95
- ❑2, Sep 1997, b&w ... 2.95
- ❑3, Nov 1997, b&w ... 2.95
- ❑4, Jan 1998, b&w ... 2.95

FOREVER AMBER
IMAGE
- ❑1/A, Jul 1999 ... 2.95
- ❑1/B, Jul 1999; alternate cover has white background ... 2.95
- ❑2, Aug 1999 ... 2.95
- ❑3, Sep 1999 ... 2.95
- ❑4, Oct 1999 ... 2.95

FOREVER MAELSTROM
DC
- ❑1, Jan 2003 ... 2.95
- ❑2, Feb 2003 ... 2.95
- ❑3, Mar 2003 ... 2.95
- ❑4, Apr 2003 ... 2.95
- ❑5, May 2003 ... 2.95
- ❑6, Jun 2003 ... 2.95

FOREVER NOW
ENTERTAINMENT
- ❑1 ... 1.50
- ❑2 ... 1.50

FOREVER PEOPLE, THE
DC
- ❑1, Mar 1971; JK (w); JK (a); O: Forever People. Darkseid ... 30.00
- ❑2, May 1971; JK (w); JK (a); 1: Desaad. 1: Mantis (DC). Darkseid .. 20.00
- ❑3, Jul 1971; JK (w); JK (a); 1: Glorious Godfrey. Darkseid ... 16.00
- ❑4, Sep 1971; JK (w); JK (a); Darkseid 16.00
- ❑5, Nov 1971; Giant-size JK (w); JK (a) 16.00
- ❑6, Jan 1972; Giant-size; JK (w); JK (a); A: Sandy. A: Sandman. Darkseid ... 10.00
- ❑7, Mar 1972 JK (w); JK (a) ... 10.00
- ❑8, May 1972; JK (w); JK (a); Darkseid 10.00
- ❑9, Jul 1972 JK (w); JK (a) ... 10.00
- ❑10, Jul 1972 JK (w); JK (a) ... 10.00
- ❑11, Nov 1972 JK (w); JK (a); 1: The Pursuer. ... 10.00

FOREVER PEOPLE (MINI-SERIES)
DC
- ❑1, Feb 1988 ... 2.00
- ❑2, Mar 1988 ... 2.00
- ❑3, Apr 1988 ... 2.00
- ❑4, May 1988 ... 2.00
- ❑5, Jun 1988 ... 2.00
- ❑6, Jul 1988 ... 2.00

FOREVER WARRIORS
CFD
- ❑1, May 1997 ... 2.95

FORGE
CROSSGEN
- ❑1, May 2002 ... 9.95
- ❑2, Jun 2002 ... 9.95
- ❑3, Jul 2002 ... 9.95
- ❑4, Aug 2002 ... 11.95
- ❑5, Sep 2002 ... 11.95
- ❑6, Oct 2002 ... 11.95
- ❑7, Nov 2002 ... 11.95
- ❑8, Dec 2002 ... 7.95
- ❑9, Jan 2003 ... 7.95
- ❑10, Feb 2003 ... 7.95
- ❑11, Mar 2003 ... 7.95
- ❑12, Apr 2003 ... 7.95
- ❑13, May 2003 ... 7.95

FORGOTTEN REALMS (DC)
DC
- ❑1, Sep 1989 ... 1.50
- ❑2, Oct 1989 ... 1.00
- ❑3, Nov 1989 ... 1.00
- ❑4, Dec 1989 ... 1.00

N-MINT

- ❑5, Jan 1990 ... 1.00
- ❑6, Feb 1990 ... 1.00
- ❑7, Mar 1990 ... 1.00
- ❑8, Apr 1990 ... 1.00
- ❑9, May 1990 ... 1.00
- ❑10, Jun 1990 ... 1.00
- ❑11, Jul 1990 ... 1.00
- ❑12, Aug 1990 ... 1.00
- ❑13, Sep 1990 ... 1.00
- ❑14, Oct 1990 ... 1.00
- ❑15, Nov 1990 ... 1.00
- ❑16, Dec 1990 ... 1.00
- ❑17, Jan 1991 ... 1.00
- ❑18, Feb 1991 ... 1.00
- ❑19, Mar 1991 ... 1.00
- ❑20, Apr 1991 ... 1.00
- ❑21, May 1991 ... 1.00
- ❑22, Jun 1991 ... 1.00
- ❑23, Jul 1991 ... 1.00
- ❑24, Aug 1991 ... 1.00
- ❑25, Sep 1991 ... 1.00
- ❑Annual 1, ca. 1990 ... 1.50

FORGOTTEN REALMS: THE GRAND TOUR
TSR
- ❑1; no cover price ... 1.00

FOR LOVERS ONLY
CHARLTON
- ❑60, Aug 1971 ... 20.00
- ❑61, Oct 1971 ... 10.00
- ❑62, Dec 1971 ... 10.00
- ❑63, Feb 1972 ... 10.00
- ❑64, Apr 1972; Shirley Jones pin-up . 10.00
- ❑65, Jun 1972 ... 10.00
- ❑66, Aug 1972 ... 10.00
- ❑67, Oct 1972; Bobby Sherman pictures ... 10.00
- ❑68, Dec 1972 ... 10.00
- ❑69, Feb 1973 ... 10.00
- ❑70, Apr 1973 ... 10.00
- ❑71, Jun 1973 ... 10.00
- ❑72, Aug 1973 ... 10.00
- ❑73, Oct 1973 ... 10.00
- ❑74, Dec 1973 ... 10.00
- ❑75, Sep 1974 ... 10.00
- ❑76, Nov 1974 ... 10.00
- ❑77, ca. 1975 ... 10.00
- ❑78, ca. 1975 ... 10.00
- ❑79, Jun 1975 ... 10.00
- ❑80, ca. 1975 ... 10.00
- ❑81, Oct 1975 ... 10.00
- ❑82, Dec 1975 ... 10.00
- ❑83, ca. 1976 ... 10.00
- ❑84, ca. 1976 ... 10.00
- ❑85, ca. 1976 ... 10.00
- ❑86, ca. 1976 ... 10.00
- ❑87, Nov 1976 ... 10.00

FORMERLY KNOWN AS T HE JUSTICE LEAGUE
DC
- ❑1, Sep 2003 ... 2.50
- ❑2, Oct 2003 ... 2.50
- ❑3, Nov 2003 ... 2.50
- ❑4, Dec 2003 ... 2.50
- ❑5, Jan 2004 ... 2.50
- ❑6, Feb 2004 ... 2.50

FORT: PROPHET OF THE UNEXPLAINED
DARK HORSE
- ❑1, Jun 2002 ... 2.99
- ❑2, Jul 2002 ... 2.99
- ❑3, Aug 2002 ... 2.99
- ❑4, Sep 2002 ... 2.99

FORTUNE AND GLORY
ONI
- ❑1, Dec 1999, b&w ... 4.95
- ❑2, Feb 2000, b&w ... 4.95
- ❑3, Apr 2000, b&w ... 4.95

Magicman was one of ACG's super-heroes.

N-MINT

FORTUNE'S FOOL, THE STORY OF JINXER
CRANIUM
- ❑0, Jul 1999 ... 2.95

FORTUNE'S FRIENDS: HELL WEEK
ARIA
- ❑1; graphic novel ... 6.95

FORTY WINKS
ODD JOBS LIMITED
- ❑1, Nov 1997 ... 2.95
- ❑2, Dec 1997 ... 2.95
- ❑3, Mar 1998 ... 2.95
- ❑4, Jun 1998 ... 2.95

FORTY WINKS CHRISTMAS SPECIAL
PEREGRINE ENTERTAINMENT
- ❑1, Aug 1998, b&w ... 2.95

FORTY WINKS SUPER SPECIAL EDITION: TV PARTY TONITE!
PEREGRINE ENTERTAINMENT
- ❑1, Apr 1999, b&w ... 2.95

FOTON EFFECT, THE
ACED
- ❑1, Oct 1986 ... 1.50
- ❑2 ... 1.50
- ❑3 ... 1.50

FOUL!
TRAITORS GAIT
- ❑1 ... 3.00

4
MARVEL
- ❑1, Oct 2000; Universe X tie-in; Sue Richards restored to life ... 3.99

4-D MONKEY, THE
DR. LEUNG'S
- ❑1 1988 ... 2.00
- ❑2 1988 ... 2.00
- ❑3 1988 ... 2.00
- ❑4 1989 ... 2.00
- ❑5 1989 ... 2.00
- ❑6 1989 ... 2.00
- ❑7 1989 ... 2.00
- ❑8 1989 ... 2.00
- ❑9 1990 ... 2.00
- ❑10 1990 ... 2.00
- ❑11 1990 ... 2.00
- ❑12 1990 ... 2.00

FOUR HORSEMEN
DC / VERTIGO
- ❑1, Feb 2000 ... 2.50
- ❑2, Mar 2000 ... 2.50
- ❑3, Apr 2000 ... 2.50
- ❑4, May 2000 ... 2.50

FOUR KUNOICHI, THE: BLOODLUST
LIGHTNING
- ❑1, Dec 1996, b&w; Standard edition 2.75
- ❑1/Nude; Nude cover ... 9.95
- ❑1/Platinum; Platinum edition ... 9.95
- ❑1/PLND; Platinum Nude edition ... 4.00

FOUR KUNOICHI: ENTER THE SINJA
LIGHTNING
- ❑1, Feb 1997, b&w ... 2.95

N-MINT

411
Marvel
- ❑1, Jun 2003; cardstock cover 3.50
- ❑2, Jul 2003; cardstock cover 3.50

FOUR-STAR BATTLE TALES
DC
- ❑1, Feb 1973; Reprints 8.00
- ❑2, May 1973; Reprints 5.00
- ❑3, Aug 1973; Reprints 5.00
- ❑4, Oct 1973; Reprints 5.00
- ❑5, Nov 1973; Reprints 5.00

FOUR STAR SPECTACULAR
DC
- ❑1, Apr 1976; Giant-size 7.50
- ❑2, Jun 1976; Giant-size 5.00
- ❑3, Aug 1976; Giant-size; Bicentennial #15 .... 5.00
- ❑4, Oct 1976; Giant-size 5.00
- ❑5, Dec 1976; Giant-size 5.00
- ❑6, Feb 1977; Giant-size 5.00

FOURTH WORLD (JACK KIRBY'S...)
DC
- ❑1, Mar 1997 JBy (w); JBy (a) 2.50
- ❑2, Apr 1997 JBy (w); JBy (a) 2.00
- ❑3, May 1997 JBy (w); JBy (a) 2.00
- ❑4, Jun 1997 JBy (w); JBy (a) 2.00
- ❑5, Jul 1997 JBy (w); JBy (a) 2.00
- ❑6, Aug 1997 JBy (w); JBy (a) 2.00
- ❑7, Sep 1997 JBy (w); JBy (a) 2.00
- ❑8, Oct 1997; JBy (w); JBy (a); Genesis 2.00
- ❑9, Nov 1997 JBy (w); JBy (a) 2.00
- ❑10, Dec 1997; JBy (w); JBy (a); Face cover 2.00
- ❑11, Jan 1998 JBy (w); JBy (a) 2.00
- ❑12, Feb 1998 JBy (w); JBy (a) 2.00
- ❑13, Mar 1998 JBy (w); JBy (a) 2.00
- ❑14, Apr 1998; JBy (w); JBy (a); Darkseid and Ares escape Source Wall . 2.00
- ❑15, May 1998 JBy (w); JBy (a) 2.00
- ❑16, Jun 1998 JBy (w); JBy (a) 2.00
- ❑17, Jul 1998 JBy (w); JBy (a) 2.00
- ❑18, Aug 1998 JBy (w); JBy (a) 2.00
- ❑19, Sep 1998; JBy (w); JBy (a); Return of Supertown 2.25
- ❑20, Oct 1998 JBy (a); A: Superman. 2.25

FOURTH WORLD GALLERY, THE
DC
- ❑1 1996; pin-ups based on Jack Kirby creations 3.50

FOUR WOMEN
DC / Homage
- ❑1, Dec 2001 .... 2.95
- ❑2, Jan 2002 .... 2.95
- ❑3, Feb 2002 .... 2.95
- ❑4, Mar 2002 .... 2.95
- ❑5, Apr 2002 .... 2.95

FOX AND THE CROW
DC
- ❑36, Oct 1956 .... 85.00
- ❑37, Dec 1956 .... 85.00
- ❑38, Feb 1957 .... 85.00
- ❑39, Mar 1957 .... 85.00
- ❑40, Apr 1957 .... 85.00
- ❑41, Jun 1957 .... 60.00
- ❑42, Aug 1957 .... 60.00
- ❑43, Sep 1957 .... 60.00
- ❑44, Oct 1957 .... 60.00
- ❑45, Dec 1957 .... 60.00
- ❑46, Feb 1958 .... 60.00
- ❑47, Mar 1958 .... 60.00
- ❑48, Apr 1958 .... 60.00
- ❑49, Jun 1958 .... 60.00
- ❑50, Aug 1958 .... 60.00
- ❑51, Sep 1958 .... 60.00
- ❑52, Oct 1958 .... 60.00
- ❑53 .... 60.00
- ❑54, Mar 1959 .... 60.00
- ❑55, May 1959 .... 60.00
- ❑56, Jul 1959 .... 60.00
- ❑57, Sep 1959 .... 60.00
- ❑58, Nov 1959 .... 60.00
- ❑59, Jan 1960 .... 60.00
- ❑60, Mar 1960 .... 60.00
- ❑61, May 1960 .... 60.00
- ❑62, Jul 1960 .... 42.00
- ❑63, Sep 1960 .... 42.00
- ❑64, Nov 1960 .... 42.00
- ❑65, Jan 1961 .... 42.00
- ❑66, Mar 1961 .... 42.00
- ❑67, May 1961 .... 42.00
- ❑68, Jul 1961 .... 42.00
- ❑69, Sep 1961 .... 42.00
- ❑70, Nov 1961 .... 42.00
- ❑71, Jan 1962 .... 42.00
- ❑72, Mar 1962 .... 42.00
- ❑73, May 1962 .... 42.00
- ❑74, Jul 1962 .... 42.00
- ❑75, Sep 1962 .... 42.00
- ❑76, Nov 1962 .... 42.00
- ❑77, Jan 1963 .... 42.00
- ❑78, Mar 1963 .... 42.00
- ❑79, May 1963 .... 42.00
- ❑80, Jul 1963 .... 42.00
- ❑81, Sep 1963 .... 26.00
- ❑82, Nov 1963 .... 26.00
- ❑83, Jan 1964 .... 26.00
- ❑84, Mar 1964 .... 26.00
- ❑85, May 1964 .... 26.00
- ❑86, Jul 1964 .... 26.00
- ❑87, Sep 1964 .... 26.00
- ❑88, Nov 1964 .... 26.00
- ❑89, Jan 1965 .... 26.00
- ❑90, Feb 1965 .... 26.00
- ❑91, May 1965 .... 26.00
- ❑92, Jul 1965 .... 26.00
- ❑93, Sep 1965 .... 26.00
- ❑94, Nov 1965 .... 26.00
- ❑95, Dec 1965 O: Stanley and His Monster. 1: Stanley and His Monster. ... 50.00
- ❑96, Mar 1966 .... 22.00
- ❑97, May 1966 .... 22.00
- ❑98, Jul 1966 .... 22.00
- ❑99, Sep 1966 .... 22.00
- ❑100, Nov 1966 .... 22.00
- ❑101, Jan 1967 .... 18.00
- ❑102, Mar 1967 .... 18.00
- ❑103, May 1967 .... 18.00
- ❑104, Jul 1967 .... 18.00
- ❑105, Sep 1967 A: Stanley and His Monster. 18.00
- ❑106, Nov 1967 .... 18.00
- ❑107, Jan 1968 .... 18.00
- ❑108, Mar 1968; Series continued in Stanley and His Monster 18.00

FOX COMICS
Fantagraphics
- ❑24, b&w 2.95
- ❑25, b&w 2.95
- ❑26, b&w 2.95
- ❑Special 1, b&w; Australian; Special . 2.95

FOX COMICS LEGENDS SERIES
Fantagraphics
- ❑1, Jul 1992, b&w; Three Stooges 2.50
- ❑2, b&w; Elvis 2.50

FOXFIRE (MALIBU)
Malibu / Ultraverse
- ❑1, Feb 1996 .... 1.50
- ❑2, Mar 1996 .... 1.50
- ❑3, Apr 1996 .... 1.50
- ❑4, May 1996 .... 1.50

FOXFIRE (NIGHT WYND)
Nightwynd
- ❑1, b&w 2.50
- ❑2, b&w 2.50
- ❑3, b&w 2.50

FOX KIDS FUNHOUSE
Acclaim
- ❑1; digest; The Tick, Life with Louie, Bobby's World 4.50
- ❑2 .... 4.50

FRACTION
DC / Focus
- ❑1, Jun 2004 .... 2.50
- ❑2, Jul 2004 .... 2.50
- ❑3, Aug 2004 .... 2.50
- ❑4, Sep 2004 ....

FRACTURED FAIRY TALES
Gold Key
- ❑1, Oct 1962 .... 75.00

FRAGGLE ROCK (STAR)
Marvel / Star
- ❑1, Apr 1985 .... 1.50
- ❑2, Jun 1985 .... 1.25
- ❑3, Aug 1985 .... 1.25
- ❑4, Oct 1985 .... 1.25
- ❑5, Dec 1985 .... 1.25
- ❑6, Feb 1986 .... 1.25
- ❑7, Apr 1986 .... 1.25
- ❑8, Jun 1986 .... 1.25

FRAGGLE ROCK (MARVEL)
Marvel
- ❑1, Apr 1988 .... 1.50
- ❑2, Jun 1988 .... 1.00
- ❑3, Jun 1988 .... 1.00
- ❑4, Jul 1988 .... 1.00
- ❑5, Aug 1988 .... 1.00

FRAGMENTS
Screaming Cat
- ❑1 .... 2.50

FRANCIS, BROTHER OF THE UNIVERSE
Marvel
- ❑1 .... 1.50

FRANK (NEMESIS)
Nemesis
- ❑1, Apr 1994; newsstand 1.75
- ❑1/Direct ed., Apr 1994; variant cover: direct sale 2.50
- ❑2, May 1994; newsstand 1.75
- ❑2/Direct ed., May 1994; direct sale .. 2.50
- ❑3, Jun 1994; newsstand 1.75
- ❑3/Direct ed., Jun 1994; direct sale ... 2.50
- ❑4, Jul 1994; newsstand 1.75
- ❑4/Direct ed., Jul 1994; direct sale 2.50

FRANK (FANTAGRAPHICS)
Fantagraphics
- ❑1, Sep 1996, b&w 2.95
- ❑2, Dec 1997, b&w 3.95

FRANK FRAZETTA FANTASY ILLUSTRATED
Frank Frazetta Fantasy Illustrated
- ❑1, Spr 1998 .... 7.00
- ❑1/Variant, Spr 1998; alternate cover 7.00
- ❑2, Sum 1998; Battle Chasers story .. 6.00
- ❑2/Variant, Sum 1998; alternate cover 6.00
- ❑3, Fal 1998 .... 6.00
- ❑3/Variant, Fal 1998; alternate cover . 6.00
- ❑4, Win 1998 .... 5.99
- ❑4/Variant, Win 1998; alternate cover 6.00
- ❑5, Mar 1999 .... 5.99
- ❑5/Variant, Mar 1999; alternate cover 7.50
- ❑6, May 1999 .... 6.00
- ❑6/Variant, May 1999; alternate cover 6.00
- ❑7, Jul 1999 .... 5.99
- ❑7/Variant, Jul 1999; alternate cover . 5.99

FRANK IN THE RIVER
Tundra
- ❑1; 'Tantalizing Stories Presents Frank in the River' 2.95

FRANK THE UNICORN
Fragments West
- ❑1, Sep 1986 .... 2.00
- ❑2, Nov 1986 .... 2.00
- ❑3, Jan 1987 .... 2.00
- ❑4 .... 2.00
- ❑5 .... 2.00
- ❑6 .... 2.00
- ❑7 .... 2.00

N-MINT

❑8 .... 2.00
❑9 .... 2.00

FRANK ZAPPA: VIVA LA BIZARRE
Revolutionary

❑1, Feb 1994, b&w 3.00

FRANKENSTEIN (DELL)
Dell

❑1, Mar 1963 .... 35.00
❑2 .... 25.00
❑3, Dec 1966 .... 15.00
❑4, Mar 1967 .... 15.00

FRANKENSTEIN (THE MONSTER OF...)
Marvel

❑1, Jan 1973 MP (a); O: Frankenstein's Monster. 24.00
❑2, Mar 1973 MP (w); MP (a); O: Bride of Frankenstein. 12.00
❑3, May 1973 .... 9.00
❑4, Jul 1973 .... 9.00
❑5, Sep 1973 .... 9.00
❑6, Oct 1973; Cover changes titles to "The Frankenstein Monster" 7.00
❑7, Nov 1973 .... 7.00
❑8, Jan 1974 A: Dracula. 10.00
❑9, Mar 1974; A: Dracula. Marvel Value Stamp #68: Son of Satan 10.00
❑10, May 1974; Marvel Value Stamp #69: Marvel Girl 6.00
❑11, Jul 1974; V: Ivan. Marvel Value Stamp #12: Daredevil 5.00
❑12, Sep 1974; The monster comes to the modern day; Marvel Value Stamp #59: Golem 5.00
❑13, Nov 1974; Marvel Value Stamp #60: Ka-Zar 5.00
❑14, Jan 1975; Marvel Value Stamp #90: Hercules 5.00
❑15, Mar 1975; VM, KJ (a); Back-up story Reprints Tales of Suspense #10 .... 5.00
❑16, May 1975; 1: Veronica Frankenstein. 1: Berserker. Marvel Value Stamp #8: Captain America 5.00
❑17, Jul 1975; V: Berserker. Monster regains speech 5.00
❑18, Sep 1975 .... 5.00

FRANKENSTEIN (ETERNITY)
Eternity

❑1, b&w 2.00
❑2, b&w 2.00
❑3, Aug 1989, b&w 2.00

FRANKENSTEIN (MARY SHELLEY'S...)
Topps

❑1, Oct 1994 .... 2.95
❑2 .... 2.95
❑3 .... 2.95
❑4 .... 2.95

FRANKENSTEIN/DRACULA WAR, THE
Topps

❑1, Feb 1995 .... 2.50
❑2 .... 2.50
❑3 .... 2.50

FRANKENSTEIN MOBSTER
Image

❑0, Oct 2003 .... 2.95
❑1, Dec 2003 .... 2.95
❑2, Feb 2004 .... 2.95
❑3, May 2004 .... 2.95

FRANKENSTEIN: OR THE MODERN PROMETHEUS
Caliber

❑1 .... 2.95

FRAY
Dark Horse

❑1, Jun 2001 .... 3.00
❑2, Jul 2001 .... 2.99
❑3, Aug 2001 .... 2.99
❑4, Sep 2001 .... 2.99
❑5, Oct 2001 .... 2.99
❑6, Nov 2001 .... 2.99

N-MINT

❑7, Apr 2003 .... 2.99
❑8, ca. 2003 .... 2.99

FREAK FORCE
Image

❑1, Dec 1993 KG, EL (w); 1: Freak Force. 2.00
❑2, Jan 1994 .... 1.95
❑3, Feb 1994 .... 1.95
❑4, Mar 1994 A: Vanguard. 1.95
❑5, Apr 1994 .... 1.95
❑6, Jun 1994; Identity of Mighty Man revealed 1.95
❑7, Jul 1994 .... 1.95
❑8, Aug 1994 .... 2.50
❑9, Sep 1994 A: Cyber Force. 2.50
❑10, Oct 1994 .... 2.50
❑11, Nov 1994 .... 2.50
❑12, Dec 1994 .... 2.50
❑13, Jan 1995; Jerry Ordway pin-up 2.50
❑13/A, Jan 1995; alternate cover 2.50
❑14, Feb 1995 .... 2.50
❑15, Mar 1995 A: Maxx. 2.50
❑16, Apr 1995 .... 2.50
❑17, Jun 1995 .... 2.50
❑18, Jul 1995 .... 2.50

FREAK FORCE (MINI-SERIES)
Image

❑1, Apr 1997 .... 2.95
❑2, May 1997 .... 2.95
❑3, Jul 1997 .... 2.95

FREAK OUT ON INFANT EARTHS
Blackthorne

❑1, Jan 1987 .... 2.00
❑2 .... 2.00

FREAKS
Fantagraphics / Eros

❑1 .... 2.25
❑2 .... 2.25
❑3 .... 2.25

FREAKS' AMOUR
Dark Horse

❑1 .... 3.95
❑2 .... 3.95
❑3 .... 3.95

FREAKS OF THE HEARTLAND
Dark Horse

❑1, Jan 2004 .... 2.99
❑2, Mar 2004 .... 2.99
❑3, May 2004 .... 2.99

FRED & BIANCA CENSORSHIP SUCKS SPECIAL
Comics Interview

❑1, b&w 2.25

FRED & BIANCA MOTHER'S DAY MASSACRE
Comics Interview

❑1, b&w 2.25

FRED & BIANCA VALENTINE'S DAY MASSACRE
Comics Interview

❑1, b&w 2.25

FRED THE CLOWN
Hotel Fred

❑1, Sep 2001 .... 2.95
❑2, Jan 2002 .... 2.95

FREDDY KRUEGER'S NIGHTMARE ON ELM STREET
Marvel

❑1, Oct 1989, b&w; magazine RB, AA, TD (a); O: Freddy Krueger. 4.50
❑2, Nov 1989, b&w; magazine AA, TD (a) 4.00

FREDDY'S DEAD: THE FINAL NIGHTMARE
Innovation

❑1 .... 2.50
❑1/3D; part 3-D 2.50
❑2 .... 2.50

Following the events of *Justice League of America* #107 and #108, the Quality super-heroes who had teamed up as The Freedom Fighters got their own series.

N-MINT

❑3 .... 2.50
❑3/3D; 3-D version of #3; Requires glasses provided at movie showings 2.50

FREDERIC REMINGTON: THE MAN WHO PAINTED THE WEST
Tome

❑1, b&w 2.95

FRED HEMBECK DESTROYS THE MARVEL UNIVERSE
Marvel

❑1, Jul 1989 .... 1.50

FRED HEMBECK SELLS THE MARVEL UNIVERSE
Marvel

❑1, Oct 1990 FH (w); FH (a) 1.50

FRED THE POSSESSED FLOWER
Happy Predator

❑1 .... 2.95
❑2 .... 2.95
❑3 .... 2.95
❑4 .... 2.95
❑5 .... 2.95
❑6 .... 2.95

FREE CEREBUS
Aardvark-Vanaheim

❑1; giveaway 1.00

FREE LAUGHS
Deschaine

❑1, b&w 1.00

FREE SPEECHES
Oni

❑1, Aug 1998; collects Nadine Strossen, Dave Sim, Neil Gaiman, and Frank Miller speeches; Fundraiser for Comic Book Legal Defense Fund 2.95

FREE-VIEW
Acclaim

❑1, Mar 1993 VM (a) 1.00

FREEBOOTERS/YOUNG GODS/ PARADOXMAN PREVIEW
Dark Horse

❑1 .... 1.00

FREEDOM FIGHTERS
DC

❑1, Apr 1976; RE (a); 1: Silver Ghost. V: Silver Ghost. Freedom Fighters arrive on Earth-1 .... 5.00
❑2, Jun 1976 V: Silver Ghost. 3.50
❑3, Aug 1976; A: Wonder Woman. Bicentennial #8 .... 3.50
❑4, Oct 1976 A: Wonder Woman. 3.00
❑5, Dec 1976 .... 3.00
❑6, Feb 1977 .... 2.50
❑7, Apr 1977 .... 2.50
❑8, Jun 1977 V: Crusaders. 2.50
❑9, Aug 1977 V: Crusaders. 2.50
❑10, Oct 1977 O: Doll Man. V: Cat-Man. 2.50
❑11, Dec 1977 O: Ray. 2.50
❑12, Feb 1978 O: Firebrand I (Rod Reilly). 2.50
❑13, Apr 1978 O: Black Condor. 2.50
❑14, Jun 1978 A: Batwoman. A: Batgirl. 2.50
❑15, Aug 1978; O: Phantom Lady. events continue in Secret Society of Super Villains #16 .... 2.50

N-MINT

FREEFLIGHT
THINKBLOTS

❑1, Apr 1994 .... 2.95

FREEJACK
NOW

❑1, Apr 1992; newsstand 1.95
❑1/Direct ed., Apr 1992; direct-sale edition 2.50
❑2, May 1992; newsstand 1.95
❑2/Direct ed., May 1992; direct-sale 2.50
❑3, Jun 1992; newsstand 1.95
❑3/Direct ed., Jun 1992; direct-sale 2.50

FREEMIND
FUTURE

❑1 2002 .... 3.50
❑2 2002 .... 3.50
❑3 2003 .... 3.50
❑4 2003 .... 3.50
❑5, Apr 2003 .... 3.50
❑6, May 2003 .... 3.50
❑7, Jul 2003 .... 2.99

FREEWAY NINJA HANZO
SLEEPYHOUSE

❑1; Heavyweight premiere issue 3.50

FREEX
MALIBU / ULTRAVERSE

❑1, Jul 1993 1: Freex. 1: Pressure. 2.00
❑1/Hologram, Jul 1993; 1: Freex. 1: Pressure. Hologram cover; "Ultra Limited" 5.00
❑2, Aug 1993 1: Rush. 2.00
❑3, Sep 1993 1: Bloodhounds. 2.00
❑4, Oct 1993; Rune 2.50
❑5, Nov 1993 .... 1.95
❑6, Dec 1993; Break-Thru 1.95
❑7, Jan 1994 O: Pressure. O: Hardcase. 1.95
❑8, Feb 1994 .... 1.95
❑9, Mar 1994 O: Sweetface. 1: Contrary. 1.95
❑10, Apr 1994 O: Boomboy. 1.95
❑11, May 1994 O: Plug. 1.95
❑12, Aug 1994 1: The Guardian. 1.95
❑13, Sep 1994 1: Prometheus. 1.95
❑14, Oct 1994 1: The Savior. 1.95
❑15, Jan 1995; 1: Eliminator. 1: Manic. 1: Oyabun. Flip-book with Ultraverse Premiere #9 .... 3.50
❑16, Jan 1995 .... 1.95
❑17, Feb 1995 A: Rune. 2.50
❑18, Feb 1995 1: A.J. Analla. 1: Tulath. 2.50
❑Giant Size 1; 1: Pixx. 2.50

FRENCH ICE
RENEGADE

❑1, b&w 2.00
❑2, Apr 1987, b&w 2.00
❑3, May 1987, b&w 2.00
❑4, Jun 1987, b&w 2.00
❑5, Jul 1987, b&w 2.00
❑6, Sep 1987, b&w 2.00
❑7, Oct 1987, b&w 2.00
❑8, Nov 1987, b&w 2.00
❑9, Dec 1987, b&w 2.00
❑10, Jan 1988, b&w 2.00
❑11, Feb 1988, b&w 2.00
❑12, Mar 1988, b&w 2.00
❑13, Apr 1988, b&w 2.00

FRENCH TICKLERS
KITCHEN SINK

❑1, Oct 1989, b&w 2.00
❑2, Oct 1989, b&w 2.00
❑3, Oct 1989, b&w 2.00

FRENZY
INDEPENDENT

❑1 .... 1.00
❑1/A 1.00

FRESCAZIZIS
LAST GASP

❑1 .... 1.00

N-MINT

FRESH BLOOD FUNNY BOOK, THE
LAST GASP

❑1 .... 1.25

FRIENDLY GHOST, CASPER, THE
HARVEY

❑1, Aug 1958 .... 190.00
❑2, Sep 1958 .... 100.00
❑3, Oct 1958 .... 85.00
❑4, Nov 1958 .... 55.00
❑5, Jan 1959 .... 55.00
❑6, Feb 1959 .... 46.00
❑7, Mar 1959 .... 46.00
❑8, Apr 1959 .... 46.00
❑9, May 1959 .... 46.00
❑10, Jun 1959 .... 46.00
❑11, Jul 1959 .... 36.00
❑12, Aug 1959 .... 36.00
❑13, Sep 1959 .... 36.00
❑14, Oct 1959 .... 36.00
❑15, Nov 1959 .... 36.00
❑16, Dec 1959 .... 36.00
❑17, Jan 1960 .... 36.00
❑18, Feb 1960 .... 36.00
❑19, Mar 1960 .... 36.00
❑20, Apr 1960 .... 36.00
❑21, May 1960 .... 25.00
❑22, Jun 1960 .... 25.00
❑23, Jul 1960 .... 25.00
❑24, Aug 1960 .... 25.00
❑25, Sep 1960 .... 25.00
❑26, Oct 1960 .... 25.00
❑27, Nov 1960 .... 25.00
❑28, Dec 1960 .... 25.00
❑29, Jan 1961 .... 25.00
❑30, Feb 1961 .... 25.00
❑31, Mar 1961 .... 18.00
❑32, Apr 1961 .... 18.00
❑33, May 1961 .... 18.00
❑34, Jun 1961 .... 18.00
❑35, Jul 1961 .... 18.00
❑36, Aug 1961 .... 18.00
❑37, Sep 1961 .... 18.00
❑38, Oct 1961 .... 18.00
❑39, Nov 1961 .... 18.00
❑40, Dec 1961 .... 18.00
❑41, Jan 1962 .... 15.00
❑42, Feb 1962 .... 15.00
❑43, Mar 1962 .... 15.00
❑44, Apr 1962 .... 15.00
❑45, May 1962 .... 15.00
❑46, Jun 1962 .... 15.00
❑47, Jul 1962 .... 15.00
❑48, Aug 1962 .... 15.00
❑49, Sep 1962 .... 15.00
❑50, Oct 1962 .... 15.00
❑51, Nov 1962 .... 12.00
❑52, Dec 1962 .... 12.00
❑53, Jan 1963 .... 12.00
❑54, Feb 1963 .... 12.00
❑55, Mar 1963 .... 12.00
❑56, Apr 1963 .... 12.00
❑57, May 1963 .... 12.00
❑58, Jun 1963 .... 12.00
❑59, Jul 1963 .... 12.00
❑60, Aug 1963 .... 12.00
❑61, Sep 1963 .... 10.00
❑62, Oct 1963 .... 10.00
❑63, Nov 1963 .... 10.00
❑64, Dec 1963 .... 10.00
❑65, Jan 1964 .... 10.00
❑66, Feb 1964 .... 10.00
❑67, Mar 1964 .... 10.00
❑68, Apr 1964 .... 10.00
❑69, May 1964 .... 10.00
❑70, Jun 1964 .... 10.00
❑71, Jul 1964 .... 8.00
❑72, Aug 1964 .... 8.00
❑73, Sep 1964 .... 8.00
❑74, Oct 1964 .... 8.00
❑75, Nov 1964 .... 8.00
❑76, Dec 1964 .... 8.00

N-MINT

❑77, Jan 1965 .... 8.00
❑78, Feb 1965 .... 8.00
❑79, Mar 1965 .... 8.00
❑80, Apr 1965 .... 8.00
❑81, May 1965 .... 7.00
❑82, Jun 1965 .... 7.00
❑83, Jul 1965 .... 7.00
❑84, Aug 1965 .... 7.00
❑85, Sep 1965 .... 7.00
❑86, Oct 1965 .... 7.00
❑87, Nov 1965 .... 7.00
❑88, Dec 1965 .... 7.00
❑89, Jan 1966 .... 7.00
❑90, Feb 1966 .... 6.00
❑91, Mar 1966 .... 6.00
❑92, Apr 1966 .... 6.00
❑93, May 1966 .... 6.00
❑94, Jun 1966 .... 6.00
❑95, Jul 1966 .... 6.00
❑96, Aug 1966 .... 6.00
❑97, Sep 1966 .... 6.00
❑98, Oct 1966 .... 6.00
❑99, Nov 1966 .... 6.00
❑100, Dec 1966 .... 6.00
❑101, Jan 1967 .... 5.00
❑102, Feb 1967 .... 5.00
❑103, Mar 1967 .... 5.00
❑104, Apr 1967 .... 5.00
❑105, May 1967 .... 5.00
❑106, Jun 1967 .... 5.00
❑107, Jul 1967 .... 5.00
❑108, Aug 1967 .... 5.00
❑109, Sep 1967 .... 5.00
❑110, Oct 1967 .... 5.00
❑111, Nov 1967 .... 5.00
❑112, Dec 1967 .... 5.00
❑113, Jan 1968 .... 5.00
❑114, Feb 1968 .... 5.00
❑115, Mar 1968 .... 5.00
❑116, Apr 1968 .... 5.00
❑117, May 1968 .... 5.00
❑118, Jun 1968 .... 5.00
❑119, Jul 1968 .... 5.00
❑120, Aug 1968 .... 5.00
❑121, Sep 1968 .... 4.00
❑122, Oct 1968 .... 4.00
❑123, Nov 1968 .... 4.00
❑124, Dec 1968 .... 4.00
❑125, Jan 1969 .... 4.00
❑126, Feb 1969 .... 4.00
❑127, Mar 1969 .... 4.00
❑128, Apr 1969 .... 4.00
❑129, May 1969 .... 4.00
❑130, Jun 1969 .... 4.00
❑131, Jul 1969 .... 4.00
❑132, Aug 1969 .... 4.00
❑133, Sep 1969 .... 4.00
❑134, Oct 1969 .... 4.00
❑135, Nov 1969 .... 4.00
❑136, Dec 1969 .... 4.00
❑137, Jan 1970 .... 4.00
❑138, Feb 1970 .... 4.00
❑139, Mar 1970 .... 4.00
❑140, Apr 1970 .... 4.00
❑141, May 1970 .... 3.00
❑142, Jun 1970 .... 3.00
❑143, Jul 1970 .... 3.00
❑144, Aug 1970 .... 3.00
❑145, Sep 1970 .... 3.00
❑146, Oct 1970 .... 3.00
❑147, Nov 1970 .... 3.00
❑148, Dec 1970 .... 3.00
❑149, Jan 1971 .... 3.00
❑150, Feb 1971 .... 3.00
❑151, Mar 1971 .... 3.00
❑152, Apr 1971 .... 3.00
❑153, May 1971 .... 3.00
❑154, Jun 1971 .... 3.00
❑155, Jul 1971 .... 3.00
❑156, Aug 1971 .... 3.00
❑157, Sep 1971 .... 3.00

	N-MINT
❑158, Oct 1971	3.00
❑159, Nov 1971	3.00
❑160, Mar 1972	3.00
❑161, May 1972	3.00
❑162, Jul 1972	3.00
❑163, Sep 1972	3.00
❑164, Nov 1972	3.00
❑165, Jan 1973	3.00
❑166, Mar 1973	3.00
❑167, May 1973	3.00
❑168, Jul 1973	3.00
❑169, Sep 1973	3.00
❑170, Nov 1973	2.00
❑171, Jan 1974	2.00
❑172, Mar 1974	2.00
❑173, May 1974	2.00
❑174, Jul 1974	2.00
❑175, Sep 1974	2.00
❑176, Nov 1974	2.00
❑177, Jan 1975	2.00
❑178, Mar 1975	2.00
❑179, May 1975	2.00
❑180, Jul 1975	2.00
❑181, Sep 1975	2.00
❑182, Nov 1975	2.00
❑183, Jan 1976	2.00
❑184, Mar 1976	2.00
❑185, Apr 1976	2.00
❑186, Jun 1976	2.00
❑187, Aug 1976	2.00
❑188, Oct 1976	2.00
❑189, Dec 1976	2.00
❑190, Feb 1977	2.00
❑191, Apr 1977	2.00
❑192, Jun 1977	2.00
❑193, Aug 1977	2.00
❑194, Oct 1977	2.00
❑195, Dec 1977	2.00
❑196, Feb 1978	2.00
❑197, Apr 1978	2.00
❑198, Jun 1978	2.00
❑199, Aug 1978	2.00
❑200, Oct 1978	2.00
❑201, Dec 1978	2.00
❑202, Feb 1979	2.00
❑203, Apr 1979	2.00
❑204, Jun 1979	2.00
❑205, Aug 1979	2.00
❑206, Oct 1979	2.00
❑207, Dec 1979	2.00
❑208, Feb 1980	2.00
❑209, Apr 1980	2.00
❑210, Jun 1980	2.00
❑211, Aug 1980	2.00
❑212, Oct 1980	2.00
❑213, Dec 1980	2.00
❑214, Feb 1981	2.00
❑215, Apr 1981	2.00
❑216, Jun 1981	2.00
❑217, Aug 1981	2.00
❑218, Oct 1981	2.00
❑219, Dec 1981	2.00
❑220, Feb 1982	2.00
❑221, Apr 1982	2.00
❑222, Jun 1982	2.00
❑223, Aug 1982	2.00
❑224, Oct 1982	2.00
❑225	2.00
❑226, Nov 1983	2.00
❑227, Dec 1983	2.00
❑228, Jan 1984	2.00
❑229, Feb 1984	2.00
❑230, Mar 1984	2.00
❑231, Apr 1984	2.00
❑232, May 1984	2.00
❑233, Jun 1984	2.00
❑234, Jul 1984	2.00
❑235, Aug 1984	2.00
❑236, Sep 1984	2.00
❑237, Oct 1984	2.00
❑238, Jan 1985	2.00
❑239, Mar 1985	2.00
❑240, May 1985	2.00
❑241, Jul 1985	2.00
❑242, Sep 1985	2.00
❑243, Nov 1985	2.00
❑244, Jan 1986	2.00
❑245, Mar 1986	2.00
❑246, Jul 1986	2.00
❑247 1986	2.00
❑248, Oct 1986	2.00
❑249	2.00
❑250, Mar 1987	2.00
❑251, Apr 1987	2.00
❑252, May 1987	2.00
❑253, Jun 1987; Series continued in Casper the Friendly Ghost #254	2.00

FRIENDS
RENEGADE

	N-MINT
❑1, May 1987, b&w	2.00
❑2, b&w	2.00
❑3, b&w	2.00

FRIENDS OF MAXX
IMAGE

	N-MINT
❑1, Apr 1996; Dude Japan	2.95
❑2, Nov 1996; Broadminded	2.95
❑3, Mar 1997	2.95

FRIGHT
ATLAS-SEABOARD

	N-MINT
❑1, Jun 1975 O: Son of Dracula.	2.50

FRIGHT (ETERNITY)
ETERNITY

	N-MINT
❑1	2.00
❑2	2.00
❑3	2.00
❑4	2.00
❑5	2.00
❑6	2.00
❑7	2.00
❑8	2.00
❑9, Apr 1989	2.00
❑10, May 1989	2.00
❑11, Jun 1989	2.00
❑12, Jul 1989	2.00

FRIGHT NIGHT
NOW

	N-MINT
❑1, Oct 1988; Adapts movie	2.50
❑2, Nov 1988; Adapts movie	2.00
❑3, Dec 1988	2.00
❑4, Feb 1989	2.00
❑5, Mar 1989	2.00
❑6, Apr 1989	2.00
❑7, May 1989	2.00
❑8, Jun 1989	2.00
❑9, Jul 1989	2.00
❑10, Aug 1989	2.00
❑11, Sep 1989	2.00
❑12, Oct 1989	2.00
❑13, Nov 1989	2.00
❑14, Dec 1989	2.00
❑15, Jan 1990	2.00
❑16, Feb 1990	2.00
❑17, Mar 1990	2.00
❑18, Apr 1990	2.00
❑19, May 1990	2.00
❑20, Jun 1990	2.00
❑21, Jul 1990	2.00
❑22, Aug 1990	2.00

FRIGHT NIGHT 1993 HALLOWEEN ANNUAL
NOW

	N-MINT
❑1; 3-D	2.95

FRIGHT NIGHT 3-D
NOW

	N-MINT
❑1, Jun 1992; with glasses	2.95
❑2, Fal 1992; Dracula	2.95

FRIGHT NIGHT 3-D WINTER SPECIAL
NOW

	N-MINT
❑1, Win 1993; Brainbats	2.95

Alan Moore and Eddy Campbell's *From Hell* was collected as a trade paperback and hardcover book in 2000.

© 1992 Alan Moore and Eddy Campbell (Kitchen Sink).

FRIGHT NIGHT II GRAPHIC NOVEL
NOW

	N-MINT
❑1	3.95

FRINGE
CALIBER

	N-MINT
❑1, b&w	2.50
❑2, b&w	2.50
❑3, b&w	2.50
❑4, b&w	2.50
❑5, b&w	2.50
❑6, b&w	2.50
❑7, b&w	2.50
❑8, b&w	2.50

FROGMEN, THE
DELL

	N-MINT
❑2, May 1962; Continued from Four Color Comics #1258	34.00
❑3, Sep 1962	26.00
❑4, Feb 1963	20.00
❑5, May 1963 ATh (a)	22.00
❑6, Aug 1963	20.00
❑7, Nov 1963	18.00
❑8, Feb 1964	18.00
❑9, May 1964	18.00
❑10, Aug 1964	18.00
❑11, Nov 1964	18.00

FROM BEYONDE
STUDIO INSIDIO

	N-MINT
❑1, b&w	2.25

FROM BEYOND THE UNKNOWN
DC

	N-MINT
❑1, Nov 1969	35.00
❑2, Jan 1970	18.00
❑3, Mar 1970	13.00
❑4, May 1970	13.00
❑5, Jul 1970	13.00
❑6, Sep 1970	10.00
❑7, Nov 1970 JKu (c)	12.00
❑8, Jan 1971	12.00
❑9, Mar 1971	12.00
❑10, May 1971 CS (c)	12.00
❑11, Jul 1971	10.00
❑12, Sep 1971 JKu (c)	10.00
❑13, Nov 1971	10.00
❑14, Jan 1972 JKu (c)	10.00
❑15, Mar 1972	10.00
❑16, May 1972 MA, CI (a)	10.00
❑17, Jul 1972	10.00
❑18, Sep 1972	8.00
❑19, Nov 1972	8.00
❑20, Jan 1973	8.00
❑21, Mar 1973; reprints from Strange Adventures #23, #149, and #159	8.00
❑22, May 1973	8.00
❑23, Aug 1973	8.00
❑24, Oct 1973	8.00
❑25, Dec 1973	8.00

FROM DUSK TILL DAWN
BIG

	N-MINT
❑1	4.95
❑1/Deluxe	9.95

FROM HELL
TUNDRA

	N-MINT
❑1, Mar 1991 AMo (w)	6.00
❑1-2, Feb 1992 AMo (w)	5.00

N-MINT

❑1-3; AMo (w); 3rd printing (Kitchen Sink) 5.00
❑1-4; 4th printing (Kitchen Sink) 4.95
❑2 AMo (w) 5.00
❑2-2; AMo (w); 2nd printing (Kitchen Sink) 5.00
❑2-3 AMo (w) 5.00
❑3, Dec 1993 AMo (w) 5.00
❑3-2 AMo (w) 5.00
❑3-3 AMo (w) 5.00
❑4, Mar 1994 AMo (w) 5.00
❑4-2 AMo (w) 5.00
❑4-3 AMo (w) 5.00
❑5, Jun 1994 AMo (w) 4.95
❑6, Nov 1994 AMo (w) 4.95
❑7, Apr 1995 AMo (w) 4.95
❑8, Jul 1995 AMo (w) 4.95
❑9, Apr 1996 AMo (w) 4.95
❑10, Aug 1996 AMo (w) 4.95
❑11, Sep 1998 AMo (w) 4.95

FROM HELL: DANCE OF THE GULL CATCHERS
KITCHEN SINK

❑1; sequel to From Hell 4.95

FROM THE DARKNESS
ADVENTURE

❑1 .... 3.00
❑2 .... 2.50
❑3, b&w 2.50
❑4, b&w 2.50

FROM THE DARKNESS BOOK II: BLOOD VOWS
CRY FOR DAWN

❑1 .... 2.50
❑2 .... 2.50
❑3 .... 2.50

FRONTIER
SLAVE LABOR

❑1, Jul 1994 .... 2.95

FRONTIERS '86 PRESENTS
FRONTIERS

❑1; Crusaders 1.50
❑2; Crusaders 1.50

FRONTLINE COMBAT (RCP)
GEMSTONE

❑1, Aug 1995; Reprints Frontline Combat (EC) #1 .... 2.00
❑2, Nov 1995; Reprints Frontline Combat (EC) #2 .... 2.00
❑3, Feb 1996; Reprints Frontline Combat (EC) #3 .... 2.00
❑4, May 1996; Reprints Frontline Combat (EC) #4 .... 2.00
❑5, Aug 1996; Reprints Frontline Combat (EC) #5 .... 2.50
❑6, Nov 1996; Reprints Frontline Combat (EC) #6 .... 2.50
❑7, Feb 1997; Reprints Frontline Combat (EC) #7 .... 2.50
❑8, May 1997; Reprints Frontline Combat (EC) #8 .... 2.50
❑9, Aug 1997; Reprints Frontline Combat (EC) #9 .... 2.50
❑10, Nov 1997; Reprints Frontline Combat (EC) #10 .... 2.50
❑11, Feb 1998; Reprints Frontline Combat (EC) #11 .... 2.50
❑12, May 1998; Reprints Frontline Combat (EC) #12 .... 2.50
❑13, Aug 1998; Reprints Frontline Combat (EC) #13 .... 2.50
❑14, Nov 1998; Reprints Frontline Combat (EC) #14 .... 2.50
❑15, Feb 1999; Reprints Frontline Combat (EC) #15 .... 2.50
❑Annual 1; Collects Frontline Combat #1-5 .... 10.95
❑Annual 2; Collects Frontline Combat #6-10 .... 12.95

FROST
CALIBER

❑1, b&w 1.95

FROSTBITER: WRATH OF THE WENDIGO
CALIBER

❑1 .... 2.95
❑2 .... 2.95
❑3 .... 2.95

FROST: THE DYING BREED
CALIBER

❑1, b&w 2.50
❑2, b&w 2.50
❑3, b&w 2.50

FROZEN EMBRYO
SLAVE LABOR

❑1, Dec 1992 .... 2.95

F-3 BANDIT
ANTARCTIC

❑1, Jan 1995; mini-poster 2.95
❑2, Mar 1995; trading card 2.95
❑3, May 1995; trading card 2.95
❑4, Jul 1995; trading card 2.95
❑5, Sep 1995; trading card 2.95
❑6, Nov 1995 .... 2.95
❑7, Jan 1996 .... 2.95
❑8, Mar 1996 .... 2.95
❑9, May 1996, b&w 2.95
❑10, Jul 1996, b&w; trading card 2.95

F-TROOP
GOLD KEY

❑1, Aug 1966 .... 50.00
❑2, Nov 1966 .... 40.00
❑3, Feb 1967 .... 36.00
❑4, Apr 1967 .... 36.00
❑5, May 1967 .... 36.00
❑6, Jun 1967 .... 32.00
❑7, Aug 1967 .... 32.00

FUGITIVE
CALIBER

❑1, ca. 1989, b&w; No indicia 2.50

FUGITOID
MIRAGE

❑1 1985; Teenage Mutant Ninja Turtles tie-in; Continued from TMNT #4; continued in TMNT #5 .... 3.00

FULL METAL FICTION
LONDON NIGHT

❑1, Mar 1997 .... 3.95

FULL METAL PANIC
ADV MANGA

❑1, ca 2003 .... 9.99
❑2, ca 2003 .... 9.99

FULL THROTTLE
AIRCEL

❑1, b&w 2.95
❑2, b&w 2.95

FUN BOYS SPRING SPECIAL
TUNDRA

❑1, b&w 1.95

FUN COMICS (BILL BLACK'S...)
AC

❑1, b&w; magazine format 2.00
❑2, b&w; magazine format 2.00
❑3, magazine format 2.00
❑4, Mar 1983; Captain Paragon, Nightfall 2.00

FUN HOUSE
MN DESIGN

❑1; photos 6.50

FUN HOUSE (J.R. WILLIAMS'...)
STARHEAD

❑1, Nov 1993, b&w; Collections of comics, strips... .... 3.95

FUN-IN
GOLD KEY

❑1, Feb 1970 .... 16.00
❑2 1970 .... 10.00
❑3 1970 .... 9.00
❑4, Nov 1970 .... 9.00
❑5, Jan 1971; Motormouse and Autocat, Dastardly and Muttley 8.00
❑6, Mar 1971; Dastardly and Muttley, It's the Wolf 8.00
❑7, May 1971; Motormouse and Autocat, Dastardly and Muttley, It's the Wolf 6.00
❑8, Jul 1971 .... 6.00
❑9, Oct 1971 .... 6.00
❑10, Jan 1972 .... 6.00
❑11, Apr 1974 .... 5.00
❑12, Jun 1974 .... 5.00
❑13, Aug 1974 .... 5.00
❑14, Oct 1974 .... 5.00
❑15 .... 5.00

FUNKY PHANTOM
GOLD KEY

❑1, Mar 1972 .... 24.00
❑2, Jun 1972 .... 15.00
❑3, Sep 1972 .... 10.00
❑4, Dec 1972 .... 10.00
❑5, Mar 1973 .... 10.00
❑6, Jun 1973 .... 8.00
❑7, Sep 1973 .... 8.00
❑8, Dec 1973 A: April. A: Skip. A: Augie. A: Elmo. A: Prissy Atwater. 8.00
❑9, Mar 1974 .... 8.00
❑10, Jun 1974 .... 8.00
❑11, Sep 1974 .... 6.00
❑12, Dec 1974 .... 6.00
❑13, Mar 1975 .... 6.00

FUNNY STUFF STOCKING STUFFER
DC

❑1, Mar 1985 .... 1.25

FUNNYTIME FEATURES
EENIEWEENIE

❑1, Jul 1994, b&w 2.50
❑1-2, b&w 2.50
❑2, ca. 1994, b&w 2.50
❑3, ca. 1994, b&w 2.50
❑4, ca. 1995, b&w 2.50
❑5, ca. 1995, b&w 2.50
❑6, ca. 1995, b&w 2.50
❑7, ca. 1995 .... 2.50
❑8, ca. 1995, b&w 2.50

FUNTASTIC WORLD OF HANNA-BARBERA
MARVEL

❑1, Dec 1977 .... 13.00
❑2, Mar 1978 .... 9.00
❑3, Jun 1978 .... 6.00

FURIES (AVATAR)
AVATAR

❑0, Feb 1997 .... 3.00
❑0/Nude, Mar 1997; Nude cover 3.00

FURIES, THE (CARBON-BASED)
CARBON-BASED

❑1, May 1996, b&w 2.75
❑2, Jul 1996, b&w 2.75
❑3, Sep 1996, b&w 2.75
❑4, Nov 1996, b&w 2.75
❑5, Jan 1997, b&w 2.75
❑6, Mar 1997, b&w 2.75
❑7, ca. 1997 .... 2.75
❑8, Sep 1997 .... 2.75

FURKINDRED, THE
MU

❑1, Jan 1992, b&w 6.95
❑2, Nov 1992, b&w 7.95

FURRLOUGH
ANTARCTIC

❑1, Nov 1991 .... 4.00
❑2, Feb 1992 .... 3.50
❑3, May 1992 .... 3.50
❑4, Jul 1992 .... 3.00
❑5, Nov 1992 .... 3.00
❑6, Jan 1993 .... 3.00
❑7, Mar 1993 .... 3.00
❑8, May 1993 .... 3.00
❑9, Jul 1993 .... 3.00
❑10, Sep 1993 .... 3.00
❑11, Nov 1993 .... 2.75

N-MINT

- ❑12, Dec 1993 .... 2.75
- ❑13, Jan 1994 .... 2.75
- ❑14, Feb 1994 .... 2.75
- ❑15, Mar 1994 .... 2.75
- ❑16, Apr 1994 .... 2.75
- ❑17, May 1994 .... 2.75
- ❑18, Jun 1994 .... 2.75
- ❑19, Jul 1994 .... 2.75
- ❑20, Aug 1994 .... 2.75
- ❑21, Sep 1994 .... 2.75
- ❑22, Oct 1994 .... 2.75
- ❑23, Nov 1994; Giant-size 3.50
- ❑24, Dec 1994 .... 2.75
- ❑25, Jan 1995 .... 2.75
- ❑26, Feb 1995 .... 2.75
- ❑27, Mar 1995 .... 2.75
- ❑28, Apr 1995 .... 2.75
- ❑29, May 1995 .... 2.75
- ❑30, Jun 1995 .... 2.75
- ❑31, Jul 1995 .... 2.75
- ❑32, Aug 1995 .... 2.75
- ❑33, Sep 1995 .... 2.75
- ❑34, Oct 1995 .... 2.75
- ❑35, Nov 1995; fourth anniversary special 3.50
- ❑36, Dec 1995 .... 2.95
- ❑37, Jan 1996 .... 2.95
- ❑38, Feb 1996 .... 2.95
- ❑39, Mar 1996 .... 2.95
- ❑40, Apr 1996 .... 2.95
- ❑41, May 1996 .... 2.95
- ❑42, Jun 1996 .... 2.95
- ❑43, Jul 1996 .... 2.95
- ❑44, Aug 1996 .... 2.95
- ❑45, Sep 1996 .... 2.95
- ❑46, Oct 1996 .... 2.95
- ❑47, Nov 1996 .... 2.95
- ❑48, Dec 1996 .... 2.95
- ❑49, Jan 1997 .... 2.95
- ❑50, Feb 1997; Giant-size 3.95
- ❑51, Mar 1997 .... 2.95
- ❑52, Apr 1997 .... 2.95
- ❑53, May 1997 .... 2.95
- ❑54, Jun 1997 .... 2.95
- ❑55, Jul 1997 .... 2.95
- ❑56, Aug 1997 .... 2.95
- ❑57, Sep 1997 .... 2.95
- ❑58, Oct 1997 .... 2.95
- ❑59, Nov 1997 .... 2.95
- ❑60, Dec 1997 .... 2.95
- ❑61, Jan 1998 .... 2.95
- ❑62, Feb 1998 .... 2.95
- ❑63, Mar 1998 .... 2.95
- ❑64, Apr 1998 .... 2.95
- ❑65, May 1998 .... 2.95
- ❑66, Jun 1998 .... 2.95
- ❑67, Jul 1998 .... 2.95
- ❑68, Aug 1998 .... 2.95
- ❑69, Sep 1998 .... 2.95
- ❑70, Oct 1998 .... 2.95
- ❑71, Nov 1998 .... 2.95
- ❑72, Dec 1998 .... 2.95
- ❑73, Jan 1999 .... 2.95
- ❑79, Jul 1999 .... 2.95
- ❑80, Aug 1999 .... 2.95
- ❑81, Sep 1999 .... 2.95
- ❑82, Oct 1999 .... 2.95
- ❑83, Nov 1999 .... 2.95
- ❑84, Dec 1999 .... 2.95
- ❑85, Jan 2000 .... 2.95
- ❑86, Feb 2000 .... 2.95
- ❑87, Mar 2000 .... 2.95
- ❑88, Apr 2000 .... 2.95
- ❑89, May 2000 .... 2.95
- ❑90, Jun 2000 .... 2.95
- ❑91, Jul 2000 .... 2.95
- ❑92, Aug 2000 .... 2.95
- ❑93, Sep 2000 .... 2.95
- ❑94, Oct 2000 .... 2.95
- ❑95, Nov 2000 .... 2.95
- ❑96, Dec 2000 .... 2.95

N-MINT

- ❑97, Jan 2001 .... 2.95
- ❑98, Feb 2001 .... 2.95
- ❑99, Mar 2001 .... 2.95
- ❑100, Apr 2001 .... 2.95
- ❑101, May 2001 .... 2.95
- ❑102, Jun 2001 .... 2.95
- ❑103, Jul 2001 .... 2.99
- ❑104, Aug 2001 .... 2.99
- ❑105, Sep 2001 .... 2.99
- ❑106, Oct 2001 .... 2.99
- ❑107, Nov 2001 .... 2.99
- ❑108, Dec 2001 .... 2.99
- ❑109, Jan 2002 .... 2.99
- ❑110, Feb 2002 .... 2.99
- ❑111, Mar 2002 .... 2.99
- ❑112, Apr 2002 .... 2.99
- ❑113, May 2002 .... 2.99
- ❑114, Jun 2002 .... 2.99
- ❑115, Jul 2002 .... 2.99
- ❑116, Aug 2002 .... 2.99
- ❑117, Sep 2002 .... 2.99
- ❑118, Oct 2002 .... 2.99
- ❑119, Nov 2002 .... 2.99
- ❑120, Dec 2002 .... 2.99
- ❑121, Jan 2003 .... 2.99
- ❑122, Feb 2003 .... 2.99
- ❑123, Mar 2003 .... 2.99
- ❑124, Apr 2003 .... 2.99

FURTHER ADVENTURES OF CYCLOPS AND PHOENIX, THE
MARVEL

- ❑1, Jun 1996 .... 1.95
- ❑2, Jul 1996 .... 1.95
- ❑3, Aug 1996 .... 1.95
- ❑4, Sep 1996 .... 1.95

FURTHER ADVENTURES OF INDIANA JONES, THE
MARVEL

- ❑1, Jan 1983 JBy, TD (a) 2.50
- ❑2, Feb 1983 JBy, TD (a) 2.00
- ❑3, Mar 1983 .... 2.00
- ❑4, Apr 1983 .... 2.00
- ❑5, May 1983 .... 2.00
- ❑6, Jun 1983 .... 2.00
- ❑7, Jul 1983 .... 2.00
- ❑8, Aug 1983 .... 2.00
- ❑9, Sep 1983 .... 2.00
- ❑10, Oct 1983 .... 2.00
- ❑11, Nov 1983 .... 2.00
- ❑12, Dec 1983 .... 2.00
- ❑13, Jan 1984 .... 2.00
- ❑14, Feb 1984 .... 2.00
- ❑15, Mar 1984 .... 2.00
- ❑16, Apr 1984 .... 2.00
- ❑17, May 1984 .... 2.00
- ❑18, Jun 1984 .... 2.00
- ❑19, Jul 1984 .... 2.00
- ❑20, Aug 1984 .... 2.00
- ❑21, Sep 1984 .... 2.00
- ❑22, Oct 1984 .... 2.00
- ❑23, Nov 1984 .... 2.00
- ❑24, Dec 1984 .... 2.00
- ❑25, Jan 1985 SD (a) 2.00
- ❑26, Feb 1985 SD (a) 2.00
- ❑27, Mar 1985 SD (a) 2.00
- ❑28, Apr 1985 SD (a) 2.00
- ❑29, May 1985 SD (a) 2.00
- ❑30, Jul 1985 SD (a) 2.00
- ❑31, Sep 1985 SD (a) 2.00
- ❑32, Nov 1985 SD (a) 2.00
- ❑33, Jan 1986 .... 2.00
- ❑34, Mar 1986 .... 2.00

FURTHER ADVENTURES OF NYOKA THE JUNGLE GIRL, THE
AC

- ❑1 .... 2.25
- ❑2 .... 2.25
- ❑3, b&w 2.25
- ❑4, b&w 2.25
- ❑5 .... 2.50

College student Ron Raymond and Professor Martin Stein were merged into the nuclear-powered Firestorm when a bomb exploded near the duo, who had been tied to a nuclear reactor.

© 1982 DC Comics.

N-MINT

FURTHER ADVENTURES OF YOUNG JEFFY DAHMER, THE
BONEYARD

- ❑1, b&w 3.00

FURTHER FATTENING ADVENTURES OF PUDGE, GIRL BLIMP, THE
STAR*REACH

- ❑1; Comic size 4.00
- ❑1/A; large size 5.00
- ❑2; Comic size 4.00
- ❑3; Comic size 4.00

FURY (DELL)
DELL

- ❑1, Aug 1962 .... 25.00

FURY (1ST SERIES)
MARVEL

- ❑1, May 1994 O: S.H.I.E.L.D.. O: Hydra. O: Nick Fury. 3.00

FURY (2ND SERIES)
MARVEL / MAX

- ❑1, Nov 2001 .... 2.99
- ❑2, Dec 2001 .... 2.99
- ❑3, Jan 2002 .... 2.99
- ❑4, Feb 2002 .... 2.99
- ❑5, Mar 2002 .... 2.99
- ❑6, Apr 2002 .... 2.99

FURY/AGENT 13
MARVEL

- ❑1, Jun 1998; gatefold summary 2.99
- ❑2, Jul 1998; gatefold summary; Fury returns to Marvel universe 2.99

FURY/BLACK WIDOW: DEATH DUTY
MARVEL

- ❑1, Feb 1995; prestige format 5.95

FURY OF FIRESTORM, THE
DC

- ❑1, Jun 1982 PB (a); O: Firestorm. 1: Lorraine Reilly. 1: Black Bison. 2.50
- ❑2, Jul 1982 PB (a) 1.75
- ❑3, Aug 1982 PB (a); A: Killer Frost. 1.75
- ❑4, Sep 1982 PB (a); A: Justice League of America. A: Killer Frost. 1.75
- ❑5, Oct 1982 PB (a); A: Pied Piper. 1.75
- ❑6, Nov 1982; PB (a); Master of the Universe preview insert 1.50
- ❑7, Dec 1982 PB (a); 1: Plastique. 1.50
- ❑8, Jan 1983 A: Typhoon. 1.50
- ❑9, Feb 1983 A: Typhoon. 1.50
- ❑10, Mar 1983 PB (a); A: Hyena. 1.50
- ❑11, Apr 1983 PB (a) 1.25
- ❑12, May 1983 PB (a) 1.25
- ❑13, Jun 1983 PB (a) 1.25
- ❑14, Jul 1983 PB (a); 1: Mica (Enforcer II). 1: Enforcer I (Leroy Merkyn). 1.25
- ❑15, Aug 1983 PB (a); A: Multiplex. 1.25
- ❑16, Sep 1983 PB (a) 1.25
- ❑17, Oct 1983 PB, GT (a); 1: Firehawk. 1.25
- ❑18, Nov 1983 GT (a); 1: Enforcer II (Mica). 1.25
- ❑19, Jan 1984 GC (a); V: Goldenrod. 1.25
- ❑20, Feb 1984 1: Louise Lincoln. A: Firehawk. V: Killer Frost. 1.25
- ❑21, Mar 1984 D: Killer Frost I (Crystal Frost). V: Killer Frost. 1.00
- ❑22, Apr 1984 PB (a); O: Firestorm. 1.00
- ❑23, May 1984 V: Byte. 1.00

N-MINT

❑24, Jun 1984 1: Bug. 1: Blue Devil. 1: Byte. ... 1.00
❑25, Jul 1984 1: Silver Deer. V: Black Bison. ... 1.00
❑26, Aug 1984 V: Black Bison. ... 1.00
❑27, Sep 1984 ... 1.00
❑28, Oct 1984 1: Slipknot. V: Slipknot. 1.00
❑29, Nov 1984 1: Mindboggler. 1: Breathtaker (villain). V: Stratos. ... 1.00
❑30, Dec 1984 GK (c); V: Mindboggler. 1.00
❑31, Jan 1985 V: Mindboggler. 1.00
❑32, Feb 1985 A: Phantom Stranger. 1.00
❑33, Mar 1985 1.00
❑34, Apr 1985 1: Killer Frost II (Louise Lincoln). V: Killer Frost. ... 1.00
❑35, May 1985 V: Killer Frost. V: Plastique. ... 1.00
❑36, Jun 1985 V: Killer Frost. V: Plastique. ... 1.00
❑37, Jul 1985 ... 1.00
❑38, Aug 1985 ... 1.00
❑39, Sep 1985 ... 1.00
❑40, Oct 1985 ... 1.00
❑41, Nov 1985; Crisis ... 1.00
❑42, Dec 1985; Crisis ... 1.00
❑43, Jan 1986 ... 1.00
❑44, Feb 1986 V: Typhoon. ... 1.00
❑45, Mar 1986 ... 1.00
❑46, Apr 1986 A: Blue Devil. ... 1.00
❑47, May 1986 A: Blue Devil. V: Multiplex. ... 1.00
❑48, Jun 1986 1: Moonbow. ... 1.00
❑49, Jul 1986 ... 1.00
❑50, Aug 1986 ... 1.00
❑51, Sep 1986 ... 1.00
❑52, Oct 1986 ... 1.00
❑53, Nov 1986 ... 1.00
❑54, Dec 1986 ... 1.00
❑55, Jan 1987; A: Cosmic Boy. V: Brimstone. Legends ... 1.00
❑56, Feb 1987; A: Hawk. Legends ... 1.00
❑57, Mar 1987 ... 1.00
❑58, Apr 1987 1: Parasite II. V: Parasite. 1.00
❑59, May 1987 A: Firehawk. V: Parasite. 1.00
❑60, Jun 1987 ... 1.00
❑61, Jul 1987; V: Typhoon. regular cover ... 1.00
❑61/A, Jul 1987; V: Typhoon. Alternate cover (test cover) ... 4.00
❑62, Aug 1987 ... 1.00
❑63, Sep 1987 A: Captain Atom. ... 1.00
❑64, Oct 1987; A: Suicide Squad. series continues as Firestorm, the Nuclear Man ... 1.00
❑Annual 1, ca. 1983 ... 2.00
❑Annual 2, ca. 1984; text story ... 1.50
❑Annual 3, ca. 1985 ... 1.50
❑Annual 4, ca. 1986 ... 1.50
❑Annual 5, ca. 1987; A: Suicide Squad. 1: Firestorm (new); Title changes to Firestorm Annual ... 1.50

FURY OF HELLINA
LIGHTNING

❑1, Jan 1995, b&w ... 2.75

FURY OF S.H.I.E.L.D.
MARVEL

❑1, Apr 1995; HC (w); chromium cover 2.50
❑2, May 1995 HC (w); A: Iron Man. .. 2.00
❑3, Jun 1995 HC (w); A: Iron Man. ... 2.00
❑4, Jul 1995; HC (w); polybagged with decoder ... 2.50

FUSED
IMAGE

❑1, Mar 2002 ... 2.95
❑2, Jul 2002 ... 2.95
❑3, Oct 2002 ... 2.95
❑4, Jan 2003 ... 2.95

FUSED (DARK HORSE)
DARK HORSE

❑1, Jan 2004 ... 2.99
❑2, Feb 2004 ... 2.99
❑3, Feb 2004 ... 2.99
❑4, Mar 2004 ... 2.99

N-MINT

FUSION
ECLIPSE

❑1, Jan 1987, b&w ... 2.00
❑2, Mar 1987, b&w ... 2.00
❑3, May 1987, b&w ... 2.00
❑4, Jul 1987, b&w ... 2.00
❑5, Sep 1987, b&w ... 2.00
❑6, Nov 1987, b&w ... 2.00
❑7, Jan 1988, b&w ... 2.00
❑8, Mar 1988, b&w ... 2.00
❑9, May 1988, b&w ... 2.00
❑10, Jul 1988, b&w ... 2.00
❑11, Sep 1988, b&w ... 2.00
❑12, Nov 1988, b&w ... 2.00
❑13, Jan 1989, b&w ... 2.00
❑14, Mar 1989, b&w ... 2.00
❑15, May 1989, b&w ... 2.00
❑16, Jul 1989, b&w ... 2.00
❑17, Sep 1989, b&w ... 2.00

FUTABA-KUN CHANGE
IRONCAT

❑1 ... 2.95
❑2 ... 2.95
❑3 ... 2.95

FUTABA-KUN CHANGE (VOL. 3)
IRONCAT

❑1, Jul 1999 ... 2.95
❑2 ... 2.95
❑3 ... 2.95
❑4 ... 2.95

FUTURAMA
SLAVE LABOR

❑1, Apr 1989, b&w ... 2.00
❑2, Jun 1989, b&w ... 2.00
❑3, Aug 1989, b&w ... 2.00

FUTURAMA (BONGO)
BONGO

❑1, ca. 2000 ... 2.50
❑1-2, ca 2000 ... 2.50
❑2 2001 ... 2.50
❑3 2001 ... 2.50
❑4 2001 ... 2.50
❑5 2001 ... 2.50
❑6 2001 ... 2.50
❑7 2002 ... 2.50
❑8 2002; Fake CGC cover ... 2.50
❑9 2002 ... 2.50
❑10 2002 ... 2.50
❑11 2003 ... 2.50
❑12 2003 ... 2.50
❑13 2003 ... 2.50
❑14, Jul 2003 ... 2.50
❑15, Oct 2003 ... 2.99
❑16, Feb 2004 ... 2.99
❑17, May 2004 ... 2.99

FUTURE BEAT
OASIS

❑1, Jul 1986 ... 1.50
❑2 ... 1.50

FUTURE COP: L.A.P.D.
DC / WILDSTORM

❑1, Jan 1999; magazine-sized ... 4.95
❑Ashcan 1 1998 ... 1.00

FUTURE COURSE
REOCCURRING IMAGES

❑1 ... 2.95

FUTURETECH
MUSHROOM

❑1, Feb 1995, b&w; 2nd Printing (first printing published by BlackLine Studios, Oct 94) ... 3.50

FUTURIANS BY DAVE COCKRUM, THE
LODESTONE

❑1, Oct 1985; DC (w); DC (a); 1: Doctor Zeus. 1: Hammerhand. 2: The Futurians. Story continued from Marvel Graphic Novel #9 ... 2.00
❑2, Dec 1985 DC (w); DC (a) ... 2.00
❑3, Apr 1986 DC (w); DC (a) ... 2.00

N-MINT

FUTURIANS (VOL. 2)
AARDWOLF

❑1, Aug 1995, b&w ... 2.95

FUZZY BUZZARD AND FRIENDS
HALL OF HEROES

❑1, Apr 1995 ... 2.50

G

G-8 AND HIS BATTLE ACES
BLAZING

❑1, Oct 1966 ... 1.50

GABRIEL
CALIBER

❑1, ca. 1995, b&w; prestige format; One-shot; prestige format; b&w 3.95

!GAG!
HARRIER

❑1 1987 ... 3.50
❑2, Jul 1987 ... 3.00
❑3 1987 ... 3.00
❑4 1987; magazine ... 3.00
❑5 1988; magazine ... 3.00
❑6 1988; magazine ... 3.00
❑7 1988; magazine ... 3.00

GAG REFLEX (SKIP WILLIAMSON'S...)
WILLIAMSON

❑1, Jan 1994, b&w ... 2.95

GAIJIN (MATRIX)
MATRIX

❑1, Feb 1987 ... 1.75

GAIJIN (CALIBER)
CALIBER

❑1, b&w ... 3.50

GAJIT GANG, THE
AMAZING

❑1 ... 1.95

GALACTIC
DARK HORSE

❑1, Aug 2003 ... 2.99
❑2, Oct 2003 ... 2.99
❑3, Oct 2003 ... 2.99

GALACTICA: THE NEW MILLENNIUM
REALM

❑1, Sep 1999 ... 2.99

GALACTIC GLADIATORS
PLAYDIGM

❑1 2001 ... 2.95
❑2 2001 ... 2.95
❑3 2002 ... 2.95
❑4 2002 ... 2.95

GALACTIC GUARDIANS
MARVEL

❑1, Jul 1994 ... 1.50
❑2, Aug 1994 ... 1.50
❑3, Sep 1994 ... 1.50
❑4, Oct 1994 ... 1.50

GALACTIC PATROL
ETERNITY

❑1, Jul 1990, b&w ... 2.25
❑2, b&w ... 2.25
❑3, b&w ... 2.25
❑4, b&w ... 2.25
❑5, b&w ... 2.25

GALACTUS THE DEVOURER
MARVEL

❑1, Sep 1999 BSz (a) ... 3.50
❑2, Oct 1999 ... 3.50
❑3, Nov 1999 ... 3.50
❑4, Dec 1999 JB (a) ... 3.50
❑5, Jan 2000 ... 3.50
❑6, Feb 2000 ... 3.50

N-MINT

GALAXINA
AIRCEL

❑1 1991, b&w 2.95
❑2 1991, b&w 2.95
❑3 1991, b&w 2.95
❑4 1991 .... 2.95

GALAXION
HELIKON

❑1, May 1997, b&w 2.75
❑2, Jul 1997, b&w 2.75
❑3, Sep 1997, b&w 2.75
❑4, Nov 1997, b&w 2.75
❑5, Jan 1998, b&w 2.75
❑6, Mar 1998, b&w 2.75
❑7 1998 .... 2.75
❑8 1998 .... 2.75
❑9 1999 .... 2.75
❑10 1999 .... 2.75
❑11, Nov 1999 .... 2.75
❑Special 1, May 1998, b&w 1.00

GALAXY GIRL
DYNAMIC

❑1, b&w 2.50

GALLEGHER BOY REPORTER
GOLD KEY

❑1, May 1965 .... 15.00

GALL FORCE: ETERNAL STORY
CPM

❑1, Mar 1995 .... 2.95
❑2, May 1995 .... 2.95
❑3, Jul 1995 .... 2.95
❑4, Sep 1995 .... 2.95

GAMBIT (1ST SERIES)
ETERNITY

❑1, Sep 1988, b&w 1.95

GAMBIT (2ND SERIES)
ORACLE

❑1, Sep 1986 .... 1.50
❑2, Nov 1986 .... 1.50

GAMBIT (3RD SERIES)
MARVEL

❑1, Dec 1993; foil cover 3.00
❑1/Gold, Dec 1993; Gold promotion edition 4.00
❑2, Jan 1994 .... 2.50
❑3, Feb 1994 .... 2.50
❑4, Mar 1994 .... 2.50

GAMBIT (4TH SERIES)
MARVEL

❑1, Sep 1997; gatefold summary 2.50
❑2, Oct 1997; gatefold summary 2.50
❑3, Nov 1997 .... 2.50
❑4, Dec 1997 .... 2.50

GAMBIT (5TH SERIES)
MARVEL

❑1, Feb 1999 A: X-Men. A: X-Cutioner. 3.00
❑1/A, Feb 1999; A: X-Men. A: X-Cutioner. DFE alternate cover 4.00
❑1/B, Feb 1999; A: X-Men. A: X-Cutioner. DFE alternate cover 4.00
❑1/C, Feb 1999; A: X-Men. A: X-Cutioner. Marvel Authentix printed sketch cover; 600 printed 6.00
❑1/D, Feb 1999, White cover with sepiatone sketch art 4.00
❑2, Mar 1999 A: Storm. 2.50
❑3, Apr 1999 A: Courier. A: Mengo Brothers. 2.50
❑4, May 1999 .... 2.50
❑5, Jun 1999 .... 1.99
❑6, Jul 1999; early adventure 1.99
❑7, Aug 1999 .... 1.99
❑8, Sep 1999 .... 1.99
❑9, Oct 1999 .... 1.99
❑10, Nov 1999 .... 1.99
❑11, Dec 1999 .... 1.99
❑12, Jan 2000 .... 2.25
❑13, Feb 2000 .... 2.25
❑14, Mar 2000 .... 2.25
❑15, Apr 2000 .... 2.25

N-MINT

❑16, May 2000 .... 2.25
❑17, Jun 2000 .... 2.25
❑18, Jul 2000 .... 2.25
❑19, Aug 2000 .... 2.25
❑20, Sep 2000 .... 2.25
❑21, Oct 2000 .... 2.25
❑22, Nov 2000 .... 2.25
❑23, Dec 2000 .... 2.25
❑24, Jan 2001 .... 2.25
❑25, Feb 2001; double-sized 2.99
❑Annual 1999, Sep 1999 .... 3.50
❑Giant Size 1, Feb 1998; Giant sized . 4.00

GAMBIT AND BISHOP
MARVEL

❑1, Mar 2001 .... 2.25
❑2, Apr 2001 .... 2.25
❑3, May 2001 .... 2.25
❑4, Jun 2001 .... 2.25
❑5, May 2001 .... 2.25

GAMBIT AND BISHOP ALPHA
MARVEL

❑1, Feb 2001 .... 2.25

GAMBIT AND BISHOP GENESIS
MARVEL

❑1, Mar 2001, reprints Uncanny X-Men #266, Uncanny X-Men #283, and X-Men (2nd series) #8 .... 3.50

GAMBIT & THE X-TERNALS
MARVEL

❑1, Mar 1995 .... 2.00
❑2, Apr 1995 .... 2.00
❑3, May 1995 .... 2.00
❑4, Jun 1995; AM (a); The Age of Apocalypse 2.00

GAME BOY
VALIANT

❑1 .... 1.95
❑2 .... 1.95
❑3 .... 1.95
❑4 .... 1.95

GAME GUYS!
WONDER

❑1 .... 2.50

GAMERA
DARK HORSE

❑1, Aug 1996 .... 2.95
❑2, Sep 1996 .... 2.95
❑3, Oct 1996 .... 2.95
❑4, Nov 1996 .... 2.95

GAMMARAUDERS
DC

❑1, Jan 1989 .... 1.25
❑2, Mar 1989 .... 1.25
❑3, Apr 1989 .... 1.25
❑4, May 1989 .... 1.25
❑5, Jul 1989 .... 1.25
❑6, Aug 1989 .... 1.25
❑7, Sep 1989 .... 2.00
❑8, Oct 1989 .... 2.00
❑9, Nov 1989 .... 2.00
❑10, Dec 1989 .... 2.00

GAMORRA SWIMSUIT SPECIAL
IMAGE

❑1, Jun 1996; pin-ups 2.50

GANGBANG GIRLS: ALL WET
ANGEL

❑1 .... 3.00

GANGLAND
DC / VERTIGO

❑1, Jun 1998; cover overlay 2.95
❑2, Jul 1998 .... 2.95
❑3, Aug 1998 .... 2.95
❑4, Sep 1998 .... 2.95

GANTAR: THE LAST NABU
TARGET

❑1, Dec 1986 .... 1.75
❑2, Feb 1987 .... 1.75
❑3, Apr 1987, b&w 1.75
❑4 .... 1.75

Before it started its super-hero line, Valiant published several series featuring Nintendo characters.

© 1990 Voyager Communications (Valiant) and Nintendo.

N-MINT

❑5 .... 1.75
❑6 .... 1.75
❑7 .... 1.75

GARGOYLE
MARVEL

❑1, Jun 1985 BWr (c); BWr (a) 1.50
❑2, Jul 1985 .... 1.50
❑3, Aug 1985 .... 1.50
❑4, Sep 1985 .... 1.50

GARGOYLES
MARVEL

❑1, Feb 1995; enhanced cover 2.50
❑2, Mar 1995 .... 1.50
❑3, Apr 1995 .... 1.50
❑4, May 1995 .... 1.50
❑5, Jun 1995 .... 1.50
❑6, Jul 1995 .... 1.50
❑7, Aug 1995 .... 1.50
❑8, Sep 1995 .... 1.50
❑9, Oct 1995 .... 1.50
❑10, Nov 1995 .... 1.50
❑11, Dec 1995 .... 1.50

GAROU: THE LONE WOLF
BARE BONES

❑1, Jul 1999 .... 2.00

GARRISON'S GORILLAS
DELL

❑1, Jan 1968 .... 21.00
❑2, Apr 1968 .... 14.00
❑3, Jul 1968 .... 14.00
❑4, Oct 1968 .... 14.00
❑5, Oct 1969; Reprints #1 .... 12.00

GASP!
QUEBECOR

❑1 1994; PF (w); PF (a); Previews Tyrant, Rare Bit Fiends, Wandering Star, and more. Contains new Buck Godot, Zap Gun for Hire story. 1.00

GATECRASHER: RING OF FIRE
BLACK BULL

❑1, Mar 2000; Yellow cover with five figures 2.50
❑1/A, Mar 2000; Green cover with two figures 2.50
❑2, Apr 2000 .... 2.50
❑3, May 2000 .... 2.50
❑3/A, May 2000; variant cover 2.50
❑4, Jun 2000 .... 2.50
❑4/A, Jun 2000; Variant (woman in lingerie, shipped 1:4) 2.50

GATEKEEPER
GATEKEEPER

❑1, b&w 2.50

GATES OF EDEN
FANTACO

❑1, ca. 1982, b&w 3.50

GATES OF PANDRAGON
IANUS

❑1, b&w 2.25

GATEWAY TO HORROR (BASIL WOLVERTON'S...)
DARK HORSE

❑1, Aug 1987, b&w 1.75

Condition price index: Multiply "NM prices" above by: **0.83 for Very Fine/Near Mint**
0.66 for Very Fine • 0.33 for Fine • 0.2 for Very Good • 0.125 for Good

N-MINT

GATHERING OF TRIBES
KC Arts
❑1; giveaway; no cover price 1.00

GAUNTLET, THE
Aircel
❑1, Jul 1992 .... 3.00
❑2, Aug 1992 .... 3.00
❑3, Sep 1992 .... 3.00
❑4, Oct 1992 .... 3.00
❑5, Nov 1992 .... 3.00
❑6, Dec 1992 .... 3.00
❑7, Jan 1993 .... 3.00
❑8, Feb 1993 .... 3.00

GAY COMICS (BOB ROSS)
Bob Ross
❑1, 'Gay Comix'; Published by Kitchen Sink 12.50
❑2, ca. 1981; 'Gay Comix'; Published by Kitchen Sink 8.00
❑3; 'Gay Comix'; Published by Kitchen Sink 6.00
❑4; 'Gay Comix'; Published by Kitchen Sink 6.00
❑5; 'Gay Comix'; Published by Kitchen Sink 6.00
❑6; Bob Ross begins as publisher 4.50
❑7 .... 4.50
❑8 .... 4.50
❑9, Win 1986 .... 4.50
❑10 .... 3.50
❑11, ca. 1987; Wee-Wee's Gayhouse 3.50
❑12, Spr 1988 .... 3.50
❑13, Sum 1991 .... 3.50
❑14, ca. 1991 .... 3.50
❑15; Title changes to 'Gay Comics' ... 3.50
❑16, Sum 1992; Desert Peach story . 3.50
❑17, ca. 1992 .... 3.00
❑18 .... 3.00
❑19, Sum 1993; Alison Bechdel Special 3.00
❑20; super-heroes 3.00
❑21 .... 3.00
❑22, Sum 1994; Funny Animals Special with Omaha the Cat Dancer story .. 5.00
❑23, Sum 1996; Funny Animals Special 5.00
❑24, Fal 1996 A: The Maxx. 5.00
❑25, ca. 1997 .... 3.50
❑Special 1 .... 3.00

GAZILLION
Image
❑1, Nov 1998 .... 2.50
❑1/Variant, Nov 1998; alternate cover; framed 2.50

GD MINUS 18
Antarctic
❑1, Feb 1998, b&w; Gold Digger Special 2.95

GEAR
Fireman
❑1, Nov 1998 .... 2.95
❑2, Dec 1998 .... 2.95
❑3, Jan 1999 .... 2.95
❑4, Feb 1999 .... 2.95
❑5, ca. 1999 .... 2.95
❑6, Apr 1999 .... 2.95

GEAR STATION, THE
Image
❑1, Mar 2000 .... 2.50
❑2, Apr 2000 .... 2.50
❑3, Jun 2000 .... 2.50
❑4, Jul 2000 .... 2.50
❑5, Nov 2000 .... 2.95

GEEKSVILLE
3 Finger Prints
❑1, Aug 1999, b&w 3.00
❑2, Oct 1999, b&w 3.00
❑3, Dec 1999, b&w 2.75

N-MINT

GEEKSVILLE (VOL. 2)
Image
❑0, Mar 2000, b&w 3.00
❑1, May 2000, b&w 3.00
❑2, Jul 2000, b&w 2.95
❑3, Sep 2000, b&w 2.95
❑4, Nov 2000, b&w 2.95
❑5, Jan 2001 .... 2.95
❑6, Mar 2001 .... 2.95

GEISHA
Oni
❑1, Sep 1998 .... 2.95
❑2, Oct 1998 .... 2.95
❑3, Nov 1998 .... 2.95
❑4, Dec 1998 .... 2.95

GEMINAR
Image
❑Special 1, Jul 2000 .... 4.95

GEMINI BLOOD
DC / Helix
❑1, Sep 1996 .... 2.25
❑2, Oct 1996 .... 2.25
❑3, Nov 1996 .... 2.25
❑4, Dec 1996 .... 2.25
❑5, Jan 1997 .... 2.25
❑6, Feb 1997 .... 2.25
❑7, Mar 1997 .... 2.25
❑8, Apr 1997 .... 2.25
❑9, May 1997 .... 2.25

GEN-ACTIVE
WildStorm
❑1, May 2000; Superchick Smackdown cover 3.95
❑1/A, May 2000; Woman with knife on cover 3.95
❑2, Aug 2000; Group cover 3.95
❑2/A, Aug 2000; Woman kicking on cover 3.95
❑3, Nov 2000 .... 3.95
❑4, Feb 2001 .... 3.95
❑5, May 2001 .... 3.95
❑6, Aug 2001 .... 3.95

GENE DOGS
Marvel
❑1, Oct 1993; four trading cards; Polybagged 2.75
❑2, Nov 1993 .... 1.75
❑3, Dec 1993 .... 1.75
❑4, Jan 1994 .... 1.75

GENERATION HEX
DC / Amalgam
❑1, Jun 1997 .... 1.95

GENERATION NEXT
Marvel
❑1, Mar 1995 .... 1.95
❑2, Apr 1995 .... 1.95
❑3, May 1995; Age of Apocalypse 1.95
❑4, Jun 1995 .... 1.95

GENERATION X
Marvel
❑-1, Jul 1997; JRo (w); A: Stan Lee. Flashback 2.00
❑0.5, ca. 1998 .... 2.50
❑0.5/Ltd., ca. 1998 .... 3.00
❑1, Nov 1994; enhanced cover 3.00
❑2, Dec 1994 .... 1.75
❑2/Deluxe, Dec 1994; Deluxe edition . 2.00
❑3, Jan 1995 .... 1.75
❑3/Deluxe, Jan 1995; Deluxe edition . 2.00
❑4, Feb 1995; Holiday Spectacular 1.75
❑4/Deluxe, Feb 1995; Deluxe edition; Holiday Spectacular 2.00
❑5, Jul 1995 .... 2.00
❑6, Aug 1995 .... 2.00
❑7, Sep 1995 .... 2.00
❑8, Oct 1995 .... 2.00
❑9, Nov 1995 AM (a) 2.00
❑10, Dec 1995 AM (a); A: Wolverine. A: Omega Red. A: Banshee. V: Omega Red. 2.00
❑11, Jan 1996 AM (a) 2.00

N-MINT

❑12, Feb 1996 AM (a); V: Emplate. 2.00
❑13, Mar 1996 V: Emplate. 2.00
❑14, Apr 1996 .... 2.00
❑15, May 1996 AM (a) 2.00
❑16, Jun 1996 .... 2.00
❑17, Jul 1996 .... 2.00
❑18, Aug 1996 .... 2.00
❑19, Sep 1996 .... 2.00
❑20, Oct 1996 A: Howard the Duck. .. 2.00
❑21, Nov 1996 A: Howard the Duck. . 2.00
❑22, Dec 1996 A: Nightmare. 2.00
❑23, Jan 1997 .... 2.00
❑24, Feb 1997 .... 2.00
❑25, Mar 1997; Giant-size; wraparound cover 3.00
❑26, Apr 1997 .... 2.00
❑27, May 1997 .... 2.00
❑28, Jun 1997 .... 2.00
❑29, Aug 1997; gatefold summary; JRo (w); AM (a); Operation Zero Tolerance 2.00
❑30, Sep 1997; gatefold summary; Operation Zero Tolerance 2.00
❑31, Oct 1997; gatefold summary; JRo (w); Operation Zero Tolerance 2.00
❑32, Nov 1997; gatefold summary V: Circus of Crime. 2.00
❑33, Dec 1997; gatefold summary 2.00
❑34, Jan 1998; gatefold summary; V: White Queen. 2.00
❑35, Feb 1998; gatefold summary 2.00
❑36, Mar 1998; gatefold summary 2.00
❑37, Apr 1998; gatefold summary 2.00
❑38, May 1998; gatefold summary 2.00
❑39, Jun 1998; gatefold summary 2.00
❑40, Jul 1998; gatefold summary 2.00
❑41, Aug 1998; gatefold summary 2.00
❑42, Sep 1998; gatefold summary 2.00
❑43, Oct 1998; gatefold summary; White Queen powerless 2.00
❑44, Nov 1998; gatefold summary 2.00
❑45, Dec 1998; gatefold summary; White Queen regains powers 2.00
❑46, Dec 1998; gatefold summary 2.00
❑47, Jan 1999; gatefold summary; A: Forge. 2.00
❑48, Feb 1999 A: Jubilee. 2.00
❑49, Mar 1999 A: Maggott. 2.00
❑50, Apr 1999 A: Dark Beast. 3.00
❑50/Autographed, Apr 1999 A: Dark Beast. 3.00
❑51, May 1999 .... 2.00
❑52, Jun 1999 .... 2.00
❑53, Jul 1999 .... 2.00
❑54, Aug 1999 .... 2.00
❑55, Sep 1999 .... 2.00
❑56, Oct 1999 .... 2.00
❑57, Nov 1999 .... 2.99
❑58, Dec 1999 .... 1.99
❑59, Jan 2000 .... 1.99
❑60, Feb 2000 .... 2.25
❑61, Mar 2000 .... 2.25
❑62, Apr 2000 .... 2.25
❑63, May 2000 .... 2.25
❑64, Jun 2000 .... 2.25
❑65, Jul 2000 .... 2.25
❑66, Aug 2000 .... 2.25
❑67, Sep 2000 .... 2.25
❑68, Oct 2000 .... 2.25
❑69, Nov 2000 .... 2.25
❑70, Dec 2000 .... 2.25
❑71, Jan 2001 .... 2.25
❑72, Feb 2001 .... 2.25
❑73, Mar 2001 .... 2.25
❑74, Apr 2001 .... 2.25
❑75, May 2001 .... 2.99
❑Annual 1995, ca. 1995; wraparound cover 3.95
❑Annual 1996, ca. 1996; MG (w); Generation X '96; wraparound cover 2.99
❑Annual 1997, ca. 1997; gatefold summary; Generation X '97; wraparound cover 2.99

N-MINT

❑Annual 1998, ca. 1998; gatefold summary; Generation X/Dracula '98; wraparound cover ... 3.50
❑Annual 1999, ca. 1999 ... 3.50
❑Special 1, Feb 1998 A: Nanny. A: Orphan-Maker. ... 3.50
❑Ashcan 1; ashcan edition; 'Collector's Preview ... 0.75
❑Holiday 1, Feb 1998; Giant-size; Holiday Special ... 3.50

GENERATION X/GEN13
MARVEL

❑1, ca. 1997; crossover with Image; wraparound cover ... 4.00
❑1/A, ca. 1997; variant cover ... 3.50

GENERATION X UNDERGROUND
MARVEL

❑1, May 1998, b&w; cardstock cover 2.50

GENERIC COMIC, THE
MARVEL

❑1, Apr 1984 ... 2.50

GENERIC COMIC, THE (COMICS CONSPIRACY)
COMICS CONSPIRACY

❑1, Jan 2001 ... 1.95
❑2, May 2001 ... 1.95
❑3, ca. 2001 ... 1.95
❑4, ca. 2001 ... 1.95
❑5 ... 1.95
❑5/Variant; Special cover ... 5.95
❑6, Feb 2002 ... 1.95
❑7, Apr 2002 ... 1.95
❑8, Jun 2002 ... 1.95
❑9 ... 1.95

GENESIS (MALIBU)
MALIBU

❑0, Oct 1993; foil cover ... 3.50

GENESIS (DC)
DC

❑1, Oct 1997 ... 1.95
❑2, Oct 1997 ... 1.95
❑3, Oct 1997 ... 1.95
❑4, Oct 1997 ... 1.95

GENETIX
MARVEL

❑1, Oct 1993; wraparound cover ... 2.75
❑2, Nov 1993 ... 1.75
❑3, Dec 1993 ... 1.75
❑4, Jan 1994 ... 1.75
❑5, Feb 1994 ... 1.75
❑6, Mar 1994 ... 1.75

GENOCIDE
RENEGADE TRIBE

❑1, Aug 1994 ... 2.95
❑1-2, Aug 1994 ... 2.95

GENOCYBER
VIZ

❑1 1993, b&w; Japanese ... 2.75
❑2 1993, b&w; Japanese ... 2.75
❑3, b&w; Japanese ... 2.75
❑4, b&w; Japanese ... 2.75
❑5, b&w; Japanese ... 2.75

GEN OF HIROSHIMA
EDUCOMICS

❑1, Jan 1980 ... 2.00
❑2, ca. 1981 ... 2.00

GENSAGA
EXPRESS / ENTITY

❑1 ... 2.50

GEN12
IMAGE

❑1, Feb 1998 ... 2.50
❑2, Mar 1998 ... 2.50
❑3, Apr 1998 ... 2.50
❑4, May 1998 ... 2.50
❑5, Jun 1998 ... 2.50

N-MINT

GEN13 (MINI-SERIES)
IMAGE

❑0, Sep 1994 ... 3.50
❑0.5, Mar 1994; Wizard promotional edition ... 2.00
❑0.5/A, Mar 1994 ... 5.00
❑1, Feb 1994; 1: Grunge (full appearance). 1: Burnout (full appearance). 1: Freefall (full appearance). first printing ... 4.00
❑1/A, Oct 1997; 3-D; 1: Grunge (full appearance). 1: Burnout (full appearance). 1: Freefall (full appearance). alternate cover; with glasses ... 4.95
❑1/B, Oct 1997; 3-D; 1: Grunge (full appearance). 1: Burnout (full appearance). 1: Freefall (full appearance). with glasses ... 5.00
❑1/C; 1: Grunge (full appearance). 1: Burnout (full appearance). 1: Freefall (full appearance). Fairchild flexing on cover ... 4.00
❑1-2, Jun 1994 1: Grunge (full appearance). 1: Burnout (full appearance). 3.00
❑2, Mar 1994 ... 3.00
❑3, Apr 1994 A: Pitt. ... 3.00
❑4, May 1994, b&w; A: Pitt. wraparound cover ... 2.50
❑5, Jul 1994 ... 2.50
❑5/A, Jul 1994; alternate cover ... 2.50
❑Ashcan 1 ... 4.00

GEN13
IMAGE

❑-1, Jan 1997; American Entertainment exclusive ... 3.00
❑0, Sep 1994 JLee (a) ... 3.00
❑1/3D, Feb 1998; 3D Edition; 1: Trance. 1: The Bounty Hunters. 1: Alex Fairchild. with glasses ... 4.95
❑1/A, Mar 1995; 1: Trance. 1: The Bounty Hunters. 1: Alex Fairchild. Cover 1 of 13: Charge!; ommon ... 3.00
❑1/B, Mar 1995; 1: Trance. 1: The Bounty Hunters. 1: Alex Fairchild. Cover 2 of 13: Thumbs Up; common 3.00
❑1/C, Mar 1995; 1: Trance. 1: The Bounty Hunters. 1: Alex Fairchild. Cover 3 of 13: Li'l GEN13 ... 3.00
❑1/D, Mar 1995; 1: Trance. 1: The Bounty Hunters. 1: Alex Fairchild. Cover 4 of 13: Barbari-GEN ... 3.00
❑1/E, Mar 1995; 1: Trance. 1: The Bounty Hunters. 1: Alex Fairchild. Cover 5 of 13: Your Friendly Neighborhood Grunge ... 3.00
❑1/F, Mar 1995; 1: Trance. 1: The Bounty Hunters. 1: Alex Fairchild. Cover 6 of 13: Gen13 Goes Madison Avenue ... 3.00
❑1/G, Mar 1995; 1: Trance. 1: The Bounty Hunters. 1: Alex Fairchild. Cover 7 of 13: Lin-GEN-re ... 3.50
❑1/H, Mar 1995; 1: Trance. 1: The Bounty Hunters. 1: Alex Fairchild. Cover 8 of 13: GEN-et Jackson ... 3.50
❑1/I, Mar 1995; 1: Trance. 1: The Bounty Hunters. 1: Alex Fairchild. Cover 9 of 13: That's the Way We Became the GEN13 ... 3.00
❑1/J, Mar 1995; 1: Trance. 1: The Bounty Hunters. 1: Alex Fairchild. Cover 10 of 13: All Dolled Up ... 3.00
❑1/K, Mar 1995; 1: Trance. 1: The Bounty Hunters. 1: Alex Fairchild. Cover 11 of 13: Verti-GEN ... 3.00
❑1/L, Mar 1995; 1: Trance. 1: The Bounty Hunters. 1: Alex Fairchild. Cover 12 of 13: Picto-Fiction ... 3.00
❑1/M, Mar 1995; 1: Trance. 1: The Bounty Hunters. 1: Alex Fairchild. Cover 13 of 13: Do-It-Yourself-Cover 3.00
❑1-2; Encore edition; Fairchild in French maid outfit on cover ... 2.50
❑2, May 1995; 1: Helmut. Flip cover . 2.50
❑3, Jul 1995 ... 2.50
❑4, Jul 1995; 1: Lucius. indicia says Jul, cover says Aug ... 2.50
❑5, Oct 1995 ... 2.50
❑6, Nov 1995 1: Frostbite. 1: The Order of the Cross. ... 2.50

Gen[13] #13/A, #13/B, and #13/C were collected in a prestige-format one-shot.

© 1996 Image.

N-MINT

❑7, Jan 1996; 1: Copycat. 1: Evo. indicia says Jan, cover says Dec ... 2.50
❑8, Feb 1996 1: Powerhaus. 1: Sublime. 2.50
❑9, Mar 1996 1: Absolom. ... 2.50
❑10, Apr 1996 1: Sigma. ... 2.50
❑11, May 1996 ... 2.50
❑11/A, May 1996; European Tour Edition 3.00
❑12, Aug 1996 ... 2.50
❑13/A, Nov 1996 A: Archie, Jughead, Betty, Veronica, Reggie. ... 1.50
❑13/B, Nov 1996; A: TMNTs, Bone, Beanworld, Spawn, Madman. cover says Oct, indicia says Sep ... 1.50
❑13/C, Nov 1996 A: Madman, Maxx, Shi, Francine, Katchoo, Monkeyman, O'Brien, Hellboy. ... 1.50
❑13/CS, Nov 1996; Collected Edition of #13A, B, and C A: Maxx. A: Madman. A: Hellboy. A: Bone. A: Shi. A: Teenage Mutant Ninja Turtles. A: Spawn. 6.95
❑13/D, Nov 1996; Collected Edition of #13A, B, and C; A: Maxx. A: Madman. A: Hellboy. A: Bone. A: Shi. A: Teenage Mutant Ninja Turtles. A: Spawn. Variant cover collected edition ... 6.95
❑14, Nov 1996 ... 2.50
❑15, Dec 1996 JLee (w) ... 2.50
❑16, Jan 1997 JLee (w) ... 2.50
❑17, Feb 1997 ... 2.50
❑18, Apr 1997 ... 2.50
❑19, May 1997 ... 2.50
❑20, Jun 1997 ... 2.50
❑21, Aug 1997; in space ... 2.50
❑22, Sep 1997 ... 2.50
❑23, Oct 1997 ... 2.50
❑24, Nov 1997 ... 2.50
❑25, Dec 1997 ... 3.50
❑25/A, Dec 1997; Alternate cover; white background ... 3.50
❑25/B, Dec 1997; chromium cover ... 3.50
❑25/CS, Dec 1997; Voyager pack ... 4.00
❑26, Feb 1998 ... 2.50
❑26/A, Feb 1998; Alternate cover; fight scene ... 2.50
❑27, Mar 1998 ... 2.50
❑28, Apr 1998 ... 2.50
❑29, May 1998 ... 2.50
❑30, Jun 1998 ... 2.50
❑30/A, Jun 1998; alternate swimsuit cover ... 2.50
❑31, Jul 1998 ... 2.50
❑32, Aug 1998 ... 2.50
❑33, Sep 1998; Planetary preview ... 2.50
❑34, Oct 1998 ... 2.50
❑34/A, Oct 1998; Variant cover depicts Fairchild posing black background . 2.50
❑35, Nov 1998 ... 2.50
❑36, Dec 1998 ... 2.50
❑36/A, Dec 1998; KN (c); KN (a); Variant cover depicts corn dogs ... 2.50
❑37, Mar 1999 ... 2.50
❑38, Apr 1999 ... 2.50
❑38/Variant, Apr 1999; Variant cover depicts Grunge w/popcorn ... 2.50
❑39, May 1999 ... 2.50
❑40, Jun 1999 ... 2.50
❑40/Variant, Jun 1999; Variant cover depicts Roxy in shower ... 2.50
❑41, Jul 1999 ... 2.50
❑42, Aug 1999 ... 2.50
❑43, Sep 1999 ... 2.50

N-MINT

❑44, Oct 1999 A: Mr. Majestic. 2.50
❑45, Nov 1999 .... 2.50
❑46, Dec 2000 .... 2.50
❑47, Jan 2000 .... 2.50
❑48, Feb 2000 .... 2.50
❑49, Mar 2000 .... 2.50
❑50, Apr 2000; Giant-size 3.95
❑51, May 2000 .... 2.50
❑52, Jun 2000 .... 2.50
❑53, Jul 2000 .... 2.50
❑54, Aug 2000 .... 2.50
❑55, Sep 2000 .... 2.50
❑56, Oct 2000 .... 2.50
❑57, Nov 2000 .... 2.50
❑58, Dec 2000 .... 2.50
❑59, Jan 2001 .... 2.50
❑60, Feb 2001 .... 2.50
❑61, Mar 2001 .... 2.50
❑62, Apr 2001 .... 2.50
❑63, May 2001 .... 2.50
❑64, Jun 2001 .... 2.50
❑65, Jul 2001 .... 2.50
❑66, Aug 2001 JLee (a) 2.50
❑67, Sep 2001 .... 2.50
❑68, Oct 2001 .... 2.50
❑69, Nov 2001 .... 2.50
❑70, Dec 2001 .... 2.50
❑71, Jan 2002 .... 2.50
❑72, Feb 2002 .... 2.50
❑73, Mar 2002 .... 2.50
❑74, Apr 2002 .... 2.50
❑75, May 2002 .... 2.50
❑76, Jun 2002 .... 2.50
❑77, Jul 2002 .... 2.50
❑3D 1; European Tour Edition 5.00
❑3D 1/A; double-sized; Fairchild holding open dinosaur mouth on cover 5.00
❑Annual 1, May 1997; 1997 Annual .. 2.95
❑Annual 1999, Mar 1999; wraparound cover; continues in DV8 Annual 1999 3.50
❑Annual 2000, Dec 2000 .... 3.50

GEN13 (WILDSTORM)
WildStorm

❑0, Sep 2002 .... 1.00
❑1, Nov 2002 .... 2.95
❑2, Dec 2002 .... 2.95
❑3, Jan 2003 .... 2.95
❑4, Feb 2003 .... 2.95
❑5, Mar 2003 JLee (c) 2.95
❑6, Apr 2003 .... 2.95
❑7, May 2003 .... 2.95
❑8, Jun 2003 .... 2.95
❑9, Jul 2003 .... 2.95
❑10, Aug 2003 .... 2.95
❑11, Sep 2003 .... 2.95
❑12, Oct 2003 .... 2.95
❑13, Nov 2003 .... 2.95
❑14, Dec 2003 .... 2.95
❑15, Jan 2004 .... 2.95
❑16, Feb 2004 .... 2.95

GEN13: A CHRISTMAS CAPER
WildStorm

❑1, Jan 2000 .... 5.95

GEN13: BACKLIST
Image

❑1, Nov 1996; collects Gen13 #1/2, Gen13 #0, Gen13 #1, Gen13: The Unreal World, and WildStorm! #1 . 2.50

GEN13 BIKINI PIN-UP SPECIAL
Image

❑1; American Entertainment Exclusive 5.00

GEN13 BOOTLEG
Image

❑1/A, Nov 1996; Team standing, Fairchild front on cover 3.00
❑1/B; Team falling 3.00
❑2, Dec 1996 .... 2.50
❑3, Jan 1997 .... 2.50
❑4, Feb 1997 .... 2.50
❑5, Mar 1997 .... 2.50
❑6, Apr 1997 .... 2.50
❑7, May 1997 JRo (w) 2.50
❑8, Jun 1997; manga-style story 2.50
❑9, Jul 1997; manga-style story; action movie references 2.50
❑10, Aug 1997; manga-style story; video game references 2.50
❑11, Sep 1997 .... 2.50
❑12, Oct 1997 .... 2.50
❑13, Nov 1997 .... 2.50
❑14, Dec 1997 .... 2.50
❑15, Jan 1998 .... 2.50
❑16, Feb 1998 .... 2.50
❑17/A, Mar 1998; alternate cover; videogame 2.50
❑17/B, Mar 1998; alternate cover; videogame 2.50
❑18/A, May 1998; Surfing cover 2.50
❑18/B, May 1998; Beach cover 2.50
❑19, Jun 1998 .... 2.50
❑20, Jul 1998 .... 2.50
❑Annual 1, Feb 1998 .... 2.95

GEN13: CARNY FOLK
WildStorm

❑1, Jan 2000 .... 3.50

GEN13/FANTASTIC FOUR
WildStorm

❑1, Mar 2001 .... 5.95

GEN13/GENERATION X
Image

❑1/A, Jul 1997; crossover with Marvel 2.95
❑1/B, Jul 1997; alternate cover; crossover with Marvel 2.95
❑1/C, Jul 1997; 3D Edition; Limited cover 5.00
❑1/D, Jul 1997; 3D Edition; alternate cover; crossover with Marvel; with glasses 5.00
❑1/E, Jul 1997; San Diego Comic-Con edition 4.00

GEN13: GOING WEST
DC / WildStorm

❑1, Jun 1999 .... 2.50

GEN13: GRUNGE SAVES THE WORLD
DC / WildStorm

❑1, May 1999; prestige format 5.95

GEN13 INTERACTIVE
Image

❑1, Oct 1997 .... 2.50
❑2, Nov 1997 .... 2.50
❑3, Jan 1998; cover says Dec, indicia says Jan 2.50

GEN13: LONDON, NEW YORK, HELL
DC / WildStorm

❑1, Aug 2001, Collects Gen13 Anl #1, Gen13: Bootleg Anl #1 .... 6.95

GEN13: MAGICAL DRAMA QUEEN ROXY
Image

❑1, Oct 1998 .... 3.50
❑1/A, Oct 1998; alternate cover 4.00
❑1/B, Oct 1998; DFE alternate cover .. 4.00
❑2, Nov 1998 .... 3.50
❑2/A, Nov 1998; alternate cover 3.50
❑3, Dec 1998 .... 3.50
❑3/A, Dec 1998; alternate cover 3.50

GEN13/MAXX
Image

❑1, Dec 1995 .... 3.50

GEN13: MEDICINE SONG
WildStorm

❑1 .... 5.95

GEN13/MONKEYMAN & O'BRIEN
Image

❑1, Jun 1998 .... 2.50
❑1/A, Jun 1998; alternate cover 3.00
❑1/B, Jun 1998; Variant chromium cover 3.00
❑1/C, Jun 1998; Monkeyman holding team on cover, blue/gold background 3.00
❑2, Aug 1998 .... 2.50
❑2/A, Aug 1998; alternate cover 2.50

GEN13: ORDINARY HEROES
Image

❑1, Feb 1996 .... 2.50
❑2, Jul 1996 .... 2.50

GEN13 RAVE
Image

❑1, Mar 1995; wraparound cover 3.00

GEN13: SCIENCE FRICTION
WildStorm

❑1, Jun 2001 .... 5.95

GEN13: THE UNREAL WORLD
Image

❑1, Jul 1996 .... 2.50

GEN13: WIRED
DC / WildStorm

❑1, Apr 1999 .... 2.50

GEN13 YEARBOOK '97
Image

❑1, Jun 1997; Yearbook-style info on team 2.50

GEN13 'ZINE
Image

❑1, Dec 1996, b&w; digest 2.00

GENTLE BEN
Dell

❑1, Feb 1968 .... 30.00
❑2, May 1968 .... 20.00
❑3, Aug 1968 .... 20.00
❑4, Nov 1968 .... 20.00
❑5, Oct 1969; Same cover as #1 .... 20.00

GENUS
Antarctic / Venus

❑1, May 1993; Antarctic publishes 3.50
❑2, Sep 1993 .... 3.00
❑3, Nov 1993 .... 3.00
❑4, Jan 1994 .... 3.00
❑5, Mar 1994 .... 3.00
❑6, May 1994 .... 3.00
❑7, Jul 1994 .... 3.00
❑8, Sep 1994 .... 3.00
❑9, Nov 1994 .... 3.00
❑10, Jan 1995 .... 3.00
❑11, Mar 1995 .... 2.95
❑12, May 1995 .... 2.95
❑13, Jul 1995 .... 2.95
❑14, Sep 1995 .... 2.95
❑15, Nov 1995 .... 2.95
❑16, Jan 1996 .... 2.95
❑17, Mar 1996 .... 2.95
❑18, May 1996 .... 2.95
❑19, Jul 1996 .... 2.95
❑20, Sep 1996 .... 2.95
❑21, Nov 1996 .... 2.95
❑22, Jan 1997 .... 2.95
❑23, Apr 1997; all-skunk issue; Radio Comix publishes 2.95
❑24, Jun 1997 .... 2.95
❑25, Aug 1997 .... 2.95
❑26, Oct 1997 .... 2.95
❑27, Dec 1997 .... 2.95
❑28, Feb 1998 .... 2.95
❑29, Apr 1998 .... 2.95
❑30, Jun 1998 .... 2.95
❑31, Aug 1998 .... 2.95
❑32, Oct 1998 .... 2.95
❑33, Dec 1998 .... 2.95
❑34, Feb 1999 .... 2.95
❑35, Apr 1999 .... 2.95
❑36, Jun 1999 .... 2.95
❑37, Aug 1999 .... 2.95
❑38, Oct 1999 .... 2.95
❑39, Dec 1999 .... 2.95
❑40, Feb 2000 .... 2.95
❑41, Apr 2000 .... 2.95
❑42, Jun 2000 .... 2.95
❑43, Aug 2000 .... 2.95
❑44, Oct 2000 .... 2.95

N-MINT

❑45, Dec 2000 ... 2.95
❑46, Feb 2001 ... 2.95
❑47, Apr 2001 ... 2.95
❑48, Jun 2001 ... 2.99
❑49, Aug 2001 ... 2.99
❑50, Oct 2001 ... 2.99
❑51, Dec 2001 ... 2.99
❑52, Feb 2002 ... 2.99
❑53, Apr 2002 ... 2.99
❑54, Jun 2002 ... 2.99
❑55, Aug 2002 ... 2.99
❑56, Oct 2002 ... 2.99
❑57, Dec 2002 ... 2.99
❑58, Feb 2003 ... 3.50

GENUS GREATEST HITS
ANTARCTIC

❑1, Apr 1996 ... 4.50
❑2, May 1997 ... 4.95

GENUS SPOTLIGHT
RADIO

❑1, Jul 1998; Skunkworks ... 2.95
❑2, Nov 1998; Skunkworks ... 2.95

GEOBREEDERS
CPM MANGA

❑1, Mar 1999 ... 2.95
❑2, Apr 1999 ... 2.95
❑3, May 1999 ... 2.95
❑4, Jun 1999 ... 2.95
❑5, Jul 1999 ... 2.95
❑6, Aug 1999 ... 2.95
❑7, Sep 1999 ... 2.95
❑8, Oct 1999 ... 2.95
❑9, Nov 1999 ... 2.95
❑10, Dec 1999 ... 2.95
❑11, Jan 2000 ... 2.95
❑12, Feb 2000 ... 2.95
❑13, Mar 2000 ... 2.95
❑14, Apr 2000 ... 2.95
❑15, May 2000 ... 2.95
❑16, Jun 2000 ... 2.95
❑17, Jul 2000 ... 2.95
❑18, Aug 2000 ... 2.95
❑19, Sep 2000 ... 2.95
❑20, Oct 2000 ... 2.95
❑21, Nov 2000 ... 2.95
❑22, Dec 2000 ... 2.95
❑23, Jan 2001 ... 2.95
❑24, Feb 2001 ... 2.95
❑25, Mar 2001 ... 2.95
❑26, Apr 2001 ... 2.95
❑27, May 2001 ... 2.95
❑28, Jun 2001 ... 2.95
❑29, Jul 2001 ... 2.95
❑30, Aug 2001 ... 2.95
❑31, Sep 2001 ... 2.95

GEOMANCER
VALIANT

❑1, Nov 1994; Chromium wraparound cover ... 3.75
❑2, Dec 1994 ... 2.25
❑3, Jan 1995 ... 2.25
❑4, Feb 1995 ... 2.25
❑5, Mar 1995 ... 2.25
❑6, Apr 1995 ... 2.25
❑7, May 1995 ... 2.25
❑8, Jun 1995 ... 2.25

GEORGE OF THE JUNGLE
GOLD KEY

❑1, Feb 1969; George, Tom Slick, and Super Chicken stories ... 35.00
❑2, Oct 1969; George, Tom Slick, and Super Chicken stories ... 24.00

GEPETTO FILES, THE
QUICK TO FLY

❑1, Sep 1998 ... 3.00

GERIATRIC GANGRENE JUJITSU GERBILS
PLANET-X

❑1, b&w ... 1.50
❑2 ... 1.50

N-MINT

GERIATRICMAN
C&T

❑1, b&w ... 1.75

GE ROUGE
VEROTIK

❑0.5, Oct 1998 ... 2.95
❑1, Feb 1997 ... 2.95
❑2, Apr 1997 ... 2.95
❑3, Jul 1997 ... 2.95

GERTIE THE DINOSAUR COMICS
GERTIE THE DINOSAUR

❑1, Jul 2000 ... 2.95

GESTALT (NEC)
NEW ENGLAND

❑1, Apr 1993, b&w ... 1.95
❑2 ... 1.95

GESTALT (CALIBER)
CALIBER

❑0 ... 2.95

GET ALONG GANG
MARVEL / STAR

❑1, May 1985 ... 1.00
❑2, Jul 1985 ... 1.00
❑3, Sep 1985 ... 1.00
❑4, Nov 1985 ... 1.00
❑5, Jan 1986 ... 1.00
❑6, Mar 1986 ... 1.00

GET LOST (VOL. 2)
NEW COMICS

❑1, Oct 1987, b&w ... 1.95
❑2, ca. 1988, b&w ... 1.95
❑3, ca. 1988, b&w ... 1.95

GET REAL COMICS
TIDES CENTER

❑1 ... 1.95

GET SMART
DELL

❑1, Jun 1966 ... 45.00
❑2, Sep 1966 ... 30.00
❑3, Nov 1966 ... 22.00
❑4, Jan 1967 ... 22.00
❑5, Mar 1967 ... 22.00
❑6, Apr 1967 ... 20.00
❑7, Jun 1967 ... 20.00
❑8, Sep 1967; Cover from #1 reprinted ... 20.00

GHETTO BITCH
FANTAGRAPHICS / EROS

❑1, b&w ... 2.75

GHETTO BLASTERS, THE
WHIPLASH

❑1, Sep 1997, b&w ... 2.50

GHOST
DARK HORSE

❑1, Apr 1995 ... 3.00
❑2, May 1995 ... 2.50
❑3, Jun 1995 ... 2.50
❑4, Jul 1995 ... 2.50
❑5, Aug 1995 ... 2.50
❑6, Sep 1995 ... 2.50
❑7, Oct 1995 ... 2.50
❑8, Nov 1995 ... 2.50
❑9, Dec 1995 ... 2.50
❑10, Jan 1996 ... 2.50
❑11, Feb 1996 ... 2.50
❑12, Mar 1996; preview of Ghost/Hellboy crossover ... 2.50
❑13, Apr 1996 ... 2.50
❑14, May 1996 ... 2.50
❑15, Jun 1996 ... 2.50
❑16, Jul 1996 ... 2.50
❑17, Aug 1996 ... 2.50
❑18, Sep 1996 ... 2.50
❑19, Nov 1996 ... 2.50
❑20, Dec 1996 ... 2.50
❑21, Jan 1997 ... 2.50
❑22, Feb 1997 ... 2.50
❑23, Mar 1997 ... 2.50
❑24, Apr 1997 ... 2.50

The misadventures of C.O.N.T.R.O.L. Agent 86 came to comics in Dell's *Get Smart* series.

© 1966 Dell.

N-MINT

❑25, May 1997; Giant-size; 48-page special; photo front and back covers ... 3.95
❑26, Jun 1997 ... 2.95
❑27, Jul 1997 ... 2.95
❑28, Aug 1997 ... 2.95
❑29, Sep 1997; flip-book with Timecop story ... 2.95
❑30, Oct 1997 ... 2.95
❑31, Nov 1997 ... 2.95
❑32, Dec 1997 ... 2.95
❑33, Jan 1998 ... 2.95
❑34, Feb 1998 ... 2.95
❑35, Mar 1998 ... 2.95
❑36, Apr 1998 ... 2.95
❑Special 1, Jul 1994; Ghost Special ... 3.95
❑Special 2, Jun 1998; Immortal Coil ... 3.95
❑Special 3, Dec 1998; Scary Monsters ... 3.95

GHOST (VOL. 2)
DARK HORSE

❑1, Sep 1998 ... 3.50
❑2, Oct 1998 ... 3.00
❑3, Nov 1998 ... 3.00
❑4, Dec 1998 ... 3.00
❑5, Jan 1999 ... 3.00
❑6, Feb 1999 ... 2.95
❑7, Mar 1999 ... 2.95
❑8, Apr 1999 ... 2.95
❑9, May 1999 ... 2.95
❑10, Jun 1999 A: Vortex. ... 2.95
❑11, Jul 1999 ... 2.95
❑12, Sep 1999 ... 2.95
❑13, Oct 1999 ... 2.95
❑14, Nov 1999 ... 2.95
❑15, Dec 1999 ... 2.95
❑16, Jan 2000 ... 2.95
❑17, Feb 2000 ... 2.95
❑18, Mar 2000 ... 2.95
❑19, Apr 2000 ... 2.95
❑20, Jun 2000 ... 2.95
❑21, Jul 2000 A: X. ... 2.95
❑22, Aug 2000 ... 2.95

GHOST AND THE SHADOW
DARK HORSE

❑1, Dec 1995 ... 2.95

GHOST/BATGIRL
DARK HORSE

❑1, Aug 2000 ... 2.95
❑2, Oct 2000 ... 2.99
❑3, Nov 2000 ... 2.95
❑4, Dec 2000 ... 2.95

GHOSTBUSTERS
FIRST

❑1, Feb 1986 ... 1.50
❑2, Mar 1986 ... 1.50
❑3, May 1986 ... 1.50
❑4, Jun 1986 ... 1.50
❑5, Aug 1986 ... 1.50
❑6, Sep 1986 ... 1.50

GHOSTBUSTERS II
NOW

❑1, Oct 1989 ... 2.00
❑2, Nov 1989 ... 2.00
❑3, Dec 1989 ... 2.00

N-MINT

GHOSTDANCING
DC / VERTIGO

❑1, Mar 1995 .... 1.95
❑2, Apr 1995 .... 1.95
❑3, Jun 1995 .... 2.50
❑4, Jul 1995 .... 2.50
❑5, Aug 1995 .... 2.50
❑6, Sep 1995 .... 2.50

GHOST HANDBOOK
DARK HORSE

❑1, Aug 1999; background on characters 2.95

GHOST/HELLBOY SPECIAL
DARK HORSE

❑1, May 1996 .... 2.50
❑2, Jun 1996 .... 2.50

GHOST IN THE SHELL
DARK HORSE / MANGA

❑1, Mar 1995 .... 25.00
❑2, Apr 1995 .... 14.00
❑3, Apr 1995 .... 10.00
❑4, Jun 1995 .... 10.00
❑5, Jul 1995 .... 8.00
❑6, Aug 1995 .... 8.00
❑7, Sep 1995 .... 7.00
❑8, Oct 1995 .... 7.00

GHOST IN THE SHELL 2: MAN/MACHINE INTERFACE
DARK HORSE

❑1, Feb 2003 .... 3.99
❑1/Hologram, Feb 2003; Holo cover . 10.00
❑2, Feb 2003 .... 3.50
❑2/A, Apr 2003; New cover painting . 3.50
❑3, Apr 2003 .... 3.50
❑4, May 2003 .... 3.50
❑5, Jul 2003 .... 3.50
❑6, Aug 2003 .... 3.50
❑7, Sep 2003 .... 3.50
❑8, Oct 2003 .... 3.50
❑9, Nov 2003 .... 3.50
❑10, Dec 2003 .... 3.50
❑11, Dec 2003 .... 3.50

GHOST MANOR (1ST SERIES)
CHARLTON

❑1, Jul 1968 .... 12.00
❑2, Sep 1968 .... 7.00
❑3, Nov 1968 .... 7.00
❑4, Jan 1969 .... 7.00
❑5, Mar 1969 .... 7.00
❑6, May 1969 .... 6.00
❑7, Jul 1969 .... 6.00
❑8, Sep 1969 .... 6.00
❑9, Nov 1969 .... 6.00
❑10, Jan 1970 .... 6.00
❑11, Mar 1970 .... 5.00
❑12, May 1970 .... 5.00
❑13, Jul 1970 .... 5.00
❑14, Sep 1970 .... 5.00
❑15, Nov 1970 .... 5.00
❑16, Jan 1971 .... 5.00
❑17, Mar 1971 .... 5.00
❑18, May 1971 .... 5.00
❑19, Jul 1971; Series continued in Ghostly Haunts #20 .... 5.00

GHOST MANOR (2ND SERIES)
CHARLTON

❑1, Oct 1971 O: Ghost Manor. 10.00
❑2, Dec 1971 .... 6.00
❑3, Feb 1972 .... 6.00
❑4, Apr 1972 .... 6.00
❑5, Jun 1972 .... 6.00
❑6, Aug 1972 .... 6.00
❑7, Oct 1972 .... 6.00
❑8, Nov 1972 WW (a) 7.50
❑9, Feb 1973 .... 5.00
❑10, Mar 1973 .... 5.00
❑11, Apr 1973 .... 4.00
❑12, Jun 1973 .... 4.00
❑13, Jul 1973 .... 4.00
❑14, Sep 1973 .... 4.00

N-MINT

❑15, Oct 1973 .... 4.00
❑16, Dec 1973 .... 4.00
❑17, Jan 1974 .... 4.00
❑18, May 1974 .... 4.00
❑19, Jul 1974 .... 4.00
❑20, Sep 1974 .... 4.00
❑21, Nov 1974 .... 4.00
❑22, Mar 1975 .... 4.00
❑23, May 1975 .... 4.00
❑24, Jul 1975 .... 4.00
❑25, Sep 1975 .... 4.00
❑26, Nov 1975 .... 4.00
❑27, Jan 1976 .... 4.00
❑28, Mar 1976 .... 4.00
❑29, Jun 1976 .... 4.00
❑30, Aug 1976 .... 4.00
❑31, Oct 1976 .... 3.00
❑32, Dec 1976 .... 3.00
❑33, Sep 1977 .... 3.00
❑34, Nov 1977 .... 3.00
❑35, Feb 1978 .... 3.00
❑36, Mar 1978 .... 3.00
❑37, May 1978 .... 3.00
❑38, Jun 1978 .... 3.00
❑39, Oct 1978 .... 3.00
❑40, Dec 1978; Warren Sattler credits 3.00
❑41, Feb 1979 .... 3.00
❑42, Mar 1979 .... 3.00
❑43, Jun 1979 .... 3.00
❑44, Jul 1979 .... 3.00
❑45, Sep 1979 .... 3.00
❑46, Oct 1979 .... 3.00
❑47, Nov 1979 .... 3.00
❑48, Jan 1979 .... 3.00
❑49, Mar 1980 .... 3.00
❑50, May 1980 .... 3.00
❑51, Jul 1980 .... 3.00
❑52, Sep 1980 .... 3.00
❑53, Nov 1980 .... 3.00
❑54, Jan 1981 .... 3.00
❑55, Mar 1981 .... 3.00
❑56, May 1981 .... 3.00
❑57, Jul 1981 .... 3.00
❑58, Aug 1981 .... 3.00
❑59, Oct 1981 .... 3.00
❑60, Dec 1981 .... 3.00
❑61, Feb 1982 .... 3.00
❑62, Apr 1982 .... 3.00
❑63, Jun 1982 .... 3.00
❑64, Aug 1982 .... 3.00
❑65, Oct 1982 .... 3.00
❑66, Dec 1982 .... 3.00
❑67, Feb 1983 .... 3.00
❑68, Apr 1983 .... 3.00
❑69, Jul 1983 .... 3.00
❑70, Sep 1983 .... 3.00
❑71, Nov 1983 .... 3.00
❑72, Jan 1984 .... 3.00
❑73, Mar 1984 .... 3.00
❑74, May 1984 .... 3.00
❑75, Jul 1984 .... 3.00
❑76, Sep 1984 .... 3.00
❑77, Nov 1984 .... 3.00

GHOST RIDER, THE
MARVEL

❑1, Feb 1967; O: Ghost Rider. 1: Ghost Rider. Western; back-up reprints story from Kid Colt Outlaw #105 ... 28.00
❑2, Apr 1967; V: Tarantula. Western; back-up reprints story from Kid Colt Outlaw #99 .... 20.00
❑3, Jun 1967; Western; back-up reprints story from Kid Colt Outlaw #116 .... 20.00
❑4, Aug 1967; A: Tarantula. V: Sting-Ray a.k.a. Scorpion. Western; back-up reprints story from Two-Gun Kid #69 12.50
❑5, Sep 1967; V: Tarantula. Western . 12.50
❑6, Oct 1967; V: Towering Oak. Western 12.50
❑7, Nov 1967; Western 12.50

N-MINT

GHOST RIDER (VOL. 1)
MARVEL

❑1, Aug 1973 GK (a); 1: Son of Satan (partially shown). 125.00
❑2, Oct 1973 .... 26.00
❑3, Dec 1973 JM (a) 25.00
❑4, Feb 1974 JM (a) 25.00
❑5, Apr 1974; Marvel Value Stamp #24: Falcon 25.00
❑6, Jun 1974; Marvel Value Stamp #74: Stranger 20.00
❑7, Aug 1974; Marvel Value Stamp #20: Brother Voodoo 20.00
❑8, Oct 1974; JM (a); 1: Inferno. A: Roxanne. Marvel Value Stamp #48: Kraven 14.00
❑9, Dec 1974; Marvel Value Stamp #81: Rhino 14.00
❑10, Feb 1975; A: Hulk. Reprints Marvel Spotlight #5 .... 14.00
❑11, Apr 1975; SB, GK, KJ (a); A: Hulk. Marvel Value Stamp #66: General Ross 12.00
❑12, Jun 1975 D: Phantom Eagle. 12.00
❑13, Aug 1975 .... 12.00
❑14, Oct 1975 .... 12.00
❑15, Dec 1975 .... 12.00
❑16, Feb 1976 .... 12.00
❑17, Apr 1976 .... 12.00
❑17/30 cent, Apr 1976; 30 cent regional price variant 20.00
❑18, Jun 1976 A: Spider-Man. 12.00
❑18/30 cent, Jun 1976, A: Spider-Man. 30 cent regional price variant 20.00
❑19, Aug 1976 .... 12.00
❑19/30 cent, Aug 1976; 30 cent regional price variant 20.00
❑20, Oct 1976 JBy, GK, KJ (a); A: Daredevil. 9.00
❑21, Dec 1976 D: Eel I (Leopold Stryke). 7.00
❑22, Feb 1977 1: Enforcer (Marvel). .. 7.00
❑23, Apr 1977 O: Water Wizard. 1: Water Wizard. 7.00
❑24, Jun 1977 .... 7.00
❑25, Aug 1977 .... 7.00
❑26, Oct 1977 .... 7.00
❑27, Dec 1977 .... 7.00
❑28, Feb 1978 .... 7.00
❑29, Apr 1978 .... 7.00
❑30, Jun 1978 .... 7.00
❑31, Aug 1978 .... 6.00
❑32, Oct 1978 .... 6.00
❑33, Dec 1978 .... 6.00
❑34, Feb 1979 .... 6.00
❑35, Apr 1979 .... 6.00
❑36, Jun 1979 .... 6.00
❑37, Aug 1979 .... 6.00
❑38, Oct 1979 .... 6.00
❑39, Dec 1979 .... 6.00
❑40, Jan 1980 .... 6.00
❑41, Feb 1980 .... 6.00
❑42, Mar 1980 .... 6.00
❑43, Apr 1980 .... 6.00
❑44, May 1980 .... 6.00
❑45, Jun 1980 .... 6.00
❑46, Jul 1980 .... 6.00
❑47, Aug 1980 .... 6.00
❑48, Sep 1980 .... 6.00
❑49, Oct 1980 .... 6.00
❑50, Nov 1980; Giant-size DP (a); A: Night Rider. 4.00
❑51, Dec 1980 .... 3.00
❑52, Jan 1981 .... 3.00
❑53, Feb 1981 .... 3.00
❑54, Mar 1981 .... 3.00
❑55, Apr 1981 .... 3.00
❑56, May 1981 1: Night Rider II (Hamilton Slade). 3.00
❑57, Jun 1981 .... 3.00
❑58, Jul 1981 .... 3.00
❑59, Aug 1981 .... 3.00
❑60, Sep 1981 .... 3.00
❑61, Oct 1981 .... 3.00

N-MINT

❑62, Nov 1981 .... 3.00
❑63, Dec 1981 .... 3.00
❑64, Jan 1982 .... 3.00
❑65, Feb 1982 .... 3.00
❑66, Mar 1982 .... 3.00
❑67, Apr 1982 .... 3.00
❑68, May 1982 O: Ghost Rider (Johnny Blaze). 5.00
❑69, Jun 1982 .... 2.50
❑70, Jul 1982 .... 2.50
❑71, Aug 1982 .... 2.50
❑72, Sep 1982 1: Fire-Eater. 2.50
❑73, Oct 1982 .... 2.50
❑74, Nov 1982 1: Centurius. 2.50
❑75, Dec 1982 .... 2.50
❑76, Jan 1983 .... 2.50
❑77, Feb 1983 O: Zarathos. O: Centurius. 2.50
❑78, Mar 1983 .... 2.50
❑79, Apr 1983 .... 2.50
❑80, May 1983 O: Centurius. 2.50
❑81, Jun 1983; D: Ghost Rider. Zarathos leaves Johnny Blaze-end of Ghost Rider I 4.00

GHOST RIDER (VOL. 2)
MARVEL

❑-1, Jul 1997; Flashback 1.95
❑1, May 1990 O: Ghost Rider II (Dan Ketch). 1: Ghost Rider II (Dan Ketch). 1: Deathwatch. 4.00
❑1-2, Sep 1990; O: Ghost Rider II (Dan Ketch). 1: Ghost Rider II (Dan Ketch). 1: Deathwatch. 2nd Printing (gold) 2.25
❑2, Jun 1990 1: Blackout II. 3.00
❑3, Jul 1990 V: Blackout. V: Kingpin. V: Deathwatch. 3.00
❑4, Aug 1990; V: Mr. Hyde. Scarcer .. 3.00
❑5, Sep 1990 JLee (c); JLee (a); A: Punisher. 3.00
❑5/Variant, Jun 1994; JLee (c); JLee (a); A: Punisher. Die-cut cover 3.00
❑5-2, Sep 1990; JLee (c); JLee (a); A: Punisher. 2nd printing (gold) 1.50
❑6, Oct 1990 A: Punisher. 2.50
❑7, Nov 1990 V: Scarecrow. 2.00
❑8, Dec 1990 .... 2.00
❑9, Jan 1991 A: X-Factor. 2.00
❑10, Feb 1991 .... 2.00
❑11, Mar 1991 .... 1.50
❑12, Apr 1991 A: Doctor Strange. 1.50
❑13, May 1991 1: Snowblind. A: Doctor Strange. 1.50
❑14, Jun 1991; Johnny Blaze; Ghost Rider vs. Johnny Blaze 1.50
❑15, Jul 1991; glow in the dark cover 2.00
❑15-2; 2nd Printing (gold); glow in the dark cover 2.00
❑16, Aug 1991 A: Hobgoblin. A: Spider-Man. A: Johnny Blaze. 1.75
❑17, Sep 1991 A: Hobgoblin. A: Spider-Man. 1.75
❑18, Oct 1991; Painted cover 1.75
❑19, Nov 1991 .... 1.75
❑20, Dec 1991 .... 1.75
❑21, Jan 1992 .... 1.75
❑22, Feb 1992 .... 1.75
❑23, Mar 1992 V: Deathwatch. 1.75
❑24, Apr 1992 D: Snowblind. V: Deathwatch. 1.75
❑25, May 1992; Pop-up centerfold, double-sized 2.00
❑26, Jun 1992 A: X-Men. 1.75
❑27, Jul 1992 A: X-Men. 1.75
❑28, Aug 1992 1: Lilith II. 2.50
❑29, Sep 1992 JKu (a); A: Wolverine. A: Beast. 1.75
❑30, Oct 1992 JKu (a); V: Nightmare. 1.75
❑31, Nov 1992 JKu (a) 2.50
❑32, Dec 1992 .... 1.75
❑33, Jan 1993 AW (a) 1.75
❑34, Feb 1993 .... 1.75
❑35, Mar 1993 AW (a) 1.75
❑36, Apr 1993 .... 1.75
❑37, May 1993 .... 1.75
❑38, Jun 1993 .... 1.75

N-MINT

❑39, Jul 1993 .... 1.75
❑40, Aug 1993; black cover 2.25
❑41, Sep 1993 .... 1.75
❑42, Oct 1993; A: Deathwatch. A: Centurius. A: Ghostie. A: John Blaze. Neon cover 1.75
❑43, Nov 1993 .... 1.75
❑44, Dec 1993; Neon cover 1.75
❑45, Jan 1994; Spot-varnished cover 1.75
❑46, Feb 1994 .... 1.75
❑47, Mar 1994 .... 1.75
❑48, Apr 1994 A: Spider-Man. 1.75
❑49, May 1994 .... 1.75
❑50, Jun 1994; Giant-size; foil cover . 2.50
❑50/Variant, Jun 1994; Giant-size; Die-cut cover 2.95
❑51, Jul 1994 .... 1.95
❑52, Aug 1994 .... 1.95
❑53, Sep 1994 .... 1.95
❑54, Oct 1994 .... 1.95
❑55, Nov 1994 .... 1.95
❑56, Dec 1994 .... 1.95
❑57, Jan 1995 A: Wolverine. 1.95
❑58, Feb 1995 .... 1.95
❑59, Mar 1995 .... 1.95
❑60, Apr 1995 .... 1.95
❑61, May 1995; Giant-size 2.50
❑62, Jun 1995 .... 1.95
❑63, Jul 1995 .... 1.95
❑64, Aug 1995 .... 1.95
❑65, Sep 1995 .... 1.95
❑66, Oct 1995 D: Blackout. 1.95
❑67, Nov 1995 A: Gambit. 1.95
❑68, Dec 1995 A: Gambit. A: Wolverine. 1.95
❑69, Jan 1996 .... 1.95
❑70, Feb 1996 .... 1.95
❑71, Mar 1996 .... 1.95
❑72, Apr 1996 .... 1.95
❑73, May 1996 V: Snowblind. 1.95
❑74, Jun 1996 .... 1.95
❑75, Jul 1996 .... 1.50
❑76, Aug 1996 .... 1.50
❑77, Sep 1996 A: Doctor Strange. 1.50
❑78, Oct 1996 .... 1.50
❑79, Nov 1996 .... 1.50
❑80, Dec 1996 .... 1.50
❑81, Jan 1997 A: Howard the Duck. .. 1.50
❑82, Feb 1997 A: Devil Dinosaur. A: Howard the Duck. A: Moonboy. 1.50
❑83, Mar 1997 .... 1.95
❑84, Apr 1997 .... 1.95
❑85, May 1997 A: Scarecrow. 1.95
❑86, Jun 1997 .... 1.95
❑87, Aug 1997; gatefold summary 1.95
❑88, Sep 1997; gatefold summary 1.95
❑89, Oct 1997; gatefold summary 1.95
❑90, Nov 1997; gatefold summary 1.95
❑91, Dec 1997; gatefold summary 1.95
❑92, Jan 1998; gatefold summary 1.95
❑93, Feb 1998; Giant-size 2.99
❑Annual 1, ca. 1993; trading card 2.95
❑Annual 2, ca. 1994 V: Scarecrow. ... 2.95

GHOST RIDER (VOL. 3)
MARVEL

❑1, Aug 2001 .... 2.99
❑2, Sep 2001 .... 2.99
❑3, Oct 2001 .... 2.99
❑4, Nov 2001 .... 2.99
❑5, Dec 2001 .... 2.99
❑6, Jan 2002 .... 2.99

GHOST RIDER & CABLE: SERVANTS OF THE DEAD
MARVEL

❑1, Sep 1991; cardstock cover; no indicia; Reprints Ghost Rider/Cable series from Marvel Comics Presents 3.95

GHOST RIDER AND THE MIDNIGHT SONS MAGAZINE
MARVEL

❑1 .... 3.95

The spirit of vengeance took over teen-age Dan Ketch's body and became the second Ghost Rider in *Ghost Rider* (Vol. 2).

© 1990 Marvel Comics.

N-MINT

GHOST RIDER/BALLISTIC
MARVEL

❑1, Feb 1997; crossover with Top Cow; continues in Ballistic/Wolverine 2.95

GHOST RIDER/BLAZE: SPIRITS OF VENGEANCE
MARVEL

❑1, Aug 1992; without poster 1.50
❑1/CS, Aug 1992 .... 2.75
❑2, Sep 1992 .... 1.75
❑3, Oct 1992 .... 1.75
❑4, Nov 1992 .... 1.75
❑5, Dec 1992; Venom 1.75
❑6, Jan 1993 .... 1.75
❑7, Feb 1993 .... 1.75
❑8, Mar 1993 .... 1.75
❑9, Apr 1993 .... 1.75
❑10, May 1993 .... 1.75
❑11, Jun 1993 .... 1.75
❑12, Jul 1993; Glow-in-the-dark cover 2.75
❑13, Aug 1993; black cover 2.25
❑14, Sep 1993 .... 1.75
❑15, Oct 1993; Neon ink cover; Blaze's new costume and powers 1.75
❑16, Nov 1993 .... 1.75
❑17, Dec 1993; Neon inks on cover ... 1.75
❑18, Jan 1994; Spot-varnished cover 1.75
❑19, Feb 1994 .... 1.75
❑20, Mar 1994 .... 1.75
❑21, Apr 1994 .... 1.75
❑22, May 1994 .... 1.75
❑23, Jun 1994 .... 1.95

GHOST RIDER/CAPTAIN AMERICA: FEAR
MARVEL

❑1, Oct 1992; Fold-out cover 5.95

GHOST RIDER: CROSSROADS
MARVEL

❑1, Dec 1995; enhanced wraparound cardstock cover 3.95

GHOST RIDER: HIGHWAY TO HELL
MARVEL

❑1, Aug 2001 .... 3.50

GHOST RIDER POSTER MAGAZINE
MARVEL

❑1 .... 4.95

GHOST RIDER: THE HAMMER LANE
MARVEL

❑1, Aug 2001 .... 2.99
❑2, Sep 2001 .... 2.99
❑3, Oct 2001 .... 2.99
❑4, Nov 2001 .... 2.99
❑5, Dec 2001 .... 2.99
❑6, Jan 2002 .... 2.99

GHOST RIDER 2099
MARVEL

❑1, May 1994 O: Ghost Rider 2099. 1: Ghost Rider 2099. .... 2.00
❑1/CS, May 1994; Polybagged with trading card 2.50
❑2, Jun 1994; Polybagged with poster 1.50
❑3, Jul 1994 .... 1.50
❑4, Aug 1994 .... 1.50
❑5, Sep 1994 .... 1.50
❑6, Oct 1994 .... 1.50
❑7, Nov 1994 A: Spider-Man 2099. ... 1.50

	N-MINT
❑8, Dec 1994	1.50
❑9, Jan 1995	1.50
❑10, Feb 1995	1.50
❑11, Mar 1995	1.50
❑12, Apr 1995	1.50
❑13, May 1995	1.95
❑14, Jun 1995	1.95
❑15, Jul 1995 1: Heartbreaker.	1.95
❑16, Aug 1995	1.95
❑17, Sep 1995	1.95
❑18, Oct 1995	1.95
❑19, Nov 1995	1.95
❑20, Dec 1995 A: L-Cypher. A: Heartbreaker. A: Archfiends. A: Zero Cochrane.	1.95
❑21, Jan 1996	1.95
❑22, Feb 1996	1.95
❑23, Mar 1996	1.95
❑24, Apr 1996	1.95
❑25, May 1996; double-sized; wraparound cover	2.50

GHOST RIDER; WOLVERINE; PUNISHER: THE DARK DESIGN
MARVEL

❑1, Dec 1991; squarebound; Double fold-out cover	5.95

GHOSTS
DC

❑1, Oct 1971 TD, JA (a)	73.00
❑2, Dec 1971 TD (a)	25.00
❑3, Feb 1972 TD (w)	17.00
❑4, Apr 1972	17.00
❑5, Jun 1972	17.00
❑6, Aug 1972	10.00
❑7, Sep 1972	10.00
❑8, Oct 1972	10.00
❑9, Nov 1972	10.00
❑10, Jan 1973	10.00
❑11, Feb 1973	8.00
❑12, Mar 1973	8.00
❑13, Apr 1973	8.00
❑14, May 1973	8.00
❑15, Jun 1973	8.00
❑16, Jul 1973	8.00
❑17, Aug 1973	8.00
❑18, Sep 1973	8.00
❑19, Oct 1973	8.00
❑20, Nov 1973	8.00
❑21, Dec 1973	6.00
❑22, Jan 1974	6.00
❑23, Feb 1974	6.00
❑24, Mar 1974	6.00
❑25, Apr 1974	6.00
❑26, May 1974	6.00
❑27, Jun 1974	6.00
❑28, Jul 1974	6.00
❑29, Aug 1974	6.00
❑30, Sep 1974	6.00
❑31, Oct 1974	5.00
❑32, Nov 1974	5.00
❑33, Dec 1974	5.00
❑34, Jan 1975	5.00
❑35, Feb 1975	5.00
❑36, Mar 1975	5.00
❑37, Apr 1975	5.00
❑38, May 1975	5.00
❑39, Jun 1975	5.00
❑40, Jul 1975; giant	6.00
❑41, Aug 1975	5.00
❑42, Sep 1975	5.00
❑43, Oct 1975	5.00
❑44, Nov 1975	5.00
❑45, Jan 1976	5.00
❑46, Mar 1976	5.00
❑47, Jun 1976	5.00
❑48 1976; Bicentennial #2	5.00
❑49 1976	5.00
❑50, Nov 1976	5.00
❑51, Jan 1977	4.00
❑52 1977	4.00
❑53 1977	4.00
❑54, May 1977	4.00
❑55 1977	4.00
❑56, Sep 1977	4.00
❑57, Oct 1977	4.00
❑58, Nov 1977	4.00
❑59, Dec 1977	4.00
❑60, Jan 1978	4.00
❑61, Feb 1978	4.00
❑62, Mar 1978	4.00
❑63, Apr 1978	4.00
❑64, May 1978	4.00
❑65, Jun 1978	4.00
❑66, Jul 1978	4.00
❑67, Aug 1978	4.00
❑68, Sep 1978	4.00
❑69, Oct 1978	4.00
❑70, Nov 1978	4.00
❑71, Dec 1978	3.00
❑72, Jan 1979	3.00
❑73, Feb 1979	3.00
❑74, Mar 1979	3.00
❑75, Apr 1979	3.00
❑76, May 1979	3.00
❑77, Jun 1979	3.00
❑78, Jul 1979	3.00
❑79, Aug 1979	3.00
❑80, Sep 1979	3.00
❑81, Oct 1979	3.00
❑82, Nov 1979	3.00
❑83, Dec 1979	3.00
❑84, Jan 1980	3.00
❑85, Feb 1980	3.00
❑86, Mar 1980	3.00
❑87, Apr 1980	3.00
❑88, May 1980	3.00
❑89, Jun 1980	3.00
❑90, Jul 1980	3.00
❑91, Aug 1980	3.00
❑92, Sep 1980	3.00
❑93, Oct 1980	3.00
❑94, Nov 1980	3.00
❑95, Dec 1980	3.00
❑96, Jan 1981	3.00
❑97, Feb 1981 A: Spectre.	3.00
❑98, Mar 1981 A: Spectre.	3.00
❑99, Apr 1981 A: Spectre.	3.00
❑100, May 1981	3.00
❑101, Jun 1981	3.00
❑102, Jul 1981	3.00
❑103, Aug 1981	3.00
❑104, Sep 1981	3.00
❑105, Oct 1981	3.00
❑106, Nov 1981	3.00
❑107, Dec 1981	3.00
❑108, Jan 1982	3.00
❑109, Feb 1982	3.00
❑110, Mar 1982	3.00
❑111, Apr 1982	3.00
❑112, May 1982	3.00

GHOST SHIP
SLAVE LABOR

❑1, Mar 1996, b&w; cardstock cover	3.50
❑2, Jun 1996, b&w; cardstock cover	2.95
❑3, Oct 1996, b&w; cardstock cover	2.95

GHOSTS OF DRACULA
ETERNITY

❑1, Sep 1991, b&w	2.50
❑2, b&w	2.50
❑3, b&w	2.50
❑4, b&w	2.50
❑5, b&w	2.50

GHOST SPY
IMAGE

❑1, Aug 2004	2.95

GHOST STORIES
DELL

❑1, Sep 1962	36.00
❑2, Apr 1963	20.00
❑3, Jul 1963	14.00
❑4, Oct 1963	14.00
❑5, Jan 1964	14.00
❑6, Apr 1964	10.00
❑7, Jul 1964	10.00
❑8, Oct 1964	10.00
❑9, Jan 1965	10.00
❑10, Apr 1965	10.00
❑11, Aug 1965	7.00
❑12, Dec 1965	7.00
❑13, Mar 1966	7.00
❑14, Jun 1966	7.00
❑15, Sep 1966	7.00
❑16, Dec 1966	7.00
❑17, Mar 1967	6.00
❑18, May 1967	6.00
❑19, Aug 1967	6.00
❑20, Nov 1967	6.00
❑21, Oct 1968	5.00
❑22, Oct 1969	5.00
❑23, Jan 1970	5.00
❑24, May 1970	5.00
❑25, Jul 1970	5.00
❑26, Oct 1970	5.00
❑27, Jan 1971	5.00
❑28, Apr 1971	5.00
❑29, Jul 1971	5.00
❑30, Oct 1971	5.00
❑31, Jan 1972	5.00
❑32, Apr 1972	5.00
❑33, Jul 1972	5.00
❑34, Oct 1972	5.00
❑35, Jan 1973	5.00
❑36, Jul 1973	5.00
❑37, Oct 1973	5.00

GHOST STORIES (DARK HORSE)
DARK HORSE

❑1; Collects Comics' Greatest World, Arcadia Week 3: Ghost; Ghost Special; X #8	8.95

GHOULS
ETERNITY

❑1, b&w	2.25

GIANTKILLER
DC

❑1, Aug 1999	2.50
❑2, Sep 1999	2.50
❑3, Oct 1999	2.50
❑4, Nov 1999	2.50
❑5, Dec 1999	2.50
❑6, Jan 2000	2.50

GIANTKILLER A TO Z
DC

❑1, Aug 1999; no indicia; biographical monster information	2.50

GIANT-SIZE AMAZING SPIDER-MAN
MARVEL

❑1, Aug 1999; cardstock cover; reprints stories from Spider-Man Adventures #6, #11, #12, and Marvel Tales #205	4.50

GIANT-SIZE AVENGERS
MARVEL

❑1, Aug 1974 RB (a); 1: Whizzer I (Robert Frank). D: Miss America.	24.00
❑2, Nov 1974; DC (a); O: Rama-Tut. D: Swordsman. reprints Fantastic Four #19 (Rama-Tut)	16.00
❑3, Feb 1975; DC (a); O: Immortus. O: Kang. A: Wonder Man. A: Zemo. A: Human Torch. A: Frankenstein's Monster. continued from Avengers #132; reprints Avengers #2; Marvel Value Stamp #41: Gladiator	18.00
❑4, Jun 1975; DH (a); Wedding of Vision and Scarlet Witch	18.00
❑5, Dec 1975	10.00

GIANT-SIZE CAPTAIN AMERICA
MARVEL

❑1 O: Captain America.	14.00

GIANT-SIZE CAPTAIN MARVEL
MARVEL

❑1 A: Hulk. A: Captain America.	10.00

N-MINT

GIANT-SIZE CHILLERS (1ST SERIES)
MARVEL

❑1, Jun 1974; GC (a); 1: Lilith. Dracula ... 13.00

GIANT-SIZE CHILLERS (2ND SERIES)
MARVEL

❑1 ... 9.00
❑2, Aug 1975 ... 6.00
❑3 ... 6.00

GIANT-SIZE CONAN
MARVEL

❑1, Sep 1974; TS, BB, GK (a); 1: Bélit. ... 6.00
❑2, Dec 1974 TS, GK (a) ... 4.00
❑3, Apr 1975 GK (a) ... 4.00
❑4, Jun 1975 GK (a) ... 4.00
❑5, Jun 1975 ... 4.00

GIANT-SIZE CREATURES
MARVEL

❑1, Jul 1974; DP (a); O: Tigra. 1: Tigra. Marvel Value Stamp A-34 (Mr. Fantastic) ... 10.00

GIANT-SIZE DAREDEVIL
MARVEL

❑1, ca. 1975 ... 8.00

GIANT-SIZE DEFENDERS
MARVEL

❑1, Jul 1974; JSn (a); A: Silver Surfer. Silver Surfer ... 7.00
❑2, Oct 1974; GK, KJ (a); Son of Satan ... 5.00
❑3, Jan 1975; DN, JSn, JM, DA (a); 1: Korvac. Marvel Value Stamp #48: Kraven ... 5.00
❑4, Apr 1975 DH (a) ... 4.00
❑5, Jul 1975 DH (a); A: Guardians of the Galaxy. ... 4.00

GIANT-SIZE DOC SAVAGE
MARVEL

❑1, Jan 1975; RA (a); reprints Doc Savage (Marvel) #1 and 2; adapts Man of Bronze ... 6.00

GIANT-SIZE DOCTOR STRANGE
MARVEL

❑1, ca. 1975; GT, DA (a); Reprints stories from Strange Tales #164, 165, 166, 167, 168 ... 6.00

GIANT-SIZE DRACULA
MARVEL

❑2, Sep 1974; Series continued from Giant-Size Chillers (1st Series) #1; SL (w); DH (a) ... 6.00
❑3, Dec 1974 DH (a) ... 5.00
❑4, Mar 1975 DH (a) ... 5.00
❑5, Jun 1975; JBy (a); Marvel Value Stamp #55: Medusa ... 5.00

GIANT-SIZE FANTASTIC FOUR
MARVEL

❑1, May 1974; published as Giant-Size Super-Stars; SL (w); RB, JK (a); A: Fantastic Four. A: Hulk. Thing battles Hulk ... 15.00
❑2, Aug 1974; Title changes to Giant-Size Fantastic Four; GK (c); JB (a); A: Willie Lumpkin. V: Tempus. also reprints Fantastic Four #13 ... 8.00
❑3, Nov 1974; RB (a); also reprints Fantastic Four #21 ... 7.00
❑4, Feb 1975; RB (c); JK, SL (w); JB, JK (a); O: Madrox the Multiple Man. 1: Madrox the Multiple Man. A: Professor X. A: Medusa. Marvel Value Stamp #2: Hulk ... 8.00
❑5, May 1975; reprints Fantastic Four Annual #5 and Fantastic Four #15 . ... 6.00
❑6, Oct 1975; reprints Fantastic Four Annual #6 ... 6.00

GIANT-SIZE HULK
MARVEL

❑1, Jan 1975; reprints Hulk Annual #1 ... 6.00

GIANT-SIZE INVADERS
MARVEL

❑1, Jun 1975 O: the Sub-Mariner. O: Invaders. 1: Invaders. ... 5.00

N-MINT

GIANT-SIZE IRON MAN
MARVEL

❑1, ca. 1975 ... 7.50

GIANT-SIZE KID COLT
MARVEL

❑1, A: Rawhide Kid. ... 16.00
❑2, GK (c) ... 12.00
❑3, Jul 1975 GK (c); A: Night Rider ("Ghost Rider"). ... 12.00

GIANT-SIZE MAN-THING
MARVEL

❑1, Aug 1974 SD, JK, MP (a); V: Glob. ... 8.00
❑2 ... 6.00
❑3, Feb 1975; Marvel Value Stamp #77: Swordsman ... 6.00
❑4, May 1975; FB (a); Howard the Duck; Marvel Value Stamp #36: Ancient One ... 10.00
❑5, Aug 1975; FB (a); Howard the Duck ... 8.00

GIANT-SIZE MARVEL TRIPLE ACTION
MARVEL

❑1, May 1975 ... 5.00
❑2, Jul 1975 ... 4.00

GIANT-SIZE MASTER OF KUNG FU
MARVEL

❑1, Sep 1974 PG, CR (a) ... 8.00
❑2, Dec 1974 ... 5.00
❑3, Mar 1975; Marvel Value Stamp #71: Vision ... 4.00
❑4, Jun 1975; JK (a); Yellow Claw ... 4.00

GIANT-SIZE MINI COMICS
ECLIPSE

❑1, Aug 1986, b&w ... 2.00
❑2, Oct 1986, b&w ... 2.00
❑3, Dec 1986, b&w ... 2.00
❑4, Feb 1987, b&w ... 2.00

GIANT SIZE MINI-MARVELS: STARRING SPIDEY
MARVEL

❑1, Feb 2002 ... 3.50

GIANT SIZE OFFICIAL PRINCE VALIANT
PIONEER

❑1, b&w; Hal Foster ... 3.95

GIANT-SIZE POWER MAN
MARVEL

❑1, ca. 1975 ... 4.00

GIANT-SIZE SPIDER-MAN
MARVEL

❑1, Jul 1974; JR (c); RA (a); A: Dracula. reprints story from Strange Tales Annual #2 ... 36.00
❑2, Oct 1974; JR (c); GK, RA (a); A: Shang-Chi. reprints story from Amazing Spider-Man Annual #3 ... 12.00
❑3, Jan 1975; GK (c); RA (a); A: Doc Savage. also reprints story from Amazing Spider-Man #16 ... 12.00
❑4, Apr 1975 GK (c); RA (a); 1: Moses Magnum (Magnum Force). A: Punisher. ... 38.00
❑5, Jul 1975 GK (c); RA (a); A: Man-Thing. V: Lizard. ... 12.00
❑6, Sep 1975; reprints Amazing Spider-Man Annual #4 ... 12.00

GIANT SIZE SPIDER-MAN (2ND SERIES)
MARVEL

❑1, Dec 1998; reprints stories from Marvel Team-Up ... 4.00

GIANT-SIZE SUPER-HEROES
MARVEL

❑1, Jun 1974; GK (a); A: Man-Wolf. A: Spider-Man. A: Morbius. "How Stan..." Reprints Amazing Spider-Man Annual #1 ... 16.00

GIANT-SIZE SUPER-STARS
MARVEL

❑1, May 1974 ... 5.00

Stories featuring Captain America and The Incredible Hulk appeared in the only issue of *Giant-Size Captain Marvel.*

© 1975 Marvel Comics.

N-MINT

GIANT-SIZE SUPER-VILLAIN TEAM-UP
MARVEL

❑1, Mar 1975 ... 7.00
❑2, Jun 1975; Doctor Doom, Sub-Mariner ... 6.00

GIANT-SIZE THOR
MARVEL

❑1, Jul 1975 GK (a) ... 20.00

GIANT-SIZE WEREWOLF BY NIGHT
MARVEL

❑2, Oct 1974; Title changes to Giant Size Werewolf by Night; SD (a); Frankenstein reprint ... 6.00
❑3, Jan 1975 GK (a) ... 5.00
❑4, Apr 1975 GK (a) ... 5.00
❑5 GK (a) ... 5.00

GIANT-SIZE X-MEN
MARVEL

❑1, Sum 1975 GK, DC (a); O: Storm. O: Nightcrawler. 1: X-Men (new). 1: Thunderbird. 1: Colossus. 1: Storm. 1: Nightcrawler. 1: Illyana Rasputin. ... 800.00
❑2, Nov 1975; GK, KJ (a); reprints X-Men #57-59 ... 80.00

GIANT THB PARADE
HORSE

❑1, b&w; over-sized ... 5.00

G.I. COMBAT (DC)
DC

❑44, Jan 1957; DC begins publishing; previous issues published by Quality ... 350.00
❑45, Feb 1957 ... 225.00
❑46, Mar 1957 ... 115.00
❑47, Apr 1957 ... 100.00
❑48, May 1957 ... 100.00
❑49, Jun 1957 ... 100.00
❑50, Jul 1957 (c) ... 100.00
❑51, Aug 1957 ... 85.00
❑52, Sep 1957 (c) ... 85.00
❑53, Oct 1957 ... 85.00
❑54, Nov 1957 ... 85.00
❑55, Dec 1957 ... 85.00
❑56, Jan 1958 (c) ... 85.00
❑57, Feb 1958 ... 85.00
❑58, Mar 1958 ... 85.00
❑59, Apr 1958 ... 85.00
❑60, May 1958 ... 85.00
❑61, Jun 1958 ... 70.00
❑62, Jul 1958 ... 70.00
❑63, Aug 1958 ... 70.00
❑64, Sep 1958 ... 70.00
❑65, Oct 1958 ... 70.00
❑66, Nov 1958 ... 70.00
❑67, Dec 1958 1: Tank Killer. ... 110.00
❑68, Jan 1959 ... 70.00
❑69, Feb 1959 ... 70.00
❑70, Mar 1959 ... 70.00
❑71, Apr 1959 ... 70.00
❑72, May 1959 ... 70.00
❑73, Jun 1959 ... 70.00
❑74, Jul 1959 ... 70.00
❑75, Aug 1959 ... 70.00
❑76, Sep 1959 ... 70.00
❑77, Oct 1959 ... 70.00
❑78, Nov 1959 ... 70.00
❑79, Dec 1959 ... 70.00

	N-MINT
❑80, Mar 1960	70.00
❑81, May 1960	70.00
❑82, Jul 1960 JKu (a)	70.00
❑83, Sep 1960 RA (a); 1: Charlie Cigar. 1: Little Al. 1: Big Al.	70.00
❑84, Nov 1960	70.00
❑85, Jan 1961	70.00
❑86, Mar 1961	70.00
❑87, May 1961 1: Haunted Tank.	260.00
❑88, Jul 1961	55.00
❑89, Sep 1961	55.00
❑90, Nov 1961	55.00
❑91, Jan 1962	55.00
❑92, Mar 1962	55.00
❑93, May 1962	55.00
❑94, Jul 1962	55.00
❑95, Sep 1962	55.00
❑96, Nov 1962	55.00
❑97, Jan 1963	55.00
❑98, Mar 1963	55.00
❑99, May 1963	55.00
❑100, Jul 1963	55.00
❑101, Sep 1963	45.00
❑102, Nov 1963	45.00
❑103, Jan 1964; RH (c); JKu (a); Painted cover	45.00
❑104, Mar 1964; Sgt. Mule back-up	45.00
❑105, May 1964 JKu (c)	45.00
❑106, Jul 1964 JKu (c)	45.00
❑107, Sep 1964 JKu (c); JKu (a)	45.00
❑108, Nov 1964 JKu (c)	45.00
❑109, Jan 1965 JKu (c)	45.00
❑110, Mar 1965 JKu (c); JKu (a)	45.00
❑111, May 1965 JKu (c)	38.00
❑112, Jul 1965 JKu (c)	38.00
❑113, Sep 1965 (c)	38.00
❑114, Nov 1965 RH (c); O: Haunted Tank.	75.00
❑115, Jan 1966 (c)	28.00
❑116, Mar 1966 JKu (c); A: Johnny Cloud.	28.00
❑117, May 1966 JKu (c)	28.00
❑118, Jul 1966 (c)	28.00
❑119, Sep 1966	28.00
❑120, Nov 1966 (c); A: Johnny Cloud. A: Sgt. Rock.	28.00
❑121, Jan 1967 (c)	22.00
❑122, Mar 1967 JKu (c)	22.00
❑123, May 1967 (c)	22.00
❑124, Jul 1967	22.00
❑125, Sep 1967 RH (c)	22.00
❑126, Nov 1967 RH (c)	22.00
❑127, Jan 1968 JKu (c)	22.00
❑128, Mar 1968 (c)	22.00
❑129, May 1968 RH (c)	22.00
❑130, Jul 1968 RH (c); A: Attila the Hun's ghost.	22.00
❑131, Sep 1968	22.00
❑132, Nov 1968	22.00
❑133, Jan 1969 JKu (c)	22.00
❑134, Mar 1969 JKu (c)	22.00
❑135, May 1969 JKu (c)	22.00
❑136, Jul 1969	22.00
❑137, Sep 1969 JKu (c)	22.00
❑138, Nov 1969 1: Losers.	22.00
❑139, Jan 1970 JKu (c)	22.00
❑140, Mar 1970	22.00
❑141, May 1970 JKu (c)	8.00
❑142, Jul 1970	8.00
❑143, Sep 1970 JKu (c)	8.00
❑144, Nov 1970 JKu (c)	8.00
❑145, Jan 1971	8.00
❑146, Mar 1971; Giant-size	10.00
❑147, May 1971; Giant-size (c)	10.00
❑148, Jul 1971; Giant-size	10.00
❑149, Sep 1971; JKu (c); Sgt. Rock back-up	10.00
❑150, Nov 1971; JKu (c); RH (a); 1: New Haunted Tank.	10.00
❑151, Jan 1972 JKu (c)	8.00
❑152, Mar 1972 JKu (c)	8.00
❑153, May 1972 JKu (c)	8.00
❑154, Jul 1972 JKu (c)	8.00
❑155, Sep 1972	8.00
❑156, Nov 1972	8.00
❑157, Jan 1973 JKu (c)	8.00
❑158, Feb 1973 (c)	8.00
❑159, Mar 1973 JKu (c)	8.00
❑160, May 1973	8.00
❑161, Jun 1973 JKu (c)	7.00
❑162, Jul 1973 JKu (c)	7.00
❑163, Aug 1973	7.00
❑164, Sep 1973 (c)	7.00
❑165, Oct 1973	7.00
❑166, Nov 1973 (c)	7.00
❑167, Dec 1973 (c)	7.00
❑168, Jan 1974 (c)	7.00
❑169, Feb 1974	7.00
❑170, Mar 1974 (c)	7.00
❑171, Jun 1974 JKu (c)	7.00
❑172, Aug 1974 (c)	7.00
❑173, Oct 1974 JKu (c)	7.00
❑174, Dec 1974 JKu (c)	7.00
❑175, Feb 1975 JKu (c)	7.00
❑176, Mar 1975 JKu (c)	7.00
❑177, Apr 1975	7.00
❑178, May 1975 JKu (c)	7.00
❑179, Jun 1975 JKu (c)	7.00
❑180, Jul 1975 JKu (c)	7.00
❑181, Aug 1975	5.00
❑182, Sep 1975	5.00
❑183, Oct 1975 JKu (c)	5.00
❑184, Nov 1975 JKu (c)	5.00
❑185, Dec 1975	5.00
❑186, Jan 1976	5.00
❑187, Feb 1976 JKu (c)	5.00
❑188, Mar 1976 (c)	5.00
❑189, Apr 1976 (c)	5.00
❑190, May 1976	5.00
❑191, Jun 1976	5.00
❑192, Jul 1976; Bicentennial #27; O.S.S. stories begin	5.00
❑193, Aug 1976 JKu (c)	5.00
❑194, Sep 1976	5.00
❑195, Oct 1976 JKu (c)	5.00
❑196, Nov 1976 JKu (c)	5.00
❑197, Dec 1976 JKu (c)	5.00
❑198, Jan 1977 JKu (c)	5.00
❑199, Feb 1977 JKu (c)	5.00
❑200, Mar 1977 JKu (c)	5.00
❑201, Apr 1977 JKu (c)	3.50
❑202, Jun 1977 JKu (c)	3.50
❑203, Aug 1977 JKu (c)	3.50
❑204, Oct 1977 JKu (c)	3.50
❑205, Dec 1977 JKu (c)	3.50
❑206, Feb 1978	3.50
❑207, Apr 1978	3.50
❑208, Jun 1978	3.50
❑209, Aug 1978 JKu (c)	3.50
❑210, Oct 1978	3.50
❑211, Dec 1978 JKu (c)	3.50
❑212, Feb 1979 JKu (c)	3.50
❑213, Apr 1979 JKu (c)	3.50
❑214, Jun 1979	3.50
❑215, Aug 1979	3.50
❑216, Oct 1979	3.50
❑217, Dec 1979	3.50
❑218, Feb 1980	3.50
❑219, Apr 1980 JKu (c)	3.50
❑220, Jun 1980 JKu (c)	3.50
❑221, Aug 1980	3.50
❑222, Oct 1980 JKu (c)	3.50
❑223, Nov 1980 JKu (c)	3.50
❑224, Dec 1980 JKu (c)	3.50
❑225, Jan 1981	3.50
❑226, Feb 1981 JKu (c)	3.50
❑227, Mar 1981 JKu (c)	3.50
❑228, Apr 1981 JKu (c)	3.50
❑229, May 1981 JKu (c)	3.50
❑230, Jun 1981 JKu (c)	3.50
❑231, Jul 1981 JKu (c)	3.50
❑232, Aug 1981 JKu (c); 1: Kana.	3.50
❑233, Sep 1981 JKu (c)	3.50
❑234, Oct 1981 JKu (c)	3.50
❑235, Nov 1981 JKu (c)	3.50
❑236, Dec 1981 JKu (c)	3.50
❑237, Jan 1982 JKu (c)	3.50
❑238, Feb 1982 JKu (c)	3.50
❑239, Mar 1982 JKu (c)	3.50
❑240, Apr 1982 JKu (c)	3.50
❑241, May 1982 JKu (c)	3.50
❑242, Jun 1982 JKu (c); 1: The Mercenaries.	3.50
❑243, Jul 1982 JKu (c)	3.50
❑244, Aug 1982 JKu (c); A: Mercenaries.	3.50
❑245, Sep 1982 JKu (c)	3.50
❑246, Oct 1982; 30th anniversary JKu (c); A: Ninja. A: Johnny Cloud. A: Gunner & Sarge. A: Sgt. Rock. A: Captain Storm. A: Falcon. A: Haunted Tank.	3.50
❑247, Nov 1982 JKu (c)	3.50
❑248, Dec 1982 JKu (c)	3.50
❑249, Jan 1983 JKu (c)	3.50
❑250, Feb 1983 JKu (c)	3.50
❑251, Mar 1983 JKu (c)	2.50
❑252, Apr 1983 JKu (c)	2.50
❑253, May 1983 JKu (c)	2.50
❑254, Jun 1983 JKu (c)	2.50
❑255, Jul 1983 JKu (c)	2.50
❑256, Aug 1983 JKu (c)	2.50
❑257, Sep 1983 JKu (c)	2.50
❑258, Oct 1983 JKu (c)	2.50
❑259, Nov 1983 JKu (c)	2.50
❑260, Dec 1983 JKu (c)	2.50
❑261, Jan 1984 JKu (c)	2.50
❑262, Feb 1984 JKu (c)	2.50
❑263, Mar 1984 JKu (c)	2.50
❑264, Apr 1984 JKu (c)	2.50
❑265, May 1984 JKu (c)	2.50
❑266, Jun 1984 JKu (c)	2.50
❑267, Jul 1984 JKu (c); KG (a)	2.50
❑268, Aug 1984 JKu (c)	2.50
❑269, Sep 1984 JKu (c)	2.50
❑270, Oct 1984 JKu (c)	2.50
❑271, Nov 1984 JKu (c)	2.50
❑272, Dec 1984 JKu (c)	2.50
❑273, Jan 1985 JKu (c)	2.50
❑274, Feb 1985 JKu (c); A: Monitor. A: Attila.	2.50
❑275, Mar 1985 JKu (c)	2.50
❑276, Apr 1985 JKu (c)	2.50
❑277, May 1985 JKu (c)	2.50
❑278, Jul 1985 JKu (c)	2.50
❑279, Sep 1985 JKu (c)	2.50
❑280, Nov 1985 JKu (c)	2.50
❑281, Jan 1986 JKu (c)	2.50
❑282, Mar 1986; JKu (c); Mercenaries	2.50
❑283, May 1986; JKu (c); Mercenaries	2.50
❑284, Jul 1986; JKu (c); Mercenaries	2.50
❑285, Sep 1986; JKu (c); Mercenaries	2.50
❑286, Nov 1986; JKu (c); Mercenaries	2.50
❑287, Jan 1987; JKu (c); Haunted Tank	2.50
❑288, Mar 1987; JKu (c); Haunted Tank	2.50

GIDEON HAWK
BIG SHOT

	N-MINT
❑1, Jan 1995, b&w	2.00
❑2, Mar 1995, b&w	2.00
❑3, Jun 1995, b&w	2.00

GIDGET
DELL

	N-MINT
❑1, Apr 1966	100.00

GIFT, THE: A FIRST PUBLISHING HOLIDAY SPECIAL
FIRST

	N-MINT
❑1, Nov 1990	5.95

GIFTS OF THE NIGHT
DC / VERTIGO

	N-MINT
❑1, Feb 1999	2.95
❑2, Mar 1999	2.95
❑3, Apr 1999	2.95
❑4, May 1999	2.95

GIGANTOR
ANTARCTIC / VERTIGO

	N-MINT
❑1, Jan 2000	2.50

N-MINT

GIGOLO
Fantagraphics / Eros
- ❑1 ... 2.95
- ❑2, Nov 1995 ... 2.95

G.I. GOVERNMENT ISSUED
Paranoid
- ❑1, Aug 1994 ... 2.00
- ❑2, Aug 1994 ... 2.00

G.I. JACKRABBITS
Excalibur
- ❑1, Dec 1986 ... 1.50

GI JOE (VOL. 1)
Dark Horse
- ❑1, Dec 1995 FM (c); FM (a); 1: Tall Sally. 1: Short Fuse. ... 2.00
- ❑2, Jan 1996 ... 2.00
- ❑3, Mar 1996 ... 2.00
- ❑4, Apr 1996 ... 2.00

GI JOE (VOL. 2)
Dark Horse
- ❑1, Jun 1996 ... 2.50
- ❑2, Jul 1996 ... 2.50
- ❑3, Aug 1996 ... 2.50
- ❑4, Sep 1996 ... 2.50

G.I. JOE (IMAGE)
Image
- ❑1, Sep 2001 ... 3.00
- ❑1-2, Sep 2001 ... 2.95
- ❑2, ca. 2001 ... 2.95
- ❑3, ca. 2002 ... 2.95
- ❑4, ca. 2002 ... 3.50
- ❑5, ca. 2002; Duke vs. Major Bludd ... 2.95
- ❑6, ca. 2002 ... 2.95
- ❑7, ca. 2002 ... 2.95
- ❑8, ca. 2002 ... 2.95
- ❑9, ca. 2002 ... 2.95
- ❑10, ca. 2002 ... 2.95
- ❑11, ca. 2002 ... 2.95
- ❑12, Nov 2002 ... 2.95
- ❑13, Dec 2002 ... 2.95
- ❑14, Jan 2003 ... 2.95
- ❑15, Feb 2003 ... 2.95
- ❑16, Mar 2003 ... 2.95
- ❑17, Apr 2003 ... 2.95
- ❑18, Jun 2003 ... 2.95
- ❑19, Jul 2003 ... 2.95
- ❑20, Aug 2003 ... 2.95
- ❑21, Aug 2003 ... 2.95
- ❑22, Nov 2003 ... 2.95
- ❑23, Nov 2003 ... 2.95
- ❑24, Nov 2003 ... 2.95
- ❑25, Dec 2003 ... 2.95

G.I. JOE (DEVIL'S DUE)
Devil's Due
- ❑26, Mar 2004 ... 2.95
- ❑27, Apr 2004 ... 2.95
- ❑28, May 2004 ... 2.95
- ❑29, Jun 2004 ... 2.95
- ❑30, Jul 2004 ... 2.95

G.I. JOE AND THE TRANSFORMERS
Marvel
- ❑1, Jan 1987 HT (a) ... 1.00
- ❑2, Feb 1987 ... 1.00
- ❑3, Mar 1987 ... 1.00
- ❑4, Apr 1987 ... 1.00

G.I. JOE: BATTLE FILES
Image
- ❑1 2002 ... 5.95
- ❑2 2002 ... 5.95
- ❑3 2002 ... 5.95

G.I. JOE COMICS MAGAZINE
Marvel
- ❑1, Dec 1986; digest ... 3.00
- ❑2, Feb 1987; digest ... 2.00
- ❑3, Apr 1987; digest ... 2.00
- ❑4, Jun 1987; digest ... 2.00
- ❑5, Aug 1987; digest ... 2.00
- ❑6, Oct 1987; digest ... 2.00
- ❑7, Dec 1987; digest ... 2.00

N-MINT

- ❑8, Feb 1988; digest ... 2.00
- ❑9, Apr 1988; digest ... 2.00
- ❑10, Jun 1988; digest ... 2.00
- ❑11, Aug 1988; digest ... 2.00
- ❑12, Oct 1988; digest ... 2.00
- ❑13, Dec 1988; digest ... 2.00

G.I. JOE EUROPEAN MISSIONS
Marvel
- ❑1, Jun 1988 ... 1.50
- ❑2, Jul 1988 ... 1.50
- ❑3, Aug 1988 ... 1.50
- ❑4, Sep 1988 ... 1.50
- ❑5, Oct 1988 ... 1.50
- ❑6, Nov 1988 ... 1.50
- ❑7, Dec 1988 ... 1.50
- ❑8, Jan 1989 ... 1.50
- ❑9, Feb 1989 ... 1.50
- ❑10, Mar 1989 ... 1.50
- ❑11, Apr 1989 ... 1.50
- ❑12, May 1989 ... 1.75
- ❑13, Jun 1989 ... 1.75
- ❑14, Jul 1989 ... 1.75
- ❑15, Aug 1989 ... 1.75

G.I. JOE: FRONTLINE
Image
- ❑1, Oct 2002 ... 2.95
- ❑2, Nov 2002 ... 2.95
- ❑3, Dec 2002 ... 2.95
- ❑4, Jan 2003 ... 2.95
- ❑5, Feb 2003 ... 2.95
- ❑6, Mar 2003 ... 2.95
- ❑7, Apr 2003 ... 2.95
- ❑8, Jul 2003 ... 2.95
- ❑9, Jul 2003 ... 2.95
- ❑10, Jul 2003 ... 2.95
- ❑11, Aug 2003 ... 2.95
- ❑12, Aug 2003 ... 2.95
- ❑13, Aug 2003 ... 2.95
- ❑14, Sep 2003 ... 2.95
- ❑15, Oct 2003 ... 2.95
- ❑16, Nov 2003 ... 2.95
- ❑17, Nov 2003 ... 2.95
- ❑18, Dec 2003 ... 2.95

G.I. JOE IN 3-D
Blackthorne
- ❑1, Jul 1987 ... 3.00
- ❑2, Oct 1987 ... 2.50
- ❑3, Jan 1988 ... 2.50
- ❑4, Apr 1988 ... 2.50
- ❑5, Jul 1988 ... 2.50
- ❑6, Oct 1988 ... 2.50

G.I. JOE ORDER OF BATTLE
Marvel
- ❑1, Dec 1986; The Official G.I. Joe Handbook ... 1.25
- ❑2, Jan 1987; Rocky Balboa ... 1.25
- ❑3, Feb 1987 ... 1.25
- ❑4, Mar 1987 ... 1.25

G.I. JOE, A REAL AMERICAN HERO
Marvel
- ❑1, Jun 1982; Giant-size HT (a) ... 10.00
- ❑2, Aug 1982 ... 4.00
- ❑2-2, Aug 1982 ... 2.00
- ❑3, Sep 1982 HT, JAb (a) ... 4.00
- ❑3-2, Sep 1982 ... 2.00
- ❑4, Oct 1982 BH (c); HT, JAb (a) ... 4.00
- ❑4-2, Oct 1982 ... 2.00
- ❑5, Nov 1982 HT, JAb (a) ... 4.00
- ❑5-2, Nov 1982 ... 2.00
- ❑6, Dec 1982 HT (a) ... 4.00
- ❑6-2, Dec 1982 ... 1.00
- ❑7, Jan 1983 HT (a) ... 4.00
- ❑7-2, Jan 1983 ... 1.00
- ❑8, Feb 1983 HT (a) ... 4.00
- ❑8-2, Feb 1983 ... 1.00
- ❑9, Mar 1983 ... 4.00
- ❑9-2, Mar 1983 ... 1.00
- ❑10, Apr 1983 ... 6.00
- ❑10-2, Apr 1983 ... 1.00
- ❑11, May 1983 ... 4.00

Two Hasbro licenses came together in the four-issue *G.I. Joe and the Transformers.*

© 1987 Marvel Comics and Hasbro.

N-MINT

- ❑11-2, May 1983 ... 1.00
- ❑12, Jun 1983 ... 4.00
- ❑12-2, Jun 1983 ... 1.00
- ❑13, Jul 1983 ... 4.00
- ❑13-2, Jul 1983 ... 1.00
- ❑14, Aug 1983 ... 4.00
- ❑14-2, Aug 1983 ... 1.00
- ❑15, Sep 1983 ... 4.00
- ❑15-2, Sep 1983 ... 1.00
- ❑16, Oct 1983 ... 4.00
- ❑16-2, Oct 1983 ... 1.00
- ❑17, Nov 1983 ... 4.00
- ❑17-2, Nov 1983 ... 1.00
- ❑18, Dec 1983 ... 4.00
- ❑18-2, Dec 1983 ... 1.00
- ❑19, Jan 1984 ... 6.00
- ❑19-2, Jan 1984 ... 1.00
- ❑20, Feb 1984 ... 4.00
- ❑20-2, Feb 1984 ... 1.00
- ❑21, Mar 1984; "silent" issue ... 15.00
- ❑21-2, Mar 1984 ... 1.00
- ❑22, Apr 1984 ... 4.00
- ❑22-2, Apr 1984 ... 1.00
- ❑23, May 1984 ... 4.00
- ❑23-2, May 1984 ... 1.00
- ❑24, Jun 1984 ... 4.00
- ❑24-2, Jun 1984 ... 1.00
- ❑25, Jul 1984 ... 4.00
- ❑25-2, Jul 1984 ... 1.00
- ❑26, Aug 1984 O: Snake Eyes. ... 4.00
- ❑26-2, Aug 1984 O: Snake Eyes. ... 1.00
- ❑27, Sep 1984 O: Snake Eyes. ... 4.00
- ❑27-2, Sep 1984 O: Snake Eyes. ... 1.00
- ❑28, Oct 1984 ... 4.00
- ❑28-2, Oct 1984 ... 1.00
- ❑29, Nov 1984 ... 4.00
- ❑29-2, Nov 1984 ... 1.00
- ❑30, Dec 1984 ... 4.00
- ❑30-2, Dec 1984 ... 1.00
- ❑31, Jan 1985 ... 4.00
- ❑31-2, Jan 1985 ... 1.00
- ❑32, Feb 1985 ... 4.00
- ❑32-2, Feb 1985 ... 1.00
- ❑33, Mar 1985 ... 4.00
- ❑33-2, Mar 1985 ... 1.00
- ❑34, Apr 1985 ... 4.00
- ❑34-2, Apr 1985 ... 1.00
- ❑35, May 1985 ... 4.00
- ❑35-2, May 1985 ... 1.00
- ❑36, Jun 1985 ... 4.00
- ❑36-2, Jun 1985 ... 1.00
- ❑37, Jul 1985 ... 4.00
- ❑38, Aug 1985 ... 4.00
- ❑39, Sep 1985 ... 4.00
- ❑40, Oct 1985 ... 4.00
- ❑41, Nov 1985 ... 4.00
- ❑42, Dec 1985 ... 4.00
- ❑43, Jan 1986 ... 4.00
- ❑44, Feb 1986 ... 4.00
- ❑45, Mar 1986 ... 4.00
- ❑46, Apr 1986 ... 4.00
- ❑47, May 1986 ... 4.00
- ❑48, Jun 1986 ... 4.00
- ❑49, Jul 1986 ... 4.00
- ❑50, Aug 1986; Double-size ... 4.00
- ❑51, Sep 1986 ... 4.00
- ❑52, Oct 1986 ... 4.00

N-MINT

❑53, Nov 1986 4.00
❑54, Dec 1986 4.00
❑55, Jan 1987 4.00
❑56, Feb 1987 3.00
❑57, Mar 1987 3.00
❑58, Apr 1987 3.00
❑59, May 1987 3.00
❑60, Jun 1987 TMc (a) 3.00
❑61, Jul 1987 3.00
❑62, Aug 1987 3.00
❑63, Sep 1987 3.00
❑64, Oct 1987 3.00
❑65, Nov 1987 3.00
❑66, Dec 1987 3.00
❑67, Jan 1988 3.00
❑68, Feb 1988 3.00
❑69, Mar 1988 3.00
❑70, Apr 1988 3.00
❑71, May 1988 3.00
❑72, Jun 1988 3.00
❑73, Jul 1988 3.00
❑74, Aug 1988 3.00
❑75, Sep 1988 3.00
❑76, Sep 1988 3.00
❑77, Oct 1988 3.00
❑78, Oct 1988 3.00
❑79, Nov 1988 3.00
❑80, Nov 1988 3.00
❑81, Dec 1988 3.00
❑82, Jan 1989 3.00
❑83, Feb 1989 3.00
❑84, Mar 1989 3.00
❑85, Apr 1989 3.00
❑86, May 1989 3.00
❑87, Jun 1989 3.00
❑88, Jul 1989 3.00
❑89, Aug 1989 3.00
❑90, Sep 1989 3.00
❑91, Oct 1989 3.00
❑92, Nov 1989 3.00
❑93, Nov 1989 3.00
❑94, Dec 1989 3.00
❑95, Dec 1989 3.00
❑96, Jan 1990 3.00
❑97, Feb 1990 3.00
❑98, Mar 1990 3.00
❑99, Apr 1990 3.00
❑100, May 1990; Giant size 3.00
❑101, Jun 1990 3.00
❑102, Jul 1990 3.00
❑103, Aug 1990 3.00
❑104, Sep 1990 3.00
❑105, Oct 1990 3.00
❑106, Nov 1990 3.00
❑107, Dec 1990 3.00
❑108, Jan 1991; Dossiers begin 3.00
❑109, Feb 1991 3.00
❑110, Mar 1991 3.00
❑111, Apr 1991 3.00
❑112, May 1991 3.00
❑113, Jun 1991 3.00
❑114, Jul 1991 1: Metal-Head. 3.00
❑115, Aug 1991 3.00
❑116, Sep 1991 3.00
❑117, Oct 1991 3.00
❑118, Nov 1991 3.00
❑119, Dec 1991 HT (a) 3.00
❑120, Jan 1992 3.00
❑121, Feb 1992 3.00
❑122, Mar 1992 3.00
❑123, Apr 1992 3.00
❑124, May 1992 3.00
❑125, Jun 1992 3.00
❑126, Jul 1992 3.00
❑127, Sep 1992 3.00
❑128, Sep 1992 3.00
❑129, Oct 1992 3.00
❑130, Nov 1992 3.00
❑131, Dec 1992 3.00
❑132, Jan 1993 3.00
❑133, Feb 1993 3.00

N-MINT

❑134, Mar 1993 A: Snake Eyes. 3.00
❑135, Apr 1993; Polybagged with trading card; Team members are regrouped into three strike teams 3.00
❑136, May 1993; trading card 3.00
❑137, Jun 1993; trading card 3.00
❑138, Jul 1993; trading card 3.00
❑139, Aug 1993; Transformers 3.00
❑140, Sep 1993; Transformers 3.00
❑141, Oct 1993 A: Transformers: Generation 2. A: Megatron. A: Cobra Commander. 3.00
❑142, Nov 1993; Transformers 3.00
❑143, Dec 1993 3.00
❑144, Jan 1994 3.00
❑145, Feb 1994 3.00
❑146, Mar 1994 3.00
❑147, Apr 1994 3.00
❑148, May 1994 3.00
❑149, Jun 1994 3.00
❑150, Jul 1994; Giant-size 3.00
❑151, Aug 1994 3.00
❑152, Sep 1994 7.00
❑153, Oct 1994 7.00
❑154, Nov 1994 7.00
❑155, Dec 1994 16.00
❑Yearbook 1, Mar 1985; Yearbook (annual) #1 2.50
❑Yearbook 2, Mar 1986; Yearbook (annual) #2 2.00
❑Yearbook 3, Mar 1987; Yearbook (annual) #3 2.00
❑Yearbook 4, Feb 1988; Yearbook (annual) #4 1.50
❑Special 1, Feb 1995 TMc (c) 20.00

G.I. JOE: RELOADED
DEVIL'S DUE

❑1, May 2004 5.00
❑2, Jun 2004 3.00
❑3, Jul 2004 3.00

G.I. JOE SPECIAL MISSIONS
MARVEL

❑1, Oct 1986 1.50
❑2, Dec 1986 1.00
❑3, Feb 1987 1.00
❑4, Apr 1987 1.00
❑5, Jun 1987 1.00
❑6, Aug 1987 1.00
❑7, Oct 1987 1.00
❑8, Dec 1987 1.00
❑9, Feb 1988 1.00
❑10, Apr 1988 1.00
❑11, Jun 1988 1.00
❑12, Aug 1988 1.00
❑13, Sep 1988 1.00
❑14, Oct 1988 BMc (c); HT (a) 1.00
❑15, Nov 1988 1.00
❑16, Dec 1988 BMc (c); HT (a) 1.00
❑17, Jan 1989 1.00
❑18, Feb 1989 1.00
❑19, Mar 1989 1.00
❑20, Apr 1989 BMc (c); HT (a) 1.00
❑21, May 1989 1.00
❑22, Jun 1989 1.00
❑23, Jul 1989 1.00
❑24, Aug 1989 1.00
❑25, Sep 1989 1.00
❑26, Oct 1989 HT (a) 1.00
❑27, Nov 1989 1.00
❑28, Nov 1989 HT (a) 1.00

G.I. JOE/TRANSFORMERS
IMAGE

❑1, Jul 2003 2.95
❑2, Aug 2003 2.95
❑3, Sep 2003 2.95
❑4, Oct 2003 2.95
❑5, Dec 2003 2.95
❑6, Dec 2003 2.95

GILGAMESH II
DC

❑1 1989; prestige format 3.95
❑2 1989; prestige format 3.95

N-MINT

❑3 1989; prestige format 3.95
❑4 1989; prestige format 3.95

GIMME
HEAD IMPORTS

❑1 3.00

G.I. MUTANTS
ETERNITY

❑1, ca. 1987 1.95
❑2, ca. 1987 1.95
❑3, ca. 1987 1.95
❑4, ca. 1987 1.95

GINGER FOX
COMICO

❑1, Sep 1988; Yellow 1.75
❑2, Oct 1988 1.75
❑3, Nov 1988 1.75
❑4, Dec 1988 1.75

GIN-RYU
BELIEVE IN YOURSELF

❑1, Mar 1995 2.75
❑2, May 1995 2.75
❑3 2.75
❑3/Ashcan 1.00
❑4, Oct 1995 2.75

GIPSY
NBM

❑1 10.95
❑2 10.95

G.I. R.A.M.B.O.T.
WONDER COLOR

❑1, Apr 1987 1.95

GIRL, THE
RIP OFF

❑1, Feb 1991, b&w 2.50
❑1-2, Oct 1992, b&w 2.50
❑2, May 1991, b&w 2.50
❑3, Aug 1991, b&w 2.50
❑4, Dec 1991, b&w 2.50

GIRL
DC / VERTIGO

❑1, Jul 1996 2.50
❑2, Aug 1996 2.50
❑3, Sep 1996 2.50

GIRL CALLED...WILLOW!, A
ANGEL

❑1, Fal 1996, b&w 2.95

GIRL CALLED...WILLOW! SKETCHBOOK, A
ANGEL

❑1, b&w; pin-ups and rough pencil sketches; wraparound cover 2.95

GIRL CRAZY
DARK HORSE

❑1, May 1996, b&w 2.95
❑2, Jul 1996, b&w 2.95
❑3, Jul 1996, b&w 2.95

GIRL FROM U.N.C.L.E., THE
GOLD KEY

❑1, Jan 1967; 10197-701; pin-up on back cover 36.00
❑2, Apr 1967 24.00
❑3, Jun 1967 20.00
❑4, Aug 1967 15.00
❑5, Oct 1967 15.00

GIRL GENIUS
STUDIO FOGLIO

❑1, Feb 2001, b&w; PF (c); PF (w); PF (a); cardstock cover 2.95
❑Ashcan 1, Oct 2000, b&w; PF (c); PF (w); PF (a); No cover price; preview of upcoming series; smaller than normal comic book 1.00
❑2 2001 PF (c); PF (w); PF (a) 2.95
❑3 2001 PF (c); PF (w); PF (a) 2.95
❑4 2001 PF (c); PF (w); PF (a) 3.95
❑5 2001 PF (c); PF (w); PF (a) 3.95
❑6 2002 PF (c); PF (w); PF (a) 3.95
❑7 2002 PF (c); PF (w); PF (a) 3.95
❑8 2002 PF (c); PF (w); PF (a) 3.95

N-MINT

❑9 2003 .... 3.95
❑10 2004 .... 3.95
❑11 2004 .... 3.95

GIRLHERO
HIGH DRIVE

❑1, Aug 1993, b&w 3.00
❑2, Feb 1994, b&w 3.00
❑3, Jul 1994, b&w 3.00

GIRL ON GIRL COLLEGE KINK: NEW YEAR'S BABES
ANGEL

❑1 .... 3.00

GIRL ON GIRL: FEEDIN' TIME
ANGEL

❑1 .... 3.00

GIRL ON GIRL: TICKLISH
ANGEL

❑1 .... 3.00

GIRLS' LOVE STORIES
DC

❑45, Jan 1957 .... 38.00
❑46, Mar 1957 .... 38.00
❑47, May 1957 .... 38.00
❑48, Jul 1957 .... 38.00
❑49, Sep 1957 .... 38.00
❑50, Nov 1957 .... 30.00
❑51, Dec 1957 .... 30.00
❑52, Feb 1958 .... 30.00
❑53, Mar 1958 .... 30.00
❑54, May 1958 .... 30.00
❑55, Jun 1958 .... 30.00
❑56, Aug 1958 .... 30.00
❑57, Sep 1958 .... 30.00
❑58, Nov 1958 .... 30.00
❑59, Dec 1958 .... 30.00
❑60, Feb 1959 .... 30.00
❑61, Mar 1959 .... 30.00
❑62, May 1959 .... 30.00
❑63, Jun 1959 .... 30.00
❑64, Aug 1959 .... 30.00
❑65, Sep 1959 .... 30.00
❑66, Nov 1959 .... 30.00
❑67, Dec 1959 .... 30.00
❑68, Feb 1960 .... 30.00
❑69, Mar 1960 .... 30.00
❑70, May 1960 .... 30.00
❑71, Jun 1960 .... 30.00
❑72, Aug 1960 .... 25.00
❑73, Sep 1960 .... 25.00
❑74, Oct 1960 .... 25.00
❑75, Nov 1960 .... 25.00
❑76, Feb 1961 .... 25.00
❑77, Mar 1961 .... 25.00
❑78, May 1961 .... 25.00
❑79, Jun 1961 .... 25.00
❑80, Jul 1961 .... 25.00
❑81, Sep 1961 .... 25.00
❑82, Oct 1961 .... 25.00
❑83, Nov 1961 .... 25.00
❑84, Jan 1962 .... 25.00
❑85, Feb 1962 .... 25.00
❑86, Apr 1962 .... 25.00
❑87, May 1962 .... 25.00
❑88, Jul 1962 .... 25.00
❑89, Sep 1962 .... 25.00
❑90, Oct 1962 .... 25.00
❑91, Nov 1962 .... 25.00
❑92, Jan 1963 .... 25.00
❑93, Feb 1963 .... 25.00
❑94, Apr 1963 .... 25.00
❑95, May 1963 .... 20.00
❑96, Jul 1963 .... 20.00
❑97, Sep 1963 .... 20.00
❑98, Oct 1963 .... 20.00
❑99, Nov 1963 .... 20.00
❑100, Jan 1964 .... 20.00
❑101, Feb 1964 .... 20.00
❑102, Apr 1964 .... 20.00
❑103, May 1964 .... 20.00
❑104, Jul 1964 .... 20.00

N-MINT

❑105, Sep 1964 .... 20.00
❑106, Oct 1964 .... 17.00
❑107, Nov 1964 .... 17.00
❑108, Jan 1965 .... 17.00
❑109, Feb 1965 .... 17.00
❑110, Apr 1965 .... 17.00
❑111, May 1965 .... 17.00
❑112, Jul 1965 .... 15.00
❑113, Sep 1965 .... 15.00
❑114, Oct 1965 .... 15.00
❑115, Nov 1965 .... 15.00
❑116, Jan 1966 .... 15.00
❑117, Feb 1966 .... 15.00
❑118, Apr 1966 .... 15.00
❑119, May 1966 .... 15.00
❑120, Jul 1966 .... 15.00
❑121, Sep 1966 .... 15.00
❑122, Oct 1966 .... 15.00
❑123, Nov 1966 .... 15.00
❑124, Jan 1967 .... 14.00
❑125, Feb 1967 .... 14.00
❑126, Apr 1967 .... 14.00
❑127, May 1967 .... 14.00
❑128, Jul 1967 .... 14.00
❑129, Sep 1967 .... 14.00
❑130, Oct 1967 .... 14.00
❑131, Nov 1967 .... 14.00
❑132, Jan 1968 .... 14.00
❑133, Feb 1968 .... 14.00
❑134, Apr 1968 .... 14.00
❑135, May 1968 .... 14.00
❑136, Jul 1968 .... 14.00
❑137, Sep 1968 .... 14.00
❑138, Oct 1968 .... 14.00
❑139, Nov 1968 .... 14.00
❑140, Jan 1969 .... 14.00
❑141, Feb 1969 .... 14.00
❑142, Apr 1969 .... 14.00
❑143, May 1969 .... 14.00
❑144, Jul 1969 .... 9.00
❑145, Sep 1969 .... 9.00
❑146, Oct 1969 .... 9.00
❑147, Nov 1969 .... 9.00
❑148, Jan 1970 .... 9.00
❑149, Feb 1970 .... 9.00
❑150, Apr 1970 .... 9.00
❑151, May 1970 .... 9.00
❑152, Jul 1970 .... 9.00
❑153, Sep 1970 .... 9.00
❑154, Oct 1970 .... 9.00
❑155, Nov 1970 .... 9.00
❑156, Jan 1971 .... 9.00
❑157, May 1971 .... 9.00
❑158, Jun 1971 .... 9.00
❑159, Jul 1971 .... 9.00
❑160, Aug 1971 .... 9.00
❑161, Sep 1971 .... 9.00
❑162, Oct 1971 .... 9.00
❑163, Nov 1971 .... 9.00
❑164, Dec 1971 .... 9.00
❑165, Jan 1972 .... 7.00
❑166, Feb 1972 .... 7.00
❑167, Mar 1972 .... 7.00
❑168, Apr 1972 .... 7.00
❑169, May 1972 .... 7.00
❑170, Jun 1972 .... 7.00
❑171, Jul 1972 .... 7.00
❑172, Aug 1972 .... 7.00
❑173, Sep 1972 .... 7.00
❑174, Oct 1972 .... 7.00
❑175, Dec 1972 .... 7.00
❑176, Feb 1973 .... 7.00
❑177, May 1973 .... 7.00
❑178, Aug 1973 .... 7.00
❑179, Oct 1973 .... 7.00
❑180, Dec 1973 .... 7.00

GIRLS OF '95: GOOD, BAD & DEADLY
LOST CAUSE

❑1, Feb 1996 .... 3.95

The short-lived *Man from U.N.C.L.E.* spin-off, *The Girl from U.N.C.L.E.* spawned its own Gold Key series.

© 1967 CBS Television and Western Publishing (Gold Key)

N-MINT

GIRLS OF NINJA HIGH SCHOOL
ANTARCTIC

❑1, b&w 3.75
❑2, b&w 3.75
❑3, Apr 1993, b&w 3.75
❑4, Apr 1994, b&w; 1994 Annual 3.95
❑5, Apr 1995; 1995 Annual 4.50
❑6, ca. 1996; 1996 Annual 3.95
❑7, May 1997; 1997 Annual 3.95
❑8/A, May 1998; 1998 Annual 3.95
❑8/B, May 1998; 1998 Annual; alternate cover (manga-style) 3.95
❑9, Apr 1999; Nylon Menaces: Dandelion; Minerva: Blind Spot; back cover pin-up 2.99

GIRL SQUAD X
FANTACO

❑1, b&w 2.95

GIRL TALK
FANTAGRAPHICS

❑4, Sum 1996, b&w 3.50

GIRL: THE RULE OF DARKNESS
CRY FOR DAWN

❑1, b&w 2.50

GIRL: THE SECOND COMING
NBM

❑1 .... 10.95

GIRL WHO WOULD BE DEATH, THE
DC / VERTIGO

❑1, Dec 1998 .... 2.50
❑2, Jan 1999 .... 2.50
❑3, Feb 1999 .... 2.50
❑4, Mar 1999 .... 2.50

GIVE ME LIBERTY! (RIP OFF)
RIP OFF

❑1, Jan 1976 .... 4.00

GIVE ME LIBERTY
DARK HORSE

❑1, Jun 1990; prestige format 5.00
❑2, Sep 1990; prestige format 5.00
❑3, Dec 1990; prestige format 5.00
❑4, Apr 1991; prestige format 5.00

G.I. WAR TALES
DC

❑1, Mar 1973 .... 12.00
❑2, Jun 1973; Reprints stories from Star Spangled War Stories #134, G.I. Combat #133 .... 7.00
❑3, Aug 1973; JKu, RH (a); Reprints stories from All American Men of War #55, 38 .... 6.00
❑4, Oct 1973 .... 6.00

GIZMO (MIRAGE)
MIRAGE

❑1, Feb 1986, b&w 1.50
❑2, Mar 1986, b&w 1.50
❑3, Apr 1986, b&w 1.50
❑4, May 1986, b&w 1.50
❑5, Mar 1987, b&w 1.50
❑6, Jul 1987, b&w 1.50

GIZMO (CHANCE)
CHANCE

❑1 .... 2.50

N-MINT

GIZMO AND THE FUGITOID
MIRAGE
- ❑1, Jun 1989, b&w ... 2.00
- ❑2, Jun 1989, b&w ... 2.00

GLADIATOR/SUPREME
MARVEL
- ❑1, Mar 1997 ... 4.99

GLAMOROUS GRAPHIX PRESENTS
GLAMOROUS GRAPHIX
- ❑1, Jan 1996, b&w; Becky Sunshine; pin-ups ... 3.95

GLASS JAW (VOL. 2)
CLAY HEELED
- ❑1; no date ... 2.95

GLOBAL FORCE
SILVERLINE
- ❑1 ... 1.95
- ❑2 ... 1.95

GLOBAL FREQUENCY
DC / WILDSTORM
- ❑1, Dec 2002 ... 2.95
- ❑2, Jan 2003 ... 2.95
- ❑3, Feb 2003 ... 2.95
- ❑4, Mar 2003 ... 2.95
- ❑5, Apr 2003 ... 2.95
- ❑6, May 2003 ... 2.95
- ❑7, Jun 2003 ... 2.95
- ❑8, Jul 2003 ... 2.95
- ❑9, Sep 2003 ... 2.95
- ❑10, Sep 2003 ... 2.95
- ❑11, Mar 2004 ... 2.95
- ❑12, Aug 2004 ... 2.95
- ❑13, Aug 2004; Re-print ... 2.95

GLOOMCOOKIE
SLAVE LABOR
- ❑1, Jun 1999 ... 4.00
- ❑2, Sep 1999 ... 3.50
- ❑3, Dec 1999 ... 3.00
- ❑4, Mar 2000 ... 2.95
- ❑5, Jun 2000 ... 2.95
- ❑6, Oct 2000 ... 2.95
- ❑7, Apr 2001 ... 2.95
- ❑8, Jun 2001 ... 2.95
- ❑9, Sep 2001 ... 2.95
- ❑10, Dec 2001 ... 2.95
- ❑11, Feb 2002 ... 2.95
- ❑12, Apr 2002 ... 2.95

GLORIANNA
PRESS THIS
- ❑1, b&w ... 3.95

GLORY
IMAGE
- ❑0, Feb 1996 ... 2.50
- ❑1, Mar 1995 ... 2.50
- ❑1/A, Mar 1995; Image publishes; alternate cover ... 2.50
- ❑2, Apr 1995 ... 2.50
- ❑3, May 1995 ... 2.50
- ❑4, Jun 1995 ... 2.50
- ❑4/A, Jun 1995; Variant cover ... 2.50
- ❑5, Aug 1995; polybagged with trading card ... 2.50
- ❑6, Sep 1995 ... 2.50
- ❑7, Oct 1995 ... 2.50
- ❑8, Nov 1995; Babewatch ... 2.50
- ❑9, Jan 1996; polybagged with Glory card ... 2.50
- ❑10, Mar 1996 ... 2.50
- ❑11, Apr 1996 ... 2.50
- ❑12, May 1996; double-sized anniversary issue ... 3.50
- ❑12/A, May 1996; double-sized anniversary issue; alternate cover ... 3.50
- ❑13, Jun 1996 ... 2.50
- ❑14, Jul 1996 ... 2.50
- ❑15, Sep 1996 ... 2.50
- ❑16, Oct 1996; Maximum begins as publisher ... 2.50
- ❑17, Nov 1996 ... 2.50
- ❑18, Dec 1996 ... 2.50
- ❑19, Jan 1997 ... 2.50
- ❑20, Feb 1997 ... 2.50
- ❑21, ca. 1997 ... 2.50
- ❑22, ca. 1997 ... 2.50
- ❑23, ca. 1997 ... 2.50

GLORY & FRIENDS BIKINI FEST
IMAGE
- ❑1, Sep 1995; pin-ups ... 2.50
- ❑1/Variant, Sep 1995; alternate cover; pin-ups ... 2.50

GLORY & FRIENDS CHRISTMAS SPECIAL
IMAGE
- ❑1, Dec 1995 ... 2.50

GLORY & FRIENDS LINGERIE SPECIAL
IMAGE
- ❑1, Sep 1995; pin-ups ... 2.95
- ❑1/Variant, Sep 1995; alternate cover; pin-ups ... 2.95

GLORY/ANGELA: ANGELS IN HELL
IMAGE
- ❑1, Apr 1996; flipbook with Darkchylde preview ... 2.50

GLORY/AVENGELYNE
IMAGE
- ❑1/A, Oct 1995; no title information on cover ... 3.95
- ❑1/B, Oct 1995; no title information on cover ... 3.95

GLORY/CELESTINE: DARK ANGEL
IMAGE
- ❑1, Sep 1996 ... 2.50
- ❑2, Oct 1996 ... 2.50

GLYPH
LABOR OF LOVE
- ❑1, b&w; magazine ... 4.95
- ❑2, b&w; magazine ... 4.95
- ❑3, b&w; magazine ... 4.95

G-MEN
CALIBER
- ❑1, b&w ... 2.50

GNATRAT: THE DARK GNAT RETURNS
PRELUDE
- ❑1 1986, b&w; Batman parody; continues in Darerat/Tadpole ... 1.95

GNATRAT: THE MOVIE
INNOVATION
- ❑1, b&w; Batman parody ... 2.25

G'N'R'S GREATEST HITS
REVOLUTIONARY
- ❑1, Oct 1993, b&w ... 2.50

GO-GO
CHARLTON
- ❑1, Jun 1966 ... 40.00
- ❑2, Aug 1966 ... 30.00
- ❑3, Oct 1966 ... 30.00
- ❑4, Dec 1966 ... 30.00
- ❑5, Feb 1967 ... 30.00
- ❑7, Jun 1967 ... 30.00
- ❑8, Jun 1967 ... 30.00
- ❑9, Oct 1967 A: Miss Bikini Luv. ... 30.00

GOBBLEDYGOOK (1ST SERIES)
MIRAGE
- ❑1 1: The Teenage Mutant Ninja Turtles. ... 110.00
- ❑2 ... 70.00

GOBBLEDYGOOK (2ND SERIES)
MIRAGE
- ❑1, Dec 1986, b&w ... 5.00

GOBLIN LORD
GOBLIN
- ❑1, Oct 1996 ... 2.50
- ❑2 ... 2.50
- ❑3, Feb 1997 ... 2.50

GOBLIN MAGAZINE, THE
WARREN
- ❑1 ... 8.50
- ❑2 ... 5.00
- ❑3, Nov 1982 AN (a) ... 5.00
- ❑4 ... 5.00

GOBLIN MARKET
TOME
- ❑1, b&w; poem ... 2.50

GOBLIN STUDIOS
GOBLIN
- ❑1 ... 2.25
- ❑2 ... 2.25
- ❑3 ... 2.25
- ❑4 ... 2.25
- ❑5, Aug 1995 ... 2.25

GO BOY 7 HUMAN ACTION MACHINE
DARK HORSE
- ❑1, Jul 2003 ... 2.99
- ❑2, Aug 2003 ... 2.99
- ❑3, Oct 2003 ... 2.99
- ❑4, Nov 2003 ... 2.99
- ❑5, Mar 2004 ... 2.99

GODDESS
DC / VERTIGO
- ❑1, Jun 1995 ... 2.95
- ❑2, Jul 1995 ... 2.95
- ❑3, Aug 1995 ... 2.95
- ❑4, Sep 1995 ... 2.95
- ❑5, Oct 1995 ... 2.95
- ❑6, Nov 1995 ... 2.95
- ❑7, Dec 1995 ... 2.95
- ❑8, Jan 1996 ... 2.95

GODDESS (TWILIGHT TWINS)
TWILIGHT TWINS
- ❑1, b&w; Zolastraya ... 2.00

GODHEAD
ANUBIS
- ❑1 ... 4.00
- ❑1/Ltd.; limited edition 1: Jhatori. ... 4.00
- ❑2 ... 6.00
- ❑2/Ltd.; Numbered, Limited edition (1500 printed) ... 6.00
- ❑3 ... 6.00

GODS & TULIPS
WESTHAMPTON
- ❑1 ... 3.00

GODS FOR HIRE
HOT
- ❑1, Dec 1986 ... 2.00
- ❑2, Jan 1987 ... 2.00

GOD'S HAMMER
CALIBER
- ❑1, b&w ... 2.50
- ❑2, b&w ... 2.50
- ❑3, b&w ... 2.50

GOD'S SMUGGLER
SPIRE
- ❑1; Based on the book "God's Smuggler" by Brother Andrew ... 6.00

GODWHEEL
MALIBU / ULTRAVERSE
- ❑0, Jan 1995; Flip cover ... 2.50
- ❑1, Jan 1995; Flip cover ... 2.50
- ❑1/Ashcan; Wizard ashcan edition; Flip cover; 1: Primevil ... 2.50
- ❑2, Feb 1995; Flip cover ... 2.50
- ❑3, Feb 1995; Flip cover; Marvel, Malibu universes cross ... 2.50

GODZILLA
MARVEL
- ❑1, Aug 1977 HT, JM (a) ... 12.00
- ❑1/35 cent, Aug 1977; HT, JM (a); 35 cent regional price variant ... 15.00
- ❑2, Sep 1977 ... 6.00
- ❑2/35 cent, Sep 1977; 35 cent regional price variant ... 15.00
- ❑3, Oct 1977 A: Champions. ... 5.00

N-MINT

- ❑3/35 cent, Oct 1977; A: Champions. 35 cent regional price variant 15.00
- ❑4, Nov 1977 1: Doctor Demonicus. V: Batragon. 5.00
- ❑5, Dec 1977 O: Doctor Demonicus. . 5.00
- ❑6, Jan 1978 .... 4.00
- ❑7, Feb 1978 V: Red Ronin. 4.00
- ❑8, Mar 1978 V: Red Ronin. 4.00
- ❑9, Apr 1978 .... 4.00
- ❑10, May 1978 .... 4.00
- ❑11, Jun 1978 V: Red Ronin, Yetrigar. 3.00
- ❑12, Jul 1978 .... 3.00
- ❑13, Aug 1978 .... 3.00
- ❑14, Sep 1978 .... 3.00
- ❑15, Oct 1978 .... 3.00
- ❑16, Nov 1978 .... 3.00
- ❑17, Dec 1978; Godzilla shrunk by Henry Pym's gas 3.00
- ❑18, Jan 1979 .... 3.00
- ❑19, Feb 1979 HT (a) 3.00
- ❑20, Mar 1979 A: Fantastic Four. 3.00
- ❑21, Apr 1979 A: Devil Dinosaur. 3.00
- ❑22, May 1979 A: Devil Dinosaur. 3.00
- ❑23, Jun 1979 A: Avengers. 3.00
- ❑24, Jul 1979 A: Spider-Man. V: Fantastic Four. V: Avengers. 3.00

GODZILLA (MINI-SERIES)
DARK HORSE

- ❑1, Jul 1987, b&w; manga 4.00
- ❑2, Aug 1987, b&w; manga 3.00
- ❑3, Sep 1987, b&w; manga 3.00
- ❑4, Oct 1987, b&w; manga 3.00
- ❑5, Nov 1987, b&w; manga 3.00
- ❑6, Dec 1987, b&w; manga 3.00

GODZILLA (DARK HORSE)
DARK HORSE

- ❑0, May 1995; reprints and expands story from Dark Horse Comics #10 and 11 .... 4.00
- ❑1, Jun 1995 .... 3.00
- ❑2, Jul 1995 .... 3.00
- ❑3, Aug 1995 V: Bagorah, the Bat Monster. 3.00
- ❑4, Sep 1995 V: Bagorah, the Bat Monster. 3.00
- ❑5, Oct 1995 .... 3.00
- ❑6, Nov 1995 .... 2.95
- ❑7, Dec 1995 .... 2.95
- ❑8, Jan 1996 .... 2.95
- ❑9, Mar 1996 .... 2.95
- ❑10, Apr 1996; Godzilla vs. Spanish Armada 2.95
- ❑11, May 1996; Godzilla travels through time to sink the Titanic 2.95
- ❑12, Jun 1996 .... 2.95
- ❑13, Jun 1996 V: Burtannus. 2.95
- ❑14, Jul 1996 .... 2.95
- ❑15, Aug 1996 V: Lord Howe Monster. 2.95
- ❑16, Sep 1996 .... 2.95

GODZILLA COLOR SPECIAL
DARK HORSE

- ❑1, Aug 1992 .... 4.00

GODZILLA, KING OF THE MONSTERS SPECIAL
DARK HORSE

- ❑1/A, Aug 1987 .... 3.00
- ❑1/B; misprinted cover; fewer than 100 3.00

GODZILLA VS. BARKLEY
DARK HORSE

- ❑1 .... 3.00

GODZILLA VERSUS HERO ZERO
DARK HORSE

- ❑1, Jul 1995 .... 2.50

GO GIRL!
IMAGE

- ❑1, Aug 2000 .... 3.50
- ❑2, Nov 2000 .... 3.50
- ❑3, Nov 2001 .... 3.50
- ❑4, Aug 2001 .... 3.50
- ❑5, Dec 2001 .... 3.50

N-MINT

GOG (VILLAINS)
DC

- ❑1, Feb 1998; New Year's Evil 1.95

GOING HOME
AARDVARK-VANAHEIM

- ❑1; no date 2.00

GOJIN
ANTARCTIC

- ❑1, Apr 1995 .... 2.95
- ❑2, Jun 1995 .... 2.95
- ❑3, Aug 1995 .... 2.95
- ❑3/A, Aug 1995; alternate cover 2.95
- ❑4, b&w 2.95
- ❑5, b&w 2.95
- ❑6, b&w 2.95
- ❑7, b&w 2.95
- ❑8, Jun 1996, b&w 2.95

GOLD DIGGER
ANTARCTIC

- ❑1, Sep 1992 .... 35.00
- ❑2, Nov 1992 .... 20.00
- ❑3, Jan 1993 .... 15.00
- ❑4, Mar 1993 .... 13.00

GOLD DIGGER (2ND SERIES)
ANTARCTIC

- ❑1, Jul 1993 .... 5.00
- ❑2, Aug 1993 .... 4.00
- ❑3, Sep 1993 .... 4.00
- ❑4, Oct 1993 .... 4.00
- ❑5, Nov 1993; has issue #0 on cover; production mistake 4.00
- ❑6, Dec 1993 .... 4.00
- ❑7, Jan 1994 .... 4.00
- ❑8, Feb 1994 .... 4.00
- ❑9, Mar 1994 .... 4.00
- ❑10, Apr 1994 .... 4.00
- ❑11, May 1994 .... 4.00
- ❑12, Jun 1994 .... 4.00
- ❑13, Jul 1994 .... 4.00
- ❑14, Aug 1994 .... 4.00
- ❑15, Sep 1994 .... 4.00
- ❑16, Oct 1994 .... 4.00
- ❑17, Nov 1994 .... 4.00
- ❑18, Dec 1994 .... 4.00
- ❑19, Feb 1995 .... 4.00
- ❑20, Apr 1995 .... 4.00
- ❑21, May 1995 .... 3.50
- ❑22, Jun 1995 .... 3.50
- ❑23, Jul 1995 .... 3.50
- ❑24, Aug 1995 .... 3.50
- ❑25, Oct 1995 .... 3.50
- ❑26, Nov 1995 .... 3.50
- ❑27, Dec 1995 .... 3.50
- ❑28, Feb 1996 .... 3.50
- ❑29, Apr 1996 .... 3.50
- ❑30, Jul 1996 .... 3.50
- ❑31, Aug 1996 .... 3.50
- ❑32, Oct 1996 .... 3.50
- ❑33, Dec 1996 .... 3.50
- ❑34, Feb 1997 .... 3.50
- ❑35, Apr 1997 .... 3.50
- ❑36, Jul 1997 .... 3.50
- ❑37, Aug 1997 .... 3.50
- ❑38, Jan 1998; cover says Nov 97, indicia says Jan 98 .... 3.50
- ❑39, Mar 1998 .... 3.50
- ❑40, May 1998 .... 3.50
- ❑41, Jun 1998 .... 3.50
- ❑42, Jul 1998 .... 3.50
- ❑43, Aug 1998 .... 3.50
- ❑44, Sep 1998 .... 3.50
- ❑45, Oct 1998 .... 3.50
- ❑46, Dec 1998 .... 3.50
- ❑47, Jan 1999 .... 3.50
- ❑48, Feb 1999 .... 3.50
- ❑49, Apr 1999 .... 3.50
- ❑50, Jun 1999 .... 3.50
- ❑50/CS, Jun 1999; poster edition 5.99
- ❑Annual 1, Sep 1995 .... 3.95
- ❑Annual 2, Sep 1996, b&w 3.95

Frank Miller and Dave Gibbons' Martha Washington, the heroine of *Give Me Liberty*, went on to other adventures.

© 1990 Frank Miller, Dave Gibbons, and Dark Horse.

N-MINT

- ❑Annual 3, Sep 1997, b&w; 1997 Annual 3.95
- ❑Annual 4, Sep 1998, b&w; 1998 Annual 3.95
- ❑GN 1; Graphic Novel 10.95
- ❑Special 1; Special edition; Reprints Gold Digger Vol. 1 #1 .... 3.00

GOLD DIGGER (3RD SERIES)
ANTARCTIC

- ❑1, Jul 1999; new color series 4.00
- ❑2, Aug 1999 .... 3.00
- ❑3, Sep 1999 .... 3.00
- ❑4, Oct 1999 .... 3.00
- ❑5, Nov 1999 .... 3.00
- ❑6, Dec 1999 .... 3.00
- ❑7, Jan 2000 .... 3.00
- ❑8, Feb 2000 .... 3.00
- ❑9, Mar 2000 .... 3.00
- ❑10, Apr 2000 .... 3.00
- ❑11, May 2000 .... 3.00
- ❑12, Jun 2000 .... 3.00
- ❑13, Jul 2000 .... 3.00
- ❑14, Aug 2000 .... 3.00
- ❑15, Oct 2000 .... 3.00
- ❑16, Nov 2000 .... 3.00
- ❑17, Dec 2000 .... 3.00
- ❑18, Jan 2000 .... 3.00
- ❑19, Feb 2001 .... 3.00
- ❑20, Mar 2001 .... 3.00
- ❑21, Apr 2001 .... 2.95
- ❑22, May 2001 .... 2.95
- ❑23, Jun 2001 .... 2.95
- ❑24, Jul 2001 .... 2.95
- ❑25, Aug 2001 .... 2.95
- ❑26, Nov 2001 .... 2.99
- ❑27, Dec 2001 .... 2.99
- ❑28, Jan 2002 .... 2.99
- ❑29, Feb 2002 .... 2.99
- ❑30, Mar 2002 .... 2.99
- ❑31, Apr 2002 .... 2.99
- ❑32, May 2002 .... 2.99
- ❑33, Jun 2002 .... 2.99
- ❑34, Jul 2002 .... 2.99
- ❑35, Aug 2002 .... 2.99
- ❑36, Oct 2002 .... 2.99
- ❑37, Nov 2002 .... 2.99
- ❑38, Dec 2002 .... 2.99
- ❑39, Jan 2003 .... 3.50
- ❑40, Feb 2003 .... 3.50
- ❑41, Mar 2003 .... 3.50
- ❑42, Apr 2003 .... 3.50
- ❑43, May 2003 .... 3.50
- ❑44, Jun 2003 .... 3.50
- ❑45, Oct 2003 .... 2.99
- ❑46, Oct 2003 .... 2.99
- ❑47, Nov 2003 .... 2.99
- ❑48, Dec 2003 .... 2.99
- ❑49, Jan 2004 .... 2.99
- ❑50, Feb 2004 .... 2.99
- ❑51, Mar 2004 .... 2.99
- ❑52, May 2004 .... 2.99
- ❑Annual 4, Sep 2003 .... 4.95

GOLD DIGGER: BETA
ANTARCTIC

- ❑1, Feb 1998 .... 2.95

N-MINT

GOLD DIGGER: EDGE GUARD
RADIO

❑1, Aug 2000 .... 2.95
❑2, Sep 2000 .... 2.95
❑3, Oct 2000 .... 2.95
❑4, Nov 2000 .... 2.95
❑5, Dec 2000 .... 2.95

GOLD DIGGER MANGAZINE
ANTARCTIC

❑1, Mar 1994 .... 2.99
❑1-2, Apr 1999 .... 2.99

GOLD DIGGER PERFECT MEMORY
ANTARCTIC

❑1, Jul 1996, b&w; story synopses, character profiles, and other material 4.50

GOLD DIGGER SWIMSUIT END OF SUMMER SPECIAL
ANTARCTIC

❑1, Jul 2003 .... 4.50

GOLD DIGGER SWIMSUIT SPECIAL
ANTARCTIC

❑1, May 2000 ....
❑2, May 2003; 2003 Swimsuit special 4.50
❑3, May 2004; 2004 Swimsuit special 4.50

GOLDEN AGE, THE
DC

❑1, ca. 1993; JRo (w); PS (a); Elseworlds 5.50
❑2, Jan 1993; JRo (w); PS (a); O: Dynaman. Elseworlds 5.50
❑3, ca. 1993; JRo (w); PS (a); Elseworlds 5.50
❑4, ca. 1993; JRo (w); PS (a); D: Dynaman. D: Ultra-Humanite. D: Hawkman. D: Doll Man. D: Miss America. Elseworlds 5.50

GOLDEN AGE OF TRIPLE-X, THE
REVISIONARY

❑1, b&w 3.50

GOLDEN AGE OF TRIPLE-X: JOHN HOLMES SPECIAL "JOHNNY DOES PARIS"
RE-VISIONARY

❑1 .... 2.95

GOLDEN AGE SECRET FILES
DC

❑1, Feb 2001 .... 4.95

GOLDEN AGE SHEENA, THE
AC

❑1 .... 9.95

GOLDEN DRAGON
SYNCHRONICITY

❑1 .... 1.50

GOLDEN FEATURES (JERRY IGER'S...)
BLACKTHORNE

❑1 .... 2.00
❑2 .... 2.00
❑3, Jun 1986 .... 2.00
❑4, Aug 1986 .... 2.00
❑5, Oct 1986 .... 2.00
❑6 .... 2.00

GOLDEN WARRIOR
INDUSTRIAL DESIGN

❑1, Mar 1997, b&w 2.95

GOLDEN WARRIOR ICZER ONE
ANTARCTIC

❑1, Apr 1994, b&w 2.95
❑2, May 1994, b&w 2.95
❑3, Jun 1994, b&w 2.95
❑4, Jul 1994, b&w 2.95
❑5, Aug 1994, b&w 2.95

GOLD KEY SPOTLIGHT
GOLD KEY

❑1, May 1976; Tom, Dick, and Harriet 6.00
❑2 1976 .... 4.00
❑3 1976 .... 4.00
❑4 1977 .... 4.00
❑5 1977 .... 4.00
❑6, Jun 1977; Dagar 4.00
❑7 1977 .... 4.00
❑8 1977 .... 4.00
❑9 1977 .... 4.00
❑10 1977 .... 4.00
❑11 1978 .... 4.00

GOLDYN 3-D
BLACKTHORNE

❑1 .... 2.00

GOLGOTHIKA
CALIBER

❑1, Nov 1996, b&w 2.95
❑2, ca. 1996, b&w 2.95
❑3, ca. 1996, b&w 2.95
❑4, b&w 2.95

GOLGO 13
LEAD

❑1, b&w 1.00
❑2 .... 1.50

GOLGO 13 (2ND SERIES)
VIZ

❑1, b&w 4.95
❑2, b&w 4.95
❑3, b&w 4.95

GO-MAN!
CALIBER

❑1, Nov 1989, b&w 2.50
❑2, b&w 2.50
❑3, b&w 2.50
❑4, b&w 2.50

GOMER PYLE
GOLD KEY

❑1, Jul 1966 .... 40.00
❑2, Jan 1967 .... 25.00
❑3, Oct 1967 .... 25.00

GON
DC / PARADOX PRESS

❑1, b&w; digest 5.95
❑2, b&w; digest 5.95
❑3, b&w; digest 5.95
❑4, b&w; digest 5.95
❑5, b&w; digest 6.95

GONAD THE BARBARIAN
ETERNITY

❑1 .... 2.25

GON COLOR SPECTACULAR
DC / PARADOX PRESS

❑1; prestige format 5.95

GON UNDERGROUND
DC / PARADOX PRESS

❑1 .... 7.95

GOOD-BYE, CHUNKY RICE
TOP SHELF

❑1, Oct 1999, b&w; graphic novel 14.95

GOOD GIRL ART QUARTERLY
AC

❑1, Jul 1990; new & reprints 3.95
❑2, Fal 1990 .... 3.95
❑3, Win 1991 .... 3.95
❑4, Spr 1991 .... 3.95
❑5, Sum 1991 .... 3.95
❑6, Fal 1991; Fall 1991 .... 3.95
❑7, Win 1992 .... 3.95
❑8, Spr 1992 .... 3.95
❑9, Sum 1992 .... 3.95
❑10, Fal 1992 .... 3.95
❑11, Win 1993 .... 3.95
❑12, Spr 1993 .... 3.95
❑13, Sum 1993 .... 3.95
❑14, Fal 1993 .... 3.95
❑15, Win 1994 .... 3.95
❑16, Spr 1994 .... 3.95
❑17, Sum 1994 .... 3.95
❑18, Fal 1994 .... 3.95
❑19, Win 1995 .... 6.95

GOOD GIRLS
FANTAGRAPHICS

❑1, Apr 1987, b&w 2.00
❑2, Oct 1987 .... 2.00
❑3 1988 .... 2.00
❑4, Feb 1989 .... 2.00
❑6, Jun 1991, b&w 2.00

GOOD GUYS, THE
DEFIANT

❑1, Nov 1993; Giant-size 2.50
❑2, Dec 1993 .... 2.50
❑3, Jan 1994 .... 2.50
❑4, Feb 1994 .... 2.50
❑5, Mar 1994 .... 2.50
❑6, Apr 1994 .... 2.50
❑7, May 1994 .... 2.50
❑8, Jun 1994 .... 2.50
❑9, Jul 1994 .... 2.50
❑10, Aug 1994 .... 2.50
❑11, Sep 1994 .... 2.50
❑12, Oct 1994 .... 2.50

GOODY GOOD COMICS
FANTAGRAPHICS

❑1, Jun 2000 .... 2.95

GOOFY ADVENTURES
DISNEY

❑1, Jun 1990 .... 2.50
❑2, Jul 1990 .... 1.50
❑3, Aug 1990 .... 1.50
❑4, Sep 1990 .... 1.50
❑5, Oct 1990 .... 1.50
❑6, Nov 1990 .... 1.50
❑7, Dec 1990; Three Musketeers 1.50
❑8, Jan 1991 .... 1.50
❑9, Feb 1991; FG (a); James Bond parody 1.50
❑10, Mar 1991 .... 1.50
❑11, Apr 1991 .... 1.50
❑12, May 1991 .... 1.50
❑13, Jun 1991 .... 1.50
❑14, Jul 1991 .... 1.50
❑15, Aug 1991; Super-Goof 1.50
❑16, Sep 1991; Sherlock Holmes parody 1.50
❑17, Oct 1991 GC (a) 1.50

GOON, THE (1ST SERIES)
AVATAR

❑1 1998 .... 15.00
❑2 1999 .... 10.00
❑3 1999 .... 10.00

GOON, THE (2ND SERIES)
ALBATROSS EXPLODING

❑1 2002 .... 10.00
❑1/Variant 2002; Sketch cover, limited convention edition 10.00
❑2 2002 .... 5.00
❑3 2002; Norman Rockwell tribute cover 5.00
❑4 2002 .... 5.00

GOON, THE (3RD SERIES)
DARK HORSE

❑1 2003 .... 2.99
❑2 2003 .... 2.99
❑3, Oct 2003 .... 2.99
❑4, Dec 2003 .... 2.99
❑5, Feb 2004 .... 2.99
❑6, Apr 2004 .... 2.99
❑7, Aug 2004 .... 2.99

GOON PATROL
PINNACLE

❑1 .... 1.75

GORDON YAMAMOTO AND THE KING OF THE GEEKS
HUMBLE

❑1, Oct 1997, b&w 2.95

GORE SHRIEK
FANTACO

❑1, ca. 1986, b&w; 1st Greg Capullo story 3.00
❑2, b&w 3.00

N-MINT

❑3, b&w 3.00
❑4, b&w 3.00
❑5 3.50
❑6 3.50
❑Annual 1, b&w 4.95

GORE SHRIEK (VOL. 2)
FANTACO

❑1, b&w 2.50
❑2, b&w 2.50
❑3, b&w 2.50

GORE SHRIEK DELECTUS
FANTACO

❑1 8.95

GORGANA'S GHOUL GALLERY
AC

❑1, b&w 2.95
❑2 2.95

GORGON
VENUS

❑1, Jun 1996 2.95
❑2, Jun 1996 2.95
❑3, Jun 1996 2.95
❑4, Jun 1996 2.95
❑5, Aug 1996 2.95

GORILLA GUNSLINGER
MOJO

❑0; Sampler 1.00

GOTCHA!
RIP OFF

❑1, Sep 1991, b&w 2.50

G.O.T.H.
VEROTIK

❑1 3.00
❑2, Mar 1996 3.00
❑3, Jun 1996 3.00

GOTHAM CENTRAL
DC

❑1, Jan 2003 2.50
❑2, Feb 2003 2.50
❑3, Mar 2003 2.50
❑4, Apr 2003 2.50
❑5, May 2003 2.50
❑6, Jun 2003 2.50
❑7, Jul 2003 2.50
❑8, Aug 2003 2.50
❑9, Sep 2003 2.50
❑10, Oct 2003 2.50
❑11, Nov 2003 2.50
❑12, Dec 2003 2.50
❑13, Jan 2004 2.50
❑14, Feb 2004 2.50
❑15, Mar 2004 2.50
❑16, Apr 2004 2.50
❑17, May 2004 2.50
❑18, Jun 2004 2.50
❑20, Aug 2004 2.50
❑21, Sep 2004

GOTHAM GIRLS
DC

❑1, Oct 2002 2.25
❑2, Nov 2002 2.25
❑3, Dec 2002 2.25
❑4, Jan 2003 2.25
❑5, Feb 2003 2.25

GOTHAM NIGHTS
DC

❑1, Mar 1992 2.00
❑2, Apr 1992 2.00
❑3, May 1992 2.00
❑4, Jun 1992 2.00

GOTHAM NIGHTS II
DC

❑1, Mar 1995 2.00
❑2, Apr 1995 2.00
❑3, May 1995 2.00
❑4, Jun 1995 2.00

N-MINT

GOTHIC
5TH PANEL

❑1, Apr 1997, b&w 2.50
❑2 2.50

GOTHIC MOON
ANARCHY BRIDGEWORKS

❑1 5.95

GOTHIC NIGHTS
REBEL

❑1, b&w 2.00
❑2 2.00

GOTHIC RED
BONEYARD

❑1 2.95
❑3, Mar 1997, b&w 2.95

GOTHIC SCROLLS, THE: DRAYVEN
DAVDEZ

❑1, Dec 1997 2.95
❑2, Feb 1998 2.50
❑3, Mar 1998 2.50
❑Ashcan 1, Aug 1997; Preview edition; cover says Sep, indicia says Aug 1.50

GRACKLE, THE
ACCLAIM

❑1, Jan 1997, b&w 2.95
❑2, Feb 1997, b&w 2.95
❑3, Mar 1997, b&w 2.95
❑4, Apr 1997, b&w 2.95

GRAFFITI KITCHEN
TUNDRA

❑1 2.95

GRAFIK MUZIK
CALIBER

❑1, b&w A: Madman. 15.00
❑2, ca. 1991 10.00
❑3 6.00
❑4 6.00

GRAMMAR PATROL, THE
CASTEL

❑1 2.00

GRAPHIC
FANTACO

❑1 3.95

GRAPHIC HEROES IN HOUSE OF CARDS
GRAPHIC STAFFING

❑1; personalized promotional piece for temporary graphics employees 1.00

GRAPHIC STORY MONTHLY
FANTAGRAPHICS

❑1, b&w 4.00
❑2, b&w 3.50
❑3, b&w 3.50
❑4, b&w 3.50
❑5, b&w 3.50
❑6, b&w 3.50
❑7 3.50

GRAPHIQUE MUSIQUE
SLAVE LABOR

❑1, Dec 1989, b&w 8.00
❑2, Mar 1990, b&w 8.00
❑3, May 1990, b&w 8.00

GRATEFUL DEAD COMIX
KITCHEN SINK

❑1 6.00
❑2 5.00
❑3 5.00
❑4 5.00
❑5 5.00
❑6 5.00
❑7 5.00

GRATEFUL DEAD COMIX (VOL. 2)
KITCHEN SINK

❑1; comic-book size 3.95
❑2, Apr 1994 3.95

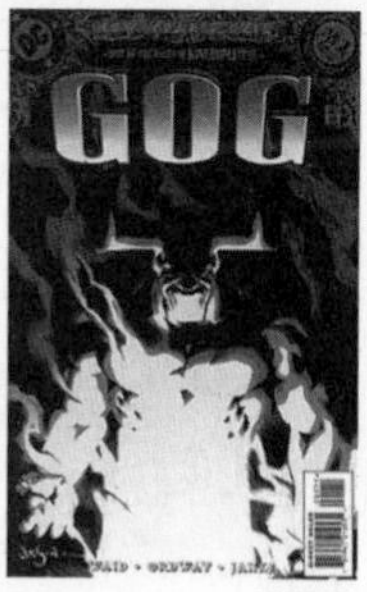

The Kingdom was spun out of events in *Gog (Villains)*.
© 1998 DC Comics.

N-MINT

GRAVEDIGGERS
ACCLAIM

❑1, Nov 1996, b&w 2.95
❑2, Dec 1996, b&w 2.95
❑3, Jan 1997, b&w 2.95
❑4, Feb 1997, b&w 2.95

GRAVEDIGGER TALES
AVALON

❑1, b&w 2.95

GRAVESTONE
MALIBU

❑1 2.25
❑2 2.25
❑3, Sep 1993; Genesis 2.25
❑4 2.25
❑5; Genesis 2.25
❑6; Genesis 2.25
❑7, Feb 1994; Genesis; last issue 2.25

GRAVESTOWN
ARIEL

❑1, Oct 1997 2.95

GRAVE TALES
HAMILTON

❑1, Oct 1991, b&w 3.95
❑2, b&w 3.95
❑3, b&w 3.95

GRAY AREA
IMAGE

❑1, Aug 2004 5.95

GREASE MONKEY
KITCHEN SINK

❑1, Oct 1995 3.50
❑2, Oct 1995 3.50

GREASE MONKEY (IMAGE)
IMAGE

❑1, Jan 1998 2.95
❑2, Mar 1998 2.95

GREAT ACTION COMICS
I.W.

❑8 70.00
❑9 70.00

GREAT AMERICAN WESTERN
AC

❑1, ca. 1988 2.00
❑2 1988 2.95
❑3 2.95
❑4 3.50
❑5 5.00

GREAT BIG BEEF
ERR

❑97, Jun 1996, b&w 2.00
❑98, Jan 1997, b&w; cover says Apr, indicia says Jan 2.00
❑99, Sep 1997, b&w 2.00

GREATEST AMERICAN COMIC BOOK
OCEAN

❑1; Spider-Man parody; Batman 2.55

GREATEST DIGGS OF ALL TIME!
RIP OFF

❑1, Feb 1991, b&w 2.00

GREAT GALAXIES
ZUB

❑0, b&w 1: The Warp Patrol. 2.95
❑1, b&w O: Captain Dean. 2.50

N-MINT

❑2, b&w 2.50
❑3, b&w 2.50
❑4, b&w 2.50
❑5, b&w 2.50
❑6/Ashcan; Flip book with Telluria Ashcan #6 0.50

GREAT GAZOO, THE
CHARLTON

❑1, Aug 1973 20.00
❑2 1973 12.00
❑3 1974 10.00
❑4, Jun 1974 10.00
❑5, Aug 1974 10.00
❑6, Oct 1974 10.00
❑7, Dec 1974 10.00
❑8, Feb 1975 10.00
❑9, Apr 1975 10.00
❑10, Jun 1975 10.00
❑11 1975 10.00
❑12, Sep 1975 10.00
❑13, Nov 1975 10.00
❑14, Jan 1976 10.00
❑15, Mar 1976 10.00
❑16, May 1976 10.00
❑17, Jul 1976 10.00
❑18, Sep 1976 10.00
❑19, Nov 1976 10.00
❑20, Jan 1977 10.00

GREAT MORONS IN HISTORY
REVOLUTIONARY

❑1, Oct 1993, b&w; Dan Quayle 2.50

GREAT SOCIETY COMIC BOOK, THE
PARALLAX

❑1 16.00
❑2 12.00

GREEENLOCK
AIRCEL

❑1, b&w 2.50

GREEN ARROW
DC

❑0, Oct 1994 1: Connor Hawke (as adult). 3.00
❑1, Feb 1988; MGr (c); MGr (w); DG (a); Painted cover 4.00
❑2, Mar 1988; MGr (c); MGr (w); DG (a); Painted cover 2.00
❑3, Apr 1988; MGr (c); MGr (w); FMc, DG (a); Painted cover 2.00
❑4, May 1988 MGr (c); MGr (w) 2.00
❑5, Jun 1988 2.00
❑6, Jul 1988 2.00
❑7, Aug 1988 2.00
❑8, Sep 1988 2.00
❑9, Oct 1988 2.00
❑10, Nov 1988 MGr (c) 2.00
❑11, Dec 1988 MGr (c) 1.50
❑12, Dec 1988 MGr (c) 1.50
❑13, Jan 1989 1.50
❑14, Jan 1989 1.50
❑15, Feb 1989 1.50
❑16, Mar 1989 1.50
❑17, Apr 1989 1.50
❑18, May 1989 1.50
❑19, Jun 1989 1.50
❑20, Jul 1989 1.50
❑21, Aug 1989 1: Connor Hawke (baby). 2.50
❑22, Aug 1989 1.50
❑23, Sep 1989 1.50
❑24, Sep 1989 1.50
❑25, Oct 1989 1.50
❑26, Nov 1989 1.50
❑27, Dec 1989 A: Warlord. 1.50
❑28, Jan 1990 A: Warlord. 1.50
❑29, Feb 1990 1.50
❑30, Mar 1990 1.50
❑31, Apr 1990 1.50
❑32, May 1990 1.50
❑33, Jun 1990 1.50
❑34, Jul 1990 1.50
❑35, Aug 1990; Black Arrow 1.50
❑36, Sep 1990; Black Arrow 1.50
❑37, Sep 1990; Black Arrow 1.50
❑38, Oct 1990; Black Arrow 1.50
❑39, Nov 1990 1.50
❑40, Dec 1990 MGr (a) 1.50
❑41, Dec 1990 1.50
❑42, Jan 1991 1.50
❑43, Feb 1991 1.50
❑44, Mar 1991 1.50
❑45, Apr 1991 1.50
❑46, May 1991 1.50
❑47, Jun 1991 1.50
❑48, Jun 1991 1.50
❑49, Jul 1991 1.50
❑50, Aug 1991; Giant-size 2.50
❑51, Aug 1991 1.50
❑52, Sep 1991 1.50
❑53, Oct 1991 1.50
❑54, Nov 1991 1.50
❑55, Dec 1991 MGr (w) 1.50
❑56, Jan 1992 1.50
❑57, Feb 1992 1.50
❑58, Mar 1992 1.50
❑59, Apr 1992 1.50
❑60, May 1992 1.50
❑61, May 1992 FS (a) 1.50
❑62, Jun 1992 FS (a) 1.50
❑63, Jun 1992 1.50
❑64, Jul 1992 1.50
❑65, Aug 1992 1.50
❑66, Sep 1992 1.50
❑67, Oct 1992 1.50
❑68, Nov 1992 1.50
❑69, Dec 1992 MGr (w) 1.75
❑70, Jan 1993 1.75
❑71, Feb 1993 1.75
❑72, Mar 1993 1.75
❑73, Apr 1993 1.75
❑74, May 1993 1.75
❑75, Jun 1993; Giant-size 2.50
❑76, Jul 1993 O: Green Lantern and Green Arrow. 1.75
❑77, Aug 1993 1.75
❑78, Sep 1993 1.75
❑79, Oct 1993 1.75
❑80, Nov 1993 MGr (w) 1.75
❑81, Dec 1993 JA (a) 1.75
❑82, Jan 1994 JA (a) 1.75
❑83, Feb 1994 JA (a) 1.75
❑84, Mar 1994 JA (a) 1.75
❑85, Apr 1994 JA (a); A: Deathstroke. 1.75
❑86, May 1994; JA (a); Catwoman 1.75
❑87, Jun 1994 JA (a) 1.95
❑88, Jul 1994 JA (a); A: JLA. 1.95
❑89, Aug 1994 1.95
❑90, Sep 1994; Zero Hour 2.25
❑91, Nov 1994 JA (a) 1.95
❑92, Dec 1994 JA (a) 1.95
❑93, Jan 1995 JA (a) 1.95
❑94, Feb 1995 JA (a) 1.95
❑95, Mar 1995 JA (a) 1.95
❑96, Apr 1995 3.00
❑97, Jun 1995 3.00
❑98, Jul 1995 JA (a) 3.00
❑99, Aug 1995 JA (a) 3.00
❑100, Sep 1995; Giant-size; enhanced cover 7.00
❑101, Oct 1995; D: Green Arrow I (Oliver Queen). Later disproved 18.00
❑102, Nov 1995; Underworld Unleashed 2.25
❑103, Dec 1995 A: Green Lantern. 2.25
❑104, Jan 1996 2.25
❑105, Feb 1996 A: Robin. 2.25
❑106, Mar 1996 2.25
❑107, Apr 1996 2.25
❑108, May 1996 A: Thorn. 2.25
❑109, Jun 1996 JA (a) 2.25
❑110, Jul 1996 2.25
❑111, Aug 1996 2.25
❑112, Sep 1996 2.25
❑113, Oct 1996 2.25
❑114, Nov 1996; Final Night 2.25
❑115, Dec 1996 A: Shado, Black Canary. 2.25
❑116, Jan 1997 A: Black Canary, Oracle, Shado. 2.25
❑117, Feb 1997 A: Black Canary. 2.25
❑118, Mar 1997 2.25
❑119, Apr 1997 A: Warlord. 2.25
❑120, May 1997 A: Warlord. 2.25
❑121, Jun 1997 2.25
❑122, Jul 1997 2.25
❑123, Aug 1997 JA (a) 2.25
❑124, Sep 1997 2.25
❑125, Oct 1997; Giant-size; continues in Green Lantern #92 3.50
❑126, Nov 1997 2.50
❑127, Dec 1997; Face cover 2.50
❑128, Jan 1998 2.50
❑129, Feb 1998 2.50
❑130, Mar 1998; cover forms triptych with Flash #135 and Green Lantern #96 2.50
❑131, Apr 1998 2.50
❑132, May 1998 2.50
❑133, Jun 1998 A: JLA. 2.50
❑134, Jul 1998; A: Batman. continues in Detective Comics #723 2.50
❑135, Aug 1998 V: Lady Shiva. 2.50
❑136, Sep 1998 A: Hal Jordan. 2.50
❑137, Oct 1998 A: Superman. 4.00
❑1000000, Nov 1998 3.00
❑Annual 1, Sep 1988 A: Batman. 3.50
❑Annual 2, Aug 1989 A: Question. 3.00
❑Annual 3, Dec 1990 A: Question. 3.00
❑Annual 4, Jun 1991; 50th Anniversary; Robin Hood 3.00
❑Annual 5, ca. 1994 TVE, FS (a); A: Batman. 3.00
❑Annual 6, ca. 1994 1: Hook. 3.50
❑Annual 7, ca. 1994; Year One 3.95

GREEN ARROW (MINI-SERIES)
DC

❑1, May 1983 DG (a); O: Green Arrow. 3.00
❑2, Jun 1983 DG, TVE (a) 2.50
❑3, Jul 1983 DG (a) 2.00
❑4, Aug 1983 DG (a) 2.00

GREEN ARROW (2ND SERIES)
DC

❑1, Apr 2001; MW (c); KSm (w); Return of Oliver Queen 6.00
❑2, May 2001 MW (c); KSm (w) 6.00
❑3, Jun 2001 MW (c); KSm (w) 3.00
❑4, Jul 2001 MW (c); KSm (w) 3.00
❑5, Aug 2001 MW (c); KSm (w) 3.00
❑6, Sep 2001 MW (c); KSm (w) 3.00
❑7, Oct 2001 MW (c); KSm (w) 2.50
❑8, Nov 2001 MW (c); KSm (w) 2.50
❑9, Dec 2001 MW (c); KSm (w) 2.50
❑10, Jan 2002 MW (c); KSm (w) 2.50
❑11, Feb 2002 MW (c); KSm (w) 2.50
❑12, Mar 2002 MW (c); KSm (w) 2.50
❑13, Apr 2002 MW (c); KSm (w) 2.50
❑14, Aug 2002 MW (c); KSm (w) 2.50
❑15, Sep 2002 MW (c); KSm (w) 2.50
❑16, Oct 2002 MW (c) 2.50
❑17, Nov 2002 MW (c) 2.50
❑18, Dec 2002 MW (c) 2.50
❑19, Jan 2003 MW (c) 2.50
❑20, Mar 2003 MW (c) 2.50
❑21, Apr 2003 MW (c) 2.50
❑22, May 2003 MW (c) 2.50
❑23, Jun 2003; MW (c); Continues in Green Lantern #162 2.50
❑24, Jun 2003; MW (c); Continues in Green Lantern #163 2.50
❑25, Jul 2003; MW (c); Continues in Green Lantern #164 2.50
❑26, Jul 2003 MW (c) 2.50
❑27, Aug 2003 2.50
❑28, Sep 2003 2.50
❑29, Oct 2003 2.50
❑30, Nov 2003 2.50
❑31, Dec 2003 2.50

N-MINT

❑32, Jan 2004 .... 2.50
❑33, Feb 2004 .... 2.50
❑34, Mar 2004 .... 2.50
❑35, Apr 2004 .... 2.50
❑36, May 2004 .... 2.50
❑37, Jun 2004 .... 2.50
❑38, Jul 2004 .... 2.50
❑39, Aug 2004 .... 2.50
❑40, Sep 2004 .... 2.50

GREEN ARROW: THE LONGBOW HUNTERS
DC

❑1, Aug 1987 MGr (w); MGr (a); 1: Shado. 3.50
❑1-2, Aug 1987 MGr (w); MGr (a); 1: Shado. 3.00
❑1-3, Aug 1987 MGr (w); MGr (a); 1: Shado. 3.00
❑2, Sep 1987 MGr (w); MGr (a) 3.00
❑3, Oct 1987 MGr (w); MGr (a) 3.00

GREEN ARROW: THE WONDER YEAR
DC

❑1, Feb 1993 MGr (w); GM, MGr (a) . 2.00
❑2, Mar 1993 MGr (w); GM, MGr (a) 2.00
❑3, Apr 1993 MGr (w); GM, MGr (a) . 2.00
❑4, May 1993 MGr (w); GM, MGr (a) 2.00

GREEN CANDLES
DC / PARADOX

❑1, ca. 1995, b&w; digest 5.95
❑2, ca. 1995, b&w; digest 5.95
❑3, ca. 1995, b&w; digest 5.95

GREENER PASTURES
KRONOS

❑1 .... 2.50
❑1-2, Jan 1997 .... 2.50
❑2, Oct 1994 .... 2.50
❑3, Feb 1995 .... 2.50
❑4, Dec 1995 .... 2.50
❑4.5, Feb 1996 .... 1.95
❑5, Aug 1996 .... 2.95
❑6, Nov 1996 .... 2.95
❑7, Feb 1997 .... 2.95

GREEN GOBLIN
MARVEL

❑1, Oct 1995; enhanced cardstock cover 2.95
❑2, Nov 1995 .... 1.95
❑3, Dec 1995; Story continued from Amazing Scarlet Spider #2 .... 1.95
❑4, Jan 1996 .... 1.95
❑5, Feb 1996 .... 1.95
❑6, Mar 1996 .... 1.95
❑7, Apr 1996 .... 1.95
❑8, May 1996 .... 1.95
❑9, Jun 1996 .... 1.95
❑10, Jul 1996 .... 1.95
❑11, Aug 1996 .... 1.95
❑12, Sep 1996 .... 1.95
❑13, Oct 1996 .... 1.95

GREEN-GREY SPONGE-SUIT SUSHI TURTLES
MIRAGE

❑1; parody; cardstock cover 3.50

GREENHAVEN
AIRCEL

❑1 .... 2.00
❑2 .... 2.00
❑3; Continued in Elflord #21 .... 2.00

GREEN HORNET (GOLD KEY)
GOLD KEY

❑1, Feb 1967 .... 120.00
❑2, May 1967 .... 80.00
❑3, Aug 1967 .... 80.00

GREEN HORNET, THE (VOL. 1)
NOW

❑1, Nov 1989 JSo (c); JSo (a); O: Green Hornet I. O: 1940s Green Hornet. .. 3.50
❑1-2, Apr 1990; prestige format; O: The Green Hornet. perfect bound 3.95
❑2, Dec 1989 .... 2.50

N-MINT

❑3, Jan 1990 .... 2.00
❑4, Feb 1990 SR (c) 2.00
❑5, Mar 1990 .... 2.00
❑6, Apr 1990 .... 2.00
❑7, May 1990; BSz (c); 1: new Kato. Mishi becomes new Kato 2.00
❑8, Jun 1990 .... 2.00
❑9, Jul 1990 .... 2.00
❑10, Aug 1990 .... 2.00
❑11, Sep 1990 .... 2.00
❑12, Oct 1990 .... 2.00
❑13, Nov 1990 .... 2.00
❑14, Feb 1991 .... 2.00

GREEN HORNET, THE (VOL. 2)
NOW

❑1, Sep 1991 .... 2.00
❑2, Oct 1991 .... 2.00
❑3, Nov 1991 .... 2.00
❑4, Dec 1991 .... 2.00
❑5, Jan 1992 .... 2.00
❑6, Feb 1992 .... 2.00
❑7, Mar 1992 .... 2.00
❑8, Apr 1992 .... 2.00
❑9, May 1992 .... 2.00
❑10, Jun 1992 .... 2.00
❑11, Jul 1992 .... 2.00
❑12, Aug 1992; bagged; with button . 2.50
❑13, Sep 1992 .... 1.95
❑14, Oct 1992 .... 1.95
❑15, Nov 1992 .... 1.95
❑16, Dec 1992 .... 1.95
❑17, Jan 1993 .... 1.95
❑18, Feb 1993 .... 1.95
❑19, Mar 1993 .... 1.95
❑20, Apr 1993 .... 1.95
❑21, May 1993 .... 1.95
❑22, Jun 1993; newsstand, trading card; newsstand; Has UPC, Comics Code seal 2.95
❑22/Direct ed., Jun 1993; alternate cover; direct sale; trading card; No Comics Code seal 2.95
❑23, Jul 1993 .... 2.95
❑24, Aug 1993 .... 1.95
❑25, Sep 1993 .... 1.95
❑26, Oct 1993 .... 1.95
❑27, Nov 1993 .... 2.95
❑28, Dec 1993 .... 1.95
❑29, Jan 1994 .... 1.95
❑30, Feb 1994 .... 1.95
❑31, Mar 1994 .... 1.95
❑32, Apr 1994 .... 1.95
❑33, May 1994 .... 1.95
❑34, Jun 1994 .... 1.95
❑35, Jul 1994 .... 1.95
❑36, Aug 1994 .... 1.95
❑37, Sep 1994 .... 1.95
❑38, Nov 1994 .... 2.50
❑39, Dec 1994 .... 1.95
❑40, Jan 1995 .... 2.50
❑Annual 1, Dec 1992 .... 2.50
❑Annual 1994, Oct 1994 .... 2.95

GREEN HORNET ANNIVERSARY SPECIAL
NOW

❑1, Aug 1992; bagged; with button ... 2.50
❑2, Sep 1992 .... 1.95
❑3, Oct 1992 .... 1.95

GREEN HORNET, THE: DARK TOMORROW
NOW

❑1, Jun 1993 .... 2.50
❑2, Jul 1993 .... 2.50
❑3, Aug 1993 .... 2.50

GREEN HORNET, THE: SOLITARY SENTINEL
NOW

❑1, Dec 1992 .... 2.50
❑2, Jan 1993 .... 2.50
❑3, Feb 1993 .... 2.50

Songs composed and performed by The Grateful Dead were the basis for the stories in *Grateful Dead Comix.*

N-MINT

GREEN LANTERN (2ND SERIES)
DC

❑1, Aug 1960 GK (a); O: Green Lantern II (Hal Jordan). 1: the Guardians. ... 2900.00
❑2, Oct 1960 GK (a); 1: Qward. 1: Pieface. 775.00
❑3, Dec 1960 GK (a) 475.00
❑4, Feb 1961 GK (a) 350.00
❑5, Apr 1961 GK (a); 1: Hector Hammond. 350.00
❑6, Jun 1961 GK (a); 1: Tomar. 300.00
❑7, Aug 1961 GK (a); O: Sinestro. 1: Sinestro. 250.00
❑8, Oct 1961 GK (a) 250.00
❑9, Dec 1961 GK (a) 250.00
❑10, Jan 1962 GK (a) 250.00
❑11, Mar 1962 GK (a); 1: The Green Lantern Corps. 180.00
❑12, Apr 1962 GK (a); 1: Doctor Polaris. 180.00
❑13, Jun 1962 GK (a); A: Flash II (Barry Allen). 185.00
❑14, Jul 1962 GK (a); 1: Sonar. 150.00
❑15, Sep 1962 GK (a) 145.00
❑16, Oct 1962 GK (a); O: Star Sapphire. 1: Star Sapphire. 1: Zamarons. 145.00
❑17, Dec 1962 GK (a) 135.00
❑18, Jan 1963 GK (a) 135.00
❑19, Mar 1963 GK (a) 135.00
❑20, Apr 1963 GK (a); A: Flash II (Barry Allen). 135.00
❑21, Jun 1963 GK (a); O: Doctor Polaris. 120.00
❑22, Jul 1963 GK (a) 120.00
❑23, Sep 1963 GK (a); 1: Tattooed Man. 120.00
❑24, Oct 1963 GK (a); O: The Shark. 1: The Shark. 120.00
❑25, Dec 1963 GK (a) 120.00
❑26, Jan 1964 GK (a) 120.00
❑27, Mar 1964 GK (a) 120.00
❑28, Apr 1964 GK (a); 1: Goldface. ... 120.00
❑29, Jun 1964 GK (a); 1: Black Hand. A: Justice League of America. 120.00
❑30, Jul 1964 GK (a) 100.00
❑31, Sep 1964 GK (a) 70.00
❑32, Oct 1964 GK (a) 70.00
❑33, Dec 1964 GK (a) 70.00
❑34, Jan 1965 GK (a) 70.00
❑35, Mar 1965 GK (a) 70.00
❑36, Apr 1965 GK (a) 70.00
❑37, Jun 1965 GK (a); 1: Evil Star. 70.00
❑38, Jul 1965 GK (a) 70.00
❑39, Sep 1965 GK (a) 70.00
❑40, Oct 1965 O: the Guardians. 1: Krona. A: Green Lantern I (Alan Scott). 320.00
❑41, Dec 1965 GK (a); A: Star Sapphire. 50.00
❑42, Jan 1966 GK (a) 50.00
❑43, Mar 1966 GK (a); 1: Major Disaster. A: Flash II (Barry Allen). 50.00
❑44, Apr 1966 GK (a) 50.00
❑45, Jun 1966 GK (a); 1: Prince Peril. A: Green Lantern I (Alan Scott). 50.00
❑46, Jul 1966 GK (a) 50.00
❑47, Sep 1966 GK (a) 50.00
❑48, Oct 1966 GK (a) 50.00
❑49, Dec 1966 GK (a) 50.00
❑50, Jan 1967 GK (a) 50.00
❑51, Mar 1967 .... 40.00
❑52, Apr 1967 A: Green Lantern I (Alan Scott). 40.00
❑53, Jun 1967 .... 40.00

N-MINT

- ❑54, Jul 1967 ..... 40.00
- ❑55, Sep 1967 ..... 40.00
- ❑56, Oct 1967 ..... 40.00
- ❑57, Dec 1967 ..... 40.00
- ❑58, Jan 1968 ..... 40.00
- ❑59, Mar 1968 1: Guy Gardner. 110.00
- ❑60, Apr 1968 ..... 40.00
- ❑61, Jun 1968 A: Green Lantern I (Alan Scott). 40.00
- ❑62, Jul 1968 ..... 40.00
- ❑63, Sep 1968 ..... 40.00
- ❑64, Oct 1968 ..... 40.00
- ❑65, Dec 1968 ..... 40.00
- ❑66, Jan 1969 ..... 40.00
- ❑67, Mar 1969 ..... 40.00
- ❑68, Apr 1969 ..... 40.00
- ❑69, Jun 1969 ..... 40.00
- ❑70, Jul 1969 GK (a) 40.00
- ❑71, Sep 1969 GK (a) 24.00
- ❑72, Oct 1969 GK (a) 24.00
- ❑73, Dec 1969 GK (a) 24.00
- ❑74, Jan 1970 GK (a) 24.00
- ❑75, Mar 1970 GK (a) 24.00
- ❑76, Apr 1970; NA (a); A: Green Arrow. Green Lantern/Green Arrow series 200.00
- ❑77, Jun 1970; NA (a); A: Green Arrow. Green Lantern/Green Arrow series 75.00
- ❑78, Jul 1970; NA (a); A: Green Arrow. Green Lantern/Green Arrow series 75.00
- ❑79, Sep 1970; NA (a); A: Green Arrow. Green Lantern/Green Arrow series 58.00
- ❑80, Oct 1970; NA (a); A: Green Arrow. Green Lantern/Green Arrow series 58.00
- ❑81, Dec 1970; NA (a); A: Green Arrow. Green Lantern/Green Arrow series 45.00
- ❑82, Mar 1971; NA (a); A: Green Arrow. Green Lantern/Green Arrow series 45.00
- ❑83, May 1971; NA (a); A: Green Arrow. Green Lantern/Green Arrow series; Anti-drug issue 45.00
- ❑84, Jul 1971; BWr, NA (a); Green Arrow; Green Lantern/Green Arrow series 45.00
- ❑85, Sep 1971; NA (a); Green Arrow; Anti-drug issue; Green Lantern/Green Arrow series 45.00
- ❑86, Nov 1971; NA (a); Green Lantern/Green Arrow series; Green Arrow; Anti-drug issue 60.00
- ❑87, Jan 1972; NA, GK (a); 1: John Stewart. A: Green Arrow. Guy Gardner cameo; Green Lantern/Green Arrow series 50.00
- ❑88, Mar 1972 GK (a); A: Green Arrow. 20.00
- ❑89, May 1972; NA (a); A: Green Arrow. Green Lantern/Green Arrow series 30.00
- ❑90, Sep 1976; MGr (w); MGr (a); A: Green Arrow. Green Lantern/Green Arrow series 10.00
- ❑91, Nov 1976 MGr (a) 10.00
- ❑92, Dec 1976 MGr (a) 10.00
- ❑93, Feb 1977 MGr (a) 9.00
- ❑94, Apr 1977 MGr (a) 9.00
- ❑95, Jun 1977 MGr (a) 9.00
- ❑96, Aug 1977 MGr (a) 9.00
- ❑97, Oct 1977 MGr (a) 9.00
- ❑98, Nov 1977 MGr (a) 9.00
- ❑99, Dec 1977 MGr (a) 9.00
- ❑100, Jan 1978; 100th anniversary issue MGr (a); 1: Air Wave II (Harry "Hal" Jordan). 10.00
- ❑101, Feb 1978; McGinty 9.00
- ❑102, Mar 1978 MGr (a); A: Green Arrow. 4.00
- ❑103, Apr 1978 MGr (a); A: Green Arrow. 4.00
- ❑104, May 1978 MGr (a); A: Green Arrow. 4.00
- ❑105, Jun 1978 MGr (a); A: Green Arrow. 4.00
- ❑106, Jul 1978 MGr (a); A: Green Arrow. 4.00
- ❑107, Aug 1978 MGr (a); A: Green Arrow. 4.00
- ❑108, Sep 1978; MGr (a); A: Green Arrow. Golden Age Green Lantern back-up 4.00
- ❑109, Oct 1978; MGr (a); A: Green Arrow. Golden Age Green Lantern back-up 4.00
- ❑110, Nov 1978 MGr (a); A: Green Arrow. 4.00
- ❑111, Dec 1978 MGr (a); A: Green Arrow. 4.00
- ❑112, Jan 1979 O: Green Lantern I (Alan Scott). 8.00
- ❑113, Feb 1979 ..... 3.00
- ❑114, Mar 1979 ..... 3.00
- ❑115, Apr 1979 ..... 3.00
- ❑116, May 1979; Guy Gardner becomes a Green Lantern 8.00
- ❑117, Jun 1979 ..... 3.00
- ❑118, Jul 1979 ..... 3.00
- ❑119, Aug 1979 ..... 2.50
- ❑120, Sep 1979 ..... 2.50
- ❑121, Oct 1979 ..... 2.50
- ❑122, Nov 1979 A: Guy Gardner. 3.50
- ❑123, Dec 1979; Guy Gardner as Green Lantern 6.00
- ❑124, Jan 1980 ..... 2.50
- ❑125, Feb 1980 ..... 2.50
- ❑126, Mar 1980 ..... 2.50
- ❑127, Apr 1980 JSa (a) 2.50
- ❑128, May 1980 JSa (a) 2.50
- ❑129, Jun 1980 JSa (a) 2.50
- ❑130, Jun 1980 JSa (a) 2.50
- ❑131, Aug 1980 JSa (a) 2.25
- ❑132, Sep 1980 JSa (a) 2.25
- ❑133, Oct 1980 JSa (a); A: Doctor Polaris. 2.25
- ❑134, Nov 1980 JSa (a); A: Doctor Polaris. 2.25
- ❑135, Dec 1980 JSa (a); A: Doctor Polaris. 2.25
- ❑136, Jan 1981 JSa (a) 2.50
- ❑137, Feb 1981 JSa (a); 1: Citadel. 2.50
- ❑138, Mar 1981 JSa (a) 2.50
- ❑139, Apr 1981 JSa (a) 2.50
- ❑140, May 1981 JSa (a) 2.00
- ❑141, Jun 1981 JSa (a); 1: Broot. 1: Harpis. 1: Omega Men. 1: Auron. 1: Kalista. 1: Demonia. 1: Primus. 3.00
- ❑142, Jul 1981 JSa (a); 1: The Gordanians. A: Omega Men. 2.50
- ❑143, Aug 1981 JSa (a); A: Omega Men. 2.50
- ❑144, Sep 1981 JSa (a); A: Omega Men. 2.50
- ❑145, Oct 1981 JSa (a) 2.00
- ❑146, Nov 1981 JSa (a) 2.00
- ❑147, Dec 1981 JSa (a) 2.00
- ❑148, Jan 1982 JSa (a) 2.00
- ❑149, Feb 1982 JSa (a) 2.00
- ❑150, Mar 1982; 150th anniversary issue JSa (a) 5.00
- ❑151, Apr 1982 ..... 2.00
- ❑152, May 1982 ..... 2.00
- ❑153, Jun 1982 ..... 2.00
- ❑154, Jul 1982 ..... 2.00
- ❑155, Aug 1982 ..... 2.00
- ❑156, Sep 1982 ..... 2.00
- ❑157, Oct 1982 ..... 2.00
- ❑158, Nov 1982 ..... 2.00
- ❑159, Dec 1982 ..... 2.00
- ❑160, Jan 1983; Omega Men 2.00
- ❑161, Feb 1983; Omega Men 1.50
- ❑162, Mar 1983; KB (w); KP (a); Back-up story is Kurt Busiek's first major comics work 1.50
- ❑163, Apr 1983 KP (a) 1.50
- ❑164, May 1983 KP (a); 1: The Green Man. 1.50
- ❑165, Jun 1983 KP (a) 1.50
- ❑166, Jul 1983 ..... 1.50
- ❑167, Aug 1983 DaG, GT (a); 1: Spider Guild. 1.50
- ❑168, Sep 1983 ..... 1.50
- ❑169, Oct 1983 ..... 1.50
- ❑170, Nov 1983 GK (c) 1.50
- ❑171, Dec 1983 ..... 1.50
- ❑172, Jan 1984 ..... 1.50
- ❑173, Feb 1984 DG (a); 1: Javelin. A: Monitor. V: Javelin. 1.50
- ❑174, Mar 1984 DG (a) 1.50
- ❑175, Apr 1984 DG (a); A: Flash. V: Shark. 1.50
- ❑176, May 1984 DG (a); 1: Demolition Team. V: Shark. 1.50
- ❑177, Jun 1984 GK (c); V: Hector Hammond. 1.50
- ❑178, Jul 1984 DG (a); 1: The Predator (Carol Ferris). A: Monitor. V: Demolition Team. 1.50
- ❑179, Aug 1984 DG (a); A: Predator. V: Demolition Team. 1.50
- ❑180, Sep 1984 DG (a); A: Superman. A: Green Arrow. A: Flash. 1.50
- ❑181, Oct 1984; DG (a); Hal Jordan quits as Green Lantern 1.50
- ❑182, Nov 1984; DG (a); John Stewart becomes new Green Lantern; retells origin 1.50
- ❑183, Dec 1984 ..... 1.50
- ❑184, Jan 1985; GK (a); reprints origin of Guy Gardner 1.50
- ❑185, Feb 1985 KB (w); DG (a) 1.50
- ❑186, Mar 1985 DG (a); V: Eclipso. 1.50
- ❑187, Apr 1985 ..... 1.50
- ❑188, May 1985; John Stewart reveals ID to public 1.50
- ❑189, Jun 1985 V: Sonar. 1.50
- ❑190, Jul 1985 V: Predator. 1.50
- ❑191, Aug 1985 ..... 1.50
- ❑192, Sep 1985 ..... 1.50
- ❑193, Oct 1985 ..... 1.50
- ❑194, Nov 1985; Crisis; Guy Gardner returns; Guy Gardner vs. Hal Jordan 2.50
- ❑195, Dec 1985; Crisis; Guy Gardner becomes new Green Lantern of Earth 4.00
- ❑196, Jan 1986; Crisis 1.50
- ❑197, Feb 1986; Crisis; Guy Gardner vs. John Stewart 1.50
- ❑198, Mar 1986; Crisis; giant; Hal Jordan returns as Green Lantern 1.50
- ❑199, Apr 1986; Crisis; Hal Jordan returns as GL 1.50
- ❑200, May 1986; Crisis; Guardians join Zamarons 2.00
- ❑201, Jun 1986; Crisis aftermath 1.50
- ❑202, Jul 1986 ..... 1.50
- ❑203, Aug 1986 O: Ch'p. 1.50
- ❑204, Sep 1986 ..... 1.50
- ❑205, Oct 1986; Series continues as Green Lantern Corps 1.50
- ❑Special 1, Dec 1988 ..... 2.50
- ❑Special 2, ca. 1989 ..... 2.50

GREEN LANTERN (3RD SERIES)
DC

- ❑0, Oct 1994; O: Green Lantern (Kyle Rayner). V: Hal Jordan. Oa destroyed 3.50
- ❑1, Jun 1990 PB (a) 7.00
- ❑2, Jul 1990 PB (a) 2.50
- ❑3, Aug 1990; Hal vs. Guy 2.00
- ❑4, Sep 1990 ..... 2.00
- ❑5, Oct 1990 ..... 2.00
- ❑6, Nov 1990 ..... 1.50
- ❑7, Dec 1990 ..... 1.50
- ❑8, Jan 1991 ..... 1.50
- ❑9, Feb 1991 A: G'Nort. 1.50
- ❑10, Mar 1991 A: G'Nort. 1.50
- ❑11, Apr 1991 A: G'Nort. 1.50
- ❑12, May 1991 A: G'Nort. 1.50
- ❑13, Jun 1991; Giant-size 2.25
- ❑14, Jul 1991 ..... 1.50
- ❑15, Aug 1991 ..... 1.50
- ❑16, Sep 1991 ..... 1.50
- ❑17, Oct 1991 ..... 1.50
- ❑18, Nov 1991 ..... 1.50
- ❑19, Dec 1991; Giant-size; GK (c); PB, JSa, RT (a); 50th anniversary issue; Giant-size 2.00
- ❑20, Jan 1992 PB (a) 1.50
- ❑21, Feb 1992 PB (a) 1.50
- ❑22, Mar 1992 PB (a) 1.50
- ❑23, Apr 1992 PB (a) 1.50
- ❑24, May 1992 PB (a) 1.50
- ❑25, Jun 1992; Giant size; Hal Jordan vs. Guy Gardner 2.25
- ❑26, Jul 1992 ..... 1.50
- ❑27, Aug 1992 ..... 1.25
- ❑28, Sep 1992 ..... 1.25

	N-MINT
❑29, Sep 1992	1.25
❑30, Oct 1992 A: Flash. V: Gorilla Grodd.	1.25
❑31, Oct 1992 A: Flash. V: Hector Hammond. V: Gorilla Grodd.	1.25
❑32, Nov 1992	1.25
❑33, Nov 1992	1.25
❑34, Dec 1992	1.25
❑35, Jan 1993	1.25
❑36, Feb 1993	1.25
❑37, Mar 1993	1.25
❑38, Apr 1993; A: Adam Strange.	1.25
❑39, May 1993 A: Adam Strange.	1.25
❑40, May 1993 A: Darkstar.	1.25
❑41, Jun 1993	1.25
❑42, Jun 1993	1.25
❑43, Jul 1993	1.25
❑44, Aug 1993 RT (c); RT (a)	1.25
❑45, Sep 1993	1.25
❑46, Oct 1993 A: Superman. V: Mongul.	4.00
❑47, Nov 1993 A: Green Arrow.	2.00
❑48, Jan 1994	5.00
❑49, Feb 1994	5.00
❑50, Mar 1994; Double-size; 1: Green Lantern IV (Kyle Rayner). D: Sinestro. D: Kilowog. Glow-in-the-dark cover	5.00
❑51, May 1994; New costume	3.00
❑52, Jun 1994 V: Mongul.	2.00
❑53, Jul 1994 A: Superman.	2.00
❑54, Aug 1994 V: Major Force.	2.00
❑55, Sep 1994; A: Green Lantern I. A: Alan Scott. Zero Hour	2.00
❑56, Nov 1994	2.00
❑57, Dec 1994; A: New Titans. continues in New Titans #116	2.00
❑58, Jan 1995	2.00
❑59, Feb 1995 V: Doctor Polaris.	2.00
❑60, Mar 1995 A: Guy Gardner. V: Major Force.	2.00
❑61, Apr 1995 A: Darkstar. V: Kalibak.	2.00
❑62, May 1995	2.00
❑63, Jun 1995	2.00
❑64, Jul 1995	2.00
❑65, Aug 1995; continues in Darkstars #34	2.00
❑66, Sep 1995; teams with Flash	2.00
❑67, Oct 1995	2.00
❑68, Nov 1995; A: Donna Troy. Underworld Unleashed	2.00
❑69, Dec 1995; Underworld Unleashed	2.00
❑70, Jan 1996 A: John Stewart.	2.00
❑71, Feb 1996 A: Robin. A: Sentinel. A: Batman.	2.00
❑72, Mar 1996 A: Captain Marvel.	2.00
❑73, Apr 1996 A: Wonder Woman.	2.00
❑74, Jun 1996	2.00
❑75, Jul 1996	2.00
❑76, Jul 1996	2.00
❑77, Aug 1996	2.00
❑78, Sep 1996	2.00
❑79, Oct 1996 V: Sonar.	2.00
❑80, Nov 1996; V: Doctor Light. Final Night	2.00
❑81, Dec 1996; Funeral of Hal Jordan; Memorial for Hal Jordan	3.00
❑81/Variant, Dec 1996; Embossed cover; Funeral of Hal Jordan; Kane back-up story; reprints origin; Memorial for Hal Jordan	4.00
❑82, Jan 1997	1.75
❑83, Feb 1997	1.75
❑84, Mar 1997	1.75
❑85, Apr 1997	1.75
❑86, May 1997 A: Jade. A: Obsidian.	1.75
❑87, Jun 1997 A: Martian Manhunter. A: Access.	1.75
❑88, Jul 1997	1.75
❑89, Aug 1997	1.75
❑90, Sep 1997	1.75
❑91, Oct 1997; V: Desaad. Genesis	1.75
❑92, Nov 1997; concludes in Green Arrow #126	1.75

	N-MINT
❑93, Dec 1997; A: Deadman. Face cover	1.95
❑94, Jan 1998 A: Superboy.	1.95
❑95, Feb 1998	1.95
❑96, Mar 1998; cover forms triptych with Flash #135 and Green Arrow #130	1.95
❑97, Apr 1998 V: Grayven.	1.95
❑98, May 1998 1: Cary Wren as Green Lantern. A: Legion of Super-Heroes.	1.95
❑99, Jun 1998	1.95
❑100/A, Jul 1998; Hal Jordan cover (Kyle Rayner cover inside)	2.95
❑100/Autographed, Jul 1998	4.00
❑100/B, Jul 1998; Kyle Rayner cover (Hal Jordan cover inside)	2.95
❑101, Aug 1998	1.95
❑102, Aug 1998 V: Kalibak.	1.95
❑103, Sep 1998 A: JLA.	1.95
❑104, Sep 1998 A: Green Arrow.	1.95
❑105, Oct 1998 V: Parallax.	1.95
❑106, Oct 1998; Hal returned to past	1.95
❑107, Dec 1998; Kyle gives a ring to Jade	1.99
❑108, Jan 1999; Wonder Woman	1.99
❑109, Feb 1999; Green Lantern IV (Jade)	1.99
❑110, Mar 1999 A: Green Lantern (Alan Scott). A: Green Arrow. A: Conner Hawke.	1.99
❑111, Apr 1999 A: Fatality. A: John Stewart. V: Fatality.	1.99
❑112, May 1999; Kyle returns	1.99
❑113, Jun 1999	1.99
❑114, Jul 1999	1.99
❑115, Aug 1999 A: Plastic Man. A: Booster Gold.	1.99
❑116, Sep 1999 A: Plastic Man. A: Booster Gold.	1.99
❑117, Oct 1999 V: Manhunter.	1.99
❑118, Nov 1999; A: Enchantress. Day of Judgment	1.99
❑119, Dec 1999 A: new Spectre.	1.99
❑120, Jan 2000	1.99
❑121, Feb 2000	1.99
❑122, Mar 2000	1.99
❑123, Apr 2000	1.99
❑124, May 2000	1.99
❑125, Jun 2000	1.99
❑126, Jul 2000	1.99
❑127, Aug 2000	1.99
❑128, Sep 2000	2.25
❑129, Oct 2000	2.25
❑130, Nov 2000	2.25
❑131, Dec 2000	2.25
❑132, Jan 2001	2.25
❑133, Feb 2001	2.25
❑134, Mar 2001	2.25
❑135, Apr 2001	2.25
❑136, May 2001	2.25
❑137, Jun 2001	2.25
❑138, Jul 2001	2.25
❑139, Aug 2001	2.25
❑140, Sep 2001	2.25
❑141, Oct 2001	2.25
❑142, Nov 2001	2.25
❑143, Dec 2001; Joker: Last Laugh crossover	2.25
❑144, Jan 2002	2.25
❑145, Feb 2002	2.25
❑146, Mar 2002	2.25
❑147, Apr 2002	2.25
❑148, May 2002	2.25
❑149, Jun 2002	2.25
❑150, Jul 2002	3.50
❑151, Aug 2002	2.25
❑152, Sep 2002	2.25
❑153, Oct 2002	2.25
❑154, Nov 2002 JLee (c)	2.25
❑155, Dec 2002	2.25
❑156, Jan 2003	2.25
❑157, Feb 2003	2.25
❑158, Mar 2003	2.25
❑159, Apr 2003	2.25

The Flash and Green Lantern teamed up for many Silver Age adventures.

© 1962 National Periodical Publications (DC).

	N-MINT
❑160, May 2003	2.25
❑161, May 2003	2.25
❑162, Jun 2003; Continued from Green Arrow #23	2.25
❑163, Jun 2003; Continued from Green Arrow #24	2.25
❑164, Jul 2003; Continued from Green Arrow #25	2.25
❑165, Jul 2003	2.25
❑166, Aug 2003	2.25
❑167, Sep 2003	2.25
❑168, Oct 2003	2.25
❑169, Nov 2003	2.25
❑170, Dec 2003	2.25
❑171, Jan 2004	2.25
❑172, Feb 2004	2.25
❑173, Mar 2004	2.25
❑174, Apr 2004	2.25
❑175, May 2004	2.25
❑176, Jun 2004	8.00
❑177, Jul 2004	4.00
❑178, Aug 2004	2.25
❑179, Sep 2004	
❑1000000, Nov 1998; One Million	3.00
❑Annual 1, ca. 1992	3.00
❑Annual 2, ca. 1993 O: Nightblade. 1: Nightblade.	2.50
❑Annual 3, ca. 1994; Elseworlds	3.00
❑Annual 4, ca. 1995; Year One; Kyle and Hal switch places	3.50
❑Annual 5, ca. 1996; Legends of the Dead Earth	2.95
❑Annual 6, Oct 1997; Pulp Heroes; John Carter of Mars theme	3.95
❑Annual 7, Oct 1998; Ghosts	2.95
❑Annual 8, Oct 1999; KG (w); JLApe	2.95
❑Annual 9, Oct 2000; 1: Sala. Planet DC	3.50
❑Annual 1963; MA, ATh, GK (a); published in 1998 in style of 1963 annuals; cardstock cover	4.95
❑Giant Size 1, Dec 1998; 80-Page Giant A: G'Nort.	4.95
❑Giant Size 2, Jun 1999; 80-Page Giant MWa (w); A: Plastic Man. A: Guy Gardner. A: Deadman. A: Impulse. A: Zatanna. A: Big Barda. A: Aquaman.	4.95
❑Giant Size 3, Aug 2000	5.95
❑3D 1, Dec 1998 V: Doctor Light.	4.50
❑3D 1/Ltd., Dec 1998; V: Doctor Light. Signed	16.95

GREEN LANTERN/ADAM STRANGE
DC

❑1, Oct 2000	2.50

GREEN LANTERN/ATOM
DC

❑1, Oct 2000	2.50

GREEN LANTERN: BRIGHTEST DAY, BLACKEST NIGHT
DC

❑1, Aug 2002	5.95

GREEN LANTERN: CIRCLE OF FIRE
DC

❑1, Oct 2000	4.95
❑2, Oct 2000	4.95

GREEN LANTERN CORPS, THE
DC

❑205, Oct 1986; Series continued from Green Lantern (2nd Series) #204	1.50
❑206, Nov 1986	1.50

N-MINT

❑207, Dec 1986; Legends 1.50
❑208, Jan 1987 ..... 1.50
❑209, Feb 1987 ..... 1.50
❑210, Mar 1987 ..... 1.50
❑211, Apr 1987 ..... 1.50
❑212, May 1987 ..... 1.50
❑213, Jun 1987 ..... 1.50
❑214, Jul 1987 ..... 1.50
❑215, Aug 1987 ..... 1.50
❑216, Sep 1987 ..... 1.50
❑217, Oct 1987 ..... 1.50
❑218, Nov 1987 ..... 1.50
❑219, Dec 1987 ..... 1.50
❑220, Jan 1988; Millennium 1.50
❑221, Feb 1988; Millennium 1.50
❑222, Mar 1988 ..... 1.50
❑223, Apr 1988 ..... 1.50
❑224, May 1988; Giant-size GK (a) ... 1.50
❑Annual 1 1985 ..... 2.50
❑Annual 2 1986 ..... 2.25
❑Annual 3 1987 KB (w) 2.00

GREEN LANTERN CORPS QUARTERLY
DC

❑1, Sum 1992 ..... 2.50
❑2, Aut 1992; Hector Hammond vs. Alan Scott 2.50
❑3, Win 1992 ..... 2.50
❑4, Spr 1993; Alan Scott vs. Solomon Grundy 2.50
❑5, Sum 1993 ..... 2.50
❑6, Aut 1993; Alan Scott vs. New Harlequin 2.95
❑7, Win 1993 ..... 2.95
❑8, Spr 1994; Jack Chance vs. Lobo . 2.95

GREEN LANTERN: DRAGON LORD
DC

❑1, Jun 2001 ..... 4.95
❑2, Jul 2001 ..... 4.95
❑3, Aug 2001 ..... 4.95

GREEN LANTERN: EMERALD DAWN
DC

❑1, Dec 1989 O: Green Lantern II (Hal Jordan). 2.00
❑2, Jan 1990 ..... 1.50
❑3, Feb 1990 ..... 1.50
❑4, Mar 1990 KG (w) 1.50
❑5, Apr 1990 ..... 1.50
❑6, May 1990 ..... 1.50

GREEN LANTERN: EMERALD DAWN II
DC

❑1, Apr 1991 KG (w) 1.50
❑2, May 1991 KG (w) 1.00
❑3, Jun 1991 KG (w) 1.00
❑4, Jul 1991 KG (w) 1.00
❑5, Aug 1991 KG (w) 1.00
❑6, Sep 1991 KG (w) 1.00

GREEN LANTERN: EMERALD TWILIGHT NEW DAWN
DC

❑1, ca. 2003 ..... 19.95

GREEN LANTERN: EVIL'S MIGHT
DC

❑1, Oct 2002 ..... 5.95
❑2, Nov 2002 ..... 5.95
❑3, Dec 2002 ..... 5.95

GREEN LANTERN/FIRESTORM
DC

❑1, Oct 2000 ..... 2.50

GREEN LANTERN/FLASH: FASTER FRIENDS
DC

❑1; prestige format; concludes in Flash/ Green Lantern: Faster Friends 4.95

GREEN LANTERN GALLERY
DC

❑1, Dec 1996; pin-ups 3.50

N-MINT

GREEN LANTERN: GANTHET'S TALE
DC

❑1 1992; prestige format; enhanced cover; Larry Niven 5.95

GREEN LANTERN/GREEN ARROW
DC

❑1, Oct 1983 DG, NA (a) 4.00
❑2, Nov 1983 DG, NA (a) 3.50
❑3, Dec 1983 DG, NA (a) 3.50
❑4, Jan 1984 DG, NA (a) 3.50
❑5, Feb 1984 BWr, DG, NA (a) 3.50
❑6, Mar 1984 DG, NA (a) 3.50
❑7, Apr 1984 DG, NA (a) 3.50

GREEN LANTERN/GREEN LANTERN
DC

❑1, Oct 2000 ..... 2.50

GREEN LANTERN: MOSAIC
DC

❑1, Jun 1992 ..... 1.25
❑2, Jul 1992 ..... 1.25
❑3, Aug 1992 ..... 1.25
❑4, Sep 1992 ..... 1.25
❑5, Oct 1992 ..... 1.25
❑6, Nov 1992 ..... 1.25
❑7, Dec 1992 ..... 1.25
❑8, Jan 1993 ..... 1.25
❑9, Feb 1993 ..... 1.25
❑10, Mar 1993 ..... 1.25
❑11, Apr 1993 ..... 1.25
❑12, May 1993 ..... 1.25
❑13, Jun 1993 ..... 1.25
❑14, Jul 1993 ..... 1.25
❑15, Aug 1993 ..... 1.25
❑16, Sep 1993 ..... 1.25
❑17, Oct 1993 ..... 1.25
❑18, Nov 1993 ..... 1.25

GREEN LANTERN: 1001 EMERALD NIGHTS
DC

❑1, May 2001, Elseworlds 6.95

GREEN LANTERN: OUR WORLDS AT WAR
DC

❑1, Aug 2001, hardcover 2.95

GREEN LANTERN PLUS
DC

❑1, Dec 1996 ..... 2.95

GREEN LANTERN/POWER GIRL
DC

❑1, Oct 2000 ..... 2.50

GREEN LANTERN SECRET FILES
DC

❑1, Jul 1998; background on all Green Lanterns 4.95
❑2, Sep 1999; background on all Green Lanterns 4.95
❑3, Jul 2002 ..... 4.95

GREEN LANTERN/SENTINEL: HEART OF DARKNESS
DC

❑1, Mar 1998; covers form triptych ... 1.95
❑2, Apr 1998; covers form triptych ... 1.95
❑3, May 1998; covers form triptych .. 1.95

GREEN LANTERN/SILVER SURFER: UNHOLY ALLIANCES
DC

❑1 1995; prestige format; crossover with Marvel 4.95

GREEN LANTERN/SUPERMAN: LEGEND OF THE GREEN FLAME
DC

❑1 2000 ..... 5.95

GREEN LANTERN: THE NEW CORPS
DC

❑1, ca. 1999; prestige format 4.95
❑1/Autographed, ca. 1999 ..... 8.00
❑2, ca. 1999; prestige format 4.95

N-MINT

GREEN LANTERN VS. ALIENS
DC

❑1, Sep 2000 ..... 3.00
❑2, Oct 2000 ..... 3.00
❑3, Nov 2000 ..... 3.00
❑4, Dec 2000 ..... 3.00

GREEN LANTERN: WILLWORLD
DC

❑1; hardcover 24.95
❑2, ca. 2003 ..... 17.95

GREENLEAF IN EXILE
CAT'S PAW

❑1 ..... 2.95
❑2 ..... 2.95
❑3 ..... 2.95
❑4 ..... 2.95
❑5 ..... 2.95
❑6 ..... 2.95

GREENLOCK
AIRCEL

❑1, Mar 1991, b&w 2.50

GREEN PLANET
CHARLTON

❑1, ca. 1962 ..... 26.00

GREEN SKULL, THE
KNOWN ASSOCIATES

❑1 ..... 2.50

GREGORY
DC / PIRANHA

❑1, b&w 7.95
❑1-2 ..... 7.95
❑2; Herman Vermin's Very Own Best-selling & Critically Acclaimed Book with Gregory 4.95
❑3 ..... 7.95
❑3/Gold; Gold logo edition (limited printing) 9.00
❑4, b&w; Fat Boy 4.95

GREMLIN TROUBLE
ANTI-BALLISTIC

❑1 1: Remi-el. 1: Xynophylyen, The Chief Imp. 1: Cypher. 3.50
❑2 ..... 3.00
❑3 ..... 3.00
❑4 1: Prince Frothbar of the Mountain Fairies. 3.00
❑5 ..... 3.00
❑6 ..... 2.95
❑7 ..... 2.95
❑8; 1: Goblin General Grafsnout. 1: Tuberian Nebulian Cruiser ship. Instigation of the Gremlin-Goblin War 2.95
❑9 1: Dr. Brandy Schwarzchild. 1: Candy Tsai and the Moist Towelettes. 1: Dr. Pi Yukawa. 2.95
❑10 ..... 2.95
❑11 ..... 2.95
❑12 1: Ballpoint P. Greml. 2.95
❑13 ..... 2.95
❑14 ..... 2.95
❑15 ..... 2.95
❑16 ..... 2.95
❑17 ..... 2.95
❑19 ..... 2.95
❑18 ..... 2.95

GRENDEL (1ST SERIES)
COMICO

❑1, Mar 1983, b&w MW (a) 45.00
❑2, ca. 1983, b&w MW (a) 35.00
❑3, Feb 1984, b&w MW (a) 26.00

GRENDEL (2ND SERIES)
COMICO

❑1, Oct 1986 MW (w); MW (a) 5.00
❑1-2 MW (w); MW (a) 2.50
❑2, Nov 1986 MW (w); MW (a) 4.00
❑3, Dec 1986 MW (w); MW (a) 3.50
❑4, Jan 1987 DSt (c); MW (w) 3.50
❑5, Feb 1987 MW (w); MW (a) 3.50
❑6, Mar 1987 MW (w); MW (a) 3.00
❑7, Apr 1987 MW (w); MW (a) 3.00
❑8, May 1987 MW (w); MW (a) 3.00

N-MINT

❑9, Jun 1987 MW (w); MW (a) 3.00
❑10, Jul 1987 MW (w); MW (a) 3.00
❑11, Aug 1987 MW (w); MW (a) 3.00
❑12, Sep 1987 MW (w); MW (a); D: Grendel. 3.00
❑13, Oct 1987; MW (w); MW (a); new Grendel 3.00
❑14, Nov 1987; MW (w); MW (a); new Grendel 3.00
❑15, Dec 1987; MW (w); MW (a); new Grendel 3.00
❑16, Jan 1988; MW (w); MW (a); Mage begins 4.00
❑17, Feb 1988 MW (w); MW (a) 2.50
❑18, Apr 1988 MW (w); MW (a) 3.00
❑19, May 1988 MW (w); MW (a) 2.50
❑20, Jun 1988 MW (w); MW (a) 2.50
❑21, Jul 1988 MW (w); MW (a) 2.50
❑22, Aug 1988 MW (w); MW (a) 2.50
❑23, Sep 1988 MW (w); MW (a) 2.50
❑24, Oct 1988 MW (w); MW (a) 2.50
❑25, Nov 1988 MW (w); MW (a) 2.50
❑26, Dec 1988 MW (w); MW (a) 2.50
❑27, Jan 1989 MW (w); MW (a) 2.50
❑28, Feb 1989 MW (w); MW (a) 2.50
❑29, Mar 1989 MW (w); MW (a) 2.50
❑30, Apr 1989 MW (w); MW (a) 2.50
❑31, May 1989 MW (w); MW (a) 2.50
❑32, Jun 1989 MW (w); MW (a) 2.50
❑33, Jul 1989; Giant-size MW (w); MW (a) 3.75
❑34, Aug 1989 MW (w); MW (a) 2.50
❑35, Sep 1989 MW (w); MW (a) 2.50
❑36, Oct 1989 MW (w); MW (a) 2.50
❑37, Nov 1989 MW (w); MW (a) 2.50
❑38, Dec 1989 MW (w); MW (a) 2.50
❑39, Jan 1990 MW (w); MW (a) 2.50
❑40, Feb 1990; MW (w); MW (a); flip book with Grendel Tales Special Preview 3.50

GRENDEL: BLACK, WHITE, & RED
DARK HORSE

❑1, Nov 1998 MW (w) 4.00
❑2, Dec 1998 MW (w) 4.00
❑3, Jan 1999 MW (w) 4.00
❑4, Feb 1999 MW (w) 4.00

GRENDEL CLASSICS
DARK HORSE

❑1, Jul 1995; cardstock cover 3.95
❑2, Aug 1995; cardstock cover 3.95

GRENDEL CYCLE
DARK HORSE

❑1, Oct 1995; prestige format; background information on the various series including a timeline 5.95

GRENDEL: DEVIL BY THE DEED
COMICO

❑1; MW (a); graphic novel; reprints Comico one-shot; cardstock cover 4.00
❑1/Ltd.; MW (a); Limited to 2000 ...... 8.00
❑1-2, Jul 1993; MW (a); reprints Comico one-shot; cardstock cover 3.95

GRENDEL: DEVIL CHILD
DARK HORSE

❑1, Jun 1999; cardstock cover 2.95
❑2, Aug 1999; cardstock cover 2.95

GRENDEL: DEVIL QUEST
DARK HORSE

❑1, Nov 1995; prestige format 4.95

GRENDEL: DEVIL'S LEGACY
COMICO

❑1, Mar 2000 .... 2.95
❑2, Apr 2000 .... 2.95
❑3, Apr 2000 .... 2.95
❑4, Jun 2000 .... 2.95
❑5, Jul 2000 .... 2.95
❑6, Aug 2000 .... 2.95
❑7, Sep 2000 .... 2.95
❑8, Oct 2000 .... 2.95
❑9, Nov 2000 .... 2.95
❑10, Dec 2000 .... 2.95

N-MINT

❑11, Jan 2001 .... 2.95
❑12, Feb 2001 .... 2.95

GRENDEL: DEVIL'S REIGN
DARK HORSE

❑1, May 2004 .... 3.50
❑2, Aug 2004 .... 3.50

GRENDEL: DEVIL'S VAGARY
COMICO

❑1 .... 8.00

GRENDEL: GOD & THE DEVIL
DARK HORSE

❑1, Feb 2003 .... 3.50
❑2, Mar 2003 .... 3.50
❑3, Apr 2003 .... 3.50
❑4, May 2003 .... 3.50
❑5, Jun 2003 .... 3.50
❑6, Jul 2003 .... 3.50
❑7, Aug 2003 .... 3.50
❑8, Sep 2003 .... 3.50
❑9, Nov 2003 .... 3.50
❑10, Dec 2003 .... 4.99

GRENDEL: PAST PRIME
DARK HORSE

❑1, Jul 2000 .... 14.95

GRENDEL: RED, WHITE & BLACK
DARK HORSE

❑1, Sep 2002 .... 4.99
❑2, Oct 2002 .... 4.99
❑3, Nov 2002 .... 4.99
❑4, Dec 2002 .... 4.99

GRENDEL TALES: DEVILS AND DEATHS
DARK HORSE

❑1, Oct 1994 .... 2.95
❑2, Nov 1994 .... 2.95

GRENDEL TALES: DEVIL'S CHOICES
DARK HORSE

❑1, Mar 1995 .... 2.95
❑2, Apr 1995 .... 2.95
❑3, May 1995 .... 2.95
❑4, Jun 1995 .... 2.95

GRENDEL TALES: DEVIL'S HAMMER
DARK HORSE

❑1, Feb 1994 .... 2.95
❑2, Mar 1994 .... 2.95
❑3, Apr 1994 .... 2.95

GRENDEL TALES: FOUR DEVILS, ONE HELL
DARK HORSE

❑1, Aug 1993; JRo (w); cardstock cover 3.00
❑2, Sep 1993; JRo (w); cardstock cover 3.00
❑3, Oct 1993; JRo (w); cardstock cover 3.00
❑4, Oct 1993; JRo (w); cardstock cover 3.00
❑5, Dec 1993; JRo (w); cardstock cover 3.00
❑6, Jan 1994; JRo (w); cardstock cover; Grendel-Prime returns 3.00

GRENDEL TALES: HOMECOMING
DARK HORSE

❑1, Dec 1994; cardstock cover 2.95
❑2, Jan 1995; cardstock cover 2.95
❑3, Feb 1995; cardstock cover 2.95

GRENDEL TALES: THE DEVIL IN OUR MIDST
DARK HORSE

❑1, May 1994 .... 2.95
❑2, Jun 1994 .... 2.95
❑3, Jul 1994 .... 2.95
❑4, Aug 1994 .... 2.95
❑5, Sep 1994 .... 2.95

GRENDEL TALES: THE DEVIL MAY CARE
DARK HORSE

❑1, Dec 1995; cardstock cover 2.95
❑2, Jan 1996; cardstock cover 2.95
❑3, Feb 1996; cardstock cover 2.95
❑4, Mar 1996; cardstock cover 2.95

Kyle Rayner was given the last Green Lantern ring after Hal Jordan had wiped out the remainder of The Green Lantern Corps in *Green Lantern* (3rd series) #50.
© 1994 DC Comics.

N-MINT

❑5, Apr 1996; cardstock cover 2.95
❑6, May 1996; cardstock cover 2.95

GRENDEL TALES: THE DEVIL'S APPRENTICE
DARK HORSE

❑1, Sep 1997 .... 2.95
❑2, Oct 1997 .... 2.95
❑3, Nov 1997 .... 2.95

GRENDEL: THE DEVIL INSIDE
COMICO

❑1, Sep 2001; Dark Horse publishes .
❑2, Oct 2001 ....
❑3, Nov 2001 ....

GRENDEL: WAR CHILD
DARK HORSE

❑1, Aug 1992; MW (w); MW (a); Part 41 of Grendel total series 3.50
❑2, Sep 1992; MW (w); Part 42 of Grendel total series 3.00
❑3, Oct 1992; MW (w); Part 43 of Grendel total series 3.00
❑4, Nov 1992; MW (w); Part 44 of Grendel total series 3.00
❑5, Dec 1992; MW (w); Part 45 of Grendel total series 3.00
❑6, Jan 1993; MW (w); Part 46 of Grendel total series 2.50
❑7, Jan 1993; MW (w); Part 47 of Grendel total series 2.50
❑8, Mar 1993; MW (w); Part 48 of Grendel total series 2.50
❑9, Apr 1993; MW (w); Part 49 of Grendel total series 2.50
❑10, Jun 1993; Double-size; MW (w); Part 50 of Grendel total series 3.75

GREY
VIZ

❑1, Oct 1989; Introduction by Harlan Ellison 4.00
❑2, Nov 1989 .... 3.50
❑3, Dec 1989 .... 3.50
❑4, Jan 1989 .... 3.50
❑5, Feb 1989 .... 3.50
❑6, Mar 1989 .... 3.25
❑7, Apr 1989 .... 3.25
❑8, May 1989 .... 3.25
❑9, Jun 1989 .... 3.25

GREY LEGACY
FRAGILE ELITE

❑1, b&w 2.75

GREYLORE
SIRIUS COMICS

❑1, Dec 1985 .... 1.50
❑2, Jan 1986 .... 1.50
❑3, Jan 1986 .... 1.50
❑4, Jan 1986 .... 1.50
❑5, Jan 1986 .... 1.50

GREYMATTER
ALAFFINITY

❑1, Oct 1993 .... 2.95
❑2, Nov 1993 .... 2.95
❑3, Dec 1993 .... 2.95
❑4, Jan 1994, b&w 2.95
❑5, Apr 1994, b&w 2.95
❑6, Sep 1994, b&w; cover forms diptych with #7 .... 2.95
❑7, Oct 1994, b&w; cover forms diptych with #6 .... 2.95

N-MINT

❑8, Mar 1995 2.95
❑9, Dec 1995 2.95
❑10, Mar 1996 2.95
❑11, Jun 1996 2.95

GREYSHIRT: INDIGO SUNSET
DC / America's Best Comics

❑1, Dec 2001 3.50
❑2, Jan 2002 3.50
❑3, Feb 2002 3.50
❑4, Apr 2002 3.50
❑5, Jun 2002 3.50
❑6, Aug 2002 3.50

GRIFFIN, THE (SLAVE LABOR)
Slave Labor

❑1, Jul 1988, b&w 1.75
❑1-2, Apr 1989, b&w 1.75
❑2, Dec 1988 1.75
❑3, Apr 1989 1.75

GRIFFIN, THE (DC)
DC

❑1, Nov 1991 4.95
❑2, Dec 1991 4.95
❑3, Jan 1991 4.95
❑4, Feb 1991 4.95
❑5, Mar 1991 4.95
❑6, Apr 1991 4.95

GRIFFIN, THE (AMAZE INK)
Slave Labor

❑1, May 1997 2.95

GRIFFITH OBSERVATORY
Fantagraphics

❑1 4.95

GRIFTER AND THE MASK
Dark Horse

❑1, Sep 1996; crossover with Image . 2.50
❑2, Oct 1996; crossover with Image . 2.50

GRIFTER/BADROCK
Image

❑1/A, Oct 1995 2.50
❑1/B, Oct 1995; alternate cover 2.50
❑2/A, Nov 1995; flipbook with Badrock #2A 2.50
❑2/B, Nov 1995; flipbook with Badrock #2A 2.50

GRIFTER: ONE SHOT
Image

❑1, Jan 1995 4.95

GRIFTER/SHI
Image

❑1, Apr 1996; cover says Mar, indicia says Apr; crossover with Crusade . 2.95
❑2, May 1996; crossover with Crusade 2.95

GRIFTER (VOL. 1)
Image

❑1, May 1995; bound-in trading cards 2.50
❑1/Direct ed., May 1995; Direct Market edition 2.50
❑2, Jun 1995 2.00
❑3, Jul 1995; indicia says Jul, cover says Aug 2.00
❑4, Aug 1995 2.00
❑5, Oct 1995; indicia says Oct, cover says Jun 2.00
❑6, Nov 1995 2.00
❑7, Dec 1995 2.00
❑8, Jan 1996 2.00
❑9, Feb 1996 2.00
❑10, Mar 1996 2.00

GRIFTER (VOL. 2)
Image

❑1, Jul 1996 2.50
❑2, Aug 1996 2.50
❑3, Sep 1996 2.50
❑4, Oct 1996 2.50
❑5, Nov 1996 2.50
❑6, Dec 1996; cover says Nov, indicia says Dec 2.50
❑7, Jan 1997 2.50
❑8, Feb 1997 2.50
❑9, Mar 1997 2.50
❑10, Apr 1997 2.50
❑11, May 1997 2.50
❑12, Jun 1997 2.50
❑13, Jul 1997 2.50
❑14, Aug 1997 2.50

GRIM GHOST, THE
Atlas-Seaboard

❑1, Jan 1975 O: Grim Ghost. 1: Grim Ghost. 2.50
❑2, Mar 1975 2.00
❑3, Jul 1975 2.00

GRIMJACK
First

❑1, Aug 1984 2.50
❑2, Sep 1984 2.00
❑3, Oct 1984 2.00
❑4, Nov 1984 2.00
❑5, Dec 1984 2.00
❑6, Jan 1985 2.00
❑7, Feb 1985 2.00
❑8, Mar 1985 2.00
❑9, Apr 1985 2.00
❑10, May 1985 2.00
❑11, Jun 1985 2.00
❑12, Jul 1985 2.00
❑13, Aug 1985 2.00
❑14, Sep 1985 2.00
❑15, Oct 1985 2.00
❑16, Nov 1985 2.00
❑17, Dec 1985 2.00
❑18, Jan 1986 2.00
❑19, Feb 1986 2.00
❑20, Mar 1986 2.00
❑21, Apr 1986 1.50
❑22, May 1986 1.50
❑23, Jun 1986 1.50
❑24, Jul 1986 1.50
❑25, Aug 1986 1.50
❑26, Sep 1986 TS (a); A: Teenage Mutant Ninja Turtles. 3.00
❑27, Oct 1986 1.50
❑28, Nov 1986 1.50
❑29, Dec 1986 1.50
❑30, Jan 1987; Dynamo Joe 1.50
❑31, Feb 1987 1.50
❑32, Mar 1987 1.50
❑33, Apr 1987 1.50
❑34, May 1987 1.50
❑35, Jun 1987 1.50
❑36, Jul 1987 D: Grimjack. 1.50
❑37, Aug 1987 1.50
❑38, Sep 1987 1.50
❑39, Oct 1987 1.50
❑40, Nov 1987 1.95
❑41, Dec 1987 1.95
❑42, Jan 1988 1.95
❑43, Feb 1988 1.95
❑44, Mar 1988 1.95
❑45, Apr 1988 1.95
❑46, May 1988 1.95
❑47, Jun 1988 1.95
❑48, Jul 1988 1.95
❑49, Aug 1988 1.95
❑50, Sep 1988 1.95
❑51, Oct 1988 1.95
❑52, Nov 1988 1.95
❑53, Dec 1988 1.95
❑54, Jan 1989 1.95
❑55, Feb 1989; new Grimjack 1.95
❑56, Mar 1989 1.95
❑57, Apr 1989 1.95
❑58, May 1989 1.95
❑59, Jun 1989 1.95
❑60, Jul 1989 1.95
❑61, Aug 1989 1.95
❑62, Sep 1989 1.95
❑63, Oct 1989 1.95
❑64, Nov 1989 1.95
❑65, Dec 1989 1.95
❑66, Jan 1990 1.95
❑67, Feb 1990 1.95
❑68, Mar 1990 1.95
❑69, Apr 1990 1.95
❑70, May 1990 1.95
❑71, Jun 1990 2.00
❑72, Jul 1990 2.00
❑73, Aug 1990 2.00
❑74, Sep 1990 2.00
❑75, Oct 1990; Giant 75th issue 3.50
❑76, Nov 1990 2.00
❑77, Dec 1990 2.00
❑78, Jan 1991 2.00
❑79, Feb 1991 2.00
❑80, Mar 1991 2.00
❑81, Apr 1991 2.00

GRIMJACK CASEFILES
First

❑1, Nov 1990 1.95
❑2, Dec 1990 1.95
❑3, Jan 1991 1.95
❑4, Feb 1991 1.95
❑5, Mar 1991 1.95

GRIMLOCK
Empyre

❑1, Jan 1996, b&w 2.95
❑2, b&w; no cover date 2.95

GRIMMAX
Defiant

❑0, Aug 1994; DC (a); no cover price 1.00

GRIMM'S GHOST STORIES
Gold Key

❑1, Jan 1972 14.00
❑2, Mar 1972 8.00
❑3, May 1972 8.00
❑4, Jul 1972 8.00
❑5, Sep 1972 AW (a) 8.00
❑6, Nov 1972; Misprinted editions duplicated stories 6.00
❑7, Jan 1973 6.00
❑8, Mar 1973 AW (a) 6.00
❑9, May 1973 6.00
❑10, Jul 1973 6.00
❑11, Aug 1973 4.00
❑12, Sep 1973 4.00
❑13, Nov 1973 4.00
❑14, Jan 1974 4.00
❑15, Mar 1974 4.00
❑16, May 1974 4.00
❑17, Jul 1974 4.00
❑18, Aug 1974 4.00
❑19, Sep 1974 4.00
❑20, Nov 1974 4.00
❑21, Jan 1975 4.00
❑22, Mar 1975 4.00
❑23, May 1975 4.00
❑24, Jul 1975 4.00
❑25, Aug 1975 4.00
❑26, Sep 1975 4.00
❑27, Nov 1975 4.00
❑28, Jan 1976 4.00
❑29, Mar 1976 4.00
❑30, May 1976 4.00
❑31, Jul 1976 3.00
❑32, Aug 1976 3.00
❑33, Sep 1976 3.00
❑34, Oct 1976 3.00
❑35, Nov 1976 3.00
❑36 1977 3.00
❑37, May 1977 3.00
❑38 1977 3.00
❑39 1977 3.00
❑40 1977 3.00
❑41, Oct 1977 BMc (a) 3.00
❑42, Nov 1977 3.00
❑43 1978 3.00
❑44, May 1978 3.00
❑45, Jul 1978 3.00
❑46, Sep 1978 3.00
❑47, Oct 1978 3.00
❑48, Nov 1978 3.00
❑49, Mar 1979 3.00

N-MINT

❑50, May 1979 3.00
❑51, Jul 1979 3.00
❑52, Sep 1979 3.00
❑53, Oct 1979 3.00
❑54, Nov 1979 3.00
❑55, Apr 1981 3.00
❑56, Oct 1981 3.00
❑57, Dec 1981 3.00
❑58, Feb 1982 3.00
❑59, May 1982 3.00
❑60 3.00

GRINGO
CALIBER

❑1, b&w 1.95

GRIPS
SILVERWOLF

❑1, Sep 1986 3.00
❑1/Ltd.; Signed, Numbered edition (limited to 350) 9.95
❑2, Oct 1986 2.50
❑3, Nov 1986 2.50
❑4, Dec 1986 2.50

GRIPS (VOL. 2)
GREATER MERCURY

❑1 2.00
❑2, Apr 1990, b&w 2.00
❑3, Jun 1990 2.00
❑4, Aug 1990 2.00
❑5, Oct 1990, b&w 2.00
❑6, Nov 1990 2.00
❑7, Dec 1990, b&w 2.00
❑8, ca. 1991 1.95
❑9, ca. 1991 1.95
❑10, Dec 1991, b&w 2.50
❑11 2.50
❑12 2.50

GRIP: THE STRANGE WORLD OF MEN
DC / VERTIGO

❑1, Jan 2002 2.50
❑2, Feb 2002 2.50
❑3, Mar 2002 2.50
❑4, Apr 2002 2.50
❑5, May 2002 2.50

GRIT BATH
FANTAGRAPHICS

❑1, b&w 2.50
❑2; no cover price 2.50
❑3, Aug 1994; no cover price 2.50

GROO (IMAGE)
IMAGE

❑1, Dec 1994 SA (c); ME (w); SA (a) 3.00
❑2, Jan 1995; SA (c); ME (w); SA (a); indicia says issue #1 2.50
❑3, Feb 1995 SA (c); ME (w); SA (a) 2.50
❑4, Mar 1995 SA (c); ME (w); SA (a) 2.00
❑5, Apr 1995 SA (c); ME (w); SA (a) 2.00
❑6, May 1995 SA (c); ME (w); SA (a) 2.00
❑7, Jun 1995 SA (c); ME (w); SA (a) 2.00
❑8, Jul 1995 SA (c); ME (w); SA (a) 2.00
❑9, Aug 1995 SA (c); ME (w); SA (a) 2.25
❑10, Sep 1995 SA (c); ME (w); SA (a) 2.25
❑11, Oct 1995 SA (c); ME (w); SA (a) 2.25
❑12, Nov 1995 SA (c); ME (w); SA (a) 2.25

GROO (DARK HORSE)
DARK HORSE

❑1, Jan 1998 SA (c); ME (w); SA (a) 2.95
❑2, Feb 1998 SA (c); ME (w); SA (a) 2.95
❑3, Mar 1998 SA (c); ME (w); SA (a) 2.95
❑4, Apr 1998 SA (c); ME (w); SA (a) 2.95

GROO AND RUFFERTO (SERGIO ARAGONÉS')
DARK HORSE

❑1, Dec 1998; Rufferto sent through time SA (c); ME (w); SA (a) 2.95
❑2, Jan 1999 SA (c); ME (w); SA (a) 2.95
❑3, Feb 1999 SA (c); ME (w); SA (a) 2.95
❑4, Mar 1999 SA (c); ME (w); SA (a) 2.95

N-MINT

GROO CHRONICLES, THE
MARVEL / EPIC

❑1, Jun 1989; squarebound SA (c); ME (w); SA (a) 3.50
❑2 1989; squarebound SA (c); ME (w); SA (a) 3.50
❑3 1989; squarebound SA (c); ME (w); SA (a) 3.50
❑4; squarebound SA (c); ME (w); SA (a) 3.50
❑5; squarebound SA (c); ME (w); SA (a) 3.50
❑6, Feb 1990; squarebound SA (c); ME (w); SA (a) 3.50

GROO: DEATH & TAXES (SERGIO ARAGONÉS'...)
DARK HORSE

❑1, Dec 2001 SA (c); ME (w); SA (a) 2.99
❑2, Jan 2002 SA (c); ME (w); SA (a) 2.99
❑3, Feb 2002 SA (c); ME (w); SA (a) 2.99
❑4, Mar 2002 SA (c); ME (w); SA (a) 2.99

GROO: MIGHTIER THAN THE SWORD (SERGIO ARAGONÉS')
DARK HORSE

❑1, Jan 2000 SA (c); ME (w); SA (a) 2.95
❑2, Feb 2000 SA (c); ME (w); SA (a) 2.95
❑3, Mar 2000 SA (c); ME (w); SA (a) 2.95
❑4, Apr 2000 SA (c); ME (w); SA (a) 2.95

GROO SPECIAL
ECLIPSE

❑Special 1, Oct 1984 SA (c); ME (w); SA (a) 3.00

GROO THE WANDERER (SERGIO ARAGONÉS')
PACIFIC

❑1, Dec 1982 SA (c); ME (w); SA (a); 1: Groo. 1: Minstrel. 1: Sage. 6.50
❑2, Feb 1983 ME (w); SA (a) 4.50
❑3, Apr 1983 ME (w); SA (a) 3.75
❑4, Sep 1983 ME (w); SA (a) 3.50
❑5, Oct 1983 ME (w); SA (a) 3.00
❑6, Dec 1983 ME (w); SA (a) 3.00
❑7, Feb 1984 ME (w); SA (a) 3.00
❑8, Apr 1984 ME (w); SA (a) 3.00

GROO THE WANDERER
MARVEL / EPIC

❑1, Mar 1985 SA (c); ME (w); SA (a); 1: Minstrel. 5.00
❑2, Apr 1985 SA (c); ME (w); SA (a) 4.00
❑3, May 1985 SA (c); ME (w); SA (a) 3.50
❑4, Jun 1985 SA (c); ME (w); SA (a) 3.00
❑5, Jul 1985 SA (c); ME (w); SA (a) 3.00
❑6, Aug 1985 SA (c); ME (w); SA (a) 3.00
❑7, Sep 1985 SA (c); ME (w); SA (a) 3.00
❑8, Oct 1985 SA (c); ME (w); SA (a) 3.00
❑9, Nov 1985 SA (c); ME (w); SA (a) 3.00
❑10, Dec 1985 SA (c); ME (w); SA (a) 3.00
❑11, Jan 1986 SA (c); ME (w); SA (a) 2.50
❑12, Feb 1986 SA (c); ME (w); SA (a) 2.50
❑13, Mar 1986 SA (c); ME (w); SA (a) 2.50
❑14, Apr 1986 SA (c); ME (w); SA (a) 2.50
❑15, May 1986 SA (c); ME (w); SA (a) 2.50
❑16, Jun 1986 SA (c); ME (w); SA (a) 2.50
❑17, Jul 1986 SA (c); ME (w); SA (a) 2.50
❑18, Aug 1986 SA (c); ME (w); SA (a) 2.50
❑19, Sep 1986 SA (c); ME (w); SA (a) 2.50
❑20, Oct 1986 SA (c); ME (w); SA (a) 2.50
❑21, Nov 1986 SA (c); ME (w); SA (a) 2.50
❑22, Dec 1986 SA (c); ME (w); SA (a) 2.50
❑23, Jan 1987 SA (c); ME (w); SA (a) 2.50
❑24, Feb 1987 SA (c); ME (w); SA (a) 2.50
❑25, Mar 1987 SA (c); ME (w); SA (a) 2.50
❑26, Apr 1987 SA (c); ME (w); SA (a) 2.50
❑27, May 1987 SA (c); ME (w); SA (a) 2.50
❑28, Jun 1987 SA (c); ME (w); SA (a) 2.50
❑29, Jul 1987 SA (c); ME (w); SA (a) 2.50
❑30, Aug 1987 SA (c); ME (w); SA (a) 2.50
❑31, Sep 1987 SA (c); ME (w); SA (a) 2.00
❑32, Oct 1987 SA (c); ME (w); SA (a) 2.00
❑33, Nov 1987 SA (c); ME (w); SA (a) 2.00
❑34, Dec 1987 SA (c); ME (w); SA (a) 2.00
❑35, Jan 1988 SA (c); ME (w); SA (a) 2.00
❑36, Feb 1988 SA (c); ME (w); SA (a) 2.00

Marc Hempel's vocabulary-challenged protagonist had a quartet of books that were reprinted in 2004.

N-MINT

❑37, Mar 1988 SA (c); ME (w); SA (a) 2.00
❑38, Apr 1988 SA (c); ME (w); SA (a) 2.00
❑39, May 1988 SA (c); ME (w); SA (a) 2.00
❑40, Jun 1988 SA (c); ME (w); SA (a) 2.00
❑41, Jul 1988 SA (c); ME (w); SA (a) 2.00
❑42, Aug 1988 SA (c); ME (w); SA (a) 2.00
❑43, Sep 1988 SA (c); ME (w); SA (a) 2.00
❑44, Oct 1988 SA (c); ME (w); SA (a) 2.00
❑45, Nov 1988 SA (c); ME (w); SA (a) 2.00
❑46, Dec 1988 SA (c); ME (w); SA (a) 2.00
❑47, Jan 1989 SA (c); ME (w); SA (a) 2.00
❑48, Feb 1989 SA (c); ME (w); SA (a) 2.00
❑49, Mar 1989 SA (c); ME (w); SA (a); A: Chakaal. 2.00
❑50, Apr 1989; Giant-size SA (c); ME (w); SA (a); A: Chakaal. 3.00
❑51, May 1989 SA (c); ME (w); SA (a); A: Chakaal. 2.00
❑52, Jun 1989 SA (c); ME (w); SA (a); A: Chakaal. 2.00
❑53, Jul 1989 SA (c); ME (w); SA (a); A: Chakaal. 2.00
❑54, Aug 1989 SA (c); ME (w); SA (a) 2.00
❑55, Sep 1989 SA (c); ME (w); SA (a) 2.00
❑56, Oct 1989 SA (c); ME (w); SA (a) 2.00
❑57, Nov 1989 SA (c); ME (w); SA (a) 2.00
❑58, Nov 1989 SA (c); ME (w); SA (a) 2.00
❑59, Dec 1989 SA (c); ME (w); SA (a) 2.00
❑60, Dec 1989 SA (c); ME (w); SA (a) 2.00
❑61, Jan 1990 SA (c); ME (w); SA (a) 2.00
❑62, Feb 1990 SA (c); ME (w); SA (a) 2.00
❑63, Mar 1990 SA (c); ME (w); SA (a) 2.00
❑64, Apr 1990 SA (c); ME (w); SA (a) 2.00
❑65, May 1990 SA (c); ME (w); SA (a) 2.00
❑66, Jun 1990 SA (c); ME (w); SA (a) 2.00
❑67, Jul 1990 SA (c); ME (w); SA (a) 2.00
❑68, Aug 1990 SA (c); ME (w); SA (a) 2.00
❑69, Sep 1990 SA (c); ME (w); SA (a) 2.00
❑70, Oct 1990 SA (c); ME (w); SA (a) 2.00
❑71, Nov 1990 SA (c); ME (w); SA (a) 1.50
❑72, Dec 1990 SA (c); ME (w); SA (a) 1.50
❑73, Jan 1991 SA (c); ME (w); SA (a) 1.50
❑74, Feb 1991 SA (c); ME (w); SA (a) 1.50
❑75, Mar 1991 SA (c); ME (w); SA (a) 1.50
❑76, Apr 1991 SA (c); ME (w); SA (a) 1.50
❑77, May 1991 SA (c); ME (w); SA (a) 1.50
❑78, Jun 1991; SA (c); ME (w); SA (a); bookburners 1.50
❑79, Jul 1991 SA (c); ME (w); SA (a) 1.50
❑80, Aug 1991 SA (c); ME (w); SA (a) 1.50
❑81, Sep 1991 SA (c); ME (w); SA (a) 1.50
❑82, Oct 1991 SA (c); ME (w); SA (a) 1.50
❑83, Nov 1991 SA (c); ME (w); SA (a) 1.50
❑84, Dec 1991 SA (c); ME (w); SA (a) 1.50
❑85, Jan 1992 SA (c); ME (w); SA (a) 1.50
❑86, Feb 1992 SA (c); ME (w); SA (a) 1.50
❑87, Mar 1992 SA (c); ME (w); SA (a) 2.25
❑88, Apr 1992 SA (c); ME (w); SA (a) 2.25
❑89, May 1992 SA (c); ME (w); SA (a) 2.25
❑90, Jun 1992 SA (c); ME (w); SA (a) 2.25
❑91, Jul 1992 SA (c); ME (w); SA (a) 2.25
❑92, Aug 1992; SA (c); ME (w); SA (a); Groo finds fountain of youth 2.25
❑93, Sep 1992; SA (c); ME (w); SA (a); Groo finds fountain of youth 2.25
❑94, Oct 1992 SA (c); ME (w); SA (a) 2.25
❑95, Nov 1992 SA (c); ME (w); SA (a) 2.25
❑96, Dec 1992 SA (c); ME (w); SA (a) 2.25
❑97, Jan 1993 SA (c); ME (w); SA (a) 2.25

N-MINT

❑98, Feb 1993 SA (c); ME (w); SA (a) 2.25
❑99, Mar 1993 SA (c); ME (w); SA (a) 2.25
❑100, Apr 1993; 100th anniversary issue; SA (c); ME (w); SA (a); Groo learns to read 2.95
❑101, May 1993 SA (c); ME (w); SA (a) 2.25
❑102, Jun 1993 SA (c); ME (w); SA (a) 2.25
❑103, Aug 1993 SA (c); ME (w); SA (a) 2.25
❑104, Sep 1993 SA (c); ME (w); SA (a); O: Rufferto (Groo's Dog). 2.25
❑105, Oct 1993 SA (c); ME (w); SA (a) 2.25
❑106, Nov 1993 SA (c); ME (w); SA (a) 2.25
❑107, Dec 1993 SA (c); ME (w); SA (a) 2.25
❑108, Jan 1994 SA (c); ME (w); SA (a) 2.25
❑109, Feb 1994 SA (c); ME (w); SA (a) 2.25
❑110, Mar 1994 SA (c); ME (w); SA (a) 2.25
❑111, Apr 1994 SA (c); ME (w); SA (a) 2.25
❑112, May 1994 SA (c); ME (w); SA (a) 2.25
❑113, Jun 1994 SA (c); ME (w); SA (a) 2.25
❑114, Jul 1994 SA (c); ME (w); SA (a) 2.25
❑115, Aug 1994 SA (c); ME (w); SA (a) 2.25
❑116, Sep 1994 SA (c); ME (w); SA (a) 2.25
❑117, Oct 1994 SA (c); ME (w); SA (a) 2.25
❑118, Nov 1994 SA (c); ME (w); SA (a) 2.25
❑119, Dec 1994 SA (c); ME (w); SA (a) 2.25
❑120, Jan 1995 SA (c); ME (w); SA (a) 2.25

GROOTLORE
FANTAGRAPHICS

❑1, b&w 2.00
❑2, b&w 2.00

GROOTLORE (VOL. 2)
FANTAGRAPHICS

❑1, May 1991, b&w 2.00
❑2, b&w 2.00
❑3 2.25

GROOVY
MARVEL

❑1, Mar 1968 A: Monkees. 25.00
❑2, May 1968 16.00
❑3, Jul 1968; Marvel Comics Group Publisher 16.00

GROSS POINT
DC

❑1, Aug 1997 2.50
❑2, Sep 1997 2.50
❑3, Oct 1997 2.50
❑4, Nov 1997 2.50
❑5, Dec 1997 2.50
❑6, Dec 1997 2.50
❑7, Jan 1998 2.50
❑8, Feb 1998 2.50
❑9, Mar 1998 2.50
❑10, Apr 1998 2.50
❑11, May 1998 2.50
❑12, Jun 1998 2.50
❑13, Jul 1998 2.50
❑14, Aug 1998 2.50

GROUND POUND! COMIX
BLACKTHORNE

❑1, Jan 1987 2.00

GROUND ZERO
ETERNITY

❑1, Oct 1991, b&w 2.50
❑2, b&w 2.50

GROUP LARUE, THE (MIKE BARON'S...)
INNOVATION

❑1, Aug 1989 1.95
❑2 1.95
❑3 1.95
❑4 1.95

GRRL SCOUTS (JIM MAHFOOD'S...)
ONI

❑1, Mar 1999, b&w 2.95
❑2, Jun 1999, b&w 2.95
❑3, Sep 1999, b&w 2.95

GRRL SCOUTS: WORK SUCKS
IMAGE

❑1, Feb 2003 2.95
❑2, Mar 2003 2.95
❑3, Apr 2003 2.95
❑4, Jun 2003 2.95

GRRRL SQUAD
AMAZING AARON

❑1, Mar 1999, b&w 2.95

GRUN
HARRIER

❑1, Jun 1987 1.95
❑2, Aug 1987 1.95
❑3, Oct 1987 1.95
❑4 1.95

GRUNTS
MIRAGE

❑1, Nov 1987, b&w 2.00

GUARDIAN, THE
SPECTRUM

❑1, Mar 1984 1.00
❑2, Jun 1984 1.00

GUARDIAN ANGEL
IMAGE

❑1, May 2002 2.95
❑2, Jul 2002

GUARDIAN KNIGHTS: DEMON'S KNIGHT
LIMELIGHT

❑1, b&w; no indicia 2.95
❑2, b&w; no indicia 2.95

GUARDIANS
MARVEL

❑1, Sep 2004 2.99

GUARDIANS OF METROPOLIS, THE
DC

❑1, Nov 1994 1.50
❑2, Dec 1994 1.50
❑3, Jan 1995 1.50
❑4, Feb 1995 1.50

GUARDIANS OF THE GALAXY
MARVEL

❑1, Jun 1990 2.00
❑2, Jul 1990 V: The Stark. 2.00
❑3, Aug 1990 2.00
❑4, Sep 1990 A: Firelord. 2.00
❑5, Oct 1990 TMc (c); TMc (a); V: Force. 2.00
❑6, Nov 1990 A: Captain America's shield. 1.50
❑7, Dec 1990 1: Malevolence. V: Malevolence. 1.50
❑8, Jan 1991 1: Rancor. 1.50
❑9, Feb 1991 RL (c); RL (a); O: Rancor. 1: Replica. V: Rancor. 1.50
❑10, Mar 1991 JLee (c); JLee (a) 1.50
❑11, Apr 1991 1: Phoenix. 1.50
❑12, May 1991 V: Overkill. 1.50
❑13, Jun 1991 1: Spirit of Vengeance. 2.00
❑14, Jul 1991 A: Spirit of Vengeance. 2.00
❑15, Aug 1991 JSn (c); JSn (a); 1: Protege. 1.50
❑16, Sep 1991; Giant-size 1.75
❑17, Oct 1991; 1: Talon (Cameo) 1.50
❑18, Nov 1991; 1: Talon (Full appearance) 1.50
❑19, Dec 1991 1: Talon. 1.50
❑20, Jan 1992; A: Captain America's shield. Vance Astro becomes Major Victory 1.50
❑21, Feb 1992 V: Rancor. 1.50
❑22, Mar 1992 1.50
❑23, Apr 1992 1.50
❑24, May 1992 A: Silver Surfer. 1.50
❑25, Jun 1992; V: Galactus. regular cover 2.50
❑25/Variant, Jun 1992; V: Galactus. foil cover 2.50
❑26, Jul 1992 O: Guardians of the Galaxy. 1.50
❑27, Aug 1992 O: Talon. 1.50
❑28, Sep 1992; V: Doctor Octopus. Infinity War 1.50
❑29, Oct 1992; Infinity War 1.50
❑30, Nov 1992 1.25
❑31, Dec 1992 1.25
❑32, Jan 1993 A: Dr. Strange. A: Doctor Strange. 1.25
❑33, Feb 1993 1.25
❑34, Mar 1993; Yellowjacket joins team 1.25
❑35, Apr 1993; 1: Galactic Guardians. regular cover 1.25
❑35/Variant, Apr 1993; 1: Galactic Guardians. sculpted cover 2.95
❑36, May 1993 V: Dormammu. 1.25
❑37, Jun 1993 D: Doctor Strange. 1.25
❑38, Jul 1993 A: Beyonder. 1.25
❑39, Aug 1993; Holo-grafix cover; Rancor vs. Doom 2.95
❑40, Sep 1993 V: Composite. 1.25
❑41, Oct 1993 A: Inhumans. A: Starhawk. A: Composite. A: Loki. V: Loki. 1.25
❑42, Nov 1993 1.25
❑43, Dec 1993 1: Woden. 1.25
❑44, Jan 1994 1.25
❑45, Feb 1994 1.25
❑46, Mar 1994 1.25
❑47, Apr 1994; Protege vs. Beyonder 1.25
❑48, May 1994 V: Overkill. 1.50
❑49, Jun 1994 A: Celestial. 1.50
❑50, Jul 1994; Giant-size 2.00
❑50/Variant, Jul 1994; Giant-size; foil cover 2.95
❑51, Aug 1994 1.50
❑52, Sep 1994 1.50
❑53, Oct 1994; Drax vs. Wolfhound 1.50
❑54, Nov 1994; final fate of Spider-Man 1.50
❑55, Dec 1994 V: Ripjak. 1.50
❑56, Jan 1995 V: Ripjak. 1.50
❑57, Feb 1995 A: Bubonicus. 1.50
❑58, Mar 1995 1.50
❑59, Apr 1995 A: Silver Surfer. 1.50
❑60, May 1995 A: Silver Surfer. 1.50
❑61, Jun 1995 1.50
❑62, Jul 1995; Giant-size 2.50
❑Annual 1, Jul 1991; Korvac Quest 3.00
❑Annual 2, ca. 1992 HT, BWi (a) 2.50
❑Annual 3, ca. 1993; 1: Cuchulain. trading card 2.95
❑Annual 4, ca. 1994; 1994 Annual; ca. 1994 2.95

GUERRILLA GROUNDHOG
ECLIPSE

❑1, Jan 1987, b&w 1.50
❑2, Mar 1987 1.50

GUERRILLA WAR
DELL

❑12; Series continued from Jungle War Stories #11 10.00
❑13 10.00
❑14, Mar 1966 10.00

GUFF!
DARK HORSE

❑1, Apr 1998, b&w; bound-in Meanie Babies card 1.95

GUMBY 3-D
BLACKTHORNE

❑1 2.50
❑2 2.50
❑3 2.50
❑4 2.50
❑5 2.50
❑6 2.50
❑7 2.50

GUMBY'S SUMMER FUN SPECIAL
COMICO

❑1, Jul 1987 2.50

GUMBY'S WINTER FUN SPECIAL
COMICO

❑1 2.50

GUNDAM: THE ORIGIN
VIZ

❑1, Apr 2002 7.95
❑2, Jul 2002 7.95

N-MINT

GUNDAM WING: BLIND TARGET
VIZ

❑1, Feb 2001 .... 2.95
❑2, Mar 2001 .... 2.95
❑3, Apr 2001 .... 2.95
❑4, May 2001 .... 2.95

GUNDAM WING: EPISODE ZERO
VIZ

❑1, Apr 2001 .... 2.95
❑2, May 2001 .... 2.95
❑3, Jun 2001 .... 2.95
❑4, Jul 2001 .... 2.95
❑5, Aug 2001 .... 2.95
❑6, Sep 2001 .... 2.95
❑7, Oct 2001 .... 2.95
❑8, Nov 2001 .... 2.95

GUN FIGHTERS IN HELL
REBEL

❑1 .... 2.25
❑2 .... 2.25
❑3, b&w 2.25
❑4 .... 2.25
❑5 .... 2.25

GUNFIRE
DC

❑0, Oct 1994; Continued in Gunfire #6 2.00
❑1, May 1994 .... 2.00
❑2, Jun 1994 .... 2.00
❑3, Jul 1994 .... 2.00
❑4, Aug 1994 .... 2.00
❑5, Sep 1994; Continued in Gunfire #0 2.00
❑6, Nov 1994 .... 2.00
❑7, Dec 1994 .... 2.00
❑8, Jan 1995 .... 2.00
❑9, Feb 1995 .... 2.00
❑10, Mar 1995 .... 2.00
❑11, Apr 1995 .... 2.00
❑12, May 1995 .... 2.00
❑13, Jun 1995 .... 2.25

GUN FURY
AIRCEL

❑1, Jan 1989, b&w 1.95
❑2, Feb 1989, b&w 1.95
❑3, Mar 1989, b&w 1.95
❑4, Apr 1989, b&w 1.95
❑5, May 1989, b&w 1.95
❑6, Jun 1989, b&w 1.95
❑7, Jul 1989, b&w 1.95
❑8, Aug 1989, b&w 1.95
❑9, Sep 1989, b&w 1.95
❑10, Oct 1989, b&w 1.95

GUN FURY RETURNS
AIRCEL

❑1, Sep 1990, b&w 2.25
❑2, Oct 1990, b&w 2.25
❑3, Nov 1990, b&w 2.25
❑4, Dec 1990, b&w 2.25

GUNG HO
AVALON

❑1, b&w 2.95

GUNHAWKS
MARVEL

❑1, Oct 1972 1: Reno Jones and Kid Cassidy. 9.00
❑2, Dec 1972 .... 6.00
❑3, Feb 1973 .... 5.00
❑4, Apr 1973 .... 5.00
❑5, Jun 1973 V: Reverend Mr. Graves. 5.00
❑6, Aug 1973 D: Kid Cassidy. 5.00
❑7, Oct 1973; Title changes to Gunhawk 5.00

GUNHED
VIZ

❑1; Japanese 5.50
❑2; Japanese 5.50
❑3; Japanese 5.50

GUNNER
GUN DOG

❑1, Mar 1999 .... 2.95

N-MINT

GUN RUNNER
MARVEL

❑1, Oct 1993; four cards; Polybagged; wraparound cover 2.75
❑2, Nov 1993 .... 1.75
❑3, Dec 1993 .... 1.75
❑4, Jan 1994 .... 1.75
❑5, Feb 1994 .... 1.75
❑6, Mar 1994 .... 1.75

GUNSMITH CATS
DARK HORSE / MANGA

❑1, Sep 1995 .... 3.00
❑2, Sep 1995 .... 2.50
❑3, Sep 1995 .... 2.50
❑4, Sep 1995 .... 3.00
❑5, Sep 1995 .... 3.00
❑6, Oct 1995 .... 3.00
❑7, Nov 1995 .... 3.00
❑8, Dec 1995 .... 3.00
❑9, Jan 1996 .... 3.00
❑10, Feb 1996 .... 3.00

GUNSMITH CATS: BAD TRIP
DARK HORSE / MANGA

❑1, Jun 1998 .... 2.95
❑2, Jun 1998 .... 2.95
❑3, Aug 1998 .... 2.95
❑4, Sep 1998 .... 2.95
❑5, Oct 1998 .... 2.95
❑6, Nov 1998 .... 2.95

GUNSMITH CATS: BEAN BANDIT
DARK HORSE / MANGA

❑1, Jan 1999 .... 2.95
❑2, Feb 1999 .... 2.95
❑3, Mar 1999 .... 2.95
❑4, Apr 1999 .... 2.95
❑5, May 1999 .... 2.95
❑6, Jun 1999 .... 2.95
❑7, Jul 1999 .... 2.95
❑8, Aug 1999 .... 2.95
❑9, Sep 1999 .... 2.95

GUNSMITH CATS: GOLDIE VS. MISTY
DARK HORSE / MANGA

❑1, Nov 1997 .... 2.95
❑2, Dec 1997 .... 2.95
❑3, Jan 1998 .... 2.95
❑4, Feb 1998 .... 2.95
❑5, Mar 1998 .... 2.95
❑6, Apr 1998 .... 2.95
❑7, May 1998 .... 2.95

GUNSMITH CATS: KIDNAPPED
DARK HORSE / MANGA

❑1, Nov 1999 .... 2.95
❑2, Dec 1999 .... 2.95
❑3, Jan 2000 .... 2.95
❑4, Feb 2000 .... 2.95
❑5, Mar 2000 .... 2.95
❑6, Apr 2000 .... 2.95
❑7, May 2000 .... 2.95
❑8, Jun 2000 .... 2.95
❑9, Jul 2000 .... 2.95
❑10, Aug 2000 .... 2.95

GUNSMITH CATS: MISTER V
DARK HORSE / MANGA

❑1, Oct 2000 .... 3.50
❑2, Nov 2000 .... 3.50
❑3, Dec 2000 .... 3.50
❑4, Jan 2001 .... 3.50
❑5, Feb 2001 .... 3.50
❑6, Mar 2001 .... 3.50
❑7, Apr 2001 .... 3.50
❑8, May 2001 .... 3.50
❑9, Jun 2001 .... 3.50
❑10, Jul 2001 .... 3.50
❑11, Aug 2001 .... 3.50

GUNSMITH CATS: SHADES OF GRAY
DARK HORSE / MANGA

❑1, May 1997 .... 2.95
❑2, Jun 1997 .... 2.95
❑3, Jul 1997 .... 2.95

The longest-running *Groo* series (so far) was published by Epic.

© 1986 Sergio Aragonés and Mark Evanier (Epic).

N-MINT

❑4, Aug 1997 .... 2.95
❑5, Sep 1997 .... 2.95

GUNSMITH CATS SPECIAL
DARK HORSE

❑1, Nov 2001 .... 2.99

GUNSMITH CATS: THE RETURN OF GRAY
DARK HORSE / MANGA

❑1, Aug 1996 .... 2.95
❑2, Sep 1996 .... 2.95
❑3, Oct 1996 .... 2.95
❑4, Nov 1996 .... 2.95
❑5, Dec 1996 .... 2.95
❑6, Jan 1997 .... 2.95
❑7, Feb 1997 .... 2.95

GUNSMOKE (GOLD KEY)
GOLD KEY

❑1, Feb 1969 .... 30.00
❑2, Apr 1969 .... 20.00
❑3, Jun 1969 .... 20.00
❑4, Aug 1969 .... 20.00
❑5, Nov 1969 .... 20.00
❑6, Feb 1970 .... 20.00

GUNS OF SHAR-PEI
CALIBER

❑1, b&w 2.95
❑2, b&w 2.95
❑3, b&w 2.95

GUNS OF THE DRAGON
DC

❑1, Oct 1998 .... 2.50
❑2, Nov 1998 .... 2.50
❑3, Dec 1998 .... 2.50
❑4, Jan 1999 .... 2.50

GUN THAT WON THE WEST, THE
WINCHESTER

❑1; giveaway 24.00

GUN THEORY
MARVEL / EPIC

❑1, Oct 2003 .... 2.50
❑2, Nov 2003 .... 2.50
❑3 .... 0.00
❑4 .... 0.00

GUNWITCH, THE: OUTSKIRTS OF DOOM
ONI

❑1 2001 .... 2.95

GUTWALLOW
NUMBSKULL

❑1, Feb 1998, b&w 2.95
❑2, Apr 1998 .... 2.95
❑3, Jun 1998 .... 2.95
❑4, Aug 1998 .... 2.95
❑5, Oct 1998 .... 2.95
❑6, Feb 1999 .... 2.95
❑7, Apr 1999 .... 2.95
❑8, Jul 1999 .... 2.95
❑9, Sep 1999 .... 2.95
❑10, Dec 1999 .... 2.95
❑11, Mar 2000 .... 2.95
❑12, Jun 2000 .... 2.95

GUTWALLOW (VOL. 2)
NUMBSKULL

❑1, Nov 2000 .... 2.95

N-MINT

- ❑2, Feb 2001 .... 2.95
- ❑3, Jun 2001 .... 2.95

GUY GARDNER
DC

- ❑1, Oct 1992 JSa (a) 2.00
- ❑2, Nov 1992 JSa (a) 1.75
- ❑3, Dec 1992; JSa (a); (almost) wordless story 1.50
- ❑4, Jan 1993 JSa (a) 1.50
- ❑5, Feb 1993 JSa (a) 1.50
- ❑6, Mar 1993 JSa (a) 1.25
- ❑7, Apr 1993 JSa (a) 1.25
- ❑8, May 1993 JSa (a) 1.25
- ❑9, Jun 1993 JSa (a) 1.25
- ❑10, Jul 1993 JSa (a) 1.25
- ❑11, Aug 1993 JSa (a) 1.25
- ❑12, Sep 1993 JSa (a) 1.25
- ❑13, Oct 1993 JSa (a) 1.25
- ❑14, Nov 1993 JSa (a) 1.25
- ❑15, Dec 1993 .... 1.50
- ❑16, Jan 1994; Series continued in Guy Gardner: Warrior #17 .... 1.50

GUY GARDNER REBORN
DC

- ❑1, ca. 1992 .... 4.95
- ❑2, ca. 1992 .... 4.95
- ❑3, ca. 1992 .... 4.95

GUY GARDNER: WARRIOR
DC

- ❑0, Oct 1994 O: Guy Gardner's Warrior persona. 1.75
- ❑17, Feb 1994; Title changes to Guy Gardner: Warrior; Series continued from Guy Gardner #16 .... 1.50
- ❑18, Mar 1994 .... 1.50
- ❑19, Apr 1994 .... 1.50
- ❑20, May 1994 .... 1.50
- ❑21, Jun 1994 V: Parallax. 1.50
- ❑22, Jul 1994 .... 1.50
- ❑23, Aug 1994 .... 1.50
- ❑24, Sep 1994; Zero Hour 1.50
- ❑25, Nov 1994; Giant-size 2.50
- ❑26, Dec 1994 .... 1.50
- ❑27, Jan 1995 .... 1.50
- ❑28, Feb 1995 .... 1.50
- ❑29, Mar 1995; Giant-size 1.50
- ❑29/Variant, May 1995; Giant-size; enhanced foldout cover 2.95
- ❑30, Apr 1995 .... 1.50
- ❑31, Jun 1995 .... 1.75
- ❑32, Jul 1995 .... 1.75
- ❑33, Aug 1995 .... 1.75
- ❑34, Sep 1995 .... 1.75
- ❑35, Oct 1995 .... 1.75
- ❑36, Nov 1995 .... 1.75
- ❑37, Dec 1995; Underworld Unleashed 1.75
- ❑38, Jan 1996 .... 1.75
- ❑39, Feb 1996; Christmas party at Warriors 1.75
- ❑40, Mar 1996 .... 1.75
- ❑41, Apr 1996 .... 1.75
- ❑42, May 1996; Guy becomes a woman 1.75
- ❑43, Jun 1996 .... 1.75
- ❑44, Jul 1996 V: Major Force. 1.75
- ❑Annual 1, ca. 1995; Year One; 1995 Annual 3.50
- ❑Annual 2, ca. 1996; JSa (a); Legends of the Dead Earth; 1996 Annual 2.95

GUY PUMPKINHEAD
SAINT GRAY

- ❑1 .... 2.50

GUZZI LEMANS
ANTARCTIC

- ❑1, Aug 1996, b&w 2.95
- ❑2, Oct 1996, b&w 2.95

GYRE
ABACULUS

- ❑1, Dec 1997, b&w 3.50
- ❑2, Feb 1998, b&w 2.95
- ❑3, Apr 1998 .... 2.95
- ❑Ashcan 1; Preview of Gyre #1 .... 0.50
- ❑Special 1 .... 4.50

GYRE: TRADITIONS & INTERRUPTIONS
ABACULUS

- ❑1, b&w; Promotional book for series 1.00

GYRO COMICS
RIP OFF

- ❑1, ca. 1988, b&w 2.00
- ❑2, ca. 1988, b&w 2.00
- ❑3, ca. 1988, b&w 2.00

H

HACKER FILES, THE
DC

- ❑1, Aug 1992 TS (a); 1: Jack Marshall. 2.25
- ❑2, Sep 1992 TS (a) 1.95
- ❑3, Oct 1992 TS (a) 1.95
- ❑4, Nov 1992 TS (a) 1.95
- ❑5, Dec 1992 TS (a) 1.95
- ❑6, Jan 1993 TS (a) 1.95
- ❑7, Feb 1993 TS (a) 1.95
- ❑8, Mar 1993 TS (a) 1.95
- ❑9, Apr 1993 TS (a) 1.95
- ❑10, May 1993 TS (a) 1.95
- ❑11, Jun 1993 TS (a) 1.95
- ❑12, Jul 1993 TS (a) 1.95

HACKMASTERS OF EVERKNIGHT
KENZER AND COMPANY

- ❑1, May 2000, b&w 3.50
- ❑2, Jul 2000, b&w 2.95
- ❑3, Sep 2000, b&w 2.95
- ❑4, Nov 2000, b&w 2.95
- ❑5, Jan 2001, b&w 2.95
- ❑6, Mar 2001, b&w 2.95
- ❑7, May 2001, b&w 2.95
- ❑8, Jul 2001, b&w 2.95

HAIRBAT
SCREAMING RICE

- ❑1, b&w 2.50
- ❑2, b&w 2.50
- ❑3, b&w 2.50
- ❑4, b&w 2.50

HAIRBAT (VOL. 2)
SLAVE LABOR

- ❑1, Jul 1995, b&w 2.95

HAIR BEAR BUNCH, THE
GOLD KEY

- ❑1, Feb 1972 .... 10.00
- ❑2, May 1972 .... 7.00
- ❑3, Aug 1972 .... 6.00
- ❑4, Nov 1972 .... 6.00
- ❑5, Feb 1973 .... 6.00
- ❑6, May 1973 .... 4.00
- ❑7, Aug 1973 .... 4.00
- ❑8, Nov 1973 .... 4.00
- ❑9, Feb 1974 .... 4.00

HAIRBUTT THE HIPPO
RAT RACE

- ❑1, ca. 1992, b&w 2.95
- ❑2, ca. 1993, b&w 2.95
- ❑3, ca. 1993, b&w 2.95

HAIRBUTT THE HIPPO CRIME FILES
RAT RACE

- ❑1, Dec 1995, b&w 3.50
- ❑2, ca. 1996, b&w 3.50
- ❑3, ca. 1996, b&w 3.50
- ❑4, ca. 1996, b&w 3.50
- ❑5, ca. 1996, b&w 3.50
- ❑6, ca. 1996, b&w 3.50

HAIRBUTT THE HIPPO: PRIVATE EYE
RATRACE

- ❑1, Spr 1997, b&w; no indicia 2.95
- ❑2, Sum 1997, b&w; no indicia 2.95
- ❑3, ca. 1997, b&w 2.95

HALIFAX EXPLOSION
HALIFAX

- ❑1, Apr 1997, b&w 2.50

HALL OF FAME
J.C.

- ❑1 .... 1.50
- ❑2 .... 1.50
- ❑3 .... 1.50

HALL OF HEROES
HALL OF HEROES

- ❑1, May 1997, b&w 2.50
- ❑2 .... 2.50
- ❑3 .... 2.50

HALL OF HEROES HALLOWEEN SPECIAL
HALL OF HEROES

- ❑1, Oct 1997, b&w 2.50

HALL OF HEROES PRESENTS (1ST SERIES)
HALL OF HEROES

- ❑1, Aug 1993 .... 2.50
- ❑2, Sep 1993 .... 2.50
- ❑3, Nov 1993 .... 2.50

HALL OF HEROES PRESENTS (2ND SERIES)
HALL OF HEROES

- ❑0/A, Mar 1997, b&w; Slingers cover 2.50
- ❑0/B, Mar 1997, b&w; Salamandroid cover 2.50
- ❑0/C, Mar 1997, b&w; The Fuzz cover 2.50
- ❑1, Jul 1996, b&w 2.50
- ❑2, Sep 1996, b&w 2.50
- ❑3/A, b&w; no indicia 2.50
- ❑3/B; alternate b cover with Nazi swastika in background 2.50
- ❑4, May 1997; Turaxx 2.50
- ❑5, Sep 1997; The Becoming; extra-wide 2.50

HALLOWED KNIGHT
SHEA

- ❑1, Apr 1997, b&w 2.95
- ❑2, Sep 1997, b&w 2.95
- ❑2/Autographed; Signed 2.95

HALLOWEEN
CHAOS

- ❑1, Nov 2000; based on movie 2.95

HALLOWEEN HORROR
ECLIPSE

- ❑1, Oct 1987; JD (a);a.k.a. Seduction of the Innocent #7 .... 2.00

HALLOWEEN MEGAZINE
MARVEL

- ❑1, Dec 1996; reprints stories from Tomb of Dracula 2.99

HALLOWEEN TERROR
ETERNITY

- ❑1, b&w 2.50

HALLS OF HORROR (JOHN BOLTON'S...)
ECLIPSE

- ❑1, Jun 1985 .... 1.75
- ❑2, Jun 1985 .... 1.75
- ❑3 .... 1.75

HALO, AN ANGEL'S STORY
SIRIUS

- ❑1, Apr 1996 .... 2.95
- ❑2, May 1996 .... 2.95
- ❑3, Jun 1996 .... 2.95
- ❑4, Jul 1996 .... 2.95

HAMMER, THE
DARK HORSE

- ❑1, Oct 1997 .... 2.95
- ❑2, Nov 1997 .... 2.95
- ❑3, Dec 1997 .... 2.95
- ❑4, Jan 1998 .... 2.95

N-MINT

HAMMER, THE: THE OUTSIDER
Dark Horse

❑1, Feb 1999 .... 2.95
❑2, Mar 1999 .... 2.95
❑3, Apr 1999 .... 2.95

HAMMER, THE: UNCLE ALEX
Dark Horse

❑1, Aug 1998 .... 2.95

HAMMERLOCKE
DC

❑1, Sep 1992 .... 1.75
❑2, Oct 1992 .... 1.75
❑3, Nov 1992 .... 1.75
❑4, Dec 1992 .... 1.75
❑5, Jan 1993 .... 1.75
❑6, Feb 1993 .... 1.75
❑7, Mar 1993 .... 1.75
❑8, Apr 1993 .... 1.75
❑9, May 1993 .... 1.75

HAMMER OF GOD
First

❑1 .... 1.95
❑2 .... 1.95
❑3 .... 1.95
❑4 .... 1.95

HAMMER OF GOD: BUTCH
Dark Horse

❑1, May 1994 .... 2.50
❑2, Jul 1994 .... 2.50
❑3, Aug 1994 .... 2.50

HAMMER OF GOD: PENTATHLON
Dark Horse

❑1 .... 2.50

HAMMER OF GOD: SWORD OF JUSTICE
First

❑1 .... 4.95
❑2 .... 4.95

HAMMER OF THE GODS: HAMMER HITS CHINA
Image

❑1, Feb 2003 .... 2.95
❑2, May 2003 .... 2.95
❑3, Oct 2003 .... 2.95

HAMSTER VICE (BLACKTHORNE)
Blackthorne

❑1 .... 1.50
❑2 .... 1.50
❑3 .... 1.50
❑4 .... 1.50
❑5 .... 1.50
❑6 .... 1.50
❑7 .... 1.50
❑8, Jul 1987 .... 1.50
❑9 .... 1.50
❑3D 1, Nov 1986 .... 2.50
❑3D 2, Feb 1987; a.k.a. Blackthorne 3-D #15 .... 2.50

HAMSTER VICE (ETERNITY)
Eternity

❑1, Apr 1989, b&w 1.95
❑2, b&w 1.95

HAND SHADOWS
Doyan

❑1 .... 1.50
❑2, Nov 1986 .... 1.50

HANDS OFF!
Ward Sutton

❑1, b&w 2.95

HANDS OF THE DRAGON
Atlas-Seaboard

❑1, Jun 1975 .... 3.00

HANNA-BARBERA ALL-STARS
Archie

❑1, Oct 1995 .... 2.00
❑2, Dec 1995 .... 2.00
❑3, Feb 1996 .... 2.00
❑4, Apr 1996 .... 2.00

N-MINT

HANNA-BARBERA BANDWAGON
Gold Key

❑1, Oct 1962 .... 70.00
❑2, Jan 1963 .... 50.00
❑3, Apr 1963 .... 50.00

HANNA-BARBERA BIG BOOK
Harvey

❑1, Jun 1993 .... 1.95
❑3 .... 2.50

HANNA-BARBERA GIANT SIZE
Harvey

❑2, Nov 1992 .... 2.25

HANNA-BARBERA PARADE
Charlton

❑2 .... 18.00
❑3 .... 15.00
❑4 .... 13.00
❑5 1972 .... 14.00
❑6, Apr 1972; A: Wilma Flintstone. A: Fred Flintstone. A: Pebbles Flintstone. Dixie cameo; Pixie cameo 12.00
❑7, May 1972 .... 12.00
❑8 .... 12.00
❑9 .... 12.00
❑10 .... 12.00

HANNA-BARBERA PRESENTS
Archie

❑1, Nov 1995; Atom Ant and Secret Squirrel 1.50
❑2, Jan 1996; Wacky Races 1.50
❑3, Mar 1996; Yogi Bear 1.50
❑4, May 1996; Quick Draw McGraw and Magilla Gorilla 1.50
❑5, Jul 1996 .... 1.50
❑6, Aug 1996; Superstar Olympics 1.50
❑8, Oct 1996; Frankenstein Jr. and the Impossibles 1.50

HANNA-BARBERA PRESENTS ALL-NEW COMICS
Harvey

❑1; giveaway promo 1.00

HANNA-BARBERA SUPER TV HEROES
Gold Key

❑1, Apr 1968; Herculoids 58.00
❑2, Jul 1968; Birdman 36.00
❑3, Oct 1968; Shazzan, Space Ghost, Moby Dick, Birdman, Young Samson and Goliath 36.00
❑4, Jan 1969; Herculoids, Birdman, Shazzan, Moby Dick, Mighty Mightor 30.00
❑5, Apr 1969 .... 30.00
❑6, Jul 1969; Space Ghost 35.00
❑7, Oct 1969; Space Ghost 35.00

HANSI, THE GIRL WHO LOVED THE SWASTIKA
Spire

❑1, ca. 1973 .... 28.00

HAP HAZARD
Fandom House

❑1, b&w 2.00

HAPPENSTANCE JACK, III
-Ism

❑1, May 1998 .... 3.00

HAPPY
Wonder Comics

❑1, b&w 2.00

HAPPY BIRTHDAY GNATRAT!
Dimension

❑1 .... 1.95

HAPPY BIRTHDAY MARTHA WASHINGTON
Dark Horse / Legend

❑1, Mar 1995; FM (w); DaG (a);cardstock cover 3.00

HAPPYDALE: DEVILS IN THE DESERT
DC / Vertigo

❑1; prestige format 6.95
❑2; prestige format 6.95

The computer network of the DC universe was defined in *The Hacker Files*.

© 1993 DC Comics.

N-MINT

HAPPY DAYS
Gold Key

❑1, Mar 1979 .... 15.00
❑2, May 1979 .... 8.00
❑3, Jul 1979 .... 8.00
❑4, Sep 1979 .... 8.00
❑5 1979 .... 8.00
❑6, Feb 1980 .... 8.00

HARBINGER
Valiant

❑0, Feb 1993; O: Sting. sendaway; Special issue given as a premium from coupons in Harbinger #1-6 .... 4.00
❑0/Pink, Feb 1993; Pink variant ....
❑0-2, Feb 1993; O: Sting. Included with Harbinger trade paperback 4.00
❑1, Jan 1992 O: Harbinger. 1: Flamingo. 1: Zeppelin. 1: Sting. 1: Kris. 1: Torque. 1: Harbinger kids. 15.00
❑2, Feb 1992 .... 6.00
❑3, Mar 1992 V: Ax. 4.00
❑4, Apr 1992; Scarce 4.00
❑5, May 1992 A: Solar. 4.00
❑6, Jun 1992 D: Torque. 3.00
❑7, Jul 1992 .... 2.50
❑8, Aug 1992; FM (c); FM (a);Unity 2.50
❑9, Sep 1992; Unity; Birth of Magnus 2.50
❑10, Oct 1992 1: H.A.R.D Corps. 2.50
❑11, Nov 1992 A: H.A.R.D Corps. 2.50
❑12, Dec 1992 .... 2.50
❑13, Jan 1993; Dark Knight cover 2.50
❑14, Feb 1993 .... 2.50
❑15, Mar 1993 .... 2.50
❑16, Apr 1993 .... 2.50
❑17, May 1993 .... 2.50
❑18, Jun 1993 1: Screen. 2.50
❑19, Jul 1993 .... 2.50
❑20, Aug 1993 .... 2.50
❑21, Sep 1993 .... 2.50
❑22, Oct 1993 A: Archer & Armstrong. 2.50
❑23, Nov 1993 .... 2.50
❑24, Dec 1993 .... 2.50
❑25, Jan 1994; Giant-size; D: Rock. V: Harada. Sting vs. Harada; Harada put into coma; Sting loses powers 3.50
❑26, Feb 1994; 1: Sonix. 1: Anvil. 1: Amazon. 1: Microwave. 1: Jolt. new team; Zephyr rejoins Harbinger foundation 2.50
❑27, Mar 1994 .... 2.50
❑28, Apr 1994 .... 2.50
❑29, May 1994; trading card 2.50
❑30, Jun 1994 A: H.A.R.D.Corps. 2.50
❑31, Aug 1994 A: H.A.R.D.Corps. 2.50
❑32, Sep 1994 A: Eternal Warrior. 2.50
❑33, Oct 1994 A: Doctor Eclipse. 2.50
❑34, Nov 1994; Chaos Effect 2.50
❑35, Dec 1994 .... 2.50
❑36, Jan 1995 A: Magnus. 2.50
❑37, Feb 1995; Painted cover 2.50
❑38, Mar 1995 .... 2.50
❑39, Apr 1995 .... 2.50
❑40, May 1995 .... 2.50
❑41, Jun 1995 .... 2.50

HARBINGER: ACTS OF GOD
Acclaim

❑1 .... 3.95

N-MINT

HARBINGER FILES
VALIANT

❑1, Aug 1994 .... 2.50
❑2, Feb 1995 .... 2.50

HARDBALL
AIRCEL

❑1 1991 .... 2.95
❑2 1991 .... 2.95
❑3, Aug 1991 .... 2.95
❑4 1991 .... 2.95

HARD BOILED
DARK HORSE

❑1, Sep 1990 .... 4.95
❑2, Dec 1990 .... 5.95
❑3, Mar 1992 .... 5.95

HARDCASE
MALIBU / ULTRAVERSE

❑1, Jun 1993 1: NM-E. 1: Nicholas Lone (Solitaire). 1: Hardcase. 2.50
❑1/Hologram, Jun 1993; Holographic cover 5.00
❑1/Ltd., Jun 1993; Ultrafoil limited edition 3.00
❑2, Jul 1993; 1: Choice. trading card 2.00
❑3, Aug 1993 1: The Needler. 1: Gun Nut. 1: Trouble. 2.00
❑4, Sep 1993; O: Hardcase. Fold-out cover 2.00
❑5, Oct 1993; Rune 2.00
❑6, Nov 1993 .... 1.95
❑7, Dec 1993; Break-Thru 1.95
❑8, Jan 1994 A: Solution. 1.95
❑9, Feb 1994 BA (a) 1.95
❑10, Mar 1994 .... 1.95
❑11, Apr 1994 .... 1.95
❑12, May 1994 .... 1.95
❑13, Jun 1994 1: Karr. 1: Wynn. 1.95
❑14, Jul 1994 .... 1.95
❑15, Aug 1994 .... 1.95
❑16, Oct 1994; KB (w); Flip book with Ultraverse Premiere #7 .... 3.50
❑17, Nov 1994 1: The Genius. 1.95
❑18, Dec 1994 .... 1.95
❑19, Jan 1995 1: Trauma. 1: Bismark. 1.95
❑20, Feb 1995 .... 2.50
❑21, Mar 1995 .... 2.50
❑22, Apr 1995 D: Trouble. 2.50
❑23, May 1995 .... 2.50
❑24, Jun 1995 .... 2.50
❑25, Jul 1995 .... 2.50
❑26, Aug 1995 .... 2.95

HARDCORE STATION
DC

❑1, Jul 1998 .... 2.50
❑2, Aug 1998 .... 2.50
❑3, Sep 1998 .... 2.50
❑4, Oct 1998 .... 2.50
❑5, Nov 1998 .... 2.50
❑6, Dec 1998 .... 2.50

H.A.R.D. CORPS, THE
VALIANT

❑1, Dec 1992; JL (c);Fold-out cover 4.00
❑1/Gold, Dec 1992; Gold (promotional) edition; Fold-out cover 7.00
❑2, Jan 1993 .... 3.00
❑3, Feb 1993 BL (w) 2.50
❑4, Apr 1993 .... 2.50
❑5, Apr 1993 A: Bloodshot. 2.25
❑6, May 1993 .... 2.25
❑7, Jun 1993 V: Spider-Aliens. 2.25
❑8, Jul 1993 .... 2.25
❑9, Aug 1993 .... 2.25
❑10, Sep 1993 A: Turok. 2.25
❑11, Oct 1993 .... 2.25
❑12, Nov 1993 .... 2.25
❑13, Dec 1993 D: Superstar. 2.25
❑14, Jan 1994 .... 2.25
❑15, Feb 1994 .... 2.25
❑16, Mar 1994 .... 2.25
❑17, Apr 1994 V: Armorines. 2.25
❑18, May 1994; trading card 2.25
❑19, Jun 1994; Harada awakes from coma 2.25
❑20, Jul 1994 A: Harbinger. 2.25
❑21, Sep 1994 .... 2.25
❑22, Oct 1994 .... 2.25
❑23, Nov 1994; Chaos Effect 2.25
❑24, Dec 1994 .... 2.25
❑25, Jan 1995 .... 2.25
❑26, Feb 1995 .... 2.25
❑27, Mar 1995 .... 2.25
❑28, Apr 1995 .... 2.25
❑29, May 1995 .... 2.25
❑30, Jun 1995 .... 2.25

HARDKORR
AIRCEL

❑1, Jun 1991, b&w 2.50
❑2, Jul 1991, b&w 2.50
❑3, Aug 1991, b&w 2.50
❑4, Sep 1991, b&w 2.50

HARD LOOKS
DARK HORSE

❑1 1992, b&w 2.50
❑2 1992, b&w 2.50
❑3 1992, b&w 2.50
❑4, b&w 2.50
❑5, b&w 2.50
❑6, b&w 2.95
❑7, b&w 2.95
❑8, b&w 2.95
❑9, b&w 2.95
❑10, b&w 3.50

HARD ROCK COMICS
REVOLUTIONARY

❑1, Mar 1992, b&w; Metallica; early 5.00
❑2, Apr 1992, b&w; Motley Crue 4.00
❑3, May 1992, b&w; Jane's Addiction 3.00
❑4, Jun 1992, b&w; Nirvana 4.00
❑5, Jul 1992, b&w; Kiss: Tales From the Tours 8.00
❑5-2, Jul 1992; Kiss: Tales From the Tours 5.00
❑6, Sep 1992, b&w; Def Leppard II 2.50
❑7, Oct 1992, b&w; Red Hot Chili Peppers 2.50
❑8, Nov 1992, b&w; Soundgarden, Pearl Jam 2.50
❑9, Dec 1992, b&w; Queen II 2.50
❑10, Jan 1993, b&w; Birth of Punk 2.50
❑11, Feb 1993, b&w; Pantera 2.50
❑12, Mar 1993, b&w; Hendrix 2.50
❑13, Apr 1993, b&w; Dead Kennedys 3.00
❑14, May 1993, b&w; Van Halen II 2.50
❑15, Jun 1993, b&w; Megadeath, Motorhead; Dave Mustaine interview 2.50
❑16, Jul 1993, b&w; Joan Jett, Lita Ford 2.50
❑17; never published; British Metal 2.50
❑18, Sep 1993, b&w; Queensryche II 2.50
❑19, Oct 1993, b&w; Tesla, Spirit, UKJ 2.50
❑20, Nov 1993, b&w; Ratt, P-Funk, Sweet 2.50

HARD TIME
DC / FOCUS

❑1, Apr 2004 .... 2.50
❑2, May 2004 .... 2.50
❑3, Jun 2004 .... 2.50
❑4, Jul 2004 .... 2.50
❑5, Aug 2004 .... 2.50
❑6, Sep 2004

HARDWARE
DC / MILESTONE

❑1, Apr 1993; O: Hardware. 1: Reprise. 1: Edwin Alva. 1: Hardware. newsstand 1.50
❑1/CS, Apr 1993; O: Hardware. 1: Reprise. 1: Edwin Alva. 1: Hardware. bagged 2.95
❑1/Platinum, Apr 1993; Platinum (promotional) edition; O: Hardware. 1: Reprise. 1: Edwin Alva. 1: Hardware. no cover price; platinum 3.00
❑2, May 1993 1: Barraki Young. 1.50
❑3, May 1993 1: Systematic. 1.50
❑4, Jun 1993 .... 1.50
❑5, Jul 1993 1: Deacon Stuart. 1: Deathwish. 1.50
❑6, Aug 1993 .... 1.50
❑7, Sep 1993 O: Deathwish. 1.50
❑8, Oct 1993 .... 1.50
❑9, Nov 1993 1: Technique. 1.50
❑10, Dec 1993 RB (a); 1: Harm. 1: Transit. 1.50
❑11, Jan 1994 1: Shadowspire. 1: Dharma. 1: The Star Chamber. 1.50
❑12, Feb 1994 RB (a) 1.50
❑13, Mar 1994 .... 1.50
❑14, Apr 1994 .... 1.50
❑15, May 1994 .... 1.50
❑16, Jun 1994; Giant-size 1: Hardware Version 2.0. .... 2.50
❑16/Variant, Jun 1994; Giant-size; 1: Hardware Version 2.0. Fold-out cover 3.95
❑17, Jul 1994 A: Steel. 1.50
❑18, Aug 1994 A: Steel. 1.75
❑19, Sep 1994 .... 1.75
❑20, Oct 1994 KP (a) 1.75
❑21, Nov 1994 .... 1.75
❑22, Dec 1994 .... 1.75
❑23, Jan 1995 .... 1.75
❑24, Feb 1995 .... 1.75
❑25, Mar 1995; Giant-size 2.95
❑26, Apr 1995 .... 1.75
❑27, May 1995 .... 1.75
❑28, Jun 1995 .... 1.75
❑29, Jul 1995; cover has both.99 and 2.50 cover price 2.50
❑30, Aug 1995 .... 2.50
❑31, Sep 1995 D: Edwin Alva. 2.50
❑32, Oct 1995 .... 2.50
❑33, Nov 1995 HC (c) 2.50
❑34, Dec 1995 .... 2.50
❑35, Jan 1996 .... 2.50
❑36, Feb 1996 .... 2.50
❑37, Mar 1996 .... 2.50
❑38, Apr 1996 .... 2.50
❑39, May 1996 .... 2.50
❑40, Jun 1996 KP (a) 2.50
❑41, Jul 1996 .... 2.50
❑42, Aug 1996 .... 2.50
❑43, Sep 1996 .... 2.50
❑44, Oct 1996 .... 2.50
❑45, Nov 1996; return of Edwin Alva 2.50
❑46, Dec 1996 .... 2.50
❑47, Jan 1997 .... 2.50
❑48, Feb 1997 .... 2.50
❑49, Mar 1997 .... 2.50
❑50, Apr 1997; Giant-size 3.95

HARDWIRED
BANGTRO

❑1, May 1994 .... 2.25

HARDY BOYS
GOLD KEY

❑1, Apr 1970 .... 28.00
❑2, Jul 1970 .... 18.00
❑3, Oct 1970 .... 18.00
❑4, Jan 1971 .... 18.00

HARI KARI
BLACK OUT

❑0; indicia says "#0 #1" 2.95
❑1 .... 2.95

HARI KARI: LIVE & UNTAMED
BLACKOUT

❑0 .... 2.95
❑0/Variant; variant cover 4.00
❑1 .... 2.95

HARI KARI PRIVATE GALLERY
BLACKOUT

❑0; Pin-Ups 2.95

HARI KARI: REBIRTH
BLACK OUT

❑1 .... 2.95

N-MINT

HARI KARI RESURRECTION
BLACKOUT

❑1 ... 2.95

HARI KARI: THE BEGINNING
BLACK OUT

❑1 ... 2.95

HARI KARI: THE DIARY OF KARI SUN
BLACKOUT

❑0.5; prose accompanied with pin-ups ... 2.95

HARI KARI: THE SILENCE OF EVIL
BLACK OUT

❑0 ... 2.95

HARLEM GLOBETROTTERS
GOLD KEY

❑1, Apr 1972 ... 13.00
❑2, Jul 1972 ... 9.00
❑3, Oct 1972 A: Curly. A: Gip. A: Pabs. A: Geese. A: Granny. A: Dribbles. A: B.J.. A: Meadowlark. ... 7.00
❑4, Jan 1973 ... 7.00
❑5, Apr 1973 ... 7.00
❑6, Jul 1973 ... 5.00
❑7, Oct 1973 ... 5.00
❑8, Jan 1974 ... 5.00
❑9, Apr 1974 ... 5.00
❑10, Jul 1974 ... 5.00
❑11, Oct 1974 ... 5.00
❑12, Jan 1975 ... 5.00

HARLEM HEROES
FLEETWAY-QUALITY

❑1, b&w ... 1.95
❑2, b&w ... 1.95
❑3, b&w ... 1.95
❑4, b&w ... 1.95
❑5, b&w ... 1.95
❑6, b&w ... 1.95

HARLEQUIN
CALIBER

❑1, May 1993, b&w ... 2.95

HARLEY & IVY: LOVE ON THE LAM
DC

❑1, Nov 2001, b&w ... 5.95

HARLEY QUINN
DC

❑1, Dec 2000 ... 3.50
❑2, Jan 2001 ... 3.00
❑3, Feb 2001 A: Catwoman. ... 3.00
❑4, Mar 2001 ... 3.00
❑5, Apr 2001 ... 3.00
❑6, May 2001 ... 2.50
❑7, Jun 2001 ... 2.50
❑8, Jul 2001 ... 2.50
❑9, Aug 2001 ... 2.50
❑10, Sep 2001 ... 2.50
❑11, Oct 2001 ... 2.25
❑12, Nov 2001 ... 2.95
❑13, Dec 2001; Joker: Last Laugh crossover ... 2.25
❑14, Jan 2002 ... 2.25
❑15, Feb 2002 ... 2.25
❑16, Mar 2002 A: Poison Ivy. ... 2.25
❑17, Apr 2002 ... 2.25
❑18, May 2002 ... 2.25
❑19, Jun 2002 A: Superman. ... 2.25
❑20, Jul 2002 ... 2.25
❑21, Aug 2002 ... 2.25
❑22, Sep 2002 ... 2.25
❑23, Oct 2002 ... 2.50
❑24, Nov 2002 ... 2.50
❑25, Dec 2002 ... 2.50
❑26, Jan 2003 ... 2.50
❑27, Feb 2003 ... 2.50
❑28, Mar 2003 ... 2.50
❑29, Apr 2003 ... 2.50
❑30, May 2003 ... 2.50
❑31, Jun 2003 ... 2.50
❑32, Jul 2003 ... 2.50
❑33, Aug 2003 ... 2.50
❑34, Sep 2003 ... 2.50
❑35, Oct 2003 ... 2.50

N-MINT

❑36, Nov 2003 ... 2.50
❑37, Dec 2003 ... 2.50
❑38, Jan 2004 ... 2.50

HARLEY QUINN: OUR WORLDS AT WAR
DC

❑1, Oct 2001, b&w ... 2.95

HARLEY RIDER
HUNGNESS

❑1 ... 2.00

HAROLD HEDD (LAST GASP)
LAST GASP ECO-FUNNIES

❑1 ... 8.00
❑2 ... 4.00

HAROLD HEDD IN "HITLER'S COCAINE"
KITCHEN SINK

❑1 ... 4.00
❑2 ... 4.00

HARPY PIN-UP SPECIAL
PEREGRINE ENTERTAINMENT

❑1, May 1998, b&w ... 3.00

HARPY PREVIEW
GROUND ZERO

❑1, Oct 1996, b&w ... 3.00

HARPY: PRIZE OF THE OVERLORD
GROUND ZERO

❑1, Dec 1996, b&w ... 3.00
❑2, Feb 1997, b&w ... 3.00
❑3, Apr 1997, b&w; cover says Blood of the Demon ... 3.00
❑4 ... 3.00
❑5 ... 3.00
❑6 ... 3.00

HARRIER PREVIEW
HARRIER

❑1 ... 1.00

HARRIERS
EXPRESS / ENTITY

❑1; Foil stamped cover ... 2.95
❑2 ... 2.95
❑3 ... 2.95

HARROWERS, THE (CLIVE BARKER'S)
MARVEL / EPIC

❑1, Dec 1993; glow in the dark cover ... 2.95
❑2, Jan 1994 ... 2.50
❑3, Feb 1994 ... 2.50
❑4, Mar 1994 ... 2.50
❑5, Apr 1994 ... 2.50
❑6, May 1994 ... 2.50

HARRY THE COP
SLAVE LABOR

❑1, Apr 1992, b&w ... 2.95
❑1-2, Oct 1992, b&w ... 2.95

HARSH REALM
HARRIS

❑1, Feb 1994 ... 2.95
❑2, Mar 1994 ... 2.95
❑3, Apr 1994 ... 2.95
❑4, May 1994 ... 2.95
❑5, Jun 1994 ... 2.95
❑6, Jul 1994 ... 2.95

HARTE OF DARKNESS
ETERNITY

❑1, b&w ... 2.50
❑2, b&w ... 2.50
❑3, b&w ... 2.50
❑4, b&w ... 2.50

HARVEY
MARVEL

❑1, Oct 1970; humor ... 20.00
❑2, Dec 1970; humor ... 12.00
❑3, Jun 1972; humor ... 8.00
❑4, Aug 1972; humor ... 6.00
❑5, Oct 1972; humor ... 6.00
❑6, Dec 1972; humor ... 6.00

With implants allowing them to mimic super-abilities, The H.A.R.D. Corps resisted The Harada Corporation's attempts at world domination.

© 1992 Voyager Communications (Valiant).

N-MINT

HATE
FANTAGRAPHICS

❑1, Sum 1990, b&w ... 8.00
❑1-2 ... 3.50
❑1-3 ... 2.00
❑2, Fal 1990 ... 5.00
❑2-2 ... 3.00
❑2-3 ... 2.50
❑3, Win 1990 ... 4.00
❑3-2 ... 2.50
❑3-3 ... 2.50
❑4, Spr 1991 ... 4.00
❑4-2 ... 2.00
❑5, Sum 1991 ... 4.00
❑5-2 ... 2.00
❑6, Fal 1991 ... 4.00
❑7, Win 1991 ... 3.00
❑8, Spr 1992 ... 3.00
❑9, Sum 1992 ... 3.00
❑10, Fal 1992 ... 3.00
❑11, Win 1993 ... 2.50
❑12, Spr 1993 ... 2.50
❑13, ca. 1993 ... 2.50
❑14, ca. 1993 ... 2.50
❑15, ca. 1994 ... 2.50
❑16, ca. 1994; color story ... 2.95
❑17, ca. 1995 ... 2.95
❑18, Apr 1995 ... 2.95
❑19, Jun 1995 ... 2.95
❑20, Sep 1995; color and b&w ... 2.95
❑21, Dec 1995 ... 2.95
❑22, Apr 1996 ... 2.95
❑23, Jun 1996 ... 2.95
❑24, Sep 1996 ... 2.95
❑25, Dec 1996 ... 2.95
❑26, Mar 1997 ... 2.95
❑27, May 1997 ... 2.95
❑28, Jul 1997 ... 2.95
❑29, Jan 1998 ... 2.95
❑30, Jun 1998; color and b&w ... 2.95

HATEBALL
FANTAGRAPHICS

❑1; giveaway ... 1.00

HATE JAMBOREE!
FANTAGRAPHICS

❑1, Oct 1998; newsprint cover ... 3.95

HAUNTED, THE
CHAOS

❑1, Jan 2002 ... 2.95
❑1/Ltd.; premium edition; Limited to 3,000 copies ... 2.95
❑2, Feb 2002 ... 2.95
❑3, Mar 2002 ... 2.95
❑4, Apr 2002 ... 2.95

HAUNTED MAN, THE
DARK HORSE

❑1, Mar 2000 ... 2.95
❑2 ... 2.95
❑3 ... 2.95

HAUNT OF FEAR, THE (GLADSTONE)
GLADSTONE

❑1, May 1991 ... 2.50
❑2, Jul 1991 ... 2.50

N-MINT

HAUNT OF FEAR (RCP)
COCHRAN

- ❑1, Sep 1991; Giant-size; Reprints Haunt of Fear #14, Weird Fantasy #13 .... 2.00
- ❑2, Nov 1991; Giant-size 2.00
- ❑3, Jan 1992; Giant-size 2.00
- ❑4, Mar 1992; Giant-size 2.00
- ❑5, May 1992; Giant-size 2.00

HAUNT OF FEAR, THE (RCP)
GEMSTONE

- ❑1, Nov 1992; Reprints The Haunt of Fear (EC) #1 .... 2.00
- ❑2, Feb 1993; Reprints The Haunt of Fear (EC) #2 .... 2.00
- ❑3, May 1993; Reprints The Haunt of Fear (EC) #3 .... 2.00
- ❑4, Aug 1993; Reprints The Haunt of Fear (EC) #4 .... 2.00
- ❑5, Nov 1993; Reprints The Haunt of Fear (EC) #5 .... 2.00
- ❑6, Feb 1994; Reprints The Haunt of Fear (EC) #6 .... 2.00
- ❑7, May 1994; Reprints The Haunt of Fear (EC) #7 .... 2.00
- ❑8, Aug 1994; Reprints The Haunt of Fear (EC) #8 .... 2.00
- ❑9, Nov 1994; Reprints The Haunt of Fear (EC) #9 .... 2.00
- ❑10, Feb 1995; Reprints The Haunt of Fear (EC) #10 .... 2.00
- ❑11, May 1995; Reprints The Haunt of Fear (EC) #11 .... 2.00
- ❑12, Aug 1995; Reprints The Haunt of Fear (EC) #12 .... 2.00
- ❑13, Nov 1995; Reprints The Haunt of Fear (EC) #13 .... 2.00
- ❑14, Feb 1996; O: The Old Witch. Reprints The Haunt of Fear (EC) #14 2.00
- ❑15, May 1996; Reprints The Haunt of Fear (EC) #15 .... 2.00
- ❑16, Aug 1996; GE, JKa, GI (w); GE, JKa, GI (a);Ray Bradbury story; Reprints The Haunt of Fear (EC) #16; Ray Bradbury adaptation 2.50
- ❑17, Nov 1996; GE, JKa, GI (w); GE, JKa, GI (a);Reprints The Haunt of Fear (EC) #17 .... 2.50
- ❑18, Feb 1997; GE, JKa, GI (w); GE, JKa, GI (a);Ray Bradbury story; Reprints The Haunt of Fear (EC) #18 2.50
- ❑19, May 1997; GE, JKa, GI (w); GE, JKa, GI (a);Reprints The Haunt of Fear (EC) #19; Mentioned in Seduction of the Innocent "A comic book baseball game" 2.50
- ❑20, Aug 1997; Reprints The Haunt of Fear (EC) #20 .... 2.50
- ❑21, Nov 1997; Reprints The Haunt of Fear (EC) #21 .... 2.50
- ❑22, Feb 1998; Reprints The Haunt of Fear (EC) #22 .... 2.50
- ❑23, May 1998; Reprints The Haunt of Fear (EC) #23 .... 2.50
- ❑24, Aug 1998; Reprints The Haunt of Fear (EC) #24 .... 2.50
- ❑25, Nov 1998; Reprints The Haunt of Fear (EC) #25 .... 2.50
- ❑26, Feb 1999; JKa, GI (w); JKa, GI (a);Reprints The Haunt of Fear (EC) #26 .... 2.50
- ❑27, May 1999; GE, JKa, GI (w); Reprints The Haunt of Fear (EC) #27 2.50
- ❑28, Aug 1999; BK, JKa, GI (w); BK, JKa, GI (a);Reprints The Haunt of Fear (EC) #28 .... 2.50
- ❑Annual 1; Reprints The Haunt of Fear #1-5 .... 8.95
- ❑Annual 2; Reprints The Haunt of Fear #6-10 .... 9.95
- ❑Annual 3; Reprints The Haunt of Fear #11-15 .... 10.95
- ❑Annual 4; Reprints The Haunt of Fear #16-20 .... 10.50
- ❑Annual 5; Reprints The Haunt of Fear #21-25 .... 11.95
- ❑Annual 6; JKa, GI (w); JKa, GI (a);Reprints The Haunt of Fear #26-28 .... 8.95

N-MINT

HAUNT OF HORROR
MARVEL

- ❑1, May 1974 .... 8.00
- ❑2, Jul 1974 .... 6.00
- ❑3, Sep 1974 .... 5.00
- ❑4, Nov 1974 .... 5.00
- ❑5, Jan 1975 .... 5.00

HAVEN: THE BROKEN CITY
DC

- ❑1, Feb 2002 .... 2.50
- ❑2, Mar 2002 .... 2.50
- ❑3, Apr 2002 .... 2.50
- ❑4, May 2002 .... 2.50
- ❑5, Jun 2002 .... 2.50
- ❑6, Jul 2002 .... 2.50
- ❑7, Aug 2002 .... 2.50
- ❑8, Sep 2002 .... 2.50
- ❑9, Oct 2002 .... 2.50

HAVOC, INC.
RADIO

- ❑1, Mar 1998 .... 2.95
- ❑2, Jun 1998 .... 2.95
- ❑3, Sep 1998 .... 2.95
- ❑4, Dec 1998 .... 2.95
- ❑5 1999 .... 2.95
- ❑6 1999 .... 2.95
- ❑7 .... 2.95
- ❑8, Jul 2000 .... 2.95
- ❑9 .... 2.95

HAVOK & WOLVERINE: MELTDOWN
MARVEL / EPIC

- ❑1, Mar 1989 .... 4.00
- ❑2, ca. 1989 .... 4.00
- ❑3, ca. 1989 .... 4.00
- ❑4, Oct 1989 .... 4.00

HAWAIIAN DICK
IMAGE

- ❑1, Dec 2002 .... 2.95
- ❑2, Feb 2003 .... 2.95
- ❑3, Apr 2003 .... 2.95

HAWK & THE DOVE, THE (1ST SERIES)
DC

- ❑1, Aug 1968 SD (a) 30.00
- ❑2, Oct 1968 DG (w); SD (a) 20.00
- ❑3, Dec 1968 DG (w); GK (a) 18.00
- ❑4, Feb 1969 DG (w); GK (a) 18.00
- ❑5, Mar 1969 DG (w); GK (a); A: Teen Titans. 18.00
- ❑6, Jun 1969 DG, GK (w); GK (a) 18.00

HAWK AND DOVE (2ND SERIES)
DC

- ❑1, Oct 1988 RL (a); 1: Dove II. 3.00
- ❑2, Nov 1988 RL (a) 2.50
- ❑3, Dec 1988 RL (a) 2.00
- ❑4, Win 1988 RL (a) 2.00
- ❑5, Hol 1989; RL (a); O: Dove. Hol 1989 2.00

HAWK AND DOVE (3RD SERIES)
DC

- ❑1, Jun 1989 .... 1.50
- ❑2, Jul 1989 .... 1.00
- ❑3, Aug 1989 .... 1.00
- ❑4, Sep 1989 .... 1.00
- ❑5, Oct 1989 .... 1.00
- ❑6, Nov 1989 .... 1.00
- ❑7, Dec 1989 .... 1.00
- ❑8, Jan 1990 .... 1.00
- ❑9, Feb 1990 .... 1.00
- ❑10, Mar 1990 .... 1.00
- ❑11, Apr 1990 .... 1.00
- ❑12, May 1990 A: New Titans. 1.00
- ❑13, Jun 1990 .... 1.00
- ❑14, Jul 1990 .... 1.00
- ❑15, Aug 1990 .... 1.00
- ❑16, Sep 1990 .... 1.00
- ❑17, Oct 1990 .... 1.00
- ❑18, Nov 1990 .... 1.00
- ❑19, Dec 1990 .... 1.00
- ❑20, Jan 1991 .... 1.00
- ❑21, Feb 1991 .... 1.00

N-MINT

- ❑22, Mar 1991 .... 1.00
- ❑23, Apr 1991 .... 1.00
- ❑24, May 1991 .... 1.00
- ❑25, Jun 1991; Giant-size 2.00
- ❑26, Aug 1992 O: Hawk and Dove. 1.25
- ❑27, Sep 1991 .... 1.25
- ❑28, Oct 1991; Giant-size; War of the Gods 2.00
- ❑Annual 1, Oct 1990; Titans West 2.00
- ❑Annual 2, Sep 1991; Armageddon 2001 .... 2.00

HAWK AND DOVE (4TH SERIES)
DC

- ❑1, Nov 1997 .... 2.50
- ❑2, Dec 1997 .... 2.50
- ❑3, Jan 1998 .... 2.50
- ❑4, Feb 1998 .... 2.50
- ❑5, Mar 1998 .... 2.50

HAWK & WINDBLADE
WARP

- ❑1, Aug 1997 .... 2.95
- ❑2, Sep 1997 .... 2.95

HAWKEYE (1ST SERIES)
MARVEL

- ❑1, Sep 1983 O: Hawkeye. 2.50
- ❑2, Oct 1983 .... 2.00
- ❑3, Nov 1983 1: Oddball. 2.00
- ❑4, Dec 1983 .... 2.00

HAWKEYE (2ND SERIES)
MARVEL

- ❑1, Jan 1994 .... 1.75
- ❑2, Feb 1994 .... 1.75
- ❑3, Mar 1994 .... 1.75
- ❑4, Apr 1994 .... 1.75

HAWKEYE (3RD SERIES)
MARVEL

- ❑1, Dec 2003 .... 2.99
- ❑2, Jan 2004 .... 2.99
- ❑3, Feb 2004 .... 2.99
- ❑4, Mar 2004 .... 2.99
- ❑5, Apr 2004 .... 2.99
- ❑6, May 2004 .... 2.99
- ❑7, Jun 2004 .... 2.99
- ❑8, Aug 2004 .... 2.99

HAWKEYE: EARTH'S MIGHTIEST MARKSMAN
MARVEL

- ❑1, Oct 1998 .... 2.99

HAWKMAN (1ST SERIES)
DC

- ❑1, May 1964 MA (a) 350.00
- ❑2, Jul 1964 MA (a) 140.00
- ❑3, Sep 1964 MA (a) 85.00
- ❑4, Nov 1964 MA (a); O: Zatanna. 1: Zatanna. 140.00
- ❑5, Jan 1965 MA (a) 85.00
- ❑6, Mar 1965 MA (a) 65.00
- ❑7, May 1965; MA (a);reprint from Mystery in Space #87 .... 65.00
- ❑8, Jul 1965 MA (a) 65.00
- ❑9, Sep 1965; MA (a); A: Atom. Atom & Hawkman learn identities 65.00
- ❑10, Nov 1965 MA (a) 65.00
- ❑11, Jan 1966 MA (a) 50.00
- ❑12, Mar 1966 MA (a) 50.00
- ❑13, May 1966 MA (a) 50.00
- ❑14, Jul 1966 MA (a) 50.00
- ❑15, Sep 1966 MA (a) 50.00
- ❑16, Nov 1966 MA (a) 36.00
- ❑17, Jan 1967 MA (a) 36.00
- ❑18, Mar 1967; MA (a); A: Adam Strange. V: Manhawks. Part 1 .... 36.00
- ❑19, May 1967; MA (a);Part 2 .... 36.00
- ❑20, Jul 1967 MA (a) 32.00
- ❑21, Sep 1967 MA (a) 32.00
- ❑22, Nov 1967 DD (a) 32.00
- ❑23, Jan 1968 DD (a) 32.00
- ❑24, Mar 1968; DD (a);Reprint story . 32.00
- ❑25, May 1968; DD (a);Golden Age Hawkman reprint 32.00

N-MINT

❑26, Jul 1968; DD (a);reprints 2-page Kirby story 32.00
❑27, Sep 1968 DD (a) 32.00

HAWKMAN (2ND SERIES)
DC

❑1, Aug 1986 RHo (a) 2.50
❑2, Sep 1986 RHo (a); V: Shadow Thief. 2.00
❑3, Oct 1986 RHo (a); V: Shadow Thief. 2.00
❑4, Nov 1986 RHo (a); A: Zatanna. 1.50
❑5, Dec 1986 RHo (a); V: Lionmane. 1.50
❑6, Jan 1987 RHo (a); V: Lionmane. 1.50
❑7, Feb 1987 V: Darkwing. 1.50
❑8, Mar 1987 V: Darkwing. 1.50
❑9, Apr 1987 .... 1.50
❑10, May 1987 A: Superman. 1.50
❑11, Jun 1987 .... 1.50
❑12, Jul 1987 .... 1.50
❑13, Aug 1987 .... 1.50
❑14, Sep 1987 .... 1.50
❑15, Oct 1987 .... 1.50
❑16, Nov 1987 .... 1.50
❑17, Dec 1987 .... 1.50
❑Special 1, Mar 1986 RHo (w); RHo (a) 1.50

HAWKMAN (3RD SERIES)
DC

❑0, Oct 1994 O: Hawkman (new). 2.50
❑1, Sep 1993; JDu (a);foil cover 2.50
❑2, Oct 1993 JDu (a) 1.75
❑3, Nov 1993 JDu (a) 1.75
❑4, Dec 1993 JDu (a) 1.75
❑5, Jan 1994 .... 1.75
❑6, Feb 1994 .... 1.75
❑7, Mar 1994 LMc (a) 1.75
❑8, Apr 1994 LMc (a) 1.75
❑9, May 1994 .... 1.75
❑10, Jun 1994 .... 1.75
❑11, Jul 1994 A: Carter Hall. 1.75
❑12, Aug 1994 .... 1.95
❑13, Sep 1994; Zero Hour 1.95
❑14, Nov 1994 .... 1.95
❑15, Dec 1994 A: Aquaman. 1.95
❑16, Jan 1995 A: Wonder Woman. 1.95
❑17, Feb 1995 .... 1.95
❑18, May 1995 .... 1.95
❑19, Apr 1995 .... 1.95
❑20, May 1995 .... 1.95
❑21, Jun 1995 V: Shadow Thief. V: Gentleman Ghost. 2.25
❑22, Jul 1995 .... 2.25
❑23, Aug 1995 .... 2.25
❑24, Sep 1995 .... 2.25
❑25, Oct 1995 .... 2.25
❑26, Nov 1995; A: Scarecrow. Underworld Unleashed 2.25
❑27, Dec 1995; A: Neuron. A: Silent Knight. Underworld Unleashed 2.25
❑28, Jan 1996 V: Dr. Polaris. V: Doctor Polaris. 2.25
❑29, Feb 1996 A: Vandal Savage. 2.25
❑30, Mar 1996 .... 2.25
❑31, Apr 1996 .... 2.25
❑32, Jun 1996 .... 2.25
❑33, Jul 1996 A: Arion. D: Hawkman. 2.25
❑Annual 1, ca. 1993 JDu (a); 1: Mongrel. 3.50
❑Annual 2, ca. 1995; Year One 3.95

HAWKMAN (4TH SERIES)
DC

❑1, May 2002 .... 3.00
❑2, Jun 2002 .... 2.50
❑3, Jul 2002 .... 2.50
❑4, Aug 2002 .... 2.50
❑5, Sep 2002 .... 2.50
❑6, Oct 2002 JRo (w) 2.50
❑7, Nov 2002 JRo (w) 2.50
❑8, Dec 2002 .... 2.50
❑9, Jan 2003 .... 2.50
❑10, Feb 2003 .... 2.50
❑11, Mar 2003 .... 2.50
❑12, Apr 2003 .... 2.50
❑13, May 2003 .... 2.50
❑14, Jun 2003 .... 2.50
❑15, Jul 2003 .... 2.50
❑16, Aug 2003 .... 2.50
❑17, Sep 2003 .... 2.50
❑18, Oct 2003 .... 2.50
❑19, Nov 2003 .... 2.50
❑20, Dec 2003 .... 2.50
❑21, Jan 2004 .... 2.50
❑22, Jan 2004 .... 2.50
❑23, Feb 2004 .... 2.50
❑24, Mar 2004 .... 2.50
❑25, Apr 2004 .... 2.50
❑26, May 2004 .... 2.50
❑27, Jun 2004 .... 2.50
❑28, Jul 2004 .... 2.50
❑29, Aug 2004 .... 2.50
❑30, Sep 2004 .... 2.50

HAWKMAN SECRET FILES AND ORIGINS
DC

❑1, Oct 2002, b&w 4.95

HAWKMOON: THE JEWEL IN THE SKULL
FIRST

❑1, May 1986 .... 1.75
❑2, Jul 1986 .... 1.75
❑3, Sep 1986 .... 1.75
❑4, Nov 1986 .... 1.75

HAWKMOON: THE MAD GOD'S AMULET
FIRST

❑1, Jan 1987 .... 1.75
❑2, Feb 1987 .... 1.75
❑3, Mar 1987 .... 1.75
❑4, Apr 1987 .... 1.75

HAWKMOON: THE RUNESTAFF
FIRST

❑1, ca. 1988 .... 2.00
❑2, ca. 1988 .... 2.00
❑3, ca. 1988 .... 2.00
❑4, ca. 1988 .... 2.00

HAWKMOON: THE SWORD OF THE DAWN
FIRST

❑1, Sep 1987 .... 1.75
❑2, Nov 1987 .... 1.75
❑3, Jan 1988 .... 1.75
❑4, Mar 1988 .... 1.75

HAWKSHAWS
IMAGE

❑1, Mar 2000, b&w 2.95

HAWK, STREET AVENGER
TAURUS

❑1, Jun 1996, b&w 2.50

HAWKWORLD (MINI-SERIES)
DC

❑1, Aug 1989; O: Hawkman. New costume 4.00
❑2, Sep 1989 .... 4.00
❑3, Oct 1989 .... 4.00

HAWKWORLD
DC

❑1, Jun 1990 .... 2.50
❑2, Jul 1990 .... 2.00
❑3, Aug 1990 .... 2.00
❑4, Sep 1990 .... 2.00
❑5, Oct 1990 .... 2.00
❑6, Dec 1990 .... 2.00
❑7, Jan 1991 .... 2.00
❑8, Feb 1991 .... 2.00
❑9, Mar 1991 .... 2.00
❑10, Apr 1991 .... 2.00
❑11, May 1991 .... 1.50
❑12, Jun 1991 .... 1.50
❑13, Jul 1991 .... 1.50
❑14, Aug 1991 .... 1.50
❑15, Sep 1991; War of the Gods 1.50
❑16, Oct 1991; War of the Gods 1.50
❑17, Nov 1991 .... 1.50

The Old Witch's origin story can be found in Russ Cochran's reprint of *Haunt of Fear,* which includes *Haunt of Fear* #14 and *Weird Fantasy* #13.

© 1991 Russ Cochran and E.C.

N-MINT

❑18, Dec 1991 .... 1.50
❑19, Jan 1992 .... 1.50
❑20, Feb 1992 .... 1.50
❑21, Mar 1992 .... 1.50
❑22, Apr 1992 .... 1.50
❑23, May 1992 .... 1.50
❑24, Jul 1992 .... 1.50
❑25, Aug 1992 .... 1.50
❑26, Sep 1992 .... 1.50
❑27, Oct 1992 1: The White Dragon. 1.75
❑28, Nov 1992 JDu (a) 1.75
❑29, Dec 1992 .... 1.75
❑30, Jan 1993 1: Count Viper. 1: The Netherworld. 1.75
❑31, Feb 1993 .... 1.75
❑32, Mar 1993 .... 1.75
❑Annual 1, Dec 1990 A: Flash. 3.00
❑Annual 2, Aug 1991 .... 2.95
❑Annual 2-2, Aug 1991; silver 2.95
❑Annual 3, ca. 1992; LMc (a);Eclipso 2.95

HAYWIRE
DC

❑1, Oct 1988 .... 1.25
❑2, Nov 1988 .... 1.25
❑3, Dec 1988 .... 1.25
❑4, Dec 1988 .... 1.25
❑5, Jan 1989 .... 1.25
❑6, Jan 1989 .... 1.25
❑7, Mar 1989 .... 1.25
❑8, Apr 1989 .... 1.25
❑9, May 1989 .... 1.25
❑10, Jun 1989 .... 1.25
❑11, Jul 1989 .... 1.25
❑12, Aug 1989 .... 1.25
❑13, Sep 1989 .... 1.25

HAZARD
IMAGE

❑1, Jun 1996 .... 1.75
❑2, Jul 1996; cover says Jun, indicia says Jul 1.75
❑3, Jul 1996 .... 1.75
❑4, Aug 1996 .... 1.75
❑5, Sep 1996 .... 1.75
❑6, Oct 1996; cover says Sep, indicia says Oct 2.25
❑7, Nov 1996 .... 2.25

HAZARD! (MOTION)
MOTION

❑1, b&w; Breakneck Blvd. 2.50

HAZARD! (RECKLESS VISION)
RECKLESS VISION

❑1, b&w; first Breakneck Blvd. Story 2.50

H-BOMB
ANTARCTIC

❑1, Apr 1993, b&w 2.95

HEADBANGER
PARODY

❑1 .... 2.50

HEADBUSTER
ANTARCTIC

❑1, Sep 1998, b&w 2.95

HEADHUNTERS
IMAGE

❑1, Apr 1997, b&w; cover says Mar, indicia says Apr 2.95

Condition price index: Multiply "NM prices" above by: **0.83 for Very Fine/Near Mint**
0.66 for Very Fine • 0.33 for Fine • 0.2 for Very Good • 0.125 for Good

N-MINT

❑2, May 1997, b&w ... 2.95
❑3, Jun 1997, b&w ... 2.95

HEADLESS HORSEMAN
ETERNITY

❑1, b&w ... 2.25
❑2, b&w ... 2.25

HEADMAN
INNOVATION

❑1 ... 2.50

HEALTH
DAVID TOMPKINS

❑1 ... 1.00
❑2 ... 1.50
❑3 ... 1.50
❑4 ... 2.00
❑5 ... 2.00
❑6 ... 5.00

HEAP
SKYWALD

❑1, Sep 1971 TS, JAb (a) ... 16.00

HEARTBREAK COMICS
ECLIPSE

❑1, b&w; magazine ... 3.95

HEARTBREAKERS
DARK HORSE

❑1, Apr 1996 ... 2.95
❑2, May 1996 ... 2.95
❑3, Jun 1996 ... 2.95
❑4, Jul 1996 ... 2.95

HEARTLAND
DC / VERTIGO

❑1, Mar 1997 ... 4.95

HEART OF DARKNESS
HARDLINE

❑1 ... 2.95

HEART OF EMPIRE
DARK HORSE

❑1, Apr 1999 ... 2.95
❑2, May 1999 ... 2.95
❑3, Jun 1999 ... 2.95
❑4, Jul 1999 ... 2.95
❑5, Aug 1999 ... 2.95
❑6, Sep 1999 ... 2.95
❑7, Oct 1999 ... 2.95
❑8, Nov 1999 ... 2.95
❑9, Dec 1999 ... 2.95

HEARTS OF DARKNESS
MARVEL

❑1, Dec 1991; Ghost Rider, Wolverine, and Punisher vs. Blackheart ... 4.95

HEART THROBS
DC

❑44 1956 ... 18.00
❑45 1957 ... 18.00
❑46 1957 ... 18.00
❑47, May 1957; DC begins as publisher ... 125.00
❑48, Jul 1957 ... 65.00
❑49, Sep 1957 ... 60.00
❑50, Nov 1957 ... 60.00
❑51, Jan 1958 ... 48.00
❑52, Mar 1958 ... 48.00
❑53, May 1958 ... 48.00
❑54, Jul 1958 ... 48.00
❑55, Sep 1958 ... 48.00
❑56, Nov 1958 ... 48.00
❑57, Jan 1959 ... 48.00
❑58, Feb 1959 ... 48.00
❑59, May 1959 ... 48.00
❑60, Jul 1959 ... 48.00
❑61, Sep 1959 ... 38.00
❑62, Nov 1959 ... 38.00
❑63, Jan 1960 ... 38.00
❑64, Mar 1960 ... 38.00
❑65, May 1960 ... 38.00
❑66, Jul 1960 ... 38.00
❑67, Sep 1960 ... 38.00
❑68, Nov 1960 ... 38.00
❑69, Jan 1961 ... 38.00
❑70, Mar 1961 ... 38.00
❑71, May 1961 ... 27.00
❑72, Jul 1961 ... 27.00
❑73, Sep 1961 ... 27.00
❑74, Nov 1961 ... 27.00
❑75, Jan 1962 ... 27.00
❑76, Mar 1962 ... 27.00
❑77, May 1962 ... 27.00
❑78, Jul 1962 ... 27.00
❑79, Sep 1962 ... 27.00
❑80, Nov 1962 ... 27.00
❑81, Jan 1963 ... 20.00
❑82, Mar 1963 ... 20.00
❑83, May 1963 ... 20.00
❑84, Jul 1963 ... 20.00
❑85, Sep 1963 ... 20.00
❑86, Nov 1963 ... 20.00
❑87, Jan 1964 ... 20.00
❑88, Mar 1964 ... 20.00
❑89, May 1964 ... 20.00
❑90, Jul 1964 ... 20.00
❑91, Sep 1964 ... 16.00
❑92, Nov 1964 ... 16.00
❑93, Jan 1965 ... 16.00
❑94, Mar 1965 ... 16.00
❑95, May 1965 ... 16.00
❑96, Jul 1965 ... 16.00
❑97, Sep 1965 ... 16.00
❑98, Nov 1965 ... 16.00
❑99, Jan 1966 ... 16.00
❑100, Mar 1966 ... 16.00
❑101, May 1966; A: The Beatles. Beauty column begins; Beatles mentioned on cover ... 60.00
❑102, Jul 1966 ... 13.00
❑103, Sep 1966; 3 Girls: Their Lives, Their Loves ... 13.00
❑104, Nov 1966 ... 13.00
❑105, Jan 1967; Mod fashion column debuts; 3 Girls: Their Lives, Their Loves ... 13.00
❑106, Mar 1967 ... 13.00
❑107, May 1967 ... 13.00
❑108, Jul 1967; 3 Girls: Their Lives, Their Loves ... 13.00
❑109, Sep 1967 ... 13.00
❑110, Nov 1967 ... 13.00
❑111, Jan 1968 ... 10.00
❑112, Mar 1968 ... 10.00
❑113, May 1968 ... 10.00
❑114, Jul 1968 ... 10.00
❑115, Sep 1968 ... 10.00
❑116, Nov 1968 ... 10.00
❑117, Jan 1969 ... 10.00
❑118, Mar 1969 ... 10.00
❑119, May 1969 ... 10.00
❑120, Jul 1969 ... 10.00
❑121, Sep 1969 ... 10.00
❑122, Nov 1969 ... 10.00
❑123, Jan 1970 ... 10.00
❑124, Mar 1970 ... 10.00
❑125, May 1970 ... 10.00
❑126, Jul 1970 ... 10.00
❑127, Sep 1970 ... 10.00
❑128, Nov 1970 ... 10.00
❑129, Jan 1971 ... 10.00
❑130, Mar 1971 ... 10.00
❑131, May 1971 ... 9.00
❑132, Jul 1971 ... 9.00
❑133, Sep 1971 ... 9.00
❑134, Oct 1971 ... 9.00
❑135, Nov 1971 ... 9.00
❑136, Dec 1971 ... 9.00
❑137, Jan 1972 ... 9.00
❑138, Feb 1972 ... 9.00
❑139, Mar 1972 ... 9.00
❑140, Apr 1972 ... 9.00
❑141, May 1972 ... 9.00
❑142, Jun 1972 ... 9.00
❑143, Jul 1972 ... 9.00
❑144, Aug 1972 ... 9.00
❑145, Sep 1972 ... 9.00
❑146, Oct 1972; Series continues as Love Stories ... 9.00

HEARTTHROBS (VERTIGO)
DC / VERTIGO

❑1, Jan 1999 ... 2.95
❑2, Feb 1999 ... 2.95
❑3, Mar 1999 ... 2.95
❑4, Apr 1999 ... 2.95

HEATHCLIFF
MARVEL / STAR

❑1, Apr 1985 ... 1.50
❑2, Jun 1985 ... 1.00
❑3, Aug 1985 ... 1.00
❑4, Oct 1985 ... 1.00
❑5, Dec 1985 ... 1.00
❑6, Feb 1986 ... 1.00
❑7, Apr 1986 ... 1.00
❑8, Jun 1986 ... 1.00
❑9, Aug 1986 ... 1.00
❑10, Sep 1986 ... 1.00
❑11, Oct 1986 ... 1.00
❑12, Nov 1986 ... 1.00
❑13, Dec 1986 ... 1.00
❑14, Feb 1987 ... 1.00
❑15, Apr 1987 ... 1.00
❑16, Jun 1987 ... 1.00
❑17, Aug 1987 ... 1.00
❑18, Sep 1987 ... 1.00
❑19, Oct 1987 ... 1.00
❑20, Nov 1987 ... 1.00
❑21, Dec 1987 ... 1.00
❑22, Feb 1988 ... 1.00
❑23, Apr 1988 ... 1.00
❑24, Jun 1988 ... 1.00
❑25, Aug 1988 ... 1.00
❑26, Sep 1988 ... 1.00
❑27, Oct 1988 ... 1.00
❑28, Nov 1988 ... 1.00
❑29, Dec 1988 ... 1.00
❑30, Feb 1989 ... 1.00
❑31, Mar 1989 ... 1.00
❑32, Apr 1989 ... 1.00
❑33, May 1989 ... 1.00
❑34, Jun 1989 ... 1.00
❑35, Jul 1989 ... 1.00
❑36, Aug 1989 ... 1.00
❑37, Sep 1989 ... 1.00
❑38, Oct 1989 ... 1.00
❑39, Nov 1989 ... 1.00
❑40, Nov 1989 ... 1.00
❑41, Dec 1989 ... 1.00
❑42, Dec 1989 ... 1.00
❑43, Jan 1990 ... 1.00
❑44, Feb 1990 ... 1.00
❑45, Mar 1990 ... 1.00
❑46, Apr 1990 ... 1.00
❑47, May 1990; Batman parody ... 1.00
❑48, Jun 1990 ... 1.00
❑49, Jul 1990 ... 1.00
❑50, Aug 1990; Giant-size; giant ... 1.50
❑51, Sep 1990 ... 1.00
❑52, Oct 1990 ... 1.00
❑53, Nov 1990 ... 1.00
❑54, Dec 1990 ... 1.00
❑55, Jan 1991 ... 1.00
❑56, Feb 1991 ... 1.00
❑Annual 1, ca. 1987 ... 1.25

HEATHCLIFF'S FUNHOUSE
MARVEL / STAR

❑1, May 1987 ... 1.25
❑2, Jun 1987 ... 1.00
❑3, Jul 1987 ... 1.00
❑4, Aug 1987 ... 1.00
❑5, Sep 1987 ... 1.00
❑6, Oct 1987 ... 1.00
❑7, Nov 1987 ... 1.00
❑8, Dec 1987 ... 1.00
❑9, Jan 1988 ... 1.00
❑10, Feb 1988 ... 1.00

HEATSEEKER
FANTACO

❑1 ... 5.95

N-MINT

HEAVEN LLC
IMAGE

❑1, ca 2004 .... 12.95

HEAVEN'S DEVILS
IMAGE

❑1, Oct 2003 .... 2.95
❑2, Nov 2003 .... 3.50
❑3, Apr 2004 .... 3.50

HEAVEN SENT
ANTARCTIC

❑1, Jan 2004 .... 2.99
❑2 2004 .... 2.99
❑3, May 2004 .... 2.99

HEAVEN'S WAR
IMAGE

❑0, ca. 2003 .... 12.95

HEAVY ARMOR
FANTASY GENERAL

❑1 .... 1.70
❑2 .... 1.70
❑3, b&w 1.70

HEAVY HITTERS
MARVEL / EPIC

❑Annual 1 1993 .... 3.75

HEAVY LIQUID
DC / VERTIGO

❑1, Oct 1999 .... 5.95
❑2, Nov 1999 .... 5.95
❑3, Dec 1999 .... 5.95
❑4, Jan 2000 .... 5.95
❑5, Feb 2000 .... 5.95

HEAVY METAL MONSTERS
REVOLUTIONARY

❑1, Jan 1992, b&w 3.00
❑2, ca. 1993; 3-D 3.95

HECKLE AND JECKLE (GOLD KEY)
GOLD KEY

❑1, Nov 1962 .... 36.00
❑2, Jan 1963 .... 18.00
❑3, Dec 1962 .... 16.00
❑4, Feb 1963 .... 16.00

HECKLE AND JECKLE (DELL)
DELL

❑1, May 1966 .... 25.00
❑2, Oct 1966 .... 13.00
❑3, Aug 1967 .... 13.00

HECKLER, THE
DC

❑1, Sep 1992 .... 1.25
❑2, Oct 1992; Generic issue 1.25
❑3, Nov 1992 .... 1.25
❑4, Dec 1992 .... 1.25
❑5, Jan 1993 .... 1.25
❑6, Feb 1993 .... 1.25

HECTIC PLANET
SLAVE LABOR

❑6, Nov 1993; previously titled Pirate Corp$! 2.50
❑6-2, Jan 1996 .... 2.75

HECTOR HEATHCOTE
GOLD KEY

❑1, Mar 1964; Based on Terrytoons cartoon series 30.00

HEDGE KNIGHT
IMAGE

❑1, Aug 2003 .... 2.95
❑2, Sep 2003 .... 2.95
❑2/A, Sep 2003; Vallejo cover 5.95
❑3, Feb 2004 .... 2.95

HEE HAW
CHARLTON

❑1, Aug 1970 .... 13.00
❑2, Oct 1970 .... 8.00
❑3, Dec 1970 .... 6.00
❑4, Feb 1971 .... 6.00
❑5, Apr 1971 .... 6.00
❑6, Jun 1971 .... 6.00
❑7, Aug 1971 .... 6.00

N-MINT

HEIRS OF ETERNITY
IMAGE

❑1, Apr 2003 .... 2.95
❑2, Jun 2003 .... 2.95
❑3, Jul 2003 .... 2.95
❑4, Aug 2003 .... 2.95
❑5, Sep 2003 .... 2.95

HE IS JUST A RAT
EXCLAIM! BRAND COMICS

❑1, Spr 1995 .... 2.75
❑2, Fal 1995 .... 2.75
❑3, Spr 1996 .... 2.75
❑4, Fal 1996 .... 2.75
❑5, Spr 1997 .... 2.75

HELL
DARK HORSE

❑1, Jul 2003 .... 2.99
❑2, Sep 2003 .... 2.99
❑3, Oct 2003 .... 2.99
❑4, Mar 2004 .... 2.99

HELLBENDER
ETERNITY

❑1, b&w; Shuriken 2.25

HELLBLAZER
DC

❑1, Jan 1988 .... 7.00
❑2, Feb 1988 .... 5.00
❑3, Mar 1988 .... 4.00
❑4, Apr 1988 .... 4.00
❑5, May 1988 .... 4.00
❑6, Jun 1988 .... 4.00
❑7, Jul 1988 .... 4.00
❑8, Aug 1988 AA (a) 4.00
❑9, Sep 1988; AA (a); A: Swamp Thing. Continues in Swamp Thing #76 .... 4.00
❑10, Oct 1988; A: Swamp Thing, Abby. Continues from Swamp Thing #76 .... 4.00
❑11, Nov 1988 .... 3.50
❑12, Dec 1988 .... 3.50
❑13, Dec 1988; References to British comics 3.50
❑14, Jan 1989 .... 3.00
❑15, Jan 1989 .... 3.00
❑16, Feb 1989 .... 3.00
❑17, Apr 1989 .... 3.00
❑18, May 1989 AA (a) 3.00
❑19, Jun 1989 AA (a) 3.00
❑20, Jul 1989 AA (a) 3.00
❑21, Aug 1989 AA (a) 2.50
❑22, Sep 1989 AA (a) 2.50
❑23, Oct 1989 A: Sherlock Holmes. 2.50
❑24, Nov 1989 .... 2.50
❑25, Jan 1990 .... 2.50
❑26, Feb 1990 .... 2.50
❑27, Mar 1990 NG (w) 9.00
❑28, Apr 1990 D: Thomas Constantine. 3.00
❑29, May 1990 .... 3.00
❑30, Jun 1990 .... 3.00
❑31, Jul 1990 .... 3.00
❑32, Aug 1990 .... 3.00
❑33, Sep 1990 .... 3.00
❑34, Oct 1990 .... 3.00
❑35, Nov 1990 .... 3.00
❑36, Dec 1990 .... 3.00
❑37, Jan 1991 .... 3.00
❑38, Feb 1991 .... 3.00
❑39, Mar 1991 .... 3.00
❑40, Apr 1991 .... 3.50
❑41, May 1991; 1st Garth Ennis story 6.00
❑42, Jun 1991 .... 4.00
❑43, Jul 1991 .... 4.00
❑44, Aug 1991 .... 4.00
❑45, Sep 1991 .... 4.00
❑46, Oct 1991 .... 4.00
❑47, Nov 1991 .... 3.00
❑48, Dec 1991 .... 3.00
❑49, Jan 1992 .... 3.00
❑50, Feb 1992; Giant-size 4.00
❑51, Mar 1992 .... 3.00
❑52, Apr 1992 .... 3.00
❑53, May 1992 .... 3.00

Incarnations of Hawkman (and such predecessors as The Silent Knight) were merged into one being in *Hawkman* #0.
© 1994 DC Comics.

N-MINT

❑54, Jun 1992 .... 3.00
❑55, Jul 1992 .... 3.00
❑56, Aug 1992 .... 3.00
❑57, Sep 1992 .... 3.00
❑58, Oct 1992 .... 3.00
❑59, Nov 1992 .... 3.00
❑60, Dec 1992 .... 3.00
❑61, Jan 1993 .... 3.00
❑62, Feb 1993 D: Talks About Life AIDS-awareness insert. 3.00
❑63, Mar 1993 .... 3.00
❑64, Apr 1993 .... 3.00
❑65, May 1993 .... 3.00
❑66, Jun 1993 .... 3.00
❑67, Jul 1993 .... 3.00
❑68, Aug 1993 .... 3.00
❑69, Sep 1993 .... 3.00
❑70, Oct 1993 .... 3.00
❑71, Nov 1993 .... 3.00
❑72, Dec 1993 .... 3.00
❑73, Jan 1994 .... 3.00
❑74, Feb 1994 .... 3.00
❑75, Mar 1994; Double-size 3.50
❑76, Apr 1994 .... 3.00
❑77, May 1994 .... 3.00
❑78, Jun 1994 .... 3.00
❑79, Jul 1994 .... 3.00
❑80, Aug 1994 .... 3.00
❑81, Sep 1994 .... 3.00
❑82, Oct 1994 .... 3.00
❑83, Nov 1994 .... 3.00
❑84, Dec 1994 .... 3.00
❑85, Jan 1995 .... 3.00
❑86, Feb 1995 .... 3.00
❑87, Mar 1995 .... 3.00
❑88, Apr 1995 .... 3.00
❑89, May 1995 .... 3.00
❑90, Jun 1995 .... 3.00
❑91, Jul 1995 .... 3.00
❑92, Aug 1995 .... 3.00
❑93, Sep 1995 .... 3.00
❑94, Oct 1995 .... 3.00
❑95, Nov 1995 .... 3.00
❑96, Dec 1995 .... 3.00
❑97, Jan 1996 .... 3.00
❑98, Feb 1996 .... 3.00
❑99, Mar 1996 .... 3.00
❑100, Apr 1996 .... 3.00
❑101, May 1996 .... 2.50
❑102, Jun 1996 .... 2.50
❑103, Jul 1996 .... 2.50
❑104, Aug 1996 .... 2.50
❑105, Sep 1996 .... 2.50
❑106, Oct 1996 .... 2.50
❑107, Nov 1996 .... 2.50
❑108, Dec 1996 .... 2.50
❑109, Jan 1997 .... 2.50
❑110, Feb 1997 .... 2.50
❑111, Mar 1997 .... 2.50
❑112, Apr 1997 .... 2.50
❑113, May 1997 .... 2.50
❑114, Jun 1997 .... 2.50
❑115, Jul 1997 .... 2.50
❑116, Aug 1997 .... 2.50
❑117, Sep 1997 .... 2.50
❑118, Oct 1997 .... 2.50
❑119, Nov 1997 .... 2.50

N-MINT

❑120, Dec 1997; Giant-size A: Alan Moore. 2.50
❑121, Jan 1998 2.50
❑122, Feb 1998 2.50
❑123, Mar 1998 2.50
❑124, Apr 1998 2.50
❑125, May 1998 2.50
❑126, Jun 1998 2.50
❑127, Jul 1998 2.50
❑128, Aug 1998 2.50
❑129, Sep 1998 2.50
❑130, Oct 1998 2.50
❑131, Nov 1998 2.50
❑132, Dec 1998 2.50
❑133, Jan 1999 2.50
❑134, Feb 1999 2.50
❑135, Mar 1999 2.50
❑136, Apr 1999 2.50
❑137, May 1999 2.50
❑138, Jun 1999 2.50
❑139, Jul 1999 2.50
❑140, Aug 1999 2.50
❑141, Oct 1999 2.50
❑142, Nov 1999 2.50
❑143, Dec 1999 2.50
❑144, Jan 2000 2.50
❑145, Feb 2000 2.50
❑146, Mar 2000 2.50
❑147, Apr 2000 2.50
❑148, May 2000 2.50
❑149, Jun 2000 2.50
❑150, Jul 2000 2.50
❑151, Aug 2000 2.50
❑152, Sep 2000 2.50
❑153, Oct 2000 2.50
❑154, Nov 2000 2.50
❑155, Dec 2000 2.50
❑156, Jan 2001 2.50
❑157, Feb 2001 2.50
❑158, Mar 2001 2.50
❑159, Apr 2001 2.50
❑160, May 2001 2.50
❑161, Jun 2001 2.50
❑162, Jul 2001 2.50
❑163, Aug 2001 2.50
❑164, Sep 2001 2.50
❑165, Oct 2001 2.50
❑166, Nov 2001 2.50
❑167, Dec 2001 2.50
❑168, Jan 2002 2.50
❑169, Feb 2002 2.50
❑170, Mar 2002 2.50
❑171, Apr 2002 2.50
❑172, May 2002 2.50
❑173, Jun 2002 2.50
❑174, Aug 2002 2.50
❑175, Sep 2002 2.50
❑176, Oct 2002 2.75
❑177, Dec 2002 2.75
❑178, Jan 2003 2.75
❑179, Feb 2003 2.75
❑180, Mar 2003 2.75
❑181, Apr 2003 2.75
❑182, May 2003 2.75
❑183, Jun 2003 2.75
❑184, Jul 2003 2.75
❑185, Aug 2003 2.75
❑186, Sep 2003 2.75
❑187, Oct 2003 2.75
❑188, Nov 2003 2.75
❑189, Dec 2003 2.75
❑190, Jan 2004 2.75
❑191, Feb 2004 2.75
❑192, Mar 2004 2.75
❑193, Apr 2004 2.75
❑194, May 2004 2.75
❑195, Jun 2004 2.75
❑196, Jul 2004 2.75
❑197, Aug 2004 2.75
❑198, Sep 2004

N-MINT

❑Annual 1, Oct 1989 BT (a) 6.00
❑Special 1, Jan 1993 5.00

HELLBLAZER SPECIAL: BAD BLOOD
DC / VERTIGO

❑1, Sep 2000 2.95
❑2, Oct 2000 2.95
❑3, Nov 2000 2.95
❑4, Dec 2000 2.95

HELLBLAZER SPECIAL: LADY CONSTANTINE
DC / VERTIGO

❑1, Feb 2003 2.95
❑2, Mar 2003 2.95
❑3, Apr 2003 2.95
❑4, May 2003 2.95

HELLBLAZER/THE BOOKS OF MAGIC
DC / VERTIGO

❑1, Dec 1997 3.50
❑2, Jan 1998 3.50

HELLBOY: ALMOST COLOSSUS
DARK HORSE / LEGEND

❑1, Jun 1997 2.95
❑2, Jul 1997 2.95

HELLBOY: ART OF THE MOVIE
DARK HORSE

❑1, ca 2004 24.95

HELLBOY: BOX FULL OF EVIL
DARK HORSE / MAVERICK

❑1, Aug 1999 2.95
❑2, Sep 1999 2.95

HELLBOY CHRISTMAS SPECIAL
DARK HORSE

❑1, Dec 1997 4.00

HELLBOY: CONQUEROR WORM
DARK HORSE / MAVERICK

❑1, May 2001 2.99
❑2, Jun 2001 2.99
❑3, Jul 2001 2.99
❑4, Aug 2001 2.99

HELLBOY, THE CORPSE AND THE IRON SHOES
DARK HORSE / LEGEND

❑1; collects the story serialized in the distributor catalog Advance Comics #75-82 3.50

HELLBOY JR.
DARK HORSE

❑1, Oct 1999 2.95
❑2, Nov 1999 2.95

HELLBOY JR. HALLOWEEN SPECIAL
DARK HORSE

❑1, Oct 1997; Hellboy Jr. pinup; wrap-around cover 3.95

HELLBOY: SEED OF DESTRUCTION
DARK HORSE / LEGEND

❑1, Mar 1994 O: Hellboy. 1: Monkey-man & O'Brien (in back-up story). 6.00
❑2, Apr 1994 4.00
❑3, May 1994 4.00
❑4, Jun 1994 4.00

HELLBOY: THE THIRD WISH
DARK HORSE

❑1, Jul 2002 2.90
❑2, Aug 2002 2.90

HELLBOY: THE WOLVES OF SAINT AUGUST
DARK HORSE / LEGEND

❑1; prestige format; collects the story from Dark Horse Presents #88-91 4.95

HELLBOY: WAKE THE DEVIL
DARK HORSE / LEGEND

❑1, Jun 1996; Silent as the Grave back-up 4.00
❑2, Jul 1996; Silent as the Grave back-up 3.50
❑3, Aug 1996; Silent as the Grave back-up 3.50

N-MINT

❑4, Sep 1996; Silent as the Grave back-up 3.50
❑5, Oct 1996; Silent as the Grave back-up 3.50

HELLBOY: WEIRD TALES
DARK HORSE

❑1, Feb 2003 2.99
❑2, Apr 2003 2.99
❑3, Jun 2003 2.99
❑4, Aug 2003 2.99
❑5, Oct 2003 2.99
❑6, Dec 2003 2.99
❑7, Feb 2004 2.99
❑8, Apr 2004 2.99

HELL CAR COMIX
ALTERNATING CRIMES

❑1, Fal 1998 2.95

HELLCAT
MARVEL

❑1, Sep 2000 2.99
❑2 2.99
❑3 2.99

HELL CITY, HELL
DIABLO MUSICA

❑1; shrinkwrapped with CD-ROM 2.25

HELLCOP
IMAGE

❑1, Aug 1998; cover says Oct, indicia says Aug 2.50
❑1/A, Aug 1998; Alternate cover; Man kneeling with gun, woman, faces in background 2.50
❑2, Nov 1998 2.50
❑2/A, Nov 1998; alternate cover 2.50
❑3, Jan 1999 2.50
❑4, Mar 1999 2.50

HELL ETERNAL
DC / VERTIGO

❑1; prestige format 6.95

HELLGIRL: DEMONSEED
KNIGHT

❑1, Mar 1995 2.95

HELLHOLE
IMAGE

❑1, Jul 1999 2.50
❑2, Oct 1999 2.50
❑3, Dec 1999 2.50

HELLHOUNDS
IMAGE

❑1, Aug 2003 2.95
❑2, Sep 2003 2.95
❑3, Oct 2003 2.95
❑4, Feb 2004 2.95

HELLHOUNDS: PANZER CORPS
DARK HORSE

❑1, b&w 2.50
❑2, b&w 2.50
❑3, Apr 1994, b&w 2.50
❑4, May 1994, b&w 2.50
❑5, Jun 1994, b&w 2.50
❑6, Jul 1994, b&w 2.50

HELLHOUND: THE REDEMPTION QUEST
MARVEL / EPIC

❑1, Dec 1993 2.25
❑2, Jan 1994 2.25
❑3, Feb 1994 2.25
❑4, Mar 1994 2.25

HELLINA
LIGHTNING

❑1, Sep 1994, b&w 2.75

HELLINA 1997 PIN-UP SPECIAL
LIGHTNING

❑1, Feb 1997; b&w pin-ups; cover version A 3.50

HELLINA/CATFIGHT
LIGHTNING

❑1, Oct 1995, b&w 3.00

N-MINT

❑1/A, Oct 1995; Olive metallic edition 3.00
❑1-2, Aug 1997, b&w; reprints Hellina, Catfight 2.95

HELLINA: CHRISTMAS IN HELL
LIGHTNING

❑1, Dec 1996, b&w 2.95
❑1/A, Dec 1996; nude cover A 4.00
❑1/B, Dec 1996; nude cover B 4.00

HELLINA/CYNDER
LIGHTNING

❑1, Sep 1997 2.95

HELLINA/DOUBLE IMPACT
LIGHTNING

❑1, Feb 1996 2.75
❑1/A, Feb 1996; crossover with High Impact 3.00
❑1/B, Feb 1996; alternate cover 3.00
❑1/Nude, Feb 1996; Nude edition with certificate of authenticity; polybagged nude cover 4.00
❑1/Platinum; Platinum edition 3.00

HELLINA: GENESIS
LIGHTNING

❑1, Apr 1996, b&w; bagged with Hellina poster 3.50

HELLINA: HEART OF THORNS
LIGHTNING

❑2, Sep 1996 2.75
❑2/Nude, Sep 1996; nude cover edition; nude cover edition 4.00

HELLINA: HELLBORN
LIGHTNING

❑1, Dec 1997, b&w 2.95

HELLINA: HELL'S ANGEL
LIGHTNING

❑1, Nov 1996, b&w 2.75
❑2, Dec 1996, b&w 2.75

HELLINA: IN THE FLESH
LIGHTNING

❑1, Aug 1997, b&w 2.95

HELLINA: KISS OF DEATH
LIGHTNING

❑1, Jul 1995, b&w 2.75
❑1/Gold; Gold edition 3.00
❑1/Nude, Jul 1995, b&w; Nude edition 4.00
❑1-2, Mar 1997; Encore edition; alternate cover 2.95

HELLINA: NAKED DESIRE
LIGHTNING

❑1, May 1997 2.95

HELLINA/NIRA X
LIGHTNING

❑1, Aug 1996; crossover with Entity . 3.00

HELLINA: SKYBOLT TOYZ LIMITED EDITION
LIGHTNING

❑1/A, Aug 1997, b&w; reprints Hellina #1 1.50
❑1/B, Aug 1997; alternate cover 1.50

HELLINA: TAKING BACK THE NIGHT
LIGHTNING

❑1 4.50

HELLINA: WICKED WAYS
LIGHTNING

❑1/A, Nov 1995, b&w; alternate cover; polybagged 2.75
❑1/B, Nov 1995; polybagged 3.00
❑1/Nude, Nov 1995; polybagged; Cover C 9.95
❑1/Silver; silver edition 2.75

HELLRAISER (CLIVE BARKER'S)
MARVEL / EPIC

❑Holiday 1; Nude edition with certificate of authenticity; Dark Holiday Special 4.95
❑Summer 1; Giant-size 5.95
❑Spring 1; Spring Special 6.95

N-MINT

HELLRAISER III: HELL ON EARTH
MARVEL / EPIC

❑1 5.00

HELLRAISER POSTERBOOK (CLIVE BARKER'S)
MARVEL / EPIC

❑1 4.95

HELLRAISER: SPRING SLAUGHTER
MARVEL / EPIC

❑1 6.95

HELLSAINT
BLACK DIAMOND

❑1, Mar 1998 2.50

HELL'S ANGEL
MARVEL

❑1, Jul 1993 1.75
❑2, Aug 1993 1.75
❑3, Sep 1993 1.75
❑4, Oct 1993 1.75
❑5, Nov 1993; Series continued as Dark Angel #6 1.75

HELLSHOCK (MINI-SERIES)
IMAGE

❑1, Jul 1994 2.00
❑2, Aug 1994 2.00
❑3, Oct 1994 O: Hellshock. 2.00
❑4; Pin-up by Adam Kubert and Jae Lee 2.00
❑4/A, Nov 1994; variant cover 2.00
❑4/B, Nov 1994 BSz (c) 1.95
❑Ashcan 1; ashcan 1.00

HELLSHOCK
IMAGE

❑1, Jan 1997 2.95
❑1/A, Jan 1997 2.95
❑2, Feb 1997 2.95
❑3, Mar 1997 2.95
❑4; Never published? 2.95
❑5; Never published? 2.95
❑6; Never published? 2.95
❑7; Never published? 3.95

HELLSPAWN
IMAGE

❑1, Aug 2000 BMB (w) 3.00
❑2, Sep 2000 BMB (w) 2.50
❑3, Oct 2000 BMB (w) 2.50
❑4, Nov 2000 BMB (w) 2.50
❑5, Jan 2001 BMB (w) 2.50
❑6, Feb 2001 BMB (w) 2.50
❑7, Apr 2001 TMc (a) 2.50
❑8, May 2001 2.50
❑9, Jun 2001 2.50
❑10, Jul 2001 2.50
❑11, Aug 2001 2.50
❑12, Sep 2001 2.50
❑13, May 2002 2.50
❑14 2002 2.50
❑15, Feb 2003 2.50
❑16, Apr 2003 2.50

HELLSPOCK
EXPRESS / PARODY

❑1, b&w 2.95

HELLSTALKER
REBEL CREATIONS

❑1 2.25
❑2, Jul 1989 2.25

HELLSTORM: PRINCE OF LIES
MARVEL

❑1, Apr 1993; parchment cover 2.95
❑2, May 1993 2.00
❑3, Jun 1993 2.00
❑4, Jul 1993 2.00
❑5, Aug 1993 2.00
❑6, Sep 1993 2.00
❑7, Oct 1993; Book 1 2.00
❑8, Nov 1993; Book 1 2.00
❑9, Dec 1993; Book 1 2.00
❑10, Jan 1994; Book 1 2.00
❑11, Feb 1994 2.00
❑12, Mar 1994 2.00

Occult dabbler John Constantine received his own series in 1988 and his own film in 2004.

© 1988 DC Comics.

N-MINT

❑13, Apr 1994 2.00
❑14, May 1994 2.00
❑15, Jun 1994 2.00
❑16, Jul 1994 2.00
❑17, Aug 1994 2.00
❑18, Sep 1994 2.00
❑19, Oct 1994 2.00
❑20, Nov 1994 2.00
❑21, Dec 1994 2.00

HELM PREMIERE
HELM

❑1, Mar 1995, b&w; Preview edition . 2.95

HELP (VOL. 1)
WARREN

❑1, ca. 1964 HK (w) 45.00
❑2, ca. 1964 HK (w) 28.00
❑3, ca. 1964 HK (w) 20.00
❑4, ca. 1964 HK (w) 20.00
❑5, ca. 1964 HK (w) 20.00
❑6, ca. 1964 HK (w) 20.00
❑7, ca. 1964 HK (w) 20.00
❑8, ca. 1964 HK (w) 20.00
❑9, ca. 1964 HK (w) 20.00
❑10, ca. 1964 HK (w) 20.00
❑11, ca. 1964 HK (w) 20.00
❑12, HK (w) 20.00

HELP (VOL. 2)
WARREN

❑1 HK (w) 26.00
❑2 HK (w) 16.00
❑3 HK (w) 16.00

HELSING
CALIBER

❑1, b&w 2.95
❑1/A; cover has woman in black standing 2.95
❑2, b&w 2.95

HELTER SKELTER
ANTARCTIC

❑0, May 1997, b&w 2.95
❑1, Jun 1997, b&w 2.95
❑2, Sep 1997, b&w 2.95
❑3, Nov 1997, b&w 2.95
❑4, Dec 1997, b&w 2.95
❑6, Mar 1998 2.95
❑5, Jan 1998, b&w 2.95

HELYUN: BONES OF THE BACKWOODS
SLAVE LABOR

❑1, Nov 1991, b&w 2.95

HELYUN BOOK 1
SLAVE LABOR

❑1, Aug 1990, b&w 6.95

HEMBECK
FANTACO

❑1; Best of Dateline: @!!?# 2.50
❑2, Feb 1980 FH (a) 2.50
❑3, Jun 1980 1.50
❑4, Nov 1980 1.50
❑5, Feb 1981 FH (a) 2.50
❑6, Sep 1981; Jimmy Olsen's Pal 2.25
❑7, Jan 1983; Dial H for Hembeck 1.95

N-MINT

HEMP FOR VICTORY
STARHEAD

- ❑1, Sep 1993, b&w; based on 1943 USDA film 2.50

HENRY V
CALIBER / TOME

- ❑1, b&w 2.95

HEPCATS
DOUBLE DIAMOND

- ❑1, May 1989 .... 5.00
- ❑2, Jul 1989 .... 4.00
- ❑3, Aug 1989 .... 3.00
- ❑4, Nov 1989 .... 3.00
- ❑5, Feb 1989 .... 3.00
- ❑6 .... 3.00
- ❑7 .... 3.00
- ❑8 .... 3.00
- ❑9 .... 3.00
- ❑10 .... 3.00
- ❑11, Jan 1994 .... 3.00
- ❑12, Jul 1994 .... 3.00
- ❑13 .... 3.00
- ❑14 .... 2.50
- ❑Special 1 .... 4.00
- ❑Special 2 .... 4.00

HEPCATS (ANTARCTIC)
ANTARCTIC

- ❑0, Nov 1996 .... 4.00
- ❑0/A; Comics Cavalcade Commemorative Edition 5.95
- ❑0/Deluxe, Nov 1996; Radio Hepcats edition; polybagged with compact disc 9.95
- ❑1, Dec 1996 .... 3.50
- ❑2, Jan 1997 .... 3.50
- ❑3, Feb 1997 .... 3.00
- ❑4, Mar 1997 .... 3.00
- ❑5, Apr 1997 .... 3.00
- ❑6, Jan 1998 .... 2.95
- ❑7, Mar 1998 .... 2.95
- ❑8 .... 2.95
- ❑9, Apr 1998 .... 2.95
- ❑10, May 1998 .... 2.95
- ❑11, May 1998 .... 2.95
- ❑12, Jun 1998 .... 2.95

HERBIE (DARK HORSE)
DARK HORSE

- ❑1, Oct 1992 .... 2.50
- ❑2, Nov 1992; Series cancelled 2.50

HERBIE (A+)
A-PLUS

- ❑1; Reprints (including part of Herbie #8) 2.50
- ❑2 .... 2.50
- ❑3 .... 2.50
- ❑4 .... 2.50
- ❑5 .... 2.50
- ❑6 .... 2.50

HERBIE (ACG)
ACG

- ❑1, Apr 1964 A: Castro. A: Lyndon Johnson. A: Sonny Liston. A: Khrushchev. 95.00
- ❑2, Jun 1964 A: Marie Antoinette. 60.00
- ❑3, Aug 1964 A: Churchill. 48.00
- ❑4, Sep 1964 A: Doc Holliday. A: Clantons. 48.00
- ❑5, Oct 1964 A: Frank Sinatra. A: Beatles. A: Dean Martin. 48.00
- ❑6, Dec 1964 A: Gregory Peck. A: Ava Gardner. 40.00
- ❑7, Feb 1965 A: Harry Truman. A: Mao. A: Khruschcev. 40.00
- ❑8, Mar 1965 O: Fat Fury. A: George Washington. A: Barry Goldwater. A: Lyndon Johnson. 50.00
- ❑9, Apr 1965 .... 38.00
- ❑10, Jun 1965 .... 38.00
- ❑11, Aug 1965 A: Adlai Stevenson. A: Queen Isabella. A: Columbus. A: Lyndon Johnson. 30.00
- ❑12, Sep 1965; Fat Fury story 30.00
- ❑13, Oct 1965 .... 30.00
- ❑14, Dec 1965 A: Magicman. A: Fat Fury. A: Nemesis. 30.00
- ❑15, Feb 1966 A: Josephine. A: Napoleon. 30.00
- ❑16, Mar 1966 A: Mao Tse Tung. A: Fat Fury. 30.00
- ❑17, Apr 1966 .... 30.00
- ❑18, Jun 1966 .... 30.00
- ❑19, Aug 1966 A: Cleopatra. 30.00
- ❑20, Sep 1966; Fat Fury vs. Dracula .. 30.00
- ❑21, Oct 1966 .... 30.00
- ❑22, Dec 1966; A: Charles de Gaulle. A: Queen Elizabeth. A: Ben Franklin. Fat Fury learns magic 30.00
- ❑23, Feb 1967 .... 30.00

HERCULES (CHARLTON)
CHARLTON

- ❑1, Oct 1967; Thane of Bagarth by Steve Skeates and Jim Aparo; sell-through 46.6%, according to Charlton files 14.00
- ❑2, Dec 1967; Thane of Bagarth by Steve Skeates and Jim Aparo; sell-through 40.3%, according to Charlton files 9.00
- ❑3, Feb 1968; Sell-through 36.1%, according to Charlton files 6.00
- ❑4, Jun 1968; Sell-through 37.6%, according to Charlton files 6.00
- ❑5, Jul 1968; Sell-through 33.5%, according to Charlton files 6.00
- ❑6, Sep 1968; Sell-through 35.5%, according to Charlton files 5.00
- ❑7, Nov 1968 .... 5.00
- ❑8, Dec 1968; JA (a);Thane of Bagarth by Steve Skeates and Jim Aparo; sell-through 47%, according to Charlton files 5.00
- ❑8/A, Dec 1968; Magazine-sized issue; Low distribution 10.00
- ❑9, Feb 1969; Sell-through 31.4%, according to Charlton files 5.00
- ❑10, Apr 1967; Sell-through 36.0%, according to Charlton files 5.00
- ❑11 1967; Sell-through 32.9%, according to Charlton files 5.00
- ❑12, Jul 1967; Sell-through 28%, according to Charlton files 5.00
- ❑13, Oct 1967 .... 5.00

HERCULES (VOL. 1)
MARVEL

- ❑1, Sep 1982 BL (w); BL (a) 1.50
- ❑2, Oct 1982 BL (w); BL, LMc (a) 1.50
- ❑3, Nov 1982 BL (a) 1.50
- ❑4, Dec 1982 BL (w); BL (a) 1.50

HERCULES (VOL. 2)
MARVEL

- ❑1, Mar 1984 BL (w); BL (a) 1.50
- ❑2, Apr 1984 BL (w); BL (a) 1.25
- ❑3, May 1984 BL (w); BL (a) 1.25
- ❑4, Jun 1984 BL (w); BL (a) 1.25

HERCULES: HEART OF CHAOS
MARVEL

- ❑1, Aug 1997; gatefold summary 2.50
- ❑2, Sep 1997; gatefold summary 2.50
- ❑3, Oct 1997; gatefold summary 2.50

HERCULES: OFFICIAL COMICS MOVIE ADAPTATION
ACCLAIM

- ❑1; digest; adapts movie 4.50

HERCULES PROJECT, THE
MONSTER

- ❑1, Aug 1991, b&w 1.95
- ❑2, b&w 1.95

HERCULES: THE LEGENDARY JOURNEYS
TOPPS

- ❑1, Jun 1996; wraparound cover 3.00
- ❑2, Jul 1996 .... 3.00
- ❑3/A, Aug 1996; A: Xena. art cover ... 3.00
- ❑3/B, Aug 1996 A: Xena. 3.00
- ❑3/Gold, Aug 1996; 1: Xena. Gold logo variant 3.00
- ❑4, Sep 1996 2: Xena. A: Xena. 3.00
- ❑5, Oct 1996 A: Xena. 3.00

HERCULES UNBOUND
DC

- ❑1, Nov 1975 WW, JL (a) 6.00
- ❑2, Jan 1976 .... 4.00
- ❑3, Mar 1976 .... 4.00
- ❑4, May 1976 .... 3.00
- ❑5, Jul 1976 .... 3.00
- ❑6, Sep 1976 .... 2.50
- ❑7, Nov 1976 .... 2.50
- ❑8, Jan 1977 .... 2.50
- ❑9, Mar 1977 .... 2.50
- ❑10, May 1977 .... 2.50
- ❑11, Jul 1977 .... 2.50
- ❑12, Sep 1977 .... 2.50

HERE COME THE BIG PEOPLE
EVENT

- ❑1, Sep 1997 .... 2.95
- ❑1/A, Sep 1997; Alternate cover (large woman burping man) 2.95

HERETIC, THE
DARK HORSE / BLANC NOIR

- ❑1, Nov 1996; Maximum Velocity back-up 2.95
- ❑2, Jan 1997; Maximum Velocity back-up 2.95
- ❑3, Feb 1997; Maximum Velocity back-up 2.95
- ❑4, Mar 1997; Maximum Velocity back-up 2.95

HERETICS
IGUANA

- ❑1, Nov 1993; Foil-embossed logo 2.95

HERMES VS. THE EYEBALL KID
DARK HORSE

- ❑1, Dec 1994, b&w 2.95
- ❑2, Jan 1995, b&w 2.95
- ❑3, Feb 1995, b&w 2.95

HERO
MARVEL

- ❑1, May 1990 .... 1.50
- ❑2, Jun 1990 .... 1.50
- ❑3, Jul 1990 .... 1.50
- ❑4, Aug 1990 .... 1.50
- ❑5, Sep 1990 .... 1.50
- ❑6, Oct 1990 .... 1.50

HERO ALLIANCE (WONDER COLOR)
WONDER COLOR

- ❑1, May 1987 .... 1.95

HERO ALLIANCE (INNOVATION)
INNOVATION

- ❑1, Sep 1989 .... 1.75
- ❑2, Oct 1989 .... 1.75
- ❑3, Dec 1989 .... 1.95
- ❑4, Feb 1990 .... 1.95
- ❑5, Mar 1990 .... 1.95
- ❑6, Apr 1990 .... 1.95
- ❑7, May 1990 .... 1.95
- ❑8, Jul 1990 .... 1.95
- ❑9, Sep 1990 .... 1.95
- ❑10, Oct 1990 .... 1.95
- ❑11, Nov 1990 .... 1.95
- ❑12, Dec 1990 .... 1.95
- ❑13, Mar 1991 .... 1.95
- ❑14, Apr 1991 .... 1.95
- ❑15, May 1991 .... 1.95
- ❑16, Jun 1991 .... 1.95
- ❑17, Jul 1991 .... 2.50
- ❑Annual 1, Sep 1990 .... 2.75
- ❑Special 1 .... 2.50

HERO ALLIANCE & JUSTICE MACHINE: IDENTITY CRISIS
INNOVATION

- ❑1, Oct 1990 .... 2.75

Condition price index: Multiply "NM prices" above by: **0.83 for Very Fine/Near Mint**
0.66 for Very Fine • 0.33 for Fine • 0.2 for Very Good • 0.125 for Good

N-MINT

HERO ALLIANCE: END OF THE GOLDEN AGE
INNOVATION

❑1-2, Jul 1989 ....
❑1, Jul 1989 .... 1.75
❑2, Jul 1989 .... 1.75
❑3, Aug 1989 .... 1.75

HERO ALLIANCE QUARTERLY
INNOVATION

❑1, Sep 1991 .... 2.75
❑2, Dec 1991 .... 2.75
❑3, Mar 1992 .... 2.75
❑4 .... 2.75

HEROBEAR AND THE KID
ASTONISH

❑1, ca. 1999, b&w 2.95
❑1-2, ca. 2000, b&w 2.95
❑2, ca. 2000, b&w 2.95
❑2-2, ca. 2000, b&w 2.95
❑3, ca. 2001, b&w 3.50
❑4, ca. 2002, b&w 3.50
❑5, ca. 2002, b&w 3.50

H-E-R-O (DC)
DC

❑1, Apr 2003 .... 2.50
❑2, May 2003 .... 2.50
❑1-2, Sep 2003 .... 4.95
❑3, Jun 2003 .... 2.50
❑4, Jul 2003 .... 2.50
❑5, Aug 2003 .... 2.50
❑6, Sep 2003 .... 2.50
❑7, Oct 2003 .... 2.50
❑8, Nov 2003 .... 2.50
❑9, Dec 2003 .... 2.50
❑10, Jan 2004 .... 2.50
❑11, Feb 2004 .... 2.50
❑12, Mar 2004 .... 2.50
❑13, Apr 2004 .... 2.50
❑14, May 2004 .... 2.50
❑15, Jun 2004 .... 2.50
❑16, Jul 2004 .... 2.50
❑17, Aug 2004 .... 2.50
❑18, Sep 2004 ....

HERO DOUBLE FEATURE
DC

❑1, Jun 2003; Collects Hero (DC) #1 & #2 .... 4.95

HEROES (BLACKBIRD)
BLACKBIRD

❑1 .... 3.00
❑2 .... 1.75
❑3 .... 1.75
❑4, Nov 1987 .... 2.00
❑5 .... 2.00
❑6 .... 2.00

HEROES (MILESTONE)
DC / MILESTONE

❑1, May 1996 .... 2.50
❑2, Jun 1996 .... 2.50
❑3, Jul 1996 .... 2.50
❑4, Aug 1996 .... 2.50
❑5, Sep 1996 .... 2.50
❑6, Nov 1996 .... 2.50

HEROES (MARVEL)
MARVEL

❑1, Dec 2001 .... 7.00
❑1-2, Dec 2001 .... 3.50

HEROES AGAINST HUNGER
DC

❑1, Aug 1986; JSn (w); DaG, CI, KG, JDu, GP, JK, JKu, RA, MR (a);Charity benefit comic for Ethiopian famine victims 3.00

HEROES ANONYMOUS
BONGO

❑1, Jul 2003 .... 2.99
❑2, Oct 2003 .... 2.99
❑3, Dec 2003 .... 2.99
❑4, Feb 2004 .... 2.99
❑5, Jun 2004 .... 2.99

N-MINT

HEROES FOR HIRE
MARVEL

❑1, Jul 1997; Hulk, Hercules, Iron Fist, Luke Cage, Black Knight, White Tiger; wraparound cover 2.99
❑2/A, Aug 1997; gatefold summary; Jim Hammond (original Human Torch) joins team 1.99
❑2/B, Aug 1997; gatefold summary; alternate cover; Jim Hammond (original Human Torch) joins team 1.99
❑3, Sep 1997; gatefold summary 1.99
❑4, Oct 1997; gatefold summary 1.99
❑5, Nov 1997; gatefold summary 1.99
❑6, Dec 1997; gatefold summary 1.99
❑7, Jan 1998; gatefold summary 1.99
❑8, Feb 1998; gatefold summary 1.99
❑9, Mar 1998; gatefold summary 1.99
❑10, Apr 1998; gatefold summary 1.99
❑11, May 1998; gatefold summary ... 1.99
❑12, Jun 1998; gatefold summary 2.99
❑13, Jul 1998; gatefold summary; Ant-Man inside Hammond's body 1.99
❑14, Aug 1998; gatefold summary; Black Knight vs. dragons 1.99
❑15, Sep 1998; gatefold summary 1.99
❑16, Oct 1998; gatefold summary 1.99
❑17, Nov 1998; gatefold summary 1.99
❑18, Dec 1998; gatefold summary 1.99
❑19, Jan 1999; gatefold summary 1.99
❑Annual 1998; gatefold summary; Heroes for Hire/Quicksilver '98; wraparound cover 2.99

HEROES FOR HOPE
MARVEL

❑1, Dec 1985; MGr, SL, AMo (w); BWr, GM, JB, JBy, JR2, SR, BB, FM, BA, CV (a);famine relief 5.00

HEROES FROM WORDSMITH
SPECIAL STUDIO

❑1, b&w 2.50

HEROES INCORPORATED
DOUBLE EDGE

❑1, Mar 1995 .... 2.95

HEROES, INC. PRESENTS CANNON
WALLY WOOD

❑1, ca. 1969 .... 12.50
❑2 .... 10.00

HEROES, INC. PRESENTS CANNON
ARMED SERVICES

❑1 1969 WW (w); WW (a) 12.50
❑2 .... 10.00

HEROES OF FAITH
CORETOONS

❑1, Jun 1992 .... 2.50

HEROES OF ROCK 'N FIRE
WONDER COMIX

❑1, Apr 1987 .... 1.95
❑2, Aug 1987, b&w 1.75

HEROES OF THE EQUINOX
FANTASY FLIGHT

❑1 ....

HEROES REBORN
MARVEL

❑0.5 1996; JPH (w); RL (a);With certificate of authenticity 3.00

HEROES REBORN: ASHEMA
MARVEL

❑1, Jan 2000 .... 1.99

HEROES REBORN: DOOM
MARVEL

❑1, Jan 2000 .... 1.99

HEROES REBORN: DOOMSDAY
MARVEL

❑1, Jan 2000 .... 1.99

HEROES REBORN: MASTERS OF EVIL
MARVEL

❑1, Feb 1999 .... 1.99

Herbie's super-heroic alter-ego, The Fat Fury, faced ACG's version of Dracula in *Herbie* #20.

© 1966 American Comics Group (ACG).

N-MINT

HEROES REBORN MINI COMIC
MARVEL

❑1 .... 1.00

HEROES REBORN: REBEL
MARVEL

❑1, Jan 2000 .... 1.99

HEROES REBORN: REMNANTS
MARVEL

❑1, Jan 2000 .... 1.99

HEROES REBORN: THE RETURN
MARVEL

❑1, Dec 1997 PD (w) 2.50
❑1/Variant, Dec 1997; PD (w); Franklin Richards on cover 3.00
❑2, Dec 1997 PD (w) 2.50
❑2/Variant, Dec 1997; PD (w); Spider-Man/Hulk variant cover 3.00
❑3, Dec 1997 PD (w) 2.50
❑3/Variant, Dec 1997; PD (w); Iron Man variant cover 3.00
❑4, Dec 1997 PD (w) 2.50
❑4/Variant, Dec 1997; PD (w); Reed Richards variant cover 3.00
❑Ashcan 1, Dec 1997 RL, JLee (a) 1.00

HEROES REBORN: YOUNG ALLIES
MARVEL

❑1, Jan 2000 .... 1.99

HERO FOR HIRE
MARVEL

❑1, Jun 1972 GT, JR (a); O: Power Man II (Luke Cage). 1: Diamondback. 1: Power Man II (Luke Cage). 90.00
❑2, Aug 1972 V: Diamondback. 25.00
❑3, Oct 1972 1: Mace. V: Mace. 14.00
❑4, Dec 1972 .... 12.00
❑5, Jan 1973 .... 12.00
❑6, Feb 1973 .... 12.00
❑7, Mar 1973 .... 9.00
❑8, Apr 1973 A: Doctor Doom. 9.00
❑9, May 1973 .... 9.00
❑10, Jun 1973 1: Señor Muerte I (Ramon Garcia). 8.00
❑11, Jul 1973 D: Señor Muerte I (Ramon Garcia). 9.00
❑12, Aug 1973 1: Chemistro I (Curtis Carr). 9.00
❑13, Sep 1973 V: Lionfang. 9.00
❑14, Oct 1973 O: Luke Cage. V: Big Ben. 9.00
❑15, Nov 1973; Sub-Mariner back-up 9.00
❑16, Dec 1973; O: Stiletto. D: Rackham. V: Stiletto. series continues as Power Man 9.00

HERO HOTLINE
DC

❑1, Apr 1989 KS (a) 2.00
❑2, May 1989 .... 2.00
❑3, Jun 1989 1: Snafu. 2.00
❑4, Jul 1989 .... 2.00
❑5, Aug 1989 .... 2.00
❑6, Sep 1989 .... 2.00

HEROIC
LIGHTNING

❑1 .... 1.75

HEROIC 17
PENNACLE

❑1, Sep 1993 .... 2.95

N-MINT

HEROIC TALES
Lone Star
- ❑1, Jun 1997; Amazon 2.50
- ❑2, Aug 1997; Amazon 2.50
- ❑3, Oct 1997 ..... 2.50
- ❑4, Dec 1997 ..... 2.50
- ❑5, Feb 1998 ..... 2.50
- ❑6, May 1998; Amazon and Blackheart 2.50
- ❑7, Jul 1998; Amazon and Gunslinger 2.50
- ❑8, Aug 1998; Atlas 2.50
- ❑9, Apr 2000 ..... 2.50
- ❑10, May 2000 ..... 2.50

HEROINES INC.
Avatar
- ❑1, Apr 1989, b&w 1.75

HEROMAN
Dimension
- ❑1, Oct 1986 ..... 1.75

HERO ON A STICK
Big-Baby
- ❑1 ..... 2.95

HEROS
OK
- ❑1 ..... 2.50

HERO SANDWICH
Slave Labor
- ❑1, Feb 1987 ..... 2.00
- ❑2, May 1987 ..... 1.50
- ❑3, Aug 1987 ..... 1.50
- ❑4, Jan 1988 ..... 1.75
- ❑5, Oct 1988 ..... 1.75
- ❑6, Feb 1989 ..... 1.75
- ❑7, Mar 1990 ..... 2.25
- ❑8, Jun 1991 ..... 2.50
- ❑9, May 1992 ..... 2.50

HERO ZERO
Dark Horse
- ❑0, Sep 1994 ..... 2.50

HERU, SON OF AUSAR
Ania
- ❑1, Apr 1993 ..... 1.95

HE SAID/SHE SAID COMICS
First Amendment
- ❑1; Amy Fisher/Joey Buttafuoco 3.00
- ❑2; Woody Allen/Mia Farrow 3.00
- ❑3; Bill Clinton/Gennifer Flowers 3.00
- ❑4; Tonya Harding/Jeff Gillooly 3.00
- ❑5; O.J. Simpson/Nicole Brown 3.00

HEX
DC
- ❑1, Sep 1985; O: Hex (future Jonah Hex). 1: Hex (future Jonah Hex). 1: Stiletta. continued from Jonah Hex #92 ..... 2.00
- ❑2, Oct 1985 ..... 1.50
- ❑3, Nov 1985 ..... 1.50
- ❑4, Dec 1985 ..... 1.50
- ❑5, Jan 1986 ..... 1.50
- ❑6, Feb 1986 ..... 1.50
- ❑7, Mar 1986 ..... 1.50
- ❑8, Apr 1986 ..... 1.50
- ❑9, May 1986 ..... 1.50
- ❑10, Jun 1986 A: Legion. 1.50
- ❑11, Jul 1986 A: Batman of future. ... 1.50
- ❑12, Aug 1986 A: Batman of future. .. 1.50
- ❑13, Sep 1986 1: Dogs of War. 1.50
- ❑14, Oct 1986 ..... 1.50
- ❑15, Nov 1986 KG (a) 1.50
- ❑16, Dec 1986 KG (a) 1.50
- ❑17, Jan 1987 KG (a) 1.50
- ❑18, Feb 1987 KG (a) 1.50

HEXBREAKER: A BADGER GRAPHIC NOVEL
First
- ❑1, Mar 1988 ..... 8.95

HEX OF THE WICKED WITCH
Asylum
- ❑0/A, Aug 1999 ..... 1.95
- ❑0/B, Aug 1999; Deluxe edition 3.95

N-MINT

HEY, BOSS!
Visionary
- ❑1 ..... 2.00

HEY, MISTER
Insomnia
- ❑1, May 1997, b&w 2.50
- ❑2, Nov 1997, b&w 2.50
- ❑3, Aug 1998, b&w 2.95
- ❑4, Dec 1998, b&w 2.95

HEY MISTER: AFTER SCHOOL SPECIAL
Top Shelf
- ❑1, b&w; digest; collects five-issue mini-comics series 4.95

HI-ADVENTURE HEROES
Gold Key
- ❑1, May 1969 ..... 12.00
- ❑2, Aug 1969 ..... 7.00

HIDEO LI FILES, THE
Raging Rhino
- ❑1, b&w 2.95

HIDING PLACE, THE
DC / Piranha
- ❑1 ..... 12.95

HIEROGLYPH
Dark Horse
- ❑1, Nov 1999 ..... 2.95
- ❑2, Dec 1999 ..... 2.95
- ❑3, Jan 2000 ..... 2.95
- ❑4, Feb 2000 ..... 2.95

HIGH ADVENTURE
Red Top
- ❑1, Oct 1957 ..... 40.00

HIGH CALIBER
Caliber
- ❑1, b&w; Trade Paperback 9.95
- ❑2 ..... 3.95
- ❑3 ..... 3.95
- ❑4; Giant-size; flip book with Raven Chronicles #15 ..... 3.95

HIGH CHAPARRAL, THE
Gold Key
- ❑1, Aug 1968 ..... 40.00

HIGH OCTANE THEATRE
Infiniti
- ❑1 ..... 2.50

HIGH ROADS
DC / Homage
- ❑1, Jun 2002 ..... 2.95
- ❑2, Jul 2002 ..... 2.95
- ❑3, Aug 2002 ..... 2.95
- ❑4, Sep 2002 ..... 2.95
- ❑5, Oct 2002 ..... 2.95
- ❑6, Nov 2002 ..... 2.95

HIGH SCHOOL AGENT
Sun
- ❑1 ..... 2.50

HIGH SHINING BRASS
Apple
- ❑1, b&w 2.75
- ❑2, b&w 2.75
- ❑3, b&w 2.75
- ❑4 ..... 2.75

HIGH STAKES ADVENTURES
Antarctic
- ❑1, Dec 1998 ..... 2.95
- ❑1/Deluxe, Dec 1998; Deluxe edition . 5.95

HIGHTOP NINJA
Authority
- ❑1 ..... 2.95
- ❑2 ..... 2.95
- ❑3 ..... 2.95

HIGH VOLTAGE
Black Out
- ❑0 ..... 2.95

N-MINT

HILLY ROSE
Astro
- ❑1, May 1995 ..... 3.00
- ❑1/A 3.00
- ❑2, Jul 1995 ..... 4.00
- ❑3, Oct 1995 ..... 3.00
- ❑4, Dec 1995 ..... 3.00
- ❑5, Feb 1996 ..... 3.00
- ❑6, Apr 1996 ..... 3.00
- ❑7, Aug 1996 ..... 3.00
- ❑8, Dec 1996 ..... 3.00
- ❑9, Apr 1997 ..... 3.00

HIP FLASK
Comicraft
- ❑0.5, Aug 1998; San Dego Comic-Con preview 2.95

HIS NAME IS... SAVAGE
Adventure House
- ❑1; magazine GK (a) 24.00

HISTORY OF MARVELS COMICS, THE
Marvel
- ❑1, Jul 2000 ..... 1.00

HISTORY OF THE DC UNIVERSE
DC
- ❑1, Sep 1986 GP (a) 3.25
- ❑2, Nov 1986 GP (a) 3.25

HISTORY OF VIOLENCE
DC / Paradox
- ❑1, b&w 9.95

HITCHHIKER'S GUIDE TO THE GALAXY, THE
DC
- ❑1 ..... 4.95
- ❑2, ca. 1993 ..... 4.95
- ❑3, ca. 1993 ..... 4.95

HITMAN
DC
- ❑1, Apr 1996 A: Batman. 3.00
- ❑2, Jun 1996 A: Joker. V: Joker. 3.00
- ❑3, Jul 1996 ..... 2.50
- ❑4, Aug 1996 ..... 2.50
- ❑5, Sep 1996 ..... 2.50
- ❑6, Oct 1996; cover says Part 4 of 4 . 2.50
- ❑7, Nov 1996 D: Nightfist. D: Johnny Navarone. 2.50
- ❑8, Dec 1996; O: Hitman. Final Night 2.50
- ❑9, Dec 1996 ..... 2.50
- ❑10, Jan 1997 ..... 2.50
- ❑11, Feb 1997 ..... 2.25
- ❑12, Mar 1997 A: Green Lantern. 2.25
- ❑13, Apr 1997 ..... 2.25
- ❑14, May 1997 ..... 2.25
- ❑15, Jun 1997 ..... 2.25
- ❑16, Jul 1997 A: Catwoman. 2.25
- ❑17, Aug 1997 ..... 2.25
- ❑18, Sep 1997 ..... 2.25
- ❑19, Oct 1997 ..... 2.25
- ❑20, Nov 1997 ..... 2.25
- ❑21, Dec 1997; Face cover 2.25
- ❑22, Jan 1998 ..... 2.25
- ❑23, Feb 1998 ..... 2.25
- ❑24, Mar 1998 ..... 2.25
- ❑25, Apr 1998 ..... 2.25
- ❑26, May 1998 ..... 2.25
- ❑27, Jun 1998 ..... 2.25
- ❑28, Jul 1998 ..... 2.25
- ❑29, Aug 1998 ..... 2.25
- ❑30, Sep 1998 ..... 2.50
- ❑31, Oct 1998 ..... 2.50
- ❑32, Dec 1998 ..... 2.50
- ❑33, Jan 1999 ..... 2.50
- ❑34, Feb 1999 A: Superman. 2.50
- ❑35, Mar 1999 1: Frances Monaghan. 2.50
- ❑36, Apr 1999 2: Frances Monaghan. D: Tommy's mother. 2.50
- ❑37, May 1999 ..... 2.50
- ❑38, Jun 1999 ..... 2.50
- ❑39, Jul 1999 ..... 2.50
- ❑40, Aug 1999 ..... 2.50
- ❑41, Sep 1999 ..... 2.50

N-MINT

❑42, Oct 1999 .... 2.50
❑43, Nov 1999 .... 2.50
❑44, Dec 1999 .... 2.50
❑45, Jan 2000 .... 2.50
❑46, Feb 2000 .... 2.50
❑47, Mar 2000 .... 2.50
❑48, Apr 2000 .... 2.50
❑49, May 2000 .... 2.50
❑50, Jun 2000 .... 2.50
❑51, Jul 2000 .... 2.50
❑52, Aug 2000 .... 2.50
❑53, Sep 2000 .... 2.50
❑54, Oct 2000 .... 2.50
❑55, Nov 2000 .... 2.50
❑56, Dec 2000 .... 2.50
❑57, Jan 2001 .... 2.50
❑58, Feb 2001 .... 2.50
❑59, Mar 2001 .... 2.50
❑60, Jun 2001 D: Hitman. 2.50
❑1000000, Nov 1998 .... 3.00
❑Annual 1; Pulp Heroes; 1997 Annual 3.95

HITMAN/LOBO: THAT STUPID BASTICH
DC

❑1, Sep 2000 .... 3.95

HITOMI 2
ANTARCTIC

❑1, Aug 1993, b&w 2.50
❑2, Oct 1993, b&w 2.75
❑3, Dec 1993, b&w 2.75
❑4, Feb 1994, b&w 2.75
❑5, Apr 1994, b&w 2.75
❑6, Jul 1994, b&w 2.75
❑7, Nov 1994, b&w 2.75
❑8, Mar 1995, b&w 2.75
❑9, May 1995, b&w 2.75
❑10, May 1997, b&w 3.95

HITOMI AND HER GIRL COMMANDOS
ANTARCTIC

❑1, Apr 1992, b&w 2.50
❑2, Jun 1992, b&w 2.50
❑3, Aug 1992, b&w 2.50
❑4, Oct 1992, b&w 2.50

HIT THE BEACH
ANTARCTIC

❑1, Jul 1993, b&w 2.95
❑1/Gold, Jul 1993; Deluxe edition; gold foil 4.95
❑2, Jul 1994, b&w 2.95
❑3, Jul 1995, b&w 2.95
❑4, Jul 1997, b&w 2.95
❑5, Jul 1998, b&w; regular edition 2.95
❑5/CS, Jul 1998, b&w; Special edition; polybagged with postcard 4.95
❑6, Jul 1999 .... 3.95

HOBBIT, THE (J.R.R. TOLKIEN'S...)
ECLIPSE

❑1, Aug 1989 .... 4.95
❑1-2 .... 4.95
❑2, ca. 1990 .... 4.95
❑3, ca. 1990 .... 4.95

HOCKEY MASTERS
REVOLUTIONARY

❑1, Dec 1993, b&w 2.95

HOE, THE
THUNDERBALL

❑1 .... 2.50

HOGAN'S HEROES
DELL

❑1, Jun 1966 .... 50.00
❑2, Sep 1966; Photo still doctored for cover gag 40.00
❑3, Nov 1966; Photo still doctored for cover gag 32.00
❑4, Jan 1967 .... 32.00
❑5, Mar 1967 .... 32.00
❑6, May 1967 .... 26.00
❑7, Jul 1967 .... 26.00
❑8, Sep 1967 .... 26.00
❑9, Oct 1969; Cover Reprints #1 .... 26.00

N-MINT

HOKUM & HEX
MARVEL

❑1, Sep 1993; Embossed cover 2.50
❑2, Oct 1993 .... 1.75
❑3, Nov 1993 .... 1.75
❑4, Dec 1993 .... 1.75
❑5, Jan 1994 .... 1.75
❑6, Feb 1994 .... 1.75
❑7, Mar 1994 .... 1.75
❑8, Apr 1994 .... 1.75
❑9, May 1994 .... 1.75

HOLED UP (RICH JOHNSON'S)
AVATAR

❑1, Apr 2004 .... 3.50

HOLIDAY FOR SCREAMS
MALIBU

❑1, b&w 4.95

HOLIDAY OUT
RENEGADE

❑1, Mar 1987, b&w 2.00
❑2, b&w 2.00
❑3, b&w 2.00

HOLLOW EARTH, THE
VISION

❑1, May 1996 .... 2.50
❑2, ca. 1996 .... 2.50
❑3, Jan 1997 .... 2.50

HOLLYWOOD SUPERSTARS
MARVEL / EPIC

❑1, Nov 1990 .... 2.95
❑2, Jan 1991 .... 2.25
❑3, Feb 1991 .... 2.25
❑4, Mar 1991 .... 2.25
❑5, Apr 1991 .... 2.25

HOLO BROTHERS, THE
MONSTER

❑1 1989, b&w 2.00
❑2, b&w 2.00
❑3 .... 2.25
❑4 .... 2.25
❑5 .... 2.25
❑6 .... 2.25
❑7 .... 2.25
❑8 .... 2.25
❑9 .... 2.25
❑10 .... 2.25
❑Special 1 0: Holo. Brothers. 2.25

HOLY AVENGER
SLAVE LABOR

❑1, Apr 1996 .... 4.95

HOLY CROSS
FANTAGRAPHICS

❑0, b&w 4.95
❑1 .... 2.95
❑2, Oct 1994, b&w 2.95

HOLY TERROR
IMAGE

❑1, Aug 2002, b&w 2.95

HOMAGE STUDIOS SWIMSUIT SPECIAL
IMAGE

❑1, Apr 1993; pin-ups 2.00

HOME GROWN FUNNIES
KITCHEN SINK

❑1, Jan 1971 .... 55.00
❑1-2 .... 22.00
❑1-3 .... 10.00
❑1-4 .... 6.00
❑1-5 .... 4.00
❑1-6 .... 3.00
❑1-7 .... 3.00
❑1-8 .... 3.00
❑1-9 .... 3.00
❑1-10 .... 2.50
❑1-11 .... 2.50
❑1-12 .... 2.50
❑1-13 .... 2.50

After the events of *Crisis on Infinite Earths*, Marv Wolfman and George Pérez set down the revised history of the DC universe in a two-issue prestige-format series.

© 1986 DC Comics.

N-MINT

❑1-14 .... 2.50
❑1-15 .... 2.50

HOMELANDS ON THE WORLD OF MAGIC: THE GATHERING
ACCLAIM / ARMADA

❑1; prestige format; polybagged with Homelands card 5.95

HOMER, THE HAPPY GHOST (2ND SERIES)
MARVEL

❑1, Nov 1969 DDC (c); SL (w); DDC (a) 40.00
❑2, Jan 1969; DDC (c); SL (w); DDC (a);Reprints cover from #21 of the Atlas series 30.00
❑3, Mar 1969 DDC (c); SL (w); DDC (a) 30.00
❑4, May 1970 DDC (c); SL (w); DDC (a) 30.00

HOMICIDE
DARK HORSE

❑1, Apr 1990, b&w 1.95

HOMICIDE: TEARS OF THE DEAD
CHAOS

❑1 .... 2.95

HOMO PATROL
HELPLESS ANGER

❑1, b&w 3.50

HONEYMOONERS, THE (LODESTONE)
LODESTONE

❑1, Oct 1986 .... 1.50

HONEYMOONERS, THE (TRIAD)
TRIAD

❑1, Sep 1987 .... 2.00
❑2, Sep 1987; reprints #1's indicia; photo back cover 2.00
❑3, Dec 1987; Deluxe edition; square-bound; wraparound cover 3.50
❑4, Jan 1988; photo back cover 2.00
❑5, Feb 1988; wraparound cover 2.00
❑6, Mar 1988; photo back cover 2.00
❑7, Apr 1988; wraparound cover 2.00
❑8, May 1988; wraparound cover 2.00
❑9, Jul 1988; squarebound; wrap-around cover 2.00
❑10, Apr 1989 .... 2.00
❑11, Jun 1989 .... 2.00
❑12, Aug 1989 .... 2.00
❑13 1989 .... 2.00

HONEY WEST
GOLD KEY

❑1, Sep 1966 .... 25.00

HONG KONG PHOOEY
CHARLTON

❑1, May 1975 .... 25.00
❑2, Aug 1975 .... 15.00
❑3, Oct 1975 .... 8.00
❑4, Dec 1975 .... 8.00
❑5, Feb 1976 .... 8.00
❑6, May 1976 .... 8.00
❑7, Jul 1976 .... 8.00
❑8, Sep 1976 .... 8.00
❑9, Nov 1976 .... 8.00

HONG ON THE RANGE
IMAGE

❑1, Dec 1997 .... 2.50
❑2, Jan 1998 .... 2.50
❑3, Feb 1998 .... 2.50

N-MINT

HONK!
FANTAGRAPHICS

- ❑1, Nov 1986, b&w ... 2.25
- ❑2, Jan 1987, b&w ... 2.25
- ❑3, Mar 1987, b&w ... 2.25
- ❑4, May 1987, b&w ... 2.25
- ❑5, Jul 1987, b&w ... 2.25

HONKO THE CLOWN
C&T

- ❑1, b&w ... 2.00

HONOR AMONG THIEVES
GATEWAY

- ❑1 ... 1.50

HOOD, THE
SOUTH CENTRAL

- ❑1, b&w ... 2.75

HOOD, THE (MARVEL)
MARVEL

- ❑1, Jul 2002 ... 2.99
- ❑2, Aug 2002 ... 2.99
- ❑3, Sep 2002 ... 2.99
- ❑4, Oct 2002 ... 2.99
- ❑5, Nov 2002 ... 2.99
- ❑6, Dec 2002 ... 2.99

HOOD MAGAZINE
OAKLAND

- ❑1 ... 3.00
- ❑2 ... 3.00

HOODOO
3-D ZONE

- ❑1, Nov 1988, b&w ... 2.50

HOOK
MARVEL

- ❑1, Feb 1992 CV (w); GM (a) ... 1.25
- ❑2, Feb 1992 CV (w) ... 1.25
- ❑3, Mar 1992 CV (w) ... 1.25
- ❑4, Mar 1992 CV (w) ... 1.25

HOOK (MAGAZINE)
MARVEL

- ❑1; magazine ... 2.95

HOON, THE
EENIEWEENIE

- ❑1, Jun 1995, b&w ... 2.50
- ❑2, Aug 1995, b&w ... 2.50
- ❑3, Oct 1995, b&w ... 2.50
- ❑4, Dec 1995, b&w ... 2.50
- ❑5, Feb 1996, b&w ... 2.50
- ❑6, Apr 1996, b&w ... 2.50

HOON, THE (VOL. 2)
CALIBER / TAPESTRY

- ❑1, ca. 1996, b&w ... 2.95
- ❑2, ca. 1996, b&w ... 2.95

HOPSTER'S TRACKS
BONGO

- ❑1, b&w ... 2.95
- ❑2, b&w ... 2.95

HORDE
SWING SHIFT

- ❑1, b&w ... 2.00

HORNY BIKER SLUTS
LAST GASP

- ❑1, b&w ... 2.95
- ❑2 ... 2.95
- ❑3 ... 2.95
- ❑4 1991 ... 2.95
- ❑5, b&w; b&w pin-ups, cardstock cover ... 2.95
- ❑6 ... 3.95
- ❑7 ... 3.95
- ❑8 ... 3.95
- ❑9 ... 3.95
- ❑10 ... 3.95
- ❑11 ... 3.95
- ❑12 ... 3.95
- ❑13 ... 3.95

N-MINT

HORNY COMIX & STORIES
RIP OFF

- ❑1, Apr 1991, b&w ... 2.50
- ❑2, Jul 1991, b&w ... 2.50
- ❑3, Dec 1991, b&w ... 2.50
- ❑4, May 1992, b&w ... 2.50

HORNY TAILS
NBM

- ❑1 ... 12.95

HORNY TOADS (WALLACE WOOD'S...)
FANTAGRAPHICS / EROS

- ❑1, b&w ... 2.95

HOROBI PART 1
VIZ

- ❑1, Mar 1990, b&w; Japanese ... 3.75
- ❑2, Apr 1990, b&w; Japanese ... 3.75
- ❑3, May 1990, b&w; Japanese ... 3.75
- ❑4, Jun 1990, b&w; Japanese ... 3.75
- ❑5, Jul 1990, b&w; Japanese ... 3.75
- ❑6, Aug 1990, b&w; Japanese ... 3.75
- ❑7, Sep 1990, b&w; Japanese ... 3.75
- ❑8, Oct 1990, b&w; Japanese ... 3.75

HOROBI PART 2
VIZ

- ❑1, Nov 1990, b&w; Japanese ... 4.25
- ❑2, Dec 1990, b&w; Japanese ... 4.25
- ❑3, Jan 1991, b&w; Japanese ... 4.25
- ❑4, Feb 1991, b&w; Japanese ... 4.25
- ❑5, Mar 1991, b&w; Japanese ... 4.25
- ❑6, Apr 1991, b&w; Japanese ... 4.25
- ❑7, May 1991, b&w; Japanese ... 4.25

HORRIBLE TRUTH ABOUT COMICS, THE
ALTERNATIVE

- ❑1, Jan 1999, b&w ... 2.95

HORROR HOUSE
AC

- ❑1, ca. 1994 ... 2.95

HORROR, THE ILLUSTRATED BOOK OF FEARS
NORTHSTAR

- ❑1 ... 4.00
- ❑2, Feb 1990 ... 4.00

HORROR IN THE DARK
FANTAGOR

- ❑1, b&w ... 2.00
- ❑2, b&w ... 2.00
- ❑3, b&w ... 2.00
- ❑4, b&w ... 2.00

HORRORIST, THE
DC / VERTIGO

- ❑1, Dec 1995 ... 5.95
- ❑2, Jan 1996 ... 5.95

HORROR OF COLLIER COUNTY, THE
DARK HORSE

- ❑1, Oct 1999 ... 2.95
- ❑2 ... 2.95
- ❑3 ... 2.95
- ❑4 ... 2.95
- ❑5 ... 2.95

HORRORS OF THE HAUNTER
AC

- ❑1, b&w ... 2.95

HORSE
SLAVE LABOR

- ❑1, Sep 1989, b&w ... 2.95
- ❑2 ... 2.95
- ❑3 ... 2.95

HORSEMAN
KEVLAR

- ❑0, May 1996, b&w; Commemorative edition; no cover price; published after Crusade issue #1 ... 2.95
- ❑0/Gold, May 1996; gold foil-embossed cardstock cover; published after Crusade issue #1 ... 2.95
- ❑0/Silver; no cover price or indicia; published after Crusade issue #1 ... 2.95

N-MINT

- ❑0/A, May 1996; Woman holding sword facing forward on cover ... 2.95
- ❑1, Mar 1996 ... 2.95
- ❑1/A, Nov 1996; Kevlar edition ... 2.95
- ❑2, Jan 1997, b&w; no cover price or indicia ... 2.95

HOSIE'S HEROINES
SLAVE LABOR

- ❑1, Apr 1993 ... 2.95

HOSTILE TAKEOVER
MALIBU

- ❑Ashcan 1, Sep 1994; ashcan; Ultraverse Preview ... 1.00

HOTEL HARBOUR VIEW
VIZ

- ❑1, b&w; Japanese ... 9.95

HOTHEAD PAISAN: HOMICIDAL LESBIAN TERRORIST
GIANT ASS

- ❑13 ... 3.50

HOT LINE
FANTAGRAPHICS / EROS

- ❑1, Nov 1992 ... 2.50

HOT MEXICAN LOVE COMICS
HOT MEXICAN LOVE COMICS

- ❑1 ... 3.95
- ❑2 ... 3.95

HOT N' COLD HEROES
A-PLUS

- ❑1, b&w ... 2.50
- ❑2, Mar 1991; reprints O: Nemesis, Magicman ... 2.50

HOT NIGHTS IN RANGOON
FANTAGRAPHICS / EROS

- ❑1 ... 2.95
- ❑2 1994 ... 2.95
- ❑3, Nov 1994 ... 2.95

HOT ROD RACERS
CHARLTON

- ❑1 1965 ... 30.00
- ❑2 1965 ... 20.00
- ❑3, May 1965 ... 20.00
- ❑4, Jul 1965 ... 20.00
- ❑5, Sep 1965 ... 20.00
- ❑6, Nov 1965 ... 20.00
- ❑7 1966 ... 20.00
- ❑8 1966 ... 20.00
- ❑9 1966 ... 20.00
- ❑10 1966 ... 20.00
- ❑11 1966 ... 20.00
- ❑12 1967 ... 20.00
- ❑13 1967 ... 20.00
- ❑14 1967 ... 20.00
- ❑15 1967 ... 20.00

HOT SHOTS
HOT

- ❑1, Apr 1987 ... 2.00

HOT SHOTS: AVENGERS
MARVEL

- ❑1, Oct 1995; pin-ups ... 2.95

HOT SHOTS: SPIDER-MAN
MARVEL

- ❑1, Jan 1996; pin-ups ... 2.95

HOT SHOTS: X-MEN
MARVEL

- ❑1, Jan 1996; pin-ups; Introduction by Scott Lobdell ... 2.95

HOTSPUR
ECLIPSE

- ❑1, Jun 1987 ... 1.75
- ❑2 1987 ... 1.75
- ❑3 1987 ... 1.75

HOT STUF'
SAL QUARTUCCIO

- ❑1 ... 4.00
- ❑2 ... 3.00
- ❑3, Dec 1976 RCo (w); RCo (a) ... 3.00

N-MINT

❑4, Mar 1977 ATh, GM (w); ATh, GM, EC (a) 3.00
❑5, Fal 1977 3.00
❑6, Dec 1977 MN, EC (w); MN, EC (a) 3.00
❑7 3.00
❑8, ca. 1978 3.00

HOT STUFF (VOL. 2)
HARVEY

❑1, Sep 1991 1.50
❑2, Dec 1991 1.25
❑3, Mar 1992 1.25
❑4, Jun 1992 1.25
❑5, Sep 1992 1.25
❑6, Mar 1993 1.25
❑7, May 1993 1.25
❑8, Aug 1993 1.25
❑9, Nov 1993 1.50
❑10, Jan 1994 1.50
❑11 1994 1.50
❑12, Jun 1994 1.50

HOT STUFF BIG BOOK
HARVEY

❑1, Nov 1992 1.95
❑2 1.95

HOT STUFF DIGEST
HARVEY

❑1 2.25
❑2 2.25
❑3 1.75
❑4 1.75
❑5 1.75

HOT STUFF GIANT SIZE
HARVEY

❑1, Oct 1992 2.25
❑2, Jul 1993 2.25
❑3, Oct 1993 2.25

HOT STUFF, THE LITTLE DEVIL
HARVEY

❑1, Oct 1957 150.00
❑2, Dec 1957 80.00
❑3, Feb 1958 60.00
❑4, Apr 1958 60.00
❑5, Jun 1958 60.00
❑6, Aug 1958 52.00
❑7, Sep 1958 52.00
❑8, Dec 1958 52.00
❑9, Feb 1959 52.00
❑10, Apr 1959 52.00
❑11, May 1959 40.00
❑12, Jun 1959 40.00
❑13, Jul 1959 40.00
❑14, Aug 1959 40.00
❑15, Sep 1959 40.00
❑16, Oct 1959 40.00
❑17, Nov 1959 40.00
❑18, Dec 1959 40.00
❑19, Jan 1960 40.00
❑20, Feb 1960 40.00
❑21, Mar 1960 28.00
❑22, Apr 1960 28.00
❑23, May 1960 28.00
❑24, Jun 1960 28.00
❑25, Jul 1960 28.00
❑26, Aug 1960 28.00
❑27, Sep 1960 28.00
❑28, Oct 1960 28.00
❑29, Nov 1960 28.00
❑30, Dec 1960 28.00
❑31, Jan 1961 16.00
❑32, Feb 1961 16.00
❑33, Mar 1961 16.00
❑34, Apr 1961 16.00
❑35, May 1961 16.00
❑36, Jun 1961 16.00
❑37, Jul 1961 16.00
❑38, Aug 1961 16.00
❑39, Sep 1961 16.00
❑40, Oct 1961 16.00
❑41, Nov 1961 12.00
❑42, Dec 1961 12.00

N-MINT

❑43, Jan 1962 12.00
❑44 1962 12.00
❑45 1962 12.00
❑46 1962 12.00
❑47 1962 12.00
❑48 1962 12.00
❑49 1962 12.00
❑50, Oct 1962 12.00
❑51, Dec 1962 10.00
❑52, Feb 1963 10.00
❑53, Apr 1963 10.00
❑54, Jun 1963 10.00
❑55, Aug 1963 10.00
❑56, Oct 1963 10.00
❑57, Dec 1963 10.00
❑58, Feb 1964 10.00
❑59, Apr 1964 10.00
❑60, Jun 1964 10.00
❑61, Aug 1964 10.00
❑62, Oct 1964 10.00
❑63, Dec 1964 10.00
❑64, Feb 1965 10.00
❑65, Apr 1965 10.00
❑66, Jun 1965 10.00
❑67, Aug 1965 10.00
❑68, Oct 1965 10.00
❑69, Dec 1965 10.00
❑70, Feb 1966 10.00
❑71, Apr 1966 6.00
❑72, Jun 1966 6.00
❑73, Aug 1966 6.00
❑74, Oct 1966 6.00
❑75, Dec 1966 6.00
❑76, Feb 1967 6.00
❑77, Apr 1967 6.00
❑78, Jun 1967 6.00
❑79, Aug 1967 6.00
❑80, Oct 1967 6.00
❑81, Dec 1967 6.00
❑82, Feb 1968 6.00
❑83, Apr 1968 6.00
❑84, Jun 1968 6.00
❑85, Aug 1968 6.00
❑86, Oct 1968 6.00
❑87, Dec 1968 6.00
❑88, Feb 1969 6.00
❑89 1969 6.00
❑90, May 1969 6.00
❑91, Jul 1969 6.00
❑92 1969 6.00
❑93, Oct 1969 6.00
❑94 1969 6.00
❑95, Jan 1970 6.00
❑96, Mar 1970 6.00
❑97, May 1970 6.00
❑98 1970 6.00
❑99 1970 6.00
❑100 1970 6.00
❑101 4.00
❑102 4.00
❑103, Mar 1971 4.00
❑104, May 1971 4.00
❑105, Jul 1971 4.00
❑106, Sep 1971 4.00
❑107, Nov 1971 4.00
❑108, Jan 1972 4.00
❑109, Mar 1972 4.00
❑110, May 1972 4.00
❑111, Jul 1972 4.00
❑112, Sep 1972 4.00
❑113, Nov 1972 4.00
❑114, Jan 1973 4.00
❑115, Mar 1973 4.00
❑116, May 1973 4.00
❑117, Jul 1973 4.00
❑118, Sep 1973 4.00
❑119, Nov 1973 4.00
❑120, Jan 1974 4.00
❑121, Mar 1974 3.00
❑122, May 1974 3.00
❑123, Jul 1974 3.00

Pin-ups of Marvel characters appeared in the *Hot Shots* series.

© 1995 Marvel Characters Inc.

N-MINT

❑124, Sep 1974 3.00
❑125, Nov 1974 3.00
❑126, Jan 1975 3.00
❑127, Mar 1975 3.00
❑128, May 1975 3.00
❑129, Jul 1975 3.00
❑130, Sep 1975 3.00
❑131, Nov 1975 3.00
❑132, Jan 1976 3.00
❑133, Mar 1976 3.00
❑134, May 1976 3.00
❑135, Jul 1976 3.00
❑136, Sep 1976 3.00
❑137, Nov 1976 3.00
❑138, Jan 1977 3.00
❑139, Mar 1977 3.00
❑140, May 1977 3.00
❑141, Jul 1977 2.00
❑142, Feb 1978 2.00
❑143, Apr 1978 2.00
❑144, Jun 1978 2.00
❑145, Sep 1978 2.00
❑146, Dec 1978 2.00
❑147, Feb 1979 2.00
❑148, Apr 1979 2.00
❑149, Jun 1979 2.00
❑150, Aug 1979 2.00
❑151, Oct 1979 2.00
❑152 2.00
❑153 1980 2.00
❑154, May 1980 2.00
❑155, Jul 1980 2.00
❑156, Sep 1980 2.00
❑157, Nov 1980 2.00
❑158, Jan 1981 2.00
❑159, Mar 1981 2.00
❑160, May 1981 2.00
❑161, Jul 1981 2.00
❑162, Sep 1981 2.00
❑163, Nov 1981 2.00
❑164 2.00
❑165, Oct 1986 2.00
❑166, Dec 1986 2.00
❑167, Feb 1987 2.00
❑168, Apr 1987 2.00
❑169, Jun 1987 2.00
❑170, Sep 1987 2.00
❑171 2.00
❑172 2.00
❑173, Sep 1990 2.00
❑174, Oct 1990 2.00
❑175, Nov 1990 2.00
❑176, Dec 1990 2.00
❑177, Jan 1991 2.00

HOT TAILS
FANTAGRAPHICS / EROS

❑1 3.50

HOT WHEELS
DC

❑1, Apr 1970 45.00
❑2, Jun 1970 30.00
❑3, Aug 1970 NA (c); NA (a) 24.00
❑4, Oct 1970 24.00
❑5, Dec 1970 24.00
❑6, Feb 1971 NA (c) 30.00

N-MINT

HOURMAN
DC

❑1, Apr 1999 A: Amazo. A: Justice League of America. A: Snapper Carr. V: Amazo. 2.50
❑1/Autographed A: Amazo. A: Justice League of America. A: Snapper Carr. 15.95
❑2, May 1999 A: Tomorrow Woman. 2.50
❑3, Jun 1999 2.50
❑4, Jul 1999 V: Lord of Time. 2.50
❑5, Aug 1999 A: Golden Age Hourman. 2.50
❑6, Sep 1999 V: Amazo. 2.50
❑7, Oct 1999 V: Amazo. 2.50
❑8, Nov 1999; Day of Judgment 2.50
❑9, Dec 1999 2.50
❑10, Jan 2000 2.50
❑11, Feb 2000 2.50
❑12, Mar 2000 2.50
❑13, Apr 2000 2.50
❑14, May 2000 2.50
❑15, Jun 2000 2.50
❑16, Jul 2000 2.50
❑17, Aug 2000 2.50
❑18, Sep 2000 2.50
❑19, Oct 2000 2.50
❑20, Nov 2000 2.50
❑21, Dec 2000 2.50
❑22, Jan 2001 2.50
❑23, Feb 2001 2.50
❑24, Mar 2001 2.50
❑25, Apr 2001 2.50

HOUSE II THE SECOND STORY
MARVEL

❑1, Oct 1987 2.00

HOUSE OF FRIGHTENSTEIN
AC

❑1, b&w 2.95

HOUSE OF MYSTERY
DC

❑56, Nov 1956 95.00
❑57, Dec 1956 95.00
❑58, Jan 1957 95.00
❑59, Feb 1957 95.00
❑60, Mar 1957 95.00
❑61, Apr 1957 JK (a) 95.00
❑62, May 1957 70.00
❑63, Jun 1957 JK (a) 85.00
❑64, Jul 1957 70.00
❑65, Aug 1957 JK (a) 85.00
❑66, Sep 1957 JK (a) 70.00
❑67, Oct 1957 70.00
❑68, Nov 1957 70.00
❑69, Dec 1957 70.00
❑70, Jan 1958 JK (a) 85.00
❑71, Feb 1958 65.00
❑72, Mar 1958 65.00
❑73, Apr 1958 65.00
❑74, May 1958 65.00
❑75, Jun 1958 65.00
❑76, Jul 1958 JK (a) 85.00
❑77, Aug 1958 65.00
❑78, Sep 1958 65.00
❑79, Oct 1958 65.00
❑80, Nov 1958 54.00
❑81, Dec 1958 54.00
❑82, Jan 1959 54.00
❑83, Feb 1959 54.00
❑84, Mar 1959 JK (a) 85.00
❑85, Apr 1959 JK (a) 85.00
❑86, May 1959 54.00
❑87, Jun 1959 54.00
❑88, Jul 1959 54.00
❑89, Aug 1959 54.00
❑90, Sep 1959 54.00
❑91, Oct 1959 54.00
❑92, Nov 1959 54.00
❑93, Dec 1959 54.00
❑94, Jan 1960 54.00
❑95, Feb 1960 54.00
❑96, Mar 1960 54.00
❑97, Apr 1960 54.00

N-MINT

❑98, May 1960 54.00
❑99, Jun 1960 54.00
❑100, Jul 1960 65.00
❑101, Aug 1960 45.00
❑102, Sep 1960 45.00
❑103, Oct 1960 45.00
❑104, Nov 1960 45.00
❑105, Dec 1960 45.00
❑106, Jan 1961 45.00
❑107, Feb 1961 45.00
❑108, Mar 1961 45.00
❑109, Apr 1961 45.00
❑110, May 1961 45.00
❑111, Jun 1961 45.00
❑112, Jul 1961 45.00
❑113, Aug 1961 45.00
❑114, Sep 1961 45.00
❑115, Oct 1961 45.00
❑116, Nov 1961 45.00
❑117, Dec 1961 35.00
❑118, Jan 1962 35.00
❑119, Feb 1962 35.00
❑120, Mar 1962 ATh (a) 45.00
❑121, Apr 1962 28.00
❑122, May 1962 28.00
❑123, Jun 1962 28.00
❑124, Jul 1962 28.00
❑125, Aug 1962 28.00
❑126, Sep 1962 28.00
❑127, Oct 1962 28.00
❑128, Nov 1962 28.00
❑129, Dec 1962 28.00
❑130, Jan 1963 28.00
❑131, Feb 1963 22.00
❑132, Mar 1963 22.00
❑133, Apr 1963 22.00
❑134, May 1963 22.00
❑135, Jun 1963 22.00
❑136, Jul 1963 22.00
❑137, Sep 1963 22.00
❑138, Oct 1963 22.00
❑139, Dec 1963 22.00
❑140, Jan 1964 22.00
❑141, Mar 1964 22.00
❑142, Apr 1964 22.00
❑143, Jun 1964; MM (a);J'onn J'onzz; Martian Manhunter begins 90.00
❑144, Jul 1964 48.00
❑145, Sep 1964 40.00
❑146, Oct 1964 40.00
❑147, Dec 1964 40.00
❑148, Jan 1965 40.00
❑149, Mar 1965 ATh (a) 40.00
❑150, Apr 1965 40.00
❑151, Jun 1965 40.00
❑152, Jul 1965 40.00
❑153, Sep 1965; J'onn J'onzz 40.00
❑154, Oct 1965 40.00
❑155, Dec 1965 40.00
❑156, Jan 1966 O: Dial "H" For Hero. 1: Dial "H" For Hero. 1: Robby Reed. 65.00
❑157, Mar 1966 36.00
❑158, Apr 1966 36.00
❑159, Jun 1966 36.00
❑160, Jul 1966; Dial "H" for Hero; Robby Reed becomes Plastic Man 55.00
❑161, Sep 1966; Dial "H" for Hero 32.00
❑162, Oct 1966 32.00
❑163, Dec 1966 32.00
❑164, Jan 1967 32.00
❑165, Mar 1967 32.00
❑166, Apr 1967 32.00
❑167, Jun 1967 32.00
❑168, Jul 1967 32.00
❑169, Sep 1967 1: Gem Girl. 32.00
❑170, Oct 1967 32.00
❑171, Dec 1967; Dial "H" for Hero 32.00
❑172, Feb 1968 32.00
❑173, Apr 1968 32.00
❑174, Jun 1968; NA (a);Mystery format begins 24.00
❑175, Aug 1968 NA (a); 1: Cain. 38.00

N-MINT

❑176, Oct 1968 NA (a) 24.00
❑177, Dec 1968 NA (a) 24.00
❑178, Feb 1969 NA (a) 32.00
❑179, Apr 1969; BWr, JO, NA (a);Bernie Wrightson's first professional work 40.00
❑180, Jun 1969 SA, BWr, NA, GK, WW (a) 18.00
❑181, Aug 1969 BWr, NA (a) 18.00
❑182, Oct 1969 NA, AT, WH (a) 18.00
❑183, Dec 1969 BWr, NA, WW (a) 18.00
❑184, Feb 1970 BWr, NA, GK, WW, AT (a) 18.00
❑185, Apr 1970 AW, BWr, NA, WW (a) 18.00
❑186, Jun 1970 BWr, NA (a) 40.00
❑187, Aug 1970 NA, AT, WH (a) 14.00
❑188, Oct 1970 BWr, NA (a) 21.00
❑189, Dec 1970 NA, AT (a) 15.00
❑190, Feb 1971 NA, AT (a) 15.00
❑191, Apr 1971 NA (a) 15.00
❑192, Jun 1971 GM, NA (a) 15.00
❑193, Jul 1971 BWr (a) 46.00
❑194, Sep 1971 BWr (a) 15.00
❑195, Oct 1971; BWr (a);Swamp Thing prototype? 15.00
❑196, Nov 1971 NA (a) 15.00
❑197, Dec 1971 NA (a) 15.00
❑198, Jan 1972 15.00
❑199, Feb 1972 JK, NA, WW (a) 15.00
❑200, Mar 1972 15.00
❑201, Apr 1972 SA, BWr (a) 14.00
❑202, May 1972 SA (a) 14.00
❑203, Jun 1972 14.00
❑204, Jul 1972 BWr, AN (a) 20.00
❑205, Aug 1972 12.00
❑206, Sep 1972 12.00
❑207, Oct 1972 JSn, BWr, NR, JSt (a) 30.00
❑208, Nov 1972 12.00
❑209, Dec 1972 BWr, AA (a) 10.00
❑210, Jan 1973 10.00
❑211, Feb 1973 BWr, NR, AA (a) 10.00
❑212, Mar 1973 AN (a) 10.00
❑213, Apr 1973 BWr (a) 10.00
❑214, May 1973 BWr (a) 6.00
❑215, Jun 1973 6.00
❑216, Jul 1973 6.00
❑217, Sep 1973 BWr (c) 6.00
❑218, Oct 1973 6.00
❑219, Nov 1973 BWr (a) 6.00
❑220, Dec 1973 6.00
❑221, Jan 1974 BWr (a) 6.00
❑222, Feb 1974 6.00
❑223, Mar 1974 6.00
❑224, Apr 1974; 100-page giant; BWr, NA, AN (a); A: Phantom Stranger. Phantom Stranger 20.00
❑225, Jun 1974; 100-page giant AN (a); 15.00
❑226, Aug 1974; 100-page giant BWr, NR, AA (a); A: Phantom Stranger. 15.00
❑227, Oct 1974; 100-page giant NR (a) 15.00
❑228, Dec 1974; 100-page giant NR, NA, AT (a) 15.00
❑229, Feb 1975; 100-page giant 15.00
❑230, Apr 1975 5.00
❑231, May 1975 5.00
❑232, Jun 1975 5.00
❑233, Jul 1975 5.00
❑234, Aug 1975 5.00
❑235, Sep 1975 5.00
❑236, Oct 1975 SD, BWr, NA (a) 5.00
❑237, Nov 1975 5.00
❑238, Dec 1975 5.00
❑239, Feb 1976 5.00
❑240, Apr 1976 5.00
❑241, May 1976 5.00
❑242, Jun 1976 5.00
❑243, Jul 1976; Bicentennial #10 5.00
❑244, Aug 1976 5.00
❑245, Sep 1976 5.00
❑246, Oct 1976 5.00
❑247, Nov 1976 5.00
❑248, Dec 1976 5.00
❑249, Jan 1977 5.00
❑250, Feb 1977 5.00

Condition price index: Multiply "NM prices" above by: **0.83 for Very Fine/Near Mint**
0.66 for Very Fine • 0.33 for Fine • 0.2 for Very Good • 0.125 for Good

	N-MINT
❑251, Mar 1977; NA, WW (a);giant	4.00
❑252, May 1977; NA, AN (a);giant	4.00
❑253, Jul 1977; NA, AN (a);giant	4.00
❑254, Sep 1977; SD, NA, WH (a);giant	4.00
❑255, Nov 1977; BWr (a);giant	4.00
❑256, Jan 1978; BWr (a);giant	4.00
❑257, Mar 1978; MG (a);giant	4.00
❑258, May 1978; SD (a);giant	4.00
❑259, Jul 1978; DN, MG (a);giant	4.00
❑260, Sep 1978	3.00
❑261, Oct 1978	3.00
❑262, Nov 1978	3.00
❑263, Dec 1978	3.00
❑264, Jan 1979	3.00
❑265, Feb 1979	3.00
❑266, Mar 1979	3.00
❑267, Apr 1979	3.00
❑268, May 1979	3.00
❑269, Jun 1979	3.00
❑270, Jul 1979	3.00
❑271, Aug 1979	3.00
❑272, Sep 1979	3.00
❑273, Oct 1979	3.00
❑274, Nov 1979 JO (a)	3.00
❑275, Dec 1979	3.00
❑276, Jan 1980	3.00
❑277, Feb 1980	3.00
❑278, Mar 1980	3.00
❑279, Apr 1980	3.00
❑280, May 1980	3.00
❑281, Jun 1980	3.00
❑282, Jul 1980 JSn (a)	3.00
❑283, Aug 1980	3.00
❑284, Sep 1980	3.00
❑285, Oct 1980	3.00
❑286, Nov 1980	3.00
❑287, Dec 1980	3.00
❑288, Jan 1981	3.00
❑289, Feb 1981 1: I, Vampire.	3.00
❑290, Mar 1981; I, Vampire	3.00
❑291, Apr 1981; I, Vampire	3.00
❑292, May 1981	3.00
❑293, Jun 1981; I, Vampire	3.00
❑294, Jul 1981	3.00
❑295, Aug 1981	3.00
❑296, Sep 1981	3.00
❑297, Oct 1981	3.00
❑298, Nov 1981	3.00
❑299, Dec 1981; I, Vampire	3.00
❑300, Jan 1982	3.00
❑301, Feb 1982	3.00
❑302, Mar 1982; I, Vampire	3.00
❑303, Apr 1982; I, Vampire	3.00
❑304, May 1982; I, Vampire	3.00
❑305, Jun 1982; I, Vampire	3.00
❑306, Jul 1982; I, Vampire	3.00
❑307, Aug 1982; I, Vampire	3.00
❑308, Sep 1982; I, Vampire	3.00
❑309, Oct 1982; I, Vampire	3.00
❑310, Nov 1982; I, Vampire	3.00
❑311, Dec 1982; I, Vampire	3.00
❑312, Jan 1983; I, Vampire	3.00
❑313, Feb 1983	3.00
❑314, Mar 1983; I, Vampire	3.00
❑315, Apr 1983; I, Vampire	3.00
❑316, May 1983	3.00
❑317, Jun 1983	3.00
❑318, Jul 1983; I, Vampire	3.00
❑319, Aug 1983 D: I, Vampire.	3.00
❑320, Sep 1983	3.00
❑321, Oct 1983	3.00

HOUSE OF SECRETS
DC

	N-MINT
❑1, Nov 1956 MD (a)	1400.00
❑2, Jan 1957	550.00
❑3, Mar 1957 JK (a)	450.00
❑4, May 1957 JK (a)	350.00
❑5, Jul 1957	200.00
❑6, Sep 1957	200.00
❑7, Nov 1957	200.00
❑8, Jan 1958 JK (a)	230.00
❑9, Mar 1958	200.00
❑10, Jun 1958	200.00
❑11, Aug 1958	200.00
❑12, Sep 1958 JK (a)	200.00
❑13, Oct 1958	125.00
❑14, Nov 1958	125.00
❑15, Dec 1958	125.00
❑16, Jan 1959	110.00
❑17, Feb 1959	110.00
❑18, Mar 1959	110.00
❑19, Apr 1959	110.00
❑20, May 1959	110.00
❑21, Jun 1959	85.00
❑22, Jul 1959	80.00
❑23, Aug 1959 1: Mark Merlin.	100.00
❑24, Sep 1959	80.00
❑25, Oct 1959	80.00
❑26, Nov 1959	80.00
❑27, Dec 1959	80.00
❑28, Jan 1960	80.00
❑29, Feb 1960	80.00
❑30, Mar 1960	80.00
❑31, Apr 1960	65.00
❑32, May 1960	65.00
❑33, Jun 1960	65.00
❑34, Jul 1960	65.00
❑35, Aug 1960	65.00
❑36, Sep 1960	65.00
❑37, Oct 1960	65.00
❑38, Nov 1960	65.00
❑39, Dec 1960	65.00
❑40, Jan 1961	65.00
❑41, Feb 1961	65.00
❑42, Mar 1961	65.00
❑43, Apr 1961	65.00
❑44, May 1961	65.00
❑45, Jun 1961	65.00
❑46, Jul 1961	65.00
❑47, Aug 1961	65.00
❑48, Sep 1961	65.00
❑49, Oct 1961	65.00
❑50, Nov 1961	65.00
❑51, Dec 1961	52.00
❑52, Jan 1962	52.00
❑53, Mar 1962	52.00
❑54, May 1962	52.00
❑55, Jul 1962	52.00
❑56, Sep 1962	52.00
❑57, Nov 1962	52.00
❑58, Jan 1963	52.00
❑59, Mar 1963	52.00
❑60, May 1963	52.00
❑61, Jul 1963 1: Eclipso.	80.00
❑62, Sep 1963	60.00
❑63, Nov 1963	50.00
❑64, Jan 1964	50.00
❑65, Mar 1964	50.00
❑66, May 1964; Eclipso cover	65.00
❑67, Jul 1964	40.00
❑68, Sep 1964	36.00
❑69, Nov 1964	36.00
❑70, Jan 1965	36.00
❑71, Mar 1965	36.00
❑72, May 1965; Eclipso	36.00
❑73, Jul 1965 1: Prince Ra-Man.	36.00
❑74, Sep 1965; Eclipso	36.00
❑75, Nov 1965	36.00
❑76, Jan 1966; Eclipso	36.00
❑77, Mar 1966	36.00
❑78, May 1966	36.00
❑79, Jul 1966	36.00
❑80, Sep 1966	45.00
❑81, Sep 1969; 1: Abel. Mystery format begins	45.00
❑82, Nov 1969 NA (a)	15.00
❑83, Jan 1970 ATh (a)	15.00
❑84, Mar 1970 NA (c)	15.00
❑85, May 1970 NA, GK (a)	15.00
❑86, Jul 1970 NA (c); GM (a)	15.00
❑87, Sep 1970 NA (c); BWr (a)	15.00
❑88, Nov 1970	40.00

Swamp Thing made his first appearance in *House of Secrets* #92.

	N-MINT
❑89, Jan 1971 GM (a)	15.00
❑90, Mar 1971; RB, GM, NA (a);1st Buckler DC art	15.00
❑91, May 1971 MA, NA, WW (a)	15.00
❑92, Jul 1971 DD, ME (w); BWr, DD, TD (a); 1: Swamp Thing.	425.00
❑93, Sep 1971 BWr, JA (a)	22.00
❑94, Nov 1971 ATh, BWr (a)	22.00
❑95, Jan 1972	22.00
❑96, Mar 1972	22.00
❑97, May 1972	22.00
❑98, Jul 1972	22.00
❑99, Sep 1972	22.00
❑100, Oct 1972	22.00
❑101, Nov 1972	16.00
❑102, Dec 1972	16.00
❑103, Jan 1973	16.00
❑104, Feb 1973	16.00
❑105, Mar 1973	16.00
❑106, Apr 1973	16.00
❑107, May 1973	16.00
❑108, Jun 1973	16.00
❑109, Jul 1973	16.00
❑110, Aug 1973	16.00
❑111, Sep 1973	16.00
❑112, Oct 1973	16.00
❑113, Nov 1973	7.00
❑114, Dec 1973	7.00
❑115, Jan 1974	7.00
❑116, Feb 1974	7.00
❑117, Mar 1974 AA, AN (a)	7.00
❑118, Apr 1974; This issue's Statement of Ownership was also accidentally printed in Our Fighting Forces #148	7.00
❑119, May 1974	7.00
❑120, Jun 1974	7.00
❑121, Jul 1974	7.00
❑122, Aug 1974	7.00
❑123, Sep 1974 ATh (a)	7.00
❑124, Oct 1974	7.00
❑125, Nov 1974	7.00
❑126, Dec 1974	7.00
❑127, Jan 1975	7.00
❑128, Feb 1975	7.00
❑129, Mar 1975	7.00
❑130, Apr 1975	7.00
❑131, May 1975	7.00
❑132, Jun 1975	7.00
❑133, Jul 1975	7.00
❑134, Aug 1975	7.00
❑135, Sep 1975	7.00
❑136, Nov 1975	7.00
❑137, Jan 1976	7.00
❑138, Mar 1976	7.00
❑139, May 1976	7.00
❑140, Jul 1976 O: Patchwork Man.	7.00
❑141, Sep 1976 O: Patchwork Man.	7.00
❑142, Nov 1976	5.00
❑143, Jan 1977	5.00
❑144, Mar 1977	5.00
❑145, May 1977	5.00
❑146, Jul 1977	5.00
❑147, Sep 1977	5.00
❑148, Nov 1977	5.00
❑149, Jan 1978	5.00
❑150, Mar 1978	5.00
❑151, May 1978 MG (a)	5.00
❑152, Jul 1978	5.00

	N-MINT
❑153, Sep 1978	5.00
❑154, Nov 1978; Series continued in The Unexpected	5.00

HOUSE OF SECRETS (2ND SERIES)
DC / VERTIGO

	N-MINT
❑1, Oct 1996	3.00
❑2, Nov 1996	3.00
❑3, Dec 1996	3.00
❑4, Jan 1997	3.00
❑5, Feb 1997	3.00
❑6, Mar 1997	3.00
❑7, Apr 1997	3.00
❑8, May 1997	3.00
❑9, Jun 1997	3.00
❑10, Jul 1997	3.00
❑11, Aug 1997	3.00
❑12, Sep 1997	3.00
❑13, Oct 1997	3.00
❑14, Nov 1997	3.00
❑15, Dec 1997	3.00
❑16, Feb 1998	3.00
❑17, Mar 1998; covers form triptych	3.00
❑18, Apr 1998; covers form triptych .	3.00
❑19, May 1998; covers form triptych	3.00
❑20, Jun 1998	3.00
❑21, Jul 1998	2.50
❑22, Aug 1998	2.50
❑23, Sep 1998	2.50
❑24, Nov 1998	2.50
❑25, Dec 1998	2.50

HOUSE OF YANG
CHARLTON

	N-MINT
❑1, Jul 1975	15.00
❑2, Oct 1975	10.00
❑3, Dec 1975	10.00
❑4, Feb 1976	10.00
❑5, Apr 1976	10.00
❑6, Jun 1976	10.00

HOUSEWIVES AT PLAY
FANTAGRAPHICS / EROS

	N-MINT
❑1	2.95
❑2	2.95
❑3	2.95

HOWARD THE DUCK (VOL. 1)
MARVEL

	N-MINT
❑1, Jan 1976 FB (a); 1: Beverly. A: Spider-Man.	5.00
❑2, Mar 1976 FB (a)	2.00
❑3, May 1976 JB (a)	2.00
❑3/30 cent, May 1976; JB (a);30 cent regional price variant	20.00
❑4, Jul 1976 GC (a)	2.00
❑4/30 cent, Jul 1976; GC (a);30 cent regional price variant	20.00
❑5, Sep 1976 GC (a)	2.00
❑6, Nov 1976 GC (a)	2.00
❑7, Dec 1976 GC (a)	2.00
❑8, Jan 1977 GC (a)	2.00
❑9, Feb 1977 GC (a)	2.00
❑10, Mar 1977 GC (a)	2.00
❑11, Apr 1977 GC (a)	2.00
❑12, May 1977 GC (a); 1: Kiss (rock group).	6.00
❑13, Jun 1977 GC (a); A: Kiss (rock group).	4.00
❑13/35 cent, Jun 1977; 35 cent regional price variant	15.00
❑14, Jul 1977 GC (a)	2.00
❑14/35 cent, Jul 1977; GC (a);35 cent regional price variant	15.00
❑15, Aug 1977 GC (a); 1: Doctor Bong.	2.00
❑15/35 cent, Aug 1977; GC (a); 1: Doctor Bong. 35 cent regional price variant	15.00
❑16, Sep 1977; O: Doctor Bong. all-text issue	2.00
❑16/35 cent, Sep 1977; O: Doctor Bong. 35 cent regional price variant; all-text issue	15.00
❑17, Oct 1977 GC (a); O: Doctor Bong.	2.00
❑17/35 cent, Oct 1977, GC (a); O: Doctor Bong. 35 cent regional price variant	15.00
❑18, Nov 1977 GC (a)	2.00
❑19, Dec 1977 GC (a)	2.00
❑20, Jan 1978 GC (a); V: Sudol.	2.00
❑21, Feb 1978 CI (a); V: Soofi.	2.00
❑22, Mar 1978 VM (a)	2.00
❑23, Apr 1978 VM (a)	2.00
❑24, May 1978 GC (a)	2.00
❑25, Jun 1978 GC (a); A: Ringmaster.	2.00
❑26, Jul 1978 GC (a); A: Ringmaster.	2.00
❑27, Sep 1978 GC (a); A: Ringmaster.	2.00
❑28, Nov 1978 CI (a)	2.00
❑29, Jan 1979 ME (w)	2.00
❑30, Mar 1979 GC (a); V: Doctor Bong.	2.00
❑31, May 1979 AM, GC (a); V: Doctor Bong.	2.00
❑32, Jan 1986 PS (a); O: Howard the Duck.	2.00
❑33, Sep 1986 VM (a)	2.50
❑Annual 1, Oct 1977 VM (a)	2.00

HOWARD THE DUCK (VOL. 2)
MARVEL / MAX

	N-MINT
❑1, Mar 2002	2.99
❑2, Apr 2002	2.99
❑3, May 2002	2.99
❑4, Jun 2002	2.99
❑5, Jul 2002	2.99
❑6, Aug 2002	2.99

HOWARD THE DUCK (MAGAZINE)
MARVEL

	N-MINT
❑1, Oct 1979; VM (a);contains nudity	4.00
❑2, Dec 1979 GC, KJ (a)	3.00
❑3, Feb 1980 GC (a)	3.00
❑4, Mar 1980 GC, JB, KJ (a); A: Kiss. A: Beatles.	4.00
❑5, May 1980	3.00
❑6, Jul 1980	3.00
❑7, Sep 1980 GC (a); A: Man-Thing. .	3.00
❑8, Nov 1980; GC, MR (a);Batman parody	3.00
❑9, Mar 1981	3.00

HOWARD THE DUCK HOLIDAY SPECIAL
MARVEL

	N-MINT
❑1, Feb 1997	2.50

HOWARD THE DUCK: THE MOVIE
MARVEL

	N-MINT
❑1, Dec 1986 O: Howard the Duck. ...	1.00
❑2, Jan 1987	1.00
❑3, Feb 1987	1.00

HOWL
ETERNITY

	N-MINT
❑1, b&w	2.25
❑2, b&w	2.25

HOW THE WEST WAS WON
GOLD KEY

	N-MINT
❑1, Jul 1963	18.00

HOW TO DRAW COMICS COMIC, THE
SOLSON

	N-MINT
❑1, ca. 1985	1.95

HOW TO DRAW FELIX THE CAT AND HIS FRIENDS
FELIX

	N-MINT
❑1 1992, b&w	2.25

HOW TO DRAW MANGA
ANTARCTIC

	N-MINT
❑1	4.95
❑2	4.95
❑3, Feb 2001	4.95
❑4, Mar 2001	4.95
❑5, Apr 2001	4.95
❑6, Jun 2001	4.95
❑7, Aug 2001	4.95
❑8, Sep 2001	4.95
❑9, Oct 2001	4.95
❑10, Nov 2001	4.95
❑11, Jan 2002	4.95
❑12, Feb 2002	4.95
❑13, Mar 2002	4.95
❑14, Apr 2002	4.95
❑15, May 2002	4.95
❑16, Jun 2002	4.95
❑17, Jul 2002	4.95
❑18, Aug 2002	4.95
❑19, Oct 2002	4.95
❑20 2002	4.95
❑21 2002	4.95
❑22, Feb 2003	4.95
❑23, Apr 2003	4.95
❑24, May 2003	4.95
❑25, Aug 2003	4.95

HOW TO DRAW TEENAGE MUTANT NINJA TURTLES
SOLSON

	N-MINT
❑1	2.25

HOW TO PICK UP GIRLS IF YOU'RE A COMIC BOOK GEEK
3 FINGER PRINTS

	N-MINT
❑1, Jul 1997; cardstock cover	3.95

HOW TO PUBLISH COMICS
SOLSON

	N-MINT
❑1	2.00

H.R. PUFNSTUF
GOLD KEY

	N-MINT
❑1, Oct 1970	45.00
❑2, Jan 1971	30.00
❑3, Apr 1971	30.00
❑4, Jul 1971	26.00
❑5, Oct 1971	26.00
❑6, Jan 1972	26.00
❑7, Apr 1972	20.00
❑8, Jul 1972	20.00

HUCKLEBERRY HOUND & QUICK DRAW MCGRAW GIANT-SIZE FLIP BOOK
HARVEY

	N-MINT
❑1	2.25

HUEY, DEWEY, AND LOUIE JUNIOR WOODCHUCKS
GOLD KEY

	N-MINT
❑1	36.00
❑2, Aug 1967	20.00
❑3	16.00
❑4, Jan 1970; Reprints Walt Disney's Comics #181 and 227	12.00
❑5, Apr 1970; Reprints Walt Disney's Comics #125 and 132	12.00
❑6, Jul 1970	12.00
❑7, Oct 1970	12.00
❑8, Jan 1971	12.00
❑9, Apr 1971	12.00
❑10, Jul 1971	12.00
❑11, Oct 1971	10.00
❑12, Jan 1972 CB (w)	10.00
❑13, Mar 1972	10.00
❑14, May 1972	10.00
❑15, Jul 1972	10.00
❑16, Sep 1972	10.00
❑17, Nov 1972	10.00
❑18, Jan 1973	10.00
❑19, Mar 1973	10.00
❑20, May 1973	10.00
❑21, Jul 1973	8.00
❑22, Sep 1973	8.00
❑23, Nov 1973	8.00
❑24, Jan 1974	8.00
❑25, Mar 1974	8.00
❑26, May 1974; Reprints Walt Disney's Comics #232	8.00
❑27, Jul 1974	8.00
❑28, Sep 1974	8.00
❑29, Nov 1974	8.00
❑30, Jan 1975	8.00
❑31, Mar 1975	8.00
❑32, May 1975	8.00
❑33, Jul 1975	8.00
❑34, Sep 1975	8.00
❑35, Nov 1975; Reprints Huey, Dewey and Louie Junior Woodchucks #7 ..	8.00
❑36, Jan 1976	8.00
❑37, Mar 1976	8.00

	N-MINT
❑38, May 1976	8.00
❑39, Jul 1976	8.00
❑40	8.00
❑41; Reprints Huey, Dewey and Louie Junior Woodchucks #6	6.00
❑42, Mar 1977	6.00
❑43, Apr 1977	6.00
❑44, Jun 1977	6.00
❑45, Aug 1977	6.00
❑46, Sep 1977	6.00
❑47, Dec 1977	6.00
❑48, Feb 1978	6.00
❑49, Apr 1978	6.00
❑50, Jun 1978	6.00
❑51, Aug 1978	6.00
❑52, Sep 1978	6.00
❑53, Dec 1978	6.00
❑54, Feb 1979	6.00
❑55, Apr 1979	6.00
❑56, Jun 1979	6.00
❑57, Jul 1979	6.00
❑58, Aug 1979	6.00
❑59, Sep 1979	6.00
❑60, Dec 1979	6.00
❑61, Feb 1980	4.00
❑62, Mar 1980	4.00
❑63, ca. 1980	4.00
❑64, ca. 1980	4.00
❑65, Sep 1980	4.00
❑66, ca. 1980	4.00
❑67, Jan 1981	4.00
❑68, Jun 1981	4.00
❑69, Aug 1981	4.00
❑70, ca. 1981	4.00
❑71, Dec 1981	4.00
❑72, ca. 1982	4.00
❑73	4.00
❑74	4.00
❑75	4.00
❑76	4.00
❑77	4.00
❑78	4.00
❑79, ca. 1984	4.00
❑80, ca. 1984	4.00
❑81, ca. 1984	4.00

HUGGA BUNCH
MARVEL / STAR

	N-MINT
❑1, Oct 1986	1.00
❑2, Dec 1986	1.00
❑3, Feb 1986	1.00
❑4, Apr 1986	1.00
❑5, Jun 1986	1.00
❑6, Aug 1986	1.00

HUGO
FANTAGRAPHICS

	N-MINT
❑1	1.95
❑2	1.95
❑3, Jul 1985	1.95

HULK
MARVEL

	N-MINT
❑1, Apr 1999; JBy (w); DGr (a);wraparound cover	3.50
❑1/A, Apr 1999; JBy (w); DGr (a);Sunburst cover	5.00
❑1/Autographed, Apr 1999 JBy (w); DGr (a)	4.00
❑1/Gold, Apr 1999; JBy (w); DGr (a);DFE gold foil cover	4.00
❑2, May 1999 DGr (c); JBy (w); DGr (a)	2.50
❑3, Jun 1999 DGr (c); JBy (w); DGr (a)	2.50
❑4, Jul 1999 DGr (c); JBy (w); DGr (a)	2.50
❑5, Aug 1999 JBy (w); A: Avengers.	2.50
❑6, Sep 1999 DGr (c); JBy (w); DGr (a); A: Man-Thing.	2.50
❑7, Oct 1999 DGr (c); JBy (w); DGr (a); A: Man-Thing. A: Avengers.	2.50
❑8, Nov 1999 DGr (c); EL (w); SB (a); V: Wolverine.	2.50
❑9, Dec 1999 DGr (c); JOy (w); SB (a)	2.50
❑10, Jan 2000 JOy (w); SB (a)	2.50
❑11, Feb 2000 SB (c); JOy (w); SB (a)	2.50
❑12, Mar 2000 SB (c); SB (a)	2.50
❑13, Apr 2000 SB (c); SB (a)	2.50
❑14, May 2000 SB (c); SB (a)	2.50
❑15, Jun 2000 SB (c); SB (a)	2.50
❑16, Jul 2000 SB (c); SB (a)	2.50
❑17, Aug 2000 SB (c); SB (a)	2.50
❑18, Sep 2000 SB (c); SB (a)	2.50
❑19, Oct 2000 SB (a)	2.50
❑20, Nov 2000 SB (c); SB (a)	2.50
❑21, Dec 2000	2.25
❑22, Jan 2001	2.25
❑23, Feb 2001	2.25
❑24, Mar 2001; JR2 (c); JR2, DG (a); A: Abomination. A: Thunderbolt Ross. lower cover price; part of Marvel's Slashback program	2.00
❑25, Apr 2001; double-sized JR2 (c); JR2, TP (a); A: Abomination.	2.99
❑26, May 2001	2.25
❑27, Jun 2001 JR2 (c); JR2, TP (a)	2.25
❑28, Jul 2001 (c); JR2, TP (a)	2.25
❑29, Aug 2001	2.25
❑30, Sep 2001 TP (a)	2.25
❑31, Oct 2001 TP (a)	2.25
❑32, Nov 2001 TP (a)	2.25
❑33, Dec 2001	2.25
❑34, Jan 2002 JR2, TP (a)	12.50
❑35, Feb 2002 JR2, TP (a)	6.00
❑36, Mar 2002 JR2, TP (a)	5.00
❑37, Apr 2002 JR2, TP (a)	5.00
❑38, May 2002; JR2, TP (a);Norman Rockwell spoof cover	5.00
❑39, Jun 2002, JR2, TP (a);wraparound cover	4.00
❑40, Jul 2002, TP (a);wraparound cover	4.00
❑41, Aug 2002, TP (a);wraparound cover	4.00
❑42, Aug 2002, TP (a);wraparound cover	3.00
❑43, Sep 2002, JR2 (a);wraparound cover	3.00
❑44, Oct 2002, wraparound cover	3.00
❑45, Nov 2002, wraparound cover	3.00
❑46, Dec 2002, wraparound cover	2.50
❑47, Jan 2003, wraparound cover	2.25
❑48, Feb 2003, wraparound cover	2.25
❑49, Mar 2003, wraparound cover	2.25
❑50, Apr 2003, wraparound cover	5.00
❑51, May 2003	4.00
❑52, Jun 2003	3.00
❑53, Jun 2003	3.00
❑54, Jul 2003	3.00
❑55, Aug 2003	2.00
❑56, Aug 2003	2.25
❑57, Sep 2003	2.25
❑58, Sep 2003	2.25
❑59, Oct 2003	2.25
❑60, Nov 2003	2.25
❑61, Nov 2003	2.25
❑62, Dec 2003	2.25
❑63, Jan 2004	2.25
❑64, Feb 2004	2.99
❑65, Mar 2004	2.25
❑66, Apr 2004	2.25
❑67, Apr 2004	2.99
❑68, May 2004	2.99
❑69, May 2004	2.99
❑70, Jun 2004	2.99
❑71, Jun 2004 A: . A: Tony Stark.	2.99
❑72, Jul 2004 A: Tony Stark.	2.99
❑73, Aug 2004	2.25
❑74, Sep 2004	
❑Annual 1999, Oct 1999 DGr (c); JBy (w); DGr, KJ (a)	3.50
❑Annual 2000 A: She-Hulk. A: Avengers.	3.50
❑Annual 2001, Nov 2001 (c); EL (w) .	2.99

HULK, THE
MARVEL

	N-MINT
❑10, Aug 1978; format changes to color magazine; VM (c);Title changes to The Hulk	4.00
❑11, Oct 1978 GC, TD (a)	4.00
❑12, Dec 1978 KP (a)	4.00
❑13, Feb 1979 BSz, BMc (a)	4.00
❑14, Apr 1979 BSz, BMc (a)	4.00
❑15, Jun 1979 BSz, AA, BMc (a)	4.00
❑16, Aug 1979 MZ (a)	4.00
❑17, Oct 1979 BSz, AA, KJ (a)	4.00
❑18, Dec 1979 BSz, AA, KJ (a)	4.00
❑19, Feb 1980 GC, HT, AA, JSe, BWi (a)	4.00
❑20, Apr 1980 BSz, AA (a)	4.00
❑21, Jun 1980 HC, BMc (a)	4.00
❑22, Aug 1980 HC, AA (a)	4.00
❑23, Oct 1980 JB, HC, BA, AA (a)	4.00
❑24, Dec 1980 GC, HC, AA (a)	4.00
❑25, Feb 1981 GC, HC, AA (a)	4.00
❑26, Apr 1981 JB (c); GC, AA (a)	4.00
❑27, Jun 1981 GC (a)	4.00

When the *Howard the Duck* movie was released in 1986, Marvel produced two additional issues of the ongoing series that had been canceled in 1979.

© 1986 Marvel Comics

HULK/PITT
MARVEL

	N-MINT
❑1, Dec 1996	5.99

HULK: PROJECT H.I.D.E.
MARVEL

	N-MINT
❑1, Aug 1998; No cover price; prototype for children's comic	2.00

HULK SMASH
MARVEL

	N-MINT
❑1, Mar 2001	2.99
❑2, Apr 2001	2.99

HULK: THE MOVIE ADAPTATION
MARVEL

	N-MINT
❑1, Aug 2003	3.50

HULK 2099
MARVEL

	N-MINT
❑1, Dec 1994	2.50
❑2, Jan 1995	1.50
❑3, Feb 1995	1.50
❑4, Mar 1995	1.50
❑5, Apr 1995	1.50
❑6, May 1995	1.50
❑7, Jun 1995	1.95
❑8, Jul 1995	1.95
❑9, Aug 1995	1.95
❑10, Sep 1995; continued in 2099 A.D. Apocalypse #1	1.95

HULK: UNCHAINED
MARVEL

	N-MINT
❑1, Feb 2004	2.99
❑2, Apr 2004	2.99
❑3, May 2004	2.99

HULK VERSUS THING
MARVEL

	N-MINT
❑1, Dec 1999; Reprints Fantastic Four #24, 26, 112, Marvel Features #11	3.99

HULK/WOLVERINE: 6 HOURS
MARVEL

	N-MINT
❑1, Feb 2003	2.99
❑2, Mar 2003	2.99
❑3, Apr 2003	2.99
❑4, May 2003	2.99

HUMAN DEFENSE CORPS
DC

	N-MINT
❑1, Jul 2003	2.50
❑2, Aug 2003	2.50
❑3, Sep 2003	2.50
❑4, Oct 2003	2.50

N-MINT

- ❑5, Nov 2003 ... 2.50
- ❑6, Dec 2003 ... 2.50

HUMAN FLY, THE
MARVEL

- ❑1, Sep 1977 O: Human Fly. 1: Human Fly. A: Spider-Man. ... 3.00
- ❑1/35 cent, Sep 1977; O: Human Fly. 1: Human Fly. A: Spider-Man. 35 cent regional price variant ... 15.00
- ❑2, Oct 1977 Cl (a); A: Ghost Rider. .. 2.00
- ❑2/35 cent, Oct 1977; Cl (a); A: Ghost Rider. 35 cent regional price variant ... 15.00
- ❑3, Nov 1977 ... 1.50
- ❑4, Dec 1977 ... 1.50
- ❑5, Jan 1978 ... 1.50
- ❑6, Feb 1978 ... 1.50
- ❑7, Mar 1978 ... 1.50
- ❑8, Apr 1978 ... 1.50
- ❑9, May 1978 A: Daredevil. ... 1.50
- ❑10, Jun 1978 ... 1.50
- ❑11, Jul 1978 ... 1.50
- ❑12, Aug 1978 ... 1.50
- ❑13, Sep 1978 ... 1.50
- ❑14, Oct 1978 ... 1.50
- ❑15, Nov 1978 ... 1.50
- ❑16, Dec 1978 ... 1.50
- ❑17, Jan 1979 ... 1.50
- ❑18, Feb 1979 ... 1.50
- ❑19, Mar 1979 ... 1.50

HUMAN GARGOYLES, THE
ETERNITY

- ❑1, Jun 1988, b&w ... 1.95
- ❑2, Aug 1988, b&w ... 1.95
- ❑3, b&w ... 1.95
- ❑4, b&w ... 1.95

HUMAN HEAD COMIX
ICONOGRAFIX

- ❑1, b&w ... 2.50

HUMAN POWERHOUSE, THE
PURE IMAGINATION

- ❑1, b&w ... 2.00

HUMAN REMAINS
BLACK EYE

- ❑1 ... 3.50

HUMAN TARGET
DC / VERTIGO

- ❑1, Apr 1999 ... 2.95
- ❑2, May 1999 ... 2.95
- ❑3, Jun 1999 ... 2.95
- ❑4, Jul 1999 ... 2.95

HUMAN TARGET (2ND SERIES)
DC / VERTIGO

- ❑1, Oct 2003 ... 2.95
- ❑2, Nov 2003 ... 2.95
- ❑3, Dec 2003 ... 2.95
- ❑4, Jan 2004 ... 2.95
- ❑5, Feb 2004 ... 2.95
- ❑6, Mar 2004 ... 2.95
- ❑7, Apr 2004 ... 2.95
- ❑8, May 2004 ... 2.95
- ❑9, Jun 2004 ... 2.95
- ❑10, Jul 2004 ... 2.95
- ❑11, Aug 2004 ... 2.95
- ❑12, Sep 2004 ...

HUMAN TARGET SPECIAL
DC

- ❑1, Nov 1991 ... 2.00

HUMAN TARGET: STRIKE ZONE
DC

- ❑1, ca 2004 ... 9.95

HUMAN TORCH, THE (2ND SERIES)
MARVEL

- ❑1, Sep 1974; JK (a);Torch vs. Torch Reprints Strange Tales #101; Horror Hotel Reprints The Human Torch (1st series) #33 ... 6.00
- ❑2, Nov 1974; JK (a);Reprints Torch story from Strange Tales #102 and The Human Torch (1st series) #30 ... 4.00
- ❑3, Jan 1975; SL (w); JK (a);Reprints Torch story from Strange Tales #103, Sub-Mariner #23 ... 3.00
- ❑4, Mar 1975; Reprints Torch story from Strange Tales #104, The Human Torch (1st series) #38 ... 3.00
- ❑5, May 1975; Reprints Torch story from Strange Tales #105, The Human Torch (1st series) #38 ... 3.00
- ❑6, Jul 1975; Reprints Torch story from Strange Tales #106, The Human Torch (1st series) #38 ... 3.00
- ❑7, Sep 1975; Reprints Torch story from Strange Tales #107, Sub-Mariner #35 ... 3.00
- ❑8, Nov 1975; JK (a);Reprints Torch story from Strange Tales #108, Marvel Super-Heroes #16 ... 3.00

HUMAN TORCH (3RD SERIES)
MARVEL

- ❑1, Jun 2003 ... 2.50
- ❑2, Jul 2003 ... 2.50
- ❑3, Aug 2003 ... 2.50
- ❑4, Sep 2003 ... 2.50
- ❑5, Oct 2003 ... 2.50
- ❑6, Nov 2003 ... 2.99
- ❑7, Jan 2004 ... 2.50
- ❑8, Feb 2004 ... 2.99
- ❑9, Mar 2004 ... 2.99
- ❑10, Apr 2004 ... 2.99
- ❑11, May 2004 ... 2.99
- ❑12, Jun 2004 ... 2.99

HUMANTS
LEGACY

- ❑1 ... 2.45
- ❑2 ... 2.45

HUMMINGBIRD
SLAVE LABOR

- ❑1, Jun 1996 ... 4.95

HUMONGOUS MAN
ALTERNATIVE

- ❑1, Sep 1997, b&w ... 2.25
- ❑2, Nov 1997, b&w ... 2.25

HUMOR ON THE CUTTING...EDGE
EDGE

- ❑1, b&w ... 2.95
- ❑2, b&w ... 2.95
- ❑3, b&w ... 2.95
- ❑4, b&w ... 2.95

HUNCHBACK OF NOTRE DAME, THE (DISNEY'S...)
MARVEL

- ❑1, Jul 1996; adapts movie; square binding; cardstock cover ... 4.95

HUNTER'S HEART
DC / PARADOX

- ❑1, b&w; digest ... 5.95
- ❑2, b&w; digest ... 5.95
- ❑3, b&w; digest ... 5.95

HUNTER: THE AGE OF MAGIC
DC / VERTIGO

- ❑1, Sep 2001 ... 3.50
- ❑2, Oct 2001 ... 3.00
- ❑3, Nov 2001 ... 3.00
- ❑4, Dec 2001 ... 3.00
- ❑5, Jan 2002 ... 3.00
- ❑6, Feb 2002 ... 3.00
- ❑7, Mar 2002 ... 3.00
- ❑8, Apr 2002 ... 3.00
- ❑9, May 2002 ... 3.00
- ❑10, Jun 2002 ... 3.00
- ❑11, Jul 2002 ... 2.50
- ❑12, Aug 2002 ... 2.50
- ❑13, Sep 2002 ... 2.50
- ❑14, Oct 2002 ... 2.75
- ❑15, Nov 2002 ... 2.75
- ❑16, Dec 2002 ... 2.75
- ❑17, Jan 2003 ... 2.75
- ❑18, Feb 2003 ... 2.75
- ❑19, Mar 2003 ... 2.75
- ❑20, Apr 2003 ... 2.75
- ❑21, May 2003 ... 2.75
- ❑22, Jun 2003 ... 2.75
- ❑23, Jul 2003 ... 2.75
- ❑24, Aug 2003 ... 2.75
- ❑25, Sep 2003 ... 2.75

HUNT FOR BLACK WIDOW, THE
FLEETWAY-QUALITY

- ❑1; Judge Dredd ... 2.95

HUNTING, THE
NORTHSTAR

- ❑1, Nov 1993 ... 3.95

HUNTRESS, THE
DC

- ❑1, Apr 1989 O: The Huntress III (Helena Bertinelli). 1: The Huntress III (Helena Bertinelli). ... 2.50
- ❑2, May 1989 JSa (a) ... 2.00
- ❑3, Jun 1989 ... 2.00
- ❑4, Jul 1989 ... 1.50
- ❑5, Aug 1989 ... 1.50
- ❑6, Sep 1989 ... 1.25
- ❑7, Oct 1989 ... 1.25
- ❑8, Nov 1989 ... 1.25
- ❑9, Dec 1989 ... 1.25
- ❑10, Jan 1990 ... 1.25
- ❑11, Feb 1990 ... 1.25
- ❑12, Mar 1990 ... 1.25
- ❑13, Apr 1990 ... 1.25
- ❑14, May 1990 JSa (a) ... 1.25
- ❑15, Jun 1990 ... 1.25
- ❑16, Jul 1990 ... 1.25
- ❑17, Aug 1990 A: Batman. ... 1.25
- ❑18, Sep 1990 A: Batman. ... 1.25
- ❑19, Oct 1990 A: Batman. ... 1.25

HUNTRESS, THE (MINI-SERIES)
DC

- ❑1, Jun 1994 ... 2.00
- ❑2, Jul 1994 ... 2.00
- ❑3, Aug 1994 ... 2.00
- ❑4, Sep 1994 ... 2.00

HUP
LAST GASP

- ❑1, ca. 1986, b&w ... 3.00
- ❑2 ... 3.00
- ❑3 ... 3.00
- ❑4, ca. 1992 ... 3.00

HURRICANE GIRLS
ANTARCTIC

- ❑1, Jul 1995 ... 3.50
- ❑2, Sep 1995 ... 3.50
- ❑3, Nov 1995 ... 3.50
- ❑4 ... 3.50
- ❑5 ... 3.50
- ❑6 ... 3.50
- ❑7, Aug 1996 ... 3.50

HURRICANE LEROUX
INFERNO

- ❑1 ... 2.50

HUSTLER COMIX
L.F.P.

- ❑1, Spr 1997; magazine ... 4.99
- ❑2, Sum 1997; magazine ... 4.99
- ❑3, Fal 1997; magazine ... 4.99
- ❑4, Win 1997; magazine ... 4.99

HUSTLER COMIX (VOL. 2)
L.F.P.

- ❑1, Spr 1998; magazine ... 4.99
- ❑2, May 1998; magazine ... 4.99
- ❑3, Jul 1998; magazine ... 4.99
- ❑4, Sep 1998; magazine ... 4.99
- ❑5, Nov 1998; magazine ... 4.99

HUSTLER COMIX XXX
L.F.P.

- ❑1, Jan 1999; magazine ... 5.99

HUTCH OWEN'S WORKING HARD
NEW HAT

- ❑1, b&w ... 3.95

N-MINT

HY-BREED, THE
Division

❑1, ca. 1994, b&w ... 2.25
❑2, ca. 1994, b&w ... 2.25
❑3, ca. 1994, b&w ... 2.25
❑4, b&w ... 3.00
❑5, b&w ... 2.50
❑6, b&w ... 2.50
❑7, b&w ... 2.50
❑8 ... 2.50
❑9 ... 2.50

HYBRID: ETHERWORLDS
Dimension 5

❑1 ... 2.50
❑2 ... 2.50
❑3 ... 2.50

HYBRIDS (1ST SERIES)
Continuity

❑0, Apr 1993; silver and red foil covers 1.00
❑1, Apr 1993; trading cards; diecut cardstock cover ... 2.50
❑2, Jun 1993; thermal cover; trading card ... 2.50
❑3, Aug 1993; trading card; Deathwatch 2000 dropped from indicia; Published out of sequence after #5 2.50
❑4; Published out of sequence after #5, #3 ... 2.50
❑5 ... 2.50

HYBRIDS (2ND SERIES)
Continuity

❑1, Jan 1994; Embossed cover ... 2.50

HYBRIDS: THE ORIGIN
Continuity

❑1; really Revengers: Hybrids Special #1 ... 2.50
❑2, Jul 1993; "Revengers Special" on cover ... 2.50
❑3, Sep 1993; "Revengers Special" on cover ... 2.50
❑4, Dec 1993 ... 2.50
❑5, Jan 1994 ... 2.50

HYDE-25
Harris

❑0, Apr 1995; Reprints Vampirella (Magazine) #1 in color ... 2.95

HYDROGEN BOMB FUNNIES
Rip Off

❑1 ... 5.00

HYDROPHIDIAN
NBM

❑1 ... 10.95

HYENA
Tundra

❑1, b&w ... 3.95
❑2, b&w ... 3.95
❑3, b&w ... 3.95
❑4 ... 3.95

HYPER COMIX
Kitchen Sink

❑1 ... 5.00

HYPER DOLLS
Ironcat

❑1 ... 2.95
❑2 ... 2.95

HYPER DOLLS (VOL. 2)
Ironcat

❑1 ... 2.95
❑2 ... 2.95
❑3 ... 2.95
❑4 ... 2.95
❑5 ... 2.95
❑6, Jul 1999 ... 2.95

HYPERKIND
Marvel / Razorline

❑1, Sep 1993; Foil embossed cover .. 2.50
❑2, Oct 1993 ... 1.75
❑3, Nov 1993 ... 1.75
❑4, Dec 1993 ... 1.75
❑5, Jan 1994 ... 1.75

N-MINT

❑6, Feb 1994 ... 1.75
❑7, Mar 1994 ... 1.75
❑8, Apr 1994 ... 1.75
❑9, May 1994 ... 1.75

HYPERKIND UNLEASHED!
Marvel

❑1, Aug 1994 ... 2.95

HYPERSONIC
Dark Horse

❑1, Nov 1997 ... 2.95
❑2, Dec 1997 ... 2.95
❑3, Jan 1998 ... 2.95
❑4, Feb 1998 ... 2.95

HYPER VIOLENTS
CFD

❑1, Jul 1996, b&w ... 2.95

I

I 4 N I
Mermaid

❑1 1994 ... 2.25
❑2, Feb 1995 ... 2.25

I AM LEGEND
Eclipse

❑1, b&w ... 5.95
❑2 ... 5.95
❑3 ... 5.95
❑4 ... 5.95

I BEFORE E
Fantagraphics

❑1, b&w ... 3.95
❑1-2, May 1994 ... 3.95
❑2, b&w ... 3.95

I-BOTS (ISAAC ASIMOV'S...) (1ST SERIES)
Tekno

❑1, Dec 1995 HC (w); GP (a); 1: the I•Bots. ... 2.00
❑2, Dec 1995 HC (w); GP (a) ... 2.00
❑3, Jan 1996 HC (w); GP (a) ... 2.25
❑4, Feb 1996 HC (w); GP (a) ... 2.25
❑5, Mar 1996 HC (w); GP (a) ... 2.25
❑6, Apr 1996 HC (w); GP (a) ... 2.25
❑7, May 1996 HC (w); GP (a); A: Lady Justice. ... 2.25

I-BOTS (ISAAC ASIMOV'S...) (2ND SERIES)
Big

❑1, Jun 1996 ... 2.25
❑2, Jul 1996 ... 2.25
❑3, Aug 1996 ... 2.25
❑4, Sep 1996 ... 2.25
❑5, Oct 1996 ... 2.25
❑6, Nov 1996; E.C. tribute cover ... 2.25
❑7, Dec 1996; forms triptych ... 2.25
❑8, Jan 1997; forms triptych ... 2.25
❑9, Feb 1997; forms triptych ... 2.25

ICANDY
DC / Vertigo

❑1 ... 0.00
❑2 ... 0.00
❑3 ... 0.00
❑4 ... 0.00
❑5 ... 0.00
❑6 ... 0.00

ICARUS (AIRCEL)
Aircel

❑1 1987 ... 2.00
❑2, Apr 1987 ... 2.00
❑3 1987 ... 2.00
❑4 1987 ... 2.00
❑5 1987 ... 2.00

ICARUS (KARDIA)
Kardia

❑1, Jun 1992 ... 2.25

Carl Barks plotted many of the adventures of *Huey, Dewey, and Louie Junior Woodchucks.*
© 1972 Walt Disney Productions.

N-MINT

ICE AGE ON THE WORLD OF MAGIC: THE GATHERING
Acclaim / Armada

❑1, Jul 1995; bound-in Magic card (Chub Toad) ... 2.50
❑2, Aug 1995; bound-in Chub Toad card from Ice Age ... 2.50
❑3, Sep 1995; polybagged with sheet of creature tokens ... 2.50
❑4, Oct 1995; polybagged with sheet of creature tokens ... 2.50

ICEMAN (1ST SERIES)
Marvel

❑1, Dec 1984 O: Iceman. ... 2.50
❑2, Feb 1985 ... 2.50
❑3, Apr 1985 ... 2.50
❑4, Jun 1985 ... 2.50

ICEMAN (2ND SERIES)
Marvel

❑1, Dec 2001 ... 2.99
❑2, Jan 2002 ... 2.50
❑3, Feb 2002 ... 2.50
❑4, Mar 2002 ... 2.50

ICICLE
Hero

❑1, Jul 1992, b&w ... 4.95
❑2, b&w ... 3.50
❑3, b&w ... 3.50
❑4, b&w ... 3.50
❑5, b&w ... 3.95

I COME IN PEACE
Greater Mercury

❑1 ... 1.50

ICON
DC / Milestone

❑1, May 1993 O: Rocket. O: Icon. 1: S.H.R.E.D.. 1: Rocket. 1: Icon. ... 2.00
❑1/CS, May 1993; O: Rocket. O: Icon. poster; trading card ... 2.95
❑2, Jun 1993 1: Payback. ... 1.50
❑3, Jul 1993 ... 1.50
❑4, Aug 1993; A: Blood Syndicate. Rocket's pregnant ... 1.50
❑5, Sep 1993 V: Blood Syndicate. ... 1.50
❑6, Oct 1993 V: Blood Syndicate. ... 1.50
❑7, Nov 1993 ... 1.50
❑8, Dec 1993 O: Icon. ... 1.50
❑9, Jan 1994 ... 1.50
❑10, Feb 1994 V: Holocaust. ... 1.50
❑11, Mar 1994 KB (w); 1: Todd Loomis. ... 1.50
❑12, Apr 1994 1: Gideon's Cord. ... 1.50
❑13, May 1994 1: Buck Wild. ... 1.50
❑14, Jun 1994 ... 1.50
❑15, Jul 1994 A: Superboy. ... 1.75
❑16, Aug 1994 A: Superman. ... 1.75
❑17, Sep 1994 ... 1.75
❑18, Oct 1994 ... 1.75
❑19, Nov 1994 ... 1.75
❑20, Dec 1994 A: Static. A: Wise Son. A: Dharma. A: Hardware. ... 1.75
❑21, Jan 1995 ... 1.75
❑22, Feb 1995 1: New Rocket. A: Static. A: Hardware. A: DMZ. ... 1.75
❑23, Mar 1995 ... 1.75
❑24, Apr 1995; Rocket's baby born ... 1.75
❑25, May 1995; Giant-size ... 2.95
❑26, Jun 1995 V: Oblivion. ... 1.75

N-MINT

❑27, Jul 1995; Icon returns from space 2.50
❑28, Aug 1995 2.50
❑29, Sep 1995 2.50
❑30, Oct 1995; Funeral of Buck Wild . 2.50
❑31, Nov 1995 1.00
❑32, Dec 1995 2.50
❑33, Jan 1996 2.50
❑34, Feb 1996 2.50
❑35, Mar 1996 2.50
❑36, Apr 1996 2.50
❑37, Sep 1996; Icon in the 1920s 2.50
❑38, Oct 1996 V: Holocaust. 2.50
❑39, Nov 1996 V: Holocaust. 2.50
❑40, Dec 1996 V: Blood Syndicate. 2.50
❑41, Jan 1997 2.50
❑42, Feb 1997 2.50

ICON DEVIL
SPIDER

❑1 1.50
❑2 1.50

ICON DEVIL (VOL. 2)
SPIDER

❑2, b&w 2.25

ICONOGRAFIX SPECIAL
ICONOGRAFIX

❑1, b&w 2.50

ICZER 3
CPM

❑1, Sep 1996, b&w 2.95
❑2, Oct 1996, b&w 2.95

ID
FANTAGRAPHICS / EROS

❑1, b&w 2.50
❑2, b&w 2.50
❑3, b&w 2.50
❑3-2, Jun 1995, b&w 2.95

ID4: INDEPENDENCE DAY
MARVEL

❑0, Jun 1996; prequel to movie 2.50
❑1, Jul 1996; adapts movie 1.95
❑2, Aug 1996; adapts movie 1.95

IDENTITY CRISIS
DC

❑1, Aug 2004 4.50
❑2, Sep 2004

IDENTITY DISC
MARVEL / VERTIGO

❑1, Aug 2004 2.99
❑2, Sep 2004

I DIE AT MIDNIGHT
DC / VERTIGO

❑1, ca. 2000 2.95

IDIOTLAND
FANTAGRAPHICS

❑1, b&w 2.95
❑2, b&w 2.50
❑3, b&w 2.50
❑4, b&w 2.50
❑5, b&w 2.50
❑6, Aug 1994, b&w 2.50

IDLE WORSHIP
VISCERAL

❑1 2.95

IDOL
MARVEL / EPIC

❑1 2.95
❑2 2.95
❑3 2.95

I DREAM OF JEANNIE (DELL)
DELL

❑1, Apr 1966 60.00
❑2, Dec 1966 40.00

I DREAM OF JEANNIE (AIRWAVE)
AIRWAVE

❑1, b&w 2.95

I FEEL SICK
SLAVE LABOR

❑1, Aug 1999 3.95

IGRAT
VEROTIK

❑1, Nov 1995 2.95

IGRAT ILLUSTRATIONS, THE
VEROTIK

❑1, Apr 1997; pin-ups; embossed card-stock cover 3.95

I HAD A DREAM
KING INK EMPIRE

❑1, Jun 1995 2.95

I HUNT MONSTERS
ANTARCTIC

❑1, Mar 2004 2.99
❑2, Apr 2004 2.99
❑3, May 2004 2.99

IKE AND KITZI
A CAPELLA

❑1 2.50

ILIAD
SLAVE LABOR / AMAZE INK

❑1, Dec 1997, b&w 2.95
❑2, Jan 1998, b&w 2.95

ILIAD II
MICMAC

❑1, b&w 2.00
❑2, b&w 2.00
❑3, b&w 2.00

ILLEGAL ALIENS
ECLIPSE

❑1, Sep 1999, b&w 2.50

ILLUMINATIONS (VOL. 2)
MONOLITH

❑1 2.50
❑2 2.50
❑3 2.50
❑4 2.50
❑5 2.50

ILLUMINATOR
MARVEL / NELSON

❑1, ca. 1993 4.99
❑2, ca. 1993 4.99
❑3, ca. 1993 2.95

ILLUMINATUS (EYE-N-APPLE)
EYE-N-APPLE

❑1 2.00
❑2 2.00

ILLUMINATUS! (RIP OFF)
RIP OFF

❑1, Oct 1990, b&w 2.50
❑2, Dec 1990, b&w 2.50
❑3, Apr 1991, b&w 2.50

ILLUSTRATED CLASSEX
COMIC ZONE

❑1, b&w 2.75

ILLUSTRATED DORE: BOOK OF GENESIS
TOME

❑1, b&w 2.50

ILLUSTRATED DORE: BOOK OF THE APOCRYPHA
TOME

❑1, b&w 2.50

ILLUSTRATED EDITIONS
THWACK! POW!

❑1, Feb 1995 1.95

ILLUSTRATED KAMA SUTRA, THE
NBM

❑1 12.95

ILLUSTRATED TALES (JAXON'S...)
FTR

❑1 1.95

I LOVE LUCY
ETERNITY

❑1, May 1990, b&w; strip reprint 2.95
❑2, Jun 1990, b&w; strip reprint 2.95
❑3, Jul 1990, b&w; strip reprint 2.95
❑4, Aug 1990, b&w; strip reprint 2.95
❑5, Sep 1990, b&w; strip reprint 2.95
❑6, Oct 1990, b&w; strip reprint 2.95

I LOVE LUCY BOOK TWO
ETERNITY

❑1, Nov 1990, b&w; strip reprints 2.95
❑2, Dec 1990, b&w; strip reprints 2.95
❑3, Jan 1991, b&w; strip reprints 2.95
❑4, Feb 1991, b&w; strip reprints 2.95
❑5, Mar 1991, b&w; strip reprints 2.95
❑6, Apr 1991, b&w; strip reprints 2.95

I LOVE LUCY IN 3-D
ETERNITY

❑1 3.95

I LOVE LUCY IN FULL COLOR
ETERNITY

❑1; comic book reprint; Collects I Love Lucy # 4,5,8,16 5.95

I LOVE NEW YORK
LINSNER.COM

❑1, ca. 2002; A: Dawn. 9/11 benefit issue; title appears on cover, spray painted on World Trade Center 10.00

I LOVE YOU (CHARLTON)
CHARLTON

❑7, Sep 1955; Continued from In Love #6 55.00
❑8 1955 16.00
❑9 16.00
❑10 1956 16.00
❑11 1956 14.00
❑12 1956 14.00
❑13 14.00
❑14 1957 14.00
❑15, Oct 1957 14.00
❑16 14.00
❑17 1958; Giant-size 18.00
❑18 1958 14.00
❑19 1958 14.00
❑20, Oct 1958 14.00
❑21, Jan 1959 12.00
❑22 1959 12.00
❑23 1959 12.00
❑24 1959 12.00
❑25 1959 12.00
❑26 1959 12.00
❑27 12.00
❑28 1960 12.00
❑29 1960 12.00
❑30 1960 12.00
❑31 10.00
❑32 10.00
❑33, Mar 1961 10.00
❑34, May 1961 10.00
❑35, Jul 1961 10.00
❑36, Sep 1961 10.00
❑37 1961 10.00
❑38 10.00
❑39 1962 10.00
❑40 1962 10.00
❑41 1962 10.00
❑42, Oct 1962 10.00
❑43, Dec 1963 10.00
❑44, Feb 1963 10.00
❑45, Apr 1963 10.00
❑46, Jun 1963 10.00
❑47, Aug 1963 10.00
❑48, Oct 1963 10.00
❑49, Feb 1964 10.00
❑50, Apr 1964 10.00
❑51, Jun 1964 8.00
❑52, Aug 1964 8.00
❑53, Oct 1964 8.00
❑54, Jan 1965 8.00
❑55, Mar 1965 8.00
❑56, May 1965 8.00

N-MINT

❑57, Jul 1965 8.00
❑58, Sep 1965 8.00
❑59, Nov 1965 8.00
❑60, Jan 1966; Elvis Presley story 60.00
❑61, Mar 1966 4.00
❑62, May 1966 4.00
❑63, Jul 1966 4.00
❑64, Sep 1966 4.00
❑65, Nov 1966 4.00
❑66, Feb 1967 4.00
❑67, Apr 1967 4.00
❑68, Jun 1967 4.00
❑69, Aug 1967 4.00
❑70, Oct 1967 3.00
❑71 3.00
❑72 3.00
❑73, Jun 1968 3.00
❑74, Aug 1968 3.00
❑75, Oct 1968 3.00
❑76, Dec 1968 3.00
❑77, Jan 1969 3.00
❑78, Mar 1969 3.00
❑79, May 1969 3.00
❑80, Jul 1969 3.00
❑81, Sep 1969 3.00
❑82, Nov 1969 3.00
❑83, Jan 1970 3.00
❑84, Mar 1970 3.00
❑85, May 1970 3.00
❑86, Jul 1970 3.00
❑87, Sep 1970 3.00
❑88, Nov 1970 3.00
❑89, Jan 1971 3.00
❑90, Mar 1971 3.00
❑91, May 1971 2.50
❑92, Jul 1971 2.50
❑93, Sep 1971 2.50
❑94, Nov 1971 2.50
❑95, Jan 1972 2.50
❑96, Mar 1972 2.50
❑97, May 1972 2.50
❑98, Jul 1972 2.50
❑99, Sep 1972 2.50
❑100, Dec 1972 2.50
❑101, Jan 1973 2.50
❑102, Mar 1973 2.50
❑103, May 1973 2.50
❑104, Jul 1973 2.50
❑105, Sep 1973 2.50
❑106, Nov 1973 2.50
❑107, Jun 1974 2.50
❑108, Sep 1974 2.50
❑109, Nov 1974 2.50
❑110, Jan 1975 2.50
❑111, Mar 1975 2.50
❑112, May 1975 2.50
❑113 1975 2.50
❑114, Oct 1975 2.50
❑115, Dec 1975 2.50
❑116, Feb 1976 2.50
❑117, Apr 1976 2.50
❑118, Jun 1976 2.50
❑119, Aug 1976 2.50
❑120, Oct 1976 2.50
❑121, Dec 1976; End of original run (1976) 2.50
❑122, Mar 1979; Series begins again (1979) 1.50
❑123, Jun 1979 1.50
❑124 1979 1.50
❑125 1979 1.50
❑126 1979 1.50
❑127 1.50
❑128, Feb 1980 1.50
❑129, Mar 1980 1.50
❑130, May 1980; Final issue 1.50

I LOVE YOU (AVALON)
AVALON

❑1 2.95

N-MINT

I LOVE YOU SPECIAL
AVALON

❑1, b&w 2.95

I, LUSIPHUR
MULEHIDE

❑1, b&w 20.00
❑2, b&w 12.00
❑3, b&w 15.00
❑4, b&w 12.00
❑5, b&w 10.00
❑6, b&w 8.00
❑7, b&w; series continues as Poison Elves 8.00

IMAGE
IMAGE

❑0, ca. 1993; TMc, RL, JLee, EL (w); TMc, RL, JLee, EL (a);Mail-away coupon-redemption promo from coupons in early Image comics 4.00

IMAGE INTRODUCES... BELIEVER
IMAGE

❑1, Dec 2001, b&w 2.95

IMAGE INTRODUCES... CRYPTOPIA
IMAGE

❑1, Apr 2002, b&w 2.95

IMAGE INTRODUCES... DOG SOLDIERS
IMAGE

❑1, Jun 2002, b&w 2.95

IMAGE INTRODUCES... LEGEND OF ISIS
IMAGE

❑1, Feb 2002, b&w 2.95

IMAGE INTRODUCES... PRIMATE
IMAGE

❑1/A, Sep 2001, b&w 2.95
❑1/B, Sep 2001 2.95

IMAGE OF THE BEAST, THE
LAST GASP

❑1, ca. 1979 3.00

IMAGE PLUS
IMAGE

❑1, May 1993 2.25

IMAGES OF A DISTANT SOIL
IMAGE

❑1, Feb 1997, b&w; pin-ups by various artists 2.95

IMAGES OF OMAHA
KITCHEN SINK

❑1, b&w; benefit comic; intro by Harlan Ellison; afterword by Neil Gaiman; cardstock cover 3.95
❑2, b&w; benefit comic; cardstock cover 3.95

IMAGES OF SHADOWHAWK
IMAGE

❑1, Sep 1993 1.95
❑2, Oct 1993 1.95
❑3, Jan 1994 1.95

IMAGE TWO-IN-ONE
IMAGE

❑1, Dec 2001, b&w 2.95

IMAGI-MATION
IMAGI-MATION

❑1; Gnatman 1.75
❑2; Star Wreck 1.75

I'M DICKENS... HE'S FENSTER
DELL

❑1, May 1963 25.00
❑2, Aug 1963 20.00

IMMORTAL COMBAT
EXPRESS / ENTITY

❑1, Feb 1995; Entity Illustrated Novella #5; cardstock cover 2.95

IMMORTAL DOCTOR FATE, THE
DC

❑1, Jan 1985 MN, KG, JSa (a); O: Doctor Fate. 1.50

Arrowette, the daughter of Green Arrow "ally" Little Miss Arrowette, made her first appearance in *Impulse* #28.

© 1997 DC Comics.

N-MINT

❑2, Feb 1985 KG (a) 1.50
❑3, Mar 1985 KG (a) 1.50

IMMORTAL II
IMAGE

❑1, Apr 1997, b&w; cover also says May, indicia says Apr 2.50
❑1/A, Apr 1997, b&w; cover says Immortal Two, indicia says Immortal II 2.50
❑2, Jun 1997, b&w; cover says Immortal Two, indicia says Immortal II 2.50
❑3, Aug 1997, b&w; cover says Immortal Two, indicia says Immortal II 2.50
❑4, Sep 1997, b&w; cover says Immortal Two, indicia says Immortal II 2.50
❑5, Feb 1998, b&w; cover says Immortal Two, indicia says Immortal II 2.50

IMMORTALS, THE
COMICS BY DAY

❑1 1.00

IMP
SLAVE LABOR

❑1, Jun 1994 2.95

IMPACT (RCP)
RCP

❑1, Apr 1999 2.50
❑2, May 1999 2.50
❑3, Jun 1999 2.50
❑4, Jul 1999 2.50
❑5, Aug 1999 2.50
❑Annual 1; Collects Impact (RCP) #1-5 13.50

IMPACT CHRISTMAS SPECIAL
DC / IMPACT

❑1 1991 2.50

IMPACT COMICS WHO'S WHO
DC / IMPACT

❑1 4.95
❑2 4.95
❑3; trading cards 4.95

IMPERIAL GUARD
MARVEL

❑1, Jan 1997 1.99
❑2, Feb 1997; wraparound cover 1.99
❑3, Mar 1997 1.99

IMPOSSIBLE MAN SUMMER VACATION SPECTACULAR
MARVEL

❑1, Aug 1990 2.00
❑2, Aug 1991 2.00

IMPULSE
DC

❑1, Apr 1995 MWa (w); O: Impulse. 4.00
❑2, May 1995 MWa (w) 3.50
❑3, Jun 1995 MWa (w) 2.50
❑4, Jul 1995 MWa (w); 1: White Lightning. 2.50
❑5, Aug 1995 MWa (w) 2.50
❑6, Sep 1995; MWa (w); Child abuse 2.25
❑7, Oct 1995 MWa (w) 2.25
❑8, Nov 1995; MWa (w); V: Blockbuster. Underworld Unleashed 2.25
❑9, Dec 1995 MWa (w); A: Xs. 2.25
❑10, Jan 1996; MWa (w); continues in Flash #110 2.00
❑11, Feb 1996 MWa (w); D: Johnny Quick. 2.00
❑12, Mar 1996 MWa (w) 2.00

N-MINT

❑13, May 1996 MWa (w) 2.00
❑14, Jun 1996 MWa (w); V: White Lightning. V: Trickster. 2.00
❑15, Jul 1996 MWa (w); V: White Lightning. V: Trickster. 2.00
❑16, Aug 1996; MWa (w); more of Max Mercury's past revealed 2.00
❑17, Sep 1996 MWa (w); A: Zatanna. 2.00
❑18, Oct 1996 2.00
❑19, Nov 1996 MWa (w) 2.00
❑20, Dec 1996; MWa (w); Bart plays baseball 1.75
❑21, Jan 1997 MWa (w); A: Legion. 1.75
❑22, Feb 1997 MWa (w); A: Jesse Quick. 1.75
❑23, Mar 1997; MWa (w); Impulse's mother returns 1.75
❑24, Apr 1997; MWa (w); Impulse goes to 30th century 1.75
❑25, May 1997; MWa (w); Impulse in 30th century 1.75
❑26, Jun 1997; MWa (w); Impulse returns to 20th century 1.75
❑27, Jul 1997 MWa (w) 1.75
❑28, Aug 1997 1: Arrowette. 1.75
❑29, Sep 1997 1.75
❑30, Oct 1997; Genesis; Impulse gains new powers 1.75
❑31, Nov 1997 1.75
❑32, Dec 1997; Face cover 1.95
❑33, Jan 1998 1: Jasper Pierson. V: White Lightning. 1.95
❑34, Feb 1998; Max and Impulse travel in time 1.95
❑35, Mar 1998; Max and Impulse turned into apes 1.95
❑36, Apr 1998 1.95
❑37, May 1998 1: Glory Shredder. 1.95
❑38, Jun 1998; Manchester floods 1.95
❑39, Jul 1998 A: Trickster. 1.95
❑40, Aug 1998 1.95
❑41, Sep 1998 A: Arrowette. 2.25
❑42, Oct 1998; Virtual pets 2.25
❑43, Dec 1998 2.25
❑44, Jan 1999; Halloween 2.25
❑45, Feb 1999; A: Bart's mother. Christmas 2.25
❑46, Mar 1999 A: Flash II (Barry Allen). 2.25
❑47, Apr 1999; A: Superman. Superboy cameo 2.25
❑48, May 1999 V: Riddler. 2.25
❑49, Jun 1999 2.25
❑50, Jul 1999 A: Batman. V: Joker. 2.25
❑51, Aug 1999 2.25
❑52, Sep 1999 2.25
❑53, Oct 1999 V: Inertia. V: Kalibak. 2.25
❑54, Nov 1999; Day of Judgment 2.25
❑55, Dec 1999 2.25
❑56, Jan 2000 A: Young Justice. 2.25
❑57, Feb 2000 A: Plastic Man. 2.25
❑58, Mar 2000 2.25
❑59, Apr 2000 2.25
❑60, May 2000 2.25
❑61, Jun 2000 2.25
❑62, Jul 2000 2.25
❑63, Aug 2000 2.25
❑64, Sep 2000 2.25
❑65, Oct 2000 2.50
❑66, Nov 2000 2.50
❑67, Dec 2000 2.50
❑68, Jan 2001 2.50
❑69, Feb 2001 2.50
❑70, Mar 2001 2.50
❑71, Apr 2001 2.50
❑72, May 2001 2.50
❑73, Jun 2001 2.50
❑74, Jul 2001 2.50
❑75, Aug 2001 2.50
❑76, Sep 2001 2.50
❑77, Oct 2001 2.50
❑78, Nov 2001 2.50
❑79, Dec 2001 2.50
❑80, Jan 2002 2.50
❑81, Feb 2002 2.50

N-MINT

❑82, Mar 2002 2.50
❑83, Apr 2002 2.50
❑84, May 2002 2.50
❑85, Jun 2002 2.50
❑86, Jul 2002 2.50
❑87, Aug 2002 2.50
❑88, Sep 2002 2.50
❑89, Oct 2002 2.50
❑1000000, Nov 1998 A: John Fox. 3.00
❑Annual 1, ca. 1996; MWa (w); Legends of the Dead Earth 2.95
❑Annual 2, ca. 1997; A: Vigilante. Pulp Heroes 3.95

IMPULSE/ATOM DOUBLE-SHOT
DC

❑1, Feb 1998 1.95

IMPULSE: BART SAVES THE UNIVERSE
DC

❑1; prestige format; Batman cameo; Flash I (Jay Garrick) cameo; Flash II (Barry Allen) cameo; Flash III (Wally West) cameo 5.95

IMPULSE PLUS
DC

❑1, Sep 1997; continues in Superboy Plus #2 2.95

IMP-UNITY
SPOOF

❑1, b&w; parody 2.95

INCOMPLETE DEATH'S HEAD, THE
MARVEL

❑1, Jan 1993; Giant-size; Die-cut cover 2.95
❑2, Feb 1993 1.75
❑3, Mar 1993 1.75
❑4, Apr 1993 1.75
❑5, May 1993 1.75
❑6, Jun 1993 1.75
❑7, Jul 1993 1.75
❑8, Aug 1993 1.75
❑9, Sep 1993 1.75
❑10, Oct 1993 1.75
❑11, Nov 1993 1.75
❑12, Dec 1993; double-sized 1.75

INCREDIBLE HULK, THE
MARVEL

❑-1, Jul 1997; PD (w); O: Hulk. Flashback 2.25
❑1, May 1962; JK (c); SL (w); JK (a); O: Hulk. 1: General "Thunderbolt" Ross. 1: Hulk. 1: Rick Jones. 1: Betty Ross. Hulk's skin is gray (printing mistake) 9500.00
❑2, Jul 1962; JK (c); SL (w); SD, JK (a); O: Hulk. Hulk's skin is printed in green 2100.00
❑3, Sep 1962 (c); SL (w); JK (a); O: Hulk. 1: Ringmaster. 1: Cannonball (villain). 1: The Clown. 1: Teena the Fat Lady. 1: Bruto the Strongman. 1525.00
❑4, Nov 1962 JK (c); SL (w); JK (a); O: Hulk. 1400.00
❑5, Jan 1963 JK (c); SL (w); JK (a); 1: Tyrannus. 1400.00
❑6, Mar 1963; SD (c); SL (w); SD (a); 1: Metal Master. 1: Teen Brigade. Moves to "Tales To Astonish" following this issue 1500.00
❑102, Apr 1968; GT (a); O: Hulk. Numbering continued from "Tales To Astonish" 175.00
❑103, May 1968 1: Space Parasite. 75.00
❑104, Jun 1968 V: Rhino. 60.00
❑105, Jul 1968 BEv (w); GT (a); 1: Missing Link. V: Gargoyle. 50.00
❑106, Aug 1968 HT, GT (a) 50.00
❑107, Sep 1968 HT (a); V: Mandarin. 50.00
❑108, Oct 1968 SL (w); HT, JSe (a); A: Nick Fury. 40.00
❑109, Nov 1968 (c); SL (w); HT, JSe (a) 40.00
❑110, Dec 1968 HT (c); SL (w); HT, JSe (a) 40.00
❑111, Jan 1969 HT (c); SL (w); HT, DA (a) 35.00

N-MINT

❑112, Feb 1969 HT (c); SL (w); HT, DA (a) 35.00
❑113, Mar 1969 HT (c); SL (w); HT, DA (a); V: Sandman. 35.00
❑114, Apr 1969 HT (c); SL (w); HT, DA (a) 35.00
❑115, May 1969 HT (c); SL (w); HT, DA (a) 35.00
❑116, Jun 1969 HT (c); SL (w); HT, DA (a) 32.00
❑117, Jul 1969 HT (c); SL (w); HT, DA (a) 32.00
❑118, Aug 1969 HT (c); SL (w); HT (a); A: Sub-Mariner. 32.00
❑119, Sep 1969 HT (c); SL (w); HT (a) 32.00
❑120, Oct 1969 HT (c); SL (w); HT (a) 32.00
❑121, Nov 1969 HT (c); HT (a) 30.00
❑122, Dec 1969; HT (c); HT (a); A: Thing. Hulk vs. Thing 45.00
❑123, Jan 1970 HT (c); HT (a) 20.00
❑124, Feb 1970 HT (c); SB, HT (a); V: Rhino. 20.00
❑125, Mar 1970 HT (c); HT (a); V: Absorbing Man. 20.00
❑126, Apr 1970 HT (c); HT (a) 20.00
❑127, May 1970 HT (c); HT (a); V: Mogol. 20.00
❑128, Jun 1970 HT (c); HT (a) 20.00
❑129, Jul 1970 HT (c); HT (a) 20.00
❑130, Aug 1970 HT (c); HT (a) 20.00
❑131, Sep 1970; HT (c); HT, JSe (a);Iron Man 20.00
❑132, Oct 1970 HT (c); HT, JSe (a); V: Hydra. 20.00
❑133, Nov 1970 HT (c); HT, JSe (a) 16.00
❑134, Dec 1970 HT (c); SB, HT (a) 16.00
❑135, Jan 1971 HT (c); SB, HT (a); V: Kang. 16.00
❑136, Feb 1971 HT (c); SB, HT (a); 1: Xeron. 16.00
❑137, Mar 1971 HT (c); HT (a) 16.00
❑138, Apr 1971 HT (c); HT (a) 16.00
❑139, May 1971 HT (c); HT (a) 16.00
❑140, Jun 1971 HT (c); HT (a); 1: Jarella. 16.00
❑140-2 HT (c); HT (a); 1: Jarella. 2.50
❑141, Jul 1971 HT (c); HT, JSe (a); O: Doc Samson. 1: Doc Samson. 60.00
❑142, Aug 1971 HT (c); HT, JSe (a) 16.00
❑143, Sep 1971 HT (c); JSe (a); V: Doctor Doom. 16.00
❑144, Oct 1971 HT (c); JSe (a); V: Doctor Doom. 16.00
❑145, Nov 1971; Giant-size HT (c); HT, JSe (a); O: Hulk. 16.00
❑146, Dec 1971 HT (c); HT, JSe (a) 16.00
❑147, Jan 1972 HT (c); HT, JSe (a) 16.00
❑148, Feb 1972; HT (c); HT, JSe (a); 1: Peter Corbeau 14.00
❑149, Mar 1972 HT (c); HT, JSe (a); 1: Inheritor. 14.00
❑150, Apr 1972 HT (c); HT, JSe (a); 1: Viking. A: Lorna Dane. A: Havoc. 14.00
❑151, May 1972 HT (c); HT, JSe (a) 14.00
❑152, Jun 1972 HT (c) 14.00
❑153, Jul 1972 HT (c); HT, JSe (a); A: Fantastic Four. A: Peter Parker. A: Matt Murdock. 14.00
❑154, Aug 1972 HT (c); HT, JSe (a); A: Ant-Man. V: Chameleon. 14.00
❑155, Sep 1972 HT (c); HT, JSe (a); 1: Shaper of Worlds. V: Captain Axis. 14.00
❑156, Oct 1972 HT (c); HT (a) 14.00
❑157, Nov 1972 HT (c); HT (a) 14.00
❑158, Dec 1972 HT (c); HT (a); A: Warlock. V: Rhino on Counter-Earth. 14.00
❑159, Jan 1973 V: Abomination. 14.00
❑160, Feb 1973 HT (c); HT (a) 14.00
❑161, Mar 1973 HT (c); HT (a); A: Mimic. D: Mimic. V: Beast. 14.00
❑162, Apr 1973 HT (c); HT (a); 1: Wendigo. V: Wendigo. 45.00
❑163, May 1973 HT (a); 1: Gremlin. 12.00
❑164, Jun 1973 HT (c); HT (a); 1: Captain Omen. 12.00
❑165, Jul 1973 HT (c); HT (a); V: Aquon. 12.00
❑166, Aug 1973 HT (a); 1: Zzzax. 12.00

N-MINT

❑167, Sep 1973 HT (c); HT, JAb (a); V: Modok. 12.00
❑168, Oct 1973 HT (c); HT, JAb (a); 1: Harpy. 12.00
❑169, Nov 1973 HT (c); HT, JAb (a); 1: Bi-Beast I. V: Bi-Beast I. 12.00
❑170, Dec 1973 HT (c); HT, JAb (a); D: Bi-Beast I. 12.00
❑171, Jan 1974 HT (c); HT, JAb (a); V: Abomination. V: Rhino. 12.00
❑172, Feb 1974 HT (c); HT, JAb (a); A: X-Men. 20.00
❑173, Mar 1974 HT (c); HT (a); V: Cobalt Man. 11.00
❑174, Apr 1974; HT (c); HT, JAb (a); V: Cobalt Man. Marvel Value Stamp #47: Green Goblin 11.00
❑175, May 1974; HT (c); HT, JAb (a); A: Inhumans. V: Inhumans. Marvel Value Stamp #56: Rawhide Kid 11.00
❑176, Jun 1974; HT (c); HT, JAb (a); A: Warlock. Marvel Value Stamp #67: Cyclops 11.00
❑177, Jul 1974; HT (c); HT, JAb (a); D: Warlock. Marvel Value Stamp #39: Iron Fist 15.00
❑178, Aug 1974; HT (c); HT, JAb (a); D: Warlock. Warlock returns 15.00
❑179, Sep 1974; HT (c); HT, JAb (a);Marvel Value Stamp #16: Shang-Chi 11.00
❑180, Oct 1974; HT (c); HT, JAb (a); 1: Wolverine (cameo). A: Wendigo. Marvel Value Stamp #67: Cyclops 165.00
❑181, Nov 1974; HT (c); HT, JAb (a); 1: Wolverine (full appearance). A: Wendigo. Marvel Value Stamp #54: Shanna the She-Devil 900.00
❑181/Ace; Wizard Ace Edition; acetate cover 6.00
❑182, Dec 1974; HT (c); HT (a); O: Hammer. O: Anvil. 1: Hammer. 1: Anvil. 1: Crackajack. A: Wolverine. V: Hammer. V: Anvil. Marvel Value Stamp #59: Golem 84.00
❑183, Jan 1975; V: Zzzax. Marvel Value Stamp #4: Thing 8.00
❑184, Feb 1975; HT (c); HT (a);Marvel Value Stamp #58: Mandarin 8.00
❑185, Mar 1975 HT (c); HT (a) 8.00
❑186, Apr 1975; HT (c); HT (a); 1: Devastator I (Kirov Petrovna). D: Devastator I (Kirov Petrovna). Marvel Value Stamp #11: Deathlok 8.00
❑187, May 1975 HT (c); HT, JSa (a); V: Gremlin. 8.00
❑188, Jun 1975 HT (c); HT, JSa (a); V: Gremlin. 8.00
❑189, Jul 1975 HT (c); HT, JSa (a); V: Mole Man. 8.00
❑190, Aug 1975 HT (c); HT (a); 1: Glorian. V: Toad Men. 8.00
❑191, Sep 1975 HT (c); HT, JSa (a); V: Shaper of Worlds. 8.00
❑192, Oct 1975 HT, JSa (a) 8.00
❑193, Nov 1975 GK (c); HT, JSa (a); V: Doc Samson. 8.00
❑194, Dec 1975 GK (c); SB, JSa (a) 8.00
❑195, Jan 1976 SB, JSa (a); V: Abomination. 8.00
❑196, Feb 1976 GK (c); SB, JSa (a); V: Abomination. 8.00
❑197, Mar 1976 BWr (c); SB, JSa (a); V: Man-Thing. V: Gardner. 8.00
❑198, Apr 1976 GK (c); SB, JSa (a); A: Man-Thing. 8.00
❑198/30 cent, Apr 1976; 30 cent regional variant 20.00
❑199, May 1976 RB (c); SB, JSa (a); V: Doc Samson. 8.00
❑199/30 cent, May 1976; 30 cent regional variant 20.00
❑200, Jun 1976; 200th anniversary issue RB (c); SB, JSa (a); A: Surfer and others. 16.00
❑200/30 cent, Jun 1976; 200th anniversary issue; RB (c); SB, JSa (a); A: Surfer and others. 30 cent regional variant 30.00
❑201, Jul 1976 RB, JR (c); SB, JSa (a) 7.00

N-MINT

❑201/30 cent, Jul 1976; 30 cent regional variant 20.00
❑202, Aug 1976 RB, JR (c); SB, JSa (a); A: Jarella. 7.00
❑202/30 cent, Aug 1976; RB (c); JSa (a);30 cent regional variant 20.00
❑203, Sep 1976 JR (c); SB, JSa (a); V: Psyklop. 7.00
❑204, Oct 1976 HT (c); HT, JSa (a); O: Hulk. 1: Kronus. 7.00
❑205, Nov 1976 HT (c); SB, JSa (a) 7.00
❑206, Dec 1976 DC (c); SB, JSa (a) 7.00
❑207, Jan 1977 DC (c); SB, JSa (a); A: Defenders. 7.00
❑208, Feb 1977 SB, JSa (a) 7.00
❑209, Mar 1977 SB, JSa (a); V: Absorbing Man. 7.00
❑210, Apr 1977 SB (a); A: Doctor Druid. 7.00
❑211, May 1977 SB (a); A: Doctor Druid. 7.00
❑212, Jun 1977 RB (c); SB (a); 1: Constrictor. V: Constrictor. 7.00
❑212/35 cent, Jun 1977; RB (c); SB (a); 1: Constrictor. V: Constrictor. 35 cent regional variant 15.00
❑213, Jul 1977 SB, TP (a); V: Quintronic Man. 7.00
❑213/35 cent, Jul 1977; SB, TP (a); V: Quintronic Man. 35 cent regional variant 15.00
❑214, Aug 1977; SB (a);Jack of Hearts 7.00
❑214/35 cent, Aug 1977; SB (a);Jack of Hearts; 35 cent regional variant 15.00
❑215, Sep 1977 SB (a); 1: Bi-Beast II. 7.00
❑215/35 cent, Sep 1977; SB (a); 1: Bi-Beast II. 35 cent regional variant 15.00
❑216, Oct 1977 SB (a); V: Bi-Beast II. 7.00
❑216/35 cent, Oct 1977; SB (a); V: Bi-Beast II. 35 cent regional variant 15.00
❑217, Nov 1977 JSn (c); SB (a); V: Circus of Crime. 7.00
❑218, Dec 1977; KP, GT (a);Doc Samson vs. Rhino 7.00
❑219, Jan 1978 SB (a) 5.00
❑220, Feb 1978 SB (a) 5.00
❑221, Mar 1978 SB, AA (a); A: Stingray. 5.00
❑222, Apr 1978 JSn, AA (a) 5.00
❑223, May 1978 SB (a) 5.00
❑224, Jun 1978 SB (a) 5.00
❑225, Jul 1978 SB (a) 5.00
❑226, Aug 1978 SB, JSt (a) 5.00
❑227, Sep 1978; HT (c); SB, KJ (a);Doc Samson 5.00
❑228, Oct 1978 HT, BMc (c); SB, BMc (a); O: Moonstone. 1: Moonstone. 5.00
❑229, Nov 1978 BL, HT (c); SB (a); A: Moonstone. A: Doc Samson. 5.00
❑230, Dec 1978 BL (c); BL, JM (a) 5.00
❑231, Jan 1979 HT (c); SB (a) 5.00
❑232, Feb 1979 (c); SB (a); A: Captain America. 5.00
❑233, Mar 1979 AM (c); SB (a); A: Marvel Man (Quasar). 5.00
❑234, Apr 1979; AM (c); SB, JAb (a); 1: Quasar. (Marvel Man changed name to Quasar) 5.00
❑235, May 1979 AM (c); SB (a); A: Machine Man. 5.00
❑236, Jun 1979 AM (c); SB (a); A: Machine Man. 5.00
❑237, Jul 1979 AM (c); SB, JAb (a) 5.00
❑238, Aug 1979 AM (c); SB, JAb (a) 5.00
❑239, Sep 1979 AM (c); SB (a) 5.00
❑240, Oct 1979 AM (c); SB, JSt (a) 5.00
❑241, Nov 1979 SB (a) 4.00
❑242, Dec 1979 BL (c); SB (a); V: Tyranus. 4.00
❑243, Jan 1980 AM (c); SB (a); A: Power Man and Iron Fist. 4.00
❑244, Feb 1980 AM (c); Cl (a); D: It, the Living Colossus. 4.00
❑245, Mar 1980 AM (c); SB (a) 4.00
❑246, Apr 1980 RB, JAb (c); SB (a); A: Captain Marvel. 4.00
❑247, May 1980 AM (c); SB (a); A: Jarella. 4.00

After three appearances in *Marvel Premiere* and a later one in *What If?* #9, 3-D Man made his first modern-day appearance in *Incredible Hulk* #251.

© 1980 Marvel Comics.

N-MINT

❑248, Jun 1980 MG (c); SB (a); V: Gardener. 4.00
❑249, Jul 1980 SD (c); SD (a); A: Jack Frost. 4.00
❑250, Aug 1980; Giant-sized AM (c); SB (a); 1: Sabra (cameo). A: Silver Surfer. 7.00
❑251, Sep 1980 MG (c); SB (a); A: 3-D Man. 2.50
❑252, Oct 1980 RB, FS (c); SB (a); A: Changelings. 2.50
❑253, Nov 1980 RB, FS (c); SB (a); A: Doc Samson. A: Changelings. 2.50
❑254, Dec 1980 AM (c); SB (a); O: X-Ray. O: Vector. O: U-Foes. O: Ironclad. 1: X-Ray. 1: Vector. 1: U-Foes. 1: Ironclad. 2.50
❑255, Jan 1981 AM, RB (c); SB (a); V: Thor. 2.50
❑256, Feb 1981 AM, RB (c); SB (a); O: Sabra. 1: Sabra (full). 2.50
❑257, Mar 1981 AM, TD (c); SB (a); O: Arabian Knight. 1: Arabian Knight. 2.50
❑258, Apr 1981 AM, FM (c); SB (a); O: Ursa Major. 1: Ursa Major. V: Soviet Super-Soldiers. 2.50
❑259, May 1981 AM, PB (c); AM, SB (a); O: Presence. O: Vanguard. A: Soviet Super-Soldiers. 2.50
❑260, Jun 1981 AM (c); SB (a) 2.50
❑261, Jul 1981 FM (c); SB (a); V: Absorbing Man. 2.50
❑262, Aug 1981 AM (c); SB (a) 2.50
❑263, Sep 1981 AM (c); SB (a); V: Landslide, Avalanche. 2.50
❑264, Oct 1981 FM (c); SB (a) 2.50
❑265, Nov 1981 AM (c); SB (a); 1: Shooting Star. 1: Firebird. V: Rangers. 2.50
❑266, Dec 1981 AM (c); SB (a); V: High Evolutionary. 2.50
❑267, Jan 1982 AM (c); SB (a); O: Glorian. V: Glorian. 2.50
❑268, Feb 1982 FM (c); SB (a); O: Rick Jones. 2.50
❑269, Mar 1982 AM (c); SB (a) 2.50
❑270, Apr 1982 AM (c); SB (a) 2.50
❑271, May 1982; 20th Anniversary Issue AM (c); SB (a); 1: Rocket Raccoon. 2.50
❑272, Jun 1982 SB (a); A: Alpha Flight. 2.50
❑273, Jul 1982 SB (a); A: Alpha Flight. 2.50
❑274, Aug 1982 SB (a) 2.50
❑275, Sep 1982 SB, JSt (a); V: Megalith. 2.50
❑276, Oct 1982 SB, JSt (a); V: U-Foes. 2.50
❑277, Nov 1982 SB (a); V: U-Foes. 2.50
❑278, Dec 1982; AM, SB (c); SB, JSt (a);Hulk granted amnesty 2.50
❑279, Jan 1983 2.50
❑280, Feb 1983 SB (a) 2.50
❑281, Mar 1983 SB, JSt (a) 2.50
❑282, Apr 1983 AM, JSt (c); SB, JSt (a); A: She-Hulk. 2.50
❑283, May 1983 AM (c); SB, JSt (a); A: Avengers. 2.50
❑284, Jun 1983 AM, JSt (c); SB, JSt (a); A: Avengers. V: Leader. 2.50
❑285, Jul 1983 JSt (c); SB (a) 2.50
❑286, Aug 1983 BA (c); SB (a) 2.50
❑287, Sep 1983 AM (c); SB (a) 2.50
❑288, Oct 1983 AM, JSt (c); SB, JM (a); V: Modok. 2.50

Condition price index: Multiply "NM prices" above by: **0.83 for Very Fine/Near Mint**
0.66 for Very Fine • 0.33 for Fine • 0.2 for Very Good • 0.125 for Good

N-MINT

❑289, Nov 1983 AM (c); SB, JSt (a); V: A.I.M.. 2.50
❑290, Dec 1983 AM (c); SB (a); V: Modok. V: Modame. 2.50
❑291, Jan 1984; SB (a); O: Thunderbolt Ross. Assistant Editor Month 2.50
❑292, Feb 1984 KN (c); SB, JSt (a) 2.50
❑293, Mar 1984 SB (a); V: Fantastic Four. 2.50
❑294, Apr 1984 SB (a) 2.50
❑295, May 1984; BSz (c); SB (a); V: Boomerang. Secret Wars aftermath 2.50
❑296, Jun 1984 BSz (c); SB (a); V: ROM. 2.50
❑297, Jul 1984 BSz (c); SB (a) 2.50
❑298, Aug 1984 KN (c); SB (a); A: Nightmare. 2.50
❑299, Sep 1984 SB (a); A: Doctor Strange. 2.50
❑300, Oct 1984; 300th anniversary edition; (c); SB (a); V: Everybody. Hulk banished to Crossroads 4.00
❑301, Nov 1984 BSz (c); SB (a) 2.50
❑302, Dec 1984 SB (a) 2.50
❑303, Jan 1985 SB (a) 2.50
❑304, Feb 1985 SB (a) 2.50
❑305, Mar 1985 SB (a); V: U-Foes. 2.50
❑306, Apr 1985 SB (a) 2.50
❑307, May 1985 SB (a) 2.50
❑308, Jun 1985 SB (a) 2.50
❑309, Jul 1985 SB (a) 2.50
❑310, Aug 1985 AW (c); AW (a) 2.50
❑311, Sep 1985 AW (c) 2.50
❑312, Oct 1985; BSz (c);Secret Wars II 2.50
❑313, Nov 1985 A: Alpha Flight. 2.50
❑314, Dec 1985 JBy (c); JBy (w); JBy, BWi (a); A: Doc Samson. 2.50
❑315, Jan 1986; JBy (c); JBy (w); JBy (a);Hulk and Banner separated 3.00
❑316, Feb 1986 JBy (c); JBy (w); JBy (a); A: Avengers. 3.00
❑317, Mar 1986 JBy (c); JBy (w); JBy (a) 3.00
❑318, Apr 1986 JBy (c); JBy (w); JBy (a) 3.00
❑319, May 1986; JBy (c); JBy (w); JBy (a);Wedding of Bruce Banner and Betty Ross 3.00
❑320, Jun 1986 (c); AM (w); AM (a); V: Doc Samson. 2.00
❑321, Jul 1986 AM, BWi (c); AM (w); AM (a); V: Avengers. 2.00
❑322, Aug 1986 AM (c); AM (w); AM (a) 2.00
❑323, Sep 1986 AM (c); AM (w); AM (a) 2.00
❑324, Oct 1986 AM (c); AM (w); AM (a); O: Hulk. 1: Grey Hulk (new). 5.00
❑325, Nov 1986 AM (c); AM (w); AM, BMc (a); 1: Rick Jones as green Hulk. 3.00
❑326, Dec 1986; BMc (c); AM (w); Green Hulk vs. Grey Hulk 3.50
❑327, Jan 1987 AM (c); AM (w); V: Zzzax. 2.50
❑328, Feb 1987; BMc (c); PD (w); TD (a);1st Peter David writing 2.50
❑329, Mar 1987 AM (c); AM (w); AM (a) 2.00
❑330, Apr 1987 TMc (c); AM (w); AM, TMc (a); D: Thunderbolt Ross. 5.00
❑331, May 1987; PD (w); TMc (a);2nd Peter David issue; gray Hulk revealed 5.00
❑332, Jun 1987 BMc (c); PD (w); TMc (a) 5.00
❑333, Jul 1987 (c); PD (w); TMc (a) 5.00
❑334, Aug 1987 (c); PD (w); TMc (a) 5.00
❑335, Sep 1987 BMc (c); PD (w) 2.00
❑336, Oct 1987 BMc (c); PD (w); TMc (a); A: X-Factor. 3.00
❑337, Nov 1987 BMc (c); PD (w); TMc (a); A: X-Factor. 3.00
❑338, Dec 1987 (c); PD (w); TMc (a); 1: Mercy. 3.00
❑339, Jan 1988 BMc (c); PD (w); TMc (a); A: Ashcan, Leader. 3.00
❑340, Feb 1988 TMc, BWi (c); PD (w); TMc (a); V: Wolverine. 18.00
❑341, Mar 1988 TMc (c); PD (w); TMc (a); V: Man-Bull. 4.00
❑342, Apr 1988 TMc (c); PD (w); TMc (a); A: Leader. 2.00

N-MINT

❑343, May 1988 TMc (c); PD (w); TMc (a) 2.00
❑344, Jun 1988 TMc, BWi (c); PD (w); TMc, BWi (a) 2.00
❑345, Jul 1988; Double-size TMc (c); PD (w); TMc (a) 2.00
❑346, Aug 1988 TMc, EL (c); PD (w); EL (a) 2.00
❑347, Sep 1988; PD (w); MGu (a);in Vegas 2.00
❑348, Oct 1988 MGu (c); PD (w); MGu (a); V: Absorbing Man. 2.00
❑349, Nov 1988 BMc (c); PD (w); A: Spider-Man. 2.00
❑350, Dec 1988; PD (w); Hulk vs. Thing 5.00
❑351, Jan 1989 PD (w); BWi (a) 2.00
❑352, Feb 1989 PD (w) 2.00
❑353, Mar 1989 PD (w) 2.00
❑354, Apr 1989 PD (w) 2.00
❑355, May 1989 PD (w); HT (a); A: Glorian. 2.00
❑356, Jun 1989 BMc (c); PD (w) 2.00
❑357, Jul 1989 BMc (c); PD (w) 2.00
❑358, Aug 1989 PD (w) 2.00
❑359, Sep 1989 JBy (c); PD (w) 2.00
❑360, Oct 1989 BMc (c); V: Nightmare. 2.00
❑361, Nov 1989; BMc (c); PD (w); Iron Man 2.00
❑362, Nov 1989 KN (c); PD (w); A: Werewolf by Night. 2.00
❑363, Dec 1989; GC (c); PD (w); V: Grey Gargoyle. Acts of Vengeance 2.00
❑364, Dec 1989 PD (w); V: Abomination. 2.00
❑365, Jan 1990 PD (w); V: Thing. 2.00
❑366, Feb 1990 PD (w); V: Leader. 2.00
❑367, Mar 1990; PD (w); V: Madman. 1st Dale Keown art 2.00
❑368, Apr 1990 PD (w); 1: Pantheon. V: Mr. Hyde. 2.00
❑369, May 1990 (c); PD (w); BMc (a); V: Freedom Force. 2.00
❑370, Jun 1990 BMc (c); PD (w); BMc (a); A: Doctor Strange. A: Sub-Mariner. 2.00
❑371, Jul 1990 BMc (c); PD (w); BMc (a); A: Doctor Strange. A: Sub-Mariner. 2.00
❑372, Aug 1990; PD (w); BMc (a);Green Hulk returns 3.00
❑373, Sep 1990 BMc (c); PD (w) 2.00
❑374, Oct 1990 BMc (c); PD (w); BMc (a); V: Super Skrull. 2.00
❑375, Nov 1990 BMc (c); PD (w); BMc (a); V: Super Skrull. 2.00
❑376, Dec 1990; BMc (c); PD (w); BMc (a); 1: Agamemnon (as hologram). Green Hulk vs. Grey Hulk 2.00
❑377, Jan 1991; BMc (c); PD (w); BMc (a); 1: Hulk (new, smart). Fluorescent inks on cover 2.50
❑377-2, Jan 1991; BMc (c); PD (w); BMc (a); 1: Hulk (new, smart). Fluorescent inks on cover; 2nd printing (gold) 2.00
❑377-3, Jan 1991 BMc (c); PD (w); BMc (a) 2.00
❑378, Feb 1991; BMc (c); PD (w); Rhino as Santa 2.00
❑379, Mar 1991 BMc (c); PD (w); A: Pantheon. 2.00
❑380, Apr 1991; PD (w); Doc Samson solo story 2.00
❑381, May 1991; PD (w); Hulk joins Pantheon 2.00
❑382, Jun 1991 BMc (c); PD (w) 2.00
❑383, Jul 1991 PD (w); V: Abomination. 2.00
❑384, Aug 1991; PD (w); V: Abomination. Infinity Gauntlet; tiny Hulk 2.00
❑385, Sep 1991; PD (w); Infinity Gauntlet 2.00
❑386, Oct 1991 PD (w); A: Sabra. 2.00
❑387, Nov 1991 PD (w); A: Sabra. 2.00
❑388, Dec 1991 PD (w); 1: Speedfreek. 2.00
❑389, Jan 1992 A: Man-Thing. 2.00
❑390, Feb 1992 PD (w) 2.00
❑391, Mar 1992 PD (w); A: X-Factor. 2.00
❑392, Apr 1992 PD (w); A: X-Factor. 2.00

N-MINT

❑393, May 1992; 30th Anniversary of the Hulk, Green Foil Cover PD (w); HT (a); A: X-Factor. 3.00
❑393-2, May 1992; 30th Anniversary of the Hulk; PD (w); HT (a);non-foil cover 2.50
❑394, Jun 1992 PD (w); 1: Trauma. 1.50
❑395, Jul 1992 PD (w); A: Punisher. 1.50
❑396, Aug 1992 PD (w); A: Punisher. V: Mr. Frost. V: Doctor Octopus. 1.50
❑397, Sep 1992 PD (w); V: U-Foes. 1.50
❑398, Oct 1992 PD (w); V: Leader. 1.50
❑399, Nov 1992 JDu (c); PD (w); JDu (a); D: Marlo. 1.50
❑400, Dec 1992; PD (w); JDu (a); D: Leader. Marlo revived; Prism cover 3.00
❑400-2, Dec 1992 PD (w); JDu (a) 2.50
❑401, Jan 1993 PD (w); JDu (a); 1: Agamemnon (physical). V: U-Foes. 1.50
❑402, Feb 1993 PD (w); JDu (a); A: Doc Samson. V: Juggernaut. 1.50
❑403, Mar 1993 PD (w); V: Juggernaut. 1.50
❑404, Apr 1993 PD (w); A: Avengers. V: Juggernaut. 1.50
❑405, May 1993 PD (w) 1.50
❑406, Jun 1993 PD (w); A: Doc Samson. A: Captain America. 1.50
❑407, Jul 1993 PD (w); 1: Piecemeal. 1.50
❑408, Aug 1993 PD (w); D: Perseus. V: Madman. 1.50
❑409, Sep 1993 PD (w); A: Killpower. A: Motormouth. 1.50
❑410, Oct 1993 PD (w); A: Doctor Samson. A: S.H.I.E.L.D.. A: Nick Fury. 1.50
❑411, Nov 1993 PD (w); A: Nick Fury. 1.50
❑412, Dec 1993 PD (w); A: She-Hulk. V: Bi-Beast. 1.50
❑413, Jan 1994 PD (w) 1.50
❑414, Feb 1994 PD (w); A: Silver Surfer. 1.50
❑415, Mar 1994 PD (w); A: Starjammers. 1.50
❑416, Apr 1994 PD (w) 1.50
❑417, May 1994; PD (w); Rick's bachelor party 1.50
❑418, Jun 1994; PD (w); D: Sandman. Wedding of Rick Jones and Marlo; Peter David (writer) puts himself in script 2.00
❑418/Variant, Jun 1994; PD (w); D: Sandman. Die-cut cover; Wedding of Rick Jones and Marlo; Peter David (writer) puts himself in script 3.00
❑419, Jul 1994 PD (w); V: Talos the Tamed. 1.50
❑420, Aug 1994 PD (w); D: Jim Wilson. 1.50
❑421, Sep 1994 PD (w); V: Thor. 1.50
❑422, Oct 1994 PD (w) 1.50
❑423, Nov 1994 PD (w); A: Hel. 1.50
❑424, Dec 1994 PD (w) 1.50
❑425, Jan 1995; Giant-size PD (w) 2.25
❑425/Variant, Jan 1995; Giant-size; PD (w); Hologram cover 3.50
❑426, Feb 1995; PD (w); Hulk reverts to Banner 1.50
❑426/Deluxe, Feb 1995; Deluxe edition PD (w) 1.95
❑427, Mar 1995 PD (w); A: Man-Thing. 1.50
❑427/Deluxe, Mar 1995 PD (w) 1.95
❑428, Apr 1995 PD (w); A: Man-Thing. 1.50
❑428/Deluxe, Apr 1995 PD (w) 1.95
❑429, May 1995 (c); PD (w) 1.50
❑429/Deluxe, May 1995 (c); PD (w) 1.95
❑430, Jun 1995 PD (w); V: Speedfreek. 1.95
❑431, Jul 1995 (c); PD (w); V: Abomination. 1.95
❑432, Aug 1995 (c); PD (w); V: Abomination. 1.95
❑433, Sep 1995 PD (w); A: Punisher. A: Nick Fury. 1.95
❑434, Oct 1995; (c); PD (w); AM (a); A: Howling Commandoes. Funeral of Nick Fury; OverPower cards inserted 1.95
❑435, Nov 1995; AM (c); PD (w); AM (a); V: Rhino. Casey at the Bat tribute 1.95
❑436, Dec 1995; (c); PD (w); A: Maestro. continued in Cutting Edge #1 1.95
❑437, Jan 1996 AM (c); PD (w) 1.95

Condition price index: Multiply "NM prices" above by: **0.83 for Very Fine/Near Mint**
0.66 for Very Fine • 0.33 for Fine • 0.2 for Very Good • 0.125 for Good

N-MINT

- ❑438, Feb 1996 (c); PD (w) 1.95
- ❑439, Mar 1996 (c); PD (w) 1.95
- ❑440, Apr 1996 (c); PD (w); V: Thor. 1.95
- ❑441, May 1996; (c); PD (w); A: She-Hulk. Pulp Fiction tribute cover 1.95
- ❑442, Jun 1996; (c); PD (w); A: She-Hulk. A: Doc Samson. A: Molecule Man. no Hulk 1.95
- ❑443, Jul 1996 (c); PD (w); A: Janis. 1.50
- ❑444, Aug 1996 PD (w); V: Cable. 1.50
- ❑445, Sep 1996 PD (w); A: Avengers. 1.50
- ❑446, Oct 1996; PD (w); post-Onslaught; Hulk turns savage and highly radioactive 1.50
- ❑447, Nov 1996 PD (w) 1.50
- ❑448, Dec 1996 PD (w); A: Pantheon. 1.50
- ❑449, Jan 1997 PD (w); 1: The Thunderbolts. 8.00
- ❑450, Feb 1997; Giant-size; PD (w); A: Doctor Strange. connection to Heroes Reborn universe revealed .. 5.00
- ❑451, Mar 1997; PD (w); Hulk takes over Duck Key 2.00
- ❑452, Apr 1997; PD (w); Hulk vs. Hurricane Betty 2.00
- ❑453, May 1997; PD (w); Hulk vs. Hulk 2.00
- ❑454, Jun 1997 PD (w) 2.00
- ❑455, Aug 1997; gatefold summary; PD (w); DGr (a); A: Apocalypse. V: X-Men. Thunderbolt Ross returns . 2.00
- ❑456, Sep 1997; gatefold summary; PD (w); JKu (a);Apocalypse transforms Hulk into War 2.00
- ❑457, Oct 1997; gatefold summary PD (w); V: Juggernaut. 2.00
- ❑458, Nov 1997; gatefold summary PD (w); A: Mercy. V: Mr. Hyde. 2.00
- ❑459, Dec 1997; gatefold summary PD (w); A: Mercy. V: Abomination. 2.00
- ❑460, Jan 1998; gatefold summary; (c); PD (w); The Hulk and Bruce Banner are reunited; return of Maestro 2.00
- ❑461, Feb 1998; gatefold summary PD (w); V: Destroyer. 2.00
- ❑462, Mar 1998; gatefold summary PD (w) 2.00
- ❑463, Apr 1998; gatefold summary PD (w) 2.00
- ❑464, May 1998; gatefold summary JKu (c); PD (w); JKu (a); A: Silver Surfer. 2.00
- ❑465, Jun 1998; gatefold summary (c); PD (w); A: Reed Richards. A: Tony Stark. 2.00
- ❑466, Jul 1998; gatefold summary PD (w); D: Betty Banner. 2.00
- ❑467, Aug 1998; gatefold summary; PD (w); final Peter David-written issue 2.00
- ❑468, Sep 1998; gatefold summary; 1st Joe Casey issue 2.00
- ❑469, Oct 1998; gatefold summary (c); V: Super-Adaptoid. 2.00
- ❑470, Nov 1998; gatefold summary (c); V: Circus of Crime. 2.00
- ❑471, Dec 1998; gatefold summary V: Circus of Crime. 2.00
- ❑472, Jan 1999; gatefold summary (c); A: Xantarean. 2.00
- ❑473, Feb 1999; gatefold summary A: Xanterean. A: Watchers. A: Abomination. A: Xantarean. 1.99
- ❑474, Mar 1999 (c); A: Xanterean. A: Watchers. A: Abomination. A: Thunderbolt Ross. 1.99
- ❑Annual 1, Oct 1968 JSo (c) 100.00
- ❑Annual 2, Oct 1969; SD, JK (a);Reprints from Incredible Hulk #3 and Tales to Astonish #62-66 .... 40.00
- ❑Annual 3, Jan 1971; Cover reads "King-Size Special"; JK (a); Reprints from Tales to Astonish #70-74 ...... 10.00
- ❑Annual 4, Jan 1972; HT (c); SL (w); JK, JR (a);Cover reads "Special"; Reprints from Tales to Astonish #75-77 and Not Brand Ecch #5 .... 8.00
- ❑Annual 5, ca. 1976 (c); SB, JAb (a); V: Xemnu. V: Groot. V: Diablo. V: Diablo. V: Blip. V: Taboo. V: Goom. 9.00

N-MINT

- ❑Annual 6, ca. 1977; (c); HT (a); 1: Paragon. A: Warlock. A: Doctor Strange. Doctor Strange 9.00
- ❑Annual 7, ca. 1978 JBy, BL (c); JBy (w); JBy, BL (a); A: Iceman. A: Angel. 9.00
- ❑Annual 8, ca. 1979; (c); JBy (w); SB, AA (a);Alpha Flight 5.00
- ❑Annual 9, ca. 1980 (c); AM, SD (a) . 3.00
- ❑Annual 10, ca. 1981; (c); AM (a);Captain Universe 4.00
- ❑Annual 11, ca. 1982; FM (a);1st Frank Miller Marvel pencils 3.00
- ❑Annual 12, ca. 1983 BA (c); HT, BA (a) 2.50
- ❑Annual 13, ca. 1984 .... 2.50
- ❑Annual 14, ca. 1985 .... 2.50
- ❑Annual 15, ca. 1986 V: Abomination. 2.50
- ❑Annual 16, ca. 1990; PD (w); HT (a);Lifeform 2.50
- ❑Annual 17, ca. 1991 .... 2.50
- ❑Annual 18, ca. 1992; PD (w); Return of Defenders 2.75
- ❑Annual 19, ca. 1993; 1: Lazarus. Polybagged with trading card 2.95
- ❑Annual 20, ca. 1994 .... 2.95
- ❑Annual 1997, ca. 1997; Hulk vs. Gladiator; Incredible Hulk '97 .... 2.99
- ❑Annual 1998, ca. 1998; gatefold summary; wraparound cover; Hulk/Sub-Mariner '98 .... 2.99
- ❑Ashcan 1; ashcan edition 1.00

INCREDIBLE HULK AND WOLVERINE
MARVEL

- ❑1, Oct 1986; Reprints The Incredible Hulk #181-182, other story 7.00
- ❑1-2; Reprints The Incredible Hulk #181-182, other story 4.00

INCREDIBLE HULK, THE: FUTURE IMPERFECT
MARVEL

- ❑1, Jan 1993; prestige format; PD (w); GP (a); 1: The Maestro. Embossed cover; indicia lists date as Jan 93 .. 6.00
- ❑2, Feb 1993; prestige format; PD (w); GP (a);Embossed cover; indicia lists date as Dec 92 .... 6.00

INCREDIBLE HULK: HERCULES UNLEASHED
MARVEL

- ❑1, Oct 1996; follows events of Onslaught 2.50

INCREDIBLE HULK MEGAZINE, THE
MARVEL

- ❑1, Dec 1996 .... 3.95

INCREDIBLE HULK, THE: NIGHTMERICA
MARVEL

- ❑1, Aug 2003 .... 2.99
- ❑2, Sep 2003 .... 2.99
- ❑3, Oct 2003 .... 2.99
- ❑4, Nov 2003 .... 2.99
- ❑5, Mar 2004 .... 2.99
- ❑6, Apr 2004 .... 2.99

INCREDIBLE HULK POSTER MAGAZINE
MARVEL

- ❑1/A; comics 3.95
- ❑1/B; TV show 2.00

INCREDIBLE HULK: THE END
MARVEL

- ❑1, Aug 2002 .... 5.95

INCREDIBLE HULK VERSUS QUASIMODO, THE
MARVEL

- ❑1, Mar 1983; SB (a);Based on Saturday morning cartoon 1.50

INCREDIBLE HULK VS. SUPERMAN
MARVEL

- ❑1, Jul 1999; prestige format 6.00

INCREDIBLE HULK VS. VENOM
MARVEL

- ❑1, Apr 1994 .... 3.00

Descendants and protégés of The Justice Society of America dealt with the loss of their elders following *Crisis on Infinite Earths* in *Infinity Inc.* #30.

© 1986 DC Comics.

N-MINT

INCREDIBLE MR. LIMPET, THE
DELL

- ❑1, Jun 1964 .... 25.00

INCUBUS
PALLIARD

- ❑1, b&w 2.95
- ❑2, b&w 2.95

INDEPENDENT PUBLISHER'S GROUP SPOTLIGHT
HERO

- ❑0, Aug 1993, b&w; Bagged w/ card; no cover price or indicia 3.50

INDEPENDENT VOICES
PEREGRINE ENTERTAINMENT

- ❑1, Sep 1998, b&w; SPX '98 anthology 1.95
- ❑2-2, May 2000, b&w; CBLDF benefit comic book 2.95
- ❑2, Sep 1999, b&w; CBLDF benefit comic book 2.95
- ❑3, Aug 2001 .... 2.95

INDIANA JONES AND T HE ARMS OF GOLD
DARK HORSE

- ❑1, Feb 1994 .... 2.50
- ❑2, Mar 1994 .... 2.50
- ❑3, Apr 1994 .... 2.50
- ❑4, May 1994 .... 2.50
- ❑5 .... 2.50
- ❑6, Apr 1994 .... 2.50

INDIANA JONES AND THE FATE OF ATLANTIS
DARK HORSE

- ❑1, Mar 1991; trading cards 2.50
- ❑1-2 .... 2.50
- ❑2, May 1991; trading cards 2.50
- ❑3, Jul 1991 .... 2.50
- ❑4, Sep 1991 .... 2.50

INDIANA JONES AND THE GOLDEN FLEECE
DARK HORSE

- ❑1, Jun 1994 .... 2.50
- ❑2, Jul 1994 .... 2.50

INDIANA JONES AND THE IRON PHOENIX
DARK HORSE

- ❑1, Dec 1994 .... 2.50
- ❑2, Jan 1995 .... 2.50
- ❑3, Feb 1995 .... 2.50
- ❑4, Mar 1995 .... 2.50

INDIANA JONES AND THE LAST CRUSADE
MARVEL

- ❑1, Oct 1989 .... 1.00
- ❑2, Oct 1989 .... 1.00
- ❑3, Nov 1989 .... 1.00
- ❑4, Nov 1989 .... 1.00

INDIANA JONES AND THE LAST CRUSADE (MAGAZINE)
MARVEL

- ❑1, Aug 1989, b&w; magazine 2.95

INDIANA JONES AND THE SARGASSO PIRATES
DARK HORSE

- ❑1, Dec 1995 .... 2.50
- ❑2, Jan 1996 .... 2.50

N-MINT

❑3, Feb 1996 .... 2.50
❑4, Mar 1996 .... 2.50

INDIANA JONES AND THE SHRINE OF THE SEA DEVIL
DARK HORSE

❑1, Sep 1994 .... 2.50

INDIANA JONES AND THE SPEAR OF DESTINY
DARK HORSE

❑1, Apr 1995 .... 2.50
❑2, May 1995 .... 2.50
❑3, Jun 1995 .... 2.50
❑4, Jul 1995 .... 2.50

INDIANA JONES AND THE TEMPLE OF DOOM
MARVEL

❑1, Sep 1984 .... 2.00
❑2, Oct 1984 .... 2.00
❑3, Nov 1984 .... 2.00

INDIANA JONES: THUNDER IN THE ORIENT
DARK HORSE

❑1, Sep 1993 .... 2.50
❑2, Oct 1993 .... 2.50
❑3, Nov 1993 .... 2.50
❑4, Dec 1993 .... 2.50
❑5, Mar 1994 .... 2.50
❑6, Apr 1994 .... 2.50

INDIAN SUMMER
NBM

❑1 .... 21.95

INDUSTRIAL GOTHIC
DC / VERTIGO

❑1, Dec 1995 .... 2.50
❑2, Jan 1996 .... 2.50
❑3, Feb 1996 .... 2.50
❑4, Mar 1996 .... 2.50
❑5, Apr 1996 .... 2.50

INDUSTRIAL STRENGTH PREVIEW
SILVER SKULL

❑1, b&w 1.50

INEDIBLE ADVENTURES OF CLINT THE CARROT
HOT LEG

❑1, Mar 1994, b&w 2.50

INFECTIOUS
FANTACO

❑1 .... 3.95

INFERIOR FIVE, THE
DC

❑1, Apr 1967 .... 24.00
❑2, Jun 1967 .... 16.00
❑3, Aug 1967 .... 14.00
❑4, Oct 1967 .... 14.00
❑5, Dec 1967 .... 14.00
❑6, Feb 1968 A: DC heroes. 14.00
❑7, Apr 1968 .... 14.00
❑8, Jun 1968 .... 14.00
❑9, Aug 1968 .... 14.00
❑10, Oct 1968; A: other heroes. Final issue of original run (1968) 14.00
❑11, Sep 1972; reprints Showcase #62; Series begins again (1972) 10.00
❑12, Nov 1972; reprints Showcase #63 .... 10.00

INFERNO (AIRCEL)
AIRCEL

❑1, Oct 1990, b&w 2.50
❑2, Nov 1990, b&w 2.50
❑3, Dec 1990, b&w 2.50
❑4, Jan 1991, b&w 2.50

INFERNO (CALIBER)
CALIBER

❑1, Aug 1995, b&w 2.95

INFERNO (DC)
DC

❑1, Oct 1997; spin-off from Legion of Super-Heroes 2.50
❑2, Nov 1997 .... 2.50
❑3, Jan 1998 .... 2.50
❑4, Feb 1998 .... 2.50

INFERNO: HELLBOUND
IMAGE

❑0, Jul 2002 .... 2.50
❑1, Feb 2002 .... 2.50
❑2, Aug 2002 .... 2.50
❑3, Nov 2002 .... 2.99

INFINITE KUNG FU
KAGAN MCLEOD

❑1, Aug 2000 .... 4.50
❑1-2; 2nd printing, 2002 .... 4.50

INFINITY CHARADE, THE
PARODY

❑1/A 2.50
❑1/B 2.50
❑1/Gold; Gold limited edition (1500 printed) 4.00

INFINITY CRUSADE, THE
MARVEL

❑1, Jun 1993; Gold foil cover 3.50
❑2, Jul 1993 .... 2.50
❑3, Aug 1993 .... 2.50
❑4, Sep 1993 .... 2.50
❑5, Oct 1993 .... 2.50
❑6, Nov 1993 .... 2.50

INFINITY GAUNTLET
MARVEL

❑1, Jul 1991 JSn (w); GP (a); A: Thanos. A: Spider-Man. A: Avengers. A: Silver Surfer. 3.00
❑2, Aug 1991 JSn (w); GP (a); A: Thanos. A: Spider-Man. A: Avengers. A: Silver Surfer. 2.50
❑3, Sep 1991 JSn (w); GP (a); A: Thanos. A: Spider-Man. A: Avengers. A: Silver Surfer. 2.50
❑4, Oct 1991 JSn (w); GP (a); A: Thanos. A: Spider-Man. A: Avengers. A: Silver Surfer. 2.50
❑5, Nov 1991 GP (c); JSn (w) 2.50
❑6, Dec 1991 GP (c); JSn (w) 2.50

INFINITY, INC.
DC

❑1, Mar 1984 JOy (a); O: Infinity Inc. 2.50
❑2, May 1984 JOy (a); O: ends. V: Ultra-Humanite. 2.00
❑3, Jun 1984 JOy (a); V: Solomon Grundy. 2.00
❑4, Jul 1984 JOy (a) 2.00
❑5, Aug 1984 JOy (a) 2.00
❑6, Sep 1984 JOy (a) 1.50
❑7, Oct 1984 JOy (a); A: E-2 Superman. 1.50
❑8, Nov 1984 JOy (a) 1.50
❑9, Dec 1984 JOy (a) 1.50
❑10, Jan 1985 JOy (a) 1.50
❑11, Feb 1985; more on Infinity's origin 1.25
❑12, Mar 1985; 1: Yolanda Montez. Brainwave Junior's new powers 1.25
❑13, Apr 1985 V: Thorn. 1.25
❑14, May 1985 TMc (a); 1: Chroma. 1: Marcie Cooper. 3.50
❑15, Jun 1985 TMc (a); A: Chroma. 2.50
❑16, Jul 1985 TMc (a); 1: Mr. Bones. 2.50
❑17, Aug 1985 TMc (a); 1: Helix. 2.50
❑18, Sep 1985; TMc (a); V: Helix. Crisis 2.50
❑19, Oct 1985; TMc (a); 1: Mekanique. A: Steel. A: JLA. Crisis 2.50
❑20, Nov 1985; TMc (a); 1: Rick Tyler. Crisis 2.50
❑21, Dec 1985; TMc (a); 1: Doctor Midnight (new). 1: Hourman II (Rick Tyler). Crisis 2.50
❑22, Jan 1986; TMc (a);Crisis 2.50
❑23, Feb 1986; TMc (a); V: Solomon Grundy. Crisis 2.50
❑24, Mar 1986; TMc (a);Star Spangled Kid, Jonni Thunder vs. Last Criminal; Crisis 2.50
❑25, Apr 1986; TMc (a);Crisis aftermath; Hourman II joins team; Doctor Midnight joins team; Wildcat II joins team 2.50
❑26, May 1986 TMc (a); A: Helix. 2.50
❑27, Jun 1986; TMc (a);Lyta's memories erased 2.50
❑28, Jul 1986 TMc (a); V: Mr. Bones. 2.50
❑29, Jul 1986 TMc (a); V: Helix. 2.50
❑30, Sep 1986; TMc (a);JSA mourned 2.50
❑31, Oct 1986 TMc (a); 1: Skyman. A: Jonni Thunder. 2.50
❑32, Nov 1986 TMc (a); V: Psycho Pirate. 2.50
❑33, Dec 1986 TMc (a); O: Obsidian. 2.50
❑34, Jan 1987 TMc (a); V: Global Guardians. 2.50
❑35, Feb 1987 TMc (a); V: Injustice Unlimited. 2.50
❑36, Mar 1987 TMc (a); V: Solomon Grundy. 2.50
❑37, Apr 1987 TMc (a); O: Northwing. 2.50
❑38, May 1987 .... 1.25
❑39, Jun 1987 O: Solomon Grundy. 1.25
❑40, Jul 1987 .... 1.25
❑41, Aug 1987 .... 1.25
❑42, Sep 1987; Fury leaves team 1.25
❑43, Oct 1987 .... 1.25
❑44, Nov 1987 .... 1.25
❑45, Dec 1987 A: Titans. 1.25
❑46, Jan 1988; V: Floronic Man. Millennium 1.50
❑47, Feb 1988; V: Harlequin. Millennium 1.25
❑48, Mar 1988 O: Nuklon. 1.25
❑49, Apr 1988 A: Sandman. 1.25
❑50, May 1988; Giant-size 2.50
❑51, Jun 1988 D: Skyman. 1.25
❑52, Jul 1988 V: Helix. 1.25
❑53, Aug 1988 V: Injustice Unlimited. 1.75
❑Annual 1, Nov 1985; TMc (a); O: Jade and Obsidian. Crisis 2.50
❑Annual 2, Jul 1988; crossover with Young All-Stars Annual #1 .... 2.50
❑Special 1, ca. 1987; cover forms diptych with Outsiders Special #1 .... 1.50

INFINITY OF WARRIORS, THE
OMINOUS

❑1, Oct 1994 .... 1.95

INFINITY WAR, THE
MARVEL

❑1, Jun 1992; gatefold cover 2.50
❑2, Jul 1992; gatefold cover 2.50
❑3, Aug 1992; gatefold cover 2.50
❑4, Sep 1992; gatefold cover 2.50
❑5, Oct 1992; gatefold cover 2.50
❑6, Nov 1992; gatefold cover 2.50

INFOCHAMELEON: COMPANY CULT
MEDIAWARP

❑1, Feb 1997, b&w 4.50

INHUMANOIDS, THE
MARVEL / STAR

❑1, Jan 1987 1: Earth Corps. 1.00
❑2, Mar 1987 .... 1.00
❑3, May 1987 .... 1.00
❑4, Jul 1987 .... 1.00

INHUMANS, THE
MARVEL

❑1, Oct 1975 GP (a); V: Blastaar. 7.00
❑2, Dec 1976 .... 4.00
❑3, Feb 1976 .... 4.00
❑4, Apr 1976 .... 3.50
❑4/30 cent, Apr 1976; 30 cent regional price variant 7.00
❑5, Jun 1976 .... 3.50
❑6, Aug 1976 .... 3.00
❑6/30 cent, Aug 1976; 30 cent regional price variant 20.00
❑7, Oct 1976 .... 3.00
❑8, Dec 1976 .... 3.00
❑9, Feb 1977 .... 3.00
❑10, Apr 1977 .... 3.00
❑11, Jun 1977 .... 3.00
❑11/35 cent, Jun 1977; 35 cent regional price variant 15.00
❑12, Aug 1977 V: Hulk. 3.00
❑Special 1, Apr 1990 RHo (a); O: Medusa. A: Fantastic Four. 2.50

N-MINT

INHUMANS (VOL. 2)
Marvel
❑1, Nov 1998; gatefold summary 4.00
❑1/Ltd., Nov 1998; DFE alternate cover signed 4.00
❑1/Variant, Nov 1998; DFE alternate cover 4.00
❑2/A, Dec 1998; gatefold summary; Woman in circle on cover 3.00
❑2/B, Dec 1998; gatefold summary 3.00
❑3, Jan 1999 3.00
❑4, Feb 1999 3.00
❑5, Mar 1999; Earth vs. Attilan war 3.00
❑6, Apr 1999 3.00
❑7, May 1999 3.00
❑8, Jun 1999 3.00
❑9, Jul 1999 3.00
❑10, Aug 1999 3.00
❑11, Sep 1999 3.00
❑12, Oct 1999 3.00

INHUMANS (VOL. 3)
Marvel
❑1, Jun 2000 2.99
❑2, Jul 2000 2.99
❑3, Aug 2000 2.99
❑4, Sep 2000 2.99

INHUMANS (VOL. 6)
Marvel
❑1, Jun 2003 2.50
❑2, Jul 2003 2.50
❑3, Aug 2003 2.50
❑4, Oct 2003 2.99
❑5, Nov 2003 2.99
❑6, Dec 2003 2.99
❑7, Jan 2004 2.99
❑8, Feb 2004 2.99
❑9, Mar 2004 2.99
❑10, Apr 2004 2.99
❑11, May 2004 2.99
❑12, Jun 2004 2.99

INHUMANS, THE: THE GREAT REFUGE
Marvel
❑1, May 1995 2.95

INKPUNKS QUARTERLY
Funk-O-Tron
❑1 2.95
❑2 2.95
❑3 2.95

INMATES PRISONERS OF SOCIETY
Delta
❑1, Aug 1997 2.95
❑2, Mar 1998 2.95
❑3, Jul 1998 2.95
❑4, Nov 1998 2.95

INNERCIRCLE
Mushroom
❑0.1, Feb 1995 2.50

INNER-CITY PRODUCTS
Hype
❑1, b&w 2.00

INNER CITY ROMANCE
Last Gasp
❑1 5.00
❑2 3.00
❑3 3.00
❑4 3.00
❑5 3.00

INNOCENT BYSTANDER
Ollie Ollie! Oxen Free
❑1 1: Lao Shan. 1: Balac-Soon. 2.95
❑2 2.95
❑3 2.95
❑4, Sum 1997 2.95
❑5, Win 1998 2.95
❑6, Fal 1998 2.95

INNOVATION PREVIEW SPECIAL
Innovation
❑1, Jun 1989; sampler 1.00

N-MINT

INNOVATION SPECTACULAR
Innovation
❑1, Dec 1990 2.95
❑2, Jan 1991 2.95

INNOVATION SUMMER FUN SPECIAL
Innovation
❑1 3.50

INOVATORS
Dark Moon
❑1, Apr 1995; cardstock cover 2.50

IN RAGE
CFD
❑1, ca. 1994, b&w; no cover price or indicia 2.50

INSANE
Dark Horse
❑1, Feb 1988 1.75
❑2 1.75

INSANE CLOWN POSSE
Chaos!
❑1, Jun 1999 3.00
❑1/A, Jun 1999; Tower Reocrds variant 4.00
❑2, Aug 1999 3.00
❑2/CS, Aug 1999 4.00
❑3, Oct 1999 3.00
❑3/A, Oct 1999; Tower Reocrds variant 4.00
❑4, Jan 2000; Says #1 on cover with Pendulum below issue number; polybagged with first of 12 Pendulum CDs 3.00
❑4/CS, Jan 2000 4.00
❑5 2000 3.00
❑5/CS 2000 4.00
❑6 2000 3.00
❑6/CS 4.00
❑7 2000 3.00
❑7/CS 2000 4.00
❑8 2001 3.00
❑8/CS 4.00
❑9 2001 3.00
❑9/CS 3.00
❑10 2001 3.00
❑10/CS 3.00
❑11 2001 3.00
❑11/CS 4.00
❑12 2001 3.00
❑12/CS 3.00

IN SEARCH OF THE CASTAWAYS
Gold Key
❑1, Mar 1963 20.00

INSECT MAN'S 25TH ANNIVERSARY SPECIAL
Entertainment
❑1, Mar 1991 2.00

INSIDE OUT KING, THE
Free Fall
❑1 2.95
❑1-2 2.95

INSOMNIA
Fantagraphics
❑1 2.95

INSPECTOR, THE
Gold Key
❑1, Jul 1974 20.00
❑2, Oct 1974 10.00
❑3, Jan 1974 5.00
❑4, Apr 1975 5.00
❑5, Jul 1975 5.00
❑6, Oct 1975 5.00
❑7, Jan 1976 5.00
❑8, Mar 1976 5.00
❑9, May 1976 5.00
❑10, Jul 1976 5.00
❑11, Sep 1976 5.00
❑12, Nov 1976 5.00
❑13, Feb 1977 5.00
❑14, Apr 1977 5.00
❑15, Jun 1977 5.00
❑16, Aug 1977 5.00

Golden Age stalwarts Captain America, The Human Torch, and The Sub-Mariner (with their respective sidekicks) teamed as The Invaders in 1975.

© 1975 Marvel Comics.

N-MINT

❑17, Oct 1977 5.00
❑18, Dec 1977 5.00
❑19, Feb 1978 5.00

INSTANT PIANO
Dark Horse
❑1, Aug 1994, b&w 3.95
❑2, Dec 1994, b&w 3.95
❑3, Feb 1995, b&w 3.95
❑4, Jun 1995, b&w 3.95

INTENSE!
Pure Imagination
❑2, b&w 3.00

INTERACTIVE COMICS
Adventure
❑1 4.95
❑2, b&w 4.95

INTERFACE
Marvel / Epic
❑1, Dec 1989 5.00
❑2, Feb 1990 4.00
❑3, Apr 1990 4.00
❑4, Jun 1990 4.00
❑5, Aug 1990 4.00
❑6, Oct 1990 9.00
❑7, Nov 1990 9.00
❑8, Dec 1990 9.00

INTERNATIONAL COWGIRL MAGAZINE
Iconografix
❑1, b&w 2.95
❑2, b&w 2.95

INTERPLANETARY LIZARDS OF THE TEXAS PLAINS
Leadbelly
❑0 2.50
❑1, b&w 2.00
❑2, b&w 2.00
❑3 2.00
❑8, b&w 2.50

INTERSTELLAR OVERDRIVE
Leonine
❑1 1990 1.25
❑2, Apr 1990 1.25

INTERVIEW WITH THE VAMPIRE (ANNE RICE'S...)
Innovation
❑1, ca. 1991 2.50
❑2, ca. 1991 2.50
❑3, ca. 1991 2.50
❑4, ca. 1991 2.50
❑5, ca. 1992 2.50
❑6, ca. 1992 2.50
❑7, ca. 1992 2.50
❑8, ca. 1993 2.50
❑9, ca. 1993 2.50
❑10, ca. 1993 2.50
❑11, ca. 1993 2.50
❑12, ca. 1993 2.50

IN THE DAYS OF THE ACE ROCK 'N' ROLL CLUB
Fantagraphics
❑1, b&w 4.95

N-MINT

IN THE DAYS OF THE MOB
DC

❑1, Fal 1971 ... 2.00

IN THE PRESENCE OF MINE ENEMIES
SPIRE

❑1 ... 7.00

IN THIN AIR
TOME

❑1/A, b&w; With alternate ending #1 ... 2.95
❑1/B, b&w; With alternate ending #2 ... 2.95

INTRAZONE
BRAINSTORM

❑1, Mar 1993, b&w ... 2.95
❑1/Ltd., Mar 1993; limited edition ... 5.95
❑2, Apr 1993, b&w ... 2.95
❑2/Ltd., Apr 1993; limited edition ... 5.95

INTRIGUE
IMAGE

❑1/A, Aug 1999 ... 2.50
❑1/B, Aug 1999; alternate cover with woman firing directly at reader ... 2.50
❑2/A, Sep 1999; Woman posting next to target on cover ... 2.50
❑2/B, Sep 1999; alternate cover ... 2.50
❑3, Oct 1999 ... 2.95

INTRUDER COMICS MODULE
TSR

❑1 ... 2.95
❑2 ... 2.95
❑3 ... 2.95
❑4 ... 2.95
❑5; "Intruder II" on cover ... 2.95
❑6; "Intruder II" on cover ... 2.95
❑7; Intruder II ... 2.95
❑8; Intruder II ... 2.95
❑9; Intruder II ... 2.95

INU-YASHA
VIZ

❑1, Apr 1997 ... 3.00
❑2, May 1997 ... 2.95
❑3, Jun 1997 ... 2.95
❑4, Jul 1997 ... 2.95
❑5, Aug 1997 ... 2.95
❑6, Sep 1997 ... 3.25
❑7, Oct 1997 ... 3.25
❑8, Nov 1997 ... 3.25
❑9, Dec 1997 ... 3.25
❑10, Jan 1998 ... 3.25
❑11, Feb 1998 ... 3.25
❑12, Mar 1998 ... 3.25
❑13, Apr 1998 ... 3.25
❑14, May 1998 ... 3.25
❑15, Jun 1998 ... 3.25

INU-YASHA PART 2
VIZ

❑1, Jul 1998 ... 3.25
❑2, Aug 1998 ... 3.25
❑3, Sep 1998 ... 3.25
❑4, Oct 1998 ... 3.25
❑5, Nov 1998 ... 3.25
❑6, Dec 1998 ... 3.25
❑7, Jan 1999 ... 3.25
❑8, Feb 1999 ... 3.25
❑9, Mar 1999 ... 3.25

INU-YASHA PART 3
VIZ

❑1, Apr 1999 ... 3.25
❑2, May 1999 ... 3.25
❑3, Jun 1999 ... 3.25
❑4, Jul 1999 ... 3.25
❑5, Aug 1999 ... 3.25
❑6, Sep 1999 ... 3.25
❑7, Oct 1999 ... 3.25

INU-YASHA PART 4
VIZ

❑1, Nov 1999 ... 3.25
❑2, Dec 1999 ... 3.25
❑3, Jan 2000 ... 3.25
❑4, Feb 2000 ... 3.25
❑5, Mar 2000 ... 3.25
❑6, Apr 2000 ... 3.25
❑7, May 2000 ... 3.25

INU-YASHA PART 5
VIZ

❑1, Jun 2000 ... 2.95
❑2, Jul 2000 ... 2.95
❑3, Aug 2000 ... 2.95
❑4, Sep 2000 ... 2.95
❑5, Oct 2000 ... 2.95
❑6, Nov 2000 ... 2.95
❑7, Dec 2000 ... 2.95
❑8, Jan 2001 ... 2.95
❑9, Feb 2001 ... 2.95
❑10, Mar 2001 ... 2.95
❑11, Apr 2001 ... 2.95

INU-YASHA PART 6
VIZ

❑1, May 2001 ... 2.95
❑2, Jun 2001 ... 2.95
❑3, Jul 2001 ... 2.95
❑4, Aug 2001 ... 2.95
❑5, Sep 2001 ... 2.95
❑6, Oct 2001 ... 2.95
❑7, Nov 2001 ... 2.95
❑8, Dec 2001 ... 2.95
❑9, Jan 2002 ... 2.95
❑10, Feb 2002 ... 2.95
❑11, Mar 2002 ... 2.95
❑12, Apr 2002 ... 2.95
❑13, May 2002 ... 2.95
❑14, Jun 2002 ... 2.95
❑15, Jul 2002 ... 2.95

INU-YASHA PART 7
VIZ

❑1, Aug 2002 ... 2.95
❑2, Sep 2002 ... 2.95
❑3, Oct 2002 ... 2.95
❑4, Nov 2002 ... 2.95
❑5, Dec 2002 ... 2.95
❑6, Jan 2003 ... 2.95
❑7, Feb 2003 ... 2.95

INVADERS
MARVEL

❑0 ...

INVADERS (GOLD KEY)
GOLD KEY

❑1, Oct 1967 ... 40.00
❑2, Jan 1968 ... 28.00
❑3, Jun 1968 ... 28.00
❑4, Oct 1968 ... 28.00

INVADERS, THE
MARVEL

❑1, Aug 1975; continued from Giant-Size Invaders #1; FR (a);Marvel Value Stamp #37: Watcher ... 12.00
❑2, Oct 1975 1: Mailbag. 1: Brain Drain. V: Donar. ... 7.00
❑3, Nov 1975; 1: U-Man. Captain America vs. Namor vs. Torch; Marvel Value Stamp #97: Black Knight ... 6.00
❑4, Jan 1976 O: U-Man. V: U-Man. ... 6.00
❑5, Mar 1976 1: Fin. V: Red Skull. ... 6.00
❑6, May 1976 A: Liberty Legion. ... 5.00
❑6/30 cent, May 1976; 30 cent regional price variant ... 20.00
❑7, Jul 1976 V: Baron Blood. ... 5.00
❑7/30 cent, Jul 1976; 30 cent regional price variant ... 20.00
❑8, Sep 1976 A: Union Jack. ... 5.00
❑8/30 cent, Sep 1976, A: Union Jack. 30 cent regional price variant ... 20.00
❑9, Oct 1976 O: Baron Blood. V: Baron Blood. ... 5.00
❑10, Nov 1976; V: Reaper. reprints Captain America #22 ... 4.00
❑11, Dec 1976 O: Spitfire. 1: Blue Bullet. 1: Spitfire. V: Blue Bullet. ... 4.00
❑12, Jan 1977 1: Spitfire. ... 4.00
❑13, Feb 1977 A: Golem. ... 4.00
❑14, Mar 1977 1: Spirit of '76. 1: Dyna-Mite. 1: Crusaders. ... 4.00
❑15, Apr 1977 FR, FS (a); V: Crusaders. ... 4.00
❑16, May 1977 V: Master Man. ... 4.00
❑17, Jun 1977 1: Warrior Woman. V: Warrior Woman. ... 4.00
❑17/35 cent, Jun 1977 ... 7.00
❑18, Jul 1977 1: Mighty Destroyer. ... 4.00
❑18/35 cent, Jul 1977 ... 7.00
❑19, Aug 1977; O: Union Jack II (Brian Falsworth). 1: the Sub-Mariner. 1: Union Jack II (Brian Falsworth). A: Hitler. Mighty Destroyer becomes Union Jack II; Reprints Motion Picture Funnies Weekly ... 4.00
❑19/35 cent, Aug 1977 ... 7.00
❑20, Sep 1977; O: Sub-Mariner. 1: Sub-Mariner. A: Spitfire. A: Union Jack. Reprints Sub-Mariner story from Motion Picture Funnies Weekly #1 . ... 5.00
❑20/35 cent, Sep 1977 ... 10.00
❑21, Oct 1977; FR, FS (a);Reprints Sub-Mariner story from Marvel Mystery Comics #10 ... 3.00
❑21/35 cent, Oct 1977 ... 6.00
❑22, Nov 1977 O: Toro (new origin). V: Asbestos Lady. ... 3.00
❑23, Dec 1977 1: Scarlet Scarab. V: Scarlet Scarab. ... 3.00
❑24, Jan 1978; reprints Marvel Mystery Comics #17 ... 3.00
❑25, Feb 1978 V: Scarlet Scarab. ... 2.50
❑26, Mar 1978 1: Destroyer II (Roger Aubrey). V: Agent Axis. ... 2.50
❑27, Apr 1978 ... 2.50
❑28, May 1978 1: Golden Girl. 1: Kid Commandos. 1: Human Top (David Mitchell). ... 2.50
❑29, Jun 1978 O: Invaders. 1: Teutonic Knight. V: Teutonic Knight. ... 2.50
❑30, Jul 1978 ... 2.50
❑31, Aug 1978 V: Frankenstein. ... 2.50
❑32, Sep 1978 V: Thor. ... 2.50
❑33, Oct 1978 V: Thor. ... 2.50
❑34, Nov 1978 V: Destroyer. ... 2.50
❑35, Dec 1978 A: Whizzer. ... 2.50
❑36, Jan 1979 V: Iron Cross. ... 2.50
❑37, Feb 1979 A: Liberty Legion. V: Iron Cross. ... 2.50
❑38, Mar 1979 1: Lady Lotus. A: U-Man. ... 2.50
❑39, Apr 1979 ... 2.50
❑40, May 1979 V: Baron Blood. ... 2.50
❑41, Sep 1979; Double-size V: Super Axis (Baron Blood, U-Man, Warrior Woman, Master Man). ... 3.50
❑Annual 1, ca. 1977 ... 5.00

INVADERS, THE (LTD. SERIES)
MARVEL

❑1, May 1993 ... 1.75
❑2, Jun 1993 ... 1.75
❑3, Jul 1993 ... 1.75
❑4, Aug 1993 ... 1.75

INVADERS FROM HOME
DC / PIRANHA

❑1 ... 2.50
❑2 ... 2.50
❑3 ... 2.50
❑4 ... 2.50
❑5 ... 2.50
❑6 ... 2.50

INVADERS FROM MARS
ETERNITY

❑1, Feb 1990, b&w ... 2.50
❑2, Mar 1990, b&w ... 2.50
❑3, Apr 1990, b&w ... 2.50

INVADERS FROM MARS (BOOK II)
ETERNITY

❑1, ca. 1990, b&w; sequel ... 2.50
❑2, ca. 1990, b&w; sequel ... 2.50
❑3, ca. 1990, b&w; sequel ... 2.50

N-MINT

INVASION!
DC

❑1, Jan 1989; 84 page giant KG (w); TMc (a); O: Blasters. 1: Garryn Bek. 1: Blasters. 1: Dominators. 1: Vril Dox II. 3.00
❑2, Feb 1989; 84 page giant TMc (a); 1: Strata. 1: L.E.G.I.O.N.. 1: Lyrissa Mallor. 3.00
❑3, Mar 1989; 84 page giant 3.00

INVASION (AVALON)
AVALON

❑1 2.95

INVASION '55
APPLE

❑1, Oct 1990, b&w 2.25
❑2, b&w 2.25
❑3, b&w 2.25

INVASION OF THE MIND SAPPERS
FANTAGRAPHICS

❑1, Jan 1996, b&w; cardstock cover . 8.95

INVASION OF THE SPACE AMAZONS FROM THE PURPLE PLANET
GRIZMART

❑1, May 1997, b&w 2.25
❑2, Fal 1997, b&w 2.25
❑3, Win 1997, b&w 2.25

INVERT
CALIBER

❑1, b&w 2.50

INVINCIBLE
IMAGE

❑1, Jan 2003 2.95
❑2, Feb 2003 2.95
❑3, Mar 2003 2.95
❑4, Apr 2003 2.95
❑5, Jun 2003 2.95
❑6, Oct 2003 2.95
❑7, Nov 2003 2.95
❑8, Jan 2004 2.95
❑9, Feb 2004 2.95
❑10, Mar 2004 2.95
❑11, Apr 2004 2.95
❑12, Apr 2004 2.95
❑13, Aug 2004 2.95

INVINCIBLE ED
DARK HORSE

❑1 0.00
❑2 0.00
❑3, Jul 2003 2.99
❑4, Feb 2004 2.99

INVINCIBLE FOUR OF KUNG FU & NINJA
DR. LEUNG'S

❑1 2.00
❑2 2.00
❑3 2.00
❑4 2.00
❑5 2.00

INVINCIBLE MAN
JUNKO / DARK HORSE

❑1, Sum 1998, b&w; Glossy cover; 1500 printed 5.00
❑1/Ltd., b&w; has $100 cover price; 500 printed 8.00

INVINCIBLES
CFD

❑1, May 1997 2.95

INVISIBLE 9
FLYPAPER

❑1, May 1998 2.95

INVISIBLE DIRTY OLD MAN, THE
RED GIANT

❑1 3.50

INVISIBLE PEOPLE
KITCHEN SINK

❑1 2.95
❑2 2.95
❑3 2.95

N-MINT

INVISIBLES, THE
DC / VERTIGO

❑1, Sep 1994; Giant-size 1: King Mob. 3.50
❑2, Oct 1994 2.50
❑3, Nov 1994 2.50
❑4, Dec 1994 2.00
❑5, Jan 1995; There are at least four cover variants, denoted A through D. 2.00
❑6, Feb 1995 2.00
❑7, Mar 1995 2.00
❑8, Apr 1995 2.00
❑9, Jun 1995 2.50
❑10, Jul 1995 2.50
❑11, Aug 1995 2.50
❑12, Sep 1995 2.50
❑13, Oct 1995 2.50
❑14, Nov 1995 2.50
❑15, Dec 1995 2.50
❑16, Jan 1996 2.50
❑17, Feb 1996 2.50
❑18, Mar 1996 3.00
❑19, Apr 1996 3.00
❑20, May 1996 3.00
❑21, Jun 1996 3.00
❑22, Jul 1996 3.00
❑23, Aug 1996 3.00
❑24, Sep 1996 3.00
❑25, Oct 1996 4.00

INVISIBLES, THE (VOL. 2)
DC / VERTIGO

❑1, Feb 1997 3.00
❑2, Mar 1997 2.50
❑3, Apr 1997 BB (c); BB (a) 2.50
❑4, May 1997 2.50
❑5, Jun 1997 BB (c); BB (a) 2.50
❑6, Jul 1997 2.50
❑7, Aug 1997 2.50
❑8, Sep 1997 2.50
❑9, Oct 1997 2.50
❑10, Nov 1997 BB (c); BB (a) 2.50
❑11, Dec 1997 2.50
❑12, Jan 1998 2.50
❑13, Feb 1998 2.50
❑14, Mar 1998 2.50
❑15, Apr 1998 2.50
❑16, May 1998 2.50
❑17, Aug 1998 2.50
❑18, Sep 1998 2.50
❑19, Oct 1998 2.50
❑20, Nov 1998 2.50
❑21, Jan 1999 2.50
❑22, Feb 1999 2.50

INVISIBLES, THE (VOL. 3)
DC / VERTIGO

❑12, Apr 1999; Issues count from 12 to 1 2.95
❑11, May 1999; Issues count from 12 to 1 2.95
❑10, Jun 1999; Issues count from 12 to 1 2.95
❑9, Jul 1999; Issues count from 12 to 1 2.95
❑8, Aug 1999; Issues count from 12 to 1 2.95
❑7, Oct 1999; Issues count from 12 to 1 2.95
❑6, Dec 1999; Issues count from 12 to 1 2.95
❑5, Jan 2000; Issues count from 12 to 1 2.95
❑4, Mar 2000; Issues count from 12 to 1 2.95
❑3, Apr 2000; Issues count from 12 to 1 2.95
❑2, May 2000; Issues count from 12 to 1 2.95
❑1, Jun 2000; Issues count from 12 to 1 2.95

INVISOWORLD
ETERNITY

❑1 1.95

I.N.V.U.
TOKYOPOP

❑1, Feb 2003, b&w 9.99
❑2, Feb 2003, b&w 9.99

IO
INVICTUS

❑1, Oct 1994 2.25
❑3, Win 1995, b&w; ashcan 2.25

The Controller used small discs to control his victims mentally.

© 1969 Marvel Comics.

N-MINT

I, PAPARAZZI
DC / VERTIGO

❑1 29.95

IRONCAT
IRONCAT

❑1, Jul 1999 2.95
❑2, Aug 1999 2.95

IRON CORPORAL, THE (CHARLTON)
CHARLTON

❑23, Oct 1985; Continues From Army War Heroes 1.50
❑24, Dec 1985 1.50
❑25, Feb 1985 1.50

IRON CORPORAL (AVALON)
AVALON

❑1, b&w 2.95

IRON DEVIL, THE
FANTAGRAPHICS / EROS

❑1, b&w 2.95
❑2, b&w 2.95
❑3, Mar 1994, b&w 2.95

IRON FIST
MARVEL

❑1, Nov 1975; JBy (a); A: Iron Man. Marvel Value Stamp #63: Sub-Mariner 24.00
❑2, Dec 1975 JBy (a) 12.00
❑3, Feb 1976 JBy (a) 10.00
❑4, Apr 1976 JBy (a) 8.00
❑4/30 cent, Apr 1976; JBy (a);30 cent regional price variant 20.00
❑5, Jun 1976 JBy (a) 8.00
❑5/30 cent, Jun 1976, JBy (a);30 cent regional price variant 20.00
❑6, Aug 1976 JBy (a) 6.00
❑6/30 cent, Aug 1976, JBy (a);30 cent regional price variant 20.00
❑7, Sep 1976 JBy (a) 6.00
❑8, Oct 1976 JBy (a) 6.00
❑9, Nov 1976 JBy (a) 6.00
❑10, Dec 1976 JBy (a) 6.00
❑11, Feb 1977 JBy (a) 6.00
❑12, Apr 1977 JBy (a) 6.00
❑13, Jun 1977 JBy (a); V: Boomerang. 6.00
❑13/35 cent, Jun 1977; 35¢ cover price; Limited distribution 10.00
❑14, Aug 1977 JBy (a); 1: Sabretooth. 100.00
❑14/35 cent, Aug 1977; JBy (a); 1: Sabretooth. 35¢ cover price; Limited distribution 525.00
❑15, Sep 1977 JBy (a); A: X-Men. A: Wolverine. 35.00
❑15/35 cent, Sep 1977; JBy (a); A: X-Men. 35¢ cover price; Limited distribution 75.00

IRON FIST (2ND SERIES)
MARVEL

❑1, Sep 1996 2.00
❑2, Oct 1996 1.50

IRON FIST (3RD SERIES)
MARVEL

❑1, Jul 1998; gatefold summary 2.50
❑2, Aug 1998; gatefold summary 2.50
❑3, Sep 1998; gatefold summary 2.50

Condition price index: Multiply "NM prices" above by: **0.83 for Very Fine/Near Mint**
0.66 for Very Fine • 0.33 for Fine • 0.2 for Very Good • 0.125 for Good

IRON FIST (4TH SERIES)
MARVEL

	N-MINT
❑1, May 2004	2.99
❑2, Jun 2004	2.99
❑3, Jul 2004	2.99
❑4, Aug 2004	2.99
❑5, Sep 2004	

IRON FIST: WOLVERINE
MARVEL

	N-MINT
❑1, Nov 2000	2.99
❑2, Dec 2000	2.99
❑3, Jan 2001	2.99
❑4, Feb 2001	2.99

IRONHAND OF ALMURIC
DARK HORSE

	N-MINT
❑1, b&w	2.00
❑2, b&w	2.00
❑3, b&w	2.00
❑4, b&w	2.00

IRONJAW
ATLAS-SEABOARD

	N-MINT
❑1, Jan 1975 NA (c)	1.50
❑2, Mar 1975 NA (c)	1.00
❑3, May 1975	1.00
❑4, Jul 1975 O: Ironjaw.	1.00

IRON LANTERN
MARVEL / AMALGAM

	N-MINT
❑1, Jun 1997	1.95

IRON MAN & SUB-MARINER
MARVEL

	N-MINT
❑1, Apr 1968 GC, JCr (a); O: Destiny.	120.00

IRON MAN: BAD BLOOD
MARVEL

	N-MINT
❑1, Sep 2000	2.99
❑2, Oct 2000	2.99
❑3, Nov 2000	2.99
❑4, Dec 2000	2.99

IRON MAN: CRASH
MARVEL / EPIC

	N-MINT
❑1; Computer-generated art	12.95

IRON MAN: THE IRON AGE
MARVEL

	N-MINT
❑1, Aug 1998; prestige format; retells early Iron Man adventures	5.99
❑2, Sep 1998; prestige format; retells early Iron Man adventures	5.99

IRON MAN: THE LEGEND
MARVEL

	N-MINT
❑1, Sep 1996; wraparound cover; summation of history of character	3.95

IRON MAN 2020
MARVEL

	N-MINT
❑1	5.95

IRON MANUAL
MARVEL

	N-MINT
❑1, ca. 1993; no cover date; background info on Iron Man's armor	2.00

IRON MAN (VOL. 1)
MARVEL

	N-MINT
❑1, May 1968 GC, JCr (a); O: Iron Man.	225.00
❑2, Jun 1968 JCr (a); 1: Demolisher.	60.00
❑3, Jul 1968 JCr (a)	55.00
❑4, Aug 1968 JCr (a)	50.00
❑5, Sep 1968 JCr (a)	50.00
❑6, Oct 1968 JCr, GT (a)	42.00
❑7, Nov 1968 JCr, GT (a)	42.00
❑8, Dec 1968 JCr, GT (a)	40.00
❑9, Jan 1969 JCr, GT (a); V: Hulk (robot).	40.00
❑10, Feb 1969 JCr, GT (a)	40.00
❑11, Mar 1969 V: Mandarin.	28.00
❑12, Apr 1969 O: The Controller. 1: Janice Cord.	28.00
❑13, May 1969 V: Controller.	28.00
❑14, Jun 1969 V: Night Phantom.	28.00
❑15, Jul 1969 V: Unicorn.	28.00
❑16, Aug 1969 V: Unicorn.	21.00
❑17, Sep 1969 1: Madame Masque I (Whitney Frost).	21.00
❑18, Oct 1969 O: Madame Masque I.	21.00
❑19, Nov 1969; O: Madame Masque I. Tony Stark's heart repaired	21.00
❑20, Dec 1969 V: Lucifer.	21.00
❑21, Jan 1970; 1: Crimson Dynamo III (Alex Nevsky). Tony Stark quits as Iron Man	15.00
❑22, Feb 1970 D: Janice Cord. V: Crimson Dynamo.	15.00
❑23, Mar 1970	15.00
❑24, Apr 1970 V: Minotaur.	15.00
❑25, May 1970 A: Sub-Mariner. V: Sub-Mariner.	15.00
❑26, Jun 1970 A: Val-Larr.	15.00
❑27, Jul 1970 1: Firebrand (Marvel). V: Firebrand.	15.00
❑28, Aug 1970 V: Controller.	15.00
❑29, Sep 1970	15.00
❑30, Oct 1970	15.00
❑31, Nov 1970 1: Kevin O'Brien (later Guardsman). V: Smashers.	13.00
❑32, Dec 1970 V: Mechanoid.	13.00
❑33, Jan 1971 1: Spymaster. V: Spymaster.	13.00
❑34, Feb 1971 V: Spymaster.	13.00
❑35, Mar 1971 A: Daredevil.	13.00
❑36, Apr 1971 DH (a); V: Ramrod.	13.00
❑37, May 1971	13.00
❑38, Jun 1971 V: Jonah.	13.00
❑39, Jul 1971 V: White Dragon.	13.00
❑40, Aug 1971 D: White Dragon I.	13.00
❑41, Sep 1971 V: Slasher.	10.00
❑42, Oct 1971	10.00
❑43, Nov 1971; Giant-size GT, JM (a); 1: Guardsman. V: Mikas.	20.00
❑44, Jan 1972 GT (a); V: Night Phantom.	10.00
❑45, Mar 1972 GT (a)	10.00
❑46, May 1972 GT (a); 1: Marianne Rodgers. A: Guardsman. D: Guardsman.	10.00
❑47, Jun 1972 JM (a); O: Iron Man.	20.00
❑48, Jul 1972 V: Firebrand.	10.00
❑49, Aug 1972 V: Adaptoid.	10.00
❑50, Sep 1972 V: Princess Python.	10.00
❑51, Oct 1972	14.00
❑52, Nov 1972 V: Raga.	8.00
❑53, Dec 1972 JSn (a); 1: Black Lama. V: Black Lama.	8.00
❑54, Jan 1973 1: Moondragon (as Madame MacEvil). A: Sub-Mariner. V: Sub-Mariner.	16.00
❑55, Feb 1973 JSn (a); 1: Mentor. 1: Drax the Destroyer. 1: Thanos. 1: Kronos. 1: Blood Brothers. 1: Starfox.	90.00
❑56, Mar 1973 JSn (a); 1: Fangor.	15.00
❑57, Apr 1973	8.00
❑58, May 1973 V: Mandarin.	8.00
❑59, Jun 1973	8.00
❑60, Jul 1973	8.00
❑61, Aug 1973	8.00
❑62, Sep 1973	8.00
❑63, Oct 1973	8.00
❑64, Nov 1973; survey	8.00
❑65, Dec 1973 O: Doctor Spectrum.	8.00
❑66, Feb 1974; A: Thor. Marvel Value Stamp A80	8.00
❑67, Apr 1974; A: Sunfire. Marvel Value Stamp #80: Ghost Rider	8.00
❑68, Jun 1974; GT (a); O: Iron Man. A: Sunfire. Marvel Value Stamp #29: Baron Mordo	8.00
❑69, Aug 1974; GT (a); V: Sunfire. V: Mandarin. V: Unicorn. V: Yellow Claw. Marvel Value Stamp #22: Man-Thing	8.00
❑70, Sep 1974; GT (a);Marvel Value Stamp #2: Hulk	8.00
❑71, Nov 1974; GT (a);Marvel Value Stamp #26: Mephisto	7.00
❑72, Jan 1975; GT, NA (a);comic con	7.00
❑73, Mar 1975	7.00
❑74, May 1975 V: Modok.	7.00
❑75, Jun 1975	7.00
❑76, Jul 1975 GT (a)	7.00
❑77, Aug 1975	7.00
❑78, Sep 1975; in Vietnam	7.00
❑79, Oct 1975	7.00
❑80, Nov 1975 JKu (c)	7.00
❑81, Dec 1975; Marvel Value Stamp	7.00
❑82, Jan 1976; repeats letter column from #81; Marvel Value Stamp B2	7.00
❑83, Feb 1976; HT (a); V: Red Ghost. Marvel Value Stamp B16	7.00
❑84, Mar 1976; HT (a);Marvel Value Stamp B56	7.00
❑85, Apr 1976	7.00
❑85/30 cent, Apr 1976	20.00
❑86, May 1976; 1: Blizzard. V: Blizzard. Marvel Value Stamp B84	7.00
❑86/30 cent, May 1976	20.00
❑87, Jun 1976; Marvel Value Stamp	7.00
❑87/30 cent, Jun 1976	20.00
❑88, Jul 1976; GT (a);Marvel Value Stamp 66	7.00
❑88/30 cent, Jul 1976	20.00
❑89, Aug 1976 GT (a); A: Daredevil.	7.00
❑89/30 cent, Aug 1976	20.00
❑90, Sep 1976	7.00
❑91, Oct 1976 GT (a)	7.00
❑92, Nov 1976 GT (a); V: Melter.	7.00
❑93, Dec 1976	7.00
❑94, Jan 1977 HT (a)	7.00
❑95, Feb 1977	7.00
❑96, Mar 1977; GT (a); 1: New Guardsman. Michael O'Brien becomes New Guardsman	7.00
❑97, Apr 1977	7.00
❑98, May 1977	7.00
❑99, Jun 1977 GT (a); V: Mandarin.	7.00
❑100, Jul 1977; 100th anniversary issue; JSn (c); GT (a);Mandarin	10.00
❑100/35 cent, Jul 1977	12.00
❑101, Aug 1977 GT (a); 1: Dreadknight.	5.00
❑102, Sep 1977 O: Dreadknight. 1: Dreadknight.	5.00
❑103, Oct 1977 A: Jack of Hearts.	5.00
❑104, Nov 1977	5.00
❑105, Dec 1977 GT (a); A: Jack of Hearts.	5.00
❑106, Jan 1978	5.00
❑107, Feb 1978 KP (a); V: Midas.	5.00
❑108, Mar 1978 CI (a)	5.00
❑109, Apr 1978 1: Vanguard. V: Darkstar. V: Vanguard.	5.00
❑110, May 1978 KP (a); A: Jack of Hearts.	5.00
❑111, Jun 1978; Wundagore	5.00
❑112, Jul 1978 KP, AA (a)	5.00
❑113, Aug 1978 HT (a)	5.00
❑114, Sep 1978	5.00
❑115, Oct 1978 DGr (a)	5.00
❑116, Nov 1978; BL, JR2 (a); D: Ape-Man I (Gordon Monk Keefer). D: Frog-Man I (Francois LeBlanc). D: Count Nefaria. D: Cat-Man I (Townshend Patane). D: Bird-Man I (Henry Hawk). 1st David Michelinie written issue	5.00
❑117, Dec 1978 BL, JR2 (a); 1: Beth Cabe.	5.00
❑118, Jan 1979 JBy, BL (a); 1: James Rhodes (Rhodey). 1: Mrs. Arbogast.	6.00
❑119, Feb 1979; BL, JR2 (a);Stark battles with alcohol	5.00
❑120, Mar 1979; 1: Justin Hammer. A: Sub-Mariner. Stark battles with alcohol	5.00
❑121, Apr 1979; A: Sub-Mariner. Stark battles with alcohol	5.00
❑122, May 1979; O: Iron Man. A: Sub-Mariner. Stark battles with alcohol	5.00
❑123, Jun 1979; Stark battles with alcohol	5.00
❑124, Jul 1979; JR2 (a);Stark battles with alcohol	5.00
❑125, Aug 1979; JR2 (a); A: Scott Lang (Ant-Man). Stark battles with alcohol	5.00
❑126, Sep 1979; V: Justin Hammer. Stark battles with alcohol	5.00
❑127, Oct 1979; Stark battles with alcohol	5.00

N-MINT

❑128, Nov 1979; BL, JR2 (a);Stark begins recovery from alcohol 5.00
❑129, Dec 1979 SB (a); V: Dreadnought. 4.00
❑130, Jan 1980 4.00
❑131, Feb 1980 A: Hulk. 4.00
❑132, Mar 1980 A: Hulk. 4.00
❑133, Apr 1980 BL (a); A: Hulk. A: Ant-Man. 4.00
❑134, May 1980 BL (a) 4.00
❑135, Jun 1980 BL (a); V: Titanium Man. 4.00
❑136, Jul 1980 BWi (a) 4.00
❑137, Aug 1980 BL (a) 4.00
❑138, Sep 1980 BL, TP (a); 1: Dreadnought (silver). 4.00
❑139, Oct 1980; BL (a);Bethany Cabe knows Tony is Iron Man 4.00
❑140, Nov 1980 BL (a) 4.00
❑141, Dec 1980 BL, JR2 (a) 4.00
❑142, Jan 1981 BL, JR2 (a); 1: Space Armor. 4.00
❑143, Feb 1981 BL, JR2 (a); 1: Sunturion. 4.00
❑144, Mar 1981 BL, JR2 (a); O: James Rhodes (Rhodey). 4.00
❑145, Apr 1981 BL, JR2 (a) 4.00
❑146, May 1981 BL, JR2 (a); V: Blacklash. 4.00
❑147, Jun 1981 BL, JR2 (a) 4.00
❑148, Jul 1981 BL, JR2 (a) 4.00
❑149, Aug 1981 BL, JR2 (a); V: Doctor Doom. 4.00
❑150, Sep 1981; double-sized; BL, JR2 (a); V: Doctor Doom. In Camelot 5.00
❑151, Oct 1981 BL, LMc (a); A: Ant-Man. 4.00
❑152, Nov 1981 BL, JR2 (a); 1: Stealth Armor. 4.00
❑153, Dec 1981 BL, JR2 (a) 4.00
❑154, Jan 1982 BL, JR2 (a); D: Unicorn I (Milos Masaryk). 4.00
❑155, Feb 1982 BL, JR2 (a) 4.00
❑156, Mar 1982 JR2 (a) 4.00
❑157, Apr 1982 4.00
❑158, May 1982 CI (a) 4.00
❑159, Jun 1982; PS (a);Diablo 4.00
❑160, Jul 1982; SD (a);Serpent Squad 4.00
❑161, Aug 1982; LMc (a);Moon Knight 4.00
❑162, Sep 1982 4.00
❑163, Oct 1982 LMc (a); 1: Obadiah Stane (voice only). 1: Chessmen. 1: Indries Moomji. 1: Iron Monger (voice only). 4.00
❑164, Nov 1982 BA (c); LMc, BA (a) . 4.00
❑165, Dec 1982 LMc (a) 4.00
❑166, Jan 1983 LMc (a); 1: Obadiah Stane (full appearance). 1: Iron Monger (full appearance). 4.00
❑167, Feb 1983; LMc (a);Alcohol problem returns 4.00
❑168, Mar 1983; LMc (a);Machine Man; Stark battles with alcohol 4.00
❑169, Apr 1983; LMc (a);Jim Rhodes takes over Stark's job as Iron Man; Stark battles with alcohol 4.00
❑170, May 1983; LMc (a); 1: Morley Erwin. 1: James Rhodes as Iron Man. Stark battles with alcohol 4.00
❑171, Jun 1983; LMc (a); 1: Clytemnestra Erwin. V: Thunderball. Stark battles with alcohol 2.50
❑172, Jul 1983; LMc (a); A: Captain America. Stark battles with alcohol 2.50
❑173, Aug 1983; LMc (a);Stark International becomes Stane International; Stark battles with alcohol 2.50
❑174, Sep 1983; LMc (a); V: Chessmen. S.H.I.E.L.D. acquires armor; Stark battles with alcohol 2.50
❑175, Oct 1983; LMc (a);Stark battles with alcohol 2.50
❑176, Nov 1983; LMc (a);Stark battles with alcohol 2.50
❑177, Dec 1983; LMc (a); V: Flying Tiger. Stark battles with alcohol (alcohol storyline continues through next several issues) 2.50
❑178, Jan 1984 LMc (a) 2.50

N-MINT

❑179, Feb 1984 LMc (a); V: Mandarin. 2.50
❑180, Mar 1984 LMc (a); V: Mandarin. 2.50
❑181, Apr 1984; LMc (a); V: Mandarin. Erroneously reprints 1982 Statement of Ownership 2.50
❑182, May 1984; LMc (a);alcoholism cured again 2.50
❑183, Jun 1984 LMc (a); V: Taurus. .. 2.50
❑184, Jul 1984; LMc (a);Tony Stark founds new company in California 2.50
❑185, Aug 1984 LMc (a) 2.50
❑186, Sep 1984 LMc (a); O: Vibro. 1: Vibro. V: Vibro. 2.50
❑187, Oct 1984 LMc (a); V: Vibro. 2.50
❑188, Nov 1984 DP (a); 1: Circuits Maximus. V: Brothers Grimm. 2.50
❑189, Dec 1984 LMc (a); V: Termite. 2.50
❑190, Jan 1985 LMc (a); A: Scarlet Witch. V: Termite. 2.50
❑191, Feb 1985; LMc (a);Tony Stark returns as Iron Man in original armor 2.50
❑192, Mar 1985; Iron Man (Stark) vs. Iron Man (Rhodey) 2.50
❑193, Apr 1985; LMc (a);West Coast Avengers learn Tony is Iron Man ... 2.50
❑194, May 1985 LMc (a); 1: Scourge. A: West Coast Avengers. D: Enforcer (Marvel). 2.50
❑195, Jun 1985 A: Shaman. 2.50
❑196, Jul 1985 2.50
❑197, Aug 1985; Secret Wars II 2.50
❑198, Sep 1985 SB (a); O: Obadiah Stane. O: Iron Monger. 2.50
❑199, Oct 1985; HT (a); D: Morley Erwin. James Rhodes crippled 2.50
❑200, Nov 1985; double-sized; 1: Red and white battlesuit. D: Obadiah Stane. D: Iron Monger. Tony Stark returns as Iron Man; New armor (red & white) 3.00
❑201, Dec 1985 2.00
❑202, Jan 1986 A: Ka-Zar. V: Fixer. ... 2.00
❑203, Feb 1986 2.00
❑204, Mar 1986 2.00
❑205, Apr 1986 V: Modok. 2.00
❑206, May 1986 2.00
❑207, Jun 1986 2.00
❑208, Jul 1986 2.00
❑209, Aug 1986 2.00
❑210, Sep 1986 A: Happy Hogan. 2.00
❑211, Oct 1986 2.00
❑212, Nov 1986 2.00
❑213, Dec 1986 A: Dominic Fortune. 2.00
❑214, Jan 1987; Construction of Stark Enterprises begins 2.00
❑215, Feb 1987 2.00
❑216, Mar 1987 D: Clytemnestra Erwin. 2.00
❑217, Apr 1987 1: undersea armor. .. 2.00
❑218, May 1987 BL (a); 1: Deep Sea armor. 2.00
❑219, Jun 1987 BL (a); 1: Ghost. V: Ghost. 2.00
❑220, Jul 1987 D: Spymaster. 2.00
❑221, Aug 1987 2.00
❑222, Sep 1987 2.00
❑223, Oct 1987 1: Rae LaCoste. 2.00
❑224, Nov 1987 BL (a) 2.00
❑225, Dec 1987; Giant-size 3.00
❑226, Jan 1988 2.50
❑227, Feb 1988 2.50
❑228, Mar 1988 2.50
❑229, Apr 1988 D: Gremlin a.k.a Titanium Man II. 3.00
❑230, May 1988; V: Firepower. apparent death of Iron Man 2.50
❑231, Jun 1988; V: Firepower. new armor 2.50
❑232, Jul 1988; offset 2.50
❑232/A, Jul 1988; Flexographic 2.50
❑233, Aug 1988 1: Kathy Dare. A: Ant-Man. 2.00
❑234, Sep 1988 A: Spider-Man. 2.00
❑235, Oct 1988 1.50
❑236, Nov 1988 1.50
❑237, Dec 1988 1.50

Tony Stark announced the formation of his new consulting firm, Stark Solutions, in *Iron Man* (Vol. 3) #1.

N-MINT

❑238, Jan 1989 1: Madame Masque II. 1.50
❑239, Feb 1989 1.50
❑240, Mar 1989 1.50
❑241, Apr 1989 1.50
❑242, May 1989; Stark shot by Kathy Dare 1.50
❑243, Jun 1989; BL (a);Stark crippled 2.00
❑244, Jul 1989; Giant-size; Carl Walker a.k.a. Force becomes Iron Man; New armor to allow Stark to walk again . 3.00
❑245, Aug 1989 PS (a) 1.50
❑246, Sep 1989 BL (a) 1.50
❑247, Oct 1989 BL (a) 1.50
❑248, Nov 1989; BL (a);Stark cured by implanted bio-chip 1.50
❑249, Nov 1989; BL (a);Doctor Doom 1.50
❑250, Dec 1989; double-sized; BL (a); V: Doctor Doom. Acts of Vengeance 1.75
❑251, Dec 1989; HT (a); V: Wrecker. Acts of Vengeance 1.25
❑252, Jan 1990; HT (a); V: Chemistro. Acts of Vengeance 1.25
❑253, Feb 1990 JBy (c); GC (a) 1.25
❑254, Mar 1990 BL (w); BL (a) 1.25
❑255, Apr 1990 HT (a) 1.25
❑256, May 1990 BL (w); JR2 (a) 1.25
❑257, Jun 1990 1.25
❑258, Jul 1990 JBy (w); JR2 (a) 1.50
❑259, Aug 1990 JBy (w); JR2 (a) 1.50
❑260, Sep 1990 JBy (w); JR2 (a) 1.50
❑261, Oct 1990 JBy (w); JR2 (a) 1.50
❑262, Nov 1990 JBy (w); JR2 (a) 1.50
❑263, Dec 1990 JBy (w); JR2 (a) 1.50
❑264, Jan 1991 JBy (w); JR2 (a) 1.50
❑265, Feb 1991 JBy (w); JR2 (a) 1.50
❑266, Mar 1991 JR2 (a) 1.50
❑267, Apr 1991 JBy (w) 1.50
❑268, May 1991 JBy (w); O: Iron Man. 1.50
❑269, Jun 1991 JBy (w) 1.50
❑270, Jul 1991 JBy (w) 1.50
❑271, Aug 1991 JBy (w) 1.50
❑272, Sep 1991 JBy (w) 1.50
❑273, Oct 1991 JBy (w) 1.50
❑274, Nov 1991 JBy (w); O: Fin Fang Foom. V: Fin Fang Foom. 1.50
❑275, Dec 1991; Giant-size JBy (w); V: Fin Fang Foom. V: Mandarin. V: Dragon Lords. 1.50
❑276, Jan 1992 JBy (w) 1.50
❑277, Feb 1992 JBy (w) 1.50
❑278, Mar 1992; 1: new Space Armor. Galactic Storm 1.50
❑279, Apr 1992; V: Ronan the Accuser. Galactic Storm 1.50
❑280, May 1992 A: The Stark. 1.50
❑281, Jun 1992 1: War Machine armor. 3.00
❑282, Jul 1992 2: War Machine armor. 3.00
❑283, Aug 1992 1.50
❑284, Sep 1992 O: War Machine. 1: War Machine. D: Tony Stark. 2.00
❑285, Oct 1992 1.25
❑286, Nov 1992 1.25
❑287, Dec 1992 1.25
❑288, Jan 1993; 30th anniversary special; Embossed cover; Tony Stark revived 2.50
❑289, Feb 1993 1.25
❑290, Mar 1993; Metallic ink cover; New Armor 3.50

Condition price index: Multiply "NM prices" above by: **0.83 for Very Fine/Near Mint**
0.66 for Very Fine • 0.33 for Fine • 0.2 for Very Good • 0.125 for Good

	N-MINT
❑291, Apr 1993; James Rhodes leaves to become War Machine	1.25
❑292, May 1993	1.25
❑293, Jun 1993	1.25
❑294, Jul 1993	1.25
❑295, Aug 1993	1.25
❑296, Sep 1993	1.25
❑297, Oct 1993 A: M.O.D.A.M. A: Omega Red.	1.25
❑298, Nov 1993	1.25
❑299, Dec 1993 V: Ultimo.	1.25
❑300, Jan 1994; Giant size; A: Iron Legion (all substitute Iron Men). V: Ultimo. Stark dons new (modular) armor	2.50
❑300/Variant, Jan 1994; Giant size; Special (embossed foil) cover edition; Stark dons new (modular) armor	3.95
❑301, Feb 1994	1.25
❑302, Mar 1994 A: Venom.	1.25
❑303, Apr 1994	1.25
❑304, May 1994 1: Hulkbuster Armor.	1.25
❑305, Jun 1994 A: Hulk.	1.50
❑306, Jul 1994; Stark restructures company	1.50
❑307, Aug 1994	1.50
❑308, Sep 1994	1.50
❑309, Oct 1994	1.50
❑310, Nov 1994	1.50
❑310/CS, Nov 1994; polybagged with 16-page preview, acetate print, and other items	2.95
❑311, Dec 1994	1.50
❑312, Jan 1995	1.50
❑313, Feb 1995	1.50
❑314, Mar 1995	1.50
❑315, Apr 1995 V: Titanium Man.	1.50
❑316, May 1995	1.50
❑317, Jun 1995; D: Titanium Man I. flip book with War Machine: Brothers in Arms part 3 back-up	2.50
❑318, Jul 1995	1.50
❑319, Aug 1995 O: Iron Man.	1.50
❑320, Sep 1995	1.50
❑321, Oct 1995; OverPower cards inserted	1.50
❑322, Nov 1995	1.50
❑323, Dec 1995 A: Avengers. A: Hawkeye.	1.50
❑324, Jan 1996	1.50
❑325, Feb 1996; Giant-size; wraparound cover; Tony Stark vs. young Tony Stark	3.00
❑326, Mar 1996	1.50
❑327, Apr 1996; V: Frostbite. reading of Tony Stark's will	1.50
❑328, May 1996	1.50
❑329, Jun 1996; Fujikawa International takes over Stark Enterprises	1.50
❑330, Jul 1996	1.50
❑331, Aug 1996	1.50
❑332, Sep 1996	1.50
❑Annual 1, Aug 1970; GC, DH, JK, WW, JAb (a);Reprints from Tales of Suspense #71, #79, and #80, and Tales to Astonish #82	22.00
❑Annual 2, Nov 1971	20.00
❑Annual 3, ca. 1976	10.00
❑Annual 4, ca. 1977; Cover reads "King-Size Special"	4.00
❑Annual 5, ca. 1982	3.00
❑Annual 6, ca. 1983; LMc (a); A: Eternals. D: Zuras (spirit leaves body). New Iron Man appears	3.00
❑Annual 7, ca. 1984; LMc (a); 1: Goliath III (Erik Josten). West Coast Avengers; Was formerly known as Power Man I	3.00
❑Annual 8, ca. 1986 A: X-Factor.	3.00
❑Annual 9, ca. 1987	3.00
❑Annual 10, ca. 1989; PS, DP (a);Atlantis Attacks	2.50
❑Annual 11, ca. 1990 A: Machine Man.	2.00
❑Annual 12, ca. 1991 1: Trapster II.	2.00
❑Annual 13, ca. 1992 GC (a); A: Darkhawk, Avengers West Coast.	2.00
❑Annual 14, ca. 1993; trading card	2.95
❑Annual 15, ca. 1994 GC (a); V: Controller.	2.95
❑Ashcan 1, Nov 1994; Collectors' Preview; "Iron Man & Force Works" on cover	1.95

IRON MAN (VOL. 2)
MARVEL

	N-MINT
❑1, Nov 1996; Giant-size JLee (w); O: Hulk (new). O: Iron Man (new).	3.00
❑1/A, Nov 1996; Giant-size; JLee (w); O: Iron Man (new). variant cover	3.00
❑2, Dec 1996 JLee (w); V: Hulk.	2.00
❑3, Jan 1997 JLee (w); 1: Whirlwind. A: Fantastic Four.	2.00
❑4, Feb 1997 JLee (w); V: Living Laser.	2.00
❑4/A, Feb 1997; JLee (w); variant cover	2.00
❑5, Mar 1997 JLee (w); V: Whirlwind.	1.95
❑6, Apr 1997; JLee (a); A: Onslaught. concludes in Captain America #6	1.95
❑7, May 1997 JLee (w)	1.95
❑8, Jun 1997	1.95
❑9, Jul 1997	1.95
❑10, Aug 1997; gatefold summary	1.95
❑11, Sep 1997; gatefold summary A: Doctor Doom.	1.95
❑12, Oct 1997; gatefold summary; cover forms quadtych with Fantastic Four #12, Avengers #12, and Captain America #12	3.50
❑13, Nov 1997; gatefold summary; cover forms quadtych with Fantastic Four #13, Avengers #13, and Captain America #13	2.50

IRON MAN (VOL. 3)
MARVEL

	N-MINT
❑1, Feb 1998; Giant-size; KB (w); 1: Stark Solutions. wraparound cover	3.50
❑1/A, Feb 1998; gatefold summary; KB (w); 1: Stark Solutions. wraparound cover	4.00
❑2, Mar 1998; gatefold summary KB (w)	2.00
❑2/Variant, Mar 1998; KB (w); variant cover	3.00
❑3, Apr 1998; gatefold summary KB (w)	2.00
❑4, May 1998; gatefold summary KB (w); V: Firebrand.	2.00
❑5, Jun 1998; gatefold summary KB (w); V: Firebrand.	2.00
❑6, Jul 1998; gatefold summary KB (w); A: Black Widow.	2.00
❑7, Aug 1998; gatefold summary KB (w); A: Warbird.	2.00
❑8, Sep 1998; gatefold summary; KB (w); Tony beaten	2.00
❑9, Oct 1998; gatefold summary KB (w); A: Winter Guard.	2.00
❑10, Nov 1998; gatefold summary KB (w)	2.00
❑11, Dec 1998; gatefold summary; KB (w); A: Warbird. V: War Machine armor. new home	2.00
❑12, Jan 1999; gatefold summary KB (w); A: Warbird. V: War Machine armor.	2.00
❑13, Feb 1999; double-sized KB (w); A: Controller. V: Controller.	3.00
❑13/Autographed, Feb 1999 KB (w); A: Controller.	4.00
❑14, Mar 1999; KB (w); A: Fantastic Four. A: S.H.I.E.L.D.. A: Watcher. V: Ronan. Fantastic Four crossover, part 2	1.99
❑15, Apr 1999 KB (w); V: Nitro.	1.99
❑16, May 1999 KB (w)	1.99
❑17, Jun 1999 KB (w); A: Fin Fang Foom.	1.99
❑18, Jul 1999 KB (w); A: Warbird.	1.99
❑19, Aug 1999 KB (w); V: War Machine.	1.99
❑20, Sep 1999 KB (w); V: War Machine.	1.99
❑21, Oct 1999; KB (w); 1: Inferno. continues in Thor #17	1.99
❑22, Nov 1999; KB (w); 1: Carnivore. A: Thor. continues in Peter Parker, Spider-Man #11	1.99
❑23, Dec 1999 KB (w); A: Ultimo.	1.99
❑24, Jan 2000	1.99
❑25, Feb 2000; double-sized KB (w); A: Warbird. A: Ultimo.	2.25
❑26, Mar 2000	2.25
❑27, Apr 2000	2.25
❑28, May 2000	2.25
❑29, Jun 2000	2.25
❑30, Jul 2000	2.25
❑31, Aug 2000	2.25
❑32, Sep 2000; A: Wong-Chu. concludes in Iron Man Annual 2000	2.25
❑33, Oct 2000	2.25
❑34, Nov 2000	2.25
❑35, Dec 2000	2.25
❑36, Jan 2001	2.25
❑37, Feb 2001	2.25
❑38, Mar 2001	2.25
❑39, Apr 2001	2.25
❑40, May 2001 BL, JR, ES (a)	2.25
❑41, Jun 2001	2.25
❑42, Jul 2001	2.25
❑43, Aug 2001	2.25
❑44, Sep 2001	2.25
❑45, Oct 2001	2.25
❑46, Nov 2001	3.50
❑47, Dec 2001	2.25
❑48, Jan 2002	2.25
❑49, Feb 2002	2.25
❑50, Mar 2002 MGr (w)	2.99
❑51, Apr 2002, MGr (w); wraparound cover	2.25
❑52, May 2002, MGr (w); wraparound cover	2.25
❑53, Jun 2002, MGr (w); wraparound cover	2.25
❑54, Jun 2002, MGr (w); wraparound cover	2.25
❑55, Jul 2002, MGr (w); wraparound cover	2.25
❑56, Aug 2002, MGr (w); wraparound cover	2.25
❑57, Sep 2002, MGr (w); wraparound cover	2.25
❑58, Oct 2002, MGr (w); wraparound cover	2.25
❑59, Nov 2002, MGr (w); wraparound cover	2.25
❑60, Dec 2002, MGr (w); wraparound cover	2.25
❑61, Jan 2003, MGr (w); wraparound cover	2.25
❑62, Feb 2003, MGr (w); wraparound cover	2.25
❑63, Feb 2003, MGr (w); wraparound cover	2.25
❑64, Mar 2003, MGr (w); wraparound cover	2.25
❑65, Apr 2003	2.25
❑66, May 2003	2.25
❑67, Jun 2003	2.99
❑68, Jul 2003	2.99
❑69, Aug 2003 (c)	2.99
❑70, Sep 2003	2.99
❑71, Oct 2003	2.99
❑72, Nov 2003	2.99
❑73, Dec 2003; Stark seeks cabinet post	2.99
❑74, Jan 2004; Stark nomination announced	2.99
❑75, Feb 2004	2.99
❑76, Mar 2004; A: Crimson Dynamo III (Alex Nevsky). Stark rejected by Senate subcommittee	2.99
❑77, Apr 2004	2.99
❑78, May 2004; Stark named Secretary of Defense	2.99
❑79, Jun 2004	2.99
❑80, Jun 2004; Stark visits Iraq	2.99
❑81, Jul 2004	2.99
❑82, Jul 2004; Force reconciled with Stark	2.99
❑83, Jul 2004	2.99
❑84, Aug 2004; Avengers Dissasemble Prologue	2.99

N-MINT

❑85, Aug 2004; Avengers Dissasemble Prologue 2.99
❑86, Sep 2004 .... 2.99
❑Annual 1998, ca. 1998, MWa (w); V: Modok. Iron Man/Captain America '98; wraparound cover 3.50
❑Annual 1999, Aug 1999, wraparound cover 3.50
❑Annual 2000, ca. 2000, D: Wong-Chu. wraparound cover 3.50
❑Annual 2001, ca. 2001 .... 2.99

IRON MAN/X-O MANOWAR: HEAVY METAL
MARVEL

❑1, Sep 1996; crossover with Acclaim 2.50

IRON MARSHAL
JADEMAN

❑1, Jul 1990 .... 1.75
❑2, Aug 1990 .... 1.75
❑3, Sep 1990 .... 1.75
❑4, Oct 1990 .... 1.75
❑5, Nov 1990 .... 1.75
❑6, Dec 1990 .... 1.75
❑7, Jan 1991 .... 1.75
❑8, Feb 1991 .... 1.75
❑9, Mar 1991 .... 1.75
❑10, Apr 1991 .... 1.75
❑11, May 1991 .... 1.75
❑12, Jun 1991 .... 1.75
❑13, Jul 1991 .... 1.75
❑14, Aug 1991 .... 1.75
❑15, Sep 1991 .... 1.75
❑16, Oct 1991 .... 1.75
❑17, Nov 1991 .... 1.75
❑18, Dec 1991 .... 1.75
❑19, Jan 1992 .... 1.75
❑20, Feb 1992 .... 1.75
❑21, Mar 1992 .... 1.75
❑22, Apr 1992 .... 1.75
❑23, May 1992 .... 1.75
❑24, Jun 1992 .... 1.75
❑25, Jul 1992 .... 1.75
❑26, Aug 1992 .... 1.75
❑27, Sep 1992 .... 1.75
❑28, Oct 1992 .... 1.75
❑29, Nov 1992 .... 1.75
❑30, Dec 1992 .... 1.75
❑31, Jan 1993 .... 1.75
❑32, Feb 1993 .... 1.75

IRON SAGA'S ANTHOLOGY
IRON SAGA

❑1, Jan 1987 .... 1.75

IRON WINGS
ACTION

❑1, May 1999 .... 2.50

IRON WINGS (VOL. 2)
IMAGE

❑1, Apr 2000 .... 2.50

IRONWOLF
DC

❑1, ca. 1986; Reprints IronWolf adventures from Weird Worlds #8-10 ..... 2.00

IRONWOOD
FANTAGRAPHICS / EROS

❑1, b&w 4.00
❑2, b&w 2.25
❑3, b&w 2.25
❑4, b&w 2.25
❑5, b&w 2.25
❑6, ca. 1992, b&w 2.25
❑7, Mar 1992, b&w 2.50
❑8, ca. 1992, b&w 2.50
❑9, Aug 1993, b&w 2.50
❑10, Sep 1994, b&w 2.75

I SAW IT
EDUCOMICS

❑1, b&w; Hiroshima 2.00

N-MINT

ISIS
DC

❑1, Oct 1976 .... 6.00
❑2, Dec 1976 .... 4.00
❑3, Feb 1977 .... 3.50
❑4, Apr 1977 .... 3.50
❑5, Jun 1977 .... 3.50
❑6, Aug 1977 .... 3.50
❑7, Oct 1977 O: Isis. 4.00
❑8, Dec 1977 .... 3.50

ISLAND OF DR. MOREAU, THE
MARVEL

❑1, Oct 1977 .... 3.00

ISMET
CANIS

❑1 .... 1.25
❑2 .... 1.25
❑3 .... 1.25
❑4 .... 1.25
❑5 .... 1.25

I SPY
GOLD KEY

❑1, Aug 1966; based on TV series 55.00
❑2, Apr 1967; based on TV series 40.00
❑3, Nov 1967; based on TV series 33.00
❑4, Feb 1968; based on TV series 33.00
❑5, Jun 1968; based on TV series 33.00
❑6, Sep 1968; based on TV series 33.00

ITCHY & SCRATCHY COMICS
BONGO

❑1, ca. 1993 .... 2.50
❑2, ca. 1994 .... 2.00
❑3, ca. 1994 A: Bart Simpson. 2.25
❑Holiday 1, ca. 1994; Itchy & Scratchy Holiday Hi-Jinx Special 2.00

ITCHY PLANET
FANTAGRAPHICS

❑1, Spr 1988 .... 2.25
❑2, Sum 1988 .... 2.25
❑3, Fal 1988 .... 2.25

IT'S A BIRD
DC

❑1, ca 2004 .... 24.95

IT'S ABOUT TIME
GOLD KEY

❑1, Jan 1967 .... 25.00

IT'S ONLY A MATTER OF LIFE AND DEATH
FANTAGRAPHICS

❑1, b&w 3.95

IT'S SCIENCE WITH DR. RADIUM
SLAVE LABOR

❑1, Sep 1986 .... 2.00
❑2, Jan 1987 .... 2.00
❑3, Mar 1987 .... 2.00
❑4, May 1987 .... 2.00
❑5, Jul 1987 .... 2.00
❑6, Oct 1987 .... 2.00
❑7, Feb 1988 .... 2.00
❑Special 1, Jan 1989, b&w 2.95

IT! THE TERROR FROM BEYOND SPACE
MILLENNIUM

❑1; Die-cut cover 2.50
❑2, Jan 1993 .... 2.50
❑3 .... 2.50
❑4 .... 2.50

I WANT TO BE YOUR DOG
FANTAGRAPHICS / EROS

❑1, b&w 1.95
❑2, b&w 1.95
❑3, b&w 1.95
❑4, b&w 1.95
❑5, b&w 2.25

Cain Marko's son discovered his super-powered legacy in a possible Marvel future in *J2* #1.

© 1998 Marvel Characters Inc.

N-MINT

J

J2
MARVEL

❑1, Oct 1998; gatefold summary; son of Juggernaut 2.00
❑1/A, Oct 1998; gatefold summary; Alternate cover with J2 alone in foreground 2.00
❑2, Nov 1998; gatefold summary V: X-People. 2.00
❑3, Dec 1998 A: Hulk. A: Dr. Strange. A: Doctor Strange. A: Sub-Mariner. 2.00
❑4, Jan 1999 1: Nemesus. A: Doc Magus. 2.00
❑5, Feb 1999 1: Wild Thing. A: Wolverine. A: Elektra. 2.00
❑6, Mar 1999; A: Magneta. Wild Thing story 2.00
❑7, Apr 1999; A: Cyclops. A: Uncanny X-People. A: Parody. Wild Thing story 2.00
❑8, May 1999 .... 2.00
❑9, Jun 1999 1: Big Julie. 2.00
❑10, Jul 1999 A: Wolverine. 2.00
❑11, Aug 1999 A: Sons of the Tiger. A: Iron Fist. 2.00
❑12, Oct 1999 .... 2.00

JAB
ADHESIVE

❑1 .... 2.50
❑2 .... 2.50
❑3, Spr 1993; bullet hole 2.50
❑4 .... 2.50
❑5 .... 2.50

JAB (CUMMINGS DESIGN)
CUMMINGS DESIGN GROUP

❑3, Aut 1994, b&w 2.95

JAB (FUNNY PAPERS)
FUNNY PAPERS

❑1, b&w 2.50
❑2, b&w 2.50

JACKAROO, THE
ETERNITY

❑1, Feb 1990, b&w; Australian 2.25
❑2, Mar 1990, b&w; Australian 2.25
❑3, Apr 1990, b&w; Australian 2.25

JACK FROST
AMAZING

❑1, b&w 1.95
❑2, b&w 1.95

JACK HUNTER
BLACKTHORNE

❑1, Mar 1988 .... 1.25

JACKIE JOKERS
HARVEY

❑1, Mar 1973 .... 12.00
❑2, May 1973; Richard Nixon appears on cover with Jackie 10.00
❑3, Jul 1973 .... 10.00
❑4, Sep 1973 .... 10.00

JACK OF HEARTS
MARVEL

❑1, Jan 1984 .... 1.50
❑2, Feb 1984 .... 1.50
❑3, Mar 1984 .... 1.50
❑4, Apr 1984 .... 1.50

Condition price index: Multiply "NM prices" above by: **0.83 for Very Fine/Near Mint**
0.66 for Very Fine • 0.33 for Fine • 0.2 for Very Good • 0.125 for Good

N-MINT

JACK'S LUCK RUNS OUT
Beekeeper Cartoon Amusements
- ❑1 ... 3.50

JACK STAFF
Image
- ❑1, Feb 2003 ... 0.00
- ❑2, Apr 2003 ... 2.95
- ❑3, Aug 2003 ... 2.95
- ❑4, Nov 2003 ... 2.95
- ❑5, Aug 2004 ... 3.50

JACK THE RIPPER (CALIBER)
Caliber / Tome
- ❑1 1998, b&w ... 2.95

JACK THE RIPPER
Eternity
- ❑1, b&w ... 2.25
- ❑2, b&w ... 2.25
- ❑3, b&w ... 2.25

JACQUELYN THE RIPPER
Fantagraphics
- ❑1, Oct 1994, b&w ... 2.95
- ❑2, Oct 1994, b&w ... 2.95

JACQUE'S VOICE OF DOOM
Doomed Comics
- ❑1, b&w; strip reprints ... 1.50

JADEMAN COLLECTION
Jademan
- ❑1 ... 2.50
- ❑2 ... 2.50
- ❑3, Feb 1990 ... 2.50

JADEMAN KUNG FU SPECIAL
Jademan
- ❑1; Perviews of Jademan's Titles ... 1.50

JADE WARRIORS
Image
- ❑1 ... 2.50
- ❑1/A; Painted alternate cover ... 2.50
- ❑2, Jan 2000 ... 2.50

JAGUAR, THE
DC / Impact
- ❑1, Aug 1991 O: Jaguar. 1: The Jaguar (Maria de Guzman). 1: Timon de Guzman. 1: Tracy Dickerson. 1: Maxim Ruiz. 1: Maxx-13. 1: Luiza Timmerman. ... 1.00
- ❑2, Sep 1991 ... 1.00
- ❑3, Oct 1991 V: Maxx-13. ... 1.00
- ❑4, Nov 1991 1: Victor Drago. A: Black Hood. ... 1.00
- ❑5, Dec 1991 1: Void. ... 1.00
- ❑6, Jan 1992 ... 1.00
- ❑7, Mar 1992 ... 1.00
- ❑8, Apr 1992 ... 1.00
- ❑9, May 1992; 1: Moonlighter. trading card ... 1.00
- ❑10, Jun 1992 ... 1.00
- ❑11, Jul 1992 ... 1.25
- ❑12, Aug 1992 ... 1.25
- ❑13, Sep 1992 ... 1.25
- ❑14, Oct 1992 ... 1.25
- ❑Annual 1, ca. 1992 ... 2.50

JAGUAR GOD
Verotik
- ❑0, Feb 1996 FF (c); FF (a) ... 4.00
- ❑1, Mar 1995 FF (c); FF (a) ... 4.00
- ❑2, Aug 1995 ... 4.00
- ❑3, Mar 1996 ... 3.50
- ❑4 1996 ... 3.50
- ❑5, Sep 1996 ... 3.50
- ❑6, Apr 1997 ... 2.95
- ❑7, Jun 1997 ... 2.95
- ❑8 1997 ... 2.95

JAILBAIT
Fantagraphics / Eros
- ❑1, Dec 1998 ... 2.95

JAKE THRASH
Aircel
- ❑1 ... 2.00
- ❑2 ... 2.00

JAM, THE
Slave Labor
- ❑1, Nov 1989, b&w ... 2.50
- ❑2, Jan 1990, b&w ... 2.00
- ❑3, Mar 1990, b&w ... 2.00
- ❑4, May 1990 ... 2.95
- ❑5, Mar 1991 ... 2.95
- ❑6 ... 2.50
- ❑7, Mar 1994, b&w ... 2.50
- ❑8, Feb 1995, b&w ... 2.95
- ❑9, Aug 1995, b&w ... 2.95
- ❑10, b&w ... 2.95
- ❑11, b&w ... 2.95
- ❑12 ... 2.95
- ❑13 ... 2.95

JAMAR CHRONICLES, THE
Sweat Shop
- ❑1, b&w ... 2.00

JAMES BOND 007: A SILENT ARMAGEDDON
Dark Horse
- ❑1, Mar 1993; cardstock cover ... 2.95
- ❑2, May 1993; cardstock cover ... 2.95

JAMES BOND 007/GOLDENEYE
Topps
- ❑1, Jan 1996 ... 2.95
- ❑2, Feb 1996 ... 2.95
- ❑3, Mar 1996 ... 2.95

JAMES BOND 007: SERPENT'S TOOTH
Dark Horse
- ❑1, Jul 1992; prestige format ... 4.95
- ❑2, Aug 1992; prestige format ... 4.95
- ❑3, Feb 1993; prestige format ... 4.95

JAMES BOND 007: SHATTERED HELIX
Dark Horse
- ❑1, Jun 1994 ... 2.50
- ❑2, Jul 1994 ... 2.50

JAMES BOND 007: THE QUASIMODO GAMBIT
Dark Horse
- ❑1, Jan 1995; cardstock cover ... 3.95
- ❑2, Feb 1995; cardstock cover ... 3.95
- ❑3, May 1995; cardstock cover ... 3.95

JAMES BOND FOR YOUR EYES ONLY
Marvel
- ❑1, Oct 1981 HC (a) ... 1.50
- ❑2, Nov 1981 HC (a) ... 1.50

JAMES BOND JR.
Marvel
- ❑1, Jan 1992; TV cartoon ... 1.00
- ❑2, Feb 1992; TV cartoon ... 1.00
- ❑3, Mar 1992; TV cartoon ... 1.00
- ❑4, Apr 1992; TV cartoon ... 1.00
- ❑5, May 1992; TV cartoon ... 1.00
- ❑6, Jun 1992; TV cartoon ... 1.00
- ❑7, Jul 1992; TV cartoon ... 1.00
- ❑8, Aug 1992; TV cartoon ... 1.00
- ❑9, Sep 1992; TV cartoon ... 1.00
- ❑10, Oct 1992; TV cartoon ... 1.00
- ❑11, Nov 1992; TV cartoon ... 1.00
- ❑12, Dec 1992; TV cartoon ... 1.00

JAMES BOND: PERMISSION TO DIE
Eclipse
- ❑1, Jul 1991 MGr (w); MGr (a) ... 4.00
- ❑2, Aug 1991 MGr (w); MGr (a) ... 4.00
- ❑3, Sep 1991 MGr (w); MGr (a) ... 5.00

JAM QUACKY
JQ
- ❑1, b&w ... 2.00

JAM SPECIAL, THE
Matrix
- ❑1 ... 2.50

JAM SUPER COOL COLOR-INJECTED TURBO ADVENTURE FROM HELL
Comico
- ❑1, May 1988 ... 2.50

JAM URBAN ADVENTURE, THE
Tundra
- ❑1 ... 2.95
- ❑2 ... 2.95
- ❑3 ... 2.95

JANE BONDAGE
Fantagraphics / Eros
- ❑1 ... 2.95
- ❑2, Sep 1995 ... 2.95

JANE BOND: THUNDERBALLS
Fantagraphics / Eros
- ❑1, b&w ... 2.50

JANE DOE
Raging Rhino
- ❑1, b&w ... 2.95
- ❑2, b&w ... 2.95
- ❑3, b&w ... 2.95

JANX
Es Graphics
- ❑1 ... 1.00
- ❑2 ... 1.00

J.A.P.A.N.
Outerealm
- ❑1 ... 1.80

JAR OF FOOLS PART ONE
Penny Dreadful
- ❑1, Jun 1994, b&w ... 5.95

JASON AND THE ARGONAUTS
Tome
- ❑1, b&w ... 2.50
- ❑2, b&w ... 2.50
- ❑3, b&w ... 2.50
- ❑4, b&w ... 2.50
- ❑5, b&w ... 2.50

JASON GOES TO HELL: THE FINAL FRIDAY
Topps
- ❑1, Jul 1993; glowing cover ... 2.95
- ❑2, Aug 1993 ... 2.95
- ❑3, Sep 1993 ... 2.95

JASON MONARCH
Oracle
- ❑1, b&w ... 2.00

JASON VS. LEATHERFACE
Topps
- ❑1, Oct 1995 ... 2.95
- ❑2, Nov 1995 ... 2.95
- ❑3, Dec 1995 ... 2.95

JAVA TOWN
Slave Labor
- ❑1, May 1992, b&w ... 2.95
- ❑2, Nov 1993, b&w ... 2.95
- ❑3, Jul 1994, b&w ... 2.95
- ❑4, Jul 1995, b&w ... 2.95
- ❑5, Nov 1995, b&w ... 2.95
- ❑6, Jun 1996, b&w ... 2.95

JAVERTS
Firstlight
- ❑1, ca. 1997, b&w; no cover price or indicia ... 2.95

JAX AND THE HELL HOUND
Blackthorne
- ❑1, Nov 1986 ... 1.75
- ❑2, Feb 1987 ... 1.75
- ❑3 1987 ... 1.75
- ❑4 1987 ... 1.75

JAY ANACLETO SKETCHBOOK
Image
- ❑1, Apr 1999; no cover price ... 2.00
- ❑1/A, Apr 1999; Has cover price ... 2.00

JAY & SILENT BOB
Oni
- ❑1, Jul 1998 KSm (w) ... 4.00
- ❑1/Variant, Jul 1998 KSm (w) ... 5.00
- ❑1-2, Oct 1998 KSm (w) ... 2.95
- ❑2, Oct 1998 KSm (w) ... 3.00

Condition price index: Multiply "NM prices" above by: **0.83 for Very Fine/Near Mint**
0.66 for Very Fine • 0.33 for Fine • 0.2 for Very Good • 0.125 for Good

N-MINT

❑3, Dec 1998 KSm (w) 3.00
❑4, Oct 1999 KSm (w) 3.00

JAZZ
HIGH IMPACT

❑1 1996 ..... 2.95
❑2, May 1996 ..... 2.95

JAZZ AGE CHRONICLES (EF)
EF GRAPHICS

❑1, Jan 1989 ..... 1.50
❑2, Mar 1989 ..... 1.50
❑3, May 1989 ..... 1.50

JAZZ AGE CHRONICLES (CALIBER)
CALIBER

❑1, b&w 2.50
❑2, May 1990, b&w 2.50
❑3, b&w 2.50
❑4, b&w 2.50
❑5, b&w 2.50

JAZZBO COMICS THAT SWING
SLAVE LABOR

❑1, Nov 1994 ..... 2.95
❑2, Apr 1995; Replacement God preview 2.95

JAZZ: SOLITAIRE
HIGH IMPACT

❑1, May 1998 ..... 2.95
❑1/A, May 1998; wraparound cover .. 3.50
❑1/Gold, May 1998; gold foil logo; no cover price 3.50
❑2, May 1998 ..... 3.00
❑2/A; no cover price 5.00
❑2/B; nude cover (blue background) . 5.00
❑3 ..... 3.00
❑3/A; Nude cover 5.00
❑3/B; wraparound nude cover 5.00

JCP FEATURES
J.C.

❑1, Feb 1981; DG, NA (a);THUNDER Agents 3.00

JEFFREY DAHMER: AN UNAUTHORIZED BIOGRAPHY OF A SERIAL KILLER
BONEYARD

❑1, Mar 1992 ..... 4.00
❑1-2 ..... 3.00

JEFFREY DAHMER VS. JESUS CHRIST
BONEYARD

❑1, Feb 1993; wraparound cover 4.00
❑1/Autographed 4.00

JEMM, SON OF SATURN
DC

❑1, Sep 1984 GC, KJ (a); 1: Jemm, Son of Saturn. 1.50
❑2, Oct 1984 ..... 1.00
❑3, Nov 1984 O: Jemm. 1.00
❑4, Dec 1984 ..... 1.00
❑5, Jan 1985 ..... 1.00
❑6, Feb 1985 ..... 1.00
❑7, Mar 1985 GC, KJ (a) 1.00
❑8, Apr 1985 ..... 1.00
❑9, May 1985 ..... 1.00
❑10, Jun 1985 ..... 1.00
❑11, Jul 1985 ..... 1.00
❑12, Aug 1985 ..... 1.00

JENNY FINN
ONI

❑1, Jun 1999 ..... 2.95
❑2, Sep 1999 ..... 2.95
❑3, Nov 1999 ..... 2.95
❑4, Feb 2000 ..... 2.95

JENNY SPARKS: THE SECRET HISTORY OF THE AUTHORITY
DC / WILDSTORM

❑1, Aug 2000 ..... 2.50
❑2, Sep 2000 ..... 2.50
❑3, Oct 2000 ..... 2.50
❑4, Nov 2000 ..... 2.50
❑5, Mar 2001 ..... 2.50

N-MINT

JEREMIAH: A FISTFUL OF SAND
ADVENTURE

❑1, b&w 2.50
❑2, b&w 2.50

JEREMIAH: BIRDS OF PREY
ADVENTURE

❑1, Apr 1991, b&w 2.50
❑2, Apr 1991, b&w 2.50

JEREMIAH: THE HEIRS
ADVENTURE

❑1, b&w 2.50
❑2, b&w 2.50

JERSEY DEVIL
SOUTH JERSEY REBELLION

❑1 1992; no indicia 2.25
❑2 ..... 2.95
❑3 ..... 2.25
❑4 1997 ..... 2.25
❑5 1997 ..... 2.25
❑6 1997 ..... 2.25
❑7; no indicia 2.25

JESSE JAMES
AC

❑1, b&w 3.95

JESTER'S MOON, THE
ONE SHOT

❑1, Aug 1996, b&w 1.00

JESUS COMICS (FOOLBERT STURGEON'S...)
RIP OFF

❑1 ..... 5.00
❑2 ..... 4.00
❑3 ..... 4.00

JET
AUTHORITY

❑1, Dec 1996 ..... 2.95

JET (WILDSTORM)
DC / WILDSTORM

❑1, Nov 2000 ..... 2.50
❑2, Dec 2000 ..... 2.50
❑3, Jan 2001 ..... 2.50
❑4, Feb 2001 ..... 2.50

JET BLACK
MONOLITH

❑1, Sep 1997 ..... 2.50

JET COMICS
SLAVE LABOR / AMAZE INK

❑1, Oct 1997, b&w 2.95
❑2, Feb 1998, b&w 2.95
❑3, Mar 1998 ..... 2.95

JET DREAM
GOLD KEY

❑1, Jun 1968; Painted cover 18.00

JETSONS, THE (GOLD KEY)
GOLD KEY

❑1, Jan 1963 ..... 90.00
❑2, Apr 1963 ..... 65.00
❑3, Jun 1963 ..... 48.00
❑4, Jul 1963 ..... 48.00
❑5, Sep 1963 ..... 48.00
❑6, Nov 1963 ..... 40.00
❑7, Jan 1964 ..... 40.00
❑8, Mar 1964 ..... 40.00
❑9, May 1964 ..... 40.00
❑10, Jul 1964 ..... 40.00
❑11, Sep 1964 ..... 24.00
❑12, Nov 1964 ..... 24.00
❑13, Jan 1965 ..... 24.00
❑14, Mar 1965 ..... 24.00
❑15, May 1965 ..... 24.00
❑16, Jul 1965 ..... 24.00
❑17, Sep 1965 ..... 24.00
❑18, Nov 1965 ..... 24.00
❑19, Jan 1966 ..... 24.00
❑20, Mar 1966 ..... 24.00
❑21, Jun 1966 ..... 16.00
❑22, Sep 1966 ..... 16.00
❑23, Jul 1967 ..... 16.00

While many creators have appeared on the cover of their comics, Kevin Smith is one of the few to appear as his own character, Silent Bob.

© 1998 Kevin Smith and Oni Press.

N-MINT

❑24, Oct 1967 ..... 16.00
❑25, Jan 1968 ..... 16.00
❑26, Apr 1968 ..... 16.00
❑27, Jul 1968 ..... 16.00
❑28, Oct 1968 ..... 16.00
❑29, Jan 1969 ..... 16.00
❑30, Apr 1969 ..... 16.00
❑31, Jul 1969 ..... 14.00
❑32, Oct 1969 ..... 14.00
❑33, Jan 1970 ..... 14.00
❑34, Apr 1970 ..... 14.00
❑35, Jul 1970 ..... 14.00
❑36, Oct 1970 ..... 14.00

JETSONS, THE (CHARLTON)
CHARLTON

❑1, Nov 1970 ..... 35.00
❑2, Jan 1971 ..... 22.00
❑3, Mar 1971 ..... 14.00
❑4, May 1971 ..... 14.00
❑5, Jul 1971 ..... 14.00
❑6, Sep 1971 ..... 10.00
❑7, Nov 1971 ..... 10.00
❑8, Jan 1972 ..... 10.00
❑9, Mar 1972 ..... 10.00
❑10, May 1972 ..... 10.00
❑11, Jul 1972 ..... 7.00
❑12, Sep 1972 ..... 7.00
❑13, Nov 1972 ..... 7.00
❑14, Jan 1973 ..... 7.00
❑15, Feb 1973 ..... 7.00
❑16, Apr 1973 ..... 7.00
❑17, Jun 1973 ..... 7.00
❑18, Aug 1973 ..... 7.00
❑19, Oct 1973 ..... 7.00
❑20, Dec 1973 ..... 7.00

JETSONS, THE (HARVEY)
HARVEY

❑1, Sep 1992 ..... 1.50
❑2, Jan 1993 ..... 1.50
❑3, May 1993 ..... 1.50
❑4, Sep 1993 ..... 1.50
❑5, Nov 1993 ..... 1.50

JETSONS, THE (ARCHIE)
ARCHIE

❑1, Sep 1995 A: The Flintstones. 2.00
❑2, Oct 1995 ..... 1.50
❑3, Nov 1995 ..... 1.50
❑4, Dec 1995 ..... 1.50
❑5, Jan 1996 ..... 1.50
❑6, Feb 1996 ..... 1.50
❑7, Mar 1996 ..... 1.50
❑8, Apr 1996 ..... 1.50
❑9, May 1996 ..... 1.50
❑10, Jun 1996 ..... 1.50
❑11, Jul 1996 ..... 1.50
❑12, Aug 1996 ..... 1.50

JETSONS BIG BOOK, THE
HARVEY

❑1, Nov 1992 ..... 1.95
❑2, Apr 1993 ..... 1.95
❑3, ca. 1993 ..... 1.95

JETSONS GIANT SIZE
HARVEY

❑1, Oct 1992 ..... 3.00
❑2, Mar 1993 ..... 2.50
❑3, ca. 1993 ..... 2.50

N-MINT

JEZEBEL JADE
Comico

❑1, Oct 1988; wraparound cover 2.00
❑2, Nov 1988; wraparound cover 2.00
❑3, Dec 1988; wraparound cover 2.00

JEZEBELLE
WildStorm

❑1/A, Mar 2001; Woman leaping backward on cover, two hands with energy glow 2.50
❑1/B, Mar 2001; Woman standing on cover, one hand in energy ball 2.50
❑2, Apr 2001 .... 2.50
❑3, May 2001 .... 2.50
❑4, Jun 2001 .... 2.50
❑5, Jul 2001 .... 2.50
❑6, Aug 2001 .... 2.50

JFK ASSASSINATION
Zone

❑1 .... 3.50

JHEREG
Marvel / Epic

❑1 .... 8.95

JIGABOO DEVIL
Millennium

❑0, b&w 2.95

JIGSAW
Harvey

❑1, Sep 1966 O: Jigsaw (Harvey). 1: Jigsaw (Harvey). 16.00
❑2 .... 10.00

JILL: PART-TIME LOVER
NBM

❑1 .... 11.95

JIM (VOL. 1)
Fantagraphics

❑1 .... 8.00
❑2 .... 6.00
❑3 .... 5.00
❑4 .... 5.00

JIM (VOL. 2)
Fantagraphics

❑1, Dec 1993, b&w 5.00
❑2, b&w 4.00
❑3, b&w 4.00
❑4, b&w 3.00
❑5, b&w 3.00
❑6, May 1996, b&w 3.00
❑Special 1; Frank's Real Pa Special Edition 4.00

JIMBO
Bongo / Zongo

❑1, ca. 1995, b&w 2.95
❑2, ca. 1995, b&w 2.95
❑3; indicia says #2 .... 2.95
❑4, b&w; no indicia 2.95
❑5 .... 2.95
❑6 .... 2.95
❑7 .... 2.95

JIM HARDY (2ND SERIES)
United Feature

❑1 .... 100.00
❑2, Jul 1947 .... 60.00

JIM LEE SKETCHBOOK
WildStorm

❑1 JLee (a) 40.00

JINGLE BELLE
Oni

❑1, Nov 1999, b&w 2.95
❑2, Dec 1999, b&w 2.95

JINGLE BELLE'S ALL-STAR HOLIDAY HULLABALOO
Oni

❑1, Nov 2000, b&w 4.95

JINN
Image

❑1, Feb 2000 .... 2.95
❑2, May 2000 .... 2.95
❑3, Oct 2000 .... 2.95

N-MINT

JINX
Caliber

❑1, b&w; BMB (w); BMB (a) 3.50
❑2, b&w BMB (w); BMB (a) 3.00
❑3, b&w BMB (w); BMB (a) 3.00
❑4, b&w BMB (w); BMB (a) 3.00
❑5, Nov 1996, b&w BMB (w); BMB (a) 3.00
❑6, b&w; BMB (w); BMB (a);series moves to Image 3.00
❑7 BMB (w); BMB (a) 3.00
❑8; BMB (w); BMB (a);Charity Special 4.95
❑9; Homeless Edition BMB (w); BMB (a) 4.95
❑10, b&w; BMB (w); BMB (a).......... 2.95
❑11, b&w BMB (w); BMB (a) 2.95
❑12 BMB (w); BMB (a) 3.95
❑13, b&w BMB (w); BMB (a) 3.95
❑14, b&w BMB (w); BMB (a) 3.95
❑15 BMB (w); BMB (a) 3.95
❑16; BMB (w); BMB (a);Torso 3.95
❑17; BMB (w); BMB (a);Torso 3.95
❑18; BMB (w); BMB (a);Fire 2.95
❑19; BMB (w); BMB (a);Buried Treasures 2.95
❑20, b&w; BMB (w); BMB (a);True Crime Confessions 3.95
❑21; BMB (w); BMB (a);Torso 3.95

JINX POP CULTURE HOO-HAH, THE
Image

❑1, b&w 3.95

JIZZ
Fantagraphics

❑1, b&w 2.00
❑2, b&w 2.00
❑3, b&w 2.00
❑4, b&w 2.00
❑5 .... 2.25
❑6 .... 2.25
❑7 .... 2.25
❑8 .... 2.50
❑9 .... 2.95
❑10, b&w 2.50

JLA
DC

❑1, Jan 1997; Superman, Batman, Flash, Wonder Woman, Green Lantern, Martian Manhunter, Aquaman team 6.00
❑2, Feb 1997 .... 4.00
❑3, Mar 1997 .... 4.00
❑4, Apr 1997 .... 4.00
❑5, May 1997; V: Prof. Ivo. V: T.O. Morrow. Membership drive 4.00
❑6, Jun 1997 1: Zauriel. A: Neron. A: Ghast. A: Abnegazar. 4.00
❑7, Jul 1997 .... 3.00
❑8, Aug 1997 V: Key. 3.00
❑9, Sep 1997 V: Key. 3.00
❑10, Oct 1997 V: New Injustice Gang. 3.00
❑11, Nov 1997 .... 2.50
❑12, Dec 1997 .... 2.50
❑13, Dec 1997; Face cover; Aquaman, Green Lantern, and Flash in future . 2.50
❑14, Jan 1998 .... 2.50
❑15, Feb 1998; Giant-size 2.95
❑16, Mar 1998; V: Prometheus. Watchtower blueprints 2.00
❑17, Apr 1998 V: Prometheus. 2.00
❑18, May 1998 1: Julian September. . 2.00
❑19, Jun 1998 A: Atom. 2.00
❑20, Jul 1998 V: Adam Strange. 2.00
❑21, Aug 1998 A: Aleaa. V: Adam Strange. 2.00
❑22, Sep 1998 A: Daniel (Sandman). 2.00
❑23, Oct 1998 A: Daniel. V: Star Conqueror. 2.00
❑24, Dec 1998 1: Ultramarine Corps. 2.00
❑25, Jan 1999 V: Ultramarine Corps. 2.00
❑26, Feb 1999 A: Ultra-Marines. A: Shaggy Man. V: Shaggy Man. 2.00
❑27, Mar 1999 A: Justice Society of America. V: Amazo. 2.00
❑28, Apr 1999 A: Justice Society of America. A: Triumph. 2.00

N-MINT

❑29, May 1999 JSa (w); JSa (a); A: Justice Society of America. A: Captain Marvel. 2.00
❑30, Jun 1999 A: Justice Society of America. 2.00
❑31, Jul 1999 .... 2.00
❑32, Aug 1999; DGry, MWa (w); JLA in No Man's Land 2.00
❑33, Sep 1999 MWa (w) 2.00
❑34, Oct 1999 .... 2.00
❑35, Nov 1999; A: new Spectre. Day of Judgment 2.00
❑36, Dec 1999 .... 2.00
❑37, Jan 2000 .... 2.00
❑38, Feb 2000 .... 2.00
❑39, Mar 2000 .... 2.00
❑40, Apr 2000 .... 2.00
❑41, May 2000; Giant-size 2.99
❑42, Jun 2000 .... 1.99
❑43, Jul 2000 MWa (w) 1.99
❑44, Aug 2000 MWa (w) 1.99
❑45, Sep 2000 MWa (w) 2.25
❑46, Oct 2000 MWa (w) 2.25
❑47, Nov 2000 MWa (w) 2.25
❑48, Dec 2000 MWa (w) 2.25
❑49, Jan 2001 MWa (w) 2.25
❑50, Feb 2001; Giant-size MWa (w) .. 3.75
❑51, Apr 2001 MWa (w) 2.25
❑52, May 2001 MWa (w) 2.25
❑53, Jun 2001 .... 2.25
❑54, Jul 2001 .... 2.25
❑55, Aug 2001 .... 2.25
❑56, Sep 2001 .... 2.25
❑57, Oct 2001 .... 2.25
❑58, Nov 2001 .... 2.25
❑59, Dec 2001 .... 2.25
❑60, Jan 2002 .... 2.25
❑61, Feb 2002; Giant-size 2.25
❑62, Mar 2002 .... 2.25
❑63, Apr 2002 .... 2.25
❑64, May 2002 .... 2.25
❑65, Jun 2002 .... 2.25
❑66, Jul 2002 .... 2.25
❑67, Aug 2002 .... 2.25
❑68, Sep 2002 .... 2.25
❑69, Oct 2002 .... 2.25
❑70, Oct 2002 .... 2.25
❑71, Nov 2002 .... 2.25
❑72, Nov 2002 .... 2.25
❑73, Dec 2002 .... 2.25
❑74, Dec 2002 .... 2.25
❑75, Jan 2003 .... 2.25
❑76, Feb 2003 .... 2.25
❑77, Mar 2003 .... 2.25
❑78, Apr 2003 .... 2.25
❑79, May 2003 .... 2.25
❑80, Jun 2003 .... 2.25
❑81, Jul 2003 .... 2.25
❑82, Aug 2003 .... 2.25
❑83, Sep 2003 .... 2.25
❑84, Oct 2003 .... 2.25
❑85, Oct 2003 .... 2.25
❑86, Nov 2003 .... 2.25
❑87, Nov 2003 .... 2.25
❑88, Dec 2003 .... 2.25
❑89, Dec 2003 .... 2.25
❑90, Jan 2004 .... 2.25
❑91, Feb 2004 .... 2.25
❑92, Mar 2004 .... 2.25
❑93, Apr 2004 .... 2.25
❑94, May 2004 JOy, JBy (c); JBy (w); JOy, JBy (a) 2.25
❑95, May 2004 .... 2.25
❑96, Jun 2004 .... 2.25
❑97, Jun 2004 .... 2.25
❑98, Jul 2004 .... 2.25
❑99, Jul 2004 .... 2.25
❑100, Aug 2004 .... 3.50
❑101, Sep 2004 ....
❑102, Sep 2004 ....
❑1000000, Nov 1998; One Million 3.00
❑Annual 1, ca. 1997; Pulp Heroes 4.50

N-MINT

❑Annual 2, Oct 1998; Ghosts 4.50
❑Annual 3, Sep 1999; JLApe 3.50
❑Giant Size 1, Jul 1998 .... 4.95
❑Giant Size 2, Nov 1999 .... 4.95
❑Giant Size 3, Oct 2000 .... 4.95

JLA: ACT OF GOD
DC

❑1, Jan 2001 .... 4.95
❑2, Feb 2001 .... 4.95
❑3, Mar 2001 .... 4.95

JLA: AGE OF WONDER
DC

❑1, Jun 2003 .... 5.95
❑2, Jul 2003 .... 5.95

JLA/AVENGERS
MARVEL

❑1, Nov 2003 .... 5.95
❑3, Jan 2004 .... 5.95
❑3-2, Apr 2004 .... 5.95

JLA: BLACK BAPTISM
DC

❑1, May 2001 .... 2.50
❑2, Jun 2001 .... 2.50
❑3, Jul 2001 .... 2.50
❑4, Aug 2001 .... 2.50

JLA: CREATED EQUAL
DC

❑1, ca. 2000 .... 5.95
❑2, ca. 2000 .... 5.95

JLA: DESTINY
DC

❑1, Aug 2002 .... 5.95
❑2, Sep 2002 .... 5.95
❑3, Oct 2002 .... 5.95
❑4, Nov 2002 .... 5.95

JLA: FOREIGN BODIES
DC

❑1 1999; prestige format 5.95

JLA GALLERY
DC

❑1, ca. 1997; pin-ups; wraparound cover 2.95

JLA: GATEKEEPER
DC

❑1, Dec 2001 .... 4.95
❑2, Jan 2002 .... 4.95
❑3, Feb 2002 .... 4.95

JLA: GODS AND MONSTERS
DC

❑1, Aug 2001 .... 6.95

JLA/HAVEN: ANATHEMA
DC

❑1, Nov 2002 .... 5.95

JLA/HAVEN: ARRIVAL
DC

❑1, Jan 2002 .... 5.95

JLA: HEAVEN'S LADDER
DC

❑1 .... 9.95

JLA: INCARNATIONS
DC

❑1, Jul 2001 .... 3.50
❑2, Aug 2001 .... 3.50
❑3, Sep 2001 .... 3.50
❑4, Oct 2001 .... 3.50
❑5, Nov 2001 .... 3.50
❑6, Dec 2001 .... 3.50
❑7, Feb 2002 .... 3.50

JLA IN CRISIS SECRET FILES
DC

❑1, Nov 1998; summaries of events from Crisis through One Million 4.95

JLA: OUR WORLDS AT WAR
DC

❑1, Sep 2001 .... 2.95

N-MINT

JLA: PARADISE LOST
DC

❑1, Jan 1998 .... 2.00
❑2, Feb 1998 .... 2.00
❑3, Mar 1998 .... 2.00

JLA: PRIMEVAL
DC

❑1, ca. 1999 .... 5.95

JLA: SCARY MONSTERS
DC

❑1, May 2003 .... 2.50
❑2, Jun 2003 .... 2.50
❑3, Jul 2003 .... 2.50
❑4, Aug 2003 .... 2.50
❑5, Aug 2003 .... 2.50
❑6, Sep 2003 .... 2.50

JLA SECRET FILES
DC

❑1, Sep 1997; bios of team members and key villains; timeline 4.95
❑2, Aug 1998; bios of team members and key villains 3.95
❑3, Dec 2000 .... 4.95

JLA: SECRET SOCIETY OF SUPER-HEROES
DC

❑1, ca. 2000 .... 5.95
❑2 .... 5.95

JLA: SEVEN CASKETS
DC

❑1 .... 5.95

JLA: SHOGUN OF STEEL
DC

❑1, Apr 2002 .... 6.95

JLA SHOWCASE
DC

❑Giant Size 1, Feb 2000; 80-Page Giant 4.95

JLA/SPECTRE: SOUL WAR
DC

❑1, Mar 2003 .... 5.95
❑2, Apr 2003 .... 5.95

JLA: SUPERPOWER
DC

❑1, Nov 1999; prestige format 5.95

JLA: THE ISLAND OF DR. MOREAU
DC

❑1, Oct 2002 .... 6.95

JLA: THE NAIL
DC

❑1, Aug 1998; Elseworlds 5.50
❑2, Sep 1998; Elseworlds 5.00
❑3, Oct 1998; Elseworlds 5.00

JLA/TITANS
DC

❑1, Dec 1998 .... 3.00
❑1/Ltd., Dec 1998 .... 5.00
❑2, Jan 1999 .... 3.00
❑3, Feb 1999 .... 3.00

JLA: TOMORROW WOMAN
DC

❑1, Jun 1998; Girlfrenzy; set during events of JLA #5 .... 1.95

JLA VERSUS PREDATOR
DC

❑1, ca. 2000 .... 5.95

JLA: WELCOME TO WORKING WEEK
DC

❑1, ca. 2003 .... 6.95

JLA/WILDC.A.T.S
DC

❑1, ca. 1997; prestige format; cross-over with Image; Crime Machine ... 5.95

JLA/WITCHBLADE
DC

❑1, ca. 2000 .... 5.95

Fans of the annual Justice League of America-Justice Society of America team-ups of the Silver Age got a taste once again in *JLA*'s "Crisis Times Five."

© 1999 DC Comics.

N-MINT

JLA: WORLD WITHOUT GROWN-UPS
DC

❑1, Aug 1998; prestige format; wrap-around cover 5.50
❑2, Sep 1998 .... 5.00

JLA: YEAR ONE
DC

❑1, Jan 1998 MWa (w) 3.50
❑2, Feb 1998 MWa (w) 3.00
❑3, Mar 1998 MWa (w) 3.00
❑4, Apr 1998 MWa (w) 3.00
❑5, May 1998 MWa (w); A: Doom Patrol. 3.00
❑6, Jun 1998 MWa (w) 1.95
❑7, Jul 1998 MWa (w); A: Superman. 1.95
❑8, Aug 1998 MWa (w) 1.95
❑9, Sep 1998 MWa (w) 1.95
❑10, Oct 1998 MWa (w) 1.99
❑11, Nov 1998 JSa, MWa (w); JSa (a); A: Metal Men. A: Blackhawks. A: Freedom Fighters. A: Challengers. . 1.99
❑12, Dec 1998 MWa (w) 2.95

JLA-Z
DC

❑1, Nov 2003 .... 2.50
❑2, Dec 2003 .... 2.50
❑3, Jan 2004 .... 2.50

JLX
DC / AMALGAM

❑1, Apr 1996 .... 1.95

JLX UNLEASHED
DC / AMALGAM

❑1, Jun 1997 .... 1.95

JOE DIMAGGIO
CELEBRITY

❑1; trading cards 6.95

JOE PSYCHO & MOO FROG
GOBLIN

❑1 .... 3.50
❑2, ca. 1996 .... 3.00
❑3, Sep 1997 .... 3.00
❑4 .... 3.00
❑5 .... 3.00
❑Ashcan 1, b&w; Kinko's Ashcan Edition; no cover price 1.50

JOE PSYCHO FULL COLOR EXTRAVAGARBONZO
GOBLIN

❑1, ca. 1998 .... 2.95

JOE SINN
CALIBER

❑1, b&w 2.95
❑1/Ltd.; limited edition 3.00
❑2, b&w; Final issue (others never released) 2.95

JOHN CARTER OF MARS (EDGAR RICE BURROUGHS'...)
GOLD KEY

❑1, Apr 1964 .... 30.00
❑2, Jul 1964 .... 16.00
❑3, Oct 1964 .... 16.00

JOHN CARTER, WARLORD OF MARS
MARVEL

❑1, Jun 1977 GK, DC (a); O: John Carter, Warlord of Mars. 6.00
❑1/35 cent, Jun 1977; 35 cent regional price variant 12.00

	N-MINT
❑2, Jul 1977 GK (a); V: White Apes.	4.00
❑2/35 cent, Jul 1977; 35 cent regional price variant	8.00
❑3, Aug 1977 GK, TD (a); V: White Apes.	3.00
❑4, Sep 1977 GK (a)	3.00
❑5, Oct 1977 GK (a); V: Stara Kan.	3.00
❑6, Nov 1977	2.50
❑7, Dec 1977	2.50
❑8, Jan 1978	2.50
❑9, Feb 1978	2.50
❑10, Mar 1978	2.50
❑11, Apr 1978 O: Dejah Thoris.	2.50
❑12, May 1978	2.50
❑13, Jun 1978	2.50
❑14, Jul 1978	2.50
❑15, Aug 1978	2.50
❑16, Sep 1978	2.50
❑17, Oct 1978	2.50
❑18, Nov 1978 FM (a)	2.50
❑19, Dec 1978	2.50
❑20, Jan 1979	2.50
❑21, Feb 1979	2.50
❑22, Mar 1979	2.50
❑23, Apr 1979	2.50
❑24, May 1979	2.50
❑25, Jul 1979 FM (c); FM (a)	2.50
❑26, Aug 1979 FM (c); FM (a)	2.50
❑27, Sep 1979	2.50
❑28, Oct 1979	2.50
❑Annual 1, ca. 1977	2.00
❑Annual 2, ca. 1978	2.00
❑Annual 3, ca. 1979	2.00

JOHN F. KENNEDY
DELL

❑1, Aug 1964; DG (a);12-378-410; memorial comic book; Biography	45.00
❑1-2, ca. 1964; DG (a);Biography	30.00
❑1-3, ca. 1964; DG (a);Biography	22.00

JOHN LAW DETECTIVE
ECLIPSE

❑1, Apr 1983 WE (w); WE (a)	2.00

JOHNNY ATOMIC
ETERNITY

❑1, b&w	2.50
❑2, b&w	2.50
❑3, b&w	2.50

JOHNNY COMET
AVALON

❑1, Apr 1999	2.95
❑2 1999	2.95
❑3 1999	2.95
❑4 1999	2.95
❑5 1999	2.95

JOHNNY COSMIC
THORBY

❑1; Flip-book with Spacegal Comics #2	2.95

JOHNNY DYNAMITE
DARK HORSE

❑1, Sep 1994	2.95
❑2, Oct 1994	2.95
❑3, Nov 1994	2.95
❑4, Dec 1994	2.95

JOHNNY GAMBIT
HOT

❑1, Apr 1987	1.75

JOHNNY HAZARD (PIONEER)
PIONEER

❑1, Dec 1988, b&w	2.00

JOHNNY HAZARD QUARTERLY
DRAGON LADY

❑1	5.95
❑2	5.95
❑3	5.95
❑4	5.95

JOHNNY JASON, TEEN REPORTER
DELL

❑2, Aug 1962, First issue published as Dell's Four Color #1302	20.00

JOHNNY NEMO MAGAZINE, THE
ECLIPSE

	N-MINT
❑1, Sep 1995	2.75
❑2	2.75
❑3	2.75
❑4; Exists?	2.75
❑5; Exists?	2.75
❑6; Exists?	2.75

JOHNNY THE HOMICIDAL MANIAC
SLAVE LABOR

❑1, Aug 1995, b&w A: Squee.	13.00
❑1-2, Dec 1995, b&w	4.00
❑1-3, Aug 1996, b&w	3.00
❑1-4, May 1997, b&w	3.00
❑2, Nov 1995, b&w	9.00
❑2-2, Jul 1996, b&w	3.00
❑3, Feb 1996, b&w	7.00
❑3-2, Jul 1996, b&w	3.00
❑4, May 1996, b&w	6.00
❑4-2, Apr 1997, b&w	3.00
❑5, Aug 1996, b&w	5.00
❑5-2, Apr 1997, b&w	3.00
❑6, Aug 1996, b&w	4.00
❑7, Aug 1996, b&w	4.00
❑Special 1; Limited to 2000; Reprints Johnny the Homicidal Maniac #1 with cardstock outer cover	20.00

JOHNNY THUNDER
DC

❑1, Mar 1973	12.00
❑2, May 1973	8.00
❑3, Aug 1973	8.00

JOHN STEELE, SECRET AGENT
GOLD KEY

❑1, Dec 1964	18.00

JOKER, THE
DC

❑1, May 1975 DG, IN (a); A: Two-Face.	16.00
❑2, Jul 1975	12.00
❑3, Oct 1975	8.00
❑4, Dec 1975 V: Green Arrow.	8.00
❑5, Feb 1976	8.00
❑6, Apr 1976	7.00
❑7, Jun 1976	7.00
❑8, Aug 1976; Bicentennial #7	7.00
❑9, Sep 1976 A: Catwoman.	7.00

JOKER: LAST LAUGH
DC

❑1, Dec 2001	2.95
❑2, Dec 2001	2.95
❑3, Dec 2001	2.95
❑4, Dec 2001	2.95
❑5, Dec 2001	2.95
❑6, Jan 2002	2.95

JOKER: LAST LAUGH SECRET FILES
DC

❑1, Dec 2001	5.95

JOKER/MASK
DARK HORSE

❑1, May 2000	2.95
❑2, Jun 2000	2.95
❑3, Jul 2000	2.95
❑4, Aug 2000	2.95

JOLLY JACK STARJUMPER SUMMER OF '92 ONE-SHOT, THE
CONQUEST

❑1, b&w	2.95

JONAH HEX
DC

❑1, Apr 1977	25.00
❑2, Jun 1977 1: El Papagayo. V: El Papagayo.	10.00
❑3, Aug 1977	7.00
❑4, Sep 1977	7.00
❑5, Oct 1977	7.00
❑6, Nov 1977	6.00
❑7, Dec 1977 O: Jonah Hex.	7.00
❑8, Jan 1978 O: Jonah's facial scars.	7.00
❑9, Feb 1978	5.00
❑10, Mar 1978	5.00
❑11, Apr 1978	4.00
❑12, May 1978	4.00
❑13, Jun 1978	4.00
❑14, Jul 1978	4.00
❑15, Aug 1978	4.00
❑16, Sep 1978	4.00
❑17, Oct 1978	4.00
❑18, Nov 1978	4.00
❑19, Dec 1978	4.00
❑20, Jan 1979	4.00
❑21, Feb 1979	3.00
❑22, Mar 1979	3.00
❑23, Apr 1979	3.00
❑24, May 1979	3.00
❑25, Jun 1979	3.00
❑26, Jul 1979	3.00
❑27, Aug 1979	3.00
❑28, Sep 1979	3.00
❑29, Oct 1979	3.00
❑30, Nov 1979	3.00
❑31, Dec 1979	3.00
❑32, Jan 1980	3.00
❑33, Feb 1980	3.00
❑34, Mar 1980	3.00
❑35, Apr 1980	3.00
❑36, May 1980	3.00
❑37, Jun 1980 A: Stonewall Jackson.	3.00
❑38, Jul 1980	3.00
❑39, Aug 1980	3.00
❑40, Sep 1980	3.00
❑41, Oct 1980	3.00
❑42, Nov 1980	3.00
❑43, Dec 1980	3.00
❑44, Jan 1981	3.00
❑45, Feb 1981	3.00
❑46, Mar 1981	3.00
❑47, Apr 1981	3.00
❑48, May 1981	3.00
❑49, Jun 1981	3.00
❑50, Jul 1981	3.00
❑51, Aug 1981	2.50
❑52, Sep 1981	2.50
❑53, Oct 1981	2.50
❑54, Nov 1981	2.50
❑55, Dec 1981	2.50
❑56, Jan 1982	2.50
❑57, Feb 1982; El Diablo back-up	2.50
❑58, Mar 1982; El Diablo back-up	2.50
❑59, Apr 1982; El Diablo back-up	2.50
❑60, May 1982; El Diablo back-up	2.50
❑61, Jun 1982; in China	2.50
❑62, Jul 1982; in China	2.50
❑63, Aug 1982	2.50
❑64, Sep 1982	2.50
❑65, Oct 1982	2.50
❑66, Nov 1982	2.50
❑67, Dec 1982	2.50
❑68, Jan 1983	2.50
❑69, Feb 1983	2.50
❑70, Mar 1983	2.50
❑71, Apr 1983	2.50
❑72, May 1983	2.50
❑73, Jun 1983	2.50
❑74, Jul 1983	2.50
❑75, Aug 1983 TD (a)	2.50
❑76, Sep 1983 TD (a)	2.50
❑77, Oct 1983 TD (a)	2.50
❑78, Nov 1983 TD (a)	2.50
❑79, Dec 1983	2.50
❑80, Jan 1984	2.50
❑81, Feb 1984	2.50
❑82, Mar 1984	2.50
❑83, Apr 1984	2.50
❑84, May 1984	2.50
❑85, Jun 1984 V: Gray Ghost.	2.50
❑86, Aug 1984	2.50
❑87, Oct 1984	2.50
❑88, Dec 1984	2.50
❑89, Feb 1985 V: Gray Ghost.	2.50
❑90, Apr 1985	2.50

N-MINT

❑91, Jun 1985 .... 2.50
❑92, Aug 1985; events continue in Hex 2.50

JONAH HEX AND OTHER WESTERN TALES
DC

❑1, Oct 1979 .... 7.00
❑2, Dec 1979 .... 7.00
❑3, Feb 1980 .... 7.00

JONAH HEX: RIDERS OF THE WORM AND SUCH
DC / VERTIGO

❑1, Mar 1995 .... 3.00
❑2, Apr 1995 .... 3.00
❑3, May 1995 .... 3.00
❑4, Jun 1995 .... 3.00
❑5, Jul 1995 .... 3.00

JONAH HEX: SHADOWS WEST
DC / VERTIGO

❑1, Feb 1999 .... 2.95
❑2, Mar 1999 .... 2.95
❑3, Apr 1999 .... 2.95

JONAH HEX: TWO-GUN MOJO
DC / VERTIGO

❑1, Aug 1993 .... 3.50
❑1/Silver, Aug 1993; Silver (limited promotional) edition; platinum 6.00
❑2, Sep 1993 .... 3.00
❑3, Oct 1993 .... 3.00
❑4, Nov 1993 .... 3.00
❑5, Dec 1993 .... 3.00

JONAS! (MIKE DEODATO'S...)
CALIBER

❑1 .... 2.95

JONATHAN FOX
MARIAH GRAPHICS

❑1 .... 2.00

JONES TOUCH
FANTAGRAPHICS / EROS

❑1 .... 2.75

JONNI THUNDER
DC

❑1, Feb 1985; DG (a); O: Jonni Thunder. 1: Jonni Thunder. origin 1.25
❑2, Apr 1985 DG (a) 1.25
❑3, Jun 1985 DG (a) 1.25
❑4, Aug 1985 DG (a) 1.25

JONNY DEMON
DARK HORSE

❑1, May 1994 .... 2.50
❑2, Jun 1994 .... 2.50
❑3, Jul 1994 .... 2.50

JONNY DOUBLE
DC / VERTIGO

❑1, Sep 1998 .... 2.95
❑2, Oct 1998 .... 2.95
❑3, Nov 1998 .... 2.95
❑4, Dec 1998 .... 2.95

JONNY QUEST (GOLD KEY)
GOLD KEY

❑1, Dec 1964 .... 85.00

JONNY QUEST (COMICO)
COMICO

❑1, Jun 1986 .... 3.00
❑2, Jul 1986 .... 2.50
❑3, Aug 1986 DSt (c) 2.50
❑4, Sep 1986 TY (a) 2.50
❑5, Oct 1986 DSt (c) 2.50
❑6, Nov 1986 .... 2.00
❑7, Dec 1986 .... 2.00
❑8, Jan 1987 .... 2.00
❑9, Feb 1987 MA (a) 2.00
❑10, Mar 1987 .... 2.00
❑11, Apr 1987 BSz (c); BA (a) 1.50
❑12, May 1987 .... 1.50
❑13, Jun 1987 CI (a) 1.50
❑14, Jul 1987 .... 1.50
❑15, Aug 1987 .... 1.75
❑16, Sep 1987 .... 1.75

N-MINT

❑17, Oct 1987 ME (w); SR (a) 1.75
❑18, Nov 1987 .... 1.75
❑19, Dec 1987 .... 1.75
❑20, Jan 1988 .... 1.75
❑21, Feb 1988 .... 1.75
❑22, Mar 1988 .... 1.75
❑23, Apr 1988 .... 1.75
❑24, May 1988 .... 1.75
❑25, Jun 1988 .... 1.75
❑26, Jul 1988 .... 1.75
❑27, Aug 1988 .... 1.75
❑28, Sep 1988 .... 1.75
❑29, Oct 1988 .... 1.75
❑30, Nov 1988 .... 1.75
❑31, Dec 1988 .... 1.75
❑Special 1, Sep 1988 .... 1.75
❑Special 2, Oct 1988 .... 1.75

JONNY QUEST CLASSICS
COMICO

❑1, May 1987 .... 2.00
❑2, Jun 1987 .... 2.00
❑3, Jul 1987 .... 2.00

JON SABLE, FREELANCE
FIRST

❑1, Jun 1983 MGr (w); MGr (a); 1: Sable. 3.00
❑2, Jul 1983 MGr (w); MGr (a) 2.00
❑3, Aug 1983 MGr (w); MGr (a); O: Sable. 2.00
❑4, Sep 1983 MGr (w); MGr (a); O: Sable. 2.00
❑5, Oct 1983 MGr (w); MGr (a); O: Sable. 2.00
❑6, Nov 1983 MGr (w); MGr (a); O: Sable. 2.00
❑7, Dec 1983 MGr (w); MGr (a) 2.00
❑8, Jan 1984 MGr (w); MGr (a) 2.00
❑9, Feb 1984 MGr (w); MGr (a) 2.00
❑10, Mar 1984 MGr (w); MGr (a) 2.00
❑11, Apr 1984 MGr (w); MGr (a) 2.00
❑12, May 1984 MGr (w); MGr (a) 2.00
❑13, Jun 1984 MGr (w); MGr (a) 2.00
❑14, Jul 1984 MGr (w); MGr (a) 2.00
❑15, Aug 1984 MGr (w); MGr (a) 2.00
❑16, Sep 1984 MGr (w); MGr (a) 2.00
❑17, Oct 1984 MGr (w); MGr (a) 2.00
❑18, Oct 1984 MGr (w); MGr (a) 2.00
❑19, Dec 1984 MGr (w); MGr (a) 2.00
❑20, Jan 1985 MGr (w); MGr (a) 2.00
❑21, Feb 1985 MGr (w); MGr (a) 1.75
❑22, Mar 1985 MGr (w); MGr (a) 1.75
❑23, Apr 1985 MGr (w); MGr (a) 1.75
❑24, May 1985 MGr (w); MGr (a) 1.75
❑25, Jun 1985; MGr (w); MGr (a);Shatter back-up story 1.75
❑26, Jul 1985; MGr (w); MGr (a);Shatter back-up story 1.75
❑27, Aug 1985; MGr (w); MGr (a);Shatter back-up story 1.75
❑28, Sep 1985; MGr (w); MGr (a);Shatter back-up story 1.75
❑29, Oct 1985; MGr (w); MGr (a);Shatter back-up story 1.75
❑30, Nov 1985; MGr (w); MGr (a);Shatter back-up story 1.75
❑31, Dec 1985 MGr (w); MGr (a) 1.75
❑32, Jan 1986 MGr (w); MGr (a) 1.75
❑33, Feb 1986 MGr (w); MGr (a) 1.75
❑34, Mar 1986 MGr (w); MGr (a) 1.75
❑35, Apr 1986 MGr (w); MGr (a) 1.75
❑36, May 1986 MGr (w); MGr (a) 1.75
❑37, Jun 1986 MGr (w); MGr (a) 1.75
❑38, Jul 1986 MGr (w); MGr (a) 1.75
❑39, Aug 1986 MGr (w); MGr (a) 1.75
❑40, Sep 1986 MGr (w); MGr (a) 1.75
❑41, Oct 1986 MGr (w); MGr (a) 1.75
❑42, Nov 1986 MGr (w); MGr (a) 1.75
❑43, Dec 1986 MGr (w); MGr (a) 1.75
❑44, Jan 1987 MGr (c); MGr (w); MGr (a) 1.75
❑45, Mar 1987 MGr (c); MGr (w); MGr (a) 1.75
❑46, Apr 1987 MGr (c); MGr (w); MGr (a) 1.75
❑47, May 1987 MGr (c); MGr (w); MGr (a) 1.75
❑48, Jun 1987 MGr (c); MGr (w); MGr (a) 1.75

A live-action Josie movie was released in 2001.

© 1967 Archie Publications Inc.

N-MINT

❑49, Jul 1987 MGr (c); MGr (w); MGr (a) 1.75
❑50, Aug 1987 MGr (c); MGr (w); MGr (a) 1.75
❑51, Sep 1987 MGr (c); MGr (w); MGr (a) 1.75
❑52, Oct 1987 MGr (c); MGr (w); MGr (a) 1.75
❑53, Nov 1987 MGr (c); MGr (w); MGr (a) 1.75
❑54, Dec 1987 MGr (c); MGr (w); MGr (a) 1.75
❑55, Jan 1988 MGr (c); MGr (w); MGr (a) 1.75
❑56, Feb 1988 MGr (c); MGr (w); MGr (a) 1.75

JONTAR RETURNS
MILLER

❑1, b&w 2.00
❑2, b&w 2.00
❑3, b&w 2.00
❑4, b&w 2.00

JOSIE & THE PUSSYCATS
ARCHIE

❑45, Dec 1969 .... 12.00
❑46, Feb 1970 .... 6.00
❑47, Apr 1970 .... 6.00
❑48, Jun 1970 .... 6.00
❑49, Aug 1970 .... 6.00
❑50, Sep 1970 .... 6.00
❑51, Oct 1970 .... 6.00
❑52, Dec 1970 .... 6.00
❑53, Feb 1971 .... 6.00
❑54, Apr 1971 .... 6.00
❑55, Jun 1971; Giant-size 6.00
❑56, Aug 1971; Giant-size 6.00
❑57, Sep 1971; Giant-size 6.00
❑58, Oct 1971; Giant-size 6.00
❑59, Dec 1971; Giant-size 6.00
❑60, Feb 1972; Giant-size 6.00
❑61, Apr 1972; Giant-size 5.00
❑62, Jun 1972; Giant-size 5.00
❑63, Aug 1972; Giant-size 5.00
❑64, Sep 1972; Giant-size 5.00
❑65, Oct 1972; Giant-size 5.00
❑66, Dec 1972; Giant-size 5.00
❑67, Feb 1973 .... 5.00
❑68, Apr 1973 .... 5.00
❑69, Jun 1973 .... 5.00
❑70, Aug 1973 .... 5.00
❑71, Sep 1973 .... 4.00
❑72, Oct 1973 .... 4.00
❑73, Dec 1973 .... 4.00
❑74, Feb 1974 .... 4.00
❑75, Apr 1974 .... 4.00
❑76, Jun 1974 .... 4.00
❑77, Aug 1974 .... 4.00
❑78, Sep 1974 .... 4.00
❑79, Oct 1974 .... 4.00
❑80, Dec 1974 .... 4.00
❑81, Feb 1975 .... 4.00
❑82, Jun 1975 .... 4.00
❑83, Aug 1975 .... 4.00
❑84, Sep 1975 .... 4.00
❑85, Oct 1975 .... 4.00
❑86, Dec 1975 .... 4.00
❑87, Feb 1976 .... 4.00
❑88, Apr 1976 .... 4.00
❑89, Jun 1976 .... 4.00
❑90, Aug 1976 .... 4.00
❑91, Sep 1976 .... 3.00
❑92, Oct 1976 .... 3.00
❑93, Dec 1976 .... 3.00
❑94, Feb 1977 .... 3.00

	N-MINT
❑95, Aug 1977	3.00
❑96	3.00
❑97	3.00
❑98	3.00
❑99, Aug 1979	3.00
❑100, Oct 1979	3.00
❑101, Aug 1980	3.00
❑102	3.00
❑103	3.00
❑104	3.00
❑105	3.00
❑106, Oct 1982	3.00

JOURNEY
AARDVARK-VANAHEIM

	N-MINT
❑1, Mar 1983	4.00
❑2 1983	3.00
❑3 1983	2.50
❑4 1983	2.50
❑5 1983	2.50
❑6	2.50
❑7	2.50
❑8, Mar 1984	2.50
❑9, Apr 1984	2.50
❑10, May 1984	2.50
❑11, Jun 1984	2.00
❑12, Jul 1984	2.00
❑13, Aug 1984	2.00
❑14, Sep 1984	2.00
❑15, Apr 1985	2.00
❑16, May 1985	2.00
❑17, Jun 1985	2.00
❑18, Jul 1985	2.00
❑19, Aug 1985	2.00
❑20, Sep 1985	2.00
❑21, Oct 1985	2.00
❑22, Nov 1985	2.00
❑23, Dec 1985	2.00
❑24, Jan 1986	2.00
❑25, Feb 1986	2.00
❑26, Mar 1986	2.00
❑27, Jul 1986	2.00

JOURNEY INTO MYSTERY (1ST SERIES)
MARVEL

	N-MINT
❑-1, Jul 1997; Flashback	2.25
❑39, Oct 1956	225.00
❑40, Nov 1956	225.00
❑41, Dec 1956	200.00
❑42, Jan 1957	200.00
❑43, Feb 1957	200.00
❑44, Mar 1957	200.00
❑45, Apr 1957	200.00
❑46, May 1957	200.00
❑47, Jun 1957	200.00
❑48, Sep 1957	200.00
❑49, Oct 1957	200.00
❑50, Nov 1957	160.00
❑51, Mar 1959	155.00
❑52, May 1959	155.00
❑53, Jul 1959	155.00
❑54, Sep 1959	155.00
❑55, Nov 1959	155.00
❑56, Jan 1960	155.00
❑57, Mar 1960	155.00
❑58, May 1960	155.00
❑59, Jul 1960	155.00
❑60, Sep 1960	155.00
❑61, Oct 1960	155.00
❑62, Nov 1960 1: Xemnu: "Hulk" tryout?.	250.00
❑63, Dec 1960	145.00
❑64, Jan 1961	145.00
❑65, Feb 1961	145.00
❑66, Mar 1961	145.00
❑67, Apr 1961	145.00
❑68, May 1961	145.00
❑69, Jun 1961	145.00
❑70, Jul 1961	145.00
❑71, Aug 1961	145.00
❑72, Sep 1961	140.00
❑73, Oct 1961	200.00
❑74, Nov 1961	140.00
❑75, Dec 1961	140.00
❑76, Jan 1962	140.00
❑77, Feb 1962	140.00
❑78, Mar 1962; Doctor Strange prototype	140.00
❑79, Apr 1962	140.00
❑80, May 1962	140.00
❑81, Jun 1962	140.00
❑82, Jul 1962	160.00
❑83, Aug 1962 SL (w); SD, JK (a); O: Thor.	4500.00
❑83/Golden Recor, ca. 1966; SL (w); SD, JK (a); O: Thor. 1: Thor. Golden Records reprint (with record)	75.00
❑84, Sep 1962 SL (w); SD, DH, JK (a); 1: Executioner. 1: Loki. 1: Jane Foster. 2: Thor.	725.00
❑85, Oct 1962 SL (w); SD, DH, JK (a); 1: Balder. 1: Loki. 1: Odin. 1: Tyr. 1: Heimdall.	450.00
❑86, Nov 1962 SL (w); SD, DH, JK (a); 1: Tomorrow Man. 1: Odin.	400.00
❑87, Dec 1962 SL (w); SD, JK (a)	600.00
❑88, Jan 1963 SL (w); SD, DH, JK (a); A: Loki.	250.00
❑89, Feb 1963 SL (w); SD, JK (a); O: Thor.	300.00
❑90, Mar 1963 SL (w); SD, JSt (a); 1: Carbon-Copy.	150.00
❑91, Apr 1963 JK (c); SL (w); SD, JSt (a); 1: Sandu.	130.00
❑92, May 1963 SL (w); SD, JSt (a); 1: Frigga. A: Loki.	130.00
❑93, Jun 1963 SL (w); SD, JK (a); 1: Radioactive Man (Dr. Chen Lu)-Marvel.	160.00
❑94, Jul 1963; JK (c); SL (w); SD, JSt (a);Loki	130.00
❑95, Aug 1963 JK (c); SL (w); SD, JSt (a)	130.00
❑96, Sep 1963; JK (c); SL (w); SD, JSt (a);Merlin	130.00
❑97, Oct 1963; SL (w); DH, JK (a); 1: Surtur. 1: Tales of Asgard. 1: Lava Men. V: Ymir. V: Molto.	140.00
❑98, Nov 1963 JK (c); SL (w); DH, JK (a)	110.00
❑99, Dec 1963 SL (w); DH, JK (a); 1: Mr. Hyde.	95.00
❑100, Jan 1964 JK (c); SL (w); DH, JK (a)	90.00
❑101, Feb 1964 SL (w); JK (a); A: Iron Man. A: Giant Man.	70.00
❑102, Mar 1964 SL (w); JK (a); 1: Hela. 1: Sif. 1: The Norns.	75.00
❑103, Apr 1964 SL (w); JK (a); 1: Enchantress. V: Executioner.	75.00
❑104, May 1964; SL (w); JK (a);giants	75.00
❑105, Jun 1964 SL (w); JK (a); V: Cobra. V: Hyde.	75.00
❑106, Jul 1964 JK (a); O: Balder.	75.00
❑107, Aug 1964 JK (a); O: Grey Gargoyle. 1: Grey Gargoyle.	75.00
❑108, Sep 1964 JK (a); A: Doctor Strange.	75.00
❑109, Oct 1964 JK (a); A: Magneto.	85.00
❑110, Nov 1964 JK (a); V: Loki. V: Cobra. V: Hyde.	75.00
❑111, Dec 1964 JK (a); V: Loki. V: Cobra. V: Hyde.	75.00
❑112, Jan 1965 JK (a); V: Hulk.	210.00
❑113, Feb 1965 JK (a); V: Grey Gargoyle.	75.00
❑114, Mar 1965 JK (a); O: Absorbing Man. 1: Absorbing Man.	75.00
❑115, Apr 1965 JK (a); O: Loki.	90.00
❑116, May 1965 JK (a); A: Daredevil. A: Loki.	75.00
❑117, Jun 1965 JK (a); A: Loki.	70.00
❑118, Jul 1965 JK (a); 1: The Destroyer.	70.00
❑119, Aug 1965 JK (a); 1: Warriors Three. 1: Hogun. 1: Fandrall. 1: Volstagg.	70.00
❑120, Sep 1965 JK (a)	70.00
❑121, Oct 1965 JK (a)	70.00
❑122, Nov 1965 JK (a)	70.00
❑123, Dec 1965 SL (w); JK (a)	70.00
❑124, Jan 1966 JK (a)	70.00
❑125, Feb 1966; JK (a);Series continues in Thor #126	70.00
❑503, Nov 1996; A: Lost Gods. D: Red Norvell. Series continued from Thor #502	1.50
❑504, Dec 1996 A: Ulik.	1.50
❑505, Jan 1997 A: Spider-Man. V: Wrecking Crew.	1.50
❑506, Feb 1997	1.50
❑507, Mar 1997	1.50
❑508, Apr 1997 V: Red Norvell.	1.50
❑509, May 1997; return of Loki	1.50
❑510, Jun 1997 V: Red Norvell.	1.50
❑511, Aug 1997; gatefold summary; Loki vs. Seth	1.99
❑512, Sep 1997; gatefold summary	1.99
❑513, Oct 1997; gatefold summary; SB (a);Asgardian storyline concludes	1.99
❑514, Nov 1997; gatefold summary; Shang-Chi	1.99
❑515, Dec 1997; gatefold summary; Shang-Chi	1.99
❑516, Jan 1998; gatefold summary; Shang-Chi	1.99
❑517, Feb 1998; gatefold summary; Black Widow	1.99
❑518, Mar 1998; gatefold summary; Black Widow	1.99
❑519, Apr 1998; gatefold summary; Black Widow	1.99
❑520, May 1998; gatefold summary; Hannibal King	1.99
❑521, Jun 1998; gatefold summary; Hannibal King	1.99
❑Annual 1, ca. 1965; King-Size Annual; JK (a); 1: Hercules. A: Zeus. 1: Hercules; New stories and reprints from JIM #85, 93 and 97; continues as Thor Annual	150.00

JOURNEY INTO MYSTERY (2ND SERIES)
MARVEL

	N-MINT
❑1, Oct 1972; GK, TP (a);Robert Howard adaptation: "Dig Me No Grave"	14.00
❑2, Dec 1972	5.00
❑3, Feb 1973	5.00
❑4, Apr 1973; H.P. Lovecraft adaptation: "Haunter of the Dark"	4.00
❑5, Jun 1973; Robert Bloch adaptation: "Shadow From the Steeple"	4.00
❑6, Aug 1973	3.00
❑7, Oct 1973	3.00
❑8, Dec 1973	3.00
❑9, Feb 1974	3.00
❑10, Apr 1974	3.00
❑11, Jun 1974	3.00
❑12, Aug 1974	3.00
❑13, Oct 1974	3.00
❑14, Dec 1974	3.00
❑15, Feb 1975	3.00
❑16, Apr 1975	3.00
❑17, Jun 1975	3.00
❑18, Aug 1975	3.00
❑19, Oct 1975	3.00

JOURNEYMAN
IMAGE

	N-MINT
❑1, Aug 1999	2.95
❑2, Sep 1999	2.95
❑3, Oct 1999	2.95

JOURNEYMAN/DARK AGES, THE
LUCID

	N-MINT
❑1, Sum 1997, b&w; San Diego edition	3.00

JOURNEY: WARDRUMS
FANTAGRAPHICS

	N-MINT
❑1, May 1987; sepia tones	2.00
❑1-2, Aug 1987, b&w; sepia dropped	1.75
❑2	2.00

JR. CARROT PATROL
DARK HORSE

	N-MINT
❑1, May 1989, b&w	2.00
❑2, b&w	2.00

Condition price index: Multiply "NM prices" above by: **0.83 for Very Fine/Near Mint**
0.66 for Very Fine • 0.33 for Fine • 0.2 for Very Good • 0.125 for Good

N-MINT

JSA
DC

❑1, Aug 1999 JRo (w) 3.00
❑2, Sep 1999 JRo (w); V: Mordru. 2.50
❑3, Oct 1999 JRo (w); V: Mordru. 2.50
❑4, Nov 1999; V: Mordru. identity of new Doctor Fate revealed 2.50
❑5, Dec 1999 JRo (w) 2.50
❑6, Jan 2000 .... 2.50
❑7, Feb 2000 .... 2.50
❑8, Mar 2000 .... 2.50
❑9, Apr 2000 .... 2.50
❑10, May 2000 .... 2.50
❑11, Jun 2000 .... 2.50
❑12, Jul 2000 .... 2.50
❑13, Aug 2000 .... 2.50
❑14, Sep 2000 .... 2.50
❑15, Oct 2000 .... 2.50
❑16, Nov 2000 .... 2.50
❑17, Dec 2000 .... 2.50
❑18, Jan 2001 .... 2.50
❑19, Feb 2001 .... 2.50
❑20, Mar 2001 .... 2.50
❑21, Apr 2001 .... 2.50
❑22, May 2001 .... 2.50
❑23, Jul 2001 .... 2.50
❑24, Aug 2001 .... 2.50
❑25, Sep 2001 .... 2.50
❑26, Oct 2001 .... 2.50
❑27, Nov 2001 .... 2.50
❑28, Dec 2001 .... 2.50
❑29, Jan 2002 .... 2.50
❑30, Feb 2002 .... 2.50
❑31, Mar 2002 .... 2.50
❑32, Apr 2002 .... 2.50
❑33, May 2002 KG (a) 2.50
❑34, Jun 2002 .... 2.50
❑35, Jul 2002 .... 2.50
❑36, Aug 2002 .... 2.50
❑37, Aug 2002 .... 3.50
❑38, Sep 2002 .... 2.50
❑39, Oct 2002 .... 2.50
❑40, Nov 2002 .... 2.50
❑41, Dec 2002 .... 2.50
❑42, Jan 2003 .... 2.50
❑43, Feb 2003 .... 2.50
❑44, Mar 2003 .... 2.50
❑45, Apr 2003 .... 2.50
❑46, May 2003 .... 2.50
❑47, Jun 2003 .... 2.50
❑48, Jul 2003 .... 2.50
❑49, Aug 2003 .... 2.50
❑50, Sep 2003 .... 3.95
❑51, Oct 2003 .... 2.50
❑52, Nov 2003 .... 2.50
❑53, Dec 2003 .... 2.50
❑54, Jan 2004 .... 2.50
❑55, Jan 2004 .... 2.50
❑56, Feb 2004 .... 2.50
❑57, Mar 2004 .... 2.50
❑58, Apr 2004 .... 2.50
❑59, May 2004 .... 2.50
❑60, Jun 2004 .... 2.50
❑61, Jul 2004 .... 2.50
❑62, Aug 2004 .... 2.50
❑63, Sep 2004 ....
❑Annual 1, Oct 2000; 1: Nemesis. Planet DC 3.50

JSA: ALL STARS
DC

❑1, Jul 2003 .... 2.50
❑2, Aug 2003 .... 2.50
❑3, Sep 2003 .... 2.50
❑4, Oct 2003 .... 2.50
❑5, Nov 2003 .... 2.50
❑6, Dec 2003 .... 2.50
❑7, Jan 2004 .... 3.50
❑8, Feb 2004 .... 2.50

JSA: OUR WORLDS AT WAR
DC

❑1, Sep 2001 .... 2.95

N-MINT

JSA SECRET FILES
DC

❑1, Aug 1999; background information on team's formation and members 4.95
❑2, Sep 1999 .... 4.95

JSA: THE LIBERTY FILE
DC

❑1, Feb 2000 .... 6.95
❑2, Mar 2000 .... 6.95

JSA: UNHOLY THREE
DC

❑1, Apr 2003 .... 6.95
❑2, May 2003 .... 6.95

JUDGE DREDD VERSUS ALIENS: INCUBUS
DARK HORSE

❑1, Mar 2003 .... 2.99
❑2, Apr 2003 .... 2.99
❑3, May 2003 .... 2.99
❑4, Jun 2003 .... 2.99

JUDGE CHILD
EAGLE

❑1 BB (a) 2.00
❑2 .... 2.00
❑3 .... 2.00
❑4 .... 2.00
❑5 .... 2.00

JUDGE DREDD (VOL. 1)
EAGLE

❑1, Nov 1983 BB (a); 1: Judge Dredd (in U.S.). A: Judge Death. 4.00
❑2, Dec 1983 BB (a) 3.00
❑3, Jan 1984 BB (a); A: Judge Anderson. V: Judge Death. 2.50
❑4, Feb 1984 BB (a) 2.50
❑5, Mar 1984 .... 2.50
❑6, Apr 1984 .... 2.50
❑7, May 1984 .... 2.50
❑8, Jun 1984 .... 2.50
❑9, Jul 1984 .... 2.50
❑10, Aug 1984 .... 2.50
❑11, Sep 1984 .... 2.00
❑12, Oct 1984 .... 2.00
❑13, Nov 1984 .... 2.00
❑14, Dec 1984 .... 2.00
❑15, Jan 1985; Umpty Candy 2.00
❑16, Feb 1985 V: Fink Angel. 2.00
❑17, Mar 1985 .... 2.00
❑18, Apr 1985 .... 2.00
❑19, May 1985 .... 2.00
❑20, Jun 1985 .... 2.00
❑21, Jul 1985 .... 2.00
❑22, Aug 1985 .... 2.00
❑23, Sep 1985 .... 2.00
❑24, Oct 1985 .... 2.00
❑25, Nov 1985 .... 2.00
❑26, Dec 1985 .... 2.00
❑27, Jan 1986 .... 2.00
❑28, Feb 1986 .... 2.00
❑29, Mar 1986 .... 2.00
❑30, Apr 1986 .... 2.00
❑31, May 1986 V: Judge Child. V: Mean Machine. 2.00
❑32, Jun 1986 V: Mean Machine. 2.00
❑33, Jul 1986; League of Fatties 2.00
❑34, Aug 1986 .... 2.00
❑35, Sep 1986 .... 2.00

JUDGE DREDD (VOL. 2)
FLEETWAY-QUALITY

❑1, Oct 1986 .... 3.00
❑2, Nov 1986 .... 2.50
❑3, Dec 1986 .... 2.00
❑4, Jan 1987 .... 2.00
❑5, Feb 1987; poster 2.00
❑6, Mar 1987; Christmas issue 2.00
❑7 1987 .... 2.00
❑8, Jul 1987; wraparound cover 2.00
❑9, Aug 1987 .... 2.00
❑10, Sep 1987 .... 2.00
❑11, Oct 1987 .... 2.00

After Thor disappeared into an alternate universe, his self-titled series reverted to its original title, *Journey into Mystery*, and became an anthology series.

© 1997 Marvel Characters Inc.

N-MINT

❑12; dropped publication date from cover and indicia for rest of series . 2.00
❑13 .... 2.00
❑14 BB (a) 2.00
❑15 .... 2.00
❑16 .... 2.00
❑17 .... 2.00
❑18 .... 2.00
❑19 .... 2.00
❑20 .... 2.00
❑21; double issue #21, 22 .... 2.00
❑22 .... 2.00
❑23; double issue #23, 24 .... 2.00
❑24 .... 2.00
❑25 .... 2.00
❑26 .... 2.00
❑27 .... 2.00
❑28 .... 2.00
❑29 .... 2.00
❑30 .... 2.00
❑31 .... 2.00
❑32 .... 2.00
❑33 .... 2.00
❑34 .... 2.00
❑35 .... 2.00
❑36 .... 2.00
❑37 .... 2.00
❑38 .... 2.00
❑39 .... 2.00
❑40 .... 2.00
❑41; Reprints 2000 A.D. #449; Reprints 2000 A.D. #447; Reprints 2000 A.D. #445 .... 2.00
❑42; Reprints story from 2000 A.D. #434; Reprints story from 2000 A.D. #421; Reprints story from 2000 A.D. #422 .... 2.00
❑43; Reprints story from 2000 A.D. #113-115; Reprints story from 2000 A.D. #412 .... 2.00
❑44; Reprint from 2000 A.D. #60; Reprint from 2000 A.D. #514; Reprint from 2000 A.D. #304 .... 2.00
❑45; BT (a);Reprint from 2000 A.D. #457; Reprint from 2000 A.D. #458; Reprint from 2000 A.D. #459; Reprint from 2000 A.D. #119 .... 2.00
❑46 .... 2.00
❑47 .... 2.00
❑48 .... 2.00
❑49; Stories 2000 A.D. #493; From 2000 A.D. #182; From 2000 A.D. #490; From 2000 A.D. #491 .... 2.00
❑50 .... 2.00
❑51 .... 2.00
❑52 .... 2.00
❑53; BB (a);Reprints 2000 A.D. #519; From 2000 A.D. #25 .... 2.00
❑54; Reprints 2000 A.D. #643-645; Reprints 2000 A.D. 1990 Mega-Special 2.00
❑55 .... 2.00
❑56 .... 2.00
❑57 .... 2.00
❑58 .... 2.00
❑59 .... 1.95
❑60 .... 1.95
❑61; Series continued in Judge Dredd Classics #62 .... 1.95
❑Special 1 .... 2.50

N-MINT

JUDGE DREDD (DC)
DC

- ❑1, Aug 1994 .... 3.00
- ❑2, Sep 1994 .... 2.50
- ❑3, Oct 1994 .... 2.50
- ❑4, Nov 1994 .... 2.00
- ❑5, Dec 1994 .... 2.00
- ❑6, Jan 1995 .... 2.00
- ❑7, Feb 1995 .... 2.00
- ❑8, Mar 1995 .... 2.00
- ❑9, Apr 1995; homage to Judge Dredd #1 (first series) 2.00
- ❑10, May 1995 .... 2.00
- ❑11, Jun 1995 .... 2.25
- ❑12, Jul 1995 .... 2.25
- ❑13, Aug 1995 .... 2.25
- ❑14, Sep 1995 .... 2.25
- ❑15, Oct 1995 .... 2.25
- ❑16, Nov 1995 .... 2.25
- ❑17, Dec 1995 .... 2.25
- ❑18, Jan 1996 .... 2.25

JUDGE DREDD: AMERICA
FLEETWAY-QUALITY

- ❑1 .... 2.95
- ❑2 .... 2.95

JUDGE DREDD CLASSICS
FLEETWAY-QUALITY

- ❑62 .... 1.95
- ❑63 .... 1.95
- ❑64 .... 1.95
- ❑65 .... 1.95
- ❑66 .... 1.95
- ❑67 .... 1.95
- ❑68 .... 1.95
- ❑69 .... 1.95
- ❑70 .... 1.95
- ❑71 .... 1.95
- ❑72 .... 1.95
- ❑73 .... 1.95
- ❑74 .... 1.95
- ❑75 .... 1.95
- ❑76 .... 1.95
- ❑77 .... 1.95

JUDGE DREDD: EMERALD ISLE
FLEETWAY-QUALITY

- ❑1, ca. 1991 .... 4.95

JUDGE DREDD: LEGENDS OF THE LAW
DC

- ❑1, Dec 1994 BA (a) 2.50
- ❑2, Jan 1995 BA (a) 2.00
- ❑3, Feb 1995 BA (a) 2.00
- ❑4, Mar 1995 BA (a) 2.00
- ❑5, Apr 1995 .... 2.00
- ❑6, May 1995 .... 2.00
- ❑7, Jun 1995 .... 2.25
- ❑8, Jul 1995 JBy (a) 2.25
- ❑9, Aug 1995 JBy (a) 2.25
- ❑10, Sep 1995 JBy (a) 2.25
- ❑11, Oct 1995 JBy (c) 2.25
- ❑12, Nov 1995 .... 2.25
- ❑13, Dec 1995 .... 2.25

JUDGE DREDD: RAPTAUR
FLEETWAY-QUALITY

- ❑1; Judge Dredd 2.95
- ❑2; Judge Dredd 2.95

JUDGE DREDD'S CRIME FILE (EAGLE)
EAGLE

- ❑1 .... 3.00
- ❑2 .... 3.00
- ❑3 .... 3.00
- ❑4, Nov 1985 .... 3.00
- ❑5 .... 3.00
- ❑6 .... 3.00

JUDGE DREDD'S CRIME FILE (FLEETWAY)
FLEETWAY-QUALITY

- ❑1 .... 4.25
- ❑2 .... 4.25
- ❑3 .... 4.25
- ❑4 .... 4.25

JUDGE DREDD'S HARDCASE PAPERS
FLEETWAY-QUALITY

- ❑1 .... 5.95
- ❑2 .... 5.95
- ❑3 .... 5.95
- ❑4 .... 5.95

JUDGE DREDD THE MEGAZINE
FLEETWAY-QUALITY

- ❑1 .... 4.95
- ❑2 .... 4.95
- ❑3 .... 4.95

JUDGE DREDD: THE OFFICIAL MOVIE ADAPTATION
DC

- ❑1; prestige format 5.95

J.U.D.G.E.: SECRET RAGE
IMAGE

- ❑1, Mar 2000 .... 2.95

JUDGMENT DAY (LIGHTNING)
LIGHTNING

- ❑1/A, Sep 1993; Red prism border; red foil cover 3.50
- ❑1/B, Sep 1993; purple foil cover 3.50
- ❑1/C, Sep 1993; misprint 3.50
- ❑1/D, Aug 1993; promotional copy; metallic ink 3.50
- ❑1/Gold, Sep 1993; Gold prism border; Gold foil cover 3.50
- ❑1/Platinum, Aug 1993; promotional copy; platinum 3.50
- ❑2, Oct 1993; trading card 2.95
- ❑3, Nov 1993 .... 2.95
- ❑4, Dec 1993 .... 2.95
- ❑5, Jan 1994 .... 2.95
- ❑6, Feb 1994 .... 2.95
- ❑7, Mar 1994 .... 2.95
- ❑8, Apr 1994 .... 2.95

JUDGMENT DAY
AWESOME

- ❑1, Jun 1997; Alpha 2.50
- ❑1/A, Jun 1997; Alpha; variant cover 2.50
- ❑1-2; Alpha 2.50
- ❑2, Jul 1997; Omega 2.50
- ❑2/A, Jul 1997; Omega; variant cover 2.50
- ❑3; Final Judgment 2.50
- ❑3/A; Final Judgment 2.50

JUDGMENT DAY: AFTERMATH
AWESOME

- ❑1, Jan 1998 .... 3.50
- ❑1/A; Purple cover by Evans 3.50

JUDGMENT DAY SOURCEBOOK
AWESOME

- ❑1; no cover price or indicia; American Entertainment exclusive preview of series 1.00

JUDGMENT PAWNS
ANTARCTIC

- ❑1, Feb 1997, b&w 2.95
- ❑2, Apr 1997, b&w 2.95
- ❑3, Jul 1997, b&w 2.95

JUDGMENTS
NBM

- ❑1 .... 14.95

JUDOMASTER
CHARLTON

- ❑89, Jun 1966; Series continued from Gun Master #89 .... 12.00
- ❑90, Aug 1966 .... 9.00
- ❑91, Oct 1966 A: Sarge Steel. 9.00
- ❑92, Dec 1966 .... 9.00
- ❑93, Feb 1967 .... 9.00
- ❑94, Apr 1967 .... 9.00
- ❑95, Jun 1967 FMc (w); FMc, DG (a) 9.00
- ❑96, Aug 1967 .... 9.00
- ❑97, Oct 1967 .... 9.00
- ❑98, Dec 1967 .... 9.00

JUGGERNAUT, THE
MARVEL

- ❑1, Apr 1997 .... 2.99

JUGGERNAUT, THE (2ND SERIES)
MARVEL

- ❑1, Nov 1999 .... 2.99

JUGHEAD (VOL. 2)
ARCHIE

- ❑1, Aug 1987 .... 3.00
- ❑2, Oct 1987 .... 2.00
- ❑3, Dec 1987 .... 2.00
- ❑4, Feb 1988 .... 1.50
- ❑5, Apr 1988 .... 1.50
- ❑6, Jun 1988 .... 1.50
- ❑7, Aug 1988 .... 1.50
- ❑8, Oct 1988 .... 1.50
- ❑9, Dec 1988 .... 1.50
- ❑10, Feb 1989 .... 1.50
- ❑11, Apr 1989 .... 1.50
- ❑12, Jun 1989 .... 1.50
- ❑13, Aug 1989 .... 1.50
- ❑14, Oct 1989 .... 1.50
- ❑15, Dec 1989 .... 1.50
- ❑16, Feb 1990 .... 1.50
- ❑17, Apr 1990 .... 1.50
- ❑18, Jun 1990 .... 1.50
- ❑19, Aug 1990 .... 1.50
- ❑20, Oct 1990 .... 1.50
- ❑21, Dec 1990 .... 1.50
- ❑22, Feb 1991 .... 1.50
- ❑23, Apr 1991 .... 1.50
- ❑24, Jun 1991 .... 1.50
- ❑25, Aug 1991 .... 1.50
- ❑26, Oct 1991 .... 1.50
- ❑27, Nov 1991 .... 1.50
- ❑28, Dec 1991 .... 1.50
- ❑29, Jan 1992 .... 1.50
- ❑30, Feb 1992 .... 1.50
- ❑31, Mar 1992 .... 1.50
- ❑32, Apr 1992 .... 1.50
- ❑33, May 1992 .... 1.50
- ❑34, Jun 1992 .... 1.50
- ❑35, Jul 1992 .... 1.50
- ❑36, Aug 1992 .... 1.50
- ❑37, Sep 1992 .... 1.50
- ❑38, Oct 1992 .... 1.50
- ❑39, Nov 1992 .... 1.50
- ❑40, Dec 1992 .... 1.50
- ❑41, Jan 1993 .... 1.50
- ❑42, Feb 1993 .... 1.50
- ❑43, Mar 1993 .... 1.50
- ❑44, Apr 1993 .... 1.50
- ❑45, May 1993; Series continued in Archie's Pal Jughead #46 .... 1.50

JUGHEAD AS CAPTAIN HERO
ARCHIE

- ❑1, Oct 1966 .... 28.00
- ❑2, Dec 1966 .... 15.00
- ❑3, Feb 1967 .... 10.00
- ❑4, Apr 1967 .... 7.00
- ❑5, Jun 1967 .... 7.00
- ❑6, Aug 1967 .... 7.00
- ❑7, Nov 1967 .... 7.00

JUGHEAD'S BABY TALES
ARCHIE

- ❑1, Spr 1994 .... 2.00
- ❑2, Win 1994; Continued from Baby Tales #1 .... 2.00

JUGHEAD'S DINER
ARCHIE

- ❑1, Apr 1990 .... 2.00
- ❑2, Jun 1990 .... 1.50
- ❑3, Aug 1990 .... 1.50
- ❑4, Oct 1990 .... 1.50
- ❑5, Dec 1990 .... 1.50
- ❑6, Feb 1991 .... 1.50
- ❑7, Apr 1991 .... 1.50

JUGHEAD'S DOUBLE DIGEST
ARCHIE

	N-MINT
❑1, Oct 1989	6.00
❑2, Jan 1990	4.00
❑3, ca. 1990	4.00
❑4, Aug 1990	4.00
❑5, Nov 1990	4.00
❑6, Feb 1991	3.00
❑7, May 1991	3.00
❑8, Aug 1991	3.00
❑9, Nov 1991	3.00
❑10, Feb 1992 DDC (c)	3.00
❑11, Apr 1992	3.00
❑12, Jul 1992	3.00
❑13, Oct 1992	3.00
❑14, Dec 1992	3.00
❑15, Feb 1993	3.00
❑16, ca. 1993	3.00
❑17, May 1993	3.00
❑18	3.00
❑19	3.00
❑20	3.00
❑21	3.00
❑22, ca. 1993	3.00
❑23	3.00
❑24	3.00
❑25	3.00
❑26, ca. 1994	3.00
❑27, Dec 1994	3.00
❑28, Jan 1995	3.00
❑29, Mar 1995	3.00
❑30, May 1995	3.00
❑31, Jul 1995	2.75
❑32, Sep 1995	2.75
❑33, Nov 1995	2.75
❑34, Jan 1996	2.75
❑35, Feb 1996	2.75
❑36, Apr 1996	2.75
❑37, Jun 1996	2.75
❑38, Aug 1996	2.75
❑39, Sep 1996	2.75
❑40, Nov 1996; duplicate pages at front	2.75
❑41, Jan 1997	2.75
❑42, Feb 1997	2.75
❑43, Apr 1997	2.75
❑44, Jun 1997	2.75
❑45, Jul 1997	2.75
❑46, Sep 1997	2.79
❑47, Nov 1997	2.79
❑48, Dec 1997	2.79
❑49, Feb 1998	2.79
❑50, Apr 1998	2.79
❑51, Jun 1998	2.79
❑52, Jul 1998	2.79
❑53, Aug 1998	2.79
❑54, Oct 1998	2.79
❑55, Nov 1998 DDC (a)	2.95
❑56, Jan 1999	2.95
❑57, Feb 1999	2.95
❑58, Apr 1999	2.95
❑59, Jun 1999	2.99
❑60, Jul 1999	2.99
❑61, Aug 1999	2.99
❑62, Oct 1999	2.99
❑63, Nov 1999	2.99
❑64, Jan 2000	2.99
❑65, Feb 2000	2.99
❑66, Apr 2000	2.99
❑67, May 2000	2.99
❑68, Jul 2000	3.19
❑69, Aug 2000	3.19
❑70, Oct 2000	3.19
❑71, Nov 2000	3.19
❑72, Jan 2001	3.19
❑73, Feb 2001	3.19
❑74, Mar 2001	3.19
❑75, May 2001	3.29
❑76, Jun 2001	3.29
❑77, Aug 2001	3.29
❑78, Sep 2001	3.29
❑79, Oct 2001	3.29
❑80, Nov 2001	3.59
❑81, Jan 2002	3.59
❑82, Feb 2002	3.59
❑83, Mar 2002	3.59
❑84, May 2002	3.59
❑85, Jun 2002	3.59
❑86, Aug 2002	3.59
❑87, Sep 2002	3.59
❑88, Oct 2002	3.59
❑89, Nov 2002	3.59
❑90, Jan 2003	3.59
❑91, Feb 2003	3.59
❑92, Mar 2003	3.59
❑93, May 2003	3.59
❑94, Jun 2003	3.59
❑95, Aug 2003	3.59
❑96, Sep 2003	3.59
❑97, Oct 2003	3.59
❑98, Dec 2003	3.59
❑99, Jan 2004	3.59
❑100, Mar 2004 AM (a)	3.59
❑101, Apr 2004	3.59
❑102, May 2004	3.59
❑103, Jul 2004	3.59

JUGHEAD'S JOKES
ARCHIE

	N-MINT
❑1, Aug 1967	60.00
❑2, Oct 1967	35.00
❑3, Jan 1968	25.00
❑4, Mar 1968	18.00
❑5, May 1968	18.00
❑6, Jul 1968	15.00
❑7, Sep 1968	15.00
❑8, Nov 1968	15.00
❑9, Jan 1969; Archie Giant	15.00
❑10, Mar 1969; Archie Giant	15.00
❑11, May 1969; Archie Giant	12.00
❑12, Jul 1969; Archie Giant	12.00
❑13, Sep 1969; Archie Giant	12.00
❑14, Nov 1969; Archie Giant	12.00
❑15, Jan 1970; Archie Giant	12.00
❑16, Mar 1970; Archie Giant	10.00
❑17, May 1970; Archie Giant	10.00
❑18, Jul 1970; Archie Giant	10.00
❑19, Sep 1970; Archie Giant	10.00
❑20, Nov 1970; Archie Giant	10.00
❑21, Jan 1971; Archie Giant	7.00
❑22, Mar 1971; Archie Giant	7.00
❑23, May 1971; Archie Giant	7.00
❑24, Jul 1971; Archie Giant	7.00
❑25, Sep 1971; Archie Giant	7.00
❑26, Oct 1971; Archie Giant	7.00
❑27, Jan 1972; Archie Giant	7.00
❑28, Apr 1972; Archie Giant	7.00
❑29, Jul 1972; Archie Giant	7.00
❑30, Sep 1972; Archie Giant	7.00
❑31, Oct 1972; Archie Giant	5.00
❑32, Jan 1973; Archie Giant	5.00
❑33, Apr 1973; Archie Giant	5.00
❑34, Jul 1973; Archie Giant	5.00
❑35, Sep 1973; Archie Giant	5.00
❑36, Oct 1973; Archie Giant	5.00
❑37, Jan 1974; Archie Giant	5.00
❑38, Apr 1974	5.00
❑39, Jul 1974	5.00
❑40, Sep 1974	5.00
❑41, Oct 1974	4.00
❑42, Jan 1975	4.00
❑43, Apr 1975	4.00
❑44, Jul 1975	4.00
❑45, Sep 1975	4.00
❑46, Oct 1975	4.00
❑47, Jan 1976	4.00
❑48, Apr 1976	4.00
❑49, Jul 1976	4.00
❑50, Sep 1976	4.00
❑51, Oct 1976	4.00
❑52, Jan 1977	4.00
❑53, Apr 1977	4.00
❑54, Jul 1977	4.00
❑55, Sep 1977	4.00

Charlton's Judomaster fought crime and espionage in the Pacific during World War II.

© 1966 Charlton.

	N-MINT
❑56, Oct 1977	4.00
❑57, Jan 1978	4.00
❑58, Apr 1978	4.00
❑59, Jul 1978	4.00
❑60, Sep 1978	4.00
❑61, Oct 1978	3.00
❑62, Jan 1979	3.00
❑63, Apr 1979	3.00
❑64, Jul 1979	3.00
❑65, Sep 1979	3.00
❑66, Oct 1979	3.00
❑67	3.00
❑68	3.00
❑69	3.00
❑70	3.00
❑71	3.00
❑72	3.00
❑73	3.00
❑74	3.00
❑75	3.00
❑76	3.00
❑77	3.00
❑78, Sep 1982	3.00

JUGHEAD'S PAL HOT DOG
ARCHIE

	N-MINT
❑1, Jan 1990	1.00
❑2, Jan 1990	1.00
❑3 1990	1.00
❑4 1990	1.00
❑5 1990	1.00

JUGHEAD'S TIME POLICE
ARCHIE

	N-MINT
❑1, Jul 1990	1.25
❑2, Sep 1990	1.00
❑3, Nov 1990	1.00
❑4, Jan 1991	1.00
❑5, Mar 1991 A: Abe Lincoln.	1.00
❑6, May 1991 O: Time Beanie.	1.00

JUGHEAD WITH ARCHIE DIGEST MAGAZINE
ARCHIE

	N-MINT
❑1, Mar 1974	12.00
❑2, May 1974	7.00
❑3, Jul 1974	7.00
❑4, Sep 1974	7.00
❑5, Nov 1974	7.00
❑6, Jan 1975	7.00
❑7, Mar 1975	7.00
❑8, May 1975	7.00
❑9, Jul 1975	7.00
❑10, Sep 1975	7.00
❑11, Nov 1975	4.00
❑12, Jan 1976	4.00
❑13, Mar 1976	4.00
❑14, May 1976	4.00
❑15, Jul 1976	4.00
❑16, Sep 1976	4.00
❑17, Nov 1976	4.00
❑18, Jan 1977	4.00
❑19, Mar 1977	4.00
❑20, May 1977	4.00
❑21, Jul 1977	2.50
❑22, Sep 1977	2.50
❑23, Nov 1977	2.50
❑24, Jan 1978	2.50
❑25, Mar 1978	2.50

N-MINT

❑26, May 1978 .... 2.50
❑27, Jul 1978 .... 2.50
❑28, Sep 1978 .... 2.50
❑29, Nov 1978 .... 2.50
❑30, Jan 1979 .... 2.50
❑31, Mar 1979 .... 2.50
❑32, May 1979 .... 2.50
❑33, Jul 1979 .... 2.50
❑34, Sep 1979 .... 2.50
❑35, Nov 1979 .... 2.50
❑36, Jan 1980 .... 2.50
❑37, Mar 1980 .... 2.50
❑38, May 1980 .... 2.50
❑39, Jul 1980 .... 2.50
❑40, Sep 1980 .... 2.50
❑41, Nov 1980 .... 2.50
❑42, Jan 1981 DDC (c) 2.50
❑43, Mar 1981 .... 2.50
❑44, May 1981 .... 2.50
❑45, Jul 1981 .... 2.50
❑46, Sep 1981 .... 2.50
❑47, Nov 1981 .... 2.50
❑48, Jan 1982 .... 2.50
❑49, Mar 1982 .... 2.50
❑50, May 1982 .... 2.50
❑51, Jul 1982 .... 2.00
❑52, Sep 1982 .... 2.00
❑53, Nov 1982 .... 2.00
❑54, Jan 1983 .... 2.00
❑55, Mar 1983 .... 2.00
❑56, May 1983 .... 2.00
❑57, Jul 1983 .... 2.00
❑58, Sep 1983 .... 2.00
❑59, Nov 1983 .... 2.00
❑60, Jan 1984 .... 2.00
❑61, Mar 1984 .... 2.00
❑62, May 1984 .... 2.00
❑63, Jul 1984 .... 2.00
❑64, Sep 1984 .... 2.00
❑65, Nov 1984 DDC (c) 2.00
❑66, Jan 1985 .... 2.00
❑67, Mar 1985 .... 2.00
❑68, May 1985 .... 2.00
❑69, Jul 1985 .... 2.00
❑70, Sep 1985 .... 2.00
❑71, Nov 1985 .... 2.00
❑72, Jan 1986 .... 2.00
❑73, Mar 1986 .... 2.00
❑74, May 1986 .... 2.00
❑75, Jul 1986 .... 2.00
❑76, Sep 1986 .... 2.00
❑77, Nov 1986 .... 2.00
❑78, Jan 1987 .... 2.00
❑79, Mar 1987 DDC (c) 2.00
❑80, May 1987 .... 2.00
❑81, Jul 1987 .... 2.00
❑82, Sep 1987 .... 2.00
❑83, Nov 1987 .... 2.00
❑84, Jan 1988 .... 2.00
❑85, Mar 1988 .... 2.00
❑86, May 1988 .... 2.00
❑87, Jul 1988 .... 2.00
❑88, Sep 1988 .... 2.00
❑89, Nov 1988 .... 2.00
❑90, Jan 1989 .... 2.00
❑91, Mar 1989 .... 2.00
❑92, May 1989 .... 2.00
❑93, Jul 1989 .... 2.00
❑94, Sep 1989 .... 2.00
❑95, Nov 1989 .... 2.00
❑96, Jan 1990 .... 2.00
❑97, Mar 1990 .... 2.00
❑98, May 1990 .... 2.00
❑99, Jul 1990 .... 2.00
❑100, Sep 1990 .... 2.00
❑101, Nov 1990 .... 1.75
❑102, Jan 1991 .... 1.75
❑103, Mar 1991 .... 1.75
❑104, May 1991 .... 1.75
❑105, Jul 1991 .... 1.75
❑106, Sep 1991 .... 1.75

N-MINT

❑107, Nov 1991 .... 1.75
❑108, Jan 1992 DDC (c); GC (a) 1.75
❑109, Feb 1992 DDC (c) 1.75
❑110, Apr 1992 .... 1.75
❑111, Jun 1992 .... 1.75
❑112, Aug 1992 .... 1.75
❑113, Nov 1992 .... 1.75
❑114, Feb 1993 .... 1.75
❑115, May 1993 .... 1.75
❑116, Aug 1993 .... 1.75
❑117, Nov 1993 .... 1.75
❑118, Mar 1994 .... 1.75
❑119, May 1994 .... 1.75
❑120, Aug 1994 .... 1.75
❑121, Nov 1994 .... 1.75
❑122, Jan 1995 .... 1.75
❑123, May 1995 .... 1.75
❑124, Aug 1995 .... 1.75
❑125, Oct 1995 .... 1.75
❑126, Jan 1996 .... 1.75
❑127, ca. 1996 .... 1.75
❑128, Sep 1996 .... 1.79
❑129, Oct 1996 .... 1.79
❑130, Dec 1997 .... 1.79
❑131, Feb 1997 .... 1.79
❑132, Mar 1997 .... 1.79
❑133, May 1997 .... 1.79
❑134, Jul 1997 .... 1.79
❑135, Aug 1997 .... 1.79
❑136, Oct 1997 .... 1.79
❑137, Dec 1997 .... 1.79
❑138, Jan 1998 .... 1.95
❑139, Mar 1998 .... 1.95
❑140, May 1998 .... 1.95
❑141, Jun 1998 .... 1.95
❑142, Aug 1998 .... 1.95
❑143, Oct 1998 DDC (a) 1.95
❑144, Nov 1998 .... 1.95
❑145, Dec 1998 .... 1.95
❑146, Feb 1999 .... 1.95
❑147, Apr 1999 .... 1.95
❑148, May 1999 .... 1.95
❑149, Jun 1999 .... 1.99
❑150, Aug 1999 .... 1.99
❑151, Sep 1999 .... 1.99
❑152, Nov 1999 .... 1.99
❑153, Dec 1999 .... 1.99
❑154, Feb 2000 .... 1.99
❑155, Mar 2000 .... 1.99
❑156, May 2000 .... 1.99
❑157, Jul 2000 .... 2.19
❑158, Aug 2000 .... 2.19
❑159, Sep 2000 .... 2.19
❑160, Nov 2000 .... 2.19
❑161, Dec 2000 .... 2.19
❑162, Jan 2001 .... 2.19
❑163, Feb 2001 .... 2.19
❑164, Mar 2001 .... 2.39
❑165, Jun 2001; Little Archie stories . 2.39
❑166, Jul 2001 .... 2.39
❑167, Aug 2001 .... 2.39
❑168, Oct 2001 .... 2.39
❑169, Nov 2001 .... 2.39
❑170, Jan 2002 .... 2.39
❑171, Feb 2002 .... 2.39
❑172, Mar 2002 .... 2.39
❑173, May 2002 .... 2.39
❑174, Jul 2002 .... 2.39
❑175, Aug 2002 .... 2.39
❑176, Sep 2002 .... 2.39
❑177, Nov 2002 .... 2.39
❑178, Dec 2002 .... 2.39
❑179, Jan 2003 .... 2.39
❑180, Mar 2003 .... 2.39
❑181, Apr 2003 .... 2.39
❑182, May 2003 .... 2.39
❑183, Jul 2003 .... 2.39
❑184, Aug 2003 .... 2.39
❑185, Sep 2003; Pop Tate's first name revealed as Leo 2.39
❑186, Oct 2003 .... 2.39

N-MINT

❑187, Dec 2003 .... 2.39
❑188, Jan 2004 .... 2.39
❑189, Feb 2004 .... 2.39
❑190, Apr 2004 .... 2.39
❑191, May 2004 .... 2.39
❑192, Jun 2004 .... 2.39

JUGULAR
BLACK OUT

❑0 .... 2.95

JUMPER
ZAV

❑1, b&w 3.00
❑2, b&w 3.00

JUN
DISNEY

❑1 .... 1.50

JUNCTION 17
ANTARCTIC

❑1, Aug 2003 .... 3.50
❑2 2003 .... 2.99
❑3 2003 .... 2.99
❑4, Jan 2004 .... 2.99

JUNGLE ACTION
MARVEL

❑1, Oct 1972; Reprints 8.00
❑2, Dec 1972; Reprints 5.00
❑3, Feb 1973; Reprints 5.00
❑4, Apr 1973; Reprints 5.00
❑5, Jul 1973; Black Panther begins ... 6.00
❑6, Sep 1973; Black Panther 4.00
❑7, Nov 1973; Black Panther 4.00
❑8, Jan 1974; RB, KJ (a); O: Black Panther. Black Panther 4.00
❑9, May 1974; Black Panther; Marvel Value Stamp #31 Modok 4.00
❑10, Jul 1974; Black Panther; Marvel Value Stamp #38: Red Sonja 3.00
❑11, Sep 1974; Black Panther; Marvel Value Stamp #43: Enchantress 3.00
❑12, Nov 1974; Black Panther; Marvel Value Stamp #9: Captain Marvel 3.00
❑13, Jan 1975; Black Panther; Marvel Value Stamp #33: Invisible Girl 3.00
❑14, Mar 1975; Black Panther 3.00
❑15, May 1975; Black Panther 3.00
❑16, Jul 1975; Black Panther 3.00
❑17, Sep 1975; Black Panther 3.00
❑18, Nov 1975; Black Panther 3.00
❑19, Jan 1976; 1: Baron Macabre. Black Panther 3.00
❑20, Mar 1976; Black Panther 3.00
❑21, May 1976; Black Panther 3.00
❑21/30 cent, May 1976; 30 cent regional variant; Black Panther 20.00
❑22, Jul 1976; Black Panther 3.00
❑22/30 cent, Jul 1976; 30 cent regional variant; Black Panther 20.00
❑23, Sep 1976; Black Panther; reprints Daredevil #69 .... 3.00
❑24, Nov 1976; 1: Wind Eagle. Black Panther 3.00

JUNGLE BOOK (GOLD KEY)
GOLD KEY

❑1, Mar 1968 .... 25.00

JUNGLE BOOK, THE
DISNEY

❑1/A; saddle-stitched 2.95
❑1/B; squarebound 5.95

JUNGLE BOOK, THE (NBM)
NBM

❑1 .... 16.95

JUNGLE COMICS (A-LIST)
A-LIST

❑1, Spr 1997; gatefold summary; Sheena; Reprints Sheena 3-D special #1 in color 2.95
❑2, Fal 1997; Wambi 2.95
❑3, Win 1997 .... 2.95
❑4, Mar 1998 .... 2.95
❑5, Oct 1998; Sheena 2.95

N-MINT

JUNGLE FANTASY
AVATAR

❑1, Feb 2003 .... 3.50
❑2, Mar 2003 .... 3.50
❑3, Jul 2003 .... 3.50

JUNGLE GIRLS
AC

❑1, Aug 1988, b&w 2.00
❑2 .... 2.25
❑3 .... 2.75
❑4 .... 2.75
❑5 .... 2.75
❑6 MB (a) 2.95
❑7 MB (a) 2.95
❑8, b&w 2.95
❑9, b&w 2.95
❑10, ca. 1992, b&w 2.95
❑11, ca. 1992, b&w 2.95
❑12, b&w 2.95
❑13, ca. 1993, b&w 2.95
❑14, ca. 1993, b&w 2.95
❑15, ca. 1993, b&w 2.95
❑16, b&w 2.95

JUNGLE GIRLS! (ETERNITY)
ETERNITY

❑8 .... 2.95

JUNGLE JIM (KING)
KING

❑5, Dec 1967 .... 9.00

JUNGLE JIM (CHARLTON)
CHARLTON

❑22, Feb 1969; Series continued from Jungle Jim (Dell) 24.00
❑23, Apr 1969 .... 18.00
❑24, Jun 1969 .... 18.00
❑25, Aug 1969 .... 16.00
❑26, Oct 1969 .... 16.00
❑27, Dec 1969 .... 16.00
❑28, Feb 1970 .... 16.00

JUNGLE JIM (AVALON)
AVALON

❑1; published in 1998, indicia says 1995 .... 2.95

JUNGLE LOVE
AIRCEL

❑1, b&w 2.95
❑2, b&w 2.95
❑3, b&w 2.95

JUNGLE TALES OF CAVEWOMAN
BASEMENT

❑1 .... 2.95

JUNGLE TALES OF TARZAN
CHARLTON

❑1, Jan 1965 .... 45.00
❑2, Mar 1965 .... 35.00
❑3, May 1965 .... 35.00
❑4, Jul 1965; Bill Montes and Ernie Bache credits 35.00

JUNIOR JACKALOPE
NEVADA CITY

❑1, b&w 1.50
❑2, b&w 1.50

JUNIOR WOODCHUCKS (WALT DISNEY'S...)
DISNEY

❑1, Jul 1991 .... 1.50
❑2, Aug 1991 .... 1.50
❑3, Sep 1991 .... 1.50
❑4, Oct 1991 .... 1.50

JUNK CULTURE
DC / VERTIGO

❑1, Jul 1997 .... 2.50
❑2, Aug 1997 .... 2.50

JUNKER
FLEETWAY-QUALITY

❑1 .... 2.95
❑2 .... 2.95
❑3 .... 2.95
❑4 .... 2.95

N-MINT

JUNKFOOD NOIR
OKTOBER BLACK

❑1, Jun 1996, b&w 1.95

JUNK FORCE
COMICSONE

❑1, Jan 2004 .... 9.95

JUNKYARD ENFORCER
BOXCAR

❑1, Aug 1998, b&w 2.95

JUPITER
SANDBERG

❑1 .... 2.95
❑2 .... 2.95
❑3 .... 2.95

JURASSIC LARK DELUXE EDITION
PARODY

❑1, b&w 2.95

JURASSIC PARK
TOPPS

❑0, Nov 1993; GK (a);Polybagged with trade paperback; Flip book with two prequels to the movie 2.95
❑0/Direct ed., Nov 1993; GP (c); GK (a);trading cards (came packed with trade paperback) 3.00
❑1, Jun 1993 DC (c); GK (a) 3.00
❑1/Direct ed., Jun 1993; DC (c); GK (a);trading cards 3.00
❑2, Jul 1993 GK (a) 3.00
❑2/Direct ed., Jul 1993; GK (a);trading cards 3.00
❑3, Jul 1993 GK (a) 3.00
❑3/Direct ed., Jul 1993; GK (a);trading cards 3.00
❑4, Aug 1993 GK (a) 3.00
❑4/Direct ed., Aug 1993; GK (a);hologram card 3.00

JURASSIC PARK ADVENTURES
TOPPS

❑1, Jun 1994 .... 2.00
❑2, ca. 1994 .... 2.00
❑3, ca. 1994 .... 2.00
❑4, ca. 1994 .... 2.00
❑5, ca. 1994 .... 2.00
❑6, ca. 1994 .... 2.00
❑7, ca. 1994 .... 2.00
❑8, Dec 1994 .... 2.00
❑9 .... 2.00
❑10 .... 2.00

JURASSIC PARK: RAPTOR
TOPPS

❑1, Nov 1993; Zorro #0 .... 2.95
❑2, Dec 1993; cards 2.95

JURASSIC PARK: RAPTORS ATTACK
TOPPS

❑1, Mar 1994 .... 2.50
❑2, Apr 1994 .... 2.50
❑3, May 1994 .... 2.50
❑4, Jun 1994 .... 2.50

JURASSIC PARK: RAPTORS HIJACK
TOPPS

❑1 .... 2.50
❑2 .... 2.50
❑3 .... 2.50
❑4 .... 2.50

JUST A PILGRIM
BLACK BULL

❑1, May 2001 .... 2.99
❑2, Jun 2001 .... 2.99
❑3, Jul 2001 .... 2.99
❑4, Aug 2001 .... 2.99
❑5, Sep 2001 .... 2.99

JUSTICE (MARVEL)
MARVEL

❑1, Nov 1986 1: Justice. 1.25
❑2, Dec 1986 .... 1.00
❑3, Jan 1987 .... 1.00
❑4, Feb 1987 .... 1.00
❑5, Mar 1987 .... 1.00
❑6, Apr 1987 .... 1.00

Jurassic Park #0 was only available with the *Jurassic Park* trade paperback.

© 1993 Topps

N-MINT

❑7, May 1987 .... 1.00
❑8, Jun 1987 .... 1.00
❑9, Jul 1987 .... 1.00
❑10, Aug 1987 .... 1.00
❑11, Sep 1987 .... 1.00
❑12, Oct 1987 .... 1.00
❑13, Nov 1987 .... 1.00
❑14, Dec 1987 .... 1.00
❑15, Jan 1988 .... 1.00
❑16, Feb 1988 .... 1.00
❑17, Mar 1988 .... 1.00
❑18, Apr 1988 .... 1.25
❑19, May 1988 .... 1.25
❑20, Jun 1988 .... 1.25
❑21, Jul 1988 .... 1.25
❑22, Aug 1988 .... 1.25
❑23, Sep 1988 .... 1.25
❑24, Oct 1988 .... 1.25
❑25, Nov 1988 .... 1.25
❑26, Dec 1988 .... 1.50
❑27, Jan 1989 .... 1.50
❑28, Feb 1989 .... 1.50
❑29, Mar 1989 .... 1.50
❑30, Apr 1989 PD (w); A: Psi-Force. . 1.50
❑31, May 1989 .... 1.50
❑32, Jun 1989 .... 1.50

JUSTICE (ANTARCTIC)
ANTARCTIC

❑1, May 1994, b&w 3.50

JUSTICE BRIGADE
TCB COMICS

❑1, b&w 1.50
❑2, b&w 1.50
❑3, b&w 1.50
❑4, b&w 1.50
❑5, b&w 1.50
❑6, b&w 1.50
❑7, b&w 1.50
❑8, b&w 1.50

JUSTICE: FOUR BALANCE
MARVEL

❑1, Sep 1994 .... 1.75
❑2, Oct 1994 .... 1.75
❑3, Nov 1994 .... 1.75
❑4, Dec 1994 .... 1.75

JUSTICE, INC.
DC

❑1, Jun 1975; O: The Avenger. adapts Justice Inc. novel 3.00
❑2, Aug 1975; JK (a);adapts The Skywalker 2.00
❑3, Oct 1975 JK (a); 1: Fergus MacMurdie. 2.00
❑4, Dec 1975 JKu (c); JK (a) 2.00

JUSTICE, INC. (MINI-SERIES)
DC

❑1 1989; prestige format O: The Avenger. 4.00
❑2 1989; prestige format 4.00

JUSTICE LEAGUE
DC

❑1, May 1987 1: Maxwell Lord. 3.00
❑2, Jun 1987 1: Silver Sorceress. 1: Bluejay. 1: Wandjina. 2.50
❑3, Jul 1987 V: Rocket Reds. 2.50

N-MINT

❑3/Ltd., Jul 1987; Superman logo on cover (limited edition); alternate cover ... 10.00
❑4, Aug 1987; V: Royal Flush Gang. Booster Gold joins team ... 2.50
❑5, Sep 1987; Batman vs. Guy Gardner 2.00
❑6, Oct 1987; KG (w); KG (a);Series continues in Justice League International #7 ... 2.00
❑Annual 1, ca. 1987, b&w; numbering continues with Justice League International Annual #2 ... 2.00

JUSTICE LEAGUE ADVENTURES
DC

❑1, Jan 2002 ... 2.50
❑2, Feb 2002 ... 2.00
❑3, Mar 2002 ... 2.00
❑4, Apr 2002 ... 2.00
❑5, May 2002 ... 2.00
❑6, Jun 2002 ... 2.00
❑7, Jul 2002 ... 2.00
❑8, Aug 2002 ... 2.00
❑9, Sep 2002 ... 2.00
❑10, Oct 2002 ... 2.25
❑11, Nov 2002 ... 2.25
❑12, Dec 2002 ... 2.25
❑13, Jan 2003 ... 2.25
❑14, Feb 2003 ... 2.25
❑15, Mar 2003 ... 2.25
❑16, Apr 2003 ... 2.25
❑17, May 2003 ... 2.25
❑18, Jun 2003 ... 2.25
❑19, Jul 2003 ... 2.25
❑20, Aug 2003 ... 2.25
❑21, Sep 2003 ... 2.25
❑22, Oct 2003 ... 2.25
❑23, Nov 2003 ... 2.25
❑24, Dec 2003 ... 2.25
❑25, Jan 2004 ... 2.25
❑26, Feb 2004 ... 2.25
❑27, Mar 2004 ... 2.25
❑28, Apr 2004 ... 2.25
❑29, May 2004 ... 2.25
❑30, Jun 2004 ... 2.25
❑31, Jul 2004 ... 2.25
❑32, Aug 2004 ... 2.25
❑33, Sep 2004 ... 2.25

JUSTICE LEAGUE AMERICA
DC

❑0, Oct 1994; New team begins: Wonder Woman, Flash III (Wally West), Fire, Metamorpho, Crimson Fox, Hawkman, Obsidian, Nuklon ... 2.00
❑26, May 1989; A: Huntress. Continued from Justice League International . 1.75
❑27, Jun 1989; Exorcist homage cover 1.75
❑28, Jul 1989 ... 1.75
❑29, Aug 1989 ... 1.75
❑30, Sep 1989 ... 1.75
❑31, Oct 1989 A: Justice League Europe. ... 1.75
❑32, Nov 1989 A: Justice League Europe. ... 1.75
❑33, Dec 1989 A: Kilowog. ... 1.75
❑34, Jan 1990 ... 1.75
❑35, Feb 1990 ... 1.75
❑36, Mar 1990 1: Mr. Nebula. 1: Scarlet Skier. A: G'Nort. ... 1.75
❑37, Apr 1990 ... 1.75
❑38, May 1990 V: Despero. ... 1.75
❑39, Jun 1990 V: Despero. ... 1.75
❑40, Jul 1990 V: Despero. ... 1.75
❑41, Aug 1990 ... 1.75
❑42, Sep 1990; membership drive; Return of Mr. Miracle; Orion joins team; Lightray joins team ... 1.75
❑43, Oct 1990 ... 1.75
❑44, Nov 1990 ... 1.75
❑45, Jan 1991 ... 1.75
❑46, Jan 1991; 1: General Glory. Medley art begins ... 1.75
❑47, Feb 1991 ... 1.75
❑48, Mar 1991 ... 1.75
❑49, Apr 1991 ... 1.75

N-MINT

❑50, May 1991; Double-size ... 1.75
❑51, Jun 1991 ... 1.25
❑52, Jul 1991; Guy Gardner vs. Blue Beetle ... 1.25
❑53, Aug 1991 ... 1.25
❑54, Sep 1991 ... 1.25
❑55, Oct 1991 V: Global Guardians. .. 1.25
❑56, Nov 1991; back to Happy Harbor 1.25
❑57, Dec 1991 V: Extremists. ... 1.25
❑58, Jan 1992 A: Lobo. V: Lobo. V: Despero. ... 1.25
❑59, Feb 1992 ... 1.25
❑60, Mar 1992 ... 1.25
❑61, Apr 1992; 1: Bloodwynd. V: Weapons Master. new JLA ... 1.25
❑62, May 1992 V: Weapons Master. .. 1.25
❑63, Jun 1992; Bloodwynd joins team; Guy Gardner leaves team ... 1.25
❑64, Jul 1992 V: Starbreaker. ... 1.25
❑65, Aug 1992 V: Starbreaker. ... 1.25
❑66, Sep 1992; Guy returns ... 1.25
❑67, Oct 1992 ... 1.25
❑68, Nov 1992 ... 1.25
❑69, Dec 1992; Doomsday ... 3.00
❑69-2, Dec 1992 ... 1.75
❑70, Jan 1993; cover wrapper ... 2.00
❑70-2, Jan 1993; cover wrapper; Funeral for a Friend ... 1.75
❑71, Feb 1993; black cover wrapper; Wonder Woman joins team; Ray joins team; Agent Liberty joins team; Black Condor joins team ... 2.00
❑71/Variant, Feb 1993; New team begins; Split cover ... 2.00
❑72, Mar 1993 V: Doctor Destiny. ... 1.50
❑73, Apr 1993 V: Doctor Destiny. ... 1.50
❑74, May 1993 V: Doctor Destiny. ... 1.50
❑75, Jun 1993 V: Doctor Destiny. ... 1.50
❑76, Jul 1993 ... 1.50
❑77, Jul 1993 ... 1.50
❑78, Aug 1993 RT (a); A: Jay Garrick. 1.50
❑79, Aug 1993 V: new Extremists. ... 1.50
❑80, Sep 1993; Booster gets new armor ... 1.50
❑81, Oct 1993; Ray vs. Captain Atom 1.50
❑82, Nov 1993 ... 1.50
❑83, Dec 1993 ... 1.50
❑84, Jan 1994 ... 1.50
❑85, Feb 1994 ... 1.50
❑86, Mar 1994 ... 1.50
❑87, Apr 1994 ... 1.50
❑88, May 1994 ... 1.50
❑89, Jun 1994 ... 1.50
❑90, Jul 1994 ... 1.50
❑91, Aug 1994; Funeral of Ice ... 1.50
❑92, Sep 1994; A: Triumph. Zero Hour 1.50
❑93, Nov 1994 ... 1.50
❑94, Dec 1994 ... 1.50
❑95, Jan 1995 ... 1.50
❑96, Feb 1995 ... 1.50
❑97, Mar 1995 ... 1.50
❑98, Apr 1995 ... 1.50
❑99, May 1995 ... 1.50
❑100, Jun 1995; Giant-size anniversary edition ... 2.95
❑100/Variant; Giant-size anniversary edition; Holo-grafix cover ... 3.95
❑101, Jul 1995 ... 1.75
❑102, Aug 1995 ... 1.75
❑103, Sep 1995 ... 1.75
❑104, Oct 1995 ... 1.75
❑105, Nov 1995 ... 1.75
❑106, Dec 1995; Underworld Unleashed ... 1.75
❑107, Jan 1996 ... 1.75
❑108, Feb 1996 1: Equinox. ... 1.75
❑109, Mar 1996 A: Equinox. ... 1.75
❑110, Apr 1996 A: El Diablo. ... 1.75
❑111, Jun 1996 ... 1.75
❑112, Jul 1996 ... 1.75
❑113, Aug 1996 ... 1.75
❑Annual 4, ca. 1990; Justice League Antarctica ... 3.00

N-MINT

❑Annual 5, ca. 1989; Armageddon 2001 ... 3.00
❑Annual 5-2, ca. 1990; Silver ink cover 2.50
❑Annual 6, ca. 1991; DC (a);Eclipso .. 2.50
❑Annual 7, ca. 1992; 1: Terrorsmith. Bloodlines ... 2.50
❑Annual 8, ca. 1993; Elseworlds ... 2.95
❑Annual 9, ca. 1994; Year One ... 3.50
❑Annual 10, ca. 1996; Legends of the Dead Earth; events continue in Ray #26; 1996 ... 2.95
❑Special 1, ca. 1990 ... 1.50
❑Special 2, ca. 1991 ... 2.95
❑Special 1/A, ca. 1992; Double-size; Justice League Spectacular; Green Lantern on cover ... 2.00
❑Special 1/B, ca. 1992; Double-size; Justice League Spectacular; Superman on cover ... 2.00

JUSTICE LEAGUE: A MIDSUMMER'S NIGHTMARE
DC

❑1, Sep 1996; forms triptych with other two issues ... 2.95
❑2, Oct 1996; forms triptych with other two issues ... 2.95
❑3, Nov 1996; forms triptych with other two issues ... 2.95

JUSTICE LEAGUE EUROPE
DC

❑1, Apr 1989 KG (w); KG (a); 1: Catherine Cobert. ... 2.00
❑2, May 1989 ... 1.50
❑3, Jun 1989 ... 1.50
❑4, Jul 1989 V: Queen Bee. ... 1.50
❑5, Aug 1989 A: Sapphire, Java. ... 1.50
❑6, Sep 1989 1: Crimson Fox. ... 1.50
❑7, Oct 1989 A: Justice League of America. ... 1.50
❑8, Nov 1989 A: Justice League of America. ... 1.50
❑9, Dec 1989 A: Superman. ... 1.50
❑10, Jan 1990 ... 1.50
❑11, Feb 1990; Guy Gardner vs. Metamorpho ... 1.50
❑12, Mar 1990 ... 1.50
❑13, Apr 1990 ... 1.50
❑14, May 1990 ... 1.50
❑15, Jun 1990 1: Extremists. ... 1.50
❑16, Jun 1990 V: Extremists. ... 1.50
❑17, Aug 1990 V: Extremists. ... 1.50
❑18, Sep 1990 V: Extremists. ... 1.50
❑19, Oct 1990 V: Extremists. ... 1.50
❑20, Nov 1990 ... 1.50
❑21, Dec 1990 ... 1.25
❑22, Jan 1991 ... 1.25
❑23, Feb 1991 ... 1.25
❑24, Mar 1991 ... 1.25
❑25, Apr 1991 ... 1.25
❑26, May 1991 ... 1.25
❑27, Jun 1991 ... 1.25
❑28, Jul 1991 ... 1.25
❑29, Aug 1991 ... 1.25
❑30, Sep 1991 V: Jack O'Lantern. ... 1.25
❑31, Oct 1991; evicted from JLI Embassy ... 1.25
❑32, Nov 1991 ... 1.25
❑33, Dec 1991 A: Lobo. V: Lobo. V: Despero. ... 1.25
❑34, Jan 1992 A: Lobo. V: Lobo. V: Despero. ... 1.25
❑35, Feb 1992 V: Extremists. ... 1.25
❑36, Mar 1992 ... 1.25
❑37, Apr 1992; new team ... 1.25
❑38, May 1992 ... 1.25
❑39, Jun 1992 ... 1.25
❑40, Jul 1992 ... 1.25
❑41, Aug 1992 ... 1.25
❑42, Sep 1992; Wonder Woman joins team ... 1.25
❑43, Oct 1992 ... 1.25
❑44, Oct 1992 ... 1.25
❑45, Dec 1992 ... 1.25
❑46, Jan 1993 ... 1.25

N-MINT

❑47, Feb 1993 .... 1.25
❑48, Mar 1993 A: Justice Society of America. 1.25
❑49, Apr 1993 .... 1.25
❑50, May 1993; Giant-size; A: Justice Society of America. V: Sonar. Series continues as Justice League International 2.50
❑Annual 1 A: Global Guardians. 2.00
❑Annual 2 A: Demon. A: Elongated Man. A: Anthro. A: Bat Lash. A: Hex. A: General Glory. A: Legion. 2.00
❑Annual 3; Eclipso; numbering continues as Justice League International Annual 2.50

JUSTICE LEAGUE INTERNATIONAL
DC

❑7, Nov 1987; Title changes to Justice League International; Captain Marvel leaves team; Captain Atom joins team; Rocket Red joins team 2.00
❑8, Dec 1987 .... 1.50
❑9, Jan 1988; Millennium 1.50
❑10, Feb 1988; 1: G'Nort. Millennium 1.50
❑11, Mar 1988 .... 1.25
❑12, Apr 1988 .... 1.25
❑13, May 1988 A: Suicide Squad. 1.25
❑14, Jun 1988 .... 1.25
❑15, Jul 1988 1: Manga Khan. 1: L-Ron. 1.25
❑16, Aug 1988 .... 1.25
❑17, Sep 1988 .... 1.25
❑18, Oct 1988; A: Lobo. Bonus Book 1.25
❑19, Nov 1988 A: Lobo. 1.25
❑20, Dec 1988 A: Lobo. 1.25
❑21; A: Lobo. no month of publication 1.25
❑22; Invasion!; no month of publication; Oberon solo story 1.25
❑23, Jan 1989; 1: Injustice League. V: Injustice League. Invasion! 1.25
❑24, Feb 1989; Giant-size; 1: JL Europe. Bonus Book 2.00
❑25, Apr 1989; becomes Justice League America 1.25
❑51, Jun 1993; was Justice League Europe 1.25
❑52, Jul 1993 .... 1.25
❑53, Aug 1993 .... 1.25
❑54, Sep 1993 .... 1.25
❑55, Sep 1993 .... 1.25
❑56, Oct 1993 .... 1.25
❑57, Oct 1993 .... 1.25
❑58, Nov 1993 .... 1.25
❑59, Dec 1993 .... 1.50
❑60, Jan 1994 .... 1.50
❑61, Feb 1994 .... 1.50
❑62, Mar 1994 .... 1.50
❑63, Apr 1994 .... 1.50
❑64, May 1994 .... 1.50
❑65, Jun 1994 .... 1.50
❑66, Jul 1994 .... 1.50
❑67, Aug 1994 .... 1.50
❑68, Sep 1994; A: Triumph. Zero Hour 1.50
❑Annual 2, ca. 1988, A: Joker. V: Joker. numbering continued from Justice League Annual #1 .... 2.00
❑Annual 3, ca. 1989 .... 2.00
❑Annual 4, ca. 1990 1: Lionheart. 2.50
❑Annual 5, ca. 1991; Elseworlds 2.95
❑Special 1; KG (w); KG (a);Mr. Miracle 1.50
❑Special 2; Huntress 2.95

JUSTICE LEAGUE OF AMERICA
DC

❑1, Nov 1960; O: Despero. 1: Despero. Membership consists of Flash, Wonder Woman, J'onn J'onzz, Green Lantern, Superman, Batman and Aquaman 2271.00
❑2, Jan 1961 A: Merlin. 900.00
❑3, Mar 1961 O: Kanjar Ro. 1: Kanjar Ro. 1: Hyathis. 650.00
❑4, May 1961; Green Arrow joins team; Snapper Carr 500.00
❑5, Jul 1961 O: Doctor Destiny. 1: Doctor Destiny. 400.00
❑6, Sep 1961 1: Professor Amos Fortune. 325.00

N-MINT

❑7, Nov 1961 .... 325.00
❑8, Jan 1962 .... 325.00
❑9, Feb 1962 O: Justice League of America. 525.00
❑10, Mar 1962 1: Lord of Time. 1: Felix Faust. 300.00
❑11, May 1962 .... 225.00
❑12, Jun 1962 O: Doctor Light I 1: Doctor Light I 225.00
❑13, Aug 1962 .... 225.00
❑14, Sep 1962; Atom joins Justice League of America 225.00
❑15, Nov 1962 .... 225.00
❑16, Dec 1962 .... 200.00
❑17, Feb 1963 1: Tornado Champion (Red Tornado). 200.00
❑18, Mar 1963 .... 200.00
❑19, May 1963 .... 200.00
❑20, Jun 1963 .... 200.00
❑21, Aug 1963; 1: Earth-2 (named). Return of Justice Society of America; Justice League of America teams up with Justice Society of America 380.00
❑22, Sep 1963; Return of Justice Society of America; Justice League of America teams up with Justice Society of America 310.00
❑23, Nov 1963 1: Queen Bee. 130.00
❑24, Dec 1963 .... 130.00
❑25, Feb 1964 .... 130.00
❑26, Mar 1964 .... 130.00
❑27, May 1964 .... 130.00
❑28, Jun 1964 .... 130.00
❑29, Aug 1964; O: Crime Syndicate. 1: Earth-3. 1: Crime Syndicate. A: Justice Society of America. 120.00
❑30, Sep 1964; Part 2; Justice League of America teams up with Justice Society of America against the Crime Syndicate of America 120.00
❑31, Nov 1964; Hawkman joins team 85.00
❑32, Dec 1964 O: Brainstorm. 1: Brainstorm. V: Brain Storm. 55.00
❑33, Feb 1965 .... 55.00
❑34, Mar 1965 A: Joker. V: Doctor Destiny. V: Dr. Destiny. 60.00
❑35, May 1965 .... 45.00
❑36, Jun 1965 .... 45.00
❑37, Aug 1965 1: Earth-A. A: Justice Society of America. 90.00
❑38, Sep 1965 A: Justice Society of America. 90.00
❑39, Nov 1965; 80 page giant (#16); reprints Brave and the Bold #28, 30, and Justice League of America #5 . ... 90.00
❑40, Nov 1965; social issue 45.00
❑41, Dec 1965 MA (c); MA (a); 1: The Key. V: Key. 45.00
❑42, Feb 1966 MA (c); MA (a); A: Metamorpho. 35.00
❑43, Mar 1966 MA (c); MA (a); 1: Royal Flush Gang. 35.00
❑44, May 1966 MA (c); MA (a) 35.00
❑45, Jun 1966 MA (c); MA (a); 1: Shaggy Man. V: Shaggy Man. 35.00
❑46, Aug 1966 1: Sandman I (in Silver Age). A: Justice Society of America. V: Solomon Grundy, Blockbuster. 110.00
❑47, Sep 1966 A: Justice Society of America. V: Anti-Matter Man. 70.00
❑48, Oct 1966 MA (c); MA (a) 50.00
❑49, Nov 1966 MA (c); MA (a) 45.00
❑50, Dec 1966 MA (c); MA (a) 45.00
❑51, Feb 1967 A: Elongated Man. 45.00
❑52, Mar 1967 .... 45.00
❑53, May 1967 .... 45.00
❑54, Jun 1967 .... 45.00
❑55, Aug 1967; Justice League of America teams up with Justice Society of America 90.00
❑56, Sep 1967; Justice League of America teams up with Justice Society of America 60.00
❑57, Nov 1967 .... 40.00
❑58, Dec 1967; Giant-size; G-41 .... 40.00
❑59, Dec 1968 .... 40.00
❑60, Feb 1968 .... 40.00

The Crime Syndicate and its Earth, Earth-3, were introduced in *Justice League of America* #29.

N-MINT

❑61, Mar 1968 .... 40.00
❑62, May 1968 .... 40.00
❑63, Jun 1968 .... 40.00
❑64, Aug 1968; DD (a); A: Justice Society of America. Return of Red Tornado 40.00
❑65, Sep 1968; DD (a); V: T.O.Morrow. Justice League of America teams up with Justice Society of America 40.00
❑66, Nov 1968 DD (a) 40.00
❑67, Dec 1968 DD (a) 40.00
❑68, Jan 1969 DD (a) 40.00
❑69, Feb 1969; DD (a);Wonder Woman leaves Justice League of America 20.00
❑70, Mar 1969 DD (a); A: Creeper. 20.00
❑71, May 1969; DD (a); 1: Blue Jay. Martian Manhunter leaves Justice League of America 20.00
❑72, Jun 1969 DD (a) 20.00
❑73, Aug 1969 DD (a); A: Justice Society of America. 20.00
❑74, Sep 1969; DD (a); A: Justice Society. D: Larry Lance. Black Canary goes to Earth-1 .... 20.00
❑75, Nov 1969 DD (a); 1: Black Canary II (Dinah Lance). 20.00
❑76, Dec 1969; MA, DD (a);giant; reprints #7 and #12; pin-ups of Justice Society of America and Seven Soldiers 20.00
❑77, Dec 1969 DD (a) 15.00
❑78, Feb 1970 DD (a) 15.00
❑79, Mar 1970 DD (a) 15.00
❑80, May 1970 DD (a) 15.00
❑81, Jun 1970 DD (a) 15.00
❑82, Aug 1970 DD (a) 15.00
❑83, Sep 1970 DD (a); A: Spectre. 15.00
❑84, Nov 1970 DD (a) 15.00
❑85, Dec 1970; Giant-size 25.00
❑86, Dec 1970 DD (a) 15.00
❑87, Feb 1971 DD (a); 1: Silver Sorceress. 15.00
❑88, Mar 1971 DD (a) 15.00
❑89, May 1971 DD (a) 15.00
❑90, Jun 1971 DD (a) 15.00
❑91, Aug 1971 DD (a) 15.00
❑92, Sep 1971 DD (a); 1: Starbreaker. 15.00
❑93, Nov 1971; Giant-size 15.00
❑94, Nov 1971; NA, DD (a); O: Sandman I (Wesley Dodds). 1: Merlyn. A: Deadman. Reprints Adventure Comics #40 .... 45.00
❑95, Dec 1971; DD (a); O: Doctor Midnight. O: Doctor Fate. Reprints More Fun Comics #67 and All-American Comics #25 .... 15.00
❑96, Feb 1972 DD (a); V: Cosmic Vampire. 15.00
❑97, Mar 1972 DD (a); O: Justice League of America. 15.00
❑98, May 1972 DD (a); A: Sargon. 15.00
❑99, Jun 1972 DD (a); A: Sargon. 15.00
❑100, Aug 1972; DD (a);Return of Seven Soldiers of Victory 35.00
❑101, Sep 1972; DD (a);Justice League of America teams up with Justice Society of America 15.00
❑102, Oct 1972; DD (a); D: Red Tornado. Justice League of America teams up with Justice Society of America 15.00
❑103, Dec 1972 DG, DD (a); A: Phantom Stranger. 15.00

Condition price index: Multiply "NM prices" above by: **0.83 for Very Fine/Near Mint**
0.66 for Very Fine • 0.33 for Fine • 0.2 for Very Good • 0.125 for Good

	N-MINT
❑104, Feb 1973 DG, DD (a); V: Hector Hammond. V: Shaggy Man.	15.00
❑105, May 1973; DG, DD (a);Elongated Man joins the Justice League of America	15.00
❑106, Aug 1973; DG, DD (a);Red Tornado (new) joins the Justice League of America	15.00
❑107, Oct 1973 DG, DD (a); 1: Freedom Fighters. 1: Earth-X. A: Justice Society of America.	15.00
❑108, Dec 1973 DG, DD (a); A: Justice Society of America. A: Freedom Fighters.	18.00
❑109, Feb 1974; DG, DD (a);Hawkman resigns from Justice League of America	15.00
❑110, Apr 1974; DG, DD (a);Justice Society of America pin-up	15.00
❑111, Jun 1974 DG, DD (a); V: Libra.	15.00
❑112, Aug 1974 DG, DD (a); V: Amazo.	15.00
❑113, Oct 1974 DG, DD (a)	15.00
❑114, Dec 1974; DG, DD (a); V: Anakronus. Return of Snapper Carr	15.00
❑115, Feb 1975 DG, DD (a)	15.00
❑116, Mar 1975; DG, DD (a); V: Matter Master. Return of Hawkman	15.00
❑117, Apr 1975; FMc, DD (a);Hawkman rejoins JLA	5.00
❑118, May 1975 FMc, DD (a)	5.00
❑119, Jun 1975 FMc, DD (a)	5.00
❑120, Jul 1975 FMc, DD (a); A: Adam Strange. V: Kanjar Ro.	5.00
❑121, Aug 1975 FMc, DD (a)	5.00
❑122, Sep 1975 FMc, DD (a); V: Doctor Light. V: Dr. Light.	5.00
❑123, Oct 1975 FMc, DD (a); 1: Earth-Prime (named). A: Justice Society of America.	5.00
❑124, Nov 1975 FMc, DD (a); A: Justice Society of America.	5.00
❑125, Dec 1975 FMc, DD (a)	5.00
❑126, Jan 1976; FMc, DD (a);Joker	5.00
❑127, Feb 1976 FMc, DD (a)	5.00
❑128, Mar 1976; FMc, DD (a);Wonder Woman rejoins	5.00
❑129, Apr 1976 FMc, DD (a); D: Red Tornado (new).	5.00
❑130, May 1976 FMc, DD (a)	5.00
❑131, Jun 1976 FMc, DD (a)	5.00
❑132, Jul 1976; FMc, DD (a);Bicentennial #6	5.00
❑133, Aug 1976 FMc, DD (a)	5.00
❑134, Sep 1976 FMc, DD (a)	5.00
❑135, Oct 1976 FMc, DD (a); 1: Earth-S (named).	5.00
❑136, Nov 1976 FMc, DD (a)	5.00
❑137, Dec 1976; FMc, DD (a); A: Marvel Family. Superman vs. Captain Marvel (Golden Age)	5.00
❑138, Jan 1977; double-sized FMc, DD (a)	5.00
❑139, Feb 1977; double-sized FMc, DD (a)	5.00
❑140, Mar 1977; double-sized FMc, DD (a); A: Manhunters.	5.00
❑141, Apr 1977; double-sized FMc, DD (a); A: Manhunters.	5.00
❑142, May 1977; double-sized FMc, DD (a); 1: The Construct.	5.00
❑143, Jun 1977; double-sized FMc, DD (a); 1: Privateer.	5.00
❑144, Jul 1977; double-sized FMc, DD (a); O: Justice League of America.	5.00
❑145, Aug 1977 FMc, DD (a)	5.00
❑146, Sep 1977 FMc, DD (a)	5.00
❑147, Oct 1977 FMc, DD (a); A: Legion. V: Mordru.	5.00
❑148, Nov 1977 FMc, DD (a); A: Legion. V: Mordru.	5.00
❑149, Dec 1977 FMc, DD (a); 1: Star-Tsar.	5.00
❑150, Jan 1978 FMc, DD (a); V: Key.	5.00
❑151, Feb 1978 FMc, DD (a)	4.00
❑152, Mar 1978 FMc, DD (a)	4.00
❑153, Apr 1978 FMc, DD (a); 1: Ultraa.	4.00
❑154, May 1978 FMc, DD (a); V: Doctor Destiny. V: Dr. Destiny.	4.00
❑155, Jun 1978 FMc, DD (a)	4.00

	N-MINT
❑156, Jul 1978 FMc, DD (a); A: Phantom Stranger.	4.00
❑157, Aug 1978 FMc, DD (a)	4.00
❑158, Sep 1978 FMc, DD (a)	4.00
❑159, Oct 1978 JSa (w); FMc, DD (a); A: Enemy Ace. A: Justice Society of America. A: Black Pirate. A: Viking Prince. A: Miss Liberty. A: Jonah Hex.	4.00
❑160, Nov 1978 JSa (w); FMc, DD (a); A: Enemy Ace. A: Justice Society of America. A: Black Pirate. A: Viking Prince. A: Miss Liberty. A: Jonah Hex.	4.00
❑161, Dec 1978; FMc, DD (a);Zatanna joins the Justice League of America	4.00
❑162, Jan 1979 FMc, DD (a)	4.00
❑163, Feb 1979 FMc, DD (a)	4.00
❑164, Mar 1979 FMc, DD (a)	4.00
❑165, Apr 1979 FMc, DD (a)	4.00
❑166, May 1979 FMc, DD (a); V: Secret Society of Super-Villains.	4.00
❑167, Jun 1979 FMc, DD (a)	4.00
❑168, Jul 1979 FMc, DD (a); V: Secret Society of Super-Villains.	4.00
❑169, Aug 1979 FMc, DD (a)	4.00
❑170, Sep 1979 FMc, DD (a); A: Supergirl.	4.00
❑171, Oct 1979 FMc, DD (a); A: Justice Society of America. D: Mr. Terrific.	4.00
❑172, Nov 1979 FMc, DD (a); A: Justice Society of America.	4.00
❑173, Dec 1979 FMc, DD (a); A: Black Lightning.	4.00
❑174, Jan 1980 FMc, DD (a); A: Black Lightning.	4.00
❑175, Feb 1980 FMc, DD (a); V: Doctor Destiny.	4.00
❑176, Mar 1980 FMc, DD (a); V: Doctor Destiny.	4.00
❑177, Apr 1980 FMc, DD (a); A: J'onn J'onzz. V: Despero.	4.00
❑178, May 1980 JSn (c); FMc, DD (a); V: Despero.	4.00
❑179, Jun 1980; JSn (c); FMc, DD (a);Firestorm joins the Justice League of America	4.00
❑180, Jul 1980 JSn (c); FMc, DD (a)	4.00
❑181, Aug 1980; FMc, DD (a); A: Snapper Carr. Green Arrow leaves team	4.00
❑182, Sep 1980; DC (c); FMc, DD (a); A: Felix Faust. Elongated Man back-up	4.00
❑183, Oct 1980 JSn (c); JSa (w); FMc, DD (a); A: Orion. A: Justice Society of America. A: Metron. A: Mr. Miracle. V: Icicle. V: Shade. V: Fiddler. V: Darkseid.	4.00
❑184, Nov 1980 GP (c); FMc, GP (a); A: Justice Society of America. A: New Gods. V: Darkseid. V: Injustice Society.	4.00
❑185, Dec 1980 JSn (c); FMc, GP (a); A: Justice Society of America. A: New Gods. V: Darkseid. V: Injustice Society.	4.00
❑186, Jan 1981 FMc, GP (a); V: Shaggy Man.	4.00
❑187, Feb 1981 DG (c); FMc, DH, RA (a)	4.00
❑188, Mar 1981 DG (c); FMc, DH, RA (a)	4.00
❑189, Apr 1981 BB (c); FMc, RB (a); V: Starro.	4.00
❑190, May 1981 BB (c); RB (a); V: Starro.	4.00
❑191, Jun 1981 DG (c); RB (a); V: Amazo. V: The Key.	4.00
❑192, Jul 1981 GP (a); O: Red Tornado. A: T.O. Morrow.	4.00
❑193, Aug 1981 GP (a); 1: Danette Reilly. 1: All-Star Squadron.	4.00
❑194, Sep 1981 GP (a)	4.00
❑195, Oct 1981 GP (a); A: Justice Society of America. V: Secret Society of Super-Villains.	4.00
❑196, Nov 1981 GP (a); A: Justice Society of America. V: Secret Society of Super-Villains.	4.00
❑197, Dec 1981 GP (a); A: Justice Society of America. V: Secret Society of Super-Villains.	4.00
❑198, Jan 1982 RA (c); DH (a); A: Scalphunter. A: Bat Lash. A: Cinnamon. A: Jonah Hex. V: Lord of Time.	4.00

	N-MINT
❑199, Feb 1982 GP (c); DH (a); A: Scalphunter. A: Bat Lash. A: Cinnamon. A: Jonah Hex. V: Lord of Time.	4.00
❑200, Mar 1982; Anniversary issue; CI, GP, DG, JKu, GK (a); O: JLA. A: Snapper Carr. Green Arrow rejoins	5.00
❑201, Apr 1982 GP (c); DH (a); V: Ultraa.	3.00
❑202, May 1982 GP (c); DH (a)	3.00
❑203, Jun 1982 GP (c); DH (a); V: Hector Hammond. V: New Royal Flush Gang.	3.00
❑204, Jul 1982 GP (c); DH (a); V: Hector Hammond. V: New Royal Flush Gang.	3.00
❑205, Aug 1982 GP (c); DH (a); V: Hector Hammond. V: New Royal Flush Gang.	3.00
❑206, Sep 1982 DC (c); DH, RT (a); V: Rath. V: Ghast. V: Abnegazar.	3.00
❑207, Oct 1982; GP (c); JSa (w); DH, RT (a); A: Justice Society of America. A: All-Star Squadron. V: Per Degaton. V: Crime Syndicate. Justice Society of America, Justice League of America, and All-Star Squadron team up	3.00
❑208, Nov 1982; GP (c); JSa (w); DH (a); A: Justice Society of America. A: All-Star Squadron. V: Per Degaton. V: Crime Syndicate. Justice Society of America, Justice League of America, and All-Star Squadron team up	3.00
❑209, Dec 1982; GP (c); JSa (w); DH (a); A: Justice Society of America. A: All-Star Squadron. V: Per Degaton. V: Crime Syndicate. Justice Society of America, Justice League of America, and All-Star Squadron team up	3.00
❑210, Jan 1983; RB (a);first publication of story slated for 1977 DC tabloid	3.00
❑211, Feb 1983; RB (a);first publication of story slated for 1977 DC tabloid	3.00
❑212, Mar 1983; GP (c); RB (a);concludes story slated for 1977 DC tabloid	3.00
❑213, Apr 1983 GP (c); DH, RT (a)	3.00
❑214, May 1983 GP (c); DH, RT (a)	3.00
❑215, Jun 1983 GP (c); DH, RT (a)	3.00
❑216, Jul 1983 DH (a)	3.00
❑217, Aug 1983 GP (c); D: Garn Daanuth.	3.00
❑218, Sep 1983 A: Amazo. V: Prof. Ivo.	3.00
❑219, Oct 1983 GP (c); JSa (w); JSa (a); A: Justice Society of America. A: Thunderbolt.	3.00
❑220, Nov 1983 GP (c); JSa (w); JSa (a); O: Black Canary. A: Justice Society of America. A: Sargon.	3.00
❑221, Dec 1983	3.00
❑222, Jan 1984	3.00
❑223, Feb 1984	3.00
❑224, Mar 1984 KB (w); V: Paragon.	3.00
❑225, Apr 1984	3.00
❑226, May 1984 RA (c)	3.00
❑227, Jun 1984	3.00
❑228, Jul 1984; J'onn J'onzz returns	3.00
❑229, Aug 1984	3.00
❑230, Sep 1984	3.00
❑231, Oct 1984 JSa, KB (w); JSa (a); A: Justice Society of America. A: Supergirl. A: Phantom Stranger.	3.00
❑232, Nov 1984 JSa, KB (w); JSa (a); A: Justice Society of America. A: Supergirl. V: Crime Syndicate.	3.00
❑233, Dec 1984; A: Vibe. cover forms four-part poster with issues #234-236; New team begins	3.00
❑234, Jan 1985 A: Monitor. A: Vixen.	3.00
❑235, Feb 1985 O: Steel. 1: The Cadre. V: Overmaster. V: The Cadre.	3.00
❑236, Mar 1985 A: Gypsy. V: Overmaster. V: The Cadre.	3.00
❑237, Apr 1985 A: Wonder Woman. A: Superman. A: The Flash. V: Mad Maestro.	3.00
❑238, May 1985 D: Anton Allegro.	3.00
❑239, Jun 1985; D: General Mustapha Maksai. Wonder Woman leaves Justice League	3.00
❑240, Jul 1985 KB (w); 1: Doctor Anomaly.	3.00
❑241, Aug 1985 GT (a); V: Amazo.	3.00

Condition price index: Multiply "NM prices" above by: **0.83 for Very Fine/Near Mint**
0.66 for Very Fine • 0.33 for Fine • 0.2 for Very Good • 0.125 for Good

N-MINT

- ❑242, Sep 1985 GT (a); V: Amazo. 3.00
- ❑243, Oct 1985; GT (a); V: Amazo. Aquaman leaves the Justice League of America 3.00
- ❑244, Nov 1985; JSa (w); JSa (a); A: Justice Society of America. A: Infinity, Inc.. Crisis; Steel vs. Steel 3.00
- ❑245, Dec 1985; LMc (a); A: Lord of Time. Crisis; Steel in future 3.00
- ❑246, Jan 1986; LMc (a);evicted from HQ 3.00
- ❑247, Feb 1986; LMc (a);back to Happy Harbor 3.00
- ❑248, Mar 1986; LMc (a);J'onn J'onzz solo story 3.00
- ❑249, Apr 1986 LMc (a) 3.00
- ❑250, May 1986; Giant-size; LMc (a); A: original JLA. Batman rejoins Justice League of America 3.00
- ❑251, Jun 1986 LMc (a); V: Despero. 3.00
- ❑252, Jul 1986 LMc (a); V: Despero. 3.00
- ❑253, Aug 1986 LMc (a); O: Despero. 3.00
- ❑254, Sep 1986 JO (w); LMc (a); V: Despero. 3.00
- ❑255, Oct 1986 LMc (a); O: Gypsy. ... 3.00
- ❑256, Nov 1986 LMc (a) 3.00
- ❑257, Dec 1986; LMc (a);Zatanna leaves Justice League 3.00
- ❑258, Jan 1987 LMc (a); D: Vibe. 3.00
- ❑259, Feb 1987; LMc (a);Gypsy leaves team 3.00
- ❑260, Mar 1987 LMc (a); D: Steel. 3.00
- ❑261, Apr 1987; LMc (a);group disbands 4.00
- ❑Annual 1, Oct 1983 A: John Stewart. A: Sandman. V: Doctor Destiny. V: Dr. Destiny. 4.50
- ❑Annual 2, Oct 1984 O: New JLA (Vixen, Vibe, Gypsy, Steel). 1: Gypsy. 1: New JLA (Vixen, Vibe, Gypsy, Steel). 3.50
- ❑Annual 3, Nov 1985; 1: Red Tornado (in current form). Crisis 3.50

JUSTICE LEAGUE OF AMERICA: ANOTHER NAIL
DC

- ❑1, Jul 2004 .... 5.95
- ❑2, Aug 2004 .... 5.95
- ❑3, Sep 2004 .... 5.95

JUSTICE LEAGUE OF AMERICA INDEX
ECLIPSE / INDEPENDENT

- ❑1, Apr 1986 .... 1.50
- ❑2, Apr 1986 .... 1.50
- ❑3, May 1986 .... 1.50
- ❑4, May 1986 .... 1.50
- ❑5, Oct 1986 .... 2.00
- ❑6, Nov 1986 .... 2.00
- ❑7, Jan 1987 .... 2.00
- ❑8; Title changes to Justice League of America Index 2.00

JUSTICE LEAGUE OF AMERICA SUPER SPECTACULAR
DC

- ❑1, ca. 1999 .... 5.95

JUSTICE LEAGUE QUARTERLY
DC

- ❑1, Win 1990 .... 3.00
- ❑2, Spr 1991 .... 3.00
- ❑3, Jun 1991; cover says Sum, indicia says Jun 3.00
- ❑4, Fal 1991 .... 3.00
- ❑5, Win 1991 .... 3.00
- ❑6, Spr 1992 .... 3.00
- ❑7, Sum 1992 .... 3.00
- ❑8, Sum 1992; cover says Aut, indicia says Sum; new Conglomerate 3.00
- ❑9, Win 1992 .... 3.00
- ❑10, Spr 1993 .... 3.00
- ❑11, Sum 1993 .... 3.00
- ❑12, Sum 1993; covers says Aut, indicia says Sum; Conglomerate 3.00
- ❑13, Aut 1993; cover says Win, indicia says Aut 3.00
- ❑14, Spr 1994 .... 3.00

N-MINT

- ❑15, Jun 1994; cover says Sum, indicia says Jun 3.00
- ❑16, Sep 1994 .... 3.00
- ❑17, Win 1994 .... 3.00

JUSTICE LEAGUES: JL?
DC

- ❑1, Mar 2001 .... 2.50

JUSTICE LEAGUES: JLA
DC

- ❑1, Mar 2001 .... 2.50

JUSTICE LEAGUES: JUSTICE LEAGUE OF ALIENS
DC

- ❑1, Mar 2001 .... 2.50

JUSTICE LEAGUES: JUSTICE LEAGUE OF AMAZONS
DC

- ❑1, Mar 2001 .... 2.50

JUSTICE LEAGUES:JUSTICE LEAGUE OF ARKHAM
DC

- ❑1, Mar 2001 .... 2.50

JUSTICE LEAGUES: JUSTICE LEAGUE OF ATLANTIS
DC

- ❑1, Mar 2001 .... 2.50

JUSTICE LEAGUE TASK FORCE
DC

- ❑0, Oct 1994 MWa (w); A: Triumph. . 1.75
- ❑1, Jun 1993; membership card 2.00
- ❑2, Jul 1993 .... 1.50
- ❑3, Aug 1993 .... 1.50
- ❑4, Sep 1993 .... 1.50
- ❑5, Oct 1993 .... 1.50
- ❑6, Nov 1993 .... 1.25
- ❑7, Dec 1993; transsexual J'onn J'onzz 1.50
- ❑8, Jan 1994; PD (w); transsexual J'onn J'onzz 1.50
- ❑9, Feb 1994 JPH (w); A: New Bloods. 1.50
- ❑10, Mar 1994 V: Aryan Brigade. 1.50
- ❑11, Apr 1994 V: Aryan Brigade. 1.50
- ❑12, May 1994 .... 1.50
- ❑13, Jun 1994 MWa (w) 1.50
- ❑14, Jul 1994 .... 1.50
- ❑15, Aug 1994 .... 1.50
- ❑16, Sep 1994; A: Triumph. Zero Hour 1.50
- ❑17, Nov 1994 MWa (w) 1.50
- ❑18, Dec 1994 MWa (w) 1.50
- ❑19, Jan 1995 MWa (w); V: Vandal Savage. 1.50
- ❑20, Feb 1995 .... 1.50
- ❑21, Mar 1995 .... 1.50
- ❑22, Apr 1995 .... 1.50
- ❑23, May 1995 .... 1.50
- ❑24, Jun 1995 .... 1.75
- ❑25, Jul 1995 .... 1.75
- ❑26, Aug 1995 .... 1.75
- ❑27, Sep 1995 .... 1.75
- ❑28, Oct 1995 .... 1.75
- ❑29, Nov 1995 .... 1.75
- ❑30, Dec 1995; Underworld Unleashed 1.75
- ❑31, Jan 1996 .... 1.75
- ❑32, Feb 1996 .... 1.75
- ❑33, Mar 1996 .... 1.75
- ❑34, May 1996 .... 1.75
- ❑35, Jun 1996 A: Warlord. 1.75
- ❑36, Jul 1996 .... 1.75
- ❑37, Aug 1996 .... 1.75

JUSTICE MACHINE (NOBLE)
NOBLE

- ❑1 1981 JBy (c); MGu (a) 2.50
- ❑2 TD (c); MGu (a) 2.50
- ❑3 MGu (a) 2.50
- ❑4 MGu (a) 2.50
- ❑5, Nov 1983 MGu (a) 2.50
- ❑Annual 1, Jan 1984; 1: Elementals. THUNDER Agents 5.00

The *Justice Society of America* mini-series spawned a short-lived ongoing series.

© 1991 DC Comics.

N-MINT

JUSTICE MACHINE (COMICO)
COMICO

- ❑1, Jan 1987 MGu (a) 2.50
- ❑2, Feb 1987 MGu (a) 2.00
- ❑3, Mar 1987 MGu (a) 1.75
- ❑4, Apr 1987 MGu (a) 1.75
- ❑5, May 1987 MGu (a) 1.75
- ❑6, Jun 1987 MGu (a) 1.75
- ❑7, Jul 1987 MGu (a) 1.75
- ❑8, Aug 1987 MGu (a); D: Demon. 1.75
- ❑9, Sep 1987 MGu (a) 1.75
- ❑10, Oct 1987 MGu (a) 1.75
- ❑11, Nov 1987 MGu (a) 1.75
- ❑12, Dec 1987 .... 1.75
- ❑13, Jan 1988 MGu (a) 1.75
- ❑14, Feb 1988 MGu (a) 1.75
- ❑15, Mar 1988 .... 1.75
- ❑16, Apr 1988 .... 1.75
- ❑17, May 1988 .... 1.75
- ❑18, Jun 1988 .... 1.75
- ❑19, Jul 1988 .... 1.75
- ❑20, Aug 1988 .... 1.75
- ❑21, Sep 1988 .... 1.75
- ❑22, Oct 1988 .... 1.75
- ❑23, Nov 1988 .... 1.75
- ❑24, Dec 1988 .... 1.75
- ❑25, Jan 1989 .... 1.75
- ❑26, Feb 1989 .... 1.75
- ❑27, Mar 1989 .... 1.75
- ❑28, Apr 1989 .... 1.95
- ❑29, May 1989 .... 1.95
- ❑Annual 1, Jun 1989 A: Elementals. .. 2.75

JUSTICE MACHINE, THE (INNOVATION)
INNOVATION

- ❑1, Apr 1990 .... 1.95
- ❑2, May 1990 .... 1.95
- ❑3, Jul 1990 .... 1.95
- ❑4, Sep 1990 .... 1.95
- ❑5, Nov 1990 .... 1.95
- ❑6, Jan 1991 .... 2.25
- ❑7, Apr 1991 .... 2.25

JUSTICE MACHINE, THE (MILLENNIUM)
MILLENNIUM

- ❑1, ca. 1992 .... 2.50
- ❑2, ca. 1992 .... 2.50

JUSTICE MACHINE FEATURING THE ELEMENTALS
COMICO

- ❑1, May 1986 .... 2.00
- ❑2, Jun 1986 .... 1.75
- ❑3, Jul 1986 .... 1.75
- ❑4, Aug 1986 .... 1.75

JUSTICE MACHINE SUMMER SPECTACULAR, THE
INNOVATION

- ❑1 .... 2.75

JUSTICE RIDERS
DC

- ❑1 1997; prestige format; Elseworlds; Justice League in old West 5.95

Condition price index: Multiply "NM prices" above by: **0.83 for Very Fine/Near Mint**
0.66 for Very Fine • 0.33 for Fine • 0.2 for Very Good • 0.125 for Good

N-MINT

JUSTICE SOCIETY OF AMERICA (MINI-SERIES)
DC

- ❑1, Apr 1991; Flash 2.00
- ❑2, May 1991; Black Canary 1.75
- ❑3, Jun 1991; Green Lantern 1.75
- ❑4, Jul 1991; Hawkman 1.50
- ❑5, Aug 1991; Flash, Hawkman 1.50
- ❑6, Sep 1991; Green Lantern, Black Canary 1.50
- ❑7, Oct 1991; Green Lantern, Black Canary, Hawkman, Flash, Starman 1.50
- ❑8, Nov 1991; Green Lantern, Black Canary, Hawkman, Flash, Starman 1.50

JUSTICE SOCIETY OF AMERICA
DC

- ❑1, Aug 1992 .... 1.50
- ❑2, Sep 1992 .... 1.50
- ❑3, Oct 1992 V: Ultra-Humanite. 1.50
- ❑4, Nov 1992 V: Ultra-Humanite. 1.50
- ❑5, Dec 1992 .... 1.50
- ❑6, Jan 1993 .... 1.25
- ❑7, Feb 1993; in Bahdnesia 1.25
- ❑8, Mar 1993 .... 1.25
- ❑9, Apr 1993; Alan Scott vs. Guy Gardner 1.25
- ❑10, May 1993 .... 1.25

JUSTICE SOCIETY OF AMERICA 100-PAGE SUPER SPECTACULAR
DC

- ❑1; 2000 facsimile of 1975 100-Page Super Spectacular; reprints The Flash #137 and #201, All Star Comics #57, The Brave and the Bold #62, and Adventure Comics #418 .... 6.95

JUST IMAGINE COMICS AND STORIES
JUST IMAGINE

- ❑1 1982 .... 2.00
- ❑2 1982 .... 2.00
- ❑3 1982 .... 2.00
- ❑4 1982 .... 2.00
- ❑5 1983 .... 2.00
- ❑6 1983 .... 2.00
- ❑7 1983 .... 2.00
- ❑8 1983 .... 2.00
- ❑9 .... 2.00
- ❑10 1984 .... 2.00
- ❑11 1984 .... 2.00
- ❑Special 1 1983; gophers 2.00

JUST IMAGINE'S SPECIAL
JUST IMAGINE

- ❑1, Jul 1986; 1: The Mildly Microwaved Pre-Pubescent Kung-Fu Gophers! . 1.50

JUST IMAGINE STAN LEE... SECRET FILES AND ORIGINS
DC

- ❑1, Mar 2002, DaG, JB, JOy, JBy, JKu, JLee (a) 4.95

JUST IMAGINE STAN LEE WITH CHRIS BACHALO CREATING CATWOMAN
DC

- ❑1, Jul 2002 .... 5.95

JUST IMAGINE STAN LEE WITH DAVE GIBBONS CREATING GREEN LANTERN
DC

- ❑1, Dec 2001 .... 5.95

JUST IMAGINE STAN LEE WITH GARY FRANK CREATING SHAZAM!
DC

- ❑1, May 2002 .... 5.95

JUST IMAGINE STAN LEE WITH JERRY ORDWAY CREATING JLA
DC

- ❑1, Feb 2002 .... 5.95

N-MINT

JUST IMAGINE STAN LEE WITH JIM LEE CREATING WONDER WOMAN
DC

- ❑1, Oct 2001 .... 5.95

JUST IMAGINE STAN LEE WITH JOE KUBERT CREATING BATMAN
DC

- ❑1, Sep 2001 .... 5.95

JUST IMAGINE STAN LEE WITH JOHN BUSCEMA CREATING SUPERMAN
DC

- ❑1, Nov 2001 .... 5.95

JUST IMAGINE STAN LEE WITH JOHN BYRNE CREATING ROBIN
DC

- ❑1, Apr 2002 .... 5.95

JUST IMAGINE STAN LEE WITH JOHN CASSADAY CREATING CRISIS
DC

- ❑1, Sep 2002 .... 5.95

JUST IMAGINE STAN LEE WITH KEVIN MAGUIRE CREATING THE FLASH
DC

- ❑1, Jan 2002 .... 5.95

JUST IMAGINE STAN LEE WITH SCOTT MCDANIEL CREATING AQUAMAN
DC

- ❑1, Jun 2002 .... 5.95

JUST IMAGINE STAN LEE WITH WALTER SIMONSON CREATING SANDMAN
DC

- ❑1, Aug 2002 .... 5.95

JUST TWISTED
NECROMICS

- ❑1 .... 2.00

JUSTY
VIZ

- ❑1, Dec 1988, b&w; Japanese 2.00
- ❑2, Dec 1988, b&w; Japanese 2.00
- ❑3, Jan 1989, b&w; Japanese 2.00
- ❑4, Jan 1989, b&w; Japanese 2.00
- ❑5, Feb 1989, b&w; Japanese 2.00
- ❑6, Feb 1989, b&w; Japanese 2.00
- ❑7, Mar 1989, b&w; Japanese 2.00
- ❑8, Mar 1989, b&w; Japanese 2.00
- ❑9, Apr 1989, b&w; Japanese 2.00

K

KABOOM
AWESOME

- ❑1, Sep 1997 JPH (w); 1: Kaboom. ... 2.50
- ❑1/A, Sep 1997; JPH (w); Dynamic Forces variant (marked as such); Purple Awesome logo 2.50
- ❑1/Gold, Sep 1997; Gold edition with silver logo JPH (w); 1: Kaboom. 2.50
- ❑2, Oct 1997 JPH (w) 2.50
- ❑2/Autographed, Oct 1997 JPH (w) .. 2.50
- ❑2/Gold, Oct 1997; Gold edition JPH (w) 2.50
- ❑3, Nov 1997 JPH (w) 2.50
- ❑4, Feb 1998 JPH (w) 2.50
- ❑5, Mar 1998 JPH (w) 2.50
- ❑Ashcan 1, Feb 1998; Preview edition JPH (w) 2.50
- ❑Ashcan 1/Gold, Feb 1998; Gold edition JPH (w) 2.50

KABUKI
IMAGE

- ❑0.5, Sep 2001; Speckle-foil Wizard variant 3.00
- ❑0.5/A; Speckle-foil Wizard variant ... 4.00
- ❑1, Oct 1997 .... 5.00
- ❑1/A, Oct 1997; alternate cover 5.00

N-MINT

- ❑2, Dec 1997 .... 4.00
- ❑3, Mar 1998 .... 4.00
- ❑4, Jun 1998 .... 3.50
- ❑5, Sep 1998 .... 2.95
- ❑6, Nov 1998 .... 2.95
- ❑7, Feb 1999 .... 2.95
- ❑8, Jun 1999 .... 2.95
- ❑9, Mar 2000 .... 2.95

KABUKI AGENTS
IMAGE

- ❑1, Aug 1999; Scarab 2.95
- ❑1/A, Aug 1999; Scarab alternate cover 2.95
- ❑2, Oct 1999; Scarab 2.95
- ❑3, Nov 1999; Scarab 2.95
- ❑4, Apr 2000; Scarab 2.95
- ❑5, Nov 2000; Scarab 2.95
- ❑6, Jan 2001; Scarab 2.95
- ❑7, Mar 2001; Scarab 2.95
- ❑8, Aug 2001; Scarab 2.95

KABUKI: CIRCLE OF BLOOD
CALIBER

- ❑1, Jan 1995, b&w 4.00
- ❑1/Ltd., Jan 1995; Limited edition with new, painted cover 5.00
- ❑1-2, Jul 1995, b&w; enhanced cover 3.50
- ❑2, Mar 1995, b&w 3.50
- ❑3, May 1995, b&w; reprints #1's indicia 3.50
- ❑4, Jul 1995, b&w 3.00
- ❑5, Sep 1995, b&w 3.00
- ❑6, Nov 1995, b&w 3.00
- ❑6/Ltd., Nov 1995; New painted cover, signed 10.00

KABUKI CLASSICS
IMAGE

- ❑1, Feb 1999; Squarebound; Reprints Kabuki: Fear the Reaper 3.25
- ❑2, Mar 1999; Reprints Kabuki: Dance of Death 3.00
- ❑3, Mar 1999; Squarebound 4.95
- ❑4, Apr 1999 .... 3.25
- ❑5, Jul 1999 .... 3.25
- ❑6, Jul 1999 .... 3.25
- ❑7, Aug 1999 .... 3.25
- ❑8, Sep 1999 .... 3.25
- ❑9, Oct 1999 .... 3.25
- ❑10, Nov 1999 .... 3.25
- ❑11, Dec 1999 .... 3.25
- ❑12, Mar 2000 .... 3.25

KABUKI COLOR SPECIAL
CALIBER

- ❑1, Jan 1996 MGr (a) 3.50

KABUKI: DANCE OF DEATH
LONDON NIGHT

- ❑1, Jan 1995, b&w; no cover price or indicia 3.50

KABUKI: DREAMS OF THE DEAD
CALIBER

- ❑1, Jul 1996 .... 2.95

KABUKI: FEAR THE REAPER
CALIBER

- ❑1, Nov 1994 .... 3.50

KABUKI GALLERY
CALIBER

- ❑1, Aug 1995; pin-ups 2.95
- ❑1/A, Aug 1995; Comic Cavalcade edition 15.00

KABUKI-IMAGES
IMAGE

- ❑1, Jul 1998; prestige format; pin-ups and story; Reprints Kabuki (Image) #1 with new pin-ups 4.95
- ❑2, Jan 1999; prestige format; Reprints Kabuki (Image) #2-3 .... 4.95

KABUKI (MARVEL)
MARVEL

- ❑1, Sep 2004 .... 2.99

KABUKI: MASKS OF THE NOH
IMAGE

- ❑1, May 1996, b&w 3.00
- ❑2, Jun 1996, b&w 3.00

N-MINT

❑3, Sep 1996, b&w 3.00
❑4, Jan 1997, b&w 3.00

KABUKI REFLECTIONS
IMAGE

❑1, Jul 1998; prestige format; no number on cover or in indicia 4.95
❑2, Dec 1998; prestige format 4.95
❑3, Jan 2000 .... 4.95
❑4, May 2002 .... 4.95

KABUKI: SKIN DEEP
CALIBER

❑1, Oct 1996 .... 3.50
❑2, Feb 1997 .... 3.00
❑2/A, Feb 1997; alternate cover; white background 3.00
❑2/Ltd., Feb 1997; Wraparound cover by David Mack and Alex Ross 8.00
❑3, May 1997 .... 2.95

KAFKA
RENEGADE

❑1, Apr 1987, b&w 3.00
❑2, May 1987, b&w 2.50
❑3, Jun 1987, b&w 2.50
❑4, Jul 1987, b&w 2.50
❑5, Aug 1987, b&w 2.50
❑6, Sep 1987, b&w 2.50

KAFKA: THE EXECUTION
FANTAGRAPHICS

❑1, b&w; Duranona 2.95

KAKTUS
FANTAGRAPHICS

❑1, b&w 2.50

KALAMAZOO COMIX
DISCOUNT HOBBY

❑1 .... 1.95
❑2, Win 1996 .... 1.95
❑3, Win 1996 .... 1.95
❑4, Spr 1997 .... 2.95
❑5, Dec 1997 .... 2.95

KALGAN THE GOLDEN
HARRIER

❑1, Mar 1988 .... 1.95

KAMANDI: AT EARTH'S END
DC

❑1, Jun 1993 .... 1.75
❑2, Jul 1993 .... 1.75
❑3, Aug 1993 .... 1.75
❑4, Sep 1993 .... 1.75
❑5, Oct 1993 .... 1.75
❑6, Nov 1993 .... 1.75

KAMANDI, THE LAST BOY ON EARTH
DC

❑1, Nov 1972 JK (w); JK (a); O: Kamandi. 1: Dr. Canus. 1: Ben Boxer. 25.00
❑2, Jan 1973 JK (w); JK (a) 15.00
❑3, Feb 1973; JK (w); JK (a);in Vegas 10.00
❑4, Mar 1973 JK (w); JK (a); 1: Prince Tuftan. 8.00
❑5, Apr 1973 JK (w); JK (a) 8.00
❑6, Jun 1973 JK (w); JK (a) 8.00
❑7, Jul 1973 JK (w); JK (a) 8.00
❑8, Aug 1973; JK (w); JK (a);In Washington, D.C. 8.00
❑9, Sep 1973 JK (w); JK (a) 8.00
❑10, Oct 1973 JK (w); JK (a) 8.00
❑11, Nov 1973 JK (w); JK (a) 5.00
❑12, Dec 1973 JK (w); JK (a) 5.00
❑13, Jan 1974 JK (w); JK (a) 5.00
❑14, Feb 1974 JK (w); JK (a) 5.00
❑15, Mar 1974 JK (w); JK (a) 5.00
❑16, Apr 1974 JK (w); JK (a) 5.00
❑17, May 1974 JK (w); JK (a) 5.00
❑18, Jun 1974 JK (w); JK (a) 5.00
❑19, Jul 1974; JK (w); JK (a);in Chicago 5.00
❑20, Aug 1974; JK (w); JK (a);in Chicago 5.00
❑21, Sep 1974 JK (w); JK (a) 4.00
❑22, Oct 1974 JK (w); JK (a) 4.00
❑23, Nov 1974 JK (w); JK (a) 4.00
❑24, Dec 1974 JK (w); JK (a) 4.00
❑25, Jan 1975 JK (w); JK (a) 4.00
❑26, Feb 1975 JK (w); JK (a) 4.00
❑27, Mar 1975 JK (w); JK (a) 4.00
❑28, Apr 1975 JK (w); JK (a) 4.00
❑29, May 1975; JK (w); JK (a);Superman's legend 4.00
❑30, Jun 1975 JK (w); JK (a); 1: Pyra. 4.00
❑31, Jul 1975 JK (w); JK (a) 4.00
❑32, Aug 1975; JK (w); JK (a); O: Kamandi. giant; Jack Kirby interview; New story and reprints Kamandi #1 .... 4.00
❑33, Sep 1975 JK (w); JK (a) 4.00
❑34, Oct 1975 JKu (c); JK (w); JK (a) 4.00
❑35, Nov 1975 JKu (c); JK (w); JK (a) 4.00
❑36, Dec 1975 JKu (c); JK (w); JK (a) 4.00
❑37, Jan 1976 JKu (c); JK (w); JK (a) 4.00
❑38, Feb 1976 JKu (c); JK (w); JK (a) 4.00
❑39, Mar 1976 JKu (c); JK (w); JK (a) 4.00
❑40, Apr 1976 JKu (c); JK (w); JK (a) 4.00
❑41, May 1976 JKu (c) 2.50
❑42, Jun 1976 .... 2.50
❑43, Jul 1976; Tales of the Great Disaster backup stories begin; Bicentennial #4 .... 2.50
❑44, Aug 1976 .... 2.50
❑45, Sep 1976 .... 2.50
❑46, Oct 1976; Tales of the Great Disaster backup stories end 2.50
❑47, Nov 1976 .... 2.50
❑48, Jan 1977 .... 2.50
❑49, Mar 1977 .... 2.50
❑50, May 1977; Kamandi reverts to OMAC 2.50
❑51, Jul 1977 .... 2.50
❑52, Sep 1977 .... 2.50
❑53, Nov 1977 .... 2.50
❑54, Jan 1978 .... 2.50
❑55, Mar 1978 V: Vortex Beast. 2.50
❑56, May 1978 .... 2.50
❑57, Jul 1978 .... 2.50
❑58, Sep 1978; A: Karate Kid. Karate Kid 2.50
❑59, Oct 1978; OMAC back-up begins; continues in Warlord #37 .... 4.00

KAMA SUTRA (GIRL'S...)
BLACK LACE

❑1 .... 2.95

KAMIKAZE
DC / CLIFFHANGER

❑1, Dec 2003 .... 2.95
❑2, Jan 2004 .... 2.95
❑3, Feb 2004 .... 2.95
❑4, Mar 2004 .... 2.95
❑5, Apr 2004 .... 2.95
❑6, May 2004 .... 2.95

KAMIKAZE CAT
PIED PIPER

❑1, Jul 1987 .... 1.95

KANE
DANCING ELEPHANT

❑1 .... 3.50
❑2 .... 3.50
❑3 .... 3.50
❑4 .... 3.50
❑5 .... 3.50
❑6 .... 3.50
❑7 .... 3.50
❑8 .... 3.50
❑9 .... 3.50
❑10 .... 3.50
❑11 .... 3.50
❑12 .... 3.50
❑13 .... 3.50
❑14 .... 3.50
❑15 .... 3.50
❑16 .... 3.50
❑17 .... 3.50
❑18 .... 3.50
❑19 .... 3.50
❑20 .... 3.50
❑21 .... 3.50

Kamandi found himself in a ravaged Washington, D.C., overrun with intelligent lions in *Kamandi* #8.

© 1973 National Periodical Publications (DC).

N-MINT

❑22 .... 3.50
❑23 .... 2.95
❑24 .... 2.95
❑25, Jan 1999 .... 2.95
❑26, Apr 1999 .... 2.95
❑27; Giant-size 5.00
❑28 .... 2.95
❑29 .... 2.95
❑30, Nov 2000 .... 2.95
❑31, Apr 2001 .... 2.95
❑32, Jul 2001 .... 2.95

KANSAS THUNDER
RED MENACE

❑1, b&w 2.95

KAOS
TOMMY REGALADO

❑1, Aug 1994, b&w 2.00

KAOS MOON
CALIBER

❑1 1996, b&w 2.95
❑2, Nov 1996, b&w 2.95
❑3, Jul 1997 .... 2.95
❑4 1997 .... 2.95

KAPTAIN KEEN & KOMPANY
VORTEX

❑1, Dec 1986 .... 1.75
❑2 .... 1.75
❑3 .... 1.75
❑4 .... 1.75
❑5 .... 1.75
❑6, Feb 1988 .... 1.75

KARATE GIRL
FANTAGRAPHICS / EROS

❑1, b&w 2.50
❑2, b&w 2.50

KARATE GIRL TENGU WARS
FANTAGRAPHICS / EROS

❑1 .... 2.95
❑2 .... 2.95
❑3, Jun 1995 .... 2.95

KARATE KID
DC

❑1, Apr 1976 JSa, RE (a) 3.50
❑2, Jun 1976 .... 2.50
❑3, Aug 1976 .... 2.50
❑4, Oct 1976 .... 2.00
❑5, Dec 1976 .... 2.00
❑6, Feb 1977 .... 2.00
❑7, Apr 1977 MGr (a) 2.00
❑8, Jun 1977 MGr, JSa, RE (a) 2.00
❑9, Aug 1977 .... 2.00
❑10, Oct 1977 .... 2.00
❑11, Dec 1977 .... 2.00
❑12, Feb 1978 .... 2.00
❑13, Apr 1978 .... 2.00
❑14, Jun 1978 .... 2.00
❑15, Aug 1978 .... 2.00

KARATE KREATURES
MA

❑1, Sum 1989 .... 2.00
❑2 .... 2.00

Condition price index: Multiply "NM prices" above by: **0.83 for Very Fine/Near Mint**
0.66 for Very Fine • 0.33 for Fine • 0.2 for Very Good • 0.125 for Good

N-MINT

KARE KANO
TOKYOPOP

❑1, Jan 2003, b&w; printed in Japanese format ... 9.99
❑2, Mar 2003, b&w; printed in Japanese format ... 9.99
❑3, May 2003, b&w; printed in Japanese format ... 9.99

KARZA
IMAGE

❑1, Feb 2003 ... 2.95
❑2, Apr 2003 ... 2.95
❑3, May 2003 ... 2.95
❑4, May 2003 ... 2.95

KATMANDU
ANTARCTIC

❑1, Nov 1993, b&w ... 2.75
❑2, Jan 1994, b&w ... 2.95
❑3, Apr 1994, b&w ... 2.95
❑4, Mar 1995, b&w ... 2.75
❑5, May 1995, b&w ... 2.75
❑6, Aug 1995 ... 2.75
❑7 ... 2.75
❑8, Jul 1996, b&w ... 1.95
❑9, b&w ... 1.95
❑10, b&w ... 1.95
❑11, b&w ... 1.95
❑12, b&w ... 1.95
❑13, Sep 1997, b&w ... 2.95
❑14 ... 2.95
❑15 ... 2.95
❑16, Apr 1999, b&w ... 2.95
❑17 ... 2.95
❑18 ... 2.95
❑19 ... 2.95
❑20, Apr 2000 ... 2.95
❑21, Jul 2000 ... 2.95
❑22 ... 2.95
❑23 2001 ... 2.95
❑24 2001 ... 2.95
❑25 2001 ... 2.95
❑26, Jun 2002 ... 4.99
❑27, Aug 2002 ... 4.99
❑28 ... 4.99
❑Annual 1 ... 4.99
❑Annual 2 ... 4.99
❑Annual 3, Dec 2001 ... 4.99
❑Annual 4, Dec 2002 ... 4.99

KATO OF THE GREEN HORNET
NOW

❑1, Nov 1991 ... 2.50
❑2, Dec 1991 ... 2.50
❑3 1992 ... 2.50
❑4 1992 ... 2.50

KATO OF THE GREEN HORNET II
NOW

❑1, Nov 1992 ... 2.50
❑2, Dec 1992 ... 2.50

KA-ZAR (1ST SERIES)
MARVEL

❑1, Aug 1970; SL (w); GC, JK, FS (a); 1: Ka-Zar. 1: Zabu. A: X-Men. giant; reprints X-Men #10 (first series) and Daredevil #24; Hercules back-up ... 10.00
❑2, Dec 1970; SL (w); GT, JK, JR (a); O: Ka-Zar. A: Daredevil. giant; Angel back-up; reprints Daredevil #12 and 13 ... 7.00
❑3, Mar 1971; giant; reprints Amazing Spider-Man #57 and Daredevil #14; Angel back-up continues in Marvel Tales #30 ... 7.00

KA-ZAR (2ND SERIES)
MARVEL

❑1, Jan 1974 O: Savage Land. ... 3.00
❑2, Mar 1974; DH (a);Marvel Value Stamp #28: Hawkeye ... 2.50
❑3, May 1974; DH (a);Marvel Value Stamp #46: Mysterio ... 2.50
❑4, Jul 1974; DH (a);Marvel Value Stamp #9: Captain Marvel ... 2.50
❑5, Sep 1974; DH (a);Marvel Value Stamp #18: Volstagg ... 2.50
❑6, Nov 1974; JB (a);Marvel Value Stamp #17: Black Bolt ... 2.00
❑7, Jan 1975 JB (a) ... 2.00
❑8, Mar 1975; JB (a);Marvel Value Stamp #38: Red Sonja ... 2.00
❑9, Jun 1975 JB (a) ... 2.00
❑10, Aug 1975; JB (a);Marvel Value Stamp #72: Lizard ... 2.00
❑11, Oct 1975 ... 1.50
❑12, Nov 1975; Marvel Value Stamp #95: Moleman ... 1.50
❑13, Dec 1975 ... 1.50
❑14, Feb 1976 A: Klaw. ... 1.50
❑15, Apr 1976 ... 1.50
❑15/30 cent, Apr 1976; 30 cent regional price variant ... 20.00
❑16, Jun 1976 ... 1.50
❑16/30 cent, Jun 1976; 30 cent regional price variant ... 20.00
❑17, Aug 1976 ... 1.50
❑17/30 cent, Aug 1976; 30 cent regional price variant ... 20.00
❑18, Oct 1976 ... 1.50
❑19, Dec 1976 ... 1.50
❑20, Feb 1977 A: Klaw. ... 1.50

KA-ZAR (3RD SERIES)
MARVEL

❑-1, Jul 1997; Flashback ... 2.00
❑1, May 1997 ... 2.50
❑2, Jun 1997 ... 2.00
❑2/A, Jun 1997; alternate cover ... 2.00
❑3, Jul 1997 ... 2.00
❑4, Aug 1997; gatefold summary ... 2.00
❑5, Sep 1997; gatefold summary ... 2.00
❑6, Oct 1997; gatefold summary ... 2.00
❑7, Nov 1997; gatefold summary ... 2.00
❑8, Dec 1997; gatefold summary; Spider-Man CD-ROM inserted ... 2.00
❑9, Jan 1998; gatefold summary ... 2.00
❑10, Feb 1998; gatefold summary ... 2.00
❑11, Mar 1998; gatefold summary ... 1.99
❑12, Apr 1998; gatefold summary ... 1.99
❑13, May 1998; gatefold summary ... 1.99
❑14, Jun 1998; Flip-book ... 1.99
❑15, Jul 1998; gatefold summary; blinded ... 1.99
❑16, Aug 1998; gatefold summary ... 1.99
❑17, Sep 1998; gatefold summary ... 1.99
❑18, Oct 1998; gatefold summary ... 1.99
❑19, Nov 1998; gatefold summary ... 1.99
❑20, Dec 1998; gatefold summary ... 1.99
❑Annual 1997, ca. 1997; gatefold summary; wraparound cover ... 2.99

KAZAR OF THE SAVAGE LAND
MARVEL

❑1, Feb 1997; wraparound cover ... 2.50

KA-ZAR: SIBLING RIVALRY
MARVEL

❑-1, Jul 1997; Flashback ... 1.95

KA-ZAR THE SAVAGE
MARVEL

❑1, Apr 1981 BA (a); O: Ka-Zar. ... 2.50
❑2, May 1981 BA (a) ... 2.00
❑3, Jun 1981 BA (a) ... 1.50
❑4, Jul 1981 BA (a) ... 1.50
❑5, Aug 1981 BA (a) ... 1.50
❑6, Sep 1981 BA (a) ... 1.50
❑7, Oct 1981 BA (a) ... 1.50
❑8, Nov 1981 BA (a) ... 1.50
❑9, Dec 1981 BA (a) ... 1.50
❑10, Jan 1982; BA (a);direct distribution ... 1.50
❑11, Feb 1982; BA (a); 1: Belasco. Zabu ... 1.50
❑12, Mar 1982; BA (a);panel missing ... 1.50
❑12-2 ... 1.00
❑13, Apr 1982 BA (a) ... 1.50
❑14, May 1982 BA (a) ... 1.50
❑15, Jun 1982 BA (a) ... 1.50
❑16, Jul 1982 ... 1.50
❑17, Aug 1982 ... 1.50
❑18, Sep 1982 ... 1.50
❑19, Oct 1982 BA (a) ... 1.50
❑20, Nov 1982 ... 1.50
❑21, Dec 1982 ... 1.50
❑22, Jan 1983 ... 1.50
❑23, Feb 1983 BH (a) ... 1.50
❑24, Mar 1983 BH (a) ... 1.50
❑25, Apr 1983 ... 1.50
❑26, May 1983 ... 1.50
❑27, Aug 1983 ... 1.50
❑28, Oct 1983 ... 1.50
❑29, Dec 1983; Double-size; Wedding of Ka-Zar, Shanna ... 1.50
❑30, Feb 1984 ... 1.50
❑31, Apr 1984 ... 1.50
❑32, Jun 1984 ... 1.50
❑33, Aug 1984 ... 1.50
❑34, Oct 1984 ... 1.50

KEENSPOT SPOTLIGHT
KEENSPOT

❑2002, Apr 2002 ... 1.00

KEIF LLAMA
ONI

❑1, Mar 1999 ... 2.95

KEIF LLAMA XENO-TECH
FANTAGRAPHICS

❑1 ... 2.00
❑2 ... 2.00
❑3 ... 2.00
❑4 ... 2.00
❑5 ... 2.00
❑6 ... 2.00

KELLY BELLE POLICE DETECTIVE
NEWCOMERS

❑1 ... 2.95
❑2 ... 2.95
❑3 ... 2.95

KELVIN MACE
VORTEX

❑1 ... 3.00
❑2 ... 1.75

KENDRA: LEGACY OF THE BLOOD
PERRYDOG

❑1, Feb 1987, b&w ... 2.00
❑2, Apr 1987, b&w ... 2.00

KENTS, THE
DC

❑1, Aug 1997; Clark Kent's ancestors in frontier Kansas ... 3.00
❑2, Sep 1997 ... 2.50
❑3, Oct 1997 ... 2.50
❑4, Nov 1997 ... 2.50
❑5, Dec 1997 ... 2.50
❑6, Jan 1998 ... 2.50
❑7, Feb 1998 ... 2.50
❑8, Mar 1998 ... 2.50
❑9, Apr 1998 ... 2.50
❑10, May 1998 ... 2.50
❑11, Jun 1998 ... 2.50
❑12, Jul 1998 ... 2.50

KERRY DRAKE
BLACKTHORNE

❑1, May 1986 ... 6.95
❑2, Jul 1986 ... 6.95
❑3, Dec 1986 ... 6.95
❑4, Feb 1987 ... 6.95
❑5, Jul 1987 ... 6.95

KEYHOLE
MILLENNIUM

❑1, Jun 1996 ... 2.95
❑2, Oct 1996 ... 2.95
❑3 1997 ... 2.95
❑4, May 1997 ... 2.95
❑5, Jun 1998 ... 2.95

KICKERS, INC.
MARVEL

❑1, Nov 1986 ... 0.75
❑2, Dec 1986 ... 0.75
❑3, Jan 1987 ... 0.75
❑4, Feb 1987 ... 0.75
❑5, Mar 1987 ... 0.75

	N-MINT
❑6, Apr 1987	0.75
❑7, May 1987	0.75
❑8, Jun 1987	0.75
❑9, Jul 1987	0.75
❑10, Aug 1987	0.75
❑11, Sep 1987	0.75
❑12, Oct 1987	0.75

KID ANARCHY
FANTAGRAPHICS

	N-MINT
❑1, b&w	2.50
❑2, b&w	2.75
❑3, b&w	2.75

KID BLASTOFF
SLAVE LABOR / AMAZE INK

	N-MINT
❑1, Jun 1996	2.75

KID CANNIBAL
ETERNITY

	N-MINT
❑1, Oct 1991	2.50
❑2 1991	2.50
❑3 1992	2.50
❑4 1992	2.50

KID COLT OUTLAW
MARVEL

	N-MINT
❑65, Oct 1956	48.00
❑66, Nov 1956	48.00
❑67, Dec 1956	48.00
❑68, Jan 1957	48.00
❑69, Feb 1957	48.00
❑70, Mar 1957	48.00
❑71, Apr 1957	40.00
❑72, May 1957	40.00
❑73, Jul 1957	40.00
❑74, Sep 1957	40.00
❑75, Nov 1957	40.00
❑76, Jan 1958	40.00
❑77, Mar 1958	40.00
❑78, May 1958	40.00
❑79, Jul 1958	40.00
❑80, Sep 1958	40.00
❑81, Nov 1958	40.00
❑82, Jan 1959	40.00
❑83, Mar 1959	40.00
❑84, May 1959	40.00
❑85, Jul 1959	40.00
❑86, Sep 1959	40.00
❑87, Nov 1959	40.00
❑88, Jan 1960	40.00
❑89, Mar 1960	40.00
❑90, May 1960	40.00
❑91, Jul 1960	40.00
❑92, Sep 1960	40.00
❑93, Oct 1960	40.00
❑94, Nov 1960	40.00
❑95, Dec 1960	40.00
❑96, Jan 1961	40.00
❑97, Mar 1961	40.00
❑98, May 1961	40.00
❑99, Jul 1961	40.00
❑100, Sep 1961	40.00
❑101, Nov 1961	28.00
❑102, Jan 1962	28.00
❑103, Mar 1962	28.00
❑104, May 1962	28.00
❑105, Jul 1962	28.00
❑106, Sep 1962	28.00
❑107, Nov 1962	28.00
❑108, Jan 1963	28.00
❑109, Mar 1963	28.00
❑110, May 1963 SL (w)	28.00
❑111, Jul 1963	18.00
❑112, Sep 1963 SL (w)	18.00
❑113, Nov 1963	18.00
❑114, Jan 1964 V: Iron Mask.	18.00
❑115, Mar 1964	18.00
❑116, May 1964	18.00
❑117, Jul 1964	18.00
❑118, Sep 1964 V: Scorpion. V: Bull Barton. V: Doctor Danger.	18.00
❑119, Nov 1964	18.00
❑120, Jan 1965	18.00
❑121, Mar 1965	14.00
❑122, May 1965	14.00
❑123, Jul 1965	14.00
❑124, Sep 1965 V: Phantom Raider.	14.00
❑125, Nov 1965 A: Two-Gun Kid.	14.00
❑126, Jan 1966	14.00
❑127, Mar 1966 V: Iron Mask. V: Fat Man. V: Doctor Danger.	14.00
❑128, May 1966	14.00
❑129, Jul 1966	14.00
❑130, Sep 1966; SL (w); O: Kid Colt. giant	14.00
❑131, Nov 1966; SL (w); GC (a);giant	10.00
❑132, Jan 1967; giant	10.00
❑133, Mar 1967 V: Rammer Ramkin.	10.00
❑134, May 1967	10.00
❑135, Jul 1967	10.00
❑136, Sep 1967	10.00
❑137, Nov 1967	10.00
❑138, Jan 1968	10.00
❑139, Mar 1968; series goes on hiatus	10.00
❑140, Nov 1969; Reprints begin	5.00
❑141, Dec 1969	5.00
❑142, Jan 1970	5.00
❑143, Feb 1970	5.00
❑144, Mar 1970	5.00
❑145, Apr 1970	5.00
❑146, May 1970	5.00
❑147, Jun 1970	5.00
❑148, Jul 1970	5.00
❑149, Aug 1970	5.00
❑150, Oct 1970	5.00
❑151, Dec 1970	5.00
❑152, Feb 1971	5.00
❑153, Apr 1971	5.00
❑154, Jul 1971	5.00
❑155, Sep 1971	5.00
❑156, Nov 1971	5.00
❑157, Jan 1972	5.00
❑158, Mar 1972	5.00
❑159, May 1972	5.00
❑160, Jul 1972	5.00
❑161, Aug 1972	5.00
❑162, Sep 1972	5.00
❑163, Oct 1972	5.00
❑164, Nov 1972	5.00
❑165, Dec 1972	5.00
❑166, Jan 1973	5.00
❑167, Feb 1973	5.00
❑168, Mar 1973	5.00
❑169, Apr 1973	5.00
❑170, May 1973	5.00
❑171, Jun 1973	4.00
❑172, Jul 1973	4.00
❑173, Aug 1973	4.00
❑174, Sep 1973	4.00
❑175, Oct 1973	4.00
❑176, Nov 1973	4.00
❑177, Dec 1973	4.00
❑178, Jan 1974	4.00
❑179, Feb 1974	4.00
❑180, Mar 1974	4.00
❑181, Apr 1974	4.00
❑182, May 1974	4.00
❑183, Jun 1974	4.00
❑184, Jul 1974	4.00
❑185, Aug 1974	4.00
❑186, Sep 1974	4.00
❑187, Oct 1974	4.00
❑188, Nov 1974	4.00
❑189, Dec 1974	4.00
❑190, Jan 1975	4.00
❑191, Feb 1975	4.00
❑192, Mar 1975	4.00
❑193, Apr 1975	4.00
❑194, May 1975	4.00
❑195, Jun 1975	4.00
❑196, Jul 1975	4.00
❑197, Aug 1975	4.00
❑198, Sep 1975	4.00
❑199, Oct 1975	4.00
❑200, Nov 1975	4.00

Kevin Plunder's descent into savagery was retold in *Ka-Zar the Savage* #1.

© 1981 Marvel Comics.

	N-MINT
❑201, Dec 1975	3.00
❑202, Jan 1976	3.00
❑203, Feb 1976	3.00
❑204, Mar 1976; Reprints Kid Colt Outlaw #72	3.00
❑205, Apr 1976	3.00
❑205/30 cent, Apr 1976; 30 cent regional price variant	20.00
❑206, May 1976	3.00
❑206/30 cent, May 1976; 30 cent regional price variant	20.00
❑207, Jun 1976	3.00
❑207/30 cent, Jun 1976; 30 cent regional price variant	20.00
❑208, Jul 1976	3.00
❑208/30 cent, Jul 1976; 30 cent regional price variant	20.00
❑209, Aug 1976	3.00
❑209/30 cent, Aug 1976; 30 cent regional price variant	20.00
❑210, Sep 1976	3.00
❑211, Oct 1976	3.00
❑212, Nov 1976	3.00
❑213, Dec 1976	3.00
❑214, Jan 1977	3.00
❑215, Feb 1977	3.00
❑216, Mar 1977	3.00
❑217, Apr 1977	3.00
❑218, Jun 1977	3.00
❑219, Aug 1977	3.00
❑220, Oct 1977	3.00
❑221, Dec 1977	3.00
❑222, Feb 1978	3.00
❑223, Apr 1978	3.00
❑224, Jun 1978	3.00
❑225, Aug 1978	3.00
❑226, Oct 1978	3.00
❑227, Dec 1978	3.00
❑228, Feb 1979	3.00
❑229, Apr 1979	3.00

KID DEATH & FLUFFY: HALLOWEEN SPECIAL
EVENT

	N-MINT
❑1, Oct 1997	2.95

KID DEATH & FLUFFY SPRING BREAK SPECIAL
EVENT

	N-MINT
❑1, Jun 1996	2.50

KID ETERNITY (MINI-SERIES)
DC / VERTIGO

	N-MINT
❑1, May 1991	4.95
❑2, Jul 1991	4.95
❑3, Oct 1991	4.95

KID ETERNITY
DC / VERTIGO

	N-MINT
❑1, May 1993	1.95
❑2, Jun 1993	1.95
❑3, Jul 1993	1.95
❑4, Aug 1993	1.95
❑5, Sep 1993	1.95
❑6, Oct 1993	1.95
❑7, Nov 1993	1.95
❑8, Dec 1993	1.95
❑9, Jan 1994	1.95
❑10, Feb 1994	1.95
❑11, Mar 1994	1.95
❑12, May 1994	1.95

N-MINT

❑13, Jun 1994 .... 1.95
❑14, Jul 1994 .... 1.95
❑15, Aug 1994 .... 1.95
❑16, Sep 1994 .... 1.95

KID 'N PLAY
MARVEL

❑1, Feb 1992 .... 1.25
❑2, Mar 1992 .... 1.25
❑3, Apr 1992 .... 1.25
❑4, May 1992 .... 1.25
❑5, Jun 1992 .... 1.25
❑6, Jul 1992 .... 1.25
❑7, Aug 1992 .... 1.25
❑8, Sep 1992 .... 1.25
❑9, Oct 1992 .... 1.25

KID SUPREME
IMAGE

❑1, Mar 1996; Kid Supreme with fist outstretched on cover 2.50
❑1/A, Mar 1996; Kid Supreme surounded by girls on cover 2.50
❑2, Apr 1996 .... 2.50
❑3, Jul 1996 .... 2.50
❑3/A, Jul 1996; alternate cover (green background) 2.50

KID'S WB JAM PACKED ACTION
DC

❑1, ca 2004 .... 7.99

KID TERRIFIC
IMAGE

❑1, Nov 1998, b&w 2.95

KIDZ OF THE KING
KING

❑1, Mar 1994 .... 2.95
❑2, May 1994 .... 2.95
❑3, Apr 1995 .... 2.95

KI-GORR THE KILLER
AC

❑1 .... 3.95

KIKU SAN
AIRCEL

❑1, Nov 1988 .... 1.95
❑2, Dec 1988 .... 1.95
❑3, Jan 1989 .... 1.95
❑4, Feb 1989 .... 1.95
❑5, Mar 1989 .... 1.95
❑6, Apr 1989 .... 1.95

KILGORE
RENEGADE

❑1, Nov 1987 .... 2.00
❑2 .... 2.00
❑3 .... 2.00
❑4, May 1988 .... 2.00

KILL BARNY
EXPRESS / PARODY

❑1, b&w 2.50

KILL BARNY 3
EXPRESS / PARODY

❑1, b&w 2.75

KILLBOX
ANTARCTIC

❑1, Dec 2002 .... 5.00
❑2, Jan 2003 .... 5.00
❑3, Feb 2003 .... 5.00

KILLER FLY
SLAVE LABOR

❑1, Mar 1995 .... 2.95
❑2, Jun 1995 .... 2.95
❑3, Sep 1995 .... 2.95

KILLER INSTINCT
ACCLAIM / ARMADA

❑1, Jun 1996; based on video game 2.50
❑2, Jul 1996; based on video game 2.50
❑3, Jul 1996; based on video game 2.50
❑4, Sep 1996; based on video game 2.50
❑5, Oct 1996; based on video game 2.50
❑6, Nov 1996; based on video game 2.50

N-MINT

KILLER INSTINCT TOUR BOOK
IMAGE

❑1/A; Embossed cover 3.00
❑1/B; Embossed cover 3.00
❑1/Gold; Gold edition 3.00

KILLER...TALES BY TIMOTHY TRUMAN
ECLIPSE

❑1, Mar 1985 .... 1.75

KILL IMAGE
BONEYARD

❑1, b&w; foil cover 3.50

KILLING STROKE
ETERNITY

❑1, b&w 2.50
❑2, b&w 2.50
❑3, b&w 2.50
❑4, b&w 2.50

KILL MARVEL
BONEYARD

❑1/Ltd.; Special "Marvel Can..." edition 5.00

KILLPOWER: THE EARLY YEARS
MARVEL

❑1, Sep 1993; foil cover 1.75
❑2, Oct 1993 .... 1.75
❑3, Nov 1993 .... 1.75
❑4, Dec 1993 .... 1.75

KILLRAVEN
MARVEL

❑1, Feb 2001 .... 2.99

KILLRAVEN (2ND SERIES)
MARVEL

❑1, Dec 2002 .... 2.99
❑2, Jan 2003 .... 2.99
❑3, Feb 2003 .... 2.99
❑4, Mar 2003 .... 2.99
❑5, Apr 2003 .... 2.99
❑6, May 2003 .... 2.99

KILL RAZOR SPECIAL
IMAGE

❑1, Aug 1995 .... 2.50

KILL YOUR BOYFRIEND
DC / VERTIGO

❑1, Jun 1995 .... 4.95
❑1-2, May 1998; reprints 1995 one-shot with new afterword and other new material 5.95

KILROY IS HERE
CALIBER

❑0, ca. 1994, b&w 2.95
❑1, ca. 1995, b&w 2.95
❑2, ca. 1995, b&w 2.95
❑3, ca. 1995, b&w 2.95
❑4, ca. 1995, b&w 2.95
❑5, ca. 1995, #4 on cover 2.95

KILROY: REVELATIONS
CALIBER

❑1, ca. 1994, b&w; "Black light" cover 2.95

KILROY: THE SHORT STORIES
CALIBER

❑1, ca. 1995, b&w; "Black light" cover 2.95

KILROY (VOL. 2)
CALIBER

❑1, Apr 1998 .... 2.95
❑1/A 2.95

KIMBER, PRINCE OF THE FEYLONS
ANTARCTIC

❑1, Apr 1992, b&w 2.50
❑2, Jun 1992, b&w 2.50

KIMURA
NIGHTWYND

❑1, b&w 2.50
❑2, b&w 2.50
❑3, b&w 2.50
❑4, b&w 2.50

N-MINT

KIN
IMAGE

❑1, Sep 1999 .... 2.95
❑2, Oct 1999 .... 2.95
❑3, Nov 1999 .... 2.95
❑4, Jul 2000 .... 2.95
❑5, Aug 2000 .... 2.95
❑6, Sep 2000 .... 3.95

KINDRED, THE
IMAGE

❑1, Mar 1994 .... 2.50
❑2, Apr 1994 .... 1.95
❑3, May 1994 .... 1.95
❑3/A, May 1994; alternate cover 1.95
❑4, Jul 1994 .... 2.50

KINDRED II, THE
DC / WILDSTORM

❑1, Mar 2002 .... 2.50
❑2, Apr 2002 .... 2.50
❑3, May 2002 .... 2.50
❑4, Jun 2002 .... 2.50

KINETIC
DC / FOCUS

❑1, May 2004 .... 2.50
❑2, Jun 2004 .... 2.50
❑3, Jul 2004 .... 2.50
❑4, Aug 2004 .... 2.50
❑5, Sep 2004 ....

KING ARTHUR AND THE KNIGHTS OF JUSTICE
MARVEL

❑1 .... 1.25
❑2, Jan 1994 .... 1.25
❑3, Feb 1994 .... 1.25

KING COMICS PRESENTS
KING COMICS

❑1 .... 1.95

KING CONAN
MARVEL

❑1, Mar 1980; JB (a); V: Thoth-Amon. wife & son 2.50
❑2, Jun 1980 JB (a) 1.50
❑3, Sep 1980 JB (a) 1.50
❑4, Dec 1980 V: Thoth-Amon. 1.50
❑5, Mar 1981 .... 1.50
❑6, Jun 1981 .... 1.50
❑7, Sep 1981 .... 1.50
❑8, Dec 1981 .... 1.50
❑9, Mar 1982 .... 1.50
❑10, May 1982 .... 1.50
❑11, Jul 1982 .... 1.25
❑12, Sep 1982 .... 1.25
❑13, Nov 1982 .... 1.25
❑14, Jan 1983 .... 1.25
❑15, Mar 1983 .... 1.25
❑16, May 1983 .... 1.25
❑17, Jul 1983 .... 1.25
❑18, Sep 1983 .... 1.25
❑19, Nov 1983; Series continued in Conan the King #20 .... 1.25

KING DAVID
DC / VERTIGO

❑1, May 2002 .... 19.95

KINGDOM, THE
DC

❑1, Feb 1999; MWa (w); MZ (a);Elseworlds 2.95
❑1/Autographed, Feb 1999; MWa (w); Elseworlds 8.00
❑2, Feb 1999; MWa (w); MZ (a);Elseworlds 2.95
❑2/Autographed, Feb 1999; MWa (w); MZ (a);Elseworlds 12.00

KINGDOM COME
DC

❑1, ca. 1996; MWa (w); ARo (a);Elseworlds 5.00
❑1-2, ca. 1996 ARo (a) 4.95
❑2, ca. 1996; MWa (w); ARo (a);Elseworlds 5.00

N-MINT

❑3, ca. 1996; MWa (w); ARo (a);return of Captain Marvel; Elseworlds 5.00
❑4, ca. 1996; MWa (w); ARo (a); D: Captain Marvel. Elseworlds 5.00

KINGDOM, THE: KID FLASH
DC

❑1, Feb 1999; Elseworlds 1.99

KINGDOM, THE: NIGHTSTAR
DC

❑1, Feb 1999; Elseworlds 1.99

KINGDOM, THE: OFFSPRING
DC

❑1, Feb 1999; Elseworlds 1.99

KINGDOM, THE: PLANET KRYPTON
DC

❑1, Feb 1999; Elseworlds 1.99

KINGDOM, THE: SON OF THE BAT
DC

❑1, Feb 1999; Elseworlds 1.99

KINGDOM OF THE DWARFS
COMICO

❑1 .... 4.95

KINGDOM OF THE WICKED
CALIBER

❑1 1996, b&w 2.95
❑2 1996, b&w 2.95
❑3 1996, b&w 2.95
❑4 1996, b&w 2.95

KING KONG (GOLD KEY)
GOLD KEY

❑1, Sep 1968; adapts 1932 film 12.00

KING KONG (MONSTER)
MONSTER

❑1, Feb 1991, b&w DSt (c); DSt (a) .. 2.50
❑2, ca. 1991 .... 2.50
❑3, ca. 1991 .... 2.50
❑4, ca. 1991 .... 2.50
❑5, Nov 1991 AW (c) 2.50
❑6, Mar 1992 .... 2.50

KING LEONARDO AND HIS SHORT SUBJECTS
GOLD KEY

❑1, May 1962 .... 35.00
❑2, Oct 1962 .... 25.00
❑3, Dec 1962 .... 25.00
❑4, Mar 1963 .... 25.00

KING LOUIE AND MOWGLI
GOLD KEY

❑1, Sep 1963 .... 20.00

KING OF THE DEAD
FANTACO

❑0 .... 1.95
❑1 .... 1.95
❑2 .... 1.95
❑3 .... 1.95
❑4 .... 2.95

KINGPIN
MARVEL

❑1, Nov 1997 .... 5.99

KINGPIN (2ND SERIES)
MARVEL

❑1, Aug 2003 .... 2.50
❑2, Sep 2003 .... 2.50
❑3, Oct 2003 .... 2.99
❑4, Nov 2003 .... 2.99
❑5, Dec 2003 .... 2.99
❑6, Dec 2003 .... 2.99
❑7, Feb 2004 .... 2.99

KINGS IN DISGUISE
KITCHEN SINK

❑1, Mar 1988, b&w 2.00
❑2, May 1988 .... 2.00
❑3, Jul 1988 .... 2.00
❑4, Sep 1988 .... 2.00
❑5, Mar 1989 .... 2.00
❑6, Sep 1989 .... 2.00

N-MINT

KINGS OF THE NIGHT
DARK HORSE

❑1 .... 2.25
❑2 .... 2.25

KING TIGER & MOTORHEAD
DARK HORSE

❑1, Aug 1996 .... 2.95
❑2, Sep 1996 .... 2.95

KINKI KLITT KOMICS
RIP OFF

❑1, Apr 1992, b&w 2.95
❑2, Jun 1992, b&w 2.50

KINKY HOOK, THE
FANTAGRAPHICS / EROS

❑1, b&w 2.50

KIP
HAMMER & ANVIL

❑1, b&w 2.50

KIRBY KING OF THE SERIALS
BLACKTHORNE

❑1, Jan 1989, b&w 2.00

KISS
PERSONALITY

❑1, b&w 3.50
❑2 .... 3.00
❑3 .... 3.00

KISS (DARK HORSE)
DARK HORSE

❑1, Jun 2002 .... 2.99
❑2, Aug 2002; More Beast Now than Man cover 2.99
❑2/Variant, Aug 2002 .... 2.99
❑3, Sep 2002 .... 2.99
❑3/Variant, Sep 2002 .... 2.99
❑4 2002 .... 2.99
❑4/Variant 2002 .... 2.99
❑5 2002 .... 2.99
❑5/Variant 2002 .... 2.99
❑6 2003 .... 2.99
❑6/Variant 2003 .... 2.99
❑7, Feb 2003 .... 2.99
❑8, Mar 2003 .... 2.99
❑9, Apr 2003 .... 2.99
❑10, May 2003 .... 2.99
❑11, Jul 2003 .... 2.99
❑12, Aug 2003 .... 2.99
❑13, Sep 2003 .... 2.99

KISS & TELL
PATRICIA BREEN

❑1, Dec 1995, b&w; magazine 2.75

KISS & TELL (VOL. 2)
SIRIUS

❑1, b&w 2.50

KISS CLASSICS
MARVEL

❑1; Reprints Marvel Super Special #1, #5 .... 10.00

KISSES
SPOOF

❑1, b&w 2.95

KISSING CANVAS
MN DESIGN

❑1; photos 5.50

KISS KISS BANG BANG
CROSSGEN

❑1, Feb 2004 .... 2.95
❑1-2, Mar 2004 .... 2.95
❑2, Mar 2004 .... 2.95
❑3, Apr 2004 .... 2.95
❑4, Jun 2004 .... 2.95
❑4-2, Jun 2004 .... 2.95
❑5, Aug 2004 .... 2.95

KISS OF DEATH
ACME

❑1, Apr 1987 .... 2.00

KISS OF THE VAMPIRE
BRAINSTORM

❑1 .... 2.95

A possible future for the DC universe was revealed in *Kingdom Come*.

© 1996 DC Comics.

N-MINT

KISS PRE-HISTORY
REVOLUTIONARY

❑1, Apr 1993, b&w 3.00
❑2, May 1993, b&w 3.00
❑3, Jul 1993, b&w 3.00

KISS: PSYCHO CIRCUS
IMAGE

❑1, Aug 1997 .... 1.95
❑2, Sep 1997 .... 1.95
❑3, Oct 1997 .... 1.95
❑4, Nov 1997 .... 1.95
❑5, Dec 1997 .... 1.95
❑6, Jan 1998 .... 2.25
❑7, Mar 1998 .... 2.25
❑8, Apr 1998 .... 2.25
❑9, May 1998 .... 2.25
❑10, Jun 1998; covers of #10-12 form quadtych 2.25
❑11, Jul 1998 .... 2.25
❑12, Aug 1998 .... 2.25
❑13, Oct 1998 .... 2.25
❑14, Nov 1998 .... 2.25
❑15, Dec 1998 .... 2.25
❑16, Feb 1999 .... 2.25
❑17, Mar 1999 .... 2.25
❑18, Apr 1999 .... 2.25
❑19, May 1999 .... 2.25
❑20, Jun 1999 .... 2.25
❑21, Jul 1999 .... 2.25
❑22, Aug 1999 .... 2.25
❑23, Sep 1999 .... 2.25
❑24, Oct 1999 .... 2.25
❑25, Nov 1999 .... 2.25
❑26, Jan 2000 .... 2.25
❑27, Feb 2000 .... 2.25
❑28, Apr 2000 .... 2.25
❑29, Apr 2000 .... 2.50
❑30, May 2000 .... 2.50
❑31, Jun 2000 .... 2.50
❑Special 1; Special Wizard Edition 2.00

KISS: SATAN'S MUSIC?
CELEBRITY

❑1; trading cards 4.00

KISSYFUR
DC

❑1 .... 2.00

KISS: YOU WANTED THE BEST, YOU GOT THE BEST
WIZARD

❑1 .... 1.00

KITCHEN SINK CLASSICS
KITCHEN SINK

❑1, Jan 1994, b&w; reprints Omaha #0 4.50
❑2, b&w; reprints The People's Comics 3.00
❑3, b&w; reprints Death Rattle #8 ..... 3.00

KITTY PRYDE & WOLVERINE
MARVEL

❑1, Nov 1984 AM (a) 3.00
❑2, Dec 1984 AM (a) 2.50
❑3, Jan 1985 AM (a) 2.50
❑4, Feb 1985 AM (a) 2.50
❑5, Mar 1985 AM (a) 2.50
❑6, Apr 1985 AM (a) 2.50

N-MINT

KITTY PRYDE, AGENT OF SHIELD
MARVEL

- ❑1, Dec 1997; gatefold summary 2.50
- ❑2, Jan 1998; gatefold summary 2.50
- ❑3, Feb 1998; gatefold summary 2.50

KITZ 'N' KATZ KOMIKS
PHANTASY

- ❑1 ... 1.50
- ❑2, b&w ... 1.50
- ❑3, b&w ... 1.50
- ❑4, b&w ... 1.50
- ❑5 ... 1.50
- ❑6 ... 1.50

KIWANNI: DAUGHTER OF THE DAWN
C&T

- ❑1, Feb 1988, b&w ... 2.25

KLOR
SIRIUS

- ❑1 ... 2.95
- ❑2 ... 2.95
- ❑3 ... 2.95

KNEWTS OF THE ROUND TABLE
PAN

- ❑1, Jul 1998, b&w ... 2.50
- ❑2, Sep 1998, b&w ... 2.50
- ❑3 ... 2.50
- ❑4 ... 2.50
- ❑5 ... 2.50

KNIGHT
BEAR CLAW

- ❑0, Oct 1993 ... 2.50

KNIGHTFOOL: THE FALL OF THE SPLATMAN
PARODY

- ❑1 ... 2.95

KNIGHTHAWK
ACCLAIM / WINDJAMMER

- ❑1, Sep 1995 ... 2.50
- ❑2, Sep 1995 ... 2.50
- ❑3, Oct 1995 ... 2.50
- ❑4, Oct 1995 ... 2.50
- ❑5, Nov 1995 ... 2.50
- ❑6, Nov 1995 ... 2.50

KNIGHTMARE (ANTARCTIC)
ANTARCTIC

- ❑1, Jul 1994, b&w ... 2.75
- ❑2, Sep 1994, b&w ... 2.75
- ❑3, Jan 1995, b&w ... 2.75
- ❑4, Mar 1995, b&w ... 2.75
- ❑5, Mar 1995, b&w ... 2.75
- ❑6, May 1995, b&w ... 2.75

KNIGHTMARE (IMAGE)
IMAGE

- ❑0, Aug 1995; chromium cover 3.50
- ❑1, Feb 1995 ... 2.50
- ❑2, Mar 1995 ... 2.50
- ❑3, Apr 1995 ... 2.50
- ❑4, May 1995 ... 2.50
- ❑4/A, May 1995; alternate cover 2.50
- ❑5, Jun 1995; Flip book with Warcry #1 2.50
- ❑6 ... 2.50
- ❑7 ... 2.50
- ❑8 ... 2.50

KNIGHTSHIFT
LONDON NIGHT

- ❑1 ... 3.00
- ❑2, Dec 1996 ... 3.00

KNIGHTS' KINGDOM
LEGO

- ❑1 ... 4.99

KNIGHTS OF PENDRAGON, THE (1ST SERIES)
MARVEL

- ❑1, Jul 1990 ... 2.50
- ❑2, Aug 1990 ... 2.00
- ❑3, Oct 1990 ... 2.00
- ❑4, Oct 1990 ... 2.00
- ❑5, Nov 1990 ... 2.00
- ❑6, Dec 1990 ... 2.00
- ❑7, Jan 1991 ... 2.00
- ❑8, Feb 1991 ... 2.00
- ❑9, Mar 1991 ... 2.00
- ❑10, Apr 1991 ... 2.00
- ❑11, May 1991 A: Iron Man. 2.00
- ❑12, Jun 1991 ... 2.00
- ❑13, Jul 1991 ... 2.00
- ❑14, Aug 1991 ... 2.00
- ❑15, Sep 1991 ... 2.00
- ❑16, Oct 1991 ... 2.00
- ❑17, Nov 1991 ... 2.00
- ❑18, Dec 1991 A: Iron Man. ... 2.00

KNIGHTS OF PENDRAGON (2ND SERIES)
MARVEL

- ❑1, Jul 1992 A: Iron Man. ... 2.00
- ❑2, Aug 1992 ... 1.75
- ❑3, Sep 1992 ... 1.75
- ❑4, Oct 1992 ... 1.75
- ❑5, Nov 1992; Title changes to The Knights of Pendragon; New armor . 1.75
- ❑6, Dec 1992 ... 1.75
- ❑7, Jan 1993 A: Amazing Spider-Man. 1.75
- ❑8, Feb 1993 ... 1.75
- ❑9, Mar 1993; Spider-Man ... 1.75
- ❑10, Apr 1993 ... 1.75
- ❑11, May 1993 ... 1.75
- ❑12, Jun 1993 ... 1.75
- ❑13, Jul 1993 ... 1.75
- ❑14, Aug 1993 A: Death's Head II. 1.75
- ❑15, Sep 1993 A: Death's Head II. 1.75

KNIGHTS OF THE DINNER TABLE
ALDERAC GROUP

- ❑1, Jul 1994 ... 150.00
- ❑2, Jan 1995 ... 45.00
- ❑3, Apr 1995 ... 25.00
- ❑4, Feb 1997; Gary Con issue ... 25.00
- ❑5, Mar 1997 ... 25.00
- ❑6, Apr 1997 ... 18.00
- ❑7, May 1997 ... 18.00
- ❑8, Jun 1997 ... 18.00
- ❑9, Jul 1997 ... 18.00
- ❑10, Aug 1997 ... 18.00
- ❑11, Sep 1997 ... 14.00
- ❑12, Oct 1997 ... 14.00
- ❑13, Nov 1997 ... 14.00
- ❑14, Dec 1997 ... 14.00
- ❑15, Jan 1998 ... 14.00
- ❑16, Feb 1998 ... 10.00
- ❑17, Mar 1998 ... 10.00
- ❑18, Apr 1998 ... 10.00
- ❑19, May 1998 ... 10.00
- ❑20, Jun 1998 ... 10.00
- ❑21, Jul 1998; Gary Con issue ... 10.00
- ❑22, Aug 1998 ... 6.00
- ❑23, Sep 1998 ... 6.00
- ❑24, Oct 1998 ... 6.00
- ❑25, Nov 1998 ... 6.00
- ❑26, Dec 1998 ... 6.00
- ❑27, Jan 1999 ... 6.00
- ❑28, Feb 1999 ... 6.00
- ❑29, Mar 1999 ... 6.00
- ❑30, Apr 1999 ... 6.00
- ❑31, May 1999 ... 4.00
- ❑32, Jun 1999 ... 4.00
- ❑33, Jul 1999; Wild Wild Hack ... 3.00
- ❑34, Aug 1999 ... 2.95
- ❑35, Sep 1999 ... 2.95
- ❑36, Oct 1999 ... 2.95
- ❑37, Nov 1999 ... 2.95
- ❑38, Dec 1999 ... 2.95
- ❑39, Jan 2000 ... 2.95
- ❑40, Feb 2000 ... 2.95
- ❑41, Mar 2000 ... 2.95
- ❑42, Apr 2000 ... 2.95
- ❑43, May 2000 ... 2.95
- ❑44, Jun 2000 ... 2.95
- ❑45, Jul 2000 ... 2.95
- ❑46, Aug 2000 ... 2.95
- ❑47, Sep 2000 ... 2.95
- ❑48, Oct 2000 ... 2.95
- ❑49, Nov 2000 ... 2.95
- ❑50, Dec 2000; double-sized ... 4.95
- ❑51, Jan 2001 ... 2.95
- ❑52, Feb 2001 ... 2.95
- ❑53, Mar 2001 ... 2.95
- ❑54, Apr 2001 ... 2.95
- ❑55, May 2001 ... 2.95
- ❑56, Jun 2001 ... 2.95
- ❑57, Jul 2001 ... 2.95
- ❑58, Aug 2001 ... 2.95
- ❑59, Sep 2001 ... 2.95
- ❑60, Oct 2001 ... 2.99
- ❑61, Nov 2001 ... 2.99
- ❑62, Dec 2001 ... 2.99
- ❑63, Jan 2002 ... 2.99
- ❑64, Feb 2002 ... 2.99
- ❑65, Mar 2002 ... 2.99
- ❑66, Apr 2002 ... 2.99
- ❑67, May 2002 ... 2.99
- ❑68, Jun 2002 ... 2.99
- ❑69, Jul 2002 ... 2.99
- ❑70, Aug 2002 ... 3.99
- ❑71, Sep 2002 ... 3.99
- ❑72, Oct 2002 ... 3.99
- ❑73, Nov 2002 ... 3.99
- ❑74, Dec 2002 ... 3.99
- ❑75, Jan 2003 ... 3.99
- ❑76, Feb 2003 ... 3.99
- ❑77, Mar 2003 ... 3.99
- ❑78, Apr 2003 ... 3.99
- ❑79, May 2003 ... 3.99
- ❑80, Jun 2003 ... 3.99
- ❑81, Jul 2003 ... 3.99
- ❑82, Aug 2003 ... 3.99
- ❑83, Sep 2003 ... 3.99
- ❑84, Oct 2003 ... 3.99
- ❑85, Nov 2003 ... 3.99
- ❑86, Dec 2003 ... 3.99
- ❑87, Jan 2004 ... 3.99
- ❑88, Feb 2004 ... 3.99
- ❑89, Mar 2004 ... 3.99
- ❑90, Apr 2004 ... 3.99
- ❑91, May 2004 ... 3.99

KNIGHTS OF THE DINNER TABLE: BLACK HANDS GAMING SOCIETY SPECIAL
KENZER AND COMPANY

- ❑1, ca 2003 ... 2.99
- ❑2, ca. 2004 ... 2.99

KNIGHTS OF THE DINNER TABLE: EVERKNIGHTS
KENZER AND COMPANY

- ❑1, Jul 2002 ... 2.99
- ❑2, Sep 2002 ... 2.99
- ❑3, Nov 2002 ... 2.99
- ❑4, Jan 2003 ... 2.99
- ❑5, Mar 2003 ... 2.99
- ❑6, May 2003 ... 2.99
- ❑7, Jul 2003 ... 2.99
- ❑8, Sep 2003 ... 2.99
- ❑9, Nov 2003 ... 2.99
- ❑10, Jan 2004 ... 2.99
- ❑11, Mar 2004 ... 2.99
- ❑12, May 2004 ... 2.99

KNIGHTS OF THE DINNER TABLE/ FAANS CROSSOVER SPECIAL
SIX HANDED

- ❑1, Jul 1999, b&w ... 2.95

KNIGHTS OF THE DINNER TABLE ILLUSTRATED
KENZER & COMPANY

- ❑1, Jun 2000, b&w ... 2.95
- ❑2, Aug 2000, b&w ... 2.95
- ❑3, Oct 2000, b&w ... 2.95
- ❑4, Dec 2000, b&w ... 2.95
- ❑5, Feb 2001 ... 2.95
- ❑6, Apr 2001 ... 2.95
- ❑7, Jun 2001 ... 2.95

	N-MINT
❑8, Aug 2001	2.95
❑9, Oct 2001	2.95
❑10, Dec 2001	2.99
❑11, Feb 2002	2.99
❑12, Apr 2002	2.99
❑13, Jun 2002	2.99
❑14, Aug 2002	2.99
❑15, Oct 2002	2.99
❑16, Nov 2002	2.99
❑17, Dec 2002	2.99
❑18, Jan 2003	2.99
❑19, Feb 2003	2.99
❑20, Mar 2003	2.99
❑21, Apr 2003	2.99
❑22, May 2003	2.99
❑23, Jun 2003	2.99
❑24, Jul 2003	2.99
❑25, Aug 2003	2.99
❑26, Sep 2003	2.99
❑27, Oct 2003	2.99
❑28, Nov 2003	2.99
❑29, Dec 2003	2.99
❑30, Jan 2004	2.99
❑31, Feb 2004	2.99
❑32, Mar 2004	2.99
❑33, Apr 2004	2.99
❑34, May 2004	2.99

KNIGHTS OF THE JAGUAR SUPER LIMITED ONE SHOT
IMAGE

❑1, Jan 2004	3.00

KNIGHTS ON BROADWAY
BROADWAY

❑1, Jul 1996	2.95
❑2, Aug 1996	2.95
❑3, Oct 1996	2.95

KNIGHT'S ROUND TABLE
KNIGHT

❑1, Oct 1996, b&w	2.95
❑1/A	2.95

KNIGHTSTRIKE
IMAGE

❑1, Dec 1995; polybagged with Sentinel card	2.50

KNIGHT WATCHMAN
IMAGE

❑1, Jun 1998; cover says May, indicia says Jun	2.95
❑2, Jul 1998	2.95
❑3, Aug 1998	2.95
❑4, Oct 1998	2.95

KNIGHT WATCHMAN: GRAVEYARD SHIFT
CALIBER

❑1, b&w	2.95
❑2	2.95
❑3	2.95
❑4	2.95

KNIGHT WOLF, THE
FIVE STAR

❑1	2.50
❑2	2.50
❑3	2.50

KNUCKLES
ARCHIE

	N-MINT
❑1, Apr 1997	4.00
❑2, May 1997	3.00
❑3, Jun 1997	3.00
❑4, Aug 1997	2.25
❑5, Sep 1997	2.25
❑6, Oct 1997	2.25
❑7, Dec 1997	2.25
❑8, Jan 1998	2.25
❑9, Feb 1998	2.25
❑10, Mar 1998	2.25
❑11, Apr 1998	2.25
❑12, May 1998	2.25
❑13, Jun 1998	2.25
❑14, Jul 1998	2.25
❑15, Aug 1998	2.25
❑16, Sep 1998	2.25
❑17, Oct 1998	2.25
❑18, Nov 1998	2.25
❑19, Dec 1998	2.25
❑20, Jan 1999	2.25
❑21, Feb 1999	2.25
❑22, Mar 1999; cover forms triptych with #23 and #24	2.25
❑23, Apr 1999; cover forms triptych with #22 and #24	2.25
❑24, May 1999; cover forms triptych with #22 and #23	2.25
❑25, Jun 1999	2.25
❑26, Jul 1999	2.25
❑27, Aug 1999	2.25
❑28, Sep 1999	2.25
❑29, Oct 1999; The Echidna	2.25

KNUCKLES' CHAOTIX
ARCHIE

❑1, Jan 1996	3.00

KNUCKLES THE MALEVOLENT NUN
FANTAGRAPHICS

❑1, b&w	2.25
❑2	2.25

KOBALT
DC / MILESTONE

❑1, Jun 1994	1.75
❑2, Jul 1994	1.75
❑3, Aug 1994	1.75
❑4, Sep 1994	1.75
❑5, Oct 1994	1.75
❑6, Nov 1994	1.75
❑7, Dec 1994	1.75
❑8, Jan 1995	1.75
❑9, Feb 1995	1.75
❑10, Mar 1995	1.75
❑11, Apr 1995	1.75
❑12, Jun 1995	1.75
❑13, Jul 1995	2.50
❑14, Jul 1995	2.50
❑15, Aug 1995	2.50
❑16, Sep 1995	2.50

KOBRA
DC

❑1, Mar 1976 JK (a); O: Kobra. 1: Kobra.	4.00
❑2, May 1976	3.00
❑3, Jul 1976 KG (a)	3.00
❑4, Sep 1976	3.00
❑5, Dec 1976	3.00
❑6, Feb 1977	3.00
❑7, Apr 1977	3.00

KODOCHA: SANA'S STAGE
TOKYOPOP

❑1, Jun 2002, b&w; printed in Japanese format	9.99
❑2, Jul 2002, b&w; printed in Japanese format	9.99
❑3, Sep 2002, b&w; printed in Japanese format	9.99

KOGARATSU: THE LOTUS OF BLOOD
ACME

❑1	5.95

KOMODO AND THE DEFIANTS
VICTORY

❑1	1.50
❑2	1.50

KONA
DELL

❑2, Jul 1962 A: Numbering continued from.	18.00
❑3, Sep 1962	15.00
❑4, Oct 1962; O: Anak. 1: Anak. Anak stories begin as back-up	15.00
❑5, Jan 1963	15.00
❑6, Apr 1963	12.00
❑7, Jul 1963	12.00
❑8, Oct 1963	12.00
❑9, Jan 1964	12.00
❑10, Apr 1964	12.00
❑11, Jul 1964	12.00
❑12, Oct 1964	12.00

Knights of the Dinner Table has fun with several role-playing genres, including the standard dungeon crawl, outer space adventures, and an occasional foray into the Wild West.

	N-MINT
❑13, Jan 1965	12.00
❑14, Apr 1965	12.00
❑15, Jul 1965	10.00
❑16, Oct 1965	10.00
❑17, Jan 1966	10.00
❑18, Apr 1966	10.00
❑19, Jul 1966	10.00
❑20, Oct 1966	10.00
❑21, Jan 1967	10.00

KONGA
CHARLTON

❑1, ca. 1960	75.00
❑2, Aug 1961	50.00
❑3, Oct 1961	35.00
❑4, Dec 1961	35.00
❑5, Mar 1962	25.00
❑6, May 1962	25.00
❑7, Jul 1962	25.00
❑8, Sep 1962	25.00
❑9, Nov 1962	25.00
❑10, Jan 1963	25.00
❑11, Mar 1963	16.00
❑12, May 1963	16.00
❑13, Jul 1963	16.00
❑14, Sep 1963	16.00
❑15, Nov 1963	16.00
❑16, Jan 1964	16.00
❑17, Mar 1964	16.00
❑18, Jun 1964	16.00
❑19, Sep 1964	16.00
❑20, Dec 1965	16.00
❑21, Feb 1965	14.00
❑22, May 1965	14.00
❑23, Nov 1965	14.00

KONGA'S REVENGE
CHARLTON

❑1, ca. 1963; Reprints Konga's Revenge #3; Published out of sequence	10.00
❑2, ca. 1963	7.00
❑3, ca. 1963	7.00

KONG THE UNTAMED
DC

❑1, Jul 1975 BWr (c); BWr, AA (a); O: Kong the Untamed.	4.00
❑2, Sep 1975	3.00
❑3, Nov 1975 AA (a)	3.00
❑4, Jan 1976	3.00
❑5, Mar 1976	3.00

KONNY AND CZU
ANTARCTIC

❑1, Sep 1994, b&w	2.75
❑2, Nov 1994, b&w	2.75
❑3, Jan 1995, b&w	2.75
❑4, Mar 1995, b&w	2.75

KOOLAU THE LEPER (JACK LONDON'S...)
TOME

❑1, b&w	2.50

KOOSH KINS
ARCHIE

❑1, Oct 1991	1.00
❑2, Oct 1991	1.00
❑3, Dec 1991	1.00
❑4, Feb 1992	1.00

N-MINT

KORAK, SON OF TARZAN
Gold Key

❑1, Jan 1964; RM (a);Gold Key begins publishing ... 35.00
❑2, Mar 1964 RM (a) ... 25.00
❑3, May 1964 RM (a) ... 25.00
❑4, Aug 1964 RM (a) ... 25.00
❑5, Oct 1964 RM (a) ... 25.00
❑6, Dec 1964 RM (a) ... 20.00
❑7, Mar 1965 RM (a) ... 20.00
❑8, May 1965 RM (a) ... 20.00
❑9, Jul 1965 RM (a) ... 20.00
❑10, Sep 1965 RM (a) ... 20.00
❑11, Nov 1965 RM (a) ... 20.00
❑12, Mar 1966 ... 16.00
❑13, Jun 1966 ... 16.00
❑14, Sep 1966 ... 16.00
❑15, Dec 1966 ... 16.00
❑16, Mar 1967 ... 16.00
❑17, Jun 1967 ... 16.00
❑18, Aug 1967 ... 16.00
❑19, Oct 1967 ... 16.00
❑20, Dec 1967 ... 16.00
❑21, Feb 1968 RM (a) ... 13.00
❑22, Apr 1968 ... 13.00
❑23, Jun 1968 ... 13.00
❑24, Aug 1968 ... 13.00
❑25, Oct 1968 ... 13.00
❑26, Dec 1968 ... 13.00
❑27, Feb 1969 ... 13.00
❑28, Apr 1969 ... 13.00
❑29, Jun 1969 ... 13.00
❑30, Aug 1969 ... 13.00
❑31, Oct 1969 ... 8.00
❑32, Dec 1969 ... 8.00
❑33, Jan 1970 ... 8.00
❑34, Mar 1970 ... 8.00
❑35, May 1970 ... 8.00
❑36, Jul 1970 ... 8.00
❑37, Sep 1970 ... 8.00
❑38, Nov 1970 ... 8.00
❑39, Jan 1971 ... 8.00
❑40, Mar 1971 ... 8.00
❑41, May 1971 ... 6.00
❑42, Jul 1971 ... 6.00
❑43, Sep 1971 ... 6.00
❑44, Nov 1971 ... 6.00
❑45, Jan 1972 ... 6.00
❑46, May 1972; continues Gold Key numbering; DC begins publishing . 4.00
❑47, Jul 1972 ... 2.00
❑48, Sep 1972 ... 2.00
❑49, Nov 1972 ... 2.00
❑50, Feb 1973 ... 2.00
❑51, Apr 1973 JKu (c); FT (a) ... 2.00
❑52, Jul 1973 ... 2.00
❑53, Sep 1973; JKu (c);Carson of Venus back-up ... 2.00
❑54, Nov 1973; JKu (c);Carson of Venus back-up ... 2.00
❑55, Jan 1974; JKu (c);Carson of Venus back-up ... 2.00
❑56, Mar 1974; JKu (c);Carson of Venus back-up ... 2.00
❑57, Jun 1975 ... 2.00
❑58, Aug 1975 ... 2.00
❑59, Oct 1975; Series continued in Tarzan Family #60 ... 2.00

KORE
Image

❑1, Apr 2003 ... 2.95
❑2, Jun 2003 ... 2.95
❑3, Jul 2003 ... 2.95
❑4, Sep 2003 ... 2.95
❑5, Oct 2003 ... 2.95

KORG: 70,000 B.C.
Charlton

❑1, May 1975 ... 8.00
❑2, Aug 1975 ... 5.00
❑3, Oct 1975 ... 5.00
❑4, Dec 1975 ... 5.00
❑5, Feb 1976 ... 5.00
❑6, May 1976 ... 5.00
❑7, Jul 1976 ... 5.00
❑8, Sep 1976 ... 5.00
❑9, Nov 1976 ... 5.00

KORVUS
Arrow

❑0, Jul 1999; Flip book with Spank the Monkey #1 ... 2.95
❑1 ... 2.95
❑2 ... 2.95
❑3, Spr 1998 ... 2.95

KORVUS (VOL. 2)
Arrow

❑1, Fal 1998 ... 2.95
❑2 ... 2.95

KOSMIC KAT
Image

❑1, Aug 1999 ... 2.95

KOSMIC KAT ACTIVITY BOOK
Image

❑1, Aug 1999 ... 2.95

KREE-SKRULL WAR STARRING THE AVENGERS, THE
Marvel

❑1, Sep 1983 JB, NA (a) ... 3.00
❑2, Oct 1983 JB, NA (a) ... 3.00

KREMEN
Grey Productions

❑1 ... 2.50
❑2 ... 2.50
❑3 ... 2.50

KREY
Gauntlet

❑1, b&w ... 2.50
❑2, b&w ... 2.50
❑3, b&w ... 2.50

KROFFT SUPERSHOW
Gold Key

❑1, Apr 1978 ... 6.00
❑2, May 1978 ... 4.00
❑3, Jun 1978 ... 4.00
❑4, Sep 1978 ... 4.00
❑5, Nov 1978 ... 4.00
❑6, Jan 1979 ... 4.00

KRULL
Marvel

❑1, Nov 1983 ... 1.25
❑2, Dec 1983 ... 1.25

KRUSTY COMICS
Bongo

❑1, ca. 1995 ... 2.50
❑2, ca. 1995 ... 2.50
❑3, ca. 1995 ... 2.50

KRYPTON CHRONICLES
DC

❑1, Sep 1981 CS (a); A: Superman. .. 1.50
❑2, Oct 1981 CS (a); A: Black Flame. . 1.50
❑3, Nov 1981 CS (a); O: name of Kal-El. 1.50

KULL AND THE BARBARIANS
Marvel

❑1, May 1975, b&w; magazine; Reprints Kull the Conqueror #1 and 2, Supernatural Thrillers #3 ... 5.00
❑2, Jul 1975, b&w; magazine ... 3.00
❑3, Sep 1975, b&w; magazine O: Red Sonja. ... 4.00

KULL IN 3-D
Blackthorne

❑1 ... 2.50
❑2 ... 2.50

KULL THE CONQUEROR (1ST SERIES)
Marvel

❑1, Jun 1971 WW, RA (a); O: Kull. 1: Brule the Spear-Slayer. ... 8.00
❑2, Sep 1971 JSe (a) ... 4.00
❑3, Jul 1972 JSe (a); A: Thulsa Doom. 3.50
❑4, Sep 1972 JSe (a) ... 2.50
❑5, Nov 1972 JSe (a) ... 2.50
❑6, Jan 1973 JSe (a) ... 2.50
❑7, Mar 1973 ... 2.50
❑8, May 1973 ... 2.50
❑9, Jul 1973 ... 2.50
❑10, Sep 1973; Continued as "Kull the Destroyer" ... 2.50

KULL THE CONQUEROR (2ND SERIES)
Marvel

❑1, Dec 1982; JB (a);Brule ... 2.50
❑2, Mar 1983; Misareena ... 2.00

KULL THE CONQUEROR (3RD SERIES)
Marvel

❑1, May 1983; JB (a);Iraina ... 2.00
❑2, Jul 1983 JB (a) ... 1.75
❑3, Dec 1983 JB (a) ... 1.75
❑4, Feb 1984 JB (a) ... 1.50
❑5, Aug 1984 ... 1.50
❑6, Oct 1984 ... 1.25
❑7, Dec 1984 ... 1.25
❑8, Feb 1985 ... 1.25
❑9, Apr 1985 ... 1.25
❑10, Jun 1985 ... 1.25

KULL THE DESTROYER
Marvel

❑11, Nov 1973; Continued from Kull the Conqueror (1st Series) #10 ... 2.00
❑12, Jan 1974 MP (a) ... 2.00
❑13, Mar 1974; MP (a);Marvel Value Stamp #73: Kingpin ... 2.00
❑14, May 1974; JSn, MP (a);Marvel Value Stamp #40: Loki ... 2.00
❑15, Aug 1974; SD, MP (a);series goes on hiatus; Marvel Value Stamp #42: Man Wolf ... 2.00
❑16, Aug 1976 ... 2.00
❑16/30 cent, Aug 1976; 30 cent regional price variant ... 20.00
❑17, Oct 1976 AA (a) ... 2.00
❑18, Dec 1976 AA (a) ... 2.00
❑19, Feb 1977 AA (a) ... 2.00
❑20, Apr 1977 AA (a) ... 2.00
❑21, Jun 1977 ... 2.00
❑21/35 cent, Jun 1977; 35 cent regional price variant ... 15.00
❑22, Aug 1977 ... 2.00
❑22/35 cent, Aug 1977; 35 cent regional price variant ... 15.00
❑23, Oct 1977 ... 2.00
❑23/35 cent, Oct 1977; 35 cent regional price variant ... 15.00
❑24, Dec 1977 ... 2.00
❑25, Feb 1978 ... 2.00
❑26, Apr 1978 ... 2.00
❑27, Jun 1978 ... 2.00
❑28, Aug 1978 ... 2.00
❑29, Oct 1978 A: Thulsa Doom. ... 2.00

KUNOICHI
Lightning

❑1, Sep 1996; also contains Sinja: Resurrection #1; indicia is for Sinja: Resurrection ... 3.00

KWAIDEN
Dark Horse

❑1, ca 2004 ... 14.95

KYRA
Elsewhere

❑1, b&w ... 2.00
❑2, Spr 1986, b&w ... 2.00
❑3, Sum 1986, b&w ... 2.00
❑4, Dec 1986 ... 2.00
❑5, Jun 1987 ... 2.00
❑6 1987 ... 2.00

K-Z COMICS PRESENTS
K-Z

❑1, Jun 1985 ... 1.50

N-MINT

L

LA BLUE GIRL
CPM / Bare Bear

❑1, Jul 1996, b&w; wraparound cover 2.95
❑2, Aug 1996, b&w 2.95
❑3, Sep 1996, b&w 2.95
❑4, Oct 1996, b&w 2.95
❑5, Nov 1996, b&w 2.95
❑6, Dec 1996 2.95
❑7, Jan 1997 2.95
❑8, Feb 1997 2.95
❑9, Mar 1997 2.95
❑10, Apr 1997 2.95
❑11, May 1997 2.95
❑12, Jun 1997 2.95

LABMAN
Image

❑1, Nov 1996 3.50
❑1/A, Nov 1996; alternate cover 3.50
❑1/B, Nov 1996; alternate cover 3.50
❑1/C, Nov 1996; alternate cover 3.50
❑2, Dec 1996 2.95
❑3, Jan 1997 2.95

LABMAN SOURCEBOOK
Image

❑1, Jun 1996; Limited edition giveaway from 1996 San Diego Comic-Con 1.00

LABOR FORCE
Blackthorne

❑1, Sep 1986 1.50
❑2 1.50
❑3 1.50
❑4 1.75
❑5, Mar 1987 1.75
❑6 1.75
❑7 1.75
❑8 1.75

LABOURS OF HERCULES, THE
Malan Classical Enterprises

❑1, b&w 2.95

LAB RATS
DC

❑1, Jun 2002 2.50
❑2, Jul 2002 2.50
❑3, Aug 2002 2.50
❑4, Sep 2002 2.50
❑5, Oct 2002 2.50
❑6, Nov 2002 2.50
❑7, Dec 2002 2.50

LABYRINTH OF MADNESS
TSR

❑1 1.00

LABYRINTH: THE MOVIE
Marvel

❑1, Nov 1986 JB, RT (a) 1.50
❑2, Dec 1986 JB, RT (a) 1.50
❑3, Jan 1987 JB, RT (a) 1.50

L.A. COMICS
Los Angeles

❑1 3.00
❑2 3.00

LAD, A DOG
Dell

❑2, Sep 1962, First issue published as Dell's Four Color #1303; no photo cover on this issue 30.00

LADY AND THE TRAMP
Dell

❑1, Jun 1955 25.00

LADY ARCANE
Hero Graphics

❑1, Jul 1992 4.95
❑2, b&w 3.50
❑3, b&w 3.50
❑4, b&w 2.95

N-MINT

LADY CRIME
AC

❑1, ca. 1992, b&w; Bob Powell reprints 2.75

LADY DEATH (MINI-SERIES)
Chaos!

❑0, Nov 1997 3.00
❑0.5; Wizard mail-in promotional edition 4.00
❑0.5/A; Wizard mail-in promotional edition 6.00
❑0.5/Gold; Gold edition 5.00
❑1, Jan 1994 8.00
❑1/Ltd., Jan 1994; Signed limited edition 12.00
❑1-2, Feb 1994; Commemorative edition 2.75
❑2, Feb 1994 8.00
❑3, Mar 1994 5.00
❑4, Apr 1994 4.00

LADY DEATH
Chaos!

❑1, Feb 1998 2.95
❑1/Ltd., Feb 1998; premium limited edition; no cover price 4.00
❑2, Mar 1998 2.95
❑3, Apr 1998; Signed edition 2.95
❑4, May 1998 2.95
❑5, Jun 1998 2.95
❑5/Variant, Jun 1998; variant cover 3.50
❑6, Jul 1998 2.95
❑7, Aug 1998 2.95
❑8, Sep 1998 2.95
❑9, Oct 1998 2.95
❑10, Nov 1998; cover says Oct, indicia says Nov 2.95
❑11, Dec 1998 2.95
❑12, Jan 1999 2.95
❑13, Feb 1999 2.95
❑14, Mar 1999 2.95
❑15, Apr 1999 2.95
❑16, May 1999 2.95

LADY DEATH (BRIAN PULIDO'S...)
CrossGen

❑1, Mar 2003 2.95
❑2, Apr 2003 2.95
❑3, May 2003 2.95
❑4, Jun 2003 2.95
❑5, Jul 2003 2.95
❑6, Sep 2003 2.95
❑7, Oct 2003 2.95
❑8, Oct 2003 2.95
❑9, Dec 2003 2.95
❑10, Feb 2004 2.95
❑11, Mar 2004 2.95
❑12, Apr 2004 2.95

LADY DEATH: ALIVE
Chaos

❑1, May 2001 2.95
❑1/Ltd., May 2001 2.95
❑2, Jun 2001 2.95
❑3, Jul 2001 2.95
❑4, Aug 2001 2.95

LADY DEATH AND THE WOMEN OF CHAOS! GALLERY
Chaos

❑1, Nov 1996 2.25

LADY DEATH/BAD KITTY
Chaos

❑1, Sep 2001 2.99

LADY DEATH (BRIAN PULIDO'S...): WILD HUNT
CrossGen

❑1, Apr 2004 2.95
❑2, May 2004 2.95

LADY DEATH: DARK MILLENNIUM
Chaos

❑1, Feb 2000 2.95
❑2, Mar 2000 2.95

Hanna-Barbera characters participated in Olympic-style events in *Laff-a-lympics*.

© 1978 Marvel Comics and Hanna-Barbera Productions.

N-MINT

LADY DEATH: DRAGON WARS
Chaos

❑1, Apr 1998 2.95

LADY DEATH IV: THE CRUCIBLE
Chaos!

❑0.5, Nov 1996; Wizard promotional edition 5.00
❑0.5/A; Wizard promotional edition; Cloth alternate cover 8.00
❑1, Nov 1996 3.00
❑1/A, Nov 1996; Leather edition 12.50
❑1/B, Nov 1996; All silver cover; Limited to 400; Comes with certificate of authenticity 16.00
❑1/Silver, Nov 1996; silver embossed cardstock wraparound cover 3.50
❑2, Jan 1997 2.95
❑3, Mar 1997 2.95
❑4, Apr 1997 2.95
❑5, Aug 1997 2.95
❑5/Variant, Aug 1997; Nightmare Premium Edition; no cover price 5.00
❑6, Oct 1997 2.95

LADY DEATH: HEARTBREAKER
Chaos

❑1, Mar 2002 2.99
❑2 2.99
❑3 2.99
❑4 2.99
❑Ashcan 1; ashcan edition 1.00

LADY DEATH IN LINGERIE
Chaos!

❑1, Aug 1995 2.95
❑1/Ltd., Aug 1995; foil-stamped leather premium edition; no cover price; limited to 10, 000 copies 10.00

LADY DEATH: JUDGEMENT WAR
Chaos!

❑1, Nov 1999 2.95
❑2, Dec 1999 2.95
❑3, Jan 2000 2.95

LADY DEATH: JUDGEMENT WAR PRELUDE
Chaos!

❑1, Oct 1999 2.95

LADY DEATH: RETRIBUTION
Chaos!

❑1, Aug 1998 2.95
❑1/A, Aug 1998; Painted alternate cover 3.50
❑1/Ltd., Aug 1998; premium edition 4.00

LADY DEATH SWIMSUIT SPECIAL
Chaos!

❑1, May 1994, b&w 2.50
❑1/Variant, May 1994; Red Velvet edition 8.00

LADY DEATH: THE GAUNTLET
Chaos

❑1, Apr 2002 2.99
❑2, May 2002 2.99

LADY DEATH: THE RAPTURE
Chaos!

❑1, Jun 1999 2.95
❑2, Jul 1999 2.95
❑3, Aug 1999 2.95
❑4, Sep 1999 2.95

N-MINT

LADY DEATH III: THE ODYSSEY
CHAOS!

❑-1, Apr 1996; Sneak Peek Preview; promotional piece for mini-series .. 1.50
❑1, Apr 1996; Gold foil cover 3.50
❑1/Variant, Apr 1996; foil embossed cardstock wraparound cover 5.00
❑2, May 1996 .... 3.00
❑3, Jun 1996 .... 3.00
❑4, Aug 1996 .... 3.00
❑4/A, Aug 1996; alternate cover 8.00

LADY DEATH: TRIBULATION
CHAOS!

❑1, Dec 2000 .... 2.95
❑2, Jan 2001 .... 2.95

LADY DEATH II: BETWEEN HEAVEN & HELL
CHAOS!

❑1, Mar 1995; O: Lady Death. chromium cover 3.50
❑1/A, Mar 1995; Gold edition 4.00
❑1/B, Mar 1995; Black velvet limited edition 5.00
❑1/Ltd., Mar 1995 .... 5.00
❑1-2; Commemorative edition 2.75
❑2, Apr 1995 .... 3.00
❑3, May 1995 .... 3.00
❑4, Jun 1995 .... 3.00
❑4/Variant, Jun 1995; Lady Demon chase cover 5.00

LADY DEATH/VAMPIRELLA: DARK HEARTS
CHAOS!

❑1, Mar 1999; crossover with Harris . 3.50
❑1/A, Mar 1999; Premium edition (5000 printed) 8.00

LADY DEATH VS. PURGATORI
CHAOS!

❑1/A, Dec 1999; Limited to 3,000 copies ....
❑1, Dec 1999; no cover price; red foil logo 3.00

LADY DEATH V. VAMPIRELLA
CHAOS

❑Ashcan 1, Feb 2000; Lady Death/Vampirella II Preview Book 1.00

LADY DEATH: WICKED WAYS
CHAOS!

❑1, Feb 1998 .... 2.95
❑1/Variant, Feb 1998; premium edition; white background cover 5.00

LADY DRACULA
FANTACO

❑1 .... 4.95
❑2 .... 4.95

LADY JUSTICE (VOL. 1) (NEIL GAIMAN'S...)
TEKNO

❑1, Sep 1995 1: Lady Justice. 2.00
❑2, Oct 1995 .... 2.00
❑3, Nov 1995 .... 2.00
❑4, Dec 1995; begins new story-arc with new Lady Justice 2.00
❑5, Dec 1995 .... 2.00
❑6, Jan 1996 .... 2.25
❑7, Jan 1996; stand-alone story 2.25
❑8, Feb 1996 .... 2.25
❑9, Mar 1996 .... 2.25
❑10, Apr 1996 .... 2.25
❑11, May 1996 .... 2.25

LADY JUSTICE (VOL. 2) (NEIL GAIMAN'S...)
BIG

❑1, Jun 1996 .... 2.25
❑2, Jul 1996 .... 2.25
❑3, Aug 1996 .... 2.25
❑4, Sep 1996 .... 2.25
❑5, Oct 1996 .... 2.25
❑6, Nov 1996 .... 2.25
❑7, Dec 1996 .... 2.25

N-MINT

❑8, Jan 1997 .... 2.25
❑9, Feb 1997 .... 2.25

LADY PENDRAGON GALLERY EDITION
IMAGE

❑1, Oct 1999 .... 2.95
❑1/A, Oct 1999; alternate cover 2.95

LADY PENDRAGON: MERLIN
IMAGE

❑1, Jan 2000 .... 2.95

LADY PENDRAGON/MORE THAN MORTAL
IMAGE

❑1, May 1999 .... 2.50
❑1/A, May 1999; alternate cover; white background 4.00
❑1/B, May 1999; DF alternate cover (holding spear facing forward) 5.00
❑Ashcan 1, Feb 1999, b&w; no cover price; preview of upcoming crossover 2.00

LADY PENDRAGON (VOL. 1)
MAXIMUM

❑1, Mar 1996 .... 2.50
❑1/A, Mar 1996; alternate cover 2.50
❑1/Autographed, Mar 1996 .... 6.00
❑1-2, Mar 1996; Remastered edition . 2.50
❑Ashcan 1 .... 4.00
❑Ashcan 1/Autographed 6.00

LADY PENDRAGON (VOL. 2)
IMAGE

❑0, Mar 1999; flipbook with origin back-up 2.50
❑0/A 4.00
❑1, Nov 1998 .... 3.00
❑1/A, Nov 1998; alternate cover; castle 3.00
❑1/B, Nov 1998; Dynamic Forces alternate cover; Swordswoman amid city ruins with sword pointing at sky 3.00
❑1-2, Feb 1999; Lady Pendragon Remastered; reprints #1 with corrections 2.50
❑2, Dec 1998 .... 3.00
❑2/A, Dec 1998; alternate cover 3.00
❑3, Jan 1999; crucified on cover 2.50
❑3/A, Jan 1999; manga-style cover ... 2.50
❑Ashcan 1, Jun 1998; Convention Preview Edition; no cover price 3.00

LADY PENDRAGON (VOL. 3)
IMAGE

❑1, Mar 1999 .... 2.50
❑1/A, Apr 1999; "Stormkote"-covered flip book 2.50
❑1/B, Apr 1999; European Tour Edition 4.00
❑2, Apr 1999 .... 2.50
❑2/A, Apr 1999; alternate cover; Lady Pendragon vanquished 2.50
❑3, Jul 1999 .... 2.50
❑4, Aug 1999 .... 2.50
❑5, Sep 1999 .... 2.50
❑6, Oct 1999 .... 2.50
❑7, Dec 1999; Giant-size 3.95
❑8, Feb 2000 .... 2.50
❑9, Apr 2000 .... 2.50
❑10, Aug 2000 .... 2.50

LADY RAWHIDE
TOPPS

❑1, Jul 1995 .... 2.95
❑2, Sep 1995 .... 2.95
❑3, Nov 1995 .... 2.95
❑4, Jan 1996 .... 2.95
❑5, Mar 1996 .... 2.95

LADY RAWHIDE (VOL. 2)
TOPPS

❑0.5, ca. 1996 1: Star Wolf. 5.00
❑1, Oct 1996 1: Scarlet Fever. 2.95
❑2, Dec 1996 V: Scarlet Fever. 2.95
❑3, Feb 1997 .... 2.95
❑4, Apr 1997, b&w 2.95
❑5, Jun 1997, b&w 2.95

N-MINT

❑6, Aug 1997; Exists? 2.95
❑7, Oct 1997; Exists? 2.95

LADY RAWHIDE MINI COMIC
TOPPS

❑1, Jul 1995; Wizard supplement; no cover price 1.00

LADY RAWHIDE: OTHER PEOPLE'S BLOOD
IMAGE

❑1, Mar 1999 .... 2.95
❑2, Apr 1999 .... 2.95
❑3, May 1999 .... 2.95
❑4, Jun 1999 .... 2.95
❑5, Jul 1999 .... 2.95

LADY RAWHIDE SPECIAL EDITION
TOPPS

❑1, Jun 1995; reprints Zorro #2 and 3 3.95

LADY SPECTRA & SPARKY SPECIAL
J. KEVIN CARRIER

❑1, Jan 1995 .... 2.50

LADY SUPREME
IMAGE

❑1, May 1996; aquamarine background cover 2.50
❑1/A, May 1996; brown background cover 2.50
❑2, Aug 1996; flip-book with New Men Special Preview Edition 2.50

LADY VAMPRÉ
BLACK OUT

❑0 .... 2.95
❑1 .... 2.95

LADY VAMPRÉ: PLEASURES OF THE FLESH
BLACK OUT

❑1, b&w 2.95

LADY VAMPRÉ VS. BLACK LACE
BLACK OUT

❑1, Sep 1996; Flip-book 2.95

LAFF-A-LYMPICS
MARVEL

❑1, Mar 1978; based on Hanna-Barbera animated series 18.00
❑2, Apr 1978 .... 10.00
❑3, May 1978 .... 8.00
❑4, Jun 1978 .... 8.00
❑5, Jul 1978 .... 8.00
❑6, Aug 1978 .... 6.00
❑7, Sep 1978 .... 6.00
❑8, Oct 1978 .... 6.00
❑9, Nov 1978 .... 6.00
❑10, Dec 1978 .... 6.00
❑11, Jan 1979 .... 6.00
❑12, Feb 1979 .... 6.00
❑13, Mar 1979 .... 6.00

LAFFIN' GAS
BLACKTHORNE

❑1, Jun 1986 .... 2.00
❑2 1986 .... 2.00
❑3 1986 .... 2.00
❑4 1986 .... 2.00
❑5 .... 2.00
❑6; 3-D 2.00
❑7, Mar 1987 .... 2.00
❑8 1987 .... 2.00
❑9 1987 .... 2.00
❑10 1987 .... 2.00
❑11 .... 2.00
❑12 .... 2.00

LAMENT OF THE LAMB
TOKYOPOP

❑1, May 2004 .... 9.99

LANCE BARNES: POST NUKE DICK
MARVEL / EPIC

❑1, Apr 1993; Lance accidentally destroys the world 2.50
❑2, May 1993 .... 2.50
❑3, Jun 1993 .... 2.50
❑4, Jul 1993 .... 2.50

N-MINT

LANCELOT LINK, SECRET CHIMP
Gold Key

❑1, May 1971 .... 22.00
❑2, Aug 1971 .... 14.00
❑3, Nov 1971 .... 10.00
❑4, Feb 1972 .... 10.00
❑5, May 1972 .... 10.00
❑6, Aug 1972 .... 10.00
❑7, Nov 1972 .... 10.00
❑8, Feb 1973 .... 10.00

LANCELOT STRONG, THE SHIELD
Archie / Red Circle

❑1, Jun 1983 .... 2.00
❑2, Aug 1983 .... 2.00

LANCER
Gold Key

❑1 1969 .... 25.00
❑2 1969 .... 20.00
❑3, Sep 1969 .... 20.00

LAND OF NOD, THE
Dark Horse

❑1, Jul 1997, b&w 2.95
❑2, Nov 1997, b&w 2.95
❑3, Feb 1998, b&w 2.95
❑4, Jun 1998, b&w 2.95

LAND OF OZ, THE
Arrow

❑1, Nov 1998 .... 2.95
❑2, Jan 1999 .... 2.95
❑3, Mar 1999 .... 2.95
❑4, May 1999 .... 2.95
❑5, Jul 1999 .... 2.95
❑6, Sep 1999 .... 2.95
❑7, Nov 1999 .... 2.95
❑8, Mar 2000 .... 2.95
❑9, Apr 2000 .... 2.95

LAND OF THE GIANTS
Gold Key

❑1, Nov 1968 .... 30.00
❑2, Jan 1969 .... 18.00
❑3, Mar 1969 .... 15.00
❑4 .... 15.00
❑5, Sep 1969 .... 15.00

LANDRA SPECIAL
Alchemy

❑1, b&w 2.00

LANN
Fantagraphics / Eros

❑1, b&w 2.50

LA PACIFICA
DC / Paradox

❑1, b&w; digest 4.95
❑2, b&w; digest 4.95
❑3, b&w; digest 4.95

L.A. PHOENIX
David G. Brown

❑1, Jul 1994, b&w 2.00
❑2, Jul 1995, b&w 2.00
❑3, Jul 1996, b&w 2.00

L.A. RAPTOR
Morbid

❑1 .... 2.95

LARS OF MARS 3-D
Eclipse

❑1, Apr 1987 .... 2.50

LASER ERASER & PRESSBUTTON
Eclipse

❑1, Nov 1985 .... 1.50
❑2, Dec 1985 .... 1.50
❑3 .... 1.50
❑4 .... 1.50
❑5 .... 1.50
❑6 .... 1.50
❑3D 1 .... 2.00

LASH LARUE WESTERN
AC

❑1; some color 3.50
❑Annual 1, b&w 2.95

N-MINT

LASSIE (GOLDEN PRESS)
Golden Press

❑1, ca. 1978; Giant issue reprints stories from Lassie #19, 20, 21, 37, 38, 39, and 40; reprints painted cover from Lassie #30 .... 22.00

LAST AMERICAN, THE
Marvel / Epic

❑1, Dec 1990 .... 2.25
❑2, Jan 1991 .... 2.25
❑3, Feb 1991 .... 2.25
❑4, Mar 1991 .... 2.25

LAST AVENGERS
Marvel

❑1, Nov 1995; Alterniverse story 5.95
❑2, Dec 1995; Alterniverse story 5.95

LAST DANGEROUS CHRISTMAS
Aeon

❑1, b&w; squarebound; benefit comic for neglected and abused children . 5.95

LAST DAYS OF HOLLYWOOD, U.S.A.
Morgan

❑1 .... 2.95
❑2 .... 2.95
❑3 .... 2.95
❑4 .... 2.95
❑5 .... 2.95

LAST DAYS OF THE JUSTICE SOCIETY SPECIAL
DC

❑1, ca. 1986, JSA to Ragnarok after Crisis 3.00

LAST DAZE OF THE BAT-GUY
Mythic

❑1, b&w 2.95

LAST DEFENDER OF CAMELOT, THE
Zim

❑1, b&w 1.95

LAST DITCH
Edge

❑1, b&w 2.50

LAST GASP COMICS AND STORIES
Last Gasp Eco-Funnies

❑1, ca. 1994 .... 3.95
❑2 .... 3.95
❑3, b&w 3.95
❑4 .... 3.95

LAST GENERATION, THE
Black Tie

❑1 1987 .... 1.95
❑2 .... 1.95
❑3 .... 1.95
❑4 .... 1.95
❑5 1989 .... 1.95

LAST KISS
Eclipse

❑1, ca. 1990, b&w 3.95

LAST KISS (SHANDA)
Shanda

❑1, Feb 2001 .... 4.95
❑2, Aug 2001 .... 4.95
❑3, Feb 2002 .... 4.95

LAST KNIGHT, THE
NBM

❑1 .... 15.95

LAST OF THE DRAGONS
Marvel / Epic

❑1 .... 6.95

LAST OF THE VIKING HEROES, THE
Genesis West

❑1, Mar 1987 .... 1.50
❑2, Jun 1987 .... 2.00
❑3 .... 1.75
❑4 .... 1.75
❑5/A, Jun 1988 .... 1.95
❑5/B 1988 .... 1.95
❑6 1988 .... 1.95
❑7, Jan 1989 .... 1.95

Laugh Comics offers yet another venue for the adventures of the Archie gang.

© 1977 Archie Comic Publications Inc.

N-MINT

❑8, Jul 1989 .... 1.95
❑9 .... 1.95
❑10 .... 2.50
❑11 .... 2.50
❑12 .... 2.50
❑Summer 1, Mar 1988; digest; Summer Special #1 .... 2.50
❑Summer 2; Signed, numbered edition signed by authors; Summer Special #2 2.50
❑Summer 3, Apr 1991; Wizard mail-in promotional edition; Summer Special #3 .... 2.50

LAST ONE, THE
DC / Vertigo

❑1, Jul 1993 .... 2.50
❑2, Aug 1993 .... 2.50
❑3, Sep 1993 .... 2.50
❑4, Oct 1993 .... 2.50
❑5, Nov 1993 .... 2.50
❑6, Dec 1993 .... 2.50

LAST PLANET, THE
MBS

❑1 .... 2.50

LAST SHOT
Image

❑1, Aug 2001 .... 2.95
❑2, Oct 2001 .... 2.95
❑3, Dec 2001 .... 2.95
❑4, Mar 2002 .... 2.95

LAST SHOT: FIRST DRAW
Image

❑1, May 2001 .... 2.95

LAST STARFIGHTER, THE
Marvel

❑1, Oct 1984 .... 2.00
❑2, Nov 1984 .... 2.00
❑3, Dec 1984 .... 2.00

LAST TEMPTATION, THE
Marvel Music

❑1, May 1994 .... 4.95
❑1/A, May 1994; Variant cover with white background; came with the CD 4.95
❑2, Aug 1994 .... 4.95
❑3, Dec 1994 .... 4.95

LATIGO KID WESTERN
AC

❑1, b&w 1.95

LAUGH COMICS
Archie

❑77, Oct 1956 .... 25.00
❑78, Dec 1956 .... 25.00
❑79, Feb 1957 .... 25.00
❑80, Apr 1957 .... 25.00
❑81, Jun 1957 .... 20.00
❑82, Aug 1957 .... 20.00
❑83, Oct 1957 .... 20.00
❑84, Dec 1957 .... 20.00
❑85, Feb 1958 .... 20.00
❑86, Apr 1958 .... 20.00
❑87, Jun 1958 .... 20.00
❑88, Jul 1958 .... 20.00
❑89, Aug 1958 .... 20.00
❑90, Sep 1958 .... 20.00
❑91, Oct 1958 .... 18.00
❑92, Nov 1958 .... 18.00
❑93, Dec 1958 .... 18.00

	N-MINT
❑94, Jan 1959	18.00
❑95, Feb 1959	18.00
❑96, Mar 1959	18.00
❑97, Apr 1959	18.00
❑98, May 1959	18.00
❑99, Jun 1959	18.00
❑100, Jul 1959	18.00
❑101, Aug 1959	15.00
❑102, Sep 1959	15.00
❑103, Oct 1959	15.00
❑104, Nov 1959	15.00
❑105, Dec 1959	15.00
❑106, Jan 1960	15.00
❑107, Feb 1960	15.00
❑108, Mar 1960	15.00
❑109, Apr 1960	15.00
❑110, May 1960	15.00
❑111, Jun 1960	15.00
❑112, Jul 1960	15.00
❑113, Aug 1960	15.00
❑114, Sep 1960	15.00
❑115, Oct 1960	15.00
❑116, Nov 1960	15.00
❑117, Dec 1960	15.00
❑118, Jan 1961	15.00
❑119, Feb 1961	15.00
❑120, Mar 1961	15.00
❑121, Apr 1961	15.00
❑122, May 1961	15.00
❑123, Jun 1961	15.00
❑124, Jul 1961	15.00
❑125, Aug 1961	15.00
❑126, Sep 1961	15.00
❑127, Oct 1961	15.00
❑128, Nov 1961	15.00
❑129, Dec 1961	15.00
❑130, Jan 1962	15.00
❑131, Feb 1962	12.00
❑132, Mar 1962	12.00
❑133, Apr 1962	12.00
❑134, May 1962	12.00
❑135, Jun 1962	12.00
❑136, Jul 1962	12.00
❑137, Aug 1962	12.00
❑138, Sep 1962	12.00
❑139, Oct 1962	12.00
❑140, Nov 1962	12.00
❑141, Dec 1962	12.00
❑142, Jan 1963	12.00
❑143, Feb 1963	12.00
❑144, Mar 1963	12.00
❑145, Apr 1963	12.00
❑146, May 1963	12.00
❑147, Jun 1963	12.00
❑148, Jul 1963	12.00
❑149, Aug 1963	12.00
❑150, Sep 1963	12.00
❑151, Oct 1963	12.00
❑152, Nov 1963	12.00
❑153, Dec 1963	12.00
❑154, Jan 1964	12.00
❑155, Feb 1964	12.00
❑156, Mar 1964	12.00
❑157, Apr 1964	12.00
❑158, May 1964	12.00
❑159, Jun 1964	12.00
❑160, Jul 1964	12.00
❑161, Aug 1964	12.00
❑162, Sep 1964	12.00
❑163, Oct 1964	12.00
❑164, Nov 1964	12.00
❑165, Dec 1964	12.00
❑166, Jan 1965	12.00
❑167, Feb 1965	12.00
❑168, Mar 1965	12.00
❑169, Apr 1965	12.00
❑170, May 1965	12.00
❑171, Jun 1965	9.00
❑172, Jul 1965	9.00
❑173, Aug 1965	9.00
❑174, Sep 1965	9.00

	N-MINT
❑175, Oct 1965	9.00
❑176, Nov 1965	9.00
❑177, Dec 1965	9.00
❑178, Jan 1966	9.00
❑179, Feb 1966	9.00
❑180, Mar 1966	9.00
❑181, Apr 1966	9.00
❑182, May 1966	9.00
❑183, Jun 1966	9.00
❑184, Jul 1966	9.00
❑185, Aug 1966	9.00
❑186, Sep 1966	9.00
❑187, Oct 1966	9.00
❑188, Nov 1966	9.00
❑189, Dec 1966	9.00
❑190, Jan 1967	8.00
❑191, Feb 1967	8.00
❑192, Mar 1967	8.00
❑193, Apr 1967	8.00
❑194, May 1967	8.00
❑195, Jun 1967	8.00
❑196, Jul 1967	8.00
❑197, Aug 1967	8.00
❑198, Sep 1967	8.00
❑199, Oct 1967	8.00
❑200, Nov 1967	8.00
❑201, Dec 1967	6.00
❑202, Jan 1968	6.00
❑203, Feb 1968	6.00
❑204, Mar 1968	6.00
❑205, Apr 1968	6.00
❑206, May 1968	6.00
❑207, Jun 1968	6.00
❑208, Jul 1968	6.00
❑209, Aug 1968	6.00
❑210, Sep 1968	6.00
❑211, Oct 1968	6.00
❑212, Nov 1968	6.00
❑213, Dec 1968	6.00
❑214, Jan 1969	6.00
❑215, Feb 1969	6.00
❑216, Mar 1969	6.00
❑217, Apr 1969	6.00
❑218, May 1969	6.00
❑219, Jun 1969	6.00
❑220, Jul 1969	6.00
❑221, Aug 1969	6.00
❑222, Sep 1969	6.00
❑223, Oct 1969	6.00
❑224, Nov 1969	6.00
❑225, Dec 1969	6.00
❑226, Jan 1970; Title changes to Laugh	6.00
❑227, Feb 1970	6.00
❑228, Mar 1970	6.00
❑229, Apr 1970	6.00
❑230, May 1970	6.00
❑231, Jun 1970	6.00
❑232, Jul 1970	6.00
❑233, Aug 1970	6.00
❑234, Sep 1970	6.00
❑235, Oct 1970	6.00
❑236, Nov 1970	6.00
❑237, Dec 1970	6.00
❑238, Jan 1971	6.00
❑239, Feb 1971	6.00
❑240, Mar 1971	6.00
❑241, Apr 1971	6.00
❑242, May 1971	6.00
❑243, Jun 1971	6.00
❑244, Jul 1971	6.00
❑245, Aug 1971	6.00
❑246, Sep 1971	6.00
❑247, Oct 1971	6.00
❑248, Nov 1971	6.00
❑249, Dec 1971	6.00
❑250, Jan 1972	6.00
❑251, Feb 1972	4.00
❑252, Mar 1972	4.00
❑253, Apr 1972	4.00
❑254, May 1972	4.00
❑255, Jun 1972	4.00

	N-MINT
❑256, Jul 1972	4.00
❑257, Aug 1972	4.00
❑258, Sep 1972	4.00
❑259, Oct 1972	4.00
❑260, Nov 1972	4.00
❑261, Dec 1972	4.00
❑262, Jan 1973	4.00
❑263, Feb 1973	4.00
❑264, Mar 1973	4.00
❑265, Apr 1973	4.00
❑266, May 1973	4.00
❑267, Jun 1973	4.00
❑268, Jul 1973	4.00
❑269, Aug 1973	4.00
❑270, Sep 1973	4.00
❑271, Oct 1973	4.00
❑272, Nov 1973	4.00
❑273, Dec 1973	4.00
❑274, Jan 1974	4.00
❑275, Feb 1974	4.00
❑276, Mar 1974	4.00
❑277, Apr 1974	4.00
❑278, May 1974	4.00
❑279, Jun 1974	4.00
❑280, Jul 1974	4.00
❑281, Aug 1974	4.00
❑282, Sep 1974	4.00
❑283, Oct 1974	4.00
❑284, Nov 1974	4.00
❑285, Dec 1974	4.00
❑286, Jan 1975	4.00
❑287, Feb 1975	4.00
❑288, Mar 1975	4.00
❑289, Apr 1975	4.00
❑290, May 1975	4.00
❑291, Jun 1975	4.00
❑292, Jul 1975	4.00
❑293, Aug 1975	4.00
❑294, Sep 1975	4.00
❑295, Oct 1975	4.00
❑296, Nov 1975	4.00
❑297, Dec 1975	4.00
❑298, Jan 1976	4.00
❑299, Feb 1976	4.00
❑300, Mar 1976	4.00
❑301, Apr 1976	2.50
❑302, May 1976	2.50
❑303, Jun 1976	2.50
❑304, Jul 1976	2.50
❑305, Aug 1976	2.50
❑306, Sep 1976	2.50
❑307, Oct 1976	2.50
❑308, Nov 1976	2.50
❑309, Dec 1976	2.50
❑310, Jan 1977	2.50
❑311, Feb 1977	2.50
❑312, Mar 1977	2.50
❑313, Apr 1977	2.50
❑314, May 1977	2.50
❑315, Jun 1977	2.50
❑316, Jul 1977	2.50
❑317, Aug 1977	2.50
❑318, Sep 1977	2.50
❑319, Oct 1977	2.50
❑320, Nov 1977 A: Reggie. A: Betty. A: Li'l Jinx. A: Archie. A: Mr. Lodge. A: Jughead. A: Veronica. A: Moose. A: Fat Charley.	2.50
❑321, Dec 1977	2.50
❑322, Jan 1978	2.50
❑323, Feb 1978	2.50
❑324, Mar 1978	2.50
❑325, Apr 1978	2.50
❑326, May 1978	2.50
❑327, Jun 1978	2.50
❑328, Jul 1978	2.50
❑329, Aug 1978	2.50
❑330, Sep 1978	2.50
❑331, Oct 1978	2.50
❑332, Nov 1978	2.50
❑333, Dec 1978	2.50
❑334, Jan 1979	2.50

	N-MINT
❑335, Feb 1979	2.50
❑336, Mar 1979	2.50
❑337, Apr 1979	2.50
❑338, May 1979	2.50
❑339, Jun 1979	2.50
❑340, Jul 1979	2.50
❑341, Aug 1979	2.50
❑342, Sep 1979	2.50
❑343, Oct 1979	2.50
❑344, Nov 1979	2.50
❑345, Dec 1979	2.50
❑346, Jan 1980	2.50
❑347, Feb 1980	2.50
❑348, Mar 1980	2.50
❑349, Apr 1980	2.50
❑350, May 1980	2.50
❑351, Jun 1980	2.00
❑352, Jul 1980	2.00
❑353, Aug 1980	2.00
❑354, Sep 1980	2.00
❑355, Oct 1980	2.00
❑356, Nov 1980	2.00
❑357, Dec 1980	2.00
❑358, Jan 1981	2.00
❑359, Feb 1981	2.00
❑360, Mar 1981	2.00
❑361, Apr 1981	2.00
❑362, May 1981	2.00
❑363, Jun 1981	2.00
❑364, Jul 1981	2.00
❑365, Aug 1981	2.00
❑366, Sep 1981	2.00
❑367, Oct 1981	2.00
❑368, Nov 1981	2.00
❑369, Dec 1981	2.00
❑370, Jan 1982	2.00
❑371, Feb 1982	2.00
❑372, May 1982	2.00
❑373, Jul 1982	2.00
❑374, Sep 1982	2.00
❑375, Nov 1982	2.00
❑376, Jan 1983	2.00
❑377, Apr 1983	2.00
❑378, Jul 1983	2.00
❑379, Oct 1983	2.00
❑380, Dec 1983	2.00
❑381, Feb 1984	2.00
❑382, Apr 1984	2.00
❑383, Jun 1984	2.00
❑384, Aug 1984	2.00
❑385, Oct 1984	2.00
❑386, Dec 1984	2.00
❑387, Feb 1985	2.00
❑388, Apr 1985	2.00
❑389, Jun 1985	2.00
❑390, Aug 1985	2.00
❑391, Oct 1985	2.00
❑392, Dec 1985	2.00
❑393, Feb 1986	2.00
❑394, Apr 1986	2.00
❑395, Jun 1986	2.00
❑396, Aug 1986	2.00
❑397, Oct 1986	2.00
❑398, Dec 1986	2.00
❑399, Feb 1987	2.00
❑400, Apr 1987	2.00

LAUGH (VOL. 2)
ARCHIE

	N-MINT
❑1, Jun 1987	3.00
❑2, Aug 1987	2.00
❑3, Oct 1987	2.00
❑4, Dec 1987	2.00
❑5, Feb 1988	2.00
❑6, Apr 1988	1.00
❑7, Jun 1988	1.00
❑8, Jul 1988	1.00
❑9, Aug 1988	1.00
❑10, Oct 1988	1.00
❑11, Dec 1988	1.00
❑12, Feb 1989	1.00
❑13, Apr 1989	1.00
❑14, Jun 1989	1.00
❑15, Jul 1989	1.00
❑16, Aug 1989	1.00
❑17, Oct 1989	1.00
❑18, Dec 1989	1.00
❑19, Feb 1990	1.00
❑20, Apr 1990	1.00
❑21, Jun 1990	1.00
❑22, Jul 1990	1.00
❑23, Aug 1990	1.00
❑24, Oct 1990	1.00
❑25, Dec 1990	1.00
❑26, Feb 1991	1.00
❑27, Apr 1991	1.00
❑28, Jun 1991	1.00
❑29, Aug 1991	1.00

LAUGH DIGEST MAGAZINE
ARCHIE

	N-MINT
❑1, Aug 1974 NA (a)	10.00
❑2, Jan 1976	8.00
❑3, Mar 1976	8.00
❑4, May 1976	8.00
❑5, Jul 1976	8.00
❑6, Sep 1976	4.00
❑7, Nov 1976	4.00
❑8, Jan 1977	4.00
❑9, Mar 1977	4.00
❑10, May 1977	4.00
❑11, Jul 1977	3.00
❑12, Sep 1977	3.00
❑13, Nov 1977	3.00
❑14, Jan 1978	3.00
❑15, Mar 1978	3.00
❑16, May 1978	3.00
❑17, Jul 1978	3.00
❑18, Sep 1978	3.00
❑19, Nov 1978	3.00
❑20, Jan 1979	3.00
❑21, Mar 1979	2.00
❑22, May 1979	2.00
❑23, Jul 1979	2.00
❑24, Sep 1979	2.00
❑25, Nov 1979	2.00
❑26, Jan 1980	2.00
❑27, Mar 1980	2.00
❑28, May 1980	2.00
❑29, Jul 1980	2.00
❑30, Sep 1980	2.00
❑31, Nov 1980	2.00
❑32, Jan 1981	2.00
❑33, Mar 1981	2.00
❑34, May 1981	2.00
❑35, Jul 1981	2.00
❑36, Sep 1981	2.00
❑37, Nov 1981	2.00
❑38, Jan 1982	2.00
❑39, Mar 1982	2.00
❑40, May 1982	2.00
❑41, Jul 1982	1.50
❑42, Sep 1982	1.50
❑43, Nov 1982	1.50
❑44, Jan 1983	1.50
❑45, Mar 1983	1.50
❑46, May 1983	1.50
❑47, Jul 1983	1.50
❑48, Sep 1983	1.50
❑49, Nov 1983	1.50
❑50, Jan 1984	1.50
❑51, Mar 1984	1.50
❑52, May 1984	1.50
❑53, Jul 1984	1.50
❑54, Sep 1984	1.50
❑55, Nov 1984	1.50
❑56, Jan 1985	1.50
❑57, Mar 1985	1.50
❑58, May 1985	1.50
❑59, Jul 1985	1.50
❑60, Sep 1985	1.50
❑61, Nov 1985	1.50
❑62, Jan 1986	1.50
❑63, Mar 1986	1.50

Alan Moore teamed characters from a number of literary adventures in *The League of Extraordinary Gentlemen.*

© 1999 Alan Moore (America's Best Comics).

	N-MINT
❑64, May 1986	1.50
❑65, Jul 1986	1.50
❑66, Sep 1986	1.50
❑67, Nov 1986	1.50
❑68, Jan 1987	1.50
❑69, Mar 1987	1.50
❑70, May 1987	1.50
❑71, Jul 1987	1.50
❑72, Sep 1987	1.50
❑73, Nov 1987	1.50
❑74, Jan 1988	1.50
❑75, Mar 1988	1.50
❑76, May 1988	1.50
❑77, Jul 1988	1.50
❑78, Sep 1988	1.50
❑79, Nov 1988	1.50
❑80, Jan 1989	1.50
❑81, Mar 1989	1.50
❑82, May 1989	1.50
❑83, Jul 1989	1.50
❑84, Sep 1989	1.50
❑85, Nov 1989	1.50
❑86, Jan 1990	1.50
❑87, Mar 1990	1.50
❑88, May 1990	1.50
❑89, Jul 1990	1.50
❑90, Sep 1990	1.50
❑91, Nov 1990	1.50
❑92, Jan 1991	1.50
❑93, Mar 1991	1.50
❑94, ca. 1991	1.50
❑95, ca. 1991	1.50
❑96, ca. 1991	1.50
❑97, ca. 1991	1.50
❑98	1.50
❑99, ca. 1992	1.50
❑100, ca. 1992	1.50
❑101, ca. 1992	1.50
❑102, ca. 1992	1.50
❑103, ca. 1992	1.50
❑104, ca. 1992	1.50
❑105, ca. 1992	1.50
❑106, ca. 1993	1.50
❑107, May 1993	1.50
❑108, Jul 1993	1.50
❑109, Sep 1993	1.50
❑110, Nov 1993	1.50
❑111, Dec 1994	1.50
❑112, Feb 1994	1.50
❑113, ca. 1994	1.50
❑114, ca. 1994	1.50
❑115, ca. 1994	1.50
❑116, ca. 1994	1.50
❑117, Nov 1994	1.75
❑118, Jan 1995	1.75
❑119, Mar 1995	1.75
❑120, May 1995	1.75
❑121, Jul 1995	1.75
❑122, Sep 1995	1.75
❑123, Nov 1995	1.75
❑124, Dec 1995	1.75
❑125, Feb 1996	1.75
❑126, Apr 1996	1.75
❑127, May 1996	1.75
❑128, Jul 1996	1.75
❑129, Sep 1996	1.79
❑130, Oct 1996	1.79

N-MINT

- ❑131, Dec 1996 .... 1.79
- ❑132, Feb 1997 .... 1.79
- ❑133, Apr 1997 .... 1.79
- ❑134, May 1997 .... 1.79
- ❑135, Jul 1997 .... 1.79
- ❑136, Sep 1997 .... 1.79
- ❑137, Oct 1997 .... 1.79
- ❑138, Dec 1997 .... 1.79
- ❑139, Jan 1998 .... 1.95
- ❑140, Mar 1998 .... 1.95
- ❑141, May 1998 .... 1.95
- ❑142, Jul 1998 .... 1.95
- ❑143, Aug 1998 .... 1.95
- ❑144, Oct 1998 .... 1.95
- ❑145, Nov 1998 DDC (a) 1.95
- ❑146, Jan 1999 .... 1.95
- ❑147, Mar 1999 .... 1.95
- ❑148, Apr 1999 .... 1.99
- ❑149, May 1999 .... 1.99
- ❑150, Jul 1999 .... 1.99
- ❑151, Aug 1999 .... 1.99
- ❑152, Oct 1999 .... 1.99
- ❑153, Nov 1999 .... 1.99
- ❑154, Jan 2000 .... 1.99
- ❑155, Mar 2000 .... 1.99
- ❑156, May 2000 .... 1.99
- ❑157, Jul 2000 .... 2.19
- ❑158, Aug 2000 .... 2.19
- ❑159, Oct 2000 .... 2.19
- ❑160, Nov 2000 .... 2.19
- ❑161, Dec 2000 .... 2.19
- ❑162, Jan 2001 .... 2.19
- ❑163, Feb 2001 .... 2.19
- ❑164, Apr 2001 .... 2.19
- ❑165, May 2001 .... 2.19
- ❑166, Jul 2001 .... 2.19
- ❑167, Aug 2001 .... 2.19
- ❑168, Oct 2001 .... 2.19
- ❑169, Nov 2001 .... 2.19
- ❑170, Dec 2001 .... 2.19
- ❑171, Jan 2002 .... 2.19
- ❑172, Mar 2002 .... 2.19
- ❑173, May 2002 .... 2.19
- ❑174, Jul 2002 .... 2.19
- ❑175, Aug 2002 .... 2.19
- ❑176, Sep 2002 .... 2.19
- ❑177, Nov 2002 .... 2.19
- ❑178, Dec 2002 .... 2.19
- ❑179, Jan 2003 .... 2.19
- ❑180, Feb 2003 .... 2.39
- ❑181, Mar 2003 .... 2.39
- ❑182, May 2003 .... 2.39
- ❑183, Jun 2003 .... 2.39
- ❑184, Jul 2003 .... 2.39
- ❑185, Sep 2003 .... 2.39
- ❑186, Oct 2003 .... 2.39
- ❑187, Nov 2003 .... 2.39
- ❑188, Dec 2003 .... 2.39
- ❑189, Feb 2004 .... 2.39
- ❑190, Mar 2004 .... 2.39
- ❑191, May 2004 .... 2.39
- ❑192, Jun 2004 .... 2.39
- ❑193, Jul 2004 .... 2.39

LAUNCH!
ELSEWHERE

- ❑1 .... 1.75

LAUNDRYLAND
FANTAGRAPHICS

- ❑1, b&w 2.25
- ❑2, Jun 1991, b&w 2.50
- ❑3, b&w 2.50
- ❑4, b&w 2.50

LAUREL AND HARDY (GOLD KEY)
GOLD KEY

- ❑1, Jan 1967 .... 24.00
- ❑2, Oct 1967 .... 18.00

LAUREL AND HARDY (DC)
DC

- ❑1, Aug 1972 .... 40.00

LAUREL & HARDY IN 3-D
BLACKTHORNE

- ❑1, Fal 1987; aka Blackthorne 3-D #23 .... 2.50
- ❑2, Dec 1987; aka Blackthorne 3-D #34 .... 2.50

LAVA
CROSSBREED

- ❑1 .... 2.95

LAW, THE
ASYLUM GRAPHICS

- ❑1, b&w; no publication date 1.75

LAW AND ORDER
MAXIMUM

- ❑1, Sep 1995 .... 2.50
- ❑1/A, Sep 1995; Alternate cover with women standing atop body 2.50
- ❑2, Oct 1995 .... 2.50
- ❑3, Nov 1995 .... 2.50

LAWDOG
MARVEL / EPIC

- ❑1, May 1993; Embossed cover 2.50
- ❑2, Jun 1993 .... 1.95
- ❑3, Jul 1993 .... 1.95
- ❑4, Aug 1993 .... 1.95
- ❑5, Sep 1993 .... 1.95
- ❑6, Oct 1993 .... 1.95
- ❑7, Nov 1993 .... 1.95
- ❑8, Dec 1993; trading card 1.95
- ❑9, Jan 1994 .... 1.95
- ❑10, Feb 1994 .... 1.95

LAWDOG AND GRIMROD: TERROR AT THE CROSSROADS
MARVEL / EPIC

- ❑1, Sep 1993 .... 3.50

L.A.W., THE (LIVING ASSAULT WEAPONS)
DC

- ❑1, Sep 1999 .... 2.50
- ❑2, Oct 1999 .... 2.50
- ❑3, Nov 1999 .... 2.50
- ❑4, Dec 1999 .... 2.50
- ❑5, Jan 2000 .... 2.50
- ❑6, Feb 2000 .... 2.50

LAW OF DREDD, THE
FLEETWAY-QUALITY

- ❑1; BB (a);Reprints Judge Dredd stories from 2000 A.D. #149- 1.50
- ❑2 .... 1.50
- ❑3 V: Judge Death. 1.50
- ❑4 .... 1.50
- ❑5 .... 1.50
- ❑6 .... 1.50
- ❑7 .... 1.50
- ❑8 .... 1.50
- ❑9 .... 1.75
- ❑10 .... 1.75
- ❑11 .... 1.75
- ❑12 .... 1.75
- ❑13 A: Judge Caligula. 1.75
- ❑14 .... 1.75
- ❑15 .... 1.75
- ❑16 .... 1.75
- ❑17 .... 1.75
- ❑18 .... 1.75
- ❑19 .... 1.75
- ❑20 .... 1.75
- ❑21 .... 1.75
- ❑22 .... 1.75
- ❑23 .... 1.75
- ❑24 .... 1.75
- ❑25 .... 1.75
- ❑26 .... 1.75
- ❑27 .... 1.75
- ❑28 .... 1.75
- ❑29 .... 1.75
- ❑30 .... 1.95
- ❑31 .... 1.95
- ❑32 .... 1.95
- ❑33 .... 1.95

LAZARUS CHURCHYARD
TUNDRA

- ❑1 .... 4.50
- ❑2 .... 4.50
- ❑3 .... 4.95

LAZARUS FIVE
DC

- ❑1, Jul 2000 .... 2.50
- ❑2, Aug 2000 .... 2.50
- ❑3, Sep 2000 .... 2.50
- ❑4, Oct 2000 .... 2.50
- ❑5, Nov 2000 .... 2.50

LAZARUS PITS, THE
BONEYARD

- ❑1, Feb 1993, b&w; b&w pin-ups, cardstock cover 4.00

LEAF
NAB

- ❑1 .... 1.95
- ❑1/Deluxe; deluxe 4.95
- ❑2 .... 1.95

LEAGUE OF CHAMPIONS, THE
HERO

- ❑1, Dec 1990 .... 3.00
- ❑2, Feb 1991 O: Malice (true origin). . 3.00
- ❑3, Apr 1991 .... 3.00
- ❑4, b&w 3.50
- ❑5, b&w 3.50
- ❑6, b&w 3.50
- ❑7, Nov 1992, b&w A: the Southern Knights. 3.50
- ❑8, b&w 3.50
- ❑9, b&w 3.50
- ❑10, b&w 3.50
- ❑11, b&w 3.95
- ❑12, Jul 1993 .... 2.95

LEAGUE OF EXTRAORDINARY GENTLEMEN, THE
DC / AMERICA'S BEST COMICS

- ❑1, Mar 1999 AMo (w) 6.00
- ❑1/A, Apr 1999; AMo (w); DF Alternate; 5000 copies 5.00
- ❑2, Apr 1999 AMo (w) 5.00
- ❑3, May 1999 AMo (w) 4.00
- ❑4, Nov 1999 AMo (w) 4.00
- ❑5, Jun 2000 AMo (w) 4.00
- ❑5/A, Jun 2000; AMo (w); Contained fake ad for The Marvel; All but est. 200 destroyed by DC 25.00
- ❑6, Sep 2000 AMo (w) 4.00

LEAGUE OF EXTRAORDINARY GENTLEMEN, THE (VOL. 2)
AMERICA'S BEST

- ❑1, Sep 2002 .... 4.00
- ❑2, Oct 2002 .... 3.50
- ❑3, Nov 2002 .... 3.50
- ❑4, Feb 2003 AMo (w) 3.50
- ❑5, Jul 2003 .... 3.50
- ❑6, Nov 2003 .... 3.50

LEAGUE OF JUSTICE
DC

- ❑1; prestige format; Elseworlds 5.95
- ❑2; prestige format; Elseworlds 5.95

LEAGUE OF RATS, THE
CALIBER / TOME

- ❑1, b&w 2.95

LEAGUE OF SUPER GROOVY CRIMEFIGHTERS
ANCIENT

- ❑1, Jun 2000 .... 2.95
- ❑2, Dec 2000, b&w 2.95
- ❑3 2001, b&w 2.95
- ❑4, May 2001, b&w; published after #3, but dated before 2.95
- ❑5 2001 .... 2.95

LEATHER & LACE
AIRCEL

- ❑1/A, Aug 1989, b&w; Adult version . 2.50
- ❑1/B, Aug 1989, b&w; Tame version . 1.95
- ❑2/A, Sep 1989, b&w; Adult version . 2.50

N-MINT

❑2/B, Sep 1989, b&w; Tame version . 1.95
❑3/A, Oct 1989, b&w; Adult version .. 2.50
❑3/B, Oct 1989, b&w; Tame version .. 1.95
❑4/A, Nov 1989, b&w; Adult version . 2.50
❑4/B, Nov 1989, b&w; Tame version . 1.95
❑5/A, Dec 1989, b&w; Adult version . 2.50
❑5/B, Dec 1989, b&w; Tame version . 1.95
❑6/A, Jan 1990, b&w; Adult version .. 2.50
❑6/B, Jan 1990, b&w; Tame version . 1.95
❑7/A, Feb 1990, b&w; Adult version .. 2.50
❑7/B, Feb 1990, b&w; Tame version . 1.95
❑8/A, Mar 1990, b&w; Adult version . 2.50
❑8/B, Mar 1990, b&w; Tame version . 1.95
❑9, Apr 1990, b&w 2.50
❑10, May 1990, b&w 2.50
❑11, Jun 1990, b&w 2.50
❑12, Jul 1990, b&w 2.50
❑13, Aug 1990, b&w 2.50
❑14, Sep 1990, b&w 2.50
❑15, Oct 1990, b&w 2.50
❑16, Nov 1990, b&w 2.50
❑17, Dec 1990, b&w 2.50
❑18, Jan 1991, b&w 2.50
❑19, Feb 1991, b&w 2.50
❑20, Mar 1991, b&w 2.50
❑21, Apr 1991, b&w 2.50
❑22, May 1991, b&w 2.95
❑23, Jun 1991, b&w 2.95
❑24, Jul 1991, b&w 2.95
❑25, Aug 1991, b&w 2.95

LEATHER & LACE: BLOOD, SEX, & TEARS
AIRCEL

❑1, Oct 1991, b&w 2.95
❑2, Nov 1991, b&w 2.95
❑3, Dec 1991, b&w 2.95
❑4, Jan 1992 2.95

LEATHER & LACE SUMMER SPECIAL
AIRCEL

❑1, Jun 1990, b&w 2.50

LEATHERBOY
FANTAGRAPHICS / EROS

❑1, Jul 1994 2.95
❑2, Oct 1994 2.95
❑3, Nov 1994 2.95

LEATHERFACE
ARPAD

❑1, Apr 1991 2.75

LEATHER UNDERWEAR
FANTAGRAPHICS

❑1, b&w 2.50

LEAVE IT TO BEAVER
DELL

❑-207, Jul 1962; No number; cover says 01-428-207; previous issues appeared as Dell Four Color (2nd Series) #912, #999, #1103, #1191, and #1285 100.00

LEAVE IT TO CHANCE
IMAGE

❑1, Sep 1996 JRo (w); PS (a) 3.00
❑1-2 JRo (w); PS (a) 2.50
❑2, Oct 1996 JRo (w); PS (a) 3.00
❑3, Nov 1996 JRo (w); PS (a) 3.00
❑4, Feb 1997 JRo (w); PS (a) 3.00
❑5, May 1997 JRo (w); PS (a) 3.00
❑6, Jul 1997 JRo (w); PS (a) 2.50
❑7, Oct 1997 JRo (w); PS (a) 2.50
❑8, Feb 1998 JRo (w); PS (a) 2.50
❑9, Apr 1998 JRo (w); PS (a) 2.50
❑10, Jun 1998 JRo (w); PS (a) 2.50
❑11, Sep 1998 JRo (w); PS (a) 2.95
❑12, Jun 1999 JRo (w); PS (a) 2.95

LED ZEPPELIN
PERSONALITY

❑1, b&w 2.95
❑2, b&w 2.95
❑3, b&w 2.95
❑4, b&w 2.95

N-MINT

LED ZEPPELIN EXPERIENCE, THE
REVOLUTIONARY

❑1, Aug 1992, b&w 2.50
❑2, Oct 1992, b&w 2.50
❑3, Dec 1992, b&w 2.50
❑4, Jan 1993, b&w 2.50
❑5, Feb 1993, b&w 2.50

LEFT-FIELD FUNNIES
APEX NOVELTIES

❑1 4.00

LEGACY
MAJESTIC

❑0, Aug 1993 2.25
❑0/Gold, Aug 1993 2.25
❑1, Oct 1993 2.25
❑2, Jan 1994 2.25

LEGACY (FRED PERRY'S...)
ANTARCTIC

❑1, Aug 1999 2.99

LEGACY (IMAGE)
IMAGE

❑1, May 2003 2.95
❑2, Jul 2003 2.95
❑3, Nov 2003 2.95
❑4, Apr 2004 2.95

LEGACY OF KAIN: DEFIANCE ONE SHOT
IMAGE

❑1, Jan 2004 2.99

LEGACY OF KAIN: SOUL REAVER
TOP COW

❑1, Oct 1999 2.00

LEGEND LORE (ARROW)
ARROW

❑1, b&w 2.00
❑2, b&w 2.00

LEGENDLORE (CALIBER)
CALIBER

❑1 2.95
❑2 2.95
❑3 2.95
❑4 2.95

LEGENDLORE: WRATH OF THE DRAGON
CALIBER

❑1; A.k.a. LegendLore #13 2.95
❑2; A.k.a. LegendLore #14 2.95

LEGEND OF JEDIT OJANEN ON THE WORLD OF MAGIC: THE GATHERING
ACCLAIM / ARMADA

❑1, Mar 1996; polybagged with card . 2.50
❑2, Apr 1996 2.50

LEGEND OF KAMUI, THE
ECLIPSE / VIZ

❑1, May 1987, b&w; Japanese 3.00
❑1-2 1.50
❑2, Jun 1987 2.00
❑2-2 1.50
❑3, Jun 1987 2.00
❑3-2 1.50
❑4, Jul 1987 1.50
❑5, Jul 1987 1.50
❑6, Aug 1987 1.50
❑7, Aug 1987 1.50
❑8, Sep 1987 1.50
❑9, Sep 1987 1.50
❑10, Oct 1987 1.50
❑11, Oct 1987 1.50
❑12, Nov 1987 1.50
❑13, Nov 1987 1.50
❑14, Dec 1987 1.50
❑15, Dec 1987 1.50
❑16, Jan 1988 1.50
❑17, Jan 1988 1.50
❑18, Feb 1988 1.50
❑19, Feb 1988 1.50
❑20, Mar 1988 1.50
❑21, Mar 1988 1.50

DC's first multi-title crossover after *Crisis on Infinite Earths* was *Legends*.

© 1986 DC Comics.

N-MINT

❑22, Apr 1988 1.50
❑23, Apr 1988 1.50
❑24, May 1988 1.50
❑25, May 1988 1.50
❑26, Jun 1988 1.50
❑27, Jun 1988 1.50
❑28, Jul 1988 1.50
❑29, Jul 1988 1.50
❑30, Aug 1988 1.50
❑31, Aug 1988 1.50
❑32, Sep 1988 1.50
❑33, Sep 1988 1.50
❑34, Oct 1988 1.50
❑35, Oct 1988 1.50
❑36, Nov 1988 1.50
❑37, Nov 1988 1.50

LEGEND OF LEMNEAR
CPM

❑1, Jan 1998; wraparound cover 3.00
❑2, Feb 1998 3.00
❑3, Mar 1998 3.00
❑4, Apr 1998 3.00
❑5, May 1998 3.00
❑6, Jun 1998; wraparound cover 3.00
❑7, Jul 1998; wraparound cover 3.00
❑8, Aug 1998 2.95
❑9, Sep 1998 2.95
❑10, Oct 1998 2.95
❑11, Nov 1998 2.95
❑12, Dec 1998 2.95
❑13, Jan 1999; wraparound cover 2.95
❑14, Feb 1999 2.95

LEGEND OF LILITH
IMAGE

❑0; no date 4.95

LEGEND OF MOTHER SARAH
DARK HORSE / MANGA

❑1, Apr 1995, b&w 3.50
❑2, May 1995, b&w 3.00
❑3, Jun 1995, b&w 3.00
❑4, Jul 1995, b&w 2.50
❑5, Aug 1995, b&w 2.50
❑6, Sep 1995, b&w 2.50
❑7, Oct 1995, b&w 2.50
❑8, Nov 1995, b&w 2.50

LEGEND OF MOTHER SARAH, THE: CITY OF THE ANGELS
DARK HORSE / MANGA

❑1, Oct 1997 3.95
❑2, Dec 1997 3.95
❑3, Jan 1998 3.95
❑4, Feb 1998 3.95
❑5, Mar 1998 3.95
❑6, Apr 1998 3.95
❑7, May 1998 3.95
❑8, Jun 1998 3.95
❑9, Jul 1998 3.95

LEGEND OF MOTHER SARAH, THE: CITY OF THE CHILDREN
DARK HORSE / MANGA

❑1, Jan 1996 3.95
❑2, Feb 1996 3.95
❑3, Mar 1996 3.95
❑4, Apr 1996 3.95
❑5, May 1996 3.95

N-MINT

❑6, Jun 1996 .... 3.95
❑7, Jul 1996 .... 3.95

LEGEND OF SLEEPY HOLLOW, THE
TUNDRA

❑1 .... 6.95

LEGEND OF SUPREME
IMAGE

❑1, Dec 1994 .... 2.50
❑2, Jan 1995 .... 2.50
❑3, Feb 1995 .... 2.50

LEGEND OF THE ELFLORD
DAVDEZ

❑1, Jul 1998 .... 2.95
❑2, Sep 1998 .... 2.95
❑3 .... 2.95

LEGEND OF THE HAWKMAN
DC

❑1 2000 .... 4.95
❑2 2000 .... 4.95
❑3 2000 .... 4.95

LEGEND OF THE SHIELD, THE
DC / IMPACT

❑1, Jul 1991 .... 1.50
❑2, Aug 1991 .... 1.00
❑3, Sep 1991 .... 1.00
❑4, Oct 1991 .... 1.00
❑5, Nov 1991 .... 1.00
❑6, Dec 1991 .... 1.00
❑7, Jan 1992 .... 1.00
❑8, Feb 1992 .... 1.00
❑9, Mar 1992 .... 1.00
❑10, Apr 1992 .... 1.00
❑11, May 1992; trading card 1.00
❑12, Jun 1992 .... 1.00
❑13, Jul 1992 .... 1.00
❑14, Aug 1992 .... 1.00
❑15, Sep 1992 .... 1.00
❑16, Oct 1992 .... 1.00
❑Annual 1 .... 2.50

LEGEND OF WONDER WOMAN, THE
DC

❑1, May 1986 KB (w) 1.50
❑2, Jun 1986 KB (w) 1.50
❑3, Jul 1986 KB (w) 1.50
❑4, Aug 1986 KB (w) 1.50

LEGEND OF ZELDA, THE
VALIANT

❑1, ca. 1990 .... 1.95
❑2, ca. 1990 .... 1.95
❑3, ca. 1990 .... 1.95
❑4, ca. 1990 .... 1.95
❑5, ca. 1990 .... 1.95

LEGEND OF ZELDA, THE (2ND SERIES)
VALIANT

❑1, ca. 1990 .... 1.50
❑2, ca. 1990 .... 1.50
❑3, ca. 1990 .... 1.50
❑4, ca. 1990 .... 1.50
❑5, ca. 1990 .... 1.50

LEGENDS
DC

❑1, Nov 1986 JBy (a); 1: Amanda Waller. 2.00
❑2, Dec 1986 JBy (a) 1.50
❑3, Jan 1987 JBy (a); 1: Suicide Squad (modern). 2.00
❑4, Feb 1987 JBy (a) 1.50
❑5, Mar 1987 JBy (a) 1.50
❑6, Apr 1987 JBy (a); 1: Justice League. 3.00

LEGENDS AND FOLKLORE
ZONE

❑1, b&w 2.95
❑2, ca. 1992, b&w 2.95

LEGENDS FROM DARKWOOD
ANTARCTIC

❑1, Nov 2003 .... 3.50
❑2, Jan 2004 .... 3.50
❑3, Feb 2004 .... 3.50

LEGENDS OF ELFINWILD, THE
WEHNER

❑1, b&w 1.75

LEGENDS OF KID DEATH & FLUFFY
EVENT

❑1, Feb 1997 .... 2.95

LEGENDS OF LUXURA
BRAINSTORM

❑1, Feb 1996, b&w; collects Luxura stories 2.95
❑1/Ltd., Feb 1996; Special edition; no cover price; limited to 1000 copies 4.00

LEGENDS OF NASCAR, THE
VORTEX

❑1; Bill Elliott 3.50
❑1-2; Bill Elliott 2.00
❑1-3; Bill Elliott; Indicia marks it as 2nd Printing 3.00
❑2; Richard Petty; no indicia 2.00
❑2/Variant; hologram 3.00
❑3; Ken Shrader 2.00
❑4; Bobby Allison 2.00
❑5; Sterling Marlin 2.00
❑6 .... 2.00
❑7 .... 2.00
❑8; Benny Parsons 2.00
❑9; Rusty Wallace 2.00
❑10; Talladega Story 2.00
❑11; Morgan Shepherd 2.00
❑12 .... 2.00
❑13 .... 2.00
❑14 .... 2.00
❑15 .... 2.00
❑16; Final issue (?) 2.00

LEGENDS OF THE DARK CLAW
DC / AMALGAM

❑1, Apr 1996 O: The Hyena. O: The Dark Claw. 2.00

LEGENDS OF THE DCU: CRISIS ON INFINITE EARTHS
DC

❑1, Feb 1999; A: Flash II (Barry Allen). Takes place between Crisis of Infinite Earths #4 and #5; Supergirl I (Kara Zor-El) 4.95
❑1/Autographed, Feb 1999; A: Flash II (Barry Allen). Takes place between Crisis of Infinite Earths #4 and #5; Supergirl I (Kara Zor-El) 18.95

LEGENDS OF THE DC UNIVERSE
DC

❑1, Feb 1998; Superman 3.00
❑2, Mar 1998; Superman 2.50
❑3, Apr 1998; Superman 2.50
❑4, May 1998; Wonder Woman 2.50
❑5, Jun 1998; Wonder Woman 2.50
❑6, Jul 1998; KN (a);Robin, Superman 2.25
❑7, Aug 1998; Green Lantern/Green Arrow 2.25
❑8, Sep 1998; Green Lantern/Green Arrow 2.25
❑9, Oct 1998; Green Lantern/Green Arrow 2.25
❑10, Nov 1998; O: Oracle. Batgirl 2.25
❑11, Dec 1998; O: Oracle. Batgirl 2.25
❑12, Jan 1999; JLA 2.25
❑13, Feb 1999; JLA 2.25
❑14, Mar 1999 JK, ME (w); SR (a); A: Jimmy Olsen. A: Simyan. A: Superman. A: Darkseid. A: Guardian. A: Mokkari. 2.25
❑15, Apr 1999 A: Flash II (Barry Allen). 2.25
❑16, May 1999 A: Flash II (Barry Allen). 2.25
❑17, Jun 1999 A: Flash II (Barry Allen). 2.25
❑18, Jul 1999; Kid Flash, Raven 2.25
❑19, Aug 1999; Impulse; prelude to JLApe Annuals 2.25
❑20, Sep 1999; MZ (a);Green Lantern: Abin Sur 2.25
❑21, Oct 1999; MZ (a);Green Lantern: Abin Sur 1.99
❑22, Nov 1999 .... 1.99
❑23, Dec 1999 .... 1.99
❑24, Jan 2000 .... 1.99
❑25, Feb 2000 .... 1.99
❑26, Mar 2000 .... 1.99
❑27, Apr 2000 TVE (a) 1.99
❑28, May 2000 GK, KJ (a) 1.99
❑29, Jun 2000 GK, KJ (a) 1.99
❑30, Jul 2000 .... 1.99
❑31, Aug 2000 .... 2.50
❑32, Sep 2000 .... 2.50
❑33, Oct 2000 .... 2.50
❑34, Nov 2000 .... 2.50
❑35, Dec 2000 .... 2.50
❑36, Jan 2001 .... 2.50
❑37, Feb 2001 .... 2.50
❑38, Mar 2001 .... 2.50
❑39, Apr 2001 .... 2.50
❑40, May 2001 .... 2.50
❑41, Jun 2001 .... 2.50
❑Giant Size 1, Sep 1998; Spectre, Hawkman, Teen Titans, Adam Strange, Chronos, Doom Patrol, Rip Hunter, Linear Men 4.95
❑Giant Size 2, Jan 2000 KJ (a) 4.95

LEGENDS OF THE DC UNIVERSE 3-D GALLERY
DC

❑1, Dec 1998; pin-ups 2.95

LEGENDS OF THE LEGION
DC

❑1, Feb 1998 .... 2.25
❑2, Mar 1998 .... 2.25
❑3, Apr 1998 .... 2.25
❑4, May 1998 .... 2.25

LEGENDS OF THE LIVING DEAD
FANTACO

❑1 .... 3.95

LEGENDS OF THE STARGRAZERS
INNOVATION

❑1, Aug 1989 .... 1.95
❑2 .... 1.95
❑3 .... 1.95
❑4 .... 1.95
❑5 .... 1.95
❑6 .... 1.95

LEGENDS OF THE WORLD'S FINEST
DC

❑1, ca. 1994; Prestige format 4.95
❑2, ca. 1994; Prestige format 4.95
❑3, ca. 1994; Superman, Batman
❑Prestige format. 4.95

L.E.G.I.O.N.
DC

❑1, Feb 1989; O: L.E.G.I.O.N.. 1: Stealth. L.E.G.I.O.N. '89 starts 2.50
❑2, Mar 1989 .... 2.00
❑3, Apr 1989 .... 2.00
❑4, May 1989 A: Lobo. 2.00
❑5, Jun 1989; Lobo joins team 2.00
❑6, Jul 1989 .... 1.75
❑7, Aug 1989 .... 1.75
❑8, Sep 1989 .... 1.75
❑9, Nov 1989 A: Phantom Girl. 1.75
❑10, Dec 1989 .... 1.75
❑11, Jan 1990; L.E.G.I.O.N. '90 starts 1.50
❑12, Feb 1990 A: Emerald Eye. 1.50
❑13, Mar 1990 .... 1.50
❑14, Apr 1990 .... 1.50
❑15, May 1990 .... 1.50
❑16, Jun 1990 A: Lar Gand. 1.50
❑17, Jul 1990 .... 1.50
❑18, Aug 1990 .... 1.50
❑19, Sep 1990 .... 1.50
❑20, Oct 1990 .... 1.50
❑21, Nov 1990 .... 1.50
❑22, Dec 1990 A: Lady Quark. 1.50
❑23, Jan 1991; L.E.G.I.O.N. '91 starts 2.50
❑24, Feb 1991 .... 1.50
❑25, Mar 1991 .... 1.50
❑26, Apr 1991 .... 1.50

N-MINT

❑27, May 1991 1.50
❑28, Jun 1991 KG (w) 1.50
❑29, Jul 1991 1.50
❑30, Aug 1991 1: Ig'nea. 1.50
❑31, Sep 1991; Painted cover; Lobo vs. Captain Marvel; Lobo vs. Capt. Marvel 1.50
❑32, Oct 1991 1: Ice Man. 1.50
❑33, Nov 1991 1.50
❑34, Dec 1991 1.50
❑35, Jan 1992; L.E.G.I.O.N. '92 starts 1.50
❑36, Feb 1992 1.50
❑37, Mar 1992 1.50
❑38, Apr 1992 1.50
❑39, May 1992 1.50
❑40, Jun 1992 1.50
❑41, Jul 1992 1.50
❑42, Jul 1992 1.50
❑43, Aug 1992 1.50
❑44, Aug 1992 1.50
❑45, Sep 1992 1.50
❑46, Nov 1992 1.50
❑47, Dec 1992; Lobo vs. Green Lantern (Hal Jordan) 1.50
❑48, Jan 1993; L.E.G.I.O.N. '93 starts 1.50
❑49, Feb 1993 1.75
❑50, Mar 1993; Double-size; L.E.G.I.O.N. '67 back-up 3.50
❑51, Apr 1993 1.75
❑52, May 1993 1.75
❑53, Jun 1993 1.75
❑54, Jun 1993 1.75
❑55, Jul 1993 1.75
❑56, Jul 1993 1.75
❑57, Aug 1993 1.75
❑58, Sep 1993 1.75
❑59, Oct 1993 1.75
❑60, Nov 1993 1.75
❑61, Dec 1993 1.75
❑62, Jan 1994; L.E.G.I.O.N. '94 starts 1.75
❑63, Feb 1994 1.75
❑64, Mar 1994 1.75
❑65, Apr 1994 1.75
❑66, May 1994 1.75
❑67, Jun 1994 1.75
❑68, Jul 1994 1.75
❑69, Aug 1994 A: Ultra Boy. 1.75
❑70, Sep 1994; Giant-size; Zero Hour; story continues in R.E.B.E.L.S. '94 #0; L.E.G.I.O.N. goes renegade (becomes R.E.B.E.L.S.) 2.50
❑Annual 1, ca. 1990; A: Superman. Vril Dox vs. Brainiac 2.95
❑Annual 2, ca. 1991; Armageddon 2001 2.95
❑Annual 3, ca. 1992 2.95
❑Annual 4, ca. 1993 1: Pax. 3.50
❑Annual 5, ca. 1994; Elseworlds; L.E.G.I.O.N. 007 3.50

LEGION, THE
DC

❑1, Dec 2001 3.00
❑2, Jan 2002 2.50
❑3, Feb 2002 2.50
❑4, Mar 2002 2.50
❑5, Apr 2002 2.50
❑6, May 2002 2.50
❑7, Jun 2002 2.50
❑8, Jul 2002 2.50
❑9, Aug 2002 2.50
❑10, Sep 2002 2.50
❑11, Oct 2002 2.50
❑12, Nov 2002 2.50
❑13, Dec 2002 2.50
❑14, Jan 2003 2.50
❑15, Feb 2003 2.50
❑16, Mar 2003 2.50
❑17, Apr 2003 2.50
❑18, May 2003 2.50
❑19, Jun 2003 2.50
❑20, Jul 2003 2.50
❑21, Aug 2003 2.50
❑22, Sep 2003 2.50
❑23, Oct 2003 2.50

N-MINT

❑24, Nov 2003 2.50
❑25, Dec 2003 3.95
❑26, Jan 2004 2.50
❑27, Jan 2004 2.50
❑28, Feb 2004 2.50
❑29, Mar 2004 2.50
❑30, Apr 2004 (c) 2.50
❑31, May 2004 2.50
❑32, Jun 2004 2.50
❑33, Jul 2004 2.50
❑34, Aug 2004 2.50
❑35, Sep 2004
❑36, Sep 2004

LEGION ANTHOLOGY
LIMELIGHT

❑1, b&w; manga 2.95
❑2 2.95

LEGION LOST
DC

❑1, May 2000 2.50
❑2, Jun 2000 2.50
❑3, Jul 2000 2.50
❑4, Aug 2000 2.50
❑5, Sep 2000 2.50
❑6, Oct 2000 2.50
❑7, Nov 2000 2.50
❑8, Dec 2000 2.50
❑9, Jan 2001 2.50
❑10, Feb 2001 2.50
❑11, Mar 2001 2.50
❑12, Apr 2001 2.50

LEGION MANGA ANTHOLOGY
LIMELIGHT

❑1 2.95
❑2 2.95
❑3 2.95
❑4 2.95

LEGIONNAIRES
DC

❑0, Oct 1994; MWa (w); revised Legion origin; continues in Legion of Super-Heroes #62 and Legionnaires #19 . 2.25
❑1, Apr 1993; with trading card 3.00
❑2, May 1993; V: Fatal Five. covers of issues #2-6 form one image 2.00
❑3, Jun 1993 V: Fatal Five. 2.00
❑4, Jul 1993 V: Fatal Five. 2.00
❑5, Aug 1993 V: Fatal Five. 2.00
❑6, Sep 1993 V: Fatal Five. 1.50
❑7, Oct 1993 1.50
❑8, Nov 1993; Brainiac 5 leaves team 1.50
❑9, Dec 1993 1.50
❑10, Jan 1994 1.50
❑11, Feb 1994; Kid Quantum joins team 1.50
❑12, Mar 1994 1.50
❑13, Apr 1994; Matter-Eater Lad becomes a girl 1.50
❑14, May 1994 1.50
❑15, Jun 1994 1.50
❑16, Jul 1994; Return of Dream Girl . 1.50
❑17, Aug 1994; End of an Era Conclusion 1.50
❑18, Sep 1994; Zero Hour 1.50
❑19, Nov 1994 1.50
❑20, Dec 1994 V: Mano. 1.50
❑21, Jan 1995 1: Work Force. 1.50
❑22, Feb 1995 1.50
❑23, Mar 1995 1.50
❑24, Apr 1995 1.50
❑25, May 1995 1.50
❑26, Jun 1995 1.75
❑27, Jul 1995 2.25
❑28, Aug 1995 1: Legion Espionage Squad. 2.25
❑29, Sep 1995 1: Dirk Morgna. 2.25
❑30, Oct 1995; Lightning Lad turning point 2.25
❑31, Nov 1995; Future Tense, Part 3; Superboy made honorary member; Valor released into 30th century 2.25
❑32, Dec 1995; A: Chronos. Underworld Unleashed 2.25

The Legion of Super-Heroes (3rd series) ended with "The Magic Wars," which set the stage for the fourth series, set five years in the future.

© 1989 DC Comics.

N-MINT

❑33, Jan 1996; Kinetix finds Emerald Eye; [L1996-2] 2.25
❑34, Feb 1996; [L1996-4] 2.25
❑35, Mar 1996; XS returns to 30th century; [L1996-6] 2.25
❑36, May 1996; [L1996-8] 2.25
❑37, Jun 1996; O: M'onel. [L1996-10] 2.25
❑38, Jul 1996; [L1996-12] 2.25
❑39, Aug 1996; Triad's three personalities become distinct; [L1996-14] .. 2.25
❑40, Sep 1996; [L1996-16] 2.25
❑41, Oct 1996; [L1996-18] 2.25
❑42, Nov 1996; [L1996-20] 2.25
❑43, Dec 1996; Legion try-outs; Magno joins team; Umbra joins team; Sensor joins team; [L1996-22] 2.25
❑44, Jan 1997; [L1997-1] 2.25
❑45, Feb 1997; V: Mantis Morlo. [L1997-3] 2.25
❑46, Mar 1997; [L1997-5] 2.25
❑47, Apr 1997; [L1997-7] 2.25
❑48, May 1997; V: Mordru. [L1997-9] 2.25
❑49, Jun 1997; A: Workforce. A: Heroes of Xanthu. D: Atom'x. V: Mordru. [L1997-11] 2.25
❑50, Jul 1997; Giant-size; V: Mordru. Poster; Mysa becomes young; [L1997-13] 3.95
❑51, Aug 1997; [L1997-15] 2.25
❑52, Sep 1997; Vi's new powers manifest; [L1997-17] 2.25
❑53, Oct 1997; Monstress joins team; Magno leaves team; [L1997-19] 2.25
❑54, Nov 1997; Golden Age story; [L1997-21] 2.25
❑55, Dec 1997; V: Composite Man. Face cover; [L1997-23] 2.25
❑56, Jan 1998; M'onel returns to Daxam; [L1998-1] 2.25
❑57, Feb 1998; [L1998-3] 2.25
❑58, Mar 1998; [L1998-5] 2.25
❑59, Apr 1998; [L1998-7] 2.25
❑60, May 1998; Chameleon leaves team; Sensor leaves team; Karate Kid joins team; Kid Quantum joins team; [L1998-9] 2.25
❑61, Jun 1998; A: Superman (from Time and Time Again). Multiple time shifts; [L1998-11] 2.25
❑62, Jul 1998; Dark Circle Rising, Part 1: Crossfire!; [L1998-13] 2.25
❑63, Aug 1998; Dark Circle Rising, Part 3: Resignation!; [L1998-15] 2.25
❑64, Sep 1998; Dark Circle Rising, Part 5: Enlightenment!; [L1998-17] 2.25
❑65, Oct 1998; Dark Circle falls; [L1998-19] 2.50
❑66, Dec 1998; 1: Charma. [L1998-21] 2.50
❑67, Jan 1999; A: Kono. [L1999-1] ... 2.50
❑68, Feb 1999; Monstress changes color; [L1999-3] 2.50
❑69, Mar 1999; A: Plasma. [L1999-5] 2.50
❑70, Apr 1999; Cosmic Boy vs. Domain; [L1999-7] 2.50
❑71, May 1999; V: Elements of Disaster. [L1999-9] 2.50
❑72, Jun 1999; [L1999-11] 2.50
❑73, Jul 1999; Star Boy solo; [L1999-13] 2.50
❑74, Aug 1999; [L1999-15] 2.50
❑75, Sep 1999; [L1999-17] 2.50
❑76, Oct 1999; O: Wildfire. [L1999-19] 2.50

Condition price index: Multiply "NM prices" above by: **0.83 for Very Fine/Near Mint**
0.66 for Very Fine • 0.33 for Fine • 0.2 for Very Good • 0.125 for Good

N-MINT

❑77, Nov 1999; [L1999-21] 2.50
❑78, Dec 2000; [L1999-23] 2.50
❑79, Jan 2000; [L2000-1] 2.50
❑80, Feb 2000; [L2000-3] 2.50
❑1000000, Nov 1998; set 1, 000 years after events of One Million 3.00
❑Annual 1, ca. 1994; Elseworlds; Futuristic Camelot 2.95
❑Annual 2, ca. 1995; D: Apparition. Andromeda leaves team 3.95
❑Annual 3, ca. 1996; A: Barry Allen. Legends of the Dead Earth; XS' travels in time; 1996 Annual 2.95

LEGIONNAIRES THREE
DC

❑1, Feb 1986 KG (w); V: Time Trapper. 1.25
❑2, Mar 1986 .... 1.00
❑3, Apr 1986 .... 1.00
❑4, May 1986 .... 1.00

LEGION OF MONSTERS, THE
MARVEL

❑1; magazine, b&w 6.00

LEGION OF NIGHT, THE
MARVEL

❑1, Nov 1991 .... 4.95
❑2, Dec 1991 .... 4.95

LEGION OF STUPID HEROES
ALTERNATE CONCEPTS

❑1, Jul 1997 .... 2.50
❑2, Sep 1997 .... 2.50
❑3 .... 2.50
❑4, Mar 1998 .... 2.50

LEGION OF STUPID KNIGHTS
ALTERNATE CONCEPTS

❑Special 1, Feb 1998, b&w 2.50

LEGION OF SUBSTITUTE HEROES SPECIAL
DC

❑1 KG (a) 2.00

LEGION OF SUPER-HEROES (1ST SERIES)
DC

❑1, Feb 1973; Tales of the Legion of Super-Heroes; Tommy Tomorrow reprint 14.00
❑2, Mar 1973; Tales of the Legion of Super-Heroes; Tommy Tomorrow reprint 8.00
❑3, May 1973; V: Computo. Tales of the Legion of Super-Heroes; Tommy Tomorrow reprint 7.00
❑4, Aug 1973; V: Computo. Tales of the Legion of Super-Heroes; Tommy Tomorrow reprint 7.00

LEGION OF SUPER-HEROES, THE (2ND SERIES)
DC

❑259, Jan 1980; Superboy leaves team; Continued from "Superboy and the Legion of Super-Heroes" 3.50
❑260, Feb 1980 V: Circus of Crime. .. 2.75
❑261, Mar 1980 V: Circus of Crime. .. 2.50
❑262, Apr 1980 .... 2.50
❑263, May 1980 .... 2.50
❑264, Jun 1980 .... 2.50
❑265, Jul 1980; O: Tyroc. bonus Superman story starring the TRS-80 Computer Whiz Kids (Radio Shack sponsored story) 2.50
❑266, Aug 1980; Return of Bouncing Boy; Return of Duo Damsel 2.50
❑267, Sep 1980; O: Legion Flight Rings. 2.50
❑268, Oct 1980 SD (a) 2.50
❑269, Nov 1980 V: Fatal Five. 2.50
❑270, Dec 1980; Dark Man's identity revealed 2.50
❑271, Jan 1981 O: Dark Man. 1.75
❑272, Feb 1981; O: Blok. 1: Dial 'H' for Hero (new). Blok joins Legion of Super-Heroes; Dial "H" For Hero preview story 1.75
❑273, Mar 1981 .... 1.75
❑274, Apr 1981; SD (a);Ultra Boy becomes pirate 1.75
❑275, May 1981 .... 1.75
❑276, Jun 1981 .... 1.75
❑277, Jul 1981 .... 1.75
❑278, Aug 1981 A: Reflecto. V: Grimbor. 1.75
❑279, Sep 1981; Reflecto's identity revealed 1.75
❑280, Oct 1981; Superboy rejoins 1.75
❑281, Nov 1981 SD (a); V: Molecule Master. 1.75
❑282, Dec 1981; O: Reflecto. Ultra Boy returns 1.75
❑283, Jan 1982; O: Wildfire. Wildfire story 1.75
❑284, Feb 1982 .... 1.75
❑285, Mar 1982 PB (a) 2.50
❑286, Apr 1982 PB (a); V: Doctor Regulus. V: Dr. Regulus. 2.00
❑287, May 1982 KG (a); V: Kharlak. .. 2.00
❑288, Jun 1982 KG (a) 2.00
❑289, Jul 1982 KG (a) 2.00
❑290, Aug 1982; KG (a);Great Darkness Saga, Part 1 .... 2.00
❑291, Sep 1982; KG (a);Great Darkness Saga, Part 2 .... 2.00
❑292, Oct 1982; KG (a);Great Darkness Saga, Part 3 .... 2.00
❑293, Nov 1982; KG (a);Great Darkness Saga, Part 4; Masters of the Universe preview story 2.00
❑294, Dec 1982; KG (a);Great Darkness Saga, Part 5; giant-size issue 2.00
❑295, Jan 1983 O: Universo (possible origin). A: Green Lantern Corps. 1.50
❑296, Feb 1983 .... 1.50
❑297, Mar 1983; O: Legion of Super-Heroes. Cosmic Boy solo story 1.50
❑298, Apr 1983; 1: Gemworld. 1: Dark Opal. 1: Amethyst. Amethyst, Princess of Gemworld preview story 1.50
❑299, May 1983; Invisible Kid II meets Invisible Kid I 1.50
❑300, Jun 1983; Double-size; Tales of the Adult Legion; alternate futures . 2.00
❑301, Jul 1983 .... 1.50
❑302, Aug 1983; Lightning Lad vs. Lightning Lord 1.50
❑303, Sep 1983 V: Emerald Empress. 1.50
❑304, Oct 1983; Legion Academy 1.50
❑305, Nov 1983; Shrinking Violet revealed as Durlan; real Shrinking Violet returns 1.50
❑306, Dec 1983 O: Star Boy. 1.50
❑307, Jan 1984 V: Prophet. 1.50
❑308, Feb 1984 V: Prophet. 1.50
❑309, Mar 1984 V: Prophet. 1.50
❑310, Apr 1984 V: Omen. 1.50
❑311, May 1984 .... 1.50
❑312, Jun 1984 .... 1.50
❑313, Jul 1984; series continues as Tales of the Legion of Super-Heroes 1.50
❑Annual 1, ca. 1982 KG (a); 1: Invisible Kid II (Jacques Foccart). 2.50
❑Annual 2, ca. 1983; DaG, KG (a);Wedding of Karate Kid and Princess Projectra; Karate Kid and Princess Projectra leave Legion of Super-Heroes 2.00
❑Annual 3, ca. 1984 CS (a); O: Validus. 2.00

LEGION OF SUPER-HEROES (3RD SERIES)
DC

❑1, Aug 1984; KG (w); KG (a); V: Legion of Super-Villains. Silver ink cover .. 5.00
❑2, Sep 1984 KG (a); 1: Kono. V: Legion of Super-Villains. 4.00
❑3, Oct 1984 V: Legion of Super-Villains. 4.00
❑4, Nov 1984 D: Karate Kid. V: Legion of Super-Villains. 4.00
❑5, Dec 1984 D: Nemesis Kid. 4.00
❑6, Jan 1985; 1: Laurel Gand. Spotlight on Lightning Lass 2.25
❑7, Feb 1985 .... 2.25
❑8, Mar 1985 .... 2.25
❑9, Apr 1985 .... 2.25
❑10, May 1985 .... 2.25
❑11, Jun 1985; Bouncing Boy back-up 2.00
❑12, Jul 1985 .... 2.00
❑13, Aug 1985 .... 2.00
❑14, Sep 1985; 1: Quislet. New members 2.00
❑15, Oct 1985 .... 2.00
❑16, Nov 1985; Crisis 2.00
❑17, Dec 1985 .... 2.00
❑18, Jan 1986; Crisis 2.00
❑19, Feb 1986 .... 2.00
❑20, Mar 1986 V: Tyr. 2.00
❑21, Apr 1986 V: Emerald Empress. .. 2.00
❑22, May 1986 .... 2.00
❑23, Jun 1986 .... 2.00
❑24, Jul 1986 .... 2.00
❑25, Aug 1986 .... 2.00
❑26, Sep 1986 .... 2.00
❑27, Oct 1986 V: Mordru. 2.00
❑28, Nov 1986 .... 2.00
❑29, Dec 1986 V: Starfinger. 2.00
❑30, Jan 1987 .... 2.00
❑31, Feb 1987; Karate Kid, Princess Projectra, Ferro Lad story 1.75
❑32, Mar 1987; Universo Project, Chapter 1 .... 1.75
❑33, Apr 1987; Universo Project, Chapter 2 .... 1.75
❑34, May 1987; Universo Project, Chapter 3 .... 1.75
❑35, Jun 1987; Universo Project, Chapter 4 .... 1.75
❑36, Jul 1987; Legion elections 1.75
❑37, Aug 1987; Fate of Superboy revealed; Return of Star Boy and Sun Girl 5.00
❑38, Sep 1987; D: Superboy. Death of Superboy 5.00
❑39, Oct 1987 CS (a); O: Colossal Boy. 1.75
❑40, Nov 1987 V: Starfinger. 1.75
❑41, Dec 1987 V: Starfinger. 1.75
❑42, Jan 1988; V: Laurel Kent. Millennium 1.75
❑43, Feb 1988; V: Laurel Kent. Millennium 1.75
❑44, Mar 1988 O: Quislet. 1.75
❑45, Apr 1988; Double-size; 30th Anniversary Issue 3.00
❑46, May 1988 .... 1.75
❑47, Jun 1988 V: Starfinger. 1.75
❑48, Jul 1988 V: Starfinger. 1.75
❑49, Aug 1988 V: Starfinger. 1.75
❑50, Sep 1988; Giant-size; D: Duo Damsel (half). D: Time Trapper (possible death). D: Infinite Man. Mon-El wounded 2.00
❑51, Oct 1988 .... 1.75
❑52, Nov 1988 .... 1.75
❑53, Dec 1988 .... 1.75
❑54, Win 1988; no month of publication; cover says Winter 1.75
❑55, Hol 1989; no month of publication; cover says Holiday 1.75
❑56, Jan 1989 .... 1.75
❑57, Feb 1989 .... 1.75
❑58, Mar 1989 D: Emerald Empress. . 1.75
❑59, Apr 1989 .... 1.75
❑60, May 1989 KG (a) 1.75
❑61, Jun 1989 KG (a) 1.75
❑62, Jul 1989 KG (a); D: Magnetic Kid. 1.75
❑63, Aug 1989 KG (a) 1.75
❑Annual 1, Oct 1985 KG (a) 2.00
❑Annual 2, ca. 1986 V: Validus. 2.00
❑Annual 3, ca. 1987 O: new Legion of Substitute Heroes. 2.00
❑Annual 4, ca. 1988; O: Starfinger. 1988 annual 2.50

Condition price index: Multiply "NM prices" above by: **0.83 for Very Fine/Near Mint**
0.66 for Very Fine • 0.33 for Fine • 0.2 for Very Good • 0.125 for Good

N-MINT

LEGION OF SUPER-HEROES (4TH SERIES)
DC

❑0, Oct 1994; KG (w); KG (a); O: Legion of Super-Heroes (revised). continues in Legion of Super-Heroes #62 and Legionnaires #19 ... 2.00
❑1, Nov 1989; KG (w); KG (a);Begins five years after previous series ... 2.50
❑2, Dec 1989 ... 2.00
❑3, Jan 1990 V: Roxxas. ... 2.00
❑4, Feb 1990 KG (w); KG (a); A: Mon-El. 2.00
❑5, Mar 1990 ... 2.00
❑6, Apr 1990 ... 2.00
❑7, May 1990 ... 2.00
❑8, Jun 1990; origin ... 2.00
❑9, Jul 1990 ... 2.00
❑10, Aug 1990 V: Roxxas. ... 2.00
❑11, Sep 1990 A: Matter-Eater Lad. .. 2.00
❑12, Oct 1990; Legion reformed ... 2.00
❑13, Nov 1990; poster ... 2.00
❑14, Jan 1991 ... 2.00
❑15, Feb 1991 ... 2.00
❑16, Mar 1991 ... 2.00
❑17, Apr 1991 ... 2.00
❑18, May 1991 V: Dark Circle. ... 2.00
❑19, Jun 1991 ... 2.00
❑20, Jul 1991 ... 2.00
❑21, Aug 1991 ... 1.75
❑22, Sep 1991 ... 1.75
❑23, Oct 1991 V: Lobo. ... 1.75
❑24, Dec 1991 KG (a) ... 1.75
❑25, Jan 1992 ... 1.75
❑26, Feb 1992; contains map of Legion headquarters ... 1.75
❑27, Mar 1992 V: B.I.O.N.. ... 1.75
❑28, Apr 1992 KG (a); A: Sun Boy. ... 1.75
❑29, May 1992 ... 1.75
❑30, Jun 1992; The Terra Mosaic ... 1.75
❑31, Jul 1992; The Terra Mosaic; romance cover ... 1.75
❑32, Aug 1992; The Terra Mosaic ... 1.75
❑33, Sep 1992; The Terra Mosaic; Fate of Kid Quantum ... 1.75
❑34, Oct 1992; The Terra Mosaic; Timber Wolf mini-series preview ... 1.75
❑35, Nov 1992; The Terra Mosaic; Sun Boy meets Sun Boy ... 1.75
❑36, Nov 1992; The Terra Mosaic conclusion ... 1.75
❑37, Dec 1992; Star Boy and Dream Girl return ... 1.75
❑38, Dec 1992; A: Death (Sandman). Earth destroyed ... 2.50
❑39, Jan 1993 KG (a) ... 1.75
❑40, Feb 1993 ... 1.75
❑41, Mar 1993 1: Legionnaires. ... 1.75
❑42, Apr 1993 ... 1.75
❑43, May 1993; White Witch returns ... 1.75
❑44, Jun 1993 ... 1.75
❑45, Jul 1993 ... 1.75
❑46, Aug 1993 ... 1.75
❑47, Sep 1993 V: dead heroes. ... 1.75
❑48, Oct 1993 V: Mordru. ... 1.75
❑49, Nov 1993 ... 1.75
❑50, Nov 1993; Wedding of Matter-Eater Lad and Saturn Queen ... 3.50
❑51, Dec 1993 ... 1.75
❑52, Dec 1993 O: Timber Wolf. ... 1.75
❑53, Jan 1994 V: Glorith. ... 1.75
❑54, Feb 1994; Die-cut cover ... 2.95
❑55, Mar 1994 ... 1.75
❑56, Apr 1994 ... 1.75
❑57, May 1994 ... 1.75
❑58, Jun 1994 ... 1.75
❑59, Jul 1994 ... 1.95
❑60, Aug 1994; Crossover with Legionnaires and Valor ... 1.95
❑61, Sep 1994; Zero Hour; end of original Legion of Super-Heroes ... 1.95
❑62, Nov 1994 ... 1.95
❑63, Dec 1994; 1: Athramites, new Legion headquarters. Tenzil Kem hired as chef ... 1.95

N-MINT

❑64, Jan 1995; MWa (w); Return of Ultra Boy ... 1.95
❑65, Feb 1995 ... 1.95
❑66, Mar 1995; A: Laurel Gand. Andromeda, Shrinking Violet and Kinetix join team ... 1.95
❑67, Apr 1995 ... 1.95
❑68, May 1995 ... 1.95
❑69, Jun 1995 ... 2.25
❑70, Jul 1995 ... 2.25
❑71, Aug 1995; Trom destroyed ... 2.25
❑72, Sep 1995 ... 2.25
❑73, Oct 1995 A: Mekt Ranz. ... 2.25
❑74, Nov 1995; A: Superboy. A: Scavenger. Future Tense, Part 2; Concludes in Legionnaires #31 ... 2.25
❑75, Dec 1995; A: Chronos. Underworld Unleashed ... 2.25
❑76, Jan 1996; Star Boy and Gates join team; [L1996-1] ... 2.25
❑77, Feb 1996; O: Brainiac Five. [L1996-3] ... 2.25
❑78, Mar 1996; O: Fatal Five. 1: Fatal Five. [L1996-5] ... 2.25
❑79, Apr 1996; V: Fatal Five. [L1996-7] 2.25
❑80, May 1996; [L1996-9] ... 2.25
❑81, Jun 1996; Dirk Morgna becomes Sun Boy; Brainiac 5 quits; [L1996-11] 2.25
❑82, Jul 1996; Apparition returns; [L1996-13] ... 2.25
❑83, Aug 1996; D: Leviathan. Violet possessed by Emerald Eye; [L1996-15] 2.25
❑84, Sep 1996; [L1996-17] ... 2.25
❑85, Oct 1996; A: Superman. Seven Legionnaires, Inferno, and Shvaughn Erin in 20th century; [L1996-19] ... 2.25
❑86, Nov 1996; A: Ferro. Final Night; [L1996-21] ... 2.25
❑87, Dec 1996; A: Deadman. A: Phase. [L1996-23] ... 2.25
❑88, Jan 1997; A: Impulse. [L1997-2] 2.25
❑89, Feb 1997; A: Doctor Psycho. [L1997-4] ... 2.25
❑90, Mar 1997; V: Doctor Psycho. [L1997-6] ... 2.25
❑91, Apr 1997; Legion visits several DC eras; [L1997-8] ... 2.25
❑92, May 1997; 20th century group lands in 1958 Happy Harbor; [L1997-10] ... 2.25
❑93, Jun 1997; D: Douglas Nolan. [L1997-12] ... 2.25
❑94, Jul 1997; [L1997-14] ... 2.25
❑95, Aug 1997; A: Metal Men. [L1997-16] ... 2.25
❑96, Sep 1997; Wedding of Ultra Boy and Apparition; Cosmic Boy revives; [L1997-18] ... 2.25
❑97, Oct 1997; V: Mantis. Genesis; Spark gains gravity powers; [L1997-20] ... 2.25
❑98, Nov 1997; Phase meets Apparition; [L1997-22] ... 2.25
❑99, Dec 1997; Face cover; [L1997-24] 2.25
❑100, Jan 1998; Double-size; gatefold cover; Legionnaires return from 20th century; Pin-ups; [L1998-2] ... 5.95
❑101, Feb 1998; Spark gets her lightning powers back; [L1998-4] ... 2.25
❑102, Mar 1998; A: Heroes of Xanthu. [L1998-6] ... 2.25
❑103, Apr 1998; Karate Kid quits McCauley Industries; [L1998-8] ... 2.25
❑104, May 1998; A: Kono. time shifts to 2968; [L1998-10] ... 2.25
❑105, Jun 1998; V: Time Trapper. [L1998-12] ... 2.25
❑106, Jul 1998; Dark Circle Rising, Part 2: Assassination!; [L1998-14] ... 2.25
❑107, Aug 1998; Dark Circle Rising, Part 4: Duplicity!; [L1998-16] ... 2.25
❑108, Sep 1998; Dark Circle Rising, Part 6: Revelation!; [L1998-18] ... 2.25
❑109, Oct 1998; V: Emerald Eye. [L1998-20] ... 2.50
❑110, Dec 1998; Thunder joins team; [L1998-22] ... 2.50

The anime version of E.E. "Doc" Smith's space opera was the basis for Eternity's *Lensman* series.
© 1990 Eternity.

N-MINT

❑111, Jan 1999; Karate Kid vs. M'onel; [L1999-2] ... 2.50
❑112, Feb 1999; [L1999-4] ... 2.50
❑113, Mar 1999; [L1999-6] ... 2.50
❑114, Apr 1999; 1: Bizarro Legion. [L1999-8] ... 2.50
❑115, May 1999; [L1999-10] ... 2.50
❑116, Jun 1999; Thunder vs. Pernisius; [L1999-12] ... 2.50
❑117, Jul 1999; [L1999-14] ... 2.50
❑118, Aug 1999; V: Pernisius. [L1999-16] ... 2.50
❑119, Sep 1999; M'Onel and Apparition tell a L.E.G.I.O.N. story; [L1999-18] 2.50
❑120, Oct 1999; V: Fatal Five. [L1999-20] 2.50
❑121, Nov 1999; [L1999-22] ... 2.50
❑122, Dec 1999; [L1999-24] ... 2.50
❑123, Jan 2000; [L2000-2] ... 2.50
❑1000000, Nov 1998; KG (a);set 1, 000 years after events of One Million+E12681 ... 3.00
❑Annual 1, ca. 1990 O: Glorith, Ultra Boy, Legion. ... 3.50
❑Annual 2, ca. 1991 O: Valor. ... 3.50
❑Annual 3, ca. 1992; Timber Wolf goes to 20th century ... 3.50
❑Annual 4, ca. 1993 O: Jamm. 1: Jamm. ... 3.50
❑Annual 5, ca. 1994; CS (a);Elseworlds; Legion in Oz ... 3.50
❑Annual 6, ca. 1995; O: Leviathan. O: Kinetix. Year One; 0: XS; Legion Headquarters Map; Legion Equipment ... 3.95
❑Annual 7, ca. 1996; A: Wildfire. Legends of the Dead Earth; 1996 annual 2.95

LEGION OF SUPER-HEROES INDEX
ECLIPSE / INDEPENDENT

❑1 ... 2.00
❑2, Jan 1987 ... 2.00
❑3, Feb 1987 ... 2.00
❑4, Mar 1987 ... 2.00
❑5, May 1987 ... 2.00

LEGION OF SUPER-HEROES SECRET FILES
DC

❑1, Jan 1998; bios on members and villains ... 4.95
❑2, Jun 1999; bios on members and villains; Legion constitution ... 4.95

LEGION OF THE STUPID-HEROES
BLACKTHORNE

❑1, b&w; parody ... 1.75

LEGION: SCIENCE POLICE
DC

❑1, Aug 1998 ... 2.25
❑2, Sep 1998 ... 2.25
❑3, Oct 1998 ... 2.25
❑4, Nov 1998 ... 2.25

LEGION SECRET FILES 3003
DC

❑1, Jan 2004 ... 4.95

LEGIONS OF LUDICROUS HEROES
C&T

❑1, b&w ... 2.00

N-MINT

LEGION WORLDS
DC

- ❑1, Jun 2001 ... 3.95
- ❑2, Jul 2001 ... 3.95
- ❑3, Aug 2001 ... 3.95
- ❑4, Sep 2001 ... 3.95
- ❑5, Oct 2001 ... 3.95
- ❑6, Nov 2001 ... 3.95

LEGION X-1 (VOL. 2)
GREATER MERCURY

- ❑1, Aug 1989, b&w ... 2.00
- ❑2, Aug 1989, b&w; Cover says September ... 2.00
- ❑3, Jul 1990, b&w ... 2.00

LEJENTIA
OPUS

- ❑1 ... 1.95
- ❑2 ... 2.25

LEMONADE KID
AC

- ❑1; Powell reprints ... 2.50

LENORE
SLAVE LABOR

- ❑1, Feb 1998 ... 3.25
- ❑2, Jun 1998 ... 3.00
- ❑3, Sep 1998 ... 2.95
- ❑4, Jan 1999 ... 2.95
- ❑5, Mar 1999 ... 2.95
- ❑6, Jul 1999 ... 2.95
- ❑7, Dec 1999 ... 2.95

LENSMAN
ETERNITY

- ❑1, Feb 1990, b&w ... 2.25
- ❑1/Variant, Feb 1990, b&w; Special edition; cardstock cover; Includes Episode Guide; History; Story Timeline; Cycroader info; Galactic Patrol & Eddore Organizational charts; Vital Statistics on characters, vehicles and weapons ... 3.95
- ❑2 ... 2.25
- ❑3 ... 2.25
- ❑4 ... 2.25
- ❑5 ... 2.25
- ❑6 ... 2.25

LENSMAN: WAR OF THE GALAXIES
ETERNITY

- ❑1, Nov 1990, b&w ... 2.25
- ❑2 1991, b&w ... 2.25
- ❑3 1991, b&w ... 2.25
- ❑4 1991, b&w ... 2.25
- ❑5 1991, b&w ... 2.25
- ❑6, Jun 1991, b&w ... 2.25
- ❑7, Jul 1991, b&w ... 2.25

LEONARD NIMOY
CELEBRITY

- ❑1, b&w ... 5.95

LEONARDO TEENAGE MUTANT NINJA TURTLE
MIRAGE

- ❑1, Dec 1986; continues in Teenage Mutant Ninja Turtles #10 ... 2.00

LEOPOLD AND BRINK
FAULTLINE

- ❑1, Jun 1997, b&w ... 2.50
- ❑2, Nov 1997, b&w ... 2.50
- ❑3, Jan 1998, b&w ... 2.95

LESTER GIRLS: THE LIZARD'S TRAIL
ETERNITY

- ❑1, b&w ... 2.50
- ❑2, b&w ... 2.50
- ❑3, b&w ... 2.50

LETHAL
IMAGE

- ❑1, Feb 1996 ... 2.50

LETHAL FOES OF SPIDER-MAN
MARVEL

- ❑1, Sep 1993 ... 2.00
- ❑2, Oct 1993 A: Answer. A: Hardshell. A: Doctor Octopus. A: Vulture. ... 2.00
- ❑3, Nov 1993 KP (a) ... 2.00
- ❑4, Dec 1993 ... 2.00

LETHAL STRIKE
LONDON NIGHT

- ❑0; Commemorative edition ... 5.95
- ❑0.5 ... 3.00
- ❑1, Jun 1995 ... 3.00
- ❑2 ... 3.00
- ❑3 ... 3.00
- ❑Annual 1 ... 3.00

LETHAL STRIKE/DOUBLE IMPACT: LETHAL IMPACT
LONDON NIGHT

- ❑1, May 1996; crossover with High Impact ... 3.00

LETHARGIC COMICS
ALPHA

- ❑1, b&w; Spawn/Cerebus parody cover ... 3.50
- ❑2, Feb 1994, b&w ... 3.00
- ❑3, Mar 1994, b&w ... 3.00
- ❑3.14, Apr 1994, b&w; Issue #pi ... 3.00
- ❑4, May 1994, b&w; Marvels #4 parody cover ... 3.00
- ❑5, Jul 1994, b&w; Dot-It-Yerself cover ... 3.00
- ❑6, b&w; Sin City parody cover ... 2.50
- ❑7, b&w; Spawn/Batman parody cover ... 2.50
- ❑8, b&w ... 2.50
- ❑9, Apr 1995, b&w; Bone ... 2.50
- ❑10, b&w; Sin City parody cover ... 2.50
- ❑11, Aug 1995, b&w; Milk & Cheese ... 2.50
- ❑12, b&w; A: Shi. Shi cover ... 2.50
- ❑13 ... 2.50
- ❑14 ... 2.50

LETHARGIC COMICS, WEAKLY
LETHARGIC

- ❑1, Jun 1991, b&w; 1: Guy with a Gun. 1: No Mutants. 1: Lethargic Lad. 1: Walrus Boy. 1: Him. 1: The Grad. 1: The Zit. Action Comics #601 parody cover ... 4.00
- ❑2, b&w; Detective Comics #27 parody cover ... 3.00
- ❑3, b&w; Spider-Man #1 parody cover ... 3.00
- ❑4, b&w; X-Men #1 parody cover ... 2.50
- ❑5, b&w; Dark Knight #1 parody cover ... 2.50
- ❑6, b&w; Dark Knight #4 parody cover ... 2.50
- ❑7; Crisis on Infinite Earths #12 parody cover ... 2.50
- ❑8; Avengers #4 parody cover ... 2.50
- ❑9; Spider-Man #16 parody cover; Issue reads sideways ... 2.50
- ❑10; Adventures of Captain America parody cover ... 2.50
- ❑11; Youngblood #1 parody cover ... 2.50
- ❑12, b&w; Alpha begins publishing; Superman #75 parody cover ... 2.50

LETHARGIC LAD (1ST SERIES)
CRUSADE

- ❑1, Jun 1996, b&w ... 2.95
- ❑2, Jul 1996, b&w ... 2.95
- ❑3, Sep 1996, b&w; wraparound cover; Kingdom Come parody ... 2.95

LETHARGIC LAD (2ND SERIES)
CRUSADE

- ❑1, Oct 1997; Team-up with Him ... 2.95
- ❑2, Dec 1997 ... 2.95
- ❑3, Mar 1998; Thieves & Kings ... 2.95
- ❑4, Apr 1998; Starro'David, The Captain Company (Starro and Avengers parodies); Batman origin parody ... 2.95
- ❑5, Jun 1998 ... 2.95
- ❑6, Sep 1998 ... 2.95
- ❑7, Nov 1998 ... 2.95
- ❑8, Jan 1999 ... 2.95
- ❑9, Mar 1999 ... 2.95

LEVEL X
CALIBER

- ❑1, b&w ... 3.95
- ❑2, b&w ... 3.95

LEWD MOANA
FANTAGRAPHICS / EROS

- ❑1 ... 2.95

LEX LUTHOR: THE UNAUTHORIZED BIOGRAPHY
DC

- ❑1, Jul 1989; O: Luthor. Painted cover ... 4.00

LEX TALIONIS: JUNGLE TALE ONE SHOT
IMAGE

- ❑1, Jan 2004 ... 5.95

LIAISONS DELICIEUSES
FANTAGRAPHICS / EROS

- ❑1, b&w ... 1.95
- ❑2, b&w ... 1.95
- ❑3 ... 2.25
- ❑4 ... 2.25
- ❑5 ... 2.25
- ❑6, Jun 1991 ... 2.25

LIBBY ELLIS (ETERNITY)
ETERNITY

- ❑1, Jun 1988 ... 1.95
- ❑2, Jul 1988 ... 1.95
- ❑3, Aug 1988 ... 1.95
- ❑4, Sep 1988 ... 1.95

LIBBY ELLIS (MALIBU)
MALIBU

- ❑1 ... 1.95
- ❑2 ... 1.95
- ❑3 ... 1.95
- ❑4 ... 1.95

LIBERATOR
MALIBU

- ❑1, Dec 1987, b&w ... 1.95
- ❑2, Feb 1988 ... 1.95
- ❑3, Mar 1988 ... 1.95
- ❑4, Jun 1988 ... 1.95
- ❑5, Oct 1988 ... 1.95
- ❑6, Dec 1988 ... 1.95

LIBERATOR, THE (IMAGES & REALITIES)
IMAGES & REALITIES

- ❑1 ... 2.00

LIBERTINE, THE
FANTAGRAPHICS / EROS

- ❑1, b&w ... 2.25
- ❑2 ... 2.50

LIBERTY MEADOWS
INSIGHT

- ❑1, Jun 1999; Reprints first eight weeks of Liberty Meadows ... 18.00
- ❑1=2; Reprints first eight weeks of Liberty Meadows ... 6.00
- ❑1-2; Reprints first eight weeks of Liberty Meadows ... 2.95
- ❑2, Aug 1999; Reprints weeks 9-16 of Liberty Meadows strip ... 10.00
- ❑3, Oct 1999; Reprints weeks 17-24 of Liberty Meadows strip ... 6.00
- ❑4, Nov 1999; Reprints weeks 25-32 of Liberty Meadows strip ... 6.00
- ❑5, Dec 1999; 42 strips plus 3 Sunday strip reprints ... 5.00
- ❑6, Jan 2000 ... 4.00
- ❑7, Feb 2000 ... 4.00
- ❑8, Mar 2000 ... 4.00
- ❑9, Apr 2000 ... 4.00
- ❑10, May 2000 ... 4.00
- ❑11, Jun 2000 ... 3.00
- ❑12, Jul 2000 ... 3.00
- ❑13, Aug 2000 ... 3.00
- ❑14, Sep 2000 ... 3.00
- ❑15, Nov 2000; reader requests ... 3.00
- ❑16, Dec 2000; Wiener Dog Race ... 3.00
- ❑17, Jan 2001 ... 3.00
- ❑18, Feb 2001 ... 3.00
- ❑19, Mar 2001 ... 2.95
- ❑20, May 2001 ... 2.95
- ❑21, Jul 2001 ... 2.95
- ❑22 ... 2.95
- ❑23 ... 2.95
- ❑24 ... 2.95
- ❑25 ... 2.95

N-MINT

- ❑26 .... 2.95
- ❑27, Aug 2002; Image begins as publisher 2.95
- ❑28, Oct 2002 .... 2.95
- ❑29, Dec 2002 .... 2.95
- ❑30, Feb 2003 .... 2.95
- ❑31, Apr 2003 .... 2.95
- ❑32, Jul 2003 .... 2.95
- ❑33, Aug 2003 .... 2.95
- ❑34, Oct 2003 .... 2.95
- ❑35, Jan 2004 .... 2.95
- ❑36, Apr 2004 .... 2.95

LIBERTY PROJECT, THE
ECLIPSE

- ❑1, Jun 1987 KB (w); O: The Liberty Project. 1: Cimmaron. 1: Burnout. 1: Crackshot. 1: The Liberty Project. 1: Slick. 2.00
- ❑2, Jul 1987 KB (w) 1.75
- ❑3, Aug 1987 KB (w) 1.75
- ❑4, Sep 1987 KB (w) 1.75
- ❑5, Oct 1987 KB (w) 1.75
- ❑6, Nov 1987 KB (w); A: Valkyrie. 1.75
- ❑7, Dec 1987 KB (w) 1.75
- ❑8, May 1988 KB (w) 1.75

LIBRA
ETERNITY

- ❑1, Apr 1987 .... 1.95

LIBRARIAN, THE
FANTAGRAPHICS

- ❑1, b&w 2.75

LICENSABLE BEAR
ABOUT

- ❑1, Nov 2003 .... 2.95

LICENSE TO KILL
ECLIPSE

- ❑1 .... 7.95

LIDSVILLE
GOLD KEY

- ❑1, Oct 1972 .... 20.00
- ❑2, Jan 1973 .... 14.00
- ❑3, Apr 1973 .... 12.00
- ❑4, Jul 1973 .... 12.00
- ❑5, Oct 1973 .... 12.00

LT. ROBIN CRUSOE, U.S.N.
GOLD KEY

- ❑1, Oct 1966, Cover code -601; later reprinted in Walt Disney Showcase #26 .... 20.00

L.I.F.E. BRIGADE, THE
BLUE COMET

- ❑1 .... 2.00
- ❑1-2 .... 2.00
- ❑2 .... 2.00
- ❑3; Title changes to New L.I.F.E. Brigade 2.00

LIFE OF CAPTAIN MARVEL, THE
MARVEL

- ❑1, Aug 1985; JSn (w); JSn (a);Baxter reprint 3.00
- ❑2, Sep 1985; JSn (w); JSn (a);Baxter reprint 2.50
- ❑3, Oct 1985; JSn (a);Baxter reprint . 2.50
- ❑4, Nov 1985; JSn (a);Baxter reprint 2.50
- ❑5, Dec 1985; JSn (a);Baxter reprint . 2.50

LIFE OF CHRIST, THE
MARVEL / NELSON

- ❑1, Feb 1993 .... 3.00

LIFE OF CHRIST, THE: THE EASTER STORY
MARVEL / NELSON

- ❑1 .... 3.00

LIFE OF POPE JOHN PAUL II, THE
MARVEL

- ❑1, Jan 1983 JSt (a) 2.50

LIFEQUEST
CALIBER

- ❑1 .... 2.95
- ❑2 .... 2.95

N-MINT

LIFE UNDER SANCTIONS
FANTAGRAPHICS

- ❑1, Feb 1994, b&w 2.95

LIFE, THE UNIVERSE AND EVERYTHING
DC

- ❑1; prestige format; adapts Douglas Adams book 6.95
- ❑2; prestige format; adapts Douglas Adams book 6.95
- ❑3; prestige format; adapts Douglas Adams book 6.95

LIFE WITH MILLIE
ATLAS

- ❑8, Dec 1960 .... 35.00
- ❑9, Feb 1961 .... 28.00
- ❑10, Apr 1961 .... 28.00
- ❑11, Jun 1961 .... 26.00
- ❑12, Aug 1961 .... 26.00
- ❑13, Oct 1961 .... 26.00
- ❑14, Dec 1961 .... 26.00
- ❑15, Feb 1962 .... 26.00
- ❑16, Apr 1962 .... 26.00
- ❑17, Jun 1962 .... 26.00
- ❑18, Aug 1962 .... 26.00
- ❑19, Oct 1962 .... 26.00
- ❑20, Dec 1962 .... 26.00

LIGHT AND DARKNESS WAR, THE
MARVEL / EPIC

- ❑1, Oct 1988 .... 1.95
- ❑2, Nov 1988 .... 1.95
- ❑3, Jan 1989 .... 1.95
- ❑4, Feb 1989 .... 1.95
- ❑5, Apr 1989 .... 1.95
- ❑6, Sep 1989 .... 1.95

LIGHT BRIGADE
DC

- ❑1, Apr 2004 .... 5.95
- ❑2, May 2004 .... 5.95
- ❑3, Jun 2004 .... 5.95
- ❑4, Jun 2004 .... 5.95

LIGHT FANTASTIC, THE (TERRY PRATCHETT'S...)
INNOVATION

- ❑0 .... 2.50
- ❑1, Jun 1992 .... 2.50
- ❑2 .... 2.50
- ❑3 .... 2.50
- ❑4 .... 2.50

LIGHTNING COMICS PRESENTS
LIGHTNING

- ❑1, May 1994 .... 3.50

LILI
IMAGE

- ❑0, ca. 1999 .... 4.95

LI'L KIDS
MARVEL

- ❑1, Jul 1970 .... 35.00
- ❑2, Oct 1970 .... 22.00
- ❑3, Nov 1971 .... 22.00
- ❑4, Feb 1972 .... 22.00
- ❑5, Apr 1972 .... 22.00
- ❑6, Jun 1972 .... 16.00
- ❑7, Aug 1972 .... 16.00
- ❑8, Oct 1972 .... 16.00
- ❑9 1973 .... 16.00
- ❑10, Feb 1973 .... 16.00
- ❑11, Apr 1973 .... 16.00
- ❑12, Jun 1973 .... 16.00

LILLITH: DEMON PRINCESS
ANTARCTIC

- ❑0, Mar 1998 .... 1.95
- ❑0/Variant, Mar 1998; Special limited cover (Lilith flying w/green swish) 5.00
- ❑1, Aug 1996 .... 5.00
- ❑2, Oct 1996 .... 5.00
- ❑3, Feb 1997 .... 5.00

The adventures of Archie and the gang as children were chronicled in the long-running *Little Archie*.

© 1963 Archie Publications Inc.

N-MINT

LIMITED COLLECTORS' EDITION
DC

- ❑20; really C-20; Rudolph the Red-Nosed Reindeer 32.00
- ❑21, Sum 1973; really C-21; Shazam!; reprints Golden Age Marvel Family stories 16.00
- ❑22, Fal 1973; JK, JKu (a);really C-22; Tarzan 14.00
- ❑23; really C-23; House of Mystery ... 16.00
- ❑24; really C-24; Rudolph the Red-Nosed Reindeer 26.00
- ❑25; NA (a);really C-25; Batman 28.00
- ❑27; really C-27; Shazam!; reprints Golden Age Marvel Family stories .. 16.00
- ❑29; JK (a);really C-29; Tarzan 10.00
- ❑30; really C-30; Superman 12.00
- ❑31, Nov 1974; really C-31; Superman 15.00
- ❑32, Jan 1975; really C-32; Ghosts ... 10.00
- ❑33, Feb 1975; really C-33; Rudolph the Red-Nosed Reindeer 16.00
- ❑34, Mar 1975; really C-34; Christmas With the Super-Heroes 12.00
- ❑35, May 1975; really C-35; Shazam! 10.00
- ❑36, Jul 1975; NR, JK, JKu (a);really C-36; The Bible 16.00
- ❑37, Sep 1975; really C-37; Batman .. 20.00
- ❑38, Nov 1975; really C-38; Superman 10.00
- ❑39, Nov 1975; CI, NA, DD, CCB (a);really C-39; Secret Origins of Super Villains 10.00
- ❑40, Nov 1975; really C-40; Dick Tracy 12.00
- ❑41, Jan 1976; ATh (a);really C-41; Super Friends 10.00
- ❑42, Mar 1976; really C-42; Rudolph the Red-Nosed Reindeer 10.00
- ❑43, Mar 1976; really C-43; Christmas With the Super-Heroes 10.00
- ❑44, Jul 1976; really C-44; Batman ... 12.00
- ❑45, Jul 1976; really C-45; More Secret Origins of Super-Villains 10.00
- ❑46, Sep 1976; really C-46; Justice League of America 10.00
- ❑47, Sep 1976; really C-47; Superman Salutes the Bicentennial; reprints Tomahawk stories 10.00
- ❑48, Nov 1976; really C-48; Superman vs. Flash 12.00
- ❑49, Nov 1976; really C-49; Legion ... 10.00
- ❑50; really C-50; Rudolph the Red-Nosed Reindeer; poster 10.00
- ❑51, Aug 1977; really C-51; Batman vs. Ra's Al Ghul 12.00
- ❑52; NA (a);really C-52; Best of DC ... 10.00
- ❑57; really C-57; Welcome Back, Kotter 14.00
- ❑59; Series continued in All-New Collectors' Edition; really C-59; Batman's Strangest Cases 14.00

LINCOLN-16
SKARWOOD

- ❑1, Aug 1997 .... 2.95
- ❑2, Oct 1997, b&w 2.95

LINDA CARTER, STUDENT NURSE
ATLAS

- ❑1, Sep 1961 .... 60.00
- ❑2, Nov 1961 .... 40.00
- ❑3, Jan 1962 .... 40.00
- ❑4, Mar 1962 .... 40.00
- ❑5, May 1962 .... 40.00
- ❑6, Jul 1962 .... 30.00
- ❑7, Sep 1962 .... 30.00

Condition price index: Multiply "NM prices" above by: **0.83 for Very Fine/Near Mint**
0.66 for Very Fine • 0.33 for Fine • 0.2 for Very Good • 0.125 for Good

N-MINT

❑8, Nov 1962 .... 30.00
❑9, Jan 1963 .... 30.00

LINDA LARK
DELL

❑1, Oct 1961 .... 15.00
❑2, Jan 1962 .... 10.00
❑3, Apr 1962 .... 10.00
❑4, Jul 1962 .... 10.00
❑5, Sep 1962 .... 10.00
❑6, Dec 1962 .... 10.00
❑7, Mar 1963 .... 10.00
❑8, Aug 1963 .... 10.00

LINE THE DUSTBIN FUNNIES
EAST WILLIS

❑1, Sum 1997 .... 2.95

LIONHEART
AWESOME

❑1/A, Aug 1999; JPH (w); Dynamic Forces variant 3.50
❑1/B, Aug 1999; JPH (w); Women, treasure chest on cover 3.00
❑Ashcan 1, Jul 1999; Wizard World '99 preview edition JPH (w) 3.00

LION KING, THE (DISNEY'S...)
MARVEL

❑1, Jul 1994 .... 2.50

LIPPY THE LION AND HARDY HAR HAR
GOLD KEY

❑1, Mar 1963 .... 60.00

LIPSTICK
RIP OFF

❑1, May 1992, b&w 2.50

LISA COMICS
BONGO

❑1 .... 2.25

LITA FORD: THE QUEEN OF HEAVY METAL
ROCK-IT COMICS

❑1 .... 5.00

LITTLE ARCHIE DIGEST MAGAZINE
ARCHIE

❑1 1991 .... 3.00
❑2 1991 .... 2.00
❑3 1991 .... 2.00
❑4 1991 .... 2.00
❑5 1992 .... 2.00
❑6 1992 .... 2.00
❑7 1992 .... 2.00
❑8 1992 .... 2.00
❑9 1992 .... 2.00
❑10 .... 2.00
❑11 .... 1.75
❑12 .... 1.75
❑13 .... 1.75
❑14, Aug 1995 .... 1.75
❑15, Oct 1995 .... 1.75
❑16, Jun 1996 .... 1.75
❑17, Sep 1996 .... 1.79
❑18, Mar 1997 .... 1.79
❑19, Jun 1997 .... 1.79
❑20, Sep 1997 .... 1.79
❑21, Mar 1998 .... 1.95
❑22 .... 1.95
❑23 .... 1.95
❑24 .... 1.95
❑25 .... 1.95

LITTLE ARCHIE MYSTERY
ARCHIE

❑1, Aug 1963 .... 60.00
❑2, Oct 1963 .... 42.00

LITTLE AUDREY (HARVEY, 2ND SERIES)
HARVEY

❑1, Aug 1992 .... 1.50
❑2 1992 .... 1.25
❑3 1992 .... 1.25
❑4 1992 .... 1.25
❑5 1993 .... 1.25
❑6 1993 .... 1.25
❑7 1993 .... 1.25
❑8 1993 .... 1.25
❑9 1993 .... 1.25

LITTLE AUDREY TV FUNTIME
HARVEY

❑1, Sep 1962 .... 45.00
❑2, Dec 1962 .... 28.00
❑3, Mar 1963 .... 24.00
❑4, Jun 1963 .... 20.00
❑5, Sep 1963 .... 20.00
❑6, Dec 1963 .... 16.00
❑7, Mar 1964 .... 16.00
❑8, Jun 1964 .... 16.00
❑9, Sep 1964 .... 16.00
❑10, Dec 1964 .... 16.00
❑11, Mar 1965 .... 12.00
❑12, Jun 1965 .... 12.00
❑13, Sep 1965 .... 12.00
❑14, Dec 1965 .... 12.00
❑15, Mar 1966 .... 12.00
❑16 1966 .... 12.00
❑17, Nov 1966 .... 12.00
❑18, Mar 1967 .... 12.00
❑19 1967 .... 12.00
❑20, Oct 1967 .... 12.00
❑21, Dec 1967 .... 9.00
❑22 1968 .... 9.00
❑23 1968 .... 9.00
❑24, Sep 1968 .... 9.00
❑25 .... 9.00
❑26 .... 9.00
❑27 .... 9.00
❑28, Aug 1969 .... 9.00
❑29 .... 9.00
❑30, Dec 1970 .... 9.00
❑31 .... 9.00
❑32 .... 9.00
❑33 .... 9.00

LITTLE DOT (VOL. 2)
HARVEY

❑1, Sep 1992 .... 1.50
❑2 .... 1.50
❑3, Jun 1993 .... 1.50
❑4 1993 .... 1.50
❑5, Jan 1994 .... 1.50
❑6, Apr 1994 .... 1.50
❑7, Jun 1994 .... 1.50

LITTLE DOT DOTLAND
HARVEY

❑1, Jul 1962 .... 75.00
❑2, Sep 1962 .... 40.00
❑3, Nov 1962 .... 40.00
❑4, Jan 1963 .... 35.00
❑5, Mar 1963 .... 35.00
❑6, May 1963 .... 24.00
❑7, Jul 1963 .... 24.00
❑8, Sep 1963 .... 24.00
❑9, Nov 1963 .... 24.00
❑10, Jan 1964 .... 24.00
❑11, Mar 1964 .... 20.00
❑12, May 1964 .... 20.00
❑13, Jul 1964 .... 20.00
❑14, Sep 1964 .... 20.00
❑15, Nov 1964 .... 20.00
❑16, Jan 1965 .... 20.00
❑17, Mar 1965 .... 20.00
❑18, May 1965 .... 20.00
❑19, Jul 1965 .... 20.00
❑20, Sep 1965 .... 20.00
❑21, Nov 1965 .... 16.00
❑22, Jan 1966 .... 16.00
❑23, Mar 1966 .... 16.00
❑24, May 1966 .... 16.00
❑25, Jul 1966 .... 16.00
❑26, Sep 1966 .... 16.00
❑27, Oct 1966 .... 16.00
❑28, Jan 1967 .... 16.00
❑29, Mar 1967 .... 16.00
❑30, May 1967 .... 12.00
❑31, Jul 1967 .... 12.00
❑32, Sep 1967 .... 12.00
❑33, Nov 1967 .... 12.00
❑34, Jan 1968 .... 12.00
❑35, Sep 1968 .... 12.00
❑36, Nov 1968 .... 12.00
❑37, Jan 1969 .... 12.00
❑38, Mar 1969 .... 12.00
❑39, Apr 1969 .... 12.00
❑40, Jun 1969 .... 10.00
❑41, Aug 1969 .... 10.00
❑42, Oct 1969 .... 10.00
❑43, Dec 1969 .... 10.00
❑44, Feb 1970 .... 10.00
❑45, Apr 1970 .... 10.00
❑46, Aug 1970 .... 10.00
❑47, Oct 1970 .... 10.00
❑48, Jan 1971 .... 10.00
❑49, Apr 1971 .... 10.00
❑50, Aug 1971 .... 10.00
❑51, ca. 1971 .... 10.00
❑52, ca. 1972 .... 10.00
❑53, Jun 1972 .... 10.00
❑54, Sep 1972 .... 10.00
❑55, Nov 1972 .... 8.00
❑56, Feb 1973 .... 8.00
❑57, Apr 1973 .... 8.00
❑58, Jun 1973 .... 8.00
❑59, Aug 1973 .... 8.00
❑60, Nov 1973 .... 8.00
❑61, Dec 1973; becomes Dot Dotland 8.00
❑62, Sep 1974; was Little Dot Dotland 10.00
❑63, Nov 1974 .... 10.00

LITTLE DOT IN 3-D
BLACKTHORNE

❑1 .... 2.50

LITTLE DOT'S UNCLES AND AUNTS
HARVEY

❑1, ca. 1961 .... 70.00
❑2, Aug 1962 A: Richie Rich. 42.00
❑3, Nov 1962 .... 42.00
❑4, Feb 1963 .... 36.00
❑5, May 1963 .... 36.00
❑6, Aug 1963 .... 28.00
❑7, Nov 1963 .... 28.00
❑8, Feb 1964 .... 28.00
❑9, May 1964 .... 28.00
❑10, Aug 1964 .... 28.00
❑11, Nov 1964 .... 22.00
❑12, Feb 1965 .... 22.00
❑13, May 1965 .... 22.00
❑14, Aug 1965 .... 22.00
❑15 .... 22.00
❑16 .... 22.00
❑17 1966 .... 22.00
❑18, Sep 1966 .... 22.00
❑19, Nov 1966 .... 22.00
❑20, Aug 1967 .... 22.00
❑21, Nov 1967 .... 22.00
❑22, Feb 1968 .... 22.00
❑23, Jul 1968 .... 22.00
❑24, Oct 1968 .... 22.00
❑25, Dec 1968 .... 22.00
❑26 1969 .... 22.00
❑27, Jun 1969 .... 22.00
❑28, Aug 1969 .... 22.00
❑29, Oct 1969 .... 22.00
❑30, Nov 1969 .... 22.00
❑31, Mar 1970 .... 22.00
❑32, Jun 1970 .... 22.00
❑33, Aug 1970 .... 22.00
❑34 1970 .... 22.00
❑35, Nov 1970 .... 22.00
❑36, Mar 1971 .... 14.00
❑37 1971 .... 14.00
❑38, Aug 1971 .... 14.00
❑39, Oct 1971 .... 14.00
❑40 .... 14.00
❑41 1972 .... 14.00
❑42, Jun 1972 .... 14.00
❑43 1972 .... 14.00
❑44, Dec 1972 .... 14.00

	N-MINT
❑45, Feb 1973	14.00
❑46, Apr 1973	14.00
❑47, Jun 1973	14.00
❑48, Aug 1973	14.00
❑49, Oct 1973	14.00
❑50, Dec 1973	14.00
❑51, Feb 1974	14.00
❑52, Apr 1974	14.00

LITTLE ENDLESS STORYBOOK, THE
DC / Vertigo

❑1, Aug 2001	5.95

LITTLE GLOOMY
Slave Labor

❑1, Oct 1999	2.95

LITTLE GRETA GARBAGE
Rip Off

❑1, Jul 1990, b&w	2.50
❑2, Jun 1991, b&w	2.50

LITTLE GREY MAN
Image

❑1; graphic novel	6.95

LITTLE ITALY
Fantagraphics

❑1, b&w	3.95

LITTLE JIM-BOB BIG FOOT
Jump Back

❑1, b&w	2.95
❑2, Jan 1998, b&w	2.95

LITTLE LOTTA (VOL. 1)
Harvey

❑1, Nov 1955	225.00
❑2, Jan 1956	90.00
❑3, Mar 1956	75.00
❑4, May 1956	55.00
❑5, Jul 1956	55.00
❑6, Sep 1956	40.00
❑7, Nov 1956	40.00
❑8, Jan 1957	40.00
❑9, Mar 1957	40.00
❑10, May 1957	40.00
❑11, Jul 1957	28.00
❑12, Sep 1957	28.00
❑13, Nov 1957	28.00
❑14, Jan 1958	28.00
❑15, Mar 1958	28.00
❑16, May 1958	28.00
❑17, Jul 1958	28.00
❑18, Sep 1958	28.00
❑19, Nov 1958	28.00
❑20, Feb 1959	28.00
❑21, Apr 1959	22.00
❑22, Jun 1959	22.00
❑23, Aug 1959	22.00
❑24, Oct 1959	22.00
❑25, Dec 1959	22.00
❑26, ca. 1960	22.00
❑27, ca. 1960	22.00
❑28, ca. 1960	22.00
❑29, ca. 1960	22.00
❑30, ca. 1960	22.00
❑31, ca. 1960	18.00
❑32, ca. 1961	18.00
❑33, ca. 1961	18.00
❑34, ca. 1961	18.00
❑35, ca. 1961	18.00
❑36, ca. 1961	18.00
❑37, Sep 1961	18.00
❑38, Nov 1961	18.00
❑39, Jan 1962	18.00
❑40, Mar 1962	18.00
❑41, May 1962	15.00
❑42, Jul 1962	15.00
❑43, Sep 1962	15.00
❑44, Nov 1962	15.00
❑45, Jan 1963	15.00
❑46, Mar 1963	15.00
❑47, May 1963	15.00
❑48, Jul 1963	15.00
❑49, Sep 1963	15.00
❑50, Nov 1963	15.00
❑51, Jan 1964	12.00
❑52, Mar 1964	12.00
❑53, May 1964	12.00
❑54, Jul 1964	12.00
❑55, Sep 1964	12.00
❑56, Nov 1964	12.00
❑57, Jan 1965	12.00
❑58, Mar 1965	12.00
❑59, May 1965	12.00
❑60, Jul 1965	12.00
❑61, Sep 1965	12.00
❑62, Nov 1965	12.00
❑63, Jan 1966	12.00
❑64, Mar 1966	12.00
❑65, May 1966	12.00
❑66, Jul 1966	12.00
❑67, Sep 1966	12.00
❑68, Nov 1966	12.00
❑69, Jan 1967	12.00
❑70, Mar 1967	12.00
❑71, May 1967	8.00
❑72, Jul 1967	8.00
❑73, Sep 1967	8.00
❑74, Nov 1967	8.00
❑75, Jan 1968	8.00
❑76, Mar 1968	8.00
❑77, May 1968	8.00
❑78, Jul 1968	8.00
❑79, Sep 1968	8.00
❑80, Nov 1968	8.00
❑81, Jan 1969	8.00
❑82, Mar 1969	8.00
❑83, May 1969	8.00
❑84, Jul 1969	8.00
❑85 1969	8.00
❑86, Oct 1969	8.00
❑87, Dec 1969	8.00
❑88, Jan 1970	8.00
❑89, Apr 1970	8.00
❑90, Jul 1970	8.00
❑91 1970	5.00
❑92, Oct 1970	5.00
❑93, Nov 1970	5.00
❑94, Jan 1971	5.00
❑95, Mar 1971	5.00
❑96, May 1971	5.00
❑97, Jul 1971	5.00
❑98, Sep 1971	5.00
❑99, Nov 1971	6.00
❑100, Mar 1972	6.00
❑101, May 1972	6.00
❑102, Jul 1972	6.00
❑103, Sep 1972	3.00
❑104, Nov 1972	3.00
❑105, Jan 1973	3.00
❑106, Mar 1973	3.00
❑107, May 1973	3.00
❑108, Jul 1973	3.00
❑109, Sep 1973	3.00
❑110, Nov 1973	3.00
❑111, Sep 1974	3.00
❑112, Nov 1974	3.00
❑113, Jan 1975	3.00
❑114, Mar 1975	3.00
❑115, May 1975	3.00
❑116, Jul 1975	3.00
❑117, Sep 1975	3.00
❑118, Nov 1975	3.00
❑119, Jan 1976	3.00
❑120, Mar 1976	3.00

LITTLE LOTTA (VOL. 2)
Harvey

❑1, Oct 1992	1.50
❑2, Jan 1993	1.50
❑3, Apr 1993	1.50
❑4, Jul 1993	1.50

LITTLE LOTTA FOODLAND
Harvey

❑1, Sep 1963; Giant	45.00
❑2, Dec 1963; Giant	35.00

Keith Giffen hired Lobo to wipe out everyone in the DC universe in *Lobo* #50.

© 1998 DC Comics.

	N-MINT
❑3, Mar 1964; Giant	35.00
❑4 1964; Giant	30.00
❑5 1964; Giant	30.00
❑6 1964; Giant	24.00
❑7 1965; Giant	24.00
❑8 1965; Giant	24.00
❑9 1965; Giant	24.00
❑10, Jan 1966; Giant	24.00
❑11, Apr 1966; Giant	16.00
❑12 1966; Giant	16.00
❑13 1967; Giant	16.00
❑14 1967; Giant	16.00
❑15, Oct 1968; Giant	16.00
❑16 1969; Giant	12.00
❑17 1969; Giant	12.00
❑18, Dec 1969; Giant	12.00
❑19, Sep 1970; Giant	12.00
❑20 1970; Giant	12.00
❑21, Feb 1971; Giant	8.00
❑22, May 1971; Giant	8.00
❑23, Aug 1971; Giant	8.00
❑24, Oct 1971; Giant	8.00
❑25, Dec 1971; Giant	8.00
❑26, Feb 1972; Giant	8.00
❑27, May 1972; Giant	8.00
❑28, Aug 1972; Giant	8.00
❑29, Oct 1972; Giant	8.00

LITTLE MERMAID, THE (DISNEY'S...)
Marvel

❑1, Sep 1994	2.50
❑2, Oct 1994	2.00
❑3, Nov 1994	2.00
❑4, Dec 1994	2.00
❑5, Jan 1995	2.00
❑6, Feb 1995	2.00
❑7, Mar 1995	2.00
❑8, Apr 1995	2.00
❑9, May 1995	2.00
❑10, Jun 1995	2.00
❑11, Jul 1995	2.00
❑12, Aug 1995	2.00

LITTLE MERMAID LIMITED SERIES, THE (DISNEY'S...)
Disney

❑1, Feb 1992	2.00
❑2, Mar 1992	2.00
❑3, May 1992	2.00
❑4, Jun 1992	2.00

LITTLE MERMAID (ONE-SHOT)
W.D.

❑1	3.50

LITTLE MERMAID, THE: UNDERWATER ENGAGEMENTS (DISNEY'S...)
Acclaim

❑1; flip-book digest set before movie	4.50

LITTLE MERMAID, THE (WALT DISNEY'S...)
Disney

❑1; stapled	2.50
❑1/Direct ed.; squarebound	5.95

LITTLE MISS STRANGE
Millennium

❑1	2.95

Condition price index: Multiply "NM prices" above by: **0.83 for Very Fine/Near Mint**
0.66 for Very Fine • 0.33 for Fine • 0.2 for Very Good • 0.125 for Good

N-MINT

LITTLE MISTER MAN
SLAVE LABOR

❑1, Nov 1995, b&w ... 2.95
❑2, Dec 1995, b&w ... 2.95
❑3, Feb 1996, b&w ... 2.95

LITTLE MONSTERS, THE (GOLD KEY)
GOLD KEY

❑1, Nov 1964 ... 20.00
❑2, Feb 1965 ... 12.00
❑3, Nov 1965 ... 8.00
❑4 1966 ... 8.00
❑5, Jul 1966 ... 8.00
❑6, Oct 1966 ... 6.00
❑7, Dec 1966 ... 6.00
❑8, Feb 1967 ... 6.00
❑9, Apr 1967 ... 6.00
❑10, Jun 1967 ... 5.00
❑11 ... 5.00
❑12, Dec 1970 ... 5.00
❑13, ca. 1971 ... 5.00
❑14, Sep 1971 ... 5.00
❑15, Dec 1971 ... 5.00
❑16, Mar 1972 ... 5.00
❑17, Jun 1972 ... 5.00
❑18, Sep 1972 ... 5.00
❑19, Dec 1972 ... 5.00
❑20, Mar 1973 ... 5.00
❑21, Jun 1973 ... 4.00
❑22, Sep 1973 ... 4.00
❑23, Dec 1973 ... 4.00
❑24, Mar 1974 ... 4.00
❑25, Jun 1974 ... 4.00
❑26, Sep 1974 ... 4.00
❑27, Dec 1974 ... 4.00
❑28, Mar 1975 ... 4.00
❑29, Jun 1975 ... 4.00
❑30, Sep 1975 ... 4.00
❑31, Dec 1975 ... 4.00
❑32, Feb 1976 ... 4.00
❑33, Apr 1976 ... 4.00
❑34, Jun 1976 ... 4.00
❑35, Aug 1976 ... 4.00
❑36, Oct 1976 ... 4.00
❑37, Dec 1976 ... 4.00
❑38, Feb 1977 ... 4.00
❑39, Apr 1977 ... 4.00
❑40, Jun 1977 ... 4.00
❑41, Aug 1977 ... 4.00
❑42, Oct 1977 ... 4.00
❑43, Dec 1977 ... 4.00
❑44, Feb 1978 ... 4.00

LITTLE MONSTERS
NOW

❑1, Jan 1990 ... 1.50
❑2, Feb 1990 ... 1.50
❑3, Mar 1990 ... 1.50
❑4, Apr 1990 ... 1.50
❑5, May 1990 ... 1.50
❑6, Jun 1990 ... 1.50

LITTLE NEMO IN SLUMBERLAND 3-D
BLACKTHORNE

❑1 ... 2.50

LITTLE RED HOT: BOUND
IMAGE

❑1, Jul 2001 ... 2.95
❑2, Sep 2001 ... 2.95
❑3, Nov 2001 ... 2.95

LITTLE RED HOT: CHANE OF FOOLS
IMAGE

❑1, Feb 1999 ... 2.95
❑2, Mar 1999 ... 2.95
❑3, Apr 1999 ... 2.95

LITTLE RONZO IN SLUMBERLAND
SLAVE LABOR

❑1, Jul 1987 ... 1.75

LITTLE SAD SACK
HARVEY

❑1, Oct 1964 ... 7.00
❑2, Dec 1964 ... 4.00
❑3, Feb 1964 ... 4.00
❑4, Apr 1965 ... 4.00
❑5, Jun 1965 ... 4.00
❑6, Aug 1965 ... 3.00
❑7, Oct 1965 ... 3.00
❑8, Dec 1965 ... 3.00
❑9, Feb 1966 ... 3.00
❑10, Apr 1966 ... 3.00
❑11, Jun 1966 ... 3.00
❑12, Sep 1966 ... 3.00
❑13, Nov 1966 ... 3.00
❑14, Jan 1966 ... 3.00
❑15, Mar 1966 ... 3.00
❑16, May 1966 ... 3.00
❑17, Jul 1966 ... 3.00
❑18, Sep 1966 ... 3.00
❑19, Nov 1966 ... 3.00

LITTLE SHOP OF HORRORS
DC

❑1, Mar 1987 ... 2.00

LITTLE WHITE MOUSE
CALIBER

❑1, Nov 1997, b&w ... 2.95
❑2, Jan 1998, b&w ... 2.95
❑3 1998 ... 2.95
❑4, Jan 2001 ... 2.95

LIVINGSTONE MOUNTAIN
ADVENTURE

❑1, Jul 1991, b&w ... 2.50
❑2, Aug 1991, b&w ... 2.50
❑3, Sep 1991, b&w ... 2.50
❑4, Oct 1991, b&w ... 2.50

LIZ AND BETH (VOL. 1)
FANTAGRAPHICS / EROS

❑1, b&w ... 3.00
❑2, b&w ... 3.00
❑3, b&w ... 3.00
❑4 ... 3.00

LIZ AND BETH (VOL. 2)
FANTAGRAPHICS / EROS

❑1, b&w ... 2.50
❑2, b&w ... 2.50
❑3, b&w ... 2.50
❑4 ... 2.50

LIZ AND BETH (VOL. 3)
FANTAGRAPHICS / EROS

❑1, b&w ... 2.50
❑2, b&w ... 2.50
❑3, b&w ... 2.50
❑4, b&w ... 2.50
❑5, b&w ... 2.50
❑6, b&w ... 2.50
❑7, b&w ... 2.50

LIZARD LADY
AIRCEL

❑1, b&w ... 2.95
❑2, b&w ... 2.95
❑3, b&w ... 2.95
❑4, b&w ... 2.95

LIZARDS SUMMER FUN SPECIAL
CALIBER

❑1, b&w ... 3.50

LIZZIE MCGUIRE CINE-MANGA
TOKYOPOP

❑1, May 2003, fumetti with photos from the TV show ... 7.99

LLOYD LLEWELLYN
FANTAGRAPHICS

❑1, Apr 1986 ... 2.25
❑2, Jun 1986 ... 2.25
❑3, Aug 1986 ... 2.25
❑4, Oct 1986 ... 2.25
❑5, Jan 1987 ... 2.25
❑6, Jun 1987 ... 2.25
❑Special 1 ... 2.50
❑Special 1-2 ... 2.95

LOADED
INTERPLAY

❑1 ... 1.00

LOBO (MINI-SERIES)
DC

❑1, Nov 1990 KG (a) ... 3.00
❑1-2, Nov 1990 KG (a) ... 2.00
❑2, Dec 1990 KG (a) ... 2.00
❑3, Jan 1991 KG (a) ... 2.00
❑4, Feb 1991 KG (a) ... 2.00

LOBO
DC

❑0, Oct 1994; O: Lobo. 10/94 ... 2.50
❑1, Dec 1993; foil cover ... 3.50
❑2, Feb 1994 ... 2.50
❑3, Mar 1994 ... 2.50
❑4, Apr 1994 ... 2.50
❑5, May 1994 ... 2.50
❑6, Jun 1994 ... 2.50
❑7, Jul 1994 ... 2.50
❑8, Aug 1994 ... 2.50
❑9, Sep 1994 ... 2.50
❑10, Nov 1994 ... 2.50
❑11, Dec 1994 ... 2.00
❑12, Jan 1995 ... 2.00
❑13, Feb 1995 ... 2.00
❑14, Mar 1995 ... 2.00
❑15, Apr 1995 ... 2.00
❑16, Jun 1995 ... 2.25
❑17, Jul 1995 ... 2.25
❑18, Aug 1995 ... 2.25
❑19, Sep 1995 ... 2.25
❑20, Oct 1995 ... 2.25
❑21, Nov 1995 A: Space Cabby. ... 2.25
❑22, Dec 1995; Underworld Unleashed ... 2.25
❑23, Jan 1996 ... 2.25
❑24, Feb 1996 ... 2.25
❑25, Mar 1996 ... 2.25
❑26, Apr 1996 ... 2.25
❑27, May 1996 ... 2.25
❑28, Jun 1996 ... 2.25
❑29, Jul 1996 ... 2.25
❑30, Aug 1996 ... 2.25
❑31, Sep 1996 ... 2.25
❑32, Oct 1996; Lobo's body is destroyed ... 2.25
❑33, Nov 1996 ... 2.25
❑34, Dec 1996 ... 2.25
❑35, Jan 1997 ... 2.25
❑36, Feb 1997 A: Hemingway. A: Poe. A: Mark Twain. A: Chaucer. A: Shakespeare. ... 2.25
❑37, Mar 1997 ... 2.25
❑38, Apr 1997 ... 2.25
❑39, May 1997; Lobo as a pirate ... 2.25
❑40, Jun 1997; Lobo inside a whale .. 2.25
❑41, Jul 1997 ... 2.25
❑42, Aug 1997 ... 2.25
❑43, Sep 1997 ... 2.25
❑44, Oct 1997; Genesis ... 2.25
❑45, Nov 1997 V: Jackie Chin. ... 2.25
❑46, Dec 1997; Face cover ... 2.25
❑47, Jan 1998 ... 2.25
❑48, Feb 1998 ... 2.25
❑49, Mar 1998 ... 2.25
❑50, Apr 1998 A: Keith Giffen. D: Everyone. ... 2.25
❑51, May 1998 ... 2.25
❑52, Jun 1998 ... 2.25
❑53, Jul 1998 ... 2.25
❑54, Aug 1998 ... 2.25
❑55, Sep 1998 ... 2.25
❑56, Oct 1998 ... 2.50
❑57, Dec 1998; at police convention . 2.50
❑58, Jan 1999 A: Orion. A: Superman. 2.50
❑59, Feb 1999; A: Bad Wee Bastards. in miniature world ... 2.50
❑60, Mar 1999; 1: Superbo. Lobo reforms ... 2.50
❑61, Apr 1999 2: Superbo. A: Savage Six. ... 2.50
❑62, May 1999 ... 2.50
❑63, Jun 1999 A: Demon. ... 2.50
❑64, Jul 1999 A: Demon. ... 2.50
❑1000000, Nov 1998 1: Layla. ... 3.00

N-MINT

- ❑Annual 1, ca. 1993 .... 3.50
- ❑Annual 2, ca. 1994; SA (a);Elseworlds 3.50
- ❑Annual 3, ca. 1995; Year One 3.95

LOBO: A CONTRACT ON GAWD
DC
- ❑1, Apr 1994 .... 2.00
- ❑2, May 1994 .... 2.00
- ❑3, Jun 1994 .... 2.00
- ❑4, Jul 1994 .... 2.00

LOBO: BLAZING CHAIN OF LOVE
DC
- ❑1, Sep 1992 .... 2.00

LOBO: BOUNTY HUNTING FOR FUN AND PROFIT
DC
- ❑1; prestige format 4.95

LOBO: CHAINED
DC
- ❑1, May 1997; Lobo goes to jail 2.50

LOBO CONVENTION SPECIAL
DC
- ❑1; KG (w); Set at 1993 San Diego Comic Convention 2.00

LOBO/DEADMAN: THE BRAVE AND THE BALD
DC
- ❑1, Feb 1995 .... 3.50

LOBO: DEATH AND TAXES
DC
- ❑1, Oct 1996 .... 2.25
- ❑2, Nov 1996 .... 2.25
- ❑3, Dec 1996 .... 2.25
- ❑4, Jan 1997 .... 2.25

LOBO/DEMON: HELLOWEEN
DC
- ❑1, Dec 1996 .... 2.25

LOBO: FRAGTASTIC VOYAGE
DC
- ❑1, ca. 1998; prestige format 5.95

LOBO GALLERY, THE: PORTRAITS OF A BASTICH
DC
- ❑1, Sep 1995; pin-ups 3.50

LOBO GOES TO HOLLYWOOD
DC
- ❑1, Aug 1996 .... 2.25

LOBO: INFANTICIDE
DC
- ❑1, Oct 1992 KG (w); KG (a) 2.00
- ❑2, Nov 1992 KG (w); KG (a) 2.00
- ❑3, Dec 1992 KG (w); KG (a) 2.00
- ❑4, Jan 1993 KG (w); KG (a) 2.00

LOBO: IN THE CHAIR
DC
- ❑1, Aug 1994 .... 1.95

LOBO: I QUIT
DC
- ❑1, Dec 1995; Lobo stops smoking .. 2.75

LOBO/JUDGE DREDD: PSYCHO-BIKERS VS. THE MUTANTS FROM HELL
DC
- ❑1; prestige format 4.95

LOBO/MASK
DC
- ❑1, Feb 1997; prestige format cross-over with Dark Horse 5.95
- ❑2, Mar 1997; prestige format cross-over with Dark Horse 5.95

LOBO PARAMILITARY CHRISTMAS SPECIAL
DC
- ❑1, Jan 1991 KG (w); KG (a); D: Santa Claus. 3.00

LOBO: PORTRAIT OF A VICTIM
DC
- ❑1, ca. 1993 .... 2.00

N-MINT

LOBO'S BACK
DC
- ❑1, May 1992; KG (a); 1: Ramona. Variant covers exist 2.00
- ❑2, Jun 1992 KG (a) 2.00
- ❑3, Oct 1992 KG (a) 2.00
- ❑4, Nov 1992 KG (a) 2.00

LOBO'S BIG BABE SPRING BREAK SPECIAL
DC
- ❑1, Spr 1995 .... 1.95

LOBO THE DUCK
DC / AMALGAM
- ❑1, Jun 1997 .... 1.95

LOBO: UN-AMERICAN GLADIATORS
DC
- ❑1, Jun 1993 .... 2.00
- ❑2, Jul 1993 .... 2.00
- ❑3, Aug 1993 .... 2.00
- ❑4, Sep 1993 .... 2.00

LOBO UNBOUND
DC
- ❑1, Aug 2003 .... 2.95
- ❑2, Sep 2003 .... 2.95
- ❑3, Nov 2003 .... 2.95
- ❑4, Jan 2004 .... 2.95
- ❑5, Mar 2004 .... 2.95
- ❑6, May 2004 .... 2.95

LOBOCOP
DC
- ❑1, Feb 1994 .... 2.00

LOCO VS. PULVERINE
ECLIPSE
- ❑1, Jul 1992, b&w; wraparound cover; parody 2.50

LOGAN: PATH OF THE WARLORD
MARVEL
- ❑1, Feb 1996 .... 6.00

LOGAN: SHADOW SOCIETY
MARVEL
- ❑1, Dec 1996 .... 6.00

LOGAN'S RUN (MARVEL)
MARVEL
- ❑1, Jan 1977 GP (a) 3.00
- ❑2, Feb 1977 GP (a) 2.00
- ❑3, Mar 1977 GP (a) 2.00
- ❑4, Apr 1977 GP (a) 2.00
- ❑5, May 1977 GP (a) 2.00
- ❑6, Jun 1977; TS (a); A: Thanos. New stories begin; Back-up story is first solo story featuring Thanos 3.50
- ❑7, Jul 1977 GP (a) 2.00

LOGAN'S RUN (ADVENTURE)
ADVENTURE
- ❑1; PG (c); PG (a);Introduction by William F. Nolan 2.50
- ❑2, Jul 1990 .... 2.50
- ❑3 .... 2.50
- ❑4, Oct 1990 .... 2.50
- ❑5, Mar 1991 .... 2.50
- ❑6, Apr 1991 .... 2.50

LOGAN'S WORLD
ADVENTURE
- ❑1, May 1991, b&w 2.50
- ❑2, Aug 1991, b&w 2.50
- ❑3, Sep 1991, b&w 2.50
- ❑4, Nov 1991, b&w 2.50
- ❑5, Jan 1992, b&w 2.50
- ❑6, Mar 1992, b&w 2.50

LOIS LANE
DC
- ❑1, Aug 1986 GM (a) 2.00
- ❑2, Sep 1986 GM (a) 2.00

LOKI
MARVEL
- ❑1, Sep 2004 .... 2.99
- ❑2, Sep 2004 .... 2.99

First's *Lone Wolf and Cub* featured new covers by Frank Miller and other artists.

© 1987 First.

N-MINT

LONE
DARK HORSE
- ❑1, Sep 2003 .... 2.99
- ❑2, Oct 2003 .... 2.99
- ❑3, Nov 2003 .... 2.99
- ❑4, Feb 2004 .... 2.99
- ❑5, Mar 2004 .... 2.99
- ❑6, Apr 2004 .... 2.99

LONE GUNMEN, THE
DARK HORSE
- ❑Special 1, Jun 2001 .... 2.99

LONELY NIGHTS COMICS
LAST GASP
- ❑1 .... 2.00

LONELY WAR OF WILLY SCHULTZ, THE
AVALON
- ❑1, b&w 2.95
- ❑2 .... 2.95
- ❑3 .... 2.95
- ❑4 .... 2.95

LONE RANGER, THE (PURE IMAGINATION)
PURE IMAGINATION
- ❑1 1996, b&w; reprints newspaper strip 3.00

LONE RANGER AND TONTO, THE
TOPPS
- ❑1, Aug 1994 .... 2.50
- ❑1/Variant, Aug 1994; foil edition 4.00
- ❑2, Sep 1994 .... 2.50
- ❑2/Variant, Sep 1994; limited edition 3.50
- ❑3, Oct 1994 .... 2.50
- ❑3/Variant, Oct 1994; limited edition . 3.00
- ❑4, Nov 1994 .... 2.50
- ❑4/Variant, Nov 1994; limited edition 3.00

LONE RANGER GOLDEN WEST
GOLD KEY
- ❑1, ca. 1966 .... 45.00

LONE WOLF 2100: RED FILES
DARK HORSE
- ❑1, Feb 2003 .... 2.99

LONE WOLF AND CUB
FIRST
- ❑1, May 1987; FM (c); FM (a);Introduction by Frank Miller 6.00
- ❑1-2 FM (c); FM (a) 2.50
- ❑1-3 FM (c); FM (a) 2.50
- ❑2, Jun 1987 FM (c); FM (a) 4.00
- ❑2-2, Jun 1987 FM (c); FM (a) 2.50
- ❑3, Jul 1987 FM (c); FM (a) 4.00
- ❑3-2 FM (c); FM (a) 2.50
- ❑4, Aug 1987 FM (c); FM (a) 3.00
- ❑5, Sep 1987 FM (c); FM (a) 3.00
- ❑6, Oct 1987 FM (c); FM (a); O: Lone Wolf. 3.00
- ❑7, Nov 1987 FM (c); FM (a); O: Lone Wolf. 3.00
- ❑8, Dec 1987 FM (c); FM (a) 3.00
- ❑9, Jan 1988 FM (c); FM (a) 3.00
- ❑10, Feb 1988 FM (c); FM (a) 3.00
- ❑11, Mar 1988 FM (c); FM (a) 2.50
- ❑12, Apr 1988 FM (c); FM (a) 2.50
- ❑13, May 1988 BSz (c); BSz (a) 2.50
- ❑14, Jun 1988 BSz (c); BSz (a) 2.50
- ❑15, Jul 1988 BSz (c); BSz (a) 2.50

	N-MINT
❑16, Aug 1988 BSz (c); BSz (a)	2.50
❑17, Sep 1988 BSz (c); BSz (a)	2.50
❑18, Oct 1988 BSz (c); BSz (a)	2.50
❑19, Nov 1988 BSz (c); BSz (a)	2.50
❑20, Dec 1988 BSz (c); BSz (a)	2.50
❑21, Jan 1989 BSz (c); BSz (a)	2.50
❑22, Feb 1989 BSz (c); BSz (a)	2.50
❑23, Mar 1989 BSz (c); BSz (a)	2.50
❑24, Apr 1989 BSz (c); BSz (a)	2.50
❑25, May 1989 MW (c); MW (a)	2.50
❑26, Jun 1989 MW (c); MW (a)	2.95
❑27, Jul 1989 MW (c); MW (a)	3.00
❑28, Aug 1989 MW (c); MW (a)	3.00
❑29, Sep 1989 MW (c); MW (a)	3.00
❑30, Oct 1989 MW (c); MW (a)	3.00
❑31, Jan 1990 MW (c)	3.00
❑32, Apr 1990 MW (c)	3.00
❑33, May 1990 MW (c)	3.00
❑34, Jun 1990 MW (c)	3.25
❑35, Jun 1990 MW (c)	3.25
❑36, Jul 1990 MW (c)	3.25
❑37, Aug 1990 MP (c); MP (a)	3.25
❑38, Sep 1990 MP (c); MP (a)	3.25
❑39, Oct 1990; Giant-size MP (c); MP (a)	6.00
❑40, Nov 1990 MP (c); MP (a)	3.25
❑41, Dec 1990 MP (c); MP (a)	4.00
❑42, Jan 1991 MP (c); MP (a)	4.00
❑43, Feb 1991 MP (c); MP (a)	4.00
❑44, Mar 1991 MP (c); MP (a)	4.00
❑45, Apr 1991 MP (c); MP (a)	4.00
❑46, May 1991 MP (c); MP (a)	4.00
❑47, Jun 1991 MP (c); MP (a)	4.00
❑48, Jul 1991	4.00
❑49, Aug 1991	4.00

LONE WOLF 2100
Dark Horse

❑1, May 2002	2.99
❑2, Jun 2002	2.99
❑3, Jul 2002	2.99
❑4, Aug 2002	2.99
❑5, Nov 2002	2.99
❑6, Dec 2002	2.99
❑7, Jan 2003	2.99
❑8, May 2003	2.99
❑9, Sep 2003	2.99
❑10, Oct 2003	2.99
❑11, Jan 2004	2.99

LONG, HOT SUMMER, THE
DC / Milestone

❑1, Jul 1995; enhanced cover	2.95
❑2, Aug 1995	2.50
❑3, Sep 1995	2.50

LONGSHOT
Marvel

❑1, Sep 1985 1: Longshot.	3.50
❑2, Oct 1985 1: Ricochet Rita.	3.00
❑3, Nov 1985 1: Mojo. 1: Spiral.	2.50
❑4, Dec 1985 A: Spider-Man.	2.50
❑5, Jan 1986	2.00
❑6, Feb 1986; Double-size	2.50

LONGSHOT (2ND SERIES)
Marvel

❑1, Feb 1998; wraparound cover	3.99

LONGSHOT COMICS
Slave Labor

❑1, Jun 1995	2.95
❑1-2, Feb 1996	2.95
❑2, Jul 1997, b&w	2.95

LOOKERS
Avatar

❑1	3.00
❑2	3.00

LOOKERS: SLAVES OF ANUBIS
Avatar

❑1	3.50

LOONEY TUNES: BACK IN ACTION THE MOVIE
DC

❑1, ca. 2003	3.95

LOONEY TUNES (DC)
DC

❑1, Apr 1994 A: Marvin Martian.	2.25
❑2, May 1994; Road Runner, Coyote .	2.00
❑3, Jun 1994; Baseball issue	2.00
❑4, Jul 1994 A: Witch Hazel.	2.00
❑5, Aug 1994; Coyote, Martians	1.75
❑6, Sep 1994; Tazmanian Devil	1.50
❑7, Oct 1994	1.50
❑8, Nov 1994	1.50
❑9, Dec 1994	1.50
❑10, Jan 1995; Christmas issue	1.50
❑11, Feb 1995	1.50
❑12, Mar 1995	1.50
❑13, Apr 1995; Coyote	1.50
❑14, May 1995	1.50
❑15, Jun 1995	1.50
❑16, Jul 1995; Daffy, Speedy Gonzales	1.50
❑17, Aug 1995	1.50
❑18, Sep 1995; Duck Dodgers	1.50
❑19, Oct 1995	1.50
❑20, Nov 1995; Yosemite Sam	1.50
❑21, Feb 1996; Tazmanian Devil	1.50
❑22, Apr 1996	1.50
❑23, Jun 1996	1.75
❑24, Aug 1996	1.75
❑25, Oct 1996; Indiana Itz Mine	1.75
❑26, Nov 1996; indicia says Nov, cover says Dec	1.75
❑27, Jan 1997; indicia says Jan, cover says Feb	1.75
❑28, Feb 1997; cover says Apr 96, indicia says Feb 97; Valentine's issue ..	1.75
❑29, May 1997; Coyote	1.75
❑30, Jul 1997; Twilight Zone cover	1.75
❑31, Aug 1997	1.75
❑32, Sep 1997; Hercules parody	1.75
❑33, Oct 1997; Back to School issue .	1.75
❑34, Nov 1997; Daffy versus Dinky Downunder	1.75
❑35, Dec 1997; Agent Daffy	1.95
❑36, Jan 1998; Sylvester, Tweety	1.95
❑37, Feb 1998 V: Crusher.	1.95
❑38, Mar 1998 A: Marvin Martian.	1.95
❑39, Apr 1998; Foghorn Leghorn	1.95
❑40, May 1998; Sylvester	1.95
❑41, Jun 1998; Sylvester, Porky	1.95
❑42, Jul 1998; Speedy Gonzales, Sylvester	1.95
❑43, Aug 1998; Bugs and Daffy do Magic	1.95
❑44, Sep 1998; Tweety and Sylvester	1.99
❑45, Oct 1998; Marvin Martian	1.99
❑46, Nov 1998; Bugs and Taz	1.99
❑47, Dec 1998; Christmas issue	1.99
❑48, Jan 1999 A: Rocky and Mugsy. .	1.99
❑49, Feb 1999; Pepe is stalked	1.99
❑50, Mar 1999	1.99
❑51, Apr 1999	1.99
❑52, May 1999	1.99
❑53, Jun 1999	1.99
❑54, Jul 1999	1.99
❑55, Aug 1999	1.99
❑56, Sep 1999	1.99
❑57, Oct 1999	1.99
❑58, Nov 1999	1.99
❑59, Dec 1999	1.99
❑60, Jan 2000	1.99
❑61, Feb 2000	1.99
❑62, Mar 2000	1.99
❑63, Apr 2000	1.99
❑64, May 2000	1.99
❑65, Jun 2000	1.99
❑66, Jul 2000	1.99
❑67, Aug 2000	1.99
❑68, Sep 2000	1.99
❑69, Oct 2000	1.99
❑70, Nov 2000	1.99
❑71, Dec 2000	1.99
❑72, Jan 2001	1.99
❑73, Feb 2001	1.99
❑74, Mar 2001	1.99
❑75, Apr 2001	1.99
❑76, May 2001	1.99
❑77, Jun 2001	1.99
❑78, Jul 2001	1.99
❑79, Aug 2001	1.99
❑80, Sep 2001	1.99
❑81, Oct 2001	1.99
❑82, Nov 2001	1.99
❑83, Dec 2001	1.99
❑84, Jan 2002	1.99
❑85, Feb 2002	1.99
❑86, Mar 2002	1.99
❑87, Apr 2002	1.99
❑88, May 2002	1.99
❑89, Jun 2002	1.99
❑90, Jul 2002	1.99
❑91, Aug 2002	1.99
❑92, Sep 2002	1.99
❑93, Oct 2002	2.25
❑94, Nov 2002	2.25
❑95, Dec 2002	2.25
❑96, Jan 2003	2.25
❑97, Feb 2003	2.25
❑98, Mar 2003	2.25
❑99, Apr 2003	2.25
❑100, May 2003	2.25
❑101, Jun 2003	2.25
❑102, Jul 2003	2.25
❑103, Aug 2003	2.25
❑104, Sep 2003	2.25
❑105, Oct 2003	2.25
❑106, Nov 2003	2.25
❑107, Dec 2003	2.25
❑108, Jan 2004	2.25
❑109, Feb 2004	2.25
❑110, Mar 2004	2.25
❑111, Apr 2004	2.25
❑112, May 2004	2.25
❑113, Jun 2004	2.25
❑114, Jul 2004	2.25
❑115, Aug 2004	2.25
❑116, Sep 2004	

LOOSE CANNON
DC

❑1, Jun 1995	1.75
❑2, Jul 1995	1.75
❑3, Aug 1995	1.75
❑4, Sep 1995	1.75

LOOSE TEETH
Fantagraphics

❑1, b&w	2.75
❑2, b&w	2.75
❑3, b&w	2.75

LORD FARRIS: SLAVEMASTER
Fantagraphics / Eros

❑1, Feb 1996	2.95
❑2, May 1996	2.95

LORD OF THE DEAD
Conquest

❑1, b&w	2.95

LORD PUMPKIN
Malibu / Ultraverse

❑0, Oct 1994	2.50

LORD PUMPKIN/NECROMANTRA
Malibu / Ultraverse

❑1, Apr 1995, b&w; Cover says Necromantra/Lord Pumpkin	2.95
❑2, May 1995, b&w; Cover says Necromantra/Lord Pumpkin	2.95
❑3, Jun 1995, b&w; Cover says Necromantra/Lord Pumpkin	2.95
❑4, Jul 1995, b&w; Cover says Necromantra/Lord Pumpkin	2.95

LORDS
Legend (Not Dark Horse Imprint)

❑1	2.25

N-MINT

LORDS OF MISRULE, THE (DARK HORSE)
DARK HORSE

❑1, Jan 1997, b&w ... 2.95
❑2, Feb 1997, b&w ... 2.95
❑3, Mar 1997, b&w ... 2.95
❑4, Apr 1997, b&w ... 2.95
❑5, May 1997, b&w ... 2.95
❑6, Jun 1997, b&w ... 2.95

LORDS OF MISRULE (ATOMEKA)
ATOMEKA

❑1 ... 6.95

LORDS OF THE ULTRA-REALM
DC

❑1, Jun 1987 ... 1.50
❑2, Jul 1986 ... 1.50
❑3, Aug 1986 ... 1.50
❑4, Sep 1986 ... 1.50
❑5, Oct 1986 ... 1.50
❑6, Nov 1986 ... 1.50
❑Special 1 ... 2.25

LORELEI
STARWARP

❑1, b&w ... 2.50

LORELEI OF THE RED MIST
CONQUEST

❑1, b&w ... 2.95
❑2, b&w ... 2.95

LORI LOVECRAFT: MY FAVORITE REDHEAD
CALIBER

❑1, Feb 1997 ... 3.95

LORI LOVECRAFT: REPRESSION
A V

❑1, Jun 2002 ... 2.95

LORI LOVECRAFT: THE BIG COMEBACK
CALIBER

❑1 ... 2.95

LORI LOVECRAFT: THE DARK LADY
CALIBER

❑1 ... 2.95

LORTNOC
RADIO

❑1, Aug 1998, b&w ... 2.95

LOSERS, THE
DC / VERTIGO

❑1, Aug 2003 ... 2.95
❑2, Sep 2003 ... 2.95
❑3, Oct 2003 ... 2.95
❑4, Nov 2003 ... 2.95
❑5, Dec 2003 ... 2.95
❑6, Jan 2004 ... 2.95
❑7, Feb 2004 ... 2.95
❑8, Mar 2004 ... 2.95
❑9, Apr 2004 ... 2.95
❑10, May 2004 ... 2.95
❑11, Jun 2004 ... 2.95
❑12, Jul 2004 ... 2.95
❑13, Aug 2004 ... 2.95
❑14, Sep 2004 ...

LOSERS SPECIAL
DC

❑1, Sep 1985; O: Pooch (Gunner's Dog). O: Johnny Cloud. O: Captain Storm. D: The Losers. Crisis ... 2.50

LOST AND FOUND SEASON OF THE MOST POPEJOEY (VOL. 4)
ABANNE

❑1, Oct 2001 ... 2.95

LOST ANGEL
CALIBER

❑1, b&w ... 2.95

LOST, THE (CALIBER)
CALIBER

❑1, Oct 1996, b&w ... 2.95
❑2 1996, b&w ... 2.95

N-MINT

LOST, THE (CHAOS)
CHAOS

❑1, Dec 1997, b&w ... 2.95
❑2, Jan 1998, b&w ... 2.95
❑3, Feb 1998, b&w; cover says Feb 97; a misprint ... 2.95

LOST CONTINENT
ECLIPSE

❑1, b&w; Japanese ... 3.50
❑2, b&w; Japanese ... 3.50
❑3, b&w; Japanese ... 3.50
❑4, b&w; Japanese ... 3.50
❑5, b&w; Japanese ... 3.50
❑6, b&w; Japanese ... 3.50

LOST GIRLS
KITCHEN SINK

❑1, Nov 1995; Oversized; cardstock cover ... 5.95
❑2, Feb 1996; Oversized; cardstock cover ... 5.95

LOST HEROES
DAVDEZ

❑0, Mar 1998 ... 2.95
❑1, Apr 1998 ... 2.95
❑2, May 1998 ... 2.95
❑3, Jun 1998 ... 2.95
❑4, Aug 1998 ... 2.95

LOST IN SPACE (INNOVATION)
INNOVATION

❑1, Aug 1991 ... 3.00
❑2, Nov 1991 ... 2.75
❑3, Dec 1991 ... 2.75
❑4, Feb 1992 ... 2.50
❑5, Mar 1992 ... 2.50
❑6, May 1992 ... 2.50
❑7, Jun 1992 ... 2.50
❑8, Aug 1992 ... 2.50
❑9, Oct 1992 ... 2.50
❑10, Nov 1992 ... 2.50
❑11, Dec 1992; Judy's story ... 2.50
❑12 1993 ... 2.50
❑13, Aug 1993; enhanced cardstock cover ... 4.95
❑13/Gold, Aug 1993; Gold edition; enhanced cardstock cover ... 5.00
❑14, Sep 1993 ... 2.50
❑15, Aug 1993 ... 2.50
❑16, Sep 1993 ... 2.50
❑17, Oct 1993 ... 2.50
❑18, Nov 1993 ... 2.50
❑Annual 1, ca. 1991 ... 2.95
❑Annual 2, ca. 1992 PD (w) ... 2.95
❑Special 1; amended reprint of #1 ... 2.50
❑Special 2 ... 2.50

LOST IN SPACE (DARK HORSE)
DARK HORSE

❑1, Apr 1998 ... 2.95
❑2, May 1998 ... 2.95
❑3, Jul 1998 ... 2.95

LOST IN SPACE: PROJECT ROBINSON
INNOVATION

❑1, Nov 1993 ... 2.50

LOST LAUGHTER
BAD HABIT

❑1, b&w ... 2.50
❑2, b&w ... 2.50
❑3, b&w ... 2.50
❑4, Apr 1994, b&w ... 2.50

LOST ONES, THE
IMAGE

❑1 ... 2.95

LOST ONES, THE: FOR YOUR EYES ONLY
IMAGE

❑1, Mar 2000; special preview; no price ... 1.00

LOST PLANET
ECLIPSE

❑1, May 1987 ... 2.00
❑2, Jul 1987 ... 2.00
❑3, Sep 1987 ... 2.00

Bill Mumy, who played Will Robinson on the TV series, wrote stories in Innovation's *Lost in Space* series.

© 1993 Irwin Allen Productions and Innovative Corporation (Innovation).

N-MINT

❑4, Dec 1987 ... 2.00
❑5, Feb 1988 ... 2.00
❑6, Mar 1989 ... 2.00

LOST UNIVERSE (GENE RODDENBERRY'S...)
TEKNO

❑0 ... 2.25
❑1, Apr 1995 ... 1.95
❑2, May 1995 ... 1.95
❑3, Jun 1995; trading card ... 1.95
❑3/A, Jun 1995; variant cover ... 1.95
❑4, Jul 1995; bound-in trading card ... 1.95
❑5, Aug 1995 ... 1.95
❑6, Sep 1995 ... 1.95
❑7, Oct 1995 ... 1.95

LOST WORLD, THE
MILLENNIUM

❑1, Jan 1996; cover says Mar, indicia says Jan ... 2.95
❑2, Mar 1996 ... 2.95

LOST WORLD, THE: JURASSIC PARK
TOPPS

❑1, May 1997 ... 2.95
❑2, Jun 1997 ... 2.95
❑3, Jul 1997 ... 2.95

LOUD CANNOLI
CRAZYFISH / MJ-12

❑1 ... 2.95

LOUDER THAN WORDS (SERGIO ARAGONÉS')
DARK HORSE

❑1, Jul 1997 ... 2.95
❑2, Aug 1997 ... 2.95
❑3, Sep 1997 ... 2.95
❑4, Oct 1997 ... 2.95
❑5, Nov 1997 ... 2.95
❑6, Dec 1997 ... 2.95

LOUIE THE RUNE SOLDIER
ADV MANGA

❑1, Mar 2004 ... 9.99

LOUIS RIEL
DRAWN & QUARTERLY

❑1 ... 2.95
❑2 ... 2.95
❑3 ... 2.95
❑4 ... 2.95
❑5, Sep 2000 ... 2.95

LOUIS VS. ALI
REVOLUTIONARY

❑1, Dec 1993, b&w ... 2.95

LOVE & ROCKETS
FANTAGRAPHICS

❑1, Fal 1982 ... 25.00
❑1-2 ... 4.00
❑1-3 ... 3.95
❑1-4, May 1995 ... 4.95
❑2, Spr 1983; Spring 1983 ... 12.00
❑2-2 ... 3.95
❑3 ... 9.00
❑3-2, Apr 1991 ... 3.95
❑4 ... 8.00
❑4-2, Apr 1991 ... 2.50
❑4-3 ... 3.95
❑5, Mar 1984 ... 7.00
❑5-2, May 1991 ... 2.50

N-MINT

- ❑6, May 1984 ... 5.00
- ❑6-2, May 1991 ... 2.50
- ❑7, Jul 1984 ... 5.00
- ❑7-2, May 1991 ... 2.50
- ❑8, Sep 1984 ... 5.00
- ❑8-2, Aug 1991 ... 2.50
- ❑9, Nov 1984 ... 5.00
- ❑9-2, Oct 1991 ... 2.50
- ❑10, Jan 1985 ... 5.00
- ❑10-2, Dec 1991 ... 2.95
- ❑11, Apr 1985 ... 4.00
- ❑11-2, Feb 1992 ... 2.50
- ❑12, Jul 1985 ... 4.00
- ❑12-2, Aug 1992 ... 2.50
- ❑13, Sep 1985 ... 4.00
- ❑13-2, Oct 1992 ... 2.50
- ❑14, Nov 1985 ... 4.00
- ❑14-2, Feb 1993 ... 2.50
- ❑15, Jan 1986 ... 4.00
- ❑15-2, Aug 1993 ... 2.50
- ❑16, Mar 1986 ... 3.00
- ❑16-2, Oct 1993 ... 2.95
- ❑17, Jun 1986 ... 3.00
- ❑18, Sep 1986 ... 3.00
- ❑19, Jan 1987 ... 3.00
- ❑20, Apr 1987 ... 3.00
- ❑21, Jul 1987 ... 2.25
- ❑22, Aug 1987 ... 2.25
- ❑23, Oct 1987 ... 2.25
- ❑24, Dec 1987 ... 2.25
- ❑25, Mar 1988 ... 2.25
- ❑26, Jun 1988 ... 2.25
- ❑27, Aug 1988 ... 2.25
- ❑28, Dec 1988 ... 2.95
- ❑28-2, Apr 1995 ... 2.95
- ❑29, Mar 1989 ... 2.75
- ❑29-2, Mar 1992 ... 2.25
- ❑30, Jul 1989 ... 2.95
- ❑30-2, Mar 1992 ... 2.95
- ❑31, Dec 1989 ... 2.50
- ❑31-2, Apr 1992 ... 2.50
- ❑32, May 1990 ... 2.50
- ❑33, Aug 1990 ... 2.50
- ❑34, Nov 1990 ... 2.50
- ❑35, Mar 1991 ... 2.75
- ❑36, Nov 1991 ... 2.75
- ❑37, Feb 1992 ... 2.75
- ❑38, Apr 1992 ... 2.75
- ❑39, Aug 1992 ... 2.75
- ❑40, Jan 1993 ... 3.50
- ❑41, Apr 1993 ... 2.95
- ❑42, Aug 1993 ... 2.95
- ❑43, Nov 1993 ... 2.95
- ❑44, Mar 1994 ... 2.95
- ❑45, Jul 1994 ... 2.95
- ❑46, Nov 1994 ... 2.95
- ❑47, Apr 1995 ... 2.95
- ❑48, Jul 1995 ... 2.95
- ❑49, Nov 1995 ... 2.95
- ❑50, Apr 1996, b&w ... 4.95
- ❑36896, May 1995 ... 4.95
- ❑36925, May 1996 ... 4.95

LOVE & ROCKETS BONANZA
FANTAGRAPHICS

- ❑1, Mar 1989, b&w ... 2.95
- ❑1-2, Feb 1992, b&w ... 2.95

LOVE AND ROMANCE
CHARLTON

- ❑1 1971 ... 24.00
- ❑2 1971 ... 16.00
- ❑3 1972 ... 12.00
- ❑4 1972 ... 12.00
- ❑5 1972 ... 12.00
- ❑6 1972 ... 8.00
- ❑7, Aug 1972 ... 8.00
- ❑8, Oct 1972 ... 8.00
- ❑9, Dec 1972 ... 8.00
- ❑10, Feb 1973 ... 8.00
- ❑11, Apr 1973 ... 6.00
- ❑12 1973 ... 6.00
- ❑13 1973 ... 6.00
- ❑14 1973 ... 6.00
- ❑15 1973 ... 6.00
- ❑16, Jan 1974 ... 6.00
- ❑17 1974 ... 6.00
- ❑18 1974 ... 6.00
- ❑19 1974 ... 6.00
- ❑20 1974 ... 6.00
- ❑21 1974 ... 4.00
- ❑22 1975 ... 4.00
- ❑23 1975 ... 4.00
- ❑24 1975 ... 4.00

LOVE BITES
FANTAGRAPHICS / EROS

- ❑1, b&w ... 2.25
- ❑2 ... 2.25

LOVE BITES (RADIO COMIX)
RADIO

- ❑1, Oct 2000 ... 2.95

LOVE BOMB
ABACULUS

- ❑1 ... 2.95
- ❑2 ... 2.95

LOVEBUNNY & MR. HELL: DAY IN THE LOVE LIFE
IMAGE

- ❑1, Feb 2003 ... 2.95

LOVEBUNNY & MR. HELL: SAVAGE LOVE
IMAGE

- ❑1, Apr 2003 ... 2.95

LOVECRAFT
ADVENTURE

- ❑1 ... 2.95
- ❑1/Ltd.; limited edition ... 3.00
- ❑2 ... 2.95
- ❑3 ... 2.95
- ❑4 ... 2.95

LOVE ETERNAL: A TORTURED SOUL
VLAD ENT.

- ❑1, b&w ... 2.00

LOVE FANTASY
RENEGADE

- ❑1, b&w ... 2.00

LOVE HINA
TOKYOPOP

- ❑1 2002 ... 2.95
- ❑2 2002 ... 2.95
- ❑3 2002 ... 2.95
- ❑4 2002 ... 2.95
- ❑5 2002 ... 2.95

LOVE IN TIGHTS
SLAVE LABOR

- ❑1, Nov 1998, b&w; First heart throbbin' issue ... 2.95

LOVE LETTERS IN THE HAND
FANTAGRAPHICS / EROS

- ❑1, b&w ... 2.25
- ❑2, b&w ... 2.25
- ❑3, b&w ... 2.50

LOVELY AS A LIE
ILLUSTRATION

- ❑1, Nov 1994 ... 3.25

LOVELY LADIES
CALIBER

- ❑1, b&w; pin-ups ... 3.50

LOVELY PRUDENCE
ALL THE RAGE

- ❑1, ca. 1995 ... 2.95
- ❑2, ca. 1995 ... 2.95
- ❑3, ca. 1995, b&w ... 2.95

LOVE ME TENDERLOIN
DARK HORSE

- ❑1, Jan 2004, Cal McDonald Mystery One Shot ... 2.99

LOVE STORIES
DC

- ❑147, Nov 1972; Previous issues published as Heart Throbs ... 8.00
- ❑148, Jan 1973 ... 8.00
- ❑149, Mar 1973 ... 8.00
- ❑150, Jun 1973 ... 8.00
- ❑151, Aug 1973 ... 8.00
- ❑152, Oct 1973 ... 8.00

LOVE SUCKS
ACE

- ❑1 ... 2.95

LOWLIFE
CALIBER

- ❑1, b&w ... 2.50
- ❑2, b&w ... 2.50
- ❑3, b&w ... 2.50
- ❑4, Feb 1994, b&w ... 2.50

L.T. CAPER
SPOTLIGHT

- ❑1 ... 1.75

LUBA
FANTAGRAPHICS

- ❑1, Feb 1998 ... 2.95
- ❑2, Jul 1998 ... 2.95
- ❑3, Dec 1998 ... 2.95

LUCIFER (VERTIGO)
DC / VERTIGO

- ❑1, Jun 2000 ... 3.50
- ❑2, Jul 2000 ... 3.00
- ❑3, Aug 2000 ... 3.00
- ❑4, Sep 2000 ... 3.00
- ❑5, Oct 2000 ... 3.00
- ❑6, Nov 2000 ... 2.50
- ❑7, Dec 2000 ... 2.50
- ❑8, Jan 2001 ... 2.50
- ❑9, Feb 2001 ... 2.50
- ❑10, Mar 2001 ... 2.50
- ❑11, Apr 2001 ... 2.50
- ❑12, May 2001 ... 2.50
- ❑13, Jun 2001 ... 2.50
- ❑14, Jul 2001 ... 2.50
- ❑15, Aug 2001 ... 2.50
- ❑16, Sep 2001 ... 2.50
- ❑17, Oct 2001 ... 2.50
- ❑18, Nov 2001 ... 2.50
- ❑19, Dec 2001 ... 2.50
- ❑20, Jan 2002 ... 2.50
- ❑21, Feb 2002 ... 2.50
- ❑22, Mar 2002 ... 2.50
- ❑23, Apr 2002 ... 2.50
- ❑24, May 2002 ... 2.50
- ❑25, Jul 2002 A: Death (Sandman). .. 2.50
- ❑26, Jul 2002 ... 2.50
- ❑27, Aug 2002 ... 2.50
- ❑28, Sep 2002 ... 2.50
- ❑29, Oct 2002 ... 2.50
- ❑30, Nov 2002 ... 2.50
- ❑31, Dec 2002 ... 2.50
- ❑32, Jan 2003 ... 2.50
- ❑33, Feb 2003 ... 2.50
- ❑34, Mar 2003 ... 2.50
- ❑35, Apr 2003 ... 2.50
- ❑36, May 2003 ... 2.50
- ❑37, Jun 2003 ... 2.50
- ❑38, Jul 2003 ... 2.50
- ❑39, Aug 2003 ... 2.50
- ❑40, Sep 2003 ... 2.50
- ❑41, Oct 2003 ... 2.50
- ❑42, Nov 2003 ... 2.50
- ❑43, Dec 2003 ... 2.50
- ❑44, Jan 2004 ... 2.50
- ❑45, Feb 2004 ... 2.50
- ❑46, Mar 2004 ... 2.50
- ❑47, Apr 2004 ... 2.50
- ❑48, May 2004 ... 2.50
- ❑49, Jun 2004 ... 2.50
- ❑50, Jul 2004 ... 3.50
- ❑51, Aug 2004 ... 2.50
- ❑52, Sep 2004 ...

N-MINT

LUCIFER (TRIDENT)
Trident

❑1, Jul 1990, b&w ... 1.95
❑2, b&w ... 1.95
❑3, b&w ... 1.95

LUCIFER: NIRVANA
DC / Vertigo

❑1, Oct 2002, b&w ... 5.95

LUCIFER'S HAMMER
Innovation

❑1, Nov 1993 ... 2.50
❑2 ... 2.50
❑3 ... 2.50
❑4 ... 2.50
❑5 ... 2.50
❑6 ... 2.50

LUCK OF THE DRAW
Radio

❑1, Jun 2000, b&w ... 3.95

LUCKY 7
Runaway Graphics

❑1, Apr 1993 ... 1.95

LUCKY LUKE: JESSE JAMES
Fantasy Flight

❑1 ... 8.95

LUCKY LUKE: THE STAGE COACH
Fantasy Flight

❑1 ... 8.95

LUCY SHOW
Gold Key

❑1, Jun 1963 ... 65.00
❑2, Sep 1963 ... 40.00
❑3, Dec 1963 ... 32.00
❑4, Mar 1964 ... 32.00
❑5, Jun 1964 ... 32.00

LUDWIG VON DRAKE (WALT DISNEY'S...)
Dell

❑1, Nov 1961 ... 16.00
❑2, Jan 1962 ... 10.00
❑3, Mar 1962 ... 8.00
❑4, Jun 1962 ... 8.00

LUFTWAFFE: 1946 TECHNICAL MANUAL
Antarctic

❑1, Feb 1998; Projekt Saucer ... 4.00
❑2, Apr 1999; Hitler's Kamikazes ... 4.00

LUFTWAFFE: 1946 (VOL. 1)
Antarctic

❑1, Jul 1996, b&w ... 5.00
❑2, Sep 1996, b&w ... 4.00
❑3, Nov 1996, b&w ... 4.00
❑4, Jan 1997, b&w ... 4.00
❑Annual 1, Apr 1998, b&w ... 4.00

LUFTWAFFE: 1946 (VOL. 2)
Antarctic

❑1, Mar 1997 ... 4.00
❑2, Apr 1997; contains indicia for issue #1 ... 3.50
❑3, May 1997 ... 3.50
❑4, Jul 1997 ... 3.50
❑5, Aug 1997 ... 3.00
❑6, Oct 1997 ... 3.00
❑7, Nov 1997 ... 3.00
❑8, Feb 1998; 50th "Families of Altered Wars" issue ... 3.00
❑9, Apr 1998 ... 3.00
❑10, May 1998 ... 3.00
❑11, Jun 1998 ... 3.00
❑12, Jul 1998 ... 3.00
❑13, Aug 1998 ... 3.00
❑14, Oct 1998 ... 3.00
❑15, Feb 1999 ... 3.00
❑16, Mar 1999 ... 3.00
❑Annual 1, ca. 1998; 1998 Annual ... 3.00
❑Special 1, Apr 1998; Color Special ... 4.00
❑Special 2, Feb 1997, b&w; TriebflÉgel Special; German rocketry; Triebflngel Special ... 4.00

N-MINT

LUFTWAFFE: 1946 (VOL. 3)
Antarctic

❑1, Aug 2002 ... 5.95
❑2, Oct 2002 ... 5.95
❑3, Oct 2002 ... 5.95
❑4, ca. 2002 ... 5.95
❑5, Jan 2003 ... 5.95
❑6, Feb 2003 ... 5.95
❑7, Mar 2003 ... 5.95
❑8, Apr 2003 ... 5.95
❑9, May 2003 ... 5.95
❑10, Jun 2003 ... 5.95
❑11, Jul 2003 ... 5.95
❑12, Aug 2003 ... 5.95
❑13, Nov 2003 ... 5.95
❑14, Dec 2003 ... 5.95
❑15, Dec 2003 ... 5.95
❑16, Jan 2004 ... 5.95
❑17, Feb 2004 ... 5.95

LUGER
Eclipse

❑1, Oct 1986 TY (a) ... 2.00
❑2, Dec 1986 TY (a) ... 2.00
❑3, Feb 1987 TY (a) ... 2.00

LUGH, LORD OF LIGHT
Flagship

❑1, Feb 1987 ... 1.75
❑2, Jun 1987 ... 1.75
❑3 ... 1.75
❑4 ... 1.75

LUGO
Lost Boys

❑0.5; Promotional edition ... 1.00

LUMENAGERIE
NBM

❑1 ... 11.95

LUM URUSEI*YATSURA
Viz

❑1, b&w; Japanese ... 5.00
❑2, b&w; Japanese ... 4.00
❑3, b&w; Japanese ... 4.00
❑4, b&w; Japanese ... 4.00
❑5 ... 3.50
❑6 ... 3.50
❑7 ... 3.50
❑8 ... 3.50

LUNAR DONUT
Lunar Donut

❑0, b&w; says (Honey-Glazed); cardstock cover ... 2.50
❑1, b&w; Flip-book; cover says (With Sprinkles) ... 2.50
❑2, b&w; Flip-book; cover says (Cherry-Filled) ... 2.50
❑3, b&w; Flip-book; cover says (Jelly-Filled) ... 2.50

LUNATIC BINGE
Eternity

❑1 ... 3.95
❑2 ... 3.95

LUNATIC FRINGE, THE
Innovation

❑1, Jul 1989 ... 1.75
❑2, Aug 1989 ... 1.75

LUNATIK
Marvel

❑1, Dec 1995 ... 1.95
❑2, Jan 1996 ... 1.95
❑3, Feb 1996 ... 1.95

LURID TALES
Fantagraphics / Eros

❑1, b&w ... 2.75

LUST
Fantagraphics / Eros

❑1, Apr 1997 ... 2.95
❑2, May 1997 ... 2.95
❑3, Jun 1997 ... 2.95
❑4, Jul 1997 ... 2.95

Lucifer features the earthly adventures of the retired Lord of Hell.
© 2000 DC Comics

N-MINT

❑5, Aug 1997 ... 2.95
❑6, Sep 1997 ... 2.95

LUST FOR LIFE
Slave Labor

❑1, Feb 1997, b&w ... 2.95
❑2, May 1997, b&w ... 2.95
❑3, Aug 1997, b&w ... 2.95
❑4, Jan 1998 ... 2.95

LUST OF THE NAZI WEASEL WOMEN
Fantagraphics

❑1, b&w ... 2.25
❑2, b&w ... 2.25
❑3, Jan 1991, b&w ... 2.25
❑4, b&w ... 2.25

LUX & ALBY SIGN ON AND SAVE THE UNIVERSE
Dark Horse

❑1, b&w ... 2.50
❑2, May 1993, b&w ... 2.50
❑3, Jun 1993, b&w ... 2.50
❑4, Jul 1993 ... 2.50
❑5, Aug 1993 ... 2.50
❑6, Sep 1993 ... 2.50
❑7, Oct 1993 ... 2.50
❑8, Oct 1993 ... 2.50
❑9, Dec 1993 ... 2.50

LUXURA & VAMPFIRE
Brainstorm

❑1 ... 2.95

LUXURA COLLECTION (KIRK LINDO'S...)
Brainstorm

❑1; stories and pin-ups; cardstock cover ... 4.95

LUXURA LEATHER SPECIAL
Brainstorm

❑1, Mar 1996 ... 2.95

LYCANTHROPE LEO
Viz

❑1, b&w ... 2.95
❑2, b&w ... 2.95
❑3, b&w ... 2.95
❑4, b&w ... 2.95
❑5, b&w ... 2.95
❑6, b&w ... 2.95
❑7, b&w ... 2.95

LYCEUM
Hunter

❑1, Oct 1996, b&w ... 2.95
❑2, Aug 1997, b&w ... 2.95

LYCRA-WOMAN AND SPANDEX-GIRL
Comic Zone

❑1, Dec 1992, b&w ... 2.95

LYCRA WOMAN AND SPANDEX GIRL CHRISTMAS '77 SPECIAL
Comic Zone

❑1, b&w ... 2.95

LYCRA WOMAN AND SPANDEX GIRL HALLOWEEN SPECIAL
Lost Cause

❑1, b&w ... 2.95

N-MINT

LYCRA WOMAN AND SPANDEX GIRL JURASSIC DINOSAUR SPECIAL
Comic Zone

❑1, b&w 2.95

LYCRA WOMAN AND SPANDEX GIRL SUMMER VACATION SPECIAL
Comic Zone

❑1, b&w 2.95

LYCRA WOMAN AND SPANDEX GIRL TIME TRAVEL SPECIAL
Comic Zone

❑1, b&w 2.95

LYCRA WOMAN AND SPANDEX GIRL VALENTINE SPECIAL
Comic Zone

❑1, b&w 2.95

LYNCH
Image

❑1, May 1997; no indicia 2.50

LYNCH MOB
Chaos

❑1, Jun 1994 .... 2.50
❑2, Jul 1994 .... 2.50
❑3, Aug 1994 .... 2.50
❑4, Sep 1994 .... 2.50

LYNX: AN ELFLORD TALE
Peregrine Entertainment

❑1, Mar 1999, b&w 2.95

M

M
Eclipse

❑1 .... 4.95
❑2 .... 4.95
❑3 .... 4.95
❑4 .... 5.95

MACABRE
Lighthouse

❑1 1989, b&w 2.50
❑2 1989, b&w 2.50
❑3 1989, b&w 2.50
❑4 1989 .... 2.50
❑5 1989 .... 2.50
❑6, Aug 1989 .... 2.50

MACABRE (VOL. 2)
Lighthouse

❑1 1989 .... 2.50
❑2 1989 .... 2.50

MACE: BOUNTY HUNTER
Image

❑1, Apr 2003 .... 2.99

M.A.C.H. 1
Fleetway-Quality

❑1, b&w 1: John Probe. 2.00
❑2, b&w 2.00
❑3, b&w 2.00
❑4, b&w 2.00
❑5, b&w 2.00
❑6, b&w 2.00
❑7, b&w 2.00
❑8, b&w 2.00
❑9, b&w 2.00

MACHINE, THE
Dark Horse

❑1, Nov 1994 .... 2.50
❑2, Dec 1994 .... 2.50
❑3, Jan 1995 .... 2.50
❑4, Feb 1995 .... 2.50

MACHINE MAN
Marvel

❑1, Apr 1978 JK (w); JK (a); 1: Machine Man. 2.50
❑2, May 1978 .... 2.00
❑3, Jun 1978 .... 2.00
❑4, Jul 1978 .... 2.00
❑5, Aug 1978 .... 2.00
❑6, Sep 1978 .... 2.00
❑7, Oct 1978 .... 2.00
❑8, Nov 1978 .... 2.00
❑9, Dec 1978 .... 2.00
❑10, Aug 1979 .... 2.00
❑11, Oct 1979 .... 2.00
❑12, Dec 1979 .... 2.00
❑13, Feb 1980 .... 2.00
❑14, Apr 1980 .... 2.00
❑15, Jun 1980 O: Ion. 1: Ion. 2.00
❑16, Aug 1980 1: Baron Brimstone. .. 2.00
❑17, Oct 1980 .... 2.00
❑18, Dec 1980 A: Alpha Flight. 2.00
❑19, Feb 1981; FM (c); 1: Jack O'Lantern I (Jason Macendale). Macendale becomes Hobgoblin II in Amazing Spider-Man #289 .... 12.50

MACHINE MAN (LTD. SERIES)
Marvel

❑1, Oct 1984 HT (a) 1.50
❑2, Nov 1984 HT (a); 1: Iron Man 2020. 1.50
❑3, Dec 1984 HT (a) 1.50
❑4, Jan 1985 HT (a) 1.50

MACHINE MAN/BASTION '98
Marvel

❑1, ca. 1998; gatefold summary; Marvel Annual; wraparound cover 2.99

MACHINE MAN 2020
Marvel

❑1, Aug 1994 .... 2.00
❑2, Sep 1994 .... 2.00

MACK BOLAN: THE EXECUTIONER (DON PENDLETON'S...)
Innovation

❑1, Jul 1993; enhanced cardstock cover; adapts War Against the Mafia 2.95
❑1/A, Jul 1993; Indestructible Tyvek cover 3.95
❑1/B, Jul 1993; Double-cover edition; black outer cover with red X 3.50
❑2, Aug 1993; Adapts War Against the Mafia 2.50
❑3, Nov 1993; Adapts War Against the Mafia 2.50
❑4 .... 2.50

MACKENZIE QUEEN
Matrix

❑1 .... 1.50
❑2, b&w 1.50
❑3 .... 1.50
❑4 .... 1.50
❑5 .... 1.50

MACK THE KNIFE: MONOCHROME MEMORIES
Caliber

❑1, b&w 2.50

MACROSS II
Viz

❑1, ca. 1992 .... 3.00
❑2, ca. 1992 .... 2.75
❑3, ca. 1992 .... 2.75
❑4, ca. 1992 .... 2.75
❑5, ca. 1992 .... 2.75
❑6, ca. 1992 .... 2.75
❑7, ca. 1993 .... 2.75
❑8, ca. 1993 .... 2.75
❑9, ca. 1993 .... 2.75
❑10, ca. 1993 .... 2.75

MACROSS II: T HE MICRON CONSPIRACY
Viz

❑1, b&w 3.00
❑2, b&w 2.75
❑3, b&w 2.75
❑4, b&w 2.75
❑5, b&w 2.75

MADAME XANADU
DC

❑1, Jul 1981 BB, MR (a); O: Madame Xanadu. 3.00

MADBALLS
Marvel / Star

❑1, Sep 1986 O: Madballs. 1: Madballs. 1: Colonel Corn. 1.00
❑2, Oct 1986 .... 1.00
❑3, Nov 1986 .... 1.00
❑4, Jun 1987 .... 1.00
❑5, Aug 1987 .... 1.00
❑6, Oct 1987 .... 1.00
❑7, Dec 1987 .... 1.00
❑8, Feb 1988 .... 1.00
❑9, Apr 1988 .... 1.00
❑10, Jun 1988 .... 1.00

MAD-DOG
Marvel

❑1, May 1993 .... 1.25
❑2, Jun 1993 .... 1.25
❑3, Jul 1993 .... 1.25
❑4, Aug 1993 .... 1.25
❑5, Sep 1993 .... 1.25
❑6, Oct 1993 .... 1.25

MAD DOG MAGAZINE
Blackthorne

❑1, Nov 1986 .... 1.75
❑2 .... 1.75
❑3, Mar 1987 .... 1.75

MAD DOGS
Eclipse

❑1 .... 2.50
❑2 .... 2.50
❑3 .... 2.50

MADHOUSE GLADS
Archie

❑73, May 1970; Previous issues published as Madhouse Ma-ad Freakout 3.00
❑74, Jul 1970 .... 3.00
❑75, Sep 1970 .... 3.00
❑76, Nov 1970 .... 3.00
❑77, Feb 1971 .... 3.00
❑78, May 1971 .... 5.00
❑79, Aug 1971 .... 5.00
❑80, Sep 1971 .... 5.00
❑81, Nov 1971 .... 5.00
❑82, Feb 1972 .... 5.00
❑83, May 1972 .... 5.00
❑84, Aug 1972 .... 5.00
❑85, Oct 1972 .... 5.00
❑86, Dec 1972 .... 5.00
❑87, Feb 1973 .... 5.00
❑88, May 1973 .... 5.00
❑89, Aug 1973 .... 5.00
❑90, Oct 1973 .... 5.00
❑91, Dec 1973 .... 5.00
❑92, Feb 1974 .... 5.00
❑93, May 1974 .... 3.00
❑94, Aug 1974; Later issues published as Madhouse 3.00

MADHOUSE MA-AD FREAKOUT
Archie

❑71, ca. 1969; Earlier issues published as Madhouse Ma-ad Jokes 3.00
❑72, Jan 1970; Later issues published as Madhouse Glads 3.00

MADHOUSE MA-AD JOKES
Archie

❑66, Feb 1969; Previous issues published as Archie's Madhouse 3.50
❑67, Apr 1969 .... 3.50
❑68, Jun 1969 .... 3.50
❑69, Aug 1969 .... 3.50
❑70, Oct 1969; Series continues as Madhouse Ma-ad Freakout 3.50

MADMAN
Tundra

❑1-4; Double-acetate cover ....
❑1, Mar 1992, b&w; prestige format; flip-action corners 8.00
❑1-2 .... 5.00
❑1-3; Kitchen Sink publishes 4.00
❑2, Apr 1992 .... 6.00
❑3, May 1992 .... 6.00

N-MINT

MADMAN ADVENTURES
TUNDRA

❑1, ca. 1992 ... 5.00
❑2, ca. 1993 ... 4.00
❑3, ca. 1993 ... 4.00

MADMAN COMICS
DARK HORSE

❑1, Apr 1994 FM (c); O: Madman. ... 4.00
❑2, Jun 1994 ... 3.50
❑3, Aug 1994 ... 3.50
❑4, Oct 1994 ... 3.00
❑5, Jan 1995 ... 3.00
❑6, Mar 1995 ... 3.00
❑7, May 1995 ... 3.00
❑8, Jul 1995 ... 3.00
❑9, Oct 1995 ... 3.00
❑10, Jan 1996 ARo (c) ... 2.95
❑11, Oct 1996 ... 2.95
❑12, Apr 1999; Doctor Robot back-up 2.95
❑13, May 1999; Doctor Robot back-up 2.95
❑14, Jun 1999; Doctor Robot back-up 2.95
❑15, Jul 1999; Doctor Robot back-up 2.95
❑16, Dec 1999 ... 2.95
❑17, Aug 2000 ... 2.95
❑18, Sep 2000 ... 2.95
❑19, Oct 2000 ... 2.99
❑20, Dec 2000 ... 2.99
❑Yearbook 1995, Jan 1996; Yearbook '95; collects Madman Comics #1-5 17.95

MADMAN/THE JAM
DARK HORSE

❑1, Jul 1998 ... 2.95
❑2, Aug 1998 ... 2.95

MAD MONSTER PARTY ADAPTATION
BLACK BEAR

❑1 ... 2.95
❑2 ... 2.95
❑3 ... 2.95
❑4 ... 2.95

MADONNA
PERSONALITY

❑1, b&w ... 2.95
❑1/Autographed, b&w ... 3.95
❑2, b&w ... 2.95
❑2/Autographed, b&w ... 3.95

MADONNA SEX GODDESS
FRIENDLY

❑1, ca. 1990 ... 2.95
❑2, ca. 1991 ... 2.95
❑3, ca. 1991 ... 2.95

MADONNA SPECIAL
REVOLUTIONARY

❑1, Aug 1993, b&w ... 2.50

MADONNA VS. MARILYN
CELEBRITY

❑1 ... 2.95

MAD RACCOONS
MU

❑1, Jul 1991 ... 2.50
❑2, Sep 1992 ... 2.50
❑3, Aug 1993 ... 2.50
❑4, Aug 1994 ... 2.95
❑5, Aug 1995; cardstock cover ... 2.95
❑6, Jul 1996; cardstock cover ... 2.95

MADRAVEN HALLOWEEN SPECIAL
HAMILTON

❑1, Oct 1995 ... 2.95

MAEL'S RAGE
OMINOUS

❑2, Aug 1994 ... 2.50
❑2/Variant, Aug 1994; cardstock outer cover ... 2.50

MAELSTROM
AIRCEL

❑1, Jun 1987 ... 1.70
❑2, Jul 1987 ... 1.70
❑3, Aug 1987 ... 1.70
❑4, Sep 1987 ... 1.70
❑5, Oct 1987 ... 1.50

N-MINT

❑6, Nov 1987 ... 1.50
❑7, Dec 1987 ... 1.50
❑8, Jan 1988 ... 1.50
❑9, Feb 1988 ... 1.50
❑10, Mar 1988 ... 1.50

MAGDALENA, THE
IMAGE

❑1, Apr 2000 ... 2.50
❑1/A, Apr 2000; 2000 Megacon Exclusive ... 2.50
❑1/B, Apr 2000; Alternate cover with Magdalena standing, cross at bottom center of design ... 2.50
❑2, Jun 2000 ... 2.50
❑3, Jan 2001 ... 2.50
❑3/A, Jan 2001; Alternate cover with Eruptor logo and foil additions ... 2.50

MAGDALENA (VOL. 2)
IMAGE

❑1, Jul 2003 ... 2.99
❑1/A, Jul 2003 ... 5.00
❑2, Aug 2003 ... 2.99
❑3, Oct 2003 ... 2.99
❑4, Dec 2003 ... 2.99

MAGDALENA/ANGELUS
IMAGE

❑0 ... 2.95
❑0.5, Nov 2001 ... 2.95

MAGDALENA/VAMPIRELLA
IMAGE

❑1, Jun 2003 ... 2.99

MAGE
COMICO

❑1, May 1984 MW (w); MW (a); 1: Kevin Matchstick. ... 5.00
❑2, Jul 1984 MW (w); MW (a) ... 4.00
❑3, Sep 1984 MW (w); MW (a) ... 3.00
❑4, Nov 1984 MW (w); MW (a) ... 3.00
❑5, Jan 1985 MW (w); MW (a) ... 3.00
❑6, Mar 1985; MW (w); MW (a); 1: Grendel I (Hunter Rose) (in color). Grendel ... 15.00
❑7, May 1985 MW (w); MW (a); A: Grendel I (Hunter Rose). ... 8.00
❑8, Jul 1985 MW (w); MW (a); A: Grendel I (Hunter Rose). ... 4.00
❑9, Sep 1985 MW (w); MW (a); A: Grendel I (Hunter Rose). ... 3.00
❑10, Dec 1985 MW (w); MW (a); A: Grendel I (Hunter Rose). ... 3.00
❑11, Feb 1986 MW (w); MW (a); A: Grendel I (Hunter Rose). ... 3.00
❑12, Apr 1986 MW (w); MW (a); A: Grendel I (Hunter Rose). ... 3.00
❑13, Jun 1986 MW (w); MW (a); D: Grendel I (Hunter Rose). D: Edsel. 4.00
❑14, Aug 1986 MW (w); MW (a); A: Grendel. ... 3.00
❑15, Dec 1986; Giant-size MW (w); MW (a) ... 6.00

MAGE (IMAGE)
IMAGE

❑0, Jul 1997; MW (a);American Entertainment Exclusive ... 3.00
❑0/Autographed, Jul 1997 MW (a) ... 5.00
❑1, Jul 1997 MW (w); MW (a) ... 4.00
❑1/3D, Feb 1998; 3-D edition; MW (w); MW (a);with glasses ... 4.95
❑2, Aug 1997 MW (w); MW (a) ... 3.50
❑3, Sep 1997 MW (w); MW (a) ... 3.50
❑4, Nov 1997 MW (w); MW (a) ... 3.00
❑5, Jan 1998 MW (w); MW (a) ... 3.00
❑6, Mar 1998 MW (w); MW (a) ... 2.50
❑7, Apr 1998 MW (w); MW (a) ... 2.50
❑8, Jun 1998 MW (w); MW (a) ... 2.50
❑9, Sep 1998 MW (w); MW (a) ... 2.50
❑10, Dec 1998 MW (w); MW (a) ... 2.50
❑11, Feb 1999 MW (w); MW (a) ... 2.50
❑12, Apr 1999 MW (w); MW (a) ... 2.50
❑13/A, Jun 1999; MW (a);covers form triptych ... 2.50
❑13/B, Jun 1999; MW (a);Mage cover 2.50
❑13/C, Jun 1999 MW (a) ... 2.50

Only one book in Don Pendleton's long-running Mack Bolan series was adapted by Innovation before the company went out of business.
© 1993 Mack Bolan and Innovative Corporation (Innovation).

N-MINT

❑14, Aug 1999 MW (w); MW (a) ... 2.50
❑15, Oct 1999 MW (w); MW (a) ... 2.50
❑15/Variant, Oct 1999; MW (w); MW (a);Special acetate double-cover ... 5.95

MAGGIE AND HOPEY COLOR SPECIAL
FANTAGRAPHICS

❑1, May 1997 ... 3.50

MAGGIE THE CAT
IMAGE

❑1, Jan 1996 ... 2.50
❑2, Mar 1996 ... 2.50
❑3 1996; Exists? ... 2.50
❑4 1996; Exists? ... 2.50

MAGGOTS
HAMILTON

❑1, Nov 1991, b&w ... 3.95
❑2 1992, b&w ... 3.95
❑3 1992, b&w ... 3.95

MAGICAL MATES
ANTARCTIC

❑1, Feb 1996 ... 2.95
❑2, Apr 1996 ... 2.95
❑3, Jun 1996 ... 2.95
❑4, Aug 1996 ... 2.95
❑5, Oct 1996 ... 2.95
❑6, Dec 1996 ... 2.95
❑7 1997 ... 2.95
❑8 1997 ... 2.95
❑9 1997 ... 2.95

MAGICAL NYMPHINI, THE
RIP OFF

❑1, Feb 1991, b&w ... 2.50
❑1-2 ... 2.50
❑2, Apr 1991, b&w ... 2.50
❑2-2 ... 2.50
❑3, Aug 1991, b&w ... 2.50
❑3-2 ... 2.50
❑4, Dec 1991, b&w ... 2.95
❑4-2 ... 2.95
❑5, Aug 1992, b&w ... 2.95
❑5-2 ... 2.95

MAGICAL TWILIGHT
GRAPHIC VISIONS

❑1 ... 2.95

MAGIC CARPET
SHANDA FANTASY ARTS

❑1, Apr 1999, b&w ... 4.50

MAGIC FLUTE, THE
ECLIPSE

❑1, ca. 1990; Part of Eclipse's Night Music series ... 4.95
❑2, ca. 1990 ... 4.95
❑3, ca. 1990 ... 4.95

MAGICIANS' VILLAGE
MAD MONKEY

❑1, ca. 1995 ... 2.45

MAGICMAN
A-PLUS

❑1, b&w ... 2.95

MAGIC PICKLE
ONI

❑1 2001 ... 2.95
❑2 2001 ... 2.95
❑3 2001 ... 2.95
❑4 ... 2.95

N-MINT

MAGIC PRIEST
ANTARCTIC
❑1, Jun 1998, b&w 2.95

MAGIC: THE GATHERING: ANTIQUITIES WAR
ACCLAIM / ARMADA
❑1, Nov 1995 2.50
❑2, Dec 1995 2.50
❑3, Jan 1996 2.50
❑4, Feb 1996 2.50

MAGIC: THE GATHERING: ELDER DRAGONS
ACCLAIM / ARMADA
❑1, Apr 1996 2.50
❑2, May 1996 2.50

MAGIC: THE GATHERING: GERARD'S QUEST
DARK HORSE
❑1, Mar 1998 2.95
❑2, Apr 1998 2.95
❑3, May 1998 2.95
❑4, Sep 1998 2.95

MAGIC: THE GATHERING: NIGHTMARE
ACCLAIM / ARMADA
❑1, ca. 1995 2.50

MAGIC: THE GATHERING: SHANDALAR
ACCLAIM / ARMADA
❑1, Mar 1996 2.50
❑2, Apr 1996 2.50

MAGIC: THE GATHERING: THE SHADOW MAGE
ACCLAIM / ARMADA
❑1, Jul 1995; bound-in Fireball card 2.50
❑2, Aug 1995; bound-in Blue Elemental card 2.50
❑3, Sep 1995; bagged with Magic: The Gathering tokens and counters 2.50
❑4, Oct 1995; polybagged with sheet of creature tokens 2.50

MAGIC: THE GATHERING: WAYFARER
ACCLAIM / ARMADA
❑1, Nov 1995 2.50
❑2, Dec 1995 2.50
❑3, Jan 1996 2.50
❑4, Feb 1996 2.50
❑5, Mar 1996 2.50

MAGIC WHISTLE
ALTERNATIVE
❑1, b&w 2.95
❑2, b&w 2.95

MAGIK
MARVEL
❑1, Dec 1983 TP (a) 2.25
❑2, Jan 1984 TP (a) 2.00
❑3, Feb 1984 TP (a) 2.00
❑4, Mar 1984 TP (a) 2.00

MAGIK (2ND SERIES)
MARVEL
❑1, Dec 2000 2.99
❑2, Jan 2001 2.99
❑3, Feb 2001 2.99
❑4, Mar 2001 2.99

MAGILLA GORILLA (GOLD KEY)
GOLD KEY
❑1, ca. 1964 30.00
❑2, ca. 1964 15.00
❑3, Dec 1964 12.00
❑4, ca. 1965 12.00
❑5, ca. 1965 12.00
❑6, Aug 1965 10.00
❑7, Nov 1965 10.00
❑8, Jul 1966 10.00
❑9 10.00
❑10, Dec 1968 10.00

N-MINT

MAGNA-MAN: THE LAST SUPERHERO
COMICS INTERVIEW
❑1, b&w 1.95
❑2, Sum 1988, b&w 1.95
❑3, Sum 1988, b&w 1.95

MAGNESIUM ARC
ICONOGRAFIX
❑1 3.50

MAGNETIC MEN FEATURING MAGNETO
MARVEL / AMALGAM
❑1, Jun 1997 1.95

MAGNETO
MARVEL
❑0, Sep 1993; retailer giveaway; JDu (a); O: Magneto. no cover price; Promotional give-away; Reprints "A Fire in the Sky" from X-Men Classic #19; Reprints "I Magneto" From X-Men Classic #12 3.00

MAGNETO (LTD. SERIES)
MARVEL
❑1, Nov 1996 2.00
❑2, Dec 1996 2.00
❑3, Jan 1997 2.00
❑4, Feb 1997 2.00

MAGNETO AND THE MAGNETIC MEN
MARVEL / AMALGAM
❑1, Apr 1996 1.95

MAGNETO ASCENDANT
MARVEL
❑1, Apr 1999; Reprints Magneto Stories from X-Men (1st Series) 3.99

MAGNETO: DARK SEDUCTION
MARVEL
❑1, Jun 2000 2.99

MAGNETO REX
MARVEL
❑1, Apr 1999 2.50
❑2, Jun 1999 2.50
❑3, Jul 1999 2.50

MAGNETS: ROBOT DISMANTLER
PARODY
❑1, b&w; Foil-embossed cover 2.50

MAGNUS, ROBOT FIGHTER (GOLD KEY)
GOLD KEY
❑1, Feb 1963 O: Magnus. 1: Leeja Clane. 1: Magnus. 110.00
❑2, May 1963 65.00
❑3, Aug 1963 65.00
❑4, Nov 1963 30.00
❑5, Feb 1964 30.00
❑6, May 1964; RM (a);Keys Of Knowledge: Atomic Energy #7: Atoms That Explode; Keys of Knowledge: Physical Fitness #11: Twisting and Bending 30.00
❑7, Aug 1964 30.00
❑8, Nov 1964 30.00
❑9, Feb 1965 30.00
❑10, May 1965 30.00
❑11, Aug 1965 18.00
❑12, Nov 1965 18.00
❑13, Feb 1966 1: Doctor Noel. 18.00
❑14, May 1966 18.00
❑15, Aug 1966 18.00
❑16, Nov 1966 18.00
❑17, Feb 1967 18.00
❑18, May 1967 18.00
❑19, Aug 1967 18.00
❑20, Nov 1967 18.00
❑21, Feb 1968 12.00
❑22, May 1968; O: Magnus. 1: Leeja Clane. 1: Magnus. Reprints Magnus, Robot Fighter (Gold Key) #1 12.00
❑23, Aug 1968 DS (a) 12.00
❑24, Nov 1968; Destruction of Malev-6 12.00
❑25, Feb 1969 12.00
❑26, May 1969 12.00
❑27, Aug 1969 12.00

N-MINT

❑28, Nov 1969; goes on hiatus 12.00
❑29, Nov 1971 5.00
❑30, Jan 1972 5.00
❑31, Apr 1972 5.00
❑32, Jul 1972 5.00
❑33, Oct 1972 5.00
❑34, Jan 1973 5.00
❑35, May 1974 5.00
❑36, Aug 1974 5.00
❑37, Nov 1974 5.00
❑38, Feb 1975 5.00
❑39, May 1975 5.00
❑40, Aug 1975 5.00
❑41, Nov 1975 5.00
❑42, Jan 1976 5.00
❑43, May 1976 5.00
❑44, Aug 1976 5.00
❑45, Oct 1976 5.00
❑46, Jan 1977 5.00

MAGNUS ROBOT FIGHTER (VALIANT)
VALIANT
❑0, ca. 1992; Promotional "0" edition (from redeeming coupons in issues 1-8); O: Magnus. No cover price; sendaway 8.00
❑0/A, ca. 1992; Promotional "0" edition without trading card; O: Magnus. No cover price; sendaway; without trading card 5.00
❑1, May 1991; O: Magnus. trading cards 4.00
❑2, Jul 1991 2.50
❑3, Aug 1991 1: Tekla. 2.50
❑4, Sep 1991 2.50
❑5, Oct 1991; Flip-book; 1: Rai. Flip-book with Rai #1 2.00
❑6, Nov 1991; Flip-book A: Rai. A: Solar. 2.00
❑7, Dec 1991; Flip-book A: Rai. V: Rai. 2.00
❑8, Jan 1992; Flip-book A: Rai. 2.00
❑9, Feb 1992 2.00
❑10, Mar 1992 2.00
❑11, Apr 1992 2.00
❑12, May 1992; Giant-size 1: Turok (Valiant). A: Turok. 5.00
❑13, Jun 1992 2.25
❑14, Jul 1992 2.25
❑15, Aug 1992; FM (c); FM (a);Unity 2.25
❑16, Sep 1992; Unity 2.25
❑17, Nov 1992 2.25
❑18, Nov 1992 SD (w) 2.25
❑19, Dec 1992 SD (w) 2.25
❑20, Jan 1993 2.25
❑21, Feb 1993; New logo 2.25
❑21/Gold, Feb 1993; Gold edition; New logo 3.00
❑22, Mar 1993 2.25
❑23, Apr 1993 2.25
❑24, May 1993; Story leads into Rai and the Future Force #9 2.25
❑25, Jun 1993; BL (c);Silver embossed cover 2.95
❑25/Ltd., Jun 1993; BL (c);Silver embossed cover 3.00
❑26, Jul 1993 2.25
❑27, Aug 1993 2.25
❑28, Sep 1993 2.25
❑29, Oct 1993 A: Eternal Warrior. 2.25
❑30, Nov 1993 A: X-O. 2.25
❑31, Dec 1993 2.25
❑32, Jan 1994 2.25
❑33, Feb 1994 A: Timewalker. 2.25
❑34, Mar 1994 2.25
❑35, Apr 1994 2.25
❑36, May 1994; trading card 2.25
❑37, Jun 1994 A: Starwatchers. A: Rai. 2.25
❑38, Aug 1994 2.25
❑39, Sep 1994 A: Torque. 2.25
❑40, Oct 1994 2.25
❑41, Nov 1994; Chaos Effect 2.25
❑42, Dec 1994 2.25
❑43, Jan 1995 2.25
❑44, Feb 1995 2.25

	N-MINT
❑45, Mar 1995	2.25
❑46, Apr 1995	2.25
❑47, May 1995	2.25
❑48, Jun 1995	2.25
❑49, Jul 1995	2.50
❑50, Jul 1995; Birthquake	2.25
❑51, Aug 1995; Birthquake	2.25
❑52, Aug 1995; Birthquake	2.25
❑53, Sep 1995	2.25
❑54, Sep 1995	2.25
❑55, Oct 1995	2.25
❑56, Oct 1995	2.50
❑57, Nov 1995	2.50
❑58, Nov 1995	2.50
❑59, Dec 1995	2.50
❑60, Dec 1995	2.50
❑61, Jan 1996	2.50
❑62, Jan 1996; Torque becomes a Psi-Lord	2.50
❑63, Feb 1996	2.50
❑64, Feb 1996 D: Magnus, Robot Fighter (Valiant).	2.25
❑Yearbook 1, ca. 1994; cardstock cover	3.95

MAGNUS ROBOT FIGHTER (ACCLAIM)
ACCLAIM

❑1, May 1997	2.50
❑1/Variant, May 1997; alternate painted cover	2.50
❑2, Jun 1997	2.50
❑3, Jul 1997	2.50
❑4, Aug 1997	2.50
❑5, Sep 1997	2.50
❑6, Oct 1997	2.50
❑7, Nov 1997; Gold Key homage cover	2.50
❑8, Dec 1997	2.50
❑9, Jan 1998	2.50
❑10, Feb 1998	2.50
❑11, Mar 1998	2.50
❑12, Apr 1998	2.50
❑13, Jan 1998; No cover date; indicia says Jan	2.50
❑14, Feb 1998; No cover date; indicia says Feb	2.50
❑15, Mar 1998	2.50
❑16, Apr 1998	2.50
❑17, May 1998	2.50
❑Ashcan 1, Jan 1997, b&w; No cover price; preview of upcoming series	1.00

MAGNUS ROBOT FIGHTER/NEXUS
VALIANT / DARK HORSE

❑1, Dec 1993; covers says Mar, indicia says Dec	3.00
❑2, Apr 1994 SR (a)	3.00

MAGUS
CALIBER

❑1	2.95
❑1/A; Variant cover of Girl praying in foreground, Magus behind	2.95
❑2	2.95

MAINE ZOMBIE LOBSTERMEN
MAINE STREAM COMICS

❑1, b&w	2.50
❑2, b&w	2.50
❑3, b&w	3.50

MAI, THE PSYCHIC GIRL
ECLIPSE / VIZ

❑1, May 1987, b&w; Japanese	3.50
❑1-2 1987	2.00
❑2, Jun 1987	2.50
❑2-2 1987	2.00
❑3, Jun 1987	2.50
❑4, Jul 1987	2.00
❑5, Jul 1987	2.00
❑6, Aug 1987	1.75
❑7, Aug 1987	1.75
❑8, Sep 1987	1.75
❑9, Sep 1987	1.75
❑10, Oct 1987	1.75
❑11, Oct 1987	1.75
❑12, Nov 1987	1.75

	N-MINT
❑13, Nov 1987	1.75
❑14, Dec 1987	1.75
❑15, Dec 1987	1.75
❑16, Jan 1988	1.75
❑17, Jan 1988	1.75
❑18, Feb 1988	1.75
❑19, Feb 1988	1.75
❑20, Mar 1988	1.75
❑21, Mar 1988	1.75
❑22, Apr 1988	1.75
❑23, Apr 1988	1.75
❑24, May 1988	1.75
❑25, May 1988	1.75
❑26, Jun 1988	1.75
❑27, Jun 1988	1.75
❑28, Jul 1988	1.75

MAISON IKKOKU PART 1
VIZ

❑1, Jun 1992	4.00
❑2, Jul 1992	3.50
❑3, Aug 1992	3.50
❑4, Sep 1992	3.50
❑5, Oct 1992	3.50
❑6, Nov 1992	3.50
❑7, Dec 1992	3.50

MAISON IKKOKU PART 2
VIZ

❑1, Jan 1993	3.50
❑2, Feb 1993	3.00
❑3, Mar 1993	3.00
❑4, Apr 1993	3.00
❑5, May 1993	3.00
❑6, Jun 1993	3.00

MAISON IKKOKU PART 3
VIZ

❑1, Jul 1993	3.00
❑2, Aug 1993	3.00
❑3, Sep 1993	3.00
❑4, Oct 1993	3.00
❑5, Nov 1993	3.00
❑6, Dec 1993	3.00

MAISON IKKOKU PART 4
VIZ

❑1, Jan 1994	2.95
❑2, Feb 1994	2.95
❑3, Apr 1994	2.95
❑4, May 1994	2.95
❑5, Jun 1994	2.95
❑6, Jul 1994	2.95
❑7, Aug 1994	2.95
❑8, Sep 1994	2.95
❑9, Oct 1994	2.95
❑10, Nov 1994	2.95

MAISON IKKOKU PART 5
VIZ

❑1, Nov 1995	2.95
❑2, Dec 1995	2.95
❑3, Jan 1996	3.50
❑4, Feb 1996	3.50
❑5, Mar 1996	3.50
❑6, Apr 1996	2.95
❑7, May 1996	3.50
❑8, Jun 1996	3.50
❑9, Jul 1996	2.75

MAISON IKKOKU PART 6
VIZ

❑1, Aug 1996	3.50
❑2, Sep 1996	2.95
❑3, Oct 1996	3.50
❑4, Nov 1996	3.50
❑5, Dec 1996	2.95
❑6, Jan 1997	3.50
❑7, Feb 1997	2.95
❑8, Mar 1997	2.95
❑9, Apr 1997	2.95
❑10, May 1997	2.95
❑11, Jun 1997	3.50

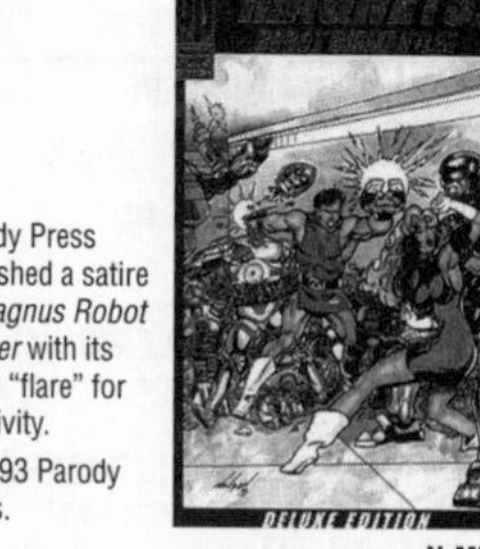

Parody Press published a satire of *Magnus Robot Fighter* with its usual "flare" for creativity.
© 1993 Parody Press.

MAISON IKKOKU PART 7
VIZ

	N-MINT
❑1, Jul 1997	3.50
❑2, Aug 1997	3.50
❑3, Sep 1997	3.25
❑4, Oct 1997	3.25
❑5, Nov 1997	3.25
❑6, Dec 1997	3.25
❑7, Jan 1998	3.25
❑8, Feb 1998	3.25
❑9, Mar 1998	3.25
❑10, Apr 1998	3.25
❑11, May 1998	3.25
❑12, Jun 1998	3.25
❑13, Jul 1998	3.25

MAISON IKKOKU PART 8
VIZ

❑1, Aug 1998	3.25
❑2, Sep 1998	3.50
❑3, Oct 1998	2.95
❑4, Nov 1998	3.50
❑5, Dec 1998	3.50
❑6, Jan 1999	3.50
❑7, Feb 1999	3.50
❑8, Mar 1999	3.25

MAISON IKKOKU PART 9
VIZ

❑1, Apr 1999	3.25
❑2, May 1999	3.25
❑3, Jun 1999	3.25
❑4, Jul 1999	3.25
❑5, Aug 1999	3.25
❑6, Sep 1999	3.25
❑7, Oct 1999	3.25
❑8, Nov 1999	3.25
❑9, Dec 1999	3.25
❑10, Jan 2000	2.95

MAJCANS, THE
P.S.

❑1	1.00

MAJOR BUMMER
DC

❑1, Aug 1997 O: Major Bummer. 1: The Gecko. 1: Major Bummer.	3.00
❑2, Sep 1997	2.50
❑3, Oct 1997	2.50
❑4, Nov 1997	2.50
❑5, Dec 1997; Face cover	2.50
❑6, Jan 1998	2.50
❑7, Feb 1998	2.50
❑8, Mar 1998	2.50
❑9, Apr 1998	2.50
❑10, May 1998	2.50
❑11, Jun 1998	2.50
❑12, Jul 1998	2.50
❑13, Aug 1998	2.50
❑14, Sep 1998	2.50
❑15, Oct 1998	2.50

MAJOR DAMAGE
INVICTUS

❑1, Oct 1994	2.25
❑2	2.25

MAJOR POWER AND SPUNKY
FANTAGRAPHICS / EROS

❑1, Oct 1994; one shot	3.50

N-MINT

MAKEBELIEVE
LIAR

❑1 .... 2.95

MALCOLM-10
ONLI

❑1, b&w 2.00

MALCOLM X (MILLENNIUM)
MILLENNIUM

❑1 .... 3.95

MALIBU ASHCAN: ULTRAFORCE
MALIBU / ULTRAVERSE

❑1, Jun 1994 .... 0.75

MALIBU SIGNATURE SERIES
MALIBU

❑1993; autograph book giveaway 0.25
❑1994; autograph book giveaway 0.25

MALICE IN WONDERLAND
FANTAGRAPHICS / EROS

❑1, Aug 1993, b&w 2.75

MALLIMALOU
CHANCE

❑1 .... 1.50

MAN AGAINST TIME
IMAGE

❑1, May 1996 .... 2.25
❑1/A, May 1996 .... 2.25
❑2, Jun 1996 .... 2.25
❑3, Jul 1996 .... 2.25
❑4, Aug 1996 .... 2.25
❑5, Sep 1996 .... 2.25
❑6, Oct 1996 .... 2.25

MAN-BAT (1ST SERIES)
DC

❑1, Dec 1975 SD (a) 6.00
❑2, Feb 1976 SD (a) 4.00

MAN-BAT (2ND SERIES)
DC

❑1, Dec 1984 .... 2.50

MAN-BAT (MINI-SERIES)
DC

❑1, Feb 1996 .... 2.50
❑2, Mar 1996 A: Killer Croc. 2.50
❑3, Apr 1996 .... 2.50

MAN CALLED A-X, THE
MALIBU / BRAVURA

❑0, Feb 1995; Published between #3 and #4 .... 2.95
❑1, Nov 1994 .... 2.95
❑1/A, Nov 1994 .... 2.95
❑2, Dec 1994 .... 2.95
❑3, Jan 1995 .... 2.95
❑4, Feb 1995 .... 2.95
❑5, Mar 1995 .... 2.95

MAN CALLED A-X, THE (DC)
DC

❑1, Oct 1997; follows events in Malibu/Bravura series 2.50
❑2, Nov 1997 .... 2.50
❑3, Dec 1997 .... 2.50
❑4, Jan 1998 .... 2.50
❑5, Feb 1998 .... 2.50
❑6, Mar 1998 .... 2.50
❑7, Apr 1998 .... 2.50
❑8, May 1998 .... 2.50

MAN CALLED LOCO, A
AVALON

❑1 .... 2.50

MANDRAKE THE MAGICIAN (KING)
KING

❑1, Sep 1966 .... 32.00
❑2, Nov 1966 .... 20.00
❑3, Jan 1967 .... 14.00
❑4, Mar 1967 .... 13.00
❑5, May 1967; Flying saucer story 13.00
❑6, Jul 1967 .... 10.00
❑7, Aug 1967 .... 10.00
❑8, Sep 1967 JJ (a) 16.00

N-MINT

❑9, Oct 1967 .... 9.00
❑10, Nov 1967 AR (a) 24.00

MANDRAKE THE MAGICIAN
MARVEL

❑1, Apr 1995; cardstock cover 2.95
❑2, May 1995; cardstock cover 2.95

MAN-EATING COW
NEC

❑1, Jul 1992 .... 4.50
❑2, Nov 1992 .... 3.50
❑3, Jan 1993 .... 3.50
❑4, Apr 1993; Scarcer 3.50
❑5, Jun 1993 .... 3.00
❑6, Aug 1993 .... 2.75
❑7, Nov 1993 .... 2.75
❑8, Jan 1994 .... 2.75
❑9 1994 A: The Tick. 3.00
❑10 1994 A: The Tick. 3.00

MAN-FROG
MAD DOG

❑1, Jul 1987, b&w 2.00
❑2, b&w 2.00

MAN FROM ATLANTIS
MARVEL

❑1, Feb 1978; Giant-size; TS (a);TV series; giant 3.00
❑2, Mar 1978 FR (a) 2.00
❑3, Apr 1978 .... 2.00
❑4, May 1978 FR (a) 2.00
❑5, Jun 1978 .... 2.00
❑6, Jul 1978 .... 2.00
❑7, Aug 1978 FR (a) 2.00

MAN FROM U.N.C.L.E., THE
GOLD KEY

❑1, Feb 1965; based on TV series 45.00
❑2, Oct 1965 .... 30.00
❑3, Nov 1965 .... 20.00
❑4, Jan 1966 .... 20.00
❑5, Mar 1966 .... 20.00
❑6, May 1966 .... 15.00
❑7, Jul 1966 .... 15.00
❑8, Sep 1966; 10146-609 .... 15.00
❑9, Nov 1966 .... 15.00
❑10, Jan 1967 .... 15.00
❑11, Mar 1967 .... 14.00
❑12, May 1967 .... 14.00
❑13, Jul 1967 .... 14.00
❑14, Sep 1967 .... 14.00
❑15, Nov 1967 .... 14.00
❑16, Jan 1968 .... 14.00
❑17, Mar 1968 .... 14.00
❑18, May 1968 .... 14.00
❑19, Jul 1968 .... 14.00
❑20, Oct 1968 .... 14.00
❑21, Jan 1969 .... 8.00
❑22, Apr 1969 .... 8.00

MAN FROM U.N.C.L.E., THE (2ND SERIES)
ENTERTAINMENT

❑1, Jan 1987, b&w 2.00
❑2, Feb 1987 .... 2.00
❑3, Apr 1987 .... 2.00
❑4, Aug 1987 .... 2.00
❑5, Dec 1987 .... 2.00
❑6, Feb 1988 .... 2.00
❑7, May 1988 .... 2.00
❑8, Jul 1988 .... 2.00
❑9, Aug 1988 .... 2.00
❑10, Sep 1988 .... 2.00
❑11, Sep 1988 .... 2.00

MAN FROM U.N.C.L.E., THE: THE BIRDS OF PREY AFFAIR
MILLENNIUM

❑1, Mar 1993 .... 2.95
❑2, Sep 1993 .... 2.95

MANGA HORROR
AVALON

❑1, b&w; reprints Ghostly Tales 2.95

N-MINT

MANGAPHILE
RADIO

❑1, Aug 1999, b&w 2.95
❑2, Oct 1999, b&w 2.95
❑3, Dec 1999, b&w 2.95
❑4, Feb 2000, b&w 2.95
❑5, Apr 2000, b&w 2.95
❑6, Jun 2000, b&w 2.95
❑7, Aug 2000, b&w 2.95

MANGA SHI
CRUSADE

❑1, Aug 1996 .... 3.00

MANGA SHI: SHISEJI
CRUSADE

❑1 .... 2.95

MANGA SHI 2000
CRUSADE

❑1, Feb 1997; flip book with Shi: Heaven and Earth preview back-up; In the Killer Skies 2.95
❑1/A, Feb 1997; "Virgin" cover without price or logo 3.00
❑1/B; Rising Sun Edition 3.00
❑2, Apr 1997 .... 2.95
❑3, Jun 1997 .... 2.95

MANGA SURPRISE!
MORNING & AFTERNOON, KODANSHA LTD.

❑1, Jul 1996, b&w 2.00

MANGA VIZION
VIZ

❑1, Mar 1995 .... 5.00
❑2, Apr 1995 .... 5.00
❑3, May 1995 .... 5.00
❑4, Jun 1995 .... 5.00
❑5, Jul 1995 .... 5.00
❑6, Aug 1995 .... 5.00
❑7, Sep 1995 .... 5.00
❑8, Oct 1995 .... 5.00
❑9, Nov 1995 .... 5.00
❑10, Dec 1995 .... 5.00

MANGA VIZION (VOL. 2)
VIZ

❑1, Jan 1996 .... 5.00
❑2, Feb 1996 .... 5.00
❑3, Mar 1996 .... 5.00
❑4, Apr 1996 .... 5.00
❑5, May 1996 .... 5.00
❑6, Jun 1996 .... 5.00
❑7, Jul 1996 .... 5.00
❑8, Aug 1996 .... 5.00
❑9, Sep 1996 .... 5.00
❑10, Oct 1996 .... 5.00
❑11, Nov 1996 .... 5.00
❑12, Dec 1996 .... 5.00

MANGA VIZION (VOL. 3)
VIZ

❑1, Jan 1997 .... 4.95
❑2, Feb 1997 .... 4.95
❑3, Mar 1997 .... 4.95
❑4, Apr 1997 .... 4.95
❑5 1997 .... 4.95
❑6 1997 .... 4.95
❑7 1997 .... 4.95
❑8 1997 .... 4.95

MANGA VIZION (VOL. 4)
VIZ

❑1 .... 4.95
❑2 .... 4.95
❑3 .... 4.95
❑4 .... 4.95
❑5 .... 4.95
❑6 .... 4.95
❑7 .... 4.95
❑8 .... 4.95

MANGA ZEN
ZEN COMICS

❑1, b&w 2.50

N-MINT

MANGAZINE
ANTARCTIC

❑1, ca. 1985, b&w; first Antarctic publication; newsprint cover; company name misspelled throughout 4.00
❑1-2 .... 2.00
❑2, ca. 1985 .... 3.50
❑3, ca. 1986 .... 1.75
❑4, ca. 1986 .... 3.50
❑5, ca. 1986 .... 3.50

MANGAZINE (VOL. 2)
ANTARCTIC

❑1, Jan 1989, b&w 3.50
❑2, Jun 1989, b&w 3.00
❑3 1989, b&w 2.00
❑4, b&w 2.00
❑5, ca. 1990, b&w 2.00
❑6 .... 3.00
❑7 .... 3.00
❑8 .... 3.00
❑9 .... 3.00
❑10, Jul 1991 .... 3.00
❑11, Sep 1991 .... 3.00
❑12, Nov 1991 .... 3.00
❑13, Jan 1992 .... 3.00
❑14, Mar 1992 .... 3.00
❑15, May 1992 .... 3.00
❑16, ca. 1992 .... 3.00
❑17, Nov 1992 .... 3.00
❑18, Nov 1992; Urusei Yatsura special issue 3.00
❑19, Jan 1993 .... 3.00
❑20, Feb 1993 .... 3.00
❑21, Mar 1993 .... 3.00
❑22, Apr 1993 .... 3.00
❑23, May 1993 .... 3.00
❑24, Jun 1993 .... 3.00
❑25, Jul 1993 .... 3.00
❑26, Aug 1993 .... 3.00
❑27, Sep 1993 .... 3.00
❑28, Oct 1993 .... 3.00
❑29, Nov 1993 .... 3.00
❑30, Dec 1993 .... 3.00
❑31, Jan 1994 .... 2.95
❑32, Feb 1994; Super Cat Nuku-Nuku 2.95
❑33, May 1994 .... 2.95
❑34, Jul 1994 .... 2.95
❑35, Sep 1994 .... 2.95
❑36, Nov 1994 .... 2.95
❑37, Jan 1995 .... 2.95
❑38, Mar 1995 .... 2.95
❑39, May 1995 .... 2.95
❑40, Sep 1995 .... 2.95
❑41, Sep 1995; Samurai Troopers 2.95
❑42, Sep 1995 .... 2.95
❑43, Sep 1995; Samurai Troopers Episode Guide, Part 2 .... 2.95
❑44, May 1996 .... 2.95

MANGLE TANGLE TALES
INNOVATION

❑1; Intro by Harlan Ellison 2.95

MANHUNTER (1ST SERIES)
DC

❑1, ca. 1984; Double-size; reprints serial from Detective Comics; Archie Goodwin 2.50

MANHUNTER (2ND SERIES)
DC

❑1, Jul 1988 O: Manhunter II (Mark Shaw). 1.50
❑2, Aug 1988 .... 1.25
❑3, Sep 1988 .... 1.25
❑4, Oct 1988 .... 1.25
❑5, Nov 1988 .... 1.25
❑6, Dec 1988 .... 1.25
❑7, Dec 1988 V: Count Vertigo. 1.25
❑8, Jan 1989; A: Flash. Invasion! 1.25
❑9, Jan 1989; A: Flash. Invasion! 1.25
❑10, Feb 1989 A: Checkmate. 1.25
❑11, Mar 1989 .... 1.25
❑12, Apr 1989 .... 1.25
❑13, May 1989 .... 1.25

N-MINT

❑14, Jun 1989 .... 1.25
❑15, Jul 1989 .... 1.25
❑16, Aug 1989 .... 1.25
❑17, Sep 1989 A: Batman. 1.25
❑18, Oct 1989 .... 1.25
❑19, Nov 1989 .... 1.25
❑20, Dec 1989 .... 1.25
❑21, Jan 1990 .... 1.25
❑22, Feb 1990 .... 1.25
❑23, Mar 1990 .... 1.25
❑24, Apr 1990 .... 1.25

MANHUNTER (3RD SERIES)
DC

❑0, Oct 1994 1: Manhunter III (Chase Lawler). 2.25
❑1, Nov 1994 O: Manhunter III (Chase Lawler). 2.25
❑2, Dec 1994 O: Manhunter III (Chase Lawler). 2.00
❑3, Jan 1995 .... 2.00
❑4, Feb 1995 .... 2.00
❑5, Mar 1995 .... 2.00
❑6, Apr 1995 .... 2.00
❑7, Jun 1995 .... 2.00
❑8, Jul 1995 .... 2.25
❑9, Aug 1995 .... 2.25
❑10, Sep 1995 .... 2.25
❑11, Oct 1995 .... 2.25
❑12, Nov 1995; Underworld Unleashed 2.25

MANHUNTER: THE SPECIAL EDITION
DC

❑1, ca. 1999; collects serial from Detective Comics plus new story 9.95

MANIC ONE-SHOT
IMAGE

❑1, Feb 2004 .... 3.50

MANIK
MILLENNIUM

❑1, Sep 1995; foil cover 2.95
❑2 1995 .... 2.95
❑3 1996 .... 2.95

MANIMAL
RENEGADE

❑1, Jan 1986, b&w 1.70

MAN IN BLACK
RECOLLECTIONS

❑1, b&w 2.00
❑2, Jul 1991, b&w 2.00

MANKIND
CHAOS

❑1, Sep 1999 .... 2.95

MANN AND SUPERMAN
DC

❑1, ca. 2000 .... 5.95

MAN OF MANY FACES
TOKYOPOP

❑1, May 2003, b&w; printed in Japanese format 9.99

MAN OF RUST
BLACKTHORNE

❑1/A, Nov 1986 .... 1.50
❑1/B, Nov 1986 .... 1.50

MAN OF STEEL, THE (MINI-SERIES)
DC

❑1, Oct 1986; JBy (w); JBy (a);newsstand 2.50
❑1/Variant, Oct 1986; JBy (w); JBy, DG (a);direct 2.50
❑1/Silver, Oct 1986; silver edition JBy (w); JBy (a) 2.50
❑2, Oct 1986 JBy (w); JBy (a) 2.50
❑2/Silver, Nov 1986; silver edition JBy (w); JBy (a) 2.50
❑3, Nov 1986 JBy (w); JBy (a); A: Batman. 2.50
❑3/Silver, Nov 1986; silver edition JBy (w); JBy (a); A: Batman. 2.50
❑4, Nov 1986 JBy (w); JBy (a) 2.50
❑4/Silver, Nov 1986; silver edition JBy (w); JBy (a) 2.50
❑5, Dec 1986 JBy (w); JBy (a) 2.50

Before he stepped out of showers on *Dallas*, Patrick Duffy played *The Man from Atlantis*.
© 1978 Marvel Comics.

N-MINT

❑5/Silver, Dec 1986; silver edition JBy (w); JBy (a) 2.50
❑6, Dec 1986 JBy (w); JBy (a) 2.50
❑6/Silver, Jan 1986; silver edition JBy (w); JBy (a) 2.50

MAN OF THE ATOM
ACCLAIM / VALIANT

❑1, Jan 1997; No cover price; preview of upcoming one-shot 1.00

MAN OF WAR (ECLIPSE)
ECLIPSE

❑1, Aug 1987 .... 1.75
❑1/Direct ed. 2.50
❑2, Dec 1987 .... 1.75
❑3, Feb 1988 .... 1.75
❑4 .... 1.75
❑5 .... 1.75

MAN OF WAR (MALIBU)
MALIBU

❑1/Direct ed., Apr 1993; Direct Market edition with different cover, no UPC code 2.50
❑1, ca. 1993 .... 1.95
❑2, ca. 1993 .... 2.50
❑3, ca. 1993 .... 2.50
❑4, ca. 1993 .... 2.50
❑5, ca. 1993 .... 2.50
❑6, ca. 1993 .... 2.25
❑7, ca. 1994 .... 2.25
❑8, ca. 1994 .... 2.25

MANOSAURS
EXPRESS / ENTITY

❑1 .... 2.95
❑2 .... 2.95

MANTECH ROBOT WARRIORS
ARCHIE

❑1, Sep 1984, O: The Mantechs. 1: The Mantechs. 1.00
❑2, Dec 1984 .... 1.00
❑3, Feb 1985 .... 1.00
❑4, May 1985 .... 1.00

MAN-THING (MINI-SERIES)
MARVEL

❑1, Sep 2004 .... 2.99

MAN-THING (VOL. 1)
MARVEL

❑1, Jan 1974 FB, VM, JM (a); 2: Howard the Duck. 10.00
❑2, Feb 1974 VM (a) 7.00
❑3, Mar 1974; VM, JAb (a); 1: FoolKiller I (Greg Everbest). Marvel Value Stamp #60: Ka-Zar 6.00
❑4, Apr 1974; VM, JAb (a); O: FoolKiller I (Greg Everbest). D: FoolKiller I (Greg Everbest). Marvel Value Stamp #17: Black Bolt 4.00
❑5, May 1974; MP (a);Marvel Value Stamp #83: Dragon Man 4.00
❑6, Jun 1974; MP (a);Marvel Value Stamp #55: Medusa 3.00
❑7, Jul 1974; MP (a);Marvel Value Stamp #19: Balder, Hogun, Fandral 3.00
❑8, Aug 1974; MP (a);Marvel Value Stamp #37: Watcher 3.00
❑9, Sep 1974; MP (a);Marvel Value Stamp #53: Grim Reaper 3.00
❑10, Oct 1974 MP (w); MP (a) 3.00
❑11, Nov 1974; MP (a);Marvel Value Stamp #28: Hawkeye 2.50

N-MINT

❑12, Dec 1974 JB, KJ (a) ... 2.50
❑13, Jan 1975; TS, JB (a);Marvel Value Stamp #54: Shanna ... 2.50
❑14, Feb 1975; AA (a);Marvel Value Stamp #64: Sif ... 2.50
❑15, Mar 1975 ... 2.50
❑16, Apr 1975 JB, TP (a) ... 2.50
❑17, May 1975 JM (a) ... 2.50
❑18, Jun 1975 JM (a) ... 2.50
❑19, Jul 1975 JM, FS (a); 1: Scavenger. 2.50
❑20, Aug 1975 JM (a) ... 2.50
❑21, Sep 1975 JM (a); O: Scavenger. 2.50
❑22, Oct 1975 JM (a); A: Howard the Duck. ... 3.00

MAN-THING (VOL. 2)
MARVEL

❑1, Nov 1979 JM, BWi (a) ... 2.50
❑2, Jan 1980 VM (a) ... 2.00
❑3, Mar 1980 JM, BWi (a) ... 2.00
❑4, May 1980 DP, BWi (a); A: Dr. Strange. ... 2.00
❑5, Jul 1980 DP, BWi (a) ... 2.00
❑6, Sep 1980 DP, BWi (a) ... 2.00
❑7, Nov 1980 DP, BWi (a) ... 2.00
❑8, Jan 1981 ... 2.00
❑9, Mar 1981 ... 2.00
❑10, May 1981 ... 2.00
❑11, Jul 1981 ... 2.00

MAN-THING (VOL. 3)
MARVEL

❑1, Dec 1997; gatefold summary; wraparound cover ... 2.99
❑2, Jan 1998; gatefold summary ... 2.99
❑3, Feb 1998; gatefold summary ... 2.99
❑4, Mar 1998; gatefold summary ... 2.99
❑5, Apr 1998; gatefold summary ... 2.99
❑6, May 1998; gatefold summary ... 2.99
❑7, Jun 1998; gatefold summary ... 2.99
❑8, Jul 1998; gatefold summary ... 2.99

MANTRA
MALIBU / ULTRAVERSE

❑1, Jul 1993; O: Mantra I (Eden Blake). 1: Boneyard. 1: Warstrike. 1: Mantra I (Eden Blake). Ultraverse ... 2.50
❑1/Ltd., Jul 1993; Ultra Limited edition 3.00
❑2, Aug 1993 ... 2.25
❑3, Sep 1993 1: Kismet Deadly. ... 2.25
❑4, Oct 1993; Rune ... 2.50
❑5, Nov 1993 ... 2.00
❑6, Dec 1993; Break-Thru ... 2.00
❑7, Jan 1994 ... 2.00
❑8, Feb 1994 ... 2.00
❑9, Mar 1994 ... 2.00
❑10, Apr 1994; Flip-book with Ultraverse Premiere #2 ... 3.50
❑11, May 1994 ... 1.95
❑12, Jun 1994 ... 1.95
❑13, Aug 1994; D: Boneyard's Wives. issue has two different covers ... 1.95
❑13/A; D: Boneyard's Wives. variant cover ... 1.95
❑14, Sep 1994 1: Mantra II (Lauren). D: Archimage. ... 1.95
❑15, Oct 1994 A: Prime. D: Notch. ... 1.95
❑16, Nov 1994 ... 1.95
❑17, Dec 1994 1: NecroMantra. V: Necro Mantra. ... 1.95
❑18, Feb 1995 ... 1.95
❑19, Mar 1995 ... 1.95
❑20, Apr 1995 1: Overlord. D: Overlord. 1.95
❑21, May 1995 ... 2.50
❑22, Jun 1995 ... 2.50
❑23, Jul 1995 ... 2.50
❑24, Aug 1995 ... 2.50
❑Giant Size 1, ca. 1994; Giant-Size Mantra #1 1: Topaz. 1: Opal Queen. 1: Sapphire Queen. ... 3.50
❑1/Hologram, Jul 1993; O: Mantra I (Eden Blake). 1: Boneyard. 1: Warstrike. 1: Mantra I (Eden Blake). Hologram cover ... 6.00

N-MINT

MANTRA (VOL. 2)
MALIBU / ULTRAVERSE

❑0, Sep 1995; O: New Mantra. # Infinity 1.50
❑0/A, Sep 1995; O: New Mantra. alternate cover ... 1.50
❑1, Oct 1995 O: Coven. 1: Coven. ... 2.00
❑2, Nov 1995 ... 1.50
❑3, Dec 1995 V: Necro Mantra. ... 1.50
❑4, Jan 1996 ... 1.50
❑5, Feb 1996 V: N-ME. ... 1.50
❑6, Mar 1996; A: Rush. Mantra gets new costume ... 1.50
❑7, Apr 1996 ... 1.50

MANTRA: SPEAR OF DESTINY
MALIBU / ULTRAVERSE

❑1, Apr 1995 ... 2.50
❑2, May 1995 ... 2.50

MANTUS FILES
ETERNITY

❑1, b&w ... 2.50
❑2, b&w ... 2.50
❑3, b&w ... 2.50
❑4, b&w ... 2.50

MANY REINCARNATIONS OF LAZARUS, THE (VOL. 2)
FISHER

❑1, Dec 1998 ... 3.00
❑Ashcan 1, b&w; no cover price ... 1.00

MANY WORLDS OF TESLA STRONG
DC

❑1, May 2003 ... 3.00

MARA
AIRCEL

❑1, May 1991 ... 2.50
❑2 ... 2.50
❑3 ... 2.50
❑4, Jan 1992 ... 2.95

MARA CELTIC SHAMANESS
FANTAGRAPHICS / EROS

❑1 ... 2.95
❑2 ... 2.95
❑3 ... 2.95
❑4 ... 2.95
❑5 ... 2.95
❑6 ... 2.95

MARA OF THE CELTS BOOK 1
RIP OFF

❑Special 1, Sep 1993, b&w ... 2.95

MARA OF THE CELTS BOOK 2
FANTAGRAPHICS / EROS

❑1 ... 2.95

MARAUDER
SILVERLINE

❑1, Jan 1998 ... 2.95
❑2 1998 ... 2.95
❑3 1998 ... 2.95
❑4 1998 ... 2.95

MARCH HARE, THE
LODESTONE

❑1, b&w ... 1.50

MARC SILVESTRI SKETCHBOOK
IMAGE

❑1, Jan 2004 ... 2.99

MARC SPECTOR: MOON KNIGHT
MARVEL

❑1, Jun 1989 ... 2.50
❑2, Jul 1989 ... 2.00
❑3, Mar 1989 ... 2.00
❑4, Sep 1989 ... 2.00
❑5, Oct 1989 ... 2.00
❑6, Nov 1989; Brother Voodoo ... 2.00
❑7, Nov 1989; Brother Voodoo ... 2.00
❑8, Dec 1989 A: Punisher. ... 3.00
❑9, Dec 1989 A: Punisher. ... 3.00
❑10, Jan 1990 1: Ringer II. ... 2.00
❑11, Feb 1990 ... 2.00
❑12, Mar 1990 ... 2.00
❑13, Apr 1990 ... 2.00
❑14, May 1990 ... 2.00

N-MINT

❑15, Jun 1990 ... 2.00
❑16, Jul 1990 ... 2.00
❑17, Aug 1990 ... 2.00
❑18, Sep 1990 ... 2.00
❑19, Oct 1990 A: Punisher. A: Spider-Man. ... 3.00
❑20, Nov 1990 A: Punisher. A: Spider-Man. ... 3.00
❑21, Dec 1990 A: Punisher. A: Spider-Man. ... 3.00
❑22, Jan 1991 ... 3.00
❑23, Feb 1991 ... 3.00
❑24, Mar 1991 ... 3.00
❑25, Apr 1991; Giant-size TP (a); A: Ghost Rider. ... 2.50
❑26, May 1991 TP (a) ... 2.00
❑27, Jun 1991 ... 2.00
❑28, Jul 1991 ... 2.00
❑29, Aug 1991 ... 2.00
❑30, Sep 1991 ... 2.00
❑31, Oct 1991 ... 2.00
❑32, Nov 1991 A: Hobgoblin. ... 3.00
❑33, Dec 1991 A: Hobgoblin. ... 3.00
❑34, Jan 1992 ... 2.00
❑35, Feb 1992 A: Punisher. ... 2.00
❑36, Mar 1992 A: Punisher. ... 2.00
❑37, Apr 1992 A: Punisher. ... 2.00
❑38, May 1992 A: Punisher. ... 2.00
❑39, Jun 1992 V: Doctor Doom. ... 2.00
❑40, Jul 1992 ... 2.00
❑41, Aug 1992 ... 2.00
❑42, Sep 1992 ... 2.00
❑43, Oct 1992 ... 2.00
❑44, Nov 1992 ... 2.00
❑45, Dec 1992 ... 2.00
❑46, Jan 1993 ... 2.00
❑47, Feb 1993 ... 2.00
❑48, Mar 1993 ... 2.00
❑49, Apr 1993 ... 2.00
❑50, May 1993; Die-cut cover ... 2.95
❑51, Jun 1993 ... 1.75
❑52, Jul 1993 ... 1.75
❑53, Aug 1993 ... 1.75
❑54, Sep 1993 ... 1.75
❑55, Oct 1993; 1: Sunstreak. 1st professional Stephen Platt art ... 2.50
❑56, Nov 1993 ... 2.50
❑57, Dec 1993 ... 2.50
❑58, Jan 1994 ... 2.00
❑59, Feb 1994 ... 2.00
❑60, Mar 1994 ... 2.00
❑Special 1, ca. 1992; Team-up with Shang-Chi, Master of Kung Fu ... 2.50

MARGIE
DELL

❑2, Sep 1962, First issue published as Dell's Four Color #1307 ... 25.00

MARILYN MONROE: SUICIDE OR MURDER?
REVOLUTIONARY

❑1, Sep 1993, b&w ... 2.50

MARINES ATTACK
CHARLTON

❑1 ... 16.00
❑2 ... 12.00
❑3 ... 9.00
❑4 ... 9.00
❑5 ... 9.00
❑6 ... 6.00
❑7 ... 6.00
❑8 ... 6.00
❑9 ... 6.00

MARIONETTE
RAVEN

❑1 1987, b&w ... 1.00
❑3, b&w ... 1.00

MARIONETTE, THE
ALPHA PRODUCTIONS

❑1, b&w ... 2.50
❑2, b&w ... 2.50
❑3 ... 2.50

N-MINT

MARK, THE (1ST SERIES)
DARK HORSE

❑1, Sep 1987 .... 2.00
❑2, Dec 1987 .... 2.00
❑3, Aug 1988 .... 2.00
❑4, Sep 1988 .... 2.00
❑5, Nov 1988 .... 2.00
❑6, Jan 1989 .... 2.00

MARK, THE (2ND SERIES)
DARK HORSE

❑1, Dec 1993 .... 2.50
❑2, Jan 1994 .... 2.50
❑3, Feb 1994 .... 2.50
❑4, Mar 1994 .... 2.50

MARKAM
GAUNTLET

❑1 .... 2.50

MARK HAZZARD: MERC
MARVEL

❑1, Nov 1986 PD (w); GM (a); 1: Mark Hazzard. 1.25
❑2, Dec 1986 .... 1.00
❑3, Jan 1987 .... 1.00
❑4, Feb 1987 .... 1.00
❑5, Mar 1987 .... 1.00
❑6, Apr 1987 .... 1.00
❑7, May 1987 .... 1.00
❑8, Jun 1987 .... 1.00
❑9, Jul 1987 .... 1.00
❑10, Aug 1987 GM (a) 1.00
❑11, Sep 1987 .... 1.00
❑12, Oct 1987 .... 1.00
❑Annual 1, Nov 1987 D: Hazzard. 1.25

MARK OF CHARON
CROSSGEN

❑1, Apr 2003 .... 2.95
❑2, May 2003 .... 2.95
❑3, Jun 2003 .... 2.95
❑4, Jul 2003 .... 2.95
❑5, Sep 2003 .... 2.95

MARKSMAN, THE
HERO

❑1, Jan 1988 .... 1.95
❑2, Feb 1988 .... 1.95
❑3, Apr 1988 .... 1.95
❑4, Jun 1988 .... 1.95
❑5, Aug 1988 .... 1.95
❑Annual 1, Dec 1988 .... 2.75

MARMALADE BOY
TOKYOPOP

❑1 2001; printed in Japanese format 2.95
❑2 2001; printed in Japanese format 2.95
❑3 2001; printed in Japanese format 2.95

MAROONED!
FANTAGRAPHICS / EROS

❑1, b&w 1.95

MARQUIS, THE: DANSE MACABRE
ONI

❑1, b&w 2.95
❑2, Jul 2000, b&w 2.95
❑3, Oct 2000, b&w 2.95

MARRIAGE OF HERCULES AND XENA, THE
TOPPS

❑1, Jul 1998 .... 2.95

MARRIED...WITH CHILDREN (VOL. 1)
NOW

❑1, Jun 1990 .... 2.50
❑1-2 .... 2.00
❑2, Jul 1990 .... 2.00
❑3, Aug 1990 .... 2.00
❑4, Sep 1990 .... 2.00
❑5, Oct 1990 .... 2.00
❑6, Nov 1990 .... 2.00
❑7, Feb 1991 .... 2.00

N-MINT

MARRIED...WITH CHILDREN (VOL. 2)
NOW

❑1, Sep 1991 .... 2.50
❑2, Oct 1991; Peggy invents bon-bon filling detector 2.25
❑3, Nov 1991; Al turns into Psychodad 2.25
❑4, Dec 1991 .... 2.00
❑5, Jan 1992 .... 2.00
❑6, Mar 1992 .... 2.00
❑7, Apr 1992 .... 2.00
❑Annual 1994, ca. 1994; Annual 2.50
❑Special 1, Jul 1992; Special; with poster 2.00

MARRIED...WITH CHILDREN: BUCK'S TALE
NOW

❑1, ca. 1994 O: Buck (the Bundy Family dog). 2.00

MARRIED...WITH CHILDREN: BUD BUNDY, FANBOY IN PARADISE
NOW

❑1 .... 2.95

MARRIED...WITH CHILDREN: FLASHBACK SPECIAL
NOW

❑1, Jan 1993; Al & Peg's First Date .. 2.00
❑2, Feb 1993; Al & Peg's Wedding 2.00
❑3, Mar 1993 .... 2.00

MARRIED...WITH CHILDREN: KELLY BUNDY
NOW

❑1, Aug 1992 .... 2.25
❑2, Sep 1992 .... 2.25
❑3, Oct 1992 .... 2.25

MARRIED...WITH CHILDREN: KELLY GOES TO KOLLEGE
NOW

❑1 .... 2.95
❑2 .... 2.95
❑3 .... 2.95

MARRIED...WITH CHILDREN: OFF BROADWAY
NOW

❑1, Sep 1993 .... 2.00

MARRIED...WITH CHILDREN: QUANTUM QUARTET
NOW

❑1, Oct 1993; parody 2.00
❑2, Nov 1993; parody 2.00
❑3, Fal 1994; The Big Wrap-Up; combines issues #3 and 4 into flipbook; no indicia; parody 2.95

MARRIED...WITH CHILDREN 3-D SPECIAL
NOW

❑1, Jun 1993 .... 2.95

MARRIED...WITH CHILDREN: 2099
NOW

❑1, Jun 1993; Terminator spoof 2.00
❑2, Jul 1993 .... 2.00
❑3, Aug 1993 .... 2.00

MARS (FIRST)
FIRST

❑1, Jan 1984 .... 1.50
❑2, Feb 1984 .... 1.25
❑3, Mar 1984 .... 1.25
❑4, Apr 1984 .... 1.25
❑5, May 1984 .... 1.25
❑6, Jun 1984 .... 1.25
❑7, Jul 1984 .... 1.25
❑8, Aug 1984 .... 1.25
❑9, Sep 1984 .... 1.25
❑10, Oct 1984 .... 1.25
❑11, Nov 1984 .... 1.25
❑12, Dec 1984 .... 1.25

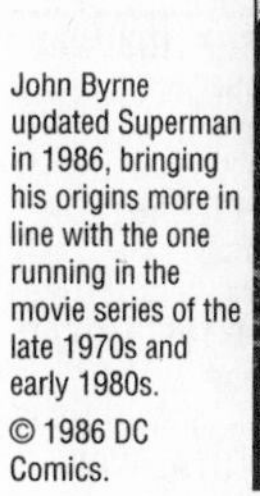

John Byrne updated Superman in 1986, bringing his origins more in line with the one running in the movie series of the late 1970s and early 1980s.

© 1986 DC Comics.

N-MINT

MARS (TOKYOPOP)
TOKYOPOP

❑1, Mar 2002, b&w; printed in Japanese format 9.99
❑2, Jun 2002, b&w; printed in Japanese format 9.99
❑3, Aug 2002, b&w; printed in Japanese format 9.99

MARS ATTACKS (VOL. 1)
TOPPS

❑1, May 1994; KG (w); KG (a);Flip-book format 4.00
❑1/Ace, May 1994; Wizard Ace Edition #11; acetate overlay cover; send-away from Wizard #65 .... 4.00
❑1/Ltd., May 1994; Limited edition promotional edition (5,000 printed); Flip-book format 4.00
❑2, Jun 1994 .... 3.00
❑3, Aug 1994 .... 3.00
❑4, Sep 1994 .... 3.00
❑5, Oct 1994 .... 3.00

MARS ATTACKS (VOL. 2)
TOPPS

❑1, Aug 1995 KG (w) 3.50
❑2, Sep 1995 .... 3.00
❑3, Oct 1995 .... 3.00
❑4, Jan 1996 .... 3.00
❑5, Jan 1996 .... 3.00
❑6, Mar 1996 .... 3.00
❑7, May 1996 .... 3.00
❑8, Jul 1996 .... 3.00

MARS ATTACKS BASEBALL SPECIAL
TOPPS

❑1, Jun 1996 .... 2.95

MARS ATTACKS HIGH SCHOOL
TOPPS

❑1, May 1997 .... 2.95
❑2, Sep 1997 .... 2.95

MARS ATTACKS IMAGE
IMAGE

❑1, Dec 1996; crossover with Topps . 2.50
❑2, Jan 1997 .... 2.50
❑3, Mar 1997 .... 2.50
❑4, Apr 1997 .... 2.50

MARS ATTACKS THE SAVAGE DRAGON
TOPPS

❑1, Dec 1996; crossover with Image; trading cards 2.95
❑2, Jan 1997; crossover with Image . 2.95
❑3, Feb 1997; crossover with Image . 2.95
❑4, Mar 1997; crossover with Image . 2.95

MARSHAL LAW
MARVEL / EPIC

❑1, Oct 1987 .... 3.50
❑2, Feb 1988 .... 2.50
❑3, Apr 1988 .... 2.50
❑4, Aug 1988 .... 2.50
❑5, Dec 1988 .... 2.50
❑6, Apr 1989 .... 2.50

MARSHAL LAW: KINGDOM OF THE BLIND
APOCALYPSE

❑1; newsstand 3.95
❑1/Direct ed.; squarebound 5.95

N-MINT

MARSHAL LAW: SECRET TRIBUNAL
DARK HORSE
- ❑1, Sep 1993; cardstock cover 2.95
- ❑2, Apr 1994; cardstock cover 2.95

MARSHAL LAW: SUPER BABYLON
DARK HORSE
- ❑1, May 1992; prestige format 4.95

MARSHAL LAW: THE HATEFUL DEAD
APOCALYPSE
- ❑1; prestige format 5.95

M.A.R.S. PATROL TOTAL WAR
GOLD KEY
- ❑3, Sep 1966; WW (a);Series continued from Total War #2 .... 12.00
- ❑4, Oct 1967 .... 9.00
- ❑5, May 1968 .... 9.00
- ❑6, Aug 1968 .... 7.50
- ❑7, Nov 1968 .... 7.50
- ❑8, Feb 1969 .... 7.50
- ❑9, May 1969 .... 7.50
- ❑10, Aug 1969 .... 7.50

MARTHA SPLATTERHEAD'S WEIRDEST STORIES EVER TOLD
MONSTER
- ❑1, b&w 3.50

MARTHA WASHINGTON GOES TO WAR
DARK HORSE / LEGEND
- ❑1, May 1994; FM (w); DaG (a);cardstock cover 3.00
- ❑2, Jun 1994; FM (w); DaG (a);cardstock cover 3.00
- ❑3, Jul 1994; FM (w); DaG (a);cardstock cover 3.00
- ❑4, Aug 1994; FM (w); DaG (a);cardstock cover 3.00
- ❑5, Nov 1994; FM (w); DaG (a);cardstock cover 3.00

MARTHA WASHINGTON SAVES THE WORLD
DARK HORSE
- ❑1, Dec 1997; FM (w); DaG (a);cardstock cover 3.00
- ❑2, Jan 1998; FM (w); DaG (a);cardstock cover 3.00
- ❑3, Feb 1998; FM (w); DaG (a);cardstock cover 3.00

MARTHA WASHINGTON: STRANDED IN SPACE
DARK HORSE / LEGEND
- ❑1, Nov 1995; FM (w); DaG (a); A: The Big Guy. reprints story from Dark Horse Presents;cardstock cover 3.00

MARTIAN MANHUNTER (MINI-SERIES)
DC
- ❑1, May 1988 O: Martian Manhunter. 1.50
- ❑2, Jun 1988 .... 1.50
- ❑3, Jul 1988 .... 1.50
- ❑4, Aug 1988 .... 1.50

MARTIAN MANHUNTER
DC
- ❑0, Oct 1998 .... 3.00
- ❑1, Dec 1998 .... 2.50
- ❑2, Jan 1999 .... 2.00
- ❑3, Feb 1999 A: Bette Noir. 2.00
- ❑4, Mar 1999 D: Karen Smith. 2.00
- ❑5, Apr 1999 JDu (a) 2.00
- ❑6, May 1999 V: JLA. 2.00
- ❑7, Jun 1999 .... 2.00
- ❑8, Jul 1999 .... 2.00
- ❑9, Aug 1999 A: JLA. 2.00
- ❑10, Sep 1999 A: Fire. 2.00
- ❑11, Oct 1999 .... 2.00
- ❑12, Nov 1999; A: Steel. A: Crimson Fox. A: Ice. A: Vibe. Day of Judgment 2.00
- ❑13, Dec 1999 .... 2.00
- ❑14, Jan 2000 .... 1.99
- ❑15, Feb 2000 .... 1.99
- ❑16, Mar 2000 .... 1.99
- ❑17, Apr 2000 .... 1.99
- ❑18, May 2000 A: JSA. 1.99
- ❑19, Jun 2000 .... 1.99
- ❑20, Jul 2000 .... 1.99
- ❑21, Aug 2000 .... 1.99
- ❑22, Sep 2000 .... 2.50
- ❑23, Oct 2000 .... 2.50
- ❑24, Nov 2000 .... 2.50
- ❑25, Dec 2000 .... 2.50
- ❑26, Jan 2001 .... 2.50
- ❑27, Feb 2001 .... 2.50
- ❑28, Mar 2001 .... 2.50
- ❑29, Apr 2001 .... 2.50
- ❑30, May 2001 .... 2.50
- ❑31, Jun 2001 .... 2.50
- ❑32, Jul 2001 .... 2.50
- ❑33, Aug 2001 .... 2.50
- ❑34, Sep 2001 .... 2.50
- ❑35, Oct 2001 .... 2.50
- ❑36, Nov 2001 .... 2.50
- ❑1000000, Nov 1998, b&w 3.00
- ❑Annual 1, ca. 1998; Ghosts 2.95
- ❑Annual 2, Oct 1999; JLApe 2.95

MARTIAN MANHUNTER: AMERICAN SECRETS
DC
- ❑1, ca. 1992; prestige format 4.95
- ❑2, ca. 1992; prestige format 4.95
- ❑3, ca. 1992; prestige format 4.95

MARTIAN MANHUNTER SPECIAL
DC
- ❑1, ca. 1996 .... 3.50

MARTIN MYSTERY
DARK HORSE
- ❑1, Mar 1999 .... 4.95
- ❑2, Apr 1999 .... 4.95
- ❑3, May 1999 .... 4.95
- ❑4, Jun 1999 .... 4.95
- ❑5, Jul 1999 .... 4.95
- ❑6, Aug 1999 .... 4.95

MARTIN THE SATANIC RACOON
GABE MARTINEZ
- ❑1 .... 1.00
- ❑2 .... 2.00

MARVEL ACTION HOUR, FEATURING IRON MAN
MARVEL
- ❑1, Nov 1994 .... 1.50
- ❑1/CS, Nov 1994; Collector's set: includes animation cel 2.95
- ❑2, Dec 1994 .... 1.50
- ❑3, Jan 1995 .... 1.50
- ❑4, Feb 1995 .... 1.50
- ❑5, Mar 1995 .... 1.50
- ❑6, Apr 1995 .... 1.50
- ❑7, May 1995 .... 1.50
- ❑8, Jun 1995 .... 1.50

MARVEL ACTION HOUR, FEATURING THE FANTASTIC FOUR
MARVEL
- ❑1, Nov 1994 .... 1.50
- ❑1/CS, Nov 1994; Collector's set: includes animation cel 2.95
- ❑2, Dec 1994 .... 1.50
- ❑3, Jan 1995 .... 1.50
- ❑4, Feb 1995 .... 1.50
- ❑5, Mar 1995 .... 1.50
- ❑6, Apr 1995 .... 1.50
- ❑7, May 1995 .... 1.50
- ❑8, Jun 1995 .... 1.50

MARVEL ACTION UNIVERSE
MARVEL
- ❑1, Jan 1989; Reprints Spider-Man and His Amazing Friends #1 .... 1.00

MARVEL ADVENTURE
MARVEL
- ❑1, Dec 1975; SL (w); GC (a);Reprints Daredevil #22 .... 3.50
- ❑2, Feb 1976; Reprints Daredevil #23 2.50
- ❑3, Apr 1976; Reprints Daredevil #24 2.50
- ❑3/30 cent, Apr 1976; 30 cent regional price variant; reprints Daredevil #24 20.00
- ❑4, Jun 1976; Reprints Daredevil #25 2.50
- ❑4/30 cent, Jun 1976; 30 cent regional price variant; reprints Daredevil #25 20.00
- ❑5, Aug 1976; Reprints Daredevil #26 2.50
- ❑5/30 cent, Aug 1976; 30 cent regional price variant; reprints Daredevil #26 20.00
- ❑6, Oct 1976; Reprints Daredevil #27 2.50

MARVEL ADVENTURES
MARVEL
- ❑1, Apr 1997 A: Hulk. V: Leader. V: Abomination. 2.00
- ❑2, May 1997 A: Spider-Man. V: Scorpion. 1.50
- ❑3, Jun 1997 A: X-Men. V: Magneto. . 1.50
- ❑4, Jul 1997 A: Hulk. V: Brotherhood of Evil Mutants. 1.50
- ❑5, Aug 1997 A: X-Men. A: Spider-Man. V: Abomination. V: Magneto. 1.50
- ❑6, Sep 1997 A: Torch. A: Spider-Man. V: Lava Men. 1.50
- ❑7, Oct 1997 A: Hulk. V: Tyrannus. 1.50
- ❑8, Nov 1997 A: X-Men. 1.50
- ❑9, Dec 1997 A: Fantastic Four. 1.50
- ❑10, Jan 1998 A: Silver Surfer. V: Gladiator. 1.50
- ❑11, Feb 1998 A: Spider-Man. V: Sandman. 1.50
- ❑12, Mar 1998 .... 1.50
- ❑13, Apr 1998 .... 1.50
- ❑14, May 1998 A: Hulk. A: Doctor Strange. A: Juggernaut. 1.50
- ❑15, Jun 1998 A: Wolverine. 1.50
- ❑16, Jul 1998 A: Silver Surfer. V: Skrulls. 1.50
- ❑17, Aug 1998 A: Iron Man. A: Spider-Man. V: Grey Gargoyle. 1.50
- ❑18, Sep 1998 .... 1.50

MARVEL AGE
MARVEL
- ❑1, Apr 1983 .... 2.00
- ❑2, May 1983 .... 1.00
- ❑3, Jun 1983; Micronauts 1.00
- ❑4, Jul 1983; Return of the Jedi; Rock & Rule graphic novel 1.00
- ❑5, Aug 1983; Daredevil; The Hobgoblin 1.00
- ❑6, Sep 1983; Cloak & Dagger 1.00
- ❑7, Oct 1983; X-Men and Micronauts Ltd. Series 1.00
- ❑8, Nov 1983; Stan Lee, Jim Shooter interviews 1.00
- ❑9, Dec 1983; Super Boxers 1.00
- ❑10, Jan 1984; Star Wars cover 1.00
- ❑11, Feb 1984; Kitty Pryde & Wolverine 1.00
- ❑12, Mar 1984; Secret Wars 1.00
- ❑13, Apr 1984; Dreadstar; Feature on coloring comics 1.00
- ❑14, May 1984; FH (w); FH (a);John Byrne; Power Pack; Six From Sirius; Fred Hembeck strips begin 1.00
- ❑15, Jun 1984; FH (w); FH (a);Archie Goodwin on Epic Comics 1.00
- ❑16, Jul 1984 FH (w); FH (a) 1.00
- ❑17, Aug 1984; FH (w); FH (a);Muppets 1.00
- ❑18, Sep 1984; FH (w); FH (a);Questprobe 1.00
- ❑19, Oct 1984; FH (w); FH (a);Star Comics 1.00
- ❑20, Nov 1984; FH (w); FH (a);Letters to Marvel Super-Hero Secret Wars 1.00
- ❑21, Dec 1984; FH (w); FH (a);Void Indigo 1.00
- ❑22, Jan 1985; FH (w); FH (a);Sol Brodsky Remembered 1.00
- ❑23, Feb 1985; FH (w); FH (a);ROM .. 1.00
- ❑24, Mar 1985 FH (w); FH (a) 1.00
- ❑25, Apr 1985; FH (w); FH (a);Rocket Raccoon; Cloak & Dagger; Gargoyle 1.00
- ❑26, May 1985; FH (w); FH (a);Starstruck 1.00
- ❑27, Jun 1985; FH (w); FH (a);Secret Wars II 1.00
- ❑28, Jul 1985 FH (w); FH (a) 1.00

N-MINT

❑29, Aug 1985; FH (w); FH (a);Vision & Scarlet Witch; West Coast Avengers (Ltd. Series) 1.00
❑30, Sep 1985 FH (w); FH (a) 1.00
❑31, Oct 1985 FH (w); FH (a) 1.00
❑32, Nov 1985 FH (w); FH (a) 1.00
❑33, Dec 1985; FH (w); FH (a);X-Factor 1.00
❑34, Jan 1986; FH (w); FH (a);G.I. Joes 1.00
❑35, Feb 1986; FH (w); FH (a);A Day in the Life of Marvel Comics 1.00
❑36, Mar 1986 FH (w); FH (a) 1.00
❑37, Apr 1986 FH (w); FH (a) 1.00
❑38, May 1986; FH (w); FH (a);He-Man 1.00
❑39, Jun 1986 FH (w); FH (a) 1.00
❑40, Jul 1986 FH (w); FH (a) 1.00
❑41, Aug 1986 FH (w); FH (a) 1.00
❑42, Sep 1986 FH (w); FH (a) 1.00
❑43, Oct 1986 FH (w); FH (a) 1.00
❑44, Nov 1986 FH (w); FH (a) 1.00
❑45, Dec 1986 FH (w); FH (a) 1.00
❑46, Jan 1987 FH (w); FH (a) 1.00
❑47, Feb 1987 FH (w); FH (a) 1.00
❑48, Mar 1987 FH (w); FH (a) 1.00
❑49, Apr 1987 FH (w); FH (a) 1.00
❑50, May 1987 FH (w); FH (a) 1.00
❑51, Jun 1987 FH (w); FH (a) 1.00
❑52, Jul 1987 FH (w); FH (a) 1.00
❑53, Aug 1987 FH (w); FH (a) 1.00
❑54, Sep 1987; FH (w); FH (a);Spider-Man wedding 1.00
❑55, Oct 1987 FH (w); FH (a) 1.00
❑56, Nov 1987 FH (w); FH (a) 1.00
❑57, Dec 1987 FH (w); FH (a) 1.00
❑58, Jan 1988 FH (w); FH (a) 1.00
❑59, Feb 1988 FH (w); FH (a) 1.00
❑60, Mar 1988 FH (w); FH (a) 1.00
❑61, Apr 1988 FH (w); FH (a) 1.00
❑62, May 1988 FH (w); FH (a) 1.00
❑63, Jun 1988 FH (w); FH (a) 1.00
❑64, Jul 1988 FH (w); FH (a) 1.00
❑65, Aug 1988 FH (w); FH (a) 1.00
❑66, Sep 1988 FH (w); FH (a) 1.00
❑67, Oct 1988 FH (w); FH (a) 1.00
❑68, Nov 1988 FH (w); FH (a) 1.00
❑69, Dec 1988 FH (w); FH (a) 1.00
❑70, Jan 1989 FH (w); FH (a) 1.00
❑71, Feb 1989 FH (w); FH (a) 1.00
❑72, Mar 1989 FH (w); FH (a) 1.00
❑73, Apr 1989 FH (w); FH (a) 1.00
❑74, May 1989 FH (w); FH (a) 1.00
❑75, Jun 1989 FH (w); FH (a) 1.00
❑76, Jul 1989; FH (w); FH (a);Atlantis Attacks 1.00
❑77, Aug 1989 FH (w); FH (a) 1.00
❑78, Sep 1989 FH (w); FH (a) 1.00
❑79, Oct 1989 FH (w); FH (a) 1.00
❑80, Nov 1989 FH (w); FH (a) 1.00
❑81, Nov 1989 FH (w); FH (a) 1.00
❑82, Dec 1989; FH (w); FH (a);Squadron Supreme 1.00
❑83, Dec 1989 FH (w); FH (a) 1.00
❑84, Jan 1990 FH (w); FH (a) 1.00
❑85, Feb 1990 FH (w); FH (a) 1.00
❑86, Mar 1990 FH (w); FH (a) 1.00
❑87, Apr 1990 FH (w); FH (a) 1.00
❑88, May 1990; FH (w); FH (a);Guardians of the Galaxy 1.00
❑89, Jun 1990 FH (w); FH (a) 1.00
❑90, Jul 1990 FH (w); FH (a) 1.00
❑91, Aug 1990 FH (w); FH (a) 1.00
❑92, Sep 1990 FH (w); FH (a) 1.00
❑93, Oct 1990 FH (w); FH (a) 1.00
❑94, Nov 1990 FH (w); FH (a) 1.00
❑95, Dec 1990; FH (w); FH (a);Captain America issue 1.00
❑96, Jan 1991 FH (w); FH (a) 1.00
❑97, Feb 1991 FH (w); FH (a) 1.00
❑98, Mar 1991 FH (w); FH (a) 1.00
❑99, Apr 1991 FH (w); FH (a) 1.00
❑100, May 1991; 100th anniversary issue FH (w); FH (a) 1.00
❑101, Jun 1991 FH (w); FH (a) 1.00
❑102, Jul 1991 FH (w); FH (a) 1.00

N-MINT

❑103, Aug 1991 FH (w); FH (a) 1.00
❑104, Sep 1991 FH (w); FH (a) 1.00
❑105, Oct 1991 FH (w); FH (a) 1.00
❑106, Nov 1991; Daredevil 300th anniversary FH (w); FH (a) 1.00
❑107, Dec 1991 FH (w); FH (a) 1.00
❑108, Jan 1992 FH (w); FH (a) 1.00
❑109, Feb 1992 FH (w); FH (a) 1.00
❑110, Mar 1992 FH (w); FH (a) 1.00
❑111, Apr 1992 FH (w); FH (a) 1.00
❑112, May 1992; Captain America 400th Anniversary FH (w); FH (a) .. 1.00
❑113, Jun 1992 FH (w); FH (a) 1.00
❑114, Jul 1992; Spider-Man's 30th anniversary FH (w); FH (a) 1.00
❑115, Aug 1992 FH (w); FH (a) 1.00
❑116, Sep 1992; FH (w); FH (a);X-Men 1.00
❑117, Oct 1992; FH (w); FH (a);2099 1.00
❑118, Nov 1992; FH (w); FH (a);with card 1.00
❑119, Dec 1992 FH (w); FH (a) 1.00
❑120, Jan 1993; Tenth anniversary special FH (w); FH (a) 1.00
❑121, Feb 1993; FH (w); FH (a);Ren & Stimpy 1.00
❑122, Mar 1993; X-Men 30th anniversary special FH (w); FH (a) 1.00
❑123, Apr 1993 FH (w); FH (a) 1.00
❑124, May 1993 FH (w); FH (a) 1.00
❑125, Jun 1993 FH (w); FH (a) 1.00
❑126, Jul 1993 FH (w); FH (a) 1.00
❑127, Aug 1993 FH (w); FH (a) 1.00
❑128, Sep 1993 FH (w); FH (a) 1.00
❑129, Oct 1993; Flip-book; GP (c); FH (w); FH, GP (a);1/2 X-Men/Avengers crossover poster; Biker Mice from Mars preview; Hellraiser/Marshal Law preview; Heavy Hitters Preview 1.25
❑130, Nov 1993; FH (w); FH (a);Marvels; poster 1.25
❑131, Dec 1993; FH (w); FH (a);Excalibur 1.25
❑132, Jan 1994; FH (w); FH (a);Force Works, ClanDestine 1.25
❑133, Feb 1994; FH (w); FH (a);X-Wedding, War Machine 1.25
❑134, Mar 1994; FH (w); FH (a);Beavis & Butt-Head 1.50
❑135, Apr 1994; FH (w); FH (a);Ghost Rider 2099; Conan the Adventurer 1.25
❑136, May 1994 FH (w); FH (a) 1.25
❑137, Jun 1994 FH (w); FH (a) 1.50
❑138, Jul 1994; Giant-size; FH (w); FH (a);remembering Jack Kirby; Spider-Man Animated Series, Blaze 1.50
❑139, Aug 1994; FH (w); FH (a);Batman and the Punisher 1.25
❑140, Sep 1994; FH (w); FH (a);Marvel Action Hour 1.25
❑Annual 1, Sep 1985 .... 1.00
❑Annual 2, Sep 1986 .... 1.00
❑Annual 3, Sep 1987 FH, JB, TD, MR (a) 1.00
❑Annual 4, Sep 1988; Wolverine 1.00

MARVEL AGE: FANTASTIC FOUR
MARVEL

❑1, Jun 2004 .... 2.99
❑2, Jul 2004 .... 2.25
❑3, Aug 2004 .... 2.25
❑4, Sep 2004 ....

MARVEL AGE PREVIEW
MARVEL

❑1, Apr 1990 .... 1.50
❑2 .... 2.25

MARVEL AGE: SPIDER-MAN
MARVEL

❑1, May 2004 .... 2.99
❑2, Jun 2004 .... 2.99
❑3, Jul 2004 .... 2.99
❑4, Jul 2004 .... 2.99
❑5, Aug 2004 .... 2.25
❑6, Aug 2004 .... 2.25
❑7, Sep 2004 .... 2.25
❑8, Sep 2004 .... 2.25

Like Daredevil, Moon Knight had his run-ins with The Punisher.

N-MINT

MARVEL AND DC PRESENT
MARVEL

❑1, Nov 1982; TD (a);X-Men & Titans; Early Marvel/DC crossover 12.00

MARVEL BOY (2ND SERIES)
MARVEL

❑1/A, Aug 2000; Dynamic Forces cover 5.00
❑1, Aug 2000 .... 2.99
❑2, Sep 2000 .... 2.99
❑3, Oct 2000 .... 2.99
❑4, Nov 2000 .... 2.99
❑5, Dec 2000 .... 2.99
❑6, Mar 2001 .... 2.99

MARVEL CHILLERS
MARVEL

❑1, Nov 1975 1: The Other (Chthon). 1: Modred the Mystic. 5.00
❑2, Jan 1976; A: Tigra. Modred 3.00
❑3, Mar 1976; O: Tigra. 1: The Darkhold. Tigra 5.00
❑4, May 1976 A: Tigra. A: Kraven. 2.50
❑4/30 cent, May 1976; 30 cent regional price variant 20.00
❑5, Jun 1976 A: Tigra. 2.50
❑5/30 cent, Jun 1976; 30 cent regional price variant 20.00
❑6, Aug 1976 JBy (a); A: Tigra. 2.50
❑6/30 cent, Aug 1976; 30 cent regional price variant 20.00
❑7, Oct 1976 A: Tigra. 2.50

MARVEL CHILLERS: SHADES OF GREEN MONSTERS
MARVEL

❑1, Mar 1997; mostly text story 2.99

MARVEL CHILLERS: THE THING IN THE GLASS CASE
MARVEL

❑1, Mar 1997; mostly text story 2.99

MARVEL CLASSICS COMICS
MARVEL

❑1, Jan 1976 NR (a) 7.00
❑2, Feb 1976 .... 5.00
❑3, Mar 1976 .... 5.00
❑4, Apr 1976 .... 5.00
❑5, May 1976 .... 5.00
❑6, Jun 1976 .... 4.00
❑7, Jul 1976 .... 4.00
❑8, Aug 1976 .... 4.00
❑9, Sep 1976 .... 4.00
❑10, Oct 1976 .... 4.00
❑11, Nov 1976 .... 4.00
❑12, Dec 1976 .... 4.00
❑13, Jan 1977 .... 4.00
❑14, Feb 1977 .... 4.00
❑15, Mar 1977 .... 4.00
❑16, Apr 1977 .... 4.00
❑17, May 1977 .... 4.00
❑18, Jun 1977 .... 4.00
❑19, Jul 1977 .... 4.00
❑20, Aug 1977 .... 4.00
❑21, Sep 1977 .... 4.00
❑22, Oct 1977 .... 4.00
❑23, Nov 1977 .... 4.00
❑24, Dec 1977 .... 4.00
❑25, Jan 1978 .... 4.00
❑26, Feb 1978 .... 4.00
❑27, Mar 1978 .... 4.00

N-MINT

❑28, Apr 1978; MG (a);Mike Golden's first professional art 8.00
❑29, May 1978 ..... 4.00
❑30, Jun 1978 ..... 4.00
❑31, Jul 1978 ..... 4.00
❑32, Aug 1978 ..... 4.00
❑33, Sep 1978 ..... 4.00
❑34, Oct 1978 AA (a) 4.00
❑35, Nov 1978 ..... 4.00
❑36, Dec 1978 BH (c) 4.00

MARVEL COLLECTIBLE CLASSICS: AMAZING SPIDER-MAN
MARVEL

❑300; TMc (a); 1: Venom. Chromium wraparound cover; Reprints Amazing Spider-Man #300 ..... 13.50
❑300/Autographed; TMc (a); 1: Venom. Chromium wraparound cover; Reprints Amazing Spider-Man #300 29.99

MARVEL COLLECTIBLE CLASSICS: AVENGERS (VOL. 3)
MARVEL

❑1, Nov 1998; Chromium wraparound cover 13.50

MARVEL COLLECTIBLE CLASSICS: X-MEN
MARVEL

❑1, Aug 1998; Chromium wraparound cover; Reprints X-Men #1 ..... 13.50
❑Giant Size 1, Nov 1998; Reprints Giant Size X-Men #1; Chromium wraparound cover 13.50

MARVEL COLLECTIBLE CLASSICS: X-MEN (VOL. 2)
MARVEL

❑1, Oct 1998; JLee (a);Chromium wraparound cover 13.50
❑1/Autographed, Oct 1998; JLee (a);Chromium wraparound cover .. 29.99

MARVEL COLLECTOR'S EDITION
MARVEL

❑1 1992; RHo (w); Spider-Man, Wolverine, Ghost Rider; Charleston Chew promotion, $.50 and a candy bar wrapper; Flip-book format 2.50

MARVEL COLLECTORS' ITEM CLASSICS
MARVEL

❑1, Feb 1966 ..... 48.00
❑2, Apr 1966 ..... 30.00
❑3, Jun 1966; reprints Fantastic Four (Vol. 1) #4, Tales of Suspense #40, Incredible Hulk #3, Tales of Suspense #49, Strange Tales #110 ..... 26.00
❑4, Aug 1966 ..... 26.00
❑5, Oct 1966 ..... 15.00
❑6, Dec 1966 ..... 15.00
❑7, Feb 1967 ..... 15.00
❑8, Apr 1967 ..... 15.00
❑9, Jun 1967 ..... 15.00
❑10, Aug 1967 ..... 15.00
❑11, Oct 1967 ..... 12.00
❑12, Dec 1967 ..... 12.00
❑13, Feb 1968 ..... 12.00
❑14, Apr 1968 ..... 12.00
❑15, Jun 1968 ..... 12.00
❑16, Aug 1968 ..... 12.00
❑17, Oct 1968 ..... 12.00
❑18, Dec 1968 ..... 12.00
❑19, Feb 1969 SL (w); DH, JK (a) 12.00
❑20, Apr 1969 ..... 12.00
❑21, Jun 1969 ..... 10.00
❑22, Aug 1969; Series continued in Marvel's Greatest Comics #23 ..... 10.00

MARVEL COMICS PRESENTS
MARVEL

❑1, Sep 1988; AM (w); AM, TS, JB, DC, KJ (a);Wolverine features begin 4.00
❑2, Sep 1988; KJ (c); AM (w); AM, TS, JB, DC, KJ (a);Wolverine 2.50
❑3, Sep 1988; JR2, BWi (c); AM (w); AM, TS, JB, DC, KJ (a);Wolverine .. 2.50

N-MINT

❑4, Oct 1988; AM, CR (c); AM (w); AM, TS, JB, DC, KJ (a);Wolverine 2.50
❑5, Oct 1988; TS, JB, DC, MGu, KJ (a);Wolverine 2.50
❑6, Nov 1988; TS, JB (a); A: Sub-Mariner. Wolverine 2.00
❑7, Nov 1988; BL (c); SD (w); TS, SD, JB, DC, KJ (a);Wolverine 2.00
❑8, Dec 1988; TS, JB (a);Wolverine .. 2.00
❑9, Dec 1988; TS, JB, KJ (a);Wolverine 2.00
❑10, Jan 1989; SD (w); TS, SD, JB, CR, KJ (a);Wolverine; Colossus features begin 2.00
❑11, Jan 1989; TS, BL (a);Colossus .. 1.50
❑12, Feb 1989; TS, DH, FS (a);Colossus, Man-Thing 1.50
❑13, Feb 1989; GC (a);Colossus 1.50
❑14, Mar 1989; SD (w); GC (a);Colossus 1.50
❑15, Mar 1989; GC (a);Colossus 1.50
❑16, Mar 1989; GC (a);Colossus 1.50
❑17, Apr 1989; TS, GC (a);Cyclops features begin 1.50
❑18, Apr 1989; JBy (w); RHo, GC, JBy (a);She-Hulk, Cyclops 1.50
❑19, May 1989; GC (a); 1: Damage Control. Cyclops 1.50
❑20, May 1989; GC (a);Cyclops 1.50
❑21, Jun 1989; GC (a);Cyclops 1.50
❑22, Jun 1989; GC, DC (a);Cyclops ... 1.50
❑23, Jul 1989; GC, DC (a);Cyclops 1.50
❑24, Jul 1989; RB, GC (a);Cyclops, Havok 1.50
❑25, Aug 1989; RB, GC (a); O: Nth Man. 1: Nth Man. Havok 1.50
❑26, Aug 1989; RB, GC, PG (a); 1: Coldblood. Havok 1.50
❑27, Sep 1989; RB, GC, PG (a);Havok 1.50
❑28, Sep 1989; RB, GC, PG (a);Havok 1.50
❑29, Sep 1989; RB, GC, PG (a);Havok 1.50
❑30, Oct 1989; RB, GC, PG (a); A: Wolverine. Havok 1.50
❑31, Oct 1989; RB, GC, PG, EL (a); O: Coldblood. Havok, Excalibur 1.50
❑32, Nov 1989; TMc (c); GC, DH, PG, EL (a);Excalibur 1.50
❑33, Nov 1989; GC, PG, JLee, EL (a);Excalibur 1.50
❑34, Dec 1989; GC, PG, EL (a);Excalibur 1.50
❑35, Dec 1989; GC, PG, EL (a); 1: Starduster. Excalibur 1.50
❑36, Jan 1989; GC, EL (a);Excalibur .. 1.50
❑37, Jan 1989; GC, EL (a);Excalibur .. 1.50
❑38, Feb 1989; JB, EL, MR (a);Excalibur 2.00
❑39, Feb 1989; BL (w); JB, BL, EL (a);Wolverine 1.50
❑40, Mar 1989; BL (w); JB, BL, DH (a);Wolverine 1.50
❑41, Mar 1990; BL (w); JB, BL, DC (a);Wolverine 1.50
❑42, Mar 1990; JB (a);Wolverine 1.50
❑43, Apr 1990; JB (a);Wolverine 1.50
❑44, Apr 1990; JB (a);Wolverine 1.50
❑45, May 1990; JB (a);Wolverine 1.50
❑46, May 1990; JB (a);Wolverine 1.50
❑47, Apr 1990; JB (a);Wolverine; cover dates, which only appeared in the indicia or in Marvel's catalog copy, actually do go backwards for a while at this point 1.50
❑48, Apr 1990; Spider-Man, Wolverine 2.00
❑49, May 1990; 1: Whiplash II. Spider-Man, Wolverine 2.00
❑50, May 1990; O: Captain Ultra. Spider-Man, Wolverine 2.00
❑51, Jun 1990; RL (a);Wolverine 2.00
❑52, Jun 1990; RL (a);Wolverine 2.00
❑53, Jul 1990; RL (a);Wolverine 2.00
❑54, Jul 1990; Wolverine & Hulk 2.50
❑55, Jul 1990; Wolverine & Hulk 2.50
❑56, Aug 1990; SD (w); Wolverine & Hulk 2.50
❑57, Aug 1990; Wolverine & Hulk 2.50
❑58, Sep 1990; SD (w); Wolverine & Hulk 2.50

N-MINT

❑59, Sep 1990; Wolverine & Hulk 2.50
❑60, Oct 1990; RHo (w); RHo (a);Wolverine & Hulk 2.50
❑61, Oct 1990; RHo (w); RHo (a);Wolverine & Hulk 2.50
❑62, Nov 1990; RHo (w); RHo (a);Wolverine 2.50
❑63, Nov 1990; RHo (w); RHo, DH (a);Wolverine 2.00
❑64, Dec 1990; Wolverine, Ghost Rider 2.00
❑65, Dec 1990; Wolverine, Ghost Rider 2.00
❑66, Dec 1990; Wolverine, Ghost Rider 2.00
❑67, Jan 1991; Wolverine, Ghost Rider 2.00
❑68, Jan 1991; PG (a);Wolverine, Ghost Rider 2.00
❑69, Feb 1991; PG (a);Wolverine, Ghost Rider 2.00
❑70, Feb 1991; PG (a);Wolverine, Ghost Rider 2.00
❑71, Mar 1991; PG (a);Wolverine, Ghost Rider 2.00
❑72, Mar 1991; PG (a);Weapon X 4.00
❑73, Mar 1991; PG, JM (a);Weapon X 3.00
❑74, Apr 1991; PG, JSa (a);Weapon X 3.00
❑75, Apr 1991; PG (a);Weapon X 3.00
❑76, May 1991; PG (a);Weapon X 3.00
❑77, May 1991; PG (a);Weapon X 3.00
❑78, Jun 1991; Weapon X 3.00
❑79, Jun 1991; JBy (a);Weapon X 3.00
❑80, Jul 1991; SD (w); SD (a);Weapon X 3.00
❑81, Jul 1991; SD (w); SD, MR (a);Weapon X; Daredevil 3.00
❑82, Aug 1991; Weapon X 3.00
❑83, Aug 1991; SD (w); EL (a);Weapon X 3.00
❑84, Sep 1991; Weapon X 3.00
❑85, Sep 1991; PD (w); RL (a); 1: Cyber. Wolverine; 1st Kieth art on Wolverine 3.00
❑86, Oct 1991; PD (w); RL (a);Wolverine 2.50
❑87, Oct 1991; PD (w); RL (a);Wolverine 2.00
❑88, Nov 1991; PD (w); Wolverine 2.00
❑89, Nov 1991; PD (w); Wolverine 2.00
❑90, Dec 1991; PD (w); A: Ghost Rider. A: Cable. Flip-book covers begin; Wolverine 2.00
❑91, Dec 1991; PD (w); A: Ghost Rider. A: Cable. Wolverine 1.50
❑92, Dec 1991; PD (w); A: Ghost Rider. A: Cable. Wolverine 1.50
❑93, Jan 1992; A: Ghost Rider. A: Cable. Wolverine 1.50
❑94, Jan 1992; A: Ghost Rider. A: Cable. Wolverine 1.50
❑95, Feb 1992; A: Ghost Rider. A: Cable. Wolverine 1.50
❑96, Feb 1992; A: Ghost Rider. A: Cable. Wolverine 1.50
❑97, Mar 1992; A: Ghost Rider. A: Cable. Wolverine 1.50
❑98, Mar 1992; Wolverine 1.50
❑99, Apr 1992; RL (w); Wolverine 1.50
❑100, Apr 1992; Anniversary issue; A: Ghost Rider. V: Doctor Doom. Wolverine 1.50
❑101, May 1992; TS, GC (a);Wolverine, Nightcrawler 1.50
❑102, May 1992; TS, GC (a);Wolverine, Nightcrawler 1.50
❑103, May 1992; TS, GC (a);Wolverine, Nightcrawler 1.50
❑104, Jun 1992; TS, GC (a);Wolverine, Nightcrawler 1.50
❑105, Jun 1992; TS, GC (a);Wolverine, Nightcrawler 1.50
❑106, Jul 1992; TS, GC (a);Wolverine, Nightcrawler 1.50
❑107, Jul 1992; TS, GC (a);Wolverine, Nightcrawler 1.50
❑108, Aug 1992; TS, GC (a);Wolverine, Ghost Rider 1.50
❑109, Aug 1992; JSn (w); A: Typhoid Mary. Wolverine, Ghost Rider 1.50
❑110, Sep 1992; JSn (w); A: Typhoid Mary. Wolverine, Ghost Rider 1.50

N-MINT

❑111, Sep 1992; JSn (w); A: Typhoid Mary. Infinity War; Wolverine, Ghost Rider 1.50
❑112, Oct 1992; JSn (w); GC (a); A: Typhoid Mary. Wolverine, Ghost Rider 1.50
❑113, Oct 1992; A: Typhoid Mary. Wolverine, Ghost Rider 1.50
❑114, Oct 1992; A: Typhoid Mary. Wolverine, Ghost Rider 1.50
❑115, Nov 1992; A: Typhoid Mary. Wolverine, Ghost Rider 1.50
❑116, Nov 1992; GK (a); A: Typhoid Mary. Wolverine, Ghost Rider 1.50
❑117, Dec 1992; 1: Ravage 2099. A: Venom. Wolverine, Ghost Rider; Ravage 2099 preview 1.50
❑118, Dec 1992; 1: Doom 2099. A: Venom. Wolverine; Doom 2099 preview 1.50
❑119, Jan 1993; A: Venom. Wolverine 1.50
❑120, Jan 1993; A: Venom. Wolverine 1.50
❑121, Feb 1993; Wolverine 1.50
❑122, Feb 1993; Wolverine 1.50
❑123, Mar 1993; Wolverine 1.50
❑124, Mar 1993; Wolverine 1.50
❑125, Apr 1993; Wolverine 1.50
❑126, Apr 1993; Wolverine 1.50
❑127, May 1993; DP (a);Wolverine ... 1.50
❑128, May 1993; Wolverine 1.50
❑129, May 1993; Wolverine 1.50
❑130, Jun 1993; Wolverine 1.50
❑131, Jun 1993; Wolverine 1.50
❑132, Jul 1993; Wolverine 1.50
❑133, Jul 1993; Wolverine 1.50
❑134, Aug 1993; Wolverine 1.50
❑135, Aug 1993; Wolverine 1.50
❑136, Sep 1993; Wolverine 1.50
❑137, Sep 1993; Wolverine 1.50
❑138, Sep 1993 EL (w); A: Masters of Silence. A: Ghost Rider. A: Wolverine. A: Wusin. A: Spellbound. A: Nightcrawler. 1.50
❑139, Oct 1993 EL (w); A: Masters of Silence. A: Ghost Rider. A: Wolverine. A: Wusin. A: Foreigner. A: Spellbound. A: Zxaxz. 1.50
❑140, Oct 1993 EL (w); O: Captain Universe. A: Masters of Silence. A: Ghost Rider. A: Wolverine. A: Wusin. A: Captain Universe. A: Spellbound. A: Zxaxz. 1.50
❑141, Nov 1993 .... 1.50
❑142, Nov 1993 .... 1.50
❑143, Dec 1993; Ghost Rider 1.75
❑144, Dec 1993; Ghost Rider 1.75
❑145, Jan 1994; Ghost Rider 1.75
❑146, Jan 1994 .... 1.75
❑147, Feb 1994 .... 1.75
❑148, Feb 1994 .... 1.75
❑149, Mar 1994 .... 1.75
❑150, Mar 1994 .... 1.75
❑151, Apr 1994 .... 1.75
❑152, Apr 1994 .... 1.75
❑153, May 1994 .... 1.75
❑154, May 1994 .... 1.75
❑155, May 1994 .... 1.75
❑156, Jun 1994 .... 1.75
❑157, Jun 1994 .... 1.75
❑158, Jul 1994 .... 1.75
❑159, Jul 1994 .... 1.75
❑160, Aug 1994 .... 1.75
❑161, Aug 1994 .... 1.75
❑162, Sep 1994 .... 1.75
❑163, Sep 1994 .... 1.75
❑164, Oct 1994 .... 1.75
❑165, Oct 1994 .... 1.75
❑166, Oct 1994 .... 1.75
❑167, Nov 1994 .... 1.75
❑168, Nov 1994 .... 1.75
❑169, Dec 1994 .... 1.75
❑170, Dec 1994 .... 1.75
❑171, Jan 1995 .... 1.75
❑172, Jan 1995 .... 1.75
❑173, Feb 1995 .... 1.75

N-MINT

❑174, Feb 1995 KG (a) 1.75
❑175, Mar 1995 KG (a) 1.75

MARVEL COMICS: 2001
MARVEL

❑1, Jul 2001 .... 1.00

MARVEL DOUBLE FEATURE
MARVEL

❑1, Dec 1973 .... 4.00
❑2, Feb 1974 .... 3.50
❑3, Apr 1974 .... 3.50
❑4, Jun 1974 .... 2.50
❑5, Aug 1974 .... 2.50
❑6, Oct 1974 .... 2.50
❑7, Dec 1974 .... 2.50
❑8, Feb 1975 .... 2.50
❑9, Apr 1975 .... 2.50
❑10, Jun 1975 .... 2.50
❑11, Aug 1975 .... 2.50
❑12, Oct 1975 .... 2.50
❑13, Dec 1975 .... 2.50
❑14, Feb 1976 .... 2.50
❑15, Apr 1976 .... 2.50
❑15/30 cent, Apr 1976; 30 cent regional price variant 20.00
❑16, Jun 1976 .... 2.50
❑16/30 cent, Jun 1976; 30 cent regional price variant 20.00
❑17, Aug 1976; Reprints Iron Man vs. Sub-Mariner #1 .... 2.50
❑18, Oct 1976; Reprints story from Iron Man #1 .... 2.50
❑19, Dec 1976 .... 2.50
❑20, Feb 1977 .... 2.50
❑21, Apr 1977 .... 2.50

MARVEL DOUBLE SHOT
MARVEL

❑1, Jan 2003; Thor/Hulk 2.99
❑2, Feb 2003; Avengers/Doom 2.99
❑3, Mar 2003; Ant-Man/Fantastic Four 2.99
❑4, Apr 2003; Dr. Strange/Iron Man .. 2.99

MARVEL ENCYCLOPEDIA
MARVEL

❑1, ca. 2003 .... 29.99
❑2, ca. 2003 .... 29.99
❑3, ca. 2003 .... 19.99
❑4, ca. 2003 .... 24.99
❑5, ca. 2004; Marvel Knights 29.99

MARVEL FANFARE
MARVEL

❑1, Mar 1982; FM (c); MG, PS, FM, TD (a); 1: Vertigo II. Spider-Man; Daredevil; Angel 4.50
❑2, May 1982; MG (a);Spider-Man; Angel; Ka-Zar; Fantastic Four 3.25
❑3, Jul 1982; DC (a);X-Men 3.25
❑4, Sep 1982; MG, PS, TD (a);X-Men; Deathlok 2.50
❑5, Nov 1982; CR, MR (a);Doctor Strange 2.50
❑6, Jan 1983; Spider-Man; Doctor Strange; Scarlet Witch 2.00
❑7, Mar 1983; DD (a);Hulk; Daredevil 2.00
❑8, May 1983; CI (a);Doctor Strange; Mowgli 2.00
❑9, Jul 1983; Man-Thing; Mowgli 2.00
❑10, Aug 1983; GP (c); GP (a);Black Widow; Mowgli 2.00
❑11, Nov 1983; GP (a);Black Widow . 2.00
❑12, Jan 1984; GP (a);Black Widow .. 2.00
❑13, Mar 1984; GP (a);Black Widow . 2.00
❑14, May 1984; Vision; Quicksilver ... 2.00
❑15, Jul 1984; Thing 2.00
❑16, Sep 1984; DC (a);Skywolf 2.00
❑17, Nov 1984; DC (a);Skywolf 2.00
❑18, Jan 1985; FM (a);Captain America 2.00
❑19, Mar 1985; JSn (a);Cloak & Dagger 2.00
❑20, May 1985; JSn (w); JSn (a);Thing; Hulk; Doctor Strange 2.00
❑21, Jul 1985; JSn (a);Thing; Hulk ... 2.00
❑22, Sep 1985; JSn (a);Thing; Hulk; Iron Man 2.00
❑23, Nov 1985; JSn (a);Thing; Hulk; Iron Man 2.00

For a Charleston Chew wrapper, 50¢, and an interminable wait, some collectors received a copy of *Marvel Collector's Edition* in 1993.

© 1993 Marvel Comics.

N-MINT

❑24, Jan 1986; Weirdworld 2.00
❑25, Mar 1986; PB (a);Dave Sim pin-up section; Weirdworld 2.00
❑26, May 1986; PB (a);Weirdworld ... 2.00
❑27, Jul 1986; Weirdworld; Spider-Man; Daredevil 2.00
❑28, Sep 1986; Alpha Flight 2.00
❑29, Nov 1986; JBy (w); JBy (a); D: Hammer. D: Anvil. Hulk 2.00
❑30, Jan 1987; BA (a);Moon Knight; Painted cover 2.00
❑31, Mar 1987; KGa (a);Captain America 2.00
❑32, May 1987; Captain America 2.00
❑33, Jul 1987; Wolverine; X-Men 2.00
❑34, Sep 1987; Warriors Three 2.00
❑35, Nov 1987; Warriors Three 2.00
❑36, Jan 1988; Warriors Three 2.00
❑37, Mar 1988; Warriors Three 2.00
❑38, Apr 1988; Moon Knight 2.00
❑39, Aug 1988; Hawkeye; Moon Knight 2.00
❑40, Oct 1988; Angel; Storm 2.00
❑41, Dec 1988; DG (a);Doctor Strange 2.00
❑42, Feb 1989; BH (a);Spider-Man 2.00
❑43, Apr 1989; Sub-Mariner; Human Torch 2.00
❑44, Jun 1989; Iron Man; Iron Man vs. Doctor Doom 2.00
❑45, Aug 1989; JBy (c);all pin-ups 2.00
❑46, Oct 1989; Fantastic Four 2.00
❑47, Nov 1989; Spider-Man; Hulk 2.00
❑48, Dec 1989; She-Hulk 2.00
❑49, Feb 1990; Doctor Strange 2.00
❑50, Apr 1990; JSa (a);X-Factor 2.25
❑51, Jun 1990; Silver Surfer 2.95
❑52, Aug 1990; Black Knight; Fantastic Four 2.25
❑53, Oct 1990; Black Knight; Doctor Strange 2.25
❑54, Dec 1990; Black Knight; Wolverine 2.25
❑55, Feb 1991; Power Pack; Wolverine 2.25
❑56, Apr 1991; CI, DH (a);Shanna the She-Devil 2.25
❑57, Jun 1991; Captain Marvel; Shanna the She-Devil 2.25
❑58, Aug 1991; Shanna the She-Devil; Vision II (android); Scarlet Witch ... 2.25
❑59, Oct 1991; RHo, TD (a);Shanna the She-Devil 2.25
❑60, Jan 1992; PS (a);Black Panther; Rogue; Daredevil 2.25

MARVEL FANFARE (2ND SERIES)
MARVEL

❑1, Sep 1996; A: Captain America. A: Deathlok. A: Falcon. Flipbook with Professor Xavier and the X-Men #11 1.50
❑2, Oct 1996 A: Wendigo. A: Hulk. A: Wolverine. 1.00
❑3, Nov 1996 A: Ghost Rider. A: Spider-Man. 1.00
❑4, Dec 1996 A: Longshot. 1.00
❑5, Jan 1997 A: Dazzler. A: Longshot. V: Spiral. 1.00
❑6, Feb 1997 A: Sabretooth. A: Power Man. A: Iron Fist. V: Sabretooth. 1.00

N-MINT

MARVEL FEATURE (1ST SERIES)
MARVEL

❑1, Dec 1971 NA (c); RA (a); O: Defenders. 1: Omegatron. 1: Defenders. D: Yandroth (physical body). 85.00
❑2, Mar 1972; BEv (a); 2: Defenders. Sub-Mariner reprint 40.00
❑3, Jun 1972; BEv (a); A: Defenders. 35.00
❑4, Jul 1972 A: Peter Parker. A: Ant-Man. 12.00
❑5, Sep 1972 A: Ant-Man. 6.00
❑6, Nov 1972 A: Ant-Man. 6.00
❑7, Jan 1973 GK (a); A: Ant-Man. 6.00
❑8, Mar 1973 O: Wasp. A: Ant-Man. . 6.00
❑9, May 1973 CR (a); A: Iron Man. A: Ant-Man. 6.00
❑10, Jul 1973 CR (a); A: Ant-Man. 6.00
❑11, Sep 1973; Thing vs. Hulk 11.00
❑12, Nov 1973 A: Thing. A: Iron Man. A: Thanos. 9.00

MARVEL FEATURE (2ND SERIES)
MARVEL

❑1, Nov 1975; DG, NA (a);Red Sonja stories begin; Reprints Savage Sword of Conan #1 ..... 5.00
❑2, Jan 1976 FT (a) 3.00
❑3, Mar 1976 ..... 3.00
❑4, May 1976 FT (a) 3.00
❑4/30 cent, May 1976; 30 cent regional price variant 20.00
❑5, Jul 1976 FT (a) 3.00
❑5/30 cent, Jul 1976; 30 cent regional price variant 20.00
❑6, Sep 1976 A: Conan. 3.00
❑7, Nov 1976; Red Sonja vs. Conan .. 3.00

MARVEL FRONTIER COMICS UNLIMITED
MARVEL

❑1, Jan 1994 ..... 2.95

MARVEL FUMETTI BOOK, THE
MARVEL

❑1, Apr 1984, b&w; photos with balloon captions 2.00

MARVEL GRAPHIC NOVEL
MARVEL

❑1, ca. 1982; JSn (w); JSn (a); D: Captain Marvel. Death of Captain Marvel 13.00
❑1-2; JSn (w); JSn (a); D: Captain Marvel. Death of Captain Marvel 6.00
❑1-3; JSn (w); JSn (a); D: Captain Marvel. Death of Captain Marvel 6.00
❑2; CR (a);Elric 7.00
❑3; JSn (w); JSn (a);Dreadstar 7.50
❑4; BMc (a); O: Sunspot. O: New Mutants. 1: Mirage II (Danielle "Dani" Moonstar). 1: New Mutants. New Mutants 12.00
❑4-2; BMc (a); O: Mirage II (Danielle "Dani" Moonstar). O: Sunspot. O: New Mutants. 1: Mirage II (Danielle "Dani" Moonstar). 1: Sunspot. 1: New Mutants. New Mutants 6.00
❑4-3; BMc (a); O: Mirage II (Danielle "Dani" Moonstar). O: Sunspot. O: New Mutants. 1: Mirage II (Danielle "Dani" Moonstar). 1: Sunspot. 1: New Mutants. New Mutants 5.00
❑5; BA (a);X-Men: God Loves, Man Kills 20.00
❑5-2; BA (a);X-Men: God Loves, Man Kills 7.00
❑5-3; BA (a);X-Men: God Loves, Man Kills 6.00
❑5-4; BA (a);X-Men: God Loves, Man Kills 6.00
❑5-5; BA (a);X-Men: God Loves, Man Kills 6.00
❑6; Star Slammers 6.00
❑7; CR (a);Killraven 6.00
❑8; JBy (a);Super Boxers 6.00
❑9; DC (w); DC (a);The Futurians 6.00
❑10; Heartburst 6.00
❑11; VM (a);Void Indigo 6.00
❑12; FS (a);Dazzler: The Movie 6.00
❑13; Starstruck 6.00
❑14; Swords of the Swashbucklers ... 6.00
❑15; CV (a);Raven Banner 6.00
❑16; Aladdin Effect 6.00
❑17; Living Monolith 6.00
❑18; JBy (w); She-Hulk 7.00
❑19; Conan the Barbarian 7.00
❑20; Greenberg the Vampire 7.00
❑21; Marada the She-Wolf 7.00
❑22; BWr (a);Amazing Spider-Man 9.00
❑23; DGr (a);Dr. Strange 7.00
❑24; Daredevil 7.50
❑25; Dracula 7.00
❑26; Alien Legion 7.00
❑27; D: The Purple Man. Avengers 6.95
❑28; Conan the Reaver 6.95
❑29; Thing vs. Hulk 8.00
❑30, A Sailor's Story 5.95
❑31; O: Wolfpack. 1: Wolfpack. Wolfpack 6.95
❑32 D: Groo. 10.00
❑33; Thor 6.95
❑34; Cloak & Dagger 6.95
❑35; Hardcover; Shadow 1941 ..... 12.95
❑36; Willow 6.95
❑37; Hercules 7.00
❑38; Silver Surfer 16.00

MARVEL GRAPHIC NOVEL: ARENA
MARVEL

❑1 ..... 5.95

MARVEL GRAPHIC NOVEL: CLOAK AND DAGGER AND POWER PACK: SHELTER FROM THE STORM
MARVEL

❑1 ..... 7.95

MARVEL GRAPHIC NOVEL: EMPEROR DOOM: STARRING THE MIGHTY AVENGERS
MARVEL

❑1 ..... 5.95

MARVEL GRAPHIC NOVEL: KA-ZAR: GUNS OF THE SAVAGE LAND
MARVEL

❑1 ..... 8.95

MARVEL GRAPHIC NOVEL: RICK MASON, THE AGENT
MARVEL

❑1 1989 ..... 9.95

MARVEL GRAPHIC NOVEL: ROGER RABBIT IN THE RESURRECTION OF DOOM
MARVEL

❑1 ..... 8.95

MARVEL GRAPHIC NOVEL: WHO FRAMED ROGER RABBIT?
MARVEL

❑1 ..... 6.95

MARVEL GUIDE TO COLLECTING COMICS, THE
MARVEL

❑1, Sep 1982; no cover price 3.00

MARVEL HALLOWEEN: SUPERNATURALS TOUR BOOK
MARVEL

❑1, Nov 1998 ..... 2.99

MARVEL: HEROES & LEGENDS
MARVEL

❑1, Oct 1996; backstory on Reed and Sue's wedding; wraparound cover . 2.95
❑2, Nov 1997; untold Avengers story; Hawkeye, Quicksilver, Scarlet Witch joins team 2.99

MARVEL HOLIDAY SPECIAL
MARVEL

❑1; SB, DC, KJ (a);no cover date or date in indicia 3.00
❑1992, Jan 1993; for 1992 holiday season 3.00
❑1993, Jan 1994; AM, MG (a);for 1993 holiday season 3.00
❑1994, Jan 1995; KB (w); GM, SB (a);for 1994 holiday season 3.00
❑1996, Jan 1997 ..... 2.95

MARVEL ILLUSTRATED: SWIMSUIT ISSUE
MARVEL

❑1, Mar 1991 ..... 3.95

MARVEL KNIGHTS
MARVEL

❑1, Jul 2000 ..... 3.50
❑1/A, Jul 2000; Daredevil close-up cover 5.00
❑2, Aug 2000 A: Ulik. 2.99
❑3, Sep 2000 A: Ulik. 2.99
❑4, Oct 2000 ..... 2.99
❑5, Nov 2000 ..... 2.99
❑6, Dec 2000 ..... 2.99
❑7, Jan 2001 ..... 2.99
❑8, Feb 2001 ..... 2.99
❑9, Mar 2001 ..... 2.99
❑10, Apr 2001 ..... 2.99
❑11, May 2001 ..... 2.99
❑12, Jun 2001 ..... 2.99
❑13, Jul 2001 ..... 2.99
❑14, Aug 2001 ..... 2.99
❑15, Sep 2001 ..... 2.99

MARVEL KNIGHTS (VOL. 2)
MARVEL

❑1, May 2002 ..... 2.99
❑2, Jun 2002 ..... 2.99
❑3, Jul 2002 ..... 2.99
❑4, Aug 2002 ..... 2.99
❑5, Sep 2002 ..... 2.99
❑6, Oct 2002 ..... 2.99

MARVEL KNIGHTS 4
MARVEL

❑1, Apr 2004 ..... 2.99
❑2, May 2004 ..... 2.99
❑3, May 2004 ..... 2.99
❑4, Jun 2004 ..... 2.99
❑5, Jun 2004 ..... 2.99
❑6, Aug 2004 ..... 2.99
❑7, Sep 2004 .....
❑8, Sep 2004 .....

MARVEL KNIGHTS DOUBLE-SHOT
MARVEL

❑1, Jun 2002 ..... 2.99

MARVEL KNIGHTS MAGAZINE
MARVEL

❑1 ..... 3.99
❑2 ..... 3.99
❑3, Jul 2001 ..... 3.99
❑4 ..... 3.99
❑5 ..... 3.99
❑6 ..... 3.99

MARVEL KNIGHTS/MARVEL BOY GENESIS EDITION
MARVEL

❑1, Jun 2000; Polybagged with Punisher (5th Series) #3 ..... 1.00

MARVEL KNIGHTS: MILLENNIAL VISIONS
MARVEL

❑1, Feb 2002 ..... 3.99

MARVEL KNIGHTS SKETCHBOOK
MARVEL

❑1; BWr (a);Bundled with Wizard #84 1.00

MARVEL KNIGHTS SPIDER-MAN
MARVEL

❑1, Jun 2004 ..... 4.00
❑2, Jul 2004 ..... 2.99
❑3, Aug 2004 ..... 2.99
❑4, Sep 2004 .....

MARVEL KNIGHTS TOUR BOOK
MARVEL

❑1, Oct 1998; previews and interviews 2.99

N-MINT

MARVEL KNIGHTS WAVE 2 SKETCHBOOK
MARVEL
❑1; Special free edition from Marvel in Wizard #90; DGry (w); Sketchbook 1.00

MARVEL MANGAVERSE
MARVEL
❑1, Jun 2002 2.25
❑2, Jul 2002 2.25
❑3, Aug 2002 2.25
❑4, Sep 2002 2.25
❑5, Oct 2002 2.25
❑6, Nov 2002 2.25

MARVEL MANGAVERSE: AVENGERS ASSEMBLE!
MARVEL
❑1, Mar 2002 2.25

MARVEL MANGAVERSE: ETERNITY TWILIGHT
MARVEL
❑1, Mar 2002 2.25
❑1/A 3.50

MARVEL MANGAVERSE: FANTASTIC FOUR
MARVEL
❑1, Mar 2002 2.25

MARVEL MANGAVERSE: GHOST RIDERS
MARVEL
❑1, Mar 2002 2.25

MARVEL MANGAVERSE: NEW DAWN
MARVEL
❑1, Mar 2002 3.50

MARVEL MANGAVERSE: PUNISHER
MARVEL
❑1, Mar 2002 2.25

MARVEL MANGAVERSE: SPIDER-MAN
MARVEL
❑1, Mar 2002 2.25

MARVEL MANGAVERSE: X-MEN
MARVEL
❑1, Mar 2002 2.25

MARVEL MASTERPIECES COLLECTION
MARVEL
❑1, May 1993 2.95
❑2, Jun 1993 2.95
❑3, Jul 1993 2.95
❑4, Aug 1993 2.95

MARVEL MASTERPIECES 2 COLLECTION, THE
MARVEL
❑1, Jul 1994; Pin-ups 2.95
❑2, Aug 1994 2.95
❑3, Sep 1994 2.95

MARVEL MILESTONE EDITION: AMAZING FANTASY
MARVEL
❑15, Mar 1992; Reprints of Amazing Fantasy # 15: Spider-man's Origin 2.95

MARVEL MILESTONE EDITION: AMAZING SPIDER-MAN
MARVEL
❑1, Jan 1993; Reprints Amazing Spider-Man #1 2.95
❑3, Mar 1995; Reprints Amazing Spider-Man #3 2.95
❑129; Reprints Amazing Spider-Man #129 2.95
❑149, Nov 1994; indicia says Marvel Milestone Edition: Amazing Spider-Man #1; Reprints Amazing Spider-Man #149 2.95

N-MINT

MARVEL MILESTONE EDITION: AVENGERS
MARVEL
❑1, Sep 1993; Reprints The Avengers #1; Thor, Iron Man, Ant-man, Wasp, Hulk 2.95
❑4, Mar 1995; Reprints The Avengers #4; Captain America Joins 2.95
❑16; Reprints The Avengers #16; New team begins: Captain America, Hawkeye, Quicksilver, and Scarlet Witch 2.95

MARVEL MILESTONE EDITION: CAPTAIN AMERICA
MARVEL
❑1, Mar 1995; Reprints Captain America #1 3.95

MARVEL MILESTONE EDITION: FANTASTIC FOUR
MARVEL
❑1, Nov 1991 2.95
❑5, Nov 1992 2.95

MARVEL MILESTONE EDITION: GIANT-SIZE X-MEN
MARVEL
❑1 1991 3.95

MARVEL MILESTONE EDITION: INCREDIBLE HULK
MARVEL
❑1, Mar 1991; Reprints Incredible Hulk #1 2.95

MARVEL MILESTONE EDITION: IRON FIST
MARVEL
❑14 2.95

MARVEL MILESTONE EDITION: IRON MAN
MARVEL
❑55, Nov 1992; Reprints Iron Man #55 2.95

MARVEL MILESTONE EDITION: TALES OF SUSPENSE
MARVEL
❑39, Nov 1994; Reprints Tales of Suspense #39 2.95

MARVEL MILESTONE EDITION: X-MEN
MARVEL
❑1 1991; reprint (first series) 2.95
❑9, Oct 1993; Reprints X-Men (1st Series) #9 2.95
❑28, Nov 1994; indicia says Marvel Milestone Edition: X-Men #1; Reprints X-Men (1st Series) #28 2.95

MARVEL MOVIE PREMIERE
MARVEL
❑1, b&w; magazine 3.00

MARVEL MUST HAVES
MARVEL
❑1, Dec 2001; Reprints Wolverine: The Origin #1, Startling Stories: Banner #1, Cable #97, Spider-Man's Tangled Web #4 3.99
❑2 3.99

MARVEL MUST HAVES: AMAZING SPIDER-MAN #30-32
MARVEL
❑1, ca. 2003; Reprints Amazing Spider-Man (Vol. 2) #30-32 3.99

MARVEL MUST HAVES: INCREDIBLE HULK #50-52
MARVEL
❑1, ca. 2003; Reprints Incredible Hulk (2nd series) #50-52 3.99

MARVEL MUST HAVES: INCREDIBLE HULK #34-36
MARVEL
❑1, ca. 2003; Reprints Incredible Hulk (2nd series) #34-36 3.99

The Roger Rabbit short "Tummy Trouble" was adapted in *Marvel Graphic Novel: Roger Rabbit in the Resurrection of Doom.*

© 1987 Marvel Comics and Walt Disney Productions.

N-MINT

MARVEL MUST HAVES: NEW X-MEN #114-116
MARVEL
❑1, ca. 2003; Reprints New X-Men #114-116 3.99

MARVEL MUST HAVES: SENTINEL #1 & #2 AND RUNAWAYS #1 & #2
MARVEL
❑1, ca. 2003; Reprints Sentinel #1-2, Runaways #1-2 3.99

MARVEL MUST HAVES: THE ULTIMATES #1-3
MARVEL
❑1, ca. 2003; Reprints The Ultimates #1-3 3.99

MARVEL MUST HAVES: TRUTH: RED, WHITE AND BLACK
MARVEL
❑1, Apr 2003 3.99

MARVEL MUST HAVES: ULTIMATE SPIDER-MAN #1-3
MARVEL
❑1, ca. 2003; Reprints Ultimate Spider-Man #1-3 3.99

MARVEL MUST HAVES: ULTIMATE VENOM
MARVEL
❑1, May 2003 3.99

MARVEL MUST HAVES: ULTIMATE WAR
MARVEL
❑1, May 2003 3.99

MARVEL MUST HAVES: ULTIMATE X-MEN #1-3
MARVEL
❑1, ca. 2003; Reprints Ultimate X-Men #1-3 3.99

MARVEL MUST HAVES: ULTIMATE X-MEN #34 & #35
MARVEL
❑1, ca. 2003; Reprints Ultimate X-Men #34-35 2.99

MARVEL MUST HAVES: WOLVERINE #1-3
MARVEL
❑1, ca. 2003; no indicia; reprints Wolverine (3rd series) #1-3 3.99

MARVEL MYSTERY COMICS (2ND SERIES)
MARVEL
❑1, Dec 1999 3.95

MARVEL NO-PRIZE BOOK, THE
MARVEL
❑1, Jan 1983; SL (w); JK (a);mistakes 3.00

MARVELOUS ADVENTURES OF GUS BEEZER AND SPIDER-MAN, THE
MARVEL
❑1, Feb 2004 2.99

MARVELOUS ADVENTURES OF GUS BEEZER: HULK
MARVEL
❑1, May 2003 2.99

N-MINT

MARVELOUS ADVENTURES OF GUS BEEZER: SPIDER-MAN
MARVEL
❑1, May 2003 .... 2.99

MARVELOUS ADVENTURES OF GUS BEEZER: X-MEN
MARVEL
❑1, May 2003 .... 2.99

MARVELOUS DRAGON CLAN
LUNAR
❑1, Jul 1994, b&w 2.50
❑2, Sep 1994, b&w 2.50

MARVELOUS WIZARD OF OZ (MGM'S...)
MARVEL / DC
❑1; treasury-sized movie adaptation . 16.00

MARVEL: PORTRAITS OF A UNIVERSE
MARVEL
❑1, Mar 1995 .... 2.95
❑2, Apr 1995 .... 2.95
❑3, May 1995 .... 2.95
❑4, Jun 1995 .... 2.95

MARVEL POSTER BOOK
MARVEL
❑1, Jan 1991 .... 2.50

MARVEL POSTER MAGAZINE
MARVEL
❑2, Dec 2001, Winter 2001 .... 3.50

MARVEL PREMIERE
MARVEL
❑1, Apr 1972 GK (a); O: Counter-Earth. O: Warlock. 18.00
❑2, May 1972; JK (a); A: Warlock. Yellow Claw 12.00
❑3, Jul 1972 A: Doctor Strange. 16.00
❑4, Sep 1972 FB (a); A: Doctor Strange. 8.00
❑5, Nov 1972 MP, CR (a); A: Doctor Strange. 6.00
❑6, Jan 1973 FB, MP (a); A: Doctor Strange. 6.00
❑7, Mar 1973 MP, CR (a); A: Doctor Strange. 6.00
❑8, May 1973 JSn (a); A: Doctor Strange. 6.00
❑9, Jul 1973 FB (a); A: Doctor Strange. 6.00
❑10, Sep 1973 FB, NA (a); A: Doctor Strange. D: The Ancient One. 9.00
❑11, Oct 1973 FB, NA (a); A: Doctor Strange. 5.00
❑12, Nov 1973 FB, NA (a); A: Doctor Strange. 5.00
❑13, Jan 1974 FB, NA (a); 1: Sise-Neg (as Cagliostro). A: Doctor Strange. 5.00
❑14, Mar 1974 FB, NA (a); A: Sise-Neg. A: Doctor Strange. 5.00
❑15, May 1974; GK (a); O: Iron Fist. 1: Iron Fist. Marvel Value Stamp #94: Electro 40.00
❑16, Jul 1974; 2: Iron Fist. 2: Iron Fist. Marvel Value Stamp #71: Vision 20.00
❑17, Sep 1974; A: Iron Fist. Marvel Value Stamp #32: Red Skull 10.00
❑18, Oct 1974; A: Iron Fist. Marvel Value Stamp #74: Stranger 10.00
❑19, Nov 1974; 1: Colleen Wing. A: Iron Fist. Marvel Value Stamp #6: Thor . 10.00
❑20, Jan 1975; A: Iron Fist. Marvel Value Stamp #73: Kingpin 10.00
❑21, Mar 1975 A: Iron Fist. 10.00
❑22, Jun 1975 A: Iron Fist. 10.00
❑23, Aug 1975; PB (a); A: Iron Fist. Marvel Value Stamp #27: Black Widow 10.00
❑24, Sep 1975; PB (a); A: Iron Fist. Marvel Value Stamp #74: Stranger 10.00
❑25, Oct 1975; JBy (a); A: Iron Fist. Marvel Value Stamp #6: Thor 15.00
❑26, Nov 1975 JK (a); A: Hercules. ... 4.00
❑27, Dec 1975 A: Satana. 4.00
❑28, Feb 1976 A: Werewolf. A: Man-Thing. A: Ghost Rider. A: Legion of Monsters. A: Morbius. 5.00
❑29, Apr 1976 JK (a); O: Whizzer. O: Red Raven. O: Thin Man. O: Blue Diamond. O: Miss America. 1: Patriot. 1: Jack Frost I. 1: Thin Man. 1: Blue Diamond. A: Liberty Legion. 3.00
❑29/30 cent, Apr 1976; JK (a); O: Whizzer. O: Red Raven. O: Thin Man. O: Blue Diamond. O: Miss America. 1: Patriot. 1: Jack Frost I. 1: Thin Man. 1: Blue Diamond. A: Liberty Legion. 30 cent regional price variant 20.00
❑30, Jun 1976 JK (a); A: Liberty Legion. 2.50
❑30/30 cent, Jun 1976; JK (a); A: Liberty Legion. 30 cent regional price variant 20.00
❑31, Aug 1976 JK (a); O: Woodgod. 1: Woodgod. 2.00
❑31/30 cent, Aug 1976; JK (a); O: Woodgod. 1: Woodgod. 30 cent regional price variant 20.00
❑32, Oct 1976; HC (a);Monark Starstalker 2.00
❑33, Dec 1976; HC (a); A: Solomon Kane. Monark 2.00
❑34, Feb 1977 HC (a); A: Solomon Kane. 2.00
❑35, Apr 1977 O: 3-D Man. 1: 3-D Man. 2.00
❑36, Jun 1977 A: 3-D Man. 2.00
❑36/35 cent, Jun 1977; A: 3-D Man. 35 cent regional price variant 15.00
❑37, Aug 1977 A: 3-D Man. 2.00
❑37/35 cent, Aug 1977; A: 3-D Man. 35 cent regional price variant 15.00
❑38, Oct 1977 1: Weirdworld. 2.00
❑38/35 cent, Oct 1977; 1: Weirdworld. 35 cent regional price variant 15.00
❑39, Dec 1977 A: Torpedo. 2.00
❑40, Feb 1978 1: Bucky II (Fred Davis). A: Torpedo. 2.00
❑41, Apr 1978 TS (a); A: Seeker 3000. 2.00
❑42, Jun 1978; A: Tigra. Tigra 2.00
❑43, Aug 1978 TS (a); 1: Paladin. 2.00
❑44, Oct 1978; KG (a); A: Jack of Hearts. 2.00
❑45, Dec 1978; A: Man-Wolf. Man-Wolf 2.00
❑46, Feb 1979; GP (a); A: Man-Wolf. War God 2.00
❑47, Apr 1979 JBy (a); 1: Ant-Man. .. 2.00
❑48, Jun 1979 JBy, BL (a); A: Ant-Man. 2.00
❑49, Aug 1979 FM (c); FM (a); A: The Falcon. 2.00
❑50, Oct 1979 1: Alice Cooper. 12.50
❑51, Dec 1979 A: Black Panther. 2.00
❑52, Feb 1980 A: Black Panther. 2.00
❑53, Apr 1980 FM (c); FM (a); A: Black Panther. 2.00
❑54, Jun 1980 GD (a); 1: Caleb Hammer. 2.00
❑55, Aug 1980 A: Wonder Man. 2.00
❑56, Oct 1980 HC, TD (a); A: Dominic Fortune. 2.00
❑57, Dec 1980 DaG (a); 1: Doctor Who (in U.S.). 3.50
❑58, Feb 1981 FM (c); FM, TD (a); A: Doctor Who. 3.00
❑59, Apr 1981 A: Doctor Who. 3.00
❑60, Jun 1981 A: Doctor Who. 3.00
❑61, Aug 1981 TS (a); A: Star-Lord. .. 2.00

MARVEL PRESENTS
MARVEL
❑1, Oct 1975 O: Bloodstone. 1: Bloodstone. 4.00
❑2, Dec 1975 O: Bloodstone. 3.00
❑3, Feb 1976 A: Guardians of the Galaxy. 4.00
❑4, May 1976 O: Nikki. 1: Nikki. A: Guardians of the Galaxy. 4.00
❑4/30 cent, May 1976; 30 cent regional price variant 20.00
❑5, Jun 1976 A: Guardians of the Galaxy. 4.00
❑5/30 cent, Jun 1976; 30 cent regional price variant 20.00
❑6, Aug 1976 A: Guardians of the Galaxy. V: Planetary Man. 3.50
❑6/30 cent, Aug 1976; 30 cent regional price variant 20.00
❑7, Nov 1976 A: Guardians of the Galaxy. 3.50
❑8, Dec 1976; A: Guardians of the Galaxy. reprints Silver Surfer #2 .... 3.50
❑9, Feb 1977 O: Starhawk II (Aleta). A: Guardians of the Galaxy. 3.50
❑10, Apr 1977 O: Starhawk II (Aleta). A: Guardians of the Galaxy. 3.50
❑11, Jun 1977 A: Guardians of the Galaxy. 3.50
❑12, Aug 1977 A: Guardians of the Galaxy. 3.50

MARVEL PREVIEW
MARVEL
❑1, Sum 1975; Man Gods From Beyond the Stars 2.50
❑2 1975 O: The Punisher. 1: Dominic Fortune. 25.00
❑3, Sep 1975; Blade the Vampire Slayer 5.00
❑4, Jan 1976 O: Star-Lord. 1: Star-Lord. 4.00
❑5; Sherlock Holmes 3.00
❑6; Sherlock Holmes 3.00
❑7, Sep 1976; 1: Rocket Raccoon. Satana 3.00
❑8, Fal 1976; A: Legion of Monsters. Morbius, Blade 5.00
❑9, Apr 1977; O: Star Hawk. Man-God 3.00
❑10, Jul 1977; JSn (a);Thor 3.00
❑11, Oct 1977; Star-Lord 3.00
❑12, Jan 1978; Haunt of Horror 3.00
❑13, Apr 1978; UFO 3.00
❑14, Aug 1978; Star-Lord 3.00
❑15, Oct 1978; Star-Lord; Joe Jusko's first major comics work 3.00
❑16, Mar 1979; Detectives 3.00
❑17, May 1979; Blackmark 3.00
❑18, Aug 1979; Star-Lord 3.00
❑19, Nov 1979 A: Kull. 3.00
❑20, Mar 1980; Bizarre Adventures ... 3.00
❑21, May 1980 A: Moon Knight. 3.00
❑22, Aug 1980; Merlin; King Arthur ... 3.00
❑23, Nov 1980; FM (a);Bizarre Adventures 3.00
❑24, Feb 1981; Paradox; Title continues as "Bizarre Adventures" with #25 3.00

MARVEL PREVIEW '93
MARVEL
❑1, ca. 1993 .... 3.95

MARVEL RIOT
MARVEL
❑1, Dec 1995; parodies Age of Apocalypse; wraparound cover 1.95

MARVELS
MARVEL
❑0, Aug 1994; KB (w); ARo (a);Collects promo art and Human Torch story from Marvel Age; Fully painted 4.00
❑1, Jan 1994; KB (w); ARo (a);wraparound acetate outer cover; Torch, Sub-Mariner, Captain America; Torch, Sub-Mariner, Capt. America; Fully painted 5.00
❑1-2, Apr 1996 KB (w); ARo (a) 2.95
❑2, Feb 1994; KB (w); ARo (a);Fully painted; wraparound acetate outer cover 5.00
❑2-2, May 1996 KB (w); ARo (a) 2.95
❑3, Mar 1994; KB (w); ARo (a);Coming of Galactus; Fully painted; wraparound acetate outer cover 5.00
❑3-2, May 1996; KB (w); ARo (a);wraparound cover 5.95
❑4, Apr 1994; KB (w); ARo (a); D: Gwen Stacy. Fully painted; wraparound acetate outer cover 5.00
❑4-2, Jun 1996; KB (w); ARo (a);wraparound cover 2.95

MARVEL SAGA
MARVEL
❑1, Dec 1985 JBy, SL (w); SB, JBy, DH, JK, JSt (a); O: X-Men. O: Fantastic Four. O: Alpha Flight. 2.50
❑2, Jan 1986 SL (w); SD, JK, BWi (a); O: Hulk. O: Spider-Man. 2.00

N-MINT

❑3, Feb 1986 O: Sub-Mariner. O: Doom. 2.00
❑4, Mar 1986 SL (w); ATh, JB, JBy, HT, JK, FM, BA, DC, BH, BWi (a); O: Thor. 2.00
❑5, Apr 1986 O: Iceman. O: Angel. 2.00
❑6, May 1986 SL (w); JB, DH, GT, JK, GK (a); O: Iron Man. O: Asgard. O: Odin. 2.00
❑7, Jun 1986 SL (w); SD, BL, JR2, DH, JK, JM (a) 2.00
❑8, Jul 1986 SL (w); SD, DH, JK (a) 2.00
❑9, Aug 1986 O: Vulture. 2.00
❑10, Sep 1986 SL (w); SD, JB, BEv, JK (a); O: Marvel Girl. O: Beast. O: Avengers. 2.00
❑11, Oct 1986 O: Molecule Man. 1.50
❑12, Nov 1986; Captain America revived 1.50
❑13, Dec 1986 FM, SL (w); SD, GC, JB, BEv, DH, SR, JK, FM, TP, KJ (a); O: Daredevil. 1.50
❑14, Jan 1987 SL (w); AM, SD, JBy, DGr, JR2, JK, JSt (a); O: Scarlet Witch. O: Quicksilver. 1.50
❑15, Feb 1987 O: Wonder Man. O: Hawkeye. 1.50
❑16, Mar 1987 SL (w); SD, GC, PS, DH, JK, GK, DA (a); O: Frightful Four. O: Dormammu. 1.50
❑17, Apr 1987 SL (w); SD, VM, DH, JK, GK, JSt (a); O: Ka-Zar. O: Leader. 1.50
❑18, May 1987 SD, SL (w); SD, DH, JK, JSo, JSt (a); O: S.H.I.E.L.D. 1.50
❑19, Jun 1987; new Avengers team 1.50
❑20, Jul 1987 1.50
❑21, Aug 1987; X-Men 1.50
❑22, Sep 1987 O: Mary Jane. 1.50
❑23, Oct 1987; Inhumans 1.50
❑24, Nov 1987 JK, SL (w); JB, JK, JSt (a); O: Galactus. 1.50
❑25, Dec 1987 JK, SL (w); JB, JK, JSt (a); O: Silver Surfer. 1.50

MARVELS COMICS: CAPTAIN AMERICA
MARVEL

❑1, Jul 2000 2.25

MARVELS COMICS: DAREDEVIL
MARVEL

❑1, Jun 2000 2.25

MARVELS COMICS: FANTASTIC FOUR
MARVEL

❑1, May 2000 2.25

MARVELS COMICS: SPIDER-MAN
MARVEL

❑1, Jul 2000 2.25

MARVELS COMICS: THOR
MARVEL

❑1, Jul 2000 2.25

MARVELS COMICS: X-MEN
MARVEL

❑1, Jun 2000 2.25

MARVEL SELECTS: FANTASTIC FOUR
MARVEL

❑1, Jan 2000 2.75

MARVEL SELECTS: SPIDER-MAN
MARVEL

❑1, Jan 2000; Reprints Amazing Spider-Man #100 2.75
❑2, Feb 2000 2.75
❑3, Mar 2000 2.75

MARVEL'S GREATEST COMICS
MARVEL

❑23, Oct 1969; Giant-size; Title continued from "Marvel Collector's Item Classics" 6.00
❑24, Dec 1969; Giant-size 6.00
❑25, Feb 1970; Giant-size 6.00
❑26, Apr 1970; Giant-size 6.00
❑27, Jun 1970; Giant-size 6.00
❑28, Aug 1970; Giant-size 6.00
❑29, Dec 1970; Giant-size; Reprints Fantastic Four #12 and 31 6.00

N-MINT

❑30, Mar 1971; Giant-size; Reprints Fantastic Four #37 and 38 6.00
❑31, Jun 1971; Giant-size; Reprints Fantastic Four #39 and 40 6.00
❑32, Sep 1971; Giant-size; Reprints Fantastic Four #41 and 42 6.00
❑33, Dec 1971; Giant-size; Reprints Fantastic Four #44 and 45 6.00
❑34, Mar 1972; Giant-size; Reprints Fantastic Four #46 and 47 6.00
❑35, Jun 1972; A: Silver Surfer. Reprints Fantastic Four #48 5.00
❑36, Jul 1972; Reprints Fantastic Four #49 5.00
❑37, Sep 1972; Reprints Fantastic Four #50 5.00
❑38, Oct 1972; Reprints Fantastic Four #51 3.50
❑39, Nov 1972; Reprints Fantastic Four #52 3.50
❑40, Jan 1973; Reprints Fantastic Four #53 3.50
❑41, Mar 1973; Reprints Fantastic Four #54 3.50
❑42, May 1973; Reprints Fantastic Four #55 3.50
❑43, Jul 1973; Reprints Fantastic Four #56 3.50
❑44, Sep 1973; Reprints Fantastic Four #61 3.50
❑45, Oct 1973; Reprints Fantastic Four #62 3.50
❑46, Nov 1973; Reprints Fantastic Four #63 3.50
❑47, Jan 1974; Reprints Fantastic Four #64 3.50
❑48, Mar 1974; Reprints Fantastic Four #65 3.50
❑49, May 1974; Reprints Fantastic Four #66 3.50
❑50, Jul 1974; JK, JSt (a); A: Warlock (Him). Reprints Fantastic Four #67 4.00
❑51, Sep 1974; Reprints Fantastic Four #68 3.00
❑52, Oct 1974; Reprints Fantastic Four #69 2.50
❑53, Nov 1974; Reprints Fantastic Four #70 2.50
❑54, Jan 1975; Reprints Fantastic Four #71 2.50
❑55, Mar 1975; Reprints Fantastic Four #73 2.50
❑56, May 1975; Reprints Fantastic Four #74 2.50
❑57, Jul 1975; Reprints Fantastic Four #75 2.50
❑58, Sep 1975; Reprints Fantastic Four #76 2.50
❑59, Oct 1975; Reprints Fantastic Four #77 2.50
❑60, Nov 1975; Reprints Fantastic Four #78 2.50
❑61, Jan 1976; Reprints Fantastic Four #79 2.50
❑62, Mar 1976; Reprints Fantastic Four #80 2.50
❑63, May 1976; Reprints Fantastic Four #81 2.50
❑63/30 cent, May 1976; 30 cent regional price variant; Reprints Fantastic Four #81 20.00
❑64, Jul 1976; Reprints Fantastic Four #82 2.50
❑64/30 cent, Jul 1976; 30 cent regional price variant; Reprints Fantastic Four #82 20.00
❑65, Sep 1976; Reprints Fantastic Four #83 2.50
❑66, Oct 1976; Reprints Fantastic Four #84 2.50
❑67, Nov 1976; Reprints Fantastic Four #85 2.50
❑68, Jan 1977; Reprints Fantastic Four #86 2.50
❑69, Mar 1977; Reprints Fantastic Four #87 2.50
❑70, May 1977; Reprints Fantastic Four #88 2.50

Kurt Busiek and Alex Ross presented a look at key events in Marvel history as seen through the eyes of a news photographer in *Marvels*.

© 1994 Marvel Comics.

N-MINT

❑71, Jul 1977; Reprints Fantastic Four #89 2.00
❑72, Sep 1977; Reprints Fantastic Four #90 2.00
❑73, Oct 1977; Reprints Fantastic Four #91 2.00
❑74, Nov 1977; Reprints Fantastic Four #92 2.00
❑75, Jan 1978; Reprints Fantastic Four #93 2.00
❑76, Mar 1978; Reprints Fantastic Four #95 2.00
❑77, May 1978; Reprints Fantastic Four #96 2.00
❑78, Jul 1978; Reprints Fantastic Four #97 2.00
❑79, Sep 1978; Reprints Fantastic Four #98 2.00
❑80, Nov 1978; Reprints Fantastic Four #99 2.00
❑81, Jan 1979; Reprints Fantastic Four #100 2.00
❑82, Mar 1979; Reprints Fantastic Four #102 2.00
❑83, Dec 1979; Reprints Fantastic Four #103 2.00
❑84, Jan 1980; Reprints Fantastic Four #104 2.00
❑85, Feb 1980; Reprints Fantastic Four #105 2.00
❑86, Mar 1980; Reprints Fantastic Four #116 2.00
❑87, Apr 1980; Reprints Fantastic Four #107 2.00
❑88, May 1980; Reprints Fantastic Four #108 2.00
❑89, Jun 1980; Reprints Fantastic Four #109 2.00
❑90, Jul 1980; Reprints Fantastic Four #110 2.00
❑91, Aug 1980; Reprints Fantastic Four #111 2.00
❑92, Sep 1980; Reprints Fantastic Four #112 2.00
❑93, Oct 1980 2.00
❑94, Nov 1980 2.00
❑95, Dec 1980 2.00
❑96, Jan 1981 2.00

MARVEL: SHADOWS & LIGHT
MARVEL

❑1, Feb 1997, b&w; Wolverine, Dracula, Doctor Strange, Captain Marvel; wraparound cover 2.95

MARVEL 1602
MARVEL

❑1, Nov 2003 3.50
❑2, Nov 2003 3.50
❑3, Dec 2003 3.50
❑4, Jan 2004 3.50
❑5, Feb 2004 3.50
❑6, Mar 2004 3.50
❑7, Apr 2004 3.50
❑8, Jun 2004 3.99

MARVEL SPECIAL EDITION FEATURING CLOSE ENCOUNTERS OF THE THIRD KIND
MARVEL

❑3, ca. 1978; treasury-sized; adapts Close Encounters of the Third Kind 9.00

N-MINT

MARVEL SPECIAL EDITION FEATURING SPECTACULAR SPIDER-MAN
MARVEL

❑1, ca. 1975; treasury-sized 12.00

MARVEL SPECIAL EDITION FEATURING STAR WARS
MARVEL

❑1, ca. 1977; treasury-sized adaption of Star Wars 14.00
❑2, ca. 1977; treasury-sized adaption of Star Wars 12.00
❑3, ca. 1978; treasury-sized; collects previous two issues 14.00

MARVEL SPECTACULAR
MARVEL

❑1, Aug 1973; SL (w); JK (a);reprints Thor #128 .... 5.00
❑2, Sep 1973; SL (w); JK (a);reprints Thor #129 .... 3.00
❑3, Oct 1973; SL (w); JK (a); 1: Tana Nile (in real form). reprints Thor #130 .... 3.00
❑4, Nov 1973; SL (w); JK (a);reprints Thor #133 .... 3.00
❑5, Jan 1974; SL (w); JK (a);reprints Thor #134 .... 3.00
❑6, Mar 1974; SL (w); JK (a);reprints Tales of Asgard from Journey Into Mystery #121 and Thor #135 .... 3.00
❑7, May 1974; SL (w); JK (a);reprints Thor #136 .... 3.00
❑8, Jul 1974; SL (w); JK (a);reprints Thor #137 .... 3.00
❑9, Sep 1974; SL (w); JK (a);reprints Thor #138 .... 3.00
❑10, Oct 1974; SL (w); JK (a);reprints Thor #139 .... 3.00
❑11, Nov 1974; SL (w); JK (a);reprints Thor #140 .... 2.50
❑12, Dec 1974; SL (w); JK (a);reprints Thor #141 .... 2.50
❑13, Jan 1975; SL (w); JK (a);reprints Thor #142 .... 2.50
❑14, Mar 1975; SL (w); JK (a);reprints Thor #143 .... 2.50
❑15, Jun 1975; SL (w); JK (a);reprints Thor #144 .... 2.50
❑16, Jul 1975; SL (w); JK (a);reprints Thor #145 .... 2.50
❑17, Sep 1975; SL (w); JK (a);reprints Thor #146 .... 2.50
❑18, Oct 1975; SL (w); JK (a);reprints Thor #147 .... 2.50
❑19, Nov 1975; SL (w); JK (a);reprints Thor #148 .... 2.50

MARVEL SPOTLIGHT (VOL. 1)
MARVEL

❑1, Nov 1971 NA, WW (a); O: Red Wolf. A: Red Wolf. 10.00
❑2, Feb 1972 NA (c); FM (a); O: Werewolf. 1: Werewolf. 36.00
❑3, May 1972 A: Werewolf. 16.00
❑4, Jun 1972 A: Werewolf. 16.00
❑5, Aug 1972 FM (c); SD, FM, MP (a); O: Ghost Rider I (Johnny Blaze). 1: Zarathos (Ghost Rider's Spirit of Vengeance). 60.00
❑6, Oct 1972 A: Ghost Rider. 22.00
❑7, Dec 1972 FM (c); FM (a); A: Ghost Rider. 18.00
❑8, Feb 1973 FM (a); A: Ghost Rider. 18.00
❑9, Apr 1973 A: Ghost Rider. 13.00
❑10, Jun 1973 A: Ghost Rider. 13.00
❑11, Aug 1973 A: Ghost Rider. 13.00
❑12, Oct 1973 SD (a); O: Son of Satan. 1: Son of Satan. 13.00
❑13, Jan 1974 O: Satana. A: Son of Satan. 7.00
❑14, Mar 1974; A: Son of Satan. Marvel Value Stamp #5: Dracula 6.00
❑15, May 1974; A: Son of Satan. Marvel Value Stamp #21: Kull 6.00
❑16, Jul 1974; A: Son of Satan. Marvel Value Stamp #83: Dragon Man 5.00
❑17, Sep 1974; A: Son of Satan. Marvel Value Stamp #45: Mantis 5.00
❑18, Oct 1974; A: Son of Satan. Marvel Value Stamp #81: Rhino 5.00
❑19, Dec 1974; A: Son of Satan. Marvel Value Stamp #14: Living Mummy .. 5.00
❑20, Feb 1975; A: Son of Satan. Marvel Value Stamp #26: Mephisto 5.00
❑21, Apr 1975 A: Son of Satan. 5.00
❑22, Jun 1975 A: Ghost Rider. A: Son of Satan. 6.00
❑23, Aug 1975 A: Son of Satan. 5.00
❑24, Oct 1975; A: Son of Satan. Last Son of Satan in Marvel Spotlight ... 5.00
❑25, Dec 1975 A: Sinbad. 3.00
❑26, Feb 1976 A: Scarecrow (Marvel). 3.00
❑27, Apr 1976 A: Sub-Mariner. 3.00
❑27/30 cent, Apr 1976; 30 cent regional price variant 20.00
❑28, Jun 1976; A: Moon Knight. 1st solo story for Moon Knight 8.00
❑28/30 cent, Jun 1976; 30 cent regional price variant 18.00
❑29, Aug 1976 JK (a); A: Moon Knight. 6.00
❑29/30 cent, Aug 1976; 30 cent regional price variant 15.00
❑30, Oct 1976 JB (a); A: Warriors Three. 3.00
❑31, Dec 1976 HC (a); A: Nick Fury. .. 3.00
❑32, Feb 1977 SB, JM (a); O: Spider-Woman I (Jessica Drew). 1: Spider-Woman I (Jessica Drew). 7.00
❑33, Apr 1977 1: Devil-Slayer. A: Deathlok. 3.00

MARVEL SPOTLIGHT (VOL. 2)
MARVEL

❑1, Jul 1979 PB (a); A: Captain Marvel. 3.00
❑2, Sep 1979 FM (c); TD (a); A: Captain Marvel. 2.00
❑3, Nov 1979 PB (a); A: Captain Marvel. 2.00
❑4, Jan 1980 FM (c); SD (a); A: Dragon Lord. 2.00
❑5, Mar 1980 FM (c); SD (a); A: Dragon Lord. A: Captain Marvel. 2.00
❑6, May 1980 TS (a); O: Star-Lord. ... 2.00
❑7, Jul 1980 TS (a); A: Star-Lord. 2.00
❑8, Sep 1980 FM, TD (a); A: Captain Marvel. 2.00
❑9, Nov 1980 SD (a); A: Captain Universe. 2.00
❑10, Jan 1981 SD (a); A: Captain Universe. 2.00
❑11, Mar 1981 SD (a); A: Captain Universe. 2.00

MARVEL SPRING SPECIAL
MARVEL

❑1, Nov 1988; Elvira 2.50

MARVEL SUPER ACTION
MARVEL

❑1, May 1977; JK (a);reprints Captain America #100 .... 4.00
❑2, Jul 1977; JK (a);Reprints Captain America #101 .... 2.50
❑3, Sep 1977; JK (a);Reprints Captain America #102 .... 2.50
❑3/35 cent, Sep 1977; 35 cent regional price variant; reprints Captain America #102 .... 15.00
❑4, Nov 1977; JK (a); O: Marvel Boy. Reprints Marvel Boy #1 .... 2.50
❑5, Jan 1978; JK (a);Reprints Captain America #103 .... 2.00
❑6, Mar 1978; JK (a);Reprints Captain America #104 .... 2.00
❑7, Apr 1978; JK (a);Reprints Captain America #105 .... 2.00
❑8, Jun 1978; JK (a);Reprints Captain America #106 .... 2.00
❑9, Aug 1978; JK (a);Reprints Captain America #107 .... 2.00
❑10, Oct 1978; JK (a);Reprints Captain America #108 .... 2.00
❑11, Dec 1978; JK (a);Reprints Captain America #109 .... 2.00
❑12, Feb 1979; JSo (a); A: Hulk. Reprints Captain America #110 ..... 2.00
❑13, Apr 1979; JSo (a);Reprints Captain America #111 .... 2.00
❑14, Dec 1979; reprints Avengers #55 1.50
❑15, Jan 1980; reprints Avengers #56 1.50
❑16, Feb 1980; reprints Avengers Annual #2 .... 1.50
❑17, Mar 1980; reprints Avengers Annual #2 .... 1.50
❑18, Apr 1980; reprints Avengers #57 1.50
❑19, May 1980; reprints Avengers #58 1.50
❑20, Jun 1980; reprints Avengers #59 1.50
❑21, Jul 1980; reprints Avengers #60 1.50
❑22, Aug 1980; reprints Avengers #61 1.50
❑23, Sep 1980; reprints Avengers #62 1.50
❑24, Oct 1980; reprints Avengers #63 1.50
❑25, Nov 1980; reprints Avengers #64 1.50
❑26, Dec 1980; reprints Avengers #65 1.50
❑27, Jan 1981; reprints Avengers #66 1.50
❑28, Feb 1981; reprints Avengers #67 1.50
❑29, Mar 1981; reprints Avengers #68 1.50
❑30, Apr 1981; reprints Avengers #69 1.50
❑31, May 1981; reprints Avengers #70 1.50
❑32, Jun 1981; reprints Avengers #71 1.50
❑33, Jul 1981; reprints Avengers #72 1.50
❑34, Aug 1981; reprints Avengers #73 1.50
❑35, Sep 1981; reprints Avengers #74 1.50
❑36, Oct 1981; reprints Avengers #75 1.50
❑37, Nov 1981; reprints Avengers #76 1.50

MARVEL SUPER ACTION (MAGAZINE)
MARVEL

❑1, Jan 1976, b&w; O: Dominic Fortune. 1: Mockingbird (as Huntress). 1: Mockingbird (as "Huntress"). 2: Dominic Fortune. Weird World and Punisher stories 30.00

MARVEL SUPER HERO CONTEST OF CHAMPIONS
MARVEL

❑1, Jun 1982; JR2 (a); 1: Shamrock. 1: Le Peregrine. 1: Blitzkrieg. 1: Talisman I. 1: Collective Man. Alpha Flight 4.00
❑2, Jul 1982; JR2 (a);X-Men 3.50
❑3, Aug 1982; JR2 (a);X-Men 3.50

MARVEL SUPER-HEROES (VOL. 1)
MARVEL

❑12, Dec 1967; O: Captain Marvel. 1: Captain Marvel. Title continued from "Fantasy Masterpieces" 45.00
❑13, Mar 1968 1: Carol Danvers. 2: Captain Marvel. 26.00
❑14, May 1968; JK (a); A: Spider-Man. Reprints 1st Kirby art at Marvel 40.00
❑15, Jul 1968; GC (a);Medusa 10.00
❑16, Sep 1968 HT (a); O: Phantom Eagle. 1: Phantom Eagle. 10.00
❑17, Nov 1968; O: Black Knight III (Dane Whitman). D: Black Knight I (Sir Percy of Scandia). Reprints All-Winners Squad #21 .... 10.00
❑18, Jan 1969 O: Vance Astro. O: Guardians of the Galaxy. 1: Vance Astro. 1: Yondu. 1: Guardians of the Galaxy. 1: Charlie-27. 1: Zarek. 22.00
❑19, Mar 1969; GT (a); A: Ka-Zar. 9.00
❑20, May 1969 A: Doctor Doom. 9.00
❑21, Jul 1969; JK (a);Reprints Avengers #3 and X-Men #2 .... 6.00
❑22, Sep 1969; JO, JK (a);Reprints X-Men #3 and Daredevil #2 .... 6.00
❑23, Nov 1969; JO, JK (a);Reprints X-Men #4 and Daredevil #3 .... 6.00
❑24, Jan 1970; JO, JK, JSt (a);Reprints X-Men #5 and Daredevil #4 .... 6.00
❑25, Mar 1970; SD, JK, WW (a);Reprints X-Men #6, Daredevil #5, and Tales to Astonish #60 .... 6.00
❑26, May 1970; SD, JK, WW (a);Reprints X-Men #7, Daredevil #6, and Tales to Astonish #67 .... 6.00
❑27, Jul 1970; JK, WW (a);Reprints X-Men #8, Daredevil #7, and Tales to Astonish #68 .... 6.00
❑28, Oct 1970; GC, WW (a);Reprints Daredevil #8, Tales of Suspense #73 and #74 .... 6.00
❑29, Jan 1971; SL (w); SD, GC, WW (a);Reprints Daredevil #9, Tales of Suspense #75 and #76 .... 6.00

N-MINT

❑30, Apr 1971; SD, GC, JR (a);Reprints Daredevil #15, Tales of Suspense #77 and #78 ..... 6.00
❑31, Nov 1971; SD, GC, JR (a);Reprints Daredevil #19, Tales of Suspense #89 and #90 ..... 6.00
❑32, Sep 1972; GC, JK (a);Reprints from Tales to Astonish begin (#69 and #77) 2.50
❑33, Nov 1972; Reprints Tales to Astonish #78 ..... 2.50
❑34, Jan 1973; Reprints Tales to Astonish #79 ..... 2.50
❑35, Mar 1973; Reprints Tales to Astonish #80 ..... 2.50
❑36, May 1973; Reprints Tales to Astonish #81 ..... 2.50
❑37, Jul 1973; Reprints Tales to Astonish #82 ..... 2.50
❑38, Sep 1973; Reprints Tales to Astonish #83 ..... 2.50
❑39, Oct 1973; Reprints Tales to Astonish #84 ..... 2.50
❑40, Nov 1973; Reprints Tales to Astonish #85 ..... 2.50
❑41, Jan 1974; Reprints Tales to Astonish #86 ..... 2.50
❑42, Mar 1974; Reprints Tales to Astonish #87 ..... 2.50
❑43, May 1974; Reprints Tales to Astonish #88 ..... 2.50
❑44, Jul 1974; Reprints Tales to Astonish #89 ..... 2.50
❑45, Sep 1974; reprints Tales to Astonish #90 ..... 2.50
❑46, Oct 1974; reprints Tales to Astonish #91; Hulk vs. Abomination 2.50
❑47, Nov 1974; reprints Tales to Astonish #92 ..... 2.50
❑48, Jan 1975; reprints Tales to Astonish #93 ..... 2.50
❑49, Mar 1975; reprints Tales to Astonish #94 ..... 2.50
❑50, May 1975; reprints Tales to Astonish #95 ..... 2.50
❑51, Jul 1975; reprints Tales to Astonish #96 ..... 2.50
❑52, Sep 1975; reprints Tales to Astonish #97 ..... 2.50
❑53, Oct 1975; reprints Tales to Astonish #98 ..... 2.50
❑54, Nov 1975; reprints Tales to Astonish #99 ..... 2.50
❑55, Jan 1976; reprints Tales to Astonish #101 ..... 2.50
❑56, Mar 1976; reprints Incredible Hulk #102 (Tales to Astonish became Incredible Hulk) 2.50
❑57, May 1976; reprints Incredible Hulk #103 ..... 2.50
❑57/30 cent, May 1976; 30 cent regional price variant; reprints Incredible Hulk #103 ..... 20.00
❑58, Jul 1976; reprints Incredible Hulk #104 ..... 2.50
❑58/30 cent, Jul 1976; 30 cent regional price variant; reprints Incredible Hulk #104 ..... 20.00
❑59, Sep 1976; reprints Incredible Hulk #105 ..... 2.50
❑60, Oct 1976; reprints Incredible Hulk #106 ..... 2.50
❑61, Nov 1976; reprints Incredible Hulk #107 ..... 2.50
❑62, Jan 1977; reprints Incredible Hulk #108 ..... 2.50
❑63, Mar 1977; reprints Incredible Hulk #109 ..... 2.50
❑64, May 1977; reprints Incredible Hulk #110 ..... 2.50
❑65, Jun 1977; reprints Incredible Hulk #111 ..... 2.50
❑66, Sep 1977; reprints Incredible Hulk #112 ..... 2.50
❑67, Oct 1977; reprints Incredible Hulk #113 ..... 2.50
❑68, Nov 1977; reprints Incredible Hulk #114 ..... 2.50
❑69, Jan 1978; reprints Incredible Hulk #115 ..... 2.50

N-MINT

❑70, Mar 1978; reprints Incredible Hulk #116 ..... 2.50
❑71, May 1978; reprints Incredible Hulk #117 ..... 2.50
❑72, Jul 1978 ..... 2.50
❑73, Aug 1978; reprints Incredible Hulk #120 ..... 2.50
❑74, Sep 1978 ..... 2.50
❑75, Oct 1978 ..... 2.50
❑76, Nov 1978; reprints Incredible Hulk #124 ..... 2.50
❑77, Dec 1978; reprints Incredible Hulk #125 ..... 2.50
❑78, Jan 1979; reprints Incredible Hulk #126 ..... 2.50
❑79, Mar 1979; reprints Incredible Hulk #127 ..... 2.50
❑80, May 1979; reprints Incredible Hulk #128 ..... 2.50
❑81, Jul 1979; reprints Incredible Hulk #129 ..... 2.00
❑82, Aug 1979; reprints Incredible Hulk #130 ..... 2.00
❑83, Sep 1979; reprints Incredible Hulk #131 ..... 2.00
❑84, Oct 1979; reprints Incredible Hulk #132 ..... 2.00
❑85, Nov 1979; reprints Incredible Hulk #133 ..... 2.00
❑86, Jan 1980; reprints Incredible Hulk #134 ..... 2.00
❑87, Mar 1980 ..... 2.00
❑88, May 1980 ..... 2.00
❑89, Jul 1980; reprints Incredible Hulk #139 ..... 2.00
❑90, Aug 1980; SB (a);reprints Avengers #88 ..... 2.00
❑91, Sep 1980; reprints Incredible Hulk #140 ..... 2.00
❑92, Oct 1980 ..... 2.00
❑93, Nov 1980 ..... 2.00
❑94, Jan 1981 ..... 2.00
❑95, Mar 1981 ..... 2.00
❑96, Apr 1981 ..... 2.00
❑97, May 1981 ..... 2.00
❑98, Jun 1981 ..... 2.00
❑99, Jul 1981; reprints Incredible Hulk #150 ..... 2.00
❑100, Aug 1981; reprints Incredible Hulk #151-152 ..... 2.00
❑101, Sep 1981; reprints Incredible Hulk #153 ..... 2.00
❑102, Oct 1981; reprints Incredible Hulk #154 ..... 2.00
❑103, Nov 1981; reprints Incredible Hulk #155 ..... 2.00
❑104, Dec 1981; reprints Incredible Hulk #156 ..... 2.00
❑105, Jan 1982; reprints Incredible Hulk #157 ..... 2.00
❑Special 1, Oct 1966; SL (w); BEv, JK (a); O: Daredevil. 1: Daredevil. One-shot from 1966; Reprints stories from Avengers #2, Daredevil #1, Marvel Mystery Comics #8; Human Torch meets Sub-Mariner 40.00

MARVEL SUPER-HEROES (VOL. 2)
MARVEL

❑1, May 1990; SD, FH, KP, MGu (a); O: Raptor. Spring 1990 ..... 3.50
❑2, Jul 1990 ..... 3.25
❑3, Oct 1990 ..... 3.25
❑4, Dec 1990 ..... 3.25
❑5, Apr 1991 SD (a) 3.25
❑6, Jul 1991 RB (a) 3.25
❑7, Oct 1991 SD (a) 3.25
❑8, Dec 1991 SD (a) 3.25
❑9, Apr 1992 KB (w); A: Cupid. 3.25
❑10, Jul 1992; Oversized format A: Sabretooth. 3.25
❑11, Oct 1992; MGu (a);Ghost Rider 3.00
❑12, Jan 1993 KB (w) 2.50
❑13, Apr 1993; KB (w); GC, DH (a);Iron Man 2.75
❑14, Jul 1993 BMc (a) 2.75
❑15, Oct 1993 KP, DH (a); A: Iron Man. A: Thor. 2.75

Early issues of *Marvel Super-Heroes* (Vol. 1) served as a testing area for proposed Marvel series.

© 1968 Marvel Comics.

N-MINT

MARVEL SUPER-HEROES MEGAZINE
MARVEL

❑1, Oct 1994 ..... 2.95
❑2, Nov 1994 ..... 2.95
❑3, Dec 1994 ..... 2.95
❑4, Jan 1995 ..... 2.95
❑5, Feb 1995 ..... 2.95
❑6, Mar 1995 ..... 2.95

MARVEL SUPER HEROES SECRET WARS
MARVEL

❑1, May 1984; MZ (a); 1: Beyonder (voice only). X-Men, Avengers, Fantastic Four in all 3.00
❑2, Jun 1984 MZ (a) 2.00
❑3, Jul 1984 MZ (a); O: Volcana. 1: Volcana. 2.00
❑4, Aug 1984 BL (a) 2.00
❑5, Sep 1984 BL (a) 2.00
❑6, Oct 1984 MZ (a); D: Wasp. 2.00
❑7, Nov 1984 MZ (a); 1: Spider-Woman II (Julia Carpenter). 3.00
❑8, Dec 1984 MZ (a); O: Spider-Man's black costume. 1: Alien costume (later Venom). 11.00
❑9, Jan 1985 MZ (a) 2.00
❑10, Feb 1985 MZ (a) 2.00
❑11, Mar 1985 MZ (a) 2.00
❑12, Apr 1985; Giant-size; MZ (a);Conclusion 2.00

MARVEL SUPER SPECIAL
MARVEL

❑1, Sep 1977; O: Kiss (rock group). Group mixed drops of their blood into the printer's ink in publicity stunt 45.00
❑2, Mar 1978; Conan 6.00
❑3, Jun 1978; Close Encounters of the Third Kind 6.00
❑4, Aug 1978; The Beatles 20.00
❑5, Dec 1978; Title changes to Marvel Super Special; Jaws 2; Kiss 25.00
❑6, Dec 1978; Kiss; Jaws 2 ..... 4.00
❑7, Dec 1978; Sgt. Pepper's Lonely Hearts Club Band 3.00
❑8; Battlestar Galactica; tabloid 6.00
❑9, Feb 1979; Conan 5.00
❑10, Jun 1979; Star-Lord 5.00
❑11, Sep 1979; Warriors of Shadow Realm; Weirdworld 4.00
❑12, Nov 1979; Warriors of Shadow Realm; Weirdworld 4.00
❑13, Jan 1980; Warriors of Shadow Realm; Weirdworld 4.00
❑14, Feb 1980; GC, TP (a);Meteor 3.00
❑15, Mar 1980; Star Trek: The Motion Picture 5.00
❑16, Aug 1980; Empire Strikes Back 6.00
❑17, Nov 1980; Xanadu 3.50
❑18, Sep 1981; Raiders of the Lost Ark 3.50
❑19, Oct 1981; For Your Eyes Only 3.50
❑20, Oct 1981; Dragonslayer 3.50
❑21, Aug 1982; Conan movie 3.50
❑22, Sep 1982; Comic size; Blade Runner 3.50
❑23, Sep 1982; Annie 3.50
❑24, Mar 1983; Dark Crystal 3.50
❑25, Aug 1983; Comic size 3.50
❑26, Sep 1983; Octopussy 3.50
❑27, Sep 1983; Return of the Jedi 3.50
❑28, Oct 1983; Krull 3.50

	N-MINT
❑29, Jul 1984; Tarzan of the Apes	3.50
❑30, Aug 1984; Indiana Jones and the Temple of Doom	3.50
❑31, Sep 1984; The Last Starfighter	3.50
❑32, Oct 1984; The Muppets Take Manhattan	3.50
❑33, Nov 1984; Buckaroo Banzai	3.50
❑34, Nov 1984; Sheena	3.50
❑35, Dec 1984; Conan the Destroyer	3.50
❑36, Apr 1985; Dune	3.50
❑37, Apr 1985; 2010	3.50
❑38, Nov 1985; Red Sonja	3.50
❑39, Mar 1985; Santa Claus: the Movie	3.50
❑40, Oct 1986; Labyrinth	3.50
❑41, Nov 1986; Howard the Duck movie adaptation	3.50

MARVEL SWIMSUIT SPECIAL
MARVEL

	N-MINT
❑1, ca. 1992; 1992; in Wakanda	4.00
❑2, ca. 1993; 1993; on Monster Island	4.50
❑3, ca. 1994	4.50
❑4, ca. 1995	5.00

MARVEL TAILS
MARVEL

	N-MINT
❑1, Nov 1983 1: Peter Porker.	1.50

MARVEL TALES (2ND SERIES)
MARVEL

	N-MINT
❑1, ca. 1964; Giant-size; SL (w); SD, JK (a); O: Iron Man. O: Ant-Man. O: Spider-Man. O: The Hulk. O: Giant-Man. 1: Spider-Man. Amazing Fantasy #15; Listed as Marvel Tales Annual #1 in indicia	165.00
❑2, ca. 1965; Giant-size; O: X-Men. Reprints Uncanny X-Men #1, Incredible Hulk #3, Avengers #1	85.00
❑3, Jul 1966; Giant-size; reprints Amazing Spider-Man #6	40.00
❑4, Sep 1966; Giant-size; SD (a);Amazing Spider-Man #7	22.00
❑5, Nov 1966; Giant-size; SD (a);Amazing Spider-Man #8	22.00
❑6, Jan 1967; Giant-size; SD (a);Amazing Spider-Man #9	16.00
❑7, Mar 1967; Giant-size; SD (a);Amazing Spider-Man #10	16.00
❑8, May 1967; Giant-size; SD (a);Amazing Spider-Man #13	16.00
❑9, Jul 1967; Giant-size; SD (a);Amazing Spider-Man #14	16.00
❑10, Sep 1967; Giant-size; SD (a);Amazing Spider-Man #15	15.00
❑11, Nov 1967; Giant-size; SD (a);Amazing Spider-Man #16	10.00
❑12, Jan 1968; Giant-size; SL (w); SD, DH (a); 1: the Trapster (Paste-Pot Pete). Reprints stories from Amazing Spider-Man #17, Strange Tales #110, Tales to Astonish #58, Tales to Astonish #98	10.00
❑13, Mar 1968; Giant-size; SD (a); O: Marvel Boy. Amazing Spider-Man #18; Reprints Marvel Boy #1	10.00
❑14, May 1968; Giant-size; SD (a);Marvel Boy; Amazing Spider-Man #19	10.00
❑15, Jul 1968; Giant-size; SD (a);Marvel Boy; Amazing Spider-Man #20	10.00
❑16, Sep 1968; Giant-size; SD (a);Marvel Boy; Amazing Spider-Man #21	10.00
❑17, Nov 1968; Giant-size; SD (a);Amazing Spider-Man #22	10.00
❑18, Jan 1969; Giant-size; SD (a);Amazing Spider-Man #23	10.00
❑19, Mar 1969; Giant-size; SD (a);Amazing Spider-Man #24	10.00
❑20, May 1969; Giant-size; SD (a);Amazing Spider-Man #25	10.00
❑21, Jul 1969; Giant-size; SD (a);Amazing Spider-Man #26	8.00
❑22, Sep 1969; Giant-size; SD (a);Amazing Spider-Man #27	8.00
❑23, Nov 1969; Giant-size	8.00
❑24, Jan 1970; Giant-size; SD (a);Amazing Spider-Man #31	8.00
❑25, Mar 1970; Giant-size; SD (a);Amazing Spider-Man #32	8.00
❑26, May 1970; Giant-size; SD (a);Amazing Spider-Man #33	8.00
❑27, Jul 1970; Giant-size; SD (a);Amazing Spider-Man #34	8.00
❑28, Oct 1970; Giant-size; SD (a);Amazing Spider-Man #35 and #36	8.00
❑29, Jan 1971; Giant-size; JR (a); O: Green Goblin. Amazing Spider-Man #39 and #40	8.00
❑30, Apr 1971; Giant-size; JR (a);Amazing Spider-Man #58 and #41; conclusion of Angel back-up from Ka-Zar #3	8.00
❑31, Jul 1971; Giant-size; SD, JR (a);Amazing Spider-Man #37 and #42	8.00
❑32, Nov 1971; Last giant-size issue JR (a)	8.00
❑33, Feb 1972; JR (a);Amazing Spider-Man #45 and #47	3.00
❑34, Apr 1972; JR (a);Amazing Spider-Man #48	3.00
❑35, Jun 1972; JR (a);Amazing Spider-Man #49	3.00
❑36, Aug 1972; JR (a);Amazing Spider-Man #51	3.00
❑37, Sep 1972; JR (a);Amazing Spider-Man #52	3.00
❑38, Oct 1972; JR (a);Amazing Spider-Man #53	3.00
❑39, Nov 1972; JR (a);Amazing Spider-Man #54	3.00
❑40, Dec 1972; JR (a);Amazing Spider-Man #55	3.00
❑41, Feb 1973; JR (a);Amazing Spider-Man #56	3.00
❑42, Apr 1973; JR (a);Amazing Spider-Man #59	3.00
❑43, Jun 1973; JR (a);Amazing Spider-Man #60	3.00
❑44, Aug 1973	3.00
❑45, Sep 1973	3.00
❑46, Oct 1973	3.00
❑47, Nov 1973	3.00
❑48, Dec 1973	3.00
❑49, Feb 1974	3.00
❑50, Apr 1974	3.00
❑51, Jun 1974	2.50
❑52, Aug 1974	2.50
❑53, Sep 1974	2.50
❑54, Oct 1974	2.50
❑55, Nov 1974	2.50
❑56, Dec 1974	2.50
❑57, Feb 1975	2.50
❑58, Apr 1975	2.50
❑59, Jun 1975	2.50
❑60, Aug 1975	2.50
❑61, Sep 1975	2.50
❑62, Oct 1975	2.50
❑63, Nov 1975	2.50
❑64, Jan 1976	2.50
❑65, Mar 1976	2.50
❑66, Apr 1976	2.50
❑67, May 1976	2.50
❑67/30 cent, May 1976; 30 cent regional price variant	20.00
❑68, Jun 1976	2.50
❑68/30 cent, Jun 1976; 30 cent regional price variant	20.00
❑69, Jul 1976	2.50
❑69/30 cent, Jul 1976; 30 cent regional price variant	20.00
❑70, Aug 1976	2.50
❑70/30 cent, Aug 1976; 30 cent regional price variant	20.00
❑71, Sep 1976	2.00
❑72, Oct 1976	2.00
❑73, Nov 1976	2.00
❑74, Dec 1976	2.00
❑75, Jan 1977	2.00
❑76, Feb 1977	2.00
❑77, Mar 1977	2.00
❑78, Apr 1977	2.00
❑79, May 1977	2.00
❑80, Jun 1977	2.00
❑80/35 cent, Jun 1977; 35 cent regional price variant	15.00
❑81, Jul 1977	2.00
❑81/35 cent, Jul 1977; 35 cent regional price variant	15.00
❑82, Aug 1977	2.00
❑82/35 cent, Aug 1977; 35 cent regional price variant	15.00
❑83, Sep 1977	2.00
❑83/35 cent, Sep 1977; 35 cent regional price variant	15.00
❑84, Oct 1977	2.00
❑84/35 cent, Oct 1977; 35 cent regional price variant	15.00
❑85, Nov 1977	2.00
❑86, Dec 1977	2.00
❑87, Jan 1978	2.00
❑88, Feb 1978	2.00
❑89, Mar 1978	2.00
❑90, Apr 1978	2.00
❑91, May 1978	2.00
❑92, Jun 1978	2.00
❑93, Jul 1978	2.00
❑94, Aug 1978	2.00
❑95, Sep 1978	2.00
❑96, Oct 1978	2.00
❑97, Nov 1978	2.00
❑98, Dec 1978 D: Gwen Stacy.	5.00
❑99, Jan 1979 D: Green Goblin.	5.00
❑100, Feb 1979 MN, SD, GK, TD (a)	2.00
❑101, Mar 1979	2.00
❑102, Apr 1979	2.00
❑103, May 1979	2.00
❑104, Jun 1979	2.00
❑105, Jul 1979	2.00
❑106, Aug 1979; 1: Punisher. 1: Jackal. Reprints Amazing Spider-Man #129	4.00
❑107, Sep 1979	2.00
❑108, Oct 1979	2.00
❑109, Nov 1979	2.00
❑110, Dec 1979	2.00
❑111, Jan 1980; Punisher	2.00
❑112, Feb 1980; Punisher	2.00
❑113, Mar 1980	2.00
❑114, Apr 1980	2.00
❑115, May 1980	2.00
❑116, Jun 1980	2.00
❑117, Jul 1980	2.00
❑118, Aug 1980	2.00
❑119, Sep 1980	2.00
❑120, Oct 1980	2.00
❑121, Nov 1980	2.00
❑122, Dec 1980	2.00
❑123, Jan 1981	2.00
❑124, Feb 1981	2.00
❑125, Mar 1981	2.00
❑126, Apr 1981	2.00
❑127, May 1981	2.00
❑128, Jun 1981	2.00
❑129, Jul 1981	2.00
❑130, Aug 1981	2.00
❑131, Sep 1981	2.00
❑132, Oct 1981	2.00
❑133, Nov 1981	2.00
❑134, Dec 1981	2.00
❑135, Jan 1982	2.00
❑136, Feb 1982	2.00
❑137, Mar 1982; O: Spider-Man. 1: Spider-Man. Reprints Amazing Fantasy #15	5.00
❑138, Apr 1982; Reprints Amazing Spider-Man #1	5.00
❑139, May 1982; Reprints Amazing Spider-Man #2	3.00
❑140, Jun 1982; Reprints Amazing Spider-Man #3	3.00
❑141, Jul 1982; Reprints Amazing Spider-Man #4	3.00
❑142, Aug 1982; Reprints Amazing Spider-Man #5	3.00
❑143, Sep 1982; Reprints Amazing Spider-Man #6	3.00
❑144, Oct 1982; Reprints Amazing Spider-Man #7	3.00

	N-MINT
❑145, Nov 1982	2.00
❑146, Dec 1982	2.00
❑147, Jan 1983	2.00
❑148, Feb 1983	2.00
❑149, Mar 1983	2.00
❑150, Apr 1983; Giant-size	2.00
❑151, May 1983	2.00
❑152, Jun 1983	2.00
❑153, Jul 1983	2.00
❑154, Aug 1983	2.00
❑155, Sep 1983	2.00
❑156, Oct 1983	2.00
❑157, Nov 1983	2.00
❑158, Dec 1983	2.00
❑159, Jan 1984	2.00
❑160, Feb 1984	2.00
❑161, Mar 1984	2.00
❑162, Apr 1984	2.00
❑163, May 1984	2.00
❑164, Jun 1984	2.00
❑165, Jul 1984	2.00
❑166, Aug 1984	2.00
❑167, Sep 1984	2.00
❑168, Oct 1984	2.00
❑169, Nov 1984	2.00
❑170, Dec 1984	2.00
❑171, Jan 1985	2.00
❑172, Feb 1985	2.00
❑173, Mar 1985	2.00
❑174, Apr 1985	2.00
❑175, May 1985	2.00
❑176, Jun 1985	2.00
❑177, Jul 1985	2.00
❑178, Aug 1985	2.00
❑179, Sep 1985	2.00
❑180, Oct 1985	2.00
❑181, Nov 1985	2.00
❑182, Dec 1985	2.00
❑183, Jan 1986	2.00
❑184, Feb 1986	2.00
❑185, Mar 1986	2.00
❑186, Apr 1986	2.00
❑187, May 1986	2.00
❑188, Jun 1986	2.00
❑189, Jul 1986	2.00
❑190, Aug 1986	2.00
❑191, Sep 1986	2.00
❑192, Oct 1986; Giant-size; Reprints Amazing Spider-Man #121-122	2.00
❑193, Nov 1986	2.00
❑194, Dec 1986	2.00
❑195, Jan 1987	2.00
❑196, Feb 1987	2.00
❑197, Mar 1987	2.00
❑198, Apr 1987	2.00
❑199, May 1987	2.00
❑200, Jun 1987; Giant-size; TMc, FM (c); FM (a);Reprints Amazing Spider-Man Annual #14	2.00
❑201, Jul 1987 TMc (c)	1.50
❑202, Aug 1987 TMc (c)	1.50
❑203, Sep 1987 TMc (c)	1.50
❑204, Oct 1987 TMc (c)	1.50
❑205, Nov 1987 TMc (c)	1.50
❑206, Dec 1987 TMc (c)	1.50
❑207, Jan 1988 TMc (c)	1.50
❑208, Feb 1988 TMc (c)	1.50
❑209, Mar 1988 TMc (c); 1: Punisher. 1: Jackal.	2.00
❑210, Apr 1988 TMc (c); A: Punisher.	2.00
❑211, May 1988 TMc (c); A: Punisher.	1.50
❑212, Jun 1988 TMc (c); A: Punisher.	1.50
❑213, Jul 1988 TMc (c); A: Punisher.	1.50
❑214, Aug 1988 TMc (c); A: Punisher.	1.50
❑215, Sep 1988 TMc (c); A: Punisher.	1.50
❑216, Oct 1988 TMc (c); A: Punisher.	1.50
❑217, Nov 1988 TMc (c); A: Punisher.	1.50
❑218, Dec 1988 TMc (c); A: Punisher.	1.50
❑219, Jan 1989 TMc (c); A: Punisher.	1.50
❑220, Feb 1989 TMc (c); A: Punisher.	1.50
❑221, Mar 1989 TMc (c); A: Punisher.	1.50
❑222, Apr 1989 TMc (c); A: Punisher.	1.50

	N-MINT
❑223, May 1989 TMc (c); TMc (a)	1.50
❑224, Jun 1989 TMc (c); TMc (a)	1.50
❑225, Jul 1989 TMc (c); TMc (a)	1.50
❑226, Aug 1989 TMc (c); TMc (a)	1.50
❑227, Sep 1989 TMc (c); TMc (a)	1.50
❑228, Oct 1989 TMc (c); TMc (a)	1.50
❑229, Nov 1989 TMc (c); TMc (a)	1.50
❑230, Nov 1989 TMc (c); TMc (a)	1.50
❑231, Dec 1989 TMc (c); TMc (a)	1.50
❑232, Dec 1989 TMc (c); TMc (a)	1.50
❑233, Jan 1990 TMc (c); TMc (a)	1.50
❑234, Feb 1990 TMc (c); TMc (a)	1.50
❑235, Mar 1990 TMc (c); TMc (a)	1.50
❑236, Apr 1990 TMc (c); TMc (a)	1.50
❑237, May 1990 TMc (c); TMc (a)	1.50
❑238, Jun 1990 TMc (c); TMc (a)	1.50
❑239, Jul 1990 TMc (c); TMc (a)	1.50
❑240, Aug 1990	1.50
❑241, Sep 1990	1.50
❑242, Oct 1990	1.50
❑243, Nov 1990	1.50
❑244, Dec 1990	1.50
❑245, Jan 1991	1.50
❑246, Feb 1991	1.50
❑247, Mar 1991	1.50
❑248, Apr 1991	1.50
❑249, May 1991 GK (a)	1.50
❑250, Jun 1991; Giant-size; FM (c); FM (a); O: Storm. Reprints Marvel Team-Up #100	1.50
❑251, Jul 1991 GK (a)	1.50
❑252, Aug 1991; GK, SL (w); GK (a); 1: Morbius. Reprints Amazing Spider-Man #101	1.50
❑253, Sep 1991; Giant-size; GK, SL (w); GK (a); O: Morbius. Reprints Amazing Spider-Man #102	1.50
❑254, Oct 1991 RA (a); A: Ghost Rider.	1.50
❑255, Nov 1991 SB (a)	1.50
❑256, Dec 1991 PB (a); A: Ghost Rider.	1.50
❑257, Jan 1992 JR2, JR (a)	1.50
❑258, Feb 1992 JR2 (a)	1.50
❑259, Mar 1992 JR2 (a)	1.50
❑260, Apr 1992 JR2, KJ (a)	1.50
❑261, May 1992 KJ (a)	1.50
❑262, Jun 1992; JBy (a); A: X-Men. X-Men	1.50
❑263, Jul 1992 JBy (a); O: Woodgod.	1.50
❑264, Aug 1992; reprints Amazing Spider-Man Annual #5	1.50
❑265, Sep 1992; reprints Amazing Spider-Man Annual #6	1.50
❑266, Oct 1992	1.50
❑267, Nov 1992	1.50
❑268, Dec 1992	1.50
❑269, Jan 1993	1.50
❑270, Feb 1993	1.50
❑271, Mar 1993; Reprints Amazing Spider-Man #257	1.50
❑272, Apr 1993	1.50
❑273, May 1993	1.50
❑274, Jun 1993	1.50
❑275, Jul 1993	1.50
❑276, Aug 1993 A: Spider-Kid.	1.50
❑277, Sep 1993 1: Silver Sable.	1.50
❑278, Oct 1993; A: Kingpin. A: Beyonder. Reprints Amazing Spider-Man #268	1.50
❑279, Nov 1993 A: Firelord.	1.50
❑280, Dec 1993	1.50
❑281, Jan 1994	1.50
❑282, Feb 1994 SB (a)	1.50
❑283, Mar 1994; double-sized; O: Spider-Man. Reprints Amazing Spider-Man #275; Hobgoblin story	1.50
❑284, Apr 1994; A: Hobgoblin. D: Fly. Reprints Amazing Spider-Man #276	1.50
❑285, May 1994; Reprints Amazing Spider-Man #277	1.50
❑286, Jun 1994; PD (a); D: Wraith. Reprints Amazing Spider-Man #278	1.50
❑286/CS, Jun 1994; PD (a); Collector's Set;Reprints Amazing Spider-Man #278	2.95

An economical way to collect early Marvel stories is through its longest-running reprint series, *Marvel Tales*.

© 1966 Marvel Comics.

	N-MINT
❑286-2, Jun 1994; set; Includes animation cel, 16 page preview	2.95
❑287, Jul 1994; cover/story; Reprints Amazing Spider-Man #279	1.50
❑288, Aug 1994; Reprints Amazing Spider-Man #280	1.50
❑289, Sep 1994; A: Jack O'Lantern. Reprints Amazing Spider-Man #281	1.50
❑290, Oct 1994; A: X-Factor. Reprints Amazing Spider-Man #282	1.50
❑291, Nov 1994; BL (a);Amazing Spider-Man #283	1.50

MARVEL TEAM-UP
MARVEL

	N-MINT
❑1, Mar 1972; GK (c); RA (a); 1: Misty Knight. V: Sandman. Spider-Man; Human Torch	150.00
❑2, May 1972; GK (c); RA, JM (a); A: Human Torch. Spider-Man; Human Torch	32.00
❑3, Jul 1972; GK (c); RA (a); A: Morbius. Spider-Man; Human Torch	32.00
❑4, Sep 1972; GK (a); A: Morbius. Spider-Man; X-Men	32.00
❑5, Nov 1972; GK (a); 1: Ballox (The Monstroid). 1: Ballox ("The Monstroid"). Spider-Man; Vision	16.00
❑6, Jan 1973; GK (a); O: Puppet Master. Spider-Man; Thing	16.00
❑7, Mar 1973; GK (c); RA, JM (a); 1: Kryllk the Cruel. Spider-Man; Thor	16.00
❑8, Apr 1973; JM (a); 1: The Man-Killer. Spider-Man; The Cat	16.00
❑9, May 1973; JR (c); RA (a); A: Iron Man. Spider-Man; Iron Man	16.00
❑10, Jun 1973; JR (c); JM (a); A: Human Torch. Spider-Man; Human Torch	16.00
❑11, Jul 1973; JR (c); JM (a); A: The Inhumans. Spider-Man; Inhumans	13.00
❑12, Aug 1973; GK (c); DP, RA (a); 1: Moondark. Spider-Man; Werewolf	13.00
❑13, Sep 1973; GK (a); A: Captain America. Spider-Man; Captain America	13.00
❑14, Oct 1973; GK, WH (a); 1: The Aquanoids. Spider-Man; Sub-Mariner	13.00
❑15, Nov 1973; GK (c); DP, RA (a); O: Orb. 1: Orb. Spider-Man; Ghost Rider	13.00
❑16, Dec 1973; GK, JM (a); O: The Basilisk I (Basil Elks). 1: The Basilisk I (Basil Elks). Spider-Man; Captain Marvel	13.00
❑17, Jan 1974; GK (a); V: Basilisk. V: Mole Man. Spider-Man; Mr. Fantastic	13.00
❑18, Feb 1974; GK (a); A: The Hulk. Human Torch; Hulk	13.00
❑19, Mar 1974; GK (a); 1: Stegron, the Dinosaur Man. Spider-Man; Ka-Zar; Marvel Value Stamp #90: Hercules	13.00
❑20, Apr 1974; GK (c); SB (a); A: Black Panther. Spider-Man; Black Panther; Marvel Value Stamp #25: Torch	13.00
❑21, May 1974; GK (c); SB (a); A: Doctor Strange. Spider-Man; Doctor Strange; Marvel Value Stamp #33: Invisible Girl	8.00
❑22, Jun 1974; JR (c); SB (a); A: Hawkeye. Spider-Man; Hawkeye; Marvel Value Stamp #92: Byrrah	8.00

Condition price index: Multiply "NM prices" above by: **0.83 for Very Fine/Near Mint**
0.66 for Very Fine • 0.33 for Fine • 0.2 for Very Good • 0.125 for Good

	N-MINT
❑23, Jul 1974; GK (a); A: X-Men. Human Torch; Iceman; X-Men; Marvel Value Stamp #28: Hawkeye	8.00
❑24, Aug 1974; GK (c); JM (a); A: Brother Voodoo. Spider-Man; Brother Voodoo; Marvel Value Stamp #90: Hercules	8.00
❑25, Sep 1974; GK (c); JM (a); A: Daredevil. Spider-Man; Daredevil; Marvel Value Stamp #87: J. Jonah Jameson	8.00
❑26, Oct 1974; GK (c); JM (a); A: Thor. Human Torch; Thor; Marvel Value Stamp #56: Rawhide Kid	8.00
❑27, Nov 1974; JSn (c); JM (a); A: The Hulk. Spider-Man; Hulk; Marvel Value Stamp #68: Son of Satan	8.00
❑28, Dec 1974; GK (c); JM (a); A: Hercules. Spider-Man; Hercules; Marvel Value Stamp #43: Enchantress	8.00
❑29, Jan 1975; JR (c); JM (a); A: Iron Man. Human Torch; Iron Man; Marvel Value Stamp #11: Deathlok	8.00
❑30, Feb 1975; GK (c); JM (a); A: Falcon. Spider-Man; The Falcon; Marvel Value Stamp #89: Hammerhead	8.00
❑31, Mar 1975; GK (c); JM (a); A: Iron Fist. Spider-Man; Iron Fist	8.00
❑32, Apr 1975; GK (c); SB (a); A: Son of Satan. Human Torch; Son of Satan	5.00
❑33, May 1975; GK (c); SB (a); V: Meteor Man. Spider-Man; Nighthawk; Marvel Value Stamp #84: Dr. Doom	5.00
❑34, Jun 1975; GK (c); SB (a); V: Meteor Man. Spider-Man; Valkyrie	5.00
❑35, Jul 1975; GK (c); SB (a); A: Doctor Strange. Human Torch; Doctor Strange	5.00
❑36, Aug 1975; SB (a); A: Frankenstein. Spider-Man; Frankenstein	5.00
❑37, Sep 1975; SB (a); A: Man-Wolf. Spider-Man; Man-Wolf	5.00
❑38, Oct 1975; SB (a); A: Beast. Spider-Man; Beast	5.00
❑39, Nov 1975; SB (a); A: Human Torch. Spider-Man; Human Torch; Marvel Value Stamp #87: J. Jonah Jameson	5.00
❑40, Dec 1975; SB (a); A: Sons of the Tiger. Spider-Man; Sons of Tiger; Human Torch;	5.00
❑41, Jan 1976; GK (c); SB (a); A: Scarlet Witch. Spider-Man; Scarlet Witch	5.00
❑42, Feb 1976; SB (a); A: Vision. Spider-Man; Scarlet Witch; Vision	5.00
❑43, Mar 1976; GK (c); SB (a); A: Doctor Doom. Spider-Man; Doctor Doom	5.00
❑44, Apr 1976; GK (c); SB (a); A: Moondragon. Spider-Man; Moondragon	5.00
❑44/30 cent, Apr 1976 A: Moondragon.	20.00
❑45, May 1976; GK (c); SB (a); A: Killraven. Spider-Man; Killraven	5.00
❑45/30 cent, May 1976 A: Killraven.	20.00
❑46, Jun 1976; RB (c); SB (a); A: Deathlok. Spider-Man; Deathlok	5.00
❑46/30 cent, Jun 1976 A: Deathlok.	20.00
❑47, Jul 1976; GK (c); V: Basilisk. Spider-Man; Thing	3.50
❑47/30 cent, Jul 1976 V: Basilisk.	20.00
❑48, Aug 1976; JR (c); SB (a); 1: Wraith. Spider-Man; Iron Man	3.50
❑48/30 cent, Aug 1976 1: Wraith.	20.00
❑49, Sep 1976; JR (c); SB (a); O: Wraith. Spider-Man; Iron Man; Doctor Strange	3.50
❑50, Oct 1976; GK (c); SB (w); SB (a); A: Iron Man. Spider-Man; Doctor Strange; Iron Man	3.50
❑51, Nov 1976; GK (c); SB (a); A: Iron Man. Spider-Man; Iron Man	3.50
❑52, Dec 1976; SB (a); A: Batroc. Spider-Man; Captain America	3.50
❑53, Jan 1977; DC (c); JBy (a); A: X-Men. A: Woodgod. Spider-Man; Hulk; Woodgod; X-Men; 1st John Byrne art on X-Men	15.00
❑54, Feb 1977; GK (c); JBy (a); A: Woodgod. Spider-Man; Hulk	4.00
❑55, Mar 1977; DC (c); JBy (a); 1: the Gardener. V: Gardener. Spider-Man; Warlock	4.00
❑56, Apr 1977; JR2 (c); SB (a); V: Blizzard. V: Electro. Spider-Man; Daredevil	4.00
❑57, May 1977; DC (c); SB (a); A: Black Widow. Spider-Man; Black Widow	4.00
❑58, Jun 1977; AM (c); SB (a); A: Ghost Rider. Spider-Man; Ghost Rider	4.00
❑58/35 cent, Jun 1977; AM (c); SB (a); A: Ghost Rider. 35 cent regional price variant; Spider-Man; Ghost Rider	15.00
❑59, Jul 1977; DC (c); JBy (a); A: Wasp. Spider-Man; Yellowjacket; The Wasp	4.00
❑59/35 cent, Jul 1977; DC (c); JBy (a); A: Wasp. 35 cent regional price variant; Spider-Man; Yellowjacket; The Wasp	15.00
❑60, Aug 1977; AM (c); JBy (a); A: Yellowjacket. Spider-Man; The Wasp	4.00
❑60/35 cent, Aug 1977; AM (c); JBy (a); A: Yellowjacket. 35 cent regional price variant; Spider-Man; The Wasp	15.00
❑61, Sep 1977; RA (c); JBy (a); V: Super-Skrull. Spider-Man; Human Torch	4.00
❑61/35 cent, Sep 1977; RA (c); JBy (a); V: Super-Skrull. 35 cent regional price variant; Spider-Man; Human Torch	15.00
❑62, Oct 1977; GK (c); JBy (a); V: Super-Skrull. Spider-Man; Ms. Marvel	4.00
❑62/35 cent, Oct 1977; GK (c); JBy (a); V: Super-Skrull. 35 cent regional price variant; Spider-Man; Ms. Marvel	15.00
❑63, Nov 1977; DC (c); JBy (a); A: Iron Fist. Spider-Man; Iron Fist	4.00
❑64, Dec 1977; DC (c); JBy (a); A: Daughters of the Dragon. Spider-Man; Daughters of the Dragon	4.00
❑65, Jan 1978; GP (c); JBy (a); 1: Arcade. 1: Captain Britain (U.S.). Spider-Man; Captain Britain	4.00
❑66, Feb 1978; JBy (a); V: Arcade. Spider-Man; Captain Britain	7.00
❑67, Mar 1978; JBy (a); A: Tigra. V: Kraven. Spider-Man; Tigra	4.00
❑68, Apr 1978; JBy (a); 1: D'Spayre. A: Man-Thing. Spider-Man; Man-Thing	4.00
❑69, May 1978; DC (c); JBy (a); A: Havok. Spider-Man; Havok	4.00
❑70, Jun 1978; JBy (a); V: Living Monolith. Spider-Man; Thor	4.00
❑71, Jul 1978; A: The Falcon. Spider-Man; The Falcon	4.00
❑72, Aug 1978; JBy (c); JM (a); A: Iron Man. Spider-Man; Iron Man	4.00
❑73, Sep 1978; KP (c); A: Daredevil. Spider-Man; Daredevil	4.00
❑74, Oct 1978; DC (c); BH (a); A: Not Ready For Prime Time Players (Saturday Night Live). Spider-Man; The Not-Ready-For-Prime-Time-Players (SNL)	4.00
❑75, Nov 1978; BH (c); JBy (a); A: Power Man. Spider-Man; Power Man	4.00
❑76, Dec 1978; JBy (c); HC (a); A: Doctor Strange. Spider-Man; Doctor Strange	4.00
❑77, Jan 1979; JR2 (c); HC (a); A: Ms. Marvel. Spider-Man; Ms. Marvel	4.00
❑78, Feb 1979; AM (c); DP (a); A: Wonder Man. Spider-Man; Wonder Man	4.00
❑79, Mar 1979; JBy (a); A: Red Sonja. Spider-Man; Red Sonja	4.00
❑80, Apr 1979; RB (c); A: Clea. Spider-Man; Doctor Strange; Clea	4.00
❑81, May 1979; AM (c); D: Satana. Spider-Man; Satana	4.00
❑82, Jun 1979; RB (c); SB (a); A: Black Widow. Spider-Man; Black Widow	4.00
❑83, Jul 1979; RB (c); SB (a); A: Nick Fury. Spider-Man; Nick Fury	4.00
❑84, Aug 1979; SB (a); A: Shang-Chi. Spider-Man; Shang-Chi	4.00
❑85, Sep 1979; AM (c); SB (a); A: Nick Fury. Spider-Man; Shang-Chi; Nick Fury; Black Widow	4.00
❑86, Oct 1979; BMc (a); A: Guardians of the Galaxy. Spider-Man; Guardians of Galaxy	4.00
❑87, Nov 1979; AM (c); GC (a); 1: Hellrazor. Spider-Man; Black Panther	4.00
❑88, Dec 1979; RB (c); SB (a); A: Invisible Girl. Spider-Man; Invisible Girl	4.00
❑89, Jan 1980; MN, RB (a); 1: Cutthroat. Spider-Man; Nightcrawler	4.00
❑90, Feb 1980; AM (c); A: Beast. Spider-Man; Beast	4.00
❑91, Mar 1980; RB (c); PB (a); A: Ghost Rider. Spider-Man; Ghost Rider	4.00
❑92, Apr 1980; AM (c); CI (a); 1: Mister Fear IV (Alan Fagan). Spider-Man; Hawkeye	4.00
❑93, May 1980; DP (c); TS, CI (a); A: Werewolf. Spider-Man; Werewolf by Night	4.00
❑94, Jun 1980; AM (c); MZ (a); A: The Shroud. Spider-Man; Shroud	4.00
❑95, Jul 1980; FM (c); FM (a); 1: Mockingbird. 1: Huntress as Mockingbird. Spider-Man	3.00
❑96, Aug 1980; A: Howard the Duck. Spider-Man; Howard the Duck	3.00
❑97, Sep 1980; CI (a); A: Spider-Woman. Hulk; Spider-Woman	3.00
❑98, Oct 1980; AM (c); A: Black Widow. Spider-Man; Black Widow	3.00
❑99, Nov 1980; FM (c); FM (a); A: Machine Man. Spider-Man; Machine Man	3.00
❑100, Dec 1980; double-sized; FM (w); JBy, FM (a); O: Karma. O: Storm. 1: Karma. Spider-Man; Fantastic Four; Black Panther	6.00
❑101, Jan 1981; A: Nighthawk. Spider-Man; Nighthawk	3.00
❑102, Feb 1981; FM (c); FS (a); A: Doctor Samson. Spider-Man; Doc Samson	3.00
❑103, Mar 1981; A: Ant-Man. Spider-Man; Ant-Man	3.00
❑104, Apr 1981; AM (c); A: The Hulk. Hulk; Ka-Zar	3.00
❑105, May 1981; AM (c); CI (a); A: . A: Power Man and Iron Fist. Power Man; Iron Fist; Hulk	3.00
❑106, Jun 1981; FM (c); HT (a); V: Scorpion. Spider-Man; Captain America	3.00
❑107, Jul 1981; HT (a); A: She-Hulk. Spider-Man; She-Hulk	3.00
❑108, Aug 1981; HT (a); A: Paladin. Spider-Man; Paladin	3.00
❑109, Sep 1981; JR2 (c); HT (a); A: Dazzler. Spider-Man; Dazzler	3.00
❑110, Oct 1981; BL (c); HT (a); A: Iron Man. Spider-Man; Iron Man	3.00
❑111, Nov 1981; HT (a); A: Devil-Slayer. Spider-Man; Devil-Slayer	3.00
❑112, Dec 1981; HT (a); A: King Kull. Spider-Man; King Kull	3.00
❑113, Jan 1982; A: Quasar. Spider-Man; Quasar	3.00
❑114, Feb 1982; A: The Falcon. Spider-Man; The Falcon	3.00
❑115, Mar 1982; A: Thor. Spider-Man; Thor	3.00
❑116, Apr 1982; A: Valkyrie. Spider-Man; Valkyrie	3.00
❑117, May 1982; 1: Professor Power. Spider-Man; Wolverine	3.00
❑118, Jun 1982; HT (a); O: Professor Power. Spider-Man; Professor X	3.00
❑119, Jul 1982; KGa (a); A: Gargoyle. Spider-Man; Gargoyle	3.00
❑120, Aug 1982; KGa (a); A: Dominic Fortune. Spider-Man; Dominic Fortune	3.00
❑121, Sep 1982; KGa (a); 1: Frog-Man II. Spider-Man; Human Torch	3.00
❑122, Oct 1982; KGa (a); A: Man-Thing. Man-Thing	3.00
❑123, Nov 1982; KGa (a); A: Daredevil. Man-Thing; Daredevil	3.00
❑124, Dec 1982; KGa (a); O: Professor Power. Spider-Man; The Beast	3.00
❑125, Jan 1983; KGa (a); A: Tigra. Spider-Man; Tigra	3.00

Condition price index: Multiply "NM prices" above by: **0.83 for Very Fine/Near Mint**
0.66 for Very Fine • 0.33 for Fine • 0.2 for Very Good • 0.125 for Good

N-MINT

- ❑126, Feb 1983; BH (a); A: Son of Satan. Spider-Man; Hulk; Power Man; Son of Satan 3.00
- ❑127, Mar 1983; KGa (a); A: The Watcher. Spider-Man; The Watcher 3.00
- ❑128, Apr 1983; A: Captain America. Spider-Man; Captain America 3.00
- ❑129, May 1983; KGa (a); A: Vision. Spider-Man; Vision; The Vision 3.00
- ❑130, Jun 1983; SB (a); A: Scarlet Witch. Spider-Man; Scarlet Witch; The Scarlet Witch 3.00
- ❑131, Jul 1983; KGa (a); A: Frogman. Spider-Man; Frogman 3.00
- ❑132, Aug 1983; A: Mr. Fantastic. Spider-Man; Mr. Fantastic 3.00
- ❑133, Sep 1983; SB (a); A: Fantastic Four. Spider-Man; Fantastic Four ... 3.00
- ❑134, Oct 1983; A: Jack of Hearts. Spider-Man; Jack of Hearts 3.00
- ❑135, Nov 1983; A: Kitty Pryde. Spider-Man; Kitty Pryde 3.00
- ❑136, Dec 1983; A: Wonder Man. Spider-Man; Wonder Man 3.00
- ❑137, Jan 1984; O: Doctor Faustus. Spider-Man; Aunt May; Franklin Richards; Assistant Editor's Month 3.00
- ❑138, Feb 1984; A: Sandman. Spider-Man; Sandman (Marvel); Nick Fury 3.00
- ❑139, Mar 1984; A: Nick Fury. Spider-Man; Sandman (Marvel); Nick Fury 3.00
- ❑140, Apr 1984; A: Black Widow. Spider-Man; Black Widow 3.00
- ❑141, May 1984; A: Daredevil. Spider-Man new costume; Daredevil 3.00
- ❑142, Jun 1984; A: Captain Marvel. Spider-Man; Captain Marvel (female, new) 3.00
- ❑143, Jul 1984; A: Starfox. Spider-Man; Starfox 3.00
- ❑144, Aug 1984; A: Moon Knight. Spider-Man; Moon Knight 3.00
- ❑145, Sep 1984; A: Iron Man. Spider-Man; Iron Man 3.00
- ❑146, Oct 1984; A: Nomad. Spider-Man; Nomad 3.00
- ❑147, Nov 1984; A: Human Torch. Spider-Man; Human Torch 3.00
- ❑148, Dec 1984; A: Thor. Spider-Man; Thor 3.00
- ❑149, Jan 1985; A: Cannonball. Spider-Man; Cannonball 3.00
- ❑150, Feb 1985; Giant-size; A: the X-Men. Spider-Man; X-Men 3.00
- ❑Annual 1, ca. 1976; DC (c); SB (a); Spider-Man; X-Men 30.00
- ❑Annual 2, ca. 1979; AM (c); SB (a);Spider-Man; Hulk 6.00
- ❑Annual 3, ca. 1980; FM (c); HT, FM (a);Hulk; Power Man; Iron Fist; Machine Man 4.00
- ❑Annual 4, ca. 1981; FM (c); FM (w); HT, FM (a);Spider-Man; Iron Fist; Power Man; Daredevil; Moon Knight 3.00
- ❑Annual 5, Nov 1981; Spider-Man; Thing; Scarlet Witch; Vision; Quasar 2.50
- ❑Annual 6, Oct 1983; New Mutants; Cloak & Dagger 2.50
- ❑Annual 7, Oct 1984; Alpha Flight 2.00

MARVEL TEAM-UP (2ND SERIES)

MARVEL

- ❑1, Sep 1997; gatefold summary; Spider-Man; Generation X; Story takes place before Generation X #32 ...... 2.00
- ❑2, Oct 1997; gatefold summary; AM (a);Spider-Man; Hercules 2.00
- ❑3, Nov 1997; gatefold summary; A: Silver Sable. Spider-Man; Sandman 2.00
- ❑4, Dec 1997; gatefold summary; Spider-Man; Man-Thing 2.00
- ❑5, Jan 1998; A: Authority. V: Authority. Spider-Man 2.00
- ❑6, Feb 1998; A: Wrecking Crew. V: Wrecking Crew. Spider-Man; Sub-Mariner 2.00
- ❑7, Mar 1998; Spider-Man; Blade 2.00
- ❑8, Apr 1998; Sub-Mariner; Doctor Strange 2.00

N-MINT

- ❑9, May 1998; Sub-Mariner; Captain America 2.00
- ❑10, Jun 1998; Sub-Mariner; Thing .. 2.00
- ❑11, Jul 1998; A: Wrecking Crew. V: Wrecking Crew. Sub-Mariner; Iron Man 2.00

MARVEL: THE LOST GENERATION

MARVEL

- ❑12, Mar 2000; #1 in sequence 2.95
- ❑11, Apr 2000; #2 in sequence 2.95
- ❑10, May 2000; #3 in sequence 2.95
- ❑9, Jun 2000; #4 in sequence 2.95
- ❑8, Jul 2000; #5 in sequence 2.95
- ❑7, Aug 2000; #6 in sequence 2.95
- ❑6, Sep 2000; #7 in sequence 2.95
- ❑5, Oct 2000; #8 in sequence 2.95
- ❑4, Nov 2000; #9 in sequence 2.95
- ❑3, Dec 2000; #10 in sequence 2.95
- ❑2, Jan 2001; #11 in sequence 2.95
- ❑1, Feb 2001; #12 in sequence 2.95

MARVEL TREASURY EDITION

MARVEL

- ❑1, ca. 1974; SD (a);The Spectacular Spider-Man 15.00
- ❑2, Dec 1974; SL (w); JK (a); 1: Galactus. 1: The Silver Surfer. A: Sub-Mariner. The Fabulous Fantastic Four; Reprints early Fantastic Four issues 10.00
- ❑3, ca. 1974; SL (w); JK (a); V: Hercules. The Mighty Thor; reprints Thor #125-130 .... 10.00
- ❑4, ca. 1975; Conan 10.00
- ❑5, ca. 1975; SL (w); JSn, HT, JSe, JSt, DA (a);reprints Hulk #3, 139, 141, Tales to Astonish #79, 100, and Marvel Feature #11 .... 10.00
- ❑6, ca. 1975; SL (w); SD, GC, FB, BEv, DA (a); O: The Ancient One. Doctor Strange 10.00
- ❑7, ca. 1975; Avengers 10.00
- ❑8, Hol 1975; SL (w); SD, GC, HT, GT, FS (a);Giant Super-Hero Holiday Grab Bag; The Incredible Hulk #147, Luke Cage, Hero for Hire #7 .... 10.00
- ❑9, ca. 1976; JB, SL (w); JB, JK (a);Giant Superhero Team-up; Reprints Prince Namor, the Sub-Mariner #8, Journey into Mystery #112, Silver Surfer (Vol. 1) #14, Daredevil #43; Namor vs. Human Torch; Daredevil vs. Captain America; Thor vs. Hulk; Silver Surfer vs. Spider-Man 10.00
- ❑10, ca. 1976; SL (w); JK (a);The Mighty Thor; Reprints Thor #154-157 .... 10.00
- ❑11, ca. 1976; FF (a);Fantastic Four .. 10.00
- ❑12, ca. 1976; Reprints Howard the Duck #1, Giant-Size Man-Thing #4, 5, with new Defenders story; FB, VM, SB, TP, KJ (a);Howard the Duck 10.00
- ❑13, ca. 1976; Giant Super-Hero Holiday Grab-Bag 10.00
- ❑14, ca. 1977; Amazing Spider-Man; reprints Amazing Spider-Man #100-102 and Not Brand Echh #6 .... 10.00
- ❑15, ca. 1977; Conan; Red Sonja 10.00
- ❑16, ca. 1977; Defenders 10.00
- ❑17, ca. 1978; SB, HT, JSe (a);The Incredible Hulk; Reprints The Incredible Hulk #121, 134, 150 .... 10.00
- ❑18, ca. 1978; Spider-Man; X-Men ... 10.00
- ❑19, ca. 1978; Conan 10.00
- ❑20 1979; Hulk; reprints Incredible Hulk #136, 137, 143, 144; pin-up gallery 10.00
- ❑21, ca. 1979; FF (a);Fantastic Four .. 10.00
- ❑22, ca. 1979; Spider-Man 10.00
- ❑23, ca. 1979; Conan 10.00
- ❑24 1979; Incredible Hulk; reprints Incredible Hulk #167-170; Wolverine and Hercules new back-up story ... 10.00
- ❑25, ca. 1980; Spider-Man and Hulk at Winter Olympics 10.00
- ❑26, ca. 1980; Hulk; Wolverine; Hercules 12.00

Marvel Team-Up #53 contains John Byrne's first X-Men art.

© 1977 Marvel Comics.

N-MINT

- ❑27, ca. 1980; Marvel Team-Up; reprints MTU #9-11 and 27; new Angel story 10.00
- ❑28, Jul 1981; A: Wonder Woman. A: Hulk. V: Parasite. V: Doctor Doom. Spider-Man and Superman 25.00

MARVEL TREASURY OF OZ

MARVEL

- ❑1, ca. 1975; adapts Baum's Land of Oz 15.00

MARVEL TREASURY SPECIAL FEATURING CAPTAIN AMERICA'S BICENTENNIAL BATTLES

MARVEL

- ❑1, ca. 1976; JK (w); JK (a);Captain America's Bicentennial Battles 16.00

MARVEL TREASURY SPECIAL, GIANT SUPERHERO HOLIDAY GRAB-BAG

MARVEL

- ❑1, ca. 1974; SL (w); GC, JK, WW, RA (a);Giant Super-Hero Holiday Grab Bag; reprints Marvel Team-Up #1, Fantastic Four #25-26, Daredevil #7, and Amazing Adventures 10.00

MARVEL TRIPLE ACTION

MARVEL

- ❑1, Feb 1972; JK, JSt (a);reprints Fantastic Four #55 and #57 .... 5.00
- ❑2, Apr 1972; JK, JSt (a);reprints Fantastic Four #58 .... 3.00
- ❑3, Jun 1972; JK, JSt (a);reprints Fantastic Four #59 .... 3.00
- ❑4, Aug 1972; JK, JSt (a);reprints Fantastic Four #60 .... 3.00
- ❑5, Sep 1972 .... 3.00
- ❑6, Oct 1972 SL (w); DH (a) 2.00
- ❑7, Nov 1972 .... 2.00
- ❑8, Jan 1973 .... 2.00
- ❑9, Feb 1973 .... 2.00
- ❑10, Apr 1973 .... 2.00
- ❑11, Jun 1973 .... 2.00
- ❑12, Aug 1973 .... 2.00
- ❑13, Sep 1973 .... 2.00
- ❑14, Oct 1973 SL (w); DH (a) 2.00
- ❑15, Nov 1973 .... 2.00
- ❑16, Jan 1974 .... 2.00
- ❑17, Mar 1974 .... 2.00
- ❑18, May 1974 .... 2.00
- ❑19, Jul 1974 .... 2.00
- ❑20, Sep 1974 .... 2.00
- ❑21, Oct 1974 .... 2.00
- ❑22, Nov 1974; SL (w); DH (a);reprints Avengers #28 .... 2.00
- ❑23, Jan 1975 .... 2.00
- ❑24, Mar 1975 .... 2.00
- ❑25, Sep 1975 .... 2.00
- ❑26, Nov 1975 .... 2.00
- ❑27, Jan 1976 .... 2.00
- ❑28, Mar 1976 .... 2.00
- ❑29, May 1976 .... 2.00
- ❑29/30 cent, May 1976; 30 cent regional price variant 20.00
- ❑30, Jul 1976 .... 2.00
- ❑30/30 cent, Jul 1976; 30 cent regional price variant 20.00
- ❑31, Sep 1976 .... 2.00
- ❑32, Nov 1976 .... 2.00
- ❑33, Jan 1977 .... 2.00
- ❑34, Mar 1977 .... 2.00
- ❑35, May 1977 .... 2.00

	N-MINT
❑36, Jul 1977	2.00
❑37, Sep 1977	2.00
❑38, Nov 1977	2.00
❑39, Jan 1978	2.00
❑40, Mar 1978	2.00
❑41, Apr 1978	2.00
❑42, Jun 1978	2.00
❑43, Aug 1978	2.00
❑44, Oct 1978	2.00
❑45, Dec 1978 A: X-Men.	2.00
❑46, Feb 1979	2.00
❑47, Apr 1979	2.00
❑Giant Size 1, ca. 1975	4.00
❑Giant Size 2, ca. 1975	4.00

MARVEL TWO-IN-ONE
Marvel

	N-MINT
❑1, Jan 1974; Man-Thing	22.00
❑2, Mar 1974; Namor; Marvel Value Stamp #63: Sub-Mariner	9.00
❑3, May 1974; A: Black Widow. Daredevil; Marvel Value Stamp #89: Hammerhead	7.00
❑4, Jul 1974; Captain America; Marvel Value Stamp #88: Leader	7.00
❑5, Sep 1974; Guardians of the Galaxy; Marvel Value Stamp #93: Silver Surfer	8.00
❑6, Nov 1974; Doctor Strange; Marvel Value Stamp #47: Green Goblin	8.00
❑7, Jan 1975; A: Doctor Strange. Valkyrie; Marvel Value Stamp #45: Mantis	5.00
❑8, Mar 1975; Ghost Rider	5.00
❑9, May 1975; Thor	5.00
❑10, Jul 1975; Black Widow	5.00
❑11, Sep 1975; Golem	3.00
❑12, Nov 1975; Iron Man; Marvel Value Stamp #45: Mantis	3.00
❑13, Jan 1976; Power Man	3.00
❑14, Mar 1976; Son of Satan	3.00
❑15, May 1976; Morbius	3.00
❑15/30 cent, May 1976; 30 cent regional price variant	20.00
❑16, Jun 1976; Ka-Zar	3.00
❑16/30 cent, Jun 1976; 30 cent regional price variant	20.00
❑17, Jul 1976; A: Basilisk I (Basil Elks). Spider-Man	3.00
❑17/30 cent, Jul 1976; 30 cent regional price variant	20.00
❑18, Aug 1976; Scarecrow; Spider-Man	3.00
❑18/30 cent, Aug 1976; 30 cent regional price variant; Scarecrow; Spider-Man	20.00
❑19, Sep 1976; Tigra	3.00
❑20, Oct 1976; Liberty Legion; continued from Marvel Two-In-One Annual #1	3.00
❑21, Nov 1976; A: Human Torch. Doc Savage	3.00
❑22, Dec 1976; Human Torch; Thor	3.00
❑23, Jan 1977; Human Torch; Thor	3.00
❑24, Feb 1977; SB (a);Black Goliath	3.00
❑25, Mar 1977; Iron Fist	3.00
❑26, Apr 1977; Nick Fury	2.00
❑27, May 1977; Deathlok	2.00
❑28, Jun 1977; Sub-Mariner	2.00
❑28/35 cent, Jun 1977; 35 cent regional price variant	15.00
❑29, Jul 1977; Shang-Chi	2.00
❑29/35 cent, Jul 1977; 35 cent regional price variant; Shang-Chi	15.00
❑30, Aug 1977 JB (a); 2: Spider-Woman I (Jessica Drew).	2.00
❑30/35 cent, Aug 1977; JB (a); 2: Spider-Woman I (Jessica Drew). 35 cent regional price variant	15.00
❑31, Sep 1977; Spider-Woman I (Jessica Drew)	2.00
❑31/35 cent, Sep 1977; 35 cent regional price variant; Spider-Woman I (Jessica Drew)	15.00
❑32, Oct 1977; Invisible Girl	2.00
❑33, Nov 1977; Mordred	2.00
❑34, Dec 1977; Nighthawk	2.00
❑35, Jan 1978; Skull the Slayer	2.00
❑36, Feb 1978; Mr. Fantastic	2.00
❑37, Mar 1978; Matt Murdock	2.00
❑38, Apr 1978; Daredevil	2.00
❑39, May 1978; Vision; Daredevil	2.00
❑40, Jun 1978; Black Panther	2.00
❑41, Jul 1978; Brother Voodoo	2.00
❑42, Aug 1978; Captain America	2.00
❑43, Sep 1978; JBy (a);Man-Thing	2.00
❑44, Oct 1978; BH (c); BH, GD (a);Hercules	2.00
❑45, Nov 1978; GD (a);Captain Marvel	2.00
❑46, Dec 1978; Hulk	2.00
❑47, Jan 1979; GD (a); 1: Machinesmith. Yancy Street Gang	2.00
❑48, Feb 1979; Jack of Hearts	2.00
❑49, Mar 1979; GD (a);Doctor Strange	2.00
❑50, Apr 1979; JBy (w); JBy, JSe, JSt (a);Thing vs. Thing	2.00
❑51, May 1979; FM, BMc (a);Beast; Wonder Man; Ms. Marvel; Nick Fury	3.00
❑52, Jun 1979; Moon Knight	2.00
❑53, Jul 1979; JBy, JSe (a);Quasar	2.00
❑54, Aug 1979; JBy, JSe (a); 1: Screaming Mimi. 1: Poundcakes. D: Deathlok I (Luther Manning).	3.50
❑55, Sep 1979; JBy, JSe (a);Giant Man II (Bill Foster)	2.00
❑56, Oct 1979; GP, GD (a); 1: Letha. Thundra	1.50
❑57, Nov 1979; GP, GD (a);Wundarr	1.50
❑58, Dec 1979; GP, GD (a);Aquarian; Quasar	1.50
❑59, Jan 1980; Human Torch	1.50
❑60, Feb 1980; GP, GD (a); 1: Impossible Woman. Impossible Man	1.50
❑61, Mar 1980; GD (a); 1: Her. Starhawk	1.50
❑62, Apr 1980; GD (a);Moondragon	1.50
❑63, May 1980; GD (a);Warlock	1.50
❑64, Jun 1980; GP, GD (a); 1: Black Mamba. 1: Anaconda. 1: Death-Adder. Stingray	1.50
❑65, Jul 1980; GP, GD (a);Triton	1.50
❑66, Aug 1980; GD (a); A: Arcade. Scarlet Witch	1.50
❑67, Sep 1980; Hyperion; Thundra	1.50
❑68, Oct 1980; A: Arcade. Angel	1.50
❑69, Nov 1980; Guardians of the Galaxy	1.50
❑70, Dec 1980; Inhumans	1.50
❑71, Jan 1981; 1: Maelstrom. 1: Gronk. 1: Phobius. 1: Helio. Mr. Fantastic	1.50
❑72, Feb 1981; Stingray	1.50
❑73, Mar 1981; Quasar	1.50
❑74, Apr 1981; Puppet Master	1.50
❑75, May 1981; O: Blastaar. Avengers	1.50
❑76, Jun 1981; O: Ringmaster. Iceman	1.50
❑77, Jul 1981; Man-Thing	1.50
❑78, Aug 1981; Wonder Man	1.50
❑79, Sep 1981; 1: Star-Dancer. Blue Diamond	1.50
❑80, Oct 1981; Ghost Rider	1.50
❑81, Nov 1981; Sub-Mariner	1.50
❑82, Dec 1981; Captain America	1.50
❑83, Jan 1982; Sasquatch	1.50
❑84, Feb 1982; Alpha Flight	1.50
❑85, Mar 1982; Giant-Man; Spider-Woman	1.50
❑86, Apr 1982; Sandman (Marvel)	1.50
❑87, May 1982; Ant-Man	1.50
❑88, Jun 1982; She-Hulk	1.50
❑89, Jul 1982; Torch; Human Torch	1.50
❑90, Aug 1982; Spider-Man	1.50
❑91, Sep 1982; Sphinx	1.50
❑92, Oct 1982; V: Ultron. Jocasta; Machine Man	1.50
❑93, Nov 1982 A: Machine Man. D: Jocasta.	1.50
❑94, Dec 1982; Power Man; Iron Fist	1.50
❑95, Jan 1983; Living Mummy	1.50
❑96, Feb 1983; Marvel Heroes; Sandman (Marvel)	1.50
❑97, Mar 1983; Iron Man	1.50
❑98, Apr 1983; Franklin Richards	1.50
❑99, May 1983; ROM	1.50
❑100, Jun 1983; Double-size; JBy (w); Ben Grimm	2.50
❑Annual 1, ca. 1976; SB (a);Liberty Legion	4.00
❑Annual 2, Dec 1977; JSn (a); 1: Lord Chaos. 1: Champion of the Universe. 1: Master Order. D: Warlock. D: Thanos. Thanos transformed to stone	16.00
❑Annual 3, Aug 1978; Nova	2.00
❑Annual 4, Oct 1979; Black Bolt	2.00
❑Annual 5, Sep 1980; Hulk	2.50
❑Annual 6, Oct 1981 1: American Eagle.	2.00
❑Annual 7, Oct 1982; 1: Champion of the Universe. Champion	2.00

MARVEL UNIVERSE
Marvel

	N-MINT
❑1, Jun 1998; gatefold summary; Invaders	2.99
❑2, Jul 1998; gatefold summary; JBy (c);Invaders	1.99
❑2/A, Jul 1998; gatefold summary; JBy (c);alternate cover; Invaders	1.99
❑3, Aug 1998; gatefold summary; Invaders	1.99
❑4, Sep 1998; gatefold summary; Monster Hunters	1.99
❑5, Oct 1998; gatefold summary; Monster Hunters	1.99
❑6, Nov 1998; gatefold summary; Monster Hunters	1.99
❑7, Dec 1998; gatefold summary; O: Mole Man. Monster Hunters	1.99

MARVEL UNIVERSE: MILLENNIAL VISIONS
Marvel

	N-MINT
❑1, Feb 2002	3.99

MARVEL UNIVERSE: THE END
Marvel

	N-MINT
❑1, May 2003 AM, JSn (c); JSn (w); AM, JSn (a)	3.50
❑2, May 2003 AM, JSn (c); JSn (w); AM, JSn (a)	3.50
❑3, Jun 2003 AM, JSn (c); JSn (w); AM, JSn (a)	3.50
❑4, Jun 2003 AM, JSn (c); JSn (w); AM, JSn (a)	3.50
❑5, Jul 2003 AM, JSn (c); JSn (w); AM, JSn (a)	3.50
❑6, Aug 2003 AM, JSn (c); JSn (w); AM, JSn (a)	3.50

MARVEL VALENTINE SPECIAL
Marvel

	N-MINT
❑1, Apr 1997; DDC (a); A: Cyclops. A: Venus. A: Daredevil. A: Spider-Man. A: Phoenix. A: Absorbing Man. romance anthology	2.00

MARVEL VERSUS DC/ DC VERSUS MARVEL
DC / Marvel

	N-MINT
❑1, Mar 1996; 1: Access (out of costume). crossover with Marvel; continues in Marvel versus DC #2; cardstock cover	4.00
❑2, Mar 1996; PD (w); crossover with DC; cardstock cover	4.00
❑3, Apr 1996; 1: Access. cardstock cover; crossover with DC; voting results; Marvel and DC universes joined; Stories continued in Amalgam titles	4.00
❑4, Apr 1996; PD (w); continued from Marvel versus DC #3; cardstock cover	4.00
❑Ashcan 1; Consumer Preview; free preview of crossover series; with trading card and ballot	1.00

MARVEL X-MEN COLLECTION, THE
Marvel

	N-MINT
❑1, Jan 1994; Pin-Ups	2.95
❑2, Feb 1994	2.95
❑3, Mar 1994	2.95

MARVEL YEAR IN REVIEW
Marvel

	N-MINT
❑1, ca. 1989	3.95
❑2, ca. 1990	3.95
❑3, ca. 1991	3.95

N-MINT

❑4, ca. 1992 ... 3.95
❑5, ca. 1993 ... 3.95
❑6, ca. 1994 ... 2.95

MARVILLE
MARVEL

❑1, Nov 2002 ... 2.25
❑2, Dec 2002 ... 2.25
❑3, Jan 2003 ... 2.25
❑4, Feb 2003 ... 2.25
❑5, Mar 2003 ... 2.25
❑6, May 2003 ... 2.25
❑7, Jul 2003; Introduction and submission guidelines to Marvel's Epic imprint ... 2.25

MARY JANE
MARVEL

❑1, Aug 2004 ... 2.25
❑2, Sep 2004 ...

MASK (1ST SERIES)
DC

❑1, Dec 1985 CS, KS (a) ... 1.00
❑2, Jan 1986 CS, KS (a) ... 1.00
❑3, Feb 1986 CS, KS (a) ... 1.00
❑4, Mar 1986 CS, KS (a) ... 1.00

MASK (2ND SERIES)
DC

❑1, Feb 1987 ... 1.00
❑2, Mar 1987 ... 1.00
❑3, Apr 1987 ... 1.00
❑4, May 1987 ... 1.00
❑5, Jun 1987 ... 1.00
❑6, Jul 1987 ... 1.00
❑7, Aug 1987 ... 1.00
❑8, Sep 1987 ... 1.00
❑9, Oct 1987 ... 1.00

MASK, THE (MINI-SERIES)
DARK HORSE

❑0, ca. 1991; Reprints Mask stories from Mayhem ... 4.95
❑1, Aug 1991 ... 4.00
❑2, Sep 1991 ... 3.50
❑3, Oct 1991 ... 3.00
❑4, Nov 1991 ... 3.00

MASK, THE
DARK HORSE

❑1, Feb 1995 ... 3.00
❑2, Mar 1995 ... 2.50
❑3, Apr 1995 ... 2.50
❑4, May 1995 ... 2.50
❑5, Jun 1995 ... 2.50
❑6, Jul 1995 ... 2.50
❑7, Aug 1995 ... 2.50
❑8, Sep 1995 ... 2.50
❑9, Oct 1995 ... 2.50
❑10, Dec 1995 A: Hero Zero, King Tiger. ... 2.50
❑11, Jan 1996 A: Barb Wire, The Machine. ... 2.50
❑12, Feb 1996 A: X, Ghost, King Tiger. ... 2.50
❑13, Mar 1996 A: Warmaker, King Tiger, Vortex. ... 2.50
❑14, Apr 1996 ... 2.50
❑15, May 1996 A: Lt. Kellaway. ... 2.50
❑16, Jun 1996 ... 2.50
❑17, Jul 1996 ... 2.50

MASK, THE: OFFICIAL MOVIE ADAPTATION
DARK HORSE

❑1, Jul 1994 ... 2.50
❑2, Aug 1994 ... 2.50

MASK RETURNS, THE
DARK HORSE

❑1, Dec 1992; with Mask mask ... 4.00
❑2, Jan 1993 ... 3.00
❑3, Feb 1993 ... 3.00
❑4, Mar 1993; Walter dons Mask ... 3.00

MASK, THE: TOYS IN THE ATTIC
DARK HORSE

❑1, Aug 1998 ... 2.95
❑2, Sep 1998 ... 2.95
❑3, Oct 1998 ... 2.95
❑4, Nov 1998 ... 2.95

MASK, THE: VIRTUAL SURREALITY
DARK HORSE

❑1, Jul 1997 ... 2.95

MASK CONSPIRACY, THE
INK & FEATHERS

❑1 ... 6.95

MASKED MAN, THE
ECLIPSE

❑1, Dec 1984 O: Masked Man. ... 2.00
❑2, Feb 1985 ... 2.00
❑3, Apr 1985 ... 2.00
❑4, Jun 1985 ... 2.00
❑5, Aug 1985 ... 2.00
❑6, Oct 1985 ... 2.00
❑7, Dec 1985 ... 2.00
❑8, Feb 1986 ... 2.00
❑9, Apr 1986 ... 2.00
❑10, b&w ... 2.00
❑11, b&w ... 2.00
❑12, Apr 1988, b&w ... 2.00

MASKED RIDER
MARVEL

❑1, Apr 1996; based on Saban television series, one-shot ... 2.95

MASKED WARRIOR X
ANTARCTIC

❑1, Apr 1996, b&w ... 3.50
❑2, Jun 1996, b&w ... 2.95
❑3, Aug 1996, b&w ... 3.50
❑4, Oct 1996, b&w ... 2.95

MASK/MARSHAL LAW, THE
DARK HORSE

❑1, Feb 1998 ... 2.95
❑2, Mar 1998; Law dons the Mask ... 2.95

MASK OF ZORRO, THE
IMAGE

❑1, Aug 1998 ... 2.95
❑1/Variant, Sep 1998; alternate cover ... 2.95
❑2, Sep 1998 ... 2.95
❑2/Variant, Sep 1998; alternate cover ... 2.95
❑3, Oct 1998; indicia says Oct ... 2.95
❑3/Variant, Oct 1998; alternate cover ... 2.95
❑3/B, Nov 1998; Variant; head-shot photo ... 2.95
❑4, Dec 1998; cover says Jan, indicia says Dec ... 2.95
❑4/Variant, Dec 1998 ... 2.95

MASKS: TOO HOT FOR TV
DC

❑1, ca. 2003 ... 4.95

MASQUE OF THE RED DEATH, THE
DELL

❑1, Oct 1964 ... 20.00

MASQUERADE
MAD MONKEY

❑1 ... 3.95
❑2 ... 3.95
❑Ashcan 1 ... 2.00

MASQUES (J.N. WILLIAMSON'S...)
INNOVATION

❑1, Jul 1992 ... 4.95
❑2 ... 4.95

MASTER OF KUNG FU
MARVEL

❑17, Apr 1974; Series continued from "Special Marvel Edition"; JSn (a); 1: Black Jack Tarr. Marvel Value Stamp #53: Grim Reaper ... 12.00
❑18, Jun 1974; PG (a);Marvel Value Stamp #62: Plunderer ... 6.00
❑19, Aug 1974; PG (a); A: Man-Thing. Man-Thing; Marvel Value Stamp #11: Deathlok ... 5.00
❑20, Sep 1974 PG (a) ... 5.00
❑21, Oct 1974; Marvel Value Stamp #62: Plunderer ... 3.00
❑22, Nov 1974; PG (a);Marvel Value Stamp #79: Kang ... 3.00

Although it says #12 on the cover, *Marvel: The Lost Generation* #12 is really the first issue in the series that traveled back in Marvel time.

© 2000 Marvel Characters Inc.

N-MINT

❑23, Dec 1974; Marvel Value Stamp #97: Black Knight ... 3.00
❑24, Jan 1975; JSn (a);Marvel Value Stamp #15: Iron Man ... 3.00
❑25, Feb 1975; PG (a);Marvel Value Stamp #41: Gladiator ... 3.00
❑26, Mar 1975 ... 3.00
❑27, Apr 1975 ... 3.00
❑28, May 1975 ... 3.00
❑29, Jun 1975 PG (a); 1: Razor-Fist I. D: Razor-Fist I. ... 3.00
❑30, Jul 1975 PG (a) ... 3.00
❑31, Aug 1975; PG (a);Marvel Value Stamp #85: Lilith ... 2.50
❑32, Sep 1975 ... 2.50
❑33, Oct 1975 PG (a); 1: Leiko Wu. ... 2.50
❑34, Nov 1975 PG (a) ... 2.50
❑35, Dec 1975 PG (a) ... 2.50
❑36, Jan 1976 ... 2.50
❑37, Feb 1976 ... 2.50
❑38, Mar 1976 PG (a) ... 2.50
❑39, Apr 1976 PG (a) ... 2.50
❑39/30 cent, Apr 1976; PG (a);30 cent regional price variant ... 20.00
❑40, May 1976 PG (a) ... 2.50
❑40/30 cent, May 1976; 30 cent regional price variant ... 20.00
❑41, Jun 1976 ... 2.50
❑41/30 cent, Jun 1976; 30 cent regional price variant ... 20.00
❑42, Jul 1976 PG (a); 1: Shockwave. ... 2.50
❑42/30 cent, Jul 1976; 30 cent regional price variant ... 20.00
❑43, Aug 1976 PG (a) ... 2.50
❑43/30 cent, Aug 1976; 30 cent regional price variant ... 20.00
❑44, Sep 1976 PG (a) ... 2.50
❑45, Oct 1976 PG (a) ... 2.50
❑46, Nov 1976 PG (a) ... 2.50
❑47, Dec 1976 PG (a) ... 2.50
❑48, Jan 1977 PG (a) ... 2.50
❑49, Feb 1977 PG (a) ... 2.50
❑50, Mar 1977 PG (a) ... 2.50
❑51, Apr 1977 PG (a) ... 2.50
❑52, May 1977 ... 2.00
❑53, Jun 1977; reprints Master of Kung Fu #20 ... 2.00
❑53/35 cent, Jun 1977 ... 4.00
❑54, Jul 1977 ... 2.00
❑54/35 cent, Jul 1977 ... 4.00
❑55, Aug 1977 ... 2.00
❑55/35 cent, Aug 1977 ... 4.00
❑56, Sep 1977 ... 2.00
❑57, Oct 1977 ... 2.00
❑58, Nov 1977 ... 2.00
❑59, Dec 1977 ... 2.00
❑60, Jan 1978; V: Dr. Doom. V: Doctor Doom. Dr. Doom ... 2.00
❑61, Feb 1978 ... 2.00
❑62, Mar 1978 ... 2.00
❑63, Apr 1978 ... 2.00
❑64, May 1978 ... 2.00
❑65, Jun 1978 ... 2.00
❑66, Jul 1978 ... 2.00
❑67, Aug 1978 ... 2.00
❑68, Sep 1978 V: The Cat. ... 2.00
❑69, Oct 1978 ... 2.00
❑70, Nov 1978 ... 2.00
❑71, Dec 1978 ... 2.00

	N-MINT
❑72, Jan 1979	2.00
❑73, Feb 1979	2.00
❑74, Mar 1979	2.00
❑75, Apr 1979	2.00
❑76, May 1979	2.00
❑77, Jun 1979 O: Zaran. 1: Zaran.	2.00
❑78, Jul 1979	2.00
❑79, Aug 1979	2.00
❑80, Sep 1979	2.00
❑81, Oct 1979	2.00
❑82, Nov 1979	2.00
❑83, Dec 1979 V: Fu Manchu.	2.00
❑84, Jan 1980	2.00
❑85, Feb 1980	2.00
❑86, Mar 1980	2.00
❑87, Apr 1980	2.00
❑88, May 1980	2.00
❑89, Jun 1980 V: Fu Manchu.	2.00
❑90, Jul 1980	2.00
❑91, Aug 1980 GD (a)	2.00
❑92, Sep 1980 GD (a)	2.00
❑93, Oct 1980 GD (a)	2.00
❑94, Nov 1980 GD (a)	2.00
❑95, Dec 1980 GD (a)	2.00
❑96, Jan 1981 GD (a)	2.00
❑97, Feb 1981 GD (a)	2.00
❑98, Mar 1981 GD (a)	2.00
❑99, Apr 1981 GD (a)	2.00
❑100, May 1981; Giant-size GD (a)	2.50
❑101, Jun 1981 GD (a)	1.50
❑102, Jul 1981 GD (a); 1: Day pencils.	1.50
❑103, Aug 1981 GD (a)	1.50
❑104, Sep 1981	1.50
❑105, Oct 1981 1: Razor-Fist II. 1: Razor-Fist III. D: Razor-Fist III.	1.50
❑106, Nov 1981 GD (a); O: Razor-Fist II. O: Razor-Fist III. A: Velcro.	1.50
❑107, Dec 1981 GD (a); A: Sata.	1.50
❑108, Jan 1982 GD (a)	1.50
❑109, Feb 1982 GD (a)	1.50
❑110, Mar 1982 GD (a)	1.50
❑111, Apr 1982 GD (a)	1.50
❑112, May 1982 GD (a)	1.50
❑113, Jun 1982 GD (a)	1.50
❑114, Jul 1982	1.50
❑115, Aug 1982 GD (a)	1.50
❑116, Sep 1982 GD (a)	1.50
❑117, Oct 1982 GD (a)	1.50
❑118, Nov 1982; double-sized GD (a); D: Fu Manchu.	1.50
❑119, Dec 1982 GD (a)	1.50
❑120, Jan 1983 GD (a)	1.50
❑121, Feb 1983	1.50
❑122, Mar 1983	1.50
❑123, Apr 1983	1.50
❑124, May 1983	1.50
❑125, Jun 1983; Double-size	2.00
❑Annual 1, ca. 1976; KP (a);1976 Annual	5.00

MASTER OF KUNG FU: BLEEDING BLACK
Marvel

❑1, Feb 1991	3.00

MASTER OF MYSTICS: THE DEMONCRAFT
Chakra

❑1	1.50
❑2	1.50

MASTER OF RAMPLING GATE, THE (ANNE RICE'S...)
Innovation

❑1, Jun 1991	6.95

MASTERS OF THE UNIVERSE: ICONS OF EVIL: BEAST MAN
Image

❑1, Jun 2003	4.95

MASTER OF THE VOID
Iron Hammer

❑1, Dec 1993	2.95

MASTERS OF THE UNIVERSE (MINI-SERIES)
DC

	N-MINT
❑1, Dec 1982 GT, AA (a)	3.00
❑2, Jan 1983	2.00
❑3, Feb 1983	2.00

MASTERS OF THE UNIVERSE
Marvel / Star

❑1, May 1986	4.00
❑2, Jul 1986	2.50
❑3, Sep 1986	2.50
❑4, Nov 1986	2.50
❑5, Jan 1987	2.50
❑6, Mar 1987	2.50
❑7, May 1987	2.50
❑8, Jul 1987	2.50
❑9, Sep 1987	2.50
❑10, Nov 1987	2.50
❑11, Jan 1988	2.50
❑12, Mar 1988	2.50
❑13, May 1988	3.00

MASTERS OF THE UNIVERSE (IMAGE)
Image

❑1, Nov 2002; Cover A	2.95
❑1/B, Nov 2002; Cover B	2.95
❑1/Gold, Nov 2002; Gold foil logo on cover	5.95
❑2, Dec 2002; Cover A	2.95
❑2/B, Dec 2002; Cover B	2.95
❑3, Jan 2003; Cover A	2.95
❑3/B, Jan 2003; Cover B	2.95
❑4, Feb 2003; Cover A	2.95
❑4/B, Feb 2003; Cover B	2.95

MASTERS OF THE UNIVERSE (VOL. 2)
Image

❑1, Mar 2003	5.95
❑1/A, Jun 2003	2.95
❑2, Apr 2003	2.95
❑3, May 2003	2.95
❑4, Jun 2003	2.95
❑4/A, Jun 2003; Edwards Holofoil cover	5.95
❑4/B, Jun 2003; Santalucia cover	2.95
❑4/C, Jun 2003; Vallejo Bell cover	5.95
❑5, Jul 2003	2.95
❑6, Aug 2003	2.95

MASTER'S SERIES
Avalon

❑1; Wally Wood War	2.50

MASTERWORKS SERIES OF GREAT COMIC BOOK ARTISTS, THE
DC / Seagate

❑1, Spr 1983; FF (a);Reprints Shining Knight stories from Adventure Comics (1950-1951)	2.50
❑2, Jul 1983 FF (a)	2.50
❑3, Oct 1983 BWr (a)	2.50

MATT CHAMPION
Metro

❑1	2.00

MATTERBABY
Antarctic

❑1, Feb 1997, b&w	2.95
❑Annual 1	2.95

MAVERICK (DELL)
Dell

❑7, Oct 1959	50.00
❑8, Jan 1960	50.00
❑9, Mar 1960	50.00
❑10, May 1960	50.00
❑11, Jul 1960	40.00
❑12, Sep 1960	40.00
❑13, Nov 1960	40.00
❑14, Jan 1961	40.00
❑15, Jun 1961	40.00
❑16, Sep 1961	30.00
❑17, Dec 1961	30.00
❑18, Mar 1962	30.00
❑19, Jun 1962	30.00

MAVERICK (MINI-SERIES)
Marvel

❑1, Jan 1997; Giant-size	2.95

MAVERICK
Marvel

❑1, Sep 1997; gatefold summary; wraparound cover	3.00
❑2, Oct 1997; gatefold summary; wraparound cover	1.95
❑2/Variant, Oct 1997; variant cover	1.95
❑3, Nov 1997; gatefold summary; A: Alpha Flight. wraparound cover	1.99
❑4, Dec 1997; gatefold summary; A: Alpha Flight. wraparound cover	1.99
❑5, Jan 1998; gatefold summary	1.99
❑6, Feb 1998; gatefold summary	1.99
❑7, Mar 1998; gatefold summary	1.99
❑8, Apr 1998; gatefold summary	1.99
❑9, May 1998; gatefold summary	1.99
❑10, Jun 1998; gatefold summary	1.99
❑11, Jul 1998; gatefold summary	1.99
❑12, Aug 1998; Giant-size	2.99

MAVERICKS (DAGGER)
Dagger

❑1, Jan 1994	2.50
❑2, Feb 1994	2.50
❑3, Mar 1994	2.50
❑4, Apr 1994	2.50
❑5, May 1994	2.50

MAVERICKS: THE NEW WAVE
Dagger

❑1	2.50
❑2	2.50
❑3	2.50

MAX BREWSTER: THE UNIVERSAL SOLDIER
Fleetway-Quality

❑1	2.95
❑2	2.95
❑3	2.95

MAX BURGER PI
Graphic Image

❑1, b&w	2.00
❑2, b&w	2.50

MAX DAMAGE: PANIC!
Head

❑1, Jul 1995, b&w	2.75

MAXIMAGE
Image

❑1, Dec 1995	2.50
❑2, Jan 1996; polybagged with card	2.50
❑3, Feb 1996	2.50
❑4, Mar 1996; continued from Glory #10	2.50
❑5, Apr 1996	2.50
❑6, May 1996	2.50
❑7, Jun 1996	2.50
❑8, Jul 1996	2.50
❑9, Aug 1996	2.50
❑10, Sep 1996	2.50

MAXIMO ONE-SHOT
Dreamwave

❑1, Feb 2004	3.95

MAXIMORTAL, THE
Tundra

❑1, Aug 1992	4.00
❑2, Oct 1992	4.00
❑3, Dec 1992 A: Holmes.	4.00
❑4, Mar 1993	4.00
❑5, May 1993	3.00
❑6, Jul 1993	3.00
❑7, Dec 1993	2.95

MAXIMUM SECURITY
Marvel

❑1, Dec 2000	2.99
❑2, Dec 2000	2.99
❑3, Jan 2001	2.99

N-MINT

MAXIMUM SECURITY DANGEROUS PLANET
MARVEL
❑1, Oct 2000; lead-in to Maximum Security 2.99

MAXIMUM SECURITY: THOR VS. EGO
MARVEL
❑1, Nov 2000; reprints Thor #133, #160, and #161; Reprints Thor #133, 160, 161 .... 2.99

MAXION
CPM MANGA
❑1, Dec 1999, b&w 2.95
❑2, Jan 2000, b&w 2.95
❑3, Feb 2000, b&w 2.95
❑4, Mar 2000, b&w 2.95
❑5, Apr 2000, b&w 2.95
❑6, May 2000, b&w 2.95
❑7, Jun 2000 .... 2.95
❑8, Jul 2000 .... 2.95
❑9, Aug 2000 .... 2.95
❑10, Sep 2000 .... 2.95
❑11, Oct 2000 .... 2.95
❑12, Nov 2000 .... 2.95
❑13, Dec 2000 .... 2.95
❑14, Jan 2001 .... 2.95
❑15, Feb 2001 .... 2.95
❑16, Mar 2001 .... 2.95
❑17, Apr 2001 .... 2.95
❑18, May 2001 .... 2.95
❑19, Jun 2001 .... 2.95
❑20, Jul 2001 .... 2.95

MAX OF THE REGULATORS
ATLANTIC
❑1 .... 1.50
❑2 .... 1.75
❑3 .... 1.75
❑4 .... 1.75

MAX REP IN THE AGE OF THE ASTROTITANS
DUMBBELL
❑1, Jun 1997, b&w 2.75
❑2, Mar 1998, b&w 2.75

MAX THE MAGNIFICENT
SLAVE LABOR
❑1, Jul 1987 .... 1.50

MAXWELL MOUSE FOLLIES
RENEGADE
❑1, Feb 1986, b&w 2.00
❑2, Apr 1986, b&w 2.00
❑3, Jun 1986, b&w 2.00
❑4, Sep 1986, b&w 2.00
❑5, Dec 1986 .... 2.00
❑6, Mar 1987 .... 2.00

MAXWELL THE MAGIC CAT
ACME
❑1 .... 4.95
❑2 .... 4.95
❑3 .... 4.95
❑4 .... 5.95

MAXX
IMAGE
❑0.5, Jun 1993; Wizard promotional edition 5.00
❑0.5/Gold, Jun 1993; Gold edition; Promotional edition in slipcover with certificate of authenticity 16.00
❑1, Mar 1993 .... 3.00
❑1/3D, Jan 1998; 3-D edition; bound-in glasses 5.00
❑1/Variant, Mar 1993; Glow-in-the-dark promotional edition; glow in the dark cover 6.00
❑2, Apr 1993 .... 3.00
❑3, May 1993 .... 2.50
❑4, Aug 1993 .... 2.50
❑5, Sep 1993 .... 2.50
❑6, Nov 1993; cover says Oct, indicia says Nov 2.50
❑7, Mar 1994 A: Pitt. 2.50
❑8, May 1994 A: Pitt. 2.50

N-MINT

❑9, Jun 1994 .... 2.50
❑10, Aug 1994 .... 2.50
❑11, Oct 1994 .... 2.00
❑12, Dec 1994 .... 2.00
❑13, Jan 1995 .... 2.00
❑14, Feb 1995 .... 2.00
❑15, Apr 1995; cover says February, indicia says Apr 2.00
❑16, Jun 1995; cover says Feb, indicia says Jun 2.00
❑17, Jul 1995 .... 2.00
❑18, Aug 1995 .... 2.00
❑19, Sep 1995 .... 2.00
❑20, Nov 1995 .... 2.00
❑21, Jan 1996 .... 2.00
❑22, Feb 1996 .... 2.00
❑23, Mar 1996 .... 2.00
❑24, May 1996 .... 2.00
❑25, Jun 1996; cover says Jul, indicia says Jun 2.00
❑26, Aug 1996 O: Mr. Gone. 2.00
❑27, Sep 1996 .... 2.00
❑28, Jan 1997 .... 2.00
❑29, Apr 1997 .... 2.00
❑30, Jun 1997 .... 2.00
❑31, Jul 1997 .... 2.00
❑32, Sep 1997 .... 2.00
❑33, Oct 1997 .... 2.00
❑34, Dec 1997 .... 2.00
❑35, Feb 1998 .... 2.00

MAXX, THE (DC)
DC
❑1, ca. 2003 .... 17.95
❑2, ca. 2004 .... 17.95

MAYHEM
DARK HORSE
❑1, May 1989, b&w 4.00
❑2, Jun 1989, b&w 3.50
❑3, Jul 1989, b&w 3.50
❑4, Aug 1989, b&w 3.50

MAYHEM (KELVA)
KELVA
❑1 .... 1.25

MAZE, THE
METAPHROG
❑1, Aug 1997, b&w; no indicia 3.75

MAZE AGENCY, THE
COMICO
❑1, Dec 1988 1: The Maze Agency. 3.00
❑2, Jan 1989 .... 2.50
❑3, Feb 1989 .... 2.50
❑4, Mar 1989 .... 2.00
❑5, Apr 1989 .... 2.00
❑6, May 1989 .... 2.00
❑7, Jun 1989 .... 2.50
❑8, Dec 1989 .... 2.00
❑9, Feb 1990; Ellery Queen 2.00
❑10, Apr 1990 .... 2.00
❑11, Apr 1990 .... 2.00
❑12, May 1990 .... 2.00
❑13, Jun 1990 .... 2.00
❑14, Jul 1990 .... 2.00
❑15, Aug 1990 .... 2.00
❑16, Oct 1990 RH (c) 2.50
❑17, Dec 1990 .... 2.50
❑18, Feb 1991 .... 2.50
❑19, Mar 1991 .... 2.50
❑20, May 1991 .... 2.50
❑21, Jun 1991 .... 2.50
❑22, Jul 1991 .... 2.50
❑23, Aug 1991 .... 2.50
❑Annual 1, Aug 1990; MP (c); Spirit parody 3.00
❑Special 1, May 1990 .... 3.00
❑Xmas 1; Special edition 3.00

'MAZING MAN
DC
❑1, Jan 1986 1: 'mazing Man. 1.00
❑2, Feb 1986 .... 1.00
❑3, Mar 1986 .... 1.00

The Thing fought an earlier version of himself in *Marvel Two-in-One* #50.
© 1979 Marvel Comics.

N-MINT

❑4, Apr 1986 .... 1.00
❑5, May 1986 .... 1.00
❑6, Jun 1986 .... 1.00
❑7, Jul 1986 1: Zoot Sputnik. 1.00
❑8, Aug 1986 .... 1.00
❑9, Sep 1986 .... 1.00
❑10, Oct 1986 .... 1.00
❑11, Nov 1986 .... 1.00
❑12, Dec 1986 FM (c) 1.00
❑Special 1, Jul 1987; Special #1 .... 2.00
❑Special 2, Apr 1988; Special #2 .... 2.00
❑Special 3, Sep 1990; Special #3 .... 2.00

MCHALE'S NAVY
DELL
❑1, May 1963 .... 40.00
❑2, Aug 1963 .... 32.00
❑3, Nov 1963 .... 26.00

M.D. (GEMSTONE)
GEMSTONE
❑1, Sep 1999 .... 2.50
❑2, Oct 1999 .... 2.50
❑3, Nov 1999 .... 2.50
❑4, Dec 1999 .... 2.50
❑5, Jan 2000 .... 2.50

M.D. GEIST
CPM
❑1, Jun 1995 .... 2.95
❑2, Jul 1995 .... 2.95
❑3, Aug 1995 .... 2.95

M.D. GEIST: GROUND ZERO
CPM
❑1, Mar 1996; prequel to M.D. Geist, Armored Trooper Votoms preview back-up 2.95
❑2, Apr 1996; prequel to M.D. Geist, Armored Trooper Votoms preview back-up 2.95
❑3, May 1996; prequel to M.D. Geist, Armored Trooper Votoms preview back-up 2.95

MEA CULPA
FOUR WALLS EIGHT WINDOWS
❑1, Oct 1990 .... 12.95

ME-A DAY WITH ELVIS
INVINCIBLE
❑1 .... 0.50

MEADOWLARK
PARODY
❑1, b&w; Shadowhawk silver foil cover parody 2.95

ME AND HER
FANTAGRAPHICS / EROS
❑1, b&w 2.00
❑1-2 .... 2.00
❑2, b&w 2.00
❑3 .... 2.00
❑Special 1, b&w; Special edition 2.50

MEAN, GREEN BONDO MACHINE
MU
❑1, Jul 1992 .... 2.50

MEAN MACHINE
FLEETWAY-QUALITY
❑1; Judge Dredd; no date of publication; Reprints Mean Machine stories from 2000 A.D. #730-736 .... 4.95

N-MINT

MEANWHILE...
CROW

- ❑1, b&w 2.95
- ❑2, b&w 2.95

MEASLES
FANTAGRAPHICS

- ❑1 1998 ..... 2.95
- ❑2 1999 ..... 2.95
- ❑3, Sum 1999 ..... 2.95
- ❑4, Sum 1999 ..... 2.95
- ❑5, Win 2000 ..... 2.95
- ❑6, Spr 2000 ..... 2.95
- ❑7 2000 ..... 2.95

MEAT CAKE (FANTAGRAPHICS)
FANTAGRAPHICS

- ❑1, b&w 2.50
- ❑2, b&w 2.50
- ❑3, b&w 2.50
- ❑4, b&w 2.50
- ❑5, Nov 1995, b&w 2.95
- ❑6, Jan 1996, b&w 2.95
- ❑7 1997, b&w 2.95
- ❑8, Jun 1998, b&w 2.95
- ❑9, Apr 1999 ..... 2.95
- ❑10 ..... 2.95
- ❑11 ..... 3.95

MEAT CAKE (ICONOGRAFIX)
ICONOGRAFIX

- ❑1, b&w 2.50

MEATFACE THE AMAZING FLESH
MONSTER

- ❑1, b&w 2.50

MECHA
DARK HORSE

- ❑1, Jun 1987 ..... 1.75
- ❑2, Aug 1987 ..... 1.75
- ❑3, Oct 1987, b&w 1.75
- ❑4, Dec 1987, b&w 1.75
- ❑5, Feb 1988, b&w 1.75
- ❑6, Apr 1988 ..... 1.75

MECHANIC, THE
IMAGE

- ❑1 1998; prestige format 5.95

MECHANICAL MAN BLUES
RADIO

- ❑1, Dec 1998, b&w 2.95

MECHANICS
FANTAGRAPHICS

- ❑1 ..... 2.00
- ❑2 ..... 2.00
- ❑3 ..... 2.00

MECHANIMALS
NOVELLE

- ❑1, b&w 3.50
- ❑2, b&w 2.50

MECHANIMOIDS SPECIAL X ANNIVERSARY
MU

- ❑1, b&w; cardstock cover 3.50

MECHANOIDS
CALIBER

- ❑1, b&w 2.50
- ❑2 ..... 2.50
- ❑3 ..... 2.50

MECH DESTROYER
IMAGE

- ❑1, Mar 2001 ..... 2.95
- ❑2, Jun 2001; Indicia lists as March issue 2.95
- ❑3, Jul 2001 ..... 2.95
- ❑4, Sep 2001 ..... 2.95

MECHOVERSE
AIRBRUSH

- ❑1; Airbrushed 1.50
- ❑2; Airbrushed 1.50
- ❑3; Airbrushed 1.50

N-MINT

MECHTHINGS
RENEGADE

- ❑1, Jul 1987, b&w 2.00
- ❑2, Sep 1987, b&w 2.00
- ❑3, Nov 1987, b&w 2.00
- ❑4, Feb 1988, b&w 2.00

MEDABOTS PART 1
VIZ

- ❑1, Apr 2002, b&w 2.75
- ❑2, Apr 2002, b&w 2.75
- ❑3, May 2002, b&w 2.75
- ❑4, May 2002, b&w 2.75

MEDABOTS PART 2
VIZ

- ❑1, Jun 2002, b&w 2.75
- ❑2, Jun 2002, b&w 2.75
- ❑3, Jul 2002, b&w 2.75
- ❑4, Jul 2002, b&w 2.75

MEDABOTS PART 3
VIZ

- ❑1, Aug 2002, b&w 2.75
- ❑2, Aug 2002, b&w 2.75
- ❑3, Sep 2002, b&w 2.75
- ❑4, Sep 2002, b&w 2.75

MEDABOTS PART 4
VIZ

- ❑1, Oct 2002, b&w 2.75
- ❑2, Oct 2002, b&w 2.75
- ❑3, Nov 2002, b&w 2.75
- ❑4, Nov 2002, b&w 2.75

MEDAL OF HONOR
DARK HORSE

- ❑1, Oct 1994 ..... 2.50
- ❑2, Nov 1994 ..... 2.50
- ❑3, Dec 1994 ..... 2.50
- ❑4, Jan 1995 ..... 2.50
- ❑5 ..... 2.50
- ❑Special 1, Apr 1994 ..... 2.50

MEDIA*STARR
INNOVATION

- ❑1, Jul 1989 ..... 1.95
- ❑2, Aug 1989 ..... 1.95
- ❑3, Sep 1989 ..... 1.95

MEDIEVAL SPAWN
IMAGE

- ❑1; three-part story; polybagged with Fan 2.00
- ❑2; three-part story; polybagged with Fan 2.00
- ❑3; three-part story; polybagged with Fan 2.00

MEDIEVAL SPAWN/WITCHBLADE
IMAGE

- ❑1, May 1996 ..... 3.00
- ❑1/American Ent; American Entertainment exclusive; Gold cover 4.00
- ❑1/Gold, May 1996; Gold edition 6.00
- ❑1/Platinum; Platinum edition 15.00
- ❑2, Jun 1996 ..... 3.50
- ❑3, Jun 1996; cover says Jul, indicia says Jun 3.00

MEDIEVAL WITCHBLADE
IMAGE

- ❑1 ..... 5.90
- ❑2 ..... 5.90
- ❑3 ..... 5.90

MEDORA
LOBSTER

- ❑1, Dec 1999 ..... 2.95

MEDUSA COMICS
TRIANGLE

- ❑1 ..... 1.50

MEGA DRAGON & TIGER
IMAGE

- ❑1, Mar 1999 ..... 2.95
- ❑2, Apr 1999 ..... 2.95
- ❑3, May 1999 ..... 2.95
- ❑4, Jun 1999 ..... 2.95
- ❑5, Jul 1999 ..... 2.95

N-MINT

MEGAHURTZ
IMAGE

- ❑1, Aug 1997, b&w 2.95
- ❑1/A, Aug 1997; no cover price 2.95
- ❑1/B, Aug 1997; no cover price 2.95
- ❑2, Sep 1997 ..... 2.95
- ❑3, Oct 1997 ..... 2.95

MEGALITH
CONTINUITY

- ❑1 1989 ..... 2.00
- ❑2 1989 ..... 2.00
- ❑3 1990 ..... 2.00
- ❑4, Nov 1990 ..... 2.00
- ❑5, Jan 1991; Rise of Magic storyline 2.50
- ❑6, Jun 1991 ..... 2.50
- ❑7, Jul 1991 ..... 2.50
- ❑8, Dec 1991 ..... 2.50
- ❑9, Mar 1992 ..... 2.50

MEGALITH (2ND SERIES)
CONTINUITY

- ❑0, Apr 1993; silver foil issue number; prelude to Deathwatch 2000 ..... 1.00
- ❑0/A, Apr 1993; red foil cover 1.00
- ❑1, Apr 1993; trading cards 2.50
- ❑2, Jun 1993; trading cards 2.50
- ❑3, Aug 1993 ..... 2.50
- ❑4, Oct 1993 ..... 2.50
- ❑5, Dec 1993 ..... 2.50
- ❑6, Dec 1993 ..... 2.50
- ❑7, Jan 1994 ..... 2.50

MEGALOMANIACAL SPIDER-MAN, THE
MARVEL

- ❑1, Jun 2002 ..... 2.99

MEGAMAN
DREAMWAVE

- ❑1, Sep 2003 ..... 2.95
- ❑1/DF, Sep 2003, Holofoil cover 5.95
- ❑2, Oct 2003 ..... 2.95
- ❑3, Nov 2003 ..... 2.95
- ❑4, Dec 2003 ..... 2.95

MEGATON
MEGATON

- ❑1, Nov 1983 MGu, GD, EL (a); 1: Megaton. A: Vanguard. 3.00
- ❑2, Oct 1985 EL (a) 2.50
- ❑3, Feb 1986 EL (w); EL (a); 1: Savage Dragon. 5.00
- ❑4, Apr 1986 ..... 2.00
- ❑5, Jun 1986 ..... 2.00
- ❑6, Dec 1986 ..... 2.00
- ❑7, Apr 1987 ..... 2.00
- ❑8, Aug 1987 ..... 2.50
- ❑Holiday 1; says 1994 on cover, 1993 in indicia 3.00

MEGATON MAN
KITCHEN SINK

- ❑1, Nov 1984 O: Megaton Man. 3.00
- ❑1-2 ..... 2.00
- ❑2, Feb 1985 ..... 2.50
- ❑3, Apr 1985 ..... 2.50
- ❑4, Jun 1985 ..... 2.50
- ❑5, Aug 1985 ..... 2.50
- ❑6, Oct 1985; Border Worlds storyline begins 2.50
- ❑7, Dec 1985 ..... 2.50
- ❑8, Feb 1986; Border Worlds back-up 2.50
- ❑9, Apr 1986 ..... 2.50
- ❑10, Jun 1986 ..... 2.50

MEGATON MAN: BOMBSHELL
IMAGE

- ❑1, Jul 1999 ..... 2.95

MEGATON MAN: HARDCOPY
IMAGE

- ❑1, Feb 1999, b&w; collects Internet strips 2.95
- ❑2, Apr 1999, b&w; collects Internet strips 2.95

N-MINT

MEGATON MAN MEETS THE UNCATEGORIZABLE X+THEMS
KITCHEN SINK

❑1, Apr 1989, b&w; X-Men parody ... 2.00

MEGAZZAR DUDE
SLAVE LABOR

❑Special 1, Nov 1991, b&w 2.95

MEKANIX
MARVEL

❑1, Dec 2002 .... 2.99
❑2, Jan 2003 .... 2.99
❑3, Feb 2003 .... 2.99
❑4, Mar 2003 .... 2.99
❑5, Apr 2003 .... 2.99
❑6, May 2003 .... 2.99

MELISSA MOORE: BODYGUARD
DRACULINA

❑1, b&w 2.95

MELODY
KITCHEN SINK

❑1, b&w 2.50
❑2, b&w 2.25
❑3, b&w 2.00
❑4, b&w 2.00
❑5, b&w 2.00
❑6, b&w 2.00
❑7, b&w 2.25
❑8, b&w 2.25

MELONPOOL CHRONICLES, THE
PARA-TROOP

❑1 .... 2.95

MELTING POT
KITCHEN SINK

❑1, Dec 1993 .... 3.50
❑2 1994 .... 3.00
❑3 1994 .... 3.00
❑4, Sep 1994 .... 3.50

MELTY FEELING
ANTARCTIC / VENUS

❑1, Oct 1996, b&w 3.50
❑2, Dec 1996, b&w 3.50
❑3, Jan 1997, b&w 3.50
❑4, Feb 1997, b&w 3.50

MELVIN MONSTER (DELL)
DELL

❑1, Apr 1965 JS (a) 60.00
❑2, Jul 1965 JS (a) 45.00
❑3, Dec 1965 JS (a) 40.00
❑4, Jul 1966 JS (a) 32.00
❑5, Oct 1966 JS (a) 32.00
❑6 1967 JS (a) 26.00
❑7 1967 JS (a) 26.00
❑8 1967 JS (a) 26.00
❑9, Aug 1967 JS (a) 26.00
❑10, Oct 1969 JS (a) 26.00

MELVIS
CHAMELEON

❑1, Jul 1994; 2,500 copies 2.00
❑2 1994 .... 2.00
❑3 1994 .... 2.00
❑4 1994 .... 2.00

MEMENTO MORI
MEMENTO MORI

❑1 1995 .... 2.00
❑2, Mar 1995, b&w; no cover price ... 2.00

MEMORIES
MARVEL / EPIC

❑1, ca. 1992, b&w; Japanese 2.50

MEMORYMAN
DAVID MARKOFF

❑1/Ashcan; Ashcan edition given as promo at 1995 San Diego Comicon 1: Memoryman. 0.50

MENAGERIE
CHROME TIGER

❑1, Nov 1987, b&w 1.95
❑2, Feb 1988, b&w 2.00

N-MINT

MENDY AND THE GOLEM
MENDY

❑1, Sep 1981 .... 2.50
❑2, Nov 1981 .... 2.00
❑3 1982 .... 2.00
❑4, Mar 1982 .... 2.00
❑5 1982 .... 2.00
❑6, Jul 1982 .... 2.00
❑7, Sep 1982; Numbered Vol. 2 #1 ... 2.00
❑8, Jan 1983; Numbered Vol. 2 #2 .... 2.00
❑9, Mar 1983; Says Vol. 2 #3 in indicia only 2.00
❑10, May 1983 .... 2.00
❑11, Jul 1983 .... 2.00
❑12, Sep 1983 .... 2.00
❑13, Nov 1983 .... 2.00
❑14, Jan 1984 .... 2.00
❑15, May 1984 .... 2.00
❑16, Sep 1984 .... 2.00
❑17, Feb 1985 .... 2.00
❑18, Mar 1985 .... 2.00
❑19, Apr 1985 .... 2.00

MEN FROM EARTH
FUTURE-FUN

❑1 .... 2.00

MEN IN BLACK, THE
AIRCEL

❑1, Jan 1990, b&w 15.00
❑2, Feb 1990, b&w 10.00
❑3, Mar 1990, b&w 8.00

MEN IN BLACK, THE (BOOK II)
AIRCEL

❑1, May 1991, b&w 14.00
❑2, Jun 1991, b&w 10.00
❑3, Jul 1991, b&w 8.00

MEN IN BLACK: FAR CRY
MARVEL

❑1, Aug 1997; Jay and Kay are reunited 3.99

MEN IN BLACK: RETRIBUTION
MARVEL

❑1, Dec 1997 .... 3.99

MEN IN BLACK: THE MOVIE
MARVEL

❑1, Oct 1997; adapts movie 3.99

MEN OF WAR
DC

❑1, Aug 1977; O: Gravedigger. 1: Gravedigger. Enemy Ace back-up .. 4.00
❑2, Sep 1977; JKu (c);Enemy Ace back-up 3.00
❑3, Nov 1977; JKu (c);Enemy Ace back-up 3.00
❑4, Jan 1978; JKu (c);Dateline: Frontline back-up 3.00
❑5, Mar 1978 .... 3.00
❑6, May 1978 .... 2.50
❑7, Jul 1978 .... 2.50
❑8, Sep 1978 .... 2.50
❑9, Oct 1978 .... 2.50
❑10, Nov 1978; JKu (c);Enemy Ace and Dateline: Frontline back-ups 2.50
❑11, Dec 1978 .... 2.50
❑12, Jan 1979 .... 2.50
❑13, Feb 1979 RT (a) 2.50
❑14, Mar 1979; JKu (c);Enemy Ace back-up 2.50
❑15, Apr 1979 JKu (c) 2.50
❑16, May 1979 .... 2.50
❑17, Jun 1979 .... 2.50
❑18, Jul 1979 .... 2.50
❑19, Aug 1979 .... 2.50
❑20, Sep 1979 JKu (c) 2.50
❑21, Oct 1979 .... 2.50
❑22, Nov 1979 .... 2.50
❑23, Dec 1979 .... 2.50
❑24, Jan 1980 .... 2.50
❑25, Feb 1980 .... 2.50
❑26, Mar 1980 .... 2.50

Introduced in *Darker Image* #1, Sam Keith's Maxx spun off into an MTV animated series and a set of action figures.

© 1993 Sam Kieth and Image.

N-MINT

MEN'S ADVENTURE COMIX
PENTHOUSE INTERNATIONAL

❑1, May 1995; Comic-sized O: Miss Adventure. 1: Hericane. 1: Miss Adventure. 6.00
❑2, Jul 1995 .... 5.00
❑3, Sep 1995 .... 5.00
❑4, Nov 1995 .... 5.00
❑5, Dec 1995 .... 5.00
❑6, Feb 1996 .... 5.00
❑7, Apr 1996 .... 5.00

MENTHU
BLACK INC!

❑1, Jan 1998 .... 2.95
❑2 1998 .... 2.95
❑3 1998 .... 2.95
❑4 1998 .... 2.95

MENZ INSANA
DC / VERTIGO

❑1; prestige format 7.95

MEPHISTO VS...
MARVEL

❑1, Apr 1987; AM (w); JB (a);Fantastic Four 2.50
❑2, May 1987; AM (w); JB (a);X-Factor 2.00
❑3, Jun 1987; JB (a);X-Men 2.00
❑4, Jul 1987; JB (a);Avengers 2.00

MERCEDES
ANGUS

❑1 1995 .... 2.95
❑2, Jan 1996 .... 2.95
❑3, Feb 1996 .... 2.95
❑4, Mar 1996 .... 2.95
❑5, Apr 1996 .... 2.95
❑6 .... 2.95
❑7 .... 2.95
❑8 .... 2.95
❑9 .... 2.95
❑10 .... 2.95
❑11 .... 2.95
❑12 .... 2.95

MERCHANTS OF DEATH
ECLIPSE

❑1, Jul 1988, b&w; magazine 3.50
❑2, b&w; magazine 3.50
❑3, b&w; magazine 3.50
❑4, b&w; magazine 3.50

MERCHANTS OF VENUS, THE
DC

❑1 .... 6.00

MERCY
DC / VERTIGO

❑1 .... 6.00

MERIDIAN
CROSSGEN

❑1, Jul 2000 .... 3.50
❑2, Aug 2000 .... 3.00
❑3, Sep 2000 .... 3.00
❑4, Oct 2000 .... 3.00
❑5, Nov 2000 .... 3.00
❑6, Dec 2000 .... 2.95
❑7, Jan 2001 .... 2.95
❑8, Feb 2001 .... 2.95
❑9, Mar 2001 .... 2.95
❑10, Apr 2001 .... 2.95
❑11, May 2001 .... 2.95

	N-MINT
❑12, Jun 2001	2.95
❑13, Jul 2001	2.95
❑14, Aug 2001	2.95
❑15, Sep 2001	2.95
❑16, Oct 2001	2.95
❑17, Nov 2001	2.95
❑18, Dec 2001	2.95
❑19, Jan 2002	2.95
❑20, Feb 2002	2.95
❑21, Mar 2002	2.95
❑22, Apr 2002	2.95
❑23, May 2002	2.95
❑24, Jun 2002	2.95
❑25, Jul 2002	2.95
❑26, Aug 2002	2.95
❑27, Sep 2002	2.95
❑28, Oct 2002	2.95
❑29, Nov 2002	2.95
❑30, Dec 2002	2.95
❑31, Jan 2003	2.95
❑32, Feb 2003	2.95
❑33, Mar 2003	2.95
❑34, Apr 2003	2.95
❑35, May 2003	2.95
❑36, Jun 2003	2.95
❑37, Jul 2003	2.95
❑38, Sep 2003	2.95
❑39, Nov 2003	2.95
❑40, Dec 2003	2.95
❑41, Jan 2004	2.95
❑42, Jan 2004	2.95
❑43, Mar 2004	2.95
❑44, Apr 2004	2.95

MERLIN
ADVENTURE

❑1, Dec 1990, b&w	2.50
❑2, Jan 1991, b&w	2.50
❑3, Feb 1991, b&w	2.50
❑4, Mar 1991, b&w	2.50
❑5, Apr 1991, b&w	2.50
❑6, May 1991, b&w	2.50

MERLIN: IDYLLS OF THE KING
ADVENTURE

❑1, b&w	2.50
❑2, b&w	2.50

MERLINREALM 3-D
BLACKTHORNE

❑1, Oct 1985	2.25

MERMAID
ALTERNATIVE

❑1, May 1998, b&w	2.95

MERMAID FOREST
VIZ

❑1, b&w	2.75
❑2, b&w	2.75
❑3, b&w	2.75
❑4, b&w	2.75

MERMAID'S DREAM
VIZ

❑1, Oct 1985, b&w	2.75
❑2, b&w	2.75
❑3, b&w	2.75

MERMAID'S GAZE
VIZ

❑1, b&w	2.75
❑2, b&w	2.75
❑3, b&w	2.75
❑4, b&w	2.75

MERMAID'S MASK
VIZ

❑1, b&w	2.75
❑2, b&w	2.75
❑3, b&w	2.75
❑4	2.75

MERMAID'S PROMISE
VIZ

❑1, b&w	2.75
❑2, b&w	2.75
❑3, b&w	2.75
❑4, b&w	2.75

MERMAID'S SCAR
VIZ

❑1, ca. 1994, b&w	2.75
❑2, b&w	2.75
❑3, b&w	2.75
❑4, b&w	2.75

MERTON OF THE MOVEMENT
LAST GASP

❑1	3.50

MESSENGER, THE
IMAGE

❑1, Jul 2000	5.95

MESSENGER 29
SEPTEMBER

❑1, b&w	2.00

MESSIAH
PINNACLE

❑1, b&w	1.50

MESSOZOIC
KITCHEN SINK

❑1	2.95

META-4
FIRST

❑1, Feb 1991	3.95
❑2, Mar 1991	2.25
❑3, Apr 1991	2.25

METABARONS, THE
HUMANOIDS

❑1, Jan 2000	4.00
❑2 2000	3.50
❑3 2000	3.50
❑4 2000	3.00
❑5, Jun 2000	3.00
❑6, Jul 2000	3.00
❑7, Aug 2000	3.00
❑8, Oct 2000	3.00
❑9, Dec 2000	3.00
❑10, Jan 2001	3.00
❑11, Feb 2001	2.95
❑12, Mar 2001	2.95
❑13, May 2001	2.95
❑14, May 2001	2.95

METACOPS
FANTAGRAPHICS / MONSTER

❑1, Feb 1991, b&w	1.95
❑2, Mar 1991, b&w	1.95
❑3, Jul 1991, b&w	1.95

METAL BIKINI
ETERNITY

❑1, Oct 1990, b&w	2.25
❑2 1990, b&w	2.25
❑3 1991, b&w	2.25
❑4 1991, b&w	2.25
❑5 1991, b&w	2.25
❑6 1991, b&w	2.25

METAL GUARDIAN FAUST
VIZ

❑1, Mar 1997	2.95
❑2, Apr 1997	2.95
❑3, May 1997	2.95
❑4, Jun 1997	2.95
❑5, Jul 1997	2.95
❑6, Aug 1997	2.95
❑7, Sep 1997	2.95
❑8, Oct 1997	2.95

METALLICA (CELEBRITY)
CELEBRITY

❑1/A	2.95
❑1/B; trading cards	6.95

METALLICA (FORBIDDEN FRUIT)
FORBIDDEN FRUIT

❑1, b&w	2.95
❑2, b&w	2.95

METALLICA (ROCK-IT)
ROCK-IT COMICS

❑1	5.00

METALLICA'S GREATEST HITS
REVOLUTIONARY

❑1, Sep 1993, b&w	2.50

METALLIX
FUTURE

❑0, May 2003	3.50
❑1 2002	3.50
❑2 2003	3.50
❑3 2003	3.50
❑4, Apr 2003	3.50
❑5, Jun 2003	3.50
❑6, Jul 2003	2.99

METAL MEN
DC

❑1, May 1963	350.00
❑2, Jul 1963	175.00
❑3, Sep 1963	110.00
❑4, Nov 1963	110.00
❑5, Jan 1964	110.00
❑6, Mar 1964	80.00
❑7, May 1964	80.00
❑8, Jul 1964	80.00
❑9, Sep 1964	80.00
❑10, Nov 1964	80.00
❑11, Jan 1965	55.00
❑12, Mar 1965	55.00
❑13, May 1965 1: Tin's girlfriend. V: Skyscraper Robot.	55.00
❑14, Jul 1965	55.00
❑15, Sep 1965	55.00
❑16, Nov 1965	55.00
❑17, Jan 1966	55.00
❑18, Mar 1966	55.00
❑19, May 1966	55.00
❑20, Jul 1966	55.00
❑21, Sep 1966	45.00
❑22, Nov 1966	45.00
❑23, Jan 1967	45.00
❑24, Mar 1967	45.00
❑25, May 1967	45.00
❑26, Jul 1967	45.00
❑27, Sep 1967 O: Metal Men.	80.00
❑28, Nov 1967	42.00
❑29, Jan 1968	42.00
❑30, Mar 1968	42.00
❑31, May 1968	24.00
❑32, Jul 1968	24.00
❑33, Sep 1968	24.00
❑34, Nov 1968	24.00
❑35, Jan 1969	24.00
❑36, Mar 1969	24.00
❑37, May 1969	24.00
❑38, Jul 1969	24.00
❑39, Sep 1969	24.00
❑40, Nov 1969	24.00
❑41, Dec 1969; series put on hiatus	24.00
❑42, Mar 1973; Series begins again (1973)	12.00
❑43, May 1973	12.00
❑44, Jul 1973; V: Missile Men. back to hiatus	12.00
❑45, May 1976; Series begins again (1976)	6.00
❑46, Jul 1976	6.00
❑47, Sep 1976 V: Plutonium Man.	6.00
❑48, Nov 1976 V: Eclipso.	6.00
❑49, Jan 1977 V: Eclipso.	6.00
❑50, Mar 1977	6.00
❑51, May 1977 V: Vox.	6.00
❑52, Jul 1977	6.00
❑53, Sep 1977	6.00
❑54, Nov 1977 A: Green Lantern.	6.00
❑55, Jan 1978 V: Missile Men.	6.00
❑56, Mar 1978 V: Inheritor.	6.00

METAL MEN (MINI-SERIES)
DC

❑1, Oct 1993; foil cover	2.50
❑2, Nov 1993	1.50
❑3, Dec 1993	1.50
❑4, Jan 1994	1.50

N-MINT

METAL MEN OF MARS & OTHER IMPROBABLE TALES
SLAVE LABOR

❑1, Jan 1989, b&w A: Tasma. A: Captain Daring. ... 2.00

METAL MILITIA
EXPRESS / ENTITY

❑1/Ashcan, ca. 1995, b&w; enhanced cover ... 1.00
❑1, Aug 1995 ... 2.50
❑1/A, Aug 1995, b&w; enhanced cover; came w/ PC game ... 6.95
❑2, Sep 1995 ... 2.50
❑3 1995 ... 2.50

METAMORPHO
DC

❑1, Aug 1965 ... 45.00
❑2, Oct 1965 ... 24.00
❑3, Dec 1965 ... 20.00
❑4, Feb 1966; Metamorpho in Mexico 16.00
❑5, Apr 1966; Metamorpho vs. Metamorpho ... 16.00
❑6, Jun 1966 ... 12.00
❑7, Aug 1966 ... 12.00
❑8, Oct 1966 V: Doc Dread. ... 12.00
❑9, Dec 1966 ... 12.00
❑10, Feb 1967 1: Element Girl. ... 14.00
❑11, Apr 1967 ... 10.00
❑12, Jun 1967 ... 10.00
❑13, Aug 1967 ... 10.00
❑14, Oct 1967 ... 10.00
❑15, Dec 1967 ... 10.00
❑16, Feb 1968 ... 10.00
❑17, Apr 1968 ... 10.00

METAMORPHO (MINI-SERIES)
DC

❑1, Aug 1993 ... 1.50
❑2, Sep 1993 ... 1.50
❑3, Oct 1993 ... 1.50
❑4, Nov 1993 ... 1.50

METAPHYSIQUE (MALIBU)
MALIBU

❑1, Apr 1995 ... 2.95
❑2, May 1995 ... 2.95
❑3, Jun 1995 ... 2.95
❑4, Aug 1995 ... 2.95
❑5, ca. 1995 ... 2.95
❑6, ca. 1995 A: Superius. ... 2.95
❑Ashcan 1 ... 1.00

METAPHYSIQUE
ECLIPSE

❑1 ... 2.50

METEOR MAN
MARVEL

❑1, Aug 1993; Movie tie-in ... 1.25
❑2, Sep 1993 ... 1.25
❑3, Oct 1993 ... 1.25
❑4, Nov 1993 ... 1.25
❑5, Dec 1993 ... 1.25
❑6, Jan 1994 ... 1.25

METEOR MAN: THE MOVIE
MARVEL

❑1, Apr 1993 ... 2.00

METROPOL A.D. (VOL. 2, TED MCKEEVER'S...)
MARVEL / EPIC

❑1, Oct 1992 ... 3.50
❑2, Nov 1992 ... 3.50
❑3, Dec 1992 ... 3.50

METROPOLIS S.C.U.
DC

❑1, Nov 1994 ... 1.50
❑2, Dec 1994 ... 1.50
❑3, Jan 1995 ... 1.50
❑4, Feb 1995 ... 1.50

METROPOL (TED MCKEEVER'S...)
MARVEL / EPIC

❑1, ca. 1991 ... 2.95
❑2, ca. 1991 ... 2.95
❑3, ca. 1991 ... 2.95
❑4, ca. 1991 ... 2.95
❑5, ca. 1991 ... 2.95
❑6, ca. 1991 ... 2.95
❑7, ca. 1991 ... 2.95
❑8, ca. 1991 ... 2.95
❑9, ca. 1991 ... 2.95
❑10, ca. 1991 ... 2.95
❑11, ca. 1992 ... 2.95
❑12, ca. 1992 ... 2.95

MEZ
C.A.P.

❑1, May 1997, b&w; Canadian cover price only ... 2.00
❑2, Mar 1998, b&w; Canadian cover price only ... 2.00

MEZZ: GALACTIC TOUR 2494
DARK HORSE

❑1, May 1994, b&w ... 2.50

M FALLING
VAGABOND

❑1 ... 3.50

MFI: THE GHOSTS OF CHRISTMAS
IMAGE

❑1, Dec 1999 ... 3.95

MIAMI MICE
RIP OFF

❑1, Apr 1986 ... 2.00
❑1-2, May 1986 ... 2.00
❑1-3, May 1986 ... 2.00
❑2, Jul 1986, b&w ... 2.00
❑3, Oct 1986, b&w ... 2.00
❑3/A, Oct 1986, b&w; flexi-disc; w/ soundsheet ... 5.00
❑4, Jan 1987, b&w ... 2.00

MICHAELANGELO CHRISTMAS SPECIAL
MIRAGE

❑1, Dec 1990, b&w ... 2.00

MICHAELANGELO TEENAGE MUTANT NINJA TURTLE
MIRAGE

❑1 ... 2.50

MICHAEL CHABON PRESENTS THE AMAZING ADVENTURES OF THE ESCAPIST
DARK HORSE

❑1, Feb 2004; based on Chabon's book The Amazing Adventures of Kavalier and Clay ... 8.95
❑2, Apr 2004 ... 8.95

MICHAEL JORDAN TRIBUTE
REVOLUTIONARY

❑1 ... 2.95

MICKEY AND DONALD (WALT DISNEY'S...)
GLADSTONE

❑1, Mar 1988 CB, DR (a) ... 2.00
❑2 1988 CB (a) ... 2.00
❑3, Jul 1988 CB (a) ... 2.00
❑4, Aug 1988 CB (a) ... 2.00
❑5, Sep 1988 WK (c); CB (a) ... 2.00
❑6, Oct 1988 CB (a) ... 2.00
❑7, Nov 1988 CB (a) ... 2.00
❑8, Dec 1988 CB (a) ... 2.00
❑9 1989 CB (a) ... 2.00
❑10 1989 CB (a) ... 2.00
❑11 1989 CB (a) ... 2.00
❑12, Aug 1989 CB (a) ... 2.00
❑13, Sep 1989 CB (a) ... 2.00
❑14, Oct 1989 CB (a) ... 2.00
❑15, Nov 1989 CB (a) ... 2.00
❑16, Jan 1990 CB (a) ... 2.00
❑17, Mar 1990 CB, FG, DR (a) ... 1.95
❑18, May 1990; WK (c); CB, FG (a);series continues as Donald and Mickey ... 1.95

MEGATON No. 1 $2.00

Creator-owned characters from Entity's *Megaton* later popped up at Image.
© 1983 Erik Larsen, Rob Liefeld, and Entity.

N-MINT

MICKEY AND GOOFY EXPLORE ENERGY
DELL

❑1, ca. 1976; giveaway; no indicia or cover price ... 2.00

MICKEY & MINNIE
W.D.

❑1 ... 3.50

MICKEY MANTLE
MAGNUM

❑1, Dec 1991 JSt (a) ... 2.00
❑2 ... 2.00

MICKEY MOUSE (WALT DISNEY'S...)
DELL / GOLD KEY/WHITMAN

❑50, Oct 1956 ... 20.00
❑51, Dec 1956 ... 16.00
❑52, Feb 1957 ... 16.00
❑53, Apr 1957 ... 16.00
❑54, Jun 1957 ... 16.00
❑55, Aug 1957 ... 16.00
❑56, Oct 1957 ... 16.00
❑57, Dec 1957 ... 16.00
❑58, Feb 1958 ... 16.00
❑59, Apr 1958 ... 16.00
❑60, Jun 1958 ... 16.00
❑61, Aug 1958 ... 15.00
❑62, Oct 1958 ... 15.00
❑63, Dec 1958 ... 15.00
❑64, Feb 1959 ... 15.00
❑65, Apr 1959 ... 15.00
❑66, Jun 1959 ... 15.00
❑67, Aug 1959 ... 15.00
❑68, Oct 1959 ... 15.00
❑69, Dec 1959 ... 15.00
❑70, Feb 1960 ... 15.00
❑71, Apr 1960 ... 14.00
❑72, Jun 1960 ... 14.00
❑73, Aug 1960 ... 14.00
❑74, Oct 1960 ... 14.00
❑75, Dec 1960 ... 14.00
❑76, Mar 1961 ... 14.00
❑77, ca. 1961 ... 14.00
❑78, Jun 1961 ... 14.00
❑79, ca. 1961 ... 14.00
❑80, Nov 1961 ... 14.00
❑81, Jan 1962 ... 12.00
❑82, Mar 1962 ... 12.00
❑83, Jun 1962 ... 12.00
❑84, Sep 1962 ... 12.00
❑85, Nov 1962 ... 12.00
❑86, Feb 1963 ... 12.00
❑87, May 1963 ... 12.00
❑88, Jul 1963 ... 12.00
❑89, Sep 1963 ... 12.00
❑90, Nov 1963 ... 12.00
❑91, Dec 1963 ... 12.00
❑92, Feb 1964 ... 12.00
❑93, ca. 1964 ... 12.00
❑94, ca. 1964 ... 12.00
❑95, Jul 1964 ... 12.00
❑96, ca. 1964 ... 12.00
❑97, Oct 1964 ... 12.00
❑98, Nov 1964 ... 12.00
❑99, Feb 1965 ... 12.00
❑100, Apr 1965 ... 12.00
❑101, Jun 1965 ... 11.00
❑102, Aug 1965 ... 11.00

N-MINT

❑103, Oct 1965 11.00
❑104, Dec 1965 11.00
❑105, Feb 1966 11.00
❑106, Apr 1966 11.00
❑107, Jun 1966 11.00
❑108, Aug 1966 11.00
❑109, Oct 1966 11.00
❑110, Dec 1966 11.00
❑111, Feb 1967 11.00
❑112, Apr 1967 11.00
❑113, Jun 1967 11.00
❑114, Aug 1967 11.00
❑115, Nov 1967 11.00
❑116, Feb 1968 11.00
❑117, May 1968 11.00
❑118, Aug 1968 11.00
❑119, Nov 1968 11.00
❑120, Feb 1969 11.00
❑121, May 1969 10.00
❑122, Aug 1969 10.00
❑123, Nov 1969 10.00
❑124, Feb 1970 10.00
❑125, May 1970 10.00
❑126, Aug 1970 10.00
❑127, Nov 1970 10.00
❑128, Feb 1971 10.00
❑129, Apr 1971 10.00
❑130, Jun 1971 10.00
❑131, Aug 1971 10.00
❑132, Oct 1971 10.00
❑133, Dec 1971 10.00
❑134, Feb 1972 10.00
❑135, Apr 1972 10.00
❑136, Jun 1972 10.00
❑137, Aug 1972 10.00
❑138, Oct 1972 10.00
❑139, Dec 1972 10.00
❑140, Feb 1973 10.00
❑141, Apr 1973 8.00
❑142, Jun 1973 8.00
❑143, Aug 1973 8.00
❑144, Sep 1973 8.00
❑145, Oct 1973 8.00
❑146, Dec 1973 8.00
❑147, Feb 1974 8.00
❑148, Apr 1974 8.00
❑149, Jun 1974 8.00
❑150, Aug 1974 8.00
❑151, Sep 1974 8.00
❑152, Oct 1974 8.00
❑153, Dec 1974 8.00
❑154, Feb 1975 8.00
❑155, Apr 1975 8.00
❑156, Jun 1975 8.00
❑157, Aug 1975 8.00
❑158, Sep 1975 8.00
❑159, Oct 1975 8.00
❑160, Nov 1975 8.00
❑161, Jan 1976 7.00
❑162, Apr 1976 7.00
❑163, Jun 1976 7.00
❑164, Aug 1976 7.00
❑165, Sep 1976 7.00
❑166, Oct 1976 7.00
❑167, Nov 1976 7.00
❑168, Dec 1976 7.00
❑169, Feb 1977 7.00
❑170, Apr 1977 7.00
❑171, May 1977 7.00
❑172, Jun 1977 7.00
❑173, Jul 1977 7.00
❑174, Aug 1977 7.00
❑175, Sep 1977 7.00
❑176, Oct 1977 7.00
❑177, Nov 1977 7.00
❑178, Dec 1977 7.00
❑179, Jan 1978 7.00
❑180, Feb 1978 7.00
❑181, Mar 1978 6.00
❑182, Apr 1978 6.00
❑183, May 1978 6.00

N-MINT

❑184, Jun 1978 6.00
❑185, Jul 1978 6.00
❑186, Aug 1978 6.00
❑187, Sep 1978 6.00
❑188, Oct 1978 6.00
❑189, Nov 1978 6.00
❑190, Dec 1978 6.00
❑191, Jan 1979 6.00
❑192, Feb 1979 6.00
❑193, Mar 1979 6.00
❑194, Apr 1979 6.00
❑195, May 1979 6.00
❑196, Jun 1979 6.00
❑197, Jul 1979 6.00
❑198, Aug 1979 6.00
❑199, Sep 1979 6.00
❑200, Oct 1979 6.00
❑201, Nov 1979 5.00
❑202, Dec 1979 5.00
❑203, Jan 1980 5.00
❑204, Feb 1980 5.00
❑205, Apr 1980 5.00
❑206, Jun 1980 5.00
❑207, Jul 1980 5.00
❑208, Aug 1980 5.00
❑209 5.00
❑210 5.00
❑211, Jun 1981 4.00
❑212, Aug 1981 4.00
❑213, Sep 1981 4.00
❑214, Dec 1981 4.00
❑215, Feb 1982 4.00
❑216 4.00
❑217 4.00
❑218 4.00
❑219, Oct 1986 FG (a) 4.00
❑220, Nov 1986 FG (a) 4.00
❑221, Dec 1986 FG (a) 3.00
❑222, Jan 1987 FG (a) 3.00
❑223, Feb 1987 FG (a) 3.00
❑224, Mar 1987 FG (a) 3.00
❑225, Apr 1987 FG (a) 3.00
❑226, May 1987 FG (a) 3.00
❑227, Jun 1987 FG (a) 3.00
❑228, Jul 1987 FG (a) 3.00
❑229, Aug 1987 FG (a) 3.00
❑230, Sep 1987 FG (a) 3.00
❑231, Oct 1987 FG (a) 3.00
❑232, Nov 1987 FG (a) 3.00
❑233, Dec 1987 FG (a) 3.00
❑234, Jan 1988 FG (a) 3.00
❑235, Mar 1988 FG (a) 3.00
❑236, Apr 1988 FG (a) 3.00
❑237, Jun 1988 FG (a) 3.00
❑238, Jul 1988 FG (a) 3.00
❑239, Aug 1988 FG (a) 3.00
❑240, Sep 1988 FG (a) 3.00
❑241, Oct 1988 FG (a) 2.00
❑242, Nov 1988 FG (a) 2.00
❑243, Dec 1988 FG (a) 2.00
❑244, Jan 1989; 60th anniversary, 100 pages; FG (a);Daily Strips compilation 2.00
❑245, Mar 1989 FG (a) 2.00
❑246, Apr 1989 FG (a) 2.00
❑247, Jun 1989 FG (a) 2.00
❑248, Jul 1989 FG (a) 2.00
❑249, Aug 1989 FG (a) 2.00
❑250, Sep 1989 FG (a) 2.00
❑251, Oct 1989 FG (a) 2.00
❑252, Nov 1989 FG (a) 2.00
❑253, Dec 1989 FG (a) 2.00
❑254, Jan 1990 FG (a) 2.00
❑255, Feb 1990 2.00
❑256, Apr 1990 2.00

MICKEY MOUSE AND FRIENDS
GEMSTONE

❑257, Sep 2003 2.95
❑258, Oct 2003 2.95
❑259, Nov 2003 2.95
❑260, Dec 2003 2.95

N-MINT

❑261, Jan 2004 2.95
❑262, Feb 2004 2.95
❑263, Mar 2004 2.95
❑264, Apr 2004 2.95
❑265, May 2004 2.95
❑266, Jun 2004 2.95

MICKEY MOUSE (ONE-SHOT)
DISNEY

❑1; in Russian 4.00

MICKEY MOUSE ADVENTURES
DISNEY

❑1, Jun 1990 2.50
❑2, Jul 1990 2.00
❑3, Aug 1990 V: Phantom Blot. 2.00
❑4, Sep 1990 2.00
❑5, Oct 1990 2.00
❑6, Nov 1990 2.00
❑7, Dec 1990 2.00
❑8, Jan 1991 JBy (c) 2.00
❑9, Feb 1991; Fantasia 2.00
❑10, Mar 1991 2.00
❑11, Apr 1991 2.00
❑12, May 1991 2.00
❑13, Jun 1991 2.00
❑14, Jul 1991 2.00
❑15, Aug 1991 2.00
❑16, Sep 1991 KB (a) 2.00
❑17, Oct 1991; Dinosaur 2.00
❑18, Nov 1991; Dinosaur 2.00

MICKEY MOUSE AND GOOFY EXPLORE ENERGY CONSERVATION
DELL

❑1, ca. 1978; giveaway; no indicia or cover price 2.00

MICKEY MOUSE DIGEST
GLADSTONE

❑1, ca. 1986 5.00
❑2, ca. 1986 4.00
❑3, ca. 1986 3.00
❑4, ca. 1986 3.00
❑5, ca. 1987 3.00

MICKEY MOUSE SURPRISE PARTY
GOLD KEY

❑1, Jan 1969 18.00

MICKEY RAT
LOS ANGELES COMIC BOOK CO.

❑1, May 1972, b&w 25.00
❑2, Oct 1972, b&w 20.00
❑3, Jul 1980, b&w 15.00
❑4, b&w 15.00

MICRA: MIND CONTROLLED REMOTE AUTOMATON
COMICS INTERVIEW

❑1, Nov 1986 1.75
❑2, Jan 1987 1.75
❑3, Feb 1987 1.75
❑4 1987 1.75
❑5 1987 1.75
❑6 1987 1.75
❑7 1987 1.75

MICROBOTS, THE
GOLD KEY

❑1, Dec 1971 10.00

MICRONAUTS (VOL. 1)
MARVEL

❑1, Jan 1979 MG (a); O: Micronauts. 1: The Micronauts. 1: Baron Karza. 1: Space Glider. 1: Biotron. 1: Marionette. 4.00
❑1-2, Jan 1979 2.00
❑2, Feb 1979 MG (a) 3.00
❑3, Mar 1979 MG (a) 2.50
❑4, Apr 1979 MG (a) 2.50
❑5, May 1979 MG (a) 2.50
❑6, Jun 1979 MG (a) 2.00
❑7, Jul 1979 MG (a); A: Man-Thing. 2.00
❑8, Aug 1979 MG (a); 1: Captain Universe. 2.25
❑9, Sep 1979 MG (a) 2.00
❑10, Oct 1979 MG (a) 2.00

Condition price index: Multiply "NM prices" above by: **0.83 for Very Fine/Near Mint**
0.66 for Very Fine • 0.33 for Fine • 0.2 for Very Good • 0.125 for Good

	N-MINT
❑11, Nov 1979 MG (a)	1.50
❑12, Dec 1979 MG (a)	1.50
❑13, Jan 1980	1.50
❑14, Feb 1980	1.50
❑15, Mar 1980 A: Fantastic Four. D: Microtron.	1.50
❑16, Apr 1980 A: Fantastic Four.	1.50
❑17, May 1980 A: Fantastic Four. D: Jasmine.	1.50
❑18, Jun 1980	1.50
❑19, Jul 1980	1.50
❑20, Aug 1980 A: Ant-Man.	1.50
❑21, Sep 1980	1.50
❑22, Oct 1980	1.50
❑23, Nov 1980 V: Molecule Man.	1.50
❑24, Dec 1980	1.50
❑25, Jan 1981 O: Baron Karza. V: Mentallo.	1.50
❑26, Feb 1981 PB (a)	1.50
❑27, Mar 1981 PB (a); D: Biotron.	1.50
❑28, Apr 1981 PB (a); A: Nick Fury.	1.50
❑29, May 1981 PB (a); A: Nick Fury.	1.50
❑30, Jun 1981 PB (a)	1.50
❑31, Jul 1981 FM (c); PB, FM (a); A: Doctor Strange.	1.50
❑32, Aug 1981 PB (a); A: Doctor Strange.	1.50
❑33, Sep 1981 PB (a); A: Doctor Strange.	1.50
❑34, Oct 1981 PB (a); A: Doctor Strange.	1.50
❑35, Nov 1981; double-sized O: Microverse. A: Doctor Strange.	1.50
❑36, Dec 1981	1.50
❑37, Jan 1982 A: X-Men. A: Nightcrawler.	1.50
❑38, Feb 1982; Direct sales (only) begin	1.50
❑39, Mar 1982	1.50
❑40, Apr 1982 A: Fantastic Four.	1.50
❑41, May 1982 V: Dr. Doom. V: Doctor Doom.	1.50
❑42, Jun 1982	1.50
❑43, Jul 1982	1.50
❑44, Aug 1982	1.50
❑45, Sep 1982	1.50
❑46, Oct 1982	1.50
❑47, Nov 1982	1.50
❑48, Dec 1982; 1st Guice	1.50
❑49, Jan 1983	1.50
❑50, Feb 1983	1.50
❑51, Mar 1983	1.50
❑52, May 1983	1.50
❑53, Jul 1983	1.50
❑54, Sep 1983	1.50
❑55, Nov 1983	1.50
❑56, Jan 1984	1.50
❑57, Mar 1984; double-sized	1.50
❑58, May 1984	1.50
❑59, Aug 1984	1.50
❑Annual 1, Dec 1979 SD (a)	2.00
❑Annual 2, Oct 1980 SD (a); V: Toymaster.	2.00
❑Special 1, Dec 1983	2.00
❑Special 2, Jan 1984	2.00
❑Special 3, Feb 1984	2.00
❑Special 4, Mar 1984	2.00
❑Special 5, Apr 1984	2.00

MICRONAUTS (VOL. 2)
MARVEL

❑1, Oct 1984; Makers	2.00
❑2, Nov 1984	1.50
❑3, Dec 1984	1.50
❑4, Jan 1985	1.50
❑5, Feb 1985	1.50
❑6, Mar 1985	1.50
❑7, Apr 1985	1.50
❑8, May 1985	1.50
❑9, Jun 1985	1.50
❑10, Jul 1985	1.50
❑11, Aug 1985	1.50
❑12, Sep 1985	1.50
❑13, Oct 1985	1.50
❑14, Nov 1985	1.50
❑15, Dec 1985	1.50
❑16, Jan 1986; Secret Wars II	1.50
❑17, Feb 1986	1.50
❑18, Mar 1986	1.50
❑19, Apr 1986	1.50
❑20, May 1986	1.50

MICRONAUTS (IMAGE)
IMAGE

❑1, ca. 2002	2.95
❑2, ca. 2002	2.95
❑3, ca. 2002	2.95
❑4, Dec 2002	2.95
❑5, Feb 2003	2.95
❑6, Mar 2003	2.95
❑7, Apr 2003	2.95
❑8, Jun 2003	2.95
❑9, Jul 2003	2.95
❑10, Aug 2003	2.95
❑11, Oct 2003	2.95

MIDDLE CLASS FANTASIES
CARTOONISTS CO-OP

❑1	3.00
❑2	3.00

MIDNIGHT
AJAX

❑1, Apr 1957	54.00
❑2 1958	38.00
❑3	26.00
❑4	26.00
❑5, Feb 1958	26.00
❑6	26.00

MIDNIGHT EYE GOKÜ
VIZ

❑1	4.95
❑2	4.95
❑3	4.95
❑4	4.95
❑5	4.95
❑6	4.95

MIDNIGHT, MASS
DC / VERTIGO

❑1, Jun 2002	2.50
❑2, Jul 2002	2.50
❑3, Aug 2002	2.50
❑4, Sep 2002	2.50
❑5, Oct 2002	2.50
❑6, Nov 2002	2.50
❑7, Dec 2002	2.50
❑8, Jan 2003	2.50

MIDNIGHT MASS
DC / VERTIGO

❑1, Mar 2004	2.95
❑2, Apr 2004	2.95
❑3, May 2004	2.50
❑4, Jun 2004	2.50
❑5, Jul 2004	2.95
❑6, Aug 2004	2.95

MIDNIGHT MEN
MARVEL / EPIC

❑1, Jun 1993; Embossed cover	2.50
❑2, Jul 1993	1.95
❑3, Aug 1993	1.95
❑4, Sep 1993	1.95

MIDNIGHT NATION
IMAGE

❑0.5; Wizard send-away promotional edition	5.00
❑0.5/Gold; Gold edition	9.00
❑1/A, Oct 2000; Cover A	4.00
❑1/B, Oct 2000; Dynamic Forces Exclusive; Cover B	5.00
❑1/C, Oct 2000	8.00
❑1/D, Oct 2000; Convention exclusive edition	4.50
❑2, Nov 2000	3.00
❑3, Dec 2000	3.00
❑4, Jan 2001	3.00
❑5, Mar 2001	3.00
❑6, Apr 2001	2.50

True origins of The Metal Men weren't revealed until more than 30 years after their initial appearance.

© 1963 National Periodical Publications Inc. (DC).

	N-MINT
❑7, May 2001	2.50
❑8, Jun 2001	2.50
❑9, Jul 2001	2.50
❑10, Aug 2001	2.50
❑11, Sep 2001	2.50
❑12, Oct 2001	2.95

MIDNIGHT PANTHER
CPM

❑1, Apr 1997	2.95
❑2, May 1997	2.95
❑3, Jun 1997	2.95
❑4, Jul 1997	2.95
❑5, Aug 1997	2.95
❑6, Sep 1997	2.95
❑7, Oct 1997	2.95
❑8, Nov 1997	2.95
❑9, Dec 1997	2.95
❑10, Jan 1998	2.95
❑11, Feb 1998	2.95
❑12, Mar 1998	2.95

MIDNIGHT PANTHER: FEUDAL FANTASY
CPM

❑1, Sep 1998; wraparound cover	2.95
❑2, Oct 1998	2.95

MIDNIGHT PANTHER: SCHOOL DAZE
CPM

❑1, Apr 1998; wraparound cover	2.95
❑2, May 1998	2.95
❑3, Jun 1998; wraparound cover	2.95
❑4, Jul 1998	2.95
❑5, Aug 1998	2.95

MIDNIGHT SCREAMS
MYSTERY GRAPHIX

❑1	2.50
❑2	2.50

MIDNIGHT SONS UNLIMITED
MARVEL

❑1, Apr 1993 KJ (a)	4.00
❑2, Jul 1993	4.00
❑3, Oct 1993 JR2 (c); JR2 (a); A: Spider-Man.	4.00
❑4, Jan 1994	3.95
❑5, Apr 1994	3.95
❑6, Jul 1994	3.95
❑7, Oct 1994	3.95
❑8, Jan 1995	3.95
❑9, May 1995 ARo (c); A: Destroyer. A: Union Jack. A: Blazing Skull.	3.95
❑Ashcan 1; Previews the Midnight Sons titles	0.75

MIDNITE
BLACKTHORNE

❑1, Nov 1986	1.75
❑2, Jan 1987	1.75
❑3, Mar 1987	1.75

MIDNITE SKULKER, THE
TARGET

❑1, Jun 1986	1.75
❑2, Aug 1986, b&w	1.75
❑3, Oct 1986	1.75
❑4, Dec 1986, b&w	1.75
❑5, Feb 1987	1.75
❑6, Apr 1987	1.75
❑7, Aug 1987	1.75

N-MINT

MIDNITE'S QUICKIES
ONE SHOT

- ❑1, b&w ... 3.50
- ❑2, b&w ... 2.95
- ❑Special 1, Oct 1997, b&w; No cover price; no indicia; published in Oct 97 ... 3.00
- ❑Special 1/A, Jan 1998, b&w; No cover price; center color poster ... 3.00
- ❑Special 1/B, Oct 1997, b&w; foil variant cover ... 3.00

MIDVALE
MU

- ❑1, b&w ... 2.50
- ❑2, Oct 1990, b&w ... 2.50

MIGHTILY MURDERED POWER RINGERS
EXPRESS / PARODY PRESS

- ❑1, b&w ... 2.50

MIGHTY ACE, THE
OMEGA 7

- ❑1 ... 2.00
- ❑2; indicia indicates 1992 copyright, probably not year of publication ... 2.00

MIGHTY ATOM, THE (2ND SERIES)
MAGAZINE ENTERPRISES

- ❑1, Nov 1957 ... 22.00
- ❑2 ... 18.00
- ❑3, Mar 1958 ... 18.00
- ❑4 ... 18.00
- ❑5 ... 18.00
- ❑6, Sep 1958 ... 18.00

MIGHTY BOMB
ANTARCTIC

- ❑1, Jul 1997, b&w ... 2.95

MIGHTY BOMBSHELLS, THE
ANTARCTIC

- ❑1, Sep 1993, b&w ... 2.75
- ❑2, Oct 1993, b&w ... 2.75

MIGHTY CARTOON HEROES
KARL ART

- ❑0 ... 2.95

MIGHTY COMICS
ARCHIE

- ❑40, Nov 1966, Series continued from Fly Man #39 ... 15.00
- ❑41, Dec 1966 ... 15.00
- ❑42, Jan 1967 ... 15.00
- ❑43, Feb 1967, 1: The Storm King. 1: The Stunner. A: The Web. A: The Shield. Black Hood appearace ... 15.00
- ❑44, Mar 1967 ... 15.00
- ❑45, Apr 1967 ... 15.00
- ❑46, May 1967 ... 15.00
- ❑47, Jun 1967 ... 15.00
- ❑48, Jul 1967 ... 15.00
- ❑49 1967 ... 15.00
- ❑50, Oct 1967 ... 15.00

MIGHTY CRUSADERS, THE (1ST SERIES)
ARCHIE

- ❑1, Nov 1965 O: The Shield. ... 24.00
- ❑2 1966 O: The Comet. ... 15.00
- ❑3, Mar 1966 O: Fly Man. ... 12.00
- ❑4, Apr 1966; "Too Many Superheroes" ... 10.00
- ❑5, Jun 1966 1: The Terrific Three. ... 10.00
- ❑6, Aug 1966 ... 10.00
- ❑7, Oct 1966 O: Fly Girl. ... 10.00

MIGHTY CRUSADERS (2ND SERIES)
ARCHIE / RED CIRCLE

- ❑4, Nov 1983, b&w; RB (w); RB (a); Previously titled All New Adventures of the Mighty Crusaders ... 1.25
- ❑5, Jan 1984, b&w ... 1.25
- ❑6, Mar 1984, b&w ... 1.25
- ❑7, May 1984, b&w ... 1.25
- ❑8, Jul 1984, b&w ... 1.25
- ❑9, Sep 1984, b&w ... 1.25
- ❑10, Dec 1984, b&w ... 1.25
- ❑11, Mar 1985, b&w ... 1.25
- ❑12, Jun 1985, b&w ... 1.25
- ❑13, Sep 1985, b&w ... 1.25

MIGHTYGUY
C&T

- ❑1, May 1987 ... 1.50
- ❑2 1987 ... 1.50
- ❑3 1987 ... 1.50
- ❑4 1987 ... 1.50
- ❑5 1987 ... 1.50

MIGHTY HERCULES, THE
GOLD KEY

- ❑1, Jul 1963 ... 40.00
- ❑2, Oct 1963 ... 40.00

MIGHTY HEROES, THE (DELL)
DELL

- ❑1, Mar 1967; O: The Mighty Heroes. based on Terrytoons feature ... 50.00
- ❑2, ca. 1967 ... 35.00
- ❑3, ca. 1967 ... 35.00
- ❑4, ca. 1967 ... 35.00

MIGHTY HEROES, THE (MARVEL)
MARVEL / PARAMOUNT

- ❑1, Jan 1998; based on Terrytoons feature ... 2.99

MIGHTY I, THE
IMAGE

- ❑1, May 1995; Image Comics Fan Club... ... 1.25
- ❑2, Jul 1995; Image Comics Fan Club... 1.25

MIGHTY MAGNOR, THE
MALIBU

- ❑1, Apr 1993 ME (w); SA (a); 1: The Mighty Magnor. ... 2.25
- ❑1/Variant, Apr 1993; ME (w); SA (a); 1: The Mighty Magnor. Pop-up cover ... 3.95
- ❑2, May 1993 ME (w); SA (a) ... 1.95
- ❑3, Jun 1993 ME (w); SA (a) ... 1.95
- ❑4, Jul 1993 ME (w); SA (a) ... 1.95
- ❑5, Dec 1993 ME (w); SA (a) ... 1.95
- ❑6, Apr 1994 ME (w); SA (a) ... 1.95

MIGHTY MARVEL WESTERN, THE
MARVEL

- ❑1, Oct 1968; giant; Rawhide Kid, Kid Colt, Two-Gun Kid ... 20.00
- ❑2, Dec 1968; giant; Rawhide Kid, Kid Colt, Two-Gun Kid ... 13.00
- ❑3, Feb 1969; giant; Rawhide Kid, Kid Colt, Two-Gun Kid ... 10.00
- ❑4, Apr 1969; giant; Rawhide Kid, Kid Colt, Two-Gun Kid ... 10.00
- ❑5, Jun 1969; giant; Rawhide Kid, Kid Colt, Two-Gun Kid ... 10.00
- ❑6, Nov 1969 ... 8.00
- ❑7, Jan 1970 ... 8.00
- ❑8, May 1970 ... 8.00
- ❑9, Jul 1970 ... 8.00
- ❑10, Sep 1970 ... 6.00
- ❑11, Nov 1970 ... 6.00
- ❑12, Jan 1971 ... 6.00
- ❑13, May 1971 ... 6.00
- ❑14, Sep 1971 ... 6.00
- ❑15, Dec 1971 ... 6.00
- ❑16, Mar 1972 ... 4.00
- ❑17, Jun 1972 ... 5.00
- ❑18, Jul 1972 ... 5.00
- ❑19, Sep 1972 ... 5.00
- ❑20, Oct 1972 ... 5.00
- ❑21, Nov 1972 ... 5.00
- ❑22, Jan 1973 ... 4.00
- ❑23, Mar 1973 ... 4.00
- ❑24, May 1973 ... 4.00
- ❑25, Jul 1973 ... 4.00
- ❑26, Sep 1973 ... 4.00
- ❑27, Oct 1973 ... 4.00
- ❑28, Dec 1973 ... 4.00
- ❑29, Jan 1974 ... 4.00
- ❑30, Mar 1974 ... 4.00
- ❑31, May 1974 ... 4.00
- ❑32, Jul 1974 ... 4.00
- ❑33, Aug 1974 ... 4.00
- ❑34, Sep 1974 ... 4.00
- ❑35, Oct 1974 ... 4.00
- ❑36, Dec 1974 ... 4.00
- ❑37, Jan 1975 ... 4.00
- ❑38, Mar 1975 ... 4.00
- ❑39, May 1975 ... 4.00
- ❑40, Jul 1975 ... 4.00
- ❑41, Sep 1975 ... 4.00
- ❑42, Oct 1975 ... 4.00
- ❑43, Dec 1975 ... 4.00
- ❑44, Mar 1976 ... 4.00
- ❑45, Jun 1976 ... 4.00
- ❑45/30 cent, Jun 1976; 30 cent regional price variant ... 20.00
- ❑46, Sep 1976 ... 4.00

MIGHTY MITES, THE (VOL. 1)
ETERNITY

- ❑1, Oct 1986; X-Men parody ... 2.00
- ❑2/A, Jan 1987; Batman parody ... 2.00
- ❑2/B, Jan 1987; Batman parody ... 2.00
- ❑3, Mar 1987 ... 2.00

MIGHTY MITES, THE (VOL. 2)
ETERNITY

- ❑1, May 1987 ... 1.95
- ❑2, Jul 1987 ... 1.95

MIGHTY MORPHIN POWER RANGERS (SABAN'S...)
MARVEL

- ❑1, Nov 1995 ... 2.50
- ❑2, Dec 1995 ... 2.00
- ❑3, Dec 1995; cover says Jan, indicia says Dec ... 2.00
- ❑4, Feb 1996 ... 2.00
- ❑5, Mar 1996 ... 2.00
- ❑6, Apr 1996 ... 2.00
- ❑7, May 1996 ... 2.00
- ❑8, Jun 1996 ... 2.00
- ❑9, Jul 1996 ... 2.00

MIGHTY MORPHIN POWER RANGERS: NINJA RANGERS/VR TROOPERS (SABAN'S...)
MARVEL

- ❑1, Dec 1995; flip book with VR Troopers back-up ... 2.50
- ❑2, Jan 1996; Power Rangers cover says Dec 95 ... 2.00
- ❑3, Feb 1996; flip book with VR Troopers back-up ... 2.00
- ❑4, Mar 1996; SD (a);flip book with VR Troopers back-up ... 2.00
- ❑5, Apr 1996; SD (a);flip book with VR Troopers back-up ... 2.00
- ❑6, May 1996 ... 2.00
- ❑7, Jun 1996 ... 2.00
- ❑8, Jul 1996 ... 2.00

MIGHTY MORPHIN POWER RANGERS SAGA (SABAN'S...)
HAMILTON

- ❑1, Dec 1994 O: the Power Rangers. 2.50
- ❑2, Jan 1995 ... 2.50
- ❑3, Feb 1995 ... 2.50

MIGHTY MORPHIN POWER RANGERS: THE MOVIE
MARVEL

- ❑1, Sep 1995 ... 2.95
- ❑1/Variant, Sep 1995; cardstock cover 3.95

MIGHTY MOUSE (SPOTLIGHT)
SPOTLIGHT

- ❑1, ca. 1987 ... 2.00
- ❑2, ca. 1987 ... 2.00

MIGHTY MOUSE (MARVEL)
MARVEL

- ❑1, Oct 1990; Dark Knight parody cover 2.00
- ❑2, Nov 1990 ... 1.50
- ❑3, Dec 1990; 1: Bat-Bat. Sub-Mariner parody ... 1.50
- ❑4, Jan 1991; GP (c);Crisis parody ... 1.50
- ❑5, Feb 1991; Crisis parody ... 1.50
- ❑6, Mar 1991; McFarlane parody ... 1.50
- ❑7, Apr 1991; computer art ... 1.50
- ❑8, May 1991 ... 1.50

Condition price index: Multiply "NM prices" above by: **0.83 for Very Fine/Near Mint**
0.66 for Very Fine • 0.33 for Fine • 0.2 for Very Good • 0.125 for Good

	N-MINT
❑9, Jun 1991	1.50
❑10, Jul 1991; Letterman parody	1.50

MIGHTY MOUSE ADVENTURE MAGAZINE
SPOTLIGHT

	N-MINT
❑1, b&w	2.00

MIGHTY MOUSE AND FRIENDS HOLIDAY SPECIAL
SPOTLIGHT

	N-MINT
❑1	2.00

MIGHTY MUTANIMALS (MINI-SERIES)
ARCHIE

	N-MINT
❑1, May 1991; TMNT spin-off	1.50
❑2 1991; TMNT spin-off	1.25
❑3 1991; TMNT spin-off	1.25

MIGHTY MUTANIMALS
ARCHIE

	N-MINT
❑1, Apr 1992	1.25
❑2, Jun 1992	1.25
❑3, Aug 1992	1.25
❑4, Sep 1992	1.25
❑5, Oct 1992	1.25
❑6, Dec 1992	1.25
❑7, Feb 1993	1.25
❑8, Apr 1993	1.25

MIGHTY SAMSON
GOLD KEY

	N-MINT
❑1, Jul 1964; O: Samson. 1: Samson. back cover pin-up	30.00
❑2, Jun 1965; 1: Terra of Jerz. back cover pin-up	18.00
❑3, Sep 1965; back cover pin-up	18.00
❑4, Dec 1965; back cover pin-up	12.00
❑5, Mar 1966; back cover pin-up	12.00
❑6, Jun 1966; back cover pin-up	10.00
❑7, Sep 1966; back cover pin-up	10.00
❑8, Dec 1966	10.00
❑9, Mar 1967; In Washington, D.C.	10.00
❑10, Jun 1967	10.00
❑11, Aug 1967	8.00
❑12, Nov 1967	8.00
❑13, Feb 1968	8.00
❑14, May 1968	8.00
❑15, Aug 1968	8.00
❑16, Nov 1968	8.00
❑17, Feb 1969	8.00
❑18, May 1969	8.00
❑19, Aug 1969; N'Yark floods	8.00
❑20, Nov 1969	8.00
❑21, Aug 1972	5.00
❑22, Dec 1973	5.00
❑23, Mar 1974	5.00
❑24, Jun 1974	5.00
❑25, Sep 1974	5.00
❑26, Dec 1974	5.00
❑27, Mar 1975	5.00
❑28, Jun 1975	5.00
❑29, Sep 1975	5.00
❑30, Dec 1975; In Macy's	5.00
❑31, Mar 1976 V: giant moths.	5.00
❑32, Apr 1982; 1982 revival	4.00

MIGHTY THOR, THE: GODSTORM
MARVEL

	N-MINT
❑1, Nov 2001	3.50
❑2, Dec 2001	3.50
❑3, Jan 2002	3.50

MIGHTY TINY
ANTARCTIC

	N-MINT
❑1, b&w	2.00
❑2, b&w	2.00
❑3, b&w	2.00
❑4, b&w	2.00
❑5	2.50

MIGHTY TINY: THE MOUSE MARINES
ANTARCTIC

	N-MINT
❑1, b&w	2.50

MIKE DANGER (VOL. 1) (MICKEY SPILLANE'S...)
TEKNO

	N-MINT
❑1, Sep 1995 FM (c)	1.95
❑2, Oct 1995	1.95
❑3, Nov 1995	1.95
❑4, Dec 1995	1.95
❑5, Dec 1995	2.25
❑6, Jan 1996	2.25
❑7, Jan 1996	2.25
❑8, Feb 1996	2.25
❑9, Mar 1996	2.25
❑10, Apr 1996	2.25
❑11, May 1996	2.25

MIKE DANGER (VOL. 2) (MICKEY SPILLANE'S...)
BIG

	N-MINT
❑1, Jun 1996	2.25
❑2, Jul 1996; Mike's head is separated from his body	2.25
❑3, Aug 1996	2.25
❑4, Sep 1996	2.25
❑5, Oct 1996	2.25
❑6, Nov 1996	2.25
❑7, Dec 1996	2.25
❑8, Jan 1997	2.25
❑9, Feb 1997	2.25
❑10, Apr 1997	2.25

MIKE MAUSER FILES
AVALON

	N-MINT
❑1 1999	2.95

MIKE MIST MINUTE MIST-ERIES
ECLIPSE

	N-MINT
❑1, Apr 1981, b&w	1.50

MIKE REGAN
HARDBOILED

	N-MINT
❑1, b&w	2.95

MIKE SHAYNE PRIVATE EYE
DELL

	N-MINT
❑1, Nov 1962	16.00
❑2, Feb 1962	10.00
❑3, May 1962	10.00

MILIKARDO KNIGHTS
MAD BADGER

	N-MINT
❑1, Mar 1997, b&w	3.00
❑2, Jan 1998, b&w	3.00

MILK
RADIO

	N-MINT
❑1, Sep 1997, b&w	2.95
❑2, Nov 1997, b&w	2.95
❑3, Jan 1998, b&w	2.95
❑4, Mar 1998, b&w	2.95
❑5, May 1998, b&w	2.95
❑6, Jul 1998, b&w	2.95
❑7, Sep 1998, b&w	2.95
❑8, Nov 1998, b&w	2.95
❑9, Jan 1999, b&w	2.95
❑10, Mar 1999, b&w	2.95
❑11, May 1999, b&w	2.95
❑12, Jul 1999, b&w	2.95
❑13, Sep 1999, b&w	2.95
❑14, Nov 1999, b&w	2.95
❑15, Jan 2000, b&w	2.95
❑16, Mar 2000, b&w	2.95
❑17, May 2000, b&w	2.95
❑18, Jul 2000, b&w	2.95
❑19, Sep 2000, b&w	2.95
❑20, Nov 2000	2.95
❑21, Jan 2001	2.99
❑22, Mar 2001	2.99
❑23, May 2001	2.99
❑24, Jul 2001	2.99
❑25, Sep 2001	2.99
❑26, Nov 2001	2.99
❑27, Jan 2002	2.99
❑28, Mar 2002	2.99
❑29, May 2002	2.99
❑30, Jul 2002	2.99
❑31, Sep 2002	2.99
❑32, Nov 2002	2.99

To celebrate his 60th anniversary, Gladstone produced a 100-page issue of *Mickey Mouse* which contained a compilation of newspaper strips and other features.

© 1989 Walt Disney Productions (Gladstone).

	N-MINT
❑33, Mar 2003	2.99
❑34, May 2003	2.99

MILK & CHEESE
SLAVE LABOR

	N-MINT
❑1, Mar 1991, b&w	65.00
❑1-2, Sep 1991, b&w	6.00
❑1-3, Sep 1992, b&w	5.00
❑1-4, Aug 1993, b&w	3.00
❑1-5, Oct 1994, b&w	3.00
❑1-6, Sep 1995, b&w	3.00
❑1-7, Feb 1997, b&w	2.75
❑2, Mar 1992, b&w; Other Number One; has Doctor Radium ad on back cover	35.00
❑2-2, Jun 1993; has Fine Dairy Products ad on back cover	5.00
❑2-3, Oct 1994; has APE II ad on back cover	4.00
❑2-4, Jan 1996	2.75
❑2-5	2.75
❑3, Aug 1992, b&w; Third #1; has Rats ad on back cover	28.00
❑3-2, May 1993; has Fine Dairy Products ad on back cover	4.00
❑3-3, Oct 1994; has APE II ad on back cover	3.00
❑3-4, Feb 1996	2.75
❑3-5	2.75
❑4, Apr 1993, b&w; Fourth #1; has Fine Dairy Products ad on back cover	16.00
❑4-2, Mar 1995; has APE II ad on back cover	3.00
❑4-3, Aug 1996	2.50
❑5, Apr 1994, b&w; First Second Issue; has APE ad on back cover	15.00
❑5-2, Nov 1994; has APE II ad on back cover	3.00
❑5-3, Feb 1996	3.00
❑5-4	2.75
❑6, Apr 1995, b&w; Six Six Six	8.00
❑6-2, Sep 1996	2.75
❑7, Jun 1997, b&w; Latest Thing!	3.00

MILLENNIUM
DC

	N-MINT
❑1, Jan 1988 JSa (a)	2.00
❑2, Jan 1988	1.50
❑3, Jan 1988	1.50
❑4, Jan 1988	1.50
❑5, Feb 1988	1.50
❑6, Feb 1988	1.50
❑7, Feb 1988	1.50
❑8, Feb 1988	1.50

MILLENNIUM 2.5 A.D.
AVALON

	N-MINT
❑1	2.95

MILLENNIUM EDITION: ACTION COMICS
DC

	N-MINT
❑1, Feb 2000	3.95

MILLENNIUM EDITION: ADVENTURE COMICS
DC

	N-MINT
❑61, Dec 2000	3.95
❑247, Nov 2000; The Legion of Super-Heroes; The 13 Superstition Arrows; Aquaman's Super Sea-Squad	2.50

N-MINT

MILLENNIUM EDITION: ALL STAR COMICS
DC
- ❑3, Jun 2000 1: the Justice Society of America. 3.95
- ❑3/Variant, Jun 2000; 1: the Justice Society of America. chromium cover 10.00
- ❑8, Feb 2001 O: Wonder Woman. 1: Wonder Woman. 3.95

MILLENNIUM EDITION: ALL-STAR WESTERN
DC
- ❑10, Apr 2000; Reprints All-Star Western #10 .... 2.50

MILLENNIUM EDITION: BATMAN
DC
- ❑1, Feb 2001 .... 3.95

MILLENNIUM EDITION: BATMAN: THE DARK KNIGHT RETURNS
DC
- ❑1, Oct 2000; Reprints Batman: The Dark Knight #1 .... 5.95

MILLENNIUM EDITION: CRISIS ON INFINITE EARTHS
DC
- ❑1, ca. 2000; Reprints Crisis on Infinite Earths #1 .... 2.50

MILLENNIUM EDITION: DETECTIVE COMICS
DC
- ❑1, Jan 2001; Reprints Detective Comics #1 .... 3.95
- ❑27, Feb 2000 .... 3.95
- ❑38, ca. 2000 .... 3.95
- ❑225, Dec 2000 .... 2.50
- ❑359, Oct 2000 .... 3.95

MILLENNIUM EDITION: FLASH COMICS
DC
- ❑1, Sep 2000; Reprints Flash Comics #1 .... 3.95

MILLENNIUM EDITION: GEN13
WILDSTORM
- ❑1; Reprints Gen13 (Mini-Series) #1 2.50

MILLENNIUM EDITION: GREEN LANTERN
DC
- ❑76, ca. 2000 .... 2.50

MILLENNIUM EDITION: HELLBLAZER
DC
- ❑1, Jul 2000; Reprints Hellblazer #1 . 2.95

MILLENNIUM EDITION: HOUSE OF MYSTERY
DC
- ❑1, Sep 2000; Reprints House of Mystery #1 .... 2.50

MILLENNIUM EDITION: HOUSE OF SECRETS
DC
- ❑92, May 2000 .... 2.50

MILLENNIUM EDITION: JLA
DC
- ❑1, ca. 2000 .... 2.50

MILLENNIUM EDITION: JUSTICE LEAGUE
DC
- ❑1, Jul 2000; Reprints Justice League #1 .... 2.50

MILLENNIUM EDITION: KINGDOM COME
DC
- ❑1, Aug 2000 .... 5.95

MILLENNIUM EDITION: MILITARY COMICS
DC
- ❑1, Oct 2000 .... 3.95

N-MINT

MILLENNIUM EDITION: MORE FUN COMICS
DC
- ❑73, Jan 2001 .... 3.95
- ❑101, Nov 2000 .... 2.95

MILLENNIUM EDITION: MYSTERIOUS SUSPENSE
DC
- ❑1, Sep 2000; 1: The Question; Reprints Mysterious Suspense #1 .... 2.50

MILLENNIUM EDITION: NEW GODS
DC
- ❑1, Jun 2000 .... 2.50

MILLENNIUM EDITION: OUR ARMY AT WAR
DC
- ❑81, Jun 2000 .... 2.50

MILLENNIUM EDITION: PLOP!
DC
- ❑1, Jul 2000; Reprints Plop! #1 .... 2.50

MILLENNIUM EDITION: POLICE COMICS
DC
- ❑1, Sep 2000; Reprints Police Comics #1 .... 3.95

MILLENNIUM EDITION: PREACHER
DC
- ❑1, Oct 2000 .... 2.95

MILLENNIUM EDITION: S ENSATION COMICS
DC
- ❑1, Oct 2000; Reprints Sensation Comics #1 .... 3.95

MILLENNIUM EDITION: SHOWCASE
DC
- ❑4, ca. 2000; Reprints Showcase #4 . 2.50
- ❑9, Jan 2001; Reprints Showcase #9 2.50
- ❑22, Dec 2000; Reprints Showcase #22 2.50

MILLENNIUM EDITION: SUPERBOY
DC
- ❑1, Feb 2001 .... 2.95

MILLENNIUM EDITION: SUPERMAN
DC
- ❑75, ca. 2000 .... 2.95

MILLENNIUM EDITION: SUPERMAN (1ST SERIES)
DC
- ❑1, Dec 2000; Reprints Superman (1st Series) #1 .... 2.95
- ❑76, ca. 2000 .... 2.95
- ❑233, Jan 2001 .... 2.50

MILLENNIUM EDITION: SUPERMAN'S PAL JIMMY OLSEN
DC
- ❑1, Apr 2000; Reprints Superman's Pal Jimmy Olsen #1 .... 2.95

MILLENNIUM EDITION: TALES CALCULATED TO DRIVE YOU MAD
DC
- ❑1, ca. 2000 .... 2.95

MILLENNIUM EDITION: THE BRAVE AND THE BOLD
DC
- ❑28, Feb 2000 .... 2.50
- ❑85, Nov 2000 .... 2.50

MILLENNIUM EDITION: THE FLASH
DC
- ❑123, May 2000; Reprints The Flash (1st Series) #1 .... 2.50

MILLENNIUM EDITION: THE MAN OF STEEL
DC
- ❑1, ca. 2000 .... 2.50

MILLENNIUM EDITION: THE NEW TEEN TITANS
DC
- ❑1, Dec 2000 .... 2.50

N-MINT

MILLENNIUM EDITION: THE SAGA OF THE SWAMP THING
DC
- ❑21, Feb 2000; Reprints Sandman #1 2.50

MILLENNIUM EDITION: THE SANDMAN
DC
- ❑1, Feb 2000; Reprints Sandman #1 . 2.95

MILLENNIUM EDITION: THE SHADOW
DC
- ❑1, Feb 2001 .... 2.50

MILLENNIUM EDITION: THE SPIRIT
DC
- ❑1, Jul 2000; Reprints The Spirit #1 .. 2.95

MILLENNIUM EDITION: WATCHMEN
DC
- ❑1, ca. 2000; Reprints Watchmen #1 2.50

MILLENNIUM EDITION: WHIZ COMICS
DC
- ❑1, Mar 2000 .... 3.95

MILLENNIUM EDITION: WILDC.A.T.S
DC
- ❑1, ca. 2000 .... 2.50

MILLENNIUM EDITION: WONDER WOMAN (1ST SERIES)
DC
- ❑1, Aug 2000; Reprints Wonder Woman (1st Series) #1 .... 3.95

MILLENNIUM EDITION: WONDER WOMAN (2ND SERIES)
DC
- ❑1, May 2000; Reprints Wonder Woman (2nd Series) #1 .... 2.50

MILLENNIUM EDITION: WORLD'S FINEST
DC
- ❑71 .... 2.50

MILLENNIUM EDITION: YOUNG ROMANCE COMICS
DC
- ❑1, Apr 2000; Reprints Young Romance (DC) #1; 1st romance comic 2.95

MILLENNIUM FEVER
DC / VERTIGO
- ❑1, Oct 1995 .... 2.50
- ❑2, Nov 1995 .... 2.50
- ❑3, Dec 1995 .... 2.50
- ❑4, Jan 1996 .... 2.50
- ❑Ashcan 1 .... 0.75

MILLENNIUM INDEX
ECLIPSE
- ❑1, Mar 1988 .... 2.00
- ❑2, Mar 1988 .... 2.00

MINDBENDERS
MBS
- ❑1 .... 2.50

MINDGAME GALLERY, THE
MINDGAME
- ❑1, b&w 1.95

MIND PROBE
RIP OFF
- ❑1, b&w 3.25

MINIMUM WAGE
FANTAGRAPHICS
- ❑1, Oct 1995 .... 2.95
- ❑2, Dec 1995 .... 2.95
- ❑3, Mar 1996 .... 2.95
- ❑4, Jun 1996; pin-ups 2.95
- ❑5, Nov 1996 .... 2.95
- ❑6, Mar 1997 .... 2.95
- ❑7, Aug 1997 .... 2.95
- ❑8, Feb 1998 .... 2.95
- ❑9, Jun 1998 .... 2.95
- ❑10, Jan 1999 .... 2.95

N-MINT

MINISTRY OF SPACE
IMAGE
- ❑1, Apr 2001 ... 2.95
- ❑2, Sep 2001 ... 2.95
- ❑3, May 2004 ... 2.95

MINK
TOKYOPOP
- ❑1, Apr 2004 ... 9.99

MINOTAUR
LABYRINTH
- ❑1, Feb 1996, b&w ... 2.50
- ❑2, Apr 1996, b&w ... 2.50
- ❑3, Jun 1996, b&w; cover says Jul, indicia says Jun ... 2.50
- ❑4, Sep 1996, b&w ... 2.50

MINX, THE
DC / VERTIGO
- ❑1, Oct 1998 ... 2.50
- ❑2, Nov 1998 ... 2.50
- ❑3, Dec 1998 ... 2.50
- ❑4, Jan 1999 ... 2.50
- ❑5, Feb 1999 ... 2.50
- ❑6, Mar 1999 ... 2.50
- ❑7, Apr 1999 ... 2.50
- ❑8, May 1999 ... 2.50

MIRACLE GIRLS
TOKYOPOP
- ❑1, ca. 2000 ... 2.95
- ❑2, ca. 2000 ... 2.95
- ❑3 ... 2.95
- ❑4 ... 2.95
- ❑5, ca. 2001 ... 2.95
- ❑6, ca. 2001 ... 2.95
- ❑7, ca. 2001 ... 2.95
- ❑8, ca. 2001 ... 2.95
- ❑9, ca. 2001 ... 2.95
- ❑10, ca. 2001 ... 2.95
- ❑11, ca. 2001 ... 2.95
- ❑12, ca. 2001 ... 2.95
- ❑13, ca. 2001 ... 2.95
- ❑14 ... 2.95
- ❑15 ... 2.95
- ❑16, ca. 2002 ... 2.95
- ❑17, ca. 2002 ... 2.95
- ❑18, ca. 2002 ... 2.95
- ❑19, ca. 2002 ... 2.95

MIRACLEMAN
ECLIPSE
- ❑1, Aug 1985 AMo (w) ... 10.00
- ❑2, Oct 1985 AMo (w) ... 8.00
- ❑3, Nov 1985 AMo (w) ... 8.00
- ❑4, Dec 1985 AMo (w) ... 8.00
- ❑5, Jan 1986 AMo (w) ... 8.00
- ❑6, Feb 1986 AMo (w) ... 8.00
- ❑7, Apr 1986 AMo (w); D: Gargunza. ... 8.00
- ❑8, Jun 1986 AMo (w); 1: The New Wave. ... 8.00
- ❑9, Jul 1986; AMo (w); birth ... 10.00
- ❑10, Dec 1986 AMo (w) ... 10.00
- ❑11, May 1987 AMo (w) ... 14.00
- ❑12, Sep 1987 AMo (w) ... 14.00
- ❑13, Nov 1987 AMo (w) ... 18.00
- ❑14, Apr 1988 AMo (w) ... 24.00
- ❑15, Nov 1988; AMo (w); Scarce ... 70.00
- ❑16, Dec 1988; AMo (w); last Moore ... 16.00
- ❑17, Jun 1990; NG (w); 1st Neil Gaiman ... 25.00
- ❑18, Aug 1990 NG (w) ... 20.00
- ❑19, Nov 1990; NG (w); cardstock cover ... 15.00
- ❑20, Mar 1991; NG (w); cardstock cover ... 15.00
- ❑21, Jul 1991 NG (w) ... 15.00
- ❑22, Aug 1991 NG (w) ... 15.00
- ❑23, Jun 1992 NG (w) ... 16.00
- ❑24, Aug 1993; scarcer ... 25.00
- ❑3D 1, Dec 1985; Giant-size; AMo (w); 3-D Special #1 ... 10.00

MIRACLEMAN: APOCRYPHA
ECLIPSE
- ❑1, Nov 1991 JRo, MW, NG (w) ... 3.00
- ❑2, Jan 1992 KB, NG (w) ... 3.00
- ❑3, Apr 1991 NG (w) ... 3.00

MIRACLEMAN FAMILY
ECLIPSE
- ❑1, May 1988 O: Young Miracleman. ... 3.00
- ❑2, Sep 1988 ... 3.00

MIRACLE SQUAD
UPSHOT
- ❑1 ... 2.00
- ❑2 ... 2.00
- ❑3, b&w ... 2.00
- ❑4, b&w ... 2.00

MIRACLE SQUAD, THE: BLOOD AND DUST
APPLE
- ❑1, Jan 1989, b&w ... 2.00
- ❑2, Mar 1989, b&w ... 2.00
- ❑3, May 1989, b&w ... 2.00
- ❑4, Jul 1989, b&w ... 2.00

MIRRORWALKER
NOW
- ❑1, Oct 1990; semi-fumetti ... 2.95
- ❑2 ... 2.95

MIRRORWORLD: RAIN
NETCO
- ❑0, Apr 1997 ... 3.25
- ❑1, Feb 1997 ... 3.25

MISADVENTURES OF BREADMAN AND DOUGHBOY, THE
HEMLOCK PARK
- ❑1, Oct 1999; no cover price ... 2.95
- ❑2 ... 2.95

MISEROTH: AMOK HELL
NORTHSTAR
- ❑1 ... 4.95
- ❑2 ... 4.95
- ❑3 ... 4.95

MISERY
IMAGE
- ❑1, Dec 1995 ... 2.95

MISPLACED
IMAGE
- ❑1, May 2003 ... 2.95
- ❑2, Aug 2003 ... 2.95

MISS FURY (ADVENTURE)
ADVENTURE
- ❑1, Nov 1991 ... 2.50
- ❑1/Ltd.; limited edition ... 4.95
- ❑2, Dec 1991 ... 2.50
- ❑3 ... 2.50
- ❑4 ... 2.50

MISS FURY (AVALON)
AVALON
- ❑1 ... 2.95
- ❑2 ... 2.95

MISSING BEINGS SPECIAL
COMICS INTERVIEW
- ❑1, b&w ... 2.25

MISSION: IMPOSSIBLE (DELL)
DELL
- ❑1, May 1967; Same cover as #5 ... 24.00
- ❑2, Sep 1967 ... 18.00
- ❑3, Dec 1967 ... 18.00
- ❑4, Oct 1968 ... 18.00
- ❑5, Oct 1969; Same cover as #1 ... 12.00

MISSION IMPOSSIBLE (MARVEL)
MARVEL
- ❑1, May 1996; prequel to movie ... 2.95

MISSIONS IN TIBET
DIMENSION
- ❑1, Jul 1995 ... 2.50

MISS PEACH
DELL
- ❑1, Oct 1963 ... 60.00

When Valiant began reviving various Gold Key characters, Mighty Samson was one of the most-requested for an update.
© 1966 Gold Key.

N-MINT

MISSPENT YOUTHS
BRAVE NEW WORDS
- ❑1 ... 2.50
- ❑2 ... 2.50
- ❑3, Jul 1991 ... 2.50

MISS VICTORY GOLDEN ANNIVERSARY SPECIAL
AC
- ❑1, Nov 1991; reprint 1: Miss Victory ... 5.00

MISTER AMERICA
ENDEAVOR
- ❑1 ... 2.95
- ❑2, Apr 1994 ... 2.95

MR. AND MRS. J. EVIL SCIENTIST
GOLD KEY
- ❑1, Nov 1963 ... 50.00
- ❑2, ca. 1964 ... 30.00
- ❑3, ca. 1965 ... 20.00
- ❑4, Sep 1966 ... 20.00

MR. AVERAGE
B.S.
- ❑1 ... 2.25
- ❑2 ... 2.25
- ❑3 ... 2.25

MR. BEAT ADVENTURES
MOORDAM
- ❑1, Jan 1997, b&w ... 2.95

MR. BEAT'S BABES AND BONGOS ANNUAL
MOORDAM
- ❑1 ... 2.95

MR. BEAT'S HOUSE OF BURNING JAZZ LOVE
MOORDAM
- ❑1, Dec 1997, b&w ... 2.95

MR. BEAT'S TWO-FISTED ATOMIC ACTION SUPER SPECIAL
MOORDAM
- ❑1, Sep 1997, b&w ... 2.95

MISTER BLANK
SLAVE LABOR / AMAZE INK
- ❑0 ... 2.95
- ❑1, May 1997 ... 2.95
- ❑2, May 1997 ... 2.95
- ❑3, Aug 1997 ... 2.95
- ❑4, Nov 1997 ... 2.95
- ❑5, Feb 1998 ... 2.95

MR. CREAM PUFF
BLACKTHORNE
- ❑1 ... 1.75

MR. DAY & MR. NIGHT
SLAVE LABOR
- ❑1, Apr 1993 ... 3.95

MR. DOOM
PIED PIPER
- ❑1, Jul 1987 ... 1.95

MISTER E
DC
- ❑1, Jun 1991 ... 2.00
- ❑2, Jul 1991 ... 2.00
- ❑3, Aug 1991 ... 2.00
- ❑4, Sep 1991 ... 2.00

Condition price index: Multiply "NM prices" above by: **0.83 for Very Fine/Near Mint**
0.66 for Very Fine • 0.33 for Fine • 0.2 for Very Good • 0.125 for Good

N-MINT

MR. FIXITT (APPLE)
APPLE
❑1, Jan 1989, b&w 1.95
❑2, Mar 1990 .... 1.95

MR. FIXITT (HEROIC)
HEROIC
❑1, b&w; trading card 2.95

MR. HERO-THE NEWMATIC MAN (1ST SERIES) (NEIL GAIMAN'S...)
TEKNO
❑1, Mar 1995; game piece; trading card 1.95
❑2, Apr 1995; game piece; trading card 1.95
❑3, May 1995; game piece; trading card 1.95
❑4, Jun 1995; coupon 1.95
❑5, Jul 1995 .... 1.95
❑6, Aug 1995 .... 1.95
❑7, Sep 1995 .... 1.95
❑8, Oct 1995 .... 1.95
❑9, Nov 1995 .... 1.95
❑10, Dec 1995 .... 1.95
❑11, Dec 1995 .... 1.95
❑12, Jan 1996 .... 2.25
❑13, Jan 1996 .... 2.25
❑14, Feb 1996 .... 2.25
❑15, Mar 1996 .... 2.25
❑16, Apr 1996 .... 2.25
❑17, May 1996 .... 2.25

MR. HERO-THE NEWMATIC MAN (2ND SERIES) (NEIL GAIMAN'S...)
BIG
❑1, Jun 1996 .... 2.25
❑2, Jul 1996 .... 2.25
❑3, Aug 1996 .... 2.25
❑4, Sep 1996 .... 2.25

MR. JIGSAW SPECIAL
OCEAN
❑1, Spr 1988; O: Mr. Jigsaw. blue paper 2.00

MR. LIZARD 3-D
NOW
❑1, May 1993; instant Mr. Lizard capsule 3.50

MR. LIZARD ANNUAL
NOW
❑1, Sep 1993; Ralph Snart capsule ... 2.95

MR. MAJESTIC
DC / WILDSTORM
❑1, Sep 1999 .... 3.00
❑2, Oct 1999 .... 2.50
❑3, Nov 1999 .... 2.50
❑4, Dec 1999 .... 2.50
❑5, Jan 2000 .... 2.50
❑6, Feb 2000 .... 2.50
❑7, Mar 2000 .... 2.50
❑8, Apr 2000 .... 2.50
❑9, May 2000 .... 2.50

MISTER MIRACLE (1ST SERIES)
DC
❑1, Apr 1971 JK (w); JK (a); 1: Oberon. 1: Mister Miracle. 24.00
❑2, Jun 1971 JK (a); 1: Doctor Bedlam. 1: Granny Goodness. 15.00
❑3, Aug 1971; JK (a); V: Doctor Bedlam. Boy Commandos reprint 12.00
❑4, Oct 1971; Giant-size; JK (a); 1: Big Barda, Boy Commandos reprint (Detective Comics #82) 11.00
❑5, Dec 1971; Giant-size; JK (a);Boy Commandos reprint (Detective Comics #76) 11.00
❑6, Feb 1972; Giant-size; JK (a); 1: Funky Flashman. 1: Lashina. 1: Female Furies. reprints Boy Commandos #1 .... 10.00
❑7, Apr 1972; Giant-size; JK (a);reprints Boy Commandos #3 ... 10.00
❑8, Jun 1972; Giant-size; JK (a);Boy Commandos reprint (Detective Comics #64) 10.00
❑9, Aug 1972 JK (a) 8.00
❑10, Oct 1972 JK (a) 8.00
❑11, Dec 1972 JK (a) 7.00
❑12, Feb 1973 JK (a) 7.00
❑13, Apr 1973 JK (a) 7.00
❑14, Jul 1973 JK (w); JK (a); 1: Madame Evil Eye. 7.00
❑15, Sep 1973 JK (a); 1: Mister Miracle II (Shilo Norman). 7.00
❑16, Nov 1973 JK (a) 7.00
❑17, Jan 1974 JK (a) 7.00
❑18, Mar 1974; JK (a);series goes on hiatus; Wedding of Mister Miracle and Barda 7.00
❑19, Sep 1977 .... 5.00
❑20, Oct 1977 .... 5.00
❑21, Dec 1977 .... 5.00
❑22, Feb 1978 .... 5.00
❑23, Apr 1978 .... 5.00
❑24, Jun 1978 .... 5.00
❑25, Sep 1978 .... 5.00
❑Special 1, ca. 1987 .... 3.50

MISTER MIRACLE (2ND SERIES)
DC
❑1, Jan 1989 O: Mister Miracle. A: Doctor Bedlam. A: Dr. Bedlam. 2.50
❑2, Feb 1989 .... 1.50
❑3, Mar 1989 .... 1.50
❑4, Apr 1989 .... 1.50
❑5, Jun 1989 .... 1.50
❑6, Jul 1989 .... 1.25
❑7, Aug 1989 .... 1.25
❑8, Sep 1989 .... 1.25
❑9, Oct 1989 1: Maxi-Man. 1.25
❑10, Nov 1989 .... 1.25
❑11, Dec 1989 .... 1.25
❑12, Jan 1990 .... 1.25
❑13, Mar 1990 A: Lobo. 1.25
❑14, Apr 1990 A: Lobo. 1.25
❑15, May 1990 .... 1.25
❑16, Jun 1990 .... 1.25
❑17, Jul 1990 .... 1.25
❑18, Aug 1990 .... 1.25
❑19, Sep 1990 .... 1.25
❑20, Oct 1990 .... 1.25
❑21, Nov 1990 .... 1.25
❑22, Dec 1990 .... 1.25
❑23, Jan 1991 .... 1.25
❑24, Feb 1991 .... 1.25
❑25, Mar 1991 .... 1.25
❑26, Apr 1991 .... 1.25
❑27, May 1991 .... 1.25
❑28, Jun 1991 .... 1.25

MISTER MIRACLE (3RD SERIES)
DC
❑1, Apr 1996 .... 1.95
❑2, May 1996 .... 1.95
❑3, Jun 1996 .... 1.95
❑4, Jul 1996 .... 1.95
❑5, Aug 1996 .... 1.95
❑6, Sep 1996 .... 1.95
❑7, Oct 1996 .... 1.95

MR. MONSTER
DARK HORSE
❑1, Feb 1988 O: Mr. Monster. 2.00
❑2, Apr 1988 .... 2.00
❑3, Jun 1988 .... 2.00
❑4, Nov 1988 .... 2.00
❑5, Mar 1989 .... 2.00
❑6, Oct 1989; has indicia for #5 .... 2.00
❑7, Apr 1990 .... 2.00
❑8, Sep 1990; Giant-size D: Mr. Monster. 5.00

MR. MONSTER ATTACKS!
TUNDRA
❑1, Aug 1992 .... 3.95
❑2, Sep 1992 .... 3.95
❑3, Oct 1992 .... 3.95

MR. MONSTER PRESENTS (CRACK-A-BOOM!)
CALIBER
❑1, Jun 1997 .... 2.95
❑2 1997 .... 2.95
❑3, Sep 1997 .... 2.95

MR. MONSTER'S GAL FRIDAY...KELLY!
IMAGE
❑1, Jan 2000 .... 3.50
❑2 .... 3.50
❑3 .... 3.50

MR. MONSTER'S HIGH-OCTANE HORROR
ECLIPSE
❑1, May 1986; A.K.A. Super Duper Special #2 .... 2.00
❑3D 1, May 1986; A.K.A. Super Duper Special #1 .... 2.50

MR. MONSTER'S HI-SHOCK SCHLOCK
ECLIPSE
❑1, Mar 1987; A.K.A. Super Duper Special #6 .... 2.00
❑2, May 1987; A.K.A. Super Duper Special #7 .... 2.00

MR. MONSTER'S HI-VOLTAGE SUPER SCIENCE
ECLIPSE
❑1, Jan 1987; A.K.A. Super Duper Special #5 .... 2.00

MR. MONSTER'S TRIPLE THREAT 3-D
3-D ZONE
❑1, Jul 1993 .... 3.95

MR. MONSTER'S TRUE CRIME
ECLIPSE
❑1, Sep 1986; A.K.A. Super Duper Special #3 .... 2.00
❑2, Oct 1986; A.K.A. Super Duper Special #4 .... 2.00

MR. MONSTER'S WEIRD TALES OF THE FUTURE
ECLIPSE
❑1; BW (w); BW (a);A.K.A. Super Duper Special #8 .... 2.00

MR. MONSTER VS. GORZILLA
IMAGE
❑1, Jul 1998; red, white, and blue 2.95

MR. MXYZPTLK (VILLAINS)
DC
❑1, Feb 1998; New Year's Evil 1.95

MR. NATURAL
KITCHEN SINK
❑1 .... 90.00
❑2, Oct 1971 .... 50.00
❑3, Jan 1977 .... 45.00
❑3-2 .... 22.00
❑3-3 .... 10.00
❑3-4 .... 4.50
❑3-5; 1980 .... 3.00
❑3-6 .... 2.50
❑3-7 .... 2.50
❑3-8 .... 2.50

MR. NIGHTMARE'S WINTER SPECIAL
MOONSTONE
❑1, Dec 1995, b&w 3.50

MR. NIGHTMARE'S WONDERFUL WORLD
MOONSTONE
❑1, Jun 1995, b&w 2.95
❑2, Aug 1995, b&w 2.95
❑3, Oct 1995, b&w 2.95
❑4, Nov 1995, b&w 2.95
❑5, Feb 1996, b&w 2.95

MISTER PLANET
MR. PLANET
❑1, b&w 3.00
❑2, b&w 3.00

MISTER SIXX
IMAGINE NATION
❑1 .... 1.95

N-MINT

MR. T AND THE T-FORCE
NOW

❑1, Jun 1993; NA (w); NA (a);trading card 3.00
❑1/Gold; Gold logo promotional edition; NA (w); NA (a);gold, advance 4.00
❑2, Sep 1993; trading card 2.00
❑3, Oct 1993; trading card 2.00
❑4, Nov 1993; trading card 2.00
❑5, Dec 1993; trading card 2.00
❑6, Jan 1994; trading card 2.00
❑7, Feb 1994; trading card 2.00
❑8, Mar 1994; trading card 2.00
❑9, Apr 1994; trading card; cover says Aug, indicia says Apr 2.00
❑10, May 1994 .... 2.00
❑11, Jun 1994 .... 2.00
❑12, Jul 1994 .... 2.00

MISTER X (VOL. 1)
VORTEX

❑1, Jun 1984 1: Mister X. 4.00
❑2, Aug 1984 .... 2.75
❑3 .... 2.75
❑4 .... 2.50
❑5 .... 2.50
❑6 .... 2.50
❑7 .... 2.50
❑8 .... 2.50
❑9 .... 2.50
❑10, Oct 1986 BSz (c) 2.50
❑11 .... 2.50
❑12, Jan 1988 .... 2.50
❑13, Mar 1988 .... 2.50
❑14 .... 2.50

MISTER X (VOL. 2)
VORTEX

❑1, b&w 3.00
❑2, b&w 2.50
❑3, b&w 2.50
❑4, b&w 2.50
❑5, b&w 2.50
❑6, b&w 2.25
❑7, b&w 2.25
❑8, b&w 2.25
❑9, b&w 2.25
❑10, b&w 2.25
❑11, b&w 2.25
❑12, b&w 2.50

MISTER X (VOL. 3)
CALIBER

❑1, ca. 1996, b&w 2.95
❑2, ca. 1996 .... 2.95
❑3, Sep 1996 .... 2.95
❑4, Dec 1996 .... 2.95

MISTRESS OF BONDAGE
FANTAGRAPHICS / EROS

❑1, b&w 2.95
❑2, b&w 2.95
❑3, b&w 2.95

MISTY
MARVEL / STAR

❑1, Dec 1985 .... 1.00
❑2, Feb 1986 .... 1.00
❑3, Apr 1986 .... 1.00
❑4, Jun 1986 .... 1.00
❑5, Aug 1986 .... 1.00
❑6, Oct 1986 .... 1.00

MISTY GIRL EXTREME
FANTAGRAPHICS / EROS

❑1, Jan 1997 .... 2.95
❑2, Feb 1997 .... 2.95

MITES
CONTINUŪM

❑1, b&w 1.50
❑2 .... 1.75

MIXXZINE
MIXX

❑1 .... 4.99
❑2 .... 4.99
❑3 .... 4.99
❑4 .... 4.99
❑5, Apr 1998; Issue #1-5 .... 4.99
❑6 .... 4.99

MOBFIRE
DC / VERTIGO

❑1, Dec 1994 .... 2.50
❑2, Jan 1995 .... 2.50
❑3, Feb 1995 .... 2.50
❑4, Mar 1995 .... 2.50
❑5, Apr 1995 A: John Constantine. 2.50
❑6, May 1995 .... 2.50
❑Ashcan 1; "Ashcan" preview given away by DC at shows 0.50

MOBILE POLICE PATLABOR PART 1
VIZ

❑1, Jul 1997, b&w 2.95
❑2, Aug 1997, b&w 2.95
❑3, Sep 1997, b&w 2.95
❑4, Oct 1997, b&w 2.95
❑5, Nov 1997, b&w 2.95
❑6, Dec 1997, b&w 2.95

MOBILE POLICE PATLABOR PART 2
VIZ

❑1, Jan 1998, b&w 2.95
❑2, Feb 1998, b&w 2.95
❑3, Mar 1998, b&w 2.95
❑4, Apr 1998, b&w 2.95
❑5, May 1998, b&w 2.95
❑6, Jun 1998, b&w 2.95

MOBILE SUIT GUNDAM 0079
VIZ

❑1, Mar 1999 .... 2.95
❑2, Apr 1999 .... 2.95
❑3, May 1999 .... 2.95
❑4, Jun 1999 .... 2.95
❑5, Jul 1999 .... 2.95
❑6, Aug 1999 .... 2.95
❑7, Sep 1999 .... 2.95
❑8, Oct 1999 .... 2.95

MOBILE SUIT GUNDAM 0083
VIZ

❑1, Nov 1999 .... 4.95
❑2, Dec 1999 .... 4.95
❑3, Jan 2000 .... 4.95
❑4, Feb 2000 .... 4.95
❑5, Mar 2000 .... 4.95
❑6, Apr 2000 .... 4.95
❑7, May 2000 .... 4.95
❑8, Jun 2000 .... 4.95
❑9, Jul 2000 .... 4.95
❑10, Aug 2000 .... 4.95
❑11, Sep 2000 .... 4.95
❑12, Oct 2000 .... 4.95
❑13, Nov 2000 .... 4.95

MOBILE SUIT GUNDAM WING: GROUND ZERO
VIZ

❑1, Jun 2000 .... 2.95

MOBSTERS AND MONSTERS MAGAZINE
ORIGINAL SYNDICATE

❑1, Jul 1995 .... 3.00

MOD
KITCHEN SINK

❑1 1: Adventures in Limbo. 5.00

MODEL
TOKYOPOP

❑1, May 2004 .... 9.99

MODEL BY DAY
RIP OFF

❑1, Jul 1990, b&w 2.50
❑2, Oct 1990, b&w 2.50

MODERN GRIMM
SYMPTOM

❑1, Dec 1996, b&w 2.75

MODERN PULP
SPECIAL STUDIO

❑1, b&w 2.75

In 2000, DC celebrated with a series of *Millennium Editions* reprinting key issues from its history.

© 2000 DC Comics.

N-MINT

MODERN ROMANS
FANTAGRAPHICS / EROS

❑1, b&w 2.25
❑2, b&w 2.25
❑3, b&w 2.25

MODEST PROPOSAL, A
TOME

❑1, b&w 2.50
❑2, b&w 2.50

MOEBIUS COMICS
CALIBER

❑1, May 1996 .... 3.00
❑2, Jul 1996 .... 3.00
❑3, Sep 1996 .... 3.00
❑4, Nov 1996 .... 3.00
❑5, Jan 1997 .... 3.00
❑6, Mar 1997 .... 3.00

MOEBIUS: EXOTICS
DARK HORSE

❑1; prestige format 6.95

MOEBIUS: H.P.'S ROCK CITY
DARK HORSE

❑1 1996; smaller than a normal comic book; squarebound 7.95

MOEBIUS: MADWOMAN OF THE SACRED HEART
DARK HORSE

❑1 .... 12.95

MOEBIUS: THE MAN FROM THE CIGURI
DARK HORSE

❑1 1996; smaller than a normal comic book; squarebound 7.95

MOGOBI DESERT RATS
STUDIO 91

❑1, Jan 1991 .... 2.25

MOJO ACTION COMPANION UNIT, THE
EXCLAIM

❑1, Spr 1997, b&w 2.75

MOJO MECHANICS
SYNDICATE

❑1, b&w 2.95
❑2 .... 2.95

MOMENT OF SILENCE, A
MARVEL

❑1, ca. 2002 ARo, JR2 (a) 3.50

MONA
KITCHEN SINK

❑1 .... 4.95

MONARCHY, THE
DC / WILDSTORM

❑1, Apr 2001 .... 2.50
❑2, Jun 2001 .... 2.50
❑3, Jul 2001 .... 2.50
❑4, Aug 2001 .... 2.50
❑5, Sep 2001 .... 2.50
❑6, Sep 2001 .... 2.50
❑7, Oct 2001 .... 2.50
❑8, Nov 2001 .... 2.50
❑9, Dec 2001 .... 2.50
❑10, Jan 2002 .... 2.50
❑11, Feb 2002 .... 2.50
❑12, Mar 2002 .... 2.50

N-MINT

MONDO 3-D
3-D Zone

❑1 ... 3.95

MONDO BONDO
LCD

❑1 ... 2.95

MONEY TALKS
Slave Labor

❑1, Jun 1996 ... 3.50
❑2, Aug 1996 ... 2.95
❑3, Oct 1996 ... 2.95
❑4, Dec 1996 ... 2.95
❑5, Feb 1997 ... 2.95

MONGREL
Northstar

❑1/A, Dec 1994, b&w ... 3.95
❑2 ... 3.95
❑3 ... 3.95

MONICA'S STORY
Alternative

❑1, Feb 1999, b&w ... 3.50

MONKEES, THE
Gold Key

❑1, Mar 1967; based on TV series ... 45.00
❑2, May 1967 ... 30.00
❑3, Jul 1967 ... 24.00
❑4, Sep 1967 ... 20.00
❑5, Oct 1967 ... 20.00
❑6, Nov 1967 ... 18.00
❑7, Dec 1967 ... 18.00
❑8, Jan 1968 ... 18.00
❑9, Feb 1968 ... 18.00
❑10, Mar 1968 ... 18.00
❑11, May 1968 ... 12.00
❑12, Jun 1968 ... 12.00
❑13, Jul 1968 ... 12.00
❑14, Aug 1968 ... 12.00
❑15, Sep 1968 ... 12.00
❑16 1969 ... 12.00
❑17 1969 ... 12.00

MONKEY BUSINESS
Parody

❑1, b&w ... 2.50
❑2; Ren & Stimpy parody ... 2.50

MONKEYMAN AND O'BRIEN
Dark Horse / Legend

❑1, Jul 1996 V: Shrewmanoid. ... 3.50
❑2, Aug 1996 V: Froglodytes. ... 3.00
❑3, Sep 1996 A: Shrewmanoid. V: Quash. ... 2.95
❑Special 1, Feb 1996 O: Monkeyman and O'Brien. ... 2.95

MONNGA
Daikaiju

❑1, Aug 1995 ... 3.95

MONOLITH
Comico

❑1, Oct 1991 ... 2.50
❑2, Nov 1991 ... 2.50
❑3 ... 2.50
❑4, Aug 1992 ... 2.50

MONOLITH, THE (DC)
DC / Vertigo

❑1, Apr 2004 ... 2.95
❑2, May 2004 ... 2.95
❑3, Jun 2004 ... 2.95
❑4, Jul 2004 ... 2.95
❑5, Aug 2004 ... 2.95
❑6, Sep 2004 ... 2.95

MONOLITH (LAST GASP)
Last Gasp

❑1 ... 3.00

MONROE
Conquest

❑1, b&w; poster; cards ... 4.95

MONSTER (BUTLER & HOGG'S...)
Slave Labor

❑1, b&w ... 2.95

N-MINT

MONSTER, THE
Ring

❑1 ... 2.00

MONSTER BOY
Monster

❑1, b&w ... 2.50

MONSTER BOY COMICS
Slave Labor

❑1, Sep 1997, b&w ... 2.95
❑2, Dec 1997, b&w ... 2.95
❑3 ... 2.95

MONSTER FIGHTERS INC.
Image

❑1, Apr 1999 ... 3.50

MONSTER FIGHTERS INC.: THE BLACK BOOK
Image

❑1, Sep 2000 ... 3.50

MONSTER FIGHTERS INC.: THE GHOSTS OF CHRISTMAS
Image

❑1, Dec 1999 ... 3.95

MONSTER FRAT HOUSE
Eternity

❑1, Oct 1989, b&w ... 2.25

MONSTER IN MY POCKET
Harvey

❑1, Mar 1991 EC (a) ... 1.50
❑2, May 1991; The Exterminator ... 1.50
❑3, Jul 1991 GK (a) ... 1.50
❑4, Sep 1991 GK (a) ... 1.50

MONSTER ISLAND
Compass

❑1, Nov 1998, b&w; wraparound cover ... 3.95

MONSTER LOVE
Kitchen Sink

❑1 ... 2.50

MONSTERMAN
Image

❑1, Sep 1997, b&w ... 2.95

MONSTER MASSACRE
Atomeka

❑1 ... 7.95

MONSTER MASSACRE SPECIAL
Blackball

❑1 ... 2.50

MONSTER MATINEE
Chaos!

❑1, Oct 1997; monster pin-ups; commentary by Forrest J. Ackerman ... 2.50
❑1/Variant, Oct 1997; premium edition; alternate logoless cover; monster pin-ups; commentary by Forrest J. Ackerman ... 2.50
❑2, Oct 1997; monster pin-ups; commentary by Forrest J. Ackerman ... 2.50
❑3, Oct 1997; monster pin-ups; commentary by Forrest J. Ackerman ... 2.50

MONSTER MENACE
Marvel

❑1, Dec 1993 SL (w); SD (a) ... 1.50
❑2, Jan 1994 SD (a) ... 1.50
❑3, Feb 1994 SD (a) ... 1.50
❑4, Mar 1994 SD, JK (a) ... 1.50

MONSTERMEN, THE (GARY GIANNI'S...)
Dark Horse

❑1, Aug 1999 ... 2.50

MONSTER POSSE
Adventure

❑1, b&w ... 2.50
❑2, Nov 1992 ... 2.50
❑3 ... 2.50

MONSTERS FROM OUTER SPACE
Adventure

❑1, Dec 1992, b&w ... 2.50
❑2, b&w ... 2.50
❑3, b&w ... 2.50

N-MINT

MONSTERS ON THE PROWL
Marvel

❑9, Feb 1971; Title changes to Monsters on the Prowl; Series continued from Chamber of Darkness #8 ... 8.00
❑10, Apr 1971 ... 5.00
❑11, Jun 1971 ... 5.00
❑12, Aug 1971 ... 5.00
❑13, Oct 1971 ... 5.00
❑14, Dec 1971 ... 5.00
❑15, Feb 1972 ... 5.00
❑16, Apr 1972; JSe (a);King Kull ... 6.00
❑17, Jun 1972 ... 4.00
❑18, Aug 1972 ... 4.00
❑19, Oct 1972 ... 4.00
❑20, Dec 1972 SD (a) ... 4.00
❑21, Feb 1973 ... 4.00
❑22, Apr 1973 ... 4.00
❑23, Jun 1973 ... 4.00
❑24, Aug 1973 ... 4.00
❑25, Sep 1973 ... 4.00
❑26, Oct 1973 ... 4.00
❑27, Nov 1974 ... 4.00
❑28, Jun 1975 ... 4.00
❑29, Aug 1975 ... 4.00
❑30, Oct 1975 ... 4.00

MONSTERS TO LAUGH WITH
Marvel

❑1, ca. 1964 ... 40.00
❑2, ca. 1964 ... 30.00
❑3, ca. 1965 ... 30.00

MONSTERS UNLEASHED
Marvel

❑1, Jul 1973, b&w; magazine ... 14.00
❑2, Sep 1973; Frankenstein ... 10.00
❑3, Nov 1973; Frankenstein, Man-Thing, Son of Satan ... 9.00
❑4, Jan 1974; Frankenstein ... 9.00
❑5, Mar 1974; Frankenstein, Man-Thing ... 9.00
❑6, May 1974; Frankenstein, Werewolf ... 7.00
❑7, Jul 1974; Frankenstein, Werewolf ... 7.00
❑8, Sep 1974; Frankenstein, Man-Thing ... 7.00
❑9, Nov 1974; Frankenstein, Man-Thing, Wendigo ... 7.00
❑10, Jan 1975; Frankenstein, Tigra ... 7.00
❑11, Mar 1975; Gabriel ... 7.00
❑Annual 1, ca. 1975 ... 7.00

MONSTER WORLD
DC / Wildstorm

❑1, Jul 2001 ... 2.50
❑2, Aug 2001 ... 2.50
❑3, Sep 2001 ... 2.50
❑4, Oct 2001 ... 2.95

MONSTROSITY
Slap Happy

❑1, Oct 1998, b&w ... 4.95

MOON BEAST
Avalon

❑1 ... 2.95

MOONCHILD
Forbidden Fruit

❑1, b&w ... 2.95
❑2, b&w ... 2.95

MOON CHILD (VOL. 2)
Forbidden Fruit

❑1, b&w ... 3.50
❑2, b&w ... 3.50
❑3, b&w ... 3.50

MOONFIGHTING
Harrier

❑1, Mar 1988, b&w ... 1.95

MOON KNIGHT (1ST SERIES)
Marvel

❑1, Nov 1980 BSz (a); O: Moon Knight. ... 3.50
❑2, Dec 1980 BSz (a) ... 2.50
❑3, Jan 1981 BSz (a) ... 2.50
❑4, Feb 1981 BSz (a) ... 2.50
❑5, Mar 1981 BSz (a) ... 2.50

N-MINT

❑6, Apr 1981 BSz (a) ... 2.50
❑7, May 1981 BSz (a) ... 2.50
❑8, Jun 1981 BSz (a); V: Moon Kings. 2.50
❑9, Jul 1981 BSz, FM (a); V: Midnight Man. ... 2.50
❑10, Aug 1981 BSz (a); V: Midnight Man. ... 2.50
❑11, Sep 1981 BSz (a); V: Creed. ... 2.50
❑12, Oct 1981 BSz, FM (a) ... 2.50
❑13, Nov 1981 BSz, FM (a); A: Daredevil. ... 2.50
❑14, Dec 1981 BSz (a) ... 2.50
❑15, Jan 1982; FM (c); BSz, FM (a); A: Thing. direct ... 2.50
❑16, Feb 1982 BSz (c); BSz (a); V: Blacksmith. ... 2.50
❑17, Mar 1982 BSz (a) ... 2.50
❑18, Apr 1982 BSz (a); V: Slayers Elite. 2.50
❑19, May 1982 BSz (a); V: Arsenal. ... 2.50
❑20, Jun 1982 BSz (a); V: Arsenal. ... 2.50
❑21, Jul 1982 BSz (c); BSz (a) ... 2.00
❑22, Aug 1982 BSz (a) ... 2.00
❑23, Sep 1982 BSz (a) ... 2.00
❑24, Oct 1982 BSz (a) ... 2.00
❑25, Nov 1982; double-sized BSz (a) 2.50
❑26, Dec 1982 BSz (a) ... 2.00
❑27, Jan 1983 FM (c) ... 2.00
❑28, Feb 1983 BSz (a) ... 2.00
❑29, Mar 1983 BSz (a) ... 2.00
❑30, Apr 1983 BSz (a) ... 2.00
❑31, May 1983 BSz (c); BSz, KN (a) . 2.00
❑32, Jul 1983 BSz (c); BSz, KN (a) ... 2.00
❑33, Sep 1983 BSz (c); BSz, KN (a) .. 2.00
❑34, Nov 1983 BSz (c); RHo, BSz (a) 2.00
❑35, Jan 1984; double-sized KN (a); A: X-Men. ... 2.50
❑36, Mar 1984 ... 2.00
❑37, May 1984 BSz (a) ... 2.00
❑38, Jul 1984 ... 2.00

MOON KNIGHT (2ND SERIES)
MARVEL

❑1, Jun 1985; Double-size O: Moon Knight. ... 2.50
❑2, Aug 1985 ... 2.00
❑3, Sep 1985 ... 2.00
❑4, Oct 1985 ... 2.00
❑5, Nov 1985 ... 2.00
❑6, Dec 1985; Painted cover ... 2.00

MOON KNIGHT (3RD SERIES)
MARVEL

❑1, Jan 1998 ... 2.50
❑2, Feb 1998 ... 2.50
❑3, Mar 1998 ... 2.50
❑4, Apr 1998 ... 2.50

MOON KNIGHT (4TH SERIES)
MARVEL

❑1, Jan 1999; says Feb on cover, Jan in indicia ... 2.99
❑2, Feb 1999 ... 2.99
❑3, Feb 1999 ... 2.99
❑4, Feb 1999 ... 2.99

MOON KNIGHT: DIVIDED WE FALL
MARVEL

❑1, ca. 1992, b&w ... 4.95

MOON KNIGHT SPECIAL
MARVEL

❑1; Shang-Chi ... 2.50

MOON KNIGHT SPECIAL EDITION
MARVEL

❑1, Nov 1983; Reprints from Hulk (magazine) BSz (a) ... 2.50
❑2, Dec 1983 BSz (a) ... 2.50
❑3, Jan 1984 BSz (a) ... 2.50

MOONSHADOW
MARVEL / EPIC

❑1, Mar 1985 O: Moonshadow. ... 3.50
❑2, May 1985 ... 2.50
❑3, Jul 1985 ... 2.50
❑4, Sep 1985 ... 2.00
❑5, Nov 1985 ... 2.00
❑6, Jan 1986 ... 2.00

N-MINT

❑7, Apr 1986 ... 2.00
❑8, Jun 1986 ... 2.00
❑9, Aug 1986 ... 2.00
❑10, Oct 1986 ... 2.00
❑11, Jan 1987 O: Moonshadow. ... 2.00
❑12, Feb 1987 ... 2.00

MOONSHADOW (VERTIGO)
DC / VERTIGO

❑1, Sep 1994 O: Moonshadow. ... 3.00
❑2, Oct 1994 ... 2.50
❑3, Nov 1994 ... 2.50
❑4, Dec 1994 ... 2.50
❑5, Jan 1995 ... 2.50
❑6, Feb 1995 ... 2.25
❑7, Mar 1995 ... 2.25
❑8, Apr 1995 ... 2.25
❑9, May 1995 ... 2.25
❑10, Jun 1995 ... 2.25
❑11, Jul 1995 O: Moonshadow. ... 2.25
❑12, Aug 1995 ... 2.95

MOON SHOT, THE FLIGHT OF APOLLO 12
PEPPER PIKE GRAPHIX

❑1, Jun 1994 ... 2.95

MOONSTRUCK
WHITE WOLF

❑1, May 1987 ... 2.00

MOONTRAP
CALIBER

❑1, b&w ... 2.00

MOONWALKER 3-D
BLACKTHORNE

❑1 ... 2.50

MORBID ANGEL
LONDON NIGHT

❑0.5, Jul 1996 ... 3.00
❑1 ... 3.00

MORBID ANGEL: PENANCE
LONDON NIGHT

❑1, Sep 1996 ... 3.95

MORBIUS REVISITED
MARVEL

❑1, Aug 1993; Reprints Fear #27 ... 2.00
❑2, Sep 1993; FR (a);Reprints Fear #28 2.00
❑3, Oct 1993; DH (a); A: Helleyes. A: Simon Stroud. Reprints Fear #29 .. 2.00
❑4, Nov 1993; GE (a);Reprints Fear #30 2.00
❑5, Dec 1993; Reprints Fear #31 ... 2.00

MORBIUS: THE LIVING VAMPIRE
MARVEL

❑1, Sep 1992; Without poster ... 1.50
❑1/CS, Sep 1992; Polybagged w/poster 3.00
❑2, Oct 1992 ... 2.00
❑3, Nov 1992 ... 2.00
❑4, Dec 1992 ... 2.00
❑5, Jan 1993 ... 2.00
❑6, Feb 1993 ... 1.75
❑7, Mar 1993 ... 1.75
❑8, Apr 1993 ... 1.75
❑9, May 1993 ... 1.75
❑10, Jun 1993 ... 1.75
❑11, Jul 1993 ... 1.75
❑12, Aug 1993; Double cover ... 2.25
❑13, Sep 1993 ... 1.75
❑14, Oct 1993 ... 1.75
❑15, Nov 1993 ... 1.75
❑16, Dec 1993; Neon ink/matte finish cover ... 1.75
❑17, Jan 1994; Spot-varnished cover ... 1.75
❑18, Feb 1994 ... 1.75
❑19, Mar 1994 ... 1.75
❑20, Apr 1994 ... 1.75
❑21, May 1994 ... 1.75
❑22, Jun 1994 ... 1.95
❑23, Jul 1994 ... 1.95
❑24, Aug 1994 ... 1.95
❑25, Sep 1994; Giant-size ... 2.50
❑26, Oct 1994 ... 1.95
❑27, Nov 1994 ... 1.95

Currency characters came to life in Slave Labor's *Money Talks*.

© 1997 Slave Labor.

N-MINT

❑28, Dec 1994 ... 1.95
❑29, Jan 1995 ... 1.95
❑30, Feb 1995 ... 1.95
❑31, Mar 1995 ... 1.95
❑32, Apr 1995 ... 1.95

MORE FETISH
BONEYARD

❑1, Nov 1993 ... 2.95

MORE SECRET ORIGINS REPLICA EDITION
DC

❑1, Dec 1999; reprints 80-Page Giant #8 ... 4.95

MORE TALES FROM GIMBLEY
HARRIER

❑1, Feb 1988 ... 1.95

MORE TALES FROM SLEAZE CASTLE
GRATUITOUS BUNNY

❑1 ... 4.00
❑2 ... 3.00
❑3 1990 ... 3.00
❑4, Jan 1991 ... 3.00
❑5, Jan 1992 ... 3.00
❑6, Jan 1993 ... 3.00

MORE THAN MORTAL
LIAR

❑1, Jun 1997 ... 3.00
❑1-2, Jun 1997 ... 2.95
❑2, Sep 1997 ... 3.00
❑2/Variant, Sep 1997; logoless cover 2.95
❑3, Dec 1997 ... 3.00
❑4, Apr 1998 ... 3.00
❑5, Dec 1999 ... 3.00
❑6, Mar 2000 ... 2.95

MORE THAN MORTAL/LADY PENDRAGON
IMAGE

❑1, Jun 1999 ... 2.50
❑1/A, Jun 1999; alternate cover ... 3.00

MORE THAN MORTAL: OTHERWORLDS
IMAGE

❑1, Jul 1999 ... 3.00
❑1/A, Jul 1999; alternate cover ... 3.00
❑2, Aug 1999; Woman and man kneeling on cover, large figure standing behind ... 3.00
❑2/A, Aug 1999; alternate cover ... 3.00
❑3, Oct 1999; Woman holding sword on cover, red top left background .. 3.00
❑3/A, Oct 1999; alternate cover ... 3.00
❑4, Dec 1999 ... 3.00

MORE THAN MORTAL: SAGAS
LIAR

❑1, Aug 1998 O: Morlock. 1: Morlock. 2.95
❑1/A, Aug 1998; variant cover for New Dimension Comics ... 3.00
❑2, Oct 1998 ... 2.95
❑3, Dec 1998 ... 2.95

MORE THAN MORTAL: TRUTHS & LEGENDS
LIAR

❑1, Jun 1998; Cover has man with glowing eye at bow of ship ... 2.95
❑1/A, Jun 1998; Variant edition ... 3.00
❑1/Ltd., Jun 1998; Variant edition ... 4.00

Condition price index: Multiply "NM prices" above by: **0.83 for Very Fine/Near Mint**
0.66 for Very Fine • 0.33 for Fine • 0.2 for Very Good • 0.125 for Good

N-MINT

❑2, Aug 1998 .... 2.95
❑3, Oct 1998 .... 2.95
❑4, Jan 1999 .... 2.95
❑5, Apr 1999 .... 2.95

MORLOCKS
MARVEL

❑1, Jun 2002 .... 2.50
❑2, Jul 2002 .... 2.50
❑3, Aug 2002 .... 2.50
❑4, Sep 2002 .... 2.50

MORLOCK 2001
ATLAS-SEABOARD

❑1, Feb 1975 AM (a); O: Morlock. 2.50
❑2, Apr 1975 AM (a) 2.00
❑3, Jul 1975 AM, SD, BWr (a); O: Midnight Men. 2.00

MORNING GLORY
RADIO

❑1, Nov 1998, b&w 2.95
❑2, Dec 1998, b&w 2.95
❑3, Jan 1999, b&w 2.95
❑4 .... 2.95
❑5, May 1999, b&w 2.95

MORNINGSTAR SPECIAL
TRIDENT

❑1, Apr 1990, b&w 2.50

MORPHING PERIOD
SHANDA

❑1 .... 4.95

MORPHOS THE SHAPECHANGER
DARK HORSE

❑1, Jul 1996; prestige format 4.95

MORPHS
GRAPHXPRESS

❑1 .... 2.00
❑2, Jul 1987 .... 2.00
❑3 .... 2.00
❑4 .... 2.00

MORRIGAN (DIMENSION X)
DIMENSION X

❑1, Aug 1993, b&w 2.75

MORRIGAN (SIRIUS)
SIRIUS

❑1, Jul 1997 .... 2.95

MORTAL COILS
RED EYE

❑1, Aug 2002 .... 2.50

MORTAL KOMBAT
MALIBU

❑1, Jul 1994, b&w; Blood and Thunder 3.00
❑1/A, Jul 1994, b&w; variant cover (Mortal Kombat logo) 3.00
❑2, Aug 1994, b&w; variant cover (Mortal Kombat logo); Blood and Thunder 3.00
❑3, Sep 1994, b&w; variant cover (Mortal Kombat logo); Blood and Thunder 3.00
❑4, Oct 1994, b&w; variant cover (Mortal Kombat logo); Blood and Thunder 3.00
❑5, Nov 1994, b&w; variant cover (Mortal Kombat logo); Blood and Thunder 3.00
❑6, b&w; variant cover (Mortal Kombat logo) 3.00

MORTAL KOMBAT: BARAKA
MALIBU

❑1, ca. 1995 .... 2.95

MORTAL KOMBAT: BATTLEWAVE
MALIBU

❑1, ca. 1995 .... 3.00
❑2, Mar 1995 .... 3.00
❑3, ca. 1995 .... 3.00
❑4, ca. 1995 .... 3.00
❑5, ca. 1995 .... 3.00
❑6, ca. 1995 .... 3.00

MORTAL KOMBAT: GORO, PRINCE OF PAIN
MALIBU

❑1, Sep 1994 .... 2.95
❑2, Oct 1994 .... 2.95
❑3, Nov 1994 .... 2.95

MORTAL KOMBAT: KITANA & MILEENA
MALIBU

❑1, ca. 1995 .... 2.95

MORTAL KOMBAT: KUNG LAO
MALIBU

❑1, ca. 1995 .... 2.95

MORTAL KOMBAT: RAYDEN & KANO
MALIBU

❑1, ca. 1995 .... 2.95
❑2, Apr 1995 .... 2.95
❑3 .... 2.95

MORTAL KOMBAT SPECIAL EDITION
MALIBU

❑1, Nov 1994 .... 2.95
❑2 1994 .... 2.95

MORTAL KOMBAT U.S. SPECIAL FORCES
MALIBU

❑1, Jan 1995 .... 3.50
❑2, Feb 1995 .... 3.50

MORTAL SOULS
AVATAR

❑1/A, Apr 2002 .... 3.50

MORTAR MAN
MARSHALL COMICS

❑1, May 1993, b&w 1.95
❑2, ca. 1993, b&w 1.95
❑3, ca. 1993 .... 1.95

MORTIGAN GOTH: IMMORTALIS
MARVEL

❑1, Sep 1993 .... 1.95
❑1/Variant, Sep 1993; foil cover 2.95
❑2, Oct 1993 .... 1.95
❑3, Jan 1994 .... 1.95
❑4, Mar 1994 .... 1.95

MORT THE DEAD TEENAGER
MARVEL

❑1, Nov 1992 .... 1.75
❑2, Dec 1992 .... 1.75
❑3, Jan 1993 .... 1.75
❑4, Mar 1993 .... 1.75

MORTY THE DOG (MU)
MU

❑1, b&w; digest 3.95
❑2, Spr 1991, b&w; digest 3.95

MORTY THE DOG (STARHEAD)
STARHEAD

❑1 .... 2.00

MOSAIC
SIRIUS

❑1/A, Mar 1999 .... 2.95
❑1/B, Mar 1999; alternate cover; smaller logos 2.95
❑2, Apr 1999 .... 2.95
❑3, May 1999 .... 2.95
❑4, Jun 1999 .... 2.95
❑5, Jul 1999 .... 2.95

MOSAIC: HELL CITY RIPPER
SIRIUS

❑1 .... 2.95
❑1/Variant; alternate cover 2.95

MOSTLY WANTED
WILDSTORM

❑1, Jul 2000 .... 2.50
❑2, Aug 2000 .... 2.50
❑3, Sep 2000 .... 2.50
❑4, Nov 2000 .... 2.50

MOTHERLESS CHILD
KITCHEN SINK

❑1 .... 2.95

MOTHER'S OATS COMIX
RIP OFF

❑1 .... 5.00
❑2 .... 3.00

MOTHER SUPERION
ANTARCTIC

❑1, Jul 1997 .... 2.95

MOTHER TERESA OF CALCUTTA
MARVEL

❑1, ca. 1984 .... 1.50

MOTLEY STORIES
DIVISION

❑1, b&w 2.75

MOTORBIKE PUPPIES, THE
DARK ZULU LIES

❑1, Jun 1992 .... 2.50
❑2; Never published? 2.50

MOTORHEAD
DARK HORSE

❑1, Aug 1995 .... 2.50
❑2, Sep 1995 .... 2.50
❑3, Oct 1995 .... 2.50
❑4, Nov 1995 .... 2.50
❑5, Dec 1995 .... 2.50
❑6, Jan 1996 .... 2.50
❑Special 1, Mar 1994 .... 3.95

MOTORMOUTH
MARVEL

❑1, Jun 1992 1: Motormouth. 2.00
❑2, Jul 1992 .... 1.75
❑3, Aug 1992; Punisher 1.75
❑4, Sep 1992 .... 1.75
❑5, Oct 1992 A: Punisher. 1.75
❑6, Nov 1992; Title changes to Motormouth & Killpower 1.75
❑7, Dec 1992 A: Cable. 1.75
❑8, Jan 1993 .... 1.75
❑9, Feb 1993 .... 1.75
❑10, Apr 1993 .... 1.75
❑11, Apr 1993 .... 1.75
❑12, May 1993 .... 1.75

MOUNTAIN
UNDERGROUND

❑1; Flipbook High School Funnies 3.00

MOUNTAIN WORLD
ICICLE RIDGE

❑1, b&w 2.00

MOUSE ON THE MOON, THE
DELL

❑1, Oct 1963 .... 15.00

MOVIE STAR NEWS
PURE IMAGINATION

❑1; DSt (c);Bettie Page photos 6.00

MOXI
LIGHTNING

❑1, Jul 1996 .... 3.00

MOXI'S FRIENDS: BOBBY JOE & NITRO
LIGHTNING

❑1, Sep 1996 .... 2.75

MOXI: STRANGE DAZE
LIGHTNING

❑1, Nov 1996, b&w 3.00

M. REX
IMAGE

❑1, Nov 1999 .... 2.95
❑1/A, Nov 1999; Alternate cover has large figure in background, boy, monkey on waterbike in foreground 2.95
❑2, Dec 1999 .... 2.95
❑Ashcan 1/A, Jul 1999; Flying car on cover 5.00
❑Ashcan 1/B, Jul 1999; Blue background on cover 5.00

MS. ANTI-SOCIAL
HELPLESS ANGER

❑1, b&w 1.75

Condition price index: Multiply "NM prices" above by: **0.83 for Very Fine/Near Mint**
0.66 for Very Fine • 0.33 for Fine • 0.2 for Very Good • 0.125 for Good

MS. CYANIDE & ICE
Black Out

	N-MINT
❑0	2.95
❑1; Sly & Furious preview	2.95

MS. FANTASTIC
Conquest

	N-MINT
❑1, b&w	2.95
❑2, b&w	2.95
❑3, b&w	2.95
❑4, b&w	2.95

MS. FANTASTIC CLASSICS
Conquest

	N-MINT
❑1, b&w	2.95

MS. FORTUNE
Image

	N-MINT
❑1, Jan 1998, b&w	2.95

MS. MARVEL
Marvel

	N-MINT
❑1, Jan 1977 JB (a); 1: Ms. Marvel.	4.00
❑2, Feb 1977	3.00
❑3, Mar 1977	3.00
❑4, Apr 1977	2.50
❑5, May 1977 A: Vision.	2.50
❑6, Jun 1977	2.50
❑6/35 cent, Jun 1977; 35 cent regional variant	15.00
❑7, Jul 1977 V: Modok. V: M.O.D.O.K..	2.50
❑7/35 cent, Jul 1977; 35 cent regional variant	15.00
❑8, Aug 1977	2.50
❑8/35 cent, Aug 1977; 35 cent regional variant	15.00
❑9, Sep 1977 1: Deathbird.	2.50
❑9/35 cent, Sep 1977; 35 cent regional variant	15.00
❑10, Oct 1977	2.50
❑10/35 cent, Oct 1977; 35 cent regional variant	15.00
❑11, Nov 1977	2.00
❑12, Dec 1977 V: Hecate.	2.00
❑13, Jan 1978	2.00
❑14, Feb 1978 1: Steeplejack II (Maxwell Plumm).	2.00
❑15, Mar 1978	2.00
❑16, Apr 1978 1: Mystique (cameo).	7.50
❑17, May 1978	4.00
❑18, Jun 1978 1: Mystique (full appearance).	9.00
❑19, Aug 1978 A: Captain Marvel.	2.50
❑20, Oct 1978; New costume	2.00
❑21, Dec 1978	2.00
❑22, Feb 1979	2.00
❑23, Apr 1979	2.00

MS. MYSTIC (PACIFIC)
Pacific

	N-MINT
❑1, Oct 1982; NA (w); NA (a); O: Ms. Mystic. origin	1.50
❑2, Feb 1984 NA (w); NA (a); O: Ayre. O: Fyre. O: Watr. O: Urth. 1: Ayre. 1: Fyre. 1: Watr. 1: Urth. 1: Urth 4.	1.50

MS. MYSTIC (CONTINUITY)
Continuity

	N-MINT
❑1, Mar 1988; reprints Ms. Mystic (Pacific) #1	2.00
❑2, Jun 1988; reprints Ms. Mystic (Pacific) #2	2.00
❑3, Jan 1989	2.00
❑4, May 1989	2.00
❑5, Aug 1990; Comics Code	2.00
❑6, Nov 1990; Comics Code	2.00
❑7, Aug 1991	2.00
❑8, Mar 1992	2.00
❑9, May 1992	2.00

MS. MYSTIC (VOL. 2)
Continuity

	N-MINT
❑1, Oct 1993	2.50
❑2, Nov 1993	2.50
❑3, Dec 1993	2.50
❑4, Jan 1994	2.50
❑5 1994; Exists?	2.50
❑6 1994; Exists?	2.50

MS. MYSTIC DEATHWATCH 2000
Continuity

	N-MINT
❑1, May 1993; Stereo diffusion cover	2.50
❑2, Jun 1993; trading card	2.50
❑3, Aug 1993; trading card; drops Deathwatch 2000 from indicia	2.50

MS. PMS
Aaaahh!!

	N-MINT
❑0, Mar 1992	2.50
❑1	2.50

MS. QUOTED TALES
Chance

	N-MINT
❑1, Feb 1983	1.50

MS. TREE
Eclipse

	N-MINT
❑1, Apr 1983; Eclipse publishes	4.00
❑2, Jun 1983	2.75
❑3, Aug 1983	2.75
❑4, Oct 1983	2.50
❑5, Nov 1983	2.50
❑6, Feb 1984	2.00
❑7, Apr 1984	2.00
❑8, May 1984	2.00
❑9, Jul 1984	2.00
❑10, Aug 1984; Aardvark-Vanaheim begins as publisher	2.00
❑11, Sep 1984	2.00
❑12, Oct 1984	2.00
❑13, Nov 1984	2.00
❑14, Dec 1984	2.00
❑15, Jan 1985	2.00
❑16, Feb 1985	2.00
❑17, Apr 1985	2.00
❑18, May 1985	2.00
❑19, Jun 1985; Renegade Press begins as publisher	2.00
❑20, Jul 1985	2.00
❑21, Sep 1985	2.00
❑22, Oct 1985; Abortion story	2.00
❑23, Nov 1985; Abortion story	2.00
❑24, Dec 1985	2.00
❑25, Jan 1986	2.00
❑26, Feb 1986	2.00
❑27, Mar 1986	2.00
❑28, Apr 1986	2.00
❑29, May 1986	2.00
❑30, Jun 1986	2.00
❑31, Jul 1986	2.00
❑32, Sep 1986	2.00
❑33, Oct 1986	2.00
❑34, Nov 1986	2.00
❑35, Dec 1986	2.00
❑36, Feb 1987	2.00
❑37, Mar 1987	2.00
❑38, Apr 1987	2.00
❑39, May 1987	2.00
❑40, Jun 1987	2.00
❑41, Oct 1987	2.00
❑42, Nov 1987	2.00
❑43, Dec 1987	2.00
❑44, Feb 1988	2.00
❑45, Apr 1988; Johnny Dynamite back-up	2.00
❑46, May 1988	2.00
❑47, Aug 1988	2.00
❑48, Nov 1988	2.00
❑49, May 1989	2.00
❑50, Jul 1989 JK (a)	2.75
❑3D 1, Aug 1985	2.50
❑3D 2, Jul 1987; Ms. Tree's 1950's Three-Dimensional Crime	2.50
❑Summer 1, Aug 1986, b&w; Variant edition	2.00

MS. TREE QUARTERLY
DC

	N-MINT
❑1, Sum 1990; MGr (a);Batman, Midnight	4.00
❑2, Aut 1990; Butcher	4.00
❑3, Spr 1991; Butcher	4.00
❑4, Sum 1991	4.00
❑5, Aut 1991	4.00

Art Adams' *Monkeyman and O'Brien* paid tribute to early issues of *The Fantastic Four* with both its covers and stories.

© 1996 Art Adams and Dark Horse.

	N-MINT
❑6, Win 1991	4.00
❑7, Spr 1992	4.00
❑8, Sum 1992	4.00
❑9, Fal 1992; Listed as Ms. Tree Special in indicia	4.00
❑10, Win 1992	3.50

MS. VICTORY SPECIAL
AC

	N-MINT
❑1	2.00

MUCHA LUCHA
DC / Vertigo

	N-MINT
❑1, Jun 2003	2.25
❑2, Jul 2003	2.25
❑3, Aug 2003	2.25

MUKTUK WOLFSBREATH: HARD-BOILED SHAMAN
DC / Vertigo

	N-MINT
❑1, Aug 1998	2.50
❑2, Sep 1998	2.50
❑3, Oct 1998	2.50

MULLKON EMPIRE (JOHN JAKES'...)
Tekno

	N-MINT
❑1, Sep 1995	1.95
❑2, Oct 1995	1.95
❑3, Nov 1995	1.95
❑4, Dec 1995	1.95
❑5, Dec 1995	1.95
❑6, Jan 1996	1.95

MULTIVERSE (MICHAEL MOORCOCK'S...)
DC / Helix

	N-MINT
❑1, Nov 1997	2.50
❑2, Dec 1997	2.50
❑3, Jan 1998	2.50
❑4, Feb 1998	2.50
❑5, Mar 1998	2.50
❑6, Apr 1998	2.50
❑7, May 1998	2.50
❑8, Jun 1998	2.50
❑9, Jul 1998	2.50
❑10, Aug 1998	2.50
❑11, Sep 1998	2.50
❑12, Oct 1998	2.50

MUMMY, THE (MONSTER)
Monster

	N-MINT
❑1, b&w	2.00
❑2, b&w	2.00
❑3, b&w	2.00
❑4, b&w	2.00

MUMMY, THE (DELL)
Dell

	N-MINT
❑1	25.00

MUMMY ARCHIVES, THE
Millennium

	N-MINT
❑1, Jan 1992	2.50

MUMMY OR RAMSES THE DAMNED, THE (ANNE RICE'S...)
Millennium

	N-MINT
❑1, Oct 1990	3.00
❑2, Dec 1990	2.50
❑3, ca. 1992	2.50
❑4, ca. 1992	2.50
❑5, ca. 1992	2.50
❑6, ca. 1992	2.50
❑7, ca. 1992	2.50

Condition price index: Multiply "NM prices" above by: **0.83 for Very Fine/Near Mint**
0.66 for Very Fine • 0.33 for Fine • 0.2 for Very Good • 0.125 for Good

N-MINT

❑8, ca. 1992 .... 2.50
❑9, ca. 1992 .... 2.50
❑10, ca. 1992 .... 2.50
❑11, ca. 1992 .... 2.50
❑12, ca. 1992 .... 2.50

MUMMY'S CURSE, THE
AIRCEL

❑1, Nov 1990, b&w 2.50
❑2, Dec 1990, b&w 2.50
❑3, Jan 1991, b&w 2.50
❑4, Feb 1991, b&w 2.50

MUMMY, THE: VALLEY OF THE GODS
CHAOS

❑1, May 2001 .... 2.99
❑2 2001 .... 2.99
❑3 2001 .... 2.99

MUNDEN'S BAR
FIRST

❑Annual 1, Apr 1988; prestige format 2.95
❑Annual 2, Mar 1991; prestige format 5.95

MUNSTERS, THE (GOLD KEY)
GOLD KEY

❑1, Jan 1965 .... 120.00
❑2, Apr 1965 .... 75.00
❑3, Jul 1965 .... 48.00
❑4, Oct 1965 .... 48.00
❑5, Jan 1966; back cover pin-up 48.00
❑6, Apr 1966 .... 34.00
❑7, Jun 1966 .... 34.00
❑8, Aug 1966 .... 34.00
❑9, Oct 1966 .... 34.00
❑10, Dec 1966 .... 34.00
❑11, Feb 1967 .... 30.00
❑12, Apr 1967 .... 30.00
❑13, Jun 1967 .... 30.00
❑14, Aug 1967; Cover reprints cover of #2, with green background rather than brown 30.00
❑15, Nov 1967; Cover the same image as #4, with yellow behind logo 30.00
❑16, Feb 1968 .... 30.00

MUNSTERS, THE (TV COMICS!)
TV COMICS

❑1, Aug 1997 .... 3.00
❑2/A, Oct 1997; blue background 3.00
❑2/B, Oct 1997; alternate cover (Marilyn); red background 3.00
❑3, Dec 1997 .... 3.00
❑4, Mar 1998 .... 3.00
❑4/Variant, Mar 1998; logoless 3.00
❑Special 1, Aug 1997; Comic Con 1997 Edition; red foil logo 3.00

MUPPET BABIES (STAR/MARVEL)
MARVEL / STAR

❑1, May 1985 .... 1.50
❑2, Jul 1985 .... 1.00
❑3, Sep 1985 .... 1.00
❑4, Nov 1985 .... 1.00
❑5, Jan 1986 .... 1.00
❑6, Mar 1986 .... 1.00
❑7, May 1986 .... 1.00
❑8, Jul 1986 .... 1.00
❑9, Sep 1986 .... 1.00
❑10, Nov 1986 .... 1.00
❑11, Jan 1987 .... 1.00
❑12, Mar 1987 .... 1.00
❑13, May 1987 .... 1.00
❑14, Jul 1987 .... 1.00
❑15, Sep 1987 .... 1.00
❑16, Nov 1987 .... 1.00
❑17, Jan 1988 .... 1.00
❑18, Mar 1988; Marvel begins as publisher 1.00
❑19, May 1988 .... 1.00
❑20, Jul 1988 .... 1.00
❑21, Sep 1988 .... 1.00
❑22, Nov 1988 .... 1.00
❑23, Jan 1989 .... 1.00
❑24, Mar 1989 .... 1.00
❑25, May 1989 .... 1.00
❑26, Jul 1989 .... 1.00

N-MINT

MUPPET BABIES (HARVEY)
HARVEY

❑1, Jun 1993 .... 1.50
❑2, Sep 1993 .... 1.50
❑3, Dec 1993 .... 1.50
❑4, Mar 1994 .... 1.50
❑5, May 1994 .... 1.50
❑6, Aug 1994 .... 1.50

MUPPET BABIES ADVENTURES
HARVEY

❑1 .... 1.25

MUPPET BABIES BIG BOOK
HARVEY

❑1 .... 1.95

MUPPETS TAKE MANHATTAN, THE
MARVEL / STAR

❑1, Nov 1984; Reprints Marvel Super Special #32 .... 1.50
❑2, Dec 1984; Reprints Marvel Super Special #32 .... 1.50
❑3, Jan 1985; Reprints Marvel Super Special #32 .... 1.50

MURCIÉLAGA SHE-BAT
HEROIC

❑1, Jan 1993, b&w 1.50
❑2, Apr 1993, b&w 2.95
❑3, Jul 1993, b&w 2.95

MURDER
RENEGADE

❑1, Aug 1986, b&w; variant cover (Mortal Kombat logo) 2.00
❑2 .... 2.00

MURDER CAN BE FUN
SLAVE LABOR

❑1, Feb 1996, b&w 4.00
❑2, May 1996, b&w 3.50
❑3, Aug 1996, b&w 3.50
❑4, Nov 1996, b&w 3.50
❑5, May 1997, b&w 3.00
❑6, Jul 1997, b&w 3.00
❑7, Sep 1997, b&w 2.95
❑8, Jan 1998, b&w 2.95
❑9, Apr 1998, b&w 2.95
❑10, Aug 1998, b&w 2.95
❑11, Nov 1998, b&w 2.95
❑12, Feb 1999, b&w 2.95

MURDER CITY
ETERNITY

❑1, b&w; Minute Movies 3.95

MURDER ME DEAD
EL CAPITÁN

❑1, Aug 2000 .... 3.00
❑2, Oct 2000 .... 3.00
❑3, Dec 2000 .... 3.00
❑4, Feb 2001 .... 3.00
❑5, Apr 2001 .... 3.00
❑6, Jun 2001 .... 3.00
❑7, Jul 2001 .... 3.00

MUSIC COMICS
PERSONALITY

❑2 .... 2.95
❑3 .... 2.95
❑4, b&w 2.50

MUSIC COMICS ON TOUR
PERSONALITY

❑1, b&w; Beatles 2.95

MUTANT ALIENS
NBM

❑1 .... 10.95

MUTANT BOOK OF THE DEAD, THE
STARHEAD

❑1, b&w 2.50

MUTANT CHRONICLES
ACCLAIM / ARMADA

❑1, May 1996; polybagged with Doom Trooper card; cardstock cover 2.95
❑2, Jun 1996; polybagged with Doom Trooper card; cardstock cover 2.95

N-MINT

❑3, Jul 1996; polybagged with Doom Trooper card; cardstock cover 2.95
❑4, Aug 1996; polybagged with Doom Trooper card; cardstock cover 2.95

MUTANT CHRONICLES SOURCEBOOK
ACCLAIM / ARMADA

❑1, Sep 1996; polybagged with card; cardstock cover 2.95

MUTANT EARTH
IMAGE

❑1/A, Apr 2002; Flip book with Realm of the Claw #1 .... 2.95
❑1/B, Apr 2002; Flip book with Realm of the Claw #1 .... 2.95
❑2/A, Jun 2002, b&w; Flip book with Realm of the Claw #2 .... 2.95
❑2/B, Jun 2002, b&w; Flip book with Realm of the Claw #2 .... 2.95
❑3/A, Sep 2002, b&w; Flip book with Realm of the Claw #3 .... 2.95
❑3/B, Sep 2002, b&w; Flip book with Realm of the Claw #3 .... 2.95
❑4/A, ca. 2002, b&w 2.95
❑4/B, ca. 2002, b&w 2.95

MUTANT MISADVENTURES OF CLOAK & DAGGER, THE
MARVEL

❑1, Oct 1988 A: X-Factor. 2.00
❑2, Dec 1988 .... 1.50
❑3, Feb 1989 .... 1.50
❑4, Apr 1989; Inferno 1.50
❑5, Jun 1989 .... 1.50
❑6, Aug 1989 .... 1.50
❑7, Oct 1989 .... 1.50
❑8, Dec 1989 .... 1.50
❑9, Jan 1990; Avengers; Acts of Vengeance 2.50
❑10, Feb 1990 .... 1.50
❑11, Apr 1990 .... 1.50
❑12, Jun 1990 .... 1.50
❑13, Aug 1990 .... 1.50
❑14, Oct 1990; Title changes to Cloak & Dagger 1.50
❑15, Dec 1990 .... 1.50
❑16, Feb 1991 .... 1.50
❑17, Apr 1991; Spider-Man crossover 1.50
❑18, Jun 1991; Spider-Man, Ghost Rider 1.50
❑19, Aug 1991; Giant-size 0: Cloak and Dagger. 2.50

MUTANTS AND MISFITS
SILVERLINE

❑1 .... 2.00

MUTANTS VS. ULTRAS: FIRST ENCOUNTERS
MALIBU / ULTRAVERSE

❑1, Nov 1995; reprints Prime vs. Hulk, Night Man vs. Wolverine, and Exiles vs. X-Men 6.95

MUTANT X (1ST SERIES)
MARVEL

❑1, Oct 1998; gatefold summary; Mutant X, Iceman, Marvel Woman standing on cover 3.00
❑1/A, Oct 1998; alternate cover 4.00
❑2, Nov 1998; gatefold summary 2.50
❑2/A, Nov 1998; gatefold summary; alternate cover 2.50
❑3, Dec 1998; gatefold summary 2.50
❑4, Jan 1999; gatefold summary 2.50
❑5, Feb 1999 A: Havok. A: Madelyne Pryor. A: Marvel Woman. A: Brute. 2.50
❑6, Mar 1999 A: Madelyne Pryor. A: Man-Spider. A: Brute. 2.00
❑7, Apr 1999 A: Havok. A: Man-Spider. A: Brute. A: Green Goblin. 2.00
❑8, May 1999 .... 2.00
❑9, Jun 1999 A: Ben Grimm. A: Havok. A: Elektra. A: Mole Man. 2.00
❑10, Jul 1999 A: X-Men. A: Magneto. 1.99
❑11, Aug 1999 .... 1.99
❑12, Sep 1999 .... 1.99
❑14, Nov 1999 .... 1.99
❑13, Sep 1999 .... 1.99

Condition price index: Multiply "NM prices" above by: **0.83 for Very Fine/Near Mint**
0.66 for Very Fine • 0.33 for Fine • 0.2 for Very Good • 0.125 for Good

	N-MINT
❑15, Dec 1999	1.99
❑16, Jan 2000	1.99
❑17, Feb 2000	2.25
❑18, Mar 2000	2.25
❑19, Apr 2000	2.25
❑20, May 2000	2.25
❑21, Jun 2000	2.25
❑22, Aug 2000	2.25
❑23, Sep 2000	2.25
❑24, Oct 2000	2.25
❑25, Nov 2000	2.25
❑26, Dec 2000	2.25
❑27, Jan 2001	2.25
❑29, Mar 2001	2.25
❑28, Feb 2001	2.25
❑30, Apr 2001	2.25
❑31, May 2001	2.25
❑32, Jun 2001	2.99
❑Annual 2001, ca. 2001 A: Beyonder.	2.99

MUTANT X (2ND SERIES)
MARVEL

❑1, Oct 2001	2.99

MUTANT X: DANGEROUS DECISIONS
MARVEL

❑1, Jun 2002	3.50

MUTANT X: ORIGIN
MARVEL

❑1, May 2002	3.50

MUTANT ZONE
AIRCEL

❑1, Oct 1991, b&w	2.50
❑2, b&w	2.50
❑3, b&w	2.50

MUTATIS
MARVEL / EPIC

❑1, ca. 1992	2.50
❑2, ca. 1992	2.50
❑3, ca. 1992	2.50

MUTATOR
CHECKER

❑1, Sum 1998	1.95
❑2 1998	1.95

MUTIES
MARVEL

❑1, Apr 2002	2.50
❑2, May 2002	2.50
❑3, Jun 2002	2.50
❑4, Jul 2002	2.50
❑5, Aug 2002	2.50
❑6, Sep 2002	2.50

MY FAITH IN FRANKIE
DC / VERTIGO

❑1, Mar 2004	2.95
❑2, Apr 2004	2.95
❑3, May 2004	2.95
❑4, Jun 2004	2.95

MY FAVORITE MARTIAN
GOLD KEY

❑1, Jan 1964	55.00
❑2, Jul 1964; Photo in small box; cover has art	35.00
❑3, Feb 1965	30.00
❑4, May 1965	30.00
❑5, Aug 1965	24.00
❑6 1966	24.00
❑7, Apr 1966	24.00
❑8, Jul 1966	24.00
❑9, Oct 1966	24.00

MY FLESH IS COOL (STEVEN GRANT'S)
AVATAR

❑1, Feb 2004	3.50

MY GREATEST ADVENTURE
DC

	N-MINT
❑1, Jan 1955	650.00
❑2, Mar 1955	350.00
❑3, May 1955	210.00
❑4, Jul 1955	210.00
❑5, Sep 1955	190.00
❑6, Nov 1955	190.00
❑7, Jan 1956	155.00
❑8, Mar 1956	155.00
❑9, May 1956	155.00
❑10, Jul 1956	155.00
❑11, Sep 1956	110.00
❑12, Nov 1956	110.00
❑13, Jan 1957	110.00
❑14, Mar 1957	110.00
❑15, May 1957	110.00
❑16, Jul 1957 JK (a)	125.00
❑17, Sep 1957 JK (a)	125.00
❑18, Nov 1957 JK (a)	125.00
❑19, Jan 1958	110.00
❑20, Mar 1958 JK (a)	125.00
❑21, May 1958 JK (a)	125.00
❑22, Jul 1958	85.00
❑23, Sep 1958	85.00
❑24, Oct 1958	85.00
❑25, Nov 1958	85.00
❑26, Dec 1958	85.00
❑27, Jan 1959	85.00
❑28, Feb 1959 JK (a)	90.00
❑29, Mar 1959	85.00
❑30, Apr 1959	85.00
❑31, May 1959	70.00
❑32, Jun 1959	70.00
❑33, Jul 1959	70.00
❑34, Aug 1959	70.00
❑35, Sep 1959	70.00
❑36, Oct 1959	70.00
❑37, Nov 1959	70.00
❑38, Dec 1959	70.00
❑39, Jan 1960	70.00
❑40, Feb 1960	70.00
❑41, Mar 1960	55.00
❑42, Apr 1960	55.00
❑43, May 1960	55.00
❑44, Jun 1960	55.00
❑45, Jul 1960	55.00
❑46, Aug 1960	55.00
❑47, Sep 1960	55.00
❑48, Oct 1960	55.00
❑49, Nov 1960	55.00
❑50, Dec 1960	55.00
❑51, Jan 1961	55.00
❑52, Feb 1961	55.00
❑53, Mar 1961	55.00
❑54, Apr 1961	55.00
❑55, May 1961	55.00
❑56, Jun 1961	55.00
❑57, Jul 1961	55.00
❑58, Aug 1961 ATh (a)	55.00
❑59, Sep 1961	55.00
❑60, Oct 1961 ATh (a)	55.00
❑61, Nov 1961 ATh (a)	55.00
❑62, Dec 1961	35.00
❑63, Jan 1962	35.00
❑64, Feb 1962	35.00
❑65, Mar 1962	35.00
❑66, Apr 1962	35.00
❑67, May 1962	35.00
❑68, Jun 1962	35.00
❑69, Jul 1962	35.00
❑70, Aug 1962	35.00
❑71, Sep 1962	35.00
❑72, Oct 1962	35.00
❑73, Nov 1962	35.00
❑74, Dec 1962	35.00
❑75, Jan 1963	35.00
❑76, Feb 1963	35.00
❑77, Mar 1963 ATh (a)	35.00
❑78, Apr 1963	35.00
❑79, May 1963	35.00
❑80, Jun 1963; O: The Doom Patrol. O: Elastic-Girl. O: Negative Man. O: Robotman. 1: The Doom Patrol. First Doom Patrol Story	300.00
❑81, Aug 1963; A: The Doom Patrol. Doom Patrol story	150.00
❑82, Sep 1963; A: The Doom Patrol. Doom Patrol story	150.00

Malibu produced several mini-series based on the popular fighting videogame *Mortal Kombat.*

© 1994 Malibu.

	N-MINT
❑83, Nov 1963; A: The Doom Patrol. Doom Patrol story	150.00
❑84, Dec 1963; A: The Doom Patrol. Doom Patrol story	150.00
❑85, Feb 1964; A: The Doom Patrol. Series continued in Doom Patrol (1st Series) #86	150.00

MY LITTLE MARGIE
CHARLTON

❑11	26.00
❑12, ca. 1956	26.00
❑13, ca. 1956	26.00
❑14, ca. 1956	26.00
❑15, ca. 1957	26.00
❑16, ca. 1957	26.00
❑17, Oct 1957	26.00
❑18, ca. 1958	26.00
❑19, ca. 1958	26.00
❑20, ca. 1958; Giant-sized issue	45.00
❑21, Oct 1958	20.00
❑22	20.00
❑23, ca. 1959	20.00
❑24, ca. 1959	20.00
❑25, ca. 1959	20.00
❑26	20.00
❑27	20.00
❑28, Mar 1960	20.00
❑29, ca. 1960	20.00
❑30, Jun 1960	20.00
❑31, ca. 1960	16.00
❑32, Oct 1960	16.00
❑33	16.00
❑34, ca. 1961	16.00
❑35, ca. 1961	16.00
❑36, ca. 1961	16.00
❑37, ca. 1961	16.00
❑38	16.00
❑39, ca. 1962	16.00
❑40, Mar 1962	12.00
❑41, ca. 1962	12.00
❑42, ca. 1962	12.00
❑43, ca. 1962	12.00
❑44	12.00
❑45	12.00
❑46, ca. 1963	12.00
❑47, ca. 1963	12.00
❑48, ca. 1963	12.00
❑49, ca. 1963	12.00
❑50	12.00
❑51, ca. 1964	9.00
❑52, ca. 1964	9.00
❑53, ca. 1964	9.00
❑54, ca. 1964 A: Beatles.	40.00

MY MONKEY'S NAME IS JENNIFER
SLAVE LABOR

❑1, May 2002	2.95

MY NAME IS CHAOS
DC

❑1, ca. 1992	5.00
❑2, ca. 1992	5.00
❑3, ca. 1992	5.00
❑4, ca. 1992	5.00

MY NAME IS HOLOCAUST
DC / MILESTONE

❑1, May 1995	2.50
❑2, Jun 1995	2.50
❑3, Jul 1995	2.50

N-MINT

❑4, Aug 1995 .... 2.50
❑5, Sep 1995 .... 2.50

MY NAME IS MUD
INCOGNITO

❑1, Sum 1994 .... 2.50

MY ONLY LOVE
CHARLTON

❑1, Jul 1975 .... 6.00
❑2, Sep 1975 .... 4.00
❑3, Nov 1975 .... 3.00
❑4, Jan 1976 .... 3.00
❑5, Mar 1976 .... 3.00
❑6, May 1976 .... 3.00
❑7, Jul 1976 .... 3.00
❑8, Sep 1976 .... 3.00
❑9, Nov 1976 .... 3.00

MYRMIDON
RED HILLS

❑1, Jul 1998, b&w 2.95

MY ROMANTIC ADVENTURES? (AVALON)
AVALON

❑1 .... 2.75

MYRON MOOSE FUNNIES
FANTAGRAPHICS

❑1 .... 1.75
❑2 .... 1.75
❑3 .... 1.75

MYSFITS, THE
BON-A-GRAM

❑1, Apr 1994 .... 2.50

MYS-TECH WARS
MARVEL

❑1, Mar 1993; Virtually all X-Men, Marvel UK characters appear 1.75
❑2, Apr 1993; Virtually all X-Men, Marvel UK characters appear 1.75
❑3, May 1993; Virtually all X-Men, Marvel UK characters appear 1.75
❑4, Jun 1993; Virtually all X-Men, Marvel UK characters appear 1.75

MYSTERIES OF SCOTLAND YARD
MAGAZINE ENTERPRISES

❑1, ca. 1954; Reprints Manhunt (5 Stories) 50.00

MYSTERIOUS SUSPENSE
CHARLTON

❑1, Oct 1968; SD (a);Question 35.00

MYSTERY DATE
LIGHTSPEED

❑1, May 1999, b&w 2.95

MYSTERY IN SPACE
DC

❑34, Oct 1956 .... 235.00
❑35, Dec 1956 .... 235.00
❑36, Feb 1957 .... 235.00
❑37, Apr 1957 .... 235.00
❑38, Jun 1957 .... 235.00
❑39, Aug 1957 .... 235.00
❑40, Oct 1957 .... 235.00
❑41, Dec 1957 .... 195.00
❑42, Feb 1958 .... 195.00
❑43, Apr 1958 .... 195.00
❑44, Jun 1958 .... 195.00
❑45, Aug 1958 .... 195.00
❑46, Sep 1958 .... 195.00
❑47, Oct 1958 .... 195.00
❑48, Dec 1958 .... 195.00
❑49, Feb 1959 .... 195.00
❑50, Apr 1959 .... 195.00
❑51, May 1959 .... 195.00
❑52, Jun 1959 .... 195.00
❑53, Aug 1959; CI (a);Adam Strange begins 1100.00
❑54, Sep 1959 CI (a) 425.00
❑55, Nov 1959 CI (a) 250.00
❑56, Dec 1959 CI (a) 175.00
❑57, Feb 1960 CI (a) 175.00
❑58, Mar 1960 CI (a) 175.00
❑59, May 1960 CI (a) 175.00
❑60, Jun 1960 CI (a) 175.00
❑61, Aug 1960; CI (a); 1: Tornado Tyrant. Later becomes Red Tornado 120.00
❑62, Sep 1960 CI (a) 120.00
❑63, Nov 1960 CI (a) 120.00
❑64, Dec 1960 CI (a) 120.00
❑65, Feb 1961 CI (a) 120.00
❑66, Mar 1961 CI (a); 1: The Star Rovers. 120.00
❑67, May 1961 CI (a) 120.00
❑68, Jun 1961 CI (a) 120.00
❑69, Aug 1961 CI (a) 120.00
❑70, Sep 1961 CI (a) 120.00
❑71, Nov 1961 CI (a) 120.00
❑72, Dec 1961 CI (a) 95.00
❑73, Feb 1962 CI (a) 95.00
❑74, Mar 1962 CI (a) 95.00
❑75, May 1962 CI (a); A: Justice League of America. 140.00
❑76, Jun 1962 CI (a) 80.00
❑77, Aug 1962 CI (a) 80.00
❑78, Sep 1962 CI (a) 80.00
❑79, Nov 1962 CI (a) 80.00
❑80, Dec 1962 CI (a) 80.00
❑81, Feb 1963 CI (a) 60.00
❑82, Mar 1963 CI (a) 60.00
❑83, May 1963 CI (a) 60.00
❑84, Jun 1963 CI (a) 60.00
❑85, Aug 1963 MA, CI (a); A: Adam Strange. 60.00
❑86, Sep 1963 CI (a) 60.00
❑87, Nov 1963 MA, CI (a); A: Hawkman. 125.00
❑88, Dec 1963 MA, CI (a); A: Hawkman. 90.00
❑89, Feb 1964 MA, CI (a); A: Hawkman. 90.00
❑90, Mar 1964 MA, CI (a); A: Hawkman. 90.00
❑91, May 1964 CI (a) 26.00
❑92, Jun 1964 .... 26.00
❑93, Aug 1964 .... 26.00
❑94, Sep 1964 .... 26.00
❑95, Nov 1964 .... 26.00
❑96, Dec 1964 .... 26.00
❑97, Feb 1965 .... 26.00
❑98, Mar 1965 .... 26.00
❑99, May 1965 .... 26.00
❑100, Jun 1965 .... 26.00
❑101, Aug 1965 .... 26.00
❑102, Sep 1965 .... 26.00
❑103, Nov 1965 .... 26.00
❑104, Dec 1965 .... 12.00
❑105, Feb 1966 .... 12.00
❑106, Mar 1966 .... 12.00
❑107, May 1966 .... 12.00
❑108, Jun 1966 .... 12.00
❑109, Aug 1966 .... 12.00
❑110, Sep 1966; Original series ends 12.00
❑111, Sep 1980; Series begins again 5.00
❑112, Oct 1980 .... 5.00
❑113, Nov 1980 .... 5.00
❑114, Dec 1980 .... 5.00
❑115, Jan 1981 .... 5.00
❑116, Feb 1981 .... 5.00
❑117, Mar 1981 .... 5.00

MYSTERY MAN, THE
SLAVE LABOR

❑1, Jul 1988, b&w 1.75
❑2, Nov 1988, b&w 1.75

MYSTERY MEN MOVIE ADAPTATION
DARK HORSE

❑1, Jul 1999 .... 2.95
❑2, Aug 1999 .... 2.95

MYSTERYMEN STORIES
BOB BURDEN

❑1, Sum 1996, b&w; prose story with illustrations 5.00

MYSTIC (CROSSGEN)
CROSSGEN

❑1, Jul 2000 .... 3.25
❑2, Aug 2000 .... 3.00
❑3, Sep 2000 .... 3.00
❑4, Oct 2000 .... 3.00
❑5, Nov 2000 .... 3.00
❑6, Dec 2000 .... 2.95
❑7, Jan 2001 .... 2.95
❑8, Feb 2001 .... 2.95
❑9, Mar 2001 .... 2.95
❑10, Apr 2001 .... 2.95
❑11, May 2001 .... 2.95
❑12, Jun 2001 .... 2.95
❑13, Jul 2001 .... 2.95
❑14, Aug 2001 .... 2.95
❑15, Sep 2001 .... 2.95
❑16, Oct 2001 .... 2.95
❑17, Nov 2001 .... 2.95
❑18, Dec 2001 .... 2.95
❑19, Jan 2002 .... 2.95
❑20, Feb 2002 .... 2.95
❑21, Mar 2002 .... 2.95
❑22, Apr 2002 .... 2.95
❑23, May 2002 .... 2.95
❑24, Jun 2002 .... 2.95
❑25, Jul 2002 .... 2.95
❑26, Aug 2002 .... 2.95
❑27, Sep 2002 .... 2.95
❑28, Oct 2002 .... 2.95
❑29, Nov 2002 .... 2.95
❑30, Dec 2002 .... 2.95
❑31, Jan 2003 .... 2.95
❑32, Feb 2003 .... 2.95
❑33, Mar 2003 .... 2.95
❑34, Apr 2003 .... 2.95
❑35, May 2003 .... 2.95
❑36, Jun 2003 .... 2.95
❑37, Jul 2003 .... 2.95
❑38, Aug 2003 .... 2.95
❑39, Sep 2003 .... 2.95
❑40, Nov 2003 .... 2.95
❑41, Nov 2003 .... 2.95
❑42, Dec 2003 .... 2.95
❑43, Jan 2004 .... 2.95

MYSTIC EDGE
ANTARCTIC

❑1, Oct 1998 .... 2.95

MYSTIC TRIGGER, THE
MAELSTROM

❑1; Tales of the Galactic Forces preview 3.25

MYSTIQUE
MARVEL

❑1, Jun 2003 .... 2.99
❑2, Jul 2003 .... 2.99
❑3, Aug 2003 .... 2.99
❑4, Sep 2003 .... 2.99
❑5, Oct 2003 .... 2.99
❑6, Nov 2003 .... 2.99
❑7, Dec 2003 .... 2.99
❑8, Jan 2004 .... 2.99
❑9, Feb 2004 .... 2.99
❑10, Mar 2004 .... 2.99
❑11, Apr 2004 .... 2.99
❑12, May 2004 .... 2.99
❑13, Jun 2004 .... 2.99
❑14, Jul 2004 .... 2.99
❑15, Jul 2004 .... 2.99
❑16, Aug 2004 .... 2.99
❑17, Sep 2004 .... 2.99

MYSTIQUE & SABRETOOTH
MARVEL

❑1, Dec 1996 .... 1.95
❑2, Jan 1997 .... 1.95
❑3, Feb 1997 .... 1.95
❑4, Mar 1997 .... 1.95

MYST: THE BOOK OF THE BLACK SHIPS
DARK HORSE

❑0, ca. 1997; American Entertainment Exclusive Edition; No cover price; based on video game 1.50
❑1, Aug 1997; based on video game 2.95
❑2, Sep 1997 .... 2.95
❑3, Oct 1997 .... 2.95
❑4, Nov 1997 .... 2.95

N-MINT

MY TERRIBLE ROMANCE
NEC

	N-MINT
❑1	2.75
❑2, Jul 1994; Reprints from Hi-School Romance #9, My Desire #4, Voodoo #16, Romantic Love #8, All True Romance #17	2.75

MYTH
FYGMOK

	N-MINT
❑1, Dec 1996, b&w; wraparound cover	2.95
❑2, Feb 1997, b&w	2.95

MYTHADVENTURES
WARP

	N-MINT
❑1, Mar 1984; Warp publishes	2.00
❑2, Jun 1984	1.50
❑3, Sep 1984	1.50
❑4, Dec 1984	1.50
❑5, Mar 1985	1.50
❑6, Jun 1985	1.50
❑7, Sep 1985	1.50
❑8, Dec 1985 PF (w); PF (a)	1.50
❑9, Mar 1986	1.50
❑10 1986; Apple begins as publisher	1.50
❑11 1986	1.50
❑12 1986	1.50

MYTH CONCEPTIONS
APPLE

	N-MINT
❑1, Nov 1987	2.00
❑2, Jan 1988	1.75
❑3, Mar 1988	1.75
❑4, May 1988	1.75
❑5, Jul 1988	1.75
❑6, Sep 1988	1.75
❑7, Nov 1988	1.75
❑8, Jan 1989	1.75

MYTHIC HEROES
CHAPTERHOUSE

	N-MINT
❑1, Sep 1996, b&w	2.50

MYTH MAKER (ROBERT E. HOWARD'S...)
CROSS PLAINS

	N-MINT
❑1, Jun 1999	6.95

MYTHOGRAPHY
BARDIC

	N-MINT
❑1, Sep 1996	4.00
❑2, Feb 1997	4.00
❑3, Apr 1997	4.00
❑4, Jun 1997	4.00
❑5, Sep 1997	4.00
❑6, Nov 1997; Barr Girls story	4.00
❑7, Feb 1998	4.00
❑8, May 1998	4.00

MYTHOS
WONDER COMIX

	N-MINT
❑1, Jan 1987	2.00
❑2, Apr 1987	2.00
❑3, Aug 1987, b&w	2.00

MYTHOS: THE FINAL TOUR
DC / VERTIGO

	N-MINT
❑1, Dec 1996; prestige format	5.95
❑2, Jan 1997; prestige format	5.95
❑3, Feb 1997; prestige format	5.95

MYTHSTALKERS
IMAGE

	N-MINT
❑1, Apr 2003	2.95
❑2, May 2003	2.95
❑3, Jun 2003	2.95
❑4, Sep 2003	2.95
❑5, Oct 2003	2.95
❑6, Dec 2003	2.95
❑7, Feb 2004	2.95
❑8, May 2004	2.95

N

NADESICO
CPM MANGA

	N-MINT
❑1, Jun 1999	2.95
❑2, Jul 1999	2.95
❑3, Aug 1999	2.95
❑4, Sep 1999	2.95
❑5, Oct 1999	2.95
❑6, Nov 1999	2.95
❑7, Dec 1999	2.95
❑8, Jan 2000	2.95
❑9, Feb 2000	2.95
❑10, Mar 2000	2.95
❑11, Apr 2000	2.95
❑12, May 2000	2.95
❑13, Jun 2000	2.95
❑14, Jul 2000	2.95
❑15, Aug 2000	2.95
❑16, Sep 2000	2.95
❑17, Oct 2000	2.95
❑18, Nov 2000	2.95
❑19, Dec 2000	2.95
❑20, Jan 2001	2.95
❑21, Feb 2001	2.95
❑22, Mar 2001	2.95
❑23, Apr 2001	2.95
❑24, May 2001	2.95
❑25, Jun 2001	2.95
❑26, Jul 2001	2.95

NAIL
DARK HORSE

	N-MINT
❑1, Aug 2004	2.99

NAIVE INTER-DIMENSIONAL COMMANDO KOALAS
ECLIPSE

	N-MINT
❑1, Oct 1986, b&w	1.50

NAKED ANGELS
FANTAGRAPHICS / EROS

	N-MINT
❑1 1996	2.95
❑2, May 1996	2.95

NAKED EYE (S.A. KING'S...)
ANTARCTIC

	N-MINT
❑1, Dec 1994, b&w	2.75
❑2, Feb 1995, b&w	2.75
❑3, Apr 1995, b&w	2.75

'NAM, THE
MARVEL

	N-MINT
❑1, Dec 1986 MG (a)	2.00
❑1-2, Dec 1986 MG (a)	1.00
❑2, Jan 1987 MG (a)	1.00
❑3, Feb 1987 MG (a)	1.00
❑4, Mar 1987	1.00
❑5, Apr 1987	1.00
❑6, May 1987 MG (a)	1.00
❑7, Jun 1987 MG (a)	1.00
❑8, Jul 1987 MG (a)	1.00
❑9, Aug 1987 D: Mike.	1.00
❑10, Sep 1987	1.00
❑11, Oct 1987	1.00
❑12, Nov 1987	1.00
❑13, Dec 1987	1.00
❑14, Jan 1988	1.00
❑15, Feb 1988	1.00
❑16, Mar 1988	1.00
❑17, Apr 1988	1.00
❑18, May 1988	1.25
❑19, Jun 1988	1.25
❑20, Jul 1988	1.25
❑21, Aug 1988	1.25
❑22, Sep 1988	1.25
❑23, Oct 1988	1.25
❑24, Nov 1988	1.25
❑25, Dec 1988	1.25
❑26, Jan 1989	1.50
❑27, Feb 1989	1.50
❑28, Mar 1989	1.50
❑29, Apr 1989	1.50
❑30, May 1989	1.50

Introduced in *Marvel Super-Heroes* #12, Carol Danvers became a female Captain Marvel in *Ms. Marvel* #1.

© 1977 Marvel Comics.

	N-MINT
❑32, Jul 1989	1.50
❑33, Aug 1989	1.50
❑34, Sep 1989	1.50
❑35, Oct 1989; A: Bob Hope. Christmas issue	1.50
❑36, Nov 1989	1.50
❑37, Nov 1989	1.50
❑38, Dec 1989	1.50
❑39, Dec 1989 A: Iron Man. A: Captain America. A: Thor.	1.50
❑40, Jan 1990	1.50
❑41, Feb 1990 A: Iron Man. A: Captain America. A: Thor.	1.50
❑42, Mar 1990	1.50
❑43, Apr 1990	1.50
❑44, May 1990	1.50
❑45, Jun 1990	1.50
❑46, Jul 1990	1.50
❑47, Aug 1990	1.50
❑48, Sep 1990	1.50
❑49, Oct 1990	1.50
❑50, Nov 1990	1.50
❑51, Dec 1990	1.50
❑52, Jan 1991 A: Frank Castle (Punisher).	1.50
❑52-2, Jan 1991 A: Frank Castle (Punisher).	1.50
❑53, Feb 1991 A: Frank Castle (Punisher).	1.50
❑53-2, Feb 1991 A: Frank Castle (Punisher).	1.50
❑54, Mar 1991 TD (a)	1.50
❑55, Apr 1991 TD (a)	1.50
❑56, May 1991	1.50
❑57, Jun 1991	1.50
❑58, Jul 1991	1.50
❑59, Aug 1991	1.50
❑60, Sep 1991	1.50
❑61, Oct 1991	1.50
❑62, Nov 1991	1.50
❑63, Dec 1991	1.50
❑64, Jan 1992	1.50
❑65, Feb 1992 RH (a)	1.75
❑66, Mar 1992	1.75
❑67, Apr 1992 A: Punisher.	1.75
❑68, May 1992 A: Punisher.	1.75
❑69, Jun 1992 A: Punisher.	1.75
❑70, Jul 1992	1.75
❑71, Aug 1992	1.75
❑72, Sep 1992	1.75
❑73, Oct 1992	1.75
❑74, Nov 1992	1.75
❑75, Dec 1992; HT (a); Tells of Mai Lai Massacre from different points of view	2.25
❑76, Jan 1993	1.75
❑77, Feb 1993	1.75
❑79, Apr 1993	1.75
❑80, May 1993	1.75
❑81, Jun 1993	1.75
❑82, Jul 1993	1.75
❑83, Aug 1993	1.75
❑84, Sep 1993; Told from Vietnamese point of view	1.75

NAMELESS, THE
IMAGE

	N-MINT
❑1, May 1997	2.95
❑2, Jun 1997	2.95
❑3, Jul 1997, b&w	2.95

N-MINT

❑4, Aug 1997, b&w 2.95
❑5, Sep 1997, b&w 2.95

NAME OF THE GAME, THE
DC

❑1/HC 29.95

NAMES OF MAGIC
DC / VERTIGO

❑1, Feb 2001 2.50
❑2, Mar 2001 2.50
❑3, Apr 2001 2.50
❑4, May 2001 2.50
❑5, Jun 2001 2.50

'NAM MAGAZINE, THE
MARVEL

❑1, Aug 1988, b&w MG (a) 3.00
❑2, Sep 1988, b&w 2.50
❑3, Oct 1988, b&w 2.50
❑4, Nov 1988, b&w 2.50
❑5, Dec 1988, b&w 2.50
❑6, Dec 1988, b&w 2.50
❑7, Jan 1989, b&w 2.50
❑8, Feb 1989, b&w 2.50
❑9, Mar 1989, b&w 2.50
❑10, Apr 1989, b&w 2.50

NAMOR
MARVEL

❑1, Jun 2003 3.00
❑2, Jun 2003 2.25
❑3, Jul 2003, color 2.25
❑4, Aug 2003, color 2.25
❑5, Oct 2003, color 2.99
❑6, Nov 2003, color 2.99
❑7, Dec 2003, color 2.99
❑8, Dec 2003, color 2.99
❑9, Jan 2004, color 2.99
❑10, Feb 2004, color 2.99
❑11, Mar 2004, color 2.99
❑12, Apr 2004 2.99

NAMOR, THE SUB-MARINER
MARVEL

❑1, Apr 1990 JBy (w); JBy (a); O: Sub-Mariner. 2.00
❑2, May 1990 JBy (w); JBy (a) 1.50
❑3, Jun 1990 JBy (a) 1.50
❑4, Jul 1990 JBy (a) 1.50
❑5, Aug 1990 JBy (a) 1.50
❑6, Sep 1990 JBy (a) 1.25
❑7, Oct 1990 JBy (a) 1.25
❑8, Nov 1990 JBy (a) 1.25
❑9, Dec 1990 JBy (a) 1.25
❑10, Jan 1991 JBy (a) 1.25
❑11, Feb 1991 JBy (a) 1.25
❑12, Mar 1991; Giant-size JBy (a); A: Human Torch. A: Captain America. A: Invaders. 1.25
❑13, Apr 1991 JBy (a) 1.00
❑14, May 1991 JBy (a) 1.00
❑15, Jun 1991 JBy (a) 1.00
❑16, Jul 1991 JBy (a) 1.00
❑17, Aug 1991 JBy (a) 1.00
❑18, Sep 1991 JBy (a) 1.00
❑19, Oct 1991 JBy (a) 1.00
❑20, Nov 1991 JBy (a) 1.00
❑21, Dec 1991 JBy (a) 1.00
❑22, Jan 1992 JBy (a) 1.00
❑23, Feb 1992 JBy (a); A: Wolverine. A: Iron Fist. 1.25
❑24, Mar 1992; JBy (a); A: Wolverine. Namor fights Wolverine 1.25
❑25, Apr 1992 JBy (a); A: Wolverine. 1.25
❑26, May 1992; 1st Jae Lee art 1.25
❑27, Jun 1992 1.25
❑28, Jul 1992 A: Iron Fist. 1.25
❑29, Aug 1992 1.25
❑30, Sep 1992 1.25
❑31, Oct 1992 1.25
❑32, Nov 1992 1.25
❑33, Dec 1992 1.25
❑34, Jan 1993 1.25
❑35, Feb 1993 1.25
❑36, Mar 1993 1.25
❑37, Apr 1993; foil cover 2.00
❑38, May 1993 1.25
❑39, Jun 1993 1.25
❑40, Jul 1993 1.25
❑41, Aug 1993 1.25
❑42, Sep 1993 A: Stingray. 1.25
❑43, Oct 1993 A: Stingray. 1.25
❑44, Nov 1993 1.25
❑45, Dec 1993 1.25
❑46, Jan 1994 1.25
❑47, Feb 1994 1.25
❑48, Mar 1994 1.25
❑49, Apr 1994 1.25
❑50, May 1994; Giant-size 1.75
❑50/Variant, May 1994; Giant-size; foil cover 2.95
❑51, Jun 1994 1.75
❑52, Jul 1994 1.50
❑53, Aug 1994 1.50
❑54, Sep 1994 1: Llyron. 1.50
❑55, Oct 1994 1.50
❑56, Nov 1994 1.50
❑57, Dec 1994 1.50
❑58, Jan 1995 V: Avengers. 1.50
❑59, Feb 1995 1.50
❑60, Mar 1995 1.50
❑61, Apr 1995 1.50
❑62, May 1995 1.50
❑Annual 1, ca. 1991 O: Namor. 2.00
❑Annual 2, ca. 1992 A: The Defenders. 2.25
❑Annual 3, ca. 1993 O: The Assassin. 2.95
❑Annual 4, ca. 1994 2.95

NANNY AND THE PROFESSOR
DELL

❑1, Aug 1970; based on TV show 16.00
❑2, Oct 1970 10.00

NANOSOUP
MILLENNIUM

❑1, ca. 1996, b&w; wraparound cover 2.95

NARCOLEPSY DREAMS
SLAVE LABOR

❑1, Feb 1995 2.95
❑2, Aug 1995 2.95
❑4; Mini-comic 1.00

NARD N' PAT
CARTOONISTS CO-OP

❑1, b&w 3.00

NASCAR ADVENTURES
VORTEX

❑1 1992; DH (a); Fred Lorenzen; regular cover 2.95
❑2 1992; Richard Petty 2.50
❑5 1992; Ernie Irvan 2.50
❑7 1992 2.50

NASCUB ADVENTURES, THE
VORTEX

❑1, Jun 1991 2.00

NASH
IMAGE

❑1, Jul 1999; regular cover 2.95
❑1/A, Jul 1999 2.95
❑1/B, Jul 1999; no cover price 2.95
❑2, Jul 1999; regular cover 2.95
❑2/A, Jul 1999 2.95
❑Ashcan 1, Jul 1999; Preview Book; regular cover 2.50
❑Ashcan 1/Varian, Jul 1999 2.50

NASTI: MONSTER HUNTER
SCHISM

❑1, b&w 1: Nasti. 2.50
❑1/Autographed; limited edition (250 printed) with certificate of authenticity 1: Nasti. 3.00
❑2, b&w 2.50
❑3, b&w 2.50
❑Ashcan 1/Ltd., b&w; No cover price; preview of upcoming comic book on newsprint 1.00

NATHANIEL DUSK
DC

❑1, Feb 1984 GC (a); 1: Nathaniel Dusk. 1.50
❑2, Mar 1984 GC (a) 1.50
❑3, Apr 1984 GC (a) 1.50
❑4, May 1984 GC (a) 1.50

NATHANIEL DUSK II
DC

❑1, Oct 1985 2.00
❑2, Nov 1985 2.00
❑3, Dec 1985 2.00
❑4, Jan 1986 2.00

NATHAN NEVER
DARK HORSE

❑1, Mar 1999 4.95
❑2, Apr 1999 4.95
❑3, May 1999 4.95
❑4, Jun 1999 4.95
❑5, Jul 1999 4.95
❑6, Aug 1999 4.95

NATIONAL COMICS (2ND SERIES)
DC

❑1, May 1999 MWa (w); A: Flash. A: Justice Society. A: Mr. Terrific. 2.00

NATIONAL INQUIRER, THE
FANTAGRAPHICS

❑1, Apr 1989

NATIONAL VELVET (DELL)
DELL

❑1, Jul 1962, Code on cover ends in -207 30.00
❑2, Oct 1962, Code on cover ends in -210 30.00

NATIONAL VELVET
DELL

❑1, Dec 1962 12.00
❑2, Mar 1963 9.00

NATION OF SNITCHES
DC / PIRANHA

❑1 4.95

NATURAL INQUIRER
FANTAGRAPHICS

❑1, Apr 1989, b&w 2.00

NATURAL SELECTION, THE
ATOM

❑1, Jan 1998, b&w 2.95
❑2, Feb 1998, b&w 2.95

NATURE OF THE BEAST
CALIBER

❑1, b&w 2.95
❑2, b&w 2.95

NAUGHTY BITS
FANTAGRAPHICS

❑1, Mar 1991, b&w 7.00
❑1-2, b&w 2.50
❑2, Jun 1991, b&w 5.00
❑3, Sep 1991, b&w 4.00
❑4, Dec 1991, b&w 3.75
❑5, Apr 1992, b&w 3.75
❑6, Aug 1992, b&w 3.00
❑7, Nov 1992, b&w 3.00
❑8, Feb 1993, b&w 3.00
❑9, Jun 1993, b&w 3.00
❑10, Oct 1993, b&w 3.00
❑11, Jan 1994, b&w 2.50
❑12, Apr 1994, b&w 2.50
❑13, Jul 1994, b&w 2.95
❑14, Oct 1994, b&w 2.95
❑15, Feb 1995, b&w 2.95
❑16, May 1995, b&w 2.95
❑17, Aug 1995, b&w 2.95
❑18, Jan 1996, b&w 2.95
❑19, Apr 1996, b&w 2.95
❑20, Aug 1996, b&w 2.95
❑21, Nov 1996, b&w 2.95
❑22, Mar 1997, b&w 2.95
❑23, Jun 1997, b&w 2.95
❑24, Oct 1997, b&w 2.95
❑25, b&w 2.95

Condition price index: Multiply "NM prices" above by: **0.83 for Very Fine/Near Mint**
0.66 for Very Fine • 0.33 for Fine • 0.2 for Very Good • 0.125 for Good

N-MINT

❑26 2.95
❑27 2.95
❑28, ca. 1999 2.95
❑29, Jul 1999, color 2.95
❑30 2.95
❑31, Apr 2000 2.95
❑32 2.95
❑33 2.95
❑34, May 2001 2.95
❑35 2.95
❑36 2.95
❑37, Dec 2002 2.95
❑38 2.95

NAUSICAÄ OF THE VALLEY OF WIND PART 1
VIZ

❑1 3.25
❑2 3.25
❑3 3.25
❑4 3.25
❑5 3.25
❑6 3.25
❑7 3.25

NAUSICAÄ OF THE VALLEY OF WIND PART 2
VIZ

❑1 2.95
❑2 2.95
❑3 2.95
❑4 3.25

NAUSICAÄ OF THE VALLEY OF WIND PART 3
VIZ

❑1 3.95
❑2 3.95
❑3 3.95

NAUSICAÄ OF THE VALLEY OF WIND PART 4
VIZ

❑1 2.75
❑2 2.75
❑3 2.75
❑4 2.75
❑5 2.75
❑6 2.75

NAUSICAÄ OF THE VALLEY OF WIND PART 5
VIZ

❑1 2.75
❑2 2.75
❑3 2.75
❑4 2.75
❑5 2.75
❑6 2.75
❑7 2.95
❑8 2.95

NAUTILUS
SHANDA FANTASY ARTS

❑1, May 1999, b&w 2.95

NAVY WAR HEROES
CHARLTON

❑1 12.00
❑2, Mar 1964, color 8.00
❑3 1964 6.00
❑4 1964 6.00
❑5, Nov 1964 6.00
❑6 6.00
❑7 6.00

NAZA
DELL

❑1, Jan 1964 15.00
❑2, Jun 1964 8.00
❑3, Sep 1964 8.00
❑4, Dec 1964 8.00
❑5, Mar 1965 8.00
❑6, Jun 1965 6.00
❑7, Sep 1965 6.00
❑8, Dec 1965 6.00
❑9, Mar 1966 6.00

N-MINT

NAZRAT
IMPERIAL

❑1 2.00
❑2 2.00
❑3 2.00
❑4 2.00
❑5 2.00
❑6, Jun 1987, b&w 2.00

NAZZ, THE
DC

❑1, Oct 1990 4.95
❑2, Nov 1990 4.95
❑3, Dec 1990 4.95
❑4, Jan 1991 4.95

NBC SATURDAY MORNING COMICS
HARVEY

❑1, Sep 1991, Toys "R" Us giveaway A: Geoffrey Giraffe. 1.50

NEAR MYTHS
RIP OFF

❑1, Jul 1990, b&w 2.50

NEAR TO NOW
FANDOM HOUSE

❑1, b&w 2.00
❑2, b&w 2.00

NEAT STUFF
FANTAGRAPHICS

❑1 5.00
❑1-2 2.50
❑2 4.00
❑2-2 2.50
❑3 3.50
❑3-2 2.50
❑4 3.00
❑4-2 2.50
❑5, Dec 1986 2.50
❑6, Apr 1987; all Bradley issue 2.50
❑7, Aug 1987 2.50
❑8, Dec 1987 2.50
❑9 1988 2.50
❑10 1988 2.50
❑11, Nov 1988 2.50
❑12 2.50
❑13 2.50
❑14 2.50
❑15 2.50

NECROMANCER
ANARCHY

❑1, b&w 2.50
❑1/Deluxe; Deluxe edition 3.50
❑2, b&w 2.50
❑2/Deluxe; Deluxe edition 3.50
❑3, b&w 2.50
❑3/Deluxe; Deluxe edition 3.50
❑4, b&w 2.50
❑4/Deluxe; Deluxe edition 3.50

NECROMANCER (2ND SERIES)
ANARCHY

❑1, b&w 2.50
❑2, b&w 2.50
❑3, b&w 2.50
❑4, b&w 2.50

NECROPOLIS
FLEETWAY-QUALITY

❑1 2.95
❑2 2.95
❑3 2.95
❑4 2.95
❑5 2.95
❑6 2.95
❑7 2.95
❑8 2.95
❑9 2.95

NECROSCOPE
MALIBU

❑1, Oct 1992 3.00
❑1-2, Dec 1992; Hologram cover 2.95
❑2, Dec 1992; bagged with tattoo 2.95
❑3, Feb 1993 2.95

Professional wrestler Kevin Nash licensed his likeness to a series of adventures from Image.

© 1999 Image.

N-MINT

❑4 2.95
❑5 2.95

NECROSCOPE BOOK II: WAMPHYRI
MALIBU

❑1 2.95
❑2, Nov 1994 2.95
❑3, Jan 1994 2.95
❑4 2.95
❑5 2.95

NECROWAR
DREAMWAVE

❑1, Jul 2003 2.95
❑2, Aug 2003 2.95
❑3, Sep 2003 2.95

NEFARISMO
FANTAGRAPHICS / EROS

❑1 2.95
❑2 2.95
❑3 2.95
❑4 2.95
❑5, May 1995 2.95
❑6, Aug 1995 2.95
❑7, Sep 1995 2.95
❑8, Oct 1995 2.95

NEGATION
CROSSGEN

❑1, Jan 2002 2.95
❑2, Feb 2002 2.95
❑3, Mar 2002 2.95
❑4, Apr 2002 2.95
❑5, May 2002 2.95
❑6, Jun 2002 2.95
❑7, Jul 2002 2.95
❑8, Aug 2002 2.95
❑9, Sep 2002 2.95
❑10, Oct 2002 2.95
❑11, Nov 2002 2.95
❑12, Dec 2002 2.95
❑13, Jan 2003 2.95
❑14, Feb 2003 2.95
❑15, Mar 2003 2.95
❑16, Apr 2003 2.95
❑17, May 2003 2.95
❑18, Jun 2003 2.95
❑19, Jul 2003 2.95
❑20, Aug 2003 2.95
❑21, Oct 2003 2.95
❑22, Nov 2003 2.95
❑23, Nov 2003 2.95
❑24, Dec 2003 2.95
❑25, Jan 2004 2.95
❑26, Feb 2004 2.95
❑27, Mar 2004 2.95

NEGATION WAR
CROSSGEN

❑1, Apr 2004 2.95
❑1-2, May 2004 2.95
❑2, May 2004 2.95

NEGATION PREQUEL
CROSSGEN

❑1, Dec 2001 2.95

NEGATIVE BURN
CALIBER

❑1, ca. 1993, b&w BB (w); BB (a); A: Flaming Carrot. 4.00
❑2, ca. 1993, b&w 4.00

Condition price index: Multiply "NM prices" above by: **0.83 for Very Fine/Near Mint**
0.66 for Very Fine • 0.33 for Fine • 0.2 for Very Good • 0.125 for Good

	N-MINT
❑3, Apr 1993, b&w A: Bone.	4.00
❑4, ca. 1993, b&w	4.00
❑5, ca. 1993, b&w	4.00
❑6, ca. 1994, b&w	4.00
❑7, ca. 1994, b&w	4.00
❑8, ca. 1994, b&w	4.00
❑9, ca. 1994, b&w AMo (w)	4.00
❑10, ca. 1994, b&w AMo (w)	4.00
❑11, ca. 1994, b&w BB, NG (w)	4.00
❑12, ca. 1994, b&w	4.00
❑13, ca. 1994, b&w BMB, AMo, NG (w); A: Strangers in Paradise.	6.50
❑14, ca. 1994, b&w	3.95
❑15, ca. 1994, b&w BB (w); BB (a)	3.95
❑16, ca. 1994, b&w	3.95
❑17, ca. 1994, b&w	3.95
❑18, ca. 1994, b&w	3.95
❑19, Jan 1995, b&w	3.95
❑20, Feb 1995, b&w	3.95
❑21, Mar 1995, b&w	3.95
❑22, Apr 1995, b&w	3.95
❑23, May 1995, b&w	3.95
❑24, Jun 1995, b&w	3.95
❑25, Jul 1995, b&w	3.95
❑26, Aug 1995, b&w	3.95
❑27, Sep 1995, b&w	3.95
❑28, Oct 1995, b&w; Dusty Star	3.95
❑29, Nov 1995, b&w	3.95
❑30, Dec 1995, b&w	3.95
❑31, Jan 1996, b&w	3.95
❑32, Feb 1996, b&w	3.95
❑33, Mar 1996, b&w	3.95
❑34, Apr 1996, b&w	3.95
❑35, May 1996, b&w	3.95
❑36, Jun 1996, b&w	3.95
❑37, Jul 1996, b&w BB, AMo (w); BMB, BB, CR (a); A: Dusty Star.	3.95
❑38, Aug 1996	3.95
❑39, Sep 1996	3.95
❑40, Oct 1996	3.95
❑41, Nov 1996	3.95
❑42, Dec 1996	3.95
❑43, Jan 1997	3.95
❑44, Feb 1997	3.95
❑45 1997	3.95
❑46 1997	3.95
❑47 1997	3.95
❑48 1997	4.95
❑49 1997	4.95
❑50 1997	6.95

NEGATIVE ONE
Eirich Olson

❑1, Sep 1999	2.95

NEIL & BUZZ IN SPACE AND TIME
Fantagraphics

❑1, Apr 1989, b&w	2.00

NEIL THE HORSE COMICS AND STORIES
Aardvark-Vanaheim

❑1, Feb 1983	2.50
❑2, Apr 1983	2.00
❑3, Jun 1983	2.00
❑4, Aug 1983	2.00
❑5, Nov 1983	2.00
❑6, Feb 1984	2.00
❑7, Apr 1984	2.00
❑8, Jun 1984	2.00
❑9, Sep 1984	2.00
❑10, Dec 1984	2.00
❑11, Apr 1985; Title changes to Neil the Horse	2.00
❑12, Jun 1985	2.00
❑13, Dec 1986	2.00
❑14, Jul 1988; giant	3.00
❑15, Aug 1988; giant	3.00

NEMESISTER
Cheeky

	N-MINT
❑1, Apr 1997, b&w; cardstock cover	2.95
❑2, Jun 1997, b&w; cardstock cover	2.95
❑3, Sep 1997, b&w; cardstock cover	2.95
❑3/Ashcan; ashcan edition	0.50
❑4, Nov 1997, b&w; cardstock cover	2.95
❑5	2.95
❑6	2.95
❑7	2.95
❑8	2.95
❑9	2.95

NEMESIS THE WARLOCK (FLEETWAY/QUALITY)
Fleetway-Quality

❑1 1989, b&w	2.00
❑2, b&w	2.00
❑3, b&w	2.00
❑4, b&w	2.00
❑5, b&w	2.00
❑6, b&w	2.00
❑7, b&w	2.00
❑8, b&w	2.00
❑9, b&w BT (a)	2.00
❑10, b&w	2.00
❑11, b&w	2.00
❑12, b&w	2.00
❑13, b&w	2.00
❑14, b&w O: Torquemada.	2.00
❑15, b&w	2.00
❑16, b&w	2.00
❑17, b&w	2.00
❑18, b&w	2.00
❑19, b&w	2.00

NEO
Excalibur

❑1, b&w	1.50

NEOMEN
Slave Labor

❑1, Oct 1987; no indicia	1.75
❑2, Jan 1988	1.75

NEON CITY
Innovation

❑1, b&w	2.25

NEON CITY: AFTER THE FALL
Innovation

❑1, b&w	2.50

NEON CYBER
Image

❑1, Aug 1999	2.50
❑1/Variant, Aug 1999; alternate cover	5.00
❑2, Sep 1999; Man facing giant on cover	2.50
❑2/Variant, Sep 1999; alternate cover	2.50
❑3, Oct 1999; alternate cover	2.50
❑4, Dec 1999	2.50
❑5, Jan 2000	2.50
❑6, Mar 2000	2.50
❑7, May 2000	2.50
❑8, Jun 2000	2.50

NEON GENESIS EVANGELION BOOK 1
Viz

❑1/A, Sep 1997	2.95
❑1/B, Sep 1997; printed in Japanese style (back to front)	2.95
❑2/A, Oct 1997	2.95
❑2/B, Oct 1997; printed in Japanese style (back to front)	2.95
❑3/A, Nov 1997	2.95
❑3/B, Nov 1997; printed in Japanese style (back to front)	2.95
❑4/A, Dec 1997	2.95
❑4/B, Dec 1997; printed in Japanese style (back to front)	2.95
❑5/A, Jan 1998	2.95
❑5/B, Jan 1998; printed in Japanese style (back to front)	2.95
❑6/A, Feb 1998	2.95
❑6/B, Feb 1998; printed in Japanese style (back to front)	2.95

NEON GENESIS EVANGELION BOOK 2
Viz

	N-MINT
❑1/A, Mar 1998	3.50
❑1/B, Mar 1998; printed in Japanese style (back to front)	3.50
❑2/A, Apr 1998	3.25
❑2/B, Apr 1998; printed in Japanese style (back to front)	3.25
❑3/A, May 1998	2.95
❑3/B, May 1998; printed in Japanese style (back to front)	2.95
❑4/A, Jun 1998	2.95
❑4/B, Jun 1998; printed in Japanese style (back to front)	2.95
❑5/A, Jul 1998	2.95
❑5/B, Jul 1998; printed in Japanese style (back to front)	2.95

NEON GENESIS EVANGELION BOOK 3
Viz

❑1/A, Aug 1998	2.95
❑1/B, Aug 1998; printed in Japanese style (back to front)	2.95
❑2/A, Sep 1998	2.95
❑2/B, Sep 1998; printed in Japanese style (back to front)	2.95
❑3/A, Oct 1998	2.95
❑3/B, Oct 1998; printed in Japanese style (back to front)	2.95
❑4/A, Nov 1998	2.95
❑4/B, Nov 1998; printed in Japanese style (back to front)	2.95
❑5/A, Dec 1998	2.95
❑5/B, Dec 1998; printed in Japanese style (back to front)	2.95
❑6/A, Jan 1999	3.25
❑6/B, Jan 1999; printed in Japanese style (back to front)	3.25

NEON GENESIS EVANGELION BOOK 4
Viz

❑1/A, Feb 1999	2.95
❑1/B, Feb 1999; printed in Japanese style (back to front)	2.95
❑2/A, Mar 1999	2.95
❑2/B, Mar 1999; printed in Japanese style (back to front)	2.95
❑3/A, Apr 1999	2.95
❑3/B, Apr 1999; printed in Japanese style (back to front)	2.95
❑4/A, May 1999	2.95
❑4/B, May 1999, printed in Japanese style (back to front)	2.95
❑5/A, Jun 1999	2.95
❑5/B, Jun 1999; printed in Japanese style (back to front)	2.95
❑6/A, Jul 1999	2.95
❑6/B, Jul 1999; printed in Japanese style (back to front)	2.95
❑7, Aug 1999	2.95
❑7/B, Aug 1999; printed in Japanese style (back to front)	2.95

NEON GENESIS EVANGELION BOOK 5
Viz

❑1, Oct 2000	2.95
❑1/B, Oct 2000; Reads back to front	2.95
❑2, Nov 2000	2.95
❑2/B, Nov 2000; Reads back to front	2.95
❑3, Dec 2000	2.95
❑3/B, Dec 2000; Reads back to front	2.95
❑4, Jan 2001	2.95
❑4/B, Jan 2001; Reads back to front	2.95
❑5, Feb 2001	2.95
❑5/B, Feb 2001; Reads back to front	2.95
❑6, Mar 2001	2.95
❑6/B, Mar 2001; Reads back to front	2.95
❑7, Apr 2001	2.95
❑7/B, May 2001; Reads back to front	2.95

NEON GENESIS EVANGELION BOOK 6
Viz

❑1, Jul 2001	3.50
❑1/B, Jul 2001; Reads back to front	3.50
❑2, Aug 2001	3.50
❑2/B, Aug 2001; Reads back to front	3.50
❑3, Sep 2001	3.50
❑3/B, Sep 2001; Reads back to front	3.50
❑4, Oct 2001	3.50
❑4/B, Oct 2001; Reads back to front	3.50

N-MINT

NEON GENESIS EVANGELION BOOK 7
VIZ
❑1, May 2002 .... 2.95
❑1/B, May 2002; Reads back to front 2.95
❑2, Jun 2002 .... 2.95
❑2/B, Jun 2002; Reads back to front . 2.95
❑3, Jul 2002 .... 2.95
❑3/B, Jul 2002; Reads back to front .. 2.95
❑4, Aug 2002 .... 2.95
❑4/B, Aug 2002; Reads back to front 2.95
❑5, Sep 2002 .... 2.95
❑5/B, Sep 2002; Reads back to front 2.95
❑6, Oct 2002 .... 3.50
❑6/B, Oct 2002; Reads back to front . 3.50

NEOTOPIA
ANTARCTIC
❑1, Jan 2003 .... 3.95
❑2, Feb 2003 .... 3.95
❑3, Apr 2003 .... 3.95
❑4, May 2003 .... 3.95
❑5, Jun 2003 .... 3.95

NEOTOPIA (VOL 2)
ANTARCTIC
❑1, Aug 2003 .... 2.99
❑2, Sep 2003 .... 2.99
❑3, Oct 2003 .... 2.99
❑4, Nov 2003 .... 2.99
❑5, Dec 2003 .... 2.99

NEOTOPIA (VOL 3)
ANTARCTIC
❑1, Feb 2004 .... 2.99
❑2, Apr 2004 .... 2.99
❑3, May 2004 .... 2.99
❑4, Jun 2004 .... 2.99

NERVE
NERVE
❑1 .... 2.00
❑2 .... 1.50
❑3 .... 1.50
❑4 .... 1.50
❑5, Apr 1987 .... 1.50
❑6 1987 .... 1.50
❑7, Jul 1987 .... 1.50
❑8; oversize 4.00

NERVOUS REX
BLACKTHORNE
❑1, Aug 1985 .... 2.00
❑2, Oct 1985 .... 2.00
❑3, Dec 1985 .... 2.00
❑4, Feb 1986 .... 2.00
❑5, Apr 1986 .... 2.00
❑6, Jun 1986 .... 2.00
❑7, Aug 1986 .... 2.00
❑8, Oct 1986 .... 2.00
❑9, Dec 1986 .... 2.00
❑10, Feb 1987 .... 2.00

NESTROBBER
BLUE SKY BLUE
❑1, Oct 1992, b&w 1.95
❑2, Jun 1994, b&w 1.95

NETHERWORLD
AMBITION
❑1, b&w 1.50

NETHERWORLDS
ADVENTURE
❑1, Aug 1988, b&w 1.95

NETMAN
INFORMATION NETWORKS
❑0, Aug 1992 .... 0.50

NEURO JACK
BIG
❑1, Aug 1996; all-digital art 2.25

NEUROMANCER: THE GRAPHIC NOVEL
MARVEL / EPIC
❑1 .... 8.95

N-MINT

NEVADA
DC / VERTIGO
❑1, May 1998 .... 2.50
❑2, Jun 1998 .... 2.50
❑3, Jul 1998 .... 2.50
❑4, Aug 1998 .... 2.50
❑5, Sep 1998 .... 2.50
❑6, Oct 1998 .... 2.50

NEVERMEN, THE
DARK HORSE
❑1, May 2000 .... 2.95
❑2, Jun 2000 .... 2.95
❑3, Jul 2000 .... 2.95

NEVERMEN: STREETS OF BLOOD
DARK HORSE
❑1, Jan 2003 .... 2.99
❑2, Feb 2003 .... 2.99
❑3, May 2003 .... 2.99

NEW ADVENTURES OF BEAUTY AND THE BEAST (DISNEY'S...)
DISNEY
❑1 .... 1.50
❑1/Direct ed. 2.00
❑2 .... 1.50

NEW ADVENTURES OF CHOLLY AND FLYTRAP, THE: TILL DEATH DO US PART
MARVEL / EPIC
❑1, Dec 1990; prestige format 4.95
❑2, Jan 1991; prestige format 4.95
❑3, Feb 1991; prestige format 4.95

NEW ADVENTURES OF FELIX THE CAT
FELIX
❑1, Oct 1992 .... 2.25
❑2 1992 .... 2.25
❑3 1992 .... 2.25
❑4 .... 2.25
❑5 1993 .... 2.25
❑6 .... 2.25
❑7 1993; becomes New Adventures of Felix the Cat and Friends 2.25

NEW ADVENTURES OF HUCK FINN, THE
GOLD KEY
❑1 .... 10.00

NEW ADVENTURES OF JESUS, THE
RIP OFF
❑1 .... 4.50

NEW ADVENTURES OF JUDO JOE, THE
ACE
❑1, Mar 1987, b&w 1.75

NEW ADVENTURES OF PINOCCHIO
DELL
❑1, Oct 1962 .... 65.00
❑2 1963 .... 50.00
❑3 1963 .... 50.00

NEW ADVENTURES OF RICK O'SHAY AND HIPSHOT
COTTONWOOD
❑1 .... 4.95
❑2 .... 4.95

NEW ADVENTURES OF SHALOMAN
MARK 1
❑1, b&w 2.00
❑2 .... 2.50
❑3 O: Shaloman. 2.50
❑4, b&w 2.50
❑5; indicia says #4 .... 2.95
❑8, b&w A: Y-Guys. 2.50
❑Special 1, b&w 2.50

NEW ADVENTURES OF SPEED RACER, THE
NOW
❑0, Nov 1993; multi-dimensional cover 3.95
❑1, Dec 1993 .... 1.95

Work by Brian Bolland appears in *Negative Burn* #15.
© Caliber and Brian Bolland.

N-MINT

❑2, Jan 1994 .... 1.95
❑3, Feb 1994 .... 1.95

NEW ADVENTURES OF SUPERBOY, THE
DC
❑1, Jan 1980 KS (a) 4.00
❑2, Feb 1980 KS (a) 1.50
❑3, Mar 1980 KS (a) 1.50
❑4, Apr 1980 KS (a) 1.50
❑5, May 1980 KS (a) 1.50
❑6, Jun 1980 KS (a) 1.50
❑7, Jul 1980; KS (a); bonus Superman story 1.50
❑8, Aug 1980 KS (a) 1.50
❑9, Sep 1980 KS (a); V: Phantom Zone villains. 1.50
❑10, Oct 1980; KS (a); Krypto back-up 1.50
❑11, Nov 1980; KS (a); Superbaby back-up 1.50
❑12, Dec 1980 KS (a) 1.50
❑13, Jan 1981 KS (a) 1.50
❑14, Feb 1981 KS (a) 1.50
❑15, Mar 1981 KS (a) 1.50
❑16, Apr 1981 KS (a) 1.50
❑17, May 1981; KS (a); Krypto back-up 1.50
❑18, Jun 1981 KS (a) 1.50
❑19, Jul 1981 KS (a) 1.50
❑20, Aug 1981 KS (a) 1.50
❑21, Sep 1981 KS (a) 1.00
❑22, Oct 1981 KS (a) 1.00
❑23, Nov 1981 KS (a) 1.00
❑24, Dec 1981 KS (a) 1.00
❑25, Jan 1982 KS (a) 1.00
❑26, Feb 1982 KS (a) 1.00
❑27, Mar 1982 KS (a) 1.00
❑28, Apr 1982; KS (a); Dial H for Hero back-up 1.00
❑29, May 1982; KS (a); Dial H for Hero back-up 1.00
❑30, Jun 1982; KS (a); Dial H for Hero back-up 1.00
❑31, Jul 1982; KS (a); Dial H for Hero back-up 1.00
❑32, Aug 1982; KS (a); Dial H for Hero back-up 1.00
❑33, Sep 1982; KS (a); Dial H for Hero back-up 1.00
❑34, Oct 1982; KS (a); 1: The Yellow Peril. Dial H for Hero back-up 1.00
❑35, Nov 1982; KS (a); Dial H for Hero back-up 1.00
❑36, Dec 1982; KS (a); Dial H for Hero back-up 1.00
❑37, Jan 1983; KS (a); Dial H for Hero back-up 1.00
❑38, Feb 1983; KS (a); Dial H for Hero back-up 1.00
❑39, Mar 1983; KS (a); Dial H for Hero back-up 1.00
❑40, Apr 1983; KS (a); Dial H for Hero back-up 1.00
❑41, May 1983; GK (c); KS (a); Dial H for Hero back-up 1.00
❑42, Jun 1983; GK (c); KS (a); Dial H for Hero back-up 1.00
❑43, Jul 1983; GK (c); KS (a); Dial H for Hero back-up 1.00
❑44, Aug 1983; GK (c); KS (a); Dial H for Hero back-up 1.00
❑45, Sep 1983; GK (c); KS (a); 1: Sunburst. Dial H for Hero back-up 1.00

N-MINT

❑46, Oct 1983; KS (a); Dial H for Hero back-up ... 1.00
❑47, Nov 1983; KS (a); Dial H for Hero back-up ... 1.00
❑48, Dec 1983; KS (a); Dial H for Hero back-up ... 1.00
❑49, Jan 1984; KS (a); Dial H for Hero back-up ... 1.00
❑50, Feb 1984; Giant-size KG, KS (a); A: Legion of Super-Heroes. ... 1.25
❑51, Mar 1984 FM (c); CS, KS (a) ... 1.00
❑52, Apr 1984 KS (a) ... 1.00
❑53, May 1984 KS (a) ... 1.00
❑54, Jun 1984 KS (a) ... 1.00

NEW ADVENTURES OF TERRY & THE PIRATES
AVALON

❑1, ca. 1998 ... 2.95
❑2 ... 2.95
❑3 ... 2.95
❑4 ... 2.95
❑5 ... 2.95
❑6 ... 2.95

NEW ADVENTURES OF THE PHANTOM BLOT (WALT DISNEY'S...)
GOLD KEY

❑1 ... 22.00
❑2; 1st appearance of Super Goof ... 18.00
❑3 ... 12.00
❑4 ... 8.00
❑5 ... 8.00
❑6 ... 8.00
❑7 ... 8.00

NEW AGE COMICS
FANTAGRAPHICS

❑1, ca. 1985; Independent comics sampler ... 1.50

NEW AMERICA
ECLIPSE

❑1, Nov 1987 TY (c) ... 2.00
❑2, Dec 1987 ... 2.00
❑3, Jan 1988 TY (c) ... 2.00
❑4, Feb 1988 ... 2.00

NEW ARCHIES, THE
ARCHIE

❑1, Oct 1987 ... 2.50
❑2, Jan 1988 ... 1.50
❑3, Feb 1988 ... 1.50
❑4, Apr 1988 ... 1.50
❑5, May 1988 ... 1.50
❑6, Jun 1988 ... 1.00
❑7, Aug 1988 ... 1.00
❑8, Sep 1988 ... 1.00
❑9, Oct 1988 ... 1.00
❑10, Dec 1988 ... 1.00
❑11, Jan 1989 ... 1.00
❑12, Feb 1989 ... 1.00
❑13, Apr 1989 ... 1.00
❑14, May 1989 ... 1.00
❑15, Jun 1989 ... 1.00
❑16, Aug 1989 ... 1.00
❑17, Sep 1989 ... 1.00
❑18, Oct 1989 ... 1.00
❑19, Dec 1989 ... 1.00
❑20, Jan 1990 ... 1.00
❑21, Feb 1990 ... 1.00
❑22, May 1990 ... 1.00

NEW BEGINNING
UNICORN

❑1, b&w ... 2.00
❑2, b&w ... 2.00
❑3, b&w ... 2.00

NEW BONDAGE FAIRIES
FANTAGRAPHICS / EROS

❑1, Nov 1996 ... 2.95
❑2, Dec 1996 ... 2.95
❑3, Jan 1997 ... 2.95
❑4, Feb 1997 ... 2.95
❑5, Mar 1997 ... 2.95
❑6, Apr 1997 ... 2.95

N-MINT

❑7, May 1997 ... 2.95
❑8, Jun 1997 ... 2.95
❑9, Jul 1997 ... 2.95
❑10, Aug 1997 ... 2.95
❑11, Sep 1997 ... 2.95
❑12, Oct 1997 ... 2.95

NEW CREW, THE
PERSONALITY

❑1; Patrick Stewart ... 2.95
❑2; Jonathan Frakes ... 2.95
❑3 ... 2.95
❑4 ... 2.95
❑5 ... 2.95
❑6 ... 2.95
❑7 ... 2.95
❑8 ... 2.95
❑9 ... 2.95
❑10 ... 2.95

NEW CRIME FILES OF MICHAEL MAUSER, PRIVATE EYE
APPLE

❑1, b&w ... 2.50

NEW DNAGENTS, THE
ECLIPSE

❑1, Oct 1985 ME (w); O: The DNAgents. ... 1.50
❑2, Nov 1985 ME (w) ... 1.25
❑3, Nov 1985 ME (w) ... 1.25
❑4, Dec 1985 ME (w) ... 1.00
❑5, Jan 1986 ME (w) ... 1.00
❑6, Feb 1986 ME (w) ... 1.00
❑7, Apr 1986 ME (w) ... 1.00
❑8, Apr 1986 ME (w) ... 1.00
❑9, Jun 1986 ME (w) ... 1.00
❑10, Jun 1986 ME (w) ... 1.00
❑11, Aug 1986 ME (w) ... 1.00
❑12, Aug 1986 ME (w) ... 1.00
❑13, Oct 1986 ME (w) ... 1.00
❑14, Nov 1986 ME (w) ... 1.00
❑15, Dec 1986 ME (w) ... 1.00
❑16, Jan 1987 ME (w) ... 1.00
❑17, Mar 1987 ME (w) ... 1.00

NEW ENGLAND GOTHIC
VISIGOTH

❑1, Dec 1986 ... 2.00
❑2, Jun 1987, b&w ... 2.00

NEWFORCE
IMAGE

❑1, Jan 1996; polybagged with Kodak card ... 2.50
❑2, Feb 1996 ... 2.50
❑3, Mar 1996 ... 2.50
❑4, Apr 1996 ... 2.50

NEW FRONTIER, THE
DARK HORSE

❑1, Oct 1992, b&w ... 2.75
❑2, Nov 1992, b&w ... 2.75
❑3, Dec 1992, b&w ... 2.75

NEW FRONTIERS
EVOLUTION

❑1, b&w ... 1.75
❑2, b&w ... 1.95

NEW GODS, THE (1ST SERIES)
DC

❑1, Mar 1971 JK (w); JK (a); 1: Orion. 1: Apokolips. 1: Metron. 1: Kalibak. 1: Highfather. 1: Lightray. ... 38.00
❑2, May 1971 JK (w); JK (a); 1: Deep Six. ... 22.00
❑3, Jul 1971 JK (w); JK (a); 1: Black Racer. ... 19.00
❑4, Sep 1971; Giant-size JK (w); JK (a) ... 16.00
❑5, Nov 1971; Giant-size JK (w); JK (a) ... 16.00
❑6, Jan 1972; Giant-size JK (w); JK (a); 1: Fastbak. ... 16.00
❑7, Mar 1972; Giant-size JK (w); JK (a); 1: Steppenwolf. ... 16.00
❑8, May 1972; Giant-size JK (w); JK (a) ... 16.00
❑9, Jul 1972; Giant-size JK (w); JK (a); 1: Forager. ... 16.00
❑10, Sep 1972 JK (w); JK (a) ... 11.00
❑11, Nov 1972 JK (w); JK (a) ... 11.00

N-MINT

❑12, Jul 1977; Series begins again ... 6.00
❑13, Aug 1977 ... 6.00
❑14, Oct 1977 ... 6.00
❑15, Dec 1977 ... 6.00
❑16, Feb 1978 ... 6.00
❑17, Apr 1978 ... 6.00
❑18, Jun 1978 ... 6.00
❑19, Aug 1978 ... 6.00

NEW GODS (2ND SERIES)
DC

❑1, Jun 1984; New Gods (Vol. 1) reprints ... 2.00
❑2, Jul 1984; New Gods (Vol. 1) reprints ... 2.00
❑3, Aug 1984; New Gods (Vol. 1) reprints ... 2.00
❑4, Sep 1984; New Gods (Vol. 1) reprints ... 2.00
❑5, Nov 1984; New Gods (Vol. 1) reprints ... 2.00
❑6, Dec 1984; reprints New Gods (Vol. 1) #11, plus new stories ... 2.00

NEW GODS (3RD SERIES)
DC

❑1, Feb 1989 ME (w) ... 2.25
❑2, Mar 1989 ME (w) ... 2.00
❑3, Apr 1989 ME (w) ... 2.00
❑4, May 1989 ME (w) ... 2.00
❑5, Jun 1989 ME (w) ... 2.00
❑6, Jul 1989 ME (w) ... 1.50
❑7, Aug 1989 ME (w) ... 1.50
❑8, Sep 1989 ME (w) ... 1.50
❑9, Oct 1989 ME (w) ... 1.50
❑10, Nov 1989 ME (w) ... 1.50
❑11, Dec 1989 ME (w) ... 1.50
❑12, Jan 1990 ME (w) ... 1.50
❑13, Feb 1990 ... 1.50
❑14, Mar 1990 ... 1.50
❑15, Apr 1990 ... 1.50
❑16, May 1990 ... 1.50
❑17, Jun 1990 ... 1.50
❑18, Jul 1990 ... 1.50
❑19, Aug 1990 ... 1.50
❑20, Sep 1990 ... 1.50
❑21, Dec 1990 ... 1.50
❑22, Jan 1991 ... 1.50
❑23, Feb 1991 ... 1.50
❑24, Mar 1991 ... 1.50
❑25, Apr 1991 ... 1.50
❑26, May 1991 ... 1.50
❑27, Jul 1991 ... 1.50
❑28, Aug 1991 ... 1.50

NEW GODS (4TH SERIES)
DC

❑1, Oct 1995 ... 2.00
❑2, Nov 1995 ... 2.00
❑3, Dec 1995 ... 2.00
❑4, Jan 1996 ... 2.00
❑5, Feb 1996 ... 2.00
❑6, Mar 1996 ... 2.00
❑7, Apr 1996 ... 2.00
❑8, Jun 1996 ... 2.00
❑9, Jul 1996 KG (a) ... 2.00
❑10, Aug 1996 A: Superman. ... 2.00
❑11, Sep 1996 ... 2.00
❑12, Nov 1996 JBy (w); JBy (a) ... 1.00
❑13, Dec 1996 JBy (w); JBy (a) ... 2.00
❑14, Jan 1997 JBy (w); JBy (a); A: Forever People. ... 2.00
❑15, Feb 1997 JBy (w); JBy (a) ... 2.00

NEW GODS SECRET FILES
DC

❑1, Sep 1998 ... 4.95

NEW GUARDIANS, THE
DC

❑1, Sep 1988; Giant-size ... 2.00
❑2, Oct 1988 ... 1.25
❑3, Nov 1988 ... 1.25
❑4, Dec 1988 ... 1.25
❑5, Dec 1988 ... 1.25
❑6, Jan 1989; Invasion! ... 1.25

N-MINT

❑7, Feb 1989; Invasion! 1.25
❑8, Apr 1989 1.25
❑9, Jun 1989 1.25
❑10, Jul 1989 1.25
❑11, Aug 1989 1.25
❑12, Sep 1989 1.25

NEW HAT
Black Eye

❑1 1.00

NEW HERO COMICS
Red Spade

❑1, b&w 1.00

NEW HORIZONS
Shanda Fantasy Arts

❑1, b&w 4.95
❑2, b&w 4.95
❑3, b&w 4.50
❑4, b&w 4.50
❑5, Apr 1999, b&w 4.50

NEW HUMANS, THE (PIED PIPER)
Pied Piper

❑1, Jul 1987, b&w 1.95
❑2 1987 1.95
❑3 1987 1.95

NEW HUMANS, THE (ETERNITY)
Eternity

❑1, Dec 1987 1.95
❑2, Jan 1988 1.95
❑3, Feb 1988 1.95
❑4, Mar 1988; Nude cover 1.95
❑5 1988 1.95
❑6 1988 1.95
❑7 1988 1.95
❑8, Sep 1988 1.95
❑9 1988 1.95
❑10 1989 1.95
❑11 1.95
❑12, Mar 1989 1.95
❑13 1.95
❑14 1.95
❑15 1.95
❑16 1.95
❑17 1.95
❑Annual 1, b&w 2.95

NEW INVADERS, THE
Marvel

❑0, Sep 2004

NEW JUSTICE MACHINE, THE
Innovation

❑1, Nov 1989 2.00
❑2, Jan 1990 2.00
❑3, Mar 1990 2.00

NEW KIDS ON THE BLOCK, THE: BACKSTAGE PASS
Harvey

❑1, ca. 1991 1.25

NEW KIDS ON THE BLOCK: CHILLIN'
Harvey

❑1, ca. 1990 1.50
❑2, Jan 1991 1.25
❑3, ca. 1991 1.25
❑4, Apr 1991 1.25
❑5, Jun 1991 1.25
❑6, Oct 1991 1.25
❑7, Dec 1991 1.25

NEW KIDS ON THE BLOCK COMIC TOUR '90
Harvey

❑1, ca. 1991 1.25

NEW KIDS ON THE BLOCK MAGIC SUMMER TOUR
Harvey

❑1, ca. 1991 1.25
❑1/Ltd., ca. 1991; limited edition 3.95

N-MINT

NEW KIDS ON THE BLOCK, THE: NKOTB
Harvey

❑1, Dec 1990 1.25
❑2, Jan 1991 1.25
❑3, Feb 1991 1.25
❑4, Mar 1991 1.25
❑5, May 1991 1.25
❑6, Jul 1991 1.25

NEW KIDS ON THE BLOCK STEP BY STEP
Harvey

❑1, ca. 1991 1.25

NEW KIDS ON THE BLOCK: VALENTINE GIRL
Harvey

❑1, ca. 1991 1.25

NEW LOVE
Fantagraphics

❑1, Aug 1996, b&w 2.95
❑2, Oct 1996, b&w 2.95
❑3, Mar 1997, b&w 2.95
❑4, Jun 1997, b&w 2.95
❑5, Sep 1997, b&w 2.95
❑6, Dec 1997, b&w 2.95

NEWMAN
Image

❑1, Jan 1996; polybagged with card; Extreme Destroyer Part 3 2.50
❑2, Feb 1996 2.50
❑3, Apr 1996 2.50
❑4, Apr 1996 2.50

NEWMEN
Image

❑1, Apr 1994 RL (w) 2.50
❑2, May 1994 2.25
❑3, Jun 1994 2.25
❑4, Jul 1994 2.25
❑5, Aug 1994 2.50
❑6, Sep 1994 2.50
❑7, Oct 1994 2.50
❑8, Nov 1994 2.50
❑9, Dec 1994; Extreme Sacrifice 2.50
❑10, Jan 1995 2.50
❑11, Feb 1995; polybagged 2.50
❑11/A, Feb 1995; Alternate cover; polybagged 2.50
❑12, Mar 1995 2.50
❑13, Apr 1995 2.50
❑14, May 1995 2.50
❑15, Jun 1995; no indicia 2.50
❑16, Jul 1995 2.50
❑16/A, Jul 1995; alternate cover 3.00
❑17, Aug 1995 2.50
❑18, Sep 1995 2.50
❑19, Oct 1995 2.50
❑20, Nov 1995; Babewatch 2.50
❑20/A, Nov 1995; Babewatch 2.50
❑21, Aug 1996 2.50
❑22, Sep 1996 2.50
❑23, Mar 1997 2.50
❑24, Apr 1997 2.50
❑25, May 1997 2.50

NEW MUTANTS, THE
Marvel

❑1, Mar 1983 BMc (a) 4.00
❑2, Apr 1983 BMc (a); V: Sentinels. 2.00
❑3, May 1983 BMc (a); V: Brood. 2.00
❑4, Jun 1983 SB (a) 1.50
❑5, Jul 1983 SB (a); A: Team America. 1.50
❑6, Aug 1983 SB (a); A: Team America. 1.50
❑7, Sep 1983 SB (a) 1.50
❑8, Oct 1983 BMc (a); O: Magma. 1.50
❑9, Nov 1983 SB (a); 1: Selene. 1.50
❑10, Dec 1983 SB (a); 1: Magma. 1.50
❑11, Jan 1984; SB (a); Assistant Editor Month 1.50
❑12, Feb 1984 SB (a) 1.50
❑13, Mar 1984 SB (a); 1: Cypher. A: Kitty Pryde. 1.50

A previously unrevealed facet of Superboy's past was uncovered in *The New Adventures of Superboy* #1.

© 1980 DC Comics.

N-MINT

❑14, Apr 1984 SB (a); A: X-Men. V: Sy'm. 1.50
❑15, May 1984 SB (a); A: X-Men. 1.50
❑16, Jun 1984 1: Warpath. 1: Hellions. 1.50
❑17, Jul 1984 SB (a); V: Hellions. 1.50
❑18, Aug 1984 BSz (a); 1: Warlock (machine). 1.50
❑19, Sep 1984 BSz (a) 1.50
❑20, Oct 1984 BSz (a) 1.50
❑21, Nov 1984; Double-size BSz (a); O: Warlock (machine). 1.50
❑22, Dec 1984 BSz (a) 1.50
❑23, Jan 1985 BSz (a); A: Cloak & Dagger. 1.50
❑24, Feb 1985 BSz (a); A: Cloak & Dagger. 1.50
❑25, Mar 1985 BSz (c); BSz (a); 1: Legion (cameo). A: Cloak & Dagger. 2.50
❑26, Apr 1985 BSz (c); BSz (a); 1: Legion (psychic). 2.50
❑27, May 1985 BSz (c); BSz (a); A: Legion. V: Legion. 2.00
❑28, Jun 1985 BSz (a); A: Legion. 2.00
❑29, Jul 1985 BSz (a); 1: Guido Carosella (Strong Guy). 2.00
❑30, Aug 1985 BSz (a) 1.50
❑31, Sep 1985 BSz (a) 1.50
❑32, Oct 1985 1.50
❑33, Nov 1985 1.50
❑34, Dec 1985 1.50
❑35, Jan 1986; BSz (a); A: Magneto. Magneto begins as leader of New Mutants 1.50
❑36, Feb 1986 BSz (a) 1.50
❑37, Mar 1986 BSz (a) 1.50
❑38, Apr 1986 1.50
❑39, May 1986 KP (a) 1.50
❑40, Jun 1986 A: Captain America. 1.50
❑41, Jul 1986 1.50
❑42, Aug 1986 1.50
❑43, Sep 1986 1.50
❑44, Oct 1986 A: Legion. 1.50
❑45, Nov 1986 1.50
❑46, Dec 1986 1.50
❑47, Jan 1987 1.50
❑48, Feb 1987 1.50
❑49, Mar 1987 1.50
❑50, Apr 1987; Double-size; Professor X returns as headmaster 1.50
❑51, May 1987 KN (a); A: Star Jammers. 1.50
❑52, Jun 1987 1.50
❑53, Jul 1987 1.50
❑54, Aug 1987 1.50
❑55, Sep 1987 1.50
❑56, Oct 1987 1.50
❑57, Nov 1987 1.50
❑58, Dec 1987; registration card 1.50
❑59, Jan 1988 2.00
❑60, Feb 1988; double-sized D: Cypher. 2.00
❑61, Mar 1988; new costumes; (conclusion) 2.00
❑62, Apr 1988 1.50
❑63, May 1988 A: X-Men. 2.00
❑64, Jun 1988 1.50
❑65, Jul 1988 1.50
❑66, Aug 1988 1.50
❑67, Sep 1988 1.50
❑68, Oct 1988 1.50
❑69, Nov 1988 1.50

N-MINT

- ❑70, Dec 1988; Inferno 1.50
- ❑71, Jan 1989; O: N'astirh. Inferno 1.50
- ❑72, Feb 1989; Inferno 1.50
- ❑73, Mar 1989; Giant-size; Inferno 2.00
- ❑74, Apr 1989 1.50
- ❑75, May 1989 1.50
- ❑76, Jun 1989 RB (a); A: X-Terminators. A: X-Factor. A: Sub-Mariner. 1.50
- ❑77, Jul 1989 RB (a) 1.50
- ❑78, Aug 1989 1.50
- ❑79, Sep 1989 1.50
- ❑80, Oct 1989 1.50
- ❑81, Nov 1989 1.50
- ❑82, Nov 1989 1.50
- ❑83, Dec 1989 1.50
- ❑84, Dec 1989; Acts of Vengeance 1.50
- ❑85, Jan 1990; TMc (c); Acts of Vengeance 1.50
- ❑86, Feb 1990; TMc (c); 1: Zero. 1: Cable (cameo). Acts of Vengeance 3.00
- ❑87, Mar 1990 TMc (c); RL, BWi (a); 1: Stryfe. 1: Cable. 6.00
- ❑87-2, Mar 1990; TMc (c); 1: Cable. 2nd printing (gold) 2.00
- ❑88, Apr 1990 TMc (c); RL (a); 2: Cable. 2.50
- ❑89, May 1990 TMc (c) 2.00
- ❑90, Jun 1990 A: Sabretooth. 2.00
- ❑91, Jul 1990 A: Sabretooth. 2.00
- ❑92, Aug 1990 BH (a) 2.00
- ❑93, Sep 1990 TMc (c); A: Wolverine. 2.00
- ❑94, Oct 1990 A: Wolverine. 2.00
- ❑95, Nov 1990 D: Warlock (machine). 2.00
- ❑95-2, Nov 1990; D: Warlock (machine). 2nd printing (gold) 2.00
- ❑96, Dec 1990 2.00
- ❑97, Jan 1991 2.00
- ❑98, Feb 1991 RL (w); RL (a); 1: Deadpool. 1: Domino II. 1: Gideon. 5.00
- ❑99, Mar 1991; RL (w); RL (a); 1: Feral. 1: Shatterstar (full appearance). A: Sunspot. Sunspot leaves 2.50
- ❑100, Apr 1991; Giant-size RL (w); RL (a); O: Shatterstar. 1: X-Force. 2.00
- ❑100-2, Apr 1991; RL (w); RL (a); 1: X-Force. 2nd printing (gold) 2.00
- ❑100-3, Apr 1991; RL (w); RL (a); 1: X-Force. 3rd printing (silver) 2.00
- ❑Annual 1, ca. 1984 BMc (a); 1: Lila Cheney. 3.00
- ❑Annual 2, Oct 1986 1: Meggan. 1: Psylocke. 4.00
- ❑Annual 3, ca. 1987 A: Impossible Man. 2.00
- ❑Annual 4, ca. 1988 2.00
- ❑Annual 5, ca. 1989 RL (a) 2.00
- ❑Annual 6, ca. 1990 1: Shatterstar (cameo). 2.50
- ❑Annual 7, ca. 1991 2.00
- ❑Special 1, Dec 1985 1.50
- ❑Summer 1; Giant-size 2.95

NEW MUTANTS (2ND SERIES)
MARVEL

- ❑1, Jul 2003 4.00
- ❑2, Aug 2003 2.50
- ❑3, Sep 2003 2.50
- ❑4, Oct 2003 2.99
- ❑5, Nov 2003 2.99
- ❑6, Dec 2003 2.99
- ❑7, Jan 2004 2.99
- ❑8, Apr 2004 2.99
- ❑9, Apr 2004 2.99
- ❑10, May 2004 2.99
- ❑11, May 2004 2.99
- ❑12, Jun 2004 2.99
- ❑13, Jun 2004 2.99

NEW MUTANTS, THE: TRUTH OR DEATH
MARVEL

- ❑1, Nov 1997; gatefold summary; original New Mutants travel through time and meet present-day counterparts 2.50
- ❑2, Dec 1997; gatefold summary 2.50
- ❑3, Jan 1998; gatefold summary 2.50

N-MINT

NEW NIGHT OF THE LIVING DEAD
FANTACO

- ❑0 2.00
- ❑1 3.95
- ❑2 3.95
- ❑3 3.95

NEW ORDER, THE
CREATIVE FORCE

- ❑1, Nov 1994 2.95

NEW PALTZ COMIX
MOODS

- ❑1 1.50
- ❑2 1974 1.50
- ❑3 1.50

NEW PARTNERS IN PERIL
BLUE COMET

- ❑1, b&w 2.25

NEW PARTNERS IN PERIL, THE (VOL. 2)
TAMI

- ❑1 2.25

NEW PEOPLE, THE
DELL

- ❑1, Jan 1970 10.00
- ❑2, May 1970 8.00

NEW POWER STARS, THE
BLUE COMET

- ❑1, b&w 2.00

NEW SHADOWHAWK, THE
IMAGE

- ❑1, Jun 1995 2.50
- ❑2, Aug 1995 2.50
- ❑3, Sep 1995 2.50
- ❑4, Nov 1995 2.50
- ❑5, Dec 1995 2.50
- ❑6, Feb 1996 2.50
- ❑7, Mar 1996 2.50

NEW STATESMEN
FLEETWAY-QUALITY

- ❑1 4.00
- ❑2 4.00
- ❑3 4.00
- ❑4 4.00
- ❑5 4.00

NEWSTIME
DC

- ❑1, May 1993; death of Superman; Death of Superman Magazine 3.25

NEWSTRALIA
INNOVATION

- ❑1, Jul 1989 2.00
- ❑2 2.00
- ❑3 2.25
- ❑4 2.25
- ❑5, b&w 2.25

NEW TALENT SHOWCASE
DC

- ❑1, Jan 1984 1.50
- ❑2, Feb 1984 1.50
- ❑3, Mar 1984 1.50
- ❑4, Apr 1984 1.50
- ❑5, May 1984 1.50
- ❑6, Jun 1984 1.50
- ❑7, Jul 1984 1.50
- ❑8, Aug 1984 1.50
- ❑9, Sep 1984 1.50
- ❑10, Oct 1984 1.50
- ❑11, Nov 1984 1.25
- ❑12, Dec 1984 1.25
- ❑13, Jan 1985 1.25
- ❑14, Feb 1985 1.25
- ❑15, Mar 1985 1.25
- ❑16, Apr 1985; Title changes to Talent Showcase 1.25
- ❑17, May 1985 1.25
- ❑18, Jun 1985 1.25
- ❑19, Jul 1985 1.25

N-MINT

NEW TEEN TITANS, THE (1ST SERIES)
DC

- ❑1, Nov 1980 GP, RT (a) 8.00
- ❑2, Dec 1980 GP, RT (a); 1: Trigon. 1: Wintergreen. 1: Deathstroke the Terminator. D: The Ravager. 5.00
- ❑3, Jan 1981 GP (a); 1: Shimmer. 1: Gizmo. 1: Mammoth. 1: Fearsome Five. 1: Psimon. V: Doctor Light. 3.00
- ❑4, Feb 1981 GP (a); A: Justice League. 3.00
- ❑5, Mar 1981 CS, RT (a); O: Raven. 1: Trigon. 3.00
- ❑6, Apr 1981 GP (w); GP (a); O: Raven. V: Trigon. 3.00
- ❑7, May 1981 GP, RT (a); O: Cyborg. V: Fearsome Five. 3.00
- ❑8, Jun 1981 GP (w); GP, RT (a); O: Kid Flash. 3.00
- ❑9, Jul 1981 GP, RT (a) 3.00
- ❑10, Aug 1981 GP, RT (a); O: Changeling. A: Deathstroke the Terminator. V: Terminator. 3.00
- ❑11, Sep 1981 GP, RT (a) 2.00
- ❑12, Oct 1981 GP, RT (a) 2.00
- ❑13, Nov 1981 GP, RT (a); A: Doom Patrol. A: Robotman. 2.00
- ❑14, Dec 1981 GP, RT (a); 1: Houngan. 1: Plasmus. 1: Phobia. A: Doom Patrol. 2.00
- ❑15, Jan 1982 GP, RT (a); A: Doom Patrol. V: Brotherhood of Evil. 2.00
- ❑16, Feb 1982 GP, RA, RT (a); 1: Yankee Poodle. 1: Pig-Iron. 1: Fastback. 1: Captain Carrot. 1: Rubberduck. 1: Alley-Kat-Abra. 2.00
- ❑17, Mar 1982 GP, RT (a); A: Francis Kane. 2.00
- ❑18, Apr 1982 GP, RT (a); 1: Maladi Maranova. A: Starfire (later Red Star). 2.00
- ❑19, May 1982 GP, RT (a); A: Hawkman. 2.00
- ❑20, Jun 1982 GP, RT (a); 1: The Disruptor. 2.00
- ❑21, Jul 1982 GC, GP, RT (a); 1: Monitor. 1: Harbinger. 1: Brother Blood. 1: Night Force. 1: Baron Winters. V: Brother Blood. 2.00
- ❑22, Aug 1982 GP, RT (a); V: Brother Blood. 2.00
- ❑23, Sep 1982 GP, RT (a); 1: Komand'r (Blackfire). 2.00
- ❑24, Oct 1982 GP, RT (a); 1: X'Hal. A: Omega Men. 2.00
- ❑25, Nov 1982; GP, CS, RT (a); 1: Masters of the Universe. A: Omega Men. Masters of the Universe preview 2.00
- ❑26, Dec 1982 GP, RT (a); 1: Terra. 2.00
- ❑27, Jan 1983; GP, RT (a); 1: Howard Rondo. Atari Force preview 2.00
- ❑28, Feb 1983 GP, RT (a); A: Terra. V: Brotherhood of Evil. 2.00
- ❑29, Mar 1983 GP, RT (a); A: Speedy. V: Brotherhood of Evil. 2.00
- ❑30, Apr 1983 GP, RT (a); A: Terra. 2.00
- ❑31, May 1983 GP, RT (a); V: Brotherhood of Evil. 2.00
- ❑32, Jun 1983 GP, RT (a); O: Kid Flash. A: Thunder and Lightning. 2.00
- ❑33, Jul 1983 GP, RT (a); D: Trident. 2.00
- ❑34, Aug 1983 GP (a); A: Deathstroke the Terminator. V: Terminator. 2.00
- ❑35, Oct 1983 GP, KP, RT (a) 2.00
- ❑36, Nov 1983 KP (a); A: Thunder and Lightning. 2.00
- ❑37, Dec 1983 GP (a); A: Outsiders. V: Doctor Light. V: Shimmer. V: Gizmo. V: Mammoth. V: Psimon. 2.00
- ❑38, Jan 1984 GP (w); GP (a); O: Wonder Girl. 2.00
- ❑39, Feb 1984; GP (w); GP (a); Dick Grayson quits as Robin; Wally West retires as Kid Flash 2.50
- ❑40, Mar 1984; GP (w); GP (a); Series continued in Tales of the Teen Titans #41 2.00
- ❑Annual 1, ca. 1982 GP (a); A: Omega Men. 3.00

Condition price index: Multiply "NM prices" above by: **0.83 for Very Fine/Near Mint**
0.66 for Very Fine • 0.33 for Fine • 0.2 for Very Good • 0.125 for Good

N-MINT

- ❑Annual 2, ca. 1983 GP (a); 1: Lyla (Harbinger). 1: Vigilante. A: Monitor. 2.00
- ❑Annual 3, ca. 1984; D: Terra. Published as Tales of the Teen Titans Annual 2.00

NEW TEEN TITANS, THE (2ND SERIES)
DC

- ❑1, Aug 1984 GP (a) 3.00
- ❑2, Oct 1984 GP (a); A: Trigon. 2.50
- ❑3, Nov 1984 GP (a); V: Trigon. 2.50
- ❑4, Jan 1985 GP (a); V: Trigon. 2.50
- ❑5, Feb 1985 GP (a); V: Trigon. 2.50
- ❑6, Mar 1985 2.00
- ❑7, Apr 1985 JL (a); O: Lilith. 2.00
- ❑8, May 1985 JL (a); A: Destiny. 2.00
- ❑9, Jun 1985 JL (a); 1: Kole. 2.00
- ❑10, Jul 1985 JL (a) 2.00
- ❑11, Aug 1985 JL (a) 2.00
- ❑12, Sep 1985 2.00
- ❑13, Oct 1985 2.00
- ❑14, Nov 1985 2.00
- ❑15, Dec 1985 2.00
- ❑16, Jan 1986 DG (a); A: Omega Men. 2.00
- ❑17, Feb 1986; Wedding of Starfire 2.00
- ❑18, Mar 1986 2.00
- ❑19, Apr 1986 2.00
- ❑20, May 1986 A: original Titans. A: Robin II (Jason Todd). 2.00
- ❑21, Jun 1986 A: Cheshire. 1.50
- ❑22, Jul 1986 1.50
- ❑23, Aug 1986 V: Hybrids. 1.50
- ❑24, Oct 1986 V: Hybrids. 1.50
- ❑25, Nov 1986 V: Hybrids. 1.50
- ❑26, Dec 1986 KGa (a) 1.50
- ❑27, Jan 1987 KGa (a); V: Brotherhood of Evil. 1.50
- ❑28, Feb 1987 V: Brother Blood. 1.50
- ❑29, Mar 1987 V: Brother Blood. 1.50
- ❑30, Apr 1987 V: Brother Blood. 1.50
- ❑31, May 1987 A: Superman. A: Batman. V: Brother Blood. 1.50
- ❑32, Jun 1987 1.50
- ❑33, Jul 1987 EL (a) 1.50
- ❑34, Aug 1987 V: Hybrid. 1.50
- ❑35, Sep 1987 PB (a) 1.50
- ❑36, Oct 1987 V: Wildebeest. 1.50
- ❑37, Nov 1987 V: Wildebeest. 1.75
- ❑38, Dec 1987 A: Infinity Inc.. V: Ultra-Humanite. 1.75
- ❑39, Jan 1988 1.75
- ❑40, Feb 1988 V: I.Q.. V: Silver Fog. V: The Gentleman Ghost. 1.75
- ❑41, Mar 1988 V: Wildebeest. 1.75
- ❑42, Apr 1988; Brother Blood's child born 1.75
- ❑43, May 1988 CS (a); V: Raven. 1.75
- ❑44, Jun 1988 V: Godiva. 1.75
- ❑45, Jul 1988 A: Dial H for Hero. 1.75
- ❑46, Aug 1988 A: Dial H for Hero. 1.75
- ❑47, Sep 1988 O: Titans. 1.75
- ❑48, Oct 1988 V: Red Star. 1.75
- ❑49, Nov 1988; V: Red Star. Series continued in New Titans #50 1.75
- ❑Annual 1, ca. 1985 1: Vanguard. A: Superman. V: Vanguard. 2.50
- ❑Annual 2, Aug 1986 JBy (a); O: Brother Blood. 1: Cheshire. A: Doctor Light. 2.75
- ❑Annual 3, ca. 1987; 1: Godiva. 1: Danny Chase. A: King Faraday. cover indicates '87 Annual, indicia says '86 2.50
- ❑Annual 4, ca. 1988; Private Lives 2.50

NEW TEEN TITANS (GIVEAWAYS AND PROMOS)
DC

- ❑1; Beverage; DC drug issue 1.00
- ❑2; IBM/DC drug issue 1.00
- ❑3; GP, DC (a); Keebler; drug issue 1.00
- ❑4; DC (a); Keebler; drug issue 1.00
- ❑5 1.00

N-MINT

NEW TITANS, THE
DC

- ❑0, Oct 1994; A: Terra. A: Nightwing. A: Impulse. A: Mirage. A: Damage. Series continued in New Titans #115; Titans get new headquarters 1.95
- ❑50, Dec 1988; GP (a); O: Wonder Girl (new origin). Series continued from New Teen Titans #49 2.00
- ❑51, Dec 1988 GP (a) 2.00
- ❑52, Jan 1989 GP (a) 2.00
- ❑53, Feb 1989 GP (a) 2.00
- ❑54, Mar 1989 GP (a) 2.00
- ❑55, Jun 1989 GP (w); GP (a); 1: Troia. 2.00
- ❑56, Jul 1989 A: Gnaark. 2.00
- ❑57, Aug 1989 GP (a); V: Wildebeest. 2.00
- ❑58, Sep 1989 GP (a) 2.00
- ❑59, Oct 1989 GP (a); V: Wildebeest. 2.00
- ❑60, Nov 1989 GP (w); GP (a); A: Tim Drake. 2.50
- ❑61, Dec 1989 GP (w); GP (a) 2.50
- ❑62, Jan 1990 A: Deathstroke the Terminator. 2.00
- ❑63, Feb 1990 A: Deathstroke the Terminator. 2.00
- ❑64, Mar 1990 A: Deathstroke the Terminator. 2.00
- ❑65, Apr 1990 A: Robin III. A: Deathstroke the Terminator. 2.00
- ❑66, May 1990 GP (w) 2.00
- ❑67, Jul 1990 GP (w) 2.00
- ❑68, Jul 1990 V: Royal Flush Gang. 2.00
- ❑69, Sep 1990 2.00
- ❑70, Oct 1990 A: Deathstroke the Terminator. 2.00
- ❑71, Nov 1990 2.00
- ❑72, Jan 1991 A: Deathstroke the Terminator. D: Golden Eagle. 2.00
- ❑73, Feb 1991 1: Phantasm. A: Deathstroke the Terminator. 2.00
- ❑74, Mar 1991 1: Pantha. A: Deathstroke the Terminator. 2.00
- ❑75, Apr 1991 A: Deathstroke the Terminator. 2.00
- ❑76, Jun 1991; A: Deathstroke the Terminator. destruction of Titans Tower 2.00
- ❑77, Jul 1991; A: Deathstroke the Terminator. Cyborg rebuilt 2.00
- ❑78, Aug 1991 A: Deathstroke the Terminator. 2.00
- ❑79, Sep 1991 A: Team Titans. A: Deathstroke the Terminator. 2.00
- ❑80, Nov 1991 KGa (a); A: Team Titans. 1.75
- ❑81, Dec 1991 CS (a); A: Pariah. 1.75
- ❑82, Jan 1992 1.75
- ❑83, Feb 1992 D: Jericho. 1.75
- ❑84, Mar 1992 O: Phantasm. D: Raven. 1.75
- ❑85, Apr 1992 1: baby Wildebeest. A: Team Titans. 1.75
- ❑86, May 1992 V: Terminator. 1.75
- ❑87, Jun 1992 1.75
- ❑88, Jul 1992 1.75
- ❑89, Aug 1992 1.75
- ❑90, Sep 1992 1.75
- ❑91, Oct 1992 A: Phantasm. 1.75
- ❑92, Nov 1992 1.75
- ❑93, Dec 1992; follow-up to Titans Sell-Out Special 1.75
- ❑94, Feb 1993; covers of #94-96 form triptych 1.75
- ❑95, Mar 1993 1.75
- ❑96, Apr 1993 1.75
- ❑97, May 1993 1.75
- ❑98, Jun 1993 1.75
- ❑99, Jul 1993 1: Arsenal. 1.75
- ❑100, Aug 1993; Giant-size; V: Evil Raven. pin-ups; foil cover; wedding of Starfire II (Koriand'r) 3.00
- ❑101, Sep 1993 1.75
- ❑102, Oct 1993 1.75
- ❑103, Nov 1993 1.75
- ❑104, Dec 1993; final fate of Cyborg 1.75
- ❑105, Dec 1993 1.75
- ❑106, Jan 1994 1.75
- ❑107, Jan 1994 1.75
- ❑108, Feb 1994 1.75

X-Force made its first appearance in *New Mutants* #100.

© 1991 Marvel Comics.

N-MINT

- ❑109, Mar 1994 1.75
- ❑110, May 1994 1.75
- ❑111, Jun 1994 1.75
- ❑112, Jul 1994 1.95
- ❑113, Aug 1994 1.95
- ❑114, Sep 1994; new team; Series continued in The New Titans #0 1.95
- ❑115, Nov 1994 1.95
- ❑116, Dec 1994 A: Green Lantern. A: Psimon. 1.95
- ❑117, Jan 1995 V: Psimon. 1.95
- ❑118, Feb 1995 A: Thunder and Lightning. 1.95
- ❑119, Mar 1995 V: Deathwing. 1.95
- ❑120, Apr 1995 A: Supergirl. 1.95
- ❑121, May 1995 1.95
- ❑122, Jun 1995 2.25
- ❑123, Jul 1995 2.25
- ❑124, Aug 1995 2.25
- ❑125, Sep 1995; Giant-size 3.50
- ❑126, Oct 1995 2.25
- ❑127, Nov 1995 2.25
- ❑128, Dec 1995 2.25
- ❑129, Jan 1996 2.25
- ❑130, Feb 1996 2.25
- ❑Annual 5, ca. 1989; See New Teen Titans Annual for previous issues; Who's Who entries 3.50
- ❑Annual 6, ca. 1990 CS (a); 1: Society of Sin. A: Starfire. 3.50
- ❑Annual 7, ca. 1991 O: Team Titans. 1: Team Titans. 3.50
- ❑Annual 8, ca. 1992 CS (a) 3.00
- ❑Annual 9, ca. 1993 O: Anima. 1: Anima. 3.00
- ❑Annual 10, ca. 1994; Elseworlds 3.00
- ❑Annual 11, ca. 1995; Year One 3.95

NEW TRIUMPH FEATURING NORTHGUARD
MATRIX

- ❑1 1.75
- ❑1-2 1.75
- ❑2, ca. 1985 1.50
- ❑3 1.50
- ❑4 1.50
- ❑5 1.50

NEW TWO-FISTED TALES, THE
E.C. / DARK HORSE

- ❑1 HK, WE (a) 5.50

NEW TWO-FISTED TALES, THE (2ND SERIES)
DARK HORSE

- ❑1, Oct 1993 4.95

NEW VAMPIRE MIYU (VOL. 1)
IRONCAT

- ❑1, Sep 1997 3.00
- ❑2, Oct 1997 3.00
- ❑3, Nov 1997 3.00
- ❑4, Dec 1997 3.00
- ❑5, Jan 1998 3.00
- ❑6, Feb 1998 3.00

NEW VAMPIRE MIYU (VOL. 2)
IRONCAT

- ❑1, Apr 1998 2.95
- ❑2, May 1998 2.95
- ❑3, Jun 1998 2.95
- ❑4, Jul 1998 2.95

Condition price index: Multiply "NM prices" above by: **0.83 for Very Fine/Near Mint**
0.66 for Very Fine • 0.33 for Fine • 0.2 for Very Good • 0.125 for Good

N-MINT

❑5, Aug 1998 ... 2.95
❑6, Sep 1998 ... 2.95

NEW VAMPIRE MIYU (VOL. 3)
IRONCAT

❑1, Oct 1998 ... 2.95
❑2, Nov 1998 ... 2.95
❑3, Dec 1998 ... 2.95
❑4, Jan 1999 ... 2.95
❑5, Feb 1999 ... 2.95
❑6, Mar 1999 ... 2.95
❑7, Apr 1999 ... 2.95

NEW VAMPIRE MIYU (VOL. 4)
IRONCAT

❑1, May 1999 ... 2.95
❑2, Jun 1999 ... 2.95
❑3, Jul 1999 ... 2.95
❑4, Aug 1999 ... 2.95
❑5, Sep 1999 ... 2.95
❑6, Oct 1999 ... 2.95

NEW WARRIORS, THE
MARVEL

❑1, Jul 1990 O: New Warriors. ... 1.50
❑1-2, Jul 1990; O: New Warriors. 2nd Printing (gold) ... 1.00
❑2, Aug 1990 O: Night Thrasher. O: Silhouette. 1: Silhouette. ... 1.25
❑3, Sep 1990 ... 1.25
❑4, Oct 1990 ... 1.25
❑5, Nov 1990 ... 1.25
❑6, Dec 1990 ... 1.25
❑7, Jan 1991 A: Punisher. ... 1.25
❑8, Feb 1991 O: Bengal. A: Punisher. ... 1.25
❑9, Mar 1991 A: Punisher. ... 1.25
❑10, Apr 1991 ... 1.25
❑11, May 1991 A: Wolverine. ... 1.25
❑12, Jun 1991 ... 1.25
❑13, Jul 1991 ... 1.25
❑14, Aug 1991 A: Namor. A: Darkhawk. ... 1.25
❑15, Sep 1991 ... 1.25
❑16, Oct 1991 ... 1.25
❑17, Nov 1991 A: Fantastic Four. ... 1.25
❑18, Dec 1991 ... 1.25
❑19, Jan 1992 ... 1.25
❑20, Feb 1992 ... 1.25
❑21, Mar 1992 ... 1.25
❑22, Apr 1992 ... 1.25
❑23, May 1992 O: Night Thrasher. O: Silhouette. O: Chord. ... 1.25
❑24, Jun 1992 O: Silhouette. O: Chord. ... 1.25
❑25, Jul 1992; O: Chord. Die-cut cover ... 2.50
❑26, Aug 1992 ... 1.25
❑27, Sep 1992 ... 1.25
❑28, Oct 1992 1: Cardinal. 1: Turbo I (Michiko "Mickey" Musashi). ... 1.25
❑29, Nov 1992 ... 1.25
❑30, Dec 1992 ... 1.25
❑31, Jan 1993 ... 1.25
❑32, Feb 1993 ... 1.25
❑33, Mar 1993 1: Turbo II (Mike Jeffries). ... 1.25
❑34, Apr 1993 ... 1.25
❑35, May 1993 ... 1.25
❑36, Jun 1993 ... 1.25
❑37, Jul 1993 ... 1.25
❑38, Aug 1993 ... 1.25
❑39, Sep 1993 ... 1.25
❑40, Oct 1993 A: Nova. A: Air-Walker. A: Super Nova. A: Firelord. ... 1.25
❑40/Variant, Oct 1993; A: Nova. A: Air-Walker. A: Super Nova. A: Firelord. Gold foil on cover ... 2.25
❑41, Nov 1993 ... 1.25
❑42, Dec 1993 ... 1.25
❑43, Jan 1994 ... 1.25
❑44, Feb 1994 ... 1.25
❑45, Mar 1994 ... 1.25
❑46, Apr 1994 ... 1.25
❑47, May 1994 ... 1.25
❑48, Jun 1994 ... 1.50
❑49, Jul 1994 ... 1.50
❑50, Aug 1994; Giant-size ... 2.00
❑50/Variant, Aug 1994; Giant-size; Glow-in-the-dark cover ... 2.95
❑51, Sep 1994 ... 1.50
❑52, Oct 1994 ... 1.50
❑53, Nov 1994 ... 1.50
❑54, Dec 1994 ... 1.50
❑55, Jan 1995 ... 1.50
❑56, Feb 1995 ... 1.50
❑57, Mar 1995 ... 1.50
❑58, Apr 1995 ... 1.50
❑59, May 1995 ... 1.50
❑60, Jun 1995; Giant-size ... 2.50
❑61, Jul 1995; Maximum Clonage Prologue ... 1.50
❑62, Aug 1995 A: Scarlet Spider. ... 1.50
❑63, Sep 1995 ... 1.50
❑64, Oct 1995 A: Night Thrasher. A: Rage. ... 1.50
❑65, Nov 1995 A: Namorita. ... 1.50
❑66, Dec 1995 A: Scarlet Spider. A: Speedball. ... 1.50
❑67, Jan 1996; concludes in Web of Scarlet Spider #3 ... 1.50
❑68, Feb 1996 A: Guardians of the Galaxy. ... 1.50
❑69, Mar 1996 D: Speedball. ... 1.50
❑70, Apr 1996 ... 1.50
❑71, May 1996 ... 1.50
❑72, Jun 1996 A: Avengers. ... 1.50
❑73, Jul 1996 ... 1.50
❑74, Aug 1996 ... 1.50
❑75, Sep 1996 ... 1.50
❑Annual 1, ca. 1991 O: Night Thrasher. ... 2.50
❑Annual 2, ca. 1992 ... 2.25
❑Annual 3, ca. 1993 ... 2.95
❑Annual 4, ca. 1994 ... 2.95
❑Ashcan 1; "Ashcan" mini-comic ... 0.75

NEW WARRIORS, THE (VOL. 2)
MARVEL

❑1, Oct 1999 ... 2.99
❑2, Nov 1999 ... 2.50
❑3, Dec 1999 ... 2.50
❑4, Jan 2000 ... 2.50
❑5, Feb 2000 ... 2.50
❑6, Mar 2000 ... 2.50
❑7, Apr 2000 ... 2.50
❑8, May 2000 ... 2.50
❑9, Jun 2000 ... 2.50
❑10, Jul 2000 ... 2.50

NEW WAVE, THE
ECLIPSE

❑1, Jun 1986 ... 2.00
❑1/A; misprint ... 2.00
❑2, Jul 1986 ... 1.50
❑3, Jul 1986 ... 1.50
❑4, Aug 1986 ... 1.00
❑5, Aug 1986 ... 1.00
❑6, Sep 1986 ... 1.00
❑7, Sep 1986 ... 1.00
❑8, Sep 1986 ... 1.00
❑9, Oct 1986 ... 1.50
❑10, Nov 1986 ... 1.50
❑11, Dec 1986 ... 1.50
❑12, Feb 1987 ... 1.50
❑13, Mar 1987 ... 1.50

NEW WAVE VERSUS THE VOLUNTEERS, THE
ECLIPSE

❑1, Apr 1987 ... 2.50
❑2, Jun 1987 ... 2.50

NEW WORLD ORDER
BLAZER

❑1, Nov 1992, b&w ... 3.00
❑2, b&w ... 2.75
❑3, b&w ... 2.75
❑4, Aug 1993, b&w ... 2.50
❑5, Jan 1994, b&w ... 2.50
❑6, May 1994, b&w 1: Skinhead. ... 2.50
❑7, Aug 1994, b&w 1: Shining. ... 2.50
❑8, Feb 1995, b&w ... 2.50

NEW WORLD ORDER (PIG'S EYE)
PIG'S EYE

❑1 ... 1.00

NEW WORLDS ANTHOLOGY
CALIBER

❑1, ca. 1996, b&w ... 2.95
❑2, Jan 1996 ... 3.95
❑3 ... 3.95
❑4 ... 3.95
❑5 ... 3.95
❑6 ... 3.95

NEW X-MEN (ACADEMY X)
MARVEL

❑1, Jul 2004; Cover says New X-Men: Academy X; indicia says New X-Men ... 2.99
❑2, Aug 2004 ... 2.99
❑3, Sep 2004 ... 2.99

NEW YORK CITY OUTLAWS
OUTLAW

❑1 ... 2.00
❑2 ... 2.00
❑3 ... 2.00
❑4 ... 2.00

NEW YORK: YEAR ZERO
ECLIPSE

❑1, Aug 1988 ... 2.00
❑2, Aug 1988 ... 2.00
❑3, Sep 1988 ... 2.00
❑4, Oct 1988 ... 2.00

NEXT MAN
COMICO

❑1, Mar 1985 O: Next Man. 1: Next Man. ... 2.00
❑2, Apr 1985 ... 2.00
❑3, Jun 1985 ... 2.00
❑4, Aug 1985 ... 2.00
❑5, Oct 1985 ... 2.00

NEXT MEN (JOHN BYRNE'S...)
DARK HORSE

❑0, Feb 1992; JBy (w); JBy (a); Reprints Next Men stories from Dark Horse Presents ... 3.00
❑1, Jan 1992; JBy (w); JBy (a); Embossed cover (silver logo) ... 3.00
❑1-2, Jan 1992; JBy (w); JBy (a); Embossed cover (gold logo) ... 2.50
❑2, Mar 1992 JBy (w); JBy (a); 1: Sathanus. ... 3.00
❑3, Apr 1992 JBy (w); JBy (a) ... 2.50
❑4, May 1992 JBy (w); JBy (a) ... 2.50
❑5, Jun 1992 JBy (w); JBy (a) ... 2.50
❑6, Jul 1992 JBy (w); JBy (a) ... 2.50
❑7, Sep 1992; JBy (w); JBy (a); 1: M4. flipbook with M4 #1 back-up story ... 2.50
❑8, Oct 1992; JBy (w); JBy (a); flipbook with M4 #2 back-up story ... 2.50
❑9, Nov 1992; JBy (w); JBy (a); flipbook with M4 #3 back-up story ... 2.50
❑10, Dec 1992; JBy (w); JBy (a); flipbook with M4 #4 back-up story ... 2.50
❑11, Jan 1993; JBy (w); JBy (a); M4 back-up story ... 2.50
❑12, Feb 1993; JBy (w); JBy (a); M4 back-up story ... 2.50
❑13, Mar 1993; JBy (w); JBy (a); M4 back-up story ... 2.50
❑14, Apr 1993; JBy (w); JBy (a); M4 back-up story ... 2.50
❑15, Jun 1993; JBy (w); JBy (a); M4 back-up story ... 3.00
❑16, Jul 1993; JBy (w); JBy (a); M4 back-up story ... 2.50
❑17, Aug 1993; FM (c); JBy (w); JBy (a); M4 back-up story ... 2.50
❑18, Sep 1993; JBy (w); JBy (a); M4 back-up story ... 2.50
❑19, Oct 1993; JBy (w); JBy (a); M4 back-up story ... 2.50
❑20, Nov 1993; JBy (w); JBy (a); M4 back-up story ... 2.50
❑21, Dec 1993; JBy (w); JBy (a); A: Hellboy. M4 back-up story ... 30.00
❑22, Jan 1994; JBy (w); JBy (a); M4 back-up story ... 2.50

	N-MINT
❑23, Mar 1994; JBy (w); JBy (a); M4 back-up story	2.50
❑24, Apr 1994; JBy (w); JBy (a); M4 back-up story	2.50
❑25, May 1994 JBy (w); JBy (a); A: Cutter and Skywise (Elfquest characters).	2.50
❑26, Jun 1994 JBy (w); JBy (a)	2.50
❑27, Aug 1994 JBy (w); JBy (a)	2.50
❑28, Sep 1994 JBy (w); JBy (a)	2.50
❑29, Oct 1994 JBy (w); JBy (a)	2.50
❑30, Dec 1994; JBy (w); JBy (a); series goes on hiatus	2.50

NEXT NEXUS, THE
FIRST

❑1, Jan 1989 SR (a)	2.00
❑2, Feb 1989 SR (a)	2.00
❑3, Mar 1989 SR (a)	2.00
❑4, Apr 1989 SR (a)	2.00

NEXT WAVE, THE
OVERSTREET

❑1; Sampling of Five Self-Published comics	2.00

NEXUS: ALIEN JUSTICE
DARK HORSE

❑1, Dec 1992	3.95
❑2, Jan 1993	3.95
❑3, Feb 1993	3.95

NEXUS LEGENDS
FIRST

❑1, May 1989; SR (a); Reprints Nexus (Vol. 2) #1 with new cover	2.50
❑2, Jun 1989; SR (a); Reprints Nexus (Vol. 2) #2 with new cover	2.00
❑3, Jul 1989; SR (a); Reprints Nexus (Vol. 2) #3 with new cover	2.00
❑4, Aug 1989 SR (a)	2.00
❑5, Sep 1989 SR (a)	2.00
❑6, Oct 1989 SR (a)	2.00
❑7, Nov 1989 SR (a)	2.00
❑8, Dec 1989 SR (a)	2.00
❑9, Jan 1990 SR (a)	2.00
❑10, Feb 1990 SR (a)	2.00
❑11, Mar 1990 SR (a)	2.00
❑12, Apr 1990 SR (a)	2.00
❑13, May 1990 SR (a)	2.00
❑14, Jun 1990 SR (a)	2.00
❑15, Jul 1990 SR (a)	2.00
❑16, Aug 1990 SR (a)	2.00
❑17, Sep 1990 SR (a)	2.00
❑18, Oct 1990 SR (a)	2.00
❑19, Nov 1990 SR (a)	2.00
❑20, Dec 1990 SR (a)	2.00
❑21, Jan 1991 SR (a)	2.00
❑22, Feb 1991 SR (a)	2.00
❑23, Mar 1991 SR (a)	2.00

NEXUS MEETS MADMAN
DARK HORSE

❑1, May 1996	2.95

NEXUS THE LIBERATOR
DARK HORSE

❑1, Aug 1992	2.50
❑2, Sep 1992	2.50
❑3, Oct 1992	2.50
❑4, Nov 1992	2.50

NEXUS: THE ORIGIN
DARK HORSE

❑1, ca. 1995	3.95

NEXUS: THE WAGES OF SIN
DARK HORSE

❑1, Mar 1995; cardstock cover	2.95
❑2, Apr 1995; cardstock cover	2.95
❑3, May 1995; cardstock cover	2.95
❑4, Jun 1995	2.95

NEXUS (VOL. 1)
CAPITAL

❑1, b&w SR (a); 1: Nexus.	15.00
❑2 SR (a)	10.00
❑3, Oct 1982 SR (a)	15.00

NEXUS (VOL. 2)
FIRST

	N-MINT
❑1 1983; SR (a); Nexus begins for first time in color	3.00
❑2 SR (a); O: Nexus.	2.50
❑3 SR (a)	2.50
❑4 SR (a)	2.50
❑5 SR (a)	2.50
❑6 SR (a)	2.00
❑7; SR (a); First Comics begins publishing	2.00
❑8 SR (a)	2.00
❑9 SR (a)	1.50
❑10 SR (a)	1.75
❑11 SR (a)	1.75
❑12 SR (a)	1.75
❑13 SR (a)	1.75
❑14 SR (a)	1.75
❑15 SR (a)	1.75
❑16 SR (a)	1.75
❑17 ES (a)	1.75
❑18 SR (a)	1.75
❑19 SR (a)	1.75
❑20 SR (a)	1.75
❑21	1.75
❑22	1.75
❑23	1.75
❑24	1.75
❑25	1.75
❑26	1.75
❑27	1.75
❑28	1.75
❑29	1.75
❑30	1.75
❑31	1.75
❑32	1.75
❑33	1.75
❑34	1.75
❑35	1.75
❑36	1.75
❑37	1.75
❑38	1.75
❑39	1.75
❑40 SR (a)	1.75
❑41	1.75
❑42	1.75
❑43 SR (a)	1.75
❑44	1.75
❑45 A: Badger.	1.75
❑46 A: Badger.	1.75
❑47 A: Badger.	1.75
❑48 A: Badger.	1.75
❑49 A: Badger.	1.75
❑50; A: Badger. Crossroads	1.75
❑51	1.95
❑52	1.95
❑53	1.95
❑54	1.95
❑55, Apr 1989	1.95
❑56, May 1989	1.95
❑57, Jun 1989	1.95
❑58, Jul 1989	1.95
❑59, Aug 1989	1.95
❑60, Sep 1989	1.95
❑61, Oct 1989	1.95
❑62, Nov 1989	1.95
❑63, Dec 1989	1.95
❑64, Jan 1990	1.95
❑65, Feb 1990	1.95
❑66, Mar 1990	1.95
❑67, Apr 1990	1.95
❑68, May 1990	1.95
❑69, Jun 1990	1.95
❑70, Jul 1990	1.95
❑71, Aug 1990	1.95
❑72, Sep 1990	1.95
❑73, Oct 1990	2.25
❑74, Nov 1990	2.25
❑75, Dec 1990	2.25
❑76, Jan 1991	2.25
❑77, Feb 1991	2.25
❑78, Mar 1991	2.25

After exploring Wonder Girl's origins yet again, the heroine received her new identity of Troia in *New Titans* #55.

© 1989 DC Comics.

	N-MINT
❑79, Apr 1991	2.25
❑80, May 1991; Final issue of First series	2.25
❑81; Number not noted in indicia (was retroactive)	3.95
❑82; Number not noted in indicia (was retroactive)	3.95
❑83; Number not noted in indicia (was retroactive)	3.95
❑84; Number not noted in indicia (was retroactive)	3.95
❑85; Number not noted in indicia (was retroactive)	2.95
❑86; Number not noted in indicia (was retroactive)	2.95
❑87; Number not noted in indicia (was retroactive)	2.95
❑88; Number not noted in indicia (was retroactive)	2.95
❑89, Jun 1996 SR (a)	2.95
❑90, Jul 1996 SR (a)	2.95
❑91, Aug 1996 SR (a)	2.95
❑92, Sep 1996 SR (a)	2.95
❑93, Apr 1997 SR (a)	2.95
❑94, May 1997 SR (a)	2.95
❑95, Jul 1997, b&w SR (a)	2.95
❑96, Aug 1997, b&w SR (a)	2.95
❑97, Sep 1997, b&w SR (a)	2.95
❑98, Oct 1997, b&w SR (a)	2.95

NFL SUPERPRO
MARVEL

❑1, Oct 1991	1.00
❑2, Nov 1991	1.00
❑3, Dec 1991	1.00
❑4, Jan 1992	1.00
❑5, Feb 1992	1.00
❑6, Mar 1992	1.00
❑7, Apr 1992	1.00
❑8, May 1992	1.00
❑9, Jun 1992	1.00
❑10, Jul 1992	1.00
❑11, Aug 1992	1.00
❑12, Sep 1992	1.00
❑Special 1, Sep 1991; Special collector's edition	3.95
❑Special 1-2, Sep 1991; Super Bowl Special	2.00

NICK FURY, AGENT OF SHIELD (1ST SERIES)
MARVEL

❑1, Jun 1968 JSo (w); JSo (a); 1: Scorpio.	55.00
❑2, Jul 1968 JSo (a); O: Centurius. 1: Centurius.	34.00
❑3, Aug 1968 JSo (w); JSo (a)	30.00
❑4, Sep 1968; O: Nick Fury. S.H.I.E.L.D. origin issue	38.00
❑5, Oct 1968 JSo (a)	35.00
❑6, Nov 1968 JSo (c); JSo, FS (a)	27.00
❑7, Dec 1968	27.00
❑8, Jan 1969 HT (a); D: Supremus.	25.00
❑9, Feb 1969 FS (a)	24.00
❑10, Mar 1969	24.00
❑11, Apr 1969	24.00
❑12, May 1969	22.00
❑13, Jul 1969 HT (a)	22.00
❑14, Aug 1969 HT (a)	18.00
❑15, Nov 1969 1: Bullseye.	49.00

Condition price index: Multiply "NM prices" above by: **0.83 for Very Fine/Near Mint**
0.66 for Very Fine • 0.33 for Fine • 0.2 for Very Good • 0.125 for Good

N-MINT

❑16, Nov 1969; Giant-size; JK (a); Reprints from Strange Tales #136-138 ..... 19.00
❑17; Giant-size; Reprints from Strange Tales #139-141 ..... 19.00
❑18, Mar 1971; Giant-size; Reprints from Strange Tales #142-144 ..... 19.00

NICK FURY, AGENT OF SHIELD (2ND SERIES)
MARVEL

❑1, Dec 1983; BH (c); BH (a); Reprints from Nick Fury, Agent of SHIELD (1st series); wraparound cover 3.00
❑2, Jan 1984; Reprints from Nick Fury, Agent of SHIELD (1st series) 3.00

NICK FURY, AGENT OF S.H.I.E.L.D. (3RD SERIES)
MARVEL

❑1, Sep 1989 BH (a) 2.25
❑2, Oct 1989; KP (a); Death's Head 1.75
❑3, Nov 1989; KP (a); Death's Head 1.75
❑4, Nov 1989; KP (a); Sgt. Fury 1.50
❑5, Dec 1989 KP (a) 1.50
❑6, Dec 1989 KP (a) 1.50
❑7, Jan 1990 KP (a) 1.50
❑8, Feb 1990 ..... 1.50
❑9, Mar 1990 KP (a) 1.50
❑10, Apr 1990 KP (a); A: Captain America. 1.50
❑11, May 1990 ..... 1.50
❑12, Jun 1990 ..... 1.50
❑13, Jul 1990; KP (a); Return of Yellow Claw 1.50
❑14, Aug 1990 KP (a) 1.50
❑15, Sep 1990 A: Fantastic Four. 1.50
❑16, Oct 1990 ..... 1.50
❑17, Nov 1990 HT (a) 1.50
❑18, Dec 1990 ..... 1.50
❑19, Jan 1991 HT (a) 1.50
❑20, Feb 1991 ..... 1.50
❑21, Mar 1991; Baron Strucker revived 1.50
❑22, Apr 1991 ..... 1.50
❑23, May 1991 ..... 1.50
❑24, Jun 1991 A: Fantastic Four. A: Captain America. 1.50
❑25, Jul 1991 ..... 1.50
❑26, Aug 1991 A: Fantastic Four. A: Avengers. 1.50
❑27, Sep 1991 A: Wolverine. 2.00
❑28, Oct 1991 A: Wolverine. 2.00
❑29, Nov 1991 A: Wolverine. 2.00
❑30, Dec 1991 A: Deathlok. 1.50
❑31, Jan 1992 A: Deathlok. 1.50
❑32, Feb 1992 A: Weapon Omega. 1.75
❑33, Mar 1992 1: new agents (Psi-Borg, Violence, Knockabout, Ivory). 1.75
❑34, Apr 1992 V: Hydra. V: Baron Strucker. 1.75
❑35, May 1992 ..... 1.75
❑36, Jun 1992 O: Constrictor. A: Cage. V: Constrictor. 1.75
❑37, Jul 1992 ..... 1.75
❑38, Aug 1992 ..... 1.75
❑39, Sep 1992 ..... 1.75
❑40, Oct 1992 ..... 1.75
❑41, Nov 1992 ..... 1.75
❑42, Dec 1992 ..... 1.75
❑43, Jan 1993 ..... 1.75
❑44, Feb 1993 ..... 1.75
❑45, Mar 1993 ..... 1.75
❑46, Apr 1993 ..... 1.75
❑47, May 1993 D: Kate Neville (Nick Fury's Girlfriend). 1.75

NICK FURY VS. S.H.I.E.L.D.
MARVEL

❑1, Jun 1988 JSo (c) 4.00
❑2, Jul 1988 BSz (c) 3.50
❑3, Mar 1988 ..... 3.50
❑4, Sep 1988 ..... 3.50
❑5, Oct 1988 ..... 3.50
❑6, Nov 1988 ..... 3.50

N-MINT

NICK HAZARD
HARRIER

❑1, Jan 1988 ..... 1.95

NICKI SHADOW
RELENTLESS

❑0, Jul 1997 ..... 1.00
❑1, Nov 1997 ..... 2.50

NICK NOYZ AND THE NUISANCE TOUR BOOK
RED BULLET

❑1, b&w 2.50

NICK RYAN THE SKULL
ANTARCTIC

❑1, Dec 1994, b&w 2.75
❑2, Jan 1995, b&w; El Gato Negro back-up feature 2.75
❑3, Feb 1995, b&w 2.75

NIGHT, THE
SLAVE LABOR / AMAZE INK

❑0, Nov 1995 ..... 1.50

NIGHTBIRD
HARRIER

❑1, May 1988, b&w 1.95
❑2 1988, b&w 1.95

NIGHT BREED (CLIVE BARKER'S)
MARVEL / EPIC

❑1, Apr 1990 ..... 3.00
❑2, May 1990 ..... 2.50
❑3, Jun 1990 ..... 2.50
❑4, Jul 1990 ..... 2.50
❑5, Sep 1990 ..... 2.50
❑6, Nov 1990 ..... 2.50
❑7, Jan 1991 ..... 2.50
❑8, Mar 1991 ..... 2.50
❑9, May 1991 ..... 2.50
❑10, Jul 1991 ..... 2.50
❑11, Sep 1991 ..... 2.25
❑12, Nov 1991 ..... 2.25
❑13, Jan 1992; Rawhead Rex 2.25
❑14, Mar 1992 ..... 2.25
❑15, May 1992 ..... 2.25
❑16, Jun 1992 ..... 2.25
❑17, Jul 1992 ..... 2.25
❑18, Aug 1992 ..... 2.25
❑19, Sep 1992 ..... 2.25
❑20, Oct 1992 ..... 2.50
❑21, Nov 1992 ..... 2.50
❑22, Dec 1992 ..... 2.50
❑23, Jan 1993 ..... 2.50
❑24, Feb 1993 ..... 2.50
❑25, Mar 1993 ..... 2.50

NIGHT BRIGADE
WONDER COMIX

❑1, Aug 1987, b&w 1.95

NIGHTCAT
MARVEL

❑1, Apr 1991 ..... 3.95

NIGHT CITY
THORBY

❑1 ..... 2.95

NIGHTCRAWLER (VOL. 1)
MARVEL

❑1, Nov 1985 DC (w); DC (a) 2.00
❑2, Dec 1985 DC (w); DC (a) 2.00
❑3, Jan 1986 DC (w); DC (a) 2.00
❑4, Feb 1986 DC (w); DC (a) 2.00

NIGHTCRAWLER (VOL. 2)
MARVEL

❑1, Jan 2002 ..... 2.50
❑2, Feb 2002 ..... 2.50
❑3, Mar 2002 ..... 2.50
❑4, Apr 2002 ..... 2.50

NIGHTCRY
CFD

❑1, b&w; cardstock cover 3.00
❑2, b&w; cardstock cover 3.00
❑3, b&w; cardstock cover 3.00
❑4, b&w; cardstock cover 3.00

N-MINT

❑5, b&w; cardstock cover 3.00
❑6, May 1996, b&w; cardstock cover 3.00

NIGHTFALL: THE BLACK CHRONICLES
HOMAGE

❑1, Dec 1999 ..... 2.95
❑2, Jan 2000 ..... 2.95
❑3, Feb 2000 ..... 2.95

NIGHT FORCE
DC

❑1, Aug 1982 GC (a); 1: Night Force. 2.50
❑2, Sep 1982 GC (a) 1.50
❑3, Oct 1982 GC (a) 1.50
❑4, Nov 1982 GC (a) 1.50
❑5, Dec 1982 GC (a) 1.50
❑6, Jan 1983 GC (a) 1.50
❑7, Feb 1983 GC (a) 1.50
❑8, Mar 1983 GC (a) 1.50
❑9, Apr 1983 GC (a) 1.50
❑10, May 1983 GC (a) 1.50
❑11, Jun 1983 GC (a) 1.50
❑12, Jul 1983 GC (a) 1.50
❑13, Aug 1983 GC (a) 1.50
❑14, Sep 1983 GC (a) 1.50

NIGHT FORCE (2ND SERIES)
DC

❑1, Dec 1996 BA (a) 2.50
❑2, Jan 1997 BA (a) 2.25
❑3, Feb 1997 BA (a) 2.25
❑4, Mar 1997 ..... 2.25
❑5, Apr 1997 ..... 2.25
❑6, May 1997 ..... 2.25
❑7, Jun 1997 ..... 2.25
❑8, Jul 1997; continues in Challengers of the Unknown #6 ..... 2.25
❑9, Aug 1997 ..... 2.25
❑10, Sep 1997 ..... 2.25
❑11, Oct 1997 ..... 2.25
❑12, Nov 1997 ..... 2.50

NIGHT GLIDER
TOPPS

❑1, Apr 1993 ..... 2.95

NIGHTHAWK
MARVEL

❑1, Sep 1998; gatefold summary 2.99
❑2, Oct 1998; gatefold summary 2.50
❑3, Nov 1998; gatefold summary 2.50

NIGHTJAR (ALAN MOORE'S)
AVATAR

❑1, Mar 2004 ..... 3.50

NIGHT LIFE
STRAWBERRY JAM

❑1 ..... 1.50
❑2 ..... 1.50
❑3, Feb 1987 ..... 1.50
❑4, Mar 1987 ..... 1.50
❑5, Apr 1987 ..... 1.50
❑6, May 1987 ..... 1.50
❑7 ..... 1.50
❑8, Nov 1991 ..... 2.50

NIGHTLINGER
GAUNTLET

❑1, b&w 2.95
❑2, b&w 2.95

NIGHT MAN, THE
MALIBU / ULTRAVERSE

❑1, Oct 1993 O: The Night Man. 1: The Night Man (in costume). 1: Death Mask. 2.50
❑1/Ltd.; Ultra-limited edition O: The Night Man. 1: The Night Man (in costume). 1: Death Mask. 25.00
❑2, Nov 1993 1: Mangle. 2.00
❑3, Dec 1993 A: Freex. 2.00
❑4, Jan 1994 O: Firearm. 2.00
❑5, Feb 1994 ..... 2.00
❑6, Mar 1994 ..... 1.95
❑7, Apr 1994 ..... 1.95
❑8, May 1994 ..... 1.95
❑9, Jun 1994 D: Teknight I. 1.95

N-MINT

❑10, Jul 1994 1: Silver Daggers. 1: Chalk. 1.95
❑11, Aug 1994 1: Teknight II. 1.95
❑12, Sep 1994 A: The Solution. 1.95
❑13, Oct 1994; no indicia 1.95
❑14, Nov 1994 JRo (w); D: Torso. 1.95
❑15, Dec 1994 .... 1.95
❑16, Feb 1995; MZ (a); flipbook with Ultraverse Premiere #11 .... 3.50
❑17, Feb 1995 1: BloodyFly. 2.50
❑18, Mar 1995 .... 2.50
❑19, Apr 1995 D: Deathmask. 2.50
❑20, May 1995 D: BloodyFly. 2.50
❑21, Jun 1995 .... 2.50
❑22, Jul 1995 A: Loki. 2.50
❑23, Aug 1995 .... 2.50
❑Annual 1, Jan 1995 .... 3.95

NIGHT MAN, THE (VOL. 2)
MALIBU / ULTRAVERSE

❑0, Sep 1995; Listed as issue #Infinity 1.50
❑0/A, Sep 1995; alternate cover 1.50
❑1, Oct 1995 .... 1.50
❑2, Nov 1995 .... 1.50
❑3, Dec 1995 .... 1.50
❑4, Dec 1995 .... 1.50

NIGHT MAN/GAMBIT, THE
MALIBU / ULTRAVERSE

❑1, Mar 1996 .... 1.95
❑2, Apr 1996 .... 1.95
❑3, May 1996 .... 1.95

NIGHT MAN VS. WOLVERINE
MALIBU / ULTRAVERSE

❑0, Aug 1995; no cover price 5.00

NIGHTMARE (ALEX NIÑO'S...)
INNOVATION

❑1, Dec 1989 .... 1.95

NIGHTMARE
MARVEL

❑1, Dec 1994 .... 1.95
❑2, Jan 1995 .... 1.95
❑3, Feb 1995 .... 1.95
❑4, Mar 1995 .... 1.95

NIGHTMARE ON ELM STREET, A (FREDDY KRUEGER'S...)
MARVEL

❑1 .... 3.00

NIGHTMARE ON ELM STREET: THE BEGINNING
INNOVATION

❑1 .... 2.50
❑2 .... 2.50

NIGHTMARES
ECLIPSE

❑1 PG (a) 2.00
❑2 PG (a) 2.00

NIGHTMARES ON ELM STREET
INNOVATION

❑1, Sep 1991 .... 2.50
❑2 .... 2.50
❑3 .... 2.50
❑4 .... 2.50
❑5 .... 2.50
❑6 .... 2.50

NIGHTMARE THEATER
CHAOS!

❑1, Nov 1997; horror anthology 2.50
❑2, Nov 1997; horror anthology 2.50
❑3, Nov 1997; horror anthology 2.50
❑4, Nov 1997; horror anthology 2.50

NIGHTMARE WALKER
BONEYARD

❑1, Jul 1996, b&w 2.95

NIGHTMARK
ALPHA PRODUCTIONS

❑1, b&w 2.25

N-MINT

NIGHTMARK: BLOOD & HONOR
ALPHA

❑1, Apr 1994 .... 2.50
❑2 .... 2.50
❑3 .... 2.50

NIGHTMARK MYSTERY SPECIAL
ALPHA

❑1, b&w 2.50

NIGHTMASK
MARVEL

❑1, Nov 1986 O: Nightmask. 1.00
❑2, Dec 1986 .... 1.00
❑3, Jan 1987 .... 1.00
❑4, Feb 1987 .... 1.00
❑5, Mar 1987 .... 1.00
❑6, Apr 1987 .... 1.00
❑7, May 1987 .... 1.00
❑8, Jun 1987 .... 1.00
❑9, Jul 1987; Mark Bagley's first major comics work 1.00
❑10, Aug 1987 .... 1.00
❑11, Sep 1987 .... 1.00
❑12, Oct 1987 .... 1.00

NIGHT MASTERS
CUSTOM PIC

❑1 1986 .... 1.50
❑2 1986 .... 1.50
❑3 1986 .... 1.50
❑4 1986 .... 1.50
❑5, Aug 1986 .... 1.50
❑6, Jan 1987 .... 1.50

NIGHT MUSIC
ECLIPSE

❑1, Dec 1984 CR (w); CR (a) 2.00
❑2, Feb 1985 CR (w); CR (a) 2.00
❑3, Mar 1985; CR (w); CR (a); Rudyard Kipling adaptation 2.00
❑4, Dec 1985 CR (a) 2.00
❑5, Dec 1985 CR (a) 2.00
❑6 CR (a) 2.00
❑7, Feb 1988 CR (w); CR (a) 2.00
❑8, ca. 1989 .... 3.95
❑9, ca. 1990 CR (a) 4.95
❑10, ca. 1990 CR (a) 4.95
❑11, ca. 1990 CR (a) 4.95

NIGHT NURSE
MARVEL

❑1, Nov 1972 .... 45.00
❑2, Jan 1973 .... 25.00
❑3, Mar 1973 .... 25.00
❑4, May 1973 .... 25.00

NIGHT OF THE LIVING DEAD
FANTACO

❑0, b&w 2.00
❑1, ca. 1991, b&w 4.95
❑2, b&w 4.95
❑3, b&w 5.95
❑4, b&w 5.95

NIGHT OF THE LIVING DEAD: AFTERMATH
FANTACO

❑1 .... 1.95

NIGHT OF THE LIVING DEAD: LONDON
FANTACO

❑1 .... 5.95
❑2 .... 5.95

NIGHT OF THE LIVING DEAD: PRELUDE
FANTACO

❑1, ca. 1991, b&w 1.50

NIGHT OF THE LIVING DEADLINE USA
DARK HORSE

❑1, Apr 1992, b&w 2.95

NIGHT RAVEN: HOUSE OF CARDS
MARVEL

❑1, Aug 1991 .... 5.95

After escaping from a government laboratory, The Next Men explored the strange, new world in which they found themselves.

© 1992 John Byrne and Dark Horse Comics.

N-MINT

NIGHT RIDER
MARVEL

❑1, Oct 1974; Reprints Ghost Rider (Western) #1 .... 5.00
❑2, Dec 1974; Reprints Ghost Rider (Western) #2 .... 3.50
❑3, Feb 1975; Reprints Ghost Rider (Western) #3 .... 3.50
❑4, Apr 1975; Reprints Ghost Rider (Western) #4 .... 3.50
❑5, Jun 1975; Reprints Ghost Rider (Western) #5 .... 3.50
❑6, Aug 1975; Reprints Ghost Rider (Western) #6 .... 3.50

NIGHT'S CHILDREN
FANTACO

❑1, b&w 3.50
❑2, b&w 3.50
❑3, b&w 3.50
❑4, b&w 3.50

NIGHT'S CHILDREN: DOUBLE INDEMNITY
FANTACO

❑1, b&w 7.95

NIGHT'S CHILDREN EROTIC FANTASIES
FANTACO

❑1 .... 4.50

NIGHT'S CHILDREN: FOREPLAY
FANTACO

❑1, b&w 4.95

NIGHT'S CHILDREN: THE VAMPIRE
MILLENNIUM

❑1 .... 2.95
❑2 .... 2.95

NIGHT'S CHILDREN: VAMPYR!
FANTACO

❑1, b&w 3.50
❑2, b&w 3.50
❑3, b&w 3.50

NIGHTSHADE
NO MERCY

❑1, Aug 1997 .... 2.50

NIGHTSHADES
LONDON NIGHT

❑1 .... 2.95

NIGHTSIDE
MARVEL

❑1, Dec 2001 .... 2.99
❑2, Jan 2002 .... 2.99
❑3, Feb 2002 .... 2.99
❑4, Mar 2002 .... 2.99

NIGHTS INTO DREAMS
ARCHIE

❑1, Feb 1998 .... 1.75
❑2, Mar 1998 .... 1.75
❑3, Apr 1998 .... 1.75
❑4, Aug 1998 .... 1.75
❑5, Sep 1998 .... 1.75
❑6, Oct 1998 .... 1.75

NIGHTSTALKERS
MARVEL

❑1, Nov 1992; Missing poster 1.00
❑1/CS 2.75
❑2, Dec 1992 .... 2.00

N-MINT

❑3, Jan 1993 .... 2.00
❑4, Feb 1993 .... 1.75
❑5, Mar 1993 .... 1.75
❑6, Apr 1993 .... 1.75
❑7, May 1993 .... 1.75
❑8, Jun 1993 .... 1.75
❑9, Jul 1993 .... 1.75
❑10, Aug 1993; Double cover 2.25
❑11, Sep 1993 .... 1.75
❑12, Oct 1993; Gold cover 1.75
❑13, Nov 1993 .... 1.75
❑14, Dec 1993; Neon ink on cover 1.75
❑15, Jan 1994; Spot-varnish cover 1.75
❑16, Feb 1994 .... 1.75
❑17, Mar 1994 .... 1.75
❑18, Apr 1994 .... 1.75

NIGHTSTREETS (ARROW)
ARROW

❑1, Jul 1986 1: Mr. Katt. 2.50
❑2, Oct 1986 .... 2.00
❑3, Jan 1987 .... 2.00
❑4, Apr 1987 .... 2.00
❑5, Jul 1987 .... 2.00

NIGHT TERRORS, THE
CHANTING MONKS

❑1 BWr (a) 2.75

NIGHT THRASHER
MARVEL

❑1, Aug 1993; foil cover 2.95
❑2, Sep 1993 .... 1.75
❑3, Oct 1993 .... 1.75
❑4, Nov 1993 .... 1.75
❑5, Dec 1993 .... 1.75
❑6, Jan 1994 .... 1.75
❑7, Feb 1994 .... 1.75
❑8, Mar 1994 .... 1.75
❑9, Apr 1994 .... 1.75
❑10, May 1994 .... 1.95
❑11, Jun 1994 .... 1.95
❑12, Jul 1994 .... 1.95
❑13, Aug 1994 .... 1.95
❑14, Sep 1994 .... 1.95
❑15, Oct 1994 .... 1.95
❑16, Nov 1994 .... 1.95
❑17, Dec 1994 .... 1.95
❑18, Jan 1995 .... 1.95
❑19, Feb 1995 .... 1.95
❑20, Mar 1995 .... 1.95
❑21, Apr 1995 .... 1.95

NIGHT THRASHER: FOUR CONTROL
MARVEL

❑1, Oct 1992 .... 2.00
❑2, Nov 1992 .... 2.00
❑3, Dec 1992 .... 2.00
❑4, Jan 1993 .... 2.00

NIGHT TRIBES
DC / WILDSTORM

❑1, Jul 1999 .... 4.95

NIGHTVEIL
AC

❑1, Feb 1984, color 2.00
❑2 .... 2.00
❑3 .... 2.00
❑4 .... 2.00
❑5 .... 2.00
❑6 .... 2.00
❑7, Mar 1987 .... 2.00
❑Special 1, Aug 1988 .... 2.00

NIGHTVEIL'S CAULDRON OF HORROR
AC

❑1, b&w 2.50
❑2 .... 2.95
❑3, Sep 1991 .... 2.95

NIGHTVENGER
AXIS

❑Ashcan 1, May 1994 .... 2.00

N-MINT

NIGHTVISION
REBEL

❑1, Nov 1996 .... 3.00
❑2 1997 .... 2.50
❑3 1997 .... 2.50
❑4 1997 .... 2.50

NIGHTVISION: ALL ABOUT EVE
LONDON NIGHT

❑1 .... 3.00

NIGHTVISION (ATOMEKA)
ATOMEKA

❑1, b&w 2.95

NIGHT VIXEN
ABC

❑0/A, b&w 3.00
❑0/B; Eurotika Edition 4.00
❑0/C; Manga Flux Edition 4.00

NIGHT WALKER
FLEETWAY-QUALITY

❑1; Reprints Luke Kirby story from 2000 A.D. 2.95
❑2; Reprints Luke Kirby story from 2000 A.D. 2.95
❑3; Reprints Luke Kirby story from 2000 A.D. 2.95

NIGHT WARRIORS: DARKSTALKERS' REVENGE THE COMIC SERIES
VIZ

❑1, Nov 1998 .... 2.95
❑2, Dec 1998 .... 3.25
❑3, Jan 1999 .... 2.95
❑4, Feb 1999 .... 2.95
❑5, Mar 1999 .... 2.95
❑6, Apr 1999 .... 2.95

NIGHTWATCH
MARVEL

❑1, Apr 1994 .... 1.50
❑1/Variant, Apr 1994; foil cover 2.95
❑2, May 1994 .... 1.50
❑3, Jun 1994 .... 1.50
❑4, Jul 1994 .... 1.50
❑5, Aug 1994 .... 1.50
❑6, Sep 1994 .... 1.50
❑7, Oct 1994 .... 1.50
❑8, Nov 1994 .... 1.50
❑9, Dec 1994 .... 1.50
❑10, Jan 1995 .... 1.50
❑11, Feb 1995 .... 1.50
❑12, Mar 1995 .... 1.50

NIGHTWING (MINI-SERIES)
DC

❑1, Sep 1995 .... 3.50
❑2, Oct 1995 .... 2.50
❑3, Nov 1995 .... 2.50
❑4, Dec 1995 .... 2.50

NIGHTWING
DC

❑0.5 .... 4.00
❑0.5/Platinum; Platinum edition 7.00
❑1, Oct 1996 .... 11.00
❑2, Nov 1996 .... 6.00
❑3, Dec 1996 .... 4.00
❑4, Jan 1997 .... 3.50
❑5, Feb 1997 .... 3.50
❑6, Mar 1997 .... 3.00
❑7, Apr 1997 .... 3.00
❑8, May 1997 .... 3.00
❑9, Jun 1997 .... 3.00
❑10, Jul 1997 V: Scarecrow. 3.00
❑11, Aug 1997 V: Scarecrow. 2.50
❑12, Sep 1997 .... 2.50
❑13, Oct 1997 .... 2.50
❑14, Nov 1997 A: Batman. 2.50
❑15, Dec 1997; A: Batman. V: Two-Face. Face cover 2.50
❑16, Jan 1998 .... 1.95
❑17, Feb 1998 .... 1.95
❑18, Mar 1998 .... 1.95
❑19, Apr 1998; continues in Batman #553 .... 1.95

N-MINT

❑20, May 1998; continues in Batman #554 .... 1.95
❑21, Jun 1998 1: Nitewing. A: Blockbuster. 1.95
❑22, Jul 1998 V: Stallion. V: Brutale. 1.95
❑23, Aug 1998; A: Lady Shiva. concludes in Green Arrow #135 .... 1.95
❑24, Sep 1998 .... 1.99
❑25, Oct 1998 .... 1.99
❑26, Dec 1998 A: Huntress. 1.99
❑27, Jan 1999 A: Huntress. 1.99
❑28, Feb 1999 1: Torque. A: Huntress. 1.99
❑29, Mar 1999 A: Huntress. 1.99
❑30, Apr 1999 A: Superman. 1.99
❑31, May 1999; Dick joins the Bludhaven police force 1.99
❑32, Jun 1999 .... 1.99
❑33, Jul 1999 .... 1.99
❑34, Aug 1999 .... 1.99
❑35, Sep 1999; No Man's Land 1.99
❑36, Oct 1999; No Man's Land 1.99
❑37, Nov 1999; No Man's Land 1.99
❑38, Dec 2000; No Man's Land 1.99
❑39, Jan 2000 .... 1.99
❑40, Feb 2000 .... 1.99
❑41, Mar 2000 .... 1.99
❑42, Apr 2000 .... 1.99
❑43, May 2000 .... 1.99
❑44, Jun 2000 .... 1.99
❑45, Jul 2000 .... 1.99
❑46, Aug 2000 .... 1.99
❑47, Sep 2000 .... 1.99
❑48, Oct 2000 .... 2.25
❑49, Nov 2000 .... 2.25
❑50, Dec 2000 .... 3.50
❑51, Jan 2001 .... 2.25
❑52, Feb 2001 A: Catwoman. 2.25
❑53, Mar 2001 DGry (w) 2.25
❑54, Apr 2001 .... 2.25
❑55, May 2001 .... 2.25
❑56, Jun 2001 .... 2.25
❑57, Jul 2001 .... 2.25
❑58, Aug 2001 .... 2.25
❑59, Sep 2001 .... 2.25
❑60, Oct 2001 .... 2.25
❑61, Nov 2001 .... 2.25
❑62, Dec 2001; Joker: Last Laugh crossover 2.25
❑63, Jan 2002 .... 2.25
❑64, Feb 2002 .... 2.25
❑65, Mar 2002 .... 2.25
❑66, Apr 2002 .... 2.00
❑67, May 2002 .... 2.00
❑68, Jun 2002 .... 2.25
❑69, Jul 2002 .... 2.25
❑70, Aug 2002 .... 2.25
❑71, Sep 2002 .... 2.25
❑72, Oct 2002 .... 2.25
❑73, Nov 2002 .... 2.25
❑74, Dec 2002 .... 2.25
❑75, Jan 2003 .... 2.00
❑76, Feb 2003 .... 2.25
❑77, Mar 2003 .... 2.25
❑78, Apr 2003 .... 2.25
❑79, May 2003 .... 2.25
❑80, Jun 2003 A: Deathstroke the Terminator. 2.25
❑81, Jul 2003 A: Deathstroke the Terminator. 2.25
❑82, Aug 2003 .... 2.25
❑83, Sep 2003 .... 2.25
❑84, Oct 2003 .... 2.25
❑85, Nov 2003 .... 2.25
❑86, Dec 2003 .... 2.25
❑87, Jan 2004 .... 2.25
❑88, Feb 2004 .... 2.25
❑89, Mar 2004 .... 2.25
❑90, Apr 2004 .... 2.25
❑91, May 2004, DGry (w) 2.25
❑92, Jun 2004 .... 2.25
❑93, Jul 2004 .... 2.25
❑94, Aug 2004 .... 2.25

N-MINT

- ❑95, Sep 204
- ❑1000000, Nov 1998 .... 3.00
- ❑Annual 1, ca. 1997; Pulp Heroes 3.95
- ❑Giant Size 1, Dec 2000 .... 5.95

NIGHTWING: ALFRED'S RETURN
DC

- ❑1, Jul 1995 .... 3.50

NIGHTWING AND HUNTRESS
DC

- ❑1, May 1998 DGry (w) 2.00
- ❑2, Jun 1998 DGry (w); BSz (a) 2.00
- ❑3, Jul 1998 .... 2.00
- ❑4, Aug 1998 .... 2.00

NIGHTWING: OUR WORLDS AT WAR
DC

- ❑1, Sep 2001 .... 2.95

NIGHTWING SECRET FILES
DC

- ❑1, Oct 1999; background information on series 4.95

NIGHTWING: THE TARGET
DC

- ❑1, Sep 2001 .... 5.95

NIGHTWOLF
ENTROPY

- ❑1 .... 1.50
- ❑2 .... 1.50

NIGHT ZERO
FLEETWAY-QUALITY

- ❑1, b&w 1.95
- ❑2, b&w 1.95
- ❑3, b&w 1.95
- ❑4, b&w 1.95

NIKKI BLADE SUMMER FUN
ABC

- ❑1/A, b&w 3.00
- ❑1/B; solo figure on cover 3.00

NIMROD, THE
FANTAGRAPHICS

- ❑1, Jun 1998, b&w 2.95
- ❑2, Aug 1998, b&w 2.95

NINA'S ALL-TIME GREATEST COLLECTORS' ITEM CLASSIC COMICS
DARK HORSE

- ❑1, Aug 1992, b&w 2.50

NINA'S NEW & IMPROVED ALL-TIME GREATEST COLLECTORS' ITEM CLASSIC COMICS
DARK HORSE

- ❑1, Feb 1994, b&w 2.50

NINE LIVES OF LEATHER CAT, THE
FORBIDDEN FRUIT

- ❑1 .... 3.50
- ❑2 .... 3.50
- ❑3 .... 3.50
- ❑4 .... 3.50
- ❑5 .... 3.50
- ❑6 .... 3.50

NINE RINGS OF WU-TANG, THE
IMAGE

- ❑0, Nov 1999; Giveaway bundled with Wizard Magazine 2.00
- ❑1/A, Nov 1999; Woman with bow reclining on cover with jungle cats 2.95
- ❑1/B, Nov 1999; Tower Records variant 2.95
- ❑2, Dec 1999 .... 2.95
- ❑3, Feb 2000 .... 2.95
- ❑4, Apr 2000 .... 2.95
- ❑5, Jul 2000 .... 2.95

1984 MAGAZINE
WARREN

- ❑1, Jun 1978 .... 6.00
- ❑2, Aug 1978 .... 4.00
- ❑3, Sep 1978 .... 4.00
- ❑4, Oct 1978 .... 4.00
- ❑5, Feb 1979 .... 4.00
- ❑6, Jun 1979 .... 4.00

N-MINT

- ❑7, Aug 1979 .... 4.00
- ❑8, Sep 1979 .... 4.00
- ❑9, Oct 1979 .... 4.00
- ❑10, Dec 1980; Series continued in 1994 #11 .... 4.00

1994 MAGAZINE
WARREN

- ❑11, Feb 1980; Series continued from 1984 #10 .... 3.00
- ❑12, Apr 1980 .... 3.00
- ❑13, Jun 1980 .... 3.00
- ❑14, Aug 1980 .... 3.00
- ❑15, Oct 1980 .... 3.00
- ❑16, Dec 1980 AN (a) 3.00
- ❑17, Feb 1981 .... 3.00
- ❑18, Apr 1981 FT (w); FT, AN (a) 3.00
- ❑19, Jun 1981 .... 3.00
- ❑20, Aug 1981 .... 3.00
- ❑21, Oct 1981 FT (w); FT, AN (a) 3.00
- ❑22, Dec 1981 .... 3.00
- ❑23, Feb 1982 .... 3.00
- ❑24, Apr 1982 .... 3.00
- ❑25, Jun 1982 .... 3.00
- ❑26, Aug 1982 .... 3.00
- ❑27, Oct 1982 .... 3.00
- ❑28, Dec 1982 .... 3.00
- ❑29, Feb 1983 .... 3.00

1963
IMAGE

- ❑1, Apr 1993, AMo (w); DaG (a); Mystery Incorporated 2.00
- ❑1/BR, Apr 1993, Promotional limited edition AMo (w); DaG (a) 3.00
- ❑1/Gold, Apr 1993, Gold edition; AMo (w); DaG (a); Profits donated to cancer research 5.00
- ❑1/Silver, Apr 1993, silver edition; AMo (w); DaG (a); Profits donated to cancer research 3.00
- ❑2, May 1993, AMo (w); No One Escapes...the Fury 2.00
- ❑3, Jun 1993, AMo (w); Tales of the Uncanny 2.00
- ❑4, Jul 1993, AMo (w); Tales From Beyond; Johnny Beyond 2.00
- ❑5, Aug 1993, AMo (w) 2.00
- ❑6, Oct 1993, AMo (w) 2.00

NINETY-NINE GIRLS
FANTAGRAPHICS / EROS

- ❑1, b&w 2.25

NINE VOLT
IMAGE

- ❑1, Jul 1997 .... 2.50
- ❑1/A, Jul 1997; alternate cover 2.50
- ❑2, Aug 1997 .... 2.50
- ❑3, Sep 1997 .... 2.50
- ❑4, Oct 1997 .... 2.50

NINJA
ETERNITY

- ❑1 1986 .... 1.80
- ❑2 1986 .... 1.80
- ❑3 1986 .... 1.80
- ❑4 1986 .... 1.80
- ❑5 1986 .... 1.95
- ❑6 1986 .... 1.95
- ❑7 1987 .... 1.95
- ❑8 1987 .... 1.95
- ❑9 1987 .... 1.95
- ❑10 1987 .... 1.95
- ❑11 1988 .... 1.95
- ❑12, Sep 1988 .... 1.95
- ❑13 1988 .... 1.95
- ❑Special 1, b&w 2.25

NINJA-BOTS SUPER SPECIAL
PIED PIPER

- ❑1 .... 1.95

The events of *Nick Fury, Agent of S.H.I.E.L.D.* (3rd series) follow the events of *Nick Fury vs. S.H.I.E.L.D.*

© 1989 Marvel Comics.

N-MINT

NINJA ELITE
ADVENTURE

- ❑1; 7-1/2x8-1/2" version with black-and-white cover 1.50
- ❑1-2; 1st printing with color covers, full comic size; 1st printing with color covers, full comic size 1.50
- ❑2, Jul 1987 .... 1.50
- ❑3, ca. 1987 .... 1.50
- ❑4, Dec 1987 .... 1.50
- ❑5, ca. 1988 .... 1.50
- ❑6, May 1988, b&w 1.50
- ❑7, Jul 1988, b&w 1.50
- ❑8, Aug 1988, b&w 1.50

NINJA FUNNIES
ETERNITY

- ❑1, Jan 1987 .... 1.50
- ❑2 .... 1.95
- ❑3 .... 1.95
- ❑4 .... 1.95
- ❑5 .... 1.95

NINJA HIGH SCHOOL
ANTARCTIC

- ❑0, May 1994, b&w; Antarctic publishes 3.00
- ❑0/Ltd., b&w; foil cover edition (500 made) 4.00
- ❑1 .... 7.00
- ❑1-2 .... 2.50
- ❑2 .... 5.00
- ❑2-2 .... 2.00
- ❑3 .... 4.00
- ❑3-2 .... 2.00
- ❑4 .... 4.00
- ❑4-2 .... 2.00
- ❑5, Jun 1988, b&w; Eternity begins publishing 4.00
- ❑6 .... 3.50
- ❑6-2 .... 2.00
- ❑7, Sep 1988 .... 3.50
- ❑8, Dec 1988 .... 3.50
- ❑9, Feb 1989 .... 3.50
- ❑10, Mar 1989 .... 3.50
- ❑11, May 1989 .... 3.00
- ❑12, ca. 1989 .... 3.00
- ❑13, ca. 1989 .... 3.00
- ❑14, ca. 1989 .... 3.00
- ❑15, ca. 1989 .... 3.00
- ❑16, b&w 2.50
- ❑17, b&w 2.50
- ❑18, b&w 2.50
- ❑19, b&w 2.50
- ❑20, b&w 2.50
- ❑21, b&w 2.50
- ❑22, b&w 2.50
- ❑23 .... 2.25
- ❑24, Apr 1991 .... 2.25
- ❑25, ca. 1991 .... 2.25
- ❑26, ca. 1991 .... 2.25
- ❑27, ca. 1991 .... 2.25
- ❑28, ca. 1991 .... 2.25
- ❑29 .... 2.25
- ❑30 .... 2.25
- ❑31, ca. 1992 .... 2.25
- ❑32, ca. 1992, b&w 2.50
- ❑33, May 1992, b&w 2.50
- ❑34, b&w 2.50
- ❑35, b&w 2.50

	N-MINT
❑36, b&w	2.50
❑37, b&w	2.50
❑38, b&w	2.50
❑39, ca. 1993, b&w	2.50
❑40, Jun 1994, b&w	2.75
❑40/Ltd., Jun 1994, b&w; gold foil logo edition (500 made)	3.00
❑41, Jul 1994, b&w	2.75
❑42, Sep 1994, b&w	2.75
❑43, Nov 1994, b&w	2.75
❑44, Jan 1995, b&w	2.75
❑45, Mar 1995, b&w	2.75
❑46, May 1995, b&w	2.75
❑47, Jul 1995, b&w	2.75
❑48, Sep 1995, b&w	2.75
❑49, Nov 1995, b&w	2.75
❑50, Jan 1996, b&w	3.95
❑51, Apr 1996, b&w	2.95
❑52, Jun 1996, b&w	2.95
❑53, Sep 1996, b&w	2.95
❑54, Nov 1996, b&w	2.95
❑55, Jan 1997, b&w	2.95
❑56, Mar 1997, b&w	2.95
❑57, May 1997, b&w	2.95
❑58, Aug 1997, b&w	2.95
❑59, Oct 1997, b&w	2.95
❑60, Dec 1997, b&w	2.95
❑61, Feb 1998, b&w	2.95
❑62, Apr 1998, b&w	2.95
❑63, Jun 1998, b&w	2.95
❑64, Aug 1998, b&w	2.95
❑65, Oct 1998, b&w	2.95
❑66, Dec 1998, b&w	2.95
❑67, Mar 1999, b&w	2.95
❑68, Apr 1999, b&w	2.95
❑69, Jun 1999, b&w	2.95
❑70 1999	2.95
❑71 1999	2.95
❑72 1999	2.95
❑73 2000	2.95
❑74 2000	2.95
❑75 2000	2.95
❑76 2000	2.95
❑77 2000	2.95
❑78 2000	2.95
❑79 2000	2.95
❑80 2001	2.95
❑81 2001	2.95
❑82 2001	2.95
❑83 2001	2.95
❑84 2001	2.95
❑85 2001	2.95
❑86 2001	2.95
❑87 2001	2.95
❑88 2001	2.95
❑89 2001	2.95
❑90 2001	2.95
❑91 2002	2.95
❑92 2002	2.95
❑93 2002	2.95
❑94 2002	2.95
❑95 2002	2.95
❑96 2002	2.95
❑97 2002	2.95
❑98 2002	2.95
❑99 2002	2.95
❑100 2002	4.95
❑101 2002	3.50
❑102 2003	3.50
❑103 2003	3.50
❑104 2003	3.50
❑105 2003	3.50
❑106, Jun 2003	3.50
❑107, Jul 2003	3.50
❑108, Aug 2003	3.50
❑109, Sep 2003	3.50
❑110, Oct 2003	3.50
❑111, Dec 2003	3.50
❑112, Jan 2004	3.50
❑113, Feb 2004	3.50
❑114, Mar 2004	3.50
❑115, Apr 2004	3.50
❑116, May 2004	2.99
❑Yearbook 1, b&w	6.00
❑Yearbook 2, b&w; 1990 Yearbook	4.95
❑Yearbook 3, b&w; 1991 Yearbook	4.95
❑Yearbook 4; 1992 Yearbook	4.95
❑Yearbook 5, Oct 1993, b&w; 1993 Yearbook	3.95
❑Yearbook 6, Oct 1994, b&w; 1994 Yearbook	3.95
❑Yearbook 7, Oct 1995, b&w; 1995 Yearbook; cover says Oct 94, indicia says Oct 95	3.95
❑Yearbook 8, Oct 1996, b&w; 1996 Yearbook	3.95
❑Yearbook 9/A, Oct 1997, b&w; 1997 Yearbook	3.95
❑Yearbook 9/B, Oct 1997, b&w; 1997 Yearbook; alternate cover; Star Trek	3.95
❑Yearbook 10/A, Oct 1998, b&w; 1998 Yearbook	2.95
❑Yearbook 10/B, Oct 1998, b&w; 1998 Yearbook; "Titanic" themed cover	2.95
❑Summer 1, Jun 1999; Comic-sized; Summer Special (1999)	2.99
❑3D 1, Jul 1992; Trade Paperback	4.50

NINJA HIGH SCHOOL FEATURING SPEED RACER
ETERNITY / NOW

	N-MINT
❑1, Sep 1993	2.95
❑2, Dec 1993	2.95

NINJA HIGH SCHOOL IN COLOR
ETERNITY

	N-MINT
❑1, Jul 1992	2.50
❑2	2.50
❑3	2.50
❑4	2.00
❑5	2.00
❑6	2.00
❑7	2.00
❑8, ca. 1993,	2.00
❑9	2.00
❑10	2.00
❑11	2.00
❑12	2.00
❑13	2.00

NINJA HIGH SCHOOL PERFECT MEMORY
ANTARCTIC

	N-MINT
❑1, b&w; sourcebook for series	5.00
❑1-2, Jun 1996	5.95
❑2, Nov 1993; 1996 version	5.95
❑2/Platinum, Nov 1993; platinum	5.00

NINJA HIGH SCHOOL SPOTLIGHT
ANTARCTIC

	N-MINT
❑1; Indicia says #29	3.50
❑2, Oct 1996	2.95
❑3, Dec 1996	3.50
❑4, May 1999; Indicia says #1	2.99

NINJA HIGH SCHOOL SWIMSUIT SPECIAL
ANTARCTIC

	N-MINT
❑1, Dec 1992; Gold edition; JDu, JSt, KJ (a); two different covers	4.00
❑2, Dec 1993; 1998 Yearbook; Annual	3.95
❑3, Dec 1994; Trade Paperback; Annual	3.95
❑4; Gold edition	3.95
❑1996, Dec 1996, b&w; Platinum edition; No cover price; pinups	3.95

NINJA HIGH SCHOOL TALKS ABOUT COMIC BOOK PRINTING
ANTARCTIC

	N-MINT
❑1, color; giveaway	1.00

NINJA HIGH SCHOOL TALKS ABOUT SEXUALLY TRANSMITTED DISEASES
ANTARCTIC

	N-MINT
❑1, color; giveaway	2.00

NINJA HIGH SCHOOL: THE PROM FORMULA
ETERNITY

	N-MINT
❑1, color	2.95
❑2, color	2.95

NINJA HIGH SCHOOL: THE SPECIAL EDITION
ETERNITY

	N-MINT
❑1, b&w	2.50
❑2, b&w	2.50
❑3, b&w	2.50
❑4	2.50

NINJA HIGH SCHOOL VERSION 2
ANTARCTIC

	N-MINT
❑1, Jul 1999	2.50
❑2, Aug 1999	2.50

NINJAK
VALIANT

	N-MINT
❑0, Jun 1995	2.50
❑0/A, Jun 1995; #00; cover forms diptych image with #0	2.50
❑1, Feb 1994; chromium cover	3.50
❑1/Gold, Feb 1994; Gold edition; wraparound chromium cover	3.50
❑2, Mar 1994	2.25
❑3, Apr 1994	2.25
❑4, May 1994; trading card	2.25
❑5, Jun 1994	2.25
❑6, Aug 1994	2.25
❑7, Sep 1994	2.25
❑8, Oct 1994; Chaos Effect	2.25
❑9, Nov 1994; new uniform	2.25
❑10, Dec 1994	2.25
❑11, Jan 1995	2.25
❑12, Feb 1995; trading card	2.25
❑13, Mar 1995; trading card	2.25
❑14, Apr 1995	2.25
❑15, May 1995	2.50
❑16, Jun 1995	2.50
❑17, Jul 1995	2.50
❑18, Jul 1995; Birthquake	2.50
❑19, Aug 1995	2.50
❑20, Aug 1995	2.50
❑21, Sep 1995	2.50
❑22, Sep 1995	2.50
❑23, Oct 1995	2.50
❑24, Oct 1995	2.50
❑25, Nov 1995	2.50
❑26, Nov 1995	2.50
❑Yearbook 1; cardstock cover	3.95

NINJAK (VOL. 2)
ACCLAIM / VALIANT

	N-MINT
❑1, Mar 1997 KB (w); O: Ninjak. 1: Ninjak II.	2.50
❑1/Variant, Mar 1997; KB (w); O: Ninjak. 1: Ninjak II. alternate painted cover	2.50
❑2, Apr 1997 KB (w)	2.50
❑3, May 1997 KB (w)	2.50
❑4, Jun 1997; KB (w); A: Colin King. real origin of Ninjak	2.50
❑5, Jul 1997 KB (w)	2.50
❑6, Aug 1997 KB (w); A: X-O Manowar.	2.50
❑7, Sep 1997 KB (w); A: X-O Manowar.	2.50
❑8, Oct 1997 KB (w); A: Colin King.	2.50
❑9, Nov 1997 KB (w)	2.50
❑10, Dec 1997 KB (w)	2.50
❑11, Jan 1998 KB (w)	2.50
❑12, Feb 1998 KB (w)	2.50
❑Ashcan 1, Nov 1996, b&w; No cover price; preview of upcoming series	1.00

NINJUTSU, ART OF THE NINJA
SOLSON

	N-MINT
❑1, b&w	2.00

NINTENDO COMICS SYSTEM
VALIANT

	N-MINT
❑1	4.95
❑2	4.95

N-MINT

NINTENDO COMICS SYSTEM (2ND SERIES)
VALIANT

❑1; Game Boy 2.00
❑2; Game Boy 2.00
❑3; Game Boy 2.00
❑4; Game Boy 2.00
❑5; Game Boy 2.00
❑6; Game Boy 2.00
❑7; Zelda 2.00
❑8; Super Mario Bros. 2.00
❑9; Super Mario Bros. 2.00

N.I.O.
ACCLAIM / VERTIGO

❑1, Nov 1998 2.50

NIRA X: ANIME
ENTITY

❑0, Jan 1997 2.75

NIRA X: ANNUAL
EXPRESS / ENTITY

❑1/A, Sep 1996, b&w; Snowman 1944 preview 2.75
❑1/B, Sep 1996, b&w; Snowman 1944 preview 9.95

NIRA X: CYBERANGEL (MINI-SERIES)
EXPRESS / ENTITY

❑1, Dec 1994; cardstock cover 3.00
❑2, Feb 1995 2.50
❑3, Apr 1995 2.50
❑4, Jun 1995 2.50
❑Ashcan 1, Sum 1994, b&w; no cover price 1.00

NIRA X: CYBERANGEL
EXPRESS / ENTITY

❑1, May 1996; 1: Delta-Void. 1: Millennia. 1: Paradoxx. 1: Quid. Gold foil logo 2.75
❑1/Ltd., May 1996; Limited commemorative edition; 1: Delta-Void. 1: Millennia. 1: Paradoxx. 1: Quid. 3000 printed 4.00
❑2, Jun 1996, b&w 1: Talon. 1: Vex. 1: Cyberhood. 1: Solace. 2.50
❑3, Jul 1996, b&w 2.50
❑4, Aug 1996, b&w 2.50

NIRA X: CYBERANGEL (3RD SERIES)
EXPRESS / ENTITY

❑1 2.50

NIRA X: CYBERANGEL - CYNDER: ENDANGERED SPECIES
EXPRESS / ENTITY

❑1 2.95
❑1/Ltd.; Commemorative edition; limited to 1500 copies; cardstock cover 12.95

NIRA X: EXODUS
AVATAR / ENTITY

❑1, Oct 1997 3.00

NIRA X: HEATWAVE
EXPRESS / ENTITY

❑1, Jul 1995; enhanced wraparound cover 3.75
❑2, Aug 1995 2.50
❑3, Sep 1995 2.50

NIRA X: SOUL SKURGE
EXPRESS / ENTITY

❑1, Nov 1996, b&w 2.75

NOBLE ARMOUR HALBERDER (JOHN AND JASON WALTRIP'S...)
ACADEMY

❑1, Jan 1997 2.95

NOBLE CAUSES: EXTENDED FAMILY ONE SHOT
IMAGE

❑1, Jun 2003 6.95

NOBLE CAUSES
IMAGE

❑1/A 2002 2.95
❑1/B 2002 2.95
❑2/A, Mar 2002 2.95
❑2/B, Mar 2002 2.95
❑3/A 2002 2.95
❑3/B 2002 2.95
❑4/A, May 2002 2.95
❑4/B, May 2002 2.95

NOBLE CAUSES: DISTANT RELATIVES
IMAGE

❑1, Aug 2003 2.95
❑2, Oct 2003 2.95
❑3, Oct 2003 2.95
❑4, Dec 2003 2.95

NOBLE CAUSES: FAMILY SECRETS
IMAGE

❑1, Oct 2002 2.95
❑2/A, Dec 2002 2.95
❑2/B, Dec 2002 2.95
❑3/A 2003 2.95
❑3/B 2003 2.95
❑4/A 2003 2.95
❑4/B 2003 2.95

NOBLE CAUSES: FIRST IMPRESSIONS
IMAGE

❑1, Sep 2001 2.95

NOBODY
ONI

❑1, Nov 1998 3.00
❑2, Dec 1998 3.00
❑3, Jan 1999 3.00
❑4, Feb 1999 3.00

NO BUSINESS LIKE SHOW BUSINESS
3-D ZONE

❑1, b&w; not 3-D 2.50

NOCTURNAL EMISSIONS
VORTEX

❑1, b&w 2.50

NOCTURNALS, THE
MALIBU / BRAVURA

❑1, Jan 1995 1: The Nocturnals. 3.50
❑2, Feb 1995 3.00
❑3, Apr 1995 3.00
❑4, Apr 1995 3.00
❑5, Jun 1995 3.00
❑6, Aug 1995 3.00

NOCTURNALS: TROLL BRIDGE
ONI

❑1, Oct 2000; b&w and orange 4.95

NOCTURNALS, THE: WITCHING HOUR
DARK HORSE

❑1, May 1998 4.95

NOCTURNE (AIRCEL)
AIRCEL

❑1, Jun 1991, b&w 2.50
❑2, Jul 1991, b&w 2.50
❑3, Aug 1991, b&w 2.50

NOCTURNE (MARVEL)
MARVEL

❑1, Jun 1995 1.50
❑2, Jul 1995; indicia says Sep 95 1.50
❑3, Aug 1995 1.50
❑4, Sep 1995 1.50

NODWICK
HENCHMAN

❑1, Feb 2000, b&w 2.95
❑2, Mar 2000, b&w 2.95
❑3 2000, b&w 2.95
❑4, Aug 2000, b&w 2.95
❑5, Oct 2000, b&w 2.95
❑6, Dec 2000, b&w 2.95
❑7, Feb 2001, b&w 2.95
❑8, Apr 2001, b&w; Action Comics #1 cover spoof 2.95
❑9, Jun 2001, b&w 2.95
❑10, Aug 2001, b&w 2.95
❑11, Oct 2001, b&w 2.95
❑12, Dec 2001, b&w 2.99
❑13, Feb 2002, b&w 2.99
❑14, Apr 2002, b&w 2.99

In an attempt to expose corruption within the Bludhaven Police Department, Dick Grayson joined the force and attended the police academy in *Nightwing* #31.

© 1999 DC Comics.

N-MINT

❑15, Jun 2002, b&w 2.99
❑16, Jul 2002, b&w 2.99
❑17, Sep 2002, b&w 2.99
❑18, Nov 2002, b&w 2.99
❑19, Jan 2003, b&w 2.99

NO ESCAPE
MARVEL

❑1, Jun 1994 1.50
❑2, Jul 1994 1.50
❑3, Aug 1994 1.50

NOG THE PROTECTOR OF THE PYRAMIDES
ONLI

❑1 2.00

NO GUTS OR GLORY
FANTACO

❑1, ca. 1991, b&w 2.95

NO HONOR
IMAGE

❑1, Feb 2001 2.50
❑2, Mar 2001 2.50
❑3, Apr 2001 2.50
❑4, May 2002 2.50

NO HOPE
SLAVE LABOR

❑1, Apr 1993 2.95
❑1-2, Feb 1995 2.95
❑2, Aug 1993 2.95
❑2-2, Apr 1994 2.95
❑3, Nov 1993 2.95
❑3-2, Apr 1994 2.95
❑4, Feb 1994 2.95
❑4-2, Oct 1994 2.95
❑5, Jun 1994 2.95
❑6, Sep 1994 2.95
❑7, Jan 1995 2.95
❑8, Apr 1995 2.95
❑9, Jul 1995 2.95

NOID IN 3-D, THE
BLACKTHORNE

❑1 2.50
❑2 2.50

NO ILLUSIONS
COMICS DEFENCE FUND

❑1; Benefit for Comics Defence Fund (UK) 1.00

NOIR (ALPHA)
ALPHA

❑1, Win 1994; text & comics 3.95

NOIR (CREATIVE FORCE)
CREATIVE FORCE

❑1, Apr 1995 4.95

NO JUSTICE, NO PIECE!
HEAD

❑1, Oct 1997, b&w; benefit anthology for CBLDF 2.95
❑2, Jul 1998, b&w; benefit anthology for CBLDF 2.95

NOLAN RYAN
CELEBRITY

❑1 2.95

NOLAN RYAN'S 7 NO-HITTERS
REVOLUTIONARY

❑1, Aug 1993, b&w 2.95

N-MINT

NOMAD (LTD. SERIES)
Marvel

❑1, Nov 1990 .... 2.00
❑2, Dec 1990 O: Nomad. 2.00
❑3, Mar 1991 .... 2.00
❑4, Feb 1991 .... 2.00

NOMAD
Marvel

❑1, May 1992; gatefold cover 2.50
❑2, Jun 1992 .... 1.75
❑3, Jul 1992; Nomad vs. U.S.Agent .. 1.75
❑4, Aug 1992 .... 1.75
❑5, Sep 1992 .... 1.75
❑6, Oct 1992 .... 1.75
❑7, Nov 1992; Infinity War 1.75
❑8, Dec 1992; L.A riots 1.75
❑9, Jan 1993 .... 1.75
❑10, Feb 1993 A: Red Wolf. 1.75
❑11, Mar 1993 .... 1.75
❑12, Apr 1993 A: Hate-Monger. 1.75
❑13, May 1993 A: Hate-Monger. 1.75
❑14, Jun 1993 A: Hate-Monger. 1.75
❑15, Jul 1993 A: Hate-Monger. 1.75
❑16, Aug 1993 A: Gambit. 1.75
❑17, Sep 1993 .... 1.75
❑18, Oct 1993 A: Dr. Faustus. 1.75
❑19, Nov 1993 .... 1.75
❑20, Dec 1993 .... 1.75
❑21, Jan 1994 A: Man-Thing. 1.75
❑22, Feb 1994 .... 1.75
❑23, Mar 1994 .... 1.75
❑24, Apr 1994 .... 1.75
❑25, May 1994 .... 1.75

NOMAN
Tower

❑1, Nov 1966 WW (c); WW (a) 40.00
❑2, Mar 1967 WW (c); WW (a) 28.00

NON
Red Ink

❑1 .... 3.00
❑2 .... 3.00
❑3 .... 3.00

NO NEED FOR TENCHI! PART 1
Viz

❑1 .... 3.00
❑2 .... 3.00
❑3 .... 3.00
❑4 .... 3.00
❑5 .... 3.00
❑6 .... 3.00
❑7 .... 3.00

NO NEED FOR TENCHI! PART 2
Viz

❑1 .... 3.00
❑2 .... 3.00
❑3 .... 3.00
❑4 .... 3.00
❑5 .... 3.00
❑6 .... 3.00
❑7 .... 3.00

NO NEED FOR TENCHI! PART 3
Viz

❑1, Jun 1996 .... 2.95
❑2, Jul 1996 .... 2.95
❑3, Aug 1996 .... 2.95
❑4, Sep 1996 .... 2.95
❑5, Oct 1996 .... 2.95
❑6, Nov 1996 .... 2.95

NO NEED FOR TENCHI! PART 4
Viz

❑1, Dec 1997 .... 2.95
❑2, Jan 1998 .... 2.95
❑3, Feb 1998 .... 2.95
❑4, Mar 1998 .... 2.95
❑5, Apr 1998 .... 2.95
❑6, May 1998 .... 2.95

N-MINT

NO NEED FOR TENCHI! PART 5
Viz

❑1, Jun 1998 .... 3.25
❑2, Jul 1998 .... 2.95
❑3, Aug 1998 .... 2.95
❑4, Sep 1998 .... 2.95
❑5, Oct 1998 .... 2.95

NO NEED FOR TENCHI! PART 6
Viz

❑1, Nov 1998 .... 3.25
❑2, Dec 1998 .... 2.95
❑3, Jan 1999 .... 3.25
❑4, Feb 1999 .... 3.25
❑5, Mar 1999 .... 3.25

NO NEED FOR TENCHI! PART 7
Viz

❑1, Apr 1999 .... 2.95
❑2, May 1999 .... 2.95
❑3, Jun 1999 .... 2.95
❑4, Jul 1999 .... 2.95
❑5, Aug 1999 .... 2.95
❑6, Sep 1999 .... 2.95

NO NEED FOR TENCHI! PART 8
Viz

❑1, Oct 1999 .... 3.25
❑2 .... 3.25
❑3 .... 3.25
❑4 .... 3.25
❑5 .... 3.25

NO NEED FOR TENCHI! PART 9
Viz

❑1, Mar 2000 .... 2.95
❑2, Apr 2000 .... 2.95
❑3, May 2000 .... 2.95
❑4, Jun 2000 .... 2.95
❑5, Jul 2000 .... 2.95
❑6, Aug 2000 .... 2.95

NO NEED FOR TENCHI! PART 10
Viz

❑1 .... 2.95
❑2 .... 2.95
❑3 .... 2.95
❑4 .... 2.95
❑5 2001 .... 2.95
❑6 2001 .... 2.95
❑7 2001 .... 2.95

NO NEED FOR TENCHI! PART 11
Viz

❑1 2001 .... 3.50
❑2 2001 .... 3.50
❑3 2001 .... 3.50
❑4 2001 .... 3.50

NO NEED FOR TENCHI! PART 12
Viz

❑1 2001 .... 2.95
❑2 2001 .... 2.95
❑3 2001 .... 2.95
❑4 .... 2.95
❑5 .... 2.95
❑6 2002 .... 2.95

NO NINJA MAN
Custom Pic

❑1 .... 1.50
❑1-2 .... 1.50

NO NO UFO
Antarctic / Venus

❑1, Aug 1996 .... 2.95
❑2, May 1997, b&w 2.95
❑3, Sep 1997, b&w 2.95
❑4, May 1998, b&w 2.95

NO PASARAN!
NBM

❑1 .... 13.95
❑2 .... 11.95

NO PROFIT FOR THE WISE
CFD

❑1, Jul 1996, b&w 2.95

N-MINT

NORB
Mu

❑1, Jan 1992 .... 8.95

NORMALMAN
Aardvark-Vanaheim

❑1, Jan 1984; Aardvark-Vanaheim publishes 2.50
❑2, Apr 1984 O: Normalman. 2.00
❑3, Jun 1984 .... 2.00
❑4, Aug 1984 .... 2.00
❑5, Oct 1984 .... 2.00
❑6, Dec 1984 .... 2.00
❑7, Feb 1985 .... 2.00
❑8, Apr 1985 .... 2.00
❑9, Jun 1985; Renegade begins as publisher 2.00
❑10, Aug 1985, color 2.00
❑11, Oct 1985, color 2.00
❑12, Dec 1985, color 2.00
❑3D 1; Double-size 2.50

NORMALMAN 3-D
Renegade

❑1, Feb 1986 .... 2.25

NORMALMAN-MEGATON MAN SPECIAL
Image

❑1, Aug 1994 .... 2.50

NORTHERN'S HEMISPHERE
Northern's Hemisphere

❑5, b&w 2.49
❑6, b&w 2.49
❑7, b&w 2.49

NORTHERN'S HEMISPHERE UNDISGUISED
Northern's Hemisphere

❑1 .... 2.50

NORTHGUARD: THE MANDES CONCLUSION
Caliber

❑1, Sep 1989, b&w 1.95
❑2, Oct 1989, b&w 1.95
❑3, Nov 1989, b&w 1.95

NORTHSTAR
Marvel

❑1, Apr 1994 .... 2.00
❑2, May 1994 .... 2.00
❑3, Jun 1994 .... 2.00
❑4, Jul 1994 .... 2.00

NORTHSTAR PRESENTS
Northstar

❑1, Oct 1994 .... 2.50
❑2 .... 2.50

NORTHWEST CARTOON COOKERY
Starhead

❑1, ca. 1995, b&w; recipes from Pacific Northwest cartoonists 2.75

NOSFERATU (DARK HORSE)
Dark Horse

❑1, Mar 1991, b&w 3.95

NOSFERATU (CALIBER)
Tome

❑1, Jul 1991, b&w 2.75
❑2, Jul 1991, b&w 2.75

NOSFERATU, PLAGUE OF TERROR
Millennium

❑1, b&w; duotone 2.50
❑2, b&w; duotone 2.50
❑3, b&w; duotone 2.50
❑4, b&w; duotone 2.50

NOSFERATU: THE DEATH MASS
Antarctic / Venus

❑1, Dec 1997, b&w 2.95
❑2, Jan 1998, b&w 2.95
❑3, Feb 1998, b&w 2.95
❑4, Mar 1998, b&w 2.95

N-MINT

NOSTRADAMUS CHRONICLES, THE: 1559-1821
TOME / VENUS

❑1 .... 2.95

NOT APPROVED CRIME
AVALON

❑1 .... 2.95

NOT BRAND ECHH
MARVEL

❑1, Aug 1967; SL (w); BEv, JK, JSe, RA (a); 1: Forbush Man (on cover). 39.00
❑2, Sep 1967 .... 18.00
❑3, Oct 1967 O: Charlie America. O: Sore. O: Bulk. 15.00
❑4, Nov 1967 .... 15.00
❑5, Dec 1967 GC (a); O: Forbush Man. 1: Forbush Man (full appearance). . 15.00
❑6, Feb 1968 .... 9.00
❑7, Apr 1968 O: Stupor-Man. O: Fantastical Four. 9.00
❑8, Jun 1968 .... 9.00
❑9, Aug 1968; Giant-size 19.00
❑10, Oct 1968; Giant-size 19.00
❑11, Dec 1968; Giant-size 19.00
❑12, Feb 1969; Giant-size 19.00
❑13, Apr 1969; Giant-size 19.00

(NOT ONLY) THE BEST OF WONDER WART-HOG
PRINT MINT

❑1 .... 15.00
❑2 .... 12.00
❑3 .... 12.00

NOT QUITE DEAD
RIP OFF

❑1, Mar 1993, b&w 2.95
❑1-2 .... 2.95
❑2, b&w 2.95
❑3 .... 2.95
❑4 .... 2.95

NOVA (1ST SERIES)
MARVEL

❑1, Sep 1976 JB, JSt (a); O: Nova I (Richard Ryder). 1: Nova I (Richard Ryder). 6.00
❑2, Oct 1976 JB, JSt (a); 1: Powerhouse. 4.00
❑3, Nov 1976 1: Diamondhead. 3.00
❑4, Dec 1976 .... 3.00
❑5, Jan 1977 .... 3.00
❑6, Feb 1977 1: The Sphinx. 3.00
❑7, Mar 1977 O: The Sphinx. 3.00
❑8, Apr 1977 .... 3.00
❑9, May 1977 .... 3.00
❑10, Jun 1977 .... 3.00
❑10/35 cent, Jun 1977; 35 cent regional variant 15.00
❑11, Jul 1977 .... 3.00
❑11/35 cent, Jul 1977; 35 cent regional variant 15.00
❑12, Aug 1977 A: Spider-Man. 3.00
❑12/35 cent, Aug 1977; 35 cent regional variant 15.00
❑13, Sep 1977 1: Crimebuster. 3.00
❑13/35 cent, Sep 1977; 35 cent regional variant 15.00
❑14, Oct 1977 .... 3.00
❑14/35 cent, Oct 1977; 35 cent regional variant 15.00
❑15, Nov 1977 .... 3.00
❑16, Dec 1977 V: Yellow Claw. 3.00
❑17, Jan 1978 .... 3.00
❑18, Mar 1978 .... 3.00
❑19, May 1978 O: Blackout I (Marcus Daniels). 1: Blackout I (Marcus Daniels). 3.00
❑20, Jul 1978 .... 3.00
❑21, Sep 1978; 1: Harris Moore (Comet). Only appears as Harris Moore 3.00
❑22, Nov 1978 O: Comet (Harris Moore). 1: Comet (Harris Moore). . 3.00
❑23, Jan 1979 .... 3.00

N-MINT

❑24, Mar 1979 O: Crimebuster. 3.00
❑25, May 1979 .... 3.00

NOVA (2ND SERIES)
MARVEL

❑1, Jan 1994 .... 2.25
❑1/Variant, Jan 1994; Special cover .. 2.95
❑2, Feb 1994 .... 2.00
❑3, Mar 1994 A: Spider-Man. 1.75
❑4, Apr 1994 .... 1.75
❑5, May 1994 .... 1.75
❑6, Jun 1994 .... 1.95
❑7, Jul 1994 .... 1.95
❑8, Aug 1994 .... 1.95
❑9, Sep 1994 .... 1.95
❑10, Oct 1994 .... 1.95
❑11, Nov 1994 V: new Fantastic Four. 1.95
❑12, Dec 1994 .... 1.95
❑13, Jan 1995 .... 1.95
❑14, Feb 1995 .... 1.95
❑15, Mar 1995 .... 1.95
❑16, Apr 1995 .... 1.95
❑17, May 1995 .... 1.95
❑18, Jun 1995 .... 1.95

NOVA (3RD SERIES)
MARVEL

❑1, May 1999; wraparound cover 2.99
❑2, Jun 1999 .... 1.99
❑3, Jul 1999 .... 1.99
❑4, Aug 1999 .... 1.99
❑5, Sep 1999 .... 1.99
❑6, Oct 1999 .... 1.99
❑7, Nov 1999 .... 1.99

NOVA HUNTER
RYAL

❑1 .... 2.50
❑1/Autographed; Autographed limited edition 4.00

NOW COMICS PREVIEW
NOW

❑1 1: Thunderstar. 1: Valor. 1: Vector. 1: Syphons. 1: Ralph Snart. 1.00

NOWHERESVILLE
CALIBER

❑1, ca. 1995, b&w 3.50

NOWHERESVILLE: DEATH BY STARLIGHT
CALIBER

❑1, b&w 2.95
❑2, b&w 2.95
❑3, b&w; flip book with Wordsmith #7 back-up 2.95
❑4 .... 2.95

NOWHERESVILLE: THE HISTORY OF COOL
CALIBER

❑1 .... 2.95

NOW, ON A MORE SERIOUS NOTE...
DAWN

❑1, Sum 1994, b&w; no cover price . 2.00

NOW WHAT?!
NOW

❑1 .... 3.00
❑2 .... 2.00
❑3 .... 2.00
❑4 .... 2.00
❑5 .... 2.00
❑6 .... 2.00
❑7 .... 2.00
❑8 .... 2.00
❑9 .... 2.00
❑10 .... 2.00
❑11 .... 2.00

NTH MAN, THE ULTIMATE NINJA
MARVEL

❑1, Aug 1989 .... 1.00
❑2, Sep 1989 .... 1.00
❑3, Oct 1989 .... 1.00
❑4, Nov 1989 .... 1.00
❑5, Nov 1989 .... 1.00

Ninjak's second series featured the adventures of a video-game playing teen-ager.

© 1997 Acclaim

N-MINT

❑6, Dec 1989 .... 1.00
❑7, Dec 1989 .... 1.00
❑8, Jan 1990 .... 1.00
❑9, Feb 1990 .... 1.00
❑10, Mar 1990 .... 1.00
❑11, Apr 1990 .... 1.00
❑12, May 1990 .... 1.00
❑13, Jun 1990 .... 1.00
❑14, Jul 1990 .... 1.00
❑15, Aug 1990 .... 1.00
❑16, Sep 1990 .... 1.00

NUANCE
MAGNETIC INK

❑1, b&w 2.75
❑2, b&w 2.75
❑3, b&w 2.75

NUCLEAR WAR!
NEC

❑1 .... 3.50
❑2, Nov 2000 .... 3.50

NULL PATROL
ESCAPE VELOCITY

❑1 .... 1.50
❑2 .... 1.50

NUMIDIAN FORCE
KAMITE

❑4 .... 2.00

NURSES, THE
GOLD KEY

❑1, Apr 1963 .... 50.00
❑2, Jul 1963 .... 40.00
❑3, Oct 1963 .... 30.00

NURTURE THE DEVIL
FANTAGRAPHICS

❑2, Jul 1994, b&w 2.50
❑3, Dec 1994, b&w 2.50

NUT RUNNERS
RIP OFF

❑1, Sep 1991, b&w 2.50
❑2, Jan 1992, b&w 2.50

NUTS & BOTS
EXCEL GRAPHICS

❑1, Aug 1998, b&w; magazine 3.95

NYC MECH
IMAGE

❑1, Apr 2004 .... 2.95
❑2, Aug 2004 .... 2.95

NYGHT SCHOOL
BRAINSTORM

❑2, b&w 2.95

NYX
MARVEL

❑1, Dec 2003 .... 4.00
❑2, Jan 2004 .... 4.00
❑3, Feb 2004 .... 15.00
❑4, Jul 2004 .... 2.99

N-MINT

O

OBERGEIST: RAGNAROK HIGHWAY
IMAGE
- ❑1, May 2001 ... 2.95
- ❑2, Jun 2001 ... 2.95
- ❑3, Jul 2001 ... 2.95
- ❑4, Aug 2001 ... 2.95
- ❑5, Sep 2001 ... 2.95
- ❑6, Oct 2001 ... 2.95

OBERGEIST: THE EMPTY LOCKET
DARK HORSE
- ❑1, Mar 2002, b&w ... 2.95

OBJECTIVE FIVE
IMAGE
- ❑1, Jul 2000 ... 2.95
- ❑2, Aug 2000 ... 2.95
- ❑3, Sep 2000 ... 2.95
- ❑4, Nov 2000 ... 2.95
- ❑5, Dec 2000 ... 2.95
- ❑6, Jan 2001 ... 2.95

OBLIVION
COMICO
- ❑1, Jan 1996 ... 2.50
- ❑2, Mar 1996 ... 2.50
- ❑3, May 1996 ... 2.50

OBLIVION CITY
SLAVE LABOR
- ❑1, Mar 1991, b&w ... 2.50
- ❑2, May 1991, b&w ... 2.50
- ❑3, Jun 1991, b&w ... 2.50
- ❑4, Jun 1991, b&w ... 2.50
- ❑5, Sep 1991, b&w ... 2.50
- ❑6, Jan 1992, b&w ... 2.50
- ❑7, Apr 1992 ... 2.95
- ❑8, May 1992 ... 2.95
- ❑9, Jun 1992 ... 3.95

OBNOXIO THE CLOWN
MARVEL
- ❑1, Apr 1983; X-Men ... 2.00

OCEAN COMICS
OCEAN
- ❑1, b&w ... 1.75

OCELOT, THE
FANTAGRAPHICS / EROS
- ❑1 ... 2.75
- ❑2 ... 2.75
- ❑3 ... 2.75

OCTOBER YEN
ANTARCTIC
- ❑1, Jul 1996, b&w ... 3.50
- ❑2, Sep 1996, b&w ... 2.95
- ❑3, Nov 1996, b&w ... 2.95

OCTOBRIANA
REVOLUTION
- ❑1 ... 3.50
- ❑2 ... 2.95
- ❑3 ... 2.95
- ❑4 ... 2.95
- ❑5 ... 2.95

OCTOBRIANA: FILLING IN THE BLANKS
ARTFUL SALAMANDER
- ❑1, Win 1998, b&w ... 2.95

ODD ADVENTURE-ZINE, THE
ZAMBONI
- ❑1, Jan 1997 ... 2.95
- ❑2, Apr 1997 ... 2.95
- ❑3, Jul 1997 ... 2.95
- ❑4, Dec 1997 ... 2.95

ODDBALLZ
NBM
- ❑1 2002 ... 2.95
- ❑2 2002 ... 2.95
- ❑3 ... 2.95
- ❑4 ... 2.95

N-MINT

ODDJOB
SLAVE LABOR
- ❑1, Spr 1999, b&w ... 2.95

OEMING SKETCHBOOK
MICHAEL AVON OEMING
- ❑1 ... 5.00

OFFCASTES
MARVEL / EPIC
- ❑1; Embossed cover ... 2.50
- ❑2 ... 1.95
- ❑3 ... 1.95

OFFERINGS
CRY FOR DAWN
- ❑1, b&w ... 2.75
- ❑2, b&w ... 2.50

OFFICIAL, AUTHORIZED ZEN INTERGALACTIC NINJA SOURCEBOOK
EXPRESS / ENTITY
- ❑1, b&w ... 3.50
- ❑1-2; 94 revised edition ... 3.50

OFFICIAL BUZ SAWYER
PIONEER
- ❑1, Aug 1988, b&w ... 2.00
- ❑2, Sep 1988, b&w ... 2.00
- ❑3, Oct 1988, b&w ... 2.00
- ❑4, Nov 1988, b&w ... 2.00
- ❑5, Dec 1988, b&w ... 2.00

OFFICIAL HANDBOOK OF THE CONAN UNIVERSE
MARVEL
- ❑1, color ... 1.50
- ❑2, color; no price; sold with Conan Saga #75 ... 1.00

OFFICIAL HANDBOOK OF THE MARVEL UNIVERSE (VOL. 1)
MARVEL
- ❑1, Jan 1983, color; Abomination to Avengers Quinjet ... 2.00
- ❑2, Feb 1983, color; Baron Mordo to The Collective Man ... 2.00
- ❑3, Mar 1983, color; The Collector to Dracula ... 2.00
- ❑4, Apr 1983, color; Dragon Man to Gypsy Moth ... 2.00
- ❑5, May 1983, color; Hangman to Juggernaut ... 2.00
- ❑6, Jun 1983, color; Kang to Man-Bull ... 2.00
- ❑7, Jul 1983, color; Mandarin to Mystique ... 2.00
- ❑8, Aug 1983, color; Namorita to Pyro ... 2.00
- ❑9, Sep 1983, color; Quasar to She-Hulk ... 2.00
- ❑10, Oct 1983, color; Shi'ar to Sub-Mariner ... 2.00
- ❑11, Nov 1983, color; Subterraneans to Ursa Major ... 2.00
- ❑12, Dec 1983, color; Valkyrie to Zzzax ... 2.00
- ❑13, Feb 1984, color; Book of the Dead: Air-Walker to Man-Wolf ... 2.00
- ❑14, Mar 1984, color; Book of the Dead: Marvel Boy to Zuras ... 2.00
- ❑15, May 1984, color; Weapons, Hardware, and Paraphernalia ... 2.00

OFFICIAL HANDBOOK OF THE MARVEL UNIVERSE (VOL. 2)
MARVEL
- ❑1, Dec 1985, color; Abomination to Batroc's Brigade ... 2.00
- ❑2, Jan 1986, color; Beast to Clea ... 2.00
- ❑3, Feb 1986, color; Cloak to Doctor Octopus ... 2.00
- ❑4, Mar 1986, color; Doctor Strange to Galactus ... 2.00
- ❑5, Apr 1986, color; Gardener to Hulk ... 2.00
- ❑6, May 1986, color; Human Torch to Ka-Zar ... 2.00
- ❑7, Jun 1986, color; Khoryphos to Magneto ... 2.00
- ❑8, Jul 1986, color; Magus to Mole Man ... 2.00
- ❑9, Aug 1986, color; Molecule Man to Owl ... 2.00

N-MINT

- ❑10, Sep 1986, color; Paladin to The Rhino ... 2.00
- ❑11, Oct 1986, color; Richard Rider to Sidewinder ... 2.00
- ❑12, Nov 1986, color; Sif to Sunspot ... 2.00
- ❑13, Dec 1986, color; Super-Adaptoid to Umar ... 2.00
- ❑14, Jan 1987, color; Unicorn to Wolverine ... 2.00
- ❑15, Mar 1987, color; Wonder Man to Zzzax and Alien Races ... 2.00
- ❑16, Jun 1987, color; Book of the Dead: Air-Walker to Death-Stalker ... 2.00
- ❑17, Aug 1987, color; Book of the Dead: Destiny to Hobgoblin ... 2.00
- ❑18, Oct 1987, color; Book of the Dead: Hyperion to Nighthawk; Book of the Dead: Hyperion II to Nighthawk II ... 2.00
- ❑19, Dec 1987, color; Book of the Dead: Nuke to Obadiah Stane ... 2.00
- ❑20, Feb 1988, color; Book of the Dead: Stick to Zuras ... 2.00

OFFICIAL HANDBOOK OF THE MARVEL UNIVERSE (VOL. 3)
MARVEL
- ❑1, Jul 1989, color; Adversary to Chameleon ... 2.00
- ❑2, Aug 1989, color; Champion of the Universe to Ecstasy ... 2.00
- ❑3, Sep 1989, color; Eon to Hulk ... 2.00
- ❑4, Oct 1989, color; Human Torch I to Manikin ... 2.00
- ❑5, Nov 1989, color; Marauders to Power Princess ... 2.00
- ❑6, Nov 1989, color; Prowler to Serpent Society ... 2.00
- ❑7, Dec 1989, color; Set to Tyrak ... 2.00
- ❑8, Dec 1989, color; U-Man to Madelyne Pryor ... 2.00

OFFICIAL HANDBOOK OF THE MARVEL UNIVERSE MASTER EDITION
MARVEL
- ❑1, Dec 1990, color; Three-hole punched looseleaf format ... 4.50
- ❑2, Jan 1991, color ... 4.50
- ❑3, Feb 1991, color ... 4.50
- ❑4, Mar 1991, color ... 4.50
- ❑5, Apr 1991, color ... 4.50
- ❑6, May 1991, color ... 3.95
- ❑7, Jun 1991, color ... 3.95
- ❑8, Jul 1991, color ... 3.95
- ❑9, Aug 1991, color ... 3.95
- ❑10, Sep 1991, color ... 3.95
- ❑11, Oct 1991, color ... 3.95
- ❑12, Nov 1991, color ... 3.95
- ❑13, Dec 1991, color ... 4.50
- ❑14, Jan 1992, color ... 4.50
- ❑15, Feb 1992, color ... 4.50
- ❑16, Mar 1992, color ... 4.50
- ❑17, Apr 1992, color ... 4.50
- ❑18, May 1992, color ... 4.50
- ❑19, Jun 1992, color ... 4.50
- ❑20, Jul 1992, color ... 4.50
- ❑21, Aug 1992, color ... 4.50
- ❑22, Sep 1992, color ... 4.50
- ❑23, Oct 1992, color ... 4.50
- ❑24, Nov 1992, color ... 4.50
- ❑25, Dec 1992, color ... 4.50
- ❑26, Jan 1993, color ... 4.50
- ❑27, Feb 1993, color ... 4.50
- ❑28, Mar 1993, color ... 4.95
- ❑29, Apr 1993, color ... 4.95
- ❑30, May 1993, color ... 4.95
- ❑31, Jun 1993, color ... 4.95
- ❑32, Jul 1993, color ... 4.95
- ❑33, Aug 1993, color ... 4.95
- ❑34, Sep 1993, color ... 4.95
- ❑35, Oct 1993, color ... 4.95
- ❑36, Nov 1993, color ... 4.95

N-MINT

OFFICIAL HANDBOOK OF THE MARVEL UNIVERSE: SPIDER-MAN 2004
MARVEL

❑1, ca 2004 3.99

OFFICIAL HANDBOOK OF THE MARVEL UNIVERSE: THE AVENGERS
MARVEL

❑1, ca 2004 3.99

OFFICIAL HANDBOOK OF THE MARVEL UNIVERSE: X-MEN 2004
MARVEL

❑1, ca 2004, color 3.99

OFFICIAL HAWKMAN INDEX, THE
ECLIPSE / INDEPENDENT

❑1, Nov 1986, color 2.00
❑2, Dec 1986, color 2.00

OFFICIAL HOW TO DRAW G.I. JOE
BLACKTHORNE

❑1, Nov 1987 2.00
❑2, Jan 1988 2.00
❑3, Mar 1988 2.00

OFFICIAL HOW TO DRAW ROBOTECH
BLACKTHORNE

❑1, Feb 1987 2.00
❑2, Mar 1987 2.00
❑3, Apr 1987 2.00
❑4, May 1987 2.00
❑5, Jun 1987 2.00
❑6, Jul 1987 2.00
❑7, Aug 1987 2.00
❑8, Sep 1987 2.00
❑9, Oct 1987 2.00
❑10, Nov 1987 2.00
❑11, Dec 1987 2.00
❑12, Jan 1988 2.00
❑13, Feb 1988 2.00
❑14, Mar 1988 2.00

OFFICIAL HOW TO DRAW TRANSFORMERS
BLACKTHORNE

❑1, Sep 1987 2.00
❑2, Nov 1987 2.00
❑3, Jan 1988 2.00
❑4, Mar 1988 2.00

OFFICIAL JOHNNY HAZARD
PIONEER

❑1, Aug 1988, b&w; strips 2.00

OFFICIAL JUNGLE JIM
PIONEER

❑1, Jun 1988, b&w 2.00
❑2, Jul 1988, b&w 2.00
❑3, Aug 1988, b&w 2.00
❑4, Sep 1988, b&w 2.00
❑5, Oct 1988, b&w 2.00
❑6, Nov 1988, b&w 2.00
❑7, Dec 1988, b&w 2.00
❑8, Jan 1989, b&w 2.00
❑9, Feb 1989, b&w 2.00
❑10, Apr 1989 2.50
❑11, Apr 1989 2.50
❑12 2.50
❑13 2.50
❑14 2.50
❑15 2.50
❑16 2.50
❑Annual 1, Jan 1989, b&w 3.95

OFFICIAL JUSTICE LEAGUE OF AMERICA INDEX
ICG

❑1 2.00
❑2 2.00
❑3 2.00
❑4 2.00
❑5 2.00
❑6 2.00
❑7 2.00
❑8; Title changes to Justice League of America Index 2.00

N-MINT

OFFICIAL MANDRAKE
PIONEER

❑1, Jun 1988, b&w 2.00
❑2, Jul 1988, b&w 2.00
❑3, Aug 1988, b&w 2.00
❑4, Sep 1988, b&w 2.00
❑5, Oct 1988, b&w 2.00
❑6, Nov 1988, b&w 2.00
❑7, Dec 1988, b&w 2.00
❑8, Jan 1989, b&w 2.00
❑9, Feb 1989, b&w 2.00
❑10, Apr 1989 2.50
❑11, Apr 1989 2.50
❑12 2.50
❑13 2.50
❑14 2.50
❑15 2.50

OFFICIAL MARVEL INDEX TO MARVEL TEAM-UP
MARVEL

❑1, Jan 1986 1.25
❑2, Feb 1986 1.25
❑3, May 1986 1.25
❑4, Jul 1986 1.25
❑5, Oct 1986 1.25
❑6, Jul 1987 1.25

OFFICIAL MARVEL INDEX TO THE AMAZING SPIDER-MAN
MARVEL

❑1, Apr 1985; Indexes Amazing Fantasy #15, Amazing Spider-Man #1-29 1.25
❑2, May 1985 1.25
❑3, Jun 1985; Indexes Amazing Spider-Man#59-84, King-Size Annual #5-6, Spectacular Spider-Man #1-2 1.25
❑4, Jul 1985; Indexes Amazing Spider-Man#85-112, King-Size Annual #7-8 1.25
❑5, Aug 1985; Indexes Amazing Spider-Man#114-137, King-Size Annual #9, Giant-Sized Super-Heroes #1 1.25
❑6, Sep 1985; Indexes Amazing Spider-Man #138-155, Giant-Size Spider-Man #1-6 1.25
❑7, Oct 1985; Indexes Amazing Spider-Man #156-174; Spider-Man Annual #10-11 1.25
❑8, Nov 1985; Indexes issues #175-195, Annual #12 1.25
❑9, Dec 1985; Indexes issues #196-215, Annual #13-14 1.25

OFFICIAL MARVEL INDEX TO THE AVENGERS
MARVEL

❑1, Jun 1987 2.95
❑2, Aug 1987 2.95
❑3, Oct 1987 2.95
❑4, Dec 1987 2.95
❑5, Apr 1988 2.95
❑6, Jun 1988 2.95
❑7, Aug 1988 2.95

OFFICIAL MARVEL INDEX TO THE AVENGERS, THE (VOL. 2)
MARVEL

❑1, Oct 1994 1.95
❑2, Nov 1994; Indexes issues #61-122 1.95
❑3, Dec 1994 1.95
❑4, Jan 1995; Indexes issues #177-230 1.95
❑5, Feb 1995 1.95
❑6, Mar 1995 1.95

OFFICIAL MARVEL INDEX TO THE FANTASTIC FOUR
MARVEL

❑1, Dec 1985; Indexes Fantastic Four #1-15 1.25
❑2, Jan 1986 1.25
❑3, Feb 1986 1.25
❑4, Mar 1986; Indexes Fantastic Four #46-65, Annual #4 1.25
❑5, Apr 1986; Indexes Fantastic Four #66-84, Annual #5-6 1.25

Detailed information on Marvel's characters can be found in its *Official Handbook of the Marvel Universe* series.

© 1983 Marvel

N-MINT

❑6, May 1986; Indexes issues #85-106, Annual #7-8 1.25
❑7, Jun 1986; Indexes issues #107-125, Annual #9 1.25
❑8, Jul 1986; Indexes issues #126-141, Annual #10, Giant-Size Super-Stars #1 1.25
❑9, Aug 1986 1.25
❑10, Sep 1986; Indexes issues #161-176, Annual #11, Giant-Size Fantastic Four #4-6 1.25
❑11, Oct 1986; Indexes issues #177-198 1.25
❑12, Jan 1987; Indexes issues #199-214, Annual # 12-13 1.25

OFFICIAL MARVEL INDEX TO THE X-MEN
MARVEL

❑1, May 1987; squarebound; cardstock cover 2.95
❑2, Jul 1987 2.95
❑3, Sep 1987 2.95
❑4, Nov 1987 2.95
❑5, Mar 1988 2.95
❑6, May 1988 2.95
❑7, Jul 1988 2.95

OFFICIAL MARVEL INDEX TO THE X-MEN (VOL. 2)
MARVEL

❑1, Apr 1994 1.95
❑2, May 1994 1.95
❑3, Jun 1994 1.95
❑4, Jul 1994 1.95
❑5, Aug 1994 1.95

OFFICIAL MODESTY BLAISE, THE
PIONEER

❑1, Jul 1988, b&w 2.00
❑2, Aug 1988, b&w 2.00
❑3, Sep 1988, b&w 2.00
❑4, Oct 1988, b&w 2.00
❑5, Nov 1988, b&w 2.00
❑6, Dec 1988, b&w 2.00
❑7, Dec 1988, b&w 2.00
❑8, Jan 1989, b&w 2.00
❑Annual 1, Dec 1988, b&w 4.95

OFFICIAL PRINCE VALIANT, THE
PIONEER

❑1, b&w 2.00
❑2, b&w 2.00
❑3, Aug 1988, b&w 2.00
❑4, Sep 1988, b&w 2.00
❑5, Oct 1988, b&w 2.00
❑6, Oct 1988, b&w 2.00
❑7, Nov 1988 2.00
❑8, Dec 1988 2.00
❑9, Jan 1989 2.00
❑10, Feb 1989 2.50
❑11, Mar 1989 2.50
❑12, Apr 1989 2.50
❑13 2.50
❑14 2.50
❑15 2.50
❑16 2.50
❑17 2.50
❑18 2.50
❑Annual 1, Win 1988, b&w 3.95
❑King Size 1, Apr 1989, b&w 3.95

Condition price index: Multiply "NM prices" above by: **0.83 for Very Fine/Near Mint**
0.66 for Very Fine • 0.33 for Fine • 0.2 for Very Good • 0.125 for Good

N-MINT

OFFICIAL PRINCE VALIANT MONTHLY
Pioneer

❑1, Jun 1989, b&w 3.95
❑2, Jun 1989 ..... 3.95
❑3, ca. 1989 ..... 4.95
❑4, ca. 1989 ..... 4.95
❑5, ca. 1989 ..... 6.95
❑6 ..... 6.95
❑7 ..... 6.95
❑8 ..... 6.95

OFFICIAL RIP KIRBY
Pioneer

❑1, Aug 1988, b&w 2.00
❑2, Sep 1988, b&w 2.00
❑3, Oct 1988, b&w 2.00
❑4, Nov 1988, b&w 2.00
❑5, Dec 1988, b&w 2.00
❑6, Jan 1989, b&w 2.00

OFFICIAL SECRET AGENT, THE
Pioneer

❑1, Jun 1988, b&w 2.00
❑2, Jul 1988, b&w 2.00
❑3, Aug 1988, b&w 2.00
❑4, Sep 1988, b&w 2.00
❑5, Oct 1988, b&w 2.00
❑6, Nov 1988, b&w 2.00
❑7, Dec 1988, b&w 2.00

OFFICIAL TEEN TITANS INDEX, THE
Independent / Eclipse

❑1, Aug 1985 ..... 1.50
❑2, Sep 1985; Indexes Teen Titans #23-53, DC Super-Stars #1, Showcase #75, The Hawk and the Dove #1-6 . ..... 1.50
❑3, Oct 1985; Indexes DC Comics Presents #26, New Teen Titans #1-25, Tales of the New Teen Titans #1-4, Marvel and DC Present #1 ..... 1.50
❑4, Nov 1985 ..... 1.50
❑5, Dec 1985 ..... 1.50

OFFWORLD
Graphic Image

❑1 ..... 3.95

OF MIND AND SOUL
Rage

❑1, b&w 2.25

OF MYTHS AND MEN
Blackthorne

❑1, b&w 1.75
❑2, Mar 1987, b&w 1.75

OGENKI CLINIC
Akita

❑1, Sep 1997 ..... 3.95
❑2, Oct 1997 ..... 3.95
❑3, Nov 1997 ..... 4.50
❑4, Dec 1997 ..... 4.50
❑5, Jan 1998 ..... 4.50
❑6, Feb 1998 ..... 4.50

OGENKI CLINIC (VOL. 2)
Akita

❑1, Mar 1998 ..... 3.95
❑2, Apr 1998 ..... 3.95
❑3, May 1998 ..... 3.95
❑4, Jun 1998 ..... 3.95
❑5, Jul 1998 ..... 3.95
❑6, Aug 1998 ..... 3.95

OGENKI CLINIC (VOL. 3)
Sexy Fruit

❑1, Sep 1998; Antonio Honduras translation 3.95
❑2, Oct 1998 ..... 3.95
❑3, Nov 1998 ..... 3.95
❑4, Dec 1998 ..... 3.95
❑5, Jan 1999 ..... 3.95
❑6, Feb 1999 ..... 3.95
❑7, Mar 1999 ..... 3.95

OGENKI CLINIC (VOL. 4)
Sexy Fruit

❑1, Apr 1999 ..... 2.95
❑2, May 1999 ..... 2.95
❑3, Jun 1999 ..... 2.95
❑4, Jul 1999 ..... 2.95
❑5, Aug 1999 ..... 2.95
❑6, Sep 1999 ..... 2.95

OGENKI CLINIC (VOL. 5)
Sexy Fruit

❑1, Oct 1999 ..... 2.95
❑2, Nov 1999 ..... 2.95
❑3, Dec 1999 ..... 2.95
❑4, Jan 2000 ..... 2.95
❑5, Feb 2000 ..... 2.95
❑6, Mar 2000 ..... 2.95
❑7, Apr 2000 ..... 2.95

OGENKI CLINIC (VOL. 6)
Sexy Fruit

❑1, May 2000 ..... 2.95
❑2, Jun 2000 ..... 2.95
❑3, Jul 2000 ..... 2.95
❑4, Aug 2000 ..... 2.95
❑5, Sep 2000 ..... 2.95
❑6, Oct 2000 ..... 2.95
❑7, Nov 2000 ..... 2.95

OGENKI CLINIC (VOL. 7)
Ironcat

❑1, Dec 2000 ..... 2.95
❑2, Jan 2001 ..... 2.95
❑3, Feb 2001 ..... 2.95
❑4, Mar 2001 ..... 2.95
❑5, Apr 2001 ..... 2.95
❑6, Jun 2001 ..... 2.95
❑7, Jul 2001 ..... 2.95

OGENKI CLINIC (VOL. 8)
Ironcat

❑1, Aug 2001 ..... 2.95
❑2, Sep 2001 ..... 2.95
❑3, Oct 2001 ..... 2.95
❑4, Nov 2001 ..... 2.95
❑5, Dec 2001 ..... 2.95
❑6, Jan 2002 ..... 2.95
❑7, Feb 2002 ..... 2.95
❑8, Mar 2002 ..... 2.95

OGENKI CLINIC (VOL. 9)
Ironcat

❑1, Apr 2002 ..... 2.95
❑2, May 2002 ..... 2.95
❑3, Jun 2002 ..... 2.95
❑4, Jul 2002 ..... 2.95
❑5, Aug 2002 ..... 2.95
❑6, Sep 2002 ..... 2.95
❑7, Oct 2002 ..... 2.95
❑8, Nov 2002 ..... 2.95

OGRE
Black Diamond

❑1, Jan 1994 ..... 2.95
❑2, Mar 1994 ..... 2.95
❑3, May 1994 ..... 2.95
❑4, Jul 1994 ..... 2.95

O.G. WHIZ
Gold Key

❑1, Feb 1971, color 25.00
❑2, May 1971, color 15.00
❑3, Aug 1971, color 10.00
❑4, Nov 1971, color 10.00
❑5, Feb 1972, color 10.00
❑6, May 1972, color; Final issue of original run (1972) 10.00
❑7, May 1978, color; Series begins again (1978) 3.00
❑8, Jul 1978, color 3.00
❑9, Sep 1978, color A: Tubby. 3.00
❑10, Nov 1978, color 3.00
❑11, Jan 1979, color 3.00

OH.
B Publications

❑1; Magazine sized 2.95
❑2; Magazine sized 2.95
❑3; Magazine sized 2.95
❑4; Magazine sized 2.95
❑5; Magazine sized 2.95
❑6; Magazine sized 2.95
❑7; Magazine sized 2.95
❑8; Immola and the Luna Legion 2.95
❑9 ..... 2.95
❑10 ..... 2.95
❑11, Oct 1995 ..... 2.95
❑12 ..... 2.95
❑13 ..... 2.95
❑14 ..... 2.95
❑15 ..... 2.95
❑16 ..... 2.95
❑17 ..... 2.95
❑18 ..... 2.95
❑19 ..... 2.95
❑20 ..... 2.95
❑21 ..... 2.95
❑22 ..... 2.95

OHM'S LAW
Imperial

❑1, color 2.25
❑2, b&w; Black and White 1.95
❑3, b&w; Published out of sequence; Black and white 1.95

OH MY GODDESS!
Dark Horse

❑1, Aug 1994 1: Otaki. 1: Belldandy. 1: Tamiya. 1: Keiichi Morisato. 5.00
❑2, Sep 1994 1: Urd. 3.00
❑3, Oct 1994 ..... 3.00
❑4, Nov 1994 ..... 3.00
❑5, Dec 1994 ..... 3.00
❑6, Jan 1995 ..... 3.00
❑88, Jul 2002; Numbering continued from combined Oh My Goddess! Part II-XI series 3.50
❑89, Aug 2002 ..... 3.50
❑90, Sep 2002 ..... 3.50
❑91, Oct 2002 ..... 3.50
❑92, Nov 2002 ..... 3.50
❑93, Dec 2002 ..... 3.50
❑94, Jan 2003 ..... 3.50
❑95, Feb 2003 ..... 3.50
❑96, Apr 2003 ..... 2.99
❑97, May 2003 ..... 2.99
❑98, Jun 2003, b&w 0.00
❑99, Jul 2003, b&w 0.00
❑100, Aug 2003, b&w 0.00
❑101, Sep 2003, b&w 0.00
❑102, Oct 2003, b&w 0.00
❑103, Nov 2003, b&w 0.00
❑104, Dec 2003, b&w 0.00
❑105, Feb 2004, b&w 0.00
❑106, Mar 2004 ..... 3.50
❑107, Apr 2004 ..... 2.99
❑108, May 2004 ..... 2.99
❑109, Aug 2004 ..... 2.99

OH MY GODDESS! PART II
Dark Horse

❑1, Feb 1995 1: Skuld. 3.00
❑2, Mar 1995 ..... 3.00
❑3, Apr 1995; A: Otaki. Oh My Cartoonist! follow-up story 2.75
❑4, May 1995 ..... 2.75
❑5, Jun 1995 ..... 2.75
❑6, Jul 1995 ..... 2.75
❑7, Aug 1995 ..... 3.00
❑8, Sep 1995; The Adventures of Mini-Urd story 3.00

OH MY GODDESS! PART III
Dark Horse / Manga

❑1, Nov 1995; Cover reads "Oh My Goddess Special" 3.00
❑2, Dec 1995; Cover reads "Oh My Goddess Special" 3.00
❑3, Jan 1996; Cover reads "Oh My Goddess Special" 3.00
❑4, Feb 1996; Cover reads "Oh My Goddess Special" 3.00
❑5, Mar 1996; Cover reads "Oh My Goddess Special" 3.00
❑6, Apr 1996; Cover reads "Oh My Goddess! 1 of 6" 3.00
❑7, May 1996; Cover reads "Oh My Goddess! 2 of 6" 3.00

N-MINT

❑8, Jun 1996; Cover reads "Oh My Goddess! 3 of 6" 3.00
❑9, Jul 1996; Cover reads "Oh My Goddess! 4 of 6" 3.00
❑10, Aug 1996; Cover reads "Oh My Goddess, part 5 of 6" 3.00
❑11, Sep 1996; Cover reads "Oh My Goddess! 6 of 6" 3.00

OH MY GODDESS! PART IV
DARK HORSE / MANGA

❑1, Dec 1996; Cover reads "Oh My Goddess Special" 2.95
❑2, Jan 1997; Cover reads " Oh My Goddess! 1 of 3" 2.95
❑3, Feb 1997; Cover reads " Oh My Goddess! 2 of 3" 2.95
❑4, Mar 1997; Cover reads " Oh My Goddess! 3 of 3" 2.95
❑5, Apr 1997; Cover reads " Oh My Goddess Special" 2.95
❑6, May 1997; Cover reads " Oh My Goddess! 1 of 3" 2.95
❑7, Jun 1997 .... 2.95
❑8, Jul 1997; Cover reads " Oh My Goddess! 3 of 3" 2.95

OH MY GODDESS! PART V
DARK HORSE / MANGA

❑1, Sep 1997; Cover reads " Oh My Goddess Special" 2.95
❑2, Oct 1997; Cover reads " Oh My Goddess Special" 2.95
❑3, Nov 1997; Cover reads " Oh My Goddess Special" 3.95
❑4, Dec 1997; Cover reads " Oh My Goddess Special" 3.95
❑5, Jan 1998; Mara. Cover reads " Oh My Goddess! 1 of 2" 2.95
❑6, Feb 1998; Cover reads " Oh My Goddess! 2 of 2; 3.95
❑7, Mar 1998; Cover reads " Oh My Goddess! 1 of 2" 3.95
❑8, Apr 1998; Cover reads " Oh My Goddess! 2 of 2" 2.95
❑9, May 1998 .... 3.50
❑10, Jun 1998; Cover reads " Oh My Goddess! One-Shot" 3.95
❑11, Jul 1998; Cover reads " Oh My Goddess! One-Shot" 3.95
❑12, Aug 1998; Cover reads " Oh My Goddess! One-Shot" 3.95

OH MY GODDESS! PART VI
DARK HORSE / MANGA

❑1, Oct 1998 .... 3.50
❑2, Dec 1998 .... 2.95
❑3, Jan 1999 .... 2.95
❑4, Feb 1999 .... 2.95
❑5, Mar 1999 .... 2.95
❑6, Apr 1999 .... 2.95

OH MY GODDESS! PART VII
DARK HORSE / MANGA

❑1, May 1999 .... 2.95
❑2, Jun 1999 .... 2.95
❑3, Jul 1999 .... 2.95
❑4, Aug 1999 .... 2.95
❑5, Sep 1999 .... 2.95
❑6, Oct 1999 .... 2.95
❑7, Nov 1999 .... 2.95
❑8, Dec 1999 .... 2.95

OH MY GODDESS! PART VIII
DARK HORSE / MANGA

❑1, Jan 2000 .... 3.50
❑2, Feb 2000 .... 3.50
❑3, Mar 2000 .... 3.50
❑4, Apr 2000 .... 3.50
❑5, May 2000 .... 3.50
❑6, Jun 2000 .... 3.50

OH MY GODDESS! PART IX
DARK HORSE / MANGA

❑1, Jul 2000 .... 3.50
❑2, Aug 2000 .... 3.50
❑3, Sep 2000 .... 3.50
❑4, Oct 2000 .... 3.50
❑5, Nov 2000 .... 3.50

N-MINT

❑6, Dec 2000 .... 3.50
❑7, Jan 2001 .... 3.50

OH MY GODDESS! PART X
DARK HORSE / MANGA

❑1, Feb 2001 .... 3.50
❑2, Mar 2001 .... 3.50
❑3, Apr 2001 .... 3.50
❑4, May 2001 .... 3.50
❑5, Jun 2001 .... 3.50

OH MY GODDESS! PART XI
DARK HORSE

❑1, Aug 2001 .... 3.50
❑2, Sep 2001 .... 3.50
❑3, Oct 2001 .... 2.99
❑4, Nov 2001 .... 2.99
❑5, Dec 2001 .... 2.99
❑6, Feb 2002 .... 2.99

OH MY GODDESS!: ADVENTURES OF THE MINI-GODDESSES
DARK HORSE / MANGA

❑1, May 2000 .... 9.95

OH MY GOTH
SIRIUS / DOG STAR

❑1 1998 .... 2.95
❑2, Oct 1998 .... 2.95
❑3, Jan 1999 .... 2.95
❑4, Apr 1999 .... 2.95

OH MY GOTH: HUMANS SUCK!
SIRIUS

❑1, Jun 2000, b&w 2.95
❑2, Aug 2000, b&w 2.95

OINK: BLOOD AND CIRCUS
KITCHEN SINK

❑1 .... 4.95
❑2 .... 4.95
❑3 .... 4.95
❑4, Jul 1998 .... 4.95

OINK: HEAVEN'S BUTCHER
KITCHEN SINK

❑1, Dec 1995 .... 4.95
❑2, Feb 1996 .... 4.95
❑3, Apr 1996 .... 4.95

OJ'S BIG BUST OUT
BONEYARD

❑1, Mar 1995, b&w 3.50

OKTANE
DARK HORSE

❑1, Aug 1995 .... 2.50
❑2, Sep 1995 .... 2.50
❑3, Oct 1995 .... 2.50
❑4, Nov 1995 .... 2.50

OLDBLOOD
PARODY

❑1 .... 2.50
❑1-2 .... 2.50

OLYMPIANS, THE
MARVEL / EPIC

❑1 .... 3.95
❑2, Jan 1992 .... 3.95

OMAC
DC

❑1, Oct 1974 JK (w); JK (a); O: Omac. 1: Omac. 10.00
❑2, Dec 1974 JK (a); V: Mr. Big. 7.00
❑3, Feb 1975 JK (a) 7.00
❑4, Apr 1975 JK (a) 7.00
❑5, Jun 1975 JK (w); JK (a) 5.00
❑6, Aug 1975 JK (a) 5.00
❑7, Oct 1975 JK (a) 5.00
❑8, Dec 1975 JKu (c); JK (a) 5.00

OMAC: ONE MAN ARMY CORPS
DC

❑1, b&w; prestige format JBy (w); JBy, (a) 4.00
❑2, b&w; prestige format JBy (w); JBy (a) 4.00

Collectors of *Oh My Goddess!* should refer to the indicia to determine which issue and series they have, since several issues have had "Oh My Goddess Special" on their covers.

© 1997 Dark Horse Comics and Studio Proteus.

N-MINT

❑3, b&w; prestige format JBy (w); JBy (a) 4.00
❑4, b&w; prestige format JBy (w); JBy (a) 4.00

OMAHA: CAT DANCER
STEELDRAGON

❑1 .... 12.00
❑1/Ashcan; preview 3.00
❑1-2 .... 4.00
❑2 .... 8.00

OMAHA THE CAT DANCER (KITCHEN SINK)
KITCHEN SINK

❑0; 1: Omaha the Cat Dancer. Reprints early Omaha stories from Vootie, Bizarre Sex #9 .... 4.00
❑1, Oct 1986 .... 10.00
❑1-2 .... 4.00
❑1-3 .... 3.00
❑2, Oct 1986 .... 5.00
❑3, Oct 1986 .... 4.00
❑4, Jan 1987 .... 4.00
❑5, Mar 1987 .... 4.00
❑6, May 1987 .... 3.00
❑7, Jul 1987 .... 3.00
❑8, Oct 1987 .... 3.00
❑9, Feb 1988 .... 3.00
❑10, May 1988 .... 3.00
❑11, Dec 1988 .... 3.00
❑12 1989 .... 3.00
❑12-2 .... 2.95
❑13, Sep 1989 .... 3.00
❑13-2 .... 2.95
❑14, Mar 1990; Wendel back-up 3.00
❑15, Jan 1991 .... 3.00
❑16, Nov 1991 .... 2.95
❑17, Feb 1992 .... 2.95
❑18, Jan 1993 .... 2.95
❑19, Jun 1993 .... 2.95
❑20, Jun 1994; Final Kitchen Sink issue 2.95

OMAHA THE CAT DANCER (FANTAGRAPHICS)
FANTAGRAPHICS

❑1, Jul 1994 .... 3.00
❑2, Aug 1994 .... 3.00
❑3, Nov 1994 .... 3.00
❑4, Feb 1995 .... 3.00

O'MALLEY AND THE ALLEY CATS
GOLD KEY

❑1, Apr 1971 .... 8.00
❑2, Jul 1971 .... 6.00
❑3, Jul 1972 .... 6.00
❑4, Oct 1972 .... 4.00
❑5, Jan 1973 .... 4.00
❑6, Apr 1973 .... 4.00
❑7, Jul 1973 .... 4.00
❑8, Oct 1973 .... 4.00
❑9, Jan 1974 .... 4.00

OMAR LENNYX
MAGNECOM

❑1, b&w 2.95

OMEGA ELITE
BLACKTHORNE

❑1, b&w 3.50

N-MINT

OMEGA FORCE (SOUTH STAR)
South Star

- ❑1, Aug 1992 .... 2.00

OMEGA FORCE
Entity

- ❑1, ca. 1995 .... 2.50

OMEGA KNIGHTS
Underground

- ❑1 .... 2.00
- ❑2 .... 2.00
- ❑3 .... 2.00
- ❑4 .... 2.00
- ❑5 .... 2.00
- ❑6, Oct 1992 .... 2.00

OMEGA MAN
Omega 7

- ❑0 .... 3.00
- ❑1, b&w; Simpson trial; no indicia 4.00
- ❑Ashcan 1, color; no cover price; no indicia; sideways format 1.00

OMEGA MEN, THE
DC

- ❑1, Apr 1983 KG (a); O: Omega Men. 2.00
- ❑2, May 1983 KG (a); O: Broot. 1.50
- ❑3, Jun 1983 1: Lobo. 3.00
- ❑4, Jul 1983 1: Felicity. 1.50
- ❑5, Aug 1983 2: Lobo. 2.00
- ❑6, Sep 1983 .... 1.50
- ❑7, Oct 1983 O: Citadel. 1.50
- ❑8, Nov 1983 .... 1.50
- ❑9, Dec 1983 A: Lobo. 2.00
- ❑10, Jan 1984; 1st Lobo Full Story ... 2.00
- ❑11, Feb 1984 .... 1.25
- ❑12, Mar 1984 .... 1.25
- ❑13, Apr 1984 .... 1.25
- ❑14, May 1984 .... 1.25
- ❑15, Jun 1984 .... 1.25
- ❑16, Jul 1984 .... 1.25
- ❑17, Aug 1984 .... 1.25
- ❑18, Sep 1984 .... 1.25
- ❑19, Oct 1984 A: Lobo. 1.25
- ❑20, Nov 1984 A: Lobo. 2.00
- ❑21, Dec 1984 .... 1.25
- ❑22, Jan 1985 .... 1.25
- ❑23, Feb 1985 .... 1.25
- ❑24, Mar 1985 .... 1.25
- ❑25, Apr 1985 .... 1.25
- ❑26, May 1985 1: Elu. 1.25
- ❑27, Jun 1985 .... 1.25
- ❑28, Jul 1985 .... 1.25
- ❑29, Aug 1985 .... 1.25
- ❑30, Sep 1985 .... 1.25
- ❑31, Oct 1985; Crisis 1.25
- ❑32, Nov 1985 .... 1.25
- ❑33, Dec 1985 .... 1.25
- ❑34, Jan 1986 .... 1.25
- ❑35, Feb 1986 .... 1.25
- ❑36, Mar 1986 .... 1.25
- ❑37, Apr 1986 A: Lobo. 1.25
- ❑38, May 1986 .... 1.25
- ❑Annual 1, ca. 1984 .... 2.00
- ❑Annual 2, ca. 1985 O: Primus. 1.75

OMEGA THE UNKNOWN
Marvel

- ❑1, Mar 1976 JM (a); 1: James-Michael Starling (Omega the Unknown's counterpart). 1: Omega the Unknown. 7.00
- ❑2, May 1976 A: Hulk. 6.00
- ❑2/30 cent, May 1976; 30 cent regional price variant 20.00
- ❑3, Jul 1976 .... 3.00
- ❑3/30 cent, Jul 1976; 30 cent regional price variant 20.00
- ❑4, Sep 1976 .... 2.00
- ❑5, Nov 1976 .... 2.00
- ❑6, Jan 1977 .... 2.00
- ❑7, Mar 1977 .... 2.00
- ❑8, May 1977 1: Foolkiller II (Greg Salinger)-cameo. 2.00
- ❑9, Jul 1977 1: Foolkiller II (Greg Salinger)-full. 3.00
- ❑9/35 cent, Jul 1977; 1: Foolkiller II (Greg Salinger)-full. 35 cent regional price variant 15.00
- ❑10, Oct 1977 D: Omega the Unknown. 2.00
- ❑10/35 cent, Oct 1977; D: Omega the Unknown. 35 cent regional price variant 15.00

OMEN, THE (CHAOS)
Chaos!

- ❑1, May 1998 .... 2.95
- ❑2, Jun 1998 .... 2.95
- ❑3, Jul 1998 .... 2.95
- ❑4, Aug 1998 .... 2.95
- ❑5, Sep 1998 .... 2.95

OMEN (NORTHSTAR)
Northstar

- ❑1, b&w 2.00
- ❑2, b&w 2.00

OMEN, THE: SAVE THE CHOSEN PREVIEW
Chaos!

- ❑1, Sep 1997; preview of upcoming series 2.50

OMEN, THE: VEXED
Chaos!

- ❑1, Oct 1998 .... 2.95

OMICRON: ASTONISHING ADVENTURES ON OTHER WORLDS
Pyramid

- ❑1, b&w; flexi-disc 2.25
- ❑2, Sep 1987, b&w; flexi-disc 2.25

OMNIBUS: MODERN PERVERSITY
Blackbird

- ❑1, b&w; squarebound 3.25

OMNI COMIX
Omni

- ❑1, Mar 1995; magazine; BWi (a); Mar '95 issue of Omni inserted 4.00
- ❑2, Apr 1995; magazine; insert in Apr. '95 issue of Omni with Omni Comix #2 cover 4.00
- ❑3, Oct 1995; magazine; T.H.U.N.D.E.R. Agents story 4.95

OMNI MEN
Blackthorne

- ❑1, Apr 1989, b&w 3.50

ON A PALE HORSE
Innovation

- ❑1; Adapts Piers Anthony story from his Incarnations of Immortality series 4.95
- ❑2 .... 4.95
- ❑3 .... 4.95
- ❑4, Oct 1993 .... 4.95
- ❑5, Dec 1993 .... 4.95

ONCE UPON A TIME IN THE FUTURE
Platinum

- ❑1 .... 9.95

ONE
Tokyopop

- ❑1, Apr 2004 .... 9.99

ONE (PACIFIC)
Pacific

- ❑1, b&w; 1st Pacific title 3.00

ONE, THE
Marvel / Epic

- ❑1, Jul 1985 BA (a) 2.00
- ❑2, Sep 1985 BA (a) 2.00
- ❑3, Nov 1985 BA (a) 2.00
- ❑4, Jan 1986 BA (a) 2.00
- ❑5, Mar 1986 BA (a) 2.00
- ❑6, May 1986 BA (a) 2.00

ONE-ARM SWORDSMAN
Dr. Leung's

- ❑1 .... 1.80
- ❑2 .... 1.80
- ❑3 .... 1.80
- ❑4 .... 1.80
- ❑5 .... 1.80
- ❑6 .... 1.80
- ❑7 .... 1.80

ONE-FISTED TALES
Slave Labor

- ❑1, May 1990, b&w; brown paper wrapper 3.00
- ❑1-2, Nov 1990 .... 2.50
- ❑2, Sep 1990, b&w; brown paper wrapper (some wrappers printed red in error) 3.00
- ❑2-2, Apr 1993; no brown paper wrapper 2.95
- ❑3, Feb 1991, b&w; brown paper wrapper; Cherry cover and story 2.50
- ❑3-2, Apr 1993; no brown paper wrapper 2.50
- ❑3-3, Aug 1993; no brown paper wrapper 2.95
- ❑4, Jun 1991, b&w 2.50
- ❑4-2, Jan 1992 .... 2.95
- ❑4-3, Aug 1993; no brown paper wrapper 2.95
- ❑5, Sep 1991, b&w 3.95
- ❑5-2, Feb 1992 .... 2.95
- ❑6, Apr 1992 .... 2.95
- ❑7, Sep 1992, b&w 2.95
- ❑8, Mar 1993, b&w 2.95
- ❑9, Oct 1993, b&w 2.95
- ❑10, Feb 1994, b&w 2.95
- ❑11, Aug 1994, b&w 2.95

ONE HUNDRED AND ONE DALMATIANS (WALT DISNEY'S...)
Disney

- ❑1, ca. 1991 .... 2.50

100 BULLETS
DC / Vertigo

- ❑1, Aug 1999 .... 8.50
- ❑2, Sep 1999 .... 6.50
- ❑3, Oct 1999 .... 5.00
- ❑4, Nov 1999 .... 5.00
- ❑5, Dec 1999 .... 5.00
- ❑6, Jan 2000 .... 4.00
- ❑7, Feb 2000 .... 4.00
- ❑8, Mar 2000 .... 4.00
- ❑9, Apr 2000 .... 4.00
- ❑10, May 2000 .... 4.00
- ❑11, Jun 2000 .... 3.00
- ❑12, Jul 2000 .... 3.00
- ❑13, Aug 2000 .... 3.00
- ❑14, Sep 2000 .... 3.00
- ❑15, Oct 2000 .... 3.00
- ❑16, Nov 2000 .... 3.00
- ❑17, Dec 2000 .... 3.00
- ❑18, Jan 2001 .... 3.00
- ❑19, Feb 2001 .... 3.00
- ❑20, Mar 2001 .... 3.00
- ❑21, Apr 2001 .... 3.00
- ❑22, May 2001 .... 3.00
- ❑23, Jun 2001 .... 3.00
- ❑24, Jul 2001 .... 3.00
- ❑25, Aug 2001 .... 3.00
- ❑26, Sep 2001, DaG, FM, JLee (a) 3.00
- ❑27, Oct 2001 .... 3.00
- ❑28, Nov 2001 .... 3.00
- ❑29, Dec 2001 .... 3.00
- ❑30, Jan 2002 .... 3.00
- ❑31, Feb 2002 .... 2.50
- ❑32, Mar 2002 .... 2.50
- ❑33, Apr 2002 .... 2.50
- ❑34, May 2002 .... 2.50
- ❑35, Jun 2002 .... 2.50
- ❑36, Jul 2002 .... 2.50
- ❑37, Sep 2002 .... 2.50
- ❑38, Oct 2002 .... 2.50
- ❑39, Nov 2002 .... 2.50
- ❑40, Jan 2003 .... 2.50
- ❑41, Feb 2003 .... 2.50
- ❑42, Mar 2003 .... 2.50
- ❑43, Apr 2003 .... 2.50
- ❑44, May 2003 .... 2.50
- ❑45, Jun 2003 .... 2.50

N-MINT

❑46, Jul 2003 ... 2.50
❑47, Oct 2003 ... 2.50
❑48, Dec 2003 ... 2.50
❑49, May 2004 ... 2.50
❑50, Aug 2004 ... 3.50
❑51, Sep 2004 ... 2.50

100 DEGREES IN THE SHADE
Fantagraphics / Eros

❑1, Feb 1992, b&w ... 2.50
❑2, May 1992, b&w ... 2.50
❑3, Jul 1992, b&w ... 2.50
❑4, Oct 1992, b&w ... 2.50

100 GREATEST MARVELS OF ALL TIME, THE
Marvel

❑1, Dec 2001, color; reprints Uncanny X-Men #141, Fantastic Four (Vol. 1) #48, Amazing Spider-Man (Vol. 1) #1, Daredevil #181; cardstock cover ... 7.50
❑2, Dec 2001, color; reprints Avengers (Vol. 1) #1, Uncanny X-Men #350, Amazing Spider-Man (Vol. 1) #122, Captain America #109; cardstock cover ... 7.50
❑3, Dec 2001, color; reprints Incredible Hulk #181, X-Men #25, Amazing Spider-Man (Vol. 1) #33, Spider-Man #1; cardstock cover ... 7.50
❑4, Dec 2001, color; reprints Incredible Hulk (Vol. 1) #1, Ultimate X-Men #1, Daredevil #227, Wolverine #75; cardstock cover ... 7.50
❑5, Dec 2001, color; reprints Ultimate Spider-Man #1, X-Men (1st series) #1, Avengers (Vol. 1) #4, Amazing Spider-Man (Vol. 1) #121; cardstock cover ... 7.50
❑6, Dec 2001, color; reprints X-Men (2nd series) #1; cardstock cover ... 3.50
❑7, Dec 2001, color; reprints Giant-Size X-Men #1 ... 3.50
❑8, Dec 2001, color; reprints X-Men (1st series) #137; cardstock cover ... 3.50
❑9, Dec 2001, color; reprints Fantastic Four (Vol. 1) #1 ... 3.50
❑10, Dec 2001, color; reprints Amazing Fantasy #15 ... 3.50

101 OTHER USES FOR A CONDOM
Apple

❑1, ca. 1991 ... 4.95

101 WAYS TO END THE CLONE SAGA
Marvel

❑1, Jan 1997 ... 2.50

100%
DC / Vertigo

❑1, Aug 2002 ... 5.95
❑2, Sep 2002 ... 5.95
❑3, Oct 2002 ... 5.95
❑4, Nov 2002 ... 5.95
❑5, Dec 2002 ... 5.95

100% TRUE?
DC / Paradox Press

❑1, Sum 1996, b&w; magazine; excerpts from The Big Books of Death, Conspiracies, Weirdos, and Freaks ... 3.50
❑2, Win 1996, b&w; magazine; excerpts from The Big Books of Death, Conspiracies, Weirdos, and Freaks; Winter, 1996 issue ... 3.50

ONE MILE UP
Eclipse

❑1, b&w ... 2.50
❑2 ... 2.50

ONE MILLENNIUM
Hunter

❑1, b&w ... 2.50
❑2, b&w ... 2.50
❑3, ca. 1997, b&w ... 2.50
❑4, ca. 1997, b&w ... 2.50
❑5, ca. 1997, b&w ... 2.50

N-MINT

ONE-POUND GOSPEL
Viz

❑1 ... 3.50
❑2 ... 3.50
❑3 ... 2.95
❑4 ... 2.95

ONE-POUND GOSPEL ROUND 2
Viz

❑1, Jan 1997 ... 2.95
❑2, Feb 1997 ... 2.95
❑3, Mar 1997 ... 2.95
❑4 1997 ... 2.95
❑5 1997 ... 2.95
❑6 1997 ... 2.95

ONE-SHOT PARODY
Milky Way

❑1, ca. 1986, X-Men ... 1.50

ONE-SHOT WESTERN
Caliber

❑1, b&w ... 2.50

1001 NIGHTS OF SHEHERAZADE, THE
NBM

❑1 ... 12.95

1111
Crusade

❑1, Oct 1996, b&w; prose story with facing page illustrations; illustrated story ... 2.95

1,001 NIGHTS OF BACCHUS, THE
Dark Horse

❑1, May 1993, b&w ... 4.50

...ONE TO GO
Äardwolf

❑1 ... 2.50

ONE TRICK RIP OFF, THE
Dark Horse

❑

ONI
Dark Horse

❑1, Feb 2001 ... 2.99
❑2, Feb 2001 ... 2.99
❑3, Feb 2001 ... 2.99

ONI DOUBLE FEATURE
Oni

❑1, Jan 1998; Flip-book; KSm (w); MW (a); 1: Silent Bob. 1: Jay. Jay & Silent Bob, Milk & Cheese, Secret Broadcast ... 6.00
❑1-2, Mar 1998 ... 2.95
❑2, Feb 1998; Too Much Coffee Man, Car Crash, Secret Broadcast ... 4.00
❑3, Mar 1998; Frumpy the Clown, Bacon, Car Crash ... 3.50
❑4, Apr 1998; BSz (c); Bacon, A River in Egypt, Cheetahman; Judd Winick's first major comics work ... 3.50
❑5, May 1998 ... 3.50
❑6, Jun 1998; CR, NG (w); Only The End of the World Again, Zombie Kid ... 4.00
❑7, Jul 1998 ... 2.95
❑8, Aug 1998; Only The End of the World Again, Satchel of Weltschmerz, Pip & Norton ... 2.95
❑9, Oct 1998 ... 2.95
❑10, Nov 1998; Sam & Max, Drive-By, Road Trip ... 2.95
❑11, Feb 1999; Usagi Yojimbo, Blue Monday, Drive-By ... 2.95
❑12, May 1999; The Harpooner, Bluntman & Chronic, The Honor Rollers ... 2.95

ONIGAMI
Antarctic

❑1, Apr 1998 ... 2.95
❑2, Jun 1998 ... 2.95
❑3, Jul 1998 ... 2.95

ONI PRESS SUMMER VACATION SUPERCOLOR FUN SPECIAL
Oni

❑1, Jul 2000 ... 5.95

One-Fisted Tales #3 contained a new Cherry story by Larry Welz, who also provided the issue's cover. A brown-paper wrapper was provided on first printings to conceal the adult cover.

© 1991 Slave Labor and respective creators.

N-MINT

ONLY THE END OF THE WORLD AGAIN
Oni

❑1, May 2000 ... 6.95

ON OUR BUTTS
Aeon

❑1, Apr 1995 ... 2.95

ON RAVEN'S WINGS
Boneyard

❑1 ... 2.95
❑2, Sep 1994 ... 2.95

ONSLAUGHT: EPILOGUE
Marvel

❑1, Feb 1997 ... 2.95

ONSLAUGHT: MARVEL
Marvel

❑1, Oct 1996; MWa (w); DGr (a); wrap-around cover ... 6.00

ONSLAUGHT: X-MEN
Marvel

❑1, Aug 1996; MWa (w); DGr (a); wrap-around cover; set-up for Onslaught crossover in Marvel titles ... 5.00
❑1/Variant; MWa (w); DGr (a); variant cover ... 8.00

ON THE BUS
Slave Labor

❑1, Aug 1994 ... 2.95

ON THE ROAD TO PERDITION
DC

❑1, May 2003 ... 7.95
❑2, Jan 2004 ... 7.95
❑3, Aug 2004; Detour ... 7.95

ONYX OVERLORD
Marvel / Epic

❑1, Oct 1992 ... 2.75
❑2, Nov 1992 ... 2.75
❑3, Dec 1992 ... 2.75
❑4, Jan 1993 ... 2.75

OOMBAH, JUNGLE MOON MAN
Strawberry Jam

❑1, b&w ... 2.50

OPEN SEASON
Renegade

❑1 1987, b&w ... 2.00
❑2 1987, b&w ... 2.00
❑3 1987, b&w ... 2.00
❑4, Oct 1987, b&w ... 2.00
❑5, Dec 1987, b&w ... 2.00
❑6, Apr 1988, b&w; black issue ... 2.00
❑7, b&w ... 2.00

OPEN SORE FUNNIES
Home-Made Euthanasia

❑1 ... 1.25

OPEN SPACE
Marvel

❑1, Dec 1989 KB (w) ... 5.00
❑2, Apr 1990 ... 5.00
❑3, Jun 1990 ... 5.00
❑4, Aug 1990 ... 5.00

OPERATION: KANSAS CITY
Motion

❑1, Win 1993, b&w; Breakneck Blvd. Preview ... 2.50

N-MINT

OPERATION: KNIGHTSTRIKE
IMAGE

❑1, May 1995 ... 2.50
❑1/A, May 1995; Purple background on cover ... 2.50
❑2, Jun 1995 ... 2.50
❑2/A, Jun 1995 ... 2.50
❑3, Jul 1995 ... 2.50

OPERATION: STORMBREAKER
ACCLAIM / VALIANT

❑1, Aug 1997; cover says Jul, indicia says Aug ... 3.95

OPERATIVE: SCORPIO
BLACKTHORNE

❑1, Jan 1989, b&w ... 3.50

OPTIC NERVE
DRAWN & QUARTERLY

❑1 ... 5.00
❑2 ... 3.00
❑3 ... 3.00
❑4, Mar 1997 ... 3.00
❑5, Feb 1998 ... 3.00
❑6, Jan 1999 ... 3.00
❑7, Jun 2000; Mini-Comic ... 3.00

OPTIMISM OF YOUTH
FANTAGRAPHICS

❑1, Oct 1991 ... 12.95

ORA
SON OF A TREEBOB

❑1, Mar 1999, b&w ... 2.95

ORACLE
ORACLE

❑1, b&w GP (a) ... 3.00

ORACLE - A TRESPASSERS MYSTERY
AMAZING MONTAGE

❑1, b&w ... 4.95

ORACLE PRESENTS
ORACLE

❑1, b&w; GP (a); reprint of Oracle #1 ... 3.00
❑2, Aug 1986, b&w; Critter Corps ... 3.00

ORBIT
ECLIPSE

❑1 ... 4.95
❑2 ... 4.95
❑3 ... 4.95

ORB MAGAZINE
ORB

❑1 ... 1.25
❑2 ... 1.25
❑3 ... 1.25

ORDER, THE
MARVEL

❑1, Apr 2002, b&w ... 2.25
❑2, May 2002 ... 2.25
❑3, Jun 2002 ... 2.25
❑4, Jul 2002 ... 2.25
❑5, Aug 2002 ... 2.25
❑6, Sep 2002 ... 2.25

ORIENTAL HEROES
JADEMAN

❑1, Aug 1988 ... 1.95
❑2, Sep 1988 ... 1.95
❑3, Oct 1988 ... 1.95
❑4, Nov 1988 ... 1.95
❑5, Dec 1988 ... 1.95
❑6, Jan 1989 ... 1.95
❑7, Feb 1989 ... 1.95
❑8, Mar 1989 ... 1.95
❑9, Apr 1989 ... 1.95
❑10, May 1989 ... 1.95
❑11, Jun 1989 ... 1.95
❑12, Jul 1989 ... 1.95
❑13, Aug 1989 ... 1.95
❑14, Sep 1989 ... 1.95
❑15, Oct 1989 ... 1.95
❑16, Nov 1989 ... 1.95
❑17, Dec 1989 ... 1.95
❑18, Jan 1990 ... 1.95
❑19, Feb 1990 ... 1.95

N-MINT

❑20, Mar 1990 ... 1.95
❑21, Apr 1990 ... 1.95
❑22, May 1990 ... 1.95
❑23, Jun 1990 ... 1.95
❑24, Jul 1990 ... 1.95
❑25, Aug 1990 ... 1.95
❑26, Sep 1990 ... 1.95
❑27, Oct 1990 ... 1.95
❑28, Nov 1990 ... 1.95
❑29, Dec 1990 ... 1.95
❑30, Jan 1991 ... 1.95
❑31, Feb 1991 ... 1.95
❑32, Mar 1991 ... 1.95
❑33, Apr 1991 ... 1.95
❑34, May 1991 ... 1.95
❑35, Jun 1991 ... 1.95
❑36, Jul 1991 ... 1.95
❑37, Aug 1991 ... 1.95
❑38, Sep 1991 ... 1.95
❑39, Oct 1991 ... 1.95
❑40, Nov 1991 ... 1.95
❑41, Dec 1991 ... 1.95
❑42, Jan 1992 ... 1.95
❑43, Feb 1992 ... 1.95
❑44, Mar 1992 ... 1.95
❑45, Apr 1992 ... 1.95
❑46, May 1992 ... 1.95
❑47, Jun 1992 ... 1.95
❑48, Jul 1992 ... 1.95
❑49, Aug 1992 ... 1.95
❑50, Sep 1992 ... 1.95
❑51, Oct 1992 ... 1.95
❑52, Nov 1992 ... 1.95
❑53, Dec 1992 ... 1.95
❑54, Jan 1993 ... 1.95
❑55, Feb 1993 ... 1.95

ORIGINAL ASTRO BOY, THE
NOW

❑1, Sep 1987 ... 2.00
❑2, Oct 1987 ... 1.50
❑3, Nov 1987 ... 1.50
❑4, Dec 1987 ... 1.50
❑5, Jan 1988 ... 1.50
❑6, Feb 1988 ... 1.50
❑7, Mar 1988 ... 1.50
❑8, Apr 1988 ... 1.50
❑9, May 1988 ... 1.50
❑10, Jun 1988 ... 1.50
❑11, Aug 1988 ... 1.50
❑12, Sep 1988 ... 1.50
❑13, Oct 1988 ... 1.50
❑14, Nov 1988 ... 1.50
❑15, Jan 1989 ... 1.50
❑16, Feb 1989 ... 1.50
❑17, Mar 1989 ... 1.50
❑18, Apr 1989 ... 1.50
❑19, May 1989 ... 1.50
❑20, Jun 1989 ... 1.50

ORIGINAL BLACK CAT, THE
RECOLLECTIONS

❑1 ... 2.00
❑2, Mar 1989 ... 2.00
❑3, Sep 1990 ... 2.00
❑4, Jun 1991 ... 2.00
❑5, Jul 1991 ... 2.00
❑6, Aug 1991; reprints first Black Cat story from Pocket Comics #1 ... 2.00
❑7, Nov 1991 ... 2.00
❑8; Title changes to Black Cat for one issue only ... 2.00
❑9; Title reverts to Original Black Cat ... 2.00
❑10; Title changes to Black Cat Comics for final issue ... 1.00

ORIGINAL BOY: DAY OF ATONEMENT
OMEGA 7

❑1; no cover price; no indicia; events deal with Million Man March on Washington ... 1.95

N-MINT

ORIGINAL CREW, THE
PERSONALITY

❑1; William Shatner ... 3.00
❑2; Leonard Nimoy ... 3.00
❑3; DeForest Kelley ... 3.00
❑4 ... 2.95
❑5 ... 2.95
❑6 ... 2.95
❑7 ... 2.95
❑8 ... 2.95
❑9; Bruce Hyde ... 2.95
❑10 ... 2.95

ORIGINAL DICK TRACY, THE
GLADSTONE

❑1, Sep 1990; Mrs. Pruneface ... 2.00
❑2, Nov 1990; Influence ... 2.00
❑3, Jan 1991; Gargles ... 2.00
❑4, Mar 1991; Itchy ... 2.00
❑5, May 1991; Shoulders ... 2.00

ORIGINAL DOCTOR SOLAR, MAN OF THE ATOM, THE
VALIANT

❑1, Apr 1995 ... 2.95

ORIGINAL E-MAN
FIRST

❑1, Oct 1985 ... 2.00
❑2, Nov 1985 ... 2.00
❑3, Dec 1985 ... 2.00
❑4, Jan 1986 ... 2.00
❑5, Feb 1986 ... 2.00
❑6, Mar 1986 ... 2.00
❑7, Apr 1986 ... 2.00

ORIGINAL GHOST RIDER, THE
MARVEL

❑1, Jul 1992 ... 1.75
❑2, Aug 1992 ... 1.75
❑3, Sep 1992 ... 1.75
❑4, Oct 1992 ... 1.75
❑5, Nov 1992 ... 1.75
❑6, Dec 1992 ... 1.75
❑7, Jan 1993 ... 1.75
❑8, Feb 1993 ... 1.75
❑9, Mar 1993 ... 1.75
❑10, Apr 1993 ... 1.75
❑11, May 1993 ... 1.75
❑12, Jun 1993 ... 1.75
❑13, Jul 1993 ... 1.75
❑14, Aug 1993 ... 1.75
❑15, Sep 1993 ... 1.75
❑16, Oct 1993 ... 1.75
❑17, Nov 1993 ... 1.75
❑18, Dec 1993 ... 1.75
❑19, Jan 1994; Reprints Marvel Two-In-One #8 ... 1.75
❑20, Feb 1994 ... 1.75

ORIGINAL GHOST RIDER RIDES AGAIN, THE
MARVEL

❑1, Jul 1991; Reprinted from Ghost Rider #68 ... 1.50
❑2, Aug 1991 ... 1.50
❑3, Sep 1991 ... 1.50
❑4, Oct 1991 ... 1.50
❑5, Nov 1991 ... 1.50
❑6, Dec 1991 ... 1.50
❑7, Jan 1992 ... 1.50

ORIGINAL MAGNUS ROBOT FIGHTER, THE
VALIANT

❑1, Apr 1992; Reprints Magnus, Robot Fighter 4000 A.D. #2; cardstock cover ... 2.95

ORIGINAL MAN
OMEGA 7

❑1 ... 3.50

ORIGINAL MAN: THE MOST POWERFUL MAN IN THE UNIVERSE
OMEGA 7

❑1; Darkforce #0 as flip-side support story ... 1.95

N-MINT

ORIGINAL MYSTERYMEN PRESENTS (BOB BURDEN'S...)
DARK HORSE

❑1, Jul 1999 .... 2.95
❑2, Aug 1999 .... 2.95
❑3, Sep 1999 .... 2.95
❑4, Oct 1999 .... 2.95

ORIGINAL SAD SACK
RECOLLECTIONS

❑1, b&w 2.00

ORIGINAL SHIELD
ARCHIE

❑1, Apr 1984 .... 1.00
❑2, Jun 1984 .... 1.00
❑3, Aug 1984 .... 1.00
❑4, Oct 1984 .... 1.00

ORIGINAL SIN, THE
THWACK! POW!

❑1 .... 1.00
❑2 .... 1.00
❑3 .... 1.00

ORIGINAL STREET FIGHTER, THE
ALPHA

❑1, b&w 2.50

ORIGINAL TOM CORBETT, THE
ETERNITY

❑1, Sep 1990, b&w; Reprinted from Field Enterprises strips Tom Corbett, Space Cadet; The Mercurian Invasion 2.95
❑2, Sep 1990, b&w; Reprinted from Field Enterprises strips Tom Corbett, Space Cadet; The Mercurian Invasion; Colonists on Titan 2.95
❑3, Oct 1990, b&w; Reprinted from Field Enterprises strips Tom Corbett, Space Cadet; Colonists on Titan 2.95
❑4, Nov 1990, b&w; Reprinted from Field Enterprises strips Tom Corbett, Space Cadet; The Revolt on Mars 2.95
❑5, Dec 1990, b&w; Reprinted from Field Enterprises strips Tom Corbett, Space Cadet; Slave Plantation of Venus; Issues #6-10 were planned but never published. 2.95

ORIGINAL TUROK, SON OF STONE, THE
VALIANT

❑1, Apr 1995; cardstock cover 2.95
❑2, May 1995; Reprints of Turok, Son of Stone #24, #33; cardstock cover 2.95

ORIGINAL TZU, THE: SPIRITS OF DEATH
MURIM

❑1, Dec 1997, b&w; reprints manga series 2.95

ORIGIN OF GALACTUS
MARVEL

❑1, Feb 1996; reprints Super-Villain Classics #1 .... 2.50

ORIGIN OF THE DEFIANT UNIVERSE, THE
DEFIANT

❑1, Feb 1994 .... 1.50

ORION
DARK HORSE

❑1, Feb 1993, b&w; manga 3.95
❑2, Mar 1993, b&w; manga 2.95
❑3, Apr 1993, b&w; manga 2.95
❑4, May 1993, b&w; manga 2.95
❑5, Jun 1993, b&w; manga 2.95
❑6, Jul 1993 .... 3.95

ORION (DC)
DC

❑1, Jun 2000 .... 2.50
❑2, Jul 2000 .... 2.50
❑3, Aug 2000 .... 2.50
❑4, Sep 2000 .... 2.50
❑5, Oct 2000 .... 2.50
❑6, Nov 2000 .... 2.50
❑7, Dec 2000 .... 2.50

N-MINT

❑8, Jan 2001 .... 2.50
❑9, Feb 2001 .... 2.50
❑10, Mar 2001 .... 2.50
❑11, Apr 2001 .... 2.50
❑12, May 2001 .... 2.50
❑13, Jun 2001 .... 2.50
❑14, Jul 2001 .... 2.50
❑15, Aug 2001 .... 2.50
❑16, Sep 2001 .... 2.50
❑17, Sep 2001 .... 2.50
❑18, Oct 2001 .... 2.50
❑19, Nov 2001 .... 2.50
❑20, Dec 2001 .... 2.50
❑21, Jan 2002 .... 2.50
❑22, Feb 2002 .... 2.50
❑23, Mar 2002 .... 2.50
❑24, Apr 2002 .... 2.50
❑25, May 2002 .... 2.50

ORLAK REDUX
CALIBER

❑1, b&w 3.95

OSBORN JOURNALS
MARVEL

❑1, Feb 1997; summation of Clone Saga and return of Norman Osborn as Green Goblin 2.95

OTHELLO
TOME

❑1, b&w 3.50

OTHER BIG THING (COLIN UPTON'S...)
FANTAGRAPHICS

❑1, b&w 2.50
❑2 .... 2.25
❑3 .... 2.25
❑4, Jul 1992 .... 2.50

OTHERS, THE (IMAGE)
IMAGE

❑0, Mar 1995 .... 1.00
❑1, Apr 1995 .... 2.50
❑2, May 1995 .... 2.50
❑3, Jul 1995 .... 2.50
❑4 .... 2.50

OTHERS, THE (CORMAC)
CORMAC

❑1 .... 1.50

OTIS GOES HOLLYWOOD
DARK HORSE

❑1, Apr 1997, b&w 2.95
❑2, May 1997, b&w 2.95

OTTO SPACE!
MANIFEST DESTINY

❑1 .... 2.00
❑2 .... 2.00

OUR ARMY AT WAR
DC

❑51, Oct 1956 .... 95.00
❑52, Nov 1956 .... 95.00
❑53, Dec 1956 .... 95.00
❑54, Jan 1957 .... 95.00
❑55, Feb 1957 .... 95.00
❑56, Mar 1957 .... 95.00
❑57, Apr 1957 .... 90.00
❑58, May 1957 .... 90.00
❑59, Jun 1957 .... 90.00
❑60, Jul 1957 .... 80.00
❑61, Aug 1957 .... 80.00
❑62, Sep 1957 .... 80.00
❑63, Oct 1957 .... 80.00
❑64, Nov 1957 .... 80.00
❑65, Dec 1957 .... 80.00
❑66, Jan 1958 .... 80.00
❑67, Feb 1958 .... 80.00
❑68, Mar 1958 .... 80.00
❑69, Apr 1958 .... 80.00
❑70, May 1958 .... 80.00
❑71, Jun 1958 .... 65.00
❑72, Jul 1958 .... 65.00
❑73, Aug 1958 .... 65.00

Some of Dick Tracy's greatest cliffhanger escapes and battles were reprinted in color in Gladstone's *Original Dick Tracy* series.

N-MINT

❑74, Sep 1958 .... 65.00
❑75, Oct 1958 .... 65.00
❑76, Nov 1958 .... 65.00
❑77, Dec 1958 .... 65.00
❑78, Jan 1959 .... 65.00
❑79, Feb 1959 .... 65.00
❑80, Mar 1959 .... 65.00
❑81, Apr 1959 JKu, RA, RH, JAb (a); 1: Easy Co.. 1: Sgt. Rock. 2450.00
❑82, May 1959 2: Sgt. Rock. 625.00
❑83, Jun 1959; JKu (a); 1: Easy Company. 1st Kubert Sgt. Rock 1050.00
❑84, Jul 1959 .... 240.00
❑85, Aug 1959 O: The Ice Cream Soldier. 1: The Ice Cream Soldier. 280.00
❑86, Sep 1959 .... 240.00
❑87, Oct 1959 .... 240.00
❑88, Nov 1959 .... 240.00
❑89, Dec 1959 .... 240.00
❑90, Jan 1960 .... 240.00
❑91, Feb 1960; 1st full-length Sgt. Rock story; All-Rock issue 575.00
❑92, Mar 1960 .... 140.00
❑93, Apr 1960 .... 140.00
❑94, May 1960 .... 140.00
❑95, Jun 1960 .... 140.00
❑96, Jul 1960 .... 140.00
❑97, Aug 1960 .... 140.00
❑98, Sep 1960 .... 140.00
❑99, Oct 1960 .... 140.00
❑100, Nov 1960 .... 140.00
❑101, Dec 1960 .... 95.00
❑102, Jan 1961 .... 95.00
❑103, Feb 1961 .... 95.00
❑104, Mar 1961 .... 95.00
❑105, Apr 1961 .... 95.00
❑106, May 1961 .... 95.00
❑107, Jun 1961 .... 95.00
❑108, Jul 1961 .... 95.00
❑109, Aug 1961 .... 95.00
❑110, Sep 1961 .... 95.00
❑111, Oct 1961 .... 90.00
❑112, Nov 1961 .... 90.00
❑113, Dec 1961 .... 110.00
❑114, Jan 1962 .... 110.00
❑115, Feb 1962 .... 110.00
❑116, Mar 1962 .... 110.00
❑117, Apr 1962 .... 110.00
❑118, May 1962 .... 110.00
❑119, Jun 1962 .... 90.00
❑120, Jul 1962 .... 65.00
❑121, Aug 1962 .... 60.00
❑122, Sep 1962 .... 55.00
❑123, Oct 1962 .... 50.00
❑124, Nov 1962 .... 50.00
❑125, Dec 1962 .... 50.00
❑126, Jan 1963 .... 50.00
❑127, Feb 1963 .... 50.00
❑128, Mar 1963 O: Sgt. Rock. 225.00
❑129, Apr 1963 .... 36.00
❑130, May 1963 .... 36.00
❑131, Jun 1963 .... 36.00
❑132, Jul 1963 .... 36.00
❑133, Aug 1963 .... 36.00
❑134, Sep 1963 .... 36.00
❑135, Oct 1963 .... 30.00
❑136, Nov 1963 .... 30.00
❑137, Dec 1963 .... 30.00

	N-MINT
❑138, Jan 1964	25.00
❑139, Feb 1964	25.00
❑140, Mar 1964	25.00
❑141, Apr 1964	25.00
❑142, May 1964	25.00
❑143, Jun 1964	25.00
❑144, Jul 1964	25.00
❑145, Aug 1964	25.00
❑146, Sep 1964	25.00
❑147, Oct 1964 A: Sgt. Rock and Easy Co..	25.00
❑148, Nov 1964 A: Sgt. Rock and Easy Co..	25.00
❑149, Dec 1964	25.00
❑150, Jan 1965	25.00
❑151, Feb 1965 JKu (a); 1: Enemy Ace.	275.00
❑152, Mar 1965	35.00
❑153, Apr 1965 JKu (a); 2: Enemy Ace.	120.00
❑154, May 1965	24.00
❑155, Jun 1965 JKu (a); A: Enemy Ace (next appearance is in Showcase #57).	60.00
❑156, Jul 1965	30.00
❑157, Aug 1965 A: Enemy Ace.	24.00
❑158, Sep 1965 1: Iron Major.	35.00
❑159, Oct 1965	24.00
❑160, Nov 1965	24.00
❑161, Dec 1965	24.00
❑162, Jan 1966 A: Viking Prince.	24.00
❑163, Feb 1966 A: Viking Prince.	24.00
❑164, Feb 1966; Giant-size (80-Page Giant #G-19)	50.00
❑165, Mar 1966 V: Iron Major.	30.00
❑166, Apr 1966	24.00
❑167, May 1966	24.00
❑168, Jun 1966	40.00
❑169, Jul 1966	24.00
❑170, Aug 1966	24.00
❑171, Sep 1966	20.00
❑172, Oct 1966	20.00
❑173, Nov 1966	20.00
❑174, Dec 1966	20.00
❑175, Jan 1967	20.00
❑176, Feb 1967	20.00
❑177, Feb 1967; Giant-size (80-Page Giant #G-32)	38.00
❑178, Mar 1967	20.00
❑179, Apr 1967	20.00
❑180, May 1967	20.00
❑181, Jun 1967	20.00
❑182, Jul 1967 NA (a)	24.00
❑183, Aug 1967 NA (a)	24.00
❑184, Sep 1967	20.00
❑185, Oct 1967	20.00
❑186, Nov 1967 NA (a)	22.00
❑187, Dec 1967	20.00
❑188, Jan 1968	18.00
❑189, Feb 1968	18.00
❑190, Feb 1968	22.00
❑191, Mar 1968	18.00
❑192, Apr 1968	14.00
❑193, May 1968	14.00
❑194, Jun 1968 1: Unit 3 (kid guerrillas).	14.00
❑195, Jul 1968	14.00
❑196, Aug 1968	14.00
❑197, Sep 1968	14.00
❑198, Oct 1968	14.00
❑199, Nov 1968	20.00
❑200, Dec 1968; 200th issue	20.00
❑201, Jan 1969	10.00
❑202, Feb 1969	10.00
❑203, Feb 1969; Giant-size	22.00
❑204, Mar 1969	10.00
❑205, Apr 1969	10.00
❑206, May 1969	10.00
❑207, Jun 1969	10.00
❑208, Jul 1969	10.00
❑209, Aug 1969	10.00
❑210, Sep 1969	10.00
❑211, Oct 1969	10.00
❑212, Nov 1969	10.00
❑213, Dec 1969	10.00

	N-MINT
❑214, Jan 1970	10.00
❑215, Feb 1970	10.00
❑216, Feb 1970; Giant-size (80-Page Giant #G-80)	28.00
❑217, Mar 1970	8.00
❑218, Apr 1970	8.00
❑219, May 1970	8.00
❑220, Jun 1970	8.00
❑221, Jul 1970	7.00
❑222, Aug 1970	7.00
❑223, Sep 1970	7.00
❑224, Oct 1970	7.00
❑225, Nov 1970	7.00
❑226, Dec 1970	7.00
❑227, Jan 1971	7.00
❑228, Feb 1971	7.00
❑229, Mar 1971; Giant-size	22.00
❑230, Mar 1971	7.00
❑231, Apr 1971	7.00
❑232, May 1971	7.00
❑233, Jun 1971	7.00
❑234, Jul 1971	7.00
❑235, Aug 1971	7.00
❑236, Sep 1971	7.00
❑237, Oct 1971	10.00
❑238, Nov 1971	10.00
❑239, Dec 1971	10.00
❑240, Jan 1972	16.00
❑241, Feb 1972	10.00
❑242, Feb 1972; JKu (c); a.k.a. DC 100-Page Super Spectacular #DC-9; wraparound cover	14.00
❑243, Mar 1972	10.00
❑244, Apr 1972	10.00
❑245, May 1972	10.00
❑246, Jun 1972	10.00
❑247, Jul 1972	10.00
❑248, Aug 1972	10.00
❑249, Sep 1972	10.00
❑250, Oct 1972	10.00
❑251, Nov 1972	10.00
❑252, Dec 1972	10.00
❑253, Jan 1973	10.00
❑254, Feb 1973	10.00
❑255, Mar 1973	10.00
❑256, Apr 1973	10.00
❑257, Jun 1973	7.00
❑258, Jul 1973	7.00
❑259, Aug 1973	7.00
❑260, Sep 1973	7.00
❑261, Oct 1973	7.00
❑262, Nov 1973	7.00
❑263, Dec 1973	7.00
❑264, Jan 1974	7.00
❑265, Feb 1974	7.00
❑266, Mar 1974	7.00
❑267, Apr 1974	7.00
❑268, May 1974	7.00
❑269, Jun 1974	7.00
❑270, Jul 1974	7.00
❑271, Aug 1974	7.00
❑272, Sep 1974	7.00
❑273, Oct 1974	7.00
❑274, Nov 1974	7.00
❑275, Dec 1974	7.00
❑276, Jan 1975	7.00
❑277, Feb 1975	7.00
❑278, Mar 1975	7.00
❑279, Apr 1975	7.00
❑280, May 1975	7.00
❑281, Jun 1975	7.00
❑282, Jul 1975	7.00
❑283, Aug 1975	7.00
❑284, Sep 1975	7.00
❑285, Oct 1975	7.00
❑286, Nov 1975	7.00
❑287, Dec 1975	7.00
❑288, Jan 1976	7.00
❑289, Feb 1976	7.00
❑290, Mar 1976	7.00
❑291, Apr 1976	7.00
❑292, May 1976	7.00

	N-MINT
❑293, Jun 1976	7.00
❑294, Jul 1976	7.00
❑295, Aug 1976	7.00
❑296, Sep 1976	7.00
❑297, Oct 1976	7.00
❑298, Nov 1976	7.00
❑299, Dec 1976	7.00
❑300, Jan 1977	5.00
❑301, Feb 1977; Series is continued as "Sgt. Rock"	5.00

OUR FIGHTING FORCES
DC

	N-MINT
❑14, Oct 1956	135.00
❑15, Nov 1956	135.00
❑16, Dec 1956	115.00
❑17, Jan 1957	115.00
❑18, Feb 1957	115.00
❑19, Mar 1957	115.00
❑20, Apr 1957	115.00
❑21, May 1957	90.00
❑22, Jun 1957	90.00
❑23, Jul 1957	90.00
❑24, Aug 1957	90.00
❑25, Sep 1957	90.00
❑26, Oct 1957	90.00
❑27, Nov 1957	90.00
❑28, Dec 1957	90.00
❑29, Jan 1958	90.00
❑30, Feb 1958	90.00
❑31, Mar 1958	75.00
❑32, Apr 1958	75.00
❑33, May 1958	75.00
❑34, Jun 1958	75.00
❑35, Jul 1958	75.00
❑36, Aug 1958	75.00
❑37, Sep 1958	75.00
❑38, Oct 1958	75.00
❑39, Nov 1958	75.00
❑40, Dec 1958	75.00
❑41, Jan 1959; Unknown Soldier prototype	90.00
❑42, Feb 1959	70.00
❑43, Mar 1959	70.00
❑44, Apr 1959	70.00
❑45, May 1959 1: Gunner & Sarge.	235.00
❑46, Jun 1959	95.00
❑47, Jul 1959	80.00
❑48, Aug 1959	60.00
❑49, Sep 1959	60.00
❑50, Oct 1959	60.00
❑51, Nov 1959	35.00
❑52, Dec 1959	35.00
❑53, Feb 1960	35.00
❑54, Apr 1960	35.00
❑55, Jun 1960	35.00
❑56, Aug 1960	35.00
❑57, Oct 1960	35.00
❑58, Dec 1960	35.00
❑59, Feb 1961	35.00
❑60, Apr 1961	35.00
❑61, Jun 1961	28.00
❑62, Aug 1961	28.00
❑63, Oct 1961	28.00
❑64, Dec 1961	28.00
❑65, Jan 1962	18.00
❑66, Feb 1962	18.00
❑67, Apr 1962	18.00
❑68, Jun 1962	18.00
❑69, Jul 1962	18.00
❑70, Aug 1962	18.00
❑71, Oct 1962	15.00
❑72, Nov 1962	15.00
❑73, Jan 1963	15.00
❑74, Feb 1963	15.00
❑75, Apr 1963	15.00

Issue	N-MINT
❑76, Jun 1963	15.00
❑77, Jul 1963	15.00
❑78, Aug 1963	15.00
❑79, Oct 1963	15.00
❑80, Nov 1963	15.00
❑81, Jan 1964	10.00
❑82, Feb 1964	10.00
❑83, Apr 1964	10.00
❑84, May 1964; Gunner & Sarge	10.00
❑85, Jul 1964	10.00
❑86, Aug 1964	10.00
❑87, Oct 1964	10.00
❑88, Nov 1964	10.00
❑89, Jan 1965	10.00
❑90, Feb 1965	10.00
❑91, Apr 1965	7.00
❑92, May 1965	7.00
❑93, Jul 1965	7.00
❑94, Aug 1965	7.00
❑95, Oct 1965	7.00
❑96, Nov 1965	7.00
❑97, Dec 1965	7.00
❑98, Jan 1966	7.00
❑99, Feb 1966 1: Captain Phil Hunter.	7.00
❑100, Apr 1966 A: Captain Hunter.	6.00
❑101, Jun 1966	6.00
❑102, Aug 1966	6.00
❑103, Oct 1966	6.00
❑104, Dec 1966	6.00
❑105, Feb 1967	6.00
❑106, Apr 1967 1: Ben Hunter. 1: Hunter's Hellcats.	6.00
❑107, Jul 1967	6.00
❑108, Aug 1967 A: Lt. Hunter's Hell-cats.	6.00
❑109, Oct 1967	6.00
❑110, Dec 1967	6.00
❑111, Feb 1968	6.00
❑112, Apr 1968	6.00
❑113, Jul 1968	6.00
❑114, Aug 1968	6.00
❑115, Sep 1968	6.00
❑116, Nov 1968	6.00
❑117, Jan 1969	6.00
❑118, Mar 1969 A: Lt. Hunter's Hell-cats.	6.00
❑119, May 1969	6.00
❑120, Jul 1969	6.00
❑121, Sep 1969 1: Heller.	5.00
❑122, Nov 1969	5.00
❑123, Jan 1970; Losers series begins	5.00
❑124, Mar 1970	5.00
❑125, May 1970	5.00
❑126, Jul 1970	5.00
❑127, Sep 1970; RA (a); Losers	5.00
❑128, Nov 1970	5.00
❑129, Jan 1971	5.00
❑130, Mar 1971	5.00
❑131, May 1971	5.00
❑132, Jul 1971; Losers	5.00
❑133, Sep 1971	5.00
❑134, Nov 1971	5.00
❑135, Jan 1972	5.00
❑136, Mar 1972	5.00
❑137, May 1972; Giant-size; Losers	5.00
❑138, Jul 1972	5.00
❑139, Sep 1972	5.00
❑140, Nov 1972	5.00
❑141, Jan 1973	5.00
❑142, Mar 1973	5.00
❑143, May 1973	5.00
❑144, Jul 1973	5.00
❑145, Sep 1973	5.00
❑146, Nov 1973	5.00
❑147, Jan 1974	5.00
❑148, Mar 1974; Accidentally includes 1973 Statement of Ownership for House of Secrets	5.00
❑149, May 1974	5.00
❑150, Jul 1974	5.00
❑151, Sep 1974; Losers	4.00
❑152, Nov 1974; Losers	4.00
❑153, Feb 1975; Losers	4.00
❑154, Apr 1975; JK (a); Losers	4.00
❑155, May 1975; Losers	4.00
❑156, Jun 1975; Losers	4.00
❑157, Jul 1975; Losers	4.00
❑158, Aug 1975; JK (a); Losers	4.00
❑159, Sep 1975; JK (a); Losers	4.00
❑160, Oct 1975; JK (a); Losers	4.00
❑161, Nov 1975; Losers	4.00
❑162, Dec 1975; JK (a); Losers	4.00
❑163, Jan 1976	4.00
❑164, Feb 1976	4.00
❑165, Mar 1976	4.00
❑166, Apr 1976	4.00
❑167, Jun 1976	4.00
❑168, Aug 1976	4.00
❑169, Oct 1976	4.00
❑170, Dec 1976	4.00
❑171, Feb 1977	4.00
❑172, Apr 1977	4.00
❑173, Jun 1977	4.00
❑174, Aug 1977	4.00
❑175, Oct 1977	4.00
❑176, Dec 1977	4.00
❑177, Feb 1978	4.00
❑178, Apr 1978	4.00
❑179, Jun 1978	4.00
❑180, Aug 1978	4.00
❑181, Oct 1978	4.00

OUTBREED 999
Blackout

Issue	N-MINT
❑1, May 1994	2.95
❑2, Jul 1994	2.95
❑3, Aug 1994	2.95
❑4	2.95
❑5	2.95

OUTCAST, THE
Acclaim / Valiant

Issue	N-MINT
❑1, Dec 1995	2.50

OUTCASTS
DC

Issue	N-MINT
❑1, Oct 1987	1.75
❑2, Nov 1987	1.75
❑3, Dec 1987	1.75
❑4, Jan 1988	1.75
❑5, Feb 1988	1.75
❑6, Mar 1988	1.75
❑7, Apr 1988	1.75
❑8, May 1988	1.75
❑9, Jun 1988	1.75
❑10, Jul 1988	1.75
❑11, Aug 1988	1.75
❑12, Sep 1988	1.75

OUTER EDGE
Innovation

Issue	N-MINT
❑1, b&w	2.50

OUTER LIMITS, THE
Dell

Issue	N-MINT
❑1, Jan 1964	55.00
❑2, Apr 1964	30.00
❑3, Jul 1964	24.00
❑4, Dec 1964	20.00
❑5, Jan 1965	20.00
❑6, Apr 1965	20.00
❑7, Jul 1965	20.00
❑8, Dec 1965	20.00
❑9, Jul 1966	20.00
❑10, Oct 1966	20.00
❑11, Jan 1967	10.00

Captain Hunter made his second appearance in *Our Fighting Forces* #100. He would later lead the appropriately named Hunter's Hellcats.

Issue	N-MINT
❑12, Apr 1967	10.00
❑13, May 1967	10.00
❑14, Jul 1967	10.00
❑15, Sep 1967	10.00
❑16 1968	10.00
❑17, Oct 1968	10.00
❑18, Oct 1969	10.00

OUTER SPACE (VOL. 2)
Charlton

Issue	N-MINT
❑1	20.00

OUTER SPACE BABES, THE (VOL. 3)
Silhouette

Issue	N-MINT
❑1	2.95

OUT FOR BLOOD
Dark Horse

Issue	N-MINT
❑1, Sep 1999	2.95
❑2, Oct 1999	2.95
❑3, Nov 1999	2.95
❑4, Dec 1999	2.95

OUTLANDER
Malibu

Issue	N-MINT
❑1 1987	1.95
❑2 1987	1.95
❑3, Dec 1987, b&w	1.95
❑4, Jan 1988	1.95
❑5, Mar 1988	1.95
❑6 1988	1.95
❑7 1988	1.95

OUTLANDERS
Dark Horse

Issue	N-MINT
❑0, Dec 1988	3.00
❑1, Jan 1989	2.50
❑2, Feb 1989	2.00
❑3, Mar 1989	2.00
❑4, Apr 1989	2.00
❑5, May 1989	2.00
❑6, Jun 1989	2.00
❑7, Jul 1989	2.00
❑8, Aug 1989	2.00
❑9, Sep 1989	2.25
❑10, Oct 1989	2.25
❑11, Nov 1989	2.25
❑12, Dec 1989	2.25
❑13, Jan 1990	2.25
❑14, Feb 1990	2.25
❑15, Mar 1990	2.25
❑16, Apr 1990	2.25
❑17, May 1990	2.25
❑18, Jun 1990	2.25
❑19, Jul 1990	2.25
❑20, Aug 1990	2.25
❑21, Sep 1990	2.25
❑22, Oct 1990	2.50
❑23, Nov 1990	2.50
❑24, Dec 1990	2.50
❑25, Jan 1991	2.50
❑26, Feb 1991	2.50
❑27, Mar 1991; Giant-size special	2.95
❑28, Apr 1991	2.50
❑29, May 1991	2.50
❑30, Jun 1991	2.50

N-MINT

❑31, Jul 1991 .... 2.50
❑32, Aug 1991 .... 2.50
❑33, Sep 1991 .... 2.50
❑Special 1, b&w; manga; Epilogue 2.50

OUTLANDERS EPILOGUE
DARK HORSE

❑1, Mar 1994, b&w 2.50

OUTLAW 7
DARK HORSE

❑1, Aug 2001 .... 2.99
❑2, Sep 2001 .... 2.99
❑3, Jan 2002 .... 2.99

OUTLAW KID, THE (2ND SERIES)
MARVEL

❑1, Aug 1970 .... 12.00
❑2, Oct 1970 .... 6.00
❑3, Dec 1970 .... 3.50
❑4, Feb 1971 .... 2.50
❑5, Apr 1971 .... 2.50
❑6, Jun 1971 .... 2.50
❑7, Aug 1971 .... 2.50
❑8, Oct 1971; Giant-size 2.50
❑9, Dec 1971 .... 3.00
❑10, Jun 1972; O: Outlaw Kid. series goes on hiatus 2.00
❑11, Aug 1972 .... 2.00
❑12, Oct 1972 .... 2.00
❑13, Dec 1972 .... 2.00
❑14, Feb 1973 .... 2.00
❑15, Apr 1973 .... 2.00
❑16, Jun 1973 .... 2.00
❑17, Aug 1973 .... 2.00
❑18, Oct 1973 .... 2.00
❑19, Dec 1973 .... 2.00
❑20, Feb 1974 .... 2.00
❑21, Apr 1974 .... 2.00
❑22, Jun 1974 .... 2.00
❑23, Aug 1974 .... 2.00
❑24, Oct 1974 .... 2.00
❑25, Dec 1974 .... 2.00
❑26, Feb 1975 .... 2.00
❑27, Apr 1975 O: Outlaw Kid. 2.00
❑28, Jun 1975 .... 2.00
❑29, Aug 1975 .... 2.00
❑30, Oct 1975 .... 2.00

OUTLAW NATION (VERTIGO)
DC / VERTIGO

❑1, Nov 2000 .... 2.50
❑2, Dec 2000 .... 2.50
❑3, Jan 2001 .... 2.50
❑4, Feb 2001 .... 2.50
❑5, Mar 2001 .... 2.50
❑6, Apr 2001 .... 2.50
❑7, May 2001 .... 2.50
❑8, Jun 2001 .... 2.50
❑9, Jul 2001 .... 2.50
❑10, Aug 2001 .... 2.50
❑11, Sep 2001 .... 2.50
❑12, Oct 2001 .... 2.50
❑13, Nov 2001 .... 2.50
❑14, Dec 2001 .... 2.50
❑15, Jan 2002 .... 2.50
❑16, Feb 2002 .... 2.50
❑17, Mar 2002 .... 2.50
❑18, Apr 2002 .... 2.50
❑19, May 2002 .... 2.50

OUTLAW NATION (VOL. 2)
BONEYARD

❑1 1994 .... 4.95
❑1/Platinum; Tim Bradstreet cover 5.00

OUTLAW OVERDRIVE
BLUE COMET

❑1; Red Edition 2.95

OUTLAWS, THE (DC)
DC

❑1, Sep 1991 LMc (a) 2.00
❑2, Oct 1991 LMc (a) 2.00
❑3, Nov 1991 LMc (a) 2.00
❑4, Dec 1991 LMc (a) 2.00
❑5, Jan 1992 LMc (a) 2.00
❑6, Feb 1992 LMc (a) 2.00
❑7, Mar 1992 LMc (a) 2.00
❑8, Apr 1992 LMc (a) 2.00

OUT OF THE VORTEX (COMICS' GREATEST WORLD...)
DARK HORSE

❑1, Oct 1993; Foil embossed cover 2.00
❑2, Nov 1993 .... 2.00
❑3, Dec 1993 .... 2.00
❑4, Jan 1994 .... 2.00
❑5, Feb 1994 .... 2.00
❑6, Mar 1994 .... 2.00
❑7, Apr 1994 .... 2.00
❑8, May 1994 .... 2.00
❑9, Jun 1994 .... 2.00
❑10, Jul 1994 .... 2.00
❑11, Sep 1994 .... 2.00
❑12, Oct 1994 .... 2.00

OUT OF THIS WORLD (ETERNITY)
ETERNITY

❑1, b&w; Reprints stories from Strange Worlds #9, Strange Planets #16, Tomb of Terror #6, and Weird Tales of the Future #1 .... 3.50

OUTPOSTS
BLACKTHORNE

❑1, Jun 1997 .... 1.50

OUTSIDERS, THE (1ST SERIES)
DC

❑1, Nov 1985 .... 2.00
❑2, Dec 1985 .... 1.50
❑3, Jan 1986 .... 1.50
❑4, Feb 1986 .... 1.25
❑5, Mar 1986; Christmas Carol story 1.25
❑6, Apr 1986 .... 1.25
❑7, May 1986 .... 1.25
❑8, Jun 1986 .... 1.25
❑9, Jul 1986 .... 1.25
❑10, Aug 1986 .... 1.25
❑11, Sep 1986 .... 1.00
❑12, Oct 1986 .... 1.00
❑13, Nov 1986 .... 1.00
❑14, Dec 1986 .... 1.00
❑15, Jan 1987 .... 1.00
❑16, Feb 1987 .... 1.00
❑17, Mar 1987; Batman returns 1.00
❑18, Apr 1987 .... 1.00
❑19, May 1987 .... 1.00
❑20, Jun 1987 .... 1.00
❑21, Jul 1987 .... 1.00
❑22, Aug 1987; EC parody back-up 1.00
❑23, Sep 1987 .... 1.00
❑24, Oct 1987 .... 1.00
❑25, Nov 1987 .... 1.00
❑26, Dec 1987 .... 1.00
❑27, Jan 1988; Millennium 1.00
❑28, Feb 1988; Millennium 1.00
❑Annual 1 .... 2.50
❑Special 1; Crossover continued in Infinity Inc. SE #1 .... 1.50

OUTSIDERS (2ND SERIES)
DC

❑0, Oct 1994; New team begins 2.50
❑1/A, Nov 1993; Alpha version 2.50
❑1/B, Nov 1993; Omega version 2.50
❑2, Dec 1993 .... 2.00
❑3, Jan 1994 A: Eradicator. 2.00
❑4, Feb 1994 .... 2.00
❑5, Mar 1994 .... 2.00
❑6, Apr 1994 .... 2.00
❑7, May 1994 .... 2.00
❑8, Jun 1994 JA (a); A: Batman (Azrael). 2.00
❑9, Jul 1994 .... 2.00
❑10, Aug 1994 .... 2.00
❑11, Sep 1994 .... 2.00
❑12, Nov 1994 .... 2.00
❑13, Dec 1994 A: Superman. 2.00
❑14, Jan 1995 .... 2.00
❑15, Feb 1995 .... 2.00
❑16, Mar 1995 .... 2.00
❑17, Apr 1995 .... 2.00
❑18, May 1995 .... 2.00
❑19, Jun 1995 .... 2.25
❑20, Jul 1995 .... 2.25
❑21, Aug 1995 .... 2.25
❑22, Sep 1995 .... 2.25
❑23, Oct 1995 .... 2.25
❑24, Nov 1995 .... 2.25

OUTSIDERS (3RD SERIES)
DC

❑1, Aug 2003 .... 2.50
❑2, Sep 2003 .... 2.50
❑3, Oct 2003 .... 2.50
❑4, Nov 2003 .... 2.50
❑5, Dec 2003 .... 2.50
❑6, Jan 2004 .... 2.50
❑7, Feb 2004 .... 2.50
❑8, Mar 2004 .... 2.50
❑9, Apr 2004 .... 2.50
❑10, May 2004 .... 2.50
❑11, Jun 2004 .... 2.50
❑12, Jul 2004 .... 2.50
❑13, Aug 2004 .... 2.50
❑14, Sep 2004 ....

OVERKILL: WITCHBLADE/ALIENS/ DARKNESS/PREDATOR
IMAGE

❑1, Dec 2000 .... 5.95
❑2, Mar 2001 .... 5.95

OVERLOAD MAGAZINE
ECLIPSE

❑1, Apr 1987, b&w 1.50

OVERMEN, THE
EXCEL

❑1 .... 2.95

OVER THE EDGE
MARVEL

❑1, Nov 1995; Daredevil 1.25
❑2, Dec 1995 A: Doctor Strange. 1.00
❑3, Jan 1996; Hulk 1.00
❑4, Feb 1996; Ghost Rider 1.00
❑5, Mar 1996; Punisher 1.00
❑6, Apr 1996; Daredevil and Black Panther 1.00
❑7, May 1996; Doctor Strange vs. Nightmare 1.00
❑8, Jun 1996; Elektra 1.00
❑9, Jul 1996; Ghost Rider, John Blaze 1.00
❑10, Aug 1996; Daredevil 1.00

OVERTURE
ALL AMERICAN

❑1, b&w 2.25
❑2, Apr 1990, b&w 2.25

OWLHOOTS
KITCHEN SINK

❑1, color 2.50
❑2, color 2.50

OX COW O' WAR
SPOOF

❑1, b&w; parody 2.95

OZ
CALIBER

❑0 .... 4.00
❑1 .... 6.00
❑2 .... 4.00
❑3 .... 4.00
❑4 .... 4.00
❑5 .... 3.50
❑6 .... 3.50

	N-MINT
❑7	3.50
❑8	3.50
❑9	3.50
❑10	3.50
❑11	3.00
❑12	3.00
❑13	3.00
❑14	3.00
❑15 1996	3.00
❑16 1996	3.00
❑17, Sep 1996	3.00
❑18, Nov 1996	2.95
❑19, Jan 1997	2.95
❑20, Mar 1997	2.95
❑21 1997	2.95
❑22 1997	2.95

OZ COLLECTION (BILL BRYAN'S...)
ARROW

❑1 ... 2.95

OZ: DAEMONSTORM
CALIBER

❑1, b&w; intracompany crossover ... 3.95

OZ: ROMANCE IN RAGS
CALIBER

❑1, b&w ... 2.95
❑2, b&w ... 2.95
❑3, b&w ... 2.95

OZ SPECIAL: FREEDOM FIGHTERS
CALIBER

❑1, b&w ... 2.95

OZ SPECIAL: LION
CALIBER

❑1, b&w; continues in Oz Special: Tin Man ... 2.95

OZ SPECIAL: SCARECROW
CALIBER

❑1, b&w; continues in Oz Special: Lion ... 2.95

OZ SPECIAL: TIN MAN
CALIBER

❑1, b&w; continues in Oz Special: Freedom Fighters ... 2.95

OZ SQUAD (1ST SERIES)
BRAVE NEW WORDS

❑1, Oct 1991 ... 3.00
❑2, Jan 1992 ... 2.50
❑3 ... 2.50
❑4 ... 2.50

OZ SQUAD (2ND SERIES)
PATCHWORK

❑1 ... 3.00
❑2 ... 2.50
❑3 ... 2.50
❑4, ca. 1994 ... 2.75
❑5 ... 2.75
❑6 ... 2.95
❑7, Aug 1995 ... 2.75
❑8, Oct 1995 ... 2.75
❑9, Dec 1995 O: Tin Man. ... 2.75
❑10 O: Tin Man. ... 2.75

OZ: STRAW & SORCERY
CALIBER

❑1, Mar 1997, b&w ... 2.95
❑2 1997, b&w ... 2.95
❑3 1997, b&w ... 2.95

OZ-WONDERLAND WARS
DC

❑1, Jan 1986 ... 2.50
❑2, Feb 1986 A: Hoppy the Marvel Bunny. ... 2.50
❑3, Mar 1986 ... 2.50

OZZY OSBOURNE
ROCK-IT COMICS

❑1 ... 6.00

P

PACIFIC PRESENTS
PACIFIC

❑1, Oct 1982; SD, DSt (w); SD, DSt (a); Rocketeer; Missing Man ... 4.00
❑2, Apr 1983; SD, DSt (w); SD, DSt (a); Rocketeer; Missing Man ... 3.00
❑3, Mar 1984; SD (w); SD (a); Missing Man ... 1.50
❑4, Jun 1984 ... 1.50

PAC (PRETER-HUMAN ASSAULT CORPS)
ARTIFACTS

❑1, Oct 1993 ... 1.95

PACT, THE
IMAGE

❑1, Feb 1994 ... 1.95
❑2, Apr 1994 ... 1.95
❑3, Jun 1994 ... 1.95

PAGERS COMICS ANTHOLOGY
NO TALENT

❑1, Spr 1997 ... 2.50
❑2, Sum 1997 ... 2.50
❑3, Fal 1997 ... 2.50
❑4, Win 1997 ... 2.50
❑5, Spr 1998 ... 2.50
❑6, Sum 1998 ... 2.50

PAINKILLER JANE
EVENT

❑0, Nov 1998 O: Painkiller Jane. ... 3.95
❑0/Ltd. O: Painkiller Jane. ... 39.95
❑1, Jun 1997; MWa (w); wraparound cover ... 3.00
❑1/A, Jun 1997; MWa (w); variant cover ... 3.00
❑1/B, Jun 1997; MWa (w); Red foil ... 25.00
❑2, Jul 1997; MWa (w); Standard cover: Jane in sunglasses close-up ... 3.00
❑2/A, Jul 1997; MWa (w); variant cover; Jane running ... 3.00
❑3, Aug 1997 MWa (w) ... 3.00
❑3/A, Aug 1997; MWa (w); variant cover ... 3.00
❑4, Sep 1997 MWa (w) ... 3.00
❑4/A, Sep 1997; MWa (w); variant cover ... 3.00
❑5, Oct 1997 MWa (w) ... 3.00
❑5/A 1997; MWa (w); variant cover ... 3.00

PAINKILLER JANE/DARKCHYLDE
EVENT

❑0; European Preview book ... 4.00
❑0/Autographed; European Preview book ... 29.95
❑1, Oct 1998 ... 3.00
❑1/A, Oct 1998 ... 29.95
❑1/B, Oct 1998; DFE alternate cover ... 4.00
❑1/C, Oct 1998; Signed edition ... 39.95
❑Ashcan 1, Jul 1998; DF Exclusive; Sketches ... 5.00

PAINKILLER JANE/HELLBOY
EVENT

❑1, Aug 1998; Cover by Mike Mignola ... 2.95
❑1/Ltd., Aug 1998; Signed edition ... 29.95
❑1/A, Aug 1998; Cover by Quesada/Palmiotti ... 2.95

PAINKILLER JANE VS. THE DARKNESS: STRIPPER
EVENT

❑1, Apr 1997; four alternate covers ... 2.95
❑1/A, Apr 1997; Jane facing forward, shooting on cover ... 3.00
❑1/B, Apr 1997 ... 3.00
❑1/C, Apr 1997 ... 3.00
❑1/Ltd., Apr 1997; Signed edition ... 20.00

PAINTBALL UNIVERSE 2000
SPLATTOONS

❑1 ... 2.95

PAJAMA CHRONICLES
BLACKTHORNE

❑1 ... 1.75

Russ Cochran reprinted E.C.'s other humor title, *Panic*, in a pair of hardcover volumes and as individual comics issues.

© 1997 Russ Cochran Publications/ Gemstone Publishing.

PAKKINS' LAND
CALIBER / TAPESTRY

❑0, Jun 1997 ... 1.95
❑1, Oct 1996 ... 2.95
❑2, Dec 1996 ... 2.95
❑3, Feb 1997 ... 2.95
❑4, May 1997 ... 2.95
❑5, Jun 1997 ... 2.95
❑6, Jul 1997 ... 2.95

PAKKINS' LAND: FORGOTTEN DREAMS
CALIBER / TAPESTRY

❑1, Apr 1998 ... 2.95
❑2 ... 2.95
❑3 ... 2.95
❑4, Mar 2000; published by Image ... 2.95

PAKKINS' LAND: QUEST FOR KINGS
CALIBER / TAPESTRY

❑1 ... 2.95
❑1/A, Aug 1997 ... 2.95
❑2, Sep 1997 ... 2.95
❑2/A, Aug 1997; alternate cover ... 2.95
❑3, Nov 1997 ... 2.95
❑4, Dec 1997 ... 2.95
❑5, Jan 1998 ... 2.95
❑6, Mar 1998 ... 2.95

PALATINE, THE
GRYPHON RAMPANT

❑1 ... 2.50
❑2, Oct 1994 ... 2.50
❑3, Jan 1995 ... 2.50
❑4 ... 2.50
❑5 ... 2.50

PALESTINE
FANTAGRAPHICS

❑1, b&w ... 2.50
❑2, b&w ... 2.50
❑3, b&w ... 2.50
❑4, b&w ... 2.95
❑5 ... 2.50
❑6 ... 2.50
❑7, Sep 1994 ... 2.95
❑9, Oct 1995, b&w ... 2.95

PAL-YAT-CHEE
ADHESIVE

❑1, b&w ... 2.50

PAMELA ANDERSON UNCOVERED
POP

❑1 ... 2.95

PANDA KHAN SPECIAL
ABACUS

❑1, b&w ... 3.00

PANDEMONIUM
CHAOS!

❑1, Sep 1998 ... 2.95

PANDORA PILL, THE
ACID RAIN

❑1 ... 2.50

PANIC (RCP)
GEMSTONE

❑1, Mar 1997; Reprints Panic (EC) #1 ... 2.50
❑2, Jun 1997; Reprints Panic (EC) #2 ... 2.50
❑3, Sep 1997; Reprints Panic (EC) #3 ... 2.50
❑4, Dec 1997; Reprints Panic (EC) #4 ... 2.50
❑5, Mar 1998; Reprints Panic (EC) #5 ... 2.50

N-MINT

❑6, Jun 1998; Reprints Panic (EC) #6 2.50
❑7, Sep 1998; Reprints Panic (EC) #7 2.50
❑8, Dec 1998; Reprints Panic (EC) #8 2.50
❑9, Mar 1999 2.50
❑10, Jun 1999 2.50
❑11, Sep 1999 2.50
❑12, Dec 1999 2.50
❑Annual 1; Collects issues #1-4 10.95
❑Annual 2; Collects issues #5-8 10.95

PANTERA
Malibu / Rock-It

❑1, Aug 1994; magazine 4.00

PANTHA: HAUNTED PASSION
Harris / Rock-It

❑1 2.95

PANTHEON (ARCHER)
Archer Books & Games

❑1, Oct 1995, b&w 2.95
❑2, Jun 1997

PANTHEON (LONE STAR)
Lone Star

❑1, May 1998 2.95
❑2, Jul 1998 2.95
❑3, Sep 1998 2.95
❑4, Jan 1999 2.95
❑5, Jul 1999 2.95
❑6, Aug 1999 2.95

PANTHEON: ANCIENT HISTORY
Lone Star

❑1, Aug 1999 3.95

PAPER CINEMA: THE BOX
Grey Blossom Sequentials

❑3, Dec 1998 3.55

PAPER CINEMA: WAVES IN SPACE
Grey Blossom Sequentials

❑2, Dec 1998 3.55

PAPER DOLLS FROM THE CALIFORNIA GIRLS
Eclipse

❑1; paper dolls 5.95

PAPER TALES
CLG Comics

❑1, Sum 1993, b&w 2.50
❑2, Sum 1994, b&w 2.50

PARA-COPS
Excel

❑1 2.95

PARADAX
Vortex

❑1 1.75
❑2, Aug 1987 1.75

PARADIGM (IMAGE)
Image

❑1, Sep 2002 3.50
❑2, Oct 2002 3.50
❑3, Nov 2002 3.50
❑4, Dec 2002 3.50
❑5, Jan 2003 2.95
❑6, Feb 2003 2.95
❑7, Mar 2003 2.95
❑8, Apr 2003 2.95
❑9, May 2003 3.50
❑10, Jul 2003 3.50
❑11, Oct 2003 3.95
❑12, Dec 2003 3.95

PARADIGM
Gauntlet

❑1 2.95

PARADISE KISS
Tokyopop

❑1, May 2002, b&w; printed in Japanese format 9.99

PARADISE TOO
Abstract

❑1 2.95
❑2 2.95
❑3 2.95
❑4 2.95
❑5 2.95
❑6 2.95
❑7 2.95
❑8 2.95
❑9 2.95
❑10 2.95
❑11 2.95
❑12, Mar 2003 2.95
❑13, Jul 2003 2.95
❑14, Aug 2003 2.95

PARADISE X
Marvel

❑0, Apr 2002 4.50
❑1, May 2002 2.99
❑2, Jun 2002 2.99
❑3, Aug 2002 2.99
❑4, Sep 2002 2.99
❑5, Oct 2002 2.99
❑6, Dec 2002 2.99
❑7, ca. 2003 2.99
❑8, ca. 2003 2.99
❑9, ca. 2003 2.99
❑10, Jun 2003 2.99
❑11, Jul 2003 2.99
❑12, Aug 2003 2.99

PARADISE X: DEVILS
Marvel

❑1, Nov 2002 4.50

PARADISE X: HERALDS
Marvel

❑1, Dec 2001 3.50
❑2, Jan 2002 3.50
❑3, Feb 2002 3.50

PARADISE X: A
Marvel

❑1, Oct 2003 2.99

PARADISE X: X
Marvel

❑1, Nov 2003 2.99

PARADISE X: RAGNAROK
Marvel

❑1, Mar 2003 2.99
❑2, Apr 2003 2.99

PARADISE X: XEN
Marvel

❑1, Jul 2002 4.50

PARADOX PROJECT: GENESIS
Paradox Project

❑1, Dec 1998, b&w 2.95

PARAGON: DARK APOCALYPSE
AC

❑1 2.95
❑2 2.95
❑3 2.95
❑4 2.95

PARALLAX: EMERALD NIGHT
DC

❑1, Nov 1996; Final Night 2.95

PARANOIA (ADVENTURE)
Adventure

❑1, Oct 1991 2.95
❑2, Dec 1991 2.95
❑3, Feb 1992 2.95
❑4, Apr 1992 2.95
❑5, Jun 1992 2.95
❑6, Aug 1992 2.95

PARANOIA (CO. & SONS)
Co. & Sons

❑1 4.00

PARAPHERNALIA
Graphitti

❑1; Ordering Catalogue 2.00

PARA TROOP
Comics Conspiracy

❑0 3.95
❑1 2.95
❑2 2.95
❑3, Oct 1998 2.95
❑4, Dec 1998 2.95
❑5, Feb 1999 2.95
❑Ashcan 1; ashcan edition 2.95

PARDNERS
Cottonwood Graphics

❑1, b&w 7.95
❑2, b&w 7.95

PARIS THE MAN OF PLASTER
Harrier

❑1, May 1987 1.95
❑2 1987 1.95
❑3 1987 1.95
❑4 1987 1.95
❑5 1987 1.95
❑6 1987 1.95

PARLIAMENT OF JUSTICE
Image

❑1, Mar 2003 5.95

PARO-DEE
Parody

❑1, b&w 2.50

PARODY PRESS ANNUAL SWIMSUIT SPECIAL '93
Parody

❑1, Aug 1993 2.50

PARTICLE DREAMS
Fantagraphics

❑1, Oct 1986 2.25
❑2, Jan 1987 2.25
❑3, Apr 1987 2.25
❑4, Jun 1987 2.25
❑5 1987 2.25
❑6 1987 2.25

PARTNERS IN PANDEMONIUM
Caliber

❑1, b&w 2.50
❑2, b&w 2.50
❑3, b&w 2.50

PARTS OF A HOLE
Caliber

❑1, b&w; Brian Michael Bendis' first major comics work 2.50

PARTS UNKNOWN
Eclipse

❑1, Aug 1995, b&w 2.50
❑2, Mar 1995, b&w 2.50
❑3, Jun 1995, b&w 2.50
❑4, Oct 1995, b&w 2.50

PARTS UNKNOWN: DARK INTENTIONS
Knight

❑0, Aug 1995 2.95
❑1, Mar 1995 2.95
❑2, Jun 1995 2.95
❑3, Oct 1995 2.95
❑4 1995 2.95

PARTS UNKNOWN: HOSTILE TAKEOVER
Image

❑1, Jun 2000 2.95
❑1/Ashcan, Jun 2000; Preview edition 4.95
❑2, Jul 2000 2.95
❑2/Ashcan, Jul 2000; Preview edition 4.95
❑3, Aug 2000 2.95
❑3/Ashcan, Aug 2000; Preview edition 4.95
❑4, Sep 2000 2.95
❑4/Ashcan, Sep 2000; Preview edition 4.95

PARTS UNKNOWN II: THE NEXT INVASION
Eclipse

❑1, Dec 1993, b&w 2.95

PASSOVER
Maximum

❑1, Dec 1996 2.99

PATH, THE
CrossGen

❑1, Apr 2002 2.95
❑2, May 2002 2.95

N-MINT

❑3, Jun 2002 ... 2.95
❑4, Jul 2002 ... 2.95
❑5, Aug 2002 ... 2.95
❑6, Sep 2002 ... 2.95
❑7, Oct 2002 ... 2.95
❑8, Nov 2002 ... 2.95
❑9, Dec 2002 ... 2.95
❑10, Jan 2003 ... 2.95
❑11, Feb 2003 ... 2.95
❑12, Mar 2003 ... 2.95
❑13, Apr 2003 ... 2.95
❑14, May 2003 ... 2.95
❑15, Jun 2003 ... 2.95
❑16, Jul 2003 ... 2.95
❑17, Sep 2003 ... 2.95
❑18, Oct 2003 ... 2.95
❑19, Nov 2003 ... 2.95
❑20, Dec 2003 ... 2.95
❑21, Jan 2004 ... 2.95
❑22, Mar 2004 ... 2.95
❑23, Apr 2004 ... 2.95

PATH PREQUEL, THE
CrossGen

❑1, Mar 2002 ... 2.95

PATHWAYS TO FANTASY
Pacific

❑1, Jul 1984 JJ (a) ... 2.00

PATIENT ZERO
Image

❑1, Apr 2004 ... 2.95
❑2, May 2004 ... 2.95
❑3, Aug 2004 ... 2.95

PATRICK RABBIT
Fragments West

❑1, Sum 1988 ... 2.00
❑2 ... 2.00
❑3 ... 2.00
❑4 ... 2.00
❑5 ... 2.00
❑6 ... 2.00
❑7 ... 2.00

PATRICK STEWART
Celebrity

❑1 ... 2.95

PATRICK STEWART VS. WILLIAM SHATNER
Celebrity

❑1, b&w ... 5.95

PATRIOTS, THE
WildStorm

❑1, Jan 2000 ... 2.50
❑2, Feb 2000 ... 2.50
❑3, Mar 2000 ... 2.50
❑4, Apr 2000 ... 2.50
❑5, May 2000 ... 2.50
❑6, Jun 2000 ... 2.50
❑7, Jul 2000 ... 2.50
❑8, Aug 2000 ... 2.50
❑9, Sep 2000 ... 2.50
❑10, Oct 2000 ... 2.50

PAT SAVAGE: THE WOMAN OF BRONZE
Millennium

❑1, Oct 1992 ... 2.50

PATTY CAKE
Permanent Press

❑1, b&w ... 3.00
❑2, b&w ... 3.00
❑3, ca. 1995, b&w ... 3.00
❑4, ca. 1995, b&w ... 3.00
❑5, ca. 1996, b&w ... 3.00
❑6, ca. 1996, b&w ... 3.00
❑7, ca. 1996, b&w ... 3.00
❑8, ca. 1996, b&w ... 3.00
❑9, ca. 1996, b&w ... 3.00

PATTY CAKE (2ND SERIES)
Caliber / Tapestry

❑1, ca. 1996, b&w ... 3.00
❑2, ca. 1997, b&w ... 3.00

N-MINT

❑3, ca. 1997, b&w ... 3.00
❑Holiday 1, Dec 1996, b&w ... 3.00

PATTY CAKE & FRIENDS
Slave Labor

❑1, Nov 1997, b&w ... 3.00
❑2, Dec 1997, b&w ... 3.00
❑3, Jan 1998, b&w ... 3.00
❑4, Feb 1998, b&w ... 3.00
❑5, Mar 1998, b&w ... 3.00
❑6, Apr 1998, b&w ... 3.00
❑7, May 1998 ... 2.95
❑8, Jun 1998 ... 2.95
❑9, Aug 1998 ... 2.95
❑10, Sep 1998 ... 2.95
❑11, Nov 1998 ... 2.95
❑12 ... 2.95
❑Special 1, Oct 1997 ... 3.95

PATTY CAKE & FRIENDS (VOL. 2)
Slave Labor

❑1, Nov 2000, b&w; cardstock cover ... 4.95

PAUL THE SAMURAI
New England

❑1, Jul 1992 ... 4.00
❑2, Sep 1992 ... 3.00
❑3, Nov 1992; Scarcer ... 6.00
❑4, Jan 1993 ... 4.00
❑5, Mar 1993 ... 2.75
❑6, May 1993 ... 2.75
❑7, Jul 1993 ... 2.75
❑8, Nov 1993 ... 2.75
❑9, Mar 1994 A: The Tick. ... 2.75
❑10, May 1994 A: The Tick. ... 2.75

PAUL THE SAMURAI (MINI-SERIES)
NEC

❑1 A: The Tick. ... 3.50
❑2 ... 3.00
❑3 ... 3.00

PAYNE
Dream Catcher

❑1, Sep 1995, b&w ... 2.50

PEACEMAKER, THE
Charlton

❑1, Mar 1967 ... 10.00
❑2, May 1967; Fightin' 5 back-up story ... 6.00
❑3, Jul 1967 ... 6.00
❑4, Sep 1967 O: The Peacemaker. ... 8.00
❑5, Nov 1967 ... 6.00

PEACEMAKER (MINI-SERIES)
DC

❑1, Jan 1988 ... 1.50
❑2, Feb 1988 ... 1.50
❑3, Mar 1988 ... 1.50
❑4, Apr 1988 ... 1.50

PEACE PARTY
Blue Corn

❑1 ... 2.95

PEACE POSSE
Mellon Bank

❑1 ... 2.95

PEANUT BUTTER AND JEREMY
Alternative

❑1, Aug 2000, b&w ... 2.95

PEANUTS (DELL)
Dell

❑1, ca. 1954 ... 125.00
❑4, Feb 1960 ... 75.00
❑5, May 1960 ... 55.00
❑6, Aug 1960 ... 55.00
❑7, Nov 1960 ... 55.00
❑8, Feb 1961 ... 55.00
❑9, May 1961 ... 55.00
❑10, Aug 1961 ... 55.00
❑11, Nov 1961 ... 55.00
❑12, Feb 1962 ... 55.00
❑13, May 1962 ... 55.00

Pebbles and Bamm-Bamm featured the misadventures of Fred and Barney's children as teen-agers.
© 1974 Charlton.

N-MINT

PEANUTS (GOLD KEY)
Gold Key

❑1, May 1963 ... 125.00
❑2, Aug 1963 ... 75.00
❑3, Nov 1963 ... 75.00
❑4, Feb 1964 ... 75.00

PEBBLES AND BAMM-BAMM
Charlton

❑1, Jan 1972 ... 18.00
❑2, Mar 1972 ... 12.00
❑3, May 1972 ... 9.00
❑4, Jul 1972 ... 9.00
❑5, Aug 1972 ... 9.00
❑6, Sep 1972 ... 7.00
❑7, Oct 1972; No credits in issue ... 7.00
❑8, Nov 1972 ... 7.00
❑9 ... 7.00
❑10, ca. 1973 ... 7.00
❑11, ca. 1973 ... 5.00
❑12, ca. 1973 ... 5.00
❑13, ca. 1973 ... 5.00
❑14, ca. 1973 ... 5.00
❑15, Aug 1973 ... 5.00
❑16, Oct 1973 ... 5.00
❑17, Nov 1973 ... 5.00
❑18, Jan 1974 ... 5.00
❑19, Feb 1974 ... 5.00
❑20, Jun 1974 ... 5.00
❑21, Aug 1974 ... 4.00
❑22, Nov 1974 ... 4.00
❑23, Jan 1975 ... 4.00
❑24, Feb 1975 ... 4.00
❑25, Mar 1975 ... 4.00
❑26, ca. 1975 ... 4.00
❑27, ca. 1975 ... 4.00
❑28, ca. 1975 ... 4.00
❑29, ca. 1975 ... 4.00
❑30, Dec 1975 ... 4.00
❑31, Feb 1976 ... 3.00
❑32, Apr 1976 ... 3.00
❑33, Jun 1976 ... 3.00
❑34, Aug 1976; No credits listed ... 3.00
❑35, Oct 1976 ... 3.00
❑36, Dec 1976; No credits listed ... 3.00

PEBBLES & BAMM-BAMM (HARVEY)
Harvey

❑1, Nov 1993 ... 1.50
❑2, Jan 1994 ... 1.50
❑3, Mar 1994 ... 1.50
❑Summer 1; first edition ... 2.25

PEBBLES FLINTSTONE
Gold Key

❑1, Sep 1963 ... 75.00

PEDESTRIAN VULGARITY
Fantagraphics

❑1, b&w ... 2.50

PEEK-A-BOO 3-D
3-D Zone

❑1 ... 3.95

PEEPSHOW
Drawn & Quarterly

❑1 ... 2.50
❑2, May 1992 ... 2.50
❑3 ... 2.50
❑4 ... 2.50
❑5, Oct 1993 ... 2.95

	N-MINT
❑6, Apr 1994	2.95
❑7	2.95
❑8	2.95
❑9	2.95

PELLESTAR
ETERNITY

❑1, Sep 1987	1.95
❑2	1.95

PENDRAGON (AIRCEL)
AIRCEL

❑1, Nov 1991, b&w	2.95
❑2, Dec 1991, b&w	2.95

PENDULUM
ADVENTURE

❑1, b&w	2.50
❑2, b&w	2.50
❑3, b&w	2.50
❑4, b&w	2.50

PENDULUM'S ILLUSTRATED STORIES
PENDULUM

❑1; Moby Dick; No apparent cover price	4.95
❑2; Treasure Island	4.95
❑3; Doctor Jekyll	4.95
❑4; 20, 000 Leagues Under the Sea	4.95
❑5; Midsummer Night's Dream	4.95
❑6; Christmas Carol	4.95

PENGUIN & PENCILGUIN
FRAGMENTS WEST

❑1, Jan 1987	2.00
❑2, Feb 1987	2.00
❑3, Mar 1987	2.00
❑4, Apr 1987	2.00
❑5, May 1987	2.00
❑6, Jun 1987	2.00

PENGUIN BROS.
LABYRINTH

❑1	2.50
❑2	2.50

PENNY CENTURY
FANTAGRAPHICS

❑1, Dec 1997, b&w	2.95
❑2, Mar 1998, b&w	2.95
❑3, Sep 1998, b&w	2.95
❑4, Jan 1999, b&w	2.95
❑5, Jun 1999, b&w	2.95
❑6, Nov 1999, b&w	2.95
❑7, Jul 2000, b&w	2.95

PENTACLE: THE SIGN OF THE FIVE
ETERNITY

❑1, Feb 1991	2.25
❑2 1991	2.25
❑3 1991	2.25
❑4 1991	2.25

PENTHOUSE COMIX
PENTHOUSE INTERNATIONAL

❑1, Jun 1994	6.00
❑1-2; subtitled Special Edition 1995	4.95
❑2, Jul 1994	4.95
❑3, Sep 1994	4.95
❑4, Nov 1994	4.95
❑5, Jan 1995	4.95
❑6, Mar 1995; Comic size	4.95
❑6/A, Mar 1995; Magazine size	4.95
❑7, May 1995; Comic size	4.95
❑7/A, May 1995; Magazine size	4.95
❑8, Jul 1995	4.95
❑9, Sep 1995	4.95
❑10, Nov 1995	4.95
❑11, Jan 1996	4.95
❑12, Mar 1996; second anniversary issue	4.95
❑13, May 1996	4.95
❑14, Jul 1996	4.95
❑15, Sep 1996	4.95
❑16, Oct 1996	4.95
❑17, Nov 1996; reprints Manara's Hidden Camera	4.95
❑18, Dec 1996	4.95
❑19, Jan 1997	4.95
❑20, Feb 1997	4.95
❑21, Apr 1997	4.95
❑22, May 1997	4.95
❑23, Jun 1997	4.95
❑24, Jul 1997	4.95
❑25, Sep 1997; Sweet Chastity reprints begin	4.95
❑26, Oct 1997	4.95
❑27, Nov 1997	4.95
❑28, Jan 1998	4.95
❑29, Feb 1998	4.95
❑30, Apr 1998	4.95
❑31, May 1998	4.95
❑32, Jun 1998	4.95
❑33, Jul 1998	4.95

PENTHOUSE MAX
PENTHOUSE INTERNATIONAL

❑1, Jul 1996	4.95
❑2, Nov 1996	4.95
❑3, Spr 1997	4.95

PEOPLE ARE PHONY
SIEGEL AND SIMON

❑1	4.00

PEOPLE'S COMICS, THE
GOLDEN GATE

❑1, Sep 1972	4.00

PEP
ARCHIE

❑118, Nov 1956	28.00
❑119, Jan 1957	28.00
❑120, Mar 1957	28.00
❑121, May 1957	23.00
❑122, Jul 1957	23.00
❑123, Sep 1957	23.00
❑124, Nov 1957	23.00
❑125, Jan 1958	23.00
❑126, Mar 1958	23.00
❑127, May 1958	23.00
❑128, Jul 1958	23.00
❑129, Sep 1958	23.00
❑130, Nov 1958	23.00
❑131, Feb 1959	19.00
❑132, Apr 1959	19.00
❑133, Jun 1959	19.00
❑134, Aug 1959	19.00
❑135, Oct 1959	19.00
❑136, Dec 1959	19.00
❑137, ca. 1960	19.00
❑138, ca. 1960	19.00
❑139, ca. 1960	19.00
❑140, ca. 1960	19.00
❑141, ca. 1960	15.00
❑142, ca. 1960	15.00
❑143, ca. 1960	15.00
❑144, Jan 1961	15.00
❑145, Mar 1961	15.00
❑146, May 1961	15.00
❑147, Jun 1961	15.00
❑148, Aug 1961	15.00
❑149, Sep 1961	15.00
❑150, Oct 1961 A: Jaguar.	15.00
❑151, ca. 1961 A: The Fly.	15.00
❑152, Jan 1962 A: Jaguar.	15.00
❑153, Mar 1962 A: Fly Girl.	15.00
❑154, May 1962 A: The Fly.	15.00
❑155, Jun 1962 A: Fly Girl.	15.00
❑156, Aug 1962 A: Fly Girl.	15.00
❑157, Sep 1962 1: Kree-Nal. A: Jaguar.	15.00
❑158, Oct 1962 A: Fly Girl.	15.00
❑159, ca. 1962 A: Jaguar.	15.00
❑160, Jan 1963 A: The Fly.	15.00
❑161, Mar 1963	7.00
❑162, May 1963	7.00
❑163, Jun 1963	7.00
❑164, Aug 1963	7.00
❑165, Sep 1963	7.00
❑166, Oct 1963	7.00
❑167, ca. 1963	7.00
❑168, Jan 1964	7.00
❑169, Mar 1964	7.00
❑170, May 1964	7.00
❑171, Jun 1964	7.00
❑172, Aug 1964	7.00
❑173, Sep 1964	7.00
❑174, Oct 1964	7.00
❑175, Nov 1964	7.00
❑176, Dec 1964	7.00
❑177, Jan 1965	7.00
❑178, Feb 1965	6.00
❑179, Mar 1965	6.00
❑180, Apr 1965	6.00
❑181, May 1965	6.00
❑182, Jun 1965	6.00
❑183, Jul 1965	6.00
❑184, Aug 1965	6.00
❑185, Sep 1965	6.00
❑186, Oct 1965	6.00
❑187, Nov 1965	6.00
❑188, Dec 1965	6.00
❑189, Jan 1966	6.00
❑190, Feb 1966	6.00
❑191, Mar 1966	6.00
❑192, Apr 1966	6.00
❑193, May 1966	6.00
❑194, Jun 1966	6.00
❑195, Jul 1966	6.00
❑196, Aug 1966	6.00
❑197, Sep 1966	6.00
❑198, Oct 1966	6.00
❑199, Nov 1966	6.00
❑200, Dec 1966	6.00
❑201, Jan 1967	5.00
❑202, Feb 1967	5.00
❑203, Mar 1967	5.00
❑204, Apr 1967	5.00
❑205, May 1967	5.00
❑206, Jun 1967	5.00
❑207, Jul 1967	5.00
❑208, Aug 1967	5.00
❑209, Sep 1967	5.00
❑210, Oct 1967	5.00
❑211, Nov 1967	5.00
❑212, Dec 1967	5.00
❑213, Jan 1968	5.00
❑214, Feb 1968	5.00
❑215, Mar 1968	5.00
❑216, Apr 1968	5.00
❑217, May 1968	5.00
❑218, Jun 1968	5.00
❑219, Jul 1968	5.00
❑220, Aug 1968	5.00
❑221, Sep 1968	4.00
❑222, Oct 1968	4.00
❑223, Nov 1968	4.00
❑224, Dec 1968	4.00
❑225, Jan 1969	4.00
❑226, Feb 1969	4.00
❑227, Mar 1969	4.00
❑228, Apr 1969	4.00
❑229, May 1969	4.00
❑230, Jun 1969	4.00
❑231, Jul 1969	4.00
❑232, Aug 1969	3.50
❑233, Sep 1969	3.50
❑234, Oct 1969	3.50
❑235, Nov 1969	3.50
❑236, Dec 1969	3.50
❑237, Jan 1970	3.50
❑238, Feb 1970	3.50
❑239, Mar 1970	3.50
❑240, Apr 1970	3.50
❑241, May 1970	3.50
❑242, Jun 1970	3.50
❑243, Jul 1970	3.50
❑244, Aug 1970	3.50
❑245, Sep 1970	3.50
❑246, Oct 1970	3.50
❑247, Nov 1970	3.50
❑248, Dec 1970	3.50

	N-MINT
❑249, Jan 1971	3.50
❑250, Feb 1971	3.50
❑251, Mar 1971	1.75
❑252, Apr 1971	1.75
❑253, May 1971	1.75
❑254, Jun 1971	1.75
❑255, Jul 1971	1.75
❑256, Aug 1971	1.75
❑257, Sep 1971	1.75
❑258, Oct 1971	1.75
❑259, Nov 1971	1.75
❑260, Dec 1971	1.75
❑261, Jan 1972	1.75
❑262, Feb 1972	1.75
❑263, Mar 1972	1.75
❑264, Apr 1972	1.75
❑265, May 1972	1.75
❑266, Jun 1972	1.75
❑267, Jul 1972	1.75
❑268, Aug 1972	1.75
❑269, Sep 1972	1.75
❑270, Oct 1972	1.75
❑271, Nov 1972	1.75
❑272, Dec 1972	1.75
❑273, Jan 1973	1.75
❑274, Feb 1973	1.75
❑275, Mar 1973	1.75
❑276, Apr 1973	1.75
❑277, May 1973	1.75
❑278, Jun 1973	1.75
❑279, Jul 1973	1.75
❑280, Aug 1973	1.75
❑281, Sep 1973	1.50
❑282, Oct 1973	1.50
❑283, Nov 1973	1.50
❑284, Dec 1973	1.50
❑285, Jan 1974	1.50
❑286, Feb 1974	1.50
❑287, Mar 1974	1.50
❑288, Apr 1974	1.50
❑289, May 1974	1.50
❑290, Jun 1974	1.50
❑291, Jul 1974	1.50
❑292, Aug 1974	1.50
❑293, Sep 1974	1.50
❑294, Oct 1974	1.50
❑295, Nov 1974	1.50
❑296, Dec 1974	1.50
❑297, Jan 1975	1.50
❑298, Feb 1975	1.50
❑299, Mar 1975	1.50
❑300, Apr 1975	1.50
❑301, May 1975	1.25
❑302, Jun 1975	1.25
❑303, Jul 1975	1.25
❑304, Aug 1975	1.25
❑305, Sep 1975	1.25
❑306, Oct 1975	1.25
❑307, Nov 1975	1.25
❑308, Dec 1975	1.25
❑309, Jan 1976	1.25
❑310, Feb 1976	1.25
❑311, Mar 1976	1.25
❑312, Apr 1976	1.25
❑313, May 1976	1.25
❑314, Jun 1976	1.25
❑315, Jul 1976	1.25
❑316, Aug 1976	1.25
❑317, Sep 1976	1.25
❑318, Oct 1976	1.25
❑319, Nov 1976	1.25
❑320, Dec 1976	1.25
❑321, Jan 1977	1.25
❑322, Feb 1977	1.25
❑323, Mar 1977	1.25
❑324, Apr 1977	1.25
❑325, May 1977	1.25
❑326, Jun 1977	1.25
❑327, Jul 1977	1.25
❑328, Aug 1977	1.25
❑329, Sep 1977	1.25

	N-MINT
❑330, Oct 1977	1.25
❑331, Nov 1977	1.25
❑332, Dec 1977	1.25
❑333, Jan 1978	1.25
❑334, Feb 1978	1.25
❑335, Mar 1978	1.25
❑336, Apr 1978	1.25
❑337, May 1978	1.25
❑338, Jun 1978	1.25
❑339, Jul 1978	1.25
❑340, Aug 1978	1.25
❑341, Sep 1978	1.25
❑342, Oct 1978	1.25
❑343, Nov 1978	1.25
❑344, Dec 1978	1.25
❑345, Jan 1979	1.25
❑346, Feb 1979	1.25
❑347, Mar 1979	1.25
❑348, Apr 1979	1.25
❑349, May 1979	1.25
❑350, Jun 1979	1.25
❑351, Jul 1979	1.25
❑352, Aug 1979	1.25
❑353, Sep 1979	1.25
❑354, Oct 1979	1.25
❑355, Nov 1979	1.25
❑356, Dec 1979	1.25
❑357, Jan 1980	1.25
❑358, Feb 1980	1.25
❑359, Mar 1980	1.25
❑360, Apr 1980	1.25
❑361, May 1980	1.25
❑362, Jun 1980	1.25
❑363, Jul 1980	1.25
❑364, Aug 1980	1.25
❑365, ca. 1980	1.25
❑366, ca. 1980	1.25
❑367, ca. 1980	1.25
❑368	1.25
❑369, ca. 1981	1.25
❑370, ca. 1981	1.25
❑371, ca. 1981	1.00
❑372, ca. 1981	1.00
❑373, ca. 1981	1.00
❑374, ca. 1981	1.00
❑375, ca. 1981	1.00
❑376, ca. 1981	1.00
❑377, ca. 1981	1.00
❑378, ca. 1981	1.00
❑379, ca. 1981	1.00
❑380	1.00
❑381, ca. 1982	1.00
❑382, ca. 1982	1.00
❑383, Apr 1982	1.00
❑384	1.00
❑385	1.00
❑386	1.00
❑387	1.00
❑388	1.00
❑389, ca. 1983	1.00
❑390, ca. 1983	1.00
❑391, Nov 1983	1.00
❑392, Jan 1984	1.00
❑393, Mar 1984	1.00
❑394, May 1984	1.00
❑395, Jul 1984	1.00
❑396, Sep 1984	1.00
❑397, Nov 1984	1.00
❑398, Jan 1985	1.00
❑399, Mar 1985	1.00
❑400, May 1985	1.00
❑401, Jul 1985	1.00
❑402, Sep 1985	1.00
❑403, Nov 1985	1.00
❑404, Jan 1986	1.00
❑405, Mar 1986	1.00
❑406, May 1986	1.00
❑407, Jul 1986	1.00
❑408, Sep 1986	1.00
❑409, Nov 1986	1.00

After several years of listing its adjectiveless *Spider-Man* as *Peter Parker: Spider-Man* in distributor catalogs, Marvel finally produced such a series in 1999.

© 1999 Marvel

	N-MINT
❑410, Jan 1987	1.00
❑411, Mar 1987	1.00

PERAZIM
Antarctic

❑1, Sep 1996, b&w	2.95
❑2	2.95
❑3	2.95

PERCEVAN: THE THREE STARS OF INGAAR
Fantasy Flight

❑1	8.95

PEREGRINE, THE
Alliance

❑1, Apr 1994, b&w	2.50
❑2, Aug 1994, b&w	2.50

PERG
Lightning

❑1, Oct 1993; Glow-in the dark flip book	3.50
❑1/Gold, Oct 1993; Gold edition	3.50
❑1/Platinum, Oct 1993; Platinum edition	2.50
❑1/Variant, Oct 1993; glow cover	3.50
❑2, Nov 1993	2.50
❑2/Platinum, Nov 1993; Platinum edition	2.50
❑3, Dec 1993	2.50
❑3/Platinum, Dec 1993; Platinum edition	2.50
❑4, Jan 1994	2.50
❑4/Platinum, Jan 1994; Platinum edition; platinum	2.50
❑5, Feb 1994	2.50
❑6, Mar 1994	2.50
❑7, Apr 1994	2.50
❑8, May 1994	2.50

PERIPHERY
Arch-Type

❑1	2.95

PERRAMUS: ESCAPE FROM THE PAST
Fantagraphics

❑1, b&w	3.50
❑2, b&w	3.50
❑3, b&w	3.50
❑4, b&w	3.50

PERRY
Lightning

❑1, Oct 1997	2.95

PERRY MASON
Dell

❑1, Jun 1964	40.00
❑2, Oct 1964	40.00

PERSONALITY CLASSICS
Personality

❑1; John Wayne	2.95
❑2; Marilyn Monroe	2.95
❑3	2.95
❑4	2.95

PERSONALITY COMICS PRESENTS
Personality

❑1 1991; Paulina Porizkova	2.50
❑2, Apr 1991; Traci Lords	2.50
❑3 1991; Arnold Schwarzenegger	2.50
❑4 1991; Christina Applegate	2.50

N-MINT

❑5 1991; Patrick Swayze, Demi Moore 2.95
❑6 1991; Michael Jordan 2.95
❑7; Samantha Fox 2.95
❑8; Bettie Page, Jennifer Connelly 2.95
❑9; Kim Basinger, Michael Keaton 2.95
❑10; Gloria Estefan 2.95
❑11 2.95
❑12 2.95
❑13 2.95
❑14 2.95
❑15 2.95
❑16 2.95
❑17 2.95
❑18 2.95

PEST
Pest Comics

❑1 1.95
❑2 1.95
❑3 1.95
❑4 1.95
❑5 1.95
❑6, b&w 1.95
❑7 1.95

PET
Fantagraphics / Eros

❑1, May 1997 2.95

PETER CANNON-THUNDERBOLT
DC

❑1, Sep 1992 1.50
❑2, Oct 1992 1.50
❑3, Nov 1992 1.50
❑4, Dec 1992 1.25
❑5, Jan 1993 1.25
❑6, Feb 1993 1.25
❑7, Mar 1993 1.25
❑8, Apr 1993 1.25
❑9, May 1993 1.25
❑10, May 1993 1.25
❑11, Jul 1993 1.25
❑12, Aug 1993 1.25

PETER KOCK
Fantagraphics / Eros

❑1 1994, b&w 3.50
❑2 1994, b&w 2.75
❑3 1994, b&w 2.75
❑4, May 1994, b&w 2.75
❑5, Jul 1994, b&w 2.75
❑6, Aug 1994, b&w 2.75

PETER PAN (GOLD KEY)
Gold Key

❑1, Sep 1969; 10086-909 20.00
❑2 12.00

PETER PAN (TUNDRA)
Tundra

❑1 14.95
❑2 14.95

PETER PAN (WALT DISNEY'S...)
Disney

❑1; prestige format 5.95

PETER PAN AND THE WARLORDS OF OZ
Hand of Doom

❑1 2.95

PETER PAN & THE WARLORDS OF OZ: DEAD HEAD WATER
Hand of Doom

❑1 2.95

PETER PAN: RETURN TO NEVER-NEVER LAND
Adventure

❑1, color 2.50
❑2, color 2.50

PETER PARKER: SPIDER-MAN
Marvel

❑1, Jan 1999; JR2 (a); V: Scorpion. wraparound cover 5.00
❑1/A, Jan 1999; JR2 (a); sunburst variant cover 6.00
❑1/Autographed, Jan 1999 JR2 (a) 10.00
❑1/Variant, Jan 1999; JR2 (a); DFE alternate cover 14.00
❑2/A, Feb 1999; JR2 (a); A: Tocketts. A: Thor. Cover A 2.00
❑2/B, Feb 1999; JR2 (a); A: Tocketts. A: Thor. Cover B by Arthur Suydam 2.00
❑3, Mar 1999; JR2 (a); A: Shadrac. A: Iceman. A: Mary Jane. V: Shadrac. Continued from Amazing Spider-Man #3 4.00
❑4, Apr 1999 JR2 (a); A: Marrow. 4.00
❑5, May 1999 A: Black Cat. V: Spider-Woman. 4.00
❑6, Jun 1999 V: Kingpin. V: Bullseye. 4.00
❑7, Jul 1999 A: Blade. 4.00
❑8, Aug 1999 A: Kingpin. A: Blade. A: Morbius. 4.00
❑9, Sep 1999 V: Venom. 4.00
❑10, Oct 1999 V: Venom. 4.00
❑11, Nov 1999; continues in Juggernaut #1 4.00
❑12, Dec 1999 4.00
❑13, Jan 2000 4.00
❑14, Feb 2000 4.00
❑15, Mar 2000 4.00
❑16, Apr 2000 4.00
❑17, May 2000 4.00
❑18, Jun 2000 4.00
❑19, Jul 2000 4.00
❑20, Aug 2000 4.00
❑21, Sep 2000 4.00
❑22, Oct 2000 4.00
❑23, Nov 2000 4.00
❑24, Dec 2000 4.00
❑25, Jan 2001 4.00
❑26, Feb 2001 4.00
❑27, Mar 2001 A: Mendel Stromm. 4.00
❑28, Apr 2001 A: Mendel Stromm. 4.00
❑29, May 2001; continues in Amazing Spider-Man Annual 2001 4.00
❑30, Jun 2001 3.00
❑31, Jul 2001 3.00
❑32, Aug 2001 3.00
❑33, Sep 2001 3.00
❑34, Oct 2001 3.00
❑35, Nov 2001 3.00
❑36, Dec 2001 3.00
❑37, Jan 2002 3.00
❑38, Feb 2002 3.00
❑39, Mar 2002 3.00
❑40, Apr 2002, 3.00
❑41, May 2002 3.00
❑42, Jun 2002 3.00
❑43, Jun 2002 3.00
❑44, Jul 2002 3.00
❑45, Aug 2002 3.00
❑46, Sep 2002 3.00
❑47, Oct 2002 3.00
❑48, Nov 2002 3.00
❑49, Dec 2002 3.00
❑50, Jan 2003 3.00
❑51, Feb 2003 3.00
❑52, Mar 2003 3.00
❑53, Apr 2003 3.00
❑54, May 2003 3.00
❑55, Jun 2003 3.00
❑56, Jul 2003 A: Sandman (Marvel). 3.00
❑57, Aug 2003, color 3.00
❑Annual 1998, ca. 1998; gatefold summary; Peter Parker: Spider-Man/Elektra '98 2.99
❑Annual 1999, Aug 1999 A: Man-Thing. 3.50

PETER PORKER, THE SPECTACULAR SPIDER-HAM
Marvel / Star

❑1, May 1985 1: Spider-Ham. 1: J. Jonah Jackal. 1: Peter Porker. 1: Duck Doom. 1.00
❑2, Jul 1985 1.00
❑3, Sep 1985 1.00
❑4, Nov 1985 1.00
❑5, Jan 1986 1.00
❑6, Mar 1986 1.00
❑7, May 1986 1.00
❑8, Jul 1986 1.00
❑9, Aug 1986 1.00
❑10, Sep 1986 1.00
❑11, Oct 1986 1.00
❑12, Nov 1986 1.00
❑13, Jan 1987 1.00
❑14, Mar 1987 1.00
❑15, May 1987 1.00
❑16, Jul 1987 1.00
❑17, Sep 1987 1.00

PETER RABBIT 3-D
Eternity

❑1; Reprints from Peter Rabbit (Avon) stories 2.95

PETER THE LITTLE PEST
Marvel

❑1, Nov 1969 1: Peter, The Little Pest. 1: Little Pixie. 18.00
❑2, Jan 1970 14.00
❑3, Mar 1970 14.00
❑4, May 1970; titled Petey 14.00

PETE THE P.O.'D POSTAL WORKER
Sharkbait

❑1, Oct 1997 3.50
❑2, Jan 1998 3.00
❑3, Mar 1998 3.00
❑4, Jun 1998 3.00
❑5, Aug 1998; in England 3.00
❑6, Oct 1998 2.95
❑7, Jan 1999 V: Teddy Cougar. 2.95
❑8, Apr 1999 V: Teddy Cougar. 2.95
❑9, Jun 1999; on Jerry Ringer Show 2.95
❑10, Aug 1999 V: Y2K. 2.95

PETTICOAT JUNCTION
Dell

❑1, Oct 1964 35.00
❑2, Jan 1965 25.00
❑3, Apr 1965 25.00
❑4, Jul 1965 25.00
❑5, Oct 1965 25.00

PETWORKS VS. WILDK.A.T.S.
Parody

❑1 2.50

PHAEDRA
Express / Entity

❑1, Sep 1994, b&w; cardstock cover; third in series of Entity illustrated novellas with Zen Intergalactic Ninja 2.95

PHAGE: SHADOWDEATH (NEIL GAIMAN'S...)
Big

❑1, Jun 1996 2.25
❑2, Aug 1996 2.25
❑3, Sep 1996 2.25
❑4, Sep 1996 2.25
❑5, Oct 1996 2.25
❑6, Nov 1996 2.25

PHANTACEA: PHASE ONE
McPherson

❑1 5.00

PHANTASMAGORIA
Tome

❑1, b&w 2.50

PHANTASY AGAINST HUNGER
Tiger

❑1 BSz, JO, GC, BA, JR (a) 2.00

PHANTOM 2040
Marvel

❑1, May 1995 1.50
❑2, Jun 1995 1.50
❑3, Jul 1995; Poster 1.50
❑4, Aug 1995; Poster 1.50

PHANTOM, THE (2ND SERIES)
DC

❑1, May 1988 LMc (a); O: Phantom. 2.00
❑2, Jun 1988 2.00
❑3, Jul 1988 2.00
❑4, Aug 1988 2.00

PHANTOM, THE (3RD SERIES)
DC

	N-MINT
❑1, May 1989	2.00
❑2, Jun 1989	1.50
❑3, Jul 1989	1.50
❑4, Aug 1989	1.50
❑5, Sep 1989	1.50
❑6, Oct 1989	1.50
❑7, Nov 1989	1.50
❑8, Dec 1989	1.50
❑9, Jan 1989	1.50
❑10, Feb 1989	1.50
❑11, Mar 1990	1.50
❑12, Apr 1990	1.50
❑13, May 1990	1.50

PHANTOM, THE (4TH SERIES)
WOLF

	N-MINT
❑0/Ltd.; limited edition subscribers' issue	3.50
❑1 1992	2.50
❑2 1992	2.25
❑3 1992	2.25
❑4 1992	2.25
❑5 1992	2.25
❑6 1992	2.25
❑7 1992	1.95
❑8 1992	1.95

PHANTOM FORCE
IMAGE

	N-MINT
❑0, Mar 1994	2.50
❑1, Dec 1993	2.50
❑2, Apr 1994	2.50
❑3, May 1994	2.50
❑4, Jun 1994	2.50
❑5, Jul 1994	2.50
❑6, Aug 1994	2.50
❑7, Sep 1994	2.50
❑8, Oct 1994	2.50
❑Ashcan 1; ashcan	2.50

PHANTOM FORCE (GENESIS WEST)
GENESIS WEST

	N-MINT
❑0	2.50

PHANTOM GUARD
IMAGE

	N-MINT
❑1, Oct 1997	2.50
❑1/A, Oct 1997; alternate cover (white background)	2.50
❑2, Oct 1997	2.50
❑3, Dec 1997	2.50
❑4, Jan 1998	2.50
❑4/Variant, Jan 1998; chromium cover	2.50
❑5, Feb 1998	2.50
❑6, Mar 1998	2.50

PHANTOM JACK
IMAGE

	N-MINT
❑1, Apr 2004	2.95
❑2, May 2004	2.95
❑3, Aug 2004	2.95
❑4, Aug 2004	2.95

PHANTOM OF FEAR CITY
CLAYPOOL

	N-MINT
❑1, May 1993	2.50
❑2, Jul 1993	2.50
❑3, Aug 1993	2.50
❑4, Oct 1993	2.50
❑5, Nov 1993	2.50
❑6, Jan 1994	2.50
❑7, Apr 1994	2.50
❑8, Jul 1994	2.50
❑9, Sep 1994	2.50
❑10, Nov 1994	2.50
❑11, Feb 1995	2.50
❑12, May 1995	2.50

PHANTOM OF THE OPERA (ETERNITY)
ETERNITY

	N-MINT
❑1, b&w	2.00

PHANTOM OF THE OPERA (INNOVATION)
INNOVATION

	N-MINT
❑1, Dec 1991	6.95

PHANTOM QUEST CORP.
PIONEER

	N-MINT
❑1, Mar 1997, b&w; wraparound cover	2.95

PHANTOM STRANGER, THE (2ND SERIES)
DC

	N-MINT
❑1, May 1969 A: Doctor 13.	95.00
❑2, Aug 1969 A: Doctor 13.	33.00
❑3, Oct 1969 A: Doctor 13.	33.00
❑4, Dec 1969 NA (a); 1: Tala. A: Doctor 13.	33.00
❑5, Feb 1970 A: Doctor 13.	20.00
❑6, Apr 1970 A: Doctor 13.	20.00
❑7, Jun 1970 NA (c); JA (a); A: Doctor 13.	20.00
❑8, Aug 1970 A: Doctor 13.	16.00
❑9, Oct 1970 A: Doctor 13.	16.00
❑10, Dec 1970 A: Doctor 13.	16.00
❑11, Feb 1971	16.00
❑12, Apr 1971 A: Doctor 13.	18.00
❑13, Jun 1971 A: Doctor 13.	18.00
❑14, Aug 1971 A: Doctor 13.	18.00
❑15, Oct 1971; Giant-size A: Doctor 13.	18.00
❑16, Dec 1971; Giant-size JA (a); A: Doctor 13. A: Mark Merlin.	18.00
❑17, Feb 1972; Giant-size A: Doctor 13.	18.00
❑18, Apr 1972; Giant-size 1: Cassandra Craft. A: Doctor 13. A: Mark Merlin.	15.00
❑19, Jun 1972; Giant-size A: Doctor 13. A: Mark Merlin.	15.00
❑20, Aug 1972	15.00
❑21, Oct 1972 A: Doctor 13.	15.00
❑22, Dec 1972 A: Doctor 13.	9.00
❑23, Feb 1973 1: The Spawn of Frankenstein.	9.00
❑24, Apr 1973 A: The Spawn of Frankenstein.	9.00
❑25, Jul 1973 A: The Spawn of Frankenstein.	9.00
❑26, Sep 1973 A: Doctor 13. A: The Spawn of Frankenstein.	9.00
❑27, Nov 1973 A: The Spawn of Frankenstein.	9.00
❑28, Jan 1974 A: The Spawn of Frankenstein.	9.00
❑29, Mar 1974 A: The Spawn of Frankenstein.	9.00
❑30, May 1974 A: The Spawn of Frankenstein.	9.00
❑31, Jul 1974 A: Black Orchid.	9.00
❑32, Sep 1974 A: Black Orchid.	9.00
❑33, Nov 1974 A: Deadman.	9.00
❑34, Jan 1975 A: Black Orchid. A: Doctor 13.	9.00
❑35, Mar 1975 A: Black Orchid.	9.00
❑36, May 1975 A: Black Orchid.	9.00
❑37, Jul 1975	9.00
❑38, Sep 1975 A: Black Orchid.	9.00
❑39, Nov 1975 A: Deadman.	9.00
❑40, Jan 1976 A: Deadman.	9.00
❑41, Mar 1976 A: Deadman.	9.00

PHANTOM STRANGER, THE (MINI-SERIES)
DC

	N-MINT
❑1, Oct 1987	3.00
❑2, Nov 1987	2.50
❑3, Dec 1987	2.50
❑4, Jan 1988	2.50

PHANTOM, THE: THE GHOST WHO WALKS (LEE FALK'S...)
MARVEL

	N-MINT
❑1, Feb 1995; cardstock cover	2.95
❑2, Mar 1995; cardstock cover	2.95
❑3, Apr 1995; cardstock cover	2.95

PHANTOM ZONE, THE
DC

	N-MINT
❑1, Jan 1982 GC (a)	1.50
❑2, Feb 1982 GC (a)	1.25
❑3, Mar 1982 GC (a)	1.25
❑4, Apr 1982 GC (a)	1.25

Phantom Force was one of the last series in which Jack Kirby was actively involved.

© 1993 Image and Jack Kirby.

PHASE ONE
VICTORY

	N-MINT
❑1, Oct 1986	1.50
❑2	1.50
❑3	1.50
❑4	1.50
❑5	1.50

PHATHOM
BLATANT

	N-MINT
❑1	2.95

PHATWARS
BON

	N-MINT
❑1	2.00

PHAZE
ECLIPSE

	N-MINT
❑1, Apr 1988	2.25
❑2, Oct 1988	2.25

PHENOMERAMA
CALIBER

	N-MINT
❑1	2.95

PHIGMENTS
AMAZING

	N-MINT
❑1, b&w	1.95
❑2	1.95

PHILBERT DESANEX' DREAMS
RIP OFF

	N-MINT
❑1, b&w	2.95

PHILISTINE, THE
ONE SHOT

	N-MINT
❑1, Sep 1993, b&w	2.50
❑2, Apr 1994, b&w	2.50
❑3, Sep 1994, b&w	2.50
❑4	2.50
❑5	2.50
❑6	2.50

PHINEUS: MAGICIAN FOR HIRE
PIFFLE

	N-MINT
❑1, Oct 1994, b&w; wraparound cover	2.95

PHOBOS
FLASHPOINT

	N-MINT
❑1, Jan 1994	2.50

PHOEBE & THE PIGEON PEOPLE
KITCHEN SINK

	N-MINT
❑1	3.00

PHOEBE: ANGEL IN BLACK
ANGEL

	N-MINT
❑1	2.95

PHOENIX
ATLAS-SEABOARD

	N-MINT
❑1, Mar 1975 O: Phoenix (Atlas character).	5.00
❑2, Jun 1975	4.00
❑3, Oct 1975	2.00
❑4 1975	2.00

PHOENIX RESTAURANT
FANDOM HOUSE

	N-MINT
❑1, b&w	3.50

PHOENIX RESURRECTION, THE: AFTERMATH
MALIBU / ULTRAVERSE

	N-MINT
❑1, Jan 1996; continues in Foxfire #1	3.95

N-MINT

PHOENIX RESURRECTION, THE: GENESIS
MALIBU / ULTRAVERSE

❑1, Dec 1995; Giant-size; wraparound cover; continues in The Phoenix Resurrection: Revelations; Phoenix force returns ... 3.95
❑2 ... 3.95

PHOENIX RESURRECTION, THE: RED SHIFT
MALIBU / ULTRAVERSE

❑0, Mar 1996; collects the seven flip-book chapters plus one new chapter ... 2.50
❑0/Ltd., Dec 1995; American Entertainment Edition; no cover price ... 2.50

PHOENIX RESURRECTION, THE: REVELATIONS
MALIBU / ULTRAVERSE

❑1, Dec 1995; wraparound cover; continues in The Phoenix Resurrection: Aftermath ... 3.95

PHOENIX SQUARE
SLAVE LABOR

❑1, Aug 1997, b&w ... 2.95
❑2, Nov 1997 ... 2.95

PHOENIX: THE UNTOLD STORY
MARVEL

❑1, Apr 1984; JBy (a); X-Men #137 with unpublished alternate ending ... 8.00

PHONY PAGES, THE (TERRY BEATTY'S...)
RENEGADE

❑1, Apr 1986; Parody of Famous Comic Strips ... 2.00
❑2, May 1986; Parody of Famous Comic Books ... 2.00

PICTURE TAKER, THE
SLAVE LABOR

❑1, Jan 1998, b&w ... 2.95

PIE
WOW COOL

❑1, b&w ... 2.95

PIECE OF STEAK, A
TOME

❑1, b&w ... 2.50

PIECES
5TH PANEL

❑1, Apr 1997, b&w ... 2.50
❑2, Jul 1997, b&w ... 2.50
❑3 ... 2.50

PIED PIPER GRAPHIC ALBUM
PIED PIPER

❑1; Hero Alliance ... 6.95
❑2; < Never Published > ... 6.95
❑3; Beast Warriors ... 6.95

PIED PIPER OF HAMELIN
TOME

❑1, b&w ... 2.95

PIGEONMAN
ABOVE & BEYOND

❑1 ... 2.95

PIGEON-MAN, THE BIRD-BRAIN
FERRY TAIL

❑1, Apr 1993, b&w ... 2.50

PIGHEAD
WILLIAMSON

❑1, b&w ... 2.95

PILGRIM'S PROGRESS, THE
MARVEL / NELSON

❑1; adaptation ... 9.99

PINEAPPLE ARMY
VIZ

❑1, Dec 1988 ... 1.75
❑2, Dec 1988 ... 1.75
❑3, Jan 1989 ... 1.75
❑4, Jan 1989 ... 1.75
❑5, Feb 1989 ... 1.75
❑6, Feb 1989 ... 1.75
❑7, Mar 1989 ... 1.75

N-MINT

❑8, Mar 1989 ... 1.75
❑9, Apr 1989 ... 1.75
❑10, Apr 1989 ... 1.75

PINHEAD
MARVEL / EPIC

❑1, Dec 1993; Embossed foil cover ... 2.95
❑2, Jan 1994 ... 2.50
❑3, Feb 1994 ... 2.50
❑4, Mar 1994 ... 2.50
❑5, Apr 1994 ... 2.50
❑6, May 1994 ... 2.50

PINHEAD VS. MARSHAL LAW: LAW IN HELL
MARVEL / EPIC

❑1, Nov 1993; foil cover ... 2.95
❑2, Dec 1993; foil cover ... 2.95

PINK DUST
KITCHEN SINK

❑1, Aug 1998 ... 3.50

PINK FLOYD
PERSONALITY

❑1, b&w ... 2.95
❑2, b&w ... 2.95

PINK FLOYD EXPERIENCE
REVOLUTIONARY

❑1, Jun 1991, b&w ... 2.50
❑2, Aug 1991, b&w ... 2.50
❑3, Oct 1991, b&w ... 2.50
❑4, Dec 1991, b&w ... 2.50
❑5, Feb 1992, b&w ... 2.50

PINK PANTHER, THE (GOLD KEY)
GOLD KEY

❑1, Apr 1971 ... 25.00
❑2, Jul 1971 ... 15.00
❑3, Oct 1971 ... 12.00
❑4, Jan 1972 ... 12.00
❑5, Mar 1972 ... 12.00
❑6, May 1972 ... 8.00
❑7, Jul 1972 ... 8.00
❑8, Sep 1972 ... 8.00
❑9, Nov 1972 ... 8.00
❑10, Jan 1973 ... 8.00
❑11, Mar 1973 ... 6.00
❑12, May 1973 ... 6.00
❑13, Jul 1973 ... 6.00
❑14, Sep 1973 ... 6.00
❑15, Oct 1973 ... 6.00
❑16, Nov 1973 ... 6.00
❑17, Jan 1974 ... 6.00
❑18, Mar 1974 ... 6.00
❑19, May 1974 ... 6.00
❑20, Jul 1974 ... 6.00
❑21, Sep 1974 ... 4.00
❑22, Oct 1974 ... 4.00
❑23, Nov 1974 ... 4.00
❑24, Jan 1975 ... 4.00
❑25, Mar 1975 ... 4.00
❑26, May 1975 ... 4.00
❑27, Jul 1975 ... 4.00
❑28, Sep 1975 ... 4.00
❑29, Oct 1975 ... 4.00
❑30, Nov 1975 ... 4.00
❑31, Jan 1976 ... 4.00
❑32, Mar 1976 ... 4.00
❑33, Apr 1976 ... 4.00
❑34, May 1976 ... 4.00
❑35, Jun 1976 ... 4.00
❑36, Jul 1976 ... 4.00
❑37, Sep 1976 ... 4.00
❑38, Oct 1976 ... 4.00
❑39, Nov 1976 ... 4.00
❑40, Jan 1977 ... 4.00
❑41, Mar 1977 ... 2.50
❑42, Apr 1977 ... 2.50
❑43, May 1977 ... 2.50
❑44, Jun 1977 ... 2.50
❑45, Jul 1977 ... 2.50
❑46, Sep 1977 ... 2.50
❑47, Oct 1977 ... 2.50
❑48, Nov 1977 ... 2.50

N-MINT

❑49, Jan 1978 ... 2.50
❑50, Mar 1978 ... 2.50
❑51, Apr 1978 ... 2.50
❑52, May 1978 ... 2.50
❑53, Jun 1978 ... 2.50
❑54, Jul 1978 ... 2.50
❑55, Aug 1978 ... 2.50
❑56, Sep 1978 ... 2.50
❑57, Oct 1978 ... 2.50
❑58, Nov 1978 ... 2.50
❑59, Dec 1978 ... 2.50
❑60, Jan 1979 ... 2.50
❑61, Feb 1979 ... 2.50
❑62, Mar 1979 ... 2.50
❑63, Apr 1979 ... 2.50
❑64, May 1979 ... 2.50
❑65, Jun 1979 ... 2.50
❑66, Jul 1979 ... 2.50
❑67, Aug 1979 ... 2.50
❑68, Sep 1979 ... 2.50
❑69, Oct 1979 ... 2.50
❑70, Nov 1979 ... 2.50
❑71, Dec 1979 ... 2.50
❑72, Jan 1980 ... 2.50
❑73, Feb 1980 ... 2.50
❑74, ca. 1980 ... 2.50
❑75, Aug 1980 ... 2.50
❑76, Oct 1981 ... 2.50
❑77, Dec 1981 ... 2.50
❑78, Jan 1981 ... 2.50
❑79, Jul 1981 ... 2.50
❑80, Sep 1981 ... 2.50
❑81, Feb 1982 ... 2.50
❑82 (c); (w); (a) ... 2.50
❑83 (c); (w); (a) ... 2.50
❑84 (c); (w); (a) ... 2.50
❑85 (c); (w); (a) ... 2.50
❑86 (c); (w); (a) ... 2.50
❑87, ca. 1984 ... 2.50

PINK PANTHER (HARVEY)
HARVEY

❑1, Nov 1993 ... 1.50
❑2, Dec 1993 ... 1.50
❑3, Jan 1994 ... 1.50
❑4, Feb 1994 ... 1.50
❑5, Mar 1994 ... 1.50
❑6, Apr 1994 ... 1.50
❑7, May 1994 ... 1.50
❑8, Jun 1994 ... 1.50
❑9, Jul 1994 ... 1.50
❑SS 1, ca. 1993; Super Special ... 2.25

PINKY AND THE BRAIN
DC

❑1, Jul 1996; based on animated series ... 2.50
❑2, Aug 1996 ... 2.00
❑3, Sep 1996 ... 2.00
❑4, Oct 1996; Oz parody ... 1.75
❑5, Nov 1996; Western parody issue ... 1.75
❑6, Dec 1996; Ed Wood parody issue ... 1.75
❑7, Jan 1997; Faust parody ... 1.75
❑8, Feb 1997 ... 1.75
❑9, Mar 1997 ... 1.75
❑10, Apr 1997 ... 1.75
❑11, May 1997; Fantasia parody ... 1.75
❑12, Jun 1997; surfing parody ... 1.75
❑13, Jul 1997 ... 1.75
❑14, Aug 1997 ... 1.75
❑15, Sep 1997; Bikers ... 1.75
❑16, Oct 1997 ... 1.75
❑17, Nov 1997 ... 1.75
❑18, Dec 1997; Manga parody ... 1.95
❑19, Jan 1998; Brain plays Santa ... 1.95
❑20, Feb 1998 ... 1.95
❑21, Mar 1998 ... 1.95
❑22, May 1998 ... 1.95
❑23, Jun 1998; Jaws parody cover ... 1.95
❑24, Jul 1998; Zorro parody ... 1.95
❑25, Aug 1998 ... 1.95
❑26, Oct 1998; Demi Moore parody issue ... 1.95

N-MINT

❑27, Nov 1998 .... 1.99
❑Holiday 1, Jan 1996; Giant-size 1.50

PINOCCHIO AND THE EMPEROR OF THE NIGHT
MARVEL

❑1, Mar 1988 .... 1.25

PINOCCHIO SPECIAL (WALT DISNEY'S...)
GLADSTONE

❑1, Mar 1990 WK (a) 1.50

PINT-SIZED X-BABIES
MARVEL

❑1, Aug 1998; gatefold summary 2.99

PIPSQUEAK PAPERS (WALLACE WOOD'S...)
FANTAGRAPHICS / EROS

❑1, b&w 2.75

PIRACY (RCP)
GEMSTONE

❑1, Mar 1998 .... 2.50
❑2, Apr 1998 .... 2.50
❑3, May 1998 .... 2.50
❑4, Jun 1998 .... 2.50
❑5, Jul 1998 .... 2.50
❑6, Aug 1998 .... 2.50
❑7, Sep 1998 .... 2.50

PIRANHA IS LOOSE!
SPECIAL STUDIO

❑1, b&w 2.75
❑2, b&w 2.75

PIRATE CORPS
ETERNITY

❑1 .... 2.50
❑2 .... 2.50
❑3, Dec 1987 .... 2.50
❑4, Feb 1988 .... 2.50

PIRATE CORP$! (2ND SERIES)
SLAVE LABOR

❑1, Jun 1989 .... 2.50
❑1-2, Aug 1993; has Fine Dairy Products ad on back cover 2.50
❑2, Sep 1989 .... 2.50
❑2-2, Feb 1993; has Fine Dairy Products ad on back cover 2.50
❑3, Feb 1991 .... 2.50
❑3-2, Feb 1993; has Fine Dairy Products ad on back cover 2.50
❑4, Apr 1992 .... 2.50
❑4-2, Sep 1993; has Fine Dairy Products ad on back cover 2.50
❑5, Dec 1992 .... 2.50
❑5-2, Apr 1994 .... 2.50
❑Special 1, Mar 1989, b&w; has Futurama ad on back cover 1.95
❑Special 1-2, Aug 1993; has Fine Dairy Products ad on back cover 2.95

PIRATE QUEEN, THE
COMAX

❑1, b&w 3.00

PIRATES OF DARK WATER, THE
MARVEL

❑1, Nov 1991 .... 1.00
❑2, Dec 1991 .... 1.00
❑3, Jan 1992 .... 1.00
❑4, Feb 1992 .... 1.00
❑5, Mar 1992 .... 1.00
❑6, Apr 1992 .... 1.00
❑7, May 1992 .... 1.25
❑8, Jun 1992 .... 1.25
❑9, Jul 1992 .... 1.25

P.I.'S, THE: MICHAEL MAUSER AND MS. TREE
FIRST

❑1, Jan 1985; MGr, JSa (a); Ms. Tree, E-Man 1.50
❑2, Mar 1985 JSa (a) 1.50
❑3, May 1985 JSa (a) 1.50

N-MINT

PISTOLERO
ETERNITY

❑1, b&w 3.95

PI: THE BOOK OF ANTS
ARTISAN ENTERTAINMENT

❑1, b&w; based on movie 2.95

PITT
IMAGE

❑0.5 .... 1.50
❑1, Jan 1993 .... 1.95
❑1/Gold, Jan 1993; Gold edition 1.95
❑2, Jul 1993 .... 1.95
❑3, Feb 1994 .... 1.95
❑4, Apr 1994 .... 1.95
❑5, Jun 1994 .... 1.95
❑6, Sep 1994 .... 1.95
❑7, Dec 1994 .... 1.95
❑8, Apr 1994 .... 1.95
❑9, Aug 1995 .... 1.95
❑10 1996 .... 1.95
❑11 1996 .... 1.95
❑12, Dec 1996 .... 1.95
❑13, Mar 1997 .... 1.95
❑14, Jun 1997 .... 2.50
❑15, Sep 1997 .... 2.50
❑16, Dec 1997 .... 2.50
❑17, Mar 1998 .... 2.50
❑18, Jun 1998 .... 2.50
❑19, Sep 1998 .... 2.50
❑20, Oct 1998; Published by Full Bleed Studios 2.50

PITT, THE
MARVEL

❑1 .... 3.25

PITT CREW
FULL BLEED

❑1 .... 3.00

PITT: IN THE BLOOD
FULL BLEED

❑1, Aug 1996 .... 2.50

PIXY JUNKET
VIZ

❑1, b&w 2.75
❑2, b&w 2.75
❑3, b&w 2.75
❑4, b&w 2.75
❑5, b&w 2.75
❑6, b&w 2.75

P.J. WARLOCK
ECLIPSE

❑1, Nov 1986, b&w 2.00
❑2, Jan 1987, b&w 2.00
❑3, Mar 1987, b&w 2.00

PLACES THAT ARE GONE
AEON

❑1, Jul 1994 .... 2.75
❑2, Aug 1994 .... 2.75

PLAGUE
TOME

❑1, b&w 2.95

PLAN 9 FROM OUTER SPACE
ETERNITY

❑1, b&w 4.95
❑1-2 .... 5.95

PLAN 9 FROM OUTER SPACE: THIRTY YEARS LATER
ETERNITY

❑1, Jan 1991, b&w 2.50
❑2, b&w 2.50
❑3, b&w 2.50

PLANET 29
CALIBER

❑1, b&w 2.50
❑2, b&w 2.50

PLANETARY
DC / WILDSTORM

❑1, Apr 1999 .... 8.00
❑2, May 1999 .... 3.00

The Planet of the Apes license was one of the most successful for Malibu's Adventure imprint.

© 1990 20th Century Fox Film Corporation and Malibu Comics.

N-MINT

❑3, Jun 1999 .... 3.00
❑4, Jul 1999 .... 2.50
❑5, Sep 1999 .... 2.50
❑6, Nov 1999 .... 2.50
❑7, Jan 2000 .... 2.50
❑8, Feb 2000 .... 2.50
❑9, Apr 2000 .... 2.50
❑10, Jun 2000 .... 2.50
❑11, Sep 2000 .... 2.50
❑12, Jan 2001 .... 2.50
❑13, Feb 2001 .... 2.50
❑14, Jun 2001 .... 2.50
❑15, Jul 2001 .... 2.50
❑16, Oct 2003 .... 2.95
❑17, Dec 2003 .... 2.95
❑18, Feb 2004 .... 2.95
❑19, May 2004 .... 2.95
❑20, Sep 2004 ....

PLANETARY/BATMAN: NIGHT ON EARTH
DC / WILDSTORM

❑1, ca. 2003 .... 5.95

PLANETARY/JLA: TERRA OCCULTA
WILDSTORM

❑1, Nov 2002 .... 5.95

PLANETARY/THE AUTHORITY: RULING THE WORLD
DC / WILDSTORM

❑1 .... 5.95

PLANET COMICS (BLACKTHORNE)
BLACKTHORNE

❑1, Apr 1988 .... 2.00
❑2, Jun 1988 .... 2.00
❑3, Aug 1988 .... 2.00

PLANET COMICS (A-LIST)
A-LIST

❑1, Spr 1997 .... 2.95
❑2, Fal 1997, b&w 2.95
❑3, Win 1997, color 2.95

PLANET COMICS (AVALON)
AVALON

❑1 .... 5.95

PLANET LADDER
TOKYOPOP

❑1, Mar 2002, b&w; printed in Japanese format 9.99
❑2, Jul 2002, b&w; printed in Japanese format 9.99

PLANET OF GEEKS
STARHEAD

❑1, b&w 2.75

PLANET OF TERROR (BASIL WOLVERTON'S...)
DARK HORSE

❑1, Jul 1987 BW (w); BW (a) 2.00

PLANET OF THE APES (1ST SERIES)
MARVEL

❑1, Aug 1974, b&w; magazine; Special "split-cover"; adapts first movie plus new story 20.00
❑1-2; No special cover 5.00
❑2, Oct 1974, b&w; magazine; adapts first movie plus new story 10.00
❑3, Dec 1974, b&w; magazine; adapts first movie plus new stories 9.00

Condition price index: Multiply "NM prices" above by: **0.83 for Very Fine/Near Mint**
0.66 for Very Fine • 0.33 for Fine • 0.2 for Very Good • 0.125 for Good

N-MINT

❑4, Jan 1975, b&w; magazine; adapts first movie plus new stories 8.00
❑5, Feb 1975, b&w; magazine; adapts first movie plus new stories 8.00
❑6, Mar 1975, b&w; magazine; concludes first movie adaptations plus new stories 6.00
❑7, Apr 1975, b&w; magazine 5.00
❑8, May 1975, b&w; magazine 5.00
❑9, Jun 1975 5.00
❑10, Jul 1975 5.00
❑11, Aug 1975 5.00
❑12, Sep 1975 5.00
❑13, Aug 1975 5.00
❑14, Nov 1975 5.00
❑15, Dec 1975 5.00
❑16, Jan 1976 D: Zira. D: Cornelius. 5.00
❑17, Feb 1976 5.00
❑18, Mar 1976 5.00
❑19, Apr 1976, b&w; magazine 5.00
❑20, May 1976, b&w; magazine 5.00
❑21, Jun 1976, b&w; magazine 5.00
❑22, Jul 1976, b&w; magazine 5.00
❑23, Aug 1976, b&w; magazine 5.00
❑24, Sep 1976, b&w; magazine 5.00
❑25, Oct 1976, b&w; magazine 5.00
❑26, Nov 1976, b&w; magazine 5.00
❑27, Dec 1976, b&w; magazine 5.00
❑28, Jan 1977, b&w; magazine 5.00
❑29, Feb 1977, b&w; magazine 5.00
❑Annual 1 5.00

PLANET OF THE APES (2ND SERIES)
ADVENTURE

❑1, Apr 1990; extra cover in pink, yellow, or green 4.00
❑1/Ltd., Apr 1990; limited 4.00
❑1-2 2.50
❑2, Jun 1990 3.00
❑3, Jul 1990 3.00
❑4, Aug 1990 3.00
❑5, Sep 1990 3.00
❑6, Oct 1990 3.00
❑7, Nov 1990 3.00
❑8, Dec 1990; Christmas 3.00
❑9, Jan 1991 3.00
❑10, Mar 1991 3.00
❑11, Apr 1991 2.50
❑12, May 1991; Wedding of Alexander and Coure 2.50
❑13, Jun 1991 2.50
❑14, Jul 1991 2.50
❑15, Aug 1991 2.50
❑16, Sep 1991 2.50
❑17, Oct 1991 2.50
❑18, Nov 1991 2.50
❑19, Dec 1991 2.50
❑20, Jan 1992 2.50
❑21, Feb 1992 2.50
❑22, Apr 1992; sequel to Conquest of the Planet of the Apes 2.50
❑23, May 1992 2.50
❑24, Jul 1992 2.50
❑Annual 1, b&w 3.50

PLANET OF THE APES (3RD SERIES)
DARK HORSE

❑1, Jun 2001 2.99
❑1/Variant, Jun 2001 2.99
❑2, Jul 2001 2.99
❑2/Variant, Jul 2001 2.99
❑3, Aug 2001 2.99
❑3/Variant, Aug 2001 2.99

PLANET OF THE APES (4TH SERIES)
DARK HORSE

❑1, Sep 2001 2.99
❑1/Variant, Sep 2001 2.99
❑2, Oct 2001 2.99
❑2/Variant, Oct 2001 2.99
❑3, Nov 2001 2.99
❑3/Variant, Nov 2001 2.99
❑4, Dec 2001 2.99
❑4/Variant, Dec 2001 2.99
❑5, Jan 2002 2.99

N-MINT

❑5/Variant, Jan 2002 2.99
❑6, Feb 2002 2.99
❑6/Variant, Feb 2002 2.99

PLANET OF THE APES: BLOOD OF THE APES
ADVENTURE

❑1, Nov 1991, b&w 2.50
❑2, Dec 1991, b&w 2.50
❑3, Jan 1992, b&w 2.50
❑4, Feb 1992, b&w 2.50

PLANET OF THE APES: FORBIDDEN ZONE
ADVENTURE

❑1 2.50
❑2 2.50
❑3 2.50
❑4 2.50

PLANET OF THE APES: SINS OF THE FATHER
ADVENTURE

❑1, Mar 1992, b&w 2.50

PLANET OF THE APES: URCHAK'S FOLLY
ADVENTURE

❑1, Jan 1991, b&w 2.50
❑2, Feb 1991, b&w 2.50
❑3, Mar 1991, b&w 2.50
❑4, Apr 1991, b&w 2.50

PLANET OF VAMPIRES
ATLAS-SEABOARD

❑1, Apr 1975 NA (c); PB (a) 2.00
❑2, Jul 1975 NA (c) 1.50
❑3, Jul 1975 1.50

PLANET PATROL
EDGE / SEABOARD

❑1 2.95

PLANET TERRY
MARVEL / STAR

❑1, Apr 1985 O: Planet Terry. 1: Planet Terry. 1.00
❑2, May 1985 1.00
❑3, Jun 1985 1.00
❑4, Jul 1985 1.00
❑5, Aug 1985 1.00
❑6, Sep 1985 1.00
❑7, Oct 1985 1.00
❑8, Nov 1985 1.00
❑9, Dec 1985 1.00
❑10, Jan 1986 1.00
❑11, Feb 1986 1.00
❑12, Mar 1986 1.00

PLANET-X
ETERNITY

❑1, b&w 2.50

PLANET X REPRINT COMIC
PLANET X

❑1, ca. 1987, reprints adaptation of The Man from Planet X; no cover price 2.00

PLASM
DEFIANT

❑0; bound in Diamond Previews 1.00

PLASMA BABY
CALIBER

❑1, b&w 2.50
❑2, b&w 2.50
❑3, b&w 2.50

PLASMER
MARVEL

❑1, Nov 1993; four trading cards 2.50
❑2, Dec 1993 1.95
❑3, Jan 1994 1.95
❑4, Feb 1994 1.95

PLASTIC FORKS
MARVEL / EPIC

❑1, ca. 1990 4.95
❑2, ca. 1990 4.95
❑3, ca. 1990 4.95

N-MINT

❑4, ca. 1990 4.95
❑5, ca. 1990 4.95

PLASTIC LITTLE
CPM

❑Ashcan 1, Jun 1997 3.00
❑1, Aug 1997 2.95
❑2, Sep 1997 2.95
❑3, Oct 1997 2.95
❑4, Nov 1997 2.95
❑5, Dec 1997 2.95

PLASTIC MAN (DC)
DC

❑1, Dec 1966 GK (a); O: Plastic Man. 50.00
❑2, Feb 1967 28.00
❑3, Apr 1967 22.00
❑4, Jun 1967 22.00
❑5, Aug 1967 22.00
❑6, Oct 1967 15.00
❑7, Dec 1967 A: Plas' father (Plastic Man 1). A: Woozy Winks. 15.00
❑8, Feb 1968 15.00
❑9, Apr 1968 15.00
❑10, Jun 1968; series goes on hiatus until 1976 15.00
❑11, Mar 1976; Series begins again: 1976 4.00
❑12, May 1976 4.00
❑13, Jul 1976 4.00
❑14, Sep 1976 4.00
❑15, Nov 1976 4.00
❑16, Mar 1977 4.00
❑17, May 1977 4.00
❑18, Jul 1977 4.00
❑19, Sep 1977 4.00
❑20, Nov 1977 4.00

PLASTIC MAN (2ND SERIES)
DC

❑1, Feb 2004 2.95
❑2, Mar 2004 2.95
❑3, Apr 2004 2.95
❑4, May 2004 2.95
❑5, Jun 2004 2.95
❑6, Jul 2004 2.95
❑7, Aug 2004 2.95
❑8, Sep 2004

PLASTIC MAN (MINI-SERIES)
DC

❑1, Nov 1988 PF (w); O: Plastic Man. 1.25
❑2, Dec 1988 PF (w) 1.25
❑3, Jan 1989 PF (w) 1.25
❑4, Feb 1989 PF (w) 1.25

PLASTIC MAN LOST ANNUAL
DC

❑1, Feb 2004 6.95

PLASTIC MAN SPECIAL
DC

❑1, Aug 1999 3.95

PLASTRON CAFÉ
MIRAGE

❑1, Dec 1992 2.25
❑2, Feb 1993 2.25
❑3, May 1993 2.25
❑4, Jul 1993 2.25

PLATINUM.44
COMAX

❑1, b&w 2.95

PLATINUM GRIT
DEAD NUMBAT

❑1 3.50
❑2 3.50
❑3 3.50
❑4, Feb 1995, b&w 3.50
❑5 3.50
❑6 3.50

PLAYBEAR
FANTAGRAPHICS / EROS

❑1 2.95
❑2, ca. 1995 2.95
❑3, Aug 1995 2.95

Condition price index: Multiply "NM prices" above by: **0.83 for Very Fine/Near Mint**
0.66 for Very Fine • 0.33 for Fine • 0.2 for Very Good • 0.125 for Good

N-MINT

PLAYGROUND
CALIBER

❑1, b&w 2.50

PLAYGROUNDS
FANTAGRAPHICS

❑1, b&w 2.00

PLEASURE & PASSION (ALAZAR'S...)
BRAINSTORM

❑1, Oct 1997 ..... 2.95

PLEASURE BOUND
FANTAGRAPHICS / EROS

❑1, Feb 1996 ..... 2.95

PLOP!
DC

❑1, Oct 1973 BW (c); SA, BWr (a) 12.00
❑2, Dec 1973 SA (a) 8.00
❑3, Feb 1974, color SA (a) 8.00
❑4, Apr 1974 SA, BW, FR (a) 7.00
❑5, Jun 1974 SA (a) 7.00
❑6, Aug 1974 SA (a) 6.00
❑7, Oct 1974 SA (a) 6.00
❑8, Dec 1974 SA (a) 6.00
❑9, Feb 1975 SA, BW, FR (a) 6.00
❑10, Mar 1975 JO (w); SA, BW, RE (a) 6.00
❑11, Apr 1975 SA (a) 5.00
❑12, May 1975 SA (a) 5.00
❑13, Jun 1975 SA (a) 5.00
❑14, Jul 1975 SA (a) 5.00
❑15, Aug 1975 SA (a) 5.00
❑16, Sep 1975 SA (a) 5.00
❑17, Oct 1975 SA (a) 5.00
❑18, Dec 1975 SA (a) 5.00
❑19, Feb 1976 SA (a) 5.00
❑20, Apr 1976 SA (a) 5.00
❑21, Jun 1976; Giant-size SA (a) 5.00
❑22, Aug 1976; Giant-size SA (a) 5.00
❑23, Oct 1976; Giant-size; Wally Wood's Lord of the Rings parody 5.00
❑24, Dec 1976; Giant-size SA (a) 8.00

POCAHONTAS (DISNEY'S...)
MARVEL

❑1, Jul 1995; prestige format one-shot 4.95

POE
CHEESE

❑1, Sep 1996 ..... 2.50
❑2, Oct 1996 ..... 2.50
❑3, Nov 1996 ..... 2.50
❑4, Dec 1996 ..... 2.50
❑5, Feb 1997, b&w 2.50
❑6, Apr 1997, b&w 2.50
❑7 ..... 2.50
❑8 ..... 2.50
❑9 ..... 2.50
❑10 ..... 2.50
❑11 ..... 2.50

POE (VOL. 2)
SIRIUS

❑1, Oct 1997, b&w 2.50
❑2, Nov 1997, b&w 2.50
❑3, Dec 1997 ..... 2.50
❑4, Jan 1998 ..... 2.50
❑5, Feb 1998 ..... 2.50
❑6, Mar 1998 ..... 2.50
❑7, May 1998 ..... 2.50
❑8, Jun 1998 ..... 2.50
❑9, Jul 1998 ..... 2.50
❑10, Aug 1998 ..... 2.50
❑11, Sep 1998 ..... 2.50
❑12, Oct 1998 ..... 2.50
❑13, Nov 1998 ..... 2.50
❑14, Jan 1999 ..... 2.50
❑15, Feb 1999 ..... 2.50
❑16, Mar 1999 ..... 2.50
❑17, Apr 1999 ..... 2.50
❑18, Aug 1999 ..... 2.50
❑19 ..... 2.50
❑20 ..... 2.50
❑21, Jan 2000 ..... 2.95
❑22, Mar 2000 ..... 2.95
❑23, May 2000 ..... 2.95

N-MINT

❑24, Jul 2000 ..... 2.95
❑Special 1, Dec 1998; Color Special 2.95

POETS PROSPER: RHYME & REVELRY
TOME

❑1 ..... 3.50

POINT BLANK (WILDSTORM)
WILDSTORM

❑1, Oct 2002 ..... 2.95
❑2, Nov 2002 ..... 2.95
❑3, Dec 2002 ..... 2.95
❑4, Jan 2003 ..... 2.95
❑5, Feb 2003 ..... 2.95

POINT-BLANK
ECLIPSE

❑1, b&w 2.95
❑2, b&w 2.95

POISON ELVES (MULEHIDE)
MULEHIDE

❑8; magazine-sized; Series continued from I, Lusiphur #7 ..... 15.00
❑9; magazine-sized 12.00
❑10; magazine-sized 12.00
❑11 ..... 10.00
❑12, Oct 1993 ..... 10.00
❑13, Dec 1993 ..... 10.00
❑14, Feb 1994 ..... 10.00
❑15, Apr 1994; Scarcer 10.00
❑15-2 ..... 2.50
❑16, Jun 1994 ..... 8.00
❑17 ..... 8.00
❑17-2 ..... 2.50
❑18 ..... 5.00
❑19 ..... 5.00
❑20 ..... 5.00
❑Deluxe 1, ca. 2001; Poison Elves: The Mulehide Years 34.95

POISON ELVES (SIRIUS)
SIRIUS

❑1, May 1995, b&w 6.00
❑1-2 ..... 2.50
❑2, Jun 1995, b&w 4.00
❑3, Jul 1995, b&w 4.00
❑4, Aug 1995, b&w 3.00
❑5, Oct 1995 ..... 3.00
❑6, Nov 1995 ..... 3.00
❑7, Dec 1995 ..... 2.50
❑8, Jan 1996 ..... 2.50
❑9 1996 ..... 2.50
❑10, Feb 1996 ..... 2.50
❑11, Mar 1996 ..... 2.50
❑12, Apr 1996 ..... 2.50
❑13, May 1996 ..... 2.50
❑14, Jun 1996 ..... 2.50
❑15 1996 ..... 2.50
❑16, Sep 1996 ..... 2.50
❑17, Oct 1996 ..... 2.50
❑18, Nov 1996 ..... 2.50
❑19, Dec 1996 ..... 2.50
❑20, Jan 1997 ..... 2.50
❑21, Feb 1997 ..... 2.50
❑22, Mar 1997 ..... 2.50
❑23, Apr 1997 ..... 2.50
❑24, May 1997 ..... 2.50
❑25, Jul 1997 ..... 2.50
❑26, Aug 1997 ..... 2.50
❑27, Sep 1997 ..... 2.50
❑28, Oct 1997 ..... 2.50
❑29, Nov 1997 ..... 2.50
❑30, Dec 1997 ..... 2.50
❑31, Jan 1998 ..... 2.50
❑32, Feb 1998 ..... 2.50
❑33, Mar 1998 ..... 2.50
❑34, Apr 1998 ..... 2.50
❑35, May 1998 ..... 2.50
❑36, Jun 1998 ..... 2.50
❑37, Jul 1998 ..... 2.50
❑38, Aug 1998 ..... 2.50
❑39, Sep 1998 ..... 2.50
❑40, Oct 1998 ..... 2.50

Drew Hayes' *Poison Elves* was formerly known as *I, Lusiphur.*

© 1994 Drew Hayes.

N-MINT

❑41, Nov 1998 ..... 2.50
❑42, Dec 1998 ..... 2.50
❑43, Jan 1999 ..... 2.50
❑44, Feb 1999 ..... 2.50
❑45, Mar 1999 ..... 2.50
❑46, Jun 1999 ..... 2.95
❑47, Jul 1999 ..... 2.50
❑48, Aug 1999 ..... 2.50
❑49, Sep 1999 ..... 2.50
❑50, Oct 1999 ..... 2.50
❑51, Nov 1999 ..... 2.50
❑52, Dec 1999 ..... 2.50
❑53, Jan 2000 ..... 2.95
❑54, Feb 2000 ..... 2.95
❑55, Mar 2000 ..... 2.95
❑56, Apr 2000 ..... 2.95
❑57, May 2000 ..... 2.95
❑58, Jun 2000 ..... 2.95
❑59, Jul 2000 ..... 2.95
❑60, Aug 2000 ..... 2.95
❑61, Sep 2000 ..... 2.95
❑62, Nov 2000 ..... 2.95
❑63, Jan 2001 ..... 2.95
❑64, Mar 2001 ..... 2.95
❑65, May 2001 ..... 2.95
❑66, Jul 2001 ..... 2.95
❑67, Sep 2001 ..... 2.95
❑68, Nov 2001 ..... 2.95
❑69, Jan 2002 ..... 2.95
❑70, Mar 2002 ..... 2.95
❑71, Feb 2003 ..... 2.95
❑72, Mar 2003 ..... 2.95
❑73, May 2003 ..... 2.95
❑74, Aug 2003 ..... 2.95
❑75, Dec 2003 ..... 2.95
❑76, Mar 2004 ..... 2.95
❑77, Mar 2004 ..... 2.95
❑78, May 2004 ..... 2.95
❑Special 1, ca 1998; Color Special 3.00

POIZON
LONDON NIGHT

❑0 ..... 3.00
❑0/Nude 3.50
❑0.5 ..... 3.00
❑1, Feb 1996 ..... 3.00
❑1/A; Green Death edition 15.00
❑1/Nude 5.00
❑2, Apr 1996 ..... 3.00
❑3, Jun 1996 ..... 3.00

POKÉMON: THE ELECTRIC TALE OF PIKACHU
VIZ

❑1, Nov 1998 1: Pikachu. 3.50
❑1-2 ..... 3.25
❑1-3, Mar 1999 ..... 3.25
❑2, Dec 1998 ..... 3.25
❑2-2 ..... 3.25
❑3, Jan 1999 ..... 3.25
❑4, Feb 1999 ..... 3.25

POKÉMON PART 2
VIZ

❑1, Mar 1999 ..... 3.25
❑2, Apr 1999 ..... 3.25
❑3, May 1999 ..... 3.25
❑4, Jun 1999 ..... 2.95

N-MINT

POKÉMON PART 3
VIZ

- ❑1, Jul 1999 ... 3.50
- ❑2, Aug 1999 ... 3.50
- ❑3, Sep 1999 ... 3.50
- ❑4, Oct 1999 ... 3.50

POKÉMON ADVENTURES
VIZ

- ❑1, Sep 1999; Mysterious Mew ... 5.95
- ❑2, Oct 1999; Wanted: Pikachu ... 5.95
- ❑3, Nov 1999 ... 5.95
- ❑4, Dec 1999 ... 5.95
- ❑5, Jan 2000 ... 5.95

POKÉMON ADVENTURES PART 2
VIZ

- ❑1 2000 ... 2.95
- ❑2 2000 ... 2.95
- ❑3 2000 ... 2.95
- ❑4 2000 ... 2.95
- ❑5 2000 ... 2.95
- ❑6 2000 ... 2.95

POKÉMON ADVENTURES PART 3
VIZ

- ❑1 2000 ... 2.95
- ❑2 2000 ... 2.95
- ❑3 2000 ... 2.95
- ❑4 2000 ... 2.95
- ❑5 2000 ... 2.95
- ❑6, Jan 2001 ... 2.95
- ❑7, Feb 2001 ... 2.95

POKÉMON ADVENTURES PART 4
VIZ

- ❑1, Mar 2001 ... 2.95
- ❑2, Apr 2001 ... 2.95
- ❑3, May 2001 ... 4.95
- ❑4, Jun 2001 ... 4.95

POKÉMON ADVENTURES PART 5
VIZ

- ❑1, Jul 2001; Cover logo reads "Yellow Caballero" ... 4.95
- ❑2, Aug 2001; Cover logo reads "Yellow Caballero" ... 4.95
- ❑3, Sep 2001; Cover logo reads "Yellow Caballero" ... 4.95
- ❑4, Oct 2001; Cover logo reads "Yellow Caballero" ... 4.95
- ❑5, Nov 2001; Cover logo reads "Yellow Caballero" ... 4.95

POKÉMON ADVENTURES PART 6
VIZ

- ❑1, Dec 2001; Cover logo reads "Yellow Caballero" ... 4.95
- ❑2, Jan 2002; Cover logo reads "Yellow Caballero" ... 4.95
- ❑3, Feb 2002; Cover logo reads "Yellow Caballero" ... 4.95
- ❑4, Mar 2002; Cover logo reads "Yellow Caballero" ... 4.95

POKÉMON ADVENTURES PART 7
VIZ

- ❑1, Apr 2002; Cover logo reads "Yellow Caballero" ... 4.95
- ❑2, May 2002; Cover logo reads "Yellow Caballero" ... 4.95
- ❑3, Jun 2002; Cover logo reads "Yellow Caballero" ... 4.95
- ❑4, Jul 2002; Cover logo reads "Yellow Caballero" ... 4.95
- ❑5, Aug 2002; Cover logo reads "Yellow Caballero" ... 4.95

POLICE ACADEMY
MARVEL

- ❑1, Oct 1989 ... 1.00
- ❑2, Nov 1989 ... 1.00
- ❑3, Dec 1989 ... 1.00
- ❑4, Jan 1990 ... 1.00
- ❑5, Feb 1990 ... 1.00
- ❑6, Mar 1990 ... 1.00

N-MINT

POLICE ACTION (2ND SERIES)
ATLAS-SEABOARD

- ❑1, Feb 1975 ... 2.00
- ❑2, Apr 1975 ... 1.50
- ❑3, Jun 1975 ... 1.50

POLIS
BRAVE NEW WORDS

- ❑1, b&w ... 2.50
- ❑2, b&w ... 2.50

POLLY AND HER PALS
ETERNITY

- ❑1, Oct 1990, b&w; strip reprints ... 2.95
- ❑2 1990, b&w; strip reprints ... 2.95
- ❑3 1991, b&w; strip reprints ... 2.95
- ❑4 1991, b&w; strip reprints ... 2.95
- ❑5 1991, b&w; strip reprints ... 2.95

PONYTAIL
DELL

- ❑-209, Sep 1962; Counted as #1 of the ongoing series ... 12.00
- ❑2, Jun 1963 ... 8.00
- ❑3, Sep 1963 ... 8.00
- ❑4, Dec 1963 ... 8.00
- ❑5, Mar 1964 ... 8.00
- ❑6, Jun 1964 ... 8.00
- ❑7, Sep 1964 ... 8.00
- ❑8, Dec 1964 ... 8.00
- ❑9, Mar 1965 ... 8.00
- ❑10, Jun 1965 ... 8.00
- ❑11, Sep 1965 ... 8.00
- ❑12, Dec 1965; Last Dell issue; moves to Charlton ... 8.00

PONYTAIL (CHARLTON)
CHARLTON

- ❑13, Nov 1969; First Charlton issue .. 6.00
- ❑14, Jan 1970 ... 4.00
- ❑15, Mar 1970 ... 4.00
- ❑16, May 1970 ... 4.00
- ❑17, Jul 1970 ... 4.00
- ❑18, Sep 1970 ... 4.00
- ❑19, Nov 1970 ... 4.00
- ❑20, Jan 1971 ... 4.00

POOT
FANTAGRAPHICS

- ❑1, Win 1997 ... 2.95
- ❑2, Spr 1998 ... 2.95
- ❑3, Sum 1998 ... 2.95
- ❑4, Win 1998 ... 3.95

POPCORN!
DISCOVERY

- ❑1, b&w; cardstock cover ... 3.95

POPCORN PIMPS
FANTAGRAPHICS

- ❑1, Jun 1996, b&w; squarebound ... 8.95

POPEYE (HARVEY)
HARVEY

- ❑1 ... 1.50
- ❑2 ... 1.50
- ❑3, Mar 1994 ... 1.50
- ❑4 1994 ... 1.50
- ❑5, Jun 1994 ... 1.50
- ❑6, Jul 1994 ... 1.50
- ❑Summer 1 ... 2.25

POPEYE SPECIAL
OCEAN

- ❑1, Sum 1987 O: Popeye. ... 2.00
- ❑2, Sep 1988 ... 2.00

POP LIFE
FANTAGRAPHICS

- ❑1, Oct 1998 ... 3.95
- ❑2, Mar 1999 ... 3.95

POPPLES
MARVEL / STAR

- ❑1, Dec 1986 ... 1.00
- ❑2, Feb 1987 ... 1.00
- ❑3, Apr 1987 ... 1.00
- ❑4, Jun 1987 ... 1.00

N-MINT

PORK KNIGHT: THIS LITTLE PIGGY
SILVER SNAIL

- ❑1 ... 2.00

PORNOTOPIA
RADIO

- ❑1, Aug 1999 ... 2.95

PORT
SILVERWOLF

- ❑1, b&w ... 1.50
- ❑2, b&w ... 1.50

PORTABLE LOWLIFE
AEON

- ❑1, Jul 1993; prestige format ... 4.95

PORTALS OF ELONDAR
STORYBOOK

- ❑1, Jul 1996, b&w ... 2.95

PORTIA PRINZ OF THE GLAMAZONS
ECLIPSE

- ❑1, Dec 1986, b&w ... 2.00
- ❑2, Feb 1987, b&w ... 2.00
- ❑3, Apr 1987, b&w ... 2.00
- ❑4, Jun 1987, b&w ... 2.00
- ❑5, Aug 1987, b&w ... 2.00
- ❑6, Oct 1987, b&w ... 2.00

PORTRAIT OF A YOUNG MAN AS A CARTOONIST
HAMMER & ANVIL

- ❑1, Oct 1996 ... 2.95
- ❑2, Dec 1996 ... 2.95
- ❑3, Feb 1997 ... 2.95
- ❑4, Apr 1997 ... 2.95
- ❑5, Jun 1997 ... 2.95
- ❑6, Aug 1997 ... 2.95
- ❑7, Oct 1997 ... 2.95
- ❑8, Jan 1998 ... 2.95

POSSESSED
DC / CLIFFHANGER

- ❑1, Sep 2003 ... 2.95
- ❑2, Oct 2003 ... 2.95
- ❑3, Nov 2003 ... 2.95
- ❑4, Dec 2003 ... 2.95
- ❑5, Jan 2004 ... 2.95
- ❑6, Mar 2004 ... 2.95

POSSIBLEMAN
BLACKTHORNE

- ❑1, Jan 1987 ... 1.75
- ❑2, Apr 1987 ... 1.75

POST APOCALYPSE
SLAVE LABOR

- ❑1, Dec 1994 ... 2.95

(POST-ATOMIC) CYBORG GERBILS
TRIGON

- ❑1, Aug 1986 ... 2.50
- ❑2 ... 2.50

POST BROTHERS
RIP OFF

- ❑19, Apr 1991, b&w; Series continued from Those Annoying Post Brothers #18 ... 2.50
- ❑20, Jun 1991, b&w ... 2.50
- ❑21, Aug 1991, b&w ... 2.50
- ❑22, Oct 1991, b&w ... 2.50
- ❑23, Oct 1991, b&w ... 2.50
- ❑24, Dec 1991, b&w ... 2.50
- ❑25, Feb 1992, b&w ... 2.50
- ❑26, Apr 1992, b&w ... 2.50
- ❑27, Jun 1992, b&w ... 2.50
- ❑28, Aug 1992, b&w ... 2.50
- ❑29, Oct 1992, b&w ... 2.50
- ❑30, Dec 1992, b&w ... 2.50
- ❑31, Feb 1993, b&w ... 2.50
- ❑32, Apr 1993, b&w ... 2.50
- ❑33, Jun 1993, b&w; Listed as "Those Annoying Post Brothers" ... 2.50
- ❑34, Aug 1993, b&w ... 2.50
- ❑35, Oct 1993, b&w ... 2.50
- ❑36, Dec 1993, b&w ... 2.50

N-MINT

❑37, Feb 1994, b&w ... 2.50
❑38, Apr 1994, b&w; series continues as Those Annoying Post Bros. ... 2.50

POTENTIAL
SLAVE LABOR

❑1, Mar 1998, b&w; magazine-sized ... 3.50
❑2 ... 3.50
❑3, Sep 1998 ... 4.95
❑4, Feb 1999 ... 3.50

POUND, THE
RADIO

❑1, Mar 2000, b&w ... 2.95

POUNDED
ONI

❑1 2002 ... 2.95
❑2 2002 ... 2.95
❑3 2002 ... 2.95

POWDER BURN
ANTARCTIC

❑1, Mar 1999, b&w ... 2.99
❑1/A, Mar 1999, b&w; wraparound cover ... 2.99
❑1/CS, Mar 1999; Collector's Set ... 5.99

POWER, THE
AIRCEL

❑1, Mar 1991, b&w ... 2.25
❑2, Apr 1991, b&w ... 2.25
❑3, May 1991, b&w ... 2.25
❑4, Jun 1991, b&w ... 2.25

POWER & GLORY
BRAVURA / MALIBU

❑1/A, Feb 1994; HC (w); HC (a); Alternate cover (marked) ... 2.50
❑1/B, Feb 1994; HC (w); HC (a); Alternate cover (marked) ... 2.50
❑1/Ltd., Feb 1994; serigraph cover ... 2.50
❑1/Variant, Feb 1994; blue foil ... 3.00
❑2, Mar 1994 HC (w); HC (a) ... 2.50
❑3, Apr 1994 HC (w); HC (a) ... 2.50
❑4, May 1994 HC (w); HC (a) ... 2.50
❑WS 1, Dec 1994; Giant-size; HC (w); HC (a); Winter Special #1 ... 2.95

POWER BRIGADE
MOVING TARGET / MALIBU

❑1 ... 1.75

POWER COMICS (POWER)
POWER

❑1, Aug 1977; 1st Dave Sim aardvark ... 2.00
❑1-2 ... 2.00
❑2, Sep 1977 ... 2.00
❑3, Oct 1977 ... 2.00
❑4, Nov 1977 ... 2.00
❑5, Dec 1977 ... 2.00

POWER COMICS (ECLIPSE)
ECLIPSE

❑1, Mar 1988, b&w ... 2.00
❑2, May 1988, b&w ... 2.00
❑3, Jul 1988, b&w ... 2.00
❑4, Sep 1988, b&w ... 2.00

POWER COMPANY, THE
DC

❑1, Apr 2002 ... 3.00
❑2, May 2002 ... 2.50
❑3, Jun 2002 ... 2.50
❑4, Jul 2002 ... 2.50
❑5, Aug 2002 ... 2.50
❑6, Sep 2002 ... 2.50
❑7, Oct 2002 ... 2.75
❑8, Nov 2002 ... 2.75
❑9, Dec 2002 KB (w) ... 2.75
❑10, Jan 2003 KB (w) ... 2.75
❑11, Feb 2003 KB (w) ... 2.75
❑12, Mar 2003 KB (w) ... 2.75
❑13, Apr 2003 ... 2.75
❑14, May 2003 ... 2.75
❑15, Jun 2003 ... 2.75
❑16, Jul 2003 ... 2.75
❑17, Aug 2003 ... 2.75
❑18, Sep 2003 ... 2.75

N-MINT

POWER COMPANY, THE: BORK
DC

❑1, Mar 2002 ... 2.50

POWER COMPANY, THE: JOSIAH POWER
DC

❑1, Mar 2002 ... 2.50

POWER COMPANY, THE: MANHUNTER
DC

❑1, Mar 2002 ... 2.50

POWER COMPANY, THE: SAPPHIRE
DC

❑1, Mar 2002 ... 2.50

POWER COMPANY, THE: SKYROCKET
DC

❑1, Mar 2002 ... 2.50

POWER COMPANY, THE: STRIKER Z
DC

❑1, Mar 2002 ... 2.50

POWER COMPANY, THE: WITCHFIRE
DC

❑1, Mar 2002 ... 2.50

POWER DEFENSE
MILLER

❑1, b&w ... 2.50

POWER FACTOR (1ST SERIES)
WONDER

❑1, May 1986; Wonder Color Publisher ... 1.95
❑2, Jun 1986; Pied Piper Publisher ... 1.95

POWER FACTOR (2ND SERIES)
INNOVATION

❑1, Oct 1990 ... 1.95
❑2, Dec 1990 ... 2.25
❑3, Feb 1991 ... 2.25
❑Special 1, Jan 1991 ... 2.75

POWER GIRL
DC

❑1, Jun 1988 ... 1.00
❑2, Jul 1988 ... 1.00
❑3, Aug 1988 ... 1.00
❑4, Sep 1988 ... 1.00

POWERLESS
MARVEL

❑1, Aug 2004 ... 2.99
❑2, Sep 2004 ...

POWER LINE
MARVEL / EPIC

❑1, May 1988 BSz (c); BSz (a) ... 1.50
❑2, Jul 1988 ... 1.50
❑3, Sep 1988 ... 1.50
❑4, Nov 1988 ... 1.50
❑5, Jan 1989 ... 1.50
❑6, Mar 1989 ... 1.50
❑7, May 1989 GM (a) ... 1.50
❑8, Jul 1989 ... 1.50

POWER LORDS
DC

❑1, Dec 1983 O: Power Lords. 1: Power Lords. ... 1.00
❑2, Jan 1984 ... 1.00
❑3, Feb 1985 ... 1.00

POWER MAN & IRON FIST
MARVEL

❑17, Feb 1974; GT (a); A: Iron Man. Title continued from "Hero For Hire" ... 8.00
❑18, Apr 1974; Marvel Value Stamp #3: Conan ... 5.00
❑19, Jun 1974; Marvel Value Stamp #64: Sif ... 5.00
❑20, Aug 1974; Marvel Value Stamp #1: Spider-Man ... 5.00
❑21, Oct 1974; V: Power Man. Marvel Value Stamp #73: Kingpin ... 4.00
❑22, Dec 1974 ... 4.00
❑23, Feb 1975; Marvel Value Stamp #3: Conan ... 4.00

Mary Marvel and Tawky Tawny's origins were updated in *Power of Shazam* #4.

© 1995 DC Comics.

N-MINT

❑24, Apr 1975; 1: Black Goliath. V: Circus of Crime. Marvel Value Stamp #27: Black Widow ... 4.00
❑25, Jun 1975 V: Circus of Crime. ... 4.00
❑26, Aug 1975 ... 4.00
❑27, Oct 1975 GP (a) ... 4.00
❑28, Dec 1975 ... 4.00
❑29, Feb 1976 ... 4.00
❑30, Apr 1976 ... 4.00
❑30/30 cent, Apr 1976; 30 cent regional price variant ... 20.00
❑31, May 1976 NA (a) ... 4.00
❑31/30 cent, May 1976; 30 cent regional price variant ... 20.00
❑32, Jun 1976 ... 3.00
❑32/30 cent, Jun 1976; 30 cent regional price variant ... 20.00
❑33, Jul 1976 ... 3.00
❑33/30 cent, Jul 1976; 30 cent regional price variant ... 20.00
❑34, Aug 1976 ... 3.00
❑34/30 cent, Aug 1976; 30 cent regional price variant ... 20.00
❑35, Sep 1976 ... 3.00
❑36, Oct 1976 ... 3.00
❑37, Nov 1976 1: Chemistro II (Archibald "Arch" Morton). ... 3.00
❑38, Dec 1976 ... 3.00
❑39, Jan 1977 ... 3.00
❑40, Feb 1977 ... 3.00
❑41, Mar 1977 1: Thunderbolt (William Carver as...). ... 3.00
❑42, Apr 1977 ... 3.00
❑43, May 1977 ... 3.00
❑44, Jun 1977 ... 3.00
❑44/35 cent, Jun 1977; 35 cent regional price variant ... 15.00
❑45, Jul 1977 JSn (a); A: Mace. ... 3.00
❑45/35 cent, Jul 1977; JSn (a); A: Mace. 35 cent regional price variant ... 15.00
❑46, Aug 1977 GT (a); 1: Zzax. ... 3.00
❑46/35 cent, Aug 1977; GT (a); 1: Zzax. 35 cent regional price variant ... 15.00
❑47, Oct 1977 A: Iron Fist. ... 3.00
❑48, Dec 1977 JBy (a); 1: Power Man and Iron Fist. ... 4.00
❑49, Feb 1978; JBy (a); A: Iron Fist. series continues as Power Man & Iron Fist ... 3.00
❑50, Apr 1978 JBy (a) ... 3.00
❑51, Jun 1978 ... 3.00
❑52, Aug 1978 ... 3.00
❑53, Oct 1978 O: Nightshade. ... 4.00
❑54, Dec 1978 O: Iron Fist. ... 4.00
❑55, Feb 1979 ... 4.00
❑56, Apr 1979 O: Señor Suerte II (Jaime Garcia). 1: Señor Suerte II (Jaime Garcia). ... 3.00
❑57, Jun 1979 A: X-Men. ... 5.00
❑58, Aug 1979 1: El Aguila. ... 3.00
❑59, Oct 1979 BL (a) ... 3.00
❑60, Dec 1979 BL (a) ... 3.00
❑61, Feb 1980 BL (a) ... 3.00
❑62, Apr 1980 BL (a); D: Thunderbolt. ... 3.00
❑63, Jun 1980 BL (a) ... 3.00
❑64, Aug 1980 BL (a) ... 3.00
❑65, Oct 1980 BL (a); V: El Aguila. ... 3.00
❑66, Dec 1980 FM (c); FM (a); 2: Sabretooth. ... 12.00
❑67, Feb 1981 FM (c); FM (a) ... 2.00

	N-MINT
❑68, Apr 1981 FM (c); FM (a)	2.00
❑69, May 1981	2.00
❑70, Jun 1981 FM (c); FM (a); O: Colleen Wing.	2.00
❑71, Jul 1981 FM (c); FM (a)	2.00
❑72, Aug 1981 FM (c); FM (a)	2.00
❑73, Sep 1981 FM (c); FM (a); A: ROM.	2.00
❑74, Oct 1981 FM (c)	2.00
❑75, Nov 1981; origins	2.00
❑76, Dec 1981 FM (a)	2.00
❑77, Jan 1982 A: Daredevil.	2.00
❑78, Feb 1982 A: Sabretooth. V: El Aguila.	2.00
❑79, Mar 1982	2.00
❑80, Apr 1982 FM (c); FM (a); V: Montenegro.	2.00
❑81, May 1982	2.00
❑82, Jun 1982	2.00
❑83, Jul 1982	2.00
❑84, Aug 1982 A: Sabretooth.	6.00
❑85, Sep 1982	2.00
❑86, Oct 1982 A: Moon Knight.	2.00
❑87, Nov 1982 A: Moon Knight.	2.00
❑88, Dec 1982	2.00
❑89, Jan 1983	2.00
❑90, Feb 1983; KB (w); A: Unus the Untouchable. V: Unus. Kurt Busiek's first Marvel work	2.00
❑91, Mar 1983	2.00
❑92, Apr 1983 KB (w); 1: Eel II (Edward Lavell). V: Hammerhead.	2.00
❑93, May 1983 KB (w); V: Chemistro.	2.00
❑94, Jun 1983 KB (w); 1: Chemistro III (Calvin Carr).	2.00
❑95, Jul 1983 KB (w)	2.00
❑96, Aug 1983 KB (w); V: Chemistro.	2.00
❑97, Sep 1983 KB (w); V: Fera.	2.00
❑98, Oct 1983 KB (w)	2.00
❑99, Nov 1983 KB (w); V: Fera.	2.00
❑100, Dec 1983; Giant-size KB (w); V: Khan.	2.00
❑101, Jan 1984	2.00
❑102, Feb 1984 KB (w)	2.00
❑103, Mar 1984	2.00
❑104, Apr 1984	2.00
❑105, May 1984 KB (w)	2.00
❑106, Jun 1984	2.00
❑107, Jul 1984	2.00
❑108, Aug 1984	2.00
❑109, Sep 1984 V: Reaper.	2.00
❑110, Oct 1984	2.00
❑111, Nov 1984	2.00
❑112, Dec 1984	2.00
❑113, Jan 1985 D: Solarr.	2.00
❑114, Feb 1985	2.00
❑115, Mar 1985	2.00
❑116, Apr 1985	2.00
❑117, May 1985	2.00
❑118, Jul 1985	2.00
❑119, Sep 1985	2.00
❑120, Nov 1985	2.00
❑121, Jan 1986; Secret Wars II	2.00
❑122, Mar 1986	2.00
❑123, May 1986	2.00
❑124, Jul 1986	2.00
❑125, Sep 1986 D: Iron Fist (H'yithri double).	2.00
❑Annual 1, Jan 1976	3.50

POWER OF PRIME
MALIBU / ULTRAVERSE

	N-MINT
❑1, Jul 1995; story continues in Prime #25 and #26	2.50
❑2, Aug 1995	2.50
❑3, Sep 1995	2.50
❑4, Nov 1995	2.50

POWER OF SHAZAM, THE
DC

	N-MINT
❑1, Mar 1995 JOy (w)	3.00
❑2, Apr 1995 JOy (w); V: Arson Fiend.	2.00
❑3, May 1995 JOy (w)	2.00
❑4, Jun 1995; JOy (w); Return of Mary Marvel, Tawky Tawny	2.00
❑5, Jul 1995 JOy (w)	2.00
❑6, Aug 1995; JOy (w); Return of Captain Nazi; Freddy Freeman and grandfather injured	2.00
❑7, Sep 1995; JOy (w); Return of Captain Marvel Jr.	2.00
❑8, Oct 1995 JOy (w); CS (a); A: Minuteman. A: Bulletman. A: Spy Smasher.	2.00
❑9, Nov 1995 JOy (w)	2.00
❑10, Dec 1995 JOy (w); O: Satanus. O: Blaze. O: Black Adam. O: Rock of Eternity. O: Shazam.	2.00
❑11, Jan 1996; JOy (w); A: Bulletman. Return of Ibis; Return of Uncle Marvel; Return of Marvel Family	1.75
❑12, Feb 1996 JOy (w); O: Seven Deadly Foes of Man.	1.75
❑13, Mar 1996 JOy (w)	1.75
❑14, Apr 1996; JOy (w); GK (a); 1: Chain Lightning. Captain Marvel Jr. solo story	1.75
❑15, Jun 1996 JOy (w)	1.75
❑16, Jul 1996 JOy (w)	1.75
❑17, Aug 1996 JOy (w)	1.75
❑18, Sep 1996 JOy (w)	1.75
❑19, Oct 1996; JOy (w); GK, JSa (a); A: Minuteman. Captain Marvel Jr. vs. Captain Nazi	1.75
❑20, Nov 1996; JOy (w); A: Superman. Final Night	1.75
❑21, Dec 1996 JOy (w); A: Plastic Man.	1.75
❑22, Jan 1997 JOy (w); A: Batman.	1.75
❑23, Feb 1997 JOy (w); V: Mr. Atom.	1.75
❑24, Mar 1997 JOy (w); A: C.C. Batson. A: Baron Blitzkrieg. A: Spy Smasher.	1.75
❑25, Apr 1997; V: Ibac. C.C. Batson as Captain Marvel	1.75
❑26, May 1997; Shazam attempts to set time right again	1.75
❑27, Jun 1997; A: Waverider. time is restored to proper course	1.75
❑28, Jul 1997 DG (a)	1.75
❑29, Aug 1997 A: Hoppy the Marvel Bunny.	1.75
❑30, Sep 1997; V: Mr. Finish. Mary receives new costume	1.75
❑31, Oct 1997; Genesis; Billy and Mary reveal their identities to the Bromfields	1.95
❑32, Nov 1997 1: Windshear.	1.95
❑33, Dec 1997; JOy (w); Face cover	1.95
❑34, Jan 1998 JOy (w); A: Gangbuster.	1.95
❑35, Feb 1998; A: Starman. continues in Starman #40	1.95
❑36, Mar 1998 A: Starman.	1.95
❑37, Apr 1998; JOy (w); CM3 vs. Doctor Morpheus; CM3 vs. Dr. Morpheus	1.95
❑38, May 1998	1.95
❑39, Jun 1998	1.95
❑40, Jul 1998	1.95
❑41, Aug 1998 D: Mr. Mind.	1.95
❑42, Sep 1998 A: Chain Lightning.	1.95
❑43, Oct 1998; kids on life support	2.50
❑44, Dec 1998 A: Black Adam. A: Thunder.	2.50
❑45, Jan 1999 A: Justice League of America.	2.50
❑46, Feb 1999 JOy (w); JOy (a); A: Superman. A: Black Adam. V: Superman.	2.50
❑47, Mar 1999 JOy (w); JOy (a); A: Black Adam.	2.50
❑1000000, Nov 1998 JOy (w); JOy (a)	3.00
❑Annual 1, ca. 1996; JOy (w); 1996; Legends of the Dead Earth	2.95

POWER OF STRONG MAN
AC

	N-MINT
❑1, b&w	2.50

POWER OF THE ATOM
DC

	N-MINT
❑1, Aug 1988	1.00
❑2, Sep 1988	1.00
❑3, Oct 1988	1.00
❑4, Nov 1988; Bonus Book #8	1.00
❑5, Dec 1988	1.00
❑6, Win 1988	1.00
❑7, Hol 1988; Invasion!	1.00
❑8, Jan 1989; Invasion!	1.00
❑9, Feb 1989	1.00
❑10, Mar 1989	1.00
❑11, Apr 1989	1.00
❑12, May 1989	1.00
❑13, Jun 1989	1.00
❑14, Jul 1989	1.00
❑15, Aug 1989	1.00
❑16, Sep 1989	1.00
❑17, Oct 1989	1.00
❑18, Nov 1989	1.00

POWER PACHYDERMS
MARVEL

	N-MINT
❑1, Sep 1989; one-shot parody	1.00

POWER PACK
MARVEL

	N-MINT
❑1, Aug 1984; Giant-size O: Mass Master. O: Power Pack. O: Lightspeed. 1: Mass Master. 1: Power Pack. 1: Lightspeed. V: Snarks.	2.00
❑2, Sep 1984	1.50
❑3, Oct 1984	1.00
❑4, Nov 1984	1.00
❑5, Dec 1984	1.00
❑6, Jan 1985 A: Spider-Man.	1.00
❑7, Feb 1985 A: Cloak & Dagger.	1.00
❑8, Mar 1985 A: Cloak & Dagger.	1.00
❑9, Apr 1985 BA (a)	1.00
❑10, May 1985 BA (a)	1.00
❑11, Jun 1985	1.00
❑12, Jul 1985 A: X-Men.	1.00
❑13, Aug 1985 BA (a)	1.00
❑14, Sep 1985	1.00
❑15, Oct 1985	1.00
❑16, Nov 1985 1: Kofi.	1.00
❑17, Dec 1985	1.00
❑18, Jan 1986 BA (a)	1.00
❑19, Feb 1986; Giant-size BA (a); A: Wolverine.	1.50
❑20, Mar 1986 A: New Mutants.	1.00
❑21, Apr 1986 BA (a)	1.00
❑22, May 1986	1.00
❑23, Jun 1986	1.00
❑24, Jul 1986	1.00
❑25, Aug 1986	1.25
❑26, Oct 1986 A: Cloak & Dagger.	1.00
❑27, Dec 1986 A: Wolverine. A: Sabretooth.	4.00
❑28, Feb 1987 A: Fantastic Four. A: Avengers.	1.00
❑29, Apr 1987; Giant-size A: Hobgoblin. A: Spider-Man.	1.00
❑30, Jun 1987	1.00
❑31, Aug 1987 1: Trash.	1.00
❑32, Oct 1987	1.00
❑33, Nov 1987	1.00
❑34, Jan 1988	1.00
❑35, Feb 1988; Fall of Mutants	1.00
❑36, Apr 1988	1.00
❑37, May 1988	1.00
❑38, Jul 1988	1.00
❑39, Aug 1988	1.00
❑40, Sep 1988	1.00
❑41, Nov 1988	1.00
❑42, Dec 1988 A: Inferno.	1.00
❑43, Jan 1989 A: Inferno.	1.00
❑44, Mar 1989 A: Inferno.	1.50
❑45, Apr 1989	1.50
❑46, May 1989 A: Punisher.	1.50
❑47, Jul 1989	1.50
❑48, Sep 1989	1.50
❑49, Oct 1989	1.50
❑50, Nov 1989; Giant-size	2.00
❑51, Dec 1989 1: Numinus.	1.50
❑52, Dec 1989	1.50
❑53, Jan 1990	1.50
❑54, Feb 1990	1.50
❑55, Apr 1990 A: Mysterio.	1.50
❑56, Jun 1990	1.50
❑57, Jul 1990	1.50

N-MINT

❑58, Sep 1990 A: Galactus. 1.50
❑59, Oct 1990 .... 1.50
❑60, Nov 1990 .... 1.50
❑61, Dec 1990 .... 1.50
❑62, Jan 1991 .... 2.00
❑Holiday 1, Feb 1992; magazine-sized 2.50

POWER PACK (VOL. 2)
MARVEL

❑1, Aug 2000 .... 2.99

POWER PLAYS (AC)
AC

❑1, b&w 1.75
❑2, Fal 1985, b&w 1.75

POWER PLAYS (EXTRAVA-GANDT)
EXTRAVA-GANDT

❑1, b&w 2.00
❑2 .... 2.00
❑3, b&w 2.00

POWERPUFF GIRLS, THE
DC

❑1, May 2000 .... 5.00
❑2, Jun 2000 .... 3.00
❑3, Jul 2000 .... 2.50
❑4, Aug 2000 .... 2.00
❑5, Sep 2000 .... 1.99
❑6, Oct 2000 .... 1.99
❑7, Nov 2000 .... 1.99
❑8, Dec 2000 .... 1.99
❑9, Jan 2001 .... 1.99
❑10, Feb 2001 .... 1.99
❑11, Mar 2001 .... 1.99
❑12, Apr 2001 .... 1.99
❑13, May 2001 .... 1.99
❑14, Jun 2001 .... 1.99
❑15, Jul 2001 .... 1.99
❑16, Aug 2001 .... 1.99
❑17, Sep 2001 .... 1.99
❑18, Oct 2001 .... 1.99
❑19, Nov 2001 .... 1.99
❑20, Dec 2001 .... 1.99
❑21, Jan 2002 .... 1.99
❑22, Feb 2002 .... 1.99
❑23, Mar 2002 .... 1.99
❑24, Apr 2002 .... 1.99
❑25, May 2002 JBy (a) 1.99
❑26, Jun 2002 .... 1.99
❑27, Jul 2002 .... 1.99
❑28, Aug 2002 .... 1.99
❑29, Oct 2002 .... 2.25
❑30, Nov 2002 .... 2.25
❑31, Dec 2002 .... 2.25
❑32, Jan 2003 .... 2.25
❑33, Feb 2003 .... 2.25
❑34, Mar 2003 .... 2.25
❑35, Apr 2003 .... 2.25
❑36, May 2003 .... 2.25
❑37, Jun 2003 .... 2.25
❑38, Jul 2003 .... 2.25
❑39, Aug 2003 .... 2.25
❑40, Sep 2003 .... 2.25
❑41, Oct 2003 .... 2.25
❑42, Nov 2003 .... 2.25
❑43, Dec 2003 .... 2.25
❑44, Jan 2004 .... 2.25
❑45, Feb 2004 .... 2.25
❑46, Mar 2004 .... 2.25
❑47, Apr 2004 .... 2.25
❑48, May 2004 .... 2.25
❑49, Jun 2004 .... 2.25
❑50, Jul 2004 .... 2.25
❑51, Aug 2004 .... 2.25
❑52, Sep 2004 ....

POWERPUFF GIRLS DOUBLE WHAMMY, THE
DC

❑1, Dec 2000; Collects stories from Powerpuff Girls #1-2, Dexter's Laboratory #7 .... 5.00

N-MINT

POWER RANGERS TURBO: INTO THE FIRE
ACCLAIM

❑1 .... 4.50

POWER RANGERS ZEO
IMAGE

❑1, Sep 1996 .... 2.50
❑2, Oct 1996 .... 2.50

POWERS
IMAGE

❑1, Apr 2000 BMB (w) 7.00
❑2, May 2000 BMB (w) 6.00
❑3, Jun 2000; BMB (w); #1 in indicia 5.00
❑4, Aug 2000 BMB (w) 3.50
❑5, Sep 2000 BMB (w) 4.00
❑6, Oct 2000 BMB (w) 4.00
❑7, Nov 2000 BMB (w) 4.00
❑8, Dec 2001 BMB (w) 4.00
❑9, Jan 2001 BMB (w) 4.00
❑10, Mar 2001 BMB (w) 4.00
❑11, Apr 2001 BMB (w) 2.95
❑12, Jun 2001 BMB (w) 2.95
❑13, Jun 2001 BMB (w) 2.95
❑14, Jul 2001 BMB (w) 2.95
❑15, Aug 2001 BMB (w) 2.95
❑16, Sep 2001 BMB (w) 2.95
❑17, Oct 2001 BMB (w) 2.95
❑18, Nov 2001 BMB (w) 2.95
❑19, Dec 2001 BMB (w) 2.95
❑20, Jan 2002 BMB (w) 2.95
❑21, ca. 2002 .... 2.95
❑22, ca. 2002 .... 2.95
❑23, ca. 2002 .... 2.95
❑24, ca. 2002 .... 2.95
❑25, ca. 2002 .... 2.95
❑26, Dec 2002 .... 2.95
❑27, Feb 2003 .... 2.95
❑28, Jan 2003 .... 2.95
❑29, Feb 2003 .... 2.95
❑30, Mar 2003 .... 2.95
❑31, Apr 2003 .... 2.95
❑32, Jun 2003, color 2.95
❑33, Aug 2003, color 2.95
❑34, Oct 2003, color 2.95
❑35, Nov 2003, color 2.95
❑36, Jan 2004, color 2.95
❑37, Apr 2004 .... 2.95
❑Annual 1 BMB (w) 3.95

POWERS COLORING/ACTIVITY BOOK
IMAGE

❑1, Feb 2001 .... 1.50

POWERS (MARVEL)
MARVEL

❑1, Sep 2004 .... 2.99
❑2, Sep 2004 .... 2.99

POWERS THAT BE
BROADWAY

❑1, Nov 1995; 1: Fatale. 1: Star Seed. Fatale and Star Seed; 1st comic from Broadway Comics 2.25
❑2, Dec 1995; Star Seed 2.50
❑2/Ashcan, Sep 1995, b&w; giveaway preview edition; Star Seed 1.00
❑3, Jan 1996; Star Seed 2.50
❑3/Ashcan, Oct 1995, b&w; giveaway preview edition; Star Seed 1.00
❑4, Feb 1996; Star Seed 2.50
❑5, Apr 1996; 1: Marnie. V: Gina and Charlotte. Star Seed 2.50
❑6, May 1996; 1: Ajax. Star Seed 2.95
❑7, Jul 1996; Title changes to Star Seed 2.95
❑8 1996 .... 2.95
❑9, Oct 1996 .... 2.95

PRAIRIE MOON AND OTHER STORIES
DARK HORSE

❑1, b&w; Rick Geary 2.25

PREACHER
DC / VERTIGO

❑1, Apr 1995 1: Jesse Custer. 13.00
❑2, May 1995 1: The Saint of Killers. 6.00

Broadway Comics' first publication was *Powers That Be* #1 featuring the first appearances of both Fatale (pictured) and Star Seed.
© 1995 Broadway Entertainment.

N-MINT

❑3, Jun 1995 .... 5.00
❑4, Jul 1995 .... 5.00
❑5, Aug 1995 .... 5.00
❑6, Sep 1995 .... 3.50
❑7, Oct 1995 .... 3.50
❑8, Nov 1995 .... 3.50
❑9, Dec 1995 .... 3.50
❑10, Jan 1996 .... 3.50
❑11, Feb 1996 .... 3.00
❑12, Mar 1996 .... 3.00
❑13, Apr 1996 .... 3.00
❑14, Jun 1996 .... 3.00
❑15, Jul 1996 .... 3.00
❑16, Aug 1996 .... 2.50
❑17, Sep 1996 .... 2.50
❑18, Oct 1996 .... 2.50
❑19, Nov 1996 .... 2.50
❑20, Dec 1996 .... 2.50
❑21, Jan 1997 .... 2.50
❑22, Feb 1997 .... 2.50
❑23, Mar 1997 .... 2.50
❑24, Apr 1997 .... 2.50
❑25, May 1997 O: Cassidy. 2.50
❑26, Jun 1997 O: Cassidy. 2.50
❑27, Jul 1997 .... 2.50
❑28, Aug 1997 .... 2.50
❑29, Sep 1997 A: You-Know-Who. 2.50
❑30, Oct 1997 A: You-Know-Who. 2.50
❑31, Nov 1997 .... 2.50
❑32, Dec 1997 .... 2.50
❑33, Jan 1998 .... 2.50
❑34, Feb 1998 .... 2.50
❑35, Mar 1998 .... 2.50
❑36, Apr 1998 .... 2.50
❑37, May 1998 .... 2.50
❑38, Jun 1998 A: You-Know-Who. 2.50
❑39, Jul 1998; Jesse loses an eye; Starr loses a leg 2.50
❑40, Aug 1998 .... 2.50
❑41, Sep 1998; six months later; Jesse becomes sheriff of Salvation, Texas 2.50
❑42, Oct 1998 1: Odin Quincannon. .. 2.50
❑43, Nov 1998; Jesse's mother's story 2.50
❑44, Dec 1998 .... 2.50
❑45, Jan 1999 .... 2.50
❑46, Feb 1999 .... 2.50
❑47, Mar 1999 .... 2.50
❑48, Apr 1999 D: Odin Quincannon. .. 2.50
❑49, May 1999 .... 2.50
❑50, Jun 1999; Giant-size JLee (a) 3.75
❑51, Jul 1999; 100 Bullets preview ... 4.00
❑52, Aug 1999 .... 4.00
❑53, Sep 1999 .... 4.00
❑54, Oct 1999 .... 4.00
❑55, Nov 1999 .... 4.00
❑56, Dec 1999 .... 4.00
❑57, Jan 2000 .... 4.00
❑58, Feb 2000 .... 4.00
❑59, Mar 2000 .... 4.00
❑60, Apr 2000 .... 4.00
❑61, May 2000 .... 4.00
❑62, Jun 2000 .... 4.00
❑63, Jul 2000 .... 4.00
❑64, Aug 2000 .... 4.00
❑65, Sep 2000 .... 4.00
❑66, Oct 2000; Giant-size 3.75

Condition price index: Multiply "NM prices" above by: **0.83 for Very Fine/Near Mint**
0.66 for Very Fine • 0.33 for Fine • 0.2 for Very Good • 0.125 for Good

N-MINT

PREACHER SPECIAL: CASSIDY: BLOOD & WHISKEY
DC / VERTIGO
❑1, Feb 1998; prestige format 5.95

PREACHER SPECIAL: ONE MAN'S WAR
DC / VERTIGO
❑1, Mar 1998 O: Starr. 5.00

PREACHER SPECIAL: SAINT OF KILLERS
DC / VERTIGO
❑1, Aug 1996 .... 3.00
❑2, Sep 1996 .... 3.00
❑3, Oct 1996 .... 3.00
❑4, Nov 1996 .... 3.00

PREACHER SPECIAL: TALL IN THE SADDLE
DC / VERTIGO
❑1, Feb 2000 .... 4.95

PREACHER SPECIAL: THE GOOD OLD BOYS
DC / VERTIGO
❑1, Aug 1997 .... 4.95

PREACHER SPECIAL: THE STORY OF YOU-KNOW-WHO
DC / VERTIGO
❑1, Dec 1996 .... 4.95

PRECIOUS METAL
ARTS INDUSTRIA
❑1, b&w 2.50

PREDATOR
DARK HORSE
❑1, Jun 1989, color 5.00
❑1-2 .... 2.50
❑2, Sep 1989 .... 3.50
❑3, Dec 1989 .... 3.00
❑4, Mar 1990 .... 3.00

PREDATOR 2
DARK HORSE
❑1, Feb 1991 .... 3.00
❑2, Jun 1991 .... 3.00

PREDATOR: BAD BLOOD
DARK HORSE
❑1, Dec 1993 .... 2.50
❑2, Feb 1994 .... 2.50
❑3, May 1994 .... 2.50
❑4, Jun 1994 .... 2.50

PREDATOR: BIG GAME
DARK HORSE
❑1, Mar 1991; trading cards 2.50
❑2, Apr 1991; no trading cards despite cover advisory 2.50
❑3, May 1991; trading cards 2.50
❑4, Jun 1991 .... 2.50

PREDATOR: CAPTIVE
DARK HORSE
❑1, Apr 1998 .... 2.95

PREDATOR: COLD WAR
DARK HORSE
❑1, Sep 1991 .... 2.50
❑2, Oct 1991 .... 2.50
❑3, Nov 1991 .... 2.50
❑4, Dec 1991 .... 2.50

PREDATOR: DARK RIVER
DARK HORSE
❑1, Jul 1996 .... 2.95
❑2, Aug 1996 .... 2.95
❑3, Sep 1996 .... 2.95
❑4, Oct 1996 .... 2.95

PREDATOR: HELL & HOT WATER
DARK HORSE
❑1, Apr 1997; uninked pencils 2.95
❑2, May 1997; uninked pencils 2.95
❑3, Jun 1997; uninked pencils 2.95

PREDATOR: HELL COME A WALKIN'
DARK HORSE
❑1, Feb 1998; Predator in Civil War ... 2.95
❑2, Mar 1998; Predator in Civil War .. 2.95

PREDATOR: HOMEWORLD
DARK HORSE
❑1, Mar 1999 .... 2.95
❑2, Apr 1999 .... 2.95
❑3, May 1999 .... 2.95
❑4, Jun 1999 .... 2.95

PREDATOR: INVADERS FROM THE FOURTH DIMENSION
DARK HORSE
❑1, Jul 1994 .... 3.95

PREDATOR: JUNGLE TALES
DARK HORSE
❑1, Mar 1995; collects Predator: Rite of Passage from DHC #1 and 2; Predator: The Pride of Nghasa from DHC #10-12 .... 2.95

PREDATOR: KINDRED
DARK HORSE
❑1, Dec 1996 .... 2.50
❑2, Jan 1997 .... 2.50
❑3, Feb 1997 .... 2.50
❑4, Mar 1997 .... 2.50

PREDATOR: NEMESIS
DARK HORSE
❑1, Dec 1997 .... 2.95
❑2, Jan 1998 .... 2.95

PREDATOR: PRIMAL
DARK HORSE
❑1, Jul 1997; Predator vs. bears 2.95
❑2, Aug 1997; Predator vs. bears 2.95

PREDATOR: RACE WAR
DARK HORSE
❑0, Apr 1993 .... 2.50
❑1, Feb 1993 .... 2.50
❑2, Mar 1993 .... 2.50
❑3, Aug 1993 .... 2.50
❑4, Oct 1993 .... 2.50

PREDATOR: STRANGE ROUX
DARK HORSE
❑1, Nov 1996; recipe for Strange Roux in back 2.95

PREDATOR: THE BLOODY SANDS OF TIME
DARK HORSE
❑1, Feb 1992; Predator in WW I 2.75
❑2, Feb 1992; Predator in WW I 2.75

PREDATOR VERSUS JUDGE DREDD
DARK HORSE / EGMONT
❑1, Oct 1997 .... 2.50
❑2, Nov 1997 .... 2.50
❑3, Dec 1997 .... 2.50

PREDATOR VS. MAGNUS ROBOT FIGHTER
DARK HORSE / VALIANT
❑1, Nov 1992 .... 3.00
❑1/Platinum, Nov 1992; Platinum promotional edition 4.00
❑2, Dec 1993; trading cards 3.00

PREDATOR: XENOGENESIS
DARK HORSE
❑1, Aug 1999 .... 2.95
❑2, Sep 1999 .... 2.95
❑3, Oct 1999 .... 2.95
❑4, Nov 1999 .... 2.95

PREMIERE
DIVERSITY
❑1; 1500 printed 2.75
❑1/Gold; Gold limited edition (175 printed) 4.00
❑1/Ltd.; Limited edition (175 printed) 3.00
❑2 .... 2.75

PRESERVATION OF OBSCURITY, THE
LUMP OF SQUID
❑1 .... 2.75
❑2 .... 2.75

PRESSED TONGUE (DAVE COOPER'S...)
FANTAGRAPHICS
❑1, b&w 2.95
❑3, Dec 1994, b&w 2.95

PRESTO KID, THE
AC
❑1, b&w 2.50

PRE-TEEN DIRTY-GENE KUNG-FU KANGAROOS
BLACKTHORNE
❑1, Aug 1986 A: TMNT. 2.00
❑2, Nov 1986 .... 2.00
❑3 1987 .... 2.00

PREY
MONSTER
❑1, b&w 2.25
❑2, b&w 2.25
❑3, b&w 2.25

PREY FOR US SINNERS
FANTACO
❑1 .... 4.95

PREZ
DC
❑1, Sep 1973 .... 8.00
❑2, Nov 1973 .... 4.00
❑3, Jan 1974 .... 4.00
❑4, Mar 1974 .... 4.00

PRIDE & JOY
DC / VERTIGO
❑1, Jul 1997 .... 2.50
❑2, Aug 1997 .... 2.50
❑3, Sep 1997 .... 2.50
❑4, Oct 1997 .... 2.50

PRIEST
MAXIMUM
❑1, Aug 1996 .... 2.99
❑2, Sep 1996 .... 2.99
❑3, Oct 1996 .... 2.99

PRIMAL
DARK HORSE
❑1 .... 2.50
❑2 .... 2.50

PRIMAL FORCE
DC
❑0, Oct 1994 .... 1.95
❑1, Nov 1994 .... 1.95
❑2, Dec 1994 .... 1.95
❑3, Jan 1995 .... 1.95
❑4, Feb 1995 .... 1.95
❑5, Mar 1995 .... 1.95
❑6, Apr 1995 .... 1.95
❑7, May 1995 .... 1.95
❑8, Jun 1995 .... 2.25
❑9, Jul 1995 .... 2.25
❑10, Aug 1995 .... 2.25
❑11, Sep 1995 .... 2.25
❑12, Oct 1995 .... 2.25
❑13, Nov 1995; Underworld Unleashed 2.25
❑14, Dec 1995 .... 2.25

PRIMAL RAGE
SIRIUS
❑1, Aug 1996, b&w 2.50
❑2, Oct 1996, b&w 2.50
❑3, Dec 1996, b&w 2.50
❑4, Feb 1997, b&w 2.50

PRIME (VOL. 1)
MALIBU / ULTRAVERSE
❑0.5; Wizard promotional edition 2.50
❑1, Jun 1993; 1: Prime. 1: Doctor Gross. Ultraverse 2.50
❑1/Hologram; Holographic promotional edition 1: Prime. 1: Doctor Gross. 5.00
❑1/Ltd., Jun 1993; "Ultra-Limited" edition; 1: Prime. 1: Doctor Gross. foil stamped; $1.95 on cover 2.50
❑2, Jul 1993; Ultraverse; trading card 1.95
❑3, Aug 1993 O: Prime. 1.95

N-MINT

❑4, Sep 1993; 1: Maxi-Man. A: Prototype II (Jimmy Ruiz). V: Prototype. two different covers 1.95
❑5, Oct 1993; Rune 1.95
❑6, Nov 1993 .... 1.95
❑7, Dec 1993; Break-Thru 1.95
❑8, Jan 1994 O: Freex. A: Mantra. 1.95
❑9, Feb 1994 .... 1.95
❑10, Mar 1994 A: Firearm. 1.95
❑11, Apr 1994 .... 1.95
❑12, May 1994; flip-book with Ultraverse Premiere #3 .... 3.50
❑13, Jul 1994; Freex preview; two different covers 1.95
❑13/A; variant cover 1.95
❑14, Sep 1994 1: Papa Verité 1.95
❑15, Oct 1994 GP (a) 1.95
❑16, Nov 1994 1: TurboCharge. 1.95
❑17, Dec 1994 .... 1.95
❑18, Dec 1994 .... 1.95
❑19, Jan 1995 DC (a) 1.95
❑20, Mar 1995 1: Phade. 1.95
❑21, Apr 1995 JSa (a); A: Chelsea Clinton. 1.95
❑22, May 1995 .... 1.95
❑23, Jun 1995 .... 1.95
❑24, Jun 1995 .... 1.95
❑25, Jul 1995; O: Prime. continued from Power of Prime #1 .... 1.95
❑26, Aug 1995; O: Prime. continues in Power of Prime #2 .... 1.95
❑Annual 1, Oct 1994; 1: new Prime. A: Hardcase. Prime: Gross and Disgusting 3.95
❑Ashcan 1; ashcan edition 1.00

PRIME (VOL. 2)
MALIBU / ULTRAVERSE

❑0, Sep 1995; Black September; #Infinity 1.50
❑0/A, Sep 1995; Black September; alternate cover 1.50
❑1, Oct 1995; Spider-Prime 1.50
❑2, Nov 1995 .... 1.50
❑3, Dec 1995 .... 1.50
❑4, Jan 1996; Kevin rejoins Prime body 1.50
❑5, Feb 1996 .... 1.50
❑6, Mar 1996 .... 1.50
❑7, Apr 1996 .... 1.50
❑8, May 1996 .... 1.50
❑9, Jun 1996 .... 1.50
❑10, Jul 1996 .... 1.50
❑11, Aug 1996 .... 1.50
❑12, Sep 1996 .... 1.50
❑13, Oct 1996 .... 1.50
❑14, Nov 1996 .... 1.50
❑15, Dec 1996 .... 1.50

PRIME/CAPTAIN AMERICA
MALIBU / ULTRAVERSE

❑1, Mar 1996 .... 3.95

PRIME CUTS
FANTAGRAPHICS

❑1, Jan 1987 .... 3.50
❑2, Mar 1987 .... 3.50
❑3, May 1987 .... 3.50
❑4 1987 .... 3.50
❑5 1987 .... 3.50
❑6 1987 .... 3.50
❑7 1988 .... 3.95
❑8, Apr 1988 .... 3.95
❑9 1988 .... 3.95
❑10 1988 .... 3.95

PRIME CUTS (MIKE DEODATO'S...)
CALIBER

❑1 .... 2.95

PRIMER
COMICO

❑1, b&w 1: Slaughterman. 1: Skrog. 1: Az. 5.00
❑2 1982 MW (w); MW (a); 1: Argent. 1: Grendel I (Hunter Rose). 55.00
❑3 .... 4.00

N-MINT

❑4 1982, b&w 1: Firebringer. 1: Laserman. 4.00
❑5 1983; 1: The Maxx (original). 1st professional art by Sam Kieth 50.00
❑6 1: Evangeline. 5.00

PRIMER (VOL. 2)
COMICO

❑1, May 1996 .... 2.95

PRIME SLIME TALES
MIRAGE

❑1 1986, b&w; Published By Mirage Studio 1.50
❑2; Published By Mirage Studio 1.50
❑3, Nov 1986; Published By Now Comics 1.50
❑4, Jan 1987; Published By Now Comics 1.50

PRIME VS. THE INCREDIBLE HULK
MALIBU

❑0, Jul 1995; no cover price 5.00

PRIMITIVE CRETIN
FANTAGRAPHICS

❑

PRIMITIVES
SPARETIME

❑1, Jan 1995, b&w 2.50
❑2, May 1995, b&w 2.50
❑3, Oct 1995, b&w 2.50

PRIMORTALS (VOL. 1) (LEONARD NIMOY'S...)
TEKNO

❑1, Mar 1995 .... 1.95
❑2, Apr 1995 .... 1.95
❑3, May 1995 .... 1.95
❑4, Jun 1995 .... 1.95
❑5, Jul 1995 .... 1.95
❑6, Aug 1995 .... 1.95
❑7, Sep 1995 .... 1.95
❑8, Oct 1995 .... 1.95
❑9, Nov 1995 .... 1.95
❑10, Dec 1995 .... 1.95
❑11, Dec 1995 .... 1.95
❑12, Jan 1996 .... 2.25
❑13, Mar 1996 .... 2.25
❑14, Apr 1996 .... 2.25
❑15, May 1996 .... 2.25
❑16 .... 2.25

PRIMORTALS (VOL. 2) (LEONARD NIMOY'S...)
BIG

❑0, Jun 1996 .... 2.25
❑1, Jul 1996 .... 2.25
❑2, Aug 1996 .... 2.25
❑3, Sep 1996 .... 2.25
❑4, Oct 1996 .... 2.25
❑5, Nov 1996 .... 2.25
❑6, Dec 1996 .... 2.25
❑7, Jan 1997 .... 2.25
❑8, Feb 1997, b&w 2.25

PRIMORTALS ORIGINS (LEONARD NIMOY'S...)
TEKNO

❑1, Jun 1995 .... 2.25
❑2 .... 2.25

PRIMUS
CHARLTON

❑1, Feb 1972 .... 7.00
❑2 1972 .... 4.00
❑3 1972 .... 4.00
❑4, Jun 1972 .... 4.00
❑5 1972 .... 3.00
❑6 1972 .... 3.00
❑7, Oct 1972 .... 3.00

PRINCE: ALTER EGO
PIRANHA MUSIC

❑1, Dec 1991 .... 2.00

The original Grendel, Hunter Rose, made his first appearance in *Primer* #2

© 1985 Matt Wagner.

N-MINT

PRINCE AND THE NEW POWER GENERATION: THREE CHAINS OF GOLD
DC / PIRANHA

❑1 .... 3.50

PRINCE AND THE PAUPER
DELL

❑1, Jul 1962; 01-654-207 .... 15.00

PRINCE AND THE PAUPER, THE (DISNEY'S...)
DISNEY

❑1; squarebound 5.95

PRINCE NAMOR, THE SUB-MARINER
MARVEL

❑1, Sep 1984 .... 1.50
❑2, Oct 1984 .... 1.50
❑3, Nov 1984 .... 1.50
❑4, Dec 1984 .... 1.50

PRINCE NIGHTMARE
AAAARGH!

❑1 .... 2.95

PRINCESS KARANAM AND THE DJINN OF THE GREEN JUG
MU

❑1, b&w 2.50

PRINCESS PRINCE
CPM MANGA

❑1, Oct 2000 .... 2.95
❑1/A, Oct 2000; alternate wraparound cover 2.95
❑2, Nov 2000 .... 2.95
❑3, Dec 2000 .... 2.95
❑4, Jan 2001 .... 2.95
❑5, Feb 2001 .... 2.95
❑6, Mar 2001 .... 2.95
❑7, Apr 2001 .... 2.95
❑8, May 2001 .... 2.95
❑9, Jun 2001 .... 2.95
❑10, Jul 2001 .... 2.95

PRINCESS SALLY
ARCHIE

❑1, Apr 1995 .... 1.50
❑2, May 1995 .... 1.50
❑3, Jun 1995 .... 1.50

PRINCE VALIANT (MARVEL)
MARVEL

❑1, Dec 1994; cardstock cover 3.95
❑2, Jan 1995; cardstock cover 3.95
❑3, Feb 1995; cardstock cover 3.95
❑4, Mar 1995; cardstock cover 3.95

PRINCE VALIANT MONTHLY
PIONEER

❑1, b&w 4.95
❑2, b&w 4.95
❑3, b&w 4.95
❑4, b&w 4.95

PRINCE VANDAL
TRIUMPHANT

❑1; Unleashed! 2.50
❑2; Unleashed! 2.50
❑3 .... 2.50
❑4 .... 2.50
❑5 .... 2.50
❑6 .... 2.50

N-MINT

PRIORITY: WHITE HEAT
AC

❑1, Mar 1987 .... 1.75
❑2 .... 1.75

PRISONER, THE
DC

❑1, Dec 1988; a 4.00
❑2, Jan 1989; b 4.00
❑3, Jan 1989; c 4.00
❑4, Feb 1989; d 4.00

PRISONER OF CHILLON
TOME

❑1, b&w 2.95

PRISONOPOLIS
MEDIAWARP

❑1, Feb 1997, b&w 2.75
❑2, Apr 1997, b&w 2.75
❑3, Jun 1997 .... 2.75
❑4, Aug 1997 .... 2.75

PRIVATE BEACH: FUN AND PERILS IN THE TRUDYVERSE
ANTARCTIC

❑1, Jan 1995, b&w 2.75
❑2, Mar 1995, b&w 2.75
❑3, May 1995, b&w 2.75

PRIVATE COMMISSIONS (GRAY MORROW'S...)
FORBIDDEN FRUIT

❑1, b&w 2.95
❑2, b&w 2.95

PRIVATEERS
VANGUARD

❑1 .... 1.50
❑2 .... 1.50

PRIVATE EYES
ETERNITY

❑1, Sep 1988, b&w; Saint reprints 1.95
❑2, Nov 1988, b&w; Saint reprints 1.95
❑3, Jan 1989, b&w; Saint reprints 1.95
❑4, May 1989 .... 2.95
❑5, Aug 1989 .... 3.50
❑6 .... 3.95

PRO, THE
IMAGE

❑1, Jul 2002 .... 5.95

PRO ACTION MAGAZINE (VOL. 2)
MARVEL / NFL PROPERTIES

❑1, Jul 1994 .... 2.95
❑2, Sep 1994 .... 2.95
❑3, Nov 1994; magazine with bound-in Spider-Man comic book 2.95

PROBE
IMPERIAL

❑1 .... 2.00
❑2 .... 2.00
❑3 .... 2.00

PROF. COFFIN
CHARLTON

❑19, Oct 1985 WH (w); JSa, JAb, WH (a) 2.00
❑20, Dec 1985 .... 2.00
❑21, Feb 1986 TS, JSa, WH (a) 2.00

PROFESSIONAL, THE: GOLGO 13
VIZ

❑1, color; Japanese 4.95
❑2, color; Japanese 4.95
❑3, color; Japanese 4.95

PROFESSOR OM
INNOVATION

❑1, May 1990 .... 2.50

PROFESSOR XAVIER AND THE X-MEN
MARVEL

❑1, Nov 1995; JDu (a); retells origin of team and first mission 1.50
❑2, Dec 1995; JDu (a); A: Vanisher. retells first Vanisher story 1.50
❑3, Jan 1996; retells first Blob story 1.50
❑4, Feb 1996; retells first meeting with Brotherhood of Evil Mutants 1.25
❑5, Mar 1996; retells first meeting with Brotherhood of Evil Mutants 1.25
❑6, Apr 1996 .... 1.25
❑7, May 1996; Sub-Mariner vs. Magneto 1.25
❑8, Jun 1996 .... 1.25
❑9, Jul 1996 .... 1.25
❑10, Aug 1996 V: Avengers. 1.25
❑11, Sep 1996; A: Ka-Zar. Flipbook with Marvel Fanfare (2nd series) #1 .... 1.00
❑12, Oct 1996 V: Juggernaut. 1.00
❑13, Nov 1996 V: Juggernaut. 1.00
❑14, Dec 1996 .... 1.00
❑15, Jan 1997 V: Magneto. V: Stranger. 1.00
❑16, Feb 1997 V: Sentinels. 1.00
❑17, Mar 1997 .... 1.00
❑18, Apr 1997 V: Sentinels. 1.00

PROFOLIO
ALCHEMY

❑1, b&w 1.50
❑2; some color 2.50
❑3, b&w 2.50

PROFOLIO (VOL. 3)
ALCHEMY

❑1 .... 5.95

PROGENY
CALIBER

❑1, b&w 4.95

PROGRAM ERROR: BATTLEBOT
PHANTASY

❑1 .... 2.00

PROJECT, THE
DC / PARADOX PRESS

❑1, ca. 1997, b&w; digest; short story collection 5.95
❑2, ca. 1997, b&w; digest; short story collection 5.95

PROJECT A-KO
MALIBU

❑1, Mar 1994 .... 2.95
❑2, Mar 1994 .... 2.95
❑3, May 1994 .... 2.95
❑4, Jun 1994 .... 2.95

PROJECT A-KO 2
CPM

❑1, Apr 1995 .... 2.95
❑2, Jun 1995 .... 2.95
❑3, Aug 1995 .... 2.95

PROJECT A-KO VERSUS
CPM

❑1, Oct 1995 .... 2.95
❑2, Dec 1995 .... 2.95
❑3, Feb 1996 .... 2.95
❑4, Apr 1996 .... 2.95
❑5, Jun 1996 .... 2.95

PROJECT ARMS
VIZ

❑1, Sep 2002 .... 3.25
❑2, Oct 2002 .... 3.25
❑3, Nov 2002 .... 3.25
❑4, Dec 2002 .... 3.25
❑5, Jan 2003 .... 3.25

PROJECT: DARK MATTER
DIMM COMICS

❑1, Apr 1996, b&w 2.50
❑2, Jun 1996, b&w; cardstock cover 2.50
❑3, b&w; cardstock cover 2.50
❑4, Sep 1997, b&w 2.50

PROJECT: GENERATION
TRUTH

❑1, Jun 2000; Distributed at San Diego Comic-Con 1.00
❑2, Sep 2000; Fall, 2000 .... 1.00

PROJECT: HERO
VANGUARD

❑1, Aug 1987 .... 1.50
❑2 .... 1.50

PROJECT SEX
FANTAGRAPHICS / EROS

❑1, b&w 2.50

PROJECT X
KITCHEN SINK

❑1; Eastman/Bisley; bagged Thump'n Guts; poster; trading card 2.95

PROMETHEA
DC / AMERICA'S BEST COMICS

❑1, Aug 1999 .... 3.50
❑2, Sep 1999 .... 2.95
❑3, Oct 1999 .... 2.95
❑4, Nov 1999 .... 2.95
❑5, Dec 1999 .... 2.95
❑6, Mar 2000 .... 2.95
❑7, Apr 2000 .... 2.95
❑8, May 2000 .... 2.95
❑9, Sep 2000 .... 2.95
❑10, Oct 2000 .... 2.95
❑11, Dec 2000 .... 2.95
❑12, Feb 2001 .... 2.95
❑13, Apr 2001 .... 2.95
❑14, May 2001 .... 2.95
❑15, Jun 2001 .... 2.95
❑16, Jul 2001 .... 2.95
❑17, Aug 2001 .... 2.95
❑18, Sep 2001 .... 2.95
❑19, Oct 2001 .... 2.95
❑20, Nov 2001 .... 2.95
❑21 2002 .... 2.95
❑22, Nov 2002 .... 2.95
❑23, Dec 2002 .... 3.50
❑24, ca. 2003 .... 2.95
❑25, May 2003 .... 2.95
❑26, Aug 2003 .... 2.95
❑27, Nov 2003 .... 2.95
❑28, Feb 2004 .... 2.95
❑29, May 2004 .... 2.95
❑30, Jul 2004 .... 2.95

PROMETHEUS' GIFT
CAT-HEAD

❑1, b&w 2.25

PROMETHEUS (VILLAINS)
DC

❑1, Feb 1998; New Year's Evil 1.95

PROMISE
VIZ

❑1, b&w; squarebound 5.95

PROPELLERMAN
DARK HORSE

❑1, ca. 1993 .... 2.95
❑2, ca. 1993 .... 2.95
❑3, ca. 1993 .... 2.95
❑4, ca. 1993 .... 2.95
❑5, ca. 1994 .... 2.95
❑6, ca. 1994 .... 2.95
❑7, ca. 1994 .... 2.95
❑8, ca. 1994 .... 2.95

PROPHECY OF THE SOUL SORCERER
ARCANE

❑1, May 1999 .... 2.95
❑2, Jun 1999 .... 2.95
❑3, Jul 1999 .... 2.95
❑Ashcan 1, Oct 1998 .... 2.00

PROPHECY OF THE SOUL SORCERER PREVIEW ISSUE
ARCANE

❑1 .... 2.00

PROPHECY OF THE SOUL SORCERER (VOL. 2)
ARCANE

❑1, Mar 2000 .... 2.95
❑2, Apr 2000 .... 2.95
❑3, May 2000 .... 2.95

PROPHET
IMAGE

❑0, Jul 1994 .... 3.00
❑0/A, Jul 1994; San Diego Comic-Con edition 3.00

N-MINT

❑1, Oct 1993 RL (w); O: Prophet. 3.00
❑1/Gold, Oct 1993; Gold edition 3.00
❑2, Nov 1993 FM (c); FM (a) 2.50
❑3, Jan 1994 .... 2.50
❑4, Feb 1994 .... 2.50
❑4/Variant, Feb 1994; Variant cover by Platt 3.00
❑5, Apr 1994 .... 2.50
❑6, Jun 1994 .... 2.50
❑7, Sep 1994 .... 2.50
❑8, Nov 1994 .... 2.50
❑9, Dec 1994 .... 2.50
❑10, Jan 1995 .... 2.50

PROPHET (VOL. 2)
Image

❑1/A, Aug 1995 .... 3.50
❑1/B, Aug 1995 .... 3.50
❑1/C, Aug 1995; enhanced wraparound cover 3.50
❑2/A, Sep 1995 .... 2.50
❑2/B, Sep 1995; alternate cover 2.50
❑3, Nov 1995 .... 2.50
❑4, Feb 1996 .... 2.50
❑5, Feb 1996 .... 2.50
❑6, Apr 1996 .... 2.50
❑7, May 1996 .... 2.50
❑8, Jul 1996 .... 2.50
❑Annual 1/A, Sep 1995; polybagged with PowerCardz 2.50
❑Annual 1/B, Sep 1995; polybagged with PowerCardz 2.50

PROPHET (VOL. 3)
Awesome

❑1, Mar 2000; Flip cover (McFarlane cover on back side) 2.99
❑1/A, Mar 2000; Red background, woman standing with sword, large man in background 2.99

PROPHET BABEWATCH
Image

❑1, Dec 1995; cover says #1, indicia says #2 .... 2.50

PROPHET/CABLE
Maximum

❑1, Jan 1997; crossover with Marvel 3.50
❑2, Mar 1997; cover says #1, indicia says #2; crossover with Marvel; #1 on cover, #2 in indicia 3.50

PROPHET/CHAPEL: SUPER SOLDIERS
Image

❑1/A, May 1996 .... 2.50
❑1/B, May 1996; alternate cover (b&w) 2.50
❑2, Jun 1996 .... 2.50

PROPOSITION PLAYER
DC / Vertigo

❑1, Dec 1999 .... 2.50
❑2, Jan 2000 .... 2.50
❑3, Feb 2000 .... 2.50
❑4, Mar 2000 .... 2.50
❑5, Apr 2000 .... 2.50
❑6, May 2000 .... 2.50

PROTECTORS HANDBOOK
Malibu

❑1 .... 2.50

PROTECTORS, THE (MALIBU)
Malibu

❑1, Sep 1992; Split cover (in various colors) 1.95
❑1/CS, Sep 1992; with poster and wrapper 2.50
❑2, Oct 1992; with poster 2.50
❑3, Nov 1992 .... 2.50
❑4, Dec 1992 .... 2.50
❑5/A, Jan 1993; bullet hole; bagged .. 2.50
❑5/B, Jan 1993; Embossed cover; bullet hole 2.50
❑5/C, Jan 1993; Die-cut cover; bullet hole 2.95
❑6, Feb 1993 .... 2.50
❑6/CS, Feb 1993; with poster 2.50
❑7, Mar 1993 .... 2.50

N-MINT

❑8, Apr 1993 .... 2.50
❑9, May 1993 .... 2.50
❑10, Jun 1993 .... 2.50
❑11, Jul 1993 .... 2.50
❑12, Aug 1993 .... 2.50
❑13, Sep 1993; Genesis 2.25
❑14, Oct 1993 .... 2.25
❑15, Nov 1993 .... 2.25
❑16, Dec 1993 .... 2.25
❑17, Jan 1994 .... 2.25
❑18, Feb 1994 .... 2.25
❑19, Mar 1994; Genesis 2.50
❑20 .... 2.50

PROTECTORS, THE (NEW YORK)
New York

❑1 .... 1.70
❑2 .... 1.70

PROTHEUS (MIKE DEODATO'S...)
Caliber

❑1 .... 2.95
❑2 .... 2.95

PROTISTA CHRONICLES, THE
Xulu

❑1; no cover price 2.00

PROTOTYKES HOLIDAY SPECIAL/ HERO ILLUSTRATED HOLIDAY SPECIAL
Dark Horse

❑1 .... 1.00
❑2 JBy (w); JBy (a) 1.00

PROTOTYPE
Malibu / Ultraverse

❑0, Aug 1994; O: Prototype I (Bob Campbell). Reprints origin story from Malibu Sun plus new story ... 1.95
❑1, Aug 1993; 1: Prototype II (Jimmy Ruiz). 1: Prototype I (Bob Campbell). 1: Glare. 1: Veil. Ultraverse; 1st appear 2.50
❑1/Hologram; Hologram cover limited edition; 1: Prototype II (Jimmy Ruiz). 1: Prototype I (Bob Campbell). 1: Glare. 1: Veil. hologram 5.00
❑2, Sep 1993 1: Backstabber. A: Prime. 1.95
❑3, Oct 1993; Giant-size; Rune 2.50
❑4, Nov 1993 1: Wrath. 1.95
❑5, Dec 1993; A: Strangers. Break-Thru; Continued in Strangers #7 ... 1.95
❑6, Jan 1994 1: Arena. 1.95
❑7, Feb 1994 .... 1.95
❑8, Mar 1994 .... 1.95
❑9, Apr 1994 .... 1.95
❑10, May 1994 .... 1.95
❑11, Jun 1994 .... 1.95
❑12, Jul 1994 .... 1.95
❑13, Aug 1994; KB (w); flipbook with Ultraverse Premiere #6 .... 3.50
❑14, Oct 1994 .... 1.95
❑15, Nov 1994 .... 1.95
❑16, Dec 1994 1: Wild Popes. 1.95
❑17, Jan 1995 .... 1.95
❑18, Feb 1995 .... 2.50
❑Giant Size 1, ca. 1994; Giant-Size edition 2.50

PROWLER (ECLIPSE)
Eclipse

❑1, Jul 1987 .... 1.75
❑2, Aug 1987 .... 1.75
❑3, Sep 1987 .... 1.75
❑4, Oct 1987 .... 1.75

PROWLER (MARVEL)
Marvel

❑1, Nov 1994 .... 1.75
❑2, Dec 1994 .... 1.75
❑3, Jan 1995 .... 1.75
❑4, Feb 1995 .... 1.75

PROWLER IN "WHITE ZOMBIE", THE
Eclipse

❑1, Oct 1988, b&w 2.00

Almost 30 years after his debut, reluctant hero Hobey Brown got his own solo mini-series with *The Prowler* #1.

N-MINT

PRO WRESTLING'S TRUE FACTS
Dan Pettiglio

❑1, Apr 1994, b&w 2.95

PROXIMITY EFFECT
Image

❑1, ca 2004 .... 9.99

PRUDENCE & CAUTION
Defiant

❑1, May 1994; Double-size; English and Spanish versions 3.25
❑2, Jun 1994 .... 2.50
❑3, Jul 1994 .... 2.50
❑4, Aug 1994 .... 2.50
❑5, Sep 1994 .... 2.50
❑6, Oct 1994 .... 2.50

PRYDE & WISDOM
Marvel

❑1, Sep 1996 .... 1.95
❑2, Oct 1996 .... 1.95
❑3, Nov 1996 .... 1.95

PSI-FORCE
Marvel

❑1, Nov 1986 .... 1.00
❑2, Dec 1986 .... 1.00
❑3, Jan 1987 .... 1.00
❑4, Feb 1987 .... 1.00
❑5, Mar 1987 .... 1.00
❑6, Apr 1987 .... 1.00
❑7, May 1987 BH (a) 1.00
❑8, Jun 1987 .... 1.00
❑9, Jul 1987 BH (a) 1.00
❑10, Aug 1987 .... 1.00
❑11, Sep 1987 BH (a) 1.00
❑12, Oct 1987 BH (a) 1.00
❑13, Nov 1987 .... 1.00
❑14, Dec 1987 BH (a) 1.00
❑15, Jan 1988 .... 1.00
❑16, Feb 1988 .... 1.00
❑17, Mar 1988 .... 1.00
❑18, Apr 1988 .... 1.00
❑19, May 1988 .... 1.25
❑20, Jun 1988 .... 1.25
❑21, Jul 1988 .... 1.25
❑22, Aug 1988 .... 1.25
❑23, Sep 1988 .... 1.25
❑24, Oct 1988 .... 1.25
❑25, Nov 1988 .... 1.25
❑26, Dec 1988 .... 1.25
❑27, Jan 1989 .... 1.25
❑28, Feb 1989 .... 1.25
❑29, Mar 1989 .... 1.25
❑30, Apr 1989 .... 1.25
❑31, May 1989 .... 1.25
❑32, Jun 1989 .... 1.25
❑Annual 1, ca. 1987 .... 1.25

PSI-JUDGE ANDERSON
Fleetway-Quality

❑1 .... 2.00
❑2 .... 2.00
❑3 .... 2.00
❑4 .... 2.00
❑5 .... 2.00
❑6 .... 2.00
❑7 .... 2.00
❑8 .... 2.00
❑9 .... 2.00

	N-MINT
❑10	2.00
❑11	2.00
❑12	2.00
❑13	2.00
❑14	2.00
❑15	2.00

PSI-JUDGE ANDERSON: ENGRAMS
FLEETWAY-QUALITY

❑1, b&w	1.95
❑2, b&w	1.95

PSI-JUDGE ANDERSON: PSIFILES
FLEETWAY-QUALITY

❑1	2.95

PSI-LORDS
VALIANT

❑1, Sep 1994; Valiant Vision; chromium wrap-around cover	3.50
❑1/Gold, Sep 1994; Gold edition; no cover price	5.00
❑2, Oct 1994; Valiant Vision	2.25
❑3, Nov 1994; Valiant Vision; Chaos Effect	2.25
❑4, Dec 1994	2.25
❑5, Jan 1995	2.25
❑6, Feb 1995	2.25
❑7, Mar 1995	2.25
❑8, Apr 1995 V: Destroyer.	2.25
❑9, May 1995	2.25
❑10, Jun 1995	2.25

PSYBA-RATS, THE
DC

❑1, Apr 1995 D: Channelman.	2.50
❑2, May 1995	2.50
❑3, Jun 1995	2.50

PSYCHIC ACADEMY
TOKYOPOP

❑1, Mar 2004	9.99

PSYCHO, THE
DC

❑1, Sep 1991	4.95
❑2, Oct 1991	4.95
❑3, Dec 1991	4.95

PSYCHO (ALFRED HITCHCOCK'S...)
INNOVATION

❑1	2.50
❑2	2.50
❑3	2.50

PSYCHOANALYSIS (GEMSTONE)
GEMSTONE

❑1, Aug 1999	2.50
❑2, Sep 1999	2.50
❑3, Oct 1999	2.50
❑4, Nov 1999	2.50
❑Annual 1; Collects series	10.95

PSYCHOBLAST
FIRST

❑1, Nov 1987	1.75
❑2, Dec 1987	1.75
❑3, Jan 1988	1.75
❑4, Feb 1988	1.75
❑5, Mar 1988	1.75
❑6, Apr 1988	1.75
❑7, May 1988	1.75
❑8, Jun 1988	1.75
❑9, Jul 1988	1.75

PSYCHO KILLERS
COMIC ZONE

❑1, b&w; Charles Manson	4.00
❑1-2; Charles Manson	3.00
❑2, b&w; David Berkowitz ("The Son of Sam")	3.50
❑2-2; David Berkowitz ("The Son of Sam")	3.00
❑3, b&w; Ed Gein	3.50
❑3-2; Ed Gein	2.95
❑4; Henry Lee Lucas	2.95
❑5; Jeffrey Dahmer	3.25
❑6; Richard Ramirez ("The Night-stalker")	2.95
❑7; Judias Buenoano	2.95
❑8; John Wayne Gacy	2.95
❑9; Ted Bundy	2.95
❑10; Dean Corll ("The Candy Man")	2.95
❑11; The Hillside Strangler; A lawsuit was filed and resulted in this book being taken off the market	3.50
❑12; The Boston Strangler	2.95
❑13; Andrei Chikatilo	2.95
❑14; Aileen Wuornos	2.95
❑15; Charles Starkweather	2.95

PSYCHO KILLERS PMS SPECIAL
ZONE

❑1	3.25

PSYCHOMAN
REVOLUTIONARY

❑1	2.50

PSYCHONAUT
FANTAGRAPHICS

❑1, Mar 1996, b&w	3.95
❑3, b&w; flipbook with The Pursuers	3.50

PSYCHONAUTS
MARVEL / EPIC

❑1	4.95
❑2	4.95
❑3	4.95
❑4	4.95

PSYCHO-PATH
VENUSIAN

❑1	2.00
❑2, Sep 1990, b&w	2.00

PSYCHOTIC ADVENTURES ILLUSTRATED
LAST GASP

❑1	3.00
❑2	3.00
❑3	3.00

PSYENCE FICTION
ABACULUS

❑0.5, Sum 1998, b&w; Ashcan preview edition	1.00
❑1	2.95

PSYLOCKE & ARCHANGEL: CRIMSON DAWN
MARVEL

❑1, Aug 1997; gatefold summary; gatefold cover	2.50
❑2, Sep 1997; gatefold summary	2.50
❑3, Oct 1997; gatefold summary	2.50
❑4, Nov 1997; gatefold summary	2.50

PTERANOMAN
KITCHEN SINK

❑1, Aug 1990; Donald Simpson	2.00

PUBLIC ENEMIES (ETERNITY)
ETERNITY

❑1, b&w	3.95
❑2, b&w	3.95

PUBO
DARK HORSE

❑1, Nov 2003	3.50
❑2, Jan 2004	3.50
❑3, Mar 2004	0.00

PUFFED
IMAGE

❑1, Jul 2003	2.95
❑2, Aug 2003	2.95
❑3, Sep 2003	2.95

PUKE & EXPLODE
NORTHSTAR

❑1	2.50
❑2	2.50

PULP (VOL. 1)
VIZ

❑1, Dec 1997	5.95

PULP (VOL. 2)
VIZ

❑1, Jan 1998	5.95
❑2, Feb 1998	5.95
❑3, Mar 1998	5.95
❑4, Apr 1998	5.95
❑5, May 1998	5.95
❑6, Jun 1998	5.95
❑7, Jul 1998	5.95
❑8, Aug 1998	5.95
❑9, Sep 1998	5.95
❑10, Oct 1998	5.95
❑11, Nov 1998	5.95
❑12, Dec 1998	5.95

PULP (VOL. 3)
VIZ

❑1, Jan 1999	5.95
❑2, Feb 1999	5.95
❑3, Mar 1999	5.95
❑4, Apr 1999	5.95
❑5, May 1999	5.95
❑6, Jun 1999	5.95
❑7, Jul 1999	5.95
❑8, Aug 1999	5.95
❑9, Sep 1999	5.95
❑10, Oct 1999	5.95
❑11, Nov 1999	5.95
❑12, Dec 1999	5.95

PULP (VOL. 4)
VIZ

❑1, Jan 2000	5.95
❑2, Feb 2000	5.95
❑3, Mar 2000	5.95
❑4, Apr 2000	5.95
❑5, May 2000	5.95
❑6, Jun 2000	5.95

PULP (VOL. 5)
VIZ

❑1	5.95
❑2	5.95
❑3	5.95
❑4	5.95
❑5	5.95
❑6	5.95
❑7	5.95
❑8	5.95
❑9	5.95
❑10	5.95
❑11	5.95
❑12	5.95

PULP (VOL. 6)
VIZ

❑1	5.95
❑2	5.95
❑3	5.95
❑4	5.95
❑5	5.95
❑6	5.95
❑7	5.95
❑8	5.95

PULP ACTION
AVALON

❑1	2.95
❑2	2.95
❑3	2.95
❑4	2.95
❑5	2.95
❑6	2.95
❑7	2.95
❑8	2.95

PULP DREAMS
FANTAGRAPHICS / EROS

❑1, b&w	2.50

PULP FANTASTIC
DC / VERTIGO

❑1, Feb 2000	2.50
❑2, Mar 2000	2.50
❑3, Apr 2000	2.50

PULP FICTION
A LIST

❑1, Spr 1997, b&w; reprints Golden Age material	2.50
❑2, Fal 1997, b&w; reprints Golden Age material	2.50

N-MINT

❑3, Win 1997, b&w; reprints Golden Age material 2.50
❑4 .... 2.50
❑5 .... 2.95
❑6 .... 2.95

PULP WESTERN
AVALON

❑1 .... 2.95

PULSE, THE
BLACKJACK

❑1, Jun 1997, b&w; no cover price ... 2.00

PULSE
MARVEL

❑1, Apr 2004, BMB (w) 5.00
❑2, May 2004, BMB (w) 3.00
❑3, Jul 2004, BMB (w) 2.99
❑4, Sep 2004 ....

PUMA BLUES, THE
AARDVARK ONE

❑1, Jun 1986; 10,000 copies printed; Aardvark One International Publisher 2.00
❑1-2 .... 2.00
❑2, Sep 1986; 10,000 copies printed 2.00
❑3, Dec 1986; 19,000 copies printed 2.00
❑4, Feb 1987; 13,000 copies printed . 1.70
❑5, Mar 1987; 13,000 copies printed 1.70
❑6, Apr 1987; 13,000 copies printed . 1.70
❑7, May 1987; 12,000 copies printed 1.70
❑8, May 1987 .... 1.70
❑9, Jul 1987 .... 1.70
❑10, Aug 1987 .... 1.70
❑11, Sep 1987 .... 1.70
❑12, Oct 1987 .... 1.70
❑13, Nov 1987 .... 1.70
❑14, Dec 1987 .... 1.70
❑15, Jan 1988 .... 1.70
❑16, Feb 1988 .... 1.70
❑17, Mar 1988 .... 1.70
❑18, Apr 1988; self-published 1.70
❑19 1988; self-published 1.70
❑20 1988; AMo (w); self-published ... 1.70
❑21 1988, b&w; Mirage Studio Publisher 1.70
❑22 1988, b&w 1.70
❑23, b&w 1.70

PUMMELER
PARODY

❑1, b&w; Foil embossed cover; Punisher parody 2.95

PUMMELER $2099
PARODY

❑1; Gold Trimmed Foil Cover 2.95

PUMPKINHEAD: THE RITES OF EXORCISM
DARK HORSE

❑1, ca. 1992 .... 2.50
❑2, ca. 1992 .... 2.50
❑3, ca. 1992 .... 2.50
❑4, ca. 1992 .... 2.50

PUNISHER (1ST SERIES)
MARVEL

❑1, Jan 1986; Double-size 13.00
❑2, Feb 1986 MZ (a) 7.00
❑3, Mar 1986 MZ (a) 7.00
❑4, Apr 1986 MZ (a) 6.00
❑5, May 1986 MZ (a) 6.00

PUNISHER, THE (2ND SERIES)
MARVEL

❑1, Jul 1987 .... 7.00
❑2, Aug 1987 KJ (a) 4.00
❑3, Oct 1987 KJ (a) 4.00
❑4, Nov 1987 .... 3.00
❑5, Jan 1988 .... 3.00
❑6, Feb 1988 .... 3.00
❑7, Mar 1988 .... 3.00
❑8, May 1988 .... 3.00
❑9, Jun 1988 .... 3.00
❑10, Aug 1988 A: Daredevil. 4.00
❑11, Sep 1988 .... 2.00

N-MINT

❑12, Oct 1988 .... 2.00
❑13, Nov 1988 .... 2.00
❑14, Dec 1988 A: Kingpin. 2.00
❑15, Jan 1989 A: Kingpin. 2.00
❑16, Feb 1989 A: Kingpin. 2.00
❑17, Mar 1989 .... 2.00
❑18, Apr 1989 V: Kingpin. 2.00
❑19, May 1989 .... 2.00
❑20, Jun 1989 .... 2.00
❑21, Jul 1989 EL (a) 2.00
❑22, Aug 1989 EL (a) 2.00
❑23, Sep 1989 EL (a) 2.00
❑24, Oct 1989 EL (a); 1: Shadowmasters. 2.00
❑25, Nov 1989; Giant-sized EL (a); A: Shadowmasters. 2.00
❑26, Nov 1989 RH (a) 2.00
❑27, Dec 1989 .... 2.00
❑28, Dec 1989; Acts of Vengeance 2.00
❑29, Jan 1990; Acts of Vengeance 2.00
❑30, Feb 1990 .... 2.00
❑31, Mar 1990 .... 2.00
❑32, Apr 1990 .... 2.00
❑33, May 1990 .... 2.00
❑34, Jun 1990 .... 2.00
❑35, Jul 1990; Jigsaw Puzzle 2.00
❑36, Aug 1990; Jigsaw Puzzle 2.00
❑37, Aug 1990; Jigsaw Puzzle 2.00
❑38, Sep 1990; Jigsaw Puzzle 2.00
❑39, Sep 1990; Jigsaw Puzzle 2.00
❑40, Oct 1990; Jigsaw Puzzle 2.00
❑41, Oct 1990 .... 1.50
❑42, Nov 1990 .... 1.50
❑43, Dec 1990 .... 1.50
❑44, Jan 1991 .... 1.50
❑45, Feb 1991 .... 1.50
❑46, Mar 1991 .... 1.50
❑47, Apr 1991 .... 1.50
❑48, May 1991 .... 1.50
❑49, Jun 1991 .... 1.50
❑50, Jul 1991; double-sized 2.00
❑51, Aug 1991 .... 1.50
❑52, Sep 1991 .... 1.50
❑53, Oct 1991 .... 1.50
❑54, Nov 1991 .... 1.50
❑55, Nov 1991 .... 1.50
❑56, Dec 1991 .... 1.50
❑57, Dec 1991; Two covers: outer wraparound cover, inner photo cover 2.00
❑58, Jan 1992 .... 1.50
❑59, Jan 1992; Punisher becomes black 1.50
❑60, Feb 1992 VM (a); A: Luke Cage. 1.50
❑61, Mar 1992 VM (a); A: Luke Cage. 1.50
❑62, Apr 1992; VM (a); Punisher becomes white again 1.50
❑63, May 1992 .... 1.25
❑64, Jun 1992 .... 1.25
❑65 1992 .... 1.25
❑66 1992 .... 1.25
❑67 1992 .... 1.25
❑68 1992 .... 1.25
❑69, Sep 1992 .... 1.25
❑70 1992 .... 1.25
❑71, Oct 1992 .... 1.25
❑72, Nov 1992 .... 1.25
❑73, Dec 1992 .... 1.25
❑74, Jan 1993 .... 1.25
❑75, Feb 1993; Embossed cover 2.75
❑76, Mar 1993 .... 1.50
❑77, Apr 1993 VM (a) 1.50
❑78, May 1993 VM (a) 1.50
❑79, Jun 1993 .... 1.50
❑80, Jul 1993 .... 1.50
❑81, Aug 1993 .... 1.25
❑82, Sep 1993 .... 1.25
❑83, Oct 1993 .... 1.25
❑84, Nov 1993 .... 1.25
❑85, Dec 1993 .... 1.25
❑86, Jan 1994; Giant-size 2.95
❑87, Feb 1994 .... 1.25

Stripped of any supernatural trappings, Frank Castle returned to his "guy with a gun" roots in *The Punisher* (5th series).

© 2000 Marvel Characters Inc.

N-MINT

❑88, Mar 1994 .... 1.25
❑89, Apr 1994 RH (a) 1.25
❑90, May 1994 RH (a) 1.25
❑91, Jun 1994 RH (a) 1.50
❑92, Jul 1994 RH (a) 1.50
❑93, Aug 1994 .... 1.50
❑94, Sep 1994 .... 1.50
❑95, Oct 1994 .... 1.50
❑96, Nov 1994 .... 1.50
❑97, Dec 1994 .... 1.50
❑98, Jan 1995 .... 1.50
❑99, Feb 1995 .... 1.50
❑100, Mar 1995; Giant-size 2.95
❑100/Variant, Mar 1995; Giant-size; foil cover 3.95
❑101, Apr 1995 .... 4.00
❑102, May 1995 .... 1.50
❑103, Jun 1995 .... 1.50
❑104, Jul 1995 .... 1.50
❑Annual 1, ca. 1988 .... 3.50
❑Annual 2, ca. 1989; JLee (a); A: Moon Knight. V: Moon Knight. Atlantis Attacks 2.50
❑Annual 3, ca. 1990 .... 2.50
❑Annual 4, ca. 1991 JLee (a) 2.00
❑Annual 5, ca. 1992; PD (w); VM (a); System Bytes 2.25
❑Annual 6 1993; 1993 Annual; Polybagged 2.95
❑Annual 7, ca. 1994 .... 2.95

PUNISHER (3RD SERIES)
MARVEL

❑1, Nov 1995; foil cover 2.95
❑2, Dec 1995 A: Hatchetman. 1.95
❑3, Dec 1995 .... 1.95
❑4, Feb 1996 A: Daredevil. V: Jigsaw. 1.95
❑5, Mar 1996 PB (a) 1.95
❑6, Apr 1996 PB (a) 1.95
❑7, May 1996 .... 1.95
❑8, Jun 1996 .... 1.95
❑9, Jul 1996 .... 1.95
❑10, Aug 1996 V: Jigsaw. 1.95
❑11, Sep 1996; S.H.I.E.L.D. helicarrier crashes 1.95
❑12, Oct 1996 V: X-Cutioner. 1.95
❑13, Nov 1996 V: X-Cutioner. 1.95
❑14, Dec 1996 V: X-Cutioner. 1.50
❑15, Jan 1997 V: X-Cutioner. 1.50
❑16, Feb 1997 V: X-Cutioner. 1.50
❑17, Mar 1997 .... 1.95
❑18, Apr 1997 .... 1.95

PUNISHER, THE (4TH SERIES)
MARVEL

❑1, Nov 1998; gatefold summary 3.00
❑1/Variant, Nov 1998; DFE alternate cover 6.00
❑2, Dec 1998; gatefold summary 2.99
❑3, Jan 1999 .... 2.99
❑4, Feb 1999 .... 2.99

PUNISHER (5TH SERIES)
MARVEL

❑1, Apr 2000 .... 4.00
❑1/Variant, Apr 2000; White background on cover 8.50
❑2, May 2000 .... 3.50
❑2/Variant, May 2000; White background on cover 6.00

N-MINT

- ❑3, Jun 2000; Polybagged with Marvel Knights/Marvel Boy Genesis Edition 3.50
- ❑4, Jul 2000 3.00
- ❑5, Aug 2000 3.00
- ❑6, Sep 2000 2.99
- ❑7, Oct 2000 2.99
- ❑8, Nov 2000 1: The Russian. 2.99
- ❑9, Dec 2000 2.99
- ❑10, Jan 2001 2.99
- ❑11, Feb 2001 1: The Vigilante Squad. D: The Russian. 2.99
- ❑12, Mar 2001 D: Ma Gnucci. 2.99

PUNISHER, THE (6TH SERIES)
MARVEL

- ❑1, Aug 2001 2.99
- ❑2, Sep 2001 2.99
- ❑3, Oct 2001 2.99
- ❑4, Nov 2001 2.99
- ❑5, Dec 2001 2.99
- ❑6, Jan 2002 2.99
- ❑7, Feb 2002; Silent issue 2.99
- ❑8, Mar 2002 2.99
- ❑9, Apr 2002 2.99
- ❑10, May 2002 2.99
- ❑11, Jun 2002 2.99
- ❑12, Jul 2002 2.99
- ❑13, Aug 2002 2.99
- ❑14, Sep 2002 2.99
- ❑15, Oct 2002 2.99
- ❑16, Nov 2002 2.99
- ❑17, Nov 2002 2.99
- ❑18, Dec 2002 2.99
- ❑19, Jan 2003 2.99
- ❑20, Feb 2003 2.99
- ❑21, Mar 2003 2.99
- ❑22, Apr 2003 2.99
- ❑23, May 2003 2.99
- ❑24, Jun 2003 2.99
- ❑25, Jun 2003 2.99
- ❑26, Jul 2003 2.99
- ❑27, Jul 2003 2.99
- ❑28, Aug 2003 2.99
- ❑29, Sep 2003 2.99
- ❑30, Oct 2003 2.99
- ❑31, Nov 2003 2.99
- ❑32, Nov 2003 2.99
- ❑33, Dec 2003 2.99
- ❑34, Dec 2003 2.99
- ❑35, Jan 2004 2.99
- ❑36, Jan 2004 2.99
- ❑37, Feb 2004 2.99

PUNISHER, THE (7TH SERIES)
MARVEL / MAX

- ❑1, Mar 2004 2.99
- ❑2, Mar 2004 2.99
- ❑3, Apr 2004 2.99
- ❑4, May 2004 2.99
- ❑5, Jun 2004 2.99
- ❑6, Jul 2004 2.99
- ❑7, Aug 2004 2.99
- ❑8, Aug 2004 2.99
- ❑9, Sep 2004

PUNISHER, THE: A MAN NAMED FRANK
MARVEL

- ❑1, Jun 1994 6.95

PUNISHER ANNIVERSARY MAGAZINE, THE
MARVEL

- ❑1 4.95

PUNISHER ARMORY, THE
MARVEL

- ❑1, Jul 1990; weapons 2.00
- ❑2, Jun 1991 2.00
- ❑3, Apr 1991 2.00
- ❑4 2.00
- ❑5 1992 2.00
- ❑6 2.00
- ❑7, Sep 1993 2.00
- ❑8, Dec 1993 2.00

N-MINT

- ❑9 2.00
- ❑10, Nov 1994 2.00

PUNISHER BACK TO SCHOOL SPECIAL
MARVEL

- ❑1, Nov 1992; 1992 3.50
- ❑2, Oct 1993; BSz (c); BSz (a); 1993 . 3.00
- ❑3, Oct 1994; 1994 3.00

PUNISHER/BATMAN: DEADLY KNIGHTS
MARVEL

- ❑1, Oct 1994 4.95

PUNISHER/BLACK WIDOW: SPINNING DOOMSDAY'S WEB
MARVEL

- ❑1 9.95

PUNISHER: BLOODLINES
MARVEL

- ❑1, ca. 1991; prestige format 5.95

PUNISHER: DIE HARD IN THE BIG EASY
MARVEL

- ❑1, ca. 1992; prestige format one-shot 4.95

PUNISHER, THE: EMPTY QUARTER
MARVEL

- ❑1, Nov 1994; prestige format one-shot 6.95

PUNISHER: G-FORCE
MARVEL

- ❑1, ca. 1992; squarebound with cardstock cover 4.95

PUNISHER HOLIDAY SPECIAL
MARVEL

- ❑1, Jan 1993; foil cover 3.00
- ❑2, Jan 1994 3.00
- ❑3, Jan 1995 3.00

PUNISHER INVADES THE 'NAM: FINAL INVASION
MARVEL

- ❑1, Feb 1994 6.95

PUNISHER KILLS THE MARVEL UNIVERSE
MARVEL

- ❑1, Nov 1995 20.00
- ❑1-2, Mar 2000 5.95

PUNISHER MAGAZINE, THE
MARVEL

- ❑1, Sep 1989, b&w; Reprints Punisher (Ltd. Series) #1 in black & white ... 3.00
- ❑2, Oct 1989, b&w; Reprints Punisher (Ltd. Series) #2-3 in black & white 2.50
- ❑3, Nov 1989, b&w; Reprints Punisher (Ltd. Series) #4-5 in black & white 2.50
- ❑4, Dec 1989, b&w; Reprints Punisher #1-2 in black & white 2.50
- ❑5, Dec 1989, b&w; Reprints Punisher #3-4 in black & white 2.50
- ❑6, Jan 1990, b&w; Reprints Punisher #5-6 in black & white 2.50
- ❑7, Feb 1990, b&w; Reprints Punisher #7-8 in black & white 2.50
- ❑8, Mar 1990, b&w 2.50
- ❑9, Apr 1990, b&w 2.50
- ❑10, May 1990, b&w 2.50
- ❑11, Jun 1990, b&w 2.50
- ❑12, Jul 1990, b&w 2.50
- ❑13, Aug 1990, b&w 2.50
- ❑14, Sep 1990, b&w; Reprints Punisher War Journal #1-2 2.50
- ❑15, Oct 1990, b&w 2.50
- ❑16, Nov 1990, b&w 2.50

PUNISHER MEETS ARCHIE, THE
MARVEL

- ❑1, Aug 1994; enhanced cover 4.00
- ❑1/Variant, Aug 1994; Die-cut cover . 4.50

PUNISHER MOVIE SPECIAL, THE
MARVEL

- ❑1, Jun 1990 5.95

N-MINT

PUNISHER, THE: NO ESCAPE
MARVEL

- ❑1, ca. 1990, prestige format 4.95

PUNISHER, THE: OFFICIAL MOVIE ADAPTATION
MARVEL

- ❑1, May 2004 0.00
- ❑2, May 2004 0.00
- ❑3, May 2004 0.00

PUNISHER, THE: ORIGIN MICRO CHIP
MARVEL

- ❑1, Jul 1993 O: Micro Chip. 2.00
- ❑2, Aug 1993 2.00

PUNISHER/PAINKILLER JANE
MARVEL

- ❑1, Jan 2001; cardstock cover 3.50

PUNISHER: P.O.V.
MARVEL

- ❑1, ca. 1991 JSn (w); BWr, BW (a) ... 5.00
- ❑2, ca. 1991 JSn (w); BWr, BW (a) ... 5.00
- ❑3, ca. 1991 JSn (w); BWr, BW (a) ... 5.00
- ❑4, ca. 1991 JSn (w); BWr, BW (a) ... 5.00

PUNISHER SUMMER SPECIAL
MARVEL

- ❑1, Aug 1991 VM (a) 3.00
- ❑2, Aug 1992 3.00
- ❑3 1993 2.50
- ❑4, Jul 1994 2.95

PUNISHER: THE END
MARVEL

- ❑1, Jun 2004 4.50

PUNISHER: THE GHOSTS OF INNOCENTS
MARVEL

- ❑1, ca. 1993 5.95
- ❑2, ca. 1993 5.95

PUNISHER: THE MOVIE
MARVEL

- ❑1, May 2004 2.99
- ❑2, May 2004 2.99
- ❑3, May 2004 2.99

PUNISHER: THE PRIZE
MARVEL

- ❑1, ca. 1990; prestige format 4.95

PUNISHER 2099
MARVEL

- ❑1, Feb 1993; foil cover 1.75
- ❑2, Mar 1993 1.25
- ❑3, Apr 1993 1.25
- ❑4, May 1993 1.25
- ❑5, Jun 1993 1.25
- ❑6, Jul 1993 1.25
- ❑7, Aug 1993 1.25
- ❑8, Sep 1993 1.25
- ❑9, Oct 1993 1.25
- ❑10, Nov 1993 1.25
- ❑11, Dec 1993 1.25
- ❑12, Jan 1994 1.25
- ❑13, Feb 1994 1.25
- ❑14, Mar 1994 1.25
- ❑15, Apr 1994 1.25
- ❑16, May 1994 1.50
- ❑17, Jun 1994 1.50
- ❑18, Jul 1994 1.50
- ❑19, Aug 1994 1.50
- ❑20, Sep 1994 1.50
- ❑21, Oct 1994 1.50
- ❑22, Nov 1994 1.50
- ❑23, Dec 1994 1.50
- ❑24, Jan 1995 1.50
- ❑25, Feb 1995; Giant-size 2.25
- ❑25/Variant, Feb 1995; Embossed cover 2.95
- ❑26, Mar 1995 1.50
- ❑27, Apr 1995 1.50
- ❑28, May 1995 1.95
- ❑29, Jun 1995 1.95
- ❑30, Jul 1995 1.95

N-MINT

❑31, Aug 1995 .... 1.95
❑32, Sep 1995 .... 1.95
❑33, Oct 1995 .... 1.95
❑34, Nov 1995; continues in 2099 A.D. Apocalypse #1 .... 1.95

PUNISHER VS. DAREDEVIL
MARVEL

❑1, Jun 2000 .... 3.50

PUNISHER WAR JOURNAL, THE
MARVEL

❑1, Nov 1988 JLee (a); O: Punisher. . 5.00
❑2, Dec 1988 JLee (a); A: Daredevil. . 3.00
❑3, Feb 1989 JLee (a); A: Daredevil. . 3.00
❑4, Mar 1989 JLee (a) 3.00
❑5, May 1989 JLee (a) 3.00
❑6, Jun 1989 JLee (a); A: Wolverine. 3.00
❑7, Jul 1989 JLee (a); A: Wolverine. . 3.00
❑8, Sep 1989 JLee (a) 1.50
❑9, Oct 1989 JLee (a) 1.50
❑10, Nov 1989 JLee (a) 1.50
❑11, Dec 1989 JLee (a) 1.50
❑12, Dec 1989; JLee (a); Acts of Vengeance 1.50
❑13, Dec 1989; JLee (a); Acts of Vengeance 1.50
❑14, Jan 1990 RH (a); A: Spider-Man. 1.50
❑15, Feb 1990 RH (a); A: Spider-Man. 1.50
❑16, Mar 1990 .... 1.50
❑17, Apr 1990 JLee (a) 1.50
❑18, May 1990 JLee (a) 1.50
❑19, Jun 1990 JLee (a) 1.50
❑20, Jul 1990 .... 1.50
❑21, Aug 1990 .... 1.50
❑22, Sep 1990 .... 1.50
❑23, Oct 1990 .... 1.75
❑24, Nov 1990 .... 1.75
❑25, Dec 1990 .... 1.75
❑26, Jan 1991 .... 1.75
❑27, Feb 1991 .... 1.75
❑28, Mar 1991 .... 1.75
❑29, Apr 1991 A: Ghost Rider. 1.75
❑30, May 1991 A: Ghost Rider. 1.75
❑31, Jun 1991; Painted cover 1.75
❑32, Jul 1991 .... 1.75
❑33, Aug 1991 .... 1.75
❑34, Sep 1991 .... 1.75
❑35, Oct 1991 .... 1.75
❑36, Nov 1991 .... 1.75
❑37, Dec 1991 .... 1.75
❑38, Jan 1992 .... 1.75
❑39, Feb 1992 .... 1.75
❑40, Mar 1992 .... 1.75
❑41, Apr 1992 .... 1.75
❑42, May 1992 .... 1.75
❑43, Jun 1992 VM (a) 1.75
❑44, Jul 1992 VM (a) 1.75
❑45, Aug 1992 .... 1.75
❑46, Sep 1992 .... 1.75
❑47, Oct 1992 .... 1.75
❑48, Nov 1992 .... 1.75
❑49, Dec 1992 .... 1.75
❑50, Jan 1993; 1: Punisher 2099. Embossed cover; Punisher 2099 Preview 2.95
❑51, Feb 1993 .... 1.75
❑52, Mar 1993 .... 1.75
❑53, Apr 1993 .... 1.75
❑54, May 1993 .... 1.75
❑55, Jun 1993 .... 1.75
❑56, Jul 1993 .... 1.75
❑57, Aug 1993 A: Ghost Rider. A: Daredevil. 1.75
❑58, Sep 1993 A: Ghost Rider. A: Daredevil. 1.75
❑59, Oct 1993 A: Max. 1.75
❑60, Nov 1993 A: Cage. 1.75
❑61, Dec 1993; Giant-size; Embossed foil cover 2.95
❑62, Jan 1994 .... 1.75
❑63, Feb 1994 .... 1.75
❑64, Mar 1994; regular cover 2.25
❑64/Variant, Mar 1994; Die-cut cover 2.00

N-MINT

❑65, Apr 1994 .... 3.00
❑66, May 1994 BA (a); A: Captain America. 1.95
❑67, Jun 1994 .... 1.95
❑68, Jul 1994 .... 1.95
❑69, Aug 1994 .... 1.95
❑70, Sep 1994 .... 1.95
❑71, Oct 1994 .... 1.95
❑72, Nov 1994 .... 1.95
❑73, Dec 1994 .... 1.95
❑74, Jan 1995 .... 1.95
❑75, Feb 1995; Giant-size 4.00
❑76, Mar 1995; New Punisher (Lynn Michaels) begins 3.00
❑77, Apr 1995 .... 1.95
❑78, May 1995 .... 1.95
❑79, Jun 1995 D: Microchip. 1.95
❑80, Jul 1995 D: Stone Cold. 1.95

PUNISHER WAR ZONE, THE
MARVEL

❑1, Mar 1992; JR2 (a); Die-cut cover 2.50
❑2, Apr 1992 JR2 (a) 1.75
❑3, May 1992 JR2 (a) 1.75
❑4, Jun 1992 JR2 (a) 1.75
❑5, Jul 1992 JR2 (a) 1.75
❑6, Aug 1992 JR2 (a) 1.75
❑7, Sep 1992 JR2 (a) 1.75
❑8, Oct 1992 JR2 (a) 1.75
❑9, Nov 1992 .... 1.75
❑10, Dec 1992 .... 1.75
❑11, Jan 1993 .... 1.75
❑12, Feb 1993 .... 1.75
❑13, Mar 1993 .... 1.75
❑14, Apr 1992 .... 1.75
❑15, May 1993 .... 1.75
❑16, Jun 1993 .... 1.75
❑17, Jul 1993 .... 1.75
❑18, Aug 1993 .... 1.75
❑19, Sep 1993 A: Wolverine. 1.75
❑20, Oct 1993 .... 1.75
❑21, Nov 1993 .... 1.75
❑22, Dec 1993 .... 1.75
❑23, Jan 1994; Giant-size; VM (a); D: Rapido. Embossed foil cover 2.95
❑24, Feb 1994 JB, VM (a) 1.75
❑25, Mar 1994 JB, VM (a) 2.25
❑26, Apr 1994 JB (a) 1.75
❑27, May 1994 JB (a) 1.75
❑28, Jun 1994 JB (a) 1.95
❑29, Jul 1994 JB (a) 1.95
❑30, Aug 1994 JB (a) 1.95
❑31, Sep 1994 JKu (a) 1.95
❑32, Oct 1994 JKu (a) 1.95
❑33, Nov 1994 JKu (a) 1.95
❑34, Dec 1994 JKu (a) 1.95
❑35, Jan 1995 JKu (a) 1.95
❑36, Feb 1995 JKu (a) 1.95
❑37, Mar 1995 O: Max (The Punisher's dog). 1.95
❑38, Apr 1995 .... 1.95
❑39, May 1995 .... 1.95
❑40, Jun 1995 .... 1.95
❑41, Jul 1995 .... 1.95
❑Annual 1, ca. 1993; JB (a); trading card; pin-up gallery 2.95
❑Annual 2, ca. 1994 D: Roc. 2.95

PUNISHER/WOLVERINE AFRICAN SAGA
MARVEL

❑1, ca. 1988 .... 5.95

PUNISHER, THE: YEAR ONE
MARVEL

❑1, Dec 1994 .... 2.50
❑2, Jan 1995 .... 2.50
❑3, Feb 1995 .... 2.50
❑4, Mar 1995 .... 2.50

PUNX
ACCLAIM / VALIANT

❑1, Nov 1995 .... 2.50
❑2, Dec 1995 .... 2.50
❑3, Jan 1996 .... 2.50

The Punisher's diary inspired its own title in *Punisher War Journal*.

© 1988 Marvel Comics.

N-MINT

PUNX (MANGA) SPECIAL
ACCLAIM / VALIANT

❑1, Mar 1996; to be read from back to front 2.50

PUPPET MASTER
ETERNITY

❑1, color 2.50
❑2, color 2.50
❑3, color 2.50
❑4, color 2.50

PUPPET MASTER: CHILDREN OF THE PUPPET MASTER
ETERNITY

❑1, color 2.50
❑2, color 2.50

PURE IMAGES
PURE IMAGINATION

❑1; some color 2.50
❑2; some color 2.50
❑3; monsters; some color 2.50
❑4; monsters; some color 2.50

PURGATORI
CHAOS!

❑0.5, Dec 2000 .... 2.95
❑1, Oct 1998 .... 3.00
❑2, Nov 1998 V: Lady Death. 2.95
❑3, Dec 1998 .... 2.95
❑4, Jan 1999 .... 2.95
❑5, Feb 1999 .... 2.95
❑6, Mar 1999 .... 2.95
❑7, Apr 1999 V: Dracula. 2.95
❑Ashcan 1; ashcan preview; no cover price 3.00

PURGATORI: EMPIRE
CHAOS

❑1, May 2000 .... 2.95
❑2, Jun 2000 .... 2.95
❑3, Jul 2000 .... 2.95

PURGATORI: GODDESS RISING
CHAOS!

❑1, Jul 1999 .... 2.95
❑1/Ltd.; limited edition 2.95
❑2, Aug 1999 .... 2.95
❑3, Sep 1999 .... 2.95
❑4, Dec 1999 .... 2.95

PURGATORI: THE DRACULA GAMBIT
CHAOS!

❑1, Aug 1997 .... 2.95
❑1/Variant, Aug 1997; Centennial Premium Edition; no cover price 3.00

PURGATORI: THE DRACULA GAMBIT SKETCHBOOK
CHAOS!

❑1, Jul 1997; b&w preliminary sketches 2.95

PURGATORI: THE VAMPIRES MYTH
CHAOS!

❑-1, Aug 1996 .... 1.50
❑1, Aug 1996; Red foil embossed 3.50
❑1/Ltd., Aug 1996; premium edition; limited to 10, 000 copies; wrap-around acetate cover 5.00
❑1/Variant, Oct 1996; "Krome" edition (color) 8.00
❑2, Oct 1996 .... 3.00
❑3, Dec 1996 .... 2.95

N-MINT

❑4, Feb 1997 .... 2.95
❑5, Apr 1997 .... 2.95
❑6, Jun 1997 .... 2.95

PURGATORY USA
Slave Labor

❑1, Mar 1989, b&w; Ed Brubaker's first published work 2.00

PURGE
Ania

❑0 .... 1.95
❑1, Aug 1993 .... 1.95

PURGE (AMARA)
Amara

❑0; Preview edition 1.50

PURPLE CLAW MYSTERIES
AC

❑1, b&w 2.95

PURR
Blue Eyed Dog

❑1 .... 8.00

PUSSYCAT
Marvel

❑1, ca. 1968, b&w; magazine BWa, WW (a) 150.00

PVP
Dork Storm

❑1, Mar 2001 .... 2.95

PVP (IMAGE)
Image

❑1, Mar 2003 .... 2.95
❑2, May 2003 .... 2.95
❑3, Jul 2003 .... 2.95
❑4, Oct 2003 .... 2.95
❑5, Dec 2003 .... 2.95
❑6, May 2004 .... 2.95
❑7, Aug 2004 .... 2.95

Q

Q-LOC
Chiasmus

❑1, Aug 1994 .... 2.50

QUACK!
Star*Reach

❑1, Jul 1976, b&w FB, HC, ME (w); FB, HC, DSt, ME (a) 2.50
❑2, Jan 1977, b&w SA (w); SA (a) 2.50
❑3, Apr 1977, b&w 2.50
❑4, Jun 1977, b&w 2.50
❑5, Sep 1977, b&w 2.50
❑6, Dec 1977, b&w FB (w); FB (a) 2.50

QUADRANT
Quadrant

❑1, ca. 1983, b&w 1.95
❑2, ca. 1984, b&w 1.95
❑3, ca. 1984, b&w 1.95
❑4, ca. 1985, b&w 1.95
❑5, ca. 1985, b&w 1.95
❑6, ca. 1985, b&w; no cover date 1.95
❑7, ca. 1986, b&w 1.95
❑8, ca. 1986, b&w 1.95

QUADRO GANG, THE
Nonsense Unlimited

❑1, b&w 1.25

QUAGMIRE
Kitchen Sink

❑1, Sum 1970, b&w 3.00

QUAGMIRE U.S.A.
Antarctic

❑1, Mar 1994, b&w 2.75
❑2, May 1994, b&w 2.75
❑3, Jul 1994, b&w 2.75

QUAGMIRE U.S.A. (VOL 2)
Antarctic

❑1, Feb 2004 .... 2.99
❑2, Apr 2004 .... 2.99
❑3, Jun 2004 .... 2.99

N-MINT

QUALITY SPECIAL
Fleetway-Quality

❑1; Strontium Dog 2.00
❑2; Midnight Surfer 2.00

QUANTUM & WOODY
Acclaim / Valiant

❑0/American Ent, American Entertainment exclusive 3.00
❑1, Jun 1997 .... 2.50
❑1/A, Jun 1997, Painted cover 2.50
❑2, Jul 1997 .... 2.50
❑3, Aug 1997 1: The Goat. 2.50
❑4, Sep 1997 .... 2.50
❑5, Oct 1997 .... 2.50
❑6, Nov 1997 .... 2.50
❑7, Dec 1997 .... 2.50
❑8, Jan 1998 .... 2.50
❑9, Feb 1998, A: Troublemakers. 2.50
❑10, Mar 1998 .... 2.50
❑11, Apr 1998 .... 2.50
❑12, Jan 1998, indicia says Jan; no cover date 2.50
❑13, Feb 1998, indicia says Feb; no cover date 2.50
❑14, Mar 1998 .... 2.50
❑15, Apr 1998 .... 2.50
❑16, May 1998 .... 2.50
❑17, Jun 1998 .... 2.50
❑Ashcan 1, Feb 1997, b&w preview of series; no cover price 1.00

QUANTUM CREEP
Parody

❑1, b&w 2.50

QUANTUM LEAP
Innovation

❑1, Sep 1991 O: Doctor Sam Beckett (Quantum Leap). 1: Doctor Sam Beckett (Quantum Leap). 5.00
❑2, Dec 1991 .... 4.00
❑3, Mar 1992; Sam as Santa 4.00
❑4, Apr 1992; Sam on game show 4.00
❑5, May 1992; Superman theme cover 4.00
❑6, Sep 1992 .... 3.00
❑7, Oct 1992 .... 3.00
❑8, Dec 1992 .... 3.00
❑9, Feb 1993 .... 3.00
❑10, Apr 1993 .... 2.50
❑11, May 1993 .... 2.50
❑12, Jun 1993 .... 2.50
❑13, Aug 1993; Time and Space Special #1; foil-enhanced cardstock cover 2.95
❑Annual 1 1992 .... 2.95
❑Special 1, Oct 1992; reprints #1 .... 2.50

QUASAR
Marvel

❑1, Oct 1989 .... 1.50
❑2, Nov 1989 .... 1.00
❑3, Nov 1989 .... 1.00
❑4, Dec 1989 .... 1.00
❑5, Dec 1989; Acts of Vengeance 1.00
❑6, Jan 1990; Acts of Vengeance 1.00
❑7, Feb 1990; Spider-Man has cosmic powers 1.00
❑8, Mar 1990 .... 1.00
❑9, Apr 1990 .... 1.00
❑10, May 1990 .... 1.00
❑11, Jun 1990, Phoenix 1.00
❑12, Jul 1990 .... 1.00
❑13, Aug 1990 .... 1.00
❑14, Sep 1990 .... 1.00
❑15, Oct 1990 .... 1.00
❑16, Nov 1990 .... 1.00
❑17, Dec 1990 .... 1.00
❑18, Jan 1991 .... 1.00
❑19, Feb 1991 .... 1.00
❑20, Mar 1991, Fantastic Four 1.00
❑21, Apr 1991 .... 1.00
❑22, May 1991 .... 1.00
❑23, Jun 1991 .... 1.00
❑24, Jul 1991 .... 1.00
❑25, Aug 1991, new costume 1.00
❑26, Sep 1991, Infinity Gauntlet 1.00

N-MINT

❑27, Oct 1991, Infinity Gauntlet 1.00
❑28, Nov 1991 .... 1.00
❑29, Dec 1991 .... 1.00
❑30, Jan 1992 .... 1.00
❑31, Feb 1992,, New Universe 1.25
❑32, Mar 1992, Galactic Storm 1.25
❑33, Apr 1992, Galactic Storm; Cover says #2 .... 1.25
❑34, May 1992, Galactic Storm 1.25
❑35, Jun 1992, Galactic Storm 1.25
❑36, Jul 1992 .... 1.25
❑37, Aug 1992 .... 1.25
❑38, Sep 1992, Infinity War 1.25
❑39, Oct 1992, Infinity War 1.25
❑40, Nov 1992, Infinity War 1.25
❑41, Dec 1992 .... 1.25
❑42, Jan 1993 .... 1.25
❑43, Feb 1993 .... 1.25
❑44, Mar 1993 .... 1.25
❑45, Apr 1993 .... 1.25
❑46, May 1993 .... 1.25
❑47, Jun 1993 .... 1.75
❑48, Jul 1993 .... 1.25
❑49, Aug 1993 .... 1.25
❑50, Sep 1993, Giant-size; Holo-grafix cover 2.95
❑51, Oct 1993 .... 1.25
❑52, Nov 1993 .... 1.25
❑53, Dec 1993 .... 1.25
❑54, Jan 1994 .... 1.25
❑55, Feb 1994 .... 1.25
❑56, Mar 1994 .... 1.25
❑57, Apr 1994 .... 1.25
❑58, May 1994 .... 1.25
❑59, Jun 1994 .... 1.25
❑60, Jul 1994 .... 1.25
❑Special 1, Mar 1992, reprints Quasar #32 .... 1.25
❑Special 2, Apr 1992, reprints Quasar #33 .... 1.25
❑Special 3, May 1992, reprints Quasar #34 .... 1.25

QUEEN & COUNTRY
Oni

❑1, Mar 2001, b&w 2.95
❑2, May 2001, b&w 2.95
❑3, Jul 2001, b&w 2.95
❑4, Sep 2001, b&w 2.95
❑5, Nov 2001, b&w 2.95
❑6, Jan 2002, b&w 2.95
❑7, Mar 2002, b&w 2.95
❑8, May 2002, b&w 2.95
❑9, Jun 2002, b&w 2.95
❑10, Jul 2002, b&w 2.95
❑11, Aug 2002, b&w 2.95
❑12, Sep 2002, b&w 2.95
❑13, Jan 2003, b&w 2.95
❑14, Feb 2003, b&w 2.95
❑15, Apr 2003, b&w 2.95

QUEEN & COUNTRY: DECLASSIFIED
Oni

❑1, Nov 2002, b&w 2.95
❑2, Dec 2002, b&w 2.95
❑3, Jan 2003, b&w 2.95

QUEEN OF THE DAMNED (ANNE RICE'S...)
Innovation

❑1, ca. 1991 .... 2.50
❑2, ca. 1992 .... 2.50
❑3, ca. 1992 .... 2.50
❑4, ca. 1992 .... 2.50
❑5, ca. 1992 .... 2.50
❑6, ca. 1993 .... 2.50
❑7, ca. 1993 .... 2.50
❑8, Jul 1993 .... 2.50
❑9, Sep 1993 .... 2.50
❑10, Nov 1993 .... 2.50
❑11, Dec 1993 .... 2.50
❑12, Jan 1994 .... 2.50

QUEEN'S GREATEST HITS
Revolutionary

	N-MINT
❑1, Nov 1993, b&w	2.50

QUEST FOR CAMELOT
DC

	N-MINT
❑1, Jul 1998	4.95

QUEST FOR DREAMS LOST
Literacy Volunteers

	N-MINT
❑1, ca. 1987, b&w; The Realm story	2.00

QUESTION, THE
DC

	N-MINT
❑1, Feb 1987, Painted cover	2.00
❑2, Mar 1987	1.75
❑3, Apr 1987	1.75
❑4, May 1987	1.50
❑5, Jun 1987	1.50
❑6, Jul 1987	1.50
❑7, Aug 1987	1.50
❑8, Sep 1987	1.50
❑9, Oct 1987	1.50
❑10, Nov 1987	1.50
❑11, Dec 1987	1.50
❑12, Jan 1988	1.50
❑13, Feb 1988	1.50
❑14, Mar 1988	1.50
❑15, Apr 1988	1.50
❑16, May 1988	1.50
❑17, Jun 1988, Rorschach, Green Arrow	1.50
❑18, Jul 1988, Green Arrow	1.50
❑19, Aug 1988	1.50
❑20, Oct 1988	1.50
❑21, Nov 1988	1.50
❑22, Dec 1988	1.50
❑23, Win 1988	1.50
❑24, Jan 1989	1.50
❑25, Feb 1989	1.50
❑26, Mar 1989	1.50
❑27, Jun 1989	1.50
❑28, Jul 1989	1.50
❑29, Aug 1989	1.50
❑30, Sep 1989	1.50
❑31, Oct 1989	1.50
❑32, Nov 1989	1.50
❑33, Dec 1989	1.50
❑34, Jan 1990	1.50
❑35, Mar 1990	1.50
❑36, Apr 1990	1.50
❑Annual 1, ca. 1988, Batman, Green Arrow	2.00
❑Annual 2, ca. 1989, Green Arrow	2.50

QUESTION QUARTERLY, THE
DC

	N-MINT
❑1, Aut 1990	2.50
❑2, Sum 1991	2.50
❑3, Aut 1991	2.50
❑4, Win 1991	2.95
❑5, Spr 1992	2.95

QUESTION RETURNS, THE
DC

	N-MINT
❑1, Feb 1997	3.50

QUEST OF THE TIGER WOMAN, THE
Millennium

	N-MINT
❑1	2.95

QUEST PRESENTS
Quest

	N-MINT
❑1, Jul 1983 JD (a)	1.50
❑2, Sep 1983 JD (a)	1.50
❑3, Nov 1983 JD (a)	1.50

QUESTPROBE
Marvel

	N-MINT
❑1, Aug 1984, color; JR (a); O: Chief Examiner. 1: Chief Examiner. Hulk	1.50
❑2, Jan 1985, color; AM (w); AM, JM (a); Spider-Man	1.50
❑3, Nov 1985, color; Human Torch; Thing	1.50

QUICK DRAW MCGRAW (DELL)
Dell

	N-MINT
❑2, Apr 1960	15.00
❑3, Jul 1960	10.00
❑4, Oct 1960	10.00
❑5, Jan 1961	10.00
❑6, Apr 1961	10.00
❑7, Jul 1961	10.00
❑8, Oct 1961	8.00
❑9, Jan 1962	8.00
❑10, Apr 1962	8.00
❑11, Jul 1962	8.00
❑12, Oct 1962	8.00
❑13, Feb 1963	6.00
❑14, ca. 1963	6.00
❑15, Jun 1969	10.00

QUICK DRAW MCGRAW (CHARLTON)
Charlton

	N-MINT
❑1, Nov 1970	10.00
❑2, Jan 1971	7.00
❑3, Mar 1971	5.00
❑4, May 1971	5.00
❑5, Jul 1971	5.00
❑6, Sep 1971	4.00
❑7, Nov 1971	4.00
❑8, Jan 1972	4.00

QUICKEN FORBIDDEN
Cryptic

	N-MINT
❑1, ca. 1996, b&w	3.25
❑2, ca. 1996, b&w	3.00
❑3, ca. 1997, b&w	3.00
❑4, ca. 1997, b&w	3.00
❑5, ca. 1998, b&w	3.00
❑6, ca. 1998, b&w	3.00
❑7, ca. 1999, b&w	3.00
❑8, ca. 1999, b&w	3.00
❑9, ca. 2000, b&w	3.00
❑10, ca. 2000, b&w	2.95

QUICKSILVER
Marvel

	N-MINT
❑1, Nov 1997, gatefold summary; wraparound cover	2.99
❑2, Dec 1997, gatefold summary	1.99
❑3, Jan 1998, gatefold summary	1.99
❑4, Feb 1998, gatefold summary	1.99
❑5, Mar 1998, gatefold summary	1.99
❑6, Apr 1998, gatefold summary	1.99
❑7, May 1998, gatefold summary	1.99
❑8, Jun 1998, gatefold summary; in Savage Land	1.99
❑9, Jul 1998, gatefold summary	1.99
❑10, Aug 1998, gatefold summary; concludes in Avengers #7	1.99
❑11, Sep 1998, gatefold summary	1.99
❑12, Oct 1998, double-sized	1.99
❑13, Nov 1998, gatefold summary	1.99

QUINCY LOOKS INTO HIS FUTURE
General Electric

	N-MINT
❑1; giveaway; King Features strip	2.00

QUIT YOUR JOB
Alternative

	N-MINT
❑1, b&w	6.95

QUIVERS
Caliber

	N-MINT
❑1, ca. 1991, b&w	2.95
❑2, ca. 1991, b&w	2.95

Q-UNIT
Harris

	N-MINT
❑1, Dec 1993; trading card; Poly-bagged with "layered reality cyber-card"	2.95

A pair of childhood friends were reunited by the acquisition of super-powers in *Quantum & Woody*.
© 1997 Acclaim.

R

RABBIT
Sharkbait

	N-MINT
❑1	2.50

RABID
Fantaco

	N-MINT
❑1	5.95

RABID ANIMAL KOMIX
Krankin' Komix

	N-MINT
❑1	2.95
❑2	2.95

RABID RACHEL
Miller

	N-MINT
❑1, b&w	2.00

RACE AGAINST TIME
Dark Angel

	N-MINT
❑1, Jun 1997	2.50
❑2, Aug 1997	2.50

RACE OF SCORPIONS (MINI-SERIES)
Dark Horse

	N-MINT
❑1, Mar 1990, b&w	4.50
❑2, Sep 1990, b&w	4.50

RACE OF SCORPIONS
Dark Horse

	N-MINT
❑1, Jul 1991, b&w	2.25
❑2, Aug 1991	2.50
❑3, Sep 1992	2.50
❑4, Oct 1991	2.50

RACER X
Now

	N-MINT
❑1, Sep 1988	2.00
❑2, Oct 1988	1.75
❑3, Nov 1988	1.75
❑4, Jan 1989	1.75
❑5, Feb 1989	1.75
❑6, Mar 1989	1.75
❑7, Apr 1989	1.75
❑8, May 1989; Comics Code	1.75
❑9, Jun 1989; Comics Code	1.75
❑10, Jul 1989; Comics Code	1.75
❑11, Aug 1989; Comics Code	1.75

RACER X (VOL. 2)
Now

	N-MINT
❑1, Sep 1989	2.00
❑2, Oct 1989	1.75
❑3, Nov 1989	1.75
❑4, Dec 1989	1.75
❑5, Jan 1990	1.75
❑6, Feb 1990	1.75
❑7, Mar 1990	1.75
❑8, Apr 1990	1.75
❑9, May 1990	1.75
❑10, Jun 1990	1.75

RACER X (3RD SERIES)
WildStorm

	N-MINT
❑1, Oct 2000	2.95
❑2, Nov 2000	2.95
❑3, Dec 2000	2.95

RACER X PREMIERE
Now

	N-MINT
❑1, Aug 1988	3.50

N-MINT

RACK & PAIN
DARK HORSE
❑1, Mar 1994; Dark Horse 2.50
❑2, Apr 1994 .... 2.50
❑3, May 1994 .... 2.50
❑4, Jun 1994 .... 2.50

RACK & PAIN: KILLERS
CHAOS
❑1 1996; Chaos 2.95
❑2 1996 .... 2.95
❑3 1996 .... 2.95
❑4 1996 .... 2.95

RADICAL DREAMER
BLACKBALL
❑0, May 1994; poster comic 2.50
❑1, Jun 1994; poster comic 2.00
❑2, Jul 1994; poster comic 2.95
❑3, Sep 1994; poster comic 2.50
❑4, Nov 1994; foldout comic on card-stock 2.50

RADICAL DREAMER (VOL. 2)
MARK'S GIANT ECONOMY SIZE
❑1, Jun 1995, b&w 2.95
❑2, Jul 1995, b&w 2.95
❑3, Aug 1995, b&w 2.95
❑4, Sep 1995, b&w 2.95
❑5, Dec 1995, b&w 2.95

RADIOACTIVE MAN
BONGO
❑1, ca. 1993; O: Radioactive Man. glow cover 5.00
❑88; 2nd issue 5.00
❑216; 3rd issue 3.00
❑412, ca. 1994; 4th issue 3.00
❑679; 5th issue 3.00
❑1000, Jan 1995; 6th issue 3.00

RADIOACTIVE MAN (VOL. 2)
BONGO
❑1; #100 on cover 2.50
❑2, Nov 2000; #222 on cover 2.50
❑3; #136 on cover ....

RADIOACTIVE MAN 80 PAGE COLOSSAL
BONGO
❑1, ca. 1995 .... 4.95

RADIO BOY
ECLIPSE
❑1, b&w 1.50

RADISKULL & DEVIL DOLL: RADISKULL LOVE-HATE ONE SHOT
IMAGE
❑1, Apr 2003 .... 2.95

RADIX
IMAGE
❑1, Dec 2001 .... 2.95
❑2, Feb 2002 .... 2.95

RADREX
BULLET
❑1, Jan 1990 .... 2.25

RAGAMUFFINS
ECLIPSE
❑1, Jan 1985 GC (a) 2.00

RAGE
ANARCHY BRIDGEWORKS
❑1 .... 2.95

RAGGEDY ANN AND ANDY (2ND SERIES)
DELL
❑1, Oct 1964 .... 35.00
❑2 .... 20.00
❑3 .... 20.00

RAGGEDYMAN
CULT
❑1, b&w 2.50
❑1/Variant, b&w; Prism cover 2.75
❑2, b&w 1.95
❑3, b&w 1.95
❑4, b&w BT (c); BT (a) 2.50

N-MINT

❑5, Jul 1993, b&w 2.50
❑6 .... 2.50

RAGING ANGELS
CLASSIC HIPPIE
❑1, b&w 2.50

RAGMAN
DC
❑1, Sep 1976 JKu (a); O: Ragman. 1: Ragman. 5.00
❑2, Nov 1976 JKu (a) 3.00
❑3, Jan 1977 JKu (a) 3.00
❑4, Mar 1977 JKu (a) 3.00
❑5, Jul 1977 JKu (a) 3.00

RAGMAN (MINI-SERIES)
DC
❑1, Oct 1991 KG (w); PB (a) 2.00
❑2, Nov 1991 PB (a) 2.00
❑3, Dec 1991 PB (a); O: Ragman. 2.00
❑4, Jan 1992 PB (a) 2.00
❑5, Feb 1992 PB (a) 2.00
❑6, Mar 1992 PB (a) 2.00
❑7, Apr 1992 KG (w); KG, PB, RT (a) 2.00
❑8, May 1992 RT (a); A: Batman. 2.00

RAGMAN: CRY OF THE DEAD
DC
❑1, Aug 1993 .... 2.00
❑2, Sep 1993 .... 1.75
❑3, Oct 1993 .... 1.75
❑4, Nov 1993 .... 1.75
❑5, Dec 1993 .... 1.75
❑6, Jan 1994 .... 1.75

RAGMOP
PLANET LUCY
❑1 .... 2.75
❑1-2, Dec 1995 .... 3.10
❑2 .... 2.75
❑2-2, Dec 1995 .... 2.95
❑3, Oct 1995 .... 2.95
❑4, Dec 1995 .... 2.95
❑5, Feb 1996 .... 2.95
❑6, Apr 1996 .... 2.95
❑7, Jun 1996 .... 2.95

RAGMOP (VOL. 2)
IMAGE
❑1, Sep 1997, b&w; synopsis of first series 2.95
❑2, Nov 1997, b&w 2.95
❑3, Feb 1998 .... 2.95

RAGNAROK GUY
SUN
❑1 .... 2.50

RAHRWL
NORTHSTAR
❑1; Limited edition original print (1988). 32 pages. 500 copies produced 2.50
❑1-2; New edition with redrawn art, 2 additional pages; Splash page identifies it as a new printing 2.25

RAI
VALIANT
❑0, Nov 1992; BL (w); O: Rai. 1: Bloodshot. 1: Rai (new). series continues as Rai and the Future Force; Foretells future of Valiant Universe 4.00
❑1, Mar 1992 .... 5.00
❑2, Apr 1992 .... 4.00
❑3, May 1992 .... 4.00
❑4, Jun 1992; Scarcer 4.00
❑5, Jul 1992 .... 2.25
❑6, Aug 1992 FM (c) 2.25
❑7, Sep 1992; D: Rai (original). Unity 2.25
❑8, Oct 1992; Unity epilogue; Series continued in Rai and the Future Force #9 .... 2.25
❑25, Oct 1994; Series continued from Rai and the Future Force #24 .... 2.25
❑26, Nov 1994; Chaos Effect 2.25
❑27, Dec 1994 .... 2.25
❑28, Jan 1995 .... 2.25
❑29, Feb 1995 .... 2.25

N-MINT

❑30, Mar 1995 .... 2.25
❑31, Apr 1995 .... 2.25
❑32, May 1995 .... 2.25
❑33, Jun 1995 .... 2.25

RAI AND THE FUTURE FORCE
VALIANT
❑9, May 1993; BL (w); A: X-O Commando. A: Eternal Warrior. A: Magnus. Series continued from Rai #8; gatefold cover; first Sean Chen work 2.50
❑9/Gold, May 1993; BL (w); Gold 3.50
❑9/Ltd., May 1993; Signed, limited edition; BL (w); Series continued from Rai #8 .... 3.00
❑10, Jun 1993 .... 2.25
❑11, Jul 1993 .... 2.25
❑12, Aug 1993 .... 2.25
❑13, Sep 1993 .... 2.25
❑14, Oct 1993 A: X-O Manowar armor. 2.25
❑15, Nov 1993 .... 2.25
❑16, Dec 1993 .... 2.25
❑17, Jan 1994 .... 2.25
❑18, Feb 1994 .... 2.25
❑19, Mar 1994 .... 2.25
❑20, Apr 1994; Spylocke revealed as spider-alien 2.25
❑21, May 1994; trading card; series continues as Rai 2.25
❑22, Jun 1994 D: Rai. 2.25
❑23, Aug 1994 .... 2.25
❑24, Sep 1994; new Rai; Series continued in Rai #25 .... 2.25

RAI COMPANION
VALIANT
❑1; no cover price 1.00

RAIDERS OF THE LOST ARK
MARVEL
❑1, Sep 1981 JB, KJ (a) 2.00
❑2, Oct 1981 JB, KJ (a) 2.00
❑3, Nov 1981 JB, KJ (a) 2.00

RAIDER 3000
GAUNTLET
❑1, b&w 2.95
❑2, b&w 2.95

RAIJIN COMICS
GUTSOON
❑1, Dec 2002 .... 4.95
❑2, Dec 2002 .... 4.95
❑3, Dec 2002 .... 4.95
❑4, Dec 2002 .... 4.95
❑5, Jan 2003 .... 4.95
❑6, Jan 2003 .... 4.95
❑7, Jan 2003 .... 4.95
❑8, Jan 2003 .... 4.95
❑9, Feb 2003 .... 4.95
❑10, Feb 2003 .... 4.95
❑11, Feb 2003 .... 4.95
❑12, Feb 2003 .... 4.95
❑13, Mar 2003 .... 4.95
❑14, Mar 2003 .... 4.95
❑15, Mar 2003 .... 4.95
❑16, Mar 2003 .... 4.95
❑17, Apr 2003 .... 4.95
❑18, Apr 2003 .... 4.95
❑19, Apr 2003 .... 4.95
❑20, Apr 2003 .... 4.95
❑21, May 2003 .... 4.95
❑22, May 2003 .... 4.95
❑23, May 2003 .... 4.95
❑24, May 2003 .... 4.95
❑25, Jun 2003 .... 4.95
❑26, Jun 2003 .... 4.95
❑27, Jun 2003 .... 4.95
❑28, Jun 2003 .... 4.95
❑29, Jul 2003 .... 4.95
❑30, Jul 2003 .... 4.95
❑31, Jul 2003 .... 4.95
❑32, Jul 2003 .... 4.95
❑33, Aug 2003 .... 4.95
❑34, Aug 2003 .... 4.95
❑35, Aug 2003 .... 4.95

N-MINT

❑36, Aug 2003 .... 4.95
❑37, Sep 2003 .... 5.95
❑38, Oct 2003 .... 5.95
❑39, Nov 2003 .... 5.95
❑40, Dec 2003 .... 5.95
❑41, Jan 2004 .... 5.95

RAIKA
SUN

❑1 .... 2.50
❑2 .... 2.50
❑3 .... 2.50
❑4 .... 2.50
❑5 .... 2.50
❑6 .... 2.50
❑7 .... 2.50
❑8 .... 2.50
❑9 .... 2.50
❑10 .... 2.50
❑11 .... 2.50
❑12 .... 2.50
❑13 .... 2.50
❑14 .... 2.50
❑15 .... 2.50
❑16 .... 2.50
❑17 .... 2.50
❑18 .... 2.50
❑19 .... 2.50
❑20 .... 2.50

RAIN
TUNDRA

❑1; Introduction by Stephen R. Bissette 1.95
❑2 .... 1.95
❑3 .... 1.95
❑4 .... 1.95
❑5 .... 1.95
❑6 .... 1.95

RAINBOW BRITE AND THE STAR STEALER
DC

❑1, ca. 1985; Official movie adaption 1.00

RAK
RAK GRAPHICS

❑1, b&w 5.00

RAKEHELL
DRACULINA

❑1 .... 2.50

RALFY ROACH
BUGGED OUT

❑1, Jun 1993 .... 2.95

RALPH SNART ADVENTURES (VOL. 1)
NOW

❑1, Jun 1986 O: Ralph Snart. 1: Ralph Snart. 3.00
❑2, Jul 1986 .... 2.00
❑3, Aug 1986 .... 2.00

RALPH SNART ADVENTURES (VOL. 2)
NOW

❑1, Nov 1986 .... 2.00
❑2, Dec 1986 .... 1.50
❑3, Jan 1987 .... 1.50
❑4, Feb 1987 .... 1.50
❑5, Mar 1987 .... 1.50
❑6, Apr 1987 .... 1.50
❑7, May 1987 .... 1.50
❑8, Jun 1987 .... 1.50
❑9, Jul 1987 .... 1.50

RALPH SNART ADVENTURES (VOL. 3)
NOW

❑1, Sep 1988 .... 2.00
❑1/3D, Nov 1992; bagged with no cards 2.95
❑1/CS, Nov 1992; 3-D; bagged with 12 cards 3.50
❑2, Oct 1988 .... 1.75
❑3, Nov 1988 .... 1.75
❑4, Jan 1989 .... 1.75
❑5, Feb 1989 .... 1.75

N-MINT

❑6, Mar 1989 .... 1.75
❑7, Apr 1989 .... 1.75
❑8, May 1989 .... 1.75
❑9, Jun 1989 .... 1.75
❑10, Jul 1989 .... 1.75
❑11, Aug 1989 .... 1.75
❑12, Sep 1989 .... 1.75
❑13, Oct 1989 .... 1.75
❑14, Nov 1989 .... 1.75
❑15, Dec 1989 .... 1.75
❑16, Jan 1990 .... 1.75
❑17, Feb 1990 .... 1.75
❑18, Mar 1990 .... 1.75
❑19, Apr 1990 .... 1.75
❑20, May 1990 .... 1.75
❑21, Jun 1990 .... 1.75
❑22, Jul 1990 .... 1.75
❑23, Aug 1990; cover says May, indicia says Aug 1.75
❑24, Sep 1990; prestige format; with glasses 2.95
❑25, Oct 1990; The Early Years 1.75
❑26, Nov 1990 .... 1.75

RALPH SNART ADVENTURES (VOL. 4)
NOW

❑1, May 1992 .... 2.50
❑2, Jun 1992 .... 2.50
❑3, Jul 1992 .... 2.50

RALPH SNART ADVENTURES (VOL. 5)
NOW

❑1, Jul 1993 .... 2.50
❑2, Aug 1993 .... 2.50
❑3, Sep 1993 .... 2.50
❑4, Oct 1993 .... 2.50
❑5, Nov 1993 .... 2.50

RALPH SNART: THE LOST ISSUES
NOW

❑1, Apr 1993 .... 2.50
❑2, May 1993 .... 2.50
❑3, Jun 1993 .... 2.50

RAMBLIN' DAWG
EDGE

❑1, Jul 1994 .... 2.95

RAMBO
BLACKTHORNE

❑1, Oct 1988, b&w 2.00

RAMBO III
BLACKTHORNE

❑1 .... 2.00
❑3D 1 .... 2.50

RAMM
MEGATON

❑1, May 1987 .... 1.50
❑2 .... 1.50

RAMPAGING HULK
MARVEL

❑1, Aug 1998, b&w; Giant-size 1.99
❑2, Sep 1998; gatefold summary 1.99
❑2/A, Sep 1998; gatefold summary; variant cover 1.99
❑3, Oct 1998; gatefold summary 1.99
❑4, Nov 1998; gatefold summary 1.99
❑5, Dec 1998; gatefold summary 1.99
❑6, Jan 1999; gatefold summary 1.99

RAMPAGING HULK (MAGAZINE)
MARVEL

❑1, Jan 1977, b&w; JB, AA (a); Bloodstone back-up 12.00
❑2, Apr 1977; AA (a); O: the X-Men. Bloodstone back-up 14.00
❑3, Jun 1977; SB, AA (a); Bloodstone/Iron Man back-up story 5.00
❑4, Aug 1977; JSn (c); JSn, VM, AN (a); 1: Exo-Mind. Bloodstone/Iron Man back-up story 5.00
❑5, Oct 1977; JSn (c); VM, KP, AA, BWi (a); A: Sub-Mariner. Bloodstone back-up 5.00

Bart Simpson's favorite super-hero had a six-issue mini-series in 1994, with each issue poking fun at a different comics era.

© 1994 20th Century Fox Film Corporation and Bongo Comics.

N-MINT

❑6, Dec 1977; KP, TD (a); Bloodstone back-up 4.00
❑7, Feb 1978; JSn (c); JSn, KP, JM, BWi (a); A: Man-Thing. Man-Thing back-up 4.00
❑8, Apr 1978; HT, AA (a); A: Avengers. Bloodstone back-up 4.00
❑9, Jun 1978; SB, TD (a); Shanna back-up 4.00

RANA 7
NGNG

❑1 .... 2.95
❑2 .... 2.95
❑3 .... 2.95
❑4 .... 2.95

RANA 7: WARRIORS OF VENGEANCE
NGNG

❑1, Dec 1995 .... 2.50
❑2, Mar 1996 .... 2.50

RANDY O'DONNELL IS THE M@N
IMAGE

❑1, May 2001 .... 2.95
❑2, Jul 2001 .... 2.95
❑3, Sep 2001 .... 2.95

RANGO
DELL

❑1, Aug 1967 .... 25.00

RANK & STINKY
PARODY

❑1, b&w 2.50
❑1-2; Rank & Stinky Eencore Eedition 2.50
❑Special 1, b&w 2.75

RANMA 1/2
VIZ

❑1, ca. 1991; 1: Kasumi Tendo. 1: Nabiki. 1: Soun Tendo. Comic in color 25.00
❑2, ca. 1991 .... 10.00
❑3, ca. 1991 .... 8.00
❑4, ca. 1991; Comics become B&W .. 6.00
❑5, ca. 1991 .... 6.00
❑6, ca. 1991 .... 5.00
❑7, ca. 1991 .... 5.00

RANMA 1/2 PART 2
VIZ

❑1, Jan 1992 .... 7.00
❑2, Feb 1992 .... 5.00
❑3, Mar 1992 .... 4.00
❑4, Apr 1992 .... 4.00
❑5, May 1992 .... 4.00
❑6, Jun 1992 .... 3.50
❑7, Jul 1992 .... 3.50
❑8, Aug 1992 1: Shampoo. 3.50
❑9, Sep 1992 O: Shampoo. 3.50
❑10, Oct 1992 .... 3.50
❑11, Nov 1992 .... 3.50

RANMA 1/2 PART 3
VIZ

❑1, Dec 1992 .... 3.00
❑2, Jan 1993 .... 3.00
❑3, Feb 1993 .... 3.00
❑4, Mar 1993 .... 3.00
❑5, Apr 1993 .... 3.00
❑6, May 1993 .... 3.00
❑7, Jun 1993 .... 3.00
❑8, Jul 1993 .... 3.00

N-MINT

❑9, Aug 1993 ... 3.00
❑10, Sep 1993 ... 3.00
❑11, Oct 1993 ... 3.00
❑12, Nov 1993 ... 3.00
❑13, Dec 1993 ... 3.00

RANMA 1/2 PART 4
VIZ

❑1, Jan 1994 1: Happosai. ... 3.00
❑2, Feb 1994 ... 3.00
❑3, Mar 1994 ... 3.00
❑4, Apr 1994 ... 3.00
❑5, May 1994 ... 3.00
❑6, Jun 1994 ... 3.00
❑7, Jul 1994 A: ... 3.00
❑8, Aug 1994 ... 3.00
❑9, Sep 1994 ... 3.00
❑10, Oct 1994 ... 3.00
❑11, Nov 1994 ... 3.00

RANMA 1/2 PART 5
VIZ

❑1, Dec 1994 1: Ukyo Kuonji. ... 3.00
❑2, Jan 1995 ... 3.00
❑3, Feb 1995 ... 3.00
❑4, Mar 1995 ... 3.00
❑5, Apr 1995 ... 3.00
❑6, May 1995 1: Mousse (as duck). ... 3.00
❑7, Jun 1995 ... 3.00
❑8, Jul 1995 ... 3.00
❑9, Aug 1995 ... 3.00
❑10, Sep 1995 ... 3.00
❑11, Oct 1995 ... 3.00
❑12, Nov 1995 ... 3.00

RANMA 1/2 PART 6
VIZ

❑1, Dec 1996 ... 2.95
❑2, Jan 1997 ... 2.95
❑3, Feb 1997 ... 2.95
❑4, Mar 1997 ... 2.95
❑5, Apr 1997 ... 2.95
❑6, May 1997 ... 2.95
❑7, Jun 1997 ... 2.95
❑8, Jul 1997 ... 2.95
❑9, Aug 1997 ... 2.95
❑10, Sep 1997 ... 2.95
❑11, Oct 1997 ... 2.95
❑12, Nov 1997 ... 2.95
❑13, Dec 1997 ... 2.95
❑14, Jan 1998 ... 2.95

RANMA 1/2 PART 7
VIZ

❑1, Feb 1998 ... 2.95
❑2, Mar 1998 ... 2.95
❑3, Apr 1998 ... 2.95
❑4, May 1998 ... 2.95
❑5, Jun 1998 ... 2.95
❑6, Jul 1998 ... 2.95
❑7, Aug 1998 ... 2.95
❑8, Sep 1998 ... 2.95
❑9, Oct 1998 ... 2.95
❑10, Nov 1998 ... 2.95
❑11, Dec 1998 ... 2.95
❑12, Jan 1999 ... 2.95
❑13, Feb 1999 ... 2.95
❑14, Mar 1999 ... 2.95

RANMA 1/2 PART 8
VIZ

❑1, Apr 1999 ... 2.95
❑2, May 1999 ... 2.95
❑3, Jun 1999 ... 2.95
❑4, Jul 1999 ... 2.95
❑5, Aug 1999 ... 2.95
❑6, Sep 1999 ... 2.95
❑7, Sep 1999 ... 2.95
❑8, Oct 1999 ... 2.95
❑9, Nov 1999 ... 2.95
❑10, Dec 1999 ... 2.95
❑11, Jan 2000 ... 2.95
❑12, Feb 2000 ... 2.95
❑13, Mar 2000 ... 2.95

N-MINT

RANMA 1/2 PART 9
VIZ

❑1, May 2000 ... 2.95
❑2, Jun 2000 ... 2.95
❑3, Jul 2000 ... 2.95
❑4, Aug 2000 ... 2.95
❑5, Sep 2000 ... 2.95
❑6, Oct 2000 ... 2.95
❑7, Nov 2000 ... 2.95
❑8, Dec 2000 ... 2.95
❑9, Jan 2001 ... 2.95
❑10, Feb 2001 ... 2.95
❑11, Mar 2001 ... 2.95

RANMA 1/2 PART 10
VIZ

❑1, Apr 2001 ... 2.95
❑2, May 2001 ... 2.95
❑3, Jun 2001 ... 2.95
❑4, Jul 2001 ... 2.95
❑5, Aug 2001 ... 2.95
❑6, Sep 2001 ... 2.95
❑7, Oct 2001 ... 2.95
❑8, Nov 2001 ... 2.95
❑9, Dec 2001 ... 2.95
❑10, Jan 2002 ... 2.95
❑11, Feb 2002 ... 2.95

RANMA 1/2 PART 11
VIZ

❑1, Mar 2002 ... 2.95
❑2, Apr 2002 ... 2.95
❑3, May 2002 ... 2.95
❑4, Jun 2002 ... 2.95
❑5, Jul 2002 ... 2.95
❑6, Aug 2002 ... 2.95
❑7, Sep 2002 ... 2.95
❑8, Oct 2002 ... 2.95
❑9, Nov 2002 ... 2.95
❑10, Dec 2002 ... 2.95
❑11, Jan 2003 ... 2.95

RANMA 1/2 PART 12
VIZ

❑1, Mar 2003 ... 2.95

RANT
BONEYARD

❑1, Nov 1994, b&w JJ (a) ... 2.95
❑2, Feb 1995, b&w JJ (a) ... 2.95
❑3 JJ (a) ... 2.95
❑Ashcan 1; JJ (a); Ashcan version of issue #1. Black and white cover ... 2.50

RAPHAEL TEENAGE MUTANT NINJA TURTLE
MIRAGE

❑1, Nov 1987; Oversized ... 2.50
❑1-2 ... 1.50

RARE BREED
CHRYSALIS

❑1, Nov 1995 ... 2.50
❑2, Mar 1996 ... 2.50

RASCALS IN PARADISE
DARK HORSE

❑1, Aug 1994; magazine ... 4.00
❑2, Oct 1994; magazine ... 4.00
❑3, Dec 1994; magazine ... 4.00

RAT BASTARD
CRUCIAL

❑1, Jun 1997 ... 2.50
❑1/Ashcan, Jun 1997; Black and white ashcan edition ... 2.50
❑2, Nov 1997 ... 2.00
❑3, Apr 1998 ... 2.00
❑4, Jul 1998 ... 2.00
❑5, Oct 1998 ... 1.95
❑6, Jul 1999 ... 1.95

RATED X
AIRCEL

❑1, Apr 1991, b&w ... 2.95
❑2, b&w ... 2.95
❑3, b&w ... 2.95
❑Special 1, b&w ... 2.95

N-MINT

RAT FINK COMICS
WORLD OF FANDOM

❑1, b&w ... 2.50
❑2, b&w ... 2.50
❑3, b&w ... 2.50

RAT FINK COMIX (ED "BIG DADDY" ROTH'S...)
STARHEAD

❑1 ... 2.00

RATFOO
SPIT WAD

❑1, Sep 1997, b&w ... 2.95

RAT PATROL
DELL

❑1, Mar 1967 ... 40.00
❑2, Apr 1967 ... 40.00
❑3, May 1967 ... 40.00
❑4, Aug 1967 ... 40.00
❑5, Nov 1967 ... 40.00
❑6, Oct 1969; Same cover as #1, slightly recolored ... 25.00

RAT PREVIEW (JUSTIN HAMPTON'S...)
AEON / BACKBONE PRESS

❑1, May 1997, b&w; ashcan-sized; no cover price ... 1.00

RATS!
SLAVE LABOR

❑1, Aug 1992, b&w ... 2.50

RAVAGE 2099
MARVEL

❑1, Dec 1992; Metallic ink cover; foil cover ... 1.75
❑2, Jan 1993 ... 1.25
❑3, Feb 1993 ... 1.25
❑4, Mar 1993 ... 1.25
❑5, Apr 1993 ... 1.25
❑6, May 1993 ... 1.25
❑7, Jun 1993 ... 1.25
❑8, Jul 1993 ... 1.25
❑9, Aug 1993 ... 1.25
❑10, Sep 1993 ... 1.25
❑11, Oct 1993 ... 1.25
❑12, Nov 1993 ... 1.25
❑13, Dec 1993 ... 1.25
❑14, Jan 1994 ... 1.25
❑15, Feb 1994 ... 1.25
❑16, Mar 1994 ... 1.25
❑17, Apr 1994 ... 1.25
❑18, May 1994 ... 1.25
❑19, Jun 1994 ... 1.50
❑20, Jul 1994 ... 1.50
❑21, Aug 1994 ... 1.50
❑22, Sep 1994 ... 1.50
❑23, Oct 1994 ... 1.50
❑24, Nov 1994 ... 1.50
❑25, Dec 1994 ... 2.25
❑25/Variant, Dec 1994; enhanced cover ... 2.95
❑26, Jan 1995 ... 1.50
❑27, Feb 1995 ... 1.50
❑28, Mar 1995 ... 1.50
❑29, Apr 1995 ... 1.50
❑30, May 1995 ... 1.50
❑31, Jun 1995 ... 1.95
❑32, Jul 1995 ... 1.95
❑33, Aug 1995 ... 1.95

RAVEN
RENAISSANCE

❑1, Sep 1993 ... 2.50
❑2, Nov 1993 ... 2.50
❑3, Apr 1994 ... 2.50
❑4, Aug 1994 ... 2.75

RAVEN CHRONICLES
CALIBER

❑1, Jul 1995, b&w ... 2.95
❑2, b&w ... 2.95
❑3, b&w ... 2.95
❑4, b&w ... 2.95
❑5 ... 2.95

N-MINT

❑6 2.95
❑7 2.95
❑8 2.95
❑9 2.95
❑10 2.95
❑11 2.95
❑12 2.95
❑13 2.95
❑14 2.95
❑15; Giant-size; flip book with High Caliber 3.95

RAVENS AND RAINBOWS
PACIFIC

❑1, Dec 1983 1.50

RAVENWIND
PARIAH

❑1, Jun 1996, b&w 2.50

RAVER
MALIBU

❑1, Apr 1993; foil cover 2.95
❑2 1993 1.95
❑3 1993 1.95

RAW CITY
DRAMENON

❑1 3.00

RAWHIDE (DELL)
DELL

❑0, Aug 1962, No issue number: Cover code ends in -208, indicating this issue is from August 1962 200.00

RAWHIDE (GOLD KEY)
GOLD KEY

❑1, Jul 1963 175.00
❑2, Jan 1964 150.00

RAWHIDE KID (1ST SERIES)
MARVEL

❑11, Nov 1956 110.00
❑12, Jan 1957 110.00
❑13, Mar 1957 110.00
❑14, May 1957 110.00
❑15, Jul 1957 110.00
❑16, Sep 1957; series goes on hiatus 110.00
❑17, Aug 1960 JK (a); O: Rawhide Kid. 380.00
❑18, Oct 1960 95.00
❑19, Dec 1960 95.00
❑20, Feb 1961 95.00
❑21, Apr 1961 95.00
❑22, Jun 1961 90.00
❑23, Aug 1961 JK (a); O: Rawhide Kid. 180.00
❑24, Oct 1961 90.00
❑25, Dec 1961 90.00
❑26, Feb 1962 90.00
❑27, Apr 1962 90.00
❑28, Jun 1962 90.00
❑29, Aug 1962 90.00
❑30, Oct 1962 90.00
❑31, Dec 1962 75.00
❑32, Feb 1963 75.00
❑33, Apr 1963 75.00
❑34, Jun 1963 75.00
❑35, Aug 1963 75.00
❑36, Oct 1963 75.00
❑37, Dec 1963 75.00
❑38, Feb 1964 75.00
❑39, Apr 1964 75.00
❑40, Jun 1964 A: Two-Gun Kid. 75.00
❑41, Aug 1964 75.00
❑42, Oct 1964 75.00
❑43, Dec 1964 75.00
❑44, Feb 1965 75.00
❑45, Apr 1965 JK (a); O: Rawhide Kid. 90.00
❑46; Jun 1965 60.00
❑47, Aug 1965 34.00
❑48, Oct 1965 V: Marko the Manhunter. 34.00
❑49, Dec 1965 V: Masquerader. 34.00
❑50, Feb 1966 A: Kid Colt. V: Masquerader. 34.00
❑51, Apr 1966 V: Aztecs. 34.00
❑52, Jun 1966 34.00
❑53, Aug 1966 34.00

N-MINT

❑54, Oct 1966 34.00
❑55, Dec 1966 V: Plunderers. 34.00
❑56, Feb 1967 V: Peacemaker. 34.00
❑57, Apr 1967 V: Enforcerers (not Spider-Man villains). 34.00
❑58, Jun 1967 34.00
❑59, Aug 1967 V: Drako. 34.00
❑60, Oct 1967 34.00
❑61, Dec 1967 A: Wild Bill Hickock. A: Calamity Jane. 25.00
❑62, Feb 1968 V: Drako. 25.00
❑63, Apr 1968 25.00
❑64, Jun 1968; Kid Colt back-up 25.00
❑65, Aug 1968 25.00
❑66, Oct 1968; Two-Gun Kid back-up 25.00
❑67, Dec 1968 25.00
❑68, Feb 1969 V: Cougar. 25.00
❑69, Apr 1969 25.00
❑70, Jun 1969 25.00
❑71, Aug 1969 16.00
❑72, Oct 1969 16.00
❑73, Dec 1969 16.00
❑74, Feb 1970 16.00
❑75, Apr 1970 16.00
❑76, May 1970 16.00
❑77, Jun 1970 16.00
❑78, Jul 1970 16.00
❑79, Aug 1970 16.00
❑80, Oct 1970 16.00
❑81, Nov 1970 16.00
❑82, Dec 1970 16.00
❑83, Jan 1971 16.00
❑84, Feb 1971 16.00
❑85, Mar 1971 16.00
❑86, Apr 1971 JK (a); O: Rawhide Kid. 16.00
❑87, May 1971 14.00
❑88, Jun 1971 14.00
❑89, Jul 1971 14.00
❑90, Aug 1971 14.00
❑91, Sep 1971 14.00
❑92, Oct 1971 14.00
❑93, Nov 1971 12.00
❑94, Dec 1971 12.00
❑95, Jan 1972 12.00
❑96, Feb 1972 12.00
❑97, Mar 1972 12.00
❑98, Apr 1972 12.00
❑99, May 1972 12.00
❑100, Jun 1972 O: Rawhide Kid. 16.00
❑101, Jul 1972 11.00
❑102, Aug 1972 11.00
❑103, Sep 1972 11.00
❑104, Oct 1972 11.00
❑105, Nov 1972 11.00
❑106, Dec 1972 11.00
❑107, Jan 1973 11.00
❑108, Feb 1973 11.00
❑109, Mar 1973 11.00
❑110, Apr 1973 11.00
❑111, May 1973 11.00
❑112, Jun 1973 11.00
❑113, Jul 1973 11.00
❑114, Aug 1973 7.00
❑115, Sep 1973 7.00
❑116, Oct 1973 7.00
❑117, Nov 1973 7.00
❑118, Jan 1974 7.00
❑119, Mar 1974 7.00
❑120, May 1974 7.00
❑121, Jul 1974; reprints 6.00
❑122, Sep 1974; reprints 6.00
❑123, Nov 1974; reprints 6.00
❑124, Jan 1975; reprints 6.00
❑125, Mar 1975; reprints 6.00
❑126, May 1975; reprints 6.00
❑127, Jul 1975; reprints 6.00
❑128, Sep 1975; reprints 6.00
❑129, Oct 1975; reprints 6.00
❑130, Nov 1975; reprints 6.00
❑131, Jan 1976; reprints 6.00
❑132, Mar 1976; reprints 6.00
❑133, May 1976; reprints 6.00

Now collected many issues of *Ralph Snart Adventures* in a hardcover book in 2004.

© 1986 Marc Hansen (Now)

N-MINT

❑133/30 cent, May 1976; 30 cent regional price variant; reprints 20.00
❑134, Jul 1976; reprints 6.00
❑134/30 cent, Jul 1976; 30 cent regional price variant; reprints 20.00
❑135, Sep 1976; reprints 6.00
❑136, Nov 1976; reprints 6.00
❑137, Jan 1977; reprints 6.00
❑138, Mar 1977; reprints 6.00
❑139, May 1977; reprints 6.00
❑140, Jul 1977; reprints 6.00
❑141, Sep 1977; reprints 6.00
❑142, Nov 1977; reprints 6.00
❑143, Jan 1978; reprints 6.00
❑144, Mar 1978; reprints 6.00
❑145, May 1978; reprints 6.00
❑146, Jul 1978; reprints 6.00
❑147, Sep 1978; reprints 6.00
❑148, Nov 1978; reprints 6.00
❑149, Jan 1979; reprints 6.00
❑150, Mar 1979; reprints 6.00
❑151, May 1979; Reprints Rawhide Kid #99 6.00
❑Special 1, Sep 1971 12.00

RAWHIDE KID (2ND SERIES)
MARVEL

❑1, Aug 1985 JBy (c); JBy, HT, JSe (a); O: Rawhide Kid. 1.50
❑2, Sep 1985 KP (c); JBy, HT, JSe (a) 1.50
❑3, Oct 1985 KP (c); JBy, HT, JSe (a) 1.50
❑4, Nov 1985 KP (c); JBy, HT, JSe (a) 1.50

RAWHIDE KID (3RD SERIES)
MARVEL / MAX

❑1, Apr 2003 JSe (a) 5.00
❑2, May 2003 JSe (a) 4.00
❑3, May 2003 JSe (a) 3.00
❑4, Jun 2003 JSe (a) 3.00
❑5, Jun 2003 JSe (a) 2.99

RAW MEDIA ILLUSTRATED
ABC

❑1, May 1998; wet T-shirt cover 3.25
❑1/Nude, May 1998; nude cover 3.25

RAW MEDIA MAGS
REBEL

❑1, b&w 5.00
❑2, b&w 5.00
❑3, b&w 5.00
❑4, May 1994, b&w 5.00

RAW PERIPHERY
SLAVE LABOR

❑1, b&w 2.95

RAY, THE (MINI-SERIES)
DC

❑1, Feb 1992 O: The Ray II (Ray Terrill). 3.00
❑2, Mar 1992 2.00
❑3, Apr 1992 1.50
❑4, May 1992 1.50
❑5, Jun 1992 1.50
❑6, Jul 1992 1.50

RAY, THE
DC

❑0, Oct 1994 1.95
❑1, May 1994 1.75
❑1/Variant, May 1994; foil cover 2.95
❑2, Jun 1994 1.75
❑3, Jul 1994 1.75

Condition price index: Multiply "NM prices" above by: **0.83 for Very Fine/Near Mint**
0.66 for Very Fine • 0.33 for Fine • 0.2 for Very Good • 0.125 for Good

	N-MINT
❑4, Aug 1994	1.95
❑5, Sep 1994	1.95
❑6, Nov 1994	1.95
❑7, Dec 1994	1.95
❑8, Jan 1995	1.95
❑9, Feb 1995	1.95
❑10, Mar 1995	1.95
❑11, Apr 1995	1.95
❑12, May 1995	1.95
❑13, Jun 1995	2.25
❑14, Jul 1995	2.25
❑15, Aug 1995	2.25
❑16, Sep 1995	2.25
❑17, Oct 1995	2.25
❑18, Nov 1995; Underworld Unleashed	2.25
❑19, Dec 1995; Underworld Unleashed	2.25
❑20, Jan 1996	2.25
❑21, Feb 1996	2.25
❑22, Mar 1996	2.25
❑23, May 1996	2.25
❑24, Jun 1996	2.25
❑25, Jul 1996; Ray in the future	3.50
❑26, Aug 1996; continued from events in JLA Annual #10	2.25
❑27, Sep 1996	2.25
❑28, Oct 1996; secrets of both Ray's pasts revealed	2.25
❑Annual 1, ca. 1995	3.95

RAY BRADBURY COMICS
TOPPS

❑1, Feb 1993 AW (w)	3.50
❑2, Apr 1993 MW, HK (w); MW, HK (a)	3.50
❑3, Jun 1993	3.50
❑4, Aug 1993	3.50
❑5, Oct 1993; Final issue (#6 canceled)	3.50
❑Special 1, ca. 1994; CR, JKa (w); Illustrated Man	3.50

RAY BRADBURY COMICS: MARTIAN CHRONICLES
TOPPS

❑1, Jun 1994	3.25

RAY BRADBURY COMICS: TRILOGY OF TERROR
TOPPS

❑1, May 1994 WW (a)	3.25

RAY-MOND
DEEP-SEA

❑1	2.95
❑2	2.95

RAYNE
SHEET HAPPIES

❑1, Jul 1995, b&w	2.50
❑2, Apr 1996, b&w; cover says Mar, indicia says Apr	2.50
❑3, Aug 1996, b&w	2.50
❑4, Jul 1997, b&w	2.95

RAZOR
LONDON NIGHT

❑0	3.00
❑0/A; Direct Market edition	4.00
❑0-2	3.00
❑0.5; Promotional giveaway 1: Poizon.	3.00
❑1, Aug 1992	4.00
❑1-2	3.00
❑2	3.00
❑2/Platinum; Platinum edition	4.00
❑2/Variant	5.00
❑3	3.00
❑3/CS	4.00
❑4	3.00
❑4/Platinum	4.00
❑5	3.00
❑5/Platinum; Platinum edition	4.00
❑6	3.00
❑7	3.00
❑8	3.00
❑9	3.00
❑10 0: Stryke.	3.00
❑11, Sep 1994, b&w	3.00
❑12, b&w; Series continued in Razor Uncut #13	3.00
❑Annual 1, ca. 1993 1: Shi.	15.00
❑Annual 1/Gold; Gold limited edition 1: Shi.	20.00
❑Annual 2, b&w	3.50

RAZOR & SHI SPECIAL
LONDON NIGHT

❑1; Crossover with Crusade	3.00
❑1/Platinum; Platinum edition	4.00

RAZOR ARCHIVES
LONDON NIGHT

❑1, May 1997	3.95
❑2, Jun 1997	5.00
❑3	5.00
❑4, Jul 1997	5.00

RAZOR: BURN
LONDON NIGHT

❑1	3.00
❑2	3.00
❑3	3.00
❑4	3.00

RAZOR/CRY NO MORE
LONDON NIGHT

❑1 1995, b&w	3.95

RAZOR/DARK ANGEL: THE FINAL NAIL
LONDON NIGHT

❑1	2.95

RAZORGUTS
MONSTER

❑1, b&w	2.25
❑2, Feb 1992, b&w	2.25
❑3, b&w	2.25
❑4, b&w	2.25

RAZORLINE: THE FIRST CUT
MARVEL

❑1; sampler; Previews Hokum & Hex, Hyperkind, Saint Sinner, and Ectokid	1.00

RAZOR/MORBID ANGEL
LONDON NIGHT

❑1, Aug 1996	3.00
❑2, Nov 1996	3.00
❑3, Dec 1996	3.00

RAZOR'S EDGE
INNOVATION

❑1, b&w	2.50

RAZOR: THE SUFFERING
LONDON NIGHT

❑1	3.00
❑1/A; "Director's Cut"	3.00
❑2	3.00
❑2/A; "Director's Cut"	3.00
❑3	3.00

RAZOR: TORTURE
LONDON NIGHT

❑0, Dec 1995; enhanced wraparound cover; polybagged with card and catalog	3.95
❑1 1996	3.00
❑1/Variant 1996; alternate cover with no cover price	3.00
❑2 1996	3.00
❑2/Variant 1996; no cover price	3.00
❑3, Apr 1996	3.00
❑4, May 1996	3.00
❑5, Jun 1996	3.00
❑6, Jul 1996	3.00

RAZOR: UNCUT
LONDON NIGHT

❑13 1995; Series continued from Razor #12	3.00
❑14 1995	3.00
❑15 1995	3.00
❑16 1995	3.00
❑17 1995	3.00
❑18, Dec 1995	3.00
❑19 1995	3.00
❑20 1995, b&w	3.00
❑21, May 1996, b&w	3.00
❑22 1996, b&w	3.00
❑23 1996	3.00
❑24 1996	3.00
❑25 1996	3.00
❑26, Sep 1996	3.00
❑27, Oct 1996	3.00
❑28, Oct 1996	3.00
❑29, Nov 1996	3.00
❑30, Dec 1996	3.00
❑31, Jan 1997	3.00
❑32, Feb 1997	3.00
❑33, Feb 1997	3.00
❑34, Mar 1997	3.00
❑35, Apr 1997	3.00
❑36, May 1997	3.00
❑37, Jun 1997	3.00
❑38, Jul 1997	3.00
❑39, Aug 1997	3.00
❑40, Sep 1997	3.00
❑41, Oct 1997	3.00
❑42, Nov 1997	3.00
❑43, Dec 1997	3.00
❑44 1998	3.00
❑45 1998	3.00
❑46 1998	3.00
❑47 1998	3.00
❑48 1998	3.00
❑49 1998	3.00
❑50 1999	3.00
❑51, Mar 1999	3.00

RAZOR (VOL. 2)
LONDON NIGHT

❑1, Oct 1996, chromium cover	3.00
❑2, Nov 1996	3.00
❑3, Dec 1996	3.00
❑4, Mar 1997	3.00
❑5, Apr 1997	3.00
❑6, May 1997	3.00
❑7, Jun 1997	3.00

RAZOR/WARRIOR NUN AREALA: FAITH
LONDON NIGHT

❑1, May 1996; one-shot crossover with Antarctic	3.95

RAZORWIRE
5TH PANEL

❑1, Jun 1996, b&w	1.50
❑2, Jul 1997, b&w	1.50

REACTION: THE ULTIMATE MAN
STUDIO ARCHEIN

❑1	2.95

REACTO-MAN
B-MOVIE

❑1	1.50
❑2	1.50
❑3	1.50

REACTOR GIRL
TRAGEDY STRIKES

❑1, b&w	2.50
❑2	2.95
❑3	2.95
❑4	2.95
❑5	2.95

REAGAN'S RAIDERS
SOLSON

❑1, ca. 1986	2.00
❑2, ca. 1986	2.00
❑3, ca. 1987	2.00

REAL ADVENTURES OF JONNY QUEST, THE
DARK HORSE

❑1, Sep 1996; based on 1996 animated series	3.00
❑2, Oct 1996	2.95
❑3, Nov 1996	2.95
❑4, Dec 1996	2.95
❑5, Jan 1997	2.95
❑6, Feb 1997	2.95
❑7, Mar 1997	2.95
❑8, May 1997	2.95

N-MINT

- ❑9, Jun 1997 2.95
- ❑10, Jul 1997 2.95
- ❑11, Aug 1997 2.95
- ❑12, Sep 1997 2.95

REAL BOUT HIGH SCHOOL
TOKYOPOP

- ❑1, Mar 2002, b&w; printed in Japanese format 9.99
- ❑2, Jun 2002, b&w; printed in Japanese format 9.99

REAL DEAL MAGAZINE
REAL DEAL

- ❑5, b&w; magazine 2.00

REAL GHOSTBUSTERS SUMMER SPECIAL
NOW

- ❑1, Sum 1993 2.95

REAL GHOSTBUSTERS, THE (VOL. 1)
NOW

- ❑1, Aug 1988; Ghostbusters movie adaptation 2.00
- ❑2, Sep 1988 1.75
- ❑3, Oct 1988 1.75
- ❑4, Nov 1988 1.75
- ❑5, Jan 1989 1.75
- ❑6, Feb 1989 1.75
- ❑7, Mar 1989 1.75
- ❑8, Apr 1989 1.75
- ❑9, May 1989 1.75
- ❑10, Jun 1989 1.75
- ❑11, Jul 1989 1.75
- ❑12, Aug 1989 1.75
- ❑13, Sep 1989 1.75
- ❑14, Oct 1989 1.75
- ❑15, Nov 1989 1.75
- ❑16, Dec 1989 1.75
- ❑17, Jan 1990 1.75
- ❑18, Feb 1990 1.75
- ❑19, Mar 1990 1.75
- ❑20, Apr 1990 1.75
- ❑21, May 1990 1.75
- ❑22, Jun 1990 1.75
- ❑23, Jul 1990 1.75
- ❑24, Aug 1990 1.75
- ❑25, Sep 1990 1.75
- ❑26, Oct 1990 1.75
- ❑27, Nov 1990 1.75
- ❑28, Dec 1990; Final issue? 1.75
- ❑3D 1; gatefold summary 2.95

REAL GHOSTBUSTERS (VOL. 2)
NOW

- ❑1, Nov 1991 1.75
- ❑1/3D, Oct 1991; polybagged; w/ glasses 2.95
- ❑2, Dec 1991 1.75
- ❑3, Jan 1992 1.75
- ❑4, Feb 1992 1.75
- ❑Annual 1992, Mar 1992 1.00
- ❑Annual 1993, Dec 1992; 3-D 2.95

REAL GIRL
FANTAGRAPHICS

- ❑1, b&w; Magazine sized 2.50
- ❑2, b&w 2.50
- ❑3, b&w 2.95
- ❑4, b&w 2.95
- ❑5, b&w 3.50
- ❑6, b&w 3.50
- ❑7, Aug 1994, b&w 3.50

REAL LIFE
FANTAGRAPHICS

- ❑1, b&w 2.50

REALLY FANTASTIC ALIEN SEX FRENZY (CYNTHIA PETAL'S...)
FANTAGRAPHICS / EROS

- ❑1, b&w 3.95

REALM HANDBOOK, THE
CALIBER

- ❑1 2.95

N-MINT

REALM OF THE CLAW
IMAGE

- ❑0, Oct 2003 5.95
- ❑1/A; Flip book with Mutant Earth #1/A 2.95
- ❑1/B, Flip book with Mutant Earth #1/B 2.95
- ❑1/C, Nov 2003 2.95
- ❑2, Jun 2002; Flip book with Mutant Earth #2 2.95
- ❑2/A, Jan 2004 2.95

REALM OF THE DEAD
CALIBER

- ❑1 2.95
- ❑2 2.95
- ❑3 2.95

REALM, THE (VOL. 1)
ARROW

- ❑1, ca. 1986 5.00
- ❑2, ca. 1986; repeats indicia for #1 2.00
- ❑3, ca. 1986 2.00
- ❑4, Sep 1986 1: Deadworld. 4.00
- ❑5 1.75
- ❑6 1.75
- ❑7 1.75
- ❑8 1.75
- ❑9 1.75
- ❑10 1.75
- ❑11 1.75
- ❑12 1.75
- ❑13 1.95
- ❑14, Feb 1989, b&w 1.95
- ❑15, Apr 1989, b&w 1.95
- ❑16, May 1989, b&w 2.50
- ❑17 2.50
- ❑18 2.50
- ❑19; no publication date 2.50
- ❑20, Dec 1990 2.50
- ❑21; no publication date 2.50

REALM, THE (VOL. 2)
CALIBER

- ❑1, b&w 2.95
- ❑2, b&w 2.95
- ❑3, b&w 2.95
- ❑4, b&w 2.95
- ❑5, b&w 2.95
- ❑6, b&w 2.95
- ❑7, b&w 2.95
- ❑8, b&w 2.95
- ❑9, b&w 2.95
- ❑10, b&w 2.95
- ❑11, b&w 2.95
- ❑12, b&w 2.95
- ❑13, b&w 2.95

REAL SCHMUCK
STARHEAD

- ❑1, b&w 2.95

REAL SMUT
FANTAGRAPHICS / EROS

- ❑1, b&w 2.50
- ❑2, b&w 2.50
- ❑3, b&w 2.50
- ❑4, b&w 2.75
- ❑5, b&w 2.75
- ❑6, b&w 2.50

REAL STUFF
FANTAGRAPHICS

- ❑1, b&w 3.00
- ❑2, b&w 2.75
- ❑3, b&w 2.50
- ❑4, b&w 2.50
- ❑5, b&w 2.50
- ❑6, b&w 2.50
- ❑7, b&w 2.50
- ❑8, b&w 2.50
- ❑9, b&w 2.50
- ❑10, b&w 2.95
- ❑11, b&w 2.50
- ❑12, b&w 2.50
- ❑13, b&w 2.50
- ❑14, b&w 2.50
- ❑15, b&w 2.50

The Rawhide Kid, running almost 25 years, was one of Marvel's longest-running Western titles.

© 1955 Atlas Magazines (later Marvel).

N-MINT

- ❑16, b&w 2.50
- ❑17, b&w 2.50
- ❑18 2.50
- ❑19, Jul 1994, b&w 2.50
- ❑20, Oct 1994, b&w 2.95

REAL WAR STORIES
ECLIPSE

- ❑1 2.00
- ❑1-2, Feb 1988 2.00
- ❑2, Jan 1991 4.95

REAL WEIRD WAR
AVALON

- ❑1; "Real Weird War" on cover 2.95

REAL WEIRD WEST
AVALON

- ❑1 2.95

REALWORLDS: BATMAN
DC

- ❑1 5.95

REALWORLDS: JUSTICE LEAGUE OF AMERICA
DC

- ❑1, Jul 2000 5.95

REALWORLDS: SUPERMAN
DC

- ❑1 5.95

REALWORLDS: WONDER WOMAN
DC

- ❑1, Jun 2000 5.95

RE-ANIMATOR (AIRCEL)
AIRCEL

- ❑1, color 2.95
- ❑2, color 2.95
- ❑3, color 2.95

RE-ANIMATOR: DAWN OF THE RE-ANIMATOR
ADVENTURE

- ❑1, b&w 2.50
- ❑2, Apr 1992 2.50
- ❑3, May 1992 2.50
- ❑4 2.50

RE-ANIMATOR IN FULL COLOR
ADVENTURE

- ❑1, Nov 1991 2.95
- ❑2 2.95
- ❑3, Apr 1992 2.95

R.E.B.E.L.S.
DC

- ❑0, Oct 1994, story continued from L.E.G.I.O.N. '94 #70 1.95
- ❑1, Nov 1994 1.95
- ❑2, Dec 1994 1.95
- ❑3, Jan 1995 1.95
- ❑4, Feb 1995 1.95
- ❑5, Mar 1995 1.95
- ❑6, Apr 1995 1.95
- ❑7, May 1995 1.95
- ❑8, Jun 1995 2.25
- ❑9, Jul 1995 2.25
- ❑10, Aug 1995 2.25
- ❑11, Sep 1995, color; return of Captain Comet 2.25
- ❑12, Oct 1995 2.25
- ❑13, Nov 1995, Underworld Unleashed 2.25

N-MINT

❑14, Dec 1995, color; Title changes to R.E.B.E.L.S. '96 ..... 2.25
❑15, Jan 1996, color 2.25
❑16, Feb 1996, color 2.25
❑17, Mar 1996, color 2.25

REBEL SWORD
DARK HORSE

❑1, Oct 1994, b&w 2.50
❑2, Nov 1994, b&w 2.50
❑3, Dec 1994, b&w 2.50
❑4, Jan 1995, b&w 2.50
❑5, Feb 1995, b&w 2.50

RECOLLECTIONS SAMPLER
RECOLLECTIONS

❑1, b&w 1.00

RECORD OF LODOSS WAR: CHRONICLES OF THE HEROIC KNIGHT
CPM MANGA

❑1, Sep 2000, b&w 2.95
❑2, Oct 2000, b&w 2.95
❑3, Nov 2000 ..... 2.95
❑4, Dec 2000 ..... 2.95
❑5, Jan 2001 ..... 2.95
❑6, Feb 2001 ..... 2.95
❑7, Mar 2001 ..... 2.95
❑8, Apr 2001 ..... 2.95
❑9, May 2001 ..... 2.95
❑10, Jun 2001 ..... 2.95
❑11, Jul 2001 ..... 2.95

RECORD OF LODOSS WAR: THE GREY WITCH
CPM

❑1, Nov 1998; wraparound cover 2.95
❑2, Dec 1998 ..... 2.95
❑3, Jan 1999; wraparound cover 2.95
❑4, Feb 1999 ..... 2.95
❑5, Mar 1999 ..... 2.95
❑6, Apr 1999 ..... 2.95
❑7, May 1999 ..... 2.95
❑8, Jun 1999 ..... 2.95
❑9, Jul 1999 ..... 2.95
❑10, Aug 1999 ..... 2.95
❑11, Sep 1999 ..... 2.95
❑12, Oct 1999 ..... 2.95
❑13, Nov 1999 ..... 2.95
❑14, Dec 1999 ..... 2.95
❑15, Jan 2000 ..... 2.95
❑16, Feb 2000 ..... 2.95
❑17, Mar 2000 ..... 2.95
❑18, Apr 2000 ..... 2.95
❑19, May 2000 ..... 2.95
❑20, Jun 2000 ..... 2.95
❑21, Jul 2000 ..... 2.95
❑22, Aug 2000 ..... 2.95

RECTUM ERRRECTUM
BONEYARD

❑1 ..... 3.95

RED (DC)
DC / HOMAGE

❑1, Sep 2003 ..... 2.95
❑2, Oct 2003 ..... 2.95
❑3, Feb 2004 ..... 2.95

REDBLADE
DARK HORSE

❑1; gatefold cover 2.50
❑2 ..... 2.50
❑3 ..... 2.50

RED CIRCLE SORCERY
RED CIRCLE

❑6, Apr 1974; Series continued from Chilling Adventures in Sorcery #5 . 6.00
❑7, Jun 1974 ..... 4.00
❑8, Aug 1974 GM, FT (a) 4.00
❑9, Oct 1974 ..... 4.00
❑10, Dec 1974 WW, JAb (a) 4.00
❑11, Feb 1975 ..... 4.00

N-MINT

REDDEVIL
AC

❑1, color; no indicia 2.95

RED DIARIES, THE
CALIBER

❑1 ..... 3.95
❑2 ..... 3.95
❑3 ..... 3.95
❑4 ..... 3.95

RED DRAGON
COMICO

❑1, Jun 1996 ..... 2.95

REDEEMER, THE
IMAGES & REALITIES

❑1 ..... 2.95

REDEEMERS, THE
ANTARCTIC

❑1, Dec 1997, b&w 2.95

RED FLANNEL SQUIRREL, THE
SIRIUS

❑1, Oct 1997, b&w 2.95

REDFOX
HARRIER

❑1, Jan 1986; 1: Redfox. Harrier publishes 4.00
❑1-2; 1: Redfox. Harrier publishes 1.75
❑2, Mar 1986 ..... 3.00
❑3, May 1986 ..... 2.50
❑4, Jul 1986 ..... 1.75
❑5, Sep 1986 ..... 1.75
❑6, Nov 1986 ..... 1.75
❑7, Jan 1987 ..... 1.75
❑8, Mar 1987 ..... 1.75
❑9, May 1987 ..... 1.75
❑10, Jul 1987; Last Harrier issue 1.75
❑11, Sep 1987; Valkyrie begins publishing 2.00
❑12, Nov 1987 ..... 2.00
❑13, Jan 1988 ..... 2.00
❑14, Mar 1988 ..... 2.00
❑15, May 1988; Luther Arkwright cameo 2.00
❑16, Jun 1988 ..... 2.00
❑17, Aug 1988 ..... 2.00
❑18, Oct 1988 ..... 2.00
❑19, Feb 1989 ..... 2.00
❑20, Jun 1989 NG (w) 2.00

RED HEAT
BLACKTHORNE

❑1, Jul 1988, b&w 2.00
❑1/3D, Jul 1988 ..... 2.50

REDMASK OF THE RIO GRANDE
AC

❑1, color 2.95
❑2 ..... 2.95
❑3; 3-D effects; 3-D effects 2.95

RED MOON
MILLENNIUM

❑1, Mar 1995, b&w 2.95
❑2 ..... 2.95

RED PLANET PIONEER
INESCO

❑1 ..... 2.95

RED RAZORS: A DREDDWORLD ADVENTURE
FLEETWAY-QUALITY

❑1 ..... 2.95
❑2 ..... 2.95
❑3 ..... 2.95

RED REVOLUTION, THE
CALIBER / TOME

❑1, b&w 2.95

RED ROCKET 7
DARK HORSE / LEGEND

❑1, Aug 1997 ..... 2.95
❑2, Sep 1997 ..... 2.95
❑3, Oct 1997 ..... 2.95
❑4, Nov 1997 ..... 2.95

N-MINT

❑5, Jan 1998 ..... 2.95
❑6, Mar 1998 ..... 3.95
❑7, Jun 1998 ..... 3.95

RED SONJA (VOL. 1)
MARVEL

❑1, Nov 1976 FT (a); O: Red Sonja. ... 7.00
❑2, Jan 1977 FT (a) 3.00
❑3, May 1977 FT (a) 3.00
❑4, Jul 1977 FT (a) 3.00
❑4/35 cent, Jul 1977; 35 cent regional variant 15.00
❑5, Sep 1977 FT (a) 3.00
❑6, Nov 1977 WP (w); FT (a) 3.00
❑7, Jan 1978 FT (a) 1.50
❑8, Mar 1978 FT (a) 1.50
❑9, May 1978 FT (a) 1.50
❑10, Jul 1978 FT (a) 1.50
❑11, Sep 1978 FT (a) 1.50
❑12, Nov 1978 ..... 1.50
❑13, Jan 1979 ..... 1.50
❑14, Mar 1979 ..... 1.50
❑15, May 1979 ..... 1.50

RED SONJA (VOL. 2)
MARVEL

❑1, Feb 1983 TD (a) 1.00
❑2, Mar 1983 ..... 1.00

RED SONJA (VOL. 3)
MARVEL

❑1, Aug 1983; giant 1.50
❑2, Oct 1983; giant 1.50
❑3, Dec 1983; giant 1.50
❑4, Feb 1984; giant 1.50
❑5, Jan 1985 PB (a) 1.50
❑6, Feb 1985 PB (a) 1.50
❑7, Mar 1985 ..... 1.50
❑8, Apr 1985 ..... 1.50
❑9, May 1985 ..... 1.50
❑10, Aug 1985 ..... 1.50
❑11, Nov 1985 ..... 1.50
❑12, Feb 1986 ..... 1.50
❑13 ..... 1.50

RED SONJA: SCAVENGER HUNT
MARVEL

❑1, Dec 1995 ..... 2.95

RED SONJA: THE MOVIE
MARVEL

❑1, Nov 1985 ..... 1.25
❑2, Dec 1985 ..... 1.25

RED STAR, THE
IMAGE

❑1, Jun 2000 ..... 3.50
❑2, Jul 2000 ..... 3.00
❑3, Oct 2000 ..... 2.95
❑4, Jan 2001 ..... 2.95
❑5, Feb 2001 ..... 2.95
❑6, Mar 2001 ..... 2.95
❑7, Apr 2001 ..... 2.95
❑8/A 2.95
❑8/B .....
❑9, Jun 2002 .....

THE RED STAR (VOL 2)
CROSSGEN

❑1, Feb 2003 ..... 2.95
❑2, Jun 2003 ..... 2.95
❑3, Oct 2003 ..... 2.99
❑4, Mar 2004 ..... 2.99

RED TOKYO: STORM WARNING
DC

❑1, ca 2004 ..... 14.95

RED TORNADO
DC

❑1, Jul 1985 KB (w); CI (a) 1.00
❑2, Aug 1985 KB (w); CI (a) 1.00
❑3, Sep 1985 KB (w); CI (a) 1.00
❑4, Oct 1985 KB (w); CI (a) 1.00

Condition price index: Multiply "NM prices" above by: **0.83 for Very Fine/Near Mint**
0.66 for Very Fine • 0.33 for Fine • 0.2 for Very Good • 0.125 for Good

N-MINT

RED WOLF
MARVEL

❑1, May 1972 1: Red Wolf. 1: Lobo (Marvel). 7.00
❑2, Jul 1972 .... 4.00
❑3, Sep 1972 .... 4.00
❑4, Nov 1972 V: Man-Bear. 4.00
❑5, Jan 1973 .... 4.00
❑6, Mar 1973 .... 3.00
❑7, May 1973 .... 3.00
❑8, Jul 1973 .... 3.00
❑9, Sep 1973 .... 3.00

REESE'S PIECES
ECLIPSE

❑1, ca. 1986 .... 1.75
❑2, ca. 1986 .... 1.75

RE:GEX
AWESOME

❑0, Dec 1998; Woman with swords standing over figures 2.50
❑0/A, Jan 1999; Man with swords standing over figures 2.50
❑1 1998 .... 2.50
❑1/A; White background; Two women with swords on cover 2.50

REGGIE'S REVENGE
ARCHIE

❑1, Spr 1994, color 2.00
❑2, Fal 1994, color 2.00
❑3, Spr 1995, color 2.00

REGULATORS
IMAGE

❑1, Jun 1995 .... 2.50
❑2, Jul 1995 .... 2.50
❑3, Aug 1995 .... 2.50
❑4 .... 2.50

REHD
ANTARCTIC

❑0, Jun 2003 .... 2.50

REID FLEMING
BOSWELL

❑1 1: Reid Fleming. 10.00
❑1-2 .... 4.00

REID FLEMING, WORLD'S TOUGHEST MILKMAN
ECLIPSE

❑1, Oct 1986 .... 6.00
❑1-2 .... 3.00
❑1-3 .... 2.00
❑1-4 .... 2.00
❑1-5 .... 2.00
❑1-6; 1996 .... 2.95
❑2, Mar 1987 .... 3.00
❑2-2 .... 2.00
❑2-3, Mar 1989 .... 2.00
❑3, Dec 1988; Indicia says #2:3 .... 2.00
❑4, Nov 1989 .... 2.00
❑5, Nov 1990 .... 2.00
❑6 .... 2.00
❑7, Jan 1997 .... 2.95
❑8, Aug 1997 .... 2.95
❑9, Apr 1998 .... 2.95

REIGN OF THE DRAGONLORD
ETERNITY

❑1, Oct 1986 .... 1.80
❑2 .... 1.80

REIGN OF THE ZODIAC
DC / HOMAGE

❑1, Oct 2003 .... 2.75
❑2, Nov 2003 .... 2.75
❑3, Dec 2003 .... 2.75
❑4, Jan 2004 .... 2.75
❑5, Feb 2004 .... 2.75
❑6, Mar 2004 .... 2.75
❑7, Apr 2004 .... 2.75
❑8, May 2004 .... 2.75

REIKI WARRIORS
REVOLUTIONARY

❑1, Aug 1993, b&w 2.95

N-MINT

RELATIVE HEROES
DC

❑1, Mar 2000 .... 2.50
❑2, Apr 2000 .... 2.50
❑3, May 2000 .... 2.50
❑4, Jun 2000 .... 2.50
❑5, Jul 2000 .... 2.50
❑6, Aug 2000 .... 2.50

RELENTLESS PURSUIT
SLAVE LABOR

❑1, Jan 1989, b&w 1.75
❑2, May 1989, b&w 1.75
❑3, Sep 1989, b&w 2.95
❑4, Jan 1990, b&w 3.95

RELOAD
DC / HOMAGE

❑1, May 2003 .... 2.95
❑2, Jul 2003 .... 2.95
❑3, Sep 2003 .... 2.95

RELOAD/MEK
DC / WILDSTORM

❑1, ca. 2004 .... 14.95

REMARKABLE WORLDS OF PHINEAS B. FUDDLE, THE
PARADOX

❑1, Jul 2000 .... 5.95
❑2, Aug 2000 .... 5.95
❑3, Sep 2000 .... 5.95
❑4, Oct 2000 .... 5.95

REN & STIMPY SHOW
MARVEL

❑1/A, Dec 1992; Ren scratch&sniff card 2.50
❑1/B, Dec 1992; Stimpy scratch&sniff card 2.50
❑1-2; No air fouler 2.25
❑1-3; No air fouler 2.25
❑2, Jan 1993 .... 2.00
❑2-2 .... 1.75
❑3, Feb 1993 .... 2.00
❑3-2 .... 1.75
❑4, Mar 1993 A: Muddy Mudskipper. 2.00
❑5, Apr 1993; in space 2.00
❑6, May 1993 A: Spider-Man. 1.75
❑7, Jun 1993; Kid Stimpy 1.75
❑8, Jul 1993; Maltese Stimpy 1.75
❑9, Aug 1993 .... 1.75
❑10, Sep 1993 .... 1.75
❑11, Oct 1993 .... 1.75
❑12, Nov 1993; Stimpy cloned 1.75
❑13, Dec 1993; Halloween issue 1.75
❑14, Jan 1994 .... 1.75
❑15, Feb 1994; Christmas issue 1.75
❑16, Mar 1994; Elvis parody 1.75
❑17, Apr 1994 .... 1.75
❑18, May 1994; Powdered Toast Man 1.75
❑19, Jun 1994 .... 1.95
❑20, Jul 1994 A: Muddy Mudskipper. 1.95
❑21, Aug 1994 .... 1.95
❑22, Sep 1994 .... 1.95
❑23, Oct 1994; wrestling 1.95
❑24, Nov 1994; box top collecting 1.95
❑25, Dec 1994 V: Dogzilla. 1.95
❑25/Variant, Dec 1994; enhanced cover 2.95
❑26, Jan 1995 A: Sven Hoek. 1.95
❑27, Feb 1995 .... 1.95
❑28, Mar 1995 A: Filthy the monkey. 1.95
❑29, Apr 1995 .... 1.95
❑30, May 1995; Ren's birthday 1.95
❑31, Jun 1995 .... 1.95
❑32, Jul 1995 .... 1.95
❑33, Aug 1995 .... 1.95
❑34, Sep 1995 .... 1.95
❑35, Oct 1995 .... 1.95
❑36, Nov 1995 .... 1.95
❑37, Dec 1995; aliens 1.95
❑38, Jan 1996 .... 1.95
❑39, Feb 1996 .... 1.95
❑40, Mar 1996 .... 1.95

Jonny Quest's second animated series was the basis for Dark Horse's comics series.

© 1996 Hanna-Barbera Productions and Dark Horse.

N-MINT

❑41, Apr 1996 .... 1.95
❑42, May 1996 .... 1.95
❑43, Jun 1996 .... 1.95
❑44, Jul 1996 .... 1.95
❑Special 1, Jul 1994 .... 2.95
❑Special 2, Oct 1994; Summer Jobs 3.00
❑Special 3, Oct 1994; Masters of Time and Space! 3.00
❑Holiday 1, Feb 1995 .... 2.95

REN & STIMPY SHOW, THE: RADIO DAZE
MARVEL

❑1, Nov 1995; based on audio release of same name 1.95

REN & STIMPY SHOW SPECIAL, THE: AROUND THE WORLD IN A DAZE
MARVEL

❑1, Jan 1996 .... 2.95

REN & STIMPY SHOW SPECIAL: EENTERACTIVE
MARVEL

❑1, Jul 1995 .... 2.95

REN & STIMPY SHOW SPECIAL: FOUR SWERKS
MARVEL

❑1, Jan 1995 .... 2.95

REN & STIMPY SHOW SPECIAL: POWDERED TOAST MAN
MARVEL

❑1, Apr 1994; O: Crusto. Powdered Toast Man 3.00

REN & STIMPY SHOW SPECIAL: POWDERED TOASTMAN'S CEREAL
MARVEL

❑1, Apr 1995 .... 2.95

REN & STIMPY SHOW SPECIAL: SPORTS
MARVEL

❑1, Oct 1995 .... 2.95

RENEGADE, THE
RIP OFF

❑1, Aug 1991, b&w 2.50

RENEGADE!, THE (MAGNECOM)
MAGNECOM

❑1, Dec 1993 .... 2.95

RENEGADE RABBIT
PRINTED MATTER

❑1 .... 1.75
❑2 .... 1.75
❑3 .... 1.75
❑4 .... 1.75
❑5; Cerebus parody 1.75

RENEGADE ROMANCE
RENEGADE

❑1, b&w 3.50
❑2, b&w 3.50

RENEGADES, THE
AGE OF HEROES

❑1 .... 1.00
❑2 .... 1.00

RENEGADES OF JUSTICE, THE
BLUE MASQUE

❑1, ca. 1995, b&w 2.50
❑2, ca. 1995, b&w 2.50

N-MINT

RENFIELD
CALIBER

❑1, ca. 1994 ... 2.95
❑1/Ltd.; Limited special edition with second cover ... 5.95
❑2, ca. 1994 ... 2.95
❑3, ca. 1995 ... 2.95
❑Ashcan 1, b&w; no cover price ... 1.00

RENNIN COMICS (JIM CHADWICK'S...)
RESTLESS MUSE

❑1, Sum 1997, b&w ... 2.95

REPLACEMENT GOD
HANDICRAFT

❑6, Dec 1998 ... 6.95

REPLACEMENT GOD, THE
SLAVE LABOR / AMAZE INK

❑1, Jun 1995, b&w ... 6.00
❑1-2, Dec 1995, b&w ... 3.00
❑2, Sep 1995, b&w ... 3.50
❑3, Dec 1995, b&w ... 3.00
❑4, Apr 1996, b&w ... 2.95
❑5, Jul 1996, b&w ... 2.95
❑6, Sep 1996, b&w ... 2.95
❑7, Dec 1996, b&w ... 2.95
❑8, b&w ... 2.95

REPLACEMENT GOD AND OTHER STORIES, THE
IMAGE

❑1, May 1997, b&w; flip-book with Knute's Escapes back-up ... 2.95
❑2, Jul 1997, b&w; flip-book with Harris Thermidor back-up ... 2.95
❑3, Sep 1997, b&w; flip-book with Knute's Escapes back-up ... 2.95
❑4, Nov 1997, b&w; flip-book with Knute's Escapes back-up ... 2.95
❑5, Jan 1998, b&w; flip-book with Knute's Escapes back-up ... 2.95

REPORTER
REPORTER

❑1 ... 3.00

REQUIEM FOR DRACULA
MARVEL

❑1; Reprints Tomb of Dracula #69, 70 ... 2.00

RESCUEMAN
BEST

❑1, b&w ... 2.95

RESCUERS DOWN UNDER, THE (DISNEY'S...)
DISNEY

❑1 ... 2.95

RESIDENT EVIL
IMAGE

❑1, Mar 1998 ... 5.50
❑2, Jun 1998 ... 5.00
❑3, Sep 1998 ... 5.00
❑4, Dec 1998 ... 5.00
❑5, Feb 1999 ... 5.00

RESIDENT EVIL: CODE VERONICA
DC / WILDSTORM

❑1, Aug 2002 ... 14.95
❑2, Oct 2002 ... 14.95
❑3, Dec 2002 ... 14.95

RESIDENT EVIL: FIRE AND ICE
WILDSTORM

❑1, Dec 2000 ... 2.50
❑2, Jan 2001 ... 2.50
❑3, Feb 2001 ... 2.50
❑4, May 2001 ... 2.50

RESISTANCE, THE
WILDSTORM

❑1, Nov 2002 ... 2.95
❑2, Dec 2002 ... 2.95
❑3, Jan 2003 ... 2.95
❑4, Feb 2003 ... 2.95
❑5, Mar 2003 ... 2.95
❑6, Apr 2003 ... 2.95
❑7, May 2003 ... 2.95
❑8, Jun 2003 ... 2.95

RESTAURANT AT THE END OF THE UNIVERSE, THE
DC

❑1 1994; prestige format ... 6.95
❑2 1994; prestige format ... 6.95
❑3 1994; prestige format ... 6.95

RESURRECTION MAN
DC

❑1, May 1997; Lenticular disc on cover ... 3.00
❑2, Jun 1997 A: Justice League of America. ... 2.50
❑3, Jul 1997 ... 2.50
❑4, Aug 1997 BG (a) ... 2.50
❑5, Sep 1997 BG (a) ... 2.50
❑6, Oct 1997; Genesis; Resurrection Man powerless ... 2.50
❑7, Nov 1997 BG (a); A: Batman. ... 2.50
❑8, Dec 1997; BG (a); Face cover ... 2.50
❑9, Jan 1998 BG (a); A: Hitman. ... 2.50
❑10, Feb 1998 BG (a); A: Hitman. ... 2.50
❑11, Mar 1998 BG (a); O: Resurrection Man. ... 2.50
❑12, Apr 1998 BG (a) ... 2.50
❑13, May 1998 ... 2.50
❑14, Jun 1998 BG (a) ... 2.50
❑15, Jul 1998 ... 2.50
❑16, Aug 1998 A: Supergirl. ... 2.50
❑17, Sep 1998 A: Supergirl. ... 2.50
❑18, Oct 1998 A: Deadman. A: Phantom Stranger. ... 2.50
❑19, Dec 1998 ... 2.50
❑20, Jan 1999 ... 2.50
❑21, Feb 1999 A: Justice League of America. V: Major Force. ... 2.50
❑22, Mar 1999 ... 2.50
❑23, Apr 1999; Mitch as a woman ... 2.50
❑24, May 1999 A: Animal Man. A: Ray. A: Cave Carson. A: Ballistic. A: Vandal Savage. A: Vigilante. ... 2.50
❑25, Jun 1999 A: Forgotten Heroes. .. 2.50
❑26, Jul 1999 A: Immortal Man. ... 2.50
❑27, Aug 1999 D: Immortal Man. ... 2.50
❑1000000, Nov 1998 ... 3.00

RETALIATOR, THE
ECLIPSE

❑1, b&w ... 2.50
❑2, b&w ... 2.50
❑3, b&w ... 2.50
❑4, b&w ... 2.50
❑5 ... 2.50

RETIEF
ADVENTURE

❑1, b&w ... 2.25
❑2, b&w ... 2.25
❑3, b&w ... 2.25
❑4, b&w ... 2.25
❑5, b&w ... 2.25
❑6, b&w ... 2.25

RETIEF AND THE WARLORDS
ADVENTURE

❑1, b&w ... 2.50
❑2, b&w ... 2.50
❑3, b&w ... 2.50
❑4, b&w ... 2.50

RETIEF: DIPLOMATIC IMMUNITY
ADVENTURE

❑1, b&w ... 2.50
❑2, b&w ... 2.50

RETIEF: GRIME AND PUNISHMENT
ADVENTURE

❑1, Nov 1991, b&w ... 2.50

RETIEF (KEITH LAUMER'S...)
MAD DOG

❑1, Apr 1987 ... 2.00
❑2, Jun 1987 ... 2.00
❑3, Aug 1987 ... 2.00
❑4, Oct 1987 ... 2.00
❑5, Jan 1988 ... 2.00
❑6, Mar 1988 ... 2.00

RETIEF OF THE C.D.T.
MAD DOG

❑1, b&w ... 2.00

RETIEF: THE GARBAGE INVASION
ADVENTURE

❑1, b&w ... 2.50

RETIEF: THE GIANT KILLER
ADVENTURE

❑1, b&w ... 2.50

RETRO 50'S COMIX
EDGE

❑1, b&w ... 2.95
❑2, b&w ... 2.95
❑3, b&w; free fly ... 3.50

RETRO COMICS
AC

❑0, b&w; Cardstock cover; Cat-Man .. 5.95
❑1, b&w; Cardstock cover; Fighting Yank ... 5.95
❑2, b&w; Cardstock cover; Miss Victory ... 5.95
❑3; Original Cat-Man and Kitten ... 5.95

RETRO-DEAD
BLAZER

❑1, Nov 1995, b&w ... 2.95

RETROGRADE
ETERNITY

❑1 ... 1.95
❑2 ... 1.95
❑3 ... 1.95

RETURN OF DISNEY'S ALADDIN, THE
DISNEY

❑1 ... 1.50
❑2 ... 1.50

RETURN OF GIRL SQUAD X
FANTACO

❑1 ... 4.95

RETURN OF GORGO
CHARLTON

❑2, Sum 1963 ... 75.00
❑3, Fal 1964 ... 75.00

RETURN OF HAPPY THE CLOWN, THE
CALIBER

❑1, b&w ... 3.50
❑2, ca. 1995, b&w ... 2.95

RETURN OF HERBIE, THE
AVALON

❑1, b&w; reprints and new story (originally scheduled for Dark Horse's Herbie #3) ... 2.50

RETURN OF LUM URUSEI*YATSURA, THE
VIZ

❑1, Oct 1994, b&w ... 3.00
❑2, Nov 1994, b&w ... 3.00
❑3, Dec 1994, b&w ... 3.00
❑4, Jan 1995, b&w ... 3.00
❑5, Feb 1995, b&w ... 3.00
❑6, Mar 1995, b&w ... 3.00
❑7, ca. 1995 ... 2.75
❑8, ca. 1995 ... 2.75

RETURN OF LUM URUSEI*YATSURA, PART 2, THE
VIZ

❑1, Apr 1995, b&w ... 3.00
❑2, May 1995, b&w ... 3.00
❑3, Jun 1995, b&w ... 3.00
❑4, Jul 1995, b&w ... 3.00
❑5, Aug 1995, b&w ... 3.00
❑6, Sep 1995, b&w ... 3.00
❑7, Oct 1995, b&w ... 3.00
❑8, Nov 1995, b&w ... 3.00
❑9, Dec 1995, b&w ... 3.00
❑10, Jan 1996, b&w ... 3.00
❑11, Feb 1996, b&w ... 3.00

N-MINT

- ❑12, Mar 1996, b&w 3.00
- ❑13, Apr 1996, b&w 3.00

RETURN OF LUM URUSEI*YATSURA, PART 3, THE
Viz

- ❑1, May 1996, b&w 2.95
- ❑2, Jun 1996, b&w 2.95
- ❑3, Jul 1996, b&w 2.95
- ❑4, Aug 1996, b&w 2.95
- ❑5, Sep 1996, b&w 2.95
- ❑6, Oct 1996, b&w 2.95
- ❑7, Nov 1996, b&w 2.95
- ❑8, Dec 1996, b&w 2.95
- ❑9, Jan 1997, b&w 2.95
- ❑10, Feb 1997, b&w 2.95
- ❑11, Mar 1997, b&w 2.95

RETURN OF LUM URUSEI*YATSURA, PART 4, THE
Viz

- ❑1, Apr 1997, b&w 2.95
- ❑2, May 1997, b&w 2.95
- ❑3, Jun 1997, b&w 2.95
- ❑4, Jul 1997, b&w 2.95
- ❑5, Aug 1997, b&w 2.95
- ❑6, Sep 1997, b&w 2.95
- ❑7, Oct 1997, b&w 2.95
- ❑8, Nov 1997, b&w 2.95
- ❑9, Dec 1997, b&w 2.95
- ❑10, Jan 1998, b&w 2.95
- ❑11, Feb 1998, b&w 2.95

RETURN OF MEGATON MAN, THE
Kitchen Sink

- ❑1, Jul 1988 2.50
- ❑2 2.50
- ❑3 2.50

RETURN OF TARZAN, THE (EDGAR RICE BURROUGHS'...)
Dark Horse

- ❑1, Apr 1997; adapts Burroughs novel 2.95
- ❑2, May 1997; adapts Burroughs novel 2.95
- ❑3, Jun 1997; back cover has reproductions of New Story Magazine covers; adapts Burroughs novel; ... 2.95

RETURN OF THE SKYMAN
Ace

- ❑1, Sep 1987 1.75

RETURN OF VALKYRIE, THE
Eclipse

- ❑1 9.95

RETURN TO JURASSIC PARK
Topps

- ❑1, Apr 1995 2.50
- ❑2, May 1995 2.50
- ❑3, Jun 1995 2.95
- ❑4, Jul 1995 2.95
- ❑5, Aug 1995 2.95
- ❑6, Sep 1995 2.95
- ❑7, Nov 1995 2.95
- ❑8, Jan 1996 2.95
- ❑9 2.95

RETURN TO THE EVE
Monolith

- ❑1 2.50

REVELATIONS (DARK HORSE)
Dark Horse

- ❑1/Ashcan, Mar 1995 KG (w) 1.00

REVELATIONS (GOLDEN REALM)
Golden Realm Unlimited

- ❑1 2.75

REVELATIONS (CLIVE BARKER'S)
Eclipse

- ❑1 7.95

REVELATION: THE COMIC BOOK
Draw Near

- ❑1, b&w; No cover price; based on Book of Revelation 3.56
- ❑2, b&w; based on Book of Revelation 3.56
- ❑3, b&w; based on Book of Revelation 3.56
- ❑4, b&w; based on Book of Revelation 3.56

N-MINT

- ❑5 3.56
- ❑6 3.56

REVELRY IN HELL
Fantagraphics / Eros

- ❑1, b&w 2.50

REVENGE OF THE PROWLER
Eclipse

- ❑1, Feb 1988 2.00
- ❑2, Mar 1988 2.50
- ❑3, Apr 1988 2.00
- ❑4, Jun 1988 2.00

REVENGERS, THE
Continuity

- ❑1, Sep 1985; Revengers Featuring Armor and Silver Streak, The 2.00
- ❑2, Jun 1986; Origin of Armor 2.00
- ❑3, Feb 1987 2.00
- ❑Special 1, Nov 1993 4.95

REVENGERS FEATURING MEGALITH
Continuity

- ❑1, Apr 1985; newsstand 2.00
- ❑1/Direct ed., Apr 1985 2.00
- ❑2, Sep 1985; Revengers Featuring Megalith 2.00
- ❑3, Nov 1986 2.00
- ❑4, Mar 1988 2.00
- ❑5, Mar 1988 2.00
- ❑6, Mar 1988 2.00

REVENGERS: HYBRIDS SPECIAL
Continuity

- ❑1, Jul 1992; continues in Hybrids: The Origin #2 4.95

REVEREND ABLACK: ADVENTURES OF THE ANTICHRIST
Creativeforce Designs

- ❑1 2.50
- ❑2, Jul 1996, b&w 2.50

REVOLVER
Fleetway-Quality

- ❑1 2.50
- ❑2 2.50
- ❑3 2.50
- ❑4 2.50
- ❑5 2.50
- ❑6 2.50
- ❑7 2.50

REVOLVER (ROBIN SNYDER'S...)
Renegade

- ❑1, Nov 1985; SD (a); Sci-Fi Adventure 2.00
- ❑2, Dec 1985; Sci-Fi Adventure 2.00
- ❑3, Jan 1986; SD (w); SD (a); Sci-Fi Adventure 2.00
- ❑4, Feb 1986; Fantastic Fables 2.00
- ❑5, Mar 1986; Fantastic Fables 2.00
- ❑6, Apr 1986; Fantastic Fables 2.00
- ❑7, May 1986 2.00
- ❑8, Jun 1986 2.00
- ❑9, Jul 1986 2.00
- ❑10, Aug 1986; Murder 2.00
- ❑11, Sep 1986; Murder 2.00
- ❑12, Oct 1986; Murder 2.00
- ❑Annual 1, ca. 1986, b&w ATh (c) 2.00

REVOLVING DOORS
Blackthorne

- ❑1, Oct 1986 1.75
- ❑2 1.75
- ❑3 1.75

REX MUNDI
Image

- ❑1, Feb 2003 2.95
- ❑2, Mar 2003 2.95
- ❑3, Apr 2003 2.95
- ❑4, Jun 2003 2.95
- ❑5, Sep 2003 2.95
- ❑6, Oct 2003 2.95
- ❑7, Dec 2003 2.95
- ❑8, Jan 2004 2.95
- ❑9, May 2004 2.95
- ❑10, Aug 2004 2.95

Reid Fleming returned to comics in 1997.

© 1997 David Boswell (Deep Sea)

N-MINT

RHAJ
Mu

- ❑1, b&w 2.00
- ❑2, b&w 2.00
- ❑3, b&w 2.00
- ❑4 2.25

RHANES OF TERROR, THE
Buffalo Nickel

- ❑1, Oct 1999 2.99
- ❑2 2.99
- ❑3 2.99
- ❑4 2.99

RHUDIPRRT, PRINCE OF FUR
Mu

- ❑1, b&w 2.00
- ❑2, b&w 2.00
- ❑3 2.00
- ❑4, Nov 1990 2.25
- ❑5, Jun 1991 2.50
- ❑6, Nov 1991 2.50
- ❑7, b&w 2.50
- ❑8, Jan 1994 2.50

RIB
Dilemma

- ❑1, Apr 1996, b&w 1.95

RIBIT!
Comico

- ❑1 1.95
- ❑2 1.95
- ❑3 1.95
- ❑4 1.95

RICHARD DRAGON
DC

- ❑1, Jul 2004 2.50
- ❑2, Aug 2004 2.50
- ❑3, Sep 2004

RICHARD DRAGON, KUNG-FU FIGHTER
DC

- ❑1, Apr 1975, O: Richard Dragon, Kung Fu Fighter. 1: Richard Dragon, Kung Fu Fighter. 6.00
- ❑2, Jul 1975, JSn (a) 2.00
- ❑3, Sep 1975 2.00
- ❑4, Nov 1975 2.00
- ❑5, Jan 1976 2.00
- ❑6, Mar 1976 2.00
- ❑7, Apr 1976 2.00
- ❑8, May 1976 2.00
- ❑9, Jun 1976 2.00
- ❑10, Jul 1976 2.00
- ❑11, Sep 1976 1.50
- ❑12, Nov 1976 1.50
- ❑13, Feb 1977 1.50
- ❑14, Apr 1977 1.50
- ❑15, Jun 1977 1.50
- ❑16, Aug 1977 1.50
- ❑17, Oct 1977 1.50
- ❑18, Nov 1977 1.50

RICHARD SPECK
Boneyard

- ❑1, Mar 1993 2.75

RICHIE RICH (1ST SERIES)

HARVEY

	N-MINT
❑1, Nov 1960	3050.00
❑2, Jan 1961	850.00
❑3, Mar 1961	440.00
❑4, May 1961	310.00
❑5, Jul 1961	310.00
❑6, Sep 1961	200.00
❑7, Nov 1961	200.00
❑8, Jan 1962	200.00
❑9, Mar 1962	200.00
❑10, May 1962	165.00
❑11, Jul 1962	100.00
❑12, Sep 1962	100.00
❑13, Oct 1962	100.00
❑14, Nov 1962	100.00
❑15, Jan 1963	100.00
❑16, Mar 1963	75.00
❑17, May 1963	75.00
❑18, Jul 1963	75.00
❑19, Sep 1963	75.00
❑20, Nov 1963	75.00
❑21, Jan 1964	50.00
❑22, Mar 1964	50.00
❑23, May 1964	50.00
❑24, Jul 1964	50.00
❑25, Sep 1964	50.00
❑26, Oct 1964	50.00
❑27, Nov 1964	50.00
❑28, Dec 1964	50.00
❑29, Jan 1965	50.00
❑30, Feb 1965	50.00
❑31, Mar 1965	35.00
❑32, Apr 1965	35.00
❑33, May 1965	35.00
❑34, Jun 1965	35.00
❑35, Jul 1965	35.00
❑36, Aug 1965	35.00
❑37, Sep 1965	35.00
❑38, Oct 1965	35.00
❑39, Nov 1965	35.00
❑40, Dec 1965	35.00
❑41, Jan 1966	22.00
❑42, Feb 1966	22.00
❑43, Mar 1966	22.00
❑44, Apr 1966	22.00
❑45, May 1966	22.00
❑46, Jun 1966	22.00
❑47, Jul 1966	22.00
❑48, Aug 1966	22.00
❑49, Sep 1966	22.00
❑50, Oct 1966	17.00
❑51, Nov 1966	17.00
❑52, Dec 1966	17.00
❑53, Jan 1967	17.00
❑54, Feb 1967	17.00
❑55, Mar 1967	17.00
❑56, Apr 1967	17.00
❑57, May 1967	17.00
❑58, Jun 1967	17.00
❑59, Jul 1967	17.00
❑60, Aug 1967	17.00
❑61, Sep 1967	13.00
❑62, Oct 1967	13.00
❑63, Nov 1967	13.00
❑64, Dec 1967	13.00
❑65, Jan 1968	13.00
❑66, Feb 1968	13.00
❑67, Mar 1968	13.00
❑68, Apr 1968	13.00
❑69, May 1968	13.00
❑70, Jun 1968	13.00
❑71, Jul 1968	8.00
❑72, Aug 1968	8.00
❑73, Sep 1968	8.00
❑74, Oct 1968	8.00
❑75, Nov 1968	8.00
❑76, Dec 1968	8.00
❑77, Jan 1969	8.00
❑78, Feb 1969	8.00
❑79, Mar 1969	8.00
❑80, Apr 1969	8.00
❑81, May 1969	8.00
❑82, Jun 1969	8.00
❑83, Jul 1969	8.00
❑84, Aug 1969	8.00
❑85, Sep 1969	8.00
❑86, Oct 1969	8.00
❑87, Nov 1969	8.00
❑88, Dec 1969	8.00
❑89, Jan 1970	6.00
❑90, Feb 1970	6.00
❑91, Mar 1970	6.00
❑92, Apr 1970	6.00
❑93, May 1970	6.00
❑94, Jun 1970	6.00
❑95, Jul 1970	6.00
❑96, Aug 1970	6.00
❑97, Sep 1970	6.00
❑98, Oct 1970	6.00
❑99, Nov 1970	6.00
❑100, Dec 1970	6.00
❑101, Jan 1971	4.00
❑102, Feb 1971	4.00
❑103, Mar 1971	4.00
❑104, Apr 1971	4.00
❑105, May 1971	4.00
❑106, Jun 1971	4.00
❑107, Jul 1971	4.00
❑108, Aug 1971	4.00
❑109, Sep 1971	4.00
❑110, Oct 1971	4.00
❑111, Nov 1971	4.00
❑112, Jan 1972	4.00
❑113, Mar 1972	4.00
❑114, May 1972	4.00
❑115, Jul 1972	4.00
❑116, Sep 1972	4.00
❑117, Nov 1972	4.00
❑118, Jan 1973	4.00
❑119, Mar 1973	4.00
❑120, May 1973	4.00
❑121, Jul 1973	4.00
❑122, Sep 1973	4.00
❑123, Nov 1973	4.00
❑124, Jan 1974	4.00
❑125, Mar 1974	4.00
❑126, May 1974	4.00
❑127, Jul 1974	4.00
❑128, Sep 1974	4.00
❑129, Nov 1974	4.00
❑130, Jan 1975	4.00
❑131, Mar 1975	4.00
❑132, May 1975	4.00
❑133, Jul 1975	4.00
❑134, Sep 1975	4.00
❑135, Oct 1975	4.00
❑136, Nov 1975	4.00
❑137, Dec 1975	4.00
❑138, Jan 1976	4.00
❑139, Feb 1976	4.00
❑140, Mar 1976	4.00
❑141, Apr 1976	4.00
❑142, May 1976	4.00
❑143, Jun 1976	4.00
❑144, Jul 1976	4.00
❑145, Aug 1976	4.00
❑146, Sep 1976	4.00
❑147, Oct 1976	4.00
❑148, Nov 1976	4.00
❑149, Dec 1976	4.00
❑150, Jan 1977	4.00
❑151, Feb 1977	3.00
❑152, Mar 1977	3.00
❑153, Apr 1977	3.00
❑154, May 1977	3.00
❑155, Jun 1977	3.00
❑156, Jul 1977	3.00
❑157, Aug 1977	3.00
❑158, Sep 1977	3.00
❑159, Oct 1977	3.00
❑160, Nov 1977	3.00
❑161, Dec 1977	3.00
❑162, Jan 1978	3.00
❑163, Feb 1978	3.00
❑164, Mar 1978	3.00
❑165, Apr 1978	3.00
❑166, May 1978	3.00
❑167, Jun 1978	3.00
❑168, Jul 1978	3.00
❑169, Aug 1978	3.00
❑170, Sep 1978	3.00
❑171, Oct 1978	3.00
❑172, Nov 1978	3.00
❑173, Dec 1978	3.00
❑174, Jan 1979	3.00
❑175, Feb 1979	3.00
❑176, Mar 1979	3.00
❑177, Apr 1979	3.00
❑178, May 1979	3.00
❑179, Jun 1979	3.00
❑180, Jul 1979	3.00
❑181, Aug 1979	3.00
❑182, Sep 1979	3.00
❑183, Oct 1979	3.00
❑184, Nov 1979	3.00
❑185, Dec 1979	3.00
❑186, Jan 1980	3.00
❑187, Feb 1980	3.00
❑188, Mar 1980	3.00
❑189, Apr 1980	3.00
❑190, May 1980	3.00
❑191, Jun 1980	3.00
❑192, Jul 1980	3.00
❑193, Aug 1980	3.00
❑194, Sep 1980	3.00
❑195, Oct 1980	3.00
❑196, Nov 1980	3.00
❑197, Dec 1980	3.00
❑198, Jan 1981	3.00
❑199, Feb 1981	3.00
❑200, Mar 1981	3.00
❑201, Apr 1981	1.75
❑202, May 1981	1.75
❑203, Jun 1981	1.75
❑204, Jul 1981	1.75
❑205, Aug 1981	1.75
❑206, Sep 1981	1.75
❑207, Oct 1981	1.75
❑208, Nov 1981	1.75
❑209, Dec 1981	1.75
❑210, Jan 1982	1.75
❑211, Feb 1982	1.75
❑212, Mar 1982	1.75
❑213, Apr 1982	1.75
❑214, May 1982	1.75
❑215, Jun 1982	1.75
❑216, Jul 1982	1.75
❑217, Aug 1982	1.75
❑218, Oct 1982	1.75
❑219, Oct 1986	1.75
❑220, Nov 1986	1.75
❑221, Dec 1986	1.75
❑222, Jan 1987	1.75
❑223, Feb 1987	1.75
❑224, Mar 1987	1.75
❑225, Apr 1987	1.75
❑226, May 1987	1.75
❑227, Jun 1987	1.75
❑228, Jul 1987	1.75
❑229, Aug 1987	1.75
❑230, Sep 1987	1.75
❑231, Nov 1987	1.75
❑232 1988	1.75
❑233, Apr 1988	1.75
❑234, Jun 1988	1.75
❑235, Aug 1988	1.75
❑236 1988	1.75
❑237 1989	1.75
❑238 1989	1.75
❑239, Jul 1989	1.75
❑240, Sep 1989	1.75
❑241, Oct 1989	1.75

	N-MINT
❑242, Dec 1989	1.75
❑243, Feb 1990	1.75
❑244, Mar 1990	1.75
❑245, Apr 1990	1.75
❑246, May 1990	1.75
❑247, Jun 1990	1.75
❑248, Jul 1990	1.75
❑249, Aug 1990	1.75
❑250, Sep 1990	1.75
❑251, Oct 1990	1.75
❑252, Nov 1990	1.75
❑253, Dec 1990	1.75
❑254, Jan 1991	1.75

RICHIE RICH (2ND SERIES)
HARVEY

	N-MINT
❑1, Mar 1991	5.00
❑2, May 1991	3.00
❑3, Jul 1991	1.50
❑4, Sep 1991	1.50
❑5, Nov 1991	1.50
❑6, Jan 1992	1.50
❑7, Mar 1992	1.50
❑8, May 1992	1.50
❑9, Jul 1992	1.50
❑10, Sep 1992	1.50
❑11, Nov 1992	1.00
❑12, Jan 1993	1.00
❑13, Mar 1993	1.00
❑14, May 1993	1.00
❑15, Jul 1993	1.00
❑16, Sep 1993	1.00
❑17, Nov 1993	1.00
❑18, Jan 1994	1.00
❑19, Feb 1994	1.00
❑20, Mar 1994	1.00
❑21, Apr 1994	1.00
❑22, May 1994	1.00
❑23, Jun 1994	1.00
❑24, Jul 1994	1.00
❑25, Aug 1994	1.00
❑26, Sep 1994	1.00
❑27, Oct 1994	1.00
❑28, Nov 1994	1.00

RICHIE RICH ADVENTURE DIGEST MAGAZINE
HARVEY

	N-MINT
❑1, May 1992	2.00
❑2, Feb 1993	1.75
❑3, Jun 1993	1.75
❑4, Oct 1993	1.75
❑5, Feb 1994	1.75
❑6, Jun 1994	1.75

RICHIE RICH AND BILLY BELLHOPS
HARVEY

	N-MINT
❑1, Oct 1977	5.00

RICHIE RICH AND CADBURY
HARVEY

	N-MINT
❑1, Oct 1977	15.00
❑2, Sep 1978	10.00
❑3, Oct 1978	10.00
❑4, color	10.00
❑5 1979	10.00
❑6 1979	10.00
❑7, May 1979	10.00
❑8 1979	10.00
❑9 1979	10.00
❑10, color	10.00
❑11 1980	5.00
❑12 1980	5.00
❑13 1980	4.00
❑14 1980	4.00
❑15	4.00
❑16 1981	4.00
❑17 1981	4.00
❑18, Aug 1981	4.00
❑19 1981	4.00
❑20	3.00
❑21	3.00
❑22, May 1982	3.00
❑23, Jul 1982	3.00

	N-MINT
❑24, Jul 1990	3.00
❑25, Sep 1990	3.00
❑26, Oct 1990	3.00
❑27, Nov 1990	3.00
❑28, Dec 1990	3.00
❑29, Jan 1991	3.00

RICHIE RICH & CASPER
HARVEY

	N-MINT
❑1, Aug 1974	12.00
❑2, Oct 1974	6.00
❑3, Dec 1974	4.00
❑4, Feb 1975	4.00
❑5, Apr 1975	4.00
❑6, Jun 1975	3.00
❑7, Aug 1975	3.00
❑8, Oct 1975	3.00
❑9, Dec 1975	3.00
❑10, Feb 1976	3.00
❑11, Apr 1976	2.00
❑12, Jun 1976	2.00
❑13, Aug 1976	2.00
❑14, Oct 1976	2.00
❑15, Dec 1977	2.00
❑16, Feb 1977	2.00
❑17, Apr 1977	2.00
❑18, Jun 1977	2.00
❑19, Aug 1977	2.00
❑20, Oct 1977	2.00
❑21, Dec 1977	2.00
❑22, Feb 1978	2.00
❑23, Apr 1978	2.00
❑24, Jul 1978	2.00
❑25, Sep 1978	2.00
❑26, Nov 1978	2.00
❑27 1979	2.00
❑28 1979	2.00
❑29 1979	2.00
❑30 1979	2.00
❑31 1979	2.00
❑32, Feb 1980	2.00
❑33, Apr 1980	2.00
❑34, Jun 1980	2.00
❑35, Sep 1980	2.00
❑36, Nov 1980	2.00
❑37, Dec 1980	2.00
❑38, Mar 1981	2.00
❑39 1981	2.00
❑40, Sep 1981	2.00
❑41, Nov 1981	2.00
❑42 1982	2.00
❑43 1982	2.00
❑44 1982	2.00
❑45, Sep 1982	2.00

RICHIE RICH AND CASPER IN 3-D
BLACKTHORNE

	N-MINT
❑1/A	2.50
❑1/B, Spanish; Burger King	2.50

RICHIE RICH & DOLLAR, THE DOG
HARVEY

	N-MINT
❑1, Sep 1977	5.00
❑2	3.00
❑3 1978	2.00
❑4 1978	2.00
❑5 1978	2.00
❑6	1.50
❑7, Apr 1979	1.50
❑8, Jun 1979	1.50
❑9 1979	1.50
❑10 1979	1.50
❑11	1.50
❑12 1980	1.50
❑13 1980	1.50
❑14 1980	1.50
❑15 1980	1.50
❑16	1.50
❑17 1981	1.50
❑18, May 1981	1.50
❑19 1981	1.50
❑20	1.50
❑21	1.50

The Forgotten Heroes, including Animal Man and Cave Carson, rejoined their leader, The Immortal Man, as *Resurrection Man* neared its end.

	N-MINT
❑22 1982	1.50
❑23, Jun 1982	1.50
❑24, Aug 1982	1.50

RICHIE RICH AND DOT
HARVEY

	N-MINT
❑1, ca. 1974	20.00

RICHIE RICH AND GLORIA
HARVEY

	N-MINT
❑1, Sep 1977	10.00
❑2 1978	8.00
❑3, Aug 1978	8.00
❑4, Oct 1978	8.00
❑5	8.00
❑6 1979	8.00
❑7 1979	8.00
❑8 1979	8.00
❑9 1979	8.00
❑10	8.00
❑11	5.00
❑12	5.00
❑13 1980	5.00
❑14 1980	5.00
❑15 1980	5.00
❑16 1980	5.00
❑17	5.00
❑18, Mar 1981	5.00
❑19, Jun 1981	5.00
❑20, Aug 1981	4.00
❑21, Oct 1981	4.00
❑22	4.00
❑23, Mar 1982	4.00
❑24 1982	4.00
❑25, Sep 1982	4.00

RICHIE RICH AND HIS GIRLFRIENDS
HARVEY

	N-MINT
❑1, Apr 1979 (c); (w); (a)	10.00
❑2 (c); (w); (a)	8.00
❑3 (c); (w); (a)	8.00
❑4 1980 (c); (w); (a)	8.00
❑5 1980 (c); (w); (a)	8.00
❑6, Oct 1980 (c); (w); (a)	8.00
❑7 (c); (w); (a)	8.00
❑8 (c); (w); (a)	8.00
❑9 1981 (c); (w); (a)	8.00
❑10 1981 (c); (w); (a)	8.00
❑11 1981 (c); (w); (a)	5.00
❑12, Dec 1981 (c); (w); (a)	5.00
❑13 1982 (c); (w); (a)	5.00
❑14 1982 (c); (w); (a)	5.00
❑15 1982 (c); (w); (a)	5.00
❑16, Dec 1982 (c); (w); (a)	5.00

RICHIE RICH AND HIS MEAN COUSIN REGGIE
HARVEY

	N-MINT
❑1, Apr 1979	10.00
❑2 1979	5.00
❑3, Jan 1980	5.00

RICHIE RICH & JACKIE JOKERS
HARVEY

	N-MINT
❑1, Nov 1973	18.00
❑2, Jan 1974	10.00
❑3, Mar 1974	6.00
❑4, May 1974	6.00
❑5, Jul 1974	6.00
❑6, Sep 1974	4.00
❑7, Nov 1974	4.00

	N-MINT
❑8, Jan 1975	4.00
❑9, Mar 1975	4.00
❑10, May 1975	4.00
❑11, Sep 1975	3.00
❑12, Nov 1975	3.00
❑13, Jan 1976	3.00
❑14, Mar 1976	3.00
❑15, May 1976	3.00
❑16, Jul 1976	3.00
❑17, Sep 1976	3.00
❑18, Nov 1976	3.00
❑19, Jan 1977; Welcome Back Kotter parody	3.00
❑20, Apr 1977	3.00
❑21, Jun 1977	3.00
❑22, Aug 1977	3.00
❑23, Oct 1977	3.00
❑24, Dec 1977	3.00
❑25, Feb 1978	3.00
❑26, Apr 1978	3.00
❑27, Jun 1978	3.00
❑28, Aug 1978	3.00
❑29, Oct 1978	3.00
❑30, Feb 1979	3.00
❑31, Apr 1979	2.00
❑32, Jun 1979	2.00
❑33, Aug 1979	2.00
❑34, Oct 1979	2.00
❑35, Dec 1979	2.00
❑36, Feb 1980	2.00
❑37, Apr 1980	2.00
❑38, Jul 1980	2.00
❑39, Sep 1980	2.00
❑40, Nov 1980	2.00
❑41, Jan 1981	2.00
❑42, Apr 1981	2.00
❑43, Jun 1981	2.00
❑44, Aug 1981	2.00
❑45, Nov 1981	2.00
❑46, Feb 1982	2.00
❑47, May 1982	2.00
❑48, Dec 1982	2.00

RICHIE RICH AND PROFESSOR KEENBEAN
HARVEY

	N-MINT
❑1, Sep 1990	1.00
❑2, Nov 1990	1.00

RICHIE RICH AND THE NEW KIDS ON THE BLOCK
HARVEY

	N-MINT
❑1, Feb 1991	1.50

RICHIE RICH AND TIMMY TIME
HARVEY

	N-MINT
❑1, ca. 1977	8.00

RICHIE RICH BANK BOOKS
HARVEY

	N-MINT
❑1, Oct 1972	24.00
❑2, Dec 1972	10.00
❑3, Feb 1973	6.00
❑4, Apr 1973	6.00
❑5, Jun 1973	6.00
❑6, Aug 1973	4.00
❑7, Oct 1973	4.00
❑8, Dec 1973	4.00
❑9, Feb 1974	4.00
❑10, Apr 1974	4.00
❑11, Jun 1974	3.00
❑12, Aug 1974	3.00
❑13, Oct 1974	3.00
❑14, Dec 1974	3.00
❑15, Feb 1975	3.00
❑16, Apr 1975	3.00
❑17, Jun 1975	3.00
❑18, Aug 1975	3.00
❑19, Oct 1975	3.00
❑20, Dec 1975	3.00
❑21, Feb 1976	2.00
❑22, Apr 1976	2.00
❑23, Jun 1976	2.00
❑24, Aug 1976	2.00
❑25, Oct 1976	2.00
❑26, Dec 1976	2.00
❑27, Feb 1977	2.00
❑28, Apr 1977	2.00
❑29, Jun 1977	2.00
❑30, Aug 1977	2.00
❑31, Sep 1977	2.00
❑32, Nov 1977	2.00
❑33, Jan 1978	2.00
❑34, Mar 1978	2.00
❑35, May 1978	2.00
❑36, Aug 1978	2.00
❑37, Oct 1978	2.00
❑38, Jan 1979	2.00
❑39, Mar 1979	2.00
❑40, May 1979	2.00
❑41, Jul 1979	2.00
❑42 1979	2.00
❑43 1979	2.00
❑44, Dec 1979	2.00
❑45, Mar 1980	2.00
❑46, May 1980	2.00
❑47, Aug 1980	2.00
❑48, Oct 1980	2.00
❑49, Nov 1980	2.00
❑50 1981	2.00
❑51, Apr 1981	2.00
❑52, Jun 1981	2.00
❑53, Aug 1981	2.00
❑54, Oct 1981	2.00
❑55 1981	2.00
❑56 1982	2.00
❑57 1982	2.00
❑58, Jul 1982	2.00
❑59, Sep 1982	2.00

RICHIE RICH BEST OF THE YEARS
HARVEY

	N-MINT
❑1, ca. 1977	10.00
❑2, ca. 1978	6.00
❑3, ca. 1979	6.00
❑4, ca. 1979	6.00
❑5, ca. 1980	6.00
❑6, ca. 1980	6.00

RICHIE RICH BIG BOOK (VOL. 2)
HARVEY

	N-MINT
❑1, Nov 1992	1.95
❑2, May 1993	1.95

RICHIE RICH BIG BUCKS
HARVEY

	N-MINT
❑1, Apr 1991	2.00
❑2, Jun 1991	1.25
❑3, Aug 1991	1.25
❑4 1991	1.25
❑5 1991	1.25
❑6 1992	1.25
❑7 1992	1.25
❑8 1992	1.25

RICHIE RICH BILLIONS
HARVEY

	N-MINT
❑1, Oct 1974	12.00
❑2 1974	7.00
❑3 1975	6.00
❑4 1975	5.00
❑5 1975	5.00
❑6 1975	4.00
❑7 1975	4.00
❑8 1976	4.00
❑9 1976	4.00
❑10 1976	4.00
❑11 1976	3.00
❑12, Sep 1976	3.00
❑13 1976	3.00
❑14 1977	3.00
❑15 1977	3.00
❑16 1977	3.00
❑17 1977	3.00
❑18 1977	3.00
❑19, Oct 1977	3.00
❑20 1977	3.00
❑21 1978	3.00
❑22 1978	3.00
❑23, May 1978	3.00
❑24, Jul 1978	3.00
❑25, Sep 1978	3.00
❑26, Nov 1978	3.00
❑27 1979	3.00
❑28, Feb 1979	3.00
❑29, Apr 1979	3.00
❑30, Jun 1979	3.00
❑31 1979	2.00
❑32 1979	2.00
❑33 1980	2.00
❑34 1980	2.00
❑35 1980	2.00
❑36 1980	2.00
❑37 1980	2.00
❑38, Dec 1980	2.00
❑39, Feb 1981	2.00
❑40, Apr 1981	2.00
❑41 1981	2.00
❑42 1981	2.00
❑43 1981	2.00
❑44 1981	2.00
❑45 1982	2.00
❑46, May 1982	2.00
❑47 1982	2.00
❑48 1982	2.00

RICHIE RICH CASH
HARVEY

	N-MINT
❑1, Sep 1974	10.00
❑2, Nov 1974	6.00
❑3, Jan 1975	4.00
❑4, Mar 1975	4.00
❑5, May 1975	4.00
❑6, Jul 1975	4.00
❑7, Sep 1975	4.00
❑8, Nov 1975	4.00
❑9, Jan 1976	4.00
❑10, Mar 1976	4.00
❑11 1976	3.00
❑12 1976	3.00
❑13, Aug 1976	3.00
❑14, Oct 1976	3.00
❑15, Dec 1976	3.00
❑16, Feb 1977	3.00
❑17, Apr 1977	3.00
❑18, Jun 1977	3.00
❑19, Aug 1977	3.00
❑20 1977	3.00
❑21 1977	3.00
❑22, Mar 1978	3.00
❑23, May 1978	3.00
❑24, Jul 1978	3.00
❑25, Sep 1978	3.00
❑26, Dec 1978	3.00
❑27 1979	3.00
❑28 1979	3.00
❑29 1979	3.00
❑30 1979	3.00
❑31, Sep 1979	2.00
❑32 1979	2.00
❑33 1980	2.00
❑34 1980	2.00
❑35, Jun 1980	2.00
❑36, Sep 1980	2.00
❑37, Nov 1980	2.00
❑38, Jan 1981	2.00
❑39, Mar 1981	2.00
❑40, May 1981	2.00
❑41, Jul 1981	2.00
❑42, Sep 1981	2.00
❑43, Nov 1981	2.00
❑44 1982	2.00
❑45, Apr 1982	2.00
❑46, Jun 1982	2.00
❑47, Aug 1982	2.00

RICHIE RICH CASH MONEY
HARVEY

	N-MINT
❑1, ca. 1992	1.50
❑2, ca. 1992	1.50

Condition price index: Multiply "NM prices" above by: **0.83 for Very Fine/Near Mint**
0.66 for Very Fine • 0.33 for Fine • 0.2 for Very Good • 0.125 for Good

RICHIE RICH DIAMONDS
HARVEY

	N-MINT
❑1, Aug 1972	15.00
❑2, Oct 1972	9.00
❑3, Dec 1972	7.00
❑4, Feb 1973	7.00
❑5, Apr 1973	7.00
❑6, Jun 1973	5.00
❑7, Aug 1973	5.00
❑8, Oct 1973	5.00
❑9, Dec 1973	5.00
❑10, Feb 1974	5.00
❑11, Apr 1974	4.00
❑12, Jun 1974	4.00
❑13, Aug 1974	4.00
❑14, Oct 1974	4.00
❑15, Dec 1974	4.00
❑16, Feb 1975	4.00
❑17, Apr 1975	4.00
❑18, Jun 1975	4.00
❑19, Aug 1975	4.00
❑20, Oct 1975	4.00
❑21, Dec 1975	4.00
❑22, Feb 1976	4.00
❑23, Apr 1976	4.00
❑24, Jun 1976	4.00
❑25, Aug 1976	4.00
❑26, Oct 1976	4.00
❑27, Dec 1976	4.00
❑28, Feb 1977	4.00
❑29, Mar 1977	4.00
❑30, May 1977	4.00
❑31, Jul 1977	3.00
❑32, Sep 1977	3.00
❑33, Nov 1977	3.00
❑34, Jan 1978	3.00
❑35, Mar 1978	3.00
❑36, May 1978	3.00
❑37, Jul 1978	3.00
❑38, Sep 1978	3.00
❑39, Nov 1978	3.00
❑40, Jan 1979	3.00
❑41, Mar 1979	2.00
❑42, May 1979	2.00
❑43 1979	2.00
❑44 1979	2.00
❑45	2.00
❑46 1980	2.00
❑47 1980	2.00
❑48 1980	2.00
❑49 1980	2.00
❑50, Nov 1980	2.00
❑51 1981	2.00
❑52 1981	2.00
❑53 1981	2.00
❑54 1981	2.00
❑55, Nov 1981	2.00
❑56 1982	2.00
❑57 1982	2.00
❑58, Jun 1982	2.00
❑59, Aug 1982	2.00

RICHIE RICH DIGEST MAGAZINE
HARVEY

	N-MINT
❑1, Oct 1986	4.00
❑2, Nov 1986	3.00
❑3, Dec 1986	3.00
❑4, Jan 1987	3.00
❑5, Feb 1987	3.00
❑6, Mar 1987	3.00
❑7, Apr 1987	3.00
❑8	3.00
❑9	3.00
❑10	3.00
❑11	2.00
❑12	2.00
❑13	2.00
❑14	2.00
❑15	2.00
❑16	2.00
❑17	2.00
❑18	2.00
❑19	2.00
❑20, Apr 1990	2.00
❑21, Jun 1990	2.00
❑22, Aug 1990	2.00
❑23 1990	2.00
❑24 1990	2.00
❑25	2.00
❑26	2.00
❑27	2.00
❑28 1991	2.00
❑29, May 1991	2.00
❑30 1991	2.00
❑31	2.00
❑32	2.00
❑33, Feb 1992	2.00
❑34, Jun 1992	2.00
❑35, Sep 1992	2.00
❑36, Jan 1993	2.00
❑37, May 1993	2.00
❑38, Sep 1993	2.00
❑39	2.00
❑40	2.00
❑41, Jul 1994	2.00
❑42, Oct 1994	2.00

RICHIE RICH DIGEST STORIES
HARVEY

	N-MINT
❑1	10.00
❑2	5.00
❑3	5.00
❑4	5.00
❑5	5.00
❑6	5.00
❑7	5.00
❑8	5.00
❑9	5.00
❑10	5.00
❑11	3.00
❑12	3.00
❑13	3.00
❑14	3.00
❑15	3.00
❑16	3.00
❑17	3.00

RICHIE RICH DIGEST WINNERS
HARVEY

	N-MINT
❑1	10.00
❑2	5.00
❑3	5.00
❑4	5.00
❑5	5.00

RICHIE RICH DOLLARS & CENTS
HARVEY

	N-MINT
❑1, Aug 1963	200.00
❑2	80.00
❑3	60.00
❑4	60.00
❑5	60.00
❑6	24.00
❑7	24.00
❑8	24.00
❑9	24.00
❑10	24.00
❑11	16.00
❑12	16.00
❑13	16.00
❑14, Aug 1966	16.00
❑15, Oct 1966	16.00
❑16, Dec 1966	16.00
❑17, Feb 1967	16.00
❑18, Apr 1967	16.00
❑19, Jun 1967	16.00
❑20, Oct 1967	16.00
❑21, Dec 1967	10.00
❑22, Feb 1968	10.00
❑23, Apr 1968	10.00
❑24, Jun 1968	10.00
❑25, Aug 1968	10.00
❑26, Oct 1968	10.00
❑27, Dec 1968	10.00
❑28, Feb 1969	10.00

Richie Rich may have been wealthy, but he didn't flaunt his fortune; instead, he used it to help others.

	N-MINT
❑29, Apr 1969	10.00
❑30, May 1969	10.00
❑31, Jul 1969	8.00
❑32, Sep 1969	8.00
❑33, Nov 1969	8.00
❑34, Jan 1970	8.00
❑35, Mar 1970	8.00
❑36, May 1970	8.00
❑37, Jul 1970	8.00
❑38, Sep 1970	8.00
❑39, Nov 1970	8.00
❑40, Jan 1971	8.00
❑41, Mar 1971	6.00
❑42, May 1971	6.00
❑43, Jul 1971	6.00
❑44, Sep 1971	6.00
❑45, Nov 1971	6.00
❑46, Jan 1972	6.00
❑47, Mar 1972	6.00
❑48, May 1972	6.00
❑49, Jun 1972	6.00
❑50, Aug 1972	6.00
❑51, Oct 1972	4.00
❑52, Dec 1972	4.00
❑53, Feb 1973	4.00
❑54, Apr 1973	4.00
❑55, Jun 1973	4.00
❑56, Aug 1973	4.00
❑57, Oct 1973	4.00
❑58, Dec 1973	4.00
❑59, Feb 1974	4.00
❑60, Apr 1974	4.00
❑61, Jun 1974	2.50
❑62, Aug 1974	2.50
❑63, Oct 1974	2.50
❑64, Dec 1974	2.50
❑65, Feb 1975	2.50
❑66, Apr 1975	2.50
❑67, Jun 1975	2.50
❑68, Aug 1975	2.50
❑69, Oct 1975	2.50
❑70, Dec 1975	2.50
❑71, Feb 1976	2.00
❑72, Apr 1976	2.00
❑73, Jun 1976	2.00
❑74, Aug 1976	2.00
❑75, Sep 1976	2.00
❑76, Nov 1976	2.00
❑77, Jan 1977	2.00
❑78, Mar 1977	2.00
❑79, May 1977	2.00
❑80, Jul 1977	2.00
❑81, Sep 1977	2.00
❑82, Oct 1977	2.00
❑83, Dec 1977	2.00
❑84, Feb 1978	2.00
❑85, Apr 1978	2.00
❑86, Jun 1978	2.00
❑87, Aug 1978	2.00
❑88, Oct 1978	2.00
❑89	2.00
❑90 1979	2.00
❑91 1979	1.25
❑92 1979	1.25
❑93 1979	1.25
❑94 1979	1.25
❑95	1.25

Issue	N-MINT
☐96, Apr 1980	1.25
☐97 1980	1.25
☐98, Sep 1980	1.25
☐99, Nov 1980	1.25
☐100, Jan 1981	1.25
☐101, Mar 1981	1.25
☐102, May 1981	1.25
☐103 1981	1.25
☐104 1981	1.25
☐105 1981	1.25
☐106 1982	1.25
☐107, Apr 1982	1.25
☐108, Jun 1982	1.25
☐109, Aug 1982	1.25

RICHIE RICH FORTUNES
HARVEY

Issue	N-MINT
☐1, Sep 1971	25.00
☐2, Nov 1971	10.00
☐3, Jan 1972	7.00
☐4, Mar 1972	7.00
☐5, May 1972	7.00
☐6, Jul 1972	5.00
☐7, Sep 1972	5.00
☐8, Jan 1973	5.00
☐9, Mar 1973	5.00
☐10, May 1973	5.00
☐11, Jul 1973	4.00
☐12, Sep 1973	4.00
☐13, Nov 1973	4.00
☐14, Jan 1974	4.00
☐15, Mar 1974	4.00
☐16, May 1974	4.00
☐17, Jul 1974	4.00
☐18, Sep 1974	4.00
☐19, Nov 1974	4.00
☐20, Jan 1975	4.00
☐21, Mar 1975	3.00
☐22, May 1975	3.00
☐23, Jul 1975	3.00
☐24, Sep 1975	3.00
☐25, Nov 1975	3.00
☐26, Jan 1976	3.00
☐27, Mar 1976	3.00
☐28, May 1976	3.00
☐29, Jul 1976	3.00
☐30, Sep 1976	3.00
☐31, Nov 1976	3.00
☐32, Jan 1977	3.00
☐33, Mar 1977	3.00
☐34, May 1977	3.00
☐35, Jul 1977	3.00
☐36, Sep 1977	3.00
☐37, Nov 1977	3.00
☐38, Jan 1978	3.00
☐39, Mar 1978	3.00
☐40, May 1978	3.00
☐41, Jul 1978	2.00
☐42, Sep 1978	2.00
☐43, Dec 1978	2.00
☐44, Feb 1979	2.00
☐45, Apr 1979	2.00
☐46, Jun 1979	2.00
☐47, Aug 1979	2.00
☐48, Oct 1979	2.00
☐49, Dec 1979	2.00
☐50, Mar 1980	2.00
☐51, May 1980	2.00
☐52, Aug 1980	2.00
☐53, Oct 1980	2.00
☐54, Nov 1980	2.00
☐55, Mar 1981	2.00
☐56, May 1981	2.00
☐57, Jul 1981	2.00
☐58, Sep 1981	2.00
☐59, Nov 1981	2.00
☐60, Jan 1982	2.00
☐61, Mar 1982	2.00
☐62, Jun 1982	2.00
☐63, Aug 1982	2.00

RICHIE RICH GEMS
HARVEY

Issue	N-MINT
☐1, Sep 1974	10.00
☐2, Nov 1974	6.00
☐3, Jan 1975	4.00
☐4, Mar 1975	4.00
☐5, May 1975	4.00
☐6, Jul 1975	3.00
☐7, Sep 1975	3.00
☐8, Nov 1975	3.00
☐9, Jan 1976	3.00
☐10, Mar 1976	3.00
☐11, May 1976	2.00
☐12, Jul 1976	2.00
☐13, Sep 1976	2.00
☐14, Nov 1976	2.00
☐15, Jan 1977	2.00
☐16, Mar 1977	2.00
☐17, May 1977	2.00
☐18, Jul 1977	2.00
☐19, Sep 1977	2.00
☐20, Nov 1977	2.00
☐21, Jan 1978	2.00
☐22, Mar 1978	2.00
☐23 1978	2.00
☐24, Nov 1978	2.00
☐25, Jan 1979	2.00
☐26, Jul 1979	2.00
☐27, Sep 1979	2.00
☐28 1979	2.00
☐29, Feb 1980	2.00
☐30 1980	2.00
☐31, Jul 1980	2.00
☐32, Sep 1980	2.00
☐33, Nov 1980	2.00
☐34, Jan 1981	2.00
☐35, Mar 1981	2.00
☐36, May 1981	2.00
☐37, Aug 1981	2.00
☐38, Oct 1981	2.00
☐39, Dec 1981	2.00
☐40, Feb 1982	2.00
☐41, Apr 1982	2.00
☐42 1982	2.00
☐43, Sep 1982	2.00

RICHIE RICH GIANT SIZE
HARVEY

Issue	N-MINT
☐1	2.25
☐2	2.25
☐3	2.25
☐4	2.25

RICHIE RICH GOLD AND SILVER
HARVEY

Issue	N-MINT
☐1, Sep 1975	10.00
☐2 1975	6.00
☐3 1976	4.00
☐4 1976	4.00
☐5 1976	4.00
☐6 1976	3.00
☐7, Aug 1976	3.00
☐8, Oct 1976	3.00
☐9, Dec 1976	3.00
☐10, Feb 1977	3.00
☐11 1977	2.00
☐12 1977	2.00
☐13, Jul 1977	2.00
☐14, Sep 1977	2.00
☐15, Nov 1977	2.00
☐16, Jan 1978	2.00
☐17, Mar 1978	2.00
☐18, May 1978	2.00
☐19, Jul 1978	2.00
☐20, Sep 1978	2.00
☐21, Nov 1978	2.00
☐22, Jan 1979	2.00
☐23, Mar 1979	2.00
☐24, May 1979	2.00
☐25, Jul 1979	2.00
☐26, Sep 1979	2.00
☐27	2.00
☐28	2.00
☐29	2.00
☐30	2.00
☐31	2.00
☐32	2.00
☐33	2.00
☐34	2.00
☐35	2.00
☐36	2.00
☐37	2.00
☐38	2.00
☐39 1982	2.00
☐40, May 1982	2.00
☐41 1982	2.00
☐42, Oct 1982	2.00

RICHIE RICH GOLD NUGGETS DIGEST MAGAZINE
HARVEY

Issue	N-MINT
☐1	2.50
☐2	2.00
☐3, Apr 1991	2.00
☐4	2.00

RICHIE RICH HOLIDAY DIGEST
HARVEY

Issue	N-MINT
☐1	3.00
☐2	2.00
☐3	2.00
☐4	2.00
☐5	2.00

RICHIE RICH INVENTIONS
HARVEY

Issue	N-MINT
☐1, Oct 1977	10.00
☐2, May 1978	6.00
☐3	6.00
☐4	6.00
☐5	6.00
☐6	6.00
☐7	6.00
☐8	6.00
☐9	6.00
☐10	6.00
☐11	4.00
☐12	4.00
☐13	4.00
☐14	4.00
☐15	4.00
☐16	4.00
☐17	4.00
☐18, Apr 1981	4.00
☐19, Jun 1981	4.00
☐20, Aug 1981	3.00
☐21, Oct 1981	3.00
☐22, Feb 1981	3.00
☐23, Apr 1982	3.00
☐24, Jun 1982	3.00
☐25, Aug 1982	3.00
☐26, Oct 1982	3.00

RICHIE RICH JACKPOTS
HARVEY

Issue	N-MINT
☐1, Oct 1972	30.00
☐2, Dec 1972	12.00
☐3, Feb 1973	8.00
☐4, Apr 1973	8.00
☐5, Jun 1973	8.00
☐6, Aug 1973	6.00
☐7, Oct 1973	6.00
☐8, Dec 1973	6.00
☐9, Feb 1974	4.00
☐10, Apr 1974	4.00
☐11, Jun 1974	4.00
☐12, Aug 1974	4.00
☐13, Oct 1974	4.00
☐14, Dec 1974	4.00
☐15, Feb 1975	4.00
☐16, Apr 1975	4.00
☐17, Jun 1975	4.00
☐18, Aug 1975	4.00
☐19, Oct 1975	4.00
☐20, Dec 1975	4.00
☐21, Feb 1976	3.00
☐22, Apr 1976	3.00

	N-MINT
❑23, Jun 1976	3.00
❑24, Aug 1976	3.00
❑25, Oct 1976	3.00
❑26, Dec 1976	3.00
❑27, Feb 1977	3.00
❑28, Apr 1977	3.00
❑29, Jun 1977	3.00
❑30, Aug 1977	3.00
❑31, Oct 1977	3.00
❑32, Dec 1977	3.00
❑33, Feb 1978	3.00
❑34, Apr 1978	3.00
❑35, Jun 1978	3.00
❑36, Aug 1978	3.00
❑37, Oct 1978	3.00
❑38, Dec 1978	3.00
❑39, Feb 1979	3.00
❑40, Apr 1979	3.00
❑41, Jun 1979	2.00
❑42, Aug 1979	2.00
❑43, Oct 1979	2.00
❑44 1980	2.00
❑45, Apr 1980	2.00
❑46, Jun 1980	2.00
❑47, Aug 1980	2.00
❑48, Oct 1980	2.00
❑49, Dec 1980	2.00
❑50, Feb 1981	2.00
❑51, Apr 1981	2.00
❑52, Jun 1981	2.00
❑53, Aug 1981	2.00
❑54, Oct 1981	2.00
❑55 1982	2.00
❑56, Apr 1982	2.00
❑57, Jun 1982	2.00
❑58, Aug 1982	2.00

RICHIE RICH MILLION DOLLAR DIGEST
HARVEY

	N-MINT
❑1, Nov 1986	5.00
❑2, Jan 1987	3.00
❑3, Mar 1987	3.00
❑4, May 1987	3.00
❑5, Jul 1987	3.00
❑6, Sep 1987	3.00
❑7, Nov 1987	3.00
❑8 1988	3.00
❑9 1988	3.00
❑10 1988	3.00
❑11	2.00
❑12 1989	2.00
❑13, Aug 1989	2.00
❑14 1989	2.00
❑15	2.00
❑16 1990	2.00
❑17 1990	2.00
❑18 1990	2.00
❑19	2.00
❑20 1991	2.00
❑21 1991	2.00
❑22, Aug 1991	2.00
❑23	2.00
❑24 1992	2.00
❑25 1992	2.00
❑26, Jul 1992	2.00
❑27, Nov 1992	2.00
❑28, Mar 1993	2.00
❑29, Jul 1993	2.00
❑30, Nov 1993	2.00
❑31, Mar 1994	2.00
❑32, May 1994	2.00
❑33, Aug 1994	2.00
❑34, Nov 1994	2.00

RICHIE RICH MILLIONS
HARVEY

	N-MINT
❑1, Sep 1961	90.00
❑2, Sep 1962	50.00
❑3, Dec 1962	35.00
❑4, Mar 1963	28.00
❑5, Jun 1963	28.00
❑6, Sep 1963	20.00
❑7, Dec 1963	20.00
❑8, Mar 1964	16.00
❑9, Jun 1964	16.00
❑10, Sep 1964	16.00
❑11, Dec 1964	13.00
❑12, Mar 1965	13.00
❑13, Jun 1965	13.00
❑14, Sep 1965	13.00
❑15, Dec 1965	13.00
❑16, Mar 1966	13.00
❑17, May 1966	13.00
❑18, Jul 1966	13.00
❑19, Sep 1966	13.00
❑20, Oct 1966	13.00
❑21, Jan 1967	9.00
❑22, Mar 1967	9.00
❑23, Jun 1967	9.00
❑24, Aug 1967	9.00
❑25, Oct 1967	9.00
❑26, Dec 1967	9.00
❑27, Feb 1968	9.00
❑28, Apr 1968	9.00
❑29, Jun 1968	9.00
❑30, Aug 1968	9.00
❑31, Oct 1968	7.00
❑32, Dec 1968	7.00
❑33, Feb 1969	7.00
❑34, Apr 1969	7.00
❑35, May 1969	7.00
❑36, Jul 1969	7.00
❑37, Sep 1969	7.00
❑38, Nov 1969	7.00
❑39, Jan 1970	7.00
❑40, Mar 1970	7.00
❑41, May 1970	5.00
❑42, Jul 1970	5.00
❑43, Sep 1970	5.00
❑44, Nov 1970	5.00
❑45, Jan 1971	5.00
❑46, Mar 1971	5.00
❑47, May 1971	5.00
❑48, Jul 1971	5.00
❑49, Sep 1971	5.00
❑50, Nov 1971	5.00
❑51, Jan 1972	4.00
❑52, Mar 1972	4.00
❑53, May 1972	4.00
❑54, Jul 1972	4.00
❑55, Sep 1972	4.00
❑56, Nov 1972	4.00
❑57, Jan 1973	4.00
❑58, Mar 1973	4.00
❑59, May 1973	4.00
❑60, Jul 1973	4.00
❑61, Sep 1973	3.00
❑62, Nov 1973	3.00
❑63, Jan 1974	3.00
❑64, Mar 1974	3.00
❑65, May 1974	3.00
❑66, Jul 1974	3.00
❑67, Sep 1974	3.00
❑68, Nov 1974	3.00
❑69, Jan 1975	3.00
❑70, Mar 1975	3.00
❑71, May 1975	3.00
❑72, Jul 1975	3.00
❑73, Sep 1975	3.00
❑74, Nov 1975	3.00
❑75, Jan 1976	3.00
❑76, Mar 1976	3.00
❑77, May 1976	3.00
❑78, Jul 1976	3.00
❑79, Sep 1976	3.00
❑80, Nov 1976	3.00
❑81, Jan 1977	2.50
❑82, Mar 1977	2.50
❑83, May 1977	2.50
❑84, Jul 1977	2.50
❑85, Sep 1977	2.50
❑86, Nov 1977	2.50
❑87, Jan 1978	2.50

Many Richie Rich ancillary titles have monetary names.

© 1976 Harvey Comics

	N-MINT
❑88, Mar 1978	2.50
❑89, May 1978	2.50
❑90, Aug 1978	2.50
❑91, Oct 1978	2.00
❑92, Dec 1978	2.00
❑93, Feb 1979	2.00
❑94, Apr 1979	2.00
❑95, Jun 1979	2.00
❑96, Aug 1979	2.00
❑97, Oct 1979	2.00
❑98, Dec 1979	2.00
❑99, Mar 1980	2.00
❑100, May 1980	2.00
❑101, Aug 1980	1.50
❑102, Oct 1980	1.50
❑103, Dec 1981	1.50
❑104, Feb 1981	1.50
❑105, Apr 1981	1.50
❑106, Jun 1981	1.50
❑107, Aug 1981	1.50
❑108, Oct 1981	1.50
❑109 1981	1.50
❑110, Apr 1982	1.50
❑111, Jun 1982	1.00
❑112, Aug 1982	1.00
❑113, Oct 1982	1.00

RICHIE RICH MONEY WORLD
HARVEY

	N-MINT
❑1, Sep 1972	46.00
❑2, Nov 1972	18.00
❑3, Jan 1973	15.00
❑4, Mar 1973	10.00
❑5, May 1973	10.00
❑6, Jul 1973	8.00
❑7, Sep 1973	8.00
❑8, Nov 1973	8.00
❑9, Jan 1974	8.00
❑10, Mar 1974	8.00
❑11, May 1974	5.00
❑12, Jul 1974	5.00
❑13, Sep 1974	5.00
❑14, Nov 1974	5.00
❑15, Jan 1975	5.00
❑16, Mar 1975	5.00
❑17, May 1975	5.00
❑18, Jul 1975	5.00
❑19, Sep 1975	5.00
❑20, Nov 1975	5.00
❑21, Jan 1976	4.00
❑22, Mar 1976	4.00
❑23, May 1976	4.00
❑24, Jul 1976	4.00
❑25, Sep 1976	4.00
❑26, Nov 1976	4.00
❑27, Jan 1977	4.00
❑28, Mar 1977	4.00
❑29, May 1977	4.00
❑30, Jul 1977	4.00
❑31, Sep 1977	3.00
❑32, Nov 1977	3.00
❑33, Jan 1978	3.00
❑34, Mar 1978	3.00
❑35, May 1978	3.00
❑36, Aug 1978	3.00
❑37, Oct 1978	3.00
❑38, Jan 1979	3.00
❑39, Mar 1979	3.00

	N-MINT
❑40, Jun 1979	3.00
❑41, Aug 1979	3.00
❑42, Sep 1979	3.00
❑43, Nov 1979	3.00
❑44, Jan 1980	3.00
❑45, Apr 1980	3.00
❑46, Jun 1980	3.00
❑47, Sep 1980	3.00
❑48, Oct 1980	3.00
❑49, Dec 1980	3.00
❑50, Feb 1981	3.00
❑51, Apr 1981	3.00
❑52, Jun 1981	3.00
❑53, Aug 1981	3.00
❑54, Oct 1981	3.00
❑55, Mar 1982	3.00
❑56 1982	3.00
❑57 1982	3.00
❑58 1982	3.00
❑59, Sep 1982	3.00

RICHIE RICH MONEY WORLD DIGEST
HARVEY

	N-MINT
❑1, Apr 1991	2.00
❑2, Dec 1991	1.75
❑3, Apr 1992	1.75
❑4, Aug 1992	1.75
❑5, Dec 1992	1.75
❑6, Apr 1993	1.75
❑7, Aug 1993	1.75
❑8, Dec 1993	1.75

RICHIE RICH (MOVIE ADAPTATION)
MARVEL

	N-MINT
❑1, Feb 1995, color	2.95

RICHIE RICH PROFITS
HARVEY

	N-MINT
❑1, Oct 1974	25.00
❑2, Dec 1974	15.00
❑3, Feb 1975	15.00
❑4, Apr 1975	10.00
❑5, Jun 1975	10.00
❑6, Aug 1975	10.00
❑7, Oct 1975	10.00
❑8, Dec 1975	10.00
❑9, Feb 1976	10.00
❑10, Apr 1976	10.00
❑11, Jun 1976	8.00
❑12, Aug 1976	8.00
❑13, Oct 1976	8.00
❑14, Dec 1976	8.00
❑15, Feb 1977	8.00
❑16, Apr 1977	8.00
❑17, Jun 1977	8.00
❑18, Aug 1977	8.00
❑19, Oct 1977	8.00
❑20, Dec 1977	6.00
❑21, Feb 1978	6.00
❑22, Apr 1978	6.00
❑23, Jun 1978	6.00
❑24 1978	6.00
❑25 1978	6.00
❑26, Jan 1979	6.00
❑27 1979	6.00
❑28 1979	6.00
❑29 1979	6.00
❑30 1979	5.00
❑31, Oct 1979	5.00
❑32, Dec 1979	5.00
❑33, Feb 1980	5.00
❑34, Apr 1980	5.00
❑35, Jul 1980	5.00
❑36, Sep 1980	5.00
❑37, Nov 1980	5.00
❑38, Jan 1981	5.00
❑39, Mar 1981	5.00
❑40, May 1981	4.00
❑41, Jul 1981	4.00
❑42, Sep 1981	4.00
❑43, Nov 1981	4.00
❑44, Feb 1982	4.00
❑45, Apr 1982	4.00
❑46, Jun 1982	4.00
❑47, Sep 1982	4.00

RICHIE RICH RELICS
HARVEY

	N-MINT
❑1, Jan 1988	2.50
❑2, May 1988	2.50
❑3, Sep 1988	2.50
❑4, Jan 1989	2.50

RICHIE RICH RICHES
HARVEY

	N-MINT
❑1, Jul 1972	28.00
❑2, Sep 1972	13.00
❑3, Nov 1972	8.00
❑4, Jan 1973	8.00
❑5, Mar 1973	8.00
❑6, May 1973	5.00
❑7, Jul 1973	5.00
❑8, Sep 1973	5.00
❑9, Nov 1973	5.00
❑10, Jan 1974	5.00
❑11, Mar 1974	4.00
❑12, May 1974	4.00
❑13, Jul 1974	4.00
❑14, Sep 1974	4.00
❑15, Nov 1974	4.00
❑16, Jan 1975	4.00
❑17, Mar 1975	4.00
❑18, May 1975	4.00
❑19, Jul 1975	4.00
❑20, Sep 1975	4.00
❑21, Nov 1975	3.00
❑22, Jan 1976	3.00
❑23, Mar 1976	3.00
❑24, May 1976	3.00
❑25, Jul 1976	3.00
❑26, Sep 1976	3.00
❑27, Nov 1976	3.00
❑28, Jan 1977	3.00
❑29, Mar 1977	3.00
❑30, May 1977	3.00
❑31, Jul 1977	2.00
❑32, Sep 1977	2.00
❑33, Nov 1977	2.00
❑34, Jan 1978	2.00
❑35, Mar 1978	2.00
❑36, May 1978	2.00
❑37, Jul 1978	2.00
❑38, Oct 1978	2.00
❑39, Dec 1978	2.00
❑40, Feb 1979	2.00
❑41, Apr 1979	2.00
❑42, Jun 1979	2.00
❑43, Aug 1979	2.00
❑44, Oct 1979	2.00
❑45, Dec 1979	2.00
❑46, Feb 1980	2.00
❑47, May 1980	2.00
❑48, Aug 1980	2.00
❑49, Oct 1980	2.00
❑50, Dec 1980	2.00
❑51, Feb 1981	2.00
❑52, Apr 1981	2.00
❑53, Jun 1981	2.00
❑54, Aug 1981	2.00
❑55 1981	2.00
❑56 1981	2.00

RICHIE RICH SUCCESS STORIES
HARVEY

	N-MINT
❑1, Nov 1964	240.00
❑2, Feb 1965	75.00
❑3, May 1965	50.00
❑4, Aug 1965	40.00
❑5, Nov 1965	40.00
❑6, Feb 1966	30.00
❑7, May 1966	30.00
❑8, Jul 1966	30.00
❑9, Aug 1966	30.00
❑10, Oct 1966	30.00
❑11, Dec 1966	18.00
❑12, Feb 1967	18.00
❑13, Apr 1967	18.00
❑14, Jun 1967	18.00
❑15, Aug 1967	18.00
❑16, Nov 1967	18.00
❑17, Jan 1968	18.00
❑18, Mar 1968	18.00
❑19, May 1968	18.00
❑20, Jul 1968	18.00
❑21, Sep 1968	14.00
❑22, Nov 1968	14.00
❑23, Jan 1969	14.00
❑24, Mar 1969	14.00
❑25, Apr 1969	14.00
❑26, Jun 1969	12.00
❑27, Aug 1969	12.00
❑28, Oct 1969	12.00
❑29, Dec 1969	12.00
❑30, Feb 1970	12.00
❑31, Apr 1970	8.00
❑32, Jun 1970	8.00
❑33, Aug 1970	8.00
❑34, Oct 1970	8.00
❑35, Dec 1970	8.00
❑36, Feb 1971	8.00
❑37, Apr 1971	8.00
❑38, Jun 1971	8.00
❑39, Aug 1971	8.00
❑40, Oct 1971	8.00
❑41, Dec 1971	5.00
❑42, Feb 1972	5.00
❑43, Apr 1972	5.00
❑44, Jun 1972	5.00
❑45, Aug 1972	5.00
❑46, Oct 1972	5.00
❑47, Dec 1972	5.00
❑48, Feb 1973	5.00
❑49, Apr 1973	5.00
❑50, Jun 1973	5.00
❑51, Aug 1973	5.00
❑52, Oct 1973	5.00
❑53, Dec 1973	5.00
❑54, Feb 1974	5.00
❑55, Apr 1974	5.00
❑56, Jun 1974	5.00
❑57, Aug 1974	5.00
❑58, Oct 1974	5.00
❑59, Dec 1974	5.00
❑60, Feb 1975	5.00
❑61, Apr 1975	5.00
❑62, Jun 1975	5.00
❑63, Aug 1975	5.00
❑64, Oct 1975	5.00
❑65, Dec 1975	5.00
❑66, Feb 1976	5.00
❑67, Apr 1976	5.00
❑68, Jun 1976	5.00
❑69, Aug 1976	5.00
❑70, Oct 1976	5.00
❑71, Dec 1976	3.00
❑72, Feb 1977	3.00
❑73, Mar 1977	3.00
❑74, May 1977	3.00
❑75, Jul 1977	3.00
❑76, Sep 1977	3.00
❑77, Oct 1977	3.00
❑78, Dec 1977	3.00
❑79, Feb 1978	3.00
❑80, Apr 1978	3.00
❑81, Jun 1978	3.00
❑82, Aug 1978	3.00
❑83, Oct 1978	3.00
❑84, Dec 1978	3.00
❑85, Jan 1979	3.00
❑86, Mar 1979	3.00
❑87, May 1979	3.00
❑88, Jul 1979	3.00
❑89, Sep 1979	3.00
❑90, Nov 1979	3.00
❑91, Jan 1980	3.00
❑92, Apr 1980	3.00
❑93, Jun 1980	3.00
❑94, Sep 1980	3.00

	N-MINT
❑95, Nov 1980	3.00
❑96, Jan 1981	3.00
❑97, Mar 1981	3.00
❑98, May 1981	3.00
❑99, Jul 1981	3.00
❑100, Sep 1981	3.00
❑101, Dec 1981	2.00
❑102, Feb 1982	2.00
❑103, May 1982	2.00
❑104, Jul 1982	2.00
❑105, Sep 1982	2.00

RICHIE RICH VACATION DIGEST
HARVEY

	N-MINT
❑1992, Oct 1992; #1 on cover	1.75
❑1993, Oct 1993; #1 on cover	1.75

RICHIE RICH VACATIONS DIGEST
HARVEY

	N-MINT
❑1, Oct 1980	10.00
❑2, Dec 1980	5.00
❑3, Feb 1981	5.00
❑4, Apr 1981	5.00
❑5, Jun 1981	5.00
❑6, Aug 1981	5.00
❑7, Oct 1981	5.00
❑8, Dec 1981	5.00

RICHIE RICH VAULTS OF MYSTERY
HARVEY

	N-MINT
❑1, Nov 1974	10.00
❑2, Jan 1975	7.00
❑3, Mar 1975	5.00
❑4, May 1975	5.00
❑5, Jul 1975	5.00
❑6, Sep 1975	4.00
❑7, Nov 1975	4.00
❑8, Jan 1976	4.00
❑9, Mar 1976	4.00
❑10, May 1976	4.00
❑11, Jul 1976	3.00
❑12, Sep 1976	3.00
❑13, Nov 1976	3.00
❑14, Jan 1977	3.00
❑15, Mar 1977	3.00
❑16, May 1977	3.00
❑17, Jul 1977	3.00
❑18, Sep 1977	3.00
❑19, Nov 1977	3.00
❑20, Jan 1978	3.00
❑21, Mar 1978	2.00
❑22, May 1978	2.00
❑23, Jul 1978	2.00
❑24, Sep 1978	2.00
❑25, Nov 1978	2.00
❑26, Jan 1979	2.00
❑27, Mar 1979	2.00
❑28, May 1979	2.00
❑29, Jul 1979	2.00
❑30, Sep 1979	2.00
❑31, Nov 1979	2.00
❑32, Jan 1980	2.00
❑33, Apr 1980	2.00
❑34, Jun 1980	2.00
❑35, Aug 1980	2.00
❑36, Oct 1980	2.00
❑37, Dec 1980	2.00
❑38, Feb 1981	2.00
❑39, Apr 1981	2.00
❑40, Jun 1981	2.00
❑41 1981	2.00
❑42 1981	2.00
❑43 1981	2.00
❑44 1982	2.00
❑45 1982	2.00
❑46 1982	2.00
❑47, Sep 1982	2.00

RICHIE RICH ZILLIONZ
HARVEY

	N-MINT
❑1, Oct 1976	12.00
❑2 1979	6.00
❑3 1977	4.00
❑4 1977	4.00
❑5, Aug 1977	4.00
❑6, Oct 1977	3.00
❑7, Dec 1977	3.00
❑8, Feb 1978	3.00
❑9, Apr 1978	3.00
❑10, Jul 1978	3.00
❑11, Sep 1978	2.00
❑12, Nov 1978	2.00
❑13, Jan 1979	2.00
❑14, Mar 1979	2.00
❑15, May 1979	2.00
❑16, Jul 1979	2.00
❑17, Sep 1979	2.00
❑18, Nov 1979	2.00
❑19, Jan 1980	2.00
❑20, Mar 1980	2.00
❑21, May 1980	2.00
❑22 1980	2.00
❑23, Oct 1980	2.00
❑24 1980	2.00
❑25 1981	2.00
❑26 1981	2.00
❑27 1981	2.00
❑28 1981	2.00
❑29 1981	2.00
❑30 1982	2.00
❑31 1982	2.00
❑32 1982	2.00
❑33, Sep 1982	2.00

RIDE
IMAGE

	N-MINT
❑1, Aug 2004	2.95

RIFLEMAN, THE
DELL

	N-MINT
❑2, Jan 1960	85.00
❑3, Apr 1960	85.00
❑4, Jul 1960	70.00
❑5, Oct 1960	70.00
❑6, Jan 1961	70.00
❑7, Jun 1961	70.00
❑8, Sep 1961	70.00
❑9, Dec 1961	70.00
❑10, Jan 1962	70.00
❑11, Apr 1962	55.00
❑12, Jul 1962	55.00
❑13, Nov 1962	55.00
❑14, Feb 1963	55.00
❑15, May 1963	55.00
❑16, Aug 1963	55.00
❑17, Nov 1963	55.00
❑18, Apr 1964	55.00
❑19, Jul 1964	55.00
❑20, Oct 1964	55.00

RIMA, THE JUNGLE GIRL
DC

	N-MINT
❑1, May 1974 O: Rima, the Jungle Girl.	9.00
❑2, Jul 1974 JKu (c); NR, JKu, AN (a); O: Rima, the Jungle Girl.	7.00
❑3, Sep 1974 JKu (c); NR, JKu, AN (a); O: Rima, the Jungle Girl.	7.00
❑4, Nov 1974 O: Rima, the Jungle Girl.	7.00
❑5, Jan 1975	7.00
❑6, Mar 1975	7.00
❑7, May 1975	7.00

RIME OF THE ANCIENT MARINER, THE (TOME)
TOME

	N-MINT
❑1, b&w	3.95

RIMSHOT
RIP OFF

	N-MINT
❑1, Jun 1990, b&w	2.00
❑2, Feb 1991, b&w	2.00
❑3, Jul 1991, b&w	2.50

RING OF ROSES
DARK HORSE

	N-MINT
❑1, b&w	2.50
❑2, b&w	2.50
❑3, b&w	2.50
❑4, b&w	2.50

There are almost as many Richie Rich titles as there are dollars in the Rich vaults.

© 1976 Harvey Comics

RING OF THE NIBELUNG, THE
DC

	N-MINT
❑1, ca. 1989	4.95
❑2	4.95
❑3	4.95
❑4	4.95

RING OF THE NIBELUNG, THE (DARK HORSE)
DARK HORSE

	N-MINT
❑1, Feb 2000	2.95
❑2, Mar 2000	2.95
❑3, Apr 2000	2.95
❑4, May 2000	2.95

RING OF THE NIBELUNG, THE (VOL. 2)
DARK HORSE

	N-MINT
❑1, Aug 2000	2.95
❑2, Sep 2000	2.95
❑3, Oct 2000	2.99

RING OF THE NIBELUNG, THE (VOL. 3)
DARK HORSE

	N-MINT
❑1, Dec 2000	2.99
❑2, Jan 2001	2.99
❑3, Feb 2001	2.99

RING OF THE NIBELUNG, THE (VOL. 4)
DARK HORSE

	N-MINT
❑1, Jun 2001	2.99
❑2, Jul 2001	2.99
❑3, Aug 2001	2.99
❑4, Sep 2001	2.99

RINGO KID, THE
MARVEL

	N-MINT
❑1, Jan 1970; SL (w); AW (a); Reprint from Ringo Kid Western	12.00
❑2, Mar 1970 JSe (a)	8.00
❑3, May 1970	5.00
❑4, Jul 1970	5.00
❑5, Sep 1970	5.00
❑6, Nov 1970	5.00
❑7, Jan 1971	5.00
❑8, Mar 1971	5.00
❑9, May 1971	5.00
❑10, Jul 1971	5.00
❑11, Sep 1971	4.00
❑12, Nov 1971	4.00
❑13, Jan 1972	4.00
❑14, Mar 1972	4.00
❑15, May 1972	4.00
❑16, Jul 1972	4.00
❑17, Sep 1972	4.00
❑18, Nov 1972	4.00
❑19, Jan 1973	4.00
❑20, Mar 1973	4.00
❑21, May 1973	4.00
❑22, Jul 1973	4.00
❑23, Sep 1973	4.00
❑24, Nov 1973	4.00
❑25, Nov 1975	4.00
❑26, Jan 1976	4.00
❑27, Mar 1976	4.00
❑27/30 cent, Mar 1976; 30 cent regional price variant	20.00
❑28, May 1976	4.00

N-MINT

❑28/30 cent, May 1976; 30 cent regional price variant 20.00
❑29, Jul 1976 ..... 4.00
❑30, Sep 1976 ..... 4.00

RIN TIN TIN & RUSTY
GOLD KEY

❑1, Nov 1963 ..... 50.00

RIO AT BAY
DARK HORSE

❑1, Aug 1992 ..... 2.95
❑2, Aug 1992 ..... 2.95

RIO CONCHOS
GOLD KEY

❑1; Adapts film 22.00

RIO GRAPHIC NOVEL
COMICO

❑1, May 1987 ..... 8.95

RIO KID
ETERNITY

❑1, b&w 2.50
❑2, b&w 2.50
❑3, b&w 2.50

RION 2990
RION

❑1, b&w 1.50
❑2, b&w 1.50
❑3 ..... 1.50
❑4 ..... 1.50

RIOT, ACT 1
VIZ

❑1, Oct 1995 ..... 2.75
❑2, Nov 1995 ..... 2.75
❑3, Dec 1995 ..... 2.75
❑4, Jan 1996 ..... 2.95
❑5, Feb 1996 ..... 2.95
❑6, Mar 1996 ..... 2.95

RIOT, ACT 2
VIZ

❑1, Apr 1996 ..... 2.95
❑2, May 1996 ..... 2.95
❑3, Jun 1996 ..... 2.95
❑4, Jul 1996 ..... 2.95
❑5, Aug 1996 ..... 2.95
❑6, Sep 1996 ..... 2.95
❑7, Oct 1996 ..... 2.95

RIOT GEAR
TRIUMPHANT

❑1, Sep 1993 ..... 2.50
❑1/Ashcan, Sep 1993; Ashcan edition (color) 2.50
❑2, Oct 1993 ..... 2.50
❑3, Nov 1993 ..... 2.50
❑4, Dec 1993; Unleashed! 2.50
❑5, Jan 1994 ..... 2.50
❑6, Feb 1994 ..... 2.50
❑7, Mar 1994 ..... 2.50
❑8, Apr 1994 ..... 2.50
❑9, May 1994 ..... 2.50
❑10, Jun 1994 ..... 2.50
❑11, Jul 1994; Final issue? 2.50
❑Ashcan 1, color; ashcan 2.50

RIOT GEAR: VIOLENT PAST
TRIUMPHANT

❑1, Feb 1994 ..... 2.50
❑2, Feb 1994; 14,000 printed 2.50

RIPCLAW (VOL. 1)
IMAGE

❑0.5; Wizard promotional edition 2.00
❑0.5/Gold; Gold edition 2.50
❑1, Apr 1995 ..... 2.50
❑2, Jun 1995 ..... 2.50
❑3, Jul 1995 ..... 2.50
❑4, Aug 1995 ..... 2.50

RIPCLAW (VOL. 2)
IMAGE

❑1, Dec 1995 ..... 2.50
❑2, Jan 1996 ..... 2.50
❑3, Feb 1996 ..... 2.50
❑4, Mar 1996 ..... 2.50

N-MINT

❑5, Apr 1996 ..... 2.50
❑6, Jun 1996 ..... 2.50
❑Special 1, Oct 1995; Special Edition #1 ..... 2.50

R.I.P. COMICS MODULE
TSR

❑1 ..... 2.95
❑2 ..... 2.95
❑3 ..... 2.95
❑4 ..... 2.95
❑5; Brasher 2.95
❑6; Brasher 2.95
❑7; Brasher 2.95
❑8; Brasher 2.95

R.I.P.D.
DARK HORSE

❑1, Oct 1999 ..... 2.95
❑2, Nov 1999 ..... 2.95
❑3, Dec 1999 ..... 2.95
❑4, Jan 2000 ..... 2.95

RIPFIRE
MALIBU

❑0, Jan 1995 ..... 2.50

RIP HUNTER...TIME MASTER
DC

❑1, Mar 1961 ..... 350.00
❑2, May 1961 ..... 140.00
❑3, Jul 1961 ..... 115.00
❑4, Sep 1961 ..... 95.00
❑5, Nov 1961 ..... 95.00
❑6, Jan 1962 ATh (a) 85.00
❑7, Mar 1962 ATh (a) 85.00
❑8, May 1962 ..... 70.00
❑9, Jul 1962 ..... 70.00
❑10, Sep 1962 ..... 70.00
❑11, Nov 1962 ..... 70.00
❑12, Jan 1963 ..... 70.00
❑13, Mar 1963 ..... 70.00
❑14, May 1963 ..... 70.00
❑15, Jul 1963 ..... 70.00
❑16, Sep 1963 ..... 58.00
❑17, Nov 1963 ..... 58.00
❑18, Jan 1964 ..... 58.00
❑19, Mar 1964 ..... 58.00
❑20, May 1964 ..... 58.00
❑21, Jul 1964 ..... 48.00
❑22, Sep 1964 ..... 48.00
❑23, Nov 1964 ..... 48.00
❑24, Jan 1965 ..... 48.00
❑25, Mar 1965 ..... 48.00
❑26, May 1965 ..... 40.00
❑27, Jul 1965 ..... 40.00
❑28, Sep 1965 ..... 40.00
❑29, Nov 1965 ..... 40.00

RIP IN TIME
FANTAGOR

❑1, b&w 2.00
❑2, b&w 2.00
❑3, b&w 2.00
❑4, b&w 2.00
❑5, b&w 2.00

RIPLEY'S BELIEVE IT OR NOT! (DARK HORSE)
DARK HORSE

❑1, May 2002 ..... 2.99
❑2, Oct 2002 ..... 2.99
❑3 2003 ..... 2.99
❑4 2003 ..... 2.99

RIPLEY'S BELIEVE IT OR NOT!: BEAUTY & GROOMING
SCHANES

❑1 ..... 2.50

RIPLEY'S BELIEVE IT OR NOT!: CHILD PRODIGIES
SCHANES

❑1 ..... 2.50

N-MINT

RIPLEY'S BELIEVE IT OR NOT!: CRUELTY
SCHANES PRODUCTS

❑1, Jun 1993, b&w; says Crime & Murder on cover; reprints newspaper cartoons 2.50
❑2, Jun 1993, b&w; says Crime & Murder on cover; reprints newspaper cartoons 2.50

RIPLEY'S BELIEVE IT OR NOT!: FAIRY TALES & LITERATURE
SCHANES

❑1 ..... 2.50

RIPLEY'S BELIEVE IT OR NOT!: FEATS OF WONDER
SCHANES

❑1 ..... 2.50

RIPLEY'S BELIEVE IT OR NOT!: SPORTS FEATS
SCHANES PRODUCTS

❑1, Jun 1993, b&w; reprints newspaper cartoons 2.50

RIPLEY'S BELIEVE IT OR NOT!: STRANGE DEATHS
SCHANES PRODUCTS

❑1, Jun 1993, b&w; reprints newspaper cartoons 2.50

RIPLEY'S BELIEVE IT OR NOT TRUE WAR STORIES
GOLD KEY

❑1, ca. 1966; #3 in overall series; Continued in Ripley's Believe It or Not #4 ..... 24.00

RIP OFF COMIX
RIP OFF

❑1 ..... 25.00
❑2 ..... 16.00
❑3 ..... 12.00
❑4, Nov 1978 ..... 8.00
❑5, Sep 1979 ..... 6.00
❑6, Mar 1980 ..... 6.00
❑6-2, Jan 1980; 2nd printing (1980) 2.50
❑7, Nov 1980 ..... 6.00
❑8, May 1981; 1981 ..... 5.00
❑9, Sep 1981; 1981 ..... 5.00
❑10, Mar 1982 ..... 5.00
❑11, Oct 1982 ..... 4.00
❑12, Apr 1983 ..... 4.00
❑13 ..... 4.00
❑14, Apr 1987 ..... 4.00
❑15, Jul 1987 ..... 4.00
❑16, Oct 1987 ..... 4.00
❑17, Jan 1988 ..... 4.00
❑18, Apr 1988 ..... 4.00
❑19, Jul 1988 ..... 4.00
❑20, Oct 1988 ..... 4.00
❑21, Jan 1989; 20th Anniversary 4.00
❑22, Apr 1989 ..... 4.00
❑23, Jul 1989 ..... 4.00
❑24, Oct 1989; San Diego Con 3.25
❑25, Jan 1990 ..... 3.25
❑26, Apr 1990 ..... 3.25
❑27, Jul 1990 ..... 3.95
❑28, Oct 1990 ..... 3.50
❑29, Jan 1991 ..... 3.50
❑30, Apr 1991 ..... 3.50
❑31, Mar 1992 ..... 3.50

RIPPER
AIRCEL

❑1 ..... 2.50
❑2 ..... 2.50
❑3 ..... 2.50
❑4 ..... 2.50
❑5 ..... 2.50
❑6 ..... 2.50

RIPPER LEGACY, THE
CALIBER

❑1 ..... 2.95
❑2 ..... 2.95
❑3 ..... 2.95

N-MINT

RIPTIDE
Image

❑1, Sep 1995 .... 2.50
❑2, Oct 1995 .... 2.50

RISE OF APOCALYPSE
Marvel

❑1, Oct 1996; wraparound cover 1.95
❑2, Nov 1996; wraparound cover 1.95
❑3, Dec 1996; wraparound cover 1.95
❑4, Jan 1997; wraparound cover 1.95

RISING STARS
Image

❑0, Apr 2000; Wizard promotional edition 5.00
❑0/Gold 1999; Gold logo variant from Wizard promotion 12.00
❑0.5, Jul 2001 .... 2.95
❑1, Aug 1999; Standard edition; Team standing over coffin 3.50
❑1/A, Aug 1999; Holofoil edition 8.00
❑1/B, Aug 1999; chromium cover 10.00
❑1/C, Aug 1999; Gold "Monster Edition"; Team with burning figure kneeling in foreground 6.00
❑1/D, Aug 1999; Gold "Monster Edition"; Children running to house 6.00
❑1/E, Aug 1999; Gold "Monster Edition"; Battle scene with blonde woman in foreground 6.00
❑1/F, Aug 1999; Gold "Monster Edition"; Team standing over coffin 6.00
❑1/G, Aug 1999; Another Universe/Wizard World variant (boy standing in foreground looking at large glowing sphere, Wizard World/AU markings) 3.50
❑1/H, Aug 1999; No "Monster Edition" logo; Battle scene with blonde woman in foreground 3.50
❑2, Oct 1999 .... 3.00
❑2/A, Dec 1999; Dynamic Forces variant cover 4.00
❑2/B, Dec 1999; Dynamic Forces gold variant cover (Dynamic Forces seal on cover) 7.00
❑3, Dec 1999 .... 3.00
❑4 2000 .... 3.00
❑5, Mar 2000 .... 2.50
❑6, Apr 2000 .... 2.50
❑7, May 2000 .... 2.50
❑8 2000 .... 2.50
❑9, Aug 2000 .... 2.50
❑10, Oct 2000 .... 2.50
❑11, Nov 2000 .... 2.50
❑12, Jan 2001 .... 2.50
❑13, Mar 2001 .... 2.50
❑14, May 2001 .... 2.50
❑15, Jun 2001; BA (a); Flip-book with Universe preview 2.50
❑16, Jul 2001 BA (a) 2.50
❑17, Jan 2002 BA (a) 2.50
❑18, Jan 2002 .... 2.50
❑19, Sep 2002 BA (a) 2.50
❑20, Oct 2002 BA (a) 2.99
❑21, Jan 2003 .... 2.99
❑Ashcan 1, Oct 2000; Convention Exclusive preview 6.00
❑Ashcan 1/A, Mar 1999; Prelude edition 2.95

RISING STARS: BRIGHT
Image

❑1, Feb 2003 .... 2.99
❑2, Mar 2003 .... 2.99
❑3, Apr 2003 .... 2.99

RISING STARS: VISITATIONS
Image

❑1 .... 8.99

RIVERDALE HIGH
Archie

❑1, Aug 1990 .... 1.50
❑2, Oct 1990 .... 1.00
❑3, Dec 1990 .... 1.00
❑4, Feb 1990 .... 1.00
❑5, Apr 1990 .... 1.00

N-MINT

RIVETS & RUBY
Radio

❑1, Feb 1998 .... 2.95
❑2, Apr 1998 .... 2.95
❑3, Jul 1998 .... 2.95
❑4 .... 2.95

RIVIT
Blackthorne

❑1 .... 1.75

ROACH KILLER
NBM

❑1 .... 11.95

ROACHMILL (BLACKTHORNE)
Blackthorne

❑1, Dec 1986 .... 2.00
❑2, Feb 1987 .... 2.00
❑3, Apr 1987 .... 2.00
❑4, Jun 1987 .... 2.00
❑5, Sep 1987 .... 2.00
❑6, Oct 1987 .... 2.00

ROACHMILL (DARK HORSE)
Dark Horse

❑1, May 1988 .... 2.00
❑2, Jun 1988 .... 1.75
❑3, Sep 1988 .... 1.75
❑4, Nov 1988 .... 1.75
❑5, Apr 1989 .... 1.75
❑6, Jun 1989 .... 1.75
❑7, Oct 1989 .... 1.75
❑8, Jan 1990; indicia says Jan 89; a misprint 1.75
❑9, Apr 1990 .... 1.95
❑10, Dec 1990; trading cards 1.95

ROADKILL
Lighthouse

❑1, b&w 2.00
❑2, b&w 2.00

ROADKILL: A CHRONICLE OF THE DEADWORLD
Caliber

❑1; text 2.95

ROAD TRIP
Oni

❑1, Aug 2000, b&w; collects story from Oni Double Feature #9 and #10 .... 2.95

ROADWAYS
Cult

❑1, May 1994, b&w 2.75
❑2, Jun 1994, b&w 2.75
❑3 .... 2.75
❑4 .... 2.75

ROARIN' RICK'S RARE BIT FIENDS
King Hell

❑1, Jul 1994; Dave Sim 2.95
❑2, Aug 1994; Neil Gaiman 2.95
❑3, Sep 1994; Neil Gaiman 2.95
❑4, Oct 1994 .... 2.95
❑5, Nov 1994 .... 2.95
❑6, Dec 1994 .... 2.95
❑7, Jan 1995 .... 2.95
❑8, Feb 1995 .... 2.95
❑9, Mar 1995 .... 2.95
❑10, Apr 1995 .... 2.95
❑11, May 1995 .... 2.95
❑12, Jun 1995 .... 2.95
❑13, Aug 1995 .... 2.95
❑14, Sep 1995 .... 2.95
❑15, Nov 1995 .... 2.95
❑16, Dec 1995 .... 2.95
❑17, Jan 1996 .... 2.95
❑18, Mar 1996 .... 2.95
❑19, ca. 1996 .... 2.95
❑20, ca. 1996 .... 2.95
❑21, ca. 1996; Subtleman 2.95

ROBBIN' $3000
Parody

❑1, b&w 2.50

While Harvey was best-known for its Richie Rich comics, Marvel published the adaptation of the feature film starring Macauley Culkin.

© 1995 Marvel and Harvey Comics.

N-MINT

ROB HANES
WCG

❑1, Jan 1991, b&w 2.50

ROB HANES ADVENTURES
WCG

❑1, Oct 2000 .... 2.50

ROBIN (MINI-SERIES)
DC

❑1, Jan 1991; 1: King Snake. poster 3.00
❑1-2, Jan 1991; 1: King Snake. (no poster); (no poster) 1.50
❑1-3; 1: King Snake. (no poster); (no poster) 1.50
❑2, Feb 1991 .... 2.50
❑2-2, Feb 1991 .... 1.50
❑3, Mar 1991 .... 2.00
❑4, Apr 1991 V: Lady Shiva. 2.00
❑5, May 1991 V: King Shark. 2.00
❑Annual 1, ca. 1992; Eclipso 2.50
❑Annual 2, ca. 1993 1: Razorsharp. 2.50

ROBIN
DC

❑0, Oct 1994 O: Robin I (Dick Grayson). O: Robin III (Timothy Drake). O: Robin II (Jason Todd). 2.00
❑1, Nov 1993 1: Shotgun Smith. 4.00
❑1/Variant, Nov 1993; Embossed cover 3.50
❑2, Jan 1994 .... 2.00
❑3, Feb 1994 .... 2.00
❑4, Mar 1994 A: Spoiler. 2.00
❑5, Apr 1994 .... 2.00
❑6, May 1994 A: Huntress. 2.00
❑7, Jun 1994 .... 2.00
❑8, Jul 1994 .... 2.00
❑9, Aug 1994 .... 2.00
❑10, Sep 1994; Zero Hour; Tim Drake Robin teams with Dick Grayson Robin 2.00
❑11, Nov 1994 .... 1.75
❑12, Dec 1994 .... 1.75
❑13, Jan 1995 .... 1.75
❑14, Feb 1995 .... 1.75
❑14/Variant, Feb 1995; enhanced cardstock cover 2.50
❑15, Mar 1995 .... 1.75
❑16, Apr 1995 .... 1.75
❑17, Jun 1995 .... 2.00
❑18, Jul 1995 .... 2.00
❑19, Aug 1995 V: Ulysses. 2.00
❑20, Sep 1995 V: Ulysses. 2.00
❑21, Oct 1995; Ninja camp 2.00
❑22, Nov 1995; Ninja camp 2.00
❑23, Dec 1995; V: Killer Moth a.k.a. Charaxes. Underworld Unleashed 2.00
❑24, Jan 1996; V: Killer Moth a.k.a. Charaxes. Underworld Unleashed 2.00
❑25, Feb 1996; anti-guns issue 2.00
❑26, Mar 1996 .... 2.00
❑27, Mar 1996 .... 2.00
❑28, Apr 1996 .... 2.00
❑29, May 1996 .... 2.00
❑30, Jun 1996 .... 2.00
❑31, Jul 1996 A: Wildcat. 2.00
❑32, Aug 1996 .... 2.00
❑33, Sep 1996 .... 2.00
❑34, Oct 1996; self-contained story 2.00
❑35, Nov 1996; A: Spoiler. Final Night 2.00

	N-MINT
❑36, Dec 1996 V: Toyman. V: Ulysses.	2.00
❑37, Jan 1997 V: Toyman. V: Ulysses.	2.00
❑38, Feb 1997	2.00
❑39, Mar 1997	2.00
❑40, Apr 1997	1.95
❑41, May 1997	1.95
❑42, Jun 1997	1.95
❑43, Jul 1997	1.95
❑44, Aug 1997 A: Spoiler.	1.95
❑45, Sep 1997; self-contained story	1.95
❑46, Oct 1997; self-contained story	1.95
❑47, Nov 1997 A: Nightwing. A: Batman. V: Ulysses.	1.95
❑48, Dec 1997; Face cover	1.95
❑49, Jan 1998 A: King Snake.	1.95
❑50, Feb 1998; Giant-size A: King Snake. A: Lady Shiva.	2.95
❑51, Mar 1998	1.95
❑52, Apr 1998; continues in Batman: Blackgate-Isle of Men #1	1.95
❑53, May 1998	1.95
❑54, Jun 1998; A: Spoiler. Aftershock	1.95
❑55, Jul 1998; continues in Nightwing #23	1.95
❑56, Aug 1998; A: Spoiler. Tim breaks up with Ariana	1.95
❑57, Sep 1998; Spoiler and Robin date	1.99
❑58, Oct 1998 V: Steeljacket.	1.99
❑59, Dec 1998 V: Steeljacket.	1.99
❑60, Jan 1999	1.99
❑61, Feb 1999	1.99
❑62, Mar 1999; A: Flash III (Wally West). Tim relocates to Keystone City	1.99
❑63, Apr 1999 A: Riddler. A: Superman. A: Flash III (Wally West). A: Captain Boomerang.	1.99
❑64, May 1999 A: Flash III (Wally West). V: Riddler. V: Captain Boomerang.	1.99
❑65, Jun 1999; Spoiler's child is born	1.99
❑66, Jul 1999; Tim returns to Gotham	1.99
❑67, Aug 1999; A: Nightwing. No Man's Land	1.99
❑68, Sep 1999; V: Ratcatcher. No Man's Land	1.99
❑69, Oct 1999; V: Ratcatcher. No Man's Land	1.99
❑70, Nov 1999	1.99
❑71, Dec 1999	1.99
❑72, Jan 2000	1.99
❑73, Feb 2000	1.99
❑74, Mar 2000	1.99
❑75, Apr 2000; Giant-size	2.95
❑76, May 2000	1.99
❑77, Jun 2000	1.99
❑78, Jul 2000	1.99
❑79, Aug 2000	2.25
❑80, Sep 2000	2.25
❑81, Oct 2000	2.25
❑82, Nov 2000	2.25
❑83, Dec 2000	2.25
❑84, Jan 2001	2.25
❑85, Feb 2001 A: Joker.	2.25
❑86, Mar 2001	2.25
❑87, Apr 2001	2.25
❑88, May 2001	2.25
❑89, Jun 2001	2.25
❑90, Jul 2001	2.25
❑91, Aug 2001	2.25
❑92, Sep 2001	2.25
❑93, Oct 2001	2.25
❑94, Nov 2001	2.25
❑95, Dec 2001	2.25
❑96, Jan 2002	2.25
❑97, Feb 2002	2.25
❑98, Mar 2002; Bruce Wayne, Murderer? Part 6	2.25
❑99, Apr 2002; Bruce Wayne, Murderer? Part 11	2.25
❑100, May 2002; Giant-size	3.50
❑101, Jun 2002	2.25
❑102, Jul 2002	2.25
❑103, Aug 2002	2.25
❑104, Sep 2002	2.25
❑105, Oct 2002	2.25
❑106, Nov 2002	2.25
❑107, Dec 2002	2.25
❑108, Jan 2003	2.25
❑109, Feb 2003	2.25
❑110, Mar 2003	2.25
❑111, Apr 2003	2.25
❑112, May 2003	2.25
❑113, Jun 2003	2.25
❑114, Jul 2003	2.25
❑115, Aug 2003	2.25
❑116, Sep 2003	2.25
❑117, Oct 2003	2.25
❑118, Nov 2003	2.25
❑119, Dec 2003	2.25
❑120, Jan 2004	2.25
❑121, Feb 2004	2.25
❑122, Mar 2004	2.25
❑123, Apr 2004	2.25
❑124, May 2004	2.25
❑125, Jun 2004	2.25
❑126, Jul 2004	2.25
❑127, Aug 2004	2.25
❑128, Sep 2004	
❑1000000, Nov 1998 A: Robin the Toy Wonder.	3.00
❑Annual 3, ca. 1994; Elseworlds	2.95
❑Annual 4, ca. 1995; Year One	3.95
❑Annual 5, ca. 1996; Legends of the Dead Earth	2.95
❑Annual 6, ca. 1997; Pulp Heroes	3.95
❑Giant Size 1, Sep 2000; Eighty Page Giant	5.95

ROBIN II
DC

	N-MINT
❑1, Oct 1991; CR (a); newsstand; no hologram	1.00
❑1/A, Oct 1991; CR (a); Robin Hologram; Joker in straight jacket	1.75
❑1/B, Oct 1991; CR (a); Joker Holding cover; Robin Hologram	1.75
❑1/C, Oct 1991; CR (a); Robin Hologram; Batman cover	1.75
❑1/CS, Oct 1991; set of all covers; extra hologram	10.00
❑1/D, Oct 1991; CR (a); Joker standing cover; Robin Hologram	1.75
❑2, Nov 1991; Normal cover; newsstand; no hologram	1.00
❑2/A, Nov 1991; Joker w/mallet cover; Batman Hologram	1.75
❑2/B, Nov 1991; Joker w/dart board cover; Batman Hologram	1.75
❑2/C, Nov 1991; Joker w/dagger cover; Batman Hologram	1.75
❑2/CS, Nov 1991	9.00
❑3, Nov 1991; Normal cover; newsstand; no hologram	1.00
❑3/A, Nov 1991; Robin Swinging cover; Joker Hologram	1.50
❑3/B, Nov 1991; Joker Hologram; Robin perched	1.50
❑3/CS, Nov 1991	6.00
❑4, Dec 1991; Normal cover; newsstand, no hologram	1.00
❑4/A, Dec 1991; Bat signal hologram	1.50
❑4/CS, Dec 1991	4.25
❑Deluxe 1; boxed with hologram cards (limited to 25, 000); Deluxe set; Contains all issues and variations in bookshelf binder	30.00

ROBIN PLUS
DC

	N-MINT
❑1, Dec 1996	2.95
❑2, Dec 1997; continues in Scare Tactics #10	2.95

ROBIN 3000
DC

	N-MINT
❑1, ca. 1992	4.95
❑2, ca. 1992	4.95

ROBIN: YEAR ONE
DC

	N-MINT
❑1, Dec 2000	4.95
❑2, Jan 2001	4.95
❑3, Feb 2001	4.95
❑4, Mar 2001	4.95

ROBIN/ARGENT DOUBLE-SHOT
DC

	N-MINT
❑1, Feb 1998	1.95

ROBIN III: CRY OF THE HUNTRESS
DC

	N-MINT
❑1, Dec 1992; newsstand	1.25
❑1/Variant, Dec 1992; moving cover	2.50
❑2, Jan 1993; newsstand	1.25
❑2/Variant, Jan 1993; moving cover	2.50
❑3, Jan 1993; newsstand	1.25
❑3/Variant, Jan 1993; moving cover	2.50
❑4, Feb 1993; newsstand	1.25
❑4/Variant, Feb 1993; moving cover	2.50
❑5, Feb 1993; newsstand	1.25
❑5/Variant, Feb 1993; moving cover	2.50
❑6, Mar 1993; newsstand	1.25
❑6/Variant, Mar 1993; moving cover	2.50

ROBIN HOOD (DELL)
DELL

	N-MINT
❑1, ca. 1963	20.00

ROBIN HOOD (ETERNITY)
ETERNITY

	N-MINT
❑1, Aug 1989, b&w	2.25
❑2, Sep 1991, b&w	2.25
❑3, b&w	2.25
❑4, b&w	2.25

ROBIN HOOD (ECLIPSE)
ECLIPSE

	N-MINT
❑1, Jul 1991	2.50
❑2, Sep 1991	2.50
❑3, Dec 1991	2.50

ROBIN RED AND THE LUTINS
ACE

	N-MINT
❑1, Nov 1986	1.75
❑2, Jan 1987	1.75

ROBINSONIA
NBM

	N-MINT
❑1	11.95

ROBOCOP (MAGAZINE)
MARVEL

	N-MINT
❑1, Oct 1987	2.50

ROBOCOP (MARVEL)
MARVEL

	N-MINT
❑1, Mar 1990	3.00
❑2, Apr 1990	2.00
❑3, May 1990	1.50
❑4, Jun 1990	1.50
❑5, Jul 1990	1.50
❑6, Aug 1990	1.50
❑7, Sep 1990	1.50
❑8, Oct 1990	1.50
❑9, Nov 1990	1.50
❑10, Dec 1990	1.50
❑11, Jan 1991	1.50
❑12, Feb 1991	1.50
❑13, Mar 1991	1.50
❑14, Apr 1991	1.50
❑15, May 1991	1.50
❑16, Jun 1991	1.50
❑17, Jul 1991	1.50
❑18, Aug 1991	1.50
❑19, Sep 1991	1.50
❑20, Oct 1991	1.50
❑21, Nov 1991	1.50
❑22, Dec 1991	1.50
❑23, Jan 1992	1.50

ROBOCOP (MOVIE ADAPTATION)
MARVEL

	N-MINT
❑1, Jul 1990; prestige format	4.95

N-MINT

ROBOCOP 2
MARVEL
- ❑1, Aug 1990; comic book ... 1.50
- ❑2, Sep 1990; comic book ... 1.50
- ❑3, Sep 1990; comic book ... 1.50

ROBOCOP 2 (MAGAZINE)
MARVEL
- ❑1, Aug 1990, b&w; magazine ... 2.50

ROBOCOP 3
DARK HORSE
- ❑1, Jul 1993 ... 2.50
- ❑2, Sep 1993 ... 2.50
- ❑3, Nov 1993 ... 2.50

ROBOCOP (FRANK MILLER'S)
AVATAR
- ❑1, Aug 2003 ... 3.50
- ❑1/Platinum, Aug 2003 ... 3.75
- ❑2, Oct 2003 ... 3.50
- ❑3, Nov 2003 ... 3.50
- ❑3/Platinum, Nov 2003 ... 3.75
- ❑4, Dec 2003 ... 3.50
- ❑5, Feb 2004 ... 3.50

ROBOCOP: MORTAL COILS
DARK HORSE
- ❑1, Sep 1993 ... 2.50
- ❑2, Oct 1993 ... 2.50
- ❑3, Nov 1993 ... 2.50
- ❑4, Dec 1993 ... 2.50

ROBOCOP: PRIME SUSPECT
DARK HORSE
- ❑1, Oct 1992 ... 2.50
- ❑2, Nov 1992 ... 2.50
- ❑3, Dec 1992 ... 2.50
- ❑4, Jan 1993 ... 2.50

ROBOCOP: ROULETTE
DARK HORSE
- ❑1, Dec 1993 ... 2.50
- ❑2, Jan 1994 ... 2.50
- ❑3, Feb 1994 ... 2.50
- ❑4, Mar 1994 ... 2.50

ROBOCOP VERSUS THE TERMINATOR
DARK HORSE
- ❑1, ca. 1992 FM (w) ... 3.00
- ❑1/Platinum, ca. 1992; Platinum promotional edition FM (w) ... 4.00
- ❑2, ca. 1992 FM (w) ... 2.50
- ❑3, ca. 1992 FM (w) ... 2.50
- ❑4, ca. 1992 FM (w) ... 2.50

ROBO DOJO
DC / WILDSTORM
- ❑1, Apr 2002 ... 2.95
- ❑2, May 2002 ... 2.95
- ❑3, Jun 2002 ... 2.95
- ❑4, Jul 2002 ... 2.95
- ❑5, Aug 2002 ... 2.95
- ❑6, Sep 2002 ... 2.95

ROBO-HUNTER
EAGLE
- ❑1 ... 1.50
- ❑2 DaG (a) ... 1.25
- ❑3 DaG (a) ... 1.25
- ❑4 DaG (a) ... 1.25
- ❑5 ... 1.25

ROBOTECH
ANTARCTIC
- ❑1, Mar 1997 ... 2.95
- ❑2, May 1997 ... 2.95
- ❑3, Jul 1997 ... 2.95
- ❑4, Sep 1997 ... 2.95
- ❑5, Nov 1997 ... 2.95
- ❑6, Jan 1998 ... 2.95
- ❑7, Mar 1998 ... 2.95
- ❑8, May 1998 ... 2.95
- ❑9, Jul 1998 ... 2.95
- ❑10, Sep 1998 ... 2.95
- ❑11, Nov 1998 ... 2.95
- ❑Annual 1, Apr 1998, b&w ... 2.95

N-MINT

ROBOTECH (WILDSTORM)
DC / WILDSTORM
- ❑0, Feb 2003 ... 2.50
- ❑1, Feb 2003 ... 2.95
- ❑2, Mar 2003 ... 2.95
- ❑3, Apr 2003 ... 2.95
- ❑4, May 2003 ... 2.95
- ❑5, Jun 2003 ... 2.95
- ❑6, Jul 2003 ... 2.95

ROBOTECH: AMAZON WORLD-ESCAPE FROM PRAXIS
ACADEMY
- ❑1, Dec 1994 ... 2.95

ROBOTECH: CLASS REUNION
ANTARCTIC
- ❑1, Dec 1998, b&w ... 3.95

ROBOTECH: CLONE
ACADEMY
- ❑0 ... 2.95
- ❑1 ... 2.95
- ❑2 ... 2.95
- ❑3 ... 2.95
- ❑4 ... 2.95
- ❑5 ... 2.95
- ❑Special 1 ... 3.50

ROBOTECH: COVERT-OPS
ANTARCTIC
- ❑1, Aug 1998, b&w ... 2.95
- ❑2, Sep 1998, b&w ... 2.95

ROBOTECH: CYBER WORLD: SECRETS OF HAYDON IV
ACADEMY
- ❑1 ... 2.95

ROBOTECH DEFENDERS
DC
- ❑1, Jan 1985 MA (a) ... 2.00
- ❑2, Apr 1985; MA (a); three-issue series was finished in two issues ... 2.00

ROBOTECH: ESCAPE
ANTARCTIC
- ❑1, May 1998, b&w ... 2.95

ROBOTECH: FINAL FIRE
ANTARCTIC
- ❑1, Dec 1998, b&w ... 2.95

ROBOTECH: FIREWALKERS
ETERNITY
- ❑1 ... 2.50

ROBOTECH GENESIS
ETERNITY
- ❑1, color; trading cards ... 2.50
- ❑1/Ltd.; limited ... 5.95
- ❑2 ... 2.50
- ❑3 ... 2.50
- ❑4; trading cards ... 2.50
- ❑5; trading cards ... 2.50
- ❑6 ... 2.50

ROBOTECH IN 3-D
COMICO
- ❑1, Jul 1985 ... 2.50

ROBOTECH: INVASION
DC / WILDSTORM
- ❑1, Mar 2004 ... 2.95
- ❑2, Apr 2004 ... 2.95
- ❑3, May 2004 ... 2.95
- ❑4, Jun 2004 ... 2.95
- ❑5, Jul 2004 ... 2.95

ROBOTECH: INVID WAR
ETERNITY
- ❑1, May 1992, b&w ... 2.50
- ❑2, b&w ... 2.50
- ❑3, b&w ... 2.50
- ❑4, b&w ... 2.50
- ❑5, b&w ... 2.50
- ❑6, b&w ... 2.50
- ❑7, b&w ... 2.50
- ❑8, b&w ... 2.50
- ❑9, b&w ... 2.50
- ❑10, b&w ... 1.25

Gold Key's *Ripley's Believe It or Not!* expanded on the single-panel newspaper cartoons to bring readers longer tales of the strange, the bizarre, and the unexpected.

© 1976 Gold Key.

N-MINT

- ❑11, b&w ... 1.25
- ❑12, b&w ... 1.25
- ❑13, b&w ... 1.25
- ❑14 ... 2.50
- ❑15 ... 2.50
- ❑16 ... 2.50
- ❑17 ... 2.50
- ❑18 ... 2.50

ROBOTECH: INVID WAR AFTERMATH
ETERNITY
- ❑1, b&w ... 2.50
- ❑2, b&w ... 2.50

ROBOTECH: LOVE & WAR
DC / WILDSTORM
- ❑1, Aug 2003 ... 2.95
- ❑2, Sep 2003 ... 2.95
- ❑3, Oct 2003 ... 2.95
- ❑4, Nov 2003 ... 2.95
- ❑5, Dec 2003 ... 2.95
- ❑6, Jan 2004 ... 2.95

ROBOTECH MASTERS
COMICO
- ❑1, Jul 1985 ... 2.00
- ❑2, Sep 1985 ... 1.50
- ❑3, Nov 1985 ... 1.50
- ❑4, Nov 1985 ... 1.50
- ❑5 ... 1.50
- ❑6 1986 ... 1.50
- ❑7 1986 ... 1.50
- ❑8 1986 ... 1.50
- ❑9 1986 ... 1.50
- ❑10, Aug 1986 ... 1.50
- ❑11 ... 1.50
- ❑12 ... 1.50
- ❑13 ... 1.50
- ❑14 1987 ... 1.50
- ❑15 1987 ... 1.50
- ❑16 1987 ... 1.50
- ❑17 1987 ... 1.50
- ❑18 1987 ... 1.50
- ❑19 1987 ... 1.50
- ❑20 1987 ... 1.50
- ❑21 ... 1.50
- ❑22 ... 1.50
- ❑23 1988 ... 1.50

ROBOTECH: MECHANGEL
ACADEMY
- ❑1 ... 2.95
- ❑2 ... 2.95
- ❑3 ... 2.95

ROBOTECH: MEGASTORM
ANTARCTIC
- ❑1, Aug 1998; wraparound cover ... 7.95

ROBOTECH: RETURN TO MACROSS
ETERNITY
- ❑1, Mar 1993, b&w ... 3.00
- ❑2, b&w ... 2.50
- ❑3, b&w ... 2.50
- ❑4, b&w ... 2.50
- ❑5, b&w ... 2.50
- ❑6, b&w ... 2.50
- ❑7, b&w ... 2.50
- ❑8, b&w ... 2.50
- ❑9, b&w ... 2.50
- ❑10, Jan 1994, b&w ... 2.50
- ❑11 ... 2.50

	N-MINT
❑12	2.50
❑13	2.50
❑14	2.50
❑15	2.50
❑16	2.50
❑17	2.50
❑18	2.50
❑19	2.50
❑20	2.50
❑21	2.50
❑22	2.50
❑23	2.50
❑24	2.50
❑25	2.50
❑26	2.50
❑27	2.50
❑28	2.50
❑29	2.50
❑30	2.50
❑31	2.50
❑32, May 1996	2.95

ROBOTECH: SENTINELS - RUBICON
ANTARCTIC

	N-MINT
❑1, Jun 1998, b&w	2.95
❑2	2.95
❑3	2.95
❑4	2.95
❑5	2.95
❑6	2.95
❑7	2.95

ROBOTECH SPECIAL
COMICO

	N-MINT
❑1, May 1988	2.50

ROBOTECH THE GRAPHIC NOVEL
COMICO

	N-MINT
❑1	5.95

ROBOTECH: THE MACROSS SAGA
COMICO

	N-MINT
❑1, Dec 1984; "Macross" this issue	8.00
❑2, ca. 1985; Title changes to Robotech: The Macross Saga	4.00
❑3, ca. 1985	3.00
❑4, ca. 1985	3.00
❑5, ca. 1985	3.00
❑6, Sep 1985	2.00
❑7, Nov 1985	2.00
❑8	2.00
❑9, ca. 1986	2.00
❑10, ca. 1986	2.00
❑11, ca. 1986	2.00
❑12, ca. 1986	2.00
❑13, ca. 1986	2.00
❑14, ca. 1986	2.00
❑15, ca. 1986	2.00
❑16, ca. 1986	2.00
❑17, ca. 1986	2.00
❑18	2.00
❑19	2.00
❑20	2.00
❑21	2.00
❑22, ca. 1987	2.00
❑23, ca. 1987	2.00
❑24, ca. 1987	2.00
❑25, ca. 1987	2.00
❑26, ca. 1987	2.00
❑27, ca. 1987	2.00
❑28	2.00
❑29	2.00
❑30	2.00
❑31	2.00
❑32	2.00
❑33, ca. 1988	2.00
❑34, ca. 1988	2.00
❑35	2.00
❑36, ca. 1989	2.00

ROBOTECH: THE NEW GENERATION
COMICO

	N-MINT
❑1, Jul 1985	2.00
❑2, Sep 1985	1.50
❑3 1985	1.50
❑4 1985	1.50
❑5, Jan 1986	1.50
❑6, Mar 1986	1.50
❑7 1986	1.50
❑8 1986	1.50
❑9, Jul 1986	1.50
❑10	1.50
❑11	1.50
❑12	1.50
❑13	1.50
❑14	1.50
❑15 1987	1.50
❑16 1987	1.50
❑17 1987	1.50
❑18 1987	1.50
❑19 1987	1.50
❑20	1.50
❑21	1.50
❑22	1.50
❑23	1.50
❑24	1.50
❑25 1988; last	1.50

ROBOTECH II: INVID WORLD, ASSAULT ON OPTERA
ACADEMY

	N-MINT
❑1, Oct 1994	2.95

ROBOTECH II: THE SENTINELS
ETERNITY

	N-MINT
❑1, Nov 1988	3.50
❑1-2	2.00
❑2, Dec 1988	2.50
❑3, Jan 1989	2.50
❑3-2, Feb 1989	2.00
❑4, Mar 1989	2.25
❑5, Apr 1989	2.25
❑6, May 1989	2.00
❑7, Jun 1989	2.00
❑8, Jul 1989	2.00
❑9, Sep 1989	2.00
❑10, Oct 1989	2.00
❑11, Oct 1989	2.00
❑12, Nov 1989	2.00
❑13, Dec 1989	2.00
❑14, Jan 1990	2.00
❑15	2.00
❑16, Apr 1990	1.95

ROBOTECH II: THE SENTINELS BOOK II
ETERNITY

	N-MINT
❑1, May 1990	2.25
❑2, Aug 1990	2.25
❑3, Oct 1990	2.25
❑4	2.25
❑5 1991	2.25
❑6 1991	2.25
❑7 1991	2.25
❑8 1991	2.25
❑9 1991	2.25
❑10 1991	2.25
❑11	2.25
❑12	2.50
❑13, Mar 1992	2.50
❑14	2.50
❑15	2.50
❑16	2.50
❑17	2.50
❑18	2.50
❑19	2.50
❑20	2.50

ROBOTECH II: THE SENTINELS BOOK III
ETERNITY

	N-MINT
❑1	2.50
❑2	2.50
❑3	2.50
❑4	2.50
❑5	2.50
❑6	2.50

ROBOTECH II: THE SENTINELS BOOK IV
ACADEMY

	N-MINT
❑1	2.95
❑2	2.95
❑3	2.95
❑4	2.95
❑5	2.95
❑6, May 1996	2.95

ROBOTECH II: THE SENTINELS CYBERPIRATES
ETERNITY

	N-MINT
❑1	2.25
❑2	2.25
❑3	2.25
❑4	2.25

ROBOTECH II: THE SENTINELS SCRIPT BOOK
ETERNITY

	N-MINT
❑1, b&w	9.95

ROBOTECH II: THE SENTINELS SPECIAL
ETERNITY

	N-MINT
❑1, Apr 1989	1.95
❑2	1.95

ROBOTECH II: THE SENTINELS SWIMSUIT SPECTACULAR
ETERNITY

	N-MINT
❑1	2.95

ROBOTECH II: THE SENTINELS: THE ILLUSTRATED HANDBOOK
ETERNITY

	N-MINT
❑1	2.50
❑2	2.50
❑3	2.50

ROBOTECH II: THE SENTINELS THE MALCONTENT UPRISINGS
MALIBU / ETERNITY

	N-MINT
❑1	2.00
❑2	2.00
❑3	2.00
❑4	2.00
❑5	2.00
❑6	2.00
❑7	2.00
❑8	2.00
❑9	2.00
❑10	2.00
❑11	2.00
❑12	2.00

ROBOTECH II: THE SENTINELS: THE UNTOLD STORY
ETERNITY

	N-MINT
❑1, b&w	2.50

ROBOTECH II: THE SENTINELS WEDDING SPECIAL
ETERNITY

	N-MINT
❑1, Apr 1989	2.00
❑2, May 1989	2.00

ROBOTECH: VERMILION
ANTARCTIC

	N-MINT
❑1, Aug 1997	2.95
❑2, Oct 1997	2.95
❑3, Dec 1997	2.95
❑4, Feb 1997	2.95

ROBOTECH WARRIORS
ACADEMY

	N-MINT
❑1, Feb 1995	2.95

ROBOTECH: WINGS OF GIBRALTAR
ANTARCTIC

	N-MINT
❑1, Aug 1998	2.95
❑2, Sep 1998	2.95

ROBOTIX
MARVEL

	N-MINT
❑1, Feb 1986 HT (w); HT (a); 1: The Terrokors. 1: The Protectons.	1.00

Condition price index: Multiply "NM prices" above by: **0.83 for Very Fine/Near Mint**
0.66 for Very Fine • 0.33 for Fine • 0.2 for Very Good • 0.125 for Good

N-MINT

ROBO WARRIORS
CFW

- ❑1 ... 1.75
- ❑2; 0: Citation; Origin of Citation ... 1.95
- ❑3 ... 1.95
- ❑4 ... 1.95
- ❑5 ... 1.95
- ❑6 ... 1.95
- ❑7 ... 1.95
- ❑8; Reiki becomes Mister No ... 1.95

ROBYN OF SHERWOOD
CALIBER

- ❑1, Mar 1998, b&w ... 2.95

ROCKERS
RIP OFF

- ❑1, Jul 1988, b&w ... 2.00
- ❑2, Oct 1988, b&w ... 2.00
- ❑3, Jan 1989, b&w ... 2.00
- ❑4, Feb 1989, b&w ... 2.00
- ❑5, May 1989, b&w ... 2.00
- ❑6, Jun 1989, b&w ... 2.00
- ❑7, Sep 1989, b&w ... 2.00
- ❑8, Feb 1990, b&w ... 2.00

ROCKETEER 3-D COMIC, THE
DISNEY

- ❑1, Jun 1991; with audiotape; Based on The Rocketeer movie ... 5.00

ROCKETEER ADVENTURE MAGAZINE, THE
COMICO

- ❑1, Jul 1988; DSt (w); CV, DSt (a); Comico publishes ... 5.00
- ❑2, Jul 1989 DSt (w); DSt (a) ... 3.50
- ❑3, Jan 1995; DSt (w); DSt (a); Dark Horse publishes ... 3.00

ROCKETEER SPECIAL EDITION, THE
ECLIPSE

- ❑1, Nov 1984 ... 1.50

ROCKETEER, THE: THE OFFICIAL MOVIE ADAPTATION
DISNEY

- ❑1 1991; No cover date; stapled ... 2.95
- ❑1/Direct ed. 1991; No cover date; squarebound ... 5.95

ROCKETMAN: KING OF THE ROCKET MEN
INNOVATION

- ❑1 ... 2.50
- ❑2 ... 2.50
- ❑3 ... 2.50
- ❑4 ... 2.50

ROCKET RACCOON
MARVEL

- ❑1, May 1985 ... 1.00
- ❑2, Jun 1985 ... 1.00
- ❑3, Jul 1985 ... 1.00
- ❑4, Aug 1985 ... 1.00

ROCKET RANGER
ADVENTURE

- ❑1, Sep 1991, color ... 2.95
- ❑2, Dec 1991, b&w ... 2.95
- ❑3 1992, b&w ... 2.95
- ❑4 1992, b&w ... 2.95
- ❑5, Jul 1992, b&w ... 2.95
- ❑6 ... 2.95

ROCK FANTASY
ROCK FANTASY

- ❑1; Pink Floyd ... 3.00
- ❑2; Rolling Stones ... 3.00
- ❑3; Led Zeppelin ... 3.00
- ❑4; New Kids on the Block; Stevie Nicks ... 3.00
- ❑5; Guns 'n Roses ... 3.00
- ❑6; Monstrosities of Rock ... 3.00
- ❑7; The Sex Pistols ... 3.00
- ❑8; Alice Cooper ... 3.00
- ❑9; Van Halen ... 3.00
- ❑10; Kiss ... 3.00
- ❑11; Jimi Hendrix ... 3.00
- ❑12; Def Leppard ... 3.00

N-MINT

- ❑13; David Bowie ... 3.00
- ❑14; The Doors ... 3.00
- ❑15; Pink Floyd II ... 3.00
- ❑16; Double-size; The Great Gig in the Sky ... 5.00
- ❑17; Rock Vixens ... 3.00

ROCKHEADS
SOLSON

- ❑1 ... 1.95

ROCKIN' BONES
NEW ENGLAND

- ❑1, b&w ... 2.75
- ❑2, b&w ... 2.75
- ❑3, b&w ... 2.75
- ❑Holiday 1; Xmas Special ... 2.75

ROCKINFREAKAPOTAMUS PRESENTS THE RED HOT CHILI PEPPERS ILLUSTRATED LYRICS
TELLTALE

- ❑1, Jul 1997, b&w; magazine-sized ... 3.95

ROCKIN ROLLIN MINER ANTS
FATE

- ❑1, Oct 1991 ... 2.25

ROCKMEEZ, THE
JZINK COMICS

- ❑1, Oct 1992 ... 2.50
- ❑2, Nov 1992 ... 2.50
- ❑3 ... 2.50
- ❑4 ... 2.50

ROCK 'N' ROLL COMICS
REVOLUTIONARY

- ❑1, Jun 1989; Guns 'N' Roses ... 6.00
- ❑1-2, Jul 1989 ... 4.00
- ❑1-3, Aug 1989 ... 1.95
- ❑1-4, Sep 1989 ... 1.95
- ❑1-5, Oct 1989 ... 1.95
- ❑1-6, Nov 1989 ... 1.95
- ❑1-7, Dec 1989; Color, completely different than first six printings ... 1.95
- ❑2, Aug 1989; Metallica ... 3.00
- ❑2-2, Sep 1989; Metallica ... 1.95
- ❑2-3, Sep 1989; Metallica ... 1.95
- ❑2-4, Sep 1989; Metallica ... 1.95
- ❑2-5, Sep 1989; Metallica ... 1.95
- ❑2-6, color; Metallica; 50% new material added ... 1.95
- ❑3, Sep 1989; Bon Jovi; Banned by Great Southern Co.; Rare ... 10.00
- ❑3-2, Oct 1989 ... 1.95
- ❑4, Oct 1989; Motley Crue; Banned by Great Southern Co.; 15,000 copies burned by Great Southern ... 50.00
- ❑4-2, Oct 1989; 2nd printing (no Ace Backwords); Banned by Great Southern Co. ... 3.00
- ❑5, Nov 1989; Def Leppard ... 1.95
- ❑5-2, Nov 1989; Def Leppard ... 1.50
- ❑6, Dec 1989; Rolling Stones ... 1.95
- ❑6-2, Jan 1990; Rolling Stones ... 1.50
- ❑6-3, Jan 1990; Rolling Stones ... 1.50
- ❑6-4, Feb 1990; Rolling Stones ... 1.50
- ❑7, Jan 1990; The Who ... 1.95
- ❑7-2, Feb 1990; The Who ... 1.50
- ❑7-3, Mar 1990; The Who ... 1.50
- ❑8, Feb 1990; Skid Row; Never published: banned by injunction from Great Southern Company ... 1.50
- ❑9, Mar 1990; Kiss ... 5.00
- ❑9-2, Apr 1990; Kiss ... 1.95
- ❑9-3, May 1990; Kiss ... 1.95
- ❑10, Apr 1990; Two different versions printed, one with Whitesnake on cover, one with Warrant ... 1.95
- ❑10-2, May 1990; Whitesnake only on cover ... 1.50
- ❑11, May 1990; Aerosmith ... 1.95
- ❑12, Jun 1990; New Kids on the Block ... 1.95
- ❑12-2, Aug 1990; New Kids On the Block ... 1.50
- ❑13, Jul 1990; Led Zeppelin ... 1.95
- ❑14, Aug 1990; Sex Pistols ... 1.95
- ❑15, Sep 1990, color; Poison ... 1.95

The origins of all three Robins (Dick Grayson, Jason Todd, and Tim Drake) were retold in *Robin* #0.

© 1994 DC Comics.

N-MINT

- ❑16, Oct 1990, color; Van Halen ... 1.95
- ❑17, Nov 1990, color; Madonna ... 3.00
- ❑18, Dec 1990; Alice Cooper; Full color ... 1.95
- ❑19, Apr 1991, b&w; Public Enemy, 2 Live Crew ... 2.50
- ❑20, Apr 1991, b&w; Queensryche ... 2.50
- ❑21, Jan 1991, b&w; Prince ... 2.50
- ❑22, Feb 1991, color; AC/DC ... 2.50
- ❑23, Mar 1991, b&w; Living Colour ... 2.50
- ❑24, Mar 1991; Anthrax b&w ... 2.50
- ❑25, May 1991, b&w; ZZ Top ... 2.50
- ❑26, May 1991; Doors ... 2.50
- ❑27, Jun 1991; Doors ... 2.50
- ❑28, Jun 1991; Ozzy Osbourne; Black Sabbath ... 2.50
- ❑29, Jul 1991; Ozzy Osbourne; Black Sabbath ... 2.50
- ❑30, Jul 1991; The Cure ... 2.50
- ❑31, Aug 1991; Vanilla Ice ... 2.50
- ❑32, Aug 1991; Frank Zappa ... 2.50
- ❑33, Sep 1991; Guns 'N' Roses II ... 2.50
- ❑34, Sep 1991; Black Crowes ... 2.50
- ❑35, Oct 1991; R.E.M. ... 2.50
- ❑36, Oct 1991; Michael Jackson ... 2.50
- ❑37, Nov 1991; Ice-T ... 2.50
- ❑38, Nov 1991; Rod Stewart ... 2.50
- ❑39, Dec 1991; The Fall of the New Kids ... 2.50
- ❑40, Dec 1991; NWA; Ice Cube ... 2.50
- ❑41, Jan 1992; Paula Abdul ... 2.50
- ❑42, Jan 1992; Metallica II ... 2.50
- ❑43, Feb 1992; Guns N' Roses: Tales from the Tour ... 2.50
- ❑44, Feb 1992; Scorpions ... 2.50
- ❑45, Mar 1992; Grateful Dead ... 2.50
- ❑46, Apr 1992; Grateful Dead II ... 2.50
- ❑47, May 1992; Grateful Dead III ... 2.50
- ❑48, Jun 1992; Queen ... 2.50
- ❑49, Jul 1992; Rush ... 2.50
- ❑50, Aug 1992; Bob Dylan ... 2.50
- ❑51, Sep 1992; Bob Dylan II ... 2.50
- ❑52, Oct 1992; Bob Dylan III ... 2.50
- ❑53, Nov 1992; Bruce Springsteen ... 2.50
- ❑54, Dec 1992; U2 ... 2.50
- ❑55, Jan 1993; U2 II ... 2.50
- ❑56, Feb 1993; David Bowie ... 2.50
- ❑57, Mar 1993; Aerosmith ... 2.50
- ❑58, Apr 1993; Kate Bush ... 2.50
- ❑59, May 1993; Eric Clapton ... 2.50
- ❑60, Jun 1993; Genesis ... 2.50
- ❑61, Jul 1993; Yes ... 2.50
- ❑62, Aug 1993; Elton John ... 2.50
- ❑63, Sep 1993; Janis Joplin ... 2.50
- ❑64, Oct 1993; '60s San Francisco ... 2.50
- ❑65, Nov 1993; Sci-Fi Space Rockers ... 2.50

ROCK N' ROLL COMICS MAGAZINE
REVOLUTIONARY

- ❑1 ... 2.95
- ❑2 ... 2.95
- ❑3 ... 2.95
- ❑4 ... 2.95
- ❑5, Oct 1990; Aerosmith/Rolling Stones ... 2.95

ROCKOLA
MIRAGE

- ❑1 ... 1.50

Condition price index: Multiply "NM prices" above by: **0.83 for Very Fine/Near Mint**
0.66 for Very Fine • 0.33 for Fine • 0.2 for Very Good • 0.125 for Good

N-MINT

ROCKO'S MODERN LIFE
MARVEL

- ❑1, Jun 1994; TV cartoon 1.95
- ❑2, Jul 1994 .... 1.95
- ❑3, Aug 1994 .... 1.95
- ❑4, Sep 1994 .... 1.95
- ❑5, Oct 1994 .... 1.95
- ❑6, Nov 1994 .... 1.95
- ❑7, Dec 1994 .... 1.95

ROCKY AND HIS FIENDISH FRIENDS
GOLD KEY

- ❑1, Oct 1962 .... 100.00
- ❑2, Dec 1962 .... 75.00
- ❑3, Mar 1963 .... 75.00
- ❑4, Jun 1963 .... 60.00
- ❑5, Sep 1963 .... 60.00

ROCKY HORROR PICTURE SHOW, THE: THE COMIC BOOK
CALIBER

- ❑1, Jul 1990, color 7.00
- ❑1-2; new cover 3.00
- ❑2, Aug 1990, color 4.00
- ❑3, Jan 1991, color 4.00

ROCKY LANE WESTERN (AC)
AC

- ❑1, b&w 2.50
- ❑2, b&w 5.95
- ❑Annual 1, b&w 2.95

ROEL
SIRIUS

- ❑1, Feb 1997, b&w; cardstock cover . 2.95

ROGAN GOSH
DC / VERTIGO

- ❑1 .... 6.95

ROGER FNORD
RIP OFF

- ❑1, Apr 1992, b&w 2.50

ROGER RABBIT
DISNEY

- ❑1, Jun 1990 1: Dick Flint. 2.00
- ❑2, Jul 1990 .... 1.75
- ❑3, Aug 1990 .... 1.75
- ❑4, Sep 1990 .... 1.75
- ❑5, Oct 1990 .... 1.75
- ❑6, Nov 1990 .... 1.50
- ❑7, Dec 1990 .... 1.50
- ❑8, Jan 1991 .... 1.50
- ❑9, Feb 1991 .... 1.50
- ❑10, Mar 1991 .... 1.50
- ❑11, Apr 1991 .... 1.50
- ❑12, May 1991 .... 1.50
- ❑13, Jun 1991 .... 1.50
- ❑14, Jul 1991 .... 1.50
- ❑15, Aug 1991 .... 1.50
- ❑16, Sep 1991 .... 1.50
- ❑17, Oct 1991 .... 1.50
- ❑18, Nov 1991 .... 1.50
- ❑Special 1 .... 3.50

ROGER RABBIT IN 3-D
DISNEY

- ❑1; with glasses; 3-D Zone reprints .. 2.50

ROGER RABBIT'S TOONTOWN
DISNEY

- ❑1, Aug 1991 .... 1.50
- ❑2, Sep 1991; Winsor McCay tribute 1.50
- ❑3, Oct 1991 .... 1.50
- ❑4, Nov 1991 .... 1.50
- ❑5, Dec 1991; Weasels solo story 1.50

ROGER WILCO
ADVENTURE

- ❑1, color 2.95
- ❑2, Apr 1992, b&w 2.95

ROG-2000
PACIFIC

- ❑1 .... 2.00

N-MINT

ROGUE (MARVEL)
MARVEL

- ❑1, Jan 1995; enhanced cover 2.95
- ❑2, Feb 1995; enhanced cover 2.95
- ❑3, Mar 1995; enhanced cover 2.95
- ❑4, Apr 1995; enhanced cover 2.95

ROGUE (VOL. 2)
MARVEL

- ❑1, Sep 2001 .... 2.50
- ❑2, Oct 2001 .... 2.50
- ❑3, Nov 2001 .... 2.50
- ❑4, Dec 2001 .... 2.50

ROGUE (MINI-SERIES)
MARVEL

- ❑1, Sep 2004 .... 2.99

ROGUE (MONSTER)
MONSTER

- ❑1, b&w 1.95

ROGUE SATELLITE COMICS
SLAVE LABOR

- ❑1, Aug 1996, b&w 2.95
- ❑2, b&w 2.95
- ❑3, Mar 1997, b&w 2.95
- ❑Special 1, b&w 2.95

ROGUES GALLERY
DC

- ❑1; pin-ups 3.50

ROGUES, THE (VILLAINS)
DC

- ❑1, Feb 1998; New Year's Evil 1.95

ROGUE TROOPER (1ST SERIES)
FLEETWAY-QUALITY

- ❑1 DaG (a) 2.00
- ❑2 DaG (a) 2.00
- ❑3 DaG (a) 2.00
- ❑4 .... 2.00
- ❑5 DaG (a) 2.00
- ❑6 .... 1.75
- ❑7 AMo (w) 1.75
- ❑8 .... 1.75
- ❑9 .... 1.75
- ❑10 .... 1.75
- ❑11 .... 1.50
- ❑12 .... 1.50
- ❑13 .... 1.50
- ❑14 .... 1.50
- ❑15 .... 1.50
- ❑16 .... 1.50
- ❑17 .... 1.50
- ❑18 .... 1.50
- ❑19 .... 1.50
- ❑20 .... 1.50
- ❑21; double issue #21/22 .... 1.50
- ❑23; double issue #23/24 .... 1.50
- ❑25 .... 1.50
- ❑26 .... 1.50
- ❑27 .... 1.50
- ❑28 .... 1.50
- ❑29 .... 1.50
- ❑30 .... 1.75
- ❑31 .... 1.75
- ❑32 .... 1.75
- ❑33 .... 1.75
- ❑34 .... 1.75
- ❑35 .... 1.75
- ❑36 .... 1.75
- ❑37 .... 1.75
- ❑38 .... 1.75
- ❑39 .... 1.75
- ❑40 .... 1.75
- ❑41 .... 1.75
- ❑42 .... 1.75
- ❑43 .... 1.75
- ❑44 .... 1.75
- ❑45 .... 1.75
- ❑46 .... 1.75
- ❑47 .... 1.75
- ❑48 .... 1.75
- ❑49 .... 1.75

N-MINT

ROGUE TROOPER (2ND SERIES)
FLEETWAY-QUALITY

- ❑1 .... 2.95
- ❑2 .... 2.95
- ❑3 .... 2.95
- ❑4 .... 2.95
- ❑5 .... 2.95
- ❑6 .... 2.95
- ❑7 .... 2.95
- ❑8 .... 2.95
- ❑9 .... 2.95

ROJA FUSION
ANTARCTIC

- ❑1, Apr 1995 .... 2.95

ROLAND: DAYS OF WRATH
TERRA MAJOR

- ❑1, Jul 1999 .... 2.95

ROLLERCOASTER
FANTAGRAPHICS

- ❑1, Sep 1996, b&w; magazine; cardstock cover 3.95

ROLLERCOASTERS SPECIAL EDITION
BLUE COMET

- ❑1 .... 2.00

ROLLING STONES
PERSONALITY

- ❑1, b&w 2.95
- ❑2, b&w 2.95
- ❑3, b&w 2.95

ROLLING STONES: VOODOO LOUNGE
MARVEL / MARVEL MUSIC

- ❑1; prestige format one-shot 6.95

ROM
MARVEL

- ❑1, Dec 1979 SB (a); O: ROM. 1: ROM. 5.00
- ❑2, Jan 1980 FM (c); SB, FM (a) 2.00
- ❑3, Feb 1980 FM (c); SB, FM (a); 1: Firefall. 2.00
- ❑4, Mar 1980 SB (a) 1.50
- ❑5, Apr 1980 SB (a) 1.50
- ❑6, May 1980 SB (a) 1.50
- ❑7, Jun 1980 SB (a) 1.50
- ❑8, Jul 1980 SB (a) 1.50
- ❑9, Aug 1980 SB (a) 1.50
- ❑10, Sep 1980 SB (a) 1.50
- ❑11, Oct 1980 SB (a) 1.25
- ❑12, Nov 1980 SB (a) 1.25
- ❑13, Dec 1980 SB (a) 1.25
- ❑14, Jan 1981 SB (a) 1.25
- ❑15, Feb 1981 SB (a) 1.25
- ❑16, Mar 1981 SB (a) 1.25
- ❑17, Apr 1981 FM (c); SB, FM (a); A: X-Men. 1.50
- ❑18, May 1981 FM (c); SB, FM (a); A: X-Men. 1.50
- ❑19, Jun 1981 SB, JSt (a); A: X-Men. 1.25
- ❑20, Jul 1981 SB, JSt (a) 1.25
- ❑21, Aug 1981 SB, JSt (a) 1.25
- ❑22, Sep 1981 SB, JSt (a) 1.25
- ❑23, Oct 1981 SB, JSt (a); A: Power Man. 1.25
- ❑24, Nov 1981 SB, JSt (a); D: Crimebuster. D: Powerhouse. D: Nova-Prime. D: Comet (Harris Moore). D: Protector. 1.50
- ❑25, Dec 1981; Giant-size SB, JSt (a) 1.50
- ❑26, Jan 1982 .... 1.25
- ❑27, Feb 1982 .... 1.25
- ❑28, Mar 1982 .... 1.25
- ❑29, Apr 1982 .... 1.25
- ❑30, May 1982 .... 1.25
- ❑31, Jun 1982 .... 1.25
- ❑32, Jul 1982 .... 1.25
- ❑33, Aug 1982 .... 1.25
- ❑34, Sep 1982 .... 1.25
- ❑35, Oct 1982 .... 1.25
- ❑36, Nov 1982 .... 1.25
- ❑37, Dec 1982 .... 1.25
- ❑38, Jan 1983 .... 1.25
- ❑39, Feb 1983 .... 1.25
- ❑40, Mar 1983 .... 1.25

N-MINT

❑41, Apr 1983 .... 1.25
❑42, May 1983 .... 1.25
❑43, Jun 1983 .... 1.25
❑44, Jul 1983 1: Devastator II. 1.25
❑45, Aug 1983 .... 1.25
❑46, Sep 1983 .... 1.25
❑47, Oct 1983 .... 1.25
❑48, Nov 1983 .... 1.25
❑49, Dec 1983 .... 1.25
❑50, Jan 1984; double-sized SB (a); A: Skrulls. D: Torpedo. 1.25
❑51, Feb 1984 .... 1.25
❑52, Mar 1984 .... 1.25
❑53, Apr 1984 .... 1.25
❑54, May 1984 .... 1.25
❑55, Jun 1984 .... 1.25
❑56, Jul 1984 A: Alpha Flight. 1.25
❑57, Aug 1984 A: Alpha Flight. 1.25
❑58, Sep 1984; Dire Wraiths 1.25
❑59, Oct 1984 SD (a) 1.25
❑60, Nov 1984 SD (a) 1.25
❑61, Dec 1984 SD (a) 1.25
❑62, Jan 1985 SD (a) 1.25
❑63, Feb 1985 SD (a) 1.25
❑64, Mar 1985 .... 1.25
❑65, Apr 1985 .... 1.25
❑66, May 1985 .... 1.25
❑67, Jun 1985 .... 1.25
❑68, Jul 1985 .... 1.25
❑69, Aug 1985 .... 1.25
❑70, Sep 1985 .... 1.25
❑71, Oct 1985 D: The Unseen. 1.25
❑72, Nov 1985; Secret Wars II 1.25
❑73, Dec 1985 .... 1.25
❑74, Jan 1986 D: Seeker. 1.25
❑75, Feb 1986 D: Trapper. D: Scanner. 1.25
❑Annual 1, ca. 1982; Stardust 1.50
❑Annual 2, ca. 1983 .... 1.25
❑Annual 3, ca. 1984 A: New Mutants. 1.50
❑Annual 4, ca. 1985 A: Gladiator. D: Pulsar. 1.25

ROMANCER
MOONSTONE

❑1, Dec 1996, b&w 2.95

ROMAN HOLIDAYS
GOLD KEY

❑1, Feb 1973 .... 20.00
❑2, May 1973 .... 10.00
❑3, Aug 1973 .... 10.00

ROMANTIC TAILS
HEAD

❑1, Aug 1998, b&w 2.95

ROMP ONE SHOT
IMAGE

❑1, Jan 2004 .... 6.95

RONALD MCDONALD
CHARLTON

❑1, Sep 1970 .... 52.00
❑2, Nov 1970 .... 35.00
❑3, Jan 1971 .... 35.00
❑4, Mar 1971 .... 35.00

RONIN
DC

❑1, Jul 1983 FM (w); FM (a) 4.00
❑2, Sep 1983 FM (w); FM (a) 3.00
❑3, Nov 1983 FM (w); FM (a) 3.00
❑4, Jan 1984 FM (w); FM (a) 3.00
❑5, Jan 1984 FM (w); FM (a) 3.00
❑6, Aug 1984; FM (w); FM (a); Scarcer 5.00

ROOK, THE
HARRIS

❑1, Jun 1995 .... 2.95
❑2 1995 .... 2.95

ROOK MAGAZINE, THE
WARREN

❑1, Oct 1979 .... 4.00
❑2, Feb 1980 .... 2.50
❑3, Jun 1980 .... 2.50
❑4, Aug 1980 .... 2.50
❑5, Oct 1980 .... 2.50

N-MINT

❑6, Dec 1980 .... 2.50
❑7, Feb 1981 .... 2.50
❑8, Apr 1981 .... 2.50
❑9, Jun 1981 .... 2.50
❑10, Aug 1981 .... 2.50
❑11, Oct 1981 .... 2.00
❑12, Dec 1981 .... 2.00
❑13, Feb 1982 .... 2.00
❑14, Apr 1982 .... 2.00

ROOM 222
DELL

❑1, Jan 1970, color 30.00
❑2, Mar 1970, color 20.00
❑3, Jul 1970, color 20.00
❑4, Jan 1971 .... 20.00

ROOTER
CUSTOM

❑1, Aug 1996 .... 2.95
❑2, Dec 1996 .... 2.95
❑3, Feb 1997 .... 2.95
❑4, May 1997 .... 2.95
❑5, Jul 1997 .... 2.95
❑6, Oct 1997 .... 2.95

ROOTER (VOL. 2)
CUSTOM

❑1, b&w 2.95

ROOTS OF THE OPPRESSOR
NORTHSTAR

❑1, b&w 2.95

ROOTS OF THE SWAMP THING
DC

❑1, Jul 1986 .... 2.00
❑2, Aug 1986 .... 2.00
❑3, Sep 1986; reprints Swamp Thing #5 and #6 and House of Mystery #191 .... 2.00
❑4, Oct 1986; reprints Swamp Thing #7 and #8 and House of Mystery #221 2.00
❑5, Nov 1986; Reprints stories from Swamp Thing #9, #10, House of Mystery #92 .... 2.00

ROSCOE! THE DAWG, ACE DETECTIVE
RENEGADE

❑1, Jul 1987, b&w 2.00
❑2, Oct 1987, b&w 2.00
❑3, Nov 1987, b&w 2.00
❑4, Jan 1988, b&w 2.00

ROSE & THORN
DC / WILDSTORM

❑1, Feb 2004 .... 2.95
❑2, Mar 2004 .... 2.95
❑3, Apr 2004 .... 2.95
❑4, May 2004 .... 2.95
❑5, Jun 2004 .... 2.95
❑6, Jul 2004 .... 2.95

ROSE
HERO

❑1 .... 3.50
❑2 .... 2.95
❑3 .... 3.95
❑4 .... 3.95
❑5, Dec 1993 .... 2.95

ROSE & GUNN
BISHOP

❑3, May 1995, b&w 2.95
❑4, Jun 1995, b&w 2.95
❑5, Aug 1995, b&w 2.95

ROSE & GUNN CREATOR'S CHOICE
BISHOP

❑1, Sep 1995, b&w 2.95

ROSWELL: LITTLE GREEN MAN
BONGO

❑1, ca. 1996 .... 3.50
❑2, ca. 1996 .... 3.00
❑3, ca. 1996 V: Professor Von Sphinkter. 3.00
❑4, ca. 1997 D: Shorty George. 3.00

Rock 'n' Roll Comics #19 contained a back-up story on Tipper Gore's Parent's Music Resource Committee.

© 1991 Revolutionary Comics.

N-MINT

❑5, ca. 1998 .... 3.00
❑6, ca. 1999 .... 3.00

ROTOGIN JUNKBOTZ
IMAGE

❑0, Mar 2003 .... 2.50
❑1, May 2003 .... 2.95
❑2, Aug 2003 .... 2.95
❑3, Oct 2003 .... 2.95

ROUGH RAIDERS
BLUE COMET

❑1 .... 2.00
❑2 .... 2.00
❑3 .... 2.00
❑Annual 1 .... 2.50

ROULETTE
CALIBER

❑1, b&w 2.50

ROUTE 666
CROSSGEN

❑1, Jun 2002 .... 2.95
❑2, Jul 2002 .... 2.95
❑3, Aug 2002 .... 2.95
❑4, Sep 2002 .... 2.95
❑5, Oct 2002 .... 2.95
❑6, Nov 2002 .... 2.95
❑7, Dec 2002 .... 2.95
❑8, Jan 2003 .... 2.95
❑9, Feb 2003 .... 2.95
❑10, Mar 2003 .... 2.95
❑11, Apr 2003 .... 2.95
❑12, May 2003 .... 2.95
❑13, Jul 2003 .... 2.95
❑14, Aug 2003 .... 2.95
❑15, Oct 2003 .... 2.95
❑16, Nov 2003 .... 2.95
❑17, Dec 2003 .... 2.95
❑18, Dec 2003 .... 2.95
❑19, Jan 2004 .... 2.95
❑20, Mar 2004 .... 2.95
❑21, Apr 2004 .... 2.95
❑22, May 2004 .... 2.95

ROVERS, THE
MALIBU

❑1, Sep 1987 .... 1.95
❑2 1987 .... 1.95
❑3 1987 .... 1.95
❑4 1988 .... 1.95
❑5 1988 .... 1.95
❑6 1988, b&w 1.95
❑7 1988, b&w 1.95

ROYAL ROY
MARVEL / STAR

❑1, May 1985 1: Royal Roy. 1.00
❑2, Jul 1985 .... 1.00
❑3, Sep 1985 .... 1.00
❑4, Nov 1985 .... 1.00
❑5, Jan 1986 .... 1.00
❑6, Mar 1986 .... 1.00

ROY ROGERS WESTERN
AC

❑1, b&w 4.95

ROY ROGERS WESTERN CLASSICS
AC

❑1; some color 2.95
❑2; some color 2.95

N-MINT

❑3; some color 3.95
❑4; some color 3.95
❑5; photos 2.95

RUBBER BLANKET
RUBBER BLANKET

❑1, b&w 5.75
❑2 7.75
❑3 7.95

RUBES REVUE, THE
FRAGMENTS WEST

❑1, b&w 2.00

RUBY SHAFT'S TALES OF THE UNEXPURGATED
FANTAGRAPHICS / EROS

❑1, b&w 2.50

RUCK BUD WEBSTER AND HIS SCREECHING COMMANDOS
PYRAMID

❑1, b&w 1.60

RUFF AND REDDY
DELL

❑4, Jan 1960; Previous issues appeared as Four Color #937, #981, and #1038 40.00
❑5, Apr 1960 40.00
❑6, Jul 1960 40.00
❑7, Oct 1960 40.00
❑8, Jan 1961 40.00
❑9, Apr 1961 30.00
❑10, Jul 1961 30.00
❑11, Oct 1961 30.00
❑12, Jan 1962 30.00

RUGRATS COMIC ADVENTURES
NICKELODEON MAGAZINES

❑1 1997 3.50
❑2 1997 3.00
❑3 1998 3.00
❑4 1998 3.00
❑5 1998 3.00
❑6 1998 3.00
❑7 1998 3.00
❑8, Jun 1998; magazine; no cover price 3.00
❑9 1998 3.00
❑10, Aug 1998; magazine; no cover price 3.00

RUGRATS COMIC ADVENTURES (VOL. 2)
NICKELODEON MAGAZINES

❑1, Sep 1998; magazine; no cover price 3.00

RUINS
MARVEL

❑1, Aug 1995; Acetate cover overlaying cardstock inner cover 4.95
❑2, Sep 1995; Acetate cover overlaying cardstock inner cover 4.95

RUMBLE GIRLS: SILKY WARRIOR TANSIE
IMAGE

❑1, Apr 2000 3.50
❑2, Jun 2000 3.50
❑3, Jul 2000 3.50
❑4, Aug 2000 3.50
❑5, Nov 2000 3.50
❑6, Jan 2001 3.50

RUMIC WORLD
VIZ

❑1, b&w; Fire Tripper 3.25
❑2, b&w; Laughing Target 3.50

RUMMAGE $2099
PARODY

❑1; foil cover 2.95

RUNAWAY, THE
DELL

❑1, Oct 1964 16.00

RUNAWAY: A KNOWN ASSOCIATES MYSTERY
KNOWN ASSOCIATES

❑1, b&w 2.50

N-MINT

RUNAWAYS
MARVEL

❑1, Jul 2003 2.50
❑2, Aug 2003 2.50
❑3, Sep 2003 2.50
❑4, Oct 2003 2.50
❑5, Nov 2003 2.99
❑6, Nov 2003 2.99
❑7, Dec 2003 2.50
❑8, Jan 2004 2.99
❑9, Feb 2004 2.99
❑10, Mar 2004 2.99
❑11, Apr 2004 2.99
❑12, Apr 2004 2.99
❑13, May 2004 2.99
❑14, Jun 2004 2.99
❑15, Jul 2004 2.99
❑16, Aug 2004 2.99

RUN, BUDDY, RUN
GOLD KEY

❑1, Jun 1967 15.00

RUNE
MALIBU / ULTRAVERSE

❑0, Jan 1994; Promotional edition (from redeeming coupons in early Ultraverse comics); no cover price 3.00
❑1, Jan 1994 2.00
❑1/Variant, Jan 1994; Foil limited edition; silver foil logo 2.00
❑2, Feb 1994 1.95
❑3, Mar 1994; 1: Ripfire. 1: Elven. Flip-book with Ultraverse Premiere #1 .. 3.50
❑4, Jun 1994 1.95
❑5, Sep 1994 1.95
❑6, Dec 1994 1.95
❑7, Feb 1995 1.95
❑8, Feb 1995 1.95
❑9, Apr 1995 D: Sybil. D: Master Oshi. D: Tantalus. 1.95
❑Giant Size 1, Jan 1995; Giant-size Rune #1 O: Rune. 1: Sybil. 1: Master Oshi. 1: Tantalus. D: El Gato. 2.50

RUNE (VOL. 2)
MALIBU / ULTRAVERSE

❑0, Sep 1995; Black September; Rune #Infinity; black cover 1.50
❑0/Variant, Sep 1995; alternate cover; Rune #Infinity 2.00
❑1, Oct 1995 A: Gemini. A: Adam Warlock. A: Annihilus. 1.50
❑2, Nov 1995 1.50
❑3, Dec 1995 1.50
❑4, Jan 1996 1.50
❑5, Feb 1996 1.50
❑6, Mar 1996 1.50
❑7, Apr 1996 1.50

RUNE: HEARTS OF DARKNESS
MALIBU

❑1, Sep 1996; Flip-book 1.50
❑2, Oct 1996; Flip-book 1.50
❑3, Nov 1996; Flip-book 1.50

RUNE/SILVER SURFER
MARVEL

❑1, Apr 1995; newsstand edition; crossover 3.00
❑1/Direct ed., Apr 1995; Direct Market edition; crossover; Squarebound with glossier paper 6.00

RUNE VS. VENOM
MALIBU / ULTRAVERSE

❑1, Dec 1995 3.95

RUNE/WRATH
MALIBU / ULTRAVERSE

❑1; gold foil ashcan 1.00

RUSE
CROSSGEN

❑1, Nov 2001 2.95
❑2, Dec 2001 2.95
❑3, Jan 2002 2.95
❑4, Feb 2002 2.95
❑5, Mar 2002 2.95
❑6, Apr 2002 2.95

N-MINT

❑7, May 2002 2.95
❑8, Jun 2002 2.95
❑9, Jul 2002 2.95
❑10, Aug 2002 2.95
❑11, Sep 2002 2.95
❑12, Oct 2002 2.95
❑13, Nov 2002 2.95
❑14, Dec 2002 2.95
❑15, Jan 2003 2.95
❑16, Feb 2003 2.95
❑17, Mar 2003 2.95
❑18, Apr 2003 2.95
❑19, May 2003 2.95
❑20, Jun 2003 2.95
❑21, Jul 2003 2.95
❑22, Aug 2003 2.95
❑23, Sep 2003 2.95
❑24, Nov 2003 2.95
❑25, Nov 2003 2.95
❑26, Jan 2004 2.95

RUSE: ARCHARD'S AGENTS: DEADLY DARE
CROSSGEN

❑1, Mar 2004 2.95

RUSE: ARCHARD'S AGENTS: PUGILISTIC PETE
CROSSGEN

❑1, Oct 2003 2.95

RUSH LIMBAUGH MUST DIE
BONEYARD

❑1, Nov 1993, b&w 5.00

RUST
NOW

❑1, Jul 1987 2.00
❑2, Aug 1987 2.00
❑3, Sep 1987 2.00
❑4, Nov 1987 2.00
❑5, Dec 1987 2.00
❑6, Jan 1988 2.00
❑7, Feb 1988 2.00
❑8, Mar 1988 2.00
❑9, Apr 1988 2.00
❑10, May 1988 2.00
❑11, Jul 1988 2.00
❑12, Aug 1988; Terminator preview .. 2.00
❑13, Sep 1988 2.00

RUST (2ND SERIES)
NOW

❑1, Feb 1989 2.00
❑2, Mar 1989 2.00
❑3, Apr 1989 2.00
❑4, May 1989 2.00
❑5, Jun 1989 2.00
❑6, Aug 1989 2.00
❑7, Sep 1989 2.00

RUST (3RD SERIES)
ADVENTURE

❑1, Apr 1992, Adventure Comics 2.95
❑1/Ltd., Apr 1992; limited edition; Cardstock cover; rust-colored foil logo 4.95
❑2, Jun 1992 2.95
❑3, Aug 1992 2.95
❑4, Sep 1992 2.95

RUST (4TH SERIES)
CALIBER

❑1 2.95
❑2 2.95

RUULE: GANGLORDS OF CHINATOWN
BECKETT

❑1, Nov 2003
❑2, Dec 2003
❑3, Jan 2004
❑4, Feb 2004
❑5, Mar 2004

N-MINT

S

SABAN POWERHOUSE
ACCLAIM

❑1, ca. 1997; digest; Power Rangers Turbo, Masked Rider, Samurai Pizza Cats; no indicia 4.50
❑2, ca. 1997; digest; Power Rangers Turbo, Masked Rider, Samurai Pizza Cats, BettleBorgs 4.50

SABAN PRESENTS POWER RANGERS TURBO VS. BEETLEBORGS METALLIX
ACCLAIM

❑1, ca. 1997; digest 4.50

SABINA
FANTAGRAPHICS / EROS

❑1 2.95
❑2 2.95
❑3 2.95
❑4 2.95
❑5 2.95
❑6 2.95
❑7, Jul 1996 2.95

SABLE
FIRST

❑1, Mar 1988 2.00
❑2, Apr 1988 2.00
❑3, May 1988 2.00
❑4, Jun 1988 2.00
❑5, Jul 1988 2.00
❑6, Aug 1988 2.00
❑7, Sep 1988 2.00
❑8, Oct 1988 2.00
❑9, Nov 1988 2.00
❑10, Dec 1988 2.00
❑11, Jan 1989 2.00
❑12, Feb 1989 2.00
❑13, Mar 1989 2.00
❑14, Apr 1989 2.00
❑15, May 1989 2.00
❑16, Jun 1989 2.00
❑17, Jul 1989 2.00
❑18, Aug 1989 2.00
❑19, Sep 1989 2.00
❑20, Oct 1989 2.00
❑21, Nov 1989 2.00
❑22, Dec 1989 2.00
❑23, Jan 1990 2.00
❑24, Feb 1990 2.00
❑25, Mar 1990 2.00
❑26, Apr 1990 2.00
❑27, May 1990 2.00

SABLE (MIKE GRELL'S...)
FIRST

❑1, Mar 1990; MGr (w); MGr (a); Reprints Jon Sable, Freelance #1 2.00
❑2, Apr 1990 MGr (w); MGr (a) 2.00
❑3, May 1990 MGr (w); MGr (a) 2.00
❑4, Jun 1990 MGr (w); MGr (a) 2.00
❑5, Jul 1990 MGr (w); MGr (a) 2.00
❑6, Aug 1990 MGr (w); MGr (a) 2.00
❑7, Sep 1990 MGr (w); MGr (a) 2.00
❑8, Oct 1990 MGr (w); MGr (a) 2.00
❑9, Nov 1990 MGr (w); MGr (a) 2.00
❑10, Dec 1990 MGr (w); MGr (a) 2.00

SABRA BLADE
DRACULINA

❑1, Dec 1994, b&w 2.50
❑1/Variant, Dec 1994, b&w; alternate two-color cover 2.50

SABRE
ECLIPSE

❑1, Aug 1982 PG (a); 1: Sabre. 2.50
❑2, Oct 1982 PG (a) 2.00
❑3, Dec 1982 PG (a) 2.00
❑4, Mar 1983 2.00
❑5, Jul 1983 2.00
❑6, Oct 1983 2.00
❑7, Dec 1983 2.00
❑8, Feb 1984 2.00

N-MINT

❑9, Apr 1984 2.00
❑10, Jun 1984 1.75
❑11, Aug 1984 1.75
❑12, Jan 1985 1.75
❑13, Apr 1985 1.75
❑14, Aug 1985 1.75

SABRETOOTH
MARVEL

❑1, Aug 1993; Die-cut cover 3.00
❑2, Sep 1993 3.00
❑3, Oct 1993; A: Mystique. cardstock cover 3.00
❑4, Nov 1993 3.00
❑Special 1, Jan 1995; Special edition; enhanced wraparound cover 4.95

SABRETOOTH CLASSIC
MARVEL

❑1, May 1994; reprints Power Man & Iron Fist #66 2.00
❑2, Jun 1994; KGa (a); reprints Power Man & Iron Fist #78 1.50
❑3, Jul 1994; reprints Power Man & Iron Fist #84 1.50
❑4, Aug 1994; reprints Peter Parker, The Spectacular Spider-Man #116 . 1.50
❑5, Sep 1994; RB, BMc (a); reprints Peter Parker, The Spectacular Spider-Man #119 1.50
❑6, Oct 1994; reprints X-Factor #10 .. 1.50
❑7, Nov 1994; SB (a); reprints The Mighty Thor #374 1.50
❑8, Dec 1994; reprints Power Pack #27 1.50
❑9, Jan 1995; reprints Uncanny X-Men #212 1.50
❑10, Feb 1995; reprints Uncanny X-Men #213 1.50
❑11, Mar 1995; SB (a); reprints Daredevil #238 1.50
❑12, Apr 1995; reprints back-up stories from Classic X-Men #10 and Marvel Super-Heroes (no issue given) 1.50
❑13, May 1995; reprints Uncanny X-Men #219 1.50
❑14, Jun 1995; reprints Uncanny X-Men #221 1.50
❑15, Jul 1995; reprints Uncanny X-Men #222 1.50

SABRETOOTH: MARY SHELLEY OVERDRIVE
MARVEL

❑1, Aug 2002 2.99
❑2, Sep 2002 2.99
❑3, Oct 2002 2.99
❑4, Nov 2002 2.99

SABRINA
ARCHIE

❑1, May 1997, DDC (a); Photo worked into cover art 2.50
❑2, Jun 1997, Photo worked into cover art 2.00
❑3, Jul 1997, Photo worked into cover art 2.00
❑4, Aug 1997, Photo worked into cover art 1.50
❑5, Sep 1997, Photo worked into cover art 1.50
❑6, Oct 1997, Photo worked into cover art 1.50
❑7, Nov 1997, Photo worked into cover art 1.50
❑8, Dec 1997, Photo worked into cover art 1.50
❑9, Jan 1998, Photo worked into cover art 1.75
❑10, Feb 1998, Photo worked into cover art 1.75
❑11, Mar 1998, Photo worked into cover art 1.75
❑12, Apr 1998, Photo worked into cover art 1.75
❑13, May 1998, Photo worked into cover art 1.75
❑14, Jun 1998, Photo worked into cover art 1.75
❑15, Jul 1998, Photo worked into cover art 1.75

The success of the ABC television show led Archie to start a new *Sabrina* comics series in 1997.

N-MINT

❑16, Aug 1998, Photo worked into cover art 1.75
❑17, Sep 1998, A: Josie & the Pussycats. Photo worked into cover art .. 1.75
❑18, Oct 1998, Photo worked into cover art 1.75
❑19, Nov 1998, DDC (a); Photo worked into cover art; back to the '60s 1.75
❑20, Dec 1998, Photo worked into cover art 1.75
❑21, Jan 1999, Photo worked into cover art 1.75
❑22, Feb 1999, Photo worked into cover art 1.75
❑23, Mar 1999, Photo worked into cover art (hidden in crowd) 1.75
❑24, Apr 1999, Photo is inset on cover 1.79
❑25, May 1999, Photo worked into cover art 1.79
❑26, Jun 1999, Photo is inset on cover 1.79
❑27, Jul 1999, Photo is inset on cover 1.79
❑28, Aug 1999, A: Sonic. Photo is inset on cover; continues in Sonic Super Special #10 1.79
❑29, Sep 1999, Photo is inset on cover 1.79
❑30, Oct 1999, Photo is inset on cover 1.79
❑31, Nov 1999, Photo is inset on cover 1.79
❑32, Dec 1999, DDC (c); Photo appears in inset 1.79

SABRINA (VOL. 2)
ARCHIE

❑1, Jan 2000, based on the animated series 1.99
❑2, Feb 2000 1.99
❑3, Mar 2000 1.99
❑4, Apr 2000 1.99
❑5, May 2000 1.99
❑6, Jun 2000 1.99
❑7, Jul 2000 1.99
❑8, Aug 2000 1.99
❑9, Sep 2000 1.99
❑10, Oct 2000 1.99
❑11, Nov 2000 1.99
❑12, Dec 2000 1.99
❑13, Jan 2001 1.99
❑14, Feb 2001 1.99
❑15, Mar 2001 1.99
❑16, Apr 2001 1.99
❑17, May 2001 1.99
❑18, Jun 2001 1.99
❑19, Jul 2001 1.99
❑20, Aug 2001 1.99
❑21, Sep 2001 1.99
❑22, Oct 2001 1.99
❑23, Nov 2001 1.99
❑24, Dec 2001 1.99
❑25, Jan 2002 1.99
❑26, Jan 2002 1.99
❑27, Feb 2002 1.99
❑28, Mar 2002 1.99
❑29, Apr 2002 1.99
❑30, May 2002 1.99
❑31, Jun 2002 1.99
❑32, Jul 2002 1.99
❑33, Aug 2002 1.99
❑34, Sep 2002 1.99
❑35, Oct 2002 1.99
❑36, Nov 2002 1.99
❑37, Dec 2002 1.99

N-MINT

❑38, Jan 2003 1.99
❑39, Jan 2003 2.19
❑40, Feb 2003 2.19
❑41, Mar 2003 2.19
❑42, Apr 2003 2.19
❑43, May 2003 2.19
❑44, Jun 2003 2.19
❑45, Jul 2003 2.19
❑46, Aug 2003 2.19
❑47, Sep 2003 2.19
❑48, Oct 2003 2.19
❑49, Nov 2003 2.19
❑50, Dec 2003 2.19
❑51, Dec 2003 2.19
❑52, Jan 2004 2.19
❑53, Feb 2004 2.19
❑54, Mar 2004 2.19
❑55, Apr 2004 2.19
❑56, May 2004 2.19
❑57, Jul 2004 2.19

SABRINA ONLINE
VISION

❑2 3.50

SABRINA THE TEENAGE WITCH
ARCHIE

❑1, Apr 1971, Giant-size 45.00
❑2, Jul 1971, Giant-size 20.00
❑3, Sep 1971, Giant-size 12.00
❑4, Dec 1971, Giant-size 12.00
❑5, Feb 1972, Giant-size 12.00
❑6, Jun 1972, Giant-size 10.00
❑7, Aug 1972, Giant-size 10.00
❑8, Sep 1972, Giant-size 10.00
❑9, Oct 1972, Giant-size 10.00
❑10, Feb 1973, Giant-size 10.00
❑11, Apr 1973, Giant-size 8.00
❑12, Jun 1973, Giant-size 8.00
❑13, Aug 1973, Giant-size 8.00
❑14, Sep 1973, Giant-size 8.00
❑15, Oct 1973, Giant-size 8.00
❑16, Dec 1973, Giant-size 8.00
❑17, Feb 1974, Giant-size 8.00
❑18, Apr 1974, color 6.00
❑19, Jun 1974, color 6.00
❑20, Aug 1974, color 6.00
❑21, Sep 1974, color 5.00
❑22, Oct 1974, color 5.00
❑23, Feb 1975, color 5.00
❑24, Apr 1975, color 5.00
❑25, Jun 1975, color 5.00
❑26, Aug 1975, color 5.00
❑27, Sep 1975, color 5.00
❑28, Oct 1975, color 5.00
❑29, Dec 1975, color 5.00
❑30, Feb 1976, color 5.00
❑31, Apr 1976, color 4.00
❑32, Jun 1976, color 4.00
❑33, Aug 1976, color 4.00
❑34, Sep 1976, color 4.00
❑35, Oct 1976, color A: Betty. A: Ethel. A: Jughead. A: Veronica. 4.00
❑36, Dec 1977, color 4.00
❑37, Feb 1977, color 4.00
❑38, May 1977, color 4.00
❑39, Jun 1977, color 4.00
❑40, Aug 1977, color 4.00
❑41, Sep 1977, color 4.00
❑42, Oct 1977, color 4.00
❑43, Dec 1977, color 4.00
❑44, Feb 1978, color 4.00
❑45, May 1978, color 4.00
❑46, Jun 1978, color 4.00
❑47, Aug 1978, color 4.00
❑48, Sep 1978, color 4.00
❑49, Oct 1978, color 4.00
❑50, Dec 1978, color 4.00
❑51, Feb 1979, color 3.00
❑52, May 1979, color 3.00
❑53, Jun 1979, color 3.00
❑54, Aug 1979, color 3.00
❑55, Sep 1979, color 3.00
❑56, Oct 1979, color 3.00
❑57, Dec 1979, color 3.00
❑58, Feb 1980, color 3.00
❑59, Apr 1980, color 3.00
❑60, Jun 1980, color 3.00
❑61, Aug 1980, color 2.00
❑62, Sep 1980, color 2.00
❑63, Oct 1980, color 2.00
❑64, Dec 1980, color 2.00
❑65, Feb 1981, color 2.00
❑66, Apr 1981, color 2.00
❑67, Jun 1981, color 2.00
❑68, Aug 1981, color 2.00
❑69, Oct 1981, color 2.00
❑70, Dec 1981, color 2.00
❑71, Feb 1982, color 2.00
❑72, Apr 1982, color 2.00
❑73, Jun 1982, color 2.00
❑74, Aug 1982, color 2.00
❑75, Oct 1982, color 2.00
❑76, Dec 1982, color 2.00
❑77, Feb 1983, color 2.00
❑Holiday 1, ca. 1993, "Sabrina's Halloween Spoook-Tacular" 2.00
❑Holiday 2, ca. 1994 2.00
❑Holiday 3, ca. 1995 2.00

SABRINA THE TEENAGE WITCH (2ND SERIES)
ARCHIE

❑1, ca. 1996, color 2.00

SACHS & VIOLENS
MARVEL / EPIC

❑1, Nov 1993; PD (w); GP (a); Embossed cover 3.00
❑1/Platinum, Nov 1993; Platinum promotional edition; PD (w); GP (a); Embossed cover 3.00
❑2, May 1994 PD (w); GP (a) 2.25
❑3, Jun 1994; PD (w); GP (a); Sex, nudity 2.25
❑4, Jul 1994 PD (w); GP (a) 2.25

SACRIFICED TREES
MANSION

❑1 3.00

SADE/RAZOR
LONDON NIGHT

❑1-2 3.00

SAD SACK
HARVEY

❑63, Oct 1956 8.00
❑64, Nov 1956 8.00
❑65, Dec 1956 8.00
❑66, Jan 1957 8.00
❑67, Feb 1957 8.00
❑68, Mar 1957 8.00
❑69, Apr 1957 8.00
❑70, May 1957 8.00
❑71, Jun 1957 6.00
❑72, Jul 1957 6.00
❑73, Aug 1957 6.00
❑74, Sep 1957 6.00
❑75, Oct 1957 6.00
❑76, Nov 1957 6.00
❑77, Dec 1957 6.00
❑78, Jan 1958 6.00
❑79, Feb 1958 6.00
❑80, Mar 1958 6.00
❑81, ca. 1958 6.00
❑82, ca. 1958 6.00
❑83, ca. 1958 6.00
❑84, ca. 1958 6.00
❑85, ca. 1958 6.00
❑86, ca. 1958 6.00
❑87, ca. 1958 6.00
❑88, Dec 1958 6.00
❑89, Jan 1959 6.00
❑90, Feb 1959 6.00
❑91, Mar 1959 4.00
❑92, Apr 1959 4.00
❑93, May 1959 4.00
❑94, Jun 1959 4.00
❑95, Jul 1959 4.00
❑96, Aug 1959 4.00
❑97, Sep 1959 4.00
❑98, Oct 1959 4.00
❑99, Nov 1959 4.00
❑100, Dec 1959 4.00
❑101, Jan 1960 2.50
❑102, Feb 1960 2.50
❑103, Mar 1960 2.50
❑104, Apr 1960 2.50
❑105, May 1960 2.50
❑106, Jun 1960 2.50
❑107, Jul 1960 2.50
❑108, Aug 1960 2.50
❑109, Sep 1960 2.50
❑110, Oct 1960 2.50
❑111, Nov 1960 2.50
❑112, Dec 1960 2.50
❑113, Jan 1961 2.50
❑114, Feb 1961 2.50
❑115, Mar 1961 2.50
❑116, Apr 1961 2.50
❑117, May 1961 2.50
❑118, Jun 1961 2.50
❑119, Jul 1961 2.50
❑120, Aug 1961 2.50
❑121, Sep 1961 2.50
❑122, Oct 1961 2.50
❑123, Nov 1961 2.50
❑124, Dec 1961 2.50
❑125, Jan 1962 2.50
❑126, Feb 1962 2.50
❑127, Mar 1962 2.50
❑128, Apr 1962 2.50
❑129, May 1962 2.50
❑130, Jun 1962 2.50
❑131, Jul 1962 2.50
❑132, Aug 1962 2.50
❑133, Sep 1962 2.50
❑134, Oct 1962 2.50
❑135, Nov 1962 2.50
❑136, Dec 1962 2.50
❑137, Jan 1963 2.50
❑138, Feb 1963 2.50
❑139, Mar 1963 2.50
❑140, Apr 1963 2.50
❑141, May 1963 2.50
❑142, Jun 1963 2.50
❑143, Jul 1963 2.50
❑144, Aug 1963 2.50
❑145, Sep 1963 2.50
❑146, Oct 1963 2.50
❑147, Nov 1963 2.50
❑148, Dec 1963 2.50
❑149, Jan 1964 2.50
❑150, Feb 1964 2.50
❑151, Mar 1964 2.00
❑152, Apr 1964 2.00
❑153, May 1964 2.00
❑154, Jun 1964 2.00
❑155, Jul 1964 2.00
❑156, Aug 1964 2.00
❑157, Sep 1964 2.00
❑158, Oct 1964 2.00
❑159, Nov 1964 2.00
❑160, Dec 1964 2.00
❑161, Jan 1965 2.00
❑162, Feb 1965 2.00
❑163, Mar 1965 2.00
❑164, Apr 1965 2.00
❑165, May 1965 2.00
❑166, Jun 1965 2.00
❑167, Jul 1965 2.00
❑168, Aug 1965 2.00
❑169, Sep 1965 2.00
❑170, Oct 1965 2.00
❑171, Nov 1965 2.00
❑172, Dec 1965 2.00
❑173, Jan 1966 2.00
❑174, Feb 1966 2.00
❑175, Mar 1966 2.00

	N-MINT
❑176, Apr 1966	2.00
❑177, May 1966	2.00
❑178, Jun 1966	2.00
❑179, Jul 1966	2.00
❑180, Aug 1966	2.00
❑181, Sep 1966	2.00
❑182, Oct 1966	2.00
❑183, Nov 1966	2.00
❑184, Dec 1966	2.00
❑185, Jan 1967	2.00
❑186, Feb 1967	2.00
❑187, Mar 1967	2.00
❑188, Apr 1967	2.00
❑189, May 1967	2.00
❑190, Jun 1967	2.00
❑191, Jul 1967	2.00
❑192, Aug 1967	2.00
❑193, Sep 1967	2.00
❑194, Oct 1967	2.00
❑195, Nov 1967	2.00
❑196, Dec 1967	2.00
❑197, Jan 1968	2.00
❑198, Mar 1968	2.00
❑199, May 1968	2.00
❑200, Jul 1968	2.00
❑201, Sep 1968	1.50
❑202, Oct 1968	1.50
❑203, Nov 1968	1.50
❑204, Jan 1969	1.50
❑205, Mar 1969	1.50
❑206, May 1969	1.50
❑207, Jul 1969	1.50
❑208, Sep 1969	1.50
❑209, Oct 1969	1.50
❑210, Nov 1969	1.50
❑211, Jan 1970	1.50
❑212, Mar 1970	1.50
❑213, May 1970	1.50
❑214, Jul 1970	1.50
❑215, Sep 1970	1.50
❑216, Oct 1970	1.50
❑217, Nov 1970	1.50
❑218, Jan 1971	1.50
❑219, Mar 1971	1.50
❑220, May 1971	1.50
❑221, Jul 1971	1.50
❑222, Sep 1971	1.50
❑223, Nov 1971	1.50
❑224, Jan 1972	1.50
❑225, Mar 1972	1.50
❑226, May 1972	1.50
❑227, Jul 1972	1.50
❑228, Sep 1972	1.50
❑229, Nov 1972	1.50
❑230, Jan 1973	1.50
❑231, Mar 1973	1.50
❑232, May 1973	1.50
❑233, Jul 1973	1.50
❑234, Sep 1973	1.50
❑235, Nov 1973	1.50
❑236, Jan 1974	1.50
❑237, Mar 1974	1.50
❑238, May 1974	1.50
❑239, Jul 1974	1.50
❑240, Sep 1974	1.50
❑241, Nov 1974	1.50
❑242, Jan 1975	1.50
❑243, Mar 1975	1.50
❑244, May 1975	1.50
❑245, Jul 1975	1.50
❑246, Sep 1975	1.50
❑247, Nov 1975	1.50
❑248, Jan 1976	1.50
❑249, Mar 1976	1.50
❑250, May 1976	1.50
❑251, Jul 1976	1.50
❑252, Sep 1976	1.50
❑253, Nov 1976	1.50
❑254, Jan 1977	1.50
❑255, Mar 1977	1.50
❑256, May 1977	1.50

	N-MINT
❑257, Jul 1977	1.50
❑258, Sep 1977	1.50
❑259, Nov 1977	1.50
❑260, Jan 1978	1.50
❑261, Mar 1978	1.50
❑262, May 1978	1.50
❑263, Jul 1978	1.50
❑264, Sep 1978	1.50
❑265, Nov 1978	1.50
❑266, Jan 1979	1.50
❑267, Mar 1979	1.50
❑268, May 1979	1.50
❑269, Jul 1979	1.50
❑270, Sep 1979	1.50
❑271, Nov 1979	1.50
❑272, Jan 1980	1.50
❑273, Mar 1980	1.50
❑274, May 1980	1.50
❑275, Jul 1980	1.50
❑276, Sep 1980	1.50
❑277, Nov 1980	1.50
❑278, Jan 1981	1.50
❑279, Mar 1981	1.50
❑280, May 1981	1.50
❑281, Jul 1981	1.50
❑282, Sep 1981	1.50
❑283, Nov 1981	1.50
❑284, Jan 1982	1.50
❑285, Mar 1982	1.50
❑286, May 1982	1.50
❑287, Jul 1982	1.50
❑288, ca. 1992	2.75
❑289, ca. 1992	2.75
❑290, ca. 1992, b&w	1.50
❑291, ca. 1993	1.50
❑292, ca. 1993	1.50
❑293, ca. 1993	1.50
❑3D 1, ca. 1954; Harvey 3-D Hits	125.00

SAD SACK & THE SARGE
HARVEY

	N-MINT
❑1, Sep 1957	80.00
❑2, Nov 1957	45.00
❑3, Jan 1958	30.00
❑4, Mar 1958	30.00
❑5 1958	30.00
❑6, Jun 1958	20.00
❑7 1958	20.00
❑8 1958	20.00
❑9, Oct 1958	20.00
❑10, Dec 1958	20.00
❑11, Feb 1959	16.00
❑12, Apr 1959	16.00
❑13, Jun 1959	16.00
❑14, Aug 1959	16.00
❑15, Oct 1959	16.00
❑16, Dec 1959	16.00
❑17, Feb 1960	16.00
❑18, Apr 1960	16.00
❑19, Jun 1960	16.00
❑20, Aug 1960	16.00
❑21, Oct 1960	12.00
❑22, Dec 1960	12.00
❑23, Feb 1961	12.00
❑24, Apr 1961	12.00
❑25, Jun 1961	12.00
❑26, Aug 1961	12.00
❑27, Oct 1961	12.00
❑28, Dec 1961	12.00
❑29, Feb 1962	12.00
❑30, Apr 1962	12.00
❑31, Jun 1962	9.00
❑32, Aug 1962	9.00
❑33, Oct 1962	9.00
❑34, Dec 1962	9.00
❑35, Feb 1963	9.00
❑36, Apr 1963	9.00
❑37, Jun 1963	9.00
❑38, Aug 1963	9.00
❑39, Oct 1963	9.00
❑40, Dec 1963	9.00
❑41, Feb 1964	7.00

Sad Sack featured the misadventures of the world's most inept Army private. © 1967 Harvey Comics

	N-MINT
❑42, Apr 1964	7.00
❑43, Jun 1964	7.00
❑44, Aug 1964	7.00
❑45, Oct 1964	7.00
❑46, Dec 1964	7.00
❑47, Feb 1965	7.00
❑48, Apr 1965	7.00
❑49, Jun 1965	7.00
❑50, Aug 1965	6.00
❑51, Oct 1965	6.00
❑52, Dec 1965	6.00
❑53, Feb 1966	6.00
❑54, Apr 1966	6.00
❑55, Jun 1966	6.00
❑56, Aug 1966	6.00
❑57, Sep 1966	6.00
❑58, Oct 1966	6.00
❑59, Dec 1966	6.00
❑60, Feb 1967	6.00
❑61, Apr 1967	5.00
❑62, Jun 1967	5.00
❑63, Aug 1967	5.00
❑64, Oct 1967	5.00
❑65, Dec 1967	5.00
❑66, Feb 1968	5.00
❑67, Apr 1968	5.00
❑68, Jun 1968	5.00
❑69, Aug 1968	5.00
❑70, Oct 1968	5.00
❑71, Dec 1968	5.00
❑72, Jan 1969	5.00
❑73 1969	5.00
❑74, May 1969	5.00
❑75, Jun 1969	5.00
❑76, Jul 1969	5.00
❑77, Sep 1969	5.00
❑78, Oct 1969	5.00
❑79, Dec 1969	5.00
❑80, Feb 1970	5.00
❑81, Apr 1970	3.00
❑82, Jun 1970	3.00
❑83, Aug 1970	3.00
❑84, Oct 1970	3.00
❑85, Nov 1970	3.00
❑86, Jan 1971	3.00
❑87, Feb 1971	3.00
❑88, Apr 1971	3.00
❑89, Jun 1971	3.00
❑90, Aug 1971	3.00
❑91, Oct 1971; Giant size A: The General. A: Slob Slobinski.	4.00
❑92, Dec 1971; Giant size	4.00
❑93, Feb 1972; Giant size	4.00
❑94, Apr 1972; Giant size	4.00
❑95, Jun 1972; Giant size	4.00
❑96, Aug 1972; Giant size	4.00
❑97, Oct 1972	3.00
❑98, Dec 1972	3.00
❑99, Feb 1973	3.00
❑100, Apr 1973	3.00
❑101, Jun 1973	2.00
❑102, Aug 1973	2.00
❑103, Oct 1973	2.00
❑104, Dec 1973	2.00
❑105, Feb 1974	2.00
❑106, Apr 1974	2.00
❑107, Jun 1974	2.00

N-MINT

- ❑108, Aug 1974 ... 2.00
- ❑109, Oct 1974 ... 2.00
- ❑110, Dec 1974 ... 2.00
- ❑111, Feb 1975 ... 2.00
- ❑112, Apr 1975 ... 2.00
- ❑113, Jun 1975 ... 2.00
- ❑114, Aug 1975 ... 2.00
- ❑115, Oct 1975 ... 2.00
- ❑116, Dec 1975 ... 2.00
- ❑117, Feb 1976 ... 2.00
- ❑118, Apr 1976 ... 2.00
- ❑119, Jun 1976 ... 2.00
- ❑120, Aug 1976 ... 2.00
- ❑121, Oct 1976 ... 2.00
- ❑122, Dec 1976 ... 2.00
- ❑123, Feb 1977 ... 2.00
- ❑124, Apr 1977 ... 2.00
- ❑125, Jun 1977 ... 2.00
- ❑126, Aug 1977 ... 2.00
- ❑127, Oct 1977 ... 2.00
- ❑128, Dec 1977 ... 2.00
- ❑129, Feb 1978 ... 2.00
- ❑130, Apr 1978 ... 2.00
- ❑131, Jun 1978 ... 2.00
- ❑132, Aug 1978 ... 2.00
- ❑133, Oct 1978 ... 2.00
- ❑134, Dec 1978 ... 2.00
- ❑135, Feb 1979 ... 2.00
- ❑136, Apr 1979 ... 2.00
- ❑137, Jun 1979 ... 2.00
- ❑138, Aug 1979 ... 2.00
- ❑139, Oct 1979 ... 2.00
- ❑140, Dec 1979 ... 2.00
- ❑141, Feb 1980 ... 2.00
- ❑142, Apr 1980 ... 2.00
- ❑143, Jun 1980 ... 2.00
- ❑144, Aug 1980 ... 2.00
- ❑145, Oct 1980 ... 2.00
- ❑146, Dec 1980 ... 2.00
- ❑147, Feb 1981 ... 2.00
- ❑148, Apr 1981 ... 2.00
- ❑149, Jun 1981 ... 2.00
- ❑150, Aug 1981 ... 2.00
- ❑151, Oct 1981 ... 2.00
- ❑152, Dec 1981 ... 2.00
- ❑153, Feb 1982 ... 2.00
- ❑154, Apr 1982 ... 2.00
- ❑155, Jun 1982 ... 2.00

SAD SACK ARMY LIFE PARADE
HARVEY

- ❑1, Oct 1963; Giant-size ... 35.00
- ❑2, Feb 1964; Giant-size ... 20.00
- ❑3, May 1964; Giant-size ... 15.00
- ❑4, Aug 1964; Giant-size ... 12.00
- ❑5, Nov 1964; Giant-size ... 12.00
- ❑6, Feb 1965; Giant-size ... 10.00
- ❑7, May 1965; Giant-size ... 10.00
- ❑8, Aug 1965; Giant-size ... 10.00
- ❑9, Nov 1965; Giant-size ... 10.00
- ❑10, Feb 1966; Giant-size ... 10.00
- ❑11, May 1966; Giant-size ... 8.00
- ❑12, Jul 1966; Giant-size ... 8.00
- ❑13, Sep 1966; Giant-size ... 8.00
- ❑14, Oct 1966; Giant-size ... 8.00
- ❑15, Jan 1967; Giant-size ... 8.00
- ❑16, Mar 1967; Giant-size ... 8.00
- ❑17 1967; Giant-size ... 8.00
- ❑18, Nov 1967; Giant-size ... 8.00
- ❑19, Feb 1968; Giant-size ... 8.00
- ❑20, May 1968; Giant-size ... 8.00
- ❑21, Aug 1968; Giant-size ... 6.00
- ❑22 1969; Giant-size ... 6.00
- ❑23, Feb 1969; Giant-size ... 6.00
- ❑24, Apr 1969; Giant-size ... 6.00
- ❑25, Aug 1969; Giant-size ... 6.00
- ❑26, Oct 1969; Giant-size ... 6.00
- ❑27, Dec 1969; Giant-size ... 6.00
- ❑28, Feb 1970; Giant-size ... 6.00
- ❑29, Apr 1970; Giant-size ... 6.00
- ❑30, Aug 1970; Giant-size ... 6.00
- ❑31, Oct 1970; Giant-size ... 5.00
- ❑32, Dec 1970; Giant-size ... 5.00
- ❑33, Feb 1971; Giant-size ... 5.00
- ❑34, Apr 1971; Giant-size ... 5.00
- ❑35, Aug 1971; Giant-size ... 5.00
- ❑36, Oct 1971; Giant-size ... 5.00
- ❑37, Dec 1971; Giant-size ... 5.00
- ❑38, Feb 1972; Giant-size ... 5.00
- ❑39, Apr 1972; Giant-size ... 5.00
- ❑40, Jun 1972; Giant-size ... 5.00
- ❑41, Aug 1972; Giant-size ... 4.00
- ❑42, Oct 1972; Giant-size ... 4.00
- ❑43, Dec 1972; Giant-size ... 4.00
- ❑44, Feb 1973; Giant-size ... 4.00
- ❑45, Apr 1973; Giant-size ... 4.00
- ❑46, Jun 1973; Giant-size ... 4.00
- ❑47, Aug 1973; Giant-size ... 4.00
- ❑48, Oct 1973; Giant-size ... 4.00
- ❑49, Dec 1973; Giant-size ... 4.00
- ❑50, Feb 1974; Giant-size ... 4.00
- ❑51, Apr 1974; Giant-size ... 2.50
- ❑52, Jun 1974; Giant-size ... 2.50
- ❑53, Aug 1974 ... 2.50
- ❑54, Oct 1974 ... 2.50
- ❑55, Dec 1974 ... 2.50
- ❑56, Feb 1975 ... 2.50
- ❑57, Apr 1975 ... 2.50
- ❑58, Jul 1975 ... 2.50
- ❑59 1975 ... 2.50
- ❑60, Nov 1975 ... 2.50
- ❑61, ca. 1976 ... 2.50

SAD SACK AT HOME FOR THE HOLIDAYS
LORNE-HARVEY

- ❑1, ca. 1992 ... 2.00

SAD SACK IN 3-D
BLACKTHORNE

- ❑1, ca. 1988 ... 2.00

SAD SACK LAUGH SPECIAL
HARVEY

- ❑1, Win 1958; Giant-size ... 90.00
- ❑2, Spr 1959; Giant-size ... 45.00
- ❑3, Sum 1959; Giant-size ... 25.00
- ❑4, ca. 1960; Giant-size ... 25.00
- ❑5, Jul 1960; Giant-size ... 25.00
- ❑6, ca. 1960; Giant-size ... 25.00
- ❑7, ca. 1960; Giant-size ... 25.00
- ❑8, ca. 1960; Giant-size ... 25.00
- ❑9, ca. 1961; Giant-size ... 25.00
- ❑10, ca. 1961; Giant-size ... 25.00
- ❑11, ca. 1962; Giant-size ... 20.00
- ❑12, ca. 1962; Giant-size ... 20.00
- ❑13, ca. 1962; Giant-size ... 20.00
- ❑14, ca. 1962; Giant-size ... 20.00
- ❑15, Jan 1963; Giant-size ... 20.00
- ❑16 1963; Giant-size ... 20.00
- ❑17 1963; Giant-size ... 20.00
- ❑18, Oct 1963; Giant-size ... 20.00
- ❑19; Giant-size ... 20.00
- ❑20, Apr 1964; Giant-size ... 20.00
- ❑21, Jul 1964; Giant-size ... 15.00
- ❑22, Sep 1964; Giant-size ... 15.00
- ❑23, Dec 1964; Giant-size ... 15.00
- ❑24, Mar 1965; Giant-size ... 15.00
- ❑25, Jun 1965; Giant-size ... 15.00
- ❑26, Sep 1965; Giant-size ... 15.00
- ❑27, Dec 1965; Giant-size ... 15.00
- ❑28, Mar 1966; Giant-size ... 15.00
- ❑29, Jun 1966; Giant-size ... 15.00
- ❑30, Aug 1966; Giant-size ... 15.00
- ❑31 1966; Giant-size ... 12.00
- ❑32, Oct 1966; Giant-size ... 12.00
- ❑33, Dec 1966; Giant-size ... 12.00
- ❑34, Feb 1967; Giant-size ... 12.00
- ❑35, Apr 1967; Giant-size ... 12.00
- ❑36, Jun 1967; Giant-size ... 12.00
- ❑37, Oct 1967; Giant-size ... 12.00
- ❑38, Nov 1967; Giant-size ... 12.00
- ❑39 1968; Giant-size ... 12.00
- ❑40, Apr 1968; Giant-size ... 12.00
- ❑41, Jun 1968; Giant-size ... 10.00
- ❑42, Aug 1968; Giant-size ... 10.00
- ❑43, Oct 1968; Giant-size ... 10.00
- ❑44, Dec 1968; Giant-size ... 10.00
- ❑45, Feb 1969; Giant-size ... 10.00
- ❑46, Apr 1969; Giant-size ... 10.00
- ❑47, May 1969; Giant-size ... 10.00
- ❑48, Jul 1969; Giant-size ... 10.00
- ❑49, Sep 1969; Giant-size ... 10.00
- ❑50, Nov 1969; Giant-size ... 10.00
- ❑51, Jan 1970; Giant-size ... 10.00
- ❑52, Mar 1970; Giant-size ... 10.00
- ❑53, May 1970; Giant-size ... 10.00
- ❑54, Jul 1970; Giant-size ... 10.00
- ❑55, Sep 1970; Giant-size ... 10.00
- ❑56, Nov 1970; Giant-size ... 10.00
- ❑57, Jan 1971; Giant-size ... 10.00
- ❑58, Mar 1971; Giant-size ... 10.00
- ❑59, May 1971; Giant-size ... 10.00
- ❑60, Jul 1971; Giant-size ... 10.00
- ❑61, Sep 1971; Giant-size ... 8.00
- ❑62, Nov 1971; Giant-size ... 8.00
- ❑63, Jan 1972; Giant-size ... 8.00
- ❑64, Mar 1972; Giant-size ... 8.00
- ❑65, May 1972; Giant-size ... 8.00
- ❑66, Jul 1972; Giant-size ... 8.00
- ❑67, Sep 1972; Giant-size ... 8.00
- ❑68, Nov 1972; Giant-size ... 8.00
- ❑69, Jan 1973; Giant-size ... 8.00
- ❑70, Mar 1973; Giant-size ... 8.00
- ❑71, May 1973; Giant-size ... 8.00
- ❑72, Jul 1973; Giant-size ... 8.00
- ❑73, Sep 1973; Giant-size ... 8.00
- ❑74, Nov 1973; Giant-size ... 8.00
- ❑75, Jan 1974; Giant-size ... 8.00
- ❑76, Mar 1974; Giant-size ... 8.00
- ❑77, May 1974; Giant-size ... 8.00
- ❑78, Jul 1974 ... 8.00
- ❑79, Sep 1974 ... 8.00
- ❑80, Nov 1974 ... 8.00
- ❑81, Jan 1975 ... 6.00
- ❑82, Mar 1975 ... 6.00
- ❑83, Jun 1975 ... 6.00
- ❑84, Aug 1975 ... 6.00
- ❑85, Oct 1975 ... 6.00
- ❑86, Dec 1975 ... 6.00
- ❑87, Feb 1976 ... 6.00
- ❑88, Apr 1976 ... 6.00
- ❑89, Jun 1976 ... 6.00
- ❑90, Aug 1976 ... 6.00
- ❑91, Oct 1976 ... 6.00
- ❑92, Dec 1976 ... 6.00
- ❑93, Feb 1977 ... 6.00

SAD SACK NAVY, GOBS 'N' GALS
HARVEY

- ❑1, Aug 1972 ... 12.00
- ❑2, Oct 1972 ... 8.00
- ❑3, Dec 1972 ... 6.00
- ❑4, Feb 1973 ... 6.00
- ❑5, Apr 1973 ... 6.00
- ❑6, Jun 1973 ... 4.00
- ❑7, Aug 1973 ... 4.00
- ❑8, Oct 1973 ... 4.00

SAD SACK'S FUNNY FRIENDS
HARVEY

- ❑1, Dec 1955 ... 50.00
- ❑2, Feb 1956 ... 34.00
- ❑3, Apr 1956 ... 22.00
- ❑4, Jun 1956 ... 20.00
- ❑5, ca. 1957 ... 20.00
- ❑6, ca. 1957 ... 16.00
- ❑7, ca. 1957 ... 16.00
- ❑8, ca. 1957 ... 16.00
- ❑9, ca. 1957 ... 16.00
- ❑10, ca. 1958 ... 16.00
- ❑11, ca. 1958 ... 12.00
- ❑12, ca. 1958 ... 12.00
- ❑13, ca. 1958 ... 12.00
- ❑14, ca. 1959 ... 12.00
- ❑15, ca. 1959 ... 12.00
- ❑16, ca. 1959 ... 12.00
- ❑17, ca. 1959 ... 12.00

N-MINT

❑18, ca. 1959 .... 12.00
❑19, ca. 1960 .... 12.00
❑20, ca. 1960 .... 12.00
❑21, May 1960 .... 10.00
❑22, Jul 1960 .... 10.00
❑23, Sep 1960 .... 10.00
❑24, Nov 1960 .... 10.00
❑25, Jan 1961 .... 10.00
❑26, Mar 1961 .... 10.00
❑27, May 1961 .... 10.00
❑28, Jul 1961 .... 10.00
❑29, Sep 1961 .... 10.00
❑30, Nov 1961 .... 10.00
❑31, Jan 1962 .... 8.00
❑32, Mar 1962 .... 8.00
❑33, May 1962 .... 8.00
❑34, Jul 1962 .... 8.00
❑35, Sep 1962 .... 8.00
❑36, Nov 1962 .... 8.00
❑37, Jan 1963 .... 8.00
❑38, Mar 1963 .... 8.00
❑39, May 1963 .... 8.00
❑40, Jul 1963 .... 8.00
❑41, Sep 1963 .... 5.00
❑42, Nov 1963 .... 5.00
❑43, Jan 1964 .... 5.00
❑44, Mar 1964 .... 5.00
❑45, May 1964 .... 5.00
❑46, Jul 1964 .... 5.00
❑47, Sep 1964 .... 5.00
❑48, Nov 1964 .... 5.00
❑49, Jan 1965 .... 5.00
❑50, Mar 1965 .... 5.00
❑51, May 1965 .... 3.00
❑52, Jul 1965 .... 3.00
❑53, Sep 1965 .... 3.00
❑54, Nov 1965 .... 3.00
❑55, Jan 1966 .... 3.00
❑56, Mar 1966 .... 3.00
❑57, May 1966 .... 3.00
❑58, Jul 1966 .... 3.00
❑59, Sep 1966 .... 3.00
❑60, Nov 1966 .... 3.00
❑61, Jan 1967 .... 3.00
❑62, Mar 1967 .... 3.00
❑63, May 1967 .... 3.00
❑64 1967 .... 3.00
❑65, Aug 1967 .... 3.00
❑66, Oct 1967 .... 3.00
❑67, Jan 1968 .... 3.00
❑68, Mar 1968 .... 3.00
❑69, May 1968 .... 3.00
❑70 1968 .... 3.00
❑71 1968 .... 3.00
❑72, Jan 1969 .... 3.00
❑73, Apr 1969 .... 3.00
❑74, Aug 1969 .... 3.00
❑75, Oct 1969 .... 3.00

SAD SAD SACK WORLD
HARVEY

❑1, Oct 1964; Giant-size 45.00
❑2, ca. 1965; Giant-size 20.00
❑3, ca. 1965; Giant-size 20.00
❑4, ca. 1966; Giant-size 20.00
❑5, Oct 1966; Giant-size 20.00
❑6, Dec 1966; Giant-size 20.00
❑7, Apr 1967; Giant-size 20.00
❑8, Jun 1967; Giant-size 20.00
❑9, Aug 1967; Giant-size 20.00
❑10 1967; Giant-size 20.00
❑11, Dec 1967; Giant-size 15.00
❑12 1968; Giant-size 15.00
❑13 1968; Giant-size 15.00
❑14 1968; Giant-size 15.00
❑15, Nov 1968; Giant-size 15.00
❑16, Mar 1969; Giant-size 15.00
❑17, Jun 1969; Giant-size 15.00
❑18, Sep 1969; Giant-size 15.00
❑19, Nov 1969; Giant-size 15.00
❑20, Jan 1970; Giant-size 15.00
❑21 1970; Giant-size 15.00

N-MINT

❑22 1970; Giant-size 15.00
❑23, Oct 1970; Giant-size 15.00
❑24, ca. 1971; Giant-size 15.00
❑25, ca. 1971; Giant-size 15.00
❑26, ca. 1971; Giant-size 15.00
❑27, Sep 1971; Giant-size 15.00
❑28, ca. 1971; Giant-size 15.00
❑29, ca. 1972; Giant-size 15.00
❑30, Mar 1972; Giant-size 15.00
❑31, ca. 1972; Giant-size 12.00
❑32, ca. 1972; Giant-size 12.00
❑33, ca. 1972; Giant-size 12.00
❑34, ca. 1973; Giant-size 12.00
❑35, Mar 1973; Giant-size 12.00
❑36, ca. 1973; Giant-size 12.00
❑37, ca. 1973; Giant-size 12.00
❑38, ca. 1973; Giant-size 12.00
❑39, Oct 1973; Giant-size 12.00
❑40, Dec 1973 .... 12.00
❑41, Feb 1973 .... 10.00
❑42, Apr 1973 .... 10.00
❑43, Jun 1973 .... 10.00
❑44, Aug 1973 .... 10.00
❑45, Oct 1973 .... 10.00
❑46, Dec 1973 .... 10.00

SAFEST PLACE IN THE WORLD, THE
DARK HORSE

❑1, ca. 1993 .... 2.50

SAFETY-BELT MAN
SIRIUS

❑1, Jun 1994, b&w 2.50
❑2, Oct 1994, b&w 2.50
❑3, Feb 1995, b&w 2.50
❑4, Jun 1995, b&w; color centerfold; Linsner back-up story 2.50
❑5, Aug 1995, b&w 2.50
❑6, Oct 1995, b&w 2.50

SAFETY-BELT MAN: ALL HELL
SIRIUS

❑1, Jun 1996 .... 2.95
❑2, Jun 1996 .... 2.95
❑3 1996 .... 2.95
❑4, Sep 1996 .... 2.95
❑5, Jan 1997 .... 2.95
❑6, Aug 1997 .... 2.95

SAFFIRE
IMAGE

❑1, Apr 2000 .... 2.95
❑2, Dec 2000 .... 2.95
❑3, Feb 2001 .... 2.95

SAGA
ODYSSEY

❑1, b&w 1.95

SAGA OF CRYSTAR, THE CRYSTAL WARRIOR
MARVEL

❑1, May 1983 O: Crystar. 1: Crystar. 2.00
❑2, Jul 1983 1: Ika. 1.00
❑3, Sep 1983 A: Doctor Strange. 1.00
❑4, Nov 1983 .... 1.00
❑5, Jan 1984 .... 1.00
❑6, Mar 1984 A: Nightcrawler. 1.00
❑7, May 1984 .... 1.00
❑8, Jul 1984 .... 1.00
❑9, Sep 1984 .... 1.00
❑10, Nov 1984 .... 1.00
❑11, Feb 1985; Double-size A: Alpha Flight. 1.00

SAGA OF RA'S AL GHUL
DC

❑1, Jan 1988 .... 2.50
❑2, Feb 1988 .... 2.50
❑3, Mar 1988 .... 2.50
❑4, Apr 1988 .... 2.50

SAGA OF SEVEN SUNS, THE
DC / WILDSTORM

❑1, ca. 2004 .... 24.95

Early adventures pitting Batman against Ra's al Ghul were reprinted in *Saga of Ra's al Ghul.*

N-MINT

SAGA OF THE MAN ELF, THE
TRIDENT

❑1, Aug 1989 .... 2.25
❑2 1989 .... 2.25
❑3 1989 .... 2.25
❑4 1990 .... 2.25
❑5 1990 .... 2.25

SAGA OF THE ORIGINAL HUMAN TORCH
MARVEL

❑1, Apr 1990 .... 1.50
❑2, May 1990 .... 1.50
❑3, Jun 1990 .... 1.50
❑4, Jul 1990 .... 1.50

SAGA OF THE SUB-MARINER
MARVEL

❑1, Nov 1988 RB (a); O: Sub-Mariner. 1.50
❑2, Dec 1988 .... 1.50
❑3, Jan 1989 .... 1.50
❑4, Feb 1989 A: Human Torch. 1.50
❑5, Mar 1989 A: Human Torch. A: Captain America. A: Invaders. 1.50
❑6, Apr 1989 A: Torch. A: Human Torch. A: Captain America. A: Invaders. 1.50
❑7, May 1989 A: Fantastic Four. 1.50
❑8, Jun 1989 A: Fantastic Four. A: Avengers. 1.50
❑9, Jul 1989 A: Fantastic Four. A: Avengers. 1.50
❑10, Aug 1989 .... 1.50
❑11, Sep 1989 .... 1.50
❑12, Oct 1989 .... 1.50

SAGA OF THE SWAMP THING, THE
DC

❑1, May 1982 TY (a); O: Swamp Thing. 3.00
❑2, Jun 1982 TY (a) 2.00
❑3, Jul 1982 TY (a) 2.00
❑4, Aug 1982 TY (a) 2.00
❑5, Sep 1982 TY (a) 2.00
❑6, Oct 1982 TY (a) 2.00
❑7, Nov 1982 TY (a) 2.00
❑8, Dec 1982 TY (a) 2.00
❑9, Jan 1983 JDu (a) 2.00
❑10, Feb 1983 TY (a) 2.00
❑11, Mar 1983 TY (a) 2.00
❑12, Apr 1983 TY (a) 2.00
❑13, May 1983 .... 2.00
❑14, Jun 1983 .... 2.00
❑15, Jul 1983 .... 2.00
❑16, Aug 1983 .... 2.00
❑17, Oct 1983 .... 2.00
❑18, Nov 1983 BWr (a) 2.00
❑19, Dec 1983 .... 2.00
❑20, Jan 1984; AMo (w); Alan Moore scripts begin 15.00
❑21, Feb 1984 AMo (w); O: Swamp Thing. O: Swamp Thing (new origin). 12.00
❑22, Mar 1984 AMo (w) 6.00
❑23, Apr 1984 AMo (w) 6.00
❑24, May 1984 AMo (w); A: Justice League. 6.00
❑25, Jun 1984 AMo (w) 6.00
❑26, Jul 1984 AMo (w) 4.00
❑27, Aug 1984 AMo (w) 4.00
❑28, Sep 1984 AMo (w) 4.00
❑29, Oct 1984 AMo (w) 4.00
❑30, Nov 1984 AMo (w); AA (a) 4.00
❑31, Dec 1984 AMo (w) 4.00

Condition price index: Multiply "NM prices" above by: **0.83 for Very Fine/Near Mint**
0.66 for Very Fine • 0.33 for Fine • 0.2 for Very Good • 0.125 for Good

N-MINT

❑32, Jan 1985 AMo (w) 4.00
❑33, Feb 1985 3.00
❑34, Mar 1985 AMo (w) 5.00
❑35, Apr 1985 AMo (w) 3.00
❑36, May 1985 AMo (w); BWr (a) 3.00
❑37, Jun 1985 AMo (w); 1: John Constantine. 30.00
❑38, Jul 1985; AMo (w); 2: John Constantine. Series continues as Swamp Thing 15.00
❑39, Aug 1985 AMo (w); A: John Constantine. 9.00
❑40, Sep 1985 AMo (w); A: John Constantine. 9.00
❑41, Oct 1985 AMo (w) 4.00
❑42, Nov 1985 AMo (w) 4.00
❑43, Dec 1985 AMo (w) 4.00
❑44, Jan 1986 AMo (w) 4.00
❑45, Feb 1986; AMo (w); AA (a); Series continued as "Swamp Thing (2nd Series) #46" 4.00
❑Annual 1, ca. 1982; TD (a); 3.00
❑Annual 2, ca. 1985 AMo (w); A: Demon. A: Spectre. A: Deadman. A: Phantom Stranger. 4.00
❑Annual 3, ca. 1987; A: Congorilla. 2.50

SAIGON CHRONICLES
Avalon

❑1 2.95

SAILOR MOON COMIC
Mixxzine

❑1, Oct 1998; Continued from MixxZine 15.00
❑1/A, Oct 1998; San Diego lmited edition version 12.00
❑2, Nov 1998 8.00
❑3, Dec 1998; D: Kunzite. Destruction of the Moon Kingdom (flashback) 8.00
❑4, Jan 1999 8.00
❑5, Feb 1999 6.00
❑6, Mar 1999 6.00
❑7, Apr 1999 6.00
❑8, May 1999 5.00
❑9, Jun 1999 4.00
❑10, Jul 1999 3.00
❑11, Aug 1999 3.00
❑12, Sep 1999 3.00
❑13, Oct 1999 3.00
❑14, Nov 1999 3.00
❑15, Dec 1999 3.00
❑16, Jan 2000 3.00
❑17, Feb 2000 3.00
❑18, Mar 2000 3.00
❑19, Apr 2000 3.00
❑20, May 2000 3.00
❑21, Jun 2000 3.00
❑22, Jul 2000 3.00
❑23, Aug 2000 3.00
❑24, Sep 2000 3.00
❑25, Oct 2000 3.00
❑26, Nov 2000 3.00
❑27, Dec 2000 3.00
❑28, Jan 2001 3.00
❑29, Feb 2001 3.00
❑30, Mar 2001 3.00
❑31, Apr 2001 2.95
❑32, May 2001 2.95
❑33, Jun 2001 2.95

SAILOR MOON SUPERS
Mixx

❑1 9.95

SAILOR'S STORY, A
Marvel

❑1 5.95

SAILOR'S STORY, A: WINDS, DREAMS, AND DRAGONS
Marvel

❑1 6.95

SAINT ANGEL
Image

❑0, Mar 2000 2.95
❑1, Jun 2000 3.95
❑2, Oct 2000 3.95
❑3, Dec 2000 3.95
❑4, Mar 2001 3.95

ST. GEORGE
Marvel / Epic

❑1, Jun 1988 BSz (c); BSz, KJ (a) 1.50
❑2, Aug 1988 1.50
❑3, Oct 1988 1.50
❑4, Dec 1988 1.50
❑5, Feb 1989 1.50
❑6, Apr 1989 1.50
❑7, Jun 1989 1.50
❑8, Aug 1989 1.50

SAINT GERMAINE
Caliber

❑1, ca. 1997, b&w 2.95
❑2 2.95
❑3 2.95
❑4 2.95
❑5 2.95

SAINTS, THE
Saturn

❑0, Apr 1995, b&w 2.50
❑1, Fal 1996, b&w 2.50

SAINT SINNER
Marvel

❑1, Oct 1993; foil cover 2.50
❑2, Nov 1993 1.75
❑3, Dec 1993 1.75
❑4, Jan 1994 1.75
❑5, Feb 1994 1.75
❑6, Mar 1994 1.75
❑7, Apr 1994 1.75
❑8, Apr 1994 1.75

ST. SWITHIN'S DAY
Trident

❑1, ca. 1990, b&w 3.00
❑1-2, Mar 1998, b&w 2.95

ST. SWITHIN'S DAY (ONI)
Oni

❑1, Mar 1998 2.95

SAIYUKI
Tokyopop

❑1, Mar 2004 9.99

SALIMBA
Blackthorne

❑1, b&w 3.50
❑3D 1, Aug 1986, b&w 2.50
❑3D 2, Sep 1986 2.50

SALLY FORTH
Fantagraphics / Eros

❑1 2.95
❑1-2, Jun 1995 2.95
❑2, Oct 1993 2.95
❑3, Feb 1994 2.95
❑4, Apr 1994 2.95
❑5, Jul 1994 2.95
❑6, Sep 1994, b&w 2.95
❑7, Nov 1994 2.95
❑8, Jan 1995 2.95

SAM & MAX, FREELANCE POLICE
Marvel / Epic

❑1 2.25

SAM AND MAX, FREELANCE POLICE SPECIAL, THE
Fishwrap

❑1, ca. 1987, b&w 1.75

SAM & MAX FREELANCE POLICE SPECIAL
Comico

❑1, ca. 1989 2.75

SAM & MAX FREELANCE POLICE SPECIAL COLOR COLLECTION
Marvel / Epic

❑1 4.95

SAM AND TWITCH
Image

❑1, Aug 1999 2.50
❑2, Sep 1999 2.50
❑3, Oct 1999 2.50
❑4, Nov 1999 2.50
❑5, Dec 1999 2.50
❑6, Jan 2000 2.50
❑7, Feb 2000 2.50
❑8, Mar 2000 2.50
❑9, Apr 2000 2.50
❑10, May 2000 2.50
❑11, Jun 2000 2.50
❑12, Jul 2000 2.50
❑13, Aug 2000 2.50
❑14, Sep 2000 2.50
❑15, Oct 2000 2.50
❑16, Nov 2000 2.50
❑17, Dec 2000 2.50
❑18, Jan 2001 2.50
❑19, Feb 2001 2.50
❑20, Mar 2001 2.50
❑21, Apr 2001 2.50
❑22, May 2001 2.50
❑23, Jan 2002 2.50
❑24, Aug 2003 2.50
❑25, Oct 2003 2.50
❑26, Feb 2004 2.50

SAM BRONX AND THE ROBOTS
Eclipse

❑1; hardcover 6.95

SAMBU GASSHO (A CHORUS IN THREE PARTS)
Bodo Genki

❑1, Aug 1994, b&w; no cover price 1.00

SAMMY: TOURIST TRAP
Image

❑1, Feb 2003 2.95
❑2, Mar 2003 2.95
❑3, May 2003 2.95
❑4, May 2003 2.95

SAMMY VERY SAMMY DAY ONE SHOT
Image

❑1, Aug 2004 5.95

SAM SLADE, ROBO-HUNTER
Fleetway-Quality

❑1 2.00
❑2 DaG (a) 1.50
❑3 DaG (a) 1.50
❑4 DaG (a) 1.50
❑5 DaG (a) 1.50
❑6 AMo (w) 1.50
❑7 1.50
❑8 DaG (a) 1.50
❑9 1.50
❑10 1.50
❑11, no year of publication 1.50
❑12 DaG (a) 1.50
❑13 DaG (a) 1.50
❑14 DaG (a) 1.50
❑15 1.50
❑16 1.50
❑17 DaG (a) 1.50
❑18 DaG (a) 1.50
❑19 1.50
❑20 1.50
❑21; double issue #21/22 1.50
❑22 1.50
❑23; double issue #23/24 1.50
❑24 1.50
❑25 1.50
❑26 1.50
❑27 1.50
❑28 1.50
❑29 1.50
❑30 1.50
❑31 1.50
❑32 1.50
❑33 1.50

SAMSON
Samson

❑0.5, Jan 1995; no indicia 2.50

Condition price index: Multiply "NM prices" above by: **0.83 for Very Fine/Near Mint**
0.66 for Very Fine • 0.33 for Fine • 0.2 for Very Good • 0.125 for Good

N-MINT

SAM STORIES: LEGS
IMAGE / QUALITY

❑1, Dec 1999 ... 2.50

SAMURAI
AIRCEL

❑1, Jan 1986 ... 3.00
❑1-2 ... 2.00
❑1-3 ... 2.00
❑2, Feb 1986 ... 2.00
❑3, Mar 1986 ... 2.00
❑4, Apr 1986 ... 2.00
❑5, May 1986 ... 2.00
❑6, Jun 1986 ... 2.00
❑7, Jul 1986 ... 2.00
❑8, Aug 1986 ... 2.00
❑9, Sep 1986 ... 2.00
❑10, Oct 1986 ... 2.00
❑11, Nov 1986 ... 2.00
❑12, Dec 1986 ... 2.00
❑13, Jan 1987; 1st Dale Keown art ... 3.00
❑14, Feb 1987 ... 3.00
❑15, Mar 1987 ... 3.00
❑16, Apr 1987 ... 3.00
❑17, May 1987 ... 2.00
❑18, Jun 1987 ... 2.00
❑19, Jul 1987 ... 2.00
❑20, Aug 1987 ... 2.00
❑21, Sep 1987 ... 2.00
❑22, Oct 1987 ... 2.00
❑23, Nov 1987 ... 2.00

SAMURAI (VOL. 2)
AIRCEL

❑1, Dec 1987 ... 2.00
❑2, Jan 1988 ... 2.00
❑3, Feb 1988 ... 2.00

SAMURAI (VOL. 3)
AIRCEL

❑1 1988 ... 1.95
❑2 1988 ... 1.95
❑3 1988 ... 1.95
❑4 1988 ... 1.95
❑5 1988 ... 1.95
❑6, Dec 1988 ... 1.95
❑7, Jan 1989 ... 1.95

SAMURAI (VOL. 4)
WARP

❑1, May 1997, b&w ... 2.95

SAMURAI 7
GAUNTLET

❑1, b&w ... 2.50
❑2, b&w ... 2.50
❑3, b&w ... 2.50

SAMURAI CAT
MARVEL / EPIC

❑1, Jun 1991 ... 2.25
❑2, Aug 1991 ... 2.25
❑3, Sep 1991 ... 2.25

SAMURAI COMPILATION BOOK
AIRCEL

❑1, b&w ... 4.95
❑2, b&w ... 4.95

SAMURAI: DEMON SWORD
NIGHT WYND

❑1 ... 2.50
❑2 ... 2.50
❑3 ... 2.50
❑4 ... 2.50

SAMURAI FUNNIES
SOLSON

❑1; Texas chainsaw ... 2.00
❑2; Samurai 13th ... 2.00

SAMURAI GUARD
COLBURN

❑1, Nov 1999 ... 2.50
❑2, Jun 2000 ... 2.50
❑Ashcan 1 ... 1.00

N-MINT

SAMURAI JACK SPECIAL
DC

❑1, Sep 2002 ... 3.95
❑1-2, Jul 2004; reprint ... 3.95

SAMURAI JAM
SLAVE LABOR

❑1, Jan 1994 ... 2.95
❑2, Apr 1994 ... 2.95
❑3, Jun 1994 ... 2.95
❑4, Sep 1994 ... 2.95

SAMURAI: MYSTIC CULT
NIGHTWYND

❑1, b&w ... 2.50
❑2, b&w ... 2.50
❑3, b&w ... 2.50
❑4, b&w ... 2.50

SAMURAI PENGUIN
SLAVE LABOR

❑1, Jun 1986, b&w ... 1.50
❑2, Aug 1986, b&w ... 1.50
❑3, Feb 1987, b&w; pink logo version also exist ... 1.50
❑4, May 1987, b&w ... 1.50
❑5, Sep 1987, b&w ... 1.50
❑6, Mar 1988 ... 1.95
❑7, Jul 1988 ... 1.75
❑8, May 1989 ... 1.75

SAMURAI PENGUIN: FOOD CHAIN FOLLIES
SLAVE LABOR

❑1, Apr 1991 ... 5.95

SAMURAI SQUIRREL
SPOTLIGHT

❑1 ... 1.75
❑2 ... 1.75

SAMURAI: VAMPIRE'S HUNT
NIGHTWYND

❑1, b&w ... 2.50
❑2, b&w ... 2.50
❑3, b&w ... 2.50
❑4, b&w ... 2.50

SAMUREE (1ST SERIES)
CONTINUITY

❑1, May 1987 ... 2.00
❑2, Aug 1987 ... 2.00
❑3, May 1988 ... 2.00
❑4, Jan 1989 ... 2.00
❑5, Apr 1989 ... 2.00
❑6, Aug 1989 ... 2.00
❑7, Feb 1990 ... 2.00
❑8, Nov 1990 ... 2.00
❑9, Jan 1991 ... 2.00

SAMUREE (2ND SERIES)
CONTINUITY

❑1, May 1993 ... 2.50
❑2, Sep 1993 ... 2.50
❑3, Dec 1993 ... 2.50
❑4, Jan 1994 ... 2.50

SAMUREE (3RD SERIES)
ACCLAIM / WINDJAMMER

❑1, Oct 1995 ... 2.50
❑2, Nov 1995 ... 2.50

SANCTUARY PART 1
VIZ

❑1, Jun 1993, b&w ... 6.00
❑2, Jul 1993, b&w ... 5.00
❑3, Aug 1993 ... 5.00
❑4, Sep 1993 ... 5.00
❑5, Oct 1993 ... 5.00
❑6, Nov 1993 ... 5.00
❑7, Dec 1993 ... 5.00
❑8, Jan 1994 ... 5.00
❑9, Feb 1994 ... 5.00

SANCTUARY PART 2
VIZ

❑1, Mar 1994 ... 5.00
❑2, Apr 1994 ... 5.00
❑3, May 1994 ... 5.00
❑4, Jun 1994 ... 5.00

Much like Gold Key's Magnus, Sam Slade hunts down rogue robots.
© 1987 Fleetway/ Quality

N-MINT

❑5, Jul 1994 ... 5.00
❑6, Aug 1994 ... 5.00
❑7, Sep 1994 ... 5.00
❑8, Oct 1994 ... 5.00
❑9, Nov 1994 ... 5.00

SANCTUARY PART 3
VIZ

❑1, Dec 1994, b&w ... 3.25
❑2, Jan 1995, b&w ... 3.25
❑3, Feb 1995, b&w ... 3.25
❑4, Mar 1995, b&w ... 3.25
❑5, Apr 1995, b&w ... 3.25
❑6, May 1995, b&w ... 3.25
❑7, Jun 1995, b&w ... 3.25
❑8, Jul 1995, b&w ... 3.25

SANCTUARY PART 4
VIZ

❑1, Aug 1995 ... 3.25
❑2, Sep 1995 ... 3.25
❑3, Oct 1995 ... 3.25
❑4, Nov 1995 ... 3.25
❑5, Dec 1995 ... 3.25
❑6, Jan 1996 ... 3.50
❑7, Feb 1996 ... 3.50

SANCTUARY PART 5
VIZ

❑1, Mar 1996 ... 3.50
❑2, Apr 1996 ... 3.50
❑3, May 1996 ... 3.50
❑4, Jun 1996 ... 3.50
❑5, Jul 1996 ... 3.50
❑6, Aug 1996 ... 3.50
❑7, Sep 1996 ... 3.50
❑8, Oct 1996 ... 3.50
❑9, Nov 1996 ... 3.50
❑10, Dec 1996 ... 3.50
❑11, Jan 1997 ... 3.50
❑12, Feb 1997 ... 3.50
❑13, Mar 1997 ... 3.50

SANCTUM
BLACKSHOE

❑1/Ltd.; Limited edition from 1999 San Diego Comic-Con ... 3.95

SAN DIEGO COMIC-CON COMICS
DARK HORSE

❑1, ca. 1992; con giveaway; 1992 Comic-Con ... 3.25
❑2, Aug 1993; con giveaway; 1993 Comic-Con ... 2.95
❑3, Aug 1994; con giveaway; 1994 Comic-Con ... 2.50
❑4, Aug 1995; 1995 Comic-Con ... 2.50

SANDMADAM
SPOOF

❑1, b&w ... 2.95

SANDMAN, THE
DC

❑1, Win 1974 JK (a) ... 8.00
❑1/A, Win 1974; variant cover ... 10.00
❑2, May 1975 JK (a) ... 5.00
❑3, Jul 1975 JK (a) ... 4.00
❑4, Sep 1975 JK (a); A: Demon. ... 4.00
❑5, Nov 1975 JK (a) ... 4.00
❑6, Jan 1976 JK (a) ... 4.00

N-MINT

SANDMAN
DC

❑1, Jan 1989; Giant-size NG (w); 1: Sandman III (Morpheus). 21.00
❑2, Feb 1989 NG (w); A: Abel. A: Cain. 11.00
❑3, Mar 1989 NG (w); A: John Constantine. 11.00
❑4, Apr 1989 NG (w); A: Demon. 3.50
❑5, May 1989 NG (w) 3.50
❑6, Jun 1989 NG (w) 3.50
❑7, Jul 1989 NG (w) 3.50
❑8, Aug 1989; Regular edition, no indicia in inside front cover; NG (w); 1: Death (Sandman). Regular edition, no indicia in inside front cover 12.00
❑8/Ltd., Aug 1989; limited edition; NG (w); 1: Death (Sandman). 1000 copies; Has indicia in inside front cover, editorial by Karen Berger 35.00
❑9, Sep 1989 NG (w) 3.50
❑10, Nov 1989 NG (w) 3.50
❑11, Dec 1989 NG (w) 3.50
❑12, Jan 1990 NG (w) 3.50
❑13, Feb 1990 NG (w) 3.50
❑14, Mar 1990 NG (w) 3.50
❑15, Apr 1990 NG (w) 2.50
❑16, Jun 1990 NG (w) 2.50
❑17, Jul 1990 NG (w) 2.50
❑18, Aug 1990 NG (w) 2.50
❑19, Sep 1990; NG (w); CV (a); properly printed; Midsummer Night's Dream 2.50
❑19/A, Sep 1990; NG (w); CV (a); pages out of order; Midsummer Night's Dream 2.50
❑20, Oct 1990 NG (w); D: Element Girl. 2.50
❑21, Nov 1990 NG (w) 2.50
❑22, Jan 1991 NG (w); 1: Daniel (new Sandman). 3.50
❑23, Feb 1991 NG (w) 2.50
❑24, Mar 1991 NG (w) 2.50
❑25, Apr 1991 NG (w) 2.50
❑26, May 1991 NG (w) 2.50
❑27, Jun 1991 NG (w) 2.50
❑28, Jul 1991 NG (w) 2.50
❑29, Aug 1991 NG (w) 2.50
❑30, Sep 1991 NG (w) 2.50
❑31, Oct 1991 NG (w) 2.50
❑32, Nov 1991 NG (w) 2.50
❑33, Dec 1991 NG (w) 2.50
❑34, Jan 1992 NG (w) 2.50
❑35, Feb 1992 NG (w) 2.50
❑36, Apr 1992; Giant-size NG (w) 3.00
❑37, May 1992 NG (w) 2.50
❑38, Jun 1992 NG (w) 2.50
❑39, Jul 1992 NG (w) 2.50
❑40, Aug 1992 NG (w) 2.50
❑41, Sep 1992 NG (w) 2.50
❑42, Oct 1992 NG (w) 2.50
❑43, Nov 1992 NG (w) 2.50
❑44, Dec 1992 NG (w) 2.50
❑45, Jan 1993 NG (w) 2.50
❑46, Feb 1993; NG (w); Brief Lives 2.50
❑47, Mar 1993 NG (w) 2.50
❑48, Apr 1993 NG (w) 2.50
❑49, May 1993 NG (w) 2.50
❑50, Jun 1993; Double-size; NG (w); CR (a); Bronze ink 4.50
❑50/Gold, Jun 1993; Gold edition NG (w); CR (a) 20.00
❑51, Jul 1993 NG (w); BT, DG (a) 2.50
❑52, Aug 1993 NG (w); BT (a) 2.50
❑53, Sep 1993 NG (w); BT (a) 2.50
❑54, Oct 1993 NG (w); BT (a); O: Prez Rickard. 2.50
❑55, Nov 1993 NG (w) 2.50
❑56, Dec 1993 NG (w); BT (a) 2.50
❑57, Feb 1994 NG (w) 2.50
❑58, Mar 1994 NG (w) 2.50
❑59, Apr 1994 NG (w) 2.50
❑60, Jun 1994 NG (w) 2.50
❑61, Jul 1994 NG (w) 2.50
❑62, Aug 1994 NG (w); CV (a) 2.50
❑63, Sep 1994 NG (w) 2.50
❑64, Nov 1994 NG (w) 2.50

N-MINT

❑65, Dec 1994 NG (w) 2.50
❑66, Jan 1995 NG (w) 2.50
❑67, Mar 1995 NG (w) 2.50
❑68, May 1995 NG (w) 2.50
❑69, Jul 1995 NG (w); D: Sandman III (Morpheus). 3.00
❑70, Aug 1995 NG (w) 2.50
❑71, Sep 1995 NG (w) 2.50
❑72, Nov 1995; NG (w); burial of Dream 2.50
❑73, Dec 1995 NG (w); A: Hob Gadling. 2.50
❑74, Jan 1996 NG (w) 2.50
❑75, Mar 1996; NG (w); CV (a); A: William Shakespeare. contains timeline 4.00
❑Special 1, ca. 1991; Orpheus special edition; NG (w); BT (a); Glow-in-the-dark cover 5.00

SANDMAN, THE: A GALLERY OF DREAMS
DC / VERTIGO

❑1, ca. 1994 2.95

SANDMAN: ENDLESS NIGHTS
DC / VERTIGO

❑1, Nov 2003 2.95

SANDMAN MIDNIGHT THEATRE
DC / VERTIGO

❑1, Sep 1995; prestige format; Morpheus meets Wesley Dodds 6.95

SANDMAN MYSTERY THEATRE
DC / VERTIGO

❑1, Apr 1993 MW (w) 4.00
❑2, May 1993 MW (w) 3.00
❑3, Jun 1993 MW (w) 3.00
❑4, Jul 1993 MW (w) 3.00
❑5, Aug 1993 MW (w) 3.00
❑6, Sep 1993 MW (w) 3.00
❑7, Oct 1993 MW (w) 3.00
❑8, Nov 1993 MW (w) 3.00
❑9, Dec 1993 MW (w) 3.00
❑10, Jan 1994 MW (w) 3.00
❑11, Feb 1994 MW (w) 2.75
❑12, Mar 1994 MW (w) 2.75
❑13, Apr 1994 MW (w) 2.75
❑14, May 1994 MW (w) 2.75
❑15, Jun 1994 MW (w) 2.75
❑16, Jul 1994 MW (w) 2.75
❑17, Aug 1994 MW (w) 2.75
❑18, Sep 1994 MW (w) 2.75
❑19, Oct 1994 MW (w) 2.75
❑20, Nov 1994 MW (w) 2.75
❑21, Dec 1994 MW (w) 2.50
❑22, Jan 1995 MW (w) 2.50
❑23, Feb 1995 MW (w) 2.50
❑24, Mar 1995 MW (w) 2.50
❑25, Apr 1995 MW (w) 2.50
❑26, May 1995 MW (w) 2.50
❑27, Jun 1995 MW (w) 2.50
❑28, Jul 1995 MW (w) 2.50
❑29, Aug 1995 MW (w) 2.50
❑30, Sep 1995 MW (w) 2.50
❑31, Oct 1995 MW (w) 2.50
❑32, Nov 1995 MW (w) 2.50
❑33, Dec 1995 MW (w) 2.50
❑34, Jan 1996 MW (w) 2.50
❑35, Feb 1996 MW (w) 2.50
❑36, Mar 1996 MW (w) 2.50
❑37, Apr 1996 MW (w) 2.50
❑38, May 1996 MW (w) 2.50
❑39, Jun 1996 MW (w) 2.50
❑40, Jul 1996 MW (w) 2.50
❑41, Aug 1996 MW (w) 2.50
❑42, Sep 1996 MW (w) 2.50
❑43, Oct 1996 MW (w); A: Crimson Avenger. 2.50
❑44, Nov 1996 MW (w) 2.50
❑45, Dec 1996 MW (w); A: Blackhawk. 2.50
❑46, Jan 1997 MW (w) 2.50
❑47, Feb 1997 MW (w) 2.50
❑48, Mar 1997 MW (w) 2.50
❑49, Apr 1997 MW (w) 2.50
❑50, May 1997; Giant-size MW (w) 3.50

N-MINT

❑51, Jun 1997 MW (w) 2.50
❑52, Jul 1997 MW (w) 2.50
❑53, Aug 1997 MW (w) 2.50
❑54, Sep 1997 MW (w) 2.50
❑55, Oct 1997 MW (w) 2.50
❑56, Nov 1997 MW (w) 2.50
❑57, Dec 1997 MW (w) 2.50
❑58, Jan 1998 MW (w) 2.50
❑59, Feb 1998 MW (w) 2.50
❑60, Mar 1998 MW (w) 2.50
❑61, Apr 1998 2.50
❑62, May 1998 2.50
❑63, Jul 1998 2.50
❑64, Aug 1998 2.50
❑65, Sep 1998 2.50
❑66, Oct 1998 2.50
❑67, Nov 1998 2.50
❑68, Dec 1998 2.50
❑69, Jan 1999 2.50
❑70, Feb 1999 2.50
❑Annual 1 MW (w) 4.00

SANDMAN PRESENTS, THE: BAST
DC / VERTIGO

❑1, Mar 2003 2.95
❑2, Apr 2003 2.95
❑3, May 2003 2.95

SANDMAN PRESENTS, THE: LOVE STREET
DC / VERTIGO

❑1, Jul 1999; John Constantine in the '60s 2.95
❑2, Aug 1999 2.95
❑3, Sep 1999 2.95

SANDMAN PRESENTS: LUCIFER
DC / VERTIGO

❑1, Mar 1999 2.95
❑2, Apr 1999 2.95
❑3, May 1999 2.95

SANDMAN PRESENTS: PETREFAX
DC / VERTIGO

❑1, Mar 2000 2.95
❑2, Apr 2000 2.95
❑3, May 2000 2.95
❑4, Jun 2000 2.95

SANDMAN PRESENTS: TALLER TALES
DC / VERTIGO

❑1, ca. 2003 19.95

SANDMAN PRESENTS, THE: DEADBOY DETECTIVES
DC / VERTIGO

❑1, Aug 2001 2.50
❑2, Sep 2001 2.50
❑3, Oct 2001 2.50
❑4, Nov 2001 2.50

SANDMAN PRESENTS, THE: EVERYTHING YOU ALWAYS WANTED TO KNOW ABOUT DREAMS...BUT WERE AFRAID TO ASK
DC / VERTIGO

❑1, Jul 2001 3.95

SANDMAN PRESENTS: THE FURIES
DC / WILDSTORM

❑1, ca. 2004 17.95

SANDMAN PRESENTS: THESSALY - WITCH FOR HIRE
DC / VERTIGO

❑1, Apr 2004 2.95
❑2, May 2004 2.95
❑3, Jun 2004 2.95
❑4, Jul 2004 2.95

SANDMAN PRESENTS, THE: THE CORINTHIAN
DC / VERTIGO

❑1, Dec 2001 2.50
❑2, Jan 2002 2.50
❑3, Feb 2002 2.50

N-MINT

SANDMAN PRESENTS, THE: THE THESSALIAD
DC / VERTIGO
❑1, Mar 2002 .... 2.50
❑2, Apr 2002 .... 2.50
❑3, May 2002 .... 2.50
❑4, Jun 2002 .... 2.50

SANDS, THE
BLACK EYE
❑1, b&w; smaller than a normal comic book 2.50
❑2, b&w; smaller than a normal comic book 2.50
❑3, Feb 1997, b&w; smaller than a normal comic book 2.50

SANDSCAPE
DREAMWAVE
❑1, Jan 2003 .... 2.95
❑2, Feb 2003 .... 2.95
❑3, Apr 2003 .... 2.95
❑4, Jun 2003 .... 2.95

SAN FRANCISCO COMIC BOOK, THE
SAN FRANCISCO COMIC BOOK CO.
❑1, Jan 1970 .... 6.00
❑2 .... 4.00
❑3 .... 4.00
❑4 .... 4.00
❑5 .... 4.00
❑6 .... 4.00
❑7 .... 4.00

SANTA CLAUS ADVENTURES (WALT KELLY'S...)
INNOVATION
❑1 .... 6.95

SANTA CLAWS (ETERNITY)
ETERNITY
❑1, b&w 2.95

SANTA CLAWS (THORBY)
THORBY
❑1 .... 2.95

SANTANA
MALIBU / ROCK-IT
❑1, May 1994; magazine TY (a) 5.00

SANTA THE BARBARIAN
MAXIMUM
❑1, Dec 1996 .... 2.99

SAPPHIRE
AIRCEL
❑1, Feb 1990 .... 2.95
❑2, Mar 1990 .... 2.95
❑3, Apr 1990 .... 2.50
❑4, May 1990 .... 2.50
❑5, Jun 1990 .... 2.50
❑6, Jul 1990 .... 2.50
❑7, Aug 1990 .... 2.50
❑8 .... 2.50
❑9, Sep 1990 .... 2.50

SAP TUNES
FANTAGRAPHICS
❑1, b&w 2.50
❑2, b&w 2.50

SARAH-JANE HAMILTON PRESENTS SUPERSTARS OF EROTICA
RE-VISIONARY
❑1 .... 2.95

SARGE SNORKEL
CHARLTON
❑1, Oct 1973 .... 8.00
❑2, Dec 1973 .... 5.00
❑3, Jun 1974 .... 4.00
❑4, Sep 1974 .... 4.00
❑5, Nov 1974 .... 4.00
❑6, Jan 1975 .... 3.00
❑7, Mar 1975 .... 3.00
❑8, May 1975 .... 3.00
❑9, Jul 1975 .... 3.00
❑10, Sep 1975 .... 3.00
❑11, Nov 1975 .... 3.00
❑12, Jan 1976 .... 3.00

N-MINT

❑13, Mar 1976 .... 3.00
❑14, May 1976 .... 3.00
❑15, Aug 1976 .... 3.00
❑16, Oct 1976 .... 3.00
❑17, Dec 1976 .... 3.00

SARGE STEEL
CHARLTON
❑1, Dec 1964 .... 15.00
❑2, Feb 1965 .... 10.00
❑3, May 1965 .... 8.00
❑4, Jul 1965 .... 8.00
❑5, Sep 1965 .... 8.00
❑6, Nov 1965 .... 6.00
❑7, Apr 1966 .... 6.00
❑8, Oct 1966 .... 6.00
❑9 .... 6.00

SATANIKA
VEROTIK
❑0, ca. 1995 .... 4.00
❑1, Jan 1995 .... 5.00
❑2 1995 .... 4.00
❑3 1995 .... 4.00
❑4 1996 .... 3.00
❑5, Oct 1996 .... 3.00
❑6, Jan 1997 .... 2.95
❑7, Apr 1997 .... 2.95
❑8, Sep 1997 .... 2.95
❑9, Mar 1998 .... 2.95
❑10, Dec 1998 .... 2.95
❑11, May 1999 .... 3.95

SATANIKA ILLUSTRATIONS, THE
VEROTIK
❑1, Sep 1996; Cardstock cover; pin-ups 3.95

SATAN PLACE
THUNDERHILL
❑1 .... 3.50

SATAN'S SIX
TOPPS
❑1, Apr 1993; trading card; Wolff and Byrd, Counselors of the Macabre backup story 2.95
❑2, May 1993; trading cards 2.95
❑3, Jun 1993; trading cards 2.95
❑4, Jul 1993; trading cards 2.95

SATAN'S SIX: HELLSPAWN
TOPPS
❑1, Jun 1994; Inside index lists it as issue #2 .... 2.50
❑2, Jun 1994 .... 2.50
❑3, Jul 1994 .... 2.50

SATURDAY MORNING: THE COMIC
MARVEL
❑1, Apr 1996 .... 1.95

SATURDAY NITE
ANSON JEW
❑1, b&w 2.95

SAUCY LITTLE TART
FANTAGRAPHICS / EROS
❑1, Dec 1995 .... 2.95

SAURIANS: UNNATURAL SELECTION
CROSSGEN
❑1, Feb 2002 .... 2.95
❑2, Mar 2002 .... 2.95

SAVAGE COMBAT TALES
ATLAS-SEABOARD
❑1, Feb 1975 O: Sgt. Stryker's Death Squad. 2.00
❑2, Apr 1975 .... 1.50
❑3, Jul 1975 .... 1.50

SAVAGE DRAGON, THE (MINI-SERIES)
IMAGE
❑1, Jul 1992; four cover logo variants (bottom of logo is white, blue, green, or yellow) 3.00
❑2, Oct 1992; Centerfold Savage Dragon poster 2.50
❑3, Dec 1992; Centerfold Savage Dragon poster 2.50

For several years, Dark Horse produced a comic book to be given away at the San Diego Comic-Con showcasing several of the company's features.

© 1993 Dark Horse Comics.

N-MINT

SAVAGE DRAGON, THE
IMAGE
❑0.5, ca. 1997 EL (w); EL (a) 3.00
❑0.5/Platinum, ca. 1997; Platinum edition EL (w); EL (a) 4.00
❑1, Jun 1993 EL (w); EL (a) 3.00
❑2, Jul 1993; EL (w); EL (a); A: Teenage Mutant Ninja Turtles. Flip book with Vanguard #0 .... 3.00
❑3, Aug 1993; EL (w); EL (a); Mighty Man back-up feature 2.50
❑4, Sep 1993 EL (w); EL (a) 2.25
❑5, Oct 1993 EL (w); EL (a) 2.25
❑6, Nov 1993 EL (w); EL (a) 2.25
❑7, Jan 1994 EL (w); EL (a) 2.25
❑8, Mar 1994 EL (w); EL (a) 2.00
❑9, Apr 1994 EL (w); EL (a) 2.00
❑10, May 1994; EL (w); EL (a); alternate cover; newsstand version 2.00
❑10/Direct ed., May 1994 EL (w); EL (a) 2.00
❑11, Jul 1994 EL (w); EL (a) 2.00
❑12, Aug 1994; EL (w); EL (a); She Dragon 2.00
❑13, Jun 1995 EL (w); EL (a); 1: Condition Red. 2.50
❑13/A, Jun 1995; JLee (w); JLee, EL (a); Image X month version 2.50
❑14, Oct 1994 EL (w); EL (a) 1.95
❑15, Dec 1994 EL (w); EL (a) 2.50
❑16, Jan 1995; EL (w); EL (a); Savage Dragon on cover 2.50
❑17/A, Feb 1995; EL (w); EL (a); One figure on cover; two different interior pages 2.50
❑17/B, Feb 1995 EL (w); EL (a) 2.50
❑18, Mar 1995 EL (w); EL (a) 2.50
❑19, Apr 1995 EL (w); EL (a) 2.50
❑20, Jul 1995 EL (w); EL (a) 2.50
❑21, Aug 1995 EL (w); EL (a) 2.50
❑22, Sep 1995 EL (w); EL (a); A: Teenage Mutant Ninja Turtles. 2.50
❑23, Oct 1995 EL (w); EL (a) 2.50
❑24, Dec 1995 EL (w); EL (a) 2.50
❑25, Jan 1996; double-sized EL (w); EL (a) 3.95
❑25/A, Jan 1996; double-sized; EL (w); EL (a); alternate cover 3.95
❑26, Mar 1996 EL (w); EL (a) 2.50
❑27, Apr 1996 EL (w); EL (a) 2.50
❑27/A, Apr 1996; EL (w); EL (a); alternate cover only available at WonderCon 2.50
❑28, May 1996 EL (w); EL (a); A: Maxx. 2.50
❑29, Jul 1996 EL (w); EL (a); A: Wildstar. 2.50
❑30, Aug 1996 EL (w); EL (a); A: Spawn. 2.50
❑31, Sep 1996; EL (w); EL (a); censored version says God is good inside Image logo on cover; God vs. The Devil 2.50
❑31/A, Sep 1996; EL (w); EL (a); God vs. The Devil; uncensored version 2.50
❑32, Oct 1996 EL (w); EL (a) 2.50
❑33, Nov 1996; EL (w); EL (a); Birth of Dragonís son 2.50
❑34, Dec 1996 EL (w); EL (a); A: Hellboy. 2.50
❑35, Feb 1997 EL (w); EL (a); A: Hellboy. 2.50
❑36, Mar 1997 EL (w); EL (a); 1: Zeek. 2.50
❑37, Apr 1997 EL (w); EL (a) 2.50

	N-MINT
❑38, May 1997 EL (w); EL (a)	2.50
❑39, Jun 1997 EL (w); EL (a)	2.50
❑40, Jul 1997 EL (w); EL (a)	2.50
❑40/A, Jul 1997 EL (w); EL (a)	2.50
❑41, Sep 1997 EL (w); EL (a); A: Wildstar. A: Monkeyman. A: Femforce. A: E-Man. A: Zot. A: Megaton. A: Madman. A: Vampirella. A: Hellboy. A: DNAgents.	2.50
❑42, Oct 1997 EL (w); EL (a)	2.50
❑43, Nov 1997 EL (w); EL (a)	2.50
❑44, Dec 1997 EL (w); EL (a)	2.50
❑45, Jan 1998 EL (w); EL (a)	2.50
❑46, Feb 1998 EL (w); EL (a)	2.50
❑47, Mar 1998 EL (w); EL (a)	2.50
❑48, Apr 1998 EL (w); EL (a)	2.50
❑49, May 1998 EL (w); EL (a)	2.50
❑50, Jun 1998 JPH, EL (w); TMc, RL, EL (a)	5.95
❑51/A, Jul 1998; EL (w); EL (a); red logo	2.50
❑51/B, Jul 1998; EL (w); EL (a); yellow logo	2.50
❑52, Aug 1998 EL (w); EL (a)	2.50
❑53, Sep 1998 EL (w); EL (a)	2.50
❑54, Oct 1998 EL (w); EL (a)	2.50
❑55, Nov 1998 EL (w); EL (a)	2.50
❑56, Dec 1998 EL (w); EL (a)	2.50
❑57, Jan 1999 EL (w); EL (a)	2.50
❑58, Feb 1999 EL (w); EL (a)	2.50
❑59, Mar 1999 EL (w); EL (a)	2.50
❑60, Apr 1999 EL (w); EL (a)	2.50
❑61, May 1999 EL (w); EL (a)	2.50
❑62, Jun 1999 EL (w); EL (a)	2.50
❑63, Jun 1999 EL (w); EL (a)	2.50
❑64, Jul 1999 EL (w); EL (a)	2.50
❑65, Aug 1999 EL (w); EL (a)	2.50
❑66, Aug 1999 EL (w); EL (a)	2.50
❑67, Sep 1999 EL (w); EL (a)	2.50
❑68, Oct 1999 EL (w); EL (a)	2.50
❑69, Nov 1999 EL (w); EL (a)	2.50
❑70, Dec 1999 EL (w); EL (a)	2.50
❑71, Jan 2000 EL (w); EL (a)	2.50
❑72, Feb 2000 EL (w); EL (a); A: Mighty Man.	2.95
❑73, Mar 2000 EL (w); EL (a)	2.95
❑74, Apr 2000 EL (w); EL (a)	2.95
❑75, May 2000; Giant-size EL (w); EL (a)	5.95
❑76, Jun 2000 EL (w); EL (a)	2.95
❑77, Jul 2000 EL (w); EL (a)	2.95
❑78, Aug 2000 EL (w); EL (a)	2.95
❑79, Sep 2000 EL (w); EL (a)	2.95
❑80, Oct 2000 EL (w); EL (a)	2.95
❑81, Nov 2000 EL (w); EL (a)	2.95
❑82, Dec 2000 EL (w); EL (a)	2.95
❑83, Jan 2001 EL (w); EL (a); A: Madman.	2.95
❑84, Feb 2001 EL (w); EL (a)	2.95
❑85, Mar 2001 EL (w); EL (a); A: Madman.	2.95
❑86, Apr 2001 EL (w); EL (a); A: Mighty Man.	2.95
❑87, May 2001 EL (w); EL (a)	2.95
❑88, Jun 2001 EL (w); EL (a)	2.95
❑89, Jul 2001 EL (w); EL (a)	2.95
❑90, Aug 2001 EL (w); EL (a)	2.95
❑91, Sep 2001 EL (a)	2.95
❑92, Oct 2001 EL (w); EL (a)	2.95
❑93, Nov 2001 EL (a); A: SuperPatriot.	2.95
❑94, Dec 2001 EL (w); EL (a)	2.95
❑95, Jan 2002 EL (w); EL (a)	2.95
❑96, Feb 2002 EL (w); EL (a)	2.95
❑97, Mar 2002 EL (w); EL (a)	2.95
❑98, Apr 2002 EL (w); EL (a)	2.95
❑99, May 2002 EL (w); EL (a)	2.95
❑100, Jun 2002 EL (w); JOy, EL (a)	8.95
❑101, Jul 2002 EL (w); EL (a)	2.95
❑102, Aug 2002 EL (w); EL (a)	2.95
❑103, Sep 2002 EL (w); EL (a)	2.95
❑104, Oct 2002 EL (w); EL (a)	2.95
❑105, Nov 2002 EL (w); EL (a)	2.95
❑106, Apr 2002 EL (w); EL (a)	2.95
❑107, May 2003 EL (w); EL (a)	2.95
❑108, Jul 2003	2.95
❑109, Jul 2003	2.95
❑110, Sep 2003	2.95
❑111, Oct 2003	2.95
❑112, Nov 2003	2.95
❑113, Feb 2004	2.95
❑114, May 2004	2.95

SAVAGE DRAGON ARCHIVES
IMAGE

	N-MINT
❑1, Jun 1998	2.95
❑2, Oct 1998; Reprints Graphic Fantasy #2	2.95
❑3, Dec 1998	2.95
❑4, Jan 1999	2.95

SAVAGE DRAGONBERT: FULL FRONTAL NERDITY
IMAGE

	N-MINT
❑1, Oct 2002	5.95

SAVAGE DRAGON COMPANION
IMAGE

	N-MINT
❑1 2002	2.95

SAVAGE DRAGON/DESTROYER DUCK, THE
IMAGE

	N-MINT
❑1, Nov 1996	3.95

SAVAGE DRAGON/HELLBOY
IMAGE

	N-MINT
❑1, Oct 2002	5.95

SAVAGE DRAGON/MARSHAL LAW, THE
IMAGE

	N-MINT
❑1, Jul 1997, b&w; indicia says Savage Dragon/Marshall Law	2.95
❑2, Aug 1997, b&w	2.95

SAVAGE DRAGON: RED HORIZON
IMAGE

	N-MINT
❑1, Feb 1997	2.50
❑2, Apr 1997	2.50
❑3, May 1997	2.50

SAVAGE DRAGON: SEX & VIOLENCE
IMAGE

	N-MINT
❑1, Aug 1997	2.50
❑2, Sep 1997	2.50

SAVAGE DRAGON/TEENAGE MUTANT NINJA TURTLES CROSSOVER
MIRAGE

	N-MINT
❑1, Sep 1993	2.50

SAVAGE DRAGON VS. THE SAVAGE MEGATON MAN, THE
IMAGE

	N-MINT
❑1, Mar 1993 EL (w); EL (a)	2.00
❑1/Gold, Mar 1993; EL (a); Gold foil cover	3.00

SAVAGE FISTS OF KUNG FU
MARVEL

	N-MINT
❑1 AM, JSn, JB, HT, DG, DA (a); O: The Sons of the Dragon.	8.00

SAVAGE FUNNIES
VISION

	N-MINT
❑1, Jul 1996	1.95
❑2, Jul 1996	1.95

SAVAGE HENRY
VORTEX

	N-MINT
❑1, Jan 1987	2.00
❑2, Feb 1987	2.00
❑3, Apr 1987	2.00
❑4 1987	2.00
❑5 1987	2.00
❑6, Jul 1988	2.00
❑7, Sep 1988, b&w	2.00
❑8, Dec 1988	2.00
❑9, Feb 1989	2.00
❑10	2.00
❑11 1990	2.00
❑12 1990	2.00
❑13 1990; Last Vortex issue	2.00
❑14, Mar 1991, b&w; Rip Off begins as publisher	2.50
❑15, May 1991, b&w	2.50
❑16, Jul 1991, b&w	2.50
❑17, Sep 1991, b&w	2.50
❑18, Nov 1991, b&w	2.50
❑19, Jan 1992, b&w	2.50
❑20, Mar 1992, b&w	2.50
❑21, May 1992, b&w	2.50
❑22, Jul 1992, b&w	2.50
❑23, Sep 1992, b&w	2.50
❑24, Nov 1992, b&w	2.50
❑25, Jan 1993, b&w	2.50
❑26, Mar 1993, b&w	2.50
❑27, May 1993	2.50
❑28, Jul 1993, b&w	2.50
❑29, Sep 1993, b&w	2.50
❑30, Nov 1993, b&w; 1993	2.50

SAVAGE HENRY (ICONOGRAFIX)
CALIBER / ICONOGRAFIX

	N-MINT
❑1, b&w	2.95
❑2, b&w	2.95
❑3, b&w	2.95

SAVAGE HENRY: HEADSTRONG
CALIBER

	N-MINT
❑1, ca. 1995, b&w	2.95
❑2, ca. 1995, b&w	2.95
❑3, ca. 1995, b&w	2.95

SAVAGE HULK, THE
MARVEL

	N-MINT
❑1, Jan 1996; prestige format	6.95

SAVAGE NINJA
CADILLAC

	N-MINT
❑1	1.00

SAVAGE RETURN OF DRACULA, THE
MARVEL

	N-MINT
❑1, ca. 1992; Reprints Tomb of Dracula #1, 2	2.00

SAVAGES (PEREGRINE)
PEREGRINE

	N-MINT
❑1, ca. 2001	2.95

SAVAGES
COMAX

	N-MINT
❑1, b&w	2.50

SAVAGE SHE-HULK, THE
MARVEL

	N-MINT
❑1, Feb 1980 SL (w); JB (a); O: She-Hulk. 1: She-Hulk.	5.00
❑2, Mar 1980 1: Dan Zapper Ridge. 1: Morris Walters.	3.00
❑3, Apr 1980	2.50
❑4, May 1980	2.50
❑5, Jun 1980	2.50
❑6, Jul 1980 A: Iron Man.	2.00
❑7, Aug 1980	2.00
❑8, Sep 1980 A: Man-Thing.	2.00
❑9, Oct 1980	2.00
❑10, Nov 1980	2.00
❑11, Dec 1980	2.00
❑12, Jan 1981 V: Gemini.	2.00
❑13, Feb 1981 FS (a); A: Man-Wolf.	2.00
❑14, Mar 1981 FS (a); A: Man-Wolf. A: Hellcat.	2.00
❑15, Apr 1981 FS (a)	2.00
❑16, May 1981 FS (a)	2.00
❑17, Jun 1981 V: Man-Elephant.	2.00
❑18, Jul 1981 V: Grappler.	2.00
❑19, Aug 1981	2.00
❑20, Sep 1981	2.00
❑21, Oct 1981	2.00
❑22, Nov 1981 (c); FS (a); V: Radius.	2.00
❑23, Dec 1981 FS (a)	2.00
❑24, Jan 1982 AM (a)	2.00
❑25, Feb 1982; Giant-size	2.00

SAVAGE SWORD OF CONAN
MARVEL

	N-MINT
❑1, Aug 1974, b&w GK (w); JB, NA, GK, RA, BS (a); O: Red Sonja. O: Blackmark.	60.00
❑2, Oct 1974 HC (a); A: Kull.	28.00
❑3, Dec 1974	16.00
❑4, Feb 1975	12.00

	N-MINT
❑5, Apr 1975	12.00
❑6, Jun 1975	12.00
❑7, Aug 1975	12.00
❑8, Oct 1975	12.00
❑9, Dec 1975	12.00
❑10, Feb 1976	12.00
❑11, Apr 1976	8.00
❑12, Jun 1976	8.00
❑13, Aug 1976	8.00
❑14, Sep 1976	8.00
❑15, Oct 1976	8.00
❑16, Dec 1976	8.00
❑17, Feb 1977	8.00
❑18, Apr 1977	8.00
❑19, Jun 1977	8.00
❑20, Jul 1977	8.00
❑21, Aug 1977	6.00
❑22, Sep 1977	6.00
❑23, Oct 1977	6.00
❑24, Nov 1977	6.00
❑25, Dec 1977	6.00
❑26, Jan 1978	6.00
❑27, Mar 1978	6.00
❑28, Apr 1978	6.00
❑29, May 1978	6.00
❑30, Jun 1978	5.00
❑31, Jul 1978	5.00
❑32, Aug 1978	5.00
❑33, Sep 1978	5.00
❑34, Oct 1978 1: Garth.	5.00
❑35, Nov 1978	5.00
❑36, Dec 1978	5.00
❑37, Feb 1979	5.00
❑38, Mar 1979 JB, TD (a)	5.00
❑39, Apr 1979	5.00
❑40, May 1979	5.00
❑41, Jun 1979 JB, TD (a)	5.00
❑42, Jul 1979 JB, TD (a)	5.00
❑43, Aug 1979	5.00
❑44, Sep 1979 SB, TD (a)	5.00
❑45, Oct 1979	5.00
❑46, Nov 1979 TD (a)	5.00
❑47, Dec 1979 JB, GK (a)	5.00
❑48, Jan 1980 JB, TD (a)	5.00
❑49, Feb 1980	5.00
❑50, Mar 1980 JB, TD (a)	5.00
❑51, Apr 1980	3.00
❑52, May 1980 JB, TD (a)	3.00
❑53, Jun 1980 JB (a)	3.00
❑54, Jul 1980 JB (a)	3.00
❑55, Aug 1980 JB, AA (a)	3.00
❑56, Sep 1980 JB, TD, GD (a)	3.00
❑57, Oct 1980 JB, TD (a)	3.00
❑58, Nov 1980 JB, TD, KGa (a)	3.00
❑59, Dec 1980 AA (a)	3.00
❑60, Jan 1981 JB (a)	3.00
❑61, Feb 1981 GD (w); JB (a)	3.00
❑62, Mar 1981 JB (a)	3.00
❑63, Apr 1981 GK (w); JB, GK, TP, BMc (a)	3.00
❑64, May 1981 ATh, GK (w); ATh, JB, GK (a)	3.00
❑65, Jun 1981 JB, GK (a)	3.00
❑66, Jul 1981 JB (a)	3.00
❑67, Aug 1981 GK (w); JB, GK, AA (a)	3.00
❑68, Sep 1981 GD (a)	3.00
❑69, Oct 1981 GD (a)	3.00
❑70, Nov 1981 JB (a)	3.00
❑71, Dec 1981 JB (a)	3.00
❑72, Jan 1982 JB (a)	3.00
❑73, Feb 1982 JB (a)	3.00
❑74, Mar 1982 JB, VM, GD (a)	3.00
❑75, Apr 1982 AA (a)	3.00
❑76, May 1982 JB, AA (a)	3.00
❑77, Jun 1982 JB (a)	3.00
❑78, Jul 1982 JB, DG (a)	3.00
❑79, Aug 1982 JB (a)	3.00
❑80, Sep 1982 JB, AA (a)	3.00
❑81, Oct 1982 JB (a)	3.00
❑82, Nov 1982 AA (a)	3.00
❑83, Dec 1982 NA, AA (a); A: Red Sonja.	3.00

	N-MINT
❑84, Jan 1983 VM (a)	3.00
❑85, Feb 1983 GK (a)	3.00
❑86, Mar 1983 GK (a)	3.00
❑87, Apr 1983 JB (a)	3.00
❑88, May 1983 JB (a)	3.00
❑89, Jun 1983 GK (w); NR, AA (a)	3.00
❑90, Jul 1983 NR, JB (a)	3.00
❑91, Aug 1983 JB, VM (a)	3.00
❑92, Sep 1983 JB (a)	3.00
❑93, Oct 1983 JB (a)	3.00
❑94, Nov 1983 VM (a)	3.00
❑95, Dec 1983 JB (a)	3.00
❑96, Jan 1984 JB (a)	3.00
❑97, Feb 1984	3.00
❑98, Mar 1984 JB (a)	3.00
❑99, Apr 1984 JB (a)	3.00
❑100, May 1984 JB (a)	3.00
❑101, Jun 1984 JB (a)	2.50
❑102, Jul 1984	2.50
❑103, Aug 1984 GD (a)	2.50
❑104, Sep 1984 VM, GD (a)	2.50
❑105, Oct 1984	2.50
❑106, Nov 1984 GD (a)	2.50
❑107, Dec 1984	2.50
❑108, Jan 1985	2.50
❑109, Feb 1985	2.50
❑110, Mar 1985	2.50
❑111, Apr 1985	2.50
❑112, May 1985	2.50
❑113, Jun 1985	2.50
❑114, Jul 1985	2.50
❑115, Aug 1985 VM (a)	2.50
❑116, Sep 1985 SB (a)	2.50
❑117, Oct 1985	2.50
❑118, Nov 1985	2.50
❑119, Dec 1985	2.50
❑120, Jan 1986	2.50
❑121, Feb 1986	2.50
❑122, Mar 1986	2.50
❑123, Apr 1986	2.50
❑124, May 1986	2.50
❑125, Jun 1986	2.50
❑126, Jul 1986	2.50
❑127, Aug 1986	2.50
❑128, Sep 1986	2.50
❑129, Oct 1986	2.50
❑130, Nov 1986	2.50
❑131, Dec 1986	2.50
❑132, Jan 1987	2.50
❑133, Feb 1987	2.50
❑134, Mar 1987	2.50
❑135, Apr 1987	2.50
❑136, May 1987	2.50
❑137, Jun 1987	2.50
❑138, Jul 1987	2.50
❑139, Aug 1987	2.50
❑140, Sep 1987	2.50
❑141, Oct 1987	2.50
❑142, Nov 1987	2.50
❑143, Dec 1987	2.50
❑144, Jan 1988	2.50
❑145, Feb 1988 A: Red Sonja.	2.50
❑146, Mar 1988	2.50
❑147, Apr 1988	2.50
❑148, May 1988	2.50
❑149, Jun 1988	2.50
❑150, Jul 1988	2.50
❑151, Aug 1988	2.50
❑152, Sep 1988	2.50
❑153, Oct 1988 LMc (a); A: Red Sonja.	2.50
❑154, Nov 1988	2.50
❑155, Dec 1988	2.50
❑156, Jan 1989	2.50
❑157, Feb 1989	2.50
❑158, Mar 1989	2.50
❑159, Apr 1989	2.50
❑160, May 1989	2.50
❑161, Jun 1989	2.50
❑162, Jul 1989	2.50
❑163, Aug 1989	2.50
❑164, Sep 1989	2.50

Erik Larsen's *Savage Dragon* is Image's longest-running title with the same creator at the helm.

	N-MINT
❑165, Oct 1989	2.50
❑166, Nov 1989	2.50
❑167, Dec 1989	2.50
❑168, Jan 1990	2.50
❑169, Feb 1990	2.50
❑170, Mar 1990	2.50
❑171, Apr 1990	2.50
❑172, May 1990	2.50
❑173, Jun 1990	2.50
❑174, Jul 1990; Series continues as Savage Sworld of Conan the Barbarian	2.25
❑175, Aug 1990	2.25
❑176, Sep 1990	2.25
❑177, Oct 1990	2.25
❑178, Nov 1990	2.25
❑179, Dec 1990 A: Red Sonja.	2.25
❑180, Jan 1991	2.25
❑181, Feb 1991	2.25
❑182, Mar 1991	2.25
❑183, Apr 1991	2.25
❑184, May 1991 AA (a)	2.25
❑185, Jun 1991	2.25
❑186, Jul 1991	2.25
❑187, Aug 1991 A: Red Sonja.	2.25
❑188, Sep 1991	2.25
❑189, Oct 1991	2.25
❑190, Nov 1991	2.25
❑191, Dec 1991	2.25
❑192, Jan 1992	2.25
❑193, Feb 1992	2.25
❑194, Mar 1992	2.25
❑195, Apr 1992	2.25
❑196, May 1992	2.25
❑197, Jun 1992	2.25
❑198, Jul 1992	2.25
❑199, Aug 1992	2.25
❑200, Sep 1992	2.25
❑201, Oct 1992	2.25
❑202, Nov 1992	2.25
❑203, Dec 1992	2.25
❑204, Jan 1993	2.25
❑205, Feb 1993	2.25
❑206, Mar 1993	2.25
❑207, Apr 1993 JB (a)	2.25
❑208, May 1993 JB (a)	2.25
❑209, Jun 1993 JB (a)	2.25
❑210, Jul 1993 JB (a)	2.25
❑211, Aug 1993	2.25
❑212, Sep 1993	2.25
❑213, Oct 1993	2.25
❑214, Nov 1993; Adapted from Robert E. Howard's "Red Nails"	2.25
❑215, Dec 1993	2.25
❑216, Jan 1994	2.25
❑217, Feb 1994	2.25
❑218, Mar 1994	2.25
❑219, Apr 1994	2.25
❑220, May 1994	2.25
❑221, May 1994, b&w	2.25
❑222, Jun 1994, b&w	2.25
❑223, Jul 1994, b&w	2.25
❑224, Aug 1994, b&w	2.25
❑225, Sep 1994, b&w	2.25
❑226, Oct 1994, b&w	2.25
❑227, Nov 1994, b&w	2.25
❑228, Dec 1994, b&w	2.25
❑229, Jan 1995, b&w	2.25

N-MINT

❑230, Feb 1995, b&w 2.25
❑231, Mar 1995, b&w 2.25
❑232, Apr 1995, b&w 2.25
❑233, May 1995, b&w 2.25
❑234, Jun 1995, b&w 2.25
❑235, Jul 1995, b&w 2.25
❑Annual 1, ca. 1975, b&w; reprinted from Conan the Barbarian (1st series) #10 and 13; Kull the Conqueror #3; Monsters on the Prowl #16 1.25
❑Special 1, ca. 1975 6.00

SAVAGE SWORD OF MIKE
FANDOM HOUSE

❑1, b&w 2.00

SAVAGE TALES (1ST SERIES)
MARVEL

❑1, May 1971; b&w magazine SL (w); GM, GC, JB, JR, BS (a); O: Man-Thing. 1: Man-Thing. A: Conan. 88.00
❑2, Oct 1973; AW, BWr, GM, FB (a); "Crusader" reprinted from The Black Knight #1 32.00
❑3, Feb 1974; AW, FB, JSt (a); Continues "Red Nails" story from issue #2 20.00
❑4, May 1974 NA, GK (a) 20.00
❑5, Jul 1974 NA, GK (a) 12.00
❑6, Sep 1974 10.00
❑7, Nov 1974 10.00
❑8, Jan 1975 10.00
❑9, Mar 1975 10.00
❑10, May 1975 10.00
❑11, Jul 1975 10.00
❑12, Sum 1975 8.00
❑Annual 1, ca. 1975, b&w GK (a); O: Ka-Zar. 8.00

SAVAGE TALES (2ND SERIES)
MARVEL

❑1, Oct 1985, b&w; magazine; MG (a); 1st 'Nam story 4.00
❑2, Dec 1985; JSe (a); 2nd 'Nam story 3.00
❑3, Feb 1986 2.50
❑4, Apr 1986; 'Nam 2.50
❑5, Jun 1986 JSe (a) 2.50
❑6, Aug 1986 2.00
❑7, Oct 1986 2.00
❑8, Dec 1986 2.00
❑9, Feb 1987 2.00

SAVANT GARDE
IMAGE

❑1, Mar 1997 2.50
❑2, Apr 1997 1: Innuendo. 2.50
❑3, May 1997 2.50
❑4, Jun 1997 2.50
❑5, Jul 1997 2.50
❑6, Aug 1997 2.50
❑7, Sep 1997 2.50
❑Fan ed. 1, Feb 1997 1.00
❑Fan ed. 2, Mar 1997 1.00
❑Fan ed. 3, Apr 1997 1.00

SAVED BY THE BELL
HARVEY

❑1, May 1992 1.25
❑2, Jun 1992 1.25
❑3, Jul 1992 1.25
❑4, Aug 1992 1.25
❑5, Sep 1992 1.25

SAVIOUR
TRIDENT

❑1 1989, b&w 4.00
❑2, Feb 1990, b&w 1.95
❑3 1990, b&w 2.50
❑4 1990, b&w 2.50
❑5 1990, b&w 2.50

SB NINJA HIGH SCHOOL
ANTARCTIC

❑1/A, Aug 1992, b&w 2.50
❑1/B, Aug 1992, b&w; trading card 4.95
❑2/A, b&w 2.95
❑2/B, b&w; trading card 4.95
❑3/A, Sep 1994, b&w 2.75
❑3/B, Sep 1994, b&w; trading card 4.95
❑4, Feb 1995, b&w 2.75
❑5, May 1995, b&w 2.75
❑6, Aug 1995, b&w 2.75
❑7, Nov 1995, b&w 2.75

SCAB
FANTACO

❑1, b&w 3.50
❑2, b&w 3.50

SCALES OF THE DRAGON
SUNDRAGON

❑1, Mar 1997, b&w; Flip-book 1.95

SCAMP (WALT DISNEY...)
GOLD KEY / WHITMAN

❑1, ca. 1968 8.00
❑2, Mar 1969 4.00
❑3, ca. 1970 4.00
❑4, Nov 1970 4.00
❑5, Feb 1971 4.00
❑6, Oct 1971 3.00
❑7 1972 3.00
❑8 1972 3.00
❑9, Nov 1972 3.00
❑10, Feb 1973 3.00
❑11, Jun 1973 2.50
❑12, Jul 1973 2.50
❑13, Sep 1973 2.50
❑14, Nov 1973 2.50
❑15, Jan 1974 2.50
❑16, Mar 1974 2.50
❑17, May 1974 2.50
❑18, Jul 1974 2.50
❑19, Sep 1974 2.50
❑20, Nov 1974 2.50
❑21, Jan 1975 2.00
❑22, Mar 1975 2.00
❑23, May 1975 2.00
❑24, Jul 1975 2.00
❑25, Sep 1975 2.00
❑26, Nov 1975 2.00
❑27, Jan 1976 2.00
❑28, Mar 1976 2.00
❑29, May 1976 2.00
❑30, Jul 1976 2.00
❑31, Sep 1976 2.00
❑32, Nov 1976 2.00
❑33, Jan 1977 2.00
❑34, Mar 1977 2.00
❑35, May 1977 2.00
❑36, Jul 1977 2.00
❑37, Sep 1977 2.00
❑38, Nov 1977 2.00
❑39, Jan 1978 2.00
❑40, Mar 1978 2.00
❑41, May 1978 2.00
❑42, Jul 1978 2.00
❑43, Sep 1978 2.00
❑44, Nov 1979 2.00
❑45, Jan 1979 (c); (w); (a) 2.00

SCAN
ICONOGRAFIX

❑1, b&w 2.95
❑2, b&w 2.95

SCANDALS
THORBY

❑1 2.95

SCANDAL SHEET
ARRIBA

❑1, b&w 2.50

SCARAB
DC / VERTIGO

❑0, Mar 1994 1.95
❑1, Nov 1993 1.95
❑2, Dec 1993 1.95
❑3, Jan 1994 1.95
❑4, Feb 1994 1.95
❑5, Mar 1994 1.95
❑6, Apr 1994 1.95
❑7, May 1994 1.95
❑8, Jun 1994 1.95

SCARAMOUCH
INNOVATION

❑1, b&w 2.25
❑2, b&w 2.25

SCARECROW OF ROMNEY MARSH, THE
GOLD KEY

❑1, Apr 1964, No number; code on cover box ends in "404" 30.00
❑2, Jul 1965 20.00
❑3, Oct 1965 20.00

SCARECROW (VILLAINS)
DC

❑1, Feb 1998; New Year's Evil 1.95

SCARE TACTICS
DC

❑1, Dec 1996 2.25
❑2, Jan 1997; Road Trip 2.25
❑3, Feb 1997 2.25
❑4, Mar 1997 2.25
❑5, Apr 1997; Valentine's Day Nightmare 2.25
❑6, May 1997 2.25
❑7, Jun 1997 2.25
❑8, Jul 1997 2.25
❑9, Aug 1997; series goes on hiatus; story continues in Impulse Plus #1 2.25
❑10, Jan 1998 2.25
❑11, Feb 1998 2.25
❑12, Mar 1998; Phil transforms 2.25

SCARLET CRUSH
AWESOME

❑1, Jan 1998 2.50
❑2, Feb 1998 2.50

SCARLET IN GASLIGHT
ETERNITY

❑1, Mar 1988, b&w; Sherlock Holmes vs. Dracula 1.95
❑2, Apr 1988 1.95
❑3, May 1988 1.95
❑4, Jun 1988 1.95

SCARLET KISS: THE VAMPYRE
ALL AMERICAN

❑1, b&w 2.95

SCARLET SCORPION/DARKSHADE
AC

❑1, Jul 1995 3.50
❑2 1995 3.50

SCARLET SPIDER
MARVEL

❑1, Nov 1995 GK (a) 2.00
❑2, Dec 1995; JR2 (a); concludes in Spectacular Scarlet Spider #2 2.00

SCARLET SPIDER UNLIMITED
MARVEL

❑1, Nov 1995 3.95

SCARLETT
DC

❑1, Jan 1993 3.00
❑2, Feb 1993 2.00
❑3, Mar 1993 2.00
❑4, Apr 1993 1.75
❑5, May 1993 1.75
❑6, Jun 1993 1.75
❑7, Jul 1993 1.75
❑8, Aug 1993 1.75
❑9, Sep 1993 1.75
❑10, Oct 1993 1.75
❑11, Nov 1993 1.75
❑12, Dec 1993 1.75
❑13, Jan 1994 1.75
❑14, Feb 1994 1.75

SCARLET THUNDER
SLAVE LABOR / AMAZE INK

❑1, Nov 1995 1.50
❑2, Feb 1996; 1st apperance Blue Streak 1.50

	N-MINT
❑3, May 1996	2.50
❑4, Dec 1996	2.50

SCARLETT PILGRIM
LAST GASP

❑1	1.00

SCARLET WITCH
MARVEL

❑1, Jan 1994	1.75
❑2, Feb 1994	1.75
❑3, Mar 1994	1.75
❑4, Apr 1994	1.75

SCARLET ZOMBIE, THE
COMAX

❑1, b&w	2.95

SCARS (WARREN ELLIS')
AVATAR

❑1, Jan 2003	3.50
❑2, Feb 2003	3.50
❑2/A, Feb 2003; Wrap Cover	3.95
❑3, Mar 2003	3.50
❑4, Apr 2003	3.50
❑5, May 2003	3.50
❑5/A, May 2003; Wrap Cover	3.95
❑6, Jun 2003	3.50
❑6/A, Jun 2003; Wrap Cover	3.95

SCARY BOOK, THE
CALIBER

❑1, b&w	2.50
❑2, b&w	2.50

SCARY GODMOTHER
SIRIUS

❑1, May 2001	2.95

SCARY GODMOTHER: BLOODY VALENTINE
SIRIUS

❑1, Feb 1998	3.95

SCARY GODMOTHER HOLIDAY SPOOKTACULAR
SIRIUS

❑1, Nov 1998, b&w; wraparound cover	2.95

SCARY GODMOTHER: WILD ABOUT HARRY
SIRIUS

❑1, ca. 2000, b&w	2.95
❑2, ca. 2000, b&w	2.95

SCARY TALES
CHARLTON

❑1, Aug 1975 O: Countess Von Bludd. 1: Countess Von Bludd.	5.00
❑2, Oct 1975	3.00
❑3, Dec 1975	3.00
❑4, Feb 1976	3.00
❑5, Apr 1976	3.00
❑6, Jun 1976	2.50
❑7, Sep 1976	2.50
❑8, Nov 1976	2.50
❑9, Jan 1977	2.50
❑10, Sep 1977	2.50
❑11, Jan 1978	2.00
❑12, Mar 1978	2.00
❑13, Apr 1978	2.00
❑14, May 1978	2.00
❑15, Jul 1978	2.00
❑16, Oct 1978	2.00
❑17, Dec 1978	2.00
❑18, Feb 1979	2.00
❑19, Apr 1979	2.00
❑20, Jun 1979	2.00
❑21, Aug 1980	2.00
❑22, Oct 1980	2.00
❑23, Dec 1980	2.00
❑24, Feb 1981	2.00
❑25, Apr 1981	2.00
❑26, Jun 1981	2.00
❑27, Aug 1981	2.00
❑28, Oct 1981	2.00
❑29, Dec 1981	2.00
❑30, Feb 1982	2.00
❑31, Apr 1982	2.00
❑32, Jun 1982	2.00
❑33, Aug 1982	2.00
❑34, Oct 1982	2.00
❑35, Dec 1982	2.00
❑36, Feb 1983	2.00
❑37, Apr 1983	2.00
❑38, Jun 1983	2.00
❑39, Aug 1983	2.00
❑40, Oct 1983	2.00
❑41, Dec 1983	2.00
❑42, Feb 1984	2.00
❑43, Apr 1984	2.00
❑44, Jun 1984	2.00
❑45, Aug 1984	2.00
❑46, Oct 1984	2.00

SCATTERBRAIN
DARK HORSE

❑1, Jun 1998	2.95
❑2, Jul 1998	2.95
❑3, Aug 1998	2.95
❑4, Sep 1998	2.95

SCAVENGERS (FLEETWAY/QUALITY)
FLEETWAY-QUALITY

❑1, Feb 1988; Judge Dredd	1.25
❑2, Mar 1988; Judge Dredd	1.25
❑3, Apr 1988; Judge Dredd	1.25
❑4, May 1988; Judge Dredd	1.25
❑5, Jun 1988	1.25
❑6, Jul 1988	1.50
❑7, Aug 1988	1.50
❑8, Sep 1988	1.50
❑9, Oct 1988	1.50
❑10, Nov 1988	1.50
❑11, Dec 1988	1.50
❑12, Jan 1989	1.50
❑13 1989	1.50
❑14 1989	1.50

SCAVENGERS (TRIUMPHANT)
TRIUMPHANT

❑0, Mar 1994; giveaway	1.00
❑0/A, Mar 1994; 18, 000-copy edition	2.50
❑0/B, Mar 1994; 5000-copy edition	2.50
❑1, Jul 1993	2.50
❑1/Ashcan, Jul 1993; ashcan edition	2.50
❑2, Aug 1993	2.50
❑3, Sep 1993	2.50
❑4, Oct 1993	2.50
❑5, Nov 1993; D: Jack Hanal. Unleashed!	2.50
❑6, Dec 1993; Unleashed!	2.50
❑7, Jan 1994	2.50
❑8, Feb 1994	2.50
❑9, Mar 1994	2.50
❑10, Apr 1994	2.50
❑11, May 1994	2.50

SCC CONVENTION SPECIAL
SUPER CREW

❑1; 1994 Convention Special	2.25

SCENARIO A
ANTARCTIC

❑1, Jul 1998, b&w	2.95
❑2, Sep 1998, b&w	2.95

SCENE OF THE CRIME
DC / VERTIGO

❑1, May 1999	2.50
❑2, Jun 1999	2.50
❑3, Jul 1999	2.50
❑4, Aug 1999	2.50

SCHIZO
ANTARCTIC

❑1, Dec 1994, b&w	3.50
❑2, Jan 1996, b&w	3.95
❑3, Mar 1998, b&w	3.95

SCIENCE AFFAIR, A
ANTARCTIC

❑1, Mar 1994, b&w	2.75
❑1/Gold, Mar 1994; Gold edition	3.00
❑2, May 1994, b&w	2.75

A teen-age group of monsters, led by a conspiracy theorist, took to the road in search of their origins in *Scare Tactics*.

© 1996 DC Comics.

SCIENCE FICTION CLASSICS
DRAGON LADY

	N-MINT
❑1; Twin Earths	5.95

SCI-FI
ROUGH COPY

❑1	2.95

SCIMIDAR
ETERNITY

❑1, Jun 1988, b&w	2.50
❑2 1988, b&w	2.50
❑3 1988, b&w	2.50
❑4/A, Dec 1988; "mild" cover	2.00
❑4/B, Dec 1988; "hot" cover	2.00

SCIMIDAR BOOK II
ETERNITY

❑1, May 1989, b&w	3.00
❑1-2	3.00
❑2, b&w	3.00
❑3, b&w	3.00
❑4, b&w	3.00

SCIMIDAR BOOK III
ETERNITY

❑1, b&w	3.00
❑1-2	3.00
❑2, b&w	3.00
❑3, b&w	3.00
❑4, b&w	3.00

SCIMIDAR BOOK IV: "WILD THING"
ETERNITY

❑1	3.00
❑1/Nude; Nude cover	3.00
❑2, b&w	3.00
❑3, b&w	3.00
❑4, b&w	3.00

SCIMIDAR BOOK V: "LIVING COLOR"
ETERNITY

❑1, b&w	2.50
❑1/Nude, b&w; Nude cover	2.50
❑2, b&w	2.50
❑3, b&w	2.50
❑4, b&w	2.50

SCIMIDAR (CFD)
CFD

❑1, b&w	2.95
❑3	2.75

SCIMIDAR PIN-UP BOOK
ETERNITY

❑1, unstapled	3.75

SCION
CROSSGEN

❑1, Jul 2000	2.95
❑2, Aug 2000	2.95
❑3, Sep 2000	2.95
❑4, Oct 2000	2.95
❑5, Nov 2000	2.95
❑6, Dec 2000	2.95
❑7, Jan 2001	2.95
❑8, Feb 2001	2.95
❑9, Mar 2001	2.95
❑10, Apr 2001	2.95
❑11, May 2001	2.95
❑12, Jun 2001	2.95
❑13, Jul 2001	2.95
❑14, Aug 2001	2.95
❑15, Sep 2001	2.95

N-MINT

❑16, Oct 2001 ... 2.95
❑17, Nov 2001 ... 2.95
❑18, Dec 2001 ... 2.95
❑19, Jan 2002 ... 2.95
❑20, Feb 2002 ... 2.95
❑21, Mar 2002 ... 2.95
❑22, Apr 2002 ... 2.95
❑23, May 2002 ... 2.95
❑24, Jun 2002 ... 2.95
❑25, Jul 2002 ... 2.95
❑26, Aug 2002 ... 2.95
❑27, Sep 2002 ... 2.95
❑28, Oct 2002 ... 2.95
❑29, Nov 2002 ... 2.95
❑30, Dec 2002 ... 2.95
❑31, Jan 2003 ... 2.95
❑32, Feb 2003 ... 2.95
❑33, Mar 2003 ... 2.95
❑34, Apr 2003 ... 2.95
❑35, May 2003 ... 2.95
❑36, Jun 2003 ... 2.95
❑37, Jul 2003 ... 2.95
❑38, Aug 2003 ... 2.95
❑39, Oct 2003 ... 2.95
❑40, Nov 2003 ... 2.95
❑42, Jan 2004 ... 2.95
❑41, Dec 2003 ... 2.95
❑43, Apr 2004 ... 2.95

SCI-SPY
DC / VERTIGO

❑1, Apr 2002 ... 2.50
❑2, May 2002 ... 2.50
❑3, Jun 2002 ... 2.50
❑4, Jul 2002 ... 2.50
❑5, Aug 2002 ... 2.50
❑6, Sep 2002 ... 2.50

SCI-TECH
DC / WILDSTORM

❑1, Sep 1999 ... 2.50
❑2, Oct 1999 ... 2.50
❑3, Nov 1999 ... 2.50
❑4, Dec 1999 ... 2.50

SCOOBY-DOO (MARVEL)
MARVEL

❑1, Oct 1977 ... 12.00
❑2, Dec 1977 ... 7.00
❑3, Feb 1978 ... 7.00
❑4, Apr 1978 ... 7.00
❑5, Jun 1978 ... 4.00
❑6, Aug 1978 ... 4.00
❑7, Oct 1978 ... 4.00
❑8, Dec 1978 ... 4.00
❑9, Feb 1979 ... 4.00

SCOOBY-DOO (HARVEY)
HARVEY

❑1, ca. 1992 ... 1.50
❑2, ca. 1992 ... 1.50
❑3, ca. 1992 ... 1.50
❑Giant Size 1, ca. 1992 ... 2.25
❑Giant Size 2, ca. 1992 ... 2.25
❑Special 1 ... 1.95
❑Special 2 ... 1.95

SCOOBY-DOO (ARCHIE)
ARCHIE

❑1, Oct 1995 ... 1.50
❑2, Nov 1995 ... 1.50
❑3, Dec 1995 ... 1.50
❑4, Jan 1996 ... 1.50
❑5, Feb 1996 ... 1.50
❑6, Mar 1996 ... 1.50
❑7, Apr 1996 ... 1.50
❑8, May 1996 ... 1.50
❑10, Jul 1996 ... 1.50
❑11, Aug 1996 ... 1.50
❑12, Sep 1996 ... 1.50
❑14, Nov 1996 ... 1.50
❑15, Dec 1996 ... 1.50
❑16, Jan 1997 ... 1.50
❑17, Feb 1997 ... 1.50
❑18, Mar 1997 ... 1.50
❑19, Apr 1997 ... 1.50
❑20, May 1997 ... 1.50
❑21, Jun 1997 ... 1.50

SCOOBY-DOO (DC)
DC

❑1, Aug 1997 JSa (a) ... 2.50
❑2, Sep 1997 ... 2.00
❑3, Oct 1997 JSa (a) ... 2.00
❑4, Nov 1997 ... 2.00
❑5, Dec 1997 JSa (a) ... 2.00
❑6, Jan 1998 A: Stetson Rogers (Shaggy's cousin). ... 2.00
❑7, Feb 1998 ... 2.00
❑8, Mar 1998 ... 2.00
❑9, Apr 1998 ... 2.00
❑10, May 1998 ... 2.00
❑11, Jun 1998 ... 2.00
❑12, Jul 1998; JSa (a); mystery at a comic-book convention ... 2.00
❑13, Aug 1998 ... 2.00
❑14, Sep 1998 ... 2.00
❑15, Oct 1998 ... 2.00
❑16, Nov 1998 A: Groovy Ghoulie. ... 2.00
❑17, Dec 1998 ... 2.00
❑18, Jan 1999 ... 2.00
❑19, Feb 1999 JSa (a) ... 2.00
❑20, Mar 1999 JSa (a); A: Mystery, Inc.. ... 2.00
❑21, Apr 1999 JSa (a); A: Mystery, Inc.. 1.99
❑22, May 1999 ... 1.99
❑23, Jun 1999 JSa (a) ... 1.99
❑24, Jul 1999 DP (a) ... 1.99
❑25, Aug 1999 DP (a) ... 1.99
❑26, Sep 1999 JSa (a) ... 1.99
❑27, Oct 1999 JSa (a) ... 1.99
❑28, Nov 1999 JSa (a) ... 1.99
❑29, Dec 1999 JSa, DP (a) ... 1.99
❑30, Jan 2000 JSa (a) ... 1.99
❑31, Feb 2000 ... 1.99
❑32, Mar 2000 ... 1.99
❑33, Apr 2000 ... 1.99
❑34, May 2000 JSa (a) ... 1.99
❑35, Jun 2000 JSa (a) ... 1.99
❑36, Jul 2000 ... 1.99
❑37, Aug 2000 JSa (a) ... 1.99
❑38, Sep 2000 JSa (a) ... 1.99
❑39, Oct 2000 JSa (a) ... 1.99
❑40, Nov 2000 ... 1.99
❑41, Dec 2000 JSa (a) ... 1.99
❑42, Jan 2001 JSa (a) ... 1.99
❑43, Feb 2001 JSa (a) ... 1.99
❑44, Mar 2001 JSa (a) ... 1.99
❑45, Apr 2001 JSa (a) ... 1.99
❑46, May 2001 DDC (w); JSa (a) ... 1.99
❑47, Jun 2001 JSa (a) ... 1.99
❑48, Jul 2001 JSa (a) ... 1.99
❑49, Aug 2001 ... 1.99
❑50, Sep 2001 JSa (a); A: Speed Buggy. A: Funky Phantom. ... 1.99
❑51, Oct 2001 DDC (a) ... 1.99
❑52, Nov 2001 JSa (a) ... 1.99
❑53, Dec 2001 JSa (a) ... 1.99
❑54, Jan 2002 JSa (a) ... 1.99
❑55, Feb 2002 JSa (a) ... 1.99
❑56, Mar 2002 JSa (a) ... 1.99
❑57, Apr 2002 JSa (a) ... 1.99
❑58, May 2002 ... 1.99
❑59, Jun 2002 JSa (a) ... 1.99
❑60, Jul 2002 JSa (a) ... 1.99
❑61, Aug 2002 JSa (a) ... 1.99
❑62, Sep 2002 JSa (a) ... 1.99
❑63, Oct 2002 JSa (a) ... 1.99
❑64, Nov 2002 ... 1.99
❑65, Dec 2002 JSa (a) ... 2.25
❑66, Jan 2003 ... 2.25
❑67, Feb 2003 ... 2.25
❑68, Mar 2003 ... 2.25
❑69, Apr 2003 ... 2.25
❑70, May 2003 ... 2.25
❑71, Jun 2003 ... 2.25
❑72, Jul 2003 ... 2.25
❑73, Aug 2003 ... 2.25
❑74, Sep 2003 ... 2.25
❑75, Oct 2003 ... 2.25
❑76, Nov 2003 ... 2.25
❑77, Dec 2003 ... 2.25
❑78, Jan 2004 ... 2.25
❑79, Feb 2004 ... 2.25
❑80, Mar 2004 ... 2.25
❑81, Apr 2004 ... 2.25
❑82, May 2004 ... 2.25
❑83, Jun 2004 ... 2.25
❑84, Jul 2004 ... 2.25
❑85, Aug 2004 ... 2.25
❑86, Sep 2004 ...
❑Summer 1, Aug 2001 JSa (a) ... 3.95
❑Special 1, Oct 1999; JSa, EC (a); Spooky Spectacular ... 3.95
❑Special 2, Oct 2000 JSa (a) ... 3.95

SCOOBY-DOO BIG BOOK
HARVEY

❑1 1992 ... 1.95
❑2 ... 1.95

SCOOBY-DOO DOLLAR COMIC
DC

❑1, Oct 2003 ... 1.00

SCOOBY DOO, WHERE ARE YOU? (GOLD KEY)
GOLD KEY

❑1, Mar 1970 ... 60.00
❑2, Jun 1970 ... 24.00
❑3, Sep 1970 ... 24.00
❑4, Dec 1970 ... 24.00
❑5, Mar 1971 ... 24.00
❑6, Jun 1971 ... 24.00
❑7, Aug 1971 ... 24.00
❑8, Oct 1971 ... 24.00
❑9, Dec 1971 ... 18.00
❑10, Feb 1972 ... 18.00
❑11, Apr 1972 ... 18.00
❑12, Jun 1972 ... 18.00
❑13, Aug 1972 ... 18.00
❑14, Oct 1972 ... 18.00
❑15, Dec 1972 ... 18.00
❑16, ca. 1973 ... 18.00
❑17, ca. 1973 ... 18.00
❑18, ca. 1973 ... 18.00
❑19, Jul 1973 ... 18.00
❑20, Aug 1973 ... 12.00
❑21, Oct 1973 ... 12.00
❑22, Dec 1973 ... 12.00
❑23, Feb 1974 ... 12.00
❑24, Apr 1974 ... 12.00
❑25, Jun 1974 ... 12.00
❑26, ca. 1974 ... 12.00
❑27, ca. 1974 ... 12.00
❑28, ca. 1974 ... 12.00
❑29, Dec 1974 ... 12.00
❑30, ca. 1975 ... 12.00

SCOOBY DOO, WHERE ARE YOU? (CHARLTON)
CHARLTON

❑1, Apr 1975 ... 15.00
❑2, Jun 1975 ... 10.00
❑3, Aug 1975 ... 7.00
❑4, Oct 1975 ... 7.00
❑5, Dec 1975 ... 7.00
❑6, Feb 1976 ... 6.00
❑7, Apr 1976 ... 6.00
❑8, Jun 1976 ... 6.00
❑9, Aug 1976 ... 6.00
❑10, Oct 1976 ... 6.00
❑11, Dec 1976 ... 5.00

SCOOTERMAN
WELLZEE

❑1, Apr 1996, b&w ... 2.75
❑2, Dec 1996, b&w; poster ... 2.75
❑3, Jul 1997, b&w ... 2.75

SCORCHED EARTH
TUNDRA

❑1, Apr 1991 ... 2.95

N-MINT

❑2, Jun 1991 ... 2.95
❑3, Aug 1991 ... 2.95

SCORCHY
Forbidden Fruit

❑1, b&w ... 3.50

SCORE, THE
DC / Piranha

❑1, ca. 1989 ... 4.95
❑2, ca. 1989 ... 4.95
❑3, ca. 1989 ... 4.95
❑4, ca. 1989 ... 4.95

SCORN: DEADLY REBELLION
SCC Entertainment

❑0, Jul 1996, b&w ... 2.95

SCORN: HEATWAVE
SCC Entertainment

❑1, Jan 1997, b&w; follows events in Scorn: Deadly Rebellion ... 3.95

SCORPIA
Miller

❑1 ... 2.50
❑2 ... 2.50

SCORPION, THE
Atlas-Seaboard

❑1, Feb 1975 HC (c); HC (w); HC (a); 1: The Scorpion I (Moro Frost). ... 3.00
❑2, Apr 1975 BWr (a) ... 1.50
❑3, Jul 1975 1: The Scorpion II (David Harper). ... 1.50

SCORPION
Annruel

❑1, b&w ... 2.50

SCORPION CORPS
Dagger

❑1, Nov 1993 ... 2.50
❑2, Dec 1993 ... 2.50
❑3, Jan 1994 ... 2.50
❑4, Feb 1994 ... 2.50
❑5, Mar 1994 ... 2.50
❑6, Apr 1994 ... 2.50
❑7, May 1994 ... 2.50
❑8, Jun 1994 ... 2.50
❑9, Jul 1994 ... 2.50
❑10, Aug 1994 ... 2.50

SCORPION KING, THE
Dark Horse

❑1, Mar 2002 ... 2.99
❑2, Apr 2002 ... 2.99

SCORPION MOON
Express / Entity

❑1, Oct 1994, b&w; Cardstock cover; 4th in a series of Entity illustrated novellas with Zen Intergalactic Ninja ... 2.95

SCORPIO RISING
Marvel

❑1, Oct 1994; prestige format one-shot ... 5.95

SCORPIO ROSE
Eclipse

❑1, Jan 1983 MR (a); O: Scorpio Rose. 1: Scorpio Rose. 1: Doctor Orient. 2.00
❑2, Oct 1983 MR (a) ... 2.00

SCOUT
Eclipse

❑1, Nov 1985 ... 2.00
❑2, Dec 1985 ... 2.00
❑3, Jan 1985 ... 2.00
❑4, Feb 1986 ... 2.00
❑5, Mar 1986 ... 2.00
❑6, Apr 1986 ... 2.00
❑7, May 1986 ... 2.00
❑8, Jun 1986 ... 2.00
❑9, Jul 1986; Airboy preview ... 2.00
❑10, Aug 1986 ... 2.00
❑11, Sep 1986 ... 1.75
❑12, Oct 1986 ... 1.75
❑13, Nov 1986 ... 1.75
❑14, Dec 1986 ... 1.75
❑15, Jan 1987 ... 1.75
❑16, Feb 1987; 3-D ... 2.50

N-MINT

❑17, Mar 1987 ... 1.75
❑18, Apr 1987 ... 1.75
❑19, May 1987; flexidisc ... 3.00
❑20, Jun 1987 ... 1.75
❑21, Jul 1987 ... 1.75
❑22, Aug 1987 ... 1.75
❑23, Sep 1987 ... 1.75
❑24, Oct 1987 ... 1.75

SCOUT HANDBOOK
Eclipse

❑1 ... 1.75

SCOUT: WAR SHAMAN
Eclipse

❑1, Mar 1988 ... 2.00
❑2, May 1988 ... 2.00
❑3, Jun 1988 ... 2.00
❑4, Jul 1988 ... 2.00
❑5, Aug 1988 ... 2.00
❑6, Sep 1988 ... 2.00
❑7, Oct 1988 ... 2.00
❑8, Nov 1988 ... 2.00
❑9, Dec 1988 ... 2.00
❑10, Jan 1989 ... 2.00
❑11, Feb 1989 ... 2.00
❑12, Mar 1989 ... 2.00
❑13, Apr 1989 ... 2.00
❑14, May 1989 ... 2.00
❑15, Jun 1989 ... 2.00
❑16, Jul 1989 D: Scout. ... 2.00

SCRAP CITY PACK RATS
Out of the Blue

❑1, b&w ... 1.50
❑2, b&w ... 1.50
❑3, b&w ... 1.50
❑4, b&w ... 1.75
❑5 1986, b&w ... 1.75

SCRATCH
Outside

❑1 1986 ... 1.75
❑2 1986 ... 1.75
❑3 1987 ... 1.75
❑4, Apr 1987 ... 1.75
❑5 1987 ... 1.75
❑6 1987 ... 1.75

SCRATCH (DC)
DC

❑1, Aug 2004 ... 2.50
❑2, Sep 2004 ... 2.50

SCREAMERS
Fantagraphics / Eros

❑1 1995 ... 2.95
❑2 1995 ... 2.95
❑3, Oct 1995 ... 2.95

SCREEN MONSTERS
Zone

❑1 ... 2.95

SCREENPLAY
Slave Labor

❑1, Jun 1989, b&w ... 1.75

SCREWBALL SQUIRREL
Dark Horse

❑1, Jul 1995; Wolf & Red back-up ... 2.50
❑2, Aug 1995; Droopy back-up ... 2.50
❑3, Sep 1995; Wolf & Red back-up ... 2.50

SCREW COMICS
Fantagraphics / Eros

❑1, b&w ... 3.50

SCRUBS IN SCRUBLAND: THE REFLEX
Scrubland

❑1, b&w ... 2.50

SCUD: TALES FROM THE VENDING MACHINE
Fireman

❑1, Jan 1998 ... 3.00
❑2, Mar 1998 ... 2.50
❑3, May 1998 ... 2.50
❑4, Jul 1998 ... 2.50

DC is the most recent publisher to present comics adventures of Scooby, Shaggy, and the gang.
© 1997 DC Comics and Hanna-Barbera Productions.

N-MINT

SCUD: THE DISPOSABLE ASSASSIN
Fireman

❑1, Feb 1994, b&w 1: Scud. ... 10.00
❑1-2 1: Scud. ... 2.95
❑1-3 1997 1: Scud. ... 2.95
❑2, May 1994, b&w ... 4.00
❑3, b&w ... 4.00
❑4, b&w ... 4.00
❑5, b&w ... 4.00
❑6, b&w ... 2.95
❑7, b&w ... 2.95
❑8 1995, b&w ... 2.95
❑9, b&w ... 2.95
❑10, b&w ... 2.95
❑11 ... 2.95
❑12 ... 2.95
❑13 ... 2.95
❑14, Nov 1996 ... 2.95
❑15, Apr 1997 ... 2.95
❑16, Jun 1997 ... 2.95
❑17, Aug 1997 ... 2.95
❑18, Nov 1997 ... 2.95
❑19, Dec 1997 ... 2.95
❑20, Feb 1998 ... 2.95

SCUM OF THE EARTH
Aircel

❑1, b&w ... 2.50
❑2, b&w ... 2.50

SEA DEVILS
DC

❑1, Oct 1961 RH (a) ... 300.00
❑2, Dec 1961 ... 175.00
❑3, Feb 1962 RH (a) ... 120.00
❑4, Apr 1962 ... 85.00
❑5, Jun 1962 ... 85.00
❑6, Aug 1962 ... 55.00
❑7, Oct 1962 ... 55.00
❑8, Dec 1962 ... 55.00
❑9, Feb 1963 ... 55.00
❑10, Apr 1963 ... 55.00
❑11, Jun 1963 ... 38.00
❑12, Aug 1963 ... 38.00
❑13, Oct 1963 GC, JKu (a) ... 42.00
❑14, Dec 1963 ... 38.00
❑15, Feb 1964 ... 38.00
❑16, Apr 1964 ... 38.00
❑17, Jun 1964 ... 38.00
❑18, Aug 1964 ... 38.00
❑19, Oct 1964 ... 38.00
❑20, Dec 1964 ... 38.00
❑21, Feb 1965 ... 28.00
❑22, Apr 1965 ... 28.00
❑23, Jun 1965 ... 28.00
❑24, Aug 1965 ... 28.00
❑25, Oct 1965 ... 28.00
❑26, Dec 1965 ... 28.00
❑27, Feb 1966 ... 28.00
❑28, Apr 1966 ... 28.00
❑29, Jun 1966 ... 28.00
❑30, Aug 1966 ... 28.00
❑31, Oct 1966 ... 28.00
❑32, Dec 1966 ... 28.00
❑33, Feb 1967 ... 28.00
❑34, Apr 1967 ... 28.00
❑35, Jun 1967 ... 28.00

N-MINT

SEADRAGON, THE
ELITE

❑1, May 1986 .... 1.75
❑2, Jun 1986 .... 1.75
❑3, Aug 1986 .... 1.75
❑4 1986 .... 1.75
❑5 1986 .... 1.75
❑6 1986 .... 1.75

SEAGUY
DC

❑1, Jul 2004 .... 2.95
❑2, Aug 2004 .... 2.95
❑3, Sep 2004 .... 2.95

SEA HUNT
DELL

❑4, Mar 1960; numbering continues from Dell Four Color 30.00
❑5, Jun 1960 .... 30.00
❑6, Sep 1960 .... 30.00
❑7, Dec 1960 .... 25.00
❑8, Mar 1961; no cover price 25.00
❑9, Jun 1961 .... 25.00
❑10, Sep 1961 .... 20.00
❑11, Dec 1961 .... 20.00
❑12, Mar 1962 .... 20.00
❑13, Jun 1962 .... 20.00

SEALS
STUDIO ARIES

❑Ashcan 1, May 2000, b&w; preview 1.00

SEAQUEST
NEMESIS

❑1, Mar 1994; KP (a); cardstock cover; based on TV show 2.50
❑2 1994 .... 2.25
❑3 1994 .... 2.25

SEARCHERS, THE
CALIBER

❑1 1996, b&w 2.95
❑2 1996, b&w 2.95
❑3, ca. 1996, b&w 2.95
❑4, ca. 1996, b&w 2.95

SEARCHERS, THE: APOSTLE OF MERCY
CALIBER

❑1, ca. 1997, b&w; Giant-size 2.95
❑2, ca. 1997, b&w 3.95

SEBASTIAN O
DC / VERTIGO

❑1, May 1993 .... 2.00
❑2, Jun 1993 .... 2.00
❑3, Jul 1993 .... 2.00

SEBASTIAN (WALT DISNEY'S...)
DISNEY

❑1 .... 2.00
❑2 .... 2.00

SECOND CITY
HARRIER

❑1, Oct 1986 .... 1.95
❑2, Dec 1986 .... 1.95
❑3, Feb 1987 .... 1.95
❑4, Apr 1987 .... 1.95

SECOND LIFE OF DOCTOR MIRAGE, THE
VALIANT

❑1, Nov 1993 BL (w); O: Doctor Mirage. A: Master Darque. D: Gwen Mirage. 2.50
❑1/Gold, Nov 1993; Gold edition 3.00
❑2, Dec 1993 .... 2.50
❑3, Jan 1994 .... 2.50
❑4, Feb 1994 .... 2.50
❑5, Mar 1994 A: Shadowman. 2.50
❑6, Apr 1994 .... 2.50
❑7, May 1994; V: Doctor Eclipse. trading card 2.50
❑8, Jun 1994 .... 2.50
❑9, Aug 1994 .... 2.50
❑10, Sep 1994 .... 2.50
❑11, Oct 1994; Chaos Effect 2.50
❑12, Nov 1994 .... 2.50
❑13, Dec 1994 A: Walt Willey. 2.50
❑14, Jan 1995 .... 2.50
❑15, Feb 1995 .... 2.50
❑16, Mar 1995 .... 2.50
❑17, Apr 1995 .... 2.50
❑18, May 1995 .... 2.50

SECOND RATE HEROES
FOUNDATION

❑1, b&w 2.50
❑2, b&w 2.50

SECRET AGENT (CHARLTON)
CHARLTON

❑9, Oct 1966; 1: Mr. Ize!. Series continued from Sarge Steel #8 .... 8.00
❑10, Oct 1967 .... 6.00

SECRET AGENT (GOLD KEY)
GOLD KEY

❑1, Nov 1966 .... 40.00
❑2, Jan 1968 .... 25.00

SECRET AGENTS
PERSONALITY

❑1, b&w 2.95
❑2, b&w 2.95
❑3, b&w 2.95

SECRET CITY SAGA (JACK KIRBY'S...)
TOPPS

❑0, Apr 1993 .... 2.95
❑1, May 1993; trading cards 2.95
❑2, Jun 1993; trading cards 2.95
❑3, Jul 1993; trading cards 2.95
❑4, Aug 1993; trading cards 2.95

SECRET DEFENDERS
MARVEL

❑1, Mar 1993; Story continued from Doctor Strange #50; foil cover 2.50
❑2, Apr 1993 .... 1.75
❑3, May 1993 .... 1.75
❑4, Jun 1993 .... 1.75
❑5, Jul 1993 A: Punisher. 1.75
❑6, Aug 1993 .... 1.75
❑7, Sep 1993 .... 1.75
❑8, Oct 1993 A: Captain America. A: Spider-Man. A: Scarlet Witch. A: Doctor Strange. A: Xanadu. 1.75
❑9, Nov 1993 .... 1.75
❑10, Dec 1993 .... 1.75
❑11, Jan 1994 .... 1.75
❑12, Feb 1994; foil cover 2.50
❑13, Mar 1994 .... 1.75
❑14, Apr 1994 .... 1.75
❑15, May 1994 .... 1.75
❑16, Jun 1994 .... 1.95
❑17, Jul 1994 .... 1.95
❑18, Aug 1994 .... 1.95
❑19, Sep 1994 .... 1.95
❑20, Oct 1994 .... 1.95
❑21, Nov 1994 .... 1.95
❑22, Dec 1994 .... 1.95
❑23, Jan 1995 .... 1.95
❑24, Feb 1995 V: original Defenders. 1.95
❑25, Mar 1995; Giant-size 2.50

SECRET DOORS
DIMENSION

❑1, b&w 1.50

SECRET FANTASIES
BULLSEYE

❑1, digest 2.25
❑2, b&w; normal-sized; cardstock cover 2.95

SECRET FILES
ANGEL

❑0, Jun 1996, b&w 2.95
❑0/Nude, Jun 1996, b&w; nude cover edition; cardstock cover 4.00
❑1, Fal 1996, b&w 2.95

SECRET FILES AND ORIGINS GUIDE TO THE DC UNIVERSE 2000
DC

❑1, Mar 2000 .... 4.95

SECRET FILES & ORIGINS GUIDE TO THE DC UNIVERSE 2001-2002
DC

❑1, Feb 2002 .... 4.95

SECRET FILES: INVASION DAY
ANGEL

❑1 .... 5.00
❑1/Nude 5.00
❑2 .... 5.00
❑2/Nude 5.00

SECRET FILES PRESIDENT LUTHOR
DC

❑1, Mar 2001 .... 4.95

SECRET FILES: THE STRANGE CASE
ANGEL

❑1 .... 2.95

SECRET KILLERS, THE
BRONZE MAN

❑1, Oct 1997, b&w 2.95
❑2 1997, b&w 2.95
❑3 1998, b&w 2.95
❑4 1998, b&w; becomes Exit from Shadow; indicia indicates name change 2.95

SECRET MESSAGES
NBM

❑1 2001 .... 2.95
❑2 .... 2.95
❑3 .... 2.95
❑4 .... 2.95
❑5 .... 2.95

SECRET ORIGINS (1ST SERIES)
DC

❑Annual 1, Aug 1961, color; second issue published as 80 Page Giant #8; CI, JK (a); reprints Silver Age origins of the Superman/Batman team, Adam Strange, Green Lantern, Challengers of the Unknown, Green Arrow, Wonder Woman, Manhunter from Mars, and the Flash 400.00

SECRET ORIGINS (2ND SERIES)
DC

❑1, Mar 1973 CI, JKu (a); O: Superman. O: Flash. O: Batman. 14.00
❑2, May 1973 .... 8.00
❑3, Aug 1973 O: Wonder Woman. O: Wildcat. 7.00
❑4, Oct 1973 O: Kid Eternity. O: Vigilante. 7.00
❑5, Dec 1973 .... 6.00
❑6, Feb 1974 .... 6.00
❑7, Oct 1974 O: Robin I (Dick Grayson). O: Aquaman. 6.00

SECRET ORIGINS (3RD SERIES)
DC

❑1, Apr 1986 O: Superman. 5.00
❑2, May 1986 O: Blue Beetle. 2.00
❑3, Jun 1986 O: Captain Marvel. 2.00
❑4, Jul 1986 O: Firestorm. 2.00
❑5, Aug 1986 O: The Crimson Avenger. 2.00
❑6, Sep 1986 O: Halo. O: Batman (Golden Age). 2.00
❑7, Oct 1986 O: Sandman II (Dr. Garrett Sanford). O: Green Lantern (Guy Gardner). 2.00
❑8, Nov 1986 O: Doll Man. O: Shadow Lass. 2.00
❑9, Dec 1986 O: Flash I (Jay Garrick). O: Skyman. O: Stripsey. 2.00
❑10, Jan 1987; O: Phantom Stranger. Legends 2.00
❑11, Feb 1987 JOy (c); O: Power Girl. O: Hawkman (Golden Age). 2.00
❑12, Mar 1987 O: The Fury (Golden Age). O: Challengers of the Unknown. 2.00
❑13, Apr 1987 O: Johnny Thunder. O: Nightwing. O: Whip. 2.00
❑14, May 1987; O: Suicide Squad. Legends 2.00
❑15, Jun 1987 O: Spectre. O: Deadman. 2.00
❑16, Jul 1987 O: Hourman I (Rex Tyler). O: Warlord. 2.00

Condition price index: Multiply "NM prices" above by: **0.83 for Very Fine/Near Mint**
0.66 for Very Fine • 0.33 for Fine • 0.2 for Very Good • 0.125 for Good

N-MINT

❑17, Aug 1987 O: Adam Strange. O: Doctor Occult. 2.00
❑18, Sep 1987 O: Creeper. O: Green Lantern I (Alan Scott). 2.00
❑19, Oct 1987 JK (c); MA (a); O: Uncle Sam. O: Guardian. 2.00
❑20, Nov 1987 O: Doctor Mid-Nite (Golden Age). O: Batgirl. 2.00
❑21, Dec 1987 O: Black Condor. O: Jonah Hex. 2.00
❑22, Jan 1988; O: Manhunters. Millennium 2.00
❑23, Feb 1988; O: Floronic Man. O: Guardians of the Universe. Millennium 2.00
❑24, Mar 1988 O: Blue Devil. O: Doctor Fate. 2.00
❑25, Apr 1988 O: The Atom (Golden Age). O: the Legion of Super-Heroes. 2.00
❑26, May 1988 O: Miss America. O: Black Lightning. 2.00
❑27, Jun 1988 O: Zatara. O: Zatanna. 2.00
❑28, Jul 1988 O: Nightshade. O: Midnight. 2.00
❑29, Aug 1988 O: The Atom (Silver Age). O: Red Tornado (Golden Age). O: Mr. America. 2.00
❑30, Sep 1988 O: Plastic Man. O: Elongated Man. 2.00
❑31, Oct 1988 O: Justice Society of America. 2.00
❑32, Nov 1988 O: Justice League of America. 2.00
❑33, Dec 1988 O: Icemaiden. O: Green Flame. O: Mr. Miracle. 2.00
❑34, Dec 1988 O: Rocket Red. O: G'Nort. O: Captain Atom. 2.00
❑35, Jan 1989 O: Booster Gold. O: Martian Manhunter. O: Max Lord. 2.00
❑36, Jan 1989 O: Green Lantern (Silver Age). O: Poison Ivy. 2.00
❑37, Feb 1989 O: Doctor Light. O: Legion of Substitute Heroes. 2.00
❑38, Mar 1989 O: Speedy. O: Green Arrow. 2.00
❑39, Apr 1989 O: Animal Man. O: Man-Bat. 2.00
❑40, May 1989 O: Gorilla Grodd. O: Congorilla. O: Detective Chimp. 2.00
❑41, Jun 1989 O: Flash's Rogue's Gallery. 2.00
❑42, Jul 1989 O: Grim Ghost. O: Phantom Girl. 2.00
❑43, Aug 1989 O: Chris KL-99. O: Hawk. O: Dove. O: Cave Carson. 2.00
❑44, Sep 1989 O: Clayface III. O: Clayface I. O: Clayface IV. O: Clayface II. 2.00
❑45, Oct 1989 O: Blackhawk. O: El Diablo. 2.00
❑46, Dec 1989; Blueprints of Teen Titans Headquarters, Legion of Super-Heroes Headquarters 2.00
❑47, Feb 1990 O: Karate Kid. O: Chemical King. O: Ferro Lad. 2.00
❑48, Apr 1990 O: Rex the Wonder Dog. O: Ambush Bug. O: Trigger Twins. O: Stanley and His Monster. 2.00
❑49, Jun 1990 O: Newsboy Legion. O: Bouncing Boy. O: Silent Knight. 2.00
❑50, Aug 1990; 100 Page giant O: Robin I (Dick Grayson). O: Johnny Thunder (cowboy). O: Space Museum. O: Black Canary. O: Earth-2. O: Dolphin. 2.00
❑Annual 1, ca. 1987 JBy (c); O: The Doom Patrol. 2.00
❑Annual 2, ca. 1988 O: Flash III (Wally West). O: Flash II (Barry Allen). 2.00
❑Annual 3, ca. 1989 O: Teen Titans. 1: Flamebird. 2.00
❑Giant Size 1, Dec 1998 O: Wonder Girl. O: Robin III (Tim Drake). O: Superboy. O: Impulse. O: Spoiler. O: Arrowette. O: Secret. 4.95
❑Special 1, Oct 1989 O: Riddler. O: Two-Face. O: Penguin. 2.00

N-MINT

SECRET ORIGINS OF KRANKIN' KOMIX
KRANKIN' KOMIX

❑1, Nov 1996 .... 1.00

SECRET ORIGINS OF SUPER-VILLAINS
DC

❑Giant Size 1, Dec 1999 .... 4.95

SECRET ORIGINS OF THE WORLD'S GREATEST SUPER HEROES
DC

❑1, ca. 1989 .... 4.95

SECRET ORIGINS REPLICA EDITION
DC

❑1, Feb 2000; Cardstock fold-out cover; reprints Secret Origins #1 (1st series) 4.95

SECRET PLOT
FANTAGRAPHICS / EROS

❑1, Oct 1997 .... 2.95
❑2, Nov 1997 .... 2.95

SECRET SIX
DC

❑1, May 1968; O: The Secret Six. 1: The Secret Six. splash page is cover 30.00
❑2, Jul 1968 .... 15.00
❑3, Sep 1968 .... 12.00
❑4, Nov 1968 .... 12.00
❑5, Jan 1969 .... 12.00
❑6, Mar 1969 .... 15.00
❑7, May 1969 .... 20.00

SECRET SOCIETY OF SUPER-VILLAINS
DC

❑1, Jun 1976 O: Secret Society. 7.00
❑2, Aug 1976 A: Captain Comet. 3.50
❑3, Oct 1976 .... 3.50
❑4, Dec 1976 .... 3.50
❑5, Feb 1977 .... 3.50
❑6, Apr 1977 .... 2.50
❑7, Jun 1977 .... 2.50
❑8, Aug 1977 .... 2.50
❑9, Sep 1977 .... 2.50
❑10, Oct 1977 .... 2.50
❑11, Dec 1977 .... 2.50
❑12, Jan 1978 .... 2.50
❑13, Mar 1978 .... 2.50
❑14, May 1978 .... 2.50
❑15, Jul 1978 .... 2.50

SECRETS OF DRAWING COMICS (RICH BUCKLER'S...)
SHOWCASE

❑1, Jan 1994 .... 2.50
❑2 .... 2.50
❑3 .... 2.50
❑4 .... 2.50

SECRETS OF SINISTER HOUSE
DC

❑5, Jun 1972; Continues from Sinister House of Secret Love #4 .... 5.00
❑6, Aug 1972 .... 4.00
❑7, Nov 1972 .... 4.00
❑8, Dec 1972 .... 4.00
❑9, Feb 1973 .... 4.00
❑10, Mar 1973 NA (a) 6.00
❑11, Apr 1973 .... 4.00
❑12, Jun 1973 .... 4.00
❑13, Aug 1973 .... 4.00
❑14, Oct 1973 .... 4.00
❑15, Dec 1973 .... 4.00
❑16, Feb 1974 .... 4.00
❑17, Apr 1974 .... 4.00
❑18, Jun 1974 GK (a) 4.00

SECRETS OF THE LEGION OF SUPER-HEROES
DC

❑1, Jan 1981 O: the Legion of Super-Heroes. 2.00
❑2, Feb 1981 .... 2.00
❑3, Mar 1981 .... 2.00

Scud, the Disposable Assassin inspired a videogame of the same name.

© 1994 Fireman Press.

N-MINT

SECRETS OF THE VALIANT UNIVERSE
VALIANT

❑1, May 1994; Wizard Magazine promo; BL, BH (w); DP, BH (a); no price; bagged with Wizard Special . 2.00
❑2, Oct 1994; BH (w); Chaos Effect ... 2.25
❑3, Oct 1995; BL (w); future Rai; indicia says Oct; cover says Feb 2.25

SECRETS OF YOUNG BRIDES (1ST SERIES)
CHARLTON

❑5, ca. 1957 .... 25.00
❑6, ca. 1957 .... 20.00
❑7, ca. 1958 .... 20.00
❑8, ca. 1958 .... 20.00
❑9, ca. 1958 .... 20.00
❑10, ca. 1958 .... 20.00
❑11, ca. 1958 .... 20.00
❑12, ca. 1959 .... 20.00
❑13, ca. 1959 .... 20.00
❑14, ca. 1959 .... 20.00
❑15, ca. 1959 .... 20.00
❑16, ca. 1959 .... 20.00
❑17, ca. 1959 .... 20.00
❑18, Mar 1960 .... 20.00
❑19, May 1960 .... 20.00
❑20, Jul 1960 .... 20.00
❑21, Sep 1960 .... 20.00
❑22, Nov 1960 .... 20.00
❑23, Jan 1961 .... 20.00
❑24, ca. 1961 .... 15.00
❑25, ca. 1961 .... 15.00
❑26, ca. 1961 .... 15.00
❑27, ca. 1961 .... 15.00
❑28, ca. 1961 .... 15.00
❑29, ca. 1962 .... 15.00
❑30, ca. 1962 .... 15.00
❑31, ca. 1962 .... 15.00
❑32, ca. 1962 .... 15.00
❑33, ca. 1962 .... 15.00
❑34, ca. 1962 .... 15.00
❑35, ca. 1963 .... 10.00
❑36, ca. 1963 .... 10.00
❑37, ca. 1963 .... 10.00
❑38, ca. 1963 .... 10.00
❑39, ca. 1963 .... 10.00
❑40, ca. 1964 .... 10.00
❑41, ca. 1964 .... 10.00
❑42, ca. 1964 .... 10.00
❑43, ca. 1964 .... 10.00
❑44, Oct 1964 .... 10.00

SECRETUM SECRETORUM
TWILIGHT TWINS

❑0 .... 3.50

SECRET WAR
MARVEL

❑1, Apr 2004, color (c); BMB (w) 10.00
❑1-2, Jul 2004; Commorative Edition 3.99
❑2, Jul 2004 .... 6.00

SECRET WARS II
MARVEL

❑1, Jul 1985 A: X-Men. A: New Mutants. 2.00
❑2, Aug 1985 A: Fantastic Four. A: Spider-Man. A: Power Man. A: Iron Fist. D: Hate-Monger III (H.M. Unger). .. 1.50
❑3, Sep 1985 .... 1.50

N-MINT

❑4, Oct 1985 O: Kurse. 1: Kurse. A: Kursei. V: Avengers. 1.50
❑5, Nov 1985 O: Boomer (Boom Boom). 1: Boomer (Boom Boom). V: X-Men. V: Fantastic Four. V: New Mutants. V: Avengers. 2.50
❑6, Dec 1985 1.50
❑7, Jan 1986 V: All villains. 1.50
❑8, Feb 1986 O: Beyonder. 1.50
❑9, Mar 1986; double-sized D: Beyonder. 1.50

SECRET WEAPONS
VALIANT

❑1, Sep 1993; O: Doctor Eclipse. 1: Doctor Eclipse. Serial number contest 2.25
❑1/Gold, Sep 1993; Gold edition 2.00
❑2, Oct 1993 2.25
❑3, Nov 1993 2.25
❑4, Dec 1993 2.25
❑5, Jan 1994 A: Ninjak. 2.25
❑6, Feb 1994 2.25
❑7, Mar 1994 A: X-O Manowar. A: Turok. 2.25
❑8, Apr 1994 V: Harbinger. 2.25
❑9, May 1994; A: Bloodshot. trading card 2.25
❑10, Jun 1994 2.25
❑11, Aug 1994; A: Bloodshot. Enclosed in manila envelope "For Your Eyes Only" cover; bagged cover 2.25
❑12, Sep 1994 A: Bloodshot. 2.25
❑13, Oct 1994; Chaos Effect 2.25
❑14, Nov 1994 2.25
❑15, Dec 1994 2.25
❑16, Jan 1995 2.25
❑17, Feb 1995 2.25
❑18, Mar 1995 A: Ninjak. 2.25
❑19, Apr 1995 2.25
❑20, May 1995; (see Bloodshot #28) 2.25
❑21, May 1995 2.25

SECTAURS
MARVEL

❑1, Jun 1985 1.00
❑2, Aug 1985 1.00
❑3, Oct 1985 1.00
❑4, Dec 1985 1.00
❑5, Mar 1986 1.00
❑6, May 1986 1.00
❑7, Jul 1986 1.00
❑8, Sep 1986 1.00

SECTION 12
MYTHIC

❑1, b&w 2.95

SECTION ZERO
IMAGE

❑1, Jun 2000 2.50
❑2, Jul 2000 2.50
❑3, Sep 2000 2.50

SEDUCTION
ETERNITY

❑1, b&w 2.50

SEDUCTION OF THE INNOCENT (ECLIPSE)
ECLIPSE

❑1, Nov 1985; DSt (w); MM, ATh, TY (a); Reprints from Adventures into Darkness #6, Out of the Shadows #7, Fantastic Worlds #7, Out of the Shadows #9 2.50
❑2, Dec 1985 MA, ATh, MB, NC, RMo (a) 2.00
❑3, Jan 1986 MA, ATh (w); ATh (a) 2.00
❑4, Feb 1986 ATh (w); ATh, NC (a) 2.00
❑5, Mar 1986 ATh (w); ATh, TY (a) 2.00
❑6, Apr 1986 ATh, GT, FF, RA (w) 2.00
❑3D 1, ca. 1985 DSt (c); DSt (w); MM (a) 2.50
❑3D 2, ca. 1986 BWr (c); ATh, MB, NC (a) 2.50

N-MINT

SEEKER
CALIBER

❑1, Apr 1994, b&w 2.50
❑2 1994, b&w 2.95

SEEKERS INTO THE MYSTERY
DC / VERTIGO

❑1, Jan 1996 2.50
❑2, Feb 1996 2.50
❑3, Mar 1996 2.50
❑4, Apr 1996 2.50
❑5, Jun 1996 2.50
❑6, Jul 1996 2.50
❑7, Aug 1996 2.50
❑8, Sep 1996 2.50
❑9, Oct 1996 2.50
❑10, Nov 1996 2.50
❑11, Dec 1996 2.50
❑12, Jan 1997 2.50
❑13, Feb 1997 2.50
❑14, Mar 1997 2.50
❑15, Apr 1997 2.95

SEEKER 3000
MARVEL

❑1, Jun 1998; wraparound cover 2.99
❑2, Jul 1998; wraparound cover 2.99
❑3, Aug 1998; wraparound cover 2.99
❑4, Sep 1998; wraparound cover 2.99

SEEKER 3000 PREMIERE
MARVEL

❑1, Jun 1998; reprints Marvel Premiere #41 1.50

SEEKER: VENGEANCE
SKY

❑1, Nov 1993 2.50
❑1/Gold, Nov 1993; Gold edition 3.00
❑2 1994 2.50

SELF-LOATHING COMICS
FANTAGRAPHICS

❑1 1996 2.95
❑2, May 1997 2.95

SEMPER FI
MARVEL

❑1, Dec 1988 JSe (a) 1.25
❑2, Jan 1989 JSe (a) 1.25
❑3, Feb 1989 JSe (a) 1.25
❑4, Mar 1989 JSe (a) 1.25
❑5, Apr 1989 JSe (a) 1.25
❑6, May 1989 JSe (a) 1.25
❑7, Jun 1989 JSe (a) 1.25
❑8, Jul 1989 JSe (a) 1.25
❑9, Aug 1989 JSe (a) 1.25

SENSATIONAL SHE-HULK, THE
MARVEL

❑1, May 1989 JBy (w); JBy (a) 2.50
❑2, Jun 1989 JBy (w); JBy (a); V: Toad Men. 2.00
❑3, Jul 1989 JBy (w); JBy (a); A: Spider-Man. 2.00
❑4, Aug 1989 JBy (w); JBy (a); O: Blonde Phantom. A: Blonde Phantom. 2.00
❑5, Sep 1989 JBy (w); JBy (a) 2.00
❑6, Oct 1989 JBy (w); JBy (a); A: Razorback. 2.00
❑7, Nov 1989 JBy (w); JBy (a); A: Razorback. 2.00
❑8, Nov 1989 JBy (w); JBy (a); A: Nick St. Christopher. 2.00
❑9, Dec 1989 V: Madcap. 1.75
❑10, Dec 1989 1.75
❑11, Jan 1990 1.75
❑12, Feb 1990 1.75
❑13, Mar 1990 1.75
❑14, Apr 1990 A: Howard the Duck. 1.75
❑15, May 1990 A: Howard the Duck. 1.75
❑16, Jun 1990 A: Howard the Duck. 1.75
❑17, Jul 1990 A: Howard the Duck. 1.75
❑18, Aug 1990 1.75
❑19, Sep 1990 A: Nosferata the She-Bat. 1.75
❑20, Oct 1990 1.75

N-MINT

❑21, Nov 1990; Blonde Phantom 1.75
❑22, Dec 1990; Blonde Phantom 1.75
❑23, Jan 1991; Blonde Phantom 1.75
❑24, Feb 1991; Death's Head 1.75
❑25, Mar 1991; Hercules 1.75
❑26, Apr 1991 1.75
❑27, May 1991; white inside covers 1.75
❑28, Jun 1991 1.75
❑29, Jul 1991 1.75
❑30, Aug 1991 1.75
❑31, Sep 1991 JBy (w); JBy (a) 1.75
❑32, Oct 1991 JBy (w); JBy (a) 1.75
❑33, Nov 1991 JBy (w); JBy (a) 1.75
❑34, Dec 1991 JBy (w); JBy (a) 1.75
❑35, Jan 1992 JBy (w); JBy (a) 1.75
❑36, Feb 1992 JBy (w); JBy (a); A: Wyatt Wingfoot. 1.75
❑37, Mar 1992 JBy (w); JBy (a) 1.75
❑38, Apr 1992 JBy (w); JBy (a); V: Mahkizmo. 1.75
❑39, May 1992 JBy (w); JBy (a); A: Thing. V: Mahkizmo. 1.75
❑40, Jun 1992 JBy (w); JBy (a) 1.75
❑41, Jul 1992 JBy (w); JBy (a) 1.75
❑42, Aug 1992 JBy (w); JBy (a) 1.75
❑43, Sep 1992 JBy (w); JBy (a) 1.75
❑44, Oct 1992 JBy (w); JBy (a) 1.75
❑45, Nov 1992 JBy (w); JBy (a) 1.75
❑46, Dec 1992 JBy (w); JBy (a) 1.75
❑47, Jan 1993 1.75
❑48, Feb 1993 JBy (w); JBy (a) 1.75
❑49, Mar 1993 JBy (w); JBy (a) 1.75
❑50, Apr 1993; Double-size; JBy, FM (w); WP, JBy, HC, DG, FM (a); Green foil cover 2.95
❑51, May 1993; Savage She-Hulk vs. Sensational She-Hulk 1.75
❑52, Jun 1993 1.75
❑53, Jul 1993 1.75
❑54, Aug 1993 DC (a) 1.75
❑55, Sep 1993 1.75
❑56, Oct 1993 A: Hulk. 1.75
❑57, Nov 1993 A: Hulk. 1.75
❑58, Dec 1993 A: Tommy the Gopher. V: Electro. 1.75
❑59, Jan 1994 1.75
❑60, Feb 1994 A: Millie the Model. 1.75

SENSATIONAL SHE-HULK IN CEREMONY, THE
MARVEL

❑1, ca. 1989; leg shaving 3.95
❑2, ca. 1989 3.95

SENSATIONAL SPIDER-MAN, THE
MARVEL

❑-1, Jul 1997; Flashback 2.00
❑0, Jan 1996; O: Spider-Man. 1: Armada. enhanced wraparound cardstock cover with lenticular animation card attached; new costume 5.00
❑1, Feb 1996; Series picks up subscribers from Web of Spider-Man 2.00
❑1/CS, Feb 1996 4.00
❑2, Mar 1996 2.00
❑2/CS, Feb 1996 2.95
❑3, Apr 1996 2.00
❑4, May 1996; Ben Reilly revealed as Spider-Man 2.00
❑5, Jun 1996 V: Molten Man. 2.00
❑6, Jul 1996 2.00
❑7, Aug 1996 2.00
❑8, Sep 1996 V: Looter. 2.00
❑9, Oct 1996 A: Swarm. 2.00
❑10, Nov 1996 2.00
❑11, Dec 1996 2.00
❑11/CS, Dec 1996 6.99
❑12, Jan 1997 V: Trapster. 2.00
❑13, Feb 1997 A: Ka-Zar. A: Shanna. 2.00
❑14, Mar 1997 A: Ka-Zar. A: Shanna. A: Hulk. 2.00
❑15, Apr 1997 A: Ka-Zar. A: Shanna. A: Hulk. 2.00
❑16, May 1997 V: Prowler. 2.00
❑17, Jun 1997 V: Vulture. 2.00

N-MINT

❑18, Aug 1997; gatefold summary 2.00
❑19, Sep 1997; gatefold summary V: Living Pharaoh. 2.00
❑20, Oct 1997; gatefold summary 2.00
❑21, Nov 1997; gatefold summary 1.99
❑22, Dec 1997; gatefold summary A: Doctor Strange. 1.99
❑23, Jan 1998; gatefold summary 1.99
❑24, Feb 1998; gatefold summary V: Hydro-Man. 1.99
❑25, Mar 1998; double-sized 2.99
❑25/A, Mar 1998; double-sized; Wanted poster cover 2.99
❑26, Apr 1998; gatefold summary; V: Hydro-Man. V: Sandman. Identity Crisis 1.99
❑27, May 1998; gatefold summary 1.99
❑27/A, May 1998; gatefold summary; variant cover 1.99
❑28, Jun 1998; gatefold summary; A: Hornet. 1.99
❑29, Jul 1998; gatefold summary; A: Black Cat. 1.99
❑30, Aug 1998; gatefold summary 1.99
❑31, Sep 1998; gatefold summary; V: Rhino. 1.99
❑32, Oct 1998; gatefold summary 1.99
❑33, Nov 1998; gatefold summary; V: Override. 1.99
❑Annual 1996, ca. 1996; O: Kraven the Hunter. 3.00

SENSATION COMICS (2ND SERIES)
DC

❑1, May 1999; Justice Society Returns; Hawkgirl; Speed Saunders 1.99

SENSEI
FIRST

❑1, May 1989 .... 2.75
❑2 1989 .... 2.75
❑3 1989 .... 2.75
❑4, Dec 1989 .... 2.75

SENTAI
ANTARCTIC

❑1, Feb 1994, b&w; The Journal of Asian SF and Fantasy 2.95
❑2, Apr 1994, b&w; The Journal of Asian SF and Fantasy 2.95
❑3, Jul 1994, b&w; The Journal of Asian SF and Fantasy 2.95
❑4, Sep 1994, b&w; The Journal of Asian SF and Fantasy 2.95
❑5, Nov 1994; The Journal of Asian SF and Fantasy 2.95
❑6, Feb 1995, b&w; The Journal of Asian SF and Fantasy 2.95
❑7, Apr 1995, b&w; The Journal of Asian SF and Fantasy 2.95

SENTINEL (HARRIER)
HARRIER

❑1, Dec 1986 .... 1.95
❑2, Feb 1987 .... 1.95
❑3, Apr 1987 .... 1.95
❑4, Jun 1987 .... 1.95

SENTINEL (MARVEL)
MARVEL

❑1, Jun 2003 .... 2.99
❑2, Jul 2003 .... 2.99
❑3, Aug 2003 .... 2.50
❑4, Sep 2003 .... 2.50
❑5, Oct 2003 .... 2.50
❑6, Nov 2003 .... 2.99
❑7, Dec 2003 .... 2.50
❑8, Dec 2003 .... 2.99
❑9, Jan 2004 .... 2.99
❑10, Feb 2004 .... 2.99
❑11, Mar 2004 .... 2.99
❑12, Apr 2004 .... 2.99

SENTINELS OF JUSTICE (2ND SERIES)
AC

❑1; Avenger 4.00
❑2; Jet Girl 5.95
❑3; Yankee Girl 4.00

N-MINT

SENTINELS OF JUSTICE COMPACT
AC

❑1 .... 3.95
❑2 .... 3.95
❑3 .... 3.95

SENTINELS PRESENTS...CRYSTAL WORLD, THE: PRISONERS OF SPHERIS
ACADEMY

❑1 .... 2.95

SENTRY, THE
MARVEL

❑1, Sep 2000 .... 2.99
❑2, Oct 2000 .... 2.99
❑3, Nov 2000 .... 2.99
❑4, Dec 2000 .... 2.99
❑5, Jan 2001 .... 2.99

SENTRY/FANTASTIC FOUR
MARVEL

❑1, Feb 2001 .... 2.99

SENTRY/HULK
MARVEL

❑1, Feb 2001 .... 2.99

SENTRY SPECIAL
INNOVATION

❑1, Jun 1991 .... 2.75

SENTRY/SPIDER-MAN
MARVEL

❑1, Feb 2001 .... 2.99

SENTRY/THE VOID
MARVEL

❑1, Feb 2001 .... 2.99

SENTRY/X-MEN
MARVEL

❑1, Feb 2001 .... 2.99

SEPULCHER
ILLUSTRATION

❑1, Mar 2000 .... 2.99
❑2, May 2000 .... 2.99

SEQUENTIAL
I DON'T GET IT

❑1 2000 .... 2.95
❑2 2000 .... 2.95
❑3, Jun 1999 .... 2.95

SERAPHIM
INNOVATION

❑1, May 1990 .... 2.50
❑2 1990 .... 2.50
❑3 1990 .... 2.50

SGT. FROG
TOKYOPOP

❑1, Mar 2004 .... 9.99

SGT. FURY
MARVEL

❑1, May 1963 1: General Samuel Happy Sam Sawyer. 1: General Samuel "Happy Sam" Sawyer. 1: Dum Dum Dugan. 1: Sgt. Nick Fury. 1175.00
❑2, Jul 1963 .... 400.00
❑3, Sep 1963 A: Reed Richards. 225.00
❑4, Nov 1963 D: Junior Juniper. 225.00
❑5, Jan 1964 SL (w); JK (a); 1: Baron Strucker. 225.00
❑6, Mar 1964 .... 150.00
❑7, May 1964 SL (w); JK (a) 150.00
❑8, Jul 1964 1: Percival Pinkerton. V: Doctor Zemo (later Baron Zemo). 150.00
❑9, Aug 1964 .... 150.00
❑10, Sep 1964 1: Captain Savage. 150.00
❑11, Oct 1964 .... 80.00
❑12, Nov 1964 .... 80.00
❑13, Dec 1964 SL (w); JK (a); A: Captain America. 400.00
❑13-2 SL (w); JK (a); A: Captain America. 2.00
❑14, Jan 1965 A: Baron Strucker. 60.00
❑15, Feb 1965 1: Hans Rooten. 60.00
❑16, Mar 1965 .... 60.00
❑17, Apr 1965 .... 50.00

The first issue of *Secrets of the Valiant Universe* was polybagged with a *Wizard Special* focusing on the company.

© 1994 Voyager Communications Inc. (Valiant).

N-MINT

❑18, May 1965 D: Pamela Hawley. 50.00
❑19, Jun 1965 .... 50.00
❑20, Jul 1965 .... 30.00
❑21, Aug 1965 .... 30.00
❑22, Sep 1965 .... 30.00
❑23, Oct 1965 .... 30.00
❑24, Nov 1965 SL (w) 30.00
❑25, Dec 1965 .... 30.00
❑26, Jan 1966 .... 30.00
❑27, Feb 1966; Explanation of Sgt. Fury's eye patch 30.00
❑28, Mar 1966 V: Baron Strucker. 30.00
❑29, Apr 1966 V: Baron Strucker. 30.00
❑30, May 1966 .... 30.00
❑31, Jun 1966 .... 30.00
❑32, Jul 1966 .... 25.00
❑33, Aug 1966 .... 25.00
❑34, Sep 1966 O: General Samuel Happy Sam Sawyer. O: Howling Commandos. O: General Samuel "Happy Sam" Sawyer. 25.00
❑35, Oct 1966; Eric Koenig joins Howling Commandos 25.00
❑36, Nov 1966 .... 25.00
❑37, Dec 1966 .... 25.00
❑38, Jan 1967 .... 25.00
❑39, Feb 1967 .... 20.00
❑40, Mar 1967 .... 20.00
❑41, Apr 1967 .... 15.00
❑42, May 1967 .... 15.00
❑43, Jun 1967 .... 15.00
❑44, Jul 1967 JSe (a) 15.00
❑45, Aug 1967 .... 15.00
❑46, Sep 1967 .... 15.00
❑47, Oct 1967; Fury on furlough 15.00
❑48, Nov 1967; JSe (a); return of Blitz Squad 15.00
❑49, Dec 1967; JSe (a); Howlers in Pacific 15.00
❑50, Jan 1968; JSe (a); Howlers in Pacific 15.00
❑51, Feb 1968 .... 15.00
❑52, Mar 1968; in Treblinka 15.00
❑53, Apr 1968 .... 15.00
❑54, May 1968 .... 15.00
❑55, Jun 1968 .... 15.00
❑56, Jul 1968 .... 14.00
❑57, Aug 1968 TS, JSe (a) 14.00
❑58, Sep 1968 .... 14.00
❑59, Oct 1968 .... 14.00
❑60, Nov 1968 .... 14.00
❑61, Dec 1968 .... 14.00
❑62, Jan 1969 O: Sgt. Fury. 14.00
❑63, Feb 1969 .... 14.00
❑64, Mar 1969; Story continued from Captain Savage and his Leatherneck Raiders #11 .... 12.00
❑65, Apr 1969 .... 12.00
❑66, May 1969 .... 12.00
❑67, Jun 1969 JSe (c) 12.00
❑68, Jul 1969; Fury goes home on leave 12.00
❑69, Aug 1969 1: Jacob Fury (later becomes Scorpio). 12.00
❑70, Sep 1969 1: Missouri Marauders. 12.00
❑71, Oct 1969 .... 12.00
❑72, Nov 1969 .... 12.00
❑73, Dec 1969 .... 12.00
❑74, Jan 1970 .... 12.00
❑75, Feb 1970 .... 12.00

	N-MINT
❑76, Mar 1970; Fury's father vs. The Red Baron	12.00
❑77, Apr 1970	12.00
❑78, May 1970	12.00
❑79, Jun 1970	12.00
❑80, Sep 1970	12.00
❑81, Nov 1970	12.00
❑82, Dec 1970	12.00
❑83, Jan 1971; Dum-Dum Dugan vs. Man-Mountain McCoy	12.00
❑84, Feb 1971	12.00
❑85, Mar 1971	12.00
❑86, Apr 1971	12.00
❑87, May 1971	12.00
❑88, Jun 1971 A: Patton.	12.00
❑89, Jul 1971	12.00
❑90, Aug 1971	12.00
❑91, Sep 1971	12.00
❑92, Oct 1971; Giant-size	12.00
❑93, Dec 1971	12.00
❑94, Jan 1972	12.00
❑95, Feb 1972; JK (a); reprints Sgt. Fury #2	12.00
❑96, Mar 1972	12.00
❑97, Apr 1972	12.00
❑98, May 1972 1: Dugan's Deadly Dozen.	12.00
❑99, Jun 1972	12.00
❑100, Jul 1972 A: Gary Friedrich. A: Dick Ayers. A: Martin Goodman. A: Captain America. A: Stan Lee.	20.00
❑101, Sep 1972 O: the Howling Commandos.	12.00
❑102, Sep 1972	10.00
❑103, Oct 1972	8.00
❑104, Nov 1972 A: Combat Kelly and Deadly Dozen.	8.00
❑105, Dec 1972	8.00
❑106, Jan 1973	8.00
❑107, Feb 1973	8.00
❑108, Mar 1973	8.00
❑109, Apr 1973	8.00
❑110, May 1973	8.00
❑111, Jun 1973	6.00
❑112, Jul 1973 V: Baron Strucker.	6.00
❑113, Aug 1973	6.00
❑114, Sep 1973	6.00
❑115, Oct 1973	6.00
❑116, Nov 1973	6.00
❑117, Jan 1974	6.00
❑118, Mar 1974; V: Rommel. Marvel Value Stamp #93; Silver Surfer	6.00
❑119, May 1974; Marvel Value Stamp #79: Kang	6.00
❑120, Jul 1974; Marvel Value Stamp #98: Puppet Master	6.00
❑121, Sep 1974	6.00
❑122, Oct 1974	5.00
❑123, Nov 1974	5.00
❑124, Jan 1975	5.00
❑125, Mar 1975	5.00
❑126, May 1975	5.00
❑127, Jul 1975	5.00
❑128, Sep 1975	5.00
❑129, Oct 1975	5.00
❑130, Nov 1975	5.00
❑131, Jan 1976	5.00
❑132, Mar 1976	4.00
❑133, May 1976	4.00
❑133/30 cent, May 1976; 30 cent regional price variant	20.00
❑134, Jul 1976	4.00
❑134/30 cent, Jul 1976; 30 cent regional price variant	20.00
❑135, Sep 1976	4.00
❑136, Oct 1976	4.00
❑137, Nov 1976	4.00
❑138, Jan 1977	4.00
❑139, Mar 1977	4.00
❑140, May 1977	4.00
❑141, Jul 1977	4.00
❑142, Sep 1977	4.00
❑143, Nov 1977	4.00
❑144, Jan 1978	4.00
❑145, Mar 1978	4.00
❑146, May 1978	4.00
❑147, Jul 1978	4.00
❑148, Sep 1978	4.00
❑149, Nov 1978	4.00
❑150, Jan 1979	4.00
❑151, Mar 1979	4.00
❑152, Jun 1979	3.00
❑153, Aug 1979	3.00
❑154, Oct 1979	3.00
❑155, Dec 1979	3.00
❑156, Feb 1980	3.00
❑157, Apr 1980	3.00
❑158, Jun 1980	3.00
❑159, Aug 1980	3.00
❑160, Oct 1980	3.00
❑161, Dec 1980	3.00
❑162, Feb 1981	3.00
❑163, Apr 1981	3.00
❑164, Jun 1981	3.00
❑165, Aug 1981	3.00
❑166, Oct 1981	3.00
❑167, Dec 1981; Reprints Sgt. Fury #1	3.00
❑Annual 1, ca. 1965; Korea; reprints from Sgt. Fury #4 and 5	125.00
❑Annual 2, Aug 1966; O: S.H.I.E.L.D.. D-Day	55.00
❑Annual 3, Aug 1966; Cover reads "King-Size Special"; Vietnam	30.00
❑Annual 4, Apr 1968; Cover reads "King-Size Special"; Battle of the Bulge	22.00
❑Annual 5, Aug 1969; Cover reads "King-Size Special"; reprints from Sgt. Fury #6 and 7	10.00
❑Annual 6, Aug 1970; Cover reads "King-Size Special";	9.00
❑Annual 7, ca. 1971; Cover reads "King-Size Special";	9.00

SGT. ROCK
DC

	N-MINT
❑302, Mar 1977; Series continued from "Our Army At War"	14.00
❑303, Apr 1977	9.00
❑304, May 1977	9.00
❑305, Jun 1977	9.00
❑306, Jul 1977	9.00
❑307, Aug 1977	9.00
❑308, Sep 1977	9.00
❑309, Oct 1977	9.00
❑310, Nov 1977	9.00
❑311, Dec 1977	8.00
❑312, Jan 1978	8.00
❑313, Feb 1978	8.00
❑314, Mar 1978	8.00
❑315, Apr 1978	8.00
❑316, May 1978	8.00
❑317, Jun 1978	8.00
❑318, Jul 1978	8.00
❑319, Aug 1978	8.00
❑320, Sep 1978	8.00
❑321, Oct 1978	6.00
❑322, Nov 1978	6.00
❑323, Dec 1978	6.00
❑324, Jan 1979	6.00
❑325, Feb 1979	6.00
❑326, Mar 1979	6.00
❑327, Apr 1979	6.00
❑328, May 1979	6.00
❑329, Jun 1979	6.00
❑330, Jul 1979	6.00
❑331, Aug 1979	5.00
❑332, Sep 1979	5.00
❑333, Oct 1979	5.00
❑334, Nov 1979	5.00
❑335, Dec 1979	5.00
❑336, Jan 1980	5.00
❑337, Feb 1980	5.00
❑338, Mar 1980	5.00
❑339, Apr 1980	5.00
❑340, May 1980	5.00
❑341, Jun 1980	5.00
❑342, Jul 1980	4.00
❑343, Aug 1980	4.00
❑344, Sep 1980	4.00
❑345, Oct 1980	4.00
❑346, Nov 1980	4.00
❑347, Dec 1980	4.00
❑348, Jan 1981	4.00
❑349, Feb 1981	4.00
❑350, Mar 1981	4.00
❑351, Apr 1981	3.00
❑352, May 1981	3.00
❑353, Jun 1981	3.00
❑354, Jul 1981	3.00
❑355, Aug 1981	3.00
❑356, Sep 1981	3.00
❑357, Oct 1981	3.00
❑358, Nov 1981	3.00
❑359, Dec 1981	3.00
❑360, Jan 1982	3.00
❑361, Feb 1982	3.00
❑362, Mar 1982	3.00
❑363, Apr 1982	3.00
❑364, May 1982	3.00
❑365, Jun 1982	3.00
❑366, Jul 1982	3.00
❑367, Aug 1982	3.00
❑368, Sep 1982 JKu (a)	3.00
❑369, Oct 1982	3.00
❑370, Nov 1982	3.00
❑371, Dec 1982	2.50
❑372, Jan 1983	2.50
❑373, Feb 1983	2.50
❑374, Mar 1983	2.50
❑375, Apr 1983	2.50
❑376, May 1983	2.50
❑377, Jun 1983 A: Worry Wart.	2.50
❑378, Jul 1983; Christmas	2.50
❑379, Aug 1983	2.50
❑380, Sep 1983	2.50
❑381, Oct 1983	2.50
❑382, Nov 1983	2.50
❑383, Dec 1983	2.50
❑384, Jan 1984	2.50
❑385, Feb 1984	2.50
❑386, Mar 1984	2.50
❑387, Apr 1984	2.50
❑388, May 1984	2.50
❑389, Jun 1984	2.50
❑390, Jul 1984	2.50
❑391, Aug 1984	2.00
❑392, Sep 1984	2.00
❑393, Oct 1984	2.00
❑394, Nov 1984	2.00
❑395, Dec 1984 JKu (a)	2.00
❑396, Jan 1985; RH (a); children in war	2.00
❑397, Feb 1985	2.00
❑398, Mar 1985	2.00
❑399, Apr 1985	2.00
❑400, May 1985	2.00
❑401, Jun 1985	2.00
❑402, Jul 1985	2.00
❑403, Aug 1985	2.00
❑404, Sep 1985 V: Iron Major.	2.00
❑405, Oct 1985	2.00
❑406, Nov 1985	2.00
❑407, Dec 1985	2.00
❑408, Feb 1986; Shelly Mayer tribute	2.00
❑409, Apr 1986	2.00
❑410, Jun 1986	2.00
❑411, Aug 1986	2.00
❑412, Oct 1986	2.00
❑413, Dec 1986	2.00
❑414, Feb 1987; Christmas	2.00
❑415, Apr 1987	2.00
❑416, Jun 1987	2.00
❑417, Aug 1987; looking into future	2.00
❑418, Oct 1987; looking into future	2.00
❑419, Dec 1987	2.00
❑420, Feb 1988	2.00
❑421, Apr 1988	2.00
❑422, Jul 1988	2.00
❑Annual 1	4.00

Condition price index: Multiply "NM prices" above by: **0.83 for Very Fine/Near Mint**
0.66 for Very Fine • 0.33 for Fine • 0.2 for Very Good • 0.125 for Good

N-MINT

❑Annual 2, Sep 1982 .... 4.00
❑Annual 3, Aug 1983 .... 3.00
❑Annual 4, Aug 1984 .... 3.00

SGT. ROCK (2ND SERIES)
DC
❑14, Jul 1991; Series continued from Sgt. Rock Special #13 .... 2.00
❑15, Aug 1991 .... 2.00
❑16, Sep 1991 .... 2.00
❑17, Oct 1991 .... 2.00
❑18, Nov 1991 .... 2.00
❑19, Dec 1991 .... 2.00
❑20, Jan 1992 .... 2.00
❑21, Feb 1992 .... 2.00
❑22, Mar 1992 .... 2.00
❑Special 1, Oct 1992; 1992 Special ... 2.95
❑Special 2, ca. 1994; Commemorates 50th anniversary of the Battle of the Bulge; 1994 Special 2.95

SGT. ROCK SPECIAL
DC
❑1, Sep 1988 A: Viking Prince. 3.00
❑2, Dec 1988 .... 2.50
❑3, Mar 1989 .... 2.50
❑4, Jun 1989 .... 2.50
❑5, Sep 1989 .... 2.50
❑6, Dec 1989 .... 2.50
❑7, Mar 1990; reprints Our Fighting Forces #153 .... 2.50
❑8, Jun 1990 .... 2.50
❑9, Sep 1990 .... 2.50
❑10, Dec 1990 .... 2.50
❑11, Mar 1991 .... 2.50
❑12, May 1991 .... 2.50
❑13, Jun 1991 .... 2.50

SGT. ROCK'S PRIZE BATTLE TALES REPLICA EDITION
DC
❑1, ca. 2000 .... 5.95

SERGIO ARAGONÉS DESTROYS DC
DC
❑1, Jun 1996 .... 3.50

SERGIO ARAGONÉS MASSACRES MARVEL
MARVEL
❑1, Jun 1996; wraparound cover 3.50

SERGIO ARAGONÉS STOMPS STAR WARS
DARK HORSE
❑1, Feb 2000 .... 2.95

SERINA
ANTARCTIC
❑1, Mar 1996, b&w 2.95
❑2, May 1996, b&w 2.95
❑3, Jul 1996 .... 2.95

SERIUS BOUNTY HUNTER
BLACKTHORNE
❑1, Nov 1987, b&w 1.75
❑2, Jan 1988, b&w 1.75
❑3, Mar 1988, b&w 1.75

SERPENTINA
LIGHTNING
❑1/A, Feb 1998, b&w 2.95
❑1/B, Feb 1998; Alternate cover 2.95

SERPENTYNE
NIGHTWYND
❑1, b&w 2.50
❑2, b&w 2.50
❑3, b&w 2.50

SERRA ANGEL ON THE WORLD OF MAGIC: THE GATHERING
ACCLAIM / ARMADA
❑1, Aug 1996; polybagged with oversized Serra Angel card 5.95

SETH THROB UNDERGROUND ARTIST
SLAVE LABOR
❑1, Mar 1994 .... 2.95
❑2, May 1994 .... 2.95

N-MINT

❑3, Aug 1994 .... 2.95
❑4, Dec 1994 .... 2.95
❑5, Mar 1995 .... 2.95
❑6, Jun 1995 .... 2.95
❑7, Sep 1995 .... 2.95

SETTEI
ANTARCTIC
❑1, Feb 1993, b&w 7.95
❑2, Apr 1993, b&w 7.95

SETTEI SUPER SPECIAL FEATURING: PROJECT A-KO
ANTARCTIC
❑1, Feb 1994, color 2.95

SEVEN BLOCK
MARVEL / EPIC
❑1, ca. 1995, b&w; prestige format ... 4.50

SEVEN GUYS OF JUSTICE, THE
FALSE IDOL
❑1, Apr 2000 .... 2.00
❑2, ca. 2000 .... 2.00
❑3, ca. 2000 .... 2.00
❑4, ca. 2000 .... 2.00
❑5, ca. 2000 .... 2.00
❑6, ca. 2001 .... 2.00
❑7, ca. 2001 .... 2.00
❑8, ca. 2001 .... 2.00
❑9, ca. 2001 .... 2.00
❑10, ca. 2001 .... 2.00

777: WRATH/FAUST FEARBOOK
REBEL
❑1 .... 14.20

SEVEN MILES A SECOND
DC / VERTIGO
❑1, ca. 1996; prestige format 7.95

7TH MILLENNIUM
ALLIED
❑1 .... 2.50
❑2 .... 2.50
❑3 .... 2.50
❑4 .... 2.50

7TH SYSTEM, THE
SIRIUS
❑1, Jan 1998, b&w 2.95
❑2, Feb 1998, b&w 2.95
❑3, Jul 1998, b&w 2.95
❑4, Dec 1998, b&w 2.95
❑6, Feb 1999, b&w 2.95
❑5, ca. 1999 .... 2.95

77 SUNSET STRIP (DELL)
DELL
❑1, Jul 1962, color 150.00

77 SUNSET STRIP (GOLD KEY)
GOLD KEY
❑1, Nov 1962, color 100.00
❑2, Feb 1963, color 100.00

SEWAGE DRAGOON, THE
PARODY
❑1 .... 2.50
❑1-2 .... 2.50

SEX & DEATH
ACID RAIN
❑1, b&w 3.95

SEX AND DEATH (ACID RAIN)
ACID RAIN
❑1 .... 2.50

SEXCAPADES
FANTAGRAPHICS / EROS
❑1, Dec 1996 .... 2.95
❑2, Jan 1997 .... 2.95
❑3, Feb 1997 .... 2.95

SEX DRIVE
M.A.I.N.
❑1 .... 3.00

SEXECUTIONER
FANTAGRAPHICS / EROS
❑1, b&w 2.50

Long-time Fury foe Baron Strucker made his first appearance in *Sgt. Fury* #5.
© 1964 Marvel Comics.

N-MINT

❑2, b&w 2.50
❑3, b&w 2.50

SEXHIBITION
FANTAGRAPHICS / EROS
❑1 .... 2.95
❑2 .... 2.95
❑3 .... 2.95
❑4, Feb 1996 .... 2.95

SEX IN THE SINEMA
COMIC ZONE
❑1, b&w 2.95
❑2, b&w 2.95
❑3, b&w 2.95
❑4, b&w 2.95

SEX, LIES AND MUTUAL FUNDS OF THE YUPPIES FROM HELL
MARVEL
❑1 .... 2.95

SEX MACHINE
FANTAGRAPHICS / EROS
❑1, b&w 2.50
❑2, b&w 2.95
❑3, Dec 1997, b&w 2.95

SEXPLOITATION CINEMA: A CARTOON HISTORY
REVISIONARY
❑1, Nov 1998, b&w 3.50

SEX TREK: THE NEXT INFILTRATION
FRIENDLY
❑1, b&w 2.95

SEX WAD
FANTAGRAPHICS / EROS
❑1 .... 2.95
❑2 .... 2.95

SEX WARRIOR
DARK HORSE
❑1 .... 2.50
❑2 .... 2.50

SEXX WARS
IMMORTAL
❑1 .... 2.95

SEXY STORIES FROM THE WORLD RELIGIONS
LAST GASP
❑1 .... 2.50

SEXY SUPERSPY
FORBIDDEN FRUIT
❑1, b&w 2.95
❑2, b&w 2.95
❑3, b&w 2.95
❑4, b&w 2.95
❑5, b&w 2.95
❑6, b&w 2.95
❑7, b&w 2.95

SEXY WOMEN
CELEBRITY
❑1 .... 2.95
❑2 .... 2.95

SFA SPOTLIGHT
SHANDA FANTASY ARTS
❑1 .... 2.95
❑2 .... 2.95
❑3 .... 2.95

N-MINT

❑4, May 1999, b&w 2.95
❑5, May 1999, b&w; Zebra Comics 4.50

SHADE, THE
DC

❑1, Apr 1997 JRo (w) 2.50
❑2, May 1997 JRo (w) 2.50
❑3, Jun 1997 JRo (w); A: Jay Garrick. 2.50
❑4, Jul 1997 JRo (w) 2.50

SHADE, THE CHANGING MAN (1ST SERIES)
DC

❑1, Jul 1977 SD (w); SD (a); O: Shade. 1: Shade. 4.00
❑2, Sep 1977 SD (a) 3.00
❑3, Nov 1977 SD (a) 3.00
❑4, Jan 1978 SD (a) 3.00
❑5, Mar 1978 SD (a) 3.00
❑6, May 1978 SD (a); V: Khaos. 3.00
❑7, Jul 1978 SD (a) 3.00
❑8, Sep 1978 SD (a) 3.00

SHADE, THE CHANGING MAN (2ND SERIES)
DC

❑1, Jul 1990 1: Kathy George. 1: American Scream. 3.00
❑2, Aug 1990 2.00
❑3, Sep 1990 2.00
❑4, Oct 1990 2.00
❑5, Nov 1990 2.00
❑6, Dec 1990 2.00
❑7, Jan 1991 2.00
❑8, Feb 1991 2.00
❑9, Mar 1991 2.00
❑10, Apr 1991 2.00
❑11, May 1991 2.00
❑12, Jun 1991 2.00
❑13, Jul 1991 2.00
❑14, Aug 1991 2.00
❑15, Sep 1991 2.00
❑16, Oct 1991 2.00
❑17, Nov 1991 2.00
❑18, Dec 1991 2.00
❑19, Jan 1992 2.00
❑20, Jan 1992 2.00
❑21, Mar 1992 2.00
❑22, Apr 1992 2.00
❑23, May 1992 2.00
❑24, Jun 1992 2.00
❑25, Jul 1992 2.00
❑26, Aug 1992 2.00
❑27, Sep 1992 2.00
❑28, Oct 1992 2.00
❑29, Nov 1992 2.00
❑30, Dec 1992 2.00
❑31, Jan 1993 2.00
❑32, Feb 1993 Death Talks About Aids insert. 2.00
❑33, Mar 1993; Vertigo line starts 2.00
❑34, Apr 1993 2.00
❑35, May 1993 2.00
❑36, Jun 1993 2.00
❑37, Jul 1993 2.00
❑38, Aug 1993 2.00
❑39, Sep 1993 2.00
❑40, Oct 1993 2.00
❑41, Nov 1993 2.00
❑42, Dec 1993 2.00
❑43, Jan 1994 2.00
❑44, Feb 1994 2.00
❑45, Mar 1994 2.00
❑46, Apr 1994 2.00
❑47, May 1994 2.00
❑48, Jun 1994 2.00
❑49, Jul 1994 2.00
❑50, Aug 1994; Giant-size 3.00
❑51, Sep 1994 2.00
❑52, Oct 1994 2.00
❑53, Nov 1994 2.00
❑54, Dec 1994 2.00
❑55, Jan 1995 2.00
❑56, Feb 1995 2.00

N-MINT

❑57, Mar 1995 2.00
❑58, Apr 1995 2.00
❑59, May 1995 2.25
❑60, Jun 1995 2.25
❑61, Jul 1995 2.25
❑62, Aug 1995 2.25
❑63, Sep 1995 2.25
❑64, Oct 1995 2.25
❑65, Nov 1995 2.25
❑66, Dec 1995 2.25
❑67, Jan 1996 2.25
❑68, Feb 1996 2.25
❑69, Mar 1996 2.25
❑70, Apr 1996 2.25

SHADES AND ANGELS
CANDLE LIGHT

❑1, b&w 2.95

SHADES OF BLUE
AMP

❑1, Jul 1999, b&w 2.50
❑2 2.50

SHADES OF GRAY
LADY LUCK

❑1, ca. 1994 2.50
❑2 2.50
❑3 2.50
❑4 2.50
❑5 2.50
❑6 2.50
❑7 2.50
❑8 2.50
❑9 2.50
❑10 2.50
❑11 2.50

SHADES OF GRAY COMICS AND STORIES
TAPESTRY

❑1, ca. 1996 2.95
❑2 2.95
❑3 2.95
❑4 2.95

SHADE SPECIAL
AC

❑1, Oct 1984 1.50

SHADO: SONG OF THE DRAGON
DC

❑1, ca. 1992 MGr (w) 5.00
❑2, ca. 1992 MGr (w) 5.00
❑3, ca. 1992 MGr (w) 5.00
❑4, ca. 1992 MGr (w) 5.00

SHADOW, THE (1ST SERIES)
ARCHIE

❑1, Aug 1964 30.00
❑2, Sep 1964 18.00
❑3, Nov 1964 18.00
❑4, Jan 1965 18.00
❑5, Mar 1965, O: Radiation Rogue. 1: Radiation Rogue. 18.00
❑6, May 1965 18.00
❑7, Jul 1965 18.00
❑8, Sep 1965 18.00

SHADOW, THE (2ND SERIES)
DC

❑1, Nov 1973 12.00
❑2, Jan 1974 8.00
❑3, Mar 1974 BWr (a) 8.00
❑4, May 1974 6.00
❑5, Jul 1974 4.00
❑6, Sep 1974 5.00
❑7, Nov 1974 4.00
❑8, Jan 1975 4.00
❑9, Mar 1975 FMc, FR (a) 4.00
❑10, May 1975 4.00
❑11, Jul 1975 A: The Avenger. 4.00
❑12, Sep 1975 4.00

N-MINT

SHADOW, THE (3RD SERIES)
DC

❑1, May 1986; HC (w); HC (a); The Shadow returns 3.00
❑2, Jun 1986 HC (w); HC (a) 2.00
❑3, Jul 1986 HC (w); HC (a) 2.00
❑4, Aug 1986 HC (w); HC (a) 2.00

SHADOW, THE (4TH SERIES)
DC

❑1, Aug 1987 BSz (a) 2.50
❑2, Sep 1987 BSz (a) 2.00
❑3, Oct 1987 BSz (a) 2.00
❑4, Nov 1987 BSz (a) 2.00
❑5, Dec 1987 BSz (a) 2.00
❑6, Jan 1988 BSz (a) 2.00
❑7, Feb 1988 2.00
❑8, Mar 1988 2.00
❑9, Apr 1988 2.00
❑10, May 1988 2.00
❑11, Jun 1988 2.00
❑12, Jul 1988 2.00
❑13, Aug 1988 D: Shadow. 2.00
❑14, Sep 1988 2.00
❑15, Oct 1988 2.00
❑16, Nov 1988 2.00
❑17, Dec 1988 A: Avenger. 2.00
❑18, Dec 1988 A: Avenger. 2.00
❑19, Jan 1989; Shadow alive again 2.00
❑Annual 1, ca. 1987; EC parody 2.50
❑Annual 2, ca. 1988 2.50

SHADOW, THE (MOVIE ADAPTATION)
DARK HORSE

❑1, Jun 1994 2.50
❑2, Jul 1994 2.50

SHADOW AGENTS
ARMAGEDDON

❑1, May 1991 2.50

SHADOW AND DOC SAVAGE, THE
DARK HORSE

❑1, Jul 1995 2.95
❑2, Aug 1995 2.95

SHADOW AND THE MYSTERIOUS 3, THE
DARK HORSE

❑1, Sep 1994 2.95

SHADOWBLADE
HOT

❑1 1.75

SHADOW, THE: BLOOD AND JUDGMENT
DC

❑1 12.95

SHADOW CABINET
DC / MILESTONE

❑0, Jan 1994; Giant-size 2.50
❑1, Jun 1994 1.75
❑2, Jul 1994 1.75
❑3, Aug 1994 1.75
❑4, Sep 1994 1.75
❑5, Oct 1994 1.75
❑6, Nov 1994 1.75
❑7, Dec 1994 1.75
❑8, Jan 1995 1.75
❑9, Feb 1995 1.75
❑10, Mar 1995 1.75
❑11, Apr 1995 1.75
❑12, May 1995 1.75
❑13, Jun 1995 2.50
❑14, Jul 1995 2.50
❑15, Aug 1995 2.50
❑16, Sep 1995 2.50
❑17, Oct 1995 2.50

SHADOW COMIX SHOWCASE
SHADOW COMIX

❑1, May 1996 2.95

SHADOW CROSS
DARKSIDE

❑1, Oct 1995 2.75

N-MINT

SHADOW EMPIRES: FAITH CONQUERS
DARK HORSE

❑1, Aug 1994 .... 3.25
❑2, Sep 1994 .... 3.00
❑3, Oct 1994 .... 3.00
❑4, Nov 1994 .... 3.00

SHADOWGEAR
ANTARCTIC

❑1, Feb 1999 .... 2.99
❑2, Mar 1999 .... 2.99
❑3, Apr 1999 .... 2.99

SHADOWHAWK (VOL. 1)
IMAGE

❑1, Aug 1992; 1: Shadowhawk. Embossed cover 3.00
❑1/A, Aug 1992; Newsstand edition (no gold stamp); 1: Shadowhawk. Embossed cover 2.00
❑2, Oct 1992 1: Arson. A: Spawn. 2.50
❑3, Dec 1992; 1: The Others. 1: Liquefier. Glow-in-the-dark cover 2.50
❑4, Mar 1993 A: Savage Dragon. 2.00

SHADOWHAWK (VOL. 2)
IMAGE

❑1, May 1993; diecut foil cover 3.50
❑1/Gold, May 1993; Gold 3.00
❑2, Jul 1993; 1: Hawk's Shadow. ShadowHawk's identity revealed; Foil-embossed cover 2.00
❑2/Gold, Jul 1993; Gold edition 3.00
❑3, Aug 1993; 1: The Pact. 1: J.P. Slaughter. Cover perforated to allow folding out into poster 2.95

SHADOWHAWK (VOL. 3)
IMAGE

❑0, Oct 1994; RL (w); RL (a); O: Shadowhawk. A: Mist. A: Bloodstrike. A: Mars Gunther. cover says September 2.50
❑1, Nov 1993; 1: Valentine. Foil-embossed cover 2.50
❑2, Dec 1993 1: U.S. Male. 2.00
❑3, Feb 1994; Fold-up cover 2.95
❑4, Mar 1994 .... 2.95
❑12, Aug 1994; (Numbering sequence follows from total of all ShadowHawk books published to this point) 1.95
❑13, Sep 1994 A: WildC.A.T.s. 1.95
❑14, Oct 1994 A: 1963 heroes. 2.50
❑15, Nov 1994 A: The Others. 2.50
❑16, Jan 1995 A: Supreme. 2.50
❑17, Mar 1995 A: Spawn. 2.50
❑18, May 1995 D: Shadowhawk. 2.50
❑Special 1, Dec 1994; Flip-book KB (w) 3.50

SHADOWHAWK GALLERY
IMAGE

❑1, Apr 1994 .... 2.00

SHADOWHAWK SAGA, THE
IMAGE

❑1 .... 1.00

SHADOWHAWKS OF LEGEND
IMAGE

❑1, Nov 1995 .... 4.95

SHADOWHAWK-VAMPIRELLA
IMAGE / HARRIS

❑2, Feb 1995; crossover; continued from Vampirella - Shadowhawk #1 .... 4.95

SHADOW, THE: HELL'S HEAT WAVE
DARK HORSE

❑1, Apr 1995 .... 2.95
❑2, May 1995 .... 2.95
❑3, Jun 1995 .... 2.95

SHADOW HOUSE
SHADOW HOUSE

❑1, Aug 1997, b&w 2.95
❑2, Oct 1997, b&w 2.95
❑3, Dec 1997, b&w 2.95
❑4, Feb 1998, b&w 2.95

N-MINT

SHADOWHUNT SPECIAL
IMAGE

❑1/A, Apr 1996; Part 1 of five-part crossover 2.50
❑1/B, Apr 1996; alternate cover; Part 1 of five-part crossover 2.50

SHADOW, THE: IN THE COILS OF LEVIATHAN
DARK HORSE

❑1, Oct 1993 .... 2.95
❑2, Dec 1993 .... 2.95
❑3, Feb 1994 .... 2.95
❑4, Apr 1994 .... 2.95

SHADOW LADY (MASAKAZU KATSURA'S...)
DARK HORSE / MANGA

❑1, Oct 1998 1: Shadow Lady. 3.00
❑2, Nov 1998 1: Bright Honda. 2.50
❑3, Dec 1998 .... 2.50
❑4, Jan 1999 .... 2.50
❑5, Feb 1999 .... 2.50
❑6, Mar 1999 .... 2.50
❑7, Apr 1999 .... 2.50
❑8, May 1999 .... 2.50
❑9, Jun 1999 .... 2.50
❑10, Jul 1999 .... 2.50
❑11, Aug 1999 .... 2.50
❑12, Sep 1999 .... 2.50
❑13, Oct 1999 .... 2.50
❑14, Nov 1999 .... 2.50
❑15, Dec 1999 .... 2.50
❑16, Jan 2000 .... 2.50
❑17, Feb 2000 .... 2.50
❑18, Mar 2000 .... 2.50
❑19, Apr 2000 .... 2.50
❑20, May 2000 .... 2.50
❑21, Jun 2000 .... 2.50
❑22, Jul 2000 .... 2.50
❑23, Aug 2000 .... 2.50
❑24, Sep 2000 .... 2.50
❑Special 1, Oct 2000 .... 3.99

SHADOWLAND
FANTAGRAPHICS

❑1, b&w 2.25
❑2, b&w 2.25

SHADOWLINE SPECIAL
IMAGE

❑1 .... 1.00

SHADOWLORD/TRIUNE
JET CITY

❑1, Win 1986 .... 1.50

SHADOWMAN
VALIANT

❑0, Apr 1994; BH (c); BH (w); BH (a); O: Shadowman II (Jack Boniface). O: Shadowman I (Maxim St. James). Chromium cover 2.50
❑0/Gold, Apr 1994; Gold edition BH (a); O: Shadowman II (Jack Boniface). O: Shadowman I (Maxim St. James). 4.00
❑0/Variant, Apr 1994; BH (a); O: Shadowman II (Jack Boniface). O: Shadowman I (Maxim St. James). chromium cover 3.95
❑1, May 1992 O: Shadowman II (Jack Boniface). 1: Shadowman II (Jack Boniface). 3.00
❑2, Jun 1992 .... 3.00
❑3, Jul 1992 .... 2.50
❑4, Aug 1992; FM (c); FM (a); Unity . 2.50
❑5, Sep 1992; BL (w); Unity 2.50
❑6, Oct 1992 BH (w) 2.50
❑7, Nov 1992 BH (w) 2.50
❑8, Dec 1992 BH (w); 1: Master Darque. V: Master Darque. 2.50
❑9, Jan 1993 .... 2.50
❑10, Feb 1993 BH (c); BH (w); BH (a) 2.50
❑11, Mar 1993 BH (c); BH (w); BH (a) 2.50
❑12, Apr 1993 BH (c); BH (w); BH (a); V: Master Darque. 2.50
❑13, May 1993 .... 2.50
❑14, Jun 1993 BH (c); BH (w); BH (a) 2.50

After making her first appearance in *Green Arrow: The Longbow Hunters*, Shado got her own four-issue mini-series.

© 1992 DC Comics.

N-MINT

❑15, Jul 1993 BH (c); BH (w); BH (a) 2.50
❑16, Aug 1993 BH (c); BH (w); BH (a); 1: Doctor Mirage. 3.00
❑17, Sep 1993; BH (c); BH (w); BH (a); A: Archer & Armstrong. Serial number contest 2.50
❑18, Oct 1993 BH (c); BH (w); BH (a) 2.50
❑19, Nov 1993; BH (c); BH (w); BH (a); A: Aerosmith. Aerosmith 2.50
❑20, Dec 1993 BH (c); BH (w); BH (a) 2.50
❑21, Jan 1994 BH (c); BH (w); BH (a); V: Master Darque. 2.50
❑22, Feb 1994 BH (c); BH (w); BH (a) 2.50
❑23, Mar 1994 BH (c); BH (w); BH (a); A: Doctor Mirage. 2.50
❑24, Apr 1994 BH (c); BH (w); BH (a) 2.50
❑25, Apr 1994; BH (c); BH (w); BH (a); trading card 2.50
❑26, Jun 1994 BH (c); BH (w); BH (a) 2.50
❑27, Aug 1994 BH (c); BH (w); BH (a) 2.50
❑28, Sep 1994 BH (c); BH (w); BH (a) 2.50
❑29, Oct 1994; BH (c); BH (w); BH (a); Chaos Effect 2.50
❑30, Nov 1994 BH (c); BH (w); BH (a) 2.50
❑31, Dec 1994 BH (c); BH (w); BH (a) 2.50
❑32, Jan 1994 BH (c); BH (w); BH (a) 2.50
❑33, Feb 1994 BH (c); BH (w); BH (a) 2.50
❑34, Mar 1994 BH (c); BH (w); BH (a) 2.50
❑35, Apr 1995 BH (c) 2.50
❑36, May 1995 BH (c) 2.50
❑37, Jun 1995 BH (a) 2.50
❑38, Jul 1995 BH (c); BH (w); BH (a) 2.50
❑39, Aug 1995 BH (w); BH (a) 2.50
❑40, Sep 1995 BH (w); BH (a) 2.50
❑41, Oct 1995 BH (w); BH (a) 2.50
❑42, Nov 1995 BH (c); BH (w); BH (a) 2.50
❑43, Dec 1995 BH (c); BH (w); BH (a) 2.50
❑Yearbook 1, Dec 1994 .... 3.95

SHADOWMAN (VOL. 2)
ACCLAIM

❑1, Mar 1997 .... 2.50
❑1/Variant, Mar 1997; Painted cover . 2.50
❑2, Apr 1997 .... 2.50
❑3, May 1997 .... 2.50
❑4, Jun 1997 .... 2.50
❑5, Jul 1997 .... 2.50
❑5/Ashcan, Mar 1997, b&w; No cover price; preview of upcoming issue .. 1.00
❑6, Aug 1997 .... 2.50
❑7, Sep 1997 .... 2.50
❑8, Oct 1997 .... 2.50
❑9, Nov 1997 .... 2.50
❑10, Dec 1997 .... 2.50
❑11, Jan 1998 .... 2.50
❑12, Feb 1998 .... 2.50
❑13, Mar 1998; Goat Month 2.50
❑14, Apr 1998 .... 2.50
❑15, Jan 1998; No cover date; indicia says Jan 2.50
❑16, Feb 1998; No cover date; indicia says Feb 2.50
❑Ashcan 1, Nov 1996, b&w; No cover price; preview of upcoming series . 1.00

SHADOWMAN (VOL. 3)
ACCLAIM

❑1, Jul 1999 .... 3.95
❑2, Aug 1999 .... 3.95
❑3, Sep 1999 .... 3.95
❑4, Oct 1999 .... 3.95

N-MINT

SHADOW MASTER
PSYGNOSIS / MANGA

❑0; Preview ... 1.00

SHADOWMASTERS
MARVEL

❑1, Oct 1989 O: Shadowmasters. ... 4.00
❑2, Nov 1989 ... 4.00
❑3, Dec 1989 ... 4.00
❑4, Jan 1990 ... 4.00

SHADOWMEN
TRIDENT

❑1, b&w ... 2.25
❑2, b&w ... 2.25

SHADOW OF THE BATMAN
DC

❑1, Dec 1985 ... 3.00
❑2, Jan 1986 ... 2.00
❑3, Feb 1986 ... 2.00
❑4, Mar 1986 ... 2.00
❑5, Apr 1986 ... 2.00

SHADOW OF THE TORTURER, THE (GENE WOLFE'S...)
INNOVATION

❑1, ca. 1991 ... 2.50
❑2, ca. 1991 ... 2.50
❑3, ca. 1991 ... 2.50
❑4, ca. 1992 ... 2.50
❑5, ca. 1992 ... 2.50
❑6, ca. 1992 ... 2.50

SHADOW RAVEN
POC-IT

❑1, Jun 1995 ... 2.50

SHADOW REAVERS
BLACK BULL

❑1, Oct 2001 ... 2.99
❑2, Nov 2001 ... 2.99

SHADOW REIGNS
AIX C.C.

❑0, Dec 1997 ... 2.95

SHADOW RIDERS
MARVEL

❑1, Jun 1992; Embossed cover ... 2.50
❑2, Jul 1992 ... 1.75
❑3, Aug 1992 ... 1.75
❑4, Sep 1992 ... 1.75

SHADOWS
IMAGE

❑1, Mar 2003 ... 2.95
❑2, Apr 2003 ... 2.95
❑3, Aug 2003 ... 2.95
❑4, Dec 2003 ... 2.95

SHADOWS & LIGHT
MARVEL

❑1, Feb 1998, b&w ... 2.99
❑2, Apr 1998, b&w ... 2.99
❑3, Jul 1998, b&w ... 2.99

SHADOW'S EDGE, THE
LION

❑1 ... 3.95

SHADOWS FALL
DC / VERTIGO

❑1, Nov 1994 ... 2.95
❑2, Dec 1994 ... 2.95
❑3, Jan 1995 ... 2.95
❑4, Feb 1995 ... 2.95
❑5, Mar 1995 ... 2.95
❑6, Apr 1995 ... 2.95

SHADOWS FROM THE GRAVE
RENEGADE

❑1, b&w ... 2.00
❑2, Mar 1988, b&w ... 2.00

SHADOW SLASHER
POCKET CHANGE

❑1 ... 2.50

SHADOW SLAYER
ETERNITY

❑0 ... 1.95

N-MINT

SHADOWSTAR
SHADOWSTAR

❑1 ... 2.00
❑2, Nov 1985 ... 2.00
❑3, Dec 1985; first Slave Labor comic book ... 2.00

SHADOW STATE
BROADWAY

❑1, Dec 1995; DC (a); 1: BloodS.C.R.E.A.M.. enhanced card-stock cover; BloodS.C.R.E.A.M., Fatale ... 2.50
❑2, Jan 1996; Till Death Do Us Part; Fatale ... 2.50
❑3, Mar 1996; Till Death Do Us Part .. 2.50
❑4, Apr 1996; Till Death Do Us Part .. 2.50
❑5, May 1996; Till Death Do Us Part . 2.50
❑6, Jun 1996 ... 2.95
❑7, Jul 1996 ... 2.95
❑Ashcan 1, Sep 1995, b&w; giveaway preview edition; Till Death Do Us Part, Fatale ... 1.00

SHADOW STRIKES!, THE
DC

❑1, Sep 1989 ... 2.50
❑2, Oct 1989 ... 2.25
❑3, Nov 1989 ... 2.00
❑4, Dec 1989 ... 2.00
❑5, Jan 1990 A: Doc Savage. ... 2.00
❑6, Feb 1990 A: Doc Savage. ... 2.00
❑7, Mar 1990 ... 2.00
❑8, Apr 1990 V: Shiwan Khan. ... 2.00
❑9, May 1990 V: Shiwan Khan. ... 2.00
❑10, Jun 1990 V: Shiwan Khan. ... 2.00
❑11, Aug 1990 ... 2.00
❑12, Sep 1990 ... 2.00
❑13, Oct 1990 ... 2.00
❑14, Dec 1990 ... 2.00
❑15, Jan 1991 ... 2.00
❑16, Feb 1991 ... 2.00
❑17, Mar 1991 ... 2.00
❑18, Apr 1991 ... 2.00
❑19, May 1991 ... 2.00
❑20, Jun 1991 ... 2.00
❑21, Jul 1991 ... 2.00
❑22, Aug 1991 ... 2.00
❑23, Sep 1991 ... 2.00
❑24, Oct 1991 ... 2.00
❑25, Nov 1991 ... 2.00
❑26, Dec 1991 ... 2.00
❑27, Jan 1992 ... 2.00
❑28, Feb 1992 ... 2.00
❑29, Mar 1992 ... 2.00
❑30, Apr 1992 ... 2.00
❑31, May 1992 ... 2.00
❑Annual 1, Dec 1989 DS (a) ... 3.50

SHADOWTOWN
ICONOGRAFIX

❑1 ... 2.50

SHADOWTOWN: BLACK FIST RISING
MADHEART

❑1, b&w ... 2.50

SHADOW WAR OF HAWKMAN, THE
DC

❑1, May 1985 RHo, AA (a) ... 1.50
❑2, Jun 1985 RHo (a) ... 1.25
❑3, Jul 1985 RHo (a); A: Elongated Man. A: Aquaman. ... 1.25
❑4, Aug 1985 RHo (a) ... 1.25

SHADOW WARRIOR
GATEWAY

❑1, b&w ... 1.95

SHAIANA
EXPRESS / ENTITY

❑1, Jul 1995, b&w; enhanced cover .. 2.50
❑2 ... 2.50
❑3 ... 2.50

SHALOMAN
MARK 1

❑1, b&w ... 1.75
❑2, b&w ... 1.75

N-MINT

❑3, b&w ... 1.75
❑4, b&w ... 1.75
❑5, b&w ... 1.75
❑6, b&w ... 1.75
❑7, b&w ... 1.75
❑8, b&w ... 1.75
❑9, b&w ... 1.75

SHAMAN
CONTINUITY

❑0 NA, AN (a) ... 2.00

SHAMAN'S TEARS
IMAGE

❑0, Dec 1995; MGr (w); MGr (a); says 1996 indicia; meant 1995 ... 2.50
❑1, May 1993; MGr (w); MGr (a); foil cover ... 2.50
❑1/Platinum, May 1993; Platinum edition MGr (a) ... 4.00
❑2, Jul 1993; MGr (w); MGr (a); cover says Aug; indicia says Jul ... 2.50
❑3, Nov 1994 MGr (w); MGr (a) ... 1.95
❑3/Ashcan; MGr (w); MGr (a); Limited "ashcan" run of Shaman's Tears #3 ... 3.00
❑4, Dec 1994; MGr (w); MGr (a); Title moves back to Image ... 1.95
❑5, Jan 1995 MGr (w); MGr (a) ... 1.95
❑6, Feb 1995 MGr (w); MGr (a) ... 1.95
❑7, May 1995 MGr (w); MGr (a) ... 1.95
❑8, May 1995 MGr (w); MGr (a) ... 1.95
❑9, Jun 1995 MGr (w); MGr (a) ... 1.95
❑10, Jul 1995 MGr (w); MGr (a) ... 1.95
❑11, Aug 1995 MGr (w); MGr (a) ... 1.95
❑12, Aug 1995 MGr (w); MGr (a) ... 1.95

SHANDA THE PANDA
MU

❑1, May 1992, b&w ... 2.50

SHANDA THE PANDA (2ND SERIES)
ANTARCTIC

❑1, Jun 1993 ... 2.50
❑2, Aug 1993 ... 2.50
❑3, Oct 1993 ... 2.75
❑4, Dec 1993 ... 2.75
❑5, Aug 1994 ... 2.75
❑6, Nov 1994 ... 2.75
❑7, Jan 1995 ... 2.75
❑8, Feb 1995 ... 2.75
❑9, May 1995 ... 2.75
❑10, Jul 1995 ... 2.75
❑11, Sep 1995 ... 2.75
❑12, Nov 1995 ... 2.75
❑13, Jan 1996 ... 2.75
❑14, Mar 1996 ... 2.75
❑15, May 1996 ... 2.75
❑16, Jul 1996 ... 1.95
❑17 ... 1.95
❑18 ... 1.95
❑19, May 1997 ... 1.95
❑20, Jul 1997 ... 1.95
❑21, Sep 1997; Demi Moore spoof cover ... 2.95
❑22 ... 2.95
❑23, Jan 1999 ... 2.95
❑24, Apr 1999 ... 2.95
❑25, Jul 1999; Giant-size ... 4.95
❑26, Nov 1999 ... 2.95
❑27, Feb 2000 ... 2.95
❑28, May 2000 ... 2.95
❑29, Aug 2000 ... 2.95
❑30, Nov 2000 ... 2.95
❑31, Feb 2001 ... 2.99
❑32, May 2001 ... 2.99
❑33, Aug 2001 ... 2.99
❑34, Nov 2001 ... 4.99
❑35, Aug 2002 ... 4.99
❑36, ca. 2002 ... 4.99
❑37, ca. 2003 ... 4.99
❑Annual 1 ... 4.00
❑Annual 2 ... 4.00
❑Annual 3 ... 4.50
❑Annual 4 ... 4.95

N-MINT

SHANG CHI: MASTER OF KUNG FU
MARVEL

❑1, Nov 2002 .... 2.99
❑2, Dec 2002 .... 2.99
❑3, Jan 2003 .... 2.99
❑4, Feb 2003 .... 2.99
❑5, Mar 2003 .... 2.99
❑6, Apr 2003 .... 2.99

SHANGHAI: BIG MACHINE
BRICK HOUSE DIGITAL

❑1, ca. 2000 .... 2.95

SHANGHAIED: THE SAGA OF THE BLACK KITE
ETERNITY

❑1 .... 2.00
❑2 .... 2.00
❑3 .... 2.00

SHANGRI LA
IMAGE

❑1, ca. 2004 .... 7.95

SHANNA THE SHE-DEVIL
MARVEL

❑1, Dec 1972 GT (a); 1: Shanna the She-Devil. 23.00
❑2, Feb 1973 JSo (c); JSo (a) 6.00
❑3, Apr 1973 .... 3.50
❑4, Jun 1973 .... 3.50
❑5, Aug 1973 .... 3.50

SHAOLIN
BLACK TIGER

❑1 .... 2.95
❑2 .... 2.95
❑3 .... 2.95
❑4 .... 2.95
❑5 .... 2.95

SHAOLIN SISTERS
TOKYOPOP

❑1, Feb 2003, b&w; printed in Japanese format 9.99
❑2, Apr 2003, b&w; printed in Japanese format 9.99

SHAQUILLE O'NEAL VS. MICHAEL JORDAN
PERSONALITY

❑1 .... 2.95
❑2 .... 2.95

SHARDS
ASCENSION

❑1, Feb 1994 .... 2.50

SHARKY
IMAGE

❑1/A, Feb 1998 .... 2.50
❑1/B, Feb 1998; back cover pin-up ... 2.50
❑1/C, Feb 1998; signing tour edition . 2.50
❑1/D, Feb 1998; no cover price; The $1,000,000 variant 2.50
❑2/A, Apr 1998 .... 2.50
❑2/B, Apr 1998; alternate wraparound cover (with Savage Dragon) 2.50
❑3, May 1998 .... 2.50
❑4, Jul 1998; gives date of publication as Late; Group charging on cover, "The Bad Guy!" inset 2.50
❑4/A, Jul 1998 .... 2.50

SHATTER (1ST SERIES)
FIRST

❑1, Jun 1985; 1: Shatter. This is the first computer-generated comic book ... 2.50
❑1-2; 1: Shatter. This is the first computer-generated comic book 2.00

SHATTER (2ND SERIES)
FIRST

❑1, Dec 1985; first computer-drawn comic book; Continued from Shatter one-shot 2.50
❑2, Feb 1986 .... 2.00
❑3, Jun 1986 .... 2.00
❑4, Aug 1986 .... 2.00
❑5, Oct 1986 .... 2.00
❑6, Dec 1986 .... 2.00

N-MINT

❑7, Feb 1987 .... 2.00
❑8, Apr 1987 .... 2.00
❑9, Jun 1987 .... 2.00
❑10, Aug 1987 .... 2.00
❑11, Oct 1987 .... 2.00
❑12, Dec 1987 .... 2.00
❑13, Feb 1988 .... 2.00
❑14, Apr 1988 .... 2.00

SHATTERED EARTH
ETERNITY

❑1, Nov 1988 .... 1.95
❑2, Dec 1988 .... 1.95
❑3, Jan 1989 .... 1.95
❑4, Mar 1989 .... 1.95
❑5 1989 .... 1.95
❑6 1989 .... 1.95
❑7 1989 .... 1.95
❑8 1989 .... 1.95
❑9 1989 .... 1.95

SHATTERED IMAGE
IMAGE

❑1, Aug 1996 .... 2.50
❑2, Oct 1996; incorrect cover date 2.50
❑3, Nov 1996; cover says Oct, indicia says Nov 2.50
❑4, Dec 1996 .... 2.50

SHATTERPOINT
ETERNITY

❑1, b&w; Broid 2.25
❑2, b&w; Broid 2.25
❑3, b&w; Broid 2.25
❑4, b&w; Broid 2.25

SHAZAM!
DC

❑1, Feb 1973 CCB (a); O: Captain Marvel (Golden Age). 16.00
❑2, Apr 1973 CCB (a) 5.00
❑3, Jun 1973 CCB (a) 5.00
❑4, Jul 1973 CCB (a) 4.00
❑5, Sep 1973 CCB (a) 3.00
❑6, Oct 1973 CCB (a) 3.00
❑7, Nov 1973 CCB (a) 3.00
❑8, Dec 1973; 100 Page giant; CCB (a); scheduled as DC 100-Page Super-Spectacular #DC-23 .... 14.00
❑9, Jan 1974 CCB (a) 2.50
❑10, Feb 1974; BO (a); V: Aunt Minerva. Mary Marvel back-up 2.50
❑11, Mar 1974 .... 3.00
❑12, Jun 1974; 100 Page giant 9.00
❑13, Aug 1974; 100 Page giant 9.00
❑14, Oct 1974; 100 Page giant KS (a); A: Monster Society. 9.00
❑15, Dec 1974; 100 Page giant A: Lex Luthor. 9.00
❑16, Feb 1975; 100 Page giant V: Seven Deadly Sins. 9.00
❑17, Apr 1975; 100 Page giant 9.00
❑18, Jun 1975 .... 3.00
❑19, Aug 1975 .... 3.00
❑20, Oct 1975 .... 3.00
❑21, Dec 1975 CCB (w) 3.00
❑22, Feb 1976 V: King Kull. 3.00
❑23, Win 1976 .... 3.00
❑24, Spr 1976 .... 3.00
❑25, Oct 1976 O: Isis. 1: Isis. 3.00
❑26, Dec 1976 .... 3.00
❑27, Feb 1977 .... 3.00
❑28, Apr 1977 V: Black Adam. 2.00
❑29, Jun 1977 V: Ibac. 3.00
❑30, Aug 1977 .... 3.00
❑31, Oct 1977 A: Minute Man. 3.00
❑32, Dec 1977 .... 3.00
❑33, Feb 1978 V: Mr. Atom. 3.00
❑34, Apr 1978; O: Captain Marvel Jr.. Captain Marvel Jr. vs. Captain Nazi 3.00
❑35, Jun 1978 .... 3.00

SHAZAM! AND THE SHAZAM FAMILY
DC

❑Annual 1, Sep 2002 .... 5.95

Michael Kaluta presented the first several adventures of The Shadow in the pulp character's first DC series.
© 1973 National Periodical Publications Inc. (DC).

N-MINT

SHAZAM: THE NEW BEGINNING
DC

❑1, Apr 1987 O: Captain Marvel (Golden Age)-new origin. 2.00
❑2, May 1987 V: Black Adam. 2.00
❑3, Jun 1987 .... 2.00
❑4, Jul 1987 .... 2.00

SHEBA
SICK MIND

❑1, Jul 1996, b&w 2.50
❑2, Nov 1996, b&w 2.50
❑3, Feb 1997, b&w 2.50
❑4, Sep 1997, b&w 2.50

SHEBA (2ND SERIES)
SIRIUS

❑1, Dec 1997, b&w 2.50
❑2, Mar 1998, b&w 2.50
❑3, Jun 1998, b&w 2.50
❑4, Sep 1998, b&w 2.50
❑5 1999, b&w 2.50
❑6, May 1999, b&w 2.95
❑7 .... 2.95
❑8 .... 2.95

SHEBA PANTHEON
SIRIUS

❑1, Aug 1998, b&w; collects strips and character bios 2.50

SHE BUCCANEER
MONSTER

❑1, b&w 2.25
❑2, b&w 2.25

SHE-CAT
AC

❑1, Jun 1989, b&w 2.50
❑2, Apr 1990, b&w 2.50
❑3, May 1990, b&w 2.50
❑4, Jun 1990, b&w 2.50

SHEEDEVA
FANTAGRAPHICS / EROS

❑1, Aug 1994, b&w 2.95
❑2, Nov 1994, b&w 2.95

SHEENA
MARVEL

❑1, Dec 1984 GM (a) 2.00
❑2, Feb 1985 GM (a) 2.00

SHEENA 3-D SPECIAL
BLACKTHORNE

❑1, May 1985 .... 2.00

SHEENA-QUEEN OF THE JUNGLE
LONDON NIGHT

❑1/A, ca. 1998; Alligator cover 5.00
❑1/B, ca. 1998; Leopard cover 5.00
❑1/C, ca. 1998; Zebra cover 5.00
❑1/D, ca. 1998; Ministry Edition 3.00
❑1/Ltd., ca. 1998; White leather edition 15.00

SHEENA, QUEEN OF THE JUNGLE 3-D
BLACKTHORNE

❑1, May 1985, b&w DSt (a) 2.50

SHE-HULK
MARVEL

❑1, May 2004 .... 2.99
❑2, Jun 2004 .... 2.99
❑3, Jul 2004 .... 2.99
❑4, Aug 2004 .... 2.99
❑5, Sep 2004 ....

N-MINT

SHEILA TRENT: VAMPIRE HUNTER
DRACULINA

❑1 .... 2.50
❑2 .... 2.50

SHELL SHOCK
MIRAGE

❑1 .... 12.95

SHERLOCK HOLMES (DC)
DC

❑1, Oct 1975 .... 6.00

SHERLOCK HOLMES (ETERNITY)
ETERNITY

❑1, b&w; strip reprints 2.00
❑2 1988, b&w; strip reprints 2.00
❑3 1988, b&w; strip reprints 2.00
❑4 1988, b&w; strip reprints 2.00
❑5 1988, b&w; strip reprints 2.00
❑6 1988, b&w; strip reprints 2.00
❑7 1988, b&w; strip reprints 2.00
❑8, Jan 1989, b&w; strip reprints 2.00
❑9 1989, b&w; strip reprints 2.00
❑10 1989, b&w; strip reprints 2.00
❑11 1989, b&w; strip reprints 2.00
❑12 1989, b&w; strip reprints 2.00
❑13 1989, b&w; strip reprints 2.00
❑14 1989, b&w; strip reprints 2.00
❑15 1989, b&w; strip reprints 2.00
❑16 1989 .... 2.25
❑17 1989 .... 2.25
❑18 1990 .... 2.25
❑19 1990 .... 2.25
❑20 1990 .... 2.25
❑21 1990 .... 2.50
❑22 1990 .... 2.50
❑23 1990 .... 2.75

SHERLOCK HOLMES (AVALON)
AVALON

❑1, ca. 1997, b&w 2.95

SHERLOCK HOLMES: ADVENTURES OF THE OPERA GHOST
CALIBER

❑1 .... 2.95
❑2 .... 2.95

SHERLOCK HOLMES CASEBOOK
ETERNITY

❑1; Originally published as New Adventures of Sherlock Holmes 2.25
❑2; Originally published as New Adventures of Sherlock Holmes 2.25

SHERLOCK HOLMES: DR. JEKYLL & MR. HOLMES
CALIBER / TOME

❑1 1998, b&w 2.95

SHERLOCK HOLMES IN THE CASE OF THE MISSING MARTIAN
ETERNITY

❑1, Jul 1990, b&w 2.25
❑2, Aug 1990, b&w 2.25
❑3, Sep 1990, b&w 2.25
❑4, Oct 1990, b&w 2.25

SHERLOCK HOLMES IN THE CURIOUS CASE OF THE VANISHING VILLAIN
ATOMEKA

❑1 .... 4.50

SHERLOCK HOLMES MYSTERIES
MOONSTONE

❑1 .... 2.95

SHERLOCK HOLMES OF THE '30S
ETERNITY

❑1, b&w; strip reprints 2.95
❑2, b&w; strip reprints 2.95
❑3, b&w; strip reprints 2.95
❑4, b&w; strip reprints 2.95
❑5, b&w; strip reprints 2.95
❑6, b&w; strip reprints 2.95
❑7, b&w; strip reprints 2.95

N-MINT

SHERLOCK HOLMES READER
TOME

❑1 1998 .... 3.95

SHERLOCK HOLMES: RETURN OF THE DEVIL
ADVENTURE

❑1, Sep 1992, b&w 2.50
❑2 1992, b&w 2.50

SHERLOCK JR.
ETERNITY

❑1, b&w; strip reprints 2.50
❑2, Sep 1990, b&w; strip reprints 2.50
❑3, b&w; strip reprints 2.50

SHERMAN'S MARCH THROUGH ATLANTA TO THE SEA
HERITAGE COLLECTION

❑1; retells Civil War story; wraparound cover 3.50

SHEVA'S WAR
DC / VERTIGO

❑1, Oct 1998 .... 2.95
❑2, Nov 1998 .... 2.95
❑3, Dec 1998 .... 2.95
❑4, Jan 1999 .... 2.95
❑5, Feb 1999 .... 2.95

SHI
CRUSADE

❑0, ca. 1996; Flipbook with Wolverine/Shi Night of Justice Preview 2.99
❑0.5, ca. 1996; Wizard promotional edition with COA 3.00

SHI: ART OF WAR TOUR BOOK
CRUSADE

❑1, ca. 1998 .... 4.95

SHI: BLACK, WHITE, AND RED
CRUSADE

❑1, Mar 1998 .... 2.95
❑2, May 1998 .... 2.95

SHI/CYBLADE: THE BATTLE FOR INDEPENDENTS
CRUSADE

❑1, Sep 1995; 1: The Atomik Angels. A: Cerebus. A: Bone. crossover; concludes Image's Cyblade/Shi: The Battle for Independents #1; Numerous other independent characters appear 4.00
❑1/Variant, Sep 1995; alternate cover; crossover; concludes Image's Cyblade/Shi: The Battle for Independents #1 .... 5.00

SHI/DAREDEVIL: HONOR THY MOTHER
CRUSADE

❑1, Jan 1997; flipbook with TCB Sneak Attack Edition #1; crossover with Marvel 2.95
❑1/Ltd., Jan 1997; "Banzai" edition 6.00

SHIDIMA
IMAGE

❑0/A, Oct 2001 .... 2.95
❑0/B, Oct 2001 .... 2.95
❑1/A, Jan 2001; Many figures on cover, man center holding rope 2.95
❑1/B, Jan 2001; Four figures on cover, man front holding sword 2.95
❑2, Mar 2001 .... 2.95
❑3, May 2001 .... 2.95
❑4 2001 .... 2.95

SHI: EAST WIND RAIN
CRUSADE

❑1, Nov 1997; Painted cover 3.50
❑2, Feb 1998 .... 3.50
❑Ashcan 1, Jul 1997; No cover price; Sneak Teaser Preview 1.00

SHIELD
MARVEL

❑1, Feb 1973; SL (w); DH, JK (a); Nick Fury reprints from Strange Tales ... 13.00
❑2, Apr 1973; DH, JK (a); Nick Fury reprints from Strange Tales 5.00

N-MINT

❑3, Jun 1973; JB, JK (a); Nick Fury reprints from Strange Tales 5.00
❑4, Aug 1973; SL (w); JK (a); Nick Fury reprints from Strange Tales 5.00
❑5, Oct 1973; JSo (a); Nick Fury reprints from Strange Tales 5.00

SHIELD (ARCHIE)
ARCHIE / RED CIRCLE

❑1, Jun 1983 .... 1.00
❑2, Aug 1983 .... 1.00
❑3, Dec 1983, Title changes to Steel Sterling 1.00

SHI: HEAVEN & EARTH
CRUSADE

❑1, Jul 1997 .... 2.95
❑1/A, Jul 1997; alternate cover 2.95
❑2, Nov 1997 .... 2.95
❑2/A, Nov 1997; logoless cover 2.95
❑3, Jan 1998 .... 2.95
❑4 .... 2.95
❑4/A, Apr 1998; alternate cover (Shi facing right) 2.95
❑Ashcan 1, ca. 1997; Special Teaser Preview 2.95

SHI: KAIDAN
CRUSADE

❑1, Oct 1996, b&w; Japanese ghost stories 2.95
❑1/A, Oct 1996, b&w; alternate wraparound cover with no cover copy; Japanese ghost stories 3.00

SHILOH: THE DEVIL'S OWN DAY
HERITAGE COLLECTION

❑1; retells Civil War battle; wraparound cover 3.50

SHI: MASQUERADE
CRUSADE

❑1, Mar 1998; wraparound painted cover 3.50

SHIMMER
AVATAR

❑1 .... 3.50

SHI: NIGHTSTALKERS
CRUSADE

❑1, Sep 1997 .... 3.50

SHION: BLADE OF THE MINSTREL
VIZ

❑1, Sep 1990, b&w 9.95

SHI: PANDORA'S BOX
AVATAR

❑1, Apr 2003 .... 3.50

SHIP OF FOOLS (IMAGE)
IMAGE

❑0, Aug 1997, b&w 2.95
❑1, Oct 1997, b&w 2.95
❑2, Dec 1997, b&w 2.95
❑3, Feb 1998, b&w 2.95

SHIP OF FOOLS (CALIBER)
CALIBER

❑1, b&w 3.00
❑2 .... 3.00
❑3, b&w 3.00
❑4 .... 3.00
❑5 .... 3.00
❑6 .... 3.00

SHIPWRECKED!
DISNEY

❑1 .... 5.95

SHI: REKISHI
CRUSADE

❑1, Jan 1997; flipbook with Shi: East Wind Rain Sneak Attack Edition #1 .... 2.95
❑2, Apr 1997 .... 2.95

SHI: SEMPO
AVATAR

❑1, Aug 2003 .... 3.50
❑2, Oct 2003 .... 3.50

N-MINT

SHI: SENRYAKU
CRUSADE

❑1, Aug 1995 .... 3.25
❑1/Variant, Aug 1995; Variant "virgin" cover with no type 4.00
❑2, Oct 1995 .... 3.00
❑3, Dec 1995 .... 3.00

SHI: THE BLOOD OF SAINTS
CRUSADE

❑1, Nov 1996 .... 2.95
❑Fan ed. 1, Nov 1996; Promotional edition from FAN magazine 2.00

SHI: THE SERIES
CRUSADE

❑1, Aug 1997 .... 3.50
❑1/A, Aug 1997; Sneak preview edition with photo cover with Tia Carrera; Sneak preview edition 3.50
❑2, Sep 1997 .... 3.00
❑3, Oct 1997 .... 3.00
❑4, Nov 1997 .... 3.00
❑5, Dec 1997 .... 3.00
❑6, Jan 1998 .... 2.95
❑7, Feb 1998; manga-style cover 2.95
❑8, Mar 1998 .... 2.95
❑9, Apr 1998 .... 2.95
❑9/A, Apr 1998; alternate cover (full moon in background) 2.95
❑9/B, Apr 1998; alternate cover (Shi on her back) 2.95
❑9/C, Apr 1998; alternate cover (manga-style) 2.95
❑10, May 1998 .... 2.95
❑10/A, May 1998; alternate cover (in water) 2.95
❑10/B, May 1998; alternate cover (cherry blossoms) 2.95
❑10/C, May 1998; alternate cover (drawing sword) 2.95
❑11, Jun 1998, b&w 2.95
❑12, Jul 1998 .... 2.95
❑13, Aug 1998 .... 2.95
❑14, Aug 1998 .... 2.95
❑15, Sep 1998 .... 2.95
❑16, Sep 1998 .... 2.95

SHI: THE WAY OF THE WARRIOR
CRUSADE

❑0.5 .... 3.00
❑0.5/Platinum 4.00
❑1, Mar 1994 .... 6.00
❑1/A, Mar 1994 .... 5.00
❑4-2; acetate cover 3.00
❑1/B, Mar 1994; "Fan Appreciation Edition" #1 with no logo on cover 8.00
❑1/C, Mar 1994; Commemorative edition from the 1994 San Diego Comic Con; Gold logo on cover 8.00
❑2, Jun 1994 .... 5.00
❑2/A, Jun 1994; Fan appreciation edition #2 .... 3.00
❑2/Ashcan, Jun 1994; Ashcan promotional edition of Shi: The Way of the Warrior #2 .... 5.00
❑2/B, Jun 1994; San Diego Comicon edition 6.00
❑3, Oct 1994 .... 4.00
❑4 1995 .... 4.00
❑5, Apr 1995 1: Tomoe. 3.00
❑5/Variant, Apr 1995 1: Tomoe. 5.00
❑6 1995 .... 3.00
❑6/A 1995; Fan Appreciation Edition . 3.00
❑6/Ashcan 1995; Commemorative edition from 1995 San Diego Comic Con 4.00
❑7, Mar 1996; back-up crossover with Lethargic Lad 3.00
❑7/Variant, Mar 1996; chromium edition; No cover price; back-up crossover with Lethargic Lad; limited to 5, 000 copies 4.00
❑8, Jun 1996 .... 3.00
❑8/A, Jun 1996; Combo Gold Club version; 5000 publisher; With certificate of Authenticity 5.00
❑9, Sep 1996 .... 3.00
❑10, Oct 1996; wraparound cover 3.00

N-MINT

❑11, Dec 1996 .... 3.00
❑12, Apr 1997; contains Angel Fire preview 3.00
❑Fan ed. 1, Jan 1995; Included with Fan magazine 1.00
❑Fan ed. 2; Overstreet Fan promotional edition #2 .... 1.00
❑Fan ed. 3; Overstreet Fan promotional edition #3 .... 1.00

SHI/VAMPIRELLA
CRUSADE

❑1, Oct 1997; crossover with Harris . 2.95

SHI VS. TOMOE
CRUSADE

❑1, Aug 1996; Foil wrap-around cover, color 3.95
❑1/Ltd., Aug 1996; Preview sold at San Diego Comic Con, black and white 5.00

SHI: YEAR OF THE DRAGON
CRUSADE

❑1, Sep 2000 .... 2.99

SHOCK & SPANK THE MONKEYBOYS SPECIAL
ARROW

❑1, b&w 2.50

SHOCKROCKETS
IMAGE

❑1, Apr 2000 .... 2.50
❑2, May 2000 .... 2.50
❑3, Jun 2000 .... 2.50
❑4, Jul 2000 .... 2.50
❑5, Aug 2000 .... 2.50
❑6, Oct 2000 .... 2.50

SHOCK SUSPENSTORIES (RCP)
GEMSTONE

❑1, Sep 1992; JO, JKa, GI (a); Reprints Shock SuspenStories #1; Ray Bradbury adaptation; Electrocution cover 2.00
❑2, Dec 1992; Reprints Shock SuspenStories #2 .... 2.00
❑3, Mar 1993; Reprints Shock SuspenStories #3 .... 2.00
❑4, Jun 1993; JO, WW, JKa (a); Reprints Shock SuspenStories #4 . 2.00
❑5, Sep 1993; JO, WW, JKa (a); Reprints Shock SuspenStories #5 . 2.00
❑6, Dec 1993; JO, WW, JKa, GI (w); JO, WW, JKa, GI (a); Reprints Shock SuspenStories #6 .... 2.00
❑7, Mar 1994; AF (c); JO, WW, JKa, GI (w); GE, JO, JK, WW, JKa, GI (a); Reprints Shock SuspenStories #7 . 2.00
❑8, Jun 1994; AF (c); GE, AW, WW, JKa (w); GE, AW, WW, JKa (a); Reprints Shock SuspenStories #8 .... 2.00
❑9, Sep 1994; JO, WW, JKa (w); JO, WW, JKa (a); Reprints Shock SuspenStories #9 .... 2.00
❑10, Dec 1994; JO, WW, JKa (w); JO, WW, JKa (a); Reprints Shock SuspenStories #10 .... 2.00
❑11, Mar 1995; Reprints Shock SuspenStories #11 .... 2.00
❑12, Jun 1995; Reprints Shock SuspenStories #12 .... 2.00
❑13, Sep 1995; Reprints Shock SuspenStories #13 .... 2.00
❑14, Dec 1995; Reprints Shock SuspenStories #14 .... 2.00
❑15, Mar 1996; GE, WW, JKa (w); GE, WW, JKa (a); Reprints Shock SuspenStories #15; Cannibalism story 2.00
❑16, Jun 1996; GE, JO, JKa (w); GE, JO, JKa (a); Reprints Shock SuspenStories #16 .... 2.00
❑17, Sep 1996; GE, JO, JKa (w); GE, JO, JKa (a); Reprints Shock SuspenStories #17 .... 2.50
❑18, Dec 1996; GE, BK, JKa (w); GE, BK, JKa (a); Reprints Shock SuspenStories #18 .... 2.50
❑Annual 1; Reprints Shock SuspenStories #1-5 .... 8.95
❑Annual 2; JO, WW, JKa, GI (w); JO, WW, JKa, GI (a); Reprints Shock SuspenStories #6-10 .... 9.95

A movie version of Billy Tucci's *Shi*, starring Tia Carrere, was in development a few years ago.

N-MINT

❑Annual 3; Reprints Shock SuspenStories #11-14 .... 8.95
❑Annual 4; GE, BK, JKa (w); GE, BK, JKa (a); Reprints Shock SuspenStories #15-18 .... 9.95

SHOCK THE MONKEY
MILLENNIUM

❑1 .... 2.95
❑2, b&w 3.95

SHOCK THERAPY
HARRIER

❑1, Nov 1986 .... 1.95
❑2, Dec 1986 .... 1.95
❑3, Jan 1987 .... 1.95
❑4, Feb 1987 .... 1.95
❑5, Mar 1987 .... 1.95

SHOGUN WARRIORS
MARVEL

❑1, Feb 1979 HT (a); 1: Shogun Warriors. 4.00
❑2, Mar 1979 .... 2.00
❑3, Apr 1979 .... 2.00
❑4, May 1979 .... 2.00
❑5, Jun 1979 .... 2.00
❑6, Jul 1979 .... 2.00
❑7, Aug 1979 .... 2.00
❑8, Sep 1979 .... 2.00
❑9, Oct 1979 .... 2.00
❑10, Nov 1979 .... 2.00
❑11, Dec 1979 .... 1.50
❑12, Jan 1980 .... 1.50
❑13, Feb 1980 .... 1.50
❑14, Mar 1980 .... 1.50
❑15, Apr 1980 .... 1.50
❑16, May 1980 D: Followers. 1.50
❑17, Jun 1980 .... 1.50
❑18, Jul 1980 .... 1.50
❑19, Aug 1980 A: Fantastic Four. 1.50
❑20, Sep 1980 A: Fantastic Four. 1.50

SHOJO ZEN
ZEN

❑1 .... 2.50

SHONEN JUMP
VIZ

❑0, Aug 2002; Promo give-away preview; Translated by Andy Nakatani and Bill Flanagan 5.00
❑1 2002; Giant anthology, reads back to front 4.95
❑2 2003; Giant anthology, reads back to front 4.95
❑3 2003; Giant anthology, reads back to front 4.95
❑4 2003; Giant anthology, reads back to front 4.95
❑5 2003; Giant anthology, reads back to front 4.95
❑6 2003; Giant anthology, reads back to front 4.95
❑7, Jul 2003; Giant anthology, reads back to front 4.95

SHOOTY BEAGLE
FANTAGRAPHICS / EROS

❑1, b&w 2.25
❑2, b&w 2.25
❑3, b&w 2.25

N-MINT

SHORT ON PLOT!
Mu

❑1, b&w 2.50

SHORT ORDER
Head

❑1 20.00
❑2, Jan 1974 15.00

SHORTS (PAT KELLEY'S...)
Antarctic

❑1, Oct 1997 2.95
❑2 2.95

SHORTSTOP SQUAD
Ultimate Sports Force

❑1, ca. 1999; Barry Larkin apperance 3.95

SHOTGUN MARY (1ST SERIES)
Antarctic

❑1, Sep 1995 4.00
❑1/CS, Sep 1995; CD edition 9.95
❑1/Variant, Sep 1995; alternate cover 2.95
❑2 1995 3.00
❑3 1995; Exists? 3.00
❑Ashcan 1, Sep 1995; ashcan edition 2.95

SHOTGUN MARY (2ND SERIES)
Antarctic

❑1, Mar 1998 2.95
❑1/Variant, Mar 1998; Limited edition cover (purple); Limited edition cover (purple) 4.00
❑2, May 1998 2.95
❑3, Jul 1998 2.95

SHOTGUN MARY: BLOOD LORE
Antarctic

❑1, Feb 1997 2.95
❑2, Apr 1997 2.95
❑3, Jun 1997 2.95
❑4, Aug 1997 2.95

SHOTGUN MARY: DEVILTOWN
Antarctic

❑1, Jul 1996 2.95
❑1/Ltd., ca. 1996; Commemorative edition 5.40

SHOTGUN MARY SHOOTING GALLERY
Antarctic

❑1, Jun 1996 2.95

SHOTGUN MARY: SON OF THE BEAST
Antarctic

❑1, Oct 1997 2.95

SHOUJO
Antarctic

❑1, Jun 2003 5.95
❑2, Aug 2003 5.95
❑3, Oct 2003 5.95

SHOWCASE
DC

❑1, Apr 1956; Fire Fighters 2850.00
❑2, Jun 1956; JKu, RH (a); Kings of Wild 800.00
❑3, Aug 1956; RH (a); Frogmen 775.00
❑4, Oct 1956; CI, JKu (a); O: Flash II (Barry Allen). 1: Flash II (Barry Allen). Begins DC Silver Age revival of heroes 26000.00
❑5, Dec 1956 MM (a); A: Manhunters. 925.00
❑6, Feb 1957 JK (c); JK (a); O: Challengers of the Unknown. 1: Challengers of the Unknown. 3600.00
❑7, Apr 1957 JK (c); JK (a); 2: Challengers of the Unknown. 1800.00
❑8, Jun 1957 CI (a); O: Captain Cold. 1: Captain Cold. 2: Flash II (Barry Allen). 11500.00
❑9, Aug 1957 RMo (a); A: Lois Lane. 7200.00
❑10, Oct 1957 A: Lois Lane. 2600.00
❑11, Dec 1957 JK (c); JK (a); A: Challengers of the Unknown. 1625.00
❑12, Feb 1958 JK (c); JK (a); A: Challengers of the Unknown. 1625.00
❑13, Apr 1958 CI (a); O: Mr. Element. 1: Mr. Element. A: Flash II (Barry Allen). 4200.00
❑14, Jun 1958, color; CI (a); O: Doctor Alchemy. 1: Doctor Alchemy. A: Flash II (Barry Allen). 4200.00
❑15, Aug 1958 1: Space Ranger. 1650.00
❑16, Oct 1958 2: Space Ranger. 900.00
❑17, Dec 1958 GK (c); O: Adam Strange. 1: Adam Strange. 2200.00
❑18, Feb 1959 GK (c); 1: Rann. 1100.00
❑19, Apr 1959 GK (c); A: Adam Strange. 1100.00
❑20, Jun 1959, 1: Rip Hunter. 850.00
❑21, Aug 1959 2: Rip Hunter. 450.00
❑22, Oct 1959 GK (a); O: Green Lantern II (Hal Jordan). 1: Green Lantern II (Hal Jordan). 1: Carol Ferris. 5600.00
❑23, Dec 1959 GK (a); 1: Invisible Destroyer. 1600.00
❑24, Feb 1960 GK (a); A: Green Lantern II. 1500.00
❑25, Apr 1960 JKu (a); A: Rip Hunter. 275.00
❑26, Jun 1960 JKu (a); A: Rip Hunter. 275.00
❑27, Aug 1960 RH (a); 1: Sea Devils. 700.00
❑28, Oct 1960 RH (a); 2: Sea Devils. 350.00
❑29, Dec 1960 RH (a); A: Sea Devils. 350.00
❑30, Feb 1961 O: Aquaman. 750.00
❑31, Apr 1961 A: Aquaman. 340.00
❑32, Jun 1961 A: Aquaman. 340.00
❑33, Aug 1961 A: Aquaman. 325.00
❑34, Oct 1961 GK (a); O: Atom II (Ray Palmer). 1: Atom II (Ray Palmer). 1250.00
❑35, Dec 1961 MA, GK (a); 2: Atom II (Ray Palmer). 650.00
❑36, Feb 1962 MA, GK (a); A: Atom II (Ray Palmer). 475.00
❑37, Apr 1962 1: Metal Men. 525.00
❑38, Jun 1962 A: Metal Men. 350.00
❑39, Aug 1962 1: Chemo. A: Metal Men. 300.00
❑40, Oct 1962 A: Metal Men. 300.00
❑41, Dec 1962 O: Tommy Tomorrow. 150.00
❑42, Feb 1963 A: Tommy Tomorrow. 150.00
❑43, Apr 1963; James Bond, Agent 007; movie adaptation 450.00
❑44, Jun 1963 A: Tommy Tomorrow. 100.00
❑45, Aug 1963 JKu (a); O: Sgt. Rock. 275.00
❑46, Oct 1963 A: Tommy Tomorrow. 95.00
❑47, Dec 1963 A: Tommy Tomorrow. 95.00
❑48, Feb 1964 A: Cave Carson. 65.00
❑49, Apr 1964 A: Cave Carson. 65.00
❑50, Jun 1964 MA, CI (a); A: King Faraday. 65.00
❑51, Aug 1964 MA, CI (a); A: King Faraday. 65.00
❑52, Oct 1964 A: Cave Carson. 65.00
❑53, Dec 1964 JKu, RH (a); A: G.I. Joe. 80.00
❑54, Feb 1965 JKu, RH (a); A: G.I. Joe. 80.00
❑55, Apr 1965; MA (a); O: Doctor Fate. Hourman 220.00
❑56, Jun 1965; MA (a); 1: Psycho-Pirate II (Roger Hayden). Doctor Fate, Hourman 100.00
❑57, Aug 1965 JKu (a); A: Enemy Ace. 120.00
❑58, Oct 1965 JKu (a); A: Enemy Ace. 120.00
❑59, Dec 1965 NC (a); A: Teen Titans. 115.00
❑60, Feb 1966 MA (a); O: The Spectre. 225.00
❑61, Apr 1966 MA (a); A: Spectre. 100.00
❑62, Jun 1966 JO (a); O: Inferior Five. 1: Earth-12. 1: Dumb Bunny. 1: Merryman. 1: Awkwardman. 1: Blimp. 1: White Feather. 1: Inferior Five. 70.00
❑63, Aug 1966 JO (a); A: Inferior Five. 40.00
❑64, Oct 1966 MA (a); A: Spectre. 110.00
❑65, Dec 1966; A: Inferior Five. X-Men parody 40.00
❑66, Feb 1967 1: B'wana Beast. 21.00
❑67, Apr 1967 A: B'wana Beast. 21.00
❑68, Jun 1967 A: Maniaks. 21.00
❑69, Aug 1967 A: Maniaks. 21.00
❑70, Oct 1967 A: Binky. 21.00
❑71, Dec 1967 A: Maniaks. 21.00
❑72, Feb 1968; ATh, JKu (a); A: Johnny Thunder. Trigger Twins, Texas Rangers 21.00
❑73, Apr 1968; SD (a); O: Creeper. 1: Creeper. Profiles of Don Segall and Steve Ditko 85.00
❑74, May 1968; 1: Anthro. Profile of Howie Post 38.00
❑75, Jun 1968 SD, DG (w); SD (a); O: Dove I (Don Hall). O: Hawk I (Hank Hall). 1: Dove I (Don Hall). 1: Hawk I (Hank Hall). 62.00
❑76, Aug 1968 1: Bat Lash. 45.00
❑77, Sep 1968 1: Angel & Ape. 45.00
❑78, Nov 1968 1: Jonny Double. 34.00
❑79, Dec 1968 1: Dolphin. 45.00
❑80, Feb 1969 NA (c); A: Phantom Stranger. 45.00
❑81, Mar 1969; Windy & Willy 30.00
❑82, May 1969 1: Nightmaster. 45.00
❑83, Jun 1969 BWr (a); A: Nightmaster. 40.00
❑84, Aug 1969 BWr (a); A: Nightmaster. 40.00
❑85, Sep 1969 JKu (a); A: Firehair. 12.00
❑86, Nov 1969 JKu (a); A: Firehair. 12.00
❑87, Dec 1969 JKu (a); A: Firehair. 12.00
❑88, Feb 1970; Jason's Quest 8.00
❑89, Mar 1970; Jason's Quest 8.00
❑90, May 1970 A: Manhunter 2070. 7.00
❑91, Jun 1970 A: Manhunter 2070. 7.00
❑92, Aug 1970 A: Manhunter 2070. 7.00
❑93, Sep 1970 A: Manhunter 2070. 7.00
❑94, Aug 1977 JSa, JA (a); O: Doom Patrol II. 1: Celsius. 1: Doom Patrol II. 10.00
❑95, Oct 1977 JSa, JA (a); A: The Doom Patrol. 8.00
❑96, Dec 1977 JSa, JA (a); A: The Doom Patrol. 8.00
❑97, Feb 1978 A: Power Girl. 5.00
❑98, Mar 1978 JSa (a); O: Power Girl. 5.00
❑99, Apr 1978 A: Power Girl. 5.00
❑100, May 1978; Double-size; JSa (a); all-star issue 5.00
❑101, Jun 1978 JK (c); AM, MA (a); A: Hawkman. 5.00
❑102, Jul 1978 JK (c); AM, MA (a); A: Hawkman. 5.00
❑103, Aug 1978 JK (c); AM, MA (a); A: Hawkman. 5.00
❑104, Sep 1978; OSS Spies 5.00

SHOWCASE '93
DC

❑1, Jan 1993; Catwoman, Cyborg, Blue Devil 2.25
❑2, Feb 1993; Catwoman, Cyborg, Blue Devil 2.25
❑3, Mar 1993; Catwoman, Flash, Blue Devil 2.25
❑4, Apr 1993; Catwoman, Geo-Force, Blue Devil 2.00
❑5, May 1993; Robin, Peacemaker, Blue Devil 2.00
❑6, Jun 1993; Robin, Peacemaker, Blue Devil 2.00
❑7, Jul 1993; Two-Face, Deathstroke, Jade, Obsidian, Peacemaker 2.50
❑8, Aug 1993; KJ (a); Two-Face, Batman, Deadshot, Fire and Ice 2.50
❑9, Sep 1993; JRo (w); Huntress, Peacemaker, Shining Knight 2.00
❑10, Oct 1993; Huntress, Deathstroke, Katana 2.00
❑11, Nov 1993; BMc (a); Nightwing, Robin, Kobra Kronicles 2.00
❑12, Dec 1993; KG, BMc (a); Nightwing, Robin, Green Lantern, Creeper 2.00

SHOWCASE '94
DC

❑1, Jan 1994; Joker, New Gods, Gunfire 1.95
❑2, Feb 1994; Joker 1.95
❑3, Mar 1994; Arkham Asylum, Blue Beetle, Psyba-Rats 1.95
❑4, Apr 1994; Arkham Asylum, Blue Beetle, Psyba-Rats 1.95
❑5, May 1994; Huntress, Loose Cannon, Bloodwynd 1.95
❑6, Jun 1994; Robin 1.95
❑7, Jul 1994; Penguin, Arsenal, Terrorsmith 1.95
❑8, Aug 1994; Scarface, Zero Hour Prelude 1.95

N-MINT

❑9, Sep 1994; Scarface, Zero Hour Prelude 1.95
❑10, Oct 1994; Azrael, Zero Hour, Black Condor 1.95
❑11, Nov 1994; Man-Bat, Starfire, Black Condor 1.95
❑12, Dec 1994 .... 1.95

SHOWCASE '95
DC

❑1, Jan 1995; Supergirl, Alan Scott, Argus 2.50
❑2, Feb 1995; Supergirl, Metal Men, Argus 2.50
❑3, Mar 1995; Eradicator, Claw, The Question 2.50
❑4, Apr 1995 .... 2.50
❑5, Jun 1995 .... 2.50
❑6, Jul 1995; Bibbo, Lobo, Science Police, Legionnaires 2.95
❑7, Aug 1995; Mongul, Arion, New Gods 2.95
❑8, Sep 1995; Mongul, Spectre, Arsenal 2.95
❑9, Oct 1995; Lois Lane, Lobo, Martian Manhunter 2.95
❑10, Nov 1995; Gangbuster, Ferrin Colos, Hi-Tech 2.95
❑11, Nov 1995; Agent Liberty; Arkham Asylum; Hi-Tech 2.95
❑12, Dec 1995; Supergirl, Maitresse, The Shade 2.95

SHOWCASE '96
DC

❑1, Jan 1996; Steel and Guy Gardner: Warrior, Aqualad, Metropolis S.C.U. 2.95
❑2, Feb 1996; Steel and Guy Gardner: Warrior, Circe, Metallo 2.95
❑3, Mar 1996; Lois Lane and Black Canary, Doctor Fate and The Shade, Lightray 2.95
❑4, Apr 1996; Guardian and Firebrand, Doctor Fate and The Shade, The Demon 2.95
❑5, Jun 1996; Green Arrow and Thorn, Doctor Fate and The Shade, New Gods 2.95
❑6, Jul 1996; Superboy and The Demon, Firestorm, The Atom 2.95
❑7, Aug 1996; Gangbuster and The Power of Shazam!, Fire, Firestorm 2.95
❑8, Sep 1996; Superboy and Superman, Legionnaires, Supergirl 2.95
❑9, Oct 1996; Shadowdragon and Lady Shiva, Doctor Light, Martian Manhunter 2.95
❑10, Nov 1996; Bibbo, Ultra Boy, Captain Comet 2.95
❑11, Dec 1996; Brainiac vs. Legion, Wildcat, Scare Tactics 2.95
❑12, Win 1996; Brainiac vs. Legion, Jesse Quick, King Faraday 2.95

SHRED
CFW

❑1 .... 2.25
❑2 .... 2.25
❑3 .... 2.25
❑4 .... 2.25
❑5 .... 2.25
❑6 .... 2.25
❑7 .... 2.25
❑8 .... 2.25

SHREK
DARK HORSE

❑1, Sep 2003 .... 2.99
❑2, Dec 2003 .... 2.99
❑3, Dec 2003 .... 2.99

SHRIEK
FANTACO

❑1, b&w 4.95
❑2, b&w 4.95
❑Special 1, b&w 3.50
❑Special 2, b&w; Dangerbrain 3.50
❑Special 3, b&w 3.50

N-MINT

SHRIKE
VICTORY

❑1, May 1987, b&w 1.50
❑2 .... 1.50

SHROUD, THE
MARVEL

❑1, Mar 1994 .... 1.75
❑2, Apr 1994 .... 1.75
❑3, May 1994 .... 1.75
❑4, Jun 1994 .... 1.75

SHUGGA
FANTAGRAPHICS / EROS

❑1, b&w 2.50
❑2, b&w 2.50

SHURIKEN (VICTORY)
VICTORY

❑1, Win 1985; Win-85 .... 1.50
❑2, Fal 1985; Fal-85 .... 1.50
❑3 .... 1.50
❑4, Nov 1986 .... 1.50
❑5 1987 .... 1.50
❑6, Feb 1987 .... 1.50
❑7, Mar 1987 .... 1.50
❑8, Apr 1987 .... 1.50

SHURIKEN (ETERNITY)
ETERNITY

❑1, Jun 1991, b&w 2.50
❑2, ca. 1991, b&w 2.50
❑3, ca. 1991, b&w 2.50
❑4, ca. 1991, b&w 2.50
❑5, ca. 1991, b&w 2.50
❑6, ca. 1992, b&w 2.50

SHURIKEN (BLACKTHORNE)
BLACKTHORNE

❑1 .... 7.95

SHURIKEN: COLD STEEL
ETERNITY

❑1, Jul 1989, b&w; 16 pgs. 1.50
❑2, Aug 1989 .... 1.95
❑3, Sep 1989 .... 1.95
❑4, Oct 1989 .... 1.95
❑5, Nov 1989 .... 1.95
❑6, Dec 1989 .... 1.95

SHURIKEN TEAM-UP
ETERNITY

❑1, ca. 1989, b&w; Shuriken, Libra, Kokutai 1.95

SHUT UP AND DIE!
IMAGE

❑1, Jan 1998 .... 2.95
❑2, Mar 1998 .... 2.95
❑3, May 1998 .... 2.95
❑4, Aug 1998 .... 2.95
❑5, ca. 1999 .... 2.95

SICK SMILES
AIIIE!

❑1, Jun 1994 .... 2.50
❑2, Jul 1994 .... 2.50
❑3, ca. 1994 .... 2.50
❑4, ca. 1994 .... 2.50
❑5, ca. 1994 .... 2.50
❑6, ca. 1995 .... 2.50
❑7, ca. 1995 .... 2.50
❑8, Apr 1995 .... 2.95

SIDEKICKS
FANBOY

❑1, Jun 2000 .... 2.75

SIDEKICKS: THE SUBSTITUTE
ONI

❑1, Jul 2002 .... 2.95

SIDE SHOW
MATURE MAGIC

❑1 .... 1.75

SIDESHOW COMICS
PAN GRAPHICS

❑1, b&w BT (a) 1.75
❑2, b&w 1.75
❑3 .... 1.75

Showcase was the testing ground for several Silver Age revivals of Golden Age characters.

© 1956 National Periodical Publications Inc. (DC).

N-MINT

❑4 .... 1.75
❑5 .... 1.75

SIEGE
IMAGE

❑1, Jan 1997 .... 2.50
❑2, Feb 1997 .... 2.50
❑3, Mar 1997 .... 2.50
❑4, Apr 1997 .... 2.50

SIEGEL AND SHUSTER: DATELINE 1930S
ECLIPSE

❑1, Nov 1984 .... 1.75
❑2, Sep 1985 .... 1.75

SIEGE OF THE ALAMO
TOME

❑1, Jul 1991, b&w 2.50

SIGHT UNSEEN
FANTAGRAPHICS

❑1, Apr 1997, b&w; collects story from The Stranger and The Philadelphia Weekly; wraparound cover 2.95

SIGIL
CROSSGEN

❑1, Jul 2000 .... 3.25
❑2, Aug 2000 .... 3.00
❑3, Sep 2000 .... 3.00
❑4, Oct 2000 .... 3.00
❑5, Nov 2000 .... 3.00
❑6, Dec 2000 .... 2.95
❑7, Jan 2001 .... 2.95
❑8, Feb 2001 .... 2.95
❑9, Mar 2001 .... 2.95
❑10, Apr 2001 .... 2.95
❑11, May 2001 .... 2.95
❑12, Jun 2001 .... 2.95
❑13, Jul 2001 .... 2.95
❑14, Aug 2001 .... 2.95
❑15, Sep 2001 .... 2.95
❑16, Oct 2001 .... 2.95
❑17, Nov 2001 .... 2.95
❑18, Dec 2001 .... 2.95
❑19, Jan 2002 .... 2.95
❑20, Feb 2002 .... 2.95
❑21, Mar 2002 .... 2.95
❑22, Apr 2002 .... 2.95
❑23, May 2002 .... 2.95
❑24, Jun 2002 .... 2.95
❑25, Jul 2002 .... 2.95
❑26, Aug 2002 .... 2.95
❑27, Sep 2002 .... 2.95
❑28, Oct 2002 .... 2.95
❑29, Nov 2002 .... 2.95
❑30, Dec 2002 .... 2.95
❑31, Jan 2003 .... 2.95
❑32, Feb 2003 .... 2.95
❑33, Mar 2003 .... 2.95
❑34, Apr 2003 .... 2.95
❑35, May 2003 .... 2.95
❑36, Jun 2003 .... 2.95
❑37, Jul 2003 .... 2.95
❑38, Aug 2003 .... 2.95
❑39, Oct 2003 .... 2.95
❑40, Nov 2003 .... 2.95
❑41, Nov 2003 .... 2.95
❑42, Dec 2003 .... 2.95

N-MINT

SIGMA
IMAGE

❑1, Apr 1996 .... 2.50
❑2, May 1996 .... 2.50
❑3, Jun 1996 .... 2.50

SILBUSTER
ANTARCTIC

❑1, Jan 1994 .... 2.95
❑2, Feb 1994 .... 2.95
❑3, Mar 1994 .... 2.95
❑4, Apr 1994 .... 2.95
❑5, Oct 1994 .... 2.95
❑6, Nov 1994 .... 2.95
❑7, Dec 1994 .... 2.95
❑8, Jan 1995 .... 2.95
❑9, Feb 1995 .... 2.95
❑10, Aug 1995 .... 2.95
❑11, Oct 1995 .... 2.95
❑12, Oct 1995 .... 2.95
❑13, Oct 1995 .... 2.95
❑14, Oct 1995 .... 2.95
❑15, May 1996 .... 2.95
❑16, Jul 1996 .... 2.95
❑17, Sep 1996 .... 2.95
❑18, Sep 1996 .... 2.95
❑19, Jan 1997 .... 2.95

SILENCERS (CALIBER)
CALIBER

❑1, Jul 1991, b&w 2.50
❑2 1991, b&w 2.50
❑3 1991, b&w 2.50
❑4 1991, b&w 2.50

SILENCERS (MOONSTONE)
MOONSTONE

❑1 2003 .... 3.50
❑2 2003 .... 3.50

SILENT CITY, THE
KITCHEN SINK

❑1, Oct 1995, b&w; oversized graphic novel 24.95

SILENT INVASION, THE
RENEGADE

❑1, Apr 1986, b&w 2.00
❑2, Jun 1986, b&w 2.00
❑3, Aug 1986, b&w 2.75
❑4, Oct 1986, b&w 2.75
❑5, Dec 1986, b&w 2.75
❑6, Feb 1987, b&w 2.75
❑7, May 1987, b&w 2.75
❑8, Jul 1987, b&w 2.75
❑9, Sep 1987, b&w 2.75
❑10, Nov 1987, b&w 2.75
❑11, Jan 1988, b&w 2.75
❑12, Mar 1988, b&w 2.75

SILENT INVASION, THE: ABDUCTIONS
CALIBER

❑1, May 1998, b&w 2.95

SILENT MOBIUS PART 1
VIZ

❑1, ca. 1991 .... 4.95
❑2, ca. 1991 .... 4.95
❑3, ca. 1991 .... 4.95
❑4, ca. 1991 .... 4.95
❑5, ca. 1991 .... 4.95
❑6, ca. 1991 .... 4.95

SILENT MOBIUS PART 2
VIZ

❑1, ca. 1992 .... 4.95
❑2, ca. 1992 .... 4.95
❑3, ca. 1992 .... 4.95
❑4, ca. 1992 .... 4.95
❑5, ca. 1992 .... 4.95

SILENT MOBIUS PART 3
VIZ

❑1, ca. 1992 .... 2.75
❑2, ca. 1992 .... 2.75
❑3, ca. 1992 .... 2.75
❑4, ca. 1992 .... 2.75
❑5, ca. 1992 .... 2.75

SILENT MOBIUS PART 4
VIZ

❑1, ca. 1992 .... 2.75
❑2, ca. 1992 .... 2.75
❑3, ca. 1992 .... 2.75
❑4, ca. 1992 .... 2.75
❑5, ca. 1992 .... 2.75

SILENT MOBIUS PART 5: INTO THE LABYRINTH
VIZ

❑1, May 1999 .... 2.95
❑2, Jun 1999 .... 2.95
❑3, Jul 1999 .... 2.95
❑4, Aug 1999 .... 2.95
❑5, Sep 1999 .... 2.95
❑6, Oct 1999 .... 2.95

SILENT MOBIUS PART 6: KARMA
VIZ

❑1, Nov 1999 .... 3.25
❑2, Dec 1999 .... 3.25
❑3, Jan 2000 .... 3.25
❑4, Feb 2000 .... 3.25
❑5, Mar 2000 .... 3.25
❑6, Apr 2000 .... 3.25
❑7, May 2000 .... 3.25

SILENT MOBIUS PART 7: CATASTROPHE
VIZ

❑1, Jun 2000 .... 2.95
❑2, Jul 2000 .... 2.95
❑3, Aug 2000 .... 2.95
❑4, Sep 2000 .... 2.95
❑5, Oct 2000 .... 2.95
❑6, Nov 2000 .... 2.95

SILENT MOBIUS PART 8: LOVE & CHAOS
VIZ

❑1, Dec 2000 .... 2.95
❑2, Jan 2000 .... 2.95
❑3, Feb 2000 .... 2.95
❑4, Mar 2001 .... 2.95
❑5, Apr 2001 .... 2.95
❑6, May 2001 .... 2.95
❑7, Jun 2001 .... 2.95

SILENT MOBIUS PART 9: ADVENT
VIZ

❑1, Jul 2001 .... 2.95
❑2, Aug 2001 .... 2.95
❑3, Sep 2001 .... 2.95
❑4, Oct 2001 .... 2.95
❑5, Nov 2001 .... 2.95
❑6, Dec 2001 .... 2.95

SILENT MOBIUS PART 10: TURNABOUT
VIZ

❑1, Jan 2002 .... 2.95
❑2, Feb 2002 .... 2.95
❑3, Mar 2002 .... 2.95
❑4, Apr 2002 .... 2.95
❑5, May 2002 .... 2.95
❑6, Jun 2002 .... 2.95

SILENT MOBIUS PART 11: BLOOD
VIZ

❑1, Jul 2002 .... 2.95
❑2, Aug 2002 .... 2.95
❑3, Sep 2002 .... 2.95
❑4, Oct 2002 .... 2.95
❑5, Nov 2002 .... 2.95

SILENT MOBIUS PART 12: HELL
VIZ

❑1, Dec 2002 .... 2.95
❑2, Jan 2003 .... 2.95

SILENT RAPTURE
AVATAR

❑1, ca. 1997 .... 3.00
❑2, ca. 1997 .... 3.00

SILENT SCREAMERS: NOSFERATU
IMAGE

❑1, Oct 2000 .... 4.95

SILENT WINTER/PINEAPPLEMAN
LIMELIGHT

❑1 .... 2.95

SILKE
DARK HORSE

❑1, Jan 2001 .... 2.95
❑2, Feb 2001 .... 2.99
❑3, Mar 2001 .... 2.99
❑4, Apr 2001 .... 2.99

SILKEN GHOST
CROSSGEN

❑1, Jun 2003 .... 2.95
❑2, Jul 2003 .... 2.95
❑3, Aug 2003 .... 2.95
❑4, Oct 2003 .... 2.95
❑5, Oct 2003 .... 2.95

SILLY-CAT
JOE CHIAPPETTA

❑1, Dec 1997 .... 1.00

SILLY DADDY
JOE CHIAPPETTA

❑1 .... 2.75
❑2, Sep 1995, b&w; flipbook with King Cat back-up 2.75
❑3 .... 2.75
❑4 .... 2.75
❑5 .... 2.75
❑6 .... 2.75
❑7 .... 2.75
❑8 .... 2.75
❑9 .... 2.75
❑10, Mar 1996, b&w 2.75
❑11 1996, b&w 2.75
❑12, b&w 2.75
❑13, b&w 2.75
❑14, b&w; no cover price 2.75
❑15 .... 2.75
❑16 .... 2.75
❑17 .... 2.75
❑18 .... 2.75

SILVER
COMICOLOR

❑1, Oct 1996 .... 2.00

SILVER AGE
DC

❑1, Jul 2000 .... 2.50
❑Giant Size 1, Jul 2000 .... 5.95

SILVER AGE: CHALLENGERS OF THE UNKNOWN
DC

❑1, Jul 2000 .... 2.50

SILVER AGE: DIAL H FOR HERO
DC

❑1, Jul 2000 .... 2.50

SILVER AGE: DOOM PATROL
DC

❑1, Jul 2000 .... 2.50

SILVER AGE: FLASH
DC

❑1, Jul 2000 .... 2.50

SILVER AGE: GREEN LANTERN
DC

❑1, Jul 2000 .... 2.50

SILVER AGE: JUSTICE LEAGUE OF AMERICA
DC

❑1, Jul 2000 .... 2.50

SILVER AGE SECRET FILES
DC

❑1, Jul 2000 .... 4.95

SILVER AGE: SHOWCASE
DC

❑1, Jul 2000 .... 2.50

N-MINT

SILVER AGE: TEEN TITANS
DC

❑1, Jul 2000 .... 2.50

SILVER AGE: THE BRAVE AND THE BOLD
DC

❑1, Jul 2000 .... 2.50

SILVERBACK
COMICO

❑1, Oct 1989 .... 2.50
❑2, Nov 1989 .... 2.50
❑3, Dec 1989 .... 2.50

SILVERBLADE
DC

❑1, Sep 1987 .... 1.25
❑2, Oct 1987 .... 1.25
❑3, Nov 1987 .... 1.25
❑4, Dec 1987 .... 1.25
❑5, Jan 1988 .... 1.25
❑6, Feb 1988 .... 1.25
❑7, Mar 1988 .... 1.25
❑8, May 1988 .... 1.25
❑9, Jun 1988 .... 1.25
❑10, Jul 1988 .... 1.25
❑11, Aug 1988 .... 1.25
❑12, Sep 1988 .... 1.25

SILVER CROSS
ANTARCTIC

❑1, Nov 1997 .... 2.95
❑2, Jan 1998 .... 2.95
❑3, Mar 1998 .... 2.95

SILVERFAWN
CALIBER

❑1 .... 1.95

SILVERHAWKS
MARVEL / STAR

❑1, Aug 1987 .... 1.00
❑2, Oct 1987 .... 1.00
❑3, Dec 1987 .... 1.00
❑4, Feb 1988 .... 1.00
❑5, Apr 1988 .... 1.00
❑6, Jun 1988 .... 1.00
❑7, Jul 1988 .... 1.00

SILVERHEELS
PACIFIC

❑1, Dec 1983 .... 1.50
❑2, Mar 1984 .... 1.50
❑3, May 1984 .... 1.50

SILVER SABLE
MARVEL

❑1, Jun 1992; Embossed cover 2.00
❑2, Jul 1992 .... 1.50
❑3, Aug 1992 .... 1.50
❑4, Sep 1992 .... 1.50
❑5, Oct 1992 .... 1.25
❑6, Nov 1992 A: Deathlok. 1.25
❑7, Dec 1992 A: Deathlok. 1.25
❑8, Jan 1993 .... 1.25
❑9, Feb 1993 O: Wild Pack. 1.25
❑10, Mar 1993 A: Punisher. 1.25
❑11, Apr 1993 .... 1.25
❑12, May 1993 .... 1.25
❑13, Jun 1993 .... 1.25
❑14, Jul 1993 .... 1.25
❑15, Aug 1993 .... 1.25
❑16, Sep 1993 .... 1.25
❑17, Oct 1993; A: New Outlaws. A: Baron Von Strucker. A: Crippler. Infinity Crusade crossover 1.25
❑18, Nov 1993 .... 1.25
❑19, Dec 1993 .... 1.25
❑20, Jan 1994 .... 1.25
❑21, Feb 1994 .... 1.25
❑22, Mar 1994 .... 1.25
❑23, Apr 1994 A: Daredevil. V: Deadpool. 1.25
❑24, May 1994 .... 1.50
❑25, Jun 1994; Giant-size 2.00
❑26, Jul 1994 .... 1.50
❑27, Aug 1994 .... 1.50
❑28, Sep 1994 .... 1.50
❑29, Oct 1994 .... 1.50
❑30, Nov 1994 .... 1.50
❑31, Dec 1994 .... 1.50
❑32, Jan 1995 .... 1.50
❑33, Feb 1995 .... 1.50
❑34, Mar 1995 .... 1.50
❑35, Apr 1995 .... 1.50

SILVER SCREAM
RECOLLECTIONS

❑1, b&w 2.00
❑2, b&w 2.00
❑3, b&w 2.00

SILVER STAR
PACIFIC

❑1, Feb 1983 .... 1.00
❑2, Apr 1983 .... 1.00
❑3, Jun 1983 .... 1.00
❑4, Aug 1983 .... 1.00
❑5, Nov 1983 .... 1.00
❑6, Jan 1984 .... 1.00

SILVER STAR (JACK KIRBY'S...)
TOPPS

❑1, Oct 1993; trading cards 2.95
❑2 .... 2.50
❑3 .... 2.50
❑4 .... 2.50

SILVERSTORM (AIRCEL)
AIRCEL

❑1 1990, b&w 2.25
❑2 1990, b&w 2.25
❑3, Jul 1990, b&w 2.25
❑4 1990, b&w 2.25

SILVERSTORM (SILVERLINE)
SILVERLINE

❑1, Oct 1998 .... 2.95
❑2 1999 .... 2.95
❑3 1999 .... 2.95
❑4 1999 .... 2.95

SILVER SURFER, THE (VOL. 1)
MARVEL

❑1, Aug 1968; Giant-size; SL (w); GC, JB (a); O: Silver Surfer. adaptation from Tales of Suspense #53 .... 375.00
❑2, Oct 1968; Giant-size; SL (w); JB (a); adaptation from Amazing Adult Fantasy #8 .... 160.00
❑3, Dec 1968; Giant-size; SL (w); JB (a); 1: Mephisto. A: Thor. adaptation from Amazing Adult Fantasy #7 .... 135.00
❑4, Feb 1969; Giant-size; SL (w); JB (a); Scarce; adaptation from Amazing Adult Fantasy #9 .... 255.00
❑5, Apr 1969; Giant-size; SL (w); JB (a); adaptation from Tales to Astonish #26 .... 70.00
❑6, Jun 1969; Giant-size; SL (w); JB (a); adaptation from Amazing Adult Fantasy #13 .... 70.00
❑7, Aug 1969; Giant-size; SL (w); JB (a); adaptation from Amazing Adult Fantasy #12 .... 70.00
❑8, Sep 1969 SL (w); JB (a) 80.00
❑9, Oct 1969 SL (w); JB (a) 60.00
❑10, Nov 1969 SL (w); JB (a) 53.00
❑11, Dec 1969 SL (w); JB (a) 53.00
❑12, Jan 1970 SL (w); JB (a) 53.00
❑13, Feb 1970 SL (w); JB (a) 53.00
❑14, Mar 1970 SL (w); JB (a); A: Spider-Man. 100.00
❑15, Apr 1970 SL (w); JB (a) 54.00
❑16, May 1970 SL (w); JB (a) 54.00
❑17, Jun 1970 SL (w); JB (a) 54.00
❑18, Sep 1970; SL (w); JK (a); A: Inhumans. Inhumans 54.00

SILVER SURFER, THE (VOL. 2)
MARVEL / EPIC

❑1, Dec 1988 SL (w) 3.00
❑2, Jan 1989 SL (w) 2.50

Some of Jerry Siegel and Joe Shuster's other, lesser-known work was reprinted in Eclipse's two-issue series.

© 1985 Eclipse Comics.

N-MINT

SILVER SURFER, THE (VOL. 3)
MARVEL

❑-1, Jul 1997; A: Stan Lee. Flashback 3.00
❑0.5, ca. 1998; Wizard promotional edition (mail-in) 3.00
❑0.5/Platinum, ca. 1998; Wizard promotional edition (mail-in) 6.00
❑1, Jul 1987; Double-size MR (a) 7.00
❑2, Aug 1987 .... 6.00
❑3, Sep 1987 .... 4.00
❑4, Oct 1987 A: Mantis. 4.00
❑5, Nov 1987 O: Skrulls. A: Mantis. 4.00
❑6, Dec 1987 .... 3.50
❑7, Jan 1988 .... 3.50
❑8, Feb 1988 .... 3.50
❑9, Mar 1988 .... 3.50
❑10, Apr 1988 .... 3.50
❑11, May 1988 JSa (a); 1: Reptyl. 3.00
❑12, Jun 1988 .... 3.00
❑13, Jul 1988 .... 3.00
❑14, Aug 1988 .... 3.00
❑15, Sep 1988 .... 4.00
❑16, Oct 1988 A: Fantastic Four. 3.00
❑17, Nov 1988 .... 3.00
❑18, Dec 1988 .... 3.00
❑19, Jan 1989 .... 3.00
❑20, Feb 1989 .... 3.00
❑21, Mar 1989 .... 3.00
❑22, Apr 1989 .... 3.00
❑23, May 1989 .... 3.00
❑24, Jun 1989 .... 3.00
❑25, Jul 1989; Giant-size V: new Super-Skrull. 3.50
❑26, Aug 1989 .... 2.50
❑27, Sep 1989 .... 2.50
❑28, Oct 1989 .... 2.50
❑29, Nov 1989 .... 2.50
❑30, Nov 1989 .... 2.50
❑31, Dec 1989; Giant-size 3.00
❑32, Dec 1989 .... 2.00
❑33, Jan 1990 .... 2.00
❑34, Feb 1990 A: Thanos. 5.00
❑35, Mar 1990; A: Thanos. Drax the Destroyer resurrected 3.50
❑36, Apr 1990 A: Thanos. 3.00
❑37, May 1990 A: Thanos. 3.00
❑38, Jun 1990 A: Thanos. A: Silver Surfer vs. Thanos. 3.00
❑39, Jul 1990 A: Thanos. 2.00
❑40, Aug 1990 .... 2.00
❑41, Sep 1990 .... 2.00
❑42, Oct 1990 .... 2.00
❑43, Nov 1990 .... 2.00
❑44, Dec 1990 .... 2.00
❑45, Jan 1991 .... 2.00
❑46, Feb 1991; A: Adam Warlock. Return of Adam Warlock 2.50
❑47, Mar 1991 A: Warlock. 2.50
❑48, Apr 1991 .... 2.00
❑49, May 1991 .... 2.00
❑50, Jun 1991; JSn (w); O: Silver Surfer. Silver embossed cover 5.00
❑50-2, Jun 1991; JSn (w); O: Silver Surfer. Silver embossed cover 2.00
❑50-3, Jun 1991; JSn (w); O: Silver Surfer. Silver embossed cover 2.00
❑51, Jul 1991 .... 2.00
❑52, Aug 1991 A: Firelord. A: Drax. 2.00
❑53, Aug 1991 .... 2.00

	N-MINT
❑54, Sep 1991	2.00
❑55, Sep 1991	2.00
❑56, Oct 1991	2.00
❑57, Oct 1991 A: Thanos.	2.00
❑58, Nov 1991	2.00
❑59, Nov 1991	2.00
❑60, Dec 1991	2.00
❑61, Jan 1992	2.00
❑62, Feb 1992	2.00
❑63, Mar 1992	2.00
❑64, Apr 1992	2.00
❑65, May 1992	2.00
❑66, Jun 1992 1: Avatar.	2.00
❑67, Jul 1992	2.00
❑68, Aug 1992	2.00
❑69, Aug 1992 1: Morg.	2.00
❑70, Sep 1992 O: Morg.	2.00
❑71, Sep 1992	2.00
❑72, Oct 1992	2.00
❑73, Oct 1992	2.00
❑74, Nov 1992	2.00
❑75, Nov 1992; D: Nova (female). silver foil cover	3.50
❑76, Dec 1992	1.50
❑77, Jan 1993	1.50
❑78, Feb 1993	1.50
❑79, Mar 1993	1.50
❑80, Apr 1993	1.50
❑81, May 1993	1.50
❑82, Jun 1993	1.75
❑83, Jul 1993	1.50
❑84, Aug 1993	1.50
❑85, Sep 1993; A: Wonder Man. A: Storm. A: Goddess. Infinity Crusade	1.50
❑85/CS, Sep 1993; A: Wonder Man. A: Storm. A: Goddess. "Dirtbag special"; Polybagged with Dirt #4; Infinity Crusade crossover	2.95
❑86, Oct 1993	1.50
❑87, Nov 1993	1.50
❑88, Jan 1994	1.50
❑89, Feb 1994	1.50
❑90, Mar 1994; Giant-size	1.95
❑91, Apr 1994	1.25
❑92, May 1994	1.50
❑93, Jun 1994	1.50
❑94, Jul 1994	1.50
❑95, Aug 1994 A: Fantastic Four.	1.50
❑96, Sep 1994 A: Fantastic Four. A: Hulk.	1.50
❑97, Oct 1994	1.50
❑98, Nov 1994	1.50
❑99, Dec 1994	1.50
❑100, Jan 1995; Giant-size	2.50
❑100/Variant, Jan 1995; Giant-size; enhanced cover	3.95
❑101, Feb 1995	1.50
❑102, Mar 1995	1.50
❑103, Apr 1995	1.50
❑104, May 1995	1.50
❑105, Jun 1995 V: Super-Skrull.	1.50
❑106, Jul 1995; Relinquishes Power Cosmic	1.50
❑107, Aug 1995	1.50
❑108, Sep 1995; Regains Power Cosmic	1.50
❑109, Oct 1995	1.50
❑110, Nov 1995	1.50
❑111, Dec 1995 GP (w)	1.50
❑112, Jan 1996	1.95
❑113, Feb 1996	1.95
❑114, Mar 1996 GP (w)	1.95
❑115, Apr 1996	1.95
❑116, May 1996	1.95
❑117, Jun 1996	1.95
❑118, Jul 1996	1.95
❑119, Aug 1996	1.95
❑120, Sep 1996	1.95
❑121, Oct 1996	1.95
❑122, Nov 1996 GP (w); V: Captain Marvel.	1.95
❑123, Dec 1996; Surfer returns to Earth	1.95
❑124, Jan 1997 A: Kymaera.	1.50
❑125, Feb 1997; Giant-size; V: Hulk. wraparound cover	2.99
❑126, Mar 1997 A: Doctor Strange.	1.99
❑127, Apr 1997	1.95
❑128, May 1997 A: Spider-Man, Daredevil.	1.99
❑129, Jun 1997	1.99
❑130, Aug 1997; gatefold summary	1.99
❑131, Sep 1997; gatefold summary	1.99
❑132, Oct 1997; gatefold summary	1.99
❑133, Nov 1997; gatefold summary A: Puppet Master.	1.99
❑134, Dec 1997; gatefold summary	1.99
❑135, Jan 1998; gatefold summary A: Agatha Harkness.	1.99
❑136, Feb 1998; gatefold summary	1.99
❑137, Mar 1998; gatefold summary A: Agatha Harkness.	1.99
❑138, Apr 1998; gatefold summary A: Thing.	1.99
❑139, May 1998; gatefold summary	1.99
❑140, Jun 1998; gatefold summary	1.99
❑141, Jul 1998; gatefold summary	1.99
❑142, Aug 1998; gatefold summary	1.99
❑143, Sep 1998; gatefold summary V: Psycho-Man.	1.99
❑144, Oct 1998; gatefold summary	1.99
❑145, Oct 1998; gatefold summary	1.99
❑146, Nov 1998; gatefold summary	1.99
❑Annual 1, ca. 1988	4.00
❑Annual 2, ca. 1989	3.00
❑Annual 3, ca. 1990	2.50
❑Annual 4, ca. 1991 O: The Silver Surfer.	2.50
❑Annual 5, ca. 1992 O: Nebula.	2.50
❑Annual 6, ca. 1993; 1: Legacy. A: Terrax. A: Jack of Hearts. A: Ronan the Accuser. A: Ganymede. trading card; Polybagged	2.95
❑Annual 7, ca. 1994	2.95
❑Annual 1997, ca. 1997; wraparound cover	2.99
❑Annual 1998, ca. 1998; gatefold summary; V: Millennius. Silver Surfer/Thor '98; wraparound cover	2.99

SILVER SURFER (VOL 4)
MARVEL

	N-MINT
❑1, Sep 2003	2.25
❑2, Dec 2003	2.99
❑3, Jan 2004	2.99
❑4, Feb 2004	2.99
❑5, Mar 2004	2.25
❑6, Apr 2004	2.25
❑7, May 2004	2.99
❑8, Jun 2004	2.99
❑9, Jul 2004	2.99
❑10, Aug 2004	2.99
❑11, Sep 2004	

SILVER SURFER (ONE-SHOT)
MARVEL

	N-MINT
❑1, Jun 1982 JBy, SL (w); JBy (a)	12.00

SILVER SURFER: DANGEROUS ARTIFACTS
MARVEL

	N-MINT
❑1, Jun 1996	3.95

SILVER SURFER: INNER DEMONS
MARVEL

	N-MINT
❑1, Apr 1998; collects Silver Surfer #123, 125, 126	3.50

SILVER SURFER: JUDGMENT DAY
MARVEL

	N-MINT
❑1, Oct 1988; hardcover	14.95

SILVER SURFER: LOFTIER THAN MORTALS
MARVEL

	N-MINT
❑1, Oct 1999	2.50
❑2, Nov 1999	2.50

SILVER SURFER/SUPERMAN
MARVEL

	N-MINT
❑1, Nov 1996; prestige format; crossover with DC	5.95

SILVER SURFER VS. DRACULA
MARVEL

	N-MINT
❑1, ca. 1994; Reprints Tomb of Dracula #50	1.75

SILVER SURFER/WARLOCK: RESURRECTION
MARVEL

	N-MINT
❑1, Mar 1993	2.50
❑2, Apr 1993	2.50
❑3, May 1993	2.50
❑4, Jun 1993	2.50

SILVER SURFER/WEAPON ZERO
MARVEL

	N-MINT
❑1, Apr 1997; crossover with Image	2.95

SILVER SWEETIE, THE
SPOOF

	N-MINT
❑1, b&w	2.95

SILVERWING SPECIAL
NOW

	N-MINT
❑1, Jan 1987	1.00

SIMON AND KIRBY CLASSICS
PURE IMAGINATION

	N-MINT
❑1, Nov 1986; new Vagabond Prince and reprints from Stuntman #1, All-New #13 and Green Hornet #39	2.00

SIMON CAT IN TAXI
SLAB-O-CONCRETE

	N-MINT
❑1; Post card comics	1.50

SIMPSON'S COMIC MADNESS
BONGO

	N-MINT
❑1, ca 2003	14.95

SIMPSONS COMICS
BONGO

	N-MINT
❑1, ca. 1993; Fantastic Four #1 homage cover; Bart Simpsons' Creepy Crawly Tales back-up	5.00
❑2, ca. 1994; V: Sideshow Bob. Patty & Selma's Ill-Fated Romance Comics back-up	4.00
❑3, ca. 1994; Krusty, Agent of K.L.O.W.N. back-up	3.00
❑4, ca. 1994; infinity cover; trading card; Gnarly Adventures of Busman back-up	3.00
❑5, ca. 1994; wraparound cover	3.00
❑6, ca. 1994; Chief Wiggum's Pre-Code Crime Comics back-up	2.50
❑7, ca. 1994; McBain Comics back-up	2.50
❑8, ca. 1995; Edna; Queen of the Jungle back-up	2.50
❑9, ca. 1995; Lisa's diary; Barney Gumble back-up	2.50
❑10, ca. 1995; Apu's Kwik-E Comics back-up	2.50
❑11, ca. 1995; evil Flanders; Homer on the Range back-up	2.25
❑12, ca. 1995; White-Knuckled War Stories back-up	2.25
❑13, ca. 1995; Jimbo Jones' Wedgie Comics back-up	2.25
❑14, ca. 1995; Cantankerous Coot Classics back-up	2.25
❑15, ca. 1995; Heinous Funnies back-up	2.25
❑16, ca. 1996; Bongo Grab Bag back-up	2.25
❑17, ca. 1996; Headlight Comics back-up	2.25
❑18, ca. 1996; Milhouse Comics back-up	2.25
❑19, ca. 1996; Roswell back-up	2.25
❑20, ca. 1996; Roswell back-up; Bad homage cover	2.25
❑21, ca. 1996; Roswell back-up	2.25
❑22, ca. 1996; Burns and Apu team up; Roswell back-up	2.25
❑23, ca. 1996; Reverend Lovejoy's Hellfire Comics back-up	2.25
❑24, ca. 1996; Li'l Homey back-up	2.25
❑25, ca. 1996; Marge gets her own talk show; Itchy & Scratchy back-up	2.25
❑26, ca. 1996; Speed parody	2.25
❑27, ca. 1996; Homer gets smart	2.25

N-MINT

- ❑28, ca. 1997; Krusty founds his own country 2.25
- ❑29, ca. 1997; Homer becomes a pro wrestler 2.25
- ❑30, ca. 1997; Burns clones Smithers 2.25
- ❑31, ca. 1997; Homer thinks he's Radioactive Man 2.25
- ❑32, ca. 1997; Krusty's coffee bar 2.95
- ❑33, ca. 1997; Alternate Springfield 2.25
- ❑34, ca. 1997; Burns sponsors Bart as a snowboarder 2.25
- ❑35, ca. 1998; Marge opens a daycare 2.25
- ❑36, ca. 1998; The return of the geeks 2.25
- ❑37, ca. 1998; El Grampo 2.25
- ❑38, ca. 1998; Burns makes addictive donuts 2.25
- ❑39, ca. 1998; Homer and Comic Book Guy on trial 2.25
- ❑40, ca. 1998; Krusty does live show from Simpsons house; Lard Lad back-up 2.50
- ❑41, ca. 1999 2.50
- ❑42, ca. 1999; The Homer Show; Slobberwacky back-up 2.50
- ❑43, ca. 1999; story told backwards; Poochie back-up 2.50
- ❑44, ca. 1999; Lisa substitutes; Bartman back-up 2.50
- ❑45, ca. 1999; Hot Dog On A Schtick 2.50
- ❑46, ca. 1999 A: Sideshow Bob. 2.50
- ❑47, ca. 2000 2.50
- ❑48, ca. 2000 2.50
- ❑49, ca. 2000 2.50
- ❑50, ca. 2000; Giant-size 2.50
- ❑51, ca. 2000; Cletus back-up 2.50
- ❑52, ca. 2000 2.50
- ❑53, ca. 2000; Ned Flanders back-up 2.50
- ❑54, ca. 2000 2.50
- ❑55, ca. 2001 2.50
- ❑55-2, ca 2001 2.50
- ❑56, ca. 2001 2.50
- ❑56-2, ca 1002 2.50
- ❑57, ca. 2001 2.50
- ❑58, ca. 2001 2.50
- ❑59, ca. 2001 2.50
- ❑60, ca. 2001 2.50
- ❑61, ca. 2001 2.50
- ❑62, ca. 2001 2.50
- ❑63, ca. 2001 2.50
- ❑64, ca. 2001 2.50
- ❑65 2.50
- ❑66, ca. 2002 2.50
- ❑67, ca. 2002 2.50
- ❑68, ca. 2002 2.50
- ❑69, ca. 2002 2.50
- ❑70, ca. 2002 2.50
- ❑71, ca. 2002 2.50
- ❑72, ca. 2002 2.50
- ❑73, ca. 2002 2.50
- ❑74, ca. 2002 2.50
- ❑75, ca. 2002 2.50
- ❑76, ca. 2002 2.50
- ❑77 2.50
- ❑78, ca. 2003 2.50
- ❑79, ca. 2003 2.50
- ❑80, ca. 2003 2.50
- ❑81, ca. 2003 2.50
- ❑82, ca. 2003 2.50
- ❑83, Jun 2003 2.50
- ❑84, Jul 2003 2.50
- ❑85, Aug 2003 2.99
- ❑86, Sep 2003 2.99
- ❑87, Oct 2003 2.99
- ❑88, Nov 2003 2.99
- ❑89, Dec 2003 2.99
- ❑90, Jan 2004 2.99
- ❑91, Feb 2004 2.99
- ❑92, Mar 2004 2.99
- ❑93, Apr 2004 2.99
- ❑94, May 2004 2.99
- ❑95, Jun 2004 2.99

N-MINT

SIMPSONS COMICS AND STORIES
WELSH

- ❑1, ca. 1993; O: Bartman. 1: The Simpsons. with poster 4.00

SIMPSONS COMICS (MAGAZINE)
BONGO

- ❑1, Mar 1997 4.00
- ❑2, Apr 1997 3.25
- ❑3, May 1997 3.25
- ❑4, Jun 1997 3.25
- ❑5, Jul 1997 3.25
- ❑6, Aug 1997 3.25
- ❑7, Sep 1997 3.25
- ❑8, Oct 1997 3.25
- ❑9, Nov 1997 3.25
- ❑10, Dec 1997 3.25
- ❑11, Jan 1998 3.25
- ❑12, Feb 1998 3.25
- ❑13, Mar 1998 3.25
- ❑14, Apr 1998 3.25
- ❑15, May 1998 3.25
- ❑16, Jun 1998 3.25
- ❑17, Jul 1998 3.25
- ❑18, Aug 1998 3.25
- ❑19, Sep 1998 3.25
- ❑20, Oct 1998 3.25
- ❑21, Nov 1998 3.25
- ❑22, Dec 1998 3.25
- ❑23, Jan 1999 3.25
- ❑24, Feb 1999 3.25
- ❑25, Mar 1999; Reprints Bartman #1 3.25

SIMPSONS COMICS PRESENTS BART SIMPSON
BONGO

- ❑1 2000 2.50
- ❑2 2000 2.50
- ❑3 2001 2.50
- ❑4 2001 2.50
- ❑5 2001 2.50
- ❑6 2001 2.50
- ❑7 2002 2.50
- ❑8 2002 2.50
- ❑9 2002 2.50
- ❑10 2002 2.50
- ❑11 2003 2.50
- ❑12 2003 2.50
- ❑13, Sep 2003 2.99
- ❑14, Oct 2003 2.99
- ❑15, Dec 2003 2.99
- ❑16, Feb 2004 2.99
- ❑17, Apr 2004 2.99
- ❑18, Jun 2004 2.99

SIMULATORS, THE
NEATLY CHISELED FEATURES

- ❑1 2.50

SIN
TRAGEDY STRIKES

- ❑1, b&w 2.95
- ❑2, b&w 2.95
- ❑3, b&w 2.95

SINBAD
ADVENTURE

- ❑1, Nov 1989, b&w; cardstock cover 2.25
- ❑2, Dec 1989, b&w; cardstock cover 2.25
- ❑3, Jan 1990, b&w; cardstock cover 2.25
- ❑4, Mar 1990, b&w 2.25

SINBAD BOOK II
ADVENTURE

- ❑1, Mar 1991, b&w 2.50
- ❑2, Apr 1991, b&w 2.50
- ❑3, May 1991, b&w 2.50
- ❑4, Jun 1991, b&w 2.50

SIN CITY (COZMIC)
COZMIC

- ❑1 1.50

SIN CITY: A DAME TO KILL FOR
DARK HORSE

- ❑1-2, Jul 1994 2.95
- ❑1, Nov 1993, b&w FM (w); FM (a) 3.50

The Silver Surfer's origin was recounted in the first issue of his first solo series.

© 1968 Marvel Comics.

N-MINT

- ❑2, Jan 1994, b&w FM (w); FM (a) 3.25
- ❑3, Feb 1994, b&w FM (w); FM (a) 3.00
- ❑4, Mar 1994, b&w FM (w); FM (a) 3.00
- ❑5, Apr 1994, b&w FM (w); FM (a) 3.00
- ❑6, May 1994, b&w FM (w); FM (a) 3.00

SIN CITY: FAMILY VALUES
DARK HORSE

- ❑1, Oct 1997, b&w FM (w); FM (a) 15.00
- ❑1/A, Oct 1997; FM (w); FM (a); Cover has Roller-skating girl 15.00

SIN CITY: HELL AND BACK
DARK HORSE / MAVERICK

- ❑1, Jul 1999, b&w; cardstock cover 2.95
- ❑2, Aug 1999, b&w; cardstock cover 2.95
- ❑3, Sep 1999, b&w; cardstock cover 2.95
- ❑4, Oct 1999, b&w; cardstock cover 2.95
- ❑5, Nov 1999, b&w; cardstock cover 2.95
- ❑6, Dec 1999, b&w; cardstock cover 2.95
- ❑7, Jan 2000, b&w; cardstock cover 2.95
- ❑8, b&w; cardstock cover 2.95
- ❑9, Apr 2000, b&w; cardstock cover 2.95

SIN CITY: JUST ANOTHER SATURDAY NIGHT
DARK HORSE

- ❑0.5, Aug 1997; Wizard promotional edition FM (w); FM (a) 3.00
- ❑1, Oct 1998, b&w FM (w); FM (a) 2.50

SIN CITY: LOST, LONELY, & LETHAL
DARK HORSE / LEGEND

- ❑1, Dec 1996; Cardstock cover; b&w and blue 2.95

SIN CITY: SEX & VIOLENCE
DARK HORSE

- ❑1, Mar 1997, b&w; cardstock cover 2.95

SIN CITY: SILENT NIGHT
DARK HORSE / LEGEND

- ❑1, Nov 1995, b&w; cardstock cover 2.95

SIN CITY: THAT YELLOW BASTARD
DARK HORSE / LEGEND

- ❑1, Feb 1996 2.95
- ❑2, Mar 1996 2.95
- ❑3, Apr 1996 2.95
- ❑4, May 1996 2.95
- ❑5, Jun 1996 2.95
- ❑6, Jul 1996 2.95

SIN CITY: THE BABE WORE RED AND OTHER STORIES
DARK HORSE

- ❑1, Nov 1994, color 2.95

SIN CITY: THE BIG FAT KILL
DARK HORSE

- ❑1, Nov 1994, b&w 2.95
- ❑2, Dec 1994, b&w; cardstock cover 2.95
- ❑3, Jan 1995, b&w; cardstock cover 2.95
- ❑4, Feb 1995, b&w; cardstock cover 2.95
- ❑5, Mar 1995, b&w; cardstock cover 2.95

SINDY
FORBIDDEN FRUIT

- ❑1, b&w 2.95
- ❑2, b&w 2.95
- ❑3, b&w 2.95
- ❑4, b&w 2.95
- ❑5, b&w 2.95

N-MINT

SINERGY
CALIBER

- ❑1, ca. 1994, b&w 2.95
- ❑1/Ltd., ca. 1994; limited edition 5.95
- ❑2, ca. 1994, b&w 2.95
- ❑2/Ltd., ca. 1994; limited edition 5.95
- ❑3, ca. 1994, b&w 2.95
- ❑3/Ltd., ca. 1994; limited edition 5.95
- ❑4, ca. 1994, b&w 2.95
- ❑4/Ltd., ca. 1994; limited edition 5.95
- ❑5, ca. 1994, b&w 2.95
- ❑5/Ltd., ca. 1994; limited edition 5.95

SINISTER HOUSE OF SECRET LOVE, THE
DC

- ❑1, Oct 1971 .... 70.00
- ❑2, Dec 1971 JO (w); TD (a) 35.00
- ❑3, Feb 1972 .... 45.00
- ❑4, Apr 1972; TD (a); Series continued in Secrets of Sinister House #5 .... 35.00

SINISTER ROMANCE
HARRIER

- ❑1, b&w 2.00
- ❑2, b&w 2.00
- ❑3, b&w 1.95
- ❑4, b&w 1.95

SINJA: DEADLY SINS
LIGHTNING

- ❑1 .... 3.00
- ❑1/A; Commemorative edition 5.95
- ❑1/B; Nude edition 9.95

SINJA: RESURRECTION
LIGHTNING

- ❑1, Aug 1996; flipbook with Kunoichi #1; indicia says Sinja: Resurrection; cover says Kunoichi 3.00

SINNAMON (VOL. 1)
CATFISH

- ❑1, Dec 1995 .... 2.50

SINNAMON (VOL. 2)
CATFISH

- ❑1 1996 .... 2.75
- ❑2 1996 .... 2.75
- ❑3 1996 .... 2.75
- ❑4 1996 .... 2.75
- ❑4/Variant 1996; Variant cover edition (500 printed) 5.00
- ❑5 1996 .... 2.75
- ❑5/Variant 1996; Variant cover edition (500 printed) 4.00
- ❑6 1996 .... 2.75
- ❑7 1996 .... 2.75
- ❑8 1996; Sinnamon vs. Aerobica 2.75

SINNER
FANTAGRAPHICS

- ❑1 .... 2.95
- ❑2 .... 2.95
- ❑3 .... 2.95
- ❑4 .... 2.95
- ❑5 .... 2.95

SINNERS, THE
DC / PIRANHA

- ❑1 .... 9.95

SINNIN!
FANTAGRAPHICS / EROS

- ❑1, b&w 2.25
- ❑2, b&w 2.25

SIN OF THE MUMMY
FANTAGRAPHICS / EROS

- ❑1, b&w 2.50

SINS OF YOUTH: AQUABOY/LAGOON MAN
DC

- ❑1, May 2000 .... 2.50

SINS OF YOUTH: BATBOY AND ROBIN
DC

- ❑1, May 2000 .... 2.50

N-MINT

SINS OF YOUTH: JLA, JR.
DC

- ❑1, May 2000 .... 2.50

SINS OF YOUTH: KID FLASH/IMPULSE
DC

- ❑1, May 2000 .... 2.50

SINS OF YOUTH SECRET FILES
DC

- ❑1, May 2000 .... 4.95

SINS OF YOUTH: STARWOMAN AND THE JSA (JUNIOR SOCIETY)
DC

- ❑1, May 2000 .... 2.50

SINS OF YOUTH: SUPERMAN, JR./SUPERBOY, SR.
DC

- ❑1, May 2000 .... 2.50

SINS OF YOUTH: THE SECRET/DEADBOY
DC

- ❑1, May 2000 .... 2.50

SINS OF YOUTH: WONDER GIRLS
DC

- ❑1, May 2000 .... 2.50

SINTHIA
LIGHTNING

- ❑1/A, Oct 1997 .... 2.95
- ❑1/B, Oct 1997; alternate cover 2.95
- ❑1/Platinum, Oct 1997; Platinum edition 4.00
- ❑2/A, Jan 1998 .... 3.00
- ❑2/B, Jan 1998 .... 3.00

SIR CHARLES BARKLEY AND THE REFEREE MURDERS
HAMILTON

- ❑1, ca. 1993 .... 9.95

SIREN (MALIBU)
MALIBU / ULTRAVERSE

- ❑0, Sep 1995; Black September; #Infinity 1.50
- ❑0/A, Sep 1995; alternate cover 1.50
- ❑1, Oct 1995 .... 1.50
- ❑2, Nov 1995 .... 1.50
- ❑3, Dec 1995; continues in Siren Special #1 .... 1.50
- ❑Special 1, Feb 1996 .... 1.95

SIREN: SHAPES
IMAGE

- ❑1, May 1998 .... 2.95
- ❑2, Sep 1998 .... 2.95
- ❑3, Nov 1998 .... 2.95

SIRENS OF THE LOST WORLD
COMAX

- ❑1, b&w 2.95

SIRIUS GALLERY
SIRIUS

- ❑1, ca. 1997 .... 3.00
- ❑2, Apr 1999; cardstock cover; pin-ups 3.00
- ❑3, Jun 2000; no cover price; pin-ups 3.00

SISTER ARMAGEDDON
DRACULINA

- ❑1 1: Sister Armageddon. 2.75
- ❑2, b&w 2.75
- ❑3, b&w 3.00
- ❑4 .... 3.00

SISTERHOOD OF STEEL
MARVEL / EPIC

- ❑1, Dec 1984 .... 2.00
- ❑2, Feb 1985 .... 2.00
- ❑3, Apr 1985 .... 2.00
- ❑4, Jun 1985 .... 2.00
- ❑5, Aug 1985 .... 2.00
- ❑6, Oct 1985 .... 2.00
- ❑7, Dec 1985 .... 2.00
- ❑8, Feb 1986 .... 2.00

N-MINT

SISTER RED
COMICSONE

- ❑1, Feb 2004 .... 9.95
- ❑2, Apr 2004 .... 9.95

SISTERS OF DARKNESS
ILLUSTRATION

- ❑1/A 1997; Adult cover 3.25
- ❑1/B 1997; tame cover 3.25
- ❑2/A 1997; Adult cover 3.25
- ❑2/B 1997; tame cover 3.25
- ❑3, Aug 1997 .... 3.25

SISTERS OF MERCY
MAXIMUM

- ❑1, Dec 1995 .... 2.50
- ❑1/A, Dec 1995; alternate cover 2.50
- ❑2 1996 .... 2.50
- ❑3 1996 .... 2.50
- ❑4 1996 .... 2.50
- ❑5 1996 .... 2.50

SISTERS OF MERCY (VOL. 2)
LONDON NIGHT

- ❑0, Mar 1997 .... 1.50

SISTERS OF MERCY: WHEN RAZORS CRY CRIMSON TEARS
NO MERCY

- ❑1, Oct 1996 .... 2.50

SISTER VAMPIRE
ANGEL

- ❑1 .... 2.95

6, THE
VIRTUAL

- ❑1, Oct 1996 .... 2.50
- ❑2, Nov 1996 .... 2.50
- ❑3, Dec 1996 .... 2.50

6, THE: LETHAL ORIGINS
VIRTUAL

- ❑1, May 1996; digest 3.99

SIX DEGREES
HERETIC

- ❑1, b&w 3.50
- ❑1/Autographed 6.00
- ❑2, b&w 2.95
- ❑3, b&w 2.95
- ❑4, b&w 2.95
- ❑5, b&w 2.95

SIX FROM SIRIUS
MARVEL / EPIC

- ❑1, Jul 1984 PG (a) 2.00
- ❑2, Aug 1984 PG (a) 2.00
- ❑3, Sep 1984 PG (a) 2.00
- ❑4, Oct 1984 PG (a) 2.00

SIX FROM SIRIUS 2
MARVEL / EPIC

- ❑1, Feb 1986 PG (a) 2.00
- ❑2, Mar 1986 PG (a) 2.00
- ❑3, Apr 1986 PG (a) 2.00
- ❑4, May 1986 PG (a) 2.00

SIX-GUN HEROES (CHARLTON)
CHARLTON

- ❑40, ca. 1956 .... 55.00
- ❑41, ca. 1956 .... 48.00
- ❑42, ca. 1957 .... 48.00
- ❑43, ca. 1957 .... 48.00
- ❑44, ca. 1957 .... 48.00
- ❑45, ca. 1957 .... 48.00
- ❑46, ca. 1957 .... 48.00
- ❑47, Jul 1958 .... 48.00
- ❑48, Sep 1958 .... 48.00
- ❑49, Nov 1958 .... 48.00
- ❑50, Feb 1959 .... 48.00
- ❑51, ca. 1959 .... 32.00
- ❑52, Jul 1959 .... 32.00
- ❑53, Sep 1959 .... 32.00
- ❑54, Nov 1959 .... 32.00
- ❑55, Jan 1959 .... 32.00
- ❑56, Mar 1960 .... 32.00
- ❑57, May 1960 .... 32.00
- ❑58, Jul 1960 .... 32.00

	N-MINT
❑59, Sep 1960	32.00
❑60, Nov 1960	32.00
❑61, Jan 1961	22.00
❑62, Mar 1961	22.00
❑63, May 1961	22.00
❑64, Jul 1961	22.00
❑65, Sep 1961	22.00
❑66, Dec 1961	22.00
❑67, ca. 1962	22.00
❑68, ca. 1962	22.00
❑69, Jul 1962; Gunmaster, Wyatt Earp, and Annie Oakley	22.00
❑70, Sep 1962	22.00
❑71, Nov 1962	16.00
❑72, Jan 1963	16.00
❑73, Mar 1963	16.00
❑74, May 1963	16.00
❑75, Jul 1963	16.00
❑76, Sep 1963	16.00
❑77, Nov 1963; Gunmaster, Wyatt Earp, and Annie Oakley	16.00
❑78, Jan 1964	16.00
❑79, Mar 1964	16.00
❑80, Sep 1964	16.00
❑81, Nov 1964	16.00
❑82, Jan 1965	16.00
❑83, Mar 1965	16.00

SIX MILLION DOLLAR MAN, THE
CHARLTON

❑1, Jun 1976 JSa (a); O: The Six Million Dollar Man. 1: The Six Million Dollar Man (in comics).	12.00
❑2, Aug 1976; JSa (a); Nicola Cuti, Joe Staton credits; Action figure tie-in .	6.00
❑3, Oct 1976; JSa (a); Nicola Cuti, Joe Staton credits	5.00
❑4, Dec 1977	5.00
❑5, Oct 1977	5.00
❑6, Feb 1978	4.00
❑7, Mar 1978; Boyette and Himes credits	4.00
❑8, May 1978	4.00
❑9, Jun 1978	4.00

SIX MILLION DOLLAR MAN, THE (MAGAZINE)
CHARLTON

❑1	10.00
❑2	8.00
❑3	5.00
❑4	5.00
❑5	5.00
❑6	5.00
❑7	5.00

666: THE MARK OF THE BEAST
FLEETWAY-QUALITY

❑1, ca. 1986	2.50
❑2, ca. 1986	2.00
❑3, ca. 1986	2.00
❑4, ca. 1986	2.00
❑5, ca. 1986	2.00
❑6, ca. 1986	2.00
❑7, ca. 1986	2.00
❑8, ca. 1986	2.00
❑9, ca. 1986	2.00
❑10, ca. 1987	2.00
❑11, ca. 1987	2.00
❑12, ca. 1987; AMo (w); Alan Moore special	2.00
❑13, ca. 1987	2.00
❑14, ca. 1987	2.00
❑15, ca. 1987	2.00
❑16, ca. 1987	2.00
❑17, ca. 1987	2.00
❑18, ca. 1987	2.00

SIX STRING SAMURAI
AWESOME

❑1, Sep 1998	2.95

SIXTY NINE
FANTAGRAPHICS / EROS

❑1, ca. 1993	2.75
❑2	2.75

	N-MINT
❑3	2.75
❑4, Jul 1994, b&w	2.75

SIZZLE THEATRE
SLAVE LABOR

❑1, Aug 1991, b&w	2.50

SIZZLIN' SISTERS
FANTAGRAPHICS / EROS

❑1 1997	2.95
❑2, Aug 1997	2.95

SKATEMAN
PACIFIC

❑1, Nov 1983	1.50

SKELETON GIRL
SLAVE LABOR

❑1, Dec 1995	2.95
❑2, Apr 1996	2.95
❑3, Sep 1996	2.95

SKELETON HAND
AVALON

❑1	2.99

SKELETON KEY
AMAZE INK

❑1, Jul 1995	2.00
❑2, Aug 1995	2.00
❑3, Sep 1995	2.00
❑4, Oct 1995	2.00
❑5, Nov 1995	2.00
❑6, Dec 1995	2.00
❑7, Jan 1996	2.00
❑8, Feb 1996	2.00
❑9, Mar 1996	2.00
❑10, Apr 1996	2.00
❑11, May 1996	1.75
❑12, Jun 1996	1.75
❑13, Jul 1996	1.75
❑14, Aug 1996	1.75
❑15, Sep 1996; cover says Aug, indicia says Sep	1.75
❑16, Oct 1996	1.75
❑17, Nov 1996	1.75
❑18, Dec 1996	1.75
❑19, Jan 1997	1.75
❑20, Feb 1997	1.75
❑21, Mar 1997	1.75
❑22, Apr 1997	1.75
❑23, May 1997	1.75
❑24, Jun 1997	1.75
❑25, Jul 1997	1.75
❑26, Aug 1997	1.75
❑27, Sep 1997	1.75
❑28, Oct 1997	1.75
❑29, Nov 1997	1.75
❑30, Dec 1997	1.75

SKELETON WARRIORS
MARVEL

❑1, Apr 1995	1.50
❑2, May 1995	1.50
❑3, Jun 1995	1.50
❑4, Jul 1995	1.50

SKETCHBOOK SERIES, THE
TUNDRA

❑1; Melting Pot	3.95
❑2; Totleben	3.95
❑3; Zulli	3.95
❑4	3.95
❑5	3.95
❑6; Screaming Masks	3.95
❑7	3.95
❑8; Forg	3.95
❑9	3.95
❑10	4.95

SKIDMARKS
TUNDRA

❑0, b&w	2.95
❑1, b&w	2.95
❑2, b&w	2.95
❑3, b&w	2.95

Wonder Woman and Wonder Girl switched ages in *Sins of Youth: Wonder Girls.*

© 2000 DC Comics.

SKIM LIZARD
PUPPY TOSS

	N-MINT
❑1	2.95

SKIN
TUNDRA

❑1	8.95

SKIN GRAFT
ICONOGRAFIX

❑1, b&w	3.50

SKIN GRAFT: THE ADVENTURES OF A TATTOOED MAN
DC / VERTIGO

❑1, Jul 1993	2.50
❑2, Aug 1993	2.50
❑3, Sep 1993	2.50
❑4, Oct 1993	2.50

SKINHEADS IN LOVE
FANTAGRAPHICS / EROS

❑1, b&w	2.25

SKINNERS
IMAGE

❑1/A	2.95
❑1/B	2.95
❑1/C	2.95

SKIN13
EXPRESS / PARODY

❑0.5/A, Oct 1995, b&w; Amazing SKIN Thir-Teen; reprints Skin13 #1	2.50
❑0.5/B, Oct 1995, b&w; Barbari-SKIN; reprints Skin13 #1	2.50
❑0.5/C, Oct 1995, b&w; SKIN-et Jackson; reprints Skin13 #1	2.50
❑0.5/A-2	2.50
❑0.5/B-2	2.50
❑0.5/C-2	2.50
❑1/A, b&w	2.50
❑1/B, b&w; Heavy Metal-style cover ..	2.50
❑1/C, b&w; Spider-Man #1-style cover	2.50

SKIZZ
FLEETWAY-QUALITY

❑1	1.95
❑2	1.95
❑3	1.95

SKREEMER
DC

❑1, May 1989	2.00
❑2, Jun 1989	2.00
❑3, Jul 1989	2.00
❑4, Aug 1989	2.00
❑5, Sep 1989	2.00
❑6, Oct 1989	2.00

SKROG
COMICO

❑1, b&w	1.50

SKROG (YIP, YIP, YAY) SPECIAL
CRYSTAL

❑1, b&w	2.50

SKRULL KILL KREW
MARVEL

❑1, Sep 1995; cardstock cover	2.95
❑2, Oct 1995; cardstock cover	2.95
❑3, Nov 1995; cardstock cover	2.95
❑4, Dec 1995; cardstock cover	2.95
❑5, Jan 1996; cardstock cover	2.95

N-MINT

SKULKER, THE
THORBY

❑1 .... 2.95

SKULL & BONES
DC

❑1, ca. 1992 .... 4.95
❑2, ca. 1992 .... 4.95
❑3, ca. 1992 .... 4.95

SKULL COMICS
LAST GASP

❑1 .... 18.00
❑2, Jan 1970 .... 10.00
❑3 .... 6.00
❑4 .... 6.00
❑5, Jan 1972 .... 6.00
❑6, Jun 1972 .... 6.00

SKULL THE SLAYER
MARVEL

❑1, Aug 1975 GK (c); GK (a); O: Skull the Slayer. 9.00
❑2, Nov 1975 .... 1.50
❑3, Jan 1976 .... 1.50
❑4, Mar 1976 .... 1.50
❑5, May 1976 .... 1.50
❑5/30 cent, May 1976; 30 cent regional price variant 20.00
❑6, Jul 1976 .... 1.50
❑6/30 cent, Jul 1976; 30 cent regional price variant 20.00
❑7, Sep 1976 .... 1.50
❑8, Nov 1976 .... 1.50

SKUNK
MU

❑1, Dec 1993, b&w 2.50

SKUNK, THE
EXPRESS / ENTITY

❑1, ca. 1996 .... 2.75
❑2, ca. 1996 .... 2.75
❑3, Jul 1996, b&w; cover says #tree . 2.75
❑4, Sep 1996, b&w 2.75
❑5, Sep 1996, b&w; cover says Cinco de Mayo 2.75
❑6, Oct 1996, b&w; cover says #sick 2.75
❑GN 1, ca. 1996, Collects issues #1-3 4.75

SKY APE (LES ADVENTURES)
SLAVE LABOR

❑1, Jun 1997, b&w 2.95
❑2, Sep 1997, b&w 2.95
❑3, Jan 1998, b&w 2.95

SKY COMICS PRESENTS MONTHLY
SKY COMICS

❑1, b&w 2.50

SKYE BLUE
MU

❑1, b&w 2.50
❑2, b&w 2.50
❑3 .... 2.50

SKY GAL
AC

❑1; some reprint; Reprints Sky Gal stories from Jumbo Comics #68, others plus new story 3.95
❑2; some color; some reprint; Reprints Sky Gal stories from Jumbo Comics plus new story 3.95
❑3; some color; some reprint; Reprints Sky Gal stories from Jumbo Comics plus new story 3.95

SKY MASTERS
PURE IMAGINATION

❑1, ca. 1991, b&w; strip reprints 7.95

SKYNN & BONES
BRAINSTORM

❑1 .... 2.95

SKYNN & BONES: DEADLY ANGELS
BRAINSTORM

❑1 .... 2.95

N-MINT

SKYWOLF
ECLIPSE

❑1, Mar 1988 .... 2.00
❑2, May 1988 .... 2.00
❑3, Oct 1988 .... 2.00

SLACKER COMICS
SLAVE LABOR

❑1, Aug 1994 .... 3.00
❑1-2, Apr 1995 .... 2.95
❑2, Nov 1994 .... 2.95
❑3, Feb 1995 .... 2.95
❑4, May 1995 .... 2.95
❑5, Sep 1995 .... 2.95
❑6, Dec 1995 .... 2.95
❑7, Feb 1996 .... 2.95
❑8, May 1996 .... 2.95
❑9, Aug 1996 .... 2.95
❑10 1996 .... 2.95
❑11, Jan 1997 .... 2.95
❑12 1997 .... 2.95
❑13, Apr 1997 .... 2.95
❑14, May 1997; Slacker Annual; Also titled "Annual #1" 2.95
❑15 1997; no indicia 2.95
❑16, Apr 1998 .... 2.95
❑17, Jul 1998 .... 2.95
❑18, Oct 1998 .... 2.95

SLÁINE THE BERSERKER
FLEETWAY-QUALITY

❑1, Jul 1987 .... 1.50
❑2, Aug 1987 .... 1.50
❑3, Sep 1987 .... 1.50
❑4, Oct 1987 .... 1.50
❑5, Nov 1987 .... 1.50
❑6, Dec 1987 .... 1.50
❑7, Jan 1988 .... 1.50
❑8, Feb 1988 .... 1.50
❑9, Mar 1988 .... 1.50
❑10, Apr 1988 .... 1.50
❑11, May 1988 .... 1.50
❑12, Jun 1988 .... 1.50
❑13, Jul 1988 .... 1.50
❑14, Aug 1988; double issue #14/15 . 1.50
❑16, Sep 1988; double issue #16/17 . 1.50
❑18, Oct 1988 .... 1.50
❑19, Nov 1988 .... 1.50
❑20, Dec 1988 .... 1.50

SLÁINE THE HORNED GOD
FLEETWAY-QUALITY

❑1, ca. 1990 .... 3.50
❑2 .... 3.00
❑3 .... 3.00
❑4 .... 3.00
❑5 .... 3.00
❑6 .... 3.00

SLÁINE THE KING
FLEETWAY-QUALITY

❑21, Jan 1989 .... 1.50
❑22, Feb 1989 .... 1.50
❑23 1989 .... 1.50
❑24 1989 .... 1.50
❑25 1989 .... 1.50
❑26 1989 .... 1.50
❑27 1989 .... 1.50
❑28 1989 .... 1.50

SLAM DUNK KINGS
PERSONALITY

❑1, Mar 1992, b&w; Michael Jordan . 2.95
❑2 1992, b&w 2.95
❑3 1992, b&w 2.95
❑4 1992, b&w 2.95

SLAPSTICK
MARVEL

❑1, Nov 1992 .... 1.25
❑2, Dec 1992 .... 1.25
❑3, Jan 1993 .... 1.25
❑4, Feb 1993 .... 1.25

N-MINT

SLASH
NORTHSTAR

❑1, Aug 1993, b&w 2.75
❑1/Special, Aug 1993 .... 4.95
❑2 1993, b&w 2.95
❑3 1993, b&w 2.95
❑4 1993, b&w 2.95
❑5, Oct 1993 .... 2.95

SLASH MARAUD
DC

❑1, Nov 1987 PG (a) 2.25
❑2, Dec 1987 PG (a) 2.00
❑3, Jan 1988 PG (a) 2.00
❑4, Feb 1988 PG (a) 2.00
❑5, Mar 1988 PG (a) 2.00
❑6, Apr 1988 PG (a) 2.00

SLAUGHTERMAN
COMICO

❑1, b&w 3.50
❑2, b&w 3.50

SLAVE GIRL
ETERNITY

❑1, Mar 1989, b&w 2.25

SLAVE LABOR STORIES
SLAVE LABOR

❑1, Feb 1992, b&w; Doctor Radium .. 2.95
❑2, Apr 1992, b&w; Milk & Cheese ... 2.95
❑3, Jul 1992, b&w; Bill the Clown 2.95
❑4, Nov 1992, b&w; Samurai Penguin 2.95

SLAVE PIT FUNNIES
SLAVE PIT

❑1 .... 4.95

SLAYERS
CPM MANGA

❑1, Oct 1998 .... 2.95
❑2, Nov 1998 .... 2.95
❑3, Dec 1998 .... 2.95
❑4, Jan 1999 .... 2.95
❑5, Feb 1999 .... 2.95

SLEAZY SCANDALS OF THE SILVER SCREEN
KITCHEN SINK

❑1, Apr 1993, b&w; b&w pin-ups, cardstock cover 2.50

SLEDGE HAMMER
MARVEL

❑1, Feb 1988; TV tie-in 1.00
❑2, Mar 1988; TV tie-in 1.00

SLEEPER
DC / WILDSTORM

❑1, Mar 2003 .... 2.95
❑2, Apr 2003 .... 2.95
❑3, May 2003 .... 2.95
❑4, Jun 2003 .... 2.95
❑5, Jul 2003 .... 2.95
❑6, Aug 2003 .... 2.95
❑7, Oct 2003 .... 2.95
❑8, Oct 2003 .... 2.95
❑9, Nov 2003 .... 2.95
❑10, Jan 2004 .... 2.95
❑11, Feb 2004 .... 2.95
❑12, Mar 2004 .... 2.95

SLEEPER: SEASON 2
DC

❑1, Aug 2004 .... 2.95
❑2, Sep 2004 ....

SLEEPING DRAGONS
SLAVE LABOR / AMAZE INK

❑1 2000 .... 2.95
❑2 2000 .... 2.95
❑3, Mar 2001 .... 2.95
❑4, Jul 2001 .... 2.95

SLEEPWALKER
MARVEL

❑1, Jun 1991 1: Sleepwalker. 1.50
❑2, Jul 1991 1: 8-Ball. 1.00
❑3, Aug 1991 .... 1.00
❑4, Sep 1991 .... 1.00

N-MINT

- ❑5, Oct 1991 A: Spider-Man. 1.00
- ❑6, Nov 1991 A: Spider-Man. 1.00
- ❑7, Dec 1991; Infinity Gauntlet 1.00
- ❑8, Jan 1992 A: Deathlok. 1.25
- ❑9, Feb 1992 1.25
- ❑10, Mar 1992 1.25
- ❑11, Apr 1992 A: Ghost Rider. 1.25
- ❑12, May 1992 1.25
- ❑13, Jun 1992 1: Spectra. 1.25
- ❑14, Jul 1992 1.25
- ❑15, Aug 1992 1.25
- ❑16, Sep 1992 1.25
- ❑17, Oct 1992 1.25
- ❑18, Nov 1992 1.25
- ❑19, Dec 1992; Die-cut cover 2.00
- ❑20, Jan 1993 1.25
- ❑21, Feb 1993 1.25
- ❑22, Mar 1993 1.25
- ❑23, Apr 1993 1.25
- ❑24, May 1993 1.25
- ❑25, Jun 1993; Holo-grafix cover 2.95
- ❑26, Jul 1993 1.25
- ❑27, Aug 1993 1.25
- ❑28, Sep 1993 1.25
- ❑29, Oct 1993 A: Spectra. 1.25
- ❑30, Nov 1993 1.25
- ❑31, Dec 1993 1.25
- ❑32, Jan 1994 1.25
- ❑33, Feb 1994 1.25
- ❑Holiday 1, Jan 1993 2.00

SLEEPWALKING
Hall of Heroes

- ❑1, Jan 1996, b&w 2.50
- ❑1/Variant, Jan 1996, b&w; Black Magic edition; alternate logoless cover 9.95
- ❑2, Jun 1997, b&w 2.50
- ❑2/Variant, Jun 1997, b&w; alternate logoless cover 2.50
- ❑3, b&w 2.50

SLEEPY HOLLOW
DC / Vertigo

- ❑1, Jan 2000 7.95

SLEEZE BROTHERS
Marvel / Epic

- ❑1, Aug 1989 1.75
- ❑2, Sep 1989 1.75
- ❑3, Oct 1989 1.75
- ❑4, Nov 1989 1.75
- ❑5, Dec 1989 1.75
- ❑6, Jan 1990 1.75

SLEEZE BROTHERS, THE (2ND SERIES)
Marvel / Epic

- ❑1, ca. 1991 3.95

SLICE
Express / Entity

- ❑1, Oct 1996, b&w 2.75

SLIDERS
Acclaim / Armada

- ❑1, Jun 1996; DG (a); based on TV series 3.00
- ❑2, Jul 1996; DG (a); based on TV series 2.50
- ❑3, Sep 1996 2.50
- ❑4, Sep 1996 2.50
- ❑5, Oct 1996 VM (a) 2.50
- ❑6, Nov 1996 VM (a) 2.50
- ❑7, Dec 1996 VM (a) 2.50
- ❑Special 1, Nov 1996; Narcotica 3.95
- ❑Special 2, Jan 1997 3.95
- ❑Special 3, Mar 1997; Deadly Secrets 3.95

SLIGHTLY BENT COMICS
Slightly Bent

- ❑1, Fal 1998, b&w 3.00
- ❑2, Win 1999, b&w 3.00

SLIMER!
Now

- ❑1, May 1989 2.00
- ❑2, Jun 1989 2.00

N-MINT

- ❑3, Jul 1989 2.00
- ❑4, Aug 1989 1.75
- ❑5, Sep 1989 1.75
- ❑6, Oct 1989 1.75
- ❑7, Nov 1989 1.75
- ❑8, Dec 1989 1.75
- ❑9, Jan 1990 1.75
- ❑10, Feb 1990 1.75
- ❑11, Mar 1990 1.75
- ❑12, Apr 1990 1.75
- ❑13, May 1990 1.75
- ❑14, Jun 1990 1.75
- ❑15, Jul 1990 1.75
- ❑16, Aug 1990 1.75
- ❑17, Sep 1990 1.75
- ❑18, Oct 1990 1.75
- ❑19, Nov 1990 1.75

SLINGERS
Marvel

- ❑0; Wizard promotional edition 1.00
- ❑1/A, Dec 1998; gatefold summary; A: Ricochet. A: Dusk. A: Hornet. A: Prodigy. A: Black Marvel. variant cover with caption "Prodigy: Prepare for Justice!" 2.99
- ❑1/B, Dec 1998; gatefold summary; A: Ricochet. A: Dusk. A: Hornet. A: Prodigy. A: Black Marvel. Caption "Dusk Falls Over Manhattan" on cover 2.99
- ❑1/C, Dec 1998; gatefold summary; variant cover with caption "Hornet: Feel the Sting!" 2.99
- ❑1/D, Dec 1998; gatefold summary; variant cover with caption "Ricochet Springs into Action!" 2.99
- ❑2, Jan 1999; gatefold summary; Cover A 2.00
- ❑2/Variant, Jan 1999; Cover B 2.00
- ❑3, Feb 1999 A: Spider-Man. A: Prodigy. 1.99
- ❑4, Mar 1999 A: Prodigy. 1.99
- ❑5, Apr 1999 A: Black Marvel. 1.99
- ❑6, May 1999 1.99
- ❑7, Jun 1999 V: Griz. 1.99
- ❑8, Jul 1999 1.99
- ❑9, Aug 1999; Ricochet vs. Nanny and Orphanmaker 1.99
- ❑10, Sep 1999 1.99
- ❑12, Nov 1999 1.99

SLOTH PARK
Blatant

- ❑1, Jun 1998 2.95

SLOW BURN
Fantagraphics / Eros

- ❑1 2.95

SLOW DEATH
Last Gasp

- ❑1, Apr 1970 20.00
- ❑2, Jan 1970 12.00
- ❑3 10.00
- ❑4, Jan 1972 10.00
- ❑5, Jan 1973 10.00
- ❑6 6.00
- ❑7, Dec 1976 6.00
- ❑8, Jul 1977; Greenpeace issue 6.00
- ❑9 6.00
- ❑10 6.00
- ❑11 6.00

SLOWPOKE COMIX
Alternative

- ❑1, Nov 1998, b&w 2.95

SLUDGE
Malibu / Ultraverse

- ❑1, Oct 1993; Rune 2.50
- ❑1/Ltd., Oct 1993; Ultra Ltd. 3.00
- ❑2, Nov 1993 2.00
- ❑3, Dec 1993; Break-Thru 2.00
- ❑4, Jan 1994 2.00
- ❑5, Feb 1994 2.00
- ❑6, Mar 1994 1.95
- ❑7, Jun 1994 1.95
- ❑8, Jul 1994 1.95

Although each *Sliders* story arc had its own numbering, the issues also had a "whole number" which can be found in the indicia.

© 1996 20th Century Fox Film Corporation and Acclaim Comics.

N-MINT

- ❑9, Sep 1994 1.95
- ❑10, Oct 1994 1.95
- ❑11, Nov 1994 1.95
- ❑12, Dec 1994; flipbook with Ultraverse Premiere #8 3.50
- ❑13, Jan 1995 1.95

SLUDGE: RED X-MAS
Malibu / Ultraverse

- ❑1, Dec 1994 2.50

SLUG 'N' GINGER
Fantagraphics / Eros

- ❑1, b&w 2.25

SLUTBURGER STORIES
Rip Off

- ❑1, Jul 1990, b&w 2.50
- ❑2, Jul 1991, b&w 2.50

SMALL PRESS EXPO
Insight

- ❑1995, ca. 1995; Benefit Comic for American Cancer Society 2.95
- ❑1996, ca. 1996 2.95
- ❑1997, ca. 1997; Benefit comic for Comic Legal Defense Fund 2.95

SMALL PRESS SWIMSUIT SPECTACULAR
Allied

- ❑1, Jun 1995, b&w; pin-ups; benefit comic for American Cancer Society 2.95

SMALLVILLE
DC

- ❑1, May 2003 3.50
- ❑2, Jul 2003 3.50
- ❑3, Sep 2003 3.95
- ❑4, Nov 2003 3.95
- ❑5, Jan 2004 3.95
- ❑6, Mar 2004 3.95
- ❑7, May 2004 3.95
- ❑8, Jul 2004 3.95
- ❑9, Sep 2004

SMASH COMICS (2ND SERIES)
DC

- ❑1, May 1999; Justice Society Returns 1.99

SMAX
DC / America's Best Comics

- ❑1, Oct 2003 2.95
- ❑2, Nov 2003 2.95
- ❑3, Dec 2003 2.95
- ❑4, Feb 2004 2.95
- ❑5, May 2004 2.95

SMILE (MIXX)
Mixx

- ❑1, Dec 1998; Sailor Moon 3.99
- ❑2 1999 3.99
- ❑3 1999 3.99
- ❑4 1999 3.99
- ❑5 1999 3.99
- ❑6 1999 3.99
- ❑7, Dec 1999 3.99
- ❑8 3.99
- ❑9 3.99
- ❑10 3.99
- ❑11 3.99
- ❑12 3.99
- ❑13 4.99
- ❑14 4.99
- ❑15 4.99

N-MINT

❑16 ... 4.99
❑17 ... 4.99
❑18 ... 4.99
❑19 ... 4.99
❑20 ... 4.99
❑21 ... 4.99
❑22 ... 4.99
❑23 ... 4.99
❑24, Nov 2001 ... 4.99
❑25, Dec 2001 ... 4.99
❑26, Jan 2002 ... 4.99
❑27, Feb 2002 ... 4.99
❑28, Mar 2002 ... 4.99
❑29, Apr 2002 ... 4.99

SMILE (KITCHEN SINK)
KITCHEN SINK

❑1 ... 3.00

SMILEY
CHAOS

❑1, Jun 1998 ... 2.95

SMILEY ANTI-HOLIDAY SPECIAL
CHAOS!

❑1, Jan 1999 ... 2.95

SMILEY'S SPRING BREAK
CHAOS!

❑1, Apr 1999 ... 2.95

SMILEY WRESTLING SPECIAL
CHAOS!

❑1, May 1999 ... 2.95

SMILIN' ED
FANTACO

❑1 1982, b&w ... 1.25
❑2 1982, b&w ... 1.25
❑3 1982, b&w ... 1.25
❑4 1982, b&w ... 1.25

SMITH BROWN JONES
KIWI

❑1 1997 ... 4.00
❑2 1997 ... 2.95
❑3 1997 ... 2.95
❑4 1998 ... 2.95
❑5 1998 ... 2.95

SMITH BROWN JONES: ALIEN ACCOUNTANT
SLAVE LABOR

❑1, May 1998 ... 2.95
❑2, Aug 1998 ... 2.95
❑3, Nov 1998 ... 2.95
❑4, Feb 1999 ... 2.95

SMITH BROWN JONES: HALLOWEEN SPECIAL
SLAVE LABOR

❑1, Oct 1998, b&w ... 2.95

SMOKEY BEAR
GOLD KEY

❑1, Feb 1970 ... 8.00
❑2, May 1970 ... 5.00
❑3, Sep 1970 ... 4.00
❑4, Dec 1970 ... 3.00
❑5, Mar 1971 ... 3.00
❑6, Jun 1971 ... 3.00
❑7, Sep 1971 ... 3.00
❑8, Dec 1971 ... 3.00
❑9, Mar 1972 ... 3.00
❑10, Jun 1972 ... 3.00
❑11, Sep 1972 ... 3.00
❑12, Dec 1972 ... 3.00
❑13, Mar 1973 ... 3.00

SMOOT
SKIP WILLIAMSON

❑1 ... 2.95

SMURFS
MARVEL

❑1, Dec 1982 ... 4.00
❑2, Jan 1983 ... 4.00
❑3, Feb 1983 ... 4.00

N-MINT

SMUT THE ALTERNATIVE COMIC
WILTSHIRE

❑1 ... 3.00

SNACK BAR
BIG TOWN

❑1 ... 2.95

SNAGGLEPUSS
GOLD KEY

❑1, Oct 1962 ... 33.00
❑2, Dec 1962 ... 24.00
❑3, Mar 1963 ... 24.00
❑4, Jun 1963 ... 24.00

SNAKE, THE
SPECIAL STUDIO

❑1, Dec 1989, b&w ... 3.50

SNAKE EYES
FANTAGRAPHICS

❑1, b&w ... 7.95
❑2, b&w ... 7.95
❑3, b&w ... 7.95

SNAKE PLISSKEN CHRONICLES (JOHN CARPENTER'S...)
CROSSGEN

❑1/A, Jun 2003 ... 2.99
❑1/B, Jun 2003 ... 2.99
❑2, Sep 2003 ... 2.99

SNAK POSSE
HCOM

❑1, Jun 1994 ... 1.95
❑2, Jul 1994 ... 1.95

SNAP THE PUNK TURTLE
SUPER CREW

❑0.5 ... 2.25

SNARF
KITCHEN SINK

❑1, Feb 1972 ... 10.00
❑2, Aug 1972 ... 8.00
❑3, Nov 1972 WE (c); WE (a) ... 8.00
❑4, Mar 1973 ... 8.00
❑5, Mar 1974 HK (c) ... 6.00
❑6, Feb 1976 ... 6.00
❑7, Feb 1977 ... 6.00
❑8, Oct 1978 ... 6.00
❑9, Feb 1981 ... 6.00
❑10, Feb 1987 A: Omaha the Cat Dancer. ... 6.00
❑11, Feb 1989 ... 4.00
❑12 ... 4.00
❑13 ... 4.00
❑14 ... 4.00
❑15 ... 5.00

SNARL
CALIBER

❑1, b&w ... 2.50
❑2, b&w ... 2.50
❑3, b&w ... 2.50

SNOID COMICS
KITCHEN SINK

❑1, Dec 1979 ... 2.00

SNOOPER AND BLABBER DETECTIVES
GOLD KEY

❑1, Nov 1962 ... 100.00
❑2, Feb 1963 ... 75.00
❑3, May 1963 ... 75.00

S'NOT FOR KIDS
VORTEX

❑1, b&w ... 6.95

SNOWBUNI
MU

❑1, Jan 1991 ... 3.25

SNOWMAN
EXPRESS / ENTITY

❑1, Nov 1996 1: Snowman. ... 5.00
❑1/A 1996; 1: Snowman. variant cover 6.00
❑1-2, Jul 1996, b&w; 1: Snowman. no cover price; given out at 1996 Comic Con International: San Diego ... 2.50

N-MINT

❑2 1996 ... 4.00
❑2/A 1996; variant cover ... 5.00
❑2-2 1996 ... 2.50
❑3 1996 ... 3.00
❑3/A 1996; variant cover ... 3.00

SNOWMAN: 1944
ENTITY

❑1, Oct 1996 ... 2.75

SNOW WHITE
MARVEL

❑1, Jan 1995; lead story is reprint of Dell Four Color #49 ... 2.00

SNOW WHITE AND THE SEVEN DWARFS (WALT DISNEY'S...)
GLADSTONE

❑1 ... 3.50

SNUFF
BONEYARD

❑1, May 1997, b&w ... 2.95

SOAP OPERA LOVE
CHARLTON

❑1, Feb 1983 ... 12.00
❑2, Mar 1983 ... 8.00
❑3, Jun 1983 ... 8.00

SOAP OPERA ROMANCES
CHARLTON

❑1, Jul 1982; Nurse Betsy Crane ... 12.00
❑2, Sep 1982; Nurse Betsy Crane ... 8.00
❑3, Dec 1983; Nurse Betsy Crane ... 8.00
❑4, Jan 1983; Nurse Betsy Crane ... 8.00
❑5, Mar 1983; Nurse Betsy Crane ... 8.00

SOB: SPECIAL OPERATIONS BRANCH
PROMETHEAN

❑1, May 1994, b&w ... 2.25

SOCKETEER, THE
KARDIA

❑1, b&w; parody ... 2.25

SOCK MONKEY
DARK HORSE

❑1, Sep 1998, b&w ... 2.95
❑2, Oct 1998, b&w ... 2.95

SOCK MONKEY (TONY MILLIONAIRE'S...)
DARK HORSE / MAVERICK

❑1, Jul 1999, b&w ... 2.95
❑2, Aug 1999, b&w ... 2.95

SOCK MONKEY (VOL. 3) (TONY MILLIONAIRE'S...)
DARK HORSE / MAVERICK

❑1, Nov 2000 ... 2.99
❑2, Dec 2000 ... 2.99

SO DARK THE ROSE
CFD

❑1, Oct 1995 ... 2.95

SOFA JET CITY CRISIS
VISUAL ASSAULT

❑1, b&w ... 6.95

S.O.F.T. CORPS
SPOOF

❑1 ... 2.95

SOJOURN
DREAMER

❑1, May 1998 ... 2.10
❑2 ... 2.10
❑3 ... 2.10
❑4 ... 2.10
❑5 ... 2.10
❑6 ... 3.15
❑7 ... 3.15
❑8 ... 3.15
❑9 ... 3.15
❑10 ... 3.15

SOJOURN (CROSSGEN)
CROSSGEN

❑1, Aug 2001 ... 5.00
❑2, Sep 2001 ... 2.95
❑3, Oct 2001 ... 2.95

N-MINT

- ❑4, Nov 2001 ..... 2.95
- ❑5, Dec 2001 ..... 2.95
- ❑6, Jan 2002 ..... 2.95
- ❑7, Feb 2002 ..... 2.95
- ❑8, Mar 2002 ..... 2.95
- ❑9, Apr 2002 ..... 2.95
- ❑10, May 2002 ..... 2.95
- ❑11, Jun 2002 ..... 2.95
- ❑12, Jul 2002 ..... 2.95
- ❑13, Aug 2002 ..... 2.95
- ❑14, Sep 2002 ..... 2.95
- ❑15, Oct 2002 ..... 2.95
- ❑16, Nov 2002 ..... 2.95
- ❑17, Dec 2002 ..... 2.95
- ❑18, Jan 2003 ..... 2.95
- ❑19, Feb 2003 ..... 2.95
- ❑20, Mar 2003 ..... 2.95
- ❑21, Apr 2003 ..... 2.95
- ❑22, May 2003 ..... 2.95
- ❑23, Jun 2003 ..... 2.95
- ❑24, Jul 2003 ..... 2.95
- ❑25, Sep 2003 ..... 1.00
- ❑26, Sep 2003 ..... 2.95
- ❑27, Oct 2003 ..... 2.95
- ❑28, Nov 2003 ..... 2.95
- ❑29, Dec 2003 ..... 2.95
- ❑30, Jan 2004 ..... 2.95
- ❑31, Feb 2004 ..... 2.95
- ❑32, Mar 2004 ..... 2.95
- ❑33, Apr 2004 ..... 2.95
- ❑34, May 2004 ..... 2.95
- ❑34-2, Apr 2004 ..... 2.95
- ❑Special 1, Sep 2001, Collects Prequel and #1 ..... 3.95

SOJOURN PREQUEL
CROSSGEN

- ❑1, Jul 2001 ..... 5.00

SOLAR LORD
IMAGE

- ❑1, Mar 1999 ..... 2.50
- ❑2, Apr 1999 ..... 2.50
- ❑3, May 1999 ..... 2.50
- ❑4, Jun 1999 ..... 2.50
- ❑5, Jul 1999 ..... 2.50
- ❑6, Aug 1999 ..... 2.50
- ❑7, Sep 1999 ..... 2.50

SOLARMAN
MARVEL

- ❑1, Jan 1989 ..... 1.00
- ❑2, May 1990 ..... 1.00

SOLAR, MAN OF THE ATOM
VALIANT

- ❑1, Sep 1991 O: Solar. 5.00
- ❑2, Oct 1991 DP (a); O: Solar. 3.00
- ❑3, Nov 1991 O: Solar. 1: Toyo Harada. 1: Harbinger Foundation. 3.00
- ❑4, Dec 1991 O: Solar. 2.00
- ❑5, Jan 1992 EC (a) 2.00
- ❑6, Feb 1992 DP (a); V: Spider-Aliens. 2.00
- ❑7, Mar 1992 DP (a); V: X-O armor. 2.00
- ❑8, Apr 1992 ..... 2.00
- ❑9, May 1992 ..... 2.00
- ❑10, Jun 1992; 1: Eternal Warrior (cameo). All-black embossed cover 8.00
- ❑10-2 ..... 3.95
- ❑11, Jul 1992 1: Eternal Warrior (full appearance). 2.50
- ❑12, Aug 1992; FM (c); DP (a); Unity 2.50
- ❑13, Sep 1992; Unity 2.50
- ❑14, Oct 1992 1: Fred Bender. 2.25
- ❑15, Nov 1992 ..... 2.25
- ❑16, Dec 1992 D: Lyja (Valiant). 2.25
- ❑17, Jan 1993 A: X-O Manowar. 2.25
- ❑18, Feb 1993 ..... 2.25
- ❑19, Mar 1993 ..... 2.25
- ❑20, Apr 1993 ..... 2.25
- ❑21, May 1993 V: Master Darque. 2.25
- ❑22, Jun 1993 V: Master Darque. 2.25
- ❑23, Jul 1993 1: Solar the Destroyer. 2.25
- ❑24, Aug 1993 ..... 2.25
- ❑25, Sep 1993; V: Doctor Eclipse. Secret Weapons x-over 2.25
- ❑26, Oct 1993 ..... 2.25
- ❑27, Nov 1993 ..... 2.25
- ❑28, Dec 1993; Solar the Destroyer vs. spiders 2.25
- ❑29, Jan 1994; Valiant Vision 2.25
- ❑30, Feb 1994 ..... 2.25
- ❑31, Mar 1994 ..... 2.25
- ❑32, Apr 1994 ..... 2.25
- ❑33, May 1994; Valiant Vision; trading card 2.25
- ❑34, Jun 1994; Valiant Vision 2.25
- ❑35, Aug 1994; Valiant Vision 2.25
- ❑36, Sep 1994 V: Ravenus. V: Doctor Eclipse. 2.25
- ❑37, Oct 1994 V: Ravenus. V: Doctor Eclipse. 2.25
- ❑38, Nov 1994; Chaos Effect 2.25
- ❑39, Dec 1994 ..... 2.25
- ❑40, Jan 1995 ..... 2.25
- ❑41, Feb 1995 ..... 2.25
- ❑42, Mar 1995 ..... 2.25
- ❑43, Apr 1995 ..... 2.25
- ❑44, May 1995 ..... 2.25
- ❑45, Jun 1995 ..... 2.25
- ❑46, Jul 1995 DG (a) 2.50
- ❑47, Aug 1995 DG (a) 2.50
- ❑48, Sep 1995 DG (a) 2.50
- ❑49, Sep 1995 DG (a) 2.50
- ❑50, Oct 1995 DG (a) 2.50
- ❑51, Nov 1995 DG (a) 2.50
- ❑52, Nov 1995 DG (a) 2.50
- ❑53, Dec 1995 DG (a) 2.50
- ❑54, Dec 1995 DG (a) 2.50
- ❑55, Jan 1996 ..... 2.50
- ❑56, Jan 1996 ..... 2.50
- ❑57, Feb 1996 ..... 2.50
- ❑58, Feb 1996 ..... 2.50
- ❑59, Mar 1996; Texas destroyed 2.50
- ❑60, Apr 1996 ..... 2.50

SOLAR, MAN OF THE ATOM (VOL. 2)
ACCLAIM / VALIANT

- ❑1, May 1997; lays groundwork for second Valiant universe 3.95

SOLAR, MAN OF THE ATOM: HELL ON EARTH
ACCLAIM

- ❑1, Jan 1998 ..... 2.50
- ❑2, Feb 1998 ..... 2.50
- ❑3, Mar 1998 ..... 2.50
- ❑4, Apr 1998 ..... 2.50

SOLAR, MAN OF THE ATOM: REVELATIONS
ACCLAIM

- ❑1, Nov 1997 ..... 3.95

SOLAR STELLA
SIRIUS

- ❑1, Aug 2000, b&w 2.95

SOLDIERS OF FREEDOM
AC

- ❑1, Jul 1987 ..... 1.75
- ❑2, Aug 1987 ..... 1.95

SOLDIER X
MARVEL

- ❑1, Sep 2002 ..... 2.99
- ❑2, Oct 2002 ..... 2.25
- ❑3, Nov 2002 ..... 2.25
- ❑4, Dec 2002 ..... 2.25
- ❑5, Jan 2003 ..... 2.25
- ❑6, Feb 2003 ..... 2.25
- ❑7, Mar 2003 ..... 2.99
- ❑8, Apr 2003 ..... 2.99
- ❑9, May 2003 ..... 2.99
- ❑10, Jun 2003 ..... 2.99
- ❑11, Jul 2003 ..... 2.99
- ❑12, Aug 2003 ..... 2.99

Solar, Man of the Atom featured the adventures of Valiant's most powerful hero.

© 1991 Voyager Communications Inc. (Valiant).

N-MINT

SOLD OUT
FANTACO

- ❑1, ca. 1986 ..... 1.50
- ❑2, ca. 1987 ..... 1.50

SOLITAIRE
MALIBU / ULTRAVERSE

- ❑1, Nov 1993; 1: Solitaire. Comes poly-bagged with one of 4 "ace" trading cards 2.00
- ❑1/CS, Nov 1993; trading card 2.50
- ❑2, Dec 1993; Break-Thru 2.00
- ❑3, Feb 1994 O: Night Man. 2.00
- ❑4, Mar 1994 O: Solitaire. 2.00
- ❑5, Apr 1994 ..... 2.00
- ❑6, May 1994 ..... 1.95
- ❑7, Sep 1994 1: Double Edge. 1.95
- ❑8, Sep 1994 1: The Degenerate. 1.95
- ❑9, Sep 1994 D: The Degenerate. 1.95
- ❑10, Oct 1994 ..... 1.95
- ❑11, Nov 1994 ..... 1.95
- ❑12, Dec 1994 D: Jinn. D: Anton Lone. 1.95

SOLO (MARVEL)
MARVEL

- ❑1, Sep 1994 ..... 1.75
- ❑2, Oct 1994 ..... 1.75
- ❑3, Nov 1994 ..... 1.75
- ❑4, Dec 1994 ..... 1.75

SOLO (DARK HORSE)
DARK HORSE

- ❑1, Jul 1996 ..... 2.50
- ❑2, Aug 1996 ..... 2.50

SOLO AVENGERS
MARVEL

- ❑1, Dec 1987; I.D. card; 1st solo Mockingbird story 1.00
- ❑2, Jan 1988; Captain Marvel 1.00
- ❑3, Feb 1988; BH (c); BH (a); V: Batroc. Moon Knight vs. Shroud 1.00
- ❑4, Mar 1988; Black Knight 1.00
- ❑5, Apr 1988; Scarlet Witch 1.00
- ❑6, May 1988; Falcon 1.00
- ❑7, Jun 1988; Black Widow 1.00
- ❑8, Jul 1988; Hank Pym 1.00
- ❑9, Aug 1988; Hellcat 1.00
- ❑10, Sep 1988; Doctor Druid 1.00
- ❑11, Oct 1988; Hercules 1.00
- ❑12, Nov 1988 ..... 1.00
- ❑13, Dec 1988; Wonder Man 1.00
- ❑14, Jan 1989; Black Widow 1.00
- ❑15, Feb 1989 ..... 1.00
- ❑16, Mar 1989; Moondragon 1.00
- ❑17, Apr 1989; Sub-Mariner 1.00
- ❑18, May 1989; Moondragon 1.00
- ❑19, Jun 1989; Black Panther 1.00
- ❑20, Jul 1989; Moondragon; series continues as Avengers Spotlight 1.00

SOLO EX-MUTANTS
ETERNITY

- ❑1 1987 ..... 2.00
- ❑2, Feb 1988 ..... 2.00
- ❑3, Apr 1988 ..... 2.00
- ❑4 1988 ..... 2.00
- ❑5 1988 ..... 2.00
- ❑6, Jan 1989 ..... 2.00

N-MINT

SOLOMON KANE
MARVEL

❑1, Sep 1985; Double-size ... 1.50
❑2, Nov 1985 ... 1.25
❑3, Jan 1986 ... 1.25
❑4, Mar 1986 ... 1.25
❑5, May 1986 ... 1.25
❑6, Jul 1986 AW (a) ... 1.25

SOLOMON KANE IN 3-D
BLACKTHORNE

❑1 ... 2.50

SOLSON CHRISTMAS SPECIAL
SOLSON

❑1, ca. 1986; JLee (a); Samurai Santa; 1st Jim Lee art ... 3.00

SOLSON'S COMIC TALENT STARSEARCH
SOLSON

❑1 ... 1.50
❑2 ... 1.50

SOLUS
CROSSGEN

❑1, Apr 2003 ... 2.95
❑2, May 2003 ... 2.95
❑3, Jun 2003 ... 2.95
❑4, Jul 2003 ... 2.95
❑5, Aug 2003 ... 2.95
❑6, Oct 2003 ... 2.95
❑7, Nov 2003 ... 2.95
❑8, Dec 2003 ... 2.95

SOLUTION, THE
MALIBU / ULTRAVERSE

❑0, Jan 1994; Promotional (coupon redemption) edition; no cover price ... 2.50
❑1, Sep 1993; 1: Quattro. 1: The Solution. 1: Outrage. 1: Dropkick. 1: Tech. 1: Shadowmage. ... 2.00
❑1/Ltd., Sep 1993; Ultra-Limited foil edition; 1: Quattro. 1: The Solution. 1: Outrage. 1: Dropkick. 1: Tech. 1: Shadowmage. ... 3.00
❑2, Oct 1993; Rune ... 2.50
❑3, Nov 1993 ... 2.00
❑4, Dec 1993; Break-Thru ... 2.00
❑5, Jan 1994; O: The Strangers. Dropkick solo story ... 1.95
❑6, Feb 1994 O: The Solution. O: Tech. 1.95
❑7, Mar 1994 O: The Solution. ... 1.95
❑8, Apr 1994 O: The Solution. ... 1.95
❑9, Jun 1994 ... 1.95
❑10, Jul 1994 ... 1.95
❑11, Aug 1994 ... 1.95
❑12, Oct 1994 ... 1.95
❑13, Oct 1994 ... 1.95
❑14, Dec 1994 ... 1.95
❑15, Jan 1995 ... 1.95
❑16, Jan 1995; MZ (a); flipbook with Ultraverse Premiere #10 ... 3.50
❑17, Feb 1995 ... 2.50

SOMEPLACE STRANGE
MARVEL / EPIC

❑1 ... 6.95

SOMERSET HOLMES
PACIFIC

❑1, Sep 1983 BA (a) ... 2.50
❑2, Nov 1983 BA (a) ... 2.00
❑3, Feb 1984 BA (a) ... 2.00
❑4, Apr 1984 BA (a) ... 2.00
❑5, Nov 1984 BA (a) ... 2.00
❑6, Dec 1984 BA (a) ... 2.00

SOME TALES FROM GIMBLEY
HARRIER

❑1, Jun 1987 ... 1.95

SOMETHING
STRICTLY UNDERGROUND

❑1 ... 2.95

SOMETHING DIFFERENT
WOOGA CENTRAL

❑1, b&w ... 2.00

N-MINT

❑2, Spr 1992 ... 2.00
❑3, Win 1993, flexidisc ... 2.00

SOMETHING WICKED
IMAGE

❑1, Nov 2003 ... 2.95
❑2, Dec 2003 ... 2.95
❑3, Apr 2004 ... 2.95

SOME TROUBLE OF A SERRIOUS NATURE
CRUSADE

❑1, Nov 2001 ... 3.50

SOMNAMBULO: SLEEP OF THE JUST
9TH CIRCLE

❑1, Aug 1996, b&w ... 2.95

SONGBOOK (ALAN MOORE'S...)
CALIBER

❑1; Collected from issues of Negative Burn ... 5.95

SONG OF MYKAL, THE: ATLANTIS FANTASYWORLD 25TH ANNIVERSARY COMIC
ATLANTIS FANTASYWORLD

❑1, Nov 2001 ... 2.99

SONG OF THE CID
TOME

❑1, b&w ... 2.95
❑2, b&w ... 2.95

SONG OF THE SIRENS
MILLENNIUM

❑1, b&w ... 2.95
❑2, b&w ... 2.95

SONGS OF BASTARDS
CONQUEST

❑1, b&w ... 2.95

SONIC & KNUCKLES: MECHA MADNESS SPECIAL
ARCHIE

❑1, color ... 2.00

SONIC & KNUCKLES SPECIAL
ARCHIE

❑1, Aug 1995, color ... 2.00

SONIC BLAST SPECIAL
ARCHIE

❑1, Oct 1996, color ... 2.00

SONIC DISRUPTORS
DC

❑1, Dec 1987 ... 1.00
❑2, Jan 1988 ... 1.00
❑3, Feb 1988 ... 1.00
❑4, Mar 1988 ... 1.00
❑5, May 1988 ... 1.00
❑6, Jun 1988 ... 1.00
❑7, Jul 1988; series goes on hiatus with unresolved storyline; Series cancelled ... 1.00

SONIC LIVE SPECIAL
ARCHIE

❑1, Knuckles back-up continues in Sonic the Hedgehog #45 ... 2.00

SONIC QUEST - THE DEATH EGG SAGA
ARCHIE

❑2, Jan 1997 ... 1.50

SONIC'S FRIENDLY NEMESIS KNUCKLES
ARCHIE

❑1, Jul 1996 ... 3.00
❑2, Aug 1996 ... 2.00
❑3, Sep 1996 ... 2.00

SONIC THE HEDGEHOG (MINI-SERIES)
ARCHIE

❑1, ca. 1993 ... 20.00
❑2, ca. 1993 ... 10.00
❑3, ca. 1993 ... 10.00

N-MINT

SONIC THE HEDGEHOG
ARCHIE

❑0, Feb 1993 ... 9.00
❑1, Jul 1993 ... 12.00
❑2, Sep 1993 ... 9.00
❑3, Oct 1993 ... 9.00
❑4, Nov 1993 ... 7.00
❑5, Dec 1993 ... 7.00
❑6, Jan 1994 ... 6.00
❑7, Feb 1994 ... 6.00
❑8, Mar 1994 ... 6.00
❑9, Apr 1994 ... 6.00
❑10, May 1994 ... 6.00
❑11, Jun 1994 ... 4.00
❑12, Jul 1994 ... 4.00
❑13, Aug 1994 ... 4.00
❑14, Sep 1994 ... 4.00
❑15, Oct 1994 ... 4.00
❑16, Nov 1994 ... 4.00
❑17, Dec 1994 ... 4.00
❑18, Jan 1995 ... 4.00
❑19, Feb 1995 ... 4.00
❑20, Mar 1995 ... 4.00
❑21, Apr 1995 ... 3.00
❑22, May 1995 ... 3.00
❑23, Jun 1995 ... 3.00
❑24, Jul 1995 ... 3.00
❑25, Aug 1995 ... 3.00
❑26, Sep 1995 ... 3.00
❑27, Oct 1995 ... 3.00
❑28, Nov 1995 ... 3.00
❑29, Dec 1995 ... 3.00
❑30, Jan 1996 ... 3.00
❑31, Feb 1996 ... 3.00
❑32, Mar 1996 ... 3.00
❑33, Apr 1996 ... 3.00
❑34, May 1996 ... 3.00
❑35, Jun 1996 ... 3.00
❑36, Jul 1996 ... 3.00
❑37, Aug 1996; Bunnie Rabbot back-up story ... 3.00
❑38, Sep 1996; Tails solo story ... 3.00
❑39, Oct 1996 ... 3.00
❑40, Nov 1996 ... 3.00
❑41, Dec 1996 ... 3.00
❑42, Jan 1997 ... 3.00
❑43, Feb 1997 ... 3.00
❑44, Mar 1997 ... 3.00
❑45, Apr 1997 ... 3.00
❑46, May 1997 ... 3.00
❑47, Jun 1997 ... 3.00
❑48, Jul 1997 ... 3.00
❑49, Aug 1997 ... 3.00
❑50, Sep 1997 ... 3.00
❑51, Oct 1997 ... 1.50
❑52, Nov 1997; noir issue ... 1.50
❑53, Dec 1997 ... 1.50
❑54, Jan 1998 ... 1.50
❑55, Feb 1998 ... 1.50
❑56, Mar 1998 ... 1.50
❑57, Apr 1998 ... 1.50
❑58, May 1998 ... 1.50
❑59, Jun 1998 ... 1.50
❑60, Jul 1998 ... 1.50
❑61, Aug 1998 ... 1.50
❑62, Sep 1998 ... 1.50
❑63, Oct 1998 ... 1.50
❑64, Nov 1998 ... 1.75
❑65, Dec 1998 ... 1.75
❑66, Jan 1999 ... 1.75
❑67, Feb 1999 ... 1.75
❑68, Mar 1999 ... 1.75
❑69, Apr 1999 ... 1.79
❑70, May 1999 ... 1.79
❑71, Jun 1999 ... 1.79
❑72, Jul 1999 ... 1.79
❑73, Aug 1999 ... 1.79
❑74, Sep 1999 ... 1.79
❑75, Oct 1999 ... 1.79
❑76, Nov 1999 ... 1.79
❑77, Dec 1999 ... 1.79

N-MINT

❑78, Jan 2000 .... 1.79
❑79, Feb 2000 .... 1.79
❑80, Mar 2000 .... 1.79
❑81, Apr 2000 .... 1.79
❑82, May 2000 .... 1.79
❑83, Jun 2000 .... 1.99
❑84, Jul 2000 .... 1.99
❑85, Aug 2000 .... 1.99
❑86, Sep 2000 .... 1.99
❑87, Oct 2000 .... 1.99
❑88, Nov 2000 .... 1.99
❑89, Dec 2000 .... 1.99
❑90, Jan 2001 .... 1.99
❑91, Feb 2001 .... 1.99
❑92, Mar 2001 .... 1.99
❑93, Apr 2001 .... 1.99
❑94, May 2001 .... 1.99
❑95, Jun 2001 .... 1.99
❑96, Jul 2001 .... 1.99
❑97, Aug 2001 .... 1.99
❑98, Sep 2001 .... 1.99
❑99, Oct 2001 .... 1.99
❑100, Nov 2001 .... 1.99
❑101, Nov 2001 .... 1.99
❑102, Dec 2001 .... 1.99
❑103, Jan 2002 .... 1.99
❑104, Feb 2002 .... 1.99
❑105, Mar 2002 .... 1.99
❑106, Apr 2002 .... 1.99
❑107, May 2002 .... 1.99
❑108, May 2002 .... 1.99
❑109, Jun 2002 .... 1.99
❑110, Jul 2002 .... 1.99
❑111, Aug 2002 .... 1.99
❑112, Sep 2002 .... 1.99
❑113, Oct 2002 .... 1.99
❑114, Nov 2002 .... 1.99
❑115, Dec 2002 .... 1.99
❑116, Jan 2003 .... 2.19
❑117, Feb 2003 .... 2.19
❑118, ca. 2003 .... 2.19
❑119, Mar 2003 .... 2.19
❑120, Apr 2003 .... 2.19
❑121, May 2003 .... 2.19
❑122, Jun 2003 .... 2.19
❑123, Jul 2003 .... 2.19
❑124, Aug 2003 .... 2.19
❑125, Sep 2003 .... 2.19
❑126, Oct 2003 .... 2.19
❑127, Nov 2003 .... 2.19
❑128, Dec 2003 .... 2.19
❑129, Jan 2004 .... 2.19
❑130, Feb 2004 .... 2.19
❑131, Mar 2004 .... 2.19
❑132, Mar 2004 .... 2.19
❑133, Apr 2004 .... 2.19
❑134, May 2004 .... 2.19
❑135, May 2004 .... 2.19
❑136, Jul 2004 .... 2.19
❑SS 1, Nov 1997 .... 2.00
❑SS 2, ca. 1997; Brave New World ... 2.00
❑SS 3, Jan 1998; Firsts 2.25
❑SS 4, Mar 1998 .... 2.25
❑SS 5, Jun 1998; Sonic Kids 2.25
❑SS 6, Sep 1998; Director's Cut; expanded version of Sonic #50 ..... 2.25
❑SS 7, Dec 1998; crossover with Image 2.25
❑SS 8, Mar 1999 .... 2.25
❑SS 9, Jun 1999 .... 2.29
❑SS 10, Sep 1999; A: Sabrina. 2.29
❑SS 11, Dec 1999 .... 2.29
❑SS 12, Apr 2000 .... 2.29
❑SS 13, Jun 2000 .... 2.29
❑SS 14, Sep 2000 .... 2.29
❑SS 15, Feb 2001 .... 2.49

SONIC THE HEDGEHOG IN YOUR FACE SPECIAL
ARCHIE

❑1 .... 2.00

N-MINT

SONIC THE HEDGEHOG TRIPLE TROUBLE SPECIAL
ARCHIE

❑1, Oct 1995 .... 2.00

SONIC VS. KNUCKLES BATTLE ROYAL SPECIAL
ARCHIE

❑1, ca. 1997 .... 2.00

SON OF AMBUSH BUG
DC

❑1, Jul 1986 KG (a) 1.50
❑2, Aug 1986 KG (a) 1.50
❑3, Sep 1986 KG (a) 1.50
❑4, Oct 1986 KG (a) 1.50
❑5, Nov 1986 KG (a) 1.50
❑6, Dec 1986 KG (a) 1.50

SON OF MUTANT WORLD
FANTAGOR

❑1, color 3.00
❑2, color 2.50
❑3, b&w; Black and white issues begin 2.00
❑4, b&w 2.00
❑5, ca. 1990, b&w 2.00

SON OF SATAN
MARVEL

❑1, Dec 1975; Marvel Value Stamp #13: Dr. Strange 15.00
❑2, Feb 1976 .... 12.00
❑3, Apr 1976 .... 8.00
❑3/30 cent, Apr 1976; 30 cent regional variant 12.00
❑4, Jun 1976 CR (a) 8.00
❑4/30 cent, Jun 1976; 30 cent regional variant 12.00
❑5, Aug 1976 .... 8.00
❑5/30 cent, Aug 1976; 30 cent regional variant 12.00
❑6, Oct 1976 .... 6.00
❑7, Dec 1976 .... 6.00
❑8, Feb 1977 .... 6.00

SON OF SUPERMAN
DC

❑1 .... 14.95

SON OF YUPPIES FROM HELL
MARVEL

❑1 .... 3.50

SONS OF KATIE ELDER
DELL

❑1, Sep 1965 .... 125.00

SOPHISTIKATS KATCH-UP KOLLECTION, THE
SILK PURRS

❑1, Jul 1995, b&w 5.95

SORCERER'S CHILDREN, THE
SILLWILL

❑1, Dec 1998 .... 2.95
❑2, Feb 1999 .... 2.95
❑3, Apr 1999 .... 2.95
❑4, Jul 1999 .... 2.95

S.O.S.
FANTAGRAPHICS

❑1, b&w 2.75

SOUL
FLASHPOINT

❑1, Mar 1994 .... 2.50
❑1/Gold, Mar 1994; Gold edition 3.00

SOULFIRE
ASPEN

❑0, May 2004 .... 2.50

SOULFIRE PREVIEW
ASPEN

❑1, Jan 2004 .... 4.00

SOUL OF A SAMURAI
IMAGE

❑1, Jun 2003 .... 5.95
❑2, Jul 2003 .... 5.95
❑3, Jan 2004 .... 5.95
❑4, Aug 2004 .... 5.95

While not as collected by super-hero comics collectors, *Sonic the Hedgehog* back issues have much higher resale value with fans of the videogame and cartoon series.

N-MINT

SOULQUEST
INNOVATION

❑1, Apr 1989 .... 3.95

SOUL SAGA
TOP COW

❑1, Feb 2000 .... 2.50
❑2, Apr 2000 .... 2.50
❑3, Aug 2000 .... 2.50
❑4, Oct 2000 .... 2.95
❑5, Apr 2001 .... 2.95

SOULSEARCHERS AND COMPANY
CLAYPOOL

❑1 1993 RHo, PD (w) 4.00
❑2 1993 PD (w) 3.00
❑3, Aug 1993; PD (w); Sandman parody 3.00
❑4, Sep 1993 PD (w) 3.00
❑5, Oct 1993 PD (w) 3.00
❑6, Feb 1994 PD (w) 2.50
❑7, May 1994 PD (w) 2.50
❑8, Jul 1994 PD (w) 2.50
❑9 1995 PD (w) 2.50
❑10, Jan 1995 PD (w) 2.50
❑11, Feb 1995 PD (w); RHo (a) 2.50
❑12, May 1995 PD (w) 2.50
❑13, Jul 1995 PD (w) 2.50
❑14, Oct 1995 PD (w) 2.50
❑15, Dec 1995 PD (w) 2.50
❑16, Feb 1996 PD (w) 2.50
❑17, Apr 1996 PD (w) 2.50
❑18, Jun 1996 PD (w) 2.50
❑19, Aug 1996 PD (w) 2.50
❑20, Oct 1996 PD (w) 2.50
❑21, Dec 1996 PD (w) 2.50
❑22, Feb 1997 PD (w) 2.50
❑23, Apr 1997 PD (w) 2.50
❑24, Jun 1997 PD (w) 2.50
❑25, Aug 1997 PD (w) 2.50
❑26, Oct 1997 PD (w) 2.50
❑27, Dec 1997 PD (w) 2.50
❑28, Feb 1998 PD (w) 2.50
❑29, Apr 1998 PD (w); DC, JM (a) 2.50
❑30, Jun 1998 PD (w) 2.50
❑31, Aug 1998; PD (w); Li'l Soulsearchers 2.50
❑32, Sep 1998 PD (w) 2.50
❑33, Nov 1998 PD (w) 2.50
❑34, Jan 1999 PD (w) 2.50
❑35, Mar 1999 PD (w) 2.50
❑36, May 1999 PD (w) 2.50
❑37, Jul 1999 PD (w) 2.50
❑38, Sep 1999 PD (w) 2.50
❑39, Nov 1999 PD (w) 2.50
❑40, Jan 2000 PD (w) 2.50
❑41, Mar 2000 PD (w) 2.50
❑42, May 2000 PD (w) 2.50
❑43, Jul 2000 PD (w); DC (a) 2.50
❑44, Sep 2000 PD (w); DC (a) 2.50
❑45, Nov 2000 .... 2.50
❑46, Jan 2001 .... 2.50
❑47, Mar 2001 .... 2.50
❑48, May 2001 .... 2.50
❑49, Jul 2001 .... 2.50
❑50, Sep 2001 .... 2.50
❑51, Nov 2001 .... 2.50
❑52, Jan 2002 .... 2.50
❑53, Mar 2002 .... 2.50

N-MINT

❑54, May 2002 .... 2.50
❑55, Jul 2002 .... 2.50
❑56, Sep 2002 .... 2.50
❑57, Nov 2002 .... 2.50
❑58, Jan 2003 .... 2.50

SOUL TREK
Spoof

❑1, b&w; parody 2.95
❑2, b&w; parody 2.95

SOULWIND
Image

❑1, Mar 1997, b&w 2.95
❑2, Apr 1997, b&w 2.95
❑3, May 1997, b&w 2.95
❑4, Jun 1997, b&w 2.95
❑5, Oct 1997, b&w 2.95
❑6, Dec 1997, b&w 2.95
❑7, Feb 1998, b&w 2.95
❑8, Apr 1998, b&w 2.95

SOUPY SALES COMIC BOOK
Archie

❑1, Jan 1965 .... 80.00

SOUTHERN BLOOD
Jm Comics

❑1, b&w 2.50
❑2, b&w 2.50

SOUTHERN CUMFORT
Fantagraphics / Eros

❑1 .... 2.95

SOUTHERN-FRIED HOMICIDE
Cremo / Shel-Tone

❑1, b&w; cardstock cover 7.95

SOUTHERN KNIGHTS
Guild

❑2, Apr 1983; Title changes to Southern Knights 2.00
❑3, Jul 1983 .... 2.00
❑4 1983 .... 2.00
❑5 1984 .... 2.00
❑6, Jun 1984 .... 2.00
❑7, Sep 1984 .... 2.00
❑8, Apr 1985 .... 2.00
❑9, Jun 1985 .... 2.00
❑10, Aug 1985 .... 2.00
❑11, Oct 1985 .... 2.00
❑12, Dec 1985 .... 2.00
❑13, Feb 1986 .... 2.00
❑14, Apr 1986 .... 2.00
❑15, Jun 1986 .... 2.00
❑16, Aug 1986 .... 2.00
❑17, Oct 1986 .... 2.00
❑18, Dec 1986 .... 2.00
❑19, Feb 1987 .... 2.00
❑20, Apr 1987 .... 2.00
❑21, Jun 1987 .... 2.00
❑22, Aug 1987 .... 2.00
❑23, Dec 1987 .... 2.00
❑24, Dec 1987 .... 2.00
❑25, Feb 1988 .... 2.00
❑26, Apr 1988 .... 2.00
❑27, Jun 1988 .... 2.00
❑28, Aug 1988 .... 2.00
❑29, Aug 1988 .... 2.00
❑30, Sep 1988 .... 2.00
❑31, Oct 1988 .... 2.00
❑32, Jan 1989 .... 2.00
❑33, Sep 1989 .... 2.00
❑34 .... 2.25
❑35, b&w GP (c) 3.50
❑36, b&w 3.50
❑Holiday 1, Oct 1988; Wizard promotional edition; Dread Halloween Special; b&w Reprint 2.25
❑Special 1, Apr 1989, b&w 2.25

SOUTHERN KNIGHTS PRIMER
Comics Interview

❑1, b&w 2.25

N-MINT

SOUTHERN SQUADRON, THE (AIRCEL)
Aircel

❑1, Aug 1990 .... 2.25
❑2, Sep 1990 .... 2.25
❑3, Sep 1990 .... 2.25
❑4, Nov 1990 .... 2.25

SOUTHERN SQUADRON (2ND SERIES)
Eternity

❑1 1991 .... 2.50
❑2 1991 .... 2.50
❑3 1991 .... 2.50
❑4 1991 .... 2.50

SOUTHERN SQUADRON: THE FREEDOM OF INFORMATION ACT
Eternity

❑1, Jan 1992; Fantastic Four #1 homage cover 2.50
❑2, Feb 1992 .... 2.50
❑3, Mar 1992 .... 2.50

SOVEREIGN SEVEN
DC

❑1, Jul 1995 .... 2.50
❑1/Variant, Jul 1995; foil edition; no cover price 4.00
❑2, Aug 1995 .... 2.00
❑3, Sep 1995 .... 2.00
❑4, Oct 1995 .... 2.00
❑5, Nov 1995 .... 2.00
❑6, Dec 1995 .... 2.00
❑7, Jan 1996 .... 2.00
❑8, Feb 1996 .... 2.00
❑9, Mar 1996 .... 2.00
❑10, Apr 1996 .... 2.00
❑11, Jun 1996 .... 1.95
❑12, Jul 1996 .... 1.95
❑13, Aug 1996 .... 1.95
❑14, Sep 1996 .... 1.95
❑15, Oct 1996 .... 1.95
❑16, Nov 1996; Final Night 1.95
❑17, Dec 1996 .... 1.95
❑18, Jan 1997; Cascade quits 1.95
❑19, Feb 1997 .... 1.95
❑20, Mar 1997 .... 1.95
❑21, Apr 1997 .... 1.95
❑22, May 1997 .... 1.95
❑23, Jun 1997 .... 1.95
❑24, Jul 1997 .... 1.95
❑25, Aug 1997 .... 1.95
❑26, Sep 1997 .... 2.25
❑27, Oct 1997; Genesis 2.25
❑28, Nov 1997 .... 2.25
❑29, Dec 1997; Face cover 2.25
❑30, Jan 1998 .... 2.25
❑31, Feb 1998 .... 2.25
❑32, Mar 1998 .... 2.25
❑33, Apr 1998 .... 2.25
❑34, May 1998 .... 2.25
❑35, Jun 1998 .... 2.25
❑36, Jul 1998 .... 2.25
❑Annual 1, ca. 1995; Year One; Big Barda 3.95
❑Annual 2, ca. 1996; Legends of the Dead Earth; 1996 Annual 2.95

SOVEREIGN SEVEN PLUS
DC

❑1, Feb 1997 .... 2.95

SOVIET SUPER SOLDIERS
Marvel

❑1, Nov 1992 .... 2.00

SPACE: 1999
Charlton

❑1, Nov 1975, JSa (c); JSa (a); O: Moonbase Alpha. 6.00
❑2, Jan 1976, JSa (c); JSa (a) 4.00
❑3, Mar 1976, JBy (c); JBy (a) 4.00
❑4, May 1976, JBy (c); JBy (a) 4.00
❑5, Jul 1976, JBy (c); JBy (a) 4.00
❑6, Sep 1976, JBy (c); JBy (a) 4.00
❑7, Nov 1976, ... 2.50

N-MINT

SPACE: 34-24-34
MN Design

❑1, b&w; photos 4.50

SPACE: ABOVE AND BEYOND
Topps

❑1, Jan 1996 .... 2.95
❑2, Feb 1996 .... 2.95
❑3, Mar 1996 .... 2.95

SPACE: ABOVE AND BEYOND: THE GAUNTLET
Topps

❑1, May 1996 .... 2.95
❑2, Jun 1996 .... 2.95

SPACE ADVENTURES
Charlton

❑1, Jul 1952 .... 240.00
❑2, Sep 1952 .... 125.00
❑3, Nov 1952 .... 105.00
❑4, Jan 1953 .... 105.00
❑5, Mar 1953 .... 105.00
❑6, May 1953 .... 90.00
❑7, Jul 1953 .... 90.00
❑8, Sep 1953 .... 90.00
❑9, Win 1954 .... 90.00
❑10, Apr 1954 SD (a) 225.00
❑11, Jun 1954 SD (a) 225.00
❑12, Aug 1954; SD (a); Steve Ditko credits 225.00
❑13, Oct 1954 .... 90.00
❑14, Dec 1954 .... 90.00
❑15, Mar 1955 .... 90.00
❑16, May 1955 .... 90.00
❑17, Jul 1955 .... 90.00
❑18, Sep 1955 .... 90.00
❑19, Nov 1955 .... 90.00
❑20, Jan 1956 .... 110.00
❑21, Mar 1956; Series continued in War at Sea #22 .... 80.00
❑23, May 1958; Series continued from Nyoka, the Jungle Girl #22 .... 100.00
❑24, Jul 1958 .... 70.00
❑25, Sep 1958, color 70.00
❑26, Nov 1958 .... 70.00
❑27, Feb 1959 .... 70.00
❑28 1959 .... 70.00
❑29, Jul 1959 .... 70.00
❑30, Sep 1959 .... 70.00
❑31, Dec 1959 .... 70.00
❑32, Jan 1960 .... 70.00
❑33, Mar 1960 SD (a); O: Captain Atom. 1: Captain Atom. 325.00
❑34, Jun 1960 SD (a); 2: Captain Atom. 150.00
❑35, Aug 1960 SD (a); A: Captain Atom. 125.00
❑36, Oct 1960 SD (a); A: Captain Atom. 125.00
❑37, Dec 1960 SD (a); A: Captain Atom. 125.00
❑38, Feb 1961 SD (a); A: Captain Atom. 125.00
❑39, Apr 1961 SD (a); A: Captain Atom. 125.00
❑40, Jun 1961 SD (a); A: Captain Atom. 125.00
❑41, Aug 1961 .... 25.00
❑42, Oct 1961 SD (a); A: Captain Atom. 75.00
❑43, Dec 1961 .... 25.00
❑44, Feb 1962 .... 25.00
❑45, May 1962 .... 25.00
❑46, Jul 1962 .... 25.00
❑47, Sep 1962 .... 25.00
❑48, Nov 1962 .... 25.00
❑49, Jan 1963 .... 25.00
❑50, Mar 1963 .... 25.00
❑51, May 1963 .... 18.00
❑52, Jul 1963 .... 18.00
❑53, Sep 1963 .... 18.00
❑54, Nov 1963 .... 18.00
❑55, Mar 1964 .... 18.00
❑56, May 1964 .... 18.00
❑57, Jul 1964 .... 18.00
❑58, Sep 1964 .... 18.00
❑59, Nov 1964 .... 18.00
❑60, Oct 1967 .... 18.00
❑61, Jul 1968 .... 12.00
❑62, Sep 1968 .... 12.00
❑63, Nov 1968 .... 12.00

N-MINT

❑64, Jan 1969 ... 12.00
❑65, Mar 1969 ... 12.00
❑66, May 1969 ... 12.00
❑67, Jul 1969 ... 12.00
❑68, May 1978 ... 12.00
❑69 1978 ... 12.00
❑70 1978 ... 12.00
❑71, Jan 1979 ... 12.00
❑72, Mar 1979 ... 12.00

SPACE ARK
AC

❑1 ... 1.75
❑2 ... 1.75
❑3, b&w ... 1.75
❑4, b&w ... 1.75
❑5, b&w ... 1.75

SPACE BANANAS
KARL ART

❑0 ... 1.95

SPACE BEAVER
TEN-BUCK

❑1, Oct 1986 ... 1.50
❑2 ... 1.50
❑3, Feb 1987 ... 1.50
❑4 1987 ... 1.50
❑5 1987 ... 1.50
❑6, Sep 1987 ... 1.50
❑7, Oct 1987 ... 1.50
❑8, Nov 1987 ... 1.50
❑9, Dec 1987 ... 1.50
❑10, Jan 1988 ... 1.50
❑11, Feb 1988 ... 1.50

SPACE CIRCUS
DARK HORSE

❑1, Jul 2000 ... 2.95
❑2, Aug 2000 ... 2.95
❑3, Sep 2000 ... 2.95
❑4, Oct 2000 ... 2.95

SPACED
UNBRIDLED AMBITION

❑1 ... 2.00
❑2 ... 2.00
❑3 ... 2.00
❑4 ... 2.00
❑5 ... 2.00
❑6 ... 2.00
❑7 ... 2.00
❑8 ... 2.00
❑9 ... 2.00
❑10, b&w; Eclipse publisher ... 2.00
❑11, b&w ... 2.00
❑12, b&w ... 2.00
❑13, b&w ... 2.00

SPACED (COMICS AND COMIX)
COMICS AND COMIX

❑1 ... 4.00

SPACED OUT (FORBIDDEN FRUIT)
FORBIDDEN FRUIT

❑1, Jul 1992 ... 2.95

SPACED OUT (PRINT MINT)
PRINT MINT

❑1 ... 3.00

SPACE FAMILY ROBINSON
GOLD KEY

❑1, Dec 1962; Low circulation ... 200.00
❑2, Mar 1963; Robinson's become lost in space ... 90.00
❑3, Jun 1963 ... 70.00
❑4, Sep 1963 ... 70.00
❑5, Dec 1963 ... 70.00
❑6, Feb 1964 ... 50.00
❑7, Apr 1964 ... 50.00
❑8, Jun 1964 ... 50.00
❑9, Aug 1964 ... 50.00
❑10, Oct 1964 ... 50.00
❑11, Dec 1964 ... 30.00
❑12, Apr 1965 ... 30.00
❑13, Jul 1965 ... 30.00
❑14, Oct 1965 ... 30.00

N-MINT

❑15, Jan 1966; Title changes to "Space Family Robinson Lost in Space" ... 30.00
❑16, Apr 1966 ... 24.00
❑17, Jul 1966 ... 24.00
❑18, Oct 1966 ... 24.00
❑19, Dec 1966 ... 24.00
❑20, Feb 1967 ... 24.00
❑21, Apr 1967 ... 20.00
❑22, Jun 1967 ... 20.00
❑23, Aug 1967 ... 20.00
❑24, Oct 1967 ... 20.00
❑25, Dec 1967 ... 20.00
❑26, Feb 1968 ... 20.00
❑27, Apr 1968 ... 20.00
❑28, Jun 1968 ... 20.00
❑29, Aug 1968 ... 20.00
❑30, Oct 1968 ... 20.00
❑31, Dec 1968 ... 20.00
❑32, Feb 1969 ... 20.00
❑33, Apr 1969 ... 20.00
❑34, Jun 1969 ... 20.00
❑35, Aug 1969 ... 20.00
❑36, Oct 1969; Final issue of original run ... 20.00
❑37, Oct 1973; Series begins again ... 20.00
❑38, Jan 1974; Title changes to "Space Family Robinson, Lost in Space on Space Station One" ... 20.00
❑39, Apr 1974 ... 20.00
❑40, Jul 1974 ... 20.00
❑41, Oct 1974 ... 20.00
❑42, Jan 1975 ... 20.00
❑43, Apr 1975 ... 20.00
❑44, Aug 1975 ... 20.00
❑45, Oct 1975 ... 10.00
❑46, Jan 1976 ... 10.00
❑47, Apr 1976 ... 10.00
❑48, Aug 1976 ... 10.00
❑49 ... 10.00
❑50 ... 10.00
❑51 ... 10.00
❑52, ca. 1977 ... 10.00
❑53, ca. 1977 ... 10.00
❑54, Dec 1977 ... 10.00
❑55, ca. 1981; Series begins again ... 6.00
❑56, Jul 1981 ... 6.00
❑57, Oct 1981 ... 6.00
❑58, Feb 1982 ... 6.00
❑59, May 1982 ... 6.00

SPACE FUNNIES
ARCHIVAL

❑1 ... 5.95

SPACEGAL COMICS
THORBY

❑1 ... 2.95
❑2; Flip-Book with Johnny Cosmic #1 ... 2.95

SPACE GHOST (GOLD KEY)
GOLD KEY

❑1, Mar 1967 ... 150.00

SPACE GHOST (COMICO)
COMICO

❑1, Dec 1987 ... 3.50

SPACE GIANTS, THE
BONEYARD

❑1 ... 2.75

SPACEGIRL COMICS
BILL JONES GRAPHICS

❑1, Nov 1995, b&w ... 2.50
❑2, Nov 1995, b&w ... 2.50

SPACEHAWK
DARK HORSE

❑1, ca. 1989 BW (w); BW (a) ... 2.00
❑2, ca. 1989 BW (w); BW (a) ... 2.00
❑3, ca. 1989 BW (w); BW (a) ... 2.25
❑4, ca. 1989 BW (w); BW (a) ... 2.25
❑5, Jan 1993 BW (w); BW (a) ... 2.50

SPACE HUSTLERS
SLAVE LABOR

❑1, Mar 1997, b&w ... 2.95

Launched long before Irwin Allen's TV show *Lost in Space*, Gold Key's *Space Family Robinson* was a clear inspiration for that series.

© 1967 Gold Key.

N-MINT

SPACE JAM
DC

❑1, Oct 1996; prestige format ... 5.95

SPACEKNIGHTS
MARVEL

❑1, Oct 2000 ... 2.99
❑2, Nov 2000 ... 2.99
❑3, Dec 2000 ... 2.99
❑4, Jan 2001 ... 2.99
❑5, Feb 2001 ... 2.99

SPACEMAN
DELL

❑2, Jun 1962 ... 40.00
❑3, Sep 1962 ... 32.00
❑4 1963 ... 24.00
❑5, Jun 1963 ... 24.00
❑6, Sep 1963 ... 24.00
❑7, Dec 1964 ... 22.00
❑8, Mar 1964 ... 22.00
❑9, ca. 1972; Reprints Space Man #1 ... 5.00
❑10, ca. 1972; Reprints Space Man #2 ... 5.00

SPACE PATROL (ADVENTURE)
ADVENTURE

❑1 ... 2.50
❑2, b&w ... 2.50
❑3 ... 2.50

SPACE SLUTZ
COMIC ZONE

❑1, b&w ... 3.95

SPACE TIME SHUFFLE A TRILOGY
ALPHA PRODUCTIONS

❑1, b&w ... 1.95
❑2, b&w ... 1.95

SPACE TRIP TO THE MOON
AVALON

❑1, ca. 1999, b&w; adapts Destination: Moon ... 2.95

SPACE USAGI
MIRAGE

❑1, Jun 1992, b&w ... 3.00
❑2, Jul 1992, b&w ... 3.00
❑3, Aug 1992, b&w ... 3.00

SPACE USAGI (VOL. 2)
MIRAGE

❑1, Nov 1993 ... 3.00
❑2, Jan 1994 ... 3.00
❑3, Mar 1994 ... 3.00

SPACE USAGI (VOL. 3)
DARK HORSE

❑1, Jan 1996, b&w ... 2.95
❑2, Feb 1996, b&w ... 2.95
❑3, Mar 1996, b&w ... 2.95

SPACE WAR
CHARLTON

❑1, Oct 1959 ... 95.00
❑2, Dec 1959 ... 55.00
❑3, Feb 1960 ... 55.00
❑4, Apr 1960 SD (a) ... 100.00
❑5, Jun 1960 SD (a) ... 100.00
❑6, Aug 1960 SD (a) ... 100.00
❑7, Oct 1960 ... 30.00
❑8, Dec 1960 SD (a) ... 100.00
❑9, Feb 1961 ... 30.00
❑10, Apr 1961 SD (a) ... 100.00
❑11, Jun 1961 ... 30.00

	N-MINT
❑12, Aug 1961	30.00
❑13, Oct 1961	30.00
❑14, Dec 1961	30.00
❑15 1962	30.00
❑16 1962	16.00
❑17 1962	16.00
❑18 1962	16.00
❑19 1962	16.00
❑20, Jan 1963	16.00
❑21, Mar 1963	16.00
❑22, May 1963	16.00
❑23, Jul 1963	16.00
❑24, Sep 1963	16.00
❑25, Nov 1963	16.00
❑26, Jan 1964	16.00
❑27, Mar 1964; Series continued in Fightin' 5 #28	16.00
❑28, Mar 1978; Series begins again (1978)	4.00
❑29, May 1978	4.00
❑30, Jun 1978	4.00
❑31, Oct 1978	4.00
❑32, ca. 1979	4.00

SPACE WAR CLASSICS
AVALON

❑1, b&w	2.95

SPACE WOLF
ANTARCTIC

❑1, b&w	2.50
❑2, b&w	2.50

SPAM
ALPHA PRODUCTIONS

❑1, b&w	1.50
❑2, b&w	1.50

SPANDEX TIGHTS
LOST CAUSE

❑1, Sep 1994, b&w	2.50
❑2, Nov 1994, b&w	2.25
❑3, b&w	2.25
❑4, Mar 1995, b&w	2.25
❑5, May 1995, b&w	2.25
❑6, Jul 1995, b&w; V: Mighty Awful Sour Rangers. false cover for Mighty Awful Sour Rangers #1	2.50

SPANDEX TIGHTS (VOL. 2)
LOST CAUSE

❑1, Jan 1997, b&w	2.95
❑2, Mar 1997, b&w	2.95
❑3, May 1997, b&w	2.95

SPANISH FLY
FANTAGRAPHICS / EROS

❑1	2.95
❑2	2.95
❑3	2.95
❑4	2.95
❑5, May 1996	2.95

SPANK
FANTAGRAPHICS / EROS

❑2, b&w	2.25
❑3, b&w	2.25
❑4, b&w	2.25

SPANK THE MONKEY
ARROW

❑1, Jul 1999, b&w	2.95

SPANNER'S GALAXY
DC

❑1, Dec 1984; mini-series	1.00
❑2, Jan 1985	1.00
❑3, Feb 1985	1.00
❑4, Mar 1985	1.00
❑5, Apr 1985	1.00
❑6, May 1985	1.00

SPARKPLUG
HEROIC

❑1, b&w	2.95
❑2, b&w; trading card	2.95
❑3	2.95

SPARKY & TIM
AARON WARNER

	N-MINT
❑1, Feb 1999	5.95

SPARROW (MILLENNIUM)
MILLENNIUM

❑1 1995, b&w	2.95
❑2, Apr 1995, b&w	2.95
❑3, May 1995, b&w	2.95
❑4, Jul 1995, b&w	2.95

SPARTAN: WARRIOR SPIRIT
IMAGE

❑1, Jul 1995	2.50
❑2, Sep 1995	2.50
❑3, Oct 1995	2.50
❑4, Nov 1995	2.50

SPARTAN X: HELL-BENT-HERO-FOR-HIRE (JACKIE CHAN'S...)
IMAGE

❑1, Mar 1998	2.95
❑2, Apr 1998	2.95
❑3, May 1998; cover says Jun, indicia says May	2.95
❑4, Jul 1998; cover says Aug, indicia says Jul	2.95

SPARTAN X: THE ARMOUR OF HEAVEN (JACKIE CHAN'S...)
TOPPS

❑1, May 1997	2.95

SPASM (PARODY PRESS)
PARODY

❑1	9.95

SPASM (ROUGH COPY)
ROUGH COPY

❑1	2.95
❑2	2.95
❑3	2.95
❑4	2.95
❑5	2.95

SPAWN
IMAGE

	N-MINT
❑1, May 1992 TMc (w); TMc (a); 1: Spawn.	5.00
❑1/A, Sep 1997, b&w; TMc (a); promo with Spawn #65	2.95
❑2, Jul 1992; TMc (w); TMc (a); 1: Violator. cover says Jun, indicia says Jul	4.00
❑3, Aug 1992 TMc (w); TMc (a)	2.50
❑4, Sep 1992; TMc (w); TMc (a); with coupon	2.50
❑5, Oct 1992 TMc (w); TMc (a)	2.50
❑6, Nov 1992 TMc (w); TMc (a); 1: Overt-Kill.	2.50
❑7, Jan 1993 TMc (w); TMc (a)	4.00
❑8, Mar 1993; AMo (w); TMc (a); cover says Feb, indicia says Mar	4.00
❑9, Mar 1993 NG (w); TMc (a); 1: Angela.	4.00
❑10, May 1993 TMc (a); A: Cerebus.	2.75
❑11, Jun 1993 FM (w); TMc (a)	2.50
❑12, Jul 1993 TMc (w); TMc (a)	2.50
❑13, Aug 1993; TMc (w); TMc (a); Spawn vs. Chapel	2.50
❑14, Sep 1993 TMc (w); TMc (a); A: Violator.	2.50
❑15, Nov 1993 TMc (w); TMc (a)	2.50
❑16, Dec 1993 TMc (a); 1: Anti-Spawn.	2.50
❑17, Jan 1994; TMc (a); 1: Anti-Spawn. Spawn vs. Anti-Spawn	3.00
❑18, Feb 1994 TMc (a)	3.00
❑19, Oct 1994; Published out of sequence with fill-in art	3.00
❑20, Nov 1994; Published out of sequence with fill-in art	3.00
❑21, May 1994 TMc (a)	3.00
❑22, Jun 1994 TMc (a)	3.00
❑23, Aug 1994 TMc (a)	3.00
❑24, Sep 1994 TMc (a)	3.00
❑25, Oct 1994	3.00
❑26, Dec 1994 TMc (a)	3.00
❑27, Jan 1995 TMc (a)	3.00
❑28, Feb 1995 TMc (a)	3.00
❑29, Mar 1995 TMc (a)	3.00
❑30, Apr 1995 TMc (a)	3.00
❑31, May 1995 TMc (w); TMc (a)	3.00
❑32, Jun 1995 TMc (w); TMc (a)	3.00
❑33, Jul 1995 TMc (w); TMc (a)	3.00
❑34, Aug 1995 TMc (w); TMc (a)	3.00
❑35, Sep 1995 TMc (w)	3.00
❑36, Oct 1995 TMc (w)	3.00
❑37, Nov 1995 TMc, AMo (w)	3.00
❑38, Dec 1995; TMc (w); TMc (a); 1: Cy-Gor. cover says Aug, indicia says Dec	3.00
❑39, Dec 1995; TMc (w); Christmas story	3.00
❑40, Jan 1996 TMc (w)	3.00
❑41, Jan 1996 TMc (w)	3.00
❑42, Feb 1996 TMc (w)	3.00
❑43, Feb 1996 TMc (w)	3.00
❑44, Mar 1996 TMc (w)	3.00
❑45, Mar 1996 TMc (w)	3.00
❑46, Apr 1996 TMc (w)	3.00
❑47, Apr 1996 TMc (w)	3.00
❑48, May 1996 TMc (w)	3.00
❑49, May 1996 TMc (w)	3.00
❑50, Jun 1996 TMc (w)	2.95
❑51, Aug 1996; TMc (w); cover says Jul, indicia says Aug	1.95
❑52, Aug 1996 TMc (w)	1.95
❑53, Sep 1996 TMc (w)	1.95
❑54, Oct 1996 TMc (w)	1.95
❑55, Nov 1996 TMc (w)	1.95
❑56, Dec 1996 TMc (w)	1.95
❑57, Jan 1997 TMc (w)	1.95
❑58, Feb 1997 TMc (w)	1.95
❑59, Mar 1997 TMc (w)	1.95
❑60, Apr 1997 TMc (w)	1.95
❑61, May 1997 TMc (w)	1.95
❑62, Jun 1997 TMc (w); A: Angela.	1.95
❑63, Jul 1997 TMc (w)	1.95
❑64, Aug 1997; TMc (w); polybagged with McFarlane Toys catalog	1.95
❑65, Sep 1997 TMc (w)	1.95
❑66, Oct 1997 TMc (w)	1.95
❑67, Nov 1997 TMc (w)	1.95
❑68, Jan 1998 TMc (w)	1.95
❑69, Jan 1998 TMc (w)	1.95
❑70, Feb 1998 TMc (w)	1.95
❑71, Apr 1998 TMc (w)	1.95
❑72, May 1998 TMc (w)	1.95
❑73, Jun 1998 TMc (w)	1.95
❑74, Jul 1998 TMc (w)	1.95
❑75, Aug 1998 TMc (c); TMc (w); TMc (a)	1.95
❑76, Sep 1998 TMc (w)	1.95
❑77, Oct 1998 TMc (w)	1.95
❑78, Nov 1998	1.95
❑79, Jan 1999 TMc (w)	1.95
❑80, Feb 1999 TMc (w)	1.95
❑81, Mar 1999 TMc (w)	1.95
❑82, Apr 1999 TMc (w)	1.95
❑83, May 1999 TMc (w)	1.95
❑84, Jun 1999 TMc (w)	1.95
❑85, Jul 1999 TMc (w)	1.95
❑86, Aug 1999 TMc (w)	1.95
❑87, Sep 1999 TMc (w)	1.95
❑88, Oct 1999 TMc (w)	1.95
❑89, Nov 1999 TMc (w)	1.95
❑90, Dec 1999 TMc (w)	1.95
❑91, Jan 2000	1.95
❑92, Feb 2000	1.95
❑93, Mar 2000 TMc (w)	1.95
❑94, Apr 2000 TMc (w)	1.95
❑95, May 2000	1.95
❑96, Jun 2000	1.95
❑97, Jul 2000 TMc (w)	1.95
❑98, Aug 2000 TMc (w)	2.50
❑99, Sep 2000 TMc (w)	2.50
❑100/A, Nov 2000; Giant-size TMc (c); TMc (w)	4.95
❑100/B, Nov 2000; Giant-size TMc (w)	4.95
❑100/C, Nov 2000; Giant-size FM (c); TMc (w)	4.95
❑100/D, Nov 2000; Giant-size TMc (w)	4.95

N-MINT

❑100/E, Nov 2000; Giant-size ARo (c); TMc (w) ... 4.95
❑100/F, Nov 2000; Giant-size TMc (w) 4.95
❑101, Dec 2000 TMc (w) ... 2.50
❑102, Jan 2001 TMc (w) ... 2.50
❑103, Feb 2001 TMc (w) ... 2.50
❑104, Feb 2001 TMc (w) ... 2.50
❑105, Feb 2001 TMc (w) ... 2.50
❑106, Mar 2001 TMc (w) ... 2.50
❑107, Apr 2001 TMc (w) ... 2.50
❑108, May 2001 ... 2.50
❑109, Jun 2001 ... 2.50
❑110, Jul 2001 ... 2.50
❑111, Aug 2001 ... 2.50
❑112, Sep 2001 ... 2.50
❑113, Oct 2001 ... 2.50
❑114, Nov 2001 ... 2.50
❑115, Dec 2001 ... 2.50
❑116, Jan 2002 ... 2.50
❑117, May 2002 ... 2.50
❑118, Jun 2002 ... 2.50
❑119, Aug 2002 ... 2.50
❑120, Sep 2002 ... 2.50
❑121 TMc (w) ... 2.50
❑122, Feb 2003 TMc (w) ... 2.50
❑123, Mar 2003 TMc (w) ... 2.50
❑124, Apr 2003 TMc (w) ... 2.50
❑125, May 2003 TMc (w) ... 2.50
❑126, Jul 2003 ... 2.50
❑127, Aug 2003 ... 2.50
❑128, Sep 2003 ... 2.50
❑129, Oct 2003 ... 2.50
❑130, Nov 2003 ... 2.50
❑131, Dec 2003 ... 2.50
❑132, Feb 2004 ... 2.50
❑133, Apr 2004, b&w ... 2.50
❑134, May 2004 ... 2.50
❑135, Aug 2004 ... 2.50
❑Annual 1, May 1999; squarebound . 4.95
❑Fan ed. 1; Promotional edition included in Overstreet Fan ... 1.00
❑Fan ed. 2; Promotional edition included in Overstreet Fan ... 1.00
❑Fan ed. 3, Oct 1996; Promotional edition included in Overstreet Fan ... 1.00

SPAWN-BATMAN
IMAGE

❑1, ca. 1994 FM (w); TMc (a) ... 4.00

SPAWN BIBLE
IMAGE

❑1, Aug 1996; background on series 1.95

SPAWN BLOOD AND SALVATION
IMAGE

❑1, Nov 1999 ... 4.95

SPAWN BLOOD FEUD
IMAGE

❑1, Jun 1995 ... 2.25
❑2, Jul 1995 ... 2.25
❑3, Aug 1995 ... 2.25
❑4, Sep 1995 ... 2.25

SPAWN MOVIE ADAPTATION
IMAGE

❑1, Dec 1997; prestige format ... 4.95

SPAWN: SIMONY ONE-SHOT
IMAGE

❑1, Apr 2004 ... 7.95

SPAWN: THE DARK AGES
IMAGE

❑1, Mar 1999 ... 3.00
❑1/Variant, Mar 1999 TMc (c); TMc (a) 2.50
❑2, Apr 1999 TMc (c); TMc (a) ... 2.50
❑3, May 1999 ... 2.50
❑4, Jun 1999 ... 2.50
❑5, Jul 1999 ... 2.50
❑6, Aug 1999 ... 2.50
❑7, Sep 1999 ... 2.50
❑8, Oct 1999 ... 2.50
❑9, Nov 1999 ... 2.50
❑10, Dec 1999 ... 2.50
❑11, Jan 2000 ... 2.50

N-MINT

❑12, Feb 2000 ... 2.50
❑13, Mar 2000 ... 2.50
❑14, Apr 2000 ... 2.50
❑15, May 2000 ... 2.50
❑16, Jun 2000 ... 2.50
❑17, Jul 2000 ... 2.50
❑18, Aug 2000 ... 2.50
❑19, Sep 2000 ... 2.50
❑20, Oct 2000 ... 2.50
❑21, Nov 2000 ... 2.50
❑22, Jan 2001 ... 2.50
❑23, Feb 2001 ... 2.50
❑24, Mar 2001 ... 2.50
❑25, Apr 2001 ... 2.50
❑26, May 2001 ... 2.50
❑27, Jun 2001 ... 2.50
❑28, Jul 2001 ... 2.50

SPAWN THE IMPALER
IMAGE

❑1, Oct 1996 ... 2.95
❑2, Nov 1996 ... 2.95
❑3, Dec 1996 ... 2.95

SPAWN THE UNDEAD
IMAGE

❑1, Jun 1999 ... 2.00
❑2, Jul 1999 ... 1.95
❑3, Aug 1999 ... 1.95
❑4, Sep 1999 ... 1.95
❑5, Oct 1999 ... 1.95
❑6, Nov 1999 ... 1.95
❑7, Dec 1999 ... 1.95
❑8, Jan 2000 ... 2.25
❑9, Feb 2000 ... 2.25

SPAWN/WILDC.A.T.S
IMAGE

❑1, Jan 1996 AMo (w) ... 3.00
❑2, Feb 1996 AMo (w) ... 2.50
❑3, Mar 1996 AMo (w) ... 2.50
❑4, Apr 1996 AMo (w) ... 2.50

SPECIAL HUGGING AND OTHER CHILDHOOD TALES
SLAVE LABOR

❑1, Apr 1989, b&w ... 1.95

SPECIAL MARVEL EDITION
MARVEL

❑1, Jan 1971; SL (w); JK (a); reprints Thor stories from Journey into Mystery #117-119; Thor reprints begin 14.00
❑2 1971; reprints Thor stories from Journey into Mystery #120-122 ... 7.00
❑3, Sep 1971; reprints Thor stories from Journey into Mystery #123-125 7.00
❑4, Feb 1972; reprints Thor #126 and #127; Thor reprints end ... 7.00
❑5, Jul 1972; Sgt. Fury reprints begin 6.00
❑6, Sep 1972 ... 6.00
❑7, Nov 1972; Sgt. Fury ... 6.00
❑8, Jan 1973 ... 6.00
❑9, Mar 1973 ... 6.00
❑10, May 1973 ... 6.00
❑11, Jul 1973 A: Captain America. ... 6.00
❑12, Sep 1973 ... 6.00
❑13, Oct 1973 SD (a) ... 6.00
❑14, Nov 1973; Sgt. Fury reprints end 6.00
❑15, Dec 1973; JSn (a); 1: Shang-Chi, Master of Kung Fu. 1: Nayland Smith. Master of Kung Fu ... 42.00
❑16, Feb 1974; JSn (a); O: Midnight. 1: Midnight. 2: Shang-Chi, Master of Kung Fu. series continues as Master of Kung Fu ... 16.00

SPECIAL WAR SERIES
CHARLTON

❑1, Aug 1965 ... 10.00
❑2, Sep 1965 ... 8.00
❑3, Oct 1965; War and Attack ... 8.00
❑4, Nov 1965 O: Judomaster. 1: Judomaster. ... 16.00

Guest writer Neil Gaiman introduced Angela in *Spawn* #9.

N-MINT

SPECIES
DARK HORSE

❑1, Jun 1995 ... 2.50
❑2, Jul 1995 ... 2.50
❑3, Aug 1995 ... 2.50
❑4, Sep 1995 ... 2.50

SPECIES: HUMAN RACE
DARK HORSE

❑1, Nov 1996 ... 2.95
❑2, Dec 1996 ... 2.95
❑3, Jan 1997 ... 2.95
❑4, Feb 1997 ... 2.95

SPECTACLES
ALTERNATIVE

❑1, Feb 1997, b&w ... 2.95
❑2, May 1997, b&w ... 2.95
❑3, Sep 1997, b&w ... 2.95
❑4, Jan 1998, b&w ... 2.95

SPECTACULAR SCARLET SPIDER
MARVEL

❑1, Nov 1995 ... 1.95
❑2, Dec 1995 ... 1.95

SPECTACULAR SPIDER-MAN (MAGAZINE)
MARVEL

❑1, Jul 1968, b&w; magazine JR (a); 1: Richard Raleigh, Man Monster. ... 90.00
❑2, Nov 1968; color magazine JR (a); V: Green Goblin. ... 75.00

SPECTACULAR SPIDER-MAN, THE
MARVEL

❑-1, Jul 1997; Flashback ... 2.00
❑1, Dec 1976; JR, SL (w); SB, JR (a); Tarantula ... 20.00
❑2, Jan 1977; JR, SL (w); SB, JR, JM (a); Kraven ... 8.00
❑3, Feb 1977 SB (a); O: Lightmaster. 1: Lightmaster. ... 5.00
❑4, Mar 1977 SB (a); V: Vulture. ... 5.00
❑5, Apr 1977 SB (a); V: Vulture. ... 5.00
❑6, May 1977 A: Morbius. V: Morbius. 4.00
❑7, Jun 1977 A: Morbius. V: Morbius. 5.00
❑8, Jul 1977 A: Morbius. V: Morbius. 5.00
❑9, Aug 1977 A: White Tiger. ... 5.00
❑9/35 cent, Aug 1977; 35 cent regional variant ... 15.00
❑10, Sep 1977 A: White Tiger. ... 3.50
❑11, Oct 1977 JM (a) ... 3.50
❑12, Nov 1977 SB (a); 1: Razorback (partial). A: Brother Power. ... 3.50
❑13, Dec 1977 SB (a); O: Razorback. 1: Razorback (full). ... 3.50
❑14, Jan 1978 SB (a); V: Hatemonger. 3.50
❑15, Feb 1978 SB (a); A: Razorback. . 3.50
❑16, Mar 1978 SB (a); V: Beetle. ... 3.50
❑17, Apr 1978 A: Iceman. A: Angel. ... 3.50
❑18, May 1978 A: Iceman. A: Angel. . 3.50
❑19, Jun 1978 V: Enforcers. ... 3.50
❑20, Jul 1978 V: Light Master. ... 3.50
❑21, Aug 1978 A: Moon Knight. ... 2.75
❑22, Sep 1978 A: Moon Knight. ... 2.75
❑23, Oct 1978 A: Moon Knight. ... 2.75
❑24, Nov 1978 ... 2.75
❑25, Dec 1978 1: Carrion I. ... 2.75
❑26, Jan 1979 A: Daredevil. ... 2.75
❑27, Feb 1979; FM, DC (a); A: Daredevil. Frank Miller's first Daredevil art 12.00

Condition price index: Multiply "NM prices" above by: **0.83 for Very Fine/Near Mint**
0.66 for Very Fine • 0.33 for Fine • 0.2 for Very Good • 0.125 for Good

	N-MINT
❑28, Mar 1979 FM (a); A: Daredevil.	12.00
❑29, Apr 1979 V: Carrion.	2.75
❑30, May 1979 V: Carrion.	2.75
❑31, Jun 1979 O: Carrion I. D: Carrion I.	2.75
❑32, Jul 1979	2.75
❑33, Aug 1979 O: Iguana.	2.75
❑34, Sep 1979 V: Lizard.	2.75
❑35, Oct 1979	2.75
❑36, Nov 1979 V: Swarm.	2.75
❑37, Dec 1979 V: Swarm.	2.75
❑38, Jan 1980 A: Morbius. V: Morbius.	2.75
❑39, Feb 1980 V: Schizoid Man.	2.75
❑40, Mar 1980 V: Lizard.	2.75
❑41, Apr 1980 V: Meteor Man.	2.75
❑42, May 1980 A: Human Torch.	2.75
❑43, Jun 1980 1: Belladonna.	2.75
❑44, Jul 1980	2.75
❑45, Aug 1980; Vulture	2.75
❑46, Sep 1980; FM (c); MZ (a); Cobra	2.75
❑47, Oct 1980	2.75
❑48, Nov 1980 FM (c)	2.75
❑49, Dec 1980; JM (a); A: Prowler. Title changes to Peter Parker, The Spectacular Spider-Man	2.75
❑50, Jan 1981; FM (c); JR2, JM (a); Smuggler	2.75
❑51, Feb 1981 FM (c); JM (a); V: Mysterio.	2.75
❑52, Mar 1981 FM (c); A: White Tiger.	2.75
❑53, Apr 1981 JM (a); V: Tinkerer.	2.75
❑54, May 1981 FM (c)	2.75
❑55, Jun 1981 FM (c); LMc (a); V: Nitro.	2.75
❑56, Jul 1981 FM (c); JM (a); 2: Jack O'Lantern II. V: Jack O'Lantern II.	5.00
❑57, Aug 1981 FM (c); JM (a)	2.75
❑58, Sep 1981 JBy (a); V: Ringer.	2.75
❑59, Oct 1981 JM (a)	2.75
❑60, Nov 1981; Giant-size FM, JM (c); JM (a); O: Spider-Man. V: Beetle.	2.75
❑61, Dec 1981 JM (a); A: Moonstone.	2.75
❑62, Jan 1982 FM (c); FM (a); V: Gold Bug.	2.75
❑63, Feb 1982 V: Molten Man.	2.75
❑64, Mar 1982 1: Cloak & Dagger.	5.00
❑65, Apr 1982 BH (a); V: Kraven.	3.00
❑66, May 1982 V: Electro.	3.00
❑67, Jun 1982 V: Kingpin.	3.00
❑68, Jul 1982 V: Robot Master.	3.00
❑69, Aug 1982 A: Cloak & Dagger.	3.00
❑70, Sep 1982 A: Cloak & Dagger.	3.00
❑71, Oct 1982; Gun control story	3.00
❑72, Nov 1982 V: Doctor Octopus.	3.00
❑73, Dec 1982 V: Owl.	3.00
❑74, Jan 1983 BH (c); BH (a); A: Black Cat.	3.00
❑75, Feb 1983; Giant-size A: Black Cat.	2.75
❑76, Mar 1983 A: Black Cat.	3.00
❑77, Apr 1983 A: Gladiator.	3.00
❑78, May 1983 V: Doctor Octopus.	3.00
❑79, Jun 1983 V: Doctor Octopus.	3.00
❑80, Jul 1983; J. Jonah Jameson solo story	3.00
❑81, Aug 1983 AM, JM (a); A: Punisher. A: Cloak & Dagger.	3.00
❑82, Sep 1983 A: Punisher. A: Cloak & Dagger.	2.75
❑83, Oct 1983 A: Punisher.	7.00
❑84, Nov 1983	3.00
❑85, Dec 1983 A: Hobgoblin (Ned Leeds). V: Hobgoblin.	5.00
❑86, Jan 1984; A: Fred Hembeck. Asst. Editor Month	3.00
❑87, Feb 1984; AM (a); reveals identity	3.00
❑88, Mar 1984 A: Black Cat. V: Mr. Hyde. V: Cobra.	3.00
❑89, Apr 1984; A: Fantastic Four. A: Kingpin. Fantastic Four apperance	3.00
❑90, May 1984; AM (a); new costume; Black Cat's new powers	3.00
❑91, Jun 1984 V: Blob.	3.00
❑92, Jul 1984 1: The Answer. V: Answer.	3.00
❑93, Aug 1984 V: Answer.	3.00
❑94, Sep 1984 A: Cloak & Dagger. V: Silvermane.	3.00
❑95, Oct 1984 A: Cloak & Dagger. V: Silvermane.	3.00
❑96, Nov 1984 A: Cloak & Dagger. V: Silvermane.	3.00
❑97, Dec 1984 V: Hermit.	3.00
❑98, Jan 1985 1: Spot. V: Kingpin.	3.00
❑99, Feb 1985 V: Spot.	3.00
❑100, Mar 1985; Giant-size V: Spot.	5.00
❑101, Apr 1985 V: Blacklash.	2.25
❑102, May 1985 V: Killer Shrike.	2.25
❑103, Jun 1985	2.25
❑104, Jul 1985 O: Rocket Racer. V: Rocket Racer.	2.25
❑105, Aug 1985 A: Wasp.	2.25
❑106, Sep 1985 A: Wasp.	2.25
❑107, Oct 1985 D: Jean DeWolff.	2.25
❑108, Nov 1985	2.25
❑109, Dec 1985	2.25
❑110, Jan 1986 A: Daredevil.	2.25
❑111, Feb 1986; Secret Wars II	2.25
❑112, Mar 1986; Christmas story	2.25
❑113, Apr 1986	2.25
❑114, May 1986	2.25
❑115, Jun 1986 A: Doctor Strange.	2.25
❑116, Jul 1986 A: Sabretooth.	3.00
❑117, Aug 1986 A: Doctor Strange.	2.00
❑118, Sep 1986	2.00
❑119, Oct 1986 A: Sabretooth.	2.00
❑120, Nov 1986	2.00
❑121, Dec 1986	2.00
❑122, Jan 1987	2.00
❑123, Feb 1987 PD (w); V: Blaze.	2.00
❑124, Mar 1987 BH (c); V: Doctor Octopus.	2.00
❑125, Apr 1987 A: Spider Woman.	2.00
❑126, May 1987 A: Spider Woman.	2.00
❑127, Jun 1987 V: Lizard.	2.00
❑128, Jul 1987 A: Silver Sable.	2.00
❑129, Aug 1987 V: Foreigner.	2.00
❑130, Sep 1987 A: Hobgoblin. V: Hobgoblin.	3.00
❑131, Oct 1987; MZ (a); Kraven	5.00
❑132, Nov 1987; Kraven	4.00
❑133, Dec 1987 BSz (a)	3.00
❑134, Jan 1988 V: Sin Eater.	2.00
❑135, Feb 1988; V: Sin Eater. V: Electro. Title returns to The Spectacular Spider-Man	2.00
❑136, Mar 1988 V: Sin Eater.	2.00
❑137, Apr 1988 V: Tarantula.	2.00
❑138, May 1988 A: Captain America. V: Tarantula.	2.00
❑139, Jun 1988 O: Tombstone.	2.00
❑140, Jul 1988 A: Punisher.	2.00
❑141, Aug 1988 A: Punisher.	2.00
❑142, Sep 1988 A: Punisher.	2.00
❑143, Oct 1988 A: Punisher.	4.00
❑144, Nov 1988; V: Boomerang. in San Diego	2.00
❑145, Dec 1988	2.00
❑146, Jan 1989; SB (a); Inferno	2.00
❑147, Feb 1989; 1: Hobgoblin III. Inferno	8.00
❑148, Mar 1989; Inferno	2.00
❑149, Apr 1989 O: Carrion II (Malcolm McBride). 1: Carrion II (Malcolm McBride).	3.00
❑150, May 1989 V: Tombstone.	2.00
❑151, Jun 1989 V: Tombstone.	2.00
❑152, Jul 1989 SB (a); V: Lobo Brothers.	2.00
❑153, Aug 1989 V: Tombstone.	2.00
❑154, Sep 1989 V: Puma.	2.00
❑155, Oct 1989 V: Tombstone.	2.00
❑156, Nov 1989 V: Banjo.	2.00
❑157, Nov 1989 V: Electro.	2.00
❑158, Dec 1989; V: Trapster. Acts of Vengeance; Spider-Man gets cosmic powers	5.00
❑159, Dec 1989; V: Brothers Grimm. Acts of Vengeance; Cosmic-powered Spider-Man	4.00
❑160, Jan 1990; V: Doctor Doom. Acts of Vengeance; Cosmic-powered Spider-Man	1.50
❑161, Feb 1990 A: Hobgoblin III. V: Hobgoblin III.	1.50
❑162, Mar 1990 A: Hobgoblin III. V: Carrion.	1.50
❑163, Apr 1990 A: Hobgoblin III. V: Hobgoblin III. V: Carrion.	1.50
❑164, May 1990 V: Beetle.	1.50
❑165, Jun 1990 D: Arranger.	1.50
❑166, Jul 1990 SB (a)	1.50
❑167, Aug 1990 SB (a)	1.50
❑168, Sep 1990; Avengers	1.50
❑169, Oct 1990; Avengers	1.50
❑170, Nov 1990; Avengers	1.50
❑171, Dec 1990 SB (a); V: Puma.	1.50
❑172, Jan 1991 V: Puma.	1.50
❑173, Feb 1991; SB (a); Doctor Octopus	1.50
❑174, Mar 1991; SB (a); Doctor Octopus	1.50
❑175, Apr 1991; SB (a); Doctor Octopus	1.50
❑176, May 1991 KB (w); SB (a); O: Corona. 1: Corona.	1.50
❑177, Jun 1991 KB (w); SB (a)	1.50
❑178, Jul 1991 SB (a); V: Vermin.	1.50
❑179, Aug 1991 SB (a); V: Vermin.	1.50
❑180, Sep 1991 SB (a); A: Green Goblin. V: Green Goblin.	1.50
❑181, Oct 1991 SB (a); A: Green Goblin. V: Green Goblin.	1.50
❑182, Nov 1991 SB (a); O: Vermin. A: Green Goblin. V: Green Goblin.	1.50
❑183, Dec 1991 SB (a); A: Green Goblin. V: Green Goblin.	1.50
❑184, Jan 1992 SB (a); A: Green Goblin.	1.50
❑185, Feb 1992 SB (a); A: Frogman.	1.50
❑186, Mar 1992 SB (a); V: Vulture.	1.50
❑187, Apr 1992 SB (a); V: Vulture.	1.50
❑188, May 1992 SB (a); V: Vulture.	1.50
❑189, Jun 1992; 30th Anniversary Issue; SB (a); O: Spider-Man. Silver hologram cover; Gatefold painted poster	4.00
❑189-2, Jun 1992; 30th Anniversary Issue SB (a); O: Spider-Man.	3.00
❑190, Jul 1992 SB (a)	1.50
❑191, Aug 1992 SB (a)	1.50
❑192, Sep 1992 SB (a)	1.50
❑193, Oct 1992 SB (a); V: Puma.	1.50
❑194, Nov 1992 SB (a); V: Vermin.	1.50
❑195, Dec 1992 SB (a); V: Vermin.	1.50
❑195/CS, Dec 1992; Polybagged with Dirt Magazine #2, cassette sampler tape; SB (a); "Dirtbag Special"	2.50
❑196, Jan 1993 SB (a); D: Vermin.	1.50
❑197, Feb 1993 SB (a); A: Spider-Man.	1.50
❑198, Mar 1993 SB (a); A: X-Men.	1.50
❑199, Apr 1993 SB (a); A: X-Men.	1.50
❑200, May 1993; SB (a); A: Green Goblin. D: Green Goblin. foil cover	4.00
❑201, Jun 1993 SB (a); A: Carnage. A: Venom.	1.50
❑202, Jul 1993 SB (a); A: Carnage. A: Venom.	1.50
❑203, Aug 1993 SB (a); A: Carnage. A: Venom.	1.50
❑204, Sep 1993 SB (a); A: Tombstone. V: Tombstone.	1.50
❑205, Oct 1993 SB (a); A: Tombstone. V: Tombstone.	1.50
❑206, Nov 1993 SB (a); V: Tombstone.	1.50
❑207, Dec 1993 SB (a); V: Shroud.	1.50
❑208, Jan 1994 SB (a); V: Shroud.	1.50
❑209, Feb 1994 SB (a); A: Punisher. V: Foreigner.	1.50
❑210, Mar 1994 SB (a); V: Foreigner.	1.50
❑211, Apr 1994 SB (a)	1.50
❑212, May 1994 SB (a)	1.50
❑213, Jun 1994 V: Typhoid Mary.	1.50
❑213/CS, Jun 1994; V: Typhoid Mary. TV preview; print	2.95
❑214, Jul 1994 V: Bloody Mary.	1.50
❑215, Aug 1994 SB (a)	1.50
❑216, Sep 1994 SB (a); V: Scorpion.	1.50
❑217, Oct 1994 A: Ben Reilly.	1.50

N-MINT

❑217/Variant, Oct 1994; Giant-size; O: Ben Reilly. A: Ben Reilly. flip-book with back-up story; enhanced cover 2.95
❑218, Nov 1994 SB (a); V: Puma. 1.50
❑219, Dec 1994 SB (a); A: Daredevil. 1.50
❑220, Jan 1995; Giant-size; flip book with illustrated story from The Ultimate Spider-Man back-up 2.50
❑221, Feb 1995 BSz, SB (a); D: Doctor Octopus. 3.00
❑222, Mar 1995 BSz, SB (a) 1.50
❑223, Apr 1995; Giant-size 2.50
❑223/Variant, Apr 1995; Giant-size; enhanced cover 2.95
❑224, May 1995 1.50
❑225, Jun 1995; Giant-size SB (a); 1: Green Goblin IV. 5.00
❑225/Variant, Jun 1995; Hologram on cover 3.95
❑226, Jul 1995; identity of clone revealed 1.50
❑227, Aug 1995 1.50
❑228, Sep 1995; continues in Web of Spider-Man #129 1.50
❑229, Oct 1995; Giant-size; BSz, SB (a); the clone retires; wraparound cover 2.50
❑229/Variant, Oct 1995; enhanced acetate outer cover; the clone retires 3.95
❑230, Jan 1996; Giant-size; V: D.K. Special cover 3.95
❑231, Feb 1996 SB (a) 1.50
❑232, Mar 1996; SB (a); New Doctor Octopus returns 1.50
❑233, Apr 1996 SB (a) 1.50
❑234, May 1996 1.50
❑235, Jun 1996; return of Will o' the Wisp 1.50
❑236, Jul 1996 V: Dragon-Man. 1.50
❑237, Aug 1996 V: Lizard. 1.50
❑238, Sep 1996 O: second Lizard. 1.50
❑239, Oct 1996 V: Lizard. 1.50
❑240, Nov 1996 1.50
❑240/A, Nov 1996, Variant cover showing pregnant Mary Jane 1.50
❑241, Dec 1996 1.50
❑242, Jan 1997 V: Chameleon. 1.50
❑243, Feb 1997 V: Chameleon. 1.50
❑244, Mar 1997 1: Kangaroo II. V: Kraven. 1.99
❑245, Apr 1997 V: Chameleon. 1.99
❑246, May 1997 V: Legion of Losers (Gibbon, Spot, Kangaroo, Grizzly). 1.99
❑247, Jun 1997 1.99
❑248, Aug 1997; gatefold summary 1.99
❑249, Sep 1997; gatefold summary; Norman Osborn buys Daily Bugle 1.99
❑250, Oct 1997; Giant-size; wraparound cover 2.99
❑251, Nov 1997; gatefold summary V: Kraven. 1.99
❑252, Dec 1997; gatefold summary V: Kraven. 1.99
❑253, Jan 1998; gatefold summary V: Kraven. V: Calypso. 1.99
❑254, Feb 1998; gatefold summary 1.99
❑255, Mar 1998; gatefold summary 1.99
❑256, Apr 1998; gatefold summary V: White Rabbit. 1.99
❑257, May 1998; gatefold summary; Identity Crisis; has second cover with The Spectacular Prodigy #1 1.99
❑258, Jun 1998; gatefold summary 1.99
❑259, Jul 1998; gatefold summary 1.99
❑260, Aug 1998; gatefold summary 1.99
❑261, Sep 1998; gatefold summary 1.99
❑262, Oct 1998; gatefold summary 1.99
❑263, Nov 1998; gatefold summary JBy (c) 1.99
❑Annual 1, Dec 1979; RB, JM (a); Doctor Octopus 5.00
❑Annual 2, Sep 1980 JM (a); O: Rapier. 1: Rapier. 4.00
❑Annual 3, Nov 1981 3.00
❑Annual 4, Nov 1984; O: Ben Parker ("Uncle Ben"). Title changes to Peter Parker, The Spectacular Spider-Man Annual 3.00

N-MINT

❑Annual 5, Oct 1985 3.00
❑Annual 6, Oct 1986; series continues as Spectacular Spider-Man Annual 3.00
❑Annual 7, ca. 1987; V: Puma. Title returns to Spectacular Spider-Man Annual 3.00
❑Annual 8, ca. 1988 4.00
❑Annual 9, ca. 1989; Atlantis Attacks 2.50
❑Annual 10, ca. 1990; SL (w); RB, TMc, RA (a); tiny Spider-Man 2.50
❑Annual 11, ca. 1991 FH (w); FH (a) 2.50
❑Annual 12, ca. 1992; A: New Warriors. Venom back-up story 2.50
❑Annual 13, ca. 1993; AM, JR (a); trading card 2.95
❑Annual 14, ca. 1994 SB (a); V: Green Goblin. 2.95
❑Annual 1997, ca. 1997; Peter Parker Spider-Man '97 2.99
❑Special 1, ca. 1995; Flip-book; A: Scarlet Spider. A: The Lizard. A: Carnage. A: Venom. Super special 3.95

SPECTACULAR SPIDER-MAN, THE (2ND SERIES)
MARVEL

❑1, Sep 2003 2.25
❑2, Sep 2003 2.25
❑3, Oct 2003 2.99
❑4, Nov 2003 2.99
❑5, Dec 2003 2.99
❑6, Jan 2004 2.99
❑7, Jan 2004 2.99
❑8, Feb 2004 2.25
❑9, Mar 2004 2.25
❑10, Apr 2004 2.25
❑11, May 2004 2.25
❑12, May 2005 2.25
❑13, Jun 2004 2.25
❑14, Jul 2004 2.99
❑15, Aug 2004 2.25
❑16, Aug 2004 2.25
❑17, Sep 2004

SPECTACULAR SPIDER-MAN SUPER SPECIAL, THE
MARVEL

❑1, Sep 1995; Flip-book; two of the stories conclude in Web of Spider-Man Super Special #1 3.95

SPECTRE, THE (1ST SERIES)
DC

❑1, Dec 1967 MA, GC (a) 125.00
❑2, Feb 1968 NA (a) 37.00
❑3, Apr 1968 NA (a) 37.00
❑4, Jun 1968 NA (a) 37.00
❑5, Aug 1968 NA (a) 37.00
❑6, Oct 1968 MA (a) 31.00
❑7, Dec 1968 MA (a) 31.00
❑8, Feb 1969 MA (a) 31.00
❑9, Apr 1969 BWr (a) 31.00
❑10, Jun 1969 31.00

SPECTRE, THE (2ND SERIES)
DC

❑1, Apr 1987 GC (a) 3.00
❑2, May 1987 2.50
❑3, Jun 1987 2.50
❑4, Jul 1987 2.50
❑5, Aug 1987 2.50
❑6, Sep 1987 GC (a) 2.25
❑7, Oct 1987 A: Zatanna. 2.25
❑8, Nov 1987 2.25
❑9, Dec 1987 2.25
❑10, Jan 1988; Millennium 2.25
❑11, Feb 1988; Millennium 2.00
❑12, Mar 1988 2.00
❑13, Apr 1988 2.00
❑14, May 1988 2.00
❑15, Jun 1988 2.00
❑16, Jul 1988 2.00
❑17, Aug 1988 1.75
❑18, Sep 1988 1.75
❑19, Oct 1988 1.75
❑20, Nov 1988 1.75

Spider-Man faced The Tarantula in the first issue of the wall-crawler's third ongoing original series, *Spectacular Spider-Man*.

© 1978 Marvel Comics.

N-MINT

❑21, Dec 1988 1.50
❑22, Dec 1988 1.50
❑23, Jan 1989; Invasion! 1.50
❑24, Feb 1989 1.50
❑25, Apr 1989 1.50
❑26, May 1989 1.50
❑27, Jun 1989 1.50
❑28, Aug 1989 1.50
❑29, Sep 1989 1.50
❑30, Oct 1989 1.50
❑31, Nov 1989 1.50
❑Annual 1, ca. 1988 A: Deadman. 2.50

SPECTRE, THE (3RD SERIES)
DC

❑0, Oct 1994 O: The Spectre. 2.50
❑1, Dec 1992; O: The Spectre. Glow-in-the-dark cover 6.00
❑2, Jan 1993 5.00
❑3, Feb 1993 4.00
❑4, Mar 1993 3.00
❑5, Apr 1993 CV (c) 3.00
❑6, May 1993 3.00
❑7, Jun 1993 3.00
❑8, Jul 1993; Glow-in-the-dark cover 3.50
❑9, Aug 1993 3.00
❑10, Sep 1993 3.00
❑11, Oct 1993 3.00
❑12, Nov 1993 3.00
❑13, Dec 1993; Glow-in-the-dark cover 3.00
❑14, Jan 1994 2.50
❑15, Feb 1994 2.50
❑16, Mar 1994 JA (a) 2.50
❑17, Apr 1994 2.50
❑18, May 1994 2.50
❑19, Jun 1994 2.50
❑20, Jul 1994 2.50
❑21, Aug 1994 2.00
❑22, Sep 1994 A: Spear of Destiny. V: Superman. 2.00
❑23, Nov 1994 2.00
❑24, Dec 1994 2.00
❑25, Jan 1995 2.00
❑26, Feb 1995 2.00
❑27, Mar 1995 2.00
❑28, Apr 1995 2.00
❑29, May 1995 2.00
❑30, Jun 1995 2.25
❑31, Jul 1995 2.25
❑32, Aug 1995 2.25
❑33, Sep 1995 2.25
❑34, Oct 1995 2.25
❑35, Nov 1995; Underworld Unleashed 2.25
❑36, Dec 1995; Underworld Unleashed 2.25
❑37, Jan 1996 2.50
❑38, Feb 1996 O: Uncle Sam. 2.50
❑39, Mar 1996 O: Shadrach. 2.50
❑40, Apr 1996 O: Captain Fear. 2.50
❑41, May 1996 2.50
❑42, Jun 1996 2.50
❑43, Jul 1996 2.50
❑44, Aug 1996 2.50
❑45, Sep 1996; homosexuality issues 2.50
❑46, Oct 1996; National Interest acquires Spear of Destiny 2.50
❑47, Nov 1996; Final Night 2.50
❑48, Dec 1996 2.50
❑49, Jan 1997 2.50

	N-MINT
❑50, Feb 1997	2.50
❑51, Mar 1997	2.50
❑52, Apr 1997	2.50
❑53, May 1997	2.50
❑54, Jun 1997	2.50
❑55, Jul 1997	2.50
❑56, Aug 1997	2.50
❑57, Sep 1997	2.50
❑58, Oct 1997	2.50
❑59, Nov 1997	2.50
❑60, Dec 1997; Face cover	2.50
❑61, Jan 1998	2.50
❑62, Feb 1998; funeral of Jim Corrigan	2.50
❑Annual 1, ca. 1995; A: Doctor Fate. Year One	3.95

SPECTRE, THE (4TH SERIES)
DC

	N-MINT
❑1, Mar 2001	3.00
❑2, Apr 2001	2.50
❑3, May 2001	2.50
❑4, Jun 2001	2.50
❑5, Jul 2001 A: Two-Face.	2.50
❑6, Aug 2001	2.50
❑7, Sep 2001	2.50
❑8, Oct 2001	2.50
❑9, Nov 2001	2.50
❑10, Dec 2001	2.50
❑11, Jan 2002	2.50
❑12, Feb 2002	2.50
❑13, Mar 2002	2.50
❑14, Apr 2002	2.50
❑15, May 2002	2.50
❑16, Jun 2002	2.50
❑17, Jul 2002	2.50
❑18, Aug 2002	2.50
❑19, Sep 2002	2.50
❑20, Oct 2002	2.75
❑21, Nov 2002	2.75
❑22, Dec 2002	2.75
❑23, Jan 2003	2.75
❑24, Feb 2003	2.75
❑25, Mar 2003	2.75
❑26, Apr 2003	2.75
❑27, May 2003	2.75

SPECTRESCOPE
SPECTRE

	N-MINT
❑1, Mar 1994; giveaway; no cover price	1.00

SPECTRUM
NEW HORIZONS

	N-MINT
❑1, Jul 1987, b&w	1.50

SPECTRUM COMICS PREVIEWS
SPECTRUM

	N-MINT
❑1, Feb 1983	3.00

SPEEDBALL
MARVEL

	N-MINT
❑1, Sep 1988 SD (w); SD (a); O: Speedball.	1.00
❑2, Oct 1988 SD (w); SD (a)	1.00
❑3, Nov 1988 SD (a)	1.00
❑4, Dec 1988 SD (a)	1.00
❑5, Jan 1989 SD (a)	1.00
❑6, Feb 1989 SD (a)	1.00
❑7, Mar 1989 SD (a)	1.00
❑8, Apr 1989 SD (a)	1.00
❑9, May 1989 SD (a)	1.00
❑10, Jun 1989 SD (a)	1.00

SPEED BUGGY
CHARLTON

	N-MINT
❑1, May 1975	12.00
❑2, Sep 1975	8.00
❑3, Nov 1975	8.00
❑4, Jan 1976	8.00
❑5, Mar 1976	8.00
❑6, May 1976	8.00
❑7, Jul 1976	8.00
❑8, Sep 1976	8.00
❑9, Nov 1976	8.00

SPEED DEMON
MARVEL / AMALGAM

	N-MINT
❑1, Apr 1996 AM (a)	2.00

SPEED FORCE
DC

	N-MINT
❑1, Nov 1997; anthology series with stories of the various Flashes	3.95

SPEED RACER (1ST SERIES)
NOW

	N-MINT
❑1, Aug 1987 O: Speed Racer.	2.50
❑1-2 O: Speed Racer.	1.50
❑2, Sep 1987	2.00
❑3, Oct 1987	2.00
❑4, Nov 1987	1.75
❑5, Dec 1987	1.75
❑6, Jan 1988	1.75
❑7, Mar 1988	1.75
❑8, Apr 1988	1.75
❑9, May 1988	1.75
❑10, Jun 1988	1.75
❑11, Jul 1988	1.75
❑12, Aug 1988	1.75
❑13, Sep 1988	1.75
❑14, Oct 1988	1.75
❑15, Nov 1988	1.75
❑16, Dec 1988	1.75
❑17, Jan 1989	1.75
❑18, Mar 1989	1.75
❑19, Apr 1989	1.75
❑20, May 1989	1.75
❑21, Jun 1989	1.75
❑22, Jul 1989	1.75
❑23, Aug 1989	1.75
❑24, Sep 1989	1.75
❑25, Oct 1989	1.75
❑26, Nov 1989	1.75
❑27, Dec 1989	1.75
❑28, Jan 1990	1.75
❑29, Feb 1990	1.75
❑30, Mar 1990	1.75
❑31, Apr 1990	1.75
❑32, May 1990	1.75
❑33, Jun 1990	1.75
❑34, Jul 1990	1.75
❑35, Aug 1990	1.75
❑36, Sep 1990	1.75
❑37, Oct 1990	1.75
❑38, Nov 1990	1.75
❑Special 1, Mar 1988 O: The Mach 5 (Speed Racer's Car).	2.50
❑Special 1-2, Sep 1988	1.75

SPEED RACER (2ND SERIES)
DC / WILDSTORM

	N-MINT
❑1, Oct 1999	2.50
❑2, Nov 1999	2.50
❑3, Dec 1999	2.50

SPEED RACER 3-D SPECIAL
NOW

	N-MINT
❑1, Jan 1993	2.95

SPEED RACER CLASSICS
NOW

	N-MINT
❑1, Oct 1988, b&w	3.75
❑2, Feb 1989, b&w	3.95

SPEED RACER FEATURING NINJA HIGH SCHOOL
NOW / ETERNITY

	N-MINT
❑1, Aug 1993; trading card	2.50
❑2, Sep 1993; two trading cards	2.50

SPEED RACER: RETURN OF THE GRX
NOW

	N-MINT
❑1, Mar 1994	1.95
❑2, Apr 1994	1.95

SPEED RACER: THE ORIGINAL MANGA
DC / WILDSTORM

	N-MINT
❑1	9.95

SPEED TRIBES
NEMICRON

	N-MINT
❑1, Aug 1998	2.95

SPELLBINDERS
FLEETWAY-QUALITY

	N-MINT
❑1, Dec 1986	1.50
❑2, Jan 1986	1.50
❑3, Feb 1986	1.50
❑4, Mar 1986	1.50
❑5, Apr 1986	1.50
❑6, May 1986	1.50
❑7, Jun 1986	1.50
❑8, Jul 1986	1.50
❑9, Aug 1986	1.50
❑10, Sep 1986	1.50
❑11, Oct 1986	1.50
❑12, Nov 1986	1.50

SPELLBOUND
MARVEL

	N-MINT
❑1, Jan 1988	1.50
❑2, Feb 1988	1.50
❑3, Feb 1988	1.50
❑4, Mar 1988	1.50
❑5, Apr 1988	1.50
❑6, Apr 1988; Double Size	2.25

SPELLCASTER
MEDUSA

	N-MINT
❑1	2.95
❑2	2.95
❑3	2.95

SPELLJAMMER
DC

	N-MINT
❑1, Sep 1990	1.75
❑2, Oct 1990	1.75
❑3, Nov 1990	1.75
❑4, Dec 1990	1.75
❑5, Jan 1991	1.75
❑6, Feb 1991	1.75
❑7, Mar 1991	1.75
❑8, Apr 1991	1.75
❑9, May 1991	1.75
❑10, Jun 1991	1.75
❑11, Jul 1991	1.75
❑12, Aug 1991	1.75
❑13, Sep 1991	1.75
❑14, Oct 1991	1.75
❑15, Nov 1991	1.75
❑16, Dec 1991	1.75
❑17, Jan 1992	1.75
❑18, Feb 1992	1.75

SPEX-7
SHADOW SHOCK

	N-MINT
❑1, Sum 1994, b&w	1.50

SPICECAPADES
FANTAGRAPHICS

	N-MINT
❑1, Spr 1999; magazine-sized; wrap-around cover; Spice Girls parody	4.95

SPICY ADULT STORIES
AIRCEL

	N-MINT
❑1, Mar 1991; pulp reprints	2.50
❑2, Apr 1991; pulp reprints	2.50
❑3, May 1991; pulp reprints	2.50
❑4; pulp reprints	2.50

SPICY TALES
ETERNITY

	N-MINT
❑1, Apr 1988, b&w	1.95
❑2, Jun 1988, b&w	1.95
❑3, Aug 1988, b&w	1.95
❑4, Oct 1988, b&w	1.95
❑5, Dec 1988, b&w	1.95
❑6, Feb 1989, b&w	1.95
❑7, b&w	1.95
❑8, b&w	1.95
❑9, b&w	1.95
❑10	1.95
❑11	1.95
❑12	1.95
❑13	1.95
❑14	2.25
❑15	2.25
❑16	2.25
❑17	2.25
❑18	2.95

	N-MINT
❑19	2.95
❑20	2.95
❑Special 1, Feb 1989, b&w	2.25
❑Special 2, b&w	2.25

SPIDER, THE
ECLIPSE

	N-MINT
❑1, Jun 1991	4.95
❑2, Aug 1991	4.95
❑3, Oct 1991	4.95

SPIDERBABY COMIX (S.R. BISSETTE'S...)
SPIDERBABY

	N-MINT
❑1, Nov 1996	3.95

SPIDER-BOY
MARVEL / AMALGAM

	N-MINT
❑1, Apr 1996	2.50

SPIDER-BOY TEAM-UP
MARVEL / AMALGAM

	N-MINT
❑1, Jun 1997	1.95

SPIDER-FEMME
SPOOF

	N-MINT
❑1; parody	2.50

SPIDER-GIRL
MARVEL

	N-MINT
❑0, Oct 1998; O: Spider-Girl. reprints What If? #105	3.00
❑0.5; Wizard promotional edition	3.00
❑1, Oct 1998; White cover with Spider-Girl facing forward	7.00
❑1/A, Oct 1998; variant cover	7.00
❑2, Nov 1998; gatefold summary A: Darkdevil.	3.00
❑3, Dec 1998; gatefold summary A: Fantastic Five.	3.00
❑4, Jan 1999 V: Dragon King.	3.00
❑5, Feb 1999 1: Spider-Venom. A: Venom.	3.00
❑6, Mar 1999 A: Ladyhawk. A: Green Goblin.	1.99
❑7, Apr 1999 A: Nova. A: Mary Jane Parker.	1.99
❑8, May 1999 A: Kingpin. V: Mr. Nobody. V: Crazy Eight.	1.99
❑9, Jun 1999 V: Killer Watt.	1.99
❑10, Jul 1999 A: Spider-Man.	1.99
❑11, Aug 1999 A: Human Torch. A: Spider-Man. V: Spider-Slayer.	1.99
❑12, Sep 1999	1.99
❑13, Oct 1999	1.99
❑14, Nov 1999	1.99
❑15, Dec 1999	1.99
❑16, Jan 2000	2.25
❑17, Feb 2000	2.25
❑18, Mar 2000	2.25
❑19, Apr 2000	2.25
❑20, May 2000	2.25
❑21, Jun 2000	2.25
❑22, Jul 2000	2.25
❑23, Aug 2000	2.25
❑24, Sep 2000	2.25
❑25, Oct 2000	2.99
❑26, Nov 2000	2.25
❑27, Dec 2000	2.25
❑28, Jan 2001	2.25
❑29, Feb 2001	2.25
❑30, Mar 2001	2.25
❑31, Apr 2001	2.25
❑32, May 2001	2.25
❑33, Jun 2001	2.25
❑34, Jul 2001	2.25
❑35, Aug 2001	2.25
❑36, Sep 2001	2.25
❑37, Oct 2001	2.25
❑38, Nov 2001	2.25
❑39, Dec 2001	2.25
❑40, Jan 2002	2.25
❑41, Feb 2002	2.25
❑42, Mar 2002	2.25
❑43, Mar 2002	2.25
❑44, Apr 2002	2.25
❑45, May 2002, wraparound cover	2.25
❑46, Jun 2002, wraparound cover	2.25
❑47, Jul 2002, wraparound cover	2.25
❑48, Aug 2002, wraparound cover	2.25
❑49, Sep 2002, wraparound cover	2.25
❑50, Oct 2002, wraparound cover	2.25
❑51, Nov 2002, wraparound cover	2.25
❑52, Dec 2002, wraparound cover	2.25
❑53, Jan 2003	2.25
❑54, Feb 2003	2.25
❑55, Mar 2003	2.25
❑56, Apr 2003	2.25
❑57, May 2003	2.25
❑58, Jun 2003	2.25
❑59, Jun 2003	2.99
❑60, Jul 2003, AW (c); AW (a)	2.99
❑61, Aug 2003, AW (c); AW (a)	2.99
❑62, Sep 2003 SB (a)	2.99
❑63, Oct 2003 SB (a)	2.99
❑64, Nov 2003 KJ (c); SB (a)	2.99
❑65, Dec 2003 KJ (c); SB (a)	2.99
❑66, Jan 2004 SB (c); SB (a)	2.99
❑67, Feb 2004, SB (c); SB (a)	2.99
❑68, Mar 2004, SB (c); SB (a)	2.99
❑69, Mar 2004,	2.99
❑70, Apr 2004,SB (a)	2.99
❑71, May 2004, SB (a)	2.99
❑72, Jun 2004, SB (a)	2.99
❑73, Jul 2004, SB (a)	2.99
❑74, Aug 2004, SB (a)	2.99
❑75, Sep 2004	8.00
❑76, Sep 2004	
❑Annual 1999, ca. 1999	3.99

SPIDER-MAN
MARVEL

	N-MINT
❑-1, Jul 1997; Flashback	2.00
❑0.5, ca. 1999	4.00
❑0.5/Platinum, ca. 1999; Platinum edition	6.00
❑1, Aug 1990; TMc (c); TMc (w); TMc (a); Green cover (newsstand)	5.00
❑1/CG, Aug 1990; TMc (c); TMc (w); TMc (a); bagged newsstand (green)	5.00
❑1/CS, Aug 1990; TMc (c); TMc (w); TMc (a); bagged silver cover	5.00
❑1/Platinum, Aug 1990; giveaway TMc (c); TMc (w); TMc (a)	42.00
❑1/Silver, Aug 1990; TMc (c); TMc (w); TMc (a); silver cover	5.00
❑1-2; TMc (c); TMc (w); TMc (a); Gold cover; UPC box	50.00
❑1/Direct ed. -2, Aug 1990; TMc (c); TMc (w); TMc (a); Gold cover; direct sale	5.00
❑2, Sep 1990; TMc (w); TMc (a); Lizard	3.00
❑3, Oct 1990; TMc (w); TMc (a); Lizard	3.00
❑4, Nov 1990; TMc (w); TMc (a); Lizard	3.00
❑5, Dec 1990; TMc (w); TMc (a); Lizard	3.00
❑6, Jan 1991 TMc (w); TMc (a); A: Hobgoblin. A: Ghost Rider. V: Hobgoblin.	3.00
❑7, Feb 1991 TMc (w); TMc (a); A: Hobgoblin. A: Ghost Rider. V: Hobgoblin.	3.00
❑8, Mar 1991 TMc (w); TMc (a); A: Wolverine. V: Wendigo.	2.50
❑9, Apr 1991 TMc (w); TMc (a); A: Wolverine. V: Wendigo.	6.00
❑10, May 1991 TMc (w); TMc (a); A: Wolverine. V: Wendigo.	4.00
❑11, Jun 1991 TMc (w); TMc (a); A: Wolverine. V: Wendigo.	2.50
❑12, Jul 1991 TMc (w); TMc (a); A: Wolverine. V: Wendigo.	2.50
❑13, Aug 1991; TMc (w); TMc (a); Spider-Man wears black costume	5.00
❑14, Sep 1991 TMc (w); TMc (a)	2.50
❑15, Oct 1991 EL (w); EL (a); A: Beast.	2.00
❑16, Nov 1991; TMc (w); TMc (a); X-Force; Sideways printing	2.00
❑17, Dec 1991 AW (a); A: Thanos. V: Thanos.	2.00
❑18, Jan 1992; EL (w); EL (a); Ghost Rider	2.00
❑19, Feb 1992 EL (w); EL (a); A: Hulk.	2.00
❑20, Mar 1992 EL (w); EL (a); A: Nova. A: Hulk. A: Solo. A: Deathlok.	2.00

The Spectre's origins and motivation were reexamined in *The Spectre* (3rd series).

	N-MINT
❑21, Apr 1992; EL (w); EL (a); A: Solo. A: Deathlok. Deathlok appearnace	2.00
❑22, May 1992 EL (w); EL (a); A: Sleepwalker. A: Hulk. A: Ghost Rider. A: Deathlok.	2.00
❑23, Jun 1992 EL (w); EL (a); A: Fantastic Four. A: Hulk. A: Ghost Rider. A: Deathlok.	2.00
❑24, Jul 1992; Infinity War	2.00
❑25, Aug 1992 A: Phoenix.	2.00
❑26, Sep 1992; 30th Anniversary Edition; O: Spider-Man. Gatefold poster; Hologram cover	4.00
❑27, Oct 1992 MR (a)	2.00
❑28, Nov 1992	2.00
❑29, Dec 1992	2.00
❑30, Jan 1993	2.00
❑31, Feb 1993	2.00
❑32, Mar 1993 BMc (a)	2.00
❑33, Apr 1993 BMc (a); A: Punisher.	2.00
❑34, May 1993 BMc (a); A: Punisher.	2.00
❑35, Jun 1993 A: Carnage. A: Venom.	2.00
❑36, Jul 1993 A: Carnage. A: Venom.	2.00
❑37, Aug 1993 AM (a); A: Carnage. A: Venom.	2.00
❑38, Sep 1993 KJ (a)	2.00
❑39, Oct 1993 KJ (a); A: Electro.	2.00
❑40, Nov 1993 KJ (a); V: Electro.	2.00
❑41, Dec 1993	2.00
❑42, Jan 1994	2.00
❑43, Feb 1994	2.00
❑44, Mar 1994	2.00
❑45, Apr 1994	2.00
❑46, May 1994	2.00
❑46/CS, May 1994; with print	3.00
❑47, Jun 1994 V: Hobgoblin.	2.00
❑48, Jul 1994 V: Hobgoblin.	2.00
❑49, Aug 1994	2.00
❑50, Sep 1994	2.50
❑50/Variant, Sep 1994; Holo-grafix cover	3.95
❑51, Oct 1994 A: Ben Reilly.	2.50
❑51/Variant, Oct 1994; Giant-size; O: Ben Reilly. A: Ben Reilly. flip-book with back-up; enhanced cover	2.95
❑52, Nov 1994; The clone vs. Venom	2.00
❑53, Dec 1994; The clone defeats Venom	2.00
❑54, Jan 1995; flip book with illustrated story from The Ultimate Spider-Man back-up	2.00
❑55, Feb 1995	2.00
❑56, Mar 1995	2.00
❑57, Apr 1995; Giant-size JR2 (a)	2.50
❑57/Variant, Apr 1995; Giant-size; enhanced cardstock cover	2.95
❑58, May 1995	2.00
❑59, Jun 1995	2.00
❑60, Jul 1995; Kaine's identity revealed	2.00
❑61, Aug 1995	2.00
❑62, Sep 1995	2.00
❑63, Oct 1995; OverPower game cards bound-in	2.00
❑64, Jan 1996 V: Poison.	2.00
❑65, Feb 1996	2.00
❑66, Mar 1996 JR2 (a)	2.00
❑67, Apr 1996 JR2 (w); AM, AW, JR2 (a)	2.00
❑68, May 1996	2.00
❑69, Jun 1996	2.00

N-MINT

❑70, Jul 1996 A: Hammerhead. 2.00
❑71, Aug 1996 JR2 (a); V: Hammerhead. 2.00
❑72, Sep 1996 JR2 (a); V: Sentinels. 2.00
❑73, Oct 1996 JR2 (a) 2.00
❑74, Nov 1996 JR2 (a); A: Daredevil. 2.00
❑75, Dec 1996; Giant-size; JR2 (a); D: Ben Reilly. wraparound cover; return of original Green Goblin 3.50
❑76, Jan 1997 JR2 (a); A: S.H.O.C.. V: S.H.O.C.. 2.00
❑77, Feb 1997 V: Morbius. 2.00
❑78, Mar 1997 JR2 (a); V: Morbius. 2.00
❑79, Apr 1997 JR2 (a); A: Morbius. V: S.H.O.C.. 2.00
❑80, May 1997 JR2 (a); A: Morbius. V: Hammerhead. 2.00
❑81, Jun 1997 JR2 (a) 2.00
❑82, Aug 1997; gatefold summary JR2 (a) 2.00
❑83, Sep 1997; gatefold summary JR2 (a) 2.00
❑84, Oct 1997; gatefold summary JR2 (a); V: Juggernaut. 2.00
❑85, Nov 1997; gatefold summary V: Shocker. 2.00
❑86, Dec 1997; gatefold summary JR2 (a); A: Trapster. V: Shocker. 2.00
❑87, Jan 1998; gatefold summary JR2 (a); V: Shocker. 2.00
❑88, Feb 1998; gatefold summary 2.00
❑89, Mar 1998; gatefold summary JR2 (a); V: Punisher. V: Shotgun. 2.00
❑90, Apr 1998; gatefold summary 1: Spidey as Dusk. V: Blastaar. 2.00
❑91, May 1998; gatefold summary; Identity Crisis 2.00
❑92, Jun 1998; gatefold summary; JR2 (a); Identity Crisis 2.00
❑93, Jul 1998; gatefold summary A: Ghost Rider. 2.00
❑94, Aug 1998; gatefold summary 2.00
❑95, Sep 1998; gatefold summary V: Nitro. 2.00
❑96, Oct 1998; gatefold summary A: Madame Web. 2.00
❑97, Nov 1998; gatefold summary JBy (c) 2.00
❑98/A, Nov 1998; gatefold summary 2.00
❑98/B, Nov 1998; gatefold summary; JBy (c); Alternate cover; series begins again as Peter Parker: Spider-Man 2.00
❑Annual 1997, ca. 1997; 1997 Annual 2.99
❑Annual 1998, ca. 1998; gatefold summary; A: Devil Dinosaur. A: Moon Boy. wraparound cover 2.99
❑Giant Size 1, Dec 1998; Giant-Sized Spider-Man 3.99
❑Holiday 1995, Hol 1995; Trade Paperback; A: Human Torch. A: Venom. 1995 Holiday Special 2.95

SPIDER-MAN ADVENTURES
MARVEL

❑1, Dec 1994; adapts animated series 1.50
❑1/Variant, Dec 1994; Adapts animated series; enhanced cover 2.95
❑2, Jan 1995; adapts animated series 1.50
❑3, Feb 1995; adapts animated series 1.50
❑4, Mar 1995; adapts animated series 1.50
❑5, Apr 1995; adapts animated series 1.50
❑6, May 1995; adapts animated series 1.50
❑7, Jun 1995; adapts animated series 1.50
❑8, Jul 1995; Adapts animated series 1.50
❑9, Aug 1995; Adapts animated series 1.50
❑10, Sep 1995; Adapts animated series 1.50
❑11, Oct 1995; Adapts animated series 1.50
❑12, Nov 1995; Adapts animated series 1.50
❑13, Dec 1995; Adapts animated series 1.50
❑14, Jan 1996; Adapts animated series 1.50
❑15, Feb 1996; Adapts animated series; Continues in Adventures of Spider-Man #1 1.50

SPIDER-MAN AND BATMAN
MARVEL

❑1, Sep 1995; prestige format 5.95

SPIDER-MAN AND DAREDEVIL SPECIAL EDITION
MARVEL

❑1, Mar 1984 2.00

SPIDER-MAN AND DOCTOR OCTOPUS: NEGATIVE EXPOSURE
MARVEL

❑1, Dec 2003, color 2.99
❑2, Jan 2004, color 2.99
❑3, Feb 2004, color; Negative Exposure 2.99
❑4, Mar 2004 2.99
❑5, Apr 2004, color 0.00

SPIDER-MAN AND HIS AMAZING FRIENDS
MARVEL

❑1, Dec 1981; DS (a); 1: Firestar. A: Iceman. A: Green Goblin. Adapted from television show 2.50

SPIDER-MAN AND MYSTERIO
MARVEL

❑1, Jan 2001; says Spider-Man: The Mysterio Manifesto on the cover 2.99
❑2, Feb 2001; says Spider-Man: The Mysterio Manifesto on the cover 2.99
❑3, Mar 2001; says Spider-Man: The Mysterio Manifesto on the cover 2.99

SPIDER-MAN AND THE DALLAS COWBOYS
MARVEL

❑1, Sep 1983; Danger in Dallas giveaway 10.00

SPIDER-MAN AND THE INCREDIBLE HULK
MARVEL

❑1, Sep 1981; Chaos in Kansas City giveaway 10.00

SPIDER-MAN & THE NEW MUTANTS
MARVEL

❑1; giveaway; child abuse 3.00

SPIDER-MAN & WOLVERINE
MARVEL

❑1, Aug 2003 2.99
❑2, Sep 2003 2.99
❑3, Oct 2003 2.99
❑4, Nov 2003 2.99

SPIDER-MAN AND X-FACTOR: SHADOWGAMES
MARVEL

❑1, May 1994 KB (w); PB (a); O: Shadow Force. 1: Shadow Force. 2.25
❑2, Jun 1994 KB (w); PB (a) 2.25
❑3, Jul 1994 KB (w); PB (a) 2.25

SPIDER-MAN/BADROCK
MAXIMUM

❑1/A, Mar 1997; first part of story 2.99
❑1/B, Mar 1997; second part of story 2.99

SPIDER-MAN/BLACK CAT: THE EVIL THAT MEN DO
MARVEL

❑1, Aug 2002 KSm (w) 2.99
❑1/DF, Aug 2002 5.00
❑2, Sep 2002 KSm (w) 2.99
❑3, Oct 2002 KSm (w) 3.00

SPIDER-MAN: BLUE
MARVEL

❑1, Jul 2002 3.50
❑2, Aug 2002 3.50
❑3, Sep 2002 3.50
❑4, Oct 2002 3.50
❑5, Nov 2002 3.50
❑6, Dec 2002 3.50

SPIDER-MAN: CHAPTER ONE
MARVEL

❑0, May 1999 2.50
❑1, Dec 1998 2.50
❑1/A, Dec 1998; DFE alternate cover 4.00
❑1/B, Dec 1998; Signed edition 14.00
❑1/C, Dec 1998; DFE alternate cover, signed 14.00
❑2/A, Dec 1998; Cover A 2.50
❑2/B, Dec 1998; Cover B 2.50
❑2/C, Dec 1998; Cover forms diptych with issue #1 DFE cover 4.00
❑3, Jan 1999 2.50
❑4, Feb 1999 2.50
❑5, Mar 1999 2.50
❑6, Apr 1999 2.50
❑7, May 1999 2.50
❑8, Jun 1999 2.50
❑9, Jul 1999 2.50
❑10, Aug 1999 2.50
❑11, Sep 1999 2.50
❑12, Oct 1999 2.50
❑Deluxe 1 29.95
❑Deluxe 1/Ltd.; #1 & #2 Pack, DFE alternate cover signed 29.95

SPIDER-MAN: CHRISTMAS IN DALLAS
MARVEL

❑1, Dec 1983; giveaway 10.00

SPIDER-MAN CLASSICS
MARVEL

❑1, Apr 1993; SL (w); SD (a); O: Spider-Man. O: Doctor Strange. 1: Spider-Man. Reprints Amazing Fantasy #15 & Strange Tales #115 2.00
❑2, May 1993; SD, SL (w); SD (a); O: Spider-Man. 1: J. Jonah Jameson. 1: Chameleon. A: Fantastic Four. Reprints Amazing Spider-Man #1 1.50
❑3, Jun 1993; SD, SL (w); SD (a); 1: Mysterio (as alien). 1: Mysterio (as "alien"). 1: Tinkerer. 1: Vulture. Reprints Amazing Spider-Man #2 1.50
❑4, Jul 1993; SD, SL (w); SD (a); O: Doctor Octopus. 1: Doctor Octopus. Reprints Amazing Spider-Man #3 1.50
❑5, Aug 1993; SD, SL (w); SD (a); O: Sandman (Marvel). 1: Betty Brant. 1: Sandman (Marvel). Reprints Amazing Spider-Man #4 1.50
❑6, Sep 1993; SD, SL (w); SD (a); A: Doctor Doom. Reprints Amazing Spider-Man #5 1.50
❑7, Oct 1993; SD, SL (w); SD (a); O: The Lizard. 1: The Lizard. Reprints Amazing Spider-Man #6 1.50
❑8, Nov 1993; SD, SL (w); SD (a); 2: The Vulture. Reprints Amazing Spider-Man #7 1.50
❑9, Dec 1993; SD, SL (w); SD (a); 1: The Living Brain. A: Human Torch. Reprints Amazing Spider-Man #8 1.50
❑10, Jan 1994; SD, SL (w); SD (a); O: Electro. 1: Electro. Reprints Amazing Spider-Man #9 1.50
❑11, Feb 1994; SD, SL (w); SD (a); 1: Big Man. 1: Enforcers. Reprints Amazing Spider-Man #10 1.50
❑12, Mar 1994; SD, SL (w); SD (a); 2: Doctor Octopus. Reprints Amazing Spider-Man #11 1.50
❑13, Apr 1994 1.25
❑14, May 1994 1.25
❑15, Jun 1994 1: Green Goblin I (Norman Osborn). 1.25
❑15/CS, Jun 1994; 1: Green Goblin I (Norman Osborn). polybagged with animation print 2.95
❑16, Jul 1994 1.25

SPIDER-MAN COLLECTORS' PREVIEW
MARVEL

❑1, Dec 1994 1.50

SPIDER-MAN COMICS MAGAZINE
MARVEL

❑1, Jan 1987; digest 1.50
❑2, Mar 1987; digest 1.50
❑3, May 1987; digest 1.50
❑4, Jul 1987; digest 1.50
❑5, Sep 1987; digest 1.50
❑6, Nov 1987; digest 1.50

N-MINT

❑7, Jan 1988; digest 1.50
❑8, Mar 1988; digest 1.50
❑9, May 1988; digest 1.50
❑10, Jul 1988; digest 1.50
❑11, Sep 1988; digest 1.50
❑12, Nov 1988; digest 1.50
❑13, Jan 1989; digest 1.50

SPIDER-MAN/DAREDEVIL
MARVEL

❑1, Oct 2002 .... 2.99

SPIDER-MAN: DEAD MAN'S HAND
MARVEL

❑1, Apr 1997; wraparound cover 2.99

SPIDER-MAN: DEATH AND DESTINY
MARVEL

❑1, Aug 2000 .... 2.99
❑2, Sep 2000 .... 2.99
❑3, Oct 2000 .... 2.99

SPIDER-MAN/DOCTOR OCTOPUS: OUT OF REACH
MARVEL

❑1, Jan 2004 .... 2.99
❑2, Feb 2004 .... 2.99
❑3, Mar 2004 .... 2.99
❑4, Apr 2004 .... 2.99
❑5, May 2004 .... 2.99

SPIDER-MAN/DOCTOR OCTOPUS: YEAR ONE
MARVEL

❑1, Aug 2004 .... 2.99
❑2, Aug 2004 .... 2.99

SPIDER-MAN/DR. STRANGE: THE WAY TO DUSTY DEATH
MARVEL

❑1, ca. 1992, No cover price; graphic novel 6.95

SPIDER-MAN: FRIENDS & ENEMIES
MARVEL

❑1, Jan 1995 .... 1.95
❑2, Feb 1995 .... 1.95
❑3, Mar 1995 .... 1.95
❑4, Apr 1995 .... 1.95

SPIDER-MAN: FUNERAL FOR AN OCTOPUS
MARVEL

❑1, Mar 1995 .... 1.50
❑2, Apr 1995 .... 1.50
❑3, May 1995 .... 1.50
❑4, Jun 1995 .... 1.50

SPIDER-MAN/GEN13
MARVEL

❑1, Nov 1996; prestige format 4.95

SPIDER-MAN: GET KRAVEN
MARVEL

❑1, Aug 2002 .... 2.25
❑2, Sep 2002 .... 2.25
❑3, Oct 2002 .... 2.25
❑4, Nov 2002 .... 2.25
❑5, Dec 2002 .... 2.25
❑6, Jan 2003 .... 2.25
❑7, Feb 2003 .... 2.25

SPIDER-MAN: HOBGOBLIN LIVES
MARVEL

❑1, Jan 1997; wraparound cover 2.50
❑2, Feb 1997; wraparound cover 2.50
❑3, Apr 1997; identity of Hobgoblin revealed; wraparound cover; True identity of Hobgoblin I revealed 2.50

SPIDER-MAN/KINGPIN: TO THE DEATH
MARVEL

❑1; prestige format 5.95

SPIDER-MAN: LEGACY OF EVIL
MARVEL

❑1, Jun 1996; retells history of Green Goblin 3.95

N-MINT

SPIDER-MAN LEGENDS
MARVEL

❑1, ca. 2003 .... 0.00
❑2, ca. 2003, color 19.99
❑3, ca. 2004, color 24.99
❑4, ca. 2004, color 13.99

SPIDER-MAN: LIFELINE
MARVEL

❑1, Apr 2001 .... 2.99
❑2, May 2001 .... 2.99
❑3, Jun 2001 .... 2.99

SPIDER-MAN: MADE MEN
MARVEL

❑1, Aug 1999 .... 5.99

SPIDER-MAN MAGAZINE
MARVEL

❑1, Win 1994 .... 2.00
❑2, Jun 1994 .... 2.00
❑3, Jul 1994 .... 2.00
❑4, Aug 1994; X-Men 2.00
❑5, Sep 1994 .... 2.00
❑6, Oct 1994; X-Men 2.00
❑7, Nov 1994 .... 2.00
❑8, Dec 1994 .... 2.00
❑9, Jan 1995; flip book with Iron Man back-up 2.00
❑10, Feb 1995; flip book with X-Men back-up 2.00

SPIDER-MAN MAGAZINE (2ND SERIES)
MARVEL

❑1, Spr 1995 .... 2.50

SPIDER-MAN: MAXIMUM CLONAGE ALPHA
MARVEL

❑1, Aug 1995; Acetate wraparound cover overlay 5.00

SPIDER-MAN: MAXIMUM CLONAGE OMEGA
MARVEL

❑1, Aug 1995; D: The Jackal. enhanced wraparound cover 5.00

SPIDER-MAN MEGAZINE
MARVEL

❑1, Oct 1994 .... 2.50
❑2, Nov 1994 .... 2.95
❑3, Dec 1994 .... 2.95
❑4, Jan 1995 .... 2.95
❑5, Feb 1995 .... 2.95
❑6, Mar 1995 .... 2.95

SPIDER-MAN 2 MOVIE ADAPTATION
MARVEL

❑1, Aug 2004 .... 3.50

SPIDER-MAN 2 MOVIE TPB
MARVEL

❑1, ca 2004 .... 12.99

SPIDER-MAN MYSTERIES
MARVEL

❑1, Aug 1998; No cover price; prototype for children's comic 1.00

SPIDER-MAN: POWER OF TERROR
MARVEL

❑1, Jan 1995 .... 1.95
❑2, Feb 1995 .... 1.95
❑3, Mar 1995 .... 1.95
❑4, Apr 1995 .... 1.95

SPIDER-MAN, POWER PACK
MARVEL

❑1, Aug 1984; Giveaway from the National Committee for Prevention of Child Abuse; JM (a); No cover price; sexual abuse 1.00

SPIDER-MAN/PUNISHER: FAMILY PLOT
MARVEL

❑1, Feb 1996 .... 2.95
❑2, Feb 1996 .... 2.95

An amalgamation of Spider-Man and Superboy led to Amalgam's *Spider-Boy*. A second one-shot, *Spider-Boy Team-Up*, introduced readers to several more characters hinted at in the earlier title.

N-MINT

SPIDER-MAN, PUNISHER, SABRETOOTH: DESIGNER GENES
MARVEL

❑1, ca. 1993, no cover price 8.95

SPIDER-MAN: QUALITY OF LIFE
MARVEL

❑1, Jul 2002 .... 2.99
❑2, Aug 2002 .... 2.99
❑3, Sep 2002 .... 2.99
❑4, Oct 2002 .... 2.99

SPIDER-MAN: REDEMPTION
MARVEL

❑1, Sep 1996; no ads 1.50
❑2, Oct 1996 .... 1.50
❑3, Nov 1996 .... 1.50
❑4, Dec 1996 .... 1.50

SPIDER-MAN: REVENGE OF THE GREEN GOBLIN
MARVEL

❑1, Oct 2000 .... 2.99
❑2, Nov 2000 .... 2.99
❑3, Dec 2000; events lead in to Amazing Spider-Man #25 and Peter Parker, Spider-Man #25 .... 2.99

SPIDER-MAN SAGA
MARVEL

❑1, Nov 1991 .... 2.95
❑2, Dec 1991 .... 2.95
❑3, Jan 1992 .... 2.95
❑4, Feb 1992 .... 2.95

SPIDER-MAN SPECIAL EDITION
MARVEL

❑1, Nov 1992; "The Trial of Venom" special edition to benefit Unicef; PD (w); A: Venom. Embossed cover 7.00

SPIDER-MAN, STORM AND POWER MAN
MARVEL

❑1, Apr 1982; Smokescreen giveaway 2.00

SPIDER-MAN SUPER SPECIAL
MARVEL

❑1, Jul 1995; Flip-book; two of the stories continue in Venom Super Special #1 .... 3.95

SPIDER-MAN: SWEET CHARITY
MARVEL

❑1, Aug 2002 .... 4.99

SPIDER-MAN TEAM-UP
MARVEL

❑1, Dec 1995 MWa (w); A: X-Men. A: Cyclops. A: Archangel. A: Hellfire Club. A: Beast. A: Phoenix. A: Psylocke. 3.00
❑2, Mar 1996 GP (w); A: Silver Surfer. 3.00
❑3, Jun 1996 A: Fantastic Four. 3.00
❑4, Sep 1996 A: Avengers. 3.00
❑5, Dec 1996 A: Howard the Duck. A: Gambit. 3.00
❑6, Mar 1997 TP, BMc (a); A: Dracula. A: Aquarian. A: Hulk. A: Doctor Strange. 3.00
❑7, Jun 1997 KB (w); SB, DG (a); A: Thunderbolts. 3.00

N-MINT

SPIDER-MAN: THE ARACHNIS PROJECT
MARVEL

- ❑1, Aug 1994 ... 2.00
- ❑2, Sep 1994 ... 2.00
- ❑3, Oct 1994 ... 2.00
- ❑4, Nov 1994 ... 2.00
- ❑5, Dec 1994 ... 2.00
- ❑6, Jan 1995 ... 2.00

SPIDER-MAN: THE CLONE JOURNAL
MARVEL

- ❑1, Mar 1995 SB (a); O: Ben Reilly. ... 3.00

SPIDER-MAN: THE DEATH OF CAPTAIN STACY
MARVEL

- ❑1, Aug 2000; Reprints Amazing Spider-Man #88-90 ... 3.50

SPIDER-MAN: THE FINAL ADVENTURE
MARVEL

- ❑1, Dec 1995; enhanced cardstock cover; clone returns to action one last time ... 3.00
- ❑2, Jan 1996; enhanced cardstock cover ... 3.00
- ❑3, Feb 1996; enhanced cardstock cover ... 3.00
- ❑4, Mar 1996; enhanced cardstock cover; Peter loses his powers ... 3.00

SPIDER-MAN: THE JACKAL FILES
MARVEL

- ❑1, Aug 1995; files on main Spider-Man characters and equipment ... 1.95

SPIDER-MAN: THE LOST YEARS
MARVEL

- ❑0, Jan 1996; JR2 (a); collects clone origin back-up stories; Collects prologue chapters to series ... 3.95
- ❑1, Aug 1995; JR2 (a); enhanced cardstock cover ... 3.00
- ❑2, Sep 1995; JR2 (a); enhanced cardstock cover ... 3.00
- ❑3, Oct 1995; JR2 (a); enhanced cardstock cover ... 3.00

SPIDER-MAN: THE MANGA
MARVEL

- ❑1, Dec 1997 ... 3.99
- ❑2, Jan 1998 ... 2.99
- ❑3, Feb 1998 ... 2.99
- ❑4, Feb 1998 ... 2.99
- ❑5, Mar 1998 ... 2.99
- ❑6, Mar 1998 ... 2.99
- ❑7 1998 ... 2.99
- ❑8, Apr 1998 ... 2.99
- ❑9, Apr 1998 ... 2.99
- ❑10, May 1998 ... 2.99
- ❑11, May 1998 ... 2.99
- ❑12, Jun 1998 ... 2.99
- ❑13, Jun 1998 ... 2.99
- ❑14, Jul 1998 ... 2.99
- ❑15, Jul 1998 ... 2.99
- ❑16, Aug 1998 ... 2.99
- ❑17, Aug 1998 ... 2.99
- ❑18, Sep 1998 ... 2.99
- ❑19, Sep 1998 ... 2.99
- ❑20, Oct 1998 ... 2.99
- ❑21, Oct 1998 ... 2.99
- ❑22, ca. 1998 ... 2.99
- ❑23, ca. 1998 ... 2.99
- ❑24, ca. 1998 ... 2.99
- ❑25, ca. 1998 ... 2.99
- ❑26, ca. 1999 ... 2.99
- ❑27, ca. 1999 ... 2.99
- ❑28, ca. 1999 ... 2.99
- ❑29, ca. 1999 ... 2.99
- ❑30, ca. 1999 ... 2.99
- ❑31, ca. 1999 ... 2.99

N-MINT

SPIDER-MAN: THE MUTANT AGENDA
MARVEL

- ❑0, Mar 1994; strip reprints; Spaces to paste in newspaper strip; cover says Feb, indicia says Mar ... 1.25
- ❑1, Mar 1994; Ties in with daily Spider-Man newspaper strip ... 1.75
- ❑2, Apr 1994 ... 1.75
- ❑3, May 1994 ... 1.75

SPIDER-MAN: THE OFFICIAL MOVIE ADAPTATION
MARVEL

- ❑1, Jun 2002 ... 5.95

SPIDER-MAN: THE PARKER YEARS
MARVEL

- ❑1, Nov 1995; retells events in the clone's life from Amazing Spider-Man #150 to the present ... 2.50

SPIDER-MAN 2099
MARVEL

- ❑1, Nov 1992; PD (w); O: Spider-Man 2099. 1: Tyler Stone. foil cover ... 3.00
- ❑1/Autographed, Nov 1992; AW (a); foil cover with certificate of authenticity ... 1.75
- ❑2, Dec 1992 PD (w); O: Spider-Man 2099. ... 1.25
- ❑3, Jan 1993 PD (w); O: Spider-Man 2099. ... 1.25
- ❑4, Feb 1993 PD (w); 1: The Specialist. 1.25
- ❑5, Mar 1993 PD (w) ... 1.25
- ❑6, Apr 1993 PD (w); 1: Vulture 2099. 1.25
- ❑7, May 1993 PD (w) ... 1.25
- ❑8, Jun 1993 PD (w) ... 1.25
- ❑9, Jul 1993 PD (w) ... 1.25
- ❑10, Aug 1993 PD (w) ... 1.25
- ❑11, Sep 1993 PD (w) ... 1.25
- ❑12, Oct 1993 PD (w) ... 1.25
- ❑13, Nov 1993 PD (w) ... 1.25
- ❑14, Dec 1993 PD (w) ... 1.25
- ❑15, Jan 1994 PD (w) ... 1.25
- ❑16, Feb 1994 PD (w) ... 1.25
- ❑17, Mar 1994 PD (w) ... 1.25
- ❑18, Apr 1994 PD (w) ... 1.25
- ❑19, May 1994 PD (w) ... 1.50
- ❑20, Jun 1994 PD (w) ... 1.50
- ❑21, Jul 1994 PD (w) ... 1.50
- ❑22, Aug 1994 PD (w) ... 1.50
- ❑23, Sep 1994 PD (w) ... 1.50
- ❑24, Oct 1994 PD (w) ... 1.50
- ❑25, Nov 1994; Giant-size PD (w) ... 2.25
- ❑25/Variant, Nov 1994; Giant-size; PD (w); enhanced cover ... 2.95
- ❑26, Dec 1994 PD (w) ... 1.50
- ❑27, Jan 1995 PD (w) ... 1.50
- ❑28, Feb 1995 PD (w) ... 1.50
- ❑29, Mar 1995 PD (w) ... 1.50
- ❑30, Apr 1995 PD (w) ... 1.50
- ❑31, May 1995 PD (w) ... 1.50
- ❑32, Jun 1995 PD (w) ... 1.95
- ❑33, Jul 1995 PD (w); A: Strange 2099. 1.95
- ❑34, Aug 1995 PD (w) ... 1.95
- ❑35, Sep 1995 PD (w) ... 1.95
- ❑35/Variant, Sep 1995; PD (w); alternate cover ... 1.95
- ❑36, Oct 1995; PD (w); Spiderman 2099 on cover ... 1.95
- ❑36/Variant, Oct 1995; PD (w); alternate cover; says Venom 2099; forms diptych ... 1.95
- ❑37, Nov 1995 PD (w) ... 1.95
- ❑37/Variant, Nov 1995; alternate cover; says Venom 2099 ... 1.95
- ❑38, Dec 1995; PD (w); Spiderman 2099 on cover ... 1.95
- ❑38/Variant, Dec 1995; PD (w); alternate cover; says Venom 2099; forms diptych ... 1.95
- ❑39, Jan 1996 PD (w) ... 1.95
- ❑40, Feb 1996 PD (w); V: Goblin 2099. 1.95
- ❑41, Mar 1996 PD (w) ... 1.95
- ❑42, Apr 1996 PD (w); BSz (a) ... 1.95
- ❑43, May 1996 PD (w) ... 1.95
- ❑44, Jun 1996 ... 1.95
- ❑45, Jul 1996 V: Goblin 2099. ... 1.95

N-MINT

- ❑46, Aug 1996; V: Vulture 2099. story continues in Fantastic Four 2099 #8 ... 1.95
- ❑Annual 1, ca. 1994; 1994 Annual ... 2.95
- ❑Special 1, Nov 1995 ... 3.95

SPIDER-MAN 2099 MEETS SPIDER-MAN
MARVEL

- ❑1, Nov 1995 ... 5.95

SPIDER-MAN UNIVERSE
MARVEL

- ❑1, Mar 2000; Reprints Peter Parker: Spider-Man #13, Webspinners #13, Spider-Woman (2nd Series) #8 ... 4.99

SPIDER-MAN UNLIMITED
MARVEL

- ❑1, May 1993 ... 4.00
- ❑2, Aug 1993 ... 4.00
- ❑3, Nov 1993; Doctor Octopus ... 4.00
- ❑4, Feb 1994; Mysterio ... 4.00
- ❑5, May 1994; Human Torch ... 4.00
- ❑6, Aug 1994 ... 4.00
- ❑7, Nov 1994; Spider-Man and clone 4.00
- ❑8, Feb 1995; Spider-Man and clone . 4.00
- ❑9, May 1995 ... 4.00
- ❑10, Sep 1995 ... 4.00
- ❑11, Jan 1996 ... 4.00
- ❑12, May 1996 ... 4.00
- ❑13, Aug 1996 ... 2.95
- ❑14, Dec 1996 ... 2.99
- ❑15, Feb 1997 ... 2.99
- ❑16, May 1997 ... 2.99
- ❑17, Aug 1997; gatefold summary ... 2.99
- ❑18, Nov 1997; gatefold summary ... 2.99
- ❑19, Feb 1998; gatefold summary ... 2.99
- ❑20, May 1998; gatefold summary ... 2.99
- ❑21, Aug 1998; gatefold summary ... 2.99
- ❑22, Nov 1998; gatefold summary ... 2.99

SPIDER-MAN UNLIMITED (2ND SERIES)
MARVEL

- ❑1, Dec 1999; based on animated television show ... 2.99

SPIDER-MAN UNLIMITED (3RD SERIES)
MARVEL

- ❑1, Mar 2004 ... 2.99
- ❑2, May 2004 ... 2.99
- ❑3, Jul 2004 ... 2.99
- ❑4, Sep 2004

SPIDER-MAN UNMASKED
MARVEL

- ❑1, Nov 1996 ... 5.95

SPIDER-MAN: VENOM AGENDA
MARVEL

- ❑1, Jan 1998; gatefold summary ... 2.99

SPIDER-MAN VS. DRACULA
MARVEL

- ❑1 RA (a) ... 2.00

SPIDER-MAN VS. PUNISHER
MARVEL

- ❑1, Jul 2000 ... 2.99

SPIDER-MAN VS. THE HULK
MARVEL

- ❑1, ca. 1979; giveaway ... 1.00

SPIDER-MAN VS. WOLVERINE
MARVEL

- ❑1, Feb 1987 D: Ned Leeds. ... 6.00
- ❑1-2, Aug 1990; D: Ned Leeds. cardstock cover ... 4.95

SPIDER-MAN: WEB OF DOOM
MARVEL

- ❑1, Aug 1994 ... 2.00
- ❑2, Sep 1994 ... 2.00
- ❑3, Oct 1994 ... 2.00

SPIDER, THE: REIGN OF THE VAMPIRE KING
ECLIPSE

- ❑1, ca. 1992 ... 4.95

N-MINT

❑2, ca. 1992 .... 4.95
❑3, ca. 1992 .... 4.95

SPIDER'S WEB, THE
BLAZING

❑1; Flip-book 1.50

SPIDER-WOMAN
MARVEL

❑1, Apr 1978 CI (a); O: Spider-Woman I (Jessica Drew). 6.00
❑2, May 1978 1: Morgan LeFay. 3.00
❑3, Jun 1978 1: Brothers Grimm. 2.50
❑4, Jul 1978 .... 2.00
❑5, Aug 1978 .... 2.00
❑6, Sep 1978 .... 1.75
❑7, Oct 1978 .... 1.75
❑8, Nov 1978 .... 1.75
❑9, Dec 1978 O: Needle. 1: Needle. 1.75
❑10, Jan 1979 .... 1.75
❑11, Feb 1979 .... 1.50
❑12, Mar 1979 D: Brothers Grimm. 1.50
❑13, Apr 1979 .... 1.50
❑14, May 1979 .... 1.50
❑15, Jun 1979 .... 1.50
❑16, Jul 1979 .... 1.50
❑17, Aug 1979 .... 1.50
❑18, Sep 1979 .... 1.50
❑19, Oct 1979 V: Werewolf. 1.50
❑20, Nov 1979 A: Spider-Man. 1.50
❑21, Dec 1979 .... 1.50
❑22, Jan 1980 .... 1.50
❑23, Feb 1980 .... 1.50
❑24, Mar 1980 TVE (a) 1.50
❑25, Apr 1980 .... 1.50
❑26, May 1980 JBy (c) 1.50
❑27, Jun 1980 .... 1.50
❑28, Jul 1980 A: Spider-Man. 1.50
❑29, Aug 1980 A: Spider-Man. 1.50
❑30, Sep 1980 1: Doctor Karl Malus. 1.50
❑31, Oct 1980 FM (c); FM (a) 1.50
❑32, Nov 1980 FM (c); FM (a) 1.50
❑33, Dec 1980 O: Turner D. Century. 1: Turner D. Century. 1.50
❑34, Jan 1981 .... 1.50
❑35, Feb 1981 .... 1.50
❑36, Mar 1981 .... 1.50
❑37, Apr 1981 1: Siryn. A: X-Men. 4.00
❑38, Jun 1981 A: X-Men. 4.00
❑39, Aug 1981 .... 1.25
❑40, Oct 1981 .... 1.25
❑41, Dec 1981 .... 1.25
❑42, Feb 1982 .... 1.25
❑43, Apr 1982 .... 1.25
❑44, Jun 1982 .... 1.25
❑45, Aug 1982 .... 1.25
❑46, Oct 1982 .... 1.25
❑47, Dec 1982 .... 1.25
❑48, Feb 1983 .... 1.25
❑49, Apr 1983 .... 1.25
❑50, Jun 1983; Giant-size D: Spider-Woman I (Jessica Drew). 4.00

SPIDER-WOMAN (2ND SERIES)
MARVEL

❑1, Nov 1993 .... 1.75
❑2, Dec 1993 .... 1.75
❑3, Jan 1994 .... 1.75
❑4, Feb 1994 .... 1.75

SPIDER-WOMAN (3RD SERIES)
MARVEL

❑1, Jul 1999 JBy (w) 2.99
❑2, Aug 1999 .... 2.99
❑3, Sep 1999 .... 1.99
❑4, Oct 1999 .... 1.99
❑5, Nov 1999 .... 1.99
❑6, Dec 1999 .... 1.99
❑7, Jan 2000 .... 1.99
❑8, Feb 2000 .... 1.99
❑9, Mar 2000 .... 1.99
❑10, Apr 2000 .... 2.25
❑11, May 2000 .... 2.25
❑12, Jun 2000 .... 2.25
❑13, Jul 2000 .... 2.25

N-MINT

❑14, Aug 2000 .... 2.25
❑15, Sep 2000 .... 2.25
❑16, Oct 2000 .... 2.25
❑17, Nov 2000 .... 2.25
❑18, Dec 2000 JBy (w) 2.25

SPIDERY-MON: MAXIMUM CARCASS
PARODY

❑1/A, b&w; Variant edition A; Covers of the three variants join together to form a mural 3.25
❑1/B, b&w; Variant edition B; Covers of the three variants join together to form a mural 3.25
❑1/C, b&w; Variant edition C; Covers of the three variants join together to form a mural 3.25

SPIDEY AND THE MINI-MARVELS
MARVEL

❑1, May 2003 .... 3.50

SPIDEY SUPER STORIES
MARVEL

❑1, Oct 1974 O: Spider-Man. 15.00
❑2, Nov 1974 .... 6.00
❑3, Dec 1974 V: Circus of Crime. 5.00
❑4, Jan 1975 .... 5.00
❑5, Feb 1975 .... 5.00
❑6, Mar 1975 .... 5.00
❑7, Apr 1975 .... 5.00
❑8, May 1975 .... 5.00
❑9, Jun 1975; V: Dr. Doom. V: Doctor Doom. Hulk 5.00
❑10, Jul 1975 .... 5.00
❑11, Aug 1975 .... 5.00
❑12, Sep 1975 .... 5.00
❑13, Oct 1975 .... 5.00
❑14, Dec 1975 A: Shanna. 5.00
❑15, Feb 1976 A: Storm. 5.00
❑16, Apr 1976 .... 5.00
❑17, Jun 1976 .... 5.00
❑18, Aug 1976 .... 5.00
❑19, Oct 1976 .... 5.00
❑20, Dec 1976 .... 5.00
❑21, Feb 1977 .... 5.00
❑22, Apr 1977 .... 5.00
❑23, Jun 1977 .... 5.00
❑24, Jul 1977 A: Thundra. 5.00
❑25, Aug 1977 .... 5.00
❑26, Sep 1977 .... 5.00
❑27, Oct 1977 .... 5.00
❑28, Nov 1977 .... 5.00
❑29, Dec 1977 V: Kingpin. 5.00
❑30, Jan 1978 V: Kang the Conqueror. 5.00
❑31, Feb 1978 .... 5.00
❑32, Mar 1978 .... 5.00
❑33, Apr 1978 A: Hulk. 5.00
❑34, May 1978 .... 5.00
❑35, Jul 1978 A: Shanna. 5.00
❑36, Sep 1978 .... 5.00
❑37, Nov 1978 .... 5.00
❑38, Jan 1979 .... 5.00
❑39, Mar 1979 A: Thanos. A: Hellcat. 5.00
❑40, May 1979 .... 5.00
❑41, Jul 1979 .... 5.00
❑42, Sep 1979 .... 5.00
❑43, Nov 1979 .... 5.00
❑44, Jan 1980 .... 5.00
❑45, Mar 1980 A: Doctor Doom. A: Silver Surfer. 5.00
❑46, May 1980 .... 5.00
❑47, Jul 1980 .... 5.00
❑48, Sep 1980 .... 5.00
❑49, Nov 1980 .... 5.00
❑50, Jan 1981 .... 5.00
❑51, Mar 1981 .... 5.00
❑52, May 1981 .... 5.00
❑53, Jul 1981 .... 5.00
❑54, Sep 1981 .... 5.00
❑55, Nov 1981 V: Kingpin. 5.00
❑56, Jan 1982 .... 5.00
❑57, Mar 1982 .... 5.00

Spidey Super Stories was produced in cooperation with the Children's Television Workshop and featured characters from both the Marvel universe and The Electric Company.

© 1975 Marvel Comics.

N-MINT

SPINELESS-MAN $2099
PARODY

❑1 .... 2.50

SPINE-TINGLING TALES (DR. SPEKTOR PRESENTS...)
GOLD KEY

❑1, May 1975 .... 3.00
❑2, Aug 1975 .... 2.00
❑3, Nov 1975 .... 2.00
❑4, Feb 1976 .... 2.00

SPINWORLD
SLAVE LABOR / AMAZE INK

❑1, Jul 1997, b&w 2.95
❑2, Aug 1997, b&w 2.95
❑3, Oct 1997, b&w 2.95
❑4, Jan 1998, b&w 2.95

SPIRAL PATH, THE
ECLIPSE

❑1, ca. 1986 .... 1.75
❑2, ca. 1986 .... 1.75

SPIRAL ZONE
DC

❑1, Feb 1988 .... 1.00
❑2, Mar 1988 .... 1.00
❑3, Apr 1988 .... 1.00
❑4, May 1988 .... 1.00

SPIRIT, THE (5TH SERIES)
HARVEY

❑1, Oct 1966; WE (c); WE (w); WE (a); O: The Spirit. Harvey 50.00
❑2, Mar 1967 WE (c); WE (w); WE (a) 42.00

SPIRIT, THE (6TH SERIES)
KITCHEN SINK

❑1, Jan 1973, b&w; WE (c); WE (w); WE (a); Krupp/Kitchen Sink publishes 14.00
❑2, Sep 1973 WE (c); WE (w); WE (a) 14.00

SPIRIT, THE (7TH SERIES)
KEN PIERCE

❑1 WE (c); WE (w); WE (a) 18.00
❑2 WE (c); WE (w); WE (a) 18.00
❑3 WE (c); WE (w); WE (a) 18.00
❑4 WE (c); WE (w); WE (a) 18.00

SPIRIT, THE (8TH SERIES)
KITCHEN SINK

❑1, Oct 1983, color; WE (w); WE (a); O: The Spirit. Kitchen Sink publishes; 5.00
❑2, Dec 1983, color; WE (w); WE (a); 4.00
❑3, Feb 1984, color; WE (w); WE (a); 4.00
❑4, Mar 1984, color; WE (w); WE (a); Reprints Police Comics #98 Spirit Story 3.50
❑5, Jun 1984, color WE (w); WE (a) 3.50
❑6, Aug 1984, color WE (w); WE (a) 3.50
❑7, Oct 1984, color WE (w); WE (a) 3.50
❑8, Feb 1985, color WE (w); WE (a) 3.50
❑9, Apr 1985, color WE (w); WE (a) 3.50
❑10, Jun 1985, color WE (w); WE (a) 2.95
❑11, Aug 1985, color WE (w); WE (a) 2.95
❑12, Oct 1985, b&w WE (w); WE (a) 2.00
❑13, Nov 1985, b&w WE (w); WE (a) 2.00
❑14, Dec 1985, b&w WE (w); WE (a) 2.00
❑15, Jan 1986, b&w; WE (w); WE (a); 2.00
❑16, Feb 1986, b&w WE (w); WE (a) 2.00
❑17, Mar 1986, b&w WE (w); WE (a) 2.00
❑18, Apr 1986, b&w WE (w); WE (a) 2.00

N-MINT

❑19, May 1986, b&w WE (w); WE (a) 2.00
❑20, Jun 1986, b&w WE (w); WE (a) 2.00
❑21, Jul 1986, b&w WE (w); WE (a) . 2.00
❑22, Aug 1986, b&w WE (w); WE (a) 2.00
❑23, Sep 1986, b&w WE (w); WE (a) 2.00
❑24, Oct 1986, b&w WE (w); WE (a) 2.00
❑25, Nov 1986, b&w WE (w); WE (a) 2.00
❑26, Dec 1986, b&w WE (w); WE (a) 2.00
❑27, Jan 1987, b&w WE (w); WE (a) 2.00
❑28, Feb 1987, b&w WE (w); WE (a) 2.00
❑29, Mar 1987, b&w WE (w); WE (a) 2.00
❑30, Apr 1987, b&w WE (w); WE (a) 2.00
❑31, May 1987, b&w WE (w); WE (a) 2.00
❑32, Jun 1987, b&w WE (w); WE (a) 2.00
❑33, Jul 1987, b&w WE (w); WE (a) . 2.00
❑34, Aug 1987, b&w WE (w); WE (a) 2.00
❑35, Sep 1987, b&w WE (w); WE (a) 2.00
❑36, Oct 1987, b&w WE (w); WE (a) 2.00
❑37, Nov 1987, b&w WE (w); WE (a) 2.00
❑38, Dec 1988, b&w WE (w); WE (a) 2.00
❑39, Jan 1988, b&w WE (w); WE (a) 2.00
❑40, Feb 1988, b&w WE (w); WE (a) 2.00
❑41, Mar 1988, b&w; WE (w); WE (a); Wertham parody 2.00
❑42, Apr 1988, b&w WE (w); WE (a) 2.00
❑43, May 1988, b&w WE (w); WE (a) 2.00
❑44, Jun 1988, b&w WE (w); WE (a) 2.00
❑45, Jul 1988, b&w WE (w); WE (a) . 2.00
❑46, Aug 1988, b&w WE (w); WE (a) 2.00
❑47, Sep 1988, b&w WE (w); WE (a) 2.00
❑48, Oct 1988, b&w WE (w); WE (a) 2.00
❑49, Nov 1988, b&w WE (w); WE (a) 2.00
❑50, Dec 1988, b&w WE (w); WE (a) 2.00
❑51, Jan 1989, b&w WE (w); WE (a) 2.00
❑52, Feb 1989, b&w WE (w); WE (a) 2.00
❑53, Mar 1989, b&w WE (w); WE (a) 2.00
❑54, Apr 1989, b&w WE (w); WE (a) 2.00
❑55, May 1989, b&w WE (w); WE (a) 2.00
❑56, Jun 1989, b&w WE (w); WE (a) 2.00
❑57, Jul 1989, b&w WE (w); WE (a) . 2.00
❑58, Aug 1989, b&w WE (w); WE (a) 2.00
❑59, Sep 1989, b&w WE (w); WE (a) 2.00
❑60, Oct 1989, b&w; WE (w); WE (a); 2.00
❑61, Nov 1989, b&w; WE (w); WE (a); 2.00
❑62, Dec 1989, b&w WE (w); WE (a) 2.00
❑63, Jan 1990, b&w WE (w); WE (a) 2.00
❑64, Feb 1990, b&w WE (w); WE (a) 2.00
❑65, Mar 1990, b&w WE (w); WE (a) 2.00
❑66, Apr 1990, b&w WE (w); WE (a) 2.00
❑67, May 1990, b&w WE (w); WE (a) 2.00
❑68, Jun 1990, b&w WE (w); WE (a) 2.00
❑69, Jul 1990, b&w WE (w); WE (a) . 2.00
❑70, Aug 1990, b&w WE (w); WE (a) 2.00
❑71, Sep 1990, b&w WE (w); WE (a) 2.00
❑72, Oct 1990, b&w WE (w); WE (a) 2.00
❑73, Nov 1990, b&w 2.00
❑74, Dec 1990, b&w 2.00
❑75, Jan 1991, b&w 2.00
❑76, Feb 1991, b&w 2.00
❑77, Mar 1991, b&w 2.00
❑78, Apr 1991, b&w 2.00
❑79, May 1991, b&w; 2.00
❑80, Jun 1991, b&w; 2.00
❑81, Jul 1991, b&w; 2.00
❑82, Aug 1991, b&w; 2.00
❑83, Sep 1991, b&w; 2.00
❑84, Oct 1991, b&w 2.00
❑85, Nov 1991, b&w; 2.00
❑86, Dec 1991, b&w 2.00
❑87, Jan 1992, b&w 2.00

SPIRIT JAM
KITCHEN SINK

❑1 5.95

SPIRIT, THE (MAGAZINE)
WARREN

❑1, Apr 1974 WE (w); WE (a) 15.00
❑2, Jun 1974 WE (w); WE (a) 8.00
❑3, Aug 1974 WE (w); WE (a) 7.00
❑4, Oct 1974 WE (w); WE (a) 5.00
❑5, Dec 1974 WE (w); WE (a) 5.00
❑6, Feb 1975 WE (w); WE (a) 5.00
❑7, Apr 1975 WE (w); WE (a) 5.00
❑8, Jun 1975 WE (w); WE (a) 5.00
❑9, Aug 1975 WE (w); WE (a) 5.00
❑10, Oct 1975 WE (w); WE (a) 5.00
❑11, Dec 1975 WE (w); WE (a) 3.00
❑12, Feb 1976 WE (w); WE (a) 3.00
❑13, Apr 1976 WE (w); WE (a) 3.00
❑14, Jun 1976 WE (w); WE (a) 3.00
❑15, Aug 1976 WE (w); WE (a) 3.00
❑16, Oct 1976 WE (w); WE (a) 3.00
❑17, Nov 1977; WE (w); WE (a); Kitchen Sink begins as publisher; wraparound covers begin 3.00
❑18, May 1978; WE (w); WE (a); Wraparound cover 3.00
❑19, Oct 1978; WE (w); WE (a); Wraparound cover 3.00
❑20, Mar 1979; WE (w); WE (a); Wraparound cover 3.00
❑21, Jul 1979; WE (w); WE (a); Wraparound cover 3.00
❑22, Dec 1979; WE (w); WE (a); Wraparound cover 3.00
❑23, Feb 1980; WE (w); WE (a); Wraparound cover 3.00
❑24, May 1980; WE (w); WE (a); Wraparound cover 3.00
❑25, Aug 1980; WE (w); WE (a); Wraparound cover 3.00
❑26, Dec 1980; WE, WW (w); WE, WW (a); Wraparound cover 3.00
❑27, Feb 1981; WE (w); WE (a); Wraparound cover 3.00
❑28, Apr 1981; WE (w); WE (a); Wraparound cover 3.00
❑29, Jun 1981; WE (w); WE (a); Wraparound cover 3.00
❑30, Jul 1981; WE (w); WE (a); Featuring more than 50 artists; Wraparound cover 3.00
❑31, Oct 1981; WE (w); WE (a); Wraparound cover 3.00
❑32, Dec 1981; WE (w); WE (a); No wraparound cover 3.00
❑33, Feb 1982; WE (w); WE (a); Wraparound cover 3.00
❑34, Apr 1982; WE (w); WE (a); No wraparound cover 3.00
❑35, Jun 1982; WE (w); WE (a); No wraparound cover 3.00
❑36, Aug 1982; WE (w); WE (a); Wraparound cover 3.00
❑37, Oct 1982; WE (w); WE (a); Wraparound cover 3.00
❑38, Dec 1982; WE (w); WE (a); Wraparound cover 3.00
❑39, Feb 1983; WE (w); WE (a); Wraparound cover 3.00
❑40, Apr 1983; WE (w); WE (a); Wraparound cover 3.00
❑41, Jun 1983; WE (w); WE (a); Wraparound cover 3.00

SPIRIT, THE: THE NEW ADVENTURES
KITCHEN SINK

❑1, Mar 1998 3.50
❑2, Apr 1998 3.50
❑3, May 1998 3.50
❑4, Jun 1998 3.50
❑5, Jul 1998 3.50
❑6, Sep 1998 3.50
❑7, Oct 1998 3.50
❑8, Nov 1998 3.50

SPIRIT: THE ORIGIN YEARS
KITCHEN SINK

❑1, May 1992 2.95
❑2, Jul 1992 2.95
❑3, Sep 1992 2.95
❑4, Nov 1992 2.95
❑5, Jan 1993 2.95
❑6, Mar 1993 2.95
❑7, May 1993 2.95
❑8, Jul 1993 2.95
❑9, Sep 1993 2.95
❑10, Dec 1993 2.95

SPIRIT OF THE TAO, THE
IMAGE

❑1, Jun 1998 2.50
❑2, Jul 1998 2.50
❑3, Aug 1998 2.50
❑4, Sep 1998 2.50
❑5, Nov 1998 2.50
❑6, Dec 1998 2.50
❑7, Feb 1999 2.50
❑8, Apr 1999 2.50
❑9, May 1999 2.50
❑10, Jun 1999 2.50
❑11, Aug 1999 2.50
❑12, Oct 1999 2.50
❑13, Nov 1999 2.50
❑Ashcan 1 1: Jasmine. 1: Lance. 5.00

SPIRIT OF THE WIND
CHOCOLATE MOUSE

❑1, b&w 2.00

SPIRIT OF WONDER
DARK HORSE / MANGA

❑1, Apr 1996, b&w 2.95
❑2, May 1996, b&w 2.95
❑3, Jun 1996, b&w 2.95
❑4, Jul 1996, b&w 2.95
❑5, Aug 1996, b&w 2.95

SPIRITS
MIND WALKER

❑3, Sep 1995, b&w 2.95

SPIRITS OF VENOM
MARVEL

❑1 9.95

SPIRIT WORLD
DC

❑1, Jul 1971 JK (w); JK (a) 35.00

SPIROU & FANTASIO: Z IS FOR ZORGLUB
FANTASY FLIGHT

❑1; graphic novel 8.95

SPITFIRE AND THE TROUBLESHOOTERS
MARVEL

❑1, Oct 1986 HT (a) 1.00
❑2, Nov 1986 1.00
❑3, Dec 1986 1.00
❑4, Jan 1987 TMc (a) 1.00
❑5, Feb 1987 1.00
❑6, Mar 1987 1.00
❑7, Apr 1987 1.00
❑8, May 1987 1.00
❑9, Jun 1987; Series continued in "Code Name: Spitfire" 1.00

SPITTIN' IMAGE
ECLIPSE

❑1; b&w parody 2.50

SPIT WAD COMICS
SPIT WAD

❑1, Jun 1983, b&w 2.50

SPLAT!
MAD DOG

❑1, b&w 2.00
❑2, Mar 1987 2.00
❑3 2.00

SPLATTER (ARPAD)
ARPAD

❑1, b&w 2.50

SPLATTER (NORTHSTAR)
NORTHSTAR

❑1, b&w 4.95
❑2, b&w 2.75
❑3, b&w 2.75
❑4, b&w 2.75
❑5, b&w 2.75
❑6, b&w 2.75
❑7, b&w 2.75
❑8 2.75
❑Annual 1 4.95

N-MINT

SPLITTING IMAGE
IMAGE

❑1, Mar 1993; parody 1.95
❑2, Apr 1993; parody 1.95

SPOOF
MARVEL

❑1, ca. 1970 ..... 6.00
❑2, Nov 1972 ..... 4.00
❑3, Jan 1973 ..... 4.00
❑4, Mar 1973 ..... 4.00
❑5, May 1973 ..... 4.00

SPOOF COMICS
SPOOF

❑0 1992, b&w; Imp-Unity 2.50
❑1 1992, b&w; Spider-Femme 2.50
❑1-2 1992, color; Spider-Femme 2.50
❑2 1992, b&w; Batbabe 2.50
❑2-2 1992, color; Batbabe 2.50
❑3, Aug 1992, b&w; Wolverbroad 2.95
❑4, Sep 1992, b&w; Superbabe 2.95
❑5, Oct 1992, b&w; Daredame 2.95
❑6 1992, b&w; X-Babes 2.95
❑7 1993, b&w; Justice Broads 2.95
❑8 1993, b&w; Fantastic Femmes 2.95
❑9 1993, b&w; Hobo 2.95
❑10 1993, b&w 2.95
❑11 1993, b&w 2.95
❑12, Mar 1993, b&w; Deathlocks 2.95

SPOOK CITY
MYTHIC

❑1, Nov 1997, b&w 2.95

SPOOKGIRL
SLAVE LABOR

❑1, ca. 2000 ..... 2.95

SPOOKY (VOL. 1)
HARVEY

❑1, Nov 1955 ..... 200.00
❑2, Jan 1956 ..... 110.00
❑3, Mar 1956 ..... 65.00
❑4, May 1956 ..... 50.00
❑5, Jul 1956 ..... 50.00
❑6, Sep 1956 ..... 35.00
❑7, Nov 1956 ..... 35.00
❑8, Jan 1957 ..... 35.00
❑9, Mar 1957 ..... 35.00
❑10, May 1957 ..... 35.00
❑11, Jul 1957 ..... 24.00
❑12, Sep 1957 ..... 24.00
❑13, Oct 1957 ..... 24.00
❑14, Nov 1957 ..... 24.00
❑15, Dec 1957 ..... 24.00
❑16, Jan 1958 ..... 24.00
❑17, Feb 1958 ..... 24.00
❑18, Mar 1958 ..... 24.00
❑19, May 1958 ..... 24.00
❑20, Jun 1958 ..... 24.00
❑21, Jul 1958 ..... 20.00
❑22, Aug 1958 ..... 20.00
❑23, Sep 1958 ..... 20.00
❑24, Oct 1958 ..... 20.00
❑25, Nov 1958 ..... 20.00
❑26, Dec 1958 ..... 20.00
❑27, Jan 1959 ..... 20.00
❑28, Feb 1959 ..... 20.00
❑29, Mar 1959 ..... 20.00
❑30, Apr 1959 ..... 18.00
❑31, May 1959 ..... 18.00
❑32, Jun 1959 ..... 18.00
❑33, Jul 1959 ..... 18.00
❑34, Aug 1959 ..... 18.00
❑35, Sep 1959 ..... 18.00
❑36, Oct 1959 ..... 18.00
❑37, Nov 1959 ..... 18.00
❑38, Dec 1959 ..... 18.00
❑39, Jan 1960 ..... 18.00
❑40, Feb 1960 ..... 15.00
❑41, Mar 1960 ..... 15.00
❑42, Apr 1960 ..... 15.00
❑43, May 1960 ..... 15.00
❑44, Jun 1960 ..... 15.00

N-MINT

❑45, Jul 1960 ..... 15.00
❑46, Aug 1960 ..... 15.00
❑47, Sep 1960 ..... 15.00
❑48, Oct 1960 ..... 15.00
❑49, Nov 1960 ..... 15.00
❑50, Dec 1960 ..... 15.00
❑51, Jan 1961 ..... 12.00
❑52, Feb 1961 ..... 12.00
❑53, Mar 1961 ..... 12.00
❑54, Apr 1961 ..... 12.00
❑55, May 1961 ..... 12.00
❑56, Jun 1961 ..... 12.00
❑57, Jul 1961 ..... 12.00
❑58, Aug 1961 ..... 12.00
❑59, Sep 1961 ..... 12.00
❑60, Oct 1961 ..... 12.00
❑61, Nov 1961 ..... 12.00
❑62, Dec 1961 ..... 12.00
❑63, Jan 1962 ..... 12.00
❑64, Feb 1962 ..... 12.00
❑65, Mar 1962 ..... 12.00
❑66, Apr 1962 ..... 12.00
❑67, May 1962 ..... 12.00
❑68, Jun 1962 ..... 12.00
❑69, Aug 1962 ..... 12.00
❑70, Oct 1962 ..... 12.00
❑71, Dec 1962 ..... 8.00
❑72, Feb 1963 ..... 8.00
❑73, Apr 1963 ..... 8.00
❑74, Jun 1963 ..... 8.00
❑75, Aug 1963 ..... 8.00
❑76, Oct 1963 ..... 8.00
❑77, Dec 1963 ..... 8.00
❑78, Feb 1964 ..... 8.00
❑79, Apr 1964 ..... 8.00
❑80, Jun 1964 ..... 8.00
❑81, Aug 1964 ..... 8.00
❑82, Oct 1964 ..... 8.00
❑83, Dec 1964 ..... 8.00
❑84, Feb 1965 ..... 8.00
❑85, Apr 1965 ..... 8.00
❑86, Jun 1965 ..... 8.00
❑87, Aug 1965 ..... 8.00
❑88, Oct 1965 ..... 8.00
❑89, Dec 1965 ..... 8.00
❑90, Feb 1966 ..... 8.00
❑91, Apr 1966 ..... 6.00
❑92, Jun 1966 ..... 6.00
❑93, Aug 1966 ..... 6.00
❑94, Oct 1966 ..... 6.00
❑95, Dec 1966 ..... 6.00
❑96, Feb 1967 ..... 6.00
❑97, Apr 1967 ..... 6.00
❑98, Jun 1967 ..... 6.00
❑99, Aug 1967 ..... 6.00
❑100, Oct 1967 ..... 6.00
❑101, Dec 1967 ..... 6.00
❑102, Feb 1968 ..... 6.00
❑103, Apr 1968 ..... 6.00
❑104, Jun 1968 ..... 6.00
❑105, Aug 1968 ..... 6.00
❑106, Oct 1968 ..... 6.00
❑107, Dec 1968 ..... 6.00
❑108, Feb 1969 ..... 6.00
❑109 1969 ..... 6.00
❑110, May 1969 ..... 6.00
❑111 1969 ..... 5.00
❑112 1969 ..... 5.00
❑113, Oct 1969 ..... 5.00
❑114 1969 ..... 5.00
❑115, Jan 1970 ..... 5.00
❑116, Mar 1970 ..... 5.00
❑117, May 1970 ..... 5.00
❑118, Jul 1970 ..... 5.00
❑119, Sep 1970 ..... 5.00
❑120, Nov 1970 ..... 5.00
❑121, Dec 1970 ..... 5.00
❑122, Feb 1971 ..... 5.00
❑123 1971 ..... 5.00
❑124, Jun 1971 ..... 5.00
❑125 1971 ..... 5.00

With a wrap-around cover featuring nudity and adult humor, Kitchen Sink's first issue of *Spirit* reprints is considered an underground comic book.

© 1973 Denis Kitchen and Will Eisner.

N-MINT

❑126, Sep 1971 ..... 5.00
❑127, Oct 1971 ..... 5.00
❑128, Dec 1971 ..... 5.00
❑129 ..... 5.00
❑130, May 1972 ..... 5.00
❑131, Jul 1972 ..... 4.00
❑132, Sep 1972 ..... 4.00
❑133, Nov 1972 ..... 4.00
❑134, Jan 1973 ..... 4.00
❑135, Mar 1973 ..... 4.00
❑136, May 1973 ..... 4.00
❑137, Jul 1973 ..... 4.00
❑138, Sep 1973 ..... 4.00
❑139, Nov 1973 ..... 4.00
❑140, Jul 1974 ..... 4.00
❑141, Sep 1974 ..... 4.00
❑142, Nov 1974 ..... 4.00
❑143, Jan 1975 ..... 4.00
❑144, Mar 1975 ..... 4.00
❑145, May 1975 ..... 4.00
❑146, Jul 1975 ..... 4.00
❑147, Sep 1975 ..... 4.00
❑148, Nov 1975 ..... 4.00
❑149, Jan 1976 ..... 4.00
❑150, Mar 1976 ..... 4.00
❑151, May 1976 ..... 4.00
❑152, Jul 1976 ..... 4.00
❑153, Sep 1976 ..... 4.00
❑154, Nov 1976 ..... 4.00
❑155, Jan 1977 ..... 4.00
❑156, Dec 1977 ..... 4.00
❑157, Feb 1978 ..... 4.00
❑158, Apr 1978 ..... 4.00
❑159, Sep 1978 ..... 4.00
❑160, Oct 1979 ..... 4.00
❑161, Sep 1980 ..... 4.00

SPOOKY (VOL. 2)
HARVEY

❑1, ca. 1991 ..... 1.25
❑2, ca. 1991 ..... 1.25
❑3, ca. 1991 ..... 1.25
❑4, ca. 1991 ..... 1.25

SPOOKY DIGEST
HARVEY

❑1 ..... 2.00
❑2 ..... 2.00

SPOOKY SPOOKTOWN
HARVEY

❑1, Sep 1961 ..... 85.00
❑2, Sep 1962 ..... 45.00
❑3, Dec 1962, color 30.00
❑4, ca. 1963 ..... 30.00
❑5, ca. 1963 ..... 30.00
❑6, ca. 1963 ..... 22.00
❑7, ca. 1963 ..... 22.00
❑8, ca. 1964 ..... 22.00
❑9, ca. 1964 ..... 22.00
❑10, ca. 1964 ..... 22.00
❑11, ca. 1964 ..... 15.00
❑12, ca. 1964 ..... 15.00
❑13, ca. 1965 ..... 15.00
❑14, ca. 1965 ..... 15.00
❑15, Sep 1965 ..... 15.00
❑16, Mar 1966 ..... 15.00
❑17, Sep 1966 ..... 15.00
❑18, ca. 1967 ..... 15.00

N-MINT

❑19, ca. 1967 ..... 15.00
❑20, May 1967 ..... 15.00
❑21, Sep 1967 ..... 8.00
❑22, Nov 1967 ..... 8.00
❑23, ca. 1968 ..... 8.00
❑24, ca. 1968 ..... 8.00
❑25, Jul 1968 ..... 8.00
❑26, ca. 1968 ..... 8.00
❑27, Dec 1968 ..... 8.00
❑28, ca. 1969 ..... 8.00
❑29, ca. 1969 ..... 8.00
❑30, ca. 1969 ..... 5.00
❑31, Oct 1969 ..... 5.00
❑32, ca. 1970 ..... 5.00
❑33, ca. 1970 ..... 5.00
❑34, ca. 1970 ..... 5.00
❑35, ca. 1970 ..... 5.00
❑36, Oct 1970 ..... 5.00
❑37, ca. 1971 ..... 5.00
❑38, ca. 1971 ..... 5.00
❑39, ca. 1971 ..... 5.00
❑40, ca. 1971 ..... 5.00
❑41, ca. 1971 ..... 3.00
❑42, Dec 1971 ..... 3.00
❑43, Mar 1972 ..... 3.00
❑44, Jun 1972 ..... 3.00
❑45, Sep 1972 ..... 3.00
❑46, Dec 1972 ..... 3.00
❑47, Feb 1973 ..... 3.00
❑48, Apr 1973 ..... 3.00
❑49, Jun 1973 ..... 3.00
❑50, Aug 1973 ..... 3.00
❑51, Oct 1973 ..... 3.00
❑52, Dec 1973 ..... 3.00
❑53, Oct 1974 ..... 3.00
❑54, Dec 1974 ..... 3.00
❑55, Feb 1975 ..... 3.00
❑56, Apr 1975 ..... 3.00
❑57, Jun 1975 ..... 3.00
❑58, Aug 1975 ..... 3.00
❑59, Oct 1975 ..... 3.00
❑60, Dec 1975 ..... 3.00
❑61, Feb 1976 ..... 3.00
❑62, Apr 1976 A: Casper. A: Nightmare. 3.00
❑63, Jun 1976 ..... 3.00
❑64, Aug 1976 ..... 3.00
❑65, Oct 1976 ..... 3.00
❑66, Dec 1976 ..... 3.00

SPOOKY THE DOG CATCHER
PAW PRINTS

❑1, Oct 1994, b&w 2.50
❑2, Jan 1995, b&w 2.50
❑3, May 1995, b&w 2.50

SPORTS CLASSICS
PERSONALITY

❑1 ..... 2.95
❑1/Ltd.; limited edition 5.95
❑2 ..... 2.95
❑3 ..... 2.95
❑4 ..... 2.95
❑5 ..... 2.95

SPORTS COMICS
PERSONALITY

❑1 ..... 2.50
❑2 ..... 2.50
❑3 ..... 2.50
❑4 ..... 2.50

SPORTS HALL OF SHAME IN 3-D
BLACKTHORNE

❑1; baseball 2.50

SPORTS LEGENDS
REVOLUTIONARY

❑1, Sep 1992, b&w; Joe Namath 2.50
❑2, Oct 1992, b&w; Gordie Howe 2.50
❑3, Nov 1992, b&w; Arthur Ashe 2.50
❑4, Dec 1992, color; Muhammad Ali . 2.50
❑5, Jan 1993, color; O.J. Simpson 2.50
❑6, Feb 1993, color; K.A. Jabbar 2.50
❑7, Mar 1993, b&w; Walter Payton 2.95
❑8, Apr 1993, b&w; Wilt Chamberlain 2.95
❑9, May 1993, b&w; Joe Louis 2.95

SPORTS LEGENDS SPECIAL - BREAKING THE COLOR BARRIER
REVOLUTIONARY

❑1, Oct 1993, b&w 2.95

SPORTS PERSONALITIES
PERSONALITY

❑1; Bo Jackson 2.95
❑2; Nolan Ryan 2.95
❑3; Rickey Henderson 2.95
❑4; Magic Johnson 2.95
❑5 ..... 2.95
❑6 ..... 2.95
❑7 ..... 2.95
❑8 ..... 2.95
❑9 ..... 2.95
❑10 ..... 2.95
❑11 ..... 2.95
❑12 ..... 2.95
❑13 ..... 2.95

SPORTS SUPERSTARS
REVOLUTIONARY

❑1, Apr 1992, b&w; Michael Jordan .. 2.50
❑2, May 1992, b&w; Wayne Gretzsky 2.50
❑3, Jun 1992, b&w; Magic Johnson .. 2.50
❑4, Jul 1992, b&w; Joe Montana 2.50
❑5, Aug 1992, b&w; Mike Tyson 2.50
❑6, Sep 1992, b&w; Larry Bird 2.50
❑7, Oct 1992, b&w; John Elway 2.50
❑8, Nov 1992, b&w; Julius Erving 2.50
❑9, Dec 1992, color; Barry Sanders .. 2.75
❑10, Jan 1993, color; Isiah Thomas .. 2.75
❑11, Feb 1992, color; Mario Lemieux 2.95
❑12, Mar 1993, b&w; Dan Marino 2.95
❑13, Apr 1993, b&w; Deion Sanders . 2.95
❑14, May 1993, b&w; Patrick Ewing . 2.95
❑15, Jun 1993, b&w; Charles Barkley 2.95
❑16, Aug 1993, b&w; Shaquille O'neal, Christian Laettner 2.95
❑Annual 1, Feb 1993, color; Michael Jordan II 2.75

SPOTLIGHT
MARVEL

❑1, Sep 1978; Huckleberry Hound 8.00
❑2, Nov 1978 ..... 6.00
❑3, Jan 1979 ..... 6.00
❑4, Mar 1979 ..... 6.00

SPOTLIGHT ON THE GENIUS THAT IS JOE SACCO
FANTAGRAPHICS

❑1, b&w 4.95

SPRING BREAK COMICS
AC

❑1, Mar 1987, b&w 1.50

SPRING-HEEL JACK
REBEL

❑1, b&w 2.25
❑2, b&w 2.25

SPRINGTIME TALES (WALT KELLY'S...)
ECLIPSE

❑1; Peter Wheat 2.50

SPUD
SPUD

❑1, Sum 1996, b&w 3.50

SPUNKY KNIGHT
FANTAGRAPHICS / EROS

❑1, May 1996 ..... 2.95
❑2, Jun 1996 ..... 2.95
❑3, Jul 1996 ..... 2.95

SPUNKY TODD: THE PSYCHIC BOY
CALIBER

❑1, b&w 2.95

SPYBOY
DARK HORSE

❑1, Oct 1999 PD (w) 3.00
❑2, Nov 1999 PD (w) 2.75
❑3, Dec 1999 PD (w) 2.75
❑4, Jan 2000 PD (w) 2.75
❑5, Feb 2000 PD (w) 2.75
❑6, Mar 2000 PD (w) 2.50
❑7, Apr 2000 PD (w) 2.50
❑8, May 2000 PD (w) 2.50
❑9, Jun 2000 PD (w) 2.50
❑10, Jul 2000 PD (w) 2.50
❑11, Aug 2000 PD (w) 2.50
❑12, Sep 2000 PD (w) 2.95
❑13, Oct 2000 PD (w) 2.95
❑14, Nov 2000 PD (w) 2.99
❑15, Jan 2001 PD (w) 2.99
❑16, Mar 2001 PD (w) 2.99
❑17, May 2001 PD (w) 2.99
❑Special 1, May 2002 ..... 4.99

SPYBOY 13: MANGA AFFAIR
DARK HORSE

❑1, Apr 2003 ..... 2.99
❑2, Jun 2003 ..... 2.99
❑3, Aug 2003 ..... 2.99

SPYBOY: FINAL EXAM
DARK HORSE

❑1, May 2004 ..... 2.99
❑2, Aug 2004 ..... 2.99

SPYBOY/YOUNG JUSTICE
DARK HORSE

❑1, Feb 2002 ..... 2.99
❑2, Mar 2002 ..... 2.99
❑3, Apr 2002 ..... 2.99

SPYKE
MARVEL / EPIC

❑1, Jul 1993; Embossed cover 2.50
❑2, Aug 1993 ..... 1.95
❑3, Sep 1993 ..... 1.95
❑4, Oct 1993 ..... 1.95

SPYMAN
HARVEY

❑1 ..... 30.00
❑2 ..... 24.00
❑3, Feb 1967 ..... 24.00

SQUADRON SUPREME
MARVEL

❑1, Sep 1985 BH (c); BH (a) 1.50
❑2, Oct 1985 BH (c); BH (a); V: Scarlet Centurion. 1.00
❑3, Nov 1985 BH (c); BH (a) 1.00
❑4, Dec 1985 BH (c); BH (a) 1.00
❑5, Jan 1986 BH (c); BH (a); V: Institute of Evil. 1.00
❑6, Feb 1986 ..... 1.00
❑7, Mar 1986 ..... 1.00
❑8, Apr 1986 BH (c); BH (a) 1.00
❑9, May 1986 D: Tom Thumb. 1.00
❑10, Jun 1986 ..... 1.00
❑11, Jul 1986 ..... 1.00
❑12, Aug 1986 ..... 1.25

SQUADRON SUPREME: NEW WORLD ORDER
MARVEL

❑1, Sep 1998 ..... 5.99

SQUALOR
FIRST

❑1, Dec 1989; 1st comics work by Stefan Petrucha 2.75
❑2, Jun 1990 ..... 2.75
❑3, Jul 1990 ..... 2.75
❑4, Aug 1990 ..... 2.75

SQUEE!
SLAVE LABOR

❑1, Apr 1997 ..... 7.00
❑1-2 1997 ..... 2.95
❑2, Jul 1997 ..... 5.00
❑3, Nov 1997 ..... 3.50
❑4, Feb 1998 ..... 3.50

SRI KRISHNA
CHAKRA

❑1 ..... 3.50

N-MINT

STACIA STORIES
Kitchen Sink

❑1, Jun 1995, b&w 2.95

STAIN
Fathom

❑1 .... 2.95

STAINLESS STEEL ARMADILLO
Antarctic

❑1, Feb 1995, b&w 2.95
❑2, Apr 1995, b&w 2.95
❑3, Jun 1995, b&w 2.95
❑4, Aug 1995, b&w 2.95
❑5, Oct 1995, b&w 2.95

STAINLESS STEEL RAT
Eagle

❑1, Oct 1985; Reprinted from 2000 A.D. #140-145 .... 2.50
❑2, Nov 1985; Reprinted from 2000 A.D. #146-151 .... 2.50
❑3, Dec 1985 .... 2.50
❑4, Jan 1986 .... 2.50
❑5, Feb 1986 .... 2.50
❑6, Mar 1986 .... 2.50

STALKER
DC

❑1, Jul 1975 SD, WW (a); O: Stalker. 1: Stalker. 5.00
❑2, Sep 1975 .... 1.50
❑3, Nov 1975 .... 1.50
❑4, Jan 1976 .... 1.50

STALKERS
Marvel / Epic

❑1, Apr 1990 .... 1.50
❑2, May 1990 .... 1.50
❑3, Jun 1990 .... 1.50
❑4, Jul 1990 .... 1.50
❑5, Aug 1990 .... 1.50
❑6, Sep 1990 .... 1.50
❑7, Oct 1990 .... 1.50
❑8, Nov 1990 .... 1.50
❑9, Dec 1990 .... 1.50
❑10, Jan 1991 .... 1.50
❑11, Feb 1991 .... 1.50
❑12, Mar 1991 .... 1.50

STALKING RALPH
Aeon

❑1, Oct 1995; cardstock cover 4.95

STAND UP COMIX (BOB RUMBA'S...)
Grey

❑1, b&w 2.50

STANLEY & HIS MONSTER
DC

❑109, May 1968 .... 20.00
❑110, Jul 1968 .... 15.00
❑111, Sep 1968 .... 15.00
❑112, Nov 1968 .... 15.00

STANLEY AND HIS MONSTER (2ND SERIES)
DC

❑1, Feb 1993 PF (w); PF (a) 2.50
❑2, Mar 1993 PF (w); PF (a) 2.00
❑3, Apr 1993 PF (w); PF (a) 2.00
❑4, May 1993 PF (w); PF (a) 2.00

STANLEY THE SNAKE WITH THE OVERACTIVE IMAGINATION
Emerald

❑1, b&w 1.50
❑2, b&w 1.50

STAR
Image

❑1, Jun 1995 .... 2.50
❑2, Jul 1995 .... 2.50
❑3, Aug 1995 .... 2.50
❑4, Oct 1995; cover says Aug, indicia says Oct 2.50

STARBIKERS
Renegade

❑1, b&w 2.00

N-MINT

STARBLAST
Marvel

❑1, Jan 1994 .... 2.00
❑2, Feb 1994 .... 1.75
❑3, Mar 1994 .... 1.75
❑4, Apr 1994 .... 1.75

STAR BLAZERS
Comico

❑1, Apr 1987 .... 2.00
❑2, ca. 1987 .... 2.00
❑3, ca. 1987 .... 2.00
❑4, ca. 1987 .... 2.00

STAR BLAZERS (VOL. 2)
Comico

❑1, ca. 1989 .... 2.00
❑2, Jun 1989 .... 2.00
❑3 1989 .... 2.50
❑4 1989 .... 2.50
❑5 1989 .... 2.50

STAR BLAZERS: THE MAGAZINE OF SPACE BATTLESHIP YAMATO
Argo

❑0 1995 .... 2.95
❑1, Mar 1995 .... 2.95

STAR BLECCH: DEEP SPACE DINER
Parody

❑1/A; Star Blecch: Deep Space Diner cover 2.50
❑1/B; Star Blecch: The Degeneration cover 2.50

STAR BRAND, THE
Marvel

❑1, Oct 1986 JR2 (a); O: Star Brand. 1: Star Brand. 1.00
❑2, Nov 1986 .... 1.00
❑3, Dec 1986 .... 1.00
❑4, Jan 1987 .... 1.00
❑5, Feb 1987 .... 1.00
❑6, Mar 1987 .... 1.00
❑7, Apr 1987 .... 1.00
❑8, May 1987 .... 1.00
❑9, Jun 1987 .... 1.00
❑10, Jul 1987 .... 1.00
❑11, Jan 1988; JBy (a); Title changes to The Star Brand 1.00
❑12, Mar 1988; JBy (a); O: Star Brand. O: New Universe (explains "White Event"). Prelude to The Pitt 1.00
❑13, May 1988 JBy (a) 1.00
❑14, Jul 1988 JBy (a) 1.00
❑15, Sep 1988 JBy (a) 1.00
❑16, Nov 1988 JBy (a) 1.00
❑17, Jan 1989 JBy (a) 1.00
❑18, Mar 1989 JBy (a) 1.00
❑19, May 1989 JBy (a) 1.00
❑Annual 1, ca. 1987 .... 1.25

STARCHILD
Taliesen

❑0, Apr 1993, b&w 4.00
❑1, b&w; wraparound cover 4.00
❑1-2 .... 2.25
❑2 1993, b&w; wraparound cover 4.00
❑2-2, Feb 1994, b&w; wraparound cover 2.50
❑2-3, Feb 1994, b&w; wraparound cover 2.50
❑3 1993, b&w; wraparound cover 3.00
❑4 1993, b&w; wraparound cover 3.00
❑5, Jan 1994, b&w; wraparound cover 3.00
❑6, Feb 1994, b&w; wraparound cover 3.00
❑7, Mar 1994, b&w; wraparound cover 2.50
❑8, Apr 1994, b&w; wraparound cover 2.50
❑9, May 1994, b&w; wraparound cover 2.50
❑10, Aug 1994, b&w; wraparound cover 2.50
❑11, Dec 1994, b&w; wraparound cover 2.50
❑12, Jun 1995, b&w; wraparound cover 2.50
❑13 .... 2.50
❑14 .... 2.50

Peter David's Spyboy is a high-school-age secret agent.
© 1999 Peter David (Dark Horse)

N-MINT

STARCHILD: CROSSROADS
Coppervale

❑1, Nov 1995, b&w 2.95
❑2, Jan 1996, b&w 2.95
❑3, Mar 1996, b&w 2.95

STARCHILD: MYTHOPOLIS
Image

❑0, Jul 1997, b&w 2.95
❑1, Sep 1997, b&w 2.95
❑2, Nov 1997, b&w 2.95
❑3, Jan 1998, b&w 2.95
❑4, Apr 1998, b&w 2.95
❑5 .... 2.95
❑6 .... 2.95

STARCHY
Excel

❑1 .... 1.95

STAR COMICS MAGAZINE
Marvel / Star

❑1, Dec 1986; digest 3.00
❑2, Feb 1987; digest 2.00
❑3, Apr 1987; digest 2.00
❑4, Jun 1987; digest 2.00
❑5, Aug 1987; digest 2.00
❑6, Oct 1987; digest 2.00
❑7, Dec 1987; digest 2.00
❑8, Feb 1988; digest 2.00
❑9, Apr 1988; digest 2.00
❑10, Jun 1988; digest 2.00
❑11, Aug 1988; digest 2.00
❑12, Oct 1988; digest 2.00
❑13, Dec 1988; digest 2.00

S.T.A.R. CORPS
DC

❑1, Nov 1993 .... 1.50
❑2, Dec 1993 .... 1.50
❑3, Jan 1994 .... 1.50
❑4, Feb 1994 .... 1.50
❑5, Mar 1994 .... 1.50
❑6, Apr 1994 .... 1.50

STAR CROSSED
DC / Helix

❑1, Jun 1997 .... 2.50
❑2, Jul 1997 .... 2.50
❑3, Aug 1997 .... 2.50

STARDUST (NEIL GAIMAN AND CHARLES VESS'...)
DC / Vertigo

❑1; prestige format 6.50
❑2; prestige format 6.00
❑3; prestige format 6.00
❑4; prestige format 6.00

STARDUSTERS
Nightwynd

❑1, b&w 2.50
❑2, b&w 2.50
❑3, b&w 2.50
❑4, b&w 2.50

STARFIRE
DC

❑1, Sep 1976 O: Starfire I. 1: Starfire I. 1.50
❑2, Nov 1976 .... 1.00
❑3, Jan 1977 .... 1.00
❑4, Mar 1977 .... 1.00
❑5, May 1977 .... 1.00

	N-MINT
❑6, Jul 1977	1.00
❑7, Sep 1977	1.00
❑8, Nov 1977	1.00

STAR FORCES
The Other Faculty / Helix

❑1	3.00

STARFORCE SIX SPECIAL
AC

❑1, Nov 1984	1.50

STARGATE
Express / Entity

❑1, Jul 1996	2.95
❑1/Variant, Jul 1996	3.50
❑2, Aug 1996; photo section back-up	2.95
❑2/Variant, Aug 1996; photo section back-up	3.50
❑3, Sep 1996; photo section back-up	2.95
❑3/Variant, Sep 1996; photo section back-up	3.50
❑4, Oct 1996; photo section back-up	2.95
❑4/Variant, Oct 1996; photo section back-up	3.50

STARGATE DOOMSDAY WORLD
Entity

❑1, Nov 1996	2.95
❑2, Dec 1996	2.95
❑3, Jan 1997	2.95

STARGATE SG1 CON SPECIAL 2003
Avatar

❑1, Sep 2003	3.95

STARGATE SG1 CON SPECIAL 2004
Avatar

❑1, Apr 2004	2.99
❑1/A, Apr 2004; Wrap/Photo Cover	3.99

STARGATE SG1: P.O.W.
Avatar

❑1, Feb 2004	3.50
❑2, Mar 2004	3.50
❑3, May 2004	3.50

STARGATE: THE NEW ADVENTURES COLLECTION
Entity

❑1, Dec 1997, b&w; Collects Stargate: One Nation Under Ra; Stargate: Underworld	5.95

STARGATE UNDERWORLD
Entity

❑1, ca. 1997	2.95

STARGODS
Antarctic

❑1, Jul 1998	2.95
❑1/CS, Jul 1998; poster; alternate cover	5.95
❑2, Sep 1998	2.95
❑2/CS, Sep 1998; poster; alternate cover	5.95

STARGODS: VISIONS
Antarctic

❑1, Dec 1998; pin-ups	2.95

STARHEAD PRESENTS
Starhead

❑1	1.00
❑2	1.00
❑3; Bad Teens	1.00

STAR HUNTERS
DC

❑1, Nov 1977	1.00
❑2, Jan 1978 BL (a)	1.00
❑3, Mar 1978 MN, BL (a)	1.00
❑4, May 1978	1.00
❑5, Jul 1978	1.00
❑6, Sep 1978	1.00
❑7, Nov 1978	1.00

STAR JACKS
Antarctic

❑1, Jun 1994, b&w	2.75

STAR JAM COMICS
Revolutionary

	N-MINT
❑1, Apr 1992, b&w; M.C. Hammer story	2.50
❑2, Jun 1992, b&w; Janet Jackson story	2.50
❑3, Aug 1992, b&w; Beverly Hills 90210 story	2.50
❑4, Sep 1992, b&w; Beverly Hills 90210 story	2.50
❑5, Oct 1992, b&w; Beverly Hills 90210 story	2.50
❑6, Nov 1992, b&w; Kriss Kross story	2.50
❑7, Dec 1992, b&w; Marky Mark story	2.50
❑8, Jan 1993, b&w; Madonna story	2.50
❑9, Feb 1993, b&w; Jennie Garth story	2.50
❑10, Mar 1993, b&w; Melrose Place story	2.50

STARJAMMERS
Marvel

❑1, Oct 1995; OverPower cards bound-in; enhanced cardstock cover	2.95
❑2, Nov 1995; enhanced cardstock cover	2.95
❑3, Dec 1995; enhanced cardstock cover	2.95
❑4, Jan 1996; enhanced cardstock cover	2.95

STARJAMMERS (VOL. 2)
Marvel

❑1, Sep 2004	2.99
❑2, Sep 2004	2.99

STARJONGLEUR, THE
Trylvertel

❑1, Aug 1986, b&w	2.00
❑2, Win 1987, b&w	2.00

STARKID
Dark Horse

❑1, Jan 1998; prequel to movie	2.95

STARK RAVEN
Endless Horizons

❑1, Sep 2000	2.95

STARLIGHT
Eternity

❑1, Oct 1987	1.95

STARLIGHT AGENCY, THE
Antarctic

❑1, Jun 1991, b&w	2.50
❑2, Aug 1991, b&w	2.50
❑3, Sep 1991, b&w	2.50

STARLION: A PAWN'S GAME
Storm

❑1, Feb 1993	2.25

STARLORD
Marvel

❑1, Dec 1996	2.50
❑2, Jan 1997	2.50
❑3, Feb 1997	2.50

STARLORD MEGAZINE
Marvel

❑1, Nov 1996; Reprints Star-Lord, The Special Edition #1; back cover pin-up	2.95

STAR-LORD, THE SPECIAL EDITION
Marvel

❑1, Feb 1982 MG, JBy (a)	2.00

STARLOVE
Forbidden Fruit

❑1, b&w	2.95
❑2, b&w	3.50

STARMAN (1ST SERIES)
DC

	N-MINT
❑1, Oct 1988 O: Starman IV (William Payton). 1: Starman IV (William Payton).	2.00
❑2, Nov 1988	1.50
❑3, Dec 1988 V: Bolt.	1.50
❑4, Win 1988 V: Power Elite.	1.50
❑5, Hol 1989; Invasion!	1.50
❑6, Jan 1989; Invasion!	1.50
❑7, Feb 1989	1.50
❑8, Mar 1989 A: Lady Quark.	1.50
❑9, Apr 1989 O: Blockbuster. A: Batman.	1.50
❑10, May 1989 O: Blockbuster. A: Batman.	1.50
❑11, Jun 1989	1.25
❑12, Jul 1989	1.25
❑13, Aug 1989	1.25
❑14, Sep 1989; Superman	1.25
❑15, Oct 1989 1: Deadline.	1.25
❑16, Nov 1989	1.25
❑17, Dec 1989; Power Girl	1.25
❑18, Jan 1990	1.25
❑19, Feb 1990	1.25
❑20, Mar 1990	1.25
❑21, Apr 1990	1.25
❑22, May 1990 V: Deadline.	1.25
❑23, Jun 1990	1.25
❑24, Jul 1990	1.25
❑25, Aug 1990	1.25
❑26, Sep 1990 1: David Knight.	2.00
❑27, Oct 1990 O: Starman III (David Knight).	1.25
❑28, Nov 1990; Superman	1.25
❑29, Dec 1990	1.25
❑30, Jan 1991	1.25
❑31, Feb 1991	1.25
❑32, Mar 1991	1.25
❑33, Apr 1991	1.25
❑34, May 1991	1.25
❑35, Jun 1991	1.25
❑36, Jul 1991	1.25
❑37, Aug 1991	1.25
❑38, Sep 1991; War of the Gods	1.25
❑39, Oct 1991	1.25
❑40, Nov 1991	1.25
❑41, Dec 1991	1.25
❑42, Jan 1992	1.25
❑43, Feb 1992	1.25
❑44, Mar 1992; Lobo	1.25
❑45, Apr 1992; Lobo	1.25

STARMAN (2ND SERIES)
DC

❑0, Oct 1994 JRo (w)	5.00
❑1, Nov 1994 JRo (w)	5.00
❑2, Dec 1994 JRo (w)	4.00
❑3, Jan 1995 JRo (w)	4.00
❑4, Feb 1995 JRo (w)	3.00
❑5, Mar 1995 JRo (w)	3.00
❑6, Apr 1995 JRo (w)	3.00
❑7, May 1995 JRo (w)	3.00
❑8, Jun 1995 JRo (w)	3.00
❑9, Jul 1995 JRo (w)	3.00
❑10, Aug 1995 JRo (w); V: Solomon Grundy.	3.00
❑11, Sep 1995 JRo (w)	2.50
❑12, Oct 1995 JRo (w)	2.50
❑13, Nov 1995; JRo (w); Underworld Unleashed	2.50
❑14, Dec 1995 JRo (w)	2.50
❑15, Jan 1996 JRo (w)	2.50
❑16, Feb 1996 JRo (w)	2.50
❑17, Mar 1996 JRo (w)	2.50
❑18, Apr 1996; JRo (w); Original Starman versus The Mist	2.50
❑19, Jun 1996; JRo (w); Times Past	2.50
❑20, Jul 1996 JRo (w); A: Wesley Dodds appearance, Dian Belmont. A: Wesley Dodds. A: Dian Belmont.	2.50
❑21, Aug 1996 JRo (w)	2.50
❑22, Sep 1996 JRo (w)	2.50
❑23, Oct 1996 JRo (w)	2.50
❑24, Nov 1996 JRo (w)	2.50
❑25, Dec 1996 JRo (w)	2.50
❑26, Jan 1997 JRo (w)	2.50
❑27, Feb 1997 JRo (w)	2.50
❑28, Mar 1997 JRo (w)	2.50
❑29, Apr 1997 JRo (w)	2.50
❑30, May 1997 JRo (w)	2.50
❑31, Jun 1997 JRo (w)	2.50
❑32, Jul 1997 JRo (w)	2.50

	N-MINT
❑33, Aug 1997 JRo (w); A: Solomon Grundy. A: Sentinel. A: Batman.	2.50
❑34, Sep 1997 JRo (w); A: Ted Knight. A: Solomon Grundy. A: Sentinel. A: Batman. A: Jason Woodrue.	2.50
❑35, Oct 1997; JRo (w); Genesis	2.50
❑36, Nov 1997 JRo (w); A: Will Payton.	2.50
❑37, Dec 1997; JRo (w); Face cover .	2.50
❑38, Jan 1998; JRo (w); 1: Baby Starman. Mist vs. Justice League Europe	2.50
❑39, Feb 1998; JRo (w); continues in Power of Shazam! #35; cover forms diptych with Starman #40	2.50
❑40, Mar 1998; JRo (w); cover forms diptych with Starman #39	2.50
❑41, Apr 1998 JRo (w); V: Doctor Phosphorus.	2.25
❑42, May 1998 JRo (w); A: Demon.	2.25
❑43, Jun 1998 JRo (w); A: Justice League of America.	2.25
❑44, Jul 1998 JRo (w); A: Phantom Lady.	2.25
❑45, Aug 1998 JRo (w)	2.25
❑46, Sep 1998 JRo (w)	2.25
❑47, Oct 1998 JRo (w)	2.50
❑48, Dec 1998 JRo (w); A: Solomon Grundy.	2.50
❑49, Jan 1999 JRo (w)	2.50
❑50, Feb 1999 JRo (w); A: Legion.	3.95
❑51, Mar 1999; JRo (w); A: Jor-El. on Krypton	2.50
❑52, Apr 1999; JRo (w); A: Turran Kha. A: Adam Strange. on Rann	2.50
❑53, May 1999; JRo (w); A: Adam Strange. on Rann	2.50
❑54, Jun 1999; JRo (w); Times Past .	2.50
❑55, Jul 1999 JRo (w); A: Space Cabbie.	2.50
❑56, Aug 1999 JRo (w)	2.50
❑57, Sep 1999; JRo (w); A: Fastbak. A: Tigorr. on Throneworld	2.50
❑58, Oct 1999 JRo (w); A: Will Payton.	2.50
❑59, Nov 1999 JRo (w)	2.50
❑60, Dec 1999; Jack returns to Earth	2.50
❑61, Jan 2000 JRo (w)	2.50
❑62, Feb 2000 JRo (w)	2.50
❑63, Mar 2000 JRo (w)	2.50
❑64, Apr 2000 JRo (w)	2.50
❑65, May 2000 JRo (w)	2.50
❑66, Jun 2000 JRo (w)	2.50
❑67, Jul 2000 JRo (w)	2.50
❑68, Aug 2000 JRo (w)	2.50
❑69, Sep 2000 JRo (w)	2.50
❑70, Oct 2000 JRo (w)	2.50
❑71, Nov 2000 JRo (w)	2.50
❑72, Dec 2000 JRo (w)	2.50
❑73, Jan 2001 JRo (w)	2.50
❑74, Feb 2001; JRo (w); RH (a); Times Past	2.50
❑75, Mar 2001 JRo (w)	2.50
❑76, Apr 2001 JRo (w)	2.50
❑77, May 2001 JRo (w)	2.50
❑78, Jun 2001 JRo (w)	2.50
❑79, Jul 2001	2.50
❑80, Aug 2001	2.50
❑1000000, Nov 1998 JRo (w)	3.00
❑Annual 1, ca. 1996; JRo (w); Legends of the Dead Earth; Shade tells stories of Ted Knight and Gavyn; 1996 Annual	3.50
❑Annual 2, ca. 1997; JRo (w); Pulp Heroes; 1997 annual	3.95
❑Giant Size 1, Jan 1999; 80 page giant JRo (w)	4.95

STARMAN: SECRET FILES
DC

❑1, Apr 1998; background on series .	4.95

STARMAN: THE MIST
DC

❑1, Jun 1998; Girlfrenzy	1.95

STAR MASTERS (MARVEL)
MARVEL

	N-MINT
❑1, Dec 1995	1.95
❑2, Jan 1996	1.95
❑3, Feb 1996; continues in Cosmic Powers Unlimited #4	1.95

STARMASTERS (AC)
AC

❑1	1.50

STAR RANGERS
ADVENTURE

❑1, Oct 1987	1.95
❑2, Nov 1987	1.95
❑3, Dec 1987	1.95

STAR*REACH
STAR*REACH

❑1, ca. 1974 JSn, HC (w); JSn, HC (a)	2.00
❑2, ca. 1975 NA (c); JSn (w); JSn, DG (a)	2.00
❑3, ca. 1975	2.00
❑4, ca. 1976	2.00
❑5, ca. 1976 FB, HC, JSa (a)	1.50
❑6, Oct 1976 JSa, GD, AN (a)	1.50
❑7, ca. 1977 JSa (a)	1.50
❑8, ca. 1977; CR (c); CR (a); Adapts Wagner's Parsifal	1.50
❑9, ca. 1977	1.50
❑10, ca. 1977	1.50
❑11, ca. 1977	1.50
❑12, ca. 1978	1.50
❑13, ca. 1978	1.50
❑14, ca. 1978	1.50
❑15, ca. 1978	1.50
❑16, ca. 1979	1.50
❑17, ca. 1979	1.50
❑18, ca. 1979	1.50

STAR*REACH CLASSICS
ECLIPSE

❑1, Mar 1984 DG (a)	2.00
❑2, Apr 1984	2.00
❑3, May 1984	2.00
❑4, Jun 1984	2.00
❑5, Jul 1984 HC (a)	2.00
❑6, Aug 1984 CR (a)	2.00

STARRIORS
MARVEL

❑1, Nov 1984	1.00
❑2, Dec 1984	1.00
❑3, Jan 1985	1.00
❑4, Feb 1985	1.00

STAR ROVERS
COMAX

❑1, b&w	2.95

STARS AND S.T.R.I.P.E.
DC

❑0, Jul 1999; JRo (w); A: Starman. 1st Geoff Johns work	2.95
❑1, Aug 1999	2.50
❑2, Sep 1999	2.50
❑3, Oct 1999 1: Skeeter.	2.50
❑4, Nov 1999; A: Captain Marvel. Day of Judgment	2.50
❑5, Dec 1999 A: Young Justice.	2.95
❑6, Jan 2000	2.95
❑7, Feb 2000	2.95
❑8, Mar 2000	2.95
❑9, Apr 2000	2.95
❑10, May 2000	2.50
❑12, Jul 2000	2.50
❑11, Jun 2000	2.50
❑13, Aug 2000	2.50
❑14, Sep 2000	2.50

STAR SEED
BROADWAY

❑7, Jul 1996; Series continued from Powers That Be #6	2.95
❑8, Aug 1996	2.95
❑9, Sep 1996	2.95

STARSHIP TROOPERS
DARK HORSE

❑1, Oct 1997	2.95
❑2, Nov 1997	2.95

Phil Foglio revived two goony '60s series with *Angel and the Ape* and *Stanley and His Monster.*

© 1993 DC Comics.

STARSHIP TROOPERS: BRUTE CREATIONS
DARK HORSE

	N-MINT
❑1, Sep 1997	2.95

STARSHIP TROOPERS: DOMINANT SPECIES
DARK HORSE

❑1, Aug 1998	2.95
❑2, Sep 1998	2.95
❑3, Oct 1998	2.95
❑4, Nov 1998	2.95

STARSHIP TROOPERS: INSECT TOUCH
DARK HORSE

❑1, May 1997; cardstock cover	2.95
❑2, Jun 1997; cardstock cover	2.95
❑3, Jul 1997; cardstock cover	2.95

STAR SLAMMERS (MALIBU)
MALIBU / BRAVURA

❑1, May 1994	2.50
❑2, Jun 1994	2.50
❑3, Aug 1994	2.50
❑4, Feb 1995	2.50
❑5	2.50

STAR SLAMMERS SPECIAL
DARK HORSE / LEGEND

❑1, Jun 1996	2.95

STARSLAYER
PACIFIC

❑1, Feb 1982 MGr (w); MGr (a); O: Starslayer. 1: Rocketeer (cameo).	2.00
❑2, Apr 1982; MGr (w); SA, MGr, DSt (a); O: Rocketeer. 1: Rocketeer (full appearance). Rocketeer backup story	4.00
❑3, Jun 1982; MGr (w); MGr, DSt (a); A: Rocketeer. Rocketeer backup story	2.00
❑4, Aug 1982 MGr (w); MGr (a)	1.00
❑5, Nov 1982 MGr, ME (w); SA, MGr (a); A: Groo.	2.00
❑6, Apr 1983 MGr (w); MGr (a)	1.00
❑7, Aug 1983; First Comics begins publishing	1.00
❑8, Sep 1983	1.00
❑9, Oct 1983	1.00
❑10, Nov 1983 1: Grimjack.	1.50
❑11, Dec 1983 A: Grimjack.	1.00
❑12, Jan 1984 A: Grimjack.	1.00
❑13, Feb 1984 A: Grimjack.	1.00
❑14, Mar 1984 A: Grimjack.	1.00
❑15, Apr 1984 A: Grimjack.	1.00
❑16, May 1984 A: Grimjack.	1.00
❑17, Jun 1984 A: Grimjack.	1.00
❑18, Jul 1984 A: Grimjack.	1.00
❑19, Aug 1984	1.00
❑20, Sep 1984	1.00
❑21, Oct 1984	1.00
❑22, Nov 1984	1.25
❑23, Dec 1984	1.25
❑24, Jan 1985	1.25
❑25, Feb 1985; The Black Flame backup story	1.25
❑26, Mar 1985	1.25
❑27, Apr 1985 TS (a)	1.25
❑28, May 1985	1.25
❑29, Jun 1985	1.25

N-MINT

❑30, Jul 1985 ..... 1.25
❑31, Aug 1985 ..... 1.25
❑32, Sep 1985 ..... 1.25
❑33, Oct 1985 ..... 1.25
❑34, Nov 1985 ..... 1.25

STARSLAYER: THE DIRECTOR'S CUT
ACCLAIM / WINDJAMMER

❑1, Jun 1995; New story and artwork 2.50
❑2, Jun 1995; Reprints Starslayer #1 2.50
❑3, Jul 1995; Reprints Starslayer #2 . 2.50
❑4, Jul 1995; Reprints Starslayer #3 . 2.50
❑5, Aug 1995; Reprints Starslayer #4 2.50
❑6, Sep 1995; cover says Aug, indicia says Sep; Reprints Starslayer #5 ... 2.50
❑7, Sep 1995; Reprints Starslayer #6 2.50
❑8, Dec 1995; New story and artwork 2.50

STAR SPANGLED COMICS (2ND SERIES)
DC

❑1, May 1999; A: Star Spangled Kid. A: Sandman. Justice Society Returns 2.00

STAR SPANGLED WAR STORIES
DC

❑50, Oct 1956 ..... 70.00
❑51, Nov 1956 ..... 60.00
❑52, Dec 1956 ..... 60.00
❑53, Jan 1957 ..... 60.00
❑54, Feb 1957 ..... 60.00
❑55, Mar 1957 ..... 60.00
❑56, Apr 1957 ..... 60.00
❑57, May 1957 ..... 60.00
❑58, Jun 1957 ..... 60.00
❑59, Jul 1957 ..... 60.00
❑60, Aug 1957 ..... 60.00
❑61, Sep 1957 ..... 60.00
❑62, Oct 1957 ..... 60.00
❑63, Nov 1957 ..... 60.00
❑64, Dec 1957 ..... 60.00
❑65, Jan 1958 ..... 60.00
❑66, Feb 1958 ..... 60.00
❑67, Mar 1958 ..... 60.00
❑68, Apr 1958 ..... 60.00
❑69, May 1958 ..... 60.00
❑70, Jun 1958 ..... 60.00
❑71, Jul 1958 ..... 55.00
❑72, Aug 1958 ..... 55.00
❑73, Sep 1958 ..... 55.00
❑74, Oct 1958 ..... 55.00
❑75, Nov 1958 ..... 55.00
❑76, Dec 1958 ..... 55.00
❑77, Jan 1959 ..... 55.00
❑78, Feb 1959 ..... 55.00
❑79, Mar 1959 ..... 55.00
❑80, Apr 1959 ..... 55.00
❑81, May 1959 ..... 55.00
❑82, Jun 1959 ..... 55.00
❑83, Jul 1959 ..... 55.00
❑84, Aug 1959 O: Mademoiselle Marie. 1: Mademoiselle Marie. 125.00
❑85, Sep 1959 A: Mademoiselle Marie. 80.00
❑86, Oct 1959 A: Mademoiselle Marie. 80.00
❑87, Nov 1959 A: Mademoiselle Marie. 80.00
❑88, Jan 1960 ..... 65.00
❑89, Mar 1960 ..... 65.00
❑90, May 1960; 1: Dinosaur Island. Island of Armored Giants (dinosaur) story 325.00
❑91, Jul 1960 ..... 45.00
❑92, Sep 1960; Dinosaurs 110.00
❑93, Nov 1960 ..... 45.00
❑94, Jan 1961; Dinosaurs 110.00
❑95, Mar 1961; Dinosaurs 110.00
❑96, May 1961; Dinosaurs 110.00
❑97, Jul 1961; Dinosaurs 110.00
❑98, Sep 1961; Dinosaurs 110.00
❑99, Nov 1961; Dinosaurs 110.00
❑100, Jan 1962; Dinosaurs 145.00
❑101, Mar 1962; Dinosaurs 60.00
❑102, May 1962; Dinosaurs 60.00
❑103, Jul 1962; Dinosaurs 60.00
❑104, Sep 1962; Dinosaurs 60.00

N-MINT

❑105, Nov 1962; Dinosaurs 60.00
❑106, Jan 1963; Dinosaurs 60.00
❑107, Mar 1963; Dinosaurs 60.00
❑108, May 1963; Dinosaurs 60.00
❑109, Jul 1963; Dinosaurs 60.00
❑110, Sep 1963; Dinosaurs 60.00
❑111, Nov 1963; Dinosaurs 60.00
❑112, Jan 1964; Dinosaurs 60.00
❑113, Mar 1964; Dinosaurs 60.00
❑114, May 1964; Dinosaurs 60.00
❑115, Jul 1964; Dinosaurs 60.00
❑116, Sep 1964; Dinosaurs 60.00
❑117, Nov 1964; Dinosaurs 60.00
❑118, Jan 1965; Dinosaurs 60.00
❑119, Mar 1965; Dinosaurs 60.00
❑120, Apr 1965; Dinosaurs 60.00
❑121, Jun 1965; Dinosaurs 60.00
❑122, Aug 1965; Dinosaurs 60.00
❑123, Oct 1965; Dinosaurs 60.00
❑124, Dec 1965; Dinosaurs 60.00
❑125, Feb 1966; Dinosaurs 60.00
❑126, Apr 1966 1: Sgt. Gorilla. 60.00
❑127, Jun 1966; Dinosaurs 60.00
❑128, Aug 1966; Dinosaurs 60.00
❑129, Oct 1966; Dinosaurs 60.00
❑130, Dec 1966; Dinosaurs 60.00
❑131, Mar 1967; Dinosaurs 60.00
❑132, May 1967; Dinosaurs 60.00
❑133, Jul 1967; Dinosaurs 60.00
❑134, Sep 1967; NA (a); Dinosaurs ... 65.00
❑135, Nov 1967; Dinosaurs 60.00
❑136, Jan 1968; Dinosaurs 60.00
❑137, Mar 1968; Dinosaurs 60.00
❑138, May 1968; JKu (a); Enemy Ace stories begin 60.00
❑139, Jul 1968 JKu (a); O: Enemy Ace. 50.00
❑140, Sep 1968; JKu (a); Enemy Ace 24.00
❑141, Nov 1968; JKu (a); Enemy Ace 24.00
❑142, Jan 1969; JKu (a); Enemy Ace 24.00
❑143, Mar 1969; Enemy Ace 24.00
❑144, May 1969; JKu, NA (a); Enemy Ace 27.00
❑145, Jul 1969; Enemy Ace 35.00
❑146, Sep 1969; Enemy Ace 20.00
❑147, Nov 1969; JKu (a); Enemy Ace 20.00
❑148, Jan 1970; Enemy Ace 20.00
❑149, Mar 1970 ..... 20.00
❑150, May 1970; JKu (a); Enemy Ace, Viking Prince 20.00
❑151, Jul 1970 JKu (a); 1: Unknown Soldier. 110.00
❑152, Sep 1970 2: The Unknown Soldier. 20.00
❑153, Nov 1970 JKu (a) 20.00
❑154, Jan 1971; JKu (a); O: Unknown Soldier. Unknown Soldier; Enemy Ace 55.00
❑155, Mar 1971; reprints Enemy Ace story 16.00
❑156, May 1971; Unknown Soldier; Enemy Ace back-up 14.00
❑157, Jul 1971; Unknown Soldier meets Easy Co.; Enemy Ace back-up 14.00
❑158, Sep 1971 ..... 14.00
❑159, Nov 1971 JKu (a) 14.00
❑160, Jan 1972 ..... 14.00
❑161, Mar 1972; Regular Enemy Ace stories end 14.00
❑162, May 1972 JKu (c) 6.00
❑163, Jul 1972 CI, JKu, DS (a) 6.00
❑164, Sep 1972 ATh (a) 6.00
❑165, Nov 1972 ..... 6.00
❑166, Jan 1973 ..... 6.00
❑167, Feb 1973 ..... 6.00
❑168, Mar 1973 TS (w) 6.00
❑169, Apr 1973 JKu (c); JKu (a) 6.00
❑170, Jun 1973 ..... 6.00
❑171, Jul 1973 JKu (c); JKu (a); O: The Unknown Soldier. 6.00
❑172, Aug 1973 ..... 6.00
❑173, Sep 1973 ..... 6.00
❑174, Oct 1973 FR (w) 6.00
❑175, Nov 1973 ..... 6.00

N-MINT

❑176, Dec 1973 FR (w); FT (a) 6.00
❑177, Jan 1974 ..... 6.00
❑178, Feb 1974 ..... 6.00
❑179, Mar 1974 ..... 6.00
❑180, Jun 1974 ..... 6.00
❑181, Aug 1974 FR (w); FT (a) 5.00
❑182, Oct 1974 FR (w) 5.00
❑183, Dec 1974 ..... 5.00
❑184, Feb 1975 SA (w); SA (a) 5.00
❑185, Mar 1975 ..... 5.00
❑186, Apr 1975 ..... 5.00
❑187, May 1975 ..... 5.00
❑188, Jun 1975 ..... 5.00
❑189, Jul 1975 JKu (c); JKu (a) 5.00
❑190, Aug 1975 JKu (c); JKu (a) 5.00
❑191, Sep 1975 ..... 5.00
❑192, Oct 1975 JKu (c); JKu (a) 5.00
❑193, Nov 1975 ..... 5.00
❑194, Dec 1975 ..... 5.00
❑195, Jan 1976 ..... 5.00
❑196, Feb 1976 ..... 5.00
❑197, Mar 1976 ..... 5.00
❑198, Apr 1976 ..... 5.00
❑199, May 1976 ..... 5.00
❑200, Jul 1976 JKu (a); A: Mademoiselle Marie. 5.00
❑201, Sep 1976 JKu (c); JKu (a) 5.00
❑202, Nov 1976 ..... 5.00
❑203, Jan 1977 JKu (c); JKu (a) 5.00
❑204, Mar 1977; BMc (a); Series continues as Unknown Soldier 5.00

STARSTONE
AIRCEL

❑1, b&w 1.70
❑2, b&w 1.70
❑3, b&w 1.70

STARSTREAM
GOLD KEY / WHITMAN

❑1, ca. 1976 ..... 3.00
❑2 1976; Stories by Science-Fiction writers 3.00
❑3 1976 ..... 3.00
❑4 1976 JAb (a) 3.00

STARSTRUCK (EPIC)
MARVEL / EPIC

❑1, Feb 1985 ..... 2.50
❑2, Apr 1985 ..... 2.00
❑3, Jun 1985 ..... 2.00
❑4, Aug 1985 ..... 2.00
❑5, Oct 1985 ..... 2.00
❑6, Feb 1986 ..... 2.00

STARSTRUCK (DARK HORSE)
DARK HORSE

❑1, Aug 1990, b&w 2.95
❑2 1990, b&w 2.95
❑3, Jan 1991, b&w 2.95
❑4, Mar 1991; trading cards 2.95

STARTLING CRIME ILLUSTRATED
CALIBER

❑1, b&w 2.95

STARTLING STORIES: BANNER
MARVEL

❑1, Sep 2001 ..... 2.99
❑2, Oct 2001 ..... 2.99
❑3, Nov 2001 ..... 2.99
❑4, Dec 2001 ..... 2.99

STARTLING STORIES: THE THING
MARVEL

❑1, ca. 2003 ..... 3.50

STARTLING STORIES: THE THING -- NIGHT FALLS ON YANCY STREET
MARVEL

❑1, Jun 2003 ..... 3.50
❑2, Jul 2003 ..... 3.50
❑3, Aug 2003 ..... 3.50
❑4, Sep 2003 ..... 3.50

N-MINT

STAR TREK (1ST SERIES)
GOLD KEY

❑1, Oct 1967; wraparound photo cover 300.00
❑2, Jun 1968 .... 90.00
❑3, Dec 1968 .... 80.00
❑4, Jun 1969 .... 60.00
❑5, Sep 1969 .... 55.00
❑6, Dec 1969 .... 55.00
❑7, Mar 1970 .... 48.00
❑8, Sep 1970 .... 40.00
❑9, Feb 1971; last photo cover 40.00
❑10, May 1971; William Shatner and Leonard Nimoy photos in small boxes on cover 36.00
❑11, Aug 1971; William Shatner and Leonard Nimoy photos in small boxes on cover 25.00
❑12, Nov 1971; William Shatner and Leonard Nimoy photos in small boxes on cover 25.00
❑13, Feb 1972; William Shatner and Leonard Nimoy photos in small boxes on cover 25.00
❑14, May 1972; William Shatner and Leonard Nimoy photos in small boxes on cover 25.00
❑15, Aug 1972; William Shatner and Leonard Nimoy photos in small boxes on cover 25.00
❑16, Nov 1972; William Shatner and Leonard Nimoy photos in small boxes on cover 25.00
❑17, Feb 1973; William Shatner and Leonard Nimoy photos in small boxes on cover 25.00
❑18, May 1973; William Shatner and Leonard Nimoy photos in small boxes on cover 25.00
❑19, Jul 1973; William Shatner and Leonard Nimoy photos in small boxes on cover 25.00
❑20, Sep 1973; William Shatner and Leonard Nimoy photos in small boxes on cover 25.00
❑21, Nov 1973; William Shatner and Leonard Nimoy photos in small boxes on cover 25.00
❑22, Jan 1974; William Shatner and Leonard Nimoy photos in small boxes on cover 25.00
❑23, Mar 1974; William Shatner and Leonard Nimoy photos in small boxes on cover 25.00
❑24, May 1974; William Shatner and Leonard Nimoy photos in small boxes on cover 20.00
❑25, Jul 1974; William Shatner and Leonard Nimoy photos in small boxes on cover 20.00
❑26, Sep 1974; William Shatner and Leonard Nimoy photos in small boxes on cover 20.00
❑27, Nov 1974; William Shatner and Leonard Nimoy photos in small boxes on cover 20.00
❑28, Jan 1975; William Shatner and Leonard Nimoy photos in small boxes on cover 20.00
❑29, Mar 1975; William Shatner and Leonard Nimoy photos in small boxes on cover 20.00
❑30, May 1975; William Shatner and Leonard Nimoy photos in small boxes on cover 20.00
❑31, Jul 1975; William Shatner and Leonard Nimoy photos in small boxes on cover 15.00
❑32, Aug 1975; William Shatner and Leonard Nimoy photos in small boxes on cover 15.00
❑33, Sep 1975; William Shatner and Leonard Nimoy photos in small boxes on cover 15.00
❑34, Oct 1975; William Shatner and Leonard Nimoy photos in small boxes on cover 15.00
❑35, Nov 1975; William Shatner and Leonard Nimoy photos in small boxes on cover 15.00

N-MINT

❑36, Mar 1976; William Shatner and Leonard Nimoy photos in small boxes on cover 15.00
❑37, May 1976; William Shatner and Leonard Nimoy photos in small boxes on cover 15.00
❑38, Jul 1976; William Shatner and Leonard Nimoy photos in small boxes on cover 15.00
❑39, Aug 1976; William Shatner and Leonard Nimoy photos in small boxes on cover 15.00
❑40, Sep 1976; William Shatner and Leonard Nimoy photos in small boxes on cover 15.00
❑41, Nov 1976; William Shatner and Leonard Nimoy photos in small boxes on cover 12.00
❑42, Jan 1977; William Shatner and Leonard Nimoy photos in small boxes on cover 12.00
❑43, Feb 1977; William Shatner and Leonard Nimoy photos in small boxes on cover 12.00
❑44, May 1977; William Shatner and Leonard Nimoy photos in small boxes on cover 12.00
❑45, Jul 1977 .... 12.00
❑46, Aug 1977 .... 12.00
❑47, Sep 1977 .... 12.00
❑48, Oct 1977 .... 12.00
❑49, Nov 1977 .... 12.00
❑50, Jan 1978 .... 12.00
❑51, Mar 1978; A: Professor Whipple. William Shatner and Leonard Nimoy photo in small box on cover 12.00
❑52, May 1978; William Shatner and Leonard Nimoy photo in small box on cover 12.00
❑53, Jul 1978; William Shatner and Leonard Nimoy photo in small box on cover 12.00
❑54, Aug 1978 .... 12.00
❑55, Sep 1978 .... 12.00
❑56, Oct 1978 .... 12.00
❑57, Nov 1978 .... 12.00
❑58, Dec 1978 .... 12.00
❑59, Jan 1979 .... 12.00
❑60, Feb 1979 .... 10.00
❑61, Mar 1979 .... 10.00

STAR TREK (2ND SERIES)
MARVEL

❑1, Apr 1980; DC, KJ (a); adapts Star Trek: The Motion Picture 5.00
❑2, May 1980; DC, KJ (a); adapts Star Trek: The Motion Picture 3.00
❑3, Jun 1980; DC, KJ (a); adapts Star Trek: The Motion Picture 2.00
❑4, Jul 1980 .... 2.00
❑5, Aug 1980 .... 2.00
❑6, Sep 1980 .... 2.00
❑7, Oct 1980 .... 2.00
❑8, Nov 1980 .... 2.00
❑9, Dec 1980 .... 2.00
❑10, Jan 1981; Starfleet files 2.00
❑11, Feb 1981 .... 2.00
❑12, Mar 1981 .... 2.00
❑13, Apr 1981 A: McCoy's daughter. 2.00
❑14, Jun 1981 .... 2.00
❑15, Aug 1981 .... 2.00
❑16, Oct 1981 .... 2.00
❑17, Dec 1981 .... 2.00
❑18, Feb 1982 .... 2.00

STAR TREK (3RD SERIES)
DC

❑1, Feb 1984; TS (a); 1: Bearclaw. Part 1 .... 4.00
❑2, Mar 1984; TS (a); Part 2 .... 3.00
❑3, Apr 1984; TS (a); Part 3 .... 3.00
❑4, May 1984; TS (a); Part 4 .... 3.00
❑5, Jun 1984 TS (a) 3.00
❑6, Jul 1984 TS (a) 2.50
❑7, Aug 1984 TS (a); O: Saavik. 2.50
❑8, Nov 1984 TS (a); V: Romulans. 2.50
❑9, Dec 1984; TS (a); New Frontiers, Part 1; Return of Mirror Universe .. 2.50

In addition to a Groo appearance, *Starslayer* #2 contains the first full appearance of Dave Stevens' Rocketeer.

© 1982 Dave Stevens and Pacific.

N-MINT

❑10, Jan 1985; TS (a); New Frontiers, Part 2 .... 2.50
❑11, Feb 1985; TS (a); New Frontiers, Part 3; The two Spocks mind-meld 2.00
❑12, Mar 1985; TS (a); New Frontiers, Part 4; Mirror Universe Enterprise's engineering hull destroyed 2.00
❑13, Apr 1985; TS (a); New Frontiers, Part 5 .... 2.00
❑14, May 1985; TS (a); New Frontiers, Part 6 .... 2.00
❑15, Jun 1985; TS (a); New Frontiers, Part 7 .... 2.00
❑16, Jul 1985; TS (a); New Frontiers, Part 8; Kirk receives command of Excelsior 2.00
❑17, Aug 1985 TS (a) 2.00
❑18, Sep 1985 TS (a) 2.00
❑19, Oct 1985; TS, DS (a); Written by Walter Koenig 2.00
❑20, Nov 1985 TS (a) 2.00
❑21, Dec 1985 TS (a) 2.00
❑22, Jan 1986; TS (a); return of Redjac 2.00
❑23, Feb 1986; TS (a); return of Redjac 2.00
❑24, Mar 1986; TS (a); Part 1 .... 2.00
❑25, Apr 1986; TS (a); Part 2 .... 2.00
❑26, May 1986 TS (a) 2.00
❑27, Jun 1986 TS (a) 2.00
❑28, Jul 1986 TS, GM (a) 2.00
❑29, Aug 1986 TS (a) 2.00
❑30, Sep 1986 TS (a) 2.00
❑31, Oct 1986 TS (a) 2.00
❑32, Nov 1986 TS (a) 2.00
❑33, Dec 1986; 20th Anniversary of Star Trek issue; original Enterprise meets Excelsior 2.00
❑34, Jan 1987; The Doomsday Bug, part 1 .... 2.00
❑35, Feb 1987; GM (a); The Doomsday Bug, part 2 .... 2.00
❑36, Mar 1987; The Doomsday Bug, part 3; returns to Vulcan 2.00
❑37, Apr 1987; CS (a); follows events of Star Trek IV 2.00
❑38, May 1987 .... 2.00
❑39, Jun 1987; return of Harry Mudd 2.00
❑40, Jul 1987 A: Harry Mudd. 2.00
❑41, Aug 1987 V: Orion pirates. 2.00
❑42, Sep 1987 .... 2.00
❑43, Oct 1987; The Return of the Serpent, part 1 .... 2.00
❑44, Nov 1987; The Return of the Serpent, part 2 .... 2.00
❑45, Dec 1987; The Return of the Serpent, part 3 .... 2.00
❑46, Jan 1988 .... 2.00
❑47, Feb 1988 .... 2.00
❑48, Mar 1988; PD (w); 1: Moron. first Peter David script 2.00
❑49, Apr 1988 PD (w) 2.00
❑50, May 1988; Giant-size PD (w) 2.00
❑51, Jun 1988 PD (w) 2.00
❑52, Jul 1988; PD (w); Dante's Inferno 2.00
❑53, Aug 1988 PD (w) 2.00
❑54, Sep 1988; PD (w); Return of Finnegan 2.00
❑55, Oct 1988 PD (w) 2.00
❑56, Nov 1988; PD (w); set during first five-year mission 2.00
❑Annual 1, ca. 1985; Kirk's first mission on The Enterprise 2.00

N-MINT

❑Annual 2, ca. 1986; A: Captain Pike. The final mission of the first five-year mission 2.00
❑Annual 3, ca. 1988; CS (a); Scotty's romances 2.00

STAR TREK (4TH SERIES)
DC

❑1, Oct 1989 PD (w) 5.00
❑2, Nov 1989 .... 4.00
❑3, Dec 1989 .... 3.00
❑4, Jan 1990 1: R.J. Blaise. 3.00
❑5, Feb 1990 .... 2.50
❑6, Mar 1990 .... 2.50
❑7, Apr 1990 .... 2.50
❑8, May 1990 V: Sweeney. 2.50
❑9, Jun 1990 V: Sweeney. 2.50
❑10, Jul 1990; A: Areel Shaw. A: Samuel Cogsley. The Trial of James T. Kirk 2.50
❑11, Aug 1990; A: Bella Oxmyx. A: Leonard James Akaar. The Trial of James T. Kirk 2.00
❑12, Sep 1990; The Trial of James T. Kirk 2.00
❑13, Oct 1990; The Return of the Worthy 2.00
❑14, Dec 1990; The Return of the Worthy 2.00
❑15, Jan 1991; PD (w); The Return of the Worthy; final Peter David issue 2.00
❑16, Feb 1991; Written by J. Michael Straczynski 2.00
❑17, Mar 1991; Part 1 .... 2.00
❑18, Apr 1991; Part 2 .... 2.00
❑19, May 1991; Peter David 2.00
❑20, Jun 1991; Gods' Gauntlet, part 1 .... 2.00
❑21, Jul 1991; Gods' Gauntlet, part 2 .... 2.00
❑22, Aug 1991; Return of Harry Mudd, Part 1 .... 2.00
❑23, Sep 1991; A: Harry Mudd. Return of Harry Mudd, Part 2 .... 2.00
❑24, Oct 1991; 25th anniversary of Star Trek; A: Harry Mudd. Return of Harry Mudd, Part 3; 25th Anniversary issue; Text pieces by Chris Claremont, Michael Jan Friedman, Peter David and Howard Weinstein 3.00
❑25, Nov 1991 A: Saavik. A: Captain Styles. 2.00
❑26, Dec 1991 .... 2.00
❑27, Jan 1992 .... 2.00
❑28, Feb 1992 .... 2.00
❑29, Mar 1992 .... 2.00
❑30, Apr 1992; Veritas, part 1 .... 2.00
❑31, May 1992; Veritas, part 2 .... 2.00
❑32, Jun 1992; Veritas, part 3 .... 2.00
❑33, Jul 1992; Veritas, part 4 .... 2.00
❑34, Aug 1992 JDu (a) 2.00
❑35, Sep 1992; The Tabukan Syndrome, Part 1 .... 2.00
❑36, Sep 1992; The Tabukan Syndrome, Part 2 .... 2.00
❑37, Oct 1992; The Tabukan Syndrome, Part 3 .... 2.00
❑38, Oct 1992; The Tabukan Syndrome, Part 4 .... 2.00
❑39, Nov 1992; The Tabukan Syndrome, Part 5 .... 2.00
❑40, Nov 1992; The Tabukan Syndrome, Part 6 .... 2.00
❑41, Dec 1992 .... 2.00
❑42, Jan 1993; Part 1 .... 2.00
❑43, Feb 1993; Part 2 .... 2.00
❑44, Mar 1993 .... 2.00
❑45, Apr 1993; Return of Trelane 2.00
❑46, May 1993; Deceptions, part 1 .... 2.00
❑47, May 1993; Deceptions, part 2 .... 2.00
❑48, Jun 1993; Deceptions, part 3 .... 2.00
❑49, Jun 1993; Part 1 .... 2.00
❑50, Jul 1993; Giant-size anniversary special; A: Gary Seven. Part 2; Double-sized issue 3.50
❑51, Aug 1993 .... 2.00
❑52, Sep 1993 .... 2.00
❑53, Oct 1993; TS (a); Time Crime, Part 1 .... 2.00

N-MINT

❑54, Nov 1993; TS (a); Time Crime, Part 2 .... 2.00
❑55, Dec 1993; TS (a); Time Crime, Part 3 .... 2.00
❑56, Jan 1994; Time Crime, Part 4 .... 2.00
❑57, Feb 1994; Time Crime, Part 5 .... 2.00
❑58, Mar 1994; Part 1; Chekov's first days on the Enterprise; cover forms triptych with issues #59 and 60 .... 2.00
❑59, Apr 1994; Part 2; Chekov's first days on the Enterprise; cover forms triptych with issues #57 and 58 .... 2.00
❑60, Jun 1994; Part 3; Chekov's first days on the Enterprise; cover forms triptych with issues #57 and 58 .... 2.00
❑61, Jul 1994; return to Talos IV 2.00
❑62, Aug 1994; Part 1 .... 2.00
❑63, Sep 1994; Part 2 .... 2.00
❑64, Oct 1994; follows events of Where No Man Has Gone Before 2.00
❑65, Nov 1994 .... 2.00
❑66, Dec 1994; Part 1 .... 2.00
❑67, Jan 1995; Part 2 .... 2.00
❑68, Feb 1995; Part 3 .... 2.00
❑69, Mar 1995; Part 1 .... 2.00
❑70, Apr 1995; Part 2 .... 2.00
❑71, May 1995 .... 2.50
❑72, Jun 1995 .... 2.50
❑73, Jul 1995; Part 1 .... 2.50
❑74, Aug 1995; Part 2 .... 2.50
❑75, Sep 1995 .... 3.95
❑76, Oct 1995 .... 2.50
❑77, Nov 1995 .... 2.50
❑78, Dec 1995; The Chosen, Part 1 .... 2.50
❑79, Jan 1996; The Chosen, Part 2 .... 2.50
❑80, Feb 1996; The Chosen, Part 3 .... 2.50
❑Annual 1, ca. 1990; PD (w); Story by George Takei 3.50
❑Annual 2, ca. 1991; Kirk at Starfleet Academy 3.25
❑Annual 3, ca. 1992 .... 3.50
❑Annual 4, ca. 1993; Spock on Enterprise with Captain Pike 3.50
❑Annual 5, ca. 1994; 1994 Annual 3.95
❑Annual 6, ca. 1995; D: Gary Seven. Convergence, Part 1; continues in Star Trek: TNG Annual #6; 1995 Annual 3.95
❑Special 1, Spr 1994 .... 3.50
❑Special 2, Win 1994 .... 3.50
❑Special 3, Win 1995 .... 3.95

STAR TREK: DEEP SPACE NINE (MALIBU)
MALIBU

❑0, Jan 1995; premium limited edition; QVC offer 3.00
❑1/A, Aug 1993; Newsstand cover; Part 1 .... 3.00
❑1/B, Aug 1993; line-drawing cover; Part 1 .... 3.00
❑1/C, Aug 1993; deluxe edition (black/foil); Part 1 .... 4.00
❑2, Sep 1993; trading card 2.50
❑3, Oct 1993 .... 2.50
❑4, Nov 1993 .... 2.50
❑5, Dec 1993 .... 2.50
❑6, Jan 1994 .... 2.50
❑7, Feb 1994 .... 2.50
❑8, May 1994 .... 2.50
❑9, Jun 1994 .... 2.50
❑10, Jun 1994 .... 2.50
❑11, Jul 1994 .... 2.50
❑12, Jul 1994 .... 2.50
❑13, Aug 1994 .... 2.50
❑14, Sep 1994 .... 2.50
❑15, Sep 1994 .... 2.50
❑16, Nov 1994 .... 2.50
❑17, Dec 1994 .... 2.50
❑18, Jan 1995 .... 2.50
❑19, Feb 1995 .... 2.50
❑20, Mar 1995 .... 2.50
❑21, Apr 1995 .... 2.50
❑22, May 1995 .... 2.50
❑23, May 1995; The Secret of the Lost Orb, Part 1 .... 2.50

N-MINT

❑24, Jun 1995; The Secret of the Lost Orb, Part 2 .... 2.50
❑25, Jul 1995; The Secret of the Lost Orb, Part 3; Double-sized issue 3.50
❑26, Jul 1995 .... 2.50
❑27, Aug 1995 .... 2.50
❑28, Sep 1995 .... 2.50
❑29, Oct 1995 .... 2.50
❑30, Nov 1995 .... 2.50
❑31, Dec 1995 .... 3.95
❑32, Jan 1996 .... 3.50
❑Annual 1, ca. 1995 .... 3.95
❑Ashcan 1; limited edition ashcan 5.00
❑Special 1, ca. 1995 .... 3.50

STAR TREK: DEEP SPACE NINE (MARVEL)
MARVEL / PARAMOUNT

❑1, Nov 1996; DS9 is drawn into the wormhole 2.00
❑2, Dec 1996 .... 2.00
❑3, Jan 1997 .... 2.00
❑4, Feb 1997 .... 2.00
❑5, Mar 1997 .... 2.00
❑6, Apr 1997 .... 2.00
❑7, May 1997 .... 2.00
❑8, Aug 1997 .... 2.00
❑9, Sep 1997 .... 2.00
❑10, Oct 1997 .... 2.00
❑11, Nov 1997; gatefold summary; Telepathy War, Part 1; Crossover with ST: Starfleet Academy, ST: Telepathy War one-shot, ST Unlimited and ST: Voyager 2.00
❑12, Dec 1997; gatefold summary; Telepathy War, Part 2; Crossover with ST: Starfleet Academy, ST: Telepathy War one-shot, ST Unlimited and ST: Voyager 2.00
❑13, Jan 1998; gatefold summary 2.00
❑14, Feb 1998; gatefold summary A: Tribbles. 2.00
❑15, Mar 1998; gatefold summary 2.00

STAR TREK: DEEP SPACE NINE, THE CELEBRITY SERIES: BLOOD AND HONOR
MALIBU

❑1, May 1995; Written by Mark Lenard 2.95

STAR TREK: DEEP SPACE NINE HEARTS AND MINDS
MALIBU

❑1, Jun 1994; an original Deep Space Nine mini series 2.50
❑2, Jul 1994 .... 2.50
❑3, Aug 1994 .... 2.50
❑4, Sep 1994 .... 2.50

STAR TREK: DEEP SPACE NINE: LIGHTSTORM
MALIBU

❑1, Dec 1994 .... 3.50

STAR TREK: DEEP SPACE NINE: N-VECTOR
DC / WILDSTORM

❑1, Aug 2000 .... 2.50
❑2, Sep 2000 .... 2.50
❑3, Oct 2000 .... 2.50
❑4, Nov 2000 .... 2.50

STAR TREK: DEEP SPACE NINE: RULES OF DIPLOMACY
MALIBU

❑1, Aug 1995; Co-Author Aron Eisenberg plays "Nog" in series 2.95

N-MINT

STAR TREK: DEEP SPACE NINE/STAR TREK: THE NEXT GENERATION
MALIBU

❑1, Oct 1994; part two of a four-part crossover with DC; Deep Space Nine/ The Next Generation crossover, Part 2; Continued from Star Trek: The Next Generation/Star Trek: Deep Space Nine #1; Continues in Star Trek: The Next Generation/Star Trek: Deep Space Nine #2 ..... 2.50
❑2, Nov 1994; part three of a four-part crossover with DC; Deep Space Nine/ The Next Generation crossover, Part 4; Continued from Star Trek: The Next Generation/Star Trek: Deep Space Nine #2 ..... 2.50
❑Ashcan 1; No cover price; Ashcan preview; flip-book with DC's Star Trek: The Next Generation/Star Trek: Deep Space Nine Ashcan 1.00

STAR TREK: DEEP SPACE NINE: TEROK NOR
MALIBU

❑0, Jan 1995 ..... 2.95

STAR TREK: DEEP SPACE NINE, THE MAQUIS
MALIBU

❑1, Feb 1995; Soldier of Peace, Part 1 2.50
❑2, Mar 1995; Soldier of Peace, Part 2 2.50
❑3, Apr 1995; Soldier of Peace, Part 3 2.50

STAR TREK: DEEP SPACE NINE, ULTIMATE ANNUAL
MALIBU

❑1, ca. 1995 ..... 5.95

STAR TREK: DEEP SPACE NINE, WORF SPECIAL
MALIBU

❑0, Dec 1995 ..... 3.95

STAR TREK: DIVIDED WE FALL
DC

❑1, Jul 2001 ..... 2.95
❑2, Aug 2001 ..... 2.95
❑3, Sep 2001 ..... 2.95
❑4, Oct 2001 ..... 2.95

STAR TREK: EARLY VOYAGES
MARVEL / PARAMOUNT

❑1, Feb 1997; Christopher Pike as Enterprise captain 2.99
❑2, Mar 1997; Battle with the Klingons 1.99
❑3, Apr 1997; prequel to The Cage 1.99
❑4, May 1997; Yeoman Colt's POV on The Cage 1.99
❑5, Jun 1997; Part 1 ..... 1.99
❑6, Jul 1997; Part 2 ..... 1.99
❑7, Aug 1997; gatefold summary; Pike vs. Kaaj 1.99
❑8, Sep 1997; gatefold summary 1.99
❑9, Oct 1997; gatefold summary 1.99
❑10, Nov 1997; gatefold summary; Part 1 ..... 1.99
❑11, Dec 1997; gatefold summary; Part 2 ..... 1.99
❑12, Jan 1998; gatefold summary; Part 1 ..... 1.99
❑13, Feb 1998; gatefold summary; Part 2 ..... 1.99
❑14, Mar 1998; gatefold summary; Pike vs. Kirk 1.99
❑15, Apr 1998; gatefold summary 1.99
❑16, May 1998; gatefold summary; Pike goes undercover 1.99
❑17, Jun 1998; gatefold summary 1.99

STAR TREK: ENTER THE WOLVES
WILDSTORM / PARAMOUNT

❑1, ca. 2001 ..... 5.99

STAR TREK: FIRST CONTACT
MARVEL / PARAMOUNT

❑1, Nov 1996; prestige format; Movie adaptation; cardstock cover 5.95

N-MINT

STAR TREK GENERATIONS
DC

❑1; Movie adaptation; Newstand edition 3.95
❑1/Prestige; Movie adaptation; Prestige format one-shot 5.95

STAR TREKKER
ANTARCTIC

❑1, Dec 1992, b&w; parody (never distributed) 2.95

STAR TREK: MIRROR MIRROR
MARVEL / PARAMOUNT

❑1, Feb 1997; one-shot sequel to original series episode 3.99

STAR TREK MOVIE SPECIAL
DC

❑3, ca. 1984; Movie adaptation 2.00
❑4, ca. 1987; Movie adaptation 2.00
❑5, ca. 1989; Movie adaptation 2.00

STAR TREK: NEW FRONTIER: DOUBLE TIME
DC / WILDSTORM

❑1, Nov 2000; Captain Calhoun on the USS Excalibur 5.95

STAR TREK: OPERATION ASSIMILATION
MARVEL / PARAMOUNT

❑1, Apr 1997; Romulans as Borg 2.99

STAR TREK VI: THE UNDISCOVERED COUNTRY
DC

❑1, ca. 1992; The Undiscovered Country Movie adaptation; Newsstand edition 2.95
❑1/Direct ed., ca. 1992; prestige format; The Undiscovered Country Movie adaptation 5.95

STAR TREK SPECIAL
WILDSTORM

❑1 2001; Prestige format; stories for Star Trek, Next Generation, Deep Space Nine and Voyager 6.95

STAR TREK: STARFLEET ACADEMY
MARVEL / PARAMOUNT

❑1, Dec 1996 A: Nog. 2.00
❑2, Jan 1997 ..... 2.00
❑3, Feb 1997 ..... 2.00
❑4, Mar 1997; Part 1 ..... 2.00
❑5, Apr 1997 D: Kamilah. 2.00
❑6, May 1997 ..... 2.00
❑7, Jun 1997 ..... 2.00
❑8, Jul 1997; return of Charlie X 2.00
❑9, Aug 1997; gatefold summary; A: Pike. on Talos IV 2.00
❑10, Sep 1997; gatefold summary 2.00
❑11, Oct 1997; gatefold summary; cadets on trial for going to Talos IV 2.00
❑12, Nov 1997; gatefold summary; Part 1; Crossover with ST: Deep Space Nine, ST: Telepathy War one-shot; ST Unlimited and ST: Voyager 2.00
❑13, Dec 1997; gatefold summary 2.00
❑14, Jan 1998; gatefold summary; Part 1 ..... 2.00
❑15, Feb 1998; gatefold summary; Part 2 ..... 2.00
❑16, Mar 1998; gatefold summary; Part 3 ..... 2.00
❑17, Apr 1998; gatefold summary 2.00
❑18/A, May 1998; English language edition 2.00
❑18/B, May 1998; Klingon language edition 2.00
❑19, Jun 1998; gatefold summary 2.00

STAR TREK: TELEPATHY WAR
MARVEL / PARAMOUNT

❑1, Nov 1997; concludes crossover between ST: Deep Space Nine, ST: Starfleet Academy; ST Unlimited, and ST: Voyager 2.99

The first several issues of Gold Key's *Star Trek* feature photo covers with the series' cast.

© 1967 Gold Key and Desilu Productions.

N-MINT

STAR TREK: THE MODALA IMPERATIVE
DC

❑1, Jul 1991 ..... 2.50
❑2, Aug 1991 ..... 2.00
❑3, Aug 1991 ..... 2.00
❑4, Sep 1991 ..... 2.00

STAR TREK: THE NEXT GENERATION (MINI-SERIES)
DC

❑1, Feb 1988 ..... 3.00
❑2, Mar 1988 ..... 2.00
❑3, Apr 1988 ..... 2.00
❑4, May 1988 ..... 2.00
❑5, Jun 1988 D: Geordi. 2.00
❑6, Jul 1988 ..... 2.00

STAR TREK: THE NEXT GENERATION
DC

❑1, Oct 1989 ..... 5.00
❑2, Nov 1989 ..... 4.00
❑3, Dec 1989 ..... 3.00
❑4, Jan 1990 ..... 3.00
❑5, Feb 1990 ..... 3.00
❑6, Mar 1990 ..... 2.50
❑7, Apr 1990 ..... 2.50
❑8, May 1990 ..... 2.50
❑9, Jun 1990 ..... 2.50
❑10, Jul 1990 ..... 2.50
❑11, Aug 1990 ..... 2.50
❑12, Sep 1990 ..... 2.50
❑13, Oct 1990 ..... 2.50
❑14, Dec 1990 ..... 2.50
❑15, Jan 1991 V: Ferengi. 2.50
❑16, Feb 1991 ..... 2.50
❑17, Mar 1991 ..... 2.50
❑18, Apr 1991 ..... 2.50
❑19, May 1991 ..... 2.50
❑20, Jun 1991 ..... 2.50
❑21, Jul 1991 ..... 2.00
❑22, Aug 1991 ..... 2.00
❑23, Sep 1991 ..... 2.00
❑24, Oct 1991; double-sized; Double-sized 25th Anniversary issue 2.00
❑25, Nov 1991; Giant-size 2.00
❑26, Dec 1991 ..... 2.00
❑27, Jan 1992 ..... 2.00
❑28, Feb 1992; Return of K'ehleyr 2.00
❑29, Mar 1992 ..... 2.00
❑30, Apr 1992 ..... 2.00
❑31, May 1992 ..... 2.00
❑32, Jun 1992 ..... 2.00
❑33, Jul 1992; Q turns the crew into Klingons 2.00
❑34, Jul 1992 ..... 2.00
❑35, Aug 1992 ..... 2.00
❑36, Aug 1992 ..... 2.00
❑37, Sep 1992 ..... 2.00
❑38, Sep 1992 ..... 2.00
❑39, Oct 1992 ..... 2.00
❑40, Nov 1992 ..... 2.00
❑41, Dec 1992 ..... 2.00
❑42, Jan 1993 ..... 2.00
❑43, Feb 1993 ..... 2.00
❑44, Mar 1993 ..... 2.00
❑45, Apr 1993 ..... 2.00
❑46, May 1993 ..... 2.00

N-MINT

- ❑47, Jun 1993; Worst of Both Worlds, Part 1 ..... 2.00
- ❑48, Jul 1993; Worst of Both Worlds, Part 2 ..... 2.00
- ❑49, Aug 1993; Worst of Both Worlds, Part 3 ..... 2.00
- ❑50, Sep 1993; Giant-size; Worst of Both Worlds, Part 4; Double-sized issue 3.50
- ❑51, Oct 1993 ..... 2.00
- ❑52, Oct 1993; Dixon Hill story 2.00
- ❑53, Nov 1993 ..... 2.00
- ❑54, Nov 1993 ..... 2.00
- ❑55, Dec 1993 ..... 2.00
- ❑56, Jan 1994 ..... 2.00
- ❑57, Mar 1994 ..... 2.00
- ❑58, Apr 1994 ..... 2.00
- ❑59, May 1994 ..... 2.00
- ❑60, Jun 1994 ..... 2.00
- ❑61, Jul 1994 ..... 2.00
- ❑62, Aug 1994 ..... 2.00
- ❑63, Sep 1994 ..... 2.00
- ❑64, Oct 1994 ..... 2.00
- ❑65, Nov 1994 ..... 2.00
- ❑66, Dec 1994 ..... 2.00
- ❑67, Jan 1995 ..... 2.00
- ❑68, Feb 1995 ..... 2.00
- ❑69, Mar 1995 ..... 2.00
- ❑70, Apr 1995 ..... 2.00
- ❑71, May 1995 ..... 2.00
- ❑72, Jun 1995; War and Madness, Part 1 ..... 2.50
- ❑73, Jul 1995; War and Madness, Part 2 ..... 2.50
- ❑74, Aug 1995; War and Madness, Part 3 ..... 2.50
- ❑75, Sep 1995; Giant-size; V: Borg. War and Madness, Part 4; Double-sized issue 3.95
- ❑76, Oct 1995 ..... 2.50
- ❑77, Nov 1995 ..... 2.50
- ❑78, Dec 1995 ..... 2.50
- ❑79, Jan 1996; Q transforms the crew into androids 2.50
- ❑80, Feb 1996 ..... 2.50
- ❑Annual 1, ca. 1990; Q story written by deLancie; Stardate back-up feature (puts comics & books in conjunction with TV series); 1990 Annual 3.50
- ❑Annual 2, ca. 1991; 1991 Annual 3.50
- ❑Annual 3, ca. 1992; 1992 Annual 3.50
- ❑Annual 4, ca. 1993; 1993 Annual 3.50
- ❑Annual 5, ca. 1994; 1994 Annual 3.50
- ❑Annual 6, ca. 1995; Part 2; continued from Star Trek Annual #6; 1995 Annual 3.95
- ❑Special 1, ca. 1993; 1993 Special 3.50
- ❑Special 2, Sum 1994; Captain Bateson of the Bozeman; 1994 Special 3.95
- ❑Special 3, Win 1995; 1995 Special 3.95

STAR TREK: THE NEXT GENERATION/ DEEP SPACE NINE
DC

- ❑1, Dec 1994; crossover with Malibu; Deep Space Nine/The Next Generation crossover, Part 1; Continues in Star Trek: Deep Space Nine/The Next Generation #1 ..... 2.50
- ❑2, Jan 1995; crossover with Malibu; Deep Space Nine/The Next Generation crossover, Part 4; Continued from Star Trek: Deep Space Nine/The Next Generation #1; Continues in Star Trek: Deep Space Nine/The Next Generation #2 ..... 2.50
- ❑Ashcan 1; No cover price; flip-book with Malibu's Deep Space Nine/Star Trek: The Next Generation Ashcan 1.00

STSTAR TREK: THE NEXT GENERATION: ILL WIND
DC

- ❑1, Nov 1995 ..... 2.50
- ❑2, Dec 1995 ..... 2.50
- ❑3, Jan 1996 ..... 2.50
- ❑4, Feb 1996 ..... 2.50

STAR TREK: THE NEXT GENERATION: PERCHANCE TO DREAM
DC / WILDSTORM

- ❑1, Feb 2000 ..... 2.50
- ❑2, Mar 2000 ..... 2.50
- ❑3, Apr 2000 ..... 2.50
- ❑4, May 2000 ..... 2.50

STAR TREK: THE NEXT GENERATION: RIKER
MARVEL / PARAMOUNT

- ❑1, Jul 1998 ..... 3.50

STAR TREK:THE NEXT GENERATION: SHADOWHEART
DC

- ❑1, Dec 1994 ..... 1.95
- ❑2, Jan 1995 ..... 1.95
- ❑3, Feb 1995 ..... 1.95
- ❑4, Mar 1995 ..... 1.95

STAR TREK: THE NEXT GENERATION: THE KILLING SHADOWS
DC / WILDSTORM

- ❑1, Nov 2000 ..... 2.50
- ❑2, Dec 2000 ..... 2.50
- ❑3, Jan 2001 ..... 2.50
- ❑4, Feb 2001 ..... 2.50

STAR TREK: THE NEXT GENERATION: THE MODALA IMPERATIVE
DC

- ❑1, Sep 1991; Incorrect date in indicia 1.75
- ❑2, Aug 1991 ..... 1.75
- ❑3, Aug 1991 ..... 1.75
- ❑4, Oct 1991 ..... 1.75

STAR TREK: THE NEXT GENERATION: THE SERIES FINALE
DC

- ❑1, ca. 1994; adapts final TV episode 3.95

STAR TREK UNLIMITED
MARVEL / PARAMOUNT

- ❑1, Nov 1996; Original crew story; Next Generation story 3.00
- ❑2, Jan 1997; Original crew story; Next Generation story 3.00
- ❑3, Apr 1997; Original crew story; Next Generation story 3.00
- ❑4, May 1997; Original crew story; Next Generation story; Original series and Next Generation stories crossover 3.00
- ❑5, Sep 1997; Original series and Next Generation stories crossover; Original crew story; Next Generation story 3.00
- ❑6, Nov 1997; Part 4; Crossover with ST: Deep Space Nine, ST: Starfleet Academy, ST: Telepathy War one-shot and ST: Voyager 3.00
- ❑7, Jan 1998 ..... 3.00
- ❑8, Mar 1998; Kang vs. Sulu 3.00
- ❑9, May 1998; Chekov wins a Klingon cruiser 3.00
- ❑10, Jul 1998 ..... 3.00

STAR TREK: UNTOLD VOYAGES
MARVEL / PARAMOUNT

- ❑1, Mar 1998 ..... 2.50
- ❑2, Apr 1998 ..... 2.50
- ❑3, May 1998 ..... 2.50
- ❑4, Jun 1998; Sulu takes command 2.50
- ❑5, Jul 1998 ..... 3.50

STAR TREK: VOYAGER
MARVEL / PARAMOUNT

- ❑1, Nov 1996 ..... 2.00
- ❑2, Dec 1996 ..... 2.00
- ❑3, Jan 1997 ..... 2.00
- ❑4, Feb 1997 ..... 2.00
- ❑5, Mar 1997 ..... 2.00
- ❑6, Apr 1997 ..... 2.00
- ❑7, May 1997 ..... 2.00
- ❑8, Jun 1997 ..... 2.00
- ❑9, Sep 1997; gatefold summary 2.00
- ❑10, Oct 1997; gatefold summary; replays events at Wolf 359 ..... 2.00
- ❑11, Nov 1997; gatefold summary V: Leviathan. 2.00
- ❑12, Dec 1997; gatefold summary 2.00
- ❑13, Jan 1998; gatefold summary; Part 5; Crossover with ST: Deep Space Nine, ST: Starfleet Academy, ST: Telepathy War one-shot and ST Unlimited 2.00
- ❑14, Feb 1998; gatefold summary 1: Seven of Nine. 2.00
- ❑15, Mar 1998; gatefold summary 2.00

STAR TREK: VOYAGER: AVALON RISING
DC

- ❑1, Sep 2000 ..... 5.95

STAR TREK: VOYAGER: FALSE COLORS
DC / WILDSTORM

- ❑1, Jan 2000 ..... 5.95

STAR TREK: VOYAGER: SPLASHDOWN
MARVEL / PARAMOUNT

- ❑1, Apr 1998; gatefold summary 2.50
- ❑2, May 1998; gatefold summary 2.50
- ❑3, Jun 1998; gatefold summary 2.50
- ❑4, Jul 1998; gatefold summary; final Marvel Star Trek comic book 2.50

STAR TREK: VOYAGER: THE PLANET KILLER
DC / WILDSTORM

- ❑1, Mar 2001 ..... 2.95
- ❑2, Apr 2001 ..... 2.95
- ❑3, May 2001 ..... 2.95

STAR TREK/X-MEN
MARVEL / PARAMOUNT

- ❑1, Dec 1996; X-Men meet original Enterprise crew 5.00

STAR TREK/X-MEN: SECOND CONTACT
MARVEL / PARAMOUNT

- ❑1, May 1998, A: Kang. X-Men meet Next Generation crew; Sentinels; continues in Star Trek: The Next Generation/X-Men: Planet X novel 5.00
- ❑1/Variant, May 1998 ..... 4.99

STAR WARS
MARVEL

- ❑1, Jul 1977 HC (a) 14.00
- ❑1/35 cent, Jul 1977; HC (a); 35 cent regional price variant; Rare variation; Price is in a square area, and UPC code appears with no line drawn through it 260.00
- ❑1-2; HC (a); "Reprint" in upper-left corner and UPC code appears with a line drawn through it 4.00
- ❑2, Aug 1977 HC (a) 9.00
- ❑2/35 cent, Aug 1977; HC (a); 35 cent regional price variant 30.00
- ❑2-2; HC (a); Has blank square where UPC code would go 3.50
- ❑3, Sep 1977 HC (a) 6.00
- ❑3/35 cent, Sep 1977; HC (a); 35 cent regional price variant 30.00
- ❑3-2; HC (a); Has blank square where UPC code would go 3.50
- ❑4, Oct 1977; HC (a); low distribution 6.00
- ❑4/35 cent, Oct 1977; 35 cent regional price variant 30.00
- ❑4-2; HC (a); Has blank square where UPC code would go 3.50
- ❑5, Nov 1977 HC (a) 6.00
- ❑5-2; HC (a); Has blank square where UPC code would go 3.50
- ❑6, Dec 1977 HC (a) 6.00
- ❑6-2; HC (a); Has blank square where UPC code would go 3.50
- ❑7, Jan 1978 HC (a) 6.00
- ❑7-2; HC (a); Has blank square where UPC code would go 3.00
- ❑8, Feb 1978 HC (a) 4.00
- ❑8-2; HC (a); Has blank square where UPC code would go 3.00
- ❑9, Mar 1978 HC (a) 4.00
- ❑9-2; HC (a); Has blank square where UPC code would go 3.00

	N-MINT
❑10, Apr 1978 HC (a)	4.00
❑11, May 1978	4.00
❑12, Jun 1978	4.00
❑13, Jul 1978 CI (a)	4.00
❑14, Aug 1978 CI (a)	4.00
❑15, Sep 1978 CI (a); D: Crimson Jack.	4.00
❑16, Oct 1978 1: Valance the bounty hunter.	4.00
❑17, Nov 1978; AM, HT (a); low distribution; Tatooine adventure set before first movie	4.00
❑18, Dec 1978; low distribution	4.00
❑19, Jan 1979; CI, BWi (a); low distribution	4.00
❑20, Feb 1979 CI, BWi (a)	4.00
❑21, Mar 1979 CI, GD (a)	4.00
❑22, Apr 1979 CI, BWi (a)	4.00
❑23, May 1979 CI, BWi (a)	4.00
❑24, Jun 1979; CI, BWi (a); flashback to before first movie	4.00
❑25, Jul 1979 CI, GD (a)	4.00
❑26, Aug 1979 CI, GD (a)	4.00
❑27, Sep 1979 CI, BWi (a)	4.00
❑28, Oct 1979 CI, BWi (a); A: Jabba the Hutt (not movie version).	4.00
❑29, Nov 1979 CI, BWi (c); CI, BWi (a); A: Darth Vader.	4.00
❑30, Dec 1979 CI, GD (a)	4.00
❑31, Jan 1980; CI, BWi (c); CI, BWi (a); return to Tatooine	3.00
❑32, Feb 1980 CI, BWi (a)	3.00
❑33, Mar 1980 CI, GD (a)	3.00
❑34, Apr 1980 CI, BWi (a); D: Baron Tagge.	3.00
❑35, May 1980 CI, GD (a); A: Darth Vader. A: Luke Skywalker.	3.00
❑36, Jun 1980 CI, GD (a)	3.00
❑37, Jul 1980; CI, GD (a); 1st Vader/Luke duel	3.00
❑38, Aug 1980; MG (w); MG (a); living spaceship	3.00
❑39, Sep 1980; AW (a); Empire Strikes Back adaptation	3.00
❑40, Oct 1980; AW (a); Empire Strikes Back adaptation	3.00
❑41, Nov 1980; AW (a); Empire Strikes Back adaptation	3.00
❑42, Dec 1980; AW (a); Empire Strikes Back adaptation	3.00
❑43, Jan 1981; AW (a); Empire Strikes Back adaptation	3.00
❑44, Feb 1981; AW (a); Empire Strikes Back adaptation	3.00
❑45, Mar 1981; first post-Empire Strikes Back story	3.00
❑46, Apr 1981	3.00
❑47, May 1981 FM (c); FM (a)	3.00
❑48, Jun 1981	3.00
❑49, Jul 1981; low distribution	3.00
❑50, Aug 1981; double-sized AW, TP (a)	3.00
❑51, Sep 1981 A: Death of Star II. A: Tarkin. A: Star II appearance. D: Death of Star II.	3.00
❑52, Oct 1981 A: Death of Star II. A: Tarkin. A: Star II appearance. D: Death of Star II.	3.00
❑53, Nov 1981	3.00
❑54, Dec 1981	3.00
❑55, Jan 1982	3.00
❑56, Feb 1982	3.00
❑57, Mar 1982	3.00
❑58, Apr 1982; Return to Cloud City .	3.00
❑59, May 1982	3.00
❑60, Jun 1982	3.00
❑61, Jul 1982	3.00
❑62, Aug 1982; Luke kicked out of Alliance	3.00
❑63, Sep 1982	3.00
❑64, Oct 1982 BA (c); BA (a)	3.00
❑65, Nov 1982	3.00
❑66, Dec 1982	3.00
❑67, Jan 1983	3.00
❑68, Feb 1983	3.00
❑69, Mar 1983	3.00
❑70, Apr 1983	3.00

	N-MINT
❑71, May 1983	3.00
❑72, Jun 1983	3.00
❑73, Jul 1983	3.00
❑74, Aug 1983	3.00
❑75, Sep 1983	3.00
❑76, Oct 1983	3.00
❑77, Nov 1983	3.00
❑78, Dec 1983	3.00
❑79, Jan 1984	3.00
❑80, Feb 1984	3.00
❑81, Mar 1984; first post-Return of the Jedi story	3.00
❑82, Apr 1984	3.00
❑83, May 1984	3.00
❑84, Jun 1984	3.00
❑85, Jul 1984	3.00
❑86, Aug 1984	3.00
❑87, Sep 1984	3.00
❑88, Oct 1984	3.00
❑89, Nov 1984	3.00
❑90, Dec 1984	3.00
❑91, Jan 1985	3.00
❑92, Feb 1985; Giant-size	3.00
❑93, Mar 1985	3.00
❑94, Apr 1985	3.00
❑95, May 1985	3.00
❑96, Jun 1985	3.00
❑97, Jul 1985	3.00
❑98, Aug 1985	3.00
❑99, Sep 1985	3.00
❑100, Oct 1985; Giant-size	3.00
❑101, Nov 1985	3.00
❑102, Dec 1985	3.00
❑103, Jan 1986	3.00
❑104, Mar 1986	3.00
❑105, May 1986	3.00
❑106, Jul 1986	3.00
❑107, Sep 1986	19.00
❑Annual 1, Dec 1979	8.00
❑Annual 2, ca. 1982	5.00
❑Annual 3, ca. 1983	5.00

STAR WARS (MAGAZINE)
Dark Horse

	N-MINT
❑1, Oct 1992	5.00
❑2	4.00
❑3	3.00
❑4	3.00
❑5	3.00
❑6	3.00
❑7	3.00
❑8	3.00
❑9	3.00
❑10	3.00

STAR WARS (DARK HORSE)
Dark Horse

	N-MINT
❑0, Jun 1999; HC (a); American Entertainment exclusive	10.00
❑1, Dec 1998	4.00
❑2, Jan 1999	3.00
❑3, Feb 1999	3.00
❑4, Mar 1999	3.00
❑5, Apr 1999	3.00
❑6, May 1999	3.00
❑7, Jun 1999	2.50
❑8, Jul 1999	2.50
❑9, Aug 1999	2.50
❑10, Sep 1999	2.50
❑11, Oct 1999	2.50
❑12, Nov 1999	2.50
❑13, Dec 1999	2.50
❑14, Jan 2000	2.50
❑15, Feb 2000	2.50
❑16, Mar 2000	2.50
❑17, Apr 2000	2.50
❑18, May 2000	2.50
❑19, Jun 2000 JDu (a)	2.50
❑20, Jul 2000 JDu (a)	2.50
❑21, Aug 2000 JDu (a)	2.50
❑22, Sep 2000 JDu (a)	2.50
❑23, Oct 2000	2.50
❑24, Nov 2000	2.50

Marvel revisited *Star Trek*'s Mirror Universe in the one-shot *Star Trek: Mirror, Mirror.*

© 1997 Paramount and Marvel Comics.

	N-MINT
❑25, Dec 2000	2.50
❑26, Jan 2001	2.50
❑27, Feb 2001	2.99
❑28, Mar 2001	2.99
❑29, Apr 2001	2.99
❑30, May 2001	2.99
❑31, Jun 2001	2.99
❑32, Jul 2001 JDu (a)	2.99
❑33, Aug 2001 JDu (a)	2.99
❑34, Sep 2001 JDu (a)	2.99
❑35, Oct 2001	2.99
❑36, Nov 2001	2.99
❑37, Dec 2001	2.99
❑38, Jan 2002	2.99
❑39, Feb 2002	2.99
❑40, Mar 2002	2.99
❑41, Apr 2002	2.99
❑42, May 2002	2.99
❑43, Jun 2002	2.99
❑44, Jul 2002 JDu (a)	2.99
❑45, Aug 2002	2.99
❑46, Sep 2002	2.99
❑47, Oct 2002	2.99
❑48, Nov 2002	2.99
❑49, Dec 2002	2.99
❑50, Jan 2003	5.99
❑51 2003	2.99
❑52 2003	2.99
❑53 2003	2.99
❑54, Jun 2003, color	2.99
❑55, Jul 2003, color	2.99
❑56, Jul 2003, color	2.99
❑57, Sep 2003, color	2.99
❑58, Dec 2003, color	2.99
❑59, Dec 2003, color	2.99
❑60, Jan 2004, color	2.99
❑61, Feb 2004, color	2.99
❑62, Mar 2004	2.99
❑63, Apr 2004	2.99
❑64, Apr 2004	2.99
❑65, Aug 2004	2.99
❑66, Aug 2004	2.99

STAR WARS: A NEW HOPE MANGA
Dark Horse

	N-MINT
❑1, Jul 1998	9.95
❑2, Jul 1998	9.95
❑3, Sep 1998	9.95
❑4, Oct 1998	9.95

STAR WARS: A NEW HOPE: THE SPECIAL EDITION
Dark Horse

	N-MINT
❑1, Jan 1997	2.95
❑2, Feb 1997	2.50
❑3, Mar 1997	2.50
❑4, Apr 1997	2.50

STAR WARS: BOBA FETT
Dark Horse

	N-MINT
❑0.5, Dec 1997; Wizard mail-in edition	3.00
❑0.5/Gold, Dec 1997; Gold edition	5.00
❑1, Dec 1995; cardstock cover	3.95
❑2, Sep 1996; cardstock cover	3.95
❑3, Aug 1997; cardstock cover	3.95

STAR WARS: BOBA FETT: AGENT OF DOOM
Dark Horse

	N-MINT
❑1, Nov 2000	2.99

N-MINT

STAR WARS: BOBA FETT: ENEMY OF THE EMPIRE
DARK HORSE
- ❑1, Jan 1999 ... 2.95
- ❑2, Feb 1999 ... 2.95
- ❑3, Mar 1999 ... 2.95
- ❑4, Apr 1999 ... 2.95

STAR WARS: BOBA FETT: TWIN ENGINES OF DESTRUCTION
DARK HORSE
- ❑1, Jan 1997 ... 2.95

STAR WARS: CHEWBACCA
DARK HORSE
- ❑1, Jan 2000 ... 2.95
- ❑2, Feb 2000 ... 2.95
- ❑3, Mar 2000 ... 2.95
- ❑4, Apr 2000 ... 2.95

STAR WARS: CRIMSON EMPIRE
DARK HORSE
- ❑1, Dec 1997 PG (a) ... 6.00
- ❑2, Jan 1998 PG (a) ... 5.00
- ❑3, Feb 1998 PG (a) ... 5.00
- ❑4, Mar 1998 PG (a) ... 5.00
- ❑5, Apr 1998 PG (a) ... 5.00
- ❑6, May 1998 PG (a) ... 5.00

STAR WARS: CRIMSON EMPIRE II: COUNCIL OF BLOOD
DARK HORSE
- ❑1, Nov 1998 PG (a) ... 4.00
- ❑2, Dec 1998 PG (a) ... 2.95
- ❑3, Jan 1999 PG (a) ... 2.95
- ❑4, Feb 1999 PG (a) ... 2.95
- ❑5, Mar 1999 PG (a) ... 2.95
- ❑6, Apr 1999 PG (a) ... 2.95

STAR WARS: DARK EMPIRE
DARK HORSE
- ❑1, Dec 1991; cardstock cover ... 6.00
- ❑1-2, Aug 1992 ... 3.00
- ❑2, Feb 1992; cardstock cover ... 4.00
- ❑2-2, Aug 1992 ... 3.00
- ❑3, Apr 1992; cardstock cover ... 4.00
- ❑3-2 ... 3.00
- ❑4, Apr 1992; cardstock cover ... 4.00
- ❑5, Aug 1992; cardstock cover ... 3.00
- ❑6, Oct 1992; cardstock cover ... 3.00
- ❑Ashcan 1, Mar 1996; newsprint preview of trade paperback collection of mini-series; wraparound cover ... 1.00

STAR WARS: DARK EMPIRE II
DARK HORSE
- ❑1, Dec 1994; cardstock cover ... 2.95
- ❑2, Jan 1995; cardstock cover ... 2.95
- ❑3, Feb 1995; cardstock cover ... 2.95
- ❑4, Mar 1995; cardstock cover ... 2.95
- ❑5, Apr 1995; cardstock cover ... 2.95
- ❑6, May 1995; cardstock cover ... 2.95

STAR WARS: DARK FORCE RISING
DARK HORSE
- ❑1, May 1997; adapts Timothy Zahn novel; cardstock cover ... 2.95
- ❑2, Jun 1997; adapts Timothy Zahn novel; cardstock cover ... 2.95
- ❑3, Jul 1997; adapts Timothy Zahn novel; cardstock cover ... 2.95
- ❑4, Aug 1997; adapts Timothy Zahn novel; cardstock cover ... 2.95
- ❑5, Sep 1997; adapts Timothy Zahn novel; cardstock cover ... 2.95
- ❑6, Oct 1997; adapts Timothy Zahn novel; cardstock cover ... 2.95

STAR WARS: DARTH MAUL
DARK HORSE
- ❑1, Sep 2000 ... 2.95
- ❑1/Variant, Sep 2000 ... 2.95
- ❑2, Oct 2000 ... 2.99
- ❑2/Variant, Oct 2000 ... 2.99
- ❑3, Nov 2000 ... 2.99
- ❑3/Variant, Nov 2000 ... 2.99
- ❑4, Dec 2000 ... 2.99
- ❑4/Variant, Dec 2000 ... 2.99

N-MINT

STAR WARS: DROIDS (VOL. 1)
DARK HORSE
- ❑1, Apr 1994; enhanced cover ... 3.00
- ❑2, May 1994 ... 2.75
- ❑3, Jun 1994 ... 2.75
- ❑4, Jul 1994 ... 2.50
- ❑5, Aug 1994 ... 2.50
- ❑6, Sep 1994 ... 2.50
- ❑Special 1, Jan 1995; Special edition; Reprints serial from Dark Horse Comics ... 2.50

STAR WARS: DROIDS (VOL. 2)
DARK HORSE
- ❑1, Apr 1995 ... 2.50
- ❑2, May 1995 ... 2.50
- ❑3, Jun 1995 ... 2.50
- ❑4, Jul 1995 ... 2.50
- ❑5, Sep 1995 ... 2.50
- ❑6, Oct 1995 ... 2.50
- ❑7, Nov 1995 ... 2.50
- ❑8, Dec 1995 ... 2.50

STAR WARS: EMPIRE
DARK HORSE
- ❑1, Sep 2002 ... 2.99
- ❑2, Oct 2002 ... 2.99
- ❑3, Nov 2002 ... 2.99
- ❑4, Dec 2002 ... 2.99
- ❑5, Jan 2003 ... 2.99
- ❑6 2003 ... 2.99
- ❑7 2003 ... 2.99
- ❑8 2003 ... 2.99
- ❑9, Jul 2003 ... 2.99
- ❑10, Jul 2003 ... 2.99
- ❑11, Sep 2003 ... 2.99
- ❑12, Oct 2003 ... 2.99
- ❑13, Dec 2003 ... 2.99
- ❑14, Dec 2003 ... 2.99
- ❑15, Dec 2003 ... 2.99
- ❑16, Jan 2004 ... 2.99
- ❑17, Mar 2004 ... 2.99
- ❑18, Apr 2004 ... 2.99
- ❑19, May 2004 ... 2.99
- ❑20, May 2004 ... 2.99
- ❑21, Aug 2004 ... 2.99

STAR WARS: EMPIRE'S END
DARK HORSE
- ❑1, Oct 1995; cardstock cover ... 2.95
- ❑2, Nov 1995; cardstock cover ... 2.95

STAR WARS: EPISODE I ANAKIN SKYWALKER
DARK HORSE
- ❑1, May 1999; cardstock cover ... 2.95
- ❑1/Variant, May 1999 ... 2.95

STAR WARS: EPISODE I OBI-WAN KENOBI
DARK HORSE
- ❑1, May 1999; cardstock cover ... 2.95
- ❑1/Variant, May 1999 ... 2.95

STAR WARS: EPISODE I QUEEN AMIDALA
DARK HORSE
- ❑1, Jun 1999; cardstock cover ... 2.95
- ❑1/Variant, Jun 1999 ... 2.95

STAR WARS: EPISODE I QUI-GON JINN
DARK HORSE
- ❑1, Jun 1999; cardstock cover ... 2.95
- ❑1/Variant, Jun 1999 ... 2.95

STAR WARS: EPISODE I THE PHANTOM MENACE
DARK HORSE
- ❑1, May 1999; cardstock cover ... 2.95
- ❑1/Variant, May 1999 ... 2.95
- ❑2, May 1999; cardstock cover ... 2.95
- ❑2/Variant, May 1999 ... 2.95
- ❑3, May 1999; cardstock cover ... 2.95
- ❑3/Variant, May 1999 ... 2.95
- ❑4, May 1999; cardstock cover ... 2.95
- ❑4/Variant, May 1999 ... 2.95

N-MINT

STAR WARS: EPISODE II: ATTACK OF THE CLONES
DARK HORSE
- ❑1 ... 3.99
- ❑1/Variant ... 3.99
- ❑2 ... 3.99
- ❑2/Variant ... 3.99
- ❑3 ... 3.99
- ❑3/Variant ... 3.99
- ❑4 ... 3.99
- ❑4/Variant ... 3.99

STAR WARS HANDBOOK
DARK HORSE
- ❑1, Jul 1998; X-Wing Rogue Squadron profiles ... 2.95
- ❑2, Jul 1999; Crimson Empire profiles 2.95

STAR WARS: HEIR TO THE EMPIRE
DARK HORSE
- ❑1, Oct 1995 ... 2.95
- ❑2, Nov 1995 ... 2.95
- ❑3, Dec 1995 ... 2.95
- ❑4, Jan 1996 ... 2.95
- ❑5, Mar 1996 ... 2.95
- ❑6, Apr 1996 ... 2.95

STAR WARS IN 3-D
BLACKTHORNE
- ❑1, Dec 1987; a.k.a. Blackthorne in 3-D #30 ... 2.50

STAR WARS: INFINITIES: A NEW HOPE
DARK HORSE
- ❑1, May 2001 ... 2.99
- ❑2, Jun 2001 ... 2.99
- ❑3, Jul 2001 ... 2.99
- ❑4, Aug 2001 ... 2.99

STAR WARS: INFINITIES: RETURN OF THE JEDI
DARK HORSE
- ❑1, Dec 2003 ... 2.99
- ❑2, Jan 2004 ... 2.99
- ❑3, Mar 2004 ... 2.99
- ❑4, Mar 2004 ... 2.99

STAR WARS: INFINITIES: THE EMPIRE STRIKES BACK
DARK HORSE
- ❑1, Jul 2002 ... 2.99
- ❑2, Aug 2002 ... 2.99
- ❑3, Sep 2002 ... 2.99
- ❑4, Oct 2002 ... 2.99

STAR WARS: JABBA THE HUTT
DARK HORSE
- ❑1, Apr 1995 ... 2.50
- ❑2, Jun 1995 ... 2.50
- ❑3, Aug 1995 ... 2.50
- ❑4, Feb 1996 ... 2.50

STAR WARS: JANGO FETT: OPEN SEASONS
DARK HORSE
- ❑1, Apr 2002 ... 2.99
- ❑2, May 2002 ... 2.99
- ❑3, Jun 2002 ... 2.99
- ❑4, Jul 2002 ... 2.99

STAR WARS: JEDI - AAYLA SECURA
DARK HORSE
- ❑1, Aug 2003 ... 4.99

STAR WARS: JEDI ACADEMY: LEVIATHAN
DARK HORSE
- ❑1, Oct 1998 ... 2.95
- ❑2, Nov 1998 ... 2.95
- ❑3, Dec 1998 ... 2.95
- ❑4, Jan 1999 ... 2.95

STAR WARS: JEDI COUNCIL: ACTS OF WAR
DARK HORSE
- ❑1, Jun 2000 ... 2.95
- ❑2, Jul 2000 ... 2.95
- ❑3, Aug 2000 ... 2.95
- ❑4, Sep 2000 ... 2.95

N-MINT

STAR WARS: JEDI - DOOKU CLONE WARS
Dark Horse
- ❑1, Dec 2003 ... 4.99

STAR WARS: JEDI - MACE WINDU
Dark Horse
- ❑1, Feb 2003 ... 4.99

STAR WARS: JEDI QUEST
Dark Horse
- ❑1, Sep 2001 ... 2.99
- ❑2, Oct 2001 ... 2.99
- ❑3, Nov 2001 ... 2.99
- ❑4, Dec 2001 ... 2.99

STAR WARS: JEDI - SHAAK TI
Dark Horse
- ❑1, May 2003 ... 4.99

STAR WARS: JEDI VS. SITH
Dark Horse
- ❑1, Apr 2001 ... 2.99
- ❑2, May 2001 ... 2.99
- ❑3, Jun 2001 ... 2.99
- ❑4, Jul 2001 ... 2.99
- ❑5, Aug 2001 ... 2.99
- ❑6, Sep 2001 ... 2.99

STAR WARS: MARA JADE
Dark Horse
- ❑1, Aug 1998 ... 3.00
- ❑2, Sep 1998 2: Mara Jade. ... 2.95
- ❑3, Oct 1998 ... 2.95
- ❑4, Nov 1998; Darth Vader cameo; Luke Skywalker cameo; Emperor Palpatine cameo ... 2.95
- ❑5, Dec 1998 ... 2.95
- ❑6, Jan 1999 ... 2.95

STAR WARS: QUI-GON & OBI-WAN: LAST STAND ON ORD MANTELL
Dark Horse
- ❑1/A, Dec 2000; Obi-Wan leaping on cover, Qui-Gon standing ... 2.99
- ❑1/B, Dec 2000; Qui-gon and Obi-Wan standing on cover, Obi-Wan has light sabre out ... 2.99
- ❑1/C, Dec 2000 ... 2.99
- ❑2/A, Feb 2001; Drawn cover ... 2.99
- ❑2/B, Feb 2001 ... 2.99
- ❑3/A, Mar 2001; Drawn cover ... 2.99
- ❑3/B, Mar 2001 ... 2.99

STAR WARS: QUI-GON & OBI-WAN: THE AURORIENT EXPRESS
Dark Horse
- ❑1, Feb 2002 ... 2.99
- ❑2, May 2002 ... 2.99

STAR WARS: RETURN OF THE JEDI
Marvel
- ❑1, Oct 1983; AW (a); Reprints Marvel Super Special #27 ... 4.00
- ❑2, Nov 1983; AW (a); Reprints Marvel Super Special #27 ... 4.00
- ❑3, Dec 1983; AW (a); Reprints Marvel Super Special #27 ... 4.00
- ❑4, Jan 1984; AW (a); Reprints Marvel Super Special #27 ... 4.00

STAR WARS: RIVER OF CHAOS
Dark Horse
- ❑1, Jun 1995 ... 2.50
- ❑2, Jul 1995 ... 2.50
- ❑3, Sep 1995 ... 2.50
- ❑4, Nov 1995 ... 2.50

STAR WARS: SHADOWS OF EMPIRE: EVOLUTION
Dark Horse
- ❑1, Feb 1998 ... 2.95
- ❑2, Mar 1998 ... 2.95
- ❑3, Apr 1998 ... 2.95
- ❑4, May 1998 ... 2.95
- ❑5, Jun 1998 ... 2.95

N-MINT

STAR WARS: SHADOWS OF THE EMPIRE
Dark Horse
- ❑1, May 1996 ... 2.95
- ❑2, Jun 1996 ... 2.95
- ❑3, Jul 1996 ... 2.95
- ❑4, Aug 1996 ... 2.95
- ❑5, Sep 1996 ... 2.95
- ❑6, Oct 1996 ... 2.95

STAR WARS: SHADOW STALKER
Dark Horse
- ❑1, Sep 1997 ... 2.95

STAR WARS: SPLINTER OF THE MIND'S EYE
Dark Horse
- ❑1, Dec 1995 ... 2.50
- ❑2, Feb 1996 ... 2.50
- ❑3, Apr 1996 ... 2.50
- ❑4, Jun 1996 ... 2.50

STAR WARS: STARFIGHTE: CROSSBONES
Dark Horse
- ❑1, Jan 2002 ... 2.99
- ❑2, Feb 2002 ... 2.99
- ❑3, Mar 2002 ... 2.99

STAR WARS: TAG & BINK ARE DEAD
Dark Horse
- ❑1, Oct 2001 ... 2.99
- ❑2, Nov 2001 ... 2.99

STAR WARS TALES
Dark Horse
- ❑1, Sep 1999 ... 4.95
- ❑2, Dec 1999 ... 4.95
- ❑3, Mar 2000 ... 4.95
- ❑4, Jun 2000 ... 4.95
- ❑5, Sep 2000 ... 5.95
- ❑5/PH, Sep 2000 ... 5.95
- ❑6, Dec 2000 ... 5.95
- ❑7, Mar 2001 ... 5.99
- ❑8, Jun 2001 ... 5.99
- ❑9, Sep 2001 ... 5.99
- ❑10, Dec 2001 ... 5.99
- ❑11, Mar 2002 ... 5.99
- ❑12, Jun 2002 ... 5.99
- ❑13, Sep 2002 ... 5.99
- ❑14, Dec 2002 ... 5.99
- ❑15, Mar 2003 ... 5.99
- ❑16, Jun 2003 ... 5.99
- ❑17, Oct 2003 ... 5.99
- ❑18, Dec 2003 ... 5.99
- ❑19, Apr 2004 ... 5.99
- ❑20, Aug 2004 ... 5.99

STAR WARS TALES-A JEDI'S WEAPON
Dark Horse
- ❑1 ... 1.00

STAR WARS: TALES: A JEDI'S WEAPON
Dark Horse
- ❑1, May 2002 ... 2.00

STAR WARS: TALES FROM MOS EISLEY
Dark Horse
- ❑1, Mar 1996 ... 2.95

STAR WARS: TALES OF THE JEDI
Dark Horse
- ❑1, Oct 1993 ... 4.00
- ❑2, Nov 1993 ... 3.50
- ❑3, Dec 1993 ... 3.25
- ❑4, Jan 1994 ... 2.50
- ❑5, Feb 1994 ... 2.50

STAR WARS: TALES OF THE JEDI: DARK LORDS OF THE SITH
Dark Horse
- ❑1, Oct 1994 ... 3.00
- ❑2, Nov 1994 ... 3.00
- ❑3, Dec 1994 ... 3.00
- ❑4, Jan 1995 ... 3.00

Star Wars: Dark Empire could easily be Episode VII in the movie saga.

N-MINT

- ❑5, Feb 1995 ... 3.00
- ❑6, Mar 1995 ... 3.00

STAR WARS: TALES OF THE JEDI: FALL OF THE SITH EMPIRE
Dark Horse
- ❑1, Jun 1997; Man with marionettes on cover ... 2.95
- ❑1/A, Jun 1997; Variant cover, flame in background ... 2.95
- ❑2, Jul 1997 ... 2.95
- ❑3, Aug 1997 ... 2.95
- ❑4, Sep 1997 ... 2.95
- ❑5, Oct 1997 ... 2.95

STAR WARS: TALES OF THE JEDI: REDEMPTION
Dark Horse
- ❑1, Jul 1998 ... 2.95
- ❑2, Aug 1998 ... 2.95
- ❑3, Sep 1998 ... 2.95
- ❑4, Oct 1998 ... 2.95
- ❑5, Nov 1998 ... 2.95

STAR WARS: TALES OF THE JEDI: THE FREEDON NADD UPRISING
Dark Horse
- ❑1, Aug 1994 ... 2.50
- ❑2, Sep 1994 ... 2.50

STAR WARS: TALES OF THE JEDI: THE GOLDEN AGE OF THE SITH
Dark Horse
- ❑0, ca. 1996 ... 0.99
- ❑1, Oct 1996 ... 2.95
- ❑2, Nov 1996 ... 2.95
- ❑3, Dec 1996 ... 2.95
- ❑4, Jan 1997 ... 2.95
- ❑5, Feb 1997 ... 2.95

STAR WARS: TALES OF THE JEDI: THE SITH WAR
Dark Horse
- ❑1, Aug 1995 ... 2.50
- ❑2, Sep 1995 ... 2.50
- ❑3, Oct 1995 ... 2.50
- ❑4, Nov 1995 ... 2.50
- ❑5, Dec 1995 ... 2.50
- ❑6, Jan 1996 ... 2.50

STAR WARS: THE BOUNTY HUNTERS: AURRA SING
Dark Horse
- ❑1, Jul 1999 ... 2.95

STAR WARS: THE BOUNTY HUNTERS: KENIX KIL
Dark Horse
- ❑1, Oct 1999; one shot ... 2.95

STAR WARS: THE BOUNTY HUNTERS: SCOUNDREL'S WAGES
Dark Horse
- ❑1, Aug 1999 ... 2.95

STAR WARS: THE EMPIRE STRIKES BACK: MANGA
Dark Horse
- ❑1, Jan 1999 ... 9.95
- ❑2, Feb 1999 ... 9.95
- ❑3, Mar 1999 ... 9.95
- ❑4, Apr 1999 ... 9.95

N-MINT

STAR WARS: THE JABBA TAPE
DARK HORSE

❑1, Dec 1998 .... 2.95

STAR WARS: THE LAST COMMAND
DARK HORSE

❑1, Nov 1997 .... 3.50
❑2, Dec 1997 .... 3.00
❑3, Feb 1998 .... 3.00
❑4, Mar 1998 .... 3.00
❑5, Apr 1998 .... 3.00
❑6, Jul 1998 .... 2.95

STAR WARS: THE PROTOCOL OFFENSIVE
DARK HORSE

❑1, Sep 1997; prestige format; Co-written by Anthony Daniels, C-3PO 4.95

STAR WARS: UNDERWORLD: THE YAVIN VASSILIKA
DARK HORSE

❑1/A, Dec 2000; Drawn cover with Han Solo, Lando Calrisian, and Boba Fett 2.99
❑1/B, Dec 2000; Painted cover with Jabba the Hutt 2.99
❑2/A, Jan 2001 .... 2.99
❑2/B, Jan 2001 .... 2.99
❑3/A, Feb 2001; Drawn cover with Han Solo, Lando Calrisian, and Boba Fett 2.99
❑3/B, Feb 2001 .... 2.99
❑4/A, Mar 2001 .... 2.99
❑4/B, Mar 2001 .... 2.99
❑5/A, Apr 2001 .... 2.99
❑5/B, Apr 2001 .... 2.99

STAR WARS: UNION
DARK HORSE

❑1, Nov 1999 .... 14.00
❑2, Dec 1999 .... 10.00
❑3, Jan 2000 .... 7.00
❑4, Feb 2000; Wedding of Luke Skywalker & Mara Jade 5.00

STAR WARS: VADER'S QUEST
DARK HORSE

❑1, Feb 1999 .... 2.95
❑2, Mar 1999 .... 2.95
❑3, Apr 1999 .... 2.95
❑4, May 1999 .... 2.95

STAR WARS: VALENTINES STORY
DARK HORSE

❑1, Feb 2003 .... 3.50

STAR WARS: X-WING ROGUE SQUADRON
DARK HORSE

❑0.5, Feb 1997; Wizard mail-in edition 3.00
❑0.5/Platinum, Feb 1997; Platinum edition 5.00
❑1, Jul 1995 .... 4.00
❑2, Aug 1995 .... 3.50
❑3, Sep 1995 .... 3.50
❑4, Oct 1995 .... 3.50
❑5, Feb 1996 .... 3.00
❑6, Mar 1996 .... 3.00
❑7, Apr 1996 .... 3.00
❑8, Jun 1996 .... 3.00
❑9, Jul 1996 .... 3.00
❑10, Jul 1996 .... 3.00
❑11, Aug 1996 .... 3.00
❑12, Sep 1996 .... 3.00
❑13, Oct 1996 .... 3.00
❑14, Dec 1996 .... 3.00
❑15, Jan 1997 .... 3.00
❑16, Feb 1997 .... 3.00
❑17, Mar 1997 .... 3.00
❑18, Apr 1997 .... 3.00
❑19, May 1997 .... 3.00
❑20, Jun 1997 .... 3.00
❑21, Aug 1997 .... 3.00
❑22, Sep 1997 .... 3.00
❑23, Oct 1997 .... 3.00
❑24, Nov 1997 .... 3.00
❑25, Dec 1997; Giant-size O: Baron Fel. 4.00
❑26, Jan 1998 .... 2.95
❑27, Feb 1998 .... 2.95
❑28, Mar 1998 .... 2.95
❑29, Apr 1998 .... 2.95
❑30, May 1998 .... 2.95
❑31, Jun 1998 .... 2.95
❑32, Jul 1998 .... 2.95
❑33, Aug 1998 .... 2.95
❑34, Sep 1998 .... 2.95
❑35, Nov 1998 .... 2.95
❑Special 1, Aug 1995; promotional giveaway with Kellog's Apple Jacks 1.00

STAR WEEVILS
RIP OFF

❑1 .... 1.00

STAR WESTERN
AVALON

❑1 .... 5.95
❑2; John Wayne feature 5.95
❑3; Clint Eastwood feature 5.95
❑4 .... 5.95
❑5 .... 5.95

S.T.A.T.
MAJESTIC

❑1, Dec 1993 .... 2.25
❑1/Variant, Dec 1993; foil cover 2.25

STATIC
DC / MILESTONE

❑1, Jun 1993 1: Hotstreak. 1: Frieda Goren. 1: Static. 2.00
❑1/CS, Jun 1993; 1: Hotstreak. 1: Frieda Goren. 1: Static. poster; trading card; Collector's Set 3.00
❑1/Silver, Jun 1993; Silver (limited promotional) edition 1: Hotstreak. 1: Frieda Goren. 1: Static. 3.00
❑2, Jul 1993 O: Static. 1: Tarmack. 1.50
❑3, Aug 1993 .... 1.50
❑4, Sep 1993 1: Don Giacomo Cornelius. 1.50
❑5, Oct 1993 1: Commando X. 1.50
❑6, Nov 1993 .... 1.50
❑7, Dec 1993 .... 1.50
❑8, Jan 1994; Shadow War 1.50
❑9, Feb 1994 1: Virus. 1.50
❑10, Mar 1994 1: Puff. 1: Coil. 1.50
❑11, Apr 1994 .... 1.50
❑12, May 1994 1: Snakefinger. 1.50
❑13, Jun 1994 .... 1.50
❑14, Aug 1994; Giant-size 2.50
❑15, Sep 1994 .... 1.75
❑16, Oct 1994 1: Joyride. 1.75
❑17, Nov 1994 .... 1.75
❑18, Dec 1994 .... 1.75
❑19, Jan 1995 .... 1.75
❑20, Feb 1995 .... 1.75
❑21, Mar 1995 A: Blood Syndicate. ... 1.75
❑22, Apr 1995 .... 1.75
❑23, Jun 1995 .... 1.75
❑24, Jul 1995 .... 1.75
❑25, Jul 1995; Double-size 3.95
❑26, Aug 1995 .... 2.50
❑27, Sep 1995 .... 2.50
❑28, Oct 1995 .... 2.50
❑29, Nov 1995 .... 2.50
❑30, Dec 1995 D: Larry. 2.50
❑31, Jan 1996 GK (a) 0.99
❑32, Feb 1996 .... 2.50
❑33, Mar 1996 .... 2.50
❑34, Apr 1996 .... 2.50
❑35, May 1996 .... 2.50
❑36, Jun 1996 .... 2.50
❑37, Jul 1996 .... 2.50
❑38, Aug 1996 .... 2.50
❑39, Sep 1996 .... 2.50
❑40, Oct 1996 KP (a) 2.50
❑41, Nov 1996 .... 2.50
❑42, Dec 1996 .... 2.50
❑43, Jan 1997 .... 2.50
❑44, Feb 1997 .... 2.50
❑45, Mar 1997 .... 2.50
❑46, Apr 1997 .... 2.50
❑47, May 1997 .... 2.50

STATIC SHOCK!: REBIRTH OF THE COOL
DC / MILESTONE

❑1, Jan 2001 .... 2.50
❑2, Feb 2001 .... 2.50
❑3, Mar 2001 .... 2.50
❑4, Apr 2001 .... 2.50

STAY PUFFED
IMAGE

❑1, Jan 2004 .... 3.50

STEALTH FORCE
MALIBU

❑1, Jul 1987 .... 1.95
❑2, Aug 1987 .... 1.95
❑3, Sep 1987 .... 1.95
❑4, Oct 1987 .... 1.95
❑5, Nov 1987 .... 1.95
❑6, Dec 1987 .... 1.95
❑7, Jan 1988 .... 1.95
❑8, Feb 1988; Eternity begins as publisher 1.95

STEALTH SQUAD
PETRA

❑0 .... 2.50
❑1 .... 2.50
❑2 .... 2.50
❑3 .... 2.50
❑4 .... 2.50

STEAMPUNK
WILDSTORM

❑1, Apr 2000 .... 2.50
❑2, May 2000 .... 2.50
❑3, Jun 2000 .... 2.50
❑4, Jul 2000 .... 2.50
❑5, Oct 2000 .... 2.50
❑6, Jan 2001 .... 2.50
❑7, Apr 2001 .... 2.50
❑8, Jun 2001 .... 2.50
❑9, Sep 2001 .... 2.50
❑10, Jan 2002 .... 2.50
❑11, Apr 2002 .... 2.50
❑12, Jul 2002 .... 3.50

STEAMPUNK: CATECHISM
WILDSTORM

❑1, Jan 2000 .... 2.50

STECH
SILVERWOLF

❑1, Dec 1986, b&w 1.50

STEED AND MRS. PEEL
ECLIPSE

❑1, Dec 1990 .... 5.00
❑2, May 1991 .... 5.00
❑3 .... 5.00

STEEL
DC

❑0, Oct 1994 .... 1.50
❑1, Feb 1994 .... 1.50
❑2, Mar 1994 .... 1.50
❑3, Apr 1994 .... 1.50
❑4, May 1994 .... 1.50
❑5, Jun 1994 .... 1.50
❑6, Jul 1994 A: Hardware. 1.50
❑7, Aug 1994 A: Icon. A: Hardware. .. 1.50
❑8, Sep 1994 .... 1.50
❑9, Nov 1994 .... 1.50
❑10, Dec 1994 .... 1.50
❑11, Jan 1995 .... 1.50
❑12, Feb 1995 .... 1.50
❑13, Mar 1995 .... 1.50
❑14, Apr 1995 .... 1.50
❑15, May 1995 .... 1.50
❑16, Jun 1995 .... 1.95
❑17, Jul 1995 .... 1.95
❑18, Aug 1995 .... 1.95
❑19, Sep 1995 .... 1.95
❑20, Oct 1995 .... 1.95
❑21, Nov 1995; Underworld Unleashed 1.95

N-MINT

❑22, Dec 1995 A: Supergirl. A: Eradicator. 1.95
❑23, Jan 1996 1.95
❑24, Feb 1996 1.95
❑25, Mar 1996 1.95
❑26, May 1996 1.95
❑27, Jun 1996 1.95
❑28, Jul 1996 V: Plasmus. 1.95
❑29, Aug 1996 1.95
❑30, Sep 1996 1.95
❑31, Oct 1996 1.95
❑32, Nov 1996 V: Blockbuster. 1.95
❑33, Dec 1996 1.95
❑34, Jan 1997; TP (a); A: Margot. new armor 1.95
❑35, Feb 1997 TP (a) 1.95
❑36, Mar 1997 TP (a) 1.95
❑37, Apr 1997 1.95
❑38, May 1997 1.95
❑39, Jun 1997 TP (a) 1.95
❑40, Jul 1997 1: new hammer. 2.25
❑41, Aug 1997 1.95
❑42, Sep 1997 TP (a) 1.95
❑43, Oct 1997; TP (a); A: Superman. Genesis 1.95
❑44, Nov 1997 1.95
❑45, Dec 1997; TP (a); Face cover 1.95
❑46, Jan 1998 TP (a); A: Superboy. 1.95
❑47, Feb 1998 2.50
❑48, Mar 1998 BSz (a) 2.50
❑49, Apr 1998 TP (a) 2.50
❑50, May 1998; TP (a); A: Superman. Millennium Giants 2.50
❑51, Jun 1998 2.50
❑52, Jul 1998 TP (a) 2.50
❑Annual 1, ca. 1994; Elseworlds 2.95
❑Annual 2, ca. 1995; Year One 3.95

STEEL ANGEL
GAUNTLET

❑1 2.50

STEEL CLAW, THE
FLEETWAY-QUALITY

❑1, Dec 1986 1.50
❑2, Jan 1987 1.50
❑3, Feb 1987 1.50
❑4, Mar 1987 1.50
❑5, Apr 1987 1.50

STEELDRAGON STORIES
STEELDRAGON

❑1 1.50

STEELE DESTINIES
NIGHTSCAPES

❑1, Apr 1995, b&w 2.95
❑2, Jun 1995, b&w 2.95
❑3, Sep 1995, b&w 2.95

STEELGRIP STARKEY
MARVEL / EPIC

❑1, Jun 1986 1.75
❑2, Aug 1986 1.75
❑3, Nov 1986 1.75
❑4, Dec 1986 1.75
❑5, Jan 1987 1.75
❑6, May 1987 1.75

STEEL PULSE
TRUE FICTION

❑1, Mar 1986, b&w 2.00
❑2, b&w 2.00
❑3, b&w 2.00
❑4 3.50

STEEL STERLING
ARCHIE / RED CIRCLE

❑4, Jan 1984; Red Circle publishes 1.00
❑5, Mar 1984; Archie publishes 1.00
❑6, May 1984 1.00
❑7, Jul 1984 1.00

STEEL, THE INDESTRUCTIBLE MAN
DC

❑1, Mar 1978 DH (a); O: Steel. 1: Steel. 5.00
❑2, Apr 1978 2.00
❑3, Jun 1978 2.00

N-MINT

❑4, Sep 1978 2.00
❑5, Nov 1978 2.00

STEEL: THE OFFICIAL COMIC ADAPTATION OF THE WARNER BROS. MOTION PICTURE
DC

❑1, Sep 1997; prestige format 4.95

STEELTOWN ROCKERS
MARVEL

❑1, Apr 1990 1.00
❑2, May 1990 1.00
❑3, Jun 1990 1.00
❑4, Jul 1990 1.00
❑5, Aug 1990 1.00
❑6, Sep 1990 1.00

STELLAR COMICS
STELLAR

❑1 2.50

STELLAR LOSERS
ANTARCTIC

❑1, Feb 1993, b&w 2.50
❑2, Apr 1993, b&w 2.50
❑3, Jun 1993, b&w 2.50

STEPHEN DARKLORD
RAK

❑1, b&w 1.75
❑2, b&w 1.75
❑3, b&w 1.75

STEPS TO A DRUG FREE LIFE
DAVID G. BROWN

❑1, Feb 1998; promotional comic done for the Alcohol and Drug Council of Greater L.A. and Share Inc. 1.00

STERN WHEELER
SPOTLIGHT

❑1 1.75

STEVEN
KITCHEN SINK

❑1, b&w 3.00
❑2, b&w 3.00
❑3, May 1999, b&w 3.00
❑4, b&w 3.00
❑5 3.50
❑6, b&w 3.50
❑7 3.50
❑8, Dec 1996, b&w; over-sized; card-stock cover 3.50

STEVEN PRESENTS DUMPY
FANTAGRAPHICS

❑1, May 1999, b&w 2.95

STEVEN'S COMICS
DK PRESS / YELL COMICS

❑3, b&w 3.00
❑1 1.00
❑2 2.00
❑4 3.50

STEVE ZODIAK AND THE FIREBALL XL-5
GOLD KEY

❑1, Jan 1964 65.00

STEWART THE RAT
ABOUT

❑1, Feb 2003 3.95

STICKBOY (FANTAGRAPHICS)
FANTAGRAPHICS

❑1, b&w 2.50
❑1-2 2.75
❑2, b&w 2.50
❑3, b&w 2.50
❑4, Nov 1990, b&w 2.95
❑5, Feb 1992, b&w 2.50

STICKBOY (REVOLUTIONARY)
REVOLUTIONARY

❑1 2.95
❑2 2.95
❑3 2.95
❑4, Nov 1990 2.95

Static was the first Milestone character to get his own animated series with *Static Shock!* on Kids WB!
© 1993 Milestone Media.

N-MINT

STICKBOY (STARHEAD)
STARHEAD

❑1, b&w 2.50
❑2, b&w 2.50
❑3, b&w 2.50
❑4, b&w 2.50
❑5, b&w 2.50
❑6, b&w 2.50

STIG'S INFERNO
VORTEX

❑1, ca. 1989 2.00
❑2 1989 2.00
❑3 1989 3.50
❑4 1989 3.50
❑5 1989 1.75
❑6 1989, b&w 1.50
❑7 1989, b&w 1.50

STIMULATOR
FANTAGRAPHICS / EROS

❑1, b&w 2.50

STING
ARTLINE

❑1; flip book with Killer Synthetic Toads 2.50

STING OF THE GREEN HORNET
NOW

❑1, Jun 1992; bagged with poster 2.50
❑1/CS, Jun 1992 2.75
❑2, Jul 1992 2.50
❑2/CS, Jul 1992; bagged with poster 2.75
❑3, Aug 1992 2.50
❑3/CS, Aug 1992; bagged with poster 2.75
❑4, Sep 1992 2.50
❑4/CS, Sep 1992; stitched with poster 2.75

STINKTOOTH
STINKTOOTH

❑1, Nov 1991 1.00

STINZ (1ST SERIES)
FANTAGRAPHICS

❑1, Aug 1989, b&w 4.00
❑2, Oct 1989, b&w 3.00
❑3, ca. 1989, b&w 3.00
❑4, Feb 1990, b&w; Moves to Brave New Words 2.50
❑5, ca. 1990; Published by Brave New Words 2.50

STINZ (2ND SERIES)
BRAVE NEW WORDS

❑1, ca. 1990, b&w 2.50
❑3, ca. 1991 2.50
❑2, ca. 1991, b&w 2.50

STINZ (3RD SERIES)
MU

❑1, Oct 1994 2.50
❑2, Oct 1994 2.50
❑3, Feb 1995 2.50
❑4, Oct 1995 2.95
❑5, Jan 1997; Last Mu issue; moves to A Fine Line 4.95
❑6, Jun 1998; First A Fine Line Press issue 5.50
❑7, Aug 1998 4.95

STONE
IMAGE

❑1, Aug 1998 2.50
❑1/A, Aug 1998; Variant cover with white background 2.50

N-MINT

❑1/B, Aug 1998; Variant cover with side view of Stone, jewel showing in arm-band ... 2.50
❑2, Sep 1998 ... 2.50
❑2/A, Sep 1998; DFE chrome cover; reprints indicia from #1 ... 6.00
❑2/B, Sep 1998; alternate cover (white border) ... 4.00
❑3, Nov 1998 ... 2.50
❑4, Apr 1999 ... 2.50

STONE (VOL. 2)
IMAGE

❑1, Aug 1999 ... 2.50
❑1/Variant, Aug 1999; Chrome cover 6.95
❑2, Sep 1999 ... 2.50
❑3, Dec 1999 ... 2.50

STONE COLD STEVE AUSTIN
CHAOS

❑1, Oct 1999; cover says Nov, indicia says Oct ... 2.95
❑2, Nov 1999 ... 2.95
❑3, Dec 1999 ... 2.95
❑4, Jan 2000 ... 2.95

STONE PROTECTORS
HARVEY

❑1, May 1994 ... 1.50
❑2 ... 1.50
❑3, Sep 1994 ... 1.50

STONEWALL IN THE SHENANDOAH
HERITAGE COLLECTION

❑1; wraparound cover ... 3.50

STONEY BURKE
DELL

❑1, Jun 1963 ... 25.00
❑2, Sep 1963 ... 20.00

STORIES FROM BOSNIA
DRAWN AND QUARTERLY

❑1, b&w; Oversized; cardstock cover 3.95

STORM
MARVEL

❑1, Feb 1996; enhanced cardstock cover ... 2.95
❑2, Mar 1996; enhanced cardstock cover ... 2.95
❑3, Apr 1996; enhanced cardstock cover ... 2.95
❑4, May 1996; enhanced cardstock cover ... 2.95

STORMQUEST
CALIBER / SKY

❑1, Nov 1994 ... 1.95
❑2, Dec 1994 ... 1.95
❑3, ca. 1995 ... 1.95
❑4, ca. 1995 ... 1.95
❑5, ca. 1995 ... 1.95
❑6, ca. 1955 ... 1.95

STORMWATCH
IMAGE

❑0, Aug 1993; JLee (w); 1: Backlash. 1: Flashpoint. 1: Nautica. 1: Warguard. Polybagged ... 2.50
❑1, Mar 1993 1: Hellstrike. 1: Battalion. 1: Diva. 1: Winter. 1: Strafe. 1: Storm-Watch. 1: Synergy. 1: Deathtrap. 1: Fuji. ... 2.50
❑1/Gold, Mar 1993; Gold foil cover ... 3.00
❑2, May 1993 1: Regent. 1: Cannon. 1: Fahrenheit. 1: Ion & Lance. ... 1.95
❑3, Jul 1993 1: LaSalle. A: Backlash. 1.95
❑4, Aug 1993; V: Warguard. cover says Oct ... 1.95
❑5, Nov 1993 ... 1.95
❑6, Dec 1993 ... 1.95
❑7, Feb 1994 1: Sunburst. ... 1.95
❑8, Mar 1994 1: Rainmaker. ... 1.95
❑9, Apr 1994 ... 2.50
❑10, Jun 1994 ... 1.95
❑10/A, Jun 1994; Variant edition cover; Variant edition cover ... 3.00
❑10/B, Jun 1994; variant cover ... 3.00
❑11, Aug 1994 ... 1.95
❑12, Aug 1994 ... 1.95
❑13, Sep 1994 ... 1.95
❑14, Sep 1994 ... 1.95
❑15, Oct 1994 ... 1.95
❑16, Nov 1994 ... 1.95
❑17, Dec 1994 ... 2.50
❑18, Jan 1995 ... 2.50
❑19, Feb 1995 ... 2.50
❑20, Mar 1995 ... 2.50
❑21, Apr 1995; 1: Tao. cover says #1 2.50
❑22, May 1995; bound-in trading cards 2.50
❑23, Jun 1995 ... 2.50
❑24, Jul 1995 ... 2.50
❑25, May 1994; cover says Jun 95; Images of Tomorrow; Shipped out of sequence as preview to future events (after #9) ... 2.50
❑25-2, Aug 1995 ... 2.50
❑26, Aug 1995 ... 2.50
❑27, Aug 1995 ... 2.50
❑28, Sep 1995; 1: Swift. 1: Storm Force. 1: Flint. cover forms right half of diptych with issue #29 ... 2.50
❑29, Oct 1995; indicia says Oct, cover says Nov ... 2.50
❑30, Nov 1995 ... 2.50
❑31, Dec 1995 ... 2.50
❑32, Jan 1996 ... 2.50
❑33, Feb 1996 ... 2.50
❑34, Mar 1996 ... 2.50
❑35, Apr 1996 ... 2.50
❑36, Jun 1996 ... 2.50
❑37, Jul 1996; Giant-size 1: Hawksmoor. 1: Jenny Sparks. ... 3.50
❑38, Aug 1996 ... 2.50
❑39, Aug 1996 ... 2.50
❑40, Oct 1996 ... 2.50
❑41, Oct 1996 ... 2.50
❑42, Nov 1996 ... 2.50
❑43, Dec 1996 ... 2.50
❑44/A, Jan 1997; O: Jenny Sparks. Torrid Tales cover; homages to various comics eras ... 2.50
❑44/B, Jan 1997; GK (c); O: Jenny Sparks. Pop Art Masterpiece cover 2.50
❑44/C, Jan 1997; O: Jenny Sparks. Who Watches The Weathermen cover ... 2.50
❑45, Feb 1997 ... 2.50
❑46, Mar 1997 ... 2.50
❑47, Apr 1997 ... 2.50
❑48, May 1997 ... 2.50
❑49, Jun 1997 ... 2.50
❑50, Jul 1997; Giant-size ... 4.50
❑Special 1, Jan 1994 1: Argos. ... 3.50
❑Special 2, May 1995 ... 2.50

STORMWATCH (2ND SERIES)
IMAGE

❑1, Oct 1997 ... 2.50
❑1/A, Oct 1997; alternate cover (white background) ... 2.50
❑1/B, Oct 1997; Voyager pack ... 2.50
❑2, Nov 1997 ... 2.50
❑3, Dec 1997 ... 2.50
❑4, Feb 1998 ... 2.50
❑5, Mar 1998 ... 2.50
❑5/A, Mar 1998; alternate cover; group flying ... 2.50
❑6, Apr 1998 ... 2.50
❑7, May 1998 ... 2.50
❑8, Jun 1998 ... 2.50
❑9, Jul 1998 ... 2.50
❑10, Aug 1998 ... 2.50
❑11, Sep 1998 ... 2.50
❑12, Oct 1998 ... 2.50

STORMWATCHER
ECLIPSE

❑1, Apr 1989, b&w ... 2.00
❑2, May 1989, b&w ... 2.00
❑3, b&w ... 2.00
❑4, b&w ... 2.00

STORMWATCH SOURCEBOOK
IMAGE

❑1, Jan 1994 ... 2.50

STORMWATCH: TEAM ACHILLES
WILDSTORM

❑1, Aug 2002 ... 2.95
❑2, Oct 2002 ... 2.95
❑3, Nov 2002 ... 2.95
❑4, Dec 2002 ... 2.95
❑5, Jan 2003 ... 2.95
❑6, Feb 2003 ... 2.95
❑7, Mar 2003 ... 2.95
❑8, Apr 2003 ... 2.95
❑9, May 2003 ... 2.95
❑10, Jun 2003 ... 2.95
❑11, Jul 2003 ... 2.95
❑12, Aug 2003 ... 2.95
❑13, Sep 2003 ... 2.95
❑14, Oct 2003 ... 2.95
❑15, Nov 2003 ... 2.95
❑16, Dec 2003 ... 2.95
❑17, Jan 2004 ... 2.95
❑18, Feb 2004 ... 2.95
❑19, Mar 2004 ... 2.95
❑20, May 2004 ... 2.95
❑21, Jun 2004 ... 2.95
❑22, Jul 2004 ... 2.95
❑23, Aug 2004 ... 2.95

STORY OF ELECTRONICS: THE DISCOVERY THAT CHANGED THE WORLD!
RADIO SHACK

❑1, Sep 1980 ... 2.50

STRAITJACKET STUDIOS PRESENTS
STRAITJACKET

❑0 ... 2.95

STRAND
TRIDENT

❑1, Nov 1990, b&w ... 2.50
❑2, b&w ... 2.50

STRANDED ON PLANET X
RADIO

❑1, Jun 1999 ... 2.95

STRANGE ADVENTURES
DC

❑73, Oct 1956 ... 90.00
❑74, Nov 1956 ... 90.00
❑75, Dec 1956 ... 60.00
❑76, Jan 1957 ... 90.00
❑77, Feb 1957 ... 90.00
❑78, Mar 1957 ... 90.00
❑79, Apr 1957 ... 120.00
❑80, May 1957 ... 90.00
❑81, Jun 1957 ... 80.00
❑82, Jul 1957 ... 80.00
❑83, Aug 1957 ... 80.00
❑84, Sep 1957 ... 95.00
❑85, Oct 1957 ... 80.00
❑86, Nov 1957 ... 80.00
❑87, Dec 1957 ... 80.00
❑88, Jan 1958 ... 80.00
❑89, Feb 1958 ... 80.00
❑90, Mar 1958 ... 80.00
❑91, Apr 1958 ... 76.00
❑92, May 1958 ... 72.00
❑93, Jun 1958 ... 72.00
❑94, Jul 1958 ... 64.00
❑95, Aug 1958 ... 72.00
❑96, Sep 1958 ... 52.00
❑97, Oct 1958 ... 72.00
❑98, Nov 1958 ... 60.00
❑99, Dec 1958 ... 72.00
❑100, Jan 1959; 100th anniversary issue ... 100.00
❑101, Feb 1959 ... 56.00
❑102, Mar 1959 ... 80.00
❑103, Apr 1959 ... 80.00
❑104, May 1959 1: Space Museum. .. 56.00
❑105, Jun 1959 ... 56.00
❑106, Jul 1959 ... 56.00
❑107, Aug 1959 ... 65.00
❑108, Sep 1959, color; Water (PSA) . 56.00
❑109, Oct 1959 ... 56.00

N-MINT

❑110, Nov 1959 65.00
❑111, Dec 1959 50.00
❑112, Jan 1960 46.00
❑113, Feb 1960 74.00
❑114, Mar 1960 1: Star Hawkins. 100.00
❑115, Apr 1960 50.00
❑116, May 1960 50.00
❑117, Jun 1960 1: The Atomic Knights. 525.00
❑118, Jul 1960 66.00
❑119, Aug 1960 85.00
❑120, Sep 1960 2: The Atomic Knights. 180.00
❑121, Oct 1960 62.00
❑122, Nov 1960 62.00
❑123, Dec 1960 66.00
❑124, Jan 1961 72.00
❑125, Feb 1961 62.00
❑126, Mar 1961 62.00
❑127, Apr 1961 41.00
❑128, May 1961 65.00
❑129, Jun 1961 81.00
❑130, Jul 1961 37.00
❑131, Aug 1961 34.00
❑132, Sep 1961 64.00
❑133, Oct 1961 54.00
❑134, Nov 1961 56.00
❑135, Dec 1961 55.00
❑136, Jan 1962 40.00
❑137, Feb 1962 37.00
❑138, Mar 1962 A: The Atomic Knights. 48.00
❑139, Apr 1962 40.00
❑140, May 1962 40.00
❑141, Jun 1962 48.00
❑142, Jul 1962 40.00
❑143, Aug 1962 40.00
❑144, Sep 1962 A: The Atomic Knights. 40.00
❑145, Oct 1962 40.00
❑146, Nov 1962 25.00
❑147, Dec 1962 A: The Atomic Knights. 40.00
❑148, Jan 1963 40.00
❑149, Feb 1963 25.00
❑150, Mar 1963 A: The Atomic Knights. 40.00
❑151, Apr 1963 34.00
❑152, May 1963 34.00
❑153, Jun 1963 A: The Atomic Knights. 34.00
❑154, Jul 1963 36.00
❑155, Aug 1963 34.00
❑156, Sep 1963 A: The Atomic Knights. 34.00
❑157, Oct 1963 34.00
❑158, Nov 1963 34.00
❑159, Dec 1963 34.00
❑160, Jan 1964 A: The Atomic Knights. 34.00
❑161, Feb 1964 22.00
❑162, Mar 1964 22.00
❑163, Apr 1964 22.00
❑164, May 1964 22.00
❑165, Jun 1964 22.00
❑166, Jul 1964 22.00
❑167, Aug 1964 22.00
❑168, Sep 1964 18.00
❑169, Oct 1964 22.00
❑170, Nov 1964 33.00
❑171, Dec 1964 18.50
❑172, Jan 1965 22.00
❑173, Feb 1965 30.00
❑174, Mar 1965 22.00
❑175, Apr 1965 36.00
❑176, May 1965 22.00
❑177, Jun 1965 O: Immortal Man. 1: Immortal Man. 22.00
❑178, Jul 1965 14.00
❑179, Aug 1965 22.00
❑180, Sep 1965 O: Animal Man (no costume). 1: Animal Man (no costume). 110.00
❑181, Oct 1965 14.00
❑182, Nov 1965 17.00
❑183, Dec 1965 19.00
❑184, Jan 1966 A: Animal Man. 42.00
❑185, Feb 1966 A: Immortal Man. A: Star Hawkins. 15.00
❑186, Mar 1966 16.00

N-MINT

❑187, Apr 1966 O: The Enchantress. 1: The Enchantress. 9.00
❑188, May 1966 15.00
❑189, Jun 1966 21.00
❑190, Jul 1966 1: Animal Man (in costume). 80.00
❑191, Aug 1966 9.00
❑192, Sep 1966 12.00
❑193, Oct 1966 12.00
❑194, Nov 1966 9.00
❑195, Dec 1966 A: Animal Man. 26.00
❑196, Jan 1967 12.00
❑197, Feb 1967 12.00
❑198, Mar 1967 7.00
❑199, Apr 1967 20.00
❑200, May 1967 12.00
❑201, Jun 1967 A: Animal Man. 35.00
❑202, Jul 1967 10.00
❑203, Aug 1967 10.00
❑204, Sep 1967 10.00
❑205, Oct 1967 O: Deadman. 1: Deadman. 75.00
❑206, Nov 1967 NA (a); 2: Deadman. 2: Deadman. 25.00
❑207, Dec 1967; NA (a); Deadman 20.00
❑208, Jan 1968; NA (a); Deadman 36.00
❑209, Feb 1968; NA (a); Deadman 36.00
❑210, Mar 1968; NA (a); Deadman 36.00
❑211, Apr 1968; NA (a); Deadman 32.00
❑212, Jun 1968; NA (a); Deadman 32.00
❑213, Aug 1968; NA (a); Deadman 32.00
❑214, Oct 1968; NA (a); Deadman 32.00
❑215, Dec 1968; NA (a); 1: League of Assassins. 1: Sensei. Deadman 32.00
❑216, Feb 1969; NA (a); Deadman 21.00
❑217, Apr 1969 8.00
❑218, Jun 1969 9.00
❑219, Aug 1969 6.50
❑220, Oct 1969 12.00
❑221, Dec 1969 9.00
❑222, Feb 1970; NA (a); New Adam Strange story 9.00
❑223, Apr 1970 10.00
❑224, Jun 1970 8.00
❑225, Aug 1970 8.00
❑226, Oct 1970; giant series begins 8.00
❑227, Dec 1970 JKu (c) 8.00
❑228, Feb 1971 8.00
❑229, Apr 1971 8.00
❑230, Jun 1971 8.00
❑231, Aug 1971; reprints from Strange Adventures #67, #83, #125, and #160, and Adam Strange from Mystery in Space #71 5.00
❑232, Oct 1971 5.00
❑233, Dec 1971 5.00
❑234, Feb 1972 5.00
❑235, Apr 1972 5.00
❑236, Jun 1972 5.00
❑237, Jun 1972 5.00
❑238, Oct 1972 MA, CI (a) 5.00
❑239, Dec 1972 5.00
❑240, Feb 1973 5.00
❑241, Apr 1973; Reprints Adam Strange from Mystery in Space #81 5.00
❑242, Jul 1973; Reprints Adam Strange from Mystery in Space #82 5.00
❑243, Sep 1973; reprints from Strange Adventures #131 and Adam Strange from Mystery in Space #83 5.00
❑244, Nov 1973 5.00

STRANGE ADVENTURES (MINI-SERIES)
DC / VERTIGO

❑1, Nov 1999 2.50
❑2, Dec 1999 2.50
❑3, Jan 2000 2.50
❑4, Feb 2000 2.50

STRANGE ATTRACTORS
RETROGRAFIX

❑1, May 1993 4.00
❑1-2, Jul 1994 2.75
❑2, Aug 1993 3.50

An untold tale of Steel, the Indestructible Man, was adapted into *All-Star Squadron* #8 and #9.

© 1978 DC Comics.

N-MINT

❑2-2, Jul 1993 2.75
❑3, Nov 1993 3.50
❑3-2, Jun 1993 2.75
❑4, Feb 1994 3.00
❑4-2, Jun 1994 2.75
❑5, May 1994 3.00
❑6, Aug 1994 2.50
❑7, Nov 1994 2.50
❑8, Jan 1995 2.50
❑9, Apr 1995 2.50
❑10, Jun 1995 2.50
❑11, Sep 1995 2.50
❑12, Nov 1995 2.50
❑13, Feb 1996 2.50
❑14, Jul 1996 2.50
❑15, Feb 1997 2.50

STRANGE ATTRACTORS: MOON FEVER
CALIBER

❑1, Feb 1997, b&w 2.95
❑2 1997 2.95
❑3 1997 2.95

STRANGE AVENGING TALES (STEVE DITKO'S...)
FANTAGRAPHICS

❑1, Feb 1997 2.95

STRANGE BEDFELLOWS
HIPPY

❑1 2002 5.95
❑2, Jun 2002 5.95

STRANGE BREW
AARDVARK-VANAHEIM

❑1 3.00

STRANGE COMBAT TALES
MARVEL / EPIC

❑1, Oct 1993 2.50
❑2, Nov 1993 2.50
❑3, Dec 1993 2.50
❑4, Jan 1984 2.50

STRANGE DAYS
ECLIPSE

❑1 1.50
❑2 1.50
❑3 1.50

STRANGE EMBRACE
ATOMEKA

❑1, b&w 3.95
❑2, b&w 3.95
❑3, b&w 3.95

STRANGEHAVEN
ABIOGENESIS

❑1, Jun 1995 5.00
❑2 4.00
❑3, Dec 1995 4.00
❑4, Jun 1996 2.95
❑5, Nov 1996 2.95
❑6, May 1997 2.95
❑7 2.95
❑8 1997 2.95
❑9, Jun 1998 2.95
❑10, Nov 1998 2.95
❑11, Apr 1999 2.95
❑12, Oct 1999 2.95
❑13 0.00

N-MINT

❑14 ... 0.00
❑15, May 2003 ... 2.95

STRANGE HEROES
Lone Star

❑1, Jun 2000 ... 2.95
❑2 ... 2.95

STRANGE KILLINGS: BODY ORCHARD (WARREN ELLIS')
Avatar

❑1 2002 ... 3.50
❑2 2002 ... 3.50
❑3 2002 ... 3.50
❑4 2002 ... 3.50
❑5 ... 3.50
❑6, Feb 2003 ... 3.50

STRANGE KILLINGS: NECROMANCER (WARREN EILIS')
Avatar

❑1, Mar 2004 ... 3.50
❑2, Apr 2004 ... 3.50

STRANGE KILLINGS: STRONG MEDICINE (WARREN ELLIS')
Avatar

❑1, Jul 2003 ... 3.50
❑2, Aug 2003 ... 3.50
❑2/A, Aug 2003; Wrap Cover ... 3.95
❑3, Oct 2003 ... 3.50

STRANGE LOOKING EXILE
Robert Kirby

❑1 ... 2.00
❑2 ... 2.00
❑3 ... 2.00

STRANGELOVE
Express / Entity

❑1, b&w ... 2.50
❑2, b&w ... 2.50

STRANGER IN A STRANGE LAND
Rip Off

❑1, Jun 1989, b&w ... 2.00
❑2, May 1990, b&w ... 2.00
❑3, Sep 1991, b&w ... 2.50

STRANGERS, THE
Malibu / Ultraverse

❑1, Jun 1993 O: The Strangers. 1: The Strangers. 1: The Night Man (out of costume). ... 2.00
❑1/Hologram, Jun 1993; hologram edition ... 5.00
❑1/Ltd., Jun 1993; Ultra-limited edition ... 4.00
❑2, Jul 1993; card ... 2.00
❑3, Aug 1993 1: TNTNT. ... 2.00
❑4, Sep 1993 A: Hardcase. ... 2.00
❑5, Oct 1993; Rune ... 2.50
❑6, Nov 1993 ... 1.95
❑7, Dec 1993; Break-Thru ... 1.95
❑8, Jan 1994 O: The Solution. ... 1.95
❑9, Feb 1994 ... 1.95
❑10, Mar 1994 ... 1.95
❑11, Apr 1994 ... 1.95
❑12, May 1994 ... 1.95
❑13, Jun 1994; KB (w); MGu (a); 1: Pilgrim. contains Ultraverse Premiere #4 ... 3.50
❑14, Jul 1994 1: Byter. ... 1.95
❑15, Aug 1994 1: Lightshow. 1: Generator X. 1: Rodent. ... 1.95
❑16, Sep 1994 ... 1.95
❑17, Oct 1994 A: Rafferty. ... 1.95
❑18, Nov 1994 ... 1.95
❑19, Dec 1994 ... 1.95
❑20, Jan 1995 1: Beater. 1: M.C. Zed. ... 1.95
❑21, Feb 1995 ... 1.95
❑22, Mar 1995 ... 1.95
❑23, Apr 1995 ... 1.95
❑24, May 1995 ... 1.95
❑Annual 1, Dec 1994 ... 3.95

STRANGERS (IMAGE)
Image

❑1, Mar 2003 ... 2.95
❑2, Apr 2003 ... 2.95
❑3, May 2003 ... 2.95
❑4, Jul 2003 ... 2.95
❑5, Aug 2003 ... 2.95
❑6, Sep 2003 ... 2.95

STRANGERS IN PARADISE
Antarctic

❑0, b&w ... 75.00
❑1, Nov 1993, b&w ... 65.00
❑1-2, Mar 1994, b&w ... 5.00
❑1-3, Apr 1994, b&w ... 3.00
❑2, Dec 1993, b&w ... 18.00
❑3, Feb 1994, b&w ... 18.00

STRANGERS IN PARADISE (2ND SERIES)
Abstract

❑1, Sep 1994, b&w ... 30.00
❑1/Variant; Gold logo edition ... 4.00
❑1-2, Apr 1995, b&w ... 2.75
❑2, Nov 1994, b&w ... 15.00
❑2/Variant; Gold logo edition ... 3.00
❑3, Jan 1995, b&w ... 12.00
❑3/Variant; Gold logo edition ... 3.00
❑4, Mar 1995, b&w ... 10.00
❑4/Variant; Gold logo edition ... 2.75
❑5, Jun 1995, b&w ... 10.00
❑5/Variant; Gold logo edition ... 2.75
❑6, Jul 1995, b&w ... 8.00
❑6/Variant; Gold logo edition ... 2.75
❑7, Sep 1995, b&w ... 8.00
❑7/Variant; Gold logo edition ... 2.75
❑8, Nov 1995, b&w ... 8.00
❑8/Variant; Gold logo edition ... 2.75
❑9, Jan 1996, b&w ... 8.00
❑9/Variant; Gold logo edition ... 2.75
❑10, Feb 1996, b&w ... 8.00
❑10/Variant; Gold logo edition ... 2.75
❑11, b&w ... 5.00
❑11/Variant; Gold logo edition ... 2.75
❑12, May 1996, b&w ... 5.00
❑12/Variant; Gold logo edition ... 2.75
❑13, Jun 1996, b&w ... 4.00
❑14, Jul 1996; continues in 3rd series (Image); Titled: Terry Moore's Strangers in Paradise ... 2.75
❑Special 1; Molly & Poo Special ... 3.00

STRANGERS IN PARADISE (3RD SERIES)
Homage

❑1, Oct 1996, b&w ... 4.00
❑2, Dec 1996, b&w ... 3.00
❑3, Jan 1997, b&w ... 3.00
❑4, Feb 1997, b&w ... 3.00
❑5, Apr 1997, b&w; cover says Mar, indicia says Apr ... 3.00
❑6, May 1997, b&w ... 3.00
❑7, Jul 1997, b&w ... 3.00
❑8, Aug 1997, b&w; returns to Abstract ... 3.00
❑9, Sep 1997 ... 3.00
❑10, Dec 1997 ... 3.00
❑11, Dec 1997 ... 3.00
❑12, Jan 1998 ... 3.00
❑13, Mar 1998 ... 3.00
❑14, Apr 1998 ... 3.00
❑15, Jun 1998 ... 3.00
❑16, Jul 1998 ... 3.00
❑17, Sep 1998 ... 3.00
❑18, Oct 1998 ... 3.00
❑19, Nov 1998 ... 3.00
❑20, Dec 1998 ... 3.00
❑21, Feb 1999 ... 3.00
❑22, Mar 1999 ... 3.00
❑23, Mar 1999 ... 3.00
❑24, Jun 1999 ... 3.00
❑25, Jul 1999 ... 3.00
❑26, Aug 1999 ... 3.00
❑27, Sep 1999 ... 3.00
❑28, Nov 1999 ... 3.00
❑29, Dec 1999 ... 3.00
❑30, Feb 2000, b&w ... 3.00
❑31, Mar 2000 ... 2.95
❑32, May 2000 ... 2.95
❑33, May 2000, color ... 2.95
❑34, Aug 2000 ... 2.95
❑35, Sep 2000 ... 2.95
❑36, Nov 2000 ... 2.95
❑37, Dec 2000 ... 2.95
❑38, Jan 2001 ... 2.95
❑39, Mar 2001 ... 2.95
❑40, Apr 2001 ... 2.95
❑41, Jun 2001 ... 2.95
❑42, Jul 2001 ... 2.95
❑43 2001 ... 2.95
❑44 2001 ... 2.95
❑45 2001 ... 2.95
❑46 2001 ... 2.95
❑47 2002 ... 2.95
❑48 2002 ... 2.95
❑49 2002 ... 2.95
❑50 2002 ... 2.95
❑51 2002 ... 2.95
❑52 2002 ... 2.95
❑53 2002 ... 2.95
❑54 2002 ... 2.95
❑55 2002 ... 2.95
❑56 2003 ... 2.95
❑57 2003 ... 2.95
❑58, Jun 2003 ... 3.00
❑59, Aug 2003 ... 3.00
❑60, Sep 2003 ... 3.00
❑61, Dec 2003 ... 3.00
❑62, Jan 2004 ... 3.00
❑63, Feb 2004 ... 3.00
❑64, Apr 2004 ... 3.00
❑65, May 2004 ... 2.95
❑Special 1, Feb 1999; Lyrics and Poems ... 3.00

STRANGERS IN PARADISE SOURCEBOOK
Abstract

❑1, Oct 2003 ... 2.95

STRANGER'S TALE, A
Vineyard

❑1, b&w; cardstock cover ... 2.00

STRANGER THAN FICTION
Impact

❑1 1998, b&w ... 1.99
❑2, Jul 1998, b&w ... 1.99
❑3 1998 ... 1.99
❑4 1998 ... 1.99

STRANGE SPORTS STORIES
DC

❑1, Oct 1973 FR (w); BO, DG, CS (a) . 10.00
❑2, Dec 1973 FR (w); MA, DG, CS, IN (a) ... 7.00
❑3, Feb 1974 FR (w); DG, CS (a) ... 5.00
❑4, Apr 1974 DG, IN (a) ... 5.00
❑5, Jun 1974 ... 5.00
❑6, Aug 1974 ... 5.00

STRANGE SPORTS STORIES (ADVENTURE)
Adventure

❑1 ... 2.50
❑2 ... 2.50
❑3 ... 2.50

STRANGE STORIES
Avalon

❑1, b&w; reprints John Force and Magic Man stories ... 2.95

STRANGE TALES (1ST SERIES)
Marvel

❑51, Oct 1956 ... 150.00
❑52, Nov 1956 ... 150.00
❑53, Dec 1956 ... 150.00
❑54, Jan 1957 ... 150.00
❑55, Feb 1957 ... 150.00
❑56, Mar 1957 ... 150.00
❑57, Apr 1957 ... 150.00
❑58 1957 AW (a) ... 160.00
❑59, Jul 1957 BK (a) ... 180.00
❑60, Aug 1957 ... 150.00
❑61 BK (a) ... 180.00

Condition price index: Multiply "NM prices" above by: **0.83 for Very Fine/Near Mint**
0.66 for Very Fine • 0.33 for Fine • 0.2 for Very Good • 0.125 for Good

N-MINT

❑62 1958 .... 130.00
❑63 1958 .... 130.00
❑64 1958 AW (a) 160.00
❑65 1958 .... 125.00
❑66 1958 .... 125.00
❑67, Feb 1959; Quicksilver prototype? 170.00
❑68, Apr 1959 .... 125.00
❑69, Jun 1959; Professor X prototype? 155.00
❑70, Aug 1959 .... 120.00
❑71, Oct 1959 .... 120.00
❑72, Dec 1959 .... 120.00
❑73, Feb 1960 .... 120.00
❑74, Apr 1960 .... 120.00
❑75, Jun 1960 .... 120.00
❑76, Aug 1960 .... 120.00
❑77, Oct 1960 .... 120.00
❑78, Nov 1960 .... 120.00
❑79, Dec 1960; Doctor Strange try-out character 200.00
❑80, Jan 1961 .... 120.00
❑81, Feb 1961 .... 110.00
❑82, Mar 1961 .... 110.00
❑83, Apr 1961 .... 100.00
❑84, May 1961; Magneto prototype character (?) 185.00
❑85, Jun 1961 .... 110.00
❑86, Jul 1961 .... 110.00
❑87, Aug 1961 .... 110.00
❑88, Sep 1961 .... 110.00
❑89, Oct 1961 JK (a); O: Fin Fang Foom. 1: Fin Fang Foom. 240.00
❑90, Nov 1961 .... 110.00
❑91, Dec 1961 .... 110.00
❑92, Jan 1962 .... 110.00
❑93, Feb 1962 .... 100.00
❑94, Mar 1962 .... 100.00
❑95, Apr 1962 .... 100.00
❑96, May 1962 .... 100.00
❑97, Jun 1962; Aunt May & Uncle Ben prototype characters (?) 300.00
❑98, Jul 1962 .... 100.00
❑99, Aug 1962 .... 100.00
❑100, Sep 1962 .... 100.00
❑101, Oct 1962; SD, JK (a); Human Torch features begin 700.00
❑102, Nov 1962; SD, JK (a); A: Human Torch. 290.00
❑103, Dec 1962; SD, JK (a); A: Human Torch. 230.00
❑104, Jan 1963; SD, JK (a); O: Paste-Pot Pete. 1: Paste-Pot Pete. A: 230.00
❑105, Feb 1963; SD, JK (a); A: Human Torch. 230.00
❑106, Mar 1963; SD (a); A: Fantastic Four. A: Human Torch. 170.00
❑107, Apr 1963; SD (a); Human Torch vs. Sub-Mariner 185.00
❑108, May 1963; SD, JK (a); A: Human Torch. 170.00
❑109, Jun 1963; SD, JK (a); 1: Circe (later becomes Sersi). A: Human Torch. 170.00
❑110, Jul 1963; SD (a); 1: The Ancient One. 1: Doctor Strange. 1: Wong (Doctor Strange's manservant). A: Human Torch. Human Torch, Dr. Strange 950.00
❑111, Aug 1963; SD (a); 1: Asbestos. 1: Baron Mordo. 1: Eel I (Leopold Stryke). 2: Doctor Strange. A: Human Torch. 290.00
❑112, Sep 1963 SD (a); A: Human Torch. 105.00
❑113, Oct 1963 SD (a); 1: Plantman. A: Human Torch. 105.00
❑114, Nov 1963; SD, JK (a); A: Human Torch. Villain (The Acrobat) appears, dressed as Captain America; Dr. Strange 240.00
❑115, Dec 1963; SD (a); O: Doctor Strange. A: Human Torch. 360.00
❑116, Jan 1964; Human Torch vs. Thing; Dr. Strange 80.00
❑117, Feb 1964; A: Human Torch. Dr. Strange 65.00
❑118, Mar 1964; A: Human Torch. Dr. Strange 65.00

N-MINT

❑119, Apr 1964; A: Human Torch. A: Spider-Man. Dr. Strange 85.00
❑120, May 1964; A: Human Torch. A: Iceman. Dr. Strange 80.00
❑121, Jun 1964 A: Human Torch. 80.00
❑122, Jul 1964 A: Human Torch. 80.00
❑123, Aug 1964 O: The Beetle. 1: The Beetle. A: Thing. A: Human Torch. A: Thor. 45.00
❑124, Sep 1964 A: Thing. A: Human Torch. 45.00
❑125, Oct 1964 A: Human Torch. 45.00
❑126, Nov 1964 1: Dormammu. 1: Clea. A: Human Torch. 50.00
❑127, Dec 1964 A: Human Torch. 40.00
❑128, Jan 1965 A: Human Torch. 40.00
❑129, Feb 1965 SD (a); A: Human Torch. 40.00
❑130, Mar 1965 SD (a); A: Human Torch. A: Beatles. 45.00
❑131, Apr 1965 SD (a); A: Thing. A: Human Torch. 40.00
❑132, May 1965 SD (a); A: Thing. A: Human Torch. 40.00
❑133, Jun 1965 SD (a); A: Thing. A: Human Torch. 40.00
❑134, Jul 1965; SD (a); A: Torch. A: Human Torch. A: Watcher. Last Human Torch issue 40.00
❑135, Aug 1965; SL (w); SD, JK (a); O: Nick Fury, Agent of SHIELD. 1: S.H.I.E.L.D.. 1: Nick Fury, Agent of SHIELD. 1: Hydra. Doctor Strange 80.00
❑136, Sep 1965; SD, JK (a); Doctor Strange, Nick Fury 26.00
❑137, Oct 1965; Doctor Strange, Nick Fury 26.00
❑138, Nov 1965; 1: Eternity. Doctor Strange, Nick Fury 26.00
❑139, Dec 1965; Doctor Strange, Nick Fury 26.00
❑140, Jan 1966; Doctor Strange, Nick Fury 26.00
❑141, Feb 1966; 1: The Fixer. 1: Mentallo. Doctor Strange, Nick Fury 26.00
❑142, Mar 1966; Doctor Strange, Nick Fury 26.00
❑143, Apr 1966; Doctor Strange, Nick Fury 26.00
❑144, May 1966; 1: The Druid. 1: Jasper Sitwell (SHIELD agent). Doctor Strange, Nick Fury 26.00
❑145, Jun 1966; Doctor Strange, Nick Fury 26.00
❑146, Jul 1966; 1: Advanced Idea Mechanics (A.I.M.). Doctor Strange, Nick Fury 28.00
❑147, Aug 1966; O: Kaluu. 1: Kaluu. Doctor Strange, Nick Fury 26.00
❑148, Sep 1966; BEv, JK (a); O: The Ancient One. Doctor Strange, Nick Fury 45.00
❑149, Oct 1966; BEv, JK (a); Doctor Strange, Nick Fury 26.00
❑150, Nov 1966; JB, BEv, JK (a); 1: Umar. 1st John Buscema art at Marvel 30.00
❑151, Dec 1966; BEv, JK, JSo (a); 1st Jim Steranko art at Marvel 40.00
❑152, Jan 1967; Doctor Strange, Nick Fury 24.00
❑153, Feb 1967; Doctor Strange, Nick Fury 24.00
❑154, Mar 1967; 1: Dreadnought (original). Doctor Strange, Nick Fury 24.00
❑155, Apr 1967; Doctor Strange, Nick Fury 24.00
❑156, May 1967; A: Daredevil. Doctor Strange, Nick Fury 24.00
❑157, Jun 1967; 1: Living Tribunal. Doctor Strange, Nick Fury 24.00
❑158, Jul 1967; D: Baron Strucker. Doctor Strange, Nick Fury 24.00
❑159, Aug 1967; JSo (a); O: Nick Fury, Agent of SHIELD. O: Fury. 1: Val Fontaine. A: Captain America. Doctor Strange. 30.00
❑160, Sep 1967; A: Captain America. Doctor Strange, Nick Fury 24.00

Frightful Four member Paste-Pot Pete (later The Trapster) was introduced in *Strange Tales* #104.
© 1963 Marvel Comics.

N-MINT

❑161, Oct 1967; A: Captain America. Doctor Strange, Nick Fury 24.00
❑162, Nov 1967; A: Captain America. Doctor Strange, Nick Fury 24.00
❑163, Dec 1967; Doctor Strange, Nick Fury 24.00
❑164, Jan 1968; 1: Yandroth. Doctor Strange, Nick Fury 24.00
❑165, Feb 1968; Doctor Strange, Nick Fury 24.00
❑166, Mar 1968; Doctor Strange, Nick Fury 24.00
❑167, Apr 1968; JSo, DA (a); Doctor Strange, Nick Fury 24.00
❑168, May 1968; JSo, DA (a); original series continues as Doctor Strange; Nick Fury, Agent of SHIELD series ends 24.00
❑169, Jun 1973; : . O: Brother Voodoo. 1: Brother Voodoo. second series begins; Brother Voodoo 3.50
❑170, Aug 1973; Brother Voodoo 3.50
❑171, Oct 1973; 1: Baron Samedi. Brother Voodoo 3.50
❑172, Dec 1973; Brother Voodoo 3.50
❑173, Feb 1974; GC (a); 1: Black Talon I (Desmond Drew). Brother Voodoo; Marvel Value Stamp #45: Mantis ... 3.50
❑174, Jun 1974; JB, JM (a); O: Golem. Marvel Value Stamp #44: Absorbing Man 3.50
❑175, Aug 1974; SD (a); Rep-Torr; reprints Amazing Adventures #1; Marvel Value Stamp #10: Power Man 3.50
❑176, Oct 1974; Golem; Marvel Value Stamp #94: Electro 3.50
❑177, Dec 1974; TD (a); Golem 3.50
❑178, Feb 1975; JSn (a); O: Warlock. 1: Magus. Warlock 15.00
❑179, Apr 1975; JSn (a); 1: Pip. A: Warlock. 10.00
❑180, Jun 1975; JSn (a); 1: Gamora. A: Warlock. 10.00
❑181, Aug 1975; JSn (a); A: Warlock. 10.00
❑182, Oct 1975; reprinted from Strange Tales #123 and 124 .... 3.00
❑183, Dec 1975; reprinted from Strange Tales #130 and 131 .... 3.00
❑184, Feb 1976; reprinted from Strange Tales #132 and 133 .... 3.00
❑185, Apr 1976; reprinted from Strange Tales #134 and 135 .... 3.00
❑185/30 cent, Apr 1976; 30 cent regional price variant; reprinted from Strange Tales #134 and 135 .... 20.00
❑186, Jun 1976; reprinted from Strange Tales #136 and 137 .... 3.00
❑186/30 cent, Jun 1976; 30 cent regional price variant; reprinted from Strange Tales #136 and 137 .... 20.00
❑187, Aug 1976; reprinted from Strange Tales #138 and 139 .... 3.00
❑188, Oct 1976; reprinted from Strange Tales #140 and 141 .... 3.00
❑Annual 1, ca. 1962; reprinted from Journey Into Mystery #53, 55 and 59; Strange Tales #73, 76 and 78; Tales of Suspense #7 and 9; Tales to Astonish #1,6 and 7 .... 325.00
❑Annual 2, ca. 1963; A: Human Torch. A: Spider-Man. Spider-Man new, all others reprinted from Strange Tales #67; Strange Worlds #1,2 and 3; World of Fantasy #16 .... 350.00

N-MINT

STRANGE TALES (2ND SERIES)
MARVEL

- ❑1, Apr 1987; Doctor Strange, Cloak & Dagger ... 1.50
- ❑2, May 1987 ... 1.25
- ❑3, Jun 1987 ... 1.25
- ❑4, Jul 1987 ... 1.25
- ❑5, Aug 1987 ... 1.25
- ❑6, Sep 1987 ... 1.25
- ❑7, Oct 1987; Defenders ... 1.25
- ❑8, Nov 1987 ... 1.25
- ❑9, Dec 1987 ... 1.25
- ❑10, Jan 1988 ... 1.25
- ❑11, Feb 1988 ... 1.25
- ❑12, Mar 1988; Black Cat ... 1.25
- ❑13, Apr 1988 A: Punisher. ... 1.75
- ❑14, May 1988 A: Punisher. ... 1.75
- ❑15, Jun 1988 ... 1.25
- ❑16, Jul 1988 ... 1.25
- ❑17, Aug 1988 ... 1.50
- ❑18, Sep 1988; A: X-Factor. ... 1.25
- ❑19, Oct 1988 ... 1.25

STRANGE TALES (3RD SERIES)
MARVEL

- ❑1, Nov 1994; prestige format; acetate overlay cover ... 6.95

STRANGE TALES (4TH SERIES)
MARVEL

- ❑1, Sep 1998; gatefold summary A: Werewolf. A: Man-Thing. ... 4.99
- ❑2, Oct 1998; gatefold summary A: Werewolf. A: Man-Thing. ... 4.99
- ❑3, Jan 1999 ... 4.99
- ❑4, Dec 1998 ... 4.99

STRANGE TALES: DARK CORNERS
MARVEL

- ❑1, May 1998; gatefold summary ... 3.99

STRANGE WEATHER LATELY
METAPHROG

- ❑1 1997 ... 3.50
- ❑2, Dec 1997 ... 3.50
- ❑3, Feb 1998 ... 3.50
- ❑4 1998 ... 3.50
- ❑5, Jun 1998 ... 3.50
- ❑6, Aug 1998 ... 3.50
- ❑7, Oct 1998 ... 3.00
- ❑8 1999 ... 3.00
- ❑9 1999 ... 3.00
- ❑10, May 1999 ... 3.50

STRANGE WINK (JOHN BOLTON'S...)
DARK HORSE

- ❑1, Mar 1998, b&w ... 2.95
- ❑2, Apr 1998, b&w ... 2.95
- ❑3, May 1998, b&w ... 2.95

STRANGE WORLDS (ETERNITY)
ETERNITY

- ❑1, b&w ... 3.95

STRANGE WORLDS (NORTH COAST)
NORTH COAST

- ❑1, b&w; magazine; cardstock cover ... 4.00

STRANGLING DESDEMONA
NINGEN MANGA

- ❑1, b&w ... 2.95

STRAPPED (DERRECK WAYNE JACKSON'S...)
GOTHIC IMAGES

- ❑1 ... 2.00
- ❑2 ... 2.00
- ❑3 ... 2.00
- ❑4 ... 2.00

STRATA
RENEGADE

- ❑1, Jan 1986, b&w ... 2.00
- ❑2, Mar 1986, b&w ... 2.00
- ❑3 1986 ... 2.00
- ❑4 1986 ... 2.00
- ❑5 ... 2.00

N-MINT

STRATONAUT
NIGHTWYND

- ❑1, b&w ... 2.50
- ❑2, b&w ... 2.50
- ❑3, b&w ... 2.50
- ❑4, b&w ... 2.50

STRATOSFEAR
CALIBER

- ❑1 ... 2.95

STRAWBERRY SHORTCAKE
MARVEL / STAR

- ❑1, Apr 1985 ... 1.00
- ❑2, Jun 1985 ... 1.00
- ❑3, Aug 1985 ... 1.00
- ❑4, Oct 1985 ... 1.00
- ❑5, Dec 1985 ... 1.00
- ❑6, Feb 1986 ... 1.00

STRAW MEN
ALL AMERICAN

- ❑1 1989, b&w ... 1.95
- ❑2 1989, b&w ... 1.95
- ❑3 1989, b&w ... 1.95
- ❑4, Jan 1990, b&w ... 1.95
- ❑5 1990, b&w ... 1.95
- ❑6 1990, b&w ... 1.95
- ❑7 1990, b&w ... 1.95
- ❑8 1990, b&w ... 1.95

STRAY BULLETS
EL CAPITAN

- ❑1 1995, b&w ... 4.00
- ❑1-2 ... 3.00
- ❑1-3; indicia says #3; third print ... 3.00
- ❑1-4 ... 3.00
- ❑2, Apr 1995, b&w ... 2.95
- ❑2-2 ... 2.95
- ❑2-3 ... 2.95
- ❑2-4 ... 2.95
- ❑3, May 1995, b&w ... 2.95
- ❑3-2 ... 2.95
- ❑4 1995, b&w; indicia contains information for issue #3 ... 2.95
- ❑5 1995, b&w; indicia contains information for issue #4 ... 2.95
- ❑6, Sep 1995, b&w ... 2.95
- ❑7, Nov 1995, b&w ... 2.95
- ❑8, Feb 1996, b&w ... 2.95
- ❑9, May 1996, b&w ... 2.95
- ❑10, Aug 1996, b&w ... 2.95
- ❑11, Oct 1996, b&w ... 2.95
- ❑12, Jan 1997, b&w ... 2.95
- ❑13, Apr 1997, b&w ... 2.95
- ❑14, Jun 1997, b&w ... 2.95
- ❑15, Jul 1998, b&w ... 2.95
- ❑16, Aug 1998, b&w ... 2.95
- ❑17, Nov 1998, b&w ... 2.95
- ❑18, Feb 1999, b&w ... 2.95
- ❑19, Apr 1999, b&w ... 2.95
- ❑20, Jul 1999, b&w ... 2.95
- ❑21 ... 2.95
- ❑22 ... 3.50
- ❑23 2002 ... 3.50
- ❑24 2002 ... 3.50
- ❑25 2002 ... 3.50
- ❑26 2002 ... 3.50
- ❑27 2002 ... 3.50
- ❑28 2002 ... 3.50
- ❑29 2003 ... 3.50

STRAY CATS
TWILIGHT TWINS

- ❑1, Jan 1999, b&w ... 2.50

STRAY TOASTERS
MARVEL / EPIC

- ❑1 BSz (w); BSz (a) ... 4.50
- ❑2 BSz (w); BSz (a) ... 4.50
- ❑3 BSz (w); BSz (a) ... 4.50
- ❑4 BSz (w); BSz (a) ... 4.50

STREETFIGHTER (OCEAN)
OCEAN

- ❑1, Aug 1986 1: Streetfighter. ... 2.00
- ❑2, Nov 1986 2: Streetfighter. ... 2.00

N-MINT

- ❑3, Feb 1987 ... 2.00
- ❑4, May 1987 ... 2.00

STREET FIGHTER (MALIBU)
MALIBU

- ❑1, Sep 1993 ... 2.95
- ❑1/Gold, Sep 1993; gold foil edition ... 5.00
- ❑2, Oct 1993 ... 2.95
- ❑2/Gold, Oct 1993; gold foil edition ... 4.00
- ❑3, Nov 1993 ... 2.95
- ❑3/Gold, Nov 1993; gold foil edition ... 4.00

STREET FIGHTER (IMAGE)
IMAGE

- ❑1, Sep 2003 ... 2.95
- ❑1/A-2, Sep 2003 ... 5.00
- ❑1.1, Sep 2003; Madureira cover ... 2.25
- ❑1/A, Oct 2003 ... 2.95
- ❑1/B, Nov 2003 ... 2.95
- ❑1-2, Jan 2004 ... 2.95
- ❑2, Oct 2003 ... 2.95
- ❑2/A, Nov 2003 ... 2.95
- ❑3, Nov 2003 ... 2.95
- ❑3/C, Nov 2003; Chen cover ... 5.00
- ❑3/A, Dec 2003 ... 2.95
- ❑3/B, Jan 2004 ... 2.95
- ❑4, Dec 2003 ... 2.95
- ❑4/C, Dec 2003; Chen cover ... 5.00
- ❑4/A, Jan 2004 ... 2.95
- ❑5, Feb 2004 ... 2.95
- ❑5/A, Feb 2004; Shinkiro cover ... 5.00
- ❑6, Apr 2004 ... 2.95
- ❑6/DF, Apr 2004; Foil Cover ... 5.00

STREET FIGHTER: THE BATTLE FOR SHADALOO
DC

- ❑1; polybagged with trading card and temporary tattoos ... 3.95

STREET FIGHTER II (TOKUMA SHOTEN)
TOKUMA SHOTEN

- ❑1, Apr 1994 ... 2.95

STREET FIGHTER II (VIZ)
VIZ

- ❑1, Apr 1994 ... 2.95
- ❑2, May 1994 ... 2.95
- ❑3, Jun 1994 ... 2.95
- ❑4, Jul 1994 ... 2.95
- ❑5, Aug 1994 ... 2.95
- ❑6, Sep 1994 ... 2.95
- ❑7, Oct 1994 ... 2.95
- ❑8, Nov 1994 ... 2.95

STREET FIGHTER II: THE ANIMATED MOVIE
VIZ

- ❑1 ... 2.95
- ❑2 ... 2.95
- ❑3 ... 2.95
- ❑4 ... 2.95
- ❑5 ... 2.95

STREET HEROES 2005
ETERNITY

- ❑1, Jan 1989, b&w ... 1.95
- ❑2, Feb 1989, b&w ... 1.95
- ❑3, Mar 1989, b&w ... 1.95

STREET MUSIC
FANTAGRAPHICS

- ❑1, b&w ... 2.95
- ❑2, b&w ... 2.95
- ❑3, b&w ... 2.95
- ❑4, b&w ... 2.95
- ❑5, b&w ... 2.95
- ❑6, b&w ... 2.95

STREET POET RAY (BLACKTHORNE)
BLACKTHORNE

- ❑1, Apr 1989, b&w ... 2.00
- ❑2, b&w ... 2.00

STREETS
DC

- ❑1, ca. 1993 ... 4.95

N-MINT

❑2, ca. 1993 ... 4.95
❑3, ca. 1993 ... 4.95

STREET SHARKS (MINI-SERIES)
ARCHIE

❑1, Jan 1996; based on toy line and animated series ... 1.50
❑2, Feb 1996 ... 1.50
❑3, Mar 1996 ... 1.50

STREET SHARKS
ARCHIE

❑1, May 1996 ... 1.50
❑3, Aug 1996 ... 1.50

STREET WOLF
BLACKTHORNE

❑1, Jul 1986, b&w ... 2.00
❑2, Sep 1986, b&w ... 2.00
❑3, b&w ... 2.00

STRIKE!
ECLIPSE

❑1, Aug 1987 ... 1.75
❑2, Sep 1987 ... 1.75
❑3, Oct 1987 ... 1.75
❑4, Nov 1987 ... 1.75
❑5, Dec 1987 ... 1.75
❑6, Feb 1988 ... 1.75

STRIKEBACK! (MALIBU)
MALIBU / BRAVURA

❑1, Oct 1994 ... 2.95
❑2, Nov 1994 ... 2.95
❑3, Dec 1994; Final issue; series announced as six issues, but title cancelled after Marvelís purchase of Malibu ... 2.95

STRIKEBACK! (IMAGE)
IMAGE

❑1, Jan 1996; Reprints Strikeback (Malibu) #1 with new cover ... 2.50
❑2, Feb 1996; Reprints Strikeback (Malibu) #2 with new cover ... 2.50
❑3, Mar 1996; Reprints Strikeback (Malibu) #3 with new cover ... 2.50
❑4, Apr 1996 ... 2.50
❑5, Jun 1996 ... 2.50
❑6 1996 ... 2.50

STRIKE FORCE AMERICA
COMICO

❑1, Aug 1992 ... 2.50

STRIKE FORCE AMERICA (2ND SERIES)
COMICO

❑1 ... 2.95

STRIKE FORCE LEGACY
COMICO

❑1, Oct 1993 ... 3.95

STRIKEFORCE: MORITURI
MARVEL

❑1, Dec 1986; BA (a); 1: Strikeforce: Morituri. ... 2.00
❑2, Jan 1987 BA (a) ... 1.50
❑3, Feb 1987 BA (a) ... 1.50
❑4, Mar 1987 BA (a) ... 1.75
❑5, Apr 1987 BA (a) ... 1.25
❑6, May 1987 BA (a) ... 1.25
❑7, Jun 1987 BA (a) ... 1.25
❑8, Jul 1987 BA (a) ... 1.25
❑9, Aug 1987 BA (a) ... 1.25
❑10, Sep 1987 ... 1.25
❑11, Oct 1987 BA (a) ... 1.25
❑12, Nov 1987 BA (a) ... 1.25
❑13, Dec 1987; Giant-size BA (a) ... 1.50
❑14, Jan 1988 BA (a) ... 1.25
❑15, Feb 1988 BA (a) ... 1.25
❑16, Mar 1988 ... 1.25
❑17, Apr 1988 ... 1.25
❑18, May 1988 BA (a) ... 1.25
❑19, Jun 1988 BA (a) ... 1.25
❑20, Jul 1988 BA (a) ... 1.25
❑21, Sep 1988 ... 1.25
❑22, Oct 1988 ... 1.25
❑23, Nov 1988 ... 1.25

N-MINT

❑24, Dec 1988 ... 1.50
❑25, Jan 1989 ... 1.50
❑26, Feb 1989 ... 1.50
❑27, Mar 1989 ... 1.50
❑28, Apr 1989 ... 1.50
❑29, May 1989 ... 1.50
❑30, Jun 1989 ... 1.50
❑31, Jul 1989 ... 1.50

STRIKEFORCE: MORITURI: ELECTRIC UNDERTOW
MARVEL

❑1, Dec 1989; Strikeforce: Morituri ... 3.95
❑2, Dec 1989; Strikeforce: Morituri ... 3.95
❑3, Jan 1990; Strikeforce: Morituri ... 3.95
❑4, Feb 1990; Strikeforce: Morituri ... 3.95
❑5, Mar 1990; Strikeforce: Morituri ... 3.95

STRIKER
VIZ

❑1, b&w ... 2.75
❑2, b&w ... 2.75
❑3, b&w ... 2.75
❑4, b&w ... 2.75

STRIKER: SECRET OF THE BERSERKER
VIZ

❑1, b&w ... 2.75
❑2, b&w ... 2.75
❑3, b&w ... 2.75
❑4, b&w ... 2.75

STRIKE! VERSUS SGT. STRIKE SPECIAL
ECLIPSE

❑1, May 1988 ... 1.95

STRIPPERS AND SEX QUEENS OF THE EXOTIC WORLD
FANTAGRAPHICS

❑1 ... 3.95
❑2 ... 3.95
❑3, Jun 1994, b&w; cardstock cover ... 3.95
❑4, Oct 1994, b&w ... 3.95

STRIPS
RIP OFF

❑1, Dec 1989, b&w ... 2.50
❑2, Feb 1990, b&w ... 2.50
❑3, Apr 1990, b&w ... 2.50
❑4, Jun 1990, b&w ... 2.50
❑5, Nov 1990, b&w ... 2.50
❑6, Dec 1990, b&w ... 2.50
❑7, Feb 1991, b&w ... 2.50
❑8, Mar 1991, b&w ... 2.50
❑9, Jun 1991, b&w; series goes on hiatus ... 2.50
❑10, b&w; series returns (1997); wraparound cover ... 2.95
❑11, b&w; wraparound cover ... 2.95
❑12, b&w ... 2.95
❑Special 1; reprints Rip Off issues with additional material ... 2.95
❑Special 2; reprints Rip Off issues with additional material ... 2.95

STRONG GUY REBORN
MARVEL

❑1, Sep 1997; gatefold summary ... 2.99

STRONTIUM BITCH
FLEETWAY-QUALITY

❑1 ... 2.95
❑2 ... 2.95

STRONTIUM DOG (MINI-SERIES)
EAGLE

❑1 1985 O: Johnny Alpha. ... 1.50
❑2 1985 ... 1.50
❑3 1985 ... 1.50
❑4 1985 ... 1.50

STRONTIUM DOG
FLEETWAY-QUALITY

❑1 1997 ... 1.50
❑2 1997 ... 1.25
❑3 1997 ... 1.25
❑4 1997 ... 1.25

After The Human Torch departed the series with #134, Nick Fury's secret agent adventures began in *Strange Tales* #135.

© 1965 Marvel Comics

N-MINT

❑5 1997 ... 1.25
❑6 1997 ... 1.25
❑7 1988 ... 1.25
❑8, Feb 1988 ... 1.25
❑9, Mar 1988 ... 1.25
❑10, Apr 1988 ... 1.25
❑11 1988 ... 1.25
❑12 1988 ... 1.25
❑13 1988 ... 1.50
❑14 1988; double issue #14/15 ... 1.50
❑15 1988 ... 1.50
❑16 1988; double issue #16/17 ... 1.50
❑17 1988 ... 1.50
❑18 1988 ... 1.50
❑19 ... 1.50
❑20, Dec 1988 ... 1.50
❑21, Jan 1989 ... 1.50
❑22, Feb 1989 ... 1.50
❑23 ... 1.50
❑24 ... 1.50
❑25 ... 1.50
❑26 ... 1.50
❑27 ... 1.50
❑28 ... 1.50
❑29 ... 1.50
❑Special 1; Special Edition #1; AMo (w); Reprints from 2000 A.D. #87-94 ... 1.50

STRÜDEL WAR
ROUGH COPY

❑1; Flip-book ... 2.95

STRYFE'S STRIKE FILE
MARVEL

❑1, Jan 1993; Follows X-Cutioner's Song x-over series ... 1.75
❑1-2, Jan 1993; Gold cover ... 1.75

STRYKE
LONDON NIGHT

❑0 ... 3.00
❑0/A; alternate cover ... 4.00
❑1 ... 3.00

STRYKEFORCE
IMAGE

❑1, May 2004 ... 2.99
❑2, Apr 2004 ... 2.99
❑3, Aug 2004 ... 2.99

STUDIO COMICS PRESENTS
STUDIO

❑1, May 1995; Battle Bunnies ... 2.50

STUNT DAWGS
HARVEY

❑1, Mar 1993 ... 1.25

STUPID
IMAGE

❑1, May 1993; parody ... 1.95

STUPID COMICS
ONI

❑1, Jul 2000, b&w; collects Mahfood's strips from Java Magazine ... 2.95

STUPID COMICS (IMAGE)
IMAGE

❑1, Sep 2003 ... 2.95
❑2, Oct 2003 ... 2.95

N-MINT

STUPID HEROES
MIRAGE / NEXT

- ❑1, Aug 1994 .... 2.75
- ❑2, Oct 1994 .... 2.75
- ❑3, Dec 1994 .... 2.75

STUPIDMAN
PARODY

- ❑1 .... 2.50

STUPIDMAN: BURIAL FOR A BUDDY
PARODY

- ❑1/A, b&w 2.50
- ❑1/B, b&w 2.50

STUPIDMAN: RAIN ON THE STUPIDMEN
PARODY

- ❑1/A, b&w 2.50
- ❑1/B, b&w 2.95

STUPID, STUPID RAT TAILS
CARTOON BOOKS

- ❑1, Dec 1999 .... 2.95
- ❑2, Jan 2001 .... 2.95
- ❑3, Feb 2001 .... 2.95

STYGMATA
EXPRESS / ENTITY

- ❑0 1994 .... 2.95
- ❑1, Jul 1994, b&w; enhanced cover .. 2.95
- ❑2 1994; Foil-stamped cover 2.95
- ❑3, Oct 1994, b&w 2.95

SUBHUMAN
DARK HORSE

- ❑1, Nov 1998 .... 2.95
- ❑2, Dec 1998 .... 2.95
- ❑3, Jan 1999 .... 2.95
- ❑4, Feb 1999 .... 2.95

SUBMARINE ATTACK
CHARLTON

- ❑11, May 1958 .... 24.00
- ❑12 1958 .... 16.00
- ❑13, Oct 1958; Below the Storm; Fire Ships of Antwerp (text story); Gestapo's Prize; Hidden Menace; The World Below 16.00
- ❑14 .... 16.00
- ❑15 .... 16.00
- ❑16 1959 .... 16.00
- ❑17 1959 .... 16.00
- ❑18 .... 16.00
- ❑19 .... 16.00
- ❑20 .... 16.00
- ❑21, Apr 1960, Disneyland TWA contest ad on back 12.00
- ❑22 1960 .... 12.00
- ❑23 1960 .... 12.00
- ❑24, Oct 1960, Ran contest for winning a car 12.00
- ❑25, Dec 1960 .... 12.00
- ❑26, Feb 1961 .... 12.00
- ❑27, Apr 1961 .... 12.00
- ❑28, Jun 1961 .... 12.00
- ❑29, Aug 1961, Contains contest for readers to win a swimming pool ... 12.00
- ❑30 1961 .... 12.00
- ❑31 1962 .... 9.00
- ❑32, Mar 1962 .... 9.00
- ❑33 1962 .... 9.00
- ❑34 1962 .... 9.00
- ❑35 1962 .... 9.00
- ❑36 1962 .... 9.00
- ❑37, Jan 1963 .... 9.00
- ❑38 1963 .... 9.00
- ❑39 1963 .... 9.00
- ❑40 1963 .... 9.00
- ❑41, Sep 1963 .... 7.00
- ❑42 1963 .... 7.00
- ❑43 1964 .... 7.00
- ❑44, Mar 1964 .... 7.00
- ❑45, Jun 1964 .... 7.00
- ❑46 1964 .... 7.00
- ❑47 1964 .... 7.00
- ❑48, Jan 1965 .... 7.00
- ❑49, Mar 1965 .... 7.00
- ❑50 1965 .... 7.00
- ❑51, Aug 1965 .... 7.00
- ❑52 1965 .... 7.00
- ❑53, Dec 1965 .... 7.00
- ❑54, Feb 1966 .... 7.00

SUB-MARINER, THE (VOL. 2)
MARVEL

- ❑1, May 1968 JB (a); O: Sub-Mariner. 75.00
- ❑2, Jun 1968 JB (a); A: Triton. 25.00
- ❑3, Jul 1968 JB (a); A: Triton. 15.00
- ❑4, Aug 1968 JB (a) 15.00
- ❑5, Sep 1968 JB (a); O: Tiger Shark. 1: Tiger Shark. 16.00
- ❑6, Oct 1968 JB (a) 15.00
- ❑7, Nov 1968; JB (a); 1: Ikthon. Cover is black-and-white photo of New York parade; drawing of Namor superimposed 15.00
- ❑8, Dec 1968 JB (a); V: Thing. 15.00
- ❑8-2 JB (a); V: The Thing. 1.50
- ❑9, Jan 1969 1: Lemuria. 1: Naga. 15.00
- ❑10, Feb 1969 O: Naga. 15.00
- ❑11, Mar 1969 .... 12.00
- ❑12, Apr 1969 .... 12.00
- ❑13, May 1969 .... 12.00
- ❑14, Jun 1969 A: Human Torch. D: Toro. 20.00
- ❑15, Jul 1969 .... 10.00
- ❑16, Aug 1969 1: Thakos. 8.00
- ❑17, Sep 1969 1: Kormok. 8.00
- ❑18, Oct 1969 .... 8.00
- ❑19, Nov 1969 O: Stingray. 1: Stingray. 8.00
- ❑20, Dec 1969 .... 8.00
- ❑21, Jan 1970 .... 6.00
- ❑22, Feb 1970 A: Doctor Strange. 6.00
- ❑23, Mar 1970 O: Orka. 1: Orka. 6.00
- ❑24, Apr 1970 .... 6.00
- ❑25, May 1970 O: Atlantis. 6.00
- ❑26, Jun 1970 A: Red Raven. D: Red Raven. 6.00
- ❑27, Jul 1970 SB (a); 1: Commander Kraken. 6.00
- ❑28, Aug 1970 .... 6.00
- ❑29, Sep 1970 SB (a); V: Hercules. ... 6.00
- ❑30, Oct 1970 SB (a); A: Captain Marvel. 6.00
- ❑31, Nov 1970 .... 6.00
- ❑32, Dec 1970 O: Llyra. 1: Llyra. 6.00
- ❑33, Jan 1971 SB, JM (a); 1: Namora. 6.00
- ❑34, Feb 1971; SB, JM (a); A: Hulk. A: Silver Surfer. Leads into Defenders #1 .... 12.00
- ❑35, Mar 1971 SB, JM (a); A: Hulk. A: Silver Surfer. 12.00
- ❑36, Apr 1971; BWr, SB (a); 1: The Octo-Meks. Wedding of Lady Dorma 6.00
- ❑37, May 1971 RA (a); D: Lady Dorma. 6.00
- ❑38, Jun 1971 JSe, RA (a); O: Sub-Mariner. 6.00
- ❑39, Jul 1971 RA, JM (a) 6.00
- ❑40, Aug 1971 A: Spider-Man. 6.00
- ❑41, Sep 1971 GT (a) 3.00
- ❑42, Oct 1971 GT (a) 3.00
- ❑43, Nov 1971; Giant-size 3.00
- ❑44, Dec 1971 A: Human Torch. 3.00
- ❑45, Jan 1972 .... 3.00
- ❑46, Feb 1972 GC (a) 3.00
- ❑47, Mar 1972 GC (a) 3.00
- ❑48, Apr 1972 GC (a) 3.00
- ❑49, May 1972 GC (a) 3.00
- ❑50, Jun 1972 BEv (a); 1: Namorita. . 6.00
- ❑51, Jul 1972 BEv (a) 3.00
- ❑52, Aug 1972; BEv (a); Marvel Value Stamp # 3.00
- ❑53, Sep 1972; BEv (a); Reprinted from Sub-Mariner (Vol. 1) #41 .... 3.00
- ❑54, Oct 1972; BEv (a); 1: Lorvex. Reprinted from Sub-Mariner (Vol. 1) #39 .... 3.00
- ❑55, Nov 1972 BEv (a) 3.00
- ❑56, Dec 1972 1: Tamara Rahn. 3.00
- ❑57, Jan 1973 .... 3.00
- ❑58, Feb 1973 BEv (a) 3.00
- ❑59, Mar 1973 BEv (a) 3.00
- ❑60, Apr 1973 BEv (a) 3.00
- ❑61, May 1973 .... 3.00
- ❑62, Jun 1973; Tales of Atlantis 3.00
- ❑63, Jul 1973; 1: Arkus. 1: Volpan. Tales of Atlantis 3.00
- ❑64, Aug 1973; 1: Madoxx. Tales of Atlantis 3.00
- ❑65, Sep 1973; Tales of Atlantis 3.00
- ❑66, Oct 1973; 1: Raman. Tales of Atlantis 3.00
- ❑67, Nov 1973 .... 3.00
- ❑68, Jan 1974 .... 3.00
- ❑69, Mar 1974; Marvel Value Stamp #20: Brother Voodoo 3.00
- ❑70, May 1974; Marvel Value Stamp #98: Puppet Master 3.00
- ❑71, Jul 1974; Marvel Value Stamp #52: Quicksilver 3.00
- ❑72, Sep 1974; DA (a); Marvel Value Stamp #100: Galactus 3.00
- ❑Special 1, ca. 1971; Sub-Mariner Special Edition #1; SB (a); Reprinted from Tales to Astonish #70-73 .... 6.00
- ❑Special 2, ca. 1972; Sub-Mariner Special Edition #2; BEv (a); Reprinted from Tales to Astonish #74-76 .... 6.00

SUBMISSIVE SUZANNE
FANTAGRAPHICS / EROS

- ❑1, b&w 2.50
- ❑2, b&w 2.50
- ❑3, b&w 2.95
- ❑4, b&w 2.95
- ❑5, b&w 2.95
- ❑6, Aug 1998, b&w 2.95

SUBSPECIES
ETERNITY

- ❑1, May 1991 .... 2.50
- ❑2 1991 .... 2.50
- ❑3 1991 .... 2.50
- ❑4 1991 .... 2.50

SUBSTANCE AFFECT
CRAZYFISH

- ❑1 .... 2.95

SUBSTANCE QUARTERLY
SUBSTANCE

- ❑1, Spr 1994, b&w 3.00
- ❑2, Sum 1994, b&w 3.00
- ❑3, Fal 1994, b&w 3.00

SUBTLE VIOLENTS
CRY FOR DAWN

- ❑1, ca. 1991 .... 15.00
- ❑1/A, ca. 1991; San Diego Comic-Con edition 160.00

SUBURBAN HIGH LIFE
SLAVE LABOR

- ❑1, Jun 1987 .... 1.75
- ❑1-2, Feb 1988 .... 1.75
- ❑2, Aug 1987 .... 1.75
- ❑3, Oct 1987 .... 1.75

SUBURBAN HIGH LIFE (VOL. 2)
SLAVE LABOR

- ❑1, May 1988; Oversized 5.95

SUBURBAN NIGHTMARES
RENEGADE

- ❑1, Jul 1988, b&w 2.00
- ❑2, Jul 1988, b&w 2.00
- ❑3, Aug 1988, b&w 2.00
- ❑4, Aug 1988, b&w 2.00

SUBURBAN SHE-DEVILS
MARVEL

- ❑1; Cover reads Suburban Jersey Ninja She-Devils 1.50

SUBURBAN VOODOO
FANTAGRAPHICS

- ❑1, b&w 2.50

SUCCUBUS
FANTAGRAPHICS / EROS

- ❑1, b&w 2.50

SUCKER THE COMIC
TROMA

	N-MINT
❑1	2.50

SUCKLE
FANTAGRAPHICS

	N-MINT
❑1, Jan 1996, b&w; digest	14.95

SUGAR & SPIKE
DC

	N-MINT
❑1, May 1956 O: Spike. O: Sugar.	1575.00
❑1-2, Mar 2002; Facsimile Edition	2.95
❑2, Jul 1956	575.00
❑3, Sep 1956	450.00
❑4, Nov 1956	450.00
❑5, Jan 1957	450.00
❑6, Mar 1957	300.00
❑7, May 1957	300.00
❑8, Jun 1957	300.00
❑9, Aug 1957	300.00
❑10, Sep 1957	300.00
❑11, Oct 1957	230.00
❑12, Dec 1957	230.00
❑13, Feb 1958	230.00
❑14, Mar 1958	230.00
❑15, Apr 1958; left-handedness	230.00
❑16, Jun 1958	230.00
❑17, Aug 1958	230.00
❑18, Sep 1958	230.00
❑19, Oct 1958	230.00
❑20, Dec 1958	230.00
❑21, Mar 1959	145.00
❑22, May 1959	145.00
❑23, Jul 1959	145.00
❑24, Sep 1959	145.00
❑25, Nov 1959; Halloween issue	145.00
❑26, Jan 1960; Christmas issue	145.00
❑27, Mar 1960; Valentine's issue	145.00
❑28, May 1960	145.00
❑29, Jul 1960	145.00
❑30, Sep 1960	145.00
❑31, Nov 1960; Halloween issue	110.00
❑32, Jan 1961; Christmas issue	110.00
❑33, Mar 1961	110.00
❑34, May 1961	110.00
❑35, Jul 1961 A: Grampa Plumm.	110.00
❑36, Sep 1961	110.00
❑37, Nov 1961; Halloween issue	110.00
❑38, Jan 1962; Christmas issue with Christmas cards	110.00
❑39, Mar 1962; Valentine's issue with valentines	110.00
❑40, May 1962 1: Space Sprout.	110.00
❑41, Jul 1962	75.00
❑42, Sep 1962; Vacation issue	75.00
❑43, Nov 1962; Halloween issue	75.00
❑44, Jan 1963; Christmas issue with Christmas cards	75.00
❑45, Mar 1963; Valentine's issue with valentines	75.00
❑46, May 1963; Wedding cover	75.00
❑47, Jul 1963	75.00
❑48, Sep 1963	75.00
❑49, Nov 1963; Halloween issue	75.00
❑50, Jan 1964; Christmas issue with Christmas cards	75.00
❑51, Mar 1964; Valentine's issue with valentines	58.00
❑52, May 1964	58.00
❑53, Jul 1964	58.00
❑54, Sep 1964	58.00
❑55, Nov 1964; Halloween issue	58.00
❑56, Jan 1965; Christmas issue with Christmas cards	58.00
❑57, Mar 1965; Valentine's issue with valentines	58.00
❑58, May 1965	58.00
❑59, Jul 1965	58.00
❑60, Sep 1965	58.00
❑61, Nov 1965; A: Uncle Charley. Halloween issue	48.00
❑62, Jan 1966; Christmas issue with Christmas cards	48.00
❑63, Mar 1966; Valentine's issue with valentines	48.00
❑64, May 1966	48.00
❑65, Jul 1966; Summer issue	48.00
❑66, Sep 1966	48.00
❑67, Nov 1966; Halloween issue	48.00
❑68, Jan 1967; Christmas issue	48.00
❑69, Mar 1967 1: Tornado Tot.	48.00
❑70, May 1967; Sugar & Spike become giants	48.00
❑71, Jul 1967	48.00
❑72, Sep 1967 1: Bernie the Brain.	48.00
❑73, Nov 1967	48.00
❑74, Jan 1968	48.00
❑75, Mar 1968 1: M.C.P. pellet.	48.00
❑76, May 1968	48.00
❑77, Jul 1968 A: Bernie the Brain.	48.00
❑78, Sep 1968	48.00
❑79, Nov 1968	48.00
❑80, Jan 1969 A: Bernie the Brain.	48.00
❑81, Mar 1969	34.00
❑82, May 1969; Sugar & Spike as grown-ups	34.00
❑83, Jul 1969; super-powers	34.00
❑84, Sep 1969	34.00
❑85, Oct 1969	34.00
❑86, Nov 1969	34.00
❑87, Jan 1970 1: Marvin the Midget.	34.00
❑88, Mar 1970	34.00
❑89, May 1970	34.00
❑90, Jul 1970 1: Flumsh.	34.00
❑91, Sep 1970	34.00
❑92, Nov 1970	34.00
❑93, Jan 1971	34.00
❑94, Mar 1971 1: Raymond.	34.00
❑95, May 1971	34.00
❑96, Jul 1971	34.00
❑97, Sep 1971	34.00
❑98, Nov 1971	34.00

SUGAR BUZZ
SLAVE LABOR

	N-MINT
❑1, Jan 1998, b&w	2.95
❑2 1998	2.95
❑3 1998	2.95
❑4 1998	2.95

SUGAR RAY FINHEAD
WOLF

	N-MINT
❑1	2.50
❑2	2.95
❑3	2.95
❑4	2.95
❑5; Publisher changes to Jump Back Productions	2.95
❑6, Jul 1994	2.95
❑7, Nov 1994, b&w	2.95
❑8, Feb 1995, b&w	2.95
❑9, Aug 1995, b&w	2.95
❑10, Sep 1997	2.95
❑11, Oct 1998	2.95

SUGARVIRUS
ATOMEKA

	N-MINT
❑1, b&w	3.95

SUICIDE SQUAD
DC

	N-MINT
❑1, May 1987 HC (c)	1.25
❑2, Jun 1987	1.00
❑3, Jul 1987 D: Mindboggler. V: Female Furies.	1.00
❑4, Aug 1987	1.00
❑5, Sep 1987	1.00
❑6, Oct 1987	1.00
❑7, Nov 1987	1.00
❑8, Dec 1987	1.00
❑9, Jan 1988; 1: Duchess. Millennium Week 4	1.00
❑10, Feb 1988 A: Batman.	1.00
❑11, Mar 1988 A: Speedy, Vixen.	1.00
❑12, Apr 1988	1.00
❑13, May 1988; A: Justice League International. continued from Justice League International #13; Suicide Squad view of Justice League	1.00
❑14, Jun 1988	1.00
❑15, Jul 1988	1.00
❑16, Aug 1988 A: Shade, the Changing Man.	1.00
❑17, Sep 1988 V: Jihad.	1.00
❑18, Oct 1988; Ravan vs. Bronze Tiger	1.00
❑19, Nov 1988	1.00
❑20, Dec 1988	1.00
❑21, Dec 1988	1.00
❑22, Jan 1989	1.00
❑23, Jan 1989	1.00
❑24, Feb 1989	1.00
❑25, Mar 1989	1.00
❑26, Apr 1989	1.00
❑27, May 1989	1.00
❑28, May 1989 V: Force of July.	1.00
❑29, Jun 1989	1.00
❑30, Jun 1989	1.00
❑31, Jul 1989	1.00
❑32, Aug 1989	1.00
❑33, Sep 1989	1.00
❑34, Oct 1989	1.00
❑35, Nov 1989	1.00
❑36, Dec 1989	1.00
❑37, Jan 1990	1.00
❑38, Feb 1990	1.00
❑39, Mar 1990	1.00
❑40, Apr 1990	1.00
❑41, May 1990	1.00
❑42, Jun 1990	1.00
❑43, Jul 1990	1.00
❑44, Aug 1990; Flash	1.00
❑45, Sep 1990	1.00
❑46, Oct 1990	1.00
❑47, Nov 1990	1.00
❑48, Dec 1990; Joker	1.00
❑49, Jan 1991	1.00
❑50, Feb 1991	1.50
❑51, Mar 1991	1.00
❑52, Apr 1991	1.00
❑53, May 1991	1.00
❑54, Jun 1991	1.00
❑55, Jul 1991	1.00
❑56, Aug 1991	1.00
❑57, Sep 1991	1.00
❑58, Oct 1991 A: Black Adam.	1.00
❑59, Nov 1991	1.00
❑60, Dec 1991	1.00
❑61, Jan 1992	1.00
❑62, Feb 1992	1.00
❑63, Mar 1992	1.00
❑64, Apr 1992	1.25
❑65, May 1992	1.25
❑66, Jun 1992	1.25
❑Annual 1; A: Manhunter. secret of Argent revealed	1.50

After facing off against the original Human Torch numerous times in the Golden Age, Namor found a new sparring partner in The Thing in the Silver Age.

© 1968 Marvel Comics.

SUICIDE SQUAD (2ND SERIES)
DC

	N-MINT
❑1, Nov 2001	2.50
❑2, Dec 2001	2.50
❑3, Jan 2002	2.50
❑4, Feb 2002	2.50
❑5, Mar 2002	2.50
❑6, Apr 2002	2.50
❑7, May 2002	2.50
❑8, Jun 2002	2.50
❑9, Jul 2002	2.50
❑10, Aug 2002	2.50

N-MINT

❑11, Oct 2002 ... 2.50
❑12, Nov 2002 ... 2.50

SUIKODEN III: THE SUCCESSOR OF FATE
TOKYOPOP

❑1, May 2004 ... 9.99

SUIT, THE
VIRTUAL

❑1/A, May 1996 ... 3.99
❑1, May 1996 ... 2.50
❑2/A, Jun 1997 ... 3.99
❑2, Jun 1997 ... 3.99

SULTRY TEENAGE SUPER FOXES
SOLSON

❑1, b&w ... 2.00
❑2, b&w ... 2.00

SUMMER LOVE
CHARLTON

❑46, ca. 1965 ... 95.00
❑47, Oct 1966; Beatles cover drawings in ad for Help! and Hard Days Night 70.00
❑48, ca. 1967 ... 15.00

SUNBURN
ALTERNATIVE

❑1, Aug 2000, b&w; smaller than normal comic book ... 2.95

SUN DEVILS
DC

❑1, Jul 1984 ... 1.50
❑2, Aug 1984 ... 1.50
❑3, Sep 1984 ... 1.50
❑4, Oct 1984 ... 1.50
❑5, Nov 1984 ... 1.50
❑6, Dec 1984 ... 1.50
❑7, Jan 1985 ... 1.50
❑8, Feb 1985 ... 1.50
❑9, Mar 1985 ... 1.50
❑10, Apr 1985 ... 1.50
❑11, May 1985 ... 1.50
❑12, Jun 1985 ... 1.50

SUNFIRE & BIG HERO SIX
MARVEL

❑1, Sep 1998 ... 2.50
❑2, Oct 1998 ... 2.50
❑3, Nov 1998 ... 2.50

SUNGLASSES AFTER DARK
VEROTIK

❑1, Nov 1995 ... 2.95
❑2 ... 2.95
❑3, Mar 1996 ... 2.95
❑4, Aug 1996 ... 2.95
❑5, Oct 1996 ... 2.95
❑6, Nov 1996 ... 3.95

SUNRISE
HARRIER

❑1, Dec 1986 ... 1.95
❑2, May 1987 ... 1.95

SUN-RUNNERS
PACIFIC

❑1, Feb 1984 ... 1.50
❑2, Mar 1984 ... 1.50
❑3, May 1984 ... 1.50
❑4 1984 ... 1.50
❑5 1984 ... 1.75
❑6 1984 ... 1.75
❑7 1984 ... 1.75
❑Holiday 1; Double-size ... 1.95
❑Special 1; Special edition ... 1.95

SUPERBOY (1ST SERIES)
DC

❑52, Oct 1956 ... 110.00
❑53, Dec 1956 ... 110.00
❑54, Jan 1957 ... 110.00
❑55, Mar 1957 ... 110.00
❑56, Apr 1957 ... 110.00
❑57, Jun 1957 ... 110.00
❑58, Jul 1957 ... 110.00
❑59, Sep 1957 ... 110.00
❑60, Oct 1957 ... 110.00
❑61, Dec 1957 ... 90.00
❑62, Jan 1958 ... 90.00
❑63, Mar 1958 ... 90.00
❑64, Apr 1958 ... 90.00
❑65, Jun 1958 ... 90.00
❑66, Jul 1958 ... 90.00
❑67, Sep 1958; O: Klax-Ar. 1: Klax-Ar. 90.00
❑68, Oct 1958 O: Bizarro. 1: Bizarro. . 475.00
❑69, Dec 1958 ... 70.00
❑70, Jan 1959 O: Mr. Mxyzptlk. ... 70.00
❑71, Mar 1959 ... 70.00
❑72, Apr 1959 CS (a) ... 70.00
❑73, Jun 1959 ... 70.00
❑74, Jul 1959 ... 70.00
❑75, Sep 1959 ... 70.00
❑76, Oct 1959 1: Supermonkey. ... 70.00
❑77, Dec 1959 ... 70.00
❑78, Jan 1960 O: Mr. Mxyzptlk. ... 135.00
❑79, Mar 1960 ... 70.00
❑80, Apr 1960; Superboy meets Supergirl ... 110.00
❑81, Jun 1960 ... 52.00
❑82, Jul 1960 A: Bizarro Krypto. ... 52.00
❑83, Sep 1960 O: Kryptonite Kid. 1: Kryptonite Kid. ... 52.00
❑84, Oct 1960 V: Rainbow Raider. ... 52.00
❑85, Dec 1960 ... 52.00
❑86, Jan 1961 1: Pete Ross. A: Legion of Super-Heroes. ... 125.00
❑87, Mar 1961 ... 52.00
❑88, Apr 1961 ... 52.00
❑89, Jun 1961 O: Mon-El. 1: Mon-El. 220.00
❑90, Jul 1961 CS (a) ... 48.00
❑91, Sep 1961 ... 48.00
❑92, Oct 1961 ... 48.00
❑93, Dec 1961 A: Legion of Super-Heroes. ... 48.00
❑94, Jan 1962 ... 35.00
❑95, Mar 1962 ... 35.00
❑96, Apr 1962 ... 35.00
❑97, Jun 1962 ... 35.00
❑98, Jul 1962 CS (a); O: Ultra Boy. 1: Ultra Boy. A: Legion of Super-Heroes. ... 45.00
❑99, Sep 1962 ... 35.00
❑100, Oct 1962; 100th anniversary issue 1: Phantom Zone villains. A: Legion of Super-Heroes. ... 175.00
❑101, Dec 1962 ... 16.00
❑102, Jan 1963; Superbaby back-up . 16.00
❑103, Mar 1963; Red K story ... 16.00
❑104, Apr 1963 O: Phantom Zone. ... 16.00
❑105, Jun 1963 ... 16.00
❑106, Jul 1963 ... 16.00
❑107, Sep 1963 ... 16.00
❑108, Oct 1963 ... 16.00
❑109, Dec 1963 ... 16.00
❑110, Jan 1964 ... 16.00
❑111, Mar 1964 ... 15.00
❑112, Apr 1964 ... 15.00
❑113, Jun 1964 ... 15.00
❑114, Jul 1964 ... 15.00
❑115, Sep 1964; Atomic Superboy ... 15.00
❑116, Oct 1964 ... 15.00
❑117, Dec 1964 A: Legion. ... 15.00
❑118, Jan 1965 ... 15.00
❑119, Mar 1965 ... 15.00
❑120, Apr 1965 ... 15.00
❑121, Jun 1965; Clark loses his superpowers; Jor-El back-up ... 10.00
❑122, Jul 1965 ... 10.00
❑123, Sep 1965 ... 10.00
❑124, Oct 1965 1: Insect Queen. ... 10.00
❑125, Dec 1965 O: Kid Psycho. 1: Kid Psycho. ... 10.00
❑126, Jan 1966 O: Krypto. ... 10.00
❑127, Mar 1966 ... 10.00
❑128, Apr 1966; A: Dev-Em. A: Kryptonite Kid. Imaginary Story ... 10.00
❑129, May 1966; Giant-size ... 13.00
❑130, Jun 1966; Superbaby ... 8.00
❑131, Jul 1966 ... 8.00
❑132, Sep 1966 ... 8.00
❑133, Oct 1966 A: Robin. ... 8.00
❑134, Dec 1966; Krypto back-up ... 8.00
❑135, Jan 1967 ... 8.00
❑136, Mar 1967; CS (a); A: White Kryptonite. reprints story from Adventure Comics #279 ... 8.00
❑137, Apr 1967 ... 8.00
❑138, Jun 1967; Giant-size ... 13.00
❑139, Jun 1967 ... 7.00
❑140, Jul 1967 ... 7.00
❑141, Sep 1967 ... 6.00
❑142, Oct 1967 A: Beppo. ... 6.00
❑143, Dec 1967 NA (c) ... 6.00
❑144, Jan 1968 CS (c) ... 6.00
❑145, Mar 1968 NA (c) ... 6.00
❑146, Apr 1968 NA (c) ... 6.00
❑147, Jun 1968; Giant-size; CS, JM (a); O: Saturn Girl. O: Cosmic Boy. G-47; new story w/ reprints from Superboy #93 and #98, Action Comics #276, Adventure Comics #293, and Superman #147 ... 10.00
❑148, Jun 1968 NA (c) ... 6.00
❑149, Jul 1968 NA (c) ... 6.00
❑150, Sep 1968 NA (c); JAb (a); V: Mr. Cipher. ... 6.00
❑151, Oct 1968 NA (c); JAb (a) ... 6.00
❑152, Dec 1968 NA (c); WW (a) ... 6.00
❑153, Jan 1969 NA (c); FR (w); WW (a) 6.00
❑154, Mar 1969 NA (c); WW (a) ... 6.00
❑155, Apr 1969 NA (c); WW (a) ... 6.00
❑156, Jun 1969; Giant-size ... 9.00
❑157, Jun 1969 WW (a) ... 6.00
❑158, Jul 1969 WW (a) ... 6.00
❑159, Sep 1969 WW (a) ... 6.00
❑160, Oct 1969 WW (a) ... 6.00
❑161, Dec 1969 FR (w); WW (a) ... 6.00
❑162, Jan 1970 ... 6.00
❑163, Mar 1970 NA (c) ... 6.00
❑164, Apr 1970 NA (c) ... 6.00
❑165, Jun 1970; Giant-size; CS (c); CS (a); Reprints Adventure #210 & #283, and Superman #161 ... 9.00
❑166, Jun 1970 NA (c) ... 6.00
❑167, Jul 1970 NA (c) ... 6.00
❑168, Sep 1970 NA (c) ... 6.00
❑169, Oct 1970 ... 6.00
❑170, Dec 1970 ... 6.00
❑171, Jan 1971 ... 4.00
❑172, Mar 1971 A: Legion of Super-Heroes. ... 5.00
❑173, Apr 1971 NA (c); GT, DG (a); O: Cosmic Boy. ... 4.00
❑174, Jun 1971; Giant-size; reprints Adventure #219, #225, and #262, Superboy #53 and #105 ... 7.00
❑175, Jun 1971 NA (c); MA (a) ... 4.00
❑176, Jul 1971 NA (c); MA, GT, WW (a); A: Legion of Super-Heroes. ... 4.00
❑177, Sep 1971; Giant-size MA (a) ... 4.00
❑178, Oct 1971; Giant-size NA (c); MA (a) ... 4.00
❑179, Nov 1971; Giant-size ... 4.00
❑180, Dec 1971; Giant-size ... 4.00
❑181, Jan 1972; Giant-size; reprints Adventure #355 ... 4.00
❑182, Feb 1972; Giant-size ... 4.00
❑183, Mar 1972; Giant-size ... 4.00
❑184, Apr 1972; Giant-size O: Dial "H" For Hero. O: Dial H for Hero. ... 4.00
❑185, May 1972; NC (c); CS (a); A: Legion of Super-Heroes. a.k.a. DC 100-Page Super Spectacular #185; Reprints from Adventure #208, #289 and 323, Brave and the Bold #60, Hit Comics #46, Sensation #1, and Star Spangled Comics #55; wraparound cover ... 4.00
❑186, May 1972 ... 4.00
❑187, Jun 1972 ... 4.00
❑188, Jul 1972 O: Karkan. ... 4.00
❑189, Aug 1972 ... 4.00
❑190, Sep 1972 ... 4.00
❑191, Oct 1972 O: Sunboy. ... 4.00
❑192, Dec 1972; Superbaby ... 4.00
❑193, Feb 1973 ... 4.00

	N-MINT
❑194, Apr 1973	4.00
❑195, Jun 1973; 1: Wildfire. A: Legion of Super-Heroes. Wildfire joins team	4.00
❑196, Jul 1973; last Superboy solo story	4.00
❑197, Sep 1973; MA (a); Legion of Super-Heroes stories begin	6.00
❑198, Oct 1973 V: Fatal Five.	4.00
❑199, Nov 1973	4.00
❑200, Feb 1974; Wedding of Bouncing Boy and Duo Damsel	6.00
❑201, Apr 1974	3.00
❑202, Jun 1974; 100-page giant; NC (c); MGr, DC, CS (a); New stories and reprints from Superboy #91 and Adventure #342, #344, & #345	3.00
❑203, Aug 1974 MGr (a); D: Invisible Kid I (Lyle Norg). V: Validus.	3.00
❑204, Oct 1974 MGr (a); 1: Anti Lad.	3.00
❑205, Dec 1974; MGr, DC, CS (a); reprints Superboy #88, Adventure #350 and #351	3.00
❑206, Jan 1975 MGr (a)	3.00
❑207, Feb 1975 MGr (a)	3.00
❑208, Apr 1975 MGr, CS (a)	3.00
❑209, Jun 1975 MGr (a)	3.00
❑210, Aug 1975 MGr (a); O: Karate Kid.	3.00
❑211, Sep 1975 MGr (a); A: Legion Subs.	3.00
❑212, Oct 1975; MGr (a); Matter-Eater Lad leaves team	3.00
❑213, Dec 1975 A: Miracle Machine.	3.00
❑214, Jan 1976	3.00
❑215, Mar 1976	3.00
❑216, Apr 1976 1: Tyroc.	3.00
❑217, Jun 1976 1: Laurel Kent.	3.00
❑218, Jul 1976; Tyroc joins team; Bicentennial #22	3.00
❑219, Sep 1976 V: Fatal Five.	3.00
❑220, Oct 1976	3.00
❑221, Nov 1976 O: Charma. O: Grimbor. 1: Charma. 1: Grimbor.	2.00
❑222, Dec 1976	2.00
❑223, Jan 1977 1: Pulsar Stargrave. V: Time Trapper.	2.00
❑224, Feb 1977 V: Stargrave.	2.00
❑225, Mar 1977 1: Dawnstar.	2.00
❑226, Apr 1977; Dawnstar joins team; Stargrave's identity revealed	2.00
❑227, May 1977	2.00
❑228, Jun 1977 D: Chemical King.	2.00
❑229, Jul 1977	2.00
❑230, Aug 1977; Bouncing Boy's powers restored; series continues as Superboy and the Legion of Super-Heroes	2.00
❑Annual 1, Sum 1964	140.00
❑SP 1, ca. 1980; Superboy Spectacular; giant; pin-up back cover	4.00

SUPERBOY (2ND SERIES)
DC

	N-MINT
❑1, Jan 1990 JM (a)	2.00
❑2, Feb 1990	1.50
❑3, Mar 1990	1.50
❑4, Apr 1990	1.50
❑5, May 1990	1.50
❑6, Jun 1990	1.50
❑7, Jul 1990 JM (a)	1.50
❑8, Aug 1990; Bizarro	1.50
❑9, Sep 1990 CS (a)	1.50
❑10, Oct 1990 CS (a)	1.50
❑11, Nov 1990 CS (a)	1.50
❑12, Dec 1990 CS (a)	1.50
❑13, Jan 1991; Mxyzptlk	1.50
❑14, Feb 1991 V: Brimstone.	1.50
❑15, Mar 1991	1.50
❑16, Apr 1991 A: Superman.	1.50
❑17, May 1991	1.50
❑18, Jun 1991; Series continued in Adventures of Superboy #19	1.50
❑Special 1, ca. 1992 CS (a)	2.00

SUPERBOY (3RD SERIES)
DC

	N-MINT
❑0, Oct 1994; O: Superboy (clone). Comes between issues #8 and 9	2.00
❑1, Feb 1994	2.50
❑2, Mar 1994 1: Scavenger. 1: Knockout.	2.00
❑3, Apr 1994 V: Scavenger.	2.00
❑4, May 1994	2.00
❑5, Jun 1994	2.00
❑6, Jul 1994; Worlds Collide, Part 3; crossover with Milestone Media	2.00
❑7, Aug 1994; Worlds Collide, Part 8; crossover with Milestone Media	2.00
❑8, Sep 1994; Zero Hour; meets original Superboy	2.00
❑9, Nov 1994	2.00
❑10, Dec 1994	2.00
❑11, Jan 1995	2.00
❑12, Feb 1995	2.00
❑13, Mar 1995; Watery Grave, Part 1	2.00
❑14, Apr 1995; Watery Grave, Part 2	2.00
❑15, May 1995; Watery Grave, Part 3	2.00
❑16, Jun 1995 V: Loose Cannon.	2.00
❑17, Jul 1995	2.00
❑18, Aug 1995 V: Valor.	2.00
❑19, Sep 1995; Valor enters Phantom Zone	2.00
❑20, Oct 1995 A: Green Lantern.	2.00
❑21, Nov 1995; Future Tense, Part 1; continues in Legion of Super-Heroes #74	2.00
❑22, Dec 1995; A: Killer Frost. Underworld Unleashed	2.00
❑23, Jan 1996	2.00
❑24, Feb 1996; V: Silver Sword. Knockout's past revealed	2.00
❑25, Mar 1996; Giant-size; Losin' It, Part 1; pin-up pages	3.00
❑26, Apr 1996; Losin' It, Part 2	2.00
❑27, May 1996; Losin' It, Part 3	2.00
❑28, Jun 1996; A: Supergirl. Losin' It, Part 4	2.00
❑29, Jul 1996; Losin' It, Part 5	2.00
❑30, Aug 1996; Losin' It, Part 6; Knockout captured	2.00
❑31, Sep 1996	2.00
❑32, Oct 1996 O: Superboy.	2.00
❑33, Nov 1996; Final Night	2.00
❑34, Dec 1996; Dubbilex regains powers	2.00
❑35, Jan 1997 1: The Agenda.	2.00
❑36, Feb 1997 V: Match.	2.00
❑37, Mar 1997 SB (a)	2.00
❑38, Apr 1997 SB (a)	2.00
❑39, May 1997	2.00
❑40, Jun 1997; continues in Superboy & the Ravers #10	2.00
❑41, Jul 1997	2.00
❑42, Aug 1997	2.00
❑43, Sep 1997	2.00
❑44, Oct 1997; Superboy goes to timeless island	2.00
❑45, Nov 1997 A: Legion of Super-Heroes. V: Silver Sword.	2.00
❑46, Dec 1997; Face cover	2.00
❑47, Jan 1998; A: Green Lantern. Continued from Green Lantern #94	2.00
❑48, Feb 1998	2.00
❑49, Mar 1998	2.00
❑50, Apr 1998; Last Boy on Earth, Part 1	2.00
❑51, May 1998; Last Boy on Earth, Part 2	1.95
❑52, Jun 1998; Last Boy on Earth, Part 3; Superboy returns to Hawaii	1.95
❑53, Jul 1998; Last Boy on Earth, Part 4	1.95
❑54, Aug 1998 A: Guardian.	1.95
❑55, Sep 1998 1: new Hex. V: Grokk.	1.95
❑56, Oct 1998; Mechanic takes over Cadmus	1.95
❑57, Dec 1998; Demolition Run, Part 1	1.99
❑58, Jan 1999; Demolition Run, Part 2	1.99
❑59, Feb 1999; A: Superman. A: Project: Cadmus. on Krypton	1.99

While Superboy often seemed to succumb to kryptonite or other deadly items, everyone knew he'd get better, since these were "The Adventures of Superman When He Was a Boy!"

	N-MINT
❑60, Mar 1999	1.99
❑61, Apr 1999; learns Superman's identity	1.99
❑62, May 1999 O: Black Zero.	1.99
❑63, Jun 1999 V: Doomsdays.	1.99
❑64, Jul 1999	1.99
❑65, Aug 1999 A: Metal Men. A: Steel. A: Inferno. A: Green Lantern. A: Impulse. A: Creeper. A: Robin. A: Hero Hotline. A: Damage.	1.99
❑66, Sep 1999; back to Wild Lands	1.99
❑67, Oct 1999 V: King Shark.	1.99
❑68, Nov 1999; Day of Judgment	1.99
❑69, Dec 1999	1.99
❑70, Jan 2000	1.99
❑71, Feb 2000	1.99
❑72, Mar 2000	1.99
❑73, Apr 2000	1.99
❑74, May 2000; Sins of Youth	1.99
❑75, Jun 2000	1.99
❑76, Jul 2000	1.99
❑77, Aug 2000	2.25
❑78, Sep 2000	2.25
❑79, Oct 2000	2.25
❑80, Nov 2000	2.25
❑81, Dec 2000	2.25
❑82, Jan 2001	2.25
❑83, Feb 2001	2.25
❑84, Mar 2001	2.25
❑85, Apr 2001	2.25
❑86, May 2001	2.25
❑87, Jun 2001	2.25
❑88, Jul 2001	2.25
❑89, Aug 2001	2.25
❑90, Sep 2001	2.25
❑91, Oct 2001	2.25
❑92, Nov 2001	2.25
❑93, Dec 2001; Joker: Last Laugh crossover	2.25
❑94, Jan 2002	2.25
❑95, Feb 2002	2.25
❑96, Mar 2002	2.25
❑97, Apr 2002	2.25
❑98, May 2002	2.25
❑99, Jun 2002	2.25
❑100, Jul 2002; Giant-size	3.50
❑1000000, Nov 1998; Comes between issues #56 and 57	3.00
❑Annual 1, ca. 1994; Elseworlds; concludes story from Adventures of Superman Annual #6	3.00
❑Annual 2, ca. 1995; Year One; Identity of being who Superboy was cloned from is revealed	4.00
❑Annual 3, ca. 1996; Legends of the Dead Earth	2.95
❑Annual 4, ca. 1997; Pulp Heroes	3.95

SUPERBOY AND THE LEGION OF SUPER-HEROES
DC

	N-MINT
❑231, Sep 1977; V: Fatal Five. Giant-Size	2.00
❑232, Oct 1977	2.00
❑233, Nov 1977 O: Infinite Man. 1: Infinite Man.	2.00
❑234, Dec 1977	2.00
❑235, Jan 1978	2.00
❑236, Feb 1978	2.00

N-MINT

❑237, Mar 1978; Saturn Girl leaves team; Lightning Lad leaves team ... 2.00
❑238, Apr 1978; reprints Adventure Comics #359 and 360; wraparound cover ... 2.00
❑239, May 1978 ... 2.00
❑240, Jun 1978 O: Dawnstar. V: Grimbor. ... 2.00
❑241, Jul 1978 ... 2.00
❑242, Aug 1978 ... 2.00
❑243, Sep 1978 A: Legion Subs. ... 2.00
❑244, Oct 1978; Mordru returns ... 2.00
❑245, Nov 1978; Lightning Lad and Saturn Girl rejoin ... 2.00
❑246, Dec 1978 ... 2.00
❑247, Jan 1979 ... 2.00
❑248, Feb 1979 ... 2.00
❑249, Mar 1979 ... 2.00
❑250, Apr 1979 ... 2.00
❑251, May 1979 ... 1.50
❑252, Jun 1979 ... 1.50
❑253, Jul 1979 1: Blok. V: League of Super-Assassins. ... 1.50
❑254, Aug 1979 ... 1.50
❑255, Sep 1979; Legion visits Krypton before it's destroyed ... 1.50
❑256, Oct 1979 O: Brainiac 5. ... 1.50
❑257, Nov 1979; SD (a); Return of Bouncing Boy; Return of Duo Damsel ... 1.50
❑258, Dec 1979; V: Psycho Warrior. series continues as Legion of Super-Heroes ... 1.50

SUPERBOY & THE RAVERS
DC

❑1, Sep 1996 ... 1.95
❑2, Oct 1996 ... 1.95
❑3, Nov 1996 ... 1.95
❑4, Dec 1996 ... 1.95
❑5, Jan 1997 ... 1.95
❑6, Feb 1997 ... 1.95
❑7, Mar 1997 ... 1.95
❑8, Apr 1997 ... 1.95
❑9, May 1997 ... 1.95
❑10, Jun 1997; continued from Superboy #40, continues in Superboy #41 ... 1.95
❑11, Jul 1997 ... 1.95
❑12, Aug 1997 ... 1.95
❑13, Sep 1997 ... 1.95
❑14, Oct 1997; Genesis ... 1.95
❑15, Nov 1997 ... 1.95
❑16, Dec 1997 ... 1.95
❑17, Jan 1998 ... 1.95
❑18, Feb 1998 ... 1.95
❑19, Mar 1998 ... 1.95

SUPERBOY PLUS
DC

❑1, Jan 1997 ... 2.95
❑2, Fal 1997; continues in Catwoman Plus #1 ... 2.95

SUPERBOY/RISK DOUBLE-SHOT
DC

❑1, Feb 1998 ... 1.95

SUPERBOY/ROBIN: WORLD'S FINEST THREE
DC

❑1, ca. 1996; prestige format ... 4.95
❑2, ca. 1996; prestige format ... 4.95

SUPERBOY'S LEGION
DC

❑1, Apr 2001 ... 5.95
❑2, May 2001 ... 5.95

SUPERCAR
GOLD KEY

❑1, Nov 1962 ... 250.00
❑2, Feb 1963 ... 200.00
❑3, May 1963 ... 200.00
❑4, Aug 1963 ... 200.00

SUPERCOPS
NOW

❑1, Sep 1990; double-sized ... 2.75
❑2, Oct 1990 ... 1.75

N-MINT

❑3, Nov 1990 ... 1.75
❑4, Feb 1991 ... 1.75

SUPER COPS, THE
RED CIRCLE

❑1, ca. 1974 GM (c); GM (a) ... 2.00

SUPER DC GIANT
DC

❑13, Sep 1970; really S-13; Binky ... 75.00
❑14, Sep 1970; really S-14; Westerns ... 30.00
❑15, Sep 1970; really S-15; Westerns ... 30.00
❑16, Sep 1970; really S-16; Brave & the Bold ... 30.00
❑17, Sep 1970; really S-17; Romance ... 125.00
❑18, Oct 1970; really S-18; Three Mouseketeers ... 50.00
❑19, Oct 1970; really S-19; Jerry Lewis ... 50.00
❑20, Oct 1970; really S-20; House of Mystery ... 40.00
❑21, Jan 1971; really S-21; Romance ... 175.00
❑22, Mar 1971; really S-22; Westerns ... 25.00
❑23, Mar 1971; really S-23; Unexpected ... 40.00
❑24, May 1971; CS (c); JM (a); really S-24; reprints Supergirl stories from: Action Comics #295-298 ... 30.00
❑25, Aug 1971; really S-25; Challengers of the Unknown ... 25.00
❑26, Aug 1971; really S-26; Aquaman ... 25.00
❑27, Sum 1976; Flying Saucers ... 15.00

SUPERFAN
MARK 1

❑1, b&w ... 1.95

SUPERFIST AYUMI
FANTAGRAPHICS / EROS

❑1, Oct 1996 ... 2.95
❑2, Nov 1996 ... 2.95

SUPER FRIENDS
DC

❑1, Nov 1976 ATh (a) ... 5.00
❑2, Dec 1976 ... 2.00
❑3, Feb 1977 ... 2.00
❑4, Apr 1977 ... 2.00
❑5, Jun 1977 ... 2.00
❑6, Aug 1977 ... 2.00
❑7, Oct 1977 1: Wonder Twins. 1: Tasmanian Devil. ... 2.00
❑8, Nov 1977 ... 2.00
❑9, Dec 1977 1: Iron Maiden. ... 2.00
❑10, Mar 1978 ... 2.00
❑11, May 1978 ... 1.50
❑12, Jul 1978 1: Doctor Mist. ... 1.50
❑13, Sep 1978 ... 1.50
❑14, Nov 1978 ... 1.50
❑15, Dec 1978 ... 1.50
❑16, Jan 1979 ... 1.50
❑17, Feb 1979 ... 1.50
❑18, Mar 1979 ... 1.50
❑19, Apr 1979 ... 1.50
❑20, May 1979 ... 1.50
❑21, Jun 1979 ... 1.50
❑22, Jul 1979 ... 1.50
❑23, Aug 1979 ... 1.50
❑24, Sep 1979 ... 1.50
❑25, Oct 1979 1: Fire. ... 1.50
❑26, Nov 1979 ... 1.50
❑27, Dec 1979 ... 1.50
❑28, Jan 1980 ... 1.50
❑29, Feb 1980 ... 1.50
❑30, Mar 1980 ... 1.50
❑31, Apr 1980 A: Black Orchid. ... 1.50
❑32, May 1980 ... 1.50
❑33, Jun 1980 ... 1.50
❑34, Jul 1980 ... 1.50
❑35, Aug 1980 ... 1.50
❑36, Sep 1980 ... 1.50
❑37, Oct 1980 ... 1.50
❑38, Nov 1980 ... 1.50
❑39, Dec 1980 ... 1.50
❑40, Jan 1981 ... 1.50
❑41, Feb 1981 ... 1.50
❑42, Mar 1981 1: Green Flame. ... 1.50

N-MINT

❑43, Apr 1981 ... 1.50
❑44, May 1981 ... 1.50
❑45, Jun 1981 ... 1.50
❑46, Jul 1981 ... 1.50
❑47, Aug 1981 ... 1.50
❑Special 1, ca. 1981; giveaway; says A TV Comic on cover ... 2.00

SUPERGIRL (1ST SERIES)
DC

❑1, Nov 1972 ... 15.00
❑2 ... 10.00
❑3, Feb 1973 ... 8.00
❑4, Apr 1973 ... 8.00
❑5, Jun 1973; origin of Zatana ... 8.00
❑6, Aug 1973 ... 8.00
❑7, Oct 1973 ... 8.00
❑8, Nov 1973 ... 8.00
❑9, Jan 1974 ... 8.00
❑10, Sep 1974 A: Prez. ... 8.00

SUPERGIRL (2ND SERIES)
DC

❑14, Dec 1983; Title changes to Supergirl; Series continued from "Daring New Adventures of Supergirl" ... 3.00
❑15, Jan 1984 ... 3.00
❑16, Feb 1984 CI (a); A: Ambush Bug. ... 3.00
❑17, Mar 1984 ... 3.00
❑18, Apr 1984 ... 3.00
❑19, May 1984 ... 3.00
❑20, Jun 1984 A: Teen Titans. A: Justice League of America. ... 3.00
❑21, Jul 1984 CI (a) ... 3.00
❑22, Aug 1984 CI (a) ... 3.00
❑23, Sep 1984 CI (a) ... 3.00
❑DOT 1, ca. 1984; Department of Transportation giveaway JO (w); AT (a) ... 3.00

SUPERGIRL (3RD SERIES)
DC

❑1, Sep 1996; PD (w); Matrix merges with Linda Danvers ... 10.00
❑1-2, Sep 1996 PD (w) ... 3.00
❑2, Oct 1996; PD (w); Matrix learns more of Linda Danvers' past ... 4.00
❑3, Nov 1996; PD (w); V: Gorilla Grodd. Final Night ... 3.50
❑4, Dec 1996 PD (w); V: Gorilla Grodd. ... 3.00
❑5, Jan 1997 PD (w); V: Chemo. ... 3.00
❑6, Feb 1997 PD (w); A: Superman. V: Rampage. ... 2.50
❑7, Mar 1997 PD (w) ... 2.50
❑8, Apr 1997 PD (w) ... 2.00
❑9, May 1997 PD (w); V: Tempus. ... 2.00
❑10, Jun 1997 PD (w) ... 2.00
❑11, Jul 1997 PD (w); V: Silver Banshee. ... 2.00
❑12, Aug 1997 PD (w) ... 2.00
❑13, Sep 1997 PD (w) ... 2.00
❑14, Oct 1997; PD (w); Genesis ... 2.00
❑15, Nov 1997 PD (w); V: Extremists. ... 2.00
❑16, Dec 1997; PD (w); V: Extremists. Face cover ... 2.00
❑17, Jan 1998 PD (w); V: Despero. ... 2.00
❑18, Feb 1998 PD (w); V: Despero. ... 2.00
❑19, Mar 1998 PD (w); V: Blastoff. ... 2.00
❑20, Apr 1998; PD (w); Millennium Giants ... 2.00
❑21, May 1998 PD (w) ... 2.00
❑22, Jun 1998 PD (w) ... 2.00
❑23, Jul 1998 PD (w); A: Steel. ... 2.00
❑24, Aug 1998 PD (w); A: Resurrection Man. ... 2.00
❑25, Sep 1998 PD (w) ... 2.00
❑26, Oct 1998 PD (w); O: Comet. ... 2.00
❑27, Dec 1998 PD (w); V: Female Furies. ... 2.00
❑28, Jan 1999 PD (w); V: Female Furies. ... 2.00
❑29, Feb 1999 PD (w); A: Twilight. A: Female Furies. A: Granny Goodness. ... 2.00
❑30, Mar 1999 PD (w); A: Matrix. V: Matrix. ... 2.00
❑31, Apr 1999 PD (w); V: Matrix. ... 1.99
❑32, May 1999 PD (w) ... 1.99

	N-MINT
❑33, Jun 1999 PD (w)	1.99
❑34, Jul 1999 PD (w); V: Parasite.	1.99
❑35, Aug 1999 PD (w); V: Parasite.	1.99
❑36, Sep 1999 PD (w); A: Young Justice.	1.99
❑37, Oct 1999 PD (w); A: Young Justice.	1.99
❑38, Nov 1999; PD (w); A: Zauriel. Day of Judgment	1.99
❑39, Dec 1999 PD (w)	1.99
❑40, Jan 2000 PD (w)	1.99
❑41, Feb 2000 PD (w)	1.99
❑42, Mar 2000 PD (w)	1.99
❑43, Apr 2000 PD (w)	1.99
❑44, May 2000 PD (w)	1.99
❑45, Jun 2000 PD (w)	1.99
❑46, Jul 2000 PD (w)	1.99
❑47, Aug 2000 PD (w)	2.25
❑48, Sep 2000 PD (w)	2.25
❑49, Oct 2000 PD (w)	2.25
❑50, Nov 2000; Giant-size PD (w)	3.95
❑51, Dec 2000 PD (w)	2.25
❑52, Jan 2001 PD (w)	2.25
❑53, Feb 2001 PD (w)	2.25
❑54, Mar 2001 PD (w)	2.25
❑55, Apr 2001 PD (w)	2.25
❑56, May 2001 PD (w)	2.25
❑57, Jun 2001	2.25
❑58, Jul 2001	2.25
❑59, Aug 2001	2.25
❑60, Sep 2001	2.25
❑61, Oct 2001	2.25
❑62, Nov 2001 A: Two-Face.	2.25
❑63, Dec 2001	2.25
❑64, Jan 2002	2.25
❑65, Feb 2002	2.25
❑66, Mar 2002 A: Demon.	2.25
❑67, Apr 2002 A: Demon.	2.25
❑68, May 2002	2.25
❑69, Jun 2002	2.25
❑70, Jul 2002	2.25
❑71, Aug 2002	2.25
❑72, Sep 2002	2.25
❑73, Oct 2002	2.50
❑74, Nov 2002	2.50
❑75, Dec 2002	2.50
❑75/DF	19.95
❑76, Jan 2003	2.50
❑77, Feb 2003	2.50
❑78, Mar 2003	2.50
❑79, Apr 2003	2.50
❑80, May 2003	2.50
❑1000000, Nov 1998 PD (w); A: R'E'L.	3.00
❑Annual 1, ca. 1996; DG (a); Legends of the Dead Earth	2.95
❑Annual 2, ca. 1997; Pulp Heroes	3.95

SUPERGIRL/LEX LUTHOR SPECIAL
DC

	N-MINT
❑1, ca. 1993; includes pin-up gallery; cover says Supergirl and Team Luthor	2.50

SUPERGIRL (MINI-SERIES)
DC

	N-MINT
❑1, Feb 1994	3.00
❑2, Mar 1994	2.50
❑3, Apr 1994	2.50
❑4, May 1994	2.50

SUPERGIRL MOVIE SPECIAL
DC

	N-MINT
❑1; Movie adaptation	1.25

SUPERGIRL PLUS
DC

	N-MINT
❑1, Feb 1997	2.95

SUPERGIRL/PRYSM DOUBLE SHOT
DC

	N-MINT
❑1, Feb 1998	1.95

SUPERGIRL: WINGS
DC

	N-MINT
❑1, Dec 2001	5.95

SUPER GOOF (WALT DISNEY...)
GOLD KEY

	N-MINT
❑1, ca. 1965	24.00
❑2, ca. 1967	12.00
❑3, May 1968	12.00
❑4, Sep 1968	10.00
❑5, Dec 1968	10.00
❑6, Mar 1969	10.00
❑7, Jun 1969	10.00
❑8, Sep 1969	10.00
❑9, Dec 1969	10.00
❑10, Mar 1970	10.00
❑11, Jun 1970	7.00
❑12, Feb 1970	7.00
❑13, May 1970	7.00
❑14, Aug 1970	7.00
❑15, Nov 1970	7.00
❑16, Feb 1971	7.00
❑17, May 1971	7.00
❑18, Aug 1971	7.00
❑19, Nov 1971	7.00
❑20, Feb 1972	7.00
❑21, May 1972	5.00
❑22, Aug 1972	5.00
❑23, Nov 1972	5.00
❑24 1973	5.00
❑25 1973	5.00
❑26 1973	5.00
❑27, Oct 1973	5.00
❑28 1974	5.00
❑29 1974	5.00
❑30, Jun 1974	5.00
❑31, Aug 1974	3.00
❑32, Nov 1974	3.00
❑33 1975	3.00
❑34 1975	3.00
❑35, Sep 1975	3.00
❑36, Dec 1975	3.00
❑37, Feb 1976	3.00
❑38, Jun 1976	3.00
❑39, Sep 1976	3.00
❑40, Nov 1976	3.00
❑41, Feb 1977	3.00
❑42, Jun 1977	3.00
❑43, Sep 1977	3.00
❑44, Nov 1977	3.00
❑45, Feb 1978	3.00
❑46, Apr 1978	3.00
❑47, Jun 1978	3.00
❑48, Aug 1978	3.00
❑49, Oct 1978	3.00
❑50, Dec 1978	3.00
❑51, Feb 1979	2.50
❑52, Apr 1979	2.50
❑53, Jun 1979	2.50
❑54, Aug 1979	2.50
❑55, Oct 1979	2.50
❑56, Dec 1979	2.50
❑57, Jan 1980	2.50
❑58, Mar 1980	2.50
❑59, May 1980	2.50
❑60, Jul 1980	2.50
❑61, Oct 1980	2.50
❑62, Dec 1980	2.50
❑63, Jan 1981	2.50
❑64 1981	2.50
❑65 1981	2.50
❑66, Dec 1981	2.50
❑67, Feb 1982	2.50
❑68 1982	2.50
❑69 1982	2.50
❑70 1982	2.50
❑71 1982	2.50
❑72 1983	2.50
❑73, Jul 1983	2.50
❑74 1983	2.50

SUPER GREEN BERET
MILSON

	N-MINT
❑1, Apr 1967	30.00
❑2	24.00

Karl Kesel incorporated the Hypertime concept, in which all DC adventures "happened," in a six-part story in *Superboy* #60-65.

© 1999 DC Comics.

SUPER HEROES BATTLE SUPER GORILLAS
DC

	N-MINT
❑1, Win 1976	7.00

SUPER HEROES PUZZLES AND GAMES
MARVEL

	N-MINT
❑1, Apr 1980; giveaway O: Captain America. O: Spider-Man. O: The Hulk. O: Spider-Woman.	2.00

SUPER HEROES STAMP ALBUM
USPS / DC

	N-MINT
❑1; 1900-1909	3.00
❑2; 1910-1919	3.00
❑3; 1920-1929	3.00
❑4; 1930-1939; no Snow White coverage	3.00
❑5; 1940-1949	3.00
❑6; 1950-1959; 3-D stamp	3.00
❑7; 1960-1969	3.50
❑8; 1970-1979	3.50
❑9; 1980-1989	3.50
❑10; 1990-1999	3.50

SUPER HEROES VERSUS SUPER VILLAINS
ARCHIE

	N-MINT
❑1, ca. 1966	50.00

SUPER INFORMATION HIJINKS: REALITY CHECK
TAVICAT

	N-MINT
❑1, Oct 1995, b&w	2.95
❑2, Dec 1995, b&w	2.95
❑3 1996	2.95
❑4 1996	2.95
❑5 1996	2.95

SUPER INFORMATION HIJINKS: REALITY CHECK! (2ND SERIES)
SIRIUS

	N-MINT
❑1, Sep 1996	2.95
❑2, Oct 1996	2.95
❑3, Nov 1996	2.95
❑4, Dec 1996	2.95
❑5, Jan 1997	2.95
❑6, Feb 1997	2.95
❑7, Mar 1997	2.95
❑8, Jan 1998	2.95
❑9, Mar 1998	2.95
❑10, May 1998	2.95
❑11, Jul 1998	2.95
❑12, Oct 1998	2.95

SUPERIOR SEVEN
IMAGINE THIS

	N-MINT
❑1	2.00
❑2 1992, b&w	2.00
❑3 1992, b&w	2.00
❑4	2.00
❑5	2.00

SUPERMAN (1ST SERIES)
DC

	N-MINT
❑109, Nov 1956	280.00
❑110, Jan 1957	280.00
❑111, Feb 1957	240.00
❑112, Mar 1957	240.00
❑113, May 1957	240.00
❑114, Jul 1957	240.00
❑115, Aug 1957	240.00

	N-MINT
❑116, Sep 1957	240.00
❑117, Nov 1957	240.00
❑118, Jan 1958, CS (c); (w); (a)	240.00
❑119, Feb 1958	240.00
❑120, Mar 1958	240.00
❑121, May 1958	195.00
❑122, Jul 1958	195.00
❑123, Aug 1958; Supergirl prototype	195.00
❑124, Sep 1958	195.00
❑125, Nov 1958	195.00
❑126, Jan 1959	195.00
❑127, Feb 1959 O: Titano. 1: Titano.	195.00
❑128, Apr 1959	195.00
❑129, May 1959 O: Lori Lemaris. 1: Lori Lemaris.	195.00
❑130, Jul 1959	195.00
❑131, Aug 1959	155.00
❑132, Oct 1959; A: Batman & Robin.	155.00
❑133, Nov 1959	155.00
❑134, Jan 1960	155.00
❑135, Feb 1960	155.00
❑136, Apr 1960	155.00
❑137, May 1960	155.00
❑138, Jul 1960	155.00
❑139, Aug 1960	155.00
❑140, Oct 1960 1: Bizarro Jr.. 1: Blue Kryptonite. 1: Bizarro Supergirl. A: Lex Luthor.	175.00
❑141, Nov 1960	115.00
❑142, Jan 1961	115.00
❑143, Feb 1961	115.00
❑144, Apr 1961 A: Lex Luthor.	115.00
❑145, May 1961	115.00
❑146, Jul 1961; O: Superman. Superman's life	160.00
❑147, Aug 1961 CS (a); 1: Legion of Super-Heroes (adult). 1: Legion of Super-Villains.	135.00
❑148, Oct 1961 CS (a); V: Mxyzptlk.	115.00
❑149, Nov 1961 CS (a); A: Legion of Super-Heroes.	125.00
❑150, Jan 1962	68.00
❑151, Feb 1962	68.00
❑152, Apr 1962 A: Legion of Super-Heroes.	68.00
❑153, May 1962	68.00
❑154, Jul 1962 CS (a)	68.00
❑155, Aug 1962	68.00
❑156, Oct 1962	68.00
❑157, Nov 1962 1: Gold Kryptonite.	68.00
❑158, Jan 1963 CS (a); 1: Nightwing. 1: Flamebird.	68.00
❑159, Feb 1963	68.00
❑160, Apr 1963	68.00
❑161, May 1963 D: Ma & Pa Kent.	68.00
❑162, Jul 1963 KS (c); CS, KS (a)	58.00
❑163, Aug 1963	58.00
❑164, Oct 1963 CS (a)	58.00
❑165, Nov 1963	58.00
❑166, Jan 1964	58.00
❑167, Feb 1964, CS (a); O: Brainiac (new origin). O: Braniac 5 (new origin).	58.00
❑168, Apr 1964	58.00
❑169, May 1964	58.00
❑170, Jul 1964 A: John F. Kennedy.	58.00
❑171, Aug 1964 CS (a)	58.00
❑172, Oct 1964	58.00
❑173, Nov 1964	58.00
❑174, Jan 1965	58.00
❑175, Feb 1965, Imaginary Story	58.00
❑176, Apr 1965 CS (a)	58.00
❑177, May 1965	58.00
❑178, Jul 1965	58.00
❑179, Aug 1965	58.00
❑180, Oct 1965	58.00
❑181, Nov 1965 CS (a)	55.00
❑182, Jan 1966 V: Toyman.	55.00
❑183, Jan 1966, Giant-size; Golden Age reprints	55.00
❑184, Feb 1966	55.00
❑185, Apr 1966	55.00
❑186, May 1966, CS (a)	55.00

	N-MINT
❑187, Jun 1966, Giant-size; CS, KS (a); G-23; Fortress stories; reprints from Superman #17, Action Comics #164, #233, #244, and #261, and Jimmy Olsen #53 (incl. Action covers)	60.00
❑188, Jul 1966, CS (a)	55.00
❑189, Aug 1966	55.00
❑190, Oct 1966	55.00
❑191, Nov 1966, V: D.E.M.O.N..	55.00
❑192, Jan 1967, CS (a); Imaginary Story	55.00
❑193, Feb 1967, Giant-size; reprints Action #223 and Superman #149	60.00
❑194, Feb 1967; CS (a); Reprints Superman #133	55.00
❑195, Apr 1967, CS (a)	55.00
❑196, May 1967	55.00
❑197, Jul 1967, Giant-size; All Clark Kent issue	55.00
❑198, Jul 1967, CS (a)	55.00
❑199, Aug 1967, 1st Flash/Superman race.	180.00
❑200, Oct 1967	60.00
❑201, Nov 1967 CS (a)	24.00
❑202, Dec 1967, Giant-size; Bizarro issue	30.00
❑203, Jan 1968 CS (c)	24.00
❑204, Feb 1968, color NA (c); 1: Q-energy.	24.00
❑205, Apr 1968	24.00
❑206, May 1968,	24.00
❑207, Jun 1968, Giant-size; CS, KS (a); 30th Anniversary; 80-page Giant (G-48); cover says July; reprints stories from Action Comics #265 and #266, Superman #135, and Superman's Girlfriend Lois Lane #15	24.00
❑208, Jul 1968, CS, JAb (a)	24.00
❑209, Aug 1968, CS, JAb (a)	24.00
❑210, Oct 1968 CS (a)	24.00
❑211, Nov 1968 CS, JAb (a)	24.00
❑212, Jan 1969, Giant-size; CS (a); Superbabies	50.00
❑213, Jan 1969, CS, JAb (a); A: Lex Luthor.	24.00
❑214, Feb 1969 CS, JAb (a)	24.00
❑215, Apr 1969, CS, JAb (a); Imaginary Story; Superman as widower	24.00
❑216, May 1969, CS, JAb (a); in Vietnam	24.00
❑217, Jul 1969; Giant-size CS (c); CS (a)	30.00
❑218, Jul 1969 CS, JAb (a)	20.00
❑219, Aug 1969, CS (a)	20.00
❑220, Oct 1969 CS (c); CS (a)	20.00
❑221, Nov 1969 CS (a)	20.00
❑222, Jan 1970; Giant-size CS (c); CS (a)	30.00
❑223, Jan 1970 CS (a)	20.00
❑224, Feb 1970, CS (a); Imaginary Story	20.00
❑225, Apr 1970, CS (a)	20.00
❑226, May 1970 CS (a)	20.00
❑227, Jul 1970; Giant-size CS (a)	30.00
❑228, Jul 1970 CS (c); CS, DA (a)	20.00
❑229, Aug 1970, color CS, DA (a)	20.00
❑230, Oct 1970, color; CS, DA (a); Imaginary Story	20.00
❑231, Nov 1970, color; NA, CS (c); NA, CS, DA (a); Imaginary Story; Luthor reprint: Superman's Fatal Costume	20.00
❑232, Jan 1971; Giant-size; CS (a)	30.00
❑233, Jan 1971 CS (a)	40.00
❑234, Feb 1971, color; (c); MA, CS (a); A: Sand Superman. World of Krypton back-up	18.00
❑235, Mar 1971, color MA, CS (a)	18.00
❑236, Apr 1971, color; MA, DG, CS (a); World of Krypton back-up	18.00
❑237, May 1971, color MA, CS (a)	18.00
❑238, Jun 1971, color; MA, CI (c); MA, GM, CS (a); A: Sand Superman. World of Krypton back-up	18.00
❑239, Jul 1971, color; Giant-size; MA, GM, CS (a); reprints Action #267 and #268, Superman #127 and #164	30.00

	N-MINT
❑240, Jul 1971, color; DG, CS (a); A: I-Ching. World of Krypton back-up	18.00
❑241, Aug 1971, color; MA, CS (a); A: I-Ching. A: Sand Superman. Giant; Reprints Superman #112 and #176	18.00
❑242, Sep 1971, color; CI, CS (a); A: final. Reprints Superman #96, and Strange Adventures #54	18.00
❑243, Oct 1971 CS (a)	18.00
❑244, Nov 1971, color; CS (c); MA, CS (a); Reprints Superman #181, and Strange Adventures #34	18.00
❑245, Jan 1972; CS (c); CS, MR (a); a.k.a. DC 100-Page Super-Spectacular #DC-7; back cover pin-up; reprints from All-Star Western #117, The Atom #3, Detective #66, Kid Eternity #3, Mystery in Space #89, and Superman #87, and #167	22.00
❑246, Dec 1971 CS (c); CS (a)	18.00
❑247, Jan 1972, CS (c); MA, CS (a); A: Guardians of the Universe. 1st Private Life of Clark Kent; Superman of Tomorrow back-up; Reprints Action #338	18.00
❑248, Feb 1972; CS (c); CS (a); Reprints Action #339	18.00
❑249, Mar 1972 NA, CS (a); O: Terra-Man. 1: Terra-Man.	18.00
❑250, Apr 1972 CS (a)	18.00
❑251, May 1972 MA, CS (a)	18.00
❑252, Jun 1972, color; NA (c); MA, CS (a); a.k.a. DC 100-Page Super Spectacular #DC-13; wraparound cover	60.00
❑253, Jun 1972 MA, CS (a)	18.00
❑254, Jul 1972 NA, CS (a)	22.00
❑255, Aug 1972 CS (a)	9.00
❑256, Sep 1972 CS (a)	9.00
❑257, Oct 1972 CS (a)	9.00
❑258, Nov 1972, MA, DG, CS (a); Private Life of Clark Kent back-up	9.00
❑259, Dec 1972 CS (a)	9.00
❑260, Jan 1973, MA, DC, CS (a); World of Krypton back-up	9.00
❑261, Feb 1973 CS (a); A: Star Sapphire.	9.00
❑262, Mar 1973, MA, CS (a); Private Life of Clark Kent back-up	9.00
❑263, Apr 1973 CS (a)	9.00
❑264, Jun 1973 CS (a); 1: Steve Lombard.	9.00
❑265, Jul 1973, MA, CS (a)	8.00
❑266, Aug 1973 CS (a)	8.00
❑267, Sep 1973, BO, MA, CS (a); Private Life of Clark Kent back-up	8.00
❑268, Oct 1973 CS (a)	8.00
❑269, Nov 1973 CS (a)	8.00
❑270, Dec 1973 CS (a)	8.00
❑271, Jan 1974 CS (a)	8.00
❑272, Feb 1974; NC (c); BO, GK, CS (a); Reprints Action #97, and Green Lantern (2nd series) #42	20.00
❑273, Mar 1974 BO, CS (a)	7.00
❑274, Apr 1974 BO, CS (a)	7.00
❑275, May 1974 BO, CS (a)	7.00
❑276, Jun 1974 BO, CS (a); 1: Captain Thunder.	7.00
❑277, Jul 1974, BO, CS (a); Private Life of Clark Kent back-up	7.00
❑278, Aug 1974, NC (c); BO, CS (a); Reprints Action #211 and #298, Superman #33 and #138, and World's Finest Comics #62	17.00
❑279, Sep 1974, CS (a); A: Batgirl. World of Krypton back-up	5.00
❑280, Oct 1974, BO, CS (a); Private Life of Clark Kent back-up	5.00
❑281, Nov 1974 CS (a)	5.00
❑282, Dec 1974, CS, KS (a); World of Krypton back-up	5.00
❑283, Jan 1975 CS (a)	5.00
❑284, Feb 1975; NC (c); BO, CS (a); reprints Action #304, and Superman #25, #41, #42, and #148	7.00
❑285, Mar 1975 CS (a); A: Roy Raymond.	5.00
❑286, Apr 1975 CS (a); V: Luthor. V: Parasite.	5.00

	N-MINT
❑287, May 1975, BO, CS (a); Return of Krypto; Private Life of Clark Kent back-up	4.00
❑288, Jun 1975 CS (a)	4.00
❑289, Jul 1975 CS (a)	4.00
❑290, Aug 1975 CS (a)	4.00
❑291, Sep 1975, BO, CS (a)	4.00
❑292, Oct 1975, BO, AM, CS (a); O: Lex Luthor. Private Life of Clark Kent back-up	4.00
❑293, Nov 1975, BO, CS (a)	2.50
❑294, Dec 1975 CS (a)	2.50
❑295, Jan 1976 CS (a)	2.50
❑296, Feb 1976; CS (a); Superman loses powers when not in costume	2.50
❑297, Mar 1976 CS (a)	2.50
❑298, Apr 1976, BO, CS (a)	2.50
❑299, May 1976, BO, CS (a)	2.50
❑300, Jun 1976, 300th anniversary issue BO, CS (a); O: Superman of 2001.	11.00
❑301, Jul 1976 CS (a)	2.50
❑302, Aug 1976 CS (a)	2.50
❑303, Sep 1976 CS (a)	2.50
❑304, Oct 1976 CS (a)	2.50
❑305, Nov 1976 CS (a)	2.50
❑306, Dec 1976, BO, CS (a); V: Bizarro.	2.50
❑307, Jan 1977 NA (c); CS, FS, JL (a)	2.50
❑308, Feb 1977, NA (c); CS, FS, JL (a)	2.50
❑309, Mar 1977, CS, FS (a)	2.50
❑310, Apr 1977 CS (a)	2.50
❑311, May 1977 CS (a)	2.50
❑312, Jun 1977 CS (a)	2.50
❑313, Jul 1977 NA (c); CS, DA (a)	2.50
❑314, Aug 1977 CS (a)	2.50
❑315, Sep 1977 CS (a)	2.50
❑316, Oct 1977 CS (a)	2.50
❑317, Nov 1977, NA (c); CS, DA (a); Return of Lana Lang	2.50
❑318, Dec 1977 CS (a)	2.50
❑319, Jan 1978, CS (a)	2.50
❑320, Feb 1978 CS (a)	2.50
❑321, Mar 1978, DG (c); CS (a)	2.50
❑322, Apr 1978, CS (a); V: Parasite.	2.50
❑323, May 1978, color; CS, DA (a); 1: Atomic Skull. V: Atomic Skull.	2.50
❑324, Jun 1978, color; RB, DG (c); CS (a); V: Titano.	2.50
❑325, Jul 1978, color; RB (c); CS (a)	2.50
❑326, Aug 1978 CS (a)	2.50
❑327, Sep 1978 CS (a)	2.50
❑328, Oct 1978, DG (c); CS, KS (a); Private Life of Clark Kent back-up	2.50
❑329, Nov 1978, color; DG, RA (c); CS, KS (a); Mr. and Mrs. Superman back-up	2.50
❑330, Dec 1978 CS (a)	2.50
❑331, Jan 1979 CS (a)	2.50
❑332, Feb 1979 CS (a)	2.50
❑333, Mar 1979 CS (a)	2.50
❑334, Apr 1979 CS (a)	2.50
❑335, May 1979 CS (a); V: Mxyzptlk.	2.50
❑336, Jun 1979 CS (a)	2.50
❑337, Jul 1979 CS (a)	2.50
❑338, Aug 1979, color; DG, RA (c); CS (a); Kandor enlarged	2.50
❑339, Sep 1979 CS (a)	2.50
❑340, Oct 1979 CS (a)	2.50
❑341, Nov 1979, color DG, RA (c); CS (a); A: J. Wilbur Wolfingham.	2.50
❑342, Dec 1979 CS (a)	2.50
❑343, Jan 1980 CS (a)	2.50
❑344, Feb 1980 CS (a)	2.50
❑345, Mar 1980 CS (a)	2.50
❑346, Apr 1980 CS (a)	2.50
❑347, May 1980 CS (a)	2.50
❑348, Jun 1980 CS (a)	2.50
❑349, Jul 1980 CS (a)	2.50
❑350, Aug 1980 CS (a)	2.50
❑351, Sep 1980 CS (a)	2.00
❑352, Oct 1980 CS (a)	2.00
❑353, Nov 1980 CS (a)	2.00
❑354, Dec 1980 CS (a)	2.00
❑355, Jan 1981 JSn, CS (a)	2.00

	N-MINT
❑356, Feb 1981 CS (a)	2.00
❑357, Mar 1981 CS (a)	2.00
❑358, Apr 1981, DG, RA (c); CS (a); Imaginary story	2.00
❑359, May 1981 CS (a)	2.00
❑360, Jun 1981 CS (a)	2.00
❑361, Jul 1981 CS (a)	2.00
❑362, Aug 1981, color; DG, RA (c); CS, DA (a); Lana and Lois contract deadly virus that killed Kents; Superman The In-Between Years back-up	2.00
❑363, Sep 1981, color; RB, DG (c); CS (a); A: Lex Luthor. Imaginary Story	2.00
❑364, Oct 1981, color; GP, DG (c); CS (a); Superman 2020 back-up	2.00
❑365, Nov 1981, color; DG, RA (c); CS, KS (a); A: Supergirl. Superman the In-Between Years back-up	2.00
❑366, Dec 1981 CS (a)	2.00
❑367, Jan 1982 CS (a)	2.00
❑368, Feb 1982 CS (a)	2.00
❑369, Mar 1982 CS (a); V: Parasite.	2.00
❑370, Apr 1982 CS (a)	2.00
❑371, May 1982 CS (a)	2.00
❑372, Jun 1982 CS (a)	2.00
❑373, Jul 1982 CS (a)	2.00
❑374, Aug 1982 CS (a)	2.00
❑375, Sep 1982 CS (a)	2.00
❑376, Oct 1982, color; RB (c); BO, CI, CS, DA (a); Supergirl back-up	2.00
❑377, Nov 1982 CS (a)	2.00
❑378, Dec 1982 CS (a)	2.00
❑379, Jan 1983, DG, RA (c); CS (a); A: Bizarro.	2.00
❑380, Feb 1983 CS (a)	2.00
❑381, Mar 1983 CS (a)	2.00
❑382, Apr 1983 CS (a)	2.00
❑383, May 1983 CS (a)	2.00
❑384, Jun 1983 CS (a)	2.00
❑385, Jul 1983 CS (a)	2.00
❑386, Aug 1983 CS (a)	2.00
❑387, Sep 1983 CS (a)	2.00
❑388, Oct 1983, (c); CS (a)	2.00
❑389, Nov 1983 CS (a)	2.00
❑390, Dec 1983 CS (a)	2.00
❑391, Jan 1984 CS (a)	2.00
❑392, Feb 1984 CS (a)	2.00
❑393, Mar 1984 CS (a)	2.00
❑394, Apr 1984 CS (a)	2.00
❑395, May 1984 CS (a)	2.00
❑396, Jun 1984 CS (a)	2.00
❑397, Jul 1984 CS (a)	2.00
❑398, Aug 1984, CS (a)	2.00
❑399, Sep 1984 CS (a)	2.00
❑400, Oct 1984, Giant-size; HC (c); JSo (w); JD, WP, AW, SD, BSz, BWr, JO, JOy, WE, JBy, MGr, JK, BB, FM, CS, JSo, KJ, MR (a); multiple short stories	5.00
❑401, Nov 1984 CS (a)	2.00
❑402, Dec 1984, BO, CS (a)	2.00
❑403, Jan 1985 CS (a)	2.00
❑404, Feb 1985, BO, CI (a); imaginary story	2.00
❑405, Mar 1985 CS (a)	2.00
❑406, Apr 1985 CS (a)	2.00
❑407, May 1985, JOy (c); IN (a); powers passed along	2.00
❑408, Jun 1985, AW (c); AW, CS (a); nuclear nightmare	2.00
❑409, Jul 1985, AW (c); AW, CS, KS (a)	2.00
❑410, Aug 1985, KJ (c); AW, CS (a)	2.00
❑411, Sep 1985, MA, CS (w); MA, CS (a); Julius Schwartz' birthday; MASK preview comic	2.00
❑412, Oct 1985 CS (a)	2.00
❑413, Nov 1985, KJ (c); AW, CS (a)	2.00
❑414, Dec 1985, AW, CS (a); Crisis on Infinite Earths cross-over	2.00
❑415, Jan 1986, AW, CS (a); Crisis on Infinite Earths cross-over	2.00
❑416, Feb 1986, AW, CS (a); Superman learns Luthor's connection to Einstein	2.00
❑417, Mar 1986, CS (a); imaginary story	2.00

Although many fans think it's called *Reality Check!*, both series are really *Super Information Hijinks: Reality Check!* according to the indicia.

© 1998 Tavicat and Sirius.

	N-MINT
❑418, Apr 1986, CS (a)	2.00
❑419, May 1986, CS (a)	2.00
❑420, Jun 1986 CS (a)	2.00
❑421, Jul 1986, (c); CS (a); MASK comic insert	2.00
❑422, Aug 1986, BB (c); TY, CS (a)	2.00
❑423, Sep 1986, AMo (w); GP, CS (a); series continues as Adventures of Superman; imaginary story	5.00
❑Annual 1, Oct 1960; O: Supergirl. 1: Supergirl. 1: Supergirl reprinted. Reprints Action Comics #252	600.00
❑Annual 1-2, Oct 1998, color; Replica edition; CS, KS (a); Cardstock cover; Replica Edition; reprints Giant Superman Annual #1	5.00
❑Annual 2, ca. 1960 O: Titano.	325.00
❑Annual 3, Sum 1961; Strange Lives of Superman	210.00
❑Annual 4, Win 1961 O: Legion of Super-Heroes. A: Legion of Super-Heroes.	180.00
❑Annual 5, Sum 1962, Krypton related stories	105.00
❑Annual 6, Win 1962; 1: Legion of Super-Heroes. Reprints Adventure Comics #247	90.00
❑Annual 7, Jun 1963, 25th anniversary, O: Superman-Batman team.	62.00
❑Annual 8, Sum 1963, Untold Stories and Secret Origins	46.00
❑Annual 9, ca. 1983	5.00
❑Annual 10, ca. 1984, MA, CS (a)	5.00
❑Annual 11, ca. 1985, DaG (c); AMo (w); DaG (a); A: Wonder Woman. A: Robin. A: Batman. V: Mongul.	4.00
❑Annual 12, ca. 1986, BB (c); V: Luthor's Warsuit.	3.00
❑Special 1, ca. 1983, (c); GK (w); GK (a)	4.00
❑Special 2, Apr 1984	4.00
❑Special 3, Apr 1985, IN (a); V: Amazo.	4.00

SUPERMAN (2ND SERIES)
DC

❑0, Oct 1994; ▲ 1994-38	3.00
❑1, Jan 1987, JBy (w); JBy (a); 1: Metallo (new).	4.00
❑2, Feb 1987, JBy (c); JBy (w); JBy (a)	3.50
❑3, Mar 1987, color; JBy (c); JBy (w); JBy (a); 1: Amazing Grace. crossover Legends chapter 17	3.00
❑4, Apr 1987, color JBy (c); JBy (w); JBy (a); 1: Bloodsport.	2.50
❑5, May 1987, color JBy (c); JBy (w); JBy (a)	2.50
❑6, Jun 1987, color (c); JBy (w); JBy (a)	2.00
❑7, Jul 1987, color JBy (c); JBy (w); JBy (a); O: Rampage (DC). 1: Rampage (DC).	2.00
❑8, Aug 1987, color JBy (c); JBy (w); JBy (a); A: Superboy. A: Legion of Super-Heroes.	2.00
❑9, Sep 1987, color JBy (c); JBy (w); JBy (a); A: Joker. V: Joker. V: Luthor.	3.50
❑10, Oct 1987, color JBy (c); JBy (w); JBy (a)	2.00
❑11, Nov 1987, color JBy (c); JBy (w); JBy (a); O: Mr. Mxyzptlk.	2.00
❑12, Dec 1987, color (c); JBy (w); JBy (a); O: Lori Lemaris.	2.00
❑13, Jan 1988, color; JBy (c); JBy (w); JBy (a); Millennium Week 2	2.00

Condition price index: Multiply "NM prices" above by: **0.83 for Very Fine/Near Mint**
0.66 for Very Fine • 0.33 for Fine • 0.2 for Very Good • 0.125 for Good

N-MINT

❑14, Feb 1988, color; JBy (c); JBy (w); JBy (a); A: Green Lantern. Millennium Week 6 — 2.00
❑15, Mar 1988, color JBy (c); JBy (w); JBy (a) — 2.00
❑16, Apr 1988, color JBy (c); JBy (w); JBy (a); V: Prankster. — 2.00
❑17, May 1988, color JBy (c); JBy (w); JBy (a); V: Silver Banshee. — 2.00
❑18, Jun 1988, color JBy (w) — 2.00
❑19, Jul 1988, color JBy (w); JBy (a); 1: Dreadnaught. 1: Psi-Phon. — 2.00
❑20, Aug 1988, color JBy (c); JBy (w); JBy (a); A: Doom Patrol. — 2.00
❑21, Sep 1988, color; JBy (c); JBy (w); JBy (a); Supergirl — 2.00
❑22, Oct 1988, color; (c); JBy (w); JBy (a); Supergirl — 2.00
❑23, Nov 1988, color CR (a); A: Batman. — 2.00
❑24, Dec 1988, color KGa (c); KGa (a) — 2.00
❑25, Dec 1988, color KGa (c); KGa (a) — 2.00
❑26, Jan 1989, color; KGa (c); KGa (a); Invasion! — 2.00
❑27, Jan 1989, color; KGa (c); KGa (a); Invasion! — 2.00
❑28, Feb 1989, color; KGa (c); KGa (a); in space — 2.00
❑29, Mar 1989, color; KGa (c); in space — 2.00
❑30, Apr 1989, color; KGa (c); KGa (a); in space — 2.00
❑31, May 1989, color; KGa (c); Mxyzptlk vs. Luthor — 2.00
❑32, Jun 1989, color KGa (c); KGa (a); V: Mongul. — 2.00
❑33, Jul 1989, color KGa (c); KGa (a) — 2.00
❑34, Aug 1989, color KGa (c); JOy (w); KGa (a); V: Skyhook. — 2.00
❑35, Sep 1989, color; KGa (c); JOy (w); CS, KGa (a); A: Black Racer. simultaneous stories — 2.00
❑36, Oct 1989, color JOy (c); JOy (w); JOy (a); V: Prankster. — 2.00
❑37, Nov 1989, color JOy (w); JOy (a); A: Newsboys. — 2.00
❑38, Dec 1989, color JOy (c); JOy (w) — 2.00
❑39, Jan 1990, color JOy (c); JOy (w); KGa, BMc (a) — 2.00
❑40, Feb 1990, color JOy (c); JOy (w); JOy (a) — 2.00
❑41, Mar 1990, color; JOy (c); JOy (w); JOy (a); A: Lobo. The Day of the Krypton Man part 1 — 2.00
❑42, Apr 1990, color; JOy (c); JOy (w); JOy (a); The Day of the Krypton Man part 4 — 2.00
❑43, May 1990, color JOy (c); JOy (w); JOy (a); V: Kryptonite Man. — 2.00
❑44, Jun 1990, color; JOy (c); JOy (w); JOy (a); A: Batman. Dark Knight over Metropolis — 2.00
❑45, Jul 1990, color; JOy (c); JOy (w); JOy (a); Jimmy Olsen's Diary insert — 2.00
❑46, Aug 1990, color JOy (c); JOy (w); JOy (a); A: Jade. A: Obsidian. V: Terraman. — 2.00
❑47, Sep 1990, color; (c); JOy (w); JOy (a); V: Blaze. Soul Search - Chapter 2 — 2.00
❑48, Oct 1990, color KGa, BMc (c); CS (a); A: Sinbad. — 2.00
❑49, Nov 1990, color JOy (w); JOy (a) — 2.00
❑50, Dec 1990, color; JOy (c); JOy (w); JOy, JBy, CS, KGa (a); Clark Kent proposes to Lois Lane — 4.00
❑50-2, Dec 1990, color; JOy (w); JOy, JBy, CS, KGa (a); Clark Kent proposes to Lois Lane — 1.75
❑51, Jan 1991, color; JOy (c); JOy (w); JOy (a); 1: Mister Z. V: Mr. Z. ▲ 1991-1 — 2.00
❑52, Feb 1991, color JOy (c); JOy (w); KGa (a); V: Terraman. — 2.00
❑52-2, Feb 1991 — 1.50
❑53, Mar 1991, color; JOy (c); JOy (w); JOy (a); ▲ 1991-7; Lois reacts to Superman disclosing identity — 2.50
❑53-2, Mar 1991; JOy (w); Lois reacts to Superman disclosing identity — 1.50
❑54, Apr 1991, color; JOy (c); JOy (w); JOy (a); ▲ 1991-10; Time & Time Again, Part 3; Newsboy Legion back-up — 1.75
❑55, May 1991, color; JOy (c); JOy (w); JOy (a); A: Demon. ▲ 1991-13; Time & Time Again, Part 6; Newboy Legion back-up — 1.75
❑56, Jun 1991 — 1.75
❑57, Jul 1991; Double-size; BMc (a); Krypton Man — 2.00
❑58, Aug 1991 V: Bloodhounds. — 1.50
❑59, Sep 1991 — 1.50
❑60, Oct 1991 1: Agent Liberty. V: Intergang. — 2.00
❑61, Nov 1991 A: Linear Men. A: Waverider. — 1.50
❑62, Dec 1991 — 1.50
❑63, Jan 1992 A: Aquaman. — 1.50
❑64, Feb 1992; Christmas issue — 1.50
❑65, Mar 1992 A: Guy Gardner. A: Deathstroke. A: Captain Marvel. A: Batman. A: Aquaman. — 1.50
❑66, Apr 1992 A: Guy Gardner. A: Deathstroke. A: Captain Marvel. A: Batman. A: Aquaman. — 1.50
❑67, May 1992 — 1.50
❑68, Jun 1992; Deathstroke — 1.50
❑69, Jul 1992 — 1.50
❑70, Aug 1992; Robin — 1.50
❑71, Sep 1992 — 1.50
❑72, Oct 1992 — 1.50
❑73, Nov 1992 A: Doomsday. A: Waverider. — 3.00
❑73-2 — 1.75
❑74, Dec 1992; Doomsday; ▲ 1992-74 — 4.00
❑74-2, Dec 1992; ▲ 1992-74 — 1.50
❑75, Jan 1993; D: Superman. newsstand; unbagged — 4.00
❑75/CS, Jan 1993 D: Superman. — 8.00
❑75/Platinum, Jan 1993; Platinum edition D: Superman. — 15.00
❑75-2, Jan 1993 D: Superman. — 2.00
❑75-3, Jan 1993 D: Superman. — 1.50
❑75-4, Jan 1993 D: Superman. — 1.50
❑76, Feb 1993 — 2.50
❑77, Mar 1993 — 2.50
❑78, Jun 1993 1: Cyborg Superman. — 2.00
❑78/CS, Jun 1993; 1: Cyborg Superman. Die-cut cover — 2.50
❑79, Jul 1993 — 2.00
❑80, Aug 1993; V: Mongul. Coast City destroyed; Cyborg Superman revealed as evil — 2.00
❑81, Sep 1993 — 2.00
❑82, Oct 1993; return of Superman; Reign of the Superman ends; True Superman revealed — 2.00
❑82/Variant, Oct 1993; Chromium cover; with poster; Reign of the Superman ends; True Superman revealed — 3.50
❑83, Nov 1993 — 2.00
❑84, Dec 1993 D: Adam Grant. V: Toyman. — 2.00
❑85, Jan 1994 — 2.00
❑86, Feb 1994 — 2.00
❑87, Mar 1994; Bizarro — 2.00
❑88, Apr 1994; Bizarro — 2.00
❑89, May 1994 — 2.00
❑90, Jun 1994 BA (a) — 2.00
❑91, Jul 1994 BA (a) — 2.00
❑92, Aug 1994 — 2.00
❑93, Sep 1994; Zero Hour — 2.00
❑94, Nov 1994 — 2.00
❑95, Dec 1994 A: Atom. — 2.00
❑96, Jan 1995; ▲ 1995-2 — 2.00
❑97, Feb 1995 1: Shadowdragon. — 2.00
❑98, Mar 1995 — 2.00
❑99, Apr 1995 A: Agent Liberty. — 2.00
❑100, May 1995; 100th anniversary edition; ▲ 1995-18 — 3.00
❑100/Variant, May 1995; 100th anniversary edition; enhanced cover; ▲ 1995-18 — 4.00
❑101, Jun 1995; ▲ 1995-22 — 2.00
❑102, Jul 1995 V: Captain Marvel. — 2.00
❑103, Aug 1995 V: Arclight. — 2.00
❑104, Sep 1995; Cyborg is released by Darkseid — 2.00
❑105, Oct 1995 A: Green Lantern. — 2.00
❑106, Nov 1995 — 2.00
❑107, Dec 1995 — 2.00
❑108, Jan 1996 D: Mope. — 2.00
❑109, Feb 1996; Christmas story; return of Lori Lemaris; ▲ 1996-7 — 2.00
❑110, Mar 1996; A: Plastic Man. ▲ 1996-11 — 2.00
❑111, Apr 1996; ▲ 1996-16 — 2.00
❑112, Jun 1996 — 2.00
❑113, Jul 1996 — 2.00
❑114, Aug 1996 CS (a) — 2.00
❑115, Sep 1996; Lois becomes foreign correspondent — 2.00
❑116, Oct 1996; Teen Titans preview — 2.00
❑117, Nov 1996; Final Night; ▲ 1996-42 — 2.00
❑118, Dec 1996; A: Wonder Woman. Lois decides to return to Metropolis; ▲ 1996-46 — 2.00
❑119, Jan 1997; A: Legion. ▲ 1997-1 — 2.00
❑120, Feb 1997 — 2.00
❑121, Mar 1997; ▲ 1997-10 — 2.00
❑122, Apr 1997; energy powers begin to manifest — 2.00
❑123, May 1997; New costume — 3.00
❑123/Variant, May 1997; glow-in-the-dark cardstock cover; New costume — 5.00
❑124, Jun 1997 A: Booster Gold. — 2.00
❑125, Jul 1997; A: Atom. in Kandor — 2.00
❑126, Aug 1997 A: Batman. — 2.00
❑127, Sep 1997; Superman Revenge Squad leader's identity revealed — 2.00
❑128, Oct 1997; V: Cyborg Superman. Genesis — 2.00
❑129, Nov 1997; A: Scorn. ▲ 1997-44 — 2.00
❑130, Dec 1997; Face cover — 2.00
❑131, Jan 1998; D: Mayor Berkowitz. birth of Lena Luthor — 2.00
❑132, Feb 1998 — 2.00
❑133, Mar 1998 — 2.00
❑134, Apr 1998; Millennium Giants — 2.00
❑135, May 1998; leads into Superman Forever #1; End of Superman Red/Blue — 2.00
❑136, Jul 1998 — 2.00
❑137, Aug 1998 V: Muto. — 2.00
❑138, Sep 1998 A: Kismet. V: Dominus. — 2.00
❑139, Oct 1998 V: Dominus. — 1.99
❑140, Dec 1998; in Kandor; Inventor's identity revealed — 1.99
❑141, Jan 1999 1: Outburst. — 1.99
❑142, Feb 1999 A: Outburst. — 1.99
❑143, Mar 1999 A: Supermen of America. A: Superman Robots. — 1.99
❑144, Apr 1999; Fortress destroyed — 1.99
❑145, Jun 1999; ▲ 1999-23 — 1.99
❑146, Jul 1999 A: Toyman. — 1.99
❑147, Aug 1999; Superman as Green Lantern — 1.99
❑148, Sep 1999 — 1.99
❑149, Oct 1999; SB (a); ▲ 1999-40 — 1.99
❑150, Nov 1999 — 1.99
❑150/Variant, Nov 1999; Special cover — 3.95
❑151, Dec 1999; Daily Planet reopens — 1.99
❑152, Jan 2000; JPH (w); ▲ 2000-1 — 1.99
❑153, Feb 2000; JPH (w); ▲ 2000-5 — 1.99
❑154, Mar 2000 — 1.99
❑155, Apr 2000 — 1.99
❑156, May 2000; JPH (w); ▲ 2000-18 — 1.99
❑157, Jun 2000; JPH (w); ▲ 2000-22 — 1.99
❑158, Jul 2000 — 1.99
❑159, Aug 2000 — 1.99
❑160, Sep 2000 — 2.25
❑161, Oct 2000; JPH (w); ▲ 2000-39 — 2.25
❑162, Nov 2000; JPH (w); ▲ 2000-43 — 2.25
❑163, Dec 2000; JPH (w); ▲ 2000-47 — 2.25
❑164, Jan 2001; JPH (w); ▲ 2001-1 — 2.25
❑165, Feb 2001; JPH (w); ▲ 2001-6 — 2.25

N-MINT

❑166, Mar 2001; JPH (w); ▲ 2001-10 ...... 2.25
❑167, Apr 2001; JPH (w); ▲ 2001-14 ...... 2.25
❑168, May 2001; JPH (w); ▲ 2001-18 ...... 2.25
❑169, Jun 2001; ▲ 2001-22 ...... 2.25
❑170, Jul 2001 A: Krypto. 2.25
❑171, Aug 2001 ...... 2.25
❑172, Sep 2001 JPH (w) 2.25
❑173, Oct 2001 ...... 2.25
❑174, Nov 2001; ▲ 2001-42 ...... 2.25
❑175, Dec 2001; Giant-size; ▲ 2001-46; Joker: Last Laugh crossover 3.50
❑176, Jan 2002; ▲ 2002-1 ...... 2.25
❑177, Feb 2002 ...... 2.25
❑178, Mar 2002 ...... 2.25
❑179, Apr 2002 ...... 2.25
❑180, May 2002 ...... 2.25
❑181, Jun 2002 ...... 2.25
❑182, Jul 2002 ...... 2.25
❑183, Aug 2002 ...... 2.25
❑184, Sep 2002 ...... 2.25
❑185, Oct 2002 BA (a) 2.25
❑186, Nov 2002 ...... 2.25
❑187, Dec 2002 ...... 2.25
❑188, Jan 2003; Aquaman (6th series) #1 preview 2.25
❑189, Feb 2003 ...... 2.25
❑190, Apr 2003 ...... 2.25
❑190/A, Apr 2003 ...... 3.95
❑191, May 2003 ...... 2.25
❑192, Jun 2003 ...... 2.25
❑193, Jul 2003 ...... 2.25
❑194, Aug 2003 ...... 2.25
❑195, Sep 2003 ...... 2.25
❑196, Oct 2003 ...... 2.25
❑197, Nov 2003 ...... 2.25
❑198, Dec 2003 ...... 2.25
❑199, Jan 2004 ...... 2.25
❑200, Feb 2004 ...... 3.50
❑201, Mar 2004 ...... 8.00
❑202, Apr 2004 ...... 2.25
❑203, May 2004; Jim Lee sketchbook 6.00
❑204, Jun 2004 ...... 3.00
❑205, Jul 2004 ...... 2.50
❑206, Aug 2004 ...... 2.50
❑207, Sep 2004 ...... 2.50
❑1000000, Nov 1998 ...... 3.00
❑1000000/Ltd.; Signed edition 14.99
❑Annual 1, ca. 1987 O: Titano. 4.00
❑Annual 2, ca. 1988; Private Lives 3.00
❑Annual 3, ca. 1991 ...... 2.50
❑Annual 3-2 ...... 2.00
❑Annual 3-3; silver 2.00
❑Annual 4, ca. 1992 ...... 2.50
❑Annual 5, ca. 1993 1: Myriad. 2.50
❑Annual 6, ca. 1994; Elseworlds 2.95
❑Annual 7, ca. 1995; A: Dr. Occult. A: Doctor Occult. Year One 3.95
❑Annual 8, ca. 1996; Legends of the Dead Earth; The League of Supermen 2.95
❑Annual 9, Jul 1997; A: Doc Savage. Pulp Heroes 2.95
❑Annual 10, Oct 1998; A: Phantom Zone villains. Ghosts 2.95
❑Annual 11, Oct 1999; JLApe 2.95
❑Annual 12, Aug 2000; 2000 Annual; Planet DC 3.50
❑Giant Size 1, Feb 1999; 80 page giant size 4.95
❑Giant Size 2, Jun 1999; 80 page giant size 4.95
❑Giant Size 3, Nov 2000; 80 page giant size 4.95
❑Special 1, ca. 1992; 1992 Special 4.00
❑3D 1 ...... 4.00

SUPERMAN 3-D
DC

❑1, Dec 1998 ...... 4.00

SUPERMAN ADVENTURES
DC

❑1, Nov 1996; based on animated series; follow-up to pilot episode 3.00
❑2, Dec 1996 V: Metallo. 2.50
❑3, Jan 1997 V: Brainiac. 2.50
❑4, Feb 1997 ...... 2.00
❑5, Mar 1997 V: Livewire. 2.00
❑6, Apr 1997 ...... 2.00
❑7, May 1997 V: Mala. V: Jax-ur. 2.00
❑8, Jun 1997 V: Mala. V: Jax-ur. 2.00
❑9, Jul 1997 ...... 2.00
❑10, Aug 1997 V: Toyman. 2.00
❑11, Sep 1997 ...... 2.00
❑12, Oct 1997 ...... 2.00
❑13, Nov 1997 ...... 2.00
❑14, Dec 1997; ME (w); Face cover 2.00
❑15, Jan 1998 ME (w); A: Bibbo. 2.00
❑16, Feb 1998 ...... 2.00
❑17, Mar 1998 ...... 2.00
❑18, Apr 1998 DGry (w) 2.00
❑19, May 1998 ...... 2.00
❑20, Jun 1998 ...... 2.00
❑21, Jul 1998; double-sized; adapts Supergirl episode 3.95
❑22, Aug 1998 ...... 2.00
❑23, Sep 1998 A: Livewire. V: Brainiac. 2.00
❑24, Oct 1998 V: Parasite. 2.00
❑25, Nov 1998 A: Batgirl. 2.00
❑26, Dec 1998 V: Mxyzptlk. 2.00
❑27, Jan 1999 1: Superior-Man. 2.00
❑28, Feb 1999; A: Jimmy Olsen. Jimmy and Superman switch bodies 2.00
❑29, Mar 1999; A: Bizarro. A: Lobo. Lobo apperance 2.00
❑30, Apr 1999 ...... 2.00
❑31, May 1999 ...... 2.00
❑32, Jun 1999 ...... 2.00
❑33, Jul 1999 ...... 2.00
❑34, Aug 1999 A: Doctor Fate. 2.00
❑35, Sep 1999 V: Toyman. 2.00
❑36, Oct 1999 ...... 2.00
❑37, Nov 1999 V: Multi-Face. 2.00
❑38, Dec 1999 ...... 2.00
❑39, Jan 2000 ...... 2.00
❑40, Feb 2000 ...... 2.00
❑41, Mar 2000 ...... 1.99
❑42, Apr 2000 ...... 1.99
❑43, May 2000 ...... 1.99
❑44, Jun 2000 ...... 1.99
❑45, Jul 2000 ...... 1.99
❑46, Aug 2000 ...... 1.99
❑47, Sep 2000 ...... 1.99
❑48, Oct 2000 ...... 1.99
❑49, Nov 2000 ...... 1.99
❑50, Dec 2000 ...... 1.99
❑51, Jan 2001 ...... 1.99
❑52, Feb 2001 ...... 1.99
❑53, Mar 2001 ME (w) 1.99
❑54, Apr 2001 ...... 1.99
❑55, May 2001 ...... 1.99
❑56, Jun 2001 ...... 1.99
❑57, Jul 2001 ...... 1.99
❑58, Aug 2001 ...... 1.99
❑59, Sep 2001 ...... 1.99
❑60, Oct 2001 ...... 1.99
❑61, Nov 2001 ...... 1.99
❑62, Dec 2001 ...... 1.99
❑63, Jan 2002 ...... 1.99
❑64, Feb 2002 ...... 1.99
❑65, Mar 2002 ...... 1.99
❑66, Apr 2002 ...... 1.99
❑Annual 1, ca. 1997; JSa (a); ties in with Adventures in the DC Universe Annual #1 and Batman and Robin Adventures Annual #2 ...... 3.95
❑Special 1, Feb 1998 V: Lobo. 2.95

SUPERMAN/ALIENS 2: GOD WAR
DC

❑1, May 2002 ...... 2.99
❑2, Jun 2002 ...... 2.99
❑3, Jul 2002 ...... 2.99
❑4, Aug 2002 ...... 2.99

SUPERMAN: A NATION DIVIDED
DC

❑1; prestige format; Elseworlds; Superman in Civil War 4.95

The various types of kryptonite were introduced as story needs dictated in *Superman*.

SUPERMAN & BATMAN: GENERATIONS
DC

❑1, Jan 1999; Elseworlds story 4.95
❑2, Feb 1999; Elseworlds story 4.95
❑3, Mar 1999; Elseworlds story 4.95
❑4, Apr 1999; Elseworlds story 4.95

SUPERMAN & BATMAN: GENERATIONS II
DC

❑1, Oct 2001 ...... 5.95
❑2, Nov 2001 ...... 5.95
❑3, Dec 2001 ...... 5.95
❑4, Jan 2002 ...... 5.95

SUPERMAN & BATMAN: GENERATIONS III
DC

❑1, Mar 2003 ...... 2.95
❑2, Apr 2003 ...... 2.95
❑3, May 2003 ...... 2.95
❑4, Jun 2003 ...... 2.95
❑5, Jul 2003 ...... 2.95
❑6, Aug 2003 ...... 2.95
❑7, Sep 2003 ...... 2.95
❑8, Oct 2003 ...... 2.95
❑9, Nov 2003 ...... 2.95
❑10, Dec 2003 ...... 2.95
❑11, Jan 2004 ...... 2.95
❑12, Feb 2004 ...... 2.95

SUPERMAN & BATMAN MAGAZINE
WELSH

❑1, Sum 1993; bagged with poster 3.00
❑2, Fal 1993 ...... 2.00
❑3, Win 1993; trading cards 3.00
❑4, Spr 1994 ...... 2.00
❑5, Sum 1994; magazine 2.00
❑7, Win 1995; magazine 2.00
❑8, Spr 1995; magazine 2.00

SUPERMAN AND BATMAN: WORLD'S FUNNEST
DC

❑1, ca. 2000 ...... 6.95

SUPERMAN & BUGS BUNNY
DC

❑1, Jul 2000 ...... 2.50
❑2, Aug 2000 ...... 2.50
❑3, Sep 2000 ...... 2.50
❑4, Oct 2000 ...... 2.50

SUPERMAN & SAVAGE DRAGON: CHICAGO
DC

❑1, Dec 2002 ...... 5.95

SUPERMAN/BATMAN SECRET FILES
DC

❑1, Dec 2003 ...... 4.95

SUPERMAN/BATMAN
DC

❑1, Oct 2003 ...... 5.00
❑1/RRP, Oct 2003; Retailer incentive edition (aka RRP edition); no cover price 60.00
❑2, Nov 2003 ...... 2.95
❑3, Dec 2003 ...... 2.95
❑3-2, Mar 2004 ...... 2.95
❑4, Jan 2004 ...... 2.95

N-MINT

❑5, Feb 2004 .... 2.95
❑6, Mar 2004 JPH (w) 2.95
❑7, Apr 2004 JPH (w) 2.95
❑8, May 2004 .... 8.00
❑8-2, May 2004, color; Turner sketch cover 6.00
❑8-3, May 2004, color; Wonder Woman cover by Michael Turner ... 4.00
❑8-4, Aug 2004 .... 2.95
❑9, Jun 2004 .... 2.95
❑9-2, Jul 2004; reprint 2.95
❑9-3, Aug 2004 .... 2.95
❑10, Jul 2004 .... 2.95
❑10-2, Aug 2004 .... 2.95
❑11, Sep 2004 ....

SUPERMAN: BIRTHRIGHT
DC

❑1, Sep 2003 .... 2.95
❑2, Oct 2003 .... 2.95
❑3, Nov 2003 .... 2.95
❑4, Jan 2004 .... 2.95
❑5, Feb 2004 .... 2.95
❑6, Mar 2004 .... 2.95
❑7, Apr 2004 .... 2.95
❑8, May 2004 .... 2.95
❑9, May 2004 .... 2.95
❑10, Jul 2004 .... 2.95
❑11, Aug 2004 .... 2.95
❑12, Sep 2004 ....

SUPERMAN: BLOOD OF MY ANCESTORS
DC

❑1, Nov 2003 .... 6.95

SUPERMAN: DAY OF DOOM
DC

❑1, ca. 2003 .... 9.95

SUPERMAN: DISTANT FIRES
DC

❑1, Feb 1998; prestige format; Elseworlds 5.95

SUPERMAN/DOOMSDAY: HUNTER/PREY
DC

❑1, ca. 1994; prestige format 6.00
❑2, ca. 1994; prestige format O: Doomsday. 6.00
❑3, ca. 1994; prestige format D: Doomsday. 6.00

SUPERMAN: EMPEROR JOKER
DC

❑1, Oct 2000 .... 3.50

SUPERMAN: END OF THE CENTURY
DC

❑1 .... 5.95

SUPERMAN FAMILY, THE
DC

❑164, May 1974; NC (c); CS, JM, KS (a); Series continued from Superman's Pal Jimmy Olsen; reprints from Action #339, Adventure #272, Lois Lane #51, and Jimmy Olsen #76 28.00
❑165, Jul 1974; reprints from Action #296, Jimmy Olsen #59, Lois Lane #47, Superboy #111, #133, and Superman #186 .... 13.00
❑166, Sep 1974; NC (c); Reprints w/ new Lois Lane story 13.00
❑167, Nov 1974; NC (c); KS (a); Reprints from Superboy (1st series) #100, and #124; Jimmy Olsen stories new 13.00
❑168, Jan 1975; Supergirl reprinted from Action #350; Bizarro Luthor reprinted from Adventure #293; Lois Lane story new 13.00
❑169, Mar 1975 NC (c); JM (a) 13.00
❑170, May 1975 .... 11.00
❑171, Jul 1975 .... 11.00
❑172, Sep 1975; KS (c); CS, KS (a); A: Green Lantern. Reprints from Action #364, and Jimmy Olsen #85 .... 11.00
❑173, Nov 1975 .... 11.00
❑174, Jan 1976 .... 11.00
❑175, Mar 1976 .... 11.00
❑176, May 1976 .... 11.00
❑177, Jul 1976; reprints from Jimmy Olsen #74 and Lois Lane #53 .... 11.00
❑178, Sep 1976 .... 5.00
❑179, Oct 1976 .... 5.00
❑180, Nov 1976 .... 5.00
❑181, Jan 1977 .... 3.50
❑182, Apr 1977 .... 3.50
❑183, Jun 1977 .... 3.50
❑184, Aug 1977 V: Prankster. 3.50
❑185, Oct 1977 .... 3.50
❑186, Dec 1977 A: Earth-2 Superman. 3.50
❑187, Feb 1978 A: Earth-2 Superman. 3.50
❑188, Apr 1978; Red Kryptonite 3.50
❑189, Jun 1978 .... 3.50
❑190, Aug 1978 .... 3.50
❑191, Oct 1978 .... 3.50
❑192, Dec 1978 .... 3.50
❑193, Feb 1979 .... 3.50
❑194, Apr 1979 MR (a); V: Jimmy clones. 3.50
❑195, Jun 1979 .... 3.50
❑196, Aug 1979 .... 3.50
❑197, Oct 1979 .... 3.50
❑198, Dec 1979 .... 3.50
❑199, Feb 1980 .... 3.50
❑200, Apr 1980; Imaginary Story 3.50
❑201, Jun 1980 .... 3.00
❑202, Aug 1980 .... 3.00
❑203, Oct 1980 1: Lana Lang. 3.00
❑204, Dec 1980 V: Enchantress. 3.00
❑205, Feb 1981 1: H.I.V.E.. V: Enchantress. 3.00
❑206, Apr 1981 A: Lesla-Lar. 3.00
❑207, Jun 1981 A: Legion. V: Universo. 3.00
❑208, Jul 1981; Supergirl relocates to New York 3.00
❑209, Aug 1981 .... 3.00
❑210, Sep 1981 .... 3.00
❑211, Oct 1981 .... 3.00
❑212, Nov 1981 .... 3.00
❑213, Dec 1981 1: Insect Queen (Lana Lang). 3.00
❑214, Jan 1982 .... 3.00
❑215, Feb 1982 .... 3.00
❑216, Mar 1982 .... 3.00
❑217, Apr 1982 .... 3.00
❑218, May 1982 .... 3.00
❑219, Jun 1982 V: Master Jailer. 3.00
❑220, Jul 1982 V: Master Jailer. 3.00
❑221, Aug 1982 V: Master Jailer. 3.00
❑222, Sep 1982 .... 3.00

SUPERMAN/FANTASTIC FOUR
DC

❑1 .... 9.95

SUPERMAN FOR ALL SEASONS
DC

❑1, Sep 1998; prestige format; Spring 4.95
❑2, Oct 1998; prestige format; Summer 4.95
❑3, Nov 1998; prestige format; Fall ... 4.95
❑4, Dec 1998; prestige format; Winter 4.95

SUPERMAN FOR EARTH
DC

❑1, Apr 1991 .... 4.95

SUPERMAN FOREVER
DC

❑1, Jun 1998; newsstand edition; JBy, DG (a); Superman returns to normal powers 5.50
❑1/Autographed, Jun 1998 JBy, DG (a) 30.00
❑1/Variant, Jun 1998; prestige format; lenticular animation cover; Superman returns to normal powers 7.00

SUPERMAN GALLERY, THE
DC

❑1, ca. 1993 .... 2.95

SUPERMAN/GEN13
WILDSTORM

❑1, Jun 2000 .... 2.50
❑1/A, Jun 2000; Fairchild opening shirt to show Supergirl costume on cover 2.50
❑2, Jul 2000; Supergirl/Fairchild cover 2.50
❑2/A, Jul 2000; Large figures looking down on cover 2.50
❑3, Aug 2000 .... 2.50

SUPERMAN (GIVEAWAYS)
DC

❑1; game giveaway 1.00
❑2; Pizza Hut 1.00
❑3, Jul 1980; Radio Shack 1.00
❑4; Radio Shack 1.00
❑5; Radio Shack 1.00

SUPERMAN, INC.
DC

❑1, Jan 2000 .... 6.95

SUPERMAN IV MOVIE SPECIAL
DC

❑1, Oct 1987 .... 2.00

SUPERMAN: KAL
DC

❑1; prestige format one-shot 5.95

SUPERMAN: KANSAS SIGHTING
DC

❑1, Jan 2004 .... 6.95
❑2, Feb 2004 .... 6.95

SUPERMAN: KING OF THE WORLD
DC

❑1, Jun 1999; ▲ 1999-22 .... 3.95
❑1/Gold, Jun 1999; enhanced card-stock cover; ▲ 1999-22 .... 4.95

SUPERMAN: LAST SON OF EARTH
DC

❑1, Sep 2000 .... 5.95
❑2, Oct 2000 .... 5.95

SUPERMAN: LAST STAND ON KRYPTON
DC

❑1, May 2003 .... 6.95

SUPERMAN: LEX 2000
DC

❑1, Jan 2001 .... 3.50

SUPERMAN: LOIS LANE
DC

❑1, Jun 1998; Girlfrenzy 1.95

SUPERMAN/MADMAN HULLABALOO, THE
DARK HORSE / DC

❑1, Jun 1997; crossover with DC 2.95
❑2, Jul 1997; crossover with DC 2.95
❑3, Aug 1997; crossover with DC 2.95

SUPERMAN MEETS THE QUIK BUNNY
DC

❑1; promotional giveaway from Nestle CI, DG (a) 1.00

SUPERMAN: METROPOLIS
DC

❑1, Apr 2003 .... 2.95
❑2, May 2003 .... 2.95
❑3, Jun 2003 .... 2.95
❑4, Jul 2003 .... 2.95
❑5, Aug 2003 .... 2.95
❑6, Sep 2003 .... 2.95
❑7, Oct 2003 .... 2.95
❑8, Nov 2003 .... 2.95
❑9, Dec 2003 .... 2.95
❑10, Jan 2004 .... 2.95
❑11, Feb 2004 .... 2.95
❑12, Mar 2004 .... 2.95

SUPERMAN METROPOLIS SECRET FILES
DC

❑1, Jul 2000 .... 4.95

SUPERMAN MONSTER, THE
DC

❑1 .... 5.95

SUPERMAN MOVIE SPECIAL, THE
DC

❑1, Sep 1983; GM, CS (a); adapts Superman III 2.00

N-MINT

SUPERMAN: OUR WORLDS AT WAR SECRET FILES
DC

❑1, Aug 2001 ... 5.95

SUPERMAN: PEACE ON EARTH
DC

❑1, Jan 1999; Oversized ... 9.95
❑1-2 ... 9.95

SUPERMAN PLUS
DC

❑1, Feb 1997 ... 2.95

SUPERMAN: PRESIDENT LEX
DC

❑1, ca. 2003 ... 17.95

SUPERMAN: RED SON
DC

❑1, Jun 2003 ... 5.95
❑2, Jul 2003 ... 5.95
❑3, Aug 2003 ... 5.95

SUPERMAN RED/SUPERMAN BLUE
DC

❑1, Feb 1998 ... 3.95
❑Deluxe 1, Feb 1998; one-shot with 3-D cover; Superman splits into two beings ... 4.95

SUPERMAN: SAVE THE PLANET
DC

❑1, Oct 1998; Daily Planet sold to Lex Luthor ... 2.95
❑1/Variant, Oct 1998; acetate overlay ... 3.95

SUPERMAN: SECRET FILES
DC

❑1, Jan 1998; background material ... 4.95
❑2, May 1999; background material .. 4.95

SUPERMAN: SECRET FILES 2004
DC

❑1, Aug 2004 ... 4.95

SUPERMAN: SECRET IDENTITY
DC

❑1, Mar 2004 ... 5.95
❑2, Apr 2004 ... 5.95
❑3, May 2004 ... 5.95
❑4, Jun 2004 ... 5.95

SUPERMAN'S GIRL FRIEND LOIS LANE
DC

❑1, Apr 1958 ... 2600.00
❑2, Jun 1958 ... 625.00
❑3, Aug 1958 ... 415.00
❑4, Oct 1958 ... 300.00
❑5, Nov 1958 ... 300.00
❑6, Jan 1959 ... 220.00
❑7, Feb 1959 ... 220.00
❑8, Apr 1959 CS (c); KS (a) ... 220.00
❑9, May 1959 A: Pat Boone. ... 220.00
❑10, Jul 1959 ... 220.00
❑11, Aug 1959 ... 125.00
❑12, Oct 1959 ... 125.00
❑13, Nov 1959; CS, KS (a); G-87; Reprints from issues #41, #43, #49, #54, and #57 ... 125.00
❑14, Jan 1960 ... 125.00
❑15, Feb 1960 KS (a) ... 125.00
❑16, Apr 1960 ... 125.00
❑17, May 1960 ... 125.00
❑18, Jul 1960 ... 125.00
❑19, Aug 1960 ... 215.00
❑20, Oct 1960 ... 125.00
❑21, Nov 1960 ... 86.00
❑22, Jan 1961 ... 86.00
❑23, Feb 1961 ... 86.00
❑24, Apr 1961 ... 86.00
❑25, May 1961 ... 86.00
❑26, Jul 1961 ... 86.00
❑27, Aug 1961 KS (a) ... 86.00
❑28, Oct 1961 ... 86.00
❑29, Nov 1961 ... 86.00
❑30, Jan 1962 KS (a) ... 48.00

N-MINT

❑31, Feb 1962 ... 48.00
❑32, Apr 1962 ... 48.00
❑33, May 1962 A: Phantom Zone. A: Mon-El. ... 48.00
❑34, Jul 1962 ... 48.00
❑35, Aug 1962 CS (a) ... 48.00
❑36, Oct 1962 KS (a) ... 48.00
❑37, Nov 1962 KS (a) ... 48.00
❑38, Jan 1963 ... 48.00
❑39, Feb 1963 CS (a) ... 48.00
❑40, Apr 1963 KS (a) ... 48.00
❑41, May 1963 CS, KS (a) ... 48.00
❑42, Jul 1963 ... 48.00
❑43, Aug 1963 KS (a) ... 48.00
❑44, Oct 1963 ... 48.00
❑45, Nov 1963 ... 48.00
❑46, Jan 1964 ... 48.00
❑47, Feb 1964 ... 48.00
❑48, Apr 1964 ... 48.00
❑49, May 1964 KS (a) ... 48.00
❑50, Jul 1964 ... 48.00
❑51, Aug 1964 KS (a) ... 34.00
❑52, Oct 1964 ... 34.00
❑53, Nov 1964; KS (a); How Lois fell in love with Superman ... 34.00
❑54, Jan 1965 KS (a) ... 34.00
❑55, Feb 1965 ... 34.00
❑56, Apr 1965 ... 34.00
❑57, May 1965 KS (a) ... 34.00
❑58, Jul 1965 ... 34.00
❑59, Aug 1965 ... 34.00
❑60, Oct 1965 ... 34.00
❑61, Nov 1965 KS (a) ... 34.00
❑62, Jan 1966 ... 34.00
❑63, Feb 1966; V: S.K.U.L.. Noel Neill interview ... 34.00
❑64, Apr 1966 ... 34.00
❑65, May 1966 ... 34.00
❑66, Jul 1966 ... 34.00
❑67, Aug 1966 ... 34.00
❑68, Sep 1966; Giant-size ... 44.00
❑69, Oct 1966 ... 34.00
❑70, Nov 1966; A: Catwoman. 1st Catwoman in Silver Age ... 175.00
❑71, Jan 1967 A: Catwoman. ... 105.00
❑72, Feb 1967 ... 15.00
❑73, Apr 1967 ... 15.00
❑74, May 1967 1: Bizarro Flash. ... 34.00
❑75, Jul 1967 ... 15.00
❑76, Aug 1967 ... 15.00
❑77, Sep 1967; Giant-size ... 24.00
❑78, Oct 1967 ... 15.00
❑79, Nov 1967 ... 10.00
❑80, Jan 1968 ... 10.00
❑81, Feb 1968 ... 10.00
❑82, Apr 1968 IN (a) ... 10.00
❑83, May 1968 IN (a) ... 10.00
❑84, Jul 1968 IN (a) ... 10.00
❑85, Aug 1968 IN (a) ... 10.00
❑86, Sep 1968; Giant-size; NA, KS (a); G-51; Reprints stories from Lois Lane #37 and #41 ... 16.00
❑87, Oct 1968 IN (a) ... 10.00
❑88, Nov 1968 IN (a) ... 10.00
❑89, Jan 1969; Imaginary Story; Lois marries Batman ... 10.00
❑90, Feb 1969 IN (a) ... 10.00
❑91, Apr 1969 CS (a) ... 10.00
❑92, May 1969 IN (a) ... 10.00
❑93, Jul 1969 IN (a); A: Wonder Woman. ... 10.00
❑94, Aug 1969 IN (a) ... 10.00
❑95, Sep 1969, b&w; Giant-size; KS (a); Giant-size; Reprints stories from Lois Lane #8, #27, #36, and #40 ... 25.00
❑96, Oct 1969 IN (a) ... 8.00
❑97, Nov 1969 IN (a) ... 8.00
❑98, Jan 1970 IN (a) ... 8.00
❑99, Feb 1970 IN (a) ... 8.00
❑100, Apr 1970 IN (a) ... 8.00
❑101, May 1970 IN (a) ... 8.00
❑102, Jul 1970 IN (a) ... 8.00
❑103, Aug 1970 IN (a) ... 8.00

The WB animated series was the basis for *Superman Adventures*.

© 1996 DC Comics.

N-MINT

❑104, Sep 1970; Giant-size ... 16.00
❑105, Oct 1970 O: Rose & Thorn II (Rose Forrest). 1: Rose & Thorn II (Rose Forrest). 1: The 1,000. ... 14.00
❑106, Nov 1970 ... 14.00
❑107, Dec 1970 ... 6.00
❑108, Feb 1971 ... 6.00
❑109, Apr 1971 ... 6.00
❑110, May 1971 ... 6.00
❑111, Jul 1971 ... 6.00
❑112, Aug 1971; KS (a); Reprints from Lois Lane #30 ... 6.00
❑113, Sep 1971; Giant-size; 80-page Giant (G-87) ... 14.00
❑114, Sep 1971; KS (a); Reprints from Lois Lane #61 ... 6.00
❑115, Oct 1971; BO (a); Reprints Lois Lane feature from Superman (1st series) #28, and Lady Danger feature from Sensation Comics #84 ... 6.00
❑116, Nov 1971 ... 6.00
❑117, Dec 1971 ... 6.00
❑118, Jan 1972 ... 6.00
❑119, Feb 1972 ... 6.00
❑120, Mar 1972; KS (a); Reprints from Lois Lane #43, and Superman (1st series) #29 ... 6.00
❑121, Apr 1972 ... 5.00
❑122, May 1972; CS (a); Reprints from Lois Lane #35, and Superman (1st series) #30 ... 5.00
❑123, Jun 1972 ... 5.00
❑124, Jul 1972 ... 5.00
❑125, Aug 1972 ... 5.00
❑126, Sep 1972 ... 5.00
❑127, Oct 1972 ... 5.00
❑128, Dec 1972 ... 5.00
❑129, Feb 1973 ... 5.00
❑130, Apr 1973 ... 5.00
❑131, Jun 1973; KS (a); Reprints from Lois Lane #8 ... 5.00
❑132, Jul 1973 ... 5.00
❑133, Sep 1973 ... 5.00
❑134, Oct 1973 ... 5.00
❑135, Nov 1973 ... 5.00
❑136, Jan 1974 A: Wonder Woman. .. 5.00
❑137, ca. 1974 ... 5.00
❑Annual 1, Sum 1962 ... 75.00
❑Annual 2, Sum 1963 ... 50.00

SUPERMAN: SILVER BANSHEE
DC

❑1, Dec 1998 ... 2.25
❑2, Jan 1999 ... 2.25

SUPERMAN'S METROPOLIS
DC

❑1, Jan 1997; prestige format; Elseworlds ... 5.95

SUPERMAN'S NEMESIS: LEX LUTHOR
DC

❑1, Mar 1999 ... 2.50
❑2, Apr 1999 ... 2.50
❑3, May 1999 ... 2.50
❑4, Jun 1999 ... 2.50

SUPERMAN'S PAL JIMMY OLSEN
DC

❑16, Oct 1956 ... 235.00
❑17, Dec 1956 ... 235.00
❑18, Feb 1957 ... 235.00

	N-MINT
❑19, Mar 1957 CS (c)	235.00
❑20, Apr 1957	235.00
❑21, Jun 1957	150.00
❑22, Aug 1957 CS (a)	150.00
❑23, Sep 1957	150.00
❑24, Oct 1957 CS (a)	150.00
❑25, Dec 1957	150.00
❑26, Feb 1958	150.00
❑27, Mar 1958 CS (a)	150.00
❑28, Apr 1958 CS (a)	150.00
❑29, Jun 1958	150.00
❑30, Aug 1958	150.00
❑31, Sep 1958 1: Elastic Lad (Jimmy Olsen).	100.00
❑32, Oct 1958	100.00
❑33, Dec 1958	100.00
❑34, Jan 1959	100.00
❑35, Mar 1959	100.00
❑36, Apr 1959 1: Lucy Lane.	100.00
❑37, Jun 1959	100.00
❑38, Jul 1959	100.00
❑39, Sep 1959	100.00
❑40, Oct 1959, color CS (a); A: Supergirl.	100.00
❑41, Dec 1959	75.00
❑42, Jan 1960	75.00
❑43, Mar 1960	75.00
❑44, Apr 1960	75.00
❑45, Jun 1960	75.00
❑46, Jul 1960	75.00
❑47, Sep 1960	75.00
❑48, Oct 1960 1: Superman Emergency Squad.	75.00
❑49, Dec 1960; Jimmy Olsen becomes Congorilla	75.00
❑50, Jan 1961	75.00
❑51, Mar 1961	50.00
❑52, Apr 1961	50.00
❑53, Jun 1961 CS (a)	50.00
❑54, Jul 1961	50.00
❑55, Sep 1961	50.00
❑56, Oct 1961	50.00
❑57, Dec 1961 CS (a); A: Supergirl.	30.00
❑58, Jan 1962	30.00
❑59, Mar 1962 CS (a)	30.00
❑60, Apr 1962	30.00
❑61, Jun 1962	30.00
❑62, Jul 1962; Elastic Lad in Phantom Zone	30.00
❑63, Sep 1962	30.00
❑64, Oct 1962	30.00
❑65, Dec 1962	30.00
❑66, Jan 1963	30.00
❑67, Mar 1963	30.00
❑68, Apr 1963	30.00
❑69, Jun 1963 CS (a)	30.00
❑70, Jul 1963; Silver Kryptonite	30.00
❑71, Sep 1963	25.00
❑72, Oct 1963 CS (a); A: Legion of Super-Heroes.	30.00
❑73, Dec 1963	30.00
❑74, Jan 1964 CS (a); A: Lex Luthor.	25.00
❑75, Mar 1964 A: Supergirl.	25.00
❑76, Apr 1964 A: Lightning Lass. A: Saturn Girl, Lightning Lass, Triplicate Girl. A: Triplicate Girl. A: Saturn Girl.	30.00
❑77, Jun 1964	25.00
❑78, Jul 1964	25.00
❑79, Sep 1964; Jimmy as Beatle	25.00
❑80, Oct 1964 1: Bizarro-Jimmy Olsen.	25.00
❑81, Dec 1964	25.00
❑82, Jan 1965	25.00
❑83, Mar 1965	25.00
❑84, Apr 1965; CS (a); Gorilla cover	25.00
❑85, Jun 1965 CS (a)	25.00
❑86, Jul 1965	25.00
❑87, Sep 1965 A: Legion of Super-Villains. A: Bizarro Jimmy.	25.00
❑88, Oct 1965	25.00
❑89, Dec 1965	20.00
❑90, Jan 1966	20.00
❑91, Mar 1966	16.00

	N-MINT
❑92, Apr 1966 A: Batman.	16.00
❑93, Jun 1966	16.00
❑94, Jul 1966	16.00
❑95, Aug 1966; Giant-size	25.00
❑96, Sep 1966	16.00
❑97, Oct 1966	16.00
❑98, Dec 1966	16.00
❑99, Jan 1967; Jimmy as one-man Legion	16.00
❑100, Mar 1967; Wedding of Jimmy and Lucy Lane	25.00
❑101, Apr 1967	12.00
❑102, Jun 1967	12.00
❑103, Jul 1967	12.00
❑104, Aug 1967; Giant-size; giant; Weird Adventures	35.00
❑105, Sep 1967	12.00
❑106, Oct 1967	12.00
❑107, Dec 1967 CS (a)	12.00
❑108, Jan 1968 CS (a)	12.00
❑109, Mar 1968 A: Luthor.	12.00
❑110, Apr 1968 CS (a)	12.00
❑111, Jun 1968	12.00
❑112, Jul 1968	12.00
❑113, Aug 1968; CS (a); Anti-Superman issue; Reprints from Jimmy Olsen #22, #27, and #28	25.00
❑114, Sep 1968	12.00
❑115, Oct 1968 A: Aquaman.	12.00
❑116, Dec 1968; CS (a); Reprints from Jimmy Olsen #24	12.00
❑117, Jan 1969	12.00
❑118, Mar 1969	12.00
❑119, Apr 1969	12.00
❑120, Jun 1969	10.00
❑121, Jul 1969	10.00
❑122, Aug 1969	10.00
❑123, Sep 1969	10.00
❑124, Oct 1969	10.00
❑125, Dec 1969	10.00
❑126, Jan 1970 A: Kryptonite Plus.	10.00
❑127, Mar 1970	16.00
❑128, Apr 1970	10.00
❑129, Jun 1970	10.00
❑130, Jul 1970	10.00
❑131, Aug 1970	8.00
❑132, Sep 1970	8.00
❑133, Oct 1970; JK (a); 1: Newsboy Legion. 1: Habitat. A: Newsboy Legion.	10.00
❑134, Dec 1970; 1: Darkseid.	25.00
❑135, Jan 1971 1: Project Cadmus.	12.00
❑136, Mar 1971 O: Guardian (new).	12.00
❑137, Apr 1971	12.00
❑138, Jun 1971	12.00
❑139, Jul 1971 A: Don Rickles.	12.00
❑140, Aug 1971; reprints Jimmy Olsen #69, #72, and Superman #158; G-86	12.00
❑141, Sep 1971	10.00
❑142, Oct 1971	10.00
❑143, Nov 1971 JK (a)	10.00
❑144, Dec 1971 JK (a)	10.00
❑145, Jan 1972	10.00
❑146, Feb 1972	10.00
❑147, Mar 1972	10.00
❑148, Apr 1972	10.00
❑149, May 1972 BO (a)	10.00
❑150, Jun 1972	10.00
❑151, Jul 1972	8.00
❑152, Aug 1972	7.00
❑153, Oct 1972	7.00
❑154, Nov 1972	7.00
❑155, Jan 1973	7.00
❑156, Feb 1973	7.00
❑157, Mar 1973	7.00
❑158 1973	7.00
❑159, Aug 1973	7.00
❑160, Oct 1973	7.00
❑161, Nov 1973	7.00
❑162, Dec 1973	7.00
❑163, Feb 1974; Series continues as The Superman Family	7.00

SUPERMAN SPECTACULAR
DC

	N-MINT
❑1 V: Luthor. V: Brainiac.	3.00

SUPERMAN: SPEEDING BULLETS
DC

	N-MINT
❑1, ca. 1993; prestige format; Elseworlds	4.95

SUPERMAN/TARZAN: SONS OF THE JUNGLE
DARK HORSE

	N-MINT
❑1, Oct 2001	2.99
❑2, Nov 2001	2.99
❑3, Dec 2001	2.99

SUPERMAN: THE DARK SIDE
DC

	N-MINT
❑1, Oct 1998	4.95
❑2, Nov 1998	4.95
❑3, Dec 1998	4.95

SUPERMAN: THE DOOMSDAY WARS
DC

	N-MINT
❑1, ca. 1999	4.95
❑2, ca. 1999	4.95
❑3, ca. 1999	4.95

SUPERMAN: THE EARTH STEALERS
DC

	N-MINT
❑1, May 1988	2.95

SUPERMAN: THE LAST GOD OF KRYPTON
DC

	N-MINT
❑1, Aug 1999; prestige format	4.95

SUPERMAN: THE LEGACY OF SUPERMAN
DC

	N-MINT
❑1, Mar 1993; Follows up after Superman's demise	2.50

SUPERMAN: THE MAN OF STEEL
DC

	N-MINT
❑0, Oct 1994; ▲ 1994-37	2.50
❑1, Jul 1991; 1: Cerberus. ▲ 1991-19	6.00
❑2, Aug 1991 V: Sgt. Belcher. V: Rorc.	2.50
❑3, Sep 1991; War of the Gods	2.50
❑4, Oct 1991 V: Angstrom.	2.00
❑5, Nov 1991 V: Atomic Skull.	2.00
❑6, Dec 1991	2.00
❑7, Jan 1992 V: Blockhouse. V: Jolt.	2.00
❑8, Feb 1992 V: Blockhouse. V: Jolt.	2.00
❑9, Mar 1992	2.00
❑10, Apr 1992	2.00
❑11, May 1992	1.50
❑12, Jun 1992	1.50
❑13, Jul 1992	1.50
❑14, Aug 1992 A: Robin.	1.50
❑15, Sep 1992 KG (a); A: Satanus. A: Blaze.	1.50
❑16, Oct 1992	1.50
❑17, Nov 1992 1: Doomsday (cameo).	3.00
❑18, Dec 1992; 1: Doomsday (full appearance). ▲ 1992-18	4.00
❑18-2, Dec 1992; A: Doomsday. ▲ 1992-18	2.00
❑18-3, Dec 1992; A: Doomsday. ▲ 1992-18	1.50
❑19, Jan 1993; V: Doomsday. ▲ 1993-1	3.00
❑20, Feb 1993	2.50
❑21, Mar 1993; Pa Kent has heart attack	2.50
❑22, Jun 1993 1: Steel (John Henry Irons).	2.00
❑22/Variant, Jun 1993; Die-cut cover	2.50
❑23, Jul 1993; Steel vs. Superboy	2.00
❑24, Aug 1993; Steel vs. Last Son of Krypton	2.00
❑25, Sep 1993	2.00
❑26, Oct 1993	2.00
❑27, Nov 1993	2.00
❑28, Dec 1993	2.00
❑29, Jan 1994	2.00
❑30, Feb 1994; Lobo	2.00
❑30/Variant, Feb 1994; vinyl clings cover	3.00
❑31, Mar 1994	2.00

	N-MINT
❑32, Apr 1994; Bizarro	2.00
❑33, May 1994	2.00
❑34, Jun 1994	2.00
❑35, Jul 1994; crossover with Milestone Media	2.00
❑36, Aug 1994; A: Static. A: Icon. A: Hardware. ▲ 1994-29	2.00
❑37, Sep 1994; Zero Hour	2.00
❑38, Nov 1994	2.00
❑39, Dec 1994	2.00
❑40, Jan 1995; ▲ 1995-1	2.00
❑41, Feb 1995	2.00
❑42, Mar 1995	2.00
❑43, Apr 1995 A: Mr. Miracle.	2.00
❑44, May 1995	2.00
❑45, Jun 1995	2.00
❑46, Jul 1995	2.00
❑47, Aug 1995	2.00
❑48, Sep 1995 A: Aquaman.	2.00
❑49, Oct 1995	2.00
❑50, Nov 1995; Giant-size	3.00
❑51, Dec 1995 V: Freelance.	2.00
❑52, Jan 1996 V: Cyborg.	2.00
❑53, Feb 1996 V: Brawl.	2.00
❑54, Mar 1996; A: Spectre. ▲ 1996-10	2.00
❑55, Apr 1996; D: Jeb Friedman. ▲ 1996-15	2.00
❑56, May 1996 V: Mxyzptlk.	2.00
❑57, Jun 1996 A: Golden Age Flash.	2.00
❑58, Jul 1996	2.00
❑59, Aug 1996 V: Parasite.	2.00
❑60, Sep 1996	2.00
❑61, Oct 1996; polybagged with On the Edge; ▲ 1996-41	2.00
❑62, Oct 1996; O: Superman. Final Night; ▲ 1996-45	2.00
❑63, Dec 1996; Lois rescues Clark from terrorists; ▲ 1996-50	2.00
❑64, Jan 1997; ▲ 1997-4	2.00
❑65, Mar 1997; SB (a); V: Superman Revenge Squad. ▲ 1997-9	2.00
❑66, Apr 1997	2.00
❑67, May 1997; A: Scorn. destruction of old costume	2.00
❑68, Jun 1997 V: Metallo.	2.00
❑69, Jul 1997; A: Atom. in Kandor	2.00
❑70, Aug 1997 A: Scorn. V: Saviour.	2.00
❑71, Sep 1997 1: Baud.	2.00
❑72, Oct 1997; V: Mainframe. Genesis	2.00
❑73, Nov 1997 V: Parademons.	2.00
❑74, Dec 1997; A: Sam Lane. V: Rajiv. Face cover; ▲ 1997-47	2.00
❑75, Jan 1998; A: Mike Carlin. D: Mr. Mxyzptlk. ▲ 1998-1	2.00
❑76, Feb 1998 A: Simyan. A: Morgan Edge. A: Mokkari.	2.00
❑77, Mar 1998; cover forms diptych with Action Comics #742	2.00
❑78, Apr 1998; Millennium Giants	2.00
❑79, May 1998; Millennium Giants aftermath	2.00
❑80, Jun 1998; set in late '30s	2.00
❑81, Jul 1998; set in late '30s	2.00
❑82, Aug 1998 A: Kismet. V: Dominus.	2.00
❑83, Sep 1998 A: Waverider.	2.00
❑84, Dec 1998; 1: Inventor. in Kandor	2.00
❑85, Jan 1999 V: Simyan. V: Mokkari.	2.00
❑86, Feb 1999	2.00
❑87, Mar 1999 A: Steel. A: Superboy. A: Supergirl.	2.00
❑88, May 1999 V: Robots.	2.00
❑89, Jun 1999; V: Dominus. ▲ 1999-21	2.00
❑90, Jul 1999; ▲ 1999-26	2.00
❑91, Aug 1999; ▲ 1999-31	1.99
❑92, Sep 1999; Superman as Martian Manhunter; ▲ 1999-35	1.99
❑93, Oct 1999; ▲ 1999-39	1.99
❑94, Nov 1999 A: Strange Visitor. V: Parasite.	1.99
❑95, Dec 1999; ▲ 1999-48	1.99
❑96, Jan 2000; ▲ 2000-3	1.99
❑97, Feb 2000	1.99
❑98, Mar 2000	1.99
❑99, Apr 2000; ▲ 2000-16	1.99
❑100, May 2000; Giant-size; ▲ 2000-20	2.99
❑100/Variant, May 2000; Giant-size; Special fold-out cover; ▲ 2000-20	3.99
❑101, Jun 2000	1.99
❑102, Jul 2000	1.99
❑103, Aug 2000	2.25
❑104, Sep 2000; ▲ 2000-36	2.25
❑105, Oct 2000; (c)2000-41	2.25
❑106, Nov 2000; ▲ 2000-45	2.25
❑107, Dec 2000; ▲ 2000-49	2.25
❑108, Jan 2001; ▲ 2001-4	2.25
❑109, Feb 2001; ▲ 2001-8	2.25
❑110, Mar 2001; A: Stars and S.T.R.I.P.E.. ▲ 2001-12	2.25
❑111, Apr 2001; ▲ 2001-16	2.25
❑112, May 2001; ▲ 2001-20	2.25
❑113, Jun 2001	2.25
❑114, Jul 2001	2.25
❑115, Aug 2001	2.25
❑116, Sep 2001	2.25
❑117, Oct 2001; ▲ 2001-40	2.25
❑118, Nov 2001	2.25
❑119, Dec 2001; ▲ 2001-48	2.25
❑120, Jan 2002; ▲ 2002-3	2.25
❑121, Feb 2002	2.25
❑122, Mar 2002	2.25
❑123, Apr 2002	2.25
❑124, May 2002	2.25
❑125, Jun 2002	2.25
❑126, Jul 2002	2.25
❑127, Aug 2002	2.25
❑128, Sep 2002	2.25
❑129, Oct 2002	2.25
❑130, Nov 2002	2.25
❑131, Dec 2002	2.25
❑132, Jan 2003	2.25
❑133, Feb 2003	2.25
❑134, Mar 2003	2.25
❑1000000, Nov 1998 JOy (a)	3.00
❑Annual 1, ca. 1992 A: Eclipso.	3.00
❑Annual 2, ca. 1993 1: Edge.	3.00
❑Annual 3, ca. 1994; Elseworlds	3.00
❑Annual 4, ca. 1995; A: Justice League. Year One	3.00
❑Annual 5, Nov 1996; KB (w); 1: Kaleb. Legends of the Dead Earth	3.00
❑Annual 6, Aug 1997; Pulp Heroes	3.95

SUPERMAN: THE MAN OF STEEL GALLERY
DC

❑1, Dec 1995; pin-ups	3.50

SUPERMAN: THE MAN OF TOMORROW
DC

❑1, Sum 1995	2.00
❑2, Fal 1995 A: Alpha Centurion.	2.00
❑3, Win 1995; A: how Luthor regained strength and. Underworld Unleashed	2.00
❑4, Spr 1996; A: Captain Marvel. ▲ 1996-13	2.00
❑5, Sum 1996; Wedding of Lex Luthor and Contessa	2.00
❑6, Fal 1996; V: Jackal. ▲ 1996-38	2.00
❑7, Win 1997 V: Maxima.	2.00
❑8, Sum 1997 V: Rock.	2.00
❑9, Fal 1997; Ma and Pa Kent remember Superman's career	2.00
❑10, Win 1998; Obsession vs. Maxima	2.00
❑11, Fal 1998	2.00
❑12, Win 1998	2.00
❑13, Spr 1999	2.00
❑14, Sum 1999 V: Riot.	2.00
❑15, Fal 1999; V: Neron. Day of Judgment	3.00
❑1000000, Nov 1998	3.00

SUPERMAN: THE ODYSSEY
DC

❑1, Jul 1999; prestige format	4.95

Lois Lane often found herself in zany predicaments in her attempts to prove that Clark Kent and Superman were one and the same.

SUPERMAN: THE SECRET YEARS
DC

	N-MINT
❑1, Feb 1985 FM (c); FM, CS (a)	1.50
❑2, Mar 1985; FM (c); FM, CS (a); A: Lori Lemaris. Clark reveals his secret to Billy Cramer	1.50
❑3, Apr 1985 FM (c); FM, CS (a); D: Billy Cramer.	1.50
❑4, May 1985; FM (c); FM, CS (a); Superboy becomes Superman; Clark Kent meets Perry White	1.50

SUPERMAN: THE WEDDING ALBUM
DC

❑1, Dec 1996; newsstand edition with gatefold back cover; JOy, GP, JBy, GK, CS, KGa, JM, BMc (a); Wedding of Clark Kent and Lois Lane; ▲ 1996-47	4.95
❑1/Direct ed., Dec 1996; Wedding of Clark Kent and Lois Lane; white cardstock wraparound cover with gatefold back cover	4.95
❑1/Gold, Dec 1996; Gold Foil Edition; Retailer incentive; Limited to 250 copies	10.00

SUPERMAN/THUNDERCATS
DC

❑1, ca. 2004	5.95

SUPERMAN/TOYMAN
DC

❑1; promo for toy line	1.95

SUPERMAN: UNDER A YELLOW SUN
DC

❑1, ca. 1994; prestige format one-shot	5.95

SUPERMAN VS. ALIENS
DC / DARK HORSE

❑1, Jul 1995; prestige format; crossover with Dark Horse	4.95
❑2, Aug 1995; prestige format; crossover with Dark Horse	4.95
❑3, Sep 1995; prestige format; crossover with Dark Horse	4.95

SUPERMAN VS. PREDATOR
DC / DARK HORSE

❑1, Jul 2000	4.95
❑2, Aug 2000	4.95
❑3, Sep 2000	4.95

SUPERMAN VS. THE AMAZING SPIDER-MAN
DC / MARVEL

❑1; treasury-sized; DG, RA (a); V: Lex Luthor. V: Doctor Octopus. first DC/Marvel crossover	20.00

SUPERMAN VS. THE TERMINATOR: DEATH TO THE FUTURE
DARK HORSE

❑1, Dec 1999	2.95
❑2, Jan 2000	2.95
❑3, Feb 2000	2.95
❑4, Mar 2000	2.95

SUPERMAN VILLAINS SECRET FILES
DC

❑1, Jun 1998; biographical info on Superman's Rogues Gallery	4.95

SUPERMAN VS. DARKSEIS: APOKOLIPS NOW
DC

❑1, Apr 2003	2.95

N-MINT

SUPERMAN: WAR OF THE WORLDS
DC

- ❑1, Dec 1998; prestige format one-shot; Elseworlds 5.95

SUPERMAN: "WHATEVER HAPPENED TO THE MAN OF TOMORROW?"
DC

- ❑1, Feb 1997; prestige format collection of Action Comics #583 and Superman #423 ..... 5.95

SUPERMAN: WHERE IS THY STING?
DC

- ❑1, Jul 2001 ..... 6.95

SUPERMAN/WONDER WOMAN: WHOM GODS DESTROY
DC

- ❑1, Dec 1996; prestige format; Elseworlds 4.95
- ❑2, Jan 1997; prestige format; Elseworlds 4.95
- ❑3, Feb 1997; prestige format; Elseworlds 4.95
- ❑4, Mar 1997; prestige format; Elseworlds 4.95

SUPER MANGA BLAST!
DARK HORSE

- ❑1, Mar 2000 ..... 4.95
- ❑2, Apr 2000 ..... 4.95
- ❑3, May 2000 ..... 4.95
- ❑4, Jun 2000 ..... 4.95
- ❑5, Jul 2000 ..... 4.95
- ❑6, Aug 2000 ..... 4.95
- ❑7, Sep 2000 ..... 4.95
- ❑8, Nov 2000 ..... 4.95
- ❑9, Jan 2001 ..... 4.95
- ❑10, Feb 2001 ..... 4.99
- ❑11, Mar 2001 ..... 4.99
- ❑12, May 2001 ..... 4.99
- ❑13, Jun 2001 ..... 4.99
- ❑14, Jul 2001 ..... 4.99
- ❑15, Aug 2001 ..... 4.99
- ❑16, Sep 2001 ..... 4.99
- ❑17, Oct 2001 ..... 4.99
- ❑18, Nov 2001 ..... 4.99
- ❑19, Feb 2002 ..... 5.99
- ❑20, Mar 2002 ..... 5.99
- ❑21, Apr 2002 ..... 5.99
- ❑22, May 2002 ..... 5.99
- ❑23, Jun 2002 ..... 5.99
- ❑24, Jul 2002 ..... 5.99
- ❑25, Sep 2002 ..... 5.99
- ❑26, Oct 2002 ..... 5.99
- ❑27, Nov 2002 ..... 5.99
- ❑28, Dec 2002 ..... 5.99
- ❑29, Jan 2003 ..... 5.99
- ❑30, Apr 2003 ..... 5.99
- ❑31, May 2003 ..... 5.99
- ❑32, Jun 2003 ..... 5.99
- ❑33, Jul 2003 ..... 5.99
- ❑34, Aug 2003 ..... 5.99
- ❑35, Oct 2003 ..... 5.99
- ❑36, Nov 2003 ..... 5.99
- ❑37, Jan 2004 ..... 5.99
- ❑38, Feb 2004 ..... 5.99
- ❑39, Feb 2004 ..... 5.99
- ❑40, Mar 2004 ..... 5.99
- ❑41, Mar 2004 ..... 5.99
- ❑42, May 2004 ..... 5.99

SUPER MARIO BROS. (1ST SERIES)
VALIANT

- ❑1, ca. 1991 ..... 2.00
- ❑2, ca. 1991 ..... 2.00
- ❑3, ca. 1991 ..... 2.00
- ❑4, ca. 1991 ..... 2.00
- ❑5, ca. 1991 ..... 2.00
- ❑6, ca. 1991 ..... 2.00
- ❑Special 1, ca. 1990 ..... 2.00

SUPER MARIO BROS. (2ND SERIES)
VALIANT

- ❑1, ca. 1991 ..... 2.00
- ❑2, ca. 1991 ..... 2.00
- ❑3, ca. 1991 ..... 2.00
- ❑4, ca. 1991 ..... 2.00
- ❑5, ca. 1991 ..... 2.00

SUPERMEN OF AMERICA
DC

- ❑1, Mar 1999 ..... 3.95
- ❑1/CS, Mar 1999; Collector's edition; Gatefold cardstock cover 4.95
- ❑2, Apr 1999 ..... 2.50
- ❑3, May 1999 ..... 2.50
- ❑4, Jun 1999 ..... 2.50

SUPERMODELS IN THE RAINFOREST
SIRIUS

- ❑1, Dec 1998, b&w 2.95
- ❑2, Feb 1999, b&w 2.95
- ❑3, Apr 1999 ..... 2.95

SUPERNATURAL LAW
EXHIBIT A

- ❑24, Oct 1999; was Wolff & Byrd, Counselors of the Macabre 2.50
- ❑25, Feb 2000 ..... 2.50
- ❑26, May 2000 ..... 2.50
- ❑27, Jul 2000 ..... 2.50
- ❑28, Oct 2000 ..... 2.50
- ❑29, Jul 2000 ..... 2.50
- ❑30, Mar 2001 ..... 2.50
- ❑31 ..... 2.50

SUPERNATURALS, THE
MARVEL

- ❑1/A, Dec 1998 ..... 3.99
- ❑1/B, Dec 1998 ..... 3.99
- ❑1/C, Dec 1998 ..... 3.99
- ❑1/D, Dec 1998 ..... 3.99
- ❑1/E, Dec 1998 ..... 4.50
- ❑1/Ltd., Dec 1998 ..... 29.99
- ❑2/A, Dec 1998 ..... 3.99
- ❑2/B, Dec 1998 ..... 3.99
- ❑2/C, Dec 1998 ..... 3.99
- ❑2/D, Dec 1998 ..... 3.99
- ❑2/E, Dec 1998 ..... 3.99
- ❑3/A, Dec 1998 ..... 3.99
- ❑3/B, Dec 1998 ..... 3.99
- ❑3/C, Dec 1998 ..... 3.99
- ❑3/D, Dec 1998 ..... 3.99
- ❑3/E, Dec 1998 ..... 3.99
- ❑4/A, Dec 1998 ..... 3.99
- ❑4/B, Dec 1998 ..... 3.99
- ❑4/C, Dec 1998 ..... 3.99
- ❑4/D, Dec 1998 ..... 3.99
- ❑4/E, Dec 1998 ..... 3.99
- ❑Ashcan 1; Character bios, sketches, creator bios 2.99

SUPERNATURALS TOUR BOOK, THE
MARVEL

- ❑1, Oct 1998; preview of series; cardstock cover 2.99

SUPERNATURAL THRILLERS
MARVEL

- ❑1, Dec 1972; It! (Theodore Sturgeon adaptation) 20.00
- ❑2, Feb 1973; Invisible Man 10.00
- ❑3, Apr 1973; GK (a); The Valley of the Worm 10.00
- ❑4, Jun 1973; Dr. Jekyll and Mr. Hyde 10.00
- ❑5, Aug 1973 O: Living Mummy. 1: Living Mummy. 20.00
- ❑6 1974; The Headless Horseman 10.00
- ❑7 1974 A: Living Mummy. 10.00
- ❑8 1974; A: Living Mummy. Marvel Value Stamp #36: Ancient One 10.00
- ❑9 1974; A: Living Mummy. Marvel Value Stamp #29: Baron Mordo 10.00
- ❑10 1974 A: Living Mummy. 10.00
- ❑11, Feb 1975; A: Living Mummy. Marvel Value Stamp #86: Zemo 10.00
- ❑12, Apr 1975; A: Living Mummy. Marvel Value Stamp #49: Odin 10.00
- ❑13, Jun 1975 A: Living Mummy. 10.00
- ❑14, Aug 1975 A: Living Mummy. 10.00
- ❑15, Oct 1975 TS (a); A: Living Mummy. 10.00

SUPERPATRIOT
IMAGE

- ❑1, Jul 1993 KG, EL (w) 2.00
- ❑2, Sep 1993 ..... 2.00
- ❑3, Oct 1993 ..... 2.00
- ❑4, Nov 1993; cover says Dec, indicia says Nov 2.00

SUPERPATRIOT: AMERICA'S FIGHTING FORCE
IMAGE

- ❑1, Jul 2002 ..... 2.95
- ❑2, Aug 2002 ..... 2.95
- ❑3, Sep 2002; August cover date 2.95
- ❑4, Oct 2002 ..... 2.95

SUPERPATRIOT: LIBERTY & JUSTICE
IMAGE

- ❑1, Jun 1995 ..... 2.50
- ❑2, Aug 1995 ..... 2.50
- ❑3, Sep 1995 ..... 2.50
- ❑4, Oct 1995 ..... 2.50

SUPER POWERS (1ST SERIES)
DC

- ❑1, Jul 1984 JK (c) 1.00
- ❑2, Aug 1984 JK (c) 1.00
- ❑3, Sep 1984 JK (c) 1.00
- ❑4, Oct 1984 JK (c) 1.00
- ❑5, Nov 1984 JK (c); JK (w); JK (a) 1.00

SUPER POWERS (2ND SERIES)
DC

- ❑1, Sep 1985 JK (a) 1.00
- ❑2, Oct 1985 JK (a) 1.00
- ❑3, Nov 1985 JK (a) 1.00
- ❑4, Dec 1985 JK (a) 1.00
- ❑5, Jan 1986 JK (a) 1.00
- ❑6, Feb 1986 JK (a) 1.00

SUPER POWERS (3RD SERIES)
DC

- ❑1, Sep 1986 CI (a) 1.00
- ❑2, Oct 1986 CI (a) 1.00
- ❑3, Nov 1986 CI (a) 1.00
- ❑4, Dec 1986 CI (a) 1.00

SUPER SEXXX
FANTAGRAPHICS / EROS

- ❑1, b&w 3.25

SUPER SHARK HUMANOIDS
FISH TALES

- ❑1, Apr 1992 ..... 2.75

SUPER SOLDIER
DC / AMALGAM

- ❑1, Apr 1996 ..... 1.95

SUPER SOLDIER: MAN OF WAR
DC / AMALGAM

- ❑1, Jun 1997 ..... 1.95

SUPER SOLDIERS
MARVEL

- ❑1, Apr 1993; foil cover 2.50
- ❑2, May 1993 ..... 1.75
- ❑3, Jun 1993 ..... 1.75
- ❑4, Jul 1993 ..... 1.75
- ❑5, Aug 1993 ..... 1.75
- ❑6, Sep 1993 ..... 1.75
- ❑7, Oct 1993; X-Men cameo 1.75
- ❑8, Nov 1993 ..... 1.75

SUPERSONIC SOUL PUDDIN COMICS & STORIES
FOUR CATS FUNNY BOOKS

- ❑1, Jun 1995 ..... 3.50

SUPER SONIC VS. HYPER KNUCKLES
ARCHIE

- ❑1, color 2.00

SUPERSTAR: AS SEEN ON TV
IMAGE

- ❑1, Jul 2001 ..... 5.95

SUPERSWINE
CALIBER

- ❑1, b&w 2.50
- ❑2, b&w 2.50

N-MINT

SUPER TABOO
FANTAGRAPHICS / EROS
❑1, Dec 1995 .... 2.95
❑2, Jan 1996 .... 2.95

SUPER-TEAM FAMILY
DC
❑1, Nov 1975 .... 6.00
❑2, Jan 1976 A: Speedy. A: Wildcat. A: Deadman. A: Superman. A: Green Arrow. A: Creeper. A: Batman. 4.00
❑3, Mar 1976 .... 4.00
❑4, May 1976 A: Justice Society of America. A: Superman. A: Solomon Grundy. A: Robin. A: Batman. 4.00
❑5, Jul 1976 .... 3.00
❑6, Sep 1976 .... 3.00
❑7, Nov 1976; Teen Titans 3.00
❑8, Jan 1977; A: Challengers of the Unknown. New stories begin 4.00
❑9, Mar 1977 A: Challengers of the Unknown. 4.00
❑10, May 1977 A: Challengers of the Unknown. 4.00
❑11, Jul 1977; Flash, Atom, Supergirl 3.00
❑12, Sep 1977 .... 3.00
❑13, Nov 1977; Atom, Aquaman, Captain Comet 3.00
❑14, Jan 1978 .... 3.00
❑15, Apr 1978 .... 3.00

SUPER-VILLAIN CLASSICS
MARVEL
❑1, May 1983 O: Galactus. 3.00

SUPER-VILLAIN TEAM-UP
MARVEL
❑1, Aug 1975 GE, BEv, GT (a); A: Doctor Doom. A: Sub-Mariner. 7.00
❑2, Oct 1975 SB (a); A: Doctor Doom. A: Sub-Mariner. 5.00
❑3, Dec 1975 A: Doctor Doom. A: Sub-Mariner. 4.00
❑4, Feb 1976 A: Doctor Doom. A: Sub-Mariner. 4.00
❑5, Apr 1976 1: Shroud. A: Doctor Doom. A: Sub-Mariner. 4.00
❑5/30 cent, Apr 1976 .... 8.00
❑6, Jun 1976 A: Doctor Doom. A: Sub-Mariner. 3.00
❑6/30 cent, Jun 1976 .... 6.00
❑7, Aug 1976 O: Shroud. A: Doctor Doom. A: Sub-Mariner. 3.00
❑7/30 cent, Aug 1976 .... 6.00
❑8, Oct 1976 1: Rajah. A: Doctor Doom. A: Sub-Mariner. 3.00
❑9, Dec 1976 A: Doctor Doom. A: Sub-Mariner. 3.00
❑10, Feb 1977 BH (a); A: Doctor Doom. A: Sub-Mariner. 3.00
❑11, Apr 1977 BH (a) 3.00
❑12, Jun 1977 BH (a) 3.00
❑13, Aug 1977 .... 3.00
❑14, Oct 1977 BH (a) 3.00
❑15, Nov 1977 A: Red Skull. A: Doctor Doom. 3.00
❑16, May 1979 A: Red Skull. A: Doctor Doom. 3.00
❑17, Jun 1980 A: Red Skull. A: Doctor Doom. 3.00

SUPPRESSED!
TOME
❑1, b&w 2.95

SUPREME
IMAGE
❑0, Aug 1995 RL (c); RL (a) 2.50
❑1, Nov 1992 RL (w) 2.50
❑1/Gold, Nov 1992; Gold promotional edition; Embossed cover 2.50
❑2, Feb 1993; 1: Grizlock. covers says May, indicia says Feb 2.00
❑3, Jun 1993 RL (w); 1: Khrome. 2.00
❑4, Jul 1993 .... 2.00
❑5, Aug 1993 1: Thor (Image). 2.00
❑6, Oct 1993 1: the Starguard. 2.00
❑7, Nov 1993 .... 2.00
❑8, Dec 1993 .... 2.00

N-MINT

❑9, Jan 1994 .... 2.00
❑10, Feb 1994 .... 2.00
❑11, Mar 1994 .... 2.00
❑12, Apr 1994 .... 2.00
❑13, Jun 1994 .... 2.50
❑14, Jun 1994 .... 2.50
❑15, Jul 1994 .... 2.50
❑16, Jul 1994 .... 2.50
❑17, Aug 1994 V: Pitt. 2.50
❑18, Aug 1994 .... 2.50
❑19, Sep 1994 .... 2.50
❑20, Oct 1994 A: Kid Supreme. 2.50
❑21, Nov 1994 .... 2.50
❑22, Dec 1994 .... 2.50
❑23, Jan 1995; polybagged with trading card 2.50
❑24, Feb 1995 .... 2.50
❑25, May 1994; Images of Tomorrow; Shipped out of sequence after #12 to give preview of future 2.50
❑26, Mar 1995 V: Kid Supreme. 2.50
❑27, Apr 1995 .... 2.50
❑28, May 1995 .... 2.50
❑28/A, May 1995 A: Glory. 2.50
❑28/B, May 1995 A: Glory. 2.50
❑29, Jun 1995; polybagged with Power Cardz 2.50
❑30, Jul 1995; polybagged with Power Cardz 2.50
❑31, Aug 1995 .... 2.50
❑32, Oct 1995 .... 2.50
❑33, Nov 1995; Babewatch 2.50
❑34, Dec 1995 .... 2.50
❑35, Jan 1996; polybagged with Lady Supreme card 2.50
❑36, Feb 1996 .... 2.50
❑37, Mar 1996 .... 2.50
❑37/A, Mar 1996; alternate cover 2.50
❑37/B, Mar 1996; alternate cover 2.50
❑38, Apr 1996 .... 2.50
❑39, May 1996 V: Loki. 2.50
❑40, Jul 1996 .... 2.50
❑41, Aug 1996; Newmen Special Preview Edition back-up AMo (w) 3.50
❑41/A, Aug 1996; Newmen Special Preview Edition back-up; AMo (w); alternate cover (Superman homage) 3.50
❑41/B, Aug 1996; limited edition; alternate cover (Superman homage) 15.00
❑41/C, Aug 1996; alternate cover (American Entertainment exclusive) 9.00
❑41-2 .... 2.50
❑42, Sep 1996; AMo (w); Superman homage; moves to Maximum Press 3.00
❑43, Oct 1996; AMo (w); Superman homage 3.00
❑44, Jan 1997 AMo (w) 3.00
❑45, Jan 1997 AMo (w) 2.50
❑46, Feb 1997 AMo (w); 1: Suprema. 2.50
❑47, Mar 1997 AMo (w); 1: Twilight. 2.50
❑48, Apr 1997 AMo (w) 2.50
❑49, May 1997; AMo (w); cover says Jun, indicia says May 2.50
❑50, Jun 1997; Giant-size AMo (w) 2.50
❑51, Jul 1997 AMo (w) 2.50
❑52/A, Sep 1997 AMo (w) 3.50
❑52/B, Sep 1997 AMo (w) 2.50
❑53, Sep 1997 AMo (w) 2.50
❑54, Nov 1997 AMo (w) 2.50
❑55, Nov 1997; AMo (w); GK (a); cover says Dec, indicia says Nov 2.50
❑56, Feb 1998 .... 2.50
❑Annual 1, May 1995 A: The Allies. 2.95

SUPREME: GLORY DAYS
IMAGE
❑1, Oct 1994 RL (w) 3.00
❑2, Dec 1994 RL (w) 2.50

SUPREME POWER
MARVEL
❑1, Oct 2003 .... 2.99
❑1/Special, Oct 2003 .... 4.99
❑2, Nov 2003 .... 2.99
❑3, Dec 2003 .... 2.99

One of the first Elseworlds stories to *not* feature Bruce Wayne still had a Batman theme.

N-MINT

❑4, Jan 2003 .... 2.99
❑5, Feb 2004 .... 2.99
❑6, Mar 2004 .... 2.99
❑7, Apr 2004 .... 2.99
❑8, May 2004 .... 2.99
❑9, Jun 2004 .... 2.99
❑10, Jul 2004 .... 2.99
❑11, Sep 2004 ....

SUPREME: THE RETURN
AWESOME
❑1, May 1999; continues story from Supreme #56 .... 2.99
❑2, Jun 1999; infinite Darius Daxes 2.99
❑3 .... 2.99
❑4, Mar 2000 .... 2.99
❑5, May 2000 .... 2.99
❑6, Jun 2000 .... 2.99

SUPREMIE
PARODY
❑1, b&w 2.50

SURFCRAZED COMICS
PACIFICA
❑1 .... 2.50
❑3; 3-D 3.95
❑4 .... 2.50

SURF SUMO
STAR TIGER
❑1 .... 2.95
❑1-2, Jun 1997; 2nd printing with insert noting rights had reverted to Mighty Graphics; June 1997 .... 2.95

SURGE
ECLIPSE
❑1, Jul 1984 ME (w) 1.75
❑2, Aug 1984 ME (w) 1.75
❑3, Oct 1984 ME (w) 1.75
❑4, Jan 1985 ME (w) 1.75

SURROGATE SAVIOUR
HOT BRAZEN COMICS
❑1, Sep 1995, b&w 2.50
❑2, Nov 1995, b&w 2.75
❑3, Jun 1996, b&w 2.95

SURVIVE!
APPLE
❑1, b&w 2.75

SURVIVORS (FANTAGRAPHICS)
FANTAGRAPHICS
❑1 .... 2.50
❑2 .... 2.50

SURVIVORS, THE (PRELUDE)
PRELUDE
❑1, Oct 1986 .... 1.95
❑2 .... 1.95

SURVIVORS, THE (BURNSIDE)
BURNSIDE
❑1 .... 1.95

SUSHI
SHUNGA
❑1, b&w 3.00
❑1-2 .... 2.50
❑2, b&w 3.00
❑3, b&w 3.00
❑4, b&w 3.00
❑5, b&w 3.00
❑6, b&w 3.00

	N-MINT
❑7	2.50
❑8	2.50

SUSPIRA: THE GREAT WORKING
CHAOS

	N-MINT
❑1, Mar 1997	2.95
❑2, Apr 1997	2.95
❑3, May 1997	2.95
❑4, Jun 1997	2.95

SUSSEX VAMPIRE, THE
CALIBER

	N-MINT
❑1	2.95

SUSTAH-GIRL: QUEEN OF THE BLACK AGE
ONLI

	N-MINT
❑1, b&w	2.00

SWAMP FEVER
BIG MUDDY

	N-MINT
❑1	3.00

SWAMP THING (1ST SERIES)
DC

	N-MINT
❑1, Nov 1972 BWr (a); O: Swamp Thing.	60.00
❑2, Jan 1973 BWr (a)	30.00
❑3, Mar 1973 BWr (a); 1: Patchwork Man.	20.00
❑4, May 1973 BWr (a)	20.00
❑5, Aug 1973 BWr (a)	15.00
❑6, Oct 1973 BWr (a)	15.00
❑7, Dec 1973; BWr (a); A: Batman. Batman	12.00
❑8, Feb 1974 BWr (a)	10.00
❑9, Apr 1974 BWr (a)	10.00
❑10, Jun 1974 BWr (a)	10.00
❑11, Aug 1974 NR (a)	5.00
❑12, Oct 1974 NR (a)	5.00
❑13, Dec 1974 NR (a)	5.00
❑14, Feb 1975 NR (a)	5.00
❑15, Apr 1975 NR (a)	5.00
❑16, May 1975 NR (a)	5.00
❑17, Jul 1975 NR (a)	5.00
❑18, Sep 1975 NR (a)	5.00
❑19, Oct 1975 NR (a)	5.00
❑20, Jan 1976 NR (a)	5.00
❑21, Mar 1976 NR (a)	5.00
❑22, May 1976 NR (a)	5.00
❑23, Jul 1976 NR (a)	5.00
❑24, Sep 1976 NR (a)	5.00

SWAMP THING (2ND SERIES)
DC

	N-MINT
❑46, Mar 1986; AMo (w); A: John Constantine. Crisis; Series continued from "Saga of the Swamp Thing"	4.00
❑47, Apr 1986 AMo (w); 1: Parliament of Trees.	3.00
❑48, May 1986 AMo (w)	3.00
❑49, Jun 1986 AMo (w); AA (a)	3.00
❑50, Jul 1986; Giant-size AMo (w); D: Sargon.	4.00
❑51, Aug 1986 AMo (w)	3.00
❑52, Sep 1986; AMo (w); A: Arkham Asylum. A: Joker. A: Joke. Joker	4.00
❑53, Oct 1986; AMo (w); A: Batman. Arkham Asylum story	4.50
❑54, Nov 1986 AMo (w)	3.00
❑55, Dec 1986 AMo (w)	3.00
❑56, Jan 1987 AMo (w); AA (a)	3.00
❑57, Feb 1987 AMo (w)	3.00
❑58, Mar 1987; AMo (w); Spectre preview	3.00
❑59, Apr 1987 AMo (w)	3.00
❑60, May 1987; AMo (w); new format	3.00
❑61, Jun 1987 AMo (w)	3.00
❑62, Jul 1987	3.00
❑63, Aug 1987 AMo (w)	3.00
❑64, Sep 1987; AMo (w); last with Moore	3.00
❑65, Oct 1987; 1: Sprout. Arkham Asylum	3.00
❑66, Nov 1987; Arkham Asylum	2.50
❑67, Dec 1987 1: Hellblazer.	2.50
❑68, Jan 1988	2.50
❑69, Feb 1988	2.50
❑70, Mar 1988	2.50
❑71, Apr 1988	2.50
❑72, May 1988	2.50
❑73, Jun 1988	2.50
❑74, Jul 1988	2.50
❑75, Aug 1988	2.50
❑76, Sep 1988; Continues from Hellblazer #9; continues in Hellblazer #10	2.50
❑77, Oct 1988 AA (a)	2.50
❑78, Nov 1988 AA (a)	2.50
❑79, Dec 1988 A: Superman.	2.50
❑80, Win 1988	2.50
❑81, Hol 1989; Invasion!	2.50
❑82, Jan 1989; Sgt. Rock	2.25
❑83, Feb 1989; Enemy Ace	2.25
❑84, Mar 1989 A: Sandman.	5.00
❑85, Apr 1989; Jonah Hex, Bat Lash	2.25
❑86, May 1989; Tomahawk, Rip Hunter, Demon	2.25
❑87, Jun 1989; Shining Knight, Demon	2.25
❑88, Sep 1989	2.25
❑89, Oct 1989	2.25
❑90, Dec 1989; 1: Tefé Holland. Formerly known as Sprout	2.50
❑91, Jan 1990 A: Woodgod.	2.25
❑92, Feb 1990	2.25
❑93, Mar 1990	2.25
❑94, Apr 1990	2.25
❑95, May 1990	2.25
❑96, Jun 1990	2.25
❑97, Jul 1990	2.25
❑98, Aug 1990	2.25
❑99, Sep 1990	2.25
❑100, Oct 1990; Giant-size	3.00
❑101, Nov 1990	2.25
❑102, Dec 1990	2.25
❑103, Jan 1991	2.25
❑104, Feb 1991	2.25
❑105, Mar 1991	2.25
❑106, Apr 1991	2.25
❑107, May 1991	2.25
❑108, Jun 1991	2.25
❑109, Jul 1991	2.25
❑110, Aug 1991	2.25
❑111, Sep 1991	2.25
❑112, Oct 1991	2.25
❑113, Nov 1991	2.25
❑114, Dec 1991	2.25
❑115, Jan 1992	2.25
❑116, Feb 1992	2.25
❑117, Mar 1992 JDu (a)	2.25
❑118, Apr 1992	2.25
❑119, May 1992 1: Lady Jane.	2.25
❑120, Jun 1992	2.25
❑121, Jul 1992	2.00
❑122, Aug 1992	2.00
❑123, Sep 1992	2.00
❑124, Oct 1992	2.00
❑125, Nov 1992; 20th Anniversary Issue; Arcane	3.25
❑126, Dec 1992	2.00
❑127, Jan 1993	2.00
❑128, Feb 1993; Vertigo line begins	2.00
❑129, Mar 1993	2.00
❑130, Apr 1993	2.00
❑131, May 1993	2.00
❑132, Jun 1993	2.00
❑133, Jul 1993	2.00
❑134, Aug 1993	2.00
❑135, Sep 1993	2.00
❑136, Oct 1993	2.00
❑137, Nov 1993	2.00
❑138, Dec 1993	2.00
❑139, Jan 1994	2.00
❑140, Mar 1994	2.00
❑140/Platinum, Mar 1994	6.00
❑141, Apr 1994	2.00
❑142, May 1994	2.00
❑143, Jun 1994	2.00
❑144, Jul 1994	2.00
❑145, Aug 1994	2.00
❑146, Sep 1994	2.00
❑147, Oct 1994	2.00
❑148, Nov 1994	2.00
❑149, Dec 1994	2.00
❑150, Jan 1995; Giant-size	3.00
❑151, Feb 1995	2.00
❑152, Mar 1995	2.00
❑153, Apr 1995	2.00
❑154, May 1995	2.25
❑155, Jun 1995	2.25
❑156, Jul 1995	2.25
❑157, Aug 1995	2.25
❑158, Sep 1995	2.25
❑159, Oct 1995	2.50
❑160, Nov 1995	2.50
❑161, Dec 1995	2.50
❑162, Jan 1996	2.50
❑163, Feb 1996	2.50
❑164, Mar 1996	2.50
❑165, Apr 1996 CS (a)	2.50
❑166, May 1996	2.50
❑167, Jun 1996	2.50
❑168, Jul 1996	2.50
❑169, Aug 1996 A: John Constantine.	2.50
❑170, Sep 1996	2.50
❑171, Oct 1996	2.50
❑Annual 4 A: Batman.	3.50
❑Annual 5 A: Brother Power.	3.50
❑Annual 6	2.95
❑Annual 7; Children's Crusade	3.95

SWAMP THING (3RD SERIES)
DC / VERTIGO

	N-MINT
❑1, May 2000	3.00
❑2, Jun 2000	2.50
❑3, Jul 2000	2.50
❑4, Aug 2000	2.50
❑5, Sep 2000	2.50
❑6, Oct 2000	2.50
❑7, Nov 2000	2.50
❑8, Dec 2000	2.50
❑9, Jan 2001	2.50
❑10, Feb 2001	2.50
❑11, Mar 2001	2.50
❑12, Apr 2001	2.50
❑13, May 2001	2.50
❑14, Jun 2001	2.50
❑15, Jul 2001	2.50
❑16, Aug 2001	2.50
❑17, Sep 2001	2.50
❑18, Oct 2001	2.50
❑19, Nov 2001	2.50
❑20, Dec 2001	2.50

SWAMP THING (4TH SERIES)
DC / VERTIGO

	N-MINT
❑1, May 2004	2.95
❑2, Jun 2004	2.95
❑3, Jul 2004	2.95
❑4, Aug 2004	2.95
❑5, Sep 2004	

SWAMP THING: ROOTS
DC / VERTIGO

	N-MINT
❑1; prestige format one-shot	7.95

SWAN
LITTLE IDYLLS

	N-MINT
❑1, Jun 1995, b&w	2.95
❑2, Jun 1995, b&w	2.95
❑3	2.95
❑4	2.95

SWEATSHOP
DC

	N-MINT
❑1, Jun 2003	2.95
❑2, Jul 2003	2.95
❑3, Aug 2003	2.95
❑4, Sep 2003	2.95
❑5, Oct 2003	2.95
❑6, Nov 2003	2.95

SWEET
ADEPT

	N-MINT
❑1	3.95

N-MINT

SWEETCHILDE
NEW MOON
❑1, b&w 2.95

SWEET CHILDE: LOST CONFESSIONS
ANARCHY BRIDGEWORKS
❑1 .... 2.95

SWEET LUCY
BRAINSTORM
❑1, Jun 1993, b&w 2.95
❑2, b&w 2.95

SWEET LUCY: BLONDE STEELE
BRAINSTORM
❑1 .... 2.95

SWEET LUCY COMMEMORATIVE EDITION
BRAINSTORM
❑1 .... 3.95

SWEETMEATS
ATOMEKA
❑1; b&w one-shot 3.95

SWEET XVI
MARVEL
❑1, May 1991 .... 1.00
❑2, Jun 1991 .... 1.00
❑3, Jul 1991 .... 1.00
❑4, Aug 1991 .... 1.00
❑5, Sep 1991 .... 1.00
❑6, Oct 1991 .... 1.00
❑Special 1; Back to School Special 2.25

SWERVE
SLAVE LABOR / AMAZE INK
❑1, Dec 1995 .... 1.50
❑2, Mar 1996 .... 1.50

SWIFTSURE
HARRIER
❑1, May 1985 .... 2.00
❑2 .... 2.00
❑3, Aug 1985 .... 2.00
❑4 .... 2.00
❑5, Nov 1985 .... 2.00
❑6, Jan 1986 .... 2.00
❑7, Mar 1986 .... 2.00
❑8, May 1986 .... 2.00
❑9, Jul 1986; Redfox 2.00
❑10, Sep 1986 .... 2.00
❑11, Nov 1986 .... 2.00
❑12, Jan 1987 .... 2.00
❑13, Mar 1987 .... 2.00
❑14, May 1987 .... 2.00
❑15, Jul 1987 .... 2.00
❑16, Sep 1987 .... 2.00
❑17, Nov 1987 .... 2.00
❑18, Jan 1988 .... 2.00

SWIFTSURE & CONQUEROR
HARRIER
❑1 .... 2.00
❑2 .... 1.75
❑3 .... 1.75
❑4 .... 1.75
❑5 .... 1.75
❑6 .... 1.75
❑7 .... 1.75
❑8 .... 1.75
❑9 A: Redfox. 2.50
❑10 .... 1.50
❑11 .... 1.50
❑12 .... 1.50
❑13 .... 1.95
❑14 .... 1.95
❑15 .... 1.95
❑16 .... 1.95
❑17 .... 1.95
❑18 .... 1.95

SWITCHBLADE
SILVERLINE
❑1, Dec 1997 .... 2.95

N-MINT

SWORD IN THE STONE
GOLD KEY
❑1, Feb 1964 .... 30.00

SWORD OF DAMOCLES
IMAGE
❑1, Mar 1996 .... 2.50
❑2, Jul 1996 .... 2.50

SWORD OF DRACULA
IMAGE
❑1, Oct 2003 .... 2.95
❑2, Dec 2003 .... 2.95
❑3, Apr 2004 .... 2.99
❑4, Apr 2004 .... 2.95

SWORD OF SORCERY
DC
❑1, Mar 1973; HC, NA (a); Fafhrd and The Gray Mouser 3.00
❑2, May 1973; HC (a); Fafhrd and The Gray Mouser 2.00
❑3, Aug 1973; HC (a); Fafhrd and The Gray Mouser 2.00
❑4, Oct 1973; HC (a); Fafhrd and The Gray Mouser 2.00
❑5, Dec 1973; JSe (a); Fafhrd and The Gray Mouser 2.00

SWORD OF THE ATOM
DC
❑1, Sep 1983 GK (a) 1.50
❑2, Oct 1983 GK (a) 1.50
❑3, Nov 1983 GK (a) 1.50
❑4, Dec 1983 GK (a) 1.50
❑Special 1, ca. 1984 GK (a) 1.50
❑Special 2, ca. 1985 GK (a) 1.50
❑Special 3, ca. 1988 PB (a) 1.50

SWORD OF THE SAMURAI
AVALON
❑1 1996, b&w 2.50

SWORD OF VALOR
A+
❑1 .... 2.50
❑2 .... 2.50
❑3 .... 2.50
❑4 .... 2.50

SWORDSMEN AND SAURIANS
ECLIPSE
❑1, b&w 19.95

SWORDS OF CEREBUS
AARDVARK-VANAHEIM
❑1; Reprints Cerebus #1-4 .... 5.00
❑1-2; Reprints Cerebus #1-4 .... 5.00
❑1-3; Reprints Cerebus #1-4 .... 5.00
❑2; Reprints Cerebus #5-8 .... 5.00
❑2-2; Reprints Cerebus #5-8 .... 5.00
❑3; Reprints Cerebus #9-12 .... 6.00
❑3-2; Reprints Cerebus #9-12 .... 6.00
❑3-3; Reprints Cerebus #9-12 .... 6.00
❑4; Reprints Cerebus #13-16 .... 6.00
❑4-2; Reprints Cerebus #13-16 .... 6.00
❑5; Reprints Cerebus #17-20 .... 5.00
❑6; Reprints Cerebus #21-24; first printing omitted issue #25 .... 5.00

SWORDS OF CEREBUS SUPPLEMENT
AARDVARK-VANAHEIM
❑1; giveaway to buyers of Swords of Cerebus #6 first printing; reprints Cerebus #25 .... 1.00

SWORDS OF SHAR-PEI
CALIBER
❑1, b&w 2.50
❑2, b&w 2.50

SWORDS OF TEXAS
ECLIPSE
❑1, Oct 1987 .... 1.75
❑2 .... 1.75
❑3, Jan 1988 .... 1.75
❑4, Mar 1988 .... 1.75

SWORDS OF THE SWASHBUCKLERS
MARVEL / EPIC
❑1, May 1985 .... 2.00
❑2, Jul 1985 .... 1.75

Halloween masks of the main characters in Marvel's *The Supernaturals* were randomly inserted into the first issue.

© 1998 Marvel Characters Inc.

N-MINT

❑3, Sep 1985 .... 1.75
❑4, Nov 1985 .... 1.50
❑5, Jan 1986 .... 1.50
❑6, Mar 1986 .... 1.50
❑7, May 1986 .... 1.50
❑8, Jul 1986 .... 1.50
❑9, Sep 1986 .... 1.50
❑10, Nov 1986 .... 1.50
❑11, Jan 1987 .... 1.50
❑12, Mar 1987 .... 1.50

SWORDS OF VALOR
A-PLUS
❑1, b&w 2.50
❑2, b&w 2.50
❑3, b&w 2.50
❑4, b&w 2.50

SYMBOLS OF JUSTICE
HIGH IMPACT
❑1, Jun 1995 .... 2.95

SYN
DARK HORSE
❑1, Aug 2003 .... 2.99
❑2, Oct 2003 .... 2.99
❑3, Nov 2003 .... 2.99
❑4, Jan 2004 .... 2.99
❑5, Mar 2004 .... 2.99

SYNN, THE GIRL FROM LSD
AC
❑1, Aug 1990, b&w 3.95

SYNTHETIC ASSASSIN, THE
NIGHT REALM
❑1 .... 1.50

SYPHONS
NOW
❑1, Jul 1986 O: Syphons. 1: Syphons. 2.00
❑2, Sep 1986 .... 1.50
❑3, Nov 1986 .... 1.50
❑4, Jan 1987 .... 1.50
❑5, Mar 1987 .... 1.50
❑6, Jul 1987 .... 1.50
❑7, Aug 1987 .... 1.50

SYPHONS (VOL. 2)
NOW
❑0, Dec 1993; Preview edition 1.00
❑1, May 1994 .... 2.50
❑2, Jun 1994 .... 2.50
❑3, Jul 1994 .... 2.50

SYPHONS: THE SYGATE STRATAGEM
NOW
❑1, ca. 1994 .... 2.95
❑2, ca. 1994 .... 2.95
❑3, ca. 1994 .... 2.95

SYSTEM, THE
DC / VERTIGO
❑1, May 1996 .... 2.95
❑2, Jun 1996 .... 2.95
❑3, Jul 1996 .... 2.95

SYSTEM SEVEN
ARROW
❑1, Dec 1987 .... 1.50
❑2 .... 1.50
❑3 .... 1.50

N-MINT

T

TABOO
Spiderbaby / Tundra
- ❑1, b&w 9.95
- ❑2, b&w 9.95
- ❑3, b&w 9.95
- ❑4, b&w 14.95
- ❑5 .... 14.95
- ❑6; with booklet 14.95
- ❑7; with booklet 14.95
- ❑8, Jun 1995, b&w 14.95
- ❑9 .... 14.95

TABOUX
Antarctic
- ❑1, Aug 1996 .... 3.95
- ❑2, Aug 1996 .... 3.95

TAILGUNNER JO
DC
- ❑1, Sep 1988 .... 1.25
- ❑2, Oct 1988 .... 1.25
- ❑3, Nov 1988 .... 1.25
- ❑4, Dec 1988 .... 1.25
- ❑5, Win 1988 .... 1.25
- ❑6, Jan 1989 .... 1.25

TAILS
Archie
- ❑1, Dec 1995 .... 1.50
- ❑2, Jan 1996 .... 1.50
- ❑3, Feb 1996 .... 1.50

TAINTED
DC / Vertigo
- ❑1, Feb 1995 .... 4.95

TAINTED BLOOD
Weirdling
- ❑1, Apr 1996 .... 2.95

TAKEN UNDER COMPENDIUM
Caliber
- ❑1, b&w 2.95

TAKION
DC
- ❑1, Jun 1996 .... 1.75
- ❑2, Jul 1996 .... 1.75
- ❑3, Aug 1996 .... 1.75
- ❑4, Sep 1996 .... 1.75
- ❑5, Oct 1996 .... 1.75
- ❑6, Nov 1996 .... 1.75
- ❑7, Dec 1996; Lightray returns 1.75

TALE OF HALIMA, THE
Fantagraphics / Eros
- ❑1, b&w 2.75
- ❑2, b&w 2.75

TALE OF MYA ROM, THE
Aircel
- ❑1, b&w 1.70

TALE OF ONE BAD RAT, THE
Dark Horse
- ❑1, Oct 1994; BT, NG (w); BT (a); Introduction by Neil Gaiman 4.00
- ❑2, Nov 1994 BT (w); BT (a) 3.00
- ❑3, Dec 1994 BT (w); BT (a) 3.00
- ❑4, Jan 1995 BT (w); BT (a) 3.00

TALE OF THE BODY THIEF, THE (ANNE RICE'S...)
Sicilian Dragon
- ❑1, Sep 1999 .... 2.95
- ❑2, Oct 1999 .... 2.95
- ❑3 1999 .... 2.95
- ❑4 2000 .... 2.95
- ❑5 2000 .... 2.95
- ❑6 2000 .... 2.95
- ❑7 2000 .... 2.95
- ❑8 2000 .... 2.95
- ❑9 2000 .... 2.95
- ❑10 2000 .... 2.95
- ❑11 2000 .... 2.95
- ❑12 2000 .... 2.95

N-MINT

TALES CALCULATED TO DRIVE YOU MAD
E.C.
- ❑1, ca. 1997 .... 3.99
- ❑2, ca. 1997 .... 3.99
- ❑3, ca. 1997 .... 3.99
- ❑4, ca. 1998 .... 3.99
- ❑5, ca. 1998 .... 3.99
- ❑6, Mar 1999; Reprints Mad #16-18 . 3.99
- ❑7, Nov 1999 .... 3.99
- ❑8, Jan 2000; Reprints Mad #22, 23 . 3.99

TALES FROM GROUND ZERO
Excel
- ❑1, b&w 4.95

TALES FROM NECROPOLIS
Brainstorm
- ❑1, b&w 2.95

TALES FROM SLEAZE CASTLE
Gratuitous Bunny
- ❑1 .... 2.50
- ❑2 .... 2.50
- ❑3 .... 2.50

TALES FROM THE AGE OF APOCALYPSE
Marvel
- ❑1, Dec 1996 .... 5.95

TALES FROM THE AGE OF APOCALYPSE: SINISTER BLOODLINES
Marvel
- ❑1, Dec 1997 .... 5.99

TALES FROM THE ANIVERSE (MASSIVE)
Massive
- ❑1, Jan 1992, b&w 2.25
- ❑2 1992 .... 2.25
- ❑3 1992 .... 2.25

TALES FROM THE ANIVERSE (ARROW)
Arrow
- ❑1 .... 2.00
- ❑2 .... 1.50
- ❑3 .... 1.50
- ❑4 .... 1.50
- ❑5 .... 1.50
- ❑6 .... 1.50

TALES FROM THE BOG
Aberration
- ❑1, Nov 1995, b&w 3.00
- ❑2, Feb 1996, b&w 3.00
- ❑3, Jun 1996, b&w 3.00
- ❑4, Sep 1996, b&w 3.00
- ❑5, Apr 1997, b&w 3.00
- ❑6, Jun 1997, b&w 3.00
- ❑7, Nov 1997, b&w 3.00
- ❑Ashcan 1, Sep 1995 .... 2.95

TALES FROM THE BOG (DIRECTOR'S CUT)
Aberration
- ❑1 1998, b&w 2.95

TALES FROM THE CLONEZONE
Dark Horse
- ❑1 .... 1.75

TALES FROM THE CRYPT (GLADSTONE)
Gladstone
- ❑1, Jul 1990; GE, AW, FF, BE, GI (w); GE, AW, JCr, FF, BE, JKa, GI (a); O: Crypt-Keeper. Reprints Tales From the Crypt #33, Crime SuspenStories #17 .... 3.00
- ❑2, Sep 1990; JO, JCr, JKa, GI (w); JO, JCr, JKa, GI (a); Reprints Tales From the Crypt #35, Crime SuspenStories #18 .... 2.50
- ❑3, Nov 1990; HK, JO, WW, JKa, GI (w); HK, JO, JCr, WW, JKa, GI (a); Reprints Tales From the Crypt #39, Crime SuspenStories #1 .... 2.50

N-MINT

- ❑4, Jan 1991; AF, AW, HK, JO, JCr, JKa (a); Reprints Tales From the Crypt #18, Crime SuspenStories #16 .... 2.50
- ❑5, Mar 1991; JCr, BK, JKa, GI (a); Reprints Tales From the Crypt #45, Crime SuspenStories #5 .... 2.50
- ❑6, May 1991; JCr, BK, JKa, GI (a); Reprints Tales From the Crypt #42, Crime SuspenStories #27 .... 2.50

TALES FROM THE CRYPT (COCHRAN ONE-SHOT)
Cochran
- ❑1, Jul 1991; over-sized reprint of Tales #31 and Crime SuspenStories #12 .... 3.95

TALES FROM THE CRYPT (COCHRAN)
Cochran
- ❑1 .... 2.00
- ❑2, Oct 1991 .... 2.00
- ❑3, Dec 1991 .... 2.00
- ❑4, Feb 1992 .... 2.00
- ❑5, Mar 1992 .... 2.00
- ❑6, May 1992 .... 2.00
- ❑7, Jul 1992 .... 2.00

TALES FROM THE CRYPT (RCP)
Gemstone
- ❑1, Sep 1992; AF, JCr (a); Reprints Crypt of Terror (EC) #17 .... 2.00
- ❑2, Dec 1992; Reprints Crypt of Terror (EC) #18 .... 2.00
- ❑3, Mar 1993; Reprints Crypt of Terror (EC) #19 .... 2.00
- ❑4, Jun 1993; AF, JCr, JKa, GI (a); Reprints Tales From the Crypt (EC) #20 .... 2.00
- ❑5, Sep 1993; AF, HK, WW, GI (a); Reprints Tales From the Crypt (EC) #21 .... 2.00
- ❑6, Dec 1993; AF, JCr, GI (a); Reprints Tales From the Crypt (EC) #22 .... 2.00
- ❑7, Mar 1994; AF, JCr, GI (a); Reprints Tales From the Crypt (EC) #23 .... 2.00
- ❑8, Jun 1994; AF (c); JCr, WW, GI (a); Reprints Tales From the Crypt (EC) #24 .... 2.00
- ❑9, Sep 1994; Reprints Tales From the Crypt (EC) #25 .... 2.00
- ❑10, Dec 1994; Reprints Tales From the Crypt (EC) #26 .... 2.00
- ❑11, Mar 1995; JO, JKa, GI (w); JO, JKa, GI (a); Reprints Tales From the Crypt (EC) #27 .... 2.00
- ❑12, Jun 1995; JO, JKa, GI (w); JO, JKa, GI (a); Reprints Tales From the Crypt (EC) #28 .... 2.00
- ❑13, Sep 1995; JO, JKa, GI (w); JO, JKa, GI (a); Reprints Tales From the Crypt (EC) #29 .... 2.00
- ❑14, Dec 1995; JO, JKa, GI (w); JO, JKa, GI (a); Reprints Tales From the Crypt (EC) #30 .... 2.00
- ❑15, Mar 1996; AW, JKa, GI (w); AW, JKa, GI (a); Reprints Tales From the Crypt (EC) #31 .... 2.00
- ❑16, Jun 1996; GE, GI (w); GE, GI (a); Reprints Tales From the Crypt (EC) #32 .... 2.50
- ❑17, Sep 1996; GE, JKa, GI (w); GE, JKa, GI (a); O: the The Crypt Keeper. Reprints Tales From the Crypt (EC) #33 .... 2.50
- ❑18, Dec 1996; GE, JKa, GI (w); GE, JKa, GI (a); Reprints Tales From the Crypt (EC) #34 .... 2.50
- ❑19, Mar 1997; JO, JKa, GI (w); JO, JKa, GI (a); Reprints Tales From the Crypt (EC) #35 .... 2.50
- ❑20, Jun 1997; GE, JKa, GI (w); GE, JKa, GI (a); Reprints Tales From the Crypt (EC) #36 .... 2.50
- ❑21, Sep 1997; JO, BE, GI (w); JO, BE, GI (a); Reprints Tales From the Crypt (EC) #37 .... 2.50
- ❑22, Dec 1997; BE, GI (w); BE, GI (a); Reprints Tales From the Crypt (EC) #38 .... 2.50
- ❑23, Mar 1998; JO, JKa, GI (w); JO, JKa, GI (a); Reprints Tales From the Crypt (EC) #39 .... 2.50

N-MINT

❑24, Jun 1998; GE, BK, GI (w); GE, BK, GI (a); Reprints Tales From the Crypt (EC) #40 ..... 2.50
❑25, Sep 1998; GE, JKa, GI (w); GE, JKa, GI (a); Reprints Tales From the Crypt (EC) #41 ..... 2.50
❑26, Dec 1998; Reprints Tales From the Crypt (EC) #42 ..... 2.50
❑27, Mar 1999; Reprints Tales From the Crypt (EC) #43 ..... 2.50
❑28, Jun 1999; Reprints Tales From the Crypt (EC) #44 ..... 2.50
❑29, Sep 1999; Reprints Tales From the Crypt (EC) #45 ..... 2.50
❑30, Dec 1999; Reprints Tales From the Crypt (EC) #46; material originally prepared for Crypt of Terror #1 ..... 2.50
❑Annual 1; Collects Tales From the Crypt #1-5 ..... 8.95
❑Annual 2 ..... 9.95
❑Annual 3 ..... 10.95
❑Annual 4 ..... 12.95
❑Annual 5; Collects Tales From the Crypt #37-41 ..... 13.50

TALES FROM THE EDGE!
VANGUARD

❑1, Jun 1993, b&w; Flip-book WW (a) 3.50
❑2, Sep 1993, b&w 5.00
❑3, Dec 1993, b&w 3.00
❑4, Jul 1994, b&w 3.00
❑5, ca. 1994 ..... 3.00
❑6, ca. 1995 ..... 3.00
❑7, Jul 1995, b&w 3.00
❑8, b&w 4.00
❑9, b&w 5.00
❑10, b&w 4.00
❑11, Mar 1998 ..... 5.00
❑12 ..... 4.00
❑13 ..... 3.00
❑14 ..... 5.00
❑15; BSz (a); Bill Sienkiewicz Special 5.55
❑Summer 1, Aug 1994, b&w; card-stock cover 3.50

TALES FROM THE FRIDGE
KITCHEN SINK

❑1, Jun 1973, b&w 3.00

TALES FROM THE HEART
ENTROPY

❑1 1988; no cover date 4.00
❑2 1988 ..... 3.25
❑3, Dec 1988, b&w 3.00
❑4, Jan 1989, b&w 3.00
❑5, May 1989, b&w 2.95
❑6, Oct 1989, b&w 2.95
❑7, Nov 1990 ..... 2.95
❑8, Apr 1991 ..... 2.95
❑9, Aug 1992 ..... 2.95
❑10, Mar 1993, b&w 2.95
❑11, May 1994, b&w 2.95

TALES FROM THE HEART OF AFRICA: THE TEMPORARY NATIVES
MARVEL / EPIC

❑1, Aug 1990 ..... 3.95

TALES FROM THE KIDS
DAVID G. BROWN

❑1, Apr 1996, b&w; No cover price; anthology by children; produced for L.A. Cultural Affairs Dept. 2.00

TALES FROM THE LEATHER NUN
LAST GASP

❑1 ..... 14.00

TALES FROM THE OUTER BOROUGHS
FANTAGRAPHICS

❑1, b&w 2.25
❑2, b&w 2.25
❑3, b&w 2.25
❑4, b&w 2.50
❑5, b&w 2.50

TALES FROM THE PLAGUE
ECLIPSE

❑1 ..... 3.95

N-MINT

TALES FROM THE RAVAGED LANDS
MAGI

❑0; no indicia; b&w introduction to series 2.00
❑1, b&w; no indicia or cover date 2.50
❑2, b&w; no indicia or cover date 2.50
❑3, Jan 1996, b&w 2.50
❑4, ca. 1996, b&w; no indicia or cover date 2.50
❑5, May 1996, b&w 2.50
❑6, Aug 1996, b&w 2.50

TALES FROM THE STONE TROLL CAFÉ
PLANET X

❑1, ca. 1986 ..... 1.75

TALES FROM THE TOMB
DELL

❑1, Oct 1962 ..... 125.00

TALES OF A CHECKERED MAN
D.W. BRUBAKER

❑1, b&w; no cover price 2.00

TALES OF ASGARD (VOL. 1)
MARVEL

❑1, Oct 1968; SL (w); JK (a); reprints "Tales of Asgard" stories from Journey Into Mystery #98-106 ..... 30.00

TALES OF ASGARD (VOL. 2)
MARVEL

❑1, Feb 1984; SL (w); JK (a); reprints "Tales of Asgard" stories from Journey Into Mystery #129-136 ..... 1.50

TALES OF BEATRIX FARMER
MU

❑1, Feb 1996, b&w 2.95

TALES OF BLUE & GREY
AVALON

❑1, b&w 2.95

TALES OF EVIL
ATLAS-SEABOARD

❑1, Feb 1975 ..... 5.00
❑2, Apr 1975 TS (a) 5.00
❑3, Jul 1975 RB (w); RB (a) 5.00

TALES OF GHOST CASTLE
DC

❑1, May 1975 NR (a) 9.00
❑2, Jul 1975 AN (a) 9.00
❑3, Sep 1975 ..... 9.00

TALES OF G.I. JOE
MARVEL

❑1, Jan 1988; Reprints G.I. Joe, A Real American Hero #1 ..... 1.00
❑2, Feb 1988; Reprints G.I. Joe, A Real American Hero #2 ..... 1.00
❑3, Mar 1988; Reprints G.I. Joe, A Real American Hero #3 ..... 1.00
❑4, Apr 1988; Reprints G.I. Joe, A Real American Hero #4 ..... 1.00
❑5, May 1988; Reprints G.I. Joe, A Real American Hero #5 ..... 1.00
❑6, Jun 1988; Reprints G.I. Joe, A Real American Hero #6 ..... 1.00
❑7, Jul 1988; Reprints G.I. Joe, A Real American Hero #7 ..... 1.00
❑8, Aug 1988; Reprints G.I. Joe, A Real American Hero #8 ..... 1.00
❑9, Sep 1988; Reprints G.I. Joe, A Real American Hero #9 ..... 1.00
❑10, Oct 1988; Reprints G.I. Joe, A Real American Hero #10 ..... 1.00
❑11, Nov 1988; Reprints G.I. Joe, A Real American Hero #11 ..... 1.00
❑12, Dec 1988; Reprints G.I. Joe, A Real American Hero #12 ..... 1.00
❑13, Jan 1989; Reprints G.I. Joe, A Real American Hero #13 ..... 1.00
❑14, Feb 1989; Reprints G.I. Joe, A Real American Hero #14 ..... 1.00
❑15, Mar 1989; Reprints G.I. Joe, A Real American Hero #15 ..... 1.00

The Adaptoid, an android capable of mimicking the powers and abilities of his opponents, made his first appearance in *Tales of Suspense* #82.

© 1966 Marvel Comics.

N-MINT

TALES OF JERRY
HACIENDA

❑1, b&w 2.50
❑2 ..... 2.50
❑3 ..... 2.50
❑4 ..... 2.50
❑5 ..... 2.50
❑6 ..... 2.50
❑7 ..... 2.50
❑8 ..... 2.50
❑9 ..... 2.50
❑10 ..... 2.50

TALES OF LETHARGY
ALPHA

❑1, b&w 2.50
❑2, b&w 2.50
❑3, b&w 2.50

TALES OF ORDINARY MADNESS
DARK HORSE

❑1, b&w 2.50
❑2, b&w 2.50
❑3, b&w 2.50
❑4, b&w 2.50

TALES OF SCREAMING HORROR
FANTACO

❑1, ca. 1992, b&w 3.50

TALES OF SEX AND DEATH
PRINT MINT

❑1, Apr 1971 ..... 3.00
❑2 ..... 3.00

TALES OF SHAUNDRA
RIP OFF

❑1 ..... 12.95

TALES OF SUSPENSE
MARVEL

❑1, Jan 1959 ..... 1400.00
❑2, Mar 1959 ..... 540.00
❑3, May 1959 ..... 475.00
❑4, Jul 1959 AW (a) 450.00
❑5, Sep 1959 ..... 325.00
❑6, Nov 1959 ..... 325.00
❑7, Jan 1960 1: Neptune. 325.00
❑8, Mar 1960 ..... 325.00
❑9, May 1960 1: Chondu the Mystic. 325.00
❑10, Jul 1960 ..... 325.00
❑11, Sep 1960 ..... 240.00
❑12, Nov 1960 ..... 240.00
❑13, Jan 1961 ..... 240.00
❑14, Feb 1961 1: It, the Living Colossus. 240.00
❑15, Mar 1961 ..... 240.00
❑16, Apr 1961 JK (c); SL (w); JK (a); 1: Iron Man prototype. 240.00
❑17, May 1961 ..... 240.00
❑18, Jun 1961 ..... 240.00
❑19, Jul 1961 ..... 240.00
❑20, Aug 1961 JK (c); SL (w); SD, DH, JK (a); A: It, the Living Colossus. 240.00
❑21, Sep 1961 ..... 150.00
❑22, Oct 1961 ..... 150.00
❑23, Nov 1961 ..... 150.00
❑24, Dec 1961 ..... 150.00
❑25, Jan 1962 ..... 150.00
❑26, Feb 1962 ..... 150.00
❑27, Mar 1962 ..... 150.00
❑28, Apr 1962 ..... 150.00
❑29, May 1962 ..... 150.00

	N-MINT
❑30, Jun 1962	150.00
❑31, Jul 1962 1: Doctor Doom-prototype ("The Monster in the Iron Mask")	150.00
❑32, Aug 1962 1: Doctor Strange-prototype ("Sazik the Sorcerer")	150.00
❑33, Sep 1962	135.00
❑34, Oct 1962	135.00
❑35, Nov 1962	135.00
❑36, Dec 1962	135.00
❑37, Jan 1963	135.00
❑38, Feb 1963	135.00
❑39, Mar 1963; JK (a); O: Iron Man. 1: Iron Man. Grey armor	3500.00
❑40, Apr 1963 JK (a); 1: Iron Man gold armor. 2: Iron Man.	1100.00
❑41, May 1963 JK (a)	650.00
❑42, Jun 1963 SD, DH (a); 1: Mad Pharoah.	325.00
❑43, Jul 1963 O: Kala. 1: Kala.	325.00
❑44, Aug 1963	325.00
❑45, Sep 1963 1: Pepper Potts. 1: Happy Hogan. 1: Jack Frost II (Gregor Shapanka). V: Jack Frost II (Gregor Shapanka).	325.00
❑46, Oct 1963 1: Crimson Dynamo.	210.00
❑47, Nov 1963 SL (w); SD, DH (a); O: Melter. 1: Melter.	210.00
❑48, Dec 1963; SL (w); SD (a); New armor for Iron Man (red and gold)	265.00
❑49, Jan 1964; SL (w); SD (a); A: Angel II. Watcher back-up	210.00
❑50, Feb 1964; SL (w); DH (a); 1: The Mandarin. Watcher back-up	155.00
❑51, Mar 1964; SL (w); DH (a); O: Scarecrow (Marvel). 1: Scarecrow (Marvel). Watcher back-up	105.00
❑52, Apr 1964; SL (w); DH (a); 1: Black Widow. Watcher back-up	140.00
❑53, May 1964; SL (w); DH (a); O: The Watcher. A: Black Widow. Watcher back-up	120.00
❑54, Jun 1964; SL (w); DH (a); 1: Black Knight II (Nathan Garrett). Watcher back-up	62.00
❑55, Jul 1964; SL (w); DH (a); A: The Mandarin. Watcher back-up	62.00
❑56, Aug 1964; SL (w); DH (a); 1: Unicorn I (Milos Masaryk). Watcher back-up	62.00
❑57, Sep 1964; DH (a); 1: Hawkeye. A: Black Widow. Watcher back-up	170.00
❑58, Oct 1964; DH, GT (a); A: Captain America. Watcher back-up	210.00
❑59, Nov 1964; DH, JK (a); 1: Jarvis. V: Black Knight. Captain America second feature begins	210.00
❑60, Dec 1964 JK (a)	120.00
❑61, Jan 1965 DH, JK (a)	82.00
❑62, Feb 1965; DH, JK (a); O: Mandarin. redesign of Iron Man's helmet	82.00
❑63, Mar 1965 O: Bucky. O: Captain America. A: Doctor Erskine A: General Phillips. A: Sgt. Duffy.	180.00
❑64, Apr 1965 1: Agent 13 (Peggy Carter).	72.00
❑65, May 1965 A: Red Skull.	125.00
❑66, Jun 1965; O: Red Skull. Red Skull returns	125.00
❑67, Jul 1965	52.00
❑68, Aug 1965	52.00
❑69, Sep 1965 1: Titanium Man I (Boris Bullski).	52.00
❑70, Oct 1965	52.00
❑71, Nov 1965 DH, WW (a)	42.00
❑72, Dec 1965 GT, JK (a)	42.00
❑73, Jan 1966 GC, GT, JK (a); D: Black Knight II (Nathan Garrett).	42.00
❑74, Feb 1966 GC, GT, JK (a)	42.00
❑75, Mar 1966 GC (a); 1: Second Agent 13 (Sharon Carter). 1: Batroc.	42.00
❑76, Apr 1966 JK (c); SL (w); GC, JR (a); 1: Ultimo (cameo). A: The Mandarin. A: Batroc.	42.00
❑77, May 1966 SL (w); GC (a); O: Ultimo. 1: Ultimo (full appearance). 1: Peggy Carter.	42.00
❑78, Jun 1966 JK (c); SL (w); GC, JK (a); A: Nick Fury. A: Ultimo. A: The Mandarin.	42.00
❑79, Jul 1966 GC (c); SL (w); GC, JK, JAb (a); 1: Cosmic Cube (Kubik). A: Namor. A: Red Skull.	42.00
❑80, Aug 1966; SL (w); GC, JK (a); A: Namor. A: Red Skull. Cosmic Cube; Sub-Mariner vs. Iron Man	42.00
❑81, Sep 1966 GC (c); SL (w); GC, JK (a); A: Titanium Man. A: Red Skull.	32.00
❑82, Oct 1966 JK (c); SL (w); GC, JK (a); 1: Adaptoid. A: Titanium Man. A: Scarlet Witch. A: Quicksilver.	32.00
❑83, Nov 1966 GC (c); SL (w); GC, JK (a); A: Titanium Man.	32.00
❑84, Dec 1966 JK (c); SL (w); GC, JK (a); 1: Super-Adaptoid. A: Goliath. A: Hawkeye. A: The Mandarin. A: The Wasp.	32.00
❑85, Jan 1967; GC (c); SL (w); GC, JK (a); A: Batroc. V: Mandarin. Happy substitutes as Iron Man	32.00
❑86, Feb 1967 SL (w); GC, JK (a)	32.00
❑87, Mar 1967	32.00
❑88, Apr 1967 GK (c); SL (w); GC, GK (a); A: Mole Man. A: Swordsman. A: Power Man I (Erik Josten).	32.00
❑89, May 1967 GC (c); SL (w); GC, GK (a); A: Red Skull. A: Melter.	32.00
❑90, Jun 1967 GC, GK (a); O: Byrrah.	32.00
❑91, Jul 1967 GC, GK (a)	32.00
❑92, Aug 1967 GC, GK (a)	32.00
❑93, Sep 1967 GC, GK (a)	32.00
❑94, Oct 1967 1: Modok.	32.00
❑95, Nov 1967; GC, GK (a); 1: Walter Newell (later becomes Stingray). Captain America's identity revealed	32.00
❑96, Dec 1967 GC, GK (a)	32.00
❑97, Jan 1968 SL (w); GC, JK, GK (a); 1: Whiplash. A: Black Panther.	32.00
❑98, Feb 1968 GC, GK (a); O: Whitney Frost. 1: Whitney Frost.	32.00
❑99, Mar 1968; GC, GK (a); V: Red Skull. Series continued in Captain America #100, Iron Man #1	32.00

TALES OF SUSPENSE (VOL. 2)
MARVEL

	N-MINT
❑1, Jan 1995; prestige format one-shot; acetate outer cover	6.95

TALES OF TERROR
ECLIPSE

	N-MINT
❑1, Jul 1985	2.00
❑2, Sep 1985	2.00
❑3, Nov 1985	2.00
❑4, Jan 1986	2.00
❑5, Mar 1986	2.00
❑6, May 1986	2.00
❑7, Jul 1986	2.00
❑8, Sep 1986	2.00
❑9, Nov 1986	2.00
❑10, Jan 1987	2.00
❑11, Mar 1987	2.00
❑12, May 1987	2.00
❑13, Jul 1987	2.00

TALES OF THE ARMORKINS
CO. & SONS

	N-MINT
❑1	3.00

TALES OF THE BEANWORLD
ECLIPSE

	N-MINT
❑1, ca. 1985	4.00
❑2, ca. 1985	3.00
❑3, ca. 1986	3.00
❑4, ca. 1986	3.00
❑5, ca. 1986	3.00
❑6, Apr 1987	3.00
❑7, ca. 1987	3.00
❑8, ca. 1987	3.00
❑9, ca. 1988	3.00
❑10, ca. 1988	3.00
❑11, ca. 1988	2.00
❑12, Feb 1989	2.00
❑13, ca. 1989	2.00
❑14, ca. 1989	2.00
❑15, ca. 1990	2.00
❑16, ca. 1990	2.00
❑17, ca. 1990	2.00
❑18, ca. 1991	2.00
❑19, ca. 1991	2.00
❑20, ca. 1993	2.50
❑21, ca. 1993	2.95

TALES OF THE CLOSET
HETRIC-MARTIN

	N-MINT
❑1, Sum 1987, b&w	2.50
❑2, b&w	2.50
❑3, b&w	2.50
❑4, b&w	2.50
❑5, b&w	2.50
❑6, b&w	2.50
❑7, Spr 1992	2.50
❑8, Win 1992	2.50

TALES OF THE CRIMSON LION
GARY LANKFORD

	N-MINT
❑1, Jul 1987	1.95

TALES OF THE CYBORG GERBILS
HARRIER

	N-MINT
❑1, Nov 1987	1.95

TALES OF THE DARKNESS
IMAGE

	N-MINT
❑0.5, Apr 1998, BSz (a); Female demon on cover	2.95
❑0.5/A, Apr 1998, BSz (a); Man atop demons on cover	3.00
❑1, Apr 1998	2.95
❑2, Jun 1998	2.95
❑3, Aug 1998	2.95
❑4, Dec 1998	2.95

TALES OF THE FEHNNIK (ANTARCTIC)
ANTARCTIC

	N-MINT
❑1, Aug 1995, b&w	2.95

TALES OF THE FEHNNIK (RADIO)
RADIO

	N-MINT
❑1, Jun 1998, b&w	2.95

TALES OF THE GREAT UNSPOKEN
TOP SHELF

	N-MINT
❑1, b&w; no cover price	1.00

TALES OF THE GREEN BERET
DELL

	N-MINT
❑1, Jan 1967	25.00
❑2, Mar 1967	18.00
❑3, Jun 1967	18.00
❑4, Sep 1967	18.00
❑5, ca. 1968	18.00

TALES OF THE GREEN BERETS
AVALON

	N-MINT
❑1; "The Green Berets" in the indicia	2.95
❑2; "The Green Berets" in the indicia	2.95
❑3; "The Green Berets" in the indicia	2.95
❑4	2.95
❑5	2.95
❑6	2.95
❑7; "Green Berets" in the indicia	2.95

TALES OF THE GREEN HORNET (1ST SERIES)
NOW

	N-MINT
❑1, Sep 1990	2.00
❑2, Oct 1990	2.00

TALES OF THE GREEN HORNET (2ND SERIES)
NOW

	N-MINT
❑1, Jan 1992	2.00
❑2, Feb 1992 O: The Green Hornet.	2.00
❑3, Mar 1992	2.00
❑4, Apr 1992	2.00

TALES OF THE GREEN HORNET (3RD SERIES)
NOW

	N-MINT
❑1, Sep 1992; bagged with hologram card	2.75
❑2, Oct 1992	2.50
❑3, Nov 1992	2.50

N-MINT

TALES OF THE GREEN LANTERN CORPS
DC

❑1, May 1981 FMc, JSe (a); O: Green Lantern. 1.50
❑2, Jun 1981 FMc, JSe (a) 1.25
❑3, Jul 1981 FMc, JSa, JSe (a) 1.25
❑Annual 1 1.25

TALES OF THE JACKALOPE
BLACKTHORNE

❑1 1986 2.00
❑2 1986 2.00
❑3 1986 2.00
❑4 1986 2.00
❑5 1986 2.00
❑6 1986 2.00
❑7, Feb 1987 2.00

TALES OF THE KUNG FU WARRIORS
CFW

❑1 1: Ethereal Black. 1: Squamous. 2.00
❑2 2.00
❑3 2.00
❑4 2.00
❑5 2.00
❑6 2.00
❑7 2.00
❑8 2.00
❑9 2.00
❑10 2.25
❑11 2.25
❑12 2.25
❑13 2.25
❑14, Aug 1989 1: Sumo. 2.25

TALES OF THE LEGION
DC

❑314, Aug 1984 O: White Witch. 1.25
❑315, Sep 1984 KG (w); KG (a); V: Dark Circle. 1.25
❑316, Oct 1984 O: White Witch. 1.25
❑317, Nov 1984 1.25
❑318, Dec 1984 V: Persuader. 1.25
❑319, Jan 1985 1.25
❑320, Feb 1985 1.25
❑321, Mar 1985 1.25
❑322, Apr 1985 1.25
❑323, May 1985 1.25
❑324, Jun 1985 V: Dark Circle. 1.25
❑325, Jul 1985 1.25
❑326, Aug 1985; V: Legion of Super-Villains. begins reprints of Legion of Super-Heroes (3rd series) 1.00
❑327, Sep 1985 V: Legion of Super-Villains. 1.00
❑328, Oct 1985 V: Legion of Super-Villains. 1.00
❑329, Nov 1985 D: Karate Kid. V: Legion of Super-Villains. 1.00
❑330, Dec 1985 V: Legion of Super-Villains. 1.00
❑331, Jan 1986 O: Lightning Lord. O: Lightning Lass. O: Lightning Lad. 1.00
❑332, Feb 1986 1.00
❑333, Mar 1986 1.00
❑334, Apr 1986 1.00
❑335, May 1986 1.00
❑336, Jun 1986 1.00
❑337, Jul 1986 1.00
❑338, Aug 1986 1.00
❑339, Sep 1986; Magnetic Kid, Tellus, Polar Boy, Quislet, and Sensor Girl join team 1.00
❑340, Oct 1986 V: Doctor Regulus. 1.00
❑341, Nov 1986 1.00
❑342, Dec 1986 1.00
❑343, Jan 1987 O: Wildfire. 1.00
❑344, Feb 1987 1.00
❑345, Mar 1987 1.00
❑346, Apr 1987 1.00
❑347, May 1987 V: Universo. 1.00
❑348, Jun 1987; in Phantom Zone 1.00
❑349, Jul 1987 1.00
❑350, Aug 1987; Sensor Girl's identity revealed 1.00

N-MINT

❑351, Sep 1987 V: Fatal Five. 1.00
❑352, Oct 1987 1.00
❑353, Nov 1987 1.00
❑354, Dec 1987 1.00
❑Annual 4 1.25
❑Annual 5 O: Validus. 1.25

TALES OF THE MARVELS: BLOCKBUSTER
MARVEL

❑1, Apr 1995; prestige format; acetate overlay outer cover 5.95

TALES OF THE MARVELS: INNER DEMONS
MARVEL

❑1, ca. 1995, acetate overlay outer cover 5.95

TALES OF THE MARVELS: WONDER YEARS
MARVEL

❑1, Aug 1995; wraparound acetate outer cover 4.95
❑2, Sep 1995; wraparound acetate outer cover 4.95

TALES OF THE MARVEL UNIVERSE
MARVEL

❑1, Feb 1997; wraparound cover 2.99

TALES OF THE NEW TEEN TITANS
DC

❑1, Jun 1982 GP (a); O: Cyborg. 1.50
❑2, Jul 1982 GP (a); O: Raven. 1.00
❑3, Aug 1982 GP, GD (a); O: Changeling. 1.00
❑4, Sep 1982 GP (a); O: Starfire II (Koriand'r). 1: Ryand'r. 1.00

TALES OF THE NINJA WARRIORS
CFW

❑1, b&w 2.25
❑2, b&w 2.25
❑3, b&w 2.25
❑4, b&w 2.25
❑5, b&w 2.25
❑6, b&w 2.25
❑7, b&w 2.25
❑8, b&w 2.25
❑9, b&w 2.25
❑10, b&w 2.25
❑11, b&w 2.25
❑12, b&w 2.25
❑13, b&w 2.25
❑14, b&w 2.25
❑15, b&w 2.25
❑16, b&w 2.25

TALES OF THE SUN RUNNERS
SIRIUS

❑1, Jul 1986 1.50
❑2 1986 1.95
❑3 1986 1.95

TALES OF THE TEENAGE MUTANT NINJA TURTLES
MIRAGE

❑1, May 1987 3.00
❑2, Jul 1987 2.00
❑3, Oct 1987 2.00
❑4, Feb 1988; cover says Jan, indicia says Feb 2.00
❑5, May 1988 2.00
❑6, Aug 1988 2.00
❑7, Aug 1989; cover says Apr, indicia says Aug 2.00

TALES OF THE TEEN TITANS
DC

❑41, Apr 1984; GP (a); A: Brother Blood. Series continued from New Teen Titans (1st Series) #40 2.00
❑42, May 1984 GP (a); V: Deathstroke. 2.00
❑43, Jun 1984 GP (a); V: Deathstroke. V: H.I.V.E.. 2.00
❑44, Jul 1984 GP (a); O: Jericho. 1: Nightwing. 6.00
❑45, Aug 1984 GP (a); A: Aquagirl. A: Aqualad. 1.50

Donna Troy (Wonder Girl) got married in *Tales of the Teen Titans* #50.

© 1985 DC Comics.

N-MINT

❑46, Sep 1984 GP (a); V: H.I.V.E.. 1.50
❑47, Oct 1984 GP (a); V: H.I.V.E.. 1.50
❑48, Nov 1984 GP, SR (a); V: Recombatants. 1.50
❑49, Dec 1984 CI, GP (a); V: Doctor Light. 1.50
❑50, Feb 1985; Giant-size; GP (a); Wedding of Wonder Girl 2.00
❑51, Mar 1985 1: Azrael (cameo, not Batman character). V: Cheshire. 1.50
❑52, Apr 1985 RB (a); 1: Azrael (full appearace, not Batman character). V: Cheshire. 1.50
❑53, May 1985 A: Deathstroke. 1.50
❑54, Jun 1985; RB, DG (a); A: Deathstroke. Trial of Deathstroke 1.50
❑55, Jul 1985; Changeling vs. Deathstroke 1.50
❑56, Aug 1985 V: Fearsome Five. 1.50
❑57, Sep 1985; V: Fearsome Five. Cyborg transformed 1.50
❑58, Oct 1985 A: Monitor. A: Harbinger. V: Fearsome Five. 1.50
❑59, Nov 1985; reprints DC Comics Presents #26 1.50
❑60, Dec 1985; V: Trigon. series begins reprinting New Teen Titans (second series) 1.00
❑61, Jan 1986 V: Trigon. 1.00
❑62, Feb 1986 V: Trigon. 1.00
❑63, Mar 1986 V: Trigon. 1.00
❑64, Apr 1986 V: Trigon. 1.00
❑65, May 1986 1.00
❑66, Jun 1986 O: Lilith. 1.00
❑67, Jul 1986 1.00
❑68, Aug 1986 A: Kole. 1.00
❑69, Sep 1986 1.00
❑70, Oct 1986 O: Kole. 1.00
❑71, Nov 1986 1.00
❑72, Dec 1986 A: Outsiders. 1.00
❑73, Jan 1987 1.00
❑74, Feb 1987 1.00
❑75, Mar 1987 A: Omega Men. 1.00
❑76, Apr 1987; Wedding of Starfire 1.00
❑77, May 1987 1.00
❑78, Jun 1987; new team 1.00
❑79, Jul 1987 1.00
❑80, Aug 1987 A: Cheshire, Lian. 1.00
❑81, Sep 1987 1.00
❑82, Oct 1987 1.00
❑83, Nov 1987 1.00
❑84, Dec 1987 1.00
❑85, Jan 1988 1.00
❑86, Feb 1988 V: Twister. 1.00
❑87, Mar 1988 V: Brotherhood of Evil. 1.00
❑88, Apr 1988 V: Brother Blood. 1.00
❑89, May 1988 V: Brother Blood. 1.00
❑90, Jun 1988 1.00
❑91, Jul 1988 1.00
❑Annual 4; A: Superman. V: Vanguard. reprints New Teen Titans Annual #1 1.25

TALES OF THE UNEXPECTED
DC

❑1, Feb 1956 750.00
❑2, Apr 1956 385.00
❑3, Jul 1956 275.00
❑4, Aug 1956 225.00
❑5, Sep 1956 225.00
❑6, Oct 1956 165.00

	N-MINT
❑7, Nov 1956	165.00
❑8, Dec 1956	165.00
❑9, Jan 1957	165.00
❑10, Feb 1957	165.00
❑11, Mar 1957	125.00
❑12, Apr 1957	125.00
❑13, May 1957	125.00
❑14, Jun 1957	125.00
❑15, Jul 1957	125.00
❑16, Aug 1957 JK (a)	125.00
❑17, Sep 1957	125.00
❑18, Oct 1957	125.00
❑19, Nov 1957	125.00
❑20, Dec 1957	125.00
❑21, Jan 1958	100.00
❑22, Feb 1958	100.00
❑23, Mar 1958	100.00
❑24, Apr 1958	100.00
❑25, May 1958	100.00
❑26, Jun 1958	100.00
❑27, Jul 1958	100.00
❑28, Aug 1958	100.00
❑29, Sep 1958	100.00
❑30, Oct 1958; Binky: Lost, A Free Education (PSA)	100.00
❑31, Nov 1958	85.00
❑32, Dec 1958	85.00
❑33, Jan 1959	85.00
❑34, Feb 1959	85.00
❑35, Mar 1959	85.00
❑36, Apr 1959	85.00
❑37, May 1959	85.00
❑38, Jun 1959	85.00
❑39, Jul 1959	85.00
❑40, Aug 1959; Space Ranger stories begin	650.00
❑41, Sep 1959 A: Space Ranger.	275.00
❑42, Oct 1959 A: Space Ranger.	275.00
❑43, Nov 1959; A: Space Ranger. Space Ranger cover	450.00
❑44, Dec 1959 A: Space Ranger.	200.00
❑45, Jan 1960 A: Space Ranger.	200.00
❑46, Feb 1960 A: Space Ranger.	150.00
❑47, Mar 1960 A: Space Ranger.	150.00
❑48, Apr 1960 A: Space Ranger.	150.00
❑49, May 1960 A: Space Ranger.	150.00
❑50, Jun 1960 A: Space Ranger.	150.00
❑51, Jul 1960 A: Space Ranger.	125.00
❑52, Aug 1960 A: Space Ranger.	125.00
❑53, Sep 1960 A: Space Ranger.	125.00
❑54, Oct 1960 A: Space Ranger.	125.00
❑55, Nov 1960 A: Space Ranger.	125.00
❑56, Dec 1960 A: Space Ranger.	100.00
❑57, Jan 1961 A: Space Ranger.	100.00
❑58, Feb 1961 A: Space Ranger.	100.00
❑59, Mar 1961 A: Space Ranger.	100.00
❑60, Apr 1961 A: Space Ranger.	100.00
❑61, May 1961 A: Space Ranger.	85.00
❑62, Jun 1961 A: Space Ranger.	85.00
❑63, Jul 1961 A: Space Ranger.	85.00
❑64, Aug 1961 A: Space Ranger.	85.00
❑65, Sep 1961 A: Space Ranger.	85.00
❑66, Oct 1961 A: Space Ranger.	85.00
❑67, Nov 1961 A: Space Ranger.	85.00
❑68, Dec 1961 A: Space Ranger.	85.00
❑69, Feb 1962 A: Space Ranger.	85.00
❑70, Apr 1962 A: Space Ranger.	85.00
❑71, Jun 1962 A: Space Ranger.	60.00
❑72, Aug 1962 A: Space Ranger.	60.00
❑73, Oct 1962 A: Space Ranger.	60.00
❑74, Jan 1963 A: Space Ranger.	60.00
❑75, Feb 1963 A: Space Ranger.	50.00
❑76, Apr 1963 A: Space Ranger.	50.00
❑77, Jun 1963 A: Space Ranger.	50.00
❑78, Aug 1963 A: Space Ranger.	50.00
❑79, Oct 1963 A: Space Ranger.	50.00
❑80, Dec 1963 A: Space Ranger.	50.00
❑81, Feb 1964 A: Space Ranger.	50.00
❑82, Apr 1964 A: Space Ranger.	50.00
❑83, Jun 1964	30.00
❑84, Aug 1964	30.00
❑85, Oct 1964	30.00
❑86, Dec 1964	30.00
❑87, Feb 1965	30.00
❑88, Apr 1965	30.00
❑89, Jun 1965	30.00
❑90, Aug 1965	30.00
❑91, Oct 1965	22.00
❑92, Dec 1965	22.00
❑93, Feb 1966	22.00
❑94, Apr 1966	22.00
❑95, Jun 1966	22.00
❑96, Aug 1966	22.00
❑97, Oct 1966 A: Automan.	22.00
❑98, Dec 1966	22.00
❑99, Feb 1967	22.00
❑100, Apr 1967	22.00
❑101, Jun 1967	20.00
❑102, Aug 1967	20.00
❑103, Oct 1967	20.00
❑104, Dec 1967; Series continues as The Unexpected	20.00

TALES OF THE VAMPIRES
DARK HORSE

	N-MINT
❑1, Dec 2003	2.99
❑2, Jan 2004	2.99
❑3, Feb 2004	2.99
❑4, Mar 2004	2.99
❑5, Apr 2004	2.99

TALES OF THE WITCHBLADE
IMAGE

	N-MINT
❑0.5, Jun 1997; Wizard promotional item	4.00
❑0.5/A, Jun 1997; Wizard "Certified Authentic" exclusive	8.00
❑0.5/Gold, Jun 1997; Wizard promotional item; gold logo	5.00
❑1, Nov 1996	2.95
❑1/A, Nov 1996; alternate cover; Green background with Witchblade front, arms behind back	2.95
❑1/B, Nov 1996; alternate cover (blue background with black panther)	2.95
❑1/Gold, Nov 1996; Gold edition	2.95
❑1/Platinum, Nov 1996; Platinum edition	5.00
❑2, Jun 1997	2.95
❑3, Oct 1997	2.95
❑4, Jan 1998	2.95
❑5, May 1998	2.95
❑6, Sep 1998	2.95
❑7/A, Jun 1999; Woman turning around, eyes in background on cover	2.95
❑7/B, Jun 1999; Alternate cover (woman standing before pyramid)	2.95
❑7/C	2.95
❑8, Oct 1999	2.95
❑9, Jan 2001	2.95
❑Deluxe 1; Collects Tales of the Witchblade #1-7; Witchblade: Distinctions	14.95

TALES OF THE ZOMBIE
MARVEL

	N-MINT
❑1, Aug 1973, b&w; magazine O: Zombie.	8.00
❑2, Oct 1973	5.00
❑3, Jan 1974	4.00
❑4, Mar 1974	4.00
❑5, May 1974	4.00
❑6, Jul 1974	4.00
❑7, Sep 1974	4.00
❑8, Nov 1974	4.00
❑9, Jan 1975	4.00
❑10, Mar 1975	4.00
❑Annual 1	4.00

TALES OF TOAD
PRINT MINT

	N-MINT
❑1, Apr 1970, b&w	0.00
❑2, Jan 1971, b&w	0.00
❑3, Dec 1973, b&w	0.00

TALES OF TORMENT
MIRAGE

	N-MINT
❑1, Apr 2004	2.95

TALE SPIN
DISNEY

	N-MINT
❑1, Jun 1991	1.50
❑2, Jul 1991	1.50
❑3, Aug 1991	1.50
❑4, Sep 1991	1.50
❑5, Oct 1991	1.50
❑6, Nov 1991	1.50
❑7, Jan 1991	1.50

TALE SPIN LIMITED SERIES
DISNEY

	N-MINT
❑1, Jan 1991	1.50
❑2, Feb 1991	1.50
❑3, Mar 1991	1.50
❑4, Apr 1991	1.50

TALESPIN (ONE-SHOT)
DISNEY

	N-MINT
❑1; Sky-Raker	3.50

TALES TO ASTONISH (VOL. 1)
MARVEL

	N-MINT
❑1, Jan 1959	2000.00
❑2, Mar 1959	635.00
❑3, May 1959	440.00
❑4, Jul 1959	440.00
❑5, Sep 1959	440.00
❑6, Nov 1959 SD, JSt (a)	355.00
❑7, Jan 1960	355.00
❑8, Mar 1960	355.00
❑9, May 1960	355.00
❑10, Jul 1960	355.00
❑11, Sep 1960	265.00
❑12, Oct 1960	265.00
❑13, Nov 1960	265.00
❑14, Dec 1960	265.00
❑15, Jan 1961	265.00
❑16, Feb 1961	265.00
❑17, Mar 1961	265.00
❑18, Apr 1961	265.00
❑19, May 1961	265.00
❑20, Jun 1961	265.00
❑21, Jul 1961 JK (a)	200.00
❑22, Aug 1961	200.00
❑23, Sep 1961	200.00
❑24, Oct 1961	200.00
❑25, Nov 1961	200.00
❑26, Dec 1961	200.00
❑27, Jan 1962 SD, JK (a); 1: Ant-Man (out of costume). 1: Hijacker.	3600.00
❑28, Feb 1962 SD, JK (a)	175.00
❑29, Mar 1962 SD, JK (a)	175.00
❑30, Apr 1962 SD, JK (a)	175.00
❑31, May 1962 SD, JK (a)	175.00
❑32, Jun 1962 SD, JK (a)	175.00
❑33, Jul 1962 SD, JK (a)	175.00
❑34, Aug 1962 SD, JK (a)	175.00
❑35, Sep 1962 SD, JK (a); 1: Ant-Man (in costume).	1900.00
❑36, Oct 1962 SD, JK (a)	625.00
❑37, Nov 1962 SD, JK (a)	350.00
❑38, Dec 1962 1: Egghead.	350.00
❑39, Jan 1963	350.00
❑40, Feb 1963	350.00
❑41, Mar 1963 SD, DH (a)	230.00
❑42, Apr 1963 SD, DH (a); O: The Voice. 1: The Voice.	230.00
❑43, May 1963 SD, DH (a)	230.00
❑44, Jun 1963 SD, JK (a); O: Wasp. 1: Wasp.	290.00
❑45, Jul 1963 SD, DH (a)	150.00
❑46, Aug 1963 SD, DH (a)	150.00
❑47, Sep 1963 SD, DH (a)	150.00
❑48, Oct 1963 SD, DH (a); O: Porcupine. 1: Porcupine.	150.00
❑49, Nov 1963; DH, JK (a); 1: Giant Man. Ant-Man becomes Giant Man	205.00
❑50, Dec 1963 SD, JK (a); 1: Human Top (later becomes Whirlwind).	95.00
❑51, Jan 1964 JK (a)	95.00
❑52, Feb 1964 O: Black Knight II (Nathan Garrett). 1: Black Knight II (Nathan Garrett).	95.00
❑53, Mar 1964	95.00

Condition price index: Multiply "NM prices" above by: **0.83 for Very Fine/Near Mint**
0.66 for Very Fine • 0.33 for Fine • 0.2 for Very Good • 0.125 for Good

N-MINT

❑54, Apr 1964 95.00
❑55, May 1964 95.00
❑56, Jun 1964 V: Magician. 95.00
❑57, Jul 1964 A: Spider-Man. 125.00
❑58, Aug 1964 95.00
❑59, Sep 1964; JK (c); SL (w); Giant-Man vs. Hulk 150.00
❑60, Oct 1964; JK (c); SL (w); SD (a); Giant Man/Hulk double feature begins 175.00
❑61, Nov 1964 JK (c); SL (w); SD (a) 75.00
❑62, Dec 1964 JK (c); SL (w); SD (a); 1: The Leader. 75.00
❑63, Jan 1965 JK (c); SL (w); SD (a); O: The Leader. 1: The Wrecker II. 75.00
❑64, Feb 1965 JK (c); SL (w); SD (a) 75.00
❑65, Mar 1965; JK (c); SL (w); SD (a); Giant-Man's new costume 75.00
❑66, Apr 1965 JK (c); SL (w); SD (a) 70.00
❑67, May 1965 JK (c); SL (w); SD (a) 70.00
❑68, Jun 1965 JK (c); SL (w); JK (a); V: Leader. 70.00
❑69, Jul 1965; JK (c); SL (w); JK (a); Giant Man feature ends 70.00
❑70, Aug 1965; JK (c); SL (w); JK (a); Sub-Mariner begins 100.00
❑71, Sep 1965 GC (c); SL (w); JK (a); 1: Vashti. 55.00
❑72, Oct 1965 JK (c); SL (w); JK (a) . 55.00
❑73, Nov 1965 GC (c); SL (w); JK (a) 55.00
❑74, Dec 1965 GC (c); SL (w); JK (a) 55.00
❑75, Jan 1966 GC (c); SL (w); JK (a); 1: Behemoth. 55.00
❑76, Feb 1966 GC (c); SL (w); JK, GK (a) 55.00
❑77, Mar 1966; JK, JR (c); SL (w); JK, JR (a); Banner revealed as Hulk 55.00
❑78, Apr 1966 GC (c); SL (w); BEv, JK (a) 55.00
❑79, May 1966 JK (c); SL (w); BEv, JK (a) 55.00
❑80, Jun 1966 GC (c); SL (w); BEv, JK (a) 55.00
❑81, Jul 1966 BEv, JK (c); SL (w); BEv, JK (a); 1: Boomerang. 55.00
❑82, Aug 1966; GC (c); SL (w); BEv, JK (a); Iron Man vs. Sub-Mariner; Hulk 78.00
❑83, Sep 1966; BEv, JK (c); SL (w); BEv, JK (a); Sub-Mariner, Hulk 55.00
❑84, Oct 1966 GC (c); SL (w) 55.00
❑85, Nov 1966 BEv, JK (c); SL (w); JB (a) 55.00
❑86, Dec 1966 GC (c); SL (w); JB (a) 55.00
❑87, Jan 1967 GK (c); SL (w); JB (a) 55.00
❑88, Feb 1967 GC (c); SL (w); GK (a) 55.00
❑89, Mar 1967 GK (c); SL (w); GK (a) 55.00
❑90, Apr 1967 JK (c); SL (w); GK (a); 1: The Abomination. 1: Byrrah. 55.00
❑91, May 1967; GK (c); SL (w); GK (a); Sub-Mariner story continues in Avengers #40 52.00
❑92, Jun 1967; DA (c); SL (w); A: Silver Surfer. Sub-Mariner story continued from Avengers #40 75.00
❑93, Jul 1967 SL (w); A: Silver Surfer. 75.00
❑94, Aug 1967; DA (c); SL (w); HT (a); Hulk story continues from Thor #135 50.00
❑95, Sep 1967; JK (c); SL (w); HT (a); Sub-Mariner story continues from Daredevil #24 50.00
❑96, Oct 1967 DA (c); SL (w); HT (a) 50.00
❑97, Nov 1967 JK (c); SL (w); HT (a) 50.00
❑98, Dec 1967 DA (c); SL (w); HT (a); 1: Seth (Namor's advisor). 50.00
❑99, Jan 1968 SL (w) 50.00
❑100, Feb 1968; SL (w); DA (a); Hulk vs. Sub-Mariner 75.00
❑101, Mar 1968; JK (c); SL (w); Hulk feature continued in Incredible Hulk #102; Sub-Mariner feature continued in Iron Man & Sub-Mariner #1 85.00

TALES TO ASTONISH (VOL. 2)
MARVEL

❑1, Dec 1979 JB (a) 2.00
❑2, Jan 1980 JB (a) 1.50
❑3, Feb 1980 JB (a) 1.50
❑4, Mar 1980 JB (a) 1.50
❑5, Apr 1980 JB (a) 1.50
❑6, May 1980 JB (a) 1.50

N-MINT

❑7, Jun 1980 JB (a) 1.50
❑8, Jul 1980 JB (a) 1.50
❑9, Aug 1980 JB (a) 1.50
❑10, Sep 1980 JB (a) 1.50
❑11, Oct 1980 JB (a) 1.50
❑12, Nov 1980 JB (a) 1.50
❑13, Dec 1980 JB (a) 1.50
❑14, Jan 1981 JB (a) 1.50

TALES TO ASTONISH (VOL. 3)
MARVEL

❑1, Dec 1994; prestige format one-shot; acetate outer cover 6.95

TALES TO OFFEND
DARK HORSE

❑1, Jul 1997; Lance Blastoff 2.95

TALES TOO TERRIBLE TO TELL
NEC

❑1, b&w; Reprints from Mister Mystery #13, Weird Chills #1, Weird Chills #3, Mister Mystery #16, Purple Claw #1, Strange Mysteries #7, Mister Mystery #17 2.95
❑1-2, May 1993; 2nd printing with new cover; Reprints from Mister Mystery #13, Weird Chills #1, Weird Chills #3, Mister Mystery #16, Purple Claw #1, Strange Mysteries #7, Mister Mystery #17 3.50
❑2, Mar 1991, b&w; Reprints from Strange Mysteries #6, Weird Mysteries #11, Unseen #14, Black Cat Mystery #45, Journey into Fear #5, Ghoul Tales #3, Dark Mysteries #13 3.50
❑3, Jun 1991, b&w; Reprints from Weird Chills #3, Weird Mysteries #10, Weird Chills #1, Adventures into Darkness #13, Horrific #5 3.50
❑4, Dec 1991, b&w; Reprints from Mister Mystery #13, Fantastic Fears #8, Unseen #14, Journey into Fear #12, Fantastic Fears #6, Purple Claw #1, Fantastic Fears #4, Dark Mysteries #19 3.50
❑5 1992, b&w 3.50
❑6 1992, b&w 3.50
❑7 1992, b&w 3.50

TALEWEAVER
WILDSTORM

❑1, Nov 2001 3.50
❑2, Dec 2001 2.95
❑3, Jan 2002 2.95
❑4, Feb 2002 2.95
❑5, Mar 2002 2.95
❑6, Apr 2002 2.95

TALISMEN: SCSI VOODOO
BLINK

❑1 2.75
❑2 2.75
❑3 2.75

TALK DIRTY
FANTAGRAPHICS / EROS

❑1, b&w 2.50
❑2, b&w 2.50
❑3, b&w 2.95

TALKING ORANGUTANS IN BORNEO
GT-LABS

❑1, ca. 1999, b&w; efforts to educate orangutans to communicate via sign language 3.50

TALL TAILS
GOLDEN REALM

❑1, b&w 2.00
❑2, ca. 1993 2.00
❑3 2.95
❑4 2.95
❑5 2.95
❑6 2.95
❑7 2.95

TALONZ
STOP DRAGON

❑1, Jan 1987, b&w 1.50

Superman's counterpart in the Tangent universe is The Atom.

N-MINT

TALOS OF THE WILDERNESS SEA
DC

❑1, ca. 1985 2.00

TAMMAS
PANDEMONIUM

❑1, Dec 1986 1.50

TANGENT COMICS/DOOM PATROL
DC

❑1, Dec 1997; alternate universe 2.95

TANGENT COMICS/GREEN LANTERN
DC

❑1, Dec 1997; alternate universe 2.95

TANGENT COMICS/JLA
DC

❑1, Sep 1998; alternate universe 1.95

TANGENT COMICS/METAL MEN
DC

❑1, Dec 1997; alternate universe 2.95

TANGENT COMICS/NIGHTWING
DC

❑1, Dec 1997; alternate universe 2.95

TANGENT COMICS/NIGHTWING: NIGHT FORCE
DC

❑1, Sep 1998; alternate universe 1.95

TANGENT COMICS/POWERGIRL
DC

❑1, Sep 1998; alternate universe 1.95

TANGENT COMICS/SEA DEVILS
DC

❑1, Dec 1997; alternate universe 2.95

TANGENT COMICS/SECRET SIX
DC

❑1, Dec 1997; alternate universe 2.95

TANGENT COMICS/TALES OF THE GREEN LANTERN
DC

❑1, Sep 1998; alternate universe 1.95

TANGENT COMICS/THE ATOM
DC

❑1, Dec 1997; alternate universe 2.95

TANGENT COMICS/THE BATMAN
DC

❑1, Sep 1998; alternate universe 1.95

TANGENT COMICS/THE FLASH
DC

❑1, Dec 1997; alternate universe 2.95

TANGENT COMICS/THE JOKER
DC

❑1, Dec 1997; alternate universe 2.95

TANGENT COMICS/THE JOKER'S WILD
DC

❑1, Sep 1998; alternate universe 1.95

TANGENT COMICS/THE SUPERMAN
DC

❑1, Sep 1998; alternate universe 1.95

TANGENT COMICS/THE TRIALS OF THE FLASH
DC

❑1, Sep 1998; alternate universe 1.95

N-MINT

TANGENT COMICS/WONDER WOMAN
DC

❑1, Sep 1998; alternate universe 1.95

TANGLED WEB
MARVEL

❑1, Jun 2001 .... 2.99
❑2, Jul 2001 .... 2.99
❑3, Aug 2001 .... 2.99
❑4, Sep 2001 .... 2.99
❑5, Oct 2001 .... 2.99
❑6, Nov 2001 .... 2.99
❑7, Dec 2001 .... 2.99
❑8, Jan 2002 .... 2.99
❑9, Feb 2002 .... 2.99
❑10, Mar 2002 .... 2.99
❑11, Apr 2002 .... 2.99
❑12, May 2002 .... 2.99
❑13, Jun 2002 .... 2.99
❑14, Jul 2002 .... 2.99
❑15, Aug 2002 .... 2.99
❑16, Sep 2002 .... 2.99
❑17, Oct 2002 .... 2.99
❑18, Nov 2002 .... 2.99
❑19, Dec 2002 .... 2.99
❑20, Jan 2003 .... 2.99
❑21, Feb 2003 .... 2.99
❑22, Mar 2003 .... 2.99

TANK GIRL
DARK HORSE

❑1, May 1991, b&w; 1: Tank Girl (in American comics). trading cards ... 3.50
❑2, Jun 1991, b&w 3.00
❑3, Jul 1991, b&w 3.00
❑4, Aug 1991, b&w 3.00

TANK GIRL 2
DARK HORSE

❑1, Jun 1993, b&w and color 3.00
❑2, Jul 1993, b&w and color 3.00
❑3, Aug 1993, b&w and color 3.00
❑4, Sep 1993, b&w and color 3.00

TANK GIRL: APOCALYPSE
DC / VERTIGO

❑1, Nov 1995; Tank Girl becomes pregnant 2.25
❑2, Dec 1995 .... 2.25
❑3, Jan 1996 .... 2.25
❑4, Feb 1996; Tank Girl gives birth 2.25

TANK GIRL MOVIE ADAPTATION
DC / VERTIGO

❑1; prestige format one-shot 5.95

TANK GIRL: THE ODYSSEY
DC / VERTIGO

❑1, Jun 1995 .... 2.95
❑2, Jul 1995 .... 2.95
❑3, Aug 1995 .... 2.95
❑4, Oct 1995 .... 2.95

TANK VIXENS
ANTARCTIC

❑1, Jan 1994 .... 2.95
❑2, Mar 1994 .... 2.95
❑3, ca. 1995 .... 2.95
❑4, Mar 1996 .... 2.95

TANTALIZING STORIES
TUNDRA

❑1, Oct 1992 .... 2.25
❑2, Dec 1992 .... 2.25
❑3, Feb 1993 .... 2.25
❑4, Apr 1993 .... 2.25
❑6, Jun 1993 .... 2.50

TAOLAND
SUMITEK

❑1, Nov 1994, b&w; cardstock cover 2.00
❑2, Aug 1995, b&w; cardstock cover 5.95
❑3, Sep 1995, b&w; cardstock cover 5.95
❑4, Feb 1996, b&w 5.95
❑5, Dec 1996; prestige format 5.95

N-MINT

TAOLAND ADVENTURES
ANTARCTIC

❑1, Mar 1999 .... 3.50
❑2, May 1999 .... 3.50

TAP
PROMETHEAN

❑1, Sep 1994 .... 2.95
❑2, Jan 1995 .... 2.95
❑3, Jan 1995; indicia is for issue #2 .. 2.95

TAPESTRY
SUPERIOR JUNK

❑1, b&w 1.50
❑1-2, Apr 1995 .... 1.50
❑2, Apr 1994, b&w 1.95
❑3, Jun 1994, b&w 1.95
❑4, Oct 1994, b&w 2.25
❑5, b&w 2.25

TAPPING THE VEIN
ECLIPSE

❑1; prestige format; foil-embossed logo 7.50
❑2; prestige format; KJ (a); foil-embossed logo 7.00
❑3; prestige format; foil-embossed logo 7.00
❑4; prestige format; foil-embossed logo 7.95
❑5 .... 7.95

TARGET: AIRBOY
ECLIPSE

❑1, Mar 1988; A: Clint from A.R.B.B.H.. cardstock cover 2.00

TARGET: THE CORRUPTORS
DELL

❑2, Jun 1962, First issue published as Dell's Four Color #1306 .... 25.00
❑3, Dec 1962........ 25.00

TARGITT
ATLAS-SEABOARD

❑1, Mar 1975 O: Targitt. 8.00
❑2, Jun 1975 .... 8.00
❑3, Jul 1975 .... 8.00

TAROT: WITCH OF THE BLACK ROSE
BROADSWORD

❑1, Mar 2000 .... 5.00
❑2, May 2000 .... 2.95
❑3, Jul 2000 .... 2.95
❑4, Sep 2000 .... 2.95
❑5, Nov 2000 .... 2.95
❑6, Jan 2001 .... 2.95
❑7, Mar 2001 .... 2.95
❑8, May 2001 .... 2.95
❑9, Jul 2001 .... 2.95
❑10, Sep 2001 .... 2.95
❑11, Nov 2001 .... 2.95
❑12, Jan 2002 .... 2.95
❑13, Mar 2002 .... 2.95
❑14, May 2002 .... 2.95
❑15, Jul 2002 .... 2.95
❑16, Sep 2002 .... 2.95
❑17, Nov 2002 .... 2.95
❑18, Jan 2003 .... 2.95
❑19, Mar 2003 .... 2.95
❑20, May 2003 .... 2.95

TARZAN (GOLD KEY)
GOLD KEY

❑132, Nov 1962; RM (a); Continued from Tarzan (Dell) #131 .... 14.00
❑133, Jan 1963 .... 14.00
❑134, Mar 1963 .... 14.00
❑135, May 1963 .... 14.00
❑136, Jul 1963 .... 14.00
❑137, Aug 1963 .... 14.00
❑138, Oct 1963 .... 14.00
❑139, Dec 1963 .... 14.00
❑140, Feb 1964 .... 14.00
❑141, Apr 1964 .... 14.00
❑142, Jun 1964 .... 14.00
❑143, Jul 1964 .... 14.00
❑144, Aug 1964 .... 14.00
❑145, Sep 1964 .... 14.00
❑146, Oct 1964 .... 14.00
❑147, Dec 1964 .... 14.00

N-MINT

❑148, Feb 1965 .... 14.00
❑149, Apr 1965 .... 14.00
❑150, Jun 1965 .... 14.00
❑151, Aug 1965 .... 14.00
❑152, Sep 1965 .... 14.00
❑153, Oct 1965 .... 14.00
❑154, Nov 1965 .... 14.00
❑155, Dec 1965; RM (a); O: Tarzan. adapts Tarzan of the Apes 18.00
❑156, Feb 1966; RM (a); adapts Return of Tarzan 10.00
❑157, Apr 1966; RM (a); adapts Beasts of Tarzan 10.00
❑158, Jun 1966; RM (a); adapts Son of Tarzan 10.00
❑159, Aug 1966; RM (a); adapts Jewels of Opar 10.00
❑160, Sep 1966; RM (a); adapts Jewels of Opar 10.00
❑161, Oct 1966; RM (a); adapts Jewels of Opar 10.00
❑162, Dec 1966; TV Adventures on cover 10.00
❑163, Jan 1967; RM (a); adapts Tarzan the Untamed 8.00
❑164, Feb 1967; RM (a); adapts Tarzan the Untamed 8.00
❑165, Mar 1967 .... 10.00
❑166, Apr 1967; RM (a); adapts Tarzan the Terrible 8.00
❑167, May 1967; RM (a); adapts Tarzan the Terrible 8.00
❑168, Jun 1967 .... 10.00
❑169, Jul 1967; adapts Jungle Tales of Tarzan 8.00
❑170, Aug 1967; adapts Jungle Tales of Tarzan 8.00
❑171, Sep 1967; TV Adventures 10.00
❑172, Oct 1967; RM (a); adapts Tarzan and the Golden Lion 7.00
❑173, Dec 1967; RM (a); adapts Tarzan and the Golden Lion 7.00
❑174, Feb 1968; RM (a); adapts Tarzan and the Ant Men 7.00
❑175, Apr 1968; RM (a); adapts Tarzan and the Ant Men 7.00
❑176, Jun 1968; RM (a); adapts Tarzan; Lord of the Jungle 7.00
❑177, Jul 1968; RM (a); adapts Tarzan; Lord of the Jungle 7.00
❑178, Aug 1968; reprints issue #155 7.00
❑179, Sep 1968; adapts Tarzan at the Earth's Core 7.00
❑180, Oct 1968; adapts Tarzan at the Earth's Core 7.00
❑181, Dec 1968; adapts Tarzan at the Earth's Core 7.00
❑182, Feb 1969; adapts Tarzan the Invincible 7.00
❑183, Apr 1969; adapts Tarzan the Invincible 7.00
❑184, Jun 1969; adapts Tarzan Triumphant 7.00
❑185, Jul 1969; adapts Tarzan Triumphant 7.00
❑186, Aug 1969; adapts Tarzan and the City of Gold 7.00
❑187, Sep 1969; adapts Tarzan and the City of Gold 7.00
❑188, Oct 1969; adapts Tarzan's Quest 7.00
❑189, Dec 1969; adapts Tarzan's Quest 7.00
❑190, Feb 1970; adapts Tarzan and the Forbidden City 7.00
❑191, Apr 1970; adapts Tarzan and the Forbidden City 7.00
❑192, Jun 1970; adapts Tarzan and the Foreign Legion 7.00
❑193, Jul 1970; adapts Tarzan and the Foreign Legion 7.00
❑194, Aug 1970; adapts Tarzan and the Lost Empire 7.00
❑195, Sep 1970; adapts Tarzan and the Lost Empire 7.00
❑196, Oct 1970; adapts Tarzan and the Tarzan Twins 7.00
❑197, Dec 1970 .... 7.00
❑198, Feb 1971 .... 7.00
❑199, Apr 1971 .... 7.00

N-MINT

❑200, Jun 1971 .... 7.00
❑201, Jul 1971 .... 6.00
❑202, Aug 1971; RM (a); astronauts land in jungle 6.00
❑203, Sep 1971 .... 6.00
❑204, Oct 1971 .... 6.00
❑205, Dec 1971 .... 6.00
❑206, Feb 1972; moves to DC; Series continued in Tarzan (DC) #207 .... 6.00

TARZAN (DC)
DC

❑207, Apr 1972; Giant-size; JKu (a); O: Tarzan. John Carter of Mars back-up; Series continued from Tarzan (Dell) 12.00
❑208, May 1972; JKu (a); O: Tarzan. John Carter of Mars back-up 6.00
❑209, Jun 1972; JKu (a); O: Tarzan. John Carter of Mars back-up continues in Weird Worlds #1 .... 6.00
❑210, Jul 1972 JKu (a); O: Tarzan. 6.00
❑211, Aug 1972 JKu (a) 4.00
❑212, Sep 1972 JKu (a) 4.00
❑213, Oct 1972 JKu (a) 4.00
❑214, Nov 1972; JKu (a); Beyond the Farthest Star back-up 4.00
❑215, Dec 1972; JKu (a); Beyond the Farthest Star back-up 4.00
❑216, Jan 1973; JKu (a); Beyond the Farthest Star back-up 4.00
❑217, Feb 1973; JKu (a); Beyond the Farthest Star back-up 4.00
❑218, Mar 1973; JKu (a); Beyond the Farthest Star back-up 4.00
❑219, May 1973 JKu (a) 4.00
❑220, Jun 1973 JKu (a) 4.00
❑221, Jul 1973 JKu (a) 4.00
❑222, Aug 1973 JKu (a) 4.00
❑223, Sep 1973 JKu (a) 4.00
❑224, Oct 1973 JKu (a) 4.00
❑225, Nov 1973 JKu (a) 4.00
❑226, Dec 1973 JKu (a) 4.00
❑227, Jan 1974 JKu (a) 4.00
❑228, Feb 1974 JKu (a) 4.00
❑229, Mar 1974 .... 4.00
❑230, May 1974; 100 Page giant 8.00
❑231, Jul 1974; 100 Page giant 8.00
❑232, Sep 1974; 100 Page giant 8.00
❑233, Nov 1974; 100 Page giant 8.00
❑234, Jan 1975; 100 Page giant 8.00
❑235, Mar 1975; 100 Page giant 8.00
❑236, Apr 1975 .... 3.00
❑237, May 1975 JKu (c); RM (a) 3.00
❑238, Jun 1975 .... 3.00
❑239, Jul 1975 JKu (a) 3.00
❑240, Aug 1975; JKu (a); adapts The Castaways 3.00
❑241, Sep 1975 .... 3.00
❑242, Oct 1975 .... 3.00
❑243, Nov 1975 .... 3.00
❑244, Dec 1975 .... 3.00
❑245, Jan 1976 .... 3.00
❑246, Feb 1976 .... 3.00
❑247, Mar 1976 .... 3.00
❑248, Apr 1976 .... 3.00
❑249, May 1976 .... 3.00
❑250, Jun 1976 .... 3.00
❑251, Jul 1976 .... 3.00
❑252, Aug 1976 .... 3.00
❑253, Sep 1976 .... 3.00
❑254, Oct 1976 .... 3.00
❑255, Nov 1976 .... 3.00
❑256, Dec 1976; JKu (a); adapts Tarzan the Untamed 3.00
❑257, Jan 1977 JKu (w); JKu (a) 3.00
❑258, Feb 1977 .... 3.00

TARZAN (MARVEL)
MARVEL

❑1, Jun 1977 JB (a) 3.00
❑1/35 cent, Jun 1977; JB (a); 35 cent regional price variant 15.00
❑2, Jul 1977 .... 2.00
❑2/35 cent, Jul 1977; 35 cent regional price variant 15.00
❑3, Aug 1977 .... 2.00

N-MINT

❑3/35 cent, Aug 1977; 35 cent regional price variant 15.00
❑4, Sep 1977 .... 2.00
❑4/35 cent, Sep 1977; 35 cent regional price variant 15.00
❑5, Oct 1977 .... 2.00
❑5/35 cent, Oct 1977; 35 cent regional price variant 15.00
❑6, Nov 1977 .... 1.50
❑7, Dec 1977 .... 1.50
❑8, Jan 1978 .... 1.50
❑9, Feb 1978 .... 1.50
❑10, Mar 1978 .... 1.50
❑11, Apr 1978 .... 1.50
❑12, May 1978 .... 1.50
❑13, Jun 1978 .... 1.50
❑14, Jul 1978 .... 1.50
❑15, Aug 1978 .... 1.50
❑16, Sep 1978 .... 1.50
❑17, Oct 1978 .... 1.50
❑18, Nov 1978 .... 1.50
❑19, Dec 1978 .... 1.50
❑20, Jan 1979 BH (a) 1.50
❑21, Feb 1979 .... 1.50
❑22, Mar 1979 .... 1.50
❑23, Apr 1979 .... 1.50
❑24, May 1979 BH (a) 1.50
❑25, Jun 1979 BH (a) 1.50
❑26, Jul 1979 BH (a) 1.50
❑27, Aug 1979 .... 1.50
❑28, Sep 1979 .... 1.50
❑29, Oct 1979 .... 1.50
❑Annual 1, ca. 1977 .... 2.00
❑Annual 2, ca. 1978 BH (c) 1.50
❑Annual 3, ca. 1979 .... 1.50

TARZAN (DARK HORSE)
DARK HORSE

❑1, Jul 1996 .... 3.00
❑2, Aug 1996 .... 3.00
❑3, Aug 1996 .... 3.00
❑4, Sep 1996 .... 3.00
❑5, Nov 1996 .... 3.00
❑6, Nov 1996 .... 3.00
❑7, Jan 1997 .... 3.00
❑8, Feb 1997 .... 3.00
❑9, Mar 1997 .... 3.00
❑10, Apr 1997 .... 3.00
❑11, May 1997 .... 3.00
❑12, Jun 1997 .... 2.95
❑13, Aug 1997 .... 2.95
❑14, Sep 1997 .... 2.95
❑15, Sep 1997 .... 2.95
❑16, Oct 1997 .... 2.95
❑17, Dec 1997 TY (a) 2.95
❑18, Jan 1998 .... 2.95
❑19, Feb 1998 .... 2.95
❑20, Mar 1998 .... 2.95

TARZAN (DISNEY'S...)
DARK HORSE

❑1, Jul 1999 .... 2.95
❑2, Jul 1999 .... 2.95

TARZAN AND THE JEWELS OF OPAR (EDGAR RICE BURROUGHS'...)
DARK HORSE

❑1, Jun 1999; digest; collects stories from Dell's Tarzan #159-161 plus pin-ups 10.95

TARZAN: A TALE OF MUGAMBI (EDGAR RICE BURROUGHS'...)
DARK HORSE

❑1, Jun 1995 .... 2.95

TARZAN/CARSON OF VENUS
DARK HORSE

❑1, May 1998 .... 2.95
❑2, Jun 1998 .... 2.95
❑3, Jul 1998 .... 2.95
❑4, Aug 1998 .... 2.95

TARZAN DIGEST
DC

❑1, Aut 1972 .... 3.00

The numbering of Dell's *Tarzan* series was carried on by Gold Key and, later, DC, as the series moved from publisher to publisher.

N-MINT

TARZAN FAMILY, THE
DC

❑60, Dec 1975 .... 5.00
❑61, Feb 1976 .... 5.00
❑62, Apr 1976 .... 4.00
❑63, Jun 1976 .... 4.00
❑64, Aug 1976 .... 4.00
❑65, Sep 1976 .... 4.00
❑66, Nov 1976 .... 4.00

TARZAN/JOHN CARTER: WARLORDS OF MARS
DARK HORSE

❑1, Jan 1996 .... 2.50
❑2, Apr 1996; indicia says #3, cover says #2 .... 2.50
❑3, May 1996 .... 2.50
❑4, Jul 1996 .... 2.50

TARZAN, LORD OF THE JUNGLE (GOLD KEY)
GOLD KEY

❑1, Sep 1965 .... 40.00

TARZAN: LOVE, LIES AND THE LOST CITY
MALIBU

❑1, Aug 1992; Flip-book MW (w) 3.95
❑2, Sep 1992 .... 3.95
❑3, Oct 1992 .... 3.95

TARZAN OF THE APES
MARVEL

❑1, Jul 1984 ME (w); DS (a); O: Tarzan. 3.00
❑2, Aug 1984 ME (w); DS (a); O: Tarzan. 3.00

TARZAN OF THE APES (EDGAR RICE BURROUGHS'...)
DARK HORSE

❑1, May 1999; digest; collects stories from Dell's Tarzan #155-158 and spot illustrations from Tarzan #154-156 .... 12.95

TARZAN: THE BECKONING
MALIBU

❑1, Nov 1992 .... 2.50
❑2, Dec 1992 .... 2.50
❑3, Jan 1993 .... 2.50
❑4, Feb 1993 .... 2.50
❑5, Mar 1993 .... 2.50
❑6, Apr 1993 .... 2.50
❑7, Jun 1993 .... 2.50

TARZAN: THE LOST ADVENTURE (EDGAR RICE BURROUGHS'...)
DARK HORSE

❑1, Jan 1995, b&w; squarebound 2.95
❑2, Feb 1995, b&w; squarebound 2.95
❑3, Mar 1995, b&w; squarebound 2.95
❑4, Apr 1995, b&w; squarebound 2.95

TARZAN: THE RIVERS OF BLOOD (EDGAR RICE BURROUGHS'...)
DARK HORSE

❑1, Nov 1999 .... 2.95
❑2, Dec 1999 .... 2.95
❑3, Jan 2000 .... 2.95
❑4, Feb 2000 .... 2.95

TARZAN: THE SAVAGE HEART
DARK HORSE

❑1, Apr 1999 .... 2.95
❑2, May 1999 .... 2.95

N-MINT

❑3, Jun 1999 .... 2.95
❑4, Jul 1999 .... 2.95

TARZAN THE WARRIOR
MALIBU

❑1, Mar 1992 .... 2.50
❑2, May 1992 .... 2.50
❑3, Jun 1992 .... 2.50
❑4, Aug 1992 .... 2.50
❑5, Sep 1992 .... 2.50

TARZAN VS. PREDATOR AT THE EARTH'S CORE
DARK HORSE

❑1, Jan 1996 .... 2.50
❑2, Feb 1996 .... 2.50
❑3, Mar 1996 .... 2.50
❑4, Jun 1996 .... 2.50

TARZAN WEEKLY
BYBLOS

❑1 .... 5.00

T.A.S.E.R.
COMICREATIONS

❑1, Sep 1992, b&w 2.00
❑2, Jun 1993, b&w 2.00

TASKMASTER
MARVEL

❑1, Apr 2002 .... 2.99
❑2, May 2002 .... 2.99
❑3, Jun 2002 .... 2.99
❑4, Jul 2002 .... 2.99

TASMANIAN DEVIL AND HIS TASTY FRIENDS
GOLD KEY

❑1, Nov 1962 .... 75.00

TASTY BITS
AVALON

❑1, Jul 1999 .... 2.95

TATTERED BANNERS
DC / VERTIGO

❑1, Nov 1998 .... 2.95
❑2, Dec 1998 .... 2.95
❑3, Jan 1999 .... 2.95
❑4, Feb 1999 .... 2.95

TATTOO
CALIBER

❑1 .... 2.95
❑2 .... 2.95

TATTOO MAN
FANTAGRAPHICS

❑1, b&w 2.75

TAXX, THE
EXPRESS / PARODY

❑0.5 .... 1.50
❑1, b&w 2.75

T-BIRD CHRONICLES
ME COMIX

❑1, b&w 1.50
❑2, b&w 1.50

TEAM 7
IMAGE

❑1, Oct 1994 .... 3.00
❑1/A, Oct 1994 .... 3.00
❑2, Nov 1994 .... 2.50
❑3, Dec 1994 .... 2.50
❑4, Feb 1995 .... 2.50
❑Ashcan 1, Oct 1994, b&w; ashcan promo edition 1.00

TEAM 7: DEAD RECKONING
IMAGE

❑1, Jan 1996 .... 2.50
❑2, Feb 1996 .... 2.50
❑3, Mar 1996 .... 2.50
❑4, Apr 1996 .... 2.50

TEAM 7: OBJECTIVE: HELL
IMAGE

❑1, May 1995; with card 2.50
❑2, Jun 1995 .... 2.50
❑3, Jul 1995 .... 2.50

N-MINT

TEAM AMERICA
MARVEL

❑1, Jun 1982 O: Team America. 1.00
❑2, Jul 1982 LMc (a) 1.00
❑3, Aug 1982 LMc (a) 1.00
❑4, Sep 1982 LMc (a) 1.00
❑5, Oct 1982 .... 1.00
❑6, Nov 1982 .... 1.00
❑7, Dec 1982 .... 1.00
❑8, Jan 1983 .... 1.00
❑9, Feb 1983 A: Iron Man. 1.00
❑10, Mar 1983 .... 1.00
❑11, Apr 1983 A: Ghost Rider. 1.00
❑12, May 1983; Double-size; DP (a); Marauder unmasked 1.00

TEAM ANARCHY
DAGGER

❑1, Oct 1993 .... 2.75
❑2, Nov 1993 .... 2.50
❑3, Jan 1994 .... 2.50
❑4, Feb 1994 .... 2.50
❑5, Mar 1994 .... 2.50
❑6, Apr 1994 .... 2.50
❑7, May 1994 .... 2.50

TEAM NIPPON
AIRCEL

❑1, b&w 1.95
❑2, b&w 1.95
❑3, b&w 1.95
❑4, b&w 1.95
❑5, b&w 1.95
❑6, b&w 1.95
❑7, b&w 1.95

TEAM ONE: STORMWATCH
IMAGE

❑1, Jun 1995; cover says Jul, indicia says Jun 2.50
❑2, Aug 1995 .... 2.50

TEAM ONE: WILDC.A.T.S
IMAGE

❑1, Jul 1995 .... 2.50
❑2, Sep 1995 .... 2.50

TEAM SUPERMAN
DC

❑1, Jul 1999 .... 2.95

TEAM SUPERMAN SECRET FILES
DC

❑1, May 1998; biographical info on Superboy, Supergirl, Steel, and respective villains 4.95

TEAM TITANS
DC

❑1/A, Sep 1992; Comes in five different covers 1.75
❑1/B, Sep 1992; Comes in five different covers 1.75
❑1/C, Sep 1992; Comes in five different covers 1.75
❑1/D, Sep 1992; Comes in five different covers 1.75
❑1/E, Sep 1992; Comes in five different covers 1.75
❑2, Oct 1992 .... 1.75
❑3, Nov 1992 .... 1.75
❑4, Dec 1992 .... 1.75
❑5, Feb 1993 .... 1.75
❑6, Mar 1993 .... 1.75
❑7, Apr 1993 .... 1.75
❑8, May 1993 .... 1.75
❑9, Jun 1993 .... 1.75
❑10, Jul 1993 .... 1.75
❑11, Aug 1993 .... 1.75
❑12, Sep 1993 .... 1.75
❑13, Oct 1993 .... 1.75
❑14, Nov 1993 .... 1.75
❑15, Dec 1993 .... 1.75
❑16, Jan 1994 .... 1.75
❑17, Feb 1994 .... 1.75
❑18, Mar 1994 .... 1.75
❑19, Apr 1994 .... 1.75
❑20, May 1994 .... 1.75

N-MINT

❑21, Jun 1994 .... 1.75
❑22, Jul 1994 .... 1.75
❑23, Aug 1994 .... 1.95
❑24, Sep 1994; Zero Hour 1.95
❑Annual 1 .... 3.50
❑Annual 2; Elseworlds 2.95

TEAM X
MARVEL

❑2000, Feb 1999 .... 3.50

TEAM X/TEAM 7
MARVEL

❑1, Jan 1997; crossover with Image; squarebound 4.95

TEAM YANKEE
FIRST

❑1, Jan 1989 .... 1.95
❑2, Jan 1989 .... 1.95
❑3, Jan 1989 .... 1.95
❑4, Feb 1989 .... 1.95
❑5, Feb 1989 .... 1.95
❑6, Feb 1989 .... 1.95

TEAM YOUNGBLOOD
IMAGE

❑1, Sep 1993 .... 1.95
❑2, Oct 1993 .... 1.95
❑3, Nov 1993 .... 1.95
❑4, Dec 1993 .... 1.95
❑5, Jan 1994 .... 1.95
❑6, Feb 1994 .... 1.95
❑7, Mar 1994 .... 1.95
❑8, Apr 1994 .... 1.95
❑9, May 1994 .... 1.95
❑10, Jun 1994 .... 2.50
❑11, Jul 1994 .... 1.95
❑12, Aug 1994 .... 2.50
❑13, Sep 1994 .... 2.50
❑14, Oct 1994; Riptide poses nude 2.50
❑15, Nov 1994 .... 2.50
❑16, Dec 1994; polybagged with trading card 2.50
❑17, Jan 1995; polybagged with trading card 2.50
❑18, May 1995 .... 2.50
❑19, Jun 1995 .... 2.50
❑20, Jul 1995 .... 2.50
❑21, Mar 1996 .... 2.50
❑22, Apr 1996 .... 2.50

TEARS
BONEYARD

❑1, Oct 1992, b&w 2.95
❑2, Dec 1992, b&w 2.50

TEASER AND THE BLACKSMITH
FANTAGRAPHICS

❑1, b&w 3.50

TECH HIGH
VIRTUALLY REAL ENTERPRISES

❑1, Fal 1996, b&w 2.50
❑2, Win 1996, b&w 2.50
❑3, Spr 1997, b&w 2.50

TECH JACKET
IMAGE

❑1, Nov 2003 .... 2.95
❑2, Dec 2003 .... 2.95
❑3, Jan 2003 .... 2.95
❑4, Feb 2003 .... 2.95
❑5, Apr 2003 .... 2.95
❑6, May 2003 .... 2.95

TECHNO MANIACS
INDEPENDENT

❑1 .... 1.95

TECHNOPOLIS
CALIBER

❑1 .... 2.95
❑2 .... 2.95
❑3 .... 2.95
❑4 .... 2.95

TEENAGE HOTRODDERS
CHARLTON

	N-MINT
❑1, Apr 1963	35.00
❑2, Jun 1963	20.00
❑3, Aug 1963	20.00
❑4, Oct 1963	20.00
❑5, Dec 1963	20.00
❑6, Feb 1964	20.00
❑7, May 1964	20.00
❑8, Jul 1964	20.00
❑9, Oct 1964	20.00
❑10, Dec 1964	20.00
❑11, Feb 1965	15.00
❑12, May 1965	15.00
❑13, Jul 1965	15.00
❑14, Sep 1965	15.00
❑15, Nov 1965	15.00
❑16, Jan 1966	15.00
❑17, Apr 1966	15.00
❑18, Jun 1966	15.00
❑19, Aug 1966	15.00
❑20, Oct 1966	15.00
❑21, Dec 1966	15.00
❑22, Feb 1967	15.00
❑23, May 1967	15.00
❑24, Jul 1967; Becomes Top Eliminator #25	15.00

TEEN-AGE LOVE
CHARLTON

	N-MINT
❑4 1958	30.00
❑5 1958	16.00
❑6 1958	14.00
❑7 1959	14.00
❑8 1959	14.00
❑9 1959	14.00
❑10, Sep 1959	14.00
❑11, Nov 1959	9.00
❑12, Jan 1960	9.00
❑13, Mar 1960	9.00
❑14, May 1960	9.00
❑15, Jul 1960	9.00
❑16, Sep 1960	9.00
❑17, Nov 1960	9.00
❑18, Jan 1961	9.00
❑19, Mar 1961	9.00
❑20, May 1961	9.00
❑21, Jul 1961	7.00
❑22, Sep 1961	7.00
❑23, Nov 1961	7.00
❑24 1962	7.00
❑25 1962	7.00
❑26 1962	7.00
❑27 1962	7.00
❑28 1962	7.00
❑29 1962	7.00
❑30 1963	7.00
❑31 1963	5.00
❑32 1963	5.00
❑33 1963	5.00
❑34, Oct 1963	5.00
❑35 1963 DG (c)	5.00
❑36 1964	5.00
❑37 1964	5.00
❑38, Jul 1964	5.00
❑39, Oct 1964	5.00
❑40 1964	5.00
❑41, ca. 1965	5.00
❑42, Jun 1965	5.00
❑43, Aug 1965	5.00
❑44, Oct 1965	5.00
❑45 1966	5.00
❑46, Mar 1966	5.00
❑47, May 1966	5.00
❑48, Jul 1966	5.00
❑49, Sep 1966	5.00
❑50, Nov 1966	5.00
❑51, Jan 1967	3.50
❑52, Mar 1967	3.50
❑53, May 1967	3.50
❑54, Jul 1967	3.50
❑55, Sep 1967	3.50
❑56, Nov 1967	3.50
❑57, Jan 1968	3.50
❑58, May 1968	3.50
❑59, Jul 1968	3.50
❑60, Sep 1968	3.50
❑61, Nov 1968	3.50
❑62, Jan 1969	3.50
❑63, Mar 1969	3.50
❑64, May 1969	3.50
❑65 1969	3.50
❑66 1969	3.50
❑67, Nov 1969	3.50
❑68, Jan 1970	3.50
❑69, Mar 1970	3.50
❑70, May 1970	3.50
❑71, Jul 1970	2.00
❑72, Sep 1970	2.00
❑73, Nov 1970	2.00
❑74, Jan 1971	2.00
❑75, Mar 1971	2.00
❑76, May 1971	2.00
❑77 1971	2.00
❑78 1971	2.00
❑79, Nov 1971	2.00
❑80, Dec 1971; David Cassidy pin-up	2.00
❑81, Jan 1972; Susan Dey pin-up	2.00
❑82, Feb 1972; Shirley Jones pin-up	2.00
❑83, Mar 1972	2.00
❑84, Jun 1972	2.00
❑85 1972	2.00
❑86 1972	2.00
❑87 1972	2.00
❑88, Nov 1972	2.00
❑89 1972	2.00
❑90 1973	2.00
❑91 1973	2.00
❑92, Apr 1973	2.00
❑93 1973	2.00
❑94 1973	2.00
❑95, Oct 1973	2.00
❑96, Dec 1973	2.00

TEENAGE MUTANT NINJA TURTLES (1ST SERIES)
MIRAGE

	N-MINT
❑1, ca. 1984; 1: Teenage Mutant Ninja Turtles. 1st printing-Beware of counterfeits	150.00
❑1/CF; Counterfeit of first printing; Most counterfeit copies have streak or scratch marks across center of back cover, black part of cover is slightly bluish instead of black	1.50
❑1-2, ca. 1984 1: Teenage Mutant Ninja Turtles.	15.00
❑1-3, Feb 1985 1: Teenage Mutant Ninja Turtles.	8.00
❑1-4 1985; 1: Teenage Mutant Ninja Turtles. says Reprinting the first issue on cover	4.00
❑1-5, Aug 1988; 1: Teenage Mutant Ninja Turtles. fifth printing	3.00
❑2, ca. 1984; 1st printing-Beware of counterfeits	20.00
❑2/CF; Counterfeit: Uses glossy cover stock	1.50
❑2-2 1984	6.00
❑2-3 1986	3.00
❑2-4	4.00
❑3 1985; first printing; correct	8.00
❑3/A, ca. 1985; Giveaway, rare; first printing; misprints; Laird's photo appears in white instead of blue	15.00
❑3-2	3.00
❑4, ca. 1985	4.00
❑4-2, May 1987	2.00
❑5, ca. 1985	4.00
❑5-2	2.00
❑6, ca. 1986	3.00
❑6-2	2.00
❑7, ca. 1986; First color Teenage Mutant Ninja Turtles (color insert)	5.00
❑7-2; No color story	2.00
❑8, ca. 1986 A: Cerebus.	4.00
❑9, Sep 1986	3.00

The first *Teenage Mutant Ninja Turtles* series wrapped up with the 12-part "City at War" storyline.

	N-MINT
❑10, Apr 1987, b&w	3.00
❑11, Jun 1987, b&w	4.00
❑12, Sep 1987	3.00
❑13, Feb 1988	3.00
❑14, May 1988; cover says Feb, indicia says May	3.00
❑15, Sum 1988	3.00
❑16, Sep 1988; cover says Jul, indicia says Sep	2.00
❑17, Jan 1989; cover says Nov, indicia says Jan	2.00
❑18, Feb 1989, b&w	2.00
❑18-2	2.00
❑19, Mar 1989; Return to NY	2.00
❑20, Apr 1989; Return to NY	2.00
❑21, May 1989; Return to NY	2.00
❑22, Jun 1989	2.00
❑23, Aug 1989; cover says Jul, indicia says Aug	2.00
❑24, Aug 1989	2.00
❑25, Sep 1989	2.00
❑26, Dec 1989; cover says Oct, indicia says Dec	2.00
❑27, Dec 1989; cover says Nov, indicia says Dec	2.00
❑28, Feb 1990	2.00
❑29, May 1990; cover says Mar, indicia says May	2.00
❑30, Jun 1990; cover says Apr, indicia says Jun	2.00
❑31, Jul 1990	2.00
❑32, Aug 1990	2.00
❑33 1990	2.00
❑34, Sep 1990	2.00
❑35, Mar 1991	2.00
❑36, Aug 1991	2.00
❑37, Jun 1991	2.00
❑38, Jul 1991	2.00
❑39, Sep 1991	2.00
❑40, Oct 1991	2.00
❑41, Nov 1991	2.00
❑42, Dec 1991	2.00
❑43, Jan 1992	2.00
❑44, Feb 1992	2.00
❑45, Mar 1992	2.00
❑46, Apr 1992	2.00
❑47, May 1992	2.00
❑48, Jun 1992	2.00
❑49, Jul 1992	2.00
❑50, Aug 1992, b&w; City At War	2.00
❑51, Sep 1992, b&w	2.00
❑52, Oct 1992, b&w	2.25
❑53, Nov 1992, b&w	2.25
❑54, Dec 1992, b&w	2.25
❑55, Jan 1993, b&w	2.25
❑56, Feb 1993, b&w	2.25
❑57, Mar 1993, b&w	2.25
❑58, Apr 1993, b&w	2.25
❑59, May 1993, b&w	2.25
❑60, Jun 1993, b&w	2.25
❑61, Jul 1993, b&w	2.25
❑62, Aug 1993, b&w	2.25

TEENAGE MUTANT NINJA TURTLES (2ND SERIES)
MIRAGE

	N-MINT
❑1, Oct 1993	3.00
❑2, Dec 1993	3.00
❑3, Feb 1994	3.00

	N-MINT
❑4, Apr 1994	3.00
❑5, Jun 1994	3.00
❑6, Aug 1994	2.75
❑7, Oct 1994	2.75
❑8, Nov 1994	2.75
❑9, Aug 1995	2.75
❑10, Aug 1995	2.75
❑11, Sep 1995	2.75
❑12, Sep 1995	2.75
❑13, Oct 1995	2.75
❑Special 1, Jan 1993; Special	2.95

TEENAGE MUTANT NINJA TURTLES (3RD SERIES)
IMAGE

	N-MINT
❑1, Jun 1996	3.50
❑2, Jul 1996	3.25
❑3, Sep 1996	3.25
❑4, Oct 1996	3.00
❑5, Dec 1996	3.00
❑6, Jan 1997	3.00
❑7, Feb 1997	3.00
❑8, Apr 1997	3.00
❑9, May 1997 A: Knight Watchman.	3.00
❑10, Jul 1997	3.00
❑11, Oct 1997	2.95
❑12, Dec 1997	2.95
❑13, Feb 1998	2.95
❑14, Apr 1998	2.95
❑15, May 1998	2.95
❑16, Jul 1998	2.95
❑17, Sep 1998	2.95
❑18, Oct 1998	2.95
❑19, Jan 1999	2.95
❑20, Mar 1999	2.95
❑21, May 1999	2.95
❑22, Jul 1999	2.95
❑23, Oct 1999	2.95

TEENAGE MUTANT NINJA TURTLES ADVENTURES (1ST SERIES)
ARCHIE

	N-MINT
❑1, Aug 1988	3.00
❑2, Oct 1988	2.50
❑3, Dec 1988	2.50

TEENAGE MUTANT NINJA TURTLES ADVENTURES (2ND SERIES)
ARCHIE

	N-MINT
❑1, Mar 1989	3.00
❑2, May 1989	2.50
❑3, Jul 1989	2.50
❑4, Sep 1989	2.00
❑5, Oct 1989	2.00
❑6, Nov 1989	2.00
❑7, Dec 1989	2.00
❑8, Feb 1990	2.00
❑9, Mar 1990	2.00
❑10, May 1990	2.00
❑11, Jun 1990	1.50
❑12, Jul 1990	1.50
❑13, Oct 1990	1.50
❑14, Nov 1990	1.50
❑15, Dec 1990	1.50
❑16, Jan 1991	1.50
❑17, Feb 1991	1.50
❑18, Mar 1991	1.50
❑19, Apr 1991 1: Mighty Mutanimals.	1.50
❑20, May 1991	1.50
❑21, Jun 1991	1.50
❑22, Jul 1991	1.50
❑23, Aug 1991	1.50
❑24, Sep 1991	1.50
❑25, Oct 1991	1.50
❑26, Nov 1991	1.50
❑27, Dec 1991	1.50
❑28, Jan 1992	1.50
❑29, Feb 1992	1.50
❑30, Mar 1992	1.50
❑31, Apr 1992	1.50
❑32, May 1992	1.50
❑33, Jun 1992	1.50
❑34, Aug 1992	1.50
❑35, Jul 1992	1.50
❑36, Sep 1992	1.50
❑37, Oct 1992	1.50
❑38, Nov 1992	1.50
❑39, Dec 1992	1.50
❑40, Jan 1993	1.50
❑41, Feb 1993	1.50
❑42, Mar 1993	1.50
❑43, Apr 1993	1.50
❑44, May 1993	1.50
❑45, Jun 1993	1.50
❑46, Jul 1993	1.50
❑47, Aug 1993	1.50
❑48, Sep 1993	1.50
❑49, Oct 1993	1.50
❑50, Nov 1993	1.50
❑51, Dec 1993	1.50
❑52, Jan 1994	1.50
❑53, Feb 1994	1.50
❑54, Mar 1994	1.50
❑55, Apr 1994	1.50
❑56, May 1994	1.50
❑57, Jun 1994	1.50
❑58, Jul 1994	1.50
❑59, Aug 1994	1.50
❑60, Sep 1994	1.50
❑61, Oct 1994	1.50
❑62, Nov 1994	1.50
❑63, Dec 1994	1.50
❑64, Jan 1995	1.50
❑65, Feb 1995	1.50
❑66, Mar 1995	1.50
❑67, Apr 1995	1.50
❑68, May 1995	1.50
❑69, Jun 1995	1.50
❑70, Jul 1995	1.50
❑71, Sep 1995	1.50
❑72, Oct 1995	1.50
❑Special 1, Sum 1992; Teenage Mutant Ninja Turtles Meet Archie	2.50
❑Special 2, Fal 1992	2.50
❑Special 3, Win 1992	2.50
❑Special 4, Spr 1993	2.50
❑Special 5, Sum 1993	2.50
❑Special 6, Fal 1993	2.00
❑Special 7, Win 1993	2.00
❑Special 8, Spr 1994	2.00
❑Special 9, Sum 1994	2.00
❑Special Ed 10, Fal 1994	2.00
❑Special 11	2.00

TEENAGE MUTANT NINJA TURTLES ADVENTURES (3RD SERIES)
ARCHIE

	N-MINT
❑1, Jan 1996	1.50
❑2, Feb 1996	1.50
❑3, Mar 1996	1.50

TEENAGE MUTANT NINJA TURTLES ANIMATED
DREAMWAVE

	N-MINT
❑1, Jun 2003	2.95
❑2, Jul 2003	2.95
❑3, Aug 2003	2.95
❑4, Sep 2003	2.95
❑5, Oct 2003	2.95
❑6, Nov 2003	2.95
❑7, Dec 2003	2.95

TEENAGE MUTANT NINJA TURTLES AUTHORIZED MARTIAL ARTS TRAINING MANUAL
SOLSON

	N-MINT
❑1 1986 RB (w); RB (a)	2.50
❑2 1986	2.50
❑3 1986	2.50
❑4	2.50

TEENAGE MUTANT NINJA TURTLES CLASSICS DIGEST
ARCHIE

	N-MINT
❑1, ca. 1993	2.00
❑2, ca. 1993	1.75
❑3, ca. 1994	1.75
❑4, ca. 1994	1.75
❑5, ca. 1994	1.75
❑6, ca. 1994	1.75
❑7, Dec 1994; digest	1.75
❑8	1.75

TEENAGE MUTANT NINJA TURTLES/ FLAMING CARROT CROSSOVER
MIRAGE

	N-MINT
❑1, Nov 1993	3.00
❑2, Dec 1993	3.00
❑3, Jan 1994	3.00
❑4, Feb 1994	3.00

TEENAGE MUTANT NINJA TURTLES III THE MOVIE: THE TURTLES ARE BACK...IN TIME
ARCHIE

	N-MINT
❑1; newsstand	2.50
❑1/Prestige; Prestige edition	4.95

TEENAGE MUTANT NINJA TURTLES II: THE SECRET OF THE OOZE
MIRAGE

	N-MINT
❑1	5.95

TEENAGE MUTANT NINJA TURTLES MEET THE CONSERVATION CORPS
ARCHIE

	N-MINT
❑1	2.50

TEENAGE MUTANT NINJA TURTLES MICHAELANGELO CHRISTMAS SPECIAL
MIRAGE

	N-MINT
❑1	1.75

TEENAGE MUTANT NINJA TURTLES MOVIE II
ARCHIE

	N-MINT
❑1, Jun 1991	2.50

TEENAGE MUTANT NINJA TURTLES MUTANT UNIVERSE SOURCEBOOK
ARCHIE

	N-MINT
❑1	2.00
❑2	2.00
❑3	2.00

TEENAGE MUTANT NINJA TURTLES PRESENTS: APRIL O'NEIL
ARCHIE

	N-MINT
❑1, Apr 1993	1.25
❑2, May 1993	1.25
❑3, Jun 1993	1.25

TEENAGE MUTANT NINJA TURTLES PRESENTS: DONATELLO AND LEATHERHEAD
ARCHIE

	N-MINT
❑1, Jul 1993	1.25
❑2, Aug 1993	1.25
❑3, Sep 1993	1.25

TEENAGE MUTANT NINJA TURTLES PRESENTS MERDUDE AND MICHAELANGELO
ARCHIE

	N-MINT
❑1, Oct 1993	1.25
❑2, Nov 1993	1.25
❑3, Dec 1993	1.25

TEENAGE MUTANT NINJA TURTLES-SAVAGE DRAGON CROSSOVER
MIRAGE

	N-MINT
❑1, Aug 1995	3.00

TEENAGE MUTANT NINJA TURTLES: THE MOVIE (ARCHIE)
ARCHIE

	N-MINT
❑1, Sum 1990; newsstand	2.50
❑1/Direct ed., Sum 1990; prestige format	4.95
❑1/Prestige; Prestige edition	5.95

TEENAGE MUTANT NINJA TURTLES: THE MOVIE (MIRAGE)
MIRAGE

	N-MINT
❑1, b&w	5.95

N-MINT

TEENAGENTS (JACK KIRBY'S...)
TOPPS

❑1, Aug 1993; three trading cards 2.95
❑2, Sep 1993; trading cards 2.95
❑3, Oct 1993; trading cards 2.95
❑4, Nov 1993; cards; Zorro preview .. 2.95

TEEN-AGE ROMANCE (ATLAS)
ATLAS

❑77, Sep 1960 ..... 15.00
❑78, Nov 1960 ..... 15.00
❑79, Jan 1961 ..... 15.00
❑80, Mar 1961 ..... 15.00
❑81, May 1961 ..... 15.00

TEEN-AGE ROMANCE (MARVEL)
MARVEL

❑82, Jul 1961 ..... 20.00
❑83, Sep 1961 ..... 20.00
❑84, Nov 1961 ..... 20.00
❑85, Jan 1962 ..... 20.00
❑86, Mar 1962 ..... 20.00

TEEN COMICS
PERSONALITY

❑1, ca. 1992; Beverly Hills 90210; Unauthorized biographies, text & pin-ups 2.50
❑2, ca. 1992 ..... 2.50
❑3, ca. 1992; Luke Perry; Unauthorized biography, text & pin-ups 2.50
❑4; Melrose Place; Unauthorized biographies, text & pin-ups 2.50
❑5; Marky Mark; Unauthorized biography, text & pin-ups 2.50
❑6; Madonna; Prince; Unauthorized biographies, text & pin-ups 2.50

TEEN CONFESSIONS
CHARLTON

❑1, ca. 1959 ..... 75.00
❑2 1959 ..... 40.00
❑3, Jan 1960 ..... 30.00
❑4, Mar 1960 ..... 30.00
❑5, May 1960 ..... 30.00
❑6, Jul 1960 ..... 30.00
❑7, Sep 1960 ..... 30.00
❑8, Nov 1960 ..... 30.00
❑9, Jan 1961 ..... 30.00
❑10, Mar 1961 ..... 30.00
❑11, May 1961 ..... 25.00
❑12, Jul 1961 ..... 25.00
❑13, Sep 1961 ..... 25.00
❑14, Nov 1961 ..... 25.00
❑15, Jan 1962 ..... 25.00
❑16, Mar 1962 ..... 25.00
❑17, May 1962 ..... 25.00
❑18, Jul 1962 ..... 25.00
❑19, Sep 1962 ..... 25.00
❑20, Nov 1962 ..... 25.00
❑21, Feb 1963 ..... 25.00
❑22, Apr 1963 ..... 25.00
❑23, Jun 1963 ..... 25.00
❑24, Aug 1963 ..... 25.00
❑25, Oct 1963 ..... 25.00
❑26, Dec 1963 ..... 25.00
❑27, ca. 1964 ..... 25.00
❑28, May 1964 ..... 25.00
❑29, Jul 1964 ..... 25.00
❑30, ca. 1964 ..... 25.00
❑31, ca. 1965 ..... 125.00
❑32, ca. 1965 ..... 20.00
❑33, May 1965 ..... 20.00
❑34, Jul 1965 ..... 20.00
❑35, Sep 1965 ..... 20.00
❑36, Nov 1965 ..... 20.00
❑37, Jan 1966 ..... 20.00
❑38, May 1966 ..... 20.00
❑39, Jul 1966 ..... 20.00
❑40, ca. 1966 ..... 20.00
❑41, Nov 1966 ..... 20.00
❑42, Jan 1967 ..... 20.00
❑43, Mar 1967 ..... 20.00
❑44, May 1967 ..... 20.00
❑45, Jul 1967 ..... 20.00
❑46, Sep 1967 ..... 20.00

N-MINT

❑47, Nov 1967 ..... 20.00
❑48, Jan 1968 ..... 20.00
❑49, Mar 1968 ..... 20.00
❑50, Jul 1968 ..... 20.00
❑51, Sep 1968 ..... 15.00
❑52, Nov 1968 ..... 15.00
❑53, Jan 1968 ..... 15.00
❑54, Mar 1969 ..... 15.00
❑55, ca. 1969 ..... 15.00
❑56, ca. 1969 ..... 15.00
❑57, Aug 1969 ..... 15.00
❑58, Nov 1969 ..... 15.00
❑59, ca. 1970 ..... 20.00
❑60, Feb 1970 ..... 12.00
❑61, Apr 1970 ..... 12.00
❑62, Jun 1970 ..... 12.00
❑63, Aug 1970 ..... 12.00
❑64, Oct 1970 ..... 12.00
❑65, Dec 1970 ..... 12.00
❑66, Feb 1971 ..... 12.00
❑67, Apr 1971 ..... 12.00
❑68, Jun 1971 ..... 12.00
❑69, Aug 1971 ..... 12.00
❑70, Oct 1971 ..... 12.00
❑71, Dec 1971; David Cassidy pin-up 12.00
❑72, Feb 1972 ..... 12.00
❑73, Apr 1972; Shirley Jones pin-up . 12.00
❑74, Jun 1972; Bobby Sherman pin-up 12.00
❑75, Aug 1972 ..... 12.00
❑76, Oct 1972 ..... 12.00
❑77, Dec 1972 ..... 12.00
❑78, Feb 1973; Susan Dey pin-up 12.00
❑79, Apr 1973 ..... 12.00
❑80, Jun 1973 ..... 12.00
❑81, Jul 1973 ..... 12.00
❑82, Sep 1973 ..... 12.00
❑83, Nov 1973 ..... 12.00
❑84, Jan 1974 ..... 12.00
❑85, Sep 1974 ..... 12.00
❑86, ca. 1974 ..... 12.00
❑87, Feb 1975 ..... 12.00
❑88, Apr 1975 ..... 12.00
❑89, Jun 1975 ..... 12.00
❑90, Aug 1975 ..... 12.00
❑91, Oct 1975 ..... 12.00
❑92, Dec 1975 ..... 12.00
❑93, Feb 1976 ..... 12.00
❑94, Apr 1976 ..... 12.00
❑95, Jun 1976 ..... 12.00
❑96, Aug 1976 ..... 12.00
❑97, Oct 1976 ..... 12.00

TEEN TALES: THE LIBRARY COMIC
DAVID G. BROWN

❑1, Oct 1997; promotional comic book done for the L.A. Public Library 1.00

TEEN TITANS, THE
DC

❑1, Feb 1966; NC (a); Peace Corps ... 220.00
❑2, Apr 1966 NC (a) 100.00
❑3, Jun 1966 NC (a) 40.00
❑4, Aug 1966 NC (a) 40.00
❑5, Oct 1966 NC (a) 40.00
❑6, Dec 1966 ..... 32.00
❑7, Feb 1967 ..... 32.00
❑8, Apr 1967 ..... 32.00
❑9, Jun 1967 ..... 32.00
❑10, Aug 1967 ..... 32.00
❑11, Oct 1967 ..... 28.00
❑12, Dec 1967 ..... 28.00
❑13, Feb 1968 ..... 28.00
❑14, Apr 1968 ..... 28.00
❑15, Jun 1968 ..... 28.00
❑16, Aug 1968 ..... 28.00
❑17, Oct 1968 ..... 28.00
❑18, Dec 1968 1: Starfire. 33.00
❑19, Feb 1969 ..... 33.00
❑20, Apr 1969 NA, NC (a) 33.00
❑21, Jun 1969 NA, NC (a) 33.00
❑22, Aug 1969 NA, NC (a); O: Wonder Girl. 33.00
❑23, Oct 1969 DG (w); GK (a) 18.00

The original Teen Titans regrouped in "Then & Now."

© 1997 DC Comics.

N-MINT

❑24, Dec 1969 DG (w); GK (a) 18.00
❑25, Feb 1970 DG (w); NC (a); 1: Lilith. 18.00
❑26, Apr 1970 DG (w); NC (a) 12.00
❑27, Jun 1970; DG (w); CI, GT (a); in space 12.00
❑28, Aug 1970 DG (w); NC (a) 12.00
❑29, Oct 1970 DG (w); NC (a); A: Hawk & Dove. 12.00
❑30, Dec 1970 DG (w); CI, NC (a); A: Aquagirl. 12.00
❑31, Feb 1971 DG (w); GT (a) 20.00
❑32, Apr 1971 DG (w); NC (a) 18.00
❑33, Jun 1971; DG (w); GT (a); Robin returns 18.00
❑34, Aug 1971 GT (a) 18.00
❑35, Oct 1971; Giant-size GT (a); 1: Think Freak. 18.00
❑36, Dec 1971; Giant-size GT, NC, JA (a) 18.00
❑37, Feb 1972; Giant-size GT (a) 18.00
❑38, Apr 1972; Giant-size GT (a) 18.00
❑39, Jun 1972; Giant-size GT (a) 12.00
❑40, Aug 1972 1: Black Moray. A: Aqualad. 12.00
❑41, Oct 1972 ..... 12.00
❑42, Dec 1972 ..... 12.00
❑43, Feb 1973; series goes on hiatus 12.00
❑44, Nov 1976; JO (w); 1: Guardian. V: Doctor Light. Series begins again (1976); New team: Kid Flash, Wonder Girl, Robin, Speedy, Mal 7.00
❑45, Dec 1976 IN (a) 7.00
❑46, Feb 1977 IN (a); V: Fiddler. 7.00
❑47, Apr 1977 1: Darklight I. 1: Flamesplasher I. 1: Sizematic I. 1: Darklight II. 1: Flamesplasher II. 1: Sizematic II. 7.00
❑48, Jun 1977 1: Harlequin. 1: The Bumblebee. 12.00
❑49, Aug 1977 1: Bryan the Brain. 7.00
❑50, Oct 1977; DH (a); Bat-Girl returns 20.00
❑51, Nov 1977 DH (a); A: Titans West. 6.00
❑52, Dec 1977 DH (a); A: Titans West. 6.00
❑53, Feb 1978 O: Teen Titans. 1: The Antithesis. 6.00

TEEN TITANS (2ND SERIES)
DC

❑1, Oct 1996 GP (a); O: New team of four teen-agers led by Atom. 4.00
❑2, Nov 1996 GP (a) 3.00
❑3, Dec 1996; GP (a); A: Mr. Jupiter. A: Mad Mod. V: Jugular. team gets new costumes 3.00
❑4, Jan 1997 A: Captain Marvel Jr.. A: Nightwing. A: Robin. 2.50
❑5, Feb 1997 GP (a); A: Captain Marvel Jr.. A: Supergirl. A: Nightwing. A: Robin. 2.50
❑6, Mar 1997 GP (a) 2.50
❑7, Apr 1997 GP (a) 2.50
❑8, May 1997 ..... 2.50
❑9, Jun 1997 GP (a); A: Warlord. 2.50
❑10, Jul 1997; A: Warlord. in Skartaris 2.50
❑11, Aug 1997 GP (a); A: Warlord. 2.00
❑12, Sep 1997; GP, DG, GK (a); flashback with original Titans 2.95
❑13, Oct 1997; flashback with original Titans 2.00
❑14, Nov 1997; GP (a); identity of Omen revealed 2.00
❑15, Jan 1998; GP (a); D: Joto. real identity of Omen revealed 2.00
❑16, Feb 1998 ..... 2.00

N-MINT

❑17, Mar 1998; new members join ... 2.00
❑18, Apr 1998 ... 2.00
❑19, Apr 1998; A: Superman. Millennium Giants ... 2.00
❑20, May 1998 ... 2.00
❑21, Jun 1998 ... 2.00
❑22, Jul 1998 A: Changeling. ... 2.00
❑23, Aug 1998 A: Superman. ... 1.95
❑24, Sep 1998 ... 1.95
❑Annual 1, ca. 1997; Pulp Heroes ... 3.95
❑Annual 1999, ca. 1999; published in 1999 in style of '60s Annual; card-stock cover ... 4.95

TEEN TITANS (3RD SERIES)
DC

❑1, Oct 2003 ... 12.00
❑1-2, Oct 2003 ... 5.00
❑1-3, Oct 2003 ... 4.00
❑1-4, Oct 2003; sketch cover ... 8.00
❑2, Nov 2003 ... 2.50
❑3, Dec 2003 ... 2.50
❑4, Jan 2004 ... 2.50
❑5, Feb 2004 ... 2.50
❑6, Mar 2004 ... 2.50
❑7, Apr 2004 ... 2.50
❑8, May 2004 ... 2.50
❑9, May 2004 ... 2.50
❑10, Jun 2004 ... 2.50
❑11, Jul 2004 ... 2.50
❑12, Aug 2004 ... 2.50
❑13, Sep 2004 ...

TEEN TITANS GO!
DC

❑1, Jan 2004 ... 2.25
❑2, Feb 2004 ... 2.25
❑3, Mar 2004 ... 2.25
❑4, Apr 2004 ... 2.25
❑5, May 2004 ... 2.25
❑6, Jun 2004 ... 2.25
❑7, Jul 2004 ... 2.25
❑8, Aug 2004 ... 2.25
❑9, Sep 2004 ...

TEEN TITANS/OUTSIDERS SECRET FILES
DC

❑1, Dec 2003 ... 5.95

TEEN TITANS SPOTLIGHT
DC

❑1, Aug 1986; Starfire ... 1.25
❑2, Sep 1986; Starfire ... 1.25
❑3, Oct 1986; RA (a); Jericho ... 1.25
❑4, Nov 1986; RA (a); Jericho ... 1.25
❑5, Dec 1986; RA (a); Jericho ... 1.25
❑6, Jan 1987; RA (a); Jericho ... 1.00
❑7, Feb 1987 ... 1.00
❑8, Mar 1987; Hawk ... 1.00
❑9, Apr 1987; A: Robotman. Changeling ... 1.00
❑10, May 1987; EL (a); Aqualad ... 1.00
❑11, Jun 1987; JO (a); Brotherhood of Evil ... 1.00
❑12, Jul 1987; Wonder Girl ... 1.00
❑13, Aug 1987 A: Two-Face. ... 1.00
❑14, Sep 1987; Nightwing, Batman ... 1.00
❑15, Oct 1987; EL (a); A: Komand'r. A: Ryand'r. Omega Men ... 1.00
❑16, Nov 1987 ... 1.00
❑17, Dec 1987 DH (a) ... 1.00
❑18, Jan 1988; Millennium; Aqualad . 1.00
❑19, Feb 1988; Millennium; Starfire .. 1.00
❑20, Mar 1988; Cyborg; Changeling . 1.00
❑21, Apr 1988; DS (a); original Titans 1.00

TEKKEN FOREVER
IMAGE

❑1/A, Dec 2001 ... 2.95
❑1/B ... 2.95

TEK KNIGHTS
ARTLINE

❑1, b&w ... 2.95

N-MINT

TEKNO*COMIX HANDBOOK
TEKNO

❑1, May 1996; information on various Tekno characters ... 3.95

TEKNOPHAGE (NEIL GAIMAN'S...)
TEKNO

❑1, Aug 1995 ... 1.95
❑1/Variant, Jul 1995; Steel Edition; enhanced cover ... 3.00
❑2, Sep 1995 ... 1.95
❑3, Oct 1995 BT (a) ... 1.95
❑4, Nov 1995 ... 1.95
❑5, Dec 1995 ... 1.95
❑6, Dec 1995 ... 1.95
❑7, Jan 1996 ... 2.25
❑8, Feb 1996 ... 2.25
❑9, Feb 1996 ... 2.25
❑10, Mar 1996 ... 2.25

TEKNOPHAGE VERSUS ZEERUS
BIG

❑1, Jul 1996 ... 3.25

TEKQ
GAUNTLET

❑1, b&w ... 2.95
❑2, b&w ... 2.95
❑3, b&w ... 2.95
❑4, b&w ... 2.95

TEKWORLD
MARVEL / EPIC

❑1, Sep 1992 ... 2.50
❑2, Oct 1992 ... 2.00
❑3, Nov 1992 ... 2.00
❑4, Dec 1992 ... 2.00
❑5, Jan 1993 ... 2.00
❑6, Feb 1993 ... 2.00
❑7, Mar 1993 ... 2.00
❑8, Apr 1993 ... 2.00
❑9, May 1993 ... 2.00
❑10, Jun 1993 ... 2.00
❑11, Jul 1993 ... 1.75
❑12, Aug 1993 ... 1.75
❑13, Sep 1993 ... 1.75
❑14, Oct 1993; A: Jake Cardigan. Begins adaptation of TekLords ... 1.75
❑15, Nov 1993 ... 1.75
❑16, Dec 1993 ... 1.75
❑17, Jan 1994 ... 1.75
❑18, Feb 1994 ... 1.75
❑19, Mar 1994 ... 1.75
❑20, Apr 1994 ... 1.75
❑21, May 1994 ... 1.75
❑22, Jun 1994 ... 1.75
❑23, Jul 1994 ... 1.75
❑24, Aug 1994; Partial photo cover ... 1.75

TELLOS
IMAGE

❑1, May 1999 ... 2.50
❑2, Jun 1999 ... 2.50
❑3, Jul 1999 ... 2.50
❑4, Oct 1999 ... 2.50
❑4/A, Oct 1999; alternate cover w/ moon in background ... 2.50
❑4/B, Oct 1999; alternate cover w/skeletons in bottom left ... 2.50
❑5, Dec 1999 ... 2.50
❑6, Feb 2000 ... 2.50
❑7, Apr 2000 ... 2.50
❑8, Aug 2000 ... 2.50
❑9, Sep 2000 ... 2.50
❑10, Nov 2000 ... 2.50
❑Ashcan 1; Dynamic Forces preview . 2.50

TELLOS: MAIDEN VOYAGE
IMAGE

❑1, Man atop demons on cover ... 5.95

TELLOS: SONS & MOONS
IMAGE

❑1, Dec 2002, b&w and color; Man atop demons on cover ... 5.95

N-MINT

TELLOS: THE LAST HEIST
IMAGE

❑1, Jun 2001, b&w and color; Man atop demons on cover ... 5.95

TELL TALE HEART AND OTHER STORIES
FANTAGRAPHICS

❑1, b&w ... 2.50

TELLURIA
ZUB

❑1 ... 2.50
❑2 ... 2.50
❑3 ... 2.50

TEMPEST
DC

❑1, Nov 1996; Tula returns ... 1.75
❑2, Dec 1996 ... 1.75
❑3, Jan 1997; Aqualad's true origin revealed ... 1.75
❑4, Feb 1997 ... 1.75

TEMPLATE
HEAD

❑0; flip-book with Max Damage #0 ... 2.95
❑1, Dec 1995, b&w ... 2.50
❑2, Feb 1996, b&w ... 2.50
❑3, Apr 1996, b&w ... 2.50
❑4, Jun 1996, b&w ... 2.50
❑5, Aug 1996, b&w ... 2.50
❑6, Nov 1996, b&w ... 2.50
❑7, Jul 1997, b&w ... 2.50
❑Special 1, Feb 1997, b&w ... 2.95
❑Special 1/Ashcan, Feb 1997; Ashcan preview of special #1 ... 1.00
❑Special 1/Variant, Feb 1997; alternate cover ... 2.95

TEMPLE SNARE
MU

❑1, b&w ... 2.25

TEMPTRESS: THE BLOOD OF EVE
CALIBER

❑1 ... 2.95

TEMPUS FUGITIVE
DC

❑1, ca. 1990 ... 4.95
❑2, ca. 1990 ... 4.95
❑3, ca. 1990 ... 4.95
❑4, ca. 1990 ... 4.95

TENCHI MUYO!
PIONEER

❑1, Mar 1997 ... 2.95
❑2, Mar 1997 ... 2.95
❑3, May 1997 ... 2.95
❑4, Jul 1997 ... 2.95
❑5, Aug 1997 ... 2.95
❑6 ... 2.95

TENDER LOVE STORIES
SKYWALD

❑1, Feb 1971 ... 15.00
❑2, Apr 1971 ... 10.00
❑3 ... 10.00
❑4 ... 10.00

TENTH, THE
IMAGE

❑0, Aug 1997; American Entertainment exclusive ... 3.00
❑0.5, Aug 1997; Wizard promotional edition with certificate of authenticity ... 5.00
❑1, Jan 1997; cover says Mar, indicia says Jan ... 3.00
❑1/A, Jan 1997; American Entertainment exclusive cover ... 4.00
❑2, Feb 1997; cover says Apr, indicia says Feb ... 2.50
❑3, May 1997 ... 2.50
❑4, Jun 1997 ... 2.50

TENTH, THE (2ND SERIES)
IMAGE

❑0, Aug 1997 O: The Tenth. ... 3.00
❑0/A, Aug 1997 O: The Tenth. ... 8.00

N-MINT

❑0/American Ent, Aug 1997; O: The Tenth. American Entertainment exclusive 4.00
❑1, Sep 1997 ..... 3.00
❑1/American Ent, Sep 1997; American Entertainment exclusive cover (logo at bottom right) 4.00
❑2, Oct 1997 ..... 3.00
❑3, Nov 1997 ..... 2.50
❑3/A, Nov 1997; Alternate "Adrenalyn" cover 3.00
❑3/B, Nov 1997; Wizard "Certified Authentic" limited edition 8.00
❑4, Dec 1997 ..... 2.50
❑5, Jan 1998 ..... 2.50
❑6, Feb 1998 ..... 2.50
❑7, Mar 1998 ..... 2.50
❑8, Apr 1998 ..... 2.50
❑9, Jun 1998 ..... 2.50
❑10, Jul 1998 ..... 2.50
❑10/A, Jul 1998; alternate cover (logo on right) 2.50
❑11, Aug 1998 ..... 2.50
❑11/A, Aug 1998; alternate cover (white background) 2.50
❑12, Oct 1998 ..... 2.50
❑13, Nov 1998 ..... 2.50
❑14, Jan 1999 ..... 2.50
❑14/A, Jan 1999; alternate cover (solo face) 2.50

TENTH, THE (3RD SERIES)
IMAGE

❑1, Feb 1999 ..... 2.95
❑1/A, Feb 1999; alternate cover 2.95
❑1/B, Feb 1999; DFE chromium edition; alternate cover 10.00
❑2, Apr 1999 ..... 2.50
❑3, May 1999 ..... 2.50
❑4, Jun 1999 ..... 2.50

TENTH, THE (4TH SERIES)
IMAGE

❑1, Sep 1999 ..... 2.50
❑1/A, Sep 1999; Girl wearing shirt and panties on cover 6.00
❑1/B, Sep 1999; Another Universe exclusive cover 3.00
❑2, Oct 1999 ..... 2.50
❑3, Nov 1999 ..... 2.50
❑4, Dec 1999 ..... 2.50

TENTH CONFIGURATION, THE
IMAGE

❑1, Aug 1998 ..... 2.50

10TH MUSE
IMAGE

❑1, Nov 2000 ..... 2.95
❑2/A, Jan 2001; Character leaping from right on cover 2.95
❑2/B, Jan 2001; Character leaping from left on cover 2.95
❑2/C, Jan 2001 ..... 2.95
❑3/A, Mar 2001; Drawn cover with woman summoning lightning 2.95
❑3/B, Mar 2001; Cover with green border 2.95
❑3/C, Mar 2001; Drawn cover with woman leaping forward 2.95
❑3/D, Mar 2001; Wraparound Tower Records cover with red border 2.95
❑4, Mar 2001 ..... 2.95
❑4/A, Mar 2001; Drawn cover 2.95
❑4/B, Mar 2001 ..... 2.95
❑5, Jul 2001 ..... 2.95
❑6, Sep 2001 ..... 2.95
❑7, Oct 2001 ..... 2.95
❑8/A, Nov 2001; Drawn cover 2.95
❑8/B, Nov 2001 ..... 2.95
❑9/A, Dec 2001; Drawn cover 2.95
❑9/B, Dec 2001 ..... 2.95

TENTH, THE: RESURRECTED
DARK HORSE

❑1/A, Jul 2001; Lady standing in front of glowing skulls in background on cover 2.99
❑1/B, Jul 2001; Hulking figure on cover 2.99

N-MINT

❑2, Aug 2001 ..... 2.99
❑3, Nov 2001 ..... 2.99
❑4, Feb 2002 ..... 2.99

TEN YEARS OF LOVE & ROCKETS
FANTAGRAPHICS

❑1, Sep 1992, b&w 1.50

TERMINAL CITY
DC / VERTIGO

❑1, Jul 1996 ..... 2.50
❑1/Autographed, Jul 1996; Limited to 75 copies 5.00
❑2, Aug 1996 ..... 2.50
❑3, Sep 1996 ..... 2.50
❑4, Oct 1996 ..... 2.50
❑5, Nov 1996 ..... 2.50
❑6, Dec 1996 ..... 2.50
❑7, Jan 1997 ..... 2.50
❑8, Feb 1997 ..... 2.50
❑9, Mar 1997 ..... 2.50

TERMINAL CITY: AERIAL GRAFFITI
DC / VERTIGO

❑1, Nov 1997 ..... 2.50
❑2, Dec 1997 ..... 2.50
❑3, Jan 1998 ..... 2.50
❑4, Feb 1998 ..... 2.50
❑5, Mar 1998 ..... 2.50

TERMINAL POINT
DARK HORSE

❑1, Feb 1993, b&w 2.50
❑2, Mar 1993, b&w 2.50
❑3, Apr 1993, b&w 2.50

TERMINATOR, THE (1ST SERIES)
NOW

❑1, Sep 1988; movie tie-in 2.00
❑2, Oct 1988 ..... 1.75
❑3, Nov 1988 ..... 1.75
❑4, Jan 1989 ..... 1.75
❑5, Feb 1989 ..... 1.75
❑6, Mar 1989 ..... 1.75
❑7, Apr 1989 ..... 1.75
❑8, May 1989; Comics Code 1.75
❑9, Jun 1989; Comics Code 1.75
❑10, Jul 1989; Comics Code 1.75
❑11, Aug 1989; Comics Code 1.75
❑12, Sep 1989; Comics Code 1.75
❑13, Oct 1989; Comics Code 1.75
❑14, Nov 1989; Comics Code 1.75
❑15, Dec 1989; Comics Code 1.75
❑16, Jan 1990; Comics Code 1.75
❑17, Feb 1990; Comics Code 1.75

TERMINATOR, THE (2ND SERIES)
DARK HORSE

❑1, Aug 1990 ..... 3.00
❑2, Sep 1990 ..... 3.00
❑3, Oct 1990 ..... 3.00
❑4, Nov 1990 ..... 3.00

TERMINATOR 2: JUDGMENT DAY
MARVEL

❑1, Sep 1991 KJ (a) 2.00
❑2, Sep 1991 KJ (a) 2.00
❑3, Oct 1991 KJ (a) 2.00

TERMINATOR 2: JUDGMENT DAY (MAGAZINE)
MARVEL

❑1, Sep 1991, b&w; magazine 3.00

TERMINATOR, THE (3RD SERIES)
DARK HORSE

❑1, ca. 1991; leads into 1998 series 2.95

TERMINATOR, THE (4TH SERIES)
DARK HORSE

❑1, Sep 1998; no month of publication 2.95
❑2, Oct 1998 ..... 2.95
❑3, Nov 1998 ..... 2.95
❑4, Dec 1998 ..... 2.95

TERMINATOR, THE (MAGAZINE)
TRIDENT

❑1 ..... 3.00
❑2 ..... 3.00

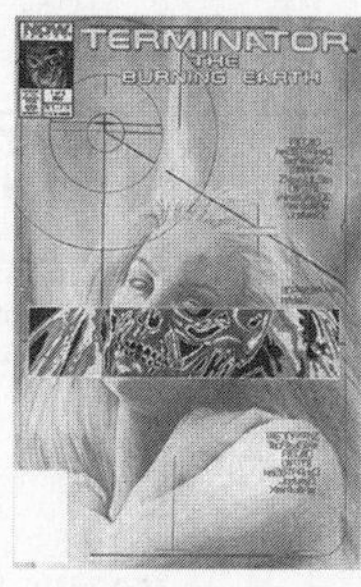

Alex Ross' earliest work can be found in *Terminator: The Burning Earth.*

N-MINT

❑3 ..... 3.00
❑4 ..... 3.00

TERMINATOR, THE: ALL MY FUTURES PAST
NOW

❑1, Aug 1990 ..... 2.50
❑2, Sep 1990 ..... 2.50

TERMINATOR: ENDGAME
DARK HORSE

❑1, Sep 1992 ..... 2.50
❑2, Oct 1992 ..... 2.50
❑3, Oct 1992 ..... 2.50

TERMINATOR: HUNTERS AND KILLERS
DARK HORSE

❑1, Mar 1992 ..... 2.50
❑2, Apr 1992 ..... 2.50
❑3, May 1992 ..... 2.50

TERMINATOR, THE: ONE SHOT
DARK HORSE

❑1, Jul 1991; prestige format; pop-up 5.95

TERMINATOR: SECONDARY OBJECTIVES
DARK HORSE

❑1, Jul 1991 ..... 2.50
❑2, Aug 1991 ..... 2.50
❑3, Sep 1991 ..... 2.50
❑4, Oct 1991 ..... 2.50

TERMINATOR, THE: THE BURNING EARTH
NOW

❑1, Mar 1990; ARo (a); 1st comics work by Alex Ross 7.50
❑2, Apr 1990 ARo (a) 5.00
❑3, May 1990 ARo (a) 5.00
❑4, Jun 1990 ARo (a) 6.00
❑5, Jul 1990 ARo (a) 6.00

TERMINATOR, THE: THE DARK YEARS
DARK HORSE

❑1, Sep 1999 ..... 2.95
❑2, Oct 1999 ..... 2.95
❑3, Nov 1999 ..... 2.95
❑4, Dec 1999 ..... 2.95

TERMINATOR, THE: THE ENEMY WITHIN
DARK HORSE

❑1, Nov 1991 ..... 2.50
❑2, Dec 1991 ..... 2.50
❑3, Jan 1992 ..... 2.50
❑4, Feb 1992 ..... 2.50

TERMINATOR 3
BECKETT

❑1, Jun 2003 ..... 5.95
❑2, Jul 2003 ..... 5.95
❑3, Aug 2003 ..... 5.95
❑4, Sep 2003 ..... 5.95
❑5, Nov 2003 ..... 5.95
❑6, Dec 2003 ..... 5.95

TERRAFORMERS
WONDER COLOR

❑1, Apr 1987 ..... 1.95
❑2 1987 ..... 1.95

N-MINT

TERRANAUTS
Fantasy General
❑1, ca. 1986 ..... 1.75

TERRA OBSCURA
DC / America's Best Comics
❑1, Aug 2003 ..... 2.95
❑2, Sep 2003 ..... 2.95
❑3, Oct 2003 ..... 2.95
❑4, Dec 2003 ..... 2.95
❑5, Jan 2004 ..... 2.95
❑6, Feb 2004 ..... 3.95

TERRARISTS
Marvel / Epic
❑1, Nov 1993 ..... 2.50
❑2, Dec 1993 ..... 2.50
❑3, Jan 1994 ..... 2.50
❑4, Feb 1994 ..... 2.50

TERRITORY, THE
Dark Horse
❑1, Jan 1999 ..... 2.95
❑2, Feb 1999 ..... 2.95
❑3, Mar 1999 ..... 2.95
❑4, Apr 1999 ..... 2.95

TERROR, THE
Leadslinger
❑1, b&w 2.50

TERRORESS
Helpless Anger
❑1, Dec 1990, b&w 2.50

TERROR, INC.
Marvel
❑1, Jul 1992 1: Terror. 2.00
❑2, Aug 1992 1: Hellfire. 1.75
❑3, Sep 1992 ..... 1.75
❑4, Oct 1992 ..... 1.75
❑5, Nov 1992 ..... 1.75
❑6, Dec 1992 A: Punisher. 1.75
❑7, Jan 1993 A: Punisher. 1.75
❑8, Feb 1993 ..... 1.75
❑9, Mar 1993 A: Wolverine. 1.75
❑10, Apr 1993 A: Wolverine. 1.75
❑11, May 1993 A: Punisher. A: Silver Sable. 1.75
❑12, Jun 1993 ..... 1.75
❑13, Jul 1993 A: Ghost Rider. 1.75

TERROR ON THE PLANET OF THE APES
Adventure
❑1 1991, b&w 2.50
❑2 1991, b&w 2.50
❑3, Aug 1991, b&w; reprints Planet of the Apes (Marvel) #3 ..... 2.50
❑4, Dec 1991, b&w; reprints Planet of the Apes (Marvel) #4 ..... 2.50

TERROR TALES
Eternity
❑1, b&w 2.50

TERRY AND THE PIRATES (AVALON)
Avalon
❑1, b&w; strip reprints 2.95
❑2 ..... 2.95

TERRY AND THE PIRATES (FEUCHTWANGER)
Sig. Feuchtwanger
❑1 ..... 25.00

TEST DIRT
Fantagraphics
❑1, b&w 2.50

TEST DRIVE
M.A.I.N.
❑1; Flip Book Previews (Side A & B) 3.00

TEX BENSON (3-D ZONE)
3-D Zone
❑1; b&w (not 3-D) 2.50
❑2; b&w (not 3-D) 2.50

TEX BENSON (METRO)
Metro
❑1, b&w 2.00
❑2 ..... 2.00
❑3 ..... 2.00
❑4 ..... 2.00

TEYKWA
Gemstone
❑1, Oct 1988, b&w 1.75

THACKER'S REVENGE
Explorer
❑1, b&w; Archie parody 2.95

THANE OF BAGARTH
Avalon
❑1 ..... 2.95

THANOS
Marvel
❑1, Dec 2003, JSn (c); JSn (w); AM, JSn (a) 2.99
❑2, Jan 2004, JSn (w); AM, JSn (a) .. 2.99
❑3, Feb 2004, JSn (w); AM, JSn (a) .. 2.99
❑4, Mar 2004, JSn (w); AM, JSn (a) . 2.99
❑5, Mar 2004 ..... 2.99
❑6, Apr 2004 ..... 2.99
❑7, May 2004, AM, JSn (c); KG (w); AM (a) 2.99
❑8, May 2004, KG (c); KG (w); AM (a) 2.99
❑9, Jun 2004, KG, KJ (c); KG (w); AM (a) 2.99
❑10, Jul 2004, KG, KJ (c); KG (w); AM (a) 2.99
❑11, Aug 2004 ..... 2.99
❑12, Sep 2004 ..... 2.99

THANOS QUEST, THE
Marvel
❑1, Sep 1990; acetate overlay outer cover 4.95
❑1-2, ca. 1991; acetate overlay outer cover 4.95
❑2, Oct 1990; acetate overlay outer cover 4.95
❑2-2, ca. 1991 ..... 4.95
❑Special 1, ca. 1999, Collects issues #1 and #2 ..... 3.99

THAT CHEMICAL REFLEX
CFD
❑1 ..... 2.50
❑2 ..... 2.50
❑3 ..... 2.50

THB
Horse
❑1, Oct 1994, b&w 12.00
❑1-2, b&w; reprints THB #1 with revised and additional material 5.50
❑2, ca. 1994, b&w 10.00
❑3, Jan 1995, b&w 8.00
❑4, Feb 1995, b&w 8.00
❑5, Mar 1995, b&w 6.00
❑6 1996 ..... 6.00
❑69, Oct 1994, b&w; promo edition; no cover price 5.00

T.H.E. CAT
Gold Key
❑1, Mar 1967 ..... 12.00
❑2, Apr 1967 ..... 10.00
❑3, Jun 1967 ..... 10.00
❑4, Oct 1967 ..... 10.00

THE COMET MAN
Marvel
❑1, Feb 1987 ..... 1.00
❑2, Mar 1987 ..... 1.00
❑3, Apr 1987 ..... 1.00
❑4, May 1987 ..... 1.00
❑5, Jun 1987 ..... 1.00
❑6, Jul 1987 ..... 1.00

THECOMICSTORE.COM PRESENTS
TheComicStore.com
❑1 ..... 1.00

THE LAST TRAIN TO DEADSVILLE: A CAL MCDONALD MYSTERY
Dark Horse
❑1, May 2004 ..... 2.99
❑2, Jun 2004 ..... 2.99
❑3, Jul 2004 ..... 2.99

THE MOTH (STEVE RUDE'S)
Dark Horse
❑1, Apr 2004 ..... 2.99
❑2, May 2004 ..... 2.99
❑3, Aug 2004 ..... 2.99

THE MOTH (STEVE RUDE'S) DOUBLE-SIZED SPECIAL
Dark Horse
❑1, May 2004 ..... 4.95

THERE'S A MADMAN IN MY MIRROR
Bench
❑1, Mar 1999; cardstock cover 3.50

THESPIAN
Dark Moon
❑1, Apr 1995 ..... 2.50

THEY CALL ME...THE SKUL
Virtual
❑1, May 1996; digest; Only issue published 2.50
❑1/A, Oct 1996; digest 3.99
❑2, Nov 1996 ..... 2.50

THEY WERE 11
Viz
❑1, b&w 2.75
❑2, b&w 2.75
❑3, b&w 2.75
❑4, b&w 2.75

THEY WERE CHOSEN TO BE THE SURVIVORS
Spectrum
❑1, Jun 1983 ..... 2.00
❑2, Sep 1983 ..... 2.00
❑3, Dec 1983 ..... 2.00
❑4, Mar 1984 ..... 2.00

THIEF
Penguin Palace
❑1, Jul 1995, b&w 2.50

THIEF OF SHERWOOD
A-Plus
❑1, b&w 2.25

THIEVES
Silverwolf
❑1, Feb 1986, b&w 1.50

THIEVES & KINGS
I Box
❑1, Sep 1994 ..... 4.00
❑1-2 ..... 2.50
❑2, Nov 1994 ..... 3.00
❑2-2 ..... 2.50
❑3, Jan 1995 ..... 3.00
❑3-2 ..... 2.35
❑4, Mar 1995 ..... 3.00
❑5, May 1995 ..... 3.00
❑6, Jul 1995 ..... 2.75
❑7, Sep 1995 ..... 2.75
❑8, Nov 1995 ..... 2.75
❑9, Jan 1996 ..... 2.75
❑10, Mar 1996 ..... 2.75
❑11, May 1996 ..... 2.50
❑12, Jul 1996 ..... 2.50
❑13, Sep 1996 ..... 2.50
❑14, Nov 1996 ..... 2.50
❑15, Jan 1997 ..... 2.50
❑16, Mar 1997 ..... 2.50
❑17, May 1997 ..... 2.50
❑18, ca. 1997 ..... 2.50
❑19, ca. 1997 ..... 2.50
❑20 ..... 2.50
❑21, ca. 1998 ..... 2.35
❑22, May 1998 ..... 2.35
❑23, Jul 1998 ..... 2.35
❑24, Sep 1998 ..... 2.35

N-MINT

❑25, Nov 1998 ... 2.50
❑26, Jan 1999 ... 2.50
❑27, Mar 1999 ... 2.50
❑28, Jul 1999 ... 2.50
❑29, Oct 1999 ... 2.50
❑30 ... 2.50
❑31, Mar 2000 ... 2.50
❑32, May 2000 ... 2.50
❑33, Aug 2000 ... 2.50
❑34, Nov 2000 ... 2.50
❑35, Feb 2001 ... 2.50
❑36, Jul 2001 ... 2.50

THING FROM ANOTHER WORLD, THE
DARK HORSE

❑1, ca. 1993; cardstock cover ... 2.95
❑2, ca. 1993; cardstock cover ... 2.95
❑3 ... 2.99
❑4 ... 2.99

THING FROM ANOTHER WORLD: CLIMATE OF FEAR
DARK HORSE

❑1, ca. 1994 ... 2.50
❑2, ca. 1994 ... 2.50
❑3, ca. 1994 ... 2.50
❑4, ca. 1994 ... 2.50

THING FROM ANOTHER WORLD, THE: ETERNAL VOWS
DARK HORSE

❑1, Dec 1993 ... 2.50
❑2, Jan 1994 ... 2.50
❑3, Feb 1994 ... 2.50
❑4, Mar 1994 ... 2.50

THING/SHE-HULK: THE LONG NIGHT
MARVEL

❑1, May 2002, b&w and color; Man atop demons on cover ... 2.99

THING, THE
MARVEL

❑1, Jul 1983 JBy (w); JBy (a); O: The Thing. ... 2.00
❑2, Aug 1983 JBy (w); JBy (a); O: The Thing. ... 1.50
❑3, Sep 1983 JBy (w); A: Inhumans. ... 1.50
❑4, Oct 1983 BA (c); JBy (w); BA (a); A: Inhumans. ... 1.50
❑5, Nov 1983 JBy (w); A: She-Hulk. A: Spider-Man. ... 1.50
❑6, Dec 1983; BA (c); JBy (w); BA (a); V: Puppet Master. all-black issue ... 1.50
❑7, Jan 1984; BA (c); BA (a); Asst. Editor Month ... 1.50
❑8, Feb 1984 JBy (w) ... 1.50
❑9, Mar 1984 JBy (w) ... 1.50
❑10, Apr 1984; JBy (w); Secret Wars ... 1.50
❑11, May 1984; JBy (w); Secret Wars aftermath ... 1.25
❑12, Jun 1984 JBy (w) ... 1.25
❑13, Jul 1984 JBy (w) ... 1.25
❑14, Aug 1984 ... 1.25
❑15, Sep 1984 ... 1.25
❑16, Oct 1984 ... 1.25
❑17, Nov 1984 ... 1.25
❑18, Dec 1984 ... 1.25
❑19, Jan 1985 JBy (w) ... 1.25
❑20, Feb 1985 JBy (w) ... 1.25
❑21, Mar 1985 JBy (w) ... 1.25
❑22, Apr 1985; returns to Earth ... 1.25
❑23, May 1985; quits Fantastic Four . 1.25
❑24, Jun 1985 D: Miracle Man (Marvel). V: Rhino. ... 1.25
❑25, Jul 1985 ... 1.25
❑26, Aug 1985 V: Taskmaster. ... 1.25
❑27, Sep 1985 ... 1.25
❑28, Oct 1985 1: Demolition Dunphy (later becomes D-Man). ... 1.25
❑29, Nov 1985 ... 1.25
❑30, Dec 1985; Secret Wars II ... 1.25
❑31, Jan 1986 ... 1.25
❑32, Feb 1986 ... 1.25
❑33, Mar 1986 D: Titania. ... 1.25
❑34, Apr 1986 D: The Sphinx. ... 1.25

N-MINT

❑35, May 1986 ... 1.25
❑36, Jun 1986 ... 1.25

3RD DEGREE, THE
NBM

❑1 ... 2.95

THIRD EYE (DARK ONE'S...)
SIRIUS

❑1 1998; prestige format; pin-ups ... 4.95
❑2, Dec 1998; pin-ups and stories; cardstock cover ... 4.95

THIRD WORLD WAR
FLEETWAY-QUALITY

❑1 ... 2.50
❑2 ... 2.50
❑3 ... 2.50
❑4 ... 2.50
❑5 ... 2.50
❑6 ... 2.50

13: ASSASSIN COMICS MODULE
TSR

❑1 ... 2.00
❑2 ... 2.00
❑3 ... 2.00
❑4 ... 2.00
❑5 ... 2.00
❑6 ... 2.00
❑7 ... 2.00
❑8 ... 2.00

13 DAYS OF CHRISTMAS, THE: A TALE OF THE LOST LUNAR BESTIARY
SIRIUS

❑1, b&w; wraparound cover ... 2.95

THIRTEEN O'CLOCK
DARK HORSE

❑1, b&w ... 2.95

THIRTEEN SOMETHING!
GLOBAL

❑1 ... 1.95

30 DAYS OF NIGHT
IDEA & DESIGN WORKS

❑1, Jun 2002 ... 65.00
❑1-2, Aug 2002 ... 15.00
❑2, Aug 2002 ... 35.00
❑3, Oct 2002 ... 10.00

30 DAYS OF NIGHT: RETURN TO BARROW
IDEA & DESIGN WORKS

❑1, ca. 2004 ... 12.00
❑2, ca. 2004 ... 8.00
❑3, ca. 2004 ... 5.00

39 SCREAMS, THE
THUNDER BAAS

❑1, ca. 1986 ... 2.00
❑2, ca. 1986 ... 2.00
❑3, ca. 1986 ... 2.00
❑4, ca. 1986 ... 2.00
❑5, ca. 1987 ... 2.00
❑6, ca. 1987 ... 2.00

32 PAGES
SIRIUS

❑1, Jan 2001 ... 2.95

THIS IS HEAT
AEON

❑1, b&w ... 2.50

THIS IS NOT AN EXIT
DRACULINA

❑1 ... 2.95
❑2 ... 2.95

THIS IS SICK!
SILVER SKULL

❑1, b&w; Zen; foil cover ... 2.95
❑2 ... 2.95

Thor picked up its numbering from *Journey into Mystery.*

© 1966 Marvel Comics

N-MINT

THOR
MARVEL

❑126, Mar 1966; SL (w); JK (a); V: Hercules. Series continued from Journey Into Mystery (Vol. 1) #125 ... 125.00
❑127, Apr 1966 SL (w); JK (a); 1: Volla. 1: Midgard Serpent. 1: Pluto. ... 45.00
❑128, May 1966 SL (w); JK (a) ... 45.00
❑129, Jun 1966 SL (w); JK (a); 1: Ares. 1: Hela. 1: Tana Nile (disguised). ... 45.00
❑130, Jul 1966 SL (w); JK (a); 1: Tana Nile (in real form). ... 45.00
❑131, Aug 1966 SL (w); JK (a) ... 45.00
❑132, Sep 1966 SL (w); JK (a); 1: Recorder. 1: Ego. V: Ego, the Living Planet. ... 45.00
❑133, Oct 1966 SL (w); JK (a) ... 45.00
❑134, Nov 1966 SL (w); JK (a); O: Man-Beast. 1: Man-Beast. 1: High Evolutionary. ... 45.00
❑135, Dec 1966 SL (w); JK (a); O: High Evolutionary. ... 45.00
❑136, Jan 1967; SL (w); JK (a); 1: Sif. Jane Foster denied immortality ... 45.00
❑137, Feb 1967 SL (w); JK (a); 1: Ulik. 45.00
❑138, Mar 1967 SL (w); JK (a) ... 45.00
❑139, Apr 1967 SL (w); JK (a) ... 45.00
❑140, May 1967 SL (w); JK (a); 1: Growing Man. V: Growing Man. ... 45.00
❑141, Jun 1967 SL (w); JK (a) ... 32.00
❑142, Jul 1967 SL (w); JK (a) ... 32.00
❑143, Aug 1967 SL (w); BEv, JK (a) .. 32.00
❑144, Sep 1967 SL (w); JK (a) ... 32.00
❑145, Oct 1967; SL (w); JK (a); Tales of Asgard back-up story ... 32.00
❑146, Oct 1967; SL (w); JK (a); O: Inhumans. A: Ringmaster. A: Circus of Crime. Origins of the Inhumans backup story ... 32.00
❑147, Dec 1967; SL (w); JK (a); O: Inhumans. Origins of the Inhumans backup story ... 32.00
❑148, Jan 1968; SL (w); JK (a); O: The Wrecker III. O: Black Bolt. 1: The Wrecker III. Origins of the Inhumans backup story ... 32.00
❑149, Feb 1968; SL (w); JK (a); O: Maximus. O: Medusa. O: Black Bolt. Origins of the Inhumans backup story 32.00
❑150, Mar 1968; SL (w); JK (a); A: Inhumans. Origins of the Inhumans backup story ... 32.00
❑151, Apr 1968; SL (w); JK (a); A: Inhumans. Origins of the Inhumans backup story ... 32.00
❑152, May 1968; SL (w); JK (a); Origins of the Inhumans backup story ... 32.00
❑153, Jun 1968 SL (w); JK (a) ... 32.00
❑154, Jul 1968 SL (w); JK (a); V: Mangog. ... 32.00
❑155, Aug 1968 SL (w); JK (a) ... 32.00
❑156, Sep 1968 SL (w); JK (a) ... 32.00
❑157, Oct 1968 SL (w); JK (a) ... 32.00
❑158, Nov 1968 SL (w); JK (a); O: Don Blake. O: Thor. ... 32.00
❑159, Dec 1968 JK (a) ... 32.00
❑160, Jan 1969; JK (a); V: Galactus. Galactus ... 32.00
❑161, Feb 1969 JK (a); V: Galactus. .. 25.00
❑162, Mar 1969 JK (a); O: Galactus. . 25.00
❑163, Apr 1969 JK (a) ... 25.00
❑164, May 1969 JK (a) ... 25.00

Condition price index: Multiply "NM prices" above by: **0.83 for Very Fine/Near Mint**
0.66 for Very Fine • 0.33 for Fine • 0.2 for Very Good • 0.125 for Good

	N-MINT
❑165, Jun 1969; JK (a); A: Him (Warlock). Warlock	40.00
❑166, Jul 1969 JK (a); A: Him (Warlock).	36.00
❑167, Aug 1969 JK (a); A: Sif.	24.00
❑168, Sep 1969 JK (a); O: Galactus.	36.00
❑169, Oct 1969; JK (a); O: Galactus. Origin of Galactus	36.00
❑170, Nov 1969 BEv, JK (a)	20.00
❑171, Dec 1969 BEv, JK (a)	20.00
❑172, Jan 1970 BEv, JK (a)	20.00
❑173, Feb 1970 BEv, JK (a)	20.00
❑174, Mar 1970 BEv, JK (a)	20.00
❑175, Apr 1970 BEv, JK (a)	20.00
❑176, May 1970 BEv (c); BEv, JK (a); V: Surtur the Fire Demon.	20.00
❑177, Jun 1970	20.00
❑178, Jul 1970	18.00
❑179, Aug 1970	18.00
❑180, Sep 1970 NA (a); V: Mephisto.	24.00
❑181, Oct 1970 NA (a); V: Mephisto. V: Loki.	23.00
❑182, Nov 1970	12.00
❑183, Dec 1970	12.00
❑184, Jan 1971 1: Infinity (as force).	12.00
❑185, Feb 1971	12.00
❑186, Mar 1971	12.00
❑187, Apr 1971	12.00
❑188, May 1971	12.00
❑189, Jun 1971	12.00
❑190, Jul 1971	12.00
❑191, Aug 1971	12.00
❑192, Sep 1971	12.00
❑193, Oct 1971 JB, SB (a); A: Silver Surfer.	55.00
❑194, Nov 1971	12.00
❑195, Dec 1971	12.00
❑196, Jan 1972	12.00
❑197, Feb 1972	12.00
❑198, Mar 1972	12.00
❑199, Apr 1972	12.00
❑200, Jun 1972; JB (a); Ragnarok	16.00
❑201, Jul 1972 JB (a)	9.00
❑202, Aug 1972 JB (a)	9.00
❑203, Sep 1972 JB (a)	9.00
❑204, Oct 1972 JB (a)	9.00
❑205, Nov 1972 JB (a)	9.00
❑206, Dec 1972 JB (a)	7.00
❑207, Jan 1973 JB (a)	7.00
❑208, Feb 1973 JB (a)	7.00
❑209, Mar 1973 JB (a); 1: Ultimus.	7.00
❑210, Apr 1973 JB (a)	7.00
❑211, May 1973 JB (a)	7.00
❑212, Jun 1973 JB (a)	7.00
❑213, Jul 1973 JB (a)	7.00
❑214, Aug 1973	7.00
❑215, Sep 1973	7.00
❑216, Oct 1973	7.00
❑217, Nov 1973	7.00
❑218, Dec 1973	7.00
❑219, Jan 1974	7.00
❑220, Feb 1974	7.00
❑221, Mar 1974; Marvel Value Stamp #1: Spider-Man	7.00
❑222, Apr 1974; Marvel Value Stamp #41: Gladiator	7.00
❑223, May 1974; Marvel Value Stamp #12: Daredevil	7.00
❑224, Jun 1974; Marvel Value Stamp #87: J. Jonah Jameson	7.00
❑225, Jul 1974; 1: Firelord. Marvel Value Stamp #17: Black Bolt	14.00
❑226, Aug 1974; Marvel Value Stamp #58: Mandarin	7.00
❑227, Sep 1974; Marvel Value Stamp #76: Dormammu	5.00
❑228, Oct 1974; Marvel Value Stamp #40: Loki	5.00
❑229, Nov 1974; Marvel Value Stamp #80: Ghost Rider	5.00
❑230, Dec 1974	5.00
❑231, Jan 1975; Marvel Value Stamp #83: Dragon Man	5.00
❑232, Feb 1975; Marvel Value Stamp #85: Lilith	5.00

	N-MINT
❑233, Mar 1975	5.00
❑234, Apr 1975	5.00
❑235, May 1975; 1: The Possessor. Marvel Value Stamp #23: Sgt. Fury	5.00
❑236, Jun 1975	5.00
❑237, Jul 1975; Marvel Value Stamp #18: Volstagg	5.00
❑238, Aug 1975; JB, JSt (a); Marvel Value Stamp #94: Electro	5.00
❑239, Sep 1975 1: Osiris. 1: Horus.	5.00
❑240, Oct 1975 1: Isis (Marvel). 1: Seth.	5.00
❑241, Nov 1975 JB (a)	5.00
❑242, Dec 1975 JB (a)	5.00
❑243, Jan 1976 JB (a)	5.00
❑244, Feb 1976 JB (a)	5.00
❑245, Mar 1976 JB (a)	5.00
❑246, Apr 1976 JB (a); A: Firelord.	5.00
❑246/30 cent, Apr 1976; 30 cent regional price variant	20.00
❑247, May 1976 JB (a); A: Firelord.	5.00
❑247/30 cent, May 1976; 30 cent regional price variant	20.00
❑248, Jun 1976 JB (a)	5.00
❑248/30 cent, Jun 1976; 30 cent regional price variant	20.00
❑249, Jul 1976; JB (a); Sif trades places with Jane	5.00
❑249/30 cent, Jul 1976; 30 cent regional price variant	5.00
❑250, Aug 1976 JB (a)	5.00
❑250/30 cent, Aug 1976; 30 cent regional price variant	5.00
❑251, Sep 1976	5.00
❑252, Oct 1976	5.00
❑253, Nov 1976	5.00
❑254, Dec 1976; Reprints Thor #159	5.00
❑255, Jan 1977	5.00
❑256, Feb 1977	5.00
❑257, Mar 1977	5.00
❑258, Apr 1977	5.00
❑259, May 1977	5.00
❑260, Jun 1977	5.00
❑260/35 cent, Jun 1977; 35 cent regional price variant	15.00
❑261, Jul 1977	5.00
❑261/35 cent, Jul 1977; 35 cent regional price variant	15.00
❑262, Aug 1977 TD (a)	5.00
❑262/35 cent, Aug 1977; TD (a); 35 cent regional price variant	15.00
❑263, Sep 1977	5.00
❑263/35 cent, Sep 1977; 35 cent regional price variant	15.00
❑264, Oct 1977	5.00
❑264/35 cent, Oct 1977; 35 cent regional price variant	15.00
❑265, Nov 1977	2.50
❑266, Dec 1977	2.50
❑267, Jan 1978	2.50
❑268, Feb 1978	2.50
❑269, Mar 1978	2.50
❑270, Apr 1978	2.50
❑271, May 1978 A: Iron Man.	2.50
❑272, Jun 1978 JB (a)	2.50
❑273, Jul 1978 1: Red Norvell.	2.50
❑274, Aug 1978 1: Sigyn. 1: Frigga. D: Balder.	2.50
❑275, Sep 1978 1: Hermod.	2.50
❑276, Oct 1978; Red Norvell named Thor	2.50
❑277, Nov 1978	2.50
❑278, Dec 1978	2.50
❑279, Jan 1979	2.50
❑280, Feb 1979	2.50
❑281, Mar 1979 A: Immortus.	3.00
❑282, Apr 1979	3.00
❑283, May 1979 A: Celestials.	3.00
❑284, Jun 1979 A: Externals.	3.00
❑285, Jul 1979	3.00
❑286, Aug 1979	3.00
❑287, Sep 1979	3.00
❑288, Oct 1979	3.00
❑289, Nov 1979	3.00
❑290, Dec 1979 V: El Toro Rojo.	3.00

	N-MINT
❑291, Jan 1980	3.00
❑292, Feb 1980	3.00
❑293, Mar 1980	3.00
❑294, Apr 1980 KP (a); O: Asgard. O: Odin. 1: Frey.	3.00
❑295, May 1980 KP (a)	3.00
❑296, Jun 1980 KP (a)	3.00
❑297, Jul 1980; KP (a); Thor as Siegfried	3.00
❑298, Aug 1980 KP (a)	3.00
❑299, Sep 1980 KP (a)	3.00
❑300, Oct 1980; KP (a); O: The Destroyer. O: Odin. D: Zuras (physical death). giant; Balder revived	8.00
❑301, Nov 1980; Thor meets other pantheons	2.00
❑302, Dec 1980	2.00
❑303, Jan 1981	2.00
❑304, Feb 1981 V: Wrecking Crew.	2.00
❑305, Mar 1981 KP (a)	2.00
❑306, Apr 1981 KP (a); O: Firelord. 1: Air-Walker (real form). D: Air-Walker (real form).	2.00
❑307, May 1981	2.00
❑308, Jun 1981 KP (a)	2.00
❑309, Jul 1981	2.00
❑310, Aug 1981 V: Mephisto.	2.00
❑311, Sep 1981	2.00
❑312, Oct 1981 KP (a); V: Tyr.	2.00
❑313, Nov 1981	2.00
❑314, Dec 1981 KP (a); 1: Shawna Lynde.	2.00
❑315, Jan 1982 KP (a)	2.00
❑316, Feb 1982	2.00
❑317, Mar 1982 KP (a)	2.00
❑318, Apr 1982 GK (a)	2.00
❑319, May 1982 KP (a)	2.00
❑320, Jun 1982 KP (a)	2.00
❑321, Jul 1982	2.00
❑322, Aug 1982 D: Darkoth.	2.00
❑323, Sep 1982	2.00
❑324, Oct 1982	2.00
❑325, Nov 1982	2.00
❑326, Dec 1982 BA (c); BA (a)	2.00
❑327, Jan 1983	2.00
❑328, Feb 1983 1: Megatak.	2.00
❑329, Mar 1983	2.00
❑330, Apr 1983 BH (c); BH (w); BH (a); O: Crusader II (Arthur Blackwood). 1: Crusader II (Arthur Blackwood).	2.00
❑331, May 1983 BH (c); BH (w); BH (a)	2.00
❑332, Jun 1983	2.00
❑333, Jul 1983 V: Dracula.	2.00
❑334, Aug 1983	2.00
❑335, Sep 1983 1: The Possessor.	2.00
❑336, Oct 1983 HT (a)	2.00
❑337, Nov 1983; O: Beta Ray Bill. 1: Beta Ray Bill. 1st Simonson Thor	7.00
❑338, Dec 1983 A: Beta Ray Bill.	3.00
❑339, Jan 1984 1: Lorelei. A: Beta Ray Bill.	4.00
❑340, Feb 1984 A: Beta Ray Bill.	2.50
❑341, Mar 1984 1: Sigurd Jarlson.	2.00
❑342, Apr 1984	2.00
❑343, May 1984	2.00
❑344, Jun 1984 1: Malekith the Dark Elf.	2.00
❑345, Jul 1984	2.00
❑346, Aug 1984	2.00
❑347, Sep 1984 1: Algrim.	2.00
❑348, Oct 1984	2.00
❑349, Nov 1984 O: Odin.	2.00
❑350, Dec 1984 A: Beta Ray Bill.	2.00
❑351, Jan 1985 A: Fantastic Four.	2.00
❑352, Feb 1985 A: Fantastic Four. A: Beta Ray Bill. A: Avengers.	2.00
❑353, Mar 1985	2.00
❑354, Apr 1985	2.00
❑355, May 1985	2.00
❑356, Jun 1985	2.00
❑357, Jul 1985	2.00
❑358, Aug 1985; Beta Ray Bill vs. Titanium Man	2.00
❑359, Sep 1985 A: Loki. D: Megatak.	2.00
❑360, Oct 1985	2.00
❑361, Nov 1985	2.00

	N-MINT
❑362, Dec 1985	2.00
❑363, Jan 1986; Secret Wars II; Thor's face scarred	2.00
❑364, Feb 1986	2.00
❑365, Mar 1986; Thor turned into frog	2.00
❑366, Apr 1986	2.00
❑367, May 1986	2.00
❑368, Jun 1986	2.00
❑369, Jul 1986	2.00
❑370, Aug 1986	2.00
❑371, Sep 1986 A: Justice Peace.	2.00
❑372, Oct 1986	2.00
❑373, Nov 1986; Mutant Massacre	2.00
❑374, Dec 1986; A: X-Factor. Mutant Massacre	3.00
❑375, Jan 1987	2.00
❑376, Feb 1987	2.00
❑377, Mar 1987	2.00
❑378, Apr 1987	2.00
❑379, May 1987	2.00
❑380, Jun 1987	2.00
❑381, Jul 1987	1.50
❑382, Aug 1987; 300th Thor issue	2.00
❑383, Sep 1987; Secret Wars II	1.50
❑384, Oct 1987 1: Dargo (future Thor).	1.50
❑385, Nov 1987 A: Hulk.	1.50
❑386, Dec 1987 1: Leir.	1.50
❑387, Jan 1988	1.50
❑388, Feb 1988	1.50
❑389, Mar 1988	1.50
❑390, Apr 1988	1.50
❑391, May 1988 1: Eric Masterson. A: Spider-Man.	2.00
❑392, Jun 1988 1: Quicksand.	1.50
❑393, Jul 1988	1.50
❑394, Aug 1988 BH (a)	1.50
❑395, Sep 1988 O: Earth-Lord. O: Wind Warrior. 1: Earth-Lord. 1: Wind Warrior.	1.50
❑396, Oct 1988	1.50
❑397, Nov 1988	1.50
❑398, Dec 1988 1: Caber.	1.50
❑399, Jan 1989	1.50
❑400, Feb 1989; A: Avengers. V: Seth and Surtur. giant	2.00
❑401, Mar 1989	1.00
❑402, Apr 1989	1.00
❑403, May 1989	1.00
❑404, Jun 1989	1.00
❑405, Jul 1989	1.00
❑406, Aug 1989	1.00
❑407, Sep 1989	1.00
❑408, Oct 1989; Eric Masterson absorbs Thor's essence; series continues as The Mighty Thor through #490	1.00
❑409, Nov 1989; Title changes to The Mighty Thor	1.00
❑410, Nov 1989	1.00
❑411, Dec 1989; 1: Night Thrasher. 1: New Warriors (cameo appearance). 1: Chord. V: Juggernaut. Acts of Vengeance	3.00
❑412, Dec 1989; 1: New Warriors (full appearance). V: Juggernaut. Acts of Vengeance	2.00
❑413, Jan 1990	1.00
❑414, Feb 1990	1.00
❑415, Mar 1990 O: Thor.	1.00
❑416, Apr 1990	1.00
❑417, May 1990	1.00
❑418, Jun 1990	1.00
❑419, Jul 1990 O: Stellaris. 1: Stellaris. 1: Black Galaxy.	1.00
❑420, Aug 1990 O: Nobilus. 1: Nobilus (partial appearance).	1.00
❑421, Aug 1990	1.00
❑422, Sep 1990 O: Nobilus. 1: Analyzer.	1.00
❑423, Sep 1990 1: Nobilus (full appearance).	1.00
❑424, Oct 1990	1.00
❑425, Oct 1990	1.00
❑426, Nov 1990	1.00
❑427, Dec 1990 A: Excalibur.	1.00
❑428, Jan 1991 A: Excalibur.	1.00

	N-MINT
❑429, Feb 1991 A: Ghost Rider.	1.00
❑430, Mar 1991 AM (a); A: Ghost Rider.	1.00
❑431, Apr 1991	1.00
❑432, May 1991; Giant size AM, JK (a); O: Thor. 1: Thor II (Eric Masterson). 1: Thor. A: 300th. D: Loki.	2.00
❑433, Jun 1991 AM (a)	2.00
❑434, Jul 1991 AM (a)	1.00
❑435, Aug 1991	1.00
❑436, Sep 1991	1.00
❑437, Oct 1991 AM (a)	1.00
❑438, Nov 1991 AM (a); V: Zarrko.	1.00
❑439, Nov 1991 AM (a)	1.00
❑440, Dec 1991 AM (a); 1: Thor Corps (Dargo, Beta Ray Bill, Eric Masterson).	1.00
❑441, Dec 1991 AM (a)	1.00
❑442, Jan 1992; AM (a); Return of Don Blake	1.00
❑443, Jan 1992 AM (a); A: Doctor Strange. A: Silver Surfer. V: Mephisto.	1.00
❑444, Feb 1992 AM (a)	1.25
❑445, Mar 1992; V: Gladiator. Galactic Storm	1.25
❑446, Apr 1992; A: Avengers. Galactic Storm	1.25
❑447, May 1992 AM (a); A: Spider-Man. A: Absorbing Man.	1.25
❑448, Jun 1992 AM (a); A: Spider-Man.	1.25
❑449, Jul 1992 AM (a); O: Bloodaxe. 1: Bloodaxe.	1.25
❑450, Aug 1992; Giant-size anniversary special AM (a); O: Loki.	2.50
❑451, Sep 1992 AM (a); V: Bloodaxe.	1.25
❑452, Oct 1992	1.25
❑453, Nov 1992 AM (a)	1.25
❑454, Nov 1992 AM (a)	1.25
❑455, Dec 1992 AM (a)	1.25
❑456, Dec 1992 AM (a)	1.25
❑457, Jan 1993; Original Thor returns	1.25
❑458, Jan 1993	1.25
❑459, Feb 1993 AM (a)	1.25
❑460, Mar 1993; JSn (w); Painted cover	1.25
❑461, Apr 1993	1.25
❑462, May 1993	1.25
❑463, Jun 1993; Infinity Crusade Crossover	1.25
❑464, Jul 1993	1.25
❑465, Aug 1993	1.25
❑466, Sep 1993	1.25
❑467, Oct 1993; A: Lady Sif. A: Valkyrie. A: Pluto. Infinity Crusade crossover	1.25
❑468, Nov 1993	1.25
❑469, Dec 1993	1.25
❑470, Jan 1994	1.25
❑471, Feb 1994	1.25
❑472, Mar 1994	1.25
❑473, Apr 1994	1.25
❑474, May 1994	1.50
❑475, Jun 1994; Giant-size O: Thor.	2.00
❑475/Variant, Jun 1994; Giant-size; O: Thor. foil cover	2.50
❑476, Jul 1994	1.50
❑477, Aug 1994	1.50
❑478, Sep 1994 A: Red Norvell.	1.50
❑479, Oct 1994	1.50
❑480, Nov 1994	1.50
❑481, Dec 1994 V: Grotesk.	1.50
❑482, Jan 1995; Giant-size	2.95
❑483, Feb 1995	1.50
❑484, Mar 1995 A: War Machine.	1.50
❑485, Apr 1995	1.50
❑486, May 1995	1.50
❑487, Jun 1995	1.50
❑488, Jul 1995	1.50
❑489, Aug 1995 V: Hulk.	1.50
❑490, Sep 1995 V: Absorbing Man.	1.50
❑491, Oct 1995; Title returns to Thor	1.50
❑492, Nov 1995 A: Enchantress.	1.50
❑493, Dec 1995 A: Enchantress.	1.50
❑494, Jan 1996	1.50
❑495, Feb 1996	1.50
❑496, Mar 1996 A: Captain America.	1.50

"Tales of Asgard" focused on Thor's supporting cast of Norse gods and goddesses.
© 1967 Marvel Comics.

	N-MINT
❑497, Apr 1996	1.50
❑498, May 1996	1.50
❑499, Jun 1996	1.50
❑500, Jul 1996; Giant-size; wrap-around cover	2.50
❑501, Aug 1996 A: Red Norvell.	1.50
❑502, Sep 1996 O: Thor.	1.50
❑Annual 2, Sep 1966; Cover reads "King Size Special"; SL (w); JK, JSt (a); reprints from Journey into Mystery #96 and #103	65.00
❑Annual 2-2 SL (w); JK, JSt (a)	2.50
❑Annual 3, Jan 1971; JK (a); A: Grey Gargoyle. A: Absorbing Man. reprints Thor stories from Journey into Mystery #113 and #114; reprints Tales of Asgard from Journey into Mystery #107-110	12.00
❑Annual 4, JK (a); Cover reads King Size Special; reprints stories from Thor #131 and 132, and Journey Into Mystery #113	10.00
❑Annual 5, ca. 1976 JB, JK (a); 1: Apollo.	8.00
❑Annual 6, ca. 1977 JB, JK (a)	8.00
❑Annual 7, ca. 1978	7.00
❑Annual 8, ca. 1979	6.00
❑Annual 9, ca. 1981 LMc (a)	3.50
❑Annual 10, ca. 1982 BH (a); O: Chthon. 1: Ahpuch. 1: Erishkegal. 1: Yama.	3.50
❑Annual 11, ca. 1983 BH (a)	3.50
❑Annual 12, ca. 1984 1: Vidar.	3.50
❑Annual 13 V: Mephisto.	3.00
❑Annual 14, ca. 1989; Title changes to The Mighty Thor Annual	2.50
❑Annual 15, ca. 1990 O: Terminus.	2.50
❑Annual 16, ca. 1991; AM, HT (a); O: Thor. 1991 Annual	2.50
❑Annual 17, ca. 1992; Citizen Kang	2.50
❑Annual 18, ca. 1993; trading card	2.95
❑Annual 19, ca. 1994	2.95

THOR (VOL. 2)
MARVEL

	N-MINT
❑1, Jul 1998; Giant-size JR2 (a)	3.50
❑1/A, Jul 1998; gatefold summary; JR2 (a); sketch cover	20.00
❑1/B, Jul 1998; gatefold summary; JR2 (a); Sunburst cover	5.00
❑1/C, Jul 1998; JR2 (a); DFE alternate cover	5.00
❑1/D, Jul 1998; JR2 (a); DFE alternate cover	8.00
❑1/E, Jul 1998; Rough Cut cover	5.00
❑2, Aug 1998; gatefold summary; JR2 (a); Thor receives new mortal identity	2.50
❑2/A, Aug 1998; JR2 (a); variant cover	2.50
❑3, Sep 1998; gatefold summary JR2 (a); V: Sedna.	2.00
❑4, Oct 1998; gatefold summary JR2 (a); A: Namor.	2.00
❑5, Nov 1998; gatefold summary JR2 (a)	2.00
❑6, Dec 1998; gatefold summary JR2 (a); A: Hercules.	2.00
❑7, Jan 1999; gatefold summary JR2 (a); A: Hercules.	2.00
❑8, Feb 1999; gatefold summary; JR2 (a); A: Spider-Man. concludes in Peter Parker; Spider-Man #2	2.00
❑9, Mar 1999 JB (a)	2.00
❑10, Apr 1999 JR2 (a); V: Perrikus.	2.00
❑11, May 1999 A: Volstagg. V: Perrikus.	1.99

N-MINT

❑12, Jun 1999; A: Hercules. A: Destroyer. A: Warriors Three. A: Replicus. V: Perrikus. wraparound cover ... 2.99
❑13, Jul 1999 V: Marnot. ... 1.99
❑14, Aug 1999 A: Iron Man. V: Absorbing Man. ... 1.99
❑15, Sep 1999 A: Warriors Three. ... 1.99
❑16, Oct 1999 ... 1.99
❑17, Nov 1999 ... 1.99
❑18, Dec 1999 ... 1.99
❑19, Jan 2000 ... 1.99
❑20, Feb 2000 ... 2.25
❑21, Mar 2000 ... 2.25
❑22, Apr 2000 ... 2.25
❑23, May 2000 ... 2.25
❑24, Jun 2000 ... 2.25
❑25, Jul 2000 ... 2.25
❑26, Aug 2000 ... 2.25
❑27, Sep 2000 ... 2.25
❑28, Oct 2000 ... 2.25
❑29, Nov 2000 A: Wrecking Crew. ... 2.25
❑30, Dec 2000 A: Malekith. A: Beta Ray Bill. ... 2.25
❑31, Jan 2001 ... 2.25
❑32, Feb 2001 ... 3.50
❑33, Mar 2001 1: Thor Girl. ... 2.25
❑34, Apr 2001 A: Gladiator. ... 2.25
❑35, May 2001 A: Gladiator. ... 2.99
❑36, Jun 2001 ... 2.25
❑37, Jul 2001 ... 2.25
❑38, Aug 2001 ... 2.25
❑39, Sep 2001 ... 2.25
❑40, Oct 2001 ... 2.25
❑41, Nov 2001 ... 2.25
❑42, Dec 2001 ... 2.25
❑43, Jan 2002 ... 2.25
❑44, Feb 2002 ... 2.25
❑45, Mar 2002 ... 2.25
❑46, Apr 2002, wraparound cover ... 2.25
❑47, May 2002, wraparound cover ... 2.25
❑48, Jun 2002, wraparound cover ... 2.25
❑49, Jul 2002, wraparound cover ... 2.25
❑50, Aug 2002, wraparound cover ... 2.25
❑51, Sep 2002, wraparound cover ... 2.25
❑52, Oct 2002, wraparound cover ... 2.25
❑53, Oct 2002, wraparound cover ... 2.25
❑54, Nov 2002, wraparound cover ... 2.25
❑55, Dec 2002, wraparound cover ... 2.25
❑56, Jan 2003, wraparound cover ... 2.25
❑57, Feb 2003, wraparound cover ... 2.25
❑58, Mar 2003, wraparound cover ... 2.25
❑59, Apr 2003 ... 2.25
❑60, May 2003 ... 2.25
❑61, May 2003 ... 2.25
❑62, Jun 2003 ... 2.99
❑63, Jun 2003 ... 2.99
❑64, Jul 2003 ... 2.99
❑65, Aug 2003 ... 2.99
❑66, Sep 2003 ... 2.99
❑67, Oct 2003 ... 2.99
❑68, Nov 2003 ... 2.99
❑69, Nov 2003 ... 2.99
❑70, Dec 2003 ... 2.99
❑71, Jan 2004 ... 2.99
❑72, Feb 2004 ... 2.99
❑73, Mar 2004 ... 2.99
❑74, Apr 2004 ... 2.99
❑75, May 2004 ... 2.99
❑76, May 2004 ... 2.99
❑77, Jun 2004 ... 2.99
❑78, Jul 2004 ... 2.99
❑79, Jul 2004 ... 2.99
❑80, Aug 2004 ... 2.99
❑81, Aug 2004 ... 2.99
❑82, Sep 2004 ...
❑Annual 1999, Mar 1999, V: Doom. set between Heroes Reborn and Heroes Return; wraparound cover ... 3.50
❑Annual 2001, Mar 2001, A: Hercules. A: Beta Ray Bill. wraparound cover ... 3.50

THOR CORPS
MARVEL

❑1, Sep 1993 ... 1.75
❑2, Oct 1993 ... 1.75
❑3, Nov 1993 ... 1.75
❑4, Dec 1993 ... 1.75

THORION OF THE NEW ASGODS
MARVEL / AMALGAM

❑1, Jun 1997 ... 1.95

THORR-SVERD
VINCENT

❑1, b&w ... 1.00
❑2, b&w ... 1.00
❑3, b&w ... 1.00

THOR: SON OF ASGARD
MARVEL

❑1, May 2004 ... 2.99
❑2, May 2004 ... 2.99
❑3, Jun 2004 ... 2.99
❑4, Jul 2004 ... 2.99
❑5, Aug 2004 ... 2.99
❑6, Sep 2004 ... 2.99

THOR: THE LEGEND
MARVEL

❑1, Sep 1996; information on Thor's career and supporting cast; wraparound cover ... 3.95

THOR: VIKINGS
MARVEL

❑1, Sep 2003; cardstock cover ... 3.50
❑2, Oct 2003; cardstock cover ... 3.50
❑3, Nov 2003; cardstock cover ... 3.50
❑4, Dec 2003; cardstock cover ... 3.50
❑5, Jan 2004 ... 3.50

THOSE ANNOYING POST BROS.
VORTEX

❑1 ... 3.00
❑2 ... 2.00
❑3 ... 2.00
❑4 ... 2.00
❑5 ... 2.00
❑6 ... 2.00
❑7 ... 2.00
❑8 ... 2.00
❑9 ... 2.00
❑10 ... 2.00
❑11 ... 2.00
❑12 ... 2.00
❑13 ... 2.00
❑14 ... 2.00
❑15 ... 2.00
❑16 ... 2.00
❑17 ... 2.00
❑18; Series continues as Post Brothers 2.00
❑39, Aug 1994, b&w; Series continued from "Post Brothers" #38 ... 2.50
❑40, Oct 1994, b&w ... 2.50
❑41, Dec 1994, b&w ... 2.50
❑42, Feb 1995, b&w ... 2.50
❑43, Jun 1995, b&w ... 2.50
❑44, Jul 1995, b&w ... 2.50
❑45, Aug 1995, b&w ... 2.50
❑46, Oct 1995, b&w ... 2.50
❑47, Nov 1995, b&w ... 2.50
❑48, Feb 1996, b&w ... 2.50
❑Annual 1, Aug 1995, b&w; cardstock cover ... 4.95

THOSE CRAZY PECKERS
U.S.COMICS

❑1, Feb 1987 ... 2.00

THOSE MAGNIFICENT MEN IN T HEIR FLYING MACHINES
GOLD KEY

❑1, Oct 1965; movie adaptation ... 25.00

THOSE UNSTOPPABLE ROGUES
ORIGINAL SYNDICATE

❑1, Mar 1995 ... 3.95

THOSE WHO HUNT ELVES
ADV MANGA

❑1, ca 2003 ... 9.99

THRAX
EVENT

❑1, Nov 1996 ... 2.95
❑2, Jan 1997 ... 2.95

THREAT!
FANTAGRAPHICS

❑1, Jun 1986, b&w ... 2.25
❑2, Jul 1986, b&w ... 2.25
❑3, Aug 1986, b&w ... 2.25
❑4, Sep 1986, b&w ... 2.25
❑5, Oct 1986, b&w ... 2.25
❑6, Nov 1986, b&w ... 2.25
❑7, Dec 1986, b&w ... 2.25
❑8, Jan 1987, b&w ... 2.25
❑9, May 1987, b&w ... 2.25
❑10, Sep 1987, b&w ... 2.25

THREE
INVINCIBLE

❑1 ... 2.00
❑2 ... 2.00
❑3 ... 2.00
❑4 ... 2.00

3-D ADVENTURE COMICS
STATS ETC.

❑1, Aug 1986 1: Statman. ... 2.00

3-D ALIEN TERROR
ECLIPSE

❑1, Jun 1986 ... 2.50

3-D EXOTIC BEAUTIES
3-D ZONE

❑1, ca. 1990 ... 3.50

3-D HEROES
BLACKTHORNE

❑1; In 3-D, glasses not included ... 2.50

3-D HOLLYWOOD
3-D ZONE

❑1; paper dolls ... 2.95

THREE DIMENSIONAL ADVENTURES
DC

❑1 ... 900.00
❑1-2; Bundled with Superman Red/ Superman Blue ... 5.00

3-D SPACE ZOMBIES
3-D ZONE

❑1 ... 3.95

3-D SUBSTANCE
3-D ZONE

❑1 ... 2.95
❑2 ... 3.95

3-D THREE STOOGES
ECLIPSE

❑1; Stuntgirl backup feature ... 2.50
❑2 ... 2.50
❑3 ... 2.50

3-D TRUE CRIME
3-D ZONE

❑1, ca. 1992 ... 3.95

3-D ZONE, THE
3-D ZONE

❑1, ca. 1986 ... 2.50
❑2, ca. 1986 ... 2.50
❑3, ca. 1987 ... 2.50
❑4, ca. 1987; Electric Fear ... 2.50
❑5, ca. 1987; Krazy Kat ... 2.50
❑6, ca. 1987; Rat Fink ... 2.50
❑7, ca. 1987; Hollywood ... 2.50
❑8, Sep 1987; High Seas ... 2.50
❑9, ca. 1987; Red Mask ... 2.50
❑10, ca. 1987; Jet ... 2.50
❑11, ca. 1987; Matt Fox ... 2.50
❑12, ca. 1987; Presidents ... 2.50
❑13, ca. 1988; Flash Gordon ... 2.50
❑14, ca. 1988; Tyranostar ... 2.50
❑15, ca. 1988; humor ... 2.50
❑16, ca. 1988; space vixens ... 2.50

N-MINT

❑17, ca. 1988; Thrilling Love 2.50
❑18, ca. 1988; ca. 1988; Spacehawk 3-D 2.50
❑19, ca. 1989; Cracked 2.50
❑20, ca. 1989; Atomic Sub 2.50

.357!
Mu

❑1, Jul 1990, b&w 2.50

3 GEEKS, THE
3 Finger Prints

❑1, Sep 1997, b&w 3.00
❑1-2, b&w 2.50
❑2, Oct 1997, b&w 2.50
❑3, Nov 1997, b&w; Brain Boy back-up 2.50
❑4, Jan 1998, b&w; Brain Boy back-up 2.50
❑5, ca. 1998, b&w 2.50
❑6, ca. 1998, b&w 2.50
❑7, ca. 1998, b&w 2.50
❑8, Sep 1998, b&w 3.50
❑9, Feb 1999, b&w; movie night 2.50
❑10, Apr 1999, b&w; Allen's birthday 2.50
❑11, Jun 1999, b&w; Allen's redemption 2.50

300
Dark Horse

❑1, May 1998, FM (w); FM (a) 3.50
❑2, Jun 1998, FM (w); FM (a) 3.50
❑3, Jul 1998, FM (w); FM (a) 3.25
❑4, Aug 1998, FM (w); FM (a) 3.25
❑5, Sep 1998 FM (w); FM (a) 3.95

3 LITTLE KITTENS: PURR-FECT WEAPONS (JIM BALENT'S...)
Broadsword

❑1, Aug 2002; 3 Kittens cover 2.95
❑1/A, Aug 2002; Catress cover 2.95
❑2, Oct 2002; 3 Kittens cover 2.95
❑2/A, Oct 2002; Jaguara cover 2.95
❑3, Dec 2002; 3 Kittens cover 2.95
❑3/A, Dec 2002; Baby Cat cover 2.95

THREE MUSKETEERS (ETERNITY)
Eternity

❑1, Dec 1988, b&w 1.95
❑2, Feb 1989, b&w 1.95
❑3, Apr 1989, b&w 1.95

THREE MUSKETEERS (MARVEL)
Marvel

❑1, Dec 1993 .... 1.50
❑2 .... 1.50

3 NINJAS KICK BACK
Now

❑1, Jun 1994 .... 1.95
❑2 .... 1.95
❑3 .... 1.95

THREE STOOGES IN 3-D
Eternity

❑1 .... 3.95

THREE STOOGES IN FULL COLOR
Eternity

❑1 .... 5.95

THREE STOOGES MEET HERCULES, THE
Dell

❑1, Aug 1962 .... 75.00

3X3 EYES
Innovation

❑1, Sep 1991, b&w; Japanese 2.50
❑2, Oct 1991, b&w; Japanese 2.25
❑3, Nov 1991, b&w; Japanese 2.25
❑4, Dec 1991, b&w; Japanese 2.25
❑5, Jan 1992, b&w; Japanese 2.25

3X3 EYES: CURSE OF THE GESU
Dark Horse / Manga

❑1, Oct 1995, b&w 2.95
❑2, Nov 1995, b&w 2.95
❑3, Dec 1995, b&w 2.95
❑4, Jan 1996, b&w 2.95
❑5, Feb 1996, b&w 2.95

N-MINT

THRESHOLD (1ST SERIES)
Sleeping Giant

❑1, Oct 1996, b&w 2.50
❑2, Nov 1996, b&w 2.50

THRESHOLD (2ND SERIES)
Sleeping Giant

❑1, Dec 1997, b&w 2.50
❑2, Mar 1998, b&w 2.50
❑3 1998 .... 2.50
❑3/Autographed 1998 .... 2.50

THRESHOLD (3RD SERIES)
Avatar

❑1, Feb 1998 .... 4.95
❑2, Mar 1998 .... 4.95
❑3, Apr 1998 .... 4.95
❑4, May 1998 .... 4.95
❑5, Jun 1998 .... 4.95
❑6, Jul 1998 .... 4.95
❑7, Aug 1998 .... 4.95
❑8, Sep 1998 .... 4.95
❑9, Oct 1998 .... 4.95
❑10, Nov 1998 .... 4.95
❑11, Dec 1998 .... 4.95
❑12, Jan 1999 .... 4.95
❑13, Feb 1999 .... 4.95
❑14, Mar 1999 .... 4.95
❑15, Apr 1999 .... 4.95
❑16, May 1999 .... 4.95
❑17, Jun 1999 .... 4.95
❑18, Jul 1999 .... 4.95
❑19, Aug 1999 .... 4.95
❑20, Sep 1999 .... 4.95
❑21, Oct 1999 .... 4.95
❑22, Nov 1999 .... 4.95
❑23, Dec 1999 .... 4.95
❑24, Jan 2000 .... 4.95
❑25, Feb 2000 .... 4.95
❑26, Mar 2000 .... 4.95
❑27, Apr 2000 .... 4.95
❑28, May 2000 .... 4.95
❑29, Jun 2000 .... 4.95
❑30, Jul 2000 .... 4.95
❑31, Aug 2000 .... 4.95
❑32, Sep 2000 .... 4.95
❑33, Oct 2000 .... 4.95
❑34, Nov 2000 .... 4.95
❑35, Dec 2000 .... 4.95
❑36, Jan 2001 .... 4.95
❑37, Feb 2001 .... 4.95
❑38, Mar 2001 .... 4.95
❑39, Apr 2001 .... 4.95
❑40, May 2001 .... 4.95
❑41, Jun 2001 .... 4.95
❑42, Jul 2001 .... 4.95
❑43, Aug 2001 .... 4.95
❑44, Sep 2001 .... 4.95
❑45, Nov 2001 .... 4.95
❑46, Jan 2002 .... 4.95
❑47, Apr 2002 .... 4.95
❑48 .... 4.95
❑49 .... 4.95
❑50, May 2003 .... 4.95

THRESHOLD OF REALITY
Maintech

❑1, Sep 1986 .... 1.00
❑2 .... 1.00
❑3 .... 1.00

THRESHOLD: THE STAMP COLLECTOR
Sleeping Giant

❑1, Mar 1997, b&w 2.50
❑2, May 1997, b&w 2.50

THRILLER
DC

❑1, Nov 1983 TVE (c); TVE (a) 2.00
❑2, Dec 1983 O: Thriller. 1.75
❑3, Jan 1984 .... 1.75
❑4, Feb 1984 .... 1.50
❑5, Mar 1984; Elvis satire 1.50
❑6, Apr 1984; Elvis satire 1.50

Thor and Doctor Doom's adventures between "Heroes Reborn" and "Heroes Return" were chronicled in *Thor Annual 1999.*

N-MINT

❑7, May 1984 .... 1.50
❑8, Jun 1984 .... 1.50
❑9, Jul 1984 .... 1.50
❑10, Aug 1984 .... 1.50
❑11, Sep 1984 .... 1.50
❑12, Oct 1984 .... 1.50

THRILLING ADVENTURE STORIES
Atlas-Seaboard

❑1, Feb 1975, b&w; magazine RH (w); FT, EC, RH (a) 5.00
❑2, Aug 1975 .... 4.00

THRILLING ADVENTURE STRIPS
Dragon Lady

❑5 1986; (formerly Best of Tribune Company) 2.95
❑6 1986 .... 2.95
❑7 1986 .... 2.95
❑8 1987 .... 2.95
❑9, Mar 1987 .... 2.95
❑10 1987 .... 2.95

THRILLING COMICS (2ND SERIES)
DC

❑1, May 1999; RH (a); A: Wildcat. A: Tigress. A: Hawkman. Manhunter apperance 2.00

THRILL KILL
Caliber

❑1, b&w 2.50

THRILLKILLER
DC

❑1, Jan 1997; Elseworlds story 2.50
❑2, Feb 1997; Elseworlds story 2.50
❑3, Mar 1997; Elseworlds story 2.50

THRILLKILLER '62
DC

❑1 1998; prestige format; Elseworlds; sequel to Thrillkiller 4.95

THRILLOGY
Pacific

❑1 .... 1.50

THUMB SCREW
Caliber

❑1, b&w 3.50
❑2, b&w 3.50
❑3, b&w 3.50

THUMP'N GUTS
Kitchen Sink

❑1; Poly-bag reads Project X, includes poster and trading card 2.95

THUN'DA, KING OF THE CONGO
AC

❑1, b&w 2.50

THUN'DA TALES (FRANK FRAZETTA'S...)
Fantagraphics

❑1, ca. 1986 .... 2.00

T.H.U.N.D.E.R.
Solson

❑1 .... 1.95

N-MINT

THUNDER AGENTS
Tower

❑1, Nov 1965 WW (c); WW (a); O: Dynamo. O: The THUNDER Squad. O: Menthor. O: NoMan. 1: Dynamo. 1: Iron Maiden. 1: The THUNDER Squad. 1: Menthor. 1: NoMan. 140.00
❑2, Jan 1966 WW (c); WW (a); 1: Lightning. D: Egghead. 75.00
❑3, Mar 1966 WW (c); WW (a) 55.00
❑4, Apr 1966 WW (a); O: Lightning. .. 55.00
❑5, Jun 1966 WW (a) 55.00
❑6, Jul 1966 WW (a) 42.00
❑7, Aug 1966 SD, WW (a); D: Menthor. 42.00
❑8, Sep 1966 WW (a); O: Raven. 1: Raven. 42.00
❑9, Oct 1966 .... 35.00
❑10, Nov 1966 .... 35.00
❑11, Mar 1967 WW (a) 38.00
❑12, Apr 1967 WW (a) 38.00
❑13, Jun 1967 WW (a); A: Undersea Agent. 38.00
❑14, Jul 1967 WW (a) 38.00
❑15, Sep 1967 WW (a) 38.00
❑16, Oct 1967 WW (a) 22.00
❑17, Dec 1967 WW (a) 22.00
❑18, Sep 1968 SD, WW (a) 22.00
❑19, Nov 1968 WW (a) 22.00
❑20, Jan 1969 WW (a); O: Dynamo. . 15.00

T.H.U.N.D.E.R. AGENTS (VOL. 2)
J.C.

❑1, May 1983 .... 2.00
❑2, Jan 1984 .... 2.00

THUNDER AGENTS (WALLY WOOD'S)
Deluxe

❑1, Nov 1984 .... 2.00
❑2, Jan 1985 .... 2.00
❑3, Nov 1985 .... 2.00
❑4, Feb 1986 .... 2.00
❑5, Oct 1986 .... 2.00

THUNDERBOLT
Charlton

❑1, Jan 1966 O: Thunderbolt. 1: Thunderbolt. 16.00
❑51, Mar 1966; Series continues after hiatus (Son of Vulcan #50?) 10.00
❑52, Jun 1966 .... 9.00
❑53, Aug 1966 .... 9.00
❑54, Oct 1966 .... 9.00
❑55, Dec 1966 .... 9.00
❑56, Feb 1967 .... 9.00
❑57, May 1967 .... 9.00
❑58, Jul 1967 .... 9.00
❑59, Sep 1967 .... 9.00
❑60, Nov 1967 .... 9.00

THUNDERBOLTS
Marvel

❑-1, Jul 1997; KB (w); A: Baron Zemo. A: Namor. Flashback 2.00
❑0, Jan 1997; KB (w); Free 1.00
❑1, Apr 1997; Giant-size; KB (w); Identities of Thunderbolts revealed 4.00
❑2, May 1997 KB (w); V: Mad Thinker. 3.00
❑2/A, May 1997, Alternate cover 3.00
❑3, Jun 1997 KB (w) 3.00
❑4, Jul 1997; KB (w); 1: Jolt. Jolt joins team 2.50
❑5, Aug 1997; gatefold summary; KB (w); Atlas vs. Growing Man 2.50
❑6, Sep 1997; gatefold summary KB (w) 2.00
❑7, Oct 1997; gatefold summary KB (w); V: Elements of Doom. 2.00
❑8, Nov 1997; gatefold summary KB (w); A: Spider-Man. 2.00
❑9, Dec 1997; gatefold summary KB (w); A: Black Widow. 2.00
❑10, Jan 1998; gatefold summary; KB (w); Thunderbolts revealed as Masters of Evil 2.00
❑11, Feb 1998; gatefold summary KB (w) 2.00
❑12, Mar 1998; gatefold summary KB (w); A: Fantastic Four. A: Avengers. 6.00
❑13, Apr 1998; gatefold summary KB (w) 2.00
❑14, May 1998; gatefold summary KB (w) 2.00
❑15, Jun 1998; gatefold summary KB (w) 2.00
❑16, Jul 1998; gatefold summary KB (w); V: Lightning Rods (formerly Great Lakes Avengers). 2.00
❑17, Aug 1998; gatefold summary KB (w); V: Graviton. 2.00
❑18, Sep 1998; gatefold summary KB (w) 2.00
❑19, Oct 1998; gatefold summary KB (w); 1: Charcoal. 2.00
❑20, Nov 1998; gatefold summary KB (w); V: new Masters of Evil. 2.00
❑21, Dec 1998; gatefold summary KB (w); A: Hawkeye. 2.00
❑22, Jan 1999; gatefold summary; KB (w); Hercules vs. Atlas 2.00
❑23, Feb 1999 KB (w); A: U.S. Agent. 2.00
❑24, Mar 1999 KB (w); A: Citizen V. .. 2.00
❑25, Apr 1999; double-sized KB (w); A: Masters of Evil. V: Masters of Evil. 2.99
❑26, May 1999; Mach-1 in prison 1.99
❑27, Jun 1999 A: Archangel. 1.99
❑28, Jul 1999 A: Archangel. V: Graviton. 1.99
❑29, Aug 1999 A: Machine Man. V: Graviton. 1.99
❑30, Sep 1999; Hawkeye and Moonstone caught in clinch 1.99
❑31, Oct 1999 .... 1.99
❑32, Nov 1999 .... 1.99
❑33, Dec 1999 .... 1.99
❑34, Jan 2000 .... 1.99
❑35, Feb 2000 .... 2.25
❑36, Mar 2000 .... 2.25
❑37, Apr 2000 .... 2.25
❑38, May 2000 .... 2.25
❑39, Jun 2000 .... 2.25
❑40, Jul 2000 .... 2.25
❑41, Aug 2000 A: Sandman. 2.25
❑42, Sep 2000 A: Wonder Man. 2.25
❑43, Oct 2000 A: Black Widow. 2.25
❑44, Nov 2000 A: Nefaria. A: Avengers. 2.25
❑45, Dec 2000 .... 2.25
❑46, Jan 2001; return of Jolt 2.25
❑47, Feb 2001 A: Captain Marvel. 2.25
❑48, Mar 2001 .... 2.25
❑49, Apr 2001 .... 2.25
❑50, May 2001; double-sized A: Citizen V. 2.99
❑51, Jun 2001 .... 2.25
❑52, Jul 2001 .... 2.25
❑53, Aug 2001 .... 2.25
❑54, Sep 2001 .... 2.25
❑55, Oct 2001 .... 2.25
❑56, Nov 2001 .... 2.25
❑57, Dec 2001 .... 2.25
❑58, Jan 2002 .... 2.25
❑59, Feb 2002 .... 2.25
❑60, Mar 2002 .... 2.25
❑61, Apr 2002 .... 2.25
❑62, May 2002 .... 2.25
❑63, Jun 2002 .... 2.25
❑64, Jul 2002 .... 2.25
❑65, Aug 2002 .... 2.25
❑66, Aug 2002 .... 2.25
❑67, Sep 2002 .... 2.25
❑68, Sep 2002 .... 2.25
❑69, Oct 2002 .... 2.25
❑70, Oct 2002 .... 2.25
❑71, Nov 2002 .... 2.25
❑72, Nov 2002 .... 2.25
❑73, Dec 2002 .... 2.25
❑74, Jan 2003 .... 2.25
❑75, Feb 2003 .... 2.25
❑76, Mar 2003 .... 2.25
❑77, Apr 2003 .... 2.99
❑78, Jun 2003 .... 2.99
❑79, Jul 2003 .... 2.25
❑80, Aug 2003 .... 2.25
❑81, Sep 2003 .... 2.25
❑Annual 1997, Aug 1997; KB (w); GC, GP, BMc (a); O: Thunderbolts. 1997 Annual; wraparound cover 3.00
❑Ashcan 1; Ashcan preview; American Entertainment 2.50

THUNDERBUNNY (1ST SERIES)
Archie / Red Circle

❑1, Jan 1984 .... 2.00

THUNDERBUNNY (2ND SERIES)
Warp

❑1, Jun 1985; O: retold. Warp publishes 2.00
❑2, Aug 1985 .... 2.00
❑3, Oct 1985 .... 2.00
❑4, Dec 1985 .... 2.00
❑5, Feb 1986 .... 2.00
❑6 1986, b&w; Apple begins publishing 2.00
❑7 1986, b&w 2.00
❑8 1987 .... 1.75
❑9 1987 .... 1.75
❑10, Jul 1987 .... 1.75
❑11, Sep 1987 A: THUNDER Agents. . 1.75
❑12, Nov 1987; last 1.75

THUNDERCATS
Marvel / Star

❑1, Dec 1985 .... 4.00
❑2, Feb 1956 .... 2.00
❑3, Apr 1986 .... 2.00
❑4, Jun 1986 .... 2.00
❑5, Aug 1986 .... 2.00
❑6, Oct 1986 .... 2.00
❑7, Dec 1986 .... 1.50
❑8, Feb 1987 .... 1.50
❑9, Mar 1987 .... 1.50
❑10, Apr 1987 .... 1.50
❑11, May 1987 .... 1.50
❑12, Jun 1987 .... 1.50
❑13, Jul 1987 .... 1.50
❑14, Aug 1987 .... 1.50
❑15, Sep 1987 .... 1.50
❑16, Oct 1987 .... 1.50
❑17, Nov 1987 .... 1.50
❑18, Dec 1987 .... 1.50
❑19, Jan 1988 .... 1.50
❑20, Feb 1988 .... 1.50
❑21, Mar 1988 .... 1.50
❑22, Apr 1988 .... 1.50
❑23, May 1988 .... 1.50
❑24, Jun 1988 .... 1.50

THUNDERCATS (WILDSTORM)
WildStorm

❑0, Oct 2002 .... 2.50
❑1, Oct 2002 .... 2.50
❑2, Nov 2002 .... 2.95
❑3, Dec 2002 .... 2.95
❑4, Jan 2003 .... 2.95
❑5, Feb 2003 .... 2.95

THUNDERCATS/BATTLE OF THE PLANETS
DC / WildStorm

❑1, ca. 2003 .... 4.95

THUNDERCATS: DOGS OF WAR
DC

❑1, Aug 2003 .... 2.95
❑2, Sep 2003 .... 2.95
❑3, Oct 2003 .... 2.95
❑4, Nov 2003 .... 2.95
❑5, Dec 2003 .... 2.95

THUNDERCATS: ENEMY'S PRIDE
DC

❑1, Aug 2004 .... 2.95
❑2, Sep 2004 ....

THUNDERCATS: HAMMERHAND'S REVENGE
DC

❑1, Dec 2003 .... 2.95
❑2, Jan 2004 .... 2.95
❑3, Feb 2004 .... 2.95
❑4, Mar 2004 .... 2.95
❑5, Apr 2004 .... 2.95

N-MINT

THUNDERCATS ORIGINS: HEROES & VILLAINS
DC

❑1, Feb 2004 .... 3.50

THUNDERCATS ORIGINS: VILLAINS & HEROES
DC

❑1, Feb 2004 .... 3.50

THUNDERCATS: RECLAIMING THUNDERA
DC

❑1, ca. 2003 .... 12.95

THUNDERCATS: THE RETURN
DC / WILDSTORM

❑1, Apr 2003 .... 2.95
❑2, May 2003 .... 2.95
❑3, Jun 2003 .... 2.95
❑4, Jul 2003 .... 2.95
❑5, Aug 2003 .... 2.95

THUNDER GIRLS
PIN & INK

❑1, Sum 1997 .... 2.95
❑2, Sum 1999 .... 2.95
❑3, Fal 1999 .... 2.95

THUNDERGOD
CRUSADE

❑1/A, Aug 1996; Alternate cover (drawn cover, man and woman clasping) .. 2.95
❑1, Aug 1996, b&w; Painted cover 2.95
❑2, Oct 1996, b&w 2.95
❑3, Dec 1996, b&w 2.95

THUNDERMACE
RAK

❑1, Mar 1986, b&w 2.00
❑2 1986 .... 1.75
❑3, Apr 1987 .... 1.75
❑4 1987 .... 1.75
❑5 1987 .... 2.00
❑6 1987 .... 2.00
❑7 1987 .... 2.00

THUNDERSAURS: THE BODACIOUS ADVENTURES OF BIFF THUNDERSAUR
INNOVATION

❑1, b&w 2.25

THUNDERSKULL! (SIDNEY MELLON'S...)
SLAVE LABOR

❑1, Aug 1989, b&w 1.95

THUNDERSTRIKE
MARVEL

❑1, Jun 1993; Prism cover 2.95
❑2, Nov 1993 .... 1.25
❑3, Dec 1993 .... 1.25
❑4, Jan 1994 .... 1.25
❑5, Feb 1994 .... 1.25
❑6, Mar 1994 .... 1.25
❑7, Apr 1994 .... 1.25
❑8, May 1994 .... 1.25
❑9, Jun 1994 .... 1.50
❑10, Jul 1994 .... 1.50
❑11, Aug 1994 .... 1.50
❑12, Sep 1994 .... 1.50
❑13, Oct 1994 .... 1.50
❑13/A, Oct 1994; flip-book with Code Blue back-up; second indicia gives title as Marvel Double Feature ... Thunderstrike/Code Blue 2.50
❑14, Nov 1994 .... 1.50
❑14/A, Nov 1994; flip-book with Code Blue back-up; second indicia gives title as Marvel Double Feature ... Thunderstrike/Code Blue 2.50
❑15, Dec 1994 .... 1.50
❑15/A, Dec 1994; flip-book with Code Blue back-up; second indicia gives title as Marvel Double Feature ... Thunderstrike/Code Blue 2.50
❑16, Jan 1995 .... 1.50

N-MINT

❑16/A, Jan 1995; flip-book with Code Blue back-up; second indicia gives title as Marvel Double Feature ... Thunderstrike/Code Blue 2.50
❑17, Feb 1995 .... 1.50
❑18, Mar 1995 .... 1.50
❑19, Apr 1995 .... 1.50
❑20, May 1995 .... 1.50
❑21, Jun 1995; Avengers #1 homage cover 1.50
❑22, Jul 1995; Identity of Bloodaxe revealed 1.50
❑23, Aug 1995 .... 1.50
❑24, Sep 1995 .... 1.50

TICK, THE
NEC

❑1, Jun 1988; Black background on cover 15.00
❑1-2 .... 3.00
❑1-3 .... 2.50
❑1-4 .... 2.25
❑1-5 .... 2.75
❑2, Sep 1988; Die-cut cover 8.00
❑2/Variant; Without die-cut cover 15.00
❑2-2 .... 3.00
❑2-3 .... 2.25
❑2-4 .... 2.25
❑2-5 .... 2.75
❑3, Dec 1988 .... 6.00
❑3-2, Nov 1989; Yellow stripe on cover saying "Encore Presentation" 3.00
❑3-3 .... 2.75
❑3-4 .... 2.75
❑4, Apr 1989 1: Paul the Samurai. 8.00
❑4-2 1: Paul the Samurai. 2.25
❑4-3 1: Paul the Samurai. 2.75
❑4-4 1: Paul the Samurai. 2.75
❑4-5 1: Paul the Samurai. 2.75
❑5, Aug 1989; Scarcer 8.00
❑5-2 .... 2.75
❑6, Nov 1989 .... 5.00
❑6-2 .... 2.75
❑6-3 .... 2.75
❑7, Feb 1990 .... 5.00
❑7-2 .... 2.75
❑7-3, Sep 1995 .... 2.75
❑8, Jul 1990; Has logo 8.00
❑8/Variant; No logo on cover 8.00
❑8-2 .... 2.75
❑9, Mar 1991 1: The Chainsaw Vigilante. 3.00
❑10, Oct 1991 .... 3.00
❑11, Aug 1992 .... 3.00
❑12, May 1993 .... 3.00
❑12/Ltd.; Gold spider foil on front 20.00
❑13, Nov 2000; Pseudo-Tick edition . 3.50
❑Special 1, Mar 1988 .... 50.00
❑Special 2, Jun 1988 .... 25.00

TICK & ARTHUR, THE
NEC

❑1, Apr 1999 .... 3.50

TICK & ARTIE
NEC

❑1/A 2002; Tick, Arthur on cover 3.50
❑1/B 2002; Bugs on cover 3.50

TICK BIG BLUE DESTINY, THE
NEC

❑1, Nov 1997; Keen Edition; Arthur and Tick with #1 posing on cover 2.95
❑1/A, Nov 1997; Wicked Keen Edition; Die-cut cover 4.95
❑1/Ashcan, ca. 1997; ashcan edition . 2.95
❑1/B, Nov 1997; Wicked Keen Edition without Die-Cut Cover; (500 printed); (500 printed) 19.00
❑2, Jan 1998 .... 2.95
❑2/Variant, Jan 1998; Tick-buster cover 2.95
❑3, Mar 1998 .... 3.50
❑4, May 1998; Justice Cover 3.50
❑4/A, May 1998; Ocean cover 3.50
❑5, Aug 1998 .... 3.50

Menthor's death in *T.H.U.N.D.E.R. Agents* #7 was poignantly portrayed.

© 1966 Tower Publications.

N-MINT

TICK BIG RED-N-GREEN CHRISTMAS SPECTACLE, THE
NEC

❑1, Dec 2001, b&w and color; Black background on cover 3.95

TICK BIG SUMMER ANNUAL, THE
NEC

❑1, Jul 1999 .... 3.50

TICK, THE: CIRCUS MAXIMUS
NEC

❑1, Mar 2000 .... 3.50
❑2, Apr 2000 .... 3.50
❑3, May 2000 .... 3.50
❑4, Jun 2000 .... 3.50

TICK, THE: HEROES OF THE CITY
NEC

❑1, Feb 1999 .... 3.50

TICK INCREDIBLE INTERNET COMIC, THE
NEC

❑1, Jul 2001, b&w and color; Black background on cover 3.95

TICK, THE: KARMA TORNADO
NEC

❑1, Oct 1993 .... 4.00
❑1-2, Jan 1997 .... 2.95
❑2, Jan 1994 .... 3.50
❑2-2, Feb 1997 .... 2.95
❑3, May 1994; Scarce 5.00
❑3-2, Mar 1997; flip book with The Tick's Back back-up 2.95
❑4, Jul 1994; Scarce 5.00
❑4-2, Apr 1997; flip book with The Tick's Back back-up 2.95
❑5, Aug 1994; Scarce 5.00
❑5-2 .... 2.95
❑6, Oct 1994 .... 4.00
❑6-2 .... 2.95
❑7 1994 .... 4.00
❑7-2 .... 2.95
❑8 1995 .... 4.00
❑8-2 .... 2.95
❑9 1995 .... 3.00
❑9-2 .... 2.95

TICK: LUNY BIN TRILOGY
NEC

❑0, Jul 1998; A.k.a. The Tick: Big Blue Destiny #6; Preview 1.50
❑1, Oct 1998 .... 3.50
❑2, Sep 1998 .... 3.50
❑3, Oct 1998 .... 3.50

TICK'S BACK, THE
NEC

❑0, Aug 1997; Red cover 2.95
❑0/A, Aug 1997; Green Cover 5.00
❑0/B, Aug 1997; Gold Tick Cover 7.50
❑0/C, Aug 1997, b&w; no logo; gold cover 10.00

TICK'S BIG BACK TO SCHOOL SPECIAL, THE
NEC

❑1, ca. 1998 .... 3.50

TICK'S BIG CRUISE SHIP VACATION SPECIAL, THE
NEC

❑1, Sep 2000 .... 3.50

N-MINT

TICK'S BIG FATHER'S DAY SPECIAL, THE
NEC
- ❑1, Jun 2000 .... 3.50

TICK'S BIG HALLOWEEN SPECIAL, THE
NEC
- ❑1, Oct 1999 .... 3.50

TICK'S BIG MOTHER'S DAY SPECIAL, THE
NEC
- ❑1, Apr 2000 .... 3.50

TICK'S BIG ROMANTIC ADVENTURE, THE
NEC
- ❑1, Feb 1998 .... 2.95

TICK'S BIG SUMMER FUN SPECIAL, THE
NEC
- ❑1, Aug 1998 .... 3.50

TICK'S BIG TAX TIME TERROR, THE
NEC
- ❑1, Apr 2000 .... 3.50

TICK'S BIG YEAR 2000 SPECIAL, THE
NEC
- ❑1, Mar 2000 .... 3.50

TICK'S BIG YULE LOG SPECIAL
NEC
- ❑1/A, Dec 1997, b&w; Tick holding Arthur on cover 3.50
- ❑1, Dec 1997, b&w 3.50
- ❑1998, Feb 1998 .... 3.50
- ❑1999, Jan 1999 .... 3.50
- ❑2000, Nov 1999 .... 3.50
- ❑2000/Ltd., Nov 1999 .... 4.95
- ❑2001 .... 3.50

TICK'S GIANT CIRCUS OF THE MIGHTY, THE
NEC
- ❑1, Sum 1992 .... 2.75
- ❑2, Sum 1992 .... 2.75

TICK'S GOLDEN AGE COMIC, THE
NEC
- ❑1/A, May 2002; Red Timely-style cover 4.95
- ❑1/B, May 2002; Standing on top of world with Eagle cover 4.95
- ❑2/A, Aug 2002; Jungle cover 4.95
- ❑2/B, Aug 2002; EC spoof cover 4.95

TICK'S MASSIVE SUMMER DOUBLE SPECTACLE, THE
NEC
- ❑1/B, Jul 2000 .... 3.50
- ❑1/A, Jul 2000 .... 3.50
- ❑1, Jul 2000 .... 3.50
- ❑2/B 2001 .... 3.50
- ❑2/A 2001 .... 3.50
- ❑2 2001 .... 3.50

TICK-TOCK FOLLIES
SLAVE LABOR
- ❑1, Dec 1996 .... 2.95

TIC TOC TOM
DETONATOR CANADA
- ❑1, Aut 1995, b&w 2.95
- ❑2, Win 1995, b&w 2.95
- ❑3, Spr 1996, b&w 2.95

TIGER 2021
ANUBIS
- ❑Ashcan 1, May 1994 .... 3.95

TIGERMAN
ATLAS-SEABOARD
- ❑1, Sep 1975 O: Tigerman. 1: Tigerman. 8.00
- ❑2, Jun 1975 SD (a) 8.00
- ❑3, Sep 1975 SD (a) 8.00

TIGERS OF TERRA
MIND-VISIONS
- ❑1, ca. 1992 .... 3.00
- ❑2, ca. 1992 .... 3.00
- ❑3, ca. 1992 .... 3.00
- ❑4, ca. 1992 .... 3.00
- ❑5, ca. 1992 .... 3.00
- ❑6, ca. 1992 .... 3.00
- ❑7, ca. 1992 .... 3.00
- ❑8, ca. 1993 .... 3.00
- ❑9, ca. 1993; two covers: a and b 3.75
- ❑10, ca. 1993, b&w 3.75
- ❑11, ca. 1993, b&w 3.95
- ❑12, Jul 1993, b&w 3.95

TIGERS OF TERRA (VOL. 2)
ANTARCTIC
- ❑0, Aug 1993 .... 2.95
- ❑1, Oct 1993 .... 3.00
- ❑2, Dec 1993 .... 3.00
- ❑3, Feb 1994 .... 3.00
- ❑4, Apr 1994 .... 3.00
- ❑5, Jul 1994 .... 3.00
- ❑6, Sep 1994 .... 3.00
- ❑7, Dec 1994 .... 3.00
- ❑8, Jan 1995 .... 3.00
- ❑9, Mar 1995 .... 3.00
- ❑10, Apr 1995 .... 3.00
- ❑11, May 1995 .... 2.75
- ❑12, Jun 1995 .... 2.75
- ❑13, Jul 1995 .... 2.75
- ❑14, Aug 1995 .... 2.75
- ❑15, Sep 1995 .... 2.75
- ❑16, Oct 1995 .... 2.75
- ❑17, Nov 1995 .... 2.75
- ❑18, Dec 1996 .... 2.95
- ❑19, Jan 1996 .... 2.95
- ❑20, Mar 1996 .... 2.95
- ❑21, May 1996 .... 2.95
- ❑22, Jul 1996 .... 2.95
- ❑23, Sep 1996 .... 2.95
- ❑24, Nov 1996 .... 3.95
- ❑25, Jan 1997 .... 2.95

TIGERS OF TERRA (VOL. 3)
ANTARCTIC
- ❑1, Jul 2000 .... 2.95

TIGERS OF TERRA: TECHNICAL MANUAL
ANTARCTIC
- ❑1, Dec 1995, b&w 2.95
- ❑2, Jun 1996, b&w 2.95

TIGER WOMAN, THE
MILLENNIUM
- ❑1, Sep 1994; no indicia 2.95
- ❑2, Apr 1995; no indicia; but title page says Tiger Woman #2, cover says Quest of the Tiger Woman #1 .... 2.95

TIGER-X
ETERNITY
- ❑1 1988, b&w; Story continued from Tiger-X Special #1 .... 2.00
- ❑2 1988, b&w 2.00
- ❑3 1988, b&w 2.00
- ❑Special 1 1988, b&w 2.25
- ❑Special 1-2, Dec 1988 .... 2.25

TIGER-X BOOK II
ETERNITY
- ❑1 1989, b&w 2.00
- ❑2 1989, b&w 2.00
- ❑3 1989, b&w 2.00
- ❑4 1989, b&w 2.00

TIGRA
MARVEL
- ❑1, May 2002 .... 2.99
- ❑2, Jun 2002 .... 2.99
- ❑3, Jul 2002 .... 2.99
- ❑4, Aug 2002 .... 2.99

TIGRESS, THE
HERO
- ❑1, Aug 1992, b&w 2.95
- ❑2, Oct 1992, b&w 2.95
- ❑3, Dec 1992, b&w 2.95
- ❑4, Feb 1993, b&w 2.95
- ❑5, Apr 1993, b&w 2.95
- ❑6, Jun 1993 .... 3.95

TIGRESS (BASEMENT)
BASEMENT
- ❑1, Jul 1998 .... 2.95

TIJUANA BIBLE, THE
STARHEAD
- ❑1, b&w 2.50
- ❑2, b&w 2.50
- ❑3, b&w 2.50
- ❑4, b&w; Bluesie Toons 2.50
- ❑5; World's Fair 2.50
- ❑6; Fuller Brush Man 2.50
- ❑7; Royalty issue 2.50
- ❑8; Hollywood women 2.50
- ❑9; An Artist's Affaire 2.50

TILAZEUS MEETS THE MESSIAH
AIIIE
- ❑1 .... 2.50

TIMBER WOLF
DC
- ❑1, Nov 1992 .... 1.50
- ❑2, Dec 1992 .... 1.50
- ❑3, Jan 1993 V: Creeper. 1.50
- ❑4, Feb 1993 .... 1.50
- ❑5, Mar 1993 .... 1.50

TIME BANDITS
MARVEL
- ❑1, Feb 1982 .... 1.50

TIME BREAKERS
DC / HELIX
- ❑1, Jan 1997 .... 2.25
- ❑2, Feb 1997 .... 2.25
- ❑3, Mar 1997 .... 2.25
- ❑4, Apr 1997 .... 2.25
- ❑5, May 1997 .... 2.25

TIME CITY
ROCKET
- ❑1, Mar 1992 .... 2.50

TIMECOP
DARK HORSE
- ❑1, Sep 1994 .... 2.50
- ❑2, Sep 1994 .... 2.50

TIMEDRIFTER (GERARD JONES'...)
INNOVATION
- ❑1, Dec 1990, b&w 2.25
- ❑2, b&w 2.25
- ❑3, b&w 2.25

TIME GATES
DOUBLE EDGE
- ❑1 .... 1.95
- ❑2 .... 1.95
- ❑3 .... 1.95

TIMEJUMP WAR, THE
APPLE
- ❑1, Oct 1989, b&w 2.25
- ❑2, b&w 2.25
- ❑3, b&w 2.25

TIME KILLERS
FLEETWAY-QUALITY
- ❑1; Tales From Beyond Space: The Men In Red 2.95
- ❑2 .... 2.95
- ❑3 .... 2.95
- ❑4 .... 2.95
- ❑5 .... 2.95
- ❑6 .... 2.95
- ❑7 .... 2.95

TIMELESS TALES (BOB POWELL'S...)
ECLIPSE
- ❑1, Mar 1989, b&w 2.00

TIMELY PRESENTS: ALL-WINNERS
MARVEL
- ❑1, Dec 1999; Reprints All-Winners Comics #19 .... 3.99

TIMELY PRESENTS: HUMAN TORCH
MARVEL
- ❑1, Feb 1999; Painted cover; Contents reprinted from Human Torch Comics #5 .... 3.99

N-MINT

TIME MACHINE, THE
Eternity

- ❑1, Apr 1990, b&w; Based on the story by H.G. Wells ... 2.50
- ❑2 1990, b&w ... 2.50
- ❑3 1990, b&w ... 2.50

TIME MASTERS
DC

- ❑1, Feb 1990 ... 2.00
- ❑2, Mar 1990 ... 1.75
- ❑3, Apr 1990 ... 1.75
- ❑4, May 1990 ... 1.75
- ❑5, Jun 1990 A: Viking Prince. ... 1.75
- ❑6, Jul 1990 A: Doctor Fate. ... 1.75
- ❑7, Aug 1990 A: Arion. ... 1.75
- ❑8, Sep 1990 ... 1.75

TIME OUT OF MIND
Graphic Serials

- ❑1 ... 2.00
- ❑2 ... 1.75
- ❑3 ... 1.75

TIMESLIP COLLECTION
Marvel

- ❑1, Nov 1998; collects short features from Marvel Vision; wraparound cover ... 2.99

TIMESLIP SPECIAL
Marvel

- ❑1, Oct 1998; cardstock cover ... 5.99

TIMESPELL
Club 408 Graphics

- ❑0, ca. 1997, b&w; cardstock cover .. 2.95
- ❑1, ca. 1998, b&w; cardstock cover .. 2.95
- ❑2, ca. 1998, b&w; cardstock cover .. 2.95
- ❑3, ca. 1998, b&w; cardstock cover .. 2.95
- ❑4, ca. 1998, b&w; cardstock cover .. 2.95
- ❑Ashcan 1, ca. 1997; no cover price; ashcan preview of upcoming series ... 1.00

TIMESPELL: THE DIRECTOR'S CUT
Club 408 Graphics

- ❑1, ca. 1998, b&w; no price on cover; reprints #1 with revisions and additions ... 2.95

TIMESPIRITS
Marvel / Epic

- ❑1, Oct 1984 TY (a) ... 2.00
- ❑2, Dec 1984 ... 1.75
- ❑3, Feb 1985 ... 1.75
- ❑4, Apr 1985 AW (a) ... 1.75
- ❑5, Jul 1985 ... 1.75
- ❑6, Sep 1985 ... 1.75
- ❑7, Dec 1985 ... 1.75
- ❑8, Mar 1986 ... 1.75

TIME TRAVELER AI
CPM Manga

- ❑1, Oct 1999, b&w ... 2.95
- ❑2, Nov 1999, b&w ... 2.95
- ❑3, Dec 1999, b&w ... 2.95
- ❑4, Jan 2000, b&w ... 2.95
- ❑5, Feb 2000, b&w ... 2.95
- ❑6, Mar 2000, b&w ... 2.95

TIME TRAVELER HERBIE
Avalon

- ❑1 ... 2.95

TIME TUNNEL, THE
Gold Key

- ❑1, Feb 1967 ... 40.00
- ❑2, Jul 1967 ... 35.00

TIME TWISTED TALES
Rip Off

- ❑1 ... 2.00

TIME TWISTERS
Fleetway-Quality

- ❑1 AMo (w); DaG (a) ... 1.50
- ❑2 AMo (w); DaG (a) ... 1.50
- ❑3 AMo (w); BT (a) ... 1.50
- ❑4 AMo (w); DaG (a) ... 1.50
- ❑5 ... 1.50
- ❑6 AMo (w) ... 1.50

N-MINT

- ❑7 AMo (w) ... 1.50
- ❑8 AMo (w); DaG (a) ... 1.50
- ❑9 AMo (w) ... 1.50
- ❑10 ... 1.50
- ❑11 ... 1.50
- ❑12 ... 1.50
- ❑13 ... 1.50
- ❑14 AMo (w); BB (a) ... 1.50
- ❑15 DaG (a) ... 1.50
- ❑16 ... 1.50
- ❑17 NG (w) ... 1.50
- ❑18 NG (w) ... 1.50
- ❑19 ... 1.50
- ❑20 ... 1.50
- ❑21 AMo (w); DaG (a) ... 1.50

TIMEWALKER
Acclaim / Valiant

- ❑0, Mar 1996 ... 2.50
- ❑1, Jan 1995; cover has Dec 94 coverdate ... 2.50
- ❑2, Feb 1995; cover has Jan coverdate 2.50
- ❑3, Mar 1995; cover has Feb coverdate 2.50
- ❑4, Apr 1995; cover has Mar coverdate 2.50
- ❑5, Apr 1995 ... 2.50
- ❑6, May 1995 ... 2.50
- ❑7, Jun 1995 ... 2.50
- ❑8, Jul 1995; Birthquake ... 2.50
- ❑9, Jul 1995; Birthquake ... 2.50
- ❑10, Aug 1995 ... 2.50
- ❑11, Aug 1995 ... 2.50
- ❑12, Sep 1995 ... 2.50
- ❑13, Sep 1995 ... 2.50
- ❑14, Oct 1995 ... 2.50
- ❑15, Oct 1995 ... 2.50
- ❑Yearbook 1, May 1995 ... 2.95

TIME WANKERS
Fantagraphics / Eros

- ❑1, Sep 1996, b&w ... 2.25
- ❑2, b&w ... 2.25
- ❑3, b&w ... 2.25
- ❑4, b&w ... 2.25
- ❑5, b&w ... 2.25

TIME WARP
DC

- ❑1, Nov 1979 DN, TS, RB, SD, DG, JA, DA (a) ... 1.25
- ❑2, Jan 1980 ... 1.25
- ❑3, Mar 1980 ... 1.25
- ❑4, May 1980 ... 1.25
- ❑5, Jul 1980 ... 1.25

TIME WARRIOR
Blazing

- ❑1 1993 ... 2.50

TIME WARRIORS: THE BEGINNING
Fantasy General

- ❑1 ... 1.50

TIM HOLT WESTERN ANNUAL
AC

- ❑1, b&w ... 2.95

TIMMY THE TIMID GHOST (1ST SERIES)
Charlton

- ❑3, ca. 1956 ... 36.00
- ❑4, ca. 1956 ... 20.00
- ❑5, ca. 1956 ... 20.00
- ❑6, Mar 1957 ... 20.00
- ❑7, ca. 1957 ... 20.00
- ❑8, Sep 1957 ... 20.00
- ❑9, ca. 1957 ... 20.00
- ❑10, ca. 1957 ... 20.00
- ❑11, Apr 1958; Big book ... 18.00
- ❑12, Oct 1958; Bog Book ... 18.00
- ❑13, Feb 1959 ... 18.00
- ❑14, Apr 1959 ... 18.00
- ❑15, Jun 1959 ... 18.00
- ❑16, Aug 1959 ... 18.00
- ❑17, Oct 1959 ... 18.00
- ❑18, Dec 1959 ... 18.00
- ❑19, Feb 1960 ... 18.00
- ❑20, Apr 1960 ... 18.00

Appropriately enough, Dark Horse adapted *Timecop*, the feature film that was based on the series that had appeared in *Dark Horse Comics* two years earlier.

© 1994 Dark Horse Comics.

N-MINT

- ❑21, Jun 1960 ... 10.00
- ❑22, Aug 1960 ... 10.00
- ❑23, Oct 1960 ... 10.00
- ❑24, Dec 1960 ... 10.00
- ❑25, Feb 1961 ... 10.00
- ❑26, Apr 1961 ... 10.00
- ❑27, ca. 1961 ... 10.00
- ❑28, ca. 1961 ... 10.00
- ❑29, ca. 1962 ... 10.00
- ❑30, ca. 1962 ... 10.00
- ❑31, Sep 1962 ... 10.00
- ❑32, ca. 1963 ... 10.00
- ❑33, Jul 1963 ... 10.00
- ❑34, Sep 1963 ... 10.00
- ❑35, Nov 1963 ... 10.00
- ❑36, Jan 1964 ... 10.00
- ❑37, Mar 1964 ... 10.00
- ❑38, May 1964 ... 10.00
- ❑39, Jun 1964 ... 10.00
- ❑40, Jul 1964 ... 10.00
- ❑41, Aug 1964 ... 10.00
- ❑42, Sep 1964 ... 10.00
- ❑43, Oct 1964 ... 10.00
- ❑44, Nov 1964 ... 10.00
- ❑45, Sep 1966 ... 10.00

TIMMY THE TIMID GHOST (2ND SERIES)
Charlton

- ❑1, Oct 1967 ... 10.00
- ❑2, Feb 1968 ... 6.00
- ❑3, Apr 1968 ... 6.00
- ❑4, Jun 1968 ... 6.00
- ❑5, Aug 1968 ... 6.00
- ❑6, Oct 1968 ... 6.00
- ❑7, Dec 1968 ... 6.00
- ❑8, Feb 1969 ... 6.00
- ❑9, Apr 1969 ... 6.00
- ❑10, Jun 1969 ... 6.00
- ❑11, Aug 1969 ... 4.00
- ❑12, Oct 1969 ... 4.00
- ❑13, Dec 1969 ... 4.00
- ❑14, Jan 1970 ... 4.00
- ❑15, Mar 1970 ... 4.00
- ❑16, May 1970 ... 4.00
- ❑17, Jul 1970 ... 4.00
- ❑18, Sep 1970 ... 4.00
- ❑19, Nov 1970 ... 4.00
- ❑20, Jan 1971 ... 4.00
- ❑21, Mar 1971 ... 4.00
- ❑22, May 1971 ... 4.00
- ❑23, Jul 1971 ... 4.00
- ❑24, Sep 1985; reprints Timmy the Timid Ghost (1st series) #7 ... 4.00
- ❑25, Nov 1985; reprints Timmy the Timid Ghost (1st series) #6 (cover reversed & recolored) ... 4.00
- ❑26, Jan 1986; reprints Timmy the Timid Ghost (1st series) #9 ... 4.00

TINCAN MAN
Image / Valiant

- ❑1, Jan 2000 ... 2.95
- ❑2, Feb 2000 ... 2.95
- ❑Ashcan 1, Dec 1999; Preview issue . 2.95

TINY DEATHS
YUGP

- ❑1 ... 1.75
- ❑2, Jan 1997 ... 1.75

N-MINT

TIPPER GORE'S COMICS AND STORIES
REVOLUTIONARY

❑1, Oct 1989, b&w ... 1.95
❑2, Jan 1990, b&w ... 1.95
❑3, Mar 1990, b&w ... 1.95
❑4, May 1990, b&w ... 1.95
❑5, Jul 1990, b&w ... 1.95

TITAN A.E.
DARK HORSE

❑1, May 2000 ... 2.95
❑2, Jun 2000 ... 2.95
❑3, Jul 2000 ... 2.95

TITANS, THE
DC

❑1, Mar 1999; DGry (w); A: H.I.V.E.. new team ... 3.00
❑1/Autographed, Mar 1999 DGry (w); A: H.I.V.E.. ... 15.95
❑2, Apr 1999 DGry (w); A: Superman. A: H.I.V.E.. ... 2.50
❑3, May 1999 DGry (w); V: Goth. ... 2.50
❑4, Jun 1999 DGry (w); V: Goth. ... 2.50
❑5, Jul 1999 DGry (w) ... 2.50
❑6, Aug 1999 DGry (w); A: Green Lantern. V: Red Panzer. ... 2.50
❑7, Sep 1999 DGry (w) ... 2.50
❑8, Oct 1999 DGry (w) ... 2.50
❑9, Nov 1999 DGry (w) ... 2.50
❑10, Dec 1999 DGry (w) ... 2.50
❑11, Jan 2000 DGry (w) ... 2.50
❑12, Feb 2000 ... 2.50
❑13, Mar 2000 ... 2.50
❑14, Apr 2000 ... 2.50
❑15, May 2000 DGry (w) ... 2.50
❑16, Jun 2000 ... 2.50
❑17, Jul 2000 ... 2.50
❑18, Aug 2000 ... 2.50
❑19, Sep 2000 DGry (w) ... 2.50
❑20, Oct 2000 DGry (w) ... 2.50
❑21, Nov 2000 ... 2.50
❑22, Dec 2000 ... 2.50
❑23, Jan 2001 ... 2.50
❑24, Feb 2001 ... 2.50
❑25, Mar 2001; Giant-size GP, NC (a) ... 3.95
❑26, Apr 2001 ... 2.50
❑27, May 2001 ... 2.50
❑28, Jun 2001 ... 2.50
❑29, Jul 2001 ... 2.50
❑30, Aug 2001 ... 2.50
❑31, Sep 2001 ... 2.50
❑32, Oct 2001 ... 2.50
❑33, Nov 2001 ... 2.50
❑34, Dec 2001 ... 2.50
❑35, Jan 2002 ... 2.50
❑36, Feb 2002 ... 2.50
❑37, Mar 2002 ... 2.50
❑38, Apr 2002 ... 2.50
❑39, May 2002 ... 2.50
❑40, Jun 2002 ... 2.50
❑41, Jul 2002 ... 2.50
❑42, Aug 2002 ... 2.50
❑43, Sep 2002 ... 2.50
❑44, Oct 2002 ... 2.75
❑45, Nov 2002 ... 2.75
❑46, Dec 2002 ... 2.75
❑47, Jan 2003 ... 2.75
❑48, Feb 2003 ... 2.75
❑49, Mar 2003 ... 2.75
❑50, Apr 2003 ... 2.75
❑Annual 1, Sep 2000; 2000 Annual; Planet DC ... 3.50

TITANS/LEGION OF SUPER-HEROES: UNIVERSE ABLAZE
DC

❑1, ca. 2000 ... 4.95
❑2, ca. 2000 ... 4.95
❑3, ca. 2000 ... 4.95
❑4 2000 ... 4.95

N-MINT

TITAN SPECIAL
DARK HORSE

❑1, Jun 1994 ... 3.95

TITANS: SCISSORS, PAPER, STONE
DC

❑1 1997; prestige format; manga-style; Elseworlds ... 4.95

TITANS SECRET FILES, THE
DC

❑1, Mar 1999 ... 4.95
❑2, Oct 2000 ... 4.95

TITANS SELL-OUT! SPECIAL
DC

❑1, Nov 1992 ... 3.50

TITANS/YOUNG JUSTICE: GRADUATION DAY
DC

❑1, Jun 2003 ... 2.50
❑2, Jul 2003 ... 2.50
❑3, Aug 2003 ... 2.50

TIYU
EXPRESS / ENTITY

❑1, Oct 1996 ... 9.95

T-MINUS-1
RENEGADE

❑1, b&w ... 2.00

TMNT MUTANT UNIVERSE SOURCEBOOK
ARCHIE

❑1, A-M ... 2.00
❑2, N-Z ... 2.00

TMNT: TEENAGE MUTANT NINJA TURTLES
MIRAGE

❑1, Dec 2001, b&w and color; Man atop demons on cover ... 2.95
❑2, Feb 2002 ... 2.95
❑3, Apr 2002 ... 2.95
❑4, Jun 2002 ... 2.95
❑5, Aug 2002 ... 2.95
❑6, Oct 2002 ... 2.95
❑7, Dec 2002 ... 2.95
❑8, Feb 2003 ... 2.95
❑9, Apr 2003 ... 2.95
❑10, Jun 2003 ... 3.95
❑11, Aug 2003 ... 2.95
❑12, Oct 2003 ... 2.95
❑13, Dec 2003 ... 2.95
❑14, Feb 2004 ... 2.95
❑15, Apr 2004 ... 2.95

TO BE ANNOUNCED
STRAWBERRY JAM

❑1, ca. 1986 ... 1.50
❑2, ca. 1986 ... 1.50
❑3, ca. 1986 ... 1.50
❑4, ca. 1986 ... 1.50
❑5, ca. 1986 ... 1.50
❑6, Feb 1987 ... 1.50
❑7, ca. 1987 ... 1.50

TODD MCFARLANE PRESENTS: KISS PSYCHO CIRCUS
IMAGE

❑1, Oct 1998; magazine; reprints #1-3 of comic book ... 6.95
❑2, Apr 1999 ... 4.95
❑3, Aug 1999 ... 4.95
❑4, Nov 1999 ... 4.95
❑5, Apr 2000 ... 4.95

TODD MCFARLANE PRESENTS: OZZY OSBOURNE
IMAGE

❑1, Jun 1999; magazine ... 4.95

TODD MCFARLANE PRESENTS: THE CROW MAGAZINE
IMAGE

❑1, Mar 2000 ... 4.95

N-MINT

TO DIE FOR
BLACKTHORNE

❑1, b&w ... 2.00
❑1/3D ... 2.50

TOKYO BABYLON
TOKYOPOP

❑1, May 2004 ... 9.99

TOKYO MEW MEW
TOKYOPOP

❑1, Apr 2003, b&w; printed in Japanese format ... 9.99

TOKYOPOP (VOL. 3)
MIXX

❑1, Aug 1999 ... 4.99
❑2, Oct 1999 ... 4.99
❑3 ... 4.99
❑4, Dec 1999 ... 4.99
❑5, Jan 2000 ... 4.99
❑6 ... 4.99
❑7 ... 4.99

TOKYOPOP (VOL. 4)
MIXX

❑1 ... 4.99
❑2, Oct 2000 ... 4.99
❑3, Nov 2000 ... 4.99

TOKYO STORM WARNING
DC / CLIFFHANGER

❑1, Aug 2003 ... 2.95
❑2, Sep 2003 ... 2.95
❑3, Dec 2003 ... 2.95

TOMAHAWK
DC

❑44, Nov 1956 ... 56.00
❑45, Jan 1957 ... 56.00
❑46, Feb 1957 ... 56.00
❑47, Mar 1957 ... 56.00
❑48, May 1957 ... 56.00
❑49, Jul 1957 ... 56.00
❑50, Aug 1957 ... 56.00
❑51, Sep 1957 ... 45.00
❑52, Nov 1957 ... 45.00
❑53, Jan 1958 ... 45.00
❑54, Feb 1958 ... 45.00
❑55, Mar 1958 ... 45.00
❑56, May 1958 ... 45.00
❑57, Jul 1958 FF (a) ... 85.00
❑58, Sep 1958 ... 40.00
❑59, Nov 1958 ... 40.00
❑60, Jan 1959 ... 40.00
❑61, Mar 1959 ... 32.00
❑62, May 1959 ... 32.00
❑63, Jul 1959 ... 32.00
❑64, Sep 1959 ... 32.00
❑65, Nov 1959 ... 32.00
❑66, Jan 1960 ... 32.00
❑67, Mar 1960 ... 32.00
❑68, May 1960 ... 32.00
❑69, Jul 1960 ... 32.00
❑70, Sep 1960 ... 32.00
❑71, Nov 1960 ... 32.00
❑72, Jan 1961 ... 32.00
❑73, Mar 1961 ... 32.00
❑74, May 1961 ... 32.00
❑75, Jul 1961 ... 32.00
❑76, Sep 1961 ... 32.00
❑77, Nov 1961 ... 32.00
❑78, Jan 1962 ... 32.00
❑79, Mar 1962 ... 32.00
❑80, May 1962 ... 32.00
❑81, Jul 1962 1: Miss Liberty. ... 25.00
❑82, Sep 1962 ... 25.00
❑83, Nov 1962 ... 25.00
❑84, Jan 1963 ... 25.00
❑85, Mar 1963 ... 25.00
❑86, May 1963 ... 25.00
❑87, Jul 1963 ... 25.00
❑88, Sep 1963 ... 25.00
❑89, Nov 1963 ... 25.00
❑90, Jan 1964 ... 25.00
❑91, Mar 1964 ... 15.00

	N-MINT
❑92, May 1964	15.00
❑93, Jul 1964	15.00
❑94, Sep 1964	15.00
❑95, Nov 1964	15.00
❑96, Jan 1965	15.00
❑97, Mar 1965	15.00
❑98, May 1965	15.00
❑99, Jul 1965	15.00
❑100, Sep 1965	15.00
❑101, Nov 1965	10.00
❑102, Jan 1966	10.00
❑103, Mar 1966	10.00
❑104, May 1966	10.00
❑105, Jul 1966	10.00
❑106, Sep 1966	10.00
❑107, Nov 1966	10.00
❑108, Jan 1967	10.00
❑109, Mar 1967	10.00
❑110, May 1967	10.00
❑111, Jul 1967	8.00
❑112, Sep 1967	8.00
❑113, Nov 1967	8.00
❑114, Jan 1968	8.00
❑115, Mar 1968	8.00
❑116, May 1968	8.00
❑117, Jul 1968	8.00
❑118, Sep 1968	8.00
❑119, Nov 1968	8.00
❑120, Jan 1969	8.00
❑121, Mar 1969	6.00
❑122, May 1969	6.00
❑123, Jul 1969	6.00
❑124, Sep 1969	6.00
❑125, Nov 1969	6.00
❑126, Jan 1970	6.00
❑127, Mar 1970	6.00
❑128, May 1970	6.00
❑129, Jul 1970	6.00
❑130, Sep 1970	6.00
❑131, Nov 1970; FF (a); Series becomes "Son of Tomahawk"	6.00
❑132, Jan 1971	6.00
❑133, Mar 1971 FT (a)	4.50
❑134, May 1971	4.50
❑135, Jul 1971 FT (a)	4.50
❑136, Sep 1971	4.50
❑137, Nov 1971	4.50
❑138, Jan 1972	4.50
❑139, Mar 1972; FF (a); says Son of Tomahawk on cover	4.50
❑140, May 1972; says Son of Tomahawk on cover	4.50

TOM & JERRY 50TH ANNIVERSARY SPECIAL
HARVEY

	N-MINT
❑1, Oct 1991	2.50

TOM & JERRY ADVENTURES
HARVEY

	N-MINT
❑1, May 1992	1.25

TOM & JERRY AND FRIENDS
HARVEY

	N-MINT
❑1, Dec 1991	1.25
❑2, Feb 1992	1.25
❑3, Apr 1992	1.25
❑4, Jul 1992	1.25

TOM & JERRY BIG BOOK
HARVEY

	N-MINT
❑1, Sep 1992	1.95
❑2	1.95

TOM & JERRY COMICS
DELL

	N-MINT
❑147, Oct 1956	7.00
❑148, Nov 1956	7.00
❑149, Dec 1956	7.00
❑150, Jan 1957	7.00
❑151, Feb 1957	6.00
❑152, Mar 1957	6.00
❑153, Apr 1957	6.00
❑154, May 1957	6.00
❑155, Jun 1957	6.00
❑156, Jul 1957	6.00
❑157, Aug 1957	6.00
❑158, Sep 1957	6.00
❑159, Oct 1957	6.00
❑160, Nov 1957	6.00
❑161, Dec 1957	6.00
❑162, Jan 1958	6.00
❑163, Feb 1958	6.00
❑164, Mar 1958	6.00
❑165, Apr 1958	6.00
❑166, May 1958	6.00
❑167, Jun 1958	6.00
❑168, Jul 1958	6.00
❑169, Aug 1958	6.00
❑170, Sep 1958	6.00
❑171, Oct 1958	5.00
❑172, Nov 1958	5.00
❑173, Dec 1958	5.00
❑174, Jan 1959	5.00
❑175, Feb 1959	5.00
❑176, Mar 1959	5.00
❑177, Apr 1959	5.00
❑178, May 1959	5.00
❑179, Jun 1959	5.00
❑180, Jul 1959	5.00
❑181, Aug 1959	5.00
❑182, Sep 1959	5.00
❑183, Oct 1959	5.00
❑184, Nov 1959	5.00
❑185, Dec 1959	5.00
❑186, Jan 1960	5.00
❑187, Feb 1960	5.00
❑188, Mar 1960	5.00
❑189, Apr 1960	5.00
❑190, May 1960	5.00
❑191, Jun 1960	4.00
❑192, Jul 1960	4.00
❑193, Aug 1960	4.00
❑194, Sep 1960	4.00
❑195, Oct 1960	4.00
❑196, Nov 1960	4.00
❑197, Dec 1960	4.00
❑198, Jan 1961	4.00
❑199, Feb 1961	4.00
❑200, Mar 1961	4.00
❑201, Apr 1961	3.00
❑202, May 1961	3.00
❑203, Jun 1961	3.00
❑204, Jul 1961	3.00
❑205, Aug 1961	3.00
❑206, Sep 1961	3.00
❑207, Oct 1961	3.00
❑208, Nov 1961	3.00
❑209, Jan 1962	3.00
❑210, Mar 1962	3.00
❑211, May 1962	3.00
❑212, Aug 1962	3.00
❑213, Nov 1962; Titled Tom and Jerry Funhouse	3.00
❑214, Feb 1963; Titled Tom and Jerry Funhouse	3.00
❑215, May 1963; Titled Tom and Jerry Funhouse	3.00
❑216, Aug 1963	3.00
❑217, Nov 1963	3.00
❑218, Feb 1964	3.00
❑219, May 1964	3.00
❑220, Aug 1964	3.00
❑221, Nov 1964	3.00
❑222, Feb 1965	3.00
❑223, Apr 1965	3.00
❑224, Jun 1965	3.00
❑225, Aug 1965	3.00
❑226, Oct 1965	3.00
❑227, Dec 1965	3.00
❑228, Feb 1966	3.00
❑229, Apr 1966	3.00
❑230, Jun 1966	3.00
❑231, Aug 1966	2.00
❑232, Oct 1966	2.00
❑233, Dec 1966	2.00
❑234, Feb 1967	2.00
❑235, Apr 1967	2.00

Scalp Hunter made several appearances, as *Tomahawk* wound down.

© 1971 National Periodical Publications Inc. (DC).

	N-MINT
❑236, Jun 1967	2.00
❑237, Aug 1967	2.00
❑238, Nov 1967	2.00
❑239, Feb 1968	2.00
❑240, May 1968	2.00
❑241, Aug 1968	2.00
❑242, Nov 1968	2.00
❑243, Feb 1969	2.00
❑244, Apr 1969	2.00
❑245, Jun 1969	2.00
❑246, Aug 1969	2.00
❑247, Oct 1969	2.00
❑248, Dec 1969	2.00
❑249, Feb 1970	2.00
❑250, Apr 1970	2.00
❑251, Jun 1970	2.00
❑252, Aug 1970	2.00
❑253, Oct 1970	2.00
❑254, Dec 1970	2.00
❑255, Feb 1971	2.00
❑256, Apr 1971	2.00
❑257, Jun 1971	2.00
❑258, Aug 1971	2.00
❑259, Sep 1971	2.00
❑260, Dec 1971	2.00
❑261, Dec 1971	2.00
❑262, Feb 1972	2.00
❑263, Apr 1972	2.00
❑264, Jun 1972	2.00
❑265, Aug 1972	2.00
❑266, Sep 1972	2.00
❑267, Oct 1972	2.00
❑268, Dec 1972	2.00
❑269, Feb 1973	2.00
❑270, Apr 1973	2.00
❑271, Jun 1973	1.50
❑272, Jul 1973	1.50
❑273, Aug 1973	1.50
❑274, Sep 1973	1.50
❑275, Oct 1973	1.50
❑276, Nov 1973	1.50
❑277, Dec 1973	1.50
❑278, Jan 1974	1.50
❑279, Feb 1974	1.50
❑280, Mar 1974	1.50
❑281, Apr 1974	1.50
❑282, May 1974	1.50
❑283, Jun 1974	1.50
❑284, Jul 1974	1.50
❑285, Aug 1974	1.50
❑286, Sep 1974	1.50
❑287, Oct 1974	1.50
❑288, Nov 1974	1.50
❑289, Dec 1974	1.50
❑290, Jan 1975	1.50
❑291, Feb 1975	1.50
❑292, Mar 1977	1.50
❑293, Apr 1977	1.50
❑294, May 1977	1.50
❑295, Jun 1977	1.50
❑296, Jul 1977	1.50
❑297, Aug 1977	1.50
❑298, Sep 1977	1.50
❑299, Oct 1977	1.50
❑300, Nov 1977	1.50
❑301, Dec 1977	1.00
❑302, Jan 1978	1.00

	N-MINT
❑303, Feb 1978	1.00
❑304, Mar 1978	1.00
❑305, Apr 1978	1.00
❑306, May 1978	1.00
❑307, Jun 1978	1.00
❑308, Jul 1978	1.00
❑309, Aug 1978	1.00
❑310, Sep 1978	1.00
❑311, Oct 1978	1.00
❑312, Nov 1978	1.00
❑313, Dec 1978	1.00
❑314, Jan 1979	1.00
❑315, Feb 1979	1.00
❑316, Mar 1979	1.00
❑317, Apr 1979	1.00
❑318, May 1979	1.00
❑319, Jun 1979	1.00
❑320, Jul 1979	1.00
❑321, Aug 1979	1.00
❑322, Sep 1979	1.00
❑323, Oct 1979	1.00
❑324, Nov 1979	1.00
❑325, Dec 1979	1.00
❑326, Jan 1980	1.00
❑327, Feb 1980	1.00
❑328, Apr 1980	1.00
❑329, Jun 1980	1.00
❑330, Aug 1980	1.00
❑331, Oct 1980	1.00
❑332, Dec 1980	1.00
❑333, Feb 1981	1.00
❑334, Apr 1981	1.00
❑335, ca. 1981	1.00
❑336, ca. 1981	1.00
❑337, ca. 1981	1.00
❑338, ca. 1982	1.00
❑339, ca. 1982	1.00
❑340, ca. 1982	1.00
❑341, ca. 1982	1.00
❑342, ca. 1982	1.00
❑343, ca. 1983	1.00
❑344, ca. 1983	1.00

TOM & JERRY DIGEST
HARVEY

❑1, ca. 1992	1.75

TOM & JERRY GIANT SIZE
HARVEY

❑1	1.95
❑2	2.25

TOM & JERRY SUMMER FUN (GOLD KEY)
GOLD KEY

❑1, Oct 1967; Droopy reprinted from Tom and Jerry Summer Fun (Dell) #1	35.00

TOM & JERRY (VOL. 2)
HARVEY

❑1, Sep 1991	1.50
❑2, Nov 1991	1.25
❑3, Jan 1992	1.25
❑4, Mar 1992	1.25
❑5, Jun 1992	1.25
❑6, Jan 1993	1.25
❑7, ca. 1993	1.25
❑8, ca. 1993	1.25
❑9, ca. 1993	1.50
❑10, Dec 1993	1.50
❑11, Jan 1994	1.50
❑12, Feb 1994	1.50
❑13, Mar 1994	1.50
❑14, Apr 1994	1.50
❑15, May 1994	1.50
❑16, Jun 1994	1.50
❑17, Jul 1994	1.50
❑18, Aug 1994	1.50
❑Annual 1, Sep 1994	2.25

TOMATO
STARHEAD

❑1, Apr 1994, b&w	2.75
❑2, Feb 1995, b&w	2.75

TOMB OF DARKNESS
MARVEL

	N-MINT
❑9, Jul 1974; Series continued from Beware #8	4.00
❑10, Sep 1974	4.00
❑11, Nov 1974	4.00
❑12, Jan 1975	4.00
❑13, Mar 1975	4.00
❑14, May 1975	4.00
❑15, Jul 1975	4.00
❑16, Sep 1975	4.00
❑17, Nov 1975	4.00
❑18, Jan 1976	4.00
❑19, Mar 1976	4.00
❑20, May 1976	4.00
❑20/30 cent, May 1976; 30 cent regional price variant	20.00
❑21, Jul 1976	4.00
❑21/30 cent, Jul 1976; 30 cent regional price variant	20.00
❑22, Sep 1976	4.00
❑23, Nov 1976	4.00

TOMB OF DRACULA
MARVEL

❑1, Apr 1972; NA (c); GC (a); O: Frank Drake. 1: Frank Drake. 1: Dracula (Marvel). Dracula revived	85.00
❑2, May 1972 GC (a)	25.00
❑3, Jul 1972 GC (a); 1: Rachel Van Helsing.	18.00
❑4, Sep 1972 GC (a)	18.00
❑5, Nov 1972 GC (a)	18.00
❑6, Jan 1973 GC (a)	18.00
❑7, Mar 1973 GC (a); 1: Edith Harker.	15.00
❑8, May 1973 GC (a)	12.00
❑9, Jun 1973 GC (a); 1: Lucas Brand.	12.00
❑10, Jul 1973 GC (a); 1: Blade the Vampire Slayer.	100.00
❑11, Aug 1973 GC (a)	10.00
❑12, Sep 1973 GC (a); A: Blade the Vampire Slayer.	12.00
❑13, Oct 1973 GC (a); O: Blade the Vampire Slayer. 1: Deacon Frost.	25.00
❑14, Nov 1973 GC (a); A: Blade the Vampire Slayer.	12.00
❑15, Dec 1973 GC (a)	10.00
❑16, Jan 1974 GC (a)	10.00
❑17, Feb 1974 GC (a); A: Blade the Vampire Slayer.	12.00
❑18, Mar 1974; GC (a); V: Werewolf by Night. Marvel Value Stamp #7: Werewolf	10.00
❑19, Apr 1974; GC (a); A: Blade the Vampire Slayer. Marvel Value Stamp #26: Mephisto	12.00
❑20, May 1974; GC (a); 1: Doctor Sun. Marvel Value Stamp #88: Leader	10.00
❑21, Jun 1974; GC (a); O: Doctor Sun. A: Blade the Vampire Slayer. Marvel Value Stamp #96: Dr. Octopus	10.00
❑22, Jul 1974; GC (a); Marvel Value Stamp #27: Black Widow	8.00
❑23, Aug 1974; GC (a); Marvel Value Stamp #50 : Black Panther	8.00
❑24, Sep 1974; GC (a); Marvel Value Stamp #57: Vulture	8.00
❑25, Oct 1974; GC (a); O: Hannibal King. 1: Hannibal King. Marvel Value Stamp #49: Odin	8.00
❑25-2, Oct 1974; GC (a); O: Hannibal King. 1: Hannibal King. (part of Marvel Value Pack)	1.50
❑26, Nov 1974; GC (a); Marvel Value Stamp #80: Ghost Rider	8.00
❑27, Dec 1974; GC, TP (a); Marvel Value Stamp #69: Marvel Girl	8.00
❑28, Jan 1975; GC, TP (a); 1: Adri Nitall. Marvel Value Stamp #57: Vulture	8.00
❑29, Feb 1975; GC, TP (a); Marvel Value Stamp #80: Ghost Rider	8.00
❑30, Mar 1975; GC (a); A: Blade the Vampire Slayer. Marvel Value Stamp #23: Sgt. Fury	10.00
❑31, Apr 1975; GC, TP (a); Marvel Value Stamp #45: Mantis	8.00
❑32, May 1975 GC (a)	8.00
❑33, Jun 1975 GC, TP (a)	7.00
❑34, Jul 1975; GC, TP (a); A: Brother Voodoo. Marvel Value Stamp #87: J. Jonah Jameson	7.00
❑35, Aug 1975; GC, TP (a); A: Brother Voodoo. Marvel Value Stamp #74: Stranger	7.00
❑36, Sep 1975 GC (a); A: Brother Voodoo.	7.00
❑37, Oct 1975; GC, TP (a); 1: Harold H. Harold. Marvel Value Stamp #12: Daredevil	7.00
❑38, Nov 1975 GC, TP (a); A: Doctor Sun.	7.00
❑39, Dec 1975; GC, TP (a); D: Dracula. Marvel Value Stamp #77: Swordsman	7.00
❑40, Jan 1976 GC, TP (a)	7.00
❑41, Feb 1976 GC (a); A: Blade the Vampire Slayer.	7.00
❑42, Mar 1976 GC (a); A: Blade the Vampire Slayer. V: Doctor Sun.	6.00
❑43, Apr 1976 GC (a)	6.00
❑43/30 cent, Apr 1976; 30 cent regional price variant	18.00
❑44, May 1976 GC (a); A: Hannibal King. A: Blade the Vampire Slayer. V: Doctor Strange.	6.00
❑44/30 cent, May 1976; 30 cent regional price variant	18.00
❑45, Jun 1976; GC (a); A: Hannibal King. Blade vs. Hannibal King	6.00
❑45/30 cent, Jun 1976; 30 cent regional price variant	18.00
❑46, Jul 1976; GC (a); A: Blade. A: Blade the Vampire Slayer. Wedding of Dracula	6.00
❑46/30 cent, Jul 1976; 30 cent regional price variant	18.00
❑47, Aug 1976 GC (a); A: Blade the Vampire Slayer.	6.00
❑47/30 cent, Aug 1976; 30 cent regional price variant	18.00
❑48, Sep 1976 GC (a); A: Hannibal King. A: Blade the Vampire Slayer.	6.00
❑49, Oct 1976 GC (a); A: Zorro. A: Tom Sawyer. A: D'Artagnan. A: Frankenstein. A: Blade the Vampire Slayer.	6.00
❑50, Nov 1976 GC (a); A: Blade the Vampire Slayer. A: Silver Surfer.	10.00
❑51, Dec 1976; GC, TP (a); 1: Janus. Blade vs. Hannibal King	6.00
❑52, Jan 1977 GC (a)	6.00
❑53, Feb 1977; GC (a); A: Son of Satan. Blade vs. Hannibal King and Deacon Frost	6.00
❑54, Mar 1977; GC, TP (a); O: Janus. A: Blade. birth of Dracula's son	6.00
❑55, Apr 1977 GC (a)	6.00
❑56, May 1977 GC (a)	6.00
❑57, Jun 1977 GC, TP (a)	6.00
❑58, Jul 1977 GC (a)	6.00
❑58/35 cent, Jul 1977; 35 cent regional price variant	12.00
❑59, Aug 1977 GC (a)	6.00
❑59/35 cent, Aug 1977; 35 cent regional price variant	12.00
❑60, Sep 1977 GC, TP (a)	6.00
❑60/35 cent, Sep 1977; 35 cent regional price variant	12.00
❑61, Nov 1977 GC (a); O: Janus.	5.00
❑62, Jan 1978 GC (a)	5.00
❑63, Mar 1978 GC (a)	5.00
❑64, May 1978 GC, TP (a)	5.00
❑65, Jul 1978 GC, TP (a)	5.00
❑66, Sep 1978 GC, TP (a)	5.00
❑67, Nov 1978 GC, TP (a); A: Lilith.	5.00
❑68, Feb 1979 GC (a)	5.00
❑69, Apr 1979 GC, TP (a)	5.00
❑70, Aug 1979; Double-size D: Dracula.	8.00

TOMB OF DRACULA (MAGAZINE)
MARVEL

❑1, Oct 1979, b&w; magazine GC (a)	8.00
❑2, Dec 1979 SD (a)	6.00
❑3, Feb 1980 GC, FM, TP (a)	6.00
❑4, Apr 1980 GC, JB, TP (a)	6.00
❑5, Jun 1980 GC, JB, TP (a)	6.00
❑6, Aug 1980 GC (a)	6.00

Condition price index: Multiply "NM prices" above by: **0.83 for Very Fine/Near Mint**
0.66 for Very Fine • 0.33 for Fine • 0.2 for Very Good • 0.125 for Good

N-MINT

TOMB OF DRACULA (LTD. SERIES)
MARVEL / EPIC

❑1, Nov 1991 AW, GC (a) 5.00
❑2, Dec 1991 AW, GC (a) 5.00
❑3, Jan 1992 AW, GC (a) 5.00
❑4, Feb 1992 AW, GC (a) 5.00

TOMB RAIDER/DARKNESS SPECIAL
IMAGE

❑1, ca. 2001; Topcowstore.com exclusive 4.00
❑1/A, ca. 2001; Topcowstore.com exclusive; Gold foil logo on cover 6.00

TOMB RAIDER: EPIPHANY
IMAGE

❑1, Jul 2003 4.99

TOMB RAIDER GALLERY, THE
IMAGE

❑1, Dec 2000 2.95

TOMB RAIDER: JOURNEYS
IMAGE

❑1, Feb 2002 2.95
❑2, Mar 2002 2.95
❑3, May 2002 2.95
❑4, Jun 2002 2.95
❑5, Aug 2002 2.95
❑6, Sep 2002 2.95
❑7, Oct 2002 2.99
❑8, Dec 2002 2.99
❑9, Feb 2003 2.99
❑10, Feb 2003 2.99
❑11, Apr 2003 2.99
❑12, May 2003 2.99

TOMB RAIDER MAGAZINE
IMAGE

❑1 4.95

TOMB RAIDER: TAKEOVER ONE SHOT
IMAGE

❑1, Dec 2003 2.99

TOMB RAIDER: THE SERIES
IMAGE

❑0, Jun 2001 2.50
❑0/A, Jun 2001; Painted cover; Dynamic Forces variant
❑0.5, Sep 2001 O: Lara Croft. 2.50
❑1/A, Dec 1999; Lara Croft crouching on rock with setting sun 2.50
❑1/B, Dec 1999; Lara in tree with temple in background 2.50
❑1/C, Dec 1999; Lara climbing mountain 2.50
❑1/D, Dec 1999; Lara standing in front of ruins 2.50
❑1/E, Dec 1999; Holofoil cover: Lara on rock, no sun in background 7.00
❑1/F, Dec 1999; Another Universe Exclusive 5.00
❑1/G, Dec 1999; Tower Records exclusive; Gold foil Tomb Raider logo; Lara on rock, no sun in background 3.00
❑1/H, Dec 1999; Tower records exclusive w/o gold logo 5.00
❑2, Jan 2000 2.50
❑2/A, Jan 2000; Tower Records: Santa cover with blue background 5.00
❑2/B, Jan 2000; Tower Records: Santa cover with yellowish holo-foil background 6.50
❑3, Feb 2000 2.50
❑3/A, Feb 2000; Monster Mart Edition; Lara kneeling on ruins, Monster Mart logo in lower right 7.00
❑3/B, Feb 2000; Gold Monster Mart edition; Lara kneeling on ruins, Monster Mart logo in lower right 6.00
❑4, Apr 2000; Lara sitting on root of tree, man standing, flames behind 2.50
❑4/A, Apr 2000; Lara in tree, DF logo at bottom left. 4.00
❑4/B, Apr 2000; Similar cover to 4, with Certificate of Authenticity 8.00
❑5, May 2000; Lara standing, dinosaur skeleton in background 2.50
❑5/A, May 2000; Dynamic Forces variant, Tomb Raider logo in upper right, DF logo below, Lara standing on Triceratops skull 6.00
❑6, Jul 2000 2.50
❑7, Jul 2000 2.50
❑7/A, Jul 2000; Museum edition, limited to 25 copies. 125.00
❑8, Oct 2000 2.50
❑9, Dec 2000; Lara sitting, faces in background 2.50
❑9/A, Dec 2000; White background, holding two guns 4.00
❑9/B, Dec 2000; Lara fighting crocodile, DF logo at top left 6.00
❑9/C, Dec 2000; Lara fighting crocodile, blue foil around DF logo at top left 6.00
❑9/D, Dec 2000; Sketch cover, black and white 10.00
❑10, Jan 2001 2.50
❑10/A, Jan 2001; Gold foil around Tomb Raider logo, includes Certificate of Authenticity 10.00
❑10/B, Jan 2001; Red foil around Tomb Raider logo, includes Certificate of Authenticity 10.00
❑11, Mar 2001 2.50
❑11/A, Mar 2001; Graham Crackers Blue Foil Edition; Limited to 2,000 copies 5.00
❑12, Apr 2001 2.50
❑13, May 2001 2.50
❑14, Jul 2001 2.50
❑15, Sep 2001 2.50
❑15/A, Sep 2001; DFE red foil cover 10.00
❑16, Oct 2001 2.50
❑17, Nov 2001 2.50
❑18, Dec 2001 2.50
❑19, Jan 2002 2.50
❑20, Feb 2002 2.50
❑21, May 2002 2.50
❑22, Jul 2002 2.50
❑23, Aug 2002 2.50
❑24, Oct 2002; Endgame Prelude 2.99
❑25, Nov 2002 2.99
❑26, Feb 2003 2.99
❑27, Feb 2003 2.99
❑28, Apr 2003 2.99
❑29, May 2003 2.99
❑30, Jun 2003 2.99
❑31, Jun 2003 2.99
❑32, Aug 2003 2.99
❑33, Sep 2003 2.99
❑34, Oct 2003 2.99
❑35, Nov 2003 2.99
❑36, Jan 2004 2.99
❑37, Feb 2004 2.99
❑38, Apr 2004 2.99
❑39, Apr 2004 2.99
❑40, May 2004 2.99
❑41, May 2004 2.99
❑42, Aug 2004 2.99
❑43, Aug 2004 2.99
❑Ashcan 1; Preview edition 5.00
❑Ashcan 1/A; Convention edition; Preview cover, with second outer cover (black & white) with Lara Croft on front, logo with white space on back 5.00

TOMB RAIDER/WITCHBLADE
IMAGE

❑1, Dec 1997; Green Cover 6.00
❑1/A, Dec 1997; Brown cover 6.00
❑1/B, Dec 1997 20.00
❑1-2, Dec 1998, titled "Tomb Raider/ Witchblade Revisited" 2.95

TOMB TALES
CRYPTIC

❑1, b&w; cardstock cover 3.00
❑2, Jun 1997, b&w; cardstock cover 3.00

TOM CORBETT
ETERNITY

❑1, Jan 1990, b&w; Original material 2.25
❑2, Feb 1990, b&w; Original material 2.25

The adventures of MGM's Tom and Jerry cartoons easily made the leap to comics.
© 1972 MGM (Dell)

N-MINT

❑3, Mar 1990, b&w; Space Academy photo inside front cover 2.25
❑4, May 1990, b&w; Interior photo of Tom (Frankie Thomas), Roger (Jan Merlin), Astro (Al Markin), Capt. Strong (Ed Bryce), and Dr. Joan Dale (Margaret Garland) [from Tom Corbett, Space Cadet (Dell) #10] 2.25

TOM CORBETT BOOK TWO
ETERNITY

❑1, Sep 1990, b&w 2.25
❑2, Oct 1990, b&w 2.25
❑3, Oct 1990, b&w 2.25
❑4, Nov 1990, b&w 2.25

TOM JUDGE: END OF DAYS
IMAGE

❑1, Sep 2003 3.99

TOM LANDRY
SPIRE

❑1, ca. 1973 3.00

TOMMI GUNN
LONDON NIGHT

❑1, May 1996 3.00

TOMMI GUNN: KILLER'S LUST
LONDON NIGHT

❑1, Feb 1997 3.00
❑1/Nude, Feb 1997; chromium cover 3.00

TOM MIX WESTERN
AC

❑1 2.95
❑2, b&w 2.50

TOMMY AND THE MONSTERS
NEW COMICS

❑1, b&w 1.95

TOMOE
CRUSADE

❑0, Mar 1996 3.00
❑0/Ltd., Mar 1996; Limited edition (5,000 printed) 4.00
❑0/Variant, Mar 1996; variant cover 3.00
❑1, Apr 1996 3.00
❑1/Ltd., Apr 1996; Limited edition (5,000 printed) 4.00
❑1-2; Fan Appreciation Edition; contains preview of Manga Shi 2000 3.00
❑2, May 1996 3.00
❑3, Jun 1996 3.00

TOMOE: UNFORGETTABLE FIRE
CRUSADE

❑1, Jun 1997; prequel to Shi: The Series 2.95
❑1/Ltd., Jun 1997; American Entertainment Exclusive Edition; No cover price; prequel to Shi: The Series 3.50

TOMOE/WITCHBLADE: FIRE SERMON
CRUSADE

❑1, Sep 1996; one-shot crossover with Image 3.95
❑1/A, Sep 1996; Avalon edition; no cover price 3.95

TOMORROW KNIGHTS
MARVEL / EPIC

❑1, Jun 1990 1.95
❑2, Jul 1990 1.50
❑3, Sep 1990 1.50
❑4, Nov 1990 1.50
❑5, Jan 1991 1.50
❑6, Mar 1991 1.50

N-MINT

TOMORROW MAN
ANTARCTIC

❑1, Aug 1993, b&w; foil cover 2.95

TOMORROW MAN & KNIGHT HUNTER: LAST RITES
ANTARCTIC

❑1, Jul 1994, b&w 2.75
❑2, Oct 1994, b&w 2.75
❑3, Dec 1994, b&w 2.75
❑4, Feb 1995, b&w 2.75
❑5, Apr 1995, b&w 2.75
❑6, Jun 1995, b&w 2.75

TOMORROW STORIES
DC / AMERICA'S BEST COMICS

❑1, Oct 1999 AMo (w); KN (a) 4.00
❑2, Nov 1999 AMo (w) 3.00
❑3, Dec 1999 AMo (w); KN (a) 2.95
❑4, Jan 2000 AMo (w); KN (a) 2.95
❑5, Feb 2000 AMo (w) 2.95
❑6, Feb 2000 AMo (w) 2.95
❑7, Apr 2000 AMo (w) 2.95
❑8, Jul 2000 AMo (w) 2.95
❑9, Feb 2001 AMo (w); O: The First American. 2.95
❑10, Jun 2001 KN (a) 2.95
❑11, Oct 2001 .... 2.95
❑12, Dec 2001 .... 2.95

TOM STRONG
DC / AMERICA'S BEST COMICS

❑1, Jun 1999 .... 4.00
❑2, Jul 1999 .... 3.00
❑3, Aug 1999 .... 2.95
❑4, Oct 1999 .... 2.95
❑5, Dec 1999 .... 2.95
❑6, Feb 2000 .... 2.95
❑7, Mar 2000 .... 2.95
❑8, Jul 2000 .... 2.95
❑9, Sep 2000 .... 2.95
❑10, Nov 2000 .... 2.95
❑11, Jan 2001 .... 2.95
❑12, Feb 2001; JLA homage cover 2.95
❑13, Mar 2001; Marvel Family homage cover 2.95
❑14, Apr 2001 .... 2.95
❑15, May 2001; Fantastic Four homage cover 2.95
❑16, Jun 2001 .... 2.95
❑17, Aug 2002 .... 2.95
❑18, Dec 2002 .... 2.95
❑19, Apr 2003 .... 2.95
❑20, Jun 2003 .... 2.95
❑21, Oct 2003 .... 2.95
❑22, Dec 2003 .... 2.95
❑23, Jan 2004 .... 2.95
❑24, Feb 2004 .... 2.95
❑25, May 2004 .... 2.95
❑26, Jul 2004 .... 2.95
❑27, Sep 2004 ....

TOM STRONG'S TERRIFIC TALES
DC / AMERICA'S BEST COMICS

❑1, Jan 2002 .... 3.50
❑2 .... 2.95
❑3 JOy (a) 2.95
❑4, Nov 2002 .... 2.95
❑5 .... 2.95
❑6, Apr 2003 .... 2.95
❑7, Jul 2003 .... 2.95
❑8, Dec 2003 .... 2.95
❑9, Apr 2004 .... 2.95
❑10, Jun 2004 .... 2.95
❑11, Sep 2004 ....

TONGUE*LASH
DARK HORSE

❑1, Aug 1996 .... 2.95
❑2, Sep 1996 .... 2.95

TONGUE*LASH II
DARK HORSE

❑1, Feb 1999 .... 2.95
❑2, Mar 1999 .... 2.95

TONY BRAVADO, TROUBLE-SHOOTER
RENEGADE

❑1, b&w 2.00
❑2, b&w 2.00
❑3, b&w 2.50
❑4, b&w 2.50

TOOL & DIE
FLASHPOINT

❑1, Mar 1994 .... 2.50

TOO MUCH COFFEE MAN
ADHESIVE

❑1, ca. 1993, b&w 12.00
❑2, b&w 8.00
❑3, b&w 6.00
❑4, b&w 5.00
❑5, b&w 5.00
❑6 .... 3.00
❑7 .... 3.00
❑8, Feb 1998 .... 3.00
❑MC 1; Mini-comic 10.00
❑MC 1-2; Mini-comic 3.00
❑MC 2; Mini-comic 8.00
❑MC 2-2; Mini-comic 3.00
❑MC 3; Mini-comic 8.00
❑MC 3-2; Mini-comic 3.00
❑MC 4; Mini-comic 6.00
❑MC 4-2; Mini-comic 3.00
❑Special 1, Jul 1997, b&w 3.00
❑Special 2; Full-Color Special Edition 3.00

TOON WARZ: THE FANDOM MENACE
SIRIUS

❑1/A, Jul 1999; Believe This Man cover 2.95
❑1/B, Jul 1999; Vain Affair cover 2.95
❑1/C, Jul 1999; Newspeak cover 2.95
❑1/D, Jul 1999; Primear cover 2.95

TOOTH AND CLAW
IMAGE

❑1, Aug 1999 .... 2.95
❑2, Sep 1999; Woman-cat holding skull on cover 2.95
❑2/A, Sep 1999; alternate cover 2.95
❑3, Oct 1999 .... 2.95
❑Ashcan 1 1999; DF Exclusive preview book 2.00

TOP 10
DC / AMERICA'S BEST COMICS

❑1, Sep 1999 .... 3.50
❑2, Oct 1999 .... 2.95
❑3, Nov 1999 .... 2.95
❑4, Dec 1999 .... 2.95
❑5, Jan 2000 .... 2.95
❑6, Feb 2000 .... 2.95
❑7, Apr 2000 .... 2.95
❑8, Jun 2000 .... 2.95
❑9, Oct 2000 .... 2.95
❑10, Jan 2001 .... 2.95
❑11, May 2001 .... 2.95
❑12, Oct 2001 .... 2.95

TOP CAT (DELL)
DELL

❑1, Dec 1961 .... 60.00
❑2, Mar 1962 .... 35.00
❑3, Jun 1962 .... 25.00
❑4, Oct 1962 .... 25.00
❑5, Jan 1963 .... 25.00
❑6, Apr 1963 .... 20.00
❑7, Jul 1963 .... 20.00
❑8, Oct 1963 .... 20.00
❑9, Jan 1964 .... 20.00
❑10, Apr 1964 .... 20.00
❑11, Jul 1964 .... 15.00
❑12, Oct 1964 .... 15.00
❑13, Jan 1965 .... 15.00
❑14, Apr 1965 .... 15.00
❑15, Jul 1965 .... 15.00
❑16, Oct 1965 .... 15.00
❑17, Jan 1966 .... 15.00
❑18 1966 .... 15.00
❑19 1966 .... 15.00
❑20 1967 .... 15.00
❑21, Dec 1967 .... 12.00
❑22, ca. 1968 .... 12.00
❑23, ca. 1968 .... 12.00
❑24, Dec 1968 .... 12.00
❑25, Mar 1969 .... 12.00
❑26, Jun 1969 .... 12.00
❑27, Sep 1969 .... 12.00
❑28, Dec 1969 .... 12.00
❑29, Mar 1970 .... 12.00
❑30, Jun 1970 .... 12.00
❑31, Sep 1970 .... 12.00

TOP CAT (CHARLTON)
CHARLTON

❑1, Nov 1970 .... 20.00
❑2, Jan 1971 .... 12.00
❑3, Mar 1971 .... 8.00
❑4, May 1971 .... 8.00
❑5, Jul 1971 .... 8.00
❑6, Sep 1971 .... 5.00
❑7, Nov 1971 .... 5.00
❑8, Dec 1971 .... 5.00
❑9, Feb 1972 .... 5.00
❑10, Apr 1972 .... 5.00
❑11, Jun 1972 .... 4.00
❑12, Aug 1972 .... 4.00
❑13, Oct 1972 .... 4.00
❑14, Nov 1972 .... 4.00
❑15, Feb 1973 .... 4.00
❑16, Mar 1973 .... 4.00
❑17, May 1973 .... 4.00
❑18, Jul 1973 .... 4.00
❑19, Sep 1973 .... 4.00
❑20, Nov 1973 .... 4.00

TOP COMICS: FLINTSTONES
GOLD KEY

❑1, ca. 1967 .... 10.00
❑2, ca. 1967 .... 10.00
❑3, ca. 1967 .... 15.00
❑4, ca. 1967 .... 15.00

TOP COMICS: FLIPPER
GOLD KEY

❑1, ca. 1967 .... 10.00

TOP COMICS: LASSIE
GOLD KEY

❑1, ca. 1967; Reprints Lassie #68; no cover price 10.00

TOP COMICS: MICKEY MOUSE
GOLD KEY

❑1, ca. 1967 .... 10.00
❑2, ca. 1967 .... 10.00
❑3, ca. 1967 .... 15.00
❑4, ca. 1967 .... 15.00

TOP COMICS: TWEETY & SYLVESTER
GOLD KEY

❑1, ca. 1967 .... 10.00
❑2, ca. 1967 .... 10.00

TOP COW 2003 COMPILATION SPECIAL
IMAGE

❑1, Mar 2003 .... 3.00

TOP COW: BOOK OF REVELATION 2003
IMAGE

❑1, Jun 2003 .... 3.99

TOP COW CLASSICS IN BLACK AND WHITE: APHRODITE IX
IMAGE

❑1, Sep 2000 .... 2.95
❑1/A, Sep 2000; Sketch cover (marked as such) ....

TOP COW CLASSICS IN BLACK AND WHITE: ASCENSCION
IMAGE

❑1/A, Apr 2000; Sketch cover (marked as such) 2.95
❑1, Apr 2000 .... 2.95

N-MINT

TOP COW CLASSICS IN BLACK AND WHITE: FATHOM
IMAGE

❑1, May 2000 .... 2.95

TOP COW CLASSICS IN BLACK AND WHITE: MAGDALENA
IMAGE

❑1, Oct 2002, b&w and color; Black background on cover 2.95

TOP COW CLASSICS IN BLACK AND WHITE: MIDNIGHT NATION
IMAGE

❑1, Mar 2001 .... 2.95

TOP COW CLASSICS IN BLACK AND WHITE: RISING STARS
IMAGE

❑1, Aug 2000 .... 2.95

TOP COW CLASSICS IN BLACK AND WHITE: THE DARKNESS
IMAGE

❑1, Mar 2000 .... 2.95

TOP COW CLASSICS IN BLACK AND WHITE: TOMB RAIDER
IMAGE

❑1, Dec 2000 .... 2.95

TOP COW CLASSICS IN BLACK AND WHITE: WITCHBLADE
IMAGE

❑1, Feb 2000 .... 2.95
❑1/A 5.00
❑25, Apr 2001 .... 2.95

TOP COW CON SKETCHBOOK 2004
IMAGE

❑1, Aug 2004 .... 3.00

TOP COW PRODUCTIONS INC./BALLISTIC STUDIOS SWIMSUIT SPECIAL
IMAGE

❑1, May 1995 .... 2.95

TOP COW SECRETS
IMAGE

❑WS 1, Jan 1996; Special Winter Lingerie Edition; pin-ups 2.95

TOP COW SPECIAL
IMAGE

❑1; Spring/Summer 2001 .... 2.95

TOP DOG
MARVEL / STAR

❑1, Apr 1985 1: Top Dog. 1.00
❑2, Jun 1985 .... 1.00
❑3, Aug 1985 .... 1.00
❑4, Oct 1985 .... 1.00
❑5, Dec 1985 .... 1.00
❑6, Feb 1986 .... 1.00
❑7, Apr 1986 .... 1.00
❑8, Jun 1986 .... 1.00
❑9, Aug 1986 .... 1.00
❑10, Oct 1986 .... 1.00
❑11, Dec 1986 .... 1.00
❑12, Feb 1987 .... 1.00
❑13, Apr 1987 .... 1.00
❑14, Jun 1987 .... 1.00

TOP ELIMINATOR
CHARLTON

❑25 1967; From Teenage Hotrodders #24 .... 10.00
❑26, Nov 1967 A: Scot Jackson and the Rod Masters. 10.00
❑27 1968 .... 10.00
❑28 1968 .... 10.00
❑29, Jul 1968 .... 10.00

TOPPS COMICS PRESENTS
TOPPS

❑0, Jul 1999; Previewed Teenagents, Silver Star, Jack Kirby's Secret City Saga, Bill the Galactic Hero, etc. 1.50
❑1, Sep 1999; giveaway 1.00

N-MINT

TOP SHELF (PRIMAL GROOVE)
PRIMAL GROOVE

❑1, Win 1995, b&w 5.00

TOP SHELF (TOP SHELF)
TOP SHELF

❑1, ca. 1996 .... 6.95
❑2, ca. 1997 .... 6.95
❑3, ca. 1997 .... 6.95
❑4, ca. 1997 .... 6.95
❑5, ca. 1998 .... 6.95
❑6, ca. 1998 .... 6.95
❑7, ca. 1998 .... 6.95

TOR (DC)
DC

❑1, Jun 1975 JKu (w); JKu (a); O: Tor. 6.00
❑2, Aug 1975 JKu (w); JKu (a) 2.00
❑3, Oct 1975 JKu (w); JKu (a) 2.00
❑4, Dec 1975 JKu (w); JKu (a) 2.00
❑5, Feb 1976 JKu (w); JKu (a) 2.00
❑6, Apr 1976 JKu (w); JKu (a) 2.00

TOR (EPIC)
MARVEL / EPIC

❑1, Jun 1993; large size 5.95
❑2, Jul 1993; large size 5.95
❑3 1993; large size 5.95
❑4 1993; large size 5.95

TOR 3-D
ECLIPSE

❑1, Jul 1986 .... 2.50
❑2, Aug 1987 .... 2.50

TORCH OF LIBERTY SPECIAL
DARK HORSE

❑1, Jan 1995 .... 2.50

TORCHY (INNOVATION)
INNOVATION

❑1, b&w 2.50
❑2, b&w 2.50
❑3, b&w 2.50
❑4, b&w 2.50
❑5, b&w 2.50
❑9, b&w; 1st Olivia cover 2.50
❑Summer 1, b&w; Summer Fun Special 2.50

TORG
ADVENTURE

❑1, b&w 2.50
❑2, Mar 1992, b&w 2.50
❑3, Apr 1992, b&w 2.50
❑4, May 1992, b&w 2.50

TORI DO
PENGUIN PALACE

❑1, Aug 1994, b&w 2.25
❑1-2, Mar 1995 .... 2.25

TO RIVERDALE AND BACK AGAIN
ARCHIE

❑1, ca. 1990 .... 2.50

TOR JOHNSON: HOLLYWOOD STAR
MONSTER

❑1, b&w 2.50

TOR LOVE BETTY
FANTAGRAPHICS / EROS

❑1, b&w 2.75

TORMENT
AIRCEL

❑1, b&w 2.95
❑2, b&w 2.95
❑3, b&w 2.95

TORPEDO
HARD BOILED

❑1, b&w 2.95
❑2, b&w 2.95
❑3, b&w 2.95
❑4, b&w 2.95

TORRID AFFAIRS
ETERNITY

❑1 1988, b&w 2.25
❑2/A, Feb 1989; tame cover 2.25
❑2/B, Feb 1989; sexy cover 2.25

"Jack B. Quick," the adventures of a boy genius, is just one of the stories in the anthology series *Tomorrow Stories.*

© 1999 America's Best Comics (DC).

N-MINT

❑3 1989 .... 2.95
❑4 1989 .... 2.95
❑5 1989 .... 2.95

TORSO
IMAGE

❑1 1999 BMB (w) 3.95
❑2 1999 BMB (w) 3.95
❑3 1999 BMB (w) 4.95
❑4 1999 BMB (w) 4.95
❑5, Jun 1999 BMB (w); BMB (a) 4.95
❑6 1999 BMB (w); BMB (a) 4.95

TORTOISE AND THE HARE, THE
LAST GASP

❑1 .... 3.00

TOTAL ECLIPSE
ECLIPSE

❑1, May 1988 .... 3.95
❑2, Aug 1988 .... 3.95
❑3, Dec 1988 .... 3.95
❑4, Jan 1989 .... 3.95
❑5, Apr 1989 .... 3.95

TOTAL ECLIPSE: THE SERAPHIM OBJECTIVE
ECLIPSE

❑1, Nov 1988 .... 1.95

TOTAL JUSTICE
DC

❑1, Oct 1996; based on Kenner action figures 2.25
❑2, Nov 1996; based on Kenner action figures 2.25
❑3, Nov 1996; based on Kenner action figures 2.25

TOTALLY ALIEN
TRIGON

❑1, b&w 2.50
❑2, b&w 2.50
❑3, b&w 2.50
❑4, b&w 2.50
❑5, b&w 2.50

TOTALLY HORSES!
PAINTED PONY

❑1; magazine; horse stories 1.95
❑2, Spr 1997; magazine; horse stories 1.95
❑3; magazine; horse stories 1.95
❑4; magazine; horse stories 1.95
❑5, Sum 1998; magazine; horse stories 1.95

TOTAL RECALL
DC

❑1, ca. 1990 .... 2.95

TOTAL WAR
GOLD KEY

❑1, Jul 1965 .... 40.00
❑2, Oct 1965; Series continued in M.A.R.S. Patrol #3 .... 35.00

TOTEMS (VERTIGO)
DC / VERTIGO

❑1, Feb 2000 .... 5.95

TOTEMS (CARTOON FROLICS)
CARTOON FROLICS

❑1 .... 2.95
❑2 .... 2.95
❑3 .... 2.95

Condition price index: Multiply "NM prices" above by: **0.83 for Very Fine/Near Mint**
0.66 for Very Fine • 0.33 for Fine • 0.2 for Very Good • 0.125 for Good

N-MINT

TOTEM: SIGN OF THE WARDOG (1ST SERIES)
Alpha Productions
❑1, b&w ... 2.25
❑2, b&w ... 2.25

TOTEM: SIGN OF THE WARDOG (2ND SERIES)
Alpha Productions
❑1, Apr 1992, b&w ... 2.50
❑2, b&w ... 2.50
❑Annual 1 ... 3.50

TOUCH
DC
❑1, Jun 2004 ... 2.50
❑2, Jul 2004 ... 2.50
❑3, Aug 2004 ... 2.50
❑4, Sep 2004 ...

TOUCH OF SILK, A TASTE OF LEATHER, A
Boneyard
❑1, Mar 1994, b&w ... 2.95

TOUCH OF SILVER, A
Image
❑1, Jan 1997, b&w; semi-autobiographical ... 2.95
❑2, Mar 1997, b&w; semi-autobiographical ... 2.95
❑3, May 1997, b&w; semi-autobiographical ... 2.95
❑4, Jul 1997, b&w; semi-autobiographical ... 2.95
❑5, Sep 1997; b&w with color section; semi-autobiographical ... 2.95
❑6, Nov 1997, b&w; semi-autobiographical ... 2.95

TOUGH GUYS AND WILD WOMEN
Eternity
❑1, Mar 1989, b&w; Saint reprints ... 2.25
❑2, b&w; Saint reprints ... 2.25

TOWER OF SHADOWS
Marvel
❑1, Sep 1969 JCr, JSo, SL (w); JB, JCr, JSo (a) ... 20.00
❑2, Nov 1969 NA (a) ... 12.00
❑3, Jan 1970 ... 12.00
❑4, Jan 1970 ... 10.00
❑5, May 1970 WW (a) ... 10.00
❑6, Jul 1970 TS, SL (w); TS, SD, GC, WW (a) ... 10.00
❑7, Sep 1970 WW (a) ... 10.00
❑8, Nov 1970 SD, WW (a) ... 10.00
❑9, Nov 1970; Series continued in Creatures On the Loose #10 ... 8.00
❑Special 1, Dec 1971 ... 10.00

TOXIC!
Apocalypse
❑1; Marshal Law ... 2.50
❑2; Marshal Law ... 2.50
❑3; Marshal Law ... 2.50
❑4; Marshal Law ... 2.50
❑5; Marshal Law; Mutomatic; The Driver ... 2.50
❑6; Marshal Law ... 2.50
❑7; Marshal Law ... 2.50
❑8; Marshal Law ... 2.50
❑9; Marshal Law ... 2.50
❑10; Marshal Law ... 2.50
❑11; Marshal Law ... 2.50
❑12; Marshal Law ... 2.50
❑13; Marshal Law ... 2.50
❑14; Marshal Law ... 2.50
❑15; Marshal Law ... 2.50
❑16; Marshal Law ... 2.50
❑17; Marshal Law ... 2.50
❑18; Marshal Law ... 2.50
❑19; Marshal Law ... 2.50

TOXIC AVENGER
Marvel
❑1, Apr 1991 O: Toxic Avenger. 1: Toxic Avenger. ... 2.00
❑2, May 1991 ... 1.50
❑3, Jun 1991 ... 1.50
❑4, Jul 1991 ... 1.50
❑5, Aug 1991 ... 1.50
❑6, Sep 1991 VM (a) ... 1.50
❑7, Oct 1991 VM (a) ... 1.50
❑8, Nov 1991 ... 1.50
❑9, Dec 1991 ... 1.50
❑10, Jan 1992 ... 1.50
❑11, Feb 1992 VM (a) ... 1.50

TOXIC CRUSADERS
Marvel
❑1, May 1992 ... 1.25
❑2, Jun 1992 ... 1.25
❑3, Jul 1992 ... 1.25
❑4, Aug 1992 ... 1.25
❑5, Sep 1992 ... 1.25
❑6, Oct 1992 ... 1.25
❑7, Nov 1992 ... 1.25
❑8, Dec 1992 ... 1.25

TOXIC GUMBO
DC / Vertigo
❑1, May 1998; prestige format ... 5.95

TOXIC PARADISE
Slave Labor
❑1, b&w; Love & Romance; cardstock cover ... 4.95

TOXINE
Nose
❑1 ... 3.00

TOYBOY
Continuity
❑1, Oct 1986 ... 2.00
❑2, Aug 1987 ... 2.00
❑3, Nov 1987 ... 2.00
❑4, Feb 1988 ... 2.00
❑5, Jun 1988 ... 2.00
❑6 1988 ... 2.00
❑7, Mar 1989 ... 2.00

TOY STORY (DISNEY'S...)
Marvel
❑1, Dec 1995 ... 4.95

TRACI LORDS: THE OUTLAW YEARS
Boneyard
❑1 ... 3.00

TRACKER
Blackthorne
❑1, May 1988, b&w ... 2.00
❑2, b&w ... 2.00

TRAGG AND THE SKY GODS
Whitman
❑1, Jun 1975 DS (a) ... 5.00
❑2, Sep 1975 ... 3.00
❑3, Dec 1975 ... 2.50
❑4, Feb 1976 ... 2.50
❑5, Apr 1976 ... 2.50
❑6, Sep 1976 ... 2.50
❑7, Nov 1976 ... 2.50
❑8, Feb 1977 ... 2.50
❑9, May 1982 ... 2.50

TRAILER TRASH
Tundra
❑1, b&w ... 2.00
❑4, b&w ... 2.95
❑7, Jun 1996, b&w ... 2.95
❑8, Nov 1996, b&w ... 2.95

TRAKK: MONSTER HUNTER
Image
❑1, Nov 2003 ... 2.95
❑2, Apr 2004 ... 2.95

TRANCERS
Eternity
❑1, Aug 1991 ... 2.50
❑2 ... 2.50

TRANQUILITY
Dreamsmith
❑1, Sep 1998, b&w ... 2.50
❑2, Oct 1998, b&w ... 2.50
❑3, Nov 1998, b&w ... 2.50

TRANQUILIZER
Luxurious
❑1 ... 2.95
❑2 ... 2.95

TRANSFORMERS, THE
Marvel
❑1, Sep 1984; 1: Transformers. "Limited Series #1" ... 10.00
❑2, Nov 1984; "Limited Series #2" ... 5.00
❑3, Jan 1985; Spider-Man; "Limited Series #3" ... 5.00
❑4, Mar 1985; "Limited Series #4" ... 3.00
❑5, Jun 1985 ... 3.00
❑6, Jul 1985 ... 3.00
❑7, Aug 1985 ... 3.00
❑8, Sep 1985 A: Dinobots. ... 3.00
❑9, Oct 1985 ... 3.00
❑10, Nov 1985 V: Devastator. ... 3.00
❑11, Dec 1985 V: Jetfire. ... 3.00
❑12, Jan 1986 ... 3.00
❑13, Feb 1986 ... 3.00
❑14, Mar 1986 ... 3.00
❑15, Apr 1986 ... 3.00
❑16, May 1986 ... 3.00
❑17, Jun 1986 ... 3.00
❑18, Jul 1986 ... 3.00
❑19, Aug 1986 ... 3.00
❑20, Sep 1986 ... 3.00
❑21, Oct 1986 1: Aerialbots. ... 2.00
❑22, Nov 1986 ... 2.00
❑23, Dec 1986 ... 2.00
❑24, Jan 1987 ... 2.00
❑25, Feb 1987 ... 2.00
❑26, Mar 1987 ... 2.00
❑27, Apr 1987 ... 2.00
❑28, May 1987 ... 2.00
❑29, Jun 1987 ... 2.00
❑30, Jul 1987 ... 2.00
❑31, Aug 1987 ... 2.00
❑32, Sep 1987 ... 2.00
❑33, Oct 1987 ... 2.00
❑34, Nov 1987 ... 2.00
❑35, Dec 1987 ... 2.00
❑36, Jan 1988 ... 2.00
❑37, Feb 1988 ... 2.00
❑38, Mar 1988 ... 2.00
❑39, Apr 1988 ... 2.00
❑40, May 1988 ... 2.00
❑41, Jun 1988 ... 2.00
❑42, Jul 1988 ... 2.00
❑43, Aug 1988 ... 2.00
❑44, Sep 1988 ... 2.00
❑45, Oct 1988 ... 2.00
❑46, Nov 1988 ... 2.00
❑47, Dec 1988 ... 2.00
❑48, Jan 1989 ... 2.00
❑49, Feb 1989 ... 2.00
❑50, Mar 1989 ... 2.00
❑51, Apr 1989 ... 2.00
❑52, May 1989 ... 2.00
❑53, Jun 1989 ... 2.00
❑54, Jul 1989 ... 2.00
❑55, Aug 1989 ... 2.00
❑56, Sep 1989 ... 2.00
❑57, Oct 1989 ... 2.00
❑58, Nov 1989 ... 2.00
❑59, Nov 1989 ... 2.00
❑60, Dec 1989 ... 2.00
❑61, Dec 1989 ... 2.00
❑62, Jan 1990 ... 2.00
❑63, Feb 1990 ... 2.00
❑64, Mar 1990 ... 2.00
❑65, Apr 1990 ... 2.00
❑66, May 1990 ... 2.00
❑67, Jun 1990 ... 2.00
❑68, Jul 1990 ... 2.00
❑69, Aug 1990 ... 2.00
❑70, Sep 1990 ... 5.00
❑71, Oct 1990 ... 5.00
❑72, Nov 1990 ... 5.00
❑73, Dec 1990 ... 5.00

	N-MINT
❑74, Jan 1991	5.00
❑75, Feb 1991; Double-size	5.00
❑76, Mar 1991	5.00
❑77, Apr 1991	10.00
❑78, May 1991	10.00
❑79, Jun 1991	10.00
❑80, Jul 1991	18.00

TRANSFORMERS: ARMADA
DREAMWAVE

	N-MINT
❑1, Jul 2002 (w)	2.95
❑1/A, Jul 2002, (w); chromium cover	2.95
❑2, Aug 2002	2.95
❑3, Oct 2002	2.95
❑4, Nov 2002	2.95
❑5, Dec 2002	2.95
❑6, Dec 2002	2.95
❑7, Jan 2003	2.95
❑7/A, Jan 2003, White background on cover	3.50
❑8, Feb 2003	2.95
❑9, Mar 2003	2.95
❑10, Apr 2003	2.95
❑11, May 2003	2.95
❑12, Jun 2003	2.95
❑13, Jul 2003	2.95
❑14, Aug 2003	2.95
❑15, Sep 2003	2.95
❑16, Oct 2003	2.95
❑17, Nov 2003	2.95
❑18, Dec 2003	2.95

TRANSFORMERS ARMADA: MORE THAN MEETS THE EYE
DARK HORSE

	N-MINT
❑1, Mar 2004	4.95
❑2, Apr 2004	4.95
❑3, May 2004	4.95

TRANSFORMERS COMICS MAGAZINE
MARVEL

	N-MINT
❑1, Jan 1987; digest	1.50
❑2, Mar 1987	1.50
❑3, May 1987	1.50
❑4, Jul 1987	1.50
❑5, Sep 1987	1.50
❑6, Nov 1987	1.50
❑7, Jan 1988	1.50
❑8, Mar 1988	1.50
❑9, May 1988	1.50
❑10, Jul 1988	1.50

TRANSFORMERS: ENERGON
DARK HORSE

	N-MINT
❑19, Jan 2004	2.95
❑20, Feb 2004	2.95
❑21, Mar 2004	2.95
❑22, Apr 2004	2.95
❑23, May 2004	2.95
❑24, Jun 2004	2.95

TRANSFORMERS/GEN13
MARVEL

	N-MINT
❑Ashcan 1	1.00

TRANSFORMERS: GENERATION 1
DREAMWAVE

	N-MINT
❑1/A, Apr 2002; Autobot cover	4.00
❑1/B, Apr 2002; Decepticon cover	4.00
❑1/C, Apr 2002; chromium cover	5.95
❑1/D, Apr 2002; Retailer Incentive Version	20.00
❑1-2, Apr 2002	2.95
❑1-3, Apr 2002	2.95
❑2/A, May 2002; Autobots cover	3.50
❑2/B, May 2002; Decepticon cover	3.50
❑2-2, May 2002	2.95
❑3/A, Jun 2002; Autobots cover	2.95
❑3/B, Jun 2002; Decepticon cover	2.95
❑4/A, Jul 2002; Autobots cover	2.95
❑4/B, Jul 2002; Decepticon cover	2.95
❑5/A, Aug 2002; Autobots cover	2.95
❑5/B, Aug 2002; Decepticon cover	2.95
❑5-2, Nov 2002	2.95
❑6/A, Oct 2002; Autobots cover	2.95
❑6/B, Oct 2002; Decepticon cover	2.95

TRANSFORMERS: GENERATION 1 (VOL 2)
DREAMWAVE

	N-MINT
❑1, Apr 2003	2.95
❑1/CF, Apr 2003; Chrome Cover	5.95
❑2, May 2003	2.95
❑3, Jun 2003	2.95
❑4, Jul 2003	2.95
❑5, Aug 2003	2.95
❑6, Oct 2003	2.95

TRANSFORMERS: GENERATION 1 (VOL 3)
DREAMWAVE

	N-MINT
❑0, Dec 2003	2.95
❑1, Feb 2004	2.95
❑2, Feb 2004	2.95
❑3, Mar 2004	2.95
❑4, Apr 2004	2.95
❑5, Jun 2004	2.95

TRANSFORMERS: GENERATION 1 PREVIEW
DREAMWAVE

	N-MINT
❑1/A, Apr 2002; Autobot cover	3.95
❑1/B, Apr 2002; Retailer Incentive Edition	3.95

TRANSFORMERS: GENERATION 2
MARVEL

	N-MINT
❑1, Nov 1993	1.75
❑1/Variant, Nov 1993; foil fold-out cover	2.95
❑2, Dec 1993	1.75
❑3, Jan 1994	1.75
❑4, Feb 1994	1.75
❑5, Mar 1994	1.75
❑6, Apr 1994	1.75
❑7, May 1994	1.75
❑8, Jun 1994	1.75
❑9, Jul 1994	1.75
❑10, Aug 1994	1.75
❑11, Sep 1994	1.75
❑12, Oct 1994; double-sized	2.25

TRANSFORMERS/G.I.JOE
DREAMWAVE

	N-MINT
❑1, Sep 2003	2.95
❑1/DF, Sep 2003	1.48
❑1/H, Sep 2003; Holofoil cover	5.95
❑2, Oct 2003	2.95
❑3, Nov 2003	2.95
❑4, Dec 2003	2.95
❑5, Jan 2004	2.95
❑6, Mar 2004	2.95

TRANSFORMERS, THE: HEADMASTERS
MARVEL

	N-MINT
❑1, Jul 1987	1.00
❑2, Sep 1987 FS (a)	1.00
❑3, Nov 1987	1.00
❑4, Jan 1988	1.00

TRANSFORMERS IN 3-D, THE
BLACKTHORNE

	N-MINT
❑1	2.50
❑2, Dec 1987	2.50
❑3, Apr 1988	2.50

TRANSFORMERS: MICROMASTERS
DREAMWAVE

	N-MINT
❑1, Jun 2004	2.95

TRANSFORMERS: MORE THAN MEETS THE EYE OFFICIAL GUIDE
DREAMWAVE

	N-MINT
❑1, Apr 2003	5.25
❑2, May 2003	5.25
❑3, Jun 2003	5.25
❑4, Jul 2003	5.25
❑5, Sep 2003	5.25
❑6, Sep 2003	5.25
❑7, Oct 2003	5.25
❑8, Nov 2003	5.25

Work by Wally Wood appeared in Marvel's *Tower of Shadows*.

© 1970 Marvel Comics.

TRANSFORMERS MOVIE
MARVEL

	N-MINT
❑1, Dec 1986	1.00
❑2, Jan 1987	1.00
❑3, Feb 1987	1.00

TRANSFORMERS: THE WAR WITHIN
DREAMWAVE

	N-MINT
❑0, Aug 2002; Preview issue; lenticular animation cover	3.00
❑1, Oct 2002	3.00
❑1/Variant, Oct 2002; lenticular animation cover	7.00
❑2, Nov 2002	2.95
❑3, Dec 2002	2.95
❑4, Jan 2003	2.95
❑5, Feb 2003	2.95
❑5/A, Feb 2003; Retailer Incentive edition; lenticular animation cover	5.00
❑6, Mar 2003	2.95

TRANSFORMERS: THE WAR WITHIN (VOL 2)
DREAMWAVE

	N-MINT
❑1, Oct 2003	2.95
❑2, Nov 2003	2.95
❑3, Dec 2003	2.95
❑4, Jan 2004	2.95
❑5, Mar 2004	2.95
❑6, Apr 2004	2.95

TRANSFORMERS UNIVERSE
MARVEL

	N-MINT
❑1, Dec 1986	1.25
❑2, Jan 1987	1.25
❑3, Feb 1987	1.25
❑4, Mar 1987	1.25

TRANSIT
VORTEX

	N-MINT
❑1, Mar 1987	1.75
❑2, May 1987	1.75
❑3, Jul 1987	1.75
❑4, Sep 1987	1.75
❑5, Nov 1987	1.75

TRANSMETROPOLITAN
DC / HELIX

	N-MINT
❑1, Sep 1997	8.00
❑2, Oct 1997	6.00
❑3, Nov 1997	4.00
❑4, Dec 1997	4.00
❑5, Jan 1998	4.00
❑6, Feb 1998	3.00
❑7, Mar 1998	3.00
❑8, Apr 1998	3.00
❑9, May 1998	3.00
❑10, Jun 1998	3.00
❑11, Jul 1998	3.00
❑12, Aug 1998	3.00
❑13, Sep 1998	2.50
❑14, Oct 1998	2.50
❑15, Nov 1998	2.50
❑16, Dec 1998	2.50
❑17, Jan 1999	2.50
❑18, Feb 1999	2.50
❑19, Mar 1999	2.50
❑20, Apr 1999	2.50
❑21, May 1999	2.50
❑22, Jun 1999	2.50
❑23, Jul 1999; 100 Bullets preview	2.50

N-MINT

- ❑24, Aug 1999 .... 2.50
- ❑25, Sep 1999 .... 2.50
- ❑26, Oct 1999 .... 2.50
- ❑27, Nov 1999 .... 2.50
- ❑28, Dec 1999 .... 2.50
- ❑29, Jan 2000 .... 2.50
- ❑30, Feb 2000 .... 2.50
- ❑31, Mar 2000 .... 2.50
- ❑32, Apr 2000 .... 2.50
- ❑33, May 2000 .... 2.50
- ❑34 2000 .... 2.50
- ❑35, Aug 2000 .... 2.50
- ❑36, Sep 2000 .... 2.50
- ❑37, Oct 2000 .... 2.50
- ❑38, Nov 2000 .... 2.50
- ❑39, Dec 2000 .... 2.50
- ❑40, Jan 2001 .... 2.50
- ❑41, Feb 2001 .... 2.50
- ❑42, Mar 2001 .... 2.50
- ❑43, Apr 2001 .... 2.50
- ❑44, May 2001 .... 2.50
- ❑45, Jun 2001 .... 2.50
- ❑46, Aug 2001 .... 2.50
- ❑47, Sep 2001 .... 2.50
- ❑48, Oct 2001 .... 2.50
- ❑49, Nov 2001 .... 2.50
- ❑50, Dec 2001 .... 2.50
- ❑51, Jan 2002 .... 2.50
- ❑52, Feb 2002 .... 2.50
- ❑53, Mar 2002 .... 2.50
- ❑54, Apr 2002 .... 2.50
- ❑55, Jun 2002 .... 2.50
- ❑56, Jul 2002 .... 2.50
- ❑57, Aug 2002 .... 2.50
- ❑58, Sep 2002 .... 2.50
- ❑59, Oct 2002 .... 2.50
- ❑60, Nov 2002 .... 2.50

TRANSMETROPOLITAN: FILTH OF THE CITY
DC / VERTIGO

- ❑1, Jul 2001, b&w and color; chromium cover 5.95

TRANSMETROPOLITAN: I HATE IT HERE
DC / VERTIGO

- ❑1, Jun 2000 .... 5.95

TRANSMUTATION OF IKE GARUDA, THE
MARVEL / EPIC

- ❑1 .... 3.95
- ❑2 .... 3.95

TRANS NUBIANS
ADEOLA

- ❑1 .... 2.95

TRASH
FLEETWAY-QUALITY

- ❑1 .... 2.95
- ❑2 .... 2.95

TRAUMA CORPS
ANUBIS

- ❑1, Feb 1994 .... 2.75

TRAVELERS, THE
SOUTH JERSEY REBELLION PRODUCTIONS

- ❑1, b&w; no indicia 2.25
- ❑2 .... 2.25
- ❑3 .... 2.25

TRAVELLER'S TALE, A
ANTARCTIC

- ❑1, b&w 2.50
- ❑2, Aug 1992, b&w 2.50
- ❑3, Oct 1992, b&w 2.50

TRAVELS OF JAIMIE MCPHEETERS, THE
GOLD KEY

- ❑1, Dec 1963 .... 12.00

TREASURE CHESTS
FANTAGRAPHICS / EROS

- ❑1, Jun 1999 .... 2.95
- ❑2 1999 .... 2.95
- ❑3 .... 2.95
- ❑4, Feb 2000 .... 2.95
- ❑5, Jul 2000 .... 2.95

TREEHOUSE OF HORROR (BART SIMPSON'S...)
BONGO

- ❑1 1995; JRo (w); Halloween stories 3.50
- ❑2 1996; infinity cover; Halloween stories 2.50
- ❑3 1997; Halloween story 2.50
- ❑4 1998; Halloween stories 2.50
- ❑5 1999; SA (a); Halloween stories; Eisner award winner 3.50
- ❑6 2000; Halloween stories 4.50
- ❑7, Oct 2001 .... 0.00
- ❑8, Oct 2002 .... 0.00
- ❑9, Oct 2003 .... 4.99

TREKKER (DARK HORSE)
DARK HORSE

- ❑1, May 1987, b&w 1.50
- ❑2, Jul 1987, b&w 1.50
- ❑3, Sep 1987 .... 1.75
- ❑4, Nov 1987 .... 1.50
- ❑5, Jan 1988 .... 1.50
- ❑6, Mar 1988 .... 1.50
- ❑7, May 1988 .... 1.50
- ❑8, Jul 1988 .... 1.50
- ❑9, Sep 1988 .... 1.50
- ❑Special 1; Color Special 2.95

TREKKER (IMAGE)
IMAGE

- ❑Special 1, Jun 1999 .... 2.95

TREK TEENS
PARODY

- ❑1, Feb 1993, b&w 2.50
- ❑1/A, Feb 1993, b&w; alternate cover 2.50

TRENCHCOAT BRIGADE
DC / VERTIGO

- ❑1, Mar 1999 .... 2.50
- ❑2, Apr 1999 .... 2.50
- ❑3, May 1999 .... 2.50
- ❑4, Jun 1999 .... 2.50

TRENCHER
IMAGE

- ❑1, May 1993 KG (w); KG (a) 2.00
- ❑2, Jun 1993 KG (a) 2.00
- ❑3, Jul 1993 KG (a) 2.00
- ❑4, Oct 1993 KG (a) 2.00

TRENCHER X-MAS BITES HOLIDAY BLOW-OUT
BLACKBALL

- ❑1, Dec 1993 .... 2.50

TRESPASSERS, THE
AMAZING MONTAGE

- ❑1 .... 2.50
- ❑2 .... 2.50
- ❑3 .... 2.50
- ❑4 .... 2.50
- ❑5 .... 2.50

TRIAD UNIVERSE
TRIAD

- ❑1, Jul 1994 .... 2.25
- ❑2, Aug 1994, b&w 2.25

TRIAL RUN
MILLER

- ❑1, b&w 2.00
- ❑2, b&w 2.00
- ❑3, b&w 2.00
- ❑4, b&w 2.00
- ❑5, b&w 2.00
- ❑6, b&w 2.00
- ❑7, b&w 2.00
- ❑14 .... 2.50
- ❑15 .... 2.50

TRIARCH
CALIBER

- ❑1, b&w 2.50
- ❑2, b&w 2.50

TRIBE
IMAGE

- ❑1, Apr 1993; Embossed cover; Only issue published by Image 2.50
- ❑1/A, Apr 1993; Special edition; foil cover 2.95
- ❑1/B, Apr 1993; Special edition; cover says Apr, indicia says Mar; gold logo 2.95
- ❑1/C, Apr 1993; gold logo; White cover 2.95
- ❑2, Sep 1993; Axis begins publishing 1.95
- ❑3, Apr 1994 .... 1.95

TRIBE (VOL. 2)
GOOD

- ❑0, Oct 1996 .... 2.95

TRICKSTER KING MONKEY
EASTERN

- ❑1 .... 1.75

TRIDENT
TRIDENT

- ❑1 1989, b&w 3.50
- ❑2 1989, b&w 3.50
- ❑3 1989, b&w 3.50
- ❑4 1990, b&w 3.50
- ❑5, Apr 1990, b&w 3.50
- ❑6 1990, b&w 3.50
- ❑7 1990, b&w 3.50
- ❑8 1990, b&w 3.50

TRIDENT SAMPLER
TRIDENT

- ❑1 .... 1.00
- ❑2 .... 1.00

TRIGGERMAN
CALIBER

- ❑1, ca. 1996, b&w 2.95
- ❑2, ca. 1997, b&w 2.95

TRIGGER TWINS
DC

- ❑1, Mar 1973; CI, RA (a); Reprints from All-Star Western #94, 81, 103 .... 5.00

TRILOGY TOUR
CARTOON

- ❑1, Sum 1997, b&w; promotional comic for Summer 1997 tour 1.50

TRILOGY TOUR II
CARTOON

- ❑1, Jun 1998, b&w and color; promotional comic for Summer 1998 tour 4.95

TRINITY ANGELS
ACCLAIM / VALIANT

- ❑1, Jul 1997 1: Rubberneck. 1: Teresa Angelina Barbella. 1: Trenchmouth. 1: Gianna Barbella. 1: Maria Barbella. 2.50
- ❑1/Variant, Jul 1997; alternate painted cover 2.50
- ❑2, Aug 1997 V: Prick. 2.50
- ❑3, Sep 1997; Justice League America #1 homage cover 2.50
- ❑4, Oct 1997 .... 2.50
- ❑5, Nov 1997; new costumes 2.50
- ❑6, Dec 1997 1: The Lounge Lizard. 2.50
- ❑7, Jan 1998; Showgirls tribute cover 2.50
- ❑8, Feb 1998 .... 2.50
- ❑9, Mar 1998 .... 2.50
- ❑10, Apr 1998 .... 2.50
- ❑11, Jan 1998; No cover date; indicia says Jan 2.50
- ❑12, Feb 1998; No cover date; indicia says Feb 2.50
- ❑Ashcan 1, Mar 1997, b&w; No cover price; preview of upcoming series 1.00

TRIPLE DARE
ALTERNATIVE

- ❑1, May 1998, b&w 2.95

N-MINT

TRIPLE•X
DARK HORSE

❑1, Dec 1994 .... 3.95
❑2, Jan 1995 .... 3.95
❑3, Feb 1995 .... 3.95
❑4, Mar 1995 .... 3.95
❑5, Apr 1995 .... 3.95
❑6, May 1995 .... 3.95
❑7, Jul 1995 .... 4.95

TRIPLE-X CINEMA: A CARTOON HISTORY
RE-VISIONARY

❑1, Mar 1997, b&w 3.50
❑2, Apr 1997, b&w 3.50
❑3, May 1997, b&w 3.50

TRIUMPH
DC

❑1, Jun 1995 .... 1.75
❑2, Jul 1995 .... 1.75
❑3, Aug 1995 .... 1.75
❑4, Sep 1995 .... 1.75

TRIUMPHANT UNLEASHED
TRIUMPHANT

❑0, ca. 1993; Unleashed Prologue 2.50
❑0/A, ca. 1993; free; Unleashed Prologue 1.00
❑0/Variant, ca. 1993; Mail-in special-cover edition. Given as promo from coupons in first 9 Triumphant books; No cover price; Unleashed Prologue; red logo; mail-away version 4.00
❑1, Nov 1993 .... 2.50

TRIUMVIRATE
CATACOMB

❑1, b&w; flipbook with Pinnacle #1 .... 2.50

TROLL
IMAGE

❑1, Dec 1993 .... 2.50

TROLL II
IMAGE

❑1, Jul 1994 .... 3.95

TROLL: HALLOWEEN SPECIAL
IMAGE

❑1, Oct 1994 .... 2.95

TROLL: ONCE A HERO
IMAGE

❑1, Aug 1994 .... 2.50

TROLLORDS: DEATH AND KISSES
APPLE

❑1 1989, b&w 2.25
❑2 1989, b&w 2.25
❑3 1989, b&w 2.25
❑4 1989, b&w 2.25
❑5 1989, b&w 2.25
❑6 .... 2.50

TROLLORDS (VOL. 1)
TRU

❑1, Feb 1986, b&w 1: Trollords. 2.00
❑1-2 1: Trollords. 1.50
❑2, ca. 1986 .... 1.50
❑3, ca. 1986 .... 1.50
❑4, ca. 1986 .... 1.50
❑5, ca. 1986 .... 1.50
❑6, ca. 1986 .... 1.50
❑7, ca. 1986 .... 1.50
❑8, ca. 1987 .... 1.50
❑9, ca. 1987 .... 1.50
❑10, ca. 1987 .... 1.50
❑11, ca. 1987 .... 1.50
❑12, ca. 1987 .... 1.50
❑13, ca. 1987 .... 1.50
❑14, ca. 1987 .... 1.50
❑15, Feb 1988 .... 1.50
❑Special 1, Feb 1987; Jerry's Big Fun Book 2.00

TROLLORDS (VOL. 2)
COMICO

❑1, ca. 1988 .... 2.00
❑2, ca. 1988 .... 2.00
❑3, ca. 1989 .... 2.00
❑4, ca. 1989 .... 2.50

TROLL PATROL
HARVEY

❑1, Jan 1993 .... 1.95

TROMBONE
KNOCKABOUT

❑1 .... 2.50

TROPO
BLACKBIRD

❑1, b&w 2.75
❑2, b&w 2.75
❑3, b&w 2.75
❑4, b&w 2.75
❑5, b&w 2.75

TROUBLE
MARVEL / EPIC

❑1, Sep 2003 .... 2.99
❑2, Oct 2003 .... 2.99
❑3, Nov 2003 .... 2.99
❑4, Dec 2003 .... 2.99
❑5, Jan 2004 .... 2.99

TROUBLE EXPRESS
RADIO

❑1, Nov 1998 .... 2.95
❑1/A, Nov 1998; Adam Warren cover 2.95
❑2, Jan 1999 .... 2.95

TROUBLE MAGNET
DC

❑1, Feb 2000 .... 2.50
❑2, Mar 2000 .... 2.50
❑3, Apr 2000 .... 2.50
❑4, May 2000 .... 2.50

TROUBLEMAKERS
ACCLAIM / VALIANT

❑1, Apr 1997; 1: Troublemakers. 1: Calamity. 1: XL. 1: Rebound. 1: Blur. cover says Mar, indicia says Apr 2.50
❑1/Variant, Apr 1997; indicia and cover dates match 2.50
❑2, May 1997; cover says Apr, indicia says May 2.50
❑3, Jun 1997 .... 2.50
❑4, Jun 1997 .... 2.50
❑5, Aug 1997 .... 2.50
❑6, Sep 1997 .... 2.50
❑7, Oct 1997 .... 2.50
❑8, Nov 1997; Cover swipe from X-Men (1st Series) #100 .... 2.50
❑9, Dec 1997; teen sex issue 2.50
❑10, Jan 1998 .... 2.50
❑11, Feb 1998 .... 2.50
❑12, Mar 1998 .... 2.50
❑13, Apr 1998 .... 2.50
❑14, Jan 1998; no cover date; indicia says Jan 2.50
❑15, Feb 1998; no cover date; indicia says Feb 2.50
❑16, Mar 1998; month of publication repeated 2.50
❑17, Mar 1998; month of publication repeated 2.50
❑18, Mar 1998; month of publication repeated 2.50
❑19, Jun 1998 .... 2.50
❑Ashcan 1, Nov 1996, b&w; no cover price; preview of upcoming series 1.00

TROUBLEMAN
IMAGE / MOTOWN

❑1, Jun 1996 .... 2.25
❑2, Jul 1996 .... 2.25
❑3, Aug 1996 .... 2.25

TROUBLESHOOTERS INC.
NIGHTWOLF

❑1, Win 1995, b&w 2.50
❑2, Spr 1995, b&w 2.50

TROUBLE WITH GIRLS, THE (VOL. 1)
MALIBU

❑1, Aug 1987, b&w 2.50
❑2, Sep 1987 .... 2.25
❑3, Oct 1987 .... 2.25

Originally billed as a limited series, the popularity of Marvel's *The Transformers* led to its continuance as an ongoing series.

© 1984 Marvel Comics and Hasbro.

N-MINT

❑4, Nov 1987 .... 2.25
❑5, Dec 1987 .... 2.25
❑6, Jan 1988 .... 2.00
❑7, Feb 1988, b&w 2.00
❑8, Mar 1988, b&w 2.00
❑9, Apr 1988, b&w 2.00
❑10, May 1988, b&w 2.00
❑11, Jun 1988, b&w 2.00
❑12, Jul 1988, b&w 2.00
❑13, Aug 1988, b&w 2.00
❑14, Sep 1988, b&w 2.00
❑Annual 1, b&w 3.25
❑Holiday 1, b&w; Mail-in special-cover edition. Given as promo from coupons in first 9 Triumphant books 2.95

TROUBLE WITH GIRLS, THE (VOL. 2)
COMICO

❑1, ca. 1989; Comico begins publishing 2.50
❑2, ca. 1989 .... 2.00
❑3, ca. 1989 .... 2.00
❑4, ca. 1989 .... 2.00
❑5, ca. 1989, b&w; Eternity begins publishing; Black & white format begins 1.95
❑6, ca. 1989, b&w 1.95
❑7, ca. 1989, b&w 1.95
❑8, ca. 1989, b&w 1.95
❑9, ca. 1990, b&w 1.95
❑10, ca. 1990, b&w 1.95
❑11, ca. 1990, b&w 1.95
❑12, ca. 1990, b&w 1.95
❑13, ca. 1990, b&w 1.95
❑14, ca. 1990, b&w 1.95
❑15, ca. 1990, b&w 2.25
❑16, ca. 1990 .... 2.25
❑17, ca. 1991 .... 2.25
❑18, ca. 1991 .... 2.25
❑19, ca. 1991 .... 2.25
❑20, ca. 1991 .... 2.25
❑21, ca. 1991 .... 2.25
❑22, ca. 1991 .... 2.25
❑23, ca. 1991 .... 2.25

TROUBLE WITH GIRLS, THE: THE NIGHT OF THE LIZARD
MARVEL / EPIC

❑1, Jun 1993; Embossed cover 2.50
❑2, Jul 1993 .... 2.25
❑3, Aug 1993 .... 2.25
❑4, Sep 1993 .... 2.25

TROUBLE WITH TIGERS
ANTARCTIC

❑1, Jan 1992, b&w 2.50
❑2, Feb 1992, b&w 2.50

TROUT FISSION
TALL TALE

❑1, Jul 1998, b&w 1.95
❑2, Oct 1998, b&w 1.95

TROY
TOME

❑1 .... 2.95

TRS-80 COMPUTER WHIZ KIDS
ARCHIE

❑1, giveaway 2.00

Condition price index: Multiply "NM prices" above by: **0.83 for Very Fine/Near Mint**
0.66 for Very Fine • 0.33 for Fine • 0.2 for Very Good • 0.125 for Good

N-MINT

TRUE ADVENTURES OF ADAM AND BRYON, THE
AMERICAN MULE

❑1, May 1998, b&w 2.50
❑2 1998 2.50
❑3 1998 2.50

TRUE CONFUSIONS
FANTAGRAPHICS

❑1, b&w 2.50

TRUE GEIN
BONEYARD

❑1, May 1993 3.00

TRUE GLITZ
RIP OFF

❑1 2.50

TRUE LOVE
ECLIPSE

❑1; DSt (c); ATh, NC (a); Reprints stories from New Romances #17, Thrilling Romances #22, #24, and Intimate Love #20 2.00
❑2; ATh, NC (a); Reprints stories from Popular Romance #22, New Romances #13, #15, and Thrilling Romances #24 2.00

TRUE NORTH, THE
COMIC LEGENDS DEFENSE FUND

❑1, ca. 1988, b&w; Cardstock cover; benefit comic 3.50

TRUE NORTH II, THE
COMIC LEGENDS DEFENSE FUND

❑1, ca. 1990; cardstock foldout cover 4.50

TRUE SIN
BONEYARD

❑1 2.95

TRUE SPY STORIES
CALIBER / TOME

❑1, b&w; bios 2.95

TRUE SWAMP
PERISTALTIC

❑1, b&w 2.50
❑2, May 1994, b&w 2.50
❑3, ca. 1994 2.50
❑4, Oct 1994, b&w 2.50
❑5, Feb 1995, b&w 2.95

TRUFAN ADVENTURES THEATRE
PARAGRAPHICS

❑1, ca. 1986, b&w 1.95
❑2, ca. 1986; 3-D 1.95

TRULY TASTELESS AND TACKY
CALIBER

❑1, b&w 2.50

TRUTH: RED, WHITE & BLACK
MARVEL

❑1, Jan 2003, cardstock cover 3.50
❑2, Feb 2003, cardstock cover 3.50
❑3, Mar 2003, cardstock cover 3.50
❑4, Apr 2003, cardstock cover 3.50
❑5, May 2003, cardstock cover 3.50
❑6, Jun 2003, cardstock cover 3.50
❑7, Jul 2003, cardstock cover 3.50

TRYPTO THE ACID DOG
RENEGADE

❑1, b&w 2.00

TSC JAMS
TSC

❑0 3.95
❑1 3.95

TSR WORLDS
DC

❑Annual 1, ca. 1990 2.00

TSUNAMI GIRL
IMAGE

❑1, Feb 1999; no month of publication 2.95
❑2, Apr 1999; no month of publication 2.95
❑3, Jun 1999 2.95

N-MINT

TSUNAMI, THE IRRESISTIBLE FORCE
EPOCH

❑1 2.00

T2: CYBERNETIC DAWN
MALIBU

❑0, Apr 1996; Flip-Book with T2 Nuclear Twilight #0 3.00
❑1, Nov 1995; immediately follows events of T2 Judgment Day 2.50
❑2, Dec 1995 2.50
❑3, Jan 1996 2.50
❑4, Feb 1996 2.50

T2: NUCLEAR TWILIGHT
MALIBU

❑0, Apr 1996; Flip-book with T2 Cybernetic Dawn #0 3.00
❑1, Nov 1995; prequel to first Terminator movie 2.50
❑2, Dec 1995 2.50
❑3, Jan 1996 2.50
❑4, Feb 1996 2.50

TUESDAY
KIM-REHR

❑1, ca. 2003, b&w 2.95
❑2, ca. 2003, b&w 2.95
❑3, ca. 2004, b&w 2.95

TUFF GHOSTS, STARRING SPOOKY
HARVEY

❑1, Jul 1962 35.00
❑2, Sep 1962 18.00
❑3, Nov 1962 18.00
❑4, Jan 1963 18.00
❑5, Mar 1963 18.00
❑6, May 1963 12.00
❑7, Jul 1963 12.00
❑8, Sep 1963 12.00
❑9, Nov 1963 12.00
❑10, Jan 1964 12.00
❑11, May 1964 10.00
❑12, Jul 1964 10.00
❑13, Nov 1964 10.00
❑14, Jan 1965 10.00
❑15, Mar 1965 10.00
❑16, May 1965 10.00
❑17, Jul 1965 10.00
❑18, Sep 1965 10.00
❑19, Nov 1965 10.00
❑20, Jan 1966 10.00
❑21, Mar 1966 10.00
❑22, May 1966 10.00
❑23, Jul 1966 10.00
❑24, Sep 1966 10.00
❑25, Nov 1966 10.00
❑26, Jan 1967 10.00
❑27, Mar 1967 10.00
❑28, May 1967 10.00
❑29, Jul 1967 10.00
❑30, Sep 1967 10.00
❑31, Nov 1967 8.00
❑32, Jan 1968 8.00
❑33, Jun 1968 8.00
❑34, Aug 1968 8.00
❑35, Oct 1968 8.00
❑36, Nov 1968 8.00
❑37, Apr 1969 8.00
❑38, Sep 1969 8.00
❑39, Nov 1969 8.00
❑40, Sep 1971 8.00
❑41, ca. 1972 6.00
❑42, Jun 1972 6.00
❑43, Oct 1972 6.00

TUG & BUSTER (ART & SOUL)
ART & SOUL

❑1, Nov 1995 3.00
❑2, Jan 1996 3.00
❑3, Mar 1996 3.00
❑4, May 1996 3.00
❑5, Aug 1996 3.00
❑6 3.00
❑7, Feb 1998 3.00

N-MINT

TUG & BUSTER (IMAGE)
IMAGE

❑1, Aug 1998, b&w 2.95

TUMBLING BOXES
FANTAGRAPHICS / EROS

❑1, Dec 1994, b&w 2.95

TUNDRA SKETCHBOOK SERIES
TUNDRA

❑1 3.95
❑2 3.95
❑3; Noodles 3.95
❑4; Rick Bryant 3.95
❑5 3.95
❑6 3.95
❑7 3.95
❑8; Forg 3.95
❑9 3.95
❑10; Skull Farmer 4.95
❑11 3.95
❑12 3.95

TUROK ADON'S CURSE
ACCLAIM

❑1 4.95

TUROK: CHILD OF BLOOD
ACCLAIM

❑1, Jan 1998 3.95

TUROK, DINOSAUR HUNTER
ACCLAIM / VALIANT

❑0, Nov 1995 2.50
❑1, Jul 1993; chromium cover 3.50
❑1/Gold, Jul 1993; Gold edition; chromium cover 40.00
❑2, Aug 1993 2.50
❑3, Sep 1993 2.50
❑4, Oct 1993 2.50
❑5, Nov 1993 2.50
❑6, Dec 1993 2.50
❑7, Jan 1994 2.50
❑8, Feb 1994 2.50
❑9, Mar 1994 2.50
❑10, Apr 1994 2.50
❑11, May 1994; trading card 2.50
❑12, Jun 1994 2.50
❑13, Aug 1994 2.50
❑14, Sep 1994 2.50
❑15, Oct 1994 2.50
❑16, Oct 1994; Chaos Effect 2.50
❑17, Nov 1994 2.50
❑18, Dec 1994 2.50
❑19, Jan 1995 2.50
❑20, Feb 1995 2.50
❑21, Mar 1995 2.50
❑22, Apr 1995 2.50
❑23, May 1995 2.50
❑24, Jun 1995; back to the Lost Land 2.50
❑25, Jul 1995 2.50
❑26, Jul 1995; Birthquake 2.50
❑27, Aug 1995 2.50
❑28, Aug 1995 2.50
❑29, Sep 1995 2.50
❑30, Sep 1995 2.50
❑31, Oct 1995 2.50
❑32, Oct 1995 2.50
❑33, Nov 1995 2.50
❑34, Nov 1995 2.50
❑35, Dec 1995; Painted cover 2.50
❑36, Dec 1995 2.50
❑37, Jan 1996 2.50
❑38, Jan 1996 2.50
❑39, Feb 1996 2.50
❑40, Mar 1996 2.50
❑41, Apr 1996 2.50
❑42, Apr 1996 2.50
❑43, May 1996 2.50
❑44, May 1996 2.50
❑45, Jun 1996 2.50
❑46, Aug 1996 2.50
❑47, Aug 1996 2.50
❑Yearbook 1; Yearbook 1 3.95

N-MINT

TUROK: SEEDS OF EVIL
ACCLAIM

❑1; newsstand edition 4.99
❑1/Direct ed.; Direct cover 4.99

TUROK/SHADOWMAN
ACCLAIM / VALIANT

❑1, Feb 1999 3.95

TUROK, SON OF STONE
DELL / GOLD KEY

❑3, May 1956; Earlier issues were Four Color #596 and #656 155.00
❑4, Jun 1956 125.00
❑5, Sep 1956 125.00
❑6, Dec 1956 110.00
❑7, Mar 1957 110.00
❑7/A, Mar 1957; Cover price variant 135.00
❑8, Jun 1957 110.00
❑9, Sep 1957 110.00
❑10, Dec 1957 110.00
❑11, Mar 1958 75.00
❑12, Jun 1958 75.00
❑13, Sep 1958 75.00
❑14, Dec 1958 75.00
❑15, Mar 1959 75.00
❑16, Jun 1959 75.00
❑17, Sep 1959 75.00
❑18, Dec 1959 75.00
❑19, Mar 1960 75.00
❑20, Jun 1960 75.00
❑21, Sep 1960 48.00
❑22, Dec 1960 48.00
❑23, Mar 1961 48.00
❑24, Jun 1961 48.00
❑25, Sep 1961 48.00
❑26, Dec 1961 48.00
❑27, Mar 1962 48.00
❑28, Jun 1962 48.00
❑29, Sep 1962 48.00
❑30, Dec 1962 48.00
❑31, Jan 1963 38.00
❑32, Mar 1963 38.00
❑33, May 1963 38.00
❑34, Jul 1963; 10030-307 38.00
❑35, Sep 1963 38.00
❑36, Nov 1963 38.00
❑37, Jan 1964 38.00
❑38, Mar 1964 38.00
❑39, May 1964 38.00
❑40, Jul 1964 38.00
❑41, Sep 1964 28.00
❑42, Nov 1964 28.00
❑43, Jan 1965 28.00
❑44, Mar 1965 28.00
❑45, May 1965 28.00
❑46, Jul 1965 28.00
❑47, Sep 1965; 10030-509 28.00
❑48, Nov 1965 28.00
❑49, Jan 1966 28.00
❑50, Mar 1966 28.00
❑51, May 1966 22.00
❑52, Jul 1966 22.00
❑53, Sep 1966 22.00
❑54, Nov 1966 22.00
❑55, Jan 1967 22.00
❑56, Mar 1967 22.00
❑57, May 1967 22.00
❑58, Jul 1967 22.00
❑59, Oct 1967 22.00
❑60, Jan 1968 22.00
❑61, Apr 1968 15.00
❑62, Jul 1968 15.00
❑63, Oct 1968 15.00
❑64, Jan 1969 15.00
❑65, Apr 1969 15.00
❑66, Jul 1969 15.00
❑67, Oct 1969 15.00
❑68, Jan 1970 15.00
❑69, Apr 1970 15.00
❑70, Jul 1970 15.00
❑71, Oct 1970 10.00
❑72, Jan 1971 10.00
❑73, Apr 1971 10.00
❑74, Jul 1971 10.00
❑75, Oct 1971 10.00
❑76, Jan 1972 10.00
❑77, Mar 1972 10.00
❑78, May 1972 10.00
❑79, Jul 1972 10.00
❑80, Sep 1972 10.00
❑81, Nov 1972 10.00
❑82, Jan 1973 10.00
❑83, Mar 1973 10.00
❑84, May 1973 10.00
❑85, Jul 1973 10.00
❑86, Sep 1973 10.00
❑87, Nov 1973 10.00
❑88, Jan 1974 10.00
❑89, Mar 1974 10.00
❑90, May 1974 10.00
❑91, Jul 1974 8.00
❑92, Sep 1974 8.00
❑93, Nov 1974 8.00
❑94, Jan 1975 8.00
❑95, Mar 1975 8.00
❑96, May 1975 8.00
❑97, Jul 1975 8.00
❑98, Aug 1975 8.00
❑99, Sep 1975 8.00
❑100, Nov 1975 8.00
❑101, Mar 1976 8.00
❑102 1976 8.00
❑103 1976 8.00
❑104 1976 8.00
❑105, Sep 1976 8.00
❑106, Nov 1976 8.00
❑107, Jan 1977 8.00
❑108, Mar 1977 8.00
❑109, May 1977 8.00
❑110, Jul 1977 8.00
❑111, Sep 1977 6.00
❑112, Nov 1977 6.00
❑113, Jan 1978 6.00
❑114, Mar 1978 6.00
❑115, May 1978 6.00
❑116, Jul 1978 6.00
❑117, Sep 1978 6.00
❑118, Nov 1978 6.00
❑119, Jan 1979 6.00
❑120, Mar 1979 6.00
❑121, May 1979 6.00
❑122, Jul 1979 6.00
❑123, Sep 1979 6.00
❑124, Nov 1979 6.00
❑125, Jan 1980 6.00
❑126, Mar 1981 6.00
❑127, Oct 1981 6.00
❑128, Dec 1981 6.00
❑129, Feb 1982 6.00
❑130, Apr 1982 6.00
❑Giant Size 1, Nov 1966 85.00

TUROK: SPRING BREAK IN THE LOST LAND
ACCLAIM / VALIANT

❑1, Jul 1997 3.95

TUROK: THE EMPTY SOULS
ACCLAIM

❑1, Apr 1997 3.95
❑1/Variant, Apr 1997; alternate painted cover 3.95
❑Ashcan 1, Nov 1996, b&w; No cover price; preview of upcoming series 1.00

TUROK THE HUNTED
ACCLAIM / VALIANT

❑1, Mar 1996 2.50
❑2, Mar 1996 2.50

TUROK, TIMEWALKER: SEVENTH SABBATH
ACCLAIM / VALIANT

❑1, Aug 1997; covers form diptych 2.50
❑2, Sep 1997; covers form diptych 2.50

All of Acclaim's November 1997 cover-dated issues paid homage to earlier comics by basing their covers on classic images. © 1997 Acclaim Comics.

N-MINT

TURTLE SOUP
MIRAGE

❑1, Sep 1987, b&w; b&w pin-ups, cardstock cover 5.00

TURTLE SOUP (2ND SERIES)
MIRAGE

❑1, Nov 1991 2.50
❑2, Dec 1991 2.50
❑3, Jan 1992 2.50
❑4, Feb 1992 2.50

TV CASPER AND COMPANY
HARVEY

❑1, Aug 1963; Harvey Giant 75.00
❑2, Oct 1963; Harvey Giant 30.00
❑3, Feb 1964; Harvey Giant 30.00
❑4; Harvey Giant 30.00
❑5; Harvey Giant 30.00
❑6; Harvey Giant 20.00
❑7 ; Harvey Giant 20.00
❑8; Harvey Giant 20.00
❑9; Harvey Giant 20.00
❑10; Harvey Giant 20.00
❑11, Mar 1966; Harvey Giant 15.00
❑12; Harvey Giant 15.00
❑13; Harvey Giant 15.00
❑14; Harvey Giant 15.00
❑15 ; Harvey Giant 15.00
❑16; Harvey Giant 15.00
❑17, Feb 1968; Harvey Giant 15.00
❑18, Apr 1968; Harvey Giant 15.00
❑19, Aug 1968; Harvey Giant 15.00
❑20, Nov 1968; Harvey Giant 15.00
❑21, Mar 1969; Harvey Giant 10.00
❑22 1969; Harvey Giant 10.00
❑23 1969; Harvey Giant 10.00
❑24 1969; Harvey Giant 10.00
❑25, Feb 1970; Harvey Giant 10.00
❑26, Apr 1970; Harvey Giant 10.00
❑27 1970; Harvey Giant 10.00
❑28 1970; Harvey Giant 10.00
❑29; Harvey Giant 10.00
❑30 1971; Harvey Giant 10.00
❑31, Apr 1971; Harvey Giant 10.00
❑32, Aug 1971; Harvey Giant 8.00
❑33, Oct 1971; Harvey Giant 8.00
❑34; Harvey Giant 8.00
❑35, Mar 1972; Harvey Giant 8.00
❑36, Aug 1972; Harvey Giant 8.00
❑37, Oct 1972; Harvey Giant 8.00
❑38, Dec 1972; Harvey Giant 8.00
❑39, Feb 1973; Harvey Giant 8.00
❑40, Apr 1973; Harvey Giant 8.00
❑41, Jun 1973; Harvey Giant 8.00
❑42, Aug 1973; Harvey Giant 8.00
❑43, Oct 1973; Harvey Giant 8.00
❑44, Dec 1973; Harvey Giant 8.00
❑45, Feb 1974; Harvey Giant 8.00
❑46, Apr 1974; Harvey Giant 8.00

TV STARS
MARVEL

❑1, Aug 1978 1: Captain Caveman (in comics). 1: Grape Ape (in comics). 6.00
❑2, Oct 1978 4.00
❑3, Dec 1978 4.00
❑4, Feb 1979 4.00

N-MINT

TV WESTERN
AC

❑1, ca. 2001, b&w; reprints stories from Range Rider #17, Roy Rogers, and Wild Bill Hickok 5.95

21
IMAGE

❑1, Feb 1996 .... 2.50
❑1/A, Feb 1996 .... 2.50
❑2, Mar 1996 .... 2.50
❑3, Apr 1996 .... 2.50

21 DOWN
DC / WILDSTORM

❑1, Nov 2002 .... 2.95
❑2, Dec 2002 .... 2.95
❑3, Jan 2003 .... 2.95
❑4, Feb 2003 .... 2.95
❑5, Mar 2003 .... 2.95
❑6, Apr 2003 .... 2.95
❑7, May 2003 .... 2.95
❑8, Jun 2003 .... 2.95
❑9, Jul 2003 .... 2.95
❑10, Jun 2003 .... 2.95
❑11, Jul 2003 .... 2.95
❑12, Sep 2003 .... 2.95

22 BRIDES
EVENT

❑1, Mar 1996 .... 2.95
❑1/Ltd., Mar 1996 .... 3.50
❑2, Jun 1996 .... 2.95
❑3, Sep 1996 .... 2.95
❑4, Jan 1997 .... 2.95
❑4/A, Jan 1997; O: Painkiller Jane. Painkiller Jane on Dinosaur cover . 3.50

TWICE-TOLD TALES OF UNSUPERVISED EXISTENCE
RIP OFF

❑1, Apr 1989, b&w 2.00

TWILIGHT (DC)
DC

❑1, ca. 1991 .... 4.95
❑2, ca. 1991 .... 4.95
❑3, ca. 1991 .... 4.95

TWILIGHT (AVATAR)
AVATAR

❑1, Mar 1997 .... 3.00
❑2 .... 3.00

TWILIGHT AVENGER, THE (ELITE)
ELITE

❑1, Jul 1986 .... 1.75
❑2, Oct 1986 .... 1.75

TWILIGHT AVENGER, THE (ETERNITY)
ETERNITY

❑1, Jul 1988, b&w 1.95
❑2, Aug 1988, b&w 1.95
❑3, Sep 1988, b&w 1.95
❑4, Nov 1988, b&w 1.95
❑5, Feb 1989, b&w 1.95
❑6, May 1989, b&w 1.95
❑7, Aug 1989, b&w 1.95
❑8, Feb 1990, b&w 1.95

TWILIGHT GIRL
CROSS PLAINS

❑1, Nov 2000 .... 2.95
❑2, Dec 2000 .... 2.95
❑3, Jan 2001 .... 2.95

TWILIGHT MAN
FIRST

❑1, Jun 1989 .... 2.75
❑2, Jul 1989 .... 2.75
❑3, Aug 1989 .... 2.75
❑4, Sep 1989 .... 2.75

TWILIGHT PEOPLE
CALIBER

❑1, b&w 2.95
❑2, b&w 2.95

N-MINT

TWILIGHT X
PORK CHOP

❑1, b&w 2.00
❑2, b&w 2.00
❑3, b&w 2.00

TWILIGHT X (VOL. 2)
ANTARCTIC

❑1, b&w 2.50
❑2, b&w 2.50
❑3, b&w 2.50
❑4, Sep 1993, b&w 2.50
❑5, Feb 1994, b&w 2.75

TWILIGHT-X: INTERLUDE
ANTARCTIC

❑1, Jul 1992, b&w 2.50
❑2, Sep 1992, b&w 2.50
❑3, Nov 1992, b&w 2.50
❑4, Jan 1993, b&w 2.50
❑5, Mar 1993, b&w 2.50
❑6, May 1993, b&w 2.50

TWILIGHT-X: INTERLUDE (VOL. 2)
ANTARCTIC

❑1, Jun 1993, b&w 2.50
❑2, Jul 1993, b&w 2.50
❑3, Aug 1993, b&w 2.50
❑4, Sep 1993, b&w 2.50
❑5, Oct 1993, b&w 2.75

TWILIGHT X QUARTERLY
ANTARCTIC

❑1, Sep 1994, b&w 2.95
❑2, Nov 1994, b&w 2.95
❑3, Feb 1995, b&w 2.95

TWILIGHT X: STORM
ANTARCTIC

❑1 2003 .... 3.50
❑2 2003 .... 3.50
❑3, May 2003 .... 3.50
❑4, Aug 2003 .... 3.50
❑5, Sep 2003 .... 3.50
❑6, Jan 2004 .... 3.50

TWILIGHT ZONE, THE (VOL. 1)
DELL

❑1, Nov 1962; published as Dell Four-Color #1173 .... 90.00
❑2, Feb 1963; published as Dell Four-Color #1174 .... 55.00
❑3, May 1963; 01-860-207 .... 42.00
❑4, Aug 1963; 01-860-210 .... 35.00
❑5, Nov 1963 .... 35.00
❑6, Feb 1964 .... 35.00
❑7, May 1964 .... 35.00
❑8, Aug 1964 .... 35.00
❑9, Nov 1964 .... 35.00
❑10, Feb 1965 .... 35.00
❑11, May 1965 .... 30.00
❑12, Aug 1965 .... 30.00
❑13, Nov 1965 .... 30.00
❑14, Feb 1966; 10016-602 .... 30.00
❑15, May 1966 .... 30.00
❑16, Jul 1966 .... 30.00
❑17, Sep 1966 .... 30.00
❑18, Nov 1966 .... 30.00
❑19, Jan 1966 .... 30.00
❑20, Mar 1966 .... 30.00
❑21, May 1967 .... 16.00
❑22, Jul 1967 .... 16.00
❑23, Oct 1967 .... 16.00
❑24, Jan 1968 .... 16.00
❑25, Apr 1968 .... 16.00
❑26, Jul 1968; 10016-807 .... 16.00
❑27, Dec 1968 .... 16.00
❑28, Mar 1969 .... 10.00
❑29, Jun 1969; 10016-906 .... 10.00
❑30, Sep 1969 .... 10.00
❑31, Dec 1969 .... 8.00
❑32, Mar 1970 .... 8.00
❑33, Jun 1970 .... 8.00
❑34, Sep 1970 .... 8.00
❑35, Dec 1970 .... 8.00
❑36, Mar 1971 .... 8.00

N-MINT

❑37, May 1971 .... 8.00
❑38, Jul 1971 .... 8.00
❑39, Sep 1971 .... 8.00
❑40, Nov 1971 .... 8.00
❑41, Jan 1972 .... 6.00
❑42, Mar 1972; 90016-203 .... 6.00
❑43, May 1972 .... 6.00
❑44, Jul 1972 .... 6.00
❑45, Sep 1972 .... 6.00
❑46, Nov 1972 .... 6.00
❑47, Jan 1973 .... 6.00
❑48, Mar 1973 .... 6.00
❑49, May 1973 .... 6.00
❑50, Jul 1973 .... 6.00
❑51, Aug 1973 .... 6.00
❑52, Sep 1973 .... 5.00
❑53, Nov 1973 .... 5.00
❑54, Jan 1974 .... 5.00
❑55, Mar 1974 .... 5.00
❑56, May 1974 .... 5.00
❑57, Jul 1974 .... 5.00
❑58, Aug 1974 .... 5.00
❑59, Sep 1974 .... 5.00
❑60, Nov 1974 .... 5.00
❑61, Jan 1975 .... 5.00
❑62, Mar 1975 .... 5.00
❑63, May 1975 .... 5.00
❑64, Jul 1975 .... 5.00
❑65, Aug 1975 .... 5.00
❑66, Sep 1975 .... 5.00
❑67, Nov 1975 .... 5.00
❑68, Jan 1976 .... 5.00
❑69, Mar 1976 .... 5.00
❑70, May 1976 .... 5.00
❑71, Jul 1976 .... 4.00
❑72, Aug 1976 .... 4.00
❑73, Sep 1976 .... 4.00
❑74, Nov 1976 .... 4.00
❑75, Jan 1977 .... 4.00
❑76, Mar 1977 .... 4.00
❑77, May 1977 .... 4.00
❑78, Jul 1977 .... 4.00
❑79, Aug 1977 .... 4.00
❑80, Sep 1977 .... 4.00
❑81, Nov 1977 .... 4.00
❑82, Jan 1978 .... 4.00
❑83, Apr 1978 .... 4.00
❑84, Jun 1978 .... 4.00
❑85, ca. 1978 .... 4.00
❑86, ca. 1978 .... 4.00
❑87, ca. 1978 .... 4.00
❑88, ca. 1978 .... 4.00
❑89, Feb 1979 .... 4.00
❑90, Apr 1979 .... 4.00
❑91, Jun 1979 .... 4.00
❑92, ca. 1982 .... 4.00

TWILIGHT ZONE, THE (VOL. 2)
NOW

❑1, Nov 1991; two covers 2.50
❑1/Direct ed.; Direct Market edition ... 2.50
❑2, Dec 1991 .... 2.25
❑3, Jan 1992 .... 2.25
❑4, Feb 1992 .... 2.00
❑5, Mar 1992 .... 2.00
❑6, Apr 1992 .... 2.00
❑7, May 1992 .... 2.00
❑8, Jun 1992 .... 2.00
❑9, Jul 1992; 3-D; Holographic cover; bagged; hologram; Partial 3-D art .. 2.95
❑9/Prestige, Jul 1992; 3-D; Holographic cover with glasses; hologram; Partial 3-D art; Extra stories 4.95
❑10, Aug 1992 .... 1.95
❑11, Sep 1992 .... 1.95
❑12, Oct 1992 .... 1.95
❑13, Nov 1992 .... 1.95
❑14, Dec 1992 .... 1.95
❑15, Jan 1993 .... 1.95
❑16, Feb 1993 .... 1.95
❑SF1, Mar 1993; hologram button; Science-Fiction Special 3.50

N-MINT

TWILIGHT ZONE, THE (VOL. 3)
Now

❑1, May 1993 .... 2.50
❑2, Jun 1993; two different covers; computer special 2.50
❑3, Jul 1993 .... 2.50
❑4, Aug 1993 .... 2.50
❑Annual 1993, Apr 1993 .... 2.50

TWILIGHT ZONE 3-D SPECIAL, THE
Now

❑1, Apr 1993; glasses 2.95

TWILIGHT ZONE PREMIERE, THE
Now

❑1, Oct 1991; Introduction by Harlan Ellison 2.50
❑1/CS; Collector's Set (polybagged, gold logo); Not code approved; Introduction by Harlan Ellison 2.95
❑1/Direct ed., Oct 1991; Introduction by Harlan Ellison 2.50
❑1/Prestige; Prestige edition; Introduction by Harlan Ellison 4.95
❑1-2; Introduction by Harlan Ellison . 2.50
❑1/Direct ed. -2; Not code-approved; Introduction by Harlan Ellison 2.50

TWIN EARTHS
R. Susor

❑1, b&w; strip reprints 5.95
❑2, b&w; strip reprints 5.95

TWIST
Kitchen Sink

❑1, b&w 2.00
❑2, May 1988 .... 2.00
❑3 .... 2.00

TWISTED
Alchemy

❑1, b&w 3.95

TWISTED 3-D TALES
Blackthorne

❑1 .... 2.50

TWISTED SISTERS
Kitchen Sink

❑1, b&w 3.50
❑2 .... 3.50
❑3 .... 3.50
❑4 .... 3.50

TWISTED TALES
Pacific

❑1, Nov 1982; AA (a); Pacific publishes 3.50
❑2, Apr 1983 VM, MP (a) 2.50
❑3, Jun 1983 .... 2.50
❑4, Aug 1983 .... 2.50
❑5 1983 VM (a) 2.50
❑6 1983 .... 2.50
❑7 1954 .... 2.50
❑8 1954; Eclipse publishes 2.50
❑9 1954 VM (a) 2.50
❑10, Dec 1984 BWr, GM (a) 2.50
❑3D 1, Aug 1986 .... 2.50

TWISTED TALES OF BRUCE JONES, THE
Eclipse

❑1 1985 .... 2.00
❑2, Jul 1986 .... 2.00
❑3, Mar 1986 .... 2.00
❑4 1986 .... 2.00

TWISTED TANTRUMS OF THE PURPLE SNIT, THE
Blackthorne

❑1 .... 1.75
❑2 .... 1.75

TWISTER
Harris

❑1; trading card 3.00

TWITCH (JUSTIN HAMPTON'S...)
Aeon

❑1 .... 2.75

N-MINT

TWO FACES OF TOMORROW, THE
Dark Horse

❑1, Aug 1997, b&w 2.95
❑2, Sep 1997, b&w; wraparound cover 2.95
❑3, Oct 1997, b&w 2.95
❑4, Nov 1997, b&w 2.95
❑5, Dec 1997, b&w 2.95
❑6, Jan 1998, b&w 2.95
❑7, Feb 1998, b&w 2.95
❑8, Mar 1998, b&w 2.95
❑9, Apr 1998, b&w 2.95
❑10, May 1998, b&w 2.95
❑11, Jun 1998, b&w 2.95
❑12, Jul 1998, b&w 2.95
❑13, Aug 1998, b&w 2.95

TWO-FISTED SCIENCE
General Tektronics Labs

❑1, b&w 2.50

TWO-FISTED TALES (RCP)
Gemstone

❑1, Oct 1992; AF, HK, JCr, WW (a); Reprints Two-Fisted Tales (EC) #18 2.00
❑2, Jan 1993; HK, JCr, JSe, WW (a); Reprints Two-Fisted Tales (EC) #19 2.00
❑3, Apr 1993; HK, JSe, WW (a); Reprints Two-Fisted Tales (EC) #20 2.00
❑4, Jul 1993; HK, JSe, WW (a); Reprints Two-Fisted Tales (EC) #21 2.00
❑5, Oct 1993; HK, JSe, WW, AT (a); Reprints Two-Fisted Tales (EC) #22 2.00
❑6, Jan 1994; HK, JSe, WW (a); Reprints Two-Fisted Tales (EC) #23 2.00
❑7, Apr 1994; HK, JSe, WW (a); Reprints Two-Fisted Tales (EC) #24 2.00
❑8, Jul 1994; Reprints Two-Fisted Tales (EC) #25 .... 2.00
❑9, Oct 1994; Reprints Two-Fisted Tales (EC) #26 .... 2.00
❑10, Jan 1995; Reprints Two-Fisted Tales (EC) #27 .... 2.00
❑11, Apr 1995; Reprints Two-Fisted Tales (EC) #28 .... 2.00
❑12, Jul 1995; Reprints Two-Fisted Tales (EC) #29 .... 2.00
❑13, Oct 1995; Reprints Two-Fisted Tales (EC) #30 .... 2.00
❑14, Jan 1996; Reprints Two-Fisted Tales (EC) #31 .... 2.00
❑15, Apr 1996; Reprints Two-Fisted Tales (EC) #32 .... 2.00
❑16, Jul 1996; Reprints Two-Fisted Tales (EC) #33 .... 2.50
❑17, Oct 1996; Reprints Two-Fisted Tales (EC) #34 .... 2.50
❑18, Jan 1997; Reprints Two-Fisted Tales (EC) #35 .... 2.50
❑19, Apr 1997; Reprints Two-Fisted Tales (EC) #36 .... 2.50
❑20, Jul 1997; Reprints Two-Fisted Tales (EC) #37 .... 2.50
❑21, Oct 1997; JSe (w); JSe (a); Reprints Two-Fisted Tales (EC) #38 2.50
❑22, Jan 1998; Reprints Two-Fisted Tales (EC) #39 .... 2.50
❑23, Apr 1998; Reprints Two-Fisted Tales (EC) #40 .... 2.50
❑24, Jul 1998; Reprints Two-Fisted Tales (EC) #41 .... 2.50
❑Annual 1; Collects Two-Fisted Tales #1-5 .... 8.95
❑Annual 2; Collects Two-Fisted Tales #6-10 .... 9.95
❑Annual 3 .... 10.95
❑Annual 4 .... 12.95
❑Annual 5 .... 13.50

TWO FOOLS
Last Gasp

❑1 .... 1.00

TWO-GUN KID
Marvel

❑33, Oct 1956 .... 60.00
❑34, Dec 1956 .... 60.00
❑35, Feb 1957 .... 60.00
❑36, Apr 1957 .... 60.00
❑37, Jun 1957 .... 60.00

Native Americans Turok and Andar found themselves in a lost valley populated by dinosaurs and cavemen in the long-running *Turok, Son of Stone*.

© 1965 Gold Key.

N-MINT

❑38, Aug 1957 .... 60.00
❑39, Dec 1957 .... 60.00
❑40, Feb 1958 .... 60.00
❑41, Apr 1958 .... 60.00
❑42, Jun 1958 .... 60.00
❑43, Aug 1958 .... 60.00
❑44, Oct 1958 .... 60.00
❑45, Dec 1958 .... 55.00
❑46, Feb 1959 .... 55.00
❑47, Apr 1959 .... 45.00
❑48, Jun 1959 .... 50.00
❑49, Aug 1959 .... 40.00
❑50, Oct 1959 .... 40.00
❑51, Dec 1959 .... 50.00
❑52, Feb 1960 .... 40.00
❑53, Apr 1960 .... 20.00
❑54, Jun 1960 .... 20.00
❑55, Aug 1960 .... 40.00
❑56, Oct 1960 .... 20.00
❑57, Dec 1960 .... 40.00
❑58, Feb 1961 O: Two-Gun Kid. 20.00
❑59, Apr 1961 .... 20.00
❑60, Nov 1962 O: Two-Gun Kid. 30.00
❑61, Jan 1963 .... 12.00
❑62, Mar 1963 .... 12.00
❑63, May 1963 .... 12.00
❑64, Jul 1963 .... 12.00
❑65, Sep 1963 .... 12.00
❑66, Nov 1963 .... 12.00
❑67, Jan 1964 .... 12.00
❑68, Mar 1964 .... 12.00
❑69, May 1964 .... 12.00
❑70, Jul 1964 .... 12.00
❑71, Sep 1964 .... 12.00
❑72, Nov 1964 V: Geronimo. 12.00
❑73, Jan 1965 .... 12.00
❑74, Mar 1965 .... 12.00
❑75, May 1965 .... 12.00
❑76, Jul 1965 .... 12.00
❑77, Sep 1965 .... 12.00
❑78, Nov 1965 .... 12.00
❑79, Jan 1966 V: Joe Goliath. 12.00
❑80, Mar 1966 V: Billy the Kid. 12.00
❑81, May 1966 .... 8.00
❑82, Jul 1966 BEv (w); BEv (a) 8.00
❑83, Sep 1966 V: Durango. 8.00
❑84, Nov 1966 .... 8.00
❑85, Jan 1967 .... 8.00
❑86, Mar 1967 V: Cole Younger. 8.00
❑87, May 1967 .... 8.00
❑88, Jul 1967 V: Rattler. 8.00
❑89, Sep 1967 A: Rawhide Kid. A: Kid Colt. 8.00
❑90, Nov 1967 .... 8.00
❑91, Jan 1968 BEv (a); V: Silver Sidewinder. 8.00
❑92, Mar 1968; series goes on hiatus 8.00
❑93, Jul 1970; Reprints begin 4.00
❑94, Sep 1970 .... 4.00
❑95, Nov 1970 .... 4.00
❑96, Jan 1971 .... 4.00
❑97, Mar 1971 .... 4.00
❑98, May 1971 .... 4.00
❑99, Jul 1971 .... 4.00
❑100, Sep 1971 .... 4.00
❑101, Nov 1971 O: Two Gun Kid. 4.00
❑102, Jan 1972 .... 4.00
❑103, Mar 1972 .... 4.00

	N-MINT
❑104, May 1972	4.00
❑105, Jul 1972	4.00
❑106, Sep 1972	4.00
❑107, Nov 1972	4.00
❑108, Jan 1973	4.00
❑109, Mar 1973	4.00
❑110, May 1973	4.00
❑111, Jul 1973	4.00
❑112, Sep 1973	4.00
❑113, Oct 1973	4.00
❑114, Nov 1973	4.00
❑115, Dec 1973	4.00
❑116, Feb 1974	4.00
❑117, Apr 1974	4.00
❑118, Jun 1974	4.00
❑119, Aug 1974	4.00
❑120, Oct 1974	4.00
❑121, Dec 1974	4.00
❑122, Feb 1975	4.00
❑123, Apr 1975	4.00
❑124, Jun 1975	4.00
❑125, Aug 1975	4.00
❑126, Oct 1975	4.00
❑127, Dec 1975	4.00
❑128, Feb 1976	4.00
❑129, Apr 1976	4.00
❑129/30 cent, Apr 1976; 30 cent regional price variant	20.00
❑130, Jun 1976	4.00
❑130/30 cent, Jun 1976; 30 cent regional price variant	20.00
❑131, Aug 1976	4.00
❑131/30 cent, Aug 1976; 30 cent regional price variant	20.00
❑132, Sep 1976	4.00
❑133, Oct 1976	4.00
❑134, Dec 1976	4.00
❑135, Feb 1977	4.00
❑136, Apr 1977	4.00

TWO-GUN KID: SUNSET RIDERS
MARVEL

	N-MINT
❑1, Nov 1995; Painted cover	6.95
❑2, Dec 1995; Painted cover	6.95

2-HEADED GIANT
A IS A

	N-MINT
❑1, Oct 1995, b&w	2.95

2 HOT GIRLS ON A HOT SUMMER NIGHT
FANTAGRAPHICS / EROS

	N-MINT
❑1, Apr 1991, b&w	3.00
❑2, May 1991, b&w	3.00
❑3, Jul 1991, b&w	3.00
❑4, Sep 1991, b&w	3.00

2 LIVE CREW COMICS
FANTAGRAPHICS / EROS

	N-MINT
❑1, b&w	2.95

TWO STEP
DC

	N-MINT
❑1, Dec 2003	2.95
❑2, Mar 2004	2.95
❑3, Jul 2004	2.95

2000 A.D. MONTHLY (1ST SERIES)
EAGLE

	N-MINT
❑1, Apr 1985 AMo (w)	2.00
❑2, May 1985 AMo (w)	2.00
❑3, Jun 1985 AMo (w)	2.00
❑4, Jul 1985 AMo (w)	2.00
❑5, Aug 1985 AMo (w)	2.00
❑6, Sep 1985 AMo (w)	2.00

2000 A.D. MONTHLY (2ND SERIES)
EAGLE

	N-MINT
❑1, Apr 1986; Judge Anderson, D.R. & Quinch, Skizz	2.00
❑2, May 1986	2.00
❑3, Jun 1986	2.00

2000 A.D. PRESENTS
FLEETWAY-QUALITY

	N-MINT
❑4, Jul 1986; Series continued from 2000 A.D. Monthly#3; Title changes to 2000 A.D. Presents; Quality begins publishing	1.50
❑5, Aug 1986	1.50
❑6, Sep 1986	1.50
❑7, Oct 1986 AMo (w); DaG (a)	1.50
❑8, Nov 1986	1.50
❑9, Dec 1986	1.50
❑10, Jan 1987	1.50
❑11, Feb 1987 DaG (a)	1.50
❑12, Dec 1987 AMo (w); DaG (a)	1.50
❑13	1.50
❑14, May 1988	1.50
❑15	1.50
❑16	1.50
❑17	1.50
❑18	1.50
❑19	1.50
❑20 DaG (a)	1.50
❑21	1.50
❑22	1.50
❑23	1.50
❑24; Series continues as 2000 A.D. Showcase	1.50
❑25; Series continues as 2000 A.D. Showcase (1st Series) #25	1.50

2000 A.D. SHOWCASE (1ST SERIES)
FLEETWAY-QUALITY

	N-MINT
❑25; Series continued from 2000 A.D. Presents #24	1.50
❑26	1.50
❑27; DaG (a); double issue #27/28	1.50
❑28; DaG (a); double issue #27/28	1.50
❑29; double issue #29/30	1.50
❑30; double issue #29/30	1.50
❑31; Zenith	1.50
❑32; Zenith	1.50
❑33; Zenith	1.50
❑34; Zenith	1.50
❑35; Zenith	1.50
❑36; Zenith	1.50
❑37; Zenith	1.50
❑38; Zenith	1.50
❑39; Zenith	1.50
❑40; Zenith	1.50
❑41; Zenith	1.50
❑42; Zenith	1.50
❑43; Zenith	1.50
❑44; Zenith	1.50
❑45; Zenith	1.50
❑46	1.50
❑47	1.50
❑48	1.75
❑49	1.75
❑50	1.75
❑51	1.75
❑52	1.75
❑53	1.75
❑54	1.75

2000 A.D. SHOWCASE (2ND SERIES)
FLEETWAY-QUALITY

	N-MINT
❑1	2.95
❑2	2.95
❑3	2.95
❑4; Axa	2.95
❑5; Axa	2.95
❑6; Strontium Dogs	2.95
❑7; Strontium Dogs	2.95
❑8	2.95
❑9	2.95
❑10	2.95
❑11	2.95

2002 TOKYOPOP MANGA SAMPLER
MIXX

	N-MINT
❑1	1.00

TWO THOUSAND MANIACS
AIRCEL

	N-MINT
❑1, b&w	2.50
❑2, b&w	2.50
❑3, b&w	2.50

2099 A.D.
MARVEL

	N-MINT
❑1, May 1995; enhanced cover	3.95

2099 A.D. APOCALYPSE
MARVEL

	N-MINT
❑1, Dec 1995; enhanced wraparound cover; continues in 2099 A.D. Genesis #1	4.95

2099 A.D. GENESIS
MARVEL

	N-MINT
❑1, Jan 1996; chromium cover	4.95

2099: MANIFEST DESTINY
MARVEL

	N-MINT
❑1, Mar 1998	5.99

2099 SPECIAL: THE WORLD OF DOOM
MARVEL

	N-MINT
❑1, May 1995	2.25

2099 UNLIMITED
MARVEL

	N-MINT
❑1, Jul 1993, 1: Hulk 2099. A: Spider-Man 2099.	3.95
❑2, Oct 1993; 1: R Gang 2099. Return of Hulk 2099	3.95
❑3, Jan 1994	3.95
❑4, Apr 1994	3.95
❑5, Jul 1994	3.95
❑6, Aug 1994	3.95
❑7, Nov 1994	3.95
❑8, Apr 1995	3.95
❑9, Jul 1995	3.95
❑10, Oct 1995	3.95
❑Ashcan 1 1993; "2099 Limited" ashcan edition from Hero magazine; foil cover	0.75

2099: WORLD OF TOMORROW
MARVEL

	N-MINT
❑1, Sep 1996; wraparound cover; 2099 anthology	2.50
❑2, Oct 1996	2.50
❑3, Nov 1996	2.50
❑4, Dec 1996	2.50
❑5, Jan 1997	2.50
❑6, Feb 1997	2.50
❑7, Mar 1997	2.50
❑8, Apr 1997	2.50

2001 NIGHTS
VIZ

	N-MINT
❑1, ca. 1990, b&w	4.00
❑2, ca. 1990, b&w	4.00
❑3, ca. 1990, b&w	4.00
❑4, ca. 1991, b&w	4.00
❑5, ca. 1991, b&w	4.00
❑6, ca. 1991, b&w	4.25
❑7, ca. 1991, b&w	4.25
❑8, ca. 1991, b&w	4.25
❑9, ca. 1991, b&w	4.25
❑10, ca. 1991, b&w	4.25

2001, A SPACE ODYSSEY
MARVEL

	N-MINT
❑1, Dec 1976, JK (w); JK (a)	5.00
❑2, Jan 1977, JK (w); JK (a)	5.00
❑3, Feb 1977, JK (w); JK (a)	5.00
❑4, Mar 1977, JK (w); JK (a)	5.00
❑5, Apr 1977, JK (w); JK (a)	5.00
❑6, May 1977, JK (w); JK (a)	5.00
❑7, Jun 1977, JK (w); JK (a)	5.00
❑7/35 cent, Jun 1977; JK (w); JK (a); 35 cent price regional variant	20.00
❑8, Jul 1977, JK (w); JK (a); O: Machine Man (as Mister Machine). 1: Machine Man (as Mister Machine).	12.00
❑9, Aug 1977, JK (w); JK (a)	5.00

N-MINT

❑10, Sep 1977, JK (w); JK (a); O: Machine Man. 5.00
❑Giant Size 1, ca. 1976; treasury-sized adaptation of movie JK (a) 12.00

2010
Marvel

❑1, Apr 1984, TP (a) 1.50
❑2, May 1984, TP (a) 1.50

2112 (JOHN BYRNE'S...)
Dark Horse

❑1, Nov 1991; prestige format 9.95
❑1-2 .... 9.95
❑1-3 .... 9.95

2020 VISIONS
DC / Vertigo

❑1, May 1997 .... 2.50
❑2, Jun 1997 .... 2.50
❑3, Jul 1997 .... 2.50
❑4, Aug 1997 .... 2.50
❑5, Sep 1997 .... 2.50
❑6, Oct 1997 .... 2.50
❑7, Nov 1997 .... 2.50
❑8, Dec 1997 .... 2.50
❑9, Jan 1998 .... 2.50
❑10, Feb 1998 .... 2.50
❑11, Mar 1998 .... 2.50
❑12, Apr 1998 .... 2.50

TWO X JUSTICE
Graphic Serials

❑1 .... 2.00

TYKES
Alternative

❑1, Nov 1997 .... 2.95
❑Ashcan 1, Jul 1997; b&w and pink; smaller than normal comic book ... 2.95

TYPHOID
Marvel

❑1, Nov 1995; wraparound cardstock cover 3.95
❑2, Dec 1995; wraparound cardstock cover 3.95
❑3, Jan 1996; wraparound cardstock cover 3.95
❑4, Feb 1996; wraparound cardstock cover 3.95

TYRANNOSAURUS TEX
Monster

❑1, Jul 1991, b&w 2.50
❑2, Sep 1991, b&w 2.50
❑3, Nov 1991 .... 2.50

TYRANT (S.R. BISSETTE'S...)
Spider Baby

❑1, Sep 1994, b&w 3.00
❑2, Nov 1994, b&w 3.00
❑3, Feb 1995, b&w 3.00
❑3/Gold, Feb 1995, b&w 3.50
❑4, Win 1996, b&w 3.00
❑5, ca. 1996, b&w 3.00
❑6, Dec 1996, b&w 3.00

TZU THE REAPER
Murim

❑1, Sep 1997 .... 2.95
❑2, Oct 1997 .... 2.95
❑3, Dec 1997 .... 2.95

U

UBERDUB
Caliber

❑1, Sep 1991 .... 2.50
❑2, Sep 1991 .... 2.50
❑3, Jan 1992 .... 2.50

UFO & OUTER SPACE
Whitman

❑14, Jun 1978; Reprints UFO Flying Saucers #3 .... 8.00
❑15, Jul 1978; Reprints UFO Flying Saucers #4 .... 6.00
❑16 1978 .... 6.00

N-MINT

❑17 1978 .... 6.00
❑18, Nov 1978 .... 6.00
❑19 1979 .... 6.00
❑20, Apr 1979 .... 6.00
❑21, Jun 1979 .... 5.00
❑22, Aug 1979 .... 5.00
❑23, Oct 1979 .... 5.00
❑24, Dec 1979 .... 5.00
❑25, Feb 1980; Reprints UFO Flying Saucers #2 .... 5.00

UFO ENCOUNTERS
Golden Press

❑1 .... 1.95

UFO FLYING SAUCERS
Gold Key

❑1, Oct 1968; giant 25.00
❑2, Nov 1970 .... 15.00
❑3, Nov 1972 .... 15.00
❑4, Nov 1974 .... 15.00
❑5, Feb 1975 .... 10.00
❑6, May 1975 .... 10.00
❑7, Aug 1975 .... 10.00
❑8, Nov 1975 .... 10.00
❑9, Jan 1976 .... 10.00
❑10 1976 .... 10.00
❑11 1976 .... 10.00
❑12, Nov 1976 .... 10.00
❑13, Jan 1977; series continues as UFO & Outer Space 10.00

ULTIMATE ADVENTURES
Marvel

❑1, ca. 2002 .... 2.25
❑2, ca. 2002 .... 2.25
❑3, Mar 2003 .... 2.25
❑4, May 2003 .... 2.25
❑5, Jul 2003 .... 2.99
❑6, Mar 2004 .... 2.99

ULTIMATE ELEKTRA AND DAREDEVIL
Marvel

❑1, Jan 2003 .... 3.00
❑2, Feb 2003 .... 2.25
❑3, Feb 2003 .... 2.25
❑4, Mar 2003 .... 2.25

ULTIMATE FANTASTIC FOUR
Marvel

❑1, Feb 2004 .... 2.25
❑2, Mar 2004 .... 2.25
❑3, Apr 2004 .... 2.25
❑4, May 2004 .... 2.25
❑5, Jun 2004 .... 2.25
❑6, Jul 2004 .... 2.25
❑7, Aug 2004 .... 2.25
❑8, Sep 2004 .... 2.25
❑9, Sep 2004 .... 2.25

ULTIMATE MARVEL MAGAZINE
Marvel

❑1, Feb 2001; reprints Ultimate Spider-Man #1 and #2 .... 6.00
❑2, Mar 2001; reprints Ultimate Spider-Man #3 and Ultimate X-Men #1 ..... 4.00
❑3, Apr 2001; reprints Ultimate Spider-Man #4 and Ultimate X-Men #2 ..... 4.00
❑4, May 2001 .... 3.99
❑5, Jun 2001 .... 3.99
❑6, Jul 2001 .... 3.99
❑7, Aug 2001 .... 3.99
❑8, Sep 2001 .... 3.99
❑9, Oct 2001 .... 3.99
❑10, Nov 2001 .... 3.99
❑11, Dec 2001 .... 3.99

ULTIMATE MARVEL TEAM-UP
Marvel

❑1, Apr 2001; BMB (w); MW (a); A: Wolverine. A: Sabretooth. A: Spider-Man. Cardstock cover; Listed in indicia as Ultimate Spider-Man and Wolverine 2.99
❑2, May 2001, BMB (w); A: Hulk. A: Spider-Man. 2.99
❑3, Jun 2001 .... 2.99
❑4, Jul 2001 .... 2.99

Several heroes from Malibu's Ultraverse teamed up as UltraForce.

N-MINT

❑5, Aug 2001 .... 2.99
❑6, Sep 2001 .... 2.99
❑7, Oct 2001 .... 3.00
❑8, Nov 2001 .... 3.00
❑9, Dec 2001 .... 3.00
❑10, Jan 2002 .... 3.00
❑11, Feb 2002 .... 3.00
❑12, Mar 2002 .... 3.00
❑13, Apr 2002 .... 3.00
❑14, May 2002 .... 3.00
❑15, Jun 2002 .... 3.00
❑16, Jul 2002 .... 3.00

ULTIMATES, THE
Marvel

❑1, Mar 2002 .... 5.00
❑2, Apr 2002 .... 2.50
❑3, May 2002 .... 2.50
❑4, Jun 2002 .... 2.25
❑5, Jul 2002 .... 2.25
❑6, Aug 2002 .... 2.25
❑7, Sep 2002 .... 2.25
❑8, Nov 2002 .... 2.25
❑9, Dec 2002 .... 2.25
❑10, Jul 2003 .... 2.25
❑11, Sep 2003 .... 2.25
❑12, Nov 2003 .... 2.25
❑13, Jun 2004 .... 3.50

ULTIMATE SIX
Marvel

❑1, Nov 2003 .... 2.99
❑2, Nov 2003 .... 2.25
❑3, Dec 2003 .... 2.25
❑4, Jan 2004 .... 2.25
❑5, Feb 2004 .... 2.25
❑6, Mar 2004 .... 2.25
❑7, Jun 2004 .... 2.25

ULTIMATE SPIDER-MAN
Marvel

❑0.5, ca. 2002; Wizard mail away incentive 8.00
❑0.5/A, ca. 2002; Wizard World East Con Edition 18.00
❑1, Oct 2000, BMB (w); O: Spider-Man. A: Mary Jane Watson. A: Norman Osborn. 65.00
❑1/A, Oct 2000; BMB (w); White background on cover-otherwise same as #1 .... 250.00
❑1/B, Oct 2000; BMB (w); Dynamic Forces cover 160.00
❑1/C, Jun 2001; BMB (w); K-B Toys Reprint 4.00
❑1/D, May 2002; BMB (w); Free Comic Book Day Edition 3.00
❑2, Dec 2000; BMB (w); Cardstock cover; Car cover 35.00
❑2/A, Dec 2000; BMB (w); Cardstock cover; Swinging cover 35.00
❑3, Jan 2001; BMB (w); O: Green Goblin. Cardstock cover; Spider-Man gets his costume 16.00
❑4, Feb 2001; BMB (w); D: Uncle Ben (off-panel). cardstock cover 8.00
❑5, Mar 2001; BMB (w); D: Uncle Ben (revealed). cardstock cover 55.00
❑6, Apr 2001; BMB (w); 1: Green Goblin (full). cardstock cover 9.00
❑7, May 2001; BMB (w); A: Green Goblin. cardstock cover 9.00

Condition price index: Multiply "NM prices" above by: **0.83 for Very Fine/Near Mint**
0.66 for Very Fine • 0.33 for Fine • 0.2 for Very Good • 0.125 for Good

N-MINT

❑8, Jun 2001, BMB (w) 8.00
❑8/DF, Jun 2001; BMB (w); alternate cover with no cover price; Dynamic Forces signed and numbered edition 10.00
❑9, Jul 2001, BMB (w) 6.00
❑10, Aug 2001, BMB (w) 6.00
❑11, Sep 2001, BMB (w) 4.00
❑12, Oct 2001, BMB (w) 4.00
❑13, Nov 2001, BMB (w) 4.00
❑14, Jan 2002; BMB (w); "3-D" cover 4.00
❑15, Feb 2002, BMB (w) 3.00
❑16, Mar 2002, BMB (w) 3.00
❑17, Apr 2002, BMB (w) 3.00
❑18, May 2002, BMB (w) 3.00
❑19, May 2002, BMB (w) 3.00
❑20, Jun 2002, BMB (w) 3.00
❑21, Jun 2002, BMB (w) 3.00
❑22, Jul 2002, BMB (w) 3.50
❑23, Aug 2002, BMB (w) 3.00
❑24, Sep 2002, BMB (w) 3.00
❑25, Oct 2002, BMB (w) 3.00
❑26, Nov 2002, BMB (w) 3.00
❑27, Nov 2002, BMB (w) 3.00
❑28, Dec 2002, BMB (w) 3.00
❑29, Dec 2002, BMB (w) 3.00
❑30, Jan 2003, BMB (w) 3.00
❑31, Jan 2003, BMB (w); D: Captain Stacy. 3.00
❑32, Feb 2003, BMB (w) 3.00
❑33, Feb 2003, BMB (w) 3.00
❑34, Mar 2003, BMB (w) 3.00
❑35, Mar 2003, BMB (w); A: Venom. 3.00
❑36, Apr 2003, BMB (w); A: Venom. 3.00
❑37, May 2003, BMB (w); A: Venom. 3.00
❑38, May 2003, BMB (w); A: Venom. 3.00
❑39, Jun 2003, BMB (w) 3.00
❑40, Jul 2003, BMB (w) 3.00
❑41, Jul 2003, BMB (w) 3.00
❑42, Aug 2003, BMB (w) 3.00
❑43, Sep 2003 BMB (w) 3.00
❑44, Oct 2003 BMB (w) 3.00
❑45, Nov 2003 BMB (w) 3.00
❑46, Nov 2003 BMB (w) 3.00
❑47, Dec 2003 BMB (w) 3.00
❑48, Dec 2003 (c); BMB (w) 3.00
❑49, Jan 2004 (c); BMB (w) 3.00
❑50, Feb 2004, BMB (w) 2.99
❑51, Feb 2004, BMB (w) 2.25
❑52, Mar 2004, BMB (w) 2.25
❑53, Apr 2004 ..... 3.00
❑54, May 2004, BMB (w) 2.25
❑55, May 2004, BMB (w) 2.25
❑56, Jun 2004, BMB (w) 2.25
❑57, Jun 2004, BMB (w) 2.25
❑54-2, Sep 2004 .....
❑58, Jul 2004, BMB (w) 2.25
❑59, Jul 2004, BMB (w) 2.25
❑60, Aug 2004 ..... 4.00
❑61, Sep 2004 ..... 2.25
❑62, Sep 2004 ..... 2.25
❑Special 1, Jul 2002 ..... 3.50

ULTIMATE WAR
MARVEL

❑1, Feb 2003, b&w and color; chromium cover 2.50
❑2, Feb 2003 ..... 3.00
❑3, Mar 2003 ..... 3.00
❑4, Apr 2003 ..... 3.00

ULTIMATE X-MEN
MARVEL

❑0.5, ca. 2002 ..... 5.00
❑1, Feb 2001; cardstock cover 14.00
❑1/A, Feb 2001 ..... 20.00
❑1/B, Feb 2001; sketch cover 40.00
❑1/C, Feb 2001; 7000 printed; DF alternate (color) cover 30.00
❑1/D, Jun 2001; Checkers Reprint 4.00
❑2, Mar 2001; cardstock cover 7.00
❑3, Apr 2001; cardstock cover 6.00
❑4, May 2001 ..... 5.00
❑5, Jun 2001 ..... 5.00
❑6, Jul 2001 ..... 4.00
❑7, Aug 2001 ..... 4.00
❑8, Sep 2001 ..... 4.00
❑9, Oct 2001 ..... 4.00
❑10, Nov 2001 ..... 4.00
❑11, Dec 2001, JKu (a) 3.00
❑12, Jan 2002 ..... 3.00
❑13, Feb 2002 ..... 3.00
❑14, Mar 2002 ..... 3.00
❑15, Apr 2002 ..... 3.00
❑16, May 2002 ..... 3.00
❑17, Jun 2002 ..... 3.00
❑18, Jul 2002 ..... 3.00
❑19, Aug 2002 ..... 3.00
❑20, Sep 2002 ..... 3.00
❑21, Oct 2002 ..... 2.50
❑22, Nov 2002 ..... 2.50
❑23, Dec 2002 ..... 2.50
❑24, Jan 2003 ..... 2.50
❑25, Jan 2003 ..... 2.50
❑26, Feb 2003, (c) 2.50
❑27, Mar 2003 ..... 2.25
❑28, Apr 2003 ..... 2.25
❑29, Apr 2003 ..... 2.25
❑30, May 2003 ..... 2.25
❑31, May 2003 ..... 2.25
❑32, Jun 2003 ..... 2.25
❑33, Jul 2003 ..... 2.25
❑34, Jul 2003, BMB (w) 2.25
❑35, Sep 2003, BMB (w) 2.25
❑36, Oct 2003, BMB (w) 2.25
❑37, Nov 2003, BMB (w) 2.25
❑38, Dec 2003, BMB (w) 2.25
❑39, Jan 2004, BMB (w) 2.25
❑40, Feb 2004 ..... 2.25
❑41, Mar 2004 ..... 2.25
❑42, Apr 2004, BMB (w) 2.25
❑43, May 2004, BMB (w) 2.25
❑44, Jun 2004, BMB (w) 2.25
❑45, Jul 2004, BMB (w) 2.25
❑46, Jul 2004 ..... 2.25
❑47, Aug 2004 ..... 2.25
❑48, Aug 2004 ..... 2.25
❑49, Sep 2004 .....

ULTRAFORCE (VOL. 1)
MALIBU / ULTRAVERSE

❑0, Sep 1994 GP (a) 2.50
❑0/Variant, Jul 1994; ashcan-sized; GP (a); no cover price 1.00
❑1, Aug 1994 GP (a); 1: Atalon. 2.50
❑1/Hologram, Aug 1994; GP (a); Hologram cover 5.00
❑2, Oct 1994 GP (c); GP (a) 1.95
❑3, Nov 1994 GP (a) 1.95
❑4, Jan 1995 GP (a) 1.95
❑5, Feb 1995 GP (a) 1.95
❑6, Mar 1995 GP (a) 2.50
❑7, Apr 1995 GP (a) 2.50
❑8, May 1995 GP (a) 2.50
❑9, Jun 1995 ..... 2.50
❑10, Jul 1995 ..... 2.50
❑Ashcan 1; Ashcan 0.75

ULTRAFORCE (VOL. 2)
MALIBU / ULTRAVERSE

❑0; #Infinity 1.50
❑0/A, Sep 1995; #infinity on cover 1.50
❑0/B, Sep 1995; alternate cover 3.50
❑0/Variant, Sep 1995; #Infinity; alternate cover 1.50
❑1, Oct 1995 ..... 1.50
❑2, Nov 1995; contains reprint of UltraForce #1 ..... 1.50
❑3, Dec 1995 ..... 1.50
❑4, Jan 1996 ..... 1.50
❑5, Feb 1996 ..... 1.50
❑6, Mar 1996 ..... 1.50
❑7, Apr 1996 ..... 1.50
❑8, May 1996 ..... 1.50
❑9, Jun 1996 ..... 1.50
❑10, Aug 1996 ..... 1.50
❑11, Aug 1996 ..... 1.50
❑12, Sep 1996 A: Exiles. 1.50
❑13, Oct 1996 ..... 1.50
❑14 1996 ..... 1.50
❑15, Dec 1996 D: Ripfire. 1.50

ULTRAFORCE/AVENGERS
MALIBU / ULTRAVERSE

❑1, Fal 1995 ..... 3.95

ULTRAFORCE/AVENGERS PRELUDE
MALIBU / ULTRAVERSE

❑1, Jul 1995; a.k.a. UltraForce #11 ..... 2.50

ULTRAFORCE/SPIDER-MAN
MALIBU / ULTRAVERSE

❑1, Jan 1996; alternate covers: 1A and 1B 3.95

ULTRAGIRL
MARVEL

❑1, Nov 1996 ..... 1.50
❑2, Dec 1996 ..... 1.50
❑3, Jan 1997; March 1997 on cover 1.50

ULTRAHAWK
D.M.S.

❑1 ..... 1.50

ULTRA KLUTZ
ONWARD

❑1, Jun 1986 ..... 2.00
❑2, Sep 1986 ..... 2.00
❑3, Oct 1986 ..... 2.00
❑4, Nov 1986 ..... 2.00
❑5, Dec 1986 ..... 2.00
❑6, Jan 1987 ..... 2.00
❑7, Feb 1987 ..... 2.00
❑8, Mar 1987 ..... 2.00
❑9, Apr 1987 ..... 2.00
❑10, May 1987 ..... 2.00
❑11, Jun 1987 ..... 2.00
❑12, Jul 1987 ..... 2.00
❑13, Aug 1987 ..... 2.00
❑14, Sep 1987 ..... 2.00
❑15, Oct 1987 ..... 2.00
❑16, Nov 1987 ..... 1.50
❑17, Dec 1987 ..... 1.50
❑18, Jan 1988 ..... 1.75
❑19, Feb 1988 ..... 1.75
❑20 1988 ..... 1.75
❑21 1988 ..... 1.75
❑22 1988 ..... 1.75
❑23, Jul 1988 ..... 2.00
❑24, Aug 1988 ..... 2.00
❑25, Sep 1988 ..... 2.00
❑26, Nov 1988 ..... 2.00
❑27, Jan 1989 ..... 2.00
❑28 1989 ..... 2.00
❑29, Jun 1990 ..... 2.00
❑30 1990 ..... 2.00
❑31, May 1991 ..... 2.00

ULTRA KLUTZ '81
ONWARD

❑1, Jun 1981 ..... 2.00

ULTRAMAN (ULTRACOMICS)
HARVEY / ULTRACOMICS

❑1, Jul 1993; O: Ultraman. newsstand 2.00
❑1/CS, Jul 1993 ..... 2.50
❑1/Direct ed., Jul 1993; trading card; no type on cover 3.50
❑2 1993; newsstand 1.75
❑2/CS 1993 ..... 2.50
❑2/Direct ed. 1993; direct sale; trading card 2.50
❑3 1993; newsstand 1.75
❑3/CS 1993 ..... 2.50
❑3/Direct ed. 1993; trading cards 2.50

ULTRAMAN (NEMESIS)
NEMESIS

❑-1, Mar 1994; negative image on cover 2.50
❑1, Apr 1994; Split cover 2.50
❑1/A, Apr 1994; alternate cover 2.25
❑2, May 1994 ..... 1.95
❑3, Aug 1994 ..... 1.95
❑4, Sep 1994 ..... 1.95
❑5 1994 ..... 1.95

ULTRAMAN CLASSIC: BATTLE OF THE ULTRA-BROTHERS
VIZ

	N-MINT
❑1, b&w	4.95
❑2, b&w	4.95
❑3, b&w	4.95
❑4, b&w	4.95
❑5, b&w	4.95

ULTRAMAN TIGA
DARK HORSE

	N-MINT
❑1, Sep 2003	3.99
❑2, Oct 2003	3.99
❑3, Nov 2003	3.99
❑4, Dec 2003	3.99
❑5, Jan 2004	3.99
❑6, Mar 2004	2.99
❑7, Apr 2004	2.99
❑8, May 2004	3.99
❑9, May 2004	3.99
❑10, Aug 2004	3.99

ULTRA MONTHLY
MALIBU

	N-MINT
❑1, Jun 1993; actually giveaway	0.50
❑2, Jul 1993; actually giveaway	0.50
❑3, Aug 1993; actually giveaway; cover says Sep, indicia says Aug	0.50
❑4, Sep 1993	0.50
❑5, Oct 1993	0.50
❑6, Nov 1993	0.50

ULTRAVERSE/AVENGERS PRELUDE
MALIBU / ULTRAVERSE

	N-MINT
❑1, Jul 1995	2.50

ULTRAVERSE DOUBLE FEATURE: PRIME AND SOLITAIRE
MALIBU / ULTRAVERSE

	N-MINT
❑1, Jan 1995	3.95

ULTRAVERSE: FUTURE SHOCK
MALIBU / ULTRAVERSE

	N-MINT
❑1, Feb 1997; final Ultraverse adventure	2.50

ULTRAVERSE ORIGINS
MALIBU / ULTRAVERSE

	N-MINT
❑1, Jan 1994; O: Prime. Origin	1.25

ULTRAVERSE PREMIERE
MALIBU / ULTRAVERSE

	N-MINT
❑0, Nov 1993	1.00

ULTRAVERSE UNLIMITED
MALIBU / ULTRAVERSE

	N-MINT
❑1, Jun 1996	2.50
❑2, Sep 1996, b&w	2.50

ULTRAVERSE YEAR ONE
MALIBU / ULTRAVERSE

	N-MINT
❑1, Sep 1994	4.95

ULTRAVERSE YEAR TWO
MALIBU / ULTRAVERSE

	N-MINT
❑1, Aug 1995	4.95

ULTRAVERSE YEAR ZERO: THE DEATH OF THE SQUAD
MALIBU / ULTRAVERSE

	N-MINT
❑1, Apr 1995	2.95
❑2, May 1995	2.95
❑3, Jun 1995	2.95
❑4, Jul 1995	2.95

UNBOUND
IMAGE

	N-MINT
❑1, Jan 1998, b&w	2.95

UNCANNY ORIGINS
MARVEL

	N-MINT
❑1, Sep 1996 O: Cyclops.	1.25
❑1/A, Sep 1996; O: Cyclops. No price on cover; variant cover	1.25
❑2, Oct 1996 O: Quicksilver.	1.00
❑3, Nov 1996 O: Archangel.	1.00
❑4, Dec 1996 O: Firelord.	1.00
❑5, Jan 1997 O: Hulk.	1.00
❑6, Feb 1997 O: Beast.	1.00
❑7, Mar 1997; O: Venom. Flip book with Untold Tales of Spider-Man #19	1.00
❑8, Apr 1997; O: Nightcrawler. Flip book with Untold Tales of Spider-Man #20	1.00
❑9, May 1997 O: Storm.	1.00
❑10, Jun 1997 O: Black Cat.	1.00
❑11, Jul 1997 O: Black Knight.	1.00
❑12, Aug 1997 O: Doctor Strange.	1.00
❑13, Sep 1997 O: Daredevil.	1.00
❑14, Oct 1997 O: Iron Fist.	1.00

UNCANNY TALES (2ND SERIES)
MARVEL

	N-MINT
❑1, Dec 1973	5.00
❑2, Feb 1974	3.50
❑3, Apr 1974	3.50
❑4, Jun 1974	3.50
❑5, Aug 1974	3.50
❑6, Oct 1974	3.50
❑7, Dec 1974	3.50
❑8, Feb 1975	3.50
❑9, Apr 1975	3.50
❑10, Jun 1975	3.50
❑11, Aug 1975	3.50
❑12, Oct 1975	3.50

UNCANNY X-MEN, THE
MARVEL

	N-MINT
❑-1, Jul 1997; Flashback	2.00
❑142, Feb 1981; JBy (a); A: Rachel Summers (Phoenix III). D: Colossus (future). D: Storm (future). D: Wolverine (future). Series continued from X-Men (1st Series) #141	25.00
❑143, Mar 1981; JBy (a); Last Byrne art on X-Men	8.00
❑144, Apr 1981 BA (c); BA (a); A: Man-Thing.	6.00
❑145, May 1981 DC (c); DC (a)	6.00
❑146, Jun 1981 DC (c); DC (a)	6.00
❑147, Jul 1981 DC (c); DC (a)	6.00
❑148, Aug 1981 DC (c); DC (a); 1: Caliban. A: Dazzler. A: Spider-Woman.	6.00
❑149, Sep 1981 DC (c); DC (a)	5.00
❑150, Oct 1981; double-sized; DC (c); DC, BWi (a); V: Magneto. Cyclops rejoins the X-Men	5.00
❑151, Nov 1981 BMc (c); BMc (a)	5.00
❑152, Dec 1981 BMc (c); BMc (a)	5.00
❑153, Jan 1982 DC (c); DC (a)	5.00
❑154, Feb 1982 DC, BWi (c); DC, BWi (a)	5.00
❑155, Mar 1982 DC, BWi (c); DC, BWi (a)	5.00
❑156, Apr 1982 DC, BWi (c); DC, BWi (a)	5.00
❑157, May 1982 DC, BWi (c); DC, BWi (a); A: Phoenix.	5.00
❑158, Jun 1982 DC, BWi (c); DC, BWi (a); A: Rogue.	6.00
❑159, Jul 1982 BSz (c); BSz, BWi (a); A: Dracula.	5.00
❑160, Aug 1982 BA, BWi (c); BA, BWi (a); 1: Magik (Illyana Rasputin as teenager).	5.00
❑161, Sep 1982 DC, BWi (c); DC, BWi (a); O: Professor X. O: Magneto.	5.00
❑162, Oct 1982; DC, BWi (c); DC, BWi (a); Wolverine solo story	6.00
❑163, Nov 1982 DC, BWi (c); DC, BWi (a)	5.00
❑164, Dec 1982 DC, BWi (c); DC, BWi (a); 1: Binary.	5.00
❑165, Jan 1983 PS (c); PS, BWi (a)	5.00
❑166, Feb 1983; Double-size PS, BWi (c); PS, BWi (a); 1: Lockheed.	5.00
❑167, Mar 1983 PS, BWi (c); PS, BWi (a); A: New Mutants.	4.00
❑168, Apr 1983 PS, BWi (c); PS, BWi (a); 1: Madelyne Pryor.	5.00
❑169, May 1983 PS, BWi (c); PS, BWi (a); 1: Morlocks. 1: Sunder.	5.00
❑170, Jun 1983 PS, BWi (c); PS, BWi (a)	5.00
❑171, Jul 1983; BWi (c); BWi (a); Rogue joins team	5.00
❑172, Aug 1983 PS (c); PS, BWi (a)	5.00
❑173, Sep 1983 BWi (c); PS (a); O: Silver Samurai.	5.00
❑174, Oct 1983 PS (c); PS, BWi (a)	5.00
❑175, Nov 1983; double-sized PS (c); PS, JR2, BWi (a)	5.00
❑176, Dec 1983 JR2 (c); JR2, BWi (a); 1: Valerie Cooper.	4.00

Uncanny X-Men picked up its numbering from *X-Men* (1st series).

	N-MINT
❑177, Jan 1984 JR2 (c); JR2 (a)	4.00
❑178, Feb 1984 DGr, JR2 (c); JR2, BWi (a)	4.00
❑179, Mar 1984 DGr, JR2 (c); DGr, JR2 (a)	4.00
❑180, Apr 1984 JR2 (c); DGr, JR2, BWi (a)	4.00
❑181, May 1984 JR2 (c); DGr, JR2 (a)	4.00
❑182, Jun 1984 JR2 (c); DGr, JR2 (a)	5.00
❑183, Jul 1984 JR2 (c); DGr, JR2 (a)	5.00
❑184, Aug 1984 DGr, JR2 (c); DGr, JR2 (a); 1: Forge. A: Rachel. A: Selene.	4.00
❑185, Sep 1984; DGr, JR2 (c); DGr, JR2 (a); Storm loses powers	4.00
❑186, Oct 1984; double-sized; Storm	4.00
❑187, Nov 1984 DGr, JR2 (c); DGr, JR2 (a)	3.00
❑188, Dec 1984 JR2 (c); DGr, JR2 (a)	3.00
❑189, Jan 1985 JR2 (c); JR2 (a)	4.00
❑190, Feb 1985 DGr, JR2 (c); DGr, JR2 (a); A: Spider-Man. A: Avengers.	4.00
❑191, Mar 1985 DGr, JR2 (c); DGr, JR2 (a); A: Captain America. A: Spider-Man. A: Avengers.	4.00
❑192, Apr 1985; DGr, JR2 (c); DGr, JR2 (a); Magus	4.00
❑193, May 1985; double-sized; DGr, JR2 (c); DGr, JR2 (a); 20th anniv.; 100th New X-Men	5.00
❑194, Jun 1985 JR2 (c); DGr, JR2 (a); A: Juggernaut. V: Juggernaut.	3.00
❑195, Jul 1985 BSz, DGr (c); DGr, JR2 (a); A: Power Pack.	3.00
❑196, Aug 1985; JR2 (c); DGr, JR2 (a); Secret Wars II	3.00
❑197, Sep 1985 DGr, JR2 (c); DGr, JR2 (a)	3.00
❑198, Oct 1985	3.00
❑199, Nov 1985 JR2 (c); DGr, JR2 (a); 1: Phoenix III (Rachel Summers).	3.00
❑200, Dec 1985; Double-size DGr, JR2 (c); DGr, JR2 (a)	5.00
❑201, Jan 1986; 1: Cable (as baby).	5.00
❑202, Feb 1986; AW, JR2 (c); AW, JR2 (a); Secret Wars II	4.00
❑203, Mar 1986; AW, JR2 (c); AW, JR2 (a); Secret Wars II	4.00
❑204, Apr 1986; Nightcrawler solo story	4.00
❑205, May 1986; A: Power Pack. Wolverine solo story	4.00
❑206, Jun 1986 AW, JR2 (c); DGr, JR2 (a); V: Freedom Force.	4.00
❑207, Jul 1986; DGr, JR2 (c); DGr, JR2 (a); Wolverine vs. Phoenix	4.00
❑208, Aug 1986 DGr, JR2 (c); DGr, JR2 (a)	4.00
❑209, Sep 1986 DGr, JR2 (c); JR2, CR (a)	4.00
❑210, Oct 1986 JR2, BWi (c); DGr, JR2 (a); 1: Marauders.	5.00
❑211, Nov 1986 AW, JR2 (c); AW, JR2 (a)	5.00
❑212, Dec 1986; DGr (c); DGr (a); A: Sabretooth. Wolverine vs. Sabretooth	6.00
❑213, Jan 1987; Wolverine vs. Sabretooth	6.00
❑214, Feb 1987 BWi (a)	3.00
❑215, Mar 1987 DGr (c); DGr (a); 1: Crimson Commando.	3.00
❑216, Apr 1987 DGr (a)	3.00
❑217, May 1987 BWi (c); A: Juggernaut.	3.00

	N-MINT
❑218, Jun 1987 BWi (c); DGr (a); V: Juggernaut.	3.00
❑219, Jul 1987; DGr (a); Havok joins X-Men	4.00
❑220, Aug 1987 DGr (c); DGr (a)	4.00
❑221, Sep 1987 DGr (c); DGr (a); 1: Mister Sinister. V: Mr. Sinister.	7.00
❑222, Oct 1987 DGr (c); DGr (a); A: Sabretooth. V: Sabretooth.	5.00
❑223, Nov 1987 DGr, KGa (c); DGr, KGa (a)	4.00
❑224, Dec 1987; BWi (c); BWi (a); registration card	3.00
❑225, Jan 1988; DGr (c); DGr (a); Fall of Mutants	3.00
❑226, Feb 1988; Double-size; DGr (c); DGr (a); Fall of Mutants; Storm regains powers	3.00
❑227, Mar 1988; DGr (c); DGr (a); Fall of Mutants	3.00
❑228, Apr 1988	3.00
❑229, May 1988 DGr (c); DGr (a); 1: The Reavers.	3.00
❑230, Jun 1988	3.00
❑231, Jul 1988 DGr (c); DGr (a)	3.00
❑232, Aug 1988 DGr (c); DGr (a)	3.00
❑233, Sep 1988 DGr (c); DGr (a)	3.00
❑234, Sep 1988 DGr (c)	3.00
❑235, Oct 1988 CR (c); CR (a)	3.00
❑236, Oct 1988 DGr (c); DGr (a)	3.00
❑237, Nov 1988	3.00
❑238, Nov 1988 DGr (c); DGr (a)	3.00
❑239, Dec 1988; DGr (c); DGr (a); Inferno	3.00
❑240, Jan 1989; DGr (c); DGr (a); A: Sabretooth. Inferno	3.00
❑241, Feb 1989; DGr (c); DGr (a); Inferno	3.00
❑242, Mar 1989; Double-size; DGr (c); DGr (a); Inferno	3.00
❑243, Apr 1989; DGr (c); Inferno	3.00
❑244, May 1989 DGr (c); DGr (a); 1: Jubilee.	5.00
❑245, Jun 1989 DGr, RL (c); DGr, RL (a)	3.00
❑246, Jul 1989 DGr (c); DGr (a)	3.00
❑247, Aug 1989 DGr (c); DGr (a)	3.00
❑248, Sep 1989; DGr, JLee (c); DGr, JLee (a); 1st Jim Lee art on X-Men	5.00
❑248-2 1989; JLee (a); 1st Jim Lee art on X-Men	1.50
❑249, Oct 1989 DGr (c); DGr (a)	3.00
❑250, Oct 1989 DGr (c)	3.00
❑251, Nov 1989 DGr (c); DGr (a)	3.00
❑252, Nov 1989 BSz, JLee (c)	2.50
❑253, Nov 1989 DGr (c)	2.50
❑254, Dec 1989 DGr (c); DGr (a); D: Sunder.	2.50
❑255, Dec 1989 DGr (c); DGr (a)	2.50
❑256, Dec 1989; JLee (c); JLee (a); Acts of Vengeance	3.00
❑257, Jan 1990; JLee (c); JLee (a); Acts of Vengeance	3.00
❑258, Feb 1990; JLee (c); JLee (a); Acts of Vengeance	3.00
❑259, Mar 1990 DGr (c); DGr (a)	3.00
❑260, Apr 1990 JLee (c); DGr (a)	3.00
❑261, May 1990 JLee (c); DGr (a)	2.50
❑262, Jun 1990	2.50
❑263, Jul 1990	2.50
❑264, Jul 1990 JLee (c)	2.50
❑265, Aug 1990	2.50
❑266, Aug 1990 1: Gambit (full appearance).	14.00
❑267, Sep 1990; JLee, BWi (c); JLee (a); Captain America, Wolverine, Black Widow team-up	6.00
❑268, Sep 1990 JLee (c); JLee (a)	6.00
❑269, Oct 1990 JLee (c); JLee (a)	3.00
❑270, Nov 1990 JLee (c); JLee (a)	4.00
❑270-2, Nov 1990; JLee (a); Gold cover	2.00
❑271, Dec 1990 JLee (c); JLee (a)	3.00
❑272, Jan 1991 JLee (c); JLee (a)	3.00
❑273, Feb 1991 JLee (c); MG, JBy, JLee, KJ (a)	3.00
❑274, Mar 1991 JLee (c); JLee (a); A: Ka-Zar. A: Magneto. A: Nick Fury.	3.00
❑275, Apr 1991; Double-size JLee (c); JLee (a)	3.00
❑275-2, Apr 1991; Double-size; JLee (a); gold logo	2.00
❑276, May 1991 JLee (c); JLee (w); JLee (a)	2.50
❑277, Jun 1991 JLee (c); JLee (w); JLee (a)	2.50
❑278, Jul 1991 PS (c); PS (a)	2.50
❑279, Aug 1991	2.50
❑280, Sep 1991; JLee (c); X-Factor crossover	2.50
❑281, Oct 1991; JBy, JLee (w); 1: Fitzroy. wraparound cover; new team	2.00
❑281-2, Oct 1991; 1: Fitzroy. 2nd printing (red); New team begins; wraparound cover	1.50
❑282, Nov 1991 JBy (w); 1: Bishop (cameo).	3.00
❑282-2, Nov 1991; 1: Bishop (cameo). Gold cover	1.25
❑283, Dec 1991 JBy (w); 1: Bishop (full).	3.00
❑284, Jan 1992 JBy (w)	2.50
❑285, Feb 1992 JBy, JLee (w); AM (a); 1: Mikhail Rasputin.	2.50
❑286, Mar 1992 JLee (c); JLee (w); JLee (a)	2.00
❑287, Apr 1992 JLee (w); BSz, JR2, BWi (a); O: Bishop.	2.50
❑288, May 1992 JBy, JLee (w); BSz (a)	2.00
❑289, Jun 1992; Bishop joins X-Men	2.00
❑290, Jul 1992	2.00
❑291, Aug 1992	2.00
❑292, Sep 1992 AM (a)	2.00
❑293, Oct 1992	2.00
❑294/CS, Nov 1992	2.00
❑295/CS, Dec 1992	1.50
❑296/CS, Jan 1993	2.00
❑297, Feb 1993	1.50
❑298, Mar 1993 AM (c); AM (a)	2.00
❑299, Apr 1993	1.50
❑300, May 1993; Double-size; DGr, JR2 (c); DGr, JR2 (a); holo-foil cover	3.00
❑301, Jun 1993 DGr, JR2 (c); DGr, JR2 (a)	1.50
❑302, Jul 1993 JR2 (c); DGr, JR2 (a)	1.50
❑303, Aug 1993 DGr (a); D: Illyana Rasputin.	3.00
❑304, Sep 1993; 30th Anniversary Issue; JR2 (c); DGr, PS, JR2, TP (a); hologram	1.50
❑305, Oct 1993 (c); JDu (a)	1.50
❑306, Nov 1993 JR2 (c); DGr, JR2 (a)	2.00
❑307, Dec 1993 DGr, JR2 (c); DGr, JR2 (a)	5.00
❑308, Jan 1994 DGr, JR2 (c); DGr, JR2 (a)	1.50
❑309, Feb 1994 DGr, JR2 (c); DGr, JR2 (a)	1.50
❑310, Mar 1994 DGr, JR2 (c); DGr, JR2 (a)	1.50
❑311, Apr 1994 JR2 (c); DGr, JR2 (a); A: Sabretooth.	1.50
❑312, May 1994 DGr (c); DGr (a)	1.50
❑313, Jun 1994 DGr (c); DGr (a)	1.50
❑314, Jul 1994 BSz (a)	1.50
❑315, Aug 1994 DGr (a)	1.50
❑316, Sep 1994 DGr (c); DGr (a)	1.50
❑316/Variant, Sep 1994; enhanced cover	1.50
❑317, Oct 1994 DGr (c); DGr (a)	1.50
❑317/Variant, Oct 1994; enhanced cover	1.50
❑318, Nov 1994	2.00
❑318/Deluxe, Nov 1994	1.50
❑319, Dec 1994 DGr (a)	2.00
❑319/Deluxe, Dec 1994	1.50
❑320, Jan 1995 MWa (w)	2.00
❑320/Deluxe, Jan 1995	1.50
❑320/Gold, Jan 1995; Wizard edition; No cover price; gold logo	2.00
❑321, Feb 1995 (c); MWa (w); DGr (a)	1.50
❑321/Deluxe, Feb 1995	2.00
❑322, Jul 1995 AM, DGr (a); V: Onslaught. V: Juggernaut.	2.00
❑323, Aug 1995 1: Sack and Vessel.	1.50
❑324, Sep 1995	2.00
❑325, Oct 1995; enhanced gatefold cardstock cover	2.00
❑326, Nov 1995	2.00
❑327, Dec 1995; AM (a); A: Magneto. Magneto's fate revealed	2.00
❑328, Jan 1996; Psylocke vs. Sabretooth	2.00
❑329, Feb 1996 JPH (w)	4.00
❑330, Mar 1996 JPH (w)	2.00
❑331, Apr 1996; Iceman vs. White Queen	2.00
❑332, May 1996 V: Ozymandias.	2.00
❑333, Jun 1996	2.00
❑334, Jul 1996 A: Juggernaut.	2.00
❑335, Aug 1996 A: Uatu. A: Apocalypse.	2.00
❑336, Sep 1996	2.00
❑337, Oct 1996	2.00
❑338, Nov 1996; Angel regains his wings	2.00
❑339, Dec 1996; A: Spider-Man. Cyclops vs. Havok	2.00
❑340, Jan 1997	2.00
❑341, Feb 1997; Cannonball vs. Gladiator	2.00
❑342, Mar 1997	2.00
❑342/A, Mar 1997; Variant cover (Rogue)	2.00
❑343, Apr 1997	2.00
❑344, May 1997	2.00
❑345, Jun 1997	2.00
❑346, Aug 1997; gatefold summary A: Spider-Man.	2.00
❑347, Sep 1997; gatefold summary AM (a)	2.00
❑348, Oct 1997; gatefold summary AM (a)	2.00
❑349, Nov 1997; gatefold summary V: Maggot.	2.00
❑350, Dec 1997; gatefold summary	2.00
❑350/Variant, Dec 1997; gatefold summary; enhanced cover	2.00
❑351, Jan 1998; gatefold summary; V: Pyro. Cecilia joins team	2.00
❑352, Feb 1998; gatefold summary	2.00
❑353, Mar 1998; gatefold summary; Rogue vs. Wolverine	3.00
❑354, Apr 1998; gatefold summary V: Sauron.	1.99
❑355, May 1998; gatefold summary A: Alpha Flight.	1.99
❑356, Jun 1998; gatefold summary	1.99
❑357, Jul 1998; gatefold summary	1.99
❑358, Aug 1998; gatefold summary	1.99
❑359, Sep 1998; gatefold summary	1.99
❑360, Oct 1998; double-sized; Kitty Pryde, Colossus, Nightcrawler rejoin team	1.99
❑360/Variant, Oct 1998; Special cover	1.99
❑361, Nov 1998; gatefold summary; Return of Gambit	1.99
❑362, Dec 1998; gatefold summary	1.99
❑363, Jan 1999; gatefold summary	4.00
❑364, Jan 1999; gatefold summary; Leinil Francis Yu's first major comics work	2.99
❑365, Mar 1999; gatefold summary; cover says Feb, indicia says Mar	1.99
❑366, Apr 1999	1.99
❑367, Apr 1999 (c)	1.99
❑368, Jun 1999; Wolverine vs. Magneto; cover says May, indicia says Jun	1.99
❑369, Jun 1999 V: Juggernaut.	1.99
❑370, Jul 1999	1.99
❑371, Aug 1999 A: Warlock.	1.99
❑372, Sep 1999	1.99
❑373, Oct 1999	1.99
❑374, Nov 1999	1.99
❑375, Dec 1999; Giant-size	1.99
❑376, Jan 2000	1.99
❑377, Feb 2000	1.99
❑378, Mar 2000	1.99
❑379, Apr 2000	2.99
❑380, May 2000	1.99
❑381, Jun 2000	2.25

Condition price index: Multiply "NM prices" above by: **0.83 for Very Fine/Near Mint**
0.66 for Very Fine • 0.33 for Fine • 0.2 for Very Good • 0.125 for Good

	N-MINT
❑381/DF, Jun 2000; Dynamic Forces chromium variant; no UPC box on cover	7.00
❑382, Jul 2000	2.25
❑383, Aug 2000; Giant-size	2.25
❑384, Sep 2000	2.25
❑385, Oct 2000	2.25
❑386, Nov 2000	2.25
❑387, Dec 2000	2.99
❑388, Jan 2001	2.25
❑389, Feb 2001	2.25
❑390, Feb 2001 D: Colossus.	2.25
❑391, Mar 2001	2.25
❑392, Apr 2001; Eve of Destruction	2.25
❑393, May 2001; Eve of Destruction	2.25
❑394, Jun 2001	2.25
❑395, Jul 2001	2.25
❑396, Aug 2001	2.25
❑397, Sep 2001	2.25
❑398, Oct 2001	2.25
❑399, Nov 2001	2.25
❑400, Dec 2001; Giant-size (c)	2.25
❑401, Jan 2002	2.25
❑402, Feb 2002	2.25
❑403, Mar 2002	2.25
❑404, Apr 2002	3.50
❑405, May 2002	2.25
❑406, Jun 2002	2.25
❑407, Jul 2002	2.25
❑408, Aug 2002	2.25
❑409, Sep 2002	2.25
❑410, Oct 2002	2.25
❑411, Oct 2002	2.25
❑412, Nov 2002 (c)	2.25
❑413, Nov 2002	2.25
❑414, Dec 2002	2.25
❑415, Jan 2003	2.25
❑416, Feb 2003	3.00
❑417, Mar 2003	2.25
❑418, Mar 2003	2.25
❑419, Apr 2003	2.25
❑420, May 2003	2.25
❑421, Jun 2003	2.25
❑422, Jun 2003	2.25
❑423, Jul 2003	2.25
❑424, Jul 2003	2.25
❑425, Aug 2003	2.25
❑426, Aug 2003	2.25
❑427, Sep 2003	2.25
❑428, Oct 2003	2.25
❑429, Oct 2003	2.25
❑430, Oct 2003	2.99
❑431, Nov 2003	2.99
❑432, Dec 2003	2.99
❑433, Jan 2004	2.99
❑434, Feb 2004	2.99
❑435, Feb 2004	2.99
❑436, Feb 2004, DGr (a)	2.99
❑437, Mar 2004	2.99
❑438, Mar 2004	2.99
❑439, Apr 2004	2.25
❑440, Apr 2004	2.99
❑441, May 2004	2.99
❑442, May 2004	2.25
❑443, Jun 2004	2.99
❑444, Jul 2004	2.99
❑445, Aug 2004	2.25
❑446, Sep 2004	
❑Annual 1, Dec 1970; JK (a); listed as X-Men in indicia, X-Men Special on cover; reprints X-Men #9 and 11	50.00
❑Annual 2, Nov 1971; Cover reads "King Size Special"; GK (c); Cover reads King Size Special; reprints X-Men #22 and 23	45.00
❑Annual 3, Jan 1980 FM (c); GP, FM (a); 1: Arkon.	14.00
❑Annual 4, Nov 1980; JR2 (a); A: Doctor Strange. series continues as Uncanny X-Men Annual	6.00
❑Annual 5, Nov 1981 BA, BMc (a); A: Fantastic Four.	5.00
❑Annual 6, Nov 1982 BSz (a); A: Dracula. D: Rachel Van Helsing.	7.00
❑Annual 7, ca. 1983 MG (a)	5.00
❑Annual 8, ca. 1984	4.00
❑Annual 9, ca. 1985	10.00
❑Annual 10, Jan 1986 1: Longshot. 1: X-babies.	8.00
❑Annual 11, ca. 1987	4.00
❑Annual 12, ca. 1988	4.00
❑Annual 13, ca. 1989; Atlantis Attacks	3.00
❑Annual 14, ca. 1990 1: Gambit (cameo).	6.00
❑Annual 15, ca. 1991; 1991 annual; ca. 1991	4.00
❑Annual 16, ca. 1992; Shattershot	2.25
❑Annual 17, ca. 1993; trading card	2.95
❑Annual 18, ca. 1994 JR2 (a)	2.95
❑Annual 1995, Nov 1995; wraparound cover	3.95
❑Annual 1996, ca. 1996; wraparound cover	2.95
❑Annual 1997, Oct 1997; 1997 Annual; wraparound cover	2.99
❑Annual 1998, ca. 1998; Uncanny X-Men/Fantastic Four '98; wraparound cover	2.99
❑Annual 2000, Feb 2001	3.50
❑Annual 2001 2001	3.50

UNCENSORED MOUSE, THE
Eternity

	N-MINT
❑1, Apr 1989, b&w; Mickey Mouse	2.50
❑2, Apr 1989; Mickey Mouse	2.50

UNCLE JOE'S COMMIE BOOK FEATURING CUTEY BUNNY
Rip Off

	N-MINT
❑1 1995, b&w	2.95

UNCLE SAM
DC / Vertigo

	N-MINT
❑1, ca. 1997; prestige format ARo (a)	5.00
❑2, ca. 1997; prestige format ARo (a)	5.00

UNCLE SCROOGE (WALT DISNEY...)
Dell / Gold Key/Whitman

	N-MINT
❑16, Dec 1956	80.00
❑17, Mar 1957	80.00
❑18, Jun 1957	80.00
❑19, Sep 1957	80.00
❑20, Dec 1957	80.00
❑21, Mar 1958	65.00
❑22, Jun 1958	65.00
❑23, Sep 1958	65.00
❑24, Dec 1958 CB (w); CB (a)	65.00
❑25, Mar 1959	65.00
❑26, Jun 1959	65.00
❑27, Sep 1959	65.00
❑28, Dec 1959	65.00
❑29, Mar 1960	65.00
❑30, Jun 1960	65.00
❑31, Sep 1960	55.00
❑32, Dec 1960	55.00
❑33, Mar 1961	55.00
❑34, Jun 1961	55.00
❑35, Sep 1961	55.00
❑36, Dec 1961; Old Number One Dime named as such	55.00
❑37, Mar 1962	55.00
❑38, Jun 1962	55.00
❑39, Sep 1962	55.00
❑40, Dec 1962; Gold Key begins as publisher	55.00
❑41, Mar 1963	45.00
❑42, May 1963	45.00
❑43, Jul 1963	45.00
❑44, Aug 1963	45.00
❑45, Oct 1963	45.00
❑46, Dec 1963	45.00
❑47, Feb 1964	45.00
❑48, Mar 1964	45.00
❑49, May 1964	45.00
❑50, Jul 1964	45.00
❑51, Aug 1964	40.00
❑52, Sep 1964	40.00
❑53, Oct 1964	40.00

Uncle Scrooge #306 contained an extra chapter in "The Life and Times of Scrooge McDuck."

© 1997 Walt Disney Productions and Gladstone.

	N-MINT
❑54, Dec 1964	40.00
❑55, Feb 1965	40.00
❑56, Mar 1965	40.00
❑57, May 1965	40.00
❑58, Jul 1965	40.00
❑59, Sep 1965	40.00
❑60, Nov 1965	40.00
❑61, Jan 1966	40.00
❑62, Mar 1966	40.00
❑63, May 1966	40.00
❑64, Jul 1966	40.00
❑65, Sep 1966	40.00
❑66, Nov 1966; Gyro reprinted from Uncle Scrooge (Walt Disney) #22	40.00
❑67, Jan 1967	40.00
❑68, Mar 1967	40.00
❑69, May 1967	40.00
❑70, Jul 1967	40.00
❑71, Oct 1967	38.00
❑72, Dec 1967; Gyro reprinted from Uncle Scrooge (Walt Disney...) #19	32.00
❑73, Feb 1968; Reprints stories from Uncle Scrooge (Walt Disney...) #33 and 36	32.00
❑74, Apr 1968	32.00
❑75, Jun 1968	32.00
❑76, Aug 1968	32.00
❑77, Oct 1968	32.00
❑78, Dec 1968	32.00
❑79, Feb 1969	32.00
❑80, Apr 1969	32.00
❑81, Jun 1969	32.00
❑82, Aug 1969; Reprints story from Uncle Scrooge (Walt Disney...) #34	32.00
❑83, Oct 1969	32.00
❑84, Dec 1969; Reprints story from Uncle Scrooge (Walt Disney...) #14	32.00
❑85, Feb 1970; Reprints story from Uncle Scrooge (Walt Disney...) #52	32.00
❑86, Apr 1970; Reprints story from Uncle Scrooge (Walt Disney...) #35	32.00
❑87, Jun 1970; Reprints story from Uncle Scrooge (Walt Disney...) #25	32.00
❑88, Aug 1970; Reprints story from Uncle Scrooge (Walt Disney...) #38	32.00
❑89, Oct 1970; Reprints story from Uncle Scrooge (Walt Disney...) #15	32.00
❑90, Dec 1970; Reprints stories from Uncle Scrooge (Walt Disney...) #37 and 35	32.00
❑91, Feb 1971; Reprints stories from Uncle Scrooge (Walt Disney...) #11 and 26	32.00
❑92, Apr 1971; Reprints stories from Uncle Scrooge (Walt Disney...) #24, 31 and 32	32.00
❑93, Jun 1971; Reprints stories from Uncle Scrooge (Walt Disney...) #34 and 36	32.00
❑94, Aug 1971; Reprints stories from Uncle Scrooge (Walt Disney...) #35 and 53	32.00
❑95, Oct 1971; Reprints stories from Uncle Scrooge (Walt Disney...) #30 and 51	32.00
❑96, Dec 1971; Reprints story from Uncle Scrooge (Walt Disney...) #47	32.00
❑97, Feb 1972; Reprints stories from Uncle Scrooge (Walt Disney...) #32	32.00
❑98, Apr 1972; Reprints story from Uncle Scrooge (Walt Disney...) #41	32.00

	N-MINT
❑99, Jun 1972; Reprints story from Uncle Scrooge (Walt Disney…) #42	32.00
❑100, Aug 1972; Reprints story from Uncle Scrooge (Walt Disney…) #30	32.00
❑101, Sep 1972; Reprints stories from Walt Disney's Comics #157 and 159	20.00
❑102, Nov 1972; Reprints stories from Uncle Scrooge (Walt Disney…) #39	20.00
❑103, Feb 1973; Reprints story from Uncle Scrooge (Walt Disney…) #16	20.00
❑104, Apr 1973; Reprints stories from Uncle Scrooge (Walt Disney…) #9 and 42	20.00
❑105, Jun 1973; Reprints stories from Four Color Comins #495 (Uncle Scrooge #3) and Uncle Scrooge (Walt Disney…) #32	20.00
❑106, Aug 1973; Reprints stories from Uncle Scrooge (Walt Disney…) #6	20.00
❑107, Sep 1973; Reprints story from Uncle Scrooge (Walt Disney…) #21	20.00
❑108, Oct 1973; Reprints story from Uncle Scrooge (Walt Disney…) #19	20.00
❑109, Dec 1973; Reprints story from Uncle Scrooge (Walt Disney…) #13	20.00
❑110, Feb 1974; Reprints story from Uncle Scrooge (Walt Disney…) #22	20.00
❑111, Jun 1974; Reprints story from Uncle Scrooge (Walt Disney…) #8	20.00
❑112, Jun 1974; Reprints story from Uncle Scrooge (Walt Disney…) #18	20.00
❑113, Aug 1974; Reprints stories from Uncle Scrooge (Walt Disney…) #24 and 44	20.00
❑114, Sep 1974; Reprints story from Uncle Scrooge (Walt Disney…) #60	20.00
❑115, Oct 1974; Reprints story from Uncle Scrooge (Walt Disney…) #58	20.00
❑116, Dec 1974; Reprints story from Uncle Scrooge (Walt Disney…) #50	20.00
❑117, Feb 1975; Reprints stories from Uncle Scrooge (Walt Disney…) #32 and 49	20.00
❑118, Apr 1975; Reprints stories from Uncle Scrooge (Walt Disney…) #54	20.00
❑119, Jun 1975; Reprints stories from Uncle Scrooge (Walt Disney…) #23 and 37	20.00
❑120, Jul 1975; Reprints stories from Uncle Scrooge (Walt Disney…) #33 and 34	20.00
❑121, Aug 1975; Reprints story from Uncle Scrooge (Walt Disney…) #55	18.00
❑122, Sep 1975; Reprints story from Uncle Scrooge (Walt Disney…) #56	18.00
❑123, Oct 1975; Reprints story from Uncle Scrooge (Walt Disney…) #57	18.00
❑124, Dec 1975; Reprints story from Uncle Scrooge (Walt Disney…) #59	18.00
❑125, Jan 1976; Reprints story from Uncle Scrooge (Walt Disney…) #68	18.00
❑126, Mar 1976; Reprints story from Uncle Scrooge (Walt Disney…) #69	18.00
❑127, Apr 1976; Reprints story from Uncle Scrooge (Walt Disney…) #61	18.00
❑128, May 1976; Reprints story from Uncle Scrooge (Walt Disney…) #62	18.00
❑129, Jun 1976; Reprints story from Uncle Scrooge (Walt Disney…) #63	18.00
❑130, Jul 1976; Reprints story from Uncle Scrooge (Walt Disney…) #65	18.00
❑131, Aug 1976; Reprints story from Uncle Scrooge (Walt Disney…) #66	18.00
❑132, Sep 1976; Reprints story from Uncle Scrooge (Walt Disney…) #10	18.00
❑133, Oct 1976; Reprints story from Uncle Scrooge (Walt Disney…) #70	18.00
❑134, Nov 1976; Reprints story from Uncle Scrooge (Walt Disney…) #64	18.00
❑135, Dec 1976; Reprints stories from Uncle Scrooge (Walt Disney…) #23 and 24	18.00
❑136, Jan 1977; Reprints stories from Uncle Scrooge (Walt Disney…) #37-39	18.00
❑137, Feb 1977; Reprints story from Uncle Scrooge (Walt Disney…) #31	18.00
❑138, Mar 1977; Reprints stories from Uncle Scrooge (Walt Disney…) #28 and 48	18.00
❑139, Apr 1977; Reprints stories from Uncle Scrooge (Walt Disney…) #45	18.00
❑140, May 1977; Reprints story from Uncle Scrooge (Walt Disney…) #43	18.00
❑141, Jun 1977; Reprints story from Uncle Scrooge (Walt Disney…) #42	12.00
❑142, Jul 1977; Reprints story from Four Color Comics #456 (Uncle Scrooge #2)	12.00
❑143, Aug 1977; Reprints stories from Uncle Scrooge (Walt Disney…) #26 and 29	12.00
❑144, Sep 1977; Reprints stories from Uncle Scrooge (Walt Disney…) #28	12.00
❑145, Oct 1977; Reprints story from Uncle Scrooge (Walt Disney…) #71	12.00
❑146, Nov 1977; Reprints story from Uncle Scrooge (Walt Disney…) #30	12.00
❑147, Dec 1977; Reprints stories from Uncle Scrooge (Walt Disney…) #34-36	12.00
❑148, Jan 1978; Reprints story from Uncle Scrooge (Walt Disney…) #11	12.00
❑149, Feb 1978; Reprints story from Uncle Scrooge (Walt Disney…) #46	12.00
❑150, Mar 1978; Reprints stories from Uncle Scrooge (Walt Disney…) #27	12.00
❑151, Apr 1978; Reprints stories from Uncle Scrooge (Walt Disney…) #25	12.00
❑152, May 1978; Reprints story from Uncle Scrooge (Walt Disney…) #52	12.00
❑153, Jun 1978; Reprints story from Uncle Scrooge (Walt Disney…) #44	12.00
❑154, Jul 1978; Reprints stories from Uncle Scrooge (Walt Disney…) #35 and 53	12.00
❑155, Aug 1978; Reprints stories from Uncle Scrooge (Walt Disney…) #11 and 30	12.00
❑156, Sep 1978; Reprints stories from Four Color Comics #456 (Uncle Scrooge #2) and Uncle Scrooge (Walt Disney…) #38	12.00
❑157, Oct 1978; Reprints stories from Uncle Scrooge (Walt Disney…) #31	12.00
❑158, Nov 1978	12.00
❑159, Dec 1978; Reprints story from Uncle Scrooge (Walt Disney…) #35	12.00
❑160, Jan 1979	12.00
❑161, Feb 1979	10.00
❑162, Mar 1979	10.00
❑163, Apr 1979	10.00
❑164, May 1979	10.00
❑165, Jun 1979	10.00
❑166, Jul 1979	10.00
❑167, Aug 1979	10.00
❑168, Sep 1979	10.00
❑169, Oct 1979	10.00
❑170, Nov 1979	10.00
❑171, Dec 1979	10.00
❑172, Jan 1980	10.00
❑173, Feb 1980	10.00
❑174, Mar 1980	10.00
❑175, Apr 1980	10.00
❑176, May 1980	10.00
❑177, Jun 1980	10.00
❑178, Jul 1980	10.00
❑179, Sep 1980	10.00
❑180, Nov 1980	10.00
❑181, Dec 1980	10.00
❑182, Jan 1981	10.00
❑183, ca. 1981	10.00
❑184, ca. 1981	10.00
❑185, Jun 1981	10.00
❑186, Jul 1981	10.00
❑187, Aug 1981	10.00
❑188, Sep 1981	10.00
❑189, Oct 1981	10.00
❑190, Nov 1981	10.00
❑191, Dec 1981	10.00
❑192, Jan 1982	10.00
❑193, Feb 1982	10.00
❑194, Spr 1982	10.00
❑195, Mar 1982	10.00
❑196, Apr 1982	10.00
❑197, May 1982	10.00
❑198, ca. 1982	15.00
❑199, May 1983	10.00
❑200, ca. 1982	10.00
❑201, ca. 1983	6.00
❑202, ca. 1983	6.00
❑203, Jul 1983	6.00
❑204, Aug 1983	6.00
❑205, Aug 1983	6.00
❑206, ca. 1984	6.00
❑207, May 1984	6.00
❑208, Jun 1984	6.00
❑209, Jul 1984	6.00
❑210, Oct 1986 CB (w); CB (a)	6.00
❑211, Nov 1986 CB (w); CB (a)	6.00
❑212, Dec 1986 CB (w); CB (a)	6.00
❑213, Jan 1987	6.00
❑214, Feb 1987	6.00
❑215, Mar 1987	6.00
❑216, Apr 1987 CB (w); CB (a)	6.00
❑217, May 1987	6.00
❑218, Jun 1987 CB (w); CB (a)	6.00
❑219, Jul 1987; DR (a); 1st Rosa Disney story	6.00
❑220, Aug 1987 CB (w); CB, DR (a)	5.00
❑221, Sep 1987 CB (w); CB (a)	5.00
❑222, Oct 1987 CB (w); CB (a)	5.00
❑223, Nov 1987 CB (w); CB (a)	5.00
❑224, Dec 1987 CB (w); CB, DR (a)	5.00
❑225, Feb 1988 CB (w); CB (a)	5.00
❑226, May 1988 CB (w); CB, DR (a)	5.00
❑227, Jul 1988 CB (w); CB (a)	5.00
❑228, Aug 1988 CB (w); CB (a)	5.00
❑229, Sep 1988 CB (w); CB (a)	5.00
❑230, Oct 1988 CB (w); CB (a)	5.00
❑231, Nov 1988 DR (c); CB (w); CB (a)	5.00
❑232, Dec 1988 CB (w); CB (a)	5.00
❑233, Feb 1989 CB (w); CB (a)	5.00
❑234, May 1989 CB (w); CB (a)	5.00
❑235, Jul 1989 CB (w); DR (a)	5.00
❑236, Aug 1989 CB (w); CB (a)	5.00
❑237, Sep 1989 CB (w); CB (a)	5.00
❑238, Oct 1989 CB (w); CB (a)	5.00
❑239, Nov 1989 CB (w); CB (a)	5.00
❑240, Dec 1989 CB (w); CB (a)	5.00
❑241, Feb 1990 CB (w); CB, DR (a)	4.00
❑242, Apr 1990; double-sized CB (w); CB (a)	4.00
❑243, Jun 1990	4.00
❑244, Jul 1990	4.00
❑245, Aug 1990	4.00
❑246, Sep 1990	4.00
❑247, Oct 1990	4.00
❑248, Nov 1990	4.00
❑249, Dec 1990	4.00
❑250, Jan 1991 CB (w); CB (a)	4.00
❑251, Feb 1991 CB (w); CB (a)	4.00
❑252, Mar 1991	4.00
❑253, Apr 1991 CB (w); CB (a)	4.00
❑254, May 1991 CB (w); CB (a)	4.00
❑255, Jun 1991 CB (w); CB (a)	4.00
❑256, Jul 1991 CB (w); CB (a)	4.00
❑257, Aug 1991	4.00
❑258, Sep 1991 CB (w); CB (a)	4.00
❑259, Oct 1991	4.00
❑260, Nov 1991	4.00
❑261, Dec 1991 DR (a)	2.50
❑262, Jan 1992 DR (a)	2.50
❑263, Feb 1992 DR (a)	2.50
❑264, Mar 1992	2.50
❑265, Apr 1992 CB (w); CB (a)	2.50
❑266, May 1992 CB (w); CB (a)	2.50
❑267, Jun 1992; CB (w); CB (a); contains Duckburg map piece 3 of 9	2.50
❑268, Jul 1992; CB (w); CB (a); contains Duckburg map piece 6 of 9	2.50
❑269, Aug 1992; CB (w); CB (a); contains Duckburg map piece 9 of 9	2.50
❑270, Sep 1992; CB (w); CB (a); Olympics	2.50
❑271, Oct 1992 CB (w); CB (a)	2.50
❑272, Nov 1992 CB (w); CB (a)	2.50
❑273, Dec 1992 CB (w); CB (a)	2.50

N-MINT

❑274, Jan 1993 CB (w); CB (a) 2.50
❑275, Feb 1993 CB (w); CB (a) 2.50
❑276, Mar 1993 DR (a) 2.50
❑277, Apr 1993 CB (w); CB (a) 2.50
❑278, May 1993 CB (w); CB (a) 2.50
❑279, Jun 1993 CB (w); CB (a) 2.50
❑280, Jul 1993 .... 2.50
❑281, Aug 1993 DR (c); CB (w); CB (a) 2.50
❑282, Oct 1993 CB (w); CB (a) 2.50
❑283, Dec 1993 CB (w); CB (a) 2.50
❑284, Feb 1994 CB (w); CB (a) 2.50
❑285, Apr 1994 DR (a) 2.50
❑286, Jun 1994 DR (a) 2.50
❑287, Aug 1994 DR (a) 2.50
❑288, Oct 1994 DR (a) 2.50
❑289, Dec 1994 DR (a) 2.50
❑290, Feb 1995 DR (a) 2.50
❑291, Apr 1995 DR (a) 2.50
❑292, Jun 1995 DR (a) 2.50
❑293, Aug 1995 DR (a) 2.50
❑294, Oct 1995; DR (a); newsprint covers begin 2.50
❑295, Dec 1995 DR (a) 2.50
❑296, Feb 1996 DR (a) 2.50
❑297, Apr 1996 DR (a) 2.50
❑298, Jun 1996 .... 2.50
❑299, Aug 1996 .... 2.50
❑300, Oct 1996 .... 2.25
❑301, Dec 1996 .... 1.50
❑302, Feb 1997; CB (w); CB (a); reprints from WDC&S #297 .... 1.50
❑303, Apr 1997; newsprint covers end 1.50
❑304, Jun 1997 CB (w); CB (a) 1.50
❑305, Aug 1997 CB (w); CB (a) 1.50
❑306, Oct 1997 DR (c); DR (w); DR (a) 1.50
❑307, Dec 1997 .... 1.50
❑308, Feb 1998 .... 1.50
❑309, May 1998; prestige format begins 6.95
❑310, Jun 1998 .... 6.95
❑311, Jul 1998 .... 6.95
❑312, Aug 1998 .... 6.95
❑313, Sep 1998 .... 6.95
❑314, Oct 1998 .... 6.95
❑315, Nov 1998 .... 6.95
❑316, Dec 1998 .... 6.95
❑317, Jan 1999 .... 6.95
❑318, Feb 1999 .... 6.95
❑319, Jul 2003......... 6.95

UNCLE SCROOGE (GEMSTONE)
GEMSTONE

❑319, Jun 2003; DR (c); CB, DR (w); CB, DR (a); Gemstone begins publishing; prestige format 6.95
❑320, Jul 2003 .... 6.95
❑321, Aug 2003 .... 6.95
❑322, Sep 2003 .... 6.95
❑323, Oct 2003 .... 6.95
❑324, Nov 2003 .... 6.95
❑325, Dec 2003 .... 6.95
❑326, Jan 2004 .... 6.95
❑327, Feb 2004 .... 6.95
❑328, Mar 2004 .... 6.95
❑329, Apr 2004 .... 6.95
❑330, May 2004 .... 6.95
❑331, Jun 2004 .... 6.95

UNCLE SCROOGE ADVENTURES
GLADSTONE

❑1, Nov 1987 CB (a) 5.00
❑2, Dec 1987 CB (a) 3.00
❑3, Jan 1988 CB (a) 2.00
❑4, Apr 1988 CB (a) 2.00
❑5, Jun 1988 DR (a) 6.00
❑6, Aug 1988 CB (a) 2.00
❑7, Sep 1988 CB (a) 2.00
❑8, Oct 1988 CB (a) 2.00
❑9, Nov 1988 DR (a) 5.00
❑10, Dec 1988 CB (a) 2.00
❑11, Jan 1989 CB (a) 2.00
❑12, Mar 1989 CB (a) 2.00
❑13, Jun 1989 DR (c); CB (a) 2.00
❑14, Aug 1989 DR (a) 5.00

N-MINT

❑15, Sep 1989 CB (a) 2.00
❑16, Oct 1989 CB (a) 2.00
❑17, Nov 1989 CB (a) 2.00
❑18, Dec 1989 CB (a) 2.00
❑19, Jan 1990 DR (c); CB (a) 2.00
❑20, Mar 1990; double-sized CB, DR (a) 5.00
❑21, May 1990; double-sized CB, DR (a) 5.00
❑22, Sep 1993 CB (a) 1.50
❑23, Nov 1993 CB (a) 2.95
❑24, Jan 1994 CB (a) 1.50
❑25, Mar 1994 DR (c); CB (a) 1.50
❑26, May 1994 CB (a) 2.95
❑27, Jul 1994 DR (a); O: Junior Woodchucks Handbook. 1.50
❑28, Sep 1994 CB (a); A: Terries and Fermies. 2.95
❑29, Nov 1994 .... 1.50
❑30, Jan 1995 .... 2.95
❑31, Mar 1995 .... 1.50
❑32, May 1995 .... 1.50
❑33, Jul 1995; CB (w); CB (a); new story 2.95
❑34, Sep 1995 .... 1.95
❑35, Nov 1995 .... 1.95
❑36, Jan 1996 .... 1.95
❑37, Mar 1996; newprint covers begin 1.50
❑38, May 1996 .... 1.50
❑39, Aug 1996 .... 1.50
❑40, Sep 1996 .... 1.50
❑41, Nov 1996 .... 1.95
❑42, Jan 1997 .... 1.95
❑43, Feb 1997; CB (a); reprints The Queen of the Wild Dog Pack from US #62 .... 1.50
❑44, Mar 1997 .... 1.50
❑45, Apr 1997 .... 1.50
❑46, May 1997; newprint covers end 1.95
❑47, Jun 1997 CB (a) 1.95
❑48, Jul 1997 .... 1.95
❑49, Aug 1997 .... 1.95
❑50, Sep 1997 CB (a) 1.95
❑51, Oct 1997 DR (a) 1.95
❑52, Nov 1997 .... 1.95
❑53, Dec 1997 .... 1.95
❑54, Feb 1998 .... 1.95

UNCLE SCROOGE AND DONALD DUCK
GOLD KEY

❑1, Jun 1965; Reprints stories from Four Color Comics #29 and 386 .... 50.00

UNCLE SCROOGE & DONALD DUCK (WALT DISNEY'S...)
GLADSTONE

❑1, Jan 1998 .... 2.00
❑2, Mar 1998 .... 2.00

UNCLE SCROOGE COMICS DIGEST
GLADSTONE

❑1, Dec 1986; CB (a); reprints 3.00
❑2, Feb 1987; CB (a); reprints 2.00
❑3, Apr 1987; CB (a); reprints 2.00
❑4, Jun 1987; CB (a); reprints 2.00
❑5, Aug 1987; CB (a); reprints 2.00

UNCLE SCROOGE GOES TO DISNEYLAND (WALT DISNEY'S...)
GLADSTONE

❑1-0 CB (a) ....
❑1, Aug 1985; CB (a); Dell Giant 275.00
❑1/A, Aug 1985; digest 5.00
❑1-2/A; digest CB (a) 5.00
❑1-2 CB (a) 6.00

UNCLE SCROOGE THE GOLDEN FLEECING (WALT DISNEY'S...)
WHITMAN

❑1 .... 8.00

UNCLE SLAM & FIRE DOG
ACTION PLANET

❑1, ca. 1997, b&w 2.95
❑2, b&w 2.95

Harvey's *Underdog* was a shorter-lived series than Charlton's.
© 1993 Harvey

N-MINT

UNCUT COMICS
UNCUT COMICS

❑1, Apr 1997, b&w; free handout; Origins 1.00
❑1/A, Feb 1997, b&w; non-slick cover 1.50
❑1/B, Feb 1997, b&w; non-slick alternate cover 1.50
❑2, May 1997, b&w; flip-book with alternate cover back-up 1.95

UNDERCOVER GENIE
DC

❑1, ca. 2003 .... 14.95

UNDERDOG (CHARLTON)
CHARLTON

❑1, Jul 1970; poster 60.00
❑2, Sep 1970 .... 38.00
❑3, Nov 1970 .... 30.00
❑4, Jan 1971 .... 30.00
❑5, Mar 1971 .... 30.00
❑6, May 1971 .... 25.00
❑7, Jul 1971 .... 25.00
❑8, Sep 1971 .... 25.00
❑9, Nov 1971 .... 25.00
❑10, Jan 1972 .... 25.00

UNDERDOG (GOLD KEY)
GOLD KEY

❑1 1975 .... 35.00
❑2 1975 .... 20.00
❑3 1975 .... 12.00
❑4 1975 .... 8.00
❑5 1976 .... 8.00
❑6 1976 .... 6.00
❑7, Jun 1976 .... 6.00
❑8, Aug 1976 .... 6.00
❑9, Oct 1976 .... 6.00
❑10, Dec 1976 .... 6.00
❑11, Feb 1976 .... 5.00
❑12, Apr 1977 .... 5.00
❑13, Jun 1977 .... 5.00
❑14, Aug 1977 .... 5.00
❑15, Oct 1977 .... 5.00
❑16, Dec 1977 .... 5.00
❑17, Feb 1978 .... 5.00
❑18, Apr 1978 .... 5.00
❑19, Jun 1978 .... 5.00
❑20, Aug 1978 .... 5.00
❑21, Oct 1978 .... 4.00
❑22, Dec 1978 .... 4.00
❑23, Feb 1979 .... 4.00

UNDERDOG (SPOTLIGHT)
SPOTLIGHT

❑1, ca. 1987 .... 2.50
❑2, ca. 1987 .... 2.50

UNDERDOG (HARVEY)
HARVEY

❑1, Nov 1993; No creator credits listed 1.50
❑2, Jan 1993; No creator credits listed 1.50
❑3, Mar 1994; No creator credits listed 1.50
❑4, May 1994; No creator credits listed 1.50
❑5, Jul 1994; No creator credits listed 1.50
❑Summer 1, Oct 1993 .... 2.25

UNDERDOG 3-D
BLACKTHORNE

❑1 .... 2.50

N-MINT

UNDERGROUND
Aircel

❑1, b&w 1.70

UNDERGROUND (ANDREW VACHSS'...)
Dark Horse

❑1, Nov 1993 3.95
❑2, Jan 1994 3.95
❑3, Mar 1994 3.95
❑4, May 1994 3.95

UNDERGROUND CLASSICS
Rip Off

❑1, Dec 1985; Fabulous Furry Freak Brothers 6.00
❑2, Feb 1986; Dealer McDope 10.00
❑2-2 1986 2.00
❑2-3 1986 2.50
❑3, Mar 1986; Dealer McDope 8.00
❑3-2 2.00
❑4, Sep 1987 2.50
❑5, Nov 1987; Wonder Warthog 7.50
❑6, Feb 1988 5.00
❑7, Apr 1988 6.00
❑8, Jun 1988 5.00
❑9, Feb 1989; Art of Greg Irons 4.00
❑10; Jesus 4.00
❑11; Jesus 4.00
❑12, Jul 1990; Shelton 3-D 5.00
❑12-2 2.95
❑13; Jesus 4.00
❑14; Jesus 4.00
❑15 4.00

UNDERSEA AGENT
Tower

❑1, Jan 1966 32.00
❑2, Apr 1966; Lt. Jones gains electrical powers 22.00
❑3, Jun 1966 18.00
❑4, Aug 1966 18.00
❑5, Oct 1966 18.00
❑6, Mar 1967 18.00

UNDERSIDE
Caliber

❑1 2.95

UNDERTAKER
Chaos

❑0, Feb 1999; Collector's issue; Wizard 3.00
❑0.5, Mar 1999 4.00
❑1, Apr 1999; Drawn cover 4.00
❑1/A, Apr 1999; DFE red foil cover 6.00
❑1/Variant, Apr 1999 4.00
❑2, May 1999 2.95
❑3, Jun 1999 2.95
❑4, Jul 1999 2.95
❑5, Aug 1999 2.95
❑6, Sep 1999 2.95
❑7, Oct 1999 2.95
❑8, Nov 1999 2.95
❑9, Dec 1999 2.95
❑10, Jan 2000 2.95
❑Holiday 1, Oct 1999; digest 2.95

UNDER TERRA
Predawn

❑2, b&w 2.45
❑3, b&w 2.45
❑4, b&w 2.45
❑5, b&w 2.45
❑6, b&w 1.75

UNDERWATER
Drawn and Quarterly

❑1, Aug 1994 2.95

UNDERWORLD (DC)
DC

❑1, Dec 1987 1.25
❑2, Jan 1988 1.25
❑3, Feb 1988 1.25
❑4, Mar 1988 1.25

UNDERWORLD (DEATH)
Death

❑1, b&w 2.00

UNDERWORLD UNLEASHED
DC

❑1, Nov 1995 MWa (w); 1: Neron. D: Mongul. D: Boomerang. D: Weather Wizard. D: Mirror Master. D: Heat Wave. D: Captain Cold. 3.50
❑2, Dec 1995 MWa (w) 3.25
❑3, Dec 1995 MWa (w) 3.25

UNDERWORLD UNLEASHED: ABYSS: HELL'S SENTINEL
DC

❑1, Dec 1995 2.95

UNDERWORLD UNLEASHED: APOKOLIPS: DARK UPRISING
DC

❑1, Nov 1995 1.95

UNDERWORLD UNLEASHED: BATMAN: DEVIL'S ASYLUM
DC

❑1 1995 2.95

UNDERWORLD UNLEASHED: PATTERNS OF FEAR
DC

❑1, Dec 1995 2.95

UNDIE DOG
Halley's

❑1, b&w 1.50

UNEXPECTED, THE
DC

❑105, Feb 1968; Series continued from Tales of the Unexpected #104 30.00
❑106, Apr 1968 18.00
❑107, Jun 1968 18.00
❑108, Aug 1968 18.00
❑109, Oct 1968 18.00
❑110, Dec 1968 18.00
❑111, Feb 1969 18.00
❑112, Apr 1969 18.00
❑113, Jun 1969 CS (a) 18.00
❑114, Aug 1969 12.00
❑115, Oct 1969 12.00
❑116, Dec 1969 12.00
❑117, Feb 1970 12.00
❑118, Apr 1970 GT (a) 12.00
❑119, Jun 1970 BWr (a) 14.00
❑120, Aug 1970 12.00
❑121, Oct 1970 BWr (a) 16.00
❑122, Dec 1970 12.00
❑123, Feb 1971 12.00
❑124, Apr 1971 12.00
❑125, Jul 1971 12.00
❑126, Aug 1971 12.00
❑127, Sep 1971 12.00
❑128, Oct 1971 BWr (a) 14.00
❑129, Nov 1971 8.00
❑130, Dec 1971 8.00
❑131, Jan 1972 DD, NC (a) 8.00
❑132, Feb 1972 8.00
❑133, Mar 1972 8.00
❑134, Apr 1972 8.00
❑135, May 1972 8.00
❑136, Jun 1972 8.00
❑137, Jul 1972 8.00
❑138, Aug 1972 8.00
❑139, Sep 1972 8.00
❑140, Oct 1972 8.00
❑141, Nov 1972 8.00
❑142, Dec 1972 8.00
❑143, Jan 1973 8.00
❑144, Feb 1973 8.00
❑145, Mar 1973 8.00
❑146, Apr 1973 8.00
❑147, Jun 1973 8.00
❑148, Jul 1973 8.00
❑149, Aug 1973 8.00
❑150, Sep 1973 8.00
❑151, Oct 1973 8.00
❑152, Nov 1973 8.00
❑153, Dec 1973 8.00
❑154, Jan 1974 8.00
❑155, Feb 1974 8.00
❑156, Mar 1974 8.00
❑157, Jun 1974; 100 Page giant 14.00
❑158, Aug 1974; 100 Page giant 14.00
❑159, Oct 1974; 100 Page giant 14.00
❑160, Dec 1974; 100 Page giant MM (a) 14.00
❑161, Feb 1975; 100 Page giant 14.00
❑162, Mar 1975; 100 Page giant 14.00
❑163, Apr 1975 5.00
❑164, May 1975 5.00
❑165, Jun 1975 5.00
❑166, Jul 1975 5.00
❑167, Aug 1975 5.00
❑168, Sep 1975 5.00
❑169 1975 5.00
❑170, Dec 1975 5.00
❑171, Feb 1976 5.00
❑172, Apr 1976 5.00
❑173, Jun 1976 5.00
❑174, Aug 1976 5.00
❑175, Oct 1976 5.00
❑176, Dec 1976 5.00
❑177, Feb 1977 5.00
❑178, Apr 1977 5.00
❑179, Jun 1977 5.00
❑180, Aug 1977 5.00
❑181, Oct 1977 5.00
❑182, Dec 1977 5.00
❑183, Feb 1978 5.00
❑184, Apr 1978 5.00
❑185, Jun 1978 5.00
❑186, Aug 1978 5.00
❑187, Oct 1978 5.00
❑188, Dec 1978 5.00
❑189, Feb 1979 5.00
❑190, Apr 1979 5.00
❑191, Jun 1979 MR (a) 6.00
❑192, Aug 1979 4.00
❑193, Oct 1979 4.00
❑194, Dec 1979 4.00
❑195, Feb 1980 4.00
❑196, Mar 1980 4.00
❑197, Apr 1980 4.00
❑198, May 1980 4.00
❑199, Jun 1980 4.00
❑200, Jul 1980 4.00
❑201, Aug 1980 4.00
❑202, Sep 1980 4.00
❑203, Oct 1980 4.00
❑204, Nov 1980 4.00
❑205, Dec 1980 4.00
❑206, Jan 1981 4.00
❑207, Feb 1981 4.00
❑208, Mar 1981 4.00
❑209, Apr 1981 4.00
❑210, May 1981 4.00
❑211, Jun 1981 4.00
❑212, Jul 1981 4.00
❑213, Aug 1981 4.00
❑214, Sep 1981 4.00
❑215, Oct 1981 4.00
❑216, Nov 1981 4.00
❑217, Dec 1981 4.00
❑218, Jan 1982 4.00
❑219, Feb 1982 4.00
❑220, Mar 1982 4.00
❑221, Apr 1982 4.00
❑222, May 1982 4.00

UNFORGIVEN, THE
Mythic

❑1 2.75

UNFUNNIES (MARK MILLAR'S)
Avatar

❑1, Jan 2004 3.50
❑2, Mar 2004 3.50

Condition price index: Multiply "NM prices" above by: **0.83 for Very Fine/Near Mint**
0.66 for Very Fine • 0.33 for Fine • 0.2 for Very Good • 0.125 for Good

N-MINT

UNFUNNY X-CONS, THE
Parody

❑1, Sep 1992; three variant covers (X, Y, Z) 2.50
❑1-2; 2nd Printing with trading card . 2.50

UNICORN ISLE
Apple

❑1, Oct 1986, b&w 2.00
❑2, Nov 1986, b&w 2.00
❑3, Dec 1986, b&w 2.00
❑4, Jan 1987 .... 2.00
❑5, Feb 1987 .... 2.00
❑6, Mar 1987 .... 2.00
❑7 .... 2.00
❑8 .... 2.00
❑9 .... 2.00
❑10 .... 2.00
❑11 .... 2.00
❑12 .... 2.00

UNICORN KING
Kz Comics

❑1, Dec 1986, b&w 2.00

UNION (MINI-SERIES)
Image

❑0, Jul 1994 .... 2.50
❑0/A, Jul 1994; Variant edition cover; alternate cover 2.50
❑1, Jun 1993; Foil-embossed cover .. 2.50
❑2, Oct 1993 .... 1.95
❑3, Dec 1993 .... 1.95
❑4, Mar 1994 .... 1.95

UNION
Image

❑1, Feb 1995 .... 2.50
❑2, Mar 1995 .... 2.50
❑3, Apr 1995 .... 2.50
❑4, May 1995; with cards 2.50
❑5, Jun 1995 .... 2.50
❑6, Jul 1995 .... 2.50
❑7, Aug 1995 .... 2.50
❑8, Oct 1995 .... 2.50
❑9, Feb 1996; Story continued in Union: Final Vengeance; covers says Dec, indicia says Feb 2.50

UNION: FINAL VENGEANCE
Image

❑1, Oct 1997; concludes story from Union #9 .... 2.50

UNION JACK
Marvel

❑1, Dec 1998; gatefold summary 2.99
❑2, Jan 1999; gatefold summary 2.99
❑3, Feb 1999 .... 2.99

UNION JACKS
Anacom

❑1, b&w 2.00

UNITY
Valiant

❑0, Aug 1992; Blue cover (regular edition); BL (a) 1.00
❑0/Ltd., Aug 1992; Red cover (limited promotional edition); BL (a) 3.00
❑1, Oct 1992 BL (w); BL (a) 2.00
❑1/Gold, Oct 1992; Gold edition BL (w); BL (a) 3.00
❑1/Platinum, Oct 1992; (w); BL (a) ... 3.00
❑Yearbook 1; A: X-O Manowar. A: Solar. a.k.a. Unity: The Lost Chapter; cardstock cover 3.95

UNITY 2000
Acclaim

❑1, Nov 1999 .... 2.50
❑2, Dec 1999 .... 2.50
❑3, Jan 2000; series canceled 2.50

UNIVERSAL MONSTERS: DRACULA
Dark Horse

❑1 1993; Based on the classic Universal pictures film 4.95

N-MINT

UNIVERSAL MONSTERS: FRANKENSTEIN
Dark Horse

❑1 1993; Based on the classic Universal pictures film 3.95

UNIVERSAL MONSTERS: THE CREATURE FROM THE BLACK LAGOON
Dark Horse

❑1, Aug 1993 .... 4.95

UNIVERSAL MONSTERS: THE MUMMY
Dark Horse

❑1 1993; Based on the classic Universal pictures film 4.95

UNIVERSAL PICTURES PRESENTS DRACULA
Dell

❑1, Sep 1963 .... 160.00

UNIVERSAL SOLDIER (NOW)
Now

❑1, Sep 1992; newsstand 1.95
❑1/Direct ed., Sep 1992; Hologram cover; direct sale 2.50
❑1/Variant, Sep 1992; Waldenbooks; has UPC box and hologram 2.50
❑2, Oct 1992; newsstand 1.95
❑2/Direct ed., Oct 1992; direct-sale ... 2.50
❑3, Nov 1992; newsstand 1.95
❑3/Direct ed., Nov 1992; uncensored 2.50

UNIVERSE
Image

❑1, Aug 2001 .... 2.50
❑2, Oct 2001 .... 2.50
❑3, Nov 2001 .... 2.50
❑4, Jan 2002 .... 2.50
❑5, Mar 2002 .... 2.50
❑6, Apr 2002 .... 2.50
❑7, Apr 2002 .... 2.50
❑8, Jul 2002 .... 4.95

UNIVERSE X
Marvel

❑0, Sep 2000; Cardstock cover; follows events of Earth X 3.99
❑1, Oct 2000; cardstock cover 3.50
❑2, Nov 2000; cardstock cover 3.50
❑3, Dec 2000; cardstock cover 3.50
❑4, Jan 2001; cardstock cover 3.50
❑5, Feb 2001; cardstock cover 3.50
❑6, Mar 2001; cardstock cover 3.50
❑7, Apr 2001; cardstock cover 3.50
❑8, May 2001; cardstock cover 3.50
❑9, Jun 2001 .... 3.50
❑10, Jul 2001 .... 3.50
❑11, Aug 2001 .... 3.50
❑12, Sep 2001 .... 3.50
❑13; X Issue 3.99

UNIVERSE X: BEASTS
Marvel

❑1, Jun 2001 .... 3.99

UNIVERSE X: CAP
Marvel

❑1, Feb 2001 ARo (c); TY (a); D: Captain America. 5.00

UNIVERSE X: IRON MEN
Marvel

❑1, Sep 2001, b&w and color; chromium cover 3.99

UNIVERSE X: OMNIBUS
Marvel

❑1, Jun 2001, b&w and color; chromium cover 3.99

UNIVERSE X: SPIDEY
Marvel

❑1, Jan 2001 ARo (c) 3.99
❑1/A, Jan 2001; ARo (c); Dynamic Forces variant 6.00

Unknown Worlds contained several fantasy stories in each issue.
© 1965 American Comics Group (ACG).

N-MINT

❑1/B, Jan 2001; ARo (c); Dynamic Forces variant sketch cover 10.00
❑1/C, Jan 2001; recalled edition with potentially libelous statement in background of one panel ARo (c) .. 60.00

UNIVERSE X: X
Marvel

❑1, Nov 2001, b&w and color; chromium cover 3.99

UNKNOWN SOLDIER
DC

❑205, May 1977 .... 5.00
❑206, Jul 1977 .... 5.00
❑207, Sep 1977 AM (c); AM, RE (a) .. 5.00
❑208, Oct 1977 .... 5.00
❑209, Nov 1977 JKu (c); FT, JKu (a) .. 5.00
❑210, Dec 1977 .... 5.00
❑211, Jan 1978 JKu (c); JKu, RH (a) . 4.00
❑212, Feb 1978 .... 4.00
❑213, Mar 1978 .... 4.00
❑214, Apr 1978 RT (a); A: Mademoiselle Marie. 4.00
❑215, May 1978 JKu (c); JKu (a) 4.00
❑216, Jun 1978 RT (a) 4.00
❑217, Jul 1978 JKu (c); JKu (a) 4.00
❑218, Aug 1978 .... 4.00
❑219, Sep 1978 JKu (c); JKu, FM, RT (a) 4.00
❑220, Oct 1978 JKu (c); JKu, RE (a) . 4.00
❑221, Nov 1978 RT (a) 4.00
❑222, Dec 1978 JKu (a) 4.00
❑223, Jan 1979 RT (a) 4.00
❑224, Feb 1979 DA, RT (a) 4.00
❑225, Mar 1979 .... 4.00
❑226, Apr 1979 JKu (c); JKu (a) 4.00
❑227, May 1979 JKu (a) 4.00
❑228, Jun 1979 JKu (a) 4.00
❑229, Jul 1979 JKu (c); JKu (a) 4.00
❑230, Aug 1979 .... 3.00
❑231, Sep 1979 JKu (c); JKu (a) 3.00
❑232, Oct 1979 JKu (c); JKu (a) 3.00
❑233, Nov 1979 JKu (c); JKu (a) 3.00
❑234, Dec 1979 .... 3.00
❑235, Jan 1980 RT (a) 3.00
❑236, Feb 1980 .... 3.00
❑237, Mar 1980 .... 3.00
❑238, Apr 1980 .... 3.00
❑239, May 1980 .... 3.00
❑240, Jun 1980 .... 3.00
❑241, Jul 1980 JKu (c); JKu (a) 3.00
❑242, Aug 1980 .... 3.00
❑243, Sep 1980 RE (a) 3.00
❑244, Oct 1980 JKu (a); A: Captain Storm. 3.00
❑245, Nov 1980 RE (a) 3.00
❑246, Dec 1980 .... 3.00
❑247, Jan 1981 JKu (c); JKu (a) 3.00
❑248, Feb 1981 O: Unknown Soldier. 5.00
❑249, Mar 1981 JKu (c); JKu (a); O: Unknown Soldier. 5.00
❑250, Apr 1981 .... 3.00
❑251, May 1981 .... 3.00
❑252, Jun 1981 JSe (a) 3.00
❑253, Jul 1981 .... 3.00
❑254, Aug 1981 .... 3.00
❑255, Sep 1981 .... 3.00
❑256, Oct 1981 .... 3.00
❑257, Nov 1981 JKu (c); JKu (a); O: Capt. Storm. A: John F. Kennedy. ... 3.00

N-MINT

❑258, Dec 1981 DS (a); A: John F. Kennedy. 3.00
❑259, Jan 1982 DS (a); A: John F. Kennedy. 3.00
❑260, Feb 1982 RE (a) 3.00
❑261, Mar 1982 RE (a) 3.00
❑262, Apr 1982 .... 3.00
❑263, May 1982 .... 3.00
❑264, Jun 1982 JKu (c); JKu, DS (a) 3.00
❑265, Jul 1982 .... 3.00
❑266, Aug 1982 .... 3.00
❑267, Sep 1982 .... 3.00
❑268, Oct 1982; JKu (c); JKu (a); D: Chat Noir. D: Hitler. D: The Unknown Soldier. Fall of Berlin 5.00

UNKNOWN SOLDIER, THE (MINI-SERIES)
DC

❑1, Win 1988 O: Unknown Soldier. ... 2.50
❑2, Hol 1988; Hol 1988 .... 2.50
❑3, Jan 1989 .... 2.50
❑4, Mar 1989 .... 2.50
❑5, Apr 1989 .... 2.50
❑6, May 1989 .... 2.50
❑7, Jul 1989 .... 2.50
❑8, Aug 1989 .... 2.50
❑9, Sep 1989 .... 2.50
❑10, Oct 1989 .... 2.50
❑11, Nov 1989 .... 2.50
❑12, Dec 1989 .... 2.50

UNKNOWN SOLDIER (MINI-SERIES)
DC / VERTIGO

❑1, Apr 1997 .... 2.50
❑2, May 1997 .... 2.50
❑3, Jun 1997 .... 2.50
❑4, Jul 1997 .... 2.50

UNKNOWN WORLDS OF FRANK BRUNNER, THE
ECLIPSE

❑1, Aug 1985 .... 1.75
❑2, Aug 1985 .... 1.75

UNKNOWN WORLDS OF SCIENCE FICTION
MARVEL

❑1, Jan 1975, b&w; magazine 3.00
❑2, Mar 1975, b&w; magazine 3.00
❑3, May 1975, b&w; magazine 3.00
❑4, Jul 1975, b&w; magazine 3.00
❑5, Sep 1975, b&w; magazine 3.00
❑6, Nov 1975, b&w; magazine 3.00
❑Special 1 1976 .... 3.00

UNLEASHED!
TRIUMPHANT

❑1 .... 2.50

UNLIMITED ACCESS
MARVEL

❑1, Dec 1997; A: Wonder Woman. A: Spider-Man. A: Juggernaut. crossover with DC 2.50
❑2, Jan 1998; A: X-Men. A: Legion of Super-Heroes. crossover with DC .. 2.00
❑3, Feb 1998; A: Justice League of America. A: Avengers. crossover with DC 2.00
❑4, Mar 1998; crossover with DC; new Amalgams 3.00

UNSUPERVISED EXISTENCE
FANTAGRAPHICS

❑1, b&w 2.00
❑2, b&w 2.00
❑3 .... 2.00
❑4 .... 2.00
❑5 .... 2.00
❑6 .... 2.00
❑7 .... 2.00
❑7-2 .... 2.00

UNTAMED
MARVEL / EPIC

❑1, Jun 1993; Embossed cover 2.50
❑2, Jul 1993 .... 1.95
❑3, Aug 1993 .... 1.95

N-MINT

UNTAMED LOVE (FRANK FRAZETTA'S...)
FANTAGRAPHICS

❑1, Nov 1987 .... 2.00

UNTOLD LEGEND OF C APTAIN MARVEL, THE
MARVEL

❑1, Apr 1997 .... 2.50
❑2, May 1997 .... 2.50
❑3, Jun 1997 .... 2.50

UNTOLD LEGEND OF THE BATMAN, THE
DC

❑1, Jul 1980 JBy, JA (a); O: Batman. . 3.00
❑2, Aug 1980 JA (a) 2.00
❑3, Sep 1980 JA (a) 2.00

UNTOLD ORIGIN OF FEMFORCE
AC

❑1 1989 .... 4.95

UNTOLD ORIGIN OF MS. VICTORY
AC

❑1, Dec 1989, b&w 2.50

UNTOLD TALES OF CHASTITY
CHAOS

❑1, Nov 2000 .... 2.95

UNTOLD TALES OF LADY DEATH
CHAOS

❑1, Nov 2000 .... 2.95

UNTOLD TALES OF PURGATORI
CHAOS

❑1, Nov 2000 .... 2.95

UNTOLD TALES OF SPIDER-MAN
MARVEL

❑-1, Jul 1997; JR (a); Flashback 1.00
❑1, Sep 1995 KB (w); O: Spider-Man. 1.50
❑2, Oct 1995 KB (w) 1.25
❑3, Nov 1995 KB (w); V: Sandman. ... 1.25
❑4, Dec 1995; KB (w); V: J. Jonah Jameson. Flip book with Avengers Unplugged #2 .... 1.00
❑5, Jan 1996 KB (w); V: Vulture. 1.00
❑6, Feb 1996 KB (w); A: Human Torch. 1.00
❑7, Mar 1996; KB (w); O: Electro. Flip book with Fantastic Four Unplugged #4 .... 1.00
❑8, Apr 1996; KB (w); V: Enforcers. Flip book with Avengers Unplugged #4 .... 1.00
❑9, May 1996 KB (w); V: Lizard. 1.00
❑10, Jun 1996 KB (w) 1.00
❑11, Jul 1996 KB (w) 1.00
❑12, Aug 1996 KB (w); O: Betty Brant. 1.00
❑13, Sep 1996 KB (w); D: Bluebird. V: Black Knight. 1.00
❑14, Oct 1996 KB (w) 1.00
❑15, Nov 1996 KB (w) 1.00
❑16, Dec 1996 KB (w); A: Mary Jane. 1.00
❑17, Jan 1997 KB (w); AW (a); O: Hawkeye. A: Hawkeye. V: Hawkeye. 1.00
❑18, Feb 1997 KB (w); AW (a); A: Headsman. V: Headsman. 1.00
❑19, Mar 1997; KB (w); AW (a); V: Doctor Octopus. Flip book with Uncanny Origins #7 .... 1.00
❑20, Apr 1997; KB (w); AW (a); O: The Vulture. V: Vulture. Flip book with Uncanny Origins #8 .... 1.00
❑21, May 1997 A: X-Men. 1.00
❑22, Jun 1997 .... 1.00
❑23, Aug 1997 V: Crime Master. 1.00
❑24, Sep 1997 BMc (a) 1.00
❑25, Oct 1997; BMc (a); V: Green Goblin. cover says Sep, indicia says Oct 1.00
❑Annual 1996, ca. 1996; KB (w); GK, KJ (a); A: Namor. A: Fantastic Four. Untold Tales of Spider-Man '96 ..... 1.95
❑Annual 1997, ca. 1997; Untold Tales of Spider-Man '97 .... 1.95

UNTOUCHABLES (DELL)
DELL

❑3, Jul 1962 .... 50.00
❑4, Aug 1962 .... 50.00

N-MINT

UNTOUCHABLES
CALIBER

❑1, Aug 1997 .... 2.95
❑2, Sep 1997 .... 2.95
❑3, Oct 1997 .... 2.95
❑4, Nov 1997 .... 2.95

UNTOUCHABLES (EASTERN)
EASTERN

❑1 .... 1.00
❑2 .... 1.00

UP FROM BONDAGE
FANTAGRAPHICS / EROS

❑1, b&w 2.95

UP FROM THE DEEP
RIP OFF

❑1, ca. 1971 .... 3.00

URBAN HIPSTER
ALTERNATIVE

❑1, Oct 1998, b&w 2.95

URBAN LEGENDS
DARK HORSE

❑1 1993, b&w 3.00

UROTSUKIDOJI: LEGEND OF THE OVERFIEND
CPM

❑1, Jul 1998 .... 2.95
❑2, Aug 1998 .... 2.95
❑3, Sep 1998 .... 2.95

URTH 4
CONTINUITY

❑1, May 1989 .... 2.00
❑2, Apr 1990 .... 2.00
❑3, Oct 1990 .... 2.00
❑4, Dec 1990 .... 2.00

URZA-MISHRA WAR ON THE WORLD OF MAGIC: THE GATHERING
ACCLAIM / ARMADA

❑1, Sep 1996; squarebound; polybagged with Soldevi Steam Beast card 5.95
❑2, Sep 1996; squarebound; polybagged with Soldevi Steam Beast and Phyrexian War Beast cards 5.95

U.S. 1
MARVEL

❑1, May 1983, HT (a); O: U.S. 1. .... 1.00
❑2, Jun 1983, HT (a) 1.00
❑3, Jul 1983, FS (a) 1.00
❑4, Aug 1983, FS (a) 1.00
❑5, Sep 1983, FS (a) 1.00
❑6, Oct 1983, FS (a) 1.00
❑7, Dec 1983, FS (a) 1.00
❑8, Feb 1984, FS (a) 1.00
❑9, Apr 1984 .... 1.00
❑10, Jun 1984, FS (a) 1.00
❑11, Aug 1984, FS (a) 1.00
❑12, Oct 1984, SD (a) 1.00

U.S.AGENT
MARVEL

❑1, Jun 1993 .... 2.00
❑2, Jul 1993 .... 2.00
❑3, Aug 1993 .... 2.00
❑4, Sep 1993 .... 2.00

USAGENT (2ND SERIES)
MARVEL

❑1, Aug 2001 .... 2.99
❑2, Sep 2001 .... 2.99
❑3, Oct 2001 .... 2.99

USAGI YOJIMBO (VOL. 1)
FANTAGRAPHICS

❑1, Jul 1987, b&w 8.00
❑1-2, Jul 1987 .... 2.50
❑2, Sep 1987, b&w 5.00
❑3, Oct 1987, b&w 5.00
❑4, Nov 1987, b&w 3.50
❑5, Jan 1988, b&w 3.50
❑6, Feb 1988, b&w 3.00
❑7, Mar 1988, b&w 3.00
❑8, May 1988, b&w 3.00

N-MINT

❑9, Jul 1988, b&w ... 3.00
❑10, Aug 1988, b&w A: Teenage Mutant Ninja Turtles. ... 3.00
❑10-2, Aug 1988 ... 2.00
❑11, Sep 1988, b&w SA (a) ... 2.50
❑12, Oct 1988, b&w ... 2.50
❑13, Jan 1989, b&w; indicia says Jan 88; a misprint ... 2.50
❑14, Jan 1989, b&w; indicia says Jan 89 ... 2.50
❑15, Mar 1989, b&w ... 2.50
❑16, May 1989, b&w ... 2.50
❑17, Jul 1989, b&w ... 2.50
❑18, Oct 1989, b&w ... 2.50
❑19, Dec 1989, b&w ... 2.50
❑20, Feb 1990, b&w ... 2.50
❑21, Apr 1990, b&w ... 2.50
❑22, May 1990, b&w ... 2.50
❑23, Jul 1990, b&w ... 2.50
❑24, Sep 1990, b&w; Lone Goat & Kid ... 2.50
❑25, Nov 1990, b&w ... 2.50
❑26, Jan 1991, b&w; indicia says Jan 90; another misprint ... 2.50
❑27, Mar 1991, b&w ... 2.50
❑28, May 1991, b&w ... 2.50
❑29, Jul 1991, b&w ... 2.50
❑30, Sep 1991, b&w; back cover reproduces front cover without logos ... 2.50
❑31, Nov 1991, b&w ... 2.50
❑32, Feb 1992, b&w ... 2.50
❑33, Apr 1992, b&w ... 2.50
❑34, Jun 1992, b&w ... 2.50
❑35, Aug 1992, b&w ... 2.50
❑36, Nov 1992, b&w ... 2.50
❑37, Feb 1993, b&w ... 2.50
❑38, Mar 1993, b&w ... 2.50
❑Special 1, Nov 1989; Color special #1 ... 3.50
❑Special 2, Oct 1991; Color special #2 ... 3.50
❑Special 3, Oct 1992; Color special #3 ... 3.50
❑Summer 1, Oct 1986, b&w; SA (a); introduction by Mark Evanier ... 4.00

USAGI YOJIMBO (VOL. 2)
MIRAGE

❑1, Mar 1993, A: Teenage Mutant Ninja Turtles. ... 4.50
❑2, May 1993 A: Teenage Mutant Ninja Turtles. ... 3.50
❑3, Jul 1993 A: Teenage Mutant Ninja Turtles. ... 3.50
❑4, Sep 1993 ... 3.50
❑5, Nov 1993 ... 3.50
❑6, Jan 1994 ... 3.00
❑7, Apr 1994 ... 3.00
❑8, Jun 1994 ... 3.00
❑9, Aug 1994 ... 3.00
❑10, Oct 1994 ... 3.00
❑11, Dec 1994 ... 2.75
❑12, Feb 1995 ... 2.75
❑13, Apr 1995 ... 2.75
❑14, Jun 1995 ... 2.75
❑15, Aug 1995 1: Lionheart (in color). ... 2.75
❑16, Oct 1995 ... 2.75

USAGI YOJIMBO (VOL. 3)
DARK HORSE

❑1, Apr 1996 ... 4.00
❑2, May 1996; Cover marked 2 of 3 ... 3.00
❑3, Jun 1996 ... 3.00
❑4, Jul 1996 ... 3.00
❑5, Aug 1996 ... 3.00
❑6, Oct 1996 ... 3.00
❑7, Nov 1996 ... 3.00
❑8, Dec 1996 ... 3.00
❑9, Jan 1997 ... 3.00
❑10, Feb 1997 ... 3.00
❑11, Mar 1997 ... 3.00
❑12, Apr 1997, b&w ... 3.00
❑13, Aug 1997, b&w ... 3.00
❑14, Sep 1997, b&w ... 2.95
❑15, Oct 1997, b&w ... 2.95
❑16, Nov 1997 ... 2.95
❑17, Jan 1998 ... 2.95
❑18, Feb 1998 ... 2.95
❑19, Mar 1998 ... 2.95

N-MINT

❑20 1998 ... 2.95
❑21, Jun 1998 ... 2.95
❑22, Jul 1998 ... 2.95
❑23, Sep 1998 ... 2.95
❑24, Oct 1998 ... 2.95
❑25, Nov 1998; Momo-Usagi-Taro ... 2.95
❑26, Jan 1999 ... 2.95
❑27, Feb 1999 ... 2.95
❑28, Apr 1999 ... 2.95
❑29, May 1999 ... 2.95
❑30, Jul 1999 ... 2.95
❑31, Sep 1999 ... 2.95
❑32, Oct 1999 ... 2.95
❑33, Nov 1999 ... 2.95
❑34, Dec 1999 ... 2.95
❑35, Jan 2000 ... 2.95
❑36, Feb 2000 ... 2.95
❑37, Apr 2000 ... 2.95
❑38, May 2000 ... 2.95
❑39, Jul 2000 ... 2.95
❑40, Aug 2000 ... 2.95
❑41, Sep 2000 ... 2.95
❑42, Oct 2000 ... 2.95
❑43, Nov 2000 ... 2.95
❑44, Dec 2000 ... 2.95
❑45, Jan 2001 ... 2.99
❑46, Mar 2001 ... 2.99
❑47, Apr 2001 ... 2.99
❑48, May 2001 ... 2.99
❑49, Jun 2001 ... 2.99
❑50, Jul 2001 ... 2.99
❑51, Aug 2001 ... 2.99
❑52, Oct 2001 ... 2.99
❑53, Dec 2001 ... 2.99
❑54, Jan 2002 ... 2.99
❑55, Feb 2002 ... 2.99
❑56, Mar 2002 ... 2.99
❑57, Apr 2002 ... 2.99
❑58, May 2002 ... 2.99
❑59, Jul 2002 ... 2.99
❑60, Aug 2002 ... 2.99
❑61, Oct 2002 ... 2.99
❑62, Nov 2002 ... 2.99
❑63 ... 2.99
❑64, Feb 2003 ... 2.99
❑65, Mar 2003 ... 2.99
❑66, Jun 2003 ... 2.99
❑67, Jul 2003 ... 2.99
❑68, Jul 2003 ... 2.99
❑69, Oct 2003 ... 2.99
❑70, Nov 2003 ... 2.99
❑71, Nov 2003 ... 2.99
❑72, Dec 2004 ... 2.99
❑73, Feb 2004 ... 2.99
❑74, Mar 2004 ... 2.99
❑75, Apr 2004 ... 2.99
❑Special 4, ca. 1997; Color Special ... 3.50

U.S. FIGHTING MEN
SUPER

❑10, ca. 1963, JSe (c) ... 15.00
❑11 ... 15.00
❑12 ... 12.00
❑13 ... 12.00
❑14 ... 12.00
❑15, ca. 1964, RH (a) ... 12.00
❑16, ca. 1964 ... 12.00
❑17, ca. 1964 ... 12.00
❑18 ... 12.00

U.S. WAR MACHINE 2.0

❑1, Sep 2003 ... 2.99
❑2, Sep 2003 ... 2.99
❑3, Sep 2003 ... 2.99

V

V
DC

❑1, Feb 1985; CI (a); Based on TV series ... 1.50
❑2, Mar 1985, CI (a) ... 1.00

While *Touch of Silver* is a semi-autobiographical account of Jim Valentino's early life, *Valentino* presents episodes of his later life, including his struggles as a beginning artist.

© 1985 Jim Valentino and Renegade.

N-MINT

❑3, Apr 1985, CI (a) ... 1.00
❑4, May 1985, CI (a) ... 1.00
❑5, Jun 1985 ... 1.00
❑6, Jul 1985, CI (a) ... 1.00
❑7, Aug 1985, CI (a) ... 1.00
❑8, Sep 1985, CI (a) ... 1.00
❑9, Oct 1985, CI (a) ... 1.00
❑10, Nov 1985, CI (a) ... 1.00
❑11, Dec 1985, CI (a) ... 1.00
❑12, Jan 1986, CI (a) ... 1.00
❑13, Feb 1986, CI (a) ... 1.00
❑14, Mar 1986, CI (a) ... 1.00
❑15, Apr 1986, CI (a) ... 1.00
❑16, May 1986, CI (a) ... 1.00
❑17, Jun 1986, DG (a) ... 1.00
❑18, Jul 1986, DG (a) ... 1.00

VAGABOND
IMAGE

❑1/A, Aug 2000; Pat Lee cover ... 2.95
❑1/B, Aug 2000 ... 2.95

VAGABOND (VIZ)
VIZ

❑1, Dec 2001 ... 4.95
❑2, Dec 2001 ... 4.95
❑3, Jan 2002 ... 4.95
❑4, Feb 2002 ... 4.95
❑5, Mar 2002 ... 4.95
❑6, Apr 2002 ... 4.95
❑7, May 2002 ... 4.95
❑8, Jun 2002 ... 4.95
❑9, Jul 2002 ... 4.95
❑10, Aug 2002 ... 4.95
❑11, Sep 2002 ... 4.95
❑12, Oct 2002 ... 4.95
❑13, Nov 2002 ... 4.95
❑14, Dec 2002 ... 4.95
❑15, Jan 2003 ... 4.95

VALENTINE
REDEYE

❑1, Sep 1997, b&w ... 2.95

VALENTINO
RENEGADE

❑1, Apr 1985, b&w ... 2.00
❑2, Apr 1987, b&w; Valentino Too ... 2.00
❑3, Apr 1988, b&w; Valentino the 3rd ... 2.00

VALERIAN
FANTASY FLIGHT

❑1, Jul 1996, b&w; Heroes of the Equinox ... 2.95

VALERIA, THE SHE-BAT (CONTINUITY)
CONTINUITY

❑1, May 1993; Promotional edition, never available for ordering; NA (w); NA (a); no cover price ... 3.00
❑2 1993; Promotional edition, never available for ordering ... 3.00
❑3 1993; Published out of sequence (after #5) ... 2.50
❑4 1993; Published out of sequence . 2.50
❑5, Nov 1993; A: Knighthawk. Tyvek wraparound cover ... 2.00

N-MINT

VALERIA THE SHE-BAT (WINDJAMMER)
ACCLAIM / WINDJAMMER

❑1, Sep 1995 .... 2.50
❑2, Sep 1995 .... 2.50

VALHALLA
ANTARCTIC

❑1, Feb 1999 .... 2.99

VALIANT EFFORTS (VOL. 2)
VALIANT COMICS

❑1, May 1991 .... 1.95

VALIANT READER
VALIANT

❑1 1993; background 0.50

VALIANT VARMINTS
SHANDA FANTASY ARTS

❑1, b&w 4.50

VALIANT VISION STARTER KIT
VALIANT

❑1, Jan 1994; comic book, glasses, poster 2.95

VALKYR
IRONCAT

❑1 .... 2.95
❑2 .... 2.95
❑3 .... 2.95

VALKYRIE (1ST SERIES)
ECLIPSE

❑1, May 1987 PG (a) 2.00
❑2, Jun 1987 PG, BA (a) 2.00
❑3, Aug 1987 PG, BA (a) 2.00

VALKYRIE (2ND SERIES)
ECLIPSE

❑1, Jul 1988 BA (a) 2.00
❑2, Aug 1988 BA (a) 2.00
❑3, Sep 1988 BA (a) 2.00

VALKYRIE (3RD SERIES)
MARVEL

❑1, Jan 1997 .... 2.95

VALLEY OF THE DINOSAURS
HARVEY

❑1, Apr 1975 .... 10.00
❑2, Jun 1975 .... 6.00
❑3, Jul 1975 .... 6.00
❑4, Oct 1975 .... 6.00
❑5, Dec 1975 .... 6.00
❑6, Feb 1976 .... 4.00
❑7, Apr 1976 .... 4.00
❑8, Jun 1976 .... 4.00
❑9, Aug 1976 .... 4.00
❑10, Oct 1976 .... 4.00
❑11, Dec 1976 .... 4.00

VALOR (DC)
DC

❑1, Nov 1992 .... 1.25
❑2, Dec 1992 .... 1.25
❑3, Jan 1993 .... 1.25
❑4, Feb 1993; Lobo 1.25
❑5, Mar 1993 .... 1.25
❑6, Apr 1993 .... 1.25
❑7, May 1993 .... 1.25
❑8, Jun 1993 .... 1.25
❑9, Jul 1993 .... 1.25
❑10, Aug 1993 .... 1.25
❑11, Sep 1993 .... 1.25
❑12, Oct 1993 .... 1.25
❑13, Nov 1993 .... 1.50
❑14, Dec 1993 .... 1.50
❑15, Jan 1994 .... 1.50
❑16, Feb 1994 .... 1.50
❑17, Mar 1994 .... 1.50
❑18, Apr 1994 .... 1.50
❑19, May 1994 .... 1.50
❑20, Jun 1994 .... 1.50
❑21, Jul 1994 .... 1.50
❑22, Aug 1994 .... 1.50
❑23, Sep 1994 .... 1.50

N-MINT

VALOR (RCP)
GEMSTONE

❑1, Oct 1998 .... 2.50
❑2, Nov 1998 .... 2.50
❑3, Dec 1998 .... 2.50
❑4, Jan 1999 .... 2.50
❑5, Feb 1999 .... 2.50

VALOR THUNDERSTAR AND HIS FIREFLIES
NOW

❑1, Dec 1986 .... 1.50
❑2 1987 .... 1.50
❑3 1987 .... 1.50

VAMPEROTICA
BRAINSTORM

❑1, b&w 8.00
❑1/Gold 1994; Gold edition 10.00
❑1/Platinum 1994; Platinum edition 10.00
❑1-2, Sep 1994 .... 4.00
❑1-3, Dec 1994 .... 3.00
❑2 1995, b&w 5.00
❑3 1995, b&w 3.00
❑4 1995, b&w 3.00
❑5 1995, b&w 3.00
❑6 1995, b&w 3.00
❑7 1995, b&w 3.00
❑8, Oct 1995, b&w 3.00
❑9, Nov 1995, b&w 3.00
❑10, Dec 1995, b&w 3.00
❑11, Jan 1996, b&w 3.00
❑12, Feb 1996, b&w 3.00
❑13, Mar 1996, b&w 3.00
❑14, Apr 1996, b&w 3.00
❑15, May 1996, b&w 3.00
❑16, Jun 1996 .... 3.00
❑16/Nude, Jun 1996; Nude cover 5.00
❑17, Jul 1996 .... 2.95
❑17/A, Jul 1996; chromium cover 4.95
❑18, Aug 1996 .... 2.95
❑18/Nude, Aug 1996; Nude cover 5.00
❑19, Sep 1996 .... 2.95
❑19/A, Sep 1996; variant cover 2.95
❑19/Nude, Sep 1996; Nude cover 5.00
❑20, Oct 1996 .... 2.95
❑20/Nude, Oct 1996; Nude cover 5.00
❑21, Nov 1996 .... 2.95
❑22, Dec 1996 .... 2.95
❑22/Nude, Dec 1996; Nude cover 5.00
❑23, Jan 1997 .... 3.00
❑24, Feb 1997 .... 3.00
❑24/Nude, Feb 1997; Nude cover 5.00
❑25, Mar 1997 .... 3.00
❑26, Apr 1997 .... 3.00
❑27, May 1997 .... 3.00
❑28, Jun 1997 .... 3.00
❑29, Jul 1997 .... 3.00
❑30, Aug 1997 .... 3.00
❑31, Sep 1997 .... 3.00
❑32, Oct 1997 .... 3.00
❑33, Nov 1997 .... 3.00
❑34, Dec 1997 .... 3.00
❑35, Jan 1998 .... 3.00
❑36, Feb 1998 .... 3.00
❑37, Mar 1998 .... 3.00
❑38, Apr 1998 .... 3.00
❑39, May 1998 .... 3.00
❑40, Jun 1998 .... 3.00
❑41, Jul 1998 .... 3.00
❑42, Aug 1998 .... 3.00
❑43, Sep 1998 .... 3.00
❑44, Oct 1998 .... 3.00
❑45, Nov 1998 .... 3.00
❑45/Variant, Nov 1998 .... 4.00
❑46, Dec 1998 .... 3.00
❑47, Jan 1999 .... 3.00
❑48, Feb 1999 .... 3.00
❑49, Mar 1999 .... 3.00
❑Annual 1; Annual #1 .... 3.95
❑Annual 1/Gold 8.00
❑SS 1; Blue cover (regular edition) 4.00

N-MINT

VAMPEROTICA MAGAZINE
BRAINSTORM

❑1 .... 4.95
❑1/Nude 6.00
❑1/Variant; Julie Strain Commemorative cover 10.00
❑2 .... 4.95
❑2/Nude 6.00
❑2/Variant 5.95
❑3 .... 4.95
❑3/Nude 6.00
❑3/Variant 6.00
❑4 .... 5.95
❑4/Nude 6.00
❑4/Variant 5.95
❑5 .... 5.95
❑5/Nude 6.00
❑6 .... 5.95
❑6/Variant 5.95
❑7 .... 5.95
❑7/Variant 5.95
❑8 .... 5.95
❑8/Variant 5.95
❑9 .... 5.95
❑9/Variant 5.95
❑10 .... 5.95
❑10/Variant 5.95
❑11 .... 2.50
❑11/Nude 3.00
❑12 .... 2.50
❑12/Nude 3.00

VAMPEROTICA PRESENTS COUNTESS VLADIMIRA
BRAINSTORM

❑1, Dec 2001, b&w 2.95

VAMPFIRE
BRAINSTORM

❑1, Sep 1996, b&w 2.95

VAMPFIRE: EROTIC ECHO
BRAINSTORM

❑1 .... 2.95
❑2, Feb 1997 .... 2.95
❑2/Nude, Feb 1997 .... 2.95

VAMPFIRE: NECROMANTIQUE
BRAINSTORM

❑1, Aug 1997 .... 2.95
❑2 .... 2.95

VAMPIRE COMPANION, THE
INNOVATION

❑1; cardstock cover 2.50
❑2; cardstock cover 2.50
❑3 .... 2.50

VAMPIRE GIRLS: BUBBLE GUM & BLOOD
ANGEL

❑1 .... 2.95
❑2 .... 2.95

VAMPIRE GIRLS: CALIFORNIA 1969
ANGEL ENTERTAINMENT

❑0, May 1996, b&w 2.95
❑0/A, b&w; nude embossed foil cardstock cover; no indicia 5.00
❑0/Nude, May 1996, b&w; Nude cover 5.00
❑1, Aug 1996, b&w 2.95

VAMPIRE GIRLS, POETS OF BLOOD: SAN FRANCISCO
ANGEL

❑1 .... 5.00
❑1/Nude 5.00
❑2; Flipbook Previews of Angel 5.00
❑2/Nude; Flipbook Previews of Angel 5.00

VAMPIRE LESTAT, THE (ANNE RICE'S...)
INNOVATION

❑1, Jan 1990 .... 5.00
❑1-2 .... 2.50
❑2, Feb 1990 .... 3.00
❑2-2 .... 2.50
❑2-3 .... 2.50

Condition price index: Multiply "NM prices" above by: **0.83 for Very Fine/Near Mint**
0.66 for Very Fine • 0.33 for Fine • 0.2 for Very Good • 0.125 for Good

	N-MINT
❑3, May 1990	3.00
❑3-2	2.50
❑4, Jun 1990	2.50
❑5, Sep 1990	2.50
❑6, Nov 1990	2.50
❑7, Jan 1991	2.50
❑8, Mar 1991	2.50
❑9, May 1991	2.50
❑10 1991	2.50
❑11 1991	2.50
❑12 1991	2.50

VAMPIRELLA (MAGAZINE)
WARREN

❑1, Sep 1969 FF (c); TS, NA (a); 1: Vampirella.	325.00
❑1-2, Oct 2001 FF (c); TS, NA (a)	
❑2, Nov 1969	125.00
❑3, Jan 1970; Scarce	200.00
❑4, Mar 1970	75.00
❑5, May 1970	75.00
❑6, Jul 1970	70.00
❑7, Sep 1970 FF (c); FF (a)	70.00
❑8, Nov 1970; Horror format begins .	70.00
❑9, Jan 1971	70.00
❑10, Mar 1971 NA (a)	30.00
❑11, May 1971 O: Pendragon. 1: Pendragon.	43.00
❑12, Jul 1971	43.00
❑13, Sep 1971	43.00
❑14, Nov 1971	43.00
❑15, Jan 1972	43.00
❑16, Apr 1972	30.00
❑17, Jun 1972	30.00
❑18, Aug 1972	30.00
❑19, Sep 1972; 1973 annual	30.00
❑20, Oct 1972	30.00
❑21, Dec 1972	30.00
❑22, Mar 1973	30.00
❑23, Apr 1973	30.00
❑24, May 1973	30.00
❑25, Jun 1973	30.00
❑26, Aug 1973	20.00
❑27, Sep 1973; 1974 annual	30.00
❑28, Nov 1973	25.00
❑29, Dec 1973	25.00
❑30, Jan 1974	25.00
❑31, Mar 1974 FF (c); FF (a)	25.00
❑32, Apr 1974	25.00
❑33, May 1974	25.00
❑34, Jun 1974	25.00
❑35, Aug 1974	25.00
❑36, Sep 1974	25.00
❑37, Oct 1974; 1975 annual	20.00
❑38, Dec 1974	20.00
❑39, Feb 1974	20.00
❑40, Mar 1975	20.00
❑41, Apr 1975	20.00
❑42, May 1975	20.00
❑43, Jun 1975	20.00
❑44, Aug 1975	20.00
❑45, Sep 1975	20.00
❑46, Oct 1975 O: Vampirella.	25.00
❑47, Dec 1975	20.00
❑48, Jan 1976	20.00
❑49, Mar 1976	20.00
❑50, Apr 1976	20.00
❑51, May 1976	17.00
❑52, Jul 1976	17.00
❑53, Aug 1976	17.00
❑54, Sep 1976	17.00
❑55, Oct 1976	17.00
❑56, Dec 1976	17.00
❑57, Jan 1977	17.00
❑58, Mar 1977 RH (a)	17.00
❑59, Apr 1977	17.00
❑60, May 1977	17.00
❑61, Jul 1977	17.00
❑62, Aug 1977	17.00
❑63, Sep 1977	17.00
❑64 1977	17.00
❑65, Dec 1977	17.00
❑66, Jan 1978	17.00
❑67, Mar 1978	17.00
❑68, Apr 1978	17.00
❑69, May 1978	17.00
❑70, Jul 1978	17.00
❑71, Aug 1978	16.00
❑72, Sep 1978	16.00
❑73 1978	16.00
❑74, Dec 1978	16.00
❑75, Jan 1979	16.00
❑76, Mar 1979	16.00
❑77 1979 RH (a)	16.00
❑78, May 1979	16.00
❑79 1979	16.00
❑80 1979	16.00
❑81 1979	16.00
❑82 1979	16.00
❑83, Dec 1979	16.00
❑84, Jan 1980	16.00
❑85, Mar 1980	16.00
❑86, Apr 1980	16.00
❑87 1980	16.00
❑88 1980	16.00
❑89 1980	16.00
❑90, Sep 1980	16.00
❑91, Oct 1980	16.00
❑92, Dec 1980	16.00
❑93, Jan 1981	16.00
❑94, Mar 1981	16.00
❑95, Apr 1981	16.00
❑96, May 1981	16.00
❑97, Jul 1981	16.00
❑98, Aug 1981	16.00
❑99, Sep 1981	16.00
❑100, Oct 1981	30.00
❑101, Dec 1981	16.00
❑102, Jan 1982	16.00
❑103, Mar 1982	16.00
❑104, Apr 1982	16.00
❑105, May 1982	16.00
❑106 1982	16.00
❑107 1982	16.00
❑108 1982	16.00
❑109 1982	16.00
❑110 1982	16.00
❑111 1983	16.00
❑112, Mar 1983	45.00
❑113 1983; 1st Harris comic; Scarce	195.00
❑Annual 1; O: Vampirella.	175.00
❑Special 1; Special edition	30.00

VAMPIRELLA
HARRIS

❑0, Dec 1994; contains Vampirella timeline; enhanced cover	5.00
❑0/A; Blue logo	5.00
❑0/Silver	5.00
❑0/Gold	15.00
❑1, Nov 1992	15.00
❑1-2	5.00
❑2, Feb 1993, A: Dracula.	12.00
❑3, Mar 1993	10.00
❑4, Jul 1993	8.00
❑5, Nov 1993	8.00

VAMPIRELLA & THE BLOOD RED QUEEN OF HEARTS
HARRIS

❑1, Sep 1996; Collects stories from Vampirella (Magazine) #49, 60, 61, 62, 65, 66, 101, and 102	9.95

VAMPIRELLA: ASCENDING EVIL
HARRIS

❑1	2.95
❑1/American Ent; American Entertainment variant cover	5.00
❑2	2.95
❑3	2.95
❑4	2.95

Anne Rice's The Vampire Lestat was eventually collected as a trade paperback.

© 1990 Innovative Corporation and Anne Rice.

VAMPIRELLA: BLOOD LUST
HARRIS

	N-MINT
❑1, Jul 1997; JRo (w); cardstock cover	5.00
❑2, Aug 1997; JRo (w); cardstock cover	5.00

VAMPIRELLA CLASSIC
HARRIS

❑1, Feb 1995; Reprints Vampirella #12 in color	2.95
❑2, Apr 1995	2.95
❑3, Jun 1995	2.95
❑4, Aug 1995	2.95
❑5, Oct 1995	2.95

VAMPIRELLA COMMEMORATIVE EDITION
HARRIS

❑1, Nov 1996	2.95

VAMPIRELLA: CROSSOVER GALLERY
HARRIS

❑1, Sep 1997; wraparound cover; pin-ups; Crossover Pin-up of Hellshock, The Savage Dragon, Kabuki, Monkeyman and O'Brien, Rascals in Paradise, Madman, Pantha, Pain Killer Jane, Shi, Cyberfrog and Salamandroid, Body Bags	2.95

VAMPIRELLA: DEATH & DESTRUCTION
HARRIS

❑1, Jul 1996	2.95
❑1/A, Jul 1996; Vampirella sitting on cover	3.00
❑1/Ltd., Jul 1996; Vampirella logo only on cover	5.00
❑2, Aug 1996	2.95
❑3, Sep 1996	2.95
❑Ashcan 1	3.00

VAMPIRELLA/DRACULA & PANTHA SHOWCASE
HARRIS

❑1, Aug 1997; Vampirella on cover; flip-book with previews of Vampirella/ Dracula and Pantha	1.50
❑1/A, Aug 1997; Pantha on cover; flip-book with previews of Vampirella/ Dracula and Pantha	1.50

VAMPIRELLA/DRACULA: THE CENTENNIAL
HARRIS

❑1, Oct 1997	5.95
❑1/A, Oct 1997	5.95
❑1/B, Oct 1997	5.95
❑2, Oct 1997	5.95

VAMPIRELLA: JULIE STRAIN SPECIAL
HARRIS

❑1	3.95
❑1/A; Chrome version	14.95
❑1/B; Holo-chrome version; 500 copies printed	24.95

VAMPIRELLA/LADY DEATH
HARRIS

❑1, Feb 1999	3.50
❑1/A, Feb 1999; Valentine edition; Red foil	5.00
❑1/Ltd., Feb 1999	10.00

Condition price index: Multiply "NM prices" above by: **0.83 for Very Fine/Near Mint**
0.66 for Very Fine • 0.33 for Fine • 0.2 for Very Good • 0.125 for Good

N-MINT

VAMPIRELLA LIVES
Harris

❑1, Dec 1996; white cardstock outer cover with cutout ... 3.50
❑1/A, Dec 1996; Cover depicts Vampirella leaning forward ... 4.00
❑1/B, Dec 1996; Cover depicts Vampirella side view ... 4.00
❑1/C, Dec 1996; Die-cut linen cover .. 10.00
❑2, Jan 1997; Vampirella bathing in blood ... 2.95
❑2/A, Jan 1997; Blue background ... 3.00
❑2/B, Jan 1997 ... 4.00
❑3, Feb 1997; Drawn cover ... 2.95
❑3/A, Feb 1997 ... 4.00

VAMPIRELLA MONTHLY
Harris

❑0; Vampirella standing, two figures in background ... 4.00
❑0/A; Vampirella bathing in blood ... 4.00
❑1, Nov 1997; Gold foil logo on cover 4.00
❑1/A, Nov 1997; Vampirella eating something bloody on cover ... 5.00
❑1/B, Nov 1997; Vampirella eating something bloody on cover; Gold marking ... 5.00
❑1/C, Nov 1997; Vampirella standing on cover, demon-eyed figures in background ... 5.00
❑1/D, Nov 1997; Vampirella standing on cover, black background, blue logo ... 5.00
❑1/E, Nov 1997; American Entertainment Edition; Vampirella reclining on skull ... 5.00
❑1/F, Nov 1997; Vampirella standing on cover, black background with foil logo ... 5.00
❑2, Dec 1997 ... 3.00
❑2/A, Dec 1997; Man shooting gun at Vampirella ... 3.00
❑3, Jan 1998 ... 3.00
❑3/A, Jan 1998; Vampirella on motorcycle (only figure on cover) ... 3.00
❑4, Feb 1998 ... 3.00
❑4/A, Feb 1998; Crimson edition ... 4.00
❑4/B, Feb 1998; Vampirella holding gun 3.00
❑5, Mar 1998 ... 3.00
❑6, Apr 1998 ... 3.00
❑7, Jun 1998 A: Shi. ... 3.00
❑7/A, Jun 1998; Vampirella with finger to mouth ... 4.00
❑7/B, Jun 1998; Shi on cover in foreground, Vampirella in background . 4.00
❑7/C, Jun 1998; Shi in background, Vampirella in foreground ... 4.00
❑7/D, Jun 1998; Vampirella and Shi on checkerboard floor, foil logo ... 6.00
❑7/E, Jun 1998; Vampirella and Shi on checkerboard floor ... 4.00
❑8, Jul 1998 A: Shi. ... 3.00
❑9, Aug 1998 A: Shi. ... 3.00
❑10, Sep 1998 ... 3.00
❑10/A, Sep 1998; Black-and-white cover 6.00
❑10/B, Sep 1998; Color cover with no words ... 5.00
❑11, Oct 1998 ... 3.00
❑12, Nov 1998 ... 3.00
❑12/A, Nov 1998; Vampirella in spiky bodysuit ... 3.00
❑12/B, Nov 1998; Vampirella hurling woman ... 3.00
❑12/Variant, Nov 1998; Like B cover . 6.00
❑13, Mar 1999 ... 3.00
❑13/A, Mar 1999; Vampirella holding heart ... 3.00
❑14, Apr 1999 ... 2.95
❑14/A, Apr 1999; Vampirella standing, figure in background ... 3.00
❑15, May 1999 ... 2.95
❑15/A, May 1999 ... 2.95
❑15/B, May 1999; alternate cover (facing away) ... 2.95
❑16, Jun 1999 ... 2.95
❑16/A, Jun 1999; Vampirella ¯ 4 other similarly clad women on cover ... 3.00
❑16/B, Jun 1999; Cover depicts Pantha standing, orange/red background .. 4.00
❑16/C, Jun 1999 ... 5.00
❑16/D, Jun 1999; Pantha drawn cover 3.00
❑16/E, Jun 1999; Cover depicts Pantha crawling, white background ... 4.00
❑16/F, Jun 1999; Cover depicts Pantha standing, blue background ... 4.00
❑17, Jul 1999 ... 2.95
❑17/A, Jul 1999; Vampirella bound on cover ... 3.00
❑17/B, Jul 1999; Cover depicts Pantha standiing, blue background ... 4.00
❑17/C, Jul 1999 ... 4.00
❑17/D, Jul 1999; Two women with giant serpent in background on cover 3.00
❑17/E, Jul 1999; Cover depicts Pantha sitting with arm outstretched, blue background ... 4.00
❑18, Aug 1999 JPH (w) ... 2.95
❑18/A, Aug 1999; Vampirella with arms outstretched on cover ... 3.00
❑18/B, Aug 1999; "Chesty" close-up Vampirella cover ... 3.00
❑19, Sep 1999; Two Vampirellas on cover ... 2.95
❑19/A, Sep 1999; Vampirella holding skull on cover ... 3.00
❑20, Oct 1999; Vampirella with gun .. 2.95
❑20/A, Oct 1999; Vampirella standing with fangs present ... 3.00
❑21, Nov 1999; Cover has tinted background ... 2.95
❑21/A, Nov 1999; Drawn cover ... 3.00
❑21/B, Nov 1999 ... 4.00
❑22, Dec 1999; Cover has red tinted background ... 4.00
❑22/A, Dec 1999; Drawn cover ... 3.00
❑22/B, Dec 1999 ... 4.00
❑23, Jan 2000; Vampirella fighting Lady Death, cover has words ... 2.95
❑23/A, Jan 2000; Wordless cover with Vampirella on knees ... 7.00
❑23/B, Jan 2000; Red-logo cover with Vampirella on knees ... 5.00
❑23/C, Jan 2000; Silver logo cover with Vampirella on knees ... 3.00
❑23/D, Jan 2000; Wordless cover with Vampirella fighting Lady Death ... 6.00
❑24, Feb 2000; Vampirella with gun, fishnet stockings in foreground on cover ... 2.95
❑24/A, Feb 2000; Reflections in sunglasses on cover ... 3.00
❑24/B, Feb 2000; Vampirella on motorcycle, other female figure at top 3.00
❑25, Mar 2000; Vampirella in chains with male figure ... 2.95
❑25/A, Mar 2000; Two women on motorcycles ... 3.00
❑26, Apr 2000; Vampirella facing Lady Death on cover ... 2.95
❑26/A, Apr 2000; Vampirella in foreground, Lady Death in background 3.00
❑Ashcan 1, Aug 1997; "Ascending Evil" on cover ... 5.00
❑Ashcan 1/A; "Holy War" on cover ... 5.00
❑Ashcan 2 ... 5.00
❑Ashcan 3 ... 5.00
❑Ashcan 3/A; Leather cover; Convention exclusive limited to 1000 copies 15.00
❑Ashcan 4 ... 3.00
❑Ashcan 5 ... 3.00
❑Ashcan 6 ... 3.00

VAMPIRELLA: MORNING IN AMERICA
Harris

❑1, b&w; distributed by Dark Horse; squarebound ... 3.95
❑2, Nov 1991, b&w; squarebound ... 3.95
❑3, Jan 1992, b&w; squarebound ... 3.95
❑4, Apr 1992, b&w; squarebound ... 3.95

VAMPIRELLA OF DRAKULON
Harris

❑0 ... 2.95
❑1, Jan 1995 ... 2.95
❑2, Mar 1995 ... 2.95
❑3, May 1995; Poly-bagged ... 2.95

VAMPIRELLA/PAINKILLER JANE
Harris

❑1, May 1998; crossover with Event; foil-enhanced cover ... 2.95
❑1/A, May 1998; Variant cover, Vampirella and Painkiller Jane on rooftop 5.00
❑1/B, May 1998; Blue cover, Vampirella and Painkiller posing (in mid-air!) . 24.95
❑1/Gold, May 1998; Gold edition ... 10.00
❑Ashcan 1, Jan 1998; no cover price 3.00

VAMPIRELLA PIN-UP SPECIAL
Harris

❑1, Oct 1995 ... 2.95
❑1/A; White background and snake on cover ... 2.95

VAMPIRELLA: SAD WINGS OF DESTINY
Harris

❑1, Sep 1996; gold edition limited to 5000; cardstock cover ... 3.95
❑1/Gold, Sep 1996; Gold mark on cover 5.00

VAMPIRELLA/SHADOWHAWK: CREATURES OF THE NIGHT
Harris

❑1, Feb 1995; crossover with Image; concludes in Shadowhawk - Vampirella #2 ... 4.95
❑2; "ShadowHawk/Vampirella" ... 4.95

VAMPIRELLA/SHI
Harris

❑1; crossover with Crusade; no cover price ... 2.95

VAMPIRELLA: SILVER ANNIVERSARY COLLECTION
Harris

❑1/A, Jan 1997; Good Girl cover ... 2.50
❑1/B, Jan 1997; Bad Girl cover ... 2.50
❑2/A, Feb 1997; Good Girl cover ... 2.50
❑2/B, Feb 1997; Bad Girl cover ... 2.50
❑3/A, Mar 1997; Good Girl cover ... 2.50
❑3/B, Mar 1997; Bad Girl cover ... 2.50
❑4/A, Apr 1997; Good Girl cover ... 2.50
❑4/B, Apr 1997; Bad Girl cover ... 2.50

VAMPIRELLA'S SUMMER NIGHTS
Harris

❑1, ca. 1992, b&w ... 3.95

VAMPIRELLA STRIKES
Harris

❑1, Oct 1995 ... 3.00
❑1/A, Oct 1995; alternate cover; marble background ... 3.00
❑1/B, Oct 1995; Cover has Vampirella with moon in background ... 3.00
❑1/C, Oct 1995; Cover has Vampirella against blue background ... 3.00
❑1/Ltd., Oct 1995 ... 10.00
❑2, Dec 1995 ... 3.00
❑3, Feb 1996 ... 3.00
❑4, Apr 1996 ... 3.00
❑5, Jun 1996 A: Eudaemon. ... 3.00
❑6, Aug 1996 ... 3.00
❑7, Oct 1996 ... 3.00
❑Annual 1, Dec 1996 ... 3.00
❑Annual 1/A, Dec 1996 ... 3.00
❑Annual 1/B, Dec 1996 ... 3.00

VAMPIRELLA 30TH ANNIVERSARY CELEBRATION
Harris

❑1 ... 3.00

VAMPIRELLA 25TH ANNIVERSARY SPECIAL
Harris

❑1, Oct 1996; prestige format ... 5.95
❑1/A, Oct 1996; Silver logo with no words on cover ... 6.00

Condition price index: Multiply "NM prices" above by: **0.83 for Very Fine/Near Mint**
0.66 for Very Fine • 0.33 for Fine • 0.2 for Very Good • 0.125 for Good

N-MINT

VAMPIRELLA VS HEMORRHAGE
HARRIS

- ❑1, Apr 1997 .... 3.50
- ❑1/A, Mar 1997; Vampirella with red hand on cover 3.50
- ❑1/Ashcan, Mar 1997; ashcan; no cover price 1.00
- ❑2, May 1997 .... 3.50
- ❑3, Jun 1997 .... 3.50

VAMPIRELLA VS PANTHA
HARRIS

- ❑1/A, Mar 1997; cardstock cover; Vampirella standing over body in street with police cars in background 3.50
- ❑1/B, Mar 1997; cardstock cover 3.50
- ❑1/C, Mar 1997; Pantha on cover with black background 3.50
- ❑Ashcan 1; "Special Showcase Edition" on cover 3.50

VAMPIRELLA/WETWORKS
HARRIS

- ❑1, Jun 1997 .... 3.00

VAMPIRE MIYU
ANTARCTIC

- ❑1, Oct 1995 .... 3.50
- ❑2, Nov 1995 .... 3.00
- ❑3, Dec 1995 .... 3.00
- ❑4, Jan 1996 .... 3.00
- ❑5, Feb 1996 .... 3.00
- ❑6, Mar 1996 .... 3.00
- ❑Ashcan 1; Ashcan promotional edition from 1995 San Diego Comic-Con 1: Vampire Miyu. 0.50

VAMPIRES LUST
CFD / BONEYARD

- ❑1, Sep 1996, b&w 2.95
- ❑1/Nude, Sep 1996; nude cover 3.95

VAMPIRE'S PRANK
ACID RAIN

- ❑1 .... 2.95

VAMPIRE TALES
MARVEL

- ❑1, Aug 1973; ME (w); BEv (a); A: Morbius. 1st full Morbius story 35.00
- ❑2, Oct 1973 1: Satana. 18.00
- ❑3, Feb 1974 .... 18.00
- ❑4, Apr 1974 .... 18.00
- ❑5, Jun 1974 .... 18.00
- ❑6, Aug 1974 A: Lilith. 18.00
- ❑7, Oct 1974 .... 18.00
- ❑8, Dec 1974 A: Blade. 20.00
- ❑9, Feb 1975 A: Blade. 20.00
- ❑10, Apr 1975 A: Blade. 20.00
- ❑11, Jun 1975 .... 20.00
- ❑Annual 1, Oct 1975 .... 10.00

VAMPIRE VERSES, THE
CFD

- ❑1, Aug 1995, b&w 2.95
- ❑1-2, Dec 2001, b&w; 2nd printing from CFD 2.95
- ❑1-3, Dec 2001, b&w; 3rd printing from Asylum Press 2.95
- ❑1/Ltd.; limited edition of 1000 copies; alternate nude cover 5.00
- ❑2, b&w 2.95
- ❑2-2, b&w; 2nd printing from Asylum Press 2.95
- ❑2-3 .... 2.95
- ❑2/Ltd.; limited edition of 1000 copies; alternate cover 5.00
- ❑3, Jun 1996, b&w 2.95
- ❑3-2, b&w; 2nd printing from Asylum Press
- ❑3/Ltd., Jun 1996; limited edition of 1000 copies; alternate nude cover 5.00
- ❑4, b&w 2.95
- ❑4-2 .... 2.95
- ❑4/Ltd.; limited edition of 1000 copies; alternate cover 5.00

VAMPIRE VIXENS
ACID RAIN

- ❑1 .... 2.75

N-MINT

VAMPIRE WORLD
ACID RAIN

- ❑1 .... 2.75

VAMPIRE YUI
IRONCAT

- ❑1, Jul 2000 .... 2.95

VAMPIRIC JIHAD
APPLE

- ❑1, b&w; cardstock cover; reprints material from Blood of Dracula #14-19 .... 4.95

VAMPORNELLA
ADAM POST

- ❑1 .... 2.95

VAMPRESS LUXURA, THE
BRAINSTORM

- ❑1, Feb 1996; wraparound cover 2.95
- ❑1/Gold, Feb 1996 .... 8.00

VAMPS
DC / VERTIGO

- ❑1, Aug 1994 .... 2.50
- ❑2, Sep 1994 .... 2.50
- ❑3, Oct 1994 .... 2.50
- ❑4, Nov 1994 .... 2.50
- ❑5, Dec 1994 .... 2.50
- ❑6, Jan 1995 .... 2.50

VAMPS: HOLLYWOOD & VEIN
DC / VERTIGO

- ❑1, Feb 1996 .... 2.50
- ❑2, Mar 1996 .... 2.50
- ❑3, Apr 1996 .... 2.50
- ❑4, May 1996 .... 2.50
- ❑5, Jun 1996 .... 2.50
- ❑6, Jul 1996 .... 2.50

VAMPS: PUMPKIN TIME
DC / VERTIGO

- ❑1, Dec 1998 .... 2.50
- ❑2, Jan 1999 .... 2.50
- ❑3, Feb 1999 .... 2.50

VAMPURADA
TAVICAT

- ❑1, Jul 1995 .... 1.95

VAMPYRES
ETERNITY

- ❑1, b&w 2.25
- ❑2, b&w 2.25
- ❑3, Mar 1989, b&w 2.25
- ❑4, b&w 2.25

VAMPYRE'S KISS
AIRCEL

- ❑1, Jun 1990, b&w 2.50
- ❑2, Jul 1990, b&w 2.50
- ❑3, Aug 1990, b&w 2.50
- ❑4, Sep 1990, b&w 2.50

VAMPYRE'S KISS, BOOK II
AIRCEL

- ❑1, b&w 2.50
- ❑2, Dec 1990, b&w 2.50
- ❑3, Feb 1991, b&w 2.50
- ❑4, Mar 1991, b&w 2.50

VAMPYRE'S KISS, BOOK III
AIRCEL

- ❑1, Aug 1991, b&w 2.50
- ❑2, b&w 2.50
- ❑3, b&w 2.50
- ❑4, b&w 2.50

VANDALA
CHAOS!

- ❑1, Aug 2000 .... 2.95

VANGUARD
IMAGE

- ❑1, Oct 1993 EL (w); EL (a) 2.00
- ❑2, Nov 1993 EL (w); EL (a) 2.00
- ❑3, Dec 1993 EL (w); EL (a); A: Savage Dragon. 2.00
- ❑4, Feb 1994 EL (w); EL (a) 2.00
- ❑5, Apr 1994 EL (w); EL (a) 2.00
- ❑6, May 1994 EL (w); EL (a) 2.00

A copy of the black-cover edition of *Venom: Lethal Protector* was the first comic book to be given a perfect 10.0 grade by the Comics Guaranty Corporation.

© 1993 Marvel Comics.

N-MINT

VANGUARD (2ND SERIES)
IMAGE

- ❑1, Oct 1996, b&w 2.95
- ❑2, Oct 1996, b&w 2.95
- ❑3, Dec 1996, b&w 2.95
- ❑4, Jan 1997, b&w; cover says Feb, indicia says Jan 2.95

VANGUARD: ETHEREAL WARRIORS
IMAGE

- ❑1, Aug 2000 .... 5.95

VANGUARD ILLUSTRATED
PACIFIC

- ❑1, Nov 1983 SR, TY (a) 1.50
- ❑2, Jan 1984 DSt (a) 1.50
- ❑3, Mar 1984 SR, TY (a) 1.50
- ❑4, Apr 1984 .... 1.50
- ❑5, May 1984 .... 1.50
- ❑6, Jun 1984 GP (a) 1.50
- ❑7 1984 GE (a); 1: Mr. Monster. 4.00

VAN HELSING ONE-SHOT
DARK HORSE

- ❑1, May 2004 .... 2.99

VANITY
PACIFIC

- ❑1, Jun 1984 .... 1.50
- ❑2, Aug 1984 .... 1.50

VANITY ANGEL
ANTARCTIC

- ❑1, Sep 1994, b&w 3.50
- ❑1-2, May 1995 .... 3.50
- ❑2, Oct 1994, b&w 3.50
- ❑2-2, Jun 1995 .... 3.50
- ❑3, Nov 1994, b&w 3.50
- ❑4, Dec 1994, b&w 3.50
- ❑5, Jan 1995, b&w 3.50
- ❑6, Feb 1995, b&w 3.50

VARCEL'S VIXENS
CALIBER

- ❑1, Feb 1990, b&w 2.50
- ❑2, b&w 2.50
- ❑3, Apr 1990, b&w 2.50

VARIATIONS ON THE THEME
SCARLET ROSE

- ❑1 .... 2.75
- ❑2 .... 2.75
- ❑3 .... 2.75
- ❑4 .... 2.75

VARICK: CHRONICLES OF THE DARK PRINCE
Q

- ❑1, Jul 1999 .... 1.95

VARIOGENESIS
DAGGER

- ❑0, Jun 1994 .... 3.50

VARLA VORTEX
BONEYARD

- ❑1 .... 2.95

VARMINTS
BLUE COMET

- ❑1 .... 2.00
- ❑Special 1; Panda Khan 2.50

Condition price index: Multiply "NM prices" above by: **0.83 for Very Fine/Near Mint**
0.66 for Very Fine • 0.33 for Fine • 0.2 for Very Good • 0.125 for Good

N-MINT

VAST KNOWLEDGE OF GENERAL SUBJECTS, A
FANTAGRAPHICS
❑1, Sep 1994, b&w 4.95

VAULT OF DOOMNATION, THE
B-MOVIE
❑1 1986, b&w 1.70

VAULT OF EVIL
MARVEL
❑1, Feb 1973 .... 8.00
❑2, Apr 1973 .... 5.00
❑3, Jun 1973 .... 5.00
❑4, Aug 1973 .... 4.00
❑5, Sep 1973 .... 4.00
❑6, Oct 1973 .... 4.00
❑7, Nov 1973 .... 4.00
❑8, Dec 1973 .... 4.00
❑9, Feb 1974 .... 4.00
❑10, Apr 1974 .... 4.00
❑11, Jun 1974 .... 3.00
❑12, Aug 1974 .... 3.00
❑13, Sep 1974 .... 3.00
❑14, Oct 1974 .... 3.00
❑15, Nov 1974 .... 3.00
❑16, Dec 1974 .... 3.00
❑17, Feb 1975 .... 3.00
❑18, Apr 1975 .... 3.00
❑19, Jun 1975 .... 3.00
❑20, Aug 1975 .... 3.00
❑21, Sep 1975 .... 3.00
❑22, Oct 1975 .... 3.00
❑23, Nov 1975 .... 3.00

VAULT OF HORROR, THE (GLADSTONE)
GLADSTONE
❑1, Aug 1990; Reprints The Vault of Horror #34, The Haunt of Fear #1 .. 2.50
❑2, Oct 1990; Reprints The Vault of Horror #27, The Haunt of Fear #17 2.50
❑3, Dec 1990; Reprints The Vault of Horror #13, The Haunt of Fear #22 2.50
❑4, Feb 1991; Reprints The Vault of Horror #23, The Haunt of Fear #13 2.50
❑5, Apr 1991; AF, JCr, WW, JKa, GI (a); Reprints The Vault of Horror #19, The Haunt of Fear #5 .... 2.50
❑6, Jun 1991; Reprints The Vault of Horror #32, Weird Fantasy #6 .... 2.50
❑7, Aug 1991; Reprints The Vault of Horror #26, Weird Fantasy #7 .... 2.50

VAULT OF HORROR (RCP)
COCHRAN
❑1, Sep 1991 .... 2.00
❑2, Nov 1991 .... 2.00
❑3, Jan 1992; Reprints Vault of Horror #26, Weird Science #7 .... 2.00
❑4, Mar 1992 .... 2.00
❑5, May 1992 .... 2.00

VAULT OF HORROR, THE (RCP)
GEMSTONE
❑1, Oct 1992; Reprints The Vault of Horror #12 .... 2.00
❑2, Jan 1993; Reprints The Vault of Horror #13 .... 2.00
❑3, Apr 1993; Reprints The Vault of Horror #14 .... 2.00
❑4, Jul 1993; Reprints The Vault of Horror #15 .... 2.00
❑5, Oct 1993; Reprints The Vault of Horror #16 .... 2.00
❑6, Jan 1994; Reprints The Vault of Horror #17 .... 2.00
❑7, Apr 1994; Reprints The Vault of Horror #18 .... 2.00
❑8, Jul 1994; Reprints The Vault of Horror #19 .... 2.00
❑9, Oct 1994; Reprints The Vault of Horror #20 .... 2.00
❑10, Jan 1995; Reprints The Vault of Horror #20 .... 2.00
❑11, Apr 1995; Reprints The Vault of Horror #21 .... 2.00
❑12, Jul 1995; Reprints The Vault of Horror #22 .... 2.00
❑13, Oct 1995; Reprints The Vault of Horror #23 .... 2.00
❑14, Jan 1996; Reprints The Vault of Horror #24 .... 2.00
❑15, Apr 1996; Reprints The Vault of Horror #25 .... 2.00
❑16, Jul 1996; Reprints The Vault of Horror #26 .... 2.50
❑17, Oct 1996; Reprints The Vault of Horror #27 .... 2.50
❑18, Jan 1997; Reprints The Vault of Horror #28 .... 2.50
❑19, Apr 1997; Reprints The Vault of Horror #29 .... 2.50
❑20, Jul 1997; Reprints The Vault of Horror #30 .... 2.50
❑21, Oct 1997; Reprints The Vault of Horror #31 .... 2.50
❑22, Jan 1998; Reprints The Vault of Horror #32 .... 2.50
❑23, Apr 1998; Reprints The Vault of Horror #33 .... 2.50
❑24, Jul 1998; Reprints The Vault of Horror #34 .... 2.50
❑25, Oct 1998 .... 2.50
❑26, Jan 1999 .... 2.50
❑27, Apr 1999 .... 2.50
❑28, Jul 1999 .... 2.50
❑29, Oct 1999 .... 2.50
❑Annual 1; Collects The Vault of Horror #1-5 .... 8.95
❑Annual 2; Collects The Vault of Horror #6-10 .... 9.95
❑Annual 3; Collects The Vault of Horror #11-15 .... 10.95
❑Annual 4 .... 12.95
❑Annual 5 .... 13.50

VAULT OF SCREAMING HORROR
FANTACO
❑1 .... 3.50

VAULT OF WHORES
FANTAGRAPHICS / EROS
❑1 .... 2.95

VECTOR
NOW
❑1, Jul 1986 .... 1.50
❑2, Sep 1986 .... 1.50
❑3, Nov 1986 .... 1.50
❑4, Jan 1987 .... 1.50

VEGAS KNIGHTS
PIONEER
❑1 .... 1.95

VEGETABLE LOVER
FANTAGRAPHICS / EROS
❑1, b&w 2.75

VEGMAN
CHECKER
❑1, Spr 1998, b&w 2.95
❑2, Sum 1998, b&w; indicia for #1 repeated inside 2.95

VELOCITY (IMAGE)
IMAGE
❑1, Nov 1995 .... 2.50
❑2, Dec 1995 .... 2.50
❑3, Jan 1996 .... 2.50

VELOCITY (ECLIPSE)
ECLIPSE
❑5, b&w 2.95

VELVET
ADVENTURE
❑1, Jan 1993, b&w 2.50
❑2, Feb 1993, b&w 2.50
❑3, Mar 1993, b&w 2.50
❑4, Apr 1993, b&w 2.50

VELVET ARTICHOKE THEATRE
VELVET ARTICHOKE
❑1, Sum 1998, b&w 2.00

VELVET TOUCH
ANTARCTIC
❑1, Oct 1993 .... 4.00
❑1/Platinum, Oct 1993; platinum 4.00
❑1-2, Apr 1995 .... 3.95
❑2, Jan 1994 .... 3.95
❑3, Jul 1994 .... 3.95
❑4, Aug 1994 .... 3.95
❑5, Oct 1994 .... 3.95
❑6, Jan 1995 .... 3.95

VENDETTA: HOLY VINDICATOR
RED BULLET
❑1, b&w; first printing limited to 500 copies 2.50
❑2, b&w; first printing limited to 500 copies 2.50
❑3, b&w; first printing limited to 3000 copies 2.50
❑4, b&w 2.50

VENGEANCE OF THE AZTECS
CALIBER
❑1, b&w 2.95
❑2, b&w 2.95
❑3, b&w 2.95
❑4 .... 2.95
❑5 .... 2.95

VENGEANCE OF VAMPIRELLA
HARRIS
❑0, Nov 1995 .... 2.95
❑0.5 .... 4.00
❑0.5/A 4.00
❑1, Apr 1994; red foil wraparound cover 3.50
❑1/A, Apr 1994; Blue foil 3.00
❑1/Gold, Apr 1994; Gold promotional edition 10.00
❑1-2; blue foil wraparound cover 3.00
❑2, May 1994 .... 3.00
❑3, Jun 1994 .... 3.00
❑4, Jul 1994 .... 3.00
❑5, Aug 1994 1: The Undead. 3.00
❑6, Sep 1994 .... 3.00
❑6/A, Sep 1994; Special Limited Edition on cover 4.00
❑7, Oct 1994 .... 3.00
❑8, Nov 1994 .... 3.00
❑9, Dec 1994 .... 3.00
❑10, Jan 1995 .... 3.00
❑11, Feb 1995; polybagged with trading card 3.00
❑12, Mar 1995; 1: Passion. cover date Feb 95 .... 3.00
❑13, Apr 1995 .... 3.00
❑14, May 1995 .... 3.00
❑14/A, May 1995; Vampirella sitting, man at top 3.00
❑15, Jun 1995 .... 3.00
❑15/A, Jun 1995; Back-to-back with man holding gun 3.00
❑16, Jul 1995 .... 3.00
❑16/A, Jul 1995; Vampirella springing, fingernails outstretched 3.00
❑17, Aug 1995 .... 3.00
❑17/A, Aug 1995; Woman with sword at right swinging at Vampirella 3.00
❑18, Sep 1995 .... 3.00
❑18/A, Sep 1995; Vampirella against purple-red background 3.00
❑19, Oct 1995 .... 3.00
❑19/A, Oct 1995; Vampirella holding heart 3.00
❑20, Nov 1995 .... 3.00
❑21, Dec 1995 .... 3.00
❑22, Jan 1996 .... 3.00
❑23, Feb 1996 .... 3.00
❑24, Mar 1996 .... 3.00
❑25, Apr 1996; cardstock cover with red foil 3.00
❑25/A; Vampirella with candles on cover 3.00
❑25/B; Blue foil on cover 5.00
❑25/Gold; Gold logo 5.00
❑25/Platinum; Platinum logo 6.00
❑25/Ashcan, Mar 1995; Preview Ashcan 5.00

VENGEANCE SQUAD
CHARLTON
❑1, Jul 1975 .... 3.00
❑2, Sep 1975 .... 2.00

N-MINT

❑3, Nov 1975 PM (a) 2.00
❑4, Jan 1976 .... 2.00
❑5, Mar 1976 .... 2.00
❑6, May 1976 .... 2.00

VENGEFUL SKYE, THE
DAVDEZ

❑1, Sum 1998 .... 2.95

VENGER ROBO
VIZ

❑1 .... 2.75
❑2 .... 2.75
❑3 .... 2.75
❑4 .... 2.75
❑5 .... 2.75
❑6 .... 2.75
❑7 .... 2.75

VENOM
MARVEL

❑1, Jun 2003 .... 2.25
❑2, Jul 2003 .... 2.25
❑3, Aug 2003 .... 2.25
❑4, Sep 2003 .... 2.99
❑5, Oct 2003 .... 2.99
❑6, Nov 2003 .... 2.25
❑7, Dec 2003 .... 2.99
❑8, Jan 2004 .... 2.99
❑9, Feb 2004 .... 2.99
❑10, Mar 2004 .... 2.99
❑11, Apr 2004 .... 2.99
❑12, May 2004 .... 2.99
❑13, Jun 2004 .... 2.99
❑14, Jul 2004 .... 2.99
❑15, Jul 2004 .... 2.99
❑16, Aug 2004 .... 2.99
❑17, Sep 2004 ....

VENOM: ALONG CAME A SPIDER
MARVEL

❑1, Jan 1996 .... 2.95
❑2, Feb 1996 .... 2.95
❑3, Mar 1996 .... 2.95
❑4, Apr 1996 .... 2.95

VENOM: CARNAGE UNLEASHED
MARVEL

❑1, Apr 1995; cardstock cover 2.95
❑2, May 1995; cardstock cover 2.95
❑3, Jun 1995; cardstock cover 2.95
❑4, Jul 1995; cardstock cover 2.95

VENOM: DEATHTRAP: THE VAULT
MARVEL

❑1; one-shot 6.95

VENOM: FINALE
MARVEL

❑1, Nov 1997; gatefold summary 2.00
❑2, Dec 1997; gatefold summary; V: Spider-Man. 2.00
❑3, Jan 1998; gatefold summary; V: Spider-Man. 2.00

VENOM: FUNERAL PYRE
MARVEL

❑1, Aug 1993; foil cover 2.95
❑2, Sep 1993 .... 2.95
❑3, Oct 1993 .... 2.95

VENOM: LETHAL PROTECTOR
MARVEL

❑1, Feb 1993; Metallic ink cover 3.00
❑1/A, Feb 1993; Black Cover printing error 75.00
❑1/Gold, Feb 1993; Gold edition 5.00
❑2, Mar 1993 A: Spider-Man. 3.00
❑3, Apr 1993 AM (a) 3.00
❑4, May 1993 A: Spider-Man. 3.00
❑5, Jun 1993 A: Spider-Man. 3.00
❑6, Jul 1993 A: Spider-Man. 3.00

VENOM: LICENSE TO KILL
MARVEL

❑1, Jun 1997 .... 2.00
❑2, Jul 1997 .... 2.00
❑3, Aug 1997; gatefold summary 2.00

N-MINT

VENOM: NIGHTS OF VENGEANCE
MARVEL

❑1, Aug 1994; red foil cover 2.95
❑2, Sep 1994; cardstock cover 2.95
❑3, Oct 1994; cardstock cover 2.95
❑4, Nov 1994; cardstock cover 2.95

VENOM: ON TRIAL
MARVEL

❑1, Mar 1997 A: Daredevil. A: Spider-Man. 2.00
❑2, Apr 1997 A: Daredevil. A: Spider-Man. 2.00
❑3, May 1997 A: Daredevil. A: Carnage. A: Spider-Man. 2.00

VENOM: SEED OF DARKNESS
MARVEL

❑-1, Jul 1997; Flashback 2.00

VENOM: SEPARATION ANXIETY
MARVEL

❑1, Dec 1994; Embossed cover 2.95
❑2, Jan 1995 .... 2.95
❑3, Feb 1995 .... 2.95
❑4, Mar 1995 .... 2.95

VENOM: SIGN OF THE BOSS
MARVEL

❑1, Sep 1997; gatefold summary 2.00
❑2, Oct 1997; gatefold summary A: Ghost Rider. 2.00

VENOM: SINNER TAKES ALL
MARVEL

❑1, Aug 1995 .... 2.95
❑2, Sep 1995 .... 2.95
❑3, Oct 1995 .... 2.95
❑4, Nov 1995 .... 2.95
❑5, Dec 1995 .... 2.95

VENOM SUPER SPECIAL
MARVEL

❑1, Aug 1995; Flip-book; two of the stories continue in Spectacular Spider-Man Super Special #1 .... 3.95

VENOM: THE ENEMY WITHIN
MARVEL

❑1, Feb 1994; Glow-in-the-dark cover 2.95
❑2, Mar 1994 .... 2.95
❑3, Apr 1994 .... 2.95

VENOM: THE HUNGER
MARVEL

❑1, Aug 1996 .... 2.00
❑2, Sep 1996 .... 2.00
❑3, Oct 1996 .... 2.00
❑4, Nov 1996 .... 2.00

VENOM: THE HUNTED
MARVEL

❑1, May 1996 .... 2.95
❑2, Jun 1996 .... 2.95
❑3, Jul 1996 .... 2.95

VENOM: THE MACE
MARVEL

❑1, May 1994; Embossed cover 2.95
❑2, Jun 1994 .... 2.95
❑3, Jul 1994 .... 2.95

VENOM: THE MADNESS
MARVEL

❑1, Nov 1993; Embossed cover 2.95
❑2, Dec 1993 .... 2.95
❑3, Jan 1994 .... 2.95

VENOM: TOOTH AND CLAW
MARVEL

❑1, Nov 1996 A: Wolverine. V: Wolverine. 2.00
❑2, Dec 1996 V: Wolverine. 2.00
❑3, Jan 1997 V: Wolverine. 2.00

VENOM VS. CARNAGE
MARVEL

❑1, Sep 2004 .... 2.99

VENTURE
AC

❑1, Aug 1986 .... 1.75
❑2 1986 .... 1.75
❑3 1987 .... 1.75

The god of bad luck was banished to Earth when he lost his last follower in DC's short-lived, but critically acclaimed, *Vext*.

© 1999 DC Comics.

N-MINT

VENTURE (IMAGE)
IMAGE

❑1, Jan 2003 .... 2.95
❑2, Feb 2003 .... 2.95
❑3, Apr 2003 .... 2.95
❑4, Sep 2003 .... 2.95

VENTURE SAN DIEGO COMIC-CON SPECIAL EDITION
VENTURE

❑1, Jul 1994, b&w 2.50

VENUMB
PARODY

❑1 1993, b&w 2.50
❑1/Deluxe 1993, b&w; enhanced cover 2.95

VENUS DOMINA
VEROTIK

❑1 .... 4.95
❑2 .... 4.95
❑3, Mar 1997 .... 4.95

VENUS INTERFACE, THE (HEAVY METAL'S...)
HM COMMUNICATIONS

❑1 .... 6.00

VENUS WARS, THE
DARK HORSE

❑1, Apr 1991, b&w; Japanese; trading cards 2.50
❑2, May 1991, b&w; Japanese; trading cards 2.25
❑3, Jun 1991, b&w; Japanese; trading cards 2.25
❑4, Jul 1991 .... 2.25
❑5, Aug 1991 .... 2.25
❑6, Sep 1991 .... 2.25
❑7, Oct 1991 .... 2.25
❑8, Nov 1991 .... 2.25
❑9, Dec 1991 .... 2.25
❑10, Jan 1992 .... 2.25
❑11, Feb 1992 .... 2.25
❑12, Mar 1992 .... 2.25
❑13, Apr 1992 .... 2.25
❑14, May 1992 .... 2.25

VENUS WARS II, THE
DARK HORSE

❑1, Jun 1992 .... 2.50
❑2, Jul 1992 .... 2.50
❑3, Aug 1992 .... 2.50
❑4, Sep 1992 .... 2.50
❑5, Oct 1992, b&w 2.50
❑6, Nov 1992, b&w 2.50
❑7, Dec 1992, b&w 2.50
❑8, Jan 1993, b&w 2.50
❑9, Feb 1993, b&w 2.50
❑10, Mar 1993, b&w 2.50
❑11, Apr 1993, b&w 2.95
❑12, May 1993, b&w 2.95
❑13, Jun 1993 .... 2.95
❑14, Jul 1993 .... 2.95
❑15, Aug 1993 .... 2.95

VERBATIM
FANTAGRAPHICS

❑1, Apr 1993, b&w 2.75
❑2, b&w 2.75

Condition price index: Multiply "NM prices" above by: **0.83 for Very Fine/Near Mint**
0.66 for Very Fine • 0.33 for Fine • 0.2 for Very Good • 0.125 for Good

N-MINT

VERDICT, THE
Eternity

- ❑1 ... 1.95
- ❑2 ... 1.95
- ❑3, Jun 1988 ... 1.95
- ❑4 1988 ... 1.95

VERMILLION
DC / Helix

- ❑1, Oct 1996 ... 2.25
- ❑2, Nov 1996 ... 2.25
- ❑3, Dec 1996 ... 2.25
- ❑4, Jan 1997 ... 2.25
- ❑5, Feb 1997 ... 2.25
- ❑6, Mar 1997 ... 2.25
- ❑7, Apr 1997 ... 2.25
- ❑8, May 1997 ... 2.25
- ❑9, Jun 1997 ... 2.25
- ❑10, Jul 1997 ... 2.25
- ❑11, Aug 1997 ... 2.25
- ❑12, Sep 1997 ... 2.25

VERONICA
Archie

- ❑1, Apr 1989 ... 2.00
- ❑2, Jul 1989 ... 1.50
- ❑3, Sep 1989 ... 1.50
- ❑4, Oct 1989 ... 1.50
- ❑5, Dec 1989 ... 1.50
- ❑6 1990 ... 1.50
- ❑7, Apr 1990 ... 1.50
- ❑8 1990 ... 1.50
- ❑9, Jul 1990 ... 1.50
- ❑10, Sep 1990 ... 1.50
- ❑11, Oct 1990 ... 1.50
- ❑12, Dec 1990 ... 1.50
- ❑13, Feb 1991 ... 1.50
- ❑14, Apr 1991 ... 1.50
- ❑15, Jun 1991 ... 1.50
- ❑16, Aug 1991 ... 1.50
- ❑17, Oct 1991 ... 1.50
- ❑18, Dec 1991 ... 1.50
- ❑19, Feb 1992 ... 1.50
- ❑20, Apr 1992 ... 1.50
- ❑21, Jun 1992 ... 1.25
- ❑22, Aug 1992 ... 1.25
- ❑23, Sep 1992 ... 1.25
- ❑24, Oct 1992 ... 1.25
- ❑25, Dec 1992 ... 1.25
- ❑26, Feb 1993 ... 1.25
- ❑27, Apr 1993 ... 1.25
- ❑28, Jun 1993 ... 1.25
- ❑29, Aug 1993 ... 1.25
- ❑30, Sep 1993 ... 1.25
- ❑31, Oct 1993 ... 1.25
- ❑32, Dec 1993 ... 1.25
- ❑33, Feb 1994 ... 1.25
- ❑34, Apr 1994 ... 1.25
- ❑35, Jun 1994 ... 1.25
- ❑36, Aug 1994 ... 1.50
- ❑37, Sep 1994 ... 1.50
- ❑38, Oct 1994 ... 1.50
- ❑39, Dec 1994 ... 1.50
- ❑40, Jan 1995 ... 1.50
- ❑41, Mar 1995 ... 1.50
- ❑42, Apr 1995 ... 1.50
- ❑43, Jun 1995 ... 1.50
- ❑44, Jul 1995 ... 1.50
- ❑45, Aug 1995 ... 1.50
- ❑46, Sep 1995 ... 1.50
- ❑47, Oct 1995 ... 1.50
- ❑48, Nov 1995 ... 1.50
- ❑49, Jan 1996 ... 1.50
- ❑50, Feb 1996 ... 1.50
- ❑51, Apr 1996 ... 1.50
- ❑52, Jun 1996 ... 1.50
- ❑53, Jul 1996 ... 1.50
- ❑54, Aug 1996 ... 1.50
- ❑55, Sep 1996 ... 1.50
- ❑56, Oct 1996 ... 1.50
- ❑57, Nov 1996 ... 1.50
- ❑58, Dec 1996 ... 1.50
- ❑59, Jan 1997 ... 1.50
- ❑60, Feb 1997 ... 1.50
- ❑61, Mar 1997 ... 1.50
- ❑62, Apr 1997 ... 1.50
- ❑63, May 1997 ... 1.50
- ❑64, Jun 1997 ... 1.50
- ❑65, Jul 1997 ... 1.50
- ❑66, Aug 1997 ... 1.50
- ❑67, Sep 1997 ... 1.50
- ❑68, Oct 1997 ... 1.50
- ❑69, Nov 1997 ... 1.50
- ❑70, Dec 1997 ... 1.50
- ❑71, Jan 1998 ... 1.50
- ❑72, Feb 1998 ... 1.50
- ❑73, Mar 1998 ... 1.50
- ❑74, Apr 1998; Veronica markets Jughead's beanie ... 1.50
- ❑75, May 1998 ... 1.50
- ❑76, Jun 1998 ... 1.50
- ❑77, Jul 1998 ... 1.50
- ❑78, Aug 1998 ... 1.50
- ❑79, Sep 1998 ... 1.75
- ❑80, Oct 1998 ... 1.75
- ❑81, Nov 1998; Veronica in Oz ... 1.75
- ❑82, Dec 1998 ... 1.75
- ❑83, Jan 1999 ... 1.75
- ❑84, Feb 1999 ... 1.75
- ❑85, Mar 1999 ... 1.75
- ❑86, Apr 1999 ... 1.79
- ❑87, May 1999 ... 1.79
- ❑88, Jun 1999 ... 1.79
- ❑89, Jul 1999 ... 1.79
- ❑90, Aug 1999 ... 1.79
- ❑91, Aug 1999 ... 1.79
- ❑92, Oct 1999 ... 1.79
- ❑93, Nov 1999 ... 1.79
- ❑94, Dec 1999 ... 1.79
- ❑95, Jan 2000 ... 1.79
- ❑96, Feb 2000 ... 1.79
- ❑97, Mar 2000 ... 1.79
- ❑98, Apr 2000 ... 1.79
- ❑99, May 2000 ... 1.99
- ❑100, Jun 2000 ... 1.99
- ❑101, Jul 2000 ... 1.99
- ❑102, Aug 2000 ... 1.99
- ❑103, Sep 2000 ... 1.99
- ❑104, Oct 2000 ... 1.99
- ❑105, Nov 2000 ... 1.99
- ❑106, Dec 2000 ... 1.99
- ❑107, Jan 2001 ... 1.99
- ❑108, Feb 2001 ... 1.99
- ❑109, Mar 2001 ... 1.99
- ❑110, Apr 2001 ... 1.99
- ❑111, May 2001 ... 1.99
- ❑112, Jun 2001 ... 1.99
- ❑113, Jul 2001 ... 1.99
- ❑114, Jul 2001 ... 1.99
- ❑115, Aug 2001 ... 1.99
- ❑116, Sep 2001 ... 1.99
- ❑117, Oct 2001 ... 1.99
- ❑118, Nov 2001 ... 1.99
- ❑119, Dec 2001 ... 1.99
- ❑120, Jan 2002 ... 1.99
- ❑121, Feb 2002 ... 1.99
- ❑122, Mar 2002 ... 1.99
- ❑123, Apr 2002 ... 1.99
- ❑124, May 2002 ... 1.99
- ❑125, Jun 2002 ... 1.99
- ❑126, Jul 2002 ... 1.99
- ❑127, Jul 2002 ... 1.99
- ❑128, Aug 2002 ... 1.99
- ❑129, Sep 2002 ... 1.99
- ❑130, Oct 2002 ... 1.99
- ❑131, Nov 2002 ... 1.99
- ❑132, Dec 2002 ... 1.99
- ❑133, Jan 2003 ... 1.99
- ❑134, Feb 2003 ... 2.19
- ❑135, Mar 2003 ... 2.19
- ❑136, Apr 2003 ... 2.19
- ❑137, May 2003 ... 2.19
- ❑138, Jun 2003 ... 2.19
- ❑139, Jul 2003 ... 2.19
- ❑140, Jul 2003 ... 2.19
- ❑141, Aug 2003 ... 2.19
- ❑142, Sep 2003 ... 2.19
- ❑143, Oct 2003 ... 2.19
- ❑144, Nov 2003 ... 2.19
- ❑145, Dec 2003 ... 2.19
- ❑146, Jan 2004 ... 2.19
- ❑147, Feb 2004 ... 2.19
- ❑148, Mar 2004 ... 2.19
- ❑149, Apr 2004 ... 2.19
- ❑150, May 2004 ... 2.19
- ❑151, Jun 2004 ... 2.19
- ❑152, Jul 2004 ... 2.19

VERONICA'S DIGEST MAGAZINE
Archie

- ❑1, ca. 1992 ... 2.00
- ❑2, ca. 1993 ... 1.75
- ❑3, ca. 1994 ... 1.75
- ❑4, Sep 1995 ... 1.75
- ❑5, Sep 1996 ... 1.75
- ❑6, Oct 1997 ... 1.79

VEROTIKA
Verotik

- ❑1 ... 4.00
- ❑2, Jan 1995 ... 3.00
- ❑3 1995 ... 3.00
- ❑4 1995 ... 3.00
- ❑5 1995 ... 3.00
- ❑6 1995 ... 3.00
- ❑7 1995 ... 3.00
- ❑8, Feb 1996 ... 3.00
- ❑9 ... 3.00
- ❑10 ... 3.00
- ❑11 ... 3.00
- ❑12 ... 3.00
- ❑13 ... 3.00
- ❑14 ... 3.00
- ❑15 ... 3.95

VEROTIK ILLUSTRATED
Verotik

- ❑1, Aug 1997 ... 6.95
- ❑2, Dec 1997 ... 6.95
- ❑3, Apr 1998 ... 6.95

VEROTIK ROGUES GALLERY OF VILLAINS
Verotik

- ❑1, Nov 1997; pin-ups ... 3.95

VERSION
Dark Horse

- ❑1.1 ... 2.50
- ❑1.2 ... 2.50
- ❑1.3 ... 2.50
- ❑1.4 ... 2.50
- ❑1.5 ... 2.50
- ❑1.6 ... 2.50
- ❑1.7 ... 2.50
- ❑1.8 ... 2.50
- ❑2.1 ... 2.95
- ❑2.2 ... 2.95
- ❑2.3 ... 2.95
- ❑2.4 ... 2.95
- ❑2.5 ... 2.95
- ❑2.6 ... 2.95
- ❑2.7 ... 2.95

VERTICAL
DC

- ❑1, Feb 2004 ... 4.95

VERTIGO GALLERY, THE: DREAMS AND NIGHTMARES
DC / Vertigo

- ❑1; MW, BSz, ATh, CV (a); pin-ups ... 4.00

VERTIGO JAM
DC / Vertigo

- ❑1, Aug 1993 ... 3.95

VERTIGO POP! BANGKOK
DC / Vertigo

- ❑1, Jul 2003 ... 2.95
- ❑2, Aug 2003 ... 2.95

N-MINT

- ❑3, Sep 2003 .... 2.95
- ❑4, Oct 2003 .... 2.95

VERTIGO POP! LONDON
DC / VERTIGO

- ❑1, ca. 2002 .... 2.95
- ❑2, ca. 2002 .... 2.95
- ❑3, ca. 2002 .... 2.95
- ❑4, Feb 2003 .... 2.95

VERTIGO POP! TOKYO
DC / VERTIGO

- ❑1, Sep 2002 .... 2.95
- ❑2, Oct 2002 .... 2.95
- ❑3, Nov 2002 .... 2.95

VERTIGO PREVIEW
DC / VERTIGO

- ❑1; Previews DC Vertigo titles 1.50

VERTIGO RAVE
DC / VERTIGO

- ❑1, Aut 1994; Aut 1994 .... 1.50

VERTIGO SECRET FILES & ORIGINS: SWAMP THING
DC / VERTIGO

- ❑1, Nov 2000 .... 4.95

VERTIGO SECRET FILES: HELLBLAZER
DC / VERTIGO

- ❑1, Aug 2000 PG (a) 4.95

VERTIGO VERITÉ: THE UNSEEN HAND
DC / VERTIGO

- ❑1, Sep 1996 .... 2.50
- ❑2, Oct 1996 .... 2.50
- ❑3, Nov 1996 .... 2.50
- ❑4, Dec 1996 .... 2.50

VERTIGO VISIONS: DOCTOR OCCULT
DC / VERTIGO

- ❑1, Jul 1994 .... 3.95

VERTIGO VISIONS: DR. THIRTEEN
DC / VERTIGO

- ❑1, Sep 1998 .... 5.95

VERTIGO VISIONS: PREZ
DC / VERTIGO

- ❑1, Sep 1995 .... 3.95

VERTIGO VISIONS: THE GEEK
DC / VERTIGO

- ❑1 .... 3.95

VERTIGO VISIONS: THE PHANTOM STRANGER
DC / VERTIGO

- ❑1, Oct 1993 .... 3.50

VERTIGO VISIONS: TOMAHAWK
DC / VERTIGO

- ❑1, Jul 1998 .... 4.95

VERTIGO VOICES: THE EATERS
DC / VERTIGO

- ❑1 .... 4.95

VERTIGO: WINTER'S EDGE
DC / VERTIGO

- ❑1, Jan 1998; prestige format anthology; wraparound cover 7.95
- ❑2, Jan 1999; wraparound cover 6.95
- ❑3, Jan 2000 .... 6.95

VERTIGO X PREVIEW
DC / VERTIGO

- ❑1, Apr 2003 .... 0.99

VERY BEST OF DENNIS THE MENACE
MARVEL

- ❑1, Apr 1982; reprints 3.00
- ❑2, Jun 1982; reprints 2.00
- ❑3, Aug 1982; reprints 2.00

VERY MU CHRISTMAS, A
MU

- ❑1, Nov 1992 .... 2.95

VERY VICKY
ICONOGRAFIX

- ❑1, b&w 2.95
- ❑1-2 .... 2.50

N-MINT

- ❑2, b&w 2.50
- ❑3, b&w 2.50
- ❑4, b&w 2.50
- ❑5, b&w 2.50
- ❑6, b&w 2.50
- ❑7, b&w 2.50
- ❑8, b&w 2.50

VESPERS
MARS MEDIA GROUP

- ❑1, Aug 1995 .... 2.50
- ❑2 ....

VEXT
DC

- ❑1, Mar 1999 .... 2.50
- ❑2, Apr 1999 .... 2.50
- ❑3, May 1999 .... 2.50
- ❑4, Jun 1999 .... 2.50
- ❑5, Jul 1999 .... 2.50
- ❑6, Aug 1999 .... 2.50

V FOR VENDETTA
DC

- ❑1, Sep 1988, AMo (w) 3.00
- ❑2, Oct 1988, AMo (w) 2.50
- ❑3, Nov 1988, AMo (w) 2.50
- ❑4, Dec 1988 .... 2.50
- ❑5, Win 1988, AMo (w) 2.50
- ❑6, Hol 1988; AMo (w); Hol 1988 .... 2.50
- ❑7, Jan 1989, AMo (w) 2.50
- ❑8, Feb 1989, AMo (w) 2.50
- ❑9, Mar 1989, AMo (w) 2.50
- ❑10, May 1989, AMo (w) 2.50

VIBE
YOUNG GUN

- ❑1, Mar 1994 .... 1.95

VIC & BLOOD
MAD DOG

- ❑1, Oct 1987, b&w 2.00
- ❑2, Feb 1988, b&w 2.00

VICIOUS
BRAINSTORM

- ❑1, b&w 2.95

VICKI
ATLAS-SEABOARD

- ❑1, Feb 1975; reprints Tippy Teen 28.00
- ❑2, Apr 1975; reprints Tippy Teen 18.00
- ❑3, Jun 1975; reprints Tippy Teen 12.00
- ❑4, Aug 1975; reprints Tippy Teen 12.00

VICKI VALENTINE
RENEGADE

- ❑1, Jul 1985, b&w 1.70
- ❑2, Nov 1985, b&w 1.70
- ❑3 1986, b&w 1.70
- ❑4 1986, b&w 1.70

VICTIM
SILVERWOLF

- ❑1, Feb 1987, b&w 1.50

VICTIMS
ETERNITY

- ❑1 1988, b&w 2.00
- ❑2 1988, b&w 2.00
- ❑3 1988, b&w 2.00
- ❑4, Jan 1989, b&w 2.00
- ❑5, Feb 1989, b&w 2.00
- ❑6 .... 2.00

VICTORIAN, THE
PENNY-FARTHING

- ❑0.5, Aug 1998; preview of upcoming series; Sketches and notes for series 1.00
- ❑1, Mar 1999 .... 3.00
- ❑2, Apr 1999 .... 2.95
- ❑3, May 1999 .... 2.95
- ❑4, Jun 1999 .... 2.95
- ❑5, Jul 1999 .... 2.95
- ❑6, Aug 1999 .... 2.95

VIC TORRY
AVALON

- ❑1 .... 2.95

The Vision and The Scarlet Witch became the proud parents of twins in *The Vision & Scarlet Witch* (Vol. 2).

© 1985 Marvel Comics.

N-MINT

VICTOR VECTOR & YONDO
FRACTAL

- ❑1, Jul 1994 .... 1.95
- ❑2 1994 .... 1.95
- ❑3 1994 .... 1.95

VICTORY (TOPPS)
TOPPS

- ❑1, Jun 1994; First and final issue (series cancelled) 2.50

VICTORY (IMAGE)
IMAGE

- ❑1, Jun 2003 .... 2.95
- ❑1/A, Jul 2003 .... 2.95
- ❑1/B, Jul 2003 .... 2.95
- ❑2, Oct 2003 .... 2.95
- ❑2/A, Oct 2003 .... 2.95
- ❑3, Dec 2003 .... 2.95
- ❑3/A, Dec 2003 .... 2.95
- ❑4, May 2004 .... 2.95

VIDEO CLASSICS
ETERNITY

- ❑1, b&w; Mighty Mouse 3.50
- ❑2, b&w; Mighty Mouse 3.50

VIDEO HIROSHIMA
AEON

- ❑1, Aug 1995, b&w 2.50

VIDEO JACK
MARVEL / EPIC

- ❑1, Sep 1987 .... 1.25
- ❑2, Nov 1987 .... 1.25
- ❑3, Mar 1988 .... 1.25
- ❑4, May 1988 .... 1.25
- ❑5, Jul 1988 .... 1.25
- ❑6, Sep 1988 .... 1.25

VIETNAM JOURNAL
APPLE

- ❑1, Nov 1987, b&w 2.00
- ❑1-2 .... 2.00
- ❑2, Jan 1988 .... 2.00
- ❑3, Mar 1988 .... 2.00
- ❑4, May 1988 .... 2.00
- ❑5, Jul 1988 .... 2.00
- ❑6, Sep 1988 .... 2.00
- ❑7, Nov 1988 .... 2.00
- ❑8, Jan 1989 .... 2.00
- ❑9, Mar 1989 .... 2.00
- ❑10, May 1989 .... 2.00
- ❑11, Jul 1989 .... 2.25
- ❑12, Sep 1989 .... 2.25
- ❑13, Nov 1989 .... 2.25
- ❑14, Jan 1990 .... 2.25
- ❑15, Mar 1990 .... 2.25
- ❑16, May 1990 .... 2.25

VIETNAM JOURNAL: BLOODBATH AT KHE SANH
APPLE

- ❑1, b&w 2.75
- ❑2, b&w 2.75
- ❑3, b&w 2.75
- ❑4, b&w 2.75

VIETNAM JOURNAL: TET '68
APPLE

- ❑1, b&w 2.75
- ❑2, b&w 2.75
- ❑3, b&w 2.75

N-MINT

❑4, b&w 2.75
❑5, b&w 2.75
❑6, b&w 2.75

VIETNAM JOURNAL: VALLEY OF DEATH
APPLE

❑1, Jun 1994, b&w 2.75

VIGILANTE, THE
DC

❑1, Nov 1983 2.00
❑2, Jan 1984 1.50
❑3, Feb 1984 1.50
❑4, Mar 1984 1.25
❑5, Apr 1984 1.25
❑6, May 1984 1.25
❑7, Jun 1984 1.25
❑8, Jul 1984 1.25
❑9, Aug 1984 1.25
❑10, Sep 1984 1.25
❑11, Oct 1984 1.25
❑12, Nov 1984 1.25
❑13, Dec 1984 1.25
❑14, Feb 1985 1.25
❑15, Mar 1985 1.25
❑16, Apr 1985 1.25
❑17, May 1985 1.25
❑18, Jun 1985 1.25
❑19, Jul 1985 1.25
❑20, Aug 1985 1.25
❑21, Sep 1985 1.25
❑22, Oct 1985; Crisis 1.25
❑23, Nov 1985 1.25
❑24, Dec 1985 1.50
❑25, Jan 1986 1.25
❑26, Feb 1986 1.25
❑27, Mar 1986 1.25
❑28, Apr 1986 1.25
❑29, May 1986 1.25
❑30, Jun 1986 1.25
❑31, Jul 1986 1.25
❑32, Aug 1986 1.25
❑33, Sep 1986 1.25
❑34, Oct 1986 1.25
❑35, Nov 1986 1.25
❑36, Dec 1986 1.25
❑37, Jan 1987 1.25
❑38, Feb 1987 1.25
❑39, Mar 1987 1.25
❑40, Apr 1987 1.25
❑41, May 1987 1.25
❑42, Jun 1987 1.25
❑43, Jul 1987 1.25
❑44, Aug 1987 1.25
❑45, Sep 1987 1.25
❑46, Oct 1987 1.25
❑47, Nov 1987 1.25
❑48, Dec 1987 1.25
❑49, Jan 1988 1.25
❑50, Feb 1988; Vigilante commits suicide 1.25
❑Annual 1, ca. 1985 2.00
❑Annual 2, ca. 1986 2.00

VIGILANTE 8: SECOND OFFENSE
CHAOS

❑1, Dec 1999 2.95

VIGILANTE: CITY LIGHTS, PRAIRIE JUSTICE
DC

❑1, Nov 1995 2.50
❑2, Dec 1995 2.50
❑3, Jan 1996 2.50
❑4, Feb 1996 2.50

VIGIL: BLOODLINE
DUALITY

❑1 2.95
❑2 2.95
❑3 2.95
❑4 2.95
❑5, Nov 1998 2.95
❑6 2.95
❑7 2.95
❑8, Jul 1999 2.95

VIGIL: DESERT FOXES
MILLENNIUM

❑1, Jul 1995, b&w 3.95
❑2, Aug 1995, b&w 3.95

VIGIL: ERUPTION
MILLENNIUM

❑1, Aug 1996, b&w 2.95
❑2 2.95

VIGIL: FALL FROM GRACE
INNOVATION

❑1, Mar 1992, b&w 2.95
❑2, b&w 2.95

VIGIL: KUKULKAN
INNOVATION

❑1 2.95

VIGIL: REBIRTH
MILLENNIUM

❑1, Nov 1994, b&w 2.95
❑2, Dec 1994, b&w 2.95

VIGIL: SCATTERSHOTS
DUALITY

❑1, Jul 1997, b&w 3.95
❑2 3.95

VIGIL: THE GOLDEN PARTS
INNOVATION

❑1, b&w 2.95

VIGIL: VAMPORUM ANIMATURI
MILLENNIUM

❑1, May 1994, b&w 3.95

VIGNETTE COMICS
HARRIER

❑1, b&w 1.95

VILE
RAGING RHINO

❑1 2.95

VILLAINS & VIGILANTES
ECLIPSE

❑1, Dec 1986 1.50
❑2, Mar 1987 1.50
❑3, Apr 1987 1.50
❑4, Apr 1987 1.50

VILLA OF THE MYSTERIES
FANTAGRAPHICS

❑1, b&w 3.95
❑2, b&w 3.95
❑3, Jul 1998, b&w 3.95

VINCENT J. MIELCAREK JR. MEMORIAL COMIC
COOPER UNION

❑1, b&w 3.00

VINTAGE COMIC CLASSICS
RECOLLECTIONS

❑1, Feb 1990; Red Demon reprint 2.00

VINTAGE MAGNUS ROBOT FIGHTER
VALIANT

❑1, Jan 1992 RM (w); RM (a); O: Magnus Robot Fighter. 2.00
❑2, Feb 1992 RM (w); RM (a) 2.00
❑3, Mar 1992 RM (w); RM (a) 2.00
❑4, Apr 1992 RM (w); RM (a) 2.00

VIOLATOR
IMAGE

❑1, May 1994 AMo (w); 1: The Admonisher. 2.50
❑2, Jun 1994 AMo (w) 2.50
❑3, Jul 1994 AMo (w) 2.50

VIOLATOR VS. BADROCK
IMAGE

❑1, May 1995 2.50
❑1/A, May 1995 2.50
❑2, Jun 1995 2.50
❑3, Jul 1995 2.50
❑4, Aug 1995 2.50

VIOLENT CASES
TITAN

❑1 NG (w) 15.00
❑1-2; NG (w); In color, with new forward by Neil Gaiman 10.00
❑1-3; NG (w); Kitchen Sink publishes; New cover (red) by Dave McKean 12.95

VIOLENT MESSIAHS
HURRICANE

❑1, Jul 1997, b&w 2.95
❑2 1997 2.95
❑3 1997 2.95

VIOLENT MESSIAHS (2ND SERIES)
IMAGE

❑0.5/A; Two pistols raised on cover 3.00
❑0.5/B; One pistol up, one down on cover 3.00
❑1, Jun 2000 2.95
❑2, Aug 2000 2.95
❑3, Sep 2000 2.95
❑4, Nov 2000 2.95
❑5, Jan 2001 2.95
❑6, Mar 2001 2.95
❑7, Jun 2001
❑8, Sep 2001

VIOLENT MESSIAHS: GENESIS
IMAGE

❑1, Dec 2001, b&w; Collects Violent Messiahs 0.5, Hurricane #1-2, plus sketches 5.95

VIOLENT MESSIAHS: LAMENTING PAIN
IMAGE

❑1, Sep 2002 2.95
❑3, Jan 2003 2.95
❑4, Sep 2003 2.95

VIOLENT TALES
DEATH

❑1, Nov 1997, b&w 2.95

VIPER
DC

❑1, Aug 1994 1.95
❑2, Sep 1994 1.95
❑3, Oct 1994 1.95
❑4, Nov 1994 1.95

VIPER FORCE
ACID RAM

❑1, Sep 1995 2.50

VIRTEX
OKTOMICA

❑0, Oct 1998 1.50
❑1, Dec 1998 2.50
❑2, Jan 1999 2.50
❑3 1999 2.50
❑Ashcan 1 1999 1.00

VIRTUA FIGHTER
MARVEL

❑1, Aug 1995 2.95

VIRTUAL BANG
IRONCAT

❑1 2.95
❑2 2.95

VIRUS
DARK HORSE

❑1, ca. 1993 2.50
❑2, ca. 1993 2.50
❑3, ca. 1993 2.50
❑4, ca. 1994 2.50

VISAGE SPECIAL EDITION
ILLUSION

❑1, Aug 1996, b&w 2.00

VISION, THE
MARVEL

❑1, Nov 1994 1.75
❑2, Dec 1994 1.75
❑3, Jan 1995 1.75
❑4, Feb 1995 1.75

N-MINT

VISION & SCARLET WITCH (VOL. 1)
MARVEL
❑1, Nov 1982 ... 1.50
❑2, Dec 1982 A: Whizzer. ... 1.50
❑3, Jan 1983 A: Wonder Man. ... 1.50
❑4, Feb 1983 A: Magneto. ... 1.50

VISION & SCARLET WITCH (VOL. 2)
MARVEL
❑1, Oct 1985 RHo (a) ... 1.50
❑2, Nov 1985 RHo (a); D: Whizzer. ... 1.25
❑3, Dec 1985 RHo (a) ... 1.25
❑4, Jan 1986 RHo (a) ... 1.25
❑5, Feb 1986 RHo (a) ... 1.25
❑6, Mar 1986 RHo (a) ... 1.25
❑7, Apr 1986 RHo (a) ... 1.25
❑8, May 1986 RHo (a) ... 1.25
❑9, Jun 1986 RHo (a) ... 1.25
❑10, Jul 1986 RHo (a) ... 1.25
❑11, Aug 1986 RHo (a); A: Spider-Man. ... 1.25
❑12, Sep 1986 RHo (a) ... 1.25

VISIONARIES
MARVEL / STAR
❑1, Jan 1988; Giant sized ... 1.00
❑2, Feb 1988 ... 1.00
❑3, Mar 1988 ... 1.00
❑4, Apr 1988 ... 1.00
❑5, May 1988 ... 1.00
❑6, Jun 1988 ... 1.00

VISIONS
CALIBER
❑1 ... 4.95

VISIONS: DAVID MACK
CALIBER
❑1 ... 5.95

VISIONS OF CURVES
FANTAGRAPHICS / EROS
❑1, Apr 1994, b&w ... 4.95
❑2 ... 4.95
❑3, May 1995; Sketchbook ... 4.95

VISIONS: R.G. TAYLOR
CALIBER
❑1, b&w ... 2.50

VISITATIONS
IMAGE
❑1, b&w; squarebound ... 6.95

VISITOR, THE
VALIANT
❑1, Apr 1995 ... 2.50
❑2, May 1995 ... 2.50
❑3, Jun 1995; Acclaim begins publishing ... 2.50
❑4, Jul 1995 ... 2.50
❑5, Jul 1995 ... 2.50
❑6, Aug 1995 ... 2.50
❑7, Aug 1995 ... 2.50
❑8, Sep 1995; The Harbinger's identity is revealed ... 2.50
❑9, Sep 1995 ... 2.50
❑10, Oct 1995 ... 2.50
❑11, Oct 1995 ... 2.50
❑12, Nov 1995 ... 2.50
❑13, Nov 1995 ... 2.50

VISITOR VS. THE VALIANT UNIVERSE, THE
VALIANT
❑1, Feb 1995; cardstock cover ... 2.95
❑2, Mar 1995; cardstock cover ... 2.95

VISUAL ASSAULT OMNIBUS
VISUAL ASSAULT
❑1, b&w ... 2.50
❑2, b&w ... 2.50
❑3, b&w; Flip-book ... 3.00

VIXEN 9
SAMSON
❑1; Flip-book; no indicia ... 2.50

VIXEN WARRIOR DIARIES
RAGING RHINO
❑1, b&w ... 2.95

N-MINT

VIXEN WARS, THE
RAGING RHINO
❑1, b&w ... 2.95
❑2, b&w ... 2.95
❑3, b&w ... 2.95
❑4, b&w ... 2.95
❑5, b&w ... 2.95
❑6 ... 2.95
❑7 ... 2.95
❑8 ... 2.95
❑9; Twisted Vixen stories begin ... 2.95
❑10; Title changes to Twisted Vixen ... 2.95

VOGUE
IMAGE
❑1, Oct 1995 ... 2.50
❑1/A, Oct 1995; alternate cover ... 2.50
❑2, Nov 1995 ... 2.50
❑3, Dec 1995 ... 2.50
❑4, Jan 1996 ... 2.50

VOID INDIGO
MARVEL / EPIC
❑1, Nov 1984; VM (a); Continued from Marvel Graphic Novel ... 2.00
❑2, Mar 1985 VM (a) ... 2.00

VOLCANIC NIGHTS
PALLIARD
❑1, b&w ... 2.95

VOLCANIC REVOLVER
ONI
❑1, Jan 1999, b&w ... 2.95
❑2, Jan 1999, b&w ... 2.95
❑3, Mar 1999, b&w ... 2.95

VOLTRON
SOLSON
❑1 ... 1.00
❑2 ... 1.00
❑3 ... 1.00

VOLTRON: DEFENDER OF THE UNIVERSE
IMAGE
❑0, May 2003 ... 2.50
❑1, May 2003 ... 2.95
❑2, Jun 2003 ... 2.95
❑3, Jul 2003 ... 2.95
❑4, Sep 2003 ... 2.95
❑5, Oct 2003 ... 2.95

VOLUNTEER COMICS SUMMER LINE-UP '96
VOLUNTEER
❑1, Sum 1996, b&w; previews ... 2.95

VOLUNTEER COMICS WINTER LINE-UP '96
VOLUNTEER
❑1, b&w; previews ... 2.95

VOLUNTEERS QUEST FOR DREAMS LOST
LITERACY
❑1, b&w; Turtles; Trollords ... 2.00

VON FANGE BROTHERS: GREEN HAIR AND RED "S'S", THE
MIKEY-SIZED COMICS
❑1, Jul 1996, b&w ... 1.75

VON FANGE BROTHERS: THE UNCOMMONS, THE
MIKEY-SIZED COMICS
❑1, Oct 1996, b&w ... 1.75

VONPYRE
EYEFUL
❑1 ... 2.95

VOODOO (IMAGE)
IMAGE
❑1, Nov 1997 ... 2.50
❑2, Dec 1997 ... 2.50
❑3, Jan 1998 ... 2.50
❑4, Mar 1998 ... 2.50

After more than 20 years with the same cover logo, Gold Key updated it for its run of *Walt Disney's Comics & Stories* beginning in the mid-1960s.
© 1965 Walt Disney Productions and Gold Key.

N-MINT

VOODOO INK
DEJA-VU
❑0, b&w ... 1.95
❑1, b&w ... 1.95
❑2, b&w ... 1.95
❑3, b&w ... 1.95
❑4, b&w ... 1.95
❑5, b&w ... 1.95

VOODOOM
ONI
❑1, Jun 2000, b&w; smaller than regular comic book ... 4.95

VOODOO•ZEALOT: SKIN TRADE
IMAGE
❑1, Aug 1995 ... 4.95

VORTEX (VORTEX)
VORTEX
❑1, Nov 1982 ... 2.00
❑2 ... 2.00
❑3, May 1983 ... 2.00
❑4 ... 2.00
❑5 ... 2.00
❑6 ... 2.00
❑7 ... 2.00
❑8 ... 2.00
❑9 ... 2.00
❑10, Sep 1984 GD (w); GD (a) ... 2.00
❑11 ... 1.75
❑12 ... 1.75
❑13 ... 1.75
❑14 ... 1.75
❑15 ... 1.75

VORTEX (COMICO)
COMICO
❑1, Oct 1991 ... 2.50
❑2 ... 2.50
❑3; Exists? ... 2.50
❑4; Exists? ... 2.50

VORTEX (HALL OF HEROES)
HALL OF HEROES
❑1, Aug 1993, b&w ... 2.50
❑2, Oct 1993 ... 2.50
❑3, Dec 1993 ... 2.50
❑4, Feb 1994 ... 2.50
❑5, Apr 1994 ... 2.50
❑6, Dec 1994 ... 2.50

VORTEX (ENTITY)
ENTITY
❑1, Jan 1996 ... 2.95

VORTEX THE WONDER MULE
CUTTING EDGE
❑1, b&w ... 2.95
❑2, b&w ... 2.95

VOX
APPLE
❑1, Jun 1989, b&w JBy (c); JBy (a) ... 2.00
❑2 ... 2.25
❑3 ... 2.25
❑4 ... 2.25
❑5 ... 2.25
❑6 ... 2.25
❑7 ... 2.25

N-MINT

VOYEUR, THE
AIRCEL

❑1, b&w ... 2.50
❑2, b&w ... 2.50
❑3, b&w ... 2.50
❑4 ... 2.95

VROOM SOCKO
SLAVE LABOR

❑1, Nov 1993; reprints strips from Deadline U.K. ... 2.50

VULGAR VINCE
THROB

❑1 ... 1.75

VULTURES OF WHAPETON
CONQUEST

❑1, b&w ... 2.95

W

W
GOOD

❑1, Nov 1996 ... 2.95

WABBIT WAMPAGE
AMAZING

❑1 ... 1.95

WACKY ADVENTURES OF CRACKY
GOLD KEY

❑1, Dec 1972 ... 5.00
❑2, Mar 1973 ... 3.00
❑3, Jun 1973 ... 2.50
❑4, Sep 1973 ... 2.50
❑5, Dec 1973 ... 2.50
❑6, Mar 1974 ... 2.00
❑7, Jun 1974 ... 2.00
❑8, Sep 1974 ... 2.00
❑9, Dec 1974 ... 2.00
❑10, Mar 1975 ... 2.00
❑11, Jun 1975 ... 2.00
❑12, Sep 1975 ... 2.00

WACKY RACES
GOLD KEY

❑1, Aug 1969 ... 40.00
❑2, Feb 1971 ... 26.00
❑3, May 1971 ... 20.00
❑4, Aug 1971 ... 20.00
❑5, Nov 1971 ... 20.00
❑6, Feb 1972 ... 20.00
❑7, May 1972 ... 20.00

WACKY SQUIRREL
DARK HORSE

❑1 1987, b&w ... 2.00
❑2 1988 ... 2.00
❑3 1988 ... 2.00
❑4, Oct 1988 ... 2.00
❑Special 1, Oct 1987; Flip-book; A: Mr. Monster. Halloween Adventure Special ... 2.00
❑Summer 1, Jul 1987; Summer Fun Special ... 2.00

WACKY WITCH
GOLD KEY

❑1, Jan 1971 ... 12.00
❑2, Apr 1971 ... 7.00
❑3, Jul 1971 ... 5.00
❑4, Oct 1971 ... 5.00
❑5, Jan 1972 ... 5.00
❑6, Apr 1972 ... 4.00
❑7, Jul 1972 ... 4.00
❑8, Oct 1972 ... 4.00
❑9, Jan 1973 ... 4.00
❑10, Apr 1973 ... 4.00
❑11, Jul 1973 ... 3.00
❑12, Oct 1973 ... 3.00
❑13, Jan 1974 ... 3.00
❑14, Apr 1974 ... 3.00
❑15, Jul 1974 ... 3.00
❑16, Oct 1974 ... 3.00
❑17, Jan 1975 ... 3.00
❑18, Apr 1975 ... 3.00
❑19, Jul 1975 ... 3.00
❑20, Oct 1975 ... 3.00
❑21, Jan 1976 ... 3.00

WAGON TRAIN (DELL)
DELL

❑4, Jan 1960 ... 38.00
❑5, Apr 1960 ... 38.00
❑6, Jul 1960 ... 38.00
❑7, Oct 1960 ... 34.00
❑8, Jan 1961 ... 34.00
❑9, Apr 1961 ... 34.00
❑10, Jul 1961 ... 25.00
❑11, Oct 1961 ... 25.00
❑12, Jan 1962 ... 25.00
❑13, Apr 1962 ... 25.00

WAGON TRAIN (GOLD KEY)
GOLD KEY

❑1, Jan 1964 ... 38.00
❑2, Apr 1964 ... 25.00
❑3, Jul 1964 ... 25.00
❑4, Oct 1964 ... 25.00

WAHH
FRANK & HANK

❑1, b&w; no indicia; cardstock cover ... 2.95
❑2, b&w; cardstock cover ... 2.95

WAHOO MORRIS
TOO HIP GOTT GO GRAPHICS

❑1, Jun 1998, b&w ... 2.75

WAHOO MORRIS (IMAGE)
IMAGE

❑1, Mar 2000 ... 2.95

WAITING FOR THE END OF THE WORLD
RODENT

❑1 ... 1.00
❑2 ... 1.00
❑3 ... 1.00

WAITING PLACE, THE
SLAVE LABOR

❑1, Apr 1997 ... 2.95
❑2, May 1997 ... 2.95
❑3, Jun 1997 ... 2.95
❑4, Jul 1997 ... 2.95
❑5, Aug 1997 ... 2.95
❑6, Sep 1997 ... 2.95

WALDO WORLD
FANTAGRAPHICS

❑1 ... 2.50
❑2 ... 2.50

WALKING DEAD, THE (IMAGE)
IMAGE

❑1, Oct 2003 ... 2.95
❑2, Nov 2003 ... 2.95
❑3, Dec 2003 ... 2.95
❑4, Jan 2004 ... 2.95
❑4/A, Feb 2004 ... 2.95
❑5, Apr 2004 ... 2.95
❑6, May 2004 ... 2.95
❑7, Apr 2004 ... 2.95
❑8, Aug 2004 ... 2.95

WALKING DEAD, THE
AIRCEL

❑1 ... 2.25
❑2 ... 2.25
❑3 ... 2.25
❑4 ... 2.25
❑Special 1, b&w ... 2.25

WALK THROUGH OCTOBER
CALIBER

❑1, ca. 1995, b&w ... 2.95

WALL OF FLESH
AC

❑1, b&w ... 3.50

WALLY THE WIZARD
MARVEL / STAR

❑1, Apr 1985 ... 1.00
❑2, May 1985 ... 1.00
❑3, Jun 1985 ... 1.00
❑4, Jul 1985 ... 1.00
❑5, Aug 1985 ... 1.00
❑6, Sep 1985 ... 1.00
❑7, Oct 1985 ... 1.00
❑8, Nov 1985 ... 1.00
❑9, Dec 1985 ... 1.00
❑10, Jan 1986 ... 1.00
❑11, Feb 1986 ... 1.00
❑12, Mar 1986 ... 1.00

WALT DISNEY COMICS DIGEST
GOLD KEY

❑1, Jun 1968 ... 60.00
❑2, Jul 1968 ... 40.00
❑3, Aug 1968 ... 40.00
❑4, Oct 1968 ... 40.00
❑5, Nov 1968 ... 40.00
❑6, Dec 1968 ... 25.00
❑7, Jan 1969 ... 25.00
❑8, Feb 1969 ... 25.00
❑9, Mar 1969 ... 25.00
❑10, Apr 1969 ... 25.00
❑11, May 1969 ... 25.00
❑12, Jun 1969 ... 25.00
❑13, Jul 1969 ... 25.00
❑14, Aug 1969 ... 20.00
❑15, Sep 1969 ... 20.00
❑16, Oct 1969 ... 20.00
❑17, Nov 1969 ... 20.00
❑18, Dec 1969 ... 20.00
❑19, Jan 1970 ... 20.00
❑20, Feb 1970 ... 20.00
❑21, Apr 1970 ... 15.00
❑22, Jun 1970 ... 15.00
❑23, Jul 1970 ... 15.00
❑24, Aug 1970 ... 15.00
❑25, Oct 1970 ... 15.00
❑26, Dec 1970 ... 15.00
❑27, Feb 1971 ... 15.00
❑28, Apr 1971 ... 15.00
❑29, Jun 1971 ... 15.00
❑30, Aug 1971 ... 15.00
❑31, Oct 1971 ... 15.00
❑32, Dec 1971 ... 15.00
❑33, Feb 1972 ... 15.00
❑34, Apr 1972 ... 15.00
❑35, Jun 1972; Feature on the 1972 film The Biscuit Eater ... 15.00
❑36, Aug 1972 ... 15.00
❑37, Oct 1972; Feature on the 1972 film Now You See Him, Now You Don't ... 15.00
❑38, Dec 1972 ... 15.00
❑39, Feb 1973 ... 15.00
❑40, Apr 1973 ... 15.00
❑41, Jun 1973 ... 15.00
❑42, Aug 1973; Mary Poppins cover . 15.00
❑43, Oct 1973 ... 15.00
❑44, Dec 1973 ... 40.00
❑45, Feb 1974 ... 15.00
❑46, Apr 1974 ... 15.00
❑47, Jun 1974 ... 15.00
❑48, Aug 1974 ... 15.00
❑49, Oct 1974 ... 15.00
❑50, Dec 1974 ... 15.00
❑51, Feb 1975 ... 10.00
❑52, Apr 1975 ... 10.00
❑53, Jun 1975 ... 10.00
❑54, Aug 1975 ... 10.00
❑55, Oct 1975 ... 10.00
❑56, Dec 1975 ... 10.00
❑57, Feb 1976 ... 10.00

WALT DISNEY GIANT
GLADSTONE

❑1, Sep 1995; newsprint cover ... 2.25
❑2, Nov 1995; newsprint cover ... 2.25
❑3, Jan 1996; newsprint cover ... 2.25
❑4, Mar 1996; Mickey Mouse; newsprint cover ... 2.25
❑5, May 1996; Mickey and Donald; newsprint cover ... 2.25

N-MINT

❑6, Jul 1996; Uncle Scrooge and the Junior Woodchucks; newsprint cover ... 2.25
❑7, Sep 1996; newsprint cover ... 2.25

WALT DISNEY'S AUTUMN ADVENTURES
DISNEY

❑1 ... 2.95
❑2 ... 2.95

WALT DISNEY'S CHRISTMAS PARADE (GOLD KEY)
GOLD KEY

❑1, ca. 1963 ... 75.00
❑2, Jan 1964 ... 50.00
❑3 1965 ... 50.00
❑4 1966 ... 50.00
❑5, Feb 1967 ... 50.00
❑6, Feb 1968 ... 50.00
❑7, Jan 1970 ... 50.00
❑8, Jan 1971 ... 50.00
❑9, Jan 1972 ... 20.00

WALT DISNEY'S CHRISTMAS PARADE (GLADSTONE)
GLADSTONE

❑1, Win 1988; cardstock cover ... 2.95
❑2, Win 1989 ... 2.95

WALT DISNEY'S CHRISTMAS PARADE (GEMSTONE)
GEMSTONE

❑1, Nov 2003 ... 8.95

WALT DISNEY'S COMICS AND STORIES
DELL

❑193, Oct 1956, CB (w); CB (a) ... 80.00
❑194, Nov 1956 CB (w); CB (a) ... 80.00
❑195, Dec 1956 CB (w); CB (a) ... 80.00
❑196, Jan 1957 CB (w); CB (a) ... 80.00
❑197, Feb 1957 CB (w); CB (a) ... 80.00
❑198, Mar 1957 CB (w); CB (a) ... 80.00
❑199, Apr 1957 CB (w); CB (a) ... 80.00
❑200, May 1957 CB (w); CB (a) ... 80.00
❑201, Jun 1957 CB (w); CB (a) ... 75.00
❑202, Jul 1957 CB (w); CB (a) ... 75.00
❑203, Aug 1957 CB (w); CB (a) ... 75.00
❑204, Sep 1957 CB (w); CB (a) ... 75.00
❑205, Oct 1957 CB (w); CB (a) ... 75.00
❑206, Nov 1957 CB (w); CB (a) ... 75.00
❑207, Dec 1957 CB (w); CB (a) ... 75.00
❑208, Jan 1958 CB (w); CB (a) ... 75.00
❑209, Feb 1958 CB (w); CB (a) ... 75.00
❑210, Mar 1958 CB (w); CB (a) ... 75.00
❑211, Apr 1958 CB (w); CB (a) ... 75.00
❑212, May 1958 CB (w); CB (a) ... 75.00
❑213, Jun 1958 CB (w); CB (a) ... 75.00
❑214, Jul 1958 CB (c); CB (w); CB (a) ... 75.00
❑215, Aug 1958 CB (w); CB (a) ... 75.00
❑216, Sep 1958 CB (w); CB (a) ... 75.00
❑217, Oct 1958 CB (w); CB (a) ... 75.00
❑218, Nov 1958 CB (w); CB (a) ... 75.00
❑219, Dec 1958 CB (w); CB (a) ... 75.00
❑220, Jan 1959 CB (w); CB (a) ... 75.00
❑221, Feb 1959 CB (w); CB (a) ... 75.00
❑222, Mar 1959 CB (w); CB (a) ... 75.00
❑223, Apr 1959 CB (w); CB (a) ... 75.00
❑224, May 1959 CB (w); CB (a) ... 75.00
❑225, Jun 1959 CB (w); CB (a) ... 75.00
❑226, Jul 1959 CB (w); CB (a) ... 75.00
❑227, Aug 1959 CB (w); CB (a) ... 75.00
❑228, Sep 1959 CB (w); CB (a) ... 75.00
❑229, Oct 1959 CB (w); CB (a) ... 75.00
❑230, Nov 1959 CB (w); CB (a) ... 75.00
❑231, Dec 1959 CB (w); CB (a) ... 75.00
❑232, Jan 1960 CB (w); CB (a) ... 75.00
❑233, Feb 1960 CB (w); CB (a) ... 75.00
❑234, Mar 1960 CB (w); CB (a) ... 75.00
❑235, Apr 1960 CB (w); CB (a) ... 75.00
❑236, May 1960 CB (w); CB (a) ... 75.00
❑237, Jun 1960 CB (w); CB (a) ... 75.00
❑238, Jul 1960 CB (w); CB (a) ... 75.00
❑239, Aug 1960 CB (w); CB (a) ... 75.00

N-MINT

❑240, Sep 1960 CB (w); CB (a) ... 75.00
❑241, Oct 1960 CB (w); CB (a) ... 60.00
❑242, Nov 1960 CB (w); CB (a) ... 60.00
❑243, Dec 1960 CB (w); CB (a) ... 60.00
❑244, Jan 1961 CB (w); CB (a) ... 60.00
❑245, Feb 1961 CB (w); CB (a) ... 60.00
❑246, Mar 1961 CB (w); CB (a) ... 60.00
❑247, Apr 1961 CB (w); CB (a) ... 60.00
❑248, May 1961 CB (w); CB (a) ... 60.00
❑249, Jun 1961 CB (w); CB (a) ... 60.00
❑250, Jul 1961 CB (w); CB (a) ... 60.00
❑251, Aug 1961 CB (w); CB (a) ... 60.00
❑252, Sep 1961 CB (w); CB (a) ... 60.00
❑253, Oct 1961 CB (w); CB (a) ... 60.00
❑254, Nov 1961 CB (w); CB (a) ... 60.00
❑255, Dec 1961 CB (w); CB (a) ... 60.00
❑256, Jan 1962 CB (w); CB (a) ... 60.00
❑257, Feb 1962 CB (w); CB (a) ... 60.00
❑258, Mar 1962 CB (w); CB (a) ... 60.00
❑259, Apr 1962 CB (w); CB (a) ... 60.00
❑260, May 1962 CB (w); CB (a) ... 60.00
❑261, Jun 1962 CB (w); CB (a) ... 50.00
❑262, Jul 1962 CB (w); CB (a) ... 50.00
❑263, Aug 1962 CB (w); CB (a) ... 50.00
❑264, Sep 1962 CB (w); CB (a) ... 50.00
❑265, Oct 1962 CB (w); CB (a) ... 50.00
❑266, Nov 1962 CB (w); CB (a) ... 50.00
❑267, Dec 1962 CB (w); CB (a) ... 50.00
❑268, Jan 1963 CB (w); CB (a) ... 50.00
❑269, Feb 1963 CB (w); CB (a) ... 50.00
❑270, Mar 1963 CB (w); CB (a) ... 50.00
❑271, Apr 1963 CB (w); CB (a) ... 50.00
❑272, May 1963 CB (w); CB (a) ... 50.00
❑273, Jun 1963 CB (w); CB (a) ... 50.00
❑274, Jul 1963 CB (w); CB (a) ... 50.00
❑275, Aug 1963 CB (w); CB (a) ... 50.00
❑276, Sep 1963 CB (w); CB (a) ... 50.00
❑277, Oct 1963 CB (w); CB (a) ... 50.00
❑278, Nov 1963 CB (w); CB (a) ... 50.00
❑279, Dec 1963 CB (w); CB (a) ... 50.00
❑280, Jan 1964 CB (w); CB (a) ... 50.00
❑281, Feb 1964 CB (w); CB (a) ... 50.00
❑282, Mar 1964 CB (w); CB (a) ... 50.00
❑283, Apr 1964 CB (w); CB (a) ... 50.00
❑284, May 1964 ... 25.00
❑285, Jun 1964 ... 25.00
❑286, Jul 1964 CB (w); CB (a) ... 28.00
❑287, Aug 1964 ... 25.00
❑288, Sep 1964 CB (w); CB (a) ... 28.00
❑289, Oct 1964 CB (w); CB (a) ... 28.00
❑290, Nov 1964 ... 25.00
❑291, Dec 1964 CB (w); CB (a) ... 28.00
❑292, Jan 1965 CB (w); CB (a) ... 28.00
❑293, Feb 1965 CB (w); CB (a) ... 28.00
❑294, Mar 1965 ... 25.00
❑295, Apr 1965 ... 25.00
❑296, May 1965 ... 25.00
❑297, Jun 1965; CB (w); CB (a); Reprints story from Uncle Scrooge #20 ... 28.00
❑298, Jul 1965; CB (w); CB (a); Reprints story from Four Color Comics #1055 (Daisy Duck's Diary) ... 28.00
❑299, Aug 1965; CB (w); CB (a); Reprints story from Walt Disney's Comics #117 ... 28.00
❑300, Sep 1965; CB (w); CB (a); Reprints story from Walt Disney's Comics #43 ... 28.00
❑301, Oct 1965; CB (w); CB (a); Reprints stories from Four Color Comics #1150 (Daisy Duck's Diary) and Walt Disney's Comics #44 ... 28.00
❑302, Nov 1965; CB (w); CB (a); Reprints story from Walt Disney's Comics #47 ... 28.00
❑303, Dec 1965; CB (w); CB (a); Reprints story from Walt Disney's Comics #49 ... 28.00
❑304, Jan 1966; CB (w); CB (a); Reprints stories from Four Color Comics #1150 (Daisy Duck's Diary) and Walt Disney's Comics #63 ... 28.00
❑305, Feb 1966; CB (w); CB (a); Reprints stories from Uncle Scrooge #25 andWalt Disney's Comics #70 ... 28.00

Many issues of *Walt Disney's Comics & Stories* reprint material from earlier issues.
© 1970 Walt Disney Productions (Gold Key)

N-MINT

❑306, Mar 1966; CB (w); CB (a); Reprints story from Walt Disney's Comics #94 ... 28.00
❑307, Apr 1966; CB (w); CB (a); Reprints story from Walt Disney's Comics #91 ... 28.00
❑308, May 1966 CB (w); CB (a) ... 28.00
❑309, Jun 1966 ... 25.00
❑310, Jul 1966 ... 25.00
❑311, Aug 1966 ... 25.00
❑312, Sep 1966 CB (w); CB (a) ... 28.00
❑313, Oct 1966 ... 14.00
❑314, Nov 1966 ... 14.00
❑315, Dec 1966 ... 14.00
❑316, Jan 1967 ... 14.00
❑317, Feb 1967 ... 14.00
❑318, Mar 1967 ... 14.00
❑319, Apr 1967 ... 14.00
❑320, May 1967 ... 14.00
❑321, Jun 1967 ... 14.00
❑322, Jul 1967 ... 14.00
❑323, Aug 1967 ... 14.00
❑324, Sep 1967 ... 14.00
❑325, Oct 1967 ... 14.00
❑326, Nov 1967 ... 14.00
❑327, Dec 1967 ... 14.00
❑328, Jan 1968; CB (w); CB (a); Reprints story from Walt Disney's Comics #148 ... 14.00
❑329, Feb 1968 ... 14.00
❑330, Mar 1968 ... 14.00
❑331, Apr 1968 ... 14.00
❑332, May 1968 ... 14.00
❑333, Jun 1968 ... 14.00
❑334, Jul 1968 ... 14.00
❑335, Aug 1968; CB (w); CB (a); Reprints story from Walt Disney's Comics #129 ... 25.00
❑336, Sep 1968 ... 14.00
❑337, Oct 1968 ... 14.00
❑338, Nov 1968 ... 14.00
❑339, Dec 1968 ... 14.00
❑340, Jan 1969 ... 14.00
❑341, Feb 1969 ... 14.00
❑342, Mar 1969; CB (w); CB (a); Reprints story from Walt Disney's Comics #131 ... 25.00
❑343, Apr 1969; CB (w); CB (a); Reprints story from Walt Disney's Comics #144 ... 25.00
❑344, May 1969; CB (w); CB (a); Reprints story from Walt Disney's Comics #127 ... 25.00
❑345, Jun 1969; CB (w); CB (a); Reprints story from Walt Disney's Comics #139 ... 25.00
❑346, Jul 1969; CB (w); CB (a); Reprints story from Walt Disney's Comics #140 ... 25.00
❑347, Aug 1969; CB (w); CB (a); Reprints story from Walt Disney's Comics #141 ... 25.00
❑348, Sep 1969; CB (w); CB (a); Reprints story from Walt Disney's Comics #155 ... 25.00
❑349, Oct 1969; CB (w); CB (a); Reprints story from Walt Disney's Comics #92 ... 25.00
❑350, Nov 1969; CB (w); CB (a); Reprints story from Walt Disney's Comics #133 ... 25.00

	N-MINT
❑351, Dec 1969; CB (w); CB (a); Reprints story from Walt Disney's Comics #147	25.00
❑351/Poster, Dec 1969; CB (w); CB (a); Reprints story from Walt Disney's Comics #147; with poster insert	30.00
❑351/No poster, Dec 1969; CB (w); CB (a); Reprints story from Walt Disney's Comics #147; poster insert removed	20.00
❑352, Jan 1970; CB (w); CB (a); Reprints story from Walt Disney's Comics #160	25.00
❑352/Poster, Jan 1970; CB (w); CB (a); Reprints story from Walt Disney's Comics #160; with poster insert	30.00
❑352/No poster, Jan 1970; CB (w); CB (a); Reprints story from Walt Disney's Comics #160; poster insert removed	20.00
❑353, Feb 1970; CB (w); CB (a); Reprints story from Walt Disney's Comics #173	25.00
❑353/Poster, Feb 1970; CB (w); CB (a); Reprints story from Walt Disney's Comics #173; with poster insert	30.00
❑353/No poster, Feb 1970; CB (w); CB (a); Reprints story from Walt Disney's Comics #173; poster insert removed	20.00
❑354, Mar 1970; CB (w); CB (a); Reprints story from Walt Disney's Comics #197	25.00
❑354/Poster, Mar 1970; CB (w); CB (a); Reprints story from Walt Disney's Comics #197; with poster insert	30.00
❑354/No poster, Mar 1970; CB (w); CB (a); Reprints story from Walt Disney's Comics #197; poster insert removed	20.00
❑355, Apr 1970; CB (w); CB (a); Reprints story from Walt Disney's Comics #206	25.00
❑355/Poster, Apr 1970; CB (w); CB (a); Reprints story from Walt Disney's Comics #206; with poster insert	30.00
❑355/No poster, Apr 1970; CB (w); CB (a); Reprints story from Walt Disney's Comics #206; poster insert removed	20.00
❑356, May 1970; CB (w); CB (a); Reprints story from Walt Disney's Comics #103	25.00
❑356/Poster, May 1970; CB (w); CB (a); Reprints story from Walt Disney's Comics #103; with poster insert	30.00
❑356/No poster, May 1970; CB (w); CB (a); Reprints story from Walt Disney's Comics #103; poster insert removed	20.00
❑357, Jun 1970; CB (w); CB (a); Reprints story from Walt Disney's Comics #145	25.00
❑357/Poster, Jun 1970; CB (w); CB (a); Reprints story from Walt Disney's Comics #145; with poster insert	30.00
❑357/No poster, Jun 1970; CB (w); CB (a); Reprints story from Walt Disney's Comics #145; poster insert removed	20.00
❑358, Jul 1970; CB (w); CB (a); Reprints story from Walt Disney's Comics #146	25.00
❑358/Poster, Jul 1970; CB (w); CB (a); Reprints story from Walt Disney's Comics #146; with poster insert	30.00
❑358/No poster, Jul 1970; CB (w); CB (a); Reprints story from Walt Disney's Comics #146; poster insert removed	20.00
❑359, Aug 1970; CB (w); CB (a); Reprints story from Walt Disney's Comics #154	25.00
❑359/Poster, Aug 1970; CB (w); CB (a); Reprints story from Walt Disney's Comics #154; with poster insert	30.00
❑359/No poster, Aug 1970; CB (w); CB (a); Reprints story from Walt Disney's Comics #154; poster insert removed	20.00
❑360, Sep 1970; CB (w); CB (a); Reprints story from Walt Disney's Comics #200	25.00
❑360/Poster, Sep 1970; CB (w); CB (a); Reprints story from Walt Disney's Comics #200; with poster insert	30.00
❑360/No poster, Sep 1970; CB (w); CB (a); Reprints story from Walt Disney's Comics #200; poster insert removed	20.00
❑361, Oct 1970; CB (w); CB (a); Reprints story from Walt Disney's Comics #158	25.00
❑362, Nov 1970; CB (w); CB (a); Reprints story from Walt Disney's Comics #180	25.00
❑363, Dec 1970; CB (w); CB (a); Reprints story from Walt Disney's Comics #126	25.00
❑364, Jan 1971; CB (w); CB (a); Reprints story from Walt Disney's Comics #172	25.00
❑365, Feb 1971; CB (w); CB (a); Reprints story from Walt Disney's Comics #149	25.00
❑366, Mar 1971; CB (w); CB (a); Reprints story from Walt Disney's Comics #150	25.00
❑367, Apr 1971; CB (w); CB (a); Reprints story from Walt Disney's Comics #151	25.00
❑368, May 1971; CB (w); CB (a); Reprints story from Walt Disney's Comics #156	25.00
❑369, Jun 1971; CB (w); CB (a); Reprints story from Walt Disney's Comics #143	25.00
❑370, Jul 1971; CB (w); CB (a); Reprints story from Walt Disney's Comics #142	25.00
❑371, Aug 1971; CB (w); CB (a); Reprints story from Walt Disney's Comics #153	25.00
❑372, Sep 1971; CB (w); CB (a); Reprints story from Walt Disney's Comics #168	25.00
❑373, Oct 1971; CB (w); CB (a); Reprints story from Walt Disney's Comics #193	25.00
❑374, Nov 1971; CB (w); CB (a); Reprints story from Walt Disney's Comics #203	25.00
❑375, Dec 1971; CB (w); CB (a); Reprints story from Walt Disney's Comics #240	25.00
❑376, Jan 1972; CB (w); CB (a); Reprints story from Walt Disney's Comics #208	25.00
❑377, Feb 1972; CB (w); CB (a); Reprints story from Walt Disney's Comics #185	25.00
❑378, Mar 1972; CB (w); CB (a); Reprints story from Walt Disney's Comics #196	25.00
❑379, Apr 1972; CB (w); CB (a); Reprints story from Walt Disney's Comics #207	25.00
❑380, May 1972; CB (w); CB (a); Reprints story from Walt Disney's Comics #211	25.00
❑381, Jun 1972; CB (w); CB (a); Reprints story from Walt Disney's Comics #202	25.00
❑382, Jul 1972; CB (w); CB (a); Reprints story from Walt Disney's Comics #213	25.00
❑383, Aug 1972; CB (w); CB (a); Reprints story from Walt Disney's Comics #215	25.00
❑384, Sep 1972; CB (w); CB (a); Reprints story from Walt Disney's Comics #177	25.00
❑385, Oct 1972; CB (w); CB (a); Reprints story from Walt Disney's Comics #187	25.00
❑386, Nov 1972; CB (w); CB (a); Reprints story from Walt Disney's Comics #209	25.00
❑387, Dec 1972; CB (w); CB (a); Reprints story from Walt Disney's Comics #205	25.00
❑388, Jan 1973; CB (w); CB (a); Reprints story from Walt Disney's Comics #136	25.00
❑389, Feb 1973; CB (w); CB (a); Reprints story from Walt Disney's Comics #253	25.00
❑390, Mar 1973; CB (w); CB (a); Reprints story from Walt Disney's Comics #239	25.00
❑391, Apr 1973; CB (w); CB (a); Reprints story from Walt Disney's Comics #137	25.00
❑392, May 1973; CB (w); CB (a); Reprints story from Walt Disney's Comics #163	25.00
❑393, Jun 1973; CB (w); CB (a); Reprints story from Walt Disney's Comics #167	25.00
❑394, Jul 1973; CB (w); CB (a); Reprints story from Walt Disney's Comics #176	25.00
❑395, Aug 1973; CB (w); CB (a); Reprints story from Walt Disney's Comics #214	25.00
❑396, Sep 1973; CB (w); CB (a); Reprints story from Walt Disney's Comics #210	25.00
❑397, Oct 1973; CB (w); CB (a); Reprints story from Walt Disney's Comics #218	25.00
❑398, Nov 1973; CB (w); CB (a); Reprints story from Walt Disney's Comics #217	25.00
❑399, Dec 1973; CB (w); CB (a); Reprints story from Walt Disney's Comics #183	25.00
❑400, Jan 1974; CB (w); CB (a); Reprints story from Walt Disney's Comics #171	25.00
❑401, Feb 1974; CB (w); CB (a); Reprints story from Walt Disney's Comics #219	14.00
❑402, Mar 1974; CB (w); CB (a); Reprints story from Walt Disney's Comics #258	14.00
❑403, Apr 1974; CB (w); CB (a); Reprints story from Walt Disney's Comics #255	14.00
❑404, May 1974; CB (w); CB (a); Reprints story from Walt Disney's Comics #223	14.00
❑405, Jun 1974; CB (w); CB (a); Reprints story from Walt Disney's Comics #259	14.00
❑406, Jul 1974; CB (w); CB (a); Reprints story from Walt Disney's Comics #191	14.00
❑407, Aug 1974; CB (w); CB (a); Reprints story from Walt Disney's Comics #221	14.00
❑408, Sep 1974; CB (w); CB (a); Reprints story from Walt Disney's Comics #229	14.00
❑409, Oct 1974; CB (w); CB (a); Reprints stories from Four Color Comics #1184 (Gyro Gearloose) and Walt Disney's Comics #249	14.00
❑410, Nov 1974; CB (w); CB (a); Reprints story from Walt Disney's Comics #216	14.00
❑411, Dec 1974; CB (w); CB (a); Reprints story from Walt Disney's Comics #254	14.00
❑412, Jan 1975; CB (w); CB (a); Reprints story from Walt Disney's Comics #220	14.00
❑413, Feb 1975; CB (w); CB (a); Reprints story from Walt Disney's Comics #294	14.00
❑414, Mar 1975; CB (w); CB (a); Reprints story from Walt Disney's Comics #269	14.00
❑415, Apr 1975; CB (w); CB (a); Reprints story from Walt Disney's Comics #265	14.00
❑416, May 1975; CB (w); CB (a); Reprints story from Walt Disney's Comics #222	14.00
❑417, Jun 1975; CB (w); CB (a); Reprints story from Walt Disney's Comics #225	14.00
❑418, Jul 1975; CB (w); CB (a); Reprints story from Walt Disney's Comics #236	14.00

	N-MINT
❑419, Aug 1975; CB (w); CB (a); Reprints story from Walt Disney's Comics #138	14.00
❑420, Sep 1975; CB (w); CB (a); Reprints story from Walt Disney's Comics #65	14.00
❑421, Oct 1975; CB (w); CB (a); Reprints story from Walt Disney's Comics #152	14.00
❑422, Nov 1975; CB (w); CB (a); Reprints story from Walt Disney's Comics #169	14.00
❑423, Dec 1975; CB (w); CB (a); Reprints story from Walt Disney's Comics #231	14.00
❑424, Jan 1976; CB (w); CB (a); Reprints story from Walt Disney's Comics #256	14.00
❑425, Feb 1976; CB (w); CB (a); Reprints story from Walt Disney's Comics #260	14.00
❑426, Mar 1976; CB (w); CB (a); Reprints story from Walt Disney's Comics #264	14.00
❑427, Apr 1976; CB (w); CB (a); Reprints story from Walt Disney's Comics #273	14.00
❑428, May 1976; CB (w); CB (a); Reprints story from Walt Disney's Comics #275	14.00
❑429, Jun 1976; CB (w); CB (a); Reprints story from Walt Disney's Comics #271	14.00
❑430, Jul 1976	10.00
❑431, Aug 1976; CB (w); CB (a); Reprints story from Walt Disney's Comics #288	12.00
❑432, Sep 1976; CB (w); CB (a); Reprints story from Walt Disney's Comics #291	12.00
❑433, Oct 1976	10.00
❑434, Nov 1976; CB (w); CB (a); Reprints story from Walt Disney's Comics #199	12.00
❑435, Dec 1976; CB (w); CB (a); Reprints story from Walt Disney's Comics #201	12.00
❑436, Jan 1977; CB (w); CB (a); Reprints story from Walt Disney's Comics #195	12.00
❑437, Feb 1977	10.00
❑438, Mar 1977	10.00
❑439, Apr 1977; CB (w); CB (a); Reprints story from Walt Disney's Comics #292	12.00
❑440, May 1977; CB (w); CB (a); Reprints story from Walt Disney's Comics #283	12.00
❑441, Jun 1977	10.00
❑442, Jul 1977; CB (w); CB (a); Reprints story from Walt Disney's Comics #312	10.00
❑443, Aug 1977; CB (w); CB (a); Reprints story from Walt Disney's Comics #297	10.00
❑444, Sep 1977	6.00
❑445, Oct 1977	6.00
❑446, Nov 1977; CB (w); CB (a); Reprints story from Walt Disney's Comics #277	10.00
❑447, Dec 1977; CB (w); CB (a); Reprints story from Walt Disney's Comics #212	10.00
❑448, Jan 1978; CB (w); CB (a); Reprints story from Walt Disney's Comics #266	10.00
❑449, Feb 1978; CB (w); CB (a); Reprints story from Walt Disney's Comics #280	10.00
❑450, Mar 1978; CB (w); CB (a); Reprints story from Walt Disney's Comics #270	10.00
❑451, Apr 1978; CB (w); CB (a); Reprints story from Walt Disney's Comics #272	10.00
❑452, May 1978; CB (w); CB (a); Reprints story from Walt Disney's Comics #274	10.00
❑453, Jun 1978; CB (w); CB (a); Reprints story from Walt Disney's Comics #206	10.00

	N-MINT
❑454, Jul 1978; CB (w); CB (a); Reprints story from Walt Disney's Comics #262	10.00
❑455, Aug 1978; CB (w); CB (a); Reprints story from Walt Disney's Comics #241	10.00
❑456, Sep 1978; CB (w); CB (a); Reprints story from Walt Disney's Comics #246	10.00
❑457, Oct 1978; CB (w); CB (a); Reprints story from Walt Disney's Comics #247	10.00
❑458, Nov 1978; CB (w); CB (a); Reprints story from Walt Disney's Comics #263	10.00
❑459, Dec 1978; CB (w); CB (a); Reprints story from Walt Disney's Comics #242	10.00
❑460, Jan 1979 CB (w); CB (a)	10.00
❑461, Feb 1979 CB (w); CB (a)	10.00
❑462, Mar 1979 CB (w); CB (a)	10.00
❑463, Apr 1979 CB (w); CB (a)	10.00
❑464, May 1979 CB (w); CB (a)	10.00
❑465, Jun 1979 CB (w); CB (a)	10.00
❑466, Jul 1979	6.00
❑467, Aug 1979 CB (w); CB (a)	10.00
❑468, Sep 1979 CB (w); CB (a)	10.00
❑469, Oct 1979 CB (w); CB (a)	10.00
❑470, Nov 1979 CB (w); CB (a)	10.00
❑471, Dec 1979 CB (w); CB (a)	10.00
❑472, Jan 1980 CB (w); CB (a)	10.00
❑473, Feb 1980 CB (w); CB (a)	10.00
❑474, Mar 1980; CB (w); CB (a); Whitman begins publishing	10.00
❑475, Apr 1980 CB (w); CB (a)	10.00
❑476, May 1980 CB (w); CB (a)	10.00
❑477, Jun 1980 CB (w); CB (a)	10.00
❑478, Jul 1980 CB (w); CB (a)	10.00
❑479, Aug 1980 CB (w); CB (a)	10.00
❑480, Sep 1980 CB (w); CB (a)	10.00
❑481, Oct 1980 CB (w); CB (a)	10.00
❑482, Nov 1980 CB (w); CB (a)	10.00
❑483, Dec 1980 CB (w); CB (a)	10.00
❑484, Jan 1981 CB (w); CB (a)	10.00
❑485, Feb 1981 CB (w); CB (a)	10.00
❑486, Mar 1981 CB (w); CB (a)	10.00
❑487 1981 CB (w); CB (a)	10.00
❑488 1981 CB (w); CB (a)	10.00
❑489 1981 CB (w); CB (a)	10.00
❑490 1981 CB (w); CB (a)	10.00
❑491, Oct 1981 CB (w); CB (a)	10.00
❑492, Nov 1981 CB (w); CB (a)	10.00
❑493, Dec 1981 CB (w); CB (a)	10.00
❑494, Jan 1981 CB (w); CB (a)	10.00
❑495, Feb 1982 CB (w); CB (a)	10.00
❑496, Feb 1982 CB (w); CB (a)	10.00
❑497, Mar 1982 CB (w); CB (a)	10.00
❑498, Apr 1982 CB (w); CB (a)	10.00
❑499, May 1982 CB (w); CB (a)	10.00
❑500, ca. 1983 CB (w); CB (a)	10.00
❑501, ca. 1983 CB (w); CB (a)	10.00
❑502, ca. 1983 CB (w); CB (a)	10.00
❑503, ca. 1983 CB (w); CB (a)	10.00
❑504, ca. 1983 CB (w); CB (a)	10.00
❑505, ca. 1983 CB (w); CB (a)	10.00
❑506, ca. 1983	10.00
❑507, ca. 1984 CB (w); CB (a)	10.00
❑508, ca. 1984 CB (w); CB (a)	10.00
❑509, ca. 1984 CB (w); CB (a)	10.00
❑510, ca. 1984 CB (w); CB (a)	10.00
❑511, ca. 1986; CB (w); CB (a); Gladstone begins publishing	15.00
❑512, Nov 1986	12.00
❑513, Dec 1986	12.00
❑514, Jan 1987	8.00
❑515, Feb 1987	8.00
❑516, Mar 1987 CB (w); CB (a)	8.00
❑517, Apr 1987	5.00
❑518, May 1987	5.00
❑519, Jun 1987 CB (w); CB (a)	14.00
❑520, Jul 1987 CB (w); CB (a)	10.00
❑521, Aug 1987 CB (w); CB, WK (a)	10.00
❑522, Sep 1987 CB (w); CB, WK (a); O: Huey, Dewey, Louie.	10.00

Near the end of its run, *Walt Disney's Comics & Stories* became a prestige-format series.

© 1996 Walt Disney Productions and Gladstone.

	N-MINT
❑523, Oct 1987; CB (w); CB, DR (a); 1st Rosa 10-page story	10.00
❑524, Nov 1987 CB (w); CB (a)	10.00
❑525, Dec 1987 CB (w); CB (a)	10.00
❑526, Jan 1988 CB (w); CB (a)	10.00
❑527, Mar 1988 CB (w); CB (a)	10.00
❑528, May 1988 CB (w); CB (a)	10.00
❑529, Jun 1988 CB (w); CB (a)	10.00
❑530, Jul 1988 CB (w); CB (a)	10.00
❑531, Aug 1988 WK (c); CB (w); CB, DR (a)	10.00
❑532, Sep 1988 CB (w); CB, DR (a)	10.00
❑533, Oct 1988 CB (w); CB (a)	10.00
❑534, Nov 1988 CB (w); CB (a)	10.00
❑535, Dec 1988 CB (w); CB (a)	10.00
❑536, Feb 1989 CB (w); CB (a)	10.00
❑537, Mar 1989; CB (w); CB (a); 1st Wm. Van Horn 10-page story	10.00
❑538, Apr 1989 WK (c); CB (w); CB (a)	10.00
❑539, Jun 1989 CB (w); CB (a)	10.00
❑540, Jul 1989 CB (w); CB (a)	10.00
❑541, Aug 1989; WK (c); CB (w); CB (a); 48 pgs.	10.00
❑542, Sep 1989 CB (w); CB (a)	10.00
❑543, Oct 1989 WK (c); CB (w); CB (a)	10.00
❑544, Nov 1989 WK (c); CB (w); CB (a)	10.00
❑545, Dec 1989 CB (w); CB (a)	10.00
❑546, Feb 1990 CB (w); CB, WK (a)	10.00
❑547, Apr 1990 CB (w); CB, DR (a)	10.00
❑548, Jun 1990; CB (w); CB (a); Disney begins publishing	10.00
❑549, Jul 1990 CB (w); CB (a)	10.00
❑550, Aug 1990; CB (w); CB (a); Milkman story	6.00
❑551, Sep 1990 CB (w); CB (a)	4.00
❑552, Oct 1990 CB (w); CB (a)	4.00
❑553, Nov 1990 CB (w); CB (a)	4.00
❑554, Dec 1990 CB (w); CB (a)	4.00
❑555, Jan 1991	3.00
❑556, Feb 1991	3.00
❑557, Mar 1991 CB (w); CB (a)	4.00
❑558, Apr 1991 CB (w); CB (a)	4.00
❑559, May 1991 CB (w); CB (a)	4.00
❑560, Jun 1991 CB (w); CB (a)	4.00
❑561, Jul 1991 CB (w); CB (a)	4.00
❑562, Aug 1991 CB (w); CB (a)	4.00
❑563, Sep 1991 CB (w); CB (a)	4.00
❑564, Oct 1991 CB (w); CB (a)	4.00
❑565, Nov 1991 CB (w); CB (a)	4.00
❑566, Dec 1991 CB (w); CB (a)	4.00
❑567, Jan 1992 CB (w); CB (a)	4.00
❑568, Feb 1992 CB (w); CB (a)	4.00
❑569, Mar 1992 CB (w); CB (a)	4.00
❑570, Apr 1992; CB (w); CB (a); Valentine centerfold	4.00
❑571, May 1992 CB (w); CB (a)	4.00
❑572, Jun 1992; CB (w); CB (a); map piece	4.00
❑573, Jul 1992; CB (w); CB (a); map piece	4.00
❑574, Aug 1992; CB (w); CB (a); map piece	5.00
❑575, Sep 1992	5.00
❑576, Oct 1992 CB (w); CB (a)	5.00
❑577, Nov 1992 CB (w); CB (a)	5.00
❑578, Dec 1992 CB (w); CB (a)	3.00
❑579, Jan 1993 CB (w); CB (a)	3.00
❑580, Feb 1993; CB (w); CB (a); strip reprint	5.00

N-MINT

❑581, Mar 1993 CB (w); CB (a) 3.00
❑582, Apr 1993 FG, WK (a) 3.00
❑583, May 1993 FG, WK (a) 3.00
❑584, Jun 1993 CB (w); CB (a) 3.00
❑585, Jul 1993 CB, FG (a) 5.00
❑586, Aug 1993 .... 3.00
❑587, Oct 1993 .... 3.00
❑588, Dec 1993 .... 3.00
❑589, Feb 1994 .... 3.00
❑590, Apr 1994 .... 3.00
❑591, Jun 1994 .... 3.00
❑592, Aug 1994 .... 3.00
❑593, Oct 1994 .... 3.00
❑594, Dec 1994 .... 3.00
❑595, Feb 1995 .... 3.00
❑596, Apr 1995 .... 3.00
❑597, Jun 1995 .... 3.00
❑598, Aug 1995 .... 4.00
❑599, Oct 1995 .... 4.00
❑600, Dec 1995; Giant-size; CB (w); CB, DR (a); reprints first Donald Duck stories by trio 6.00
❑601, Feb 1996; upgrades to prestige format 5.95
❑602, Apr 1996 .... 5.95
❑603, Jun 1996 .... 5.95
❑604, Aug 1996 .... 5.95
❑605, Oct 1996 .... 5.95
❑606, Dec 1996 .... 5.95
❑607, Jan 1996 .... 5.95
❑608, Feb 1997 .... 5.95
❑609, Mar 1997 .... 5.95
❑610, Mar 1997 .... 5.95
❑611, Apr 1997 .... 5.95
❑612, May 1997 .... 6.95
❑613, Jun 1997 .... 6.95
❑614, Jul 1997 .... 6.95
❑615, Aug 1997 .... 6.95
❑616, Sep 1997 .... 6.95
❑617, Oct 1997 .... 6.95
❑618, Nov 1997 .... 6.95
❑619, Dec 1997; Pinocchio features . 6.95
❑620, Jan 1998 .... 6.95
❑621, Feb 1998 .... 6.95
❑622, Mar 1998 .... 6.95
❑623, Apr 1998 .... 6.95
❑624, May 1998 .... 6.95
❑625, Jun 1998 .... 6.95
❑626, Jul 1998 .... 6.95
❑627, Aug 1998 .... 6.95
❑628, Sep 1998 .... 6.95
❑629, Oct 1998 .... 6.95
❑630, Nov 1998 .... 6.95
❑631, Dec 1998 .... 6.95
❑632, Jan 1999 .... 6.95
❑633, Feb 1999 .... 6.95
❑634, Jul 2003 .... 6.95

WALT DISNEY'S COMICS & STORIES (GEMSTONE)
GEMSTONE

❑634, Jun 2003 .... 6.95
❑635, Jul 2003 .... 6.95
❑636, Aug 2003 .... 6.95
❑637, Sep 2003 .... 6.95
❑638, Oct 2003 .... 6.95
❑639, Nov 2003 .... 6.95
❑640, Dec 2003 .... 6.95
❑641, Jan 2004 .... 6.95
❑642, Feb 2004 .... 6.95
❑643, Mar 2004 .... 6.95
❑644, Apr 2004 .... 6.95
❑645, May 2004 .... 6.95
❑646, Jun 2004 .... 6.95

WALT DISNEY'S COMICS AND STORIES PENNY PINCHER
GLADSTONE

❑1, May 1997 CB (a) 1.00
❑2, Jun 1997; CB (a); reprints Barks' Feud and Far Between 1.00
❑3, Jul 1997 .... 1.00
❑4, Aug 1997 .... 1.00

N-MINT

WALT DISNEY'S COMICS DIGEST
GLADSTONE

❑1, Dec 1986; CB, WK (a); Reprints story from Uncle Scrooge #5 .... 6.00
❑2 1987; CB (a); Reprints story from Uncle Scrooge #29 .... 4.00
❑3, Mar 1987; CB (a); Reprints story from Uncle Scrooge #31 .... 4.00
❑4, Apr 1987; CB (a); Reprints stories from Donald Duck #60 and Picnic Party #8 .... 4.00
❑5, May 1987; CB (a); Reprints story from Uncle Scrooge #23 .... 4.00
❑6, Jun 1987; CB (a); Reprints story from Uncle Scrooge #24 .... 4.00
❑7, Jul 1987; CB (a); Reprints stories from Four Color Comics #1025 (Vacation in Disneyland) 4.00

WALT DISNEY'S HOLIDAY PARADE
DISNEY

❑1 .... 2.95
❑2 .... 2.95

WALT DISNEY SHOWCASE
GOLD KEY

❑1, Oct 1970; Boatniks 16.00
❑2, Jan 1971; Moby Duck 10.00
❑3, Apr 1971; Bongo & Lumpjaw 9.00
❑4, Jul 1971; Pluto 9.00
❑5, Oct 1971; $1,000,000 Duck 12.00
❑6, Jan 1972; Bedknobs & Broomsticks 12.00
❑7, Apr 1972; Pluto 9.00
❑8, Jun 1972; Daisy and Donald; Goofy and Clarabelle 9.00
❑9, Aug 1972; 101 Dalmatians 10.00
❑10, Sep 1972; DS (a); Napoleon and Samantha movie adaptation 12.00
❑11, Oct 1972; Moby Duck 8.00
❑12, Dec 1972; Dumbo 8.00
❑13, Feb 1973; Pluto 8.00
❑14, Apr 1973; The World's Greatest Athlete (movie adaptation) 12.00
❑15, Jun 1973; Three Little Pigs 8.00
❑16, Jul 1973; Aristocats movie adaptation reprint 12.00
❑17, Aug 1973; Mary Poppins movie adaptation reprint 12.00
❑18, Oct 1973; Gyro Gearloose; reprints stories from Four Color Comics #1047 and 1184 (Gyro Gearloose) 12.00
❑19, Dec 1973; That Darn Cat (move adaptation) 10.00
❑20, Feb 1974; Pluto 9.00
❑21, Apr 1974; Li'l Bad Wolf and the Three Little Pigs 8.00
❑22, Jun 1974; Alice in Wonderland .. 8.00
❑23, Jul 1974; Pluto 8.00
❑24, Aug 1974; Herbie Rides Again ... 7.00
❑25, Oct 1974; Old Yeller 7.00
❑26, Dec 1974; Lt. Robin Crusoe, USN 7.00
❑27, Feb 1975; Island at the Top of the World 7.00
❑28, Apr 1975 .... 7.00
❑29, Jun 1975; Escape to Witch Mountain 7.00
❑30, Jul 1975; Magica De Spell; reprints stories from Uncles Scrooge #36 and Walt Disney's Comics #258 .... 15.00
❑31, Aug 1975; Bambi 9.00
❑32, Oct 1975; Spin and Marty 9.00
❑33, Jan 1976; Pluto 7.00
❑34, May 1976; Paul Revere's Ride .. 7.00
❑35, Aug 1976 .... 7.00
❑36, Sep 1976 .... 7.00
❑37, Nov 1976 .... 7.00
❑38, Apr 1977; Mickey and The Sleuth 7.00
❑39, Jul 1977; Mickey and The Sleuth 7.00
❑40, Sep 1977; The Rescuers (movie adaptation) 8.00
❑41, Oct 1977; Herbie Goes to Monte Carlo (movie adaptation) 8.00
❑42, Jan 1978; Mickey and The Sleuth 7.00
❑43, Apr 1978; Pete's Dragon (movie adaptation) 12.00

N-MINT

❑44, May 1978; Return From Witch Mountain (movie adaptation); Castaways 7.00
❑45, Aug 1978 .... 7.00
❑46, Oct 1978; The Cat From Outer Space 7.00
❑47, Nov 1978; Mickey Mouse Surprise Party 7.00
❑48, Jan 1979; The Wonderful Adventures of Pinocchio; The Small One . 7.00
❑49, Mar 1979; The North Avenue Irregulars (Movie adaptation); Zorro double feature 7.00
❑50, May 1979; Bedknobs & Broomsticks reprint 7.00
❑51, Jul 1979; 101 Dalmatians 7.00
❑52, Sep 1979; Unidentified Flying Oddball 7.00
❑53, Nov 1979; The Scarecrow of Romney Marsh 7.00
❑54, Jan 1980; The Black Hole 7.00

WALT DISNEY'S SPRING FEVER
DISNEY

❑1, Spr 1991 .... 2.95

WALT DISNEY'S SUMMER FUN
DISNEY

❑1 .... 2.95

WALTER
DARK HORSE

❑1, Feb 1996 .... 2.50
❑2, Mar 1996 .... 2.50
❑3, Apr 1996 .... 2.50
❑4, May 1996 .... 2.50

WALTER KITTY IN... THE HOLLOW EARTH
VISION

❑1, Jul 1996 .... 1.95
❑2, Jul 1996 .... 1.95

WALT THE WILDCAT
MOTION COMICS

❑1, Sep 1995 .... 2.50

WANDA LUWAND & THE PIRATE GIRLS
FANTAGRAPHICS / EROS

❑1, b&w 2.50

WANDERERS, THE
DC

❑1, Jun 1988 O: Aviax. O: The Wanderers. O: The Elvar. O: Re-Animage. 1: Aviax. 1: The Wanderers. 1: The Elvar. 1: Re-Animage. 1.50
❑2, Jul 1988 .... 1.50
❑3, Aug 1988 .... 1.50
❑4, Sep 1988 .... 1.50
❑5, Oct 1988 .... 1.50
❑6, Nov 1988 .... 1.50
❑7, Dec 1988 .... 1.50
❑8, Dec 1988 .... 1.50
❑9, Jan 1989 .... 1.50
❑10, Jan 1989 .... 1.50
❑11, Feb 1989 .... 1.50
❑12, Mar 1989 .... 1.50
❑13, Apr 1989 .... 1.50

WANDERING STAR
PEN AND INK

❑1, ca. 1993, b&w 8.00
❑1-2, Feb 1994 .... 4.00
❑2-2, May 1994 .... 2.00
❑1-3 .... 3.00
❑3-2, May 1994 .... 2.00
❑4-2, May 1994 .... 2.00
❑2, ca. 1993, b&w 5.00
❑5-2, May 1994 .... 2.00
❑3, ca. 1993, b&w 4.00
❑4, ca. 1993, b&w 4.00
❑5, Jan 1994, b&w 4.00
❑6, Mar 1994, b&w 3.00
❑7, Jun 1994, b&w 3.00
❑8, Oct 1994, b&w D: Graikor. 3.00
❑9, Aug 1995, b&w 3.00
❑10, Oct 1995, b&w 3.00

N-MINT

❑11, Jan 1995, b&w 2.50
❑12 1996, b&w 2.50
❑13, Jun 1996, b&w 2.50
❑14 1996, b&w 2.50
❑15 1996, b&w 2.50
❑16 1996, b&w 2.50
❑17 1996, b&w 2.50
❑18 1996, b&w 2.50
❑19, b&w 2.50
❑20, b&w 2.50
❑21 1997, b&w 2.50

WANDERING STARS
FANTAGRAPHICS

❑1 .... 2.00

WANTED (CELEBRITY)
CELEBRITY

❑1 .... 0.75
❑2 .... 0.75
❑3 .... 0.75
❑4 .... 0.75
❑5, Dec 1989 .... 0.75

WANTED
IMAGE

❑1, Dec 2003 .... 12.00
❑1/A, Dec 2003 .... 8.00
❑1/B, Dec 2003 .... 8.00
❑1/C, Apr 2004 .... 2.99
❑1/D, Apr 2004; Wizard World 5.00
❑1/E, Apr 2004; Death Row Edition ... 2.99
❑2, Jan 2004 .... 2.99
❑2/B, Apr 2004 .... 2.99
❑2/C, May 2004, Death Row Edition . 2.99
❑3, Apr 2004 .... 2.99
❑3/A, Apr 2004; Death Row Edition ... 2.99
❑4, Aug 2004 .... 2.99

WANTED: DOSSIER ONE-SHOT
IMAGE

❑1, Apr 2004 .... 2.99

WANTED, THE WORLD'S MOST DANGEROUS VILLAINS
DC

❑1, Aug 1972; reprints stories from Batman #112, World's Finest #111, and Green Lantern #1 .... 10.00
❑2, Oct 1972; reprints stories from Batman #25 and Flash #121 .... 8.00
❑3, Nov 1972; reprints stories from Action #69, More Fun #65, and Flash #100 .... 8.00
❑4, Dec 1972; 1: Solomon Grundy. reprints stories from All-American #61 and Kid Eternity #15 .... 6.00
❑5, Jan 1973; reprints stories from Green Lantern #33 and Doll Man #15 6.00
❑6, Feb 1973; reprints stories from Adventure #77 and Sensation Comics #66 and 71 .... 6.00
❑7, Apr 1973; reprints stories from More Fun #76, Flash #90, and Adventure #72 .... 6.00
❑8, Jul 1973; reprints stories from Flash #114 and More Fun #73 .... 6.00
❑9, Sep 1973; CS (a); reprints stories from Action #57 and World's Finest Comics #6 .... 6.00

WAR, THE
MARVEL

❑1, Jun 1989; Series continued from story in "The Draft" 3.50
❑2, Jul 1989 .... 3.50
❑3, Aug 1989 .... 3.50
❑4, Feb 1990 .... 3.50

WAR AGAINST CRIME (GEMSTONE)
GEMSTONE

❑1, Apr 2000; Reprints War Against Crime #1 .... 2.50
❑2, May 2000; Reprints War Against Crime #2 .... 2.50
❑3, Jun 2000; Reprints War Against Crime #3 .... 2.50
❑4, Jul 2000; Reprints War Against Crime #4 .... 2.50

N-MINT

❑5, Aug 2000; Reprints War Against Crime #5 .... 2.50
❑Annual 1, ca. 2000; Collects issues #1-5 .... 13.50

WARBLADE: ENDANGERED SPECIES
IMAGE

❑1, Jan 1995; Tri-fold cover 2.50
❑2, Feb 1995 .... 2.50
❑3, Mar 1995 .... 2.50
❑4, Apr 1995 .... 2.50

WARCAT
COCONUT

❑Ashcan 1, Oct 1997, b&w; preview of issues #1 and 2; no indicia 2.95
❑Special 1 .... 2.95

WARCHILD
MAXIMUM

❑1/A, Dec 1994; Warchild charging on cover 2.50
❑1/B, Dec 1994; Variant cover with Warchild standing, red background 2.50
❑2/A, Jan 1995; Warchild and woman on cover 2.50
❑2/B, Jan 1995; Warchild alone on cover 2.50
❑3/A, Jun 1995; Warchild crouching on cover 2.50
❑3/B, Jun 1995; Warchild standing on cover, white background 2.50
❑3/C, Jun 1995; Warchild standing on cover, red background 2.50
❑4, Aug 1995 .... 2.50

WAR CRIMINALS
COMIC ZONE

❑1, b&w 2.95

WARCRY
IMAGE

❑1 .... 2.50

WAR DANCER
DEFIANT

❑1, Feb 1994 1: War Dancer. 2.50
❑2, Mar 1994 .... 2.50
❑3, Apr 1994 .... 2.50
❑4, May 1994; Giant-size O: War Dancer. A: Charlemagne. 3.25
❑5, Jun 1994 .... 2.50
❑6, Jul 1994 .... 2.50

WARHAMMER MONTHLY
GAMES WORKSHOP

❑0, Feb 1998 .... 1.00
❑1, Mar 1998 .... 2.95
❑2, Apr 1998 .... 2.95
❑3, May 1998 .... 2.95
❑4, Jun 1998 .... 2.95
❑5, Jul 1998 .... 2.95
❑6, Aug 1998 .... 2.95
❑7, Sep 1998 .... 2.95
❑8, Oct 1998 .... 2.95
❑9, Nov 1998 .... 2.95
❑10, Dec 1998 .... 2.95
❑11, Jan 1999 .... 2.95
❑12, Feb 1999 .... 2.95
❑13, Mar 1999 .... 2.95
❑14, Apr 1999 .... 2.95
❑15, May 1999 .... 2.95
❑16, Jun 1999 .... 2.95
❑17, Jul 1999 .... 2.95
❑18, Aug 1999 .... 2.95
❑19, Sep 1999 .... 2.95
❑20, Oct 1999 .... 2.95
❑21, Nov 1999 .... 2.95
❑22, Dec 1999 .... 2.95
❑23, Jan 2000 .... 2.95
❑24, Feb 2000 .... 2.95
❑25, Mar 2000 .... 2.95
❑26, Apr 2000 .... 2.95
❑27, May 2000 .... 2.95
❑28, Jun 2000 .... 2.95
❑29, Jul 2000 .... 2.95
❑30, Aug 2000 .... 2.95
❑31, Sep 2000 .... 2.95

Walt Disney Showcase adapted Disney movies and provided a home for lesser-known Disney characters.

© 1972 Walt Disney Productions and Gold Key.

N-MINT

❑32, Oct 2000 .... 2.95
❑33, Nov 2000 .... 2.95
❑34, Dec 2000 .... 2.95
❑35, Jan 2001 .... 2.95
❑36, Feb 2001 .... 2.95
❑37, Mar 2001 .... 2.95
❑38, Apr 2001 .... 2.95
❑39, May 2001 .... 2.95
❑40, Jun 2001 .... 2.95
❑41, Jul 2001 .... 2.95
❑42, Aug 2001 .... 2.95
❑43, Sep 2001 .... 2.95
❑44, Oct 2001 .... 2.95
❑45, Nov 2001 .... 2.95
❑46, Dec 2001 .... 2.95
❑47, Jan 2002 .... 2.95
❑48, Feb 2002 .... 2.95
❑49, Mar 2002 .... 2.95
❑50, Apr 2002 .... 2.95
❑51, May 2002 .... 2.95
❑52, Jun 2002 .... 3.50
❑53, Jul 2002 .... 3.50
❑54, Aug 2002 .... 3.50
❑55, Sep 2002 .... 3.50
❑56, Oct 2002 .... 3.50
❑57, Nov 2002 .... 3.50
❑58, Dec 2002 .... 3.50
❑59, ca. 2003 .... 3.50
❑60, ca. 2003 .... 3.50
❑61, ca. 2003 .... 3.50
❑62, ca. 2003 .... 3.50
❑63, ca. 2003 .... 3.50
❑64, ca. 2003 .... 3.50
❑65, ca. 2003 .... 3.50
❑66, ca. 2003 .... 3.50
❑67, ca. 2003 .... 3.50
❑68, ca. 2003 .... 3.50
❑69, ca. 2003 .... 3.50
❑70, ca. 2003 .... 3.50
❑71, Aug 2003 .... 3.50
❑72, Sep 2003 .... 3.50
❑73, Oct 2003 .... 3.50
❑74, Nov 2003 .... 3.50
❑75, Nov 2003 .... 3.50
❑76, Hol 2004 .... 3.50
❑77, Feb 2004 .... 3.50

WARHAWKS COMICS MODULE
TSR

❑1, ca. 1990 .... 2.95
❑2, ca. 1990 .... 2.95
❑3, ca. 1990 .... 2.95
❑4, ca. 1990 .... 2.95
❑5, ca. 1990; Warhawks 2050 .... 2.95
❑6, ca. 1990; Warhawks 2050 .... 2.95
❑7, ca. 1990; Warhawks 2050 .... 2.95
❑8, ca. 1990; Warhawks 2050 .... 2.95
❑9, ca. 1990; Warhawks 2050 .... 2.95

WARHEADS
MARVEL

❑1, Jun 1992; Wolverine 1.75
❑2, Jul 1992 .... 1.75
❑3, Aug 1992 .... 1.75
❑4, Sep 1992 .... 1.75
❑5, Oct 1992 .... 1.75
❑6, Nov 1992; Death's Head II cameo 1.75
❑7, Dec 1992 .... 1.75
❑8, Jan 1993 .... 1.75

N-MINT

❑9, Feb 1993 ..... 1.75
❑10, Apr 1993 ..... 1.75
❑11, May 1993; MyS-TECH Wars Crossover 1.75
❑12, Jun 1993 ..... 1.75
❑13, Jul 1993 ..... 1.75
❑14, Aug 1993 ..... 1.75

WARHEADS: BLACK DAWN
MARVEL

❑1, Jul 1993; foil cover 2.95
❑2 1993 ..... 2.95

WAR HEROES CLASSICS
RECOLLECTIONS

❑1, b&w 2.00

WAR IS HELL
MARVEL

❑1, Jan 1973 AW (a) 15.00
❑2, Mar 1973 ..... 10.00
❑3, May 1973 ..... 10.00
❑4, Jul 1973 ..... 10.00
❑5, Sep 1973 ..... 10.00
❑6, Nov 1973 ..... 8.00
❑7, Jun 1974; SL (w); A: Sgt. Fury. Reprints Sgt. Fury #17 ..... 8.00
❑8, Aug 1974 A: Sgt. Fury. 8.00
❑9, Oct 1974 ..... 6.00
❑10, Dec 1974 ..... 6.00
❑11, Feb 1975; Marvel Value Stamp #5: Dracula 6.00
❑12, Apr 1975 ..... 6.00
❑13, Jun 1975; Marvel Value Stamp #23: Sgt. Fury 6.00
❑14, Aug 1975 ..... 6.00
❑15, Oct 1975 ..... 6.00

WARLANDS
IMAGE

❑1, Aug 1999 ..... 3.00
❑1/A, Aug 1999; alternate cover 3.00
❑1/B, Aug 1999; alternate cover 3.00
❑2, Sep 1999 ..... 2.50
❑2/A, Sep 1999; alternate cover 2.50
❑3, Nov 1999 ..... 2.50
❑4 2000 ..... 2.50
❑5, Mar 2000 ..... 2.50
❑6 2000 ..... 2.50
❑7, Jun 2000 ..... 2.50
❑8, Jul 2000 ..... 2.50
❑9, Aug 2000 ..... 2.50
❑10, Oct 2000 ..... 2.50
❑11, Nov 2000 ..... 2.50
❑12, Feb 2001 ..... 2.50
❑Deluxe 1; Darklyte 14.95

WARLANDS: DARK TIDE RISING
DREAMWAVE

❑1, Dec 2002 ..... 2.95
❑2, Jan 2003 ..... 2.95
❑3, Feb 2003 ..... 2.95
❑4, Mar 2003 ..... 2.95
❑5, Apr 2003 ..... 2.95
❑6, May 2003 ..... 2.95

WARLANDS EPILOGUE: THREE STORIES
IMAGE

❑1, Mar 2001 ..... 5.95

WARLANDS: THE AGE OF ICE
DREAMWAVE

❑0, Feb 2002 ..... 2.25
❑1, Jul 2001 ..... 2.95
❑2/A, Sep 2001; Brown logo on cover; Flip-book with Warlands: Banished Knights preview 2.95
❑2/B 2.95
❑3, Oct 2001 ..... 2.95

WARLASH
CFD

❑1, Apr 1995 ..... 2.95

N-MINT

WARLOCK (1ST SERIES)
MARVEL

❑1, Aug 1972 GK (c); GK (a); O: Warlock. 15.00
❑2, Oct 1972 ..... 8.00
❑3, Dec 1972 ..... 5.00
❑4, Feb 1973 GK (a) 5.00
❑5, Apr 1973 ..... 5.00
❑6, Jun 1973 ..... 5.00
❑7, Aug 1973 ..... 5.00
❑8, Oct 1973 ..... 5.00
❑9, Oct 1975 JSn (a); A: Thanos. 5.00
❑10, Dec 1975; JSn (a); O: Thanos. Part 1 ..... 10.00
❑11, Feb 1976; JSn (a); A: Thanos. Part 2 ..... 10.00
❑12, Apr 1976 JSn (a) 8.00
❑12/30 cent, Apr 1976; 30 cent regional price variant 15.00
❑13, Jun 1976 JSn (a) 8.00
❑13/30 cent, Jun 1976; 30 cent regional price variant 15.00
❑14, Aug 1976 JSn (a) 8.00
❑14/30 cent, Aug 1976; 30 cent regional price variant 15.00
❑15, Nov 1976 JSn (a); A: Thanos. 8.00

WARLOCK (2ND SERIES)
MARVEL

❑1, Dec 1982 JSn (a) 3.50
❑2, Jan 1983; JSn (a); Reprints Strange Tales #181, Warlock (1st Series) #9 ..... 3.00
❑3, Feb 1983 JSn (a) 3.00
❑4, Mar 1983 JSn (a) 3.00
❑5, Apr 1983 JSn, JBy (a) 3.00
❑6, May 1983 JSn (a) 3.00
❑Special 1, Dec 1982 ..... 2.50

WARLOCK (3RD SERIES)
MARVEL

❑1, May 1992; Reprints Warlock (2nd Series) #1 ..... 2.50
❑2, Jun 1992; Reprints Warlock (2nd Series) #2 ..... 2.50
❑3, Jul 1992 ..... 2.50
❑4, Aug 1992; Reprints Warlock (2nd Series) #4 ..... 2.50
❑5, Sep 1992 ..... 2.50
❑6, Oct 1992; Reprints Warlock (2nd Series) #6 ..... 2.50

WARLOCK (4TH SERIES)
MARVEL

❑1, Nov 1998; gatefold summary 3.00
❑2, Dec 1998; gatefold summary V: Captain Marvel. 3.00
❑3, Jan 1999; gatefold summary V: Drax. 3.00
❑4, Feb 1999 A: Syphonn. A: Blastaar. A: Annihilus. 3.00

WARLOCK (5TH SERIES)
MARVEL

❑1, Oct 1999 ..... 2.00
❑2, Nov 1999 ..... 1.99
❑3, Nov 1999 ..... 1.99
❑4, Dec 1999 ..... 1.99

WARLOCK AND THE INFINITY WATCH
MARVEL

❑1, Feb 1992; JSn (w); follows events of The Infinity Gauntlet 2.50
❑2, Mar 1992 JSn (w) 2.00
❑3, Apr 1992 JSn (w); A: High Evolutionary. 2.00
❑4, May 1992 JSn (w) 2.00
❑5, Jun 1992 JSn (w) 2.00
❑6, Jul 1992 JSn (w) 2.00
❑7, Aug 1992 JSn (w) 2.00
❑8, Sep 1992 JSn (w) 2.00
❑9, Oct 1992; JSn (w); O: Gamora. Infinity War 2.00
❑10, Nov 1992 JSn (w) 2.00
❑11, Dec 1992 JSn (w) 1.75
❑12, Jan 1993 ..... 1.75
❑13, Feb 1993 ..... 1.75
❑14, Mar 1993 ..... 1.75
❑15, Apr 1993 ..... 1.75
❑16, May 1993 ..... 1.75

N-MINT

❑17, Jun 1993 ..... 1.75
❑18, Jul 1993 ..... 1.75
❑19, Aug 1993 ..... 1.75
❑20, Sep 1993; A: Drax the Destroyer. A: Thor. A: Goddess. Infinity Crusade crossover 1.75
❑21, Oct 1993; JSn (w); A: Drax the Destroyer. A: Thor. A: Goddess. Infinity Crusade crossover 1.75
❑22, Nov 1993; A: Drax the Destroyer. A: Thor. A: Goddess. Infinity Crusade crossover 1.75
❑23, Dec 1993 ..... 1.75
❑24, Jan 1994 ..... 1.75
❑25, Feb 1994; diecut cover 2.95
❑26, Mar 1994 ..... 1.75
❑27, Apr 1994 ..... 1.75
❑28, May 1994 ..... 1.75
❑29, Jun 1994 ..... 1.95
❑30, Jul 1994 ..... 1.95
❑31, Aug 1994 ..... 1.95
❑32, Sep 1994 ..... 1.95
❑33, Oct 1994 ..... 1.95
❑34, Nov 1994 ..... 1.95
❑35, Dec 1994 ..... 1.95
❑36, Jan 1995 ..... 1.95
❑37, Feb 1995 ..... 1.95
❑38, Mar 1995 ..... 1.95
❑39, Apr 1995 ..... 1.95
❑40, May 1995 ..... 1.95
❑41, Jun 1995 ..... 1.95
❑42, Jul 1995 ..... 1.95

WARLOCK CHRONICLES
MARVEL

❑1, Jul 1993; Prism cover 2.95
❑2, Aug 1993; Infinity Crusade crossover 2.00
❑3, Sep 1993; Infinity Crusade crossover 2.00
❑4, Oct 1993; Infinity Crusade crossover 2.00
❑5, Nov 1993; Infinity Crusade crossover 2.00
❑6, Dec 1993 ..... 2.00
❑7, Jan 1994 ..... 2.00
❑8, Feb 1994 ..... 2.00

WARLOCK 5
AIRCEL

❑1 1986, b&w 2.00
❑2 1986, b&w 2.00
❑3, Jan 1987, b&w 2.00
❑4, Mar 1987, b&w 2.00
❑5, Apr 1987; robot skull cover 2.00
❑6 1987; woman's face on cover 2.00
❑7 1987 ..... 2.00
❑8 1987 ..... 2.00
❑9 1987 ..... 2.00
❑10 1987 ..... 2.00
❑11 1987 ..... 2.00
❑12, Dec 1987 ..... 2.00
❑13, Feb 1988 ..... 2.00
❑14, Mar 1988 ..... 2.00
❑15 1988 ..... 2.00
❑16 1988 ..... 2.00
❑17 1988 ..... 2.00
❑18 1988 ..... 2.00
❑19 1988 ..... 2.00
❑20, Dec 1988 ..... 2.00
❑21, Jan 1989 ..... 2.00
❑22, Feb 1989 ..... 2.00

WARLOCK 5 (SIRIUS)
SIRIUS

❑1, Jan 1998 ..... 2.50
❑2, Feb 1998 ..... 2.50
❑3, Mar 1998 ..... 2.50
❑4, Apr 1998 ..... 2.50

WARLOCK 5 BOOK II
AIRCEL

❑1 1989, b&w 2.00
❑2 1989, b&w 2.00
❑3 1989, b&w 2.00
❑4 1989, b&w 2.00

	N-MINT
❑5 1989, b&w	2.00
❑6 1989, b&w	2.00
❑7 1989, b&w	2.00

WARLOCKS
AIRCEL

	N-MINT
❑1 1988, b&w	2.00
❑2 1988, b&w	2.00
❑3 1988, b&w	2.00
❑4 1988, b&w	2.00
❑5 1988, b&w	2.00
❑6, Dec 1988, b&w	2.00
❑7, Jan 1989, b&w	2.00
❑8 1989, b&w	2.00
❑9 1989, b&w	2.00
❑10, b&w	2.00
❑11, Mar 1990, b&w	2.00
❑12, b&w	2.00
❑Special 1, b&w	2.25

WARLORD
DC

	N-MINT
❑1, Feb 1976 MGr (a); O: Warlord.	8.00
❑2, Apr 1976 MGr (a); 1: Machiste.	4.00
❑3, Nov 1976 MGr (a)	3.00
❑4, Jan 1977 MGr (a)	3.00
❑5, Mar 1977 MGr (a); 1: Dragonsword.	3.00
❑6, May 1977 MGr (a); 1: Mariah Romanola.	3.00
❑7, Jul 1977 MGr (a); O: Machiste.	2.00
❑8, Sep 1977 MGr (a)	2.00
❑9, Nov 1977 MGr (a)	2.00
❑10, Jan 1978; MGr (a); Deimos	2.00
❑11, Mar 1978; MGr (a); reprints 1st Issue Special	1.50
❑12, May 1978 MGr (a); 1: Aton.	1.50
❑13, Jul 1978 MGr (a)	1.50
❑14, Sep 1978 MGr (a)	1.50
❑15, Nov 1978 MGr (a); 1: Joshua Morgan (Warlord's son).	1.50
❑16, Dec 1978 MGr (a)	1.50
❑17, Jan 1979 MGr (a)	1.50
❑18, Feb 1979 MGr (a)	1.50
❑19, Mar 1979 MGr (a)	1.50
❑20, Apr 1979 MGr (a)	1.50
❑21, May 1979 MGr (a)	1.50
❑22, Jun 1979 MGr (a)	1.50
❑23, Jul 1979 MGr (a)	1.50
❑24, Aug 1979 MGr (a)	1.50
❑25, Sep 1979 MGr (a)	1.50
❑26, Oct 1979 MGr (a)	1.50
❑27, Nov 1979 MGr (a)	1.50
❑28, Dec 1979 MGr (a); 1: Mongo Ironhand. 1: Wizard World.	1.50
❑29, Jan 1980 MGr (a)	1.50
❑30, Feb 1980 MGr (a)	1.00
❑31, Mar 1980 MGr (a)	1.00
❑32, Apr 1980 MGr (a); 1: Shakira.	1.00
❑33, May 1980 MGr (a)	1.00
❑34, Jun 1980 MGr (a)	1.00
❑35, Jul 1980 MGr (a)	1.00
❑36, Aug 1980 MGr (a)	1.00
❑37, Sep 1980; MGr (a); O: Omac (new origin). Omac back-up	1.00
❑38, Oct 1980; MGr (a); 1: Jennifer Morgan (Warlord's daughter). Omac back-up	1.00
❑39, Nov 1980; MGr (a); Omac back-up	1.00
❑40, Dec 1980 MGr (a)	1.00
❑41, Jan 1981 MGr (a)	1.00
❑42, Feb 1981 MGr (a); A: Omac.	1.00
❑43, Mar 1981 MGr (a); A: Omac.	1.00
❑44, Apr 1981 MGr (a)	1.00
❑45, May 1981 MGr (a)	1.00
❑46, Jun 1981 MGr (a)	1.00
❑47, Jul 1981; MGr (a); 1: Rostov. Omac back-up	1.00
❑48, Aug 1981; Giant-size MGr, EC (a); 1: Arak. 1: Claw the Unconquered.	1.50
❑49, Sep 1981; MGr (a); 1: The Evil One. Claw back-up	1.00
❑50, Oct 1981 MGr (a)	1.00
❑51, Nov 1981; MGr (a); reprints Warlord #1; Dragonsword back-up	1.00
❑52, Dec 1981; MGr (a); Dragonsword back-up	1.00
❑53, Jan 1982; Dragonsword back-up	1.00
❑54, Feb 1982	1.00
❑55, Mar 1982; MGr (c); 1: Lady Chian. 1: Arion. Arion back-up	1.00
❑56, Apr 1982; MGr (c); Arion back-up	1.00
❑57, May 1982; MGr (c); Arion back-up	1.00
❑58, Jun 1982; MGr (c); Arion back-up	1.00
❑59, Jul 1982; MGr (c); 1: Garn Daanuth. Arion back-up	1.00
❑60, Aug 1982; MGr (c); Arion back-up	1.00
❑61, Sep 1982; MGr (c); Arion back-up	1.00
❑62, Oct 1982; MGr (c); Arion back-up	1.00
❑63, Nov 1982; MGr (c); 1: Conqueror of the Barren Earth. Arion back-up	1.00
❑64, Dec 1982; Barren Earth back-up; Masters of the Universe preview	1.00
❑65, Jan 1983	1.00
❑66, Feb 1983	1.00
❑67, Mar 1983	1.00
❑68, Apr 1983	1.00
❑69, May 1983	1.00
❑70, Jun 1983	1.00
❑71, Jul 1983	1.00
❑72, Aug 1983	1.00
❑73, Sep 1983	1.00
❑74, Oct 1983	1.00
❑75, Nov 1983	1.00
❑76, Dec 1983	1.00
❑77, Jan 1984	1.00
❑78, Feb 1984	1.00
❑79, Mar 1984	1.00
❑80, Apr 1984	1.00
❑81, May 1984	1.00
❑82, Jun 1984	1.00
❑83, Jul 1984	1.00
❑84, Aug 1984	1.00
❑85, Sep 1984	1.00
❑86, Oct 1984	1.00
❑87, Nov 1984	1.00
❑88, Dec 1984	1.00
❑89, Jan 1985	1.00
❑90, Feb 1985	1.00
❑91, Mar 1985 O: Travis Morgan. O: Warlord.	1.00
❑92, Apr 1985	1.00
❑93, May 1985	1.00
❑94, Jun 1985	1.00
❑95, Jul 1985	1.00
❑96, Aug 1985	1.00
❑97, Sep 1985	1.00
❑98, Oct 1985	1.00
❑99, Nov 1985	1.00
❑100, Dec 1985; Giant-size MGr (c)	1.00
❑101, Jan 1986 MGr (c)	1.00
❑102, Feb 1986 MGr (c)	1.00
❑103, Mar 1986 MGr (c)	1.00
❑104, Apr 1986 MGr (c)	1.00
❑105, May 1986	1.00
❑106, Jun 1986	1.00
❑107, Jul 1986	1.00
❑108, Aug 1986	1.00
❑109, Sep 1986	1.00
❑110, Oct 1986	1.00
❑111, Nov 1986	1.00
❑112, Dec 1986 MGr (c)	1.00
❑113, Jan 1987	1.00
❑114, Feb 1987; Legends	1.00
❑115, Mar 1987; Legends	1.00
❑116, Apr 1987	1.00
❑117, May 1987 MGr (c)	1.00
❑118, Jun 1987	1.00
❑119, Jul 1987	1.00
❑120, Aug 1987	1.00
❑121, Sep 1987	1.00
❑122, Oct 1987	1.00
❑123, Nov 1987	1.00
❑124, Dec 1987	1.00
❑125, Jan 1988 D: Tara.	1.00
❑126, Feb 1988	1.00
❑127, Mar 1988	1.00

Following an introductory trading-card set, *Warriors of Plasm* #1 was Defiant's first comic book.
© 1993 Defiant Comics.

	N-MINT
❑128, Apr 1988	1.00
❑129, May 1988	1.00
❑130, Jul 1988	1.00
❑131, Sep 1988; RL (a); Bonus Book #6; Rob Liefeld's first work at DC	2.00
❑132, Nov 1988	1.00
❑133, Dec 1988; Giant-size JDu (a)	1.50
❑Annual 1, ca. 1982 MGr (a)	2.00
❑Annual 2, ca. 1983	1.00
❑Annual 3, ca. 1984	1.00
❑Annual 4, ca. 1985	1.00
❑Annual 5, ca. 1986	1.00
❑Annual 6, ca. 1987	1.00

WARLORD (MINI-SERIES)
DC

	N-MINT
❑1, Jan 1992 MGr (c)	2.00
❑2, Feb 1992 MGr (c); MGr (w)	2.00
❑3, Mar 1992 MGr (c); MGr (w)	2.00
❑4, Apr 1992 MGr (c)	2.00
❑5, May 1992 MGr (c)	2.00
❑6, Jun 1992 MGr (c)	2.00

WAR MACHINE
MARVEL

	N-MINT
❑1, Apr 1994; Giant-size; newsstand	2.00
❑1/Variant, Apr 1994; Giant-size; Embossed cover	2.95
❑2, May 1994	1.50
❑3, Jun 1994	1.50
❑4, Jul 1994	1.50
❑5, Aug 1994	1.50
❑6, Sep 1994	1.50
❑7, Oct 1994	1.50
❑8, Nov 1994	1.50
❑8/CS, Nov 1994; polybagged with 16-page Marvel Action Hour preview, acetate print, coupon, sweepstakes entry form	2.95
❑9, Dec 1994	1.50
❑10, Jan 1995	1.50
❑11, Feb 1995	1.50
❑12, Mar 1995	1.50
❑13, Apr 1995	1.50
❑14, May 1995	1.50
❑15, Jun 1995; flip book with War Machine: Brothers in Arms part 2	2.50
❑16, Jul 1995	1.50
❑17, Aug 1995	1.50
❑18, Sep 1995	1.50
❑19, Oct 1995	1.50
❑20, Nov 1995	1.50
❑21, Dec 1995	1.50
❑22, Jan 1996	1.50
❑23, Feb 1996	1.50
❑24, Mar 1996	1.50
❑25, Apr 1996	1.50
❑Ashcan 1, ca. 1994; ashcan edition	0.75

WAR MACHINE (VOL. 2)
MARVEL / MAX

	N-MINT
❑1 2001	1.50
❑2, Nov 2001	1.50
❑3 2001	1.50
❑4 2001	1.50
❑5 2001	1.50
❑6 2001	1.50
❑7 2001	1.50
❑8 2001	1.50
❑9 2001	1.50

N-MINT

❑10 2002 .... 1.50
❑11 2002 .... 1.50
❑12 2002 .... 1.50

WAR MAN
MARVEL / EPIC

❑1, Nov 1993 .... 2.50
❑2, Dec 1993 .... 2.50

WAR OF THE GODS
DC

❑1, Sep 1991 .... 1.75
❑2, Oct 1991; newsstand cover 1.75
❑2/Direct ed., Oct 1991; direct sale cover 1.75
❑3, Nov 1991; newsstand cover 1.75
❑3/Direct ed., Nov 1991; direct sale cover 1.75
❑4, Dec 1991; newsstand cover 1.75
❑4/Direct ed., Dec 1991; direct sale cover 1.75

WAR OF THE WORLDS, THE (CALIBER)
CALIBER

❑1, ca. 1996 .... 2.95
❑2, ca. 1996 .... 2.95
❑3, ca. 1996 .... 2.95
❑4, ca. 1996 .... 2.95
❑5, ca. 1997 .... 2.95

WAR OF THE WORLDS (ETERNITY)
ETERNITY

❑1 .... 2.00
❑2 .... 2.00
❑3 .... 2.00
❑4 .... 2.00
❑5 .... 2.00
❑6 .... 2.00

WAR OF THE WORLDS, THE: THE MEMPHIS FRONT
ARROW

❑1, b&w; wrapraound cover 2.95
❑1/A, b&w; expanded page count 2.95
❑2 .... 2.95
❑3 .... 2.95
❑4 .... 2.95
❑5 .... 2.95

WARP
FIRST

❑1, Mar 1983; FB (a); 1: Lord Cumulus. 1: Chaos. This is the first comic published by First Comics 2.00
❑2, Apr 1983 FB (a) 1.50
❑3, May 1983 FB (a) 1.50
❑4, Jun 1983 FB (a) 1.50
❑5, Aug 1983 FB (a) 1.50
❑6, Sep 1983 FB (a) 1.50
❑7, Oct 1983 FB (a) 1.50
❑8, Nov 1983; Bill Willingham's first major comics work 1.25
❑9, Dec 1983 .... 1.25
❑10, Feb 1984 .... 1.25
❑11, Mar 1984 .... 1.25
❑12, Apr 1984 .... 1.25
❑13, May 1984 .... 1.25
❑14, Jul 1984 .... 1.25
❑15, Aug 1984 .... 1.25
❑16, Sep 1984 .... 1.25
❑17, Oct 1984 .... 1.25
❑18, Dec 1984 .... 1.25
❑19, Feb 1985 .... 1.25
❑Special 1, Jul 1983 O: Chaos. 1.00
❑Special 2, Jan 1984 .... 1.00
❑Special 3, Jun 1984; Chaos 1.00

WARP-3
EQUINOX

❑1, Mar 1990, b&w 1.50

WAR PARTY
LIGHTNING

❑1, Oct 1994 .... 2.95

N-MINT

WARP GRAPHICS ANNUAL
WARP

❑1; WP, PF (w); Elfquest, Panda Khan, Unicorn Isle, Captain Obese, Thunderbunny, MythAdventures 3.00

WARPWALKING
CALIBER

❑1, b&w 2.50
❑2, b&w 2.50
❑3, b&w 2.50
❑4, b&w 2.50

WARRIOR BUGS, THE
ARTCODA

❑1, Mar 2002 .... 2.95

WARRIOR NUN AREALA (VOL. 1)
ANTARCTIC

❑1, Dec 1994 1: Shotgun Mary. 1: Warrior Nun Areala. 5.00
❑1/Ltd., Dec 1994; Limited edition (5000 made); no cover price 5.00
❑1-2, Mar 1995 .... 3.00
❑2, Feb 1995 .... 4.00
❑3, Apr 1995 .... 4.00
❑3/CS, Apr 1995 .... 8.00
❑3/Deluxe, Apr 1995; polybagged with CD; cardstock cover 7.95
❑3/Ltd., Apr 1995; Limited edition (1000 made); no cover price 5.00

WARRIOR NUN AREALA (VOL. 2)
ANTARCTIC

❑1, Jun 1997 .... 3.00
❑1/Variant, Jun 1997; Leather edition; Print run of 700 .... 6.00
❑2, Sep 1997 .... 3.00
❑3, Nov 1997 .... 3.00
❑4, Jan 1998 .... 3.00
❑5, Mar 1998 .... 3.00
❑6, May 1998 .... 3.00

WARRIOR NUN AREALA (VOL. 3)
ANTARCTIC

❑1, Jul 1999 .... 2.50
❑2, Aug 1999 .... 2.50

WARRIOR NUN AREALA AND AVENGELYNE
ANTARCTIC

❑1/A, Dec 1996; crossover with Maximum Press 2.95
❑1/B, Dec 1996; poster edition; logoless cover and poster insert 5.95

WARRIOR NUN AREALA AND GLORY
ANTARCTIC

❑1, Sep 1997; crossover with Awesome 2.95
❑1/CS, Sep 1997; limited poster edition; crossover with Awesome 5.95

WARRIOR NUN AREALA/RAZOR: REVENGE
ANTARCTIC

❑1, Jan 1999 .... 2.99
❑1/Deluxe, Jan 1999; Deluxe Edition with painted cover 5.99

WARRIOR NUN AREALA: RESURRECTION
ANTARCTIC

❑1, Nov 1998 .... 3.00
❑1/Variant, Sum 1998; alternate logoless cover 3.00
❑2, Jan 1999 .... 3.00
❑3, Mar 1999 .... 3.00
❑4 .... 3.00
❑5 .... 3.00
❑6 .... 3.00
❑Ashcan 1, Nov 1998; b&w preview 1.00

WARRIOR NUN AREALA: RHEINT...CHTER
ANTARCTIC

❑1, Dec 1997, b&w 2.95
❑2, Apr 1998, b&w 2.95

N-MINT

WARRIOR NUN AREALA: RITUALS
ANTARCTIC

❑1, Aug 1995 .... 2.95
❑1/Variant, Aug 1995; no cover price 4.00
❑2, Oct 1995 .... 2.95
❑3, Dec 1995 .... 2.95
❑4, Feb 1996 .... 2.95
❑5, Apr 1996 .... 2.95
❑6, Jun 1996 .... 2.95

WARRIOR NUN: BLACK & WHITE
ANTARCTIC

❑1, Feb 1997 .... 3.00
❑2, Apr 1997; cover says Jan, indicia says Apr 3.00
❑3, Jun 1997 .... 3.00
❑4, Aug 1997 .... 3.00
❑5, Oct 1997 .... 3.00
❑6, Dec 1997 .... 3.00
❑7, Feb 1998 .... 3.00
❑8, Mar 1998 .... 3.00
❑9, Apr 1998 .... 3.00
❑10, May 1998 .... 3.00
❑11, Jun 1998 .... 3.00
❑12, Jul 1998 .... 3.00
❑13, Sep 1998 .... 3.00
❑14, Oct 1998 .... 3.00
❑15, Nov 1998 .... 2.95
❑16, Jan 1999 .... 2.99
❑17, Feb 1999 .... 2.99
❑18, Mar 1999 .... 2.99
❑19, Apr 1999 .... 2.99
❑20 1999 .... 2.99
❑21, Jul 1999 .... 2.50

WARRIOR NUN BRIGANTIA
ANTARCTIC

❑1, Jun 2000 .... 2.99
❑2 2000 .... 2.99
❑3 2000 .... 2.99

WARRIOR NUN DEI
ANTARCTIC

❑1; Comics Cavalcade Commemorative Edition 5.95

WARRIOR NUN DEI: AFTERTIME
ANTARCTIC

❑1, Jan 1997 .... 3.00
❑2 .... 3.00
❑3, Mar 1999 .... 3.00

WARRIOR NUN: FRENZY
ANTARCTIC

❑1, Jan 1998 .... 2.95
❑2, Jun 1998 .... 2.95

WARRIOR NUN: SCORPIO ROSE
ANTARCTIC

❑1, Sep 1996 .... 2.95
❑2, Nov 1996 .... 2.95
❑3, Jan 1997 .... 2.95
❑4, Mar 1997 .... 2.95

WARRIOR NUN VS RAZOR
ANTARCTIC

❑1, May 1996; crossover with London Night Studios 3.95

WARRIOR OF WAVERLY STREET, THE
DARK HORSE

❑1, Nov 1996 .... 2.95
❑2, Dec 1996 .... 2.95

WARRIORS
ADVENTURE

❑1, ca. 1987, b&w 2.00
❑2, Dec 1987, b&w 2.00
❑3, ca. 1988, b&w 2.00
❑4, Jul 1988, b&w 2.00
❑5, Nov 1988, b&w 2.00

WARRIORS OF PLASM
DEFIANT

❑1, Aug 1993; O: Warriors of Plasm. 1: Lorca. 1: Warriors of Plasm. First Defiant Comic (not including Warriors of Plasm #0 promotion) 2.95
❑2, Sep 1993 .... 2.95

N-MINT

❑3, Oct 1993 .... 2.95
❑4, Nov 1993 .... 2.95
❑5, Dec 1993 .... 2.50
❑6, Jan 1994 1: Prudence. 2.50
❑7, Feb 1994 .... 2.50
❑8, Mar 1994 .... 2.75
❑9, Apr 1994 .... 2.75
❑10, May 1994 .... 2.50
❑11, Jun 1994 .... 2.50
❑12, Jul 1994 .... 2.50
❑13, Aug 1994; Final issue? 2.50

WARRIORS OF PLASM GRAPHIC NOVEL
DEFIANT

❑1; Home for the Holidays 6.95

WARRIOR'S WAY
BENCH

❑1 .... 2.99
❑2, Aug 1998 .... 2.99
❑2/A, Aug 1998; alternate cover 2.99
❑3 .... 2.99

WARRIOR (ULTIMATE CREATIONS)
ULTIMATE CREATIONS

❑1, May 1996 .... 2.95
❑2 1996 .... 2.95
❑3 1997 .... 2.95
❑4 1997 .... 2.95

WAR SIRENS AND LIBERTY BELLES
RECOLLECTIONS

❑1, b&w; cardstock cover 4.95

WAR SLUTS
PRETTY GRAPHIC

❑1, b&w 3.95
❑2, b&w; cardstock cover 3.95

WAR STORY: ARCHANGEL
DC / VERTIGO

❑1, ca. 2003 .... 4.95

WAR STORY: D-DAY DODGERS
DC / VERTIGO

❑1, Dec 2001, b&w 4.95

WAR STORY: JOHANN'S TIGER
DC / VERTIGO

❑1, Nov 2001, b&w 4.95

WAR STORY: NIGHTINGALE
DC / VERTIGO

❑1, Feb 2002, b&w 4.95

WAR STORY: SCREAMING EAGLES
DC / VERTIGO

❑1, Jan 2002, b&w 4.95

WARSTRIKE
MALIBU / ULTRAVERSE

❑1, May 1994 .... 1.95
❑2, Jun 1994 .... 1.95
❑3, Jul 1994 .... 1.95
❑4, Aug 1994 .... 1.95
❑5, Sep 1994 .... 1.95
❑6, Oct 1994 .... 1.95
❑7, Nov 1994 .... 1.95
❑Giant Size 1, Dec 1994; Lord Pumpkin reborn 2.50

WARWORLD!
DARK HORSE

❑1, Feb 1989, b&w 1.75

WARZONE
EXPRESS / ENTITY

❑1, ca. 1994, b&w; enhanced cardstock cover 2.95
❑2, ca. 1994, b&w; enhanced cardstock cover 2.95
❑3, ca. 1995, b&w; enhanced cardstock cover 2.95

WARZONE 3719
POCKET CHANGE

❑1 .... 1.95

WASHMEN
NEW YORK

❑1 .... 1.70

N-MINT

WASH TUBBS QUARTERLY
DRAGON LADY

❑1 .... 4.95
❑2 .... 5.95
❑3 .... 5.95
❑4 .... 5.95
❑5 .... 5.95

WASTE L.A.: DESCENT
JOHN GAUSHELL

❑1, Jan 1996, b&w; fumetti 2.50
❑2, Mar 1996, b&w; fumetti 2.50
❑3, May 1996, b&w; fumetti 2.50

WASTELAND
DC

❑1, Dec 1987 .... 2.00
❑2, Jan 1988 .... 2.00
❑3, Feb 1988 .... 2.00
❑4, Mar 1988 .... 2.00
❑5, Apr 1988; correct cover 2.00
❑5/A, Apr 1988; cover of #6 .... 2.00
❑6, May 1988; correct cover 2.00
❑6/A, May 1988; blank cover 2.00
❑7, Jun 1988 .... 2.00
❑8, Jul 1988 .... 2.00
❑9, Aug 1988 .... 2.00
❑10, Sep 1988 .... 2.00
❑11, Oct 1988 .... 2.00
❑12, Nov 1988 JO (a) 2.00
❑13, Dec 1988 JO (a) 2.00
❑14, Win 1988 JO (a) 2.00
❑15, Hol 1988; JO (a); Hol 1988 .... 2.00
❑16, Feb 1989 JO (a) 2.00
❑17, Apr 1989 JO (a) 2.00
❑18, May 1989 JO (a) 2.00

WATCHCATS
HARRIER

❑1 .... 1.95

WATCHMEN
DC

❑1, Sep 1986 AMo (w); DaG (a); 1: Rorshach. 1: Doctor Manhattan. 1: Ozymandias. D: The Comedian. 8.00
❑2, Oct 1986 AMo (w); DaG (a) 5.00
❑3, Nov 1986 AMo (w); DaG (a) 5.00
❑4, Dec 1986 AMo (w); DaG (a); O: Doctor Manhattan. 4.00
❑5, Jan 1987 AMo (w); DaG (a) 4.00
❑6, Feb 1987 AMo (w); DaG (a); O: Rorshach. 4.00
❑7, Mar 1987 AMo (w); DaG (a) 4.00
❑8, Apr 1987 AMo (w); DaG (a) 4.00
❑9, May 1987 AMo (w); DaG (a) 4.00
❑10, Jul 1987 AMo (w); DaG (a) 4.00
❑11, Aug 1987 AMo (w); DaG (a); O: Ozymandias. 4.00
❑12, Oct 1987 AMo (w); DaG (a); D: Rorshach. 4.00

WATERWORLD: CHILDREN OF LEVIATHAN
ACCLAIM

❑1, Aug 1997; no indicia 2.50
❑2, Sep 1997 .... 2.50
❑3, Oct 1997 .... 2.50
❑4, Nov 1997 .... 2.50

WAVEMAKERS
BLIND BAT

❑1 .... 3.00

WAVE WARRIORS
ASTROBOYS

❑1 .... 2.00

WAXWORK
BLACKTHORNE

❑1, b&w 2.00
❑3D 1 .... 2.50

WAY OF THE RAT
CROSSGEN

❑1, Jun 2002 .... 2.95
❑2, Jul 2002 .... 2.95
❑3, Aug 2002 .... 2.95
❑4, Sep 2002 .... 2.95

Spider-Man outfitted himself with spider-armor in *Web of Spider-Man* #100.

© 1993 Marvel Comics.

N-MINT

❑5, Oct 2002 .... 2.95
❑6, Nov 2002 .... 2.95
❑7, Dec 2002 .... 2.95
❑8, Jan 2003 .... 2.95
❑9, Feb 2003 .... 2.95
❑10, Mar 2003 .... 2.95
❑11, Apr 2003 .... 2.95
❑12, May 2003 .... 2.95
❑13, Jun 2003 .... 2.95
❑14, May 2003 .... 2.95
❑15, Jul 2003 .... 2.95
❑16, Aug 2003 .... 2.95
❑17, Nov 2003 .... 2.95
❑18, Nov 2003 .... 2.95
❑19, Dec 2003 .... 2.95
❑20, Jan 2004 .... 2.95
❑21, Feb 2004 .... 2.95
❑22, Apr 2004 .... 2.95
❑23, May 2004 .... 2.95
❑23-2, Apr 2004 .... 2.95
❑24, May 2004 .... 2.95

WAY OUT STRIPS (FANTAGRAPHICS)
FANTAGRAPHICS

❑1 1994, b&w 2.50
❑2, May 1994, b&w 2.75
❑3, Aug 1994, b&w 2.75

WAY OUT STRIPS (TRAGEDY STRIKES)
TRAGEDY STRIKES

❑1, b&w 2.95
❑2, b&w 2.95
❑3, b&w 2.95

WAYWARD WARRIOR
ALPHA PRODUCTIONS

❑1, b&w 1.95
❑2, b&w 1.95
❑3, b&w 1.95

WCW WORLD CHAMPIONSHIP WRESTLING
MARVEL

❑1, Apr 1992 .... 1.25
❑2, May 1992 .... 1.25
❑3, Jun 1992 .... 1.25
❑4, Jul 1992 .... 1.25
❑5, Aug 1992 .... 1.25
❑6, Sep 1992 .... 1.25
❑7, Oct 1992 .... 1.25
❑8, Nov 1992 .... 1.25
❑9, Dec 1992 .... 1.25
❑10, Jan 1993 .... 1.25
❑11, Feb 1993 .... 1.25
❑12, Mar 1993 .... 1.25

WEAPON X
MARVEL

❑1, Mar 1995; Age of Apocalypse 1.95
❑2, Apr 1995; Age of Apocalypse 1.95
❑3, May 1995; Age of Apocalypse 1.95
❑4, Jun 1995; Age of Apocalypse 1.95

WEAPON X (2ND SERIES)
MARVEL

❑1, Nov 2002 .... 2.25
❑2, Dec 2002 .... 2.25
❑3, Jan 2003 .... 2.25
❑4, Feb 2003 .... 2.25
❑5, Mar 2003 .... 2.25
❑6, Apr 2003 .... 2.25

N-MINT

❑7, May 2003 ... 2.25
❑8, Jun 2003 ... 2.25
❑9, Jul 2003 ... 2.99
❑10, Aug 2003 ... 2.99
❑11, Sep 2004 ... 2.99
❑12, Oct 2003 ... 2.99
❑13, Nov 2003 ... 2.99
❑14, Dec 2003 ... 2.99
❑15, Dec 2003 ... 2.99
❑16, Jan 2004 ... 2.99
❑17, Mar 2004 ... 2.99
❑18, Apr 2004 ... 2.99
❑19, May 2004 ... 2.99
❑20, May 2004 ... 2.99
❑21, Jun 2004 ... 2.99
❑22, Jun 2004 ... 2.99
❑23, Jul 2004 ... 2.99
❑24, Jul 2004 ... 2.99
❑25, Aug 2004 ... 2.99
❑26, Sep 2004 ...

WEAPON X: THE DRAFT: KANE
MARVEL

❑1, Oct 2002 ... 2.25

WEAPON XXX: ORIGIN OF THE IMPLANTS
FRIENDLY

❑1, Jul 1992 ... 2.95
❑2 ... 2.95
❑3 ... 2.95

WEAPON ZERO
IMAGE

❑1, Jun 1995; 1: Weapon Zero. Issue #T-4 ... 3.00
❑1/Gold, Jun 1995; Gold edition; Issue #T-4; 1000 copies produced for Chicago Comicon ... 2.50
❑2, Aug 1995; Issue #T-3 ... 2.50
❑3, Sep 1995; Issue #T-2 ... 2.50
❑4, Oct 1995; Issue #T-1 ... 2.50
❑5, Dec 1995; Issue #T-0; Issue #T-0 ... 2.50

WEAPON ZERO (VOL. 2)
IMAGE

❑1, Mar 1996; indicia gives year of publication as 1995 ... 3.00
❑2, Apr 1996; indicia gives year of publication as 1995 ... 3.00
❑3, May 1996 ... 3.00
❑4, Jun 1996; indicia gives year of publication as 1995 ... 3.00
❑5, Jul 1996; indicia gives year of publication as 1995 ... 3.00
❑6, Aug 1996 ... 2.50
❑7, Sep 1996 ... 2.50
❑8, Nov 1996 ... 2.50
❑9, Dec 1996 ... 2.50
❑10, Feb 1997 ... 2.50
❑11, Apr 1997 ... 2.50
❑12, May 1997 ... 2.50
❑13, Jun 1997 ... 2.50
❑14, Sep 1997 ... 2.50
❑15, Dec 1997 ... 3.50

WEAPON ZERO/SILVER SURFER
TOP COW / IMAGE

❑1, Jan 1997; crossover with Marvel; continues in Cyblade/Ghost Rider . 2.95
❑1/A, Jan 1997; alternate cover ... 2.95

WEASEL GUY: ROAD TRIP
IMAGE

❑1, Aug 1999 ... 2.95
❑1/A, Aug 1999; alternate cover ... 2.95
❑2, Oct 1999 ... 3.50

WEASEL PATROL, THE
ECLIPSE

❑1, b&w ... 2.00

WEATHER WOMAN
CPM MANGA

❑1, Aug 2000, b&w ... 2.95
❑1/A, Aug 2000, b&w; alternate cover: Weather Woman smoking ... 2.95

N-MINT

WEAVEWORLD
MARVEL / EPIC

❑1, Dec 1991; prestige format ... 4.95
❑2, Jan 1992; prestige format ... 4.95
❑3, Feb 1992; prestige format ... 4.95

WEB, THE
DC / IMPACT

❑1, Sep 1991 1: The Web (full appearance). 1: Bill Grady. 1: Templar. ... 1.25
❑2, Oct 1991 O: The Web. 1: Gunny. 1: The Sunshine Kid. 1: Brew. 1: Powell Jennings. 1: Jump. ... 1.00
❑3, Nov 1991 1: St. James. 1: Meridian. 1.00
❑4, Dec 1991 1: Silver. ... 1.00
❑5, Jan 1992 ... 1.00
❑6, Feb 1992 ... 1.00
❑7, Apr 1992 ... 1.00
❑8, Apr 1992 1: Studs. ... 1.00
❑9, May 1992; trading card ... 1.00
❑10, Jun 1992 ... 1.25
❑11, Jul 1992 ... 1.25
❑12, Aug 1992 ... 1.25
❑13, Sep 1992 ... 1.25
❑14, Oct 1992 ... 1.25
❑Annual 1, ca. 1992; trading card ... 2.50

WEBBER'S WORLD
ALLSTAR

❑1 ... 4.95

WEB-MAN
ARGOSY

❑1; gatefold cover ... 2.50

WEB OF SCARLET SPIDER
MARVEL

❑1, Nov 1995 O: Scarlet Spider. ... 2.00
❑2, Dec 1995 A: Cyber-Slayers. ... 2.00
❑3, Jan 1996; A: Firestar. continues in New Warriors #67 ... 2.00
❑4, Feb 1996 ... 2.00

WEB OF SPIDER-MAN, THE
MARVEL

❑1, Apr 1985 ... 8.00
❑2, May 1985 ... 4.00
❑3, Jun 1985 ... 4.00
❑4, Jul 1985 V: Doctor Octopus. ... 4.00
❑5, Aug 1985 V: Doctor Octopus. ... 4.00
❑6, Sep 1985; Secret Wars II ... 4.00
❑7, Oct 1985 A: Hulk. V: Hulk. ... 4.00
❑8, Nov 1985 ... 4.00
❑9, Dec 1985 ... 4.00
❑10, Jan 1986 A: Dominic Fortune. ... 4.00
❑11, Feb 1986 ... 3.00
❑12, Mar 1986 ... 3.00
❑13, Apr 1986 ... 3.00
❑14, May 1986 ... 3.00
❑15, Jun 1986 1: The Foreigner. 1: Chance I (Nicholas Powell). ... 3.00
❑16, Jul 1986 ... 3.00
❑17, Aug 1986; V: Magma. red suit destroyed ... 3.00
❑18, Sep 1986; Venom cameo ... 3.00
❑19, Oct 1986 1: Solo. ... 3.00
❑20, Nov 1986 ... 3.00
❑21, Dec 1986 ... 3.00
❑22, Jan 1987 ... 3.00
❑23, Feb 1987 ... 3.00
❑24, Mar 1987 ... 3.00
❑25, Apr 1987 ... 3.00
❑26, May 1987 ... 3.00
❑27, Jun 1987 ... 3.00
❑28, Jul 1987 ... 3.00
❑29, Aug 1987 A: Wolverine. A: Hobgoblin II (Jason Macendale). ... 5.00
❑30, Sep 1987 O: The Rose. ... 4.00
❑31, Oct 1987 V: Kraven. ... 5.00
❑32, Nov 1987 V: Kraven. ... 5.00
❑33, Dec 1987 BSz (c) ... 3.00
❑34, Jan 1988 ... 3.00
❑35, Feb 1988 1: Tarantula II (Luis Alvarez). ... 3.00
❑36, Mar 1988 O: Tarantula II (Luis Alvarez). ... 4.00
❑37, Apr 1988 ... 3.00

N-MINT

❑38, May 1988 A: Hobgoblin II (Jason Macendale). V: Hobgoblin. ... 5.00
❑39, Jun 1988 ... 3.00
❑40, Jul 1988 ... 3.00
❑41, Aug 1988 ... 3.00
❑42, Sep 1988 ... 3.00
❑43, Oct 1988 ... 3.00
❑44, Nov 1988 A: Hulk. ... 2.50
❑45, Dec 1988 V: Vulture. ... 2.50
❑46, Jan 1989 ... 2.50
❑47, Feb 1989; V: Hobgoblin. Inferno 2.50
❑48, Mar 1989; O: Demogoblin. V: Hobgoblin. Inferno ... 8.00
❑49, Apr 1989 ... 2.00
❑50, May 1989; Giant-sized ... 2.50
❑51, Jun 1989 ... 2.00
❑52, Jul 1989 V: Chameleon. ... 2.00
❑53, Aug 1989 ... 2.00
❑54, Sep 1989 V: Chameleon. ... 2.00
❑55, Oct 1989 V: Chameleon. ... 2.00
❑56, Nov 1989 V: Rocket Racer. ... 2.00
❑57, Nov 1989 V: Skinhead. ... 2.00
❑58, Dec 1989; Acts of Vengeance ... 2.50
❑59, Dec 1989; Acts of Vengeance; Spider-Man with cosmic powers ... 8.00
❑60, Jan 1990; Acts of Vengeance ... 2.50
❑61, Feb 1990; Acts of Vengeance ... 2.50
❑62, Mar 1990 ... 2.00
❑63, Apr 1990 ... 2.00
❑64, May 1990; Acts of Vengeance ... 2.00
❑65, Jun 1990; Acts of Vengeance ... 2.00
❑66, Jul 1990 A: Green Goblin. ... 2.00
❑67, Aug 1990 A: Green Goblin. ... 2.00
❑68, Sep 1990 ... 2.00
❑69, Oct 1990 ... 2.00
❑70, Nov 1990; Spider-Hulk ... 2.00
❑71, Dec 1990 ... 2.00
❑72, Jan 1991 ... 2.00
❑73, Feb 1991 ... 2.00
❑74, Mar 1991 ... 2.00
❑75, Apr 1991 ... 2.00
❑76, May 1991 A: Fantastic Four. ... 2.00
❑77, Jun 1991 ... 2.00
❑78, Jul 1991 A: Cloak & Dagger. ... 2.00
❑79, Aug 1991 ... 2.00
❑80, Sep 1991 V: Silvermane. ... 2.00
❑81, Oct 1991 KB (w) ... 2.00
❑82, Nov 1991 KB (w) ... 2.00
❑83, Dec 1991 KB (w) ... 2.00
❑84, Jan 1992 A: Hobgoblin. ... 2.00
❑85, Feb 1992 ... 2.00
❑86, Mar 1992 ... 2.00
❑87, Apr 1992 ... 2.00
❑88, May 1992 ... 2.00
❑89, Jun 1992 ... 2.00
❑90, Jul 1992; Double-size; hologram; Poster ... 5.00
❑90-2, Jul 1992; Double-size; hologram; Poster ... 2.95
❑91, Aug 1992 ... 2.00
❑92, Sep 1992 ... 2.00
❑93, Oct 1992 ... 2.00
❑94, Nov 1992 V: Hobgoblin. ... 2.00
❑95, Dec 1992 A: Ghost Rider. A: Johnny Blaze. V: Venom. ... 2.00
❑96, Jan 1993 A: Ghost Rider. A: Johnny Blaze. V: Venom. ... 2.00
❑97, Feb 1993 ... 2.00
❑98, Mar 1993 ... 2.00
❑99, Apr 1993 V: New Enforcers. ... 2.00
❑100, May 1993; 1: Spider-Armor. foil cover ... 4.00
❑101, Jun 1993 ... 2.00
❑102, Jul 1993 ... 2.00
❑103, Aug 1993 ... 2.00
❑104, Sep 1993 ... 2.00
❑105, Oct 1993; A: Archangel. Infinity Crusade ... 2.00
❑106/CS, Nov 1993; Dirtbag special; Infinity Crusade; Polybagged with copy of Dirt Magazine, cassette tape 5.00
❑106, Nov 1993; Infinity Crusade ... 1.25

	N-MINT
❑107, Dec 1993 A: Quicksand. A: Sandman.	2.00
❑108, Jan 1994 A: Quicksand. A: Sandman.	2.00
❑109, Feb 1994	2.00
❑110, Mar 1994	2.00
❑111, Apr 1994 V: Lizard.	2.00
❑112, May 1994	2.00
❑113, Jun 1994 A: Gambit. A: Black Cat.	2.00
❑113/CS, Jun 1994; A: Gambit. A: Black Cat. TV preview; print	4.00
❑114, Jul 1994	2.00
❑115, Aug 1994	2.00
❑116, Sep 1994	2.00
❑117, Oct 1994; Flip-book A: Ben Reilly.	3.00
❑117/Variant, Oct 1994; Flip-book; O: Ben Reilly. A: Ben Reilly. foil cover	5.00
❑118, Nov 1994	3.00
❑118-2, Nov 1994; Has blank UPC code	1.50
❑119, Dec 1994; Scarlet Spider vs. Venom	2.00
❑119/CS, Dec 1994; polybagged with Marvel Milestone Edition: Amazing Spider-Man #150 and POP card for Amazing Spider-Ma; Scarlet Spider vs. Venom	6.45
❑120, Jan 1995; Giant-size; A: Morbius.	4.00
❑121, Feb 1995 V: Kaine.	2.00
❑122, Mar 1995 A: Jackal.	2.00
❑123, Apr 1995 A: Jackal.	2.00
❑124, May 1995	2.00
❑125, Jun 1995; Giant-size	2.95
❑125/Variant, Jun 1995; Giant-size; Hologram on cover	3.95
❑126, Jul 1995	1.50
❑127, Aug 1995	1.50
❑128, Sep 1995	1.50
❑129, Oct 1995 A: New Warriors.	1.50
❑129/CS	5.00
❑Annual 1, ca. 1985; Painted cover; 4th appearance Spider-Man's black costume; ca. 1985	5.00
❑Annual 2, ca. 1986 A: New Mutants.	6.00
❑Annual 3, ca. 1987; pin-ups	3.00
❑Annual 4, ca. 1988 1: Poison.	3.00
❑Annual 5, ca. 1989; O: Silver Sable. A: Fantastic Four. Atlantis Attacks	2.50
❑Annual 6, ca. 1990; V: Psycho-Man. Tiny Spidey	2.50
❑Annual 7, ca. 1991 O: Hobgoblin. O: Venom. O: Green Goblin. A: Iron Man. A: Black Panther. V: Ultron.	2.50
❑Annual 8, ca. 1992 A: New Warriors. A: Venom. V: Whiplash. V: Beetle. V: Constrictor. V: Rhino.	3.00
❑Annual 9, ca. 1993; 1: The Cadre. trading card	2.95
❑Annual 10, ca. 1994 V: Shriek.	2.95
❑SS 1, ca. 1995; Flip-book; Super Special	3.95

WEBSPINNERS: TALES OF SPIDER-MAN
Marvel

❑1/A, Jan 1999; variant cover: Spider-Man vs. Mysterio with statue against orange background	2.99
❑1, Jan 1999; gatefold summary	2.99
❑1/Autographed, Jan 1999	10.00
❑1/B, Jan 1999; gatefold summary; variant cover	2.99
❑2/A, Feb 1999	2.50
❑2/B, Feb 1999	2.50
❑3, Mar 1999	2.50
❑4, Apr 1999	2.50
❑5, May 1999	2.50
❑6, Jun 1999	2.50
❑7, Jul 1999	2.50
❑8, Aug 1999	2.50
❑9, Sep 1999	2.50
❑10, Oct 1999	2.50
❑11, Nov 1999	2.50
❑12, Dec 1999	2.50
❑13, Jan 2000	2.50
❑14, Feb 2000	2.50
❑15, Mar 2000	2.50
❑16, Apr 2000	2.50
❑17, May 2000	2.50
❑18, Jun 2000	2.50

WEDDING OF DRACULA
Marvel

❑1, Jan 1993; Reprints Tomb of Dracula #30, 45 & 46	2.00

WEDDING OF POPEYE AND OLIVE, THE
Ocean

❑1, ca. 1998, b&w	2.75

WEEZUL
Lightning

❑1/A, Aug 1996	2.75
❑1/B, Aug 1996; alternate cover	3.00

WEIRD, THE
DC

❑1, Apr 1988	1.50
❑2, May 1988	1.50
❑3, Jun 1988	1.50
❑4, Jul 1988	1.50

WEIRD (MAGAZINE)
DC / Paradox

❑1, Sum 1997, b&w; magazine; reprints material from Big Book of Conspiracies; Summer 1997	2.99

WEIRD
Avalon

❑1	2.99
❑2	2.99
❑3	2.99
❑4	2.99

WEIRDFALL
Antarctic

❑1, Jul 1995, b&w	2.75
❑2, Sep 1995, b&w	2.75
❑3, Nov 1995, b&w	2.75

WEIRD FANTASY (RCP)
Gemstone

❑1, Oct 1992 AF, HK, WW, JKa (a)	2.50
❑2, Jan 1993; AF, HK, WW, JKa (a); Reprints Weird Fantasy #14	2.00
❑3, Apr 1993 AF, HK, WW, JKa (a)	2.00
❑4, Jul 1993 AF, HK, WW, JKa (a)	2.00
❑5, Oct 1993 AF, HK, WW, JKa (w); AF, HK, WW, JKa (a)	2.00
❑6, Jan 1994 AF, HK, WW, JKa (a)	2.00
❑7, Apr 1994 AF, WW, JKa (a)	2.00
❑8, Jul 1994	2.00
❑9, Oct 1994	2.00
❑10, Jan 1995	2.00
❑11, Apr 1995	2.50
❑12, Jul 1995	2.50
❑13, Oct 1995	2.50
❑14, Jan 1996 FF (a)	2.50
❑15, Apr 1996 AW (a)	2.50
❑16, Jul 1996 AW (a)	2.50
❑17, Oct 1996 AW (a)	2.50
❑18, Jan 1997	2.50
❑19, Apr 1997; AW, JO, JSe, BE, JKa (w); AW, JO, JSe, BE, JKa (a); Reprints Weird Fantasy (EC) #19	2.50
❑20, Jul 1997; AW, JO, JSe, BE, JKa (w); AW, JO, JSe, BE, JKa (a); Reprints Weird Fantasy (EC) #20	2.50
❑21, Oct 1997; AW, JO, JSe, BE, JKa (w); AW, JO, JSe, BE, JKa (a); Reprints Weird Fantasy (EC) #21	2.50
❑22, Jan 1998; JO, BK, JKa (w); JO, BK, JKa (a); Reprints Weird Fantasy (EC) #22	2.50
❑Annual 1; Reprints Weird Fantasy #1-5	8.95
❑Annual 2; Reprints Weird Fantasy #6-10	9.95
❑Annual 3	8.95
❑Annual 4	9.95
❑Annual 5; Reprints Weird Fantasy #19-22	10.95

Weird War Tales presented the supernatural side of warfare.

© 1971 National Periodical Publications (DC).

WEIRD MELVIN
Marc Hansen Stuff!

	N-MINT
❑1, Feb 1995, b&w	2.95
❑2, Apr 1995, b&w	2.95
❑3, Jun 1995, b&w	2.95
❑4, Aug 1995, b&w	2.95
❑5, Oct 1995, b&w	2.95

WEIRD MYSTERY TALES
DC

❑1, Jul 1972 JK (a)	30.00
❑2, Sep 1972	20.00
❑3, Nov 1972	15.00
❑4, Jan 1973	12.00
❑5, Apr 1973	12.00
❑6, Jul 1973	12.00
❑7, Sep 1973	12.00
❑8, Nov 1973	12.00
❑9, Dec 1973	12.00
❑10, Mar 1974	12.00
❑11, Apr 1974	10.00
❑12, Jul 1974	10.00
❑13, Aug 1974	10.00
❑14, Oct 1974	10.00
❑15, Jan 1975	10.00
❑16, Mar 1975	10.00
❑17, Apr 1975	10.00
❑18, May 1975	10.00
❑19, Jun 1975	10.00
❑20, Jul 1975	10.00
❑21, Aug 1975	15.00
❑22, Sep 1975	10.00
❑23, Oct 1975	10.00
❑24, Nov 1975	10.00

WEIRD ROMANCE
Eclipse

❑1, ca. 1988, b&w	2.00

WEIRD SCIENCE (GLADSTONE)
Gladstone

❑1, Sep 1990; AF, GE, AW, HK, JO, WW, JKa (w); AF, GE, AW, HK, JO, WW, JKa (a); Reprints Weird Science (EC) #22; Weird Fantasy (EC) #1	2.00
❑2, Nov 1990 AW, JO, WW, JKa (a)	2.00
❑3, Jan 1991; AF, HK, WW, JKa (a); Reprints Weird Science (EC) #9, Weird Fantasy (EC) #14	2.00
❑4, Mar 1991 AF, JO, WW, JKa (a)	2.00

WEIRD SCIENCE (RCP)
Gemstone

❑1, Sep 1992; AF, HK, WW, JKa (w); AF, HK, WW, JKa (a); Reprints Weird Science (EC) #1	2.50
❑2, Dec 1992; Reprints Weird Science (EC) #2	2.00
❑3, Mar 1993; Reprints Weird Science (EC) #3	2.00
❑4, Jun 1993; AF, HK, JKa, GI (a); Reprints Weird Science (EC) #4	2.00
❑5, Sep 1993; AF, HK, WW, JKa (a); Reprints Weird Science (EC) #5	2.00
❑6, Dec 1993; AF, HK, WW, JKa (a); Reprints Weird Science (EC) #6	2.00
❑7, Mar 1994; AF (c); AF, HK, WW, JKa (a); Reprints Weird Science (EC) #7	2.00
❑8, Jun 1994; AF, WW, JKa (a); Reprints Weird Science (EC) #8	2.00
❑9, Sep 1994; Reprints Weird Science (EC) #9	2.00

	N-MINT
❑10, Dec 1994; Reprints Weird Science (EC) #10	2.00
❑11, Mar 1995; Reprints Weird Science (EC) #11	2.00
❑12, Jun 1995; Reprints Weird Science (EC) #12	2.00
❑13, Sep 1995; Reprints Weird Science (EC) #13	2.00
❑14, Dec 1995; Reprints Weird Science (EC) #14	2.00
❑15, Mar 1996; Reprints Weird Science (EC) #15	2.50
❑16, Jun 1996; Reprints Weird Science (EC) #16	2.50
❑17, Sep 1996; Reprints Weird Science (EC) #17	2.50
❑18, Dec 1996; Reprints Weird Science (EC) #18	2.50
❑19, Mar 1997; AW, JO, BE, WW (w); AW, JO, BE, WW (a); Reprints Weird Science (EC) #19	2.50
❑20, Jun 1997; AW, JO, WW, JKa (w); AW, JO, WW, JKa (a); Reprints Weird Science (EC) #20	2.50
❑21, Sep 1997; AW, JO, WW, JKa (w); AW, JO, FF, WW, JKa (a); Reprints Weird Science (EC) #21; EC editors put themselves in story	2.50
❑22, Dec 1997; GE, AW, JO, WW (w); GE, AW, JO, WW (a); Reprints Weird Science (EC) #22; Wally Wood puts himself in story	2.50
❑Annual 1; Reprints Weird Science (EC) #1-5	8.95
❑Annual 2; Reprints Weird Science (EC) #6-10	9.95
❑Annual 3; Reprints Weird Science (EC) #11-14	10.95
❑Annual 4; Reprints Weird Science (EC) #15-18	9.95
❑Annual 5; Reprints Weird Science (EC) #19-22	10.50

WEIRD SCIENCE-FANTASY (RCP)
Gemstone

	N-MINT
❑1, Nov 1992; Reprints Weird Science-Fantasy #23	2.00
❑2, Feb 1993; AF (c); AW, JO, WW, BK (w); AW, JO, WW, BK (a); Reprints Weird Science-Fantasy #24; "Upheaval" by Harlan Ellison (1st professional work by Harlan Ellison)	2.00
❑3, May 1993; AF (c); AW, JO, WW, BK (a); Reprints Weird Science-Fantasy #25	2.00
❑4, Aug 1993; UFO issue; Reprints Weird Science-Fantasy #26; Flying Saucer Report special issue	2.00
❑5, Nov 1993; JO, WW, JKa (a); Reprints Weird Science-Fantasy #27	2.00
❑6, Feb 1994; AF (c); AW, JO, WW, JKa (a); Reprints Weird Science-Fantasy #28	2.00
❑7, May 1994; FF (c); AW, JO, WW (a); Reprints Weird Science-Fantasy #29	2.00
❑8, Aug 1994	2.00
❑9, Nov 1994	2.00
❑10, Feb 1995	2.00
❑11, May 1995	2.00
❑Annual 1; Collects Weird Science-Fantasy (RCP) #1-5	8.95
❑Annual 2; Collects Weird Science-Fantasy (RCP)	12.95

WEIRD SEX
Fantagraphics / Eros

	N-MINT
❑1, Jan 1999	2.95

WEIRD SUSPENSE
Atlas-Seaboard

	N-MINT
❑1, Feb 1975 O: The Tarantula. 1: The Tarantula.	8.00
❑2, Apr 1975	8.00
❑3, Jul 1975	1.00

WEIRDSVILLE
Blindwolf

	N-MINT
❑1, Feb 1997	2.95
❑2, Apr 1997	2.95
❑3, Jun 1997	2.95
❑4, Aug 1997	2.95
❑5, Sep 1997	2.95
❑6, Dec 1997	2.95
❑7 1998	2.95
❑8, Mar 1998	2.95
❑9, Jun 1998	2.95

WEIRD TALES ILLUSTRATED
Millennium

	N-MINT
❑1	2.95
❑1/Deluxe; Deluxe edition with extra stories	4.95
❑2	2.95

WEIRD TALES OF THE MACABRE
Atlas-Seaboard

	N-MINT
❑1, Apr 1975	3.00
❑2, Apr 1975	3.00

WEIRD TRIPS MAGAZINE
Kitchen Sink

	N-MINT
❑1	4.00

WEIRD WAR TALES
DC

	N-MINT
❑1, Sep 1971 JKu (a)	125.00
❑2, Nov 1971 JKu (w); MD (a)	75.00
❑3, Jan 1972	45.00
❑4, Mar 1972 JKu (c)	30.00
❑5, May 1972	30.00
❑6, Jul 1972 JKu (c)	20.00
❑7, Sep 1972	20.00
❑8, Nov 1972 NA (c); NA, TD (a)	20.00
❑9, Dec 1972 AA (a)	20.00
❑10, Jan 1973 ATh (a)	20.00
❑11, Feb 1973	12.00
❑12, Mar 1973 DP (a)	12.00
❑13, Apr 1973 NR, TD (a)	12.00
❑14, Jun 1973	12.00
❑15, Jul 1973 DP (a)	12.00
❑16, Aug 1973 AA (a)	12.00
❑17, Sep 1973 GE (a)	12.00
❑18, Oct 1973 TD (a)	12.00
❑19, Nov 1973	12.00
❑20, Dec 1973	12.00
❑21, Jan 1974 FR (a)	8.00
❑22, Feb 1974 GE, TD (a)	8.00
❑23, Mar 1974 AA (a)	8.00
❑24, Apr 1974	8.00
❑25, May 1974 AA (a)	8.00
❑26, Jun 1974	8.00
❑27, Jul 1974	8.00
❑28, Aug 1974 AA (a)	8.00
❑29, Sep 1974	8.00
❑30, Oct 1974	8.00
❑31, Nov 1974	8.00
❑32, Dec 1974	6.00
❑33, Jan 1975	6.00
❑34, Feb 1975	6.00
❑35, Mar 1975	6.00
❑36, Apr 1975	6.00
❑37, May 1975	6.00
❑38, Jun 1975	6.00
❑39, Jul 1975 JKu (c)	6.00
❑40, Aug 1975	6.00
❑41, Sep 1975	6.00
❑42, Oct 1975 AA (a)	6.00
❑43, Nov 1975	6.00
❑44, Jan 1976 JKu (c)	6.00
❑45, Mar 1976	6.00
❑46, May 1976	6.00
❑47, Jul 1976	6.00
❑48, Sep 1976	6.00
❑49, Nov 1976 SD (a)	6.00
❑50, Jan 1977	6.00
❑51, Mar 1977 JKu (c)	5.00
❑52, Apr 1977	5.00
❑53, May 1977	5.00
❑54, Jul 1977	5.00
❑55, Sep 1977	5.00
❑56, Oct 1977	5.00
❑57, Nov 1977	5.00
❑58, Dec 1977 JKu (c); A: Hitler.	5.00
❑59, Jan 1978	5.00
❑60, Feb 1978	5.00
❑61, Mar 1978 HC, AN (a)	5.00
❑62, Apr 1978	5.00
❑63, May 1978	5.00
❑64, Jun 1978 JKu (c); FM (a)	5.00
❑65, Jul 1978	5.00
❑66, Aug 1978 TS (a)	5.00
❑67, Sep 1978 JKu (c)	5.00
❑68, Oct 1978 FM (a)	5.00
❑69, Nov 1978	5.00
❑70, Dec 1978	5.00
❑71, Jan 1979	5.00
❑72, Feb 1979	5.00
❑73, Mar 1979	5.00
❑74, Apr 1979	5.00
❑75, May 1979	5.00
❑76, Jun 1979 JKu (c)	5.00
❑77, Jul 1979	5.00
❑78, Aug 1979 JKu (c)	5.00
❑79, Sep 1979	5.00
❑80, Oct 1979 RE, RT (a)	5.00
❑81, Nov 1979	5.00
❑82, Dec 1979 DN, HC (a)	5.00
❑83, Jan 1980	5.00
❑84, Feb 1980	5.00
❑85, Mar 1980	5.00
❑86, Apr 1980	5.00
❑87, May 1980	5.00
❑88, Jun 1980	5.00
❑89, Jul 1980	5.00
❑90, Aug 1980	5.00
❑91, Sep 1980	5.00
❑92, Oct 1980 JKu (c)	5.00
❑93, Nov 1980 JKu (c); O: Creature Commandos. 1: Creature Commandos.	6.00
❑94, Dec 1980	5.00
❑95, Jan 1981	5.00
❑96, Feb 1981 JKu (c)	5.00
❑97, Mar 1981	5.00
❑98, Apr 1981	5.00
❑99, May 1981	5.00
❑100, Jun 1981; JKu (c); BH (a); Creature Commandos in War That Time Forgot	5.00
❑101, Jul 1981 1: G.I. Robot I.	5.00
❑102, Aug 1981; Creature Commandos captured by Hitler	3.50
❑103, Sep 1981 BH (a)	3.50
❑104, Oct 1981	3.50
❑105, Nov 1981; Creature Commandos	3.50
❑106, Dec 1981	3.50
❑107, Jan 1982	3.50
❑108, Feb 1982; BH (a); Creature Commandos, G.I. Robot	3.50
❑109, Mar 1982; BH (a); Creature Commandos	3.50
❑110, Apr 1982 1: Doctor Medusa. 1: Dr. Medusa.	3.50
❑111, May 1982; G.I. Robot teams with Creature Commandos	3.50
❑112, Jun 1982; Creature Commandos	3.50
❑113, Jul 1982 1: G.I. Robot II. V: Samurai Robot.	3.50
❑114, Aug 1982; A: Hitler. Creature Commandos	3.50
❑115, Sep 1982; G.I. Robot II and Creature Commandos	3.50
❑116, Oct 1982; CI (a); G.I. Robot II and Creature Commandos	3.50
❑117, Nov 1982; G.I. Robot II and Creature Commandos	3.50
❑118, Dec 1982	3.50
❑119, Jan 1983; Creature Commandos	3.50
❑120, Feb 1983; G.I. Robot	3.50
❑121, Mar 1983; Creature Commandos	3.50
❑122, Apr 1983; G.I. Robot vs. Sumo Robot	3.50
❑123, May 1983	3.50
❑124, Jun 1983	3.50

WEIRD WAR TALES (MINI-SERIES)
DC

	N-MINT
❑1, Jun 1997	2.50
❑2, Jul 1997	2.50
❑3, Aug 1997	2.50

N-MINT

❑4, Sep 1997 .... 2.50
❑Special 1, Apr 2000 .... 4.95

WEIRD WEST
FANTACO

❑1 .... 2.95
❑2 .... 2.95
❑3 .... 2.95

WEIRD WESTERN TALES
DC

❑12, Jun 1972; BWr, NA (a); Series continued from All-Star Western #11 .... 30.00
❑13, Aug 1972 NA (a) 25.00
❑14, Oct 1972 ATh (a) 20.00
❑15, Dec 1972 NA, GK (a) 20.00
❑16, Feb 1973 .... 12.00
❑17, Apr 1973 .... 12.00
❑18, Jul 1973; Jonah Hex issue 12.00
❑19, Sep 1973 .... 12.00
❑20, Nov 1973 .... 12.00
❑21, Jan 1974 .... 12.00
❑22, May 1974 .... 12.00
❑23, Jul 1974 .... 12.00
❑24, Sep 1974; blind Jonah Hex 12.00
❑25, Nov 1974 .... 12.00
❑26, Jan 1975 .... 12.00
❑27, Mar 1975 .... 12.00
❑28, May 1975 .... 12.00
❑29, Jul 1975 O: Jonah Hex. 16.00
❑30, Sep 1975 .... 6.00
❑31, Nov 1975 .... 6.00
❑32, Jan 1976 .... 6.00
❑33, Mar 1976 .... 6.00
❑34, May 1976 .... 6.00
❑35, Jul 1976 .... 6.00
❑36, Sep 1976 .... 6.00
❑37, Nov 1976 .... 6.00
❑38, Jan 1977 .... 6.00
❑39, Mar 1977 1: Scalphunter. 6.00
❑40, Jun 1977 .... 6.00
❑41, Aug 1977 .... 6.00
❑42, Oct 1977 .... 6.00
❑43, Dec 1977 .... 6.00
❑44, Feb 1978 .... 6.00
❑45, Apr 1978 .... 6.00
❑46, Jun 1978 .... 6.00
❑47, Aug 1978 .... 6.00
❑48, Oct 1978 1: Cinnamon. 6.00
❑49, Nov 1978 .... 6.00
❑50, Dec 1978 .... 6.00
❑51, Jan 1979 .... 5.00
❑52, Feb 1979 .... 5.00
❑53, Mar 1979 .... 5.00
❑54, Apr 1979 .... 5.00
❑55, May 1979 .... 5.00
❑56, Jun 1979 .... 5.00
❑57, Jul 1979 .... 5.00
❑58, Aug 1979 .... 5.00
❑59, Sep 1979 .... 5.00
❑60, Oct 1979 .... 5.00
❑61, Nov 1979 .... 5.00
❑62, Dec 1979 .... 5.00
❑63, Jan 1980 .... 5.00
❑64, Feb 1980 .... 5.00
❑65, Mar 1980 .... 5.00
❑66, Apr 1980 .... 5.00
❑67, May 1980 .... 5.00
❑68, Jun 1980 .... 5.00
❑69, Jul 1980 .... 5.00
❑70, Aug 1980 .... 5.00

WEIRD WESTERN TALES (MINI-SERIES)
DC / VERTIGO

❑1, Apr 2001 .... 2.50
❑2, May 2001 .... 2.50
❑3, Jun 2001 .... 2.50
❑4, Jul 2001 .... 2.50

WEIRD WONDER TALES
MARVEL

❑1, Dec 1973; BW (a); Reprints Mystic #6 (Eye of Doom) 10.00
❑2, Feb 1974 .... 5.00

N-MINT

❑3, Apr 1974, BEv (a) 5.00
❑4, Jun 1974, SL (w); SD (a) 2.50
❑5, Aug 1974, SL (w); SD (a) 2.50
❑6, Oct 1974, JK (a) 2.50
❑7, Dec 1974 .... 2.50
❑8, Feb 1975, SL (w) 2.50
❑9, Apr 1975 .... 2.50
❑10, Jun 1975, SD, JK (a) 2.50
❑11, Aug 1975, SL (w); SD, JK (a) 2.50
❑12, Oct 1975, SL (w); SD, MD (a) 2.50
❑13, Dec 1975, SL (w); SD, JK, RH (a) 2.50
❑14, Feb 1976, DH, JAb (a) 2.50
❑15, Apr 1976, TS (w); TS, DH (a) 2.50
❑15/30 cent, Apr 1976; 30 cent regional variant 20.00
❑16, Jun 1976, BEv, JSt (a) 2.50
❑16/30 cent, Jun 1976; 30 cent regional variant 20.00
❑17, Aug 1976, GC, BEv (a) 2.50
❑17/30 cent, Aug 1976; 30 cent regional variant 20.00
❑18, Oct 1976, BEv, JK (a) 2.50
❑19, Dec 1976; SD, JK, BK (a); Doctor Druid; Reprints from Tales to Astonish #13, Astonishing Tales #47 .... 2.50
❑20, Jan 1977; SL (w); SD, JK (a); Doctor Druid 2.50
❑21, Mar 1977; SL (w); SD (a); Doctor Druid 2.50
❑22, May 1977; SL (w); JK, JKu (a); Doctor Druid 2.50

WEIRD WORLDS
DC

❑1, Sep 1972; JKu (c); MA (a); continues John Carter of Mars from Tarzan #209 and Pellucidar from Korak 4.00
❑2, Nov 1972; JO, CI (c); MA (a); adapts Burroughs' Pellucidar and Martian novels 3.00
❑3, Jan 1973; JO (c); MA (a); adapts Burroughs' Pellucidar and Martian novels 3.00
❑4, Mar 1973; (c); adapts Burroughs' Pellucidar and Martian novels 2.50
❑5, May 1973; DGr (a); adapts Burroughs' Pellucidar and Martian novels 2.50
❑6, Aug 1973; (c); DGr (a); adapts Burroughs' Pellucidar and Martian novels 2.00
❑7, Oct 1973; HC (c); DGr (a); adapts Burroughs' Pellucidar and Martian novels; John Carter, Warlord of Mars ends 2.00
❑8, Dec 1973, HC (c); HC (w); HC (a); 1: Iron Wolf. 2.00
❑9, Feb 1974; HC (w); HC (a); Iron Wolf 2.00
❑10, Nov 1974; (w); HC (a); Iron Wolf 2.00

WELCOME BACK, KOTTER
DC

❑1, Nov 1976; BO (a); based on ABC TV series 10.00
❑2, Jan 1977; BO (c); based on ABC TV series 2.50
❑3, Mar 1977; RE (a); based on ABC TV series 2.50
❑4, May 1977; BO (c); ME (w); BO, RE (a); based on ABC TV series 2.50
❑5, Jul 1977; BO, RE (a); based on ABC TV series 2.50
❑6, Sep 1977; BO, RE (a); based on ABC TV series 2.50
❑7, Nov 1977; RE (c); BO, RE (a); based on ABC TV series 2.50
❑8, Jan 1978; BO (c); BO, RE (a); based on ABC TV series 2.50
❑9, Feb 1978; BO (c); BO, RE (a); based on ABC TV series 2.50
❑10, Mar 1978; BO (c); BO, RE (a); based on ABC TV series 2.50

WELCOME BACK TO THE HOUSE OF MYSTERY
DC / VERTIGO

❑1, Jul 1998; collects stories from House of Mystery and Plop 5.95

Early issues of *Weird Worlds* featured stories based on Edgar Rice Burroughs' Pellucidar and Mars novels.

© 1972 Edgar Rice Burroughs Estate and National Periodical Publications (DC).

N-MINT

WELCOME TO THE LITTLE SHOP OF HORRORS
ROGER CORMAN'S COSMIC COMICS

❑1, May 1995 .... 2.50
❑2, Jun 1995 .... 2.50
❑3, Jul 1995 .... 2.50

WENDEL
KITCHEN SINK

❑1, b&w 2.95

WENDY, THE GOOD LITTLE WITCH (VOL. 1)
HARVEY

❑1, Aug 1960 .... 60.00
❑2, Oct 1960 .... 40.00
❑3, Dec 1960 .... 28.00
❑4, Feb 1961 .... 28.00
❑5, Apr 1961 .... 28.00
❑6, Jun 1961 .... 22.00
❑7, Aug 1961 .... 22.00
❑8, Oct 1961 .... 22.00
❑9, Dec 1961 .... 22.00
❑10, Feb 1962 .... 22.00
❑11, Apr 1962 .... 14.00
❑12, Jun 1962 .... 14.00
❑13, Aug 1962 .... 14.00
❑14, Oct 1962 .... 14.00
❑15, Dec 1962 .... 14.00
❑16, Feb 1963 .... 12.00
❑17, Apr 1963 .... 12.00
❑18, Jun 1963 .... 12.00
❑19, Aug 1963 .... 12.00
❑20, Oct 1963 .... 12.00
❑21, Dec 1963 .... 8.00
❑22, Feb 1964 .... 8.00
❑23, Apr 1964 .... 8.00
❑24, Jun 1964 .... 8.00
❑25, Aug 1964 .... 8.00
❑26, Oct 1964 .... 6.00
❑27, Dec 1964 .... 6.00
❑28, Feb 1965 .... 6.00
❑29, Apr 1965 .... 6.00
❑30, Jun 1965 .... 6.00
❑31, Aug 1965 .... 5.00
❑32, Oct 1965 .... 5.00
❑33, Dec 1965 .... 5.00
❑34, Feb 1966 .... 5.00
❑35, Apr 1966 .... 5.00
❑36, Jun 1966 .... 5.00
❑37, Aug 1966 .... 5.00
❑38, Oct 1966 .... 5.00
❑39, Dec 1966 .... 5.00
❑40, Feb 1967 .... 5.00
❑41, Apr 1967 .... 4.00
❑42, Jun 1967 .... 4.00
❑43, Aug 1967 .... 4.00
❑44, Oct 1967 .... 4.00
❑45, Dec 1967 .... 4.00
❑46, Feb 1968 .... 4.00
❑47, Apr 1968 .... 4.00
❑48, Jun 1968 .... 4.00
❑49 1968 .... 4.00
❑50, Dec 1968 .... 4.00
❑51, Jan 1969 .... 3.00
❑52, Feb 1969 .... 3.00
❑53 1969 .... 3.00
❑54 1969 .... 3.00
❑55, Jul 1969 .... 3.00

N-MINT

❑56, Sep 1969 .... 3.00
❑57, Nov 1969 .... 3.00
❑58, Jan 1970 .... 3.00
❑59, Mar 1970 .... 3.00
❑60, May 1970 .... 3.00
❑61, Jul 1970 .... 2.00
❑62, Sep 1970 .... 2.00
❑63, Nov 1970 .... 2.00
❑64, Jan 1971 .... 2.00
❑65, Feb 1971 .... 2.00
❑66, Apr 1971 .... 2.00
❑67, Jun 1971 .... 2.00
❑68, Aug 1971 .... 2.00
❑69, Sep 1971 .... 2.00
❑70, Nov 1971 .... 2.00
❑71, Feb 1972 .... 2.00
❑72, Apr 1972 .... 2.00
❑73, Jun 1972 .... 2.00
❑74, Aug 1972 .... 2.00
❑75, Oct 1972 .... 2.00
❑76, Dec 1972 .... 2.00
❑77, Jan 1973 .... 2.00
❑78, Mar 1973 .... 2.00
❑79, May 1973 .... 2.00
❑80, Jul 1973 .... 2.00
❑81, Sep 1973 .... 2.00
❑82, Nov 1973 .... 2.00
❑83, Aug 1974 .... 2.00
❑84, Oct 1974 .... 2.00
❑85, Dec 1974 .... 2.00
❑86, Feb 1975 .... 2.00
❑87, Apr 1975 .... 2.00
❑88, Jun 1975 .... 2.00
❑89, Aug 1975 .... 2.00
❑90, Oct 1975 .... 2.00
❑91, Dec 1975 .... 2.00
❑92, Feb 1976 .... 2.00
❑93, Apr 1976 .... 2.00
❑94, Sep 1990; ; Series begins again (1990) 1.25
❑95, Oct 1990 .... 1.25
❑96, Nov 1990 .... 1.25
❑97, Dec 1990 .... 1.25

WENDY THE GOOD LITTLE WITCH (VOL. 2)
HARVEY

❑1, Apr 1991 .... 2.00
❑2 1991 .... 1.50
❑3, Aug 1991 .... 1.50
❑4, Oct 1991 .... 1.50
❑5 1992 .... 1.50
❑6 1992 .... 1.50
❑7 1992 .... 1.50
❑8, Oct 1992 .... 1.50
❑9, Jan 1993 .... 1.50
❑10, May 1993 .... 1.50
❑11 1993 .... 1.50
❑12, Dec 1993 .... 1.50
❑13, Mar 1994 .... 1.50
❑14 1994 .... 1.50
❑15, Aug 1994 .... 1.50

WENDY IN 3-D
BLACKTHORNE

❑1 .... 2.50

WENDY WHITEBREAD, UNDERCOVER SLUT
FANTAGRAPHICS / EROS

❑1, b&w 2.50
❑1-2, b&w 2.95
❑1-3, b&w 2.95
❑1-4, b&w 2.95
❑1-5, Nov 1990, b&w 3.95
❑2, b&w 2.50

WENDY WITCH WORLD
HARVEY

❑1, Oct 1961 .... 90.00
❑2, Sep 1962 .... 50.00
❑3, Dec 1962 .... 50.00
❑4, Mar 1963 .... 50.00
❑5, Jun 1963 .... 50.00

N-MINT

❑6, Sep 1963 .... 35.00
❑7, Dec 1963 .... 35.00
❑8, Mar 1964 .... 35.00
❑9, Jun 1964 .... 35.00
❑10, Sep 1964 .... 35.00
❑11, Dec 1964 .... 26.00
❑12, Mar 1965 .... 26.00
❑13, Jun 1965 .... 26.00
❑14, Sep 1965 .... 26.00
❑15, Dec 1965 .... 26.00
❑16, ca. 1966 .... 26.00
❑17, ca. 1966 .... 26.00
❑18, Nov 1966 .... 26.00
❑19, Jan 1967 .... 26.00
❑20, May 1967 .... 26.00
❑21, Aug 1967 .... 22.00
❑22, Nov 1967 .... 22.00
❑23, Jan 1968 .... 22.00
❑24, May 1968 .... 22.00
❑25, Jul 1968 .... 22.00
❑26, Sep 1968 .... 22.00
❑27, Feb 1969 .... 22.00
❑28, Apr 1969 .... 22.00
❑29, Jun 1969 .... 22.00
❑30, Aug 1969 .... 22.00
❑31, Oct 1969 .... 18.00
❑32, Dec 1969 .... 18.00
❑33, Feb 1970 .... 18.00
❑34, Apr 1970 .... 18.00
❑35, ca. 1970 .... 18.00
❑36, ca. 1970 .... 15.00
❑37, Dec 1970 .... 15.00
❑38, Feb 1971 .... 15.00
❑39, Apr 1971 .... 15.00
❑40, ca. 1971 .... 15.00
❑41, ca. 1971 .... 15.00
❑42, Dec 1971 .... 15.00
❑43, Feb 1972 .... 15.00
❑44, May 1972 .... 15.00
❑45, Sep 1972 .... 12.00
❑46, Dec 1972 .... 12.00
❑47, ca. 1973 .... 12.00
❑48, ca. 1973 .... 12.00
❑49, ca. 1973 .... 12.00
❑50, ca. 1973 .... 8.00
❑51, Oct 1973 .... 8.00
❑52, ca. 1974 .... 8.00
❑53, Sep 1974 .... 8.00

WEREWOLF
DELL

❑1, Dec 1966; TV show 8.00
❑2, Mar 1967; TV show 5.00
❑3, Apr 1967; O: Werewolf (Major Wiley Wolf). TV show 5.00

WEREWOLF (BLACKTHORNE)
BLACKTHORNE

❑1, Sep 1988, b&w 2.00
❑2 .... 2.00
❑3 .... 2.00
❑4, Jan 1989 .... 2.00

WEREWOLF AT LARGE
ETERNITY

❑1, Jun 1989, b&w 2.25
❑2, b&w 2.25
❑3, b&w 2.25

WEREWOLF BY NIGHT
MARVEL

❑1, Sep 1972, MP (c); MP (a) 30.00
❑2, Nov 1972, MP (c); MP (a) 12.00
❑3, Jan 1973, MP (c); MP (a) 8.00
❑4, Mar 1973, MP (c); MP (a) 8.00
❑5, May 1973, MP (c); MP (a) 6.00
❑6, Jun 1973, MP (a) 6.00
❑7, Jul 1973, MP, JM (a) 6.00
❑8, Aug 1973, MP (c) 6.00
❑9, Sep 1973, TS (a) 6.00
❑10, Oct 1973, TS (c); TS (a) 6.00
❑11, Nov 1973, TS, GK (a) 5.00
❑12, Dec 1973, GK, DP (a) 5.00
❑13, Jan 1974, MP (c); MP (a) 5.00

N-MINT

❑14, Feb 1974, MP (c); MP (a) 5.00
❑15, Mar 1974; MP (c); MP (a); Marvel Value Stamp #75: Morbius 5.00
❑16, Apr 1974; MP (a); Marvel Value Stamp #65: Iceman 5.00
❑17, May 1974; DP (a); Marvel Value Stamp #99: Sandman 5.00
❑18, Jun 1974, DP (a) 5.00
❑19, Jul 1974; DP (a); Marvel Value Stamp #61: Red Ghost 5.00
❑20, Aug 1974; DP (a); Marvel Value Stamp #97: Black Knight 5.00
❑21, Sep 1974; DP (a); Marvel Value Stamp #72: Lizard 4.00
❑22, Oct 1974; DP (a); Marvel Value Stamp #51: Bucky Barnes 4.00
❑23, Nov 1974; DP (a); Marvel Value Stamp #93: Silver Surfer 4.00
❑24, Dec 1974; AM, GK (c); DP (a); Marvel Value Stamp #8: Captain America 4.00
❑25, Jan 1975; DP (a); Marvel Value Stamp #63: Sub-Mariner 4.00
❑26, Feb 1975; DP (a); Marvel Value Stamp #28: Hawkeye 4.00
❑27, Mar 1975; DP (a); Marvel Value Stamp #9: Captain Marvel 4.00
❑28, Apr 1975, DP (a) 4.00
❑29, May 1975, DP (a) 4.00
❑30, Jun 1975, DP (a) 4.00
❑31, Jul 1975, DP (w); DP (a) 4.00
❑32, Aug 1975, DP (a); O: Moon Knight. 1: Moon Knight. 25.00
❑33, Sep 1975, DP (a); 2: Moon Knight. 2: Moon Knight. 15.00
❑34, Oct 1975, DP (a) 3.00
❑35, Nov 1975, DP (a) 3.00
❑36, Jan 1976, DP (c); DP (a) 3.00
❑37, Mar 1976, DP (a); A: Moon Knight. 4.00
❑38, May 1976, DP (c); DP (a) 2.50
❑38/30 cent, May 1976; 30 cent regional price variant 8.00
❑39, Jul 1976, RB (c); DP (a) 2.50
❑39/30 cent, Jul 1976; 30 cent regional price variant 8.00
❑40, Sep 1976, DP (a) 5.00
❑41, Nov 1976, DP (a) 5.00
❑42, Jan 1977, DC (c); DP (a) 10.00
❑43, Mar 1977, DP (a) 10.00

WEREWOLF BY NIGHT (VOL. 2)
MARVEL

❑1, Feb 1998 .... 3.00
❑2, Mar 1998; gatefold summary MP (c) 3.00
❑3, Apr 1998; gatefold summary 3.00
❑4, May 1998; gatefold summary (c) 3.00
❑5, Jun 1998; gatefold summary (c) . 3.00
❑6, Jul 1998; gatefold summary A: Ghost Rider. 3.00

WEREWOLF IN 3-D
BLACKTHORNE

❑1, ca. 1988 .... 2.50

WEST COAST AVENGERS
MARVEL

❑1, Oct 1985, AM, JSt (c); AM, JSt (a) 2.00
❑2, Nov 1985, AM, JSt (c); AM (a) 1.50
❑3, Dec 1985, AM, JSt (c); AM, JSt (a); V: Kraven. 1.50
❑4, Jan 1986, AM, JSt (c); AM, JSt (a); 1: Master Pandemonium. 1.00
❑5, Feb 1986, AM, JSt (c); AM, JSt (a) 1.00
❑6, Mar 1986, AM (c); AM (a) 1.00
❑7, Apr 1986, AM, JSt (c); AM, JSt (a); V: Ultron. 1.00
❑8, May 1986, AM, JSt (c); AM, JSt (a); V: Rangers. 1.00
❑9, Jun 1986, AM, JSt (c); AM, JSt (a); O: Master Pandemonium. 1.00
❑10, Jul 1986, AM, JSt (c); AM, JSt (a) 1.00
❑11, Aug 1986, AM, JSt (c); AM, JSt (a) 1.00
❑12, Sep 1986, AM, JSt (c); AM, JSt (a); 1: Halflife. 1: Quantum. V: Zzzax. 1.00
❑13, Oct 1986, AM, JSt (c); AM, JSt (a); O: Hellstorm. V: Graviton. 1.00
❑14, Nov 1986, AM, JSt (c); AM, JSt (a); 1: Hellstorm. 1.00

Condition price index: Multiply "NM prices" above by: **0.83 for Very Fine/Near Mint**
0.66 for Very Fine • 0.33 for Fine • 0.2 for Very Good • 0.125 for Good

N-MINT

❑15, Dec 1986, AM, JSt (a) 1.00
❑16, Jan 1987, AM, JSt (c); AM, JSt (a) 1.00
❑17, Feb 1987, AM, JSt (a) 1.00
❑18, Mar 1987, AM, JSt (c); AM, JSt (a) 1.00
❑19, Apr 1987, AM, JSt (a) 1.00
❑20, May 1987, AM, JSt (c); AM, JSt (a) 1.00
❑21, Jun 1987, AM, JSt (c); AM, JSt (a); A: Moon Knight. 1.00
❑22, Jul 1987, AM, JSt (c); AM (a); A: Doctor Strange. 1.00
❑23, Aug 1987, AM (c); AM, RT (a) .. 1.00
❑24, Sep 1987, AM (c); AM (a) 1.00
❑25, Oct 1987, AM (c); AM (a) 1.00
❑26, Nov 1987, AM (c); AM (a); V: Zodiac. 1.00
❑27, Dec 1987, AM (c); AM (a); V: Zodiac. 1.00
❑28, Jan 1988, AM (c); AM (a); V: Zodiac. 1.00
❑29, Feb 1988, AM (c); AM (a) 1.00
❑30, Mar 1988, AM (c); AM (w); AM (a) 1.00
❑31, Apr 1988, AM (c); AM (a); V: Arkon. 1.00
❑32, May 1988, AM (c); AM, TD (a) .. 1.00
❑33, Jun 1988, AM (c); AM (a) 1.00
❑34, Jul 1988, AM (c); AM (a); V: Quicksilver. 1.00
❑35, Aug 1988, AM (c); AM (a); V: Doctor Doom. 1.00
❑36, Sep 1988, AM (c); AM (a) 1.00
❑37, Oct 1988, AM (c); AM (a) 1.00
❑38, Nov 1988 .... 1.00
❑39, Dec 1988, AM (a) 1.00
❑40, Jan 1989, AM (c); AM, MGu (a) 1.00
❑41, Feb 1989 .... 1.00
❑42, Mar 1989, JBy (c); JBy (w); JBy (a) 1.00
❑43, Apr 1989, JBy (c); JBy (w); JBy (a) 1.00
❑44, May 1989, JBy (c); JBy (w); JBy (a); 1: U.S.Agent. 1.00
❑45, Jun 1989, JBy (c); JBy (w); JBy (a) 1.00
❑46, Jul 1989; JBy (c); JBy (w); JBy (a); 1: Great Lakes Avengers. 1: Big Bertha. Title changes to Avengers West Coast 1.00
❑Annual 1, ca. 1986; V: Quicksilver. ca. 1986; Concludes story begun in Avengers Annual #15 .... 2.00
❑Annual 2, ca. 1987; AM (c); AM (a); Begins story concluded in Avengers Annual #16; ca. 1987 .... 2.00
❑Annual 3, ca. 1988; AM (c); AM, TD (a); series continues as Avengers West Coast Annual 2.00

WEST COAST AVENGERS (LTD. SERIES)
MARVEL

❑1, Sep 1984, BH (c); BH (a); O: West Coast Avengers. 1: West Coast Avengers. 2.50
❑2, Oct 1984, BH (c); BH (a) 2.00
❑3, Nov 1984, BH (c); BH (a) 2.00
❑4, Dec 1984, BH (c); BH (a) 2.00

WESTERN ACTION
ATLAS-SEABOARD

❑1, Jun 1975 AM, JAb (a) 4.00

WESTERN GUNFIGHTERS (2ND SERIES)
MARVEL

❑1, Aug 1970; giant 10.00
❑2, Oct 1970; O: Nightwind (The Apache Kid's horse). giant 6.00
❑3, Dec 1970; giant 6.00
❑4, Mar 1971; giant 6.00
❑5, Jun 1971; giant 6.00
❑6, Sep 1971; BEv (a); D: Ghost Rider. giant 6.00
❑7, Jan 1972; O: Night Rider (Ghost Rider). 1: Lincoln Slade as Ghost Rider. D: Phantom Rider I (Carter Slade). giant 8.00
❑8, Mar 1972 .... 5.00
❑9, May 1972 .... 5.00
❑10, Jul 1972 O: Black Rider. 5.00
❑11, Sep 1972 .... 5.00
❑12, Nov 1972 O: Matt Slade. 5.00

N-MINT

❑13, Jan 1973 .... 5.00
❑14, Mar 1973 .... 5.00
❑15, May 1973 .... 5.00
❑16, Jul 1973 .... 5.00
❑17, Sep 1973 .... 4.00
❑18, Oct 1973 .... 4.00
❑19, Nov 1973 .... 4.00
❑20, Jan 1974 .... 4.00
❑21, Mar 1974 .... 4.00
❑22, May 1974 .... 4.00
❑23, Jul 1974 .... 4.00
❑24, Sep 1974 .... 4.00
❑25, Oct 1974 .... 4.00
❑26, Nov 1974 .... 4.00
❑27, Jan 1975 .... 4.00
❑28, Mar 1975 .... 4.00
❑29, May 1975 .... 4.00
❑30, Jul 1975 .... 4.00
❑31, Sep 1975 SL (w); A: Gun-Slinger. A: Apache Kid. A: Kid Colt. 4.00
❑32, Nov 1975 .... 4.00
❑33, Jan 1976 .... 4.00

WESTERN KID, THE (2ND SERIES)
MARVEL

❑1, Dec 1971 .... 9.00
❑2, Feb 1972 .... 6.00
❑3, Apr 1972 .... 6.00
❑4, Jun 1972 .... 6.00
❑5, Aug 1972 .... 6.00

WESTERN TEAM-UP
MARVEL

❑1, Nov 1973 (c); 1: The Dakota Kid. 8.00

WEST OF THE DAKOTAS
COMIC BOOK STORIES

❑1, Dec 2002 .... 4.99

WESTSIDE
ANTARCTIC

❑1, Mar 2000 .... 2.50

WEST STREET STORIES
WEST STREET

❑0, Nov 1995, b&w 2.50
❑1, Jan 1997, b&w 2.50

WETWORKS
IMAGE

❑1, Jun 1994 .... 1.95
❑1/3D, Jun 1994; 3-D edition 4.95
❑1/Ltd., Jun 1994; Special promotional edition distributed at the 1994 Chicago Comicon 1.95
❑2, Aug 1994; Standard cover: Beast attacking man 1.95
❑2/A, Aug 1994; Variant edition cover with whole team posing; alternate cover 1.95
❑3, Sep 1994 .... 1.95
❑4, Nov 1994 .... 2.50
❑5, Jan 1995 .... 2.50
❑6, Mar 1995 .... 2.50
❑7, Apr 1995 .... 2.50
❑8, May 1995; bound-in trading cards 2.50
❑8/Variant, May 1995 .... 2.50
❑9, Aug 1995 .... 2.50
❑10, Aug 1995 .... 2.50
❑11, Sep 1995 .... 2.50
❑12, Nov 1995; indicia says Nov, cover says Dec 2.50
❑13, Jan 1996 .... 2.50
❑14, Feb 1996 .... 2.50
❑15, Mar 1996 .... 2.50
❑16, Apr 1996 .... 2.50
❑17, May 1996 .... 2.50
❑18, Jul 1996 .... 2.50
❑19, Aug 1996 .... 2.50
❑20, Aug 1996 .... 2.50
❑21, Sep 1996 .... 2.50
❑22, Oct 1996 .... 2.50
❑23, Nov 1996 .... 2.50
❑24, Dec 1996 .... 2.50
❑25, Jan 1997; Giant-size; wraparound cover 3.95

Rick Jones took the full brunt of the gamma bomb blast and became a teenage Hulk in *What If?* (Vol. 1) #12.

© 1978 Marvel Comics.

N-MINT

❑25/A, Jan 1997; alternate wraparound cover (previous covers in background) 3.95
❑26, Feb 1997 .... 2.50
❑27, Mar 1997 .... 2.50
❑28, Apr 1997 .... 2.50
❑29, May 1997 .... 2.50
❑30, Jun 1997 .... 2.50
❑31, Jul 1997 .... 2.50
❑32, Aug 1997 .... 2.50
❑32/A, Aug 1997; Voyager pack; alternate cover (mostly b&w) 2.50
❑33, Sep 1997 .... 2.50
❑34, Oct 1997 .... 2.50
❑35, Nov 1997 .... 2.50
❑36, Jan 1998 .... 2.50
❑37, Feb 1998 .... 2.50
❑38, Mar 1998 .... 2.50
❑39, Apr 1998 .... 2.50
❑40, May 1998 .... 2.50
❑41, Jun 1998 .... 2.50
❑42, Jul 1998 .... 2.50
❑43, Aug 1998 .... 2.50
❑3D 1, Feb 1998; with glasses; wraparound cover 4.95

WETWORKS SOURCEBOOK
IMAGE

❑1, Oct 1994 .... 2.50

WETWORKS/VAMPIRELLA
IMAGE

❑1, Jul 1997; crossover with Harris .. 2.95
❑1/A, Jul 1997; crossover with Harris; alternate cover 2.95

WHACKED!
RIVER GROUP

❑1, Mar 1994; Tonya Harding case parody; wraparound cover 2.50

WHAM-O GIANT COMICS
WHAM-O

❑1, Apr 1967; WW (w); WW (a); Wraparound cover, oversized oversize 14 X 21 .... 100.00

WHAT IF...? (VOL. 1)
MARVEL

❑1, Feb 1977; A: Spider-Man. Spider-Man 15.00
❑2, Apr 1977; GK (c); TS, HT (a); A: Hulk. Hulk 10.00
❑3, Jun 1977; GK, JSt (c); GK (w); GK, KJ (a); A: Avengers. Avengers 8.00
❑4, Aug 1977; GK (c); FR, FS (a); A: Invaders. Invaders 8.00
❑5, Oct 1977; GT (a); O: Bucky II (Fred Davis). 1: Captain America II (William Nasland). 1: Captain America III (Jeffrey Mace). D: Captain America II (William Nasland). Captain America 8.00
❑6, Dec 1977; A: Fantastic 4. Fantastic Four 5.00
❑7, Feb 1978; GK, JSt (c); A: Spider-Man. Spider-Man 5.00
❑8, Apr 1978; GK, JR (c); JM (a); O: 'Mazing Man-Spider. Daredevil 5.00
❑9, Jun 1978; JK, GK, JSt (c); O: Marvel Boy. O: Human Robot. O: 3-D Man. O: Venus. O: Gorilla-Man. Avengers 5.00
❑10, Aug 1978; A: Thor. Thor 5.00
❑11, Oct 1978; JK, JSt (c); JK (w); JK (a); Marvel Bullpen as Fantastic Four 3.50

Condition price index: Multiply "NM prices" above by: **0.83 for Very Fine/Near Mint**
0.66 for Very Fine • 0.33 for Fine • 0.2 for Very Good • 0.125 for Good

	N-MINT
❑12, Dec 1978; SB (a); Rick Jones as Hulk	3.50
❑13, Feb 1979; JB (c); JB (a); A: Conan. Conan	5.00
❑14, Apr 1979; HT (a); A: Sgt. Fury. Sgt. Fury	3.50
❑15, Jun 1979; JSt (c); JB, JSt (a); A: Nova. Nova	3.50
❑16, Aug 1979; A: Fu Manchu. Fu Manchu	3.00
❑17, Oct 1979; Cl (a); Ghost Rider, Captain Marvel, Spider-Woman	3.50
❑18, Dec 1979; TS (a); Doctor Strange	3.00
❑19, Feb 1980; PB (a); Spider-Man	3.00
❑20, Apr 1980; AM, JSt (c); Avengers	3.00
❑21, Jun 1980; GC, BWi (a); Sub-Mariner	3.00
❑22, Aug 1980; RB, BMc (c); Doctor Doom	3.00
❑23, Oct 1980; AM (c); HT (a); Hulk	3.00
❑24, Dec 1980; JR2, BMc (c); RB, GK (a); Spider-Man	3.00
❑25, Feb 1981; (c); RB (a); O: Uni-Mind. Thor, Avengers	3.00
❑26, Apr 1981; JBy (c); HT (a); Captain America	3.00
❑27, Jul 1981; FM (c); FM (a); X-Men	5.00
❑28, Aug 1981; FM (w); TS, FM, KJ (a); A: Ghost Rider. Daredevil	8.00
❑29, Oct 1981; MG (c); RB, BMc, JSt (a); Avengers	3.00
❑30, Dec 1981; BL (c); RB, JM, JSt (a); Spider-Man clone, Inhumans	8.00
❑31, Feb 1982; BWi (c); Wolverine	8.00
❑32, Apr 1982; BL (c); FM (a); Avengers	3.00
❑33, Jun 1982; (c); BL, DP (a); Dazzler	3.00
❑34, Aug 1982; BL (c); AM, BSz, FH, BL, JR2, FM, BA (w); AM, BSz, FH, JBy, BL, JR2, FM, BA, BH, JSt, FS, BWi, JAb (a); comedy issue	3.00
❑35, Oct 1982; FM (w); SD, FM (a); A: Yellowjacket. Elektra	5.00
❑36, Dec 1982; JBy (c); JBy (w); JBy (a); Fantastic Four; Nova	3.00
❑37, Feb 1983; JSt (c); Beast; Thing; Silver Surfer	3.00
❑38, Apr 1983; Daredevil, Captain America, Vision, Scarlet Witch	3.00
❑39, Jun 1983; Thor vs. Conan	3.00
❑40, Aug 1983; (c); BG (a); Doctor Strange	3.00
❑41, Oct 1983; (c); Sub-Mariner	3.00
❑42, Dec 1983; JSt (a); Fantastic Four	3.00
❑43, Feb 1984; BH, JAb (a); Conan	3.00
❑44, Apr 1984; SB (a); Captain America	3.00
❑45, Jun 1984; (c); Hulk	3.00
❑46, Aug 1984; BSz (c); Spider-Man	3.50
❑47, Oct 1984; BSz (c); Thor, Loki	3.00
❑Special 1, Jun 1988; SD (a); Iron Man	3.00

WHAT IF...? (VOL. 2)
MARVEL

	N-MINT
❑-1, Jul 1997; Flashback; Bishop	2.00
❑1, Jul 1989; MGu (a); Avengers	4.00
❑2, Aug 1989; Daredevil	3.00
❑3, Sep 1989; AM (c); Captain America	3.00
❑4, Oct 1989; AM (c); Spider-Man	3.00
❑5, Nov 1989; Avengers	3.00
❑6, Nov 1989; X-Men	3.00
❑7, Dec 1989; RL (c); RL (a); Wolverine	3.00
❑8, Dec 1989; AM (c); Iron Man	2.50
❑9, Jan 1990; RB (c); RB (a); X-Men	2.50
❑10, Feb 1990; BMc (a); Punisher	2.50
❑11, Mar 1990; TMc (c); Fantastic Four	2.50
❑12, Apr 1990; X-Men	2.50
❑13, May 1990; JLee (c); KB (w); X-Men	2.50
❑14, Jun 1990; Captain Marvel	2.50
❑15, Jul 1990; Fantastic Four, Galactus	2.50
❑16, Aug 1990; Wolverine; Conan	3.00
❑17, Sep 1990, JR2 (c); RHo (w); RHo (a); D: Spider-Man.	2.50
❑18, Oct 1990; LMc (c); LMc (a); Fantastic Four, Doctor Doom	2.50
❑19, Nov 1990; Avengers	2.50
❑20, Dec 1990; BWi (c); Spider-Man	2.50
❑21, Jan 1991; BWi (c); D: Black Cat. Spider-Man	2.25
❑22, Feb 1991; Silver Surfer	2.25
❑23, Mar 1991; BMc (c); KB (w); X-Men	2.25
❑24, Apr 1991; vampire Wolverine	3.50
❑25, May 1991; Atlantis Attacks	3.25
❑26, Jun 1991; LMc (c); KB (w); LMc (a); Punisher	2.00
❑27, Jul 1991; Namor, Fantastic Four	2.00
❑28, Aug 1991; Captain America	2.00
❑29, Sep 1991; Captain America, Avengers	2.00
❑30, Oct 1991; Fantastic Four	2.00
❑31, Nov 1991; BMc (c); Spider-Man with cosmic powers	2.00
❑32, Dec 1991; Phoenix	2.00
❑33, Jan 1992; Phoenix	2.00
❑34, Feb 1992; JR (c); parody issue	2.00
❑35, Mar 1992; Fantastic Four; Spider-Man; Doctor Doom	2.00
❑36, Apr 1992; Avengers vs. Guardians of the Galaxy	2.00
❑37, May 1992; Wolverine	2.00
❑38, Jun 1992; MR (a); Thor	2.00
❑39, Jul 1992; Watcher	2.00
❑40, Aug 1992; X-Men	2.00
❑41, Sep 1992; Avengers vs. Galactus	2.00
❑42, Oct 1992; Spider-Man	2.00
❑43, Nov 1992; Wolverine	2.00
❑44, Dec 1992; LMc (c); KB (w); LMc (a); Venom, Punisher	2.00
❑45, Jan 1993; Ghost Rider	2.00
❑46, Feb 1993; KB (w); Cable	2.00
❑47, Mar 1993; KB (w); Magneto	2.00
❑48, Apr 1993; Daredevil	2.00
❑49, May 1993; Silver Surfer	2.00
❑50, Jun 1993; silver sculpted cover; Hulk, Wolverine	2.95
❑51, Jul 1993; Punisher, Captain America	2.00
❑52, Aug 1993; Doctor Doom	2.00
❑53, Sep 1993; Spider-Man, Hulk, Iron Man 2020	2.00
❑54, Oct 1993; A: Reed Richards. A: Fantastic Four. A: Cage. A: Death's Head II. A: War Machine. A: Captain America. A: Death's Head. A: Charnel. Death's Head	2.00
❑55, Nov 1993; Avengers	2.00
❑56, Dec 1993; Avengers	2.00
❑57, Jan 1994; Punisher	2.00
❑58, Feb 1994; Punisher, Spider-Man	2.00
❑59, Mar 1994; Wolverine/Alpha Flight	2.00
❑60, Apr 1994; KB (w); X-Men wedding	2.00
❑61, May 1994; KB (w); Spider-Man	2.00
❑62, Jun 1994; KB (w); Wolverine	2.00
❑63, Jul 1994; A: War Machine. War Machine	2.00
❑64, Aug 1994; Iron Man	2.00
❑65, Sep 1994, A: Archangel.	1.75
❑66, Oct 1994; Rogue	1.75
❑67, Nov 1994; Captain America	1.75
❑68, Dec 1994; Captain America	1.75
❑69, Jan 1995; X-Men	1.75
❑70, Feb 1995; Silver Surfer	1.75
❑71, Mar 1995; Hulk	1.50
❑72, Apr 1995; Spider-Man	1.50
❑73, May 1995; Daredevil	1.50
❑74, Jun 1995; Mr. Sinister forms The X-Men	1.50
❑75, Jul 1995; Generation X	1.50
❑76, Aug 1995; Flash Thompson as Spider-Man; last Watcher	1.50
❑77, Sep 1995; Legion	1.50
❑78, Oct 1995; New Fantastic Four remains a team	1.50
❑79, Nov 1995; Storm becomes Phoenix	1.50
❑80, Dec 1995; KGa (a); A: Maestro. Hulk becomes The Maestro	1.50
❑81, Jan 1996; Age of Apocalypse didn't end	1.50
❑82, Feb 1996; J. Jonah Jameson adopts Peter Parker	1.50
❑83, Mar 1996	1.50
❑84, Apr 1996, A: Bishop and Shard.	1.50
❑85, May 1996; Magneto ruled all mutants	1.50
❑86, Jun 1996; Scarlet Spider kills Spider-Man	1.50
❑87, Jul 1996; Sabretooth	1.50
❑88, Aug 1996; Spider-Man	1.50
❑89, Sep 1996; Fantastic Four	1.50
❑90, Oct 1996; Cyclops and Havok	1.50
❑91, Nov 1996; Hulk	1.50
❑92, Dec 1996; Joshua Guthrie and a Sentinel	1.50
❑93, Jan 1997; Wolverine	1.50
❑94, Feb 1997; Juggernaut	1.50
❑95, Mar 1997; Ghost Rider	1.95
❑96, Apr 1997; Quicksilver	1.95
❑97, May 1997; A: Doctor Doom. Black Knight	1.95
❑98, Jun 1997; Rogue, Nightcrawler	1.95
❑99, Aug 1997; gatefold summary; Spider-Man	1.99
❑100, Sep 1997; KJ (w); KJ (a); A: Fantastic 4. double-sized; gatefold summary; Gambit	1.99
❑101, Oct 1997; gatefold summary; Archangel	1.99
❑102, Nov 1997; gatefold summary; Daredevil	1.99
❑103, Dec 1997; gatefold summary (c)	1.99
❑104, Jan 1998; gatefold summary; Impossible Man with Infinity Gauntlet	1.99
❑105, Feb 1998; gatefold summary; BSz (a); O: Spider-Girl. 1: Spider-Girl. leads into Marvel 2	12.00
❑106, Mar 1998; gatefold summary	1.99
❑107, Apr 1998; gatefold summary; BSz (c); BSz (a); V: Destroyer. Thor as ruler of Asgard	1.99
❑108, May 1998; gatefold summary; Avengers vs. Carnage	1.99
❑109, Jun 1998; gatefold summary; Thing in Liddleville	1.99
❑110, Jul 1998; gatefold summary; X-Men	1.99
❑111, Aug 1998; gatefold summary; Wolverine as War	1.99
❑112, Sep 1998; gatefold summary; Ka-Zar	1.99
❑113, Oct 1998; gatefold summary; Tony Stark as Sorcerer Supreme	1.99
❑114, Nov 1998; gatefold summary; Secret Wars 25 years later	2.50

WHAT IS...THE FACE?
ACE

	N-MINT
❑1, Dec 1986	1.75
❑2, May 1987	1.75
❑3, Aug 1987	1.75

WHAT'S NEW?- THE COLLECTED ADVENTURES OF PHIL & DIXIE
PALLIARD

	N-MINT
❑1, Oct 1991, b&w and color; The Collected Adventures of Phil and Dixie	7.95
❑2, ca 1994; prestige format	7.95

WHAT'S NEW? WITH PHIL AND DIXIE
STUDIO FOGLIO

	N-MINT
❑2, Mar 2001	8.95
❑3, Apr 2000; prestige format; collects strips from The Duelist	10.95

WHAT THE-?!
MARVEL

	N-MINT
❑1, Aug 1988, AM AM, SD, JSe (a)	4.00
❑2, Sep 1988, JBy (c); AM, FH, JBy (w); AW, JBy, JSe, PF (a)	2.50
❑3, Oct 1988, KB (w); TMc, BMc, KB (a)	3.00
❑4, Nov 1988, BWi (c); FH, KB, PD (w); FH (a)	2.50
❑5, Jul 1989	2.50
❑6, Jan 1990; JBy (c); JBy (w); JBy (a); Acts of Vengeance parody	2.50
❑7, Apr 1990, JBy (c)	2.50
❑8, Jul 1990, JBy (c); KB (w)	2.50
❑9, Oct 1990; JBy (c); wraparound cover	1.75
❑10, Jan 1991; prestige format JBy (c); JBy (a)	1.75
❑11, Mar 1991, JBy (c); RL (a); O: Wolverina.	1.50

	N-MINT
❑12, May 1991 JBy (c)	1.50
❑13, Jul 1991 JBy (c)	1.50
❑14, Sep 1991 JBy (c)	1.50
❑15, Nov 1991	1.50
❑16, Jan 1992; EC parody cover	1.50
❑17, Mar 1992 KB (w)	1.50
❑18, May 1992	1.50
❑19, Jul 1992	1.50
❑20, Aug 1992	1.50
❑21, Sep 1992; JSa (a); Weapon X parody	1.50
❑22, Oct 1992 JSa (a)	1.50
❑23, Nov 1992	1.50
❑24, Dec 1992	1.50
❑25, Sum 1993; Summer Special	2.50
❑26, Fal 1993; Winter Special	2.50
❑27, Win 1993	2.50

WHEELIE AND THE CHOPPER BUNCH
CHARLTON

	N-MINT
❑1, May 1975	10.00
❑2, Jul 1975 JBy (a)	6.00
❑3, Sep 1975 JBy (a)	5.00
❑4, Nov 1975	5.00
❑5, Jan 1976	5.00
❑6, Mar 1976	5.00
❑7, May 1976	5.00

WHEEL OF WORLDS (NEIL GAIMAN'S...)
TEKNO

	N-MINT
❑0, Apr 1995; Direct Market edition; poster	2.95
❑0/CS, Apr 1995; poster	2.95
❑1, May 1996	3.25

WHEN BEANIES ATTACK
BLATANT

	N-MINT
❑1, Mar 1999	2.95
❑1/Variant, Mar 1999; Violent cover	4.95

WHERE CREATURES ROAM
MARVEL

	N-MINT
❑1, Jul 1970 JK (a)	8.00
❑2, Sep 1970 JK (a)	5.00
❑3, Nov 1970 JK (a)	5.00
❑4, Jan 1971 JK (a)	5.00
❑5, Mar 1971 JK (a)	5.00
❑6, May 1971 JK (a)	5.00
❑7, Jul 1971 JK (a)	5.00
❑8, Sep 1971 JK (a)	5.00

WHERE IN THE WORLD IS CARMEN SANDIEGO?
DC

	N-MINT
❑1, Jun 1996; based on computer game series	1.75
❑2, Sep 1996	1.75
❑3, Nov 1996	1.75
❑4, Jan 1997; all-alien issue	1.75

WHERE MONSTERS DWELL
MARVEL

	N-MINT
❑1, Jan 1970	10.00
❑2, Mar 1970	6.00
❑3, May 1970	4.00
❑4, Jul 1970	4.00
❑5, Sep 1970	4.00
❑6, Nov 1970	3.00
❑7, Jan 1971	3.00
❑8, Mar 1971	3.00
❑9, May 1971	3.00
❑10, Jul 1971 SD, SL (w); SD (a)	3.00
❑11, Sep 1971	3.00
❑12, Nov 1971; Giant-size	4.00
❑13, Jan 1972	3.00
❑14, Mar 1972	3.00
❑15, May 1972	3.00
❑16, Jul 1972	3.00
❑17, Sep 1972	3.00
❑18, Nov 1972	3.00
❑19, Jan 1973	3.00
❑20, Mar 1973	3.00
❑21, May 1973	3.00
❑22, Jul 1973	3.00
❑23, Sep 1973	3.00
❑24, Oct 1973	3.00
❑25, Nov 1973	3.00
❑26, Jan 1974	3.00
❑27, Mar 1974	3.00
❑28, May 1974	3.00
❑29, Jul 1974	3.00
❑30, Sep 1974	3.00
❑31, Oct 1974	3.00
❑32, Nov 1974	3.00
❑33, Jan 1975	3.00
❑34, Mar 1975	3.00
❑35, May 1975	3.00
❑36, Jul 1975	3.00
❑37, Sep 1975	3.00
❑38, Oct 1975	3.00

WHILE FIFTY MILLION DIED
TOME

	N-MINT
❑1, b&w; World War II	2.95

WHISPERS AND SHADOWS
OASIS

	N-MINT
❑1, b&w	1.50
❑2, b&w	1.50
❑3, b&w	1.50
❑4, b&w	1.50
❑5, b&w	1.50
❑6, b&w	1.50
❑7, b&w	1.50
❑8, b&w	1.50

WHISPER (VOL. 1)
CAPITAL

	N-MINT
❑1, Dec 1983 O: Whisper.	2.50
❑2, Mar 1984	2.00

WHISPER (VOL. 2)
FIRST

	N-MINT
❑1, Jun 1986	2.00
❑2, Aug 1986	1.50
❑3, Oct 1986	1.50
❑4, Dec 1986	1.50
❑5, Feb 1987	1.50
❑6, Apr 1987	1.50
❑7, Jun 1987	1.50
❑8, Aug 1987	1.75
❑9, Oct 1987	1.75
❑10, Dec 1987	1.75
❑11, Feb 1988	1.75
❑12, Apr 1988	1.75
❑13, Jun 1988	1.75
❑14, Jul 1988	1.75
❑15, Aug 1988	1.75
❑16, Sep 1988	1.75
❑17, Oct 1988	1.75
❑18, Nov 1988	1.95
❑19, Dec 1988	1.95
❑20, Jan 1989	1.95
❑21, Feb 1989	1.95
❑22, Mar 1989	1.95
❑23, Apr 1989	1.95
❑24, May 1989	1.95
❑25, Jun 1989	1.95
❑26, Jul 1989	1.95
❑27, Aug 1989	1.95
❑28, Sep 1989	1.95
❑29, Oct 1989	1.95
❑30, Nov 1989	1.95
❑31, Dec 1989	1.95
❑32, Jan 1990	1.95
❑33, Feb 1990	1.95
❑34, Mar 1990	1.95
❑35, Apr 1990	1.95
❑36, May 1990	1.95
❑37, Jun 1990	1.95
❑Special 1, Nov 1985; Giant-size	2.50

WHITE DEVIL
ETERNITY

	N-MINT
❑1, b&w	2.50
❑2, b&w	2.50
❑3, b&w	2.50
❑4, b&w	2.50
❑5, b&w	2.50
❑6, b&w	2.50

Greg Rucka and Steve Lieber's *Whiteout* and its sequel, *Whiteout: Melt*, have received industry awards.

© 1998 Greg Rucka and Steve Lieber (Oni).

	N-MINT
❑7, b&w	2.50
❑8, b&w	2.50

WHITE FANG
DISNEY

	N-MINT
❑1, ca. 1990; newsstand version	2.95
❑1/Direct ed., ca. 1990	5.95

WHITE LIKE SHE
DARK HORSE

	N-MINT
❑1, May 1994, b&w	2.95
❑2, Jun 1994, b&w	2.95
❑3, Jul 1994, b&w	2.95
❑4, Aug 1994, b&w	2.95

WHITE ORCHID
ATLANTIS

	N-MINT
❑1	2.95

WHITEOUT
ONI

	N-MINT
❑1, Jul 1998	2.95
❑2, Aug 1998	2.95
❑3, Sep 1998	2.95
❑4, Nov 1998	2.95

WHITEOUT: MELT
ONI

	N-MINT
❑1, Sep 1999	2.95
❑2, Oct 1999	2.95
❑3, Nov 1999	2.95
❑4, Dec 1999	2.95

WHITE RAVEN
VISIONARY

	N-MINT
❑1, ca. 1995, b&w	2.95

WHITE TRASH
TUNDRA

	N-MINT
❑1	3.95
❑2	3.95
❑3	3.95
❑4	3.95

WHIZ KIDS
IMAGE

	N-MINT
❑1, Apr 2003	4.95

WHOA, NELLIE!
FANTAGRAPHICS

	N-MINT
❑1, Jul 1996, b&w	2.95
❑2, Aug 1996, b&w	2.95
❑3, Sep 1996, b&w	2.95

WHODUNNIT?
ECLIPSE

	N-MINT
❑1, Jun 1986	2.00
❑2, Nov 1986	2.00
❑3, Apr 1987	2.00

WHO IS THE CROOKED MAN
CRUSADE

	N-MINT
❑1, Sep 1996	3.50

WHO REALLY KILLED JFK
REVOLUTIONARY

	N-MINT
❑1, Oct 1993, b&w	2.50

WHO'S WHO IN STAR TREK
DC

	N-MINT
❑1, Mar 1987	1.50
❑2, Apr 1987; McGivers-Vulcans	1.50

WHO'S WHO IN THE DC UNIVERSE
DC

	N-MINT
❑1, Aug 1990	4.95
❑2, Sep 1990	4.95
❑3, Oct 1990	4.95

N-MINT

❑4, Nov 1990 .... 4.95
❑5, Dec 1990 .... 4.95
❑6, Jan 1991 .... 4.95
❑7, Feb 1991 .... 4.95
❑8, Apr 1991 .... 4.95
❑9, May 1991 .... 4.95
❑10, Jun 1991 .... 4.95
❑11, Jul 1991 .... 4.95
❑12, Aug 1991 .... 4.95
❑13, Oct 1991 .... 4.95
❑14, Nov 1991 .... 4.95
❑15, Jan 1992 .... 4.95
❑16, Feb 1992 .... 4.95

WHO'S WHO IN THE DC UNIVERSE UPDATE 1993
DC

❑1, Dec 1992 .... 5.95
❑2, Jan 1993 .... 5.95

WHO'S WHO IN THE IMPACT UNIVERSE
DC / Impact

❑1, Sep 1991 .... 4.95
❑2, Dec 1991 .... 4.95
❑3, May 1992 .... 4.95

WHO'S WHO IN THE LEGION OF SUPER-HEROES
DC

❑1, Apr 1988; GP, RL, DC, JSa, CS (a); Absorbancy Boy through Doctor Gym'll 1.50
❑2, Jun 1988; Doctor Mayavile through High Seer 1.50
❑3, Jul 1988; Heroes of Lallor through Legion of Super-Rejects; plus Planets of the 30th Century 1.50
❑4, Aug 1988 .... 1.50
❑5, Sep 1988; Mordru through Science Police Officer Quav; Plus Tour of Legion Headquarters 1.50
❑6, Oct 1988 .... 1.50
❑7, Nov 1988 .... 1.50

WHO'S WHO: THE DEFINITIVE DIRECTORY OF THE DC UNIVERSE
DC

❑1, Mar 1985; JOy, GP, GK, MR (a); Abel through Auron 1.50
❑2, Apr 1985; JOy, GP, JK, GK, MR, JL (a); Automan through Blackhawk Plane 1.50
❑3, May 1985; DG (c); JOy, GP, JK, GK (a); Black Lightning through Byth 1.50
❑4, Jun 1985; DG (c); GP, JBy, JK, GK, DSt (a); The Cadre through Chril KL-99 .... 1.50
❑5, Jul 1985; DG (c); JOy, GP, JK, GK, MR (a); Chronos through Cyclotron 1.50
❑6, Aug 1985; DG (c); MW, JOy, JK, GK, MR, JL (a); Daily Planet through Doctor Polaris 1.50
❑7, Sep 1985; DG (c); BSz, JBy, GK, DSt (a); Doctor Psycho through Fastback 1.50
❑8, Oct 1985; DG (c); JOy, GP, JK, GK (a); Fatal Five through Garguax 1.50
❑9, Nov 1985; DG (c); BSz, GP, JK, GK (a); Garn Daanuth through Guardians of the Universe 1.50
❑10, Dec 1985; DG (c); JOy, GP, SR, JK, GK (a); Gunner & Sarge through Hyena 1.50
❑11, Jan 1986; DG (c); JOy, GP, JK, GK, MR (a); Icicle through Jonni Thunder 1.50
❑12, Feb 1986; DG (c); JOy, GP, JK, MR, JL (a); Johnny Double through Kong 1.50
❑13, Mar 1986; JSn, GP, JK, GK (a); Krona through Losers 1.50
❑14, Apr 1986; DG (c); JSn, BSz, GP, JBy, JK (a); Luther I through Masters of Disaster 1.50
❑15, May 1986; DG (c); BSz, GP, JK, MR (a); Matrix-Prime through Mister Tawky-Tawny 1.50
❑16, Jun 1986; DG (c); GP, JBy, JK, GK (a); Mr. Terrific through Nightmaster 1.50
❑17, Jul 1986; JOy, GP, JK, GK (a); Nightshade through Persuader 1.50
❑18, Aug 1986; DG (c); JOy, GP, JBy, SR, JK, DSt (a); Phantom Girl through Pursuer 1.50
❑19, Sep 1986; JBy, JK, GK, JL (a); Puzzler through Roy Raymond 1.50
❑20, Oct 1986; DG (c); JK, JL (a); Rubber Duck through Shining Knight 1.50
❑21, Nov 1986; GC, DG (c); SD, BSz, JOy, GK (a); Shrinking Violet through Starfinger 1.50
❑22, Dec 1986; JBy (c); SD, JOy, JBy, JK, GK, JL (a); Starfire I through Syonide 1.50
❑23, Jan 1987; JSa (c); MA, GK (a); Syrene through Time Trapper 1.50
❑24, Feb 1987; BSz, JBy, DG (a); Tim Trench through Universo 1.50
❑25, Mar 1987; DG (c); JKu, DS (a); Unknown Soldier through Witch Boy 1.50
❑26, Apr 1987; DG (c); MGr, RA, JL (a); Wizard through The 1000 .... 1.50

WHO'S WHO UPDATE '87
DC

❑1, Aug 1987; DG (c); KG, GP, JBy (a); All-Star Squadron through Calyst 1.50
❑2, Sep 1987; DG (c); TMc, GP, JSa (a); Catwoman II through Goldstar 1.50
❑3, Oct 1987; RHo, TMc, GP, JSa (a); Gray Man through Lionmane 1.50
❑4, Nov 1987; TMc (c); AM, PB, JBy (a); Lois Lane through Ame Starr 1.50
❑5, Dec 1987; DG, JSa (a); Reaper through Robert Campenella 1.50

WHO'S WHO UPDATE '88
DC

❑1, Aug 1988; Amazing Man through Harlequin II 1.50
❑2, Sep 1988; Icemaiden through Nightwing 1.50
❑3, Oct 1988; JOy, RL, AA, JM (a); Parliament of Trees through Trident 1.50
❑4, Nov 1988; DGr (a); Ultra-Humanite through Zuggernaut plus Supporting Characters (Abby Cable to Wade Eiling) 1.50

WHOTNOT
Fantagraphics

❑1, b&w 2.50
❑2, b&w 2.50
❑3, b&w 2.50

WICKED
Millennium

❑1 1994 .... 2.50
❑2 1995 .... 2.50
❑3, Apr 1995, b&w; cover dated Mar 2.50

WICKED, THE
Image

❑1, Dec 1999; Man, demon on cover 2.95
❑1/A, Dec 1999; Figure against red background on cover 2.95
❑1/B, Dec 1999; Girl with glowing book on cover 2.95
❑2, Feb 2000 .... 2.95
❑3, Mar 2000 .... 2.95
❑4 2000 .... 2.95
❑5, Jun 2000 .... 2.95
❑6, Jun 2000 .... 2.95
❑7, Aug 2000 .... 2.95
❑Ashcan 1, Jul 1999; Preview edition 5.00

WICKED, THE: MEDUSA'S TALE
Image

❑1, Nov 2000 .... 3.95

WIDOW
Avatar

❑0 .... 3.95
❑0/Nude, Jun 2000, b&w 3.95

WIDOW: FLESH AND BLOOD
Ground Zero

❑1, Oct 1992 .... 2.50
❑2, Dec 1992 .... 2.50
❑3, Mar 1993 .... 2.50

WIDOW: METAL GYPSIES
London Night

❑1 .... 3.95

WIINDOWS
Cult

❑1, Mar 1993, b&w; Partial prism cover 3.50
❑2, Apr 1993, b&w 3.00
❑3, May 1993, b&w 3.00
❑4, Jun 1993, b&w 2.50
❑5, Jul 1993, b&w 2.50
❑6, Aug 1993, b&w 2.50
❑7, Sep 1993, b&w 2.50
❑8, Oct 1993, b&w 2.50
❑9, Nov 1993, b&w 2.50
❑10, Dec 1993, b&w 2.50
❑11, Jan 1994, b&w 2.50
❑12, Feb 1994, b&w 2.50
❑13, Mar 1994, b&w 2.50
❑14, Apr 1994, b&w 2.50
❑15, May 1994, b&w 2.50
❑16, Jun 1994, b&w 2.50
❑17, Jun 1994, b&w 2.50

WILD ANIMALS
Pacific

❑1, ca. 1982 .... 1.50

WILD BILL HICKOK
Super

❑10, b&w 0.12
❑11, ca. 1963 .... 0.12
❑12 .... 0.12

WILD BILL PECOS
AC

❑1, ca. 1989 .... 3.50

WILDB.R.A.T.S
Fantagraphics

❑1 .... 3.25

WILDCARDS
Marvel / Epic

❑1, Sep 1990; prestige format; based on prose anthology series 4.50
❑2, Oct 1990; prestige format; based on prose anthology series 4.50
❑3, Nov 1990; prestige format; based on prose anthology series 4.50
❑4, Dec 1990; prestige format; based on prose anthology series 4.50

WILDC.A.T.S
Image

❑0, Jun 1993 .... 3.00
❑1, Aug 1992, JLee (c); JLee (w); JLee (a); 1: Maul. 1: Grifter. 1: Spartan. 1: Gnome. 1: Tri-Ad. 1: Helspont. 1: Pike. 1: WildC.A.T.s. 1: Hightower. A: 1st. 4.00
❑1/3D, Aug 1997; 3-D edition JLee (w); JLee (a) 4.95
❑1/Gold, Aug 1992; Gold edition JLee (w); JLee (a) 10.00
❑1/Variant, Aug 1992; Wizard Ace edition JLee (w); JLee (a) 5.00
❑2, Sep 1992; JLee (c); JLee (w); JLee (a); 1: Black Razor. 1: Wetworks. Coupon for Image Comics #0 enclosed; Prism cover 4.00
❑3, Dec 1992, JLee (c); JLee (w); JLee (a); A: Youngblood. 3.00
❑4, Mar 1993, JLee (w); JLee (a) 3.00
❑4/A, Mar 1993; (c); JLee (w); JLee (a); bagged; red trading card 3.00
❑5, Nov 1993, JLee (c); JLee (w); JLee (a) 2.50
❑6, Dec 1993, JLee (c); JLee (w); JLee (a) 2.50
❑6/Gold, Dec 1993; Gold edition 3.00
❑7, Jan 1994, JLee (c); JLee (w); JLee (a) 2.50
❑7/Platinum, Jan 1994; Platinum edition 3.00
❑8, Feb 1994, JLee (c); JLee (w); JLee (a); A: Cyclops and Jean Grey. 2.50
❑9, Mar 1994, JLee (c); JLee (w); JLee (a) 2.50
❑10, Apr 1994; JLee (c); JLee (a); series becomes WildC.A.T.S 2.50

	N-MINT
❑11, Jun 1994; JLee (a); Title changes to WildC.A.T.S	15.00
❑11/A, Jun 1994; variant cover	22.00
❑12, Aug 1994 1: Savant.	8.00
❑13, Sep 1994; Beavis and Butthead cameo	6.00
❑14, Sep 1994	2.50
❑15, Nov 1994	2.50
❑16, Dec 1994	2.50
❑17, Jan 1995 A: StormWatch.	2.50
❑18, Mar 1995	2.50
❑19, Apr 1995	2.50
❑20, May 1995; with cards	2.50
❑21, Jul 1995; JLee (c); AMo (w); JLee (a); 1st Moore-written issue	2.50
❑22, Aug 1995 AMo (w)	2.50
❑23, Sep 1995 AMo (w)	2.50
❑24, Nov 1995 AMo (w)	2.50
❑25, Dec 1995; AMo (w); enhanced wraparound cover	4.95
❑26, Feb 1996 AMo (w)	2.50
❑27, Mar 1996 AMo (w)	2.50
❑28, Apr 1996 AMo (w)	2.50
❑29, May 1996; AMo (w); cover says Apr, indicia says May	2.50
❑30, Jun 1996 AMo (w)	2.50
❑31, Sep 1996 AMo (w)	2.50
❑32, Jan 1997 AMo (w); JLee (a)	2.50
❑33, Feb 1997 AMo (w)	2.50
❑34, Feb 1997 AMo (w)	2.50
❑35, Mar 1997	2.50
❑36, Mar 1997	2.50
❑37, Apr 1997	2.50
❑38, May 1997	2.50
❑39, Jun 1997	2.50
❑40, Jul 1997	2.50
❑40/A, Jul 1997; alternate mostly b&w cover	2.50
❑40/B, Jul 1997; alternate mostly b&w cover	2.50
❑41, Aug 1997	2.50
❑42, Sep 1997	2.50
❑43, Oct 1997	2.50
❑44, Nov 1997	2.50
❑45, Jan 1998	2.50
❑46, Feb 1998	2.50
❑47, Mar 1998	2.50
❑47/A, Mar 1998; alternate cover with Grifter	2.50
❑47/B, Mar 1998; alternate cover with Grifter	2.50
❑48, Apr 1998	2.50
❑49, May 1998	2.50
❑50, Jun 1998; Giant-size JRo, AMo (w); JLee (a)	3.50
❑50/Variant, Jun 1998; chromium cover	3.50
❑Annual 1, Feb 1998 JRo (w)	2.95
❑Special 1, Nov 1993	3.50

WILDCATS (2ND SERIES)
DC / WILDSTORM

	N-MINT
❑1/A, Mar 1999 JLee (c)	2.50
❑1/B, Mar 1999	2.50
❑1/C, Mar 1999	2.50
❑1/D, Mar 1999	2.50
❑1/E, Mar 1999	2.50
❑1/F, Mar 1999	2.50
❑1/G, Mar 1999	6.95
❑1/H, Mar 1999; DFE alternate cover	6.95
❑1/J, Mar 1999; Euro-Edition sketch cover	29.95
❑2, May 1999	2.50
❑3, Jul 1999	2.50
❑4, Sep 1999	2.50
❑5, Nov 1999	2.50
❑6, Dec 1999	2.50
❑7 2000	2.50
❑8 2000	2.50
❑9, May 2000	2.50
❑10, Jun 2000	2.50
❑11, Jul 2000	2.50
❑12, Aug 2000	2.50
❑13, Sep 2000	2.50
❑14, Oct 2000	2.50
❑15, Nov 2000	2.50
❑16, Dec 2000	2.50
❑17, Jan 2001	2.50
❑18, Feb 2001	2.50
❑19, Mar 2001	2.50
❑20, Apr 2001	2.50
❑21, May 2001	2.50
❑22, Jun 2001	2.50
❑23, Jul 2001	2.50
❑24, Aug 2001	2.50
❑25, Sep 2001	2.50
❑26, Oct 2001	2.50
❑27, Nov 2001	2.50
❑28, Dec 2001	2.50
❑Annual 2000, Dec 2000	3.50

WILDC.A.T.S ADVENTURES
IMAGE

	N-MINT
❑1, Sep 1994 O: Warblade. O: WildC.A.T.s.	2.00
❑2, Nov 1994	2.00
❑3, Nov 1994	2.00
❑4, Dec 1994	2.50
❑5, Jan 1995	2.50
❑6, Feb 1995	2.50
❑7, Mar 1995	2.50
❑8, Apr 1995	2.50
❑9, May 1995	2.50
❑10, Jun 1995	2.50

WILDC.A.T.S ADVENTURES SOURCEBOOK
IMAGE

	N-MINT
❑1, Jan 1995	2.95

WILDC.A.T.S/ALIENS
IMAGE

	N-MINT
❑1, Aug 1998; crossover with Dark Horse; cardstock cover	4.95
❑1/A, Aug 1998; crossover with Dark Horse; alternate cardstock cover (Zealot vs. Alien)	4.95

WILDC.A.T.S (JIM LEE'S...)
IMAGE

	N-MINT
❑1, Apr 1995; no cover price; informational comic for San Diego Police Dept.	2.00

WILDCATS: LADYTRON
DC / WILDSTORM

	N-MINT
❑1, Oct 2000	5.95

WILDCATS: MOSAIC
DC / WILDSTORM

	N-MINT
❑1, Feb 2000	3.95

WILDC.A.T.S SOURCEBOOK
IMAGE

	N-MINT
❑1, Sep 1993, JLee (w)	2.50
❑1/Gold, Sep 1993; Gold edition	3.00
❑2, Nov 1994	2.50

WILDC.A.T.S TRILOGY
IMAGE

	N-MINT
❑1, Jun 1993; Foil cover	2.50
❑2, Sep 1993	1.95
❑3, Nov 1993	1.95

WILDCATS VERSION 3.0
DC / WILDSTORM

	N-MINT
❑1, Oct 2002	2.95
❑2, Nov 2002	2.95
❑3, Dec 2002	2.95
❑4, Jan 2003	2.95
❑5, Feb 2003	2.95
❑6, Mar 2003	2.95
❑7, Apr 2003	2.95
❑8, May 2003	2.95
❑9, Jun 2003	2.95
❑10, Jul 2003	2.95
❑11, Aug 2003	2.95
❑12, Sep 2003	2.95
❑13, Oct 2003	2.95
❑14, Nov 2003	2.95
❑15, Dec 2003	2.95
❑16, Jan 2004	2.95
❑17, Feb 2004	2.95

Wild Cards, an anthology prose series of super-hero stories edited by George R.R. Martin, was the basis for this four-issue Epic series.

© 1990 Epic and respective copyright holders.

	N-MINT
❑18, Mar 2004	2.95
❑19, May 2004	2.95
❑20, Jun 2004	2.95
❑21, Jul 2004	2.95
❑22, Aug 2004	2.95
❑23, Sep 2004	

WILDC.A.T.S/X-MEN: THE DARK AGE
IMAGE

	N-MINT
❑1	4.95

WILDC.A.T.S/X-MEN: THE GOLDEN AGE
IMAGE

	N-MINT
❑1; crossover with Marvel	4.50
❑1/A, Feb 1997; JLee (c); crossover with Marvel; cardstock cover; Autographed by Travis Charest	5.00
❑1/B, Feb 1997; crossover with Marvel; scroll cover; cardstock cover; Autographed by Jim Lee	8.00
❑1/C, Feb 1997; crossover with Marvel; cardstock cover	4.50
❑1/D, Sep 1997; crossover with Marvel; with glasses	6.50
❑1/F, Sep 1997, cardstock cover; crossover with Marvel; Autographed by Jim Lee	4.50
❑1/E, Sep 1997; crossover with Marvel; with glasses; scroll cover	6.50

WILDC.A.T.S/X-MEN: THE MODERN AGE
IMAGE

	N-MINT
❑1, Aug 1997; Cardstock cover with Wolverine	4.50
❑1/A, Aug 1997; crossover with Marvel; cardstock cover; Includes certificate of authenticity; Autographed by Adam Hughes	6.00
❑1/B, Aug 1997; crossover with Marvel; cardstock cover; Nightcrawler cover	4.50
❑1/C, Nov 1997; crossover with Marvel; 3-D glasses bound-in	6.50
❑1/E, Nov 1997, cardstock cover; crossover with Marvel; Includes certificate of authenticity; Autographed by James Robinson	8.00
❑1/D, Nov 1997; crossover with Marvel; Nightcrawler cover; 3-D glasses bound-in	6.50

WILDC.A.T.S/X-MEN: THE SILVER AGE
IMAGE

	N-MINT
❑1, Jun 1997; JLee (c); JLee (a); (Grifter standing center)	4.95
❑1/A, Jun 1997; NA (c); JLee (a); crossover with Marvel; cardstock cover; (Brood attacking)	4.95
❑1/B, Jun 1997; JLee (a); crossover with Marvel; cardstock cover	4.50
❑1/C, Jun 1997; 3-D edition; JLee (a); 3-D edition	6.95
❑1/E, Oct 1997; JLee (c); JLee (a); cardstock cover; crossover with Marvel; (Grifter standing center); Autographed by Jim Lee	4.50
❑1/D, Oct 1997; JLee (a); crossover with Marvel; has indicia for WildC.A.T.S/X-Men: The Modern Age 3-D; 3-D glasses bound-in	6.50

N-MINT

WILDCORE
IMAGE

❑1, Nov 1997; Three figures fighting on cover ... 2.50
❑1/A, Nov 1997; white background ... 2.50
❑1/B, Nov 1997; alternate cover: white background ... 5.00
❑2, Dec 1997; Vigor standing on cover ... 2.50
❑2/A, Dec 1997; variant cover ... 3.00
❑3, Jan 1998 ... 2.50
❑4, Mar 1998 ... 2.50
❑5, Jun 1998 ... 2.50
❑6, Jul 1998 ... 2.50
❑7, Aug 1998 ... 2.50
❑8, Oct 1998 ... 2.50
❑9, Nov 1998 ... 2.50
❑10, Dec 1998 ... 2.50
❑Ashcan 1, Oct 1997; Preview edition ... 3.00

WILD DOG
DC

❑1, Sep 1987, DG (c); DG (a) ... 1.50
❑2, Oct 1987, DG (c); DG (a) ... 1.50
❑3, Nov 1987, DG (c); DG (a) ... 1.50
❑4, Dec 1987, DG (c); DG (a) ... 1.50
❑Special 1, Nov 1989 ... 2.50

WILDFLOWER
SIRIUS

❑1, Feb 1998 ... 2.50
❑2, Apr 1998 ... 2.50
❑3, Jun 1998 ... 2.50
❑4, Aug 1998 ... 2.50
❑5, Oct 1998 ... 2.50

WILD FRONTIER
SHANDA

❑1, Jan 2000, b&w ... 2.95
❑2 ... 2.95

WILDGUARDS: CASTING CALL
IMAGE

❑1, Sep 2003 ... 2.95
❑2, Oct 2003 ... 2.95
❑3, Nov 2003 ... 2.95
❑4, Dec 2003 ... 2.95
❑5, Jan 2004 ... 2.95
❑6, May 2004 ... 2.99

WILD KINGDOM
MU

❑1, Oct 1991, b&w ... 2.50
❑2, May 1993, b&w ... 2.95
❑3, Jan 1995, b&w ... 2.95
❑4, Apr 1995, b&w; Mu Pub #249 ... 2.95
❑5, Aug 1995, b&w ... 2.95
❑6, Dec 1995, b&w ... 2.95
❑7 ... 0.00
❑8, Nov 1996, b&w; Mu Pub # 329 ... 3.50
❑9, May 1998, b&w; Mu Pub # 380 ... 0.00
❑10, Sep 1998, b&w; Mu Pub # 385 ... 0.00
❑11 ... 0.00
❑12 ... 0.00
❑13, Apr 2002, b&w; Mu Pub # 408 ... 0.00
❑14, Aug 2002, b&w; Mu Pub # 409 ... 0.00

WILD KNIGHTS
ETERNITY

❑1, Mar 1988, b&w ... 1.95
❑2, Apr 1988 ... 1.95
❑3 1988 ... 1.95
❑4 1988 ... 1.95
❑5 1988 ... 1.95
❑6 1988 ... 1.95
❑7 1988 ... 1.95
❑8, Apr 1989, b&w ... 1.95
❑9, Dec 1988 ... 1.95
❑10, Feb 1989 ... 1.95

WILD LIFE (ANTARCTIC)
ANTARCTIC

❑1, Feb 1993, b&w ... 2.50
❑2, May 1993, b&w ... 2.50
❑3, Jul 1993, b&w ... 2.50
❑4, Nov 1993, b&w ... 2.75
❑5, Feb 1994, b&w ... 2.75
❑6, Apr 1994, b&w ... 2.75
❑7, Jun 1994, b&w ... 2.75
❑8, Aug 1994, b&w ... 2.75
❑9, Oct 1994, b&w ... 2.75
❑10, Dec 1994, b&w ... 2.75
❑11, Feb 1995, b&w ... 2.75
❑12, Apr 1995, b&w ... 2.75

WILD LIFE (FANTAGRAPHICS)
FANTAGRAPHICS

❑1, Aug 1994, b&w ... 2.75
❑2, Aug 1994, b&w ... 2.75

WILDLIFERS
RADIO

❑1, Sep 1999, b&w ... 4.95

WILDMAN (GRASS GREEN'S...)
MEGATON

❑1 ... 1.50
❑2 ... 1.50

WILD PERSON IN THE WOODS
G.T. LABS

❑1 1999 ... 2.50

WILD SIDE
UNITED

❑1, Jan 1998, b&w ... 3.95
❑2 ... 0.00
❑3 ... 0.00
❑4, Oct 1998, b&w ... 3.95
❑5, Mar 1999, b&w ... 3.95
❑6, Jul 1999, b&w ... 3.95

WILDSTAR
IMAGE

❑1, Sep 1995 ... 2.50
❑1/A, Sep 1995 ... 2.50
❑2, Nov 1995 ... 2.50
❑3, Jan 1996 ... 2.50
❑4, Mar 1996 ... 2.50

WILD STARS
COLLECTOR'S

❑1, Sum 1984, b&w ... 1.00

WILD STARS (VOL. 3)
LITTLE ROCKET

❑1, Jul 2001, b&w ... 2.95
❑2, Sep 2001, b&w ... 2.95
❑3, Nov 2001, b&w ... 2.95
❑4, Jan 2002, b&w ... 2.95
❑5, Mar 2002, b&w ... 2.95
❑6, May 2002, b&w ... 2.95
❑7, Jul 2002, b&w ... 2.95

WILDSTAR: SKY ZERO
IMAGE

❑1, Mar 1993; JOy (c); JOy (a); silver foil embossed cover ... 3.00
❑1/Gold, Mar 1993; JOy (a); gold embossed cover ... 4.00
❑2, May 1993, JOy (c); JOy (a) ... 2.00
❑3, Sep 1993, JOy (c); JOy (a); A: Savage Dragon. ... 2.50
❑4, Nov 1993, JOy (c); JOy (a); A: Savage Dragon. ... 2.50

WILDSTORM!
IMAGE

❑1, Aug 1995, b&w and color; Gen13, Grifter, Deathblow, Union, Spartan ... 2.50
❑2, Oct 1995, b&w and color; cover says Sep, indicia says Oct ... 2.50
❑3, Nov 1995 ... 2.50
❑4, Dec 1995; StormWatch Showcase ... 2.50

WILDSTORM ANNUAL
DC / WILDSTORM

❑2000, Dec 2000 ... 3.50

WILDSTORM CHAMBER OF HORRORS
IMAGE

❑1, Oct 1995 ... 3.50

WILDSTORM HALLOWEEN '97
IMAGE

❑1, Oct 1997 ... 2.50

WILDSTORM RARITIES
IMAGE

❑1, Dec 1994 ... 4.95

WILDSTORM RISING
IMAGE

❑1, May 1995; with cards ... 2.50
❑2, Jun 1995; bound-in trading cards ... 1.95

WILDSTORM SAMPLER
IMAGE

❑1; giveaway; no cover price ... 1.00

WILDSTORMS PLAYER'S GUIDE
IMAGE

❑1, Mar 1996; tips on WildStorms card game ... 1.95

WILDSTORM SPOTLIGHT
IMAGE

❑1, Feb 1997; Majestic ... 2.50
❑2, Mar 1997; Loner ... 2.50
❑3, Apr 1997; Loner ... 2.50
❑4, May 1997; StormWatch; no indicia ... 2.50

WILDSTORM SUMMER SPECIAL
DC / WILDSTORM

❑1, Oct 2001 ... 5.95

WILDSTORM SWIMSUIT SPECIAL
IMAGE

❑1, Dec 1994 ... 2.95
❑2, Aug 1995; pin-ups ... 2.50
❑1997, May 1997; pin-ups; WildStorm Swimsuits '97 ... 2.50

WILDSTORM THUNDERBOOK
DC / WILDSTORM

❑1, Oct 2000 ... 6.95

WILDSTORM ULTIMATE SPORTS OFFICIAL PROGRAM
IMAGE

❑1, Aug 1997; pin-ups ... 2.50

WILDSTORM UNIVERSE 97
IMAGE

❑1, Dec 1996; information on various Wildstorm characters ... 2.50
❑2, Jan 1997; information on various Wildstorm characters ... 2.50
❑3, Feb 1997; information on various Wildstorm characters ... 2.50

WILDSTORM UNIVERSE SOURCEBOOK
IMAGE

❑1, May 1995 ... 2.50
❑2 ... 2.50

WILD THING
MARVEL

❑1, Apr 1993; Embossed cover ... 2.50
❑2, May 1993 ... 1.75
❑3, Jun 1993 ... 1.75
❑4, Jul 1993 ... 1.75
❑5, Aug 1993 ... 1.75
❑6, Sep 1993 ... 1.75
❑7, Oct 1993 ... 1.75

WILD THING (2ND SERIES)
MARVEL

❑1, Oct 1999 ... 1.99
❑2, Nov 1999 ... 1.99
❑3, Dec 1999 ... 1.99
❑4, Jan 1999 ... 1.99
❑5, Feb 2000 ... 1.99

WILD THINGS
METRO

❑1, ca. 1986, b&w ... 2.00
❑2, ca. 1987, b&w ... 2.00
❑3, ca. 1987, b&w ... 2.00

WILD THINGZ
ABC

❑0/A ... 3.00
❑0/B; swimsuit cover ... 5.95
❑0/Platinum; Virgin Special Preview; limited to 300 copies ... 3.00

WILD THINK
WILD THINK

❑1, Apr 1987 ... 2.00

N-MINT

WILD TIMES: DEATHBLOW
DC / WILDSTORM
❑1, Aug 1999; set in 1899 .... 2.50

WILD TIMES: DV8
DC / WILDSTORM
❑1, Aug 1999; set in 1944 .... 2.50

WILD TIMES: GEN13
DC / WILDSTORM
❑1, Aug 1999, b&w; set in 1969, 1972, and 1973 .... 2.50

WILD TIMES: GRIFTER
DC / WILDSTORM
❑1, Aug 1999; set in 1920s 2.50

WILD TIMES: WETWORKS
DC / WILDSTORM
❑1, Aug 1999 .... 2.50

WILD WEST (CHARLTON)
CHARLTON
❑58, Nov 1966; Series continued from Black Fury #57 .... 10.00

WILD WEST C.O.W.-BOYS OF MOO MESA, THE
ARCHIE
❑1, Mar 1993 .... 1.25
❑2, May 1993 .... 1.25
❑3, Jul 1993 .... 1.25

WILD, WILD WEST, THE (GOLD KEY)
GOLD KEY
❑1, Jun 1966; 10174-606 .... 70.00
❑2, Aug 1966 .... 45.00
❑3, Jun 1968 .... 35.00
❑4, Dec 1968 .... 35.00
❑5, Apr 1969 .... 35.00
❑6, Jul 1969 .... 35.00
❑7, Oct 1969 .... 35.00

WILD, WILD WEST, THE (MILLENNIUM)
MILLENNIUM
❑1, ca. 1990; TV 2.95
❑2, ca. 1990; TV 2.95
❑3, ca. 1991; TV 2.95
❑4, ca. 1991; TV 2.95

WILD WOMEN
PARAGON
❑1 .... 4.95

WILD ZOO
RADIO
❑1, Jul 2000, b&w 2.95
❑2 .... 0.00
❑3, Nov 2000, b&w 2.95
❑4, Jan 2001, b&w 2.95
❑5 .... 0.00
❑6, May 2001, b&w 2.95
❑7, Jul 2001, b&w 2.99
❑8, Sep 2001, b&w 3.99

WILL EISNER PRESENTS
ECLIPSE
❑1, Dec 1990, b&w; Mr. Mystic 2.50
❑2; Mr. Mystic 2.50
❑3; Mr. Mystic 2.50

WILL EISNER'S 3-D CLASSICS: SPIRIT
KITCHEN SINK
❑1, Dec 1985 .... 2.00

WILL EISNER'S QUARTERLY
KITCHEN SINK
❑1, Nov 1983 .... 2.95
❑2, Feb 1984 .... 3.50
❑3, Aug 1984 .... 2.00
❑4 1985 .... 2.00
❑5 1985 .... 2.00
❑6 1985 .... 2.00
❑7 1985 .... 2.00
❑8, Mar 1986 .... 2.00

WILLIAM SHATNER
CELEBRITY
❑1 .... 5.95

N-MINT

WILLOW (MARVEL)
MARVEL
❑1, Aug 1988, BH (c); BH (a) 1.50
❑2, Sep 1988 BH (c); BH (a) 1.50
❑3, Oct 1988 BH (c); BH (a) 1.50

WILLOW (ANGEL)
ANGEL
❑0, Jun 1996, b&w 2.95
❑0/Nude, Jun 1996; nude cardstock cover 10.00

WILL TO POWER
DARK HORSE
❑1, Jun 1994 .... 1.50
❑2, Jun 1994 .... 1.00
❑3, Jun 1994 .... 1.00
❑4, Jul 1994 1: Counterstrike. 1.00
❑5, Jul 1994 .... 1.00
❑6, Jul 1994 .... 1.00
❑7, Jul 1994 .... 1.00
❑8, Aug 1994 .... 1.00
❑9, Aug 1994 .... 1.00
❑10, Aug 1994 .... 1.00
❑11, Aug 1994 .... 1.00
❑12, Aug 1994 .... 1.00

WIMMEN'S COMIX
RENEGADE
❑1, ca. 1972; Published by Last Gasp 10.00
❑2, ca. 1973; Published by Last Gasp 8.00
❑3, ca. 1973; Published by Last Gasp 8.00
❑4, ca. 1974; Published by Last Gasp 8.00
❑5, ca. 1975; Published by Last Gasp 5.00
❑6; Published by Last Gasp 5.00
❑7, ca. 1976; Published by Last Gasp 5.00
❑8 .... 5.00
❑9 .... 4.00
❑10 .... 4.00
❑11, ca. 1987, b&w 3.00
❑12, Apr 1987; 3-D 3.00
❑13; Occult issue 3.00
❑14, Feb 1989, b&w; Disastrous Relationships 2.50
❑15, Aug 1989, b&w 2.50
❑16, Nov 1990, b&w 2.50
❑17, Aug 1992, b&w 2.50
❑18 .... 2.50

WINDBURNT PLAINS OF WONDER, THE
LOHMAN HILLS
❑1, Fal 1996; b&w Emma Davenport one-shot 11.95

WINDRAVEN
HEROIC / BLUE COMET
❑1, b&w 2.95

WINDRAVEN ADVENTURES
BLUE COMET
❑1, Jan 1993, b&w 2.95

WINDSOR
WIN-MIL
❑1 .... 1.95
❑2; Flip-cover format 1.95

WINGBIRD AKUMA-SHE
VEROTIK
❑1, Jan 1998; cardstock cover 3.95

WINGBIRD RETURNS
VEROTIK
❑1, Oct 1997; prestige format 9.95

WINGDING ORGY
FANTAGRAPHICS / EROS
❑1 .... 3.95
❑2 .... 3.95

WINGED TIGER, THE
CARTOONISTS ACROSS AMERICA
❑3, Sum 1999 .... 2.95

WINGING IT
SOLO
❑1 .... 2.00

DC and WildStorm characters crossed over in the *Wild Times* series of one-shots.
© 1999 DC Comics.

N-MINT

WINGS
MU
❑1, Sep 1992 .... 2.50

WINGS COMICS (A-LIST)
A-LIST
❑1, Spr 1997, b&w; Golden Age reprint 2.50
❑2, Fal 1997, b&w; Golden Age reprint 2.50
❑3 .... 2.95
❑4 .... 2.95

WINNIE THE POOH (WALT DISNEY...)
GOLD KEY / WHITMAN
❑1, Jan 1977 .... 12.00
❑2, May 1977 .... 6.00
❑3, Sep 1977 .... 4.00
❑4 .... 4.00
❑5 .... 4.00
❑6 .... 3.00
❑7 .... 3.00
❑8 .... 3.00
❑9 .... 3.00
❑10 .... 3.00
❑11 .... 2.50
❑12 .... 2.50
❑13 .... 2.50
❑14 .... 2.50
❑15 .... 2.50
❑16 .... 2.50
❑17 .... 2.50
❑18 .... 2.50
❑19 .... 2.50
❑20, Aug 1980 .... 2.50
❑21, Oct 1980 .... 2.50
❑22, ca. 1980 .... 2.50
❑23, Jan 1981 .... 2.50
❑24, Feb 1981 .... 2.50
❑25 1981 .... 2.50
❑26, Nov 1981 .... 2.50
❑27, Feb 1982 .... 2.50
❑28, ca. 1982 .... 2.50
❑29, ca. 1982 .... 2.50
❑30, ca. 1982 .... 2.50
❑31, ca. 1983 .... 2.50
❑32, Apr 1984 .... 2.50
❑33, ca. 1984 .... 2.50

WINNING IN THE DESERT
APPLE
❑1; booklet 2.95
❑2; booklet 2.95

WINTERSTAR
ECHO
❑1, Dec 1996, b&w 2.95

WINTERWORLD
ECLIPSE
❑1, Sep 1987 .... 2.00
❑2, Dec 1987 .... 2.00
❑3, Mar 1988 .... 2.00

WISE SON: THE WHITE WOLF
DC / MILESTONE
❑1, Nov 1996 .... 2.50
❑2, Dec 1996 .... 2.50
❑3, Jan 1997 .... 2.50
❑4, Feb 1997 .... 2.50

WISH
TOKYOPOP
❑1, Aug 2002, b&w; printed in Japanese format 9.99

Condition price index: Multiply "NM prices" above by: **0.83 for Very Fine/Near Mint**
0.66 for Very Fine • 0.33 for Fine • 0.2 for Very Good • 0.125 for Good

N-MINT

WISH UPON A STAR
WARP

❑1, May 1994; giveaway; no price 1.00

WISP
OKTOMICA

❑1, Feb 1999 ..... 2.50

WITCH
ETERNITY

❑1, b&w 1.95

WITCHBLADE
IMAGE

❑0 ..... 5.00
❑0.5; Overstreet Fan promotional edition 30.00
❑1, Nov 1995 2: Witchblade. 20.00
❑1/A, Nov 1995; Wizard Ace edition; Sketch cover variant 5.00
❑1/B, Nov 1995; Wizard Ace edition .. 15.00
❑1/C, Nov 1995; Top Cow Collection . 5.00
❑2, Jan 1996; Relatively scarce 18.00
❑2/A, Jan 1996; Wizard Ace edition .. 15.00
❑2-2; Encore edition 4.00
❑3, Mar 1996 ..... 10.00
❑4, Apr 1996 ..... 8.00
❑5, May 1996 ..... 8.00
❑6, Jun 1996 1: Julie Pezzini. 6.00
❑7, Jul 1996 ..... 6.00
❑8, Aug 1996 ..... 5.00
❑9, Sep 1996 ..... 5.00
❑9/A, Sep 1996 ..... 5.00
❑10, Nov 1996 1: The Darkness. A: Darkness. 5.00
❑10/A, Nov 1996; 1: The Darkness. A: Darkness. Alternate cover sold through Dynamic Forces: Shows two characters back-to-back 20.00
❑10/B, Nov 1996; A: Darkness. American Entertainment alternate cover . 8.00
❑10/C, Nov 1996; A: Darkness. Dynamic Forces alternate; American Entertainment alternate 8.00
❑10/D, Nov 1996; A: Darkness. Dynamic Forces alternate 8.00
❑10/Autographed, Nov 1996; 1: The Darkness. Regular cover, signed by creators and sold through Dynamic Forces; limited to 2,500 copies 27.95
❑11, Dec 1996 ..... 4.00
❑12, Mar 1997 ..... 4.00
❑13, Apr 1997 ..... 3.50
❑14, May 1997 ..... 3.50
❑14/Gold, May 1997; Gold logo edition 6.00
❑15, Jul 1997 ..... 3.50
❑16, Aug 1997 ..... 3.00
❑17, Sep 1997 ..... 3.00
❑18, Nov 1997; continues in The Darkness #9 ..... 3.00
❑18/A, Nov 1997; variant cover 2.50
❑18/American Ent, Nov 1997; American Entertainment Edition; Green variant cover 5.00
❑19, Dec 1997 ..... 3.00
❑20, Feb 1998 ..... 3.00
❑21, Mar 1998 ..... 2.50
❑22, May 1998 ..... 2.50
❑23, Jun 1998 ..... 2.50
❑24, Jul 1998 ..... 2.50
❑25, Aug 1998; Yellow background cover 3.00
❑25/A, Aug 1998; With Fathom in pool cover 4.00
❑25/B, Aug 1998; Holofoil cover 8.00
❑25/C, Aug 1998; Printer Error; Holofoil cover 15.00
❑26, Oct 1998 ..... 2.50
❑27, Nov 1998 ..... 2.50
❑28, Feb 1999 ..... 2.50
❑29, Mar 1999 ..... 2.50
❑30, Apr 1999 ..... 2.50
❑31, May 1999 ..... 2.50
❑32, Jul 1999 ..... 2.50
❑33, Aug 1999 ..... 2.50
❑34, Sep 1999 ..... 2.50
❑35, Oct 1999 ..... 2.50
❑36, Dec 1999 ..... 2.50
❑37 2000 ..... 2.50
❑38 2000 ..... 2.50
❑39, May 2000 ..... 2.50
❑40, Jun 2000 ..... 2.50
❑40/A, Jun 2000; alternate cover 2.50
❑40/Ashcan, Jun 2000; 5000 printed; Pittsburgh Convention Preview 2.50
❑41, Jul 2000 ..... 2.50
❑41/A, Jul 2000; e-Wanted alternate cover (Pezzini sitting) 3.00
❑42, Sep 2000 ..... 2.50
❑43, Nov 2000 ..... 2.50
❑44, Jan 2001 ..... 2.50
❑45, Mar 2001 ..... 2.50
❑46, May 2001 ..... 2.50
❑47, Jun 2001 ..... 2.50
❑48, Jul 2001 ..... 2.50
❑49, Aug 2001 ..... 2.50
❑50, Sep 2001; Giant-size 4.95
❑50/A, Sep 2001; DFE alternate cover 14.99
❑50/B, Sep 2001; DFE Signed alternate cover 29.99
❑50/C, Sep 2001 ..... 4.95
❑50/D, Sep 2001 ..... 5.00
❑51, Oct 2001 ..... 2.50
❑52, Nov 2001 ..... 2.50
❑53, Dec 2001 ..... 2.50
❑54, Jan 2002 ..... 2.50
❑55, Feb 2002 ..... 2.50
❑56, Jun 2002 ..... 2.50
❑57, Aug 2002 ..... 2.50
❑58, Sep 2002 ..... 2.50
❑59, Oct 2002; Endgame Prelude 2.50
❑60, Nov 2002 ..... 2.99
❑61, Feb 2002 ..... 2.99
❑62, Mar 2003 ..... 2.99
❑63, May 2003 ..... 2.99
❑64, Jun 2003 ..... 2.99
❑65, Jun 2003 ..... 2.99
❑66, Jun 2003 ..... 2.99
❑67, Aug 2003 ..... 2.99
❑68, Sep 2003 ..... 2.99
❑69, Sep 2003 ..... 2.99
❑70, Oct 2003 ..... 2.99
❑71, Nov 2003 ..... 2.99
❑72, Dec 2003 ..... 2.99
❑73, Feb 2004 ..... 2.99
❑74, May 2004 ..... 2.99
❑75, Apr 2004 ..... 4.99
❑76, Aug 2004 ..... 2.99
❑500, ca. 1998; Limited edition foil cover; Given away as premium for subscription to Wizard 5.00

WITCHBLADE (VOL. 2)
IMAGE

❑0.5, Nov 2002 ..... 2.99

WITCHBLADE/DARK MINDS: RETURN OF PARADOX
IMAGE

❑1, ca 2004 ..... 9.99

WITCHBLADE/ALIENS/THE DARKNESS/PREDATOR
DARK HORSE

❑1, Nov 2000 ..... 2.99
❑2, Dec 2000 ..... 2.99
❑3, Jan 2001 ..... 2.99

WITCHBLADE: ANIMATED ONE SHOT
IMAGE

❑1, Aug 2003 ..... 2.99

WITCHBLADE/DARKCHYLDE
IMAGE

❑1, Sep 2000 ..... 2.50

WITCHBLADE/DARKNESS SPECIAL
IMAGE

❑0.5/Platinum, Sep 2000; Promotional giveaway when applying for Wizard credit card 35.00
❑1, Dec 1999 ..... 3.95

WITCHBLADE: DESTINY'S CHILD
IMAGE

❑1, May 2000 ..... 2.95
❑2, Jul 2000 ..... 2.95
❑3, Sep 2000 ..... 2.95

WITCHBLADE/ELEKTRA
MARVEL

❑1, Mar 1997; crossover with Image; continues in Elektra/Cyblade #1 ..... 2.95
❑1/American Ent, Mar 1997; American Entertainment Edition 5.00

WITCHBLADE GALLERY
IMAGE

❑1, Nov 2000 ..... 2.95

WITCHBLADE INFINITY
IMAGE

❑1, May 1999 ..... 3.50

WITCHBLADE/LADY DEATH
IMAGE

❑1, Nov 2001 ..... 4.95

WITCHBLADE/LADY DEATH SPECIAL
IMAGE

❑1, Sep 2003 ..... 3.95

WITCHBLADE: MOVIE EDITION
IMAGE

❑1/C, Aug 2000; Witchblade.com Exclusive cover (standing in alley) . 2.50
❑1/B, Aug 2000; Witchblade.com Exclusive Holofoil cover (standing in alley, holofoil) 2.50
❑1/A, Aug 2000 ..... 2.50
❑1, Aug 2000 ..... 2.50

WITCHBLADE: NOTTINGHAM
IMAGE

❑1, Mar 2003 ..... 4.99

WITCHBLADE: OBAKEMONO
IMAGE

❑1, Jul 2002 ..... 9.95

WITCHBLADE ORIGIN
IMAGE

❑1/American Ent, Oct 1997; American Entertainment Edition 3.00

WITCHBLADE/TOMB RAIDER
IMAGE

❑0.5, Jul 2000 ..... 5.00
❑1/A, Dec 1998 ..... 4.00
❑1/B, Dec 1998; alternate cover (white background) 5.00
❑1/C, Dec 1998; Croft standing on top of Pezzini with guns crossed on cover 5.00

WITCHBLADE/WOLVERINE
IMAGE

❑1, Apr 2004 ..... 2.99

WITCHCRAFT
DC / VERTIGO

❑1, Jun 1994; covers form triptych ... 2.95
❑2, Jul 1994; Sex, violence-recommended for mature readers. 2.95
❑3, Aug 1994 ..... 2.95

WITCHCRAFT: LA TERREUR
DC / VERTIGO

❑1, Apr 1998; covers form triptych ... 2.50
❑2, May 1998; covers form triptych .. 2.50
❑3, Jun 1998; covers form triptych ... 2.50

WITCHES
MARVEL

❑1, Aug 2004 ..... 2.99
❑2, Aug 2004 ..... 2.99
❑3, Sep 2004 .....
❑4, Sep 2004 .....

WITCHES' CAULDRON: THE BATTLE OF THE CHERKASSY POCKET
HERITAGE COLLECTION

❑1, b&w 3.50

N-MINT

WITCHFINDER, THE
Image

❑1, Sep 1999; Man with torch on cover facing forward 2.95
❑1/A, Sep 1999 .... 2.95
❑1/B, Sep 1999; alternate cover 2.95
❑2, Nov 1999 .... 2.95

WITCH HUNTER
Malibu / Ultraverse

❑1, Apr 1996 .... 2.50

WITCHING, THE
DC / Vertigo

❑1, Aug 2004 .... 2.95
❑2, Sep 2004 ....

WITCHING HOUR
DC

❑1, Mar 1969, NC (c); ATh (a) 50.00
❑2, May 1969, NC (c) 25.00
❑3, Jul 1969, NC (c); BWr (a) 18.00
❑4, Sep 1969, NC (c); ATh (a) 12.00
❑5, Nov 1969, NC (c); BWr (a) 18.00
❑6, Jan 1970, NC (c) 10.00
❑7, Mar 1970, ATh (a) 8.00
❑8, May 1970, ATh, NC (a) 10.00
❑9, Jul 1970, ATh (a) 8.00
❑10, Sep 1970, GM (w); ATh, GM (a) 6.00
❑11, Nov 1970, NC (c); ATh (a) 6.00
❑12, Jan 1971, NC (c); ATh, GK (a) ... 6.00
❑13, Mar 1971, GM (a); 1: Psions. 6.00
❑14, May 1971, AW, JJ (a) 6.00
❑15, Jul 1971, NC (c); GM, WW (a) .. 5.00
❑16, Sep 1971, NC (c); GM (a) 5.00
❑17, Nov 1971, DH (a) 5.00
❑18, Jan 1972, NC (c); JA (w); JK, NC, JA (a) 5.00
❑19, Mar 1972, NC (c); NC (a) 5.00
❑20, Apr 1972, NC (c); NR, DH (a) 5.00
❑21, Jun 1972, NC (c); NC (a) 4.00
❑22, Aug 1972, NC (c) 4.00
❑23, Sep 1972, NC (c); NR, TD (a) 4.00
❑24, Oct 1972, NC (c); AA (a) 4.00
❑25, Nov 1972, NC (c); JA (a) 4.00
❑26, Dec 1972, NC (c); DD, JAb (a) .. 4.00
❑27, Jan 1973, NC (c); AA (a) 4.00
❑28, Feb 1973, NC (c) 4.00
❑29, Mar 1973, NC (c) 4.00
❑30, Apr 1973, NC (c) 4.00
❑31, Jun 1973, NC (c); AN (a) 3.00
❑32, Jul 1973, NC (c) 3.00
❑33, Aug 1973, NC (c); AA (a) 3.00
❑34, Sep 1973, NC (c); NR (a) 3.00
❑35, Oct 1973, NC (c) 3.00
❑36, Nov 1973, NC (c) 3.00
❑37, Dec 1973, NC (c) 3.00
❑39, Feb 1974, NC (c) 3.00
❑40, Mar 1974, NC (c); AN (a) 3.00
❑41, Apr 1974, NC (c) 3.00
❑42, May 1974, NC (c) 3.00
❑43, Jun 1974, NC (c) 3.00
❑44, Jul 1974, NC (c); DP (a) 3.00
❑45, Aug 1974, NC (c); DP, AN (a) 3.00
❑46, Sep 1974, NC (c) 3.00
❑47, Oct 1974, NC (c); AN (a) 3.00
❑48, Nov 1974, NC (c) 3.00
❑49, Dec 1974, NC (c) 3.00
❑50, Jan 1975, NC (c) 3.00
❑51, Feb 1975, NC (c) 2.50
❑52, Mar 1975, NC (c); DP (a) 2.50
❑53, Apr 1975 .... 2.50
❑54, May 1975 .... 2.50
❑55, Jun 1975 .... 2.50
❑56, Jul 1975 .... 2.50
❑57, Aug 1975 .... 2.50
❑58, Sep 1975 .... 2.50
❑59, Oct 1975 .... 2.50
❑60, Nov 1975, NC (c) 2.50
❑61, Jan 1976 .... 2.50
❑62, Mar 1976 .... 2.50
❑63, May 1976 .... 2.50
❑64, Jun 1976 .... 2.50
❑65, Aug 1976 .... 2.50

N-MINT

❑66, Nov 1976 .... 2.50
❑67, Jan 1977 .... 2.50
❑68, Feb 1977, RB (c) 2.50
❑69, Mar 1977, DP (a) 2.50
❑70, Apr 1977 .... 2.50
❑71, May 1977, DP (a) 2.50
❑72, Jul 1977 .... 2.50
❑73, Sep 1977 .... 2.50
❑74, Oct 1977 .... 2.50
❑75, Nov 1977 .... 2.50
❑76, Jan 1978 .... 2.50
❑77, Feb 1978 .... 2.50
❑78, Mar 1978 .... 2.50
❑79, Apr 1978 .... 2.50
❑80, May 1978, AA, CS, JAb (a) 2.50
❑81, Jun 1978, PB (a) 2.50
❑82, Jul 1978 .... 2.50
❑83, Aug 1978 .... 2.50
❑84, Sep 1978 .... 2.50
❑85, Oct 1978 .... 2.50

WITCHING HOUR, THE (VERTIGO)
DC / Vertigo

❑1, Jan 2000 .... 5.95
❑2, Feb 2000 .... 5.95
❑3, Mar 2000 .... 5.95

WITCHING HOUR, THE (ANNE RICE'S...)
Millennium

❑1, ca. 1992 .... 2.50
❑2, ca. 1993; bound-in Talamasca business card 2.50
❑3, ca. 1993 .... 2.50
❑4, ca. 1993 .... 2.50
❑5, Feb 1996 .... 2.50
❑6 .... 2.50
❑7 .... 2.50
❑8 .... 2.50
❑9 .... 2.50
❑10 .... 2.50
❑11 .... 2.50
❑12 .... 2.50
❑13 .... 2.50

WITHIN OUR REACH
Star*Reach

❑1; Spider-Man, Concrete, Gift of the Magi; Christmas benefit comic 7.95

WIZARD IN TRAINING
Upper Deck

❑0, Jan 2002 .... 2.95

WIZARD OF 4TH STREET, THE (DARK HORSE)
Dark Horse

❑1, ca. 1987, b&w 2.00
❑2, ca. 1987, b&w 2.00
❑3 .... 2.00
❑4 .... 2.00
❑5 .... 2.00
❑6 .... 2.00

WIZARD OF 4TH STREET, THE (DAVID P. HOUSE)
David P. House

❑1 .... 1.50
❑2 .... 1.50
❑3 .... 1.50

WIZARD OF TIME, THE
DPH

❑1 .... 1.50
❑2, Oct 1986 .... 1.50

WIZARDS OF THE LAST RESORT
Blackthorne

❑1, Feb 1987, b&w 1.75
❑2, Apr 1987 .... 1.75
❑3, Jun 1987 .... 1.75
❑4, Aug 1987 .... 1.75

WIZARD'S TALE, THE
Image

❑1, ca. 1997 .... 19.95
❑1/HC 29.95

Bits and pieces of Wolverine's origin were revealed in *Wolverine* #50.

© 1992 Marvel Comics.

N-MINT

WJHC
Wilson Place

❑1, Dec 1998 .... 1.95

WOGGLEBUG
Arrow

❑1 .... 2.75

WOLF & RED
Dark Horse

❑1, Apr 1995; based on Tex Avery cartoons; Droopy back-up 2.50
❑2, May 1995; based on Tex Avery cartoons; Screwball Squirrel back-up . 2.50
❑3, Jun 1995; based on Tex Avery cartoons; Droopy back-up 2.50

WOLFF & BYRD, COUNSELORS OF THE MACABRE
Exhibit A

❑1, May 1994 .... 4.00
❑2, Jul 1994 .... 3.00
❑3, Sep 1994 .... 3.00
❑4, Nov 1994 .... 3.00
❑5, Feb 1995 .... 3.00
❑6, Apr 1995 .... 2.50
❑7, Jun 1995 .... 2.50
❑8, Sep 1995 .... 2.50
❑9, Nov 1995 .... 2.50
❑10, Feb 1996 .... 2.50
❑11, Apr 1996 .... 2.50
❑12, Aug 1996 .... 2.50
❑13, Oct 1996; cover purposely upside down and backwards 2.50
❑14, Jan 1997; Anne Rice parody 2.50
❑15, Mar 1997 .... 2.50
❑16, Jul 1997 .... 2.50
❑17, Oct 1997; Halloween issue; reprint strips 2.50
❑18, Mar 1998 .... 2.50
❑19, Apr 1998 .... 2.50
❑20, May 1998 .... 2.50
❑21 1988 .... 2.50
❑22, Feb 1999 .... 2.50

WOLFF & BYRD, COUNSELORS OF THE MACABRE'S SECRETARY MAVIS
Exhibit A

❑1, Aug 1998 .... 2.95
❑2, Apr 1999 .... 2.95

WOLFPACK
Marvel

❑1, Aug 1988 O: Wolfpack. 1: Wolfpack. 1.00
❑2, Sep 1988 .... 1.00
❑3, Oct 1988 .... 1.00
❑4, Nov 1988 .... 1.00
❑5, Dec 1988 .... 1.00
❑6, Jan 1989 .... 1.00
❑7, Feb 1989 .... 1.00
❑8, Mar 1989 .... 1.00
❑9, Apr 1989 .... 1.00
❑10, May 1989 .... 1.00
❑11, Jun 1989 .... 1.00
❑12, Jul 1989 .... 1.00

WOLF RUN: A KNOWN ASSOCIATES MYSTERY
Known Associates

❑1, b&w 2.50

	N-MINT

WOLPH
BLACKTHORNE

❑1	2.00

WOLVERBROAD VS. HOBO
SPOOF

❑1, b&w; parody	2.95

WOLVERINE (LTD. SERIES)
MARVEL

❑1, Sep 1982, FM (a); A: Mariko.	12.00
❑2, Oct 1982, FM (a); 1: Yukio.	8.00
❑3, Nov 1982, FM (a)	8.00
❑4, Dec 1982, FM (a)	8.00

WOLVERINE
MARVEL

	N-MINT
❑-1, Jul 1997; A: Sabretooth. A: Carol Danvers. A: Nick Fury. Flashback; Flashback issue	2.00
❑0.5, ca. 1997; Wizard mail-away edition	3.00
❑0.5/Ltd., ca. 1997; Blue foil	8.00
❑1, Nov 1988, AW, JB (a)	10.00
❑2, Dec 1988, JB, KJ (c); JB, KJ (a)	6.00
❑3, Jan 1989, AW, JB (c); AW, JB (a)	5.00
❑4, Feb 1989, AW, JB (c); AW, JB (a); A: Roughhouse.	5.00
❑5, Mar 1989, AW, JB (c); AW, JB (a); 1: Shotgun I. 1: Harriers. 1: Battleaxe II. 1: Hardcase.	5.00
❑6, Apr 1989, AW, JB (c); AW, JB (a); A: Roughhouse.	4.00
❑7, May 1989, JB (a); A: Hulk.	5.00
❑8, Jun 1989, JB (a); A: Hulk.	5.00
❑9, Jul 1989, JB (c); PD (w); GC (a)	5.00
❑10, Aug 1989; BSz (c); BSz, JB (a); V: Sabretooth. vs. Sabretooth	8.00
❑11, Sep 1989; KN (c); PD (w); BSz, JB (a); New Costume	4.00
❑12, Sep 1989, KN (c); PD (w); BSz, JB (a)	4.00
❑13, Oct 1989, KN (c); PD (w); BSz, JB (a)	4.00
❑14, Oct 1989, KN (c); PD (w); BSz, JB (a)	4.00
❑15, Nov 1989, KN (c); PD (w); BSz, JB (a)	4.00
❑16, Nov 1989, KN (c); PD (w); BSz, JB (a)	4.00
❑17, Nov 1989, JBy (c); JBy, KJ (a); A: Roughhouse.	4.00
❑18, Dec 1989, JBy (c); JBy, KJ (a); A: Roughhouse.	4.00
❑19, Dec 1989; JBy (c); JBy, KJ (a); A: Tiger Shark. Acts of Vengeance	4.00
❑20, Jan 1990; JBy (c); JBy, KJ (a); A: Tiger Shark. Acts of Vengeance	4.00
❑21, Feb 1990, JBy, KJ (a); A: Geist.	4.00
❑22, Mar 1990, JBy (c); JBy, KJ (a); A: Geist.	4.00
❑23, Apr 1990, JBy (c); JBy (a); A: Geist.	4.00
❑24, May 1990, JLee (c); PD (w); GC (a)	3.00
❑25, Jun 1990, JLee (c); JB (a)	3.00
❑26, Jul 1990, KJ (c); TP, KJ (a)	3.00
❑27, Jul 1990, JLee (c); JB, DGr (a)	3.00
❑28, Aug 1990	3.00
❑29, Aug 1990, KJ (c); AM (a)	3.00
❑30, Sep 1990, AM (c)	3.00
❑31, Sep 1990, DGr (c); DGr (a)	2.50
❑32, Oct 1990, DGr (c); DGr (a); A: Jean Grey.	2.50
❑33, Nov 1990, DGr (c); DGr (a)	2.50
❑34, Dec 1990, DGr (c); DGr (a)	2.50
❑35, Jan 1991, DGr (c); DGr (a); A: Lady Deathstrike.	2.50
❑36, Feb 1991, DGr (a); A: Lady Deathstrike.	2.50
❑37, Mar 1991, DGr (c); DGr (a); A: Lady Deathstrike.	2.50
❑38, Apr 1991, DGr (c); DGr (a); A: Storm.	2.50
❑39, May 1991, DGr (c); DGr (a); A: Storm.	2.50
❑40, Jun 1991, DGr (a)	2.50
❑41, Jul 1991, DGr (c); DGr (a); A: Sabretooth. A: Cable. V: Sabretooth.	4.00
❑41-2, Jul 1991; A: Sabretooth. Gold cover	1.75
❑42, Jul 1991, DGr (c); DGr (a); A: Sabretooth. A: Nick Fury. A: Cable.	2.00
❑42-2, Jul 1991; A: Sabretooth. A: Nick Fury. A: Cable. Gold cover	3.50
❑43, Aug 1991, DGr (a); A: Sabretooth.	3.00
❑44, Aug 1991, PD (w); AM (a)	2.00
❑45, Sep 1991, DGr (c); DGr (a); A: Sabretooth.	2.50
❑46, Sep 1991, DGr (a); A: Sabretooth.	2.50
❑47, Oct 1991	2.50
❑48, Nov 1991; DGr (c); DGr (a); Weapons X sequel: Logan's past	2.50
❑49, Dec 1991; DGr (a); Weapons X sequel: Logan's past	2.50
❑50, Jan 1992; DGr, TP (a); 1: Shiva. diecut cover	4.00
❑51, Feb 1992, DGr (a); A: Mystique.	2.00
❑52, Mar 1992, DGr (c); DGr (a); A: Spiral.	2.00
❑53, Apr 1992, DGr (c); DGr, KJ (a); A: Mojo.	2.00
❑54, May 1992, A: Shatterstar.	2.00
❑55, Jun 1992, DGr (a); A: Cylla.	2.00
❑56, Jul 1992, DGr (c); DGr (a); A: Cylla.	2.00
❑57, Jul 1992, DGr (c); AM, DGr (a); D: Mariko Yashida.	3.00
❑58, Aug 1992, A: Terror.	2.00
❑59, Aug 1992, A: Terror.	2.00
❑60, Sep 1992, DGr (c); A: Sabretooth.	2.00
❑61, Sep 1992, A: Sabretooth.	2.00
❑62, Oct 1992, A: Sabretooth.	2.00
❑63, Nov 1992, A: Sabretooth.	2.00
❑64, Dec 1992, A: Sabretooth. D: Silver Fox.	2.00
❑65, Jan 1993	2.00
❑66, Feb 1993	2.00
❑67, Mar 1993	2.00
❑68, Apr 1993	2.00
❑69, May 1993	2.00
❑70, Jun 1993	2.00
❑71, Jul 1993, KJ (c)	2.00
❑72, Aug 1993, A: Sentinel.	2.00
❑73, Sep 1993, A: Sentinel.	2.00
❑74, Oct 1993, A: Jubilee. A: Sentinel.	2.00
❑75, Nov 1993; DGr (a); hologram; Wolverine loses adamantium skeleton	4.00
❑76, Dec 1993, AM (a); A: Lady Deathstrike.	2.00
❑77, Jan 1994, A: Lady Deathstrike.	2.00
❑78, Feb 1994, D: Cylla. D: Bloodscream.	2.00
❑79, Mar 1994	2.00
❑80, Apr 1994, AM (c); AM (a)	2.00
❑81, May 1994	2.00
❑82, Jun 1994, JKu, BMc (a)	2.00
❑83, Jul 1994	2.00
❑84, Aug 1994, AM, TP (a)	2.00
❑85, Sep 1994	2.50
❑85/Variant, Sep 1994; enhanced cover	3.50
❑86, Oct 1994	2.00
❑87, Nov 1994, DGr (a)	1.50
❑87/Deluxe, Nov 1994; Deluxe edition	2.00
❑88, Dec 1994	1.50
❑88/Deluxe, Dec 1994; Deluxe edition	2.00
❑89, Jan 1995	1.50
❑89/Deluxe, Jan 1995; Deluxe edition	2.00
❑90, Feb 1995, DGr (a)	1.50
❑90/Deluxe, Feb 1995; Deluxe edition	2.00
❑91, Jul 1995	2.00
❑92, Aug 1995, DGr (a)	2.00
❑93, Sep 1995, DGr (a); V: Juggernaut.	2.00
❑94, Oct 1995, AM (a); A: Generation X.	2.00
❑95, Nov 1995, DGr (a); A: Vindicator.	2.00
❑96, Dec 1995, DGr (a); D: Cyber.	2.00
❑97, Jan 1996, DGr (a)	2.00
❑98, Feb 1996, AM (a)	2.00
❑99, Mar 1996, DGr (a)	4.00
❑100, Apr 1996, DGr (a)	5.00
❑100/Variant, Apr 1996; enhanced cardstock cover with hologram	7.50
❑101, May 1996, DGr (c)	2.00
❑102, Jun 1996, DGr (c); DGr (a)	2.00
❑103, Jul 1996, A: Elektra.	2.00
❑104, Aug 1996, A: Elektra.	2.00
❑105, Sep 1996, A: Stick.	2.00
❑106, Oct 1996, AM (a); A: Elektra.	2.00
❑107, Nov 1996, DGr (a)	2.00
❑108, Dec 1996, DGr (a)	2.00
❑109, Jan 1997, DGr (a)	2.00
❑110, Feb 1997, A: Shaman.	2.00
❑111, Mar 1997, DGr (a)	2.00
❑112, Apr 1997, DGr (a)	2.00
❑113, May 1997	2.00
❑114, Jun 1997, V: Deathstrike.	2.00
❑115, Aug 1997; gatefold summary; (c); Operation Zero Tolerance	2.00
❑116, Sep 1997; gatefold summary; (c); Operation Zero Tolerance	2.00
❑117, Oct 1997; gatefold summary; (c); A: Jubilee. Operation Zero Tolerance	2.00
❑118, Nov 1997; gatefold summary; (c); A: Jubilee. Operation Zero Tolerance Epilogue	2.00
❑119, Dec 1997; gatefold summary (c)	2.00
❑120, Jan 1998; gatefold summary (c)	2.00
❑121, Feb 1998	2.00
❑122, Mar 1998; gatefold summary (c)	2.00
❑123, Apr 1998; gatefold summary (c); BSz (a)	2.00
❑124, May 1998; gatefold summary BSz (a); A: Captain America.	2.00
❑125, Jun 1998; gatefold summary; A: Lady Hydra. wraparound cover	3.50
❑125/A, Jun 1998; DFE alternate cover	10.00
❑125/B, Jun 1998; DFE alternate cover	10.00
❑126, Jul 1998; gatefold summary V: Lady Hydra. V: Sabretooth.	1.99
❑127, Aug 1998; gatefold summary V: Sabretooth.	1.99
❑128, Sep 1998; gatefold summary A: Shadow Cat. A: Viper. V: Sabretooth.	1.99
❑129, Oct 1998; gatefold summary (c)	1.99
❑130, Nov 1998; gatefold summary (c)	1.99
❑131, Nov 1998; gatefold summary; (c); Letterer's error resulted in ethnic slur appearing (out of context, clearly unintentional) on page 6; issue recalled but copies did reach circulation	5.00
❑131/A, Nov 1998; Corrected edition	1.99
❑132, Dec 1998; gatefold summary	1.99
❑133, Jan 1999; gatefold summary A: Warbird.	1.99
❑134, Feb 1999; gatefold summary EL (w); V: Everybody.	1.99
❑135, Feb 1999, EL (w); A: Starjammers. A: Aria.	1.99
❑136, Mar 1999, EL (w); V: Collector.	1.99
❑137, Apr 1999, EL (w); A: Starjammers. A: Collector.	1.99
❑138, May 1999, EL (w); A: Galactus.	1.99
❑139, Jun 1999, EL (w); A: Cable.	1.99
❑140, Jul 1999, EL (w); A: Nightcrawler. V: Solo. V: Cardiac.	1.99
❑141, Aug 1999, EL (w)	1.99
❑142, Sep 1999, EL (w)	1.99
❑143, Oct 1999; EL (w); wraparound cover	1.99
❑144, Nov 1999, EL (w); A: The Leader.	1.99
❑145, Dec 1999, EL (w); A: Hulk.	4.00
❑145/Nabisco, Dec 1999; Rare Nabisco variant; mail-in offer, fewer than 2,500 in circulation; cover reads "Limited Edition"	125.00
❑146, Jan 2000, EL (w)	5.00
❑147, Feb 2000, EL (w)	2.25
❑148, Mar 2000, EL (c); EL (w)	2.25
❑149, Apr 2000	2.25
❑150, May 2000; Giant-size A: Nova.	2.99
❑150/DF, May 2000; Dynamic Forces chromium variant; no "Revolution" logo	14.00
❑151, Jun 2000	2.25
❑152, Jul 2000	2.25
❑153, Aug 2000	2.25
❑154, Sep 2000, RL (c); RL (w); RL (a)	2.25

N-MINT

❑155, Oct 2000, RL (c); RL (w); RL (a); A: Deadpool. 2.25
❑156, Nov 2000, RL (w); A: Spider-Man. 2.25
❑157, Dec 2000, RL (c); RL (w); A: Mole Man. 2.25
❑158, Jan 2001; polybagged with Marvel Online CD-ROM 2.25
❑159, Feb 2001 2.25
❑160, Mar 2001 2.25
❑161, Apr 2001 2.25
❑162, May 2001 2.25
❑163, Jun 2001 2.25
❑164, Jul 2001 2.25
❑165, Aug 2001 2.25
❑166, Sep 2001 3.00
❑166/A, Sep 2001; DFE Signed, limited edition 39.99
❑167, Oct 2001 2.25
❑168, Nov 2001 2.25
❑169, Dec 2001 2.25
❑170, Jan 2002 2.25
❑171, Feb 2002 2.25
❑172, Mar 2002, A: Alpha Flight. 2.25
❑173, Apr 2002; A: Lady Deathstrike. wraparound cover 2.25
❑174, May 2002; wraparound cover 2.25
❑175, Jun 2002; A: Sabretooth. wraparound cover 2.25
❑176, Jul 2002; wraparound cover 2.25
❑177, Aug 2002; wraparound cover 2.25
❑178, Aug 2002; wraparound cover 2.25
❑179, Sep 2002; wraparound cover 2.25
❑180, Oct 2002; wraparound cover 2.25
❑181, Nov 2002; TP (a); wraparound cover 2.25
❑182, Dec 2002; TP (a); wraparound cover 2.25
❑183, Jan 2003; TP (a); A: Lady Deathstrike. wraparound cover 2.25
❑184, Feb 2003; TP (a); wraparound cover 2.25
❑185, Mar 2003; TP (a); wraparound cover 2.25
❑186, Apr 2003, A: the Punisher. 2.25
❑187, May 2003 2.25
❑188, May 2003 2.25
❑189, Jun 2003; wraparound cover 2.25
❑Annual 1995, Sep 1995 3.95
❑Annual 1996, Oct 1996; JPH (w); V: Red Ronin. wraparound cover 2.95
❑Annual 1997, ca. 1997; gatefold summary; wraparound cover 2.99
❑Annual 1999, ca. 1999, b&w and color A: Deadpool. 3.50
❑Annual 2000, ca. 2000 3.50
❑Annual 2001, ca. 2001 2.99
❑Special 1, Win 1999; Blue Print edition 2.99

WOLVERINE (VOL. 3)
MARVEL

❑1, Jul 2003 4.00
❑2, Jul 2003 3.00
❑3, Aug 2003 3.00
❑4, Aug 2003 3.00
❑5, Nov 2003 3.00
❑6, Dec 2003 TP (a) 2.99
❑7, Jan 2004 2.99
❑8, Jan 2003 2.99
❑9, Feb 2004 2.99
❑10, Mar 2004 2.25
❑11, Apr 2004 2.99
❑12, May 2004, TP (a) 2.99
❑13, Jun 2004 2.99
❑14, Jun 2004 2.99
❑15, Jul 2004, TP (a) 2.99
❑16, Aug 2004 2.25
❑17, Sep 2004

WOLVERINE AND THE PUNISHER: DAMAGING EVIDENCE
MARVEL

❑1, Oct 1993 2.00
❑2, Nov 1993 2.00
❑3, Dec 1993 2.00

N-MINT

WOLVERINE BATTLES THE INCREDIBLE HULK
MARVEL

❑1, ca. 1989; reprints Incredible Hulk #180 and #181 4.95

WOLVERINE: BLACK RIO
MARVEL

❑1, Nov 1998 5.99

WOLVERINE: BLOOD HUNGRY!
MARVEL

❑1, ca. 1993; reprint stories 6.95
❑1-2, Mar 2002, Reprints from Marvel Comics Presents #85-92 6.95

WOLVERINE: BLOODLUST
MARVEL

❑1, Dec 1990 4.95

WOLVERINE: BLOODY CHOICES
MARVEL

❑1, ca. 1993 7.95

WOLVERINE/CAPTAIN AMERICA
MARVEL

❑1, Apr 2004 2.99
❑2, Apr 2004 2.99
❑3, Apr 2004 2.99
❑4, Apr 2004 2.99

WOLVERINE: DAYS OF FUTURE PAST
MARVEL

❑1, Dec 1997; gatefold summary; Wolverine in early 21st century 2.50
❑2, Jan 1998; gatefold summary; Wolverine in early 21st century 2.50
❑3, Feb 1998; gatefold summary; Wolverine in early 21st century 2.50

WOLVERINE: DOOMBRINGER
MARVEL

❑1, Nov 1997 5.99
❑1/Variant; foil cover 14.95

WOLVERINE/DOOP
MARVEL

❑1, Jul 2003 2.99
❑2, Jul 2003 2.99

WOLVERINE: EVILUTION
MARVEL

❑1, Sep 1994; Direct Edition 5.95

WOLVERINE/GAMBIT: VICTIMS
MARVEL

❑1, Sep 1995; enhanced cardstock cover 2.95
❑2, Oct 1995; enhanced cardstock cover 2.95
❑3, Nov 1995; enhanced cardstock cover 2.95
❑4, Dec 1995; enhanced cardstock cover 2.95

WOLVERINE: GLOBAL JEOPARDY
MARVEL

❑1, Dec 1993; Embossed cover 2.95

WOLVERINE/HULK
MARVEL

❑1, Apr 2002 3.50
❑2, May 2002 3.50
❑3, Jun 2002 3.50
❑4, Jul 2002 3.50

WOLVERINE: INNER FURY
MARVEL

❑1, Nov 1992 5.95

WOLVERINE: KILLING
MARVEL

❑1, Sep 1993 5.95

WOLVERINE: KNIGHT OF TERRA
MARVEL

❑1, Aug 1995 6.95

WOLVERINE: NETSUKE
MARVEL

❑1, Nov 2002 3.99
❑2, Dec 2002 3.99
❑3, Jan 2003 3.99
❑4, Feb 2003 3.99

A magic wish for a playmate generated the first incarnation of Wonder Girl.
© 1959 National Periodical Publications Inc. (DC)

N-MINT

WOLVERINE AND NICK FURY: SCORPIO RISING
MARVEL

❑1, Oct 1994; Sequel to Wolverine/Nick Fury: The Scorpio Connection; perfect bound 4.95

WOLVERINE POSTER MAGAZINE
MARVEL

❑1; pin-ups 4.95

WOLVERINE/PUNISHER
MARVEL

❑1, May 2004 2.99
❑2, Jun 2004 2.99
❑3, Jul 2004 2.99
❑4, Aug 2004 2.99

WOLVERINE/PUNISHER REVELATION
MARVEL

❑1, Jun 1999 2.99
❑1-2, Apr 2001 2.99
❑2, Jul 1999 2.99
❑2-2, May 2001 2.99
❑3, Aug 1999 2.99
❑4, Sep 1999 2.99

WOLVERINE: RAHNE OF TERRA
MARVEL

❑1, Aug 1991; prestige format 5.95

WOLVERINE SAGA, THE
MARVEL

❑1, Sep 1989, RL (c); O: Wolverine. 4.00
❑2, Nov 1989 4.00
❑3, Dec 1989, JR2, KJ (c) 4.00
❑4, Dec 1989 4.00

WOLVERINE: SAVE THE TIGER!
MARVEL

❑1, May 1992 2.95

WOLVERINE: SNIKT!
MARVEL

❑1, Jul 2003 2.99
❑2, Aug 2003 2.99
❑3, Sep 2003 2.99
❑4, Oct 2003 0.00
❑5, Nov 2003 2.99

WOLVERINE: THE END
MARVEL

❑1, Jan 2004 10.00
❑2, Mar 2004 6.00
❑3, May 2004 3.00
❑4, Aug 2004 2.99

WOLVERINE: THE JUNGLE ADVENTURE
MARVEL

❑1, ca. 1990 4.50

WOLVERINE: THE ORIGIN
MARVEL

❑1, Nov 2001 O: Wolverine. 22.00
❑1/DF, Nov 2001; Dynamic Forces S&N w/ cert. 50.00
❑2, Dec 2001 O: Wolverine. 6.00
❑2/DF, Dec 2001; Dynamic Forces S&N w/ cert. 24.00
❑3, Jan 2002 O: Wolverine. 4.00
❑3/DF, Jan 2002; Dynamic Forces S&N w/ cert. 20.00
❑4, Feb 2002 O: Wolverine. 4.00
❑4/DF, Feb 2002; Dynamic Forces S&N w/ cert. 20.00

	N-MINT
❑5, May 2002 O: Wolverine. O: Sabretooth.	4.00
❑5/DF, May 2002; Dynamic Forces S&N w/ cert.	20.00
❑6, Jul 2002 O: Wolverine. O: Sabretooth.	4.00
❑6/DF, Jul 2002; Dynamic Forces S&N w/ cert.	20.00

WOLVERINE VS. NIGHT MAN
MARVEL

❑0; limited edition	15.00

WOLVERINE VS. SPIDER-MAN
MARVEL

❑1, Mar 1995; collects story arc from Marvel Comics Presents #48-50; cardstock cover	3.00

WOLVERINE/WITCHBLADE
IMAGE

❑1, Mar 1997	4.50
❑1/A, Mar 1997; crossover with Marvel; continues in Witchblade/Elektra	2.95

WOLVERINE: XISLE
MARVEL

❑1, Jun 2003	2.50
❑2, Jun 2003	2.50
❑3, Jun 2003	2.50
❑4, Jun 2003	2.50
❑5, Jun 2003	2.50

WOLVERTON IN SPACE
DARK HORSE

❑

WOMEN IN FUR
SHANDA FANTASY ARTS

❑2, b&w	4.50

WOMEN IN ROCK SPECIAL
REVOLUTIONARY

❑1, Dec 1993, b&w	2.50

WOMEN ON TOP
FANTAGRAPHICS / EROS

❑1, b&w	2.25

WONDERLAND
ARROW

❑1, Sum 1985	2.95
❑2, Feb 1985	2.95
❑3, Apr 1986	2.95

WONDERLANDERS, THE
OKTOMICA

❑1, Jan 1999	2.50

WONDER MAN (ONE-SHOT)
MARVEL

❑1, Mar 1986	1.50

WONDER MAN
MARVEL

❑1, Sep 1991; poster	1.50
❑2, Oct 1991, A: West Coast Avengers.	1.25
❑3, Nov 1991, 1: Splice.	1.25
❑4, Dec 1991	1.25
❑5, Jan 1992, A: Beast.	1.25
❑6, Feb 1992	1.25
❑7, Mar 1992; A: Rick Jones. Operation Galactic Storm	1.25
❑8, Apr 1992; A: the Starjammers. Operation Galactic Storm	1.25
❑9, May 1992; Operation Galactic Storm	1.25
❑10, Jun 1992	1.25
❑11, Jul 1992	1.25
❑12, Aug 1992	1.25
❑13, Sep 1992	1.25
❑14, Oct 1992; Infinity War	1.25
❑15, Nov 1992	1.25
❑16, Dec 1992	1.25
❑17, Jan 1993	1.25
❑18, Feb 1993	1.25
❑19, Mar 1993	1.25
❑20, Apr 1993	1.25
❑21, May 1993, A: Splice.	1.25
❑22, Jun 1993	1.25
❑23, Jul 1993; Covers to Wonder Man #21-24 form quadtych	1.25
❑24, Aug 1993	1.25
❑25, Sep 1993; Embossed cover	2.95
❑26, Oct 1993, A: Hulk.	1.25
❑27, Nov 1993, A: Hulk.	1.25
❑28, Dec 1993, A: Spider-Man.	1.25
❑29, Jan 1994, A: Spider-Man.	1.25
❑Annual 1, ca. 1992, KB (w)	2.25
❑Annual 2, ca. 1993; trading card	2.95

WONDERS AND ODDITIES (RICK GEARY'S...)
DARK HORSE

❑1, Dec 1988, b&w	2.00

WONDER WART-HOG, HOG OF STEEL
RIP OFF

❑1, b&w	3.00
❑2, b&w	2.50
❑3, b&w	2.50

WONDER WOMAN (1ST SERIES)
DC

❑85, Oct 1956	155.00
❑86, Nov 1956	155.00
❑87, Jan 1957	155.00
❑88, Feb 1957	155.00
❑89, Apr 1957	155.00
❑90, May 1957	155.00
❑91, Jul 1957	120.00
❑92, Aug 1957	120.00
❑93, Oct 1957	120.00
❑94, Nov 1957	120.00
❑95, Jan 1958	120.00
❑96, Feb 1958	120.00
❑97, Apr 1958	120.00
❑98, May 1958 O: Wonder Woman (new origin).	120.00
❑99, Jul 1958	120.00
❑100, Aug 1958	120.00
❑101, Oct 1958, RA (a)	90.00
❑102, Nov 1958, RA (a)	90.00
❑103, Jan 1959	90.00
❑104, Feb 1959	90.00
❑105, Apr 1959, RA (a); O: 1st Wonder Girl. O: Wonder Woman ("secret origin").	600.00
❑106, May 1959, RA (a)	80.00
❑107, Jul 1959	80.00
❑108, Aug 1959, RA (a)	80.00
❑109, Oct 1959, (c)	80.00
❑110, Nov 1959, (c)	80.00
❑111, Jan 1960	70.00
❑112, Feb 1960, A: Wonder Girl.	70.00
❑113, Apr 1960, A: Wonder Girl. Aloha, Hawaii (Public Service piece)	70.00
❑114, May 1960	70.00
❑115, Jul 1960, A: Mer-Boy.	70.00
❑116, Aug 1960, A: Wonder Girl.	70.00
❑117, Oct 1960, A: The Holiday Girls.	70.00
❑118, Nov 1960, A: Mer-Man.	70.00
❑119, Jan 1961	70.00
❑120, Feb 1961, A: Wonder Girl.	70.00
❑121, Apr 1961, 1: Wonder Family.	70.00
❑122, May 1961	70.00
❑123, Jul 1961	70.00
❑124, Aug 1961, 1: Wonder Family.	70.00
❑125, Oct 1961, A: Mer-Man.	70.00
❑126, Nov 1961, 1: Mister Genie.	70.00
❑127, Jan 1962	70.00
❑128, Feb 1962, O: Wonder Woman's Invisible Jet.	70.00
❑129, Apr 1962	70.00
❑130, May 1962	70.00
❑131, Jul 1962	56.00
❑132, Aug 1962, A: Mer-Man.	56.00
❑133, Oct 1962, A: Wonder Family.	56.00
❑134, Nov 1962, A: Wonder Girl.	56.00
❑135, Jan 1963, A: Mer-Boy.	56.00
❑136, Feb 1963	56.00
❑137, Apr 1963	56.00
❑138, May 1963, A: Wonder Family.	56.00
❑139, Jul 1963	56.00
❑140, Aug 1963, A: Mer-Boy.	56.00
❑141, Oct 1963	56.00
❑142, Nov 1963, A: Wonder Family.	56.00
❑143, Jan 1964, RA (a)	56.00
❑144, Feb 1964, RA (a)	56.00
❑145, Apr 1964, (w); A: Wonder Family.	56.00
❑146, May 1964	56.00
❑147, Jul 1964	56.00
❑148, Aug 1964	56.00
❑149, Oct 1964, A: Wonder Family.	56.00
❑150, Nov 1964, A: Bird-Boy.	50.00
❑151, Jan 1965, A: Mer-Boy.	50.00
❑152, Feb 1965, A: Mer-Boy.	50.00
❑153, Apr 1965, A: Mer-Boy.	50.00
❑154, May 1965, A: Mer-Man.	50.00
❑155, Jul 1965, A: Bird-Man.	50.00
❑156, Aug 1965	50.00
❑157, Oct 1965, A: Egg Fu.	50.00
❑158, Nov 1965, A: Egg Fu.	50.00
❑159, Jan 1966, O: Wonder Woman.	50.00
❑160, Feb 1966, A: Cheetah I (Priscilla Rich).	30.00
❑161, Apr 1966, A: Countess Draska Nishki.	30.00
❑162, May 1966, O: Wonder Woman's Secret Identity.	40.00
❑163, Jul 1966, A: Doctor Psycho.	30.00
❑164, Aug 1966	30.00
❑165, Oct 1966, RA (c); RA (a); A: Doctor Psycho.	30.00
❑166, Nov 1966, RA (c); RA (a); A: Egg Fu.	30.00
❑167, Jan 1967, RA (c); RA (a)	30.00
❑168, Feb 1967, RA (c); RA (a); A: Paula Von Gunta.	30.00
❑169, Apr 1967, RA (c); RA (a)	30.00
❑170, Jun 1967, RA (a)	30.00
❑171, Aug 1967, RA (c); RA (a); A: Mouse Man.	25.00
❑172, Oct 1967	25.00
❑173, Dec 1967	25.00
❑174, Feb 1968	25.00
❑175, Apr 1968	25.00
❑176, Jun 1968	25.00
❑177, Aug 1968, IN (c); A: Supergirl.	25.00
❑178, Oct 1968, 1: Mod Diana Prince.	25.00
❑179, Dec 1968, 1: Doctor Cyber.	25.00
❑180, Feb 1969, D: Steve Trevor (Wonder Woman's boyfriend).	25.00
❑181, Apr 1969, A: Doctor Cyber.	33.00
❑182, Jun 1969	33.00
❑183, Aug 1969	33.00
❑184, Oct 1969	33.00
❑185, Dec 1969	33.00
❑186, Feb 1970	33.00
❑187, Apr 1970, A: Doctor Cyber.	33.00
❑188, Jun 1970, A: Doctor Cyber.	33.00
❑189, Aug 1970	33.00
❑190, Oct 1970	33.00
❑191, Dec 1970	40.00
❑192, Feb 1971	40.00
❑193, Apr 1971	40.00
❑194, Jun 1971	40.00
❑195, Aug 1971	40.00
❑196, Oct 1971, DG (a); A: Cheetah.	40.00
❑197, Dec 1971, DG (c); DG (a)	40.00
❑198, Feb 1972, DG (c); DG (a)	40.00
❑199, Apr 1972, JJ (c); DH, DG (a); A: Jonny Double.	40.00
❑200, Jun 1972, JJ (c); DG (a); D: Doctor Cyber.	40.00
❑201, Aug 1972, DG (c); DG (a); A: Catwoman.	14.00
❑202, Oct 1972; DG (c); DG (a); A: Fafhrd and The Gray Mouser.	14.00
❑203, Dec 1972, DG (c); DG (a)	14.00
❑204, Feb 1973, D: I-Ching.	14.00
❑205, Apr 1973; BO, DH (a); Suggestive cover	14.00
❑206, Jun 1973, DH (a)	14.00
❑207, Aug 1973	14.00
❑208, Oct 1973, RE (a); A: Steve Trevor.	14.00
❑209, Dec 1973, RE (c); RE (a)	14.00
❑210, Feb 1974	14.00
❑211, Apr 1974, NC (c); A: Mer-Boy.	25.00
❑212, Jun 1974, CS (a); A: JLA.	11.00

	N-MINT
❑213, Aug 1974, IN (a); A: Flash.	11.00
❑214, Oct 1974, BO (c); CS, RA (a); A: Green Lantern.	30.00
❑215, Dec 1974, A: Aquaman.	11.00
❑216, Feb 1975, NC (c); A: Black Canary.	11.00
❑217, Apr 1975, MGr (c); DD, RA (a); A: Green Arrow.	11.00
❑218, Jun 1975, KS (a); A: Red Tornado.	11.00
❑219, Aug 1975, CS (a); A: Elongated Man.	7.00
❑220, Oct 1975, DG (c); DG (a); A: Atom.	7.00
❑221, Dec 1975, CS (a); A: Hawkman.	7.00
❑222, Feb 1976, A: Batman.	7.00
❑223, Apr 1976; : Steve Trevor. Return of Steve Trevor	7.00
❑224, Jun 1976, CS (a)	7.00
❑225, Aug 1976	7.00
❑226, Oct 1976	7.00
❑227, Dec 1976	7.00
❑228, Feb 1977	7.00
❑229, Mar 1977, JL (c)	7.00
❑230, Apr 1977, A: Cheetah.	7.00
❑231, May 1977, MN (c)	7.00
❑232, Jun 1977, MN (c); MN (a)	7.00
❑233, Jul 1977, GM (c); DH (a)	7.00
❑234, Aug 1977, JL (c); DH (a)	7.00
❑235, Sep 1977, JL (c); A: Doctor Mid-Nite.	7.00
❑236, Oct 1977, RB (c)	7.00
❑237, Nov 1977, RB (c); O: Wonder Woman. 1: Kung.	6.00
❑238, Dec 1977, RB (c); A: Sandman.	6.00
❑239, Jan 1978, RB (c); A: Golden Age Flash.	6.00
❑240, Feb 1978, DG, JL (c); A: Golden Age Flash.	6.00
❑241, Mar 1978, DG, JSa (c); DG, JSa (a); A: new Spectre.	6.00
❑242, Apr 1978, RB (c)	6.00
❑243, May 1978, A: Angle Man.	6.00
❑244, Jun 1978, RB (c)	6.00
❑245, Jul 1978, JSa (c)	6.00
❑246, Aug 1978, DG, JSa (c)	6.00
❑247, Sep 1978, RB, DG (c); A: Elongated Man.	6.00
❑248, Oct 1978, JL (c); D: Steve Trevor.	6.00
❑249, Nov 1978, RB, DG (c); A: Hawkgirl.	6.00
❑250, Dec 1978, RB, DG (c); 1: Orana (new Wonder Woman).	6.00
❑251, Jan 1979, DG, RA (c)	6.00
❑252, Feb 1979, DG, RA (c); 1: Stacy Macklin.	6.00
❑253, Mar 1979, DG (c)	6.00
❑254, Apr 1979, DG, RA (c); A: Angle Man.	6.00
❑255, May 1979, DG (c)	6.00
❑256, Jun 1979	6.00
❑257, Jul 1979, DG, RA (c); A: Multi-Man.	6.00
❑258, Aug 1979, DG (c)	6.00
❑259, Sep 1979, DG (c); A: Hercules.	6.00
❑260, Oct 1979, A: Hercules.	6.00
❑261, Nov 1979, DG (c); A: Hercules.	5.00
❑262, Dec 1979, DG (c); RE (a)	5.00
❑263, Jan 1980, DG (c)	5.00
❑264, Feb 1980, DG, RA (c)	5.00
❑265, Mar 1980, DG, RA (c); RE (a); A: Wonder Girl.	5.00
❑266, Apr 1980, RE (a)	5.00
❑267, May 1980, DG, RA (c); A: Animal Man.	5.00
❑268, Jun 1980, DG, RA (c); A: Animal Man.	5.00
❑269, Jul 1980, DG, RA (c); WW (a) .	4.00
❑270, Aug 1980, A: Steve Trevor.	4.00
❑271, Sep 1980, DG, RA (c); JSa (a); A: Huntress.	4.00
❑272, Oct 1980, DG, DC (c); JSa (a); A: Huntress.	4.00
❑273, Nov 1980, DG, RA (c); JSa (a); A: Solomon Grundy.	4.00
❑274, Dec 1980, JSa (a); 1: Cheetah II (Deborah Domaine).	4.00

	N-MINT
❑275, Jan 1981, RB, DG (c); JSa (a); A: Power Girl.	4.00
❑276, Feb 1981, DG, RA (c); JSa (a); A: Kobra.	4.00
❑277, Mar 1981, DG, RA (c); JSa (a); A: Kobra.	4.00
❑278, Apr 1981, DG, RA (c); JSa (a); A: Kobra.	4.00
❑279, May 1981, DG, RA (c); JSa (a)	4.00
❑280, Jun 1981, DG, RA (c); JSa (a); A: Etrigan.	3.00
❑281, Jul 1981, DG, RA (c); JSa (a); A: Joker.	5.00
❑282, Aug 1981, RB, DG (c); JSa (a); A: Joker.	5.00
❑283, Sep 1981, DG (c); JSa (a); A: Joker.	5.00
❑284, Oct 1981, GP, DG (c); JSa (a); A: Earth-2 Robin.	2.50
❑285, Nov 1981, JSa (a); A: Earth-2 Robin.	2.50
❑286, Dec 1981, DG, RA (c); JSa (a)	2.50
❑287, Jan 1982, DH, JSa, RT (a); A: New Teen Titans.	2.50
❑288, Feb 1982, GC, RT (a); 1: The Silver Swan.	2.50
❑289, Mar 1982, GC, DG (c); GC, JSa, RT (a); 1: Captain Wonder.	2.50
❑290, Apr 1982, GC, JSa, RT (a); A: Captain Wonder.	2.50
❑291, May 1982, DG, RA (c); FMc, GC (a); A: Zatanna.	2.50
❑292, Jun 1982, DG, RA (c); FMc, GC (a); A: Supergirl.	2.50
❑293, Jul 1982, DG, RA (c); FMc, GC (a); A: Raven. A: Starfire.	2.50
❑294, Aug 1982, GK (c); FMc, GC, JOy, JSa (a); A: Blockbuster.	2.50
❑295, Sep 1982, RB (c); FMc, GC, JOy, JSa (a)	2.50
❑296, Oct 1982, FMc, GC, JOy, JSa (a)	2.50
❑297, Nov 1982, FMc, GC, JSa, CS (a); 1: Aegeus.	2.50
❑298, Dec 1982, DG, FM (c); FMc, GC, JSa (a)	2.50
❑299, Jan 1983, DG (c); FMc, GC, JSa (a)	2.50
❑300, Feb 1983; Giant-size DG (c); FMc, RB, GC, KG, JDu, KP, DG, RA (a); A: New Teen Titans.	6.00
❑301, Mar 1983, DG (c); FMc, GC, DH (a)	2.50
❑302, Apr 1983, DG (c); FMc, GC (a)	2.50
❑303, May 1983, GK (c); FMc, GC (a); A: Doctor Polaris.	2.50
❑304, Jun 1983, GK (c); FMc, GC (a); A: Green Lantern.	2.50
❑305, Jul 1983, GK (c); FMc, GC (a); 1: Circe (DC).	2.50
❑306, Aug 1983, DG, JL (c); DH (a); A: Aegeus.	2.50
❑307, Sep 1983, GK (c); DH (a); A: Aegeus.	2.50
❑308, Oct 1983, DG, RA (c); DH (a); A: Black Canary.	2.50
❑309, Nov 1983, DH (a); 1: Earthworm.	2.50
❑310, Dec 1983, DG (c)	2.50
❑311, Jan 1984, DG, RA (c); DH (a) ..	2.50
❑312, Feb 1984, GK (c); DH, DS (a) ..	2.50
❑313, Mar 1984, DG (c); DH (a); A: Circe (DC).	2.50
❑314, Apr 1984, GK (c); DH (a); A: Circe (DC).	2.50
❑315, May 1984, DG (c); DH (a); A: Tezcatlipoca.	2.50
❑316, Jun 1984, DH (a); A: Tezcatlipoca.	2.50
❑317, Jul 1984, DH (a)	2.50
❑318, Aug 1984, KB (w); IN (a)	2.50
❑319, Sep 1984, DH (a); A: Doctor Cyber.	2.50
❑320, Oct 1984, DH (a); A: Doctor Cyber.	2.50
❑321, Nov 1984, DH (a); A: Doctor Cyber.	2.50
❑322, Dec 1984, DH (a); A: Eros.	2.50
❑323, Feb 1985, DH (a); A: The Monitor.	2.50

After her Silver Age incarnation was destroyed in *Crisis on Infinite Earths*, DC revived Wonder Woman with George Pérez writing and pencilling the first few issues.

© 1987 DC Comics.

	N-MINT
❑324, Apr 1985, RT (c); DH (a); A: Atomic Knight.	2.50
❑325, May 1985, DH (a); A: Atomic Knight.	2.50
❑326, Jul 1985, DH (a)	2.50
❑327, Sep 1985, DH (a); A: Tezcatlipoca.	2.50
❑328, Dec 1985; DG (c); DH (a); Crisis	2.50
❑329, Feb 1986; Giant-size; JL (c); DH (a); Crisis	2.50

WONDER WOMAN (2ND SERIES) DC

	N-MINT
❑0, Oct 1994, BB (c); O: The Amazons.	6.00
❑1, Feb 1987, GP (c); GP (w); GP (a); O: Wonder Woman (new origin). 1: Ares (DC).	4.00
❑2, Mar 1987, GP (c); GP (w); GP (a); A: Steve Trevor.	3.00
❑3, Apr 1987, GP (c); GP (w); GP (a); 1: Vanessa Kapatelis. 1: Jack Kapatelis. 1: Decay.	3.00
❑4, May 1987, GP (c); GP (w); GP (a); 2: Decay.	3.00
❑5, Jun 1987, GP (w); GP (a); V: Ares.	3.00
❑6, Jul 1987, GP (c); GP (w); GP (a); V: Ares.	2.50
❑7, Aug 1987, GP (c); GP (w); GP (a)	2.50
❑8, Sep 1987, GP (c); GP (w); GP (a)	2.50
❑9, Oct 1987, GP (c); GP (w); GP (a); 1: Cheetah.	2.50
❑10, Nov 1987; GP (c); GP (w); GP (a); gatefold	2.50
❑10/A, Nov 1987, no gatefold; gatefold	2.50
❑11, Dec 1987, GP (c); GP (w); GP (a)	2.00
❑12, Jan 1988; GP (c); GP (w); GP (a); Millennium	2.00
❑13, Feb 1988; GP (c); GP (w); GP (a); Millennium	2.00
❑14, Mar 1988, GP (c); GP (w); GP (a); A: Hercules.	2.00
❑15, Apr 1988, GP (c); GP (w); GP (a); 1: Silver Swan. 1: Ed Indelicato.	2.00
❑16, May 1988, GP (c); GP (w); GP (a); A: Silver Swan.	2.00
❑17, Jun 1988, GP (c); GP (w); GP, DG (a)	2.00
❑18, Jul 1988; GP (c); GP (w); GP, DG (a); A: Circe (DC). Bonus Book	2.00
❑19, Aug 1988, GP (c); GP (w); FMc, GP (a); A: Circe (DC).	2.00
❑20, Sep 1988, GP (c); GP (w); GP, BMc (a); A: Ed Indelicato.	2.00
❑21, Oct 1988, GP (c); GP (w); GP, BMc (a)	2.00
❑22, Nov 1988, GP (c); GP (w); GP, BMc (a)	2.00
❑23, Dec 1988, GP (c); GP (w); GP (a)	2.00
❑24, Hol 1988, GP (c); GP (w); GP (a); Hol 1988	2.00
❑25, Jan 1989; GP (c); KG, GP (w); Invasion!	2.00
❑26, Jan 1989; GP (c); KG, GP (w); Invasion!	2.00
❑27, Feb 1989, GP (c); GP (w)	2.00
❑28, Mar 1989, GP (c); GP (w); A: Cheetah.	2.00
❑29, Apr 1989, GP (c); GP (w); O: Cheetah.	2.00
❑30, May 1989, GP (c); GP (w); A: Cheetah.	2.00
❑31, Jun 1989, GP (c); GP (w); A: Cheetah.	1.75
❑32, Jul 1989, GP (c); GP (w)	1.75

Condition price index: Multiply "NM prices" above by: **0.83 for Very Fine/Near Mint**
0.66 for Very Fine • 0.33 for Fine • 0.2 for Very Good • 0.125 for Good

N-MINT

- ❑33, Aug 1989, GP (c); GP (w) 1.75
- ❑34, Sep 1989, GP (c); GP (w); A: Shim'Tar. 1.75
- ❑35, Oct 1989, GP (c); GP (w); A: Shim'Tar. 1.75
- ❑36, Nov 1989, GP (c); GP (w) 1.75
- ❑37, Dec 1989, GP (c); GP (w); A: Superman. 1.75
- ❑38, Jan 1990, GP (c); GP (w); A: Lois Lane. 1.75
- ❑39, Feb 1990, GP (c); GP (w); A: Lois Lane. 1.75
- ❑40, Mar 1990, GP (c); GP (w); A: Lois Lane. 1.75
- ❑41, Apr 1990, GP (c); GP (w); RT (a) 1.75
- ❑42, May 1990, GP (c); GP (w); RT (a); A: Silver Swan. 1.75
- ❑43, Jun 1990, GP (c); GP (w); RT (a); A: Silver Swan. 1.75
- ❑44, Jul 1990, GP (c); GP (w); RT (a); A: Silver Swan. 1.75
- ❑45, Aug 1990, GP (c); GP (w); RT (a) 1.75
- ❑46, Sep 1990, GP (c); GP (w); RT (a) 1.75
- ❑47, Oct 1990, GP (c); GP (w); RT (a); A: Troia. 1.75
- ❑48, Nov 1990, GP (c); GP (w); RT (a) 1.75
- ❑49, Dec 1990, GP (c); GP (w); A: Princess Diana. 1.75
- ❑50, Jan 1991, GP (c); GP (w); MW, SA, BB, CR, KN, RT (a) 1.75
- ❑51, Feb 1991, GP (c); GP (w); RT (a); A: Lord Hermes. 1.50
- ❑52, Mar 1991, GP (c); GP (w); KN (a) 1.50
- ❑53, Apr 1991, GP (c); GP (w); RT (a); A: Pariah. 1.50
- ❑54, May 1991, GP (c); GP (w); RT (a); A: Doctor Psycho. 1.50
- ❑55, Jun 1991, GP (c); GP (w); RT (a); A: Doctor Psycho. 1.50
- ❑56, Jul 1991, GP (c); GP (w); RT (a) 1.50
- ❑57, Aug 1991, GP (w); RT (a) 1.50
- ❑58, Sep 1991; GP (c); GP (w); RT (a); War of Gods 1.50
- ❑59, Oct 1991; GP (c); GP (w); RT (a); A: Batman. War of Gods 1.50
- ❑60, Nov 1991; GP (c); GP (w); A: Lobo. War of Gods 1.50
- ❑61, Jan 1992; GP (w); War of Gods 1.50
- ❑62, Feb 1992, GP (w); RT (a) 1.50
- ❑63, Jun 1992, BB (c); RT (a); A: Deathstroke. 1.50
- ❑64, Jul 1992, BB (c); A: . A: Ed Indelicato. 1.50
- ❑65, Aug 1992, BB (c) 1.50
- ❑66, Sep 1992, BB (c); 1: Natasha Teranova. 1.50
- ❑67, Oct 1992, BB (c); A: Natasha Teranova. 1.50
- ❑68, Nov 1992, BB (c); FMc (a); A: Natasha Teranova. 1.50
- ❑69, Dec 1992, BB (c); A: Natasha Teranova. 1.50
- ❑70, Jan 1993, BB (c); RT (a); A: Natasha Teranova. 1.50
- ❑71, Feb 1993, BB (c); RT (a); A: Natasha Teranova. 1.50
- ❑72, Mar 1993, BB (c) 1.50
- ❑73, Apr 1993, BB (c) 1.50
- ❑74, May 1993, BB (c); A: White Magician. 1.50
- ❑75, Jun 1993, BB (c) 1.50
- ❑76, Jul 1993, BB (c); A: Doctor Fate. 1.50
- ❑77, Aug 1993, BB (c); A: JLA. 1.50
- ❑78, Sep 1993, BB (c); A: Mayfly. 1.50
- ❑79, Oct 1993, BB (c); A: Flash. V: Mayfly. 1.50
- ❑80, Nov 1993, BB (c); A: Ares. 1.50
- ❑81, Dec 1993, BB (c) 1.50
- ❑82, Jan 1994, BB (c); V: Ares. 1.50
- ❑83, Feb 1994, BB (c) 1.50
- ❑84, Mar 1994, BB (c) 1.50
- ❑85, Apr 1994; BB (c); Mike Deodato Jr.'s first U.S. work 10.00
- ❑86, May 1994, BB (c) 4.00
- ❑87, Jun 1994, BB (c) 3.00
- ❑88, Jul 1994, BB (c); A: Superman. . 3.00

N-MINT

- ❑89, Aug 1994, BB (c); RT (a); A: Circe (DC). 3.00
- ❑90, Sep 1994, BB (c); A: Artemis. ... 3.00
- ❑91, Nov 1994, BB (c); A: Artemis. ... 3.00
- ❑92, Dec 1994, BB (c); A: Artemis. ... 3.00
- ❑93, Jan 1995, BB (c) 3.00
- ❑94, Feb 1995, BB (c); V: Cheshire. V: Poison Ivy. 2.00
- ❑95, Mar 1995, BB (c); V: Cheetah. V: Cheshire. V: Poison Ivy. 2.00
- ❑96, Apr 1995, BB (c); V: Joker. 2.00
- ❑97, May 1995, BB (c); V: Joker. 2.00
- ❑98, Jun 1995, BB (c) 2.00
- ❑99, Jul 1995, BB (c) 2.00
- ❑100, Jul 1995; Giant-size; D: Athena. Wonder Woman returns to old uniform 2.95
- ❑100/Variant, Jul 1995; Giant-size; (c); D: Athena. Wonder Woman returns to old uniform; enhanced cover 4.00
- ❑101, Sep 1995, JBy (c); JBy (w); JBy (a); A: Darkseid. 1.95
- ❑102, Oct 1995, JBy (c); JBy (w); JBy (a); A: Darkseid. 1.95
- ❑103, Nov 1995, JBy (c); JBy (w); JBy (a); A: Darkseid. 1.95
- ❑104, Dec 1995, JBy (c); JBy (w); JBy (a); A: Darkseid. 1.95
- ❑105, Jan 1996, JBy (c); JBy (w); JBy (a) 1.95
- ❑106, Feb 1996, JBy (c); JBy (w); JBy (a); A: Phantom Stranger. 1.95
- ❑107, Mar 1996, JBy (c); JBy (w); JBy (a); A: Demon. 1.95
- ❑108, Apr 1996, JBy (c); JBy (w); JBy (a); A: Phantom Stranger. 1.95
- ❑109, May 1996, JBy (c); JBy (w); JBy (a); V: Flash (fake). 1.95
- ❑110, Jun 1996, JBy (c); JBy (w); JBy (a); V: Sinestro (fake). 1.95
- ❑111, Jul 1996, JBy (c); JBy (w); JBy (a); V: Doomsday (fake). 1.95
- ❑112, Aug 1996, JBy (c); JBy (w); JBy (a); A: Decay. V: Doomsday (fake). 1.95
- ❑113, Sep 1996, JBy (c); JBy (w); JBy (a); A: Wonder Girl. 1.95
- ❑114, Oct 1996, JBy (c); JBy (w); JBy (a); A: Doctor Psycho. 1.95
- ❑115, Nov 1996, JBy (c); JBy (w); JBy (a); A: Cave Carson. 1.95
- ❑116, Dec 1996, JBy (c); JBy (w); JBy (a); A: Cave Carson. 1.95
- ❑117, Jan 1997, JBy (w); JBy (a); 1: Invisible Plane. 1.95
- ❑118, Feb 1997, JL (c); JBy (w); JBy (a); V: Cheetah. 1.95
- ❑119, Mar 1997, JL (c); JBy (w); JBy (a); V: Cheetah. 1.95
- ❑120, Apr 1997; 10th anniversary issue GP (c); JBy (w); JBy (a) 2.95
- ❑121, May 1997, JBy (c); JBy (w); JBy (a); A: Artemis. 1.95
- ❑122, Jun 1997, JBy (c); JBy (w); JBy (a); A: Jason Blood. 1.95
- ❑123, Jul 1997, JBy (w); JBy (a); V: Artemis. 1.95
- ❑124, Aug 1997, JL (c); JBy (w); JBy (a); V: Artemis. 1.95
- ❑125, Sep 1997; JL (c); JBy (w); JBy (a); O: Demon. A: Superman. A: Flash. A: Martian Manhunter. A: Green Lantern. A: Batman. Diana in intensive care 1.95
- ❑126, Oct 1997; JBy (c); JBy (w); JBy (a); Genesis 1.95
- ❑127, Nov 1997; JL (c); JBy (w); JBy (a); Diana is turned into a goddess and goes to Olympus 1.95
- ❑128, Dec 1997; JL (c); JBy (w); JBy (a); A: Egg Fu. Face cover 1.95
- ❑129, Jan 1998, JL (c); JBy (w); JBy (a); A: Demon. 1.95
- ❑130, Feb 1998, JBy (c); JBy (w); JBy (a); A: Justice Society of America. A: Jay Garrick. 1.95
- ❑131, Mar 1998, JBy (c); JBy (w); JBy (a); A: Justice Society of America. A: Jay Garrick. 1.95

N-MINT

- ❑132, Apr 1998, JBy (c); JBy (w); JBy (a); A: Justice Society of America. A: Jay Garrick. 1.95
- ❑133, May 1998, JBy (c); JBy (w); JBy (a); A: Justice Society of America. A: Jay Garrick. 1.95
- ❑134, Jun 1998, JBy (c); JBy (w); JBy (a); A: Dark Angel. 1.95
- ❑135, Jul 1998, JBy (c); JBy (w); JBy (a); O: Donna Troy. 1.95
- ❑136, Aug 1998; JBy (c); JBy (w); JBy (a); Diana returns to Earth; Return of Donna Troy 1.99
- ❑137, Sep 1998, RT (a) 1.99
- ❑138, Oct 1998, RT (a) 1.99
- ❑139, Dec 1998; BMc (a); Diana becomes mortal again 1.99
- ❑139/Ltd., Dec 1998; Signed edition . 14.95
- ❑140, Jan 1999, BMc (a); A: Superman. A: Batman. 1.99
- ❑141, Feb 1999, BMc (a); A: Superman. A: Batman. A: Oblivion. 1.99
- ❑142, Mar 1999, BMc (a) 1.99
- ❑143, Apr 1999, BMc (a); 1: Devastation. 1.99
- ❑144, May 1999, BMc (a); V: Devastation. 1.99
- ❑145, Jun 1999, BMc (a); V: Devastation. 1.99
- ❑146, Jul 1999, BMc (a); V: Devastation. 1.99
- ❑147, Aug 1999, BMc (a) 1.99
- ❑148, Sep 1999, BMc (a) 1.99
- ❑149, Oct 1999, BMc (a) 1.99
- ❑150, Nov 1999 .... 1.99
- ❑151, Dec 1999 .... 1.99
- ❑152, Jan 2000 .... 1.99
- ❑153, Feb 2000 .... 1.99
- ❑154, Mar 2000 .... 1.99
- ❑155, Apr 2000 .... 1.99
- ❑156, May 2000 .... 1.99
- ❑157, Jun 2000 .... 1.99
- ❑158, Jul 2000 .... 1.99
- ❑159, Aug 2000 .... 2.25
- ❑160, Sep 2000 .... 2.25
- ❑161, Oct 2000 .... 2.25
- ❑162, Nov 2000 .... 2.25
- ❑163, Dec 2000 .... 2.25
- ❑164, Jan 2001 .... 2.25
- ❑165, Feb 2001 .... 2.25
- ❑166, Mar 2001, A: Batman. 2.25
- ❑167, Apr 2001 .... 2.25
- ❑168, May 2001, GP (w) 2.25
- ❑169, Jun 2001, GP (w); GP (a) 2.25
- ❑170, Jul 2001 .... 2.25
- ❑171, Aug 2001 .... 2.25
- ❑172, Sep 2001 .... 2.25
- ❑173, Oct 2001 .... 2.25
- ❑174, Nov 2001, JLee (c) 2.25
- ❑175, Dec 2001; Joker: Last Laugh crossover 2.25
- ❑176, Jan 2002 .... 2.25
- ❑177, Feb 2002 .... 2.25
- ❑178, Mar 2002 .... 2.25
- ❑179, Apr 2002 .... 2.25
- ❑180, May 2002 .... 2.25
- ❑181, Jun 2002 .... 2.25
- ❑182, Aug 2002 .... 2.25
- ❑183, Sep 2002, (c) 2.25
- ❑184, Oct 2002 .... 2.25
- ❑185, Nov 2002, (c) 2.25
- ❑186, Dec 2002 .... 2.25
- ❑187, Feb 2003 .... 2.25
- ❑188, Mar 2003 .... 2.25
- ❑189, Apr 2003, JOy, CR (a) 2.25
- ❑190, May 2003, JOy, CR (a) 2.25
- ❑191, Jun 2003, JOy, CR (a) 2.25
- ❑192, Jul 2003, JOy, CR (a) 2.25
- ❑193, Aug 2003, JOy, CR (a) 2.25
- ❑194, Sep 2003, JOy, CR (a) 2.25
- ❑195, Oct 2003 .... 2.25
- ❑196, Nov 2003 .... 2.25
- ❑197, Dec 2003 .... 2.25
- ❑198, Jan 2004 .... 2.25
- ❑199, Feb 2004 .... 2.25
- ❑200, Mar 2004 .... 3.95
- ❑201, Apr 2004 .... 2.25

N-MINT

❑202, May 2004 ... 2.25
❑203, Jun 2004 ... 2.25
❑204, Jul 2004 ... 2.25
❑205, Aug 2004 ... 2.25
❑206, Sep 2004 ...
❑1000000, Nov 1998 ... 3.00
❑Annual 1, ca. 1988, GP (c); GP (w); GP, BB, CS, RA, BMc, JL (a) ... 2.00
❑Annual 2, Sep 1989, GP (c); GP (w); JDu, GP (a) ... 2.00
❑Annual 3, ca. 1992; KN (c); Eclipso . 2.50
❑Annual 4, ca. 1995; (c); BA (a); Year One ... 3.50
❑Annual 5, ca. 1996; DC (c); JBy (w); DC (a); Legends of the Dead Earth; 1996 Annual ... 2.95
❑Annual 6, ca. 1997; JBy (w); TP (a); A: Artemis. Pulp Heroes ... 3.95
❑Annual 7, Sep 1998; (c); RT (a); Ghosts ... 2.95
❑Annual 8, Sep 1999; JLApe ... 2.95
❑Special 1, ca. 1992, JOy (c); A: Deathstroke. ... 1.75

WONDER WOMAN: AMAZONIA
DC

❑1; Oversized; Elseworlds ... 7.95

WONDER WOMAN: BLUE AMAZON
DC / VERTIGO

❑1, Nov 2003 ... 6.95

WONDER WOMAN: DONNA TROY
DC

❑1, Jun 1998; Girlfrenzy ... 1.95

WONDER WOMAN GALLERY
DC

❑1, ca. 1996; pin-ups ... 3.50

WONDER WOMAN: OUR WORLDS AT WAR
DC

❑1, Oct 2001 ... 2.95

WONDER WOMAN PLUS
DC

❑1, Jan 1997 ... 2.95

WONDER WOMAN SECRET FILES
DC

❑1, Mar 1998; background on Wonder Woman and supporting cast ... 4.95
❑2, Jul 1999; background on Wonder Woman and supporting cast ... 4.95

WONDER WOMAN: SPIRIT OF TRUTH
DC

❑1 ... 9.95
❑1-2 ... 9.95

WONDER WOMAN: THE ONCE AND FUTURE STORY
DC

❑1, ca. 1998; prestige format one-shot; domestic violence ... 4.95

WONDERWORLD EXPRESS
THAT OTHER COMIX CO.

❑1 1984, b&w ... 2.25

WONDERWORLDS
INNOVATION

❑1 ... 3.50

WOODSTOCK: THE COMIC
MARVEL

❑1 ... 5.95

WOODSY OWL
GOLD KEY

❑1, Nov 1973 ... 8.00
❑2, Feb 1974 ... 5.00
❑3, May 1974 ... 4.00
❑4, Aug 1974 ... 4.00
❑5, Nov 1974 ... 4.00
❑6, Feb 1975 ... 3.00
❑7, May 1975 ... 3.00
❑8, Aug 1975 ... 3.00
❑9, Nov 1975 ... 3.00
❑10, Feb 1976 ... 3.00

N-MINT

WOODY WOODPECKER (WALTER LANTZ...)
DELL

❑39, Oct 1956 ... 12.00
❑40, Dec 1956 ... 12.00
❑41, Feb 1957 ... 12.00
❑42, Apr 1957 ... 12.00
❑43, Jun 1957 ... 12.00
❑44, Aug 1957 ... 12.00
❑45, Oct 1957 ... 12.00
❑46, Dec 1957 ... 12.00
❑47, Feb 1958 ... 12.00
❑48, Apr 1958 ... 12.00
❑49, Jun 1958 ... 12.00
❑50, Aug 1958 ... 12.00
❑51, Oct 1958 ... 9.00
❑52, Dec 1958 ... 9.00
❑53, Feb 1959 ... 9.00
❑54, Apr 1959 ... 9.00
❑55, Jun 1959 ... 9.00
❑56, Aug 1959 ... 9.00
❑57, Oct 1959 ... 9.00
❑58, Dec 1959 ... 9.00
❑59, Feb 1960 ... 9.00
❑60, Apr 1960 ... 9.00
❑61, Jun 1960 ... 9.00
❑62, Aug 1960 ... 9.00
❑63, Oct 1960 ... 9.00
❑64, Dec 1960 ... 9.00
❑65, Mar 1961 ... 9.00
❑66, May 1961 ... 9.00
❑67, Jul 1961 ... 9.00
❑68, Sep 1961 ... 9.00
❑69, Nov 1961 ... 9.00
❑70, Jan 1962 ... 9.00
❑71, Mar 1962 ... 9.00
❑72, Jun 1962 ... 9.00
❑73, Oct 1962; Giant-size; Gold Key begins publishing ... 25.00
❑74, Dec 1962; Giant-size ... 25.00
❑75, Mar 1963; Giant-size ... 25.00
❑76, Jun 1963 ... 15.00
❑77, Sep 1963 ... 15.00
❑78, Dec 1963 ... 15.00
❑79, Mar 1964 ... 15.00
❑80, Jun 1964 ... 15.00
❑81, Sep 1964 ... 15.00
❑82, Dec 1964 ... 15.00
❑83, Mar 1965 ... 15.00
❑84, Apr 1965 ... 15.00
❑85, Jun 1965 ... 15.00
❑86, Aug 1965 ... 15.00
❑87, Oct 1965 ... 15.00
❑88, Dec 1965 ... 15.00
❑89, Feb 1966 ... 15.00
❑90, Apr 1966 ... 15.00
❑91, Jun 1966 ... 15.00
❑92, Aug 1966 ... 15.00
❑93, Oct 1966 ... 15.00
❑94, Dec 1966 ... 15.00
❑95, Feb 1967 ... 15.00
❑96, Apr 1967 ... 15.00
❑97, Jun 1967 ... 15.00
❑98, Aug 1967 ... 15.00
❑99, Nov 1967 ... 15.00
❑100, Feb 1968 ... 15.00
❑101, May 1968 ... 10.00
❑102, Aug 1968 ... 10.00
❑103, Nov 1968 ... 10.00
❑104, Feb 1969 ... 10.00
❑105, May 1969 ... 10.00
❑106, Aug 1969 ... 10.00
❑107, Sep 1969 ... 10.00
❑108, Nov 1969 ... 10.00
❑109, Jan 1970 ... 10.00
❑110, Mar 1970 ... 10.00
❑111, May 1970 ... 10.00
❑112, Jul 1970 ... 10.00
❑113, Sep 1970 ... 10.00
❑114, Nov 1970 ... 10.00
❑115, Jan 1971 ... 10.00

Woody Woodpecker will celebrate his 65th anniversary in 2005.

© 1992 Harvey.

N-MINT

❑116, Mar 1971 ... 10.00
❑117, May 1971 ... 10.00
❑118, Jul 1971 ... 10.00
❑119, Sep 1971 ... 10.00
❑120, Nov 1971 ... 10.00
❑121, Jan 1972 ... 6.00
❑122, Mar 1972 ... 6.00
❑123, May 1972 ... 6.00
❑124, Jul 1972 ... 6.00
❑125, Sep 1972 ... 6.00
❑126, Nov 1972 ... 6.00
❑127, Jan 1973 ... 6.00
❑128, Mar 1973 ... 6.00
❑129, May 1973 ... 6.00
❑130, Jul 1973 ... 6.00
❑131, Sep 1973 ... 2.50
❑132, Oct 1973 ... 2.50
❑133, Nov 1973 ... 2.50
❑134, Jan 1974 ... 2.50
❑135, Mar 1974 ... 2.50
❑136, May 1974 ... 2.50
❑137, Jul 1974 ... 2.50
❑138, Sep 1974 ... 2.50
❑139, Oct 1974 ... 2.50
❑140, Nov 1974 ... 2.50
❑141, Jan 1975 ... 2.50
❑142, Mar 1975 ... 2.50
❑143, May 1975 ... 2.50
❑144, Jul 1975 ... 2.50
❑145, Sep 1975 ... 2.50
❑146, Oct 1975 ... 2.50
❑147, Nov 1975 ... 2.50
❑148, Jan 1976 ... 2.50
❑149, Mar 1976 ... 2.50
❑150, May 1976 ... 2.50
❑151, Jul 1976 ... 2.50
❑152, Aug 1976 ... 2.50
❑153, Sep 1976 ... 2.50
❑154, Oct 1976 ... 2.50
❑155, Dec 1976 ... 2.50
❑156, Feb 1977 ... 2.50
❑157, Apr 1977 ... 2.50
❑158, Jun 1977 ... 2.50
❑159, Aug 1977 ... 2.50
❑160, Oct 1977 ... 2.50
❑161, Dec 1977 ... 2.50
❑162, Jan 1978 ... 2.50
❑163, Feb 1978 ... 2.50
❑164, Mar 1978 ... 2.50
❑165, Apr 1978 ... 2.50
❑166, May 1978 ... 2.50
❑167, Jun 1978 ... 2.50
❑168, Jul 1978 ... 2.50
❑169, Aug 1978 ... 2.50
❑170, Sep 1978 ... 2.50
❑171, Oct 1978 ... 2.00
❑172, Nov 1978 ... 2.00
❑173, Dec 1978 ... 2.00
❑174, Jan 1979 ... 2.00
❑175, Feb 1979 ... 2.00
❑176, Mar 1979 ... 2.00
❑177, Apr 1979 ... 2.00
❑178, May 1979 ... 2.00
❑179, Jun 1979 ... 2.00
❑180, Jul 1979 ... 2.00
❑181, Aug 1979 ... 2.00
❑182, Sep 1979 ... 2.00

N-MINT

❑183, Oct 1979 ... 2.00
❑184, Nov 1979 ... 2.00
❑185, Dec 1979 ... 2.00
❑186, Jan 1980 ... 2.00
❑187, Feb 1980 ... 2.00
❑188, Mar 1980 ... 2.00
❑189 1980 ... 2.00
❑190 1980 ... 2.00
❑191 1980 ... 2.00
❑192 1981 ... 2.00
❑193 1981 ... 2.00
❑194, Oct 1981 ... 2.00
❑195, Dec 1982 ... 2.00
❑196, Feb 1982 ... 2.00
❑197, Apr 1982 ... 2.00
❑198 1982 ... 2.00
❑199 1983 ... 2.00
❑200 1984 ... 2.00
❑201 1984 ... 2.00

WOODY WOODPECKER (HARVEY)
Harvey

❑1, Sep 1991 ... 1.50
❑2, Nov 1991 ... 1.25
❑3, Jan 1992 ... 1.25
❑4, Mar 1992 ... 1.25
❑5, Jun 1992 ... 1.25
❑6, Sep 1992 ... 1.25
❑7 ... 1.25
❑8, Jun 1993 ... 1.25
❑9 ... 1.50
❑10 ... 1.50
❑11 ... 1.50
❑12 ... 1.50

WOODY WOODPECKER 50TH ANNIVERSARY SPECIAL
Harvey

❑1, Oct 1991 ... 2.50

WOODY WOODPECKER ADVENTURES
Harvey

❑1 ... 1.25
❑2 ... 1.25
❑3 ... 1.25

WOODY WOODPECKER AND FRIENDS
Harvey

❑1, Dec 1991 ... 1.25
❑2, Feb 1992 ... 1.25
❑3, Apr 1992 ... 1.25
❑4, Jun 1992 ... 1.25

WOODY WOODPECKER DIGEST
Harvey

❑1 ... 1.75

WOODY WOODPECKER GIANT SIZE
Harvey

❑1 ... 2.25

WOODY WOODPECKER'S CHRISTMAS PARADE
Gold Key

❑1, Nov 1968 ... 20.00

WOODY WOODPECKER SUMMER SPECIAL
Harvey

❑1, Oct 1990 ... 1.95

WOOFERS AND HOOTERS
Fantagraphics / Eros

❑1, b&w ... 2.50

WORDS & PICTURES
Maverick

❑1, Fal 1994, b&w ... 3.95
❑2, Spr 1995, b&w ... 3.95

WORDSMITH (RENEGADE)
Renegade

❑1, Aug 1985, b&w ... 1.70
❑2, Oct 1985, b&w ... 1.70
❑3, Dec 1985, b&w ... 1.70
❑4, Dec 1985, b&w ... 1.70
❑5, May 1986, b&w ... 1.70
❑6, Aug 1986 ... 1.70
❑7, Nov 1986 ... 2.00
❑8, Nov 1986 ... 2.00
❑9, May 1987 ... 2.00
❑10, Aug 1987 ... 2.00
❑11, Nov 1987 ... 2.00
❑12, Jan 1988 ... 2.00

WORDSMITH (CALIBER)
Caliber

❑1 1996 ... 2.95
❑2 1996 ... 2.95
❑3 1996 ... 2.95
❑4 1996 ... 2.95
❑5 1997 ... 2.95
❑6 1997 ... 2.95

WORD WARRIORS
Literacy Volunteers

❑1, b&w; Ms. Tree, Jon Sable ... 1.50

WORGARD: VIKING BERSERKIR
Stronghold

❑1, Oct 1997, b&w ... 2.95

WORKSHOP, THE
Blue Comet

❑1 ... 2.95

WORLD BANK, THE
Public Services International

❑1; educational comic; no indicia ... 2.95

WORLD BELOW, THE
Dark Horse

❑1, Mar 1999 ... 2.50
❑2, Apr 1999 ... 2.50
❑3, May 1999 ... 2.50
❑4, Jun 1999 ... 2.50

WORLD BELOW, THE: DEEPER AND STRANGER
Dark Horse

❑1, Dec 1999, b&w ... 2.95
❑2, Jan 2000, b&w ... 2.95
❑3, Feb 2000, b&w ... 2.95
❑4, Mar 2000, b&w ... 2.95

WORLD CLASS COMICS
Image

❑1, Aug 2002, b&w; hardcover ... 4.95

WORLD HARDBALL LEAGUE
Titus

❑1, Aug 1994, b&w ... 2.75
❑2, Jan 1995, b&w ... 2.75

WORLD OF ARCHIE
Archie

❑1, Aug 1992 ... 2.00
❑2, Nov 1992 ... 1.50
❑3, Feb 1993 ... 1.50
❑4, May 1993 ... 1.50
❑5, Aug 1993 ... 1.50
❑6, Nov 1993 ... 1.50
❑7, Feb 1994 ... 1.50
❑8, Apr 1994 ... 1.50
❑9, Jun 1994 ... 1.50
❑10, Aug 1994 ... 1.50
❑11, Sep 1994 ... 1.50
❑12, Nov 1994 ... 1.50
❑13, Jan 1995 ... 1.50
❑14, Mar 1995 ... 1.50
❑15, Jun 1995 ... 1.50
❑16, Sep 1995 ... 1.50
❑17, Dec 1995 ... 1.50
❑18, Mar 1996 ... 1.50
❑19, Jun 1996, DDC (a) ... 1.50
❑20, Sep 1996 ... 1.50
❑21, Dec 1996; Archie and Veronica run for class president ... 1.50
❑22, Mar 1997 ... 1.50

WORLD OF HARTZ
Tokyopop

❑1, May 2004 ... 9.99

WORLD OF KRYPTON (1ST SERIES)
DC

❑1, Jul 1979, MA, HC (a); O: Jor-El. .. 2.00
❑2, Aug 1979, HC (a) ... 2.00
❑3, Sep 1979, HC (a) ... 2.00

WORLD OF KRYPTON (2ND SERIES)
DC

❑1, Dec 1987, JBy (c); JBy (w) ... 2.00
❑2, Jan 1988, JBy (w) ... 2.00
❑3, Feb 1988, JBy (c); JBy (w) ... 2.00
❑4, Mar 1988, JBy (c); JBy (w) ... 2.00

WORLD OF METROPOLIS
DC

❑1, Aug 1988, JBy (w); FMc, DG (a) .. 1.50
❑2, Sep 1988, JBy (w); DG (a) ... 1.50
❑3, Oct 1988, JBy (w); DG (a) ... 1.50
❑4, Nov 1988, JBy (w); DG (a) ... 1.50

WORLD OF SMALLVILLE
DC

❑1, Apr 1988, JBy (w); AA, KS (a) ... 1.50
❑2, May 1988, JBy (w); AA, KS (a) ... 1.50
❑3, Jun 1988, JBy (w); AA, KS (a) ... 1.50
❑4, Jul 1988, JBy (w); AA, KS (a) ... 1.50

WORLD OF WHEELS
Charlton

❑17, Oct 1967; Previous issues published as Drag-Strip Hotrodders ... 12.00
❑18, Dec 1967 ... 12.00
❑19, Feb 1968 ... 12.00
❑20, Apr 1968 ... 12.00
❑21, Aug 1968 ... 8.00
❑22, Oct 1968 ... 8.00
❑23, Dec 1968 ... 8.00
❑24, Feb 1969 ... 8.00
❑25, Apr 1969 ... 8.00
❑26, Jun 1969 ... 8.00
❑27, Aug 1969 ... 8.00
❑28, Oct 1969 ... 8.00
❑29, Dec 1969 ... 8.00
❑30, Feb 1970 ... 8.00
❑31, Apr 1970 ... 8.00
❑32, Jun 1970 ... 8.00

WORLD OF WOOD
Eclipse

❑1, May 1986; DSt (c); WW (w); WW, DA (a); Indicia says #2 ... 2.00
❑2, May 1986; WW, DSt (c); WW (w); WW (a); Indicia for #1 corrected .. 2.00
❑3, Jun 1986; AW, WW (c); WW (w); WW (a); centaur ... 2.00
❑4, Jun 1986, WW (c); WW (w); WW (a) 2.00
❑5, Feb 1989, b&w; (c); AW, WW (a); reprints Flying Saucers #1; reprints Forbidden Worlds #3 ... 2.00

WORLD OF X-RAY, THE
Pyramid

❑1, b&w ... 1.80

WORLD OF YOUNG MASTER
New Comics

❑1, Mar 1989, b&w; Demonblade ... 1.95

WORLD'S BEST COMICS: SILVER AGE DC ARCHIVE SAMPLER
DC

❑1, Aug 2004 ... 0.99

WORLDS COLLIDE
DC / Milestone

❑1, Jul 1994 1: Rift. ... 2.50
❑1/CS, Jul 1994; 1: Rift. vinyl clings; Include press-apply stick-ons; enhanced cover ... 4.00
❑1/Platinum, Jul 1994; Platinum edition 4.00

WORLD'S FINEST
DC

❑1, ca. 1990, SR (c); DaG (w); SR (a) 5.00
❑2, ca. 1990, SR (c); DaG (w); SR (a) 4.50
❑3, ca. 1990, SR (c); DaG (w); SR (a) 4.50

WORLD'S FINEST COMICS
DC

❑84, Oct 1956 ... 235.00
❑85, Dec 1956 ... 235.00
❑86, Feb 1957 ... 235.00
❑87, Apr 1957 ... 235.00

	N-MINT
❑88, Jun 1957; A: Lex Luthor. A: Joker. Lex Luthor & The Joker team-up for the first time	235.00
❑89, Aug 1957	235.00
❑90, Oct 1957, A: Batwoman.	235.00
❑91, Dec 1957	175.00
❑92, Feb 1958	175.00
❑93, Apr 1958	175.00
❑94, Jun 1958; O: Superman-Batman team. A: Lex Luthor.	525.00
❑95, Aug 1958	175.00
❑96, Sep 1958; JK (a)	175.00
❑97, Oct 1958, JK (a)	175.00
❑98, Dec 1959, JK (a)	175.00
❑99, Feb 1959, JK (a)	175.00
❑100, Mar 1959; A: Lex Luthor. Luthor conquers Kandor	260.00
❑101, May 1959	105.00
❑102, Jun 1959	105.00
❑103, Aug 1959	105.00
❑104, Sep 1959, A: Lex Luthor. A: Batwoman.	105.00
❑105, Nov 1959	105.00
❑106, Dec 1959	105.00
❑107, Feb 1960	105.00
❑108, Mar 1960	105.00
❑109, May 1960 CS (a)	105.00
❑110, Jun 1960	105.00
❑111, Aug 1960 1: Clock King.	85.00
❑112, Sep 1960	85.00
❑113, Nov 1960	85.00
❑114, Dec 1960	85.00
❑115, Feb 1961	85.00
❑116, Mar 1961	85.00
❑117, May 1961 A: Lex Luthor. A: Batwoman.	85.00
❑118, Jun 1961	85.00
❑119, Aug 1961	85.00
❑120, Sep 1961	85.00
❑121, Nov 1961 JM (a)	85.00
❑122, Dec 1961	75.00
❑123, Feb 1962	75.00
❑124, Mar 1962	75.00
❑125, May 1962	75.00
❑126, Jun 1962 A: Lex Luthor.	75.00
❑127, Aug 1962	75.00
❑128, Sep 1962	75.00
❑129, Nov 1962 A: Lex Luthor. A: Joker.	75.00
❑130, Dec 1962 JM (a)	75.00
❑131, Feb 1963	75.00
❑132, Mar 1963	75.00
❑133, May 1963; Aqua-Girl tryout	75.00
❑134, Jun 1963 A: Miss Arrowette.	75.00
❑135, Aug 1963	75.00
❑136, Sep 1963	75.00
❑137, Nov 1963 A: Lex Luthor.	75.00
❑138, Dec 1963 JM (a)	75.00
❑139, Feb 1964	75.00
❑140, Mar 1964 A: Clayface.	75.00
❑141, May 1964; Back-up reprint stories begin	75.00
❑142, Jun 1964, CS (a); 1: Composite Superman. A: Legion of Super-Heroes.	75.00
❑143, Aug 1964 CS (a)	52.00
❑144, Sep 1964 CS (a); A: Clayface. A: Brainiac.	52.00
❑145, Nov 1964 CS (a)	52.00
❑146, Dec 1964 CS (a)	52.00
❑147, Feb 1965 CS (a)	52.00
❑148, Mar 1965; CS (a); A: Lex Luthor. A: Clayface. Congorilla back-ups begin	52.00
❑149, May 1965 CS (a)	52.00
❑150, Jun 1965 CS (a)	52.00
❑151, Aug 1965	50.00
❑152, Sep 1965	50.00
❑153, Nov 1965 A: Lex Luthor.	45.00
❑154, Dec 1965 A: Super-Sons.	45.00
❑155, Feb 1966 RMo (a)	45.00
❑156, Mar 1966 1: Bizarro Batman. A: Joker. A: Bizarro Superman.	45.00
❑157, May 1966; A: Super-Sons. Imaginary story	45.00
❑158, Jun 1966 CS (a); A: Brainiac.	45.00

	N-MINT
❑159, Aug 1966 A: Joker.	45.00
❑160, Sep 1966	45.00
❑161, Nov 1966; Giant-size G-28	45.00
❑162, Nov 1966 CS (a)	38.00
❑163, Dec 1966	38.00
❑164, Feb 1967 CS (a); A: Brainiac.	38.00
❑165, Mar 1967	38.00
❑166, May 1967 RMo (a); A: Joker.	38.00
❑167, Jun 1967; Imaginary story	38.00
❑168, Aug 1967 CS (a)	38.00
❑169, Sep 1967 CS (a)	38.00
❑170, Nov 1967; Giant-size G-40	38.00
❑171, Nov 1967	38.00
❑172, Dec 1967; CS (a); A: Lex Luthor. Imaginary story; Clark and Bruce as brothers	38.00
❑173, Feb 1968; CS (a); reprints from Action #241	38.00
❑174, Mar 1968 NA (c); JAb (a)	38.00
❑175, May 1968 NA (a)	38.00
❑176, Jun 1968 NA (a)	38.00
❑177, Aug 1968 CS (a); A: Lex Luthor. A: Joker.	38.00
❑178, Sep 1968 CS (a)	30.00
❑179, Nov 1968	30.00
❑180, Nov 1968 RA (a)	30.00
❑181, Dec 1968 RA (a)	25.00
❑182, Feb 1969 RA (a)	25.00
❑183, Mar 1969; RA (a); A: Lex Luthor. A: Brainiac. Reprints story from House of Mystery #80	25.00
❑184, May 1969	25.00
❑185, Jun 1969 RA (a)	25.00
❑186, Aug 1969 RA (a)	25.00
❑187, Sep 1969 CS (c); RA (a); O: Green Arrow.	25.00
❑188, Oct 1969; Giant-size G-64	25.00
❑189, Nov 1969 RA, RMo (a); A: Lex Luthor.	25.00
❑190, Dec 1969 A: Lex Luthor.	25.00
❑191, Feb 1970	20.00
❑192, Mar 1970	20.00
❑193, May 1970 CS (c)	20.00
❑194, Jun 1970 RA (a)	20.00
❑195, Aug 1970 RA (a)	20.00
❑196, Sep 1970 CS (a)	20.00
❑197, Nov 1970; JK (a); Giant-size G-76	20.00
❑198, Nov 1970; DD (a); Superman/Flash race	80.00
❑199, Dec 1970; DD (a); Superman/Flash race	80.00
❑200, Feb 1971 DD (a); A: Robin.	16.00
❑201, Mar 1971 DD (a); A: Doctor Fate. A: Green Lantern.	16.00
❑202, May 1971 DD (a)	16.00
❑203, Jun 1971 DD (a); A: Aquaman.	16.00
❑204, Aug 1971 MA, DD (a); A: Wonder Woman.	16.00
❑205, Sep 1971 MA, FF, DD (a); A: Teen Titans.	16.00
❑206, Nov 1971; DG (c); JM (a); Giant-size G-88	16.00
❑207, Nov 1971 GC, DD (a)	16.00
❑208, Dec 1971 NA (c); DD (a); A: Doctor Fate.	16.00
❑209, Feb 1972 DD (a); A: Hawkman.	16.00
❑210, Mar 1972 DD (a); A: Green Arrow.	16.00
❑211, May 1972 DD (a)	16.00
❑212, Jun 1972 DD (a); A: Martian Manhunter.	16.00
❑213, Sep 1972 DD (a); A: Atom.	14.00
❑214, Nov 1972 DD (a); A: Vigilante.	14.00
❑215, Jan 1973 DD (a); A: Super-Sons.	14.00
❑216, Mar 1973 MA, DD (a); A: Super-Sons.	14.00
❑217, May 1973 MA, DD (a); A: Metamorpho.	14.00
❑218, Aug 1973 DC, DD (a)	14.00
❑219, Oct 1973 DD (a)	14.00
❑220, Dec 1973 MA, DD (a)	14.00
❑221, Feb 1974 MA, DD (a); A: Super-Sons.	14.00
❑222, Apr 1974 DD (a); A: Super-Sons.	14.00

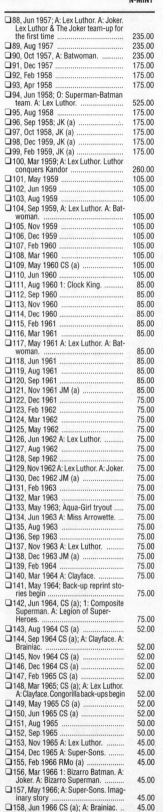

A series of stories featuring the teenage offspring of Superman and Batman were deemed "Imaginary" in the early 1980s.

© 1980 DC Comics.

	N-MINT
❑223, Jun 1974; NA, CS (a); O: Deadman. Reprints from World's Finest Comics #77 and #142	14.00
❑224, Aug 1974; Giant-size	14.00
❑225, Oct 1974; Giant-size	14.00
❑226, Dec 1974; Giant-size NA (a); A: Metamorpho.	14.00
❑227, Feb 1975; Giant-size A: Deadman.	14.00
❑228, Mar 1975; Giant-size A: Super-Sons.	14.00
❑229, Apr 1975	6.00
❑230, May 1975; Giant-size	6.00
❑231, Jul 1975 A: Super-Sons.	6.00
❑232, Sep 1975	6.00
❑233, Oct 1975	6.00
❑234, Dec 1975	6.00
❑235, Jan 1976	6.00
❑236, Mar 1976	6.00
❑237, Apr 1976	6.00
❑238, Jun 1976	6.00
❑239, Jul 1976	6.00
❑240, Sep 1976	6.00
❑241, Oct 1976	6.00
❑242, Dec 1976 A: Super-Sons.	6.00
❑243, Feb 1977	6.00
❑244, May 1977; NA (c); MN, MA, JL (a); Giant-size	6.00
❑245, Jul 1977; Giant-size; NA (c); MN, MA, GM, CS (a); A: Martian Manhunter. Giant-size	6.00
❑246, Sep 1977; NA (c); MN, MA, GM, DH, KS (a); 1: Baron Blitzkrieg. A: Justice League of America. Giant-size	6.00
❑247, Nov 1977; Giant-size; DG, JL (c); GM, KS (a); A: Justice League of America.	6.00
❑248, Jan 1978; Giant-size; DG, JL (c); GM, DG, KS (a)	6.00
❑249, Mar 1978; Giant-size; JA (c); SD (w); SD, KS (a); A: Phantom Stranger	6.00
❑250, May 1978; Giant-size; JA (c); SD (w); SD, GT (a)	6.00
❑251, Jul 1978; Giant-size; JA (c); SD (w); SD, BL, GT, RE, JAb (a); 1: Count Vertigo. A: Speedy.	6.00
❑252, Sep 1978; Giant-size; JA (c); SD (w); SD, GT, JAb (a); A: Poison Ivy	6.00
❑253, Nov 1978, Giant-size; JA (c); SD (w); DN, SD, KS (a); No ads begins; wraparound cover	6.00
❑254, Jan 1979; Giant-size; JA (c); SD (w); DN, SD, GT, KS (a)	6.00
❑255, Mar 1979; JA (c); SD (w); DN, SD, JL, KS, DA (a); A: Bulletman. A: Bulletgirl.	6.00
❑256, May 1979; DN, MA, DD, KS (a)	6.00
❑257, Jul 1979; Giant-size; JA (c); DN, FMc, RB, GT, DD, KS, RT (a); Giant-size	6.00
❑258, Sep 1979; Giant-size; DG (c); DN, RB, DG, JL, KS, RT (a)	6.00
❑259, Nov 1979; RB, DG (c); DN, MN, RB, DG, MR, KS (a); Ads begin again	6.00
❑260, Jan 1980; RB, DG (c); DN, MN, RB, DG (a); Giant-size	6.00
❑261, Mar 1980; DG, RA (c); RB, DG, RT (a); Giant-size	6.00
❑262, May 1980; DG, RA (c); DN, DG, JSa, DA, RT (a); Giant-size	6.00
❑263, Jul 1980; DG, RA (c); DN, RB, DG (a); A: Super-Sons. Giant-size	6.00
❑264, Sep 1980 DG (c); DN, RB, DG (a)	6.00
❑265, Nov 1980 JA (c); DN, DG, RE (a)	6.00

N-MINT

❑266, Jan 1981 JA (c); DN, RB (a); 1: Lady Lunar. 6.00
❑267, Mar 1981 RB, DG (c); DN, RB, DG (a); A: Challengers of the Unknown. 6.00
❑268, May 1981 DG (c); DN, RT (a) .. 6.00
❑269, Jul 1981 RB, DG (c); DN, FMc, RB, DA (a); 1: Doctor Jymbi Humm. 6.00
❑270, Aug 1981 DN, RB, RT (a) 6.00
❑271, Sep 1981 FMc, RB (a); O: Superman/Batman team in World's Finest. 4.00
❑272, Oct 1981 DG, RA (c); DN, RB (a) 4.00
❑273, Nov 1981 DN, JSa, DA (a) 4.00
❑274, Dec 1981 DG, RA (c); DN, GC (a) 4.00
❑275, Jan 1982 DN, FMc, RB, DS, DA (a) 4.00
❑276, Feb 1982 GP (c); DN, RB, CI, DS, DA (a) 4.00
❑277, Mar 1982 GP (c); DN, DH, DS, RT (a) 4.00
❑278, Apr 1982 DN, RB, DS (a); A: Hawkman. 4.00
❑279, May 1982 DN, KP (a); A: Kid Eternity. 4.00
❑280, Jun 1982 RB (c); DN, RB (a); A: Kid Eternity. 4.00
❑281, Jul 1982 GK (c); DN, IN (a); A: Kid Eternity. 4.00
❑282, Aug 1982 GK (c); FMc, CI, GK, IN (a); A: Kid Eternity. 4.00
❑283, Sep 1982 RB (c); FMc, GT, GK, IN (a); V: Composite Superman. 4.00
❑284, Oct 1982 KG (c); GT, DS (a); A: Legion. A: Composite Superman. .. 4.00
❑285, Nov 1982 DG, FM (c); RB (a); A: Zatanna. 4.00
❑286, Dec 1982 RB, DG (c); RB (a); A: Zatanna. 4.00
❑287, Jan 1983 RB, RT (c) 4.00
❑288, Feb 1983 DG (c) 4.00
❑289, Mar 1983 GK (c) 4.00
❑290, Apr 1983 KJ (c); TD (a) 4.00
❑291, May 1983 TD (a) 4.00
❑292, Jun 1983 KJ (c) 4.00
❑293, Jul 1983 KJ (c); TD (a); A: Null. A: Void. 4.00
❑294, Aug 1983 KJ (c) 4.00
❑295, Sep 1983 KJ (c); FMc (a) 4.00
❑296, Oct 1983 RA, KJ (c); RA (a) 4.00
❑297, Nov 1983 GC, KJ (c); GC (a) ... 4.00
❑298, Dec 1983 DG (c) 4.00
❑299, Jan 1984 KJ (c); GC (a) 4.00
❑300, Feb 1984; Giant-size; DG (c); GP, RA, KJ (a); A: Justice League of America. A: Titans. A: Outsiders. Giant-size 4.00
❑301, Mar 1984 KJ (c) 3.00
❑302, Apr 1984 KJ (c); DG, NA (a) 3.00
❑303, May 1984 KJ (c) 3.00
❑304, Jun 1984 KJ (c); O: Null. O: Void. 3.00
❑305, Jul 1984 KJ (c) 3.00
❑306, Aug 1984 KJ (c) 3.00
❑307, Sep 1984 KJ (c) 3.00
❑308, Oct 1984 KJ (c); KB (w); GT (a) 3.00
❑309, Nov 1984; KJ (c); KB (w); AA (a); Bonus Book 3.00
❑310, Dec 1984 KJ (c); A: Sonik. 3.00
❑311, Jan 1985 KJ (c); A: Monitor. ... 3.00
❑312, Feb 1985 AA (a) 3.00
❑313, Mar 1985 KJ (c); AA (a) 3.00
❑314, Apr 1985 KJ (c); AA (a); A: Monitor. 3.00
❑315, May 1985 .... 3.00
❑316, Jun 1985 .... 3.00
❑317, Jul 1985 .... 3.00
❑318, Aug 1985 RT (c); AA (a); A: Sonik. 3.00
❑319, Sep 1985 RT (c); AA (a) 3.00
❑320, Oct 1985 .... 3.00
❑321, Nov 1985 RB (c); AA (a); V: Chronos. 3.00
❑322, Dec 1985 KG (c); KG (a) 3.00
❑323, Jan 1986 DG (c); AA (a) 3.00

WORLD'S FINEST: OUR WORLDS AT WAR
DC

❑1, Oct 2001; Our Worlds At War; Casualties of War; Follows Action Comics #782 .... 2.95

WORLD'S FUNNIEST COMICS
MOORDAM

❑1, Mar 1998, b&w; Cray-Baby Adventures, Mr. Beat 2.95

WORLDS OF H.P. LOVECRAFT: BEYOND THE WALL OF SLEEP
TOME

❑1 .... 2.95

WORLDS OF H.P. LOVECRAFT, THE: DAGON
CALIBER

❑1, b&w 2.95

WORLDS OF H.P. LOVECRAFT: THE ALCHEMIST
TOME

❑1 .... 2.95

WORLDS OF H.P. LOVECRAFT, THE: THE MUSIC OF ERICH ZANN
CALIBER

❑1, b&w 2.95

WORLDS OF H.P. LOVECRAFT, THE: THE PICTURE IN THE HOUSE
CALIBER

❑1, b&w 2.95

WORLDS UNKNOWN
MARVEL

❑1, May 1973; GK (w); GK, AT (a); adapted from Frederik Pohl story .. 5.00
❑2, Jul 1973; VM, GK (a); adapted from L. Sprague de Camp story; adapted from Keith Laumer story 4.00
❑3, Sep 1973; WH (c); RA, WH (a); adapted from Harry Bates story 4.00
❑4, Nov 1973; JB, DG (a); adapted from Frederic Brown story 3.00
❑5, Feb 1974; JM, DA (a); adapted from A.E. Van Vogt story 3.00
❑6, Apr 1974; adapted from Theodore Sturgeon story; Marvel Value Stamp #35: Killraven 3.00
❑7, Jun 1974; GT (a); adapted from Brian Clemens screenplay; Marvel Value Stamp #32: Red Skull 3.00
❑8, Aug 1974; GT (a); Final Issue; Marvel Value Stamp #75: Morbius 3.00

WORLD'S WORST COMICS AWARDS
KITCHEN SINK

❑1 1990, b&w 2.50
❑2, Jan 1991, b&w 2.50

WORLD WAR II: 1946
ANTARCTIC

❑1, Jul 1999; FOAW #62 .... 2.50
❑2, Aug 1999; FOAW #63 .... 2.50
❑3, Sep 1999; FOAW #64 .... 2.50
❑4, Oct 1999; FOAW #65 .... 2.50
❑5, Nov 1999; FOAW #66 .... 2.50
❑6, Dec 1999; FOAW #67 .... 2.50
❑7, Jan 2000; FOAW #68 .... 2.50
❑8, Feb 2000; FOAW #69 .... 2.50
❑9, Mar 2000; FOAW #70 .... 2.50
❑10, Apr 2000; FOAW #71 .... 2.50
❑11, May 2000; FOAW #72 .... 2.50
❑12, Jun 2000; FOAW #72 .... 2.50

WORLD WAR II: 1946/FAMILIES OF ALTERED WARS
ANTARCTIC

❑1, Jul 1998, b&w; Compilation Edition 3.95
❑1-2, Oct 1998 .... 3.95
❑2, Nov 1998, b&w; has indicia from #1 .... 3.95
❑2-2, Aug 1998 .... 3.95

WORLD WITHOUT END
DC

❑1, ca. 1990 .... 2.50
❑2, ca. 1990 .... 2.50
❑3, ca. 1990 .... 2.50
❑4, ca. 1990 .... 2.50
❑5, ca. 1990 .... 2.50
❑6, ca. 1990 .... 2.50

WORON'S WORLDS
ILLUSTRATION

❑1/A 2.95
❑1/B; Adults-only cover 2.95
❑1/A-2 .... 3.25
❑1/B-2 .... 3.25
❑2/A 2.95
❑2/B; Adults-only cover 2.95
❑3/A, Nov 1994 .... 3.25
❑3/B, Nov 1994; Adults-only cover 3.25

WORST FROM MAD, THE
E.C.

❑1, ca. 1958; Magazine-sized; no number 400.00
❑2, ca. 1959; Magazine-sized 300.00
❑3, ca. 1960; Magazine-sized; has Alfred E. Neuman for president campaign poster 200.00
❑4, ca. 1961; Magazine-sized 175.00
❑5, ca. 1962; Magazine-sized; contains record 250.00
❑6, ca. 1963; Magazine-sized; contains record 250.00
❑7, ca. 1964; Magazine-sized 175.00
❑8, ca. 1965; Magazine-sized 175.00
❑9, ca. 1966; Magazine-sized; contains record 250.00
❑10, ca. 1967; Magazine-sized 175.00
❑11, ca. 1968; Magazine-sized; contains car-window stickers 175.00
❑12, ca. 1969; Magazine-sized 175.00

W.O.W. THE WORLD OF WARD
ALLIED AMERICAN ARTISTS

❑1, b&w 3.95

WRAITH, THE
OUTLANDER COMICS GROUP

❑1, Aug 1991, b&w 1.75
❑2, Oct 1991 .... 1.75

WRATH
MALIBU / ULTRAVERSE

❑1, Jan 1994, A: Mantra. 2.00
❑1/Ltd., Jan 1994; Ultra-limited edition A: Mantra. 3.00
❑2, Feb 1994 .... 2.00
❑3, Mar 1994, 1: Slayer. 2.00
❑4, Apr 1994, A: Freex. 1.95
❑5, May 1994, A: Freex. 1.95
❑6, Jun 1994 .... 1.95
❑7, Jul 1994, 1: Ogre. 1: Pierce. 1: Doc Virtual. 1.95
❑8, Oct 1994, 1: Project Patriot. A: Warstrike. A: Mantra. 1.95
❑9, Dec 1994, D: Project Patriot. 2.25
❑Giant Size 1, Aug 1994 .... 2.50

WRATH OF THE SPECTRE
DC

❑1, May 1988; Reprints from Adventure Comics #431-433, 426 .... 2.50
❑2, Jun 1988 .... 2.50
❑3, Jul 1988 .... 2.50
❑4, Aug 1988; new stories 2.50

WRETCH, THE
CALIBER

❑1, Jul 1997, b&w 2.95
❑2, Sep 1997, b&w 2.95
❑3, Nov 1997, b&w 2.95
❑4 1998, b&w 2.95
❑5, May 1998; Dedicated to Will Eisner 2.95
❑6, Jul 1998 .... 2.95

WRETCH, THE (VOL. 2)
SLAVE LABOR / AMAZE INK

❑1, Jul 1997, b&w 2.95
❑2, Sep 1997, b&w 2.95
❑3, Nov 1997, b&w 2.95
❑4, b&w 2.95

N-MINT

WRITERS' BLOC ANTHOLOGY, THE
WRITERS' BLOC
❑1 .... 3.00

WULF THE BARBARIAN
ATLAS-SEABOARD
❑1, Feb 1975, O: Wulf. 10.00
❑2, Apr 1975 .... 8.00
❑3, May 1975; indicia says July 8.00
❑4, Sep 1975 .... 8.00

WU WEI
ANGUS
❑1 .... 2.50
❑2 .... 2.50
❑3 .... 2.50
❑4 .... 2.50
❑5 .... 2.50
❑6 .... 2.50

WW 2
NEC
❑1 .... 3.50
❑2, Nov 2000 .... 3.50

WWF: WORLD WRESTLING FOUNDATION
VALIANT
❑1; 21841 .... 2.95
❑2; 21842 .... 2.95
❑3; 21843 .... 2.95
❑4; 21844 .... 2.95

WYATT EARP
MARVEL
❑1, Nov 1955 .... 120.00
❑2, Jan 1956 .... 70.00
❑3, Mar 1956 .... 50.00
❑4, May 1956 .... 50.00
❑5, Jul 1956 .... 50.00
❑6, Sep 1956 .... 50.00
❑7, Nov 1956 .... 50.00
❑8, Jan 1957 .... 50.00
❑9, Mar 1957 .... 50.00
❑10, Apr 1957 .... 50.00
❑11, May 1957 .... 42.00
❑12, Aug 1957 .... 42.00
❑13, Oct 1957 .... 42.00
❑14, Dec 1957 .... 42.00
❑15, Feb 1958 .... 42.00
❑16, Apr 1958 .... 42.00
❑17, Jun 1958 .... 42.00
❑18, Aug 1958 .... 42.00
❑19, Oct 1958 .... 42.00
❑20, Dec 1958 .... 42.00
❑21, Feb 1959 .... 30.00
❑22, Apr 1959 .... 30.00
❑23, Jun 1959 .... 30.00
❑24, Aug 1959 .... 30.00
❑25, Oct 1959 .... 30.00
❑26, Dec 1959 .... 30.00
❑27, Feb 1960 .... 30.00
❑28, Apr 1960 .... 30.00
❑29, Jun 1960; Final issue of original run 30.00
❑30, Oct 1972; Revival of old title; Series begins again 5.00
❑31, Dec 1972 SL (w) 5.00
❑32, Feb 1973 .... 5.00
❑33, Apr 1973 .... 5.00
❑34, Jun 1973 .... 5.00

WYNONNA EARP
IMAGE
❑1, Dec 1996 .... 2.50
❑2, Jan 1997 .... 2.50
❑3, Feb 1997; cover says Jan, indicia says Feb 2.50
❑4, Mar 1997 .... 2.50
❑5, Apr 1997; final issue 2.50

WYOMING TERRITORY
ARK
❑1, b&w 1.95

WYRD THE RELUCTANT WARRIOR
SLAVE LABOR
❑1, Jul 1999 .... 2.95
❑2, Aug 1999 .... 2.95

N-MINT

❑3, Sep 1999 .... 2.95
❑4, Oct 1999 .... 2.95
❑5, Nov 1999 .... 2.95
❑6, Dec 1999 .... 2.95

X

XANADU (THOUGHTS & IMAGES)
THOUGHTS & IMAGES
❑1, May 1988, b&w 2.00
❑2, Jun 1988, b&w; 1: Firepetal; 1: Gruht; 1: Kajiko Firelake; 1: Kinomon Firestar 2.00
❑3, Jul 1988, b&w 2.00
❑4, Aug 1988, b&w 2.00
❑5, Nov 1988, b&w; cover says Part Three of Five 2.00

XANADU (3-D ZONE)
3-D ZONE
❑1, b&w 2.00
❑2, b&w 2.00
❑3, b&w 2.00
❑4, b&w 2.00

XANADU: ACROSS DIAMOND SEAS
MU
❑1, Jan 1994, b&w 2.50
❑2, Feb 1994, b&w; MU PUB #205 ... 2.50
❑3, Mar 1994, b&w 2.95
❑4, Apr 1994, b&w 2.95
❑5, May 1994, b&w 2.95

XANADU COLOR SPECIAL
ECLIPSE
❑1, Dec 1988 .... 2.00

XANDER IN LOST UNIVERSE (GENE RODDENBERRY'S...)
TEKNO
❑0, Nov 1995 .... 2.25
❑1, Dec 1995 .... 2.25
❑2, Dec 1995 .... 2.25
❑3, Jan 1996 .... 2.25
❑4, Jan 1996 .... 2.25
❑5, Feb 1996 .... 2.25
❑6, Mar 1996 .... 2.25
❑7, Apr 1996 .... 2.25
❑8, May 1996; The Big Crossover, Part 5: The Big Bang 2.25

XANTH GRAPHIC NOVEL
FATHER TREE
❑1 .... 9.95

X-BABIES: MURDERAMA
MARVEL
❑1, Aug 1998 .... 2.99

X-BABIES: REBORN
MARVEL
❑1, Jan 2000 .... 3.50

X-CALIBRE
MARVEL
❑1, Mar 1995; The Age of Apocalypse 2.00
❑2, Apr 1995; cover says Jun; The Age of Apocalypse 2.00
❑3, May 1995; The Age of Apocalypse 2.00
❑4, Jun 1995; The Age of Apocalypse 2.00

XENA
BRAINSTORM
❑1, Jan 1995 .... 2.95

XENA: WARRIOR PRINCESS (VOL. 1)
TOPPS
❑0, Oct 1997 .... 2.95
❑1, Aug 1997; A: Hercules. back-up Tales of Salmoneus 2.95
❑1/A, Aug 1997 .... 2.95
❑1/American Ent, Aug 1997; American Entertainment 7.00
❑1/Variant, Aug 1997 .... 2.95
❑2, Sep 1997 .... 2.95
❑2/Variant, Sep 1997 .... 2.95

The original X-Men banded together as X-Factor to help emerging mutants control their new-found powers.
© 1986 Marvel Comics.

N-MINT

XENA: WARRIOR PRINCESS (DARK HORSE)
DARK HORSE
❑1, Sep 1999 .... 3.00
❑1/Variant, Sep 1999 .... 3.00
❑2, Oct 1999 .... 3.00
❑2/Variant, Oct 1999 .... 3.00
❑3, Nov 1999 .... 3.00
❑3/Variant, Nov 1999 .... 3.00
❑4, Dec 1999 .... 3.00
❑4/Variant, Dec 1999 .... 3.00
❑5, Jan 2000 .... 3.00
❑5/Variant, Jan 2000 .... 3.00
❑6, Feb 2000 .... 2.95
❑6/Variant, Feb 2000 .... 2.95
❑7, Mar 2000 .... 2.95
❑7/Variant, Mar 2000 .... 2.95
❑8, Apr 2000 .... 2.95
❑8/Variant, Apr 2000 .... 2.95
❑9, May 2000 .... 2.95
❑9/Variant, May 2000 .... 2.95
❑10, Jun 2000 .... 2.95
❑10/Variant, Jun 2000 .... 2.95
❑11, Jul 2000 .... 2.95
❑11/Variant, Jul 2000 .... 2.95
❑12, Aug 2000 .... 2.95
❑12/Variant, Aug 2000 .... 2.95
❑13, Sep 2000 .... 2.95
❑13/Variant, Sep 2000 .... 2.95
❑14, Oct 2000 .... 2.99
❑14/Variant, Oct 2000 .... 2.99

XENA: WARRIOR PRINCESS: AND THE ORIGINAL OLYMPICS
TOPPS
❑1, Jun 1998 .... 2.95
❑2, Jul 1998 .... 2.95
❑3, Aug 1998 .... 2.95

XENA: WARRIOR PRINCESS: BLOODLINES
TOPPS
❑1, May 1998 .... 2.95
❑2, Jun 1998 .... 2.95

XENA: WARRIOR PRINCESS/JOXER: WARRIOR PRINCE
TOPPS
❑1, Nov 1997 .... 2.95
❑1/Variant, Nov 1997 .... 2.95
❑2, Dec 1997 .... 2.95
❑2/Variant, Dec 1997 .... 2.95
❑3, Jan 1998 .... 2.95
❑3/Variant, Jan 1998 .... 2.95

XENA: WARRIOR PRINCESS: THE DRAGON'S TEETH
TOPPS
❑1, Dec 1997 .... 2.95
❑1/Variant, Dec 1997 .... 2.95
❑2, Jan 1998 .... 2.95
❑2/Variant, Jan 1998 .... 2.95
❑3, Feb 1998 .... 2.95
❑3/Variant, Feb 1998 .... 2.95

XENA: WARRIOR PRINCESS: THE ORPHEUS TRILOGY
TOPPS
❑1, Mar 1998 .... 2.95
❑1/Variant, Mar 1998 .... 2.95

N-MINT

❑2, Apr 1998 .... 2.95
❑2/Variant, Apr 1998 .... 2.95
❑3, May 1998 .... 2.95
❑3/Variant, May 1998 .... 2.95

XENA: WARRIOR PRINCESS: THE WARRIOR WAY OF DEATH
DARK HORSE

❑1, Sep 1999 .... 2.95
❑1/Variant, Sep 1999 .... 2.95
❑2, Oct 1999 .... 2.95
❑2/Variant, Oct 1999 .... 2.95

XENA: WARRIOR PRINCESS VS. CALLISTO
TOPPS

❑1, Feb 1998 .... 2.95
❑1/A, Feb 1998; No cover price 5.00
❑1/Variant, Feb 1998 .... 2.95
❑2, Mar 1998 .... 2.95
❑2/Variant, Mar 1998 .... 2.95
❑3, Mar 1998 .... 2.95
❑3/Variant, Mar 1998 .... 2.95

XENA, WARRIOR PRINCESS: WRATH OF HERA
TOPPS

❑1 .... 2.95
❑1/Variant 3.00
❑2 .... 2.95
❑2/Variant 3.00

XENA: WARRIOR PRINCESS, YEAR ONE
TOPPS

❑1, O: Xena. 5.00
❑1/Gold; O: Xena. Gold logo cover 10.00

XENE
EYEBALL SOUP DESIGNS

❑1, Jan 1996; cardstock cover 4.95
❑2, Mar 1996; cardstock cover 4.95
❑3, May 1996; cardstock cover 4.95
❑4, Jul 1996; cardstock cover 4.95

XENOBROOD
DC

❑0, Oct 1994 .... 1.50
❑1, Nov 1994 .... 1.50
❑2, Dec 1994 .... 1.50
❑3, Jan 1995 .... 1.50
❑4, Feb 1995 .... 1.50
❑5, Mar 1995 .... 1.50
❑6, Apr 1995; Final Issue 1.50

XENO-MEN
BLACKTHORNE

❑1, Nov 1987, b&w 1.75

XENON
ECLIPSE / VIZ

❑1, Dec 1987, b&w 2.00
❑2, Dec 1987, b&w 2.00
❑3, Jan 1988, b&w 2.00
❑4, Jan 1988, b&w 2.00
❑5, Feb 1988, b&w 2.00
❑6, Feb 1988, b&w 2.00
❑7, Mar 1988, b&w 2.00
❑8, Mar 1988, b&w 2.00
❑9, Apr 1988, b&w 2.00
❑10, Apr 1988, b&w 2.00
❑11, May 1988, b&w 1.50
❑12, May 1988, b&w 1.50
❑13, Jun 1988, b&w 1.50
❑14, Jun 1988, b&w 1.50
❑15, Jul 1988, b&w 1.50
❑16, Jul 1988, b&w 1.50
❑17, Aug 1988, b&w 1.50
❑18, Aug 1988, b&w 1.50
❑19, Sep 1988, b&w 1.50
❑20, Sep 1988, b&w 1.50
❑21, Oct 1988, b&w 1.50
❑22, Oct 1988, b&w 1.50
❑23, Nov 1989, b&w; Final Issue 1.50

N-MINT

XENO'S ARROW
CUP O' TEA

❑1, Feb 1999, b&w 2.50
❑2, Apr 1999 .... 2.50
❑3, Jun 1999 .... 2.50
❑4, Aug 1999 .... 2.50

XENOTECH
MIRAGE / NEXT

❑1, Aug 1994; Includes trading cards 2.75
❑1/A, Aug 1994; Variant cover with monster attacking; Includes trading cards 2.75
❑2, Oct 1994; Includes trading cards 2.75
❑3, Dec 1994; Includes trading cards 2.75

XENOZOIC TALES
KITCHEN SINK

❑1, Feb 1987, b&w 8.00
❑1-2, b&w; 2nd printing 3.00
❑2, Apr 1987, b&w 6.00
❑3, Jun 1987, b&w 6.00
❑4, Nov 1987, b&w 6.00
❑5, Feb 1988, b&w 6.00
❑6, May 1988, b&w; ca. 1988 .... 5.00
❑7, Oct 1988, b&w; ca. 1988 .... 5.00
❑8, Jan 1989, b&w; ca. 1988 .... 5.00
❑9, Sep 1989, b&w; ca. 1988 .... 5.00
❑10, Apr 1990, b&w; ca. 1989 .... 5.00
❑11, Apr 1991, b&w; ca. 1990 .... 4.00
❑12, Apr 1992, b&w; ca. 1991 .... 4.00
❑13, Dec 1994, b&w 4.00
❑14, Oct 1996, b&w; cardstock cover 4.00

XENYA
SANCTUARY

❑1, Jul 1994 .... 2.95
❑2, ca. 1994 .... 2.95
❑3, ca. 1995; no cover price 2.95

XERO
DC

❑1, May 1997 .... 2.00
❑2, Jun 1997 .... 1.75
❑3, Jul 1997 .... 1.75
❑4, Aug 1997 .... 1.75
❑5, Sep 1997 .... 1.75
❑6, Oct 1997; V: Polaris. Genesis 1.75
❑7, Nov 1997 .... 1.75
❑8, Dec 1997 Face cover 1.95
❑9, Jan 1998 .... 1.95
❑10, Feb 1998 .... 1.95
❑11, Mar 1998 .... 1.95
❑12, Apr 1998; Final Issue
❑ 1.95

X-FACTOR
MARVEL

❑-1, Jul 1997; Flashback 2.00
❑1, Feb 1986; Giant-size; BL (w); O: X-Factor. 1: Rusty Collins. Giant-size 3.00
❑2, Mar 1986, MZ (c); BL (w) 2.00
❑3, Apr 1986, BL (w) 2.00
❑4, May 1986, BL (w); KP (a); 1: Frenzy. 2.00
❑5, Jun 1986, BL (w); 1: Apocalypse (in shadows). 3.00
❑6, Jul 1986, 1: Apocalypse (full appearance). 5.00
❑7, Aug 1986, 1: Skids. 3.00
❑8, Sep 1986 .... 2.00
❑9, Oct 1989; Mutant Massacre 2.00
❑10, Nov 1989; Mutant Massacre 2.00
❑11, Dec 1989; Mutant Massacre 2.00
❑12, Jan 1987, O: Famine. 1: Famine. 2.00
❑13, Feb 1987, A: Phoenix. 2.00
❑14, Mar 1987 .... 2.00
❑15, Apr 1987 .... 2.00
❑16, May 1987, O: Skids. 2.00
❑17, Jun 1987, 1: Rictor. 2.00
❑18, Jul 1987 .... 2.00
❑19, Aug 1987 .... 2.00
❑20, Sep 1987 .... 2.00
❑21, Oct 1987 .... 2.00
❑22, Nov 1987, SB (a) 2.00
❑23, Dec 1987; 1: Archangel (cameo). registration card 5.00

N-MINT

❑24, Jan 1988, O: Apocalypse. 1: Archangel (full appearance). 8.00
❑25, Feb 1988 .... 2.00
❑26, Mar 1988 .... 2.00
❑27, Apr 1988, BWi (c) 2.00
❑28, May 1988 .... 2.00
❑29, Jun 1988 .... 2.00
❑30, Jul 1988 .... 2.00
❑31, Aug 1988 .... 2.00
❑32, Sep 1988, 1: N'astirh. A: Avengers. 2.00
❑33, Oct 1988 .... 2.00
❑34, Nov 1988 .... 2.00
❑35, Dec 1988 .... 2.00
❑36, Jan 1989; Inferno 2.00
❑37, Feb 1989; Inferno 2.00
❑38, Mar 1989; Giant-size; D: Madelyn Pryor. Inferno; Giant-size 2.00
❑39, Apr 1989; Inferno 2.00
❑40, May 1989, AM, RL (c); RL (a) 2.00
❑41, Jun 1989 .... 2.00
❑42, Jul 1989 .... 2.00
❑43, Aug 1989, PS (c); PS (a) 2.00
❑44, Sep 1989, PS (c); PS (a) 2.00
❑45, Oct 1989, PS (c); PS (a) 2.00
❑46, Nov 1989, PS (c); PS (a) 2.00
❑47, Nov 1989; AM (c); Solo Archangel story 2.00
❑48, Dec 1989, PS (c); PS (a) 2.00
❑49, Dec 1989, AM (c); PS (a) 2.00
❑50, Jan 1990; Giant-size; TMc, RL (c); RB (a); Giant-size 2.50
❑51, Feb 1990, A: Sabretooth. 2.50
❑52, Mar 1990, AM, RL (c); A: Sabretooth. 2.50
❑53, Apr 1990, AM (c); A: Sabretooth. 2.50
❑54, May 1990, AM (c); 1: Crimson. 1.50
❑55, Jun 1990, PD (w) 1.50
❑56, Jul 1990, AM (c) 1.50
❑57, Aug 1990 .... 1.50
❑58, Sep 1990, AM (c) 1.50
❑59, Oct 1990, AM (c) 1.50
❑60, Nov 1990, AM (c) 2.50
❑60-2, Nov 1990; AM (c); Gold cover 1.50
❑61, Dec 1990, AM (c) 2.50
❑62, Jan 1991, JLee (c) 2.50
❑63, Feb 1991 .... 2.50
❑64, Mar 1991 .... 2.50
❑65, Apr 1991, JLee (w) 2.50
❑66, May 1991, JLee (w) 2.50
❑67, Jun 1991, JLee (w) 2.50
❑68, Jul 1991; JLee (w); Baby Nathan is sent into future 2.50
❑69, Aug 1991; Muir Island Saga 2.50
❑70, Sep 1991; PD (w); Muir Island Epilogue 2.00
❑71, Oct 1991; AM (c); PD (w); AM (a); new team; Havok, Madrox, Polaris & Wolfsbane 2.00
❑71-2, Oct 1991; AM (c); PD (w); Havok, Madrox, Polaris & Wolfsbane 1.50
❑72, Nov 1991, AM (c); PD (w) 1.50
❑73, Dec 1991, AM (c); PD (w) 1.50
❑74, Jan 1992, AM (c); PD (w) 1.50
❑75, Feb 1992; Giant-size; (c); PD (w); Giant-size 2.00
❑76, Mar 1992, AM (c); PD (w) 1.50
❑77, Apr 1992, AM (c); PD (w) 1.50
❑78, May 1992, PD (w) 1.50
❑79, Jun 1992, KN (c); PD (w); 1: Rhapsody. 1.50
❑80, Jul 1992, AM (c); PD (w) 1.50
❑81, Aug 1992, PD (w) 1.50
❑82, Sep 1992, AM (c); PD (w) 1.50
❑83, Oct 1992, AM (c); PD (w) 1.50
❑84/CS, Nov 1992; AM (c); PD (w); Includes Caliban trading card 2.00
❑85/CS, Dec 1992; PD (w); Includes trading card 2.00
❑86/CS, Jan 1993; PD (w); Includes Dark Riders trading card 2.00
❑87, Feb 1993, AM (c); PD (w) 1.50
❑88, Mar 1993, AM (c); PD (w) 1.50
❑89, Apr 1993, AM (c); PD (w) 1.50
❑90, May 1993 .... 1.50

N-MINT

❑91, Jun 1993, AM (c) 1.50
❑92, Jul 1993; AM (c); Hologram cover; Fatal Attractions 4.00
❑93, Aug 1993, PS (c) 1.50
❑94, Sep 1993 1.50
❑95, Oct 1993, AM (c); A: Polaris. A: Random. 1.50
❑96, Nov 1993, AM (c) 1.50
❑97, Dec 1993; (c); JDu (a); Siege of Darkness preview 1.50
❑98, Jan 1994, AM (c) 1.50
❑99, Feb 1994, AM, JDu (c); JDu (a) 1.50
❑100, Mar 1994; Giant-size; (c); JDu (a); D: Multiple Man. 2.00
❑100/Variant, Mar 1994; Giant-size; (c); JDu (a); D: Multiple Man. Giant-size; foil embossed cover 3.00
❑101, Apr 1994, AM, JDu (c); JDu (a) 1.50
❑102, May 1994; (c); JDu (a); Includes trading cards 1.50
❑103, Jun 1994, JDu (c); JDu (a) 1.50
❑104, Jul 1994, AM, JDu (c); JDu (a) 1.50
❑105, Aug 1994 1.50
❑106, Sep 1994; JDu (a); wraparound cover; Phalanx Covenant 2.00
❑106/Variant, Sep 1994; JDu (a); enhanced cover; Phalanx Covenant 2.95
❑107, Oct 1994, AM, KGa (c) 1.50
❑108, Nov 1994, JDu (a) 1.50
❑108/Deluxe, Nov 1994; Deluxe edition JDu (a) 2.00
❑109, Dec 1994, AM (c); JDu (a) 1.50
❑109/Deluxe, Dec 1994; Deluxe edition AM (c); JDu (a) 2.00
❑110, Jan 1995, AM (c); JDu (a); A: Lila Cheney. 1.50
❑110/Deluxe, Jan 1995; Deluxe edition AM (c); JDu (a); A: Lila Cheney. 2.00
❑111, Feb 1995, AM (c); JDu (a) 1.50
❑111/Deluxe, Feb 1995; AM (c); JDu (a) 2.00
❑112, Jul 1995 1.95
❑113, Aug 1995 1.95
❑114, Sep 1995 1.95
❑115, Oct 1995; bound-in trading cards 1.95
❑116, Nov 1995, A: Alpha Flight. 1.95
❑117, Dec 1995, A: Cyclops. A: Wild Child. A: Havok. A: Mystique. A: Random. 1.95
❑118, Jan 1996 1.95
❑119, Feb 1996, A: Shard. 1.95
❑120, Mar 1996 1.95
❑121, Apr 1996 1.95
❑122, May 1996, AM (c) 1.95
❑123, Jun 1996 1.95
❑124, Jul 1996; Onslaught Update 1.95
❑125, Aug 1996, AM (c); AM (a) 2.95
❑126, Sep 1996; HT (a); A: real Beast. real Beast returns; Heroes Reborn Update 1.95
❑127, Oct 1996; AW (a); bound-in trading cards; Heroes Reborn Update 1.95
❑128, Nov 1996, AM (a) 1.95
❑129, Dec 1996 1.95
❑130, Jan 1997, D: Graydon Creed. 2.50
❑131, Feb 1997 1.95
❑132, Mar 1997 1.95
❑133, Apr 1997 1.95
❑134, May 1997 1.95
❑135, Jun 1997; A: Guido Carosella (Strong Guy). return of Strong Guy 1.95
❑136, Aug 1997; gatefold summary; A: Sabretooth. 1.99
❑137, Sep 1997; gatefold summary 1.99
❑138, Oct 1997; gatefold summary; (c); A: Sabretooth. V: Omega Red. 1.99
❑139, Nov 1997; gatefold summary; (c) 1.99
❑140, Dec 1997; gatefold summary; A: Xavier's Underground Enforcers. 1.99
❑141, Jan 1998; gatefold summary 1.99
❑142, Feb 1998; gatefold summary 1.99
❑143, Mar 1998; gatefold summary 1.99
❑144, Apr 1998; gatefold summary; (c); V: Random. 1.99
❑145, May 1998; gatefold summary 1.99
❑146, Jun 1998; gatefold summary; A: Multiple Man. 1.99

N-MINT

❑147, Jul 1998; gatefold summary; (c) 1.99
❑148, Aug 1998; gatefold summary; (c); A: Polaris. V: Mandroids. 1.99
❑149, Sep 1998; gatefold summary 1.99
❑Annual 1, ca. 1986, BL (c); BL (w); BL (a) 3.00
❑Annual 2, ca. 1987 3.00
❑Annual 3, ca. 1988, O: High Evolutionary. 3.00
❑Annual 4, ca. 1989, JBy (c); JBy (w); JBy (a) 2.50
❑Annual 5, ca. 1990, PD (w); A: Fantastic Four. A: New Mutants. 2.50
❑Annual 6, ca. 1991, PD (w); D: Proteus. 2.50
❑Annual 7, ca. 1992, PD (w) 2.25
❑Annual 8, ca. 1993; PD (w); A: Guido Carosella (Strong Guy). trading card 2.95
❑Annual 9, ca. 1994, KGa (a); V: Power. 2.95

X-FACTOR (VOL. 2)
MARVEL

❑1, Jun 2002 2.50
❑2, Jul 2002; Spider-Man serial 2.50
❑3, Aug 2002 2.50
❑4, Sep 2002 2.50

X-FACTOR: PRISONER OF LOVE
MARVEL

❑1, Aug 1990 4.95

X-FARCE
ECLIPSE

❑1, Jan 1992, b&w; parody 2.50

X-FARCE VS. X-CONS: X-TINCTION
PARODY

❑1 1993, b&w 2.75
❑1.5 1993, b&w; w/ trading cards 2.75

X-51
MARVEL

❑1, Sep 1999 1.99
❑2, Sep 1999 1.99
❑3, Oct 1999 1.99
❑4, Nov 1999 1.99
❑5, Dec 1999 1.99

X-FILES, THE
TOPPS

❑-2, Sep 1996; no cover price 10.00
❑-1, Sep 1996; no cover price 10.00
❑0/A; adapts pilot episode; forms diptych with Scully cover 4.00
❑0/B; adapts pilot episode; forms diptych with Mulder cover 4.00
❑0/C; adapts pilot episode 4.00
❑0.5; Wizard promotional edition 10.00
❑1, Jan 1995 8.00
❑1-2 2.50
❑2, Feb 1995 5.00
❑3, Mar 1995 4.00
❑3-2 2.50
❑4, Apr 1995 3.50
❑4-2 2.50
❑5, May 1995 3.00
❑6, Jun 1995 3.00
❑7, Jul 1995 3.00
❑8, Aug 1995 3.00
❑9, Sep 1995 3.00
❑10, Oct 1995 3.00
❑11, Nov 1995 3.00
❑12, Dec 1995 3.00
❑13, Feb 1996 3.00
❑14, Apr 1996 3.00
❑15, May 1996 3.00
❑16, May 1996 3.00
❑17, May 1996 3.00
❑18, Jun 1996 3.00
❑19, Jun 1996 3.00
❑20, Jul 1996 3.00
❑21, Aug 1996 3.00
❑22, Sep 1996 2.95
❑23, Nov 1996; Donor 2.95
❑24, Dec 1996 2.95
❑25, Jan 1997 2.95
❑26, Feb 1997 2.95
❑27, Mar 1997 2.95

More adventures of FBI agents Mulder and Scully were chronicled in Topps' *X-Files* series.

N-MINT

❑28, Apr 1997 2.95
❑29, May 1997 2.95
❑30, Jun 1997 2.95
❑31, Jul 1997 2.95
❑32, Aug 1997 2.95
❑33, Sep 1997 2.95
❑33/Variant, Sep 1997 5.00
❑34, Oct 1997 2.95
❑35, Nov 1997 2.95
❑36, Dec 1997 2.95
❑37, Jan 1998 2.95
❑38, Feb 1998 2.95
❑39, Mar 1998 2.95
❑40, Apr 1998 2.95
❑41, May 1998 2.95
❑41/Variant, Jun 1998 2.95
❑Annual 1, Aug 1995 3.95
❑Annual 2, ca. 1996; E.L.F.s 3.95
❑Ashcan 1, Jan 1995; no cover price; polybagged with Star Wars Galaxy #2 4.00
❑Special 1, Jun 1995; reprints issues #1 and 2 4.95
❑Special 2, ca. 1995; Reprints X-Files #4-6 4.95
❑Special 3, ca. 1996; Reprints X-Files #7-9 4.95
❑Special 4, Nov 1996; reprints Feelings of Unreality 4.95
❑Special 5, ca. 1997; Reprints X-Files #13, Annual #1 4.95

X-FILES COMICS DIGEST, THE
TOPPS

❑1, Dec 1995; Bradbury back-up stories 3.50
❑2, Apr 1996; Bradbury back-up stories 3.50
❑3, Sep 1996; Bradbury back-up stories 3.50

X-FILES GROUND ZERO, THE
TOPPS

❑1, Dec 1997; adapts Kevin J. Anderson novel 2.95
❑2, Jan 1998; adapts Kevin J. Anderson novel 2.95
❑3, Feb 1998; adapts Kevin J. Anderson novel 2.95
❑4, Mar 1998; adapts Kevin J. Anderson novel 2.95

X-FILES, THE: SEASON ONE
TOPPS

❑1, Jul 1997; prestige format; adapts pilot episode 4.95
❑2, Dec 1997; prestige format 4.95
❑2/A; variant cover 4.95
❑3, Oct 1997, VM (a) 4.95
❑3/A, Oct 1997; VM (a); variant cover 4.95
❑4, Dec 1997 4.95
❑5 4.95
❑6 4.95
❑7 4.95
❑8 4.95
❑9 4.95

X-FILES, THE: AFTERFLIGHT
TOPPS

❑1 5.95

X-FLIES BUG HUNT
TWIST AND SHOUT

❑1, Dec 1996 2.95
❑2, Jan 1997 2.95

	N-MINT
❑3, Feb 1997	2.95
❑4, Mar 1997	2.95

X-FLIES CONSPIRACY
Twist and Shout

	N-MINT
❑1, Mar 1996	2.95

X-FLIES SPECIAL
Twist and Shout

	N-MINT
❑1, Sep 1995	2.95

X-FORCE
Marvel

	N-MINT
❑-1, Jul 1997; AM (a); Flashback; Proudstars team up	2.00
❑1/A, Aug 1991; RL (c); RL (w); RL (a); 1: G.W. Bridge. with Cable card	2.00
❑1/B, Aug 1991; RL (c); RL (w); RL (a); 1: G.W. Bridge. with Deadpool card	2.00
❑1/C, Aug 1991; RL (c); RL (w); RL (a); 1: G.W. Bridge. with Shatterstar card	2.00
❑1/D, Aug 1991; RL (c); RL (w); RL (a); 1: G.W. Bridge. with Sunspot & Gideon card	2.00
❑1/E, Aug 1991; RL (c); RL (w); RL (a); 1: G.W. Bridge. with X-Force group card	2.00
❑1-2, Aug 1991; RL (c); RL (w); RL (a); 1: G.W. Bridge. Gold cover	1.50
❑2, Sep 1991, RL (c); RL (w); RL (a); 1: Weapon X II (Garrison Kane).	2.50
❑3, Oct 1991, RL (c); RL (w); RL (a); V: Juggernaut.	2.00
❑4, Nov 1991; (c); RL (w); RL (a); A: Spider-Man. Sideways printing	2.00
❑5, Dec 1991, RL (w); RL (a); A: Brotherhood of Evil Mutants.	2.00
❑6, Jan 1992, RL (c); RL (w); RL (a)	2.00
❑7, Feb 1992, RL (c); RL (w); RL (a)	2.00
❑8, Mar 1992, RL (c); RL (w); 1: Grizzly II.	2.00
❑9, Apr 1992, RL (c); RL (a)	2.00
❑10, May 1992, RL (w)	2.00
❑11, Jun 1992, RL (c); RL (w)	2.00
❑12, Jul 1992, RL (w)	2.00
❑13, Aug 1992	2.00
❑14, Sep 1992	2.00
❑15, Oct 1992	2.00
❑16/CS, Nov 1992; Includes Cable card	2.00
❑17/CS, Dec 1992; O: Zero. O: Stryfe. Includes trading card	2.00
❑18/CS, Jan 1993; Includes trading card	2.00
❑19, Feb 1993	1.50
❑20, Mar 1993	1.50
❑21, Apr 1993	1.50
❑22, May 1993	1.50
❑23, Jun 1993	1.50
❑24, Jul 1993	1.50
❑25, Aug 1993; Hologram cover	3.00
❑26, Sep 1993	1.50
❑27, Oct 1993, A: Mutant Liberation Front.	1.50
❑28, Nov 1993	1.50
❑29, Dec 1993, A: Arcade.	1.50
❑30, Jan 1994	1.50
❑31, Feb 1994	1.25
❑32, Mar 1994	1.25
❑33, Apr 1994	1.25
❑34, May 1994	1.50
❑35, Jun 1994, V: Nimrod.	1.50
❑36, Jul 1994	1.50
❑37, Aug 1994, AM (c)	1.50
❑38, Sep 1994; Phalanx Covenant	2.00
❑38/Variant, Sep 1994; enhanced cover; Phalanx Covenant	3.00
❑39, Oct 1994	1.50
❑40, Nov 1994	1.50
❑40/Deluxe, Nov 1994; Deluxe edition	1.95
❑41, Dec 1994	1.50
❑41/Deluxe, Dec 1994; Deluxe edition	1.95
❑42, Jan 1995	1.50
❑42/Deluxe, Jan 1995; Deluxe edition	1.95
❑43, Feb 1995	1.50
❑43/Deluxe, Feb 1995; Deluxe edition; bound-in trading cards	1.95
❑44, Jul 1995; (c); JPH (w); A: Cannonball. Cannonball leaves	1.95
❑45, Aug 1995, JPH (w)	1.95
❑46, Sep 1995, JPH (w); V: Mimic.	1.95
❑47, Oct 1995; JPH (w); bound-in trading cards	1.95
❑48, Nov 1995, JPH (w)	1.95
❑49, Dec 1995, JPH (w); A: Holocaust. A: Sebastian Shaw.	1.50
❑49/Deluxe, Dec 1995; Direct Edition JPH (w)	1.90
❑50, Jan 1996; Giant-size; (c); JPH (w); Giant-size; wraparound fold-out cover	3.00
❑50/A, Jan 1996; Giant-size; RL (c); JPH (w); Giant-size	4.00
❑50/Variant, Jan 1996; JPH (w); Giant-size; enhanced wraparound fold-out cardstock cover	1.95
❑51, Feb 1996, JPH (w); 1: Meltdown (formerly Boomer/Boom Boom).	1.95
❑52, Mar 1996, JPH (w); D: Gideon. V: Blob.	1.95
❑53, Apr 1996, JPH (w)	1.95
❑54, May 1996, JPH (w)	1.95
❑55, Jun 1996, JPH (w); V: S.H.I.E.L.D..	1.95
❑56, Jul 1996, JPH (w)	1.95
❑57, Aug 1996, JPH (w)	1.95
❑58, Sep 1996, JPH (w)	1.95
❑59, Oct 1996; (c); JPH (w); bound-in trading cards	1.95
❑60, Nov 1996, JPH (w); O: Shatterstar.	1.95
❑61, Dec 1996, JPH (w); O: Shatterstar.	1.95
❑62, Jan 1997	1.95
❑63, Feb 1997; team invades Doom's castle	1.95
❑64, Mar 1997, A: Baron Von Strucker.	1.95
❑65, Apr 1997	1.95
❑66, May 1997	1.95
❑67, Jun 1997, A: Dani Moonstar.	1.99
❑68, Aug 1997; gatefold summary; A: Vanisher.	1.99
❑69, Sep 1997; gatefold summary	1.99
❑70, Oct 1997; gatefold summary	1.99
❑71, Nov 1997; gatefold summary	1.99
❑72, Dec 1997; gatefold summary	1.99
❑73, Jan 1998; gatefold summary; D: Warpath.	1.99
❑74, Feb 1998; gatefold summary; V: Stryfe.	1.99
❑75, Mar 1998; gatefold summary; A: Cannonball.	1.99
❑76, Apr 1998; gatefold summary; Domino vs. Shatterstar	1.99
❑77, May 1998; gatefold summary	1.99
❑78, Jun 1998; gatefold summary	1.99
❑79, Jul 1998; gatefold summary; O: Reignfire.	1.99
❑80, Aug 1998; gatefold summary	1.99
❑81, Sep 1998; gatefold summary; poster	1.99
❑82, Oct 1998; gatefold summary	1.99
❑83, Nov 1998; gatefold summary	1.99
❑84, Dec 1998; gatefold summary; V: New Deviants.	1.99
❑85, Jan 1999; gatefold summary	1.99
❑86, Jan 1999; gatefold summary	1.99
❑87, Feb 1999, A: Hellions.	1.99
❑88, Mar 1999, A: Christopher Bedlam. A: Hellions. V: New Hellions.	1.99
❑89, Apr 1999, A: Armageddon Man. A: Hellions.	1.99
❑90, May 1999, (c)	1.99
❑91, Jun 1999; Siryn solo tale	1.99
❑92, Jul 1999; Domino vs. Halloween Jack	1.99
❑93, Aug 1999	1.99
❑94, Sep 1999	1.99
❑95, Oct 1999	1.99
❑96, Nov 1999	1.99
❑97, Dec 1999	2.25
❑98, Jan 2000	2.25
❑99, Feb 2000, BSz (c)	2.99
❑100, Mar 2000	2.25
❑101, Apr 2000	2.25
❑102, May 2000; Revolution	2.25
❑103, Jun 2000	2.25
❑104, Jul 2000	2.25
❑105, Aug 2000	2.25
❑106, Sep 2000	2.25
❑107, Oct 2000	2.25
❑108, Nov 2000	2.25
❑109, Dec 2000; indicia says Nov 2000	2.25
❑110, Jan 2001	2.25
❑111, Feb 2001	2.25
❑112, Mar 2001	2.25
❑113, Apr 2001	2.25
❑114, May 2001; indicia says March 01	2.25
❑115, Jun 2001	2.25
❑116, Jul 2001; indicia says May 01	2.25
❑117, Aug 2001; indicia says June 01	2.25
❑118, Sep 2001	2.25
❑119, Oct 2001	2.25
❑120, Nov 2001, A: Wolverine.	2.25
❑121, Dec 2001	2.25
❑122, Jan 2002	2.25
❑123, Feb 2002; 'Nuff Said (silent issue)	2.25
❑124, Mar 2002	2.25
❑125, Apr 2002	2.25
❑126, May 2002	2.25
❑127, Jun 2002	2.25
❑128, Jul 2002	2.25
❑129, Aug 2002	2.25
❑Annual 1, ca. 1992, BSz (a)	2.50
❑Annual 2, ca. 1993; 1: Neurotap. 1: X-Treme. 1: Stronghold. Polybagged with trading card	2.95
❑Annual 3, ca. 1994; BWi (a); 1994 Annual	2.95
❑Annual 1995, Dec 1995; JPH (w); wraparound cover; X-Force and Cable '95	3.95
❑Annual 1996, ca. 1996; wraparound cover; X-Force and Cable '96	2.99
❑Annual 1997, ca. 1997; A: Asgard. wraparound cover; X-Force and Cable '97	2.99
❑Annual 1998, Dec 1998; gatefold summary; (c); wraparound cover; X-Force/Champions '98; gatefold summary	3.50
❑Annual 1999, ca. 1999	3.50

X-FORCE/YOUNGBLOOD
Marvel

	N-MINT
❑1, Aug 1996; crossover with Image; prestige format one-shot	4.95

XIMOS: VIOLENT PAST
Triumphant

	N-MINT
❑1, Mar 1994	2.50
❑2, Mar 1994	2.50

XIOLA
Xero

	N-MINT
❑0, b&w	1.95
❑1, Oct 1994, b&w	1.95
❑2, b&w	1.95
❑3, b&w	1.95
❑Ashcan 1, b&w; no cover price	1.00

XL
Blackthorne

	N-MINT
❑1, b&w	3.50

X-LAX
Thwack! Pow!

	N-MINT
❑1, Mini-Comic	1.25

X-MAN
Marvel

	N-MINT
❑-1, Jul 1997; Flashback	2.00
❑1, Mar 1995, JPH (w)	3.00
❑1-2, Mar 1995; 2nd printing ❑	2.25
❑2, Apr 1995; JPH (w); After Xavier: Age of Apocalypse	2.50
❑3, May 1995; JPH (w); After Xavier: Age of Apocalypse	2.50
❑4, Jun 1995; JPH (w); After Xavier: Age of Apocalypse	2.50
❑5, Jul 1995, JPH (w)	2.00
❑6, Aug 1995, JPH (w)	2.00

N-MINT

❑7, Sep 1995, JPH (w) 2.00
❑8, Oct 1995; JPH (w); OverPower cards bound in 2.00
❑9, Nov 1995, JPH (w) 2.00
❑10, Dec 1995, JDu (a); V: Xavier. 2.00
❑11, Jan 1996, A: Rogue. 1.95
❑12, Feb 1996, V: Excalibur. 1.95
❑13, Mar 1996 .... 1.95
❑14, Apr 1996 .... 1.95
❑15, May 1996, A: Onslaught. 2.50
❑16, Jun 1996, V: Holocaust. 2.00
❑17, Jul 1996, V: Holocaust. 2.00
❑18, Aug 1996; Onslaught, Phase 1 .. 1.95
❑19, Sep 1996, A: Mr. Sinister. 1.95
❑20, Oct 1996; V: Abomination. bound-in trading cards 1.95
❑21, Nov 1996 .... 1.95
❑22, Dec 1996 .... 1.95
❑23, Jan 1997 .... 1.95
❑24, Feb 1997, A: Spider-Man. A: Morbius. V: Morbius. 1.95
❑25, Mar 1997; Giant-size; A: Madelyne Pryor. wraparound cover 2.99
❑26, Apr 1997 .... 1.95
❑27, May 1997 .... 1.95
❑28, Jun 1997 .... 1.95
❑29, Aug 1997; gatefold summary 1.95
❑30, Sep 1997; gatefold summary 1.95
❑31, Oct 1997; gatefold summary 1.99
❑32, Nov 1997; gatefold summary 1.99
❑33, Dec 1997; gatefold summary 1.99
❑34, Jan 1998; gatefold summary 1.99
❑35, Feb 1998; gatefold summary 1.99
❑36, Mar 1998; gatefold summary 1.99
❑37, Apr 1998; gatefold summary; A: Spider-Man. 1.99
❑38, May 1998; gatefold summary; A: Spider-Man. 1.99
❑39, Jun 1998; gatefold summary 1.99
❑40, Jul 1998; gatefold summary 1.99
❑41, Aug 1998; gatefold summary; A: Madelyne Pryor. 1.99
❑42, Sep 1998; gatefold summary; A: Madelyne Pryor. 1.99
❑43, Oct 1998; gatefold summary 1.99
❑44, Nov 1998; gatefold summary; V: Nemesis. 1.99
❑45, Dec 1998; gatefold summary 1.99
❑46, Dec 1998; gatefold summary 1.99
❑47, Jan 1999; gatefold summary 1.99
❑48, Feb 1999; gatefold summary 1.99
❑49, Mar 1999 .... 1.99
❑50, Apr 1999; A: Dark Beast. A: White Queen. Story continues from Generation X #50 .... 1.99
❑51, May 1999 .... 1.99
❑52, Jun 1999 .... 1.99
❑53, Jul 1999, A: Cyclops. A: Jean Grey. 1.99
❑54, Aug 1999 .... 1.99
❑55, Sep 1999 .... 1.99
❑56, Oct 1999, A: Spider-Man. 1.99
❑57, Nov 1999 .... 1.99
❑58, Dec 1999 .... 1.99
❑59, Jan 2000, A: Fantastic Four. 1.99
❑60, Feb 2000 .... 1.99
❑61, Mar 2000 .... 1.99
❑62, Apr 2000 .... 1.99
❑63, May 2000; Revolution 1.99
❑64, Jun 2000 .... 2.25
❑65, Jul 2000 .... 2.25
❑66, Aug 2000 .... 2.25
❑67, Sep 2000 .... 2.25
❑68, Oct 2000 .... 2.25
❑69, Nov 2000; polybagged with AOL CD-ROM 2.25
❑70, Dec 2000 .... 2.25
❑71, Jan 2001 .... 2.25
❑72, Feb 2001 .... 2.25
❑73, Mar 2001 .... 2.25
❑74, Apr 2001 .... 2.25
❑75, May 2001; double-sized 2.99
❑Annual 1996, ca. 1996; wraparound cover 2.95

N-MINT

❑Annual 1997, ca. 1997; A: Sugar Man. A: Nemesis. A: Dark Beast. wraparound cover 2.99
❑Annual 1998, ca. 1998; V: Thanos. wraparound cover; X-Man/Hulk '98 2.99

X-MAN: ALL SAINTS' DAY

MARVEL

❑1, Nov 1997 .... 5.99

X-MEN (1ST SERIES)

MARVEL

❑1, Sep 1963, SL (w); JK (a); O: X-Men. 1: X-Men. 1: Cyclops. 1: Professor X. 1: Angel II. 1: Marvel Girl. 1: Iceman. 1: Magneto. 1: Beast. 7000.00
❑2, Nov 1963, SL (w); JK (a); 1: The Vanisher. 1: Vanisher. 1900.00
❑3, Jan 1964, SL (w); JK (a); 1: The Blob. 1030.00
❑4, Mar 1964, SL (w); JK (a); 1: Toad. 1: Mastermind. 1: Scarlet Witch. 1: Quicksilver. 1: Brotherhood of Evil Mutants. 900.00
❑5, May 1964, SL (w); JK (a); A: Evil Mutants. 550.00
❑6, Jul 1964, SL (w); JK (a); A: Evil Mutants. A: Sub-Mariner. 500.00
❑7, Sep 1964, SL (w); JK (a); A: Blob. A: Evil Mutants. 475.00
❑8, Nov 1964, SL (w); JK (a); O: Unus the Untouchable. 1: Unus the Untouchable. 360.00
❑9, Jan 1965, SL (w); JK (a); 1: Lucifer. 360.00
❑10, Mar 1965, SL (w); JK (a); 1: Ka-Zar. A: Ka-Zar. 360.00
❑11, May 1965, SL (w); JK (a); 1: The Stranger. 1: Stranger. 300.00
❑12, Jul 1965, SL (w); ATh, JK (a); O: Professor X. O: Juggernaut. 1: Juggernaut. 500.00
❑13, Sep 1965, SL (w); JK, JSt (a); V: Juggernaut. 275.00
❑14, Nov 1965, SL (w); JK (a); O: Sentinels. 1: Sentinels. 250.00
❑15, Dec 1965, SL (w); JK (a); O: Beast. 190.00
❑16, Jan 1966, SL (w); JK (a); A: Sentinels. A: Master Mold. 190.00
❑17, Feb 1966, SL (w); JK (a); V: Magneto. 100.00
❑18, Mar 1966, SL (w); A: Stranger. V: Magneto. 100.00
❑19, Apr 1966, SL (w); O: Mimic. 1: Mimic. 100.00
❑20, May 1966, V: Unus. V: Lucifer. .. 100.00
❑21, Jun 1966, V: Lucifer. 90.00
❑22, Jul 1966, V: Count Nefaria. 90.00
❑23, Aug 1966, V: Count Nefaria. 90.00
❑24, Sep 1966 .... 90.00
❑25, Oct 1966, A: El Tigre. 90.00
❑26, Nov 1966, (c) 90.00
❑27, Dec 1966; V: Puppet Master. Mimic returns 90.00
❑28, Jan 1967, 1: Banshee. 155.00
❑28-2 (c); 1: Banshee. 2.00
❑29, Feb 1967, V: Super-Adaptoid. ... 90.00
❑30, Mar 1967, 1: Maha Yogi. 90.00
❑31, Apr 1967, 1: Cobalt Man. 90.00
❑32, May 1967, V: Juggernaut. 90.00
❑33, Jun 1967, V: Juggernaut. 90.00
❑34, Jul 1967, DA (a); V: Tyrannus. V: Mole Man. 90.00
❑35, Aug 1967, DA (a); 1: Changeling. A: Spider-Man. A: Banshee. 150.00
❑36, Sep 1967, RA (a); 1: Mekano. ... 65.00
❑37, Oct 1967, DH, RA (a); V: Factor Three. 65.00
❑38, Nov 1967; DA (c); DH (a); V: Blob. V: Vanisher. The Origins of the X-Men back-ups begin 80.00
❑39, Dec 1967, GT (c); DH (a); D: Mutant-Master. 90.00
❑40, Jan 1968, GT (c); DH, GT (a); V: Frankenstein. 90.00
❑41, Feb 1968, GT (c); DH, GT (a); 1: Grotesk the Sub-Human. 65.00
❑42, Mar 1968, JB (c); HT, DH, GT (a); D: Changeling (disguised as Professor X). V: Grotesk. 65.00

X-Man was the only "Age of Apocalypse" series to continue past its initial four issues.

© 1995 Marvel Characters Inc.

N-MINT

❑43, Apr 1968, JB (c); GT (a); V: Brotherhood of Evil Mutants. 65.00
❑44, May 1968; DH (c); DH, GT (a); O: Red Raven. O: Iceman. 1: Red Raven (in modern age). A: Magneto. Return of Red Raven 65.00
❑45, Jun 1968, JB (c); DH, GT (a); O: Iceman. V: Evil Mutants. 65.00
❑46, Jul 1968, DH (c); DH, GT (a); O: Iceman. V: Juggernaut. 65.00
❑47, Aug 1968, DH (c); DH (a); V: Maha Yogi. 65.00
❑48, Sep 1968, JR (c); DH (a); V: Quasimodo. 65.00
❑49, Oct 1968, JSo (c); DH, JSo (a); 1: Mesmero. 1: Polaris. 75.00
❑50, Nov 1968, JSo (c); JSo (a); V: Mesmero. 75.00
❑51, Dec 1968, JSo (c); JSo (a); V: Mesmero. 75.00
❑52, Jan 1969, DH (a); O: Lorna Dane. 65.00
❑53, Feb 1969; V: Blastaar. Barry Windsor-Smith's 1st comic book art 72.00
❑54, Mar 1969, DH (a); O: Havok. 1: Alex Summers (Havok). 1: Living Pharaoh. 72.00
❑55, Apr 1969, DH (a); O: Havok. 72.00
❑56, May 1969; NA (c); NA, TP (a); 1: Living Monolith. V: Living Monolith. Living Pharaoh becomes Living Monolith 72.00
❑57, Jun 1969, NA (c); NA, TP (a); 1: Mark II Sentinels. 72.00
❑58, Jul 1969, NA (c); NA, TP (a); 1: Havok (in costume). 100.00
❑59, Aug 1969, NA (c); NA, TP (a); 1: Dr. Karl Lykos. 69.00
❑60, Sep 1969, NA (c); NA, TP (a); O: Sauron. 1: Sauron. 69.00
❑61, Oct 1969, NA (c); NA, TP (a); V: Sauron. 69.00
❑62, Nov 1969, NA (c); NA, TP (a); 1: Piper. 1: Lupo. 1: Barbarus. A: Ka-Zar. 69.00
❑62-2, NA (a); 1: Piper. 1: Lupo. 1: Barbarus. A: Ka-Zar. 1.50
❑63, Dec 1969, NA (c); NA, TP (a); O: Piper. O: Lupo. A: Ka-Zar. V: Magneto. 69.00
❑63-2, NA (a); O: Piper. O: Lupo. A: Ka-Zar. V: Magneto. 2.00
❑64, Jan 1970, SB (c); DH, TP (a); O: Sunfire. 1: Sunfire. 69.00
❑65, Feb 1970, TP (c); NA, TP (a); A: Havok, SHIELD, Fantastic Four. D: Changeling (revealed). 69.00
❑66, Mar 1970, SB (a); A: Havok. A: Hulk. 80.00
❑67, Dec 1970; SL (w); ATh, JK, JSt (a); reprints stories from X-Men #12 and 13 .... 35.00
❑68, Feb 1971; SL (w); reprints stories from X-Men #14 and 15 .... 35.00
❑69, Apr 1971; SB (c); SL (w); reprints stories from X-Men #16 and 19 ..... 35.00
❑70, Jun 1971; SL (w); reprints stories from X-Men #17 and 18 .... 35.00
❑71, Aug 1971; reprints X-Men #20 .. 35.00
❑72, Oct 1971; reprints stories from X-Men #21 and 24 .... 35.00
❑73, Dec 1971; reprints X-Men #25 .. 35.00
❑74, Feb 1972; GK (c); reprints X-Men #26 .... 35.00
❑75, Apr 1972; reprints X-Men #27 ... 35.00
❑76, Jun 1972; GK (c); reprints X-Men #28 .... 35.00

Condition price index: Multiply "NM prices" above by: **0.83 for Very Fine/Near Mint**
0.66 for Very Fine • 0.33 for Fine • 0.2 for Very Good • 0.125 for Good

	N-MINT
❑77, Aug 1972; reprints X-Men #29 ..	35.00
❑78, Oct 1972; GK (c); reprints X-Men #30	35.00
❑79, Dec 1972; GK (c); reprints X-Men #31	35.00
❑80, Feb 1973; GK (c); reprints X-Men #32	35.00
❑81, Apr 1973; reprints X-Men #33 ..	40.00
❑82, Jun 1973; DA (a); reprints X-Men #34	40.00
❑83, Aug 1973; DA (a); reprints X-Men #35	40.00
❑84, Oct 1973; RA (a); reprints X-Men #36	40.00
❑85, Dec 1973; DH, RA (a); reprints X-Men #37	40.00
❑86, Feb 1974; DA (c); SL (w); SD, DH (a); reprints stories from X-Men #38 and Amazing Adult Fantasy #2	35.00
❑87, Apr 1974; GT (c); SL (w); SD, DH (a); reprints stories from X-Men #39 and Amazing Adult Fantasy #10	35.00
❑88, Jun 1974; GT (c); (w); DH, GT (a); reprints X-Men #40	35.00
❑89, Aug 1974; SL (w); SD, DH, GT (a); reprints stories from X-Men #41 and Amazing Adult Fantasy #11	35.00
❑90, Oct 1974; JB (c); SL (w); SD, DH, GT (a); reprints stories from X-Men #42 and Amazing Adult Fantasy #7	35.00
❑91, Dec 1974; JB (c); SL (w); SD, GT (a); reprints stories from X-Men #43 and Amazing Adult Fantasy #7	35.00
❑92, Feb 1975; DH (a); reprints stories from X-Men #44 and Mystery Tales #30	35.00
❑93, Apr 1975; JB (c); SL (w); SD, DH (a); reprints stories from X-Men #45 and Journey Into Mystery #74	35.00
❑94, Aug 1975; New X-Men begin (from Giant-Size X-Men #1); GK, DC (c); DC, BMc (a); 1: New X-Men. Old X-Men leave	500.00
❑95, Oct 1975, DC (c); DC (a); D: Thunderbird.	85.00
❑96, Dec 1975; DC (c); DC (a); 1: Moira MacTaggart.	55.00
❑97, Feb 1976; RB, DC (c); DC (a); 1: Lilandra Neramani. Cyclops vs. Havok	48.00
❑98, Apr 1976, DC (c); DC (a); A: Nick Fury. A: Matt Murdock. V: Sentinels.	48.00
❑98/30 cent, Apr 1976; 30 cent regional variant	125.00
❑99, Jun 1976, DC (c); DC (a); 1: Black Tom Cassidy.	48.00
❑99/30 cent, Jun 1976; 30 cent regional variant	125.00
❑100, Aug 1976; DC (c); DC (a); V: X-Men. Old X-Men vs. New X-Men ...	60.00
❑100/30 cent, Aug 1976; 30 cent regional variant; Old X-Men vs. New X-Men	135.00
❑101, Oct 1976, DC (c); DC (a); 1: Phoenix II (Jean Grey). A: Juggernaut. D: Jean Grey.	55.00
❑102, Dec 1976, DC (c); DC (a); O: Storm. V: Juggernaut and Black Tom.	28.00
❑103, Feb 1977, DC (c); DC (a); V: Black Tom. V: Juggernaut.	28.00
❑104, Apr 1977, DC (c); DC (a); 1: Starjammers (cameo). 1: Muir Island. V: Magneto.	28.00
❑105, Jun 1977, DC (c); BL, DC (a); A: Firelord.	28.00
❑105/35 cent, Jun 1977; 35 cent regional variant	60.00
❑106, Aug 1977, DC (c); TS, DC (a); A: Firelord.	28.00
❑106/35 cent, Aug 1977; 35 cent regional variant	60.00
❑107, Oct 1977, DC (c); DGr, DC (a); 1: Starjammers.	28.00
❑107/35 cent, Oct 1977; 35 cent regional variant	60.00
❑108, Dec 1977; DC (c); JBy (a); O: Polaris. A: Fantastic Four. 1st Byrne art on X-Men	35.00
❑109, Feb 1978, DC (c); JBy (a); 1: Weapon Alpha.	30.00

	N-MINT
❑110, Apr 1978, DC (c); DC, TD (a); A: Warhawk.	20.00
❑111, Jun 1978, DC (c); JBy (a); A: Beast, Magneto. V: Mesmero.	20.00
❑112, Aug 1978, GP, BL (c); JBy (a); V: Magneto.	20.00
❑113, Sep 1978, JBy, BL (c); JBy (w); JBy (a); V: Magneto.	20.00
❑114, Oct 1978, JBy (c); JBy (w); JBy (a); V: Sauron.	20.00
❑115, Nov 1978, JBy (c); JBy (w); JBy (a); 1: Nereel. A: Ka-Zar. V: Sauron.	20.00
❑116, Dec 1978, JBy (c); JBy (w); JBy (a); A: Ka-Zar.	16.00
❑117, Jan 1979, DC (c); JBy (w); JBy (a); O: Professor X.	16.00
❑118, Feb 1979, DC (c); JBy (w); JBy (a); 1: Mariko Yashida.	16.00
❑119, Mar 1979, DC (c); JBy (w); JBy (a); 1: Proteus (voice only).	16.00
❑120, Apr 1979, JBy (w); JBy (a); 1: Aurora. 1: Alpha Flight (cameo). 1: Snowbird. 1: Northstar. 1: Sasquatch. 1: Vindicator.	28.00
❑122, Jun 1979, DC (c); JBy (w); JBy (a); 1: Hellfire Club. V: Arcade.	12.00
❑121, May 1979, DC (c); JBy (w); JBy (a); 1: Alpha Flight (full). A: Mastermind.	28.00
❑123, Jul 1979, JBy (w); JBy (a); O: Colossus. V: Arcade.	12.00
❑124, Aug 1979, DC (c); JBy (w); JBy (a); O: Arcade. A: Arcade.	12.00
❑125, Sep 1979; DC (c); JBy (a); 1: Proteus (full appearance). Phoenix cover	12.00
❑126, Oct 1979, DC (c); JBy (a)	12.00
❑127, Nov 1979, JBy (c); JBy (w); JBy (a)	12.00
❑128, Dec 1979, GP (c); JBy (w); JBy (a); O: Proteus. D: Proteus.	12.00
❑129, Jan 1980, JBy (c); JBy (w); JBy (a); 1: Donald Pierce (the White Bishop). 1: White Queen (Emma Frost). 1: Kitty Pryde. 1: Sprite II (Kitty Pryde).	20.00
❑130, Feb 1980, JR2 (c); JBy (w); JBy (a); 1: Dazzler.	12.00
❑131, Mar 1980, JBy (c); JBy (w); JBy (a); A: Angel, White Queen. A: Dazzler.	12.00
❑132, Apr 1980, JBy (c); JBy (w); JBy (a); A: Hugh Hefner. A: Angel.	12.00
❑133, May 1980, JBy (c); JBy (w); JBy (a); 1: Dark Phoenix. 1: Senator Edward Kelly. A: Angel.	12.00
❑134, Jun 1980, JBy (c); JBy (w); JBy (a); A: Dark Phoenix.	12.00
❑135, Jul 1980, JBy (c); JBy (w); JBy (a); A: Dark Phoenix. A: Spider-Man.	12.00
❑136, Aug 1980, JBy (c); JBy (w); JBy (a)	11.00
❑137, Sep 1980; Giant-size; JBy (c); JBy (w); JBy (a); 1: Hussar. A: Angel. D: Phoenix II (Jean Grey). Giant size	14.00
❑138, Oct 1980, JBy (c); JBy (w); JBy (a); A: Angel.	8.00
❑139, Nov 1980; JBy (c); JBy (w); JBy (a); 1: Stevie Hunter. Kitty Pryde joins X-Men; New costume for Wolverine	11.00
❑140, Dec 1980, JBy (c); JBy (w); JBy (a); A: Alpha Flight.	11.00
❑141, Jan 1981; JBy (c); JBy (w); JBy (a); 1: Avalanche. 1: Rachel Summers (Phoenix III). 1: Pyro. series continues as Uncanny X-Men	11.00

X-MEN (2ND SERIES)
MARVEL

	N-MINT
❑-1, Jul 1997; O: Magneto. Flashback	3.00
❑-1/A, Jul 1997; Variant cover: "Magneto's Rage, Xavier's Hope; I had a Dream!"	2.50
❑1/A, Oct 1991; JLee (c); JLee (w); JLee (a); Storm cover	5.00
❑1/B, Oct 1991; JLee (c); JLee (w); JLee (a); Colossus cover	3.00
❑1/C, Oct 1991; JLee (c); JLee (w); JLee (a); Wolverine Cover	3.00
❑1/D, Oct 1991; JLee (c); JLee (w); JLee (a); Magneto Cover	3.00
❑1/E, Oct 1991; JLee (c); JLee (w); JLee (a); Double gatefold cover combining A-D images	5.00
❑2, Nov 1991, JLee (c); JLee (w); JLee (a)	3.00
❑3, Dec 1991, JLee (c); JLee (w); JLee (a)	3.00
❑4, Jan 1992, JLee (c); JBy, JLee (w); JLee (a); 1: Omega Red.	3.00
❑5, Feb 1992, JLee (c); JBy, JLee (w); JLee (a); 1: Maverick.	3.00
❑6, Mar 1992, JLee (c); JLee (w); JLee (a); A: Sabretooth.	3.00
❑7, Apr 1992, JLee (c); JLee (w); JLee (a)	3.00
❑8, May 1992, JLee (c); JLee (w); JLee (a); A: Ghost Rider.	3.00
❑9, Jun 1992, JLee (c); JLee (w); JLee (a); A: Ghost Rider.	3.00
❑10, Jul 1992, JLee (c); JLee (w); JLee, BWi (a); A: Longshot.	3.00
❑11, Aug 1992, JLee (c); JLee (w); JLee, BWi (a)	3.00
❑12, Sep 1992	3.00
❑13, Oct 1992	3.00
❑14/CS, Nov 1992; Apocalypse trading card	3.00
❑15/CS, Dec 1992; trading card	3.00
❑16/CS, Jan 1993; trading card	3.00
❑17, Feb 1993; indicia says February 1992	2.50
❑18, Mar 1993	2.50
❑19, Apr 1993, BWi (a)	2.50
❑20, May 1993, BWi (a)	2.50
❑21, Jun 1993	2.00
❑22, Jul 1993	2.00
❑23, Aug 1993	2.00
❑24, Sep 1993	2.00
❑25, Oct 1993; A: Magneto. Hologram cover; Wolverine loses adamantium skeleton	5.00
❑25/Gold, Oct 1993; Gold limited edition; A: Magneto. Hologram cover .	25.00
❑25/Ltd., Oct 1993; A: Magneto. Cover black and white w/ hologram	25.00
❑26, Nov 1993	2.00
❑27, Dec 1993, BWi (a)	2.00
❑28, Jan 1994, A: Sabretooth.	2.00
❑29, Feb 1994, A: Sabretooth. A: Sabretooth.	2.00
❑30, Mar 1994; Double-sized; trading cards; wedding of Jean Grey and Scott Summers	3.00
❑31, Apr 1994	1.75
❑32, May 1994; Trading cards	1.75
❑33, Jun 1994, A: Sabretooth.	1.75
❑34, Jul 1994	1.75
❑35, Aug 1994	1.75
❑36, Sep 1994	1.50
❑36/Variant, Sep 1994; Foil cover	2.00
❑37, Oct 1994	1.50
❑37/Variant, Oct 1994; enhanced cover	2.00
❑38, Nov 1994	1.50
❑38/Deluxe, Nov 1994	2.00
❑39, Dec 1994	1.50
❑39/Deluxe, Dec 1994	2.00
❑40, Jan 1995	1.50
❑40/Deluxe, Jan 1995	2.00
❑41, Feb 1995	1.50
❑41/Deluxe, Feb 1995; trading cards .	2.00
❑42, Jul 1995, PS (a)	2.00
❑43, Aug 1995, PS (a)	2.00
❑44, Sep 1995	2.00
❑45, Oct 1995; enhanced wraparound gatefold cardstock cover	2.00
❑46, Nov 1995, A: X-babies.	2.00
❑47, Dec 1995, A: Dazzler. A: X-babies.	2.00
❑48, Jan 1996, A: Sugar Man. A: alternate Beast.	2.00
❑49, Feb 1996, MWa (w)	2.00
❑50, Mar 1996; Giant-size; wraparound cover	3.00
❑50/Variant, Mar 1996; Giant-size; foil wraparound cardstock cover	4.00
❑51, Apr 1996, MWa (w)	2.00
❑52, May 1996, MWa (w)	2.00

	N-MINT
❑53, Jun 1996; MWa (w); Jean Grey vs. Onslaught	2.00
❑54, Jul 1996; MWa (w); Identity of Onslaught revealed	2.00
❑55, Aug 1996, MWa (w)	2.00
❑56, Sep 1996, MWa (w)	2.00
❑57, Oct 1996	2.00
❑58, Nov 1996; Gambit vs. Magneto	2.00
❑59, Dec 1996, A: Hercules.	2.00
❑60, Jan 1997	2.00
❑61, Feb 1997	2.00
❑62, Mar 1997, A: Shang-Chi.	2.00
❑62/A, Mar 1997; A: Shang-Chi. alternate cover	3.00
❑63, Apr 1997, A: Kingpin. A: Sebastian Shaw.	2.00
❑64, May 1997	2.00
❑65, Jun 1997	2.00
❑66, Aug 1997; gatefold summary	2.00
❑67, Sep 1997; gatefold summary	2.00
❑68, Oct 1997; gatefold summary	2.00
❑69, Nov 1997; gatefold summary	2.00
❑70, Dec 1997; gatefold summary; giant-size	2.00
❑71, Jan 1998; gatefold summary; Cyclops and Phoenix leave	2.00
❑72, Feb 1998; gatefold summary	2.00
❑73, Mar 1998; gatefold summary	2.00
❑74, Apr 1998; gatefold summary A: Abomination.	2.00
❑75, May 1998; gatefold summary; wraparound cover; giant size	2.00
❑76, Jun 1998; gatefold summary O: Maggot.	2.00
❑77, Jul 1998; gatefold summary	2.00
❑78, Aug 1998; gatefold summary	2.00
❑79, Sep 1998; gatefold summary	2.00
❑80, Oct 1998; double-sized	3.00
❑81, Nov 1998; gatefold summary	2.00
❑82, Dec 1998; gatefold summary	2.00
❑83, Jan 1999; gatefold summary BWi (a)	2.00
❑84, Feb 1999; gatefold summary A: Nina.	2.00
❑85, Feb 1999, A: Magneto.	2.00
❑86, Mar 1999, O: Joseph. A: Astra. A: Joseph. A: Acolytes. A: Magneto.	1.99
❑87, Apr 1999; A: Joseph. A: Magneto. Cover says April, indicia says May	1.99
❑88, May 1999	1.99
❑89, Jun 1999	1.99
❑90, Jul 1999, A: Galactus.	1.99
❑91, Aug 1999	1.99
❑92, Sep 1999	1.99
❑93, Oct 1999	1.99
❑94, Nov 1999; JBy (w); JBy, TP (a); double-sized	1.99
❑95, Dec 1999	1.99
❑96, Jan 2000	2.25
❑97, Feb 2000	2.25
❑98, Mar 2000	2.25
❑99, Apr 2000, PS (c)	2.99
❑100/A, May 2000; White background, team charging	2.99
❑100/B, May 2000; Nightcrawler vs. Villain cover	2.99
❑100/C, May 2000; Nightcrawler, Wolverine, Colossus, Jean Gray, Storm on cover	2.99
❑100/D, May 2000; Rogue vs. Villain on cover	2.99
❑100/E, May 2000; Team stacked cover	2.99
❑100/F, May 2000; Team in chains cover	2.99
❑100/G, May 2000; Rogue, Nightcrawler, Shadowcat, etc. charging	2.99
❑101, Jun 2000	2.25
❑102, Jul 2000	2.25
❑103, Aug 2000	2.25
❑104, Sep 2000	2.25
❑105, Oct 2000	2.99
❑106, Nov 2000; double-sized	2.25
❑107, Dec 2000	2.25
❑108, Jan 2001	2.25

	N-MINT
❑109, Feb 2001; JBy (w); JBy, DC (a); Monster sized; with reprints from X-Men (1st series) #98, 143, Uncanny X-Men #341	2.25
❑110, Mar 2001	2.25
❑111, Apr 2001, A: Magneto.	2.25
❑112, May 2001	2.25
❑113, Jun 2001; Title becomes New X-Men	2.25
❑114, Jul 2001	5.00
❑115, Aug 2001	2.25
❑116, Sep 2001	2.25
❑117, Oct 2001	2.25
❑118, Nov 2001	2.25
❑119, Dec 2001	2.25
❑120, Jan 2002	2.25
❑121, Feb 2002; 'Nuff Said month (silent issue)	2.25
❑122, Mar 2002	2.25
❑123, Apr 2002	2.25
❑124, May 2002	2.25
❑125, Jun 2002	2.25
❑126, Jul 2002	2.25
❑127, Aug 2002, BSz (a)	2.25
❑128, Aug 2002	2.25
❑129, Sep 2002	2.25
❑130, Oct 2002	2.25
❑131, Oct 2002, BSz (a)	2.25
❑132, Nov 2002	2.25
❑133, Dec 2002	2.25
❑134, Jan 2003	2.25
❑135, Feb 2003	2.25
❑136, Mar 2003	2.25
❑137, Apr 2003	2.25
❑138, May 2003	2.25
❑139, Jun 2003	2.25
❑140, Jun 2003	2.25
❑141, Jul 2003; cardstock cover	2.25
❑142, Aug 2003; cardstock cover	2.25
❑143, Aug 2003	2.25
❑144, Sep 2003	2.25
❑145, Oct 2003	2.99
❑146, Nov 2003	2.99
❑147, Nov 2003	2.99
❑148, Dec 2003	2.25
❑149, Jan 2004	2.99
❑150, Feb 2004	3.50
❑151, Mar 2004	2.99
❑152, Mar 2004	2.25
❑153, Apr 2004	2.99
❑154, May 2004	2.99
❑155, Jun 2004	2.99
❑156, Jun 2004	2.99
❑157, Jul 2004; loses "New" from title, becomes X-Men again	2.99
❑158, Aug 2004	2.25
❑159, Sep 2004	2.25
❑Annual 1, ca. 1992; JLee (c); CR, JLee (a); Rogue vs. Villain on cover	3.00
❑Annual 2, ca. 1993; (c); AM, BWi (a); 1: Empyrean. Polybagged w/ trading card; Rogue vs. Villain on cover	3.00
❑Annual 3, ca. 1994; TP, BWi (a); Rogue vs. Villain on cover	2.95
❑Annual 1995, Oct 1995; Rogue vs. Villain on cover	3.95
❑Annual 1996, Nov 1996; wraparound cover	2.99
❑Annual 1997, ca. 1997; wraparound cover	2.99
❑Annual 1998, ca. 1998; X-Men/Doctor Doom '98; wraparound cover	2.99
❑Annual 1999, Aug 1999, V: Red Skull.	3.50
❑Annual 2001, Sep 2001; Indicia says X-Men 2001	3.50
❑Ashcan 1; ashcan edition	0.75

X-MEN ADVENTURES (VOL. 1)

MARVEL

	N-MINT
❑1, Nov 1992	3.00
❑2, Dec 1992	2.00
❑3, Jan 1993	2.00
❑4, Feb 1993	2.00
❑5, Mar 1993	2.00
❑6, Apr 1993, A: Sabretooth.	2.00

Magneto and Professor X's relationship prior to the events of *X-Men* (1st series) #1 were examined in the "Flashback" issue of *X-Men* (2nd series).

	N-MINT
❑7, May 1993; Slave Island, Part 1	2.00
❑8, Jun 1993; Slave Island, Part 2	2.00
❑9, Jul 1993	2.00
❑10, Aug 1993; The Muir Island Saga, Part 1	2.00
❑11, Sep 1993; The Muir Island Saga, Part 2	1.50
❑12, Oct 1993; A: Apocalypse. The Muir Island Saga, Part 3	1.50
❑13, Nov 1993; Days of Future Past, Part 1	1.50
❑14, Dec 1993; Days of Future Past, Part 2	1.50
❑15, Jan 1994; Giant-size	1.75

X-MEN ADVENTURES (VOL. 2)

MARVEL

	N-MINT
❑1, Feb 1994	2.00
❑2, Mar 1994	1.25
❑3, Apr 1994	1.25
❑4, May 1994; Marvel Mart insert	1.25
❑5, Jun 1994	1.25
❑6, Jul 1994	1.25
❑7, Aug 1994; Time Fugitives, Part 1	1.25
❑8, Sep 1994; Time Fugitives, Part 2	1.25
❑9, Oct 1994; Includes comic insert promoting collecting football cards	1.50
❑10, Nov 1994	1.50
❑11, Dec 1994	1.50
❑12, Jan 1995	1.50
❑13, Feb 1995; Reunion, Part 2	1.50

X-MEN ADVENTURES (VOL. 3)

MARVEL

	N-MINT
❑1, Mar 1995, O: Lady Deathstrike.	2.00
❑2, Apr 1995	1.50
❑3, May 1995; The Phoenix Saga, Part 1	1.50
❑4, Jun 1995; The Phoenix Saga, Part 2	1.50
❑5, Jul 1995; The Phoenix Saga, Part 3	1.50
❑6, Aug 1995; The Phoenix Saga, Part 4	1.50
❑7, Sep 1995; The Phoenix Saga, Part 5	1.50
❑8, Oct 1995	1.50
❑9, Nov 1995	1.50
❑10, Dec 1995; A: Dazzler. A: Hellfire Club. A: Jason Wyngarde. The Dark Phoenix Saga, Part 1	1.50
❑11, Jan 1996; Dark Phoenix, Part 2	1.50
❑12, Feb 1996; Dark Phoenix, Part 3	1.50
❑13, Mar 1996	1.50

X-MEN ALPHA

MARVEL

	N-MINT
❑1, Feb 1995; MWa (w); 1: X-Men (Age of Apocalypse). enhanced cover; one-shot	3.00
❑1/Gold, Feb 1995; Gold edition; MWa (w); 1: X-Men (Age of Apocalypse)	20.00

X-MEN/ALPHA FLIGHT

MARVEL

	N-MINT
❑1, Dec 1985, PS, BWi (c); PS, BWi (a); 1: The Berserkers.	3.00
❑2, Feb 1986, PS, BWi (c); PS, BWi (a)	3.00

X-MEN/ALPHA FLIGHT (2ND SERIES)

MARVEL

	N-MINT
❑1, May 1998	2.99
❑2, Jun 1998	2.99

X-MEN/ALPHA FLIGHT: THE GIFT

MARVEL

	N-MINT
❑1, May 1998	3.99

N-MINT

X-MEN & THE MICRONAUTS
MARVEL

❑1, Jan 1984; BWi (c); BWi (a); Limited Series 3.00
❑2, Feb 1984, BWi (c); BWi (a) 2.00
❑3, Mar 1984; BWi (a); centaur
❑ 2.00
❑4, Apr 1984, BWi (c); BWi (a) 1.00

X-MEN ANNIVERSARY MAGAZINE
MARVEL

❑1, Sep 1993; Celebrates 30th anniversary of the X-Men 3.95

X-MEN ARCHIVES
MARVEL

❑1, Jan 1995; BSz (a); A: Legion. Reprints New Mutants #26; cardstock cover 2.50
❑2, Jan 1995; BSz (a); A: Legion. Reprints New Mutants #27; cardstock cover 2.50
❑3, Jan 1995; BSz (a); A: Legion. Reprints New Mutants #28; cardstock cover 2.50
❑4, Jan 1995; DC (a); A: Magneto. Reprints Uncanny X-Men #161; cardstock cover 2.50

X-MEN ARCHIVES FEATURING CAPTAIN BRITAIN
MARVEL

❑1, Jul 1995; wraparound cover; reprints Captain Britain stories from British Marvel Super Heroes #377-383 .... 2.95
❑2, Aug 1995; reprints Captain Britain stories from British Marvel Super Heroes #384-88 and The Daredevils #1 .... 2.95
❑3, Sep 1995; reprints stories from The Daredevils #2-5 .... 2.95
❑4, Oct 1995; reprints stories from The Daredevils #6-8 .... 2.95
❑5, Nov 1995; reprints stories from The Daredevils #9-11 .... 2.95
❑6, Dec 1995; reprints stories from The Mighty World of Marvel #7-10 .... 2.95
❑7, Jan 1996; reprints stories from The Mighty World of Marvel #11-13 .... 2.95

X-MEN ARCHIVES SKETCHBOOK
MARVEL

❑1, Dec 2000; character sketches 2.99

X-MEN AT THE STATE FAIR
MARVEL

❑1; JR (c); KGa (a); 1: Eques. Dallas Times-Herald 2.00

X-MEN: BOOKS OF THE ASKANI
MARVEL

❑1; wraparound cardstock cover; background info on Askani'son 2.95

X-MEN: CHILDREN OF THE ATOM
MARVEL

❑1, Nov 1999; SR (c); SR (a); prequel to X-Men (first series) #1; cardstock cover 3.00
❑2, Dec 1999; SR (c); SR (a); prequel to X-Men (first series) #1; cardstock cover 3.00
❑3, Jun 2000; SR (c); SR (a); prequel to X-Men (first series) #1; cardstock cover 3.00
❑4, Jul 2000; SR (c); PS (a); prequel to X-Men (first series) #1; cardstock cover 3.00
❑5, Aug 2000; prequel to X-Men (first series) #1; cardstock cover 2.99
❑6, Sep 2000; prequel to X-Men (first series) #1; cardstock cover 2.99

X-MEN CHRONICLES (FANTACO)
FANTACO

❑1, Jul 1981, b&w; magazine DC (c) . 2.00

X-MEN CHRONICLES (MARVEL)
MARVEL

❑1, Mar 1995; Age of Apocalypse 3.95
❑2, Jun 1995; Age of Apocalypse 3.95

N-MINT

X-MEN: CLANDESTINE
MARVEL

❑1, Oct 1996; wraparound cover 2.95
❑2, Nov 1996; wraparound cover 2.95

X-MEN CLASSIC
MARVEL

❑46, Apr 1990; JBy (w); JBy (a); Series continued from Classic X-Men #45 .... 2.00
❑47, May 1990, JBy (w); JBy (a) 2.00
❑48, Jun 1990, BA (a) 2.00
❑49, Jul 1990, DC (a) 2.00
❑50, Aug 1990, DC (a) 2.00
❑51, Sep 1990; DC (a); Reprints Uncanny X-Men #147 .... 2.00
❑52, Oct 1990; DC (a); Reprints Uncanny X-Men #148 .... 2.00
❑53, Nov 1990, DC (a) 2.00
❑54, Dec 1990, DC, BWi (a) 2.00
❑55, Jan 1991; BMc (a); Reprints Uncanny X-Men #151 .... 2.00
❑56, Feb 1991; BMc (a); Reprints Uncanny X-Men #152 .... 2.00
❑57, Mar 1991, DC (a) 2.00
❑58, Apr 1991; DC, BWi (a); Reprints Uncanny X-Men #154 .... 2.00
❑59, May 1991; DC, BWi (a); Reprints Uncanny X-Men #155 .... 2.00
❑60, Jun 1991; DC, BWi (a); Reprints Uncanny X-Men #156 .... 2.00
❑61, Jul 1991, DC, BWi (a) 2.00
❑62, Aug 1991; DC, BWi (a); Reprints Uncanny X-Men #158 .... 1.75
❑63, Sep 1991; Reprints Uncanny X-Men #159 .... 1.75
❑64, Oct 1991, BA (a) 1.75
❑65, Nov 1991; DC, BWi (a); Reprints Uncanny X-Men #161 .... 1.75
❑66, Dec 1991; DC, BWi (a); Reprints Uncanny X-Men #162 .... 1.75
❑67, Jan 1992, DC, BWi (a) 1.75
❑68, Feb 1992, DC (a) 1.75
❑69, Mar 1992; PS, BWi (a); Reprints Uncanny X-Men #165 .... 1.75
❑70, Apr 1992; Giant-size PS, BWi (a) 1.75
❑71, May 1992, PS (a) 1.50
❑72, Jun 1992; (c); PS (a); Reprints Uncanny X-Men #168 .... 1.50
❑73, Jul 1992; (c); PS (a); Reprints Uncanny X-Men #169 .... 1.50
❑74, Aug 1992, PS (a) 1.50
❑75, Sep 1992; Reprints Uncanny X-Men #171 .... 1.50
❑76, Oct 1992; Reprints Uncanny X-Men #172 .... 1.50
❑77, Nov 1992; Reprints Uncanny X-Men #173 .... 1.50
❑78, Dec 1992 .... 1.50
❑79, Jan 1993; Giant-size; Reprints Uncanny X-Men #175 .... 1.75
❑80, Feb 1993; JR2 (a); 1: Valerie Cooper. Reprints Uncanny X-Men #176 1.50
❑81, Mar 1993; JR2 (a); Reprints Uncanny X-Men #177 .... 1.50
❑82, Apr 1993; JR2 (a); Reprints Uncanny X-Men #178 .... 1.50
❑83, May 1993; JR2 (a); Reprints Uncanny X-Men #179 .... 1.50
❑84, Jun 1993; JR2 (a); Reprints Uncanny X-Men #180 .... 1.50
❑85, Jul 1993; JR2 (a); Reprints Uncanny X-Men #181 .... 1.50
❑86, Aug 1993; JR2 (a); Reprints Uncanny X-Men #182 .... 1.50
❑87, Sep 1993; JR2 (a); Reprints Uncanny X-Men #183 .... 1.50
❑88, Oct 1993; JR2 (a); 1: Forge. A: Rachel. A: Selene. Reprints Uncanny X-Men #184 .... 1.50
❑89, Nov 1993; JR2 (a); Reprints Uncanny X-Men #185; Storm loses powers 1.50
❑90, Dec 1993; double-sized; Reprints Uncanny X-Men #186 .... 1.50
❑91, Jan 1994; JR2 (a); Reprints Uncanny X-Men #187 .... 1.50
❑92, Feb 1994; JR2 (a); Reprints Uncanny X-Men #188 .... 1.50

N-MINT

❑93, Mar 1994; JR2 (a); reprints Uncanny X-Men #189 .... 1.50
❑94, Apr 1994; JR2 (a); A: Spider-Man. A: Avengers. Reprints Uncanny X-Men #190 .... 1.50
❑95, May 1994; JR2 (a); A: Spider-Man. A: Avengers. Reprints Uncanny X-Men #191 .... 1.50
❑96, Jun 1994; JR2 (a); Reprints Uncanny X-Men #192 .... 1.50
❑97, Jul 1994; double-sized; JR2 (a); giant; Reprints Uncanny X-Men #193; 100th New X-Men 1.50
❑98, Aug 1994; JR2 (a); A: Juggernaut. Reprints Uncanny X-Men #194 .... 1.50
❑99, Sep 1994; JR2 (a); A: Power-Pack. Reprints Uncanny X-Men #195 .... 1.50
❑100, Oct 1994; JR2 (a); Reprints Uncanny X-Men #196 .... 1.50
❑101, Nov 1994; JR2 (a); reprints Uncanny X-Men #197 .... 1.50
❑102, Dec 1994; reprints Uncanny X-Men #198 .... 1.50
❑103, Jan 1995; JR2 (a); 1: Phoenix III (Rachel Summers). reprints Uncanny X-Men #199 .... 1.50
❑104, Feb 1995; Double-size; JR2 (a); reprints Uncanny X-Men #200 .... 1.50
❑105, Mar 1995; 1: Cable (as baby). reprints Uncanny X-Men #201; 1st Portacio art in X-Men 1.50
❑106, Apr 1995; reprints Uncanny X-Men #202 .... 1.50
❑107, May 1995; reprints Uncanny X-Men #203 .... 1.50
❑108, Jun 1995; reprints Uncanny X-Men #204 .... 1.50
❑109, Jul 1995; reprints Uncanny X-Men #205 .... 1.50
❑110, Aug 1995; reprints Uncanny X-Men #206 .... 1.50

X-MEN CLASSICS
MARVEL

❑1, Dec 1983; TP, MZ (c); NA (a); Reprints X-Men #56-58 .... 3.50
❑2, Jan 1984; TP, MZ (c); NA (a); Reprints X-Men #59-61
❑ 3.50
❑3, Feb 1984; TP, MZ (c); NA (a); Reprints X-Men #62-63 .... 3.50

X-MEN COLLECTOR'S EDITION
MARVEL

❑2; Pizza Hut giveaway in 1993; contains fold-out poster cover 1.00

X-MEN: DECLASSIFIED
MARVEL

❑1, Oct 2000 .... 3.50

X-MEN: EARTHFALL
MARVEL

❑1, Sep 1996; wraparound cover; reprints The Brood saga 2.95

X-MEN: EVOLUTION
MARVEL

❑1, Feb 2002, DGry (w) 2.25
❑2, Mar 2002, DGry (w) 2.25
❑3, Apr 2002, DGry (w) 2.25
❑4, May 2002, DGry (w) 2.25
❑5, May 2002, DGry (w) 2.25
❑6, Jun 2002, DGry (w) 2.25
❑7, Jul 2002, DGry (w) 2.25
❑8, Aug 2002, DGry (w) 2.25
❑9, Sep 2002 .... 2.25

X-MEN FIRSTS
MARVEL

❑1, Feb 1996; reprints Avengers Annual #10, Uncanny X-Men #221 and 266, and Incredible Hulk #181 .... 4.95

X-MEN FOREVER
MARVEL

❑1, Jan 2001; cardstock cover 3.50
❑2, Feb 2001; cardstock cover 3.50
❑3, Mar 2001; cardstock cover 3.50
❑4, Apr 2001; cardstock cover 3.50
❑5, May 2001; cardstock cover 3.50
❑6, Jun 2001; cardstock cover 3.50

N-MINT

X-MEN: GOD LOVES, MAN KILLS -- SPECIAL EDITION
MARVEL

❑1, ca. 2003; wraparound cover; reprints Marvel Graphic Novel #5 .. 4.99

X-MEN: HELLFIRE CLUB
MARVEL

❑1, Jan 2000 .... 2.50
❑2, Feb 2000 .... 2.50
❑3, Mar 2000 .... 2.50
❑4, Apr 2000 .... 2.50

X-MEN: LIBERATORS
MARVEL

❑1, Nov 1998 .... 2.99
❑2, Dec 1998 .... 2.99
❑3, Jan 1999 .... 2.99
❑4, Feb 1999 .... 2.99

X-MEN: LOST TALES
MARVEL

❑1, Apr 1997; reprints back-up stories from Classic X-Men #3-5 and 12 ... 3.00
❑2, Apr 1997; reprints back-up stories from Classic X-Men #10, 17, 21, and 23 .... 3.00

X-MEN: MILLENNIAL VISIONS
MARVEL

❑1, Jul 2000, JSn, BSz, KG (a) 3.99
❑1/A, Jul 2000; JSn, BSz, KG (a); Computer-generated cover 3.50

X-MEN MOVIE ADAPTATION
MARVEL

❑1, Sep 2000 .... 5.95

X-MEN MOVIE PREMIERE PREQUEL EDITION
MARVEL

❑1, Jul 2000; Toys "R" Us giveaway ... 2.00

X-MEN MOVIE PREQUEL: MAGNETO
MARVEL

❑1, Aug 2000 .... 5.95

X-MEN MOVIE PREQUEL: ROGUE
MARVEL

❑1, Aug 2000 .... 5.95
❑1/Variant, Aug 2000 .... 5.95

X-MEN MOVIE PREQUEL: WOLVERINE
MARVEL

❑1, Aug 2000 .... 5.95
❑1/Variant, Aug 2000 .... 5.95

X-MEN MUTANT SEARCH R.U. 1?
MARVEL

❑1, Aug 1998; no cover price; prototype for children's comic 2.00

X-MEN OMEGA
MARVEL

❑1, Jun 1995; JR2, KJ (c); MWa (w); AM (a); Age of Apocalypse finale; enhanced wraparound cover 6.00
❑1/Gold; Gold edition; MWa (w); AM (a); Age of Apocalypse finale; chromium cover 25.00

X-MEN: PHOENIX
MARVEL

❑1, Dec 1999 .... 2.50
❑2, Jan 2000 .... 2.50
❑3, Feb 2000 .... 2.50

X-MEN: PHOENIX -- LEGACY OF FIRE
MARVEL

❑1, Jul 2003 .... 2.99
❑2, Aug 2003 .... 2.99
❑3, Sep 2003 .... 2.99

X-MEN POSTER MAGAZINE
MARVEL

❑1 .... 4.95
❑2 .... 4.95
❑3 .... 4.95
❑4; wraparound cover 4.95

N-MINT

X-MEN PRIME
MARVEL

❑1, Jul 1995; AM, TP, CR (a); enhanced wraparound cover with acetate overlay 5.00

X-MEN RARITIES
MARVEL

❑1, Jul 1995 .... 5.95

X-MEN: ROAD TO ONSLAUGHT
MARVEL

❑1, Oct 1996; background on Onslaught's origins 2.50

X-MEN: RONIN
MARVEL

❑1, May 2003 .... 2.99
❑2, May 2003 .... 2.99
❑3, Jun 2003 .... 2.99
❑4, Jun 2003 .... 2.99
❑5, Jul 2003 .... 2.99

X-MEN SPECIAL EDITION
MARVEL

❑1, Feb 1983; reprints Giant-Size X-Men #1; DC (a); O: Storm. O: Nightcrawler. 1: X-Men (new). 1: Thunderbird. 1: Colossus. 1: Storm. 1: Nightcrawler. 1: Illyana Rasputin. ... 4.50

X-MEN SPOTLIGHT ON...STARJAMMERS
MARVEL

❑1, May 1990 .... 4.50
❑2, Jun 1990 .... 4.50

X-MEN: SURVIVAL GUIDE TO THE MANSION
MARVEL

❑1, Aug 1993; spiralbound 6.95

X-MEN: THE EARLY YEARS
MARVEL

❑1, May 1994; SL (w); JK (a); O: X-Men. Reprints X-Men (1st Series) #1 ..... 2.50
❑2, Jun 1994; SL (w); JK (a); Reprints X-Men (1st Series) #2 .... 2.00
❑3, Jul 1994; SL (w); JK (a); Reprints X-Men (1st Series) #3 .... 2.00
❑4, Aug 1994; SL (w); JK (a); Reprints X-Men (1st Series) #4 .... 2.00
❑5, Sep 1994; SL (w); JK (a); Reprints X-Men (1st Series) #5 .... 2.00
❑6, Oct 1994; SL (w); JK (a); Reprints X-Men (1st Series) #6 .... 2.00
❑7, Nov 1994; SL (w); JK (a); Reprints X-Men (1st Series) #7 .... 2.00
❑8, Dec 1994; SL (w); JK (a); Reprints X-Men (1st Series) #8 .... 2.00
❑9, Jan 1995; SL (w); JK (a); Reprints X-Men (1st Series) #9 .... 2.00
❑10, Feb 1995; SL (w); JK (a); Reprints X-Men (1st Series) #10 .... 2.00
❑11, Mar 1995; SL (w); JK (a); Reprints X-Men (1st Series) #11 .... 2.00
❑12, Apr 1995; SL (w); ATh, JK (a); Reprints X-Men (1st Series) #12 ... 2.00
❑13, May 1995; SL (w); JK (a); Reprints X-Men (1st Series) #13 .... 2.00
❑14, Jun 1995; SL (w); JK (a); Reprints X-Men (1st Series) #14 .... 2.00
❑15, Jul 1995; SL (w); JK (a); Reprints X-Men (1st Series) #15 .... 2.00
❑16, Aug 1995; SL (w); JK (a); Reprints X-Men (1st Series) #16 .... 2.00
❑17, Sep 1995; Double-size; SL (w); JK (a); Reprints X-Men (1st Series) #17 and #18 .... 2.50

X-MEN: THE HIDDEN YEARS
MARVEL

❑1, Dec 1999 .... 3.50
❑2, Jan 2000 .... 2.50
❑3, Feb 2000 .... 2.50
❑4, Mar 2000 .... 2.50
❑5, Apr 2000 .... 2.75
❑6, May 2000 .... 2.50
❑7, Jun 2000 .... 2.50
❑8, Jul 2000 .... 2.50
❑9, Aug 2000 .... 2.50
❑10, Sep 2000 .... 2.50

Events between *X-Men* #66 and #94 (1st series) were covered in John Byrne's *X-Men: The Hidden Years.*
© 1999 Marvel Characters Inc.

N-MINT

❑11, Oct 2000 .... 2.50
❑12, Nov 2000 .... 2.50
❑13, Dec 2000 .... 2.50
❑14, Jan 2001 .... 2.50
❑15, Feb 2001 .... 2.50
❑16, Mar 2001 .... 2.50
❑17, Apr 2001 .... 2.50
❑18, May 2001 .... 2.50
❑19, Jun 2001 .... 2.50
❑20, Jul 2001 .... 2.50
❑21, Aug 2001 .... 2.50
❑22, Sep 2001 .... 2.50

X-MEN: THE MAGNETO WAR
MARVEL

❑1, Mar 1999 .... 2.99

X-MEN: THE MANGA
MARVEL

❑1, Mar 1998 .... 3.00
❑2, Apr 1998 .... 2.95
❑3, Apr 1998 .... 2.95
❑4, Apr 1998 .... 2.99
❑5, May 1998 .... 2.95
❑6, May 1998 .... 2.95
❑7, Jun 1998 .... 2.95
❑8, Jul 1998; cover says Jun, indicia says Jul 2.95
❑9, Jul 1998 .... 2.95
❑10, Aug 1998 .... 2.95
❑11, Aug 1998 .... 2.95
❑12, Sep 1998 .... 2.95
❑13, Sep 1998 .... 2.95
❑14, Oct 1998 .... 2.95
❑15, Oct 1998 .... 2.95
❑16, Nov 1998; Colossus vs. Juggernaut 3.99
❑17, Nov 1998 .... 3.99
❑18, Dec 1998 .... 3.99
❑19, Dec 1998 .... 3.99
❑20, Jan 1999 .... 3.99
❑21, Jan 1999 .... 3.99
❑22, Feb 1999 .... 3.99
❑23, Feb 1999 .... 3.99
❑24, Mar 1999 .... 3.99
❑25, Mar 1999 .... 3.99
❑26, Apr 1999; Mystique apperance .. 3.99

X-MEN: THE MOVIE SPECIAL
MARVEL

❑1 .... 1.00

X-MEN: THE SEARCH FOR CYCLOPS
MARVEL

❑1, Oct 2000; Single figure (red against black background) on cover 2.99
❑1/A, Oct 2000; Alternate cover: Blue/white split background, man with glowing eyes kneeling at right 2.99
❑2, Jan 2001 .... 2.99
❑2/A, Jan 2001 .... 2.99
❑3, Feb 2001 .... 2.99
❑4, Mar 2001 .... 2.99

X-MEN: THE ULTRA COLLECTION
MARVEL

❑1, Dec 1994; Pin-ups 2.95
❑2, Jan 1995; Pin-ups 2.95
❑3, Feb 1995; Pin-ups 2.95
❑4, Mar 1995; Pin-ups 2.95
❑5, Apr 1995; Pin-ups 2.95

Condition price index: Multiply "NM prices" above by: **0.83 for Very Fine/Near Mint**
0.66 for Very Fine • 0.33 for Fine • 0.2 for Very Good • 0.125 for Good

N-MINT

X-MEN: THE WEDDING ALBUM
MARVEL

- ❑1 1994; BSz, (a); One-shot magazine 3.00

X-MEN: TRUE FRIENDS
MARVEL

- ❑1, Sep 1999 2.99
- ❑2, Oct 1999 2.99
- ❑3, Nov 1999 2.99

X-MEN 2 MOVIE
MARVEL

- ❑1, Jun 2003; adapts X2: X-Men United 3.50

X-MEN 2 MOVIE PREQUEL: NIGHTCRAWLER
MARVEL

- ❑1, May 2003 3.50

X-MEN 2 MOVIE PREQUEL: WOLVERINE
MARVEL

- ❑1, May 2003 3.50

X-MEN 2099
MARVEL

- ❑1, Oct 1993; 1: X-Men 2099. foil cover 2.00
- ❑1/Gold, Oct 1993; Gold edition; 1: X-Men 2099. foil cover 3.00
- ❑1-2, Oct 1993; 1: X-Men 2099. foil cover 1.75
- ❑2, Nov 1993 1.50
- ❑3, Dec 1993, D: Serpentina. 1.50
- ❑4, Jan 1994 1.50
- ❑5, Feb 1994 1.50
- ❑6, Mar 1994, 1: The Freakshow. 1.25
- ❑7, Apr 1994 1.25
- ❑8, May 1994 1.50
- ❑9, Jun 1994 1.50
- ❑10, Jul 1994 1.50
- ❑11, Aug 1994 1.50
- ❑12, Sep 1994 1.50
- ❑13, Oct 1994 1.50
- ❑14, Nov 1994 1.50
- ❑15, Dec 1994 1.50
- ❑16, Jan 1995 1.50
- ❑17, Feb 1995 1.50
- ❑18, Mar 1995 1.50
- ❑19, Apr 1995 1.50
- ❑20, May 1995 1.95
- ❑21, Jun 1995 1.95
- ❑22, Jul 1995 1.95
- ❑23, Aug 1995 1.95
- ❑24, Sep 1995 1.95
- ❑25, Oct 1995 2.50
- ❑25/Variant, Oct 1995; enhanced wrap-around cardstock cover 3.95
- ❑26, Nov 1995 1.95
- ❑27, Dec 1995; A: Herod. A: Doom. Story continued from 2099 Apocalypse and Doom 2099 #36 1.95
- ❑28, Jan 1996 1.95
- ❑29, Feb 1996 1.95
- ❑30, Mar 1996; Story continued in X-Nation #1 1.95
- ❑31, Apr 1996 1.95
- ❑32, May 1996, JDu (a) 1.95
- ❑33, Jun 1996, JDu (c); JDu (a) 1.95
- ❑34, Jul 1996, JDu (c); JDu (a) 1.95
- ❑35, Aug 1996; (c); JDu (a); A: Nostromo. Final Issue 1.95
- ❑Special 1, Oct 1995 3.95

X-MEN 2099: OASIS
MARVEL

- ❑1, Aug 1996 5.95

X-MEN ULTRA III PREVIEW
MARVEL

- ❑1, Nov 1995; enhanced cardstock cover; previews Fleer card art 2.95

X-MEN UNIVERSE
MARVEL

- ❑1, Dec 1999; contains material originally published as Astonishing X-Men #1, Generation X #55, and Uncanny X-Men #373 4.99
- ❑2, Jan 2000 4.99
- ❑3, Feb 2000 4.99
- ❑4, Mar 2000 4.99
- ❑5, Apr 2000 4.99
- ❑6, May 2000 4.99
- ❑7, Jun 2000 4.99
- ❑8, Jul 2000 4.99
- ❑9, Aug 2000 4.99
- ❑10, Sep 2000 4.99
- ❑11, Oct 2000 4.99
- ❑12, Nov 2000 3.99
- ❑13, Dec 2000 3.99
- ❑14, Jan 2001 3.99
- ❑15, Feb 2001 3.99
- ❑16, Mar 2001 3.99
- ❑17, Apr 2001 3.99

X-MEN UNIVERSE: PAST, PRESENT AND FUTURE
MARVEL

- ❑1, Feb 1999 2.99

X-MEN UNLIMITED
MARVEL

- ❑1, Jun 1993 3.00
- ❑2, Sep 1993 3.00
- ❑3, Dec 1993 3.00
- ❑4, Mar 1994 3.00
- ❑5, Jun 1994 3.00
- ❑6, Sep 1994 3.00
- ❑7, Dec 1994 3.00
- ❑8, Oct 1995 3.00
- ❑9, Dec 1995 3.00
- ❑10, Mar 1996; Age of Apocalypse Beast imprisons and replaces real Beast 3.00
- ❑11, Jun 1996; Magneto and Rogue 3.00
- ❑12, Sep 1996; Onslaught: Impact; Juggernaut imprisoned in Cyttorak Gem 2.95
- ❑13, Dec 1996 2.95
- ❑14, Mar 1997 2.99
- ❑15, Jun 1997; Wolverine vs. Maverick 2.99
- ❑16, Sep 1997 2.99
- ❑17, Dec 1997 2.99
- ❑18, Mar 1998 2.99
- ❑19, Jun 1998 2.99
- ❑20, Sep 1998 2.99
- ❑21, Dec 1998 2.99
- ❑22, Mar 1999 2.99
- ❑23, Jun 1999 2.99
- ❑24, Sep 1999 2.99
- ❑25, Dec 1999 2.99
- ❑26, Mar 2000; Age of Apocalypse 2.99
- ❑27, Jun 2000 2.99
- ❑28, Sep 2000 2.99
- ❑29, Dec 2000; Maximum Security 2.99
- ❑30, Mar 2001 2.99
- ❑31, Jun 2001 2.99
- ❑32, Sep 2001 3.50
- ❑33, Dec 2001 3.50
- ❑34, May 2002 3.50
- ❑35, Jun 2002 3.50
- ❑36, Jul 2002 3.50
- ❑37, Sep 2002 3.50
- ❑38, Nov 2002 3.50
- ❑39, Jan 2003 3.50
- ❑40, Feb 2003 3.50
- ❑41, Mar 2003 3.50
- ❑42, Apr 2003 3.50
- ❑43, May 2003 3.50
- ❑44, May 2003 2.50
- ❑45, Jun 2003 2.50
- ❑46, Jun 2003 2.50
- ❑47, Jul 2003 2.50
- ❑48, Jul 2003 2.50
- ❑49, Aug 2003 2.50
- ❑50, Sep 2003 2.50

X-MEN UNLIMITED (2ND SERIES)
MARVEL

- ❑1, Apr 2004 2.99
- ❑2, Jun 2004 2.99
- ❑3, Aug 2004 2.99

X-MEN VS. DRACULA
MARVEL

- ❑1, Dec 1993; BSz (a); Reprints Uncanny X-Men Annual #6 2.00

X-MEN VS. EXILES
MALIBU

- ❑0, Oct 1995; limited edition 3.00
- ❑0/Ltd., Oct 1995; Limited edition with Certificate of Authenticity; Gold foil 5.00

X-MEN VS. THE AVENGERS
MARVEL

- ❑1, Apr 1987, 1: Titanium Man II. A: Magneto. 4.00
- ❑2, May 1987, A: Magneto. 3.00
- ❑3, Jun 1987, A: Magneto. 3.00
- ❑4, Jul 1987, KP (c); KP (a); A: Magneto. 3.00

X-MEN VS. THE BROOD
MARVEL

- ❑1, Sep 1996; wraparound cover 2.95
- ❑2, Oct 1996; wraparound cover 2.95

X-MEN/WILDC.A.T.S: THE DARK AGE
MARVEL

- ❑1/A, May 1998; cardstock cover 4.50
- ❑1/B, May 1998; alternate cardstock cover 4.50

X-MEN: WRATH OF APOCALYPSE
MARVEL

- ❑1, Feb 1996; reprints X-Factor #65-68; Nathan Summers sent into future (becomes Cable) 4.95

X-MEN: YEAR OF THE MUTANTS COLLECTOR'S PREVIEW
MARVEL

- ❑1, Feb 1995, FH (w); FH (a) 2.00

X-NATION 2099
MARVEL

- ❑1, Mar 1996; foil cover 3.95
- ❑2, Apr 1996 1.95
- ❑3, May 1996 1.95
- ❑4, Jun 1996 1.95
- ❑5, Jul 1996 1.95
- ❑6, Aug 1996; Final Issue 1.95

X/1999
VIZ

- ❑1, b&w 3.00
- ❑2, b&w 2.75
- ❑3, b&w 2.75
- ❑4, b&w 2.75
- ❑5, b&w 2.75
- ❑6, b&w 2.75

X-O DATABASE
VALIANT

- ❑1; BL (a); no cover price; polybagged with X-O TPB; armor schematics 1.00

X-O MANOWAR
VALIANT

- ❑0, Aug 1993; BL (w); O: X-O Manowar. chromium cover 3.50
- ❑0/Gold; Gold logo edition; O: X-O Manowar. chromium cover 5.00
- ❑0.5; Mini-comic from Wizard Magazine 3.00
- ❑1, Feb 1992, BL (c); BL (a); O: X-O Manowar. 1: X-O Manowar armor. 1: Aric Dacia. 2.50
- ❑2, Mar 1992, BL (c) 2.50
- ❑3, Apr 1992, BL (c); A: Solar. 2.00
- ❑4, May 1992, BL (w); 1: Shadowman (cameo, out of costume). A: Harbinger. 2.00
- ❑5, Jun 1992 2.00
- ❑6, Jul 1992, BL (c); BL (w); SD (a) 2.25
- ❑7, Aug 1992, FM (c); BL (w); FM (a) 2.25
- ❑8, Sep 1992, BL (w) 2.25
- ❑9, Oct 1992, BL (w) 2.25
- ❑10, Nov 1992, BL (w) 2.25
- ❑11, Dec 1992, BL (w) 2.25
- ❑12, Jan 1993, BL (w) 2.25
- ❑13, Feb 1993, BL (w); A: Solar. 2.25
- ❑14, Mar 1993, BL (c); BL; A: Turok. 2.25

N-MINT

❑15, Apr 1993, BL (w); A: Turok. 2.25
❑16, May 1993 .... 2.25
❑17, Jun 1993, BL (c) 2.25
❑18, Jul 1993 .... 2.25
❑19, Aug 1993 .... 2.25
❑20, Sep 1993 .... 2.25
❑21, Oct 1993, BL (c) 2.25
❑22, Nov 1993 .... 2.25
❑23, Dec 1993 .... 2.25
❑24, Jan 1994 .... 2.25
❑25, Feb 1994; with Armorines #0 .... 3.50
❑26, Mar 1994 .... 2.25
❑27, Apr 1994, A: Turok. 2.25
❑28, May 1994; trading card 2.25
❑29, Jun 1994, A: Turok. 2.25
❑30, Aug 1994, A: Solar. 2.25
❑31, Sep 1994; New armor 2.25
❑32, Oct 1994 .... 2.25
❑33, Nov 1994; BL (c); Chaos Effect . 2.25
❑34, Dec 1994 .... 2.25
❑35, Jan 1995 .... 2.25
❑36, Feb 1995 .... 2.25
❑37, Mar 1995 .... 2.25
❑38, Mar 1995 .... 2.25
❑39, Mar 1995 .... 2.25
❑40, Mar 1995 .... 2.25
❑41, Apr 1995 .... 2.25
❑42, May 1995; V: Shadowman. contains Birthquake preview 2.25
❑43, Jun 1995 .... 2.25
❑44, Jul 1995; Birthquake 2.50
❑45, Jul 1995; Birthquake 2.50
❑46, Aug 1995 .... 2.50
❑47, Aug 1995, D: Ken Clarkson. 2.50
❑48, Sep 1995 .... 2.50
❑49, Sep 1995 .... 2.50
❑50, Oct 1995; cover forms diptych with X-O Manowar #50-O 2.50
❑50/A, Oct 1995; cover forms diptych with X-O Manowar #50-X 2.50
❑51, Nov 1995 .... 2.50
❑52, Nov 1995 .... 2.50
❑53, Dec 1995 .... 2.50
❑54, Dec 1995 .... 2.50
❑55, Jan 1996 .... 2.50
❑56, Jan 1996 .... 2.50
❑57, Feb 1996 .... 2.50
❑58, Feb 1996, KG (w) 2.50
❑59, Mar 1996, KG (w) 2.50
❑60, Mar 1996, KG, BL (w) 2.50
❑61, Apr 1996, KG (w) 2.50
❑62, Apr 1996, KG (w) 2.50
❑63, May 1996; KG (w); Master Darque acquires X-O armor 2.50
❑64, May 1996, KG (w); PG (a); D: Master Darque. 2.50
❑65, Jun 1996; KG (w); X-O armor asserts control over itself 2.50
❑66, Jul 1996; BL (w); D: Ax. D: Gamin. Aric's armor rebels 2.50
❑67, Aug 1996, BL (w) 2.50
❑68, Sep 1996, BL (w) 2.50
❑Yearbook 1, Apr 1995 .... 2.95

X-O MANOWAR (VOL. 2)
ACCLAIM

❑1, Oct 1996; MWa (w); D: Rand Banion. cover says Feb, indicia says Oct 96 .. 2.50
❑1/A, Oct 1996; alternate cover 2.50
❑1/Variant, Oct 1996; MWa (w); Painted cover 2.50
❑2, Mar 1997; MWa (w); Donovan Wylie becomes X-O 2.50
❑3, Apr 1997, MWa (w) 2.50
❑4, May 1997, MWa (w) 2.50
❑5, Jun 1997, MWa (w) 2.50
❑6, Jul 1997, MWa (w); V: Magnus. .. 2.50
❑7, Aug 1997, A: New Hard Corps. ... 2.50
❑8, Sep 1997 .... 2.50
❑9, Oct 1997 .... 2.50
❑10, Nov 1997; A: Bravado. Avengers #3 homage cover 2.50
❑11, Dec 1997 .... 2.50
❑12, Jan 1998 .... 2.50

N-MINT

❑13, Feb 1998 .... 2.50
❑14, Mar 1998 .... 2.50
❑15, Apr 1998 .... 2.50
❑16, Jan 1998; V: Quantum & Woody. no cover date, indicia says Jan 2.50
❑17, Feb 1998 .... 2.50
❑18, Mar 1998; return of Rand Banion 2.50
❑19, Apr 1998, 1: Master Blaster. 2.50
❑20, May 1998 .... 2.50
❑21, Jun 1998 .... 2.50
❑Ashcan 1, Oct 1996, b&w; no cover price; preview of upcoming series . 1.00

X-O MANOWAR/IRON MAN: IN HEAVY METAL
ACCLAIM / VALIANT

❑1, Sep 1996; crossover with Marvel; concludes in Iron Man/X-O Manowar: In Heavy Metal 2.50

XOMBI
DC / MILESTONE

❑0, Jan 1994; 1: Xombi. Shadow War 2.50
❑1, Jun 1994, O: Xombi. 1: Catholic Girl. 1: Nun of the Above. 2.00
❑1/Platinum, Jun 1994; Platinum cover 3.00
❑2, Jul 1994, 1: Knight of the Spoken Fire. 1.75
❑3, Aug 1994 .... 1.75
❑4, Sep 1994 .... 1.75
❑5, Oct 1994 .... 1.75
❑6, Nov 1994 .... 1.75
❑7, Dec 1994 .... 1.75
❑8, Jan 1995 .... 1.75
❑9, Feb 1995 .... 1.75
❑10, Mar 1995 .... 1.75
❑11, Apr 1995 .... 1.75
❑12, May 1995 .... 1.75
❑13, Jun 1995 .... 1.75
❑14, Jul 1995 .... 2.50
❑15, Aug 1995 .... 2.50
❑16, Sep 1995 .... 2.50
❑17, Oct 1995 .... 0.99
❑18, Nov 1995 .... 2.50
❑19, Dec 1995 .... 2.50
❑20, Jan 1996 .... 2.50
❑21, Feb 1996; Giant-size 3.50

X: ONE SHOT TO THE HEAD
DARK HORSE

❑1, Aug 1994, b&w 2.50

X-PATROL
MARVEL / AMALGAM

❑1, Apr 1996 .... 1.95

X-PRESIDENTS
RANDOM HOUSE

❑1, Sep 2000 .... 12.95

X-RAY COMICS
SLAVE LABOR / AMALGAM

❑1, Feb 1998 .... 2.95
❑2, May 1998 .... 2.95
❑3, Apr 1998 .... 2.95

XSE
MARVEL

❑1, Nov 1996, A: Bishop and Shard. . 1.95
❑1/A, Nov 1996; A: Bishop and Shard. variant cover 2.50
❑2, Dec 1996, A: Bishop and Shard. . 1.95
❑3, Jan 1997, A: Bishop and Shard. .. 1.95
❑4, Feb 1997; A: Bishop and Shard. final issue 1.95

XSTACY: THE FIRST LOOK EDITION
FRESCO

❑1, b&w; promotional comic book sold at convention; also collects cartoons that ran in CBG 2.95

XSTACY: THE LIBRETTO
FRESCO

❑1, b&w 2.95

X-STATIX
MARVEL

❑1, Sep 2002 .... 2.99
❑2, Oct 2002 .... 2.25

The X-O Database was bundled with the *X-O Manowar* trade paperback.
© 1995 Voyager Communications Inc. (Valiant).

N-MINT

❑3, Nov 2002 .... 2.25
❑4, Dec 2002 .... 2.25
❑5, Jan 2003 .... 2.25
❑6, Feb 2003 .... 2.25
❑7, Mar 2003 .... 2.25
❑8, Apr 2003 .... 2.99
❑9, May 2003 .... 2.99
❑10, Jun 2003 .... 2.99
❑11, Aug 2003 .... 2.99
❑12, Sep 2003 .... 2.99
❑13, Oct 2003 .... 2.99
❑14, Nov 2003 .... 2.99
❑15, Dec 2003 .... 2.99
❑16, Jan 2004 .... 2.99
❑17, Feb 2004 .... 2.99
❑18, Mar 2004 .... 2.99
❑19, Apr 2004 .... 2.99
❑20, May 2004 .... 2.99
❑21, Jun 2004; vs Avengers 2.99
❑22, Jun 2004; vs. Avengers 2.99
❑23, Jul 2004 .... 2.99
❑24, Aug 2004 .... 2.99
❑25, Sep 2004 .... 2.99

X-TERMINATORS
MARVEL

❑1, Oct 1988; 1: X-Terminators. Inferno 2.00
❑2, Nov 1988; Inferno 2.00
❑3, Dec 1988; Inferno 2.00
❑4, Jan 1989; Inferno 2.00

X, THE MAN WITH X-RAY EYES
GOLD KEY

❑1, Sep 1963; Cover says "X, The Man With the X-Ray Eyes," indicia says "X, The Man With X-Ray Eyes" 50.00

X-TREME X-MEN
MARVEL

❑1, Jul 2001 .... 2.99
❑2, Aug 2001 .... 2.99
❑2/A, Aug 2001; Group Cover 2.99
❑2/B, Aug 2001; Psylocke Cover 2.99
❑3, Sep 2001 .... 2.99
❑4, Oct 2001 .... 2.99
❑5, Nov 2001 .... 2.99
❑6, Dec 2001 .... 2.99
❑7, Jan 2001 .... 2.99
❑8, Feb 2001 .... 2.99
❑9, Mar 2002 .... 2.99
❑10, Apr 2002 .... 2.99
❑11, May 2002 .... 2.99
❑12, Jun 2002 .... 2.99
❑13, Jul 2002 .... 2.99
❑14, Aug 2002 .... 2.99
❑15, Sep 2002 .... 2.99
❑16, Sep 2002 .... 2.99
❑17, Oct 2002 .... 2.99
❑18, Nov 2002 .... 2.99
❑19, Dec 2002 .... 2.99
❑20, Mar 2003 .... 2.99
❑21, Apr 2003 .... 2.99
❑22, May 2003 .... 2.99
❑23, May 2003 .... 2.99
❑24, Jun 2003 .... 2.99
❑25, Jul 2003 .... 2.99
❑26, Jul 2003 .... 2.99
❑27, Aug 2003 .... 2.99
❑28, Sep 2003 .... 2.99
❑29, Oct 2003 .... 2.99

	N-MINT
❑30, Oct 2003	2.99
❑31, Nov 2003	2.99
❑32, Dec 2003	2.99
❑33, Dec 2003	2.99
❑34, Jan 2004	2.99
❑35, Jan 2004	2.99
❑36, Feb 2004	3.50
❑37, Feb 2004	3.50
❑38, Feb 2004	3.50
❑39, Feb 2004	3.50
❑40, Mar 2004	2.99
❑41, Apr 2004	2.99
❑42, Apr 2004	2.99
❑43, May 2004	2.99
❑44, May 2004	2.99
❑45, Jun 2004	2.99
❑46, Jun 2004	2.99
❑Annual 2001, Dec 2001	4.95

X-TREME X-MEN: SAVAGE LAND
MARVEL

❑1, Nov 2001	2.99
❑2, Dec 2001	2.99
❑3, Jan 2001	2.99
❑4, Feb 2001	2.99

X-TREME X-MEN X-POSE
MARVEL

❑1, Jan 2003	2.99
❑2, Feb 2003	2.99

X-TV
COMIC ZONE

❑1, b&w	2.95
❑2, b&w	2.95

X-UNIVERSE
MARVEL

❑1, May 1995; After Xavier: The Age of Apocalypse; foil cover	3.50
❑2, Jun 1995; After Xavier: The Age of Apocalypse; foil cover	3.50

XXXENOPHILE
PALLIARD

❑1, b&w; PF (w); PF (a); It's Not Cheap, But It Is Easy	8.00
❑1-2, Jun 1989, b&w; PF (c); PF (w); PF (a); It's Not Cheap, But It Is Easy	2.50
❑2, Dec 1989, b&w PF (w); PF (a)	5.00
❑2-2, Jun 1991, b&w; PF (c); PF (w); PF (a); Tales of One Fisted Adventure; 2nd Printing	2.50
❑3, Jul 1990, b&w PF (w); PF (a)	4.00
❑3-2, Mar 1992, b&w; PF (w); PF (a); Just Plane Sex; 2nd Printing	2.50
❑4, Feb 1991, b&w; PF (w); PF (a); Practicing Safe Sex Until We Get It Right	4.00
❑4-2, b&w; PF (w); PF (a); 2nd printing	2.95
❑5, Jul 1991, b&w; PF (c); PF (w); PF (a); Bringing Good Things To Life	2.95
❑6, Feb 1992, b&w; PF (c); PF (w); PF (a); Giving The Public What I Want	2.95
❑7, Jul 1992, b&w; PF (c); PF (w); PF (a); It's Okay, It's Art	2.95
❑8, Feb 1993, b&w; PF (c); PF (w); PF (a); The Comic in the Fancy Brown Paper Wrapper	2.95
❑9, Jan 1994, b&w; PF (w); PF (a); The Adventures of Le Petit Mort	2.95
❑10, Jan 1995, b&w; PF (c); PF (w); PF (a); trading-card game cover; led to Xxxenophile card game	2.95
❑11, Sep 1998, b&w; PF (c); PF (w); PF (a); If You're so smart, why aren't you naked?; New material from Books 1-5	2.95

XXXENOPHILE PRESENTS
PALLIARD

❑1, Apr 1992, b&w	2.95
❑2, Feb 1993, b&w	2.95
❑3, Aug 1994, b&w	2.95
❑4, Jul 1995, b&w	2.95

XXX WOMEN
FANTAGRAPHICS / EROS

❑1, b&w	2.95
❑2, b&w	2.95

	N-MINT
❑3, b&w	2.95
❑4, b&w	2.95

XYZ COMICS
KITCHEN SINK

❑1, Jun 1972, b&w	25.00
❑1-2, b&w	12.00
❑1-3, b&w	8.00
❑1-4, b&w	6.00
❑1-5, b&w	6.00
❑1-6, b&w; sixth printing	5.00
❑1-7, Jan 1987, b&w; seventh printing	3.00

Y

Y2K: THE COMIC
NEC

❑1, Oct 1999	3.95

YAHOO
FANTAGRAPHICS

❑1, Oct 1988	2.50
❑2, Oct 1989; In the Company of Longhair	2.25
❑3, Apr 1990	2.00
❑4, Jan 1991; Airpower Through Victory	2.50
❑5, Dec 1991	2.50
❑6, Aug 1992; Take It Off (Topless cover)	2.50

YAKUZA
ETERNITY

❑1, Sep 1987	1.95
❑2, Nov 1987	1.95
❑3, Jan 1988	1.95
❑4, Apr 1988	1.95

YAMARA
STEVE JACKSON GAMES

❑1, b&w; magazine-sized; collects strips from Dragon	9.95

YARN MAN
KITCHEN SINK

❑1, Oct 1989, b&w	2.00

YAWN
PARODY

❑1, b&w; Spawn parody	2.50
❑1-2, b&w	2.50

YEAH!
DC / HOMAGE

❑1, Oct 1999	2.95
❑2, Nov 1999; all copies destroyed	2.95
❑3, Dec 1999	2.95
❑4, Jan 2000	2.95
❑5, Feb 2000	2.95
❑6, Mar 2000	2.95
❑7, Apr 2000	2.95
❑8, May 2000	2.95

YEAR IN REVIEW: SPIDER-MAN
MARVEL

❑1, Feb 2000	2.99

YEAR OF THE MONKEY (AARON WARNER'S...)
IMAGE / HOMAGE

❑1	2.95
❑2, Oct 1997	2.95

YELLOW SUBMARINE
GOLD KEY

❑1, Feb 1969; adapts movie; poster	110.00

YIKES! (WEISSMAN)
WEISSMAN

❑1, b&w	2.50
❑2, b&w	2.50
❑3, b&w	2.50
❑4, Win 1995, b&w	2.50
❑5; b&w with spot color	2.50

YIKES! (ALTERNATIVE)
ALTERNATIVE

❑1, Nov 1997, b&w; green and white	2.95
❑2, b&w	2.95

YIN FEI THE CHINESE NINJA
DR. LEUNG'S

	N-MINT
❑1, ca. 1988	1.80
❑2	1.80
❑3	1.80
❑4	1.80
❑5	1.80
❑6	1.80
❑7	2.00
❑8	2.00

YOGI BEAR (CHARLTON)
CHARLTON

❑1, Nov 1970	22.00
❑2	15.00
❑3	15.00
❑4, May 1971	12.00
❑5 1971	12.00
❑6 1971	12.00
❑7, Sum 1971	15.00
❑8	12.00
❑9, Feb 1972	12.00
❑10, Mar 1972	12.00
❑11 1972	8.00
❑12 1972	8.00
❑13 1972	8.00
❑14 1972	8.00
❑15	8.00
❑16	8.00
❑17	8.00
❑18, Jun 1973	8.00
❑19 1973	8.00
❑20, Oct 1973	8.00
❑21, Dec 1973	6.00
❑22, Sep 1974	6.00
❑23 1974	6.00
❑24, Feb 1975	6.00
❑25, Apr 1975	6.00
❑26, Jun 1975	6.00
❑27, Aug 1975	6.00
❑28, Oct 1975	6.00
❑29, Dec 1975	6.00
❑30, Feb 1976	6.00
❑31, Apr 1976	6.00
❑32 1976	6.00
❑33, Sep 1976	6.00
❑34	6.00
❑35	6.00

YOGI BEAR (DELL/GOLD KEY)
DELL / GOLD KEY

❑4, Sep 1961	40.00
❑5, Nov 1961	40.00
❑6, Jan 1962	40.00
❑7, Mar 1962	40.00
❑8, May 1962	40.00
❑9, Jul 1962; Last Dell issue	40.00
❑10, Oct 1962; Jellystone Jollies	55.00
❑11, Jan 1963; Jellystone Jollies (Christmas issue)	55.00
❑12, Apr 1963; Jellystone Album	30.00
❑13, Jul 1963; Surprise Party	55.00
❑14, Oct 1963	30.00
❑15, Jan 1964	30.00
❑16, Apr 1964	30.00
❑17, Jul 1964	30.00
❑18, Oct 1964	30.00
❑19, Jan 1965	30.00
❑20, Apr 1965	30.00
❑21, Jul 1965	20.00
❑22, Oct 1965	20.00
❑23, Jan 1966	20.00
❑24, Apr 1966	20.00
❑25, Jul 1966	20.00
❑26, Oct 1966	20.00
❑27, Jan 1967	20.00
❑28, Apr 1967	20.00
❑29, Jul 1967	20.00
❑30, Oct 1967	20.00
❑31, Jan 1968	20.00
❑32, Apr 1968	15.00
❑33, Jul 1968	15.00
❑34, Oct 1968	15.00

N-MINT

❑35, Jan 1969 ... 15.00
❑36, Apr 1969 ... 15.00
❑37, Jul 1969 ... 15.00
❑38, Oct 1969 ... 15.00
❑39, Jan 1970 ... 15.00
❑40, Apr 1970 ... 15.00
❑41, Jul 1970 ... 15.00
❑42, Oct 1970 ... 15.00

YOGI BEAR (MARVEL)
MARVEL

❑1, Nov 1977 ... 6.00
❑2, Jan 1978 ... 4.00
❑3, Mar 1978 ... 4.00
❑4, May 1978 ... 4.00
❑5, Jul 1978 ... 4.00
❑6, Sep 1978 ... 3.00
❑7, Nov 1978 ... 3.00
❑8, Jan 1979 ... 3.00
❑9, Mar 1979 ... 3.00

YOGI BEAR (HARVEY)
HARVEY

❑1, Sep 1992; No creator credits listed 1.50
❑2, Jan 1993; No creator credits listed 1.25
❑3, Jun 1993; No creator credits listed 1.25
❑4, Sep 1993; No creator credits listed 1.25
❑5, Dec 1993; No creator credits listed 1.25
❑6, Mar 1994; No creator credits listed 1.25

YOGI BEAR (ARCHIE)
ARCHIE

❑1, May 1997 ... 1.50

YOGI BEAR BIG BOOK
HARVEY

❑1, Nov 1992 ... 1.95
❑2, Mar 1993 ... 1.95

YOGI BEAR GIANT SIZE
HARVEY

❑1, Oct 1992 ... 2.25
❑2, Apr 1993 ... 2.25

YOSEMITE SAM
GOLD KEY / WHITMAN

❑1, Dec 1970 ... 12.00
❑2, Mar 1971 ... 9.00
❑3, Jun 1971 ... 9.00
❑4, Sep 1971 ... 9.00
❑5, Nov 1971 ... 9.00
❑6, Mar 1972 ... 7.50
❑7 1972 ... 7.50
❑8, Jun 1972 ... 7.50
❑9, Aug 1972 ... 7.50
❑10, Oct 1972 ... 7.50
❑11, Dec 1972 ... 5.00
❑12, Feb 1973 ... 5.00
❑13, Mar 1973 ... 5.00
❑14 1973 ... 5.00
❑15 1973 ... 5.00
❑16 1973 ... 5.00
❑17, Oct 1973 ... 5.00
❑18, Dec 1973 ... 5.00
❑19, Feb 1974 ... 5.00
❑20, Apr 1974 ... 5.00
❑21 1974 ... 4.00
❑22 1974 ... 4.00
❑23 1974 ... 4.00
❑24 1974 ... 4.00
❑25, Dec 1974 ... 4.00
❑26, Feb 1975 ... 4.00
❑27, Apr 1975 ... 4.00
❑28, Jun 1975 ... 4.00
❑29, Jul 1975 ... 4.00
❑30, Aug 1975 ... 4.00
❑31, Sep 1975 ... 4.00
❑32, Oct 1975 ... 4.00
❑33, Dec 1975 ... 4.00
❑34, Feb 1976 ... 4.00
❑35, Apr 1976 ... 4.00
❑36, Jun 1976 ... 4.00
❑37, Jul 1976 ... 4.00
❑38, Aug 1976 ... 4.00
❑39, Sep 1976 ... 4.00
❑40, Oct 1976 ... 4.00

N-MINT

❑41, Dec 1976 ... 4.00
❑42, Feb 1977 ... 4.00
❑43, Apr 1977 ... 4.00
❑44, Jun 1977 ... 4.00
❑45, Jul 1977 ... 4.00
❑46, Aug 1977 ... 4.00
❑47, Sep 1977 ... 4.00
❑48, Oct 1977 ... 4.00
❑49, Dec 1977 ... 4.00
❑50, Feb 1978 ... 4.00
❑51, Apr 1978 ... 2.50
❑52, Jun 1978 ... 2.50
❑53, Jul 1978 ... 2.50
❑54, Aug 1978 ... 2.50
❑55, Sep 1978 ... 2.50
❑56, Oct 1978 ... 2.50
❑57, Dec 1978 ... 2.50
❑58, Feb 1979 ... 2.50
❑59, Apr 1979 ... 2.50
❑60, Jun 1979 ... 2.50
❑61, Jul 1979 ... 2.50
❑62, Aug 1979 ... 2.50
❑63, Sep 1979 ... 2.50
❑64, Oct 1979 ... 2.50
❑65, Dec 1979 ... 2.50
❑66 1980 ... 2.50
❑67 1980 ... 2.50
❑68 1980 ... 2.50
❑69 1980 ... 2.50
❑70 1980 ... 2.50
❑71, Feb 1981 ... 2.50
❑72 1981 ... 2.50
❑73, Sep 1981 ... 2.50
❑74, Oct 1981 ... 2.50
❑75, Jan 1982 ... 2.50
❑76, Feb 1982 ... 2.50
❑77, Mar 1982 ... 2.50
❑78, Apr 1982 ... 2.50
❑79, Jul 1983 ... 2.50
❑80, Aug 1983 ... 2.50
❑81, Feb 1984 ... 2.50

YOU AND YOUR BIG MOUTH
FANTAGRAPHICS

❑1, b&w ... 2.50
❑2, b&w ... 2.50
❑3, b&w ... 2.50
❑4, Aug 1994, b&w ... 2.50

YOU CAN DRAW MANGA
ANTARCTIC

❑1, Feb 2004 ... 4.95
❑2, Mar 2004 ... 4.95
❑3, Apr 2004 ... 4.95
❑4, May 2004 ... 4.95

YOUNG ALL-STARS, THE
DC

❑1, Jun 1987; 1: Iron Munroe & Flying Fox. 1: Iron Munroe, 1: Flying Fox . 3.00
❑2, Jul 1987; Tsunami ... 2.50
❑3, Aug 1987; Flying Fox ... 2.50
❑4, Sep 1987 ... 1.75
❑5, Oct 1987; Fury ... 1.75
❑6, Nov 1987; Dyna-Mite ... 1.75
❑7, Dec 1987 ... 1.50
❑8, Jan 1988; Millennium ... 1.50
❑9, Feb 1988; Millennium ... 1.50
❑10, Mar 1988, O: Iron Munro. ... 1.50
❑11, Apr 1988, O: Iron Munro. ... 1.50
❑12, May 1988 ... 1.50
❑13, Jun 1988 ... 1.50
❑14, Jul 1988 ... 1.50
❑15, Aug 1988 ... 1.50
❑16, Sep 1988, O: Neptune Perkins. . 1.50
❑17, Oct 1988, O: Neptune Perkins. .. 1.50
❑18, Nov 1988 ... 1.50
❑19, Dec 1988 ... 1.75
❑20, Dec 1988, TD (a); O: Flying Fox. 1.75
❑21, Jan 1988 ... 1.75
❑22, Jan 1989 ... 1.75
❑23, Mar 1989 ... 1.75
❑24, Apr 1989 ... 1.75
❑25, May 1989 ... 1.75

Yosemite Sam had a long-running solo series, something his fellow Bugs Bunny foe, Elmer Fudd, never achieved.
© 1975 Gold Key.

N-MINT

❑26, Jun 1989 ... 1.75
❑27, Jul 1989 ... 1.75
❑28, Aug 1989 ... 1.75
❑29, Sep 1989 ... 1.75
❑30, Oct 1989 ... 1.75
❑31, Nov 1989 ... 1.75
❑Annual 1, ca. 1988; MGu (a); A: Infinity Inc.. 1988; Private Lives ... 2.00

YOUNGBLOOD
IMAGE

❑0, Dec 1992; RL (w); RL (a); wraparound cover ... 2.00
❑0/Gold, Dec 1992; RL (a); gold ... 4.00
❑1, Apr 1992; Flip-book; RL (w); RL (a); 1: Chapel. 1: Youngblood. 1: The Four. trading card; First comic by Image Comics ... 2.50
❑1-2, May 1992; RL (w); RL (a); 1: Chapel. 1: Youngblood. 1: The Four. gold border; First comic by Image Comics ... 2.00
❑2, Jul 1992; RL (w); RL (a); 1: Kirby. 1: Shadowhawk. 1: Darkthorn. 1: Prophet. 1: Berserkers. red logo; cover says Jun, indicia says Jul 2.50
❑2/A, Jul 1992; RL (w); RL (a); 1: Kirby. 1: Shadowhawk. 1: Darkthorn. 1: Prophet. 1: Berserkers. green logo; cover says Jun, indicia says Jul 2.50
❑3, Aug 1992; Flip-book RL (w); RL (a); 1: Showdown. 1: Supreme. ... 2.50
❑4, Feb 1993, RL (w); RL (a); 1: Pitt. 2.50
❑5, Jul 1993; backed with Brigade #4 2.00
❑6, Jun 1994 ... 3.50
❑7, Jul 1994 ... 2.50
❑8, Sep 1994 ... 2.50
❑9, Sep 1994; Image X-Month ... 2.50
❑9/A, Sep 1994; Image X-Month ... 2.50
❑10, Dec 1994, A: Spawn. D: Chapel. 2.50
❑SS 1; Super Special ... 2.99
❑Yearbook 1, Jul 1993; 1: Kanan. 1: Tyrax. ... 2.50

YOUNGBLOOD (VOL. 2)
IMAGE

❑1, Sep 1995 ... 2.50
❑2, Oct 1995 ... 2.50
❑2/A, Oct 1995; alternate cover ... 2.50
❑3, Nov 1995; Babewatch ... 2.50
❑3/A, Nov 1995; Shaft cover ... 2.50
❑3/B, Nov 1995; Cougar cover ... 2.50
❑3/C, Nov 1995; Knightsabre cover ... 2.50
❑4, Jan 1996; polybagged with Riptide card ... 2.50
❑5, Feb 1996 ... 2.50
❑5/A, Feb 1996; alternate cover ... 2.50
❑6, Mar 1996 ... 2.50
❑7, Apr 1996; Shadowhunt ... 2.50
❑8, May 1996 ... 2.50
❑9, Jun 1996 ... 2.50
❑10, Jul 1996; flipbook with Blindside #1 preview ... 2.50
❑11 ... 2.50
❑12 ... 2.50
❑13 ... 2.50
❑14 ... 2.50
❑15 ... 2.50

N-MINT

YOUNGBLOOD (VOL. 3)
AWESOME

- ❑1/A, Feb 1998; AMo (w); Blue Awesome logo, Orange Youngblood logo 2.50
- ❑1/B, Feb 1998; AMo (w); Purple Awesome and Youngblood logos 2.50
- ❑1/C, Feb 1998; AMo (w); Teal Awesome and Youngblood logos 2.50
- ❑1/D, Feb 1998; AMo (w); White Awesome logo, Yellow Youngblood logo; Shaft in foreground 2.50
- ❑1/E, Feb 1998; AMo (w); Blue Awesome logo, White Youngblood logo 2.50
- ❑1/F, Feb 1998; AMo (w); White Awesome and Youngblood logos 2.50
- ❑1/G, Feb 1998; AMo (w); White Awesome logo, Yellow Youngblood logo; Suprema in foreground 2.50
- ❑1/H, Feb 1998; AMo (w); Baby Shaft on cover; Blue Awesome logo 2.50
- ❑1/I, Feb 1998; AMo (w); Orange Awesome logo, Red Youngblood logo 2.50
- ❑1/J, Feb 1998; AMo (w); White Awesome logo, Teal Youngblood logo; Suprema in foreground 2.50
- ❑1/K, Feb 1998; AMo (w); 3 women on cover; White Awesome logo, Teal Youngblood logo 2.50
- ❑1/L, Feb 1998; AMo (w); Teal Awesome logo, Yellow Youngblood logo 2.50
- ❑1/M, Feb 1998; AMo (w); A! List exclusive; Foil logo; Three women posing on cover, leaning against wall 3.50
- ❑1/N; AMo (w); 1+ issue 2.50
- ❑2, Aug 1998, AMo (w) 2.50

YOUNGBLOOD BATTLEZONE
IMAGE

- ❑1, Apr 1993; Diagrams and schematics of team headquarters, vehicles and equipment; Cover says May, indicia says April 1.95
- ❑2, Jul 1994 2.95

YOUNGBLOOD: STRIKEFILE
IMAGE

- ❑1, Apr 1993, 1: The Allies. 1: Giger. 1: Glory. 2.50
- ❑1/Gold, Apr 1993; Gold edition 2.50
- ❑2, Jul 1993, RL (a) 2.50
- ❑2/Gold, Jul 1993; Gold edition 2.50
- ❑3, Sep 1993 2.50
- ❑4, Oct 1993 2.50
- ❑5, Jul 1994 2.50
- ❑6, Aug 1994 2.50
- ❑7, Sep 1994 2.50
- ❑8, Nov 1994; KB (w); Busiek short story; cover says Oct 2.50
- ❑9, Nov 1994 2.50
- ❑10, Dec 1994 2.50
- ❑11, Feb 1995; polybagged with card 2.50

YOUNGBLOOD/X-FORCE
IMAGE

- ❑1/A, Jul 1996; prestige format; crossover with Marvel 4.95
- ❑1/B, Jul 1996; alternate cover (black background) 4.95
- ❑1/C, Jul 1996; alternate cover 4.95

YOUNGBROADS: STRIPFILE
PARODY

- ❑1, foil cover 2.50

YOUNGBROTHER
MULTICULTURAL

- ❑1, Apr 1994 2.25

YOUNG BUG
ZOO ARSONIST

- ❑1 2.95
- ❑2 2.95
- ❑3 2.95

YOUNG CYNICS CLUB, THE
DARK HORSE

- ❑1, Mar 1993, b&w 2.50

YOUNG DEATH
FLEETWAY-QUALITY

- ❑1 2.95
- ❑2 2.95
- ❑3 2.95

YOUNG DRACULA
CALIBER

- ❑1, b&w 3.50
- ❑2, b&w 3.50
- ❑3, ca. 1993, b&w; indicia says #2 3.50

YOUNG DRACULA: PRAYER OF THE VAMPIRE
BONEYARD

- ❑1 2.95
- ❑2, Feb 1998 2.95
- ❑3 2.95
- ❑4 2.95

YOUNG GIRL ON GIRL: PASSION AND FASHION
ANGEL

- ❑1 3.00
- ❑1/Nude; Nude edition 3.95

YOUNG GUN
AC

- ❑1, b&w; reprints Billy the Kid story 2.95

YOUNG HERO
AC

- ❑1, Dec 1989, b&w; reprints Daredevil #72 (1950) 2.50
- ❑2, Aug 1990, b&w; reprints Little Wise Guys 2.75

YOUNG HEROES IN LOVE
DC

- ❑1, Jun 1997, 1: Young Heroes. 1.75
- ❑1/Ltd., Jun 1997; Wizard "Certified Authentic" edition 6.00
- ❑2, Jul 1997 1.75
- ❑3, Aug 1997, A: Superman. 1.75
- ❑4, Sep 1997 1.75
- ❑5, Oct 1997; Genesis 1.75
- ❑6, Nov 1997 1.75
- ❑7, Dec 1997; Face cover 1.95
- ❑8, Jan 1998, V: Scarecrow. 1.95
- ❑9, Feb 1998 1.95
- ❑10, Mar 1998 1.95
- ❑11, Apr 1998 1.95
- ❑12, May 1998 1.95
- ❑13, Jun 1998 1.95
- ❑14, Jul 1998 1.95
- ❑15, Aug 1998 1.95
- ❑16, Sep 1998 1.95
- ❑17, Oct 1998 2.50
- ❑1000000, Nov 1998 3.00

YOUNG INDIANA JONES CHRONICLES, THE
DARK HORSE

- ❑1, Feb 1992; A: T.E. Lawrence. Kurt Busiek (text piece) 3.00
- ❑2, Mar 1992; A: Pancho Villa. Kurt Busiek (text piece) 2.50
- ❑3, Apr 1992; GM (a); A: Teddy Roosevelt. Kurt Busiek (text piece) 2.50
- ❑4, May 1992; GM (a); Kurt Busiek (text piece) 2.50
- ❑5, Jun 1992; Kurt Busiek (text piece) 2.50
- ❑6, Jul 1992; Kurt Busiek (text piece) 2.50
- ❑7, Aug 1992; Kurt Busiek (text piece) 2.50
- ❑8, Sep 1992; Kurt Busiek (text piece) 2.50
- ❑9, Oct 1992; Kurt Busiek (text piece) 2.50
- ❑10, Dec 1992; Kurt Busiek (text piece) 2.50
- ❑11, Jan 1993; Kurt Busiek (text piece) 2.50
- ❑12, Feb 1993 2.50

YOUNG INDIANA JONES CHRONICLES, THE (2ND SERIES)
HOLLYWOOD

- ❑1, ca. 1992; reprints Dark Horse issues #1 and 2 for newsstand distribution 2.50
- ❑2, ca. 1992; reprints Dark Horse issues #3 and 4 for newsstand distribution 2.50
- ❑3 2.50

YOUNG JUSTICE
DC

- ❑1, Sep 1998, PD (w); 1: Supercycle. 1: Mighty Endowed. A: Superboy. A: Martian Manhunter. A: Impulse. A: Robin. 4.00
- ❑2, Oct 1998, PD (w); 1: Rip Roar. A: Ali Ben Styn. 3.00
- ❑3, Dec 1998, PD (w); A: Mr. Mxyzptlk. 3.00
- ❑4, Jan 1999, PD (w); 1: Harm. 1: Tora. A: Wonder Girl. A: Spirit. A: Arrowette. V: Harm. 3.00
- ❑5, Feb 1999, PD (w); V: Harm. 3.00
- ❑6, Mar 1999, PD (w); A: Wonder Woman. A: Superman. A: Justice League of America. A: Flash III (Wally West). A: Martian Manhunter. A: Green Lantern. A: Batman. A: Aquaman. A: Despero. 2.50
- ❑7, Apr 1999; PD (w); A: Nightwing. A: Max Mercury. Parent/Teacher conference 2.50
- ❑8, May 1999, A: Psyba-Rats. 2.50
- ❑9, Jun 1999, PD (w) 2.50
- ❑10, Jul 1999, PD (w) 2.50
- ❑11, Aug 1999, PD (w) 2.50
- ❑12, Sep 1999, PD (w) 2.50
- ❑13, Oct 1999, PD (w); A: Supergirl. 2.50
- ❑14, Nov 1999; PD (w); A: Harm. Day of Judgment 2.50
- ❑15, Dec 1999, PD (w) 2.50
- ❑16, Jan 2000, PD (w); 1: Old Justice. 2.50
- ❑17, Feb 2000, PD (w) 2.50
- ❑18, Mar 2000, PD (w) 2.50
- ❑19, Apr 2000, PD (w) 2.50
- ❑20, Jun 2000, PD (w); A: Li'l Lobo. A: JLA. 2.50
- ❑21, Jul 2000, PD (w) 2.50
- ❑22, Aug 2000, PD (w) 2.50
- ❑23, Sep 2000; PD (w); at Olympic Games 2.50
- ❑24, Oct 2000; PD (w); Misprinted copies exist with duplicated ad 2.50
- ❑25, Nov 2000; PD (w); at Olympic Games 2.50
- ❑26, Dec 2000, PD (w) 2.50
- ❑27, Jan 2001, PD (w) 2.50
- ❑28, Feb 2001, PD (w); A: Forever People. 2.50
- ❑29, Mar 2001, PD (w); A: Forever People. A: Darkseid. 2.50
- ❑30, Apr 2001, PD (w) 2.50
- ❑31, May 2001, PD (w) 2.50
- ❑32, Jun 2001, PD (w) 2.50
- ❑33, Jul 2001, PD (w) 2.50
- ❑34, Aug 2001, PD (w) 2.50
- ❑35, Sep 2001; PD (w); Our Worlds At War; All-Out War 2.50
- ❑36, Oct 2001; PD (w); Our Worlds At War; Casualties of War 2.50
- ❑37, Nov 2001, PD (w); A: Darkseid. A: Granny Goodness. 2.50
- ❑38, Dec 2001; PD (w); Joker: Last Laugh crossover 2.50
- ❑39, Jan 2002, PD (w) 2.50
- ❑40, Feb 2002, PD (w) 2.50
- ❑41, Mar 2002; PD (w); A: The Ray. Lifesaver/Mad insert 2.50
- ❑42, Apr 2002, PD (w); A: Spectre. 2.50
- ❑43, May 2002, PD (w) 2.50
- ❑44, Jun 2002, PD (w) 2.50
- ❑45, Jul 2002, PD (w) 2.50
- ❑46, Aug 2002, PD (w) 2.50
- ❑47, Sep 2002, PD (w) 2.50
- ❑48, Oct 2002, PD (w) 2.50
- ❑49, Nov 2002, PD (w) 2.50
- ❑50, Dec 2002, PD (w) 3.95
- ❑51, Jan 2003, PD (w) 2.50
- ❑52, Feb 2003, PD (w) 2.50
- ❑53, Mar 2003, PD (w) 2.50
- ❑54, Apr 2003 2.75
- ❑55, May 2003 2.75
- ❑1000000, Nov 1998, PD (w); 1: Young Justice Legion S. 3.00

N-MINT

❑Giant Size 1, May 1999, PD (w) 4.95
❑Special 1, Jul 1999; Young Justice in No Man's Land 3.95

YOUNG JUSTICE IN NO MAN'S LAND
DC

❑1, Jul 1999; in Gotham City 3.95

YOUNG JUSTICE: OUR WORLDS AT WAR
DC

❑1, Nov 2001; Our Worlds at War 2.95

YOUNG JUSTICE SECRET FILES
DC

❑1, Jan 1999; Includes profiles of Young Justice members; Includes timeline . 4.95

YOUNG JUSTICE: SINS OF YOUTH
DC

❑1, May 2000 ...... 2.50
❑2, May 2000 ...... 2.50

YOUNG JUSTICE: THE SECRET
DC

❑1, Jun 1998; Girlfrenzy; leads into Young Justice: World Without Grown-Ups 1.95

YOUNG LAWYERS, THE
DELL

❑1, Jan 1971 ...... 10.00
❑2, Apr 1971 ...... 10.00

YOUNG LOVE (DC)
DC

❑39, Oct 1963 ...... 30.00
❑40, Dec 1963 ...... 24.00
❑41, Feb 1964 ...... 24.00
❑42, Apr 1964 ...... 24.00
❑43, Jun 1964 ...... 24.00
❑44, Aug 1964 ...... 24.00
❑45, Oct 1964 ...... 24.00
❑46, Dec 1964 ...... 24.00
❑47, Feb 1965 ...... 24.00
❑48, Apr 1965 ...... 24.00
❑49, Jun 1965 ...... 24.00
❑50, Aug 1965 ...... 24.00
❑51, Oct 1965 ...... 20.00
❑52, Dec 1965 ...... 20.00
❑53, Feb 1966 ...... 20.00
❑54, Apr 1966 ...... 20.00
❑55, Jun 1966 ...... 20.00
❑56, Aug 1966 ...... 20.00
❑57, Oct 1966 ...... 20.00
❑58, Dec 1966 ...... 20.00
❑59, Feb 1967 ...... 20.00
❑60, Apr 1967 ...... 20.00
❑61, Jun 1967 ...... 20.00
❑62, Aug 1967 ...... 20.00
❑63, Oct 1967 ...... 20.00
❑64, Dec 1967 ...... 20.00
❑65, Feb 1968 ...... 20.00
❑66, Apr 1968 ...... 20.00
❑67, Jun 1968 ...... 20.00
❑68, Aug 1968 ...... 20.00
❑69, Sep 1968; Giant 20.00
❑70, Oct 1968 ...... 20.00
❑71, Dec 1968 ...... 14.00
❑72, Feb 1969 ...... 14.00
❑73, Apr 1969 ...... 14.00
❑74, Jun 1969 ...... 14.00
❑75, Aug 1969 ...... 14.00
❑76, Oct 1969 ...... 14.00
❑77, Dec 1969 ...... 14.00
❑78, Feb 1970 ...... 14.00
❑79, Apr 1970 ...... 14.00
❑80, Jun 1970 ...... 14.00
❑81, Aug 1970 ...... 14.00
❑82, Oct 1970 ...... 14.00
❑83, Dec 1970 ...... 14.00
❑84, Feb 1971 ...... 14.00
❑85, Apr 1971 ...... 14.00
❑86, Jun 1971 ...... 14.00
❑87, Aug 1971 ...... 14.00
❑88, Sep 1971 ...... 14.00
❑89, Oct 1971 ...... 14.00

N-MINT

❑90, Dec 1971 ...... 14.00
❑91, Jan 1972 ...... 10.00
❑92, Feb 1972 ...... 10.00
❑93, Mar 1972 ...... 10.00
❑94, Apr 1972 ...... 10.00
❑95, May 1972 ...... 10.00
❑96, Jun 1972 ...... 10.00
❑97, Jul 1972 ...... 10.00
❑98, Aug 1972 ...... 10.00
❑99, Sep 1972 ...... 10.00
❑100, Oct 1972 ...... 10.00
❑101, Nov 1972 ...... 7.00
❑102, Feb 1973 ...... 7.00
❑103, Apr 1973 ...... 7.00
❑104, Jun 1973 ...... 7.00
❑105, Sep 1973 ...... 7.00
❑106, Nov 1973 ...... 7.00
❑107, Jan 1974 ...... 25.00
❑108, Mar 1974 ...... 20.00
❑109, May 1974 ...... 20.00
❑110, Jul 1974 ...... 20.00
❑111, Sep 1974 ...... 20.00
❑112, Nov 1974 ...... 20.00
❑113, Jan 1975 ...... 20.00
❑114, Mar 1975 ...... 20.00
❑115, May 1975 ...... 12.00
❑116, Jul 1975 ...... 12.00
❑117, Sep 1975 ...... 12.00
❑118, Nov 1975 ...... 12.00
❑119, Jan 1976 ...... 12.00
❑120, Win 1976 ...... 12.00
❑121 1976 ...... 12.00
❑122 1976 ...... 12.00
❑123 1977 ...... 12.00
❑124 1977 ...... 12.00
❑125 1977 ...... 12.00
❑126, Jul 1977 ...... 12.00

YOUNG LOVERS (AVALON)
AVALON

❑1, b&w; Indicia reads "Rock and Roll Romance" 2.95

YOUNG MASTER
NEW COMICS

❑1, Nov 1987, b&w 1.75
❑2, Dec 1987, b&w 1.75
❑3, Mar 1988, b&w 1.75
❑4, May 1988, b&w 1.75
❑5, Jul 1988, b&w 1.75
❑6, Oct 1988, b&w 1.75
❑7, Jan 1989, b&w 1.75
❑8, Mar 1989, b&w 1.95
❑9, May 1989, b&w 1.95

YOUNG REBELS, THE
DELL

❑1, Jan 1971 ...... 15.00

YOUNGSPUD
SPOOF

❑1 ...... 2.95

YOUNG WITCHES, THE
FANTAGRAPHICS / EROS

❑1, May 1991, b&w 2.50
❑2, Jun 1991, b&w 2.50
❑3, Jul 1991, b&w 2.50
❑4, Sep 1991, b&w 2.50

YOUNG WITCHES, THE: LONDON BABYLON
FANTAGRAPHICS / EROS

❑1, b&w 3.50
❑2, b&w 3.50
❑3, b&w 3.50
❑4, b&w 3.50
❑5, b&w 3.50
❑6, b&w 3.50

YOUNG ZEN: CITY OF DEATH
EXPRESS / ENTITY

❑1, b&w; cardstock cover 3.25

Robin, Impulse, Superboy, Wonder Girl, Arrowette, and The Secret joined forces as Young Justice in 1998.

N-MINT

YOUNG ZEN INTERGALACTIC NINJA
EXPRESS / ENTITY

❑1, b&w; trading card 3.50
❑2, b&w 2.95

YOUR BIG BOOK OF BIG BANG COMICS
IMAGE

❑1, ca. 1998; reprints Big Bang Comics # 0, #1, #2 ...... 11.00

YOU'RE UNDER ARREST!
DARK HORSE / MANGA

❑1, Dec 1995, b&w 2.95
❑2, Jan 1996, b&w 2.95
❑3, Feb 1996, b&w 2.95
❑4, Mar 1996, b&w 2.95
❑5, Apr 1996, b&w 2.95
❑6, May 1996, b&w 2.95
❑7, Jun 1996, b&w 2.95
❑8, Jul 1996, b&w 2.95

YOUR HYTONE COMIX
APEX NOVELTIES

❑1, Feb 1971, b&w; underground 8.00

Y'S GUYS
OCTOBER

❑1, Jul 1999 ...... 2.95

Y: THE LAST MAN
DC / VERTIGO

❑1, Sep 2002 ...... 30.00
❑2, Oct 2002 ...... 15.00
❑3, Nov 2002 ...... 5.00
❑4, Dec 2002 ...... 4.00
❑5, Jan 2003 ...... 4.00
❑6, Feb 2003 ...... 2.95
❑7, Mar 2003 ...... 2.95
❑8, Apr 2003 ...... 2.95
❑9, May 2003 ...... 2.95
❑10, Jun 2003 ...... 2.95
❑11, Jul 2003 ...... 2.95
❑12, Aug 2003 ...... 2.95
❑13, Sep 2003 ...... 2.95
❑14, Oct 2003 ...... 2.95
❑15, Nov 2003 ...... 2.95
❑16, Jan 2004 ...... 2.95
❑17, Feb 2004 ...... 2.95
❑18, Mar 2004 ...... 2.95
❑19, Apr 2004 ...... 2.95
❑20, May 2004 ...... 2.95
❑21, Jun 2004 ...... 2.95
❑22, Jul 2004 ...... 2.95
❑23, Aug 2004 ...... 2.95
❑24, Sep 2004 ......

YUGGOTH CULTURES (ALAN MOORE'S)
AVATAR

❑1, Oct 2003 ...... 3.95
❑2, Nov 2003 ...... 3.95
❑3, Dec 2003 ...... 3.95

YUMMY FUR
VORTEX

❑1, Dec 1986, b&w; reprint mini-comics #1-3 ...... 6.00
❑2, b&w; reprint mini-comics #4-6; no date of publication; says #4 in indicia 5.00
❑3, Feb 1987, b&w; reprint mini-comic #7 ...... 4.00
❑4, Apr 1987, b&w 4.00

N-MINT

❑5, Jun 1987, b&w ... 4.00
❑6, Aug 1987, b&w ... 3.00
❑7, b&w ... 3.00
❑8, Nov 1987, b&w ... 3.00
❑9, b&w ... 3.00
❑10, May 1988, b&w ... 3.00
❑11, Jul 1988, b&w ... 2.50
❑12, b&w; no date of publication ... 2.50
❑13, Nov 1988, b&w ... 2.50
❑14, Jan 1989, b&w ... 2.50
❑15, Mar 1989, b&w ... 2.50
❑16, Jun 1989, b&w ... 2.50
❑17, Aug 1989, b&w ... 2.50
❑18, Oct 1989, b&w ... 2.50
❑19, Jan 1990, b&w ... 2.50
❑20, Apr 1990, b&w ... 2.50
❑21, Jun 1990, b&w ... 2.50
❑22, Sep 1990, b&w ... 2.50
❑23, Dec 1990, b&w ... 2.50
❑24 1991, b&w ... 2.50
❑25, Jul 1991, b&w ... 2.50
❑26, Oct 1991, b&w ... 2.50
❑27, b&w ... 2.50
❑28, May 1992, b&w ... 2.50
❑29, Aug 1992, b&w ... 2.50
❑30, Apr 1993, b&w ... 2.50
❑31 1993, b&w ... 2.50
❑32, Jan 1994, b&w; Drawn & Quarterly Publishes ... 2.95

YUPPIES FROM HELL
Marvel

❑1, b&w ... 2.95

YUPPIES, REDNECKS AND LESBIAN BITCHES FROM MARS
Fantagraphics / Eros

❑1, b&w ... 2.95
❑2, b&w ... 2.95
❑3, b&w ... 2.95
❑4, b&w ... 2.95
❑5, b&w ... 2.95
❑6, b&w ... 2.95
❑7, May 1998, b&w ... 2.95

Z

Z
Keystone Graphics

❑1, Nov 1994, b&w ... 2.75
❑2, Jul 1995, b&w ... 2.75
❑3, Nov 1995, b&w ... 2.75

ZAIBATSU TEARS
Limelight

❑1, b&w ... 2.95
❑2 ... 2.95
❑3 ... 2.95

ZATANNA
DC

❑1, Jul 1993 ... 2.00
❑2, Aug 1993; Zatanna gets new costume ... 2.00
❑3, Sep 1993 ... 2.00
❑4, Oct 1993 ... 2.00

ZATANNA: EVERYDAY MAGIC
DC / Vertigo

❑1, May 2003 ... 5.95

ZATANNA SPECIAL
DC

❑1, ca. 1987 ... 2.00

ZAZA THE MYSTIC (AVALON)
Avalon

❑1 ... 2.95

ZEALOT
Image

❑1, Aug 1995 ... 2.50
❑2, Oct 1995 ... 2.50
❑3, Nov 1995 ... 2.50

N-MINT

ZELL SWORDDANCER (3-D ZONE)
3-D Zone

❑1, b&w ... 2.00

ZELL, SWORDDANCER (THOUGHTS & IMAGES)
Thoughts & Images

❑1, Jul 1986, b&w ... 2.00

ZENDRA
Penny-Farthing

❑1, Jan 2002 ... 2.95
❑2, Feb 2002 ... 2.95
❑3, Mar 2002 ... 2.95
❑4, Apr 2002 ... 2.95

ZEN, INTERGALACTIC NINJA (1ST SERIES)
Zen

❑1, Nov 1987, b&w ... 3.00
❑1-2 1988 ... 2.00
❑2, b&w ... 2.00
❑3, b&w ... 2.00
❑3-2, b&w ... 2.00
❑4, b&w ... 2.00
❑5, b&w ... 2.00
❑6, b&w ... 2.00

ZEN, INTERGALACTIC NINJA (2ND SERIES)
Zen

❑1, b&w ... 2.00
❑2, b&w ... 2.00
❑3, b&w ... 2.00
❑4, b&w ... 2.00

ZEN, INTERGALACTIC NINJA (3RD SERIES)
Zen

❑1, b&w ... 2.25
❑2, b&w ... 2.25
❑3, b&w ... 2.25
❑4, b&w ... 2.25
❑5, b&w ... 2.25
❑Holiday 1, ca. 1992, b&w; Flip-book 2.95

ZEN INTERGALACTIC NINJA (4TH SERIES)
Archie

❑1, May 1992 ... 1.25
❑2 1992 ... 1.25
❑3 1992 ... 1.25

ZEN INTERGALACTIC NINJA (5TH SERIES)
Archie

❑1, Sep 1992 ... 1.25
❑2, Oct 1992 ... 1.25
❑3, Dec 1992 ... 1.25
❑4, ca. 1993 ... 1.25
❑5, ca. 1993 ... 1.25
❑6, ca. 1993 ... 1.25
❑7, ca. 1993 ... 1.25

ZEN INTERGALACTIC NINJA (6TH SERIES)
Express / Entity

❑0, Jun 1993; 1: Nira X. Gray trim around outside cover ... 3.00
❑0/A, Jun 1993, b&w; 1: Nira X. foil cover ... 2.95
❑0/B, Jun 1993, b&w; 1: Nira X. chromium cover ... 3.50
❑0/Ltd., Jun 1993, b&w; 1: Nira X. Printing limited to 3,000 copies; All-gold trim ... 3.00
❑1, ca. 1993, b&w ... 3.00
❑1/Variant, ca. 1993, b&w; Chromium, die-cut cover ... 3.95
❑2, ca. 1994, b&w ... 3.00
❑3, ca. 1994, b&w ... 3.00
❑4, ca. 1994 ... 3.00
❑Ashcan 1, ca. 1993, b&w; no cover price; contains previews of Zen: Hazardous Duty and Zen: Tour of the Universe ... 1.00
❑Spring 1, ca. 1994; Spring Spectacular 2.95

N-MINT

ZEN INTERGALACTIC NINJA ALL-NEW COLOR SPECIAL
Express / Entity

❑1, ca. 1994; Chronium Cover ... 3.50

ZEN INTERGALACTIC NINJA COLOR
Express / Entity

❑1, ca. 1994; diecut foil cover ... 3.95
❑2, ca. 1994 ... 3.95
❑3, ca. 1994 ... 3.95
❑4, ca. 1994 ... 2.50
❑5, ca. 1994 ... 2.50
❑6, ca. 1995 ... 2.50
❑7, ca. 1995; says #6a on cover, #7 in indicia ... 2.95

ZEN INTERGALACTIC NINJA COLOR (2ND SERIES)
Express / Entity

❑1, ca. 1995 ... 2.50
❑2, ca. 1995 ... 2.50

ZEN, INTERGALACTIC NINJA EARTH DAY ANNUAL
Zen

❑1, ca. 1993, b&w ... 2.95

ZEN INTERGALACTIC NINJA MILESTONE
Express / Entity

❑1, ca. 1994 ... 2.95

ZEN INTERGALACTIC NINJA STARQUEST
Express

❑1, ca. 1994, b&w ... 2.95
❑2, ca. 1994, b&w ... 2.95
❑3, ca. 1994, b&w; enhanced cover .. 2.95
❑4, ca. 1994, b&w; cardstock cover .. 2.95
❑5, ca. 1994, b&w; enhanced cover .. 2.95
❑6, ca. 1995, b&w; enhanced cover .. 2.95
❑7, ca. 1995, b&w; enhanced cover .. 2.95

ZEN INTERGALACTIC NINJA SUMMER SPECIAL: VIDEO WARRIOR
Express

❑1, ca. 1994, b&w ... 2.95

ZEN INTERGALACTIC NINJA: TOUR OF THE UNIVERSE SPECIAL, THE AIRBRUSH ART OF DAN COTE
Express / Entity

❑1, ca. 1995; enhanced cardstock cover ... 3.95

ZENITH: PHASE I
Fleetway-Quality

❑1 ... 2.00
❑2 ... 2.00
❑3 ... 2.00

ZENITH: PHASE II
Fleetway-Quality

❑1 ... 1.95
❑2 ... 1.95

ZERO
Zero Comics

❑1, Mar 1975, b&w ... 3.00
❑2, Mar 1975, b&w ... 3.00
❑3, May 1976, b&w ... 3.00

ZERO GIRL
Homage

❑1, Feb 2001 ... 2.95
❑2, Mar 2001 ... 2.95
❑3, Apr 2001 ... 2.95
❑4, May 2001 ... 2.95
❑5, Jun 2001 ... 2.95

ZERO GIRL: FULL CIRCLE
DC / Homage

❑1, Jan 2004 ... 2.95
❑2, Feb 2004 ... 2.95
❑3, Mar 2004 ... 2.95
❑4, Apr 2004 ... 2.95
❑5, May 2004 ... 2.95

N-MINT

ZERO HOUR
Dog Soup
❑1, Apr 1995, b&w; says Pat Leidy's Catfight on cover 2.95

ZERO HOUR: CRISIS IN TIME
DC
❑4, Sep 1994; JOy (a); (#1 in sequence) 2.00
❑3, Sep 1994; JOy (a); D: Atom. D: Hourman. remainder of Justice Society of America aged; (#2 in sequence) 2.00
❑2, Sep 1994; JOy (a); (#3 in sequence) 2.00
❑1, Sep 1994; JOy (a); 1: Parallax. 1: David Knight. 1: Jack Knight. Silver Age Atom de-aged; (#4 in sequence) 3.00
❑0, Sep 1994; JOy (a); V: Extant. contains Zero Hour checklist and new DC timeline foldout; (#5 in sequence) . 2.00
❑Ashcan 1, ca. 1994; Ashcan Preview 1.00

ZERO PATROL, THE (1ST SERIES)
Continuity
❑1, Nov 1984, NA (c); NA (w); NA (a); O: The Zero Patrol. 1: The Zero Patrol. . 2.00
❑2, Feb 1985, NA (c); NA (w); NA (a) 2.00

ZERO PATROL (2ND SERIES)
Continuity
❑1 1987 ..... 2.00
❑2, Nov 1987 ..... 2.00
❑3, Apr 1988 ..... 2.00
❑4, Mar 1989 ..... 2.00
❑5, May 1989 ..... 2.00

ZERO STREET
Amaze Ink
❑1, Sep 2000 ..... 2.95

ZERO TOLERANCE
First
❑1, Oct 1990 ..... 2.25
❑2, Nov 1990 ..... 2.25
❑3, Dec 1990; Vigil 2.25
❑4, Jan 1991 ..... 2.25

ZERO ZERO
Fantagraphics
❑1, Mar 1995, b&w 4.00
❑2, May 1995, b&w 4.00
❑3, Jul 1995, b&w 4.00
❑4, Aug 1995, b&w; issue number determined by back cover cartoon 4.00
❑5, Sep 1995, b&w; issue number determined by back cover cartoon 4.00
❑6, Nov 1995, b&w 4.00
❑7, Jan 1996, b&w 4.00
❑8, Mar 1996, b&w; issue number determined by back cover cartoon 5.95
❑9, May 1996, b&w; issue number determined by back cover cartoon 3.95
❑10, Jul 1996, b&w; cover says Jul 96, indicia says May 3.95
❑11, Aug 1996, b&w 3.95
❑12, Sep 1996, b&w 3.95
❑13, Nov 1996, b&w 3.95
❑14, Jan 1997, b&w 3.95
❑15, Mar 1997, b&w; Bosnia prequel 3.95
❑16, Apr 1997, b&w 3.95
❑17, Jun 1997, b&w 3.95
❑18, Jul 1997, b&w 3.95
❑19, Aug 1997, b&w 3.95
❑20, Sep 1997, b&w and color 3.95
❑21, Nov 1997, b&w 3.95
❑22, Jan 1998, b&w 3.95
❑23, Mar 1998, b&w 3.95
❑24, Sum 1998, b&w 3.95
❑25, Fal 1998, b&w 3.95
❑26, ca. 1998, b&w 3.95

ZETRAMAN
Antarctic
❑1, Sep 1991, b&w 1.95
❑2, Oct 1991, b&w 1.95
❑3, Feb 1992, b&w 1.95

ZETRAMAN: REVIVAL
Antarctic
❑1, Oct 1993 ..... 2.75

N-MINT

❑2, Dec 1993 ..... 2.75
❑3, Aug 1995 ..... 2.75

ZILLION
Eternity
❑1, Apr 1993, b&w 2.50
❑2, May 1993, b&w 2.50
❑3, Jun 1993, b&w 2.50
❑4, Jul 1993, b&w 2.50

ZIP COMICS (COZMIC)
Cozmic
❑1 ..... 4.00

ZIPPY QUARTERLY
Fantagraphics
❑1, b&w 4.95
❑2, b&w 4.95
❑3, b&w; strip reprint 3.50
❑4, b&w; strip reprint 3.50
❑5, b&w; strip reprint 3.50
❑7, Aug 1994, b&w; strip reprint 3.50
❑8, Nov 1994, b&w; strip reprint 3.50
❑12, Dec 1995, b&w; strip reprint 3.95
❑13, Aug 1996, b&w; cardstock cover; strip reprint 3.95

ZODIAC P.I.
Tokyopop
❑1, Jul 2003, b&w; printed in Japanese format 9.99

ZOIDS: CHAOTIC CENTURY
Viz
❑1, ca. 2002 ..... 6.99
❑2 ..... 6.99
❑3 ..... 6.99
❑4 ..... 6.99
❑5 ..... 6.99
❑6 ..... 6.99

ZÖLASTRÄYA AND THE BARD
Twilight Twins
❑1, Jan 1987, b&w 1.70
❑2, b&w 1.70
❑3, b&w 1.70
❑4, b&w 1.70
❑5, b&w 1.70

ZOMBIE 3-D
3-D Zone
❑1 ..... 3.95

ZOMBIE BOY (ANTARCTIC)
Antarctic
❑1, Nov 1996, b&w; wraparound cover 2.95
❑2, b&w 2.95
❑3, b&w 2.95

ZOMBIE BOY RISES AGAIN
Timbuktu
❑1, Jan 1994, b&w; Collects Zombie Boy #1 and Zombie Boy's Hoodoo Tales #1; Beverly Hillbillies cameo . 2.50

ZOMBIE BOY (TIMBUKTU)
Timbuktu
❑1, b&w 1.50

ZOMBIE LOVE
ZuZupetal
❑1 ..... 2.50
❑2 ..... 2.50
❑3 ..... 2.50

ZOMBIE WAR (TUNDRA)
Tundra
❑1 ..... 3.50

ZOMBIE WAR (FANTACO)
Fantaco
❑1, b&w 3.50
❑2, b&w 3.50

ZOMBIE WAR: EARTH MUST BE DESTROYED
Fantaco
❑1, b&w 2.95
❑1/CS, b&w; trading card 2.95
❑2, b&w 2.95
❑3, b&w 2.95
❑4, b&w 2.95

Golden Age versions of The Atom and Hourman met their ends in *Zero Hour* #3. The JSA avenged their deaths in the pages of *JSA* six years later.

© 1994 DC Comics.

N-MINT

ZOMBIEWORLD: CHAMPION OF THE WORMS
Dark Horse
❑1, Sep 1997, b&w 2.95
❑2, Oct 1997, b&w 2.95
❑3, Nov 1997, b&w 2.95

ZOMBIEWORLD: DEAD END
Dark Horse
❑1, Jan 1998, b&w 2.95
❑2, Feb 1998, b&w 2.95

ZOMBIEWORLD: EAT YOUR HEART OUT
Dark Horse
❑1, Apr 1998, b&w 2.95

ZOMBIEWORLD: HOME FOR THE HOLIDAYS
Dark Horse
❑1, Dec 1997, b&w 2.95

ZOMBIEWORLD: TREE OF DEATH
Dark Horse
❑1, Jun 1999, b&w 2.95
❑2, Aug 1999, b&w 2.95
❑3, Sep 1999, b&w 2.95
❑4, Oct 1999, b&w 2.95

ZOMBIEWORLD: WINTER'S DREGS
Dark Horse
❑1, May 1998, b&w 2.95
❑2, Jun 1998, b&w 2.95
❑3, Jul 1998, b&w 2.95
❑4, Aug 1998, b&w 2.95

ZOMBOY
Inferno
❑1, Aug 1996, b&w 2.95

ZOMOID ILLUSTORIES
3-D Zone
❑1, b&w; not 3-D 2.50

ZONE
Dark Horse
❑1, b&w 2.00

ZONE CONTINUUM, THE
Caliber
❑1, ca. 1994, b&w 2.95
❑1/A, ca. 1994, b&w; Orange background; no cover price 2.00
❑1/B, ca. 1994, b&w; Maroon background; no cover price 2.00
❑2, b&w 2.95

ZONE CONTINUUM (VOL. 2)
Caliber
❑1, b&w 2.95
❑2, b&w 2.95

ZONE ZERO
Planet Boy
❑1, b&w 2.95

ZOO FUNNIES (3RD SERIES)
Charlton
❑1, Dec 1984 ..... 2.00

ZOONIVERSE
Eclipse
❑1, Aug 1986 ..... 1.50
❑2, Oct 1986 ..... 1.50
❑3, Dec 1986 ..... 1.50
❑4, Feb 1987 ..... 1.50

	N-MINT
❑5, Apr 1987	1.50
❑6, Jun 1987	1.50

ZOOT!
FANTAGRAPHICS

	N-MINT
❑1, Nov 1992, b&w	2.50
❑2, Mar 1993, b&w	2.50
❑3, May 1993, b&w	2.50
❑4, Jul 1993, b&w	2.50
❑5, Sep 1993, b&w	2.50
❑6, Nov 1993, b&w	2.50

ZORANN: STAR-WARRIOR!
BLUE COMET

	N-MINT
❑0, May 1994, b&w; May-94	2.95
❑1, b&w	2.00

ZORI J'S 3-D BUBBLE BATH
3-D ZONE

	N-MINT
❑1, b&w	3.95

ZORI J'S SUPER-SWELL BUBBLE BATH ADVENTURE-OH BOY!
3-D ZONE

	N-MINT
❑1, b&w	2.95

ZORRO (DELL)
DELL

	N-MINT
❑8, Dec 1959	70.00
❑9, Mar 1960	70.00
❑10, Jun 1960	68.00
❑11, Sep 1960	68.00
❑12, Dec 1960	68.00
❑13, Mar 1961	65.00
❑14, Jun 1961	65.00
❑15, Sep 1961	65.00

ZORRO (GOLD KEY)
GOLD KEY

	N-MINT
❑1, Jan 1966	70.00
❑2, May 1966	38.00
❑3 1966	38.00
❑4 1966	38.00
❑5, Mar 1967	34.00
❑6, Jun 1967	34.00
❑7, Sep 1967	34.00
❑8, Dec 1967	28.00
❑9, Mar 1968	28.00

ZORRO (MARVEL)
MARVEL

	N-MINT
❑1, Dec 1990, FM (c); FM (a); O: Zorro.	3.00
❑2, Jan 1991	2.00
❑3, Feb 1991	2.00
❑4, Mar 1991	2.00
❑5, Apr 1991	2.00
❑6, May 1991	2.00
❑7, Jun 1991	2.00
❑8, Jul 1991	2.00
❑9, Aug 1991	2.00
❑10, Sep 1991, ATh (c)	2.00
❑11, Oct 1991, ATh (c)	2.00
❑12, Nov 1991; ATh (c); Final Issue	2.00

ZORRO (TOPPS)
TOPPS

	N-MINT
❑0, Nov 1993, 1: Buck Wylde.	2.50
❑1, Jan 1994, FM (c); 1: Machete.	3.50
❑2, Feb 1994, 1: Lady Rawhide (out of costume).	8.00
❑3, Mar 1994, 1: Lady Rawhide (in costume).	3.00
❑4, Apr 1994, MGr (c); 1: Moonstalker.	3.00
❑5, May 1994, JSt (c); KG (a); A: Lady Rawhide.	3.00
❑6, Jun 1994	3.00
❑7, Jul 1994, PG (c); A: Lady Rawhide.	2.50
❑8, Aug 1994, GP (c); GP (a); A: Lady Rawhide.	2.50
❑9, Sep 1994	2.50
❑10, Oct 1994, A: Lady Rawhide.	2.95
❑11, Nov 1994, A: Lady Rawhide.	2.50

ZOT!
ECLIPSE

	N-MINT
❑1, Apr 1984; (c); 1: Jenny Weaver. 1: Zot!. Color issues begin	5.00
❑2, May 1984, 1: Dekko (cameo). 1: 9-Jack-9.	2.50
❑3, Jun 1984, 1: Dekko (full).	2.50
❑4, Jul 1984, O: Zot!.	2.50
❑5, Aug 1984; Wordless panels Inside front cover in B&W	2.50
❑6, Nov 1984	2.50
❑7, Dec 1984; KB (w); DS (a); The Magic Shop back-up features begin	2.50
❑8, Mar 1985, (c)	2.50
❑9, May 1985	2.50
❑10, Jul 1985, (c)	2.50
❑10.5; Mini-comic	2.50
❑11, Jan 1987, b&w; Black & white issues begin	2.50
❑12, Mar 1987, b&w (c)	2.25
❑13, May 1987	2.25
❑14, Jul 1987	2.25
❑14.5; Adventures of Zot! in Dimension 10 1/2, The	2.25
❑15, Oct 1987	2.25
❑16, Dec 1987	2.25
❑17, Feb 1988	2.25
❑18, Apr 1988	2.25
❑19, Jun 1988	2.25
❑20, Jun 1988	2.25
❑21, Aug 1988	2.25
❑22, Oct 1988	2.25
❑23, Nov 1988	2.25
❑24, Dec 1988	2.25
❑25, Feb 1989	2.25
❑26, Apr 1989	2.25
❑27, Jun 1989	2.25
❑28, Sep 1989	2.25
❑29, Dec 1989	2.25
❑30, Mar 1990	2.25
❑31, May 1990	2.25
❑32, Jul 1990	2.25
❑33, Oct 1990	2.25
❑34, Dec 1990	2.25
❑35, Mar 1991	2.25
❑36, Jul 1991	2.95

ZU (ONE-SHOT)
MU

	N-MINT
❑1, Feb 1992	3.95

ZU
MU

	N-MINT
❑1, Jan 1995, b&w	2.95
❑2, Mar 1995, b&w	2.95
❑3, May 1995, b&w	2.95
❑4, Jul 1995, b&w	2.95
❑5, Sep 1995, b&w	2.95
❑6, Nov 1995, b&w	2.95
❑7, Jan 1996, b&w	2.95
❑8, Mar 1996, b&w	2.95
❑9, b&w	2.95
❑10, b&w	2.95
❑11, b&w	2.95
❑12, b&w	2.95
❑13, b&w	2.95
❑14, b&w	2.95
❑15, b&w	2.95
❑16, b&w	2.95
❑17, b&w	2.95
❑18, b&w	2.95
❑19, b&w	2.95

ZUGAL
BRYAN EVANS

	N-MINT
❑1	2.95

ZULUNATION
TOME

	N-MINT
❑1, b&w	2.95
❑2, b&w	2.95
❑3, b&w	2.95

ZWANNA, SON OF ZULU
DARK ZULU LIES

	N-MINT
❑1	2.00

ZZZ
ALAN BUNCE

	N-MINT
❑1, Mar 2000, b&w	2.35

Suggested Reading

Even in a volume this big, there's only so much information we can cram in. Sooner or later, you're going to want to pursue a topic further than we've had room for here. So, as you expand your quest, consider these sources of information. (Some may be out of print, but you should be able to track 'em down, thanks to the wonders of the Internet, right?)

For starters, the third edition of our own *Standard Catalog of Comic Books* contains still more information on most of the comics contained in this book, including circulation data, distributor pre-orders, and CGC-grading data. And it covers older comics, too. Copies of the softcover edition are still available for $34.99.

The ***ComicBase*** CD-ROM contains all the comics found in this edition, as well as many foreign comics. There are summaries for thousands of titles in *ComicBase*, as well. That's *www.comicbase.com* or Human Computing, 4509 Thistle Dr., San Jose, CA 95136. The latest edition (in late 2004) is 9.0.

Then, there's the comics news magazine, ***Comics Buyer's Guide***, 700 E. State St., Iola, WI 54945 (and *www.comic buyersguide.com*), which provides the latest news and updates on what's collectible, population reports, pricing reports, and the like — on comics old and new. And no magazine publishes more reviews of new comics each year!

A tireless researcher, one of the world's leading experts on comic books and strips, is Ron Goulart, and all his reference works on comics make informative *and* entertaining reading on the field. Among his most helpful works is ***The Encyclopedia of American Comics from 1897 to the Present*** (Facts on File, 1990), and, if you yearn for full-color tastes of Golden Age goodies, check out his ***Comic Book Culture: An Illustrated History*** (Collectors Press, 2000). But those are just two; buy any comics references by Goulart, if you're looking for behind-the-scenes background on Comics That Were.

The Overstreet Comic Book Price Guide, one of the leaders in the field of comics collecting, continues to publish an annual update with historical essays; the 2004 edition was its 34th. It also has information on many of the precursors of today's comic-book format. Check out *www.gem stonepub.com* or Gemstone Publishing, Inc., 1966 Greenspring Dr., Timonium, MD 21093.

The late Ernst Gerber put together incredible compendia of comic-book covers, including valuable information regarding publishing dates and the like. ***The Photo Journal Guide to Comic Books***, for example, is a two-volume set of Golden Age covers and information, packed with beautiful photos. It's not cheap, but it's a major work and rewards the browser.

Comic Book Marketplace is a magazine devoted to back-issue scholarship. More information is available from *www.eccrypt.com* and/or Russ Cochran, Publisher, P.O. Box 469, West Plains, MO 65775.

The New York Observer called ***The Comics Journal*** the "tweedy intellectual voice of the industry." That may be, but, between indictments against commercialism, it does publish many excellent long-form interviews with creators. It's available from Fantagraphics Books.

The entire CGC Census is available on the company's website, *www.cgccomics.com*. The information appears at some delay from the company's actual grading, but it still provides valuable information on what's out there and being bought and sold for noticeable bucks.

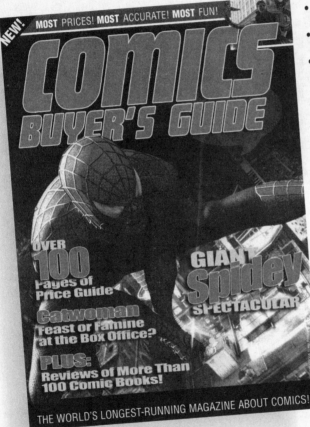